CHAMBERS

Dictionary of GREAT QUOTATIONS

CHAMBERS

First published in Great Britain in 2015 by Chambers Publishing Ltd. An Hachette UK company.

Chambers® is a registered trademark of Chambers Publishing Limited.

This third edition published in 2015 by Chambers Publishing Ltd.
First edition published 1996
Second edition published 2005

Database right Chambers Publishing Ltd (makers)

All rights reserved. No part of this publication may be reproduced, stored in a retrieval system or transmitted in any form or by any means, electronic, mechanical, photocopying, recording or otherwise, without the prior written permission of the publisher, or as expressly permitted by law, or under terms agreed with the appropriate reprographic rights organization. Enquiries concerning reproduction outside the scope of the above should be sent to the Rights Department, Chambers Publishing Ltd, at the address below.

You must not circulate this book in any other binding or cover and you must impose this same condition on any acquirer.

British Library Cataloguing in Publication Data: a catalogue record for this title is available from the British Library.
Library of Congress Catalog Card Number: on file.

ISBN 9781473608122

1

The publisher has used its best endeavours to ensure that any website addresses referred to in this book are correct and active at the time of going to press. However, the publisher and the author have no responsibility for the websites and can make no guarantee that a site will remain live or that the content will remain relevant, decent or appropriate.

The publisher has made every effort to mark as such all words which it believes to be trademarks. The publisher should also like to make it clear that the presence of a word in the book, whether marked or unmarked, in no way affects its legal status as a trademark.

Every reasonable effort has been made by the publisher to trace the copyright holders of material in this book. Any errors or omissions should be notified in writing to the publisher, who will endeavour to rectify the situation for any reprints and future editions.

Typeset by Cenveo® Publisher Services.
Printed and bound in India by Replika Press Pvt. Ltd.

Hachette UK policy is to use papers that are natural, renewable and recyclable products and made from wood grown in sustainable forests. The logging and manufacturing processes are expected to conform to the environmental regulations of the country of origin.

Carmelite House
50 Victoria Embankment
London EC4Y 0DZ
www.chambers.co.uk

Contributors to the third and previous editions

Editor of the third edition
David Pickering

Editors
Iain Campbell
Alison Jones
Stephanie Pickering
Megan Thomson

Contributors
Katherine Acheson
Julia Carlson
John Robert Colombo
Ingrid Cranfield
Don Currie
Wendy Dossett
Paul Edmonson
José Garcia
Graham Giles
W Eric Gustafson
Bruce Henstell
David Horspool
Dean Juniper
Victoria Keller
Grace Kenny
Michael Kinsella
Paul Maloney
Kenny Mathieson
Kevin McGinley
Jim Orton
Patricia Perilli
Michael Petheram
David Pickering
James Robertson
Adrian Room
Donald Rutherford
Susan Shatto
D W D Shaw
Sean Sheehan
Jane Stewart
Susan Stiles
Alan Taylor
Onno van Nijf
Wilson J Wall
Tim Winter

Political consultant
Kenneth Baker

North American consultant
Rev James B Simpson

Introduction

A quotation can come from any notable source, spoken or written, and from any language at any time. Quotations interest us especially when they express an idea or thought in an interesting or memorable way, or simply amuse us with their sharp wit. Thus this collection contains not only literary quotations from important authors both past and present, but also quotations from people in many other walks of life. As well as writers, critics, politicians and journalists, we have sought out memorable phrases from scientists, industrialists, entertainers, sportspeople, and many more, to reflect the diversity of modern life. And just as the world has changed since the last edition of this dictionary, so many of the hundreds of new quotations we have selected reflect these changes, and important global and local events.

The coverage is truly international, extending to other varieties of English and to other languages where these provide material that is readily quotable in English. Where appropriate, quotations from languages using the Roman alphabet are given in their original form and are followed by a translation. Where no specific translation has been used, we have aimed to give a good working English version.

Quotations are arranged alphabetically by author, and chronologically (as far as possible) within each author entry, with the year of the quotation put first when this is known. This enables the reader to browse through the quotes of a particular person, and see their thoughts or works as they developed over time. This chronological arrangement is specific to this dictionary, and it makes this dictionary much more than a collection of bons mots. Where possible, each entry also includes a brief biography of the author, and many quotations are supplemented by contextual notes. These will help the reader to understand and appreciate the quotations more fully.

A dependable source is given for each quotation where possible. Where quotations are known from many secondary sources with no traceable primary source they are given as 'attributed'.

The comprehensive index is arranged by keyword. This allows the reader to find quotations on a particular subject. Once you have located your keyword, each entry in the index refers the user to the author, the page number on which the quotation occurs, and the number of the quotation on the page. Quotations are numbered from 1 to 99 and then start again at 1. So a reference to BACON 47:58 points to the quotation by Francis Bacon numbered 58 on page 47. Cross-references within the text use the same system.

Our aim has been to present the most memorable comments on all aspects of human experience, but we appreciate that no selection can be definitive, and the editors would appreciate suggestions for inclusion in future editions.

Abbreviations

b.	born
bk.	book
c	century (in dates, eg 18c)
c.	circa
ch.	chapter
d.	died
fl.	floruit
l.	line
pt.	part
sc.	scene

Names of months are shortened to their first three letters.

QUOTATIONS

QUOTATIONS

Abbott, Diane Julie 1953–
British Labour politician, who became the first black woman Member of Parliament in 1987.

1 Forests of middle-aged men in dark suits…all slightly redfaced from eating and drinking too much…a nightmare of elderly white males.
1988 Of the House of Commons. In the *New York Times*, 3 Jun.

Abelard, Peter 1079–1142
French ecclesiast and theologian. At the age of 38, he fell in love with his 17-year-old pupil Héloïse; when the affair was discovered, he was castrated by her relatives. He became a monk and went on to found the monastic school of the Paraclete and to serve as Abbot of St Gildas-de-Rhuys, Brittany. Declared a heretic by his adversaries, he died on his way to defend himself.

2 *Non enim facile de his, quos plurimum diligimus, turpitudinem suspicamur.*
We do not easily suspect evil of those whom we love most.
c.1132 *Historia Calamitatum*, ch.6.

3 *Cum itaque membris his vilissimis, quæ pro summæ turpitudinis exercitio pudenda vocantur, nec proprium sustinent nomen, me divina gratia mundavit potius quam privavit, quid aliud egit quam ad puritatem munditiæ conservandam sordida removit et vitia.*
When divine grace cleansed rather than deprived me of those most vile members which from their grossly depraved activity are called 'pudenda' ['shameful'], having no proper name of their own, what else did it do but remove filth and foulness so as to preserve unblemished purity?
c.1135 Of his castration. Second letter to Héloïse.

4 *O quanta qualia sunt illa sabbata,*
Quae semper celebrat superna curia.
O what their joy and their glory must be,
Those endless sabbaths the blessèd ones see.
Hymnarius Paraclitensis, bk.1, no.29, 'Sabbato. Ad Vesperas' (translated by J M Neale).

Abercrombie, Lascelles 1881–1938
English poet and critic. He wrote several volumes of poetry in the Georgian manner, and a number of works of academic literary criticism.

5 The poet's business is not to describe things to us, or to tell us about things, but to create in our minds the very things themselves.
1932 *Poetry: Its Music and Meaning*, introduction.

Abrams, M(eyer) H(oward) 1912–
US literary critic.

6 Life without literature is a life reduced to penury. It expands you in every way. It illuminates what you're doing. It shows you possibilities you haven't thought of. It enables you to live the lives of other people than yourself. It broadens you, it makes you more human. It makes life enjoyable.
2012 In *The New York Times: Sunday Book Review*, 23 Aug.

Abse, Dannie 1923–2014
Welsh writer and physician, specialist at a London chest clinic from 1954 to 1989. Best known as a poet, he also wrote novels, plays and autobiographical works, including *A Poet in the Family* (1974) and *Goodbye, Twentieth Century* (2001).

7 I know the colour rose, and it is lovely,
But not when it ripens in a tumour;
And healing greens, leaves and grass, so springlike,
In limbs that fester are not springlike.
1968 'Pathology of Colours'.

8 So in the simple blessing of a rainbow,
In the bevelled edge of a sunlit mirror,
I have seen visible, Death's artifact
Like a soldier's ribbon on a tunic tacked.
1968 'Pathology of Colours'.

9 The theme of Death is to Poetry what Mistaken Identity is to Drama.
1984 Journal entry, Feb, collected in *Journals from the Ant-Heap* (1986).

10 We British are an aggressive nation. We seem to have become more violent this last decade: look how we drive fast and furious, with fists clenched; listen, at the stadiums, how the crowds shout, 'Kick his fuckin' head in,' or to the sirens of police cars and ambulances in the shoddy streets of Brixton or Liverpool.
1986 *Journals from the Ant-Heap*, 'Appendix 1: Authors Take Sides'.

11 I want you to go into them sober and come out drunk.
2013 Of his collection of poems *Speak, Old Parrot*.

Abu'l-'Alá Al-Ma'arri 973–1058
Syrian poet and scholar. He was blinded by smallpox in childhood and devoted himself to study, memorizing the manuscripts of Syrian libraries. As well as poems, he wrote philosophical and mystical works.

12 We live ignorant and die in errancy as we lived.
c.1000 *Luzùmiyyàt*, stanza 4 (translated by R A Nicholson in *Studies in Islamic Poetry*, 1921).

13 The world's best moment is a calm hour passed
In listening to a friend who can talk well.
c.1000 *Luzùmiyyàt*, stanza 32 (translated by R A Nicholson in *Studies in Islamic Poetry*, 1921).

14 We flee from Death's bitter cup; he follows, loving and fain.
c.1000 *Luzùmiyyàt*, stanza 36 (translated by R A Nicholson in *Studies in Islamic Poetry*, 1921).

15 Life is a malady whose one medicine is Death.
c.1000 *Luzùmiyyàt*, stanza 41 (translated by R A Nicholson in *Studies in Islamic Poetry*, 1921).

16 Consider every moment past
A thread from life's frayed mantle cast.
c.1000 *Luzùmiyyàt*, stanza 57 (translated by R A Nicholson in *Studies in Islamic Poetry*, 1921).

Abzug, Bella *originally* Bella Savitzky 1920–98
US feminist, lawyer, writer and Congresswoman. She was one of the key figures of the modern feminist movement.

17 Richard Nixon self-impeached...[and] gave us Gerald Ford as his revenge.
1976 In *Rolling Stone*, 2 Dec.

Accius 170–c.86 BC
Roman poet and playwright.

18 *Oderint, dum metuant.*
Let them hate, so long as they fear.
Quoted in Seneca *Dialogues*, 'De Ira'.

Ace, Goodman 1899–1982
US humorist, best known for his radio shows such as *The Easy Aces* (1928–45), with his wife Jane Epstein Ace. He also wrote for television comedians from 1952.

19 Derived from the words Terrible Vaudeville... We call it a medium because nothing's well done.
1954 Of T V. Letter to Groucho Marx. Collected in *The Groucho Letters* (1967).

Achebe, Chinua *originally* Albert Chinualumogo 1930–2013
Nigerian novelist, poet and essayist. His novel *Things Fall Apart* (1958) explores tensions in 19c African society. Other works include *Anthills of the Savannah* (1987, shortlisted for the Booker Prize).

20 Among the Ibo the art of conversation is regarded very highly, and proverbs are the palm-oil with which words are eaten.
1958 *Things Fall Apart*, ch.1. The title is taken from Yeats's poem 'The Second Coming'.

21 Even now they have not found the mouth with which to tell of their suffering.
1958 *Things Fall Apart*, ch.20.

22 Whenever people have asked me which among my novels is my favourite I have always evaded a direct answer, being strongly of the mind that in sheer invidiousness that question is fully comparable to asking a man to list his children in the order in which he loves them. A paterfamilias worth his salt will, if he must, speak about the peculiar attractiveness of each child.
1974 *Arrow of God*, preface to 2nd edn.

23 Americans, it seems to me, tend to protect their children from the harshness of life, in their interest. That's not the way my people rear their children. They let them experience the world as it is.
2008 In the *Philadelphia Inquirer*, 2 Apr.

24 We cannot trample upon the humanity of others without devaluing our own. The Igbo, always practical, put it concretely in their proverb *Onye ji onye n'ani ji onwe ya:* 'He who will hold another down in the mud must stay in the mud to keep him down.'
2009 *The Education of a British-Protected Child: Essays*.

Acheson, Dean Gooderham 1893–1971
US lawyer and politician. As Under-Secretary (1945–7) and then Secretary of State (1949–53) in the Truman administration, he helped to establish the Marshall Plan (1947) and the North Atlantic Treaty Organization.

25 I will undoubtedly have to seek what is happily known as gainful employment, which I am glad to say does not describe holding public office.
1952 On resigning as Secretary of State to resume his career as a lawyer. In *Time*, 22 Dec.

26 Diplomatic problems used to be discussed by ambassadors... Foreign Ministers were called... somebody thought of the summit meetings... We are nearing the moment when political meetings will be held at a divine level.
1959 Comment to reporters in Florence, Sep. Recalled in *This Vast External Realm* (1973).

27 The institution of the throne is an anachronistic, feudal institution perfectly adapted to the use of anachronistic feudal-minded groups.
Opposing US Ambassador Joseph Grew's recommendation for the Emperor's retention in postwar Japan. Quoted in Lee Giovanitti and Fred Freed *The Decision to Drop the Atomic Bomb* (1960).

28 He still had his glorious sense of words drawn from the special reservoir from which Lincoln also drew, fed by Shakespeare and those Tudor critics who wrote the first Prayer Book of Edward VI and their Jacobean successors who translated the Bible.
1961 Of Winston Churchill. *Sketches from Life of Men I Have Known*.

29 The old house carried an assurance, typically Portuguese, that nothing was urgent.
1961 On the US Embassy residence in Lisbon. *Sketches from Life of Men I Have Known*.

30 He wanted to be independent of the vagaries of butlers.
1961 Of Winston Churchill, who liked to keep a champagne bottle next to his plate. *Sketches from Life of Men I Have Known*.

31 He smiled with the spontaneity of a mechanical tiger.
1961 Of Soviet Foreign Minister V M Molotov. *Sketches from Life of Men I Have Known*.

32 He struck me as looking like a pear on top of two toothpicks.
1962 Of Charles de Gaulle, 22 Oct, after a visit during the Cuban missile crisis. Quoted in David S McLellan and David C Acheson (eds) *Among Friends: Personal Letters of Dean Gooderham Acheson* (1980).

33 Great Britain has lost an Empire and not yet found a role. The attempt to play a separate power role—that is, a role apart from Europe, based on a special relationship with the United States, on being the head of the Commonwealth—is about to be played out. Her Majesty's Government is now attempting, wisely in my opinion, to re-enter Europe.
1962 Speech at West Point military academy, 5 Dec. According to the *New York Times*, 23 Nov 1969, Prime Minister Harold Wilson later countered, 'Mr Acheson is a distinguished figure who has lost a State Department and not yet found himself a role'.

34 Fumbling silence in the White House seeps out over the country like a cold fog over a river bed where no stream runs.
1963 Letter to Harry S Truman, 28 May, alluding to the Eisenhower administration. Quoted in David S McLellan and David C Acheson (eds) *Among Friends: Personal Letters of Dean Gooderham Acheson* (1980).

35 A real Centaur—part man, part horse's ass. A rough appraisal, but curiously true.
1968 Of President Johnson. 13 Apr.

36 Like finding oneself pregnant and trying to fall in love as quickly as possible.
On the weekend of Richard M Nixon's inauguration. Quoted in Douglas Brinkley *Dean Acheson: The Cold War Years 1953–71* (1992).

37 I had shown my colors. Those who took their red straight, without a chaser of white and blue, were not mollified.
1969 *Present at the Creation.*

38 The enormity of the task...[was] just a bit less formidable than that described in the first chapter of Genesis.
1969 Of postwar restructuring. *Present at the Creation.*

39 The first requirement of a statesman is that he be dull.
1970 In the *Observer*, 21 Jun.

40 Much in life cannot be affected...but must be borne...without complaint, because complaints are a bore...and undermine the serenity essential to endurance.
Quoted in Gaddis Smith *American Secretaries of State* (1972).

41 Neither action nor style could have accomplished the result alone. Both were needed.
1975 Of Winston Churchill's charisma. *Grapes from Thorns.*

42 His speeches were prepared with that infinite capacity for taking pains, which is said to be genius.
1975 Of Winston Churchill. *Grapes from Thorns.*

43 Courageous and loyal to the tips of his stubby fingers.
1975 Of British Foreign Secretary Ernest Bevin. *Grapes from Thorns.*

44 Breathless and bewildered like an old lady at a busy intersection.
On the State Dept under Cordell Hull. Quoted in David S McLellan *Dean Acheson: The State Department Years* (1976).

45 Our name for problems is significant. We call them headaches. You take a powder and they are gone.
Quoted in David S McLellan *Dean Acheson: The State Department Years* (1976).

46 You can't argue with a river, it is going to flow. You can dam it up...put it to useful purposes...deflect it, but you can't argue with it.
On the fruitlessness of keeping Russian fishermen from waters that should be off limits. Quoted in David S McLellan *Dean Acheson: The State Department Years* (1976).

47 A memorandum is written not to inform the reader but to protect the writer.
1977 In the *Wall Street Journal*, 8 Sep.

48 The Canadians seem to be held together with string and safety pins.
Quoted in David S McLellan and David C Acheson (eds) *Among Friends: Personal Letters of Dean Gooderham Acheson* (1980).

49 Trust him as much as you would a rattlesnake with a silencer on its rattle.
1980 Advice to President Truman on J Edgar Hoover. Quoted in David S McLellan and David C Acheson (eds) *Among Friends: Personal Letters of Dean Gooderham Acheson* (1980).

50 How gently, wisely, and justly G M Young deals with him. That is not the way to write biography.
Collected in David S McClellan and David C Acheson (eds) *Among Friends: Personal Letters of Dean Gooderham Acheson* (1980). On Young's biography *Stanley Baldwin* (1952).

51 Homage to plain dumb luck.
Of the effectiveness of the US blockade of Soviet ships bringing missiles to Cuba. Quoted in Walter Isaacson and Evan Thomas *The Wise Men* (1986).

52 The Iraqi is really not whacky
Toady, perhaps, even tacky.
When they gave *him* the word
He gave *us* the bird
And joined with the Arabs, by cracky!
Limerick written during dull meeting of Foreign Ministers. Quoted in Walter Isaacson and Evan Thomas *The Wise Men* (1986).

53 Charm never made a rooster.
Of poorly-organized attempts to maintain peace by good intentions. Quoted in James B Reston *Deadline* (1991).

54 It is just as full of propaganda as a dog is full of fleas. In fact, I say it's all fleas and no dog.
Of Russian Foreign Minister Andre Vishinsky's proposal that the US should withdraw from postwar Europe. Quoted in James B Reston *Deadline* (1991).

55 With a nation, as with a boxer, one of the greatest assurances of safety is to add reach to power.
Alluding to US bases in Europe. Quoted in James B Reston *Deadline* (1991).

56 If the best minds in the world had set out to find us the worst possible location in the world to fight this damnable war, politically and militarily, the unanimous choice would have been Korea.
On the Korean War. Quoted in Joseph Goulden *Korea* (1992).

Ackerman, Diane 1948–

US poet and writer. Her poetry is published in many journals and books, which include *Wife of Light* (1978) and *Lady Faustus* (1983). She has published non-fiction and was a staff writer at the *New Yorker* from 1988 to 1994.

57 An occasion, catalyst, or tripwire...permits the poet to reach into herself and haul up whatever nugget of the human condition distracts her at the moment, something that can't be reached in any other way.
Quoted in the *New York Times*, 10 Mar 1991.

58 No matter how politely one says it, we owe our existence to the farts of blue-green algae.
2004 *An Alchemy of Mind: The Marvel and Mystery of the Brain.*

59 And yet, words are the passkeys to our souls. Without them, we can't really share the enormity of our lives.
2011 *One Hundred Names for Love: A Stroke, a Marriage, and the Language of Healing.*

Ackroyd, Peter 1949–

English novelist, biographer and critic. He has written a number of erudite and playful novels and scholarly biographies, including studies of Dickens and T S Eliot.

60 And the smell of the library was always the same—the musty odour of old clothes mixed with the keener scent of unwashed bodies, creating what the chief librarian had once described as 'the steam of the social soup'.
1987 *Chatterton*, ch.5.

61 No poet is ever completely lost. He has the secret of his childhood safe with him, like some secret cave in which he can kneel. And, when we read his poetry, we can join him there.
1987 *Chatterton*, ch.10.

62 He had a fear of the dead, and of all inanimate things, rising up around him to claim him; it is the fear of the pre-eminently solitary child and solitary man.
1990 Of Charles Dickens. *Dickens*, prologue.

63 Is it possible to be nostalgic about old fears?
1992 *English Music*, ch.1.

64 Yes, I have inherited the past because I have acknowledged it at last... And, now that I have come to

understand it, I no longer need to look back.
1992 *English Music*, ch.19.

65 Under the force of the imagination, nature itself is changed.
2008 *The Casebook of Victor Frankenstein.*

66 Suffering is intrinsic to human existence. There is no joy without its attendant pain.
2008 *The Casebook of Victor Frankenstein.*

67 Never be curious. It is the path to perdition.
2008 *The Casebook of Victor Frankenstein.*

68 Who can give more heat to the fire, or joy to heaven, or pain to hell? A ring upon a nun is like a ring in a sow's nose. Your best friend is still alive. Who is that? You. The sun is none the worse for shining on a dunghill. He must needs swim that is borne up to the chin. An hour's cold will suck out seven years of heat.
2011 *Foundation: The History of England from Its Earliest Beginnings to the Tudors.*

Acton, John Emerich Edward Dalberg, 1st Baron Acton of Aldenham 1834–1902

English historian. He sat as a Liberal MP (1859–64) and was created baron by Gladstone in 1869. In 1895 he was appointed Professor of Modern History at Cambridge.

69 Power tends to corrupt, and absolute power corrupts absolutely. Great men are almost always bad men. There is no worse heresy than that the office sanctifies the holder of it.
1887 Letter to Bishop Mandell Creighton, 3 Apr.

Adamov, Arthur 1908–70

Russian-born French playwright. A leading exponent of the Theatre of the Absurd, he was the author of such plays as *Le Professeur Taranne* (1953), *Le Ping Pong* (1955) and *Le Printemps '71* (1961).

70 The reason why Absurdist plays take place in No Man's Land with only two characters is primarily financial.
1962 Speech at Edinburgh, 13 Sep.

Adams, Abigail 1744–1818

US first lady, wife of President John Adams, and early feminist.

71 In the new code of laws which I suppose it will be necessary for you to make I desire you would remember the ladies, and be more generous and favourable to them than your ancestors. Do not put such unlimited power into the hands of the husbands. Remember all men would be tyrants if they could.
1776 Letter to John Adams, 31 Mar.

72 It is not in the still calm of life, or the repose of a pacific station, that great characters are formed... Great necessities call out great virtues.
1780 Letter to John Quincy Adams, 19 Jan.

Adams, Arthur Henry 1872–1936

New Zealand-born journalist, poet and playwright, whose first collection was *Maoriland: and Other Verses* (1899). His *London Streets* (1906) is a colonist's portrayal of the city. He returned to Sydney, Australia, as editor of *Bulletin* and *Lone Hand*.

73 The land lies desolate and stripped;
Across its waste has thinly strayed
A tattered host of eucalypt.
From whose gaunt uniform is made
A ragged penury of shade.
1913 'Written in Australia', in *The Collected Verses of Arthur H Adams.*

Adams, Charles Francis 1807–86

US diplomat and writer, congressman from Massachusetts (1858–61) and Minister to Britain during the American Civil War (1861–8).

74 It would be superfluous in me to point out to your lordship that this is war.
1863 Despatch to Earl Russell during the Civil War, 5 Sep. Quoted in C F Adams *Charles Francis Adams* (1900), ch.17.

Adams, Douglas Noël 1952–2001

English novelist and scriptwriter. His radio serial *The Hitch-Hiker's Guide to the Galaxy* (1978–80) was a cult success, and it and its sequels were also successful novels.

75 Don't Panic.
1979 *The Hitch-Hiker's Guide to the Galaxy*, preface. These words are said to be written in large friendly letters on the cover of the Guide.

76 The Answer to the Great Question Of...Life, the Universe and Everything...Is...Forty-two.
1979 *The Hitch-Hiker's Guide to the Galaxy*, ch.27.

77 'The first ten million years were the worst,' said Marvin, 'and the second ten million years, they were the worst too. The third ten million I didn't enjoy at all. After that I went into a bit of a decline.'
1980 Marvin, the paranoid android. *The Restaurant at the End of the Universe*, ch.18.

78 So Long, and Thanks for All the Fish.
1984 Title of novel.

79 It can hardly be a coincidence that no language on earth has ever produced the expression 'as pretty as an airport'.
1988 *The Long Dark Tea-Time of the Soul*, ch.1.

80 Kate's spirits sank to the very bottom of her being and began to prowl around there making a low growling noise.
1988 *The Long Dark Tea-Time of the Soul*, ch.1.

81 I love deadlines. I love the whooshing noise they make as they go by.
2001 In *The Guardian*, 14 May.

Adams, Gerry (Gerard) 1948–

Northern Irish politician. He has been President of Sinn Féin since 1983 (Vice-President 1978–83).

82 We want him to be the last British Prime Minister with jurisdiction in Ireland.
1997 On Tony Blair. In *The Irish Times*, 8 Oct.

83 Peace cannot be built on exclusion. That has been the price of the last 30 years.
1998 In the *Daily Telegraph*, 11 Apr.

84 The hardest negotiation is always with your own side.
2003 In *The Observer*, 9 Nov.

Adams, Henry Brooks 1838–1918

US historian, son of Charles Francis Adams and grandson of John Quincy Adams. His historical works include *Mont Saint Michel and Chartres* (1904), and his autobiography *The Education of Henry Adams* (published privately 1907, publicly 1918) won the 1919 Pulitzer Prize.

85 Some day science may have the existence of mankind in its power and the human race commit suicide by blowing up the race.
   1862 Letter to Charles Francis Adams, Jr, 11 Apr.

86 Politics, as a practice, whatever its professions, has always been the systematic organization of hatreds.
   1907 *The Education of Henry Adams*, ch.1.

87 All experience is an arch to build on.
   1907 *The Education of Henry Adams*, ch.6.

88 A friend in power is a friend lost.
   1907 *The Education of Henry Adams*, ch.7.

89 These questions of taste, of feeling, of inheritance, need no settlement. Everyone carries his own inch-rule of taste, and amuses himself by applying it, triumphantly, wherever he travels.
   1907 *The Education of Henry Adams*, ch.12.

90 Chaos often breeds life, when order breeds habit.
   1907 *The Education of Henry Adams*, ch.16.

91 A teacher affects eternity; he can never tell where his influence stops.
   1907 *The Education of Henry Adams*, ch.20, 'Failure'.

92 One friend in a lifetime is much; two are many; three are hardly possible. Friendship needs a certain parallelism of life, a community of thought, a rivalry of aim.
   1907 *The Education of Henry Adams*, ch.20.

93 What one knows is, in youth, of little moment; they know enough who know how to learn.
   1907 *The Education of Henry Adams*, ch.21.

94 He had often noticed that six months' oblivion amounts to newspaper death, and that resurrection is rare. Nothing is easier, if a man wants it, than rest, profound as the grave.
   1907 *The Education of Henry Adams*, ch.22.

95 Practical politics consists in ignoring the facts.
   1907 *The Education of Henry Adams*, ch.22.

96 American art, like the American language and American education, was as far as possible sexless.
   1907 *The Education of Henry Adams*, ch.25, 'The Dynamo and the Virgin'.

97 No one means all he says, and yet very few say all they mean, for words are slippery and thought is viscous.
   1907 *The Education of Henry Adams*, ch.31, 'The Grammar of Science'.

Adams, John   1735–1826

US statesman and second President, a leader of resistance to Britain and central figure in the Declaration of Independence (1776). He became the first US Vice-President under Washington (1789), and later President (1796–1800).

98 A government of laws, and not of men.
   1774 In the *Boston Gazette*, no.7. The phrase was later incorporated into the Massachusetts Constitution (1780).

99 I agree with you that in politics the middle way is none at all.
   1776 Letter to Horatio Gates, 23 Mar.

1 The second day of July 1776 will be the most memorable epoch in the history of America. It ought to be solemnised with pomp and parade, with shows, games, sports, guns, bells, bonfires and illuminations from one end of this continent to the other—from this time forward, for ever more.
   1776 Letter to his wife, 3 Jul, on the vote of Congress for independence from Britain.

2 You and I ought not to die before we have explained ourselves to each other.
   1813 Letter to Thomas Jefferson, 15 Jul.

3 What a poor, ignorant, malicious, short-sighted, crapulous mass is Tom Paine's common sense.
   1819 Letter to Thomas Jefferson, 22 Jun, referring to the Republican's treatise on independence entitled *Common Sense*.

Adams, John Quincy   1767–1848

US politician and sixth President. Ambassador to Europe and Secretary of State under Monroe, he negotiated the acquisition of Florida from Spain, before becoming President (1825). He failed to win re-election but continued to oppose slavery as a congressman.

4 *Fiat justitia, pereat coelum*. My toast would be, may our country be always successful, but whether successful or otherwise, always right.
   1816 Letter to John Adams, 1 Aug.
   ▶ See Decatur 268:64, Ferdinand I 332:73.

5 The American continents, by the free and independent condition that they have assumed and maintain, are henceforth not to be considered as subjects for future colonisation by any European powers... In the wars of the European powers in matters relating to ourselves, we have never taken any part; nor does it comport with our policy to do so.
   1823 The Monroe Doctrine, 2 Dec.

6 I inhabit a weak, frail, decayed tenement; battered by the winds and broken in on by the storms, and, from all I can learn, the landlord does not intend to repair.
   1848 Attributed, as he lay on his deathbed. Quoted in Clifton Fadiman *The Faber Book of Anecdotes* (1985).

Adams, Judge Richard   1846–1908

Irish judge. After a Law degree, he became a journalist in Cork until he was called to the Irish Bar in 1873. From 1894 he was Judge of the County Court, Limerick.

7 Look here, sir, tell me no more unnecessary lies. Such lies as your attorney advised you are necessary for the presentation of your fraudulent case I will listen to though I shall decide against you whatever you swear, but if you tell me another unnecessary lie, I'll put you in the dock.
   Presiding over Limerick County Court. Quoted in A M Sullivan *Old Ireland*.

8 You have been acquitted by a Limerick jury, and you may now leave the dock without any other stain upon your character.
   Quoted in Maurice Healy *The Old Munster Circuit*.

Adams, Samuel   1722–1803

Political leader in the American Revolution, who signed the Declaration of Independence. Clerk of the lower house of Massachusetts legislature, he was involved in the Boston Tea Party.

9 What a glorious morning is this.
   1775 On hearing gunfire at Lexington, 19 Apr. Quoted in J K Hosmer *Samuel Adams* (1886), ch.19.

Adams, Scott 1957–
US cartoonist and satirist, creator of the *Dilbert* comic strip.

10 Give a man a fish, and you'll feed him for a day. Teach a man to fish, and he'll buy a funny hat. Talk to a hungry man about fish, and you're a consultant.
2008 *Stick to Drawing Comics, Monkey Brain!: Cartoonist Ignores Helpful Advice.*

11 If an economist uses a complicated model to predict just about anything, you can ignore it. By analogy, a doctor can't tell you the exact date of your death in fifty years. But if a doctor tells you to eat less and exercise more, that's good advice even if you later get hit by a bus. Along those same lines, economists can give useful general advice on the economy, even if you know there will be surprises.
2008 Press release, 10 Sep.

12 Few things are as destructive and limiting as a worldview that assumes people are mostly rational.
2013 *How to Fail at Almost Everything and Still Win Big: Kind of the Story of My Life.*

Adamson, Harold 1906–80
US lyricist.

13 Comin' in on a wing and a prayer.
1943 Title of song. The phrase was taken from the words of a fighter pilot from his battered jet to ground control.

Adcock, (Karen) Fleur 1934–
New Zealand poet who settled in Britain in 1963. Her works include *The Eye of the Hurricane* (1964), *Selected Poems* (1983), *Poems 1960–2000* (2000) and *Dragon Talk* (2006).

14 Do not ask me for charity now:
Go away until your bones are clean.
1983 *Selected Poems,* 'Advice to a Discarded Lover'.

Addison, Joseph 1672–1719
English poet, playwright and essayist. After a Grand Tour of Europe (1699–1704), he entered Parliament as a Whig in 1708. He contributed numerous essays to the *Tatler* and was co-founder with Richard Steele of the *The Spectator* (1711).

15 Music, the greatest good that mortals know,
And all of heaven we have below.
1694 'A Song for St Cecilia's Day'.

16 For wheresoe'er I turn my ravished eyes,
Gay gilded scenes and shining prospects rise,
Poetic fields encompass me around,
And still I seem to tread on classic ground.
1704 *A Letter from Italy.*

17 A painted meadow, or a purling stream.
1704 *A Letter from Italy.*

18 'Twas then great Marlbro's mighty soul was proved.
1705 *The Campaign,* l.279.

19 And, pleased th' Almighty's orders to perform,
Rides in the whirl-wind, and directs the storm.
1705 *The Campaign,* l.291–2.

20 And those who paint 'em truest praise 'em most.
1705 *The Campaign,* l.476.

21 This republic has been much more powerful than it is at present, as it is still likelier, to sink than increase in its dominions.
1705 On Venice. *Remarks on Several parts of Italy.*

22 I remember when our whole island was shaken with an earthquake some years ago, there was an impudent mountebank who sold pills which (as he told the country people) were very good against an earthquake.
1710 In *The Tatler,* no.240, 21 Oct.

23 A reader seldom peruses a book with pleasure until he knows whether the writer of it be a black man or a fair man, of a mild or choleric disposition, married or a bachelor.
1711 In *The Spectator,* no.1, 1 Mar.

24 Thus I live in the world rather as a Spectator of mankind, than as one of the species, by which means I have made myself a speculative statesman, soldier, merchant, and artisan, without ever meddling with any practical part of life.
1711 In *The Spectator,* no.1, 1 Mar.

25 Nothing is capable of being well set to music that is not nonsense.
1711 In *The Spectator,* no.18.

26 A perfect tragedy is the noblest production of human nature.
1711 In *The Spectator,* no.39.

27 In all thy humours, whether grave or mellow,
Thou'rt such a touchy, testy, pleasant fellow;
Hast so much wit, and mirth, and spleen about thee,
There is no living with thee, nor without thee.
1711 In *The Spectator,* no.68, 18 May.

28 As Sir Roger is landlord to the whole congregation, he keeps them in very good order, and will suffer nobody to sleep in it [the church] besides himself; for if by chance he has been surprised into a short nap at sermon, upon recovering out of it, he stands up, and looks about him; and if he sees anybody else nodding, either wakes them himself, or sends his servant to them.
1711 In *The Spectator,* no.112, 9 Jul.

29 Sir Roger told them, with the air of a man who would not give his judgement rashly, that much might be said on both sides.
1711 In *The Spectator,* no.122, 20 Jul.

30 It was a saying of an ancient philosopher, which I find some of our writers have ascribed to Queen Elizabeth, who perhaps might have taken occasion to repeat it, that a good face is a letter of recommendation.
1711 In *The Spectator,* no.221, 13 Nov.

31 I have often thought, says Sir Roger, it happens very well that Christmas should fall out in the Middle of Winter.
1712 In *The Spectator,* no.269, 8 Jan.

32 A true critic ought to dwell rather upon excellencies than imperfections, to discover the concealed beauties of a writer, and communicate to the world such things as are worth their observation.
1712 In *The Spectator,* no.291, 2 Feb.

33 These widows, Sir, are the most perverse creatures in the world.
1712 In *The Spectator,* no.335, 25 Mar.

34 Mirth is short and transient, cheerfulness fixed and permanent... Mirth is like a flash of lightning that breaks through a gloom of clouds, and glitters for a

moment: cheerfulness keeps up a kind of day-light in the mind, and fills it with a steady and perpetual serenity.
1712 In The Spectator, no.381, 17 May.

35 The Knight in the triumph of his heart made several reflections on the greatness of the British Nation; as, that one Englishman could beat three Frenchmen; that we could never be in danger of Popery so long as we took care of our fleet; that the Thames was the noblest river in Europe; that London Bridge was a greater piece of work than any of the Seven Wonders of the World; with many other honest prejudices which naturally cleave to the heart of a true Englishman.
1712 In The Spectator, no.383, 20 May.

36 Wide and undetermined prospects are as pleasing to the fancy, as the speculations of eternity or infinitude are to the understanding.
1712 In The Spectator, no.412, 23 Jun.

37 An account of it would have been thought fabulous, were not the Wall itself extant.
1712 Commenting on the Great Wall of China, The Spectator, no.415, 26 Jun.

38 Through all Eternity to Thee
A joyful Song I'll raise,
For oh! Eternity's too short
To utter all thy Praise.
1712 In The Spectator, no.453, 9 Aug.

39 We have in England a particular bashfulness in every thing that regards religion.
1712 In The Spectator, no.458, 15 Aug.

40 The spacious firmament on high,
With all the blue ethereal sky,
And spangled heavens, a shining frame,
Their great Original proclaim.
Th' unwearied sun from day to day
Does his Creator's power display;
And publishes to every land
The work of an Almighty hand.
1712 In The Spectator, no.465, 23 Aug.

41 In Reason's ear they all rejoice,
And utter forth a glorious voice,
For ever singing, as they shine:
'The hand that made us is divine.'
1712 In The Spectator, no.465, 23 Aug.

42 A woman seldom asks advice before she has bought her wedding clothes.
1712 In The Spectator, no.475, 4 Sep.

43 Our disputants put me in mind of the skuttle fish, that when he is unable to extricate himself, blackens all the water about him, till he becomes invisible.
1712 In The Spectator, no.476, 5 Sept.

44 If we may believe our logicians, man is distinguished from all other creatures by the faculty of laughter.
1712 In The Spectator, no.494, 26 Sep.

45 'Tis not in mortals to command success,
But we'll do more, Sempronius; we'll deserve it.
1713 Cato, act 1, sc.2, l.43–4.

46 'Tis pride, rank pride, and haughtiness of soul;
I think the Romans call it stoicism.
1713 Cato, act 1, sc.4, l.82–3.

47 Were you with these, my prince, you'd soon forget
The pale, unripened beauties of the north.
1713 Cato, act 1, sc.4, l.134–5.

48 The woman that deliberates is lost.
1713 Cato, act 4, sc.1, l.31.

49 Curse on his virtues! they've undone his country. Such popular humanity is treason.
1713 Cato, act 4, sc.1, l.205–6.

50 What a pity is it
That we can die but once to serve our country!
1713 Cato, act 4, sc.1, l.258–9.

51 Content thyself to be obscurely good.
When vice prevails, and impious men bear sway,
The post of honour is a private station.
1713 Cato, act 4, sc.1, l.319–21.

52 It must be so—Plato, thou reason'st well!—
Else whence this pleasing hope, this fond desire,
This longing after immortality?
Or whence this secret dread, and inward horror,
Of falling into naught? Why shrinks the soul
Back on herself, and startles at destruction
'Tis the divinity that stirs within us;
'Tis heaven itself, that points out an hereafter,
And intimates eternity to man.
Eternity! thou pleasing, dreadful thought!
1713 Cato, act 5, sc.1, l.1–10.

53 From hence, let fierce contending nations know
What dire effects from civil discord flow.
1713 Cato, act 5, sc.1, closing words.

54 'We are always doing,' says he, 'something for Posterity, but I would fain see Posterity do something for us.'
1714 In The Spectator no.583, 20 Aug.

55 There is sometimes a greater judgement shewn in deviating from the rules of art, than in adhering to them; and…there is more beauty in the works of a great genius who is ignorant of all the rules of art, than in the works of a little genius, who not only knows but scrupulously observes them.
1714 In The Spectator, no.592, 10 Sep.

56 I should think myself a very bad woman, if I had done what I do for a farthing less.
1716 The Drummer, act 1, sc.1.

57 See in what peace a Christian can die.
1719 Last words, to his stepson Lord Warwick. Quoted in Edward Young Conjectures on Original Composition (1759).

58 Hunting is not a proper employment for a thinking man.
Quoted in Colin Jarman The Guinness Dictionary of Sports Quotations (1990).

Ade, George 1866–1944
US humorist and dramatist.

59 R-E-M-O-R-S-E!
Those dry Martinis did the work for me;
Last night at twelve I felt immense,
Today I feel like thirty cents.
My eyes are blurred, my coppers hot,
I'll try to eat, but I cannot.
It is no time for mirth and laughter,
The cold, grey dawn of the morning after.
1903 The Sultan of Sulu, act 2.

Adele (Adele Laurie Blue Adkins) 1988–
English singer and songwriter.

60 I don't make music for eyes, I make music for ears.
   2011 In *Rolling Stone*, 28 Apr.

Adelman, Kenneth Lee 1946–
US political scientist, director of the US Arms Control and Disarmament Agency (1983–8). His works include *The Great Universal Embrace: Arms Summitry—a skeptic's account* (1989).

61 The history of arms control is a history of great visions eventually mugged by reality.
   1986 In *Newsweek*, 1 Dec.

Adenauer, Konrad 1876–1967
German statesman. Dismissed by the Nazis (1933), he founded the Christian Democratic Union (1945) and became first Chancellor of the Federal Republic of Germany (1949–63).

62 We must free ourselves from thinking in terms of nation states. The countries of western Europe are no longer in a position to protect themselves individually. Not one of them is any longer in a position to salvage Europe's culture.
   1953 Speech, May.

Adiga, Aravind 1974–
Indian-Australian writer and journalist. His first novel, *The White Tiger*, won the 2008 Man Booker Prize.

63 See, the poor dream all their lives of getting enough to eat and looking like the rich. And what do the rich dream of? Losing weight and looking like the poor.
   2008 *The White Tiger*.

64 It's amazing. The moment you show cash, everyone knows your language.
   2008 *The White Tiger*.

65 The story of a poor man's life is written on his body, in a sharp pen.
   2008 *The White Tiger*.

66 A man's past keeps growing, even when his future has come to a full stop.
   2011 *Last Man in Tower*.

Adler, Jerry 1949–
US journalist, a senior editor at *Newsweek*.

67 She…happens to stick out a foot just as history is rushing by.
   1988 Of Fawn Hall, the secretary who helped Col Oliver North to dispose of top-secret papers, 'the archetype of the Accidental Celebrity'. In *Newsweek*, 9 Mar.

68 Norman Rockwell, the Brueghel of the 20th century bourgeoisie, the Holbein of Jell-O ads and magazine covers; by common assent, the most American artist of all.
   1993 On the opening of the Norman Rockwell Museum at Stockbridge, Massachusetts. In *Newsweek*, 12 Apr.

69 The widespread belief that Yuppies as a class would perish from Brie-cheese poisoning turned out to be over-optimistic.
   1995 'The Rise of the Overclass', in *Newsweek*, 31 Jul.

Adler, Larry (Lawrence Cecil) 1914–2001
US musician and virtuoso on the harmonica. He emigrated to Britain after being blacklisted in the US.

70 His first choice had been Yehudi Menuhin; he was lucky he got me. Menuhin on the mouth-organ is a mess.
   1984 On Henry Koster's casting for the film *Music for Millions* (1944).

Adler, Polly 1900–62
US writer.

71 A House is not a Home.
   1954 Title of a book.

Adorno, Theodor 1903–69
German social philosopher and musicologist, who emigrated to the US in 1934. His *Negative Dialectics* (1966) expounds his complex theories, but he also wrote more accessible mass-culture works.

72 In psychoanalysis nothing is true except the exaggerations.
   1966 *Negative Dialectics*.

Aelius Aristides AD 117–189
Greek orator. He spent much of his life giving rhetorical demonstrations throughout Asia Minor. He is best known for his encomium of Rome and his 'Sacred Teachings', an account of his dreams while seeking a cure in the temple of Asclepius.

73 As the character is, such is the speech.
   Pros Platona Peri Rhetorikes, bk.2, 1.392.

St Aelred of Riveaulx d.1167
English writer, historian and Cistercian monk. Raised at the court of David I of Scotland, he became Abbot of Revesby (1143) and Riveaulx (1147). He aided the England–France alliance in support of Pope Alexander II against Emperor Frederick III.

74 *Inveni fateor in rege monachum, claustrum in curia, in palatio monasterii disciplinam.*
   I confess that I found in the king a monk, in the court a cloister, and in the palace the discipline of a monastery.
   ?c.1160 Lament for David I, King of Scotland. Quoted in John Fordoun *Chronicle of Scotland* (c.1384), bk.5, ch.43.

Aeschylus c.525–c.456 BC
Greek dramatist, who served in the Athenian army at Marathon (490 BC) and probably in the navy at Salamis (480 BC). He won 13 first prizes in the dramatic contests of Athens from 484 to 458 BC, but only seven of his many works have survived.

75 Ship-destroyer, man-destroyer, city-destroyer.
   Of Helen. *Agamemnon*, 1.689.

76 Unworthy was what he did to her, worthy was what he suffered.
   Clytemnestra speaks of Agamemnon's sacrifice of their daughter Iphigeneia. *Agamemnon*, 1.1527–8 (translated by H Lloyd-Jones).

77 For by the will of the gods Fate hath held sway since ancient days.
   Persae, 1.102 (translated by H Weir Smyth).

78 Now you battle for your all.
   Persae, 1.402–5 (translated by H Weir Smyth).

79 Once to die is better than length of days in sorrow without end.
   Prometheus Vinctus, 1.750–1.

80 It's a man's job—no place for women's plans here!—what lies outside. Stay home and cause no trouble.
Septem contra Thebas, l.200–1 (translated by C M Dawson).

81 Obedience, you know, is Good Luck's mother, wedded to Salvation, they say.
Septem contra Thebas, l.224–5 (translated by C M Dawson).

82 Remember to be submissive, thou art an alien, a fugitive, and in need.
Supplices, l.202 (translated by H Weir Smyth).

Agassi, Andre 1970–

A former world no. 1 US tennis player.

83 You expect to leave the dance with the ones you came with.
2003 On his surprise at being the last star of his generation still playing. Quoted in *The Independent*, 29 Dec.

84 Now that I've won a slam, I know something very few people on earth are permitted to know. A win doesn't feel as good as a loss feels bad, and the good feeling doesn't last as long as the bad. Not even close.
2009 *Open*.

85 Big dreams, are so damn tiring.
2009 *Open*.

Agassiz, (Jean) Louis (Rodolphe) 1807–73

Swiss-born US zoologist and geologist. A professor of natural history at Neuchâtel, he came to the US (1846) to teach at Harvard University. His works include a study of fossil fish and a *Natural History of the United States* (1857–62).

86 The student must remember, for his consolation…that his failures are almost as important to the cause of science and to those who follow him in the same road, as his successes. It is much to know what we cannot do in any given direction—the first step, indeed, toward the accomplishment of what we can do.
1896 *Geological Sketches*.

87 The study of nature is interwoven with the highest mind. You should never trifle with nature.
Attributed.

Agate, James 1877–1947

English theatre critic. He wrote for the *Sunday Times* from 1923 until his death and also published a notable nine-part autobiography, *Ego* (1935–47).

88 Happy is the country which has no history, and happier still is that musical comedy about which one can find nothing to say.
1920 In the *Sunday Times*.

89 I don't know very much, but what I do know I know better than anybody, and I don't want to argue about it. I know what I think about an actor or an actress, and am not interested in what anybody else thinks. My mind is not a bed to be made and re-made.
1943 Journal entry, 9 Jun. Collected in *Ego 6* (1944).

90 Long experience has taught me that in England nobody goes to the theatre unless he or she has bronchitis.
Attributed.

91 She had a heart as big as Waterloo Station.
Of Marie Lloyd. Attributed.

Agawa, Hiroyuki 1920–

Japanese novelist. His *Citadel in Spring* (1949) is the semi-autobiographical story of a young man fighting on the losing side of World War II. Much of the story is set in Hiroshima, the city of his birth.

92 It quickly swelled into the shape of a gigantic question mark, the middle of which was a vivid crimson, and as this thunderhead-like column billowed upward through the sky, she could see a red ball of fire at its core.
1949 Of the atomic explosion, Hiroshima. *Haru no shiro* (*Citadel in Spring*, translated by Lawrence Rogers), ch.9.

Agnew, Spiro T(heodore) 1918–96

US Republican politician. As liberal Governor of Maryland he introduced anti-racial-discrimination legislation, but by 1968 had become much more conservative. He was Nixon's running mate in the 1968 election, and Vice-President (1969–73).

93 To some extent, if you've seen one city slum, you've seen them all.
1968 Election campaign speech, Detroit, 18 Oct.

94 A spirit of national masochism prevails, encouraged by an effete corps of impudent snobs who characterize themselves as intellectuals.
1969 Of media pundits. Speech, New Orleans, 19 Oct.

95 In the United States today we have more than our fair share of the nattering nabobs of negativism. They have formed their own Four H Club—the hopeless, hysterical, hypochondriacs of history.
1970 Of media pundits. Speech, San Diego, 11 Sep.

96 I was…one of the worst complications he could have had.
1980 On the effect of his no-contest plea to income-tax evasion and subsequent resignation upon Richard M Nixon. *Go Quietly or Else*.

Aguirre y Gil de Biedma, Countess of Bornos, Grandee of Spain, Esperanza 1952–

Spanish politician and former President of Madrid. In 1999 she became the first woman to serve as President of the Senate and Minister of Education and Culture in Spanish democratic history.

97 When socialism comes through the door, employment jumps out the window.
2011 In *La Razon*, 6 May.

Agustini, Delmira 1886–1914

Uruguayan poet, who was murdered by her estranged husband, who then committed suicide. Her bold sincerity and impassioned lyrics rank her among the most outstanding early modernist poets.

98 *Por todos los senderos de la noche han venido
a llorar en mi lecho.
¡Fueron tantos, son tantos!
Yo no sé cuáles viven, yo no sé cuál ha muerto.
Me lloraré a mí misma para llorarlos todos.*
They have come from all of night's pathways
to cry in my bed.
They were so many, they are so many!
I don't know who lives, I don't know who has died.
I'll cry for myself so that I can cry for all.
1924 *El rosario de Eros*, 'Mis amores' ('My lovers').

Ahmadinejad, Mahmoud 1956–

Iranian politician. He was elected President of the Islamic Republic of Iran in 2005 and re-elected in 2009, remaining in office until 2013. He attracted criticism at home and abroad for his controversial economic reforms and hostile foreign policy.

99 You cannot wash blood with blood.
2009 In *Newsweek*, 5 Oct.

St Aidan c.600–651

Irish monk, known as the Apostle of Northumbria. He was summoned from Iona by King Oswald to evangelize the north and established a community on Lindisfarne. He died in the church he had built in Bamburgh.

1 *Nam tibi carior est ille filius equae quam ille filius Dei?*
Is this son of a mare dearer to you, then, than that son of God?
c.645 To King Oswin of Deira, who had objected when Aidan gave to a beggar a horse which he had received as a gift from the king. Quoted in Bede *Historia Ecclesiastica Gentis Anglorum* (731), bk.3, ch.14.

Aitken, Jonathan William Patrick 1942–

British Conservative politician. In 1995 he sued *The Guardian* for libel following articles relating to his dealings with Saudi arms dealers. In 1999 he served a prison sentence for perjury after it was revealed he had lied repeatedly.

2 If it falls to me to start a fight to cut out the cancer of bent and twisted journalism in our country with the simple sword of truth and the trusting shield of British fair play, so be it.
1995 Press statement, 10 Apr.

Ai Weiwei 1957–

Chinese artist and political activist. In 2011 his detention on unspecified charges for 81 days by the Chinese government led to worldwide protests.

3 A society that has no ideals, that discards the principles of humanitarianism, that abandons the fundamental rights and dignity of humanity, can only survive by denying truth, fairness and justice.
2009 In *The Guardian*, 25 May.

4 A small act is worth a million thoughts.
2009 In *GlobalPost*, 23 Jun.

5 If there is one who's not free, then I am not free. If there is one who suffers, then I suffer.
2009 On Twitter, 23 Aug.

6 No outdoor sports can be more elegant than throwing stones at autocracy; no melees can be more exciting than those in cyberspace.
2010 On Twitter, 10 Mar.

7 If a nation cannot face its past, it has no future.
2011 In *Der Spiegel*, 21 Nov.

8 To express yourself needs a reason, but expressing yourself is the reason.
2011 In *Time*, 14 Dec.

9 I don't see myself as a dissident artist. I see them as a dissident government!
2012 On Twitter, 25 Jan.

10 The government computer has one button: delete.
2012 Attributed by Qichen Zhang in blog 'Ai Weiwei Says Censorship in China Will Ultimately Fail', 18 Apr.

Akers, John Fellows 1934–2014

American businessman. He joined IBM as a sales trainee in 1960 and rose to become Chairman 1986–93.

11 Each school can, once again, become what it was always meant to be—a building that has four walls with tomorrow inside.
1991 In the *Wall Street Journal*, 20 Mar.

Akihito 1933–

Emperor of Japan. He acceded to the throne in 1989.

12 I hope from the bottom of my heart that the people will, hand in hand, treat each other with compassion and overcome these difficult times.
2011 Television address following an earthquake, tsunami and nuclear crisis that devastated a large part of Japan.

Akins, Zoë 1886–1958

US poet and playwright. Her works include the play *The Greeks Had a Word for It* (1930) and the Pulitzer Prize-winning stage adaptation of Edith Wharton's novel *The Old Maid* (1935).

13 The Greeks Had a Word for It.
1930 Title of play.

Alain (Émile-Auguste Chartier) 1868–1951

French philosopher, writer and poet.

14 *Rien n'est plus dangereux qu'une idée, quand on n'a qu'une idée.*
Nothing is more dangerous than an idea, when you have only one idea.
1938 Propos sur la religion, no.74.

Alan of Lille also known as 'Alanus de Insulis' c.1114–1202

French writer and scholar. His major literary works include *De Planctu Natura* and *Anticlaudianus*.

15 *Omnis mundi creatura*
Quasi liber et pictura
Nobis est, et speculum.
Each creature of the world
Is as a book, a picture,
And a mirror to us.
c.1170 De Incarnatione Christi (*Rhythmus Alter*), l.1–3.

16 *Post nubila maxima, Phoebus.*
After the greatest clouds, the sun.
1175 Liber Parabolarum, ch.1, l.33.

17 *Qui jacet in terra non habet unde cadat.*
He who is lying on the ground has nowhere to fall.
1175 Liber Parabolarum, ch.2, l.18.

18 *Mille viae ducunt homines per sæcula Romam.*
Throughout the ages, a thousand roads lead to Rome.
1175 Liber Parabolarum, ch.3, l.56.

Al-Aswany, Alaa 1957–

Egyptian novelist and political activist. During the 'Arab Spring' that began in 2010 he played a leading role in the protests that led to the overthrow of the government of Hosni Mubarak.

19 Revolution is like a love story. When you are in love, you become a much better person. And when you are in revolution, you become a much better person.
2011 In *The Washington Post*, 4 Feb.

Alba, Duke of, Ferdinand Alvarez de Toledo 1508–82

Spanish soldier, made a general at 26 and Commander-in-Chief at 30. He led successful campaigns against the Netherlands and Portugal.

20 I have tamed men of iron in my day, shall I not easily crush these men of butter?
1567 On his appointment as Lieutenant-General to the Netherlands. Quoted in J L Motley *The Rise of the Dutch Republic* (1889), vol.2.

Albee, Edward Franklin, III 1928–

US dramatist, influenced by the Theatre of the Absurd, whose plays address the moral ambiguities of US middle-class life. His best-known work is *Who's Afraid of Virginia Woolf?* (1962), but *A Delicate Balance* (1966), *Seascape* (1975) and *Three Tall Women* (1991) all won Pulitzer Prizes.

21 JERRY: I have learned that neither kindness or cruelty by themselves, or independent of each other, create any effect beyond themselves.
1958 *The Zoo Story*.

22 JERRY: When you're a kid you use the cards as a substitute for a real experience, and when you're older you use real experience as a substitute for the fantasy.
1958 On pornographic playing cards. *The Zoo Story*.

23 BESSIE: I am sick of the disparity between things as they are and as they should be. I'm tired. I'm tired of the truth and I'm tired of lying about the truth.
1960 *The Death of Bessie Smith*.

24 Who's Afraid of Virginia Woolf?
1962 Title of play.

25 MARTHA: I have a fine sense of the ridiculous, but no sense of humour.
1962 *Who's Afraid of Virginia Woolf?*, act 1.

26 GEORGE: By God, you gotta have a swine to show you where the truffles are.
1962 *Who's Afraid of Virginia Woolf?*, act 2.

27 I am a Doctor. A.B....M.A....PH.D....ABMAPHID!...a wasting disease of the frontal lobes.
1962 Spoken by a college professor. *Who's Afraid of Virginia Woolf?*

28 American critics are like American universities...both have dull and half-dead faculties.
1969 Speech to the New York Cultural League. Reported in news summaries, 6 Nov.

29 People would rather sleep their way through life than stay awake for it.
Quoted in Joseph F McCrindle (ed) *Behind the Scenes* (1971).

Prince Albert 1819–61

Prince Consort of Queen Victoria, son of the Duke of Saxe-Coburg-Gotha. A patron of the arts and science, he planned the Great Exhibition of 1851. He died of typhoid.

30 I have had wealth, rank and power, but, if these were all I had, how wretched I should be.
1861 Attributed last words.

Alberti, Leon Battista 1404–72

Italian architect, musician, painter and humanist, dubbed 'Alberti the all-sided' by the historian Burckhardt. His work *De re aedificatoria* (c.1450), is considered the first modern work on architecture.

31 Perhaps the artist who seeks dignity above all in his 'historia', ought to represent very few figures; for as paucity of words imparts majesty to a prince, provided his thoughts and orders are understood, so the presence of only the strictly necessary numbers of bodies confers dignity on a picture.
1436 *On Painting* (translated by Cecil Grayson).

32 I prefer you to take as your model a mediocre sculpture rather than an excellent painting, for from painted objects we train our hand only to make a likeness, whereas from sculptures we learn to represent both likeness and correct incidence of light.
1436 *On Painting* (translated by Cecil Grayson).

33 I am really persuaded that if we were to inquire of all the Cities which...have fallen by Siege into the Power of new Masters, who it was that subjected and overcame them, they would tell you, the Architect; and that they were strong enough to have despised the armed Enemy, but not to withstand the Shocks of the Engines, the Violence of the Machines and the Force of other Instruments of War with which the Architect, distressed, demolished and ruinated them. On the contrary, they would inform you that their greatest Defense lay in the Art and Assistance of the Architect.
1451–2 *Architecttura* (translated by James Leoni, 1755).

Albright, Madeleine Korbel *originally* Marie Jana Korbelová 1937–

Czech-born US politician. She was the US Ambassador to the United Nations (1993–7) before serving as US Secretary of State (1997–2001), the first woman to be appointed to the role.

34 There is a special place in hell for women who don't help other women.
2006 Speech to Women's National Basketball Association All-Decade Team.

35 Armageddon is not a foreign policy.
2007 Speech at Harvard forum, 11 Apr.

36 The purpose of foreign policy is to persuade others to do what we want or, better yet, to want what we want.
2009 *Read My Pins*.

37 Journalists clamoured to know everything about our meetings, even though the negotiators were pledged to secrecy. To deflect questions, I told reporters that peace talks were comparable to mushrooms, thriving only in the dark.
2009 *Read My Pins*.

38 There are an awful lot of things going on that need understanding and explanation, but—to put it mildly—the world is a mess.
2014 On *Face the Nation*, CBS, 27 Jul.

Alcaeus c.620–c.580 BC

Greek lyric poet. He lived in Mytilene on Lesbos, and was a contemporary of Sappho. Only fragments remain of his ten books of *Odes*.

39 Brave men are a city's strongest tower of defence.
c.600 BC Attributed.

Alcott, Louisa May 1832–88

US writer. Her children's classic *Little Women* (1868) drew on her own experiences. She completed a sequel, *Good Wives*, in 1869 and wrote other novels, including *Little Men* (1871) and *Jo's Boys* (1886).

40 Christmas won't be Christmas without any presents.
   1868 *Little Women*, pt.1, ch.1.

41 Conceit spoils the finest genius…and the great charm of all power is modesty.
   1868 *Little Women*, pt.1, ch.7.

42 Housekeeping ain't no joke.
   1868 *Little Women*, pt.1, ch.11.

43 She had a womanly instinct that clothes possess an influence more powerful over many than the worth of character or the magic of manners.
   1869 *Little Women*, pt.2, ch.34.

44 Girls are so queer you never know what they mean. They say no when they mean yes, and drive a man out of his wits just for the fun of it.
   1869 *Little Women*, pt.2, ch.35.

45 What *do* girls do who haven't any mothers to help them through their troubles?
   1869 *Little Women*, pt.2, ch.46.

Alcuin 735–804

English cleric and scholar. In 771 Charlemagne summoned him to his court as tutor of the royal family. In 778 he became master of his old school at York. His numerous works include treatises on rhetoric, ethics, and theology.

46 *Nec audiendi qui solent dicere, vox populi, vox Dei, quum tumultuositas vulgi semper insaniae proxima sit.*
   We should not listen to those who like to affirm that the voice of the people is the voice of God, for the tumult of the masses is truly close to madness.
   800 Letter to Charlemagne.

Alda, Alan 1936–

US film and television actor.

47 The good thing about being a hypocrite is that you get to keep your values.
   2007 Television interview, 13 Sep.

Aldington, Richard *pseudonym of* Edward Godfree 1892–1962

English poet, novelist and biographer. He married fellow Imagist poet Hilda Doolittle ('H.D.'). His best-known work is the novel *Death of a Hero* (1929).

48 Patriotism is a lively sense of collective responsibility. Nationalism is a silly cock crowing on its own dunghill.
   1931 *The Colonel's Daughter*, pt.1, ch.6.

Aldiss, Brian Wilson 1925–

English science-fiction writer and novelist. Early novels include *The Hand-Reared Boy* (1970) and *A Soldier Erect* (1971), but his major work has been in science fiction, as a writer, critic and compiler of anthologies.

49 Science fiction is no more written for scientists than ghost stories are written for ghosts.
   1961 *Penguin Science Fiction*, introduction.

50 Keep violence in the mind
   Where it belongs.
   1969 *Barefoot in the Head*, 'Charteris'.

51 The feat represents immense achievement for the neotenic ape, species Homo sapiens. But behind this lie two old attributes of the ape—tribalism and inquisitiveness.
   1969 On space flight, in *The Guardian*.

52 Hubris clobbered by Nemesis.
   1975 His definition of science fiction. *Science Fiction Art*, introduction.

Aldrich, Henry 1647–1710

English cleric, Dean of Christ Church, Oxford. He designed the Peckwater Quadrangle and wrote the popular catch 'Hark, the bonny Christ-Church Bells', but is best remembered for his *Artis Logicae Compendium* (1691).

53 If all be true that I do think,
   There are five reasons why men drink,
   Good wine, a friend, or being dry,
   Or lest we should be by-and-by,
   Or any other reason why.
   1689 'Five Reasons for Drinking'.

Aldrin, Edwin E(ugene) Jr *known as* 'Buzz' 1930–

US astronaut, a crew member on Apollo 11 and the second man to walk on the moon.

54 Houston, Tranquillity Base here. The Eagle has landed.
   1969 Radio transmission from the moon, 20 Jul. These were the first words uttered by a human on the moon's surface.

55 Beautiful! Beautiful! Magnificent desolation.
   1969 Spoken as he stepped out of the Eagle to join Neil Armstrong on the first moon walk, 20 Jul.

Alembert, Jean le Rond d' 1717–83

French mathematician and philosopher. He wrote a major work on *Dynamics* (1743) and pioneered studies on the mechanics of rigid bodies, the motions of fluids and vibrating strings.

56 Day by day natural science accumulates new riches…
   The true system of the World has been recognized, developed and perfected… Everything has been discussed and analyzed, or at least mentioned.
   1759 *Elements of Philosophy*.

Alexander the Great 356–323 BC

King of Macedonia. He succeeded his father Philip at the age of 20, and set out to conquer the Persian Empire, campaigning as far as Afghanistan and the Indus valley. He died of a fever in Babylon, and his empire was divided between his generals.

57 Truly, if I were not Alexander, I would be Diogenes.
   Quoted in Plutarch *Alexander*, 14.3.
   ▶ See Diogenes of Sinope 286:2.

58 The end and object of conquest is to avoid doing the same thing as the conquered.
   Quoted in Plutarch *Alexander*, 40.2.

Alexander I 1777–1825

Tsar of Russia (1801–25), grandson of Catherine the Great. He spent much of his reign fighting Napoleon and founded the Holy Alliance (1815) to exclude the House of Bonaparte from power in France.

59 Napoleon thinks that I am a fool, but he who laughs last laughs longest.
   1808 Letter to his sister, 8 Oct.

Alexander II *known as* 'the Liberator' 1818–81

Tsar of Russia (1855–81). His reign was marked by the emancipation of the serfs (1861), political and military reform, the expansion of the Russian Empire into Asia and the defeat of Turkey (1877–8). He was assassinated.

60 It is better to abolish serfdom from above than to wait for it to abolish itself from below.
  1856 Speech, 30 Mar.

Alexander, Cecil Frances 1818–95

Irish hymnwriter and poet.

61 All things bright and beautiful,
  All creatures great and small,
  All things wise and wonderful,
  The Lord God made them all.
  1848 'All Things Bright and Beautiful'.

62 The rich man in his castle,
  The poor man at his gate,
  God made them, high or lowly,
  And ordered their estate.
  1848 'All Things Bright and Beautiful'.

63 Once in royal David's city
  Stood a lowly cattle-shed,
  Where a mother laid her baby
  In a manger for his bed.
  Mary was that mother mild,
  Jesus Christ her little child.
  1848 'Once in Royal David's City'.

64 There is a green hill far away,
  Without a city wall,
  Where the dear Lord was crucified,
  Who died to save us all.
  1848 'There is a Green Hill Far Away'

65 I bind into myself today
  The strong name of the Trinity,
  By invocation of the same
  The Three in One and One in Three.
  1889 'St Patrick's Breastplate', his translation from the Irish.

Alexander, Sir William c.1567–1640

Scottish courtier and poet.

66 The weaker sex, to piety more prone.
  1637 Of women. 'Doomsday', Fifth Hour.

Algren, Nelson 1909–81

US novelist, a journalist in Chicago and a migrant worker during the Depression. His hard-bitten, realist novels include *The Man with the Golden Arm* (1949).

67 A Walk on the Wild Side.
  1956 Title of novel.

68 Never play cards with a man called Doc. Never eat at a place called Mom's. And never, ever, no matter what else you do in your whole life, never sleep with anyone whose troubles are worse than your own.
  1956 In *Newsweek*, 2 Jul. Algren claimed that these were his only principles, taught him by 'a nice old Negro lady'.

69 I went out there for a thousand a week, and I worked Monday, and I got fired Wednesday. The guy that hired me was out of town Tuesday.
  In Malcolm Crowley (ed) *Writers at Work* (1958).

70 The hard necessity of bringing the judge on the bench down into the dock has been the peculiar responsibility of the writer in all ages of man.
  1961 Preface to reprint of *Chicago: City On The Make* (first published 1951).

Ali, Muhammad *formerly* Cassius Clay 1942–

US boxer. World heavyweight champion in 1964, he was stripped of his title after refusing military service on religious grounds (he was a Black Muslim). His title was restored in 1970, lost to Joe Frazier the next year and regained in 1974 and 1978. He retired in 1981.

71 I am the greatest!
  1962 In the *Louisville Times*, 16 Nov. This became his catchphrase.

72 Float like a butterfly, sting like a bee.
  c.1964 Of his boxing style. Quoted in G Sullivan *Cassius Clay* (1964), ch.8.

Allainval, Abbé d' 1700–53

French dramatist.

73 *L'embarras des richesses.*
  The Embarrassment of Riches.
  1726 Title of play.

Allen, Henry Southworth 1941–

US journalist. He is a feature writer and editor for the *Washington Post* (1970–).

74 They are a great tradition…gliding in and out of the corridors of power with the opulent calm of angelfish swimming through an aquarian castle.
  1989 Of presidential advisers. In the *Washington Post*, 3 Jan.

75 He long ago learned to eschew the little turf-dances of human encounter.
  1989 Of Brent Scowcroft, National Security Council adviser to George Bush. In the *Washington Post*, 3 Jan.

76 It is unlikely that anyone will write his biography, but he will be enshrined in 10,000 indexes.
  1989 Of Brent Scowcroft, National Security Council adviser to George Bush. In the *Washington Post*, 3 Jan.

77 Doesn't she know that numberless women have walked past mirrors hoping for a hint of Bacall's slinkiness?
  1994 Of Lauren Bacall at age 70. In the *Washington Post*, 27 Oct.

78 Edward Hopper is the great painter of American hell in the 20th century, the limner-laureate of the beauty, poignance, eternity and bone-ache disquietude of life.
  1995 In the *Washington Post*, 25 Jun.

Allen, Tim 1953–

US actor and comedian.

79 To infinity and beyond!
  1995 As the voice of Buzz Lightyear in *Toy Story* (1995, screenplay by Joss Whedon, Andrew Stanton, Joel Cohen, Joe Ranft, John Lasseter and Pete Docter).

80 Being wealthy when no one else is is like being the only one at the party with a drink.
  2011 In *Esquire*, Nov.

81 Sometimes you get the sense that the Creator is getting to that point of 'Yeah, we might have to reboot.'
  2011 In *Esquire*, Nov.

82 The ego is like a kid in the basement: it's best to keep him busy.
  2011 In *Esquire*, Nov.

Allen, Woody *pseudonym of* Allen Stewart Konigsberg
1935–

US film-maker and writer. He is best known for his comic films, which focus on the neuroses of urban life and relationships, and he has also published collections of essays and stories.

83 I think crime pays. The hours are good, you travel a lot.
   1969 *Take the Money and Run*.

84 Not only is there no God, but try getting a plumber on weekends.
   1969 'My Philosophy', in the *New Yorker*, 27 Dec.

85 TB or not TB, that is the congestion.
   1972 *Everything You Always Wanted to Know about Sex*.

86 The lion and the calf shall lie down together but the calf won't get much sleep.
   1974 'The Scrolls', in *The New Republic*, 31 Aug.

87 It's not that I'm afraid to die. I just don't want to be there when it happens.
   1975 *Death: A Comedy in One Act*.

88 It immediately doubles your chances for a date on Saturday night.
   1975 On bisexuality. In the *New York Times*, 1 Dec.

89 My one regret in life is that I am not someone else.
   Quoted as epigraph in Eric Lax *Woody Allen and His Comedy* (1975).

90 Death is an acquired trait.
   Quoted in Eric Lax *Woody Allen and His Comedy* (1975), ch.11.

91 I don't want to achieve immortality through my work… I want to achieve it through not dying.
   Quoted in Eric Lax *Woody Allen and His Comedy* (1975), ch.12.

92 And my parents finally realize that I'm kidnapped and they snap into action immediately: they rent out my room.
   Quoted in Eric Lax *Woody Allen and His Comedy* (1975).

93 On the plus side, death is one of the few things that can be done as easily lying down.
   1976 *Without Feathers*, 'Early Essays'.

94 Money is better than poverty, if only for financial reasons.
   1976 *Without Feathers*, 'Early Essays'.

95 That was the most fun I ever had without laughing.
   1977 Of sex. *Annie Hall* (with Marshall Brickman).

96 Don't knock masturbation. It's sex with someone I love.
   1977 *Annie Hall* (with Marshall Brickman).

97 I'm old fashioned. I don't believe in extra-marital relationships. I think people should mate for life, like pigeons or Catholics.
   1979 *Manhattan* (with Marshall Brickman).

98 More than at any other time in history, mankind faces a crossroads. One path leads to despair and utter hopelessness. The other, to total extinction. Let us pray we have the wisdom to choose correctly.
   1980 *Side Effects*, 'My Speech to the Graduates'.

99 Eighty percent of success is showing-up.
   Quoted in Thomas J Peters and Robert H Waterman *Among Friends* (1982).

1 I recently turned sixty. Practically a third of my life is over.
   Quoted in the *Observer*, 'Sayings of the Week', 10 Mar 1996.

2 Life does not imitate art. It imitates bad television.
   2000 In *The Guardian*, 31 Dec.

3 To a man standing on the shore, time passes quicker than to a man on a boat—especially if the man on the boat is with his wife.
   2007 *Mere Anarchy*.

4 My relationship with death remains the same—I'm strongly against it.
   2011 Press conference, Cannes Film Festival.

Allingham, Margery Louise 1904–66

English writer, creator of the fictional detective Albert Campion. She wrote a series of elegant and witty detective novels, such as *Flowers for the Judge* (1936) and *The China Governess* (1963).

5 Once sex rears its ugly 'ead it's time to steer clear.
   1936 *Flowers for the Judge*, ch.4.

Allingham, William 1824–89

Irish poet and editor of *Fraser's Magazine* (from 1874). His *Diary* (published 1907) is a rich recollection of Victorian literary life. Other works include *Day and Night Songs* (1855), illustrated by Dante Gabriel Rossetti and Millais.

6 Up the airy mountain,
   Down the rushy glen,
   We daren't go a-hunting,
   For fear of little men;
   Wee folk, good folk,
   Trooping all together;
   Green jacket, red cap,
   And white owl's feather!
   1850 'The Fairies'.

7 Four ducks on a pond,
   A grass-bank beyond,
   A blue sky of spring,
   White clouds on the wing;
   What a little thing
   To remember for years—
   To remember with tears!
   1888 'A Memory'.

Allsop, (Harold) Bruce 1912–2000

English architect, author, publisher and artist. His many books include *A Modern Theory of Architecture* (1977) and *Should Man Survive?* (1982).

8 For the normal business of living man is most at ease on the ground.
   1977 *A Modern Theory of Architecture*.

9 The phenomenon of architecture is a development of the phenomenon of man.
   1977 *A Modern Theory of Architecture*.

Almeida, Manuel Antônio de 1831–61

Brazilian writer, translator and journalist, killed in a shipwreck off the Brazilian coast while on a newspaper assignment. His *Memórias de um sargento de milícias* (1953) is considered the first great novel in Brazilian literature.

10 *Espiar a vida alheia, inquirir dos escravos o que se passava no interior das casas, era naquele tempo coisa tão comum e enraizada nos costumes, que ainda hoje, depois de passados tantos anos, restam grandes vestígios dêsse belo hábito.*
   Spying on other people's lives, asking slaves what was going on inside their houses was then so common and such

a part of our customs that today, after so many years have passed, we have many remnants of such a beautiful habit.
1853 *Memórias de um sargento de milícias* (*Memoirs of a Militia Sergeant*, 1959), ch.3.

Almodóvar, Pedro 1951–

Spanish film director. His first film to attain worldwide success was *Mujeres al Borde de un Ataque de Nervios* (1988, *Women on the Verge of a Nervous Breakdown*).

11 When I was 10, I expressly gave God one year to manifest himself. He didn't.
2004 In *The Guardian*, 7 May.

Alsop, Stewart 1914–74

US political columnist.

12 A fashionable gentleman who much concerns himself with the fashions of gentlemen is neither fashionable nor a gentleman.
1975 In *Newsweek*, 30 Jun.

Alther, Lisa *née* Reed 1944–

US novelist. She achieved success with her comic novel *Kinflicks* (1976), and explored the themes of personal and sexual identity in several subsequent books.

13 If this was adulthood, the only improvement she could detect in her situation was that now she could eat dessert without eating her vegetables.
1976 *Kinflicks*, ch.2.

14 There was nothing wrong with her that a vasectomy of the vocal chords wouldn't fix.
1976 *Kinflicks*, ch.4.

15 I happen to feel that the degree of a person's intelligence is directly reflected by the number of conflicting attitudes she can bring to bear on the same topic.
1976 *Kinflicks*, ch.7.

16 He picked her up out of the dirt and turned her into the clod she was today.
1981 *Original Sins*, pt.4, ch.1.

Altman, Robert 1925–2006

US film director. His first critical and commercial success was *M*A*S*H* (1970).

17 What's a cult? It just means not enough people to make a minority.
1981 Interview in the *Observer*, 11 Apr.

18 I'll give you the same advice I give my children: Never take advice from anybody.
2004 *Esquire*, Mar.

19 You will never see 'Altman's Great Film of the Seventies: The Director's Cut' because you have never seen a film of mine that wasn't the director's cut. I have never permitted it.
2004 In *The Independent*, 14 May.

20 Making a movie is like chipping away at a stone. You take a piece off here, you take a piece off there and when you're finished, you have a sculpture. You know that there's something in there, but you're not sure exactly what it is until you find it.
2006 In *Star Tribune*, 4 Jun.

Amado, Jorge 1912–2001

Brazilian novelist, born on a cacao plantation in Ferradas. He was imprisoned several times and exiled for leftist activities. Most of his novels are picaresque, ribald tales of lower-class Bahian city life.

21 *Ninguém no cais tem um nome só. Todos têm também um apelido ou abreviam o nome, ou o aumentam, ou lhe acrescentam qualquer coisa que recorde uma história, uma luta, um amor.*
No one on the docks has just one name. Everybody has a nickname too, or the name is shortened, or lengthened, or something is added that recalls a tale, a fight, a woman.
1936 *Mar morto* (*Sea of Death*, 1984), 'Iemanjá'.

St Ambrose c.339–397 AD

Bishop of Milan. He was much admired by St Augustine.

22 *Ubi Petrus, ibi ergo ecclesia.*
Where Peter is, there, accordingly, is the Church.
Explanatio psalmi 40.

American Library Association

23 The computer is a fast idiot, it has no imagination; it cannot originate action. It is, and will remain, only a tool to man.
1964 Statement of the American Library Association regarding the Univac computer exhibited at the New York World's Fair, 1964.

Amerine, Maynard Andrew 1911–98

US oenologist, Professor at the University of California. His works on viniculture include *Wine: An Introduction for Americans* (1965) and *Introduction to Food Science and Technology* (1973).

24 The fine wine leaves you with something pleasant; the ordinary wine just leaves.
Quoted in Clifton Fadiman *The New Joy of Wine* (1990).

Amery, Leo(pold) Charles Maurice Stennett 1873–1955

English Conservative politician. After working on *The Times* for 10 years he became an MP and served as Colonial Secretary (1919–29) and Secretary of State for India and Burma.

25 For twenty years he has held a season ticket on the line of least resistance and has gone wherever the train of events has carried him, lucidly justifying his position at whatever point he happened to find himself.
1914 Of Herbert Asquith, in *Quarterly Review*, Jul.

26 Speak for England, Arthur!
1939 Shouted to Arthur Greenwood, Labour Opposition spokesman, 2 Sep, as Greenwood began a House of Commons speech calling for the resignation of Prime Minister Neville Chamberlain, immediately preceding the declaration of World War II.

27 Cromwell said to the Long Parliament when he thought it was no longer fit to conduct the affairs of the nation, 'You have sat too long here for any good you have been doing. Depart, I say, and let us have done with you. In the name of God, go!'
1940 Remark addressed to Prime Minister Neville Chamberlain, House of Commons, 7 May.

Amin (Dada), Idi 1925–2003

Ugandan soldier and politician, an army commander who seized power in 1971 and was proclaimed President. He was deposed by exiled Ugandans with the help of the Tanzanian army in 1979 and fled to Libya.

28 Your experience will be a lesson to all of us men to be careful not to marry ladies in very high positions.
1978 Unsolicited advice to Lord Snowdon on the ending of his marriage to Princess Margaret, quoted in A Barrow *International Gossip* (1983).

Amis, Sir Kingsley 1922–95

English novelist and poet. He achieved success with his irreverent novel *Lucky Jim* (1954), and went on to write a substantial body of novels, poetry and non-fiction.

29 The light did him harm, but not as much as looking at things did; he resolved, having done it once, never to move his eyeballs again. A dusty thudding in his head made the scene before him beat like a pulse. His mouth had been used as a latrine by some small creature of the night, and then as its mausoleum.
1953 *Lucky Jim*, ch.6.

30 He thought what a pity it was that all his faces were designed to express rage or loathing. Now that something had happened that really deserved a face, he'd none to celebrate it with. As a kind of token, he made his Sex Life in Ancient Rome face.
1953 *Lucky Jim*, ch.25.

31 Man's love is of man's life a thing apart;
Girls aren't like that.
1956 'A Bookshop Idyll'.
▶ See Byron 189:1.

32 Politics is a thing that only the unsophisticated can really go for.
1957 'Socialism and the Intellectuals'.

33 Work was like cats were supposed to be: if you disliked and feared it and tried to keep out if its way, it knew at once and sought you out and jumped on your lap and climbed all over you to show how much it loved you. Please God, he thought, don't let me die in harness.
1960 *Take A Girl Like You*, ch.5.

34 More will mean worse.
1960 On expanding university intake, in *Encounter*, Jul.

35 Outside every fat man there was an even fatter man trying to close in.
1963 *One Fat Englishman*, ch.3.
▶ See also Connolly 243:13.

36 He was of the faith chiefly in the sense that the church he currently did not attend was Catholic.
1963 *One Fat Englishman*, ch.8.

37 It was no wonder that people were so horrible when they started life as children.
1963 *One Fat Englishman*, ch.14.

38 I was never an Angry Young Man. I am angry only when I hit my thumb with a hammer.
1979 Dissociating himself from that literary grouping, in *The Eton College Chronicle*, Jun.

39 The rewards for being sane may not be very many but knowing what's funny is one of them.
1984 *Stanley and the Women*, ch.2.

40 Alun's life was coming to consist more and more exclusively of being told at dictation speed what he knew.
1986 *The Old Devils*, ch.7.

41 Booze, of course, and then curtains.
1986 His response to being asked how he would spend his Booker Prize cheque, 22 Oct.

42 I wish he'd *shut up* about Flaubert.
Said about Julian Barnes. Quoted in Julian Barnes *Something to Declare* (2002).

Amis, Martin Louis 1949–

English novelist, son of Kingsley Amis. His novels include *The Rachel Papers* (1974), *London Fields* (1989), *Time's Arrow* (1991), *The Information* (1995) and *Yellow Dog* (2003).

43 The middle-management of Manhattan stared on, their faces as thin as credit cards.
1984 *Money*.

44 His name was Shadow, short for Shadow That Comes in Sight, an old Indian name, Apache or Cheyenne. I very much approved of this. You don't want dogs called Spot or Pooch. You don't want dogs called Nigel or Keith. The names of dogs should salute the mystical drama of the animal life. *Shadow*—that's a *good* name.
1984 *Money*.

45 My theory is—we don't really go that far into other people, even when we think we do. We hardly ever go in and bring them out. We just stand at the jaws of the cave, and strike a match, and ask quickly if anybody's there.
1984 *Money*.

46 New York is a jungle, they tell you. You could go further, and say that New York is a jungle. New York *is a jungle*. Beneath the columns of the old rain forest, made of melting macadam, the mean Limpopo of swamped Ninth Avenue bears an angry argosy of crocs and dragons, tiger fish, noise machines, sweating rainmakers.
1984 *Money*.

47 My belief is that everything that's written about you is actually secondary showbiz nonsense, and you shouldn't take any notice of it.
1985 Quoted in John Haffenden *Novelists in Interview* (1985).

48 When success happens to an English writer, he acquires a new typewriter. When success happens to an American writer, he acquires a new life.
1986 *The Moronic Inferno*, 'Kurt Vonnegut'.

49 Most writers need a wound, either physical or spiritual.
1987 In the *Observer*, 30 Aug.

50 How do we prevent the use of nuclear weapons? By threatening to use nuclear weapons. And we can't get rid of nuclear weapons, because of nuclear weapons.
1987 *Einstein's Monsters*, introduction.

51 Someone watches over us when we write. Mother. Teacher. Shakespeare. God.
1989 *London Fields*, ch.1.

52 And meanwhile time goes about its immemorial work of making everyone look and feel like shit.
1989 *London Fields*, ch.2.

53 But we mustn't go too far back…in anybody's life… Because if we do…then nobody is to blame for anything, and nothing matters, and everything is allowed.
1989 *London Fields*, ch.10.

54 Insects are what neurosis would sound like, if neurosis could make a noise with its nose.
1995 *The Information*, pt.3.

55 You see tragedy requires persons of heroic stature. It works on the principle of people being more than human—super-human—and also being only too human. But there just aren't many great figures around now, so the tragic mechanisms can't work.
1995 Explaining why only comedy can reflect contemporary reality. Quoted in an interview in The Scotsman, *7 Apr.*

56 We live in the age of mass loquacity. We are all writing it or at any rate talking it: the memoir, the apologia, the c.v., the *cri de coeur*.
2000 Experience.

57 Closure is a greasy little word which, moreover, describes a nonexistent condition. The truth, Venus, is that nobody gets over anything.
2006 House of Meetings.

58 Whatever else terrorism had achieved in the past few decades, it had certainly brought about a net increase in world boredom.
2009 The Second Plane: 14 Responses to September 11.

59 Love is an abstract noun, something nebulous. And yet love turns out to be the only part of us that is solid, as the world turns upside down and the screen goes black.
2009 The Second Plane: 14 Responses to September 11.

60 Screw-top wine has improved the quality of life by about ten percent, wouldn't you say?
2010 The Pregnant Widow.

61 You get the feeling that childhood does not last as long as it used to. Innocence gets harder to hold on to as the world gets older, as it accumulates more experience, more mileage and more blood on the tracks.
2012 In Smithsonian Magazine, *Sep.*

62 You use a different part of your heart with girls.
2014 In The Guardian, *22 Feb.*

Ammianus Marcellinus c.330–390 AD
Roman historian, born of Greek parents in Antioch. After a military career he moved to Rome, and devoted himself to literature. He wrote in Latin a history of the Roman Empire.

63 *Etiam parietes arcanorum soli conscii timebantur.*
Even the walls, the only sharers of secrets, were feared.
History, *14.1.7 (translated by J C Rolfe). This became a proverbial expression in the medieval tradition: 'parietes habent aures' (the walls have ears).*

Amundsen, Roald Engelbregt Gravning 1872–1928
Norwegian explorer. In 1903–6 he sailed the Northwest Passage in the smack *Gjöa*. Hearing of a British expedition to the South Pole, he made as if sailing for the Arctic but instead turned south. His party beat that of Captain Scott to the South Pole by one month.

64 Beg leave to inform you proceeding Antarctica. Amundsen.
1910 Cable sent from Madeira to Captain Robert F Scott in Melbourne, 12 Oct.

Anaxagoras c.500–428 BC
Greek philosopher. He taught in Athens, and Pericles and Euripides were among his pupils. He denied the divine nature of the celestial bodies, was banned from Athens for impiety, and died in Lampsacus.

65 The sun provides the moon with its brightness.
Fragment in Plutarch De facie in orbe lunae, *929b.*

Ancona, Ronni 1968–
Scottish comedienne and impressionist.

66 You're sitting in a room with male writers and you say something and it's ignored. You say it again and it's ignored. Then a man will say it and everyone goes 'That's brilliant'.
2004 In the Observer, *25 Apr.*

Anderson, Admiral George, Jr c.1907–1992
US Chief of Naval Operations in the Cuban missile crisis, 1962. On retirement from the Navy he served as US Ambassador to Portugal.

67 Now, Mr Secretary, if you and your deputy will go back to your offices, the Navy will run the blockade.
1962 On brandishing a manual of procedures to Pentagon officials at the time of the Cuban missile crisis. Recalled on his death, 4 Mar 1992.

Anderson, John Edward 1917–2011
US businessman.

68 You need enough cash cows to feed your pigs.
1994 On financing. In Forbes, *17 Oct.*

Anderson, Dame Judith *originally* Frances Margaret Anderson 1898–1992
Australian actress. She achieved fame in the theatre, but is best remembered for her screen role as Mrs Danvers in Alfred Hitchcock's *Rebecca* (1940). In 1984 a Broadway theatre was named after her.

69 I find myself wearing gloves more often.
On how being made a Dame of the British Empire had changed her. Attributed.

Anderson, Lindsay 1932–94
Indian-born British stage and film director. During the 1950s he made documentary films and won an Oscar for his short film *Thursday's Children* (1953). His feature film credits include *This Sporting Life* (1963), *If* (1968) and *The Whales of August* (1987).

70 Perhaps the tendency is to treat the films of one's own country like the prophets—with less than justice.
1947 Comment, quoted in Ian Christie Arrows of Desire.

Anderson, Maxwell 1888–1959
US dramatist. He wrote a large number of plays in both prose and verse, many on historical subjects.

71 What Price Glory?
1924 Title of play (with Lawrence Stallings).

72 But it's a long, long while
From May to December;
And the days grow short
When you reach September.
1938 'September Song' (music by Kurt Weill).

Anderson, Poul William 1926–2001
US science fiction and fantasy writer, author of numerous novels and short stories.

73 I have yet to see any problem, however complicated, which, when you looked at it in the right way, did not become still more complicated.
1969 In the New Scientist, *25 Sep.*

Anderson, Robert Woodruff 1917–2009

US dramatist and novelist. His plays, confronting the difficulties of human relationships, include *Tea and Sympathy* (1953) and *I Never Sang for My Father* (1968), and he also wrote several screenplays.

74 All you're supposed to do is every once in a while give the boys a little tea and sympathy.
1953 On the duties of a headmaster's wife. *Tea and Sympathy*, act 1.

Anderson, Sherwood 1876–1941

US author, who left a lucrative job as manager of a paint factory to write full-time. His *Winesburg, Ohio* (1919) is a naturalistic study of small-town America in 23 stories.

75 The moment one of the people took one of the truths to himself, called it his truth, and tried to live his life by it, he became a grotesque and the truth he embraced a falsehood.
1919 *Winesburg, Ohio*, 'The Book of the Grotesque'.

Andrade, Carlos Drummond de 1902–87

Brazilian modernist poet. Although trained in pharmacy, he turned to writing and journalism. A friend of Neruda, he shared his devotion to socialism. His writing is characteristically low-key and ironic, focusing on everyday subjects.

76 *O marciano encontrou-me na rua*
e teve miedo de minha impossibilidade humana.
Como pode existir, penseu consigo, um ser
que no existir põe sem tamanha anulação de
existência?
The Martian met me in the streets
and was frightened by my human impossibility.
He wondered how such a being could exist
who could not exist without unmaking so much
existence.
1961 *Lição de coisas*, 'Science Fiction'.

Andrade, Mário de 1893–1945

Brazilian modernist writer. His works reflect a deep interest in Brazilian folk culture, and his highly individual prose style imitates colloquial Brazilian speech.

77 *Os guerreiros de cá não buscam mavórticas damas para o enlace epitalâmico; mas antes as preferem dóceis e facilmente trocáveis por pequeninas e voláteis folhas de papel a que o vulgo chamará dinheiro—o 'curriculum vitae' da Civilização.*
The warriors here do not seek out mettlesome women for epithalamic conjunction, but prefer them docile and willing to exchange with ease their favours for those small and deliquescent leaves of paper which the masses call money—the *curriculum vitae* of Civilization.
1928 *Macunaíma* (*O Herói sem nenhum caráter*) (*Macunaima*, 1984), ch.9.

Andreas Capellanus fl. late 12c

French priest and writer, possibly chaplain to the court of Champagne. *De Amore* is his only known work.

78 *Liquide constet inter virum et uxorem amorem sibi locum vindicare non posse.*
It is clearly certain that between man and wife love can claim no place.
c.1185 *De Amore*, bk.1, ch.6, section 7.

Andrewes, Lancelot 1555–1626

English ecclesiastic, renowned for his memorable sermons. He became Bishop of Chichester, then Ely and finally Winchester.

79 It was no summer progress. A cold coming they had of it, at this time of the year; just, the worst time of the year, to take a journey, and specially a long journey, in. The ways deep, the weather sharp, the days short, the sun farthest off *in solstitio brumali*, the very dead of winter.
1622 *Of the Nativity*, sermon 15.
▶ See Eliot 318:17.

80 The nearer the Church, the further from God.
1622 *Of the Nativity*, sermon 15.

Andrews, Julie originally *Julia Elizabeth Wells* 1935–

British singer and actress. She starred in several long-running Broadway musicals, notably *My Fair Lady* (1956) and *Camelot* (1960). Her most popular films have been *Mary Poppins* (1964) and *The Sound of Music* (1965).

81 I'd like to thank all those who made this possible—especially Jack Warner.
1965 Speech at the Oscar ceremony when she won an Academy Award for her role in *Mary Poppins*, 5 Apr. Warner had rejected her for the screen role of Eliza in *My Fair Lady*, although she had played it to great acclaim on the stage, preferring Audrey Hepburn whose singing had to be dubbed. Andrews had instead taken the part in *Mary Poppins*.

Angell, Roger 1920–

US journalist. Fiction editor at the *New Yorker*, he is also known for his baseball writing.

82 Such days and moments pass, in ways that this one has not, but there's a weary strength in experience, even in the midst of horror.
2001 Reflecting on the terrorist attacks on 11 Sep. In the *New Yorker*.

Angelou, Maya originally *Maya Johnson* 1928–2014

US writer. A sexual assault on her in childhood left her mute for several years. She became a successful writer with her multi-volume autobiography. She also published several volumes of verse.

83 If growing up is painful for the Southern Black girl, being aware of her displacement is the rust on the razor that threatens the throat.
1969 *I Know Why The Caged Bird Sings*, opening section.

84 Children's talent to endure stems from their ignorance of alternatives.
1969 *I Know Why The Caged Bird Sings*, ch.17.

85 The quality of strength lined with tenderness is an unbeatable combination, as are intelligence and necessity when unblunted by formal education.
1970 *I Know Why The Caged Bird Sings*, ch.29.

86 At fifteen life had taught me undeniably that surrender, in its place, was as honorable as resistance, especially if one had no choice.
1970 *I Know Why The Caged Bird Sings*, ch.31.

87 The fact that the adult American Negro female emerges a formidable character is often met with amazement, distaste and even belligerence. It is seldom accepted as an inevitable outcome of the struggle won by survivors, and deserves respect if not enthusiastic acceptance.
1970 *I Know Why The Caged Bird Sings*, ch.34.

88 Most plain girls are virtuous because of the scarcity of opportunity to be otherwise.
1970 *I Know Why The Caged Bird Sings*, ch.35

89 It is a historical truth. No man can know where he is going unless he knows exactly where he has been and exactly how he arrived at his present place.
1972 On Africa. In the *New York Times*, 16 Apr.

90 There is a kind of strength that is almost frightening in black women. It's as if a steel rod runs right through the head down to the feet.
1973 Television interview, 21 Nov. Collected in *Conversations with Maya Angelou* (1989).

91 We had won... I thought if war did not include killing, I'd like to see one every year. Something like a festival.
1974 On the end of World War II. *Gather Together In My Name*, prologue.

92 Self-pity in its early stage is as snug as a feather mattress. Only when it hardens does it become uncomfortable.
1974 *Gather Together In My Name*, ch.6.

93 The sadness of the women's movement is that they don't allow the necessity of love. See, I don't personally trust any revolution where love is not allowed.
1975 Interview in *California Living*, 14 May. Collected in *Conversations with Maya Angelou* (1989).

94 Oh, the holiness of always being the injured party. The historically oppressed can find not only sanctity but safety in the state of victimization. When access to a better life has been denied often enough, and successfully enough, one can use the rejection as an excuse to cease all efforts.
1976 *Singin' and Swingin' and Getting Merry Like Christmas*, ch.9.

95 Life loves the liver of it.
1977 Interview in *Black Scholar*, Jan–Feb. Collected in *Conversations with Maya Angelou* (1989).

96 Something made greater by ourselves and in turn that makes us greater.
1977 Defining work. Interview in *Black Scholar*, Jan–Feb. Collected in *Conversations with Maya Angelou* (1989).

97 There is an awesome reality to Rent Day. It comes trumpeting, forcing the days before it into a wild scramble.
1981 *The Heart of a Woman*, ch.3.

98 The cliché of whites being ignorant of blacks was not only true, but understandable. Oh, but we knew them with the intimacy of a surgeon's scalpel.
1981 *The Heart of a Woman*, ch.12.

99 Genet had been right at least about one thing. Blacks should be used to play whites. For centuries we had probed their faces, the angles of their bodies, the sounds of their voices and even their odors. Often our survival had depended on the accurate reading of a white man's chuckle or the disdainful wave of a white woman's hand.
1981 *The Heart of a Woman*, ch.12.

1 Poetry is music written for the human voice.
1989 In 'The Power of the Word', Public Broadcasting Service, 15 Sep.

2 Wouldn't Take Nothing for my Journey Now.
1994 Title of book.

3 Good done anywhere is good done everywhere.
2007 In Oprah Winfrey, *O's Guide to Life*.

4 I've learned that people will forget what you said, people will forget what you did, but people will never forget how you made them feel.
2012 In *Beautifully Said Magazine*, Jul.

5 Develop enough courage so that you can stand up for yourself and then stand up for somebody else.
2012 On Facebook, 17 Sep.

6 You can only become truly accomplished at something you love.
2013 On Facebook, 9 Jun.

7 Moderation in all things. And even moderation in moderation. Don't get too much moderation, you know?
2013 In *O: The Oprah Magazine*.

8 Nothing will work unless you do.
2014 On Facebook, 2 Jan.

9 Listen to yourself and in that quietude you might hear the voice of God.
2014 On Facebook, 23 May.

Angle, Colin   1967–

US businessman. Co-founder and Chief Executive Officer of iRobot.

10 We're not using these robots to hand out flowers.
2004 On the possibility of arming military robots.

Annan, Noël Gilroy, Baron   1916–2000

English scholar, Chair of the Board of Trustees of the National Gallery (1980–5). His works include *Our Age: portrait of a generation* (1990).

11 He cultivated to perfection the sneer which he used like an oyster-knife, inserting it into the shell of his victim, exposing him with a quick-turn of the wrist, and finally flipping him over and inviting his audience to discard him as tainted and inedible.
1991 On the critic F R Leavis. *English Intellectuals Between the World Wars*.

Anne, Queen   1665–1714

Queen of Great Britain and Ireland (1702–14), the last Stuart monarch. Her reign was marked by the union of England and Scotland (1707) and the War of the Spanish Succession. After quarrelling with the Marlboroughs (Whigs), she appointed a Tory government in 1710.

12 Cricket is not illegal, for it is a manly game.
1710 Quoted in Colin Jarman *The Guinness Dictionary of Sports Quotations* (1990).

13 I have changed my Ministers but I have not changed my measures. I am still for moderation, and I will govern by it.
1711 Addressing her new Tory administration, Jan.

Anne Elizabeth Alice Louise   1950–

HRH The Princess Royal, daughter of Queen Elizabeth II and Prince Philip. She has worked on behalf of various charities, notably as President of the Save the Children Fund.

14 It could be said that the AIDS pandemic is a classic own-goal scored by the human race against itself.
1988 In the *Daily Telegraph*, 27 Jan.

Annenberg, Walter H   1908–2002

US publishing tycoon, philanthropist and former US Ambassador to Great Britain and Northern Ireland, a noted art enthusiast and collector.

15 Only when you are moved by a painting should you buy it. Being moved is what collecting is all about.
   1991 In *Connoisseur*, Feb.

16 You are asking me to sell members of my family.
   1991 In the *New York Times*, 12 Mar. Rejecting a billion-dollar Japanese offer for his art collection.

Anonymous

17 Either with it or upon it.
   Traditionally said by a Spartan mother while handing her son his shield when he went to war; he should either return with it (ie as a victor) or on it (ie dead). Plutarch *Lacaenarum Apophthegmata*, 241f.

18 *Cave canem!*
   Beware of the dog!
   Famous expression, found in mosaics and inscriptions in Pompeii and other Roman towns. See also Petronius *Satyricon*, 29.1: *Ad sinistram enim intrantibus non longe ab ostiarii cella canis ingens, catena vinctus, in pariete erat pictus superque quadrata littera scriptum cave canem* (For on the left hand as you went in, not far from the porter's office, a great dog on a chain was painted on the wall, and over him was written in large letters: 'Beware of the dog'. Translation by W H D Rouse).

19 Not everyone can sail to Corinth.
   ie, not everybody has the same opportunities. Greek proverb, which is also mentioned by Horace *Epistulae*, 1. 17.36: 'Non cuivis homini contingit adire Corinthum'.

20 Nothing in excess.
   Famous motto in Antiquity. According to Plato, the text was a temple inscription in Delphi (*Hipparchus*, 228e).

21 *Patria est ubicumque est bene.*
   One's country is wherever one does well.
   Quoted as proverbial by Cicero in *Tusculanes Disputationes*, 5. 108. The saying was attributed to the mythical figure Teucer, ancestor of the Trojans, by the Roman tragedian Pacuvius (220–c.130 BC).

22 *Ave Caesar, morituri te salutant!*
   Hail Caesar, we who are about to die salute you!
   Traditional formula for gladiators saluting the emperor. One source for the expression is Suetonius *Claudius* 21: 'Ave Imperator, morituri te salutant', ('Hail Emperor, we salute you, we who are about to die!').

23 *Candida me docuit nigras odisse puellas. Odero si potero. Si non, invitus amabo.*
   A white girl instructed me to hate black girls. I shall hate them if I can. If not, I shall love them—against my will.
   c.1c AD Graffito found in Pompeii. In *Corpus Inscriptionum Latinarum* I V, 1520.

24 *Fures fores, frugi intro!*
   Thieves out, profit in!
   c.1c AD Graffito found in Pompeii. In *Corpus Inscriptionum Latinarum* I V, 4278.

25 *Fullones ululamque cano, non arma virumque.*
   Of fullers and their wailing, I sing, not of arms and the man.
   c.1c AD Graffito found in Pompeii. In *Corpus Inscriptionum Latinarum* I V, 9131. This is a parody of the famous opening line of Virgil's *Aeneid* 1.1: 'Arma virumque cano'.

26 Enjoy another glass, for you see what the end is.
   c.2c AD Epitaph from Cos for a certain Chrysogonos. Quoted in W Peek *Griechische Versinschriften*, vol.1, no.378.

27 The glory of God is man, and the glory of man is his dress.
   c.450 *Babylonian Talmud*. Quoted in Barton Stevenson (ed) *The Macmillan Book of Proverbs, Maxims, and Famous Phrases* (1948).

28 *Gæth a wyrd swa hio scel.*
   Fate always goes as it must.
   c.800 *Beowulf*, l.455.

29 *Wyrd oft nereth*
   unfægne eorl thonne his ellen deah.
   Fate often preserves
   the undoomed warrior when his courage holds firm.
   c.800 *Beowulf*, l.572–3.

30 *Oft seldan hwær*
   æfter leodhyre lytle hwile
   bongar bugeth.
   It is very rare that,
   after the fall of a prince,
   the deadly spear rests for long.
   c.800 *Beowulf*, l.2029–31.

31 He is joyful with swift movement when a mouse sticks in his sharp paw.
   I too am joyful when I understand a dearly loved difficult problem.
   c.820 'Me and Pangur Bán', by an unidentified cat-owning scholar, translated in Gerard Murphy *Early Irish Lyrics* (1956), no.1.

32 *Lytle hwile leof beoth grene*
   thonne hie eft fealewiath, feallath on eorthan
   and forweorniath weorthiath to duste.
   For a little while the leaves are green.
   Then they turn yellow, fall to the ground,
   and perish, turning to dust.
   c.900 *Second Dialogue of Solomon and Saturn*, l.136–8.

33 *Widgongel wif word gespringeth.*
   A roving woman gives rise to gossip.
   c.900 *Maxims I*, l.64.

34 *Feoh byth frofur fira gehwylcum*
   Sceal theah manna gehwylc miclun hyt dælan.
   Money is a comfort to each man,
   But everyone should nevertheless give it away freely.
   ?c.900 *The Rune Poem*, l.1–2.

35 *Ear byth egle eorla gehwylcun.*
   The grave is ghastly to every man.
   ?c.900 *The Rune Poem*, l.90.

36 Thought shall be the harder, heart the keener, courage the greater, as our might lessens.
   c.1000 *The Battle of Maldon* (translated by R K Gordon).

37 *La flur de France as perdut.*
   The flower of France is lost.
   c.1110 *Chanson de Roland*, l.2445.

38 *Mult ad apris ki bien conuist ahan.*
   He who has suffered much learns much.
   c.1110 *Chanson de Roland*, l.2524.

39 *Man sol sô vrouwen ziehen…*
   das si üppeclîche sprüche lasen under wegen.
   Women should be trained in such a way
   that they avoid idle chatter.
   c.1200 *Das Nibelungenlied*, ch.14, l.193–4.

40 And nowe in the winter, when men kill the fat swine
   They get the bladder and blow it great and thin,
   With many beans and peason put within:
   It ratleth, soundeth, and shineth clere and fayre
   While it is throwen and caste up in the ayre,
   Each one contendeth and hath a great delite
   With foote and with hands the bladder for to smite;

If it fall to grounde, they lifte it up agayne,
But this waye to labour they count in no payne.
Medieval verse, one of the earliest descriptions of football in England.

41 *Graeca non leguntur.*
Things in Greek are not read.
Term used by medieval 'glossatores' (commentators) of the *Corpus Iuris*, indicating that the parts in Greek should be skipped. It became a traditional comment to indicate ignorance.

42 Al night by the rose, rose,
Al night by the rose I lay,
Dorst ich nought the rose stele,
And yet I bar the flour away.
c.1210–1240 Untitled lyric.

43 Sumer is icumen in,
Lhude sing cuccu!
Groweth sed, and bleweth med,
And springth the wude nu.
c.1250 'Sumer is icumen in', l.1–4.
▶ See also Pound 691:91.

44 Quhen Alysaunder oure kyng wes dede,
That Scotland led in lauche and le,
Away wes sons of alle and brede,
Off wyne and wax, of gamyn and gle;
Oure gold wes changyd in to lede.
Cryst, borne in to virgynyte,
Succour Scotland, and remede,
That stad is in perplexyte.
c.1286 Lines said to have been written after the death of Alexander II of Scotland, the earliest extant piece of Scottish verse. Quoted in the *Original Chronicle of Andrew Wyntoun* (c.1420), bk.7.

45 Lenten is come with love to toune.
c.1300 'Lenten is come', l.1.

46 *Quamdiu centum viui remanserint, nuncquam Anglorum dominio aliquatenus volumus subjugari.*
As long as one hundred of us shall remain alive, we shall never consent to subject ourselves in any degree to English dominion.
1320 *Declaration of Arbroath*, a letter sent by the barons of Scotland to Pope John XXII, asserting Scotland's independence from England and their right to defend that independence with or without the support of their sovereign.

47 Not what thou arte, ne what thou hast ben, beholdeth God with his mercyful iye; bot that thou woldest be.
c.1370 *The Cloud of Unknowing*, ch.75.

48 *Patience is a poynt, thagh it displese ofte.*
Patience is a virtue, though it often displeases.
c.1370 *Patience*, l.1.

49 Ay wolde man of happe more hente
Then moghte by ryght upon hem cleven.
Man always desires to seize more of happiness,
Than rightfully belongs to him.
c.1370 *Pearl*, l.1195–6.

50 Of alle chevalry to chose, the chef thyng alosed
Is the lel layk of luf, the lettrure of armes.
Choosing from all chivalrous actions, the chief things to praise
Are the loyal sport of love and the lore of arms.
c.1370 *Sir Gawain and the Green Knight*, l.1512–3.

51 Yif thou wolte lyve frely, lerne to dye gladly.
c.1375 *The Art of Dieing*.

52 Young men a wooing, for God that you bought,
Be well ware of wedding and think in your thought:
'Had I wist' is a thing, it serves of nought.
c.1425 *The Second Shepherd's Play*, part of the York cycle of Mystery Plays, l.91–3.

53 Now why that erthe luves erthe, wondere me thinke,
Or why that erthe for erthe sholde other swete or swinke:
For when that erthe upon erthe es broghte within brinke,
Thane shall erthe of erthe have a foulle stinke.
Now, why earth loves earth, I wonder to think,
Or why earth for earth should either sweat or labour:
For when earth upon earth comes within the grave's brink,
Then earth upon earth shall have a foul stink.
c.1450 'Erthe oute of erthe', l.19–22.

54 I wyll that my son manhede take
For reson wyll that there be thre—
A man, a madyn, and a tre.
Man for man, tre for tre,
Madyn for madyn; thus shall it be.
?c.1450 God the Father explains how Christ will atone for Adam's sin. *Towneley Annunciation Play*, l.30–5.

55 Pees maketh plente;
Plente maketh pride;
Pride make plee;
Plee maketh povert;
Povert maketh pees.
Peace makes plenty;
Plenty makes pride;
Pride makes lawsuits;
Lawsuits make poverty;
Poverty makes peace.
c.1470 Untitled lyric.

56 O God in Heaven, on you we call,
Kyrie eleison,
Help us seize our priests and kill them all,
Kyrie eleison.
1476 Satirical chant. Quoted in Gerald Strauss *Manifestations of Discontent in Germany on the Eve of the Reformation* (1971).

57 Everyman, I will go with thee, and be thy guide.
In thy most need to go by thy side.
c.1485 Knowledge speaks to Everyman. *Everyman*, l.522–3.

58 In youth open your mind, And let all learning in;
Words the head does not shape Are worthless, out and in.
Words wit has not salted, No nearer the heart than the lip,
Are nothing more than wind, A puppy's insolent yelp.
c.1500 'To a Boy'. Translated from the Irish by Michael O'Donovan ('Frank O'Connor').

59 Westron winde, when wilt thou blow,
The smalle raine downe can raine?
Christ if my love were in my armes,
And I in my bed againe.
c.1500 Untitled lyric.

60 Back and side go bare, go bare,
Both foot and hand go cold;
But, belly, God send thee good ale enough,
Whether it be new or old.
c.1575 Song, included in the play *Gammer Gurton's Needle*, act 2. William Stevenson (c.1530–75) and John Still (1543–1608) have

both been credited with authorship of the play, but the song probably predates it.

61 I cannot eat but little meat,
My stomach is not good;
But sure I think that I can drink
With him that wears a hood.
c.1575 Song, included in the play *Gammer Gurton's Needle*, act 2. 'Him that wears a hood' is either a monk or a scholar.

62 And Tib my wife, that as her life
Loveth well good ale to seek,
Full oft drinks she, till ye may see
The tears run down her cheeks.
c.1575 Song, included in the play *Gammer Gurton's Needle*, act 2.

63 Though raging stormes movis us to shake,
And wind makis waters overflow;
We yield thereto bot dois not break
And in the calm bent up we grow.

So baneist men, though princes rage,
And prisoners, be not despairit.
Abide the calm, whill that it 'suage,
For time sic causis has repairit.
1582 *The Maitland Manuscript*, 'The Reeds in the Loch Sayis'.

64 Brissit brawnis and broken banis
Stryfe discorde and waistis wanis
Crukit in eild, syne halt withal,
This are the bewteis of the fute-ball.
1582 *The Maitland Manuscript*, 'The Bewteis of the Fute-ball'.

65 *Flavit deus et dissipati sunt*
God blew and they were scattered.
1588 Inscription on medallion to commemorate the English defeat of the Spanish Armada.

66 The rose is red, the leaves are green,
God save Elizabeth, our noble queen.
1589 Lines written by a Westminster schoolboy in the margin of his copy of *Julius Caesar*. Quoted in P W Hasler (ed) *The House of Commons, 1558–1603* (vol.I), p.474.

67 My Love in her attire doth show her wit,
It doth so well become her;
For every season she hath dressings fit,
For winter, spring, and summer.
No beauty she doth miss
When all her robes are on;
But beauty's self she is
When all her robes are gone.
'Madrigal'. Collected in F Davison (ed) *Poetical Rhapsody* (1602).

68 Nose, nose, jolly red nose,
Who gave thee this jolly red nose?...
Nutmegs and ginger, cinnamon and cloves,
And they gave me this jolly red nose.
Quoted in Francis Beaumont and John Fletcher *The Knight of the Burning Pestle* (1609) but thought to be a rhyme of earlier origin.

69 Even when the courtesan farts
She does it as a favour
c.1616–1853 Collected in R H Blyth *Senryō: Japanese Satirical Verses Translated and Explained* (1949).

70 Possession is nine points of the law.
Proverb, quoted in T Draxe *Adages* (1616) no.163.

71 Too many cooks spoil the broth.
Quoted in Sir Balthazar Gerbier *Three Chief Principles of Magnificent Building* (1665).

72 O he's a ranting roving blade!
O he's a brisk and a bonnie lad!
Betide what may, my heart is glad
To see my lad wi' his white cockade.
18c 'The White Cockade'.

73 O this is no my ain house,
I ken by the biggin o't.
18c 'This is no my ain house'.

74 A good rider may often be thrown from his horse,
And climb on once again to face forward his course,
Which is how I went forward myself on my way,
And come, Christ, and give me my true judgment day.
18c Traditional Irish poem. Translated by Owen Dudley Edwards.

75 And wasna he a roguey,
A roguey, a roguey,
And wasna he a roguey,
The piper o' Dundee?
18c 'The Piper o' Dundee'.

76 The Campbells are comin', O-ho, O-ho!
c.1715 'The Campbells are comin'. Although its origins are uncertain, this song may date from John Campbell, Duke of Argyll's attack on the Jacobite army at Sheriffmuir (1715).

77 Cam ye ower frae France?
Cam ye doun by Lunnon?
Saw ye Geordie Whelps
And his bonnie woman?
Were ye at the place
Ca'd the Kittle Housie?
Saw ye Geordie's grace
Ridin' on a goosie?
c.1715 'Cam Ye Ower Frae France?', stanza 1. This Jacobite song alludes to George I and his reputed fondness for visiting brothels.

78 It made Gay Rich and Rich Gay.
c.1728 Alluding to the phenomenal success of *The Beggar's Opera*, written by John Gay and produced by John Rich.

79 O ye'll tak the high road, and I'll tak the low road,
And I'll be in Scotland afore ye,
But me and my true love will never meet again
On the bonnie, bonnie banks o' Loch Lomond
By yon bonnie banks and by yon bonnie braes,
Where the sun shines bright on Loch Lomond.
1746 'The Bonnie Banks o' Loch Lomond', chorus and stanza 1. The author was a Jacobite imprisoned in Carlisle.

80 Whaur's yer Wullie Shakespeare noo?
1756 Shout from an enthusiastic member of the audience at the first production of John Home's *Douglas* at the Canongate Theatre, Edinburgh.

81 Boston, Boston, Boston!
Thou hast naught to boast on,
But a Grand Sluice, and a high steeple;
A proud conceited ignorant people,
And a coast where souls are lost on.
1766 Comment by visitor at the opening of the Grand Sluice, Boston, Lincolnshire, 15 Oct. Quoted in Jennifer Westwood *Albion* (1985), ch. 6, 'English Shires'.

82 Some hae meat and canna eat
And some wad eat that want it;
But we hae meat and we can eat,
And sae the Lord be thankit.
c.1790 'The Selkirk Grace', sometimes attributed to Robert Burns.

83 I challenge all the men alive
To say they e'er were gladder,

Than boys all striving,
Who should kick most wind out of the bladder.
1794 Charterhouse public school song, celebrating football.

84 Here's tae us; wha's like us?
Gey few, and they're a' deid.
19c Scottish toast of uncertain origin. 'Damn' and other variations are sometimes substituted for 'gey'.

85 This stone commemorates the exploit of William Webb Ellis, who, with a fine disregard for the rules of football as played in his time, first took the ball in his arms and ran with it, thus originating the distinctive feature of the Rugby game. AD 1823.
Plaque at Rugby School.

86 What can be more palpably absurd than the prospect held out of locomotives travelling twice as fast as stagecoaches?
1825 *Quarterly Review*, Mar.

87 There was a girl in our town,
Silk an' satin was her gown,
Silk an' satin, gold an' velvet,
Guess her name, three times I've telled it.
Quoted in James Orchard Halliwell *The Nursery Rhymes of England* (1842). The answer, of course, is 'Ann'.

88 The deceased Gentleman was, we are informed, a native of Ashbourn, Derbyshire, at which place he was born in the Year of Grace, 217, and was consequently in the 1643rd year of his age. For some months the patriotic Old Man had been suffering from injuries sustained in his native town, so far back as Shrovetide in last year; he was at once removed (by appeal) to London, where he lingered in suspense till the law of death put its icy hand upon him, and claimed as another trophy to magisterial interference one who had long lived in the hearts of the people.
1860 'Death of the Right Honourable Game Football', as published in a court circular. There had been recent attempts in the courts to ban the riotous custom of 'Shrovetide football' pursued at Ashbourne, Derbyshire, and other villages.

89 What happens when a game of football is proposed at Christmas among a party of young men assembled from different schools? Alas!... The Eton man is enamoured of his own rules, and turns up his nose at Rugby as not sufficiently aristocratic; while the Rugbeian retorts that 'bullying' and 'sneaking' are not to his taste, and he is not afraid of his shins, or of a 'maul' or 'scrimmage'. On hearing this the Harrovian pricks up his ears, and though he might previously have sided with Rugby, the insinuation against the courage of those who do not allow 'shinning' arouses his ire, and causes him to refuse to lay with one who has offered it. Thus it is found impossible to get up a game.
1861 Editorial in *The Field* newspaper, illustrating the confusion before the codification of the rules of football and rugby.

90 Well-informed people know it is impossible to transmit the voice over wires and that were it possible to do so, the thing would be of no practical value.
1865 Editorial in the *Boston Post*.

91 It is a good plan, if it can previously be so arranged, to have one side with striped jerseys of one colour, say red; and the other with another, say blue. This prevents confusion and wild attempts to run after and wrest the ball from your neighbour. I have often seen this done, and the invariable apology—'I beg your pardon, I thought you were on the opposite side'.
1867 In *Routledge's Handbook of Football*.

92 In affectionate remembrance of English cricket, which died at the Oval on 29th August, 1882. Deeply lamented by a large circle of sorrowing friends and acquaintances. RIP. NB The body will be cremated and the ashes taken to Australia.
1882 Notice in *The Sporting Times*, 2 Sep, after the England cricket team's defeat by the Australians.

93 The climate of Manitoba consists of seven months of Arctic weather and five months of cold weather.
1882 *Settler's Guide to the North-West*, issued by the Northern Pacific Railway Company, New York.

94 The British 'Sphere of Influence'—the cricket ball.
Mr Punch's Book of Sport.

95 £1 per week should be ample remuneration for the best professional footballer that ever existed.
1886 In *The Field* newspaper.

96 To the Glorious, Pious, and Immortal Memory of King William the Third, Prince of Orange, who delivered us from Popes and Popery, Knaves and Knavery, Slaves and Slavery, Brass Money, and Wooden Shoes, and He that Will Not Take this Toast May He Be Damn'd, Cramm'd, and Jamm'd Down the Great Gun of Athlone, and the Gun Fired in the Pope's Belly, and the Pope Fired in the Devil's Belly, and the Devil Fired into Hell, and the Door Lock'd, and the Key Forever in the Pocket of a Stout Orangeman. And Here's a Fart for the Bishop of Cork!
c.1890 'The Orange Toast', traditional Protestant Irish.

97 These Ibsen creatures are 'neither men nor women, they are ghouls', vile, unlovable, morbid monsters, and it were well indeed for society if all such went and drowned themselves at once.
1891 In *The Gentlewoman*. Review of Henrik Ibsen's *Rosmersholm*.

98 How different, how very different, from the home life of our own dear Queen!
c.1892 Overheard from a member of the audience when Sarah Bernhardt appeared in the role of Cleopatra.

99 I don't know, darlin', but I think it was somethin' he did against the English.
1895 Unidentified Irish nurse in the US answering an infant's question on the cause of Oscar Wilde's imprisonment, reported by Kenneth Wiggins Porter.

1 The ordinary 'horseless-carriage' is at present a luxury for the wealthy; and although the price will probably fall in the future, it will never, of course, come into as common use as the bicycle.
1899 *Literary Digest*, 14 Oct.

2 Far away from where I am now there is a little gap in the hills, and beyond it the sea; and 'tis there I do be looking the whole day long, for it's the nearest thing to yourself that I can see.
c.1900 Letter from an unidentified Irish postboy to his beloved, quoted in Maurice Healy *The Old Munster Circuit*.

3 *Citius, altius, fortius.*
Swifter, higher, stronger.
Motto of the Olympic Games, c.1908. It was apparently adopted by Baron de Coubertin after he spotted it over the doorway of a French lycée, though it has also been attributed to Reverend Father Didon.

4 Skegness is so bracing.
   from 1909 Slogan in railway advertisements promoting Skegness, Lincolnshire, as a holiday resort. Quoted in Nigel Rees *Dictionary of Popular Phrases* (1990).

5 That the automobile has practically reached the limit of its development is suggested by the fact that during the past year no improvements of a radical nature have been introduced.
   1909 *Scientific American*, 2 Jan.

6 Your country needs you!
   1914 First use of British World War I recruiting slogan.

7 Berlin by Christmas.
   1914 British press.

8 Say it ain't so, Joe.
   1919 Attributed words of a young fan, to US baseball star 'Shoeless Joe' Jackson (1887–1951) who was accused of accepting bribes to throw the 1919 World Series (the 'Black Sox' scandal). Jackson always maintained his innocence, but he and seven other players were barred from baseball for life.

9 Four and twenty Yankees, feeling very dry,
   Went across the border to get a drink of rye.
   When the rye was opened, the Yanks began to sing,
   'God bless America, but God save the King!'
   c.1919 Ditty current in Canada, referring to Americans crossing the border to drink during Prohibition. The Duke of Windsor, later Edward VIII, heard it during his tour of Canada (1919) and repeated it to his father, George V, on his return, as he recalled in *A King's Story* (1951).

10 The cure of the id by the odd.
   c.1920 Popular definition of psychoanalysis.

11 Dear Sir, your astonishment's odd:
   I am always about in the Quad.
   And that's why the tree
   Will continue to be
   Since observed by Yours faithfully, God.
   c.1924 Reply to Ronald Knox's limerick. The limericks summarize Bishop George Berkeley's philosophy that everything is dependent at all times on the will of God.
   ▶ See Knox 495:18.

12 There is no woman who does not dream of being dressed in Paris.
   1925 Catalogue of the 1925 Paris Exhibition. Quoted in Colin McDowell *McDowell's Directory of Twentieth Century Fashion* (1984), ch.1.

13 There was a faith-healer of Deal
   Who said, 'Although pain isn't real,
   If I sit on a pin
   And it punctures my skin,
   I dislike what I fancy I feel.'
   Collected in *The Week-End Book* (1925).

14 Let's get out of these wet clothes and into a dry martini.
   c.1925 The origin of this line is disputed; it has been attributed to Billy Wilder, Charles Butterworth, Alexander Woollcott and Robert Benchley's press agent. It was used by Mae West in *Every Day's a Holiday* (1937 film) and by Benchley in *The Major and the Minor* (1942 film).

15 Can't act. Can't sing. Slightly bald. Can dance a little.
   c.1930 Studio executive's assessment of Fred Astaire on his first screen test.

16 Ein Reich, ein Volk, ein Führer.
   One realm, one people, one leader.
   1934 German Nazi slogan.

17 Sticks nix hick pix
   1935 Headline from *Variety*, 17 Jul. A famous example of the US trade paper's idiosyncratic form of English, referring to the unpopularity of films with rural themes in rural areas.

18 A bayonet is a weapon with a worker at each end.
   1940 British pacifist slogan during World War II.

19 A neurotic builds castles in the air, but a psychotic lives in them.
   c.1940 Popular saying.

20 *Arbeit macht frei.*
   Work liberates.
   c.1940 Legend over the gates of the concentration camp at Auschwitz, Poland.

21 Who dares, wins.
   1940s Motto of the British Special Air Service regiment.

22 Export or die.
   1940s British Board of Trade.

23 Walls have ears.
   1940s British war slogan.

24 Coughs and sneezes spread diseases. Trap the germs in your handkerchief.
   1942 British Government health slogan, quoted in J Darracott and B Loftus *Second World War Posters* (1972).

25 Went the day well?
   Title of an anthology of tributes to men and women killed in the war, used for the title of Cavalcanti's 1942 film about German soldiers invading an English village.

26 No girls, no legs, no jokes, no chance.
   1943 Review of the Rodgers and Hammerstein musical *Oklahoma!* wired to theatre critic Walter Winchell by one of his informants after its pre-Broadway tryout in New Haven. Quoted in Peter Hay *Broadway Anecdotes* (1989).

27 If only we might fall
   Like cherry blossoms in the spring
   So pure and radiant.
   c.1945 Quoted in Ivan Morris *The Nobility of Failure* (1975).

28 I like Ike.
   1947 Campaign slogan for Dwight D Eisenhower's presidential bid. Irving Berlin presented a song with this title, based on *They Like Ike* from his Broadway musical *Call Me Madam*, to an Eisenhower rally at Madison Square Garden, 8 Feb 1952.

29 Whose finger do you want on the trigger?
   1952 Headline in the *Daily Mirror*, 21 Sep, reflecting popular mistrust of both Labour and Conservative leadership in the light of the new destructive potential of the atomic bomb.

30 Massermann, the cat man,
   Makes cats neurotic.
   Are cats and humans
   Similarly symptotic?
   1952 Popular jingle. Dr Jules Massermann conducted some bizarre, behavioural experiments into animal neurosis.

31 No pain—no gain.
   Bodybuilding motto. The catchphrase may have had its origins in Adlai Stevenson's slogan 'There are no gains without pain', first voiced when accepting the Democratic nomination in 1952.

32 Piping Pebworth, Dancing Marston,
   Haunted Hillborough, Hungry Grafton,
   Dodging Exhall, Papist Wixford,
   Beggarly Broom, and Drunken Bidford.
   'Traditional Rhyme on the Vale of Avon Place-Names', quoted in Arnold Silcock, *Verse and Worse* (1952), 'Whimsies'.

33 Madly for Adlai.
1952 Campaign slogan for Adlai Stevenson's presidential bid.

34 Ban the Bomb.
1953 Used by US nuclear disarmament movement from 1953.

35 Psychology? When my daughter needs psychology I fetch her a skelp across her backside, which lifts her nigh six inches in t'air.
1955 Young Yorkshire mother's response on being asked by a local education psychologist how she felt psychology might assist her in the upbringing of her difficult daughter.

36 Cambridge has always tried to be more typical and less exotic than the other place.
1958 In *The Listener*, 14 Aug. 'The other place' has traditionally come to be used of Cambridge from an Oxford viewpoint and vice versa.

37 Life's better with the Conservatives…don't let Labour ruin it.
1959 Conservative Party general election slogan.

38 A chair should be judged by one's pants, a jewel by the light in a lady's eyes, a typewriter by the hovering fingers.
1959 On good design. In *Time*, 12 Jan.

39 Nature's way of telling you to slow down.
Of death. Quoted in *Newsweek*, 25 Apr 1960.

40 Let's get America moving again.
1960 John F Kennedy's presidential election slogan.

41 Would you buy a used car from this man?
1960 Democratic slogan to disparage Richard M Nixon in the 1960 presidential campaign. Nixon had come across badly in television debates, in contrast to the charismatic John F Kennedy.

42 Never again.
1960 Jewish Defence League.

43 GIGO: Garbage in, garbage out.
c.1960 The great and seemingly most basic principle of the computer, coined anonymously sometime early in its development.

44 I have to say Miss Brown, that your methods are outdated and incorrect. But the children love you and are learning well. Do not on any account make any changes.
c.1960 Unknown school inspector, quoted in Antony Garrard Newton Flew *Shephard's Warning. Setting schools back on course* (1994).

45 Stop The World, I Want to Get Off.
1961 From the musical by Leslie Bricusse and Anthony Newley.

46 Stretch pants—the garment that made skiing a spectator sport.
1961 In *Time*, 23 Feb.

47 All the egg heads are in one basket.
1961 Of President Kennedy's advisers. Quoted by Harold Macmillan in a letter to the Queen, 12 Apr.

48 That Was The Week That Was.
1962–3 Title of satirical BBC TV series.

49 Our little bit of grandeur is gone.
1963 Heard on a Dublin bus shortly after the assassination of John Fitzgerald Kennedy, 22 Nov, reported by Sheila O'Sullivan.

50 Make love, not war.
Flower Power movement, mid-1960s.

51 Thirteen wasted years.
1964 Labour Party general election slogan.

52 Don't report what he says, report what he means.
1964 Unwritten reporters' rule for covering Senator Barry Goldwater's campaign for presidential nomination. Quoted in Robert MacNeil *The Right Place at the Right Time* (1982).

53 Hearts and minds.
c.1965 Used by US Defense Department official with regard to winning public support for its Vietnam policy.

54 An important senior faun.
Description of Prime Minister Harold Macmillan's appearance. Quoted in John Gunther *Procession* (1965).

55 Hey, hey, LBJ! How many kids did you kill today?
1966 US anti-Vietnam war demonstrators.

56 Black is beautiful.
1966 US black civil rights movement.

57 Black power.
1966 US black civil rights slogan coined by Stokely Carmichael.

58 Magnificent magpiety.
1966 Of the art collection of cosmetic manufacturer Helena Rubinstein. *Time*, 29 Apr.

59 Bombs away with Curtis LeMay.
1967 Used by US anti-Vietnam demonstrators.

60 Burn, baby, burn!
1967 Radical cry in racial riots and fire-raising in Watts, California and Newark, New Jersey. Quoted in *Time*, 11 Aug.

61 It became necessary to destroy the town to save it.
1968 Statement issued by the US army, referring to Ben Tre in Vietnam. In the *New York Times*, 8 Feb.

62 I'm Backing Britain.
1968 Coined by publisher Robert Maxwell to encourage the public to buy British-made goods.

63 Culture is dead, now let us start creating.
1968 Graffito by Parisian students on the School of Architecture walls, May.

64 Who Else but Nelse?
1968 Campaign slogan for Nelson Rockefeller's presidential bid.

65 My mother thinks Vietnam is somewhere near Panama.
c.1968 The last words of a US soldier fatally wounded during the Vietnam War, quoted by Australian film-maker John Pilger in his 1978 film *Do you remember Vietnam?*

66 When you've got it, flaunt it.
1969 Braiff Airlines slogan.

67 Power to the people.
1969 US Black Panther movement slogan.

68 Out of the closets and into the streets.
1969 US Gay rights movement slogan.

69 Here men from the planet Earth first set foot upon the moon, July 1969 AD. We came in peace for all mankind.
1969 Text of the plaque left on the moon by the first astronauts to walk there, Buzz Aldrin and Neil Armstrong, 20 Jul.

70 Burn your bra!
1970 US feminists' slogan.

71 Yesterday's men.
1970 Labour Party general election slogan, referring to the Conservative leadership.

72 Send them a message.
1972 Governor George Wallace's presidential election slogan.

73 Nice one, Cyril.
1972 Buy-line in TV advertisement for Wonderloaf. It was adopted in 1973 as the title of a pop song by the Cockerel Chorus, addressed to Tottenham Hotspur left-back Cyril Knowles.

74 The abominable no-man.
Of Sherman Adams, Eisenhower's Chief of Staff. Quoted in William Safire *Before the Fall* (1975).

75 The Grin Will Win.
1976 Campaign slogan for Jimmy Carter's presidential bid.

76 He who has not travelled does not know the value of a man.
Arab proverb. Quoted in Ingrid Cranfield *The Challengers* (1976), preface.

77 Hypochondria is the only disease I haven't got.
1978 Graffito seen in New York.

78 Just when you thought it was safe to get back into the water.
c.1978 Publicity slogan for *Jaws 2*.

79 Sick as a parrot.
c.1978 Football cliché. The phrase may have started life as 'sick as a pierrot', an allusion to the sadfaced French Pierrot character of the 18th century, but similar phrases appear in literature as early as the 17th century.

80 To err is human; to blame it on the other party is politics.
1979 In the *Washingtonian*, Nov.

81 Labour isn't working.
1979 Used by the Conservative Party in its general election campaign, referring to high unemployment under the then Labour Government.

82 On yer bike!
1981 Catchphrase derived from Norman Tebbit's Conservative Party conference speech.

83 The Great Communicator.
1981 Tag coined for President Reagan, who was renowned for his ability to put a good spin on speeches prepared for him.

84 Britain is a Morris Minor country, but with Rolls Royce diplomacy.
1982 Remark made during the Falklands crisis by a UN delegate, Apr. Quoted in The Sunday Times Insight Team *The Falklands War* (1982).

85 See Freddy before he sees you!
1984 Publicity for the film *A Nightmare on Elm Street*.

86 It's morning again in America.
1984 Campaign slogan for Ronald Reagan's presidential campaign. Quoted in Hedrick Smith *The Power Game* (1988).

87 A desk is a dangerous place from which to view the world.
1985 Sign on desk of American Express president Louis Gerstner. Quoted in the *New York Times*, 26 Jun.

88 Cannes...is 10,000 people looking for 10 people who really count.
1986 Unknown French publicist speaking on the Cannes Film Festival. Quoted in the *New York Times*, 17 May.

89 Art comes to you proposing to give nothing but the highest quality to your moments as they pass.
Inscription on wall of entrance gallery at Dallas' Lloyd Paxton Art and Antiques. Quoted in *Architectural Digest*, May 1986.

90 Save something for the Third Act.
Show business adage applied by President Reagan to his final months in the White House. Quoted in *Time*, 16 Mar 1987.

91 The future ain't what it used to be.
1987 Anonymous Iowa farmer quoted by President Bush on NBC T V, 10 May.

92 There are checks and balances in government—the checks go to candidates and the balance to the people.
Quoted in *Sunday Morning*, CBS T V broadcast, 17 May 1987.

93 Bill was a tropical fish. His native habitat was hot water.
1987 Of William J Casey of the CIA and his role in the Iran arms sales. Quoted in the *New York Times*, 19 Jul.

94 I know one thing we did right
Was the day we started to fight,
Keep your eye on the prize,
Hold on, hold on!
Civil rights song, quoted in Juan Williams *Eye on the Prize* (1987).

95 Skinny cooks can't be trusted.
1987 Quoted by David Cobb Craig in 'Home Cooking Away From Home', *Life*, Jul.

96 Global double zero.
1987 In *Time*, 3 Aug. This arms control term was applied to Mikhail Gorbachev's agreement for mutual elimination of intermediate and shorter-range missiles in Asia and Europe.

97 Don't die of ignorance.
1987 AIDS awareness campaign slogan.

98 To go to school and finish my schooling without getting pregnant.
1987 15-year-old Detroit girl's definition of the American dream. Reported in *Newsweek*, 29 Jan.

99 Mr Elbows and Knees.
1988 Of Democratic presidential nominee Michael S Dukakis. Quoted in *Time*, 21 Nov.

1 We loved your play. We only have problems with your main character, the second act and the ending.
1988 Fan's comment to playwright Wendy Wasserstein on *The Heidi Chronicles*. Quoted in the *New York Times*, 24 Jan 1991.

2 No duties, only opportunities.
Motto of Princeton, N J, Institute for Advanced Study. Quoted in Ed Regis *Who Got Einstein's Office?* (1988).

3 Before you save the world, you've got to save your seat.
1989 On the need for legislators to keep in close touch with their constituents. Quoted in the *New York Times*, 2 Jan.

4 Life is a sexually transmitted disease.
Graffito, quoted in D J Enright *Faber Book of Fevers and Frets* (1989).

5 We're kuwaiting.
1990 NBC T V broadcast, 16 Aug. The speaker was a US serviceman posted to the Gulf after Iraq's invasion of Kuwait.

6 All the 'isms are wasms.
Attributed comment of a Foreign Office spokesman on the signing of the Molotov–Ribbentrop Pact in Aug 1939. In Peter Hennessy *Whitehall* (1990).

7 Don't iron while the strike is hot.
1991 Women's liberation slogan, quoted in PBS broadcast, 26 Jan.

8 We're here,
We're queer.
Get used to it.
1991 Motto of the homosexual liberation movement, Queer Nation, which rejected use of the term 'gay'. Quoted in the *New York Times*, 6 Apr.

9 Twelve drawers full of political cancer.
1991 FBI agent referring to the files of J Edgar Hoover. Quoted in *Newsweek*, 23 Sep.

10 A fatheaded, boneheaded, dunderheaded, blunderheaded, muttonheaded, knuckleheaded, chuckleheaded, puddingheaded, jobernowled wash-out of a cock-up.
1991 Journalist speaking of the poll tax introduced by Margaret Thatcher. Quoted in *The Economist*, 3 Dec 1994.

11 He who hath the gold maketh the rule.
1991 Inscription on plaque in Armand Hammer's bedroom. Quoted in *Regardie's*, Feb.

12 Polyester...the most valuable word to come out of the 70s, the one that defines tacky for all time.
1991 'Prettier Poly', *New York Times* editorial, 21 Mar.

13 The heraldic equivalent of a pair of furry dice bouncing around in the back of a state coach.
1992 On the title of Countess of Finchley bestowed on former Prime Minister Margaret Thatcher. In the *New Yorker*, 6 Jan.

14 The economy, stupid!
1992 Sign in the Clinton campaign headquarters which became a by-word for the central issue of the 1992 presidential campaign. Quoted in *Fortune*, 19 Oct.

15 It's easier to get a photograph of the Pope in the shower than a picture of her.
1993 On Hillary Rodham Clinton's low profile in the period between her husband's election and inauguration. In *Newsweek*, 25 Jan.

16 Behold the turtle, it only makes progress when it sticks its neck out.
Favourite saying of Harvard's president James B Conant. Quoted in James G Hershberg *James B Conant* (1993).

17 From the cradle to the grave,
Even if I misbehave,
There's a place for me
On government subsidy.
Quoted by a caller from Baltimore on Station WAMU, Washington, 15 Jun 1993.

18 Artists and poets are the raw nerve ends of humanity. By themselves they can do little to save humanity. Without them there would be little worth saving.
Inscription on headstone in Green River Cemetery, Springs NY where Jackson Pollock, Elaine de Kooning, and other artists are buried. Quoted in the *New York Times*, 17 Aug 1993.

19 To have one's credit cards cancelled is now akin to being excommunicated by the medieval church.
1993 In *Reader's Digest*, Sep.

20 Complete the mission, though I be the lone survivor. Never leave a fallen comrade to fall into the hands of the enemy.
1993 *The Ranger's Creed*, quoted in the *New York Times*, 25 Oct. The Rangers, a US Army unit, had stayed to guard the body of a pilot fatally caught in a downed helicopter in Somalia.

21 A potato candidate. The best part of him is underground.
1994 Of Adlai Stevenson and his respectable ancestors. In the *Washington Post*, 9 Jan.

22 I don't know if Mr Kissinger is a great writer, but anyone finishing this book is a great reader.
1994 Unidentified book reviewer quoted by Henry Kissinger on the publication of his 900-page *Diplomacy*. In the *Washington Post*, 11 Apr.

23 The castor oil of the Palestinian peace movement.
1994 Of PLO Chair Yassir Arafat. In NPR broadcast, 4 Jul.

24 He looks like a homeless man in a thousand dollar suit.
1994 On Senator Edward M Kennedy's campaign for re-election at age 62. In the *Washington Post*, 1 Oct.

25 If you are not the lead dog, the view never changes.
Paperweight on the desk of Richard Scott, chief executive officer, Hospital Corp of America. Quoted in *Forbes*, 10 Oct 1994.

26 The President is a walking dead man. He just doesn't know it yet.
1994 Senior legislator on President Clinton's political future as he entered the second half of his term of office. In *Nightline*, ABC TV broadcast, 6 Dec.

27 Running a cemetery is just like being President: you got a lot of people under you and nobody's listening.
Quoted by Bill Clinton, 10 Jan 1995.

28 Has he reconnected with the angry middle?
1995 Listener's question on Clinton's rapport with the middle class after the State of the Union speech. In NPR broadcast, 26 Jan.

29 I'm spending my children's inheritance.
Bumper sticker alluding to the economics of Social Security. Quoted in the *New York Times*, 24 Feb 1995.

30 Louisianans don't tolerate corruption; they demand it.
1995 In the *New York Times*, 5 Mar.

31 Welfare should be a safety-net, not a hammock.
1995 In NPR broadcast, 12 Mar.

32 To avoid criticism, say nothing, do nothing, be nothing.
Inscription on a pillow given Claudia ('Lady Bird') Johnson by her staff. Quoted in *Life*, Apr 1995.

33 Hussein isn't just sitting on the fence; he *is* the fence.
1995 Unknown US diplomat on Jordan's King Hussein prior to making peace with Palestine. Quoted in *The Times*, 22 Jul.

34 The French want to attack, the Americans want to bomb, and the British want to have another meeting.
1995 US diplomat commenting on the war in Bosnia. Quoted by William Safire in the *New York Times*, 27 Jul.

35 You can't expect the Rapid Reaction Force to be ready immediately.
1995 On the British force being sent to Bosnia. Military spokesperson interviewed on BBC Radio 4's *Today* programme.

36 Craft is the handprint of all culture.
1995 On exhibit of metal and ceramic work displayed at the White House. In *Sunday Morning*, CBS TV, 30 Apr.

37 The future's bright, the future's Orange.
1996 Advertising slogan for Orange telecommunications.

38 He may be a minister of the British Government but we are the Walt Disney Corporation and we don't roll over for anyone.
1998 An unidentified Disneyland executive commenting on reports that Peter Mandelson might use the theme park's ideas in the Millennium Dome without permission. In the *Sunday Telegraph*, 18 Jan.

39 Prudence is the other woman in Gordon's life.
1998 On Gordon Brown. Comment from unidentified aide, quoted on BBC News online, 20 Mar.

40 Hear ye! Hear ye! All persons are commanded to keep silent, on pain of imprisonment, while the House of Representatives is exhibiting to the Senate of the United States articles of impeachment against William Jefferson Clinton, President of the United States.
1999 Formal announcement. Quoted in *The Guardian*, 8 Jan.

41 He who dies with the most shoes wins.
c.2000 Advertising slogan for Nike running shoes, inspired by the earlier T-shirt slogan 'he who has the most stuff when he dies, wins'.

42 The plan is called 'shock and awe', and its goal is 'the psychological destruction of the enemy's will to frighten'.
2003 In the *New Yorker*, 10 Feb.

43 There's an app for that.
2009 Advertising slogan for the Apple iPhone.

44 We need saints without cassocks, without veils—we need saints with jeans and tennis shoes. We need saints that go to the movies that listen to music, that hang out with their friends... We need saints that drink Coca-Cola, that eat hot dogs, that surf the internet and that listen to their iPods. We need saints that love the

Eucharist, that are not afraid or embarrassed to eat a pizza or drink a beer with their friends.
c.2010 Variously attributed to Popes John Paul II, Benedict XVI and Francis.

45 We are the 99 per cent.
2011 Slogan of the Occupy Movement against corporate greed, inspired by a statistic claiming that most wealth in US society is controlled by one per cent of the population.

46 Hold the burgers, hold the fries, make our wages supersize!
2013 Slogan of fast-food workers in New York City, demanding an increase in the minimum wage.

47 Hands up! Don't shoot!
2014 Slogan adopted by protestors following the shooting by police of Michael Brown in Ferguson, Missouri, Aug.

48 *Je suis Charlie.*
I am Charlie.
2015 Slogan widely adopted in France and elsewhere in defiance after Islamic terrorists murdered 12 staff of the *Charlie Hebdo* satirical magazine in Paris, 7 Jan.

49 An apple a day keeps the doctor away.
Proverb.

50 It's 105 degrees in Saigon and rising.
Prearranged coded signal for US citizens and their dependents to assemble at evacuation points during Vietnam War. Quoted in Walter Isaacson *Kissinger* (1992).

51 It's what's in the grooves that counts.
Slogan of Tamla Motown Records.

52 Let no-one enter who does not know his geometry.
Inscription at the entrance of Plato's Academy. Reported by commentators on Aristotle (Elias *In Aristotelis categorias commentarium*, 18, 118, 18).

53 Twelve Highlanders and a bagpipe make a rebellion.
Scottish proverb.

54 Wha daur meddle wi' me?
Scots paraphrase of the Scottish royal motto, 'Nemo me impune lacessit' ('No one provokes me with impunity').

55 When the world was made, the rubbish was sent to Stockport.
Quoted in Wolfgang Mieder *Investigations of Proverbs, Proverbial Expressions, Quotations and Clichés* (1984), in turn taken from *Notes and Queries* (1871).

56 *Resta viator et lege!*
Stand still, traveller, and read!
Corpus Inscriptionum Latinarum III, 371 (From Cyzicus in Mysia).

57 Salud, Dinero, Amor…y Tiempo.
Health, Wealth, Love…and Time to enjoy them.
Traditional Spanish wedding toast.

Anouilh, Jean 1910–87

French playwright. The author of light comedies, historical pieces and tragedies, his plays include *Antigone* (1944), *Ring Round the Moon* (1947) and *Becket, or the Honour of God* (1959).

58 *Faire l'amour avec une femme qui ne vous plaît pas, c'est aussi triste que de travailler.*
To make love with a woman whom you do not like is as sad as going to work.
1931 *L'Hermine*, act 1.

59 *Je sais de quelles petitesses meurent les plus grandes amours.*
I know how pettiness ruins the greatest loves.
1931 *L'Hermine*, act 2.

60 *Nous voulons tous louer à l'année et nous ne pouvons jamais louer que pour une semaine ou pour un jour. C'est l'image de la vie.*
We would all like to lease for a year and we can only lease for a week or from day to day. That is the image of life.
1937 *Le Rendez-vous de Senlis*, act 1.

61 *Il y aura toujours un chien perdu quelque part qui m'empêchera d'être heureux.*
There will always be a lost dog somewhere that will prevent me being happy.
1938 *La Sauvage*, act 3.

62 *La mort ne fait jamais mal. La mort est douce… Ce qui fait souffrir avec certains poisons, certaines blessures maladroites, c'est la vie. C'est le reste de vie. Il faut se confier franchement à la mort comme une amie.*
Death never hurts. Death is sweet… Life is what makes us suffer with its poisons and awkward injuries. That's what remains of life. We must confide freely in death as we would in a friend.
1941 *Eurydice*, act 1.

63 *C'est bon pour les hommes de croire aux idées et de mourir pour elles.*
It is good for people to believe in ideas and die for them.
1944 *Antigone*.

64 *C'est plein de disputes, un bonheur.*
Happiness is full of strife.
1944 *Antigone*.

65 *Rien n'est vrai que ce qu'on ne dit pas.*
Nothing is true except that which is unsaid.
1944 *Antigone*.

66 *Chacun de nous a un jour, plus ou moins triste, plus ou moins lointain, où il doit enfin accepter d'être un homme.*
There will come a day for each of us, more or less sad, more or less distant, when we must accept the condition of being human.
1944 *Antigone*.

67 *Mourir, ce n'est rien. Commence donc par vivre. C'est moins drôle et c'est plus long.*
To die is nothing. Begin by living. It's less funny and lasts longer.
1946 *Roméo et Jeannette*, act 3.

68 *Vous savez bien que l'amour, c'est avant tout le don de soi!*
Above all, you must understand that love is the gift of oneself!
1949 *Ardèle*.

69 *Dieu est avec tout le monde… Et, en fin de compte, il est toujours avec ceux qui ont beaucoup d'argent et de grosses armées.*
God is on everyone's side… And, in the last analysis, he is on the side with plenty of money and large armies.
1953 *L'Alouette (The Lark)*.

St Anselm 1033–1109

Italian cleric, scholar and scholastic philosopher, author of numerous philosophical and devotional treatises. In 1078 he became Abbot of Bec, in Normandy, and in 1093 was appointed Archbishop of Canterbury.

70 *Neque enim quaero ut credem, sed credo ut intelligam.*
    For I do not seek to understand so that I may believe; but I believe so that I may understand.
    1078 *Proslogion*, ch.1 (translated by M J Charlesworth).

71 *Id quo maius non cogitari potest.*
    That than which a greater cannot be thought.
    1078 Of God. *Proslogion*, ch.3. His famous ontological argument for the existence of God. Since a being that exists is necessarily greater than a being that does not, God must by this definition exist.

Antheil, George 1900–59

US composer, of Polish descent. His controversial modernistic works included the *Jazz Symphony* (1925) and the *Ballet Mécanique* (1927), written for ten pianos and a variety of eccentric percussion instruments.

72 Art cannot hold its breath too long without dying.
    1945 *Bad Boy of Music*.

Anthony, Susan B(rownell) 1820–1906

US social reformer and women's suffrage leader. A campaigner in temperance and anti-slavery movements, she co-founded the National Women's Suffrage Association with Elizabeth Cady (1869).

73 The true Republic: men, their rights and nothing more; women, their rights and nothing less.
    1868–70 On the front of her newspaper, *The Revolution*.

74 There will never be complete equality until women themselves help to make laws and to elect lawmakers.
    In *The Arena*.

Antiphon 5c BC

Greek philosopher and sophist. Only fragments survive of his works.

75 The greatest cost, namely time.
    Quoted in Plutarch *Antonius*, 28.

Apelles 4c BC

Greek painter, probably born in Colophon on the Ionian coast of Asia Minor.

76 *Ne supra crepidam sutor iudicaret.*
    Let the cobbler stick to his last.
    Quoted in Pliny *Naturalis Historia*, 35.36.85. A cobbler who had criticized Apelles' way of rendering a sandal in one of his paintings, proceeded to criticize the rest of the painting as well. The expression became proverbial.

Apollinaire, Guillaume originally Wilhelm Apollinaris de Kostrowitzki 1880–1918

French poet and author of Polish–Italian parentage. Associated with avant-garde literary groups, he is said to have invented the word 'surrealism'.

77 *Et toi mon coeur pourquoi bats-tu*
    Comme un guetteur mélancolique
    J'observe la nuit et la mort.
    And you my heart why do you pound
    Like some melancholy watchman
    I watch the night and death.
    1899 *Le Guetteur mélancolique*, préface.

78 *Avant tout, les artistes sont des hommes qui veulent devenir inhumains.*
    Above all, artists are men who want to become inhuman.
    1913 *Les Peintres cubistes; Méditations esthétiques*, 'Sur la peinture, 1'.

79 *Un Picasso étudie un objet comme un chirurgien dissèque un cadavre.*
    A Picasso studies an object like a surgeon dissects a corpse.
    1913 *Les Peintres cubistes; Méditations esthétiques*, 'Sur la peinture, 2'.

80 *La géométrie est aux arts plastiques ce que la grammaire est à l'art de l'écrivain.*
    Geometry is to sculpture what grammar is to the art of the writer.
    1913 *Les Peintres cubistes; Méditations esthétiques*, 'Sur la peinture, 3'.

81 *Sous le pont Mirabeau coule la Seine.*
    Et nos amours, faut-il qu'il m'en souvienne?
    La joie venait toujours après la peine.
    Under Mirabeau Bridge flows the Seine.
    And our loves, must I remember them?
    Joy always came after pain.
    1913 *Les Alcools*, 'Le Pont Mirabeau'.

82 *Vienne la nuit sonne l'heure*
    Les jours s'en vont je demeure.
    Let night come, ring out the hour,
    The days go by, I remain.
    1913 *Les Alcools*, 'Le Pont Mirabeau'.

83 *Je connais gens de toutes sortes*
    Ils n'égalent pas leur destin.
    I know people of all sorts
    They do not measure up to their destiny.
    1913 *Les Alcools*, 'Marizibill'.

84 *L'art, de plus en plus, aura une patrie.*
    Art, more and more, will have a country.
    1913 'L'Esprit nouveau et les poètes', *Mercure de France*.

85 *Il est grand temps de rallumer les étoiles.*
    It's high time we relit the stars.
    1917 *Les Mamelles de Tirésias*, prologue.

86 *Perdre*
    Mais perdre vraiment
    Pour laisser place à la trouvaille
    Perdre
    La vie pour trouver la Victoire.
    To lose
    But really to lose
    And make room for discovery
    To lose
    Life so as to discover Victory.
    1918 *Calligrammes*, 'Toujours'.

Appel, Jacob M. 1973–

US author and bioethicist, best known for his short stories and plays.

87 The boss is never your friend, even if you're sleeping with him.
    2005 *Arborophilia*.

88 Nothing sells tombstones like a Girl Scout in uniform.
    2009 'Scouting for the Reaper', *Virginia Quarterly Review*.

89 Patriotism is being convinced your country is better because you were born in it.
    2012 *The Man Who Wouldn't Stand Up*.

Appleton, Sir Edward Victor 1892–1965
English physicist, Professor at London University (1924) and Cambridge (1936). He discovered the Appleton layer of electrically charged particles in the Earth's upper atmosphere, and was awarded the 1947 Nobel prize for physics.

90 You must not miss Whitehall. At one end you will find a statue of one of our kings who was beheaded; at the other, a monument to the man who did it. That is just one example of our attempts to be fair to everybody.
   1948 Speech, Stockholm, 1 Jan.

91 I do not mind what language an opera is sung in so long as it is a language I don't understand.
   1955 In the *Observer*, 28 Aug.

Appleton, Thomas Gold 1812–84
US man of letters and wit, the brother-in-law of Henry Wadsworth Longfellow. His own literary output consisted of formal poetry and pleasant essays and is collected in *Faded Leaves* (1872) and *A Sheaf of Papers* (1875).

92 Good Americans, when they die, go to Paris.
   Quoted in Oliver Wendell Holmes *The Autocrat at the Breakfast Table* (1858), ch.6. Although the speaker in Holmes's book is not identified by name, he is generally identified as Appleton.

93 Boston is a state of mind.
   Attributed. This quotation has also been attributed to Ralph Waldo Emerson and Mark Twain.

94 A Boston man is the east wind made flesh.
   Attributed.

Aquinas, St Thomas 1225–74
Italian Dominican monk and leading scholastic theologian, known as The Angelic Doctor. He was the first to attempt a complete theological system, and as Doctor of the Church his work is particularly respected in the Roman Catholic tradition.

95 *Pulchritudo enim creaturae nihil est aliud quam similitudo divinae pulchritudinis in rebus participata.*
   The beauty of creatures is nothing other than an image of the divine beauty in which things participate.
   c.1260 *Commentarium in Dionysii De Divinibus Nominibus*, bk.4, ch.5.

96 *Pange, lingua, gloriosi
   Corporis mysterium,
   Sanguinisque pretiosi,
   Quem in mundi pretium
   Fructus ventris generosi
   Rex effudit gentium.*
   Now, my tongue, the mystery telling
   Of the glorious Body sing,
   And the Blood, all price excelling,
   Which the Gentiles' Lord and King,
   In a Virgin's womb once dwelling,
   Shed for this world's ransoming.
   1263 *Pange Lingua Gloriosi*, known as the Corpus Christi hymn (translated by J M Neale et al).

97 *Tantum ergo sacramentum
   Veneremur cernui;
   Et antiquum documentum
   Novo cedat ritui.*
   Therefore we, before him bending,
   This great Sacrament revere;
   Types and shadows have their ending,
   For the newer rite is here.
   1263 *Pange Lingua Gloriosi*, known as the Corpus Christi hymn (translated by J M Neale et al).

98 *Solus homo delectatur in ipsa pulchritudine sensibilium secundum seipsam.*
   Only man delights in the beauty of sense objects for their own sake.
   c.1268 *Summa Theologia*, bk.1, question 91, article 3.

99 *Ars autem deficit ab operatione naturae.*
   Art pales when compared to the workings of nature.
   c.1272 *Summa Theologia*, bk. 3, question 66, article 4.

Arbuthnot, John 1667–1735
Scottish physician and writer, who published five satirical pamphlets against the Duke of Marlborough in 1712, under the title *The History of John Bull*.

1 Law is a bottomless pit.
   1712 *The History of John Bull*, title of pamphlet.

2 Hame's hame, be it never so hamely.
   1712 *The History of John Bull*, 'John Bull Still in His Senses', ch.3.

3 Curle (who is one of the new terrors of Death) has been writing letters to every body for memoirs of his life.
   1733 Letter to Jonathan Swift, 13 Jan.

Archer, Jeffrey Howard, Lord 1940–
English politician and writer. A Conservative MP (1969–74), he resigned from the Commons after a financial disaster and turned to fiction, becoming a best-selling author of political potboilers. In 2001 he received a four-year jail sentence on charges of perjury and perverting the course of justice.

4 Not a Penny More, Not a Penny Less.
   1975 Title of novel.

5 First Among Equals.
   1984 Title of novel.

6 I am innocent of the charge, and nothing you will say however clever you are in the wording of out-of-context pieces, however clever you are in letting people know what 'on and off the record' means, there is only one thing that matters in this court of law, sir: I have never had sexual intercourse with her. And that is the truth!
   Giving evidence at a libel trial in 1987. Quoted in Michael Crick *Jeffrey Archer: Stranger than Fiction* (1996).

Archer, Mary 1944–
English scientist. She is married to Jeffrey Archer.

7 I am cross with Jeffrey, but I have formed the judgement that he is a decent and generous spirited man over 35 years and that will not change over one weekend.
   Following the revelation that her husband planned to establish a false alibi in his 1987 libel case. In the *Observer*, 'They said what...?', 28 Nov 1999.

Archimedes c.287–212 BC
Greek mathematician, whose innovations included siege-engines and the Archimedean screw for water raising. He was killed at the Roman siege of Syracuse.

8 Give me a firm spot on which to stand, and I shall move the earth.
   Traditionally attributed to Archimedes; a variation can be found in Plutarch *Marcellus*, 14.

9 Eureka, Eureka! (I found it, I found it!).
   Vitruvius 9.9.10. Attributed, on discovering the principle of upthrust on a floating body while having a bath. Archimedes had been given the task of establishing whether there was the proper weight of gold in the crown of Hieron of Syracuse. One day when entering his bath he noticed the water which flowed over the sides as he entered and he correctly perceived that the weight of the water displaced was that of the weight of his body.

Arenas, Reinaldo 1943–90

Cuban novelist. He held several minor positions in Cuba before leaving the country in 1980 for the US. He committed suicide in New York while suffering from AIDS.

10 *Nuestro portero descubrió, o creyó descubrir, que su labor no se podía limitar a abrir la puerta del edificio, sino que él, el portero, era el señalado, el elegido, el indicado...para mostrarles a todas aquellas personas una puerta más amplia y hasta entonces invisible o inaccesible; puerta que era la de sus propias vidas.*
   Our doorman discovered (or thought he had discovered) that his tasks could not be limited to just opening the door of the building—but that he, the doorman, was the one *chosen, elected, singled out*...to show everyone who lived there a wider door, until then either invisible or inaccessible: the door to their own lives.
   1989 *El portero* (*The Doorman*, 1961), pt.1, ch.1.

Aretino, Pietro 1492–1557

Italian poet, illegitimate son of a nobleman. Banished from his native town, he wandered through Italy. His wit secured the favour of Pope Leo X, subsequently lost with the salacious *Sonetti Lussuriosi*. Later patrons included Giovanni de Medici, Francis I and Charles V. He reputedly died by falling from a stool while laughing.

11 I am a free man, I do not need to copy Petrarch or Boccaccio. My own genius is enough. Let others worry themselves about style and so cease to be themselves. Without a master, without a model, without a guide, without artifice, I go to work and earn my living, my well-being, and my fame. What do I need more? With a goose quill and a few sheets of paper I mock the universe.
   Quoted in J H Plumb (ed) *The Horizon Book of the Renaissance* (1961, new edn by Penguin, 1982).

Arguedas, José María 1911–69

Peruvian fiction writer and ethnologist. His works reflect the tensions that underlie Peruvian society, in the marginalization of native peoples. He committed suicide.

12 *Dónde está la patria, amigo? Ni en el corazón ni en la saliva.*
   Where is the country, my friend? It is not in the heart or in the saliva.
   1971 *El zorro de arriba y el zorro de abajo* ('The Upper and the Lower Fox'), ch.3.

Ariosto, Ludovico 1474–1533

Italian poet. He joined the court of Cardinal Ippolito d'Este at Ferrara in 1503, where he produced his most famous work, the Roland epic, *Orlando Furioso* (completed 1516, enlarged 1532). He also wrote comedies, satires and sonnets.

13 *Natura il fece, e poi roppe la stampa.*
   Nature made him, and then broke the mould.
   1516 *Orlando Furioso*, canto 10, stanza 84.

Aristophanes c.448–c.388 BC

Greek comic poet. Only 11 comedies survive of his 54 plays; they are characterized by exaggeration, parody and satire of contemporary political and cultural life.

14 Who brings owls to Athens?
   Avae (*The Birds*), 1.301. This ancient proverb, quoted by various authors, is the equivalent of 'to carry coals to Newcastle'.

15 Old age is second childhood.
   Nubes (*The Clouds*), 1.1417.

16 Till the wolf and the lamb be united.
   On the impossibility of peace between sworn enemies. *Pax*, 1.1076.

Aristotle 384–322 BC

Greek philosopher, scientist and physician, a student of Plato and tutor to Alexander the Great. His philosophical works include *Metaphysics*, *Politics*, *Rhetoric* and *Poetics*. His influence has been incalculable; in medieval Europe he was known simply as 'The Philosopher'.

17 All men naturally desire knowledge.
   Metaphysics, bk.1, ch.1, 980a (translated by H Tredennick).

18 It is through wonder that men now begin and originally began to philosophize; wondering in the first place at obvious perplexities, and then by gradual progression raising questions about the greater matters too.
   Metaphysics, bk.1, ch.2, 982 (translated by H Tredennick).

19 Every art and every inquiry, and similarly every action and pursuit, is thought to aim at some good; and for this reason the good has rightly been declared to be that at which all things aim.
   Nicomachean Ethics, bk.1, ch.1, 1093 (translated by Sir David Ross).

20 Human good turns out to be activity of soul exhibiting excellence, and if there is more than one sort of excellence, in accordance with the best and most complete. For one swallow does not make a summer, nor does one day; and so too one day, or a short time, does not make a man blessed and happy.
   Nicomachean Ethics, bk.1, ch.7, 1098 (translated by Sir David Ross).

21 Virtue, then, is a state of character concerned with choice, lying in a mean...it is a mean between two vices, that which depends on excess and that which depends on defect.
   Nicomachean Ethics, bk.2, ch.6, 1006 (translated by Sir David Ross).

22 For man, therefore, the life according to reason is best and pleasantest, since reason more than anything else *is* man.
   Nicomachean Ethics, bk.10, ch.7, 1178 (translated by Sir David Ross).

23 Tragedy is thus a representation of an action that is worth serious attention, complete in itself and of some amplitude...by means of pity and fear bringing about the purgation of such emotions.
   c.330 BC *Poetics*, ch.6.

24 Now a whole is that which has a beginning, a middle, and an end.
   c.330 BC *Poetics*, ch.7, referring to tragedy.

25 Man is by nature a political animal; it is his nature to live in a state.
   c.330 BC *Politics*, bk.1, ch.2, 1253a (translated by T A Sinclair).

26 Nature, as we say, does nothing without some purpose; and for the purpose of making man a political animal she has endowed him alone among the animals with the power of reasoned speech.
   c.330 BC *Politics*, bk.1, ch.2, 1253b (translated by T A Sinclair).

27 It is a bad thing that many from being rich should become poor; for men of ruined fortunes are sure to stir up revolutions.
c.330 BC *Politics*, bk.4.

28 The flute is not an instrument that has a good moral effect—it is too exciting.
c.330 BC *Politics*.

29 For that which has become habitual, becomes as it were natural.
Rhetorica, 1370a (translated by J H Freese).

30 *Amicus Plato, sed magis amica veritas.*
Plato is dear to me, but dearer still is truth.
Proverbial expression, traditionally attributed to Aristotle, going back to a passage in the *Ethica Nicomachea*, 1069a.

Arlott, (Leslie Thomas) John 1914–91

English cricket commentator and writer, a police detective before joining the BBC in 1945. His voice became the epitome of radio cricket commentary.

31 The Master: records prove the title good:
Yet figures fail you, for they cannot say
How many men whose names you never knew
Are proud to tell their sons they saw you play.

They share the sunlight of your summer day
Of thirty years; and they, with you, recall
How, through those well-wrought centuries, your hand
Reshaped the history of bat and ball.
1952 'To John Berry Hobbs on his Seventieth Birthday'.

32 Cricket, like the novel, is great when it presents men in the round, when it shows the salty quality of human nature.
1953 Quoted in Colin Jarman *The Guinness Dictionary of Sports Quotations* (1990).

33 Most games are skin-deep, but cricket goes to the bone.
1977 *Arlott and Trueman on Cricket*.

34 Cricket is a game of the most terrifying stresses with more luck about it than any other game I know. They call it a team game, but in fact it is the loneliest game of all.
Another Word from Arlott.

Arlt, Roberto 1900–42

Argentinian fiction writer, dramatist and journalist. The son of German immigrants, his works emphasize the anger and disillusionment of the urban middle class.

35 ¡Y yo, yo, Señor, no tendré nunca una querida tan linda como esa querida que lucen los cromos de los libros viciosos!
And I, Sir, I'll never have a mistress as beautiful as those in the pictures of obscene books!
1926 *El juguete rabioso* ('The Rabid Toy'), ch.2.

Armani, Giorgio 1935–

Italian fashion designer.

36 I believe that style is the only real luxury that is really desirable.
Attributed.

37 Elegance is not about being noticed, it's about being remembered.
Attributed.

Armey, Dick (Richard Keith) 1940–

US Congressman and former economics lecturer.

38 It is like relying on the Flintstones for an understanding of the Stone Age.
1994 On economic data from the Congressional Budget Office. In *Time*, 25 Nov.

39 Entitlement spending—the politics of greed wrapped in the language of love.
1994 On President Johnson's legacy to his party. In the *US News & World Report*, 12 Dec.

Armistead, Lewis Addison 1817–63

Confederate general. Commissioned in the US army from Virginia, he resigned when that state seceded. He took part in Picket's charge at Gettysburg, where he was killed.

40 Give them the cold steel, boys!
1863 Attributed, during the American Civil War.

Armstrong, Billie Joe 1972–

US singer and guitarist, lead singer with rock group Green Day.

41 A guy walks up to me and asks 'What's Punk?' So I kick over a garbage can and say 'That's punk!' So he kicks over the garbage can and says' That's Punk?', and I say 'No, that's trendy!'
2006 Quoted in Matt Doeden, *Green Day: Keeping Their Edge*.

Armstrong, Lance 1971–

US cyclist. He won the Tour de France a record six times from 1999 to 2005, but was then stripped of all his titles and banned from competitive cycling for life for drug-taking.

42 My illness was also my antidote: it cured me of laziness.
2003 Referring to his recovery from cancer in *Every Second Counts*.

43 You know when I need to die? When I'm done living. When I can't walk, can't eat, can't see, when I'm a crotchety old bastard, mad at the world. Then I can die.
2003 *Every Second Counts*.

44 I'm on my bike.
When, during a furore about drug-taking by professional cyclists, he was asked: 'What are you on?'. Quoted in Graeme Fife *Tour de France the History, the Legend, the Riders* (2000).

45 I can't say I have any regrets. It's been an excellent ride.
2011 Announcing his retirement from competitive cycling.

46 I'm a flawed character… I viewed this situation as one big lie that I repeated a lot of times.
2013 Quoted in the *Wall Street Journal* after admitting on television that he had taken performance-enhancing drugs, 18 Jan.

Armstrong, Louis known as Satchmo 1900–71

US jazz trumpeter and singer, the first major jazz virtuoso. He led studio groups such as the Hot Five and the Hot Seven as well as working with many big bands, and as a singer introduced the scat style. He toured extensively and appeared in over 50 films as a musician and entertainer.

47 Musicians don't retire; they stop when there's no more music in them.
1968 Quoted in the *Observer*, 21 Apr.

48 If you still have to ask…shame on you.
Habitual response when asked what is jazz? Quoted in M Jones *Salute to Satchmo* (1970).

49 All music is folk music. I ain't never heard no horse sing a song.
Quoted in the *New York Times*, 7 Jul 1971.

50 A lotta cats copy the Mona Lisa, but people still line up to see the original.
Alluding to his many imitators. Quoted in David Pickering *Brewer's Twentieth Century Music* (1994).

Armstrong, Neil A(lden) 1930–2012

US astronaut. A former fighter pilot, he commanded Gemini 8 (1966) and in 1969 was a crew member of Apollo 11, and the first man to walk on the moon.

51 That's one small step for a man, one giant leap forward for mankind.
1969 His words on becoming the first man to walk on the moon, 20 Jul. Armstrong claimed to have said 'That's one small step for a man...', but tape-recordings seem to confirm that he omitted the 'a', thereby causing some confusion among his listeners.

52 I believe every human has a finite number of heart-beats. I don't intend to waste any of mine running around doing exercises.
Quoted in Colin Jarman *The Guinness Dictionary of Sports Quotations* (1990).

Armstrong, Robert, Baron Armstrong of Ilminster 1927–

English civil servant. In 1970 he became principal private secretary to Prime Minister Edward Heath, and later Secretary to the Cabinet and Head of the Home Civil Service under Margaret Thatcher.

53 It contains a misleading impression, not a lie. It was being economical with the truth.
1986 On a letter, during cross-examination at the 'Spycatcher' trial, New South Wales, Australia, quoted in the *Daily Telegraph*, 19 Nov.

Arnald Amaury d.1225

French clergyman. Abbot of Citeaux (1202–12), he was the first inquisitor against the Albigensian heresy. In 1212 as Bishop of Narbonne he crusaded against the Moors in Spain.

54 Kill them all. God will recognize his own.
1209 Quoted in Caeserius of Heisterbach *Dialogus Miraculorum* (c.1233), bk.5, ch.21. Cited and translated in Jonathon Sumption *The Albigensian Crusade* (1978), ch.6.

Arnold, Matthew 1822–88

English poet and critic. His poems, mainly elegiac in mood and on pastoral themes, include 'The Forsaken Merman' (1849), 'The Scholar-Gipsy' (1853) and 'Thyrsis' (1867). His critical works include *Essays in Criticism* (1865, 1888) and *Culture and Anarchy* (1869).

55 Come, dear children, let us away;
Down and away below!
1849 *The Strayed Reveller, and Other Poems*, 'The Forsaken Merman', l.1–2.

56 Now the great winds shorewards blow;
Now the salt tides seawards flow;
Now the wild white horses play,
Champ and chafe and toss in the spray.
1849 *The Strayed Reveller, and Other Poems*, 'The Forsaken Merman', l.4–7.

57 Sand-strewn caverns, cool and deep,
Where the winds are all asleep;
Where the spent lights quiver and gleam;
Where the salt weed sways in the stream.
1849 *The Strayed Reveller, and Other Poems*, 'The Forsaken Merman', l.35–8.

58 Where great whales come sailing by,
Sail and sail, with unshut eye,
Round the world for ever and aye.
1849 *The Strayed Reveller, and Other Poems*, 'The Forsaken Merman', l.43–5.

59 Not deep the Poet sees, but wide.
1849 *The Strayed Reveller, and Other Poems*, 'Resignation', l.214.

60 Yet they, believe me, who await
No gifts from chance, have conquered fate.
1849 *The Strayed Reveller, and Other Poems*, 'Resignation', l.247–8.

61 Not milder is the general lot
Because our spirits have forgot,
In action's dizzying eddy whirled,
The something that infects the world.
1849 *The Strayed Reveller, and Other Poems*, 'Resignation', l.275–8.

62 Others abide our question. Thou art free.
We ask and ask: Thou smilest and art still,
Out-topping knowledge.
1849 *The Strayed Reveller, and Other Poems*, 'Shakespeare'.

63 And thou, who didst the stars and sunbeams know,
Self-schooled, self-scanned, self-honoured, self-secure,
Didst tread on Earth unguessed at.—Better so!
All pains the immortal spirit must endure,
All weakness which impairs, all griefs which bow,
Find their sole speech in that victorious brow.
1849 *The Strayed Reveller, and Other Poems*, 'Shakespeare'.

64 Who saw life steadily, and saw it whole:
The mellow glory of the Attic stage;
Singer of sweet Colonus, and its child.
1849 Of Sophocles. *The Strayed Reveller, and Other Poems*, 'To a Friend'.

65 France, famed in all great arts, in none supreme.
1849 *The Strayed Reveller, and Other Poems*, 'To a Republican Friend—Continued'.

66 The sea of faith
Lay like the folds of a bright girdle furled.
But now I only hear
Its melancholy, long, withdrawing roar,
Retreating, to the breath
Of the night-wind, down the vast edges drear
And naked shingles of the world.
1851 'Dover Beach', stanza 3.

67 And we are here as on a darkling plain
Swept with confused alarms of struggle and flight,
Where ignorant armies clash by night.
1851 'Dover Beach', stanza 4.

68 Be neither saint nor sophist-led, but be a man.
1852 'Empedocles on Etna', act 1, sc.2, l.136.

69 Is it so small a thing
To have enjoyed the sun,
To have lived light in the spring,
To have loved, to have thought, to have done.
1852 'Empedocles on Etna', act 1, sc.2, l.397–400.

70 Because thou must not dream, thou needst not then despair!
1852 'Empedocles on Etna', act 1, sc.2, l.426.

71 And we forget because we must
And not because we will.
1852 *Empedocles on Etna and Other Poems*, 'Absence'.

72 Only—but this is rare—
   When a beloved hand is laid in ours,
   When, jaded with the rush and glare
   Of the interminable hours,
   Our eyes can in another's eyes read clear,
   When our world-deafened ear
   Is by the tones of a loved voice caressed—
   A bolt is shot back somewhere in our breast,
   And a lost pulse of feeling stirs again.
   The eye sinks inward, and the heart lies plain,
   And what we mean, we say, and what we would, we know.
   1852 *Empedocles on Etna and Other Poems*, 'The Buried Life', l.77–87.

73 Come to me in my dreams, and then
   By day I shall be well again!
   For then the night will more than pay
   The hopeless longing of the day.
   1852 *Empedocles on Etna and Other Poems*, 'Longing' (later published as 'Faded Leaves' in *Poems: Second Series*, 1855).

74 Calm soul of all things! make it mine
   To feel, amid the city's jar,
   That there abides a peace of thine,
   Man did not make, and cannot mar.
   1852 *Empedocles on Etna and Other Poems*, 'Lines written in Kensington Garden'.

75 He spoke, and loosed our heart in tears.
   He laid us as we lay at birth
   On the cool flowery lap of earth.
   1852 Of William Wordsworth. *Empedocles on Etna and Other Poems*, 'Memorial Verses, April 1850', l.47–9.

76 With aching hands and bleeding feet
   We dig and heap, lay stone on stone;
   We bear the burden and the heat
   Of the long day, and wish 'twere done.
   Not till the hours of light return,
   All we have built do we discern.
   1852 *Empedocles on Etna and Other Poems*, 'Morality'.

77 Say, has some wet bird-haunted English lawn
   Lent it the music of its trees at dawn?
   1852 *Empedocles on Etna and Other Poems*, 'Parting', l.19–20.

78 Resolve to be thyself: and know, that he
   Who finds himself, loses his misery.
   1852 *Empedocles on Etna and Other Poems*, 'Self-Dependence', l.31–2.

79 Ah! two desires toss about
   The poet's feverish blood.
   One drives him to the world without,
   And one to solitude.
   1852 *Empedocles on Etna and Other Poems*, 'Stanzas in Memory of the Author of "Obermann"', l.93–6.

80 Still bent to make some port he knows not where,
   Still standing for some false impossible shore.
   1852 *Empedocles on Etna and Other Poems*, 'A Summer Night', l.68–9.

81 Yes! in the sea of life enisled,
   With echoing straits between us thrown,
   Dotting the shoreless watery wild,
   We mortal millions live alone.
   1852 *Empedocles on Etna and Other Poems*, 'To Marguerite—Continued', l.1–4.

82 A God, a God their severance ruled!
   And bade betwixt their shores to be
   The unplumbed, salt, estranging sea.
   1852 *Empedocles on Etna and Other Poems*, 'To Marguerite—Continued', l.22–4.

83 I am past thirty, and three parts iced over.
   1853 Letter to Arthur Hugh Clough, 12 Feb

84 Hark! ah, the Nightingale!
   The tawny-throated!
   Hark! from that moonlit cedar what a burst!
   What triumph! hark—what pain!
   1853 *Poems: A New Edition*, 'Philomela', l.1–4.

85 Eternal Passion!
   Eternal Pain!
   1853 *Poems: A New Edition*, 'Philomela', l.31–2.

86 Her cabined ample Spirit,
   It fluttered and failed for breath.
   Tonight it doth inherit
   The vasty hall of death.
   1853 *Poems: A New Edition*, 'Requiescat'.

87 Go, for they call you, Shepherd, from the hill.
   1853 *Poems: A New Edition*, 'The Scholar-Gipsy', l.1.

88 All the live murmur of a summer's day.
   1853 *Poems: A New Edition*, 'The Scholar-Gipsy', l.20.

89 Tired of knocking at Preferment's door.
   1853 *Poems: A New Edition*, 'The Scholar-Gipsy', l.35.

90 Crossing the stripling Thames at Bab-lock-hithe,
   Trailing in the cool stream thy fingers wet,
   As the slow punt swings round.
   1853 *Poems: A New Edition*, 'The Scholar-Gipsy', l.74–6.

91 Rapt, twirling in thy hand a withered spray,
   And waiting for the spark from heaven to fall.
   1853 *Poems: A New Edition*, 'The Scholar-Gipsy', l.119–20.

92 The line of festal light in Christ-Church hall.
   1853 *Poems: A New Edition*, 'The Scholar-Gipsy', l.129.

93 Thou waitest for the spark from heaven! and we,
   Light half-believers in our casual creeds...
   Who hesitate and falter life away,
   And lose tomorrow the ground won today—
   Ah, do not we, Wanderer, await it too?
   1853 *Poems: A New Edition*, 'The Scholar-Gipsy', l.171–4.

94 O born in days when wits were fresh and clear,
   And life ran gaily as the sparkling Thames:
   Before this strange disease of modern life,
   With its sick hurry, its divided aims,
   Its heads o'ertaxed, its palsied hearts, was rife—
   Fly hence, our contact fear!
   1853 *Poems: A New Edition*, 'The Scholar-Gipsy', l.201–6.

95 Still nursing the unconquerable hope,
   Still clutching the inviolable shade.
   1853 *Poems: A New Edition*, 'The Scholar-Gipsy', l.211–12.

96 Curled minion, dancer, coiner of sweet words!
   1853 *Poems: A New Edition*, 'Sohrab and Rustum', l.458.

97 No horse's cry was that, most like the roar
   Of some pained desert lion, who all day
   Hath trailed the hunter's javelin in his side,
   And comes at night to die upon the sand.
   1853 *Poems: A New Edition*, 'Sohrab and Rustum', l.501–4.

98 Truth sits upon the lips of dying men.
   1853 *Poems: A New Edition*, 'Sohrab and Rustum', l.656.

99 But the majestic river floated on,
   Out of the mist and hum of that low land,
   Into the frosty starlight.
   1853 *Poems: A New Edition*, 'Sohrab and Rustum', l.875–7.

1. Oxus, forgetting the bright speed he had
   In his high mountain cradle in Pamere,
   A foiled circuitous wanderer—till at last
   The longed-for dash of waves is heard, and wide
   His luminous home of waters opens, bright
   And tranquil, from whose floor the new-bathed stars
   Emerge, and shine upon the Aral Sea.
   1853 *Poems: A New Edition*, 'Sohrab and Rustrum', l.886–92.

2. Cruel, but composed and bland,
   Dumb, inscrutable and grand,
   So Tiberius might have sat,
   Had Tiberius been a cat.
   1855 *Poems: Second Series*, 'Poor Matthias', l.40–3.

3. For rigorous teachers seized my youth,
   And purged its faith, and trimmed its fire,
   Showed me the high, white star of Truth,
   There bade me gaze, and there aspire.
   1855 *Poems: Second Series*, 'Stanzas from the Grande Chartreuse', l.67–70.

4. Wandering between two worlds, one dead,
   The other powerless to be born,
   With nowhere yet to rest my head,
   Like these, on earth I wait forlorn.
   1855 *Poems: Second Series*, 'Stanzas from the Grande Chartreuse', l.85–8.

5. What helps it now, that Byron bore,
   With haughty scorn which mocked the smart,
   Through Europe to the Aetolian shore
   The pageant of his bleeding heart?
   That thousands counted every groan,
   And Europe made his woe her own?
   1855 *Poems: Second Series*, 'Stanzas from the Grande Chartreuse', l.133–8.

6. This truth—to prove, and make thine own:
   'Thou hast been, shalt be, art, alone.'
   1857 'Isolation. To Marguerite', l.29–30.

7. Wordsworth says somewhere that wherever Virgil seems to have composed 'with his eye on the object', Dryden fails to render him. Homer invariably composes 'with his eye on the object', whether the object be moral or a material one: Pope composes with his eye on his style, into which he translates his object, whatever it is.
   1861 *On Translating Homer*, lecture 1.

8. Of these two literatures [French and German], as of the intellect of Europe in general, the main effort, for now many years, has been a critical effort; the endeavours, in all branches of knowledge—theology, philosophy, history, art, science—to see the object as in itself it really is.
   1861 *On Translating Homer*, lecture 2.

9. [The translator] will find one English book and one only, where, as in the *Iliad* itself, perfect plainness of speech is allied with perfect nobleness; and that book is the Bible.
   1861 *On Translating Homer*, lecture 3.

10. Nothing has raised more questioning among my critics than these words—noble, the grand style... I think it will be found that the grand style arises in poetry, when a noble nature, poetically gifted, treats with simplicity or with severity a serious subject.
    1862 *On Translating Homer; Last Words*.

11. Nothing could moderate, in the bosom of the great English middle class, their passionate, absorbing, almost blood-thirsty clinging to life.
    1865 *Essays in Criticism First Series*, preface.

12. Beautiful city! so venerable, so lovely, so unravaged by the fierce intellectual life of our century, so serene!...whispering from her towers the last enchantments of the Middle Age... Home of lost causes, and forsaken beliefs, and unpopular names, and impossible loyalties!
    1865 Of Oxford. *Essays in Criticism First Series*, preface.

13. I am bound by my own definition of criticism: a disinterested endeavour to learn and propagate the best that is known and thought in the world.
    1865 *Essays in Criticism First Series*, 'The Function of Criticism at the Present Time'.

14. Philistinism!—We have not the expression in English. Perhaps we have not the word because we have so much of the thing.
    1865 *Essays in Criticism First Series*, 'Heinrich Heine'.

15. The great apostle of the Philistine, Lord Macaulay.
    1865 *Essays in Criticism First Series*, 'Joubert'.

16. The signal-elm, that looks on Ilsley downs,
    The Vale, the three lone weirs, the youthful Thames.
    1866 *New Poems*, 'Thyrsis', l.14–15. The poem is an elegy for his friend Arthur Hugh Clough, who drowned in 1861.

17. And that sweet City with her dreaming spires,
    She needs not June for beauty's heightening.
    1866 Of Oxford. *New Poems*, 'Thyrsis', l.19–20.

18. So have I heard the cuckoo's parting cry,
    From the wet field, through the vext garden trees,
    Come with the volleying rain and tossing breeze:
    'The bloom is gone, and with the bloom go I.'
    1866 *New Poems*, 'Thyrsis', l.57–60.

19. Too quick despairer, wherefore wilt thou go?
    Soon will the high Midsummer pomps come on,
    Soon will the musk carnations break and swell.
    1866 *New Poems*, 'Thyrsis', l.61–3.

20. For Time, not Corydon, hath conquered thee.
    1866 *New Poems*, 'Thyrsis', l.80.

21. The foot less prompt to meet the morning dew,
    The heart less bounding at emotion new,
    And hope, once crushed, less quick to spring again.
    1866 *New Poems*, 'Thyrsis', l.138–40.

22. It is not in the outward and visible world of material life that the Celtic genius of Wales or Ireland can at this day hope to count for much; it is in the inward world of thought and science. What it *has* been, what is *has* done, what it will be or will do, as a matter of modern politics.
    1867 'On the Study of Celtic Literature'.

23. Let us reunite ourselves with our better mind and with the world through science; and let it be one of our angelic revenges on the Philistines, who among their other sins are the guilty authors of Fenianism, to found at Oxford a chair of Celtic, and to send, through the gentle ministration of science, a message of peace to Ireland.
    1867 'On the Study of Celtic Literature'.

24. Creep into thy narrow bed,
    Creep, and let no more be said!
    Vain thy onset! all stands fast.

Thou thyself must break at last.
Let the long contention cease!
Geese are swans, and swans are geese.
Let them have it how they will!
Thou art tired; best be still.
1867 New Poems, 'The Last Word'.

25 Coldly, sadly descends
The autumn evening. The field
Strewn with its dank yellow drifts
Of withered leaves, and the elms,
Fade into dimness apace,
Silent;—hardly a shout
From a few boys late at their play!
1867 New Poems, 'Rugby Chapel, November 1857'.

26 Our society distributes itself into Barbarians, Philistines, and Populace; and America is just ourselves, with the Barbarians quite left out, and the Populace nearly.
1869 Culture and Anarchy, preface.

27 The pursuit of perfection, then, is the pursuit of sweetness and light... He who works for sweetness and light united, works to make reason and the will of God prevail.
1869 Culture and Anarchy, ch.1.

28 The men of culture are the true apostles of equality.
1869 Culture and Anarchy, ch.1.

29 That vast portion...of the working-class which, raw and half-developed has long lain half-hidden amidst its poverty and squalor, and is now issuing from its hiding-place to assert an Englishman's heaven-born privilege of doing as he likes, and is beginning to perplex us by marching where it likes, meeting where it likes, bawling what it likes, breaking what it likes—to this vast residuum we may with great propriety give the name of Populace.
1869 Culture and Anarchy, ch.3.

30 Hebraism and Hellenism—between these two points of influence moves our world.
1869 Culture and Anarchy, ch.4.

31 'He knows' says Hebraism, 'his Bible!'—whenever we hear this said, we may, without any elaborate defence of culture, content ourselves with answering simply: 'No man, who knows nothing else, knows even his Bible.'
1869 Culture and Anarchy, ch.5.

32 Culture, the acquainting ourselves with the best that has been known and said in the world, and thus with the history of the human spirit.
1873 Literature and Dogma, preface.

33 Culture is the passion for sweetness and light, and (what is more) the passion for making them prevail.
1873 Literature and Dogma, preface.

34 The true meaning of religion is thus not simply morality, but morality touched with emotion.
1873 Literature and Dogma, ch.1.

35 Conduct is three-fourths of our life and its largest concern.
1873 Literature and Dogma, ch.1.

36 The eternal *not ourselves* that makes for righteousness.
1873 Literature and Dogma, ch.8.

37 But there remains the question: what righteousness really is. The method and secret and sweet reasonableness of Jesus.
1873 Literature and Dogma, ch.12.

38 So we have the Philistine of genius in religion—Luther; the Philistine of genius in politics—Cromwell; the Philistine of genius in literature—Bunyan.
1879 Mixed Essays, 'Lord Falkland'.

39 The theatre is irresistible: organise the theatre.
1882 Irish Essays, 'The French Play in London'.

40 In poetry, no less than in life, he is 'a beautiful and ineffectual angel, beating in the void his luminous wings in vain'.
1888 Of Shelley. *Essays in Criticism Second Series,* 'Shelley'. The phrase is a quotation from his own work on Byron.

41 More and more mankind will discover that we have to turn to poetry to interpret life for us, to console us, to sustain us. Without poetry, our science will appear incomplete; and most of what now passes with us for religion and philosophy will be replaced by poetry.
1888 Essays in Criticism Second Series, 'The Study of Poetry'.

42 The difference between genuine poetry and the poetry of Dryden, Pope, and all their school, is briefly this: their poetry is conceived and composed in their wits, genuine poetry is conceived and composed in the soul.
1888 Essays in Criticism Second Series, 'Thomas Gray'.

43 Poetry is at bottom a criticism of life.
1888 Essays in Criticism Second Series, 'Wordsworth'.

44 His expression may often be called bald...but it is bald as the bare mountain tops are bald, with a baldness full of grandeur.
1888 Essays in Criticism Second Series, 'Wordsworth'.

Arnold, Thomas 1795–1842

British educator and historian, educational reformer who introduced mathematics, modern languages, and modern history into the curriculum of his day.

45 My object will be, if possible, to form Christian men, for Christian boys I can scarcely hope to make.
1828 Letter to Rev John Tucker, 2 Mar, on being appointed headmaster of Rugby School.

46 Rather than have it the principal thing in my son's mind, I would gladly have him think that the sun went around the earth, and that the stars were so many spangles set in the bright blue firmament.
1836 Letter to Dr Greenhill, 9 May.

Arnold, Thurman Wesley 1891–1969

US lawyer, Professor at Yale (1930–8), Assistant Attorney General in charge of anti-trust enforcement (1938–43) and Associate Justice at the Court of Appeals (1943–5).

47 We must protect big business from domination by fat-minded men whose principal business policy is to avoid a competitive race for efficiency... They believe in a system of soft enterprise,—soft in the way that an octopus is soft, with tentacles that stifle and suffocate.
1942 'The Abuse of Patents', in *Atlantic Monthly,* Jul.

Aron, Raymond Claude Ferdinand 1905–83

French sociologist and journalist, editor of *La France Libre* in London (1940–4).

48 To customs and beliefs, the very ones we hold sacred, sociology ruthlessly attaches the adjective 'arbitrary'.
1971 Politics and History.

49 In a way, all sociologists are akin to Marxists because of their inclination to settle everyone's accounts but their own.
1971 Politics and History.

Arras, Jean d' *also known as* Jean Blondel fl.c.1375

French writer. He collaborated with Antoine du Val and Fouquart de Cambrai on the *Évangile des Quenouilles*, which provides much information on life at the time.

50 *Bonté vaut mieux que beauté.*
Kindness is worth more than beauty.
c.1393 *Melusine.*

Asahi Shimbun

Leading mass-circulation newspaper in Japan.

51 Are we correct to have changed as much as we have? Or is Yokoi correct not to have changed at all?
1972 Editorial comment, 28 Jan, on the discovery of World War II survivor Sergeant Yokoi in the Pacific jungles.

Ascham, Roger 1515-68

English humanist, Protestant and scholar, reader in Greek at Cambridge, and tutor to Princess Elizabeth. He published a defence of archery, *Toxophilus*, in 1545, and is most famous for his treatise on humanist education, *The Schoolmaster* (1570).

52 He that will write well in any tongue, must follow this counsel of Aristotle, to speak as the common people do, to think as wise men do; and so should every man understand him, and the judgment of wise men allow him.
1545 Toxophilus, 'To all Gentlemen and Yeomen of England'.

53 Young children [are] sooner allured by love than driven by beating to attain good learning.
1570 The Schoolmaster, 'A Preface to the Reader'.

54 For [the] quick in wit and light in manners be either seldom troubled or very soon weary, in carrying a very heavy purse.
1570 The Schoolmaster, bk.2.

Ashbery, John Lawrence 1927–

US poet, critic and novelist. Poetry collections include the award-winning *Self-Portrait in a Convex Mirror* (1976).

55 Darkness falls like a wet sponge.
1956 Some Trees, 'The Picture of Little J. A. in a Prospect of Flowers', opening line.

56 And it is the colour of sand,
The darkness, as it sifts through your hand.
1962 The Tennis Court Oath, 'How Much Longer Will I Be Able To Inhabit The Divine Sepulcher...'.

57 Self-portrait in a Convex Mirror.
1976 Title of book.

58 Slated for demolition.
1979 Complete text of poem entitled 'The Cathedral Is', in As We Know.

59 Still I enjoy
The long sweetness of the simultaneity, yours and mine, ours and mine,
The mosquitoey summer night light.
1981 Shadow Train, 'Here Everything Is Still Floating'.

60 My name has gotten to be a household word—at least in certain households. I think there are now people who know my name, but don't know what I do. I'm famous for being famous.
1985 Interview in PN Review, no.46.

61 There is the view that poetry should improve your life. I think people confuse it with the Salvation Army.
1989 In the International Herald Tribune, 2 Oct.

Ashcroft, John David 1942–

US lawyer and politician, Attorney General (2001–5).

62 Why are we talking about this in the White House? History will not judge this kindly.
2008 Attributed. Referring to discussion by senior officials about torture techniques, as quoted on ABC News, 9 Apr.

63 I'm trying to think of all the reasons that are appropriate for me to refuse to answer that question.
2008 In response to a question about interrogation of terrorist suspects before the House Judiciary Committee, Jul.

Ashdown (of Norton-sub-Hamdon), Paddy Ashdown, Baron 1941–

British politician. After working with the Royal Marines (1959–71) and the diplomatic service (1971–6), he was an MP (1983–2001) and leader of the Liberal Democrats (1988–99).

64 Neil Kinnock has travelled the road to Damascus so often, I hear that he has decided to buy himself a season ticket.
1990 At the Liberal Democratic Party conference, Sep.

65 The ringmaster has altered, but the circus remains the same.
1990 On John Major's election as Conservative Party leader, in the Observer, 2 Dec.

66 I have learnt from bitter experience that when the armchair theorists and the Whitehall generals start talking of a surgical war, it is time to run for cover.
1991 Referring to plans for the Gulf War. In the Sunday Times, 27 Jan.

67 There can be no place in a 21st-century parliament for people with 15th-century titles upholding 19th-century prejudices.
1998 In The Independent, 24 Nov.

68 History teaches us these lessons for the interveners: leave your prejudices at home, keep your ambitions low, have enough resources to do the job, do not lose the golden hour, make security your first priority, involve the neighbours.
2007 On BBC radio.

Ashford, Daisy Mary Margaret 1881–1972

English writer. She wrote her only book, *The Young Visiters*, in 1890, and published the manuscript in 1919. Its childish idiosyncrasies made it a best-seller, and it was adapted for the stage in 1920, and as a musical in 1968.

69 Mr Salteena was an elderly man of 42 and was fond of asking peaple to stay with him.
1890 The Young Visiters, or Mr Salteena's Plan, ch.1.

70 You look rather rash my dear your colors don't quite match your face.
1890 The Young Visiters, or Mr Salteena's Plan, ch.2.

71 Bernard always had a few prayers in the hall and some whiskey afterwards as he was rather pious but

Mr Salteena was not very addicted to prayers so he marched up to bed.
1890 The Young Visiters, or Mr Salteena's Plan, ch.3.

72 Oh I see said the Earl but my own idear is that these things are as piffle before the wind.
1890 The Young Visiters, or Mr Salteena's Plan, ch.5.

73 I am very fond of fresh air and royalties.
1890 The Young Visiters, or Mr Salteena's Plan, ch.5.

74 The bearer of this letter is an old friend of mine not quite the right side of the blanket as they say in fact he is the son of a first rate butcher but his mother was a decent family called Hyssopps of the Glen so you see he is not so bad and is desireus of being the correct article.
1890 The Young Visiters, or Mr Salteena's Plan, ch.5.

75 My life will be sour grapes and ashes without you.
1890 The Young Visiters, or Mr Salteena's Plan, ch.8.

76 Oh Bernard muttered Ethel this is so sudden. No no cried Bernard and taking the bull by both horns he kissed her violently on her dainty face.
1890 The Young Visiters, or Mr Salteena's Plan, ch.9.

77 She had very nice feet and plenty of money.
1890 The Young Visiters, or Mr Salteena's Plan, ch.12.

Asimov, Isaac 1920–92

Russian-born US science-fiction novelist and popular scientist. A distinguished biochemist and hugely popular writer, he became a familiar media figure. His works include the 'Foundation' series (1951–3). He coined the term 'robotics'.

78 How many people is the earth able to sustain?
1971 Der Spiegel.

79 Science fiction writers foresee the inevitable, and although problems and catastrophes may be inevitable, solutions are not.
1975 'How Easy To See The Future', in Natural History, Apr.

80 If there is a category of human being for whom his work ought to speak for itself, it is the writer.
1976 Comment in D L Fitzpatrick (ed) Contemporary Novelists.

81 It is change, continuing change, inevitable change, that is the dominant factor in our society today... This, in turn, means that our statesmen, our businessmen, our everyman must take on a science fictional way of thinking.
1978 'My Own View', in R Holdstock (ed) Encyclopedia of Science Fiction (1978).

Aslet, Clive William 1955–

English journalist, editor of *Country Life* (1993–).

82 Biography is now more or less a branch of psychiatry.
1994 In Country Life, 10 Nov, reviewing Jonathan Dimbleby The Prince of Wales: A Biography (1994).

83 We expect the ticking movement of the human timepiece to be revealed.
1994 In Country Life, 10 Nov, reviewing Jonathan Dimbleby The Prince of Wales: A Biography (1994).

Asquith, Herbert Henry, 1st Earl of Oxford and Asquith 1852–1928

British Liberal politician and Prime Minister. He became an MP (1886), Home Secretary (1892–5), Chancellor (1906) and Prime Minister (1908–16). His period in office was marked by the introduction of old age pensions, the Parliament Act of 1911, the declaration of war (1914) and the Sinn Féin rebellion (1916). A coalition with Conservatives hastened his resignation. He wrote *Memories and Reflections* (1928).

84 We shall never sheath the sword which we have not lightly drawn until Belgium recovers in full measure all and more than all that she has sacrificed, until France is adequately assured against the menace of aggression, until the rights of the smaller nationalities of Europe are placed upon an unassailable foundation and until the military domination of Prussia is wholly and finally destroyed.
1914 Speech at the Guildhall, London, 9 Nov.

85 It is fitting that we should have buried the unknown Prime Minister by the side of the Unknown Soldier.
1923 Remark at the Westminster Abbey funeral of Bonar Law, 5 Nov.

86 One to mislead the public, another to mislead the Cabinet, and the third to mislead itself.
Of the three sets of figures kept by the War Office. Quoted in Alistair Horne Price of Glory (1962).

Asquith, Margot 1864–1945

Scottish society figure and wit, wife of Herbert Asquith (married 1894). Her group 'The Souls' advocated greater freedom for women. She continued her extravagant lifestyle through the war, and when Asquith was forced to resign (1916) wrote two sensational autobiographies.

87 If Kitchener is not a great man, he is, at least, a great poster.
Quoted in P Magnus Kitchener: Portrait of an Imperialist. Lady Asquith uses the phrase in her Memories (1933), but attributes it to her daughter Elizabeth.

88 She tells enough white lies to ice a wedding cake.
Of Lady Desborough. Quoted in The Listener, 11 Jun 1953.

89 David Lloyd George could not see a belt without hitting underneath it.
Quoted in The Listener, 11 Jun 1953.

90 Stafford Cripps has a brilliant mind, until he makes it up.
Quoted in The Wit of the Asquiths (published 1974).

91 F E Smith is very clever, but sometimes he lets his brains go to his head.
Quoted in The Wit of the Asquiths (published 1974).

92 The t is silent, as in Harlow.
Attributed riposte to Jean Harlow who was having trouble pronouncing her name. The line may actually have been spoken by Margot Grahame, an English actress in Hollywood in the 1930s.

93 I have no face, only two profiles clapped together.
Attributed.

Asquith of Yarnbury, (Helen) Violet Bonham-Carter, Baroness 1887–1969

English Liberal politician and publicist, daughter of Herbert Asquith. A prominent society figure, she was president of the Liberal Party Organization (1944–5) and governor of the BBC (1941–6).

94 Harold Macmillan held his party together by not allowing his left wing to see what his right wing was doing.
Attributed.

Assange, Julian Paul 1971–

Australian journalist and Internet activist, co-founder of the controversial WikiLeaks website dedicated to exposing government and corporate wrongdoing. Since 2012 he has lived at the Ecuadorian embassy in London to avoid extradition to Sweden for alleged sexual offences.

95 It is impossible to correct abuses unless we know that they're going on.
2010 Address to the Oslo Freedom Forum, 26–29 Apr.

96 Vanity in a newspaper man is like perfume on a whore; they use it to fend off a dark whiff of themselves.
2011 In Andrew O'Hagan, *Julian Assange: The Unauthorized Autobiography*.

97 Where they couldn't pick holes in our arguments they would drive horses and carriages through my character.
2011 In Andrew O'Hagan, *Julian Assange: The Unauthorized Autobiography*.

98 The internet, our greatest tool of emancipation, has been transformed into the most dangerous facilitator of totalitarianism we have ever seen. The internet is a threat to human civilization.
2012 *Cypherpunks*.

99 Man is least himself when he talks in his own person. But if you give him a mask, he will tell you the truth. Two people and a secret, the beginning of all conspiracies, more people and more secrets. But if we could find one moral man, one whistleblower, someone willing to expose those secrets, that man could topple the most powerful and most repressive of regimes.
2013 Attributed in the film *The Fifth Estate*.

Astell, Mary 1668–1731

English writer, the 'first British feminist'. Orphaned in 1684, she moved alone to London in about 1686. In *A Serious Proposal to the Ladies* (1694) she argues for the education of women. *Some Reflections Upon Marriage* (1700, 2nd edn 1706) highlights the disadvantages of marriage for women.

1 Your glass will not do you half so much service as a serious reflection of your own minds.
1694 *A Serious Proposal to the Ladies For the Advancement of their True and Greatest Interest*, 'By a Lover of Her Sex', pt.1.

2 Women are from their very Infancy debarred those advantages, with the want of which they are afterwards reproached, and nursed up in those vices which will hereafter be upbraided to them. So partial are men as to expect brick where they afford no straw.
1694 *A Serious Proposal to the Ladies For the Advancement of their True and Greatest Interest*, 'By a Lover of Her Sex', pt.1.

3 Fetters of gold are still fetters, and the softest lining can never make them so easy as liberty.
1696 *An Essay in Defence of the Female Sex*.

4 If absolute sovereignty be not necessary in a State, how comes it to be so in a family?
1706 *Some Reflections upon Marriage Occasion'd by the Duke and Duchess of Mazarine's Case which is also consider'd*, preface (1706 edn).

5 If all men are born free, how is it that all women are born slaves? as they must be if the being subjected to the inconsistent, uncertain, unknown, arbitrary will of men, be the perfect condition of slavery? and if the essence of freedom consists, as our masters say it does, in having a standing rule to live by? And why is slavery so much condemned and strove against in one case, and so highly applauded, and held so necessary and so sacred in another?
1706 *Some Reflections upon Marriage Occasion'd by the Duke and Duchess of Mazarine's Case which is also consider'd*, preface (1706 edn).

6 But if marriage be such a blessed state, how comes it, may you say, that there are so few happy marriages? Now in answer to this, is it not to be wondered that so few succeed, we should rather be surprized to find so many do, considering how imprudently men engage, the motive they act by, and the very strange conduct they observe throughout.
1706 *Some Reflections upon Marriage Occasion'd by the Duke and Duchess of Mazarine's Case which is also consider'd*, preface (1706 edn).

7 A woman indeed can't properly be said to choose, all that is allowed her, is to refuse or accept what is offered.
1706 *Some Reflections upon Marriage Occasion'd by the Duke and Duchess of Mazarine's Case which is also consider'd*, preface (1706 edn).

Astley, Sir Jacob 1579–1652

English Royalist commander, leader of Charles I's last remaining army which surrendered in March 1646.

8 O Lord! Thou knowest how busy I must be this day: if I forget thee, do not thou forget me.
1642 Prayer before the Battle of Edgehill, 23 Oct. Quoted in Sir Philip Warwick *Memoires* (1702).

9 You have now done your work and may go play, unless you will fall out amongst yourselves.
1646 Remark to his Parliamentarian captors, Mar. Quoted in Samuel Rawson Gardiner *History of the Great Civil War, 1642–9* (1911), vol.3.

Astor (of Hever Castle), Nancy Witcher Astor, Viscountess née *Langhorne* 1879–1964

US-born British politician, the first woman MP to sit in the House of Commons. She was especially interested in social problems, including women's rights and temperance.

10 I married beneath me. All women do.
1951 Speech, Oldham.

11 You will never get on in politics, my dear, with *that* hair.
Attributed remark addressed to Shirley Williams.

Asturias, Miguel Ángel 1889–1974

Guatemalan poet, novelist and diplomat, winner of the Nobel prize for literature in 1967 and the Soviet Union's Lenin Peace Prize in 1966.

12 *Como te decía al principio, nadie hace nada y, naturalmente, soy yo, es el Presidente de la República el que lo tiene que hacer todo, aunque salga como el cohetero. Con decir que si no fuera por mí no existiría la fortuna, ya que hasta de diosa ciega tengo que hacer en la lotería.*
But, as I told you, nobody ever does a thing, and so naturally it is I, the President of the Republic, who has to do everything, and take all the blame as well. You might almost say that if it weren't for me Fortune wouldn't exist, as I have even to take the part of the blind goddess in the lottery.
1946 *El señor presidente* (*The President*, 1963), pt.3, ch.37.

Atatürk, Mustapha Kemal 1880–1938

Turkish soldier and statesman, founder and first President (1923–38) of the Turkish Republic. In the subsequent social and political revolution he encouraged westernization. He took the title Atatürk, 'Father of the Turks', in 1935.

13 It was necessary to abolish the fez, emblem of ignorance, negligence, fanaticism and hatred of progress and civilization, to accept in its place the hat—the headgear worn by the whole civilized world.
1927 From his six-day speech to the Turkish Assembly, Oct.

Atkinson, Brooks 1894–1984

US journalist and theatre critic.

14 After each war there is a little less democracy to save.
1951 Once Around the Sun.

15 Thanks for tomorrow, thanks for last week, thanks for next Friday—in fact thanks for everything except last night.
Reviewing Le Roy Bailey's *Thanks for Tomorrow*. Quoted in the *New York Times*, 14 Jan 1984.

Atkinson, Kate 1951–

English author. Her bestselling works include the novel *Behind the Scenes at the Museum* (1995), which won the Whitbread Prize, and books featuring the private investigator Jackson Brodie.

16 When you had children, you measured your years in theirs. Not 'I'm forty-nine,' but 'I have a twelve-year-old child.'
2008 When Will There Be Good News?

Atkinson, Ron 1939–

English football manager. He played for Oxford United until 1971 and subsequently managed teams including West Bromwich Albion, Atlético Madrid, Manchester United, Sheffield Wednesday, Aston Villa and Coventry City, before becoming a commentator.

17 It's bloody tough being a legend.
1983 Quoted in Peter Ball and Phil Shaw *The Book of Football Quotations* (1989).

Atlas, Charles 1894–1972

US bodybuilder.

18 You too can have a body like mine!
c.1922 Advertising slogan.

Atlas, James 1949–

US writer, critic and publisher, contributor to the *New Yorker* and former editor at the *New York Times Magazine*.

19 A penumbra of somber dignity has descended over his reputation.
1985 Of Edmund Wilson. In the *New York Times*, 28 Jul, reviewing David Castronovo *Edmund Wilson* (1984).

20 To read Wilson…is to be instructed and amused in the highest sense—that is educated.
1985 Of Edmund Wilson. In the *New York Times*, 28 Jul, reviewing David Castronovo *Edmund Wilson* (1984).

Attenborough, Sir David Frederick 1926–

English naturalist and broadcaster, a respected and popular wildlife documentary maker. His series include *Life on Earth* (1979), *The Living Planet* (1984) and *Life in the Freezer* (1993).

21 Most of the animals that appeared on British television screens in 1950 did so sitting on door-mats.
1982 The Zoo Quest Expeditions.

22 If we and the rest of the backboned animals were to disappear overnight, the rest of the world would get on pretty well.
2005 Life in the Undergrowth.

23 Human beings are good at many things, but thinking about our species as a whole is not one of our strong points.
2009 How Many People Can Live on Planet Earth?, BBC *Horizon* programme.

Attlee (of Walthamstow), Clement (Richard) Attlee, 1st Earl 1883–1967

English Labour politician, Deputy Prime Minister in Churchill's war cabinet (1942–5) and Prime Minister (1945–51). During his administration the National Health Service was established and India and Burma were given independence.

24 We believe in a League system in which the whole world should be ranged against an aggressor… We do not think that you can deal with national armaments by piling up national armaments in other countries.
1935 House of Commons, 11 Mar.

25 We have seen today a gallant, civilized and democratic people betrayed and handed over to a ruthless despotism.
1938 House of Commons speech on Czechoslovakia, 3 Oct.

26 I count our progress by the extent to which what we cried in the wilderness five and thirty years ago has now become part of the assumptions of the ordinary man and woman… It is better to argue from what has been done to what may be done, rather than to suggest that very little has been accomplished.
1944 Of the Labour Party. Letter to Harold J Laski, 1 May.

27 I have been very happy…serving in a state of life to which I had never expected to be called.
1954 As It Happened.

28 Few thought he was even a starter
There were many who thought themselves smarter
But he ended PM
CH and OM
An earl and a knight of the garter.
1956 A limerick on himself, in a letter to Tom Attlee, 8 Apr.

29 Russian communism is the illegitimate child of Karl Marx and Catherine the Great.
1956 Speech, Aarhus University, 11 Apr.

30 Democracy means government by discussion, but it is only effective if you can stop people talking.
1957 Speech, Oxford, 14 Jun.

31 The House of Lords is like a glass of champagne that has stood for five days.
Attributed.

Atwood, Margaret Eleanor 1939–

Canadian writer, poet and critic. Her first book of poetry, *The Circle Game* (1966), won the Governor General's Award. Her novels include *The Edible Woman* (1969) and *The Robber Bride* (1993). She won the Booker Prize in 2000 for *The Blind Assassin*.

32 (The photograph was taken
the day after I drowned.

I am in the lake, in the center
of the picture, just under the surface.)
1966 *The Circle Game*, 'This is a Photograph of Me'.

33 we flounder, the air
ungainly in our new lungs
with sunlight streaming merciless on the shores of
morning
1966 *The Circle Game*, 'Pre-Amphibian'.

34 He stood, a point
on a sheet of green paper
proclaiming himself the center,
with no walls, no borders
anywhere; the sky no height
above him, totally un-
enclosed
and shouted:
Let me out!
1968 *The Animals in that Country*, 'Progressive Insanities of a Pioneer'.

35 Marriage is not
a house or even a tent
it is before that, and colder.
1970 *Procedures from Underground*, 'Habitation'.

36 If the national mental illness of the United States is megalomania, that of Canada is paranoid schizophrenia.
1970 *The Journals of Susanna Moodie: Poems by Margaret Atwood*, afterword.

37 We are all immigrants to this place even if we were born here: the country is too big for anyone to inhabit completely, and in the parts unknown to us we move in fear, exiles and invaders.
1970 Writing of Canada and Canadians in *The Journals of Susanna Moodie: Poems by Margaret Atwood*, afterword.

38 Possibly the symbol for America is the Frontier... The corresponding symbol for England is the Island... The central symbol for Canada...is undoubtedly Survival, *la Survivance*.
1972 *Survival: a Thematic Guide to Canadian Literature*, ch.1, 'Survival'.

39 This above all, to refuse to be a victim. Unless I can do that I am nothing.
1972 *Surfacing*.

40 Mirrors
are the perfect lovers.
1974 *You are Happy*, 'Tricks with Mirrors'.

41 You are suspended in me
beautiful and frozen, I
preserve you, in me you are safe.
1974 *You Are Happy*, 'Tricks with Mirrors'.

42 To live in prison is to live without mirrors. To live without mirrors is to live without the self.
1978 *Two-headed Poems*, 'Marrying the Hangman'.

43 I would like to be the air
that inhabits you for a moment
only. I would like to be that unnoticed
and that necessary.
1981 *True Stories*, 'Variation on the Word *Sleep*'.

44 At some time during that hour, though not for the whole hour, I forgot what things were called and saw instead what they are.
1983 *Murder in the Dark*, 'Strawberries'.

45 Canada was open for business. And closed for everything else.
1988 Essay on censorship in *The Globe and Mail*, 'The Porn Patrol', 18 Feb. Collected in Douglas Fetherling (ed) *Best Canadian Essays* (1989).

46 Who knows what evil lurks in the hearts of men? An older woman knows. But how much older do you have to get before you acquire that kind of wisdom?
1993 *The Robber Bride*, ch.48.

47 His father was self-made, but his mother was constructed by others, and such edifices are notoriously fragile.
1996 *Alias Grace*.

48 Publishing a book is often very much like being put on trial for some offence which is quite other than the one you know in your heart you've committed.
2002 *Negotiating with the Dead: A Writer on Writing*.

49 Which of us can resist the temptation of being thought indispensable?
2005 *The Penelopiad*.

50 Longed for him. Got him. Shit.
2006 'Very Short Stories', *Wired*, Nov.

51 A home filled with nothing but yourself. It's heavy, that lightness. It's crushing, that emptiness.
2006 *The Tent*.

52 I can tell you that once upon a time when I was doing public events people would ask me, 'What do you think about the arts?, What do you think of the role of women?, What do you think of men?, What do you think of all of these things?', and now they ask one thing, and that one thing is this, 'Is there hope?'.
2007 In *Turning Pages: The Life and Literature of Margaret Atwood*, 13 Sep.

53 In the spring, at the end of the day, you should smell like dirt.
2007 In *Woman's Day Magazine*, 1 Apr.

54 Maybe that's what love is, I thought: it's being pissed off.
2009 *The Year of the Flood*.

Auber, Daniel-François-Esprit 1782–1871

French composer of operas. His best-known works are *La Muette de Portici*, usually entitled *Masaniello* (1828), and *Fra Diavolo* (1830).

55 Well, there's no help for it. Ageing seems to be the only available way to live a long time.
Attributed, when a friend lamented that they were both getting older. Quoted in Clifton Fadiman *The Faber Book of Anecdotes* (1985).

Aubrey, John 1626–97

English antiquary. Only his credulous *Miscellanies* (1696) of folklore and ghost stories were printed in his lifetime, and his colourful biographical anecdotes were later collected as *Letters by Eminent Persons* (1813), better known as *Brief Lives*.

56 How these curiosities would be quite forgot, did not such idle fellows as I am put them down.
1693 *Brief Lives* (published 1813), 'Venetia Digby'.

57 He had read much, if one considers his long life; but his contemplation was much more than his reading. He was wont to say that if he had read as much as other men, he should have known no more than other men.
1693 Of Thomas Hobbes. *Brief Lives* (published 1813), 'Thomas Hobbes'.

58 His harmonical and ingenious soul did lodge in a beautiful and well proportioned body. He was a spare man.... He was so fair that they called him the *lady of Christ's College*.
1693 Of Milton. *Brief Lives* (published 1813), 'John Milton'.

59 Sir Walter, being strangely surprised and put out of his countenance at so great a table, gives his son a damned blow over the face. His son, as rude as he was, would not strike his father, but strikes over the face the gentleman that sat next to him and said 'Box about: 'twill come to my father anon.'
1693 *Brief Lives* (published 1813), 'Sir Walter Raleigh'.

60 When he killed a calf he would do it in a high style, and make a speech.
1693 *Brief Lives* (published 1813), 'William Shakespeare'. Aubrey had been misinformed that Shakespeare's father was a butcher. He was in fact a glover.

61 The first sense he had of God was when he was eleven years old at Chigwell being retired into a chamber alone: he was so suddenly surprised with a sense of inward comfort and (as he thought) an external glory in the room that he had many times said that from thence he has the Seal of Divinity and Immortality, that there was a God and that the soul of man was capable of enjoying his divine communications.
1693 Of William Penn, early Quaker. *Brief Lives* (published 1813).

Auchincloss, Louis Stanton 1917–2010
US writer and critic, who studied law. His works chronicle the life of New York City and its inhabitants, particularly the aristocracy. His works include *Venus in Sparta* (1958) and *Pursuit of the Prodigal* (1960).

62 Perfection irritates as well as it attracts, in fiction as in life.
1965 *Pioneers and Caretakers: A Study of Nine American Women Novelists*.

63 A neurotic can perfectly well be a literary genius, but his greatest danger is always that he will not recognize when he is dull.
1965 *Pioneers and Caretakers: A Study of Nine American Women Novelists*.

64 The glittering structure of her cultivation sits on her novels like a rather showy icing that detracts from the cake beneath.
1965 Of Edith Wharton. *Pioneers and Caretakers: A Study of Nine American Women Novelists*.

65 I would rather see the old reservoir on Forty-second Street or the original Madison Square Garden than I would any of the lost wonders of the ancient world.
Quoted in Carol Gelderman *Louis Auchincloss* (1993).

Auden, W(ystan) H(ugh) 1907–73
English-born US poet. His early work reflects his concern with social problems of the 1930s and his left-wing commitment. His conversion from liberal humanism to Anglo-Catholicism informs his later work. He collaborated with Christopher Isherwood in three plays and *Journey to a War* (1939).

66 Harrow the house of the dead; look shining at
New styles of architecture, a change of heart.
1930 'Sir, No Man's Enemy'.

67 Private faces in public places
Are wiser and nicer
Than public faces in private places.
1932 *The Orators*, dedication.

68 What do you think about England, this country of ours where nobody is well?
1932 *The Orators*, 'Address for a Prize Day'.

69 To ask the hard question is simple.
1933 *Poems*, no.27.

70 The sky is darkening like a stain;
Something is going to fall like rain,
And it won't be flowers.
1935 'The Witness'.

71 This is the Night Mail crossing the border
Bringing the cheque and the postal order.
1936 'Night Mail', pt.1, written to accompany a documentary by the Post Office Film Unit.

72 And none will hear the postman's knock
Without a quickening of the heart.
For who can bear to feel himself forgotten?
1936 'Night Mail', written to accompany a documentary by the Post Office Film Unit.

73 Out on the lawn I lie in bed,
Vega conspicuous overhead.
1936 *Look, Stranger*, no.2.

74 August for the people and their favourite islands.
Daily the steamers sidle up to meet
The effusive welcome of the pier.
1936 *Look, Stranger*, no.30.

75 I dread this like the dentist, rather more so:
To me Art's subject is the human clay,
And landscape but a background to a torso;
All Cézanne's apples I would give away
For one small Goya or a Daumier.
1936 'Letter to Byron', pt.3, stanza 20, collected in *Poems, Essays, Dramatic Writings 1927–1939* (1977).

76 The stars are dead. The animals will not look:
We are left alone with our day, and the time is short, and
History to the defeated
May say Alas but cannot help nor pardon.
1937 *Spain*.

77 The desires of the heart are as crooked as corkscrews,
Not to be born is the best for man;
The second-best is a formal order,
The dance's pattern; dance while you can.
1937 'Letter to William Coldstream, Esq', in *Letter from Iceland* (with Louis MacNeice).

78 All the others translate: the painter sketches
A visible world to love or reject.
1938 'The Composer' (XXXIV), collected in *The English Auden. Poems 1936–39* (1977).

79 Stop all the clocks, cut off the telephone,
Prevent the dog from barking with a juicy bone,
Silence the pianos and with muffled drum
Bring out the coffin, let the mourners come.
1939 'Stop all the clocks', *Collected Poems*. Featured in the 1994 film *Four Weddings and a Funeral*.

80 About suffering they were never wrong,
The Old Masters: how well they understood
Its human position; how it takes place
While someone else is eating or opening a window or
  just walking dully along.
1940 'Musée des Beaux Arts'.

81 I'll love you dear, I'll love you
   Till China and Africa meet
   And the river jumps over the mountain
   And the salmon sing in the street,
   I'll love you till the ocean
   Is folded and hung up to dry
   And the seven stars go squawking
   Like geese about the sky.
   1940 'As I Walked Out One Evening'.

82 But all the clocks in the city
   Began to whirr and chime:
   'O let not Time deceive you,
   You cannot conquer Time.'
   1940 'As I Walked Out One Evening'.

83 O tell me the truth about love.
   When it comes, will it come without warning
   Just as I'm picking my nose?
   Will it knock on my door in the morning,
   Or tread in the bus on my toes?
   1940 'Twelve Poems', section 12.

84 Encased in talent like a uniform,
   The rank of every poet is well known;
   They can amaze us like a thunderstorm,
   Or die so young, or live for years alone.
   1940 'The Novelist'.

85 When there was peace, he was for peace; when there was war, he went.
   1940 'The Unknown Citizen'.

86 Was he free? Was he happy? The question is absurd:
   Had anything been wrong, we should certainly have heard.
   1940 'The Unknown Citizen'.

87 Perfection, of a kind, was what he was after,
   And the poetry he invented was easy to understand.
   1940 'Epitaph On A Tyrant'.

88 When he laughed, respectable senators burst with laughter,
   And when he cried the little children died in the streets.
   1940 'Epitaph On A Tyrant'.

89 To us he is no more a person
   Now but a whole climate of opinion.
   1940 'In Memory of Sigmund Freud', stanza 17.

90 O all the instruments agree
   The day of his death was a dark cold day.
   1940 'In Memory of W.B. Yeats', pt.1.

91 You were silly like us: your gift survived it all;
   The parish of rich women, physical decay,
   Yourself; mad Ireland hurt you into poetry.
   Now Ireland has her madness and her weather still,
   For poetry makes nothing happen.
   1940 'In Memory of W.B. Yeats', pt.2.

92 Earth receive an honoured guest;
   William Yeats is laid to rest:
   Let the Irish vessel lie
   Emptied of its poetry.
   1940 'In Memory of W.B. Yeats', pt.3.

93 In the nightmare of the dark
   All the dogs of Europe bark,
   And the living nations wait,
   Each sequestered in its hate.
   1940 'In Memory of W.B. Yeats', pt.3.

94 In the deserts of the heart
   Let the healing fountain start,
   In the prison of his days
   Teach the free man how to praise.
   1940 'In Memory of W.B. Yeats', pt.3.

95 Lay your sleeping head, my love,
   Human on my faithless arm.
   1940 'Lullaby'.

96 I and the public know
   What all schoolchildren learn,
   Those to whom evil is done
   Do evil in return.
   1940 'September 1, 1939'.

97 There is no such thing as the State
   And no one exists alone;
   Hunger allows no choice
   To the citizen or the police;
   We must love one another or die.
   1940 'September 1, 1939'.

98 To the man-in-the-street, who, I'm sorry to say,
   Is a keen observer of life,
   The word 'Intellectual' suggests straight away
   A man who's untrue to his wife.
   1940 *New Year Letter* (published 1941), note to l.1277.

99 Blessed Cecilia, appear in visions
   To all musicians, appear and inspire:
   Translated Daughter, come down and startle
   Composing mortals with immortal fire.
   1941 'Anthem for St Cecilia's Day'.

1 Sob, heavy world,
   Sob as you spin
   Mantled in mist, remote from the happy.
   1944–6 *The Age of Anxiety*, pt.4, 'The Dirge'.

2 In our anguish we struggle
   To elude Him, to lie to Him, yet His love observes
   His appalling promise; His predilection
   As we wander and weep is with us to the end,
   Minding our meanings, our least matter dear to Him.
   1944–6 *The Age of Anxiety*, pt.6, Epilogue.

3 There is no love;
   There are only the various envies, all of them sad.
   1951 'In Praise of Limestone', l.58–9.

4 To save your world you asked this man to die:
   Would this man, could he see you now, ask why?
   1955 'Epitaph for the Unknown Soldier'.

5 No good opera plot can be sensible, for people do not sing when they are feeling sensible.
   Quoted in *Time*, 29 Dec 1961.

6 It is a sad fact about our culture that a poet can earn much more money writing or talking about his art than he can by practising it.
   1963 *The Dyer's Hand*, foreword.

7 Pleasure is by no means an infallible critical guide, but it is the least fallible.
   1963 *The Dyer's Hand*, 'Reading'.

8 Some books are undeservedly forgotten; none are undeservedly remembered.
   1963 *The Dyer's Hand*, 'Reading'.

9 No poet or novelist wishes he were the only one who ever lived, but most of them wish they were the only one

alive, and quite a number fondly believe that their wish has been granted.
1963 *The Dyer's Hand*, 'Writing'.

10 The true men of action in our time, those who transform the world, are not the politicians and statesmen, but the scientists... When I find myself in the company of scientists, I feel like a shabby curate who has strayed by mistake into a drawing room full of dukes.
1963 *The Dyer's Hand*, 'The Poet and the City'.

11 Man is a history-making creature who can neither repeat his past nor leave it behind.
1963 *The Dyer's Hand*, 'D.H. Lawrence'.

12 The image of myself which I try to create in my own mind in order that I may love myself is very different from the image which I try to create in the minds of others in order that they may love me.
1963 *The Dyer's Hand*, 'Hic et Ille'.

13 Among those whom I like or admire, I can find no common denominator, but among those whom I love, I can: all of them make me laugh.
1963 *The Dyer's Hand*, 'Notes on the Comic'.

14 Geniuses are the luckiest of mortals because what they must do is the same as what they most want to do.
1964 Foreword to Dag Hammarskjöld, *Markings*.

15 Some thirty inches from my nose
The frontier of my Person goes,
And all the untilled air between
Is private *pagus* or demesne.
Stranger, unless with bedroom eyes
I beckon you to fraternize,
Beware of rudely crossing it:
I have no gun, but I can spit.
1966 'Prologue: The Birth of Architecture', postscript.

16 Youth may be forgiven when it is brash or noisy, but this does not mean that brashness and noise are virtues.
1966 *Collected Shorter Poems 1927–1957*, introduction.

17 Political history is far too criminal and pathological to be a fit subject of study for the young. Children should acquire their heroes and villains from fiction.
1970 *A Certain World*.

18 All sin tends to be addictive, and the terminal point of addiction is what is called damnation.
1970 *A Certain World*, 'Hell'.

19 Of course, Behaviourism 'works'. So does torture.
1970 *A Certain World*, 'Behaviourism'.

20 To my generation no other English poet seemed so perfectly to express the sensibility of a male adolescent. If I do not now turn to him very often, I am eternally grateful to him for the joy he gave me in my youth.
1972 Of A E Housman. 'A Worcestershire Lad', collected in *Forewords and Afterwords* (1973).

21 Music is the best means we have of digesting time.
Quoted in Robert Craft *Stravinsky: Chronicle of a Friendship* (1972).

22 That singular command,
I do not understand,
Bless what there is for being,
What else am I for,
Agreeing or disagreeing?
'Precious Fire', in *Collected Poems* (1976).

23 Thou shall not sin
With statisticians nor commit
A social science.
'Under Which Lyre'.

24 My face looks like a wedding-cake left out in the rain.
Quoted in Humphrey Carpenter *W H Auden* (1981), pt.2, ch.6.

St Augustine originally Aurelius Augustinus   AD 354–430
Bishop of Hippo from 395. The son of Numidian Roman citizens (from modern Tunisia), he was converted to Christianity in 386. His works include his *Confessions* and *The City of God*.

25 *Da mihi castitatem et continentiam, sed noli modo.*
Grant me chastity and continence, but not yet.
AD **397** *Confessions*, bk.8, ch.7 (translated by Henry Chadwick).

26 *Tolle, lege, tolle, lege.*
Pick up and read, pick up and read.
AD **397** *Confessions*, bk.8, ch.12.

27 *Sero te amavi, pulchritudo tam antiqua et tam nova, sero te amavi!*
Late have I loved you, beauty so old and so new: late have I loved you.
AD **397** *Confessions*, bk.10, ch.27.

28 *Continentiam iubes; da quod iubes et iube quod vis.*
You command continence; give what you command and command what you will.
AD **397** *Confessions*, bk.10, ch.29.

29 *Quid est ergo tempus? Si nemo ex me quaerat, scio; si quaerenti explicare velim, nescio.*
What, then, is time? I know well enough what it is, provided that nobody asks me; but if I am asked what it is and try to explain, I am baffled.
AD **397** *Confessions*, bk.11, ch.14 (translated by R S Pine-Coffin).

30 *Multi quidem facilius se abstinent ut non utantur, quam temperent ut bene utantur.*
For many, total abstinence is easier than perfect moderation.
AD **401** *On the Good of Marriage*, ch.21.

31 *Dilige et quod vis fac.*
Love, and do what you like
AD **413** *In Epistolam Joannis ad Parthos*, tractatus 7, section 8.

32 What varieties man has found out in buildings, attires, husbandry, navigation, sculpture and imagery! What perfection has he shown, in the shows of theatres, in taming, killing, and catching wild beasts! What millions of inventions has he against others, and for himself in poisons, arms, engines, stratagems, and the like! What thousands of medicines for the health, of meats for the throat, of means and figures to persuade, of elegant phrases to delight, of verses for pleasure, of musical inventions and instruments! What excellent inventions are geography, arithmetic, astrology, and the rest! How large is the capacity of man, if we should stand upon particulars!
AD **427** *The City of God*.

33 All the devastation, the butchery, the plundering, the conflagrations, and all the anguish which accompanied the recent disaster at Rome were in accordance with the general practice of warfare.
AD **427** *City of God*, vol.1, ch.1, section 8.

34 If you don't believe it, you won't understand it.
Quoted in Erasmus *De Libero Arbitrio* (1523).

35 Do not plan long journeys, because whatever you believe in you have already seen. When a thing is everywhere, the way to find it is not to travel but to love.
Quoted in Ingrid Cranfield *The Challengers* (1976).

Augustus *originally* Gaius Iulius Caesar Octavianus
63 BC–AD 14

First Roman emperor, a senator's son adopted by Caesar in his will (44 BC). With Marcus Antonius and Lepidus he secured power after the battle of Philippi (42 BC) but the triumvirate collapsed and after Actium (31 BC) Caesar was sole ruler of the Roman Empire. He took the title Augustus in 27 BC and expanded the empire until the loss of three legions in Germany (AD 9).

36 *Quintili Vare, legiones redde.*
Quintilius Varus, give me back my legions.
Quoted in Suetonius, *Augustus*, section 23.

37 *Festina lente.*
Hurry slowly.
Quoted in Suetonius *Augustus*, section 25 (originally quoted in Greek, but better known in the Latin form).

38 *Acta est fabula.*
The play is over.
AD 14 Last words, attributed. In Suetonius *Augustus*, section 99.1, the scene of his death-bed is described: 'He summoned a group of friends and asked: 'Have I played my part in the farce of life well enough?' adding the verse: 'If it was any good, please applaud for the play, and send us with pleasure on our way'.'

Aung San Suu Kyi 1945–

Burmese human rights activist and a leading campaigner for the National League for Democracy before being detained in 1989 by the country's ruling military junta. She spent years under house arrest before being elected to parliament in 2012. She was awarded the Nobel peace prize in 1991.

39 There is nothing new in Third World governments seeking to justify and perpetuate authoritarian rule by denouncing liberal democratic principles as alien.
1989 *Freedom From Fear*, 'In Quest of Democracy'.

40 Regimented minds cannot grasp the concept of confrontation as an open exchange of major differences with a view to settlement through genuine dialogue.
1989 *Freedom From Fear*, 'In Quest of Democracy'.

41 In societies where men are truly confident of their own worth women are not merely tolerated, they are valued.
1995 Videotaped address at the NGO Forum on Women, Beijing, China, 31 Aug.

42 Every thought, every word, and every action that adds to the positive and the wholesome is a contribution to peace. Each and every one of us is capable of making such a contribution. Let us join hands to try to create a peaceful world where we can sleep in security and wake in happiness.
2012 Nobel Peace Prize acceptance speech, Oslo, 16 Jun.

43 'Why' is one of the most important words in any language. You have to know why the world is the way it is or you have to want to know. If you do not have this curiosity and if you do not have the intelligence in order to be able to express this curiosity in terms that others can understand then we will not be able to contribute to progress in our world.
2013 Sakharov Prize for Freedom of Thought acceptance speech, Strasbourg, 22 Oct.

Aurelius, Marcus Aurelius Antoninus AD 121–80

Roman emperor. He was consul from 140 to 161, when he succeeded Antoninus Pius to the throne. His *Meditations*, written in Greek, consist of notes made throughout his life.

44 A little flesh, a little breath, and a Reason to rule all—that is myself.
c. AD 170–180 *Meditations*, bk.2, no.2 (translated by M Staniforth).

45 Nowhere can a man find a quieter or more untroubled retreat than in his own soul.
c. AD 170–180 *Meditations*, bk.4, no.3 (translated by M Staniforth).

46 Soon you will have forgotten the world, and the world will have forgotten you.
c. AD 170–180 *Meditations*, bk.7, no.21 (translated by M Staniforth).

47 To live each day as though one's last, never flustered, never apathetic, never attitudinizing—here is perfection of character.
c. AD 170–180 *Meditations*, bk.7, no.69 (translated by M Staniforth).

Austen, Jane 1775–1817

English novelist. Her works satirized fashionable society, exploring the role of women. *Sense and Sensibility* (1811), *Pride and Prejudice* (1813), *Mansfield Park* (1814) and *Emma* (1815) were published anonymously; *Persuasion* and *Northanger Abbey* were both published posthumously (1818).

48 It was too pathetic for the feelings of Sophia and myself—we fainted alternately on the sofa.
1790 *Love and Freindship*, 'Letter the 8th'.

49 She was nothing more than a mere good-tempered, civil and obliging young woman; as such we could scarcely dislike her—she was only an Object of Contempt.
1790 *Love and Freindship*, 'Letter the 13th'.

50 We met…Dr Hall in such very deep mourning that either his mother, his wife, or himself must be dead.
1799 Letter to Cassandra Austen, 17 May.

51 On every formal visit a child ought to be of the party, by way of provisions for discourse.
1811 *Sense and Sensibility*, vol.2, ch.6.

52 It is not time or opportunity that is to determine intimacy; it is disposition alone. Seven years would be insufficient to make some people acquainted with each other, and seven days are more than enough for others.
1811 *Sense and Sensibility*, vol.2, ch.12.

53 It is a truth universally acknowledged, that a single man in possession of a good fortune, must be in want of a wife.
1813 *Pride and Prejudice*, ch.1, opening lines.

54 Her mind was less difficult to develop. She was a woman of mean understanding, little information, and uncertain temper.
1813 Of Mrs Bennet. *Pride and Prejudice*, ch.1.

55 Happiness in marriage is entirely a matter of chance.
1813 *Pride and Prejudice*, ch.6.

56 May I ask whether these pleasing attentions proceed from the impulse of the moment, or are the result of previous study?
1813 *Pride and Prejudice*, ch.14.

57 Mr Wickham is blessed with such happy manners as may ensure his making friends—whether he may be equally capable of retaining them, is less certain.
1813 *Pride and Prejudice*, ch.18.

58 From this day you must be a stranger to one of your parents.—Your mother will never see you again if you do *not* marry Mr Collins, and I will never see you again if you *do*.
1813 *Pride and Prejudice*, ch.20.

59 Without thinking highly either of men or matrimony, marriage had always been her object; it was the only honourable provision for well-educated young women of small fortune, and however uncertain of giving happiness, must be their pleasantest preservative from want.
1813 *Pride and Prejudice*, ch.22.

60 Next to being married, a girl likes to be crossed in love a little now and then. It is something to think of, and gives her a sort of distinction among her companions.
1813 *Pride and Prejudice*, ch.24.

61 What are men to rocks and mountains? Oh! what hours of transport we shall spend! And when we do return, it shall not be like other travellers, without being able to give one accurate idea of anything. We will know where we have gone—we will recollect what we have seen. Lakes, mountains, and rivers, shall not be jumbled together in our imaginations; nor, when we attempt to describe any particular scene, will we begin quarrelling about its relative situation.
1813 *Pride and Prejudice*, ch.27.

62 You ought certainly to forgive them as a Christian, but never to admit them in your sight, or allow their names to be mentioned in your hearing.
1813 *Pride and Prejudice*, ch.57.

63 For what do we live, but to make sport for our neighbours, and laugh at them in our turn?
1813 *Pride and Prejudice*, ch.57.

64 There is not one in a hundred of either sex who is not taken in when they marry. Look where I will, I see that it is so; and I feel that it must be so, when I consider that it is, of all transactions, the one in which people expect most from others, and are least honest themselves.
1814 *Mansfield Park*, ch.5.

65 Selfishness must always be forgiven you know, because there is no hope for a cure.
1814 *Mansfield Park*, ch.7.

66 We do not look in great cities for our best morality.
1814 *Mansfield Park*, ch.9.

67 Let us have no ranting tragedies. Too many characters—Not a tolerable woman's part in the play.
1814 *Mansfield Park*, ch.14.

68 A large income is the best recipe for happiness I ever heard of. It certainly may secure all the myrtle and turkey part of it.
1814 *Mansfield Park*, ch.22.

69 Shakespeare one gets acquainted with without knowing how. It is part of an Englishman's constitution. His thoughts and beauties are so spread abroad that one touches them everywhere, one is intimate with him by instinct.
1814 *Mansfield Park*, ch.34.

70 I must have a London audience. I could never preach, but to the educated; to those who were capable of estimating my composition.
1814 *Mansfield Park*, ch.34.

71 I think I may boast myself to be, with all possible vanity, the most unlearned and uninformed female who ever dared to be an authoress.
1815 Letter to Rev James Clarke, quoted in Justin Wintle and Richard Kenin (eds) *The Dictionary of Biographical Quotation* (1978).

72 She would not have him really suspect such a circumstance as her not being thought perfect by every body.
1816 *Emma*, ch.1.

73 A real, honest, old-fashioned Boarding-school, where a reasonable quantity of accomplishments were sold at a reasonable price, and where girls might be sent to be out of the way and scramble themselves into a little education, without any danger of coming back prodigies.
1816 *Emma*, ch.3.

74 One half of the world cannot understand the pleasures of the other.
1816 *Emma*, ch.9.

75 The sooner every party breaks up the better.
1816 *Emma*, ch.25.

76 I do not know whether it ought to be so, but certainly silly things do cease to be silly if they are done by sensible people in an impudent way. Wickedness is always wickedness, but folly is not always folly. It depends upon the character of those who handle it.
1816 *Emma*, ch.26.

77 Surprises are foolish things. The pleasure is not enhanced, and the inconvenience is often considerable.
1816 *Emma*, ch.26.

78 One has no great hopes from Birmingham. I always say there is something direful in the sound.
1816 Mrs Elton speaking. *Emma*, ch.36.

79 Goldsmith tells us, when a lovely woman stoops to folly, she has nothing to do but die; and when she stoops to be disagreeable, it is equally to be recommended as a clearer of ill-fame.
1816 *Emma*, ch.45.
▶ See Goldsmith 376:93.

80 What should I do with your strong, manly, spirited sketches, full of variety and glow?—How could I possibly join them on to the little bit (two inches wide) of ivory on which I work with so fine a brush, as produces little effect after much labour?
1816 Letter to J Edward Austen, 16 Dec.

81 Single women have a dreadful propensity for being poor—which is one very strong argument in favour of matrimony.
1817 Letter to Fanny Knight, 13 Mar.

82 Pictures of perfection as you know make me sick and wicked.
1817 Of heroines in novels. Letter to Fanny Knight, 23 Mar.

83 Oh! it is only a novel!...only some work in which the most thorough knowledge of human nature, the happiest delineation of its varieties, the liveliest effusions of wit and humour are conveyed to the world in the best chosen language.
1818 *Northanger Abbey*, ch.5.

84 But history, real solemn history, I cannot be interested in...it tells me nothing that does not vex or weary me...the men all so good for nothing, and hardly any women at all.
1818 *Northanger Abbey*, vol.1, ch.14.

85 Where people wish to attach, they should always be ignorant. To come with a well informed mind, is to come with an inability of administering to the vanity of others, which a sensible person would always wish to avoid. A woman especially, if she have the misfortune of knowing anything, should conceal it as well she can…imbecility in females is a great enhancement of their personal charms.
1818 *Northanger Abbey*, ch.14.

86 Vanity was the beginning and the end of Sir Walter Elliot's character; vanity of person and of situation.
1818 *Persuasion*, ch.1.

87 'My idea of good company, Mr Elliot, is the company of clever, well-informed people, who have a great deal of conversation; that is what I call good company.' 'You are mistaken,' said he gently, 'that is not good company, that is the best.'
1818 *Persuasion*, ch.16.

88 We cannot help ourselves. We live at home, quiet, confined, and our feelings prey upon us. You are forced on exertion. You have always a profession, pursuits, business of some sort or other, to take you back into the world immediately, and continual occupation and change soon weaken impressions.
1818 Of the difference between women and men. *Persuasion*, ch.23.

89 Men have every advantage of us in telling their story. Education has been theirs in so much higher a degree; the pen has been in their hands.
1818 *Persuasion*, ch.23.

90 All the privilege I claim for my own sex (it is not a very enviable one, you need not covet it) is that of loving longest, when existence or when hope is gone.
1818 *Persuasion*, ch.23.

Auster, Paul *pseudonym of* Paul Benjamin 1947–

US novelist, poet and essayist. He is best known for his novels, which include the *New York Trilogy* (1985–7), *Mr Vertigo* (1994) and *The Brooklyn Follies* (2005).

91 We construct a narrative for ourselves, and that's the thread we follow from one day to the next. People who disintegrate as personalities are the ones who lose that thread.
1989 In the *Sunday Times*, 16 Apr.

92 More often than not, our lives resemble the stuff of eighteenth-century novels.
2003 *Collected Prose*, 'The National Story Project'.

93 For only the good doubt their own goodness, which is what makes them good in the first place. The bad know they are good, but the good know nothing. They spend their lives forgiving others, but they can't forgive themselves.
2008 *Man In The Dark*.

94 Wounds are an essential part of life, and until you are wounded in some way, you cannot become a man.
2010 *Sunset Park*.

95 You think it will never happen to you, that it cannot happen to you, that you are the only person in the world to whom none of these things will ever happen, and then, one by one, they all begin to happen to you, in the same way they happen to everyone else.
2012 *Winter Journal*.

Austin, Alfred 1835–1913

English poet. Appointed Poet Laureate in 1896, he was the author of *The Season; a Satire* (1861), *The Human Tragedy* (1862), *The Conversion of Winckelmann* (1862), several volumes of poetry and an autobiography (1911).

96 Along the electric wires the message came:
'He is no better, he is much the same.'
1910 'On the Illness of the Prince of Wales'. There is some doubt about the authorship of this satiric poem, but it is usually credited to Austin.

Austin, Mary Hunter 1868–1934

US novelist, short-story writer and suffragist, best known for her fiction about the American West and portraits of Native American life. Her works include *The Land of Little Rain* (1903), *A Woman of Genius* (1912) and her autobiography, *Earth Horizon* (1932).

97 When a woman ceases to alter the fashion of her hair, you guess that she has passed the crisis of her experience.
1903 *The Land of Little Rain*, 'The Basket Maker'.

Austin, Warren R(obinson) 1877–1962

US lawyer and diplomat, a Senator (1931–46) and subsequently US representative at the United Nations (1947–53).

98 It is better that aged diplomats be bored than for young men to die.
On soporifically lengthy debates at the United Nations.

99 Jews and Arabs should settle their differences like good Christians.
Attributed.

Avison, Margaret 1918–2007

Canadian poet. Her first book of poems was *Winter Sun* (1960). Her sixth collection, *Concrete and Wild Carrot*, was published in 2002.

1 Purpose apart, perched like an umpire, dozes,
Dreams golden balls whirring through indigo.
Clay blurs the whitewash but day still encloses
The albinos, bonded in their flick and flow.
Playing in musicked gravity, the pair
Score liquid Euclids in foolscaps of air.
1960 *Winter Sun*, 'Tennis'.

Ayckbourn, Sir Alan 1939–

English playwright. Recognized as a master of farce, his plays often shrewdly observe the English class structure.

2 My mother used to say, Delia, if S-E-X ever rears its ugly head, close your eyes before you see the rest of it.
1977 *Bedroom Farce*, act 2.

Ayer, Sir Alfred Jules 1910–89

English philosopher, professor at Oxford (1947–59). His first book *Language, Truth and Logic* (1936) was an iconoclastic attack on metaphysical speculation. He wrote many more works, and was knighted in 1970.

3 The traditional disputes of philosophers are, for the most part, as unwarranted as they are unfruitful.
1936 *Language, Truth and Logic*, ch.1.

4 We shall maintain that no statement which refers to a 'reality' transcending the limits of all possible sense-experience can possibly have any literal significance.
   1936 *Language, Truth and Logic*, ch.1.

5 The criterion which we use to test the genuineness of apparent statements of fact is the criterion of verifiability. We say that a sentence is factually significant to any given person, if, and only if, he knows how to verify the proposition which it purports to express—that is, if he knows what observations would lead him, under certain conditions, to accept the proposition as being true, or reject it as being false.
   1936 *Language, Truth and Logic*, ch.1

6 Sentences which simply express moral judgements do not say anything. They are pure expressions of feeling and as such do not come under the category of truth and falsehood.
   1936 *Language, Truth and Logic*, ch.6.

7 It appears, then, that ethics, as a branch of knowledge, is nothing more than a department of psychology and sociology.
   1936 *Language, Truth and Logic*, ch.6.

8 But if science may be said to be blind without philosophy, it is true also that philosophy is virtually empty without science.
   1936 *Language, Truth and Logic*, ch.8.

Ayres, Pam 1947–

English poet and broadcaster. She established a reputation as a popular versifier, reading her own poems on everyday themes on British television in the 1970s.

9 Medicinal discovery,
   It moves in mighty leaps,
   It leapt straight past the common cold
   And gave it us for keeps.
   1976 *Some of Me Poetry*, 'Oh no, I got a cold'.

Aytoun, Sir Robert 1570–1638

Scottish poet and courtier at the court of James VI and I in London. He wrote lyrics in English and Latin, and is credited with the prototype of 'Auld Lang Syne'.

10 I loved thee once; I'll love no more—
    Thine be the grief as is the blame;
    Thou art not what thou wast before,
    What reason I should be the same?
    'To an Inconstant Mistress', stanza 1.

Aytoun, William Edmonstoune 1813–65

Scottish lawyer and humorist, who contributed many parodies and burlesque reviews to *Blackwood's*. His best-known work was *Lays of the Scottish Cavaliers and other Poems* (1848).

11 Fhairshon swore a feud
    Against the clan M'Tavish;
    Marched into their land
    To murder and to ravish;
    For he did resolve
    To extirpate the vipers,
    With four-and-twenty men
    And five-and-thirty pipers.
    1845 'The Massacre of the Macpherson', stanza 1.

12 'He is coming! he is coming!'
    Like a bridegroom from his room,
    Came the hero from his prison
    To the scaffold and the doom.
    1848 *Lays of the Scottish Cavaliers and other Poems*, 'The Execution of Montrose', stanza 14.

13 They bore within their breasts the grief
    That fame can never heal—
    The deep, unutterable woe
    Which none save exiles feel.
    1848 *Lays of the Scottish Cavaliers and other Poems*, 'The Island of the Scots', stanza 12.

b

Babbage, Charles 1792–1871

English mathematician, inventor and scientific theoretician, who developed the programmable 'analytical engine', which was able to perform computations.

1 Perhaps the most important principle on which the economy of a manufacture depends, is the division of labour amongst the persons who perform the work.
   1832 *On the Economy of Machinery and Manufactures*.

Babbitt, Bruce Edward 1938–

US lawyer, Governor of Arizona (1978–87), a Democrat and noted conservationist.

2 There is room in the west for wolves.
   1995 Statement at Yellowstone National Park in Wyoming, 12 Jan, to the House of Representatives Natural Resources Committee, on the controversial restoration of wildlife.

Babel, Isaac 1894–c.1939

Russian short-story writer.

3 No iron can stab the heart with such force as a full stop put just at the right place.
   1932 *Guy de Maupassant*.

Babeuf, François Noël 1760–97

French communist. As 'Gracchus Babeuf' during the French Revolution, he plotted to destroy the Directory (1796) and institute a communist state, but he was discovered and guillotined.

4 The French Revolution is merely the herald of a far greater and much more solemn revolution, which will be the last... The hour has come for founding the Republic of equals—that great refuge open to every man.
   Conjuration des Égaux.

Bacall, Lauren *originally* Betty Perske 1924–2014

US film actress who married Humphrey Bogart in 1945.

5 I think your whole life shows in your face and you should be proud of that.
   1988 In the *Daily Telegraph*, 2 Mar.

6 A planned life is a dead life.
2005 Interview, Aug.

Bach, Johann Sebastian 1685–1750

German composer and organist, whose polyphonic works greatly influenced the course of Western music. He composed over 200 cantatas, the *Saint John Passion* (1723), the *Saint Matthew Passion* (1729), the *Mass in B Minor* (1733), and Christmas and Easter Oratorios, as well as much keyboard and instrumental music.

7 There is nothing to it. You only have to hit the right notes at the right time and the instrument plays itself.
Of the organ. Quoted in K Geiringer The Bach Family *(1954).*

8 An agreeable harmony for the honour of God and the permissible delights of the soul.
His definition of music. Quoted in Derek Watson Music Quotations *(1991).*

Bach, Richard 1936–

US author, formerly a military pilot. He is best known for *Jonathan Livingston Seagull* (1970).

9 Heaven is not a place, and it is not a time. Heaven is being perfect.
1970 Jonathan Livingston Seagull.

10 The gull sees farthest who sees highest.
1970 Jonathan Livingston Seagull.

11 'To begin with,' he said heavily, 'you've got to understand that a seagull is an unlimited idea of freedom, an image of the Great Gull, and your whole body, from wingtip to wingtip, is nothing more than your thought itself.'
1970 Jonathan Livingston Seagull.

12 There is no such thing as a problem without a gift for you in its hands. You seek problems because you need their gifts.
1977 Illusions.

13 Argue for your limitations, and sure enough, they're yours.
1977 Illusions.

14 'I don't know they're true,' he said. 'I believe them because it's fun to believe them.'
1977 Illusions.

15 If I've learned one lesson in all my days, it's this: Life starts new, every sunrise.
2013 Travels with Puff: A Gentle Game of Life and Death.

Bacon, Francis, Viscount St Albans 1561–1626

English philosopher and statesman. Educated as a scholar and a lawyer, he entered the service of the crown and eventually became Lord Chancellor. Key works include *Essays* (1597–1625), *The Advancement of Learning* (1605), *Novum Organum* (1620) and *The New Atlantis* (1627).

16 I have taken all knowledge to be my province.
1592 Letter to Lord Burghley.

17 Knowledge is power
1597 Meditationes sacrae,*'De Haresibus' (Of Heresies).*

18 Opportunity makes a thief.
1598 Letter to the Earl of Essex.

19 For all knowledge and wonder (which is the seed of knowledge) is an impression of pleasure in itself.
1605 The Advancement of Learning, *bk.1, ch.1, section 3.*

20 So let great authors have their due, as time, which is the author of authors, be not deprived of his due, which is further and further to discover the truth.
1605 The Advancement of Learning, *bk.1, ch.4, section 12.*

21 If a man will begin with certainties, he shall end in doubts; but if he will be content to begin with doubts, he shall end in certainties.
1605 The Advancement of Learning, *bk.1, ch.5, section 8.*

22 Learned men…do many times fail to observe decency and discretion in their behaviour and carriage, so as the vulgar sort of capacities do make a judgment of them in greater matters by that which they find them wanting in smaller.
1605 The Advancement of Learning, *bk.1.*

23 Martin Luther…was enforced to awake all antiquity and to call former times to his succour to make a party against the present time, so that the ancient authors both in divinity and in humanity which had long time slept in libraries began generally to be read and revolved.
1605 The Advancement of Learning, *bk.1.*

24 Vain matter is worse than vain words.
1605 The Advancement of Learning, *bk.1.*

25 Time seemeth to be of the nature of a river or stream, which carrieth down to us that which is light and blown up, and sinketh and drowneth that which is weighty and solid.
1605 The Advancement of Learning, *bk.1.*

26 Antiquities are history defaced, or some remnants of history which have casually escaped the shipwreck of time.
1605 The Advancement of Learning, *bk.2, ch.2, section 1.*

27 [Poesy] was ever thought to have some participation of divineness, because it doth raise and erect the mind, by submitting the shows of things to the desires of the mind; whereas reason doth buckle and bow the mind unto the nature of things.
1605 The Advancement of Learning, *bk.2, ch.4, section 2.*

28 The knowledge of man is as the waters, some descending from above, and some springing from beneath; the one informed by the light of nature, the other inspired by divine revelation.
1605 The Advancement of Learning, *bk.2, ch.5, section 1.*

29 They are ill discoverers that think there is no land, when they can see nothing but sea.
1605 The Advancement of Learning, *bk.2, ch.7, section 5.*

30 A dance is a measured pace, as a verse is a measured speech.
1605 The Advancement of Learning, *bk.2, ch.16, section 5.*

31 But men must know, that in this theatre of man's life it is reserved only for God and angels to be lookers on.
1605 The Advancement of Learning, *bk.2, ch.20, section 8.*

32 We are much beholden to Machiavel and others, that write what men do, and not what they ought to do.
1605 The Advancement of Learning, *bk.2, ch.21, section 9.*

33 Did not one of the fathers in great indignation call poesy *vinum daemonum*?
1605 The Advancement of Learning, *bk.2, ch.22, section 13. The Latin translates as 'the wine of the devils'.*

34 All good moral philosophy is but an handmaid to religion.
   1605 *The Advancement of Learning*, bk.2, ch.22, section 14.

35 Of knowledge there is no satiety.
   1605 *The Advancement of Learning*, bk.2.

36 It is not granted to man to love and to be wise.
   1605 *The Advancement of Learning*, bk.2.

37 Tennis is a game of no use in itself.
   1605 *The Advancement of Learning*, bk.2.

38 Man seeketh in society comfort, use, and protection.
   1605 *The Advancement of Learning*, bk.2.

39 Fortunes...come tumbling into some men's laps.
   1605 *The Advancement of Learning*, bk.2.

40 It is in life as it is in ways, the shortest way is most commonly the foulest, and surely the fairer way is not much about.
   1605 *The Advancement of Learning*, bk.2, ch.23, section 45.

41 Empires and old women are more happy many times in their cures than learned physicians, because they are more exact and religious in holding to the composition and confection of tried medicines.
   1605 *The Advancement of Learning*, bk.4, ch.2.

42 The subtlety of nature is greater many times over than the subtlety of the senses and understanding.
   1620 *Novum Organum*, bk.1, aphorism 10.

43 *Quod enim mavult homo verum esse, id potius credit.*
   For what a man would like to be true, that he more readily believes.
   1620 *Novum Organum*, bk.1, aphorism 49.

44 Those who have handled sciences have been either men of experiment or men of dogmas. The men of experiment are like the ant; they only collect and use; the reasoners resemble spiders, who make cobwebs out of their own substance. But the bee takes a middle course; it gathers its material from the flowers of the garden and of the field, but transforms and digests by a power of its own. Not unlike this is the true business of philosophy.
   1620 *Novum Organum* bk.1, aphorism 95.

45 *Vim et virtutem et consequentias rerum inventarum notare juvat; quae non in aliis manifestius occurrunt, quam in illis tribus quae antiquis incognitae, et quarum primordia, licet recentia, obscura et ingloria sunt: Artis nimirum Imprimendi, Pulveris Tormentarii, et Acus Nauticae. Haec enim tria rerum faciem et statum in orbe terrarum mutaverunt.*
   It is well to observe the force and virtue and consequence of discoveries, and these are to be seen nowhere more conspicuously than in those three which were unknown to the ancients, and of which the origin, though recent, is obscure and inglorious; namely, printing, gunpowder and the magnet [ie the compass]. For these three have changed the whole face and state of things throughout the world.
   1620 *Novum Organum*, bk.1, aphorism 129 (translated by James Spedding).

46 *Natura enim non imperatur, nisi parendo.*
   For we cannot command Nature except by obeying her.
   1620 *Novum Organum*, bk.1, aphorism 129.

47 It would be unsound fancy and self-contradictory to expect that things which have never yet been done can be done except by means which have never yet been tried.
   1620 *Novum Organum*.

48 The lame man who keeps the right road outstrips the runner who takes a wrong one. Nay, it is obvious that when a man runs the wrong way, the more active and swift he is the further he will go astray.
   1620 *Novum Organum*.

49 *Divitiae bona ancilla, pessima domina.*
   Riches are a good handmaid, but the worst mistress.
   1623 *De Dignitiate et Augmentis Scientiarum*, Antitheta no.6 (translated by Gilbert Watts, 1640).

50 The voice of the people hath some divineness in it, else how should so many men agree to be of one mind?
   1623 *De Dignitiate et Augmentis Scientiarum*, Antitheta no.9 (translated by Gilbert Watts, 1640).

51 *Silentium, stultorum virtus.*
   Silence is the virtue of fools.
   1623 *De Dignitiate et Augmentis Scientiarum*, Antitheta no.31 (translated by Gilbert Watts, 1640).

52 The end of our foundation is the knowledge of causes, and secret motions of things; and the enlarging of the bounds of human Empire, to the effecting of all things possible.
   1624 *New Atlantis* (published posthumously, 1627).

53 Wise nature did never put her precious jewels into a garret four stories high: and therefore...exceeding tall men had ever very empty heads.
   1625 *Apophthegms*.

54 Hope is a good breakfast, but it is a bad supper.
   1625 *Apophthegms*.

55 What is truth? said jesting Pilate; and would not stay for an answer.
   1625 *Essays*, no.1, 'Of Truth'.

56 The inquiry of truth, which is the love-making, or wooing of it, the knowledge of truth, which is the presence of it, and the belief of truth, which is the enjoying of it, is the sovereign good of human nature.
   1625 *Essays*, no.1, 'Of Truth'.

57 Men fear death as children fear to go in the dark; and as that natural fear in children is increased with tales, so is the other.
   1625 *Essays*, no.2, 'Of Death'.

58 There is no passion in the mind of man so weak, but it mates and masters the fear of death. And therefore death is no such terrible enemy, when a man hath so many attendants about him that can win the combat of him. Revenge triumphs over death; love slights it; honour aspireth to it; grief flieth to it.
   1625 *Essays*, no.2, 'Of Death'.

59 It is as natural to die as to be born; and to a little infant, perhaps, the one is as painful as the other.
   1625 *Essays*, no.2, 'Of Death'.

60 Death...openeth the gate to good fame, and extinguisheth envy.
   1625 *Essays*, no.2, 'Of Death'.

61 All colours will agree in the dark.
   1625 *Essays*, no.3, 'Of Unity in Religion'.

62 Revenge is a kind of wild justice, which the more man's nature runs to, the more ought law to weed it out.
   1625 *Essays*, no.4, 'Of Revenge'.

63 The virtue of prosperity, is temperance; the virtue of adversity, is fortitude.
1625 *Essays*, no.5, 'Of Adversity'.

64 Prosperity is the blessing of the Old Testament, adversity is the blessing of the New.
1625 *Essays*, no.5, 'Of Adversity'.

65 Prosperity is not without many fears and distastes; and adversity is not without comforts and hopes.
1625 *Essays*, no.5, 'Of Adversity'.

66 Prosperity doth best discover vice, but adversity doth best discover virtue.
1625 *Essays*, no.5, 'Of Adversity'.

67 Let judges also remember that Solomon's throne was supported by lions on both sides; let them be lions, but yet lions under the throne.
1625 *Essays*, no.6, 'Of Judicature'.

68 The joys of parents are secret, and so are their griefs and fears.
1625 *Essays*, no.7, 'Of Parents and Children'.

69 Children sweeten labours, but they make misfortunes more bitter.
1625 *Essays*, no.7, 'Of Parents and Children'.

70 He that hath wife and children hath given hostages to fortune; for they are impediments to great enterprises, either of virtue or mischief. Certainly the best works, and of greatest merit for the public, have proceeded from the unmarried or childless men, which both in affection and means have married and endowed the public.
1625 *Essays*, no.8, 'Of Marriage and the Single Life'.

71 There are some others that account wife and children but as bills of charge.
1625 *Essays*, no.8, 'Of Marriage and the Single Life'.

72 The most ordinary cause of a single life is liberty, especially in certain self-pleasing and humorous minds, which are so sensible of every restraint, as they will go near to think their girdles and garters to be bonds and shackles.
1625 *Essays*, no.8, 'Of Marriage and the Single Life'.

73 Unmarried men are best friends, best masters, best servants, but not always best subjects, for they are light to run away, and almost all fugitives are of that condition.
1625 *Essays*, no.8, 'Of Marriage and the Single Life'.

74 Certainly wife and children are a kind of discipline of humanity; and single men, though they be many times more charitable, because their means are less exhaust, yet…they are more cruel and hardhearted (good to make severe inquisitors), because their tenderness is not so oft called upon.
1625 *Essays*, no.8, 'Of Marriage and the Single Life'.

75 Wives are young men's mistresses, companions for middle age, and old men's nurses.
1625 *Essays*, no.8, 'Of Marriage and the Single Life'.

76 He was reputed one of the wise men that made answer to the question when a man should marry? 'A young man not yet, an elder man not at all.'
1625 *Essays*, no.8, 'Of Marriage and the Single Life'.

77 It is often seen that bad husbands have very good wives; whether it be that it raiseth the price of their husband's kindness when it comes, or that the wives take a pride in their patience. But this never fails, if the bad husbands were of their own choosing, against their friends' consent; for then they will be sure to make good their own folly.
1625 *Essays*, no.8, 'Of Marriage and the Single Life'.

78 I had rather believe all the fables in the legend, and the Talmud, and the Alcoran, than that this universal frame is without a mind.
1625 *Essays*, no.9, 'Of Atheism'.

79 It is true, that a little philosophy inclineth Man's mind to atheism; but depth in philosophy bringeth men's minds about to religion.
1625 *Essays*, no.9 'Of Atheism'.
▶ See Berkeley 84:32.

80 For it is a true Rule that Love is ever rewarded, either with the reciproque, or with an inward and secret contempt.
1625 *Essays*, no.10, 'Of Love'.

81 The speaking in perpetual hyperbole is comely in nothing but love.
1625 *Essays*, no.10, 'Of Love'.

82 All rising to great place is by a winding stair.
1625 *Essays*, no.11, 'Of Great Place'.

83 Men in great place are thrice servants: servants of the sovereign or state, servants of fame, and servants of business.
1625 *Essays*, no.11, 'Of Great Place'.

84 It is a strange desire to seek power and to lose liberty.
1625 *Essays*, no.11, 'Of Great Place'.

85 The rising unto place is laborious, and by pains men come to greater pains; and it is sometimes base, and by indignities men come to dignities. The standing is slippery, and the regress is either a downfall, or at least an eclipse, which is a melancholy thing: *Cum non sis qui fueris, non esse cur velis vivere.*
1625 *Essays*, no.11, 'Of Great Place'. The Latin is taken from Cicero's *Familiar Letters*, and translates as: 'When you are not what you were, there is no reason to live.'

86 Certainly great persons had need to borrow other men's opinions to think themselves happy; for if they judge by their own feeling, they cannot find it; but if they think with themselves what other men think of them, and that other men would fain be as they are, then they are happy.
1625 *Essays*, no.11, 'Of Great Place'.

87 Men in great fortunes are strangers to themselves.
1625 *Essays*, no.11, 'Of Great Place'.

88 Merit and good works is the end of man's motion, and conscience of the same is the accomplishment of man's rest.
1625 *Essays*, no.11, 'Of Great Place'.

89 The vices of authority are chiefly four: delays, corruption, roughness, and facility.
1625 *Essays*, no.11, 'Of Great Place'.

90 In civil business; What first? Boldness; What second, and third? Boldness. And yet boldness is a child of ignorance and baseness.
1625 *Essays*, no.12, 'Of Boldness'.

91 There is in human nature generally more of the fool than of the wise.
1625 *Essays*, no.12, 'Of Boldness'.

Bacon

92 Mahomet made the people believe that he would call a hill to him, and from the top of it offer up his prayers for the observers of his law. The people assembled: Mahomet called the hill to come to him again and again; and when the hill stood still he was never a whit abashed, but said, 'If the hill will not come to Mahomet, Mahomet will go to the hill.'
1625 *Essays*, no.12, 'Of Boldness'.

93 New nobility is but the act of power, but ancient nobility is the act of time.
1625 *Essays*, no.14, 'Of Nobility'.

94 The surest way to prevent seditions...is to take away the matter of them.
1625 *Essays*, no.15, 'Of Seditions and Troubles'.

95 Money is like muck, not good except it be spread.
1625 *Essays*, no.15, 'Of Seditions and Troubles'.

96 The remedy is worse than the disease.
1625 *Essays*, no.15, 'Of Seditions and Troubles'.

97 It were better to have no opinion of God at all than such an opinion as is unworthy of him.
1625 *Essays*, no.17, 'Of Superstition'.

98 In all superstition wise men follow fools.
1625 *Essays*, no.17, 'Of Superstition'.

99 There is a superstition in avoiding superstition.
1625 *Essays*, no.17, 'Of Superstition'. This is directed against Puritan reformers, who decried both Catholic and Anglican rites as 'superstitious'.

1 It is a miserable state of mind to have few things to desire and many things to fear.
1625 *Essays*, no.19, 'Of Empire'.

2 In things that are tender and unpleasing, it is good to break the ice by some whose words are of less weight, and to reserve the more weighty voice to come in as by chance.
1625 *Essays*, no.22, 'Of Cunning'.

3 Nothing doth more hurt in a state than that cunning men pass for wise.
1625 *Essays*, no.22, 'Of Cunning'.

4 Be so true to thyself as thou be not false to others.
1625 *Essays*, no.23, 'Of Wisdom for a Man's Self'.

5 It is a poor centre of a man's actions, himself.
1625 *Essays*, no.23, 'Of Wisdom for a Man's Self'.

6 It is the nature of extreme self-lovers, as they will set a house on fire, and it were but to roast their eggs.
1625 *Essays*, no.23, 'Of Wisdom for a Man's Self'.

7 It is the wisdom of the crocodiles, that shed tears when they would devour.
1625 *Essays*, no.23, 'Of Wisdom for a Man's Self'.

8 As the births of living creatures at first are ill-shapen, so are all innovations, which are the births of time.
1625 *Essays*, no.24, 'Of Innovations'.

9 He that will not apply new remedies must expect new evils; for time is the greatest innovator.
1625 *Essays*, no.24, 'Of Innovations'.

10 To choose time is to save time.
1625 *Essays*, no.25, 'Of Dispatch'.

11 The French are wiser than they seem, and the Spaniards seem wiser than they are.
1625 *Essays*, no.26, 'Of Seeming Wise'.

12 It had been hard for him that spake it to have put more truth and untruth together, in a few words, than in that speech: 'Whosoever is delighted in solitude is either a wild beast, or a god.'
1625 *Essays*, no.27, 'Of Friendship'.

13 A crowd is not company, and faces are but a gallery of pictures, and talk but a tinkling cymbal, where there is no love.
1625 *Essays*, no.27, 'Of Friendship'.
▶ See Bible 126:52.

14 [Friendship] redoubleth joys, and cutteth griefs in half.
1625 *Essays*, no.27, 'Of Friendship'.

15 As if you would call a physician, that is thought good for the cure of the disease you complain of but is unacquainted with your body, and therefore may put you in the way for a present cure but overthroweth your health in some other kind; and so cure the disease and kill the patient.
1625 *Essays*, no.27, 'Of Friendship'.

16 Riches are for spending; and spending for honour and good actions.
1625 *Essays*, no.28, 'Of Expense'.

17 Neither will it be, that a people overlaid with taxes should ever become valiant and martial.
1625 *Essays*, no.29, 'Of the True Greatness of Kingdoms'.

18 Suspicions amongst thoughts are like bats amongst birds, they ever fly by twilight.
1625 *Essays*, no.31, 'Of Suspicion'.

19 There is nothing makes a man suspect much, more than to know little.
1625 *Essays*, no.31, 'Of Suspicion'.

20 If you dissemble sometimes your knowledge of that you are thought to know, you shall be thought, another time, to know that you know not.
1625 *Essays*, no.32, 'Of Discourse'.

21 When the world was young it begat more children; but now it is old it begets fewer: for I may justly account new plantations to be the children of former kingdoms.
1625 *Essays*, no.33, 'Of Plantations'.

22 If you plant where savages are, do not only entertain them with trifles and jingles, but use them justly and graciously.
1625 *Essays*, no.33, 'Of Plantations'.

23 Nature is often hidden, sometimes overcome, seldom extinguished.
1625 *Essays*, no.38, 'Of Nature in Men'.

24 Chiefly the mould of a man's fortune is in his own hands.
1625 *Essays*, no.40, 'Of Fortune'.

25 If a man look sharply, and attentively, he shall see Fortune; for though she be blind, yet she is not invisible.
1625 *Essays*, no.40, 'Of Fortune'.

26 Beauty is as summer-fruits, which are easy to corrupt, and cannot last.
1625 *Essays*, no.43, 'Of Beauty'.

27 Virtue is like a rich stone, best plain set.
1625 *Essays*, no.43, 'Of Beauty'.

28 That is the best part of beauty, which a picture cannot express.
1625 *Essays*, no.43, 'Of Beauty'.

29 There is no excellent beauty that hath not some strangeness in the proportion.
   1625 *Essays*, no.43, 'Of Beauty'.

30 God Almighty first planted a garden; and indeed, it is the purest of human pleasures.
   1625 *Essays*, no.46, 'Of Gardens'.

31 It is generally better to deal by speech than by letter.
   1625 *Essays*, no.47, 'Of Negotiating'.

32 It is better dealing with men in appetite, than with those that are where they would be.
   1625 *Essays*, no.47, 'Of Negotiating'.

33 If you would work any man, you must either know his nature and fashions, and so lead him; or his ends, and so persuade him; or his weakness and disadvantages, and so awe him, or those that have interest in him, and so govern him.
   1625 *Essays*, no.47, 'Of Negotiating'.

34 There is little friendship in the world, and least of all between equals.
   1625 *Essays*, no.48, 'Of Followers and Friends'.

35 To spend too much time in studies is sloth; to use them too much for ornament is affectation; to make judgment wholly by their rules is the humour of a scholar.
   1625 *Essays*, no.50, 'Of Studies'.

36 Read not to contradict and confute, nor to believe and take for granted, nor to find talk and discourse, but to weigh and consider.
   1625 *Essays*, no.50, 'Of Studies'.

37 Some books are to be tasted, others to be swallowed, and some few to be chewed and digested; that is, some books are to be read only in parts; others to be read but not curiously; and some few to be read wholly, and with diligence and attention. Some books also may be read by deputy, and extracts made of them by others.
   1625 *Essays*, no.50, 'Of Studies'.

38 If a man write little, he had need have a great memory; if he confer little, he had need have a present wit; and if he read little he had need have much cunning, to seem to know that he doth not.
   1625 *Essays*, no.50, 'Of Studies'.

39 Histories make men wise; poets, witty; the mathematics, subtle; natural philosophy, deep; moral, grave; logic and rhetoric, able to contend.
   1625 *Essays*, no.50, 'Of Studies'.

40 Light gains make heavy purses.
   1625 *Essays*, no.52, 'Of Ceremonies and Respects'.

41 A wise man will make more opportunities than he finds.
   1625 *Essays*, no.52, 'Of Ceremonies and Respects'.

42 It was prettily devised of Aesop, 'The fly sat upon the axletree of the chariot-wheel and said, what a dust do I raise.'
   1625 *Essays*, no.54, 'Of Vain-Glory'.

43 In the youth of a state arms do flourish; in the middle age of a state, learning; and then both of them together for a time; in the declining age of a state, mechanical arts and merchandise.
   1625 *Essays*, no.58, 'Of Vicissitude of Things'.

44 I bequeath my soul to God… For my name and memory, I leave it to men's charitable speeches, and to foreign nations, and the next age.
   1626 From his will.

45 God's first Creature, which was Light.
   New Atlantis (published 1627).

46 The end of our foundation is the knowledge of causes, and secret motions of things; and the enlarging of the bounds of human Empire, to the effecting of all things possible.
   1627 Of Solomon's House, the centre of Bacon's scientific utopia. *New Atlantis* (published 1627).

47 No man can tickle himself.
   Sylva Sylvarum (published 1627), bk.8.

48 Generally music feedeth that disposition of the spirits which it findeth.
   Sylva Sylvarum (published 1627).

49 The world's a bubble; and the life of man
   Less than a span.
   The World (published 1629).

50 Books must follow sciences, and not sciences books.
   A Proposition… Touching Amendment of the Laws of England (published 1657).

51 The government of a woman has been a rare thing at all times; felicity in such government a rarer thing still; felicity and long continuance together the rarest thing of all.
   Quoted in J E Neale *The Age of Catherine de Medici and Essays in Elizabethan History* (1963), p.217.

Bacon, Francis 1909–92

Irish-born painter, who settled in England in 1928 and began painting without formal training. His work draws on surrealism and motion photography, often evoking angst. He was a technical perfectionist, and destroyed much of his work.

52 I think of myself as a kind of pulverizing machine into which everything I look at and feel is fed. I believe that I am different from the mixed-media jackdaws who use photographs etc. more or less literally.
   On the use of photographs in his art. Quoted in John Russell *Francis Bacon* (1979).

53 Who can I tear to pieces, if not my friends?… If they were not my friends, I could not do such violence to them.
   Quoted in John Russell *Francis Bacon* (1979).

Bacon, Martha 1917–81

US educator and author

54 She soothed and solaced and celebrated, destroying her gift by maiming it to suit her hearers.
   1965 On Phillis Wheatley. In *Christian Science Monitor*, 24 Jun.

Bacon, Roger known as Doctor Mirabilis c.1214–c.1292

English philosopher, scientist and alchemist, closely associated with Oxford. His major works include the *Opus Majus*, *Opus Minor* and *Opus Tertium*. He became a Franciscan, but was rejected and persecuted for heresy.

55 All science requires mathematics…the knowledge of mathematical things is almost innate in us…this is the easiest of sciences. A fact which is obvious in that no one's brain rejects it. For laymen and people who are utterly illiterate know how to count and reckon.
   1267 *Opus Majus*, pt.4, ch.1 (translated by Robert Belle Burke, 1928).

56 Mathematics is the door and key to the sciences.
   1267 *Opus Majus*, pt.4, ch.1 (translated by Robert Belle Burke, 1928).

57 There are two modes of acquiring knowledge, namely, by reasoning and experience. Reasoning draws a conclusion and makes us grant the conclusion, but does not make the conclusion certain, nor does it remove doubt so that the mind may rest on the intuition of truth unless the mind discovers it by the path of experience.
1267 *Opus Majus* (translated by Robert Belle Burke, 1928).

Baden-Powell, Robert Stephenson Smyth, 1st Baron
1857–1941

English soldier. He became a hero for his defence of Mafeking (1899–1900) during the Boer War but is usually remembered as the founder of the Boy Scout movement in 1908 and for his book *Scouting for Boys* (1908).

58 The scouts' motto is founded on my initials, it is: BE PREPARED, which means, you are always to be in a state of readiness in mind and body to do your DUTY.
1908 *Scouting for Boys*.

59 Football, in itself, is a grand game for developing a lad physically and also morally...but it is a vicious game when it draws crowds of lads away from playing the game themselves to be merely onlookers at a few paid players.
1908 *Scouting for Boys*.

Baedeker, Karl 1801–59

German editor and publisher, famous for his foreign travel guides. The first, for Coblenz, appeared in 1829, and they continued to be published after his death.

60 On arrival at a Syrian port the traveller's passport is sometimes asked for, but an ordinary visiting-card will answer the purpose equally well.
1876 *Palestine and Syria*, 'Passports and Custom House'.

61 Oxford is on the whole more attractive than Cambridge to the ordinary visitor; and the traveller is therefore recommended to visit Cambridge first, or to omit it altogether if he cannot visit both.
1887 *Great Britain*, Route 30: 'From London to Oxford'.

Baer, George Frederick 1842–1914

US lawyer and industrialist, who led the resistance to the strike by the United Mine Workers of America in 1902.

62 The rights and interests of the laboring man will be protected and cared for, not by the labor agitators, but by the Christian men to whom God, in his infinite wisdom, has given control of the property interests of the country.
1902 Letter to the press during the Pennsylvanian miners' strike.

Bagehot, Walter 1826–77

British economist and journalist. His *English Constitution* (1867) is still considered a standard work, and *Physics and Politics* (1872), applying evolution theories to politics, greatly influenced 19c thought.

63 The essence of Toryism is enjoyment...but as far as communicating and establishing your creed are concerned—try a little pleasure. The way to keep up old customs is, to enjoy old customs; the way to be satisfied with the present state of things is, to enjoy that state of things.
1856 Essay on *Macaulay*.

64 No real English gentleman, in his secret soul, was ever sorry for the death of a political economist.
1858 *Estimates of Some Englishmen and Some Scotchmen*, 'The First Edinburgh Reviewers'.

65 Writers, like teeth, are divided into incisors and grinders.
1858 *Estimates of Some Englishmen and Some Scotchmen*, 'The First Edinburgh Reviewers'.

66 It is said that England invented the phrase, 'Her Majesty's Opposition'; that it was the first government which made a criticism of administration as much a part of the polity as administration itself.
1867 *The English Constitution*, ch.2, 'The Cabinet'.

67 *The Times* has made many ministries.
1867 *The English Constitution*, ch.2, 'The Cabinet'.

68 The fancy of the mass of men is incredibly weak; it can see nothing without a visible symbol, and there is much that it can scarcely make out with a symbol.
1867 *The English Constitution*, ch.4, 'The House of Lords'.

69 The order of nobility is of great use, too, not only in what it creates, but in what it prevents. It prevents the rule of wealth—the religion of gold. This is the obvious and natural idol of the Anglo-Saxon... From this our aristocracy preserves us.
1867 *The English Constitution*, ch.4, 'The House of Lords'.

70 A severe though not unfriendly critic of our institutions said that the cure for admiring the House of Lords was to go and look at it.
1867 *The English Constitution*, ch.4, 'The House of Lords'.

71 The great offices, whether permanent or parliamentary, which require mind now give social prestige, and almost only those. An Under-Secretary of State with £2,000 a year is a much greater man than the director of a finance company with £5,000, and the country saves the difference.
1867 *The English Constitution*, ch.4, 'The House of Lords'.

72 Nations touch at their summits.
1867 *The English Constitution*, ch.4, 'The House of Lords'.

73 The best reason why monarchy is a strong government is, that it is an intelligible government. The mass of mankind understand it, and they hardly anywhere in the world understand any other.
1867 *The English Constitution*, ch.6, 'The Monarchy'.

74 Throughout the greater part of his life George III was a kind of 'consecrated obstruction'.
1867 *The English Constitution*, ch.6, 'The Monarchy'.

75 Above all things our royalty is to be reverenced, and if you begin to poke about it you cannot reverence it... Its mystery is its life. We must not let in daylight upon magic.
1867 *The English Constitution*, ch.6, 'The Monarchy (continued)'.

76 Political economy traces in an abstract way the effects of the desire to be rich; and nations must nowadays abound in that passion if they are to have much power or respect in the world.
1876 'Preliminaries of Political Economy', collected in *Economic Studies* (1880).

77 Men of business have a solid judgment, a wonderful guessing power of what is going to happen, each in his own trade, but they have never practised themselves in reasoning out their judgments and in supporting their guesses by argument; probably if they did so, some of the finer and correcter parts of their anticipations would vanish.

1876 'Postulates of English Political Economy', in *Economic Studies* (1880).

78 Who can tell without instruction what is likely to be the effect of the new loans of England to foreign nations? We press upon half-finished and half-civilized communities incalculable sums; we are to them what the London money-dealers are to students at Oxford and Cambridge.
1876 'Postulates of English Political Economy', in *Economic Studies* (1880).

79 No man has come so near to our definition of a constitutional statesman—the powers of a first-rate man and the creed of a second-rate man.
1881 *Biographical Studies*, 'The Character of Sir Robert Peel'.

80 A constitutional statesman is in general a man of common opinion and uncommon abilities.
1881 *Biographical Studies*, 'The Character of Sir Robert Peel'.

Bailey, David 1938–

English photographer known particularly for his striking pictures of cultural icons.

81 I never cared for fashion much. Amusing little seams and witty little pleats. It was the girls I liked.
1990 In *The Independent*, 5 Nov.

82 I grew up scared of Hitler. I wanted to kill him because he spent all my childhood trying to kill me.
2001 In *The Mail on Sunday*, 14 Oct.

83 It's funny: you hate authority and then your photography takes on an authority.
2001 In *The Mail on Sunday*, 14 Oct.

Bailey, F(rancis) Lee 1933–

US criminal lawyer, who founded his own detective agency at Harvard. He defended the Boston Strangler and, more recently, he defended O J Simpson at his 1995 murder trial.

84 When you see a lawyer trying to pick a smart jury, you know he's got a strong case.
1972 In the *Los Angeles Times*, 9 Jan.

85 The guilty never escape unscathed. My fees are sufficient punishment for anyone.
1972 In the *Los Angeles Times*, 9 Jan.

86 I think my grandmother actually smelled like a cookie and that's enough to get any child's attention.
Quoted by Phyllis Hanes in *Christian Science Monitor*, 15 Jun 1988.

Bailey, Nathan d.1742

English lexicographer, best known for *An Universal Etymological English Dictionary* (1721), which gives word origins as well as definitions.

87 LONDON…the Metropolis of *Great-Britain*, founded before the City of *Rome*, walled by *Constantine* the Great, no ways inferior to the greatest in *Europe* for Riches and Greatness.
1721 *An Universal Etymological English Dictionary*.

Bailey, Philip James 1816–1902

English poet, father of the Spasmodic school. His great work *Festus* (1839) was expanded in 1889 to incorporate previously published volumes: *The Angel World* (1850), *The Mystic* (1855) and *Universal Hymn* (1867).

88 America, thou half-brother of the world;
With something good and bad of every land.
1839 *Festus*, sc.10.

Baillie, Robert 1599–1662

Scottish Presbyterian leader, an opponent of Archbishop Laud and of episcopacy. He was selected by the Scottish Church to invite Charles II to accept the covenant and crown of Scotland.

89 The Parliament of England cannot have on earth so strong pillars and pregnant supporters of all their privileges as free protestant assemblies established by law, and kept in their full freedom from the lowest to the highest—from the congregational eldership to the general synod of the nation.
A Dissuasive from the Errors of Time, 1645–6.

Bainbridge, Dame Beryl Margaret 1934–2010

English novelist and playwright. She worked as an actress and publisher's clerk before publishing *A Weekend with Claude* (1967). Her work is marked by a caustic wit and a finely turned prose style.

90 I am of the firm belief that everybody could write books and I never understand why they don't. After all, everybody speaks. Once the grammar has been learnt it is simply talking on paper and in time learning what not to say.
1976 In D L Kirkpatrick (ed) *Contemporary Novelists*.

91 Being constantly with children was like wearing a pair of shoes that were expensive and too small. She couldn't bear to throw them out, but they gave her blisters.
1977 *Injury Time*, ch.4.

92 We are essentially fragile. We don't have to wait for the sword or some other equally sensational weapon to strike us down… There are so many ways of us dying it's astonishing any of us choose old age.
1978 *Young Adolf*, ch.12.

93 I haven't the humility to find anything beneath me.
1989 *An Awfully Big Adventure*, ch.3.

94 It's all changed now, which is why it mattered to those young men from Liverpool that they should be there to support their team. What other group is going to troop their colours for them, present them with scarves and emblems?
1989 After the Hillsborough football disaster. Quoted in David Pickering *The Cassell Soccer Companion* (1994).

95 The vital accessories to my work are my reference books, such as the complete Shakespeare and a prayer book, and a large refuse bin.
1991 In *The Guardian*, 8 Aug.

96 Women are programmed to love completely, and men are programmed to spread it around.
1996 Interview in the *Daily Telegraph*, 10 Sep.

97 Bugger the writing, I'd have given anything to have had a long-lasting relationship.
2004 In *The Times*, 7 Apr.

Bairnsfather, Bruce 1888–1959

British cartoonist, a soldier in World War I and cartoonist with US troops in World War II. His works include *Fragments from France* (1916), *Bullets and Billets* (1917) and *Jeeps and Jests* (1943).

98 Well, if you knows of a better 'ole, go to it.
   1915 Caption to cartoon in *Fragments from France*. The speaker, Ol' Bill, is waist-deep in mud on the Somme. The phrase was used as the title for a 1926 US film based on the character, *The Better 'Ole*.

Baker, Colin 1943–
English actor who played Doctor Who from 1984 to 1986.

99 Love is a human emotion and the doctor isn't human. We were always told there is one golden rule: no hanky panky in the Tardis.
   2004 On playing Doctor Who. Quoted in the *Sunday Times*, 7 Mar.

Baker, Howard Henry, Jr 1925–2014
US public official, Republican senator from Tennessee and a member of the Watergate Committee (1973). He became Senate Leader and White House Chief of Staff (1987–8) under Reagan.

1 Never speak more clearly than you think.
   1987 On becoming President Reagan's third Chief of Staff. In the *New York Times*, 6 Sep.

Baker, James Addison, III 1930–
US lawyer and government official. He managed the campaigns of Ford (1976) and Bush (1980, 1988). As Secretary of State (1989–92) he initiated a round of Middle East peace talks.

2 Sometimes you move publicly, sometimes privately. Sometimes quietly, sometimes at the top of your voice. And sometimes an active policy is best advanced by doing nothing until the right time—or never.
   1990 Of statesmanship. In *Time*, 19 Mar.

Baker, John Austin 1928–2014
English cleric and theologian, Bishop of Salisbury (1982–93).

3 The crucified Jesus is the only accurate picture of God the world has ever seen.
   1970 *The Foolishness of God*.

Baker (of Dorking), Kenneth Baker, Baron 1934–
English Conservative politician and writer. He was Secretary of State for the Environment (1985) and introduced a controversial education reform bill as Secretary of State for Education (1986–9) under Margaret Thatcher. He was Home Secretary under John Major (1990–2).

4 If Conservative Backbench MPs want to get on in politics they will have to find a foothold in the narrow strip of land that lies between sycophancy and rebellion.
   1979 Queen's Speech in the House of Commons.

5 Why should Scottish and Welsh nationalism be seen as a noble thing, when in England it is seen as something dirty?
   2000 In the *Sunday Times*, 'Talking Heads', 6 Jan.

Baker, Russell Wayne 1925–
US newspaper columnist and humorist. In 1979 won a Pulitzer Prize for distinguished commentary.

6 So there he is at last. Man on the moon. The poor magnificent bungler! He can't even get to the office without undergoing the agonies of the damned, but give him a little metal, a few chemicals, some wire and twenty or thirty billion dollars and vroom! there he is, up on a rock a quarter of a million miles up in the sky.
   1969 Editoral pages, the *New York Times*, 21 Jul.

7 What is it about sociology that instantly bogs us down in fens of jargon?
   1990 In the *New York Times*, 15 Dec.

8 California's power to cloud men's minds must never be forgot. Under its spell we submitted for eight years to the governance of Ronald Reagan, who had trouble distinguishing history from old movie plots.
   1995 'Don't Look Back', in the *New York Times*, 1 Aug.

Bakunin, Mikhail Alekseyevich 1814–76
Russian anarchist. He was sent to Siberia in 1855 but escaped, and became an advocate of anarchism, speaking against Marx at the First Communist International (1868), until he was outvoted and expelled at the Hague Congress (1872).

9 From each according to his faculties, to each according to his needs; that is what we wish, sincerely and energetically.
   1870 Anarchists' declaration, signed by the 47 defendants after the failed uprising in Lyons.
   ▶ See Marx 579:43.

Balazs, Bela originally *Hubert Bauer* 1884–1949
Hungarian writer who wrote *Theory of the Film: Character and Growth of a New Art* (1953).

10 Film art has a greater influence on the minds of the general public than any other art.
   1953 *Theory of the Film: Character and Growth of a New Art* (translated by Edith Bone).

Balcon, Michael 1896–1977
British film producer.

11 In the absence of money, we'll have to make do with talent.
   Quoted in David Puttnam *Michael Balcon: The Pursuit of British Cinema* (1984), preface.

12 Well if you fellows feel so strongly in favour, on my head be it.
   Quoted in David Puttnam *Michael Balcon: The Pursuit of British Cinema* (1984), preface.

Baldwin, James Arthur 1924–87
US writer and civil rights activist. His often autobiographical novels include *Go Tell it on the Mountain* (1954) and *Just Above My Head* (1979).

13 At the root of the American Negro problem is the necessity of the American white man to find a way of living with the Negro in order to be able to live with himself.
   1953 'Stranger in a Village', in *Harper's*, Oct.

14 It seems to be typical of life in America, where opportunities, real and fancied, are thicker than anywhere else on the globe, that the second generation has no time to talk to the first.
   1955 *Notes of a Native Son*, 'Notes of a Native Son'.

15 I learned in New Jersey that to be a Negro meant, precisely, that one was never looked at but was simply at the mercy of the reflexes the color of one's skin caused in other people.
   1955 *Notes of a Native Son*, 'Notes of a Native Son'.

16 The writer's greed is appalling. He wants, or seems to want, everything and practically everybody; in

another sense, and at the same time, he needs no one at all.
1961 Nobody Knows My Name, 'Alas, Poor Richard'.

17 Children have never been very good at listening to their elders, but they have never failed to imitate them. They must, they have no other models.
1961 Nobody Knows My Name, 'Fifth Avenue, Uptown'.

18 Anyone who has ever struggled with poverty knows how extremely expensive it is to be poor.
1961 Nobody Knows My Name, 'Fifth Avenue, Uptown'.

19 Freedom is not something that anybody can be given; freedom is something people take and people are as free as they want to be.
1961 Nobody Knows My Name, 'Notes for a Hypothetical Novel'.

20 Money, it turned out, was exactly like sex, you thought of nothing else if you didn't have it and thought of other things if you did.
1961 'Black Boy Looks at the White Boy', in *Esquire*, May.

21 If the concept of God has any validity or any use, it can only be to make us larger, freer, and more loving. If God cannot do this, then it is time we got rid of Him.
1962 'Down at the Cross', in the *New Yorker*, 17 Nov.

22 The Fire Next Time.
1963 Title of book of essays. Baldwin took the phrase from the traditional spiritual, 'Home in the Rock'.

23 It comes as a great shock around the age of five, six or seven to discover that the flag to which you have pledged your allegiance, along with everybody else, has not pledged its allegiance to you. It comes as a shock to see Gary Cooper killing off the Indians and, although you are rooting for Gary Cooper, that the Indians are you.
1965 Speech at Cambridge Union, 17 Feb, arguing for the motion that 'The American Dream is at the expense of the American Negro'.

24 If they take you in the morning, they will be coming for us that night.
1971 'Open Letter to my Sister, Angela Davis', in *The New York Review of Books*, 7 Jan.

Baldwin (of Bewdley), Stanley Baldwin, 1st Earl
1867–1947

English Conservative politician, Chancellor (1922–3) and Prime Minister (1923, 1924–9 and 1935–7). His period of office was marked by the abdication of Edward VIII in 1936.

25 A lot of hard-faced men who look as if they had done very well out of the war.
1918 Of the first post-World War I Parliament. Quoted in J M Keynes *Economic Consequences of the Peace* (1919).

26 I met Curzon in Downing Street, and received the sort of greeting a corpse would give an undertaker.
1923 Of his rival for the premiership, Lord Curzon, on the death of Bonar Law. Attributed.

27 A platitude is simply a truth repeated until people get tired of hearing it.
1924 Speech in the House of Commons, 29 May.

28 There are three classes which need sanctuary more than others—birds, wild flowers, and Prime Ministers.
1925 In the *Observer*, 24 May.

29 The work of a Prime Minister is the loneliest job in the world.
1927 Speech, 9 Jan.

30 The papers conducted by Lord Rothermere and Lord Beaverbrook are not newspapers in the ordinary acceptance of the term. They are engines of propaganda for the constantly-changing policies, desires, personal wishes, and personal likes and dislikes of two men… What the proprietorship of those papers is aiming at is power, and power without responsibility—the prerogative of the harlot throughout the ages.
1931 Speech, 18 Mar. Rudyard Kipling, Baldwin's cousin, is alleged to be the original author of this famous phrase. Harold Macmillan claimed that the Duke of Devonshire (his father-in-law) responded 'Good God, that's done it, he's lost us the tarts.'

31 I think it is well also for the man in the street to realize that there is no power on earth that can protect him from being bombed. Whatever people will tell him, the bomber will always get through. The only defence is in offence, which means that you have to kill more women and children more quickly than the enemy if you want to save yourselves.
1932 Speech in the House of Commons, 10 Nov.

32 When you think about the defence of England, you no longer think of the chalk cliffs of Dover. You think of the Rhine. That is where our frontier lies today.
1934 House of Commons, 30 Jul.

33 There is a wind of nationalism and freedom blowing round the world, and blowing as strongly in Asia as elsewhere.
1934 Speech, Dec.

34 I shall be but a short time tonight. I have seldom spoken with greater regret, for my lips are not yet unsealed. Were these troubles over I would make a case, and I guarantee that not a man would go into the lobby against us.
1935 Speech in the House of Commons, 10 Dec, speaking on the Abyssinian crisis. This is often misquoted as 'My lips are sealed'.

35 You will find in politics that you are much exposed to the attribution of false motives. Never complain and never explain.
1943 Advice to Harold Nicholson.

36 When the call came for me to form a Government, one of my first thoughts was that it should be a Government of which Harrow would not be ashamed.
Attributed.

Bale, Christian (Charles Philip) 1974–

English film actor. His films include *Batman Begins* (2005), *The Fighter* (2010) and *American Hustle* (2013).

37 Always take the favour over the money.
2013 As Irving Rosenfeld in *American Hustle* (screenplay by Eric Warren Singer and David O. Russell).

Balfour, Arthur James Balfour, 1st Earl 1848–1930

Scottish Conservative politician and Prime Minister (1902–5). As Chief Secretary for Ireland (1887–91) his policy of suppression earned him the name 'Bloody Balfour', and as Foreign Secretary (1916–19) he was responsible for the Balfour Declaration, which promised Zionists a national home in Palestine.

38 I look forward to a time when Irish patriotism will as easily combine with British patriotism as Scottish patriotism combines now.
1889 Speech, Glasgow, Dec.

39 His Majesty's Government looks with favour upon the establishment in Palestine of a national home for the Jews.
   1917 The Balfour Declaration, made in a letter to Lord Rothschild, 2 Nov.

40 The General Strike has taught the working classes more in four days than years of talking could have done.
   1926 Speech in the House of Commons, 7 May.

41 I thought that he was a young man of promise, but it appears that he is a young man of promises.
   Of Winston Churchill. Quoted in Churchill *My Early Life* (1930), ch. 17.

42 Herbert Asquith's clarity is a great liability because he has nothing to say.
   Quoted by George Will in *Newsweek*, 9 Sep 1991.

43 Nothing matters very much, and very few things matter at all.
   Attributed.

44 I would rather be an opportunist and float, than go to the bottom with my principles around my neck.
   Attributed.

45 It has always been desirable to tell the truth, but seldom if ever necessary to tell the whole truth.
   Attributed.

Ball, George Wildman 1909–94

US lawyer and diplomat. As Under-Secretary of State (1961–6) he played a major part in foreign policy, particularly in the Trade Agreements of 1962. He opposed the war in Vietnam, and left government for banking in 1966.

46 Once on the tiger's back, we cannot be sure of picking the place to dismount.
   1964 Memo to Secretary of Defense Robert S McNamara, 5 Oct, on the escalation of the Vietnam War. It became known as 'the tiger's back memo'. Quoted in Deborah Shapley *Promise and Power* (1993).

47 Like giving the keys of the world's largest liquor store to a confirmed alcoholic.
   On oil profiteering that permitted an arms-buying spree by Mohammed Reza Pahlavi, last shah of Iran. Quoted in William Shawcross *The Shah's Last Ride* (1988).

48 Never to be bored, never to be frustrated, never to be alone.
   Defining what John F Kennedy wanted from the presidency. *President Kennedy* (1993).

Ball, John d.1381

English priest, one of the leaders of the Peasants' Revolt of 1381. He was executed for his part in these events.

49 When Adam delved and Eve span,
   Who was then a gentleman?
   1381 Sermon on the eve of the Peasants' Revolt. Quoted in George Holmes *The Later Middle Ages, 1272–1485* (1962), ch.7.

Ballads

50 'Oh, mother, mother, mak my bed,
   And mak it saft and narrow;
   My love has died for me to-day,
   I'll die for him tomorrow.'
   'Barbara Allen'.

51 It fell about the Lammas tide,
   When the muir-men win their hay,
   The doughty Douglas bound him to ride
   Into England, to drive a prey.
   'The Battle of Otterbourne', opening lines.

52 There was twa sisters in a bower,
   Binnorie, O Binnorie;
   There came a knight to be their wooer,
   By the bonnie mill-dams o' Binnorie.
   'Binnorie', stanza 1.

53 Ye Highlands and ye Lawlands,
   O where hae ye been?
   They hae slain the Earl of Murray
   And laid him on the green.
   'The Bonnie Earl of Murray', stanza 1.

54 He was a braw gallant,
   And he play'd at the ba';
   And the bonnie Earl of Murray
   Was the flower amang them a'.

   He was a braw gallant,
   And he play'd at the glove;
   And the bonnie Earl of Murray,
   O he was the Queen's luve.

   O lang will his lady
   Look owre the castle Doune,
   Ere she sees the Earl of Murray
   Come sounding thro' the toun.
   'The Bonnie Earl of Murray'.

55 O the broom, the bonnie, bonnie broom,
   The broom of Cowdenknowes;
   I wish I were with my dear swain,
   With his pipe and my yowes.
   'The Broom of Cowdenknowes', opening lines.

56 'A bed, a bed,' Clerk Sanders said,
   'A bed for you and me!'
   'Fye na, fye na,' said may Margaret,
   'Till anes we married be!'
   'Clerk Sanders'.

57 Is there any room at your head, Sanders?
   Is there any room at your feet?
   Or any room at your twa sides,
   Where fain, fain I would sleep?

   There is nae room at my head, Margaret,
   There is nae room at my feet;
   My bed it is the cold, cold grave;
   Among the hungry worms I sleep.
   'Clerk Sanders'.

58 She hadna sailed a league, a league,
   A league but barely three,
   When dismal grew his countenance
   And drumlie grew his e'e.
   They hadna sailed a league, a league,
   A league but barely three,
   Until she espied his cloven foot,
   And she wept right bitterlie.
   'The Demon Lover'.

59 Late at e'en, drinkin' the wine,
   And ere they paid the lawin',

They set a combat them between,
To fight it at the dawin'.

'O stay at hame, my noble lord,
O stay at hame, my marrow!
My cruel brother will you betray
On the dowie houms o' Yarrow!'
'The Dowie Houms o' Yarrow'.

60 'Yestreen I dreamed a dolefu' dream;
I ken'd here wad be sorrow!
I dreamed I pu'd the heather green,
On the dowie banks o' Yarrow.'

She gaed up yon high, high hill—
I wat she gaed wi' sorrow—
An' in the den spied nine dead men,
On the dowie houms o' Yarrow.
'The Dowie Houms o' Yarrow'.

61 'Why dois your brand sae drap wi' bluid,
Edward, Edward,
Why dois your brand sae drap wi' bluid,
And why sae sad gang ye O?'
'Edward', opening lines.

62 Then up and started our gudewife,
Gied three skips on the floor:
'Gudeman, ye've spoken the foremost word,
Get up and bar the door.'
'Get Up and Bar the Door'.

63 I wish I were where Helen lies,
Night and day on me she cries;
O that I were where Helen lies,
On fair Kirkconnell lea!
'Helen of Kirkconnell', opening lines.

64 'It's I, Jamie Telfer o' the fair Dodhead,
And a harried man I think I be!
There's naething left at the fair Dodhead
But a waefu' wife and bairnies three.'
'Jamie Telfer'.

65 'Will ye gang wi' me, Lizzy Lindsay,
Will ye gang to the Highlands wi' me?
Will ye gang wi' me, Lizzy Lindsay.
My bride and my darling to be?'
'Lizzy Lindsay', opening lines.

66 This ae nighte, this ae nighte,
—*Every nighte and alle*,
Fire and fleet and candle-lighte,
And Christe receive thy saule.
'A Lyke-Wake Dirge', opening lines.

67 Marie Hamilton's to the kirk gane,
Wi' ribbons in her hair;
The king thought mair o' Marie Hamilton
Than ony that were there.
'Marie Hamilton', opening lines.

68 'Yestreen the queen had four Maries,
The night she'll hae but three;
There was Marie Seaton, and Mari Beaton,
And Marie Carmichael, and me.'
'Marie Hamilton'.

69 The king sits in Dunfermline town,
Drinking the blude-red wine;
'O whare will I get a skeely skipper,
To sail this new ship of mine?'
'Sir Patrick Spens', opening lines.

70 'I saw the new moon late yestreen,
Wi' the auld moon in her arm;
And if we gang to sea, master,
I fear we'll come to harm.'
'Sir Patrick Spens'.

71 And lang, lang may the ladyes sit,
Wi' their fans into their hand,
Before they see Sir Patrick Spens
Come sailing to the strand!
'Sir Patrick Spens'.

72 Half-owre, half-owre to Aberdour,
'Tis fifty fathoms deep,
And there lies gude Sir Patrick Spens,
Wi' the Scots lords at his feet.
'Sir Patrick Spens'.

73 'O I forbid you, maidens a',
That wear gowd on your hair,
To come or gae by Carterhaugh,
For young Tam Lin is there.

'There's nane that gaes by Carterhaugh,
But they leave him a wad.
Either their rings or green mantles,
Or else their maidenhead.'

Janet has kilted her green kirtle
A little aboon her knee,
And she has braided her yellow hair
A little aboon her bree,
And she's awa' to Carterhaugh
As fast as she can hie.
'Tam Lin', opening stanzas.

74 True Thomas lay on Huntlie bank,
A ferlie he spied wi' his e'e,
And there he saw a ladye bright,
Come riding down by the Eildon Tree.
'Thomas the Rhymer', opening lines.

75 And see ye not yon braid, braid road,
That lies across the lily leven?
That is the path of Wickedness,
Though some call it the Road to Heaven.
'Thomas the Rhymer'.

76 There were three ravens sat on a tree,
They were as black as they might be.
The one of them said to his make,
'Where shall we our breakfast take?'
'The Three Ravens'.

77 As I was walking all alane,
I heard twa corbies making a mane;
The tane unto the tother say,
'Where sall we gang and dine to-day?'

'In behint yon auld fail dye,
I wot there lies a new-slain knight;
And naebody kens that he lies there,
But his hawk, his hound, and his lady fair.

'His hound is to the hunting gane,
His hawk to fetch the wild-fowl hame,

His lady's ta'en another mate,
So we may mak our dinner sweet.'
'The Twa Corbies', opening stanzas.

78 O'er his white banes, when they are bare,
The wind sall blaw for evermair.
'The Twa Corbies'.

79 O waly, waly up the bank,
And waly, waly doun the brae,
And waly, waly yon burn-side
Where I and my love wont to gae.

I lean'd my back unto an aik,
I thocht it was a trustie tree;
But first it bow'd, and syne it brake—
Sae my true love did lichtlie me.

O waly, waly, gin love be bonnie
A little time while it is new;
But when 'tis auld it waxeth cauld
And fades awa' like morning dew.

O wherefore should I busk my heid,
O wherefore should I kame my hair?
For my true love has me forsook,
And says he'll never lo'e me mair.
pre-1566 'Waly, Waly', opening stanzas.

80 But had I wist, before I kiss'd,
That love had been sae ill to win.
I'd lock'd my heart in a case o' gowd,
And pinn'd it wi' a siller pin.
pre-1566 'Waly, Waly', stanza 4.

81 Tom Pearce, Tom Pearce, lend me your grey mare,
All along, down along, out along lee.
For I want for to go to Widdicombe Fair,
Wi' Bill Brewer, Jan Stewer, Peter Gurney, Peter Davey,
Dan'l Whiddon, Harry Hawk,
Old Uncle Tom Cobleigh and all.
'Widdicombe Fair'.

82 There lived a wife at Usher's Well,
And a wealthy wife was she;
She had three stout and stalwart sons,
And sent them o'er the sea.
'The Wife of Usher's Well', opening lines.

83 The cock doth craw, the day doth daw,
The channerin' worm doth chide.
'The Wife of Usher's Well'.

Ballard, J(ames) G(raham)   1930–2009

British novelist and science-fiction writer, born in China. His best-known work, the novel *Empire of the Sun* (1984), draws on his childhood experiences in wartime Shanghai, then occupied by Japan.

84 The only truly alien planet is Earth.
1962 'Which Way to Inner Space', in *New Worlds*, May.

85 He believes that science fiction is the apocalyptic literature of the 20th century, the authentic language of Auschwitz, Eniwetok and Aldermaston. He also believes that inner space, not outer, is the real subject of science fiction.
1965 Author's statement contained in a biographical note to *The Drowned World*.

86 Science and technology multiply around us. To an increasing extent they dictate the languages in which we speak and think. Either we use those languages, or we remain mute.
1974 *Crash*.

Balliett, Whitney   1926–2007

US writer. He became jazz critic of the *New Yorker* in 1957, and wrote several books on music.

87 The Sound of Surprise.
1959 Title of book, much cited as a definition of jazz.

88 A bundle of biases held loosely together by a sense of taste.
1962 His definition of a critic. *Dinosaurs in the Morning*, introductory note.

Balzac, Honoré de   1799–1850

French writer, one of the great 19c realist novelists. He created a world of characters whose lives are interwoven in his *Comédie humaine* (1842).

89 Un homme n'a jamais pu élever sa maîtresse jusqu'à lui; mais une femme place toujours son amant aussi haut qu'elle.
A man can never elevate his mistress to his rank, but a woman can always place her lover as high as she.
1829 *Physiologie du mariage*.

90 Le mariage doit incessamment combattre un monstre qui dévore tout: l'habitude.
Marriage should always combat the monster that devours everything: habit.
1829 *Physiologie du mariage*.

91 La femme mariée est un esclave qu'il faut savoir mettre sur un trône.
A married woman is a slave whom one must put on a throne.
1829 *Physiologie du mariage*.

92 Un mari, comme un gouvernement, ne doit jamais avouer de faute.
A husband, like a government, never needs to admit a fault.
1829 *Physiologie du mariage*.

93 En toute chose, nous ne pouvons être jugés que par nos pairs.
In all things, we should only be judged by our peers.
1830 *La Maison du chat-qui-pelote*.

94 Dans ces grandes crises, le coeur se brise ou se bronze.
In times of crisis, the heart either breaks or boldens.
1830 *La Maison du chat-qui-pelote*.

95 Le bonheur engloutit nos forces, comme le malheur éteint nos vertus.
Happiness engulfs our strength, just as misfortune extinguishes our virtues.
1831 *La Peau de chagrin*.

96 La haine est un tonique, elle fait vivre, elle inspire la vengeance; mais la pitié tue, elle affaiblit encore notre faiblesse.
Hatred is a tonic, it makes one live, it inspires vengeance; but pity kills, it weakens our weaknesses still further.
1831 *La Peau de chagrin*.

97 *Beaucoup d'hommes ont un orgueil qui les pousse à cacher leurs combats et à ne se montrer que victorieux.*
Many men have pride that causes them to hide their combats and to only show themselves victorious.
1831 *La Recherche de l'absolu.*

98 *À lui la foi, à elle le doute, à elle le fardeau le plus lourd: la femme ne souffre-t-elle pas toujours pour deux?*
For him, faith; for her, doubt and for her the heavier load: does not the woman always suffer for both?
1831 *La Recherche de l'absolu.*

99 *L'amour n'est pas seulement un sentiment, il est un art aussi.*
Love is not only a feeling; it is also an art.
1831 *La Recherche de l'absolu.*

1 *L'amour a son instinct, il sait trouver le chemin du coeur comme le plus faible insecte marche à sa fleur avec une irrésistible volonté qui ne s'épouvante de rien.*
Love has its own instinct. It knows how to find the road to the heart just as the weakest insect moves toward its flower by an irresistible will which fears nothing.
1832 *La Femme de trente ans.*

2 *Le coeur d'une mère est un abîme au fond duquel se trouve toujours un pardon.*
A mother's heart is an abyss at the bottom of which there is always forgiveness.
1832 *La Femme de trente ans.*

3 *Les faits ne sont rien, ils n'existent pas, il ne subsiste de nous que des Idées.*
Deeds are nothing. They do not exist. Only our ideas survive.
1832 *Louis Lambert.*

4 *Nos beaux sentiments ne sont-ils pas les poésies de la volonté?*
Aren't our best feelings poetry of the will?
1835 *Le Père Goriot.*

5 *La passion est toute l'humanité. Sans elle, la religion, l'histoire, le roman, l'art seraient inutiles.*
Passion is all of humanity. Without it, religion, history, the novel and art would be useless.
1842 *La Comédie humaine,* foreword.

6 *L'homme n'est ni bon ni méchant, il naît avec des instincts et des aptitudes.*
Man is neither good nor evil; he is born with instincts and abilities.
1842 *La Comédie humaine,* foreword.

7 *L'avarice commence où la pauvreté cesse.*
Greed begins where poverty ends.
1843 *Illusions perdues,* 'Les deux poètes'.

8 *Les dettes sont jolies chez les jeunes gens de vingt-cinq ans, plus tard, personne ne les leur pardonne.*
Debts are becoming for 25-year-olds; after this, no one forgives them.
1843 *Illusions perdues,* 'Un Grand homme de province'.

Banda, Hastings Kamuzu 1898–1997

Malawian statesman, Prime Minister (1963) and President (1966; Life President from 1971).

9 I wish that I could bring Stonehenge to Nyasaland, to show that there was a time when Britain had a savage culture.
1963 In the *Observer,* 10 Mar.

Bandeira, Manuel 1886–1968

Brazilian poet, literary historian, translator and educator. He achieved enormous popularity and national acclaim.

10 *Estou farto do lirismo comedido*
Do lirismo bem comportado
Do lirismo funcionário público com livro de ponto
  expediente protocolo e manifestações de apreço ao Sr
  Diretor.
Estou farto do lirismo que pára e vai averiguar no
  dicionário o cunho vernáculo de um vocábulo.

Abaixo os puristas
I'm sick of cautious lyricism
of well-behaved lyricism
of a civil servant lyricism complete with time card office
  hours set procedures and expressions of esteem for Mr
  Boss, Sir.
I'm sick of the lyricism that has to stop in midstream to
  look up the precise meaning of a word.

Down with purists!
1930 *Libertinagem,* 'Poética' (translated as 'Poetics', 1989).

Bankhead, Tallulah 1903–68

US actress. She made her New York debut in 1918 and subsequently played a range of classical and contemporary roles, attracting notoriety for her scandalous private life. She wrote an autobiography, *Tallulah* (1952).

11 There is less in this than meets the eye.
1922 Attending a revival of Maeterlinck's play *Aglavaine and Selysette.* Quoted in Alexander Woollcott *Shouts and Murmurs* (1923), ch.4.

12 Cocaine habit-forming? Of course not. I ought to know. I've been using it for years.
1939 In conversation at the first night party of Lillian Hellman's *Little Foxes.* Recalled in *Tallulah* (1952), ch.4.

13 I'm as pure as the driven slush.
Quoted by Maurice Zolotow, in *The Saturday Evening Post,* 12 Apr 1947.

14 Darling, they've absolutely ruined your perfectly dreadful play!
1957 Greeting Tennessee Williams at the film première of his play *Orpheus Descending.* Quoted in Peter Hay *Broadway Anecdotes.*

15 Only good girls keep diaries. Bad girls don't have time.
Recalled on her death, 12 Dec 1968.

16 Nobody can be exactly like me. Sometimes even I have trouble doing it.
Attributed.

Banks, Iain Menzies 1954–2013

Scottish novelist and science-fiction writer. His works include *The Wasp Factory* (1984) and *Complicity* (1993). He wrote science-fiction novels using the name Iain M Banks.

17 They are, after all, a language; they do not so much say things about as, they are what is said.
1986 Of clothes. *The Bridge,* ch.2.

18 'You're not upset, are you, Orr?' Brooke says, pouring wine into my glass.
'Merely sober. The symptoms are similar.'
1986 *The Bridge*, ch.3.

19 The choice is not between dream and reality; it is between two different dreams.
1986 *The Bridge*, coda.

20 It was the day my grandmother exploded.
1992 *The Crow Road*, ch.1, opening words.

21 Mr Blawke always reminded me of a heron; I'm not sure why. Something to do with a sense of rapacious stillness, perhaps, and also the aura of one who knows time is on his side.
1992 Of the family lawyer. *The Crow Road*, ch.1.

22 The belief that we somehow moved on to something else—whether still recognisably ourselves, or quite thoroughly changed—might be a tribute to our evolutionary tenacity and our animal thirst for life, but not to our wisdom.
1992 On the idea of life after death. *The Crow Road*, ch.18.

23 The truth is not always useful, not always good. It's like putting your faith in water. Yes, we need the rain, but too much can sweep you away in a flood and drown you. Like all great natural, elemental forces, the truth needs to be channelled, managed, controlled and intelligently, morally allocated.
2010 *Surface Detail*.

24 All you ever were was a little bit of the universe, thinking to itself. Very specific; this bit, here, right now.
2010 *Surface Detail*.

25 One should never regret one's excesses, only one's failures of nerve.
2012 *The Hydrogen Sonata*.

26 One should never mistake pattern for meaning.
2012 *The Hydrogen Sonata*.

27 The trouble with writing fiction is that it has to make sense, whereas real life doesn't.
2013 In 'Iain Banks: The Final Interview', *The Guardian*, 14 Jun.

Banks, Lynne Reid 1929–

English novelist and playwright. Her best-known novel is her first, *The L-Shaped Room* (1960). She has also written plays for radio and television and fiction for children.

28 Jane Austen is the only novelist I know whose peculiar genius lies in taking perfectly ordinary people through ordinary situations, and transmogrifying them into fascinating fiction.
1991 In her entry in *Contemporary Novelists*, 5th edn.

29 What did I tell you when you were little girl? The only way we women can get through our lives honourably is with courage and resignation, both.
2005 *Tiger, Tiger*.

Banksy

English graffiti artist and film-maker, whose identity remains undisclosed to the general public.

30 Art should comfort the disturbed and disturb the comfortable.
Attributed.

31 I mean, they say you die twice. One time when you stop breathing and a second time, a bit later on, when somebody says your name for the last time.
2010 In *The Sun*.

32 The last time there was a naked man covered in gold paint in my house, it was me.
2011 Responding to his Oscar nomination for his documentary *Exit Through the Gift Shop*.

Bannister, Sir Roger Gilbert 1929–

English athlete and neurologist. In 1954 he ran the first 'four-minute mile' (3 mins 59.4 secs). He was knighted in 1975. After a distinguished medical career, he was appointed Master of Pembroke College, Oxford (1985–93).

33 I leapt at the tape like a man taking his last spring to save himself from the chasm that threatens to engulf him.
1955 Of the end of his record-breaking run. *First Four Minutes*.

34 I sometimes think that running has given me a glimpse of the greatest freedom a man can ever know, because it results in the simultaneous liberation of both body and mind.
1955 *First Four Minutes*.

Banting, Frederick Grant 1891–1941

Canadian physician and discoverer of insulin.

35 Diabetus. Ligate pancreatic ducts of dog. Keep dogs alive till acini degenerate leaving Islets. Try to isolate the internal secretion of these to relieve glycosuria.
1920 Note scribbled in his journal, 2.00am, 31 Oct. This led to the discovery of insulin for the treatment of diabetes, as recorded in Michael Bliss *The Discovery of Insulin* (1982).

Banville, (William) John 1945–

Irish novelist and playwright. His novel *The Sea* won the 2005 Booker Prize. Other notable works include the novels *The Book of Evidence* (1989), *The Untouchable* (1997) and *Ancient Light* (2012).

36 The first thought that occurred to me, that night when I heard the chairman of the jury announce my name, was, Just think how many people hate me at this moment. Naturally, I wanted to annoy those people even further by being arrogant.
Attributed. On winning the Booker Prize.

37 Doing what you do well is death. Your duty is to keep trying to do things that you don't do well, in the hope of learning.
2009 In *The Paris Review*, spring.

38 The sentence is the greatest invention of civilization. To sit all day long assembling these extraordinary strings of words is a marvellous thing. I couldn't ask for anything better. It's as near to godliness as I can get... The great thrill is when a sentence that starts out being completely plain suddenly begins to sing, rising far above itself and above any expectation I might have had for it. That's what keeps me going on those dark December days.
2009 In *The Paris Review*, spring.

39 The secret of survival is a defective imagination.
2009 *The Infinities*.

Barach, Alvan Leroy 1895–1977

US physician. He was Professor of Medicine at Columbia University and a pioneer in respiratory therapy.

40 An alcoholic has been lightly defined as a man who drinks more than his own doctor.
   1962 In the *Journal of the American Medical Association*, vol.181, p.393.

Baraka, Amiri *adopted name of LeRoi (Everett Leroy) Jones*
1934–2014

US poet, playwright and prose writer. He adopted a Muslim identity in 1967 after establishing his reputation as a radical and outspoken black voice.

41 Preface to a Twenty Volume Suicide Note.
   1961 Title of poetry collection.

42 A rich man told me recently that a liberal is a man who tells other people what to do with their money.
   1962 'Tokenism', in *Kulchur*, spring issue.

43 A man is either free or he is not. There cannot be any apprenticeship for freedom.
   1962 'Tokenism', in *Kulchur*, spring issue.

44 But when a man who sees the world one way becomes the slave of a man who interprets the world in exactly the opposite way, the result is, to my mind, the *worst* possible kind of slavery.
   1963 *Blues People*, ch.1.

Barbellion, W(illiam) N(ero) P(ilate) *pseudonym of Bruce Frederick Cummings* 1889–1919

English diarist. He was a self-taught biologist, and worked for the British Museum. His principal work is the self-critical *Journal of A Disappointed Man* (1919).

45 I can remember wondering as a child if I were a young Macaulay or Ruskin and secretly deciding that I was. My infant mind even was bitter with those who insisted on regarding me as a normal child and not as a prodigy.
   1919 *Journal of A Disappointed Man*, 23 Oct.

46 Give me the man who will surrender the whole world for a moss or a caterpillar, and impracticable visions for a simple human delight.
   1919 *Enjoying Life and Other Literary Remains*, 'Crying for the Moon'.

Barbirolli, Sir John 1899–1970

British conductor and cellist, conductor of the New York Philharmonic in 1937 and of the Hallé Orchestra in Manchester (1943–58). In 1950 he was awarded the Gold Medal of the Royal Philharmonic Society, and he became principal conductor of the Hallé in 1958.

47 Three farts and a raspberry, orchestrated.
   Of modern music. Quoted in M Kennedy *Barbirolli, Conductor Laureate* (1971).

48 I want you to sound like 22 women having babies without chloroform.
   To a chorus. Quoted in M Kennedy *Barbirolli, Conductor Laureate* (1971).

Barbour, John c.1316–1395

Scottish poet, prelate and scholar, the 'father of Scottish poetry'. His national epic, *The Brus*, is a narrative poem on the life of Robert I, the Bruce. He served as Archdeacon of Aberdeen from c.1357 until his death.

49 Storyss to rede ar delitabill,
   Suppos that thai be nocht but fabill.
   c.1375 *The Brus*, bk.1, l.1–2.

50 A! fredome is a noble thing!
   Fredome mayss man to haiff liking,
   Fredome all solace to man giffis:
   He levys at ess that frely levys!
   c.1375 *The Brus*, bk.1, l.225–8.

51 Luff is off sae mekill mycht,
   That it all paynis makis lycht.
   c.1375 *The Brus*, bk.2, l.520–1.

Barker, George Granville 1913–91

English poet, novelist and playwright. He was associated with Dylan Thomas and the New Apocalyptic group, but his poetry retained a distinctively individual quality.

52 Sitting as huge as Asia, seismic with laughter,
   Gin and chicken helpless in her Irish hand.
   1944 'To My Mother'.

53 Honouring itself the clay rears up
   To praise its pottering purposes,
   But, oh, much sorrow shall it sup
   Before fulfilment is.
   1954 'Goodman Jacksin and the Angel'.

54 When the guns begin to rattle
   And the men to die
   Does the Goddess of the Battle
   Smile or sigh?
   1962 'Battle Hymn of the New Republic'.

Barkley, Alben William 1877–1956

US lawyer and Democratic politician, Vice-President under Truman (1949–53).

55 The best audience is intelligent, well-educated and a little drunk.
   Recalled on his death, 30 Apr 1956.

Barlow, Joel 1754–1812

US poet. He is best remembered for his mock-heroic salute to the humble hasty-pudding (a dish of boiled Indian meal), although he considered his turgid epic *The Colombiad* (1807) his major work.

56 I sing the sweets I know, the charms I feel,
   My morning incense, and my evening meal,
   The sweets of Hasty-Pudding. Come, dear bowl,
   Glide o'er my palate, and inspire my soul.
   1796 'The Hasty-Pudding', canto 1

Barnard, Frederick R

57 One picture is worth ten thousand words.
   1927 In *Printer's Ink*, 10 Mar.

Barnes, Clive Alexander 1927–2008

English theatre critic. He wrote for the *New York Post* from 1977, directing much of his venom against the commercial Broadway stage.

58 This is the kind of show to give pornography a bad name.
   1969 Reviewing *Oh, Calcutta!*, *New York Times*, 18 Jun.

Barnes, Djuna 1892–1982

US writer, who spent a large part of her life in Europe. She is best known for her novel *Nightwood* (1936).

59 New York is the meeting place of the peoples, the only city where you can hardly find a typical American.
1916 'Greenwich Village As It Is', in *Pearson's Magazine*, Oct.

60 After all, it is not where one washes one's neck that counts but where one moistens one's throat.
1916 'Greenwich Village As It Is', in *Pearson's Magazine*, Oct.

61 Sleep demands of us a guilty immunity. There is not one of us who, given an eternal incognito, a thumbprint nowhere set against our souls, would not commit rape, murder and all abominations.
1936 Doctor. *Nightwood*, ch.5.

62 Dreams have only the pigmentation of fact.
1936 Doctor. *Nightwood*, ch.5.

63 I'm a fart in a gale of wind, a humble violet under a cow pat.
1936 Doctor. *Nightwood*, ch.5.

Barnes, Julian Patrick 1946–

English novelist, formerly a lexicographer and journalist. His best-known work is *Flaubert's Parrot* (1984), a meditation on fiction and biography. He won the 2011 Man Booker Prize for *The Sense of an Ending*.

64 We'd both been to the country and found it disappointingly empty.
1981 *Metroland*, pt.1, ch.4.

65 You can have your cake and eat it: the only trouble is you get fat.
1984 *Flaubert's Parrot*, ch.7.

66 The writer must be universal in sympathy and an outcast by nature: only then can he see clearly.
1984 *Flaubert's Parrot*, ch.10.

67 Do not imagine that Art is something which is designed to give gentle uplift and self-confidence. Art is not a *brassière*. At least, not in the English sense. But do not forget that *brassière* is the French for life-jacket.
1984 *Flaubert's Parrot*, ch.10.

68 Books are where things are explained to you; life is where things aren't... Books make sense of life. The only problem is that the lives they make sense of are other people's lives, never your own.
1984 *Flaubert's Parrot*, ch.13.

69 Women were brought up to believe that men were the answer. They weren't. They weren't even one of the questions.
1986 *Staring At The Sun*, pt.2.

70 Does history repeat itself, the first time as tragedy, the second time as farce? No, that's too grand, too considered a process. History just burps, and we taste again that raw-onion sandwich it swallowed centuries ago.
1989 *A History of the World in 10½ Chapters*, 'Parenthesis'.

71 I've always thought you are what you are and you shouldn't pretend to be anyone else. But Oliver used to correct me and explain that you are whoever it is you're pretending to be.
1991 *Talking It Over*, ch.2.

72 Love is just a system for getting someone to call you darling after sex.
1991 *Talking It Over*, ch.16.

73 Remember that cookery writers are no different from other writers: many have only one book in them (and some shouldn't have let it out in the first place).
2003 *The Pedant in the Kitchen*.

74 If a man cannot tell what he wants to do, then he must find out what he ought to do. If desire has become complicated, then hold fast to duty.
2005 *Arthur & George*.

75 This was another of our fears: that Life wouldn't turn out to be like Literature.
2011 *The Sense of an Ending*.

76 History is that certainty produced at the point where the imperfections of memory meet the inadequacies of documentation.
2011 *The Sense of an Ending*.

77 It strikes me that this may be one of the differences between youth and age: when we are young, we invent different futures for ourselves; when we are old, we invent different pasts.
2011 *The Sense of an Ending*.

78 Nature is so exact, it hurts exactly as much as it is worth, so in a way one relishes the pain, I think. If it didn't matter, it wouldn't matter.
2013 *Levels of Life*.

Barnum, P(hineas) T(aylor) 1810–91

US showman. He introduced freak shows, including General Tom Thumb (1842), in his New York museum, and in 1881 co-founded the Barnum and Bailey Circus, 'the greatest show on earth'.

79 There's a sucker born every minute.
Attributed.

Baron Cohen, Sacha (Noam) 1971–

English actor, comedian and author. He is best known as the creator of such comedic characters as Ali G, Borat Sagdiyev and General Aladeen.

80 Borat essentially works as a tool. By being anti-semitic, he lets people lower their guard and expose their own prejudice, whether it's anti-semitism or an acceptance of anti-semitism.
2006 Attributed.

Barr, Alfred Hamilton, Jr 1902–81

US art historian, first Director of the Museum of Modern Art, New York. His many works include *Cubism and Abstract Art* (1936).

81 Except the American woman, nothing interests the eye of American man more than the automobile, or seems so important to him as an object of aesthetic appreciation.
1963 In news summaries, 31 Dec.

Barrer, Bruce

82 She endured a five-year marriage to Ernest Hemingway that roughly coincided with and bore more than a passing resemblance to World War II.
1993 Of Martha Gelhorn. In the *Wall Street Journal*, 9 Mar.

Barrie, Sir J(ames) M(atthew) 1860–1937

Scottish novelist and dramatist. After journalism and several autobiographical works, he turned to playwriting in 1890, with such works as *The Admirable Crichton* (1902), *Peter Pan* (1904) and *What Every Woman Knows* (1908, published 1918).

83 The life of every man is a diary in which he means to write one story, and writes another; and his humblest

hour is when he compares the volume as it is with what he vowed to make it.
1891 *The Little Minister*, vol.1, ch.1.

84 That is ever the way. 'Tis all jealousy to the bride and good wishes to the corpse.
1901 *Quality Street* (published 1913), act 1.

85 When the first baby laughed for the first time, the laugh broke into a thousand pieces and they all went skipping about, and that was the beginning of fairies.
1904 *Peter Pan* (published 1928), act 1.

86 Every time a child says 'I don't believe in fairies' there is a little fairy somewhere that falls down dead.
1904 *Peter Pan* (published 1928), act 1.

87 To die will be an awfully big adventure.
1904 *Peter Pan* (published 1928), act 3.

88 Charm...it's a sort of a bloom on a woman. If you have it, you don't need to have anything else; and if you don't have it, it doesn't much matter what else you have.
1908 *What Every Woman Knows* (published 1918), act 1.

89 My lady, there are few more impressive sights in the world than a Scotsman on the make.
1908 *What Every Woman Knows* (published 1918), act 2.

90 I have always found that the man whose second thoughts are good is worth watching.
1908 *What Every Woman Knows* (published 1918), act 3.

91 Every man who is high up loves to think that he has done it all himself; and the wife smiles, and lets it go at that. It's our only joke. Every woman knows that.
1908 *What Every Woman Knows* (published 1918), act 4.

92 One's religion is whatever he is most interested in, and yours is Success.
1921 *The Twelve-Pound Look*.

93 I bowl so slow that if after I have delivered the ball and don't like the look of it, I can run after it and bring it back.
Quoted in Colin Jarman *The Guinness Dictionary of Sports Quotations* (1990).

94 What a polite game tennis is. The chief word in it seems to be 'sorry' and admiration of each other's play crosses the net as frequently as the ball.
Quoted in Colin Jarman *The Guinness Dictionary of Sports Quotations* (1990).

95 I am glad you have asked me. I should like you to convey when you are acting it that the man you portray has a brother in Shropshire who drinks port.
Responding to a young actor's urgent request for advice as to how he should play a minor part in one of Barrie's plays. Attributed.

Barrington, Jonah   1941–

English squash player. He was British Open Champion 1967–8 and 1970–3.

96 Squash is boxing with racquets.
Quoted in Colin Jarman *The Guinness Dictionary of Sports Quotations* (1990).

Barry, Marion Shepilov, Jr   1936–2014

US politician, Mayor of Washington, DC (1979–91, 1995–9). He was arrested and charged with possession of cocaine in 1990.

97 There are two kinds of truth...real truths and made-up truths.
1990 Of the drug charges lodged against him. In the *Washington Post*, 13 May.

Barrymore, Ethel   1879–1959

US actress, one of the most prominent members of the Drew-Barrymore acting dynasty. She made her New York debut in 1901 and went on to excel both in contemporary dramas and in Shakespearean roles. New York's Barrymore Theatre was opened in her honour in 1928.

98 For an actress to be a success she must have the face of Venus, the brains of Minerva, the grace of Terpsichore, the memory of Macaulay, the figure of Juno, and the hide of a rhinoceros.
Quoted in George Jean Nathan *The Theatre in the Fifties* (1953).

99 I never let them cough. They wouldn't dare.
1956 Of her audiences. In the *New York Post*, 7 Jun.

Barrymore, John   1882–1942

US actor of the Drew-Barrymore dynasty. He made his stage debut in 1903 and distinguished himself in Shakespearean and other roles before turning to films. Renowned for his chaotic private life, he suffered increasingly from alcoholism.

1 Die? I should say not, old fellow. No Barrymore would allow such a conventional thing to happen to him.
1942 Quoted in Lionel Barrymore *We Barrymores* (1951), ch.26.

2 My only regret in the theatre is that I could never sit out front and watch me.
Quoted in Eddie Cantor *The Way I See It* (1959), ch.2.

3 Method acting? There are quite a few methods. Mine involves a lot of talent, a glass, and some cracked ice.
Quoted in *Actors about Acting, Loving, Living, Life* (1972).

Barrymore, Lionel   1878–1954

US actor, brother of Ethel and John Barrymore. He gave up a successful stage career for the cinema in 1925, finding fame as Dr Gillespie in a series of *Dr Kildare* films (from 1938).

4 How like father—a curtain call!
1905 Attributed comment, when his father's coffin had to be raised up again after it had snagged on being lowered into the grave.

5 I've played everything but the harp.
Attributed, when asked to suggest his own epitaph.

Barth, John Simmons   1930–

US novelist. His books are much concerned with the processes of story-telling and the making of myths.

6 Everyone is necessarily the hero of his own life story.
1958 *The End of the Road*, ch.1.

7 Every life has a Scheherazadesworth of stories.
1994 *Once Upon A Time*, 'Program Note'.

Barth, Karl   1886–1968

Swiss Reformed theologian, champion of neo-orthodoxy and influential in founding the German Confessing Church, which opposed Nazism. His extensive theological output proved highly influential in 20c Christian theology.

8 Jesus Christ, as he is attested to us in Holy Scripture, is the one Word of God whom we have to hear, and whom we have to trust and obey in life and in death.
1934 *The Barmen Declaration* adopted by the Confessing Church in Germany (translated by D S Bax, 1984).

9 Humanity in its basic form is co-humanity.
   1948 *Kirchliche Dogmatik* vol.3, pt.2 (translated by H Knight as *Church Dogmatics*, 1960).

10 Basically and comprehensively, therefore, to be human is *to be with God*.
   1948 *Kirchliche Dogmatik* vol.3, pt.2 (translated by H Knight as *Church Dogmatics*, 1960).

11 It is a bad sign when Christians are frightened by 'political' sermons—as if Christian preaching could be anything but political.
   1954 *Gegen den Strom* (translated by E M Delacourt and S Godwin as 'The Christian Community and the Civil Community' in *Against the Stream*, 1954).

12 Whether the angels play only Bach in praising God I am not quite sure; I am sure, however, that *en famille* they play Mozart.
   1968 Quoted in the *New York Times*.

Barthelme, Donald 1931–89
US novelist and short story writer.

13 The distinction between children and adults, while probably useful for some purposes, is at bottom a specious one, I feel. There are only individual egos, crazy for love.
   1964 *Come Back, Dr Caligari*, 'Me and Miss Mandible'.

14 We like books that have a lot of *dreck* in them, matter which presents itself as not wholly relevant (or indeed, at all relevant), but which, carefully attended to, can supply a kind of 'sense' of what is going on. This 'sense' is not to be obtained by reading between the lines (for there is nothing there, in those white spaces), but by reading the lines themselves.
   1967 *Snow White*.

15 'Some people', Miss R. said, 'run to conceits or wisdom but I hold to the hard, brown, nutlike word. I might point out that there is enough aesthetic excitement here to satisfy anyone but a damned fool.'
   1968 *Unspeakable Practices, Unnatural Acts*, 'The Indian Uprising'.

16 Endings are elusive, middles are nowhere to be found, but worst of all is to begin, to begin, to begin.
   1968 *Unspeakable Practices, Unnatural Acts*, 'The Dolt'.

17 Doubt is a necessary precondition to meaningful action. Fear is the great mover in the end.
   1972 *Sadness*, 'The Rise of Capitalism'.

18 The self cannot be escaped, but it can be, with ingenuity and hard work, distracted.
   1972 *Sadness*, 'Daumier'.

19 Let me point out, if it has escaped your notice, that what an artist does, is fail.
   1972 *Sadness*, 'The Sandman'.

20 The world is sagging, snagging, scaling, spalling, pilling, pinging, pitting, warping, checking, fading, chipping, cracking, yellowing, leaking, stalling, shrinking, and in dynamic unbalance.
   1974 *Guilty Pleasures*, 'Down the Line with the Annual'.

21 No tale ever happened in the way we tell it. But the moral is always correct.
   1975 *The Dead Father*, ch.6.

Barthes, Roland 1915–80
French literary critic, and major theorist of semiology. He developed a modernist school of criticism which argues for the 'death' of the author, and the need for the reader to recreate the text.

22 *Je crois que l'automobile est aujourd'hui l'équivalent assez exact des grandes cathédrales gothiques: je veux dire une grande création d'époque, conçue passionnément par des artistes inconnus, consommée dans son image, sinon dans son usage, par un peuple entier qui s'approprie en elle un objet parfaitement magique.*
   Cars today are almost the exact equivalent of the great Gothic cathedrals…the supreme creation of an era, conceived with passion by unknown artists, and consummated in image if not in usage by a whole population which appropriates them as a purely magical object.
   1957 *Mythologies*, 'La nouvelle Citroën'.

23 *Le toucher est le plus démystificateur de tous les sens, à la différence de la vue, qui est le plus magique.*
   Touch is the most demystifying of all senses, different from sight which is the most magical.
   1957 *Mythologies*, 'La nouvelle Citroën'.

24 *Tout refus du langage est une mort.*
   Any refusal of language is a death.
   1957 *Mythologies*, 'Le mythe, aujourd'hui'.

25 *L'endroit le plus érotique d'un corps n'est-il pas là où le vêtement bâille?*
   Is not the most erotic part of the body wherever the clothing affords a glimpse?
   1973 *Le Plaisir du texte*.

26 *L'amoureux qui n'oublie pas quelquefois meurt par excès, fatigue et tension de mémoire (tel Werther).*
   The lover who does not forget *sometimes* dies from excess, fatigue, and the strain of memory (like Werther).
   1977 *Fragments d'un discours amoureux*.

27 *Le langage est une peau: je frotte mon langage contre l'autre.*
   Language is a skin; I rub my language against another language.
   1977 *Fragments d'un discours amoureux*, 'Déclaration'.

28 *Tout ce qui est anachronique est obscène.*
   Everything anachronistic is obscene.
   1977 *Fragments d'un discours amoureux*, 'Obscène'.

Bartley, Robert Leroy 1937–2003
US journalist. He joined the *Wall Street Journal* in 1962 as a staff writer, and rose to become Editor and Vice-President. He won a Pulitzer Prize for editorial writing in 1980.

29 You can't beat the market because it's smarter than you are. Intellectually, the only task is trying to determine what the market is telling you.
   1992 *The Seven Fat Years*, ch.3.

30 The mystery is why we even collect these figures; if we kept similar statistics for Manhattan Island, Park Avenue could lay awake at night worrying about its trade deficit.
   1992 On the balance of payments record. *The Seven Fat Years*.

Bartók, Béla 1881–1945
Hungarian composer and pianist. Much influenced by European folk music, he wrote works for piano and strings as well as music for ballet and opera. He died in poverty in the US, having emigrated in 1940.

31 The trouble is that I have to go with so much still to say.
   1945 Spoken on his deathbed. Quoted in David Pickering *Brewer's Twentieth Century Music* (1994).

32 I cannot conceive of music that expresses absolutely nothing.
   Quoted in Machlis *Introduction to Contemporary Music* (1963).

Baruch, Bernard Mannes 1870–1965

US financier and statesman. He became a powerful political influence, 'the adviser of presidents', and served on many commissions, including the American Atomic Energy Commission.

33 Let us not be deceived—we are today in the midst of a cold war.
   1947 Address to the South Carolina legislature, 16 Apr, using an expression suggested to him by editor Herbert Bayard Swope.

34 The cold war is getting warmer.
   1948 Address to a Senate committee.

35 To me old age is always fifteen years older than I am.
   1955 In *Newsweek*, 29 Aug.

Barzun, Jacques 1907–2012

French-born US scholar, Professor of History at Columbia University (1945) and Dean and Provost there (1958–67). His works include *Darwin, Marx, Wagner* (1941) and *The Use and Abuse of Art* (1974).

36 Teaching is not a lost art, but the regard for it is a lost tradition.
   1955 In *Newsweek*, 5 Dec.

37 The test and use of man's education is that he finds pleasure in the exercise of the mind.
   1958 'Science and the Humanities', in the *Saturday Evening Post*, 3 May.

38 If it were possible to talk to the unborn, one could never explain to them how it feels to be alive, for life is washed in the speechless real.
   1959 *The House of Intellect*.

39 Science is an all-pervasive energy, for it is at once a mode of thought, a source of strong emotion, and a faith as fanatical as any in history.
   1964 *Science, The Glorious Entertainment*.

40 Whoever wants to know the heart and mind of America had better learn baseball.
   Quoted in Michael Novak *The Joy of Sport* (1976), pt 1.

41 Baseball is a kind of collective chess with arms and legs in full play under sunlight.
   Quoted in Colin Jarman *The Guinness Dictionary of Sports Quotations* (1990).

42 To watch a football game is to be in prolonged neurotic doubt as to what you're seeing. It's more like an emergency happening at a distance than a game.
   Quoted in Colin Jarman *The Guinness Dictionary of Sports Quotations* (1990).

Baselitz, Georg 1938–

German avant-garde artist.

43 I have trouble with beauty.
   1995 On the effects of witnessing suffering as a child in Dresden during the war. In the *New York Times*, 21 May.

Basho, Matsuo 1644–94

Japanese poet, regarded as the founder of *haiku* as a significant poetic form, and influenced by Zen Buddhism.

44 An old pond
   A frog jumps in
   The sound of water
   c.1689 Quoted in Hugh Cortazzi *The Japanese Achievement* (1990).

45 Year by year,
   the monkey's mask
   reveals the monkey
   c.1689 *On Love and Barley: Haiku of Basho*, no.3 (translated by Lucien Stryk).

46 Year's end—
   still in straw hat
   and sandals
   c.1689 *On Love and Barley: Haiku of Basho*, no.126 (translated by Lucien Stryk).

47 Orchid—breathing
   incense into
   butterfly's wings
   c.1689 *On Love and Barley: Haiku of Basho*, no.166 (translated by Lucien Stryk).

48 Friends part
   forever—wild geese
   lost in cloud
   c.1689 *On Love and Barley: Haiku of Basho*, no.219 (translated by Lucien Stryk).

49 Learn about a pine tree from a pine tree, and about a bamboo stalk from a bamboo stalk.
   Attributed, quoted in *On Love and Barley: Haiku of Basho* (translated by Lucien Stryk), introduction.

Baskin, Leonard 1922–2000

US sculptor and graphic artist, also an influential teacher. His powerful works include *Man with a Dead Bird*.

50 Pop art is the inedible raised to the unspeakable.
   1965 In *Publisher's Weekly*, 5 Apr.
   ▶ See Wilde 941:84.

Bastard, Thomas 1566–1618

English poet.

51 Age is deformed, youth unkind,
   We scorn their bodies, they our mind.
   1598 *Chrestoleros*, bk.7, epigram 9.

Bates, H(erbert) E(rnest) 1905–74

English novelist, playwright and short-story writer. His most popular publications include *Fair Stood the Wind for France* (1944), *The Jacaranda Tree* (1949) and *The Darling Buds of May* (1958).

52 Perfick.
   1958 Pa Larkin's characteristic summation. *The Darling Buds of May*, ch.1 and passim.

Bates, Katharine Lee 1859–1929

US educator, author and poet. Her works include *College Beautiful and Other Poems* (1887), *Sunshine and Other Verses for Children* (1890), *Hermit Island* (1891) and *Fairy Gold* (1916).

53 O beautiful for spacious skies,
   For amber waves of grain,
   For purple mountain majesties

Above the fruited plain!
America! America!
God shed His grace on thee.
And crown thy good with brotherhood
From sea to shining sea.
1893 'America the Beautiful', opening lines.

Bateson, Gregory 1904–80
English-born US social scientist, with interests in anthropology and psychology.

54 Information is any difference that makes a difference.
1984 Quoted in *Scientific American*, no.41, Sep.

Batman, John 1801–39
Australian explorer, generally accepted as the founder of Melbourne, the site of which he bought from a local Aboriginal group for trinkets.

55 This will be the place for a Village.
1835 Journal entry, Jun. The phrase is often quoted as 'a fine place for a Village'.

Battelle, Phyllis 1922–
US columnist.

56 Where great-grandmothers dread to grow old.
1958 Of Hollywood. In the New York *Journal-American*, 15 Mar.

Baudelaire, Charles 1821–67
French Symbolist poet and critic. He is best known for his collection *Les Fleurs du mal* (1857), for which author, printer and publisher were prosecuted for impropriety, but was praised by critics and has exerted an influence far into the 20c.

57 *Hypocrite lecteur,—mon semblable,—mon frère!*
Hypocrite reader—my fellow man—my brother!
1857 *Les Fleurs du mal*, 'Au lecteur'.
▶ See Eliot 318:98.

58 *Je sais la douleur est la noblesse unique*
Où ne mordront jamais la terre et les enfers.
I know that pain is the one nobility
upon which Hell itself cannot encroach.
1857 *Les Fleurs du mal*, 'Bénédiction' (translated by Richard Howard, 1982).

59 *Le Poète est semblable au prince des nuées*
Qui hante la tempête et se rit de l'archer;
Exilé sur le sol au milieu des huées,
Ses ailes de géant l'empêchent de marcher.
The Poet is like that prince of the clouds
Who haunts the storms and laughs at the archer;
Exiled to the ground in the midst of jeers,
His giant wings prevent him from walking.
1857 *Les Fleurs du mal*, 'L'Albatros'—'Spleen et idéal', no.2.

60 *Les parfums, les couleurs et les sons se répondent.*
Scents, colours, and sounds echo one another.
1857 *Les Fleurs du mal*, 'Correspondances'.

61 *Ô douleur! ô douleur! Le Temps mange ma vie.*
Oh pain! Oh pain! time is eating away my life.
1857 *Les Fleurs du mal*, 'L'Ennemi'.

62 *Homme libre, toujours tu chériras la mer.*
Free man! You shall always cherish the sea.
1857 *Les Fleurs du mal*, 'L'Homme et la mer'.

63 *Quand notre coeur a fait une fois sa vendange,*
Vivre est un mal.
Once our heart has been harvested once,
Life becomes miserable.
1857 *Les Fleurs du mal*, 'Semper eadem'.

64 *Ne cherchez plus mon coeur; les bêtes l'ont mangé.*
Don't search any further for my heart; wild beasts ate it.
1857 *Les Fleurs du mal*, 'Causerie'.

65 *Là, tout n'est qu'ordre et beauté,*
Luxe, calme et volupté.
There where all is order and beauty.
Lush, calm and voluptuous.
1857 *Les Fleurs du mal*, 'L'Invitation au Voyage'.

66 *J'ai plus de souvenirs que si j'avais mille ans.*
I have more memories than if I were one thousand years old.
1857 *Les Fleurs du mal*, 'Spleen'.

67 *Souviens-toi que le Temps est un joueur avide*
Qui gagne sans tricher, à tout coup! c'est la loi.
Remember! Time, that tireless gambler, wins
on every turn of the wheel: that is the law.
1857 *Les Fleurs du mal*, 'L'Horloge' (translated by Richard Howard, 1982).

68 *Certes, je sortirai quant à moi satisfait*
D'un monde où l'action n'est pas la soeur du rêve.
Indeed, for my part, I shall be happy to leave
A world where action is not sister to the dream.
1857 *Les Fleurs du mal*, 'Le Reniement de Saint-Pierre'.

69 *Ah! Seigneur! donnez-moi la force et le courage*
De contempler mon coeur et mon corps sans dégoût.
Lord! give me the strength and the courage
To see my heart and my body without disgust.
1857 *Les Fleurs du mal*, 'Un Voyage à Cythère'.

70 *Amer savoir, celui qu'on tire du voyage!*
Bitter is the knowledge gained in travelling.
1857 *Les Fleurs du mal*, 'Le Voyage'.

71 If photography is allowed to stand in for art in some of its functions it will soon supplant or corrupt it completely thanks to the natural support it will find in the stupidity of the multitude. It must return to its real task, which is to be the servant of the sciences and the arts, but the very humble servant, like printing and shorthand which have neither created nor supplanted literature.
1859 'Salon of 1859', section 2, in *Curiosités Esthétiques* (1868).

72 Woe betide the man who goes to antiquity for the study of anything other than ideal art, logic and general method!
c.1860 Letter, published in *The Painter of Modern Life* (1863).

73 *Il est l'heure de s'enivrer! Pour n'être pas les esclaves martyrisés du Temps, enivrez-vous sans cesse! De vin, de poésie ou de vertu, à votre guise.*
This is the time for drunkenness! Be not the martyred slaves of Time, drink without stopping! Drink wine, poetry, or virtue, as you please.
1869 *Le Spleen de Paris*, 'Enivrez-vous'.

74 *Parce que le Beau est toujours étonnant, il serait absurde de supposer que ce qui est étonnant est toujours beau.*
Just because the beautiful is *always* shocking, it would be absurd to suppose that that which is shocking is *always* beautiful.
1869 *Le Spleen de Paris*, 'Salon de 1859', pt.2.

75 *L'imagination est la reine du vrai, et le possible est une des provinces du vrai.*
Imagination is the queen of the truth and the *possible* is one of the provinces of the truth.
1869 *Le Spleen de Paris*, 'Salon de 1859', pt.3.

76 *Comme l'imagination a créé le monde, elle le gouverne.*
Because imagination created the world, it governs it.
1869 *Le Spleen de Paris*, 'Salon de 1859', pt.4.

77 *Le mal se fait sans effort, naturellement, par fatalité; le bien est toujours le produit d'un art.*
Evil is done without effort, *naturally*, it's destiny; good is always a product of art.
1869 *Le Spleen de Paris*, 'Le Peintre de la vie moderne', pt.11.

78 *L'art moderne a une tendance essentiellement démoniaque.*
Modern art tends towards the demonic.
1869 *L'Art romantique*.

79 *Quand même Dieu n'existerait pas, la religion serait encore sainte et divine—Dieu est le seul être qui, pour régner, n'ait même pas besoin d'exister.*
Even if God did not exist, religion would still be holy and divine. God is the only being who, in order to reign, need not even exist.
1875 *Journaux intimes*, 'Fusées', no.1.

80 *La volupté unique et suprême de l'amour gît dans la certitude de faire le mal.*
The unique, supreme pleasure of love consists in the certainty of doing *evil*.
1875 *Journaux intimes*, 'Fusées', no.2.

81 *La femme est naturelle, c'est-à-dire abominable.*
Woman is *natural*, that is, abominable.
1887 *Mon coeur mis à nu*, pt.5.

82 *Le Dandy doit aspirer à être sublime, sans interruption. Il doit vivre et dormir devant un miroir.*
The dandy must aspire to be sublime at all times. He must live and sleep in front of a mirror.
1887 *Mon coeur mis à nu*, pt.5.

83 *Etre un homme utile m'a paru toujours quelque chose de bien hideux.*
To be useful has always seemed to me quite hideous.
1887 *Mon coeur mis à nu*, pt.9.

84 *Il faut travailler sinon par goût, au moins par désespoir, puisque, tout bien vérifié, travailler est moins ennuyeux que s'amuser.*
We should work: if not by preference, at least out of despair. All things considered, work is less boring than amusement.
1887 *Mon coeur mis à nu*, pt.18.

85 *Il y a dans tout homme, à toute heure, deux postulations simultanées, l'une vers Dieu, l'autre vers Satan.*
Every man at every moment has two simultaneous tendencies: one toward God, the other toward Satan.
1887 *Mon coeur mis à nu*, pt.19.

86 *Il n'existe que trois êtres respectables: le prêtre, le guerrier, le poète. Savoir, tuer et créer.*
There are only three respectable beings: priest, warrior, poet. To know, to kill and to create.
1887 *Mon coeur mis à nu*, pt.22.

87 *L'être le plus prostitué, c'est l'être par excellence, c'est Dieu, puisqu'il est l'ami suprême pour chaque individu, puisqu'il est le réservoir commun, inépuisable de l'amour.*
The most prostituted being, the Being par excellence, is God, since he is supreme friend to every individual, since he is the common, inexhaustible reservoir of love.
1887 *Mon coeur mis à nu*, pt.46.

88 *Je ne comprends pas qu'une main pure puisse toucher un journal sans une convulsion de dégoût.*
I cannot imagine how a pure hand can touch a newspaper without disgust.
1887 *Mon coeur mis à nu*, pt.81.

89 At its best a poem full of space and reverie.
Of portraits. Quoted in the *New York Times*, 1 Jan 1995.

90 *Il faut épater le bourgeois.*
One must astound the bourgeois.
Attributed.

Baughan, Blanche Edith   1870–1958

New Zealand writer and penal reformer, born in England where she published *Verses* (1898). She emigrated in 1900 and wrote popular verse with an increasingly local flavour.

91 Well, I'm leaving the poor old place, and it cuts as keen as a knife;
The place that's broken my heart—the place where I've lived my life.
1903 *Reuben and Other Poems*, 'The Old Place'.

Baxter, Sir Beverley (Arthur)   1891–1964

British politician and journalist. Canadian-born, he joined the Daily Express in London in 1920 and was editor-in-chief from 1929–33. He became MP for Wood Green 1935–45, and 1945–50 and MP for Southgate from 1950 until his death.

92 Beaverbrook is so pleased to be in the Government that he is like the town tart who has finally married the mayor.
1940 Remark attributed to Baxter in Sir Henry Channon *Chips: the Diaries* (1967), entry for 12 Jun.

93 A great many persons are able to become Members of this House without losing their insignificance.
1946 Speech, House of Commons.

Baxter, Richard   1615–91

English Nonconformist clergyman. Chaplain to Cromwell's army in the English Civil War, he became Royal Chaplain in 1660, but was imprisoned in 1685 for sedition in his *Paraphrase on the New Testament*.

94 Watch against inordinate sensual delight in even the lawfullest of sports. Excess of pleasure in any such vanity doth very much corrupt and befool the mind.
1678 *A Christian Directory*.

Beachcomber

▶ See J B Morton

Beamer, Todd   1968–2001

US businessman, passenger on the hijacked United Airlines Flight 93 on 11 September 2001.

95 Let's roll.
   2001 Last known words before he and other passengers tackled the hijackers.

Bearden, Romare 1914–88
US painter, whose bright, bold works deal with the experience of black Americans.

96 The canvas was always saying no to me.
   Of early attempts to perfect his medium. Recalled on his death in the *Washington Post*, 14 Mar 1988.

Beasant, Dave 1959–
English goalkeeper, he has played for teams including Wimbledon, Newcastle United and Chelsea. He became the first goalkeeper to captain a team to victory in the FA Cup, 1988.

97 I was a bit disappointed. I should have caught it really.
   1988 Of the save that made him the first goalkeeper to stop a penalty in an FA Cup Final. Quoted in Peter Ball and Phil Shaw *The Book of Football Quotations* (1989).

Beattie, Ann 1947–
US short-story writer and novelist.

98 There are things that get whispered about that writers are there to overhear.
   1987 *Best American Short Stories*, introduction.

99 Italics provide a wonderful advantage: you see, right away, that the words are in a rush. When something exists at a slant, you can't help but consider irony.
   2010 *Walks With Men: Fiction*.

Beattie, James 1735–1803
Scottish philosopher and poet, professor of moral philosophy at Aberdeen. He attacked Hume's scepticism in his *Essay on the Nature and Immutability of Truth* (1770), and wrote an autobiographical poem, *The Minstrel* (1771–4).

1 Some deemed him wondrous wise, and some believed him mad.
   1771 *The Minstrel*, bk.1, stanza 16.

2 In the deep windings of the grove no more
   The hag obscene, and grisly phantom dwell;
   Nor in the fall of mountain-stream, or roar
   Of winds, is heard the angry spirit's yell.
   1774 *The Minstrel*, bk.2, stanza 47.

Beatty, David, 1st Earl Beatty 1871–1936
British Admiral. After serving in Egypt and Sudan he became Rear Admiral in 1910. Early successes in World War I were followed by a major role in the Battle of Jutland. He commanded the fleet (1916–19) and was First Sea Lord (1919–27).

3 There's something wrong with our bloody ships today, Chatfield.
   1916 Comment at the Battle of Jutland, which ended in stalemate, 31 May. Quoted in Winston Churchill *The World Crisis 1916–1918* (1927), pt.1.

Beaumarchais, Pierre Augustin Caron de 1732–99
French writer who led a colourful life as artisan, member of the royal household, music teacher to Louis XV's daughter, speculator, secret agent in England, and munitions runner for the American colonies.

4 *Aujourd'hui, ce qui ne vaut pas la peine d'être dit, on le chante.*
   Today, what is not worth being said is sung.
   1775 *Le Barbier de Séville*, act 1, sc.2.

5 *Je me presse de rire de tout, de peur d'être obligé d'en pleurer.*
   I am quick to laugh at everything so as not to be obliged to cry.
   1775 *Le Barbier de Séville*, act 1, sc.2.

6 *On s'intéresse guère aux affaires des autres que lorsqu'on est sans inquiétude sur les siennes.*
   We hardly interest ourselves in the affairs of others when things are going well for ourselves.
   1775 *Le Barbier de Séville*.

7 *Les vices, les abus, voilà ce qui ne change point, mais se déguise en mille formes sous le masque des moeurs dominantes: leur arracher ce masque et les montrer à découvert, telle est la noble tâche de l'homme qui se voue au théâtre.*
   Vices, indulgences, these are the things which never change but which disguise themselves in a thousand forms beneath the mask of prevailing morals: to lift off this mask and expose them, this is the noble task of the person who devotes himself to the theatre.
   1784 *Le Mariage de Figaro*, préface.

8 *De toutes les choses sérieuses, le mariage étant la plus bouffonne.*
   Of all serious things, marriage is the most farcical.
   1784 *Le Mariage de Figaro*, act 1, sc.9.

9 *Boire sans soif et faire l'amour en tout temps, Madame, il n'y a que ça qui nous distingue des autres bêtes.*
   We drink when we are not thirsty and make love at any time, Madam. These are the only things which distinguish us from other animals.
   1784 *Le Mariage de Figaro*, act 2, sc.21.

10 *Les Anglais, à la vérité, ajoutent par ci, par là, quelques autres mots en conversant; mais il est bien aisé de voir que God-dam est le fond de la langue.*
   In truth, the English do add here and there other words when speaking, but it is obvious that *Goddamn* is the basis of their language.
   1784 *Le Mariage de Figaro*, act 3, sc.5.

Beaumont, Francis c.1584–1616
English dramatist, a friend of Ben Jonson and his circle, particularly John Fletcher, with whom he wrote at least 10 plays. *The Woman Hater* (1605) and *The Knight of the Burning Pestle* (c.1607) are thought to be mainly Beaumont's work.

11 What things have we seen,
   Done at the Mermaid! heard words that have been
   So nimble, and so full of subtil flame,
   As if that every one from whence they came,
   Had meant to put his whole wit in a jest,
   And had resolv'd to live a fool, the rest
   Of his dull life.
   1605 Letter to Ben Jonson, verses prefacing Jonson's *Volpone*.

12 She's private to herself, and best of knowledge
   Whom she will make so happy as to sigh for.
   c.1607 *The Knight of the Burning Pestle*, act 1.

Beaumont, Francis and Fletcher, John c.1584–1616, c.1578–1625

English dramatists.

13 It is always good
When a man has two irons in the fire.
1608 *The Faithful Friends*, act 1.

14 PHILASTER: Oh, but thou dost not know
What 'tis to die.
BELLARIO: Yes, I do know, my Lord:
'Tis less than to be born; a lasting sleep;
A quiet resting from all jealousy,
A thing we all pursue; I know besides,
It is but giving over of a game,
That must be lost.
1609 *Philaster* (published 1620), act 3, sc.1.

15 All your better deeds
Shall be in water writ, but this in marble.
1609 *Philaster* (published 1620), act 5.

16 Kiss till the cow comes home.
c.1610 *The Scornful Lady* (published 1616), act 2, sc.2.

17 There is no other purgatory but a woman.
c.1610 *The Scornful Lady* (published 1616), act 3.

18 Upon my buried body lay
Lightly gentle earth
1610–11 *The Maid's Tragedy*, act 2, sc.1.

19 Those have most power to hurt us that we love.
1610–11 *The Maid's Tragedy*, act 5.

20 The terror of his name has stretched itself
Wherever there is sun.
1611 *A King and No King*, act 2, sc.2.

21 What art thou that dost creep into my breast
And dar'st not see my face? Show forth thyself.
I feel a pair of fiery wings displayed
Hither, from thence. You shall not tarry there;
Up and begone. If thou beest love, begone.
1611 *A King and No King*, act 3, sc.1.

22 I see there's truth in no man, nor obedience
But for his own ends.
1611 *A King and No King*, act 4, sc.2.

23 You are no better than you should be.
1612 *The Coxcomb*, act 4, sc.3.

Beaverbrook, Max (William Maxwell Aitken), 1st Baron 1879–1964

Canadian-born British newspaper magnate and politician. After entering politics in 1910, he bought the *Daily Express* (1916) and made it the world's most widely read newspaper, founding the *Sunday Express* (1921). He was Minister of Supply and Lord Privy Seal during World War II.

24 Churchill on top of the wave has in him the stuff of which tyrants are made.
1928–32 *Politicians and the War*.

25 He has all the qualities that go to the making of a leader of the Conservative Party. He is not stupid, but he is very dull. He is not eloquent, but he talks well. He is not honest, politically, but he is most evangelical. He has a little money, but not much. He always conforms to the party policy.
1935 Commenting on Sir Samuel Hoare's appointment as Foreign Secretary.

26 Our cock won't fight.
1936 Of Edward VIII. Comment to Winston Churchill during the abdication crisis. Quoted in Francis Donaldson *Edward VIII* (1974).

27 I run the paper purely for the purpose of making propaganda, and with no other motive.
1947 Evidence to the Royal Commission on the Press.

28 With the publication of his private papers in 1952, he committed suicide 25 years after his death.
1956 Of Earl Haig. *Men and Power: 1917–1918*.

29 He did not seem to care which way he travelled providing he was in the driver's seat.
1963 Of Lloyd George. *The Decline and Fall of Lloyd George*, ch.7.

30 I am now in my eighty-fourth year and that is approaching the moment when I must bring out my Late Night Final.
c.1963 Quoted in A J P Taylor *Beaverbrook* (1972), ch.13.

31 Here I must say, in my eighty-sixth year, I do not feel greatly different from when I was eighty-five. This is my final word. It is time for me to become an apprentice once more. I have not settled in which direction. But somewhere, sometime soon.
1964 Address at a farewell banquet in London, hosted for him by Roy Thomson, Lord Thomson of Fleet, 25 May. He died two weeks later.

32 *News, Opinion and Advertisment must all come under the head of Entertainment to a reasonable extent—or they will not be read.* People do not read to be bored. Unless a newspaper can make its material in every department interesting it simply is not read.
Publicity handout for the *Daily Express*, quoted in A J P Taylor *Beaverbrook* (1972), ch.8.

33 Success never depended on pandering to the public taste. It has always been founded on simplicity.
Quoted in A J P Taylor *Beaverbrook* (1972), ch.13.

Beckenbauer, Franz 1945–

German footballer who captained the West German national side to European Nations Cup success in 1972 and to World Cup triumph in 1974.

34 We used to get our old players coming to watch training with football magazines in their hands. Now, more often than not, they're checking their share prices.
2001 In *World Soccer*, Nov.

Becker, Gary Stanley 1930–2014

US economist, Professor of Economics and Sociology at the University of Chicago. He won the Nobel prize for economics (1992).

35 They talk a good game, but economists hardly know enough about business cycles to figure out where they come from, let alone where they're going.
1989 'How Bad Will the Next Downturn Be?', in *Business Week*, 10 Apr.

Beckett, Dame Margaret (Mary) 1943–

English Labour politician.

36 Being effective is more important to me than being recognized.
2000 In the *Independent on Sunday*, 2 Jan.

Beckett, Samuel 1906–89

Irish author and playwright who lived mostly in France. His best-known play, *En Attendant Godot* (*Waiting for Godot*, 1955), exemplifies his absurdist view of the human condition. He was awarded the Nobel prize for literature (1969).

37 *Je ne supporterai plus d'être un homme, je n'essaierai plus.*
    I can no longer bear to be human and I will no longer try.
    1951 *Molloy, Malone Meurt.*

38 There is man in his entirety, blaming his shoe when his foot is guilty.
    1955 *Waiting for Godot*, act 1.

39 Nothing happens, nobody comes, nobody goes, it's awful!
    1955 *Waiting for Godot*, act 1.

40 He can't think without his hat.
    1955 Of Lucky. *Waiting for Godot*, act 1.

41 VLADIMIR: That passed the time.
    ESTRAGON: It would have passed in any case.
    VLADIMIR: Yes, but not so rapidly.
    1955 *Waiting for Godot*, act 1.

42 I am like that. I either forget right away or I never forget.
    1955 *Waiting for Godot*, act 2.

43 You overdo it with your carrots.
    1955 *Waiting for Godot*, act 2.

44 We are not saints, but we have kept our appointment. How many people can boast as much?
    1955 *Waiting for Godot*, act 2.

45 We are all born crazy. Some remain that way.
    1955 *Waiting for Godot*, act 2.

46 They give birth astride of a grave, the light gleams an instant, then it's night once more.
    1955 *Waiting for Godot*, act 2.

47 If I had the use of my body, I would throw it out of the window.
    1958 *Malone Dies.*

48 *Tout est faux, il n'y a personne...il n'y a rien.*
    Everything is false. There is no one...there is nothing.
    1958 *Nouvelles et textes pour rien.*

49 CLOV: Do you believe in the life to come?
    HAMM: Mine was always that.
    1958 *Endgame.*

50 *Bien choisir son moment et se taire, serait-ce le seul moyen d'avoir être et habitat?*
    To carefully choose one's moment and keep quiet, is this the only way one can be and live?
    1958 *Nouvelles et textes pour rien.*

51 Joyce was a synthesizer, trying to bring in as much as he could. I am an analyzer, trying to leave out as much as I can.
    1981 In the *New York Times*, 19 Apr.

52 Ever tried. Ever failed. No matter. Try again. Fail again. Fail better.
    1983 *Worstward Ho.*

53 I was in hospital once. There was a man in another ward, dying of throat cancer. In the silence, I could hear his screams continually. That's the only kind of form my work has.
    Attributed, in conversation with Harold Pinter.

Becket, Thomas à, Saint 1118–70

English churchman and martyr. Appointed Chancellor of England by Henry II in 1155, in 1162 he became Archbishop of Canterbury. He proved troublesome to Henry, opposing his remarriage, and was murdered in Canterbury Cathedral by four of the king's soldiers.

54 You will soon hate me as much as you love me now, for you assume an authority in the affairs of the church to which I shall never assent.
    c.1160 Remark to Henry II. Quoted in J R Green *A Short History of the English People* (1915), vol.1, ch.2, section 8.

Beckham, David 1975–

English footballer. He was appointed captain of the English national side for six years from 2000, and is a popular icon.

55 It's not easy when someone pulls your ponytail.
    2003 In *The Independent*, 29 Dec.

56 I'm very honoured to be given this honour.
    2003 On being awarded the OBE. Quoted on bbc.co.uk.

57 I showed that I wasn't just at Real Madrid to sell shirts.
    2004 On his first season at the Spanish club, 25 May.

Beckham, Victoria 1975–

English pop singer and former member of The Spice Girls. She is married to the footballer David Beckham.

58 David and I will never split. We're a business.
    2004 In *The Scotsman.*

Bede known as 'the Venerable' 673–735

English Benedictine monk, scholar and historian. His numerous works include saints' lives, hymns, grammatical treatises and biblical commentaries. His *Historia Ecclesiastica Gentis Anglorum* (731) is the single most valuable source for early English history.

59 *Talis, inquiens, mihi videtur, rex, vita hominum praesens in terris, ad comparationem eius, quod nobis incertum est, temporis, quale cum te residente, ad caenam cum ducibus ac ministris tuis tempore brumale...adveniens unus passerum domum citissime, pervolaverit; qui cum per unum ostium ingrediens, mox per aliud exierit. Ipso quidem tempore, quo intus est, hiemis tempestate non tangitur, sed tamen parvissimo spatio serenitatis ad momentum excurso, mox de hieme in hiemem regrediens, tuis oculis elabitur. Ita haec vita hominum ad modicum apparet; quid autem sequatur, quidve praecesserit, prorsus ignoramus.*
    'Such,' he said, 'O King, seems to me the present life of men on earth, in comparison with that time which to us is uncertain, as if when on a winter's night you sit feasting with your ealdormen and thegns—a single sparrow should fly swiftly into the hall, and coming in at one door, instantly fly out through another. In that time in which it is indoors it is indeed not touched by the fury of the winter, and yet, this smallest space of calmness being passed almost in a flash, from winter going into winter again, it is lost to your eyes. Somewhat like this appears the life of man; but of what follows or what went before, we are utterly ignorant.'
    731 *Historia Ecclesiastica Gentis Anglorum* (*Ecclesiastical History of the English People*, translated by B Colgrave, 1969), bk.2, ch.13.

Bee, Barnard Elliot 1823–61
Confederate General, killed at the First Battle of Bull Run.

60 There is Jackson with his Virginians, standing like a stone wall. Let us determine to die here, and we will conquer.
1861 Of General Thomas J Jackson, whose resistance stopped the Union advance at Bull Run, 21 Jul. Quoted in B Perley Poore *Perley's Reminiscences* (1886), vol.2, ch.7. 'Stonewall Jackson' became a popular nickname for the General.

Beecham, Sir Thomas 1879–1961
British conductor and impresario, famed for his outspokenness and wit, and for a dashing and romantic style of performance. He conducted frequently at Covent Garden from 1910, and founded several orchestras, including the London Philharmonic (1932) and the Royal Philharmonic (1947), with whom he made many recordings.

61 A musicologist is a man who can read music but can't hear it.
1930 Quoted in H Proctor-Gregg *Beecham Remembered* (1976).

62 The English may not like music—but they absolutely love the noise it makes.
Quoted in L Ayre *The Wit of Music* (1930).

63 It is far too large. It ought to be removed.
1940 On his first visit to Sydney, in 1940, being asked by a local journalist his opinion of the Harbour Bridge. Quoted in Gerald Moore *Am I too Loud?* (1962).

64 Good music is that which penetrates the ear with facility and quits the memory with difficulty. Magical music never leaves the memory.
1953 Television broadcast, 17 Nov.

65 Hark! The herald angels sing!
Beecham's Pills are just the thing,
Two for a woman, one for a child,
Peace on earth and mercy mild!
Quoted in Neville Cardus *Sir Thomas Beecham* (1961). Sir Thomas was heir to the Beecham pharmaceutical company.

66 The musical equivalent of the towers of St Pancras Station.
Of Elgar's First Symphony. Quoted in Neville Cardus *Sir Thomas Beecham* (1961).

67 There are two golden rules for an orchestra: start together and finish together. The public doesn't give a damn what goes on in between.
Quoted in Harold Atkins and Archie Newman *Beecham Stories* (1978).

68 Like two skeletons copulating on a corrugated tin roof.
Of the harpsichord's sound. Quoted in Harold Atkins and Archie Newman *Beecham Stories* (1978).

69 British music is in a state of perpetual promise. It might almost be said to be one long promissory note.
Quoted in Harold Atkins and Archie Newman *Beecham Stories* (1978).

70 The function of music is to release us from the tyranny of conscious thought.
Quoted in Harold Atkins and Archie Newman *Beecham Stories* (1978).

71 You have between your legs the most sensitive instrument known to man, and all you can do is scratch it.
Attributed rebuke to a female cellist. Quoted in Ian Crofton and Donald Fraser *A Dictionary of Musical Quotations* (1985).

Beerbohm, Sir (Henry) Max(imilian) 1872–1956
English writer, caricaturist and theatre critic, of Lithuanian extraction, who succeeded George Bernard Shaw as drama critic of the *Saturday Review*. His criticism was collected in *Around Theatre* (1953) and *More Theatres* (1968). He also wrote a novel, *Zuleika Dobson* (1911), an ironic romance about Oxford student life.

72 Most women are not so young as they are painted.
1894 *The Yellow Book*, vol.1.

73 Fate wrote her a most tremendous tragedy, and she played it in tights.
1894 Of Queen Caroline of Brunswick. *The Yellow Book*, vol.3.

74 There is always something rather absurd about the past.
1895 *The Yellow Book*, vol.4

75 To give an accurate and exhaustive account of the period would need a far less brilliant pen than mine.
1895 *The Yellow Book*, vol.4.

76 I have the satiric temperament: when I am laughing at anyone I am generally rather amusing, but when I am praising anyone, I am always deadly dull.
1898 In *The Saturday Review*, 28 May.

77 [At school] I was a modest, good-humoured boy. It is Oxford that has made me insufferable.
1899 *More*, 'Going Back To School'.

78 When a public man lays his hand on his heart and declares that his conduct needs no apology, the audience hastens to put up its umbrellas against the particularly severe downpour of apologies in store for it. I won't give the customary warning. My conduct shrieks aloud for apology, and you are in for a thorough drenching.
1906 'A Straight Talk' (parody of George Bernard Shaw), in the *Saturday Review*, 22 Dec.

79 She was one of those born to make chaos cosmic.
1911 *Zuleika Dobson*, ch.2.

80 Zuleika, on a desert island, would have spent most of her time in looking for a man's footprint.
1911 *Zuleika Dobson*, ch.2.

81 The dullard's envy of brilliant men is always assuaged by the suspicion that they will come to a bad end.
1911 *Zuleika Dobson*, ch.4.

82 Women who love the same man have a kind of bitter freemasonry.
1911 *Zuleika Dobson*, ch.4.

83 You will find that the woman who is really kind to dogs is always one who has failed to inspire sympathy in men.
1911 *Zuleika Dobson*, ch.6.

84 Beauty and the lust for learning have yet to be allied.
1911 *Zuleika Dobson*, ch.7.

85 You will think me lamentably crude: my experience of life has been drawn from life itself.
1911 *Zuleika Dobson*, ch.7.

86 She was one of the people who say 'I don't know anything about music really, but I know what I like.'
1911 *Zuleika Dobson*, ch.9.

87 You cannot make a man by standing a sheep on its hind-legs. But by standing a flock of sheep in that position you can make a crowd of men.
1911 *Zuleika Dobson*, ch.9.

88 The Socratic method is not a game at which two can play.
   1911 *Zuleika Dobson*, ch.15.

89 I looked out for what the metropolitan reviewers would have to say. They seemed to fall into two classes: those who had little to say and those who had nothing.
   1919 *Seven Men*, 'Enoch Soames'.

90 I have known no man of genius who had not to pay, in some affliction or defect either physical or spiritual, for what the gods had given him.
   1920 *And Even Now*, 'The Pines'.

91 Not philosophy, after all, not humanity, just sheer joyous power of song, is the primal thing in poetry.
   1920 *And Even Now*, 'The Pines'.

92 One might well say that mankind is divisible into two great classes: hosts and guests.
   1920 *And Even Now*, 'Hosts and Guests'.

93 I maintain that though you would often in the fifteenth century have heard the snobbish Roman say, in a would-be off-hand tone, 'I am dining with the Borgias tonight,' no Roman ever was able to say, 'I dined last night with the Borgias.'
   1920 *And Even Now*, 'Hosts and Guests'.

94 The critic who justly admires all kinds of things simultaneously cannot love any one of them.
   1946 'George Moore', in the *Saturday Review*, c.1912.

95 The thought of him has always slightly irritated me. Of course he was a wonderful all-round man, but the act of walking round him has always tired me.
   1956 Of William Morris. Letter to Sam Behrman, Feb.

96 Only mediocrity can be trusted to be always at its best.
   Quoted in S N Behrman *Conversations with Max* (1960), but also attributed elsewhere to Jean Giraudoux and W Somerset Maugham.

97 The one art-form that has been invented in England.
   Of the pantomime. Attributed.

98 Reminds me of a Christmas-tree decorated by a Pre-Raphaelite.
   Of the actress Ellen Terry. Attributed.

99 They were a tense and peculiar family, the Oedipuses, weren't they?
   Attributed.

Beethoven, Ludwig van 1770–1827

German composer. His prolific output included two masses, the opera *Fidelio*, nine symphonies, five piano concertos, piano sonatas and string quartets. Increasing deafness affected him and his music deeply. His influence, especially on the Romantics, was immense.

1 The immortal god of harmony.
   1801 Of Bach. Letter to Christoph Breitkopf.

2 I must confess that I live a miserable life... I live entirely in my music.
   1801 Letter to F G Wegeler.

3 *Muss es sein? Es muss sein! Es muss sein!*
   Must it be? It must be! It must be!
   1826 Written above the opening bars of the String Quartet in F Major, Op 135, his last work.

4 I still hope to create a few great works and then like an old child to finish my earthly course somewhere among kind people.
   1826 Letter to F G Wegeler.

5 *Plaudite, amici, comedia finita est.*
   Applaud, my friends, the comedy is over.
   1827 Quoted in Ian Crofton and Donald Fraser *A Dictionary of Musical Quotations* (1985), quoting the last words of Augustus as he lay dying.
   ▶ See Augustus 45:38.

6 I shall hear in heaven.
   1827 Attributed last words. Quoted in Ian Crofton and Donald Fraser *A Dictionary of Musical Quotations* (1985).

Beeton, Isabella Mary née *Mayson* 1836–65

English writer on cookery. Her *Book of Household Management* (1859–60) was published in serial form in a woman's magazine founded by her husband, the publisher Samuel Orchard Beeton.

7 There is no more fruitful source of family discontent than a housewife's badly-cooked dinners and untidy ways.
   1861 *The Book of Household Management*, preface.

8 A place for everything and everything in its place.
   1861 *The Book of Household Management*, ch.2.

Behan, Brendan Francis 1923–64

Irish playwright, twice imprisoned for IRA activities. He was released by general amnesty (1946), but was rearrested and deported in 1952. His works include *The Quare Fellow* (1956), *The Hostage* (1958) and an autobiography, *Borstal Boy* (1958).

9 When I came back to Dublin, I was courtmartialled in my absence and sentenced to death in my absence, so I said they could shoot me in my absence.
   1958 *The Hostage*, act 1.

10 My name is Behan, Brendan Behan, after Saint Brendan, who got into one of our little Irish boats called a curragh one day in the sixth century and sailed across the Atlantic and found America, and when he'd found it, like a sensible man he turned around and sailed back and left it where it fuckin' well was.
   1962 Speech in New York.

11 Bless you, Sister. May all your sons be bishops!
   1964 Addressing a nursing nun taking his pulse shortly before he died. Attributed.

12 Critics are like eunuchs in a harem. They're in there every night, they see how it should be done every night, but they can't do it themselves.
   Quoted in Gyles Brandreth *Great Theatrical Disasters* (1983).

13 I am a daylight atheist.
   Quoted in Daniel Farson *Sacred Monsters*, 'Rousting in Dublin' (1988).

14 Other people have a nationality. The Irish and the Jews have a psychosis.
   Richard's Cork Leg (1961).

Behn, Aphra née *Amis* 1640–89

English writer. She had an adventurous life, growing up in Surinam and acting as a professional spy in Antwerp. Perhaps the first professional woman author in England, her works include *Oroonoko* (1688), *The Forced Marriage* (1670) and *The Rover* (1678).

15 Variety is the soul of pleasure.
   1678 *The Rover*, pt.2, act 1.

16 Come away; poverty's catching.
   1678 *The Rover*, pt.2, act 1.

17 Money speaks sense in a language all nations understand.
   1678 *The Rover*, pt.2, act 3, sc.1.

18 A brave world, Sir, full of religion, knavery, and change:
we shall shortly see better days.
1682 *The Roundheads*, act 1, sc.1.

19 Be just, my lovely swain, and do not take
Freedoms you'll not to me allow;
Or give Amynta so much freedom back
That she may rove as well as you.

Let us then love upon the honest square,
Since interest neither have designed.
For the sly gamester, who ne'er plays me fair,
Must trick for trick expect to find.
1684 *Poems upon Several Occasions*, 'To Lysander, on some Verses he writ, and asking more for his Heart than 'twas worth'.

20 Faith, Sir, we are here to-day, and gone to-morrow.
1686 *The Lucky Chance*, act 4.

21 Love ceases to be a pleasure, when it ceases to be a secret.
1686 *The Lover's Watch*, 'Four o'Clock. General Conversation'.

22 Oh, what a dear ravishing thing is the beginning of an Amour!
1687 *The Emperor of the Moon*, act 1, sc.1.

23 They represented to me an absolute idea of the first state of innocence, before man knew how to sin.
1688 Of the Indians of Surinam. *Oroonoko, or the Royal Slave*.

24 Simple Nature is the most harmless, inoffensive, and virtuous mistress.
1688 *Oroonoko, or the Royal Slave*.

25 And though she had some decays in the face, she had none in her sense and wit.
1688 *Oroonoko, or the Royal Slave*.

26 Since Man with that inconstancy was born,
To love the absent, and the present scorn.
Why do we deck, why do we dress
For such a short-liv'd happiness?
1688 *Lycidus*, 'To Alexis in Answer to his Poem against Fruition,' stanza 3.

27 The soft, unhappy sex.
1698 *The Wandering Beauty*.

Behrman, S(amuel) N(athaniel) 1893–1973

US playwright, known for sophisticated comedies such as *No Time for Comedy* (1939) and *Lord Pengo* (1962). Other works include screenplays and biographies.

28 Early in life, Duveen...noticed that Europe had plenty of art and America had plenty of money, and his entire astonishing career was the product of that simple observation.
1952 *Duveen*, ch.1. Joseph Duveen was a highly successful US art dealer.

Belasco, David *stagename of* David Valasco 1859–1931

US actor-manager and dramatist. Nicknamed the 'Bishop of Broadway', he adapted many successful plays for the theatres he managed in New York.

29 Boxing is show-business with blood.
Quoted in Colin Jarman *The Guinness Dictionary of Sports Quotations* (1990).

Bell, Alexander Melville 1819–1905

Language instructor, father of Alexander Graham Bell.

30 Yes, Alec, it is I, your father, speaking.
1876 The first words spoken and heard on the world's first long-distance telephone call, from Alexander Melville Bell in Brantford, Ontario, Canada, to his son Alexander Graham Bell in nearby Paris, 13 km away, 10 Aug.

Bell, Bernard Iddings 1886–1958

US cleric, chaplain at the University of Chicago.

31 A good education is not so much one which prepares a man to succeed in the world, as one which enables him to sustain a failure.
1950 In *Life*, 16 Oct.

Bell, (Arthur) Clive Howard 1881–1964

English critic of art and literature, an influential member of the Bloomsbury set, husband of Vanessa Bell. His aesthetic theory emphasized form over content in art.

32 It would follow that 'significant form' was form behind which we catch a sense of ultimate reality.
1914 *Art*, pt.1, ch.3.

33 Art and Religion are, then, two roads by which men escape from circumstance to ecstasy.
1914 *Art*, pt.2, ch.1.

34 I will try to account for the degree of my aesthetic emotion. That, I conceive, is the function of the critic.
1914 *Art*, pt.3, ch.3.

35 Materially make the life of the artist sufficiently miserable to be unattractive, and no one will take to art save those in whom the divine daemon is absolute.
1914 *Art*, pt.5, ch.1.

36 Comfort came in with the middle classes.
1928 *Civilization*, ch.4.

37 Only reason can convince us of those three fundamental truths without a recognition of which there can be no effective liberty: that what we believe is not necessarily true; that what we like is not necessarily good; and that all questions are open.
1928 *Civilization*, ch.5.

Bell, Martin 1938–

English journalist and MP. After a career as a television news reporter he served as an Independent MP for Tatton from 1997 to 2001.

38 I knew when Sir Alec Guinness endorsed my campaign that the force was with us.
1997 Victory speech on winning the Tatton constituency. In *The Oxford Mail*, 2 May.

39 The great American tradition of telling truth to power was incinerated in New York on 11 September 2001.
2003 *Through Gates of Fire*.

Bell, Vanessa *née* Stephen 1879–1961

English painter and designer, sister of Virginia Woolf. She married the critic Clive Bell (1907) but left him in 1916 to live with Duncan Grant.

40 Rather lovely descriptions of scenery, don't you think?
1928 Remark to Robert Medley and Rupert Doone, when asked what she thought of D H Lawrence's *Lady Chatterley's Lover*. Recalled in Robert Medley *Drawn from the Life: a Memoir* (1983), p.91.

Bellay, Joachim du 1522–60

French poet famous for his sonnets. He was a founding member of the Pléiade and wrote its manifesto, *La défense et illustration de la langue française* (1549).

41 *Rome de Rome est le seul monument,*
   Et Rome Rome a vaincu seulement.
   Rome is the only monument left of Rome,
   And only Rome vanquished Rome.
   1558 *Antiquitez de Rome*, no.5.

42 *Rome seule pouvait à Rome ressembler,*
   Rome seule pouvait Rome fait trembler.
   Only Rome can resemble Rome,
   And Rome alone can make Rome fall.
   1558 *Antiquitez de Rome*, no.6.

43 *France, mère des arts, des armes et des lois.*
   France, mother of arts, of weapons and of laws.
   1558 *Les Regrets*, no.9.

44 *Heureux, qui comme Ulysse, a fait un beau voyage,*
   Ou comme cestuy là qui conquit la toison,
   Et puis est retourné, plein d'usage et raison,
   Vivre entre ses parents le reste de son âge!
   Happy is he who, like Ulysses, has taken a wondrous
     journey
   Or has won the Golden Fleece,
   And then returns home wise and useful
   To live in his homeland the rest of his days.
   1558 *Les Regrets*, no.31.

45 *Celuy vit seulement, lequel vit aujourdhuy.*
   Only the person who lives for today lives at all.
   1558 *Les Regrets*, no.65.

46 *Je n'écris point d'amour, n'estant point amoureux,*
   Je n'écris de beauté, n'aiant belle maistresse,
   Je n'écris de douceur, n'esprouvant que rudesse,
   Je n'écris de plaisir, me trouvant douloureux.
   I cannot write of love, as I am not in love,
   I cannot write of beauty, as I have no beautiful
     mistress,
   I cannot write of sweetness, as I experience nothing but
     hardship,
   I cannot write of pleasure, as I am always in pain.
   1558 *Les Regrets*, no.79.

Belli, Carlos Germán 1927–

Peruvian poet, translator and journalist. He travelled widely in South America, Spain, Italy and the United States. His poems are noted for their nihilistic outlook and an orderly precision of language.

47 *De los libros el luminoso plectro*
   diríase que pasa
   a ser lía del recto,
   pues después de tanto leer sin tasa
   nada ha quedado en casa.
   The luminous plectrum of books
   can be said to become
   a portion of the rectum,
   since after so much eager reading
   not a thing remains at home.
   1961 *¡Oh hada cibernética!*, 'Cuando el seso tiene la altura de un grano de arena' ('When the brain is as high as a grain of sand').

Bellini, Mario 1935–

Italian architect.

48 A design career is a process of learning better and better what you know instinctively.
   1987 In the *New York Times*, 25 Jun.

49 I designed a bench in a few moments. But, of course, it took me 25 years to do it.
   1987 In the *New York Times*, 25 Jun.

Belloc, (Joseph) Hilaire Pierre 1870–1953

French-born British writer, poet, Roman Catholic apologist and Liberal MP (1906–10). His works include *The Servile State* (1912), travel books, historical studies and religious books. He is best known for his comic and nonsensical verse for children.

50 Child! do not throw this book about;
   Refrain from the unholy pleasure
   Of cutting all the pictures out!
   Preserve it as your chiefest treasure.
   1896 *The Bad Child's Book of Beasts*, dedication.

51 A manner rude and wild
   Is common at your age.
   1896 *The Bad Child's Book of Beasts*, introduction.

52 When people call this beast to mind,
   They marvel more and more
   At such a little tail behind,
   So large a trunk before.
   1896 *The Bad Child's Book of Beasts*, 'The Elephant'.

53 I shoot the Hippopotamus
   With bullets made of platinum,
   Because if I use the leaden ones
   His hide is sure to flatten 'em.
   1896 *The Bad Child's Book of Beasts*, 'The Hippopotamus'.

54 Mothers of large families (who claim to common sense)
   Will find a Tiger will repay the trouble and expense.
   1896 *The Bad Child's Book of Beasts*, 'The Tiger'.

55 The Microbe is so very small
   You cannot make him out at all.
   1897 *More Beasts for Worse Children*, 'The Microbe'.

56 Whatever happens, we have got
   The Maxim Gun, and they have not.
   1898 *The Modern Traveller*, bk.6.

57 I am a Catholic. As far as possible I go to Mass every day. As far as possible I kneel down and tell these beads every day. If you reject me on account of my religion, I shall thank God that he has spared me the indignity of being your representative.
   1906 Election campaign speech, Salford.

58 The chief defect of Henry King
   Was chewing little bits of string.
   1907 *Cautionary Tales*, 'Henry King'.

59 Physicians of the utmost fame
   Were called at once, but when they came
   They answered, as they took their fees,
   'There is no cure for this disease.'
   1907 *Cautionary Tales*, 'Henry King'.

60 'Oh, my friends, be warned by me,
   That breakfast, dinner, lunch, and tea
   Are all the human frame requires…'
   With that the wretched child expires.
   1907 *Cautionary Tales*, 'Henry King'.

61 And always keep a hold of Nurse
For fear of finding something worse.
1907 *Cautionary Tales*, 'Jim'.

62 We had intended you to be
The next Prime Minister but three:
The stocks were sold; the Press was squared;
The Middle Class was quite prepared.
But as it is!... My language fails!
Go out and govern New South Wales!
1907 *Cautionary Tales*, 'Jim'.

63 Matilda told such Dreadful Lies,
It made one Gasp and Stretch one's Eyes;
Her Aunt, who, from her Earliest Youth,
Had kept a Strict Regard for Truth,
Attempted to Believe Matilda:
The effort very nearly killed her.
1907 *Cautionary Tales*, 'Matilda'.

64 She was not really bad at heart,
But only rather rude and wild;
She was an aggravating child.
1907 *Cautionary Tales*, 'Rebecca'.

65 Her funeral sermon (which was long
And followed by a sacred song)
Mentioned her virtues, it is true,
But dwelt upon her vices too.
1907 *Cautionary Tales*, 'Rebecca'.

66 It is the best of trades, to make songs, and the second best to sing them.
1909 *On Everything*.

67 I said to Heart, 'How goes it?' Heart replied:
'Right as a Ribstone Pippin!' But it lied.
1910 'The False Heart'.

68 When I am living in the Midlands
That are sodden and unkind.
1910 'The South Country'.

69 Everywhere the sea is a teacher of truth. I am not sure that the best thing I find in sailing is not this salt of reality.
c.1910 *The Cruise of the Nona*.

70 Do you remember an Inn,
Miranda?
Do you remember an Inn,
And the tedding and the spreading
Of the straw for a bedding,
And the fleas that tease in the High Pyrenees
And the wine that tasted of the tar?
1923 'Tarantella'.

71 When I am dead, I hope it may be said,
'His sins were scarlet, but his books were read.'
1923 'On His Books'.

72 And even now, at twenty-five,
He has to WORK to keep alive!
Yes! All day long from 10 till 4!
For half the year or even more;
With but an hour or two to spend
At luncheon with a city friend.
1930 *New Cautionary Tales*, 'Peter Goole'.

73 I am a sundial, and I make a botch
Of what is done much better by a watch.
1938 'On a Sundial'.

74 Statistics are the triumph of the quantitative method, and the quantitative method is the victory of sterility and death.
1940 *The Silence of the Sea*.

Bellow, Saul 1915–2005

Canadian-born US writer. He moved to Chicago in 1924, and was educated there. His best novels examine Jewish-American identity and the dilemma of liberal humanist values in a fast-changing world. He won the Nobel prize for literature in 1976.

75 Everyone knows there is no fineness or accuracy of suppression. If you hold down one thing you hold down the adjoining.
1953 *The Adventures of Augie March*.

76 I am an American, Chicago born—Chicago, that somber city—and go at things as I have taught myself, free-style, and will make the record in my own way: first to knock, first admitted; sometimes an innocent knock, sometimes a not so innocent.
1953 *The Adventures of Augie March*.

77 Of course, in an age of madness, to expect to be untouched by madness is a form of madness. But the pursuit of sanity can be a form of madness, too.
1959 *Henderson The Rain King*, ch.3.

78 If I am out of my mind, it's all right with me, thought Moses Herzog.
1961 *Herzog*, opening words.

79 A man may say, 'From now on I'm going to speak the truth.' But the truth hears him and runs away and hides before he's even done speaking.
1961 *Herzog*.

80 I feel that art has something to do with the achievement of stillness in the midst of chaos.
1965 Interview in *The Paris Review*, no.37, winter issue.

81 No wonder the really powerful men in our society, whether politicians or scientists, hold writers in contempt. They do it because they get no evidence from modern literature that anybody is thinking about any significant question.
1965 Interview in *The Paris Review*, no.37, winter issue.

82 I am more stupid about some things than about others; not equally stupid in all directions; I am not a well-rounded person.
1969 *Mr Sammler's Planet*, ch.2.

83 Conquered people tend to be witty.
1969 *Mr Sammler's Planet*, ch.2.

84 Mr Sammler with his screwy visions! He saw the increasing triumph of Enlightenment—Liberty, Equality, Adultery!
1969 *Mr Sammler's Planet*, ch.3.

85 There is much to be said for exotic marriages. If your husband is a bore, it takes years longer to discover.
1969 *Mr Sammler's Planet*, ch.6.

86 I think that New York is not the cultural centre of America, but the business and administrative centre of American culture.
1969 In radio interview, reported in *The Listener*, 22 May.

87 The idea, anyway, was to ward off trouble. But now the moronic inferno had caught up with me.
1975 *Humboldt's Gift*. Martin Amis used the phrase *The Moronic Inferno* as the title for a book of essays on the US (1986).

88 The only real distinction at this dangerous moment in human history and cosmic development has nothing to do with medals and ribbons. Not to fall asleep is distinguished. Everything else is mere popcorn.
1975 *Humboldt's Gift*.

89 After all these years wallowing in low seriousness—low seriousness, you understand, is high seriousness that's failed.
1975 Interview in the *Sunday Times*, 12 Jan.

90 The feeling individual appeared weak—he felt only his own weakness. But if he accepted his weakness and his separateness and descended into himself, intensifying his loneliness, he discovered his solidarity with other isolated creatures.
1976 Nobel prize lecture, Stockholm, 12 Dec.

91 A novel is balanced between a few true impressions and the multitude of false ones that make up most of what we call life.
1976 Nobel prize lecture, Stockholm, 12 Dec.

92 Tears may be intellectual, but they can never be political. They save no man from being shot, no child from being thrown alive into the furnace.
1982 *The Dean's December*, ch.12.

93 As a rule Corde avoided cemeteries and never went near the graves of his parents. He said it was just as easy for your dead to visit you, only by now he would have to hire a hall.
1982 *The Dean's December*, ch.15.

94 The secret motive of the absent-minded is to be innocent while guilty. Absent-mindedness is spurious innocence.
1987 *More Die of Heartbreak*.

95 Erotic practices have become diversified. Sex used to be a single-crop farming, like cotton or wheat; now people raise all kinds of things.
1987 *More Die of Heartbreak*.

96 The modern reader (or viewer, or listener: let's include everybody) is perilously overloaded. His attention is, to use the latest lingo, 'targeted' by powerful forces… Our consciousness is a staging area, a field of operations for all kinds of enterprises, which make free use of it.
1989 *Something To Remember Me By*, preface.

97 But Fonstein belonged to an even more advanced category…their aim is to convert weaknesses and secrets into burnable energy. A first-class man subsists on the matter he destroys, just as the stars do.
1989 *Something To Remember Me By*, 'The Bellarosa Connection'.

Bemelmans, Ludwig 1898–1962

US writer and restaurateur. He wrote food and travel books, and is best remembered for his 'Madeline' series for children.

98 In an old house in Paris
that was covered with vines
lived twelve little girls in two straight lines.
1939 *Madeline*.

99 And nobody knew so well
How to frighten Miss Clavell.
1939 *Madeline*.

1 Serves you right, you horrid brat
For what you did to that poor cat.
1956 *Madeline and the Bad Hat*.

Benaud, Richie (Richard) 1930–

Australian cricketer and broadcaster. He played in 63 Test matches (28 as captain), scoring 2201 Test runs and taking 248 wickets.

2 Cricket is a batsman's game.
1961 *Way of Cricket*.

Benchley, Robert Charles 1889–1945

US humorist and critic, a member of the famous circle of New York wits and writers known as the Algonquin Round Table. He was drama critic of *Life* and the *New Yorker*, and appeared in cameo roles in many films.

3 In America there are two classes of travel—first class, and with children.
1925 *Pluck and Luck*.

4 The surest way to make a monkey of a man is to quote him.
1936 *My Ten Years in a Quandary*.

5 I haven't been abroad in so long that I almost speak English without an accent now.
1938 *After 1903—What?*

6 One square foot less and it would be adulterous.
On the tiny office he shared with Dorothy Parker, quoted in the *New Yorker*, 5 Jan 1946.

7 My only solution for the problem of habitual accidents…is to stay in bed all day. Even then, there is always the chance that you will fall out.
1949 *Chips Off the Old Benchley*, 'Safety Second'.

8 A great many people have come up to me and asked how I manage to get so much work done and still keep looking so dissipated.
1949 *Chips Off the Old Benchley*, 'How To Get Things Done'.

9 So who's in a hurry?
On being told that the particular drink he was drinking was slow poison. Quoted in Nathaniel Benchley *Robert Benchley* (1955), ch.1.

10 STREETS FLOODED. PLEASE ADVISE.
Telegraph message to the US on arriving in Venice. Quoted in R E Drennan (ed) *Wits End* (1973).

11 Opera is where a guy gets stabbed in the back, and instead of dying, he sings.
Quoted in Ian Crofton and Donald Fraser *A Dictionary of Musical Quotations* (1985).

Bendix, Reinhard 1916–91

German-born US sociologist, Professor at the University of California, Berkeley.

12 In retrospect it always seems as if everything had to develop just the way it did. I call this view the fallacy of retrospective determinism—which looks at the modern world as a victory of the children of light over the children of darkness if we approve of the development, and of darkness over light if we condemn it.
1984 *Force, Fate, and Freedom: On Historical Sociology*.

Benedetti, Mario 1920–2009

Uruguayan fiction writer, poet and essayist, who lived in Cuba in the late 1960s. After returning to Uruguay, he helped establish a leftist coalition for future elections. With the military takeover of 1973 he was forced to leave the country.

13 está demás decirte que a esta altura
    no creo en predicadores ni en generales
    ni en las nalgas de miss universo
    ni en el arrepentimiento de los verdugos
    ni en el catecismo del confort
    ni en el flaco perdón de dios.
    It's not useless to tell you that, at this stage,
    I don't believe in preachers or generals
    or in Miss Universe's buttocks
    or in the executioner's repentance
    or in the catechism of comfort
    or in God's slim forgiving.
    1974 *Poemas de otros*, 'Credo' ('Creed').

Pope Benedict XVI *originally Joseph Aloisius Ratzinger* 1927–

German priest and theologian. He became Archbishop of Munich and Freising and a Cardinal in 1977, Prefect of the Congregation for the Doctrine of the Faith (1981) and Dean of the College of Cardinals (2002) before being elected as pope in 2005. In 2013 he became the first pope to resign since 1415 when he stepped down from the post, citing his advanced age, and was accorded the title pope emeritus.

14 History as a whole is the struggle between love and the inability to love, between love and the refusal to love.
   1997 *Salt of the Earth: The Church at the End of the Millennium—An Interview With Peter Seewald.*

15 We cannot haul 10,000 generations into the laboratory.
   2007 Arguing that evolution is not provable.

16 Failure to respect the union between a man and a woman amounts to the auto destruction of mankind.
   2008 Speech interpreted as attacking homosexuality.

17 Nations once rich in faith and vocations are losing their own identity under the harmful and destructive influence of a certain modern culture.
   2008 Speech at meeting of bishops in Rome, 5 Oct.

18 Unfortunately my guardian angel, most probably on orders from above, did not prevent this incident.
   2009 Attributed, after breaking his wrist in a fall.

19 You have suffered grievously and I am truly sorry. I know that nothing can undo the wrong you have endured. Your trust has been betrayed and your dignity has been violated.
   2010 Papal apology to victims of clerical sex abuse in Ireland.

20 Truth is not determined by a majority vote.
   Attributed.

21 Evil draws its power from indecision and concern for what other people think.
   Attributed.

22 One who has hope lives differently.
   Attributed.

Benét, Stephen Vincent 1898–1943

US poet and novelist. He wrote many evocative poems on the history and national identity of America, of which 'American Names' is the most famous.

23 I have fallen in love with American names,
   The sharp, gaunt names that never get fat,
   The snakeskin-titles of mining-claims,
   The plumed war-bonnet of Medicine Hat,
   Tucson and Deadwood and Lost Mule Flat.
   1927 'American Names'.

24 There are English counties like hunting-tunes
   Played on the keys of a postboy's horn,
   But I will remember where I was born.
   1927 'American Names'.

25 I will get me a bottle of Boston sea
   And a blue-gum nigger to sing me blues.
   I am tired of loving a foreign muse.
   1927 'American Names'.

26 I shall not rest quiet in Montparnasse.
   I shall not lie easy at Winchelsea.
   You may bury my body in Sussex grass,
   You may bury my tongue at Champmédy.
   I shall not be there, I shall rise and pass.
   Bury my heart at Wounded Knee.
   1927 'American Names'. *Bury My Heart At Wounded Knee* was used by Dee Brown as the title of a book on the Indian genocide (1971).

27 One cannot balance tragedy in the scales
   Unless one weighs it with the tragic heart.
   1928 'John Brown's Body'.

28 We thought we were done with these things but we were wrong.
   We thought, because we had power, we had wisdom.
   1935 'A Litany for Dictatorships'.

Benn, Tony (Anthony Neil Wedgwood) 1925–2014

English Labour politician. He became an MP (1950–60), and renounced his hereditary title to be re-elected to the Commons (1963–83, 1984–2001). He held various government posts, and as a left-wing representative unsuccessfully challenged Neil Kinnock for the leadership of the Labour Party in 1988.

29 The House of Lords is the British Outer Mongolia for retired politicians.
   1962 Speech made during his campaign to disclaim his hereditary peerage, 11 Feb.

30 It is as wholly wrong to blame Marx for what was done in his name, as it is to blame Jesus for what was done in his.
   Quoted in Alan Freeman *The Benn Heresy* (1982).

31 It is beginning to dawn on people that the influence of a nation is not measured by the size of its military budget, but by its industrial strength.
   1991 In *The Independent*, 18 Apr.

32 The dependence of London on Washington for the supply of our so-called independent nuclear weapons is all that remains of the 'special relationship' and…it is really a ball and chain limiting our capacity to play a more positive role in the world.
   1991 In *The Independent*, 18 Apr.
   ▶ See Churchill 226:3.

33 It is the same each time with progress. First they ignore you, then they say you are mad, then dangerous, then there's a pause, and then you can't find anyone who disagrees.
   1991 Speech at the Labour Party Conference, Oct.

34 It will be Blair, Blair, Blair just as it was Thatcher, Thatcher, Thatcher.
   1997 Replying to a student's question on the supremacy of prime ministerial power.

35 We should put the spin-doctors in spin clinics, where they can meet other spin patients and be treated by spin

consultants. The rest of us can get on with the proper democratic process.
1997 In *The Independent*, 'Quote Unquote', 25 Oct.

36 The Weetabix Years.
2004 Book title.

37 'We the peoples of the United Nations determined to save succeeding generations from the scourge of war, which twice in our lifetime has brought untold sorrow to mankind.' That was the pledge my generation gave to the younger generation and you tore it up. And it's a war crime that's been committed in Iraq, because there is no moral difference between a stealth bomber and a suicide bomber. Both kill innocent people for political reasons.
2007 In BBC topical affairs programme *Question Time*, 22 Mar.

38 Ideas are more powerful than guns.
2007 Wikinews interview, 8 Aug.

39 I think there are two ways in which people are controlled. First of all frighten people and secondly, demoralize them.
2007 Interview with Michael Moore in the film *Sicko*.

40 I got a death threat last year. Hadn't had one for years. I was so chuffed.
2009 In *The Daily Telegraph*, 12 Aug.

41 The key to any progress is to ask the question why? All the time. Why is that child poor? Why was there a war? Why was he killed? Why is he in power? And of course questions can get you into a lot of trouble, because society is trained by those who run it, to accept what goes on. Without questions we won't make any progress at all.
2013 Interview in *Creating Freedom*.

Bennard, George 1873–1958
US clergyman and hymn-writer.

42 I will cling to the old rugged cross,
And exchange it some day for a crown.
1913 'The Old Rugged Cross'.

Bennett, Alan 1934–
English writer. He came to prominence as an actor and writer in *Beyond the Fringe* (1960), and went on to write wry, mordant plays and monologues for stage and screen. He adapted his play *The Madness of George III* (1991) as an Oscar-winning film in 1995. His play *The History Boys* (2005) also won many awards.

43 Life is rather like a tin of sardines—we're all of us looking for the key.
1960 *Beyond the Fringe*.

44 I've never understood this liking for war. It panders to instincts already catered for within the scope of any respectable domestic establishment.
1968 *Forty Years On* (published 1969), act 1.

45 Memories are not shackles, Franklin, they are garlands.
1968 *Forty Years On* (published 1969), act 2.

46 The Breed never dies. Sapper, Buchan, Dornford Yates, practitioners in that school of Snobbery with Violence that runs like a thread of good-class tweed through twentieth-century literature.
1968 *Forty Years On* (published 1969), act 2. *Snobbery With Violence* was used as a book title by Colin Wilson (1971).

47 It's the one species I wouldn't mind seeing vanish from the face of the earth. I wish they were like the White Rhino—six of them left in the Serengeti National Park, and all males.
1971 Of dogs. *Getting On* (published 1972), act 1.

48 The longer I practise medicine, the more convinced I am there are only two types of cases: those that involve taking the trousers off and those that don't.
1973 *Habeas Corpus*.

49 One of the few things I have learned in life is that there is invariably something odd about women who wear ankle socks.
1977 *The Old Country*, act 1.

50 We were put to Dickens as children but it never took. That unremitting humanity soon had me cheesed off.
1977 *The Old Country*, act 2.

51 There is no such thing as a good script, only a good film, and I'm conscious that my scripts often read better than they play.
1984 *A Private Function*, introduction to published screenplay.

52 I'm going to throw caution to the winds and have a sweet sherry.
1984 Spoken by Maggie Smith as Joyce Chilvers in *A Private Function*.

53 I want a future that will live up to my past.
1984 Spoken by Maggie Smith as Joyce Chilvers in *A Private Function*.

54 They're going to have to be made to sit up and take notice. They're going to have to be made to realise who we are. My father had a chain of dry cleaners.
1984 *A Private Function*.

55 I'm not good at precise, coherent argument. But plays are suited to incoherent argument, put into the mouths of fallible people.
1991 In the *Sunday Times*, 24 Nov.

56 My claim to literary fame is that I used to deliver meat to a woman who became T. S. Eliot's mother-in-law.
1992 In the *Observer*, 26 Apr. The lady in question was the mother of Eliot's wife Valerie Fletcher; Bennett's father was the butcher in the same Yorkshire village.

57 That's a bit like asking a man crawling across the Sahara whether he would prefer Perrier or Malvern water.
2004 Reply when asked by Sir Ian McKellen if he was heterosexual or homosexual.

58 At eighty things do not occur; they recur.
2007 *The Uncommon Reader*.

59 Marriage is supposed to be a partnership. Good-looking people marry good-looking people and the others take what's left.
2011 *Smut: two unseemly stories*.

60 It is seldom at the frontier that discoveries are made but more often in the dustbin.
2012 *The Library Book*.

Bennett, (Enoch) Arnold 1867–1931
English novelist. He was also a journalist, and lived in Paris for ten years. His best-known books are those set in the pottery-making heartland of the Five Towns in the Midlands, notably the *Clayhanger* trilogy (1910–16).

61 Essential characteristic of the really great novelist: a Christ-like, all-embracing compassion.
1896 Journal entry, 15 Oct.

62 'Bah!', she said, 'With people like you, love only means one thing.' 'No,' he replied. 'It means twenty things, but it doesn't mean nineteen.'
1904 Journal entry, 20 Nov.

63 My general impression is that Englishmen act better than Frenchmen, and Frenchwomen better than Englishwomen.
1909 *Cupid and Commonsense*, preface.

64 His opinion of himself, having once risen, remained at 'set fair'.
1911 *The Card*, ch.1.

65 'Ye can call it influenza if ye like,' said Mrs Machin. 'There was no influenza in my young days. We called a cold a cold.'
1911 *The Card*, ch.8.

66 A cause may be inconvenient, but it's magnificent. It's like champagne or high heels, and one must be prepared to suffer for it.
1918 *The Title*, act 1.

67 Being a husband is a whole-time job. That is why so many husbands fail. They cannot give their entire attention to it.
1918 *The Title*, act 1.

68 Journalists say a thing that they know isn't true, in the hope that if they keep on saying it long enough it will be true.
1918 *The Title*, act 2.

69 Mr Lloyd George spoke for 17 minutes, in which period he was detected only once in the use of an argument.
1921 *Things That Have Interested Me*.

70 A test of a first-rate work, and a test of your sincerity in calling it a first-rate work, is that you finish it.
1921 *Things That Have Interested Me*, 'Finishing Books'.

71 In the meantime alcohol produces a delightful social atmosphere that nothing else can produce.
1921 *Things That Have Interested Me*, 'For and Against Prohibition'.

72 Pessimism, when you get used to it, is just as agreeable as optimism.
1921 *Things That Have Interested Me*, 'Slump Into Pessimism'.

73 The price of justice is eternal publicity.
1923 *Things That Have Interested Me* (2nd series), 'Secret Trials'.

74 Between thirty and forty a man may have reached the height of discretion without having tumbled over the top and into the feather-bed of correctitude.
1930 In the *Evening Standard*, 29 May.

75 Good taste is better than bad taste, but bad taste is better than no taste, and men without individuality have no taste—at any rate no taste that they can impose on their publics.
1930 In the *Evening Standard*, 21 Aug.

76 The thing is to produce an impression on the reader—the best you can, the truest you can, but some impression. The newest despisers of form and conventionalization produce no impression at all.
1931 Journal entry, 11 Sep.

77 The saxophone is the embodied spirit of beer.
Quoted in Derek Watson *Music Quotations* (1991).

Bennett, James Gordon, Snr 1795–1872
Scots-born US journalist. In 1835 he started the *New York Herald*, pioneering many journalistic innovations.

78 The Press is the living Jury of the Nation.
1831 In the *Courier and Enquirer*, 6 Aug.

79 An editor must always be with the people—think with them—feel with them—and he need fear nothing, he will always be right—always be strong—always *free*.
1831 In the *Courier and Enquirer*, 12 Nov.

80 This is the editorial age, and the most intellectual of all ages.
1831 In the *Courier and Enquirer*, 12 Nov.

81 What is to prevent a daily newspaper from being made the greatest organ of social life? Books have had their day—the theatres have had their day—the temple of religion has had its day. A newspaper can be made to take the lead of all these in the great movements of human thought and of human civilisation. A newspaper can send more souls to Heaven, and save more from Hell, than all the churches or chapels in New York—besides making money at the same time.
1836 In the *New York Herald*, 19 Aug.

82 I have infused life, glowing eloquence, philosophy, taste, sentiment, wit, and humor into the daily newspaper… Shakespeare is the great genius of the drama—Scott of the novel—Milton and Byron of the poem—and I mean to be the genius of the daily newspaper press.
c.1836 Quoted in Oliver Carlson *The Man Who Made News: James Gordon Bennett* (1942), ch.10.

Bennis, Warren Gameliel 1925–2014
US economist and business administrator.

83 Leaders are people who do the right things. Managers are people who do things right…a profound difference.
1994 In *Fortune*, 19 Sep.

Benson, A(rthur) C(hristopher) 1862–1925
English academic writer. He wrote a number of critical studies and biographies of eminent literary Victorians, and is remembered now for his patriotic poem 'Land of Hope and Glory', set to music by Elgar.

84 Land of Hope and Glory, Mother of the Free,
How shall we extol thee who are born of thee?
Wider still and wider shall thy bounds be set;
God who made thee mighty, make thee mightier yet.
1902 'Land of Hope and Glory'.

85 If the dullest person in the world would only put down sincerely what he or she thought about his or her life, about work and love, religion and emotion, it would be a fascinating document.
1906 'From A College Window'.

Benson, Stella 1892–1933
English novelist. Her diary was published long after her death from tuberculosis.

86 Call no man foe, but never love a stranger.
1917 *This is the End*.

Bentham, Jeremy 1748–1832
English philosopher, jurist and writer. His works include *A Fragment of Government* (1776) and *Introduction to the Principles of Morals and Legislation* (1789), which expounds his theory of hedonistic utilitarianism.

87 The community is a fictitious *body*, composed of the individual persons who are considered as constituting as it were its *members*. The interest of the community then, is what? The sum of the interests of the several members who compose it.
    1789 *An Introduction to the Principles of Morals and Legislation*, ch.1.

88 The greatest happiness of the greatest number is the foundation of morals and legislation.
    1789 *An Introduction to the Principles of Morals and Legislation*, ch.1.
    ▶ See Hutcheson 441:49.

89 All punishment is mischief: all punishment in itself is evil.
    1789 *An Introduction to the Principles of Morals and Legislation*, ch.13.

90 Every law is an evil, for every law is an infraction of liberty.
    1789 *An Introduction to the Principles of Morals and Legislation*.

91 An absolute and unlimited right over any object of property would be the right to commit nearly every crime. If I had such a right over the stick I am about to cut, I might employ it as a mace to knock down the passengers, or I might convert it into a sceptre as an emblem of royalty, or into an idol to offend the national religion.
    Principles of the Civil Code, pt.1, ch.13, final note. Collected in John Bowring (ed) *Works* (1838–43), vol.1.

92 Natural rights is simple nonsense: natural and imprescriptable rights, rhetorical nonsense—nonsense upon stilts.
    Anarchical Fallacies. Collected in J Bowring (ed) *Works* (1838–43), vol.2.

93 Publicity is the very soul of justice. It is the keenest spur to exertion, and the surest of all guards against improbity.
    Draught of a code for the organization of the judicial establishment in France. Collected in John Bowring (ed) *Works* (1838–43), vol.4.

94 He rather hated the ruling few than loved the suffering many.
    Of James Mill. Quoted in *Memories of Old Friends, being Extracts from the Journals and Letters of Caroline Fox* (1882).

95 Prose is when all the lines except the last go on to the end. Poetry is when some of them fall short of it.
    Quoted in M St J Packe *The Life of John Stuart Mill* (1954), bk.1, ch.2.

96 To be the most effectively benevolent man who ever lived.
    His ambition. Quoted in Mary Peter Mack *International Encyclopedia of the Social Sciences* (1968), vol.2.

Bentley, Edmund Clerihew 1875–1956

English writer and journalist. His books include *Biography for Beginners* (1905), *Baseless Biography* (1939) and the classic detective novel *Trent's Last Case* (1913). He is best known for his humorous verse form, named the clerihew after him.

97 The art of Biography
    Is different from Geography.
    Geography is about Maps,
    But Biography is about Chaps.
    1905 *Biography for Beginners*, introduction.

98 What I like about Clive
    Is that he is no longer alive.
    There is a great deal to be said
    For being dead.
    1905 *Biography for Beginners*, 'Clive'.

99 Sir Christopher Wren
    said, 'I am going to dine with some men.
    If anybody calls
    Say I am designing St Paul's.'
    1905 *Biography for Beginners*, 'Sir Christopher Wren'.

1   Sir Humphrey Davy
    Abominated gravy.
    He lived in the odium
    Of having discovered sodium.
    1905 *Biography for Beginners*, 'Sir Humphrey Davy'.

2   John Stuart Mill,
    By a mighty effort of will,
    Overcame his natural *bonhomie*
    And wrote 'Principles of Political Economy'.
    1905 *Biography for Beginners*, 'John Stuart Mill'.

3   Henry the Eighth
    Took a thuctheththion of mateth.
    He inthithted that the monkth
    Were a lathy lot of thkunkth.
    1929 *More Biography*, 'Henry the Eighth'.

4   George the Third
    Ought never to have occurred.
    One can only wonder
    At so grotesque a blunder.
    1929 *More Biography*, 'George the Third'.

5   When their lordships asked Bacon
    How many bribes he had taken
    He had at least the grace
    To get very red in the face.
    1939 *Baseless Biography*, 'Bacon'.

Bentley, Nicholas Clerihew 1907–78

English artist and writer, son of Edmund Clerihew Bentley. He was best known for his cartoons, and illustrations to works such as T S Eliot's *Old Possum's Book of Practical Cats* (1939). He edited several editions of *Pick of Punch* (1955–60).

6   Henry Campbell-Bannerman is remembered chiefly as the man about whom all is forgotten.
    1974 *An Edwardian Album*.

Bentsen, Lloyd Millard, Jr 1921–2006

US politician, senator for Texas (1971–93). He was the Democratic nominee for Vice-President in the 1988 elections.

7   America has just passed through…an eight-year coma in which slogans were confused with solutions and rhetoric passed for reality.
    1988 Recalling the Reagan administration as he accepted the Democratic nomination for Vice-President, 21 Jul.

8   Senator, I served with Jack Kennedy. I knew Jack Kennedy. Jack Kennedy was a friend of mine. Senator, you're no Jack Kennedy.
    1988 On his opponent Dan Quayle's contention that his congressional experience equalled that of President Kennedy when he sought the presidency. Reported in the *New York Times*, 9 Oct.

Benuzzi, Felice 1910–88

Italian diplomat, lawyer and athlete. In Jan 1943 he and two friends escaped from a POW camp at Nanyuki to climb Mt Kenya with minimal equipment and provisions, before breaking back into the camp again and giving themselves up to the British commandant.

9 I emerged at last, stumbled a few steps in the mud and then I saw it: an ethereal mountain emerging from a tossing sea of clouds framed between two dark barracks—a massive, blue-black tooth of sheer rock inlaid with azure glaciers, austere yet floating fairy-like on the near horizon. It was the first 17,000-foot peak I had ever seen.
I stood gazing until the vision disappeared among the shifting cloud banks.
For hours afterwards I remained spell-bound.
I had definitely fallen in love.
1952 *No Picnic on Mount Kenya.*

10 To remember is far worse than to forget.
1952 On being a Prisoner of War. *No Picnic on Mount Kenya.*

Bercow, John (Simon) 1963–

English Conservative politician and Speaker of the House of Commons (2009–).

11 The Minister for Children is under no obligation to behave like a child. It is not required.
2011 In the House of Commons, 4 May.

Berdyaev, Nicholas 1874–1948

Russian philosopher. He originally supported the communist revolution but subsequently found that Marxism lacked a spiritual element and abandoned it. He founded the Academy of the Philosophy of Religion in Berlin (later transferred to Paris).

12 Man found his form and his identity under the action of religious principles and energies; the confusion in which he is losing them cannot be re-ordered by purely human efforts.
1923 'Konets Rennesansa' in *Sofiya* (translated as 'The End of the Renaissance' in the *Slavonic Review*, Jun/Dec 1925).

Berendt, John 1939–

US writer, journalist and editor. He was a Pulitzer Prize finalist for general non-fiction in 1995 for *Midnight in the Garden of Good and Evil* (1994).

13 In Atlanta, the first question is 'What's your business?' In Macon, it is 'Where do you go to church?' In Augusta they want your grandmother's maiden name. But in Savannah, the first question is 'What would you like to drink?'
1994 *Midnight in the Garden of Good and Evil.*

14 Loneliness is not being alone. It's loving others to no avail.
2005 *The City of Falling Angels.*

Berenson, Bernard 1865–1959

Lithuanian-born US art critic. An authority on the Renaissance, he could identify Italian masterworks by style and technique. His works include *Venetian Painters of the Renaissance* (1894) and *Rumor and Reflection* (1952).

15 I earn it by enjoying such authority and prestige that people will not buy expensive Italian pictures without my approval.
Comment on his income, addressed to the Internal Revenue Service. Quoted in *The Making of a Legend* (1987).

Beresford, Lord Charles 1846–1919

British politician.

16 Very sorry can't come. Lie follows by post.
Telegraph to the Prince of Wales, declining a dinner invitation. Quoted in Ralph Nevill *The World of Fashion 1837–1922* (1923), ch.5.

Berg, Alban 1885–1935

Austrian composer, best known for his opera *Wozzeck* (1925), his violin concerto (1935) and the *Lyric Suite* (1926) for string quartet.

17 Why is Schoenberg's Music so Hard to Understand?
1924 Title of essay.

Berger, Bennett Maurice 1926–2005

US sociologist, Professor at the University of California, San Diego (1973–91, then emeritus).

18 Oversimplification is now a common term of reproach in academic discussions; everyone is against oversimplification. But there is no parallel term nearly as frequently used to describe the opposite phenomenon, which surely occurs as often, if not more so.
1990 *Authors of their Own Lives* (edited by Berger), introduction.

Berger, Gerhard 1959–

Austrian Formula One racing driver.

19 There was something supernatural about him. An aura, as if he came from another planet and therefore had more insight, more brain cells, more power, more energy.
1997 On Ayrton Senna. In his autobiography, *Zielgerade.*

Berger, John Peter 1926–

English writer and art critic. His writing has been strongly influenced by Marxism, and he caused a sensation by denouncing the Booker Corporation in his acceptance speech when awarded the Booker Prize for his novel *G* in 1972.

20 The five senses within whose pentagon each man is alone.
1972 *G*, pt.3, ch.5.

21 If we could all live a thousand years…we would each, at least once during that period, be considered a genius.
1972 *G*, pt.3, ch.6.

22 The camera relieves us of the burden of memory.
1978 *New Statesman*, 17 Aug.

23 It is not usually possible in a poem or a story to make the relationship between particular and universal fully explicit. Those who try to do so end up writing parables.
1979 *Pig Earth*, 'Historical Afterward'.

24 Photography, because it stops the flow of life, is always flirting with death.
1983 In the *New Statesman*, 22/29 Dec.

25 All weddings are similar but every marriage is different. Death comes to everyone but one mourns alone.
1985 *The White Bird*, 'The Storyteller'.

26 Every city has a sex and age which have nothing to do with demography.
1987 In *The Guardian*, 27 Mar.

27 Every painted image of something is also about the absence of the real thing. All painting is about the presence of absence.
1988 In *New Statesman and Society*, 15 Jul.

Bergreen, Laurence 1950–
US journalist and biographer.

28 He was not fit for marriage, only for work. A major writer, he conceded, required major torment.
1984 Of James Agee. James Agee.

Berkeley, George 1685–1753
Irish idealist philosopher and Anglican Bishop of Cloyne (1734–52). His philosophical works, such as *A Treatise Concerning the Principles of Human Knowledge* (1710), argue that things in the material world only exist when perceived in the mind.

29 I am inclined to think that the far greater part, if not all, of those difficulties which have hitherto amused philosophers, and blocked up the way to knowledge, are entirely owing to ourselves—that we have first raised a dust and then complain we cannot see.
1710 A Treatise Concerning the Principles of Human Knowledge, introduction.

30 Some truths there are so near and obvious to the mind that a man need only open his eyes to see them. Such I take this important one to be, viz. that all the choir of heaven and furniture of the earth, in a word all those bodies which compose the mighty frame of the world, have not any subsistence without a mind—that their *being* is *to be perceived or known.*
1710 A Treatise Concerning The Principles Of Human Knowledge, pt.1, section 6.

31 Whatever is immediately perceived is an idea: and can any *idea* exist out of the mind?
1713 Three Dialogues between Hylas And Philonous, first dialogue.

32 The same principles which at first lead to scepticism, pursued to a certain point bring men back to common sense.
1734 Three Dialogues between Hylas and Philonous, dialogue 3.
▶ See Bacon 51:79.

33 Whose fault is it if poor Ireland still continues poor?
1737 The Querist, pt.3.

34 Truth is the cry of all, but the game of the few.
1744 Siris.

35 It is impossible that a man who is false to his friends and neighbours should be true to the public.
1750 Maxims Concerning Patriotism.

Berlin, Irving originally Israel Baline 1888–1989
Russian-born US composer, who began as a singing waiter. He wrote lyrics and music for over 900 songs including 'Alexander's Ragtime Band' and 'White Christmas'. The musical *Annie Get Your Gun* (1946) marked the peak of his career.

36 Come on and hear,
Come on and hear
Alexander's Ragtime Band
1911 'Alexander's Ragtime Band', opening lines, featured in the 1938 film of the same title.

37 A pretty girl is like a melody
That haunts you night and day.
1919 'A Pretty Girl is Like a Melody'.

38 The song is ended
But the melody lingers on.
1927 Song from Ziegfeld Follies.

39 I'm puttin' on my top hat
Tyin' up my white tie
Brushin' off my tails
1935 'Top Hat, White Tie and Tails', performed by Fred Astaire in Top Hat.

40 There may be trouble ahead
But while there's moonlight and music and love and romance
Let's face the music and dance
1936 'Let's Face the Music and Dance', in the film Follow the Fleet.

41 I'm dreaming of a white Christmas,
Just like the ones I used to know,
Where the tree-tops glisten
And children listen
To hear sleigh bells in the snow.
1942 'I'm Dreaming of a White Christmas', in the film Holiday Inn.

42 There's No Business Like Show Business.
1946 Title of song from the film Annie Get Your Gun.

43 Listen kid, take my advice—never hate a song that has sold half a million copies.
Comment to the young Cole Porter, attributed.

44 No, for prosperity.
Attributed, when asked whether he wrote his songs for posterity.

Berlin, Sir Isaiah 1907–97
Russian-born British philosopher and historian of ideas. He was Professor of Social and Political Theory at Oxford (1957–67) and President of Wolfson College (1966–75). He served as a diplomat to Russia and the US in World War II.

45 Liberty is liberty, not equality or fairness or justice or human happiness or a quiet conscience.
1958 Two Concepts of Liberty, note.

46 The desire not to be impinged upon, to be left to oneself, has been the mark of high civilisation both on the part of individuals and communities.
1959 Four Essays on Liberty.

47 Man cannot live without seeking to describe and explain the universe.
1962 In the Sunday Times.

48 No perfect solution is, not merely in practice, but in principle, possible in human affairs, and any determined attempt to produce it is likely to lead to suffering, disillusionment and failure.
1978 The Crooked Timber of Humanity, 'The Decline of Utopian Ideals in the West'.

49 Pluralism—that is, the conception that there are many different ends that men may seek and still be fully rational, fully men, capable of understanding each other and sympathising and deriving light from each other.
1978 The Crooked Timber of Humanity, 'The Pursuit of the Ideal'.

Berlusconi, Silvio 1936–
Italian businessman and politician who has been criticized for the conflict of interest between his business interests while serving as Prime Minister. A highly controversial figure, he was convicted of tax fraud in 2013 and expelled from the Senate.

50 I heard that the game was getting dangerous, and that it was being played in the two penalty areas, with midfield being left desolately empty… And we decided to fill that immense space.

On why he founded Forza Italia, a new political party. Quoted in Paul Ginsberg *Italy and Its Discontents* (2001).

51 Let's talk about football or women.
   2003 Comment at a formal lunch at an abortive summit meeting of EU leaders, Brussels, Dec.

52 By definition, as a Prime Minister I cannot be a liar.
   2006 Italian radio broadcast, 18 Jan.

53 I am the Jesus Christ of politics. I am a patient victim, I sacrifice myself for everyone.
   2008 Launching his electoral campaign, 2 May.

54 The Left doesn't even have good taste in women. Ours are more beautiful and, moreover, all have super degrees.
   2008 During electoral campaign.

55 In absolute terms, I am the most legally persecuted man of all times, in the whole history of mankind, worldwide.
   2009 In 'Silvio Berlusconi: I am inferior to no one in history', *The Guardian*, 10 Oct.

56 I wouldn't mind being resuscitated by you.
   2009 Remark to female doctor while inspecting earthquake damage at L'Aquila.

57 I will take questions from the guys but from the girls I want telephone numbers.
   2009 Address to youth rally in Rome.

58 When asked if they would like to have sex with me, 30 per cent of women said, 'Yes', while the other 70 per cent replied, 'What, again?'
   2011 His reply when quizzed about sex allegations made against him.

Bernanos, Georges 1888–1948

French novelist who explored the role of the devil and sin in modern society. A fervent opponent of Fascism, he lost favour with conservative Catholics after publishing polemical tracts against Franco.

59 *Le désir de la prière est déjà une prière.*
   The wish for prayer is already a prayer.
   1936 *Le Journal d'un curé de campagne*, ch.2 (translated by P Morris as *Diary of a Country Priest*, 1937).

60 *L'enfer, Madame, c'est de ne plus aimer.*
   Hell, Madam, is to no longer love.
   1936 *Journal d'un curé de campagne*, ch.2.

Bernard of Chartres d. c.1130

French divine and scholar. He taught logic and grammar at Chartres school from 1114, becoming Chancellor in 1119. In 1124 he began teaching at Paris. Only fragments of his three philosophical treatises survive.

61 *Nanos gigantium humeris insidentes.*
   Dwarfs standing on the shoulders of giants.
   c.1128 Of modern scholars in relation to their ancient predecessors. Quoted in John of Salisbury *Metalogicon* (1159), bk.3, ch.4.

St Bernard of Clairvaux 1090–1153

Theologian and reformer, first abbot (1115) of the newly-founded Cistercian monastery of Clairvaux, Champagne. Renowned for his studious, ascetic life and eloquence (he spoke in support of the Second Crusade, 1146), he founded over 70 monasteries.

62 *Omnes nimirum, ex quo monachi sumus, infirmos stomachos habemus, et tam necessarium Apostoli de utendo vino consilium merito non negligimus. Modico, tamen quod ille praemissit, nescio cur praetermisso.*
   Being monks, we all naturally have a weak stomach, and we therefore justly attend to the Apostle's advice to use wine. He adds, however, the words 'a little'; I can't think why I have omitted them.
   c.1124 *Apologia ad Guillelmum*, ch.9, section 21.

63 You have been called to hold a high position, but not a safe one; a sublime position, but not a secure one. How terrible, how very terrible is the place you hold!
   c.1145 Letter to Eugenius III shortly after he had became Pope, on the dangers of the growth of papal power. Collected in B S James (ed and trans) *The Letters of St Bernard of Clairvaux* (1953).

64 *Aiunt non vos esse papam, sed me.*
   They say it is not you who are pope, but me.
   c.1145 Of his own influence within the Cistercian order. Letter to Pope Eugenius III.

65 You ordered. I obeyed… I opened my mouth; I spoke; and at once the Crusaders have multiplied to infinity. Villages and towns are now deserted. You will scarcely find one man for every seven women. Everywhere you see widows whose husbands are still alive.
   1146 Letter to Pope Eugenius III describing the effects of preaching the Second Crusade. Collected in J P Migne (ed) *Patrologia Latina*, vol.182, letter no.247.

66 *Liberavi animam meam.*
   I have freed my soul.
   c.1147 Letter to Abbot Suger.

Bernard, Claude 1813–78

French scientist, considered the founder of contemporary experimental medicine on account of his work on the digestive process and on the vasomotor mechanism.

67 Science does not permit exceptions.
   1855–6 *Lessons of Experimental Pathology*.

68 In science, the best precept is to alter and exchange our ideas as fast as science moves ahead.
   1865 *An Introduction to the Study of Experimental Medicine*, vol.1, ch.1, section 3 (translated by H C Greene).

69 Science rejects the indeterminate.
   1865 *An Introduction to the Study of Experimental Medicine*, vol.1, ch.1, section 3 (translated by H C Greene).

70 True science teaches us to doubt and, in ignorance, to refrain.
   1865 *An Introduction to the Study of Experimental Medicine*, vol.1, ch.1, section 3 (translated by H C Greene).

71 Particular facts are never scientific; only generalization can establish science.
   1865 *An Introduction to the Study of Experimental Medicine*, vol.1, ch.1, section 3 (translated by H C Greene).

Bernardin de Saint-Pierre, Jacques-Henri 1737–1814

French novelist, friend of Rousseau and enemy of many others, naturalist and precursor of the Romantics. He travelled widely in Martinique, Russia and Madagascar.

72 *Les hommes ne veulent connaître que l'histoire des grands et des rois, qui ne sert à personne.*
   Men wish to hear no stories but those about the great and powerful, which are no use to anyone.
   1788 *Paul et Virginie*.

73 Après le rare bonheur de trouver une compagne qui nous soit bien assortie, l'état le moins malheureux de la vie est sans doute de vivre seul.
After the rare happiness of finding a companion with whom we are well matched, the least unpleasant state of life is without doubt to live alone.
1788 *Paul et Virginie.*

74 La solitude rétablit aussi bien les harmonies du corps que celles de l'âme.
Solitude restores the harmonies of the body no less than those of the soul.
1788 *Paul et Virginie.*

75 On se fait une idée précise de l'ordre, mais non pas du désordre. La beauté, la vertu, le bonheur, ont des proportions; la laideur, le vice, et le malheur, n'en ont point.
We can form a precise idea of order, but not of disorder. Beauty, virtue, happiness, all have their proportions; ugliness, vice and unhappiness have none.
1788 *Paul et Virginie.*

76 Le parfum de mille roses ne plaît qu'un instant; mais la douleur que cause une seule de leurs épines dure longtemps après la piqûre.
The perfume of a thousand roses pleases only for an instant; but the pain caused by a single one of their thorns lasts a long time after the prick.
1788 *Paul et Virginie.*

77 La mort, mon fils, est un bien pour tous les hommes; elle est la nuit de ce jour inquiet qu'on appelle la vie.
Death, my son, is a good for all; it is the night of this worrisome day that one calls life.
1788 *Paul et Virginie.*

78 Artistes, poètes, écrivains, si vous copiez toujours, on ne vous copiera jamais.
Artists, poets, writers, if you copy others all the time, no one will copy you.
1790 *Mémoires sur la ménagerie.*

Bernays, Edward 1891–1995

US pioneer public relations consultant, born in Vienna. His many books include *Crystallizing Public Opinion* (1923) and *The Engineering of Consent* (1955).

79 The engineering of consent.
1955 His definition of public relations, the field he was credited with founding. *The Engineering of Consent.*

Berners, Dame Juliana or Juliana Barnes fl.14c

English nun, traditionally Prioress of Sopwell convent, St Albans. She was the author of the *Treatyse perteynynge to Hawkynge, Huntynge, Fyshynge, and Coote Armiris* (1486).

80 A greyhound should be heeded lyke a snake,
And neckyd lyke a drake,
Backed lyke a bream,
Footed lyke a catte,
Taylled lyke a ratte.
1486 *Treatyse perteynynge to Hawkynge, Huntynge, Fyshynge, and Coote Armiris.*

81 The Salmon is the most stately fish that any man may angle to in fresh water.
1486 *Treatyse perteynyne to Hawkynge, Huntynge, Fyshynge, and Coote Armiris.*

Berners-Lee, Sir Tim(othy John) 1955–

English computer scientist. He is credited with the invention of the World Wide Web and, as director of the World Wide Web Consortium, has presided over its subsequent development.

82 The original idea of the web was that it should be a collaborative space where you can communicate through sharing information.
Attributed.

83 The web does not just connect machines, it connects people.
2008 Speech to the Knight Foundation, 14 Sept.

84 These issues have crept up on us. Our rights are being infringed more and more on every side, and the danger is that we get used to it. So, I want to use the 25th anniversary for us all to do that, to take the web back into our own hands and define the web we want for the next 25 years.
2014 In *The Guardian*, 11 Mar.

Bernhardt, Sarah stage-name of Sarah Henriette Rosine Bernard 1844–1923

French actress. Hailed internationally as one of the leading theatrical performers of her generation, she made her stage debut in 1862 and went on to play many of the great tragic roles in Shakespeare, Racine, Hugo, Rostand, Sardou and others.

85 J'adore ce cricket; c'est tellement Anglais.
I do so love cricket—it's so very English.
c.1905 On being taken to see a game of football in Manchester. Quoted in R Buckle *Nijinsky* (1971).

86 For the theatre one needs long arms; it is better to have them too long than too short. An *artiste* with short arms can never, never make a fine gesture.
1907 *Memories of My Life.*

Bernini, Gianlorenzo 1598–1680

Italian sculptor, painter and architect, one of the key figures of Italian Baroque art.

87 Sometimes, in order to imitate the original, it is necessary to put something that is not in the original into a portrait in marble.
Attributed remark made to Paul Fréart, in *Diary of Cavalier Bernini's Journey in France* (1665).

Bernstein, Leonard 1918–90

US conductor, pianist and composer. He achieved fame in 1943 as conductor with the New York Philharmonic. His compositions include three symphonies, a television opera and the musical *West Side Story* (1958).

88 It would be nice to hear someone accidentally whistle something of mine, somewhere, just once.
1960 *The Joy of Music.*

Berra, Yogi Lawrence Peter 1925–

US baseball player and coach. A star with the New York Yankees, he took part in a record 14 World Series (1946–63). He went on to manage the New York Yankees, the New York Mets and the Houston Astros.

89 If the people don't want to come out to the park, nobody's gonna stop them.
Quoted in Colin Jarman *The Guinness Dictionary of Sports Quotations* (1990).

90 He made too many wrong mistakes.
Quoted in Colin Jarman *The Guinness Dictionary of Sports Quotations* (1990).

91 You can observe a lot just by watching.
Quoted in Colin Jarman *The Guinness Dictionary of Sports Quotations* (1990).

92 You can't think and hit at the same time.
Quoted in Colin Jarman *The Guinness Dictionary of Sports Quotations* (1990).

93 It ain't over 'til it's over.
Attributed.

Berry, Chuck (Charles Edward Anderson) 1926–

US black rock 'n' roll singer, whose influential hits included 'Maybelline' (1955), 'School Days' (1957), and 'Johnny B Goode' (1958). In 1959 he was charged with transporting a minor over state lines for immoral purposes and jailed for two years (1962).

94 You know my temperature's risin',
The juke box's blowin' a fuse,
My heart's beatin' rhythm,
My soul keeps a singin' the blues—
Roll over Beethoven,
Tell Tchaikovsky the news.
1956 'Roll over Beethoven'.

Berryman, John *originally* John Allyn Smith 1914–72

US poet and novelist. His reputation rests on his complex, often obscure poetry, collected in *The Dispossessed* (1948), *Homage to Mistress Bradstreet* (1953) and the extended sequence of *Dream Songs* (1964).

95 We must travel in the direction of our fears.
1942 'A Point of Age'.

96 Headstones stagger under great draughts of time
after heads pass out, and their world must reel
speechless, blind in the end
about its chilling star
1953 'Homage to Mistress Bradstreet', stanza 55.

97 Life, friends, is boring. We must not say so.
1964 'Dream Song No.14'.

98 And moreover my mother taught me as a boy
(repeatedly) 'Ever to confess you're bored
means you have no
Inner Resources.' I conclude now I have no
inner resources, because I am heavy bored.
1964 'Dream Song No.14'.

99 I seldom go to films. They are too exciting
said the Honourable Possum.
1964 'Dream Song No.53'.

1 Bats have no bankers and they do not drink
and cannot be arrested and pay no tax
and, in general, bats have it made.
1964 'Dream Song No.63'.

2 A lone letter from a young man: that is fame.
1968 'Dream Song No.342'.

3 My girls suffered during this month or so,
so did my seminars & lectures &
my poetry even. To be a *critic*, ah,
how deeper and more scientific.
1971 'Olympus'.

4 The artist is extremely lucky who is presented with the worst possible ordeal which will not actually kill him.
1972 Interview in *The Paris Review*, winter issue.

Berton, Pierre 1920–2004

Canadian writer, journalist and broadcaster. His many works include *The Mysterious North* (1956) and *Why We Act Like Canadians* (1982).

5 A Canadian is somebody who knows how to make love in a canoe.
1973 Interviewed by Dick Brown in *The Canadian*, 22 Dec.

Best, George 1946–2005

Northern Irish footballer who was the leading scorer for Manchester United in the Football League First Division in 1967–8, and in 1968 won a European Cup medal and the title of European Footballer of the Year.

6 Alcoholics Anonymous might have worked for me if I had been anonymous, but I was not. People kept asking me for my autograph.
2001 In the *Observer*, 30 Dec.

7 I *will* respect this liver. After all, it's not mine.
Referring to his liver transplant. In *Scoring at Half Time* (2003).

8 I told the assembled media that I was not the White Pele and that Pele was in fact the Black George Best.
On his arrival in the United States in 1975. In *Blessed* (2003).

9 Don't die like I did.
2005 Last words.

Bethell, (Mary) Ursula 1874–1945

New Zealand poet, born in England. Her works, celebrating detail in nature, include *From a Garden in the Antipodes* (1929) and *Day and Night: Poems 1924–1935* (1939).

10 But beside it I have planted a green Bay-tree,
—A sweet Bay, an Olive, and a Turkey Fig,
—A Fig, an Olive, and a Bay.
1929 *From a Garden in the Antipodes*, 'Detail'.

Bethmann Hollweg, Theobald von 1856–1921

German statesman, Imperial Chancellor (1909–17), who played an important part in events leading to war in 1914. Anxious for a negotiated peace, he was forced from office in 1917.

11 Just for a word 'neutrality'—a word which in wartime has so often been disregarded—just for a scrap of paper Great Britain is going to make war on a kindred nation who desires nothing better than to be friends with her.
1914 On Britain's reaction to the German invasion of neutral Belgium, 4 Aug. Quoted in *British Documents on the Origins of the War 1898–1914* (1926), vol.11.

12 If the iron dice roll, may God help us.
1914 Speech in the Reichstag.

Bethune, Norman 1890–1939

Canadian physician and revolutionary.

13 The function of the artist is to disturb. His duty is to arouse the sleeper, to shake the complacent pillars of the world. He reminds the world of its dark ancestry, and shows the world its present, and points the way to its

Betjeman

new birth. He is at once the product and the preceptor of his time.
1937 Letter from Madrid, 5 May. Quoted in Ted Allen and Sydney Gordon *The Scalpel, The Sword* (1952).

Betjeman, Sir John 1906–84

English poet, writer and broadcaster, whose nostalgic light verse, often masking an underlying melancholy, achieved great popularity. Appointed Poet Laureate in 1972, he was also a defender of traditional architecture and a perceptive social critic.

14 Oh! Chintzy, chintzy cheeriness,
Half dead and half alive.
1930 'Death in Leamington', first published in the *London Mercury*.

15 Sing on, with hymns uproarious,
Ye humble and aloof,
Look up! and oh, how glorious
He has restored the roof!
1931 *Mount Zion*, 'Hymn'.

16 Broad of Church and broad of Mind,
Broad before and broad behind,
A keen ecclesiologist,
A rather dirty Wykehamist.
1931 *Mount Zion*, 'The Wykehamist'.

17 Ghastly Good Taste, or a depressing story of the rise and fall of English architecture.
1933 Title and sub-title of book.

18 He sipped at the weak hock and seltzer
As he gazed at the London skies
Through the Nottingham lace of the curtains
Or was it his bees-winged eyes?
1937 *Continual Dew*, 'The Arrest of Oscar Wilde at The Cadogan Hotel'.

19 Spirits of well-shot woodcock, partridge, snipe,
Flutter and bear him up the Norfolk sky:
In that red house in a red mahogany book-case
The stamp collection waits with mounts long dry.
1937 *Continual Dew*, 'Death of King George V'.

20 Come, friendly bombs, and fall on Slough
It isn't fit for humans now
There isn't grass to graze a cow
Swarm over, Death!
1937 *Continual Dew*, 'Slough'.

21 Pam, I adore you, Pam, you great mountainous sports girl,
Whizzing them over the net, full of the strength of five:
That old Malvernian brother, you zephyr and khaki shorts girl,
Although he's playing for Woking,
Can't stand up to your wonderful backhand drive.
1940 *Old Lights for New Chancels*, 'Pot Pourri from a Surrey Garden'.

22 Think of what our Nation stands for,
Books from Boots' and country lanes,
Free speech, free passes, class distinction,
Democracy and proper drains.
Lord, put beneath Thy special care
One-eighty-nine Cadogan Square.
1940 *Old Lights for New Chancels*, 'In Westminster Abbey'.

23 The test of an abstract picture, for me, is not my first reaction to it, but how long I can stand it hanging on the wall of a room where I am living.
1944 *John Piper*.

24 Miss J. Hunter Dunn, Miss J. Hunter Dunn,
Furnish'd and burnish'd by Aldershot sun,
What strenuous singles we played after tea,
We in the tournament—you against me!
1945 *New Bats in Old Belfries*, 'A Subaltern's Love-Song'.

25 Miss Joan Hunter Dunn, Miss Joan Hunter Dunn,
I can hear from the car-park the dance has begun.
Oh! full Surrey twilight! importunate band!
Oh! strongly adorable tennis-girl's hand!
1945 *New Bats in Old Belfries*, 'A Subaltern's Love-Song'.

26 For a full spring-tide of blossom seethed and departed hence,
Leaving land-locked pools of jonquils by sunny garden fence.
1945 *New Bats in Old Belfries*, 'May-Day Song for North Oxford'.

27 And low the mists of evening lie
And lightly skims the midge.
1945 *New Bats in Old Belfries*, 'Henley-on-Thames'.

28 Rumbling under blackened girders, Midland, bound for Cricklewood,
Puffed its sulphur to the sunset where that Land of laundries stood.
1945 *New Bats in Old Belfries*, 'Parliament Hill Fields'.

29 Up the hill where stucco houses in Virginia creeper drown—
And my childish wave of pity, seeing children carrying down
Sheaves of drooping dandelions to the courts of Kentish Town.
1945 *New Bats in Old Belfries*, 'Parliament Hill Fields'.

30 Bournemouth is one of the few English towns one can safely call 'her'.
1949 Radio talk, later collected in *First and Last Loves* (1952), 'Bournemouth'.

31 St Endellion! St Endellion! The name is like a ring of bells.
1950 Radio talk, later collected in *First and Last Loves* (1952), 'St Endellion'.

32 Imagine the position of the modern architect. Picture the young fellow to be put into a 'profession' because trade is considered beneath him (another antiquarian prejudice). The young fellow hasn't exactly got a legal mind, like father; he's not much good at essays, so he can't write; he faints at the sight of blood so can't be a doctor. What is there for him to do? Architecture of course.
1952 *First and Last Loves*.

33 Oh prams on concrete balconies, what will your children see?
1952 *First and Last Loves*.

34 History must not be written with bias, and both sides must be given, even if there is only one side.
1952 *First and Last Loves*.

35 And girls in slacks remember Dad,
And oafish louts remember Mum.
1954 *A Few Late Chrysanthemums*, 'Christmas'.

36 And is it true? And is it true,
This most tremendous tale of all,
Seen in a stained-glass window's hue,
A Baby in an ox's stall?
The Maker of the stars and sea
Become a Child on earth for me?
1954 *A Few Late Chrysanthemums*, 'Christmas'.

37 Gaily into Ruislip Gardens
Runs the red electric train
With a thousand Ta's and Pardon's
Daintily alights Elaine.
1954 *A Few Late Chrysanthemums*, 'Middlesex'.

38 Then Harrow-on-the-Hill's a rocky island
And Harrow churchyard full of sailor's graves,
And the constant click and kissing of the trolley busses hissing
Is the level to the Wealdstone turned to waves.
1954 *A Few Late Chrysanthemums*, 'Harrow-on-the-Hill'.

39 But I'm dying now and done for,
What on earth was all the fun for?
I am ill and old and terrified and tight.
1954 *A Few Late Chrysanthemums*, 'Sun and Fun—Song of a Night-club Proprietress'.

40 Does Mum, the Persil-user, still believe
That there's no Devil and that youth is bliss?
As certain as the sun behind the Downs
And quite as plain to see, the Devil walks.
1954 *A Few Late Chrysanthemums*, 'Original Sin on the Sussex Coast'.

41 Phone for the fish knives, Norman
As Cook is a little unnerved;
You kiddies have crumpled the serviettes
And I must have things daintily served.
1954 *A Few Late Chrysanthemums*, 'How To Get On In Society'.

42 In the licorice fields at Pontefract
My love and I did meet
And many a burdened licorice bush
Was blooming round our feet;
Red hair she had and golden skin,
Her sulky lips were shaped for sin,
Her sturdy legs were flannel-slack'd,
The strongest legs in Pontefract.
1954 *A Few Late Chrysanthemums*, 'The Licorice Fields at Pontefract'.

43 In the Garden City Café with its murals on the wall
Before a talk on 'Sex and Civics' I meditated on the Fall.
1954 *A Few Late Chrysanthemums*, 'Huxley Hall'.

44 It's awf'lly bad luck on Diana
Her ponies have swallowed their bits;
She fished down their throats with a spanner
And frightened them all into fits.
1954 *A Few Late Chrysanthemums*, 'Hunter Trails'.

45 Oh wasn't it naughty of Smudges?
Oh, Mummy, I'm sick with disgust.
She threw me in front of the Judges
And my silly old collarbone's bust.
1954 *A Few Late Chrysanthemums*, 'Hunter Trails'.

46 I heard the church bells hollowing out the sky
Deep beyond deep, like never-ending stars.
1960 *Summoned By Bells*, ch.1.

47 Childhood is measured out by sounds and smells
And sights, before the dark of reason grows.
1960 *Summoned By Bells*, ch.4.

48 The dread of beatings! Dread of being late!
And, greatest dread of all, the dread of games!
1960 *Summoned by Bells*, ch.7.

Beuys, Joseph 1921–86

German avant-garde artist. Professor of Sculpture at Düsseldorf Academy (1961–71), his works were typically 'assemblages' of rubbish, deliberately anti-formal. He co-founded the German Green Party.

49 A total work of art is only possible in the context of the whole of society. Everyone will be a necessary co-creator of a social architecture, and, so long as anyone cannot participate, the ideal form of democracy has not been reached. Whether people are artists, assemblers of machines or nurses, it is a matter of participating in the whole.
1972 From an interview with G Jappe (translated by J Wheelwright), in *Studio International*, vol.184, no.950, Dec. Quoted in C Harrison and P Wood (eds) *Art in Theory 1900–1990* (1992).

Bevan, Aneurin 1897–1960

Welsh Labour politician, a miner who took a leading part in the 1926 General Strike, and a brilliant, irreverent orator. He entered politics in 1929 and joined the Labour Party (1931). As Minister of Health (1945–51), he introduced the National Health Service (1948).

50 The worst thing I can say about democracy is that it has tolerated the right honourable gentleman [Neville Chamberlain] for four and a half years.
1929 House of Commons, 23 Jul.

51 We have been the dreamers. We have been the sufferers. Now we are the builders. We want the complete political extinction of the Tory Party—and 25 years of Labour Government, for we cannot do in five years what requires to be done.
1945 Labour Party conference, Blackpool, 18 May.

52 This island is made mainly of coal and surrounded by fish. Only an organizing genius could produce a shortage of coal and a shortage of fish at the same time.
1945 Speech at Blackpool. Reported in the *Daily Herald*, 25 May.

53 No amount of cajolery, and no attempts at ethical or social seduction, can eradicate from my heart a deep and burning hatred for the Tory Party that inflicted those experiences on me. So far as I am concerned, they are lower than vermin.
1948 Speech on the inter-war depression, made at the inauguration of the National Health Service, 5 Jul.

54 In Place of Fear.
1952 Title of his book about disarmament.

55 We know what happens to people who stay in the middle of the road. They get run over.
1953 In the *Observer*, Dec.

56 A man suffering from petrified adolescence.
Of Winston Churchill. Quoted in Vincent Brome *Aneurin Bevan* (1953).

57 I am not going to spend any time whatsoever attacking the Foreign Secretary. Quite honestly, I am beginning to feel extremely sorry for him. If we complain about the tune, there is no reason to attack the monkey when the organ grinder is present.
1957 Expressing his wish to address Prime Minister Harold Macmillan rather than Selwyn Lloyd on the Suez crisis in the House of Commons, May.

58 If you carry this resolution, you will send a Foreign Secretary—whoever he may be—naked into the conference chamber. You call that statesmanship. I call it an emotional spasm.
1957 Labour Party conference speech against unilateral disarmament, Oct.

59 I read the newspapers avidly. It is my one form of continuous fiction.
1960 In *The Times*, 29 Mar.

60 Politics is a blood sport.
Quoted in Jennie Lee *My Life with Nye* (1980).

Beveridge, William Henry Beveridge, 1st Baron
1879–1963

British economist, administrator and social reformer, Director of the London School of Economics (1919–37). His *Report on Social Insurance and Allied Services* (The Beveridge Report, 1942) helped to create the Welfare State.

61 The trouble in modern democracy is that men do not approach to leadership until they have lost the desire to lead anyone.
1934 In the *Observer*, 15 Apr.

62 The object of government in peace and in war is not the glory of rulers or of races, but the happiness of the common man.
1942 *Social Insurance and Allied Services*, pt.7.

63 The most urgent tasks in Britain, once war is over, are, on the one hand, the making of a common attack on the giant evils of Want, Disease, Ignorance and Squalor, and on the other hand, the re-equipping of British industry.
1944 *Full Employment in a Free Society*.

64 The state is or can be master of money, but in a free society it is master of very little else.
1948 *Voluntary Action*, ch.12.

Bevin, Ernest 1881–1951

English Labour politician. He formed the National Transport and General Workers' Union, becoming its General Secretary (1921–40), then entered politics. He was appointed Minister of Labour and National Service in the coalition, and later Foreign Secretary (1945–51).

65 The most conservative man in the world is the British trade unionist, when you want to change him.
1927 Speech to Trade Union Congress, 8 Sep.

66 If you open that Pandora's box, you never know what Trojan 'orses will appear.
1948 Expressing doubts about the value of the newly formed Council of Europe. Recalled by his secretary Sir Roderick Barclay in Michael Charlton *The Price of Victory* (1983).

67 Well you know, Chris, we've got to give them something and I think we'll give them this talking shop in Strasbourg—the Council of Europe.
1948 Comment to Christopher Mayhew. Quoted in Michael Charlton *The Price of Victory* (1983).

68 A turn-up in a million.
On himself. Quoted in his entry by Baron Francis-Williams in the *Dictionary of National Biography* (1951–60).

69 Anything you make a mistake about, I will get you out of, and anything you do well I will take the credit for.
Attributed, to a subordinate. Quoted in A J P Taylor *From the Boer War to the Cold War: Essays on Twentieth-Century Europe* (1995).

Bezos, Jeff(rey Preston) 1964–

US entrepreneur who is best known as the founder and head of the e-commerce site Amazon, the biggest retailer on the Internet. In 2013 he added *The Washington Post* newspaper to his commercial holdings.

70 In some ways the web is the most important book in the world.
2008 Referring to the newly released Kindle e-reader.

71 We humans co-evolve with our tools. We change the tools, and the tools change us.
2009 *Newsweek*, 20 Dec.

72 The physical book really has had a 500-year run. It's probably the most successful technology ever. It's hard to come up with things that have had a longer run. If Gutenberg were alive today, he would recognize the physical book and know how to operate it immediately. Given how much change there has been everywhere else, what's remarkable is how stable the book has been for so long. But no technology, not even one as elegant as the book, lasts forever.
2009 *Newsweek*, 20 Dec.

73 We start with the customer and we work backward. We learn whatever skills we need to service the customer. We build whatever technology we need to service the customer.
2009 *Newsweek*, 20 Dec.

74 The number one rule has to be: Don't be boring.
2013 Addressing staff at *The Washington Post*, which he had just bought.

75 Amazon is not happening to book selling, the future is happening to book selling.
2013 On *60 Minutes*, CBS, 1 Dec.

Bhagavad Gita

A sacred Hindu text, part of the Mahabharata. All translations are from J Mascaro (1978).

76 As the Spirit of our mortal body wanders on in childhood and youth and old age, the Spirit wanders on to a new body: of this the sage has no doubts.
Ch.2, v.13.

77 As a man leaves an old garment and puts on one that is new, the spirit leaves his mortal body and puts on one that is new.
Ch.2, v.22.

78 Leave all things behind, and come unto me for thy salvation. I will make thee free from the bondage of sins. Fear no more.
Ch.18, v.66.

Bhutto, Bilawal Zardari 1988–

Pakistani politician. He is the grandson of former Prime Minister Zulfikar Ali Bhutto and son of President Asif Ali Zardari and Prime Minister Benazir Bhutto, later assassinated. He entered politics himself in 2007 as chairman of the Pakistan People's Party.

79 My mother always said democracy is the best revenge.
2007 Speech on accepting leadership of his mother's party, 30 Dec.

Bible (Old Testament)

All quotations are taken from the King James, or Authorized, translation of the Bible (1611).

80 In the beginning God created the heaven and the earth. And the earth was without form, and void; and darkness was upon the face of the deep. And the spirit of God moved upon the face of the waters.
Genesis 1:1–2.

81 And God said, Let there be light: and there was light.
Genesis 1:3.

82 And God called the light Day and the darkness he called Night. And the evening and morning were the first day.
Genesis 1:5.

83 And God saw that it was good.
Genesis 1:10.

84 And God said, Let us create man in our image, after our likeness: and let them have dominion over the fish of the sea, and over the fowl of the air, and over the cattle, and over all the earth, and over every creeping thing that creepeth upon the earth. So God created man in his own image, in the image of God created he him; male and female created he them. And God blessed them, and God said unto them, Be fruitful and multiply, and replenish the earth, and subdue it: and have dominion over the fish of the sea, and over the fowl of the air, and over every living thing that moveth upon the earth.
Genesis 1:26–8.

85 And on the seventh day God ended his work which he had made, and he rested on the seventh day from all his work which he had made. And God blessed the seventh day and sanctified it: because that in it he had rested from all his work which God created and made.
Genesis 2:2–3.

86 And the LORD God formed man out of the dust of the ground, and breathed into his nostrils the breath of life; and man became a living soul.
Genesis 2:7.

87 And the LORD God planted a garden eastwards in Eden; and there he put the man whom he had formed. And out of the ground made the LORD God to grow every tree that is pleasant for the sight, and good for food; the tree of life also in the midst of the garden, and the tree of knowledge of good and evil.
Genesis 2:8–9.

88 And the LORD God took the man and put him into the garden of Eden to dress it and to keep it. And the LORD God commanded the man, saying, Of every tree of the garden thou mayest freely eat: But of the tree of the knowledge of good and evil, thou shalt not eat of it: for in the day that thou eatest thereof thou shalt surely die.
Genesis 2:15–17.

89 And the LORD God said, It is not good that the man should be alone; I will make him an help meet for him.
Genesis 2:18.

90 And the LORD God caused a deep sleep to fall on Adam, and he slept: and he took one of his ribs, and closed up the flesh instead thereof; And the rib, which the LORD God had taken from man, made he a woman, and brought her unto the man. And Adam said, This is now bone of my bones, and flesh of my flesh: she shall be called Woman, because she was taken out of Man. Therefore shall a man leave his father and his mother, and shall cleave unto his wife: and they shall be one flesh.
Genesis 2:21–4.

91 Now the serpent was more subtil than any beast of the field which the LORD God had made.
Genesis 3:1.

92 And the serpent said unto the woman, Ye shall not surely die: For God doth know that in the day ye eat thereof, then your eyes shall be opened, and ye shall be as gods, knowing good and evil.
Genesis 3:4–5.

93 And when the woman saw that the tree was good for food, and that it was pleasant to the eyes, and a tree to be desired to make one wise took of the fruit thereof, and did eat, and gave also to her husband with her; and he did eat. And the eyes of them both were opened, and they knew that they were naked; and they sewed fig leaves together, and made themselves aprons. And they heard the voice of the LORD God walking in the garden in the cool of the day: and Adam and his wife hid themselves from the presence of the LORD God amongst the trees of the garden.
Genesis 3:6–8. In the Geneva Bible of 1560, the word 'aprons' was rendered 'breeches', and the version was therefore known as the Breeches Bible.

94 And he said, I heard thy voice in the garden, and I was afraid, because I was naked; and I hid myself. And he said, Who told thee that thou wast naked? Hast thou eaten of the tree, whereof I commanded thee that thou shouldst not eat?
Genesis 3:10–11.

95 And the man said, The woman whom thou gavest to be with me, she gave me of the tree, and I did eat. And the LORD God said unto the woman, What is this that thou hast done? And the woman said, The serpent beguiled me, and I did eat.
Genesis 3:12–13.

96 And the LORD God said unto the serpent, Because thou hast done this, thou art cursed above all cattle, and above every beast of the field; upon thy belly thou shalt go, and dust shalt thou eat all the days of thy life: And I will put enmity between thy seed and her seed; it shall bruise thy head, and thou shalt bruise his heel.
Genesis 3:14–15.

97 Unto the woman he said, I will greatly multiply thy sorrow and conception; in sorrow thou shalt bring forth children; and thy desire shall be for thy husband, and he shall rule over thee.
Genesis 3:16.

98 And unto Adam he said, Because thou hast hearkened unto the voice of thy wife, and hast eaten of the tree, of which I commanded thee, saying, Thou shalt not eat of it: cursed is the ground for thy sake; in sorrow shalt thou eat of it all the days of thy life.
Genesis 3:17.

99 In the sweat of thy face shalt thou eat bread, till thou return to the ground; for out of it wast thou taken: for dust thou art, and unto dust shalt return.
Genesis 3:19.

1 And the LORD God said, Behold, the man is become as one of us, to know good and evil: and now, lest he put forth his hand, and take also of the tree of life, and eat, and live for ever: Therefore the LORD God sent him forth from the garden of Eden, to till the ground from whence he was taken. So he drove out the man; and he placed at the east of the garden of Eden Cherubims, and a flaming sword which turned every way, to keep the tree of life.
Genesis 3:21–4.

2 And Adam knew Eve his wife; and she conceived and bare Cain, and said, I have gotten a man from the LORD.
Genesis 4:1.

3 And the LORD said unto Cain, Where is Abel thy brother? And he said, I know not: Am I my brother's keeper? And he said, What hast thou done? the voice of thy brother's blood crieth unto me from the ground.
Genesis 4:9.

4 My punishment is greater than I can bear.
Cain. Genesis 4:10.

5 And the LORD said unto him, Therefore whoever slayeth Cain, vengeance shall be taken on him sevenfold. And the LORD set a mark upon Cain lest any finding him should kill him.
Genesis 4:15.

6 And Cain went out from the presence of the LORD, and dwelt in the land of Nod, on the east of Eden.
Genesis 4:16.

7 And all the days of Methuselah were nine hundred sixty and nine years; and he died.
Genesis 5:27.

8 They went in two and two unto Noah into the ark, the male and the female, as God had commanded Noah.
Genesis 7:9.

9 But the dove found no rest for the sole of her foot.
Genesis 8:9.

10 And the dove came to him in the evening; and, lo, in her mouth was an olive leaf pluckt off: so Noah knew that the waters were abated from off the earth.
Genesis 8:11.

11 I will not again curse the ground any more for man's sake; for the imagination of man is evil from his youth; neither will I again smite any more every thing living, as I have done. While the earth remaineth, seedtime and harvest, and cold and heat, and summer and winter, and day and night shall not cease.
Genesis 8:21–2.

12 At the hand of every man's brother will I require the life of man. Whoso sheddeth man's blood, by man shall his blood be shed: for in the image of God made he man.
Genesis 9:5–6.

13 I do set my bow in the cloud, and it shall be for a token of a covenant between me and the earth.
Genesis 9:13.

14 He was a mighty hunter before the LORD: wherefore it is said, Even as Nimrod the mighty hunter before the LORD.
Genesis 10:9.

15 Therefore is the name of it called Babel; because the LORD did there confound the language of all the earth: and from thence did the LORD scatter them abroad upon the face of all the earth.
Genesis 11:9.

16 Now the LORD had said unto Abram, Get thee out of thy country, and from thy kindred, and from thy father's house, unto a land that I will shew thee: And I will make of thee a great nation, and I will bless thee, and make thy name great; and thou shalt be a blessing: And I will bless them that bless thee, and curse him that curseth thee: and in thee shall all families of the earth be blessed.
Genesis 12:1–3.

17 But the men of Sodom were wicked and sinners before the LORD exceedingly.
Genesis 13:13.

18 Thou shalt be buried in a good old age.
Genesis 15:15.

19 Behold, thou art with child, and shalt bear a son, and shalt call his name Ishmael; because the LORD hath heard thy affliction. And he will be a wild man; his hand will be against every man, and every man's hand against him; and he shall dwell in the presence of all his brethren.
Genesis 16:11–12.

20 And when Abram was ninety years old and nine, the LORD appeared to Abram, and said unto him, I am the Almighty God: walk before me, and be thou perfect.
Genesis 17:1.

21 And I will establish my covenant between me and thee and thy seed after thee in their generations for an everlasting covenant, to be a God unto thee, and to thy seed after thee. And I will give unto thee, and to thy seed after thee, the land wherein thou art a stranger, all the land of Canaan, for an everlasting possession; and I will be their God… Every man child among you shall be circumcised.
Genesis 17:7–10.

22 Shall not the Judge of all the earth do right.
Genesis 18:25.

23 Then the LORD rained upon Sodom and upon Gomorrah brimstone and fire from the LORD out of heaven.
Genesis 19:24.

24 But his wife looked back from behind him, and she became a pillar of salt.
Genesis 19:26.

25 Take now thy son, thine only son Isaac, whom thou lovest.
Genesis 22:2.

26 My son, God will provide himself a lamb for a burnt offering.
Genesis 22:8.

27 Esau sells his birthright for a mess of pottage.
1560 Chapter heading for Genesis 25 (in the Geneva Bible).

28 And the boys grew: and Esau was a cunning hunter, a man of the field; and Jacob was a plain man, dwelling in tents.
Genesis 25:27.

29 Esau said, Behold, I am at the point to die: and what profit shall this birthright do to me? And Jacob said, Swear to me this day: and he sware unto him: and he sold his birthright unto Jacob. Then Jacob gave Esau bread and pottage of lentiles; and he did eat and drink, and rose up, and went his way: thus Esau despised his birthright.
Genesis 25:32–4.

30 And Jacob said to Rebekah his mother, Behold, Esau my brother is a hairy man, and I am a smooth man.
Genesis 27:11.

31 Thy brother came with subtilty, and hath taken away thy blessing.
Genesis 27:35.

32 And he dreamed and behold a ladder set up on the earth, and the top of it reached to heaven: and behold the angels of God ascending and descending on it.
Genesis 28:12.

33 And Jacob awaked out of his sleep, and he said, Surely the LORD is in this place; and I knew it not.
Genesis 28:16.

34 And Jacob served seven years for Rachel; and they seemed unto him but a few days, for the love he had to her.
Genesis 29:20.

35 The LORD watch between me and thee, when we are absent one from another.
Genesis 31:49.

36 I will not let thee go, except thou bless me.
Genesis 32:26.

37 Now Israel loved Joseph more than all his children, because he was the son of his old age: and he made him a coat of many colours.
Genesis 37:3.

38 And they said to one another, Behold, this dreamer cometh.
Genesis 37:19.

39 And all his sons and all his daughters rose up to comfort him; but he refused to be comforted; and he said, For I will go down into the grave unto my son mourning. Thus his father wept for him.
Genesis 37:35.

40 And Onan knew that the seed should not be his; and it came to pass, when he went in unto his brother's wife, that he spilled it on the ground, lest that he should give seed to his brother.
Genesis 38:9.

41 And she caught him by his garment, saying, Lie with me: and he left his garment in her hand, and fled, and got him out.
Genesis 39:12.

42 And the seven thin ears devoured the seven rank and full ears. And Pharaoh awoke, and, behold, it was a dream.
Genesis 41:7.

43 Ye are spies; to see the nakedness of the land ye are come.
Genesis 42:9.

44 And he said, My son shall not go down with you; for his brother is dead, and he is left alone: if mischief befall him by the way in the which ye go, then shall ye bring down my gray hairs with sorrow to the grave.
Genesis 42:38.

45 And the famine was sore in the land.
Genesis 43:1.

46 I will give you the good of the land of Egypt, and ye shall eat the fat of the land.
Genesis 45:18.

47 So he sent his brethren away, and they departed: and he said unto them, See that ye fall not out by the way.
Genesis 45:24.

48 And Jacob said unto Pharaoh, The days of the years of my pilgrimage are an hundred and thirty years: few and evil have the days of the years of my life been, and have not attained unto the days of the years of the life of my fathers in the days of their pilgrimage.
Genesis 47:9.

49 Unstable as water, thou shalt not excel.
Genesis 49:4.

50 And he said, Who made thee a prince and a judge over us? intendest thou to kill me, as thou killedst the Egyptian?
Exodus 2:14.

51 And the angel of the LORD appeared unto him in a flame of fire out of the midst of a bush: and he looked, and, behold, the bush burned with fire, and the bush was not consumed.
Exodus 3:2.

52 And he said, Draw not nigh hither: put off thy shoes from off thy feet, for the place whereon thou standest is holy ground.
Exodus 3:5.

53 And Moses hid his face; for he was afraid to look upon God.
Exodus 3:6.

54 And I am come down to deliver them out of the hand of the Egyptians, and to bring them up out of that land unto a good land and a large, unto a land flowing with milk and honey.
Exodus 3:8.

55 And God said unto Moses, I AM THAT I AM.
Exodus 3:14.

56 But I am slow of speech, and of a slow tongue.
Exodus 4:10.

57 Let my people go.
Exodus 7:16.

58 Your lamb shall be without blemish, a male of the first year.
Exodus 12:5.

59 And thus shall ye eat it; with your loins girded, your shoes on your feet, and your staff in your hand; and ye shall eat it in haste: it is the LORD's passover. For I will pass through the land of Egypt this night, and will smite all the firstborn in the land of Egypt, both man and beast; and against all the gods of Egypt I will execute judgment: I am the LORD.
Exodus 12:11–12.

60 And Pharaoh rose up in the night, he and all his servants, and all the Egyptians; and there was a great cry in Egypt; for there was not a house where there was not one dead.
Exodus 12:30.

61 And the Egyptians were urgent upon the people, that they might send them out of the land in haste; for they said, We be all dead men.
Exodus 12:33.

62 And the LORD went before them by day in a pillar of a cloud, to lead them the way; and by night in a pillar of fire, to give them light; to go by day and night.
Exodus 13:21.

63 The LORD is a man of war: the LORD is his name.
Exodus 15:3.

64 And the children of Israel said unto them, Would to God we had died by the hand of the LORD in the land of Egypt, when we sat by the flesh pots, and when we did eat bread to the full; for ye have brought us forth to this wilderness, to kill this whole assembly with hunger.
Exodus 16:3.

Bible Exodus

65 And it came to pass, when Moses held up his hand, that Israel prevailed: and when he let down his hand, Amalek prevailed.
Exodus 17:11.

66 And God spake all these words, saying, I am the LORD thy God, which have brought thee out of the land of Egypt, out of the house of bondage.
Thou shalt have no other gods before me.
Thou shalt not make unto thee any graven image, or any likeness of any thing that is in heaven above, or that is in the earth beneath, or that is in the water under the earth:
Thou shalt not bow down thyself to them, nor serve them: for I the LORD thy God am a jealous God, visiting the iniquity of the fathers upon the children unto the third and fourth generation of them that hate me;
And shewing mercy unto thousands of them that love me, and keep my commandments.
Thou shalt not take the name of the LORD thy God in vain; for the LORD will not hold him guiltless that taketh his name in vain.
Remember the sabbath day, to keep it holy. Six days thou shalt labour and do all thy work: But the seventh day is the sabbath of the LORD thy God: in it thou shalt not do any work, thou, nor thy son, nor thy daughter, thy manservant, nor thy maidservant, nor thy cattle, nor thy stranger that is within thy gates:
For in six days the LORD made heaven and earth, the sea, and all that in them is, and rested the seventh day: wherefore the LORD blessed the sabbath day, and hallowed it.
Honour thy father and thy mother: that thy days may be long upon the land which the LORD thy God giveth thee.
Thou shalt not kill.
Thou shalt not commit adultery.
Thou shalt not steal.
Thou shalt not bear false witness against thy neighbour.
Thou shalt not covet thy neighbour's house, thou shalt not covet thy neighbour's wife, nor his manservant, nor his maidservant, nor his ox, nor his ass, nor any thing that is thy neighbour's.
Exodus 20:1–17.

67 And if any mischief follow, then thou shalt give life for life, Eye for eye, tooth for tooth, hand for hand, foot for foot. Burning for burning, wound for wound, stripe for stripe.
Exodus 21:23–4.

68 And thou shalt put in the breastplate of judgment the Urim and the Thummim; and thy shall be upon Aaron's heart, when he goeth in before the LORD: and Aaron shall bear the judgment of the children of Israel upon his heart before the LORD continually.
Exodus 28:30.

69 And he received them at their hand, and fashioned it with a graving tool, after he had made it a molten calf: and they said, These be thy gods, O Israel, which brought thee up out of the land of Egypt.
Exodus 32:4.

70 And the LORD said unto Moses, I have seen this people, and, behold, it is a stiffnecked people.
Exodus 32:9.

71 Who is on the LORD's side? let him come unto me.
Exodus 32:26.

72 And the LORD spake unto Moses face to face, as a man speaketh unto his friend.
Exodus 33:11.

73 And he said, My presence shall go with thee, and I will give thee rest. And he said unto him, If thy presence go not with me carry us not up hence.
Exodus 33:14–15.

74 And he said, I beseech thee, shew me thy glory.
Exodus 33:18.

75 And he said, I will make all my goodness pass before thee… And he said, Thou canst not see my face: for there shall no man see me, and live.
Exodus 33:19–20.

76 For I am the LORD your God: ye shall therefore sanctify yourselves, and ye shall be holy; for I am holy: neither shall ye defile yourselves with any manner of creeping thing that creepeth upon the earth.
Leviticus 11:44.

77 But the goat, on which the lot fell to be the scapegoat, shall be presented alive before the LORD, to make an atonement with him, and to let him go for a scapegoat into the wilderness.
Leviticus 16:10.

78 Thou shalt not avenge, nor bear any grudge against the children of thy people, but thou shalt love thy neighbour as thyself: I am the LORD.
Leviticus 19:18.

79 The LORD bless thee, and keep thee:
The LORD make his face shine upon thee, and be gracious unto thee:
The LORD lift up his countenance upon thee, and give thee peace.
Numbers 6:24–6.

80 And there we saw the giants, the sons of Anak, which come of the giants: and we were in our own sight as grasshoppers, and so we were in their sight.
Numbers 13:33.

81 The rod of Aaron for the house of Levi was budded, and brought forth buds, and bloomed blossoms, and yielded almonds.
Numbers 17:8.

82 And Moses made a serpent of brass, and put it upon a pole, and it came to pass, that if a serpent had bitten any man, when he beheld the serpent of brass, he lived.
Numbers 21:9.

83 And the LORD opened the mouth of the ass, and she said unto Balaam, What have I done unto thee, that thou hast smitten me these three times?
Numbers 22:28.

84 God is not a man, that he should lie; neither the son of man, that he should repent: hath he said, and shall he not do it? or hath he spoken, and shall he not make it good?
Numbers 23:19.

85 What hath God wrought!
Numbers 23:23. These words were transmitted by Samuel Morse on 24 May 1844, the first electronic telegraph message.

86 Be sure your sin will find you out.
Numbers 32:23.

87 I call heaven and earth to witness against you this day.
Deuteronomy 4:26.

88 Hear, O Israel: the LORD our God is one LORD: And thou shalt love the LORD thy God with all thy soul, and with all thy might.
Deuteronomy 6:4–5.

89 Ye shall not go after other gods, of the gods of the people which are round about you; (For the LORD thy God is a jealous God among you).
Deuteronomy 6:14–15.

90 And he humbled thee, and suffered thee to hunger, and fed thee with manna, which thou knewest not, neither did thy fathers know; that he might make thee know that man doth not live by bread only, but by every word that proceedeth out of the mouth of the LORD doth man live.
Deuteronomy 8:3.

91 Speak not thou in thine heart, after that the LORD thy God hath cast them out from before thee, saying, For my righteousness the LORD hath brought me in to possess this land: but for the wickedness of these nations the LORD doth drive them out from before thee.
Deuteronomy 9:4.

92 If there arise among you a prophet, or a dreamer of dreams, and giveth thee a sign or a wonder... Thou shalt not hearken.
Deuteronomy 13:1–3.

93 When thou cuttest down thine harvest in thy field, and hast forgot a sheaf in the field, thou shalt not go again to fetch it: it shall be for the stranger, for the fatherless, and for the widow: that the LORD thy God may bless thee in all the work of thine hands.
Deuteronomy 24:19.

94 Thou shalt not muzzle the ox when he treadeth out the corn.
Deuteronomy 25:4.

95 Cursed be he that removeth his neighbour's landmark. And all the people shall say, Amen.
Deuteronomy 27:17.

96 The secret things belong unto the LORD our God; but those things which are revealed belong unto us and our children for ever, that we may do all the words of this law.
Deuteronomy 29:29.

97 I call heaven and earth to record this day against you, that I have set before you life and death, blessing and cursing: therefore choose life, that both thou and thy seed may live.
Deuteronomy 30:19.

98 Give ear, O ye heavens, and I will speak: and hear, O earth, the words of my mouth. My doctrine shall drop as the rain, my speech shall distil as the dew, as the small rain upon the tender herb, and as the showers upon the grass.
Deuteronomy 32:1–2.

99 He found him in a desert land, and in the waste howling wilderness; he led him about, he instructed him, he kept him as the apple of his eye.
Deuteronomy 32:10.

1 Thou art waxen fat, thou art grown thick, thou art covered with fatness.
Deuteronomy 32:15.

2 As thy days, so shall thy strength be.
Deuteronomy 33:25.

3 The eternal God is thy refuge, and underneath are the everlasting arms.
Deuteronomy 33:27.

4 So Moses the servant of the LORD died there in the land of Moab... but no man knoweth of his sepulchre unto this day.
Deuteronomy 34:5–6.

5 There shall not any man be able to stand before thee all the days of thy life: as I was with Moses, so I will be with thee: I will not fail thee, nor forsake thee.
Joshua 1:5.

6 Have I not commanded thee? Be strong and of a good courage: be not afraid, neither be thou dismayed: for the LORD thy God is with thee whithersoever thou goest.
Joshua 1:9.

7 Behold, when we come into the land, thou shalt bind this line of scarlet thread in the window which thou didst let us down by.
Joshua 2:18.

8 So the people shouted when the priests blew with the trumpets: and it came to pass, when the people heard the sound of the trumpet, and the people shouted with a great shout, that the wall fell down flat, so that the people went up into the city, every man straight before him, and they took the city.
Joshua 6:20.

9 I am going the way of all the earth.
Joshua 23:14.

10 Choose you this day whom ye will serve... but as for me and my house, we will serve the LORD.
Joshua 24:15.

11 Then Jael Heber's wife took a nail of the tent, and took an hammer in her hand, and went softly unto him and smote the nail into his temples, and fastened it into the ground: for he was fast asleep and weary. So he died.
Judges 4:21.

12 He asked for water, and she brought him milk; she brought forth butter in a lordly dish. She put her hand to the nail, and her right hand to the workmen's hammer; and with the hammer she smote Sisera, she smote off his head, when she had pierced and stricken through his temples. At her feet he bowed, he fell, he lay down: at her feet he bowed he fell: where he bowed, there he fell down dead. The mother of Sisera looked out at a window, and cried through the lattice, Why is his chariot so long in coming? why tarry the wheels of his chariots?
Judges 5:25–8.

13 The sword of the LORD, and of Gideon.
Judges 7:18.

14 Then said they unto him, Say now Shibboleth: and he said Sibboleth: for he could not frame to pronounce it right. Then they took him, and slew him.
Judges 12:6.

15 And he said unto them, Out of the eater came forth meat, and out of the strong came forth sweetness. And they could not in three days expound the riddle.
Judges 14:14.

16 If ye had not plowed with my heifer, ye had not found out my riddle.
Judges 14:18.

17 He smote them hip and thigh.
Judges 15:8.

18 With the jawbone of an ass, heaps upon heaps, with the jaw of an ass have I slain a thousand men.
Judges 15:16.

19 And she said, The Philistines be upon thee, Samson. And he awoke out of his sleep, and said, I will go out as at other times before, and shake myself. And he wist not that the LORD was departed from him. But the Philistines took him, and put out his eyes, and brought him down to Gaza, and bound him with fetters of brass; and he did grind in the prison house.
Judges 16:20–21.

20 And Samson said, Let me die with the Philistines. And he bowed himself with all his might; and the house fell upon the lords, and upon all the people that were therein. So the dead which he slew at his death were more than they which he slew in his life.
Judges 16:30.

21 In those days there was no king in Israel, but every man did that which was right in his own eyes.
Judges 17:6.

22 The people arose as one man.
Judges 20:8.

23 Intreat me not to leave thee, or to return from following after thee: for whither thou goest, I will go; and where thou lodgest, I will lodge: thy people shall be my people, and thy God my God:
Where thou diest, will I die, and there will I be buried: the LORD do so to me, and more also, if ought but death part thee and me.
Ruth 1:16–17.

24 Now the Lord saith, Be it far from me; for them that honour me I will honour, and they that despise me shall be lightly esteemed.
1 Samuel 2:30.

25 The LORD called Samuel: and he answered, Here am I. And he ran unto Eli, and said, Here am I; for thou calledst me. And he said, I called not; lie down again.
1 Samuel 3:4–5.

26 Speak, LORD; for thy servant heareth.
1 Samuel 3:9.

27 Behold, I will do a thing in Israel, at which both the ears of every one that heareth it shall tingle.
1 Samuel 3:11.

28 Be strong, and quit yourselves like men.
1 Samuel 4:9.

29 And it came to pass, when he made mention of the ark of God, that he fell from off the seat backward by the side of the gate, and his neck brake, and he died: for he was an old man, and heavy.
1 Samuel 4:18.

30 Behold, thou art old, and thy sons walk not in thy ways: now make us a king to judge us like all the nations.
1 Samuel 8:5.

31 God save the king.
1 Samuel 10:24.

32 But now thy kingdom shall not continue: the LORD hath sought him a man after his own heart, and the LORD hath commanded him to be captain over his people.
1 Samuel 13:14.

33 Hath the LORD as great delight in burnt offerings and sacrifices, as in obeying the voice of the LORD? Behold, to obey is better than sacrifice, and to hearken than the fat of rams. For rebellion is as the sin of witchcraft, and stubbornness is as iniquity and idolatry.
1 Samuel 15:22–3.

34 Look not on his countenance, or on the height of his stature; because I have refused him: for the LORD seeth not as man seeth; for man looketh on the outward appearance, but the LORD looketh on the heart.
1 Samuel 16:7.

35 Now he was ruddy, and withal of a beautiful countenance, and goodly to look to. And the LORD said, Arise, anoint him: for this is he.
1 Samuel 16:12.

36 I know thy pride, and the naughtiness of thine heart.
1 Samuel 17:28.

37 David said moreover, The LORD that delivered me out of the paw of the lion, and out of the paw of the bear, he will deliver me out of the hand of this Philistine. And Saul said unto David, Go, and the LORD be with thee.
1 Samuel 17:37.

38 And he took his staff in his hand, and chose him five smooth stones out of the brook.
1 Samuel 17:40.

39 And the Philistine said unto David, Am I a dog, that thou comest to me with staves?
1 Samuel 17:43.

40 Saul hath slain his thousands, and David his ten thousands.
1 Samuel 18:7.

41 Behold, I have played the fool, and have erred exceedingly.
1 Samuel 26:21.

42 Saul and Jonathan were lovely and pleasant in their lives, and in their death they were not divided: they were swifter than eagles, they were stronger than lions… I am distressed for thee, my brother Jonathan: very pleasant hast thou been unto me: thy love to me was wonderful, passing the love of women. How are the mighty fallen, and the weapons of war perished!
2 Samuel 1:23–7.

43 And David danced before the LORD with all his might.
2 Samuel 6:14.

44 Set ye Uriah in the forefront of the hottest battle, and retire ye from him, that he may be smitten, and die.
2 Samuel 11:15.

45 But the poor man had nothing, save one little ewe lamb
2 Samuel 12:3.

46 Thou art the man.
2 Samuel 12:7.

47 For we must needs die, and are as water spilt on the ground, which cannot be gathered up again: neither doth God respect any person.
2 Samuel 14:14.

48 And when Ahithophel saw that his counsel was not followed, he saddled his ass, and arose, and gat him

49 And the king was much moved, and went up to the chamber over the gate, and wept: and as he went, thus he said, O my son Absalom, my son, my son Absalom! would God I had died for thee, O Absalom, my son, my son!
2 Samuel 18:33.

home to his house, to his city, and put his household in order, and hanged himself.
2 Samuel 17:23.

50 Nay: but I will surely buy it of thee at a price: neither will I offer burnt offerings unto the Lord my God of that which dost cost me nothing.
2 Samuel 24:24.

51 Now king David was old and stricken in years; and they covered him with clothes, but he gat no heat.
1 Kings 1:1.

52 I go the way of all the earth: be thou strong therefore, and shew thyself a man.
1 Kings 2:2.

53 I am but a little child: I know not how to go out or come in.
1 Kings 3:7.

54 But if ye shall at all turn from following me... Then will I cut off Israel out of the land which I have given them; and this house, which I have hallowed for my name, will I cast out of my sight; and Israel shall be a proverb and a byword among all people.
1 Kings 9:6–7.

55 And when the queen of Sheba heard of the fame of Solomon concerning the name of the LORD, she came to prove him with hard questions.
1 Kings 10:1.

56 I believed not the words, until I came, and mine eyes had seen it: and, behold, the half was not told me.
1 Kings 10:7.

57 But king Solomon loved many strange women.
1 Kings 11:1.

58 My little finger shall be thicker than my father's loins. And now whereas my father did lade you with a heavy yoke, I will add to your yoke: my father hath chastised you with whips, but I will chastise you with scorpions.
1 Kings 12:10–11.

59 He slept with his fathers.
1 Kings 14:20.

60 And the ravens brought him bread and flesh in the morning, and bread and flesh in the evening; and he drank of the brook.
Of Elijah. 1 Kings 17:6.

61 Elijah came unto all the people, and said, How long halt ye between two opinions? if the LORD be God, follow him: but if Baal, then follow him. And the people answered him not a word.
1 Kings 18:21.

62 Cry aloud: for he is a god; either he is talking, or he is pursuing, or he is in a journey, or peradventure he sleepeth, and must be wakened.
1 Kings 18:27.

63 There is a sound of abundance of rain.
1 Kings 18:41.

64 Behold, there ariseth a little cloud out of the sea, like a man's hand.
1 Kings 18:44.

65 Elijah...girded up his loins, and ran before Ahab.
1 Kings 18:46.

66 But he himself went a day's journey into the wilderness, and came and sat down under a juniper tree: and he requested for himself that he might die; and said, It is enough, now, O LORD, take away my life; for I am not better than my fathers.
1 Kings 19:4.

67 And, behold, the LORD passed by, and a great and strong wind rent the mountains, and brake in pieces the rocks before the LORD; but the LORD was not in the wind: and after the wind an earthquake; but the LORD was not in the earthquake: And after the earthquake a fire; but the LORD was not in the fire: and after the fire a still small voice.
1 Kings 19:11–12.

68 Elijah passed by him and cast his mantle upon him.
1 Kings 19:19.

69 In the place where dogs licked the blood of Naboth shall dogs lick thy blood, even thine. And Ahab said to Elijah, Hast thou found me, O mine enemy?
1 Kings 21:19–20.

70 A certain man drew a bow at a venture, and smote the king of Israel between the joints of the harness.
1 Kings 22:34.

71 Behold there appeared a chariot of fire, and horses of fire, and parted them both asunder; and Elijah went up by a whirlwind into heaven. And Elisha saw it, and he cried, My father, my father, the chariot of Israel, and the horsemen thereof.
2 Kings 2:11–12.

72 The spirit of Elijah doth rest on Elisha.
2 Kings 2:15.

73 Go up, thou bald head.
2 Kings 2:23.

74 Say unto her, Is it well with thee? is it well with thy husband? is it well with the child? And she answered, It is well.
2 Kings 4:26.

75 Let him come now to me, and he shall know that there is a prophet in Israel.
2 Kings 5:8.

76 Is it peace? and Jehu said, What hast thou to do with peace? turn thee behind me.
2 Kings 9:18.

77 The driving is like the driving of Jehu the son of Nimshi; for he driveth furiously.
2 Kings 9:20.

78 And when Jehu was come to Jezreel, Jezebel heard of it; and she painted her face, and tired her head, and looked out at a window.
2 Kings 9:30.

79 And he lifted up his face to the window, and said, Who is on my side? who? And there looked out to him two or three eunuchs.
2 Kings 9:32.

80 So they threw her down: and some of her blood was sprinkled on the wall, and on the horses: and he trode her under foot.
2 Kings 9:33.

Bible   2 Kings

81 And they went to bury her: but they found no more of her than the skull, and the feet, and the palms of her hands.
2 Kings 9:35.

82 Now, behold, thou trustest upon the staff of this bruised reed, even upon Egypt, on which if a man lean, it will go into his hand, and pierce it: so is Pharaoh king of Egypt unto all that trust on him.
2 Kings 18:21.

83 For we are strangers before thee, and sojourners, as were all our fathers: our days on the earth are as a shadow, and there is none abiding.
1 Chronicles 29:15.

84 And he died in a good old age, full of days, riches, and honour: and Solomon his son reigned in his stead.
1 Chronicles 29:28.

85 And king Solomon gave to the queen of Sheba all her desire, whatsoever she asked, beside that which she had brought unto the king.
2 Chronicles 9:12.

86 For the eyes of the LORD run to and fro throughout the whole earth, to shew himself strong in the behalf of them whose heart is perfect toward him. Herein thou hast done foolishly: therefore from henceforth thou shalt have wars.
2 Chronicles 16:9.

87 Be not afraid nor dismayed by reason of this great multitude; for the battle is not yours, but God's.
2 Chronicles 20:15.

88 Every one with one of his hands wrought in the work, and with the other hand held a weapon.
Nehemiah 4:17.

89 So will I go in unto the king, which is not according to the law: and if I perish, I perish.
Esther 4:16.

90 And the LORD said unto Satan, Whence comest thou? Then Satan answered the LORD, and said, From going to and fro in the earth, and from walking up and down in it.
Job 1:7.

91 Naked came I out of my mother's womb, and naked shall I return thither: the LORD gave, and the LORD hath taken away; blessed be the name of the LORD.
Job 1:21.

92 Skin for skin, yea, all that a man hath will he give for his life. But put forth thine hand now, and touch his bone and his flesh, and he will curse thee to thy face.
Job 2:4–5.

93 And he took him a potsherd to scrape himself withal; and he sat down among the ashes. Then said his wife unto him, Dost thou still retain thine integrity? curse God, and die.
Job 2:8–9.

94 Let the day perish wherein I was born, and the night in which it was said, There is a man child conceived.
Job 3:3.

95 There the wicked cease from troubling, and there the weary be at rest.
Job 3:17.

96 Shall mortal man be more just than God? shall a man be more pure than his maker?
Job 4:17.

97 Yet man is born unto trouble, as the sparks fly upward.
Job 5:7.

98 My days are swifter than a weaver's shuttle
Job 7:6.

99 Wherefore then hast thou brought me forth out of the womb? Oh that I had given up the ghost, and no eye had seen me!
Job 10:18.

1 Canst thou by searching find out God? canst thou find out the Almighty unto perfection? It is as high as heaven; what canst thou do? deeper than hell; what canst thou know? The measure thereof is longer than the earth, and broader than the sea.
Job 11:7–9.

2 No doubt but ye are the people, and wisdom shall die with you.
Job 12:2.

3 With the ancient is wisdom; and in length of days understanding.
Job 12:12.

4 Though he slay me, yet will I trust in him: but I will maintain mine own ways before him.
Job 13:15.

5 Man that is born of a woman is of few days, and full of trouble. He cometh forth like a flower, and is cut down: he fleeth also as a shadow, and continueth not.
Job 14:1–2.

6 I have heard many such things: miserable comforters are ye all.
Job 16:2.

7 I am escaped with the skin of my teeth.
Job 19:20.

8 For I know that my redeemer liveth, and that he shall stand at the latter day upon the earth: And though after my skin worms destroy this body, yet in my flesh shall I see God.
Job 19:25–6.

9 But ye should say, Why persecute we him, seeing the root of the matter is found in me?
Job 19:28.

10 Behold, my desire is, that the Almighty would answer me, and that mine adversary had written a book.
Job 31:35.

11 Great men are not always wise: neither do the aged understand judgment.
Job 32:9.

12 Therefore doth Job open his mouth in vain; he multiplieth words without knowledge.
Job 35:16.

13 Who is this that darkeneth counsel by words without knowledge? Gird up now thy loins like a man; for I will demand of thee, and answer thou me. Where wast thou when I laid the foundations of the earth? declare, if thou hast understanding.
Job 38:2–4.

14 When the morning stars sang together, and all the sons of God shouted for joy.
Job 38:7.

15 Hitherto shalt thou come, but no further: and here shall thy proud waves be stayed.
Job 38:11.

16 Hath the rain a father? or who hath begotten the drops of dew?
Job 38:28.

17 Canst thou bind the sweet influences of Pleiades, or loose the bands of Orion?
Job 38:31.

18 Hast thou given the horse strength? hast thou clothed his neck with thunder? Canst thou make him afraid as a grasshopper? the glory of his nostrils is terrible. He paweth in the valley and rejoiceth in his strength: he goeth on to meet the armed men.
Job 39:19–21.

19 He swalloweth the ground with fierceness and rage: neither believeth he that it is the sound of the trumpet. He saith among the trumpets, Ha, ha, and he smelleth the battle afar off, the thunder of the captains, and the shouting.
Job 39:24–5.

20 Behold now behemoth, which I made with thee; he eateth grass as an ox.
Job 40:15.

21 The shady trees cover him with their shadow; the willows of the brook compass him about. Behold, he drinketh up a river, and hasteth not: he trusteth that he can draw up Jordan into his mouth.
Job 40:22–3.

22 Canst thou draw out leviathan with an hook?
Job 41:1.

23 I have heard of thee by the hearing of the ear: but now mine eye seeth thee. Wherefore I abhor myself, and repent in dust and ashes.
Job 42:5–6.

24 So the LORD blessed the latter end of Job more than his beginning.
Job 42:12.

25 Blessed is the man that walketh not in the counsel of the ungodly, nor standeth in the way of sinners, nor sitteth in the seat of the scornful. But his delight is in the law of the LORD; and in his law doth he meditate day and night. And he shall be like a tree planted by the rivers of water, that bringeth forth his fruit in his season; his leaf also shall not wither; and whatsoever he doeth shall prosper. The ungodly are not so: but are like the chaff which the wind driveth away.
Psalms 1:1–4.

26 Why do the heathen rage, and the people imagine a vain thing?
Psalms 2:1.

27 He that sitteth in the heavens shall laugh: the LORD shall have them in derision.
Psalms 2:4.

28 Thou art my Son: this day have I begotten thee. Ask of me, and I shall give thee the heathen for thine inheritance, and the uttermost parts of the earth for thy possession. Thou shalt break them with a rod of iron; thou shalt dash them in pieces like a potter's vessel.
Psalms 2:7–9.

29 Stand in awe, and sin not: commune with your own heart upon your bed, and be still.
Psalms 4:4.

30 O LORD our Lord, how excellent is thy name in all the earth! who hast set thy glory above the heavens. Out of the mouth of babes and sucklings hast thou ordained strength because of thine enemies, that thou mightest still the enemy and the avenger.
Psalms 8:1–2.

31 When I consider thy heavens, the work of thy fingers, the moon and the stars, which thou hast ordained; What is man, that thou art mindful of him? and the son of man, that thou visitest him? For thou hast made him a little lower than the angels, and hast crowned him with glory and honour. Thou madest him to have dominion over the works of thy hands; thou hast put all things under his feet.
Psalms 8:3–6.

32 The fool hath said in his heart, There is no God.
Psalms 14:1.

33 They are all gone aside, they are all together become filthy: there is none that doeth good, no, not one.
Psalms 14:3.

34 LORD, who shall abide in thy tabernacle? who shall dwell in thy holy hill? He that walketh uprightly, and worketh righteousness, and speaketh the truth in his heart.
Psalms 15:1–2.

35 The lines are fallen unto me in pleasant places; yea, I have a goodly heritage.
Psalms 16:6.

36 For thou wilt not leave my soul in hell; neither wilt thou suffer thine Holy One to see corruption.
Psalms 16:10.

37 Keep me as the apple of the eye, hide me under the shadow of thy wings.
Psalms 17:8.

38 For by thee I have run through a troop; and by my God have I leaped over a wall.
Psalms 18:29.

39 He maketh my feet like hinds' feet, and setteth me upon my high places.
Psalms 18:33.

40 Some trust in chariots, and some in horses: but we will remember the name of the LORD our God.
Psalms 20:7.

41 My God, my God, why hast thou forsaken me? why art thou so far from helping me, and from the words of my roaring?
Psalms 22:1.

42 But I am a worm, and no man; a reproach of men, and despised of the people. All they that see me laugh me to scorn: they shoot out the lip, they shake the head, saying, He trusted on the LORD that he would deliver him: let him deliver him, seeing he delighted in him.
Psalms 22:6–8.

43 I am poured out like water, and all my bones are out of joint: my heart is like wax; it is melted in the midst of my bowels.
Psalms 22:14.

44 They pierced my hands and my feet. I may tell all my bones: they look *and* stare upon me. They part my garments among them, and cast lots upon my vesture.
Psalms 22:16–18.

45 The LORD is my shepherd; I shall not want. He maketh me to lie down in green pastures: he leadeth me beside the still waters. He restoreth my soul: he leadeth me in the paths of righteousness for his name's sake. Yea, though I walk through the valley of the shadow of death, I will fear no evil: for thou art with me; thy rod and thy staff they comfort me. Thou preparest a table before me in the presence of mine enemies: thou anointest my head with oil; my cup runneth over. Surely goodness and mercy shall follow me all the days of my life: and I will dwell in the house of the LORD for ever.
Psalms 23:1–6.

46 The earth is the LORD's, and the fulness thereof; the world, and they that dwell therein.
Psalms 24:1.

47 Lift up your heads, O ye gates; and be ye lift up, ye everlasting doors; and the King of glory shall come in. Who is this King of glory? The LORD strong and mighty, the LORD mighty in battle.
Psalms 24:7–8.

48 Remember not the sins of my youth, nor my transgressions.
Psalms 25:7.

49 The LORD is my light and my salvation; whom shall I fear? the LORD is the strength of my life; of whom shall I be afraid?
Psalms 27:1.

50 Though an host should encamp against me, my heart shall not fear: though war should rise against me, in this will I be confident. One thing have I desired of the LORD, that will I seek after; that I may dwell in the house of the LORD all the days of my life, to behold the beauty of the LORD, and to inquire in his temple.
Psalms 27:3–4.

51 Thou hast turned for me my mourning into dancing: thou hast put off my sackcloth, and girded me with gladness.
Psalms 30:11.

52 Into thine hand I commit my spirit: thou hast redeemed me, O LORD God of truth.
Psalms 31:5.

53 For this shall every one that is godly pray unto thee in a time when thou mayest be found: surely in the floods of great waters they shall not come nigh unto him. Thou *art* my hiding place; thou shalt preserve me from trouble; thou shalt compass me about with songs of deliverance. Selah.
Psalms 32:6–7.

54 I will instruct thee and teach thee in the way which thou shalt go: I will guide thee with mine eye. Be ye not as the horse, or as the mule, which have no understanding: whose mouth must be held in with bit and bridle, lest they come near unto thee.
Psalms 32:8–9.

55 I sought the LORD, and he heard me, and delivered me from all my fears.
Psalms 34:4.

56 O taste and see that the LORD is good: blessed is the man that trusteth in him. O fear the LORD, ye his saints: for there is no want to them that fear him. The young lions do lack, and suffer hunger: but they that seek the LORD shall not want any good thing.
Psalms 34:8–10.

57 The children of men put their trust under the shadow of thy wings.
Psalms 36:7.

58 Delight thyself also in the LORD, and he shall give thee the desires of thine heart. Commit thy way unto the LORD; trust also in him; and he shall bring *it* to pass.
Psalms 37:4–5.

59 But the meek shall inherit the earth; and shall delight themselves in the abundance of peace.
Psalms 37:11.

60 I have been young and now am old; yet have I not seen the righteous forsaken, nor his seed begging bread.
Psalms 37:25.

61 I waited patiently for the LORD, and he inclined unto me, and heard my cry. He brought me up also out of an horrible pit, out of the miry clay, and set my feet upon a rock, and established my goings.
Psalms 40:1–2.

62 Yea, mine own familiar friend, in whom I trusted, which did eat of my bread, hath lifted up his heel against me.
Psalms 41:9.

63 As the hart panteth after the water brooks, so panteth my soul after thee, O God. My soul thirsteth for God, for the living God: when shall I come and appear before God?
Psalms 42:1–2.

64 Why art thou cast down, O my soul? and why art thou disquieted in me? hope thou in God: for I shall yet praise him for the help of his countenance.
Psalms 42:5.

65 Deep calleth unto deep at the noise of thy waterspouts: all thy waves and thy billows are gone over me.
Psalms 42:7.

66 Yea, for thy sake are we killed all the day long; we are counted as sheep for the slaughter.
Psalms 44:22.

67 God is our refuge and strength, a very present help in trouble. Therefore will not we fear, though the earth be removed, and though the mountains be carried into the midst of the sea.
Psalms 46:1–2.

68 There is a river, the streams whereof shall make glad the city of God, the holy place of the tabernacles of the most High. God is in the midst of her; she shall not be moved: God shall help her, and that right early.
Psalms 46:4–5.

69 He maketh wars to cease unto the end of the earth; he breaketh the bow, and cutteth the spear in sunder; he burneth the chariot in the fire.
Be still, and know that I am God: I will be exalted among the heathen, I will be exalted in the earth.
Psalms 46:9–10.

70 Great is the LORD, and greatly to be praised in the city of our God, in the mountain of his holiness. Beautiful for situation, the joy of the whole earth, is mount Zion, on the sides of the north, the city of the great King.
Psalms 48:1–2.

71 For I acknowledge my transgressions: and my sin is ever before me. Against thee, thee only, have I sinned, and

done this evil in thy sight: that thou mightest be justified when thou speakest, and be clear when thou judgest. Behold, I was shapen in iniquity; and in sin did my mother conceive me.
Psalms 51:3–5.

72 Behold, thou desirest truth in the inward parts: and in the hidden part thou shalt make me to know wisdom. Purge me with hyssop, and I shall be clean: wash me, and I shall be whiter than snow.
Psalms 51:6–7.

73 Create in me a clean heart, O God; and renew a right spirit within me. Cast me not away from thy presence; and take not thy holy spirit from me. Restore unto me the joy of thy salvation; and uphold me with thy free spirit. Then will I teach transgressors thy ways; and sinners shall be converted unto thee.
Psalms 51:10–13.

74 Deliver me from bloodguiltiness, O God, thou God of my salvation: and my tongue shall sing aloud of thy righteousness. O Lord, open thou my lips; and my mouth shall shew forth thy praise. For thou desirest not sacrifice; else would I give it: thou delightest not in burnt offering. The sacrifices of God are a broken spirit: a broken and a contrite heart, O God, thou wilt not despise.
Psalms 51:14–17.

75 Oh that I had wings like a dove! for then would I fly away, and be at rest.
Psalms 55:6.

76 Lead me to the rock that is higher than I.
Psalms 61:2.

77 Truly my soul waiteth upon God: from him cometh my salvation. He only is my rock and my salvation; he is my defence; I shall not be greatly moved.
Psalms 62:1–2.

78 O God, thou art my God; early will I seek thee: my soul thirsteth for thee, my flesh longeth for thee in a dry and thirsty land, where no water is.
Psalms 63:1.

79 Thou crownest the year with thy goodness; and thy paths drop fatness.
Psalms 65:11.

80 God be merciful unto us, and bless us; and cause his face to shine upon us; Selah. That thy way may be known upon earth, thy saving health among all nations. Let the people praise thee, O God; let all the people praise thee.
Psalms 67:1–3.

81 Sing unto God, sing praises to his name: extol him that rideth upon the heavens by his name JAH, and rejoice before him. A father of the fatherless, and a judge of the widows, is God in his holy habitation. God setteth the solitary in families: he bringeth out those which are bound with chains: but the rebellious dwell in a dry land.
Psalms 68:4–6.

82 Thou hast ascended on high, thou hast led captivity captive: thou hast received gifts for men; yea, for the rebellious also, that the LORD God might dwell among them.
Psalms 68:18.

83 In thee, O LORD, do I put my trust: let me never be put to confusion.
Psalms 71:1.

84 Truly God is good to Israel, even to such as are of a clean heart. But as for me, my feet were almost gone; my steps had well nigh slipped. For I was envious at the foolish, when I saw the prosperity of the wicked.
Psalms 73:1–3.

85 When I thought to know this, it was too painful for me; Until I went into the sanctuary of God; then understood I their end.
Psalms 73:16–17.

86 Nevertheless I am continually with thee: thou hast holden me by my right hand. Thou shalt guide me with thy counsel, and afterward receive me to glory. Whom have I in heaven but thee? and there is none upon earth that I desire beside thee. My flesh and my heart faileth: but God is the strength of my heart, and my portion for ever.
Psalms 73:23–6.

87 I am the LORD thy God, which brought thee out of the land of Egypt: open thy mouth wide, and I will fill it.
Psalms 81:10.

88 How amiable are thy tabernacles, O LORD of hosts! My soul longeth, yea, even fainteth for the courts of the LORD: my heart and my flesh crieth out for the living God.
Yea, the sparrow hath found an house, and the swallow a nest for herself, where she may lay her young, even thine altars, O LORD of hosts, my King, and my God.
Psalms 84:1–3.

89 Who passing through the valley of Baca make it a well; the rain also filleth the pools.
They go from strength to strength, every one of them in Zion appeareth before God.
Psalms 84:6–7.

90 For a day in thy courts is better than a thousand. I had rather be a doorkeeper in the house of my God, than to dwell in the tents of wickedness.
Psalms 84:10.

91 Glorious things are spoken of thee, O city of God.
Psalms 87:3.

92 Lord, thou hast been our dwelling place in all generations. Before the mountains were brought forth, or ever thou hadst formed the earth and the world, even from everlasting to everlasting, thou art God.
Psalms 90:1–2.

93 For a thousand years in thy sight are but as yesterday when it is past, and as a watch in the night.
Psalms 90:4.

94 The days of our years are threescore years and ten; and if by reason of strength they be fourscore years, yet is their strength labour and sorrow; for it is soon cut off, and we fly away.
Psalms 90:10.

95 So teach us to number our days that we may apply our hearts unto wisdom.
Psalms 90:12.

96 Surely he shall deliver thee from the snare of the fowler, and from the noisome pestilence.

He shall cover thee with his feathers, and under his wings shalt thou trust: his truth shall be thy shield and buckler.
Thou shalt not be afraid for the terror by night; nor for the arrow that flieth by day;
Nor for the pestilence that walketh in darkness; nor for the destruction that wasteth at noonday.
A thousand shall fall at thy side, and ten thousand at thy right hand, but it shall not come nigh thee.
Psalms 91:3–7.

97 Because thou hast made the LORD, which is my refuge, even the most high, thy habitation.
Psalms 91:9.

98 They shall still bring forth fruit in old age; they shall be fat and flourishing.
Psalms 92:14.

99 He that planted the ear, shall he not hear? he that formed the eye, shall he not see?
Psalms 94:9.

1 O come let us sing unto the LORD: let us make a joyful noise to the rock of our salvation. Let us come before his presence with thanksgiving, and make a joyful noise unto him with psalms.
Psalms 95:1–2.

2 Harden not your heart, as in the provocation, and as in the day of temptation in the wilderness: When your fathers tempted me, proved me, and saw my work. Forty years long was I grieved with this generation, and said, It is a people that do err in their heart, and they have not known my ways: Unto whom I sware in my wrath that they should not enter into my rest.
Psalms 95:8–11.

3 O worship the LORD in the beauty of holiness: fear before him, all the earth.
Psalms 96:9.

4 Make a joyful noise unto the LORD, all ye lands. Serve the LORD with gladness: come before his presence with singing. Know ye that the LORD he is God: it is he that hath made us, and not we ourselves; we are his people, and the sheep of his pasture.
Psalms 100:1–3.

5 Of old hast thou laid the foundation of the earth: and the heavens are the work of thy hands.
Psalms 102:25.

6 Bless the LORD, O my soul: and all that is within me, bless his holy name. Bless the LORD, O my soul, and forget not all his benefits: Who forgiveth all thine iniquities; who healeth all thy diseases; Who redeemeth thy life from destruction; who crowneth thee with loving kindness and tender mercies; Who satisfieth thy mouth with good things; so that thy youth is renewed like the eagle's.
Psalms 103:1–5.

7 The LORD is merciful and gracious, slow to anger, and plenteous in mercy. He will not always chide: neither will he keep his anger for ever. He hath not dealt with us after our sins; nor rewarded us according to our iniquities.
Psalms 103:8–10.

8 For as the heaven is high above the earth, so great is his mercy toward them that fear him. As far as the east is from the west, so far hath he removed our transgressions from us.
Psalms 103:11–12.

9 Like as a father pitieth his children, so the LORD pitieth them that fear him. For he knoweth our frame; he remembereth that we are dust.
Psalms 103:13–14.

10 As for man, his days are as grass: as a flower of the field, so he flourisheth. For the wind passeth over it, and it is gone; and the place thereof shall know it no more.
Psalms 103:15–16.

11 He causeth the grass to grow for the cattle, and herb for the service of man: that he may bring forth food out of the earth; And wine that maketh glad the heart of man, and oil to make his face to shine, and bread which strengtheneth man's heart.
Psalms 104:14–15.

12 Man goeth forth unto his work and to his labour until the evening.
Psalms 104:23.

13 So is this great and wide sea, wherein are things creeping innumerable, both small and great beasts.
There go the ships: there is that leviathan, whom thou hast made to play therein.
These wait all upon thee; that thou mayest give them their meat in due season.
Psalms 104:25–7.

14 Their soul abhorreth all manner of meat; and they draw near unto the gates of death.
Psalms 107:18.

15 They that go down to the sea in ships, that do business in great waters;
These see the works of the LORD, and his wonders in the deep.
Psalms 107:23–4.

16 They reel to and fro, and stagger like a drunken man, and are at their wits' end.
Psalms 107:27.

17 The LORD said unto my Lord, Sit thou at my right hand, until I make thine enemies thy footstool.
Psalms 110:1.

18 The LORD hath sworn, and will not repent, Thou art a priest for ever after the order of Melchizedek.
Psalms 110:4.

19 The fear of the LORD is the beginning of wisdom.
Psalms 111:10.

20 For thou hast delivered my soul from death, mine eyes from tears, and my feet from falling. I will walk before the LORD in the land of the living. I believed, therefore have I spoken: I was greatly afflicted: I said in my haste, All men are liars.
Psalms 116:8–11.

21 Precious in the sight of the LORD is the death of his saints.
Psalms 116:15.

22 The stone which the builders refused is become the head stone of the corner. This is the LORD's doing; it is marvellous in our eyes. This is the day which the LORD hath made; we will rejoice and be glad in it.
Psalms 118:22–4.

23 Blessed be he that cometh in the name of the LORD: we have blessed you out of the house of the LORD.
Psalms 118:26.

24 Wherewithal shall a young man cleanse his way? by taking heed thereto according to thy word.
Psalms 119:9.

25 Thy word have I hid in mine heart, that I might not sin against thee.
Psalms 119:11.

26 I have more understanding than all my teachers: for thy testimonies are my meditation.
Psalms 119:99.

27 How sweet are thy words unto my taste! yea, sweeter than honey to my mouth!
Psalms 119:103.

28 Thy word is a lamp unto my feet, and a light unto my path.
Psalms 119:105.

29 The entrance of thy words giveth light; it giveth understanding unto the simple.
Psalms 119:130.

30 Great peace have they which love thy law: and nothing shall offend them.
Psalms 119:165.

31 I will lift up mine eyes unto the hills, from whence cometh my help. My help cometh from the LORD, which made heaven and earth. He will not suffer thy foot to be moved: he that keepeth thee will not slumber. Behold, he that keepeth Israel shall neither slumber nor sleep. The LORD is thy keeper: the LORD is thy shade upon thy right hand. The sun shall not smite thee by day, nor the moon by night. The LORD shall preserve thee from all evil: he shall preserve thy soul. The LORD shall preserve thy going out and thy coming in from this time forth, and even for evermore.
Psalms 121:1–8.

32 I was glad when they said unto me, Let us go into the house of the LORD.
Psalms 122:1.

33 Pray for the peace of Jerusalem: they shall prosper that love thee. Peace be within thy walls, and prosperity within thy palaces.
Psalms 122:6–7.

34 They that trust in the LORD shall be as mount Zion, which cannot be removed, but abideth for ever.
Psalms 125:1.

35 They that sow in tears shall reap in joy. He that goeth forth and weepeth, bearing precious seed, shall doubtless come again with rejoicing, bringing his sheaves with him.
Psalms 126:5–6.

36 Except the LORD build the house, they labour in vain that build it: except the LORD keep the city, the watchman waketh but in vain. It is vain for you to rise up early, to sit up late, to eat the bread of sorrows: for so he giveth his beloved sleep.
Psalms 127:1–2.

37 Lo, children are an heritage of the LORD: and the fruit of the womb is his reward. As arrows are in the hand of a mighty man; so are children of the youth. Happy is the man that hath his quiver full of them: they shall not be ashamed, but they shall speak with the enemies in the gate.
Psalms 127:3–5.

38 Thy wife shall be as a fruitful vine by the sides of thine house: thy children like olive plants round about thy table.
Psalms 128:3.

39 Out of the depths have I cried unto thee, O LORD. Lord, hear my voice: let thine ears be attentive to the voice of my supplications. If thou, LORD, shouldest mark iniquities, O LORD, who shall stand? But, there is forgiveness with thee, that thou mayest be feared.
Psalms 130:1–4.

40 Behold, how good and how pleasant it is for brethren to dwell together in unity! It is like the precious ointment upon the head, that ran down upon the beard, even Aaron's beard: that went down to the skirts of his garments; As the dew of Hermon, and as the dew that descended upon the mountains of Zion: for there the LORD commanded the blessing, even life for evermore.
Psalms 133:1–3.

41 O give thanks unto the LORD; for he is good: for his mercy endureth for ever.
Psalms 136:1.

42 By the rivers of Babylon, there we sat down, yea, we wept, when we remembered Zion. We hanged our harps upon the willows in the midst thereof. For there they that carried us away captive required of us a song; and they that wasted us required of us mirth, saying, Sing us one of the songs of Zion. How shall we sing the LORD's song in a strange land?
Psalms 137:1–4.

43 O LORD, thou hast searched me, and known me. Thou knowest my downsitting and mine uprising, thou understandest my thought afar off. Thou compassest my path and my lying down, and art acquainted with all my ways. For there is not a word in my tongue, but, lo, O LORD, thou knowest it altogether. Thou hast beset me behind and before, and laid thine hand upon me. Such knowledge is too wonderful for me; it is high, I cannot attain unto it.
Psalms 139:1–6.

44 Whither shall I go from thy spirit? or whither shall I flee from thy presence?
If I ascend up into heaven, thou art there: if I make my bed in hell, behold, thou art there.
If I take the wings of the morning, and dwell in the uttermost parts of the sea;
Even there shall thy hand lead me, and thy right hand shall hold me.
If I say, Surely the darkness shall cover me; even the night
shall be light about me.
Yea, the darkness hideth not from thee; but the night shineth as the day: the darkness and the light are both alike to thee.
Psalms 139:7–12.

45 I will praise thee; for I am fearfully and wonderfully made: marvellous are thy works; and that my soul knoweth right well. My substance was not hid from thee,

when I was made in secret, and curiously wrought in the lowest parts of the earth. Thine eyes did see my substance, yet being unperfect; and in thy book all my members were written, which in continuance were fashioned, when as yet there was none of them.
Psalms 139:14–16.

46 Search me, O God, and know my heart: try me, and know my thoughts: And see if there be any wicked way in me, and lead me in the way everlasting.
Psalms 139:23–4.

47 Set a watch, O LORD, before my mouth; keep the door of my lips.
Psalms 141:3.

48 The eyes of all wait upon thee; and thou givest them their meat in due season. Thou openest thine hand, and satisfiest the desire of every living thing.
Psalms 145:15–16.

49 He telleth the number of the stars; he calleth them all by their names.
Psalms 147:4.

50 Let the high praises of God be in their mouth, and a two-edged sword in their hand.
Psalms 149:6.

51 Wisdom crieth without; she uttereth her voice in the streets.
Proverbs 1:20.

52 Trust in the LORD with all thine heart; and lean not unto thine own understanding. In all thy ways acknowledge him, and he shall direct thy paths.
Proverbs 3:5–6.

53 For whom the LORD loveth he correcteth; even as a father the son in whom he delighteth.
Proverbs 3:12.

54 Wisdom is the principal thing; therefore get wisdom: and with all thy getting get understanding.
Proverbs 4:7.

55 Happy is the man that findeth wisdom, and the man that getteth understanding. For the merchandise of it is better than the merchandise of silver, and the gain thereof than fine gold. She is more precious than rubies: and all the things thou canst desire are not to be compared unto her. Length of days is in her right hand; and in her left hand riches and honour. Her ways are ways of pleasantness, and all her paths are peace. She is a tree of life to them that lay hold upon her: and happy is every one that retaineth her.
Proverbs 3:13–18.

56 For the lips of a strange woman drop as an honeycomb, and her mouth is smoother than oil: But her end is bitter as wormwood, sharp as a two-edged sword. Her feet go down to death; her steps take hold on hell.
Proverbs 5:3–5.

57 Let thy fountain be blessed: and rejoice with the wife of thy youth. Let her be as the loving hind and pleasant roe; let her breasts satisfy thee at all times; and be thou ravished always with her love.
Proverbs 5:18–19.

58 Go to the ant, thou sluggard; consider her ways, and be wise.
Proverbs 6:6.

59 Yet a little sleep, a little slumber, a little folding of the hands to sleep: So shall thy poverty come as one that travelleth, and thy want as an armed man.
Proverbs 6:10–11.

60 Can a man take fire in his bosom and his clothes not be burned? Can one go upon hot coals, and his feet not be burned?
Proverbs 6:27–8.

61 Wisdom hath builded her house, she hath hewn out her seven pillars.
Proverbs 9:1.

62 Stolen waters are sweet, and bread eaten in secret is pleasant.
Proverbs 9:17.

63 The rich man's wealth is his strong city: the destruction of the poor is their poverty.
Proverbs 10:15.

64 A false balance is abomination to the LORD: but a just weight is his delight.
Proverbs 11:1.

65 He that is surety for a stranger shall smart for it: and he that hateth suretiship is sure.
Proverbs 11:15.

66 A virtuous woman is a crown to her husband: but she that maketh ashamed is as rottenness in his bones.
Proverbs 12:4.

67 A wise son heareth his father's instruction: but a scorner heareth not rebuke.
Proverbs 13:1.

68 Hope deferred maketh the heart sick: but when the desire cometh, it is a tree of life.
Proverbs 13:12.

69 He that spareth his rod hateth his son: but he that loveth him chasteneth him betimes.
Proverbs 13:24.

70 There is a way which seemeth right unto a man, but the end thereof are the ways of death.
Proverbs 14:12.

71 The poor is hated even of his own neighbour: but the rich hath many friends.
Proverbs 14:20.

72 In all labour there is profit: but the talk of the lips tendeth only to penury.
Proverbs 14:23.

73 A soft answer turneth away wrath: but grievous words stir up anger.
Proverbs 15:1.

74 A merry heart maketh a cheerful countenance.
Proverbs 15:13.

75 Better is little with the fear of the LORD than great treasure and trouble therewith. Better is a dinner of herbs where love is, than a stalled ox and hatred therewith.
Proverbs 15:16–17.

76 A word spoken in due season, how good is it!
Proverbs 15:23.

77 A good report maketh the bones fat.
Proverbs 15:30.

78 Commit thy works unto the LORD, and thy thoughts shall be established.
Proverbs 16:3.

79 Pride goeth before destruction, and an haughty spirit before a fall.
Proverbs 16:18.

80 Children's children are the crown of old men; and the glory of children are their fathers.
Proverbs 17:6.

81 A friend loveth at all times, and a brother is born for adversity.
Proverbs 17:17.

82 A merry heart doeth good like a medicine: but a broken spirit drieth the bones.
Proverbs 17:22.

83 The name of the LORD is a strong tower: the righteous runneth into it, and is safe.
Proverbs 18:10.

84 A man that hath friends must shew himself friendly: and there is a friend that sticketh closer than a brother.
Proverbs 18:24.

85 He that hath pity upon the poor lendeth unto the LORD; and that which he hath given will he pay him again.
Proverbs 19:17.

86 The king's heart is in the hand of the LORD, as the rivers of water: he turneth it whithersoever he will.
Proverbs 21:1.

87 Every way of a man is right in his own eyes: but the LORD pondereth the hearts.
Proverbs 21:2.

88 It is better to dwell in a corner of the housetop, than with a brawling woman in a wide house.
Proverbs 21:9.

89 Train up a child in the way he should go: and when he is old, he will not depart from it.
Proverbs 22:6.

90 Wilt thou set thine eyes upon that which is not? for riches certainly make themselves wings; they fly away as an eagle toward heaven.
Proverbs 23:5.

91 Remove not the old landmark; and enter not into the fields of the fatherless.
Proverbs 23:10.

92 If thou faint in the day of adversity, thy strength is small.
Proverbs 24:10.

93 A word fitly spoken is like apples of gold in pictures of silver.
Proverbs 25:11.

94 Confidence in an unfaithful man in time of trouble is like a broken tooth, and a foot out of joint.
Proverbs 25:19.

95 If thine enemy be hungry, give him bread to eat; and if he be thirsty, give him water to drink: For thou shalt heap coals of fire upon his head, and the LORD shall reward thee.
Proverbs 25:21–2.

96 As a dog returneth to his vomit, so a fool returneth to his folly.
Proverbs 26:11.

97 The slothful man saith, There is a lion in the way; a lion is in the streets.
Proverbs 26:13.

98 Where no wood is, there the fire goeth out: so where there is no talebearer, the strife ceaseth.
Proverbs 26:20.

99 Boast not thyself of tomorrow; for thou knowest not what a day may bring forth.
Proverbs 27:1.

1 Wrath is cruel, and anger is outrageous; but who is able to stand before envy?
Proverbs 27:4.

2 Open rebuke is better than secret love. Faithful are the wounds of a friend; but the kisses of an enemy are deceitful.
Proverbs 27:5–6.

3 A continual dropping in a very rainy day and a contentious woman are alike.
Proverbs 27:15.

4 Hell and destruction are never full; so the eyes of man are never satisfied.
Proverbs 27:20.

5 A fool uttereth all his mind: but a wise man keepeth it in till afterwards.
Proverbs 29:11.

6 Where there is no vision, the people perish: but he that keepeth the law, happy is he.
Proverbs 29:18.

7 Who can find a virtuous woman? for her price is far above rubies.
Proverbs 31:10.

8 Favour is deceitful, and beauty is vain: but a woman that feareth the LORD, she shall be praised.
Proverbs 31:30.

9 Vanity of vanities, saith the Preacher, vanity of vanities; all is vanity. What profit hath a man of all his labour which he taketh under the sun? One generation passeth away, and another generation cometh: but the earth abideth for ever.
Ecclesiastes 1:2–4.

10 All the rivers run into the sea; yet the sea is not full; unto the place from whence the rivers come, thither they return again.
Ecclesiastes 1:7.

11 The thing that hath been, it is that which shall be; and that which is done is that which shall be done: and there is no new thing under the sun.
Ecclesiastes 1:9.

12 For in much wisdom is much grief: and he that increaseth knowledge increaseth sorrow.
Ecclesiastes 1:18.

13 I said of laughter, It is mad: and of mirth, What doeth it?
Ecclesiastes 2:2.

14 To every thing there is a season, and a time to every purpose under the heaven:
A time to be born, and a time to die; a time to plant, and a time to pluck up that which is planted;
A time to kill, and a time to heal; a time to break down, and a time to build up;

A time to weep, and a time to laugh; a time to mourn, and
a time to dance:
A time to cast away stones, and a time to gather stones
together; a time to embrace, and a time to refrain from
embracing;
A time to get, and a time to lose; a time to keep, and a
time to cast away;
A time to rend, and a time to sew; a time to keep silence,
and a time to speak;
A time to love, and a time to hate; a time of war, and a
time of peace.
Ecclesiastes 3:1–8.

15 Wherefore I perceive that there is nothing better, than
that a man should rejoice in his own works; for that is his
portion: for who shall bring him to see what shall be after him?
Ecclesiastes 3:22.

16 Wherefore I praise the dead which are already dead
more than the living which are yet alive.
Ecclesiastes 4:2.

17 Two are better than one; because they have a good
reward for their labour. For if they fall, the one will lift up
his fellow: but woe to him that is alone when he falleth;
for he hath not another to help him up.
Ecclesiastes 4:9–10.

18 And if one prevail against him, two shall withstand him;
and a threefold cord is not quickly broken.
Ecclesiastes 4:12.

19 Better is a poor and a wise child than an old and foolish
king, who will no more be admonished.
Ecclesiastes 4:13.

20 Be not rash with thy mouth, and let not thine heart be
hasty to utter any thing before God: for God is in heaven,
and thou upon earth: therefore let thy words be few.
Ecclesiastes 5:2.

21 For as the crackling of thorns under a pot, so is the
laughter of a fool: this also is vanity.
Ecclesiastes 7:6.

22 Better is the end of a thing than the beginning thereof:
and the patient in spirit is better than the proud in spirit.
Ecclesiastes 7:8.

23 Say not thou, What is the cause that the former days
were better than these? for thou dost not inquire wisely
concerning this.
Ecclesiastes 7:10.

24 There is no man that hath power over the spirit to retain
the spirit; neither hath he power in the day of death:
and there is no discharge in that war; neither shall
wickedness deliver those that are given to it.
Ecclesiastes 8:8.

25 Then I commended mirth, because a man hath no better
thing under the sun, than to eat, and to drink, and to be
merry: for that shall abide with him of his labour the days
of his life, which God giveth him under the sun.
Ecclesiastes 8:15.

26 For to him that is joined to all the living there is hope: for
a living dog is better than a dead lion. For the living
know that they shall die: but the dead know not any
thing, neither have they any more a reward; for the
memory of them is forgotten.
Ecclesiastes 9:4–5.

27 Go thy way, eat thy bread with joy, and drink thy wine
with a merry heart; for God now accepteth thy works.
Ecclesiastes 9:7.

28 Whatsoever thy hand findeth to do; do it with thy might;
for there is no work, nor device, nor knowledge, nor
wisdom, in the grave, whither thou goest.
Ecclesiastes 9:10.

29 I returned, and saw under the sun, that the race is not to
the swift, nor the battle to the strong, neither yet bread to
the wise, nor yet riches to men of understanding, nor yet
favour to men of skill; but time and chance happeneth to
them all.
Ecclesiastes 9:11

30 Dead flies cause the ointment of the apothecary to send
forth a stinking savour: so doth a little folly him that is in
reputation for wisdom and honour.
Ecclesiastes 10:1.

31 He that diggeth a pit shall fall into it; and whoso
breaketh an hedge, a serpent shall bite him.
Ecclesiastes 10:8.

32 A feast is made for laughter, and wine maketh merry: but
money answereth all things.
Ecclesiastes 10:19.

33 Curse not the king, no not in thy thought; and curse not
the rich in thy bedchamber: for a bird of the air shall
carry the voice, and that which hath wings shall tell the
matter.
Ecclesiastes 10:20.

34 Cast thy bread upon the waters: for thou shalt find it after
many days.
Ecclesiastes 11:1.

35 Rejoice, O young man, in thy youth; and let thy heart
cheer thee in the days of thy youth, and walk in the ways
of thine heart, and in the sight of thine eyes: but know
thou, that for all these things God will bring thee into
judgment.
Ecclesiastes 11:9.

36 Remember now thy Creator in the days of thy youth,
while the evil days come not, nor the years draw nigh,
when thou shalt say, I have no pleasure in them;
While the sun, or the light, or the moon, or the stars, be
not darkened, nor the clouds return after the rain:
In the day when the keepers of the house shall tremble,
and the strong men shall bow themselves, and the
grinders cease because they are few, and those that
look out of the windows be darkened,
And the doors shall be shut in the streets, when the
sound of the grinding is low, and he shall rise up at the
voice of the bird, and all the daughters of musick shall
be brought low:
Also when they shall be afraid of that which is high, and
fears shall be in the way, and the almond tree shall
flourish, and the grasshopper shall be a burden, and
desire shall fail: because man goeth to his long home,
and mourners go about the streets:
Or ever the silver cord be loosed, or the golden bowl be
broken, or the pitcher be broken at the fountain, or the
wheel broken at the cistern.
Then shall the dust return to the earth as it was: and the
spirit shall return unto God who gave it.
Ecclesiastes 12:1–7.

37 And further, by these, my son, be admonished: of making many books there is no end; and much study is a weariness of the flesh.
Ecclesiastes 12:12.

38 Fear God, and keep his commandments: for this is the whole duty of man.
Ecclesiastes 12:13.

39 The song of songs, which is Solomon's.
Song of Solomon 1:1.

40 I am the rose of Sharon, and the lily of the valleys. As the lily among thorns, so is my love among the daughters.
Song of Solomon 2:1–2.

41 He brought me to the banqueting house, and his banner over me was love.
Song of Solomon 2:4.

42 I charge you, O ye daughters of Jerusalem, by the roes, and by the hinds of the field, that ye stir not up, nor awake my love, till he please.
Song of Solomon 2:7.

43 My beloved spake, and said unto me, Rise up, my love, my fair one, and come away. For lo, the winter is past, the rain is over and gone.
Song of Solomon 2:10–11.

44 My beloved is mine, and I am his: he feedeth among the lilies.
Song of Solomon 2:16.

45 Behold, thou art fair, my love; behold, thou art fair; thou hast doves' eyes within thy locks: thy hair is as a flock of goats, that appear from mount Gilead. Thy teeth are like a flock of sheep that are even shorn, which came up from the washing; whereof every one bear twins, and none is barren among them. Thy lips are like a thread of scarlet, and thy speech is comely: thy temples are like a piece of a pomegranate within thy locks. Thy neck is like the tower of David builded for an armoury, whereon there hang a thousand bucklers, all shields of mighty men. Thy two breasts are like two young roes that are twins, which feed among the lilies. Until the day break, and the shadows flee away, I will get me to the mountain of myrrh, and to the hill of frankincense. Thou art all fair, my love; there is no spot in thee.
Song of Solomon 4:1–7.

46 A garden inclosed is my sister, my spouse; a spring shut up, a fountain sealed.
Song of Solomon 4:12.

47 My beloved put in his hand by the hole of the door, and my bowels were moved for him.
Song of Solomon 5:4.

48 How fair and how pleasant art thou, O love, for delights!
Song of Solomon 7:6.

49 Love is strong as death; jealousy is cruel as the grave: the coals thereof are coals of fire, which hath a most vehement flame. Many waters cannot quench love, neither can the floods drown it: if a man would give all the substance of his house for love, it would utterly be contemned.
Song of Solomon 8:6–7.

50 Come now, and let us reason together, saith the LORD: though your sins be as scarlet, they shall be as white as snow; though they be red like crimson, they shall be as wool.
Isaiah 1:18.

51 They shall beat their swords into plowshares, and their spears into pruninghooks: nation shall not lift up sword against nation, neither shall they learn war any more.
Isaiah 2:4.

52 What mean ye that ye beat my people to pieces, and grind the faces of the poor? saith the Lord GOD of hosts.
Isaiah 3:15.

53 Woe unto them that rise up early in the morning, that they may follow strong drink; that continue until night, till wine inflame them!
Isaiah 5:11.

54 In the year that king Uzziah died I saw also the Lord sitting upon a throne, high and lifted up, and his train filled the temple. Above it stood the seraphims: each one had six wings; with twain he covered his face, and with twain he covered his feet, and with twain he did fly. And one cried unto another, and said, Holy, holy, holy, is the LORD of hosts: the whole earth is full of his glory. And the posts of the door moved at the voice of him that cried, and the house was filled with smoke.
Isaiah 6:1–4.

55 Then said I, Woe is me! for I am undone; because I am a man of unclean lips, and I dwell in the midst of a people of unclean lips; for mine eyes have seen the King, the LORD of hosts. Then flew one of the seraphims unto me, having a live coal in his hand, which he had taken with the tongs from off the altar: And he laid it upon my mouth, and said, Lo, this hath touched thy lips; and thine iniquity is taken away, and thy sin purged. Also I heard the voice of the Lord, saying, Whom shall I send, and who will go for us? Then said I, Here am I; send me.
Isaiah 6:5–8.

56 Then said I, Lord, how long?
Isaiah 6:11.

57 Therefore the Lord himself shall give you a sign; Behold, a virgin shall conceive, and bear a son, and shall call his name Immanuel.
Isaiah 7:14.

58 And he shall be for a sanctuary; but for a stone of stumbling and for a rock of offence to both the houses of Israel, for a gin and for a snare to the inhabitants of Jerusalem.
Isaiah 8:14.

59 The people that walked in darkness have seen a great light: they that dwell in the land of the shadow of death, upon them hath the light shined.
Isaiah 9:2.

60 For unto us a child is born, unto us a son is given: and the government shall be upon his shoulder: and his name shall be called Wonderful, Counseller, The mighty God, The everlasting Father, The Prince of Peace. Of the increase of his government and peace there shall be no end, upon the throne of David, and upon his kingdom, to order it, and to establish it with judgment and with justice from henceforth even for ever. The zeal of the LORD of hosts will perform this.
Isaiah 9:6–7.

Bible Isaiah

61 And there shall come forth a rod out of the stem of Jesse, and a Branch shall grow out of his roots: And the spirit of the LORD shall rest upon him, the spirit of wisdom and understanding, the spirit of counsel and might, the spirit of knowledge and of the fear of the LORD.
Isaiah 11:1–2.

62 The wolf also shall dwell with the lamb, and the leopard shall lie down with the kid; and the calf and the young lion and the fatling together; and a little child shall lead them. And the cow and the bear shall feed; their young ones shall lie down together: and the lion shall eat straw like the ox. And the sucking child shall play on the hole of the asp, and the weaned child shall put his hand on the cockatrice' den. They shall not hurt nor destroy in all my holy mountain for the earth shall be full of the knowledge of the LORD, as the waters cover the sea.
Isaiah 11:6–9.

63 Therefore with joy shall ye draw water out of the wells of salvation.
Isaiah 12:3.

64 How art thou fallen from heaven, O Lucifer, son of the morning!
Isaiah 14:12.

65 And behold joy and gladness, slaying oxen, and killing sheep, eating flesh, and drinking wine: let us eat and drink; for to morrow we shall die.
Isaiah 22:13.

66 The earth shall reel to and fro like a drunkard, and shall be removed like a cottage; and the transgression thereof shall be heavy upon it; and it shall fall, and not rise again.
Isaiah 24:20.

67 He will swallow up death in victory; and the Lord GOD will wipe away tears from off all faces; and the rebuke of his people shall he take away from off all the earth: for the LORD hath spoken it.
Isaiah 25:8.

68 Thou wilt keep him in perfect peace, whose mind is stayed on thee.
Isaiah 26:3.

69 For precept must be upon precept, precept upon precept; line upon line, line upon line; here a little, and there a little:
For with stammering lips and another tongue will he speak to this people.
Isaiah 28:10–11.

70 We have made a covenant with death, and with hell are we at agreement.
Isaiah 28:15.

71 Behold, I lay in Zion for a foundation a stone, a tried stone, a precious corner stone, a sure foundation: he that believeth shall not make haste. Judgment also will I lay to the line, and righteousness to the plummet: and the hail shall sweep away the refuge of lies, and the waters shall overflow the hiding place.
Isaiah 28:16–17.

72 Forasmuch as this people draw near me with their mouth, and with their lips do honour me, but have removed their heart far from me, and their fear toward me is taught by the precept of men.
Isaiah 29:13.

73 In returning and rest shall ye be saved; in quietness and in confidence shall be your strength: and ye would not.
Isaiah 30:15.

74 And thine ears shall hear a word behind thee, saying, This is the way, walk ye in it, when ye turn to the right hand, and when ye turn to the left.
Isaiah 30:21.

75 And a man shall be as an hiding place from the wind, and a covert from the tempest; as rivers of water in a dry place, as the shadow of a great rock in a weary land.
Isaiah 32:2.

76 Then the eyes of the blind shall be opened, and the ears of the deaf shall be unstopped. Then shall the lame man leap as an hart, and the tongue of the dumb sing: for in the wilderness shall waters break out, and streams in the desert. And the parched ground shall become a pool, and the thirsty land springs of water: in the habitation of dragons, where each lay, shall be grass with reeds and rushes.
Isaiah 35:5–7.

77 And an highway shall be there, and a way, and it shall be called The way of holiness; the unclean shall not pass over it; but it shall be for those: the wayfaring men, though fools shall not err therein.
Isaiah 35:8.

78 Lo, thou trusted in the staff of this broken reed, on Egypt; whereon if a man lean, it will go into his hand, and pierce it: so is Pharaoh king of Egypt to all that trust in him.
Isaiah 36:6.

79 Comfort ye, comfort ye my people, saith your God.
Speak ye comfortably to Jerusalem, and cry unto her, that her warfare is accomplished, that her iniquity is pardoned: for she hath received of the LORD's hand double for all her sins.
The voice of him that crieth in the wilderness, Prepare ye the way of the LORD, make straight in the desert a highway for our God.
Every valley shall be exalted, and every mountain and hill shall be made low: and the crooked shall be made straight, and the rough places plain:
And the glory of the LORD shall be revealed, and all flesh shall see it together: for the mouth of the LORD hath spoken it.
The voice said, Cry. And he said, What shall I cry? All flesh is grass, and all the goodliness thereof is as the flower of the field:
The grass withereth, the flower fadeth: because the spirit of the LORD bloweth upon it: surely the people is grass. The grass withereth, the flower fadeth: but the word of our God shall stand for ever.
Isaiah 40:1–8.

80 He shall feed his flock like a shepherd: he shall gather the lambs with his arm, and carry them in his bosom, and shall gently lead those that are with young.
Isaiah 40:11.

81 Who hath measured the waters in the hollow of his hand, and meted out heaven with the span, and comprehended the dust of the earth in a measure, and weighed the mountains in scales, and the hills in a balance?
Isaiah 40:12.

82 Behold, the nations are as a drop of a bucket, and are counted as the small dust of the balance: behold, he taketh up the isles as a very little thing.
Isaiah 40:15.

83 To whom then will ye liken God? or what likeness will ye compare unto him?
Isaiah 40:18.

84 Have ye not known? have ye not heard? hath it not been told you from the beginning? have ye not understood from the foundations of the earth?
Isaiah 40:21.

85 Even the youths shall faint and be weary, and the young men shall utterly fall: But they that wait upon the LORD shall renew their strength; they shall mount up with wings as eagles; they shall run, and not be weary; and they shall walk, and not faint.
Isaiah 40:30–31.

86 A bruised reed shall he not break, and the smoking flax shall he not quench: he shall bring forth judgment unto truth.
Isaiah 42:3.

87 Fear not: for I have redeemed thee, I have called thee by thy name; thou art mine. When thou passest through the waters, I will be with thee; and through the rivers, they shall not overflow thee: when thou walkest through the fire, thou shalt not be burned; neither shall the flame kindle upon thee.
Isaiah 43:1–2.

88 Woe unto him that striveth with his Maker! Let the potsherd strive with the potsherds of the earth. Shall the clay say to him that fashioneth it, What makest thou? or thy work, He hath no hands?
Isaiah 45:9.

89 Can a woman forget her suckling child, that she should not have compassion on the son of her womb? yea, they may forget, yet will I not forget thee.
Isaiah 49:15.

90 How beautiful upon the mountains are the feet of him that bringeth good tidings, that publisheth peace; that bringeth good tidings of good, that publisheth salvation; that saith unto Zion, Thy God reigneth! Thy watchmen shall lift up the voice; with the voice together shall they sing: for they shall see eye to eye, when the LORD shall bring again Zion.
Isaiah 52:7–8.

91 Break forth into joy, sing together, ye waste places of Jerusalem: for the LORD hath comforted his people, he hath redeemed Jerusalem. The LORD hath made bare his holy arm in the eyes of all the nations; and all the ends of the earth shall see the salvation of our God.
Isaiah 52:9–10.

92 As many were astonished at thee; his visage was so marred more than any man, and his form more than the sons of men: So shall he sprinkle many nations; the kings shall shut their mouths at him: for that which had not been told them shall they see; and that which they had not heard shall they consider.
Isaiah 52:14–15.

93 Who hath believed our report? and to whom is the arm of the LORD revealed? For he shall grow up before him as a tender plant, and as a root out of a dry ground: he hath no form nor comeliness; and when we shall see him, there is no beauty that we should desire him. He is despised and rejected of men; a man of sorrows, and acquainted with grief: and we hid as it were our faces from him; he was despised, and we esteemed him not. Surely he hath borne our griefs, and carried our sorrows.
Isaiah 53:1–4.

94 But he was wounded for our transgressions, he was bruised for our iniquities: the chastisement of our peace was upon him; and with his stripes we are healed. All we like sheep have gone astray; we have turned every one to his own way; and the LORD hath laid on him the iniquity of us all. He was oppressed, and he was afflicted, yet he opened not his mouth: he is brought as a lamb to the slaughter, and as a sheep before her shearers is dumb, so he openeth not his mouth.
Isaiah 53:5–7.

95 He was cut off out of the land of the living: for the transgression of my people was he stricken. And he made his grave with the wicked, and with the rich in his death; because he had done no violence, neither was any deceit in his mouth.
Isaiah 53:8–9.

96 Ho, every one that thirsteth, come ye to the waters, and he that hath no money; come ye, buy, and eat; yea, come, buy wine and milk without money and without price. Wherefore do ye spend money for that which is not bread? and your labour for that which satisfieth not? hearken diligently unto me, and eat ye that which is good, and let your soul delight itself in fatness.
Isaiah 55:1–2.

97 Seek ye the LORD while he may be found, call ye upon him while he is near.
Isaiah 55:6.

98 For my thoughts are not your thoughts, neither are your ways my ways, saith the LORD. For as the heavens are higher than the earth, so are my ways higher than your ways, and my thoughts than your thoughts.
Isaiah 55:8–9.

99 For as the rain cometh down, and the snow from heaven, and returneth not thither, but watereth the earth, and maketh it bring forth and bud, that it may give seed to the sower, and bread to the eater: So shall my word be that goeth forth out of my mouth: it shall not return unto me void, but it shall accomplish that which I please, and it shall prosper in the thing whereto I sent it.
Isaiah 55:10–11.

1 For ye shall go out with joy, and be led forth with peace: the mountains and the hills shall break forth before you into singing, and all the trees of the field shall clap their hands.
Isaiah 55:12.

2 Instead of the thorn shall come up the fir tree, and instead of the brier shall come up the myrtle tree: and it shall be to the LORD for a name, for an everlasting sign that shall not be cut off.
Isaiah 55:13.

3 Peace, peace to him that is far off, and to him that is near, saith the LORD; and I will heal him.
Isaiah 57:19.

4 There is no peace, saith my God, to the wicked.
Isaiah 57:21.

5 Arise, shine; for thy light is come, and the glory of the LORD is risen upon thee.
Isaiah 60:1.

6 The Spirit of the Lord GOD is upon me; because the LORD hath anointed me to preach good tidings unto the meek; he hath sent me, to bind up the brokenhearted, to proclaim liberty to the captives, and the opening of the prison to them that are bound; To proclaim the acceptable year of the LORD, and the day of vengeance of our God; to comfort all that mourn; To appoint unto them that mourn in Zion, to give unto them beauty for ashes, the oil of joy for mourning, the garment of praise for the spirit of heaviness; that they might be called trees of righteousness, the planting of the LORD, that he might be glorified.
Isaiah 61:1–3.

7 But we are all as an unclean thing, and all our righteousnesses are as filthy rags; and we all do fade as a leaf; and our iniquities, like the wind, have taken us away.
Isaiah 64:6.

8 Stand by thyself, come not near to me; for I am holier than thou.
Isaiah 65:5.

9 For, behold, I create new heavens and a new earth: and the former shall not be remembered, nor come into mind.
Isaiah 65:17.

10 The wolf and the lamb shall feed together, and the lion shall eat straw like the bullock: and dust shall be the serpent's meat. They shall not hurt nor destroy in all my holy mountain, saith the LORD.
Isaiah 65:25.

11 Behold, I have put my words in thy mouth. See, I have this day set thee over the nations and over the kingdoms, to root out, and to pull down, and to destroy, and to throw down, to build, and to plant.
Jeremiah 1:9–10.

12 They have forsaken me the fountain of living waters, and hewed them out cisterns, broken cisterns, that can hold no water.
Jeremiah 2:13.

13 They were as fed horses in the morning: every one neighed after his neighbour's wife.
Jeremiah 5:8.

14 But this people hath a revolting and a rebellious heart; they are revolted and gone.
Jeremiah 5:23.

15 Saying, Peace, peace; when there is no peace.
Jeremiah 6:14.

16 Is this house, which is called by my name, become a den of robbers in your eyes?
Jeremiah 7:11.

17 The harvest is past, the summer is ended, and we are not saved.
Jeremiah 8:20.

18 Is there no balm in Gilead; is there no physician there?
Jeremiah 8:22.

19 Can the Ethiopian change his skin, or the leopard his spots? then may ye also do good, that are accustomed to do evil.
Jeremiah 13:23.

20 The heart is deceitful above all things, and desperately wicked: who can know it? I the LORD search the heart, I try the reins.
Jeremiah 17:9–10.

21 The LORD hath appeared of old unto me, saying, Yea, I have loved thee with an everlasting love: therefore with lovingkindness have I drawn thee.
Jeremiah 31:3.

22 A voice was heard in Ramah, lamentation, and bitter weeping; Rachel weeping for her children refused to be comforted for her children, because they were not.
Jeremiah 31:15.

23 How doth the city sit solitary, that was full of people! how is she become as a widow! she that was great among the nations, and princess among the provinces, how is she become tributary!
Lamentations 1:1.

24 Is it nothing to you, all ye that pass by? behold, and see if there be any sorrow like unto my sorrow.
Lamentations 1:12.

25 And I said, My strength and my hope is perished from the LORD: Remembering mine affliction and my misery, the wormwood and the gall.
Lamentations 3:18–19.

26 It is of the LORD'S mercies that we are not consumed, because his compassions fail not. They are new every morning: great is thy faithfulness.
Lamentations 3:22–3.

27 It is good for a man that he bear the yoke in his youth.
Lamentations 3:27.

28 The appearance of the wheels and their work was like unto the colour of a beryl: and they four had one likeness: and their appearance and their work was as it were a wheel in the middle of a wheel.
Of his vision in exile. Ezekiel 1:16.

29 For thou art not sent to a people of a strange speech and of an hard language, but to the house of Israel; Not many people of a strange speech and of an hard language, whose words thou canst not understand. Surely, had I sent thee to them, they would have hearkened unto thee.
Ezekiel 3:5–6.

30 And I will give them one heart, and I will put a new spirit within you; and I will take the stony heart out of their flesh, and will give them an heart of flesh.
Ezekiel 11:19.

31 Son of man, eat thy bread with quaking, and drink thy water with trembling and with carefulness.
Ezekiel 12:18.

32 The fathers have eaten sour grapes, and the children's teeth are set on edge.
Ezekiel 18:2.

33 I will accept you with your sweet savour, when I bring you out from the people, and gather you out of the countries wherein ye have been scattered; and I will be sanctified in you before the heathen. And ye shall know that I am the LORD, when I shall bring you into the land

of Israel, into the country for the which I lifted up mine hand to give it to your fathers. And there shall ye remember your ways, and all your doings, wherein ye have been defiled; and ye shall loath yourselves in your own sight for all your evils that ye have committed.
Ezekiel 20:41–3.

34 As I live, saith the Lord GOD, I have no pleasure in the death of the wicked; but that the wicked turn from his way and live: turn ye, turn ye from your evil ways; for why will ye die, O house of Israel?
Ezekiel 33:11.

35 The hand of the LORD was upon me, and carried me out in the spirit of the LORD, and set me down in the midst of the valley which was full of bones.
Ezekiel 37:1.

36 Son of man, can these bones live?
Ezekiel 37:3.

37 Prophesy upon these bones, and say unto them, O ye dry bones, hear the word of the LORD. Thus saith the Lord GOD unto these bones; Behold, I will cause breath to enter into you, and ye shall live: And I will lay sinews upon you, and will bring up flesh upon you, and cover you with skin, and put breath in you, and ye shall live; and ye shall know that I am the LORD.
Ezekiel 37:4–6.

38 Thou, O king, sawest, and behold a great image. This great image, whose brightness was excellent, stood before thee; and the form thereof was terrible. This image's head was of fine gold, his breast and his arms of silver, his belly and his thighs of brass. His legs of iron, his feet part of iron and part of clay. Thou sawest till that a stone was cut out without hands, which smote the image upon his feet that were of iron and clay, and brake them to pieces.
Daniel 2:31–34.

39 Then Nebuchadnezzar came near to the mouth of the burning fiery furnace, and spake, and said, Shadrach, Meshach, and Abednego, ye servants of the most high God, come forth, and come hither. Then Shadrach, Meshach, and Abednego, came forth of the midst of the fire.
Daniel 3:26.

40 The same hour was the thing fulfilled upon Nebuchadnezzar: and he was driven from men, and did eat grass as oxen, and his body was wet with the dew of heaven, till his hairs were grown like eagles' feathers, and his nails like birds' claws.
Daniel 4:33.

41 In the same hour came forth fingers of a man's hand, and wrote over against the candlestick upon the plaister of the wall of the king's palace: and the king saw the part of the hand that wrote.
Daniel 5:5.

42 And this is the writing that was written, MENE, MENE, TEKEL, UPHARSIN. This is the interpretation of the thing: MENE; God hath numbered thy kingdom, and finished it, TEKEL; Thou art weighed in the balances, and art found wanting. PERES; Thy kingdom is divided, and given to the Medes and Persians.
Daniel 5:25–8.

43 I saw in the night visions and, behold, one like the Son of man came with the clouds of heaven, and came to the Ancient of days, and they brought him near before him.
Daniel 7:13.

44 And they that be wise shall shine as the brightness of the firmament; and they that turn many to righteousness as the stars for ever and ever. But thou, O Daniel, shut up the words, and seal the book, even to the time of the end: many shall run to and fro, and knowledge shall be increased.
Daniel 12:3–4.

45 For they have sown the wind, and they shall reap the whirlwind.
Hosea 8:7.

46 When Israel was a child, then I loved him, and called my son out of Egypt.
Hosea 11:1.

47 And I will restore to you the years that the locust hath eaten, the cankerworm, and the caterpiller, and the palmerworm, my great army which I sent among you.
Joel 2:25.

48 And it shall come to pass afterward, that I will pour out my spirit upon all flesh, and your sons and your daughters shall prophesy, your old men shall dream dreams, your young men shall see visions.
Joel 2:28.

49 Beat your plowshares into swords, and your pruninghooks into spears: let the weak say, I am strong.
Joel 3:10.

50 Can two walk together, except they be agreed?
Amos 3:3.

51 The lion hath roared, who will not fear? the Lord GOD hath spoken, who can but prophesy?
Amos 3:8.

52 Therefore thus will I do unto thee, O Israel: and because I will do this unto thee, prepare to meet thy God, O Israel.
Amos 4:12.

53 Shall not the day of the LORD be darkness, and not light? even very dark, and no brightness in it?
Amos 5:20.

54 Behold, the days come, saith the Lord GOD, that I will send a famine in the land, not a famine of bread, nor a thirst for water, but of hearing the words of the LORD: And they shall wander from sea to sea, and from the north even to the east, they shall run to and fro to seek the word of the LORD, and shall not find it.
Amos 8:11–12.

55 But thou, Bethlehem, Ephratah, though thou be little among the thousands of Judah, yet out of thee shall he come forth unto me that is to be ruler in Israel.
Micah 5:2.

56 O LORD, revive thy work in the midst of the years, in the midst of the years make known; in wrath remember mercy.
Habakkuk 3:2.

57 He that earneth wages earneth wages to put it into a bag with holes.
Haggai 1:6.

Bible Zechariah

58 I lifted up mine eyes again, and looked, and behold a man with a measuring line in his hand. Then said I, Whither goest thou? And he said unto me, To measure Jerusalem, to see what is the breadth thereof, and what is the length thereof.
Zechariah 2:1–2.

59 For thus saith the LORD of hosts; After the glory hath he sent me unto the nations which spoiled you: for he that toucheth you toucheth the apple of his eye.
Zechariah 2:8.

60 Then he answered and spake unto me, saying, This is the word of the LORD unto Zerubbabel, saying, Not by might, nor by power, but by my spirit, saith the LORD of hosts.
Zechariah 4:6.

61 And I said unto them, If ye think good, give me my price; and if not, forbear. So they weighed for my price thirty pieces of silver.
Zechariah 11:12.

62 Have we not all one father, hath not one God created us? why do we deal treacherously every man against his brother, by profaning the covenant of our fathers?
Malachi 2:10.

63 Bring ye all the tithes into the storehouse, that there may be meat in mine house, and prove me now herewith, saith the LORD of hosts, if I will not open you the windows of heaven, and pour you out a blessing, that there shall not be room enough to receive it.
Malachi 3:10.

64 Then they that feared the LORD spake often one to another: and the LORD hearkened, and heard it, and a book of remembrance was written before him for them that feared the LORD, and that thought upon his name.
Malachi 3:16.

65 For, behold, the day cometh, that shall burn as an oven; and all the proud, yea, and all that do wickedly, shall be stubble: and the day that cometh shall burn them up, saith the LORD of hosts, that it shall leave them neither root nor branch. But unto you that fear my name shall the Sun of righteousness arise with healing in his wings; and ye shall go forth, and grow up as calves of the stall.
Malachi 4:1–2.

66 Behold, I will send you Elijah the prophet before the coming of the great and dreadful day of the LORD: And he shall turn the heart of the fathers to the children, and the heart of the children to their fathers, lest I come and smite the earth a curse.
Malachi 4:5–6.

Bible (Apocrypha)

67 The first wrote, Wine is the strongest. The second wrote, The king is strongest. The third wrote, Women are strongest: but above all things Truth beareth away the victory.
1 Esdras 3:10–12.

68 By this also ye must know that women have dominion over you: do ye not labour and toil, and give and bring all to the woman? Yea, a man taketh his sword, and goeth his way to rob and to steal, to sail upon the sea and upon rivers; And looketh upon a lion, and goeth in the darkness; and when he hath stolen, spoiled, and robbed, he bringeth it to his love.
1 Esdras 4:22–4.

69 Then were the entrances of this world made narrow, full of sorrow and travail: they are but few and evil, full of perils, and very painful. For the entrances of the elder world were wide and sure, and brought immortal fruit. If then they that live labour not to enter these strait and vain things, they can never receive those that are laid up for them.
2 Esdras 7:12–14.

70 For the world hath lost his youth, and the times begin to wax old.
2 Esdras 14:10.

71 Be not greedy to add money to money: but let it be as refuse in respect of our child.
Tobit 5:18.

72 For the ear of jealousy heareth all things: and the noise of murmurings is not hid.
Wisdom of Solomon 1:10.

73 Nevertheless through envy of the devil came death into the world: and they that do hold of his side do find it.
Wisdom of Solomon 2:24.

74 But the souls of the righteous are in the hand of God, and there shall no torment touch them. In the sight of the unwise they seemed to die: and their departure is taken for misery, And their going from us to be utter destruction: but they are in peace. For though they be punished in the sight of men, yet is their hope full of immortality. And having been a little chastised, they shall be greatly rewarded: for God proved them, and found them worthy for himself.
Wisdom of Solomon 3:1–5.

75 And in the time of their visitation they shall shine, and run to and fro like sparks among the stubble.
Wisdom of Solomon 3:7.

76 For the bewitching of naughtiness doth obscure things that are honest; and the wanderings of concupiscence doth undermine the simple mind. He being made perfect in a short time, fulfilled a long time.
Wisdom of Solomon 4:12–13.

77 Even so we in like manner, as soon as we were born, began to draw to our end, and had no sign of virtue to shew; but were consumed in our own wickedness. For the hope of the ungodly is like dust that is blown away with the wind; like a thin froth that is driven away with the storm; like as the smoke which is dispersed here and there with a tempest, and passeth away as the remembrance of a guest that tarrieth but a day.
Wisdom of Solomon 5:13–14.

78 For all men have one entrance into life, and the like going out.
Wisdom of Solomon 7:6.

79 For thou hast power of life and death: thou leadest to the gates of hell, and bringest up again.
Wisdom of Solomon 16:13.

80 My son, if thou come to serve the Lord, prepare thy soul for temptation.
Ecclesiasticus 2:1.

81 Saying, We will fall into the hands of the Lord, and not into the hands of men: for as his majesty is, so is his mercy.
Ecclesiasticus 2:18.

82 Be not curious in unnecessary matters: for more things are shewed unto thee than men understand.
Ecclesiasticus 3:23.

83 Be not ignorant of any thing in a great matter or a small.
Ecclesiasticus 5:15.

84 A faithful friend is the medicine of life; and they that fear the Lord shall find him.
Ecclesiasticus 6:16.

85 Laugh no man to scorn in the bitterness of his soul: for there is one which humbleth and exalteth.
Ecclesiasticus 7:11.

86 Miss not the discourse of the elders: for they also learned of their fathers, and of them thou shalt learn understanding, and to give answer as need requireth.
Ecclesiasticus 8:9.

87 Open not thine heart to every man, lest he requite thee with a shrewd turn.
Ecclesiasticus 8:19.

88 Give not thy soul unto a woman to set her foot upon thy substance.
Ecclesiasticus 9:2.

89 Forsake not an old friend; for the new is not comparable to him: a new friend is as new wine; when it is old, thou shalt drink it with pleasure.
Ecclesiasticus 9:10.

90 Many kings have sat down upon the ground; and one that was never thought of hath worn the crown.
Ecclesiasticus 11:5.

91 Judge none blessed before his death: for a man shall be known in his children.
Ecclesiasticus 11:28.

92 He that toucheth pitch shall be difiled therewith; and he that hath fellowship with a proud man shall be like unto him.
Ecclesiasticus 13:1.

93 Burden not thyself above thy power while thou livest; and have no fellowship with one that is mightier and richer than thyself: for how agree the kettle and the earthen pot together? for if the one be smitten against the other, it shall be broken.
Ecclesiasticus 13:2.

94 All flesh waxeth old as a garment: for the covenant from the beginning is, Thou shalt die the death.
Ecclesiasticus 14:17.

95 Desire not a multitude of unprofitable children, neither delight in ungodly sons.
Ecclesiasticus 16:1.

96 Be not made a beggar by banqueting upon borrowing, when thou hast nothing in thy purse: for thou shalt lie in wait for thine own life, and be talked on.
Ecclesiasticus 18:33.

97 A labouring man that is given to drunkenness shall not be rich: and he that contemneth small things shall fall by little and little.
Ecclesiasticus 19:1.

98 Wine and women will make men of understanding to fall away: and he that cleaveth to harlots will become impudent.
Ecclesiasticus 19:2.

99 If thou hast heard a word, let it die with thee; and be bold, it will not burst thee.
Ecclesiasticus 19:10.

1 As the climbing up a sandy way is to the feet of the aged, so is a wife full of words to a quiet man.
Ecclesiasticus 25:20.

2 The stroke of the whip maketh marks in the flesh: but the stroke of the tongue breaketh the bones. Many have fallen by the edge of the sword: but not so many as have fallen by the tongue.
Ecclesiasticus 28:17–18.

3 Envy and wrath shorten the life, and carefulness bringeth age before the time.
Ecclesiasticus 30:24.

4 Leave off first for manners' sake; and be not unsatiable, lest thou offend.
Ecclesiasticus 31:17.

5 Wine is as good as life to a man, if it be drunk moderately: what life is then to a man that is without wine? for it was made to make men glad.
Ecclesiasticus 31:27.

6 Let thy speech be short, comprehending much in few words; be as one that knoweth and yet holdeth his tongue.
Ecclesiasticus 32:8.

7 In all thy works keep to thyself the preeminence; leave not a stain in thine honour.
Ecclesiasticus 33:22.

8 Honour a physician with the honour due unto him for the uses which ye may have of him: for the Lord hath created him. For of the most High cometh healing, and he shall receive honour of the king.
Ecclesiasticus 38:1–2.

9 The wisdom of a learned man cometh by opportunity of leisure: and he that hath little business shall become wise. How can he get wisdom that holdeth the plough, and that glorieth in the goad, that driveth oxen, and is occupied in their labours, and whose talk is of bullocks?
Ecclesiasticus 38:24–5.

10 Let us now praise famous men, and our fathers that begat us.
Ecclesiasticus 44:1.

11 Their bodies are buried in peace; but their name liveth for evermore.
Ecclesiasticus 44:14.

12 Here then will we begin the story: only adding thus much to that which hath been said, that it is a foolish thing to make a long prologue, and to be short in the story itself.
Maccabees 2:32.

13 And when he was at the last gasp, he said, Thou like a fury takest us out of this present life, but the King of the world shall raise us up, who have died for his laws, unto everlasting life.
Maccabees 7:9.

Bible (New Testament)

14 And she shall bring forth a son, and thou shalt call his name JESUS: for he shall save his people from their sins.
St Matthew 1:21.

15 Now all this was done, that it might be fulfilled which was spoken of the Lord by the prophet, saying, Behold, a virgin shall be with child, and shall bring forth a son, and they shall call his name Emmanuel, which being interpreted is, God with us.
St Matthew 1:22–3.

16 Now when Jesus was born in Bethlehem of Judaea in the days of Herod the king, behold, there came wise men from the east to Jerusalem, Saying, Where is he that is born King of the Jews? for we have seen his star in the east, and are come to worship him.
St Matthew 2:1–2.

17 And when they were come into the house, they saw the young child with Mary his mother, and fell down, and worshipped him: and when they had opened their treasures, they presented unto him gifts; gold, and frankincense, and myrrh.
St Matthew 2:11.

18 And saying, Repent ye: for the kingdom of heaven is at hand. For this is he that was spoken of by the prophet Esaias, saying, The voice of one crying in the wilderness, Prepare ye the way of the Lord, make his paths straight.
St Matthew 3:2–3.

19 And the same John had his raiment of camel's hair, and a leathern girdle about his loins; and his meat was locusts and wild honey.
St Matthew 3:4.

20 But when he saw many of the Pharisees and Sadducees come to his baptism, he said unto them, O generation of vipers, who hath warned you to flee from the wrath to come?
St Matthew 3:7.

21 And Jesus, when he was baptized, went up straightway out of the water: and, lo, the heavens were opened unto him, and he saw the Spirit of God descending like a dove, and lighting upon him: And lo a voice from heaven, saying, This is my beloved Son, in whom I am well pleased.
St Matthew 3:16–17.

22 Then was Jesus led up of the spirit into the wilderness to be tempted of the devil. And when he had fasted forty days and forty nights, he was afterward an hungred. And when the tempter came to him, he said, If thou be the Son of God, command that these stones be made bread. But he answered and said, It is written, Man shall not live by bread alone, but by every word that proceedeth out of the mouth of God.
St Matthew 4:1–4.

23 Jesus said unto him, It is written again, Thou shalt not tempt the Lord thy God.
St Matthew 4:7.

24 Again, the devil taketh him up into an exceeding high mountain, and sheweth him all the kingdoms of the world, and the glory of them; And saith unto him, All these things will I give thee, if thou wilt fall down and worship me. Then saith Jesus unto him, Get thee hence, Satan: for it is written, Thou shalt worship the Lord thy God, and him only shalt thou serve.
St Matthew 4:8–10.

25 The people which sat in darkness saw great light; and to them which sat in the region and shadow of death light is sprung up.
St Matthew 4:16.

26 And he saith unto them, Follow me, and I will make you fishers of men.
St Matthew 4:19.

27 And seeing the multitudes, he went up into a mountain: and when he was set, his disciples came unto him: And he opened his mouth, and taught them, saying, Blessed are the poor in spirit: for theirs is the kingdom of heaven.
Blessed are they that mourn: for they shall be comforted.
Blessed are the meek: for they shall inherit the earth.
Blessed are they which do hunger and thirst after righteousness: for they shall be filled.
Blessed are the merciful: for they shall obtain mercy.
Blessed are the pure in heart: for they shall see God.
Blessed are the peacemakers: for they shall be called the children of God.
Blessed are they which are persecuted for righteousness' sake: for theirs is the kingdom of heaven.
Blessed are ye, when men shall revile you, and persecute you, and shall say all manner of evil against you falsely, for my sake.
Rejoice, and be exceeding glad: for great is your reward in heaven: for so persecuted they the prophets which were before you.
St Matthew 5:1–12.

28 Ye are the salt of the earth: but if the salt have lost his savour, wherewith shall it be salted? it is thenceforth good for nothing, but to be cast out, and to be trodden under foot of men.
St Matthew 5:13.

29 Ye are the light of the world. A city that is set on an hill cannot be hid. Neither do men light a candle, and put it under a bushel, but on a candlestick; and it giveth light unto all that are in the house. Let your light so shine before men, that they may see your good works and glorify your Father which is in heaven.
St Matthew 5:14–16.

30 Think not that I am come to destroy the law, or the prophets: I am not come to destroy, but to fulfil. For verily I say unto you, Till heaven and earth pass, one jot or one tittle shall in no wise pass from the law, till all be fulfilled.
St Matthew 5:17–18.

31 For I say unto you, That except your righteousness shall exceed the righteousness of the scribes and Pharisees, ye shall in no case enter into the kingdom of heaven.
St Matthew 5:20.

32 But I say unto you, That whosoever is angry with his brother without a cause shall be in danger of the judgment: and whosoever shall say to his brother, Raca, shall be in danger of the council: but whosoever shall say, Thou fool, shall be in danger of hell fire.
St Matthew 5:22.

33 Ye have heard that it was said by them of old time. Thou shalt not commit adultery: But I say unto you. That whosoever looketh on a woman to lust after her hath committed adultery with her already in his heart.
St Matthew 5:27–8.

34 And if thy right eye offend thee, pluck it out, and cast it from thee: for it is profitable for thee that one of thy members should perish, and not that thy whole body

should be cast into hell. And if thy right hand offend thee, cut it off, and cast it from thee: for it is profitable for thee that one of thy members should perish, and not that thy whole body should be cast into hell.
St Matthew 5:29–30.

35 Ye have heard that it hath been said, An eye for an eye, and a tooth for a tooth: But I say unto you, That ye resist not evil: but whosoever shall smite thee on thy right cheek, turn to him the other also.
St Matthew 5:38–9.

36 And whosoever shall compel thee to go a mile, go with him twain.
St Matthew 5:41.

37 Ye have heard that it hath been said, Thou shalt love thy neighbour, and hate thine enemy. But I say unto you, Love your enemies, bless them that curse you, do good to them that hate you, and pray for them which despitefully use you, and persecute you.
St Matthew 5:43–4.

38 That ye may be the children of your Father which is in heaven: for he maketh his sun to rise on the evil and on the good, and sendeth rain on the just and on the unjust.
St Matthew 5:45.

39 Be ye therefore perfect, even as your Father which is in heaven is perfect.
St Matthew 5:48.

40 Therefore when thou doest thine alms, do not sound a trumpet before thee, as the hypocrites do in the synagogues and in the streets, that they may have glory of men, Verily I say unto you, They have their reward. But when thou doest alms, let not thy left hand know what thy right hand doeth: That thine alms may be in secret: and thy Father which seeth in secret himself shall reward thee openly.
St Matthew 6:2–4.

41 But thou, when thou prayest, enter into thy closet, and when thou hast shut thy door, pray to thy Father which is in secret; and thy Father which seeth in secret shall reward thee openly. But when ye pray, use not vain repetitions, as the heathen do: for they think that they shall be heard for their much speaking.
St Matthew 6:6–7.

42 After this manner therefore pray ye: Our Father which art in heaven, Hallowed be thy name. Thy kingdom come. Thy will be done in earth, as it is in heaven. Give us this day our daily bread. And forgive us our debts, as we forgive our debtors. And lead us not into temptation, but deliver us from evil: For thine is the kingdom, and the power, and the glory, for ever. Amen.
St Matthew 6:9–13

43 Lay not up for yourselves treasures upon earth, where moth and rust doth corrupt, and where thieves break through and steal: But lay up for yourselves treasures in heaven, where neither moth nor rust doth corrupt, and where thieves do not break through nor steal: For where your treasure is, there will your heart be also.
St Matthew 6:19–21.

44 No man can serve two masters: for either he will hate the one, and love the other; or else he will hold to the one, and despise the other. Ye cannot serve God and mammon.
St Matthew 6:24.

45 Behold the fowls of the air: for they sow not, neither do they reap, nor gather into barns; yet your heavenly Father feedeth them. Are ye not much better than they? Which of you by taking thought can add one cubit unto his stature? And why take ye thought for raiment? Consider the lilies of the field, how they grow; they toil not, neither do they spin: And yet I say unto you, That even Solomon in all his glory was not arrayed like one of these.
St Matthew 6:26–9.

46 But seek ye first the kingdom of God, and his righteousness; and all these things shall be added unto you. Take therefore no thought for the morrow: for the morrow shall take thought for the things of itself. Sufficient unto the day is the evil thereof.
St Matthew 6:33–4

47 Judge not, that ye be not judged. For with what judgment ye judge, ye shall be judged: and with what measure ye mete, it shall be measured to you again.
St Matthew 7:1–2.

48 And why beholdest thou the mote that is in thy brother's eye, but considerest not the beam that is in thine own eye?
St Matthew 7:3.

49 Give not that which is holy unto the dogs, neither cast ye your pearls before swine, lest they trample them under their feet, and turn again and rend you.
St Matthew 7:6.

50 Ask, and it shall be given you; seek, and ye shall find; knock, and it shall be opened unto you: For every one that asketh receiveth; and he that seeketh findeth; and to him that knocketh it shall be opened.
St Matthew 7:7–8.

51 Or what man is there of you, whom if his son ask bread, will he give him a stone? Or if he ask a fish, will he give him a serpent? If ye then, being evil, know how to give good gifts unto your children, how much more shall your Father which is in heaven give good things to them that ask him?
St Matthew 7:9–11.

52 Enter ye in at the strait gate: for wide is the gate, and broad is the way, that leadeth to destruction, and many there be which go in thereat: Because strait is the gate, and narrow is the way, which leadeth unto life, and few there be that find it.
St Matthew 7:13–14.

53 Beware of false prophets, which come to you in sheep's clothing, but inwardly they are ravening wolves.
St Matthew 7:15.

54 Wherefore by their fruits ye shall know them.
St Matthew 7:20.

55 Not every one that saith unto me, Lord, Lord, shall enter into the kingdom of heaven; but he that doeth the will of my Father which is in heaven.
St Matthew 7:21.

56 Therefore whosoever heareth these sayings of mine, and doeth them, I will liken him unto a wise man, which built his house upon a rock: And the rain descended, and the floods came, and the winds blew, and beat upon that house; and it fell not: for it was founded upon a rock. And every one that heareth these sayings of mine,

and doeth them not, shall be likened unto a foolish man, which built his house upon the sand: And the rain descended, and the floods came, and the winds blew, and beat upon that house; and it fell: and great was the fall of it.
St Matthew 7:24–7.

57 The centurion answered and said, Lord, I am not worthy that thou shouldest come under my roof: but speak the word only, and my servant shall be healed. For I am a man under authority, having soldiers under me: and I say to this man, Go, and he goeth; and to another, Come, and he cometh; and to my servant, Do this, and he doeth it. When Jesus heard it, he marvelled, and said to them that followed, Verily I say unto you, I have not found so great faith, no, not in Israel.
St Matthew 8:8–10.

58 But the children of the kingdom shall be cast out into outer darkness: there shall be weeping and gnashing of teeth.
St Matthew 8:12.

59 And Jesus saith unto him, The foxes have holes, and the birds of the air have nests; but the Son of man hath not where to lay his head.
St Matthew 8:20.

60 But Jesus said unto him, Follow me; and let the dead bury their dead.
St Matthew 8:22.

61 And his disciples came to him, and awoke him, saying, Lord, save us: we perish. And he saith unto them, Why are ye fearful, O ye of little faith? Then he arose, and rebuked the winds and the sea; and there was a great calm. But the men marvelled, saying, What manner of man is this, that even the winds and the sea obey him!
St Matthew 8:25–7.

62 And as Jesus passed forth from thence, he saw a man, named Matthew, sitting at the receipt of custom: and he saith unto him, Follow me. And he arose, and followed him.
St Matthew 9:9.

63 But when Jesus heard that, he said unto them, They that be whole need not a physician, but they that are sick. But go ye and learn what that meaneth, I will have mercy, and not sacrifice: for I am not come to call the righteous, but sinners to repentance.
St Matthew 9:12–13.

64 No man putteth a piece of new cloth unto an old garment, for that which is put in to fill it up taketh from the garment, and the rent is made worse. Neither do men put new wine into old bottles: else the bottles break, and the wine runneth out, and the bottles perish: but they put new wine into new bottles, and both are preserved.
St Matthew 9:16–17.

65 But the Pharisees said, He casteth out devils through the prince of the devils.
St Matthew 9:34.

66 But go rather to the lost sheep of the house of Israel.
St Matthew 10:6.

67 Heal the sick, cleanse the lepers, raise the dead, cast out devils: freely ye have received, freely give.
St Matthew 10:8.

68 And whosoever shall not receive you, nor hear your words, when ye depart out of that house or city, shake off the dust of your feet.
St Matthew 10:14.

69 Behold, I send you forth as sheep in the midst of wolves: be ye therefore wise as serpents, and harmless as doves.
St Matthew 10:16.

70 The disciple is not above his master, nor the servant above his lord.
St Matthew 10:24.

71 Are not two sparrows sold for a farthing? and one of them shall not fall on the ground without your Father. But the very hairs of your head are all numbered. Fear ye not therefore, ye are of more value than many sparrows.
St Matthew 10:29–31.

72 Think not that I am come to send peace on earth: I came not to send peace, but a sword.
St Matthew 10:34.

73 He that loveth father or mother more than me is not worthy of me: and he that loveth son or daughter more than me is not worthy of me. And he that taketh not his cross, and followeth after me, is not worthy of me. He that findeth his life shall lose it: and he that loseth his life for my sake shall find it.
St Matthew 10:37–9.

74 And whosoever shall give to drink unto one of these little ones a cup of cold water only in the name of a disciple, verily I say unto you, he shall in no wise lose his reward.
St Matthew 10:42.

75 And said unto him, Art thou he that should come, or do we look for another?
St Matthew 11:3.

76 Jesus answered and said unto them, Go and shew John again those things which ye do hear and see: The blind receive their sight, and the lame walk, the lepers are cleansed, and the deaf hear, the dead are raised up, and the poor have the gospel preached to them.
St Matthew 11:4–5.

77 And as they departed, Jesus began to say unto the multitudes concerning John, What went ye out into the wilderness to see? A reed shaken with the wind? But what went ye out for to see? A man clothed in soft raiment? behold, they that wear soft clothing are in kings' houses. But what went ye out for to see? A prophet? yea, I say unto you, and more than a prophet.
St Matthew 11:7–9.

78 He that hath ears to hear, let him hear.
St Matthew 11:15.

79 And saying, We have piped unto you, and ye have not danced; we have mourned unto you, and ye have not lamented.
St Matthew 11:17.

80 But wisdom is justified of her children.
St Matthew 11:19.

81 Come unto me, all ye that labour and are heavy laden, and I will give you rest. Take my yoke upon you, and learn of me; for I am meek and lowly in heart: and ye shall find rest unto your souls. For my yoke is easy, and my burden is light.
St Matthew 11:28–30.

82 A bruised reed shall he not break, and smoking flax shall he not quench, till he send forth judgment unto victory.
St Matthew 12:20.

83 He that is not with me is against me: and he that gathereth not with me scattereth abroad.
St Matthew 12:30.

84 Wherefore I say unto you, All manner of sin and blasphemy shall be forgiven unto men: but the blasphemy against the Holy Ghost shall not be forgiven unto men.
St Matthew 12:31.

85 O generation of vipers, how can ye, being evil, speak good things? for out of the abundance of the heart the mouth speaketh.
St Matthew 12:34.

86 But he answered and said unto them, An evil and adulterous generation seeketh after a sign; and there shall no sign be given to it, but the sign of the prophet Jonas: For Jonas was three days and three nights in the whale's belly; so shall the Son of man be three days and three nights in the heart of the earth.
St Matthew 12:39–40.

87 The queen of the south shall rise up in the judgment with this generation, and shall condemn it: for she came from the uttermost parts of the earth to hear the wisdom of Solomon; and, behold, a greater than Solomon is here.
St Matthew 12:42.

88 When the unclean spirit is gone out of a man, he walketh through dry places, seeking rest, and findeth none. Then he saith, I will return into my house from whence I came out; and when he is come, he findeth it empty, swept, and garnished. Then goeth he, and taketh with himself seven other spirits more wicked than himself, and they enter in and dwell there: and the last state of that man is worse than the first. Even so shall it be also unto this wicked generation.
St Matthew 12:43–5.

89 And he stretched forth his hand toward his disciples, and said, Behold my mother and my brethren! For whosoever shall do the will of my Father which is in heaven, the same is my brother, and sister, and mother.
St Matthew 12:49–50.

90 And he spake many things unto them in parables, saying, Behold, a sower went forth to sow; And when he sowed, some seeds fell by the wayside, and the fowls came and devoured them up: Some fell upon stony places, where they had not much earth: and forthwith they sprung up, because they had no deepness of earth: And when the sun was up, they were scorched; and because they had no root, they withered away. And some fell among thorns; and the thorns sprung up, and choked them: But others fell into good ground, and brought forth fruit, some an hundredfold, some sixtyfold, some thirtyfold.
St Matthew 13:3–8.

91 He also that received seed among the thorns is he that heareth the word; and the care of this world, and the deceitfulness of riches, choke the word, and he becometh unfruitful.
St Matthew 13:22.

92 But he that received seed into the good ground is he that heareth the word, and understandeth it; which also beareth fruit, and bringeth forth, some an hundredfold, some sixty, some thirty.
St Matthew 13:23.

93 But while men slept, his enemy came and sowed tares among the wheat, and went his way.
St Matthew 13:25.

94 He said unto them, An enemy hath done this. The servants said unto him, Wilt thou then that we go and gather them up?
St Matthew 13:28.

95 Another parable put he forth unto them, saying, The kingdom of heaven is like to a grain of mustard seed which a man took, and sowed in his field: Which indeed is the least of all seeds: but when it is grown, it is the greatest among herbs, and becometh a tree, so that the birds of the air come and lodge in the branches thereof.
St Matthew 13:31–2.

96 Again the kingdom of heaven is like unto a merchant man, seeking goodly pearls: Who, when he had found one pearl of great price, went and sold all that he had, and bought it.
St Matthew 13:45–6.

97 And they were offended in him. But Jesus said unto them, A prophet is not without honour, save in his own country, and in his own house.
St Matthew 13:57.

98 And they say unto him, We have here but five loaves, and two fishes.
St Matthew 14:17.

99 And in the fourth watch of the night Jesus went unto them, walking on the sea. And when the disciples saw him walking on the sea, they were troubled, saying, It is a spirit; and they cried out for fear. But straightway Jesus spake unto them, saying, Be of good cheer; it is I; be not afraid.
St Matthew 14:25–7.

1 And immediately Jesus stretched forth his hand, and caught him, and said unto him, O thou of little faith, wherefore didst thou doubt?
St Matthew 14:31.

2 Not that which goeth into the mouth defileth a man; but that which cometh out of the mouth, this defileth a man.
St Matthew 15:11.

3 Let them alone: they be blind leaders of the blind. And if the blind lead the blind, both shall fall into the ditch.
St Matthew 15:14.

4 And she said, Truth, Lord: yet the dogs eat of the crumbs which fall from their masters' table.
St Matthew 15:27.

5 He answered and said unto them, When it is evening, ye say, It will be fair weather: for the sky is red. And in the morning, It will be foul weather to day: for the sky is red and lowring. O ye hypocrites, ye can discern the face of the sky; but can ye not discern the signs of the times?
St Matthew 16:2–3.

6 Thou art Peter, and upon this rock I will build my church; and the gates of hell shall not prevail against it. And I will give unto thee the keys of the kingdom of heaven: and whatsoever thou shalt loose on earth shall be loosed in heaven.
St Matthew 16:18–19.

Bible St Matthew

7 But he turned, and said unto Peter, Get thee behind me, Satan: thou art an offence unto me: for thou savourest not the things that be of God, but those that be of men.
St Matthew 16:23.

8 For whosoever will save his life shall lose it: and whosoever will lose his life for my sake shall find it. For what is a man profited, if he shall gain the whole world, and lose his own soul? or what shall a man give in exchange for his soul?
St Matthew 16:25–6.

9 And Jesus said unto them, Because of your unbelief: for verily I say unto you, If ye have faith as a grain of mustard seed, ye shall say unto this mountain, Remove hence to yonder place; and it shall remove; and nothing shall be impossible unto you.
St Matthew 17:20.

10 And said, Verily I say unto you, Except ye be converted, and become as little children, ye shall not enter into the kingdom of heaven.
St Matthew 18:3.

11 And whoso shall receive one such little child in my name receiveth me. But whoso shall offend one of these little ones which believe in me, it were better for him that a millstone were hanged about his neck, and that he were drowned in the depth of the sea.
St Matthew 18:5–6.

12 And if thine eye offend thee, pluck it out, and cast it from thee: it is better for thee to enter into life with one eye, rather than having two eyes to be cast into hell fire.
St Matthew 18:9.

13 For where two or three are gathered together in my name, there am I in the midst of them.
St Matthew 18:20.

14 Then came Peter to him, and said, Lord, how oft shall my brother sin against me, and I forgive him? till seven times? Jesus saith unto him, I say not unto thee, Until seven times: but, Until seventy times seven.
St Mattthew 18:21–2.

15 What therefore God hath joined together, let not man put asunder.
St Matthew 19:6.

16 Then were there brought unto him little children, that he should put his hands on them, and pray: and the disciples rebuked them. But Jesus said, Suffer little children, and forbid them not, to come unto me: for of such is the kingdom of heaven.
St Matthew 19:13–14.

17 Jesus said unto him, If thou wilt be perfect, go and sell that thou hast, and give to the poor, and thou shalt have treasure in heaven: and come and follow me. But when the young man heard that saying, he went away sorrowful: for he had great possessions.
St Matthew 19:21–2.

18 And again I say unto you, It is easier for a camel to go through the eye of a needle, than for a rich man to enter into the kingdom of God.
St Matthew 19:24.

19 When his disciples heard it, they were exceedingly amazed, saying, Who then can be saved? But Jesus beheld them, and said unto them, With men this is impossible; but with God all things are possible.
St Matthew 19:25–6.

20 But many that are first shall be last; and the last shall be first.
St Matthew 19:30.

21 And about the eleventh hour he went out, and found others standing idle, and saith unto them, Why stand ye here all the day idle?
St Matthew 20:6.

22 Is it not lawful for me to do what I will with mine own? Is thine eye evil, because I am good? So the last shall be first, and the first last: for many be called, but few chosen.
St Matthew 20:15–16.

23 And Jesus went into the temple of God, and cast out all them that sold and bought in the temple, and overthrew the tables of the moneychangers, and the seats of them that sold doves, And said unto them, It is written, My house shall be called the house of prayer; but ye have made it a den of thieves.
St Matthew 21:12–13.

24 Render therefore unto Caesar the things which are Caesar's; and unto God the things that are God's.
St Matthew 22:21.

25 For in the resurrection they neither marry, nor are given in marriage, but are as the angels of God in heaven.
St Matthew 22:30.

26 Jesus said unto him, Thou shalt love the Lord Thy God with all thy heart, and with all thy soul, and with all thy mind. This is the first and great commandment. And the second is like unto it, Thou shalt love thy neighbour as thyself. On these two commandments hang all the law and the prophets.
St Matthew 22:37–40.

27 Ye blind guides, which strain at a gnat, and swallow a camel.
St Matthew 23:24.

28 Woe unto you, scribes and Pharisees, hypocrites! for ye are like unto whited sepulchres, which indeed appear beautiful outward, but are within full of dead men's bones, and of all uncleanness.
St Matthew 23:27.

29 And ye shall hear of wars and rumours or wars: see that ye be not troubled: for all these things must come to pass, but the end is not yet. For nation shall rise against nation, and kingdom against kingdom: and there shall be famines, and pestilences, and earthquakes, in divers places.
St Matthew 24:6–7.

30 Verily I say unto you. This generation shall not pass, till all these things be fulfilled. Heaven and earth shall pass away, but my words shall not pass away.
St Matthew 24:34–5.

31 For as in the days that were before the flood they were eating and drinking, marrying and giving in marriage, until the day that Noe entered into the ark.
St Matthew 24:38.

32 Watch therefore: for ye know not what hour your Lord doth come. But know this, that if the goodman of the

house had known in what watch the thief would come, he would have watched, and would not have suffered his house to be broken up.
St Matthew 24:42–3.

33 His lord said unto him, Well done, thou good and faithful servant: thou hast been faithful over a few things, I will make thee ruler over many things: enter thou into the joy of thy lord.
St Matthew 25:21.

34 For unto every one that hath shall be given, and he shall have abundance: but from him that hath not shall be taken away even that which he hath. And cast ye the unprofitable servant into outer darkness: there shall be weeping and gnashing of teeth.
St Matthew 25:29–30.

35 When the Son of man shall come in his glory, and all the holy angels with him, then shall he sit upon the throne of his glory: And before him shall be gathered all nations: and he shall separate them one from another, as a shepherd divideth his sheep from the goats: And he shall set the sheep on his right hand, but the goats on the left.
St Matthew 25:31–3.

36 For I was an hungred, and ye gave me meat: I was thirsty, and ye gave me drink: I was a stranger, and ye took me in: Naked, and ye clothed me: I was sick, and ye visited me: I was in prison, and ye came unto me.
St Matthew 25:35–6.

37 And the King shall answer and say unto them, Verily I say unto you, Inasmuch as ye have done it unto one of the least of these my brethren, ye have done it unto me.
St Matthew 25:40.

38 For ye have the poor always with you; but me ye have not always.
St Matthew 26:11.

39 Then one of the twelve, called Judas Iscariot, went unto the chief priests, And said unto them, What will ye give me, and I will deliver him unto you? And they covenanted with him for thirty pieces of silver.
St Matthew 26:14–15.

40 And as they were eating, Jesus took bread, and blessed it, and brake it, and gave it to the disciples, and said, Take, eat; this is my body. And he took the cup, and gave thanks, and gave it to them, saying, Drink ye all of it; For this is my blood of the new testament, which is shed for many for the remission of sins.
St Matthew 26:26–8.

41 Jesus said unto him, Verily I say unto thee, That this night, before the cock crow, thou shalt deny me thrice. Peter said unto him, Though I should die with thee yet will I not deny thee. Likewise also said all the disciples.
St Matthew 26:34–5.

42 And he went a little further, and fell on his face, and prayed, saying, O my Father, if it be possible, let this cup pass from me: nevertheless not as I will, but as thou wilt.
St Matthew 26:39.

43 Watch and pray, that ye enter not into temptation: the spirit indeed is willing, but the flesh is weak.
St Matthew 26:41.

44 Then said Jesus unto him, Put up again thy sword into his place: for all they that take the sword shall perish with the sword.
St Matthew 26:52.

45 When Pilate saw that he could prevail nothing, but that rather a tumult was made, he took water, and washed his hands before the multitude, saying I am innocent of the blood of this just person: see ye to it.
St Matthew 27:24.

46 He saved others; himself he cannot save. If he be the King of Israel, let him now come down from the cross, and we will believe him.
St Matthew 27:42.

47 And about the ninth hour Jesus cried with a loud voice, saying Eli, Eli, lama sabachthani? that is to say, My God, my God, why hast thou forsaken me?
St Matthew 27:46.

48 Jesus, when he had cried again with a loud voice, yielded up the ghost. And behold, the veil of the temple was rent in twain from the top to the bottom; and the earth did quake, and the rocks rent; And the graves were opened; and many bodies of the saints which slept arose.
St Matthew 27:50–2.

49 And, lo, I am with you alway, even unto the end of the world. Amen.
St Matthew 28:20.

50 When Jesus heard it, he saith unto them, They that are whole have no need of the physician, but they that are sick: I came not to call the righteous, but sinners to repentance.
St Mark 2:17.

51 And he said unto them, The sabbath was made for man, and not man for the sabbath: Therefore the Son of man is Lord also of the sabbath.
St Mark 2:27–8.

52 And if a kingdom be divided against itself, that kingdom cannot stand. And if a house be divided against itself, that house cannot stand.
St Mark 3:24–5.

53 And he said unto them, He that hath ears to hear, let him hear.
St Mark 4:9.

54 And he said unto them, Take heed what ye hear: with what measure ye mete, it shall be measured to you: and unto you that hear shall more be given.
St Mark 4:24.

55 And he asked him, What is thy name? And he answered, saying, My name is Legion: for we are many.
St Mark 5:9.

56 And Jesus, immediately knowing in himself that virtue had gone out of him, turned him about in the press, and said, Who touched my clothes?
St Mark 5:30.

57 And were beyond measure astonished, saying, He hath done all things well: he maketh both the deaf to hear, and the dumb to speak.
St Mark 7:37.

58 And he looked up, and said, I see men as trees, walking.
St Mark 8:24.

59 And straightway the father of the child cried out, and said with tears, Lord, I believe; help thou mine unbelief.
St Mark 9:24.

60 But when Jesus saw it, he was much displeased, and said unto them, Suffer the little children to come unto me, and forbid them not: for of such is the kingdom of God.
St Mark 10:14.

61 And there came a certain poor widow, and she threw in two mites, which make a farthing. And he called unto him his disciples, and saith unto them, Verily I say unto you, That this poor widow hath cast more in, than all they which have cast into the treasury: For all they did cast in of their abundance; but she of her want did cast in all that she had, even all her living.
St Mark 12:42–4.

62 And when the centurion, which stood over against him, saw that he so cried out, and gave up the ghost, he said, Truly this man was the Son of God.
St Mark 15:39.

63 And he said unto them, Go ye into all the world, and preach the gospel to every creature.
St Mark 16:15.

64 And the angel came in unto her, and said, Hail, thou that art highly favoured, the Lord is with thee: blessed art thou among women. And when she saw him, she was troubled at his saying, and cast in her mind what manner of salutation this should be.
St Luke 1:28–9.

65 And Mary said, Behold the handmaid of the Lord; be it unto me according to thy word. And the angel departed from her.
St Luke 1:38.

66 And Mary said,
My soul doth magnify the Lord,
And my spirit hath rejoiced in God my Saviour.
For he hath regarded the low estate of his handmaiden: for, behold, from henceforth all generations shall call me blessed.
For he that is mighty hath done to me great things; and holy is his name.
And his mercy is on them that fear him from generation to generation.
He hath shewed strength with his arm; he hath scattered the proud in the imagination of their hearts.
He hath put down the mighty from their seats, and exalted them of low degree.
He hath filled the hungry with good things; and the rich he hath sent empty away.
St Luke 1:46–53.

67 And it came to pass in those days, that there went out a decree from Caesar Augustus, that all the world should be taxed.
St Luke 2:1.

68 And so it was, that, while they were there, the days were accomplished that she should be delivered. And she brought forth her firstborn son, and wrapped him in swaddling clothes, and laid him in a manger; because there was no room for them in the inn.
St Luke 2:6–7.

69 And there were in the same country shepherds abiding in the field, keeping watch over their flock by night. And, lo, the angel of the Lord came upon them, and the glory of the Lord shone round about them: and they were sore afraid. And the angel said unto them, Fear not: for, behold, I bring you good tidings of great joy, which shall be to all people. For unto you is born this day in the city of David a Saviour, which is Christ the Lord. And this shall be a sign unto you; Ye shall find the babe wrapped in swaddling clothes, lying in a manger. And suddenly there was with the angel a multitude of the heavenly host praising God, and saying, Glory to God in the highest, and on earth peace, good will toward men. And it came to pass, as the angels were gone away from them into heaven, the shepherds said one to another, Let us now go even unto Bethlehem, and see this thing which is come to pass, which the Lord hath made known unto us.
St Luke 2:8–15.

70 Lord, now lettest thou thy servant depart in peace, according to thy word: For mine eyes have seen thy salvation, Which thou hast prepared before the face of all people; A light to lighten the Gentiles, and the glory of thy people Israel.
St Luke 2:29–32.

71 And Jesus increased in wisdom and stature, and in favour with God and man.
St Luke 2:52.

72 And he said unto them, Ye will surely say unto me this proverb, Physician, heal thyself: whatsoever we have heard done in Capernaum, do also here in thy country.
St Luke 4:23.

73 Woe unto you, when all men shall speak well of you! for so did their fathers to the false prophets.
St Luke 6:26.

74 Give, and it shall be given unto you; good measure, pressed down, and shaken together, and running over, shall men give into your bosom. For with the same measure that ye mete withal it shall be measured to you again.
St Luke 6:38.

75 Wherefore I say unto thee, Her sins, which are many, are forgiven; for she loved much: but to whom little is forgiven, the same loveth little.
St Luke 7:47.

76 And he said to them all, If any man will come after me, let him deny himself, and take up his cross daily, and follow me.
St Luke 9:23.

77 And Jesus said unto him, No man, having put his hand to the plough, and looking back, is fit for the kingdom of God.
St Luke 9:62.

78 And into whatsoever house ye enter, first say, Peace be to this house. And if the son of peace be there, your peace shall rest upon it: if not, it shall turn to you again. And in the same house remain, eating and drinking such things as they give: for the labourer is worthy of his hire.
St Luke 10:5–7.

79 And he said unto them, I beheld Satan as lightning fall from heaven.
St Luke 10:18.

80 And Jesus answering said, A certain man went down from Jerusalem to Jericho, and fell among thieves, which

stripped him of his raiment, and wounded him, and departed, leaving him half dead. And by chance there came down a certain priest that way: and when he saw him, he passed by on the other side.
St Luke 10:30–31.

81 But a certain Samaritan, as he journeyed, came where he was: and when he saw him, he had compassion on him, And went to him, and bound up his wounds, pouring in oil and wine, and set him on his own beast, and brought him to an inn, and took care of him. And on the morrow when he departed, he took out two pence, and gave them to the host, and said unto him, Take care of him; and whatsoever thou spendest more, when I come again, I will repay thee.
St Luke 10:33–5.

82 And he said, He that shewed mercy on him. Then said Jesus unto him, Go, and do thou likewise.
St Luke 10:37.

83 But Martha was cumbered about much serving, and came to him, and said, Lord, dost thou not care that my sister hath left me to serve alone? bid her therefore that she help me.
And Jesus answered and said unto her, Martha, Martha, thou art careful and troubled about many things:
But one thing is needful: and Mary hath chosen that good part, which shall not be taken away from her.
St Luke 10:40–2.

84 Woe unto you, lawyers! for ye have taken away the key of knowledge.
St Luke 11:52.

85 And I will say to my soul, Soul, thou hast much goods laid up for many years; take thine ease, eat, drink, and be merry. But God said unto him, Thou fool, this night thy soul shall be required of thee.
St Luke 12:19–20.

86 For which of you, intending to build a tower, sitteth not down first, and counteth the cost, whether he have sufficient to finish it?
St Luke 14:28.

87 What man of you, having an hundred sheep, if he lose one of them, doth not leave the ninety and nine in the wilderness, and go after that which is lost, until he find it? And when he hath found it, he layeth it on his shoulders, rejoicing.
St Luke 15:4–5.

88 Either what woman having ten pieces of silver, if she lose one piece, doth not light a candle, and sweep the house, and seek diligently till she find it? And when she hath found it, she calleth her friends and her neighbours together, saying, Rejoice with me; for I have found the piece which I had lost. Likewise, I say unto you, there is joy in the presence of the angels of God over one sinner that repenteth.
St Luke 15:8–10.

89 And not many days after the younger son gathered all together, and took his journey into a far country, and there wasted his substance with riotous living.
St Luke 15:13.

90 And he would fain have filled his belly with the husks that the swine did eat: and no man gave unto him. And when he came to himself, he said, How many hired servants of my father's have bread enough and to spare, and I perish with hunger! I will arise and go to my father, and will say unto him, Father, I have sinned against heaven, and before thee, And am no more worthy to be called thy son: make me as one of thy hired servants.
St Luke 15:16–19.

91 And he arose, and came to his father. But when he was yet a great way off, his father saw him, and had compassion, and ran, and fell on his neck, and kissed him. And the son said unto him, Father, I have sinned against heaven, and in thy sight, and am no more worthy to be called thy son. But the father said to his servants, Bring forth the best robe, and put it on him; and put a ring on his hand, and shoes on his feet: And bring hither the fatted calf, and kill it: and let us eat, and be merry: For this my son was dead, and is alive again; he was lost, and is found. And they began to be merry.
St Luke 15:20–4.

92 It was meet that we should make merry, and be glad: for this thy brother was dead, and is alive again; and was lost, and is found.
St Luke 15:32.

93 And the lord commended the unjust steward, because he had done wisely: for the children of this world are in their generation wiser than the children of light.
St Luke 16:8.

94 And I say unto you, Make to yourselves friends of the mammon of unrighteousness; that, when ye fail, they may receive you into everlasting habitations.
St Luke 16:9.

95 He that is faithful in that which is least is faithful also in much: and he that is unjust in the least is unjust also in much.
St Luke 16:10.

96 There was a certain rich man, which was clothed in purple and fine linen, and fared sumptuously every day: And there was a certain beggar named Lazarus, which was laid at his gate, full of sores, And desiring to be fed with the crumbs which fell from the rich man's table: moreover the dogs came and licked his sores.
St Luke 16:19–21.

97 And it came to pass, that the beggar died, and was carried by the angels into Abraham's bosom: the rich man also died, and was buried; And in hell he lift up his eyes, being in torments, and seeth Abraham afar off, and Lazarus in his bosom.
St Luke 16:22–3.

98 And beside all this, between us and you there is a great gulf fixed: so that they which would pass from hence to you cannot; neither can they pass to us, that would come from thence.
St Luke 16:26.

99 Neither shall they say, Lo here! or, lo there! for, behold, the kingdom of God is within you.
St Luke 17:21.

1 Remember Lot's wife.
St Luke 17:32.

2 For every one that exalteth himself shall be abased; and he that humbleth himself shall be exalted.
St Luke 18:14.

3 And he answered and said unto them, I tell you that, if these should hold their peace, the stones would immediately cry out.
St Luke 19:40.

4 In your patience possess ye your souls.
St Luke 21:19.

5 Saying, Father, if thou be willing, remove this cup from me: nevertheless not my will, but thine, be done.
St Luke 22:42.

6 And the Lord turned, and looked upon Peter. And Peter remembered the word of the Lord, how he had said unto him, Before the cock crow, thou shalt deny me thrice.
St Luke 22:61.

7 Then said Jesus, Father, forgive them; for they know not what they do. And they parted his raiment, and cast lots.
St Luke 23:34.

8 And he said unto Jesus, Lord, remember me when thou comest into thy kingdom. And Jesus said unto him, Verily I say unto thee, To day shalt thou be with me in paradise.
St Luke 23:42–3.

9 And the sun was darkened, and the veil of the temple was rent in the midst.
St Luke 23:45.

10 And when Jesus had cried with a loud voice, he said, Father, into thy hands I commend my spirit: and having said thus, he gave up the ghost.
St Luke 23:46.

11 And as they were afraid, and bowed down their faces to the earth, they said unto them, Why seek ye the living among the dead? He is not here, but is risen: remember how he spake unto you when he was yet in Galilee.
St Luke 24:5–6.

12 And their words seemed to them as idle tales, and they believed them not.
St Luke 24:11.

13 And they said one to another, Did not our heart burn within us, while he talked with us by the way, and while he opened to us the scriptures?
St Luke 24:32.

14 And they gave him a piece of a broiled fish, and of an honeycomb.
St Luke 24:42.

15 In the beginning was the Word, and the Word was with God, and the Word was God. The same was in the beginning with God. All things were made by him; and without him was not anything made that was made.
St John 1:1–3.

16 In him was life; and the life was the light of men. And the light shineth in darkness; and the darkness comprehended it not.
St John 1:4–5.

17 That was the true Light, which lighteth every man that cometh into the world. He was in the world, and the world was made by him, and the world knew him not.
St John 1:9–10.

18 And the Word was made flesh, and dwelt among us, (and we beheld his glory, the glory as of the only begotten of the Father,) full of grace and truth.
St John 1:14.

19 The next day John seeth Jesus coming unto him, and saith, Behold the Lamb of God, which taketh away the sin of the world.
St John 1:29.

20 And Nathanael said unto him, Can there any good thing come out of Nazareth? Philip saith unto him, Come and see.
St John 1:46.

21 Jesus saith unto her, Woman, what have I to do with thee? mine hour is not yet come.
St John 2:4.

22 When the ruler of the feast had tasted the water that was made wine, and knew not whence it was: (but the servants which drew the water knew;) the governor of the feast called the bridegroom, And saith unto him, Every man at the beginning doth set forth good wine; and when men have well drunk, then that which is worse: but thou hast kept the good wine until now.
St John 2:9–10.

23 Jesus answered and said unto him, Verily, verily, I say unto thee, Except a man be born again, he cannot see the kingdom of God.
St John 3:3.

24 The wind bloweth where it listeth, and thou hearest the sound thereof, but canst not tell whence it cometh, and whither it goeth: so is every one that is born of the Spirit.
St John 3:8.

25 For God so loved the world, that he gave his only begotten Son, that whosoever believeth in him should not perish, but have everlasting life.
St John 3:16.

26 And this is the condemnation, that light is come into the world, and men loved darkness rather than light, because their deeds were evil.
St John 3:19.

27 He must increase, but I must decrease.
St John 3:30.

28 God is a Spirit: and they that worship him must worship him in spirit and in truth.
St John 4:24.

29 Say not ye, There are yet four months, and then cometh harvest? behold, I say unto you, Lift up your eyes, and look on the fields; for they are white already to harvest.
St John 4:35.

30 Jesus saith unto him, Rise, take up thy bed, and walk.
St John 5:8.

31 He was a burning and a shining light; and ye were willing for a season to rejoice in his light.
Of John the Baptist. St John 5:35.

32 Search the scriptures; for in them ye think ye have eternal life: and they are they which testify of me.
St John 5:39.

33 There is a lad here, which hath five barley loaves, and two small fishes: but what are they among so many?
St John 6:9.

34 And Jesus said unto them, I am the bread of life: he that cometh to me shall never hunger; and he that believeth on me shall never thirst.
St John 6:35.

35 All that the Father giveth me shall come to me; and him that cometh to me I will in no wise cast out.
St John 6:37.

36 Verily, verily, I say unto you, He that believeth on me hath everlasting life. I am that bread of life.
St John 6:47–8.

37 It is the spirit that quickeneth; the flesh profiteth nothing: the words that I speak unto you, they are spirit, and they are life.
St John 6:63.

38 So when they continued asking him, he lifted up himself, and said unto them, He that is without sin among you, let him first cast a stone at her.
St John 8:7.

39 Then spake Jesus again unto them, saying, I am the light of the world: he that followeth me shall not walk in darkness, but shall have the light of life.
St John 8:12.

40 And ye shall know the truth, and the truth shall make you free.
St John 8:32.

41 If the Son therefore shall make you free, ye shall be free indeed.
St John 8:36.

42 Ye are of your father the devil, and the lusts of the father ye will do. He was a murderer from the beginning, and abode not in the truth, because there is no truth in him. When he speaketh a lie, he speaketh of his own: for he is a liar, and the father of it.
St John 8:44.

43 Whether he be a sinner or no, I know not: one thing I know, that, whereas I was blind, now I see.
St John 9:25.

44 The thief cometh not, but for to steal, and to kill, and to destroy: I am come that they might have life, and that they might have it more abundantly.
St John 10:10.

45 I am the good shepherd: the good shepherd giveth his life for the sheep. But he that is an hireling, and not the shepherd, whose own the sheep are not, seeth the wolf coming, and leaveth the sheep, and fleeth: and the wolf catcheth them, and scattereth the sheep. The hireling fleeth, because he is an hireling, and careth not for the sheep. I am the good shepherd, and know my sheep, and am known of mine. As the Father knoweth me, even so know I the Father: and I lay down my life for the sheep. And other sheep I have which are not of this fold: them also must I bring, and they shall hear my voice; and there shall be one fold, and one shepherd.
St John 10:11–16.

46 I am the resurrection, and the life: he that believeth in me, though he were dead, yet shall he live.
St John 11:25.

47 Jesus wept.
This is the shortest verse in the Bible. St John 11:35.

48 For the poor always ye have with you; but me ye have not always.
St John 12:8.

49 That thou doest, do quickly.
Jesus to Judas. St John 13:27.

50 A new commandment I give unto you, That ye love one another; as I have loved you, that ye also love one another. By this shall all men know that ye are my disciples, if ye have love one to another.
St John 13:34–5.

51 Let not your heart be troubled: ye believe in God, believe also in me.
St John 14:1.

52 In my Father's house are many mansions: if it were not so, I would have told you. I go to prepare a place for you. And if I go and prepare a place for you, I will come again, and receive you unto myself; that where I am, there ye may be also.
St John 14:2–3.

53 Jesus saith unto him, I am the way, the truth, and the life: no man cometh unto the Father, but by me.
St John 14:6.

54 Peace I leave with you, my peace I give unto you: not as the world giveth, give I unto you, Let not your heart be troubled, neither let it be afraid.
St John 14:27.

55 This is my commandment, That ye love one another, as I have loved you. Greater love hath no man than this, that a man lay down his life for his friends.
St John 15:12–13.

56 I have yet many things to say unto you, but ye cannot bear them now.
St John 16:12.

57 These things I have spoken unto you, that in me ye might have peace. In the world ye shall have tribulation: but be of good cheer; I have overcome the world.
St John 16:33.

58 While I was with them in the world, I kept them in thy name: those that thou gavest me I have kept, and none of them is lost, but the son of perdition; that the scripture might be fulfilled.
St John 17:12.

59 Pilate saith unto him, What is truth?
St John 18:38.

60 Then said the chief priests of the Jews to Pilate, Write not, The King of the Jews; but that he said, I am King of the Jews. Pilate answered, What I have written I have written.
St John 19:21–2.

61 When Jesus therefore saw his mother, and the disciple standing by, whom he loved, he saith unto his mother, Woman, behold thy son! Then saith he to the disciple, Behold thy mother! And from that hour that disciple took her unto his own home.
St John 19:26–7.

62 He said It is finished: and he bowed his head, and gave up the ghost.
St John 19:30.

63 But one of the soldiers with a spear pierced his side, and forthwith came there out blood and water.
St John 19:34.

64 The first day of the week cometh Mary Magdalene early, when it was yet dark, unto the sepulchre, and seeth the stone taken away from the sepulchre.
St John 20:1.

65 So they ran both together: and the other disciple did outrun Peter, and came first to the sepulchre.
St John 20:4.

66 Jesus saith unto her, Woman, why weepest thou? whom seekest thou? She, supposing him to be the gardener, saith unto him, Sir, if thou have borne him hence, tell me where thou hast laid him, and I will take him away. Jesus saith unto her, Mary. She turned herself, and saith unto him, Rabboni; which is to say, Master. Jesus saith unto her, Touch me not; for I am not yet ascended to my Father: but go to my brethren, and say unto them, I ascend unto my Father, and your Father; and to my God, and your God.
St John 20:15–17. The Latin Vulgate translation of the Bible, ascribed to St Jerome, famously renders the phrase 'Do not touch me' as 'Noli me tangere'.

67 Except I shall see in his hands the print of the nails, and put my finger into the print of the nails, and thrust my hand into his side, I will not believe.
Thomas. St John 20:25.

68 Be not faithless, but believing. And Thomas answered and said unto him, My Lord and my God. Jesus saith unto him, Thomas, because thou hast seen me, thou hast believed: blessed are they that have not seen, and yet have believed.
St John 20:27–9.

69 When thou wast young, thou girdest thyself, and walkedst whither thou wouldest: but when thou shalt be old, thou shalt stretch forth thy hands, and another shall gird thee, and carry thee whither thou wouldest not.
St John 21:18.

70 It is not for you to know the times or the seasons, which the Father hath put in his own power. But ye shall receive power, after that the Holy Ghost is come upon you: and ye shall be witnesses unto me both in Jerusalem, and in all Judea, and in Samaria, and unto the uttermost part of the earth.
Acts of the Apostles 1:7–8.

71 Ye men of Galilee, why stand ye gazing up into heaven? this same Jesus, which is taken up from you into heaven, shall so come in like manner as ye have seen him go into heaven.
Acts of the Apostles 1:11.

72 And when the day of Pentecost was fully come, they were all with one accord in one place. And suddenly there came a sound from heaven as of a rushing mighty wind, and it filled all the house where they were sitting. And there appeared unto them cloven tongues like as of fire, and it sat upon each of them. And they were all filled with the Holy Ghost, and began to speak with other tongues, as the Spirit gave them utterance.
Acts of the Apostles 2:1–4.

73 Silver and gold have I none; but such as I have give I thee: In the name of Jesus Christ of Nazareth rise up and walk.
Acts of the Apostles 3:6.

74 And he leaping up stood, and walked, and entered with them into the temple, walking, and leaping, and praising God.
Acts of the Apostles 3:8.

75 Neither is there salvation in any other: for there is none other name under heaven given among men, whereby we must be saved.
Acts of the Apostles 4:12.

76 We ought to obey God rather than men.
Acts of the Apostles 5:29.

77 Then the twelve called the multitude of the disciples unto them, and said, It is not reason that we should leave the word of God, and serve tables.
Acts of the Apostles 6:2–4.

78 And the witnesses laid down their clothes at a young man's feet, whose name was Saul.
Acts of the Apostles 7:57–8.

79 Understandest thou what thou readest? And he said, How can I, except some man should guide me?
Acts of the Apostles 8:30–1.

80 Saul, Saul, why persecutest thou me? And he said, Who art thou, Lord? And the Lord said, I am Jesus whom thou persecutest: it is hard for thee to kick against the pricks.
Acts of the Apostles 9:3–5.

81 Tabitha, which by interpretation is called Dorcas: this woman was full of good works.
Acts of the Apostles 9:36.

82 And saw heaven opened, and a certain vessel descending unto him, as it had been a great sheet knit at the four corners, and let down to the earth: Wherein were all manner of fourfooted beasts of the earth, and wild beasts, and creeping things, and fowls of the air. And there came a voice to him, Rise, Peter; kill, and eat.
Acts of the Apostles 10:11–13.

83 What God hath cleansed, that call not thou common.
Acts of the Apostles 10:15.

84 Of a truth I perceive that God is no respecter of persons: But in every nation he that feareth Him, and worketh righteousness, is accepted with Him.
Acts of the Apostles 10:34–5.

85 The gods are come down to us in the likeness of men.
Acts of the Apostles 14:11.

86 Sirs, why do ye these things? We also are men of like passions with you, and preach unto you that ye should turn from these vanities unto the living God, which made heaven, and earth, and the sea, and all things that are therein.
Acts of the Apostles 14:15.

87 Sirs, what must I do to be saved? And they said, Believe on the Lord Jesus Christ, and thou shalt be saved, and thy house.
Acts of the Apostles 16:30–1.

88 But the Jews which believeth not, moved with envy, took unto them certain lewd fellows of the baser sort, and gathered a company, and set all the city on an uproar.
Acts of the Apostles 17:5.

89 These that have turned the world upside down are come hither also.
Acts of the Apostles 17:6.

90 What will this babbler say?
Acts of the Apostles 17:18.

91 Ye men of Athens, I perceive that in all things ye are too superstitious. For as I passed by, and beheld your devotions, I found an altar with this inscription, TO THE

UNKNOWN GOD. Whom therefore ye ignorantly worship, him declare I unto you.
Acts of the Apostles 17:22–3.

92 God that made the world and all things therein, seeing that he is Lord of heaven and earth, dwelleth not in temples made with hands.
Acts of the Apostles 17:24.

93 For in him we live, and move and have our being.
Acts of the Apostles 17:28.

94 And the times of this ignorance God winked at; but now commandeth all men every where to repent.
Acts of the Apostles 17:30.

95 Have ye received the Holy Ghost since ye believed? And they said unto him, We have not so much as heard whether there be any Holy Ghost.
Acts of the Apostles 19:2.

96 It is more blessed to give than to receive.
Acts of the Apostles 20:35.

97 I am a man which am a Jew of Tarsus, a city in Cilicia, a citizen of no mean city.
Acts of the Apostles 21:39.

98 The chief captain answered, With a great sum obtained I this freedom. And Paul said, But I was free born.
Acts of the Apostles 22:27–8.

99 Paul, thou art beside thyself; much learning doth make thee mad.
Acts of the Apostles 26:24.

1 Almost thou persuadest me to be a Christian.
Acts of the Apostles 26:28.

2 The just shall live by faith.
Romans 1:17.

3 Who changed the truth of God into a lie, and worshipped and served the creature more than the Creator.
Romans 1:25.

4 For when the Gentiles, which have not the law, do by nature the things contained in the law, these, having not the law, are a law unto themselves.
Romans 2:14.

5 God forbid: yea, let God be true, but every man a liar.
Romans 3:4.

6 For all have sinned, and come short of the glory of God.
Romans 3:23.

7 Because the law worketh wrath: for where no law is, there is no transgression.
Romans 4:15.

8 Who against hope believed in hope, that he might become the father of many nations.
Romans 4:18.

9 While we were yet sinners, Christ died for us.
Romans 5:8.

10 Where sin abounded, grace did much more abound.
Romans 5:20.

11 What shall we say then? Shall we continue in sin, that grace may abound? God forbid. How shall we, that are dead to sin, live any longer therein?
Romans 6:1–2.

12 Knowing that Christ being raised from the dead dieth no more; death hath no more dominion over him.
Romans 6:9.

13 For the wages of sin is death; but the gift of God is eternal life through Jesus Christ our Lord.
Romans 6:23.

14 To will is present with me; but how to perform that which is good I find not. For the good that I would I do not: but the evil which I would not, that I do.
Romans 7:19.

15 O wretched man that I am! who shall deliver me from the body of this death?
Romans 7:24.

16 There is therefore now no condemnation to them which are in Christ Jesus, who walk not after the flesh, but after the Spirit.
Romans 8:1.

17 For they that are after the flesh do mind the things of the flesh; but they that are after the Spirit the things of the Spirit. For to be carnally minded is death; but to be spiritually minded is life and peace.
Romans 8:5–6.

18 For ye have not received the spirit of bondage again to fear; but ye have received the Spirit of adoption, whereby we cry, Abba, Father. The Spirit itself beareth witness with our spirit, that we are the children of God: And if children, then heirs; heirs of God, and joint-heirs with Christ; if so be that we suffer with him, that we may be also glorified together.
Romans 8:15–17.

19 For we know that the whole creation groaneth and travaileth in pain together until now.
Romans 8:22.

20 And we know that all things work together for good to them that love God, to them who are the called according to his purpose.
Romans 8:28.

21 If God be for us, who can be against us?
Romans 8:31.

22 I am persuaded, that neither death, nor life, nor angels, nor principalities, nor powers, nor things present, nor things to come, Nor height, nor depth, nor any other creature, shall be able to separate us from the love of God, which is in Christ Jesus our Lord.
Romans 8:38–9.

23 Nay but, O man, who art thou that repliest against God? Shall the thing formed say to him that formed it, Why hast thou made me thus? Hath not the potter power over the clay, of the same lump to make one vessel unto honour, and another unto dishonour?
Romans 9:20–1.

24 I beseech you therefore, brethren, by the mercies of God, that ye present your bodies a living sacrifice, holy, acceptable unto God, which is your reasonable service.
Romans 12:1.

25 Not slothful in business; fervent in spirit; serving the Lord.
Romans 12:11.

26 Rejoice with them that do rejoice, and weep with them that weep.
Romans 12:15.

27 Mind not high things, but condescend to men of low estate. Be not wise in your own conceits. Recompense to

no man evil for evil. Provide things honest in the sight of all men. If it be possible, as much as lieth in you, live peaceably with all men. Dearly beloved, avenge not yourselves, but rather give place unto wrath: for it is written, Vengeance is mine; I will repay, saith the Lord.
Romans 12:16–19.

28 Be not overcome of evil, but overcome evil with good.
Romans 12:21.

29 Let every soul be subject unto the higher powers. For there is no power but of God: the powers that be are ordained of God.
Romans 13:1.

30 Render therefore to all their dues: tribute to whom tribute is due; custom to whom custom; fear to whom fear; honour to whom honour. Owe no man any thing, but to love one another: for he that loveth another hath fulfilled the law.
Romans 13:7–8.

31 Love worketh no ill to his neighbour: therefore love is the fulfilling of the law.
Romans 13:10.

32 Doubtful disputations.
Romans 14:1.

33 Whether we live therefore, or die, we are the Lord's.
Romans 14:8.

34 Salute one another with an holy kiss.
Romans 16:16.

35 For after that in the wisdom of God the world by wisdom knew not God, it pleased God by the foolishness of preaching to save them that believe.
1 Corinthians 1:21.

36 But God hath chosen the foolish things of the world to confound the wise; and God hath chosen the weak things of the world to confound the things which are mighty.
1 Corinthians 1:27.

37 I have planted, Apollos watered; but God gave the increase.
1 Corinthians 3:6.

38 We are made a spectacle unto the world, and to angels, and to men.
1 Corinthians 4:9.

39 What? know ye not that your body is the temple of the Holy Ghost which is in you, which ye have of God, and ye are not your own?
1 Corinthians 6:19.

40 It is better to marry than to burn.
1 Corinthians 7:9.

41 For the unbelieving husband is sanctified by the wife.
1 Corinthians 7:14.

42 But he that is married careth for the things that are of the world, how he may please his wife.
1 Corinthians 7:33.

43 I am made all things to all men, that I might by all means save some.
1 Corinthians 9:22.

44 Know ye not that they which run in a race run all, but one receiveth the prize? So run, that ye may obtain.
1 Corinthians 9:24.

45 Wherefore let him that thinketh he standeth take heed lest he fall.
1 Corinthians 10:12.

46 All things are lawful for me, but all things are not expedient: all things are lawful for me, but all things edify not.
1 Corinthians 10:23.

47 For the earth is the Lord's, and the fulness thereof.
1 Corinthians 10:26.

48 If a man have long hair, it is a shame unto him. But if a woman have long hair, it is a glory to her: for her hair is given her for a covering.
1 Corinthians 11:15.

49 The Lord Jesus the same night in which he was betrayed took bread: And when he had given thanks, he brake it, and said, Take, eat: this is my body, which is broken for you: this do in remembrance of me. After the same manner also he took the cup, when he had supped, saying, This cup is the new testament in my blood: this do ye, as oft as ye drink it, in remembrance of me. For as often as ye eat this bread, and drink this cup, ye do shew the Lord's death till he come.
1 Corinthians 11:23–6.

50 No man can say that Jesus is the Lord, but by the Holy Ghost.
1 Corinthians 12:3.

51 Now there are diversities of gifts, but the same Spirit. And there are differences of administrations, but the same Lord. And there are diversities of operations, but it is the same God which worketh all in all.
1 Corinthians 12:4–6.

52 Though I speak with the tongues of men and of angels, and have not charity, I am become as sounding brass, or a tinkling cymbal. And though I have the gift of prophecy, and understand all mysteries, and all knowledge; and though I have all faith, so that I could remove mountains, and have not charity, I am nothing. And though I bestow all my goods to feed the poor, and though I give my body to be burned, and have not charity, it profiteth me nothing. Charity suffereth long, and is kind; charity envieth not; charity vaunteth not itself, is not puffed up, Doth not behave itself unseemly, seeketh not her own, is not easily provoked, thinketh no evil; Rejoiceth not in iniquity, but rejoiceth in the truth; Beareth all things, believeth all things, hopeth all things, endureth all things. Charity never faileth: but whether there be prophecies, they shall fail; whether there be tongues, they shall cease; whether there be knowledge, it shall vanish away. For we know in part, and we prophesy in part. But when that which is perfect is come, then that which is in part shall be done away. When I was a child, I spake as a child, I understood as a child, I thought as a child: but when I became a man, I put away childish things. For now we see through a glass, darkly; but then face to face: now I know in part; but then shall I know even as also I am known. And now abideth faith, hope, charity, these three; but the greatest of these is charity.
1 Corinthians 13:1–13.

53 For if the trumpet give an uncertain sound, who shall prepare himself to the battle?
1 Corinthians 14:8.

54 Let all things be done decently and in order.
1 Corinthians 14:40.

55 And last of all he was seen of me also, as of one born out of due time. For I am the least of the apostles, that am not meet to be called an apostle, because I persecuted the church of God.
But by the grace of God I am what I am.
1 Corinthians 15:8–9.

56 If in this life only we have hope in Christ, we are of all men most miserable.
1 Corinthians 15:19.

57 But now is Christ risen from the dead, and become the first-fruits of them that slept.
For since by man came death, by man came also the resurrection of the dead.
For as in Adam all die, even so in Christ shall all be made alive.
1 Corinthians 15:20–2.

58 He must reign, till he hath put all enemies under his feet. The last enemy that shall be destroyed is death.
1 Corinthians 15:26.

59 What advantageth it me, if the dead rise not? let us eat and drink; for tomorrow we die.
1 Corinthians 15:32.
▶ *See Parker 664:15.*

60 Evil communications corrupt good manners.
1 Corinthians 15:33.

61 The first man is of the earth, earthy.
1 Corinthians 15:47.

62 Behold, I shew you a mystery; We shall not all sleep, but we shall all be changed, In a moment, in the twinkling of an eye, at the last trump: for the trumpet shall sound, and the dead shall be raised incorruptible, and we shall be changed.
1 Corinthians 15:51–2.

63 O death, where is thy sting? O grave, where is thy victory?
1 Corinthians 15:55.

64 Watch ye, stand fast in the faith, quit you like men, be strong.
1 Corinthians 16:13.

65 Not that we are sufficient of ourselves to think any thing as of ourselves; but our sufficiency is of God; Who also hath made us able ministers of the new testament; not of the letter, but of the spirit: for the letter killeth, but the spirit giveth life.
2 Corinthians 3:5–6.

66 But we have this treasure in earthen vessels.
2 Corinthians 4:7.

67 We are troubled on every side, yet not distressed; we are perplexed, but not in despair.
2 Corinthians 4:8.

68 For we know that if our earthly house of this tabernacle were dissolved, we have a building of God, an house not made with hands, eternal in the heavens.
2 Corinthians 5:1.

69 For we walk by faith, not by sight.
2 Corinthians 5:7.

70 Therefore if any man be in Christ, he is a new creature: old things are passed away; behold, all things are become new.
2 Corinthians 5:17.

71 Now then we are ambassadors for Christ.
2 Corinthians 5:20.

72 For he saith, I have heard thee in a time accepted, and in the day of salvation have I succoured thee: behold, now is the accepted time; behold, now is the day of salvation.
2 Corinthians 6:2.

73 As unknown, and yet well known; as dying, and, behold, we live; as chastened, and not killed; As sorrowful, yet alway rejoicing; as poor, yet making many rich; as having nothing, and yet possessing all things.
2 Corinthians 6:9–10.

74 So let him give; not grudgingly, or of necessity: for God loveth a cheerful giver.
2 Corinthians 9:7.

75 For ye suffer fools gladly, seeing ye yourselves are wise.
2 Corinthians 11:19.

76 And lest I should be exalted above measure through the abundance of the revelations, there was given to me a thorn in the flesh, the messenger of Satan to buffet me.
2 Corinthians 12:7.

77 My grace is sufficient for thee: for my strength is made perfect in weakness.
2 Corinthians 12:9.

78 They gave to me and Barnabas the right hands of fellowship.
Galatians 2:9.

79 There is neither Jew nor Greek, there is neither bond nor free, there is neither male nor female: for ye are all one in Christ Jesus.
Galatians 3:28.

80 Ye are fallen from grace.
Galatians 5:4.

81 But the fruit of the Spirit is love, joy, peace, longsuffering, gentleness, goodness, faith,
Meekness, temperance: against such there is no law.
Galatians 5:22–3.

82 Be not deceived; God is not mocked: for whatsoever a man soweth, that shall he also reap.
Galatians 6:7.

83 Let us not be weary in well doing: for in due season we shall reap, if we faint not.
Galatians 6:9.

84 See what a large letter I have written unto you with mine own hand.
Galatians 6:11.

85 And came and preached peace to you which were afar off, and to them that were nigh.
Ephesians 2:17.

86 Now therefore ye are no more strangers and foreigners, but fellow citizens with the saints, and of the household of God.
Ephesians 2:19.

87 Unto me, who am less than the least of all saints, is this grace given, that I should preach among the Gentiles the unsearchable riches of Christ.
Ephesians 3:8.

88 That he would grant you, according to the riches of his glory, to be strengthened with might by his Spirit in the inner man; That Christ may dwell in your hearts by faith; that ye, being rooted and grounded in love, May be able

to comprehend with all saints what is the breadth, and length, and depth, and height; And to know the love of Christ, which passeth knowledge, that ye might be filled with all the fulness of God.
Ephesians 3:16–19.

89 Now unto him that is able to do exceeding abundantly above all that we ask or think, according to the power that worketh in us, Unto him be glory in the church by Christ Jesus throughout all ages, world without end. Amen.
Ephesians 3:20–1.

90 Wherefore putting away lying, speak every man truth with his neighbour: for we are members one of another. Be ye angry, and sin not: let not the sun go down upon your wrath.
Ephesians 4:25–6.

91 Redeeming the time, because the days are evil.
Ephesians 5:16.

92 Be not drunk with wine, wherein is excess; but be filled with the Spirit.
Ephesians 5:18.

93 Ye fathers, provoke not your children to wrath.
Ephesians 6:4.

94 Not with eyeservice, as menpleasers; but as the servants of Christ, doing the will of God from the heart; With good will doing service, as to the Lord, and not to men.
Ephesians 6:6–7.

95 Put on the whole armour of God, that ye may be able to stand against the wiles of the devil. For we wrestle not against flesh and blood, but against principalities, against powers, against the rulers of the darkness of this world, against spiritual wickedness in high places. Wherefore take unto you the whole armour of God, that ye may be able to withstand in the evil day, and having done all, to stand. Stand therefore, having your loins girt about with truth, and having on the breastplate of righteousness; And your feet shod with the preparation of the gospel of peace; Above all, taking the shield of faith, wherewith ye shall be able to quench all the fiery darts of the wicked. And take the helmet of salvation, and the sword of the Spirit, which is the word of God.
Ephesians 6:11–17.

96 For to me to live is Christ, and to die is gain.
Philippians 1:21.

97 Let this mind be in you, which was also in Christ Jesus: Who, being in the form of God, thought it not robbery to be equal with God: But made himself of no reputation, and took upon him the form of a servant, and was made in the likeness of men: And being found in fashion as a man, he humbled himself, and became obedient unto death, even the death of the cross. Wherefore God also hath highly exalted him, and given him a name which is above every name: That at the name of Jesus every knee should bow, of things in heaven, and things in earth, and things under the earth; And that every tongue should confess that Jesus Christ is Lord, to the glory of God the Father.
Philippians 2:5–11.

98 Work out your own salvation with fear and trembling.
Philippians 2:12.

99 Circumcised the eighth day, of the stock of Israel, of the tribe of Benjamin, an Hebrew of the Hebrews; as touching the law, a Pharisee.
Paul lists his religious credentials. Philippians 3:5

1 But what things were gain to me, those I counted loss for Christ.
Philippians 3:7.

2 Forgetting those things which are behind, and reaching forth unto those things which are before, I press toward the mark for the prize of the high calling of God in Christ Jesus.
Philippians 3:13–14.

3 Whose end is destruction, whose God is their belly, and whose glory is in their shame, who mind earthly things.
Philippians 3:19.

4 Rejoice in the Lord alway: and again I say, Rejoice. Let your moderation be known unto all men. The Lord is at hand. Be careful for nothing; but in every thing by prayer and supplication with thanksgiving let your requests be made known unto God. And the peace of God, which passeth all understanding, shall keep your hearts and minds through Christ Jesus.
Philippians 4:4–7.

5 Finally, brethren, whatsoever things are true, whatsoever things are honest, whatsoever things are just, whatsoever things are pure, whatsoever things are lovely, whatsoever things are of good report; if there be any virtue, and if there be any praise, think on these things.
Philippians 4:8.

6 I have learned, in whatsoever state I am, therewith to be content.
Philippians 4:11.

7 I can do all things through Christ which strengtheneth me.
Philippians 4:13.

8 My God shall supply all your need according to his riches in glory by Christ Jesus.
Philippians 4:19.

9 Beware lest any man spoil you through philosophy and vain deceit, after the tradition of men, after the rudiments of the world, and not after Christ.
Colossians 2:8.

10 Set your affection on things above, not on things on the earth.
Colossians 3:2.

11 Lie not one to another, seeing that ye have put off the old man with his deeds; And have put on the new man, which is renewed in knowledge after the image of him that created him: Where there is neither Greek nor Jew, circumcision nor uncircumcision, Barbarian, Scythian, bond nor free: but Christ is all, and in all.
Colossians 3:9–11.

12 Husbands, love your wives, and be not bitter against them.
Colossians 3:19.

13 Let your speech be alway with grace, seasoned with salt, that ye may know how ye ought to answer every man.
Colossians 4:6.

14 Study to be quiet, and to do your own business, and to work with your own hands, as we commanded you.
1 Thessalonians 4:11.

15 Prove all things; hold fast that which is good.
1 Thessalonians 5:21.

16 If any would not work, neither should he eat.
2 Thessalonians 3:10.

17 This is a faithful saying, and worthy of all acceptation, that Christ Jesus came into the world to save sinners; of whom I am chief.
1 Timothy 1:15.

18 If a man desire the office of a bishop, he desireth a good work. A bishop then must be blameless, the husband of one wife, vigilant, sober, of good behaviour, given to hospitality, apt to teach; Not given to wine, no striker, not greedy of filthy lucre; but patient, not a brawler, not covetous.
1 Timothy 3:1–3.

19 But refuse profane and old wives' fables, and exercise thyself rather unto godliness.
1 Timothy 4:7–8.

20 Let no man despise thy youth.
1 Timothy 4:12.

21 Drink no longer water, but use a little wine for thy stomach's sake and thine often infirmities.
1 Timothy 5:23.

22 For we brought nothing into this world, and it is certain we can carry nothing out. And having food and raiment let us be therewith content.
1 Timothy 6:7–8.

23 For the love of money is the root of all evil.
1 Timothy 6:10.

24 Fight the good fight of faith.
1 Timothy 6:12.

25 For God hath not given us the spirit of fear; but of power, and of love, and of a sound mind.
2 Timothy 1:7.

26 I know whom I have believed, and am persuaded that he is able to keep that which I have committed unto him against that day.
2 Timothy 1:12.

27 Hold fast the form of sound words, which thou hast heard of me.
2 Timothy 1:13.

28 All scripture is given by inspiration of God, and is profitable of doctrine, for reproof, for correction, for instruction in righteousness.
2 Timothy 3:16.

29 Preach the word; be instant in season, out of season.
2 Timothy 4:2.

30 I have fought a good fight, I have finished my course, I have kept the faith.
2 Timothy 4:7.

31 The Cretans are always liars, evil beasts, slow bellies.
Titus 1:12.

32 Unto the pure all things are pure: but unto them that are defiled and unbelieving is nothing pure; but even their mind and conscience is defiled.
Titus 1:15.

33 God, who at sundry times and in divers manners spake in time past unto the fathers by the prophets, Hath in these last days spoken unto us by his Son, whom he hath appointed heir of all things, by whom he also made the worlds: Who being the brightness of his glory, and the express image of his person, and upholding all things by the word of his power, when he had by himself purged our sins, sat down on the right hand of the Majesty on high.
Hebrews 1:1–3.

34 For the word of God is quick, and powerful, and sharper than any two-edged sword, piercing even to the dividing asunder of soul and spirit.
Hebrews 4:12.

35 Ye have need that one teach you again which be the first principles of the oracles of God; and are become such as have need of milk, and not of strong meat.
Hebrews 5:12.

36 Without shedding of blood is no remission.
Hebrews 9:22.

37 It is appointed unto men once to die, but after this the judgment.
Hebrews 9:27.

38 It is a fearful thing to fall into the hands of the living God.
Hebrews 10:31.

39 Now faith is the substance of things hoped for, the evidence of things not seen.
Hebrews 11:1.

40 These all died in faith, not having received the promises, but having seen them afar off, and were persuaded of them, and embraced them, and confessed that they were strangers and pilgrims on the earth.
Hebrews 11:13.

41 But now they desire a better country, that is, an heavenly: wherefore God is not ashamed to be called their God: for he hath prepared for them a city.
Hebrews 11:16.

42 Of whom the world was not worthy.
Hebrews 11:38.

43 Wherefore seeing we also are compassed about with so great a cloud of witnesses, let us lay aside every weight, and the sin which doth so easily beset us, and let us run with patience the race that is set before us, Looking unto Jesus the author and finisher of our faith; who for the joy that was set before him endured the cross, despising the shame, and is set down at the right hand of the throne of God.
Hebrews 12:1–2.

44 For whom the Lord loveth he chasteneth.
Hebrews 12:6.

45 For our God is a consuming fire.
Hebrews 12:29.

46 Be not forgetful to entertain strangers: for thereby some have entertained angels unawares.
Hebrews 13:1–2.

47 Jesus Christ the same yesterday, and to day, and for ever.
Hebrews 13:8.

48 He that wavereth is like a wave of the sea driven with the wind and tossed. For let not that man think that he shall receive any thing of the Lord. A double minded man is unstable in all his ways.
James 1:7–8.

49 Every good gift and every perfect gift is from above, and cometh down from the Father of lights, with whom is no variableness, neither shadow of turning.
James 1:17.

50 Be ye doers of the word, and not hearers only, deceiving your own selves. For if any be a hearer of the word, and not a doer, he is like unto a man beholding his natural face in a glass: For he beholdeth himself, and goeth his way, and straightway forgetteth what manner of man he was.
James 1:22–4.

51 If any man among you seem to be religious, and bridleth not his tongue, but deceiveth his own heart, this man's religion is vain.
James 1:26.

52 Pure religion and undefiled before God and the Father is this, To visit the fatherless and widows in their affliction, and to keep himself unspotted from the world.
James 1:27.

53 Thou believest that there is one God; thou doest well: the devils also believe, and tremble.
James 2:19.

54 Faith without works is dead.
James 2:20.

55 Even so the tongue is a little member, and boasteth great things. Behold, how great a matter a little fire kindleth!
James 3:5.

56 And the tongue is a fire, a world of iniquity: so is the tongue among our members, that it defileth the whole body, and setteth on fire the course of nature; and it is set on fire of hell.
James 3:6.

57 Out of the same mouth proceedeth blessing and cursing. My brethren, these things ought not so to be. Doth a fountain send forth at the same place sweet water and bitter?
James 3:10–11.

58 Submit yourselves therefore to God, Resist the devil, and he will flee from you. Draw nigh to God, and he will draw nigh to you.
James 4:7–8.

59 What is your life? It is even a vapour, that appeareth for a little time, and then vanisheth away. For that ye ought to say, If the Lord will, we shall live, and do this, or that.
James 4:14–15.

60 Grudge not one against another, brethren, lest ye be condemned: behold, the judge standeth before the door.
James 5:9.

61 Swear not, neither by heaven, neither by the earth, neither by any other oath: but let your yea be yea; and your nay, nay.
James 5:12.

62 The effectual fervent prayer of a righteous man availeth much.
James 5:16.

63 He which converteth the sinner from the error of his way shall save a soul from death, and shall hide a multitude of sins.
James 5:20.

64 Wherefore gird up the loins of your mind, be sober, and hope to the end for the grace that is to be brought unto you at the revelation of Jesus Christ.
1 Peter 1:13.

65 For all flesh is as grass, and all the glory of man as the flower of grass. The grass withereth, and the flower thereof falleth away.
1 Peter 1:24.

66 As newborn babes, desire the sincere milk of the word, that ye may grow thereby: If so be you have tasted that the Lord is gracious.
1 Peter 2:2.

67 But ye are a chosen generation, a royal priesthood, an holy nation, a peculiar people; that ye should shew forth the praises of him who hath called you out of darkness into his marvellous light.
1 Peter 2:9.

68 Honour all men. Love the brotherhood. Fear God. Honour the king.
1 Peter 2:17.

69 For ye were as sheep going astray; but are now returned unto the Shepherd and Bishop of your souls.
1 Peter 2:25.

70 Giving honour unto the wife, as unto the weaker vessel.
1 Peter 3:7.

71 And above all things have fervent charity among yourselves: for charity shall cover the multitude of sins.
1 Peter 4:8.

72 Casting all your care upon him; for he careth for you.
1 Peter 5:6–7.

73 Be sober, be vigilant; because your adversary the devil, as a roaring lion, walketh about, seeking whom he may devour.
1 Peter 5:8.

74 The dog is turned to his own vomit again; and the sow that was washed to her wallowing in the mire.
2 Peter 2:22.

75 One day is with the Lord as a thousand years, and a thousand years as one day.
2 Peter 3:8–9.

76 But the day of the Lord will come as a thief in the night.
2 Peter 3:10–11.

77 If we say that we have no sin, we deceive ourselves, and the truth is not in us. If we confess our sins, he is faithful and just to forgive us our sins, and to cleanse us from all unrighteousness.
1 John 1:8–9.

78 If any man sin, we have an advocate with the Father, Jesus Christ the righteous.
1 John 2:1.

79 Behold, what manner of love the Father hath bestowed upon us, that we should be called the sons of God.
1 John 3:1.

80 But whoso hath this world's good, and seeth his brother have need, and shutteth up his bowels of compassion from him, how dwelleth the love of God in him?
1 John 3:17.

81 Beloved, let us love one another: for love is of God; and every one that loveth is born of God, and knoweth God. He that loveth not knoweth not God; for God is love.
1 John 4:7–8.

82 Herein is love, not that we loved God, but that he loved us, and sent his Son to be the propitiation for our sins.
1 John 4:10.

83 There is no fear in love; but perfect love casteth out fear.
1 John 4:18.

84 If a man say, I love God, and hateth his brother, he is a liar: for he that loveth not his brother whom he hath seen, how can he love God whom he hath not seen?
1 John 4:20.

85 John to the seven churches which are in Asia: Grace be unto you, and peace, from him which is, and which was, and which is to come.
Revelation 1:4.

86 Behold, he cometh with clouds; and every eye shall see him, and they also which pierced him: and all kindreds of the earth shall wail because of him. Even so, Amen.
Revelation 1:7.

87 I was in the Spirit on the Lord's day, and heard behind me a great voice, as of a trumpet, Saying, I am Alpha and Omega, the first and the last: and, What thou seest, write in a book, and send it unto the seven churches which are in Asia.
Revelation 1:10–11.

88 And in the midst of the seven candlesticks one like unto the Son of man, clothed with a garment down to the foot, and girt about the paps with golden girdle.
His head and his hairs were white like wool, as white as snow; and his eyes were as a flame of fire;
And his feet like unto fine brass, as if they burned in a furnace; and his voice as the sound of many waters.
And he had in his right hand seven stars: and out of his mouth went a sharp two-edged sword: and his countenance was as the sun shineth in his strength.
And when I saw him, I fell as his feet as dead.
Revelation 1:13–17.

89 I am he that liveth, and was dead; and, behold, I am alive for evermore, Amen; and have the keys of hell and of death.
Revelation 1:18.

90 I have somewhat against thee, because thou hast left thy first love.
Revelation 2:4.

91 Be thou faithful unto death, and I will give thee a crown of life.
Revelation 2:10.

92 And he shall rule them with a rod of iron; as the vessels of a potter shall they be broken to shivers.
Revelation 2:27.

93 Behold, I have set before thee an open door, and no man can shut it: for thou hast a little strength, and hast kept my word, and hast not denied my name.
Revelation 3:8.

94 I know thy works, that thou art neither cold nor hot: I would thou wert cold or hot. So then because thou art lukewarm, and neither cold nor hot, I will spew thee out of my mouth.
Revelation 3:15–16.

95 Behold, I stand at the door, and knock: if any man hear my voice, and open the door, I will come in to him, and will sup with him, and he with me.
Revelation 3:20.

96 And before the throne there was a sea of glass like unto crystal: and in the midst of the throne, and round about the throne, were four beasts full of eyes before and behind.
Revelation 4:6–7.

97 And the four beasts had each of them six wings about him; and they were full of eyes within: and they rest not day and night, saying, Holy, holy, holy, Lord God Almighty, which was, and is, and is to come.
Revelation 4:8.

98 Cast their crowns before the throne, saying, Thou art worthy, O Lord, to receive glory and honour and power: for thou hast created all things, and for thy pleasure they are and were created.
Revelation 4:10–11.

99 Who is worthy to open the book, and to loose the seals thereof? And no man in heaven, nor in earth, neither under the earth, was able to open the book, neither to look thereon.
Revelation 5:2–3.

1 And I looked, and behold a pale horse: and his name that sat on him was Death, and Hell followed with him.
Revelation 6:8.

2 And said to the mountains and rocks, Fall on us, and hide us from the face of him that sitteth on the throne, and from the wrath of the Lamb: For the great day of his wrath is come; and who shall be able to stand?
Revelation 6:16–17.

3 A great multitude, which no man could number, of all nations, and kindreds, and people, and tongues, stood before the throne, and before the Lamb, clothed with white robes, and palms in their hands.
Revelation 7:9.

4 These are they which came out of great tribulation, and have washed their robes, and made them white in the blood of the Lamb. Therefore are they before the throne of God, and serve him day and night in his temple: and he that sitteth on the throne shall dwell among them. They shall hunger no more, neither thirst any more; neither shall the sun light on them nor any heat. For the Lamb which is in the midst of the throne shall feed them, and shall lead them unto living fountains of waters: and God shall wipe away all tears from their eyes.
Revelation 7:14–17.

5 And when he had opened the seventh seal, there was silence in heaven about the space of half an hour.
Revelation 8:1.

6 I saw a star fall from heaven unto the earth: and to him was given the key of the bottomless pit.
Revelation 9:1.

7 And there were stings in their tails.
Revelation 9:10.

8 I took the little book out of the angel's hand, and ate it up; and it was in my mouth sweet as honey: and as soon as I had eaten it, my belly was bitter.
Revelation 10:9–10.

9 And there appeared a great wonder in heaven; a woman clothed with the sun, and the moon under her feet, and upon her head a crown of twelve stars.
Revelation 12:1.

10 And there was war in heaven: Michael and his angels fought against the dragon; and the dragon fought and his

angels, And prevailed not; neither was their place found any more in heaven. And the great dragon was cast out, that old serpent, called the Devil, and Satan, which deceiveth the whole world: he was cast out into the earth, and his angels were cast out with him.
Revelation 12:7–9.

11 And that no man might buy or sell, save he that had the mark, or the name of the beast, or the number of his name. Here is wisdom. Let him that hath understanding count the number of the beast: for it is the number of a man; and his number is Six hundred threescore and six.
Revelation 13:17–18.

12 And the smoke of their torment ascendeth up for ever and ever: and they have no rest day nor night, who worship the beast and his image, and whosoever receiveth the mark of his name.
Revelation 14:11.

13 Blessed are the dead which die in the Lord from henceforth: Yea, saith the Spirit, that they may rest from their labours; and their works do follow them.
Revelation 14:13.

14 And I saw as it were a sea of glass mingled with fire.
Revelation 15:2.

15 Behold, I come as a thief. Blessed is he that watcheth, and keepeth his garments, lest he walk naked, and they see his shame. And he gathereth them together into a place called in the Hebrew tongue Armageddon.
Revelation 16:15–16.

16 Come hither; I will shew unto thee the judgment of the great whore that sitteth upon many waters.
Revelation 17:1.

17 And upon her forehead was a name written, MYSTERY, BABYLON THE GREAT, THE MOTHER OF HARLOTS AND ABOMINATIONS OF THE EARTH.
Revelation 17:5.

18 And a mighty angel took up a stone like a great millstone, and cast it into the sea, saying, Thus with violence shall that great city Babylon be thrown down, and shall be found no more at all.
Revelation 18:21.

19 And I saw heaven opened, and behold a white horse; and he that sat upon him was called Faithful and True, and in righteousness he doth judge and make war.
Revelation 19:11.

20 And he hath on his vesture and on his thigh a name written, KING OF KINGS, AND LORD OF LORDS.
Revelation 19:16.

21 And he laid hold on the dragon, that old serpent, which is the Devil, and Satan, and bound him a thousand years, And cast him into the bottomless pit, and shut him up, and set a seal upon him, that he should deceive the nations no more, till the thousand years should be fulfilled: and after that he must be loosed a little season.
Revelation 20:2–3.

22 And I saw a great white throne, and him that sat on it, from whose face the earth and the heaven fled away; and there was found no place for them. And I saw the dead, small and great, stand before God; and the books were opened: and another book was opened, which is the book of life: and the dead were judged out of those things which were written in the books, according to their works. And the sea gave up the dead which were in it; and death and hell delivered up the dead which were in them: and they were judged every man according to their works. And death and hell were cast into the lake of fire.
Revelation 20:11–14.

23 And I saw a new heaven and a new earth: for the first heaven and the first earth were passed away; and there was no more sea. And I John saw the holy city, new Jerusalem, coming down from God out of heaven, prepared as a bride adorned for her husband.
Revelation 21:1–2.

24 And God shall wipe away all tears from their eyes; and there shall be no more death, neither sorrow, nor crying, neither shall there be any more pain: for the former things are passed away. And he that sat upon the throne said, Behold, I make all things new. And he said unto me, Write: for these words are true and faithful.
Revelation 21:4–5.

25 I will give unto him that is athirst of the fountain of the water of life freely.
Revelation 21:6.

26 And the street of the city was pure gold, as it were transparent glass.
Revelation 21:21.

27 And the gates of it shall not be shut at all by day: for there shall be no night there.
Revelation 21:25.

28 And he shewed me a pure river of water of life, clear as crystal, proceeding out of the throne of God and of the Lamb. In the midst of the street of it, and on either side of the river, was there the tree of life, which bare twelve manner of fruits, and yielded her fruit every month: and the leaves of the tree were for the healing of the nations.
Revelation 22:1–2.

29 He which testifieth these things saith, Surely I come quickly. Amen. Even so, come, Lord Jesus. The grace of our Lord Jesus Christ be with you all. Amen.
Revelation 22:20–1.

Bible (Vulgate)

A 4c translation of the Bible into Latin, commissioned by Pope Damasus and undertaken by Jerome (382–405). It became known as the *versio vulgata*, the 'common translation', and is still an official text of the Roman Catholic Church. The quotations given here are those that are well known in their Latin form.

30 *Dominus illuminatio mea, et salus mea, quem timebo?*
The Lord is the source of my light and my safety, so whom shall I fear?
Psalm 26:1.

31 *Asperges me hyssopo, et mundabor; lavabis me, et super nivem dealbabor.*
You will sprinkle me with hyssop, and I shall be made clean; you will wash me and I shall be made whiter than snow.
Psalm 50:9 (Psalm 51:7 Authorized Version).

32 *Cantate Domino canticum novum, quia mirabilia fecit.*

Sing to the Lord a new song, because he has done marvellous things.
Psalm 97:1 (Psalm 98:1 Authorized Version).
▶ See Book of Common Prayer 149:12.

33 *Jubilate Deo, omnis terra; servite Domino in laetitia.*
Sing joyfully to God, all the earth; serve the Lord with gladness.
Psalm 99:2 (Psalm 100:2 Authorized Version).
▶ See Book of Common Prayer 149:32.

34 *Beatus vir qui timet Dominum, in mandatis ejus volet nimis!*
Happy is the man who fears the Lord, who is only too willing to follow his orders.
Psalm 111:1 (Psalm 112:1 Authorized Version).

35 *Non nobis, Domine, non nobis; sed nomini tuo da gloriam.*
Not unto us, Lord, not unto us; but to thy name give glory.
Psalm 113 (2nd part):1 (Psalm 115:1 Authorized Version).

36 *Laudate Dominum, omnes gentes; laudate eum, omnes populi.*
Praise the Lord, all nations; praise him, all people.
Psalm 116:1 (Psalm 117:1 Authorized Version).

37 *Nisi Dominus aedificaverit domum, in vanum laboraverunt qui aedificant eam.*
Nisi Dominus custodierit civitatem, frustra vigilat qui custodit eam.
Unless the Lord has built the house, its builders have laboured in vain. Unless the Lord guards the city, the watchman watches in vain.
Psalm 126:1 (Psalm 127:1 Authorized Version).

38 *De profundis clamavi ad te, Domine; Domine exaudi vocem meam.*
Up from the depths I have cried to thee, Lord; Lord, hear my voice.
Psalm 129:1 (Psalm 130:1 Authorized Version).

39 *Vanitas vanitatum, dixit Ecclesiastes; vanitas vanitatum, et omnia vanitas.*
Vanity of vanities, said the preacher; vanity of vanities, and everything is vanity.
Ecclesiastes 1:2.
▶ See Bible (Old Testament) 105:9.

40 *Rorate, coeli, desuper, et nubes pluant Justum; aperiatur terra, et germinet Salvatorem.*
Drop down dew, heavens, from above, and let the clouds rain down righteousness; let the earth be opened, and a saviour spring to life.
Isaiah 45:8.

41 *Benedicite, omnia opera Domini, Domino; laudate et superexaltate eum in secula.*
Bless the Lord, all the works of the Lord; praise him and exalt him above all things for ever.
Daniel 3:57.

42 *Magnificat anima mea Dominum; et exsultavit spiritus meus in Deo salvatore meo.*
My soul doth magnify the Lord: and my spirit hath rejoiced in God my Saviour.
St Luke 1:46.
▶ See Bible (New Testament) 120:66.

43 *Esurientes implevit bonis, et divites dimisit inanes.*
He hath filled the hungry with good things: and the rich he hath sent empty away.
St Luke 1.53.
▶ See Bible (New Testament) 120:66.

44 *Nunc dimittis servum tuum, Domine, secundum verbum tuum in pace.*
Lord, now lettest thou thy servant depart in peace: according to thy word.
St Luke 2:29.
▶ See Bible (New Testament) 120:70.

45 *Pax Vobis.*
Peace be unto you.
St Luke 24:36.

46 *Quo vadis?*
Where are you going?
St John 16:5.

47 *Ecce homo.*
Behold the man.
St John 19:5.

48 *Noli me tangere.*
Do not touch me.
St John 20:17.
▶ See Bible (New Testament) 124:66.

Bickerstaffe, Isaac c.1735–c.1812

Irish playwright. An officer of marines, he was dismissed from the service and later forced to flee the country. He is credited with establishing the comic opera in English theatre.

49 And this the burthen of his song,
For ever used to be,
I care for nobody, not I,
If no one cares for me.
1762 *Love in a Village*, act 1, sc.2.

50 'Tis a sure sign that work goes on merrily, when folks sing at it.
1765 *The Maid of the Mill*, act 1, sc.1.

51 Perhaps it was right to dissemble your love,
But—why did you kick me downstairs?
1789 'An Expostulation'.

Biddle, Francis Beverley 1886–1968

US lawyer, Solicitor General (1940) and Attorney General (1941–5). He served as US judge on the Nuremberg trials of war criminals.

52 The Constitution has never greatly bothered any wartime President.
1962 *In Brief Authority*.

Biden, Joe (Joseph Robinette) 1942–

US lawyer and politician. He served as Democratic Senator for Delaware (1973–2009) before election as Vice President (2009–) under Barack Obama.

53 Rudy Giuliani—there's only three things he mentions in a sentence: a noun, a verb, and 9/11.
2007 Democratic primary debate, 30 Oct.

54 My mother's creed is the American creed: No one is better than you. You are everyone's equal, and everyone is equal to you.
2008 Acceptance speech, 27 Aug.

55 Make sure of two things. Be careful—microphones are always hot, and understand that in Washington, D.C., a gaffe is when you tell the truth. So, be careful.

2012 Speech to national conference of the National Association of Black Journalists, Washington, D.C., 20 Jun.

56 Isn't it a bitch? I mean... this vice president thing?
2014 Addressing the vice president of the student body at Harvard College, 2 Oct.

Biel, Jessica Claire 1982–

US film and television actress. Her films include *The Rules of Attraction* (2002), *The A-Team* (2010) and *Total Recall* (2012).

57 If you want a man's attention, ignore him.
2008 As Larita Whittaker in *Easy Virtue* (screenplay by Stephan Elliott and Sheridan Jobbins).

Bierce, Ambrose Gwinett 1842–c.1914

US writer and journalist, best known for his *Cynic's Word Book* (1906, retitled *The Devil's Dictionary*, 1911). His collection of stories *Tales of Soldiers and Civilians* (1892) coincided with his divorce and the death of his son in a gunfight. He is thought to have died in Mexico.

58 That sovereign of insufferables.
1882 *Wasp*, alluding to Oscar Wilde.

59 Accordion, n. An instrument in harmony with the sentiments of an assassin.
1906 *The Cynic's Word Book*. Retitled *The Devil's Dictionary* (1911).

60 Acquaintance, n. A person whom we know well enough to borrow from, but not well enough to lend to.
1906 *The Cynic's Word Book*. Retitled *The Devil's Dictionary* (1911).

61 Advice, n. The smallest current coin.
1906 *The Cynic's Word Book*. Retitled *The Devil's Dictionary* (1911).

62 Alliance, n. In international politics, the union of two thieves who have their hands so deeply inserted in each other's pocket that they cannot separately plunder a third.
1906 *The Cynic's Word Book*. Retitled *The Devil's Dictionary* (1911).

63 Ambition, n. An overmastering desire to be vilified by enemies while living and made ridiculous by friends when dead.
1906 *The Cynic's Word Book*. Retitled *The Devil's Dictionary* (1911).

64 Applause, n. The echo of a platitude.
1906 *The Cynic's Word Book*. Retitled *The Devil's Dictionary* (1911).

65 Battle, n. A method of untying with the teeth a political knot that would not yield to the tongue.
1906 *The Cynic's Word Book*. Retitled *The Devil's Dictionary* (1911).

66 Bore, n. A person who talks when you wish him to listen.
1906 *The Cynic's Word Book*. Retitled *The Devil's Dictionary* (1911).

67 Brain, n. An apparatus with which we think that we think.
1906 *The Cynic's Word Book*. Retitled *The Devil's Dictionary* (1911).

68 Calamity, n. A more than commonly plain and unmistakable reminder that the affairs of this life are not of our own ordering. Calamities are of two kinds: misfortune to ourselves, and good fortune to others.
1906 *The Cynic's Word Book*. Retitled *The Devil's Dictionary* (1911).

69 Circumlocution, n. A literary trick whereby the writer who has nothing to say breaks it gently to the reader.
1906 *The Cynic's Word Book*. Retitled *The Devil's Dictionary* (1911).

70 Conservative, n. A statesman who is enamoured of existing evils, as distinguished from the Liberal, who wishes to replace them with others.
1906 *The Cynic's Word Book*. Retitled *The Devil's Dictionary* (1911).

71 Consult, v.t. To seek another's approval of a course already decided upon.
1906 *The Cynic's Word Book*. Retitled *The Devil's Dictionary* (1911).

72 Corporation, n. An ingenious device for obtaining individual profit without individual responsibility.
1906 *The Cynic's Word Book*. Retitled *The Devil's Dictionary* (1911).

73 Cynic, n. A blackguard whose faulty vision sees things as they are, not as they ought to be.
1906 *The Cynic's Word Book*. Retitled *The Devil's Dictionary* (1911).

74 Diplomacy, n. The patriotic art of lying for one's country.
1906 *The Cynic's Word Book*. Retitled *The Devil's Dictionary* (1911).

75 Education, n. That which discloses to the wise and disguises from the foolish their lack of understanding.
1906 *The Cynic's Word Book*. Retitled *The Devil's Dictionary* (1911).

76 Egotist, n. A person of low taste, more interested in himself than in me.
1906 *The Cynic's Word Book*. Retitled *The Devil's Dictionary* (1911).

77 Faith, n. Belief without evidence in what is told by one who speaks, without knowledge, of things without parallel.
1906 *The Cynic's Word Book*. Retitled *The Devil's Dictionary* (1911).

78 Fashion, n. A despot whom the wise ridicule and obey.
1906 *The Cynic's Word Book*. Retitled *The Devil's Dictionary* (1911).

79 Future, n. That period of time in which our affairs prosper, our friends are true and our happiness is assured.
1906 *The Cynic's Word Book*. Retitled *The Devil's Dictionary* (1911).

80 History, n. An account, mostly false, of events, mostly unimportant, which are brought about by rulers, mostly knaves, and soldiers, mostly fools.
1906 *The Cynic's Word Book*. Retitled *The Devil's Dictionary* (1911).

81 Ink, n. A villainous compound...chiefly used to facilitate the infection of idiocy and promote intellectual crime.
1906 *The Cynic's Word Book*. Retitled *The Devil's Dictionary* (1911).

82 Marriage, n. The state or condition of a community consisting of a master, a mistress and two slaves, making in all, two.
1906 *The Cynic's Word Book*. Retitled *The Devil's Dictionary* (1911).

83 Mayonnaise, n. One of the sauces which serve the French in place of a state religion.
1906 *The Cynic's Word Book*. Retitled *The Devil's Dictionary* (1911).

84 Painting, n. The art of protecting flat surfaces from the weather and exposing them to the critic.
1906 *The Cynic's Word Book.* Retitled *The Devil's Dictionary* (1911).

85 Patience, n. A minor form of despair, disguised as a virtue.
1906 *The Cynic's Word Book.* Retitled *The Devil's Dictionary* (1911).

86 Peace, n. In international affairs, a period of cheating between two periods of fighting.
1906 *The Cynic's Word Book.* Retitled *The Devil's Dictionary* (1911).

87 Philosophy, n. A route of many roads leading from nowhere to nothing.
1906 *The Cynic's Word Book.* Retitled *The Devil's Dictionary* (1911).

88 Piano, n. A parlour utensil for subduing the impenitent visitor. It is operated by depressing the keys of the machine and the spirits of the audience.
1906 *The Cynic's Word Book.* Retitled *The Devil's Dictionary* (1911).

89 Positive, adj. Mistaken at the top of one's voice.
1906 *The Cynic's Word Book.* Retitled *The Devil's Dictionary* (1911).

90 Prejudice, n. A vagrant opinion without visible means of support.
1906 *The Cynic's Word Book.* Retitled *The Devil's Dictionary* (1911).

91 Saint, n. A dead sinner revised and edited.
1906 *The Cynic's Word Book.* Retitled *The Devil's Dictionary* (1911).

92 Talk, v.t. To commit an indiscretion without temptation, from an impulse without purpose.
1906 *The Cynic's Word Book.* Retitled *The Devil's Dictionary* (1911).

93 Vote, n. The instrument and symbol of a freeman's power to make a fool of himself and a wreck of his country.
1906 *The Cynic's Word Book.* Retitled *The Devil's Dictionary* (1911).

Biko, Stephen 1946–77

South African black civil rights activist, founder of the Black Consciousness Movement. In 1973 he was placed under a banning order, and detained four times. He died in police custody, allegedly as a result of beatings.

94 Whites must be made to realise that they are only human, not superior. It's the same with Blacks. They must be made to realise that they are also human, not inferior.
1977 In the *Boston Globe*, 26 Oct.

Billings, Josh *pseudonym of* Henry Wheeler Shaw 1818–85

US humorist. He became a popular success with *Josh Billings, His Sayings* (1865).

95 Man was kreated a little lower than the angells and has bin gittin a little lower ever since.
1865 *Josh Billings, His Sayings*, ch.28.

96 It ain't often that a man's reputashun outlasts his munny.
1865 *Josh Billings, His Sayings*, ch.39.

97 Mi advise to them who are about tu begin, in arnest, the jurney ov life, is tu take their harte in one hand and a club in the other.
1865 *Josh Billings, His Sayings*, ch.71.

98 Love iz like the meazles; we kant have it bad but onst, and the latter in life we hav it the tuffer it goes with us.
1874 *Josh Billings' Wit and Humour.*

Binyon, (Robert) Laurence 1869–1943

English poet and art critic. He worked at the British Museum (1913–33) and was Norton Professor of Poetry at Harvard (1933–4). He is best remembered for his patriotic elegy 'For the Fallen', which Elgar set to music.

99 With proud thanksgiving, a mother for her children,
England mourns for her dead across the sea.
Flesh of her flesh they were, spirit of her spirit,
Fallen in the cause of the free.
1914 'For the Fallen', in *The Times*, 21 Sep.

1 They shall grow not old, as we that are left grow old:
Age shall not weary them, nor the years condemn.
At the going down of the sun and in the morning
We will remember them.
1914 'For the Fallen', in *The Times*, 21 Sep.

2 Now is the time for the burning of the leaves.
1942 'The Burning of the Leaves'.

3 Rootless hope and fruitless desire are there;
Let them go to the fire, with never a look behind.
The world that was ours is a world that is ours no more.
1942 'The Burning of the Leaves'.

4 Earth cares for her own ruins, naught for ours.
Nothing is certain, only the certain spring.
1942 'The Burning of the Leaves'.

Bioy Casares, Adolfo 1914–99

Argentinian fiction writer, known for his lifelong association with Jorge Luis Borges, with whom he published several anthologies and works of fiction. His own writings are examples of fantastic literature.

5 La eternidad rotativa puede parecer atroz al espectador; es satisfactoria para sus individuos. Libres de malas noticias y de enfermedades, viven siempre como si fuera la primera vez, sin recordar las anteriores.
A circular eternity may seem atrocious to the spectator, but it is satisfactory to individuals inside. Free from bad news and disease, they always live as if it were the first time, and do not remember previous times.
1940 *La invención de Morel* (*The Invention of Morel*, 1964).

Bird, Isabella *married name* Isabella Bishop 1831–1904

English traveller. She travelled and climbed in Australasia, America and the East; then returned to England to marry. When her husband died in 1886, she set off for Tibet and in 1890 travelled between Persia and the Black Sea. In 1894–7 she again visited the Far East, founding hospitals and orphanages, and her last journey was to Africa.

6 A man who any woman might love, but who no sane woman would marry.
1879 Of Rocky Mountain Jim, her guide on her travels on horseback through the Rockies. *A Lady's Life in the Rocky Mountains.*

7 One eye was entirely gone, and the loss made one side of the face repulsive, while the other might have been modelled in marble. 'Desperado' was written in large

Birkenhead

letters all over him. I almost repented of having sought his acquaintance.
1879 Of Rocky Mountain Jim, her guide on her travels on horseback through the Rockies. *A Lady's Life in the Rocky Mountains.*

8 I am well as long as I live on horseback...sleep out-of-doors, or in a log cabin, and lead in all respects a completely unconventional life. But each time for a few days...I have become civilised, I have found myself rapidly going down again.
1879 *A Lady's Life in the Rocky Mountains.*

9 Japan offers as much novelty perhaps as an excursion to another planet.
1880 *Unbeaten Tracks in Japan: An Account of Travels on Horseback in the Interior 1880* (published 1885).

10 Appropriating the fruits of Christian civilisation, but rejecting the tree from which they spring.
1880 *Unbeaten Tracks in Japan: An Account of Travels on Horseback in the Interior 1880* (published 1885).

11 It is singular that the Japanese, who rarely commit a solecism in taste in their national costume, architecture, or decorative art, seem to be perfectly destitute of perception when they borrow ours.
1880 *Unbeaten Tracks in Japan: An Account of Travels on Horseback in the Interior 1880* (published 1885).

Birkenhead, F(rederick) E(dwin) Smith, 1st Earl of 1872–1930

English Conservative politician and lawyer, a brilliant orator. In the Irish crisis (1914) he opposed Home Rule, but helped to negotiate the Settlement of 1921. He resigned after criticism over his conduct as Secretary of State for India (1924–8) to pursue commerce.

12 The world continues to offer glittering prizes to those who have stout hearts and stout swords.
1923 Rectorial address, Glasgow University, 7 Nov.

13 We have the highest authority for believing that the meek shall inherit the Earth; though I have never found any particular corroboration of this aphorism in the records of Somerset House.
1924 *Contemporary Personalities*, 'Marquess Curzon'.

14 As a matter of fact, we both are, and the only difference between us is that I am trying to be, and you can't help it.
In response to a judge's observation that Smith was being 'extremely offensive'. Quoted in 2nd Earl of Birkenhead *Frederick Edwin Earl of Birkenhead* (1933), vol.1, ch.9.

15 It is not for me, Your Honour, to attempt to fathom the inscrutable workings of Providence.
In reply to a judge's testy inquiry 'What do you suppose I am on the Bench for, Mr Smith?'. Quoted in 2nd Earl of Birkenhead *F. E.: The Life of F. E. Smith, First Earl of Birkenhead* (1959), ch.9.

16 Possibly not, My Lord, but far better informed.
In reply to a judge who had complained 'I have read your case, Mr Smith, and I am no wiser now than I was when I started'. Quoted in 2nd Earl of Birkenhead *F. E.: The Life of F. E. Smith, First Earl of Birkenhead* (1959), ch.9.

17 I do not deal with subtleties; I am only a lawyer.
Quoted in Richard Fountain *The Wit of the Wig* (1968).

18 He has devoted the best years of his life to preparing his impromptu speeches.
Of Winston Churchill. Attributed.

Birney, Earle 1904–95

Canadian poet, professor at the universities of Toronto and, after World War II, British Columbia. His first work was *David and Other Poems* (1942).

19 And now he could only
bar himself in and wait
for the great flint to come singing into his heart.
1952 'Bushed'.

20 Through the cold time
she holds me
with evergreen
devotion
she bears up my whiteness.
1977 'She Is'.

Birns, Harold 1914–82

New York City Buildings Commissioner (1962–5).

21 OG = PLR × AEB: the opportunity for graft equals the plethora of legal requirements multiplied by the number of architects, engineers and builders.
1963 Formula for bribery in building and housing codes. In the *New York Times*, 2 Oct.

Biro, Lajos 1880–1948

Hungarian screenwriter. He worked for Alexander Korda during the 1930s on various films, including *The Private Life of Henry VIII* (1933) and *The Four Feathers* (1939).

22 The things I've done for England.
1933 Line delivered by Charles Laughton as Henry VIII to Else Lanchester as Anne of Cleves in *The Private Life of Henry VIII* (with Arthur Wimperis).

Bishop, Elizabeth 1911–79

US poet. Her work is highly regarded for its precision, elegance and imagination.

23 The ship's ignored. The iceberg rises
and sinks again; its glassy pinnacles
correct elliptics in the sky.
This is a scene where he who treads the boards
is artlessly rhetorical.
1946 'The Imaginary Iceberg'.

24 The armoured cars of dreams, contrived to let us do so many a dangerous thing.
1946 'Sleeping Standing Up'.

25 All the untidy activity continues,
awful but cheerful.
1955 'The Bight'.

26 Come like a light in the white mackerel sky,
come like a daytime comet
with a long unnebulous train of words,
from Brooklyn, over the Brooklyn Bridge, on this fine morning,
please come flying.
1955 'Invitation to Miss Marianne Moore'.

27 What childishness is it that while there's breath of life in our bodies, we are determined to rush to see the sun the other way round?
1965 'Questions of Travel'.

28 Oh, must we dream our dreams
and have them, too?
1965 'Questions of Travel'.

29 The art of losing isn't hard to master;
so many things seem filled with the intent
to be lost that their loss is no disaster.
1969 'One Art'.

Bishop, Jim 1907–87
US syndicated columnist.

30 A good writer is not, per se, a good book critic. No more so than a good drunk is automatically a good bartender.
1957 In the New York *Journal-American*, 26 Nov.

31 The peeping Tom of the sciences...men who care not where they are going: they merely want to know where everyone else has been.
1961 Of archaeology. In the New York *Journal-American*, 14 Mar.

Bismarck, Otto Edward Leopold, Fürst von (Prince of) 1815–98
Prussian statesman, Prime Minister of Prussia. He expanded territory at the expense of Denmark and Austria, forming a new German Empire of which he was Chancellor (1871–90) until he resigned, disapproving of the policies of the new Kaiser, Wilhelm II.

32 The great questions of our day cannot be solved by speeches and majority votes but by iron and blood.
1862 Speech to the Prussian Chamber, 30 Sep. He later altered the concluding words to the more commonly quoted 'blood and iron'.

33 Politics is not an exact science.
1863 Speech to the Prussian Chamber, 18 Dec.

34 Anyone who has ever looked into the glazed eyes of a soldier dying on the battlefield will think hard before starting a war.
1867 Speech, Berlin, Aug.

35 If we are to negotiate, I envisage that we shall play an essentially modest role; that of an honest broker who really intends to do business.
1878 Speech to the Reichstag, 19 Feb, on preventing war in Europe.

36 If there is ever another war in Europe, it will come out of some damned silly thing in the Balkans.
1898 Attributed deathbed remark. Quoted in the House of Commons, 16 Aug 1945.

37 My map of Africa lies in Europe. Here lies Russia and here lies France, and we are in the middle. That is my map of Africa.
Remarking on his preoccupation with European, as opposed to colonial, territorial concerns. Quoted in A J P Taylor *The Struggle for Mastery in Europe 1848–1918* (1954), p.294.

Bissell, Claude T(homas) 1916–2000
Canadian scholar and university administrator, President of the University of Toronto (1958–71).

38 It's ironical that the first people to demand free speech are the first people to deny it to others.
1969 Of student protesters who disrupted the appearance of Clark Kerr, former President of Berkeley, at the University of Toronto, 5 Feb. Recalled in *Halfway up Parnassus* (1974).

Black, Arthur 1943–
Canadian broadcaster and humorist.

39 I predict that ashtrays will become as obsolete as spitoons in our lifetime.
1989 *That Old Black Magic*, 'Smoking Can be Dangerous to Your Health'.

Black (of Crossharbour), Conrad Black, Baron 1944–
Canadian newspaper proprietor, Chairman and Chief Executive Officer of Hollinger Inc (1985–2003). In 2007 he was found guilty in a US court of fraud and obstruction of justice and sent to prison.

40 Journalists as a group, unlike all other powerful groups, require some protection from themselves, and from their own excesses.
1988 Speech, Annual Dinner of the Canadian Press, 20 Apr, reported in the *Globe and Mail* the following day.

Black, Hugo LaFayette 1886–1971
US lawyer, senator (1927–37) and Associate Justice of the US Supreme Court (1937–71). He strongly supported civil liberties.

41 Without deviation, without exception, without any ifs, buts, or whereases, freedom of speech means you shall not do something to people for views they have, express, speak, or write.
Quoted in Irving Dillard (ed) *One Man's Stand for Freedom* (1963).

Blacker, Valentine 1728–1823
Anglo-Irish soldier.

42 Put your trust in God, my boys, and keep your powder dry.
'Oliver's Advice', collected in E Hayes *Ballads of Ireland* (1856), vol.1, p.192. The words are sometimes attributed to Oliver Cromwell.
▶ See Forgy 344:19.

Blackstone, Sir William 1723–80
English jurist. Called to the bar in 1746, he became King's Counsel and MP (both 1761), Solicitor-General (1763) and a judge of the court of common pleas (1770). He published *Commentaries on the Laws of England* (1765–9).

43 It is better that ten guilty persons escape than one innocent suffer.
1769 *Commentaries on the Laws of England*, vol.4, ch.27. A puzzled visitor is apocryphally said to have remarked, 'Better for whom?'

Blainey, Geoffrey Norman 1930–
Australian economic historian and social commentator. He showed in *The Tyranny of Distance* (1966) how geographical isolation had shaped Australian history and people.

44 The Tyranny of Distance.
1966 Title of book.

Blair, Cherie 1954–
English barrister. She is married to former Prime Minister Tony Blair.

45 I am not superwoman. The reality of my daily life is that I am juggling a lot of balls in the air... And sometimes some of the balls get dropped.
2002 Statement following revelations of her links to the convicted conman Peter Foster, 10 Dec.

46 He'll be up there with Churchill.
2008 Predicting her husband's place in history.

Blair, Hamish *pseudonym of* Andrew James Fraser Blair 1872–1935
Scottish author and journalist. He moved from England to India where he founded *Empire* (1906) and the *Eastern Bureau* (1912).

He wrote a number of short stories as well as articles, sketches and light verse.

47 This bloody town's a bloody cuss—
No bloody trains, no bloody bus,
And no one cares for bloody us—
In bloody Orkney.
1952 'The Bloody Orkneys', stanza 1. First published in Arnold Silcock *Verse and Worse*, 'Queer People'.

48 Best bloody place is bloody bed,
With bloody ice on bloody head,
You might as well be bloody dead,
In bloody Orkney.
1952 'The Bloody Orkneys', last stanza. First published in Arnold Silcock *Verse and Worse*, 'Queer People'.

Blair, Tony (Anthony Charles Lynton) 1953–

Scottish-born Labour politician and barrister, Prime Minister (1997–2007). He attracted criticism for ordering troops into Iraq in 2003.

49 Labour is the Party of law and order in Britain today—tough on crime and tough on the causes of crime.
1993 Speech as Shadow Home Secretary, Labour Party Conference, Sep.

50 The art of leadership is saying no, not yes. It is very easy to say yes.
1994 In *The Mail on Sunday*, 2 Oct.

51 I didn't come into politics to change the Labour Party. I came into politics to change the country.
1995 Speech at the Labour Party Conference, 30 Sep.

52 Ask me my three main priorities for Government, and I tell you: education, education and education.
1996 Speech at the Labour Party Conference, 1 Oct.

53 People have to know that we will run from the centre and govern from the centre.
1997 Speech given to The Newspaper Society, London, 16 Mar.

54 We are not the masters. The people are the masters. We are the servants of the people… What the electorate gives, the electorate can take away.
1997 Addressing Labour MPs on the first day of the new Parliament, 7 May.

55 Sometimes I forget I'm Prime Minister. To me, I'm just Tony Blair.
1997 In *The Sun*, 29 Jul.

56 She was the people's princess and this is how she will stay.
1997 On the death of Diana, Princess of Wales. In a press statement, 1 Sep.

57 This is not the time for soundbites. I can feel the hand of history on our shoulders.
1998 On peace talks in Northern Ireland. In the *Daily Telegraph*, 8 Apr.

58 In future, welfare will be a hand-up, not a hand-out.
1999 Lecture, London, 18 Mar.

59 Britain must, and I am sure will, stand shoulder-to-shoulder with the United States of America and peaceful nations across the world in deploying every possible resource to bring to justice the people responsible, and make sure terrorism never prevails.
2001 Statement, 11 Sep.

60 Jesus was a moderniser.
Quoted in John Rentoul *Tony Blair: Prime Minister* (2001).

61 Every time I have asked us to go to war, I have hated it. I spent months trying to get Milosevic to stop ethnic cleansing in Kosovo, delaying action while we negotiated endlessly.
2003 Speech at the Labour Party Conference, 15 Feb.

62 At every stage, we should seek to avoid war. But if the threat cannot be removed peacefully, please let us not fall for the delusion that it can be safely ignored.
2003 Speech at the Labour Party Conference, 15 Feb.

63 To retreat now, I believe, would put at hazard all that we hold dearest, turn the United Nations back into a talking shop, stifle the first steps of progress in the Middle East; leave the Iraqi people to the mercy of events on which we would have relinquished all power to influence for the better.
2003 Speech to the House of Commons, 18 Mar.

64 I somehow feel I am not being entirely persuasive in certain quarters.
2004 Following protests from the public gallery during a debate on the Iraq war in the House of Commons, 4 Feb.

65 The good news is that it is easy to describe the problem in Iraq today, the bad news is it's tough to tackle it.
2004 Press conference, 22 Apr.

66 There will be no cutting and running in Iraq.
2004 Press conference, 17 May.

67 Now is not the time for a change in direction…but a change in gear.
2004 Press conference, 15 Jun.

68 Ideals survive through change. They die through inertia in the face of challenge.
2005 Speech to the European Parliament, 23 Jun.

69 It is important that those engaged in terrorism realise that our determination to defend our values and our way of life is greater than their determination to cause death and destruction to innocent people in a desire to impose extremism on the world.
2005 Statement after terrorist attacks in London, 7 Jul.

70 Let no one be in any doubt that the rules of the game are changing.
2005 Announcing new anti-terrorism measures, 5 Aug.

71 Sometimes it is better to lose and do the right thing than to win and do the wrong thing.
2005 Prime Minister's Questions, House of Commons, 9 Nov.

72 That's the art of leadership. To make sure that what shouldn't happen, doesn't happen.
2007 Interview, *Newsweek*, Feb.

73 I ask you to accept one thing. Hand on heart I did what I thought was right. I may have been wrong. That is your call.
2007 Announcing his resignation as Prime Minister, 10 May.

74 The fear of missing out means today's media, more than ever before, hunts in a pack. In these modes it is like a feral beast, just tearing people and reputations to bits. But no one dares miss out.
2007 Quoted by Reuters, 12 Jun.

75 This isn't about a lie, or a conspiracy, or a deceit, or a deception. It's a decision.
2010 Referring to his decision to go to war in Iraq.

Blake, Eubie James Hubert 1883–1983

US jazz musician.

76 If I'd known I was gonna live this long, I'd have taken better care of myself.
   1983 Quoted in the *Observer*, 13 Feb. He died 5 days after his 100th birthday.

Blake, Peter 1932–

English painter. A pioneer of the pop art movement in Britain, his most widely-known work is the cover design for the Beatles' album *Sergeant Pepper's Lonely Hearts Club Band* (1967).

77 Most artists go potty as they get older: dafter and madder as they get more celibate. So I am consciously going to do that.
   2004 In *The Guardian*, 3 Jun.

Blake, William 1757–1827

English poet, painter, engraver and mystic. His works range from the lyrical *Songs of Innocence* (1789) and *Songs of Experience* (1794) to the mystical poems of *The Marriage of Heaven and Hell* (1791). His best-known engravings are in *The Illustrations to the Book of Job* (1826).

78 Whether on Ida's shady brow,
   Or in the chambers of the East,
   The chambers of the sun that now
   From ancient melody have ceased.
   1783 *Poetical Sketches*, 'To The Muses'.

79 How have you left the ancient love
   That bards of old enjoyed in you!
   The sound is forced, the notes are few!
   1783 *Poetical Sketches*, 'To The Muses'.

80 The hills tell each other, and the listening
   Valleys hear; all our longing eyes are turned
   Up to thy holy feet visit our clime.
   Come o'er the eastern hills and let our winds
   Kiss thy perfumed garments; let us taste
   Thy morn and evening breath. Scatter thy pearls
   Upon our love-sick land that mourns for thee.
   1783 *Poetical Sketches*, 'To Spring'.

81 O thou who passest through our valleys in
   Thy strength, curb thy fierce steeds, ally the heat
   That flames from their large nostrils! thou, O Summer,
   Beneath our oaks hast slept while we beheld
   With joy thy ruddy limbs and flourishing hair.
   1783 *Poetical Sketches*, 'To Summer'.

82 O Autumn, laden with fruit, and stained
   With the blood of grape, pass not, but sit
   Beneath my shady roof; there thou may'st rest,
   And tune thy jolly voice to my fresh pipe,
   And all the daughters of the year shall dance!
   Sing now the lusty song of fruits and flowers.
   1783 *Poetical Sketches*, 'To Autumn'.

83 O Winter! bar thine adamantine doors.
   The north is thine—there hast thou built thy dark
   Deep-founded habitation. Shake not thy roofs,
   Nor bend thy pillars with thine iron car.
   1783 *Poetical Sketches*, 'To Winter'.

84 Does the eagle know what's in the pit
   Or wilt thou go ask the mole?
   Can wisdom be put in a silver rod,
   Or Love in a golden bowl.
   1789 Thel's Motto. *The Book of Thel*.

85 Piping down the valleys wild,
   Piping songs of pleasant glee,
   On a cloud I saw a child,
   And he laughing said to me,
   'Pipe a song about a lamb!'
   So I piped with merry cheer.
   'Piper, pipe that song again!'
   So I piped. He wept to hear.
   1789 *Songs of Innocence*, 'Introduction'.

86 Little lamb, who made thee?
   Dost thou know who made thee?
   Gave thee life and bid thee feed
   By the stream and o'er the mead;
   Gave thee clothing of delight,
   Softest clothing, woolly, bright;
   Gave thee such a tender voice,
   Making all the vales rejoice?
   Little lamb, who made thee?
   Dost thou know who made thee?
   1789 *Songs of Innocence*, 'The Lamb'.

87 My mother bore me in the southern wild,
   And I am black, but O! my soul is white;
   White as an angel is the English child,
   But I am black as if bereaved of light.
   1789 *Songs of Innocence*, 'The Little Black Boy'.

88 For Mercy has a human heart
   Pity a human face:
   And Love, the human form divine,
   And Peace, the human dress.
   1789 *Songs of Innocence*, 'The Divine Image'.

89 And all must love the human form,
   In heathen, Turk or Jew;
   Where mercy, Love and Pity dwell
   There God is dwelling too.
   1789 *Songs of Innocence*, 'The Divine Image'.

90 When my mother died I was very young,
   And my father sold me while yet my tongue
   Could scarcely cry weep weep weep weep.
   So your chimneys I sweep, and in soot I sleep.
   1789 *Songs of Innocence*, 'The Chimney Sweep'.

91 'Father! father! where are you going?
   O do not walk so fast.
   Speak, father, speak to your little boy,
   Or else I shall be lost.'
   1789 *Songs of Innocence*, 'The Little Boy Lost'.

92 He kissed the hand and by the hand led
   And to his mother brought,
   Who in sorrow pale, through the lonely dale,
   Her little boy weeping sought.
   1789 *Songs of Innocence*, 'The Little Boy Found'.

93 Then cherish pity, lest you drive an angel from your door.
   1789 *Songs of Innocence*, 'Holy Thursday'.

94 Without contraries is no progression. Attraction and repulsion, reason and energy, love and hate, are necessary to human existence.
   1790 *The Marriage of Heaven and Hell*, 'The Argument'.

95 Energy is Eternal Delight.
   1790 *The Marriage of Heaven and Hell*, 'The Voice of the Devil'.

96 The road of excess leads to the palace of wisdom.
   1790 *The Marriage of Heaven and Hell*, 'Proverbs of Hell'.

97 He who desires and acts not, breeds pestilence.
   1790 *The Marriage of Heaven and Hell*, 'Proverbs of Hell'.

98 Eternity is in love with the productions of time.
   1790 *The Marriage of Heaven and Hell*, 'Proverbs of Hell'.

99 Prisons are built with stones of Law, brothels with bricks of Religion.
   1790 *The Marriage of Heaven and Hell*, 'Proverbs of Hell'.

1 The tygers of wrath are wiser than the horses of instruction.
   1790 *The Marriage of Heaven and Hell*, 'Proverbs of Hell'.

2 The Pride of the peacock is the glory of God.
   The lust of the goat is the bounty of God.
   The wrath of the lion is the wisdom of God.
   The nakedness of woman is the work of God.
   1790 *The Marriage of Heaven and Hell*, 'Proverbs of Hell'.

3 Sooner murder an infant in its cradle than nurse unacted desires.
   1790 *The Marriage of Heaven and Hell*, 'Proverbs of Hell'.

4 If the doors of perception were cleansed everything would appear to man as it is, infinite.
   1790 *The Marriage of Heaven and Hell*, 'A Memorable Fancy', plate 14. Aldous Huxley used this phrase as the title of his work *The Doors of Perception* (1954).

5 Mutual forgiveness of each vice,
   Such are the Gates of Paradise.
   1793 *The Gates of Paradise*, prologue.

6 He who binds to himself a Joy
   Doth the winged life destroy;
   But he who kisses the Joy as it flies
   Lives in Eternity's sunrise.
   1793 *MS Notebooks*, p.105.

7 Never pain to tell thy love
   Love that never told can be;
   For the gentle wind does move
   Silently, invisibly.
   1793 *MS Notebooks*, p.115.

8 Hear the voice of the Bard!
   Who present, past and future sees.
   1794 *Songs of Experience*, 'Introduction'.

9 Love seeketh not itself to please,
   Nor for itself hath any care,
   But for another gives its ease,
   And builds a heaven in hell's despair.
   1794 *Songs of Experience*, 'The Clod and the Pebble'.

10 Love seeketh only self to please,
   To bind another to its delight,
   Joys in another's loss of ease
   And builds a hell in heaven's despite.
   1794 *Songs of Experience*, 'The Clod and the Pebble'.

11 Ah, sunflower, weary of time,
   Who countest the steps of the sun,
   Seeking after that sweet golden clime
   Where the traveller's journey is done;
   Where the youth pined away with desire
   And the pale virgin shrouded in snow
   Arise from their graves, and aspire
   Where my sunflower wishes to go.
   1794 *Songs of Experience*, 'Ah! Sunflower'.

12 O rose, thou art sick!
   The invisible worm
   That flies in the night,
   In the howling storm,
   Has found out thy bed
   Of crimson joy,
   And his dark secret love
   Does thy life destroy.
   1794 *Songs of Experience*, 'The Sick Rose'.

13 Is this a holy thing to see
   In a rich fruitful land,
   Babes reduced to misery,
   Fed with cold and usurous hand?
   1794 *Songs of Experience*, 'Holy Thursday'.

14 I went to the Garden of Love,
   And saw what I never had seen:
   A chapel was built in the midst
   Where I used to play on the green.
   1794 *Songs of Experience*, 'The Garden of Love'.

15 And I saw it was filled with graves,
   And tomb-stones where flowers should be;
   And priests in black gowns were walking their rounds,
   And binding with briars my joys and desires.
   1794 *Songs of Experience*, 'The Garden of Love'.

16 I wander through each charter'd street,
   Near where the charter'd Thames does flow,
   And mark in every face I meet
   Marks of weakness, marks of woe.
   1794 *Songs of Experience*, 'London'.

17 I was angry with my friend:
   I told my wrath, my wrath did end.
   I was angry with my foe:
   I told it not, my wrath did grow.
   1794 *Songs of Experience*, 'A Poison Tree'.

18 My mother groaned! my father wept.
   Into the dangerous world I leapt,
   Helpless, naked, piping loud
   Like a fiend hid in a cloud.
   1794 *Songs of Experience*, 'Infant Sorrow'.

19 Tyger! Tyger! burning bright
   In the forests of the night,
   What immortal hand or eye
   Could frame thy fearful symmetry?
   1794 *Songs of Experience*, 'The Tyger'.

20 When the stars threw down their spears,
   And watered heaven with their tears,
   Did he smile his work to see?
   Did he who made the Lamb make thee?
   1794 *Songs of Experience*, 'The Tyger'.

21 Dear Mother, dear Mother, the Church is cold,
   But the Ale-house is healthy and pleasant and warm.
   1794 *Songs of Experience*, 'The Little Vagabond'.

22 Mock on, mock on, Voltaire Rousseau;
   Mock on, mock on, 'tis all in vain!
   You throw the sand against the wind,
   And the wind blows it back again.
   1800–3 *MS Notebooks*, p.7.

23 O why was I born with a different face?
   Why was I not born like the rest of my race?
   1803 Letter to Thomas Butts, 16 Aug.

24 To see a world in a grain of sand,
   And heaven in a wild flower,

Hold infinity in the palm of your hand,
And eternity in an hour.
c.1803 *Auguries of Innocence*, l.1–4.

25 A robin red breast in a cage
Puts all Heaven in a rage.
c.1803 *Auguries of Innocence*, l.5–6.

26 Man was made for Joy and Woe,
And when this we rightly know,
Thro' the world we safely go.
Joy and Woe are woven fine,
A clothing for the soul divine.
c.1803 *Auguries of Innocence*, l.56–60.

27 The strongest poison ever known
Came from Ceasar's laurel crown.
c.1803 *Auguries of Innocence*, l.97–8.

28 The whore and gambler, by the state
Licensed build that nation's fate.
The harlot's cry from street to street
Shall weave old England's winding sheet.
c.1803 *Auguries of Innocence*, l.113–6.

29 We are led to believe a Lie
When we see with, not thro' the Eye.
c.1803 *Auguries of Innocence*, l.125–6.

30 The fields from Islington to Marybone,
To Primrose Hill and Saint John's Wood,
Were builded over with pillars of gold;
And there Jerusalem's pillars stood.
c.1804–1807 *Jerusalem*, plate 27.

31 He who would do good to another man must do it in
Minute Particulars.
General Good is the plea of the scoundrel, hypocrite,
and flatterer;
For Art and Science cannot exist but in minutely
organized Particulars.
c.1804–1807 *Jerusalem*, plate 55.

32 I gave you the end of the golden string;
Only wind it into a ball,
It will lead you in at Heaven's gate,
Built in Jerusalem's wall.
c.1804–1807 *Jerusalem*, plate 77.

33 I care not whether a man is good or evil; all that
I care
Is whether he is a wise man or a fool. Go! put off
Holiness,
And put on intellect, or my thunderous hammer shall
drive thee,
To wrath which thou condemnest, till thou obey my
voice.
c.1804–1807 *Jerusalem*, plate 91.

34 Painters are noted for being dissipated and wild.
c.1808 *Annotations to Sir Joshua Reynolds' Discourses*.

35 The man who never in his mind and thoughts travelled to
heaven is no artist.
c.1808 *Annotations to Sir Joshua Reynolds' Discourses*.

36 What has Reasoning to do with the Art of Painting?
c.1808 *Annotations to Sir Joshua Reynolds' Discourses*.

37 Knowledge of ideal beauty is not to be acquired. It is
born with us. Innate ideas are in every man, born with
him; they are truly himself.
c.1808 *Annotations to Sir Joshua Reynolds' Discourses*.

38 When Sir Joshua Reynolds died
All Nature was degraded;
The King dropp'd a tear into the Queen's ear,
And all his pictures faded.
c.1808 *Annotations to Sir Joshua Reynolds' Discourses*.

39 Thy friendship oft has made my heart to ache:
Do be my enemy—for friendship's sake.
1808–11 *MS Notebooks*, 'To H[ayley]', p.37.

40 And did those feet in ancient time
Walk upon England's mountains green?
And was the holy Lamb of God
On England's pleasant pastures seen?
1809 *Milton*, preface. Stanza 1.

41 And did the Countenance Divine
Shine forth upon our clouded hills?
And was Jerusalem builded here
Among these dark Satanic mills?
1809 *Milton*, preface. Stanza 2.

42 Bring me my bow of burning gold!
Bring me my arrows of desire!
Bring me my spear! O clouds, unfold!
Bring me my chariot of fire!
1809 *Milton*, preface. Stanza 3.

43 I will not cease from mental fight,
Nor shall my sword sleep in my hand,
Till we have built Jerusalem
In England's green and pleasant land.
1809 *Milton*, preface. Stanza 4.

44 God appears and God is light
To those poor souls who dwell in night,
But does a human form display
To those who dwell in realms of day.
1809 *Milton*, 'And Did Those Feet In Ancient Time'.

Blanc, Raymond 1949–

French chef. He has spent much of his career establishing a reputation as one of the best chefs in the UK.

45 When you cook it should be an act of love. To put a
frozen bag in the microwave for your child is an act of
hate.
2001 In *The Daily Telegraph*, 2 Oct.

Blanch, Lesley 1904–2007

English biographer, traveller and cookery writer.

46 She was an Amazon. Her whole life was spent riding at
breakneck speed towards the wilder shores of love.
1954 *The Wilder Shores of Love*, pt.2, ch.1.

Blanchflower, Danny (Robert Dennio) 1926–93

Northern Ireland-born footballer. He won numerous titles as captain of Tottenham Hotspur in the early 1960s and collected a total of 56 caps playing for Northern Ireland before retiring to become a noted football commentator and columnist.

47 We try to equalize before the others have scored.
1958 Explaining his tactics as captain of Northern Ireland.
Quoted in Colin Jarman *The Guinness Dictionary of Sports Quotations* (1990).

48 The great fallacy is that the game is first and last about
winning. It's nothing of the kind. The game is about
glory. It's about doing things in style, with a flourish,

about going out and beating the other lot, not waiting for them to die of boredom.
Quoted in Hunter Davis *The Glory Game* (1972).

Blass, Bill (William Ralph) 1922–2002
US fashion designer.

49 When in doubt wear red.
1982 In news summaries, 31 Dec.

Blavatsky, Helena Petrovna 1831–91
Russian-born mystic, founder of the Theosophical Society. Her works include *Isis Unveiled* (1877).

50 'Theosophy' is the essence of all religion and of absolute truth, a drop of which only underlies every creed.
1889 *The Key to Theosophy*.

51 Theosophy, on earth, is like the white ray of the spectrum, and each religion only one of the seven colours.
1889 *The Key to Theosophy*.

Blest Gana, Alberto 1830–1920
Chilean novelist and Ambassador to France and England. He lived in Paris until the end of his career. He pioneered the documentary social novel in Spanish American literature.

52 *Entre nosotros el dinero ha hecho desaparecer más preocupaciones de familia que en las viejas sociedades europeas. En éstas hay lo que llaman aristocracia de dinero, que jamás alcanza con su poder...a hacer olvidar enteramente la oscuridad de la cuna, al paso que en Chile...todo va cediendo su puesto a la riqueza.*
Among us, money has dissolved more worries than among ancient European societies. The latter have what they call the moneyed aristocracy, which, despite all its power, never gets to forget its humble origins; on the other hand, in Chile everything yields to wealth.
1862 *Martín Rivas*, ch.2 (translated 1918).

Blinder, Alan 1945–
US economist, Professor at Princeton University (1982–) and Vice Chair of the Federal Reserve System Board (1994–6).

53 Economists have the least influence on policy where they know the most and are most agreed...the most influence on policy where they know the least and disagree most.
1987 *Hard Heads, Soft Hearts*.

54 If you try to give an on-the-one-hand-or-the-other-hand answer, only one of the hands tends to get quoted.
1995 On economic forecasting. In the *Wall Street Journal*, 23 Jun.

55 Don't overstate your likely achievements; when in doubt, understate them.
2013 *After the Music Stopped: The Financial Crisis, the Response, and the Work Ahead*.

56 If your negligent neighbour falls asleep with a lit cigarette in his mouth, setting his house on fire, he's irresponsible and guilty. But you don't want him to perish in the blaze. Nor do you want his house setting the whole neighbourhood on fire. So you call in the fire department, even though it will cost taxpayers money.

2013 *After the Music Stopped: The Financial Crisis, the Response, and the Work Ahead*.

Bliss, Sir Arthur 1891–1975
English composer, Music Director of the BBC (1942–4) and Master of the Queen's Music (from 1953). His compositions, sometimes avant-garde, included ballets, an opera, chamber music and film scores.

57 The jazz band can be used for artificial excitement and aphrodisiac purposes, but not for spreading eternal truths.
1941 'Music Policy'.

Blix, Hans 1928–
Swedish diplomat. He was appointed Executive Chairman of the UN Monitoring, Verification and Inspection Commission for Iraq in 2000.

58 We have not found any smoking guns.
2003 Of weapons inspections in Iraq. To reporters, 9 Jan.

59 Iraq appears not to have come to a genuine acceptance—not even today—of the disarmament which was demanded of it and which it needs to carry out to win the confidence of the world and to live in peace.
2003 Security Council update on weapons inspections in Iraq, 27 Jan.

60 These reports do not contend that weapons of mass destruction remain in Iraq, but nor do they exclude that possibility. They point to lack of evidence and inconsistencies, which raise question marks, which must be straightened out, if weapons dossiers are to be closed and confidence is to arise.
2003 Security Council update on weapons inspections in Iraq, 27 Jan.

Blixen, Karen, Baroness *pseudonym Isak Dinesen* 1885–1962
Danish novelist and story teller. Her book *Out of Africa* (1938) is set on the Kenyan coffee plantation she managed with her husband (also cousin) Baron Bror Blixen. She was divorced in 1921, and returned to Denmark in 1931.

61 What is man, when you come to think upon him, but a minutely set, ingenious machine for turning, with infinite artfulness, the red wine of Shiraz into urine?
1934 *Seven Gothic Tales*, 'The Dreamers'.

62 The true aristocracy and the true proletariat of the world are both in understanding with tragedy. To them it is the fundamental principle of God, and the key, the minor key, to existence. They differ in this way from the bourgeoisie of all classes, who deny tragedy, who will not tolerate it, and to whom the word tragedy means in itself unpleasantness.
1937 *Out of Africa*, pt.5, ch.1.

Bloom, Allan 1930–92
US writer and educator, Professor of Political Science at the University of Chicago. His best-known work is *The Closing of the American Mind* (1987).

63 The liberally educated person is one who is able to resist the easy and preferred answers, not because he is obstinate but because he knows others worthy of consideration.
1987 *The Closing of the American Mind*, preface.

64 Education is the taming or demonstration of the soul's raw passions—not suppressing them or excising them, which would deprive the soul of its energy—but forming and informing them as art.
1987 *The Closing of the American Mind.*

Bloom, André Borisovich, Anthony, Metropolitan of Sourozh 1914–2003
Russian churchman and writer, Head of the Russian Orthodox Church in Great Britain and Ireland.

65 It is not the constant thought of their sins, but the vision of the holiness of God that makes the saints aware of their own sinfulness.
1966 *Living Prayer.*

66 A miracle is not the breaking of the laws of the fallen world. It is the re-establishment of the laws of the kingdom.
1966 *Living Prayer.*

Bloom, Harold 1930–
US literary critic and writer, Professor of English (1965–77) and Humanities (1974–) at Yale. His many works include *The Breaking of the Vessels* (1981).

67 The most beautiful prose paragraph yet written by any American.
1991 On the opening of ch.19 of Mark Twain's *Huckleberry Finn. The Western Canon.*

Bloomberg, Michael Rubens 1942–
US businessman and politician, Mayor of New York City (2002–13).

68 Organizing around a common interest is a fundamental part of democracy. We should no more try to take away the right of individuals to collectively bargain than we should try to take away the right to a secret ballot.
2011 In the *New York Times*, 28 Feb.

69 In our democracy, near equality is no equality. Government either treats everyone the same, or it doesn't. And right now it doesn't.
2011 Speaking about gay marriage, speech in New York, 26 May.

70 Ed, in his own way was our Moses. Just with a little less hair. He led us out of darkness and he gave us hope.
2013 Eulogy for former Mayor Ed Koch.

Blough, Roger M(iles) 1904–85
US industrialist.

71 Steel prices cause inflation like wet sidewalks cause rain.
1967 In *Forbes*, 1 Aug.

Blunden, Edmund Charles 1896–1974
English poet and critic. He served in World War I, an experience reflected both in his poetry and in his prose work *Undertones of War* (1928), but is essentially a nature poet.

72 All things they have in common, being so poor,
And their one fear, Death's shadow at the door.
Each sundown makes them mournful, each sunrise
Brings back the brightness in their failing eyes.
1920 'Almswomen'.

73 And night this toppling reed, still as the dead
The great pike lies, the murderous patriarch,
Watching the water-pit shelving and dark
Where through the plash his lithe bright vassals tread.
1920 'The Pike'.

74 Unrecorded, unrenowned,
Men from whom my ways begin,
Here I know you by your ground
But I know you not within—
There is silence, there survives
Not a moment of your lives.
1922 'Forefathers'.

75 Then is not death at watch
Within those secret waters?
What wants he but to catch
Earth's heedless sons and daughters?
1925 'The Midnight Skaters'.

76 Dance on this ball-floor thin and wan,
Use him as though you love him;
Court him, elude him, reel and pass,
And let him hate you through the glass.
1925 'The Midnight Skaters'.

77 Cuinchy…was a slaughter yard… Who that had been there for but a few hours could ever forget the sullen sorcery and mad lineaments of Cuinchy?
1928 *Undertones of War*, 'I V. The Sudden Depths'. Cuinchy, near Arras, was the scene of heavy fighting in 1914.

78 This was my country and it may be yet,
But something flew between me and the sun.
1928 'The Resignation'.

79 I have been young, and now am not too old;
And I have seen the righteous forsaken,
His health, his honour and his quality taken.
This is not what we were formerly told.
1929 'Report On Experience'.

80 Mastery in poetry consists largely in the instinct for not ruining or smothering or tinkering with moments of vision.
1930 'Leigh Hunt'.

81 I am for the woods against the world,
But are the woods for me?
1931 'The Kiss'.

82 Cricket to us was more than play,
It was a worship in the summer sun.
'Pride of the Village'. Quoted in Alan Ross (ed) *The Penguin Cricketer's Companion* (1978).

Blunkett, David 1947–
English Labour politician. Blind from birth, he became an MP in 1987 and served as Home Secretary (2001–4).

83 Let me say this very slowly indeed. Watch my lips: no selection by examination or interview under a Labour Government.
1995 Speech at the Labour Party Conference, 5 Oct.

84 They should go back home and re-create their countries which we have freed from tyranny, whether it be Kosovo or now Afghanistan. I have no sympathy whatsoever with young men in their twenties who do not get back home and rebuild their countries.
2002 On asylum seekers, 18 Sep.

85 I haven't given up on the idea that we're going to nail this individual.
2004 On the convicted football hooligan Garry Mann, who escaped his sentence when he was repatriated from Portugal before the paperwork was complete, 20 Jun.

Blythe, Ronald George 1922–

English writer. He is best known for his book *Akenfield* (1963), a portrait of an English village told in interviews with linking commentary.

86 As for the British churchman, he goes to church as he goes to the bathroom, with the minimum of fuss and with no explanation if he can help it.
1963 *The Age of Illusion*, ch.12.

87 An industrial worker would sooner have a £5 note but a countryman must have praise.
1969 *Akenfield*, ch.5.

88 Suffolk used to worship Sunday, not God.
1969 *Akenfield*, ch.6.

89 One of the reasons why old people make so many journeys into the past is to satisfy themselves that it is still there.
1979 *The View in Winter*, introduction.

Boccioni, Umberto 1882–1916

Italian artist, futurist painter and sculptor. A key figure in the drafting of the Futurist Manifesto (1910), he later turned to sculpture, attempting to convey motion and light in three-dimensional form.

90 It is necessary to destroy the pretended nobility, entirely literary and traditional, of marble and bronze… The sculptor can use twenty different materials, or even more, in a single work, provided that the plastic emotion requires it.
1912 In the *Technical Manifesto of Futurist Sculpture* (11 Apr, Milan).

Bodenheim, Maxwell 1892–1954

US writer and critic.

91 Poetry is the impish attempt to paint the color of the wind.
Quoted in Ben Hecht's play *Winkelberg* (1958).

Boethius, Anicius Manlius Severinus c.480–524 AD

Roman philosopher and statesman. Under Theodoric he became consul and later chief minister, but was accused of treason and executed. While in prison he wrote *De con-solatione philosophiae* (*The Consolation of Philosophy*, 523).

92 *Nam in omni adversitate fortunae infelicissimum est genus infortunii, fuisse felicem.*
In all adversity of fortune, the most wretched kind is once to have been happy.
523 *De consolatione philosophiae*, bk.2, pt.4 (translated by V E Watts).

Bogan, Louise 1897–1970

US poet and critic, poetry editor of the *New Yorker* for many years. Her work is intense and deeply personal.

93 Women have no wideness in them
They are provident instead,
Content in the tight hot cell of their hearts
To eat dusty bread.
1923 'Women'.

94 But childhood prolonged cannot remain a fairy-land. It becomes a hell.
1940 On Katherine Mansfield. 'Childhood's False Eden'.

95 The intellectual…is the fine nervous flower of the bourgeoisie.
1943 'Some Notes on Popular and Unpopular Poetry'.

Bogarde, Sir Dirk *originally* Derek Jules Ulric Niven van den Bogaerde 1921–99

English actor and novelist.

96 It's always full of all the people I'd hoped were dead.
On the Cannes Film Festival. Quoted in Barry Norman *And Why Not?* (2002).

Bogart, John B 1848–1921

US journalist, an early editor of the *New York Sun*.

97 When a dog bites a man, that is not news, because it happens so often. But if a man bites a dog, that is news.
Quoted in F M O'Brien *The Story of the Sun* (1918), ch.10. The phrase is often attributed to Charles A Dana.

Bohlen, Charles Eustis 1904–74

US diplomat and Soviet specialist, Ambassador to Russia (1953–7, 1959–61).

98 A non-Communist premier with Communist ministers would be like a woman trying to stay half pregnant.
Of Winston Churchill's suggestion that the West share spheres of influence with Joseph Stalin in the post-war development of the Balkans. Quoted in Walter Isaacson and Evan Thomas *The Wise Men* (1986).

99 There are two ways you can tell when a man is lying…when he says he can drink champagne all night and not get drunk…[and] when he says he understands Russians.
Quoted in the *New York Times*, 26 Dec 1993.

Boileau (Despréaux), Nicolas 1636–1711

French critic. His works include satires (1660–6), epistles, critical dissertations (particularly the influential *L'Art poétique*, 'The Art of Poetry', 1674), epigrams and translations.

1 *Si j'écris quatre mots, j'en effacerai trois.*
If I write four words, I strike out three of them.
1665 *Satire no.2 A M Molière*.

2 Often, the fear of one evil leads us into inflicting one that is worse.
1674 *L'Art poétique*.

Bok, Derek 1930–

US educator, President of Harvard University (1971–91) and Professor Emeritus there from 1991. His works include *Beyond the Ivory Tower: Social Responsibilities of the Modern University* (1982).

3 If you think education is expensive—try ignorance.
1979 In *Town and Country*, May.

Bold, Alan 1943–98

Scottish poet, biographer and critic, a prolific full-time writer and anthologizer since 1967. He wrote an award-winning biography of Hugh MacDiarmid (1989).

4 In Scotland, land of the omnipotent No.
1969 'A Memory of Death'.

5   That which once united man
    Now drives him apart. We are not helpless
    Creatures crashing onwards irresistibly to doom.
    There is time for everything and time to choose
    For everything. We are that time, that choice.
    Everybody gets what he deserves.
    1969 'June 1967 at Buchenwald'.

6   The poet lives as long as his lines are imprinted on the minds of his readers.
    1989 *MacDiarmid*, epilogue.

Bolingbroke, Henry St John, 1st Viscount
1678–1751

English Jacobite statesman, joint leader of the Tory Party. On the death of Queen Anne he fled to France, where he wrote *Reflections on Exile* (1714). He also wrote the influential *Idea of a Patriot King* (1749).

7   What a world is this, and how does fortune banter us!
    1714 Letter to Jonathan Swift, 3 Aug.

8   Faction is to party what the superlative is to the positive. Party is a political evil, and faction is the worst of all parties.
    1738 *Idea of a Patriot King*. Published in 1749.

Bolívar, Simón 1783–1830

Venezuelan soldier and statesman. He led revolutions against Spanish rule in New Granada (Colombia), Peru and Upper Peru (Bolivia). He became President of Colombia (1821–30) and of Peru (1823–9), and was a gifted prose writer.

9   *Más grande es el odio que nos ha inspirado la Península, que el mar que nos separa de ella; menos difícil es unir los dos continentes, que reconciliar los espíritus de ambos países.*
    The hate that the Iberian peninsula has inspired in us is broader than the sea which separates us from it; it is less difficult to join both continents than to join both countries' souls.
    1815 'Carta de Jamaica' (translated as *The Jamaica Letter*, 1977).

Bolles, Richard Nelson 1927–

US writer, famous for his manual for job hunters.

10 What Color is Your Parachute?
    1972 Title of a vocational guidance book published annually.

Bolt, Robert Oxton 1924–95

English playwright and screenwriter. His best-known work is the play *A Man for All Seasons* (1960). His screenplays include *Dr Zhivago* (1965) and *The Mission* (1986).

11 A Man for All Seasons.
    1960 Play title, originally said by Robert Whittington about his contemporary Sir Thomas More, the central character in Bolt's play.

12 It profits a man nothing to give his soul for the whole world…
    But for Wales—!
    1960 Thomas More. *A Man for All Seasons*.

13 To be human at all… we must stand fast a little—even at the risk of being heroes.
    1960 Thomas More. *A Man for All Seasons*.

14 The courts of Europe are a jungle, compared to which your jungles here are a well-kept garden.

1986 Line delivered by Ray Mc Anally as Cardinal Altamirano in *The Mission*.

Bolt, Usain St Leo 1986–

Jamaican sprinter. Acclaimed as the fastest runner in the history of athletics, his achievements include world records in both the 100m and 200m events and in the 4 × 100m relay as well as multiple world championship and Olympic titles.

15 It's what I came here to do, I'm now a legend.
    2012 After becoming the first man to retain the 100 and 200m titles, at the London Olympics.

Bonavia, David 1940–88

British journalist and Editor of the *Far East Economic Review*. His main field of interest was China.

16 Their civilization is based on the most forthrightly materialistic value system in the history of mankind. If they see pie in the sky, they immediately start figuring out how to get it down onto the dinner table.
    1961 *The Chinese*.

Bond, Carrie Jacobs 1862–1946

US songwriter and lyricist.

17 When you come to the end of a perfect day,
    And you sit alone with your thought,
    While the chimes ring out with a carol gay
    For the joy that the day has brought,
    Do you think what the end of a perfect day
    Can mean to a tired heart,
    When the sun goes down with a flaming ray,
    And the dear friends have to part?
    1910 'A Perfect Day'.

Bonds, Barry Lamar 1964–

US baseball player.

18 Don't talk about him no more.
    2003 On the legendary Babe Ruth, whose slugging record he broke. Quoted by Associated Press, 16 Jul.

Bone, Sir David 1874–1959

Scottish novelist. He was a high-ranking sailor, and wrote novels about the sea.

19 It's 'Damn you, Jack—I'm all right!' with you chaps.
    1910 *The Brassbounder*, ch.3.

Bonham Carter, Helena 1966–

English actress.

20 It is acting in its purest form. You have to act with your eyes.
    2001 On playing a chimp in *Planet of the Apes*. In the *Observer*, 30 Dec.

Bonhoeffer, Dietrich 1906–45

German Lutheran pastor and theologian, executed for implication in a plot against Hitler. His theology, especially his plea for 'religionless Christianity', was influential in mid- and late-20c theology.

21 The Church knows nothing of a sacredness of war. The Church which prays 'Our Father' asks God only for peace.

1932 Draft of a new Catechism with F Hildebrandt, in *Gesammelte Schriften*, vol.3 (1947, translated by E Robinson and J Bowden in *No Rusty Sword*, 1965).

22 The cross is God's truth about us, and therefore it is the only power that can make us truthful. When we know the cross we are no longer afraid of the truth.
1937 *Nachfolge* (translated as *The Cost of Discipleship*).

23 *Billige Gnade ist Gnade ohne Nachfolge, Gnade ohne Kreuz, Gnade ohne den lebendigen, menschgewordenen Jesus Christus.*
Cheap grace is grace without discipleship, grace without the cross, grace without Jesus Christ, living and incarnate.
1937 *Nachfolge* (translated as *The Cost of Discipleship*).

24 If religion is only a garment of Christianity—and even this garment has looked very different at different times—then what is religionless Christianity?
1944 Letter to Eberhardt Bethge, 30 Apr. Collected in *Widerstand und Ergebung* (1951, translated 1953).

25 Death is the supreme Festival on the road to freedom.
1945 Letter, collected in *Widerstand und Ergebung* (1951, translated 1953).

26 *Es ist der Vorzug und das Wesen der Starken, dass sie die großen Entscheidungsfragen stellen und zu ihnen klar Stellung nehmen können. Die Schwachen müssen sich immer zwischen Alternativen entscheiden, die nicht die ihren sind.*
It is the nature, and the advantage, of strong people that they can bring out the crucial questions and form a clear opinion about them. The weak always have to decide between alternatives that are not their own.
1951 *Widerstand und Ergebung*, 'Ein paar Gedanken über Verschiedenes' (translated 1953).

27 *Ein Gott, der sich von uns beweisen ließe, wäre ein Götze.*
A God who let us prove his existence would be an idol.
'Glaubst du, so hast du'. Versuch eines Lutherischen Katchismus ('If you believe it, you have it'. Attempt at a Lutheran Catechism). Quoted in E Robinson and J Bowden *No Rusty Sword* (1965).

Bono *real name* **Paul Hewson** 1960–

Irish rock singer with the band U2. He is also known for his charity campaigning and political views.

28 They didn't have Kalashnikovs but U2 tickets in their hands.
1997 Of the audience at the U2 concert in Sarajevo, 24 Sep.

29 Elvis ate America before America ate him.
2004 On Elvis Presley. In *Rolling Stone*, 15 Apr.

30 People say songs are like your children—no, they are like your parents. They tell you what to do, they tell you how to behave, they tell you how to misbehave, how to dress. Everything you do is directed by the songs.
2013 On *The Charlie Rose Show*, 16 May.

Book of Common Prayer

The idea of a new prayer book was developed initially by Thomas Cranmer during the reigns of Edward VI and Elizabeth I. The final text was published in 1662.

31 Dearly beloved brethren, the Scripture moveth us in sundry places to acknowledge and confess our manifold sins and wickedness.
Morning Prayer, Sentences of the Scriptures.

32 We have erred and strayed from thy ways like lost sheep. We have followed too much the devices and desires of our own hearts. We have offended against thy holy laws. We have left undone those things which we ought to have done. And we have done those things which we ought not to have done. And there is no health in us.
Morning Prayer, General Confession.

33 A godly, righteous, and sober life.
Morning Prayer, General Confession.

34 And forgive us our trespasses, As we forgive them that trespass against us.
Morning Prayer, the Lord's Prayer.

35 Glory be to the Father, and to the Son: and to the Holy Ghost; As it was in the beginning, is now and ever shall be: world without end. Amen.
Morning Prayer, Gloria.

36 Lord God of Sabaoth.
Morning Prayer, Te Deum.

37 I believe in God the Father Almighty, Maker of heaven and earth: And in Jesus Christ his only Son our Lord, Who was conceived by the Holy Ghost, Born of the Virgin Mary, Suffered under Pontius Pilate, Was crucified, dead, and buried: He descended into hell; The third day he rose again from the dead; He ascended into heaven, And sitteth on the right hand of God the Father Almighty; From thence he shall come to judge the quick and the dead. I believe in the Holy Ghost; The holy Catholick Church; The Communion of Saints; The Forgiveness of sins; The Resurrection of the body, And the life everlasting. Amen.
Morning Prayer, Apostle's Creed.

38 Give peace in our time, O Lord.
Morning Prayer, versicle.

39 The author of peace and lover of concord, in knowledge of whom standeth our eternal life, whose service is perfect freedom.
Morning Prayer, Second Collect, for Peace.

40 Neither run into any kind of danger.
Morning Prayer, Third Collect, for Grace.

41 Pour upon them the continual dew of thy blessing.
Morning Prayer, Prayer for the Clergy and People.

42 O God, from whom all holy desires, all good counsels, and all just works do proceed: Give unto thy servants that peace which the world cannot give.
Evening Prayer, Second Collect.

43 Lighten our darkness, we beseech thee, O Lord; and by thy great mercy defend us from all perils and dangers of this night.
Evening Prayer, Third Collect, for Aid against Perils.

44 Whosoever will be saved: before all things it is necessary that he hold the Catholic Faith.
Athanasian Creed.

45 And yet they are not three Gods: but one God.
Athanasian Creed.

46 O God the Father of heaven: have mercy upon us miserable sinners.
Litany.

47 From envy, hatred, and malice, and all uncharitableness, Good Lord, deliver us.
Litany.

48 All sorts and conditions of men.
Prayer for all Conditions of Men.

49 All who profess and call themselves Christians.
Prayer for all Conditions of Men.

50 We bless thee for our creation, preservation, and all the blessings of this life; but above all for thine inestimable love in the redemption of the world by our Lord Jesus Christ; for the means of grace, and for the hope of glory.
General Thanksgiving.

51 Almighty God, give us grace that we may cast away the works of darkness, and put upon us the armour of light, now in the time of this mortal life.
Collects, 1st Sunday in Advent.

52 Hear them, read, mark, learn, and inwardly digest them.
Of all the holy Scriptures. *Collects,* 2nd Sunday in Advent.

53 Have mercy upon all Jews, Turks, Infidels, and Hereticks, and take from them all ignorance, hardness of heart, and contempt of thy word.
Collects, Good Friday.

54 Lord of all power and might, who art the author and giver of all good things.
Collects, 7th Sunday after Trinity.

55 Serve thee with a quiet mind.
Collects, 21st Sunday after Trinity.

56 Lord, we beseech thee to keep thy household the Church in continual godliness.
Collects, 22nd Sunday after Trinity.

57 The glory that shall be revealed.
Collects, St Stephen's Day.

58 Almighty God, unto whom all hearts be open, all desires known, and from whom no secrets are hid: Cleanse the thoughts of our hearts by the inspiration of thy Holy Spirit, that we may perfectly love thee, and worthily magnify thy holy Name; through Christ our Lord. Amen.
Holy Communion, Collect.

59 For I the Lord thy God am a jealous God, and visit the sins of the fathers upon the children unto the third and fourth generation of them that hate me, and shew mercy unto thousands in them that love me and keep my commandments.
Holy Communion, Second Commandment.

60 All things visible and invisible.
Holy Communion, Nicene Creed.

61 Very God of very God, Begotten, not made, Being of one substance with the Father, By whom all things were made: Who for us men and for our salvation came down from heaven.
Holy Communion, Nicene Creed.

62 And I believe in the Holy Ghost, The Lord and giver of life, Who proceedeth from the Father and Son, Who with the Father and the Son together is worshipped and glorified, Who spake by the Prophets.
Holy Communion, Nicene Creed.

63 And I believe in one Catholick and Apostolick Church.
Holy Communion, Nicene Creed.

64 Let us pray for the whole state of Christ's Church militant here in earth.
Holy Communion, Introduction to Prayer for the Church militant.

65 Draw near with faith.
Holy Communion, Invitation.

66 Ye that do truly and earnestly repent you of your sins, and are in love and charity with your neighbours, and intend to lead a new life.
Holy Communion, Invitation.

67 We acknowledge and bewail our manifold sins and wickedness, Which we from time to time most grievously have committed, By thought, word, and deed, Against thy Divine Majesty, Provoking most justly thy wrath and indignation against us.
Holy Communion, General Confession.

68 Hear what comfortable words our Saviour Christ saith unto all that truly turn to him.
Holy Communion, Words of Encouragement.

69 It is meet and right so to do.
Holy Communion, versicles and responses.

70 Therefore with Angels, and Archangels, and with all the company of heaven, we laud and magnify thy glorious Name; evermore praising thee, and saying: Holy, holy, holy, Lord God of hosts, heaven and earth are full of thy glory: Glory be to thee, O Lord most High. Amen.
Holy Communion, Praise.

71 A full, perfect, and sufficient sacrifice, oblation, and satisfaction, for the sins of the whole world.
Holy Communion, Prayer of Consecration.

72 We do not presume to come to this thy Table, O merciful Lord, trusting in our own righteousness, but in thy manifold and great mercies. We are not worthy so much as to gather up the crumbs under thy Table. But thou art the same Lord, whose property is always to have mercy: Grant us therefore, gracious Lord, so to eat the flesh of thy dear Son Jesus Christ, and to drink his blood, that our sinful bodies may be made clean by his body, and our souls washed through his most precious blood, and that we may evermore dwell in him, and he in us. Amen.
Holy Communion, Prayer of Humble Access.

73 The Body of our Lord Jesus Christ, which was given for thee, preserve thy body and soul unto everlasting life: Take and eat this in remembrance that Christ died for thee, and feed on him in thy heart by faith with thanksgiving.
Holy Communion.

74 The Blood of our Lord Jesus Christ, which was shed for thee, preserve thy body and soul unto everlasting life: Drink this in remembrance that Christ's Blood was shed for thee, and be thankful.
Holy Communion.

75 The peace of God, which passeth all understanding, keep your hearts and minds in the knowledge and love of God, and of his Son Jesus Christ our Lord: And the blessing of God Almighty, the Father, the Son, and the Holy Ghost, be amongst you and remain with you always. Amen.
Holy Communion, Blessing.

76 O merciful God, grant that the old Adam in this Child may be so buried, that the new man may be raised up in him. Amen.
Publick Baptism of Infants, Blessing.

77 We receive this Child into the Congregation of Christ's flock, and do sign him with the sign of the Cross, in token that hereafter he shall not be ashamed to confess

the faith of Christ crucified, and manfully to fight under his banner against sin, the world, and the devil, and to continue Christ's faithful soldier and servant unto his life's end. Amen.
Publick Baptism of Infants, Reception of the Child.

78 I should renounce the devil and all his works, the pomps and vanity of this wicked world, and all the sinful lusts of the flesh.
Catechism.

79 To keep my hands from picking and stealing, and my tongue from evil-speaking, lying, and slandering.
Catechism.

80 To learn and labour truly to get mine own living, and to do my duty in that state of life, unto which it shall please God to call me.
Catechism.

81 An outward and visible sign of an inward and spiritual grace given unto us.
Catechism.

82 Children being now come to the years of discretion.
Confirmation, Preface.

83 If any of you know cause or just impediment, why these two persons should not be joined together in holy Matrimony, ye are to declare it. This is the first time of asking.
Solemnization of Matrimony, the Banns.

84 Dearly beloved, we are gathered together here in the sight of God, and in the face of this Congregation, to join together this man and this woman in holy Matrimony; which is an honourable estate, instituted of God.
Solemnization of Matrimony, Exhortation.

85 Therefore is not by any to be enterprized, nor taken in hand, unadvisedly, lightly, or wantonly, to satisfy men's carnal lusts and appetites, like brute beasts that have no understanding; but reverently, discreetly, advisedly, soberly, and in the fear of God.
Solemnization of Marriage, Exhortation.

86 First, It was ordained for the procreation of children, to be brought up in the fear and nurture of the Lord, and to the praise of his holy Name.
Solemnization of Marriage, Exhortation.

87 Thirdly, It was ordained for the mutual society, help, and comfort, that the one ought to have of the other, both in prosperity and adversity. Into which holy estate these two persons present come now to be joined.
Solemnization of Marriage, Exhortation.

88 Therefore if any man can shew any just cause, why they may not lawfully be joined together, let him now speak, or else hereafter for ever hold his peace.
Solemnization of Marriage, Exhortation.

89 Wilt thou have this woman to thy wedded wife, to live together after God's ordinance in the holy estate of Matrimony? Wilt thou love her, comfort her, honour, and keep her, in sickness and in health; and, forsaking all other, keep thee only unto her, so long as ye both shall live?
Solemnization of Marriage, Betrothal.

90 Wilt thou have this man to thy wedded husband, to live together after God's ordinance in the holy estate of Matrimony? Wilt thou obey him, and serve him, love, honour and keep him, in sickness and in health; and, forsaking all other, keep thee only unto him, so long as ye both shall live?
Solemnization of Marriage, Betrothal.

91 To have and to hold from this day forward, for better for worse, for richer for poorer, in sickness and in health, to love and to cherish, till death us do part, according to God's holy ordinance; and thereto I plight thee my troth.
Solemnization of Marriage, Betrothal.

92 To love, cherish, and to obey.
Solemnization of Marriage, Betrothal. This is the bride's form of the oath.

93 With this ring I thee wed, with my body I thee worship, and with all my worldly goods I thee endow.
Solemnization of Marriage, Wedding.

94 Those whom God hath joined together let no man put asunder.
Solemnization of Marriage, Priest's Declaration.

95 Consented together in holy wedlock.
Solemnization of Marriage, Minister's Declaration.

96 Peace be to this house.
Visitation of the Sick.

97 Almighty God, the fountain of all goodness.
Morning Prayer, Prayer for the Royal Family.

98 Man that is born of a woman hath but a short time to live, and is full of misery.
Burial of the Dead, Anthem.

99 In the midst of life we are in death.
Burial of the Dead, Anthem.

1 We therefore commit his body to the ground; earth to earth, ashes to ashes, dust to dust; in sure and certain hope of the Resurrection to eternal life, through our Lord Jesus Christ.
Burial of the Dead, Committal.

2 Why do the heathen so furiously rage together, and why do the people imagine a vain thing? The kings of the earth stand up, and the rulers take counsel together, against the Lord, and against his Anointed.
Psalm 2:1–2.

3 The Lord will abhor both the blood-thirsty and deceitful man.
Psalm 5:6.

4 Make thy way plain before my face.
Psalm 5:8.

5 Let them perish through their own imaginations.
Psalm 5:11.

6 Up, Lord, and let not man have the upper hand.
Psalm 9:19.

7 But they are all gone out of the way, they are altogether become abominable: there is none that doeth good, no not one.
Psalm 14:4.

8 The lot is fallen unto me in a fair ground: yea, I have a goodly heritage.
Psalm 16:7.
▶ See Kipling 491:48.

9 The heavens declare the glory of God: and the firmament sheweth his handywork. One day telleth another: and one night certifieth another. There is neither speech nor

language: but their voices are heard among them. Their sound is gone out into all lands: and their words into the ends of the world.
Psalm 19:1–4.

10 Thou shalt prepare a table before me against them that trouble me: thou hast anointed my head with oil, and my cup shall be full.
Psalm 23:5.

11 Into thy hands I commend my spirit.
Psalm 31:6.

12 Sing unto the Lord a new song: sing praises lustily unto him with a good courage.
Psalm 33:3.

13 I myself have seen the ungodly in great power, and flourishing like a green bay-tree. I went by, and lo, he was gone: I sought him, but his place could no where be found. Keep innocency, and take heed unto the thing that is right: for that shall bring a man peace at the last.
Psalm 37:36–8.

14 Lord, let me know mine end, and the number of my days: that I may be certified how long I have to live.
Psalm 39:5.

15 My bones are smitten asunder as with a sword: while mine enemies that trouble me cast me in the teeth; Namely, while they say daily unto me: Where is now thy God?
Psalm 42:12–13.

16 Instead of thy fathers thou shalt have children, whom thou mayest make princes in all lands.
Psalm 45:17.

17 He maketh wars to cease in all the world: he breaketh the bow, and knappeth the spear in sunder, and burneth the chariots in the fire. Be still then, and know that I am God.
Psalm 46:9–10.

18 God is gone up with a merry noise: and the Lord with the sound of the trump.
Psalm 47:5.

19 And I said, O that I had wings like a dove: for then would I flee away, and be at rest.
Psalm 55:6.

20 Be merciful unto me, O God, be merciful unto me, for my soul trusteth in thee: and under the shadow of thy wings shall be my refuge, until this tyranny be over-past.
Psalm 57:1.

21 They are as venomous as the poison of a serpent: even like the deaf adder that stoppeth her ears; Which refuseth to hear the voice of the charmer: charm he never so wisely.
Psalm 58:4–5.

22 They go to and fro in the evening: they grin like a dog, and run about through the city.
Psalm 59:6.

23 He is the God that maketh men to be of one mind in an house, and bringeth the prisoners out of captivity: but letteth the runagates continue in scarceness.
Psalm 68:6.

24 Why hop ye so, ye high hills? this is God's hill, in the which it pleaseth him to dwell: yea, the Lord will abide in it for ever.
Psalm 68:16.

25 Thou art gone up on high, thou hast led captivity captive, and received gifts for men.
Psalm 68:18.

26 Thy rebuke hath broken my heart; I am full of heaviness: I looked for some to have pity on me, but there was no man, neither found I any to comfort me. They gave me gall to eat: and when I was thirsty they gave me vinegar to drink.
Psalm 69:21–2.

27 So the Lord awaked as one out of sleep: and like a giant refreshed with wine.
Psalm 78:66.

28 O how amiable are thy dwellings, thou Lord of hosts!
Psalm 84:1.

29 Lord, thou hast been our refuge from one generation to another. Before the mountains were brought forth, or ever the earth and the world were made: thou art God from everlasting, and world without end.
Psalm 90:1–2.

30 O come, let us sing unto the Lord; let us heartily rejoice in the strength of our salvation. Let us come before his presence with thanksgiving; and shew ourselves glad in him with psalms. For the Lord is a great God; and a great King above all gods. In his hand are all the corners of the earth; and the strength of the hills is his also. The sea is his, and he made it; and his hands prepared the dry land. O come, let us worship and fall down, and kneel before the Lord our Maker. For he is the Lord our God; and we are the people of his pasture, and the sheep of his hand.
Psalm 95:1–7.

31 Today if ye will hear his voice, harden not your hearts: as in the provocation, and as in the day of temptation in the wilderness; When your fathers tempted me: proved me, and saw my works.
Psalm 95:8–9.

32 O be joyful in the Lord, all ye lands: serve the Lord with gladness, and come before his presence with a song.
Psalm 100:1.

33 Whose feet they hurt in the stocks: the iron entered into his soul.
Psalm 105:18.

34 Their soul abhorred all manner of meat: and they were even hard at death's door.
Psalm 107:18.

35 Lord, I am not high-minded: I have no proud looks.
Psalm 131:1.

36 Such knowledge is too wonderful and excellent for me: I cannot attain unto it.
Psalm 139:5.

37 I will give thanks unto thee, for I am fearfully and wonderfully made: marvellous are thy works, and that my soul knoweth right well.
Psalm 139:13.

38 O put not your trust in princes, nor in any child of man: for there is no help in them.
Psalm 146:2.

39 We therefore commit his body to the deep, to be turned into corruption, looking for the resurrection of the body, (when the Sea shall give up her dead).
Forms of Prayer to be Used at Sea, At the Burial of their Dead at Sea.

40 Holy Scripture containeth all things necessary to salvation.
Articles of Religion, VI Of the Sufficiency of the holy Scriptures for Salvation.

41 A fond thing vainly invented.
Articles of Religion, XXII Of Purgatory.

42 The Bishop of *Rome* hath no jurisdiction in this Realm of *England*.
Articles of Religion, XXXVII Of the Civil Magistrates.

43 It is lawful for Christian men, at the commandment of the Magistrate, to wear weapons, and serve in the wars.
Articles of Religion, XXXVII Of the Civil Magistrates.

44 A Man may not marry his Grandmother.
Table of Kindred and Affinity.

Bookchin, Murray pseudonym of Lewis Herber 1921–2006
US writer on social, ecological and environmental issues.

45 Once regarded as the herald of enlightenment in all spheres of knowledge, science is now increasingly seen as a strictly instrumental system of control. Its use as a system of manipulation and its role in restricting human freedom now parallel in every detail its use as a means of natural manipulation.
1982 *The Ecology of Freedom*.

Booth, John Wilkes 1839–65
US actor, usually remembered as the assassin of President Abraham Lincoln. He was hunted down and shot several days after the killing.

46 *Sic semper tyrannis!* The South is avenged!
1865 Attributed, as he shot Lincoln at Ford's Theatre, Washington DC, 14 Apr. 'Sic semper tyrannis', *Thus always to tyrants*, is the motto of the Commonwealth of Virginia.

Booth, Junius Brutus 1796–1852
English-born US actor, a leading rival of Edmund Kean in London, particularly admired as Shylock and Richard III. He continued his success after emigrating in 1821, but succumbed to alcohol-induced melancholia.

47 Where's the stage and what's the play?
Attributed, on being found drunk backstage shortly before making his first entrance.

Booth, Martin 1944–2004
English writer educated in Hong Kong. *The Dragon and the Pearl* (1994) is an account of life there.

48 At any one time, 15 per cent of the buildings of Hong Kong are being either demolished or rebuilt, renovated or restructured.
1994 *The Dragon and the Pearl*, foreword.

Boothby, Sir Robert John Graham, 1st Baron Boothby of Buchan and Rattray Head 1900–86
Scottish Conservative politician, Parliamentary Secretary to Winston Churchill (1926–9) and an original member of the Council of United Europe. His works include *The New Economy* (1943) and *I Fight to Live* (1947).

49 Of all the pygmies, Samuel Hoare was the pygmiest.
Attributed.

Boothroyd, Betty Boothroyd, Baroness 1929–
English Labour politician and first woman Speaker of the House of Commons (1992–2000).

50 My desire to get here [Parliament] was like miners' coal dust, it was under my fingers and I couldn't scrub it out.
Quoted in Glenys Kinnock and Fiona Millar (eds) *By Faith and Daring* (1993).

51 Good temper and moderation are the characteristics of parliamentary language.
1995 In *The Independent*, 9 Feb.

52 Time's up!
2000 On retiring as Speaker of the House of Commons, 26 Jul.

Borah, William Edgar 1865–1940
US Republican politician. Elected Senator for Idaho in 1906, he advocated disarmament and, as a convinced isolationist, was instrumental in blocking US entry into the League of Nations.

53 A democracy must remain at home in all matters that affect the nature of her institutions. They are of a nature to call for the undivided attention and devotion of the entire nation. We do not want the racial antipathies or national antagonisms of the Old World transformed to this continent—as they will, should we become a part of European politics. The people of this country are overwhelmingly for a policy of neutrality.
1936 Radio broadcast, 22 Feb.

Borelli, Giovanni Alfonso 1608–79
Italian mathematician and astronomer, who reasoned that celestial objects follow parabolic paths.

54 No sensible person will deny that the works of Nature are in the highest degree simple, necessary and as economical as possible. Therefore machines devised by mankind will doubtlessly likewise attain most success if they are as far as possible modelled on works of Nature.
1680 *De moto animalium*.

Borges, Jorge Luis 1899–1986
Argentinian writer. He returned to Argentina from Europe in 1921, introducing avant-garde Ultraist theories in essays and poems before publishing his intricate and fantasy-woven short stories in the 1940s. He lost his sight in the 1950s.

55 *Los metafísicos de Tlön no buscan la verdad ni siquiera la verosimilitud: buscan el asombro. Juzgan que la metafísica es una rama de la literatura fantástica.*
The metaphysicians of Tlön do not seek for the truth or even for verisimilitude, but rather for the astounding. They judge that metaphysics is a branch of fantastic literature.
1941 *Ficciones*, 'Tlön, Uqbar, Orbis Tertius' (1963).

56 *Quizá la historia universal es la historia de la diversa entonación de algunas metáforas.*
It may be that universal history is the history of the different intonations given a handful of metaphors.
1952 *Otras inquisiciones*, 'La esfera de Pascal' (translated as *The Fearful Sphere of Pascal*, 1964).

57 *En vano te hemos prodigado el océano,*
En vano el sol, que vieron los maravillados ojos de Whitman;

Has gastado los años y te has gastado,
Y todavía no has escrito el poema.
We have lavished the ocean on you in vain,
In vain the sun that was seen by Whitman's astounded eyes;
You have spent your years and you have spent yourself,
But you haven't written the poem yet.
1964 *El otro, el mismo,* 'Mateo XXV, 30' ('Matthew 25:30').

58 While we are asleep in this world, we are awake in another one; in this way, every man is two men.
Quoted in John Russell *The Meaning of Modern Art* (1974).

59 Canada is so far away it hardly exists.
1974 Response to the question, 'What do you think of when you think of Canada?', when interviewed in Buenos Aires by Canadian poet and broadcaster Robert Zend, 4 Oct.

60 The Falklands thing was a fight between two bald men over a comb.
1983 In *Time*, 14 Feb.

Borgia, Cesare 1476–1507

Italian soldier, illegitimate son of Pope Alexander VI. He served in the papal army and was created Duke of Romagna, but was defeated in 1506 under Pope Julius II. Macchiavelli praised him as a model prince, but he was commonly perceived as a cruel dictator.

61 *Aut Caesar, aut nihil.*
Either Caesar or nothing.
Motto. It goes back to a couplet composed in 1507, after Borgia's death, by Fausto Maddalena Romano: 'Borgia Caesar erat, factis et nomine Caesar, /aut nihil, aut Caesar dixit: utrumque fuit.' (Borgia was Caesar: he was Caesar in name and in fact. He said /Either Caesar, or nothing: he was both.)

Borman, Frank 1928–

US astronaut, later President of Eastern Airlines.

62 Capitalism without bankruptcy is like Christianity without hell.
1986 In *US*, 21 Apr.

63 A superior pilot uses his superior judgement to avoid situations which require the use of his superior skill.
2008 *Flying Lessons*, 8 Jan.

Born, Max 1882–1970

German-born British physicist, Professor of Physics at Göttingen until forced to leave by the Nazis. He won the Nobel prize (1954) for his insights into quantum mechanics.

64 There are two objectionable types of believers: those who believe the incredible and those who believe that 'belief' must be discarded and replaced by 'the scientific method'.
1951 *Natural Philosophy of Cause and Chance*.

65 Science…is so greatly opposed to history and tradition that it cannot be absorbed by our civilization.
1968 *My Life and Views*.

Borotra, Jean 1898–1994

French tennis player. His wins included the men's singles title at Wimbledon in 1924.

66 The only possible regret I have is the feeling that I will die without having played enough tennis.
Quoted in Colin Jarman *The Guinness Dictionary of Sports Quotations* (1990).

Borovoy, A Alan 1932–

General Counsel of the Canadian Civil Liberties Association.

67 I would renounce, therefore, the attempt to create heaven on earth, and focus instead on reducing the hell.
1988 *When Freedoms Collide: A Case for Our Civil Liberties*. His personal maxim.

68 I don't ask employers, for example, to *like* blacks or Jews or native people; I ask employers to *hire* the qualified members of these groups whether they like them or not.
1988 *When Freedoms Collide: A Case for Our Civil Liberties*.

Borrow, George Henry 1803–81

English writer and traveller. His part fictional, part factual books reflect his interest in languages and his love of Romany lore. They include *The Bible in Spain* (1843), *Lavengro* (1851), *The Romany Rye* (1857) and *Wild Wales* (1862).

69 There's night and day, brother, both sweet things; sun, moon, and stars, brother, all sweet things: there's likewise a wind on the heath. Life is very sweet, brother; who would wish to die?
1851 *Lavengro*, ch.25.

70 Fear God, and take your own part.
1857 *The Romany Rye*, ch.16.

71 I never saw such a place for merched anllad [wanton women] as Northampton.
1862 *Wild Wales*, ch.34.

72 'Scotland! a queer country that, your honour!' 'So it is,' said I; 'a queerer country I never saw in all my life.' 'And a queer set of people, your honour.' 'So they are,' said I; 'a queerer set of people than the Scotch you would scarcely see in a summer's day.'
1862 *Wild Wales*, ch.83.

Bosquet, Pierre 1810–61

French soldier, General during the Crimean War.

73 *C'est magnifique, mais ce n'est pas la guerre.*
It is magnificent, but it isn't war.
1854 On seeing the Charge of the Light Brigade at the Battle of Balaclava, 25 Oct. Quoted in Cecil Woodham Smith *The Reason Why* (1953), ch.12.

Bossidy, John Collins 1860–1928

US doctor and versifier.

74 And this is good old Boston,
The home of the bean and the cod,
Where the Lowells talk to the Cabots
And the Cabots talk only to God.
1910 Toast delivered at Holy Cross alumni dinner, Boston.

Boswell, James 1740–95

Scottish man of letters and biographer of Dr Johnson, whom he first met in 1763. Their great friendship led, after Johnson's death, to Boswell's literary masterpiece, the *Life of Samuel Johnson* (1791).

75 I think there is a blossom about me of something more distinguished than the generality of mankind.
1763 Journal entry, 20 Jan. Collected in F A Pottle (ed) *Boswell's London Journal* (1950).

76 JOHNSON: Well, we had a good talk.
BOSWELL: Yes, Sir; you tossed and gored several persons.
1768 Conversation, summer, recorded in *The Life of Samuel Johnson* (1791), vol.2.

77 I am, I flatter myself, completely a citizen of the world. In my travels through Holland, Germany, Switzerland, Italy, Corsica, France, I never felt myself from home.
1773 *Journal of a Tour to the Hebrides* (ed F A Pottle, 1936), entry for 14 Aug.

78 A man, indeed, is not genteel when he gets drunk; but most vices may be committed very genteelly: a man may debauch his friend's wife genteelly: he may cheat at cards genteelly.
1775 *The Life of Samuel Johnson* (1791), vol.2, entry for 6 Apr.

Botha, P(ieter) W(illem) 1932–2006

South African statesman, Prime Minister (1978–84) and President (1984–9). His attempts at limited constitutional reform were met with a right-wing defection from his ruling National Party (1982).

79 We simply could not go on with policies that were a failure economically and internationally, and which we could not morally justify. To allocate rights and privileges on the basis of a physical characteristic was tantamount to sinning against God.
1991 Interviewed by Donald Woods, BBC T V, Feb.

Botham, Sir Ian Terence 1955–

English cricketer. He established a record number of Test wickets (373) and scored 5,057 runs in Tests for England, including 14 Test centuries.

80 Cricket is full of theorists who can ruin your game in no time.
1980 *Ian Botham on Cricket*.

81 I want to stress again one aspect of the game which is most important. *Never argue with an umpire.*
1980 *Ian Botham on Cricket*.

Bottomley, Gordon 1874–1948

English poet and playwright. His interest in Celtic folklore is reflected in much of his work, and he is best remembered for his *Poetry of Thirty Years* (1925) and some of his plays.

82 When you destroy a blade of grass
You poison England at her roots;
Remember no man's foot can pass
Where evermore no green life shoots.
1912 'To Ironfounders and Others'.

83 Your worship is your furnaces
Which, like old idols, lost obscenes,
Have molten bowels; your vision is
Machines for making more machines.
1912 'To Ironfounders and Others'.

Boucicault, Dion(ysus Lardner) originally Dionysius Lardner Bursiquot c.1820–1890

Irish playwright, actor and director. His many works include popular melodramas such as *The Corsican Brothers* (1852), *The Colleen Bawn* (1860) and *The Shaughraun* (1875). He also promoted theatrical reforms, including the box set.

84 Men talk of killing time, while time quietly kills them.
1841 *London Assurance*, act 2, sc.1.

85 It's a mighty pleasant thing to die like this, once in a way, and hear all the good things said about ye afther you're dead and gone, when they can do you no good.
1874 Aside by Conn. *The Shaughraun*, act 3, sc.2.

86 His first holiday.
His own suggested epitaph. Attributed.

Boulanger, Nadia 1887–1979

French musician and teacher. She studied at the Paris Conservatoire (1879–1904) and wrote many vocal and instrumental works.

87 Do not take up music unless you would rather die than not do so.
Advice to her pupils. Quoted in Alan Kendall *The Tender Tyrant: Nadia Boulanger* (1976).

Boulding, Kenneth Ewart 1910–93

British-born US economist and social philosopher (or 'social ecologist'), president of the American Economic Association and professor at the Universities of Michigan and Colorado.

88 We know very little about what it is that moves great masses of men to action, and until we know more about this it is fitting for the social scientist to maintain a becoming modesty in the presence of a great deal to be modest about.
1966 *The Impact of the Social Sciences*.

89 Science might almost be redefined as the process of substituting unimportant questions which can be answered for important questions which cannot.
1969 *The Image*.

90 Almost the whole pollution–environmental problem is summed up in the proposition that all goods are generally produced jointly with bads.
1972 In Sam H Schurr (ed) *Energy, Economic Growth, and the Environment* (1972).

Boulton, Sir Harold Edwin 1859–1935

English songwriter. He compiled and wrote many collections of national songs, including the well-known 'Glorious Devon' (1902) and 'Skye Boat Song' (1908).

91 When Adam and Eve were dispossessed
Of the garden hard by Heaven,
They planted another one down in the west,
'Twas Devon, glorious Devon!
1902 'Glorious Devon'.

92 Speed, bonnie boat, like a bird on the wing,
'Onward!' the sailors cry;
Carry the lad that's born to be king
Over the sea to Skye.
1908 'Skye Boat Song'. The date and authorship of the original song are uncertain, but this is now the most famous version.

Bourassa, Henri 1868–1952

Canadian politician. He entered the Commons as an Independent Liberal (1896) and founded the Quebec Nationalist party, opposing involvement with Britain and the US. He was founding editor of *Le Devoir*, a Montreal newspaper.

93 Our special task, as French Canadians, is to insert into America the spirit of Christian France.
1918 *La Langue, Gardienne de la Foi*.

Bourdillon, F(rancis) W(illiam) 1852–1951
English poet.

94 The night has a thousand eyes,
 And the day but one;
 Yet the light of the bright world dies,
 With the dying sun.

 The mind has a thousand eyes,
 And the heart but one;
 Yet the light of a whole life dies,
 When love is done.
 1878 *Among the Flowers*, 'Light'.
 ▶ See Lyly 543:87.

Bowen, Catherine Shober née Drinker 1897–1973
US writer, biographer and essayist, whose many books include *The Lion and the Throne* (biography of Sir Edward Coke, 1957) and *Miracle at Philadelphia* (1966).

95 In writing biography, fact and fiction shouldn't be mixed. And if they are, the fiction parts should be printed in red ink, the fact parts in black ink.
 1958 In *Publisher's Weekly*, 24 Mar. Bowen's biographies were frequently partly fictionalized.

Bowen, Frank Charles 1894–1957

96 *Irish hurricane*, a flat calm with drizzling rain.
 1929 *Sea Slang, a Dictionary of the Old-Timers' Expressions and Epithets*.

Bowie, David real name David Robert Jones 1947–
English rock singer and actor. His career blossomed throughout the 1970s as he adopted a range of extreme stage images to suit a variety of musical styles and concepts.

97 You must understand that this is not a woman's dress I'm wearing. It's a man's dress.
 Quoted in Maxim Jakubowski *The Wit and Wisdom of Rock and Roll* (1983).

Bowles, Paul Frederick 1910–99
US novelist, poet, travel writer, translator and composer. He studied music in Paris, and began writing fiction after World War II. He lived in Tangier from 1952, and much of his work is set there.

98 *The Sheltering Sky*.
 1947 Title of novel.

99 Too much importance is given the writer and not enough to his work. What difference does it make who he is and what he feels, since he's merely a machine for transmission of ideas. In reality he doesn't exist—he's a cipher, a blank. A spy sent into life by the forces of death. His main objective is to get the information across the border, back into death.
 1966 Letter to James Leo Herlihy, 30 Apr.

1 The wind howls and the countryside is the colour of a lion. For a week the cicadas have been screaming; I think by now most of them have burst, for there are far fewer.
 1969 Letter to Ned Rorem, 20 Aug.

2 It was an experiment, and I think a successful one, in communal living. It worked largely because Auden ran it; he was exceptionally adept at getting the necessary money out of us when it was due.
 1972 On an artist's house in New York. *Without Stopping: An Autobiography*, ch.12.

3 My curiosity about alien cultures was avid and obsessive. I had a placid belief that it was good for me to live in the midst of people whose motives I did not understand; this unreasoned conviction was clearly an attempt to legitimize my curiosity.
 1972 *Without Stopping: An Autobiography*, ch.14.

4 The act of living had been enjoyable; at some point when I was not paying attention, it had turned into a different sort of experience, to whose grimness I had grown so accustomed that I now took it for granted.
 1972 *Without Stopping: An Autobiography*, ch.17.

5 I envy you if you're able to sustain a uniform degree of interest throughout *Ulysses*. People are always saying they do. People also claim to be clairvoyant and to levitate.
 1981 Letter to Millicent Dillon, 1 Jul.

6 The only effort worth making is the one it takes to learn the geography of one's own nature.
 1989 In the *Sunday Times*, 23 Jul.

Boycott, Geoffrey 1940–
English cricketer, who made 108 appearances for England. He scored a total of 8,114 Test runs.

7 To have some idea what it's like, stand in the outside lane of a motorway, get your mate to drive his car at you at 95 mph and wait until he's 12 yards away, before you decide which way to jump.
 1989 Of the experience of facing fast bowlers. Quoted in Helen Exley *Cricket Quotations* (1992).

8 Frankly, he had more chance of picking his nose with his toe.
 2007 Describing, as commentator, batsman Andrew Flintoff's chance of doing well against Australian spin bowlers.

Boyd, L(ouis) M(alcolm) 1927–2007
US journalist.

9 Most business meetings are staged to supply people who'd rather talk than work with people who'd rather listen than work.
 1990 'Grab Bag', in the *San Francisco Chronicle*, 7 Apr.

Boyd, William Andrew Murray 1952–
Scottish writer, born in Ghana. A lecturer in English at Oxford (1980–3) and TV critic with the *New Statesman*, he then concentrated on fiction and screenplays. His novels include *A Good Man in Africa* (1981), *Brazzaville Beach* (1990), *Any Human Heart* (2002) and *Restless* (2006).

10 Like Rome, Nkongsamba was built on seven hills, but there all similarity ended. Set in undulating tropical rain forest, from the air it resembled nothing so much as a giant pool of crapulous vomit on somebody's expansive unmown lawn.
 1981 *A Good Man in Africa*, ch.1.

11 Morgan liked to imagine the town as some immense yeast culture, left in a deep cupboard by an absent-minded lab technician, festering uncontrolled, running rampant in the ideal growing conditions.
 1981 *A Good Man in Africa*, ch.1.

12 My first act on entering this world was to kill my mother.
1988 The New Confessions, opening words.

13 The natural world is full of irregularity and random alteration, but in the antiseptic, dust-free, shadowless, brightly lit, abstract realm of the mathematicians they like their cabbages spherical, please.
1990 Brazzaville Beach, 'Cabbages Are Not Spheres'.

14 It seems to me that there are statements about the world and our lives that have no need of formal proof procedures.
1990 Brazzaville Beach, 'Fermat's Last Theorem II'.

Boyer, Charles 1899–1978

French actor who moved to Hollywood in 1929 and was particularly successful in romantic roles. His appearances include *The Garden of Allah* (1936), *Mayerling* (1937), *Love Affair* (1939) and *All This and Heaven Too* (1940).

15 Come with me to the Casbah.
1938 Although he never actually spoke this line, it was popularly associated with him as Pepe in the film *Algiers*.

Boyer, Dr Ernest L 1928–95

US educationalist, president of the Carnegie Foundation for the Advancement of Teaching (1979–95).

16 A poor surgeon hurts one person at a time. A poor teacher hurts 30.
1986 In *People*, 17 Mar.

Boyle, Danny (Daniel) 1956–

English film director, producer, screenwriter and theatre director.

17 Some of you will be baffled, I can guarantee it... I hope you enjoy that kind of Liquorice Allsorts of things. Many of you won't understand that reference, either.
2012 Addressing international journalists prior to the opening ceremony of the 2012 Olympic Games, of which he was Artistic Director.

Boyle, Peter G(erard) 1941–

Scottish academic historian.

18 They are the last drops of vintage wine from a musty old bottle.
Of Winston Churchill's letters to President Eisenhower. Quoted in Peter G Boyle (ed) *The Churchill–Eisenhower Correspondence 1953–1955* (1990).

Bracken, Peg 1918–2007

US writer and humorist. Her books include *The I Hate to Cook Book* (1960) and *I Didn't Come Here to Argue* (1969).

19 Cheese for dessert is rather like *Paradise Lost* in that everyone thinks he *ought* to like it, but still you don't notice too many people actually curling up with it.
1960 The I Hate to Cook Book, ch.9.

Bracken, Thomas 1843–98

New Zealand poet, journalist and politician, born in Ireland. He emigrated in 1869. His work, characterized by Victorian sentimentality, includes *Lays and Lyrics: God's Own Country and Other Poems* (1893).

20 Oh, God! that men would see a little clearer,
Or judge less harshly where they cannot see;
Oh, God! that men would draw a little nearer
To one another, they'd be nearer Thee,
And understood.
1905 Not Understood, and Other Poems, 'Not Understood'.

Bradbury, Malcolm Stanley 1932–2000

English novelist, critic and teacher. His novels include *The History Man* (1975) and *Rates of Exchange* (1982).

21 It had always seemed to Louis that a fundamental desire to take postal courses was being sublimated by other people into sexual activity.
1959 Eating People Is Wrong, ch.5.

22 I like the English. They have the most rigid code of immorality in the world.
1959 Eating People Is Wrong, ch.5.

23 Reading someone else's newspaper is like sleeping with someone else's wife. Nothing seems to be precisely in the right place, and when you find what you are looking for, it is not clear then how to respond to it.
1965 Stepping Westward, bk.1, ch.1.

24 My experience of ships is that on them one makes an interesting discovery about the world. One finds one can do without it completely.
1965 Stepping Westward, bk.1, ch.2.

25 They don't spend themselves in relationships until they know what the odds are; long hours spent as babies lying in the rain outside greengrocers' shops have made them tough.
1965 Stepping Westward, bk.2, ch.4.

26 English history is all about men liking their fathers, and American history is all about men hating their fathers and trying to burn down everything they ever did.
1965 Stepping Westward, bk.2, ch.5.

27 The English are polite by telling lies. The Americans are polite by telling the truth.
1965 Stepping Westward, bk.2, ch.5.

28 'We stay together, but we distrust each other.'
'Ah, yes,...but isn't that a definition of marriage?'
1975 The History Man, ch.3.

29 If God had meant us to have group sex, I guess he'd have given us all more organs.
1976 Who Do You Think You Are?, 'A Very Hospitable Person'.

30 The British have long had a taste for bad books, but they like them well written.
1981 In the *Observer*, 25 Oct.

31 In Slaka, sex is just politics with the clothes off.
1983 Rates of Exchange, pt.4, ch.3.

32 Here we have a saying: a good friend is someone who visits you when you are in prison. But a *really* good friend is someone who comes to hear your lectures.
1983 Rates of Exchange, pt.4, ch.3.

33 Conversation is never easy for the British, who are never keen to express themselves to strangers or, for that matter, anyone, even themselves.
1983 Rates of Exchange, pt.5, ch.3.

34 You probably know, the better class of Briton likes to send his children away to school until they're old and intelligent enough to come home again. Then they're too old and intelligent to want to.
1983 Rates of Exchange, pt.5, ch.3.

35 There were moments when Henry was glad he was a writer, for writers could live in their own minds and didn't have to go out at all.
1987 *Cuts*.

36 The modern novel has been many things, and functioned at many levels. It would keep D.H. Lawrence poor, and make Jilly Cooper and Jeffrey Archer rich.
1993 *The Modern British Novel*, preface.

37 The post-war period has not been marked by a great aesthetic debate about the novel comparable to that of the earlier half of the century, in part because the role of the writer and critic divided, the writer going off to the marketplace and the critic to the university (which eventually turned out to be much the same thing).
1993 *The Modern British Novel*, preface.

Bradbury, Ray(mond Douglas) 1920–2012

US science-fiction writer, one of the earliest writers in the genre to be recognized for his literary merits. His short-story collections include *The Martian Chronicles* (1950) and *The Illustrated Man* (1951); novels include *Fahrenheit 451* (1953) and *Something Wicked This Way Comes* (1962).

38 The Day it Rained Forever.
1959 Title of story.

39 Where robot mice and robot men, I said, run round in robot towns.
1977 *Where Robot Mice and Robot Men Run Round In Robot Towns*, prologue.

40 I prefer to see myself as the Janus, the two-faced god who is half Pollyanna and half Cassandra, warning of the future and perhaps living too much in the past—a combination of both.
2010 In *The Paris Review*, spring.

Bradley, Francis Herbert 1846–1924

Welsh philosopher, who spent most of his life at Oxford, a central figure of the 19c British Idealist movement. His important works are *Ethical Studies* (1876) and *Appearance and Reality* (1893).

41 Metaphysics is the finding of bad reasons for what we believe upon instinct, but to find these reasons is no less an instinct.
1893 *Appearance and Reality*, preface.

42 Where everything is bad it must be good to know the worst.
1893 *Appearance and Reality*, preface.

Bradley, Omar Nelson 1893–1981

US soldier. He played a prominent part in World War II, especially in Tunisia and Sicily. Chairman of the joint Chiefs-of-Staff in 1949, he was promoted to General in 1950.

43 We have grasped the mystery of the atom and rejected the Sermon on the Mount.
1948 Speech, 10 Nov, commemorating Armistice Day.

44 The wrong war, at the wrong place, at the wrong time—and with the wrong enemy.
1951 At the Senate inquiry into proposals to escalate the Korean war into China, May.

Bradman, Sir Don(ald George) 1908–2001

Australian cricketer and stockbroker. He played for Australia (1928–48, Captain 1936–48), scoring the highest aggregate and largest number of centuries in Tests against England. In 1949 he became the first Australian cricketer to be knighted.

45 It's hard to bat with tears in your eyes.
1948 When bowled for a duck in his final Test innings. Quoted in Colin Jarman *The Guinness Dictionary of Sports Quotations* (1990).

46 There is probably a greater premium on temperament for a batsman than for any player in any branch of sport.
1958 *The Art of Cricket*.

47 May cricket continue to flourish and spread its wings. The world can only be richer for it.
1958 *The Art of Cricket*.

48 Every ball is for me the first ball, whether my score is 0 or 200, and I never visualize the possibility of anybody getting me out.
Quoted in Colin Jarman *The Guinness Dictionary of Sports Quotations* (1990).

Bradstreet, Anne *née* Dudley 1612–72

English-born American Puritan poet. She emigrated to New England with her husband, a nonconformist minister, later Governor of Massachusetts. Her first collection was published in London by her brother-in-law without her knowledge.

49 In Criticks hands, beware thou dost not come;
And take thy way where yet thou art not known,
If for thy Father askt, say, thou hadst none:
And for thy Mother, she alas is poor,
Which caus'd her thus to send thee out of door.
1650 *The Tenth Muse Lately Sprung Up In America*, 'The Author to Her Book'.

50 I am obnoxious to each carping tongue
Who says my hand a needle better fits,
A poet's pen all scorn I should thus wrong
For such despite they cast on female wits;
If what I do prove well, it won't advance,
They'll say it's stolen, or else, it was by chance.
1678 *Several Poems Compiled with Great Variety of Wit and Learning*, 'The Prologue'.

51 If ever two were one, then surely we.
1678 *Several Poems Compiled with Great Variety of Wit and Learning*, 'To My Dear and Loving Husband'.

Brady, Nicholas F(rederick) 1930–

US financier and politician, Secretary of the Treasury (1988–93) under Presidents Reagan and Bush.

52 If you want to be vice-president, stand out here in the rain in your underwear and let everybody see what you're made of.
1988 On the need to strip the secrecy from selection of vice-presidential candidates instead of having surprise choices such as Dan Quayle. In the *Washington Post*, 28 Aug.

53 We have a habit in this country of correcting things just as they are about to correct themselves.
1989 In the *New York Times*, 1 Feb.

Bragg, Melvyn Bragg, Baron 1939–

English novelist and television arts presenter. He has written a number of novels in the realist tradition, and is well known as a television presenter, notably of the long-running arts series *The South Bank Show*.

54 Patriotism is seen not only as the last refuge of the scoundrel but as the first bolt-hole of the hypocrite.
1976 Speak For England, introduction.
▸ See Johnson 462:37.

55 There is nothing left to envy about America.
Quoted in Jonathan Freedland *Bringing Home the Revolution: How Britain Can Live in the American Dream* (1998).

Brahms, Johannes 1833–97

German Romantic composer. His compositions include four symphonies and several concertos, a large body of songs, chamber music and music for piano, and *A German Requiem* (1869).

56 When I feel the urge to compose, I begin by appealing directly to my Maker and I first ask Him the three most important questions pertaining to our life here in this world—whence, wherefore, whither.
Quoted in A Hopkins *Music All Around Me* (1967).

Bramante, Donato 1444–1514

Italian High Renaissance architect.

57 The dome of the Pantheon over the vault of the Temple of Peace.
c.1505 Description of his design for St Peter's, Rome. Quoted in Vincent Cronin *The Flowering of the Renaissance* (1969).

Bramston, James c.1694–1744

English cleric and poet.

58 What's not destroyed by Time's devouring hand? Where's Troy, and where's the Maypole in the Strand?
1729 The Art of Politics.

Brand, Jo(sephine Grace) 1957–

English comedian.

59 If we aren't supposed to eat animals, then why are they made out of meat?
2009 Looking Back in Hunger.

60 Anything is good if it's made of chocolate.
Attributed.

Brand, Russell Edward 1975–

English comedian, actor, and author.

61 Mostly orphans' tears, old clock parts, lizards' tails, spit, the concept of freedom; all up there, all shooshed up right nice and tight, like a bonfire that's never actually burned… it mutters follicular oddities into my mind.
2007 When asked what he put on his hair, Radio 1 interview, 5 Jul.

62 I want to change the world, and do something valuable and beautiful. I want people to remember me before I'm dead, and then more afterwards.
2007 My Booky Wook.

63 My modus operandi is that I'll be content with anything, as long as I know that it's the best that's personal.
2010 Booky Wook 2: This Time it's Personal.

64 I like threesomes with two women, not because I'm a cynical sexual predator. Oh no! But because I'm a romantic. I'm looking for 'The One'. And I'll find her more quickly if I audition two at a time.
Attributed.

65 Life is not a theme park, and if it is, the theme is death.
Attributed.

66 Murderers! Stop murdering. Everyone will die eventually. Just sit down and be patient.
Attributed.

Brando, Marlon 1924–2004

US film and stage actor. He found fame in stage (1947) and screen (1951) productions of *A Streetcar Named Desire*. Subsequent films include *The Wild One* (1953), *On the Waterfront* (1954), for which he won an Academy Award, *Last Tango in Paris* (1972) and *The Godfather* (1972), for which he refused to accept an Academy Award.

67 Sometimes you just get the feeling that here it is 11 o'clock in the morning and you're not in school.
1959 On playing in Western films. In the *New York Post*, 11 May.

68 An actor is a kind of guy who if you ain't talking about him ain't listening.
Quoted in Bob Thomas *Brando* (1973), ch.8.

69 He's the kind of guy that when he dies, he gives God a bad time for making him bald.
1977 On Frank Sinatra. In the *Daily Mail*, 30 Mar.

Branson, Sir Richard (Charles Nicholas) 1950–

English entrepreneur. He established his reputation initially as a music producer; the Virgin Group he founded has since expanded to include a wide range of business ventures, from music and railways to banking and airlines.

70 Screw It, Let's Do It.
2006 Book title.

71 The brave may not live forever—but the cautious do not live at all.
2013 Like a Virgin: Secrets They Won't Teach You at Business School.

72 Only a fool never changes his mind.
2013 Like a Virgin: Secrets They Won't Teach You at Business School.

73 Luck is what happens when preparation meets opportunity.
2014 The Virgin Way: How to Listen, Learn, Laugh and Lead.

74 If you want to be a millionaire, start with a billion dollars and launch a new airline.
Attributed.

Braque, Georges 1882–1963

French painter, a developer of Fauvism, and later under the influence of Picasso, of Cubism. He was badly injured in World War I.

75 *L'Art est fait pour troubler, la Science rassure.*
Art was made to disturb, science reassures.
Notebook entry. Collected in *Le Jour et la nuit: Cahiers 1917–52*.

76 *La vérité existe; on n'invente que le mensonge.*
Truth exists; only lies are invented.
Notebook entry. Collected in *Le Jour et la nuit: Cahiers 1917–52*.

Brasch, Charles 1909–73

New Zealand poet. His works include *The Land and Other People* (1939), *Ambulando* (1964) and *Home Ground* (1974). A posthumous book of *Collected Poems* was published in 1984.

77 The ruby and amethyst eyes of anemones
Glow through me, fiercer than stars.
Home Ground (1974), 'Night Cries, Wakari Hospital: Winter Anemones'.

Brathwaite, Edward Kamau originally Lawson Edward Brathwaite 1930–

West Indian poet and historian, born in Barbados. His best-known work *The Arrivants: A New World Trilogy* (1973) consists of three earlier long poems, exploring different aspects of Caribbean culture and identity.

78 It is not enough
to be pause, to be hole
to be void, to be silent
to be semicolon, to be semicolony;
1969 *Islands*, no.3 'Rebellion', pt.6 'Negus', collected as *The Arrivants: A New World Trilogy* (1973).

Bratton, John W(alter) 1867–1947

US songwriter.

79 If you go down in the woods today
You're sure of a big surprise
If you down in the woods today
You'd better go in disguise.
For every Bear that ever there was
Will gather there for certain because,
Today's the day the Teddy Bears have their Picnic.
1932 'The Teddy Bears' Picnic' (with James B Kennedy).

Braudy, Leo Beal 1941–

US academic. He became Bing Professor of Literature at the University of Southern California in 1985, and University Professor in 1997.

80 People are looking to other lives for answers to questions about their own.
1987 On the increasing popularity of biography. Quoted by Alvin P Sarnoff in *US News and World Report*, 3 Aug.

Braun, Wernher von 1912–77

German-born US rocket scientist and engineer who helped develop the liquid-fuel rocket for the Nazis, and later switched his allegiance to the US. He became technical adviser to the US rocket program and later director of development operations at NASA where he was responsible for development of the Saturn V launch vehicle.

81 Our sun is one of 100 billion stars in our galaxy. Our galaxy is one of billions of galaxies populating the universe. It would be the height of presumption to think that we are the only living things in that enormous immensity.
1960 In the *New York Times*, 29 Apr.

Brautigan, Richard 1935–84

US fabulist and poet, an icon of the 1960s counter-culture movement. His seemingly whimsical fables were also literary experiments. He committed suicide.

82 Language does not leave fossils, at least not until it has become written.
1967 *Trout Fishing In America*, 'Prelude to the Mayonnaise Chapter'.

83 The time is right to mix sentences with dirt and the sun with punctuation and rain with verbs.
1968 *Please Plant This Book*, 'Squash'.

84 If you get hung up on everybody else's hangups, then the whole world's going to be nothing more than one huge gallows.
1970 *The Abortion: An Historical Romance*.

85 Loading Mercury with a Pitchfork.
1976 Title of poetry collection.

86 They used language concentrating emotion, detail and image until they arrived at a form of dew-like steel.
1978 On Japanese poets. *June 30th–June 30th*.

Brecher, Irving 1914–2008

US screenwriter and director. He wrote the scripts for two of the Marx Brothers' later films—*At the Circus* (1939) and *Go West* (1940).

87 I'll bet your father spent the first year of your life throwing rocks at the stork.
1939 *At the Circus*.

Brecht, Bertolt Eugen Friedrich 1898–1956

German poet, playwright and theatre director, an innovator of epic theatre and the alienation effect. He fled Nazi Germany when Hitler came to power and returned to settle in East Berlin in 1947, where he directed the *Berliner Ensemble* theatre. His works include *The Threepenny Opera* (1928, with Kurt Weill), *The Life of Galileo* (1938), *Mother Courage and her Children* (1939) and *The Caucasian Chalk Circle* (1945).

88 *Und der Haifisch, der hat Zähne
Und die trägt er im Gesicht
Und Macheath, der hat ein Messer
Doch das Messer sieht man nicht.*
Oh, the shark has pretty teeth, dear,
And he shows them pearly white.
Just a jack-knife has Macheath, dear,
And he keeps it out of sight.
1928 *Die Dreigroschenoper* ('The Threepenny Opera'), prologue (translated by Ralph Manheim and John Willett, 1970).

89 *Erst kommt das Fressen, dann kommt die Moral.*
Food comes first, then morals.
1928 *Die Dreigroschenoper* ('The Threepenny Opera'), act 2, sc.3 (translated by Ralph Manheim and John Willett, 1970).

90 *Von der Wiege bis zur Bahre, zuerst die Wäsche.*
From the cradle to the grave, underwear first, last and all the time.
1928 *Die Dreigroschenoper* ('The Threepenny Opera'), act 2, sc.5 (translated by Ralph Manheim and John Willet, 1970).

91 ANDREA: *Unglücklich das Land das keine Helden hat.*
GALILEI: *Unglücklich das Land das Helden nötig hat.*
ANDREA: Unlucky the land that has no heroes.
GALILEI: Unlucky the land that has need of heroes.
1938 *Leben des Galilei* ('The Life of Galileo'), sc.13.

92 *Angesichts von Hindernissen mag die kürzeste Linie zwischen zwei Punkten die krumme sein.*
When it comes to obstacles, the shortest line between two points may be the crooked one.
1938 *Leben des Galilei* ('The Life of Galileo'), sc. 14 (translated by Howard Benton, 1980).
▶ See Lessing 524:7.

93 *Die Wissenschaft kennt nur ein Gebot: den wissenschaftlichen Beitrag.*
Science knows only one commandment: contribute to science.
1938 *Leben des Galilei* ('The Life of Galileo'), sc.14 (translated by Howard Brenton, 1980).

94 *Weil ich ihm nicht traue, sind wir befreundet.*
Because I don't trust him, we are friends.
1939 *Mutter Courage und ihre Kinder* ('Mother Courage and her Children'), sc.3.

95 Die schönsten Pläne sind schon zuschanden geworden durch die Kleinlichkeit von denen, wo sie ausführen sollten, denn die Kaiser selber können ja nix machen.
The finest plans have always been spoiled by the pettiness of those who should carry them out. Even emperors cannot do it all by themselves.
1939 *Mutter Courage und ihre Kinder* ('Mother Courage and her Children'), sc.6.

96 Der Krieg findet immer einen Ausweg.
War always finds a way.
1939 *Mutter Courage und ihre Kinder* ('Mother Courage and her Children'), sc.6.

Brenan, Gerald 1894–1987

English travel writer, born in Malta. After an itinerant early life he settled in Spain, producing *South from Granada* (1957) and *The Spanish Labyrinth* (1943) among other works.

97 Religions are kept alive by heresies, which are really sudden explosions of faith. Dead religions do not produce them.
1978 *Thoughts in a Dry Season*.

Brennan, William J(oseph), Jr 1906–97

US jurist, Associate Justice of the US Supreme Court (1956–90). He took an active role in liberal decisions handed down under Chief Justice Earl Warren.

98 Sex and obscenity are not synonymous.
1967 Ruling that established a new legal standard for obscenity, 24 Jun.

99 Death is an unusually severe and degrading punishment.
1972 Ruling to outlaw states' right to impose capital punishment, 29 Jun.

Brennus

Gallic king who captured Rome, 390 BC.

1 *Vae victis.*
Down with the defeated!
390 BC His cry on capturing Rome. Quoted in Livy *Ab urbe condita*, bk.5, ch.48, section 9.

Breslin, Jimmy 1930–

US sports journalist, writer and broadcaster. His works include *Can't Anybody Here Play This Game?* (1963). He won a Pulitzer Prize for outstanding commentary (1986).

2 They're killing the game with this phoney mystique—telling people that a guy needs the abilities of a brain surgeon to play left-guard for the Colts. Football is simply a game to keep the coalminers off the streets.
Quoted in Colin Jarman *The Guinness Dictionary of Sports Quotations* (1990).

3 Rage is the only quality which has kept me, or anybody I have ever studied, writing columns for newspapers.
1990 In *The Times*, 9 May.

Brewster, Kingman, Jr 1919–88

US educator, Professor of Law at Harvard (1950–60) and President of Yale (1963–77). He was US Ambassador to Britain (1977–81), and stayed on there as the representative of a US law firm.

4 The most fundamental value of a liberal education is that it makes life more interesting.
Recalled on his death in the *New York Times*, 9 Nov 1988.

Brezhnev, Leonid Ilyich 1906–82

Russian politician. As General Secretary of the Soviet Communist Party Central Committee after Khrushchev (1964), he became the most powerful Soviet leader, the first to hold simultaneously the position of General Secretary and President of the Supreme Soviet (1977–82).

5 She is trying to wear the trousers of Winston Churchill.
1979 Of Margaret Thatcher. Speech.

6 Whatever may divide us, Europe is our common home. A common fate has linked us through the centuries, and it continues to link us today.
1981 Speech while visiting the Federal Republic of Germany, 23 Nov.

Bricker, John W(illiam) 1893–1986

US Senator. He was Governor of Ohio (1939–45) and then Senator (1945–49). He ran as Republican vice-presidential candidate in 1944.

7 Joe, you're a dirty son of a bitch but there are times when you've got to have a son of a bitch around, and this is one of them.
c.1953 Comment to Senator Joseph R McCarthy on rescuing Republic prominence by pressing charges of Communism in government. Recalled in *This Fabulous Century* (1970).

Bridges, Robert Seymour 1844–1930

English Poet Laureate and hymn writer who qualified and practised as a doctor, and a friend of Gerard Manley Hopkins. As wartime Poet Laureate he compiled an anthology *The Spirit of Man* (1916) to lift the nation's spirits.

8 So sweet love seemed that April morn,
When first we kissed beside the thorn,
So strangely sweet, it was not strange
We thought that love could never change.

But I can tell—let truth be told—
That love will change in growing old;
Though day by day is nought to see,
So delicate his motions be.
1894 'So Sweet Loved Seemed'.

9 All my hope on God is founded
He does still my trust renew,
Me through change and chance he guideth,
Only good and only true.
God unknown,
He alone
Calls my heart to be his own.
1899 Hymn.

10 And I replied unto all these things which encompass the door of my flesh, 'Ye have told me of my god, that ye are not he: tell me something of him'. And they cried all with a great voice, 'He made us'. My questioning them was my mind's desire, and their Beauty was their answer.
1916 *The Spirit of Man: The Confessions of St Augustine*.

Bridges, (Henry) Styles 1898–1961

US Senator. He was Republican Governor of New Hampshire (1935–37) and then Senator (1937–61). He opposed the New Deal and was a supporter of Joseph McCarthy.

11 China asked for a sword, and we gave her a dull paring knife.
Of China's collapse to Communism. Quoted in David Halberstam *The Fifties* (1993).

Bridie, James *pseudonym of* Osborne Henry Mavor
1888–1951

Scottish playwright and doctor. Founder of the Glasgow Citizens' Theatre, he enjoyed considerable success with such plays as *The Anatomist* (1930) and *Daphne Laureola* (1949).

12 I sat through the first act and heard my lovely lines falling like cold porridge on a damp mattress.
   1939 *One Way of Living*, alluding to a performance of his play *Marriage is no Joke*.

Bright, John   1811–89

British radical statesman and orator, a leading member of the Anti-Corn League (1839), MP from 1843 and an enormous influence on the Unionist party. A member of the Peace Society, he denounced the Crimean War (1854).

13 The Angel of Death has been abroad throughout the land. You may almost hear the beating of his wings.
   1855 Of the Crimean War. Speech, House of Commons, 23 Feb.

14 This regard for the liberties of Europe, this care at one time for the protestant interest, this excessive love for the balance of power, is neither more nor less than a gigantic system of outdoor relief for the aristocracy of Great Britain.
   1858 Speech, Birmingham, 29 Oct.

15 England is the mother of Parliaments.
   1865 Speech, Birmingham, 18 Jan.

16 There is no nation on the continent of Europe that is less able to do harm to England, and there is no nation on the continent of Europe to whom we are less able to do harm, than Russia. We are so separate that it seems impossible that the two nations, by the use of reason or common sense at all, could possibly be brought into conflict with each other.
   1878 Speech, Birmingham, 13 Jan.

Brillat-Savarin, Jean Anthelme   1755–1826

French politician, gastronome and writer, Mayor of Belley in 1793. During the French Revolution he took refuge in Switzerland and America. His *Physiologie du goût* (1825) is an elegant and witty compendium of the art of dining.

17 *Dis-moi ce que tu manges, je te dirai ce que tu es.*
   Tell me what you eat and I will tell you what you are.
   1825 *Physiologie du goût*, aphorism 4 (translated by Anne Drayton, 1970).

18 *La découverte d'un mets nouveau fait plus pour le bonheur du genre humain que la découverte d'une étoile.*
   The discovery of a new dish does more for the happiness of mankind than the discovery of a star.
   1825 *Physiologie du goût*, aphorism 9 (translated by Anne Drayton, 1970).

19 *La volaille est pour la cuisine ce qu'est la toile pour les peintres.*
   Fowls are to the kitchen what his canvas is to the painter.
   1825 *Physiologie du goût*, pt.1, ch.6, section 34 (translated by Anne Drayton, 1970).

20 *La truffe n'est point un aphrodisiaque positif; mais elle peut, en certaines occasions, rendre les femmes plus tendres et les hommes plus aimables.*
   The truffle is not a true aphrodisiac; but in certain circumstances it can make women more affectionate and men more attentive.
   1825 *Physiologie du goût*, pt.1, ch.6, section 44 (translated by Anne Drayton, 1970).

21 *L'alcool est le monarque des liquides, et porte au dernier degré l'exaltation palatale.*
   Alcohol is the prince of liquids, and carries the palate to its highest pitch of exaltation.
   1825 *Physiologie du goût*, pt.1, ch.9, section 53 (translated by Anne Drayton, 1970).

22 *C'est aussi de tous les arts celui qui nous a rendu le service le plus important pour la vie civile.*
   It is also of all arts the one which has done the most to advance the cause of civilization.
   1825 Of cooking. *Physiologie du goût*, pt.1, ch.27, section 123 (translated by Anne Drayton, 1970).

Brinkley, David McClure   1920–2003

US news commentator who is best known for the nightly *Huntley-Brinkley Report* (1956–70), co-hosted with Chet Huntley.

23 If you turn on your set and see nothing is happening…do not call a serviceman. You have tuned in the US Senate.
   1986 On ABC TV broadcast, 1 Jun.

24 A cavalry commander…said he had just been given a thousand new men who had never seen a horse and a thousand horses who had never seen a man.
   1988 On World War II. *Washington Goes to War*.

25 [They] will fearlessly commit both parties to favor mother love and the protection of the whooping crane, and to oppose the man-eating shark and the more unpopular forms of sin.
   Of party platforms. Quoted in Marc Gunther *The House That Roone Built* (1994).

Brisbane, Arthur   1864–1936

US newspaper editor and writer. Editor of the *New York Herald*, which was owned by William Randolph Hearst, he was a proponent of 'sensationalist' journalism.

26 Never forget that if you don't hit a newspaper reader between the eyes with your first sentence, there is no need of writing a second one.
   c.1900 Quoted in Oliver Carlson *Brisbane: a Candid Biography* (1937), ch.5.

27 Hang your idea on a peg that all can read.
   c.1907 Quoted in Oliver Carlson *Brisbane: a Candid Biography* (1937), ch.7.

Britten, Baron (Edward) Benjamin, of Aldeburgh
1913–76

English composer, pianist and conductor, a student of John Ireland and Frank Bridge. His extensive output includes the opera *Peter Grimes* (1945) and other operas, songs, chamber music and orchestral works, and the *War Requiem* (1961), written for the reopening of Coventry Cathedral. With Peter Pears, he founded the Aldeburgh Festival (1948), at which much of his work was first performed.

28 I remember the first time I tried the result looked rather like the Forth Bridge.
   1964 Of his first attempts at composition. Quoted in the *Sunday Telegraph*.

Brock, Sir Isaac   1768–1812

British soldier, commander of the British and militia forces in the War of 1812.

29 Push on, brave York Volunteers!
> **1812** Last command before succumbing to a sniper's bullet in the Battle of Queenston Heights, Upper Canada (modern Ontario), 13 Oct. Quoted in C P Stacey 'Brock's Muniments', in *Books in Canada* (Aug–Sep 1980).

Brodber, Erna 1940–
Jamaican writer, critic and academic. Her works include sociological studies on women and children in Jamaica, books on Caribbean literature, and novels including *Jane and Louisa Will Soon Come Home* (1980) and *Myal* (1988).

30 Different rhymes for different times
Different styles for different climes
Someday them rogues in Whitehall
Be forced to change their tune.
> **1988** *Myal*, ch.15.

Brodkey, Harold 1930–96
US writer and journalist. He died of AIDS.

31 I have AIDS. I am surprised that I do. I have not been exposed since 1977, which is to say that my experience, my adventures in homosexuality took place largely in the 1960s and '70s, and back then I relied on time and abstinence to indicate my degree of freedom from infection—and to protect others and myself.
> **1996** *This Wild Darkness: The Story of My Death*.

32 I'm sixty-two, and it's ecological sense to die while you're still productive, die and clear a space for others, old and young.
> **1996** *This Wild Darkness: The Story of My Death*.

33 Death is not soft-mouthed, vague-footed, nearby. It is in the hall.
> **1996** *This Wild Darkness: The Story of My Death*.

34 Nothing I have ever written has been admired as much as the announcement of my death.
> Remark about his articles tracing the course of his illness in the *New Yorker*. Quoted in his obituary in *The Scotsman*, 29 Jan 1996.

Brodsky, Joseph 1940–96
Russian-born US poet. Exiled from Russia as a 'social parasite', he took US citizenship in 1977 and was awarded the Nobel prize in 1987. He latterly wrote in English, and translated his earlier Russian poems.

35 Illness and death…the only things that a tyrant has in common with his subjects… In this sense alone, a nation profits from being run by an old man.
> **1986** *Less Than One*, 'On Tyranny'.

36 The dusty catastrophe of Asia. Green only on the banner of the Prophet. Nothing grows here except mustaches.
> **1986** *Less Than One*, 'Flight From Byzantium'.

37 Racism? But isn't it only a form of misanthropy?
> **1986** *Less Than One*, 'Flight From Byzantium'.

38 Snobbery? But it's only a form of despair.
> **1986** *Less Than One*, 'Flight From Byzantium'.

39 A big step for me, and a small step for mankind.
> **1987** Response on hearing of his Nobel prize award. Quoted in his obituary in *The Scotsman*, 29 Jan 1996.
> ▶ See Armstrong 33:51.

40 Were we to choose our leaders on the basis of their reading experience and not their political programs, there would be much less grief on earth. I believe—not empirically, alas, but only theoretically—that for someone who has read a lot of Dickens to shoot his like in the name of an idea is harder than for someone who has read no Dickens.
> **1987** Nobel prize acceptance speech.

41 There are worse crimes than burning books. One of them is not reading them.
> **1991** Comment at a press conference in Washington, DC, 15 May, on accepting the US poet laureateship.

42 Russia is my home…and for everything that I have in my soul I am obligated to Russia and its people. And—this is the main thing—obligated to its language.
> **1992** In the *New York Times*, 1 Oct.

43 They should be in every room in every motel in the land.
> **1992** Of poetry books. In the *New York Times*, 1 Oct.

Brody, Hugh 1943–
British explorer, anthropologist and writer.

44 Resources left in the ground are saved, not lost.
> **1981** *Maps and Dreams: Indians and the British Columbia Frontier*.

Bronowski, Jacob 1908–74
Polish-born British mathematician, poet and humanist. He was a popular broadcaster, particularly on the BBC's *Brains Trust* and *The Ascent of Man* (1973).

45 Dissent is the native activity of the scientist, and it has got him into a good deal of trouble in the last years. But if that is cut off, what is left will not be a scientist. And I doubt whether it will be a man.
> **1953** 'The Sense of Human Dignity', lecture at Massachusetts Institute of Technology, 19 Mar.

46 Science has nothing to be ashamed of, even in the ruins of Nagasaki. The shame is theirs who appeal to other values than the human imaginative values which science has evolved.
> **1953** 'The Sense of Human Dignity', lecture at Massachusetts Institute of Technology, 19 Mar.

47 At bottom, the society of scientists is more important than their discoveries. What science has to teach us here is not its techniques but its spirit: the irresistible need to explore.
> **1956** *Science and Human Values*.

48 Man masters nature not by force but by understanding. This is why science has succeeded where magic failed: because it has looked for no spell to cast on nature.
> **1956** *Universities Quarterly*, vol.10, issue 3.

49 Sooner or later every one of us breathes an atom that has been breathed before by anyone you can think of who has lived before us—Michelangelo or George Washington or Moses.
> **1966** Quoted in the *New York Times*, 13 Oct 1969.

50 No science is immune to the infection of politics and the corruption of power.
> **1971** In *The Listener*.

51 The world can only be grasped by action, not by contemplation… The hand is the cutting edge of the mind.
> **1973** *The Ascent of Man*, ch.3.

52 That is the essence of science: ask an impertinent question and you are on the way to a pertinent answer.
> **1973** *The Ascent of Man*, ch.4.

53 Man is a singular creature. He has a set of gifts which make him unique among the animals, so that unlike them he is not a figure in the landscape—he is the shaper of the landscape.
1979 In *The Listener*.

Brontë, Anne 1820–49

English novelist and poet, younger sister of Charlotte and Emily. Her first novel *Agnes Grey* (1847) was published under the pseudonym Acton Bell. She also wrote *The Tenant of Wildfell Hall* (1848).

54 To think a soul so near divine,
Within a form, so angel fair,
United to a heart like thine,
Has gladdened once our humble sphere.
1846 'A Reminiscence', in *Poems by Currer, Ellis and Acton Bell*.

55 My soul is awakened, my spirit is soaring
And carried aloft on the wings of the breeze;
For above and around me the wild wind is roaring,
Arousing to rapture the earth and the seas.
1846 'Line Composed in a Wood on a Windy Day', in *Poems by Currer, Ellis and Acton Bell*.

56 All true histories contain instruction; though in some, the treasure may be hard to find, and when found, so trivial in quantity that the dry, shrivelled kernel scarcely compensates for the trouble of cracking the nut.
1847 *Agnes Grey*, ch.1.

57 He'll be all right when he's married, as Mama says; and reformed rakes make the best husbands, everybody knows. I only wish he were not so ugly—that's all I think about—but then there's no choice here in the country.
1847 *Agnes Grey*, ch.13.

58 What is it that constitutes virtue, Mrs Graham? Is it the circumstance of being able and willing to resist temptation; or that of having no temptation to resist?
1848 *The Tenant of Wildfell Hall*, ch.3.

Brontë, Charlotte 1816–55

English novelist and poet, elder sister of Emily and Anne. Her four novels are *Jane Eyre* (1847), *Shirley* (1849), *Villette* (1853) and *The Professor* (1857).

59 We wove a web in childhood,
A web of sunny air;
We dug a spring in infancy
Of water pure and fair;
We sowed in youth a mustard seed,
We cut an almond rod;
We are now grown up to riper age—
Are they withered in the sod?
1835 'We Wove a Web in Childhood'.

60 But two miles more and then we rest!
Well, there is still an hour of day,
And long the brightness of the west
Sit then, awhile, here in this wood
So total is the solitude,
We safely may delay.
1846 'Regret', in *Poems by Currer, Ellis and Acton Bell*.

61 Women are supposed to be very calm generally: but women feel just as men feel: they need exercise for their faculties, and a field for their efforts as much as their brothers do; they suffer from too rigid a restraint, too absolute a stagnation, precisely as men would suffer…it is thoughtless to condem them, or laugh at them, if they seek to do more than custom has pronounced necessary for their sex.
1847 *Jane Eyre*, ch.12.

62 I grant an ugly woman is a blot on the fair face of creation; but as to the gentleman, let them be solicitous to possess only strength and valour: let their motto be:—Hunt, shoot, and fight: the rest is not worth a flip.
1847 *Jane Eyre* ch.17.

63 The soul fortunately, has an interpreter—often an unconscious, but still a truthful interpreter—in the eye.
1847 *Jane Eyre*, ch.28.

64 Reader, I married him.
1847 *Jane Eyre*, ch.38.

65 Conventionality is not morality. Self-righteousness is not religion. To attack the first is not to assail the last. To pluck the mask from the face of the Pharisee, is not to lift an impious hand to the Crown of Thorns.
1848 *Jane Eyre* (2nd edn), preface.

66 Of late years an abundant shower of curates has fallen upon the north of England.
1849 *Shirley*, ch.1.

67 I describe imperfect characters. Every character in this book will be found to be more or less imperfect, my pen refusing to draw anything in the model line.
1849 *Shirley*, ch.5.

68 Old maids like the houseless and unemployed poor, should not ask for a place and an occupation in the world: the demand disturbs the happy and the rich.
1849 *Shirley*, ch.22.

69 Liberty lends us her wings and Hope guides us by her star.
1853 *Villette*, ch.6.

70 Out of association grows adhesion, and out of adhesion amalgamation.
1853 *Villette*, ch.25.

71 What animal magnetism drew thee and me together—I know not.
1857 *The Professor*, ch.1.

72 Unlawful pleasure, trenching on another's rights, is delusive and envenomed pleasure—its hollowness disappoints at the time, its poison cruelly tortures afterwards, its effects deprave forever.
1857 *The Professor*, ch.20.

Brontë, Emily Jane 1818–48

English novelist and poet, sister of Anne and Charlotte. Her poems were first published under the pseudonym Ellis Bell. Her only novel is the intense and powerful *Wuthering Heights* (1847).

73 The night is darkening round me,
The wild winds coldly blow;
But a tyrant spell has bound me
And I cannot, cannot go.
1837 'The Night is Darkening Round Me'.

74 The winter wind is loud and wild,
Come close to me, my darling child;
Forsake thy books, and mateless play;
And, while the night is gathering grey,
We'll talk its pensive hours away.

1846 'Faith and Despondency', in *Poems by Currer, Ellis and Acton Bell*.

75 No coward soul is mine,
No trembler in the world's storm-troubled sphere:
I see Heaven's glories shine,
And faith shines equal, arming me from fear.
1846 'No Coward Soul is Mine', in *Poems by Currer, Ellis and Acton Bell*.

76 Cold in the earth—and the deep snow piled above thee,
Far, far, removed, cold in the dreary grave!
Have I forgot, my only Love, to love thee,
Severed at last by Time's all-serving wave?
1846 'Remembrance', in *Poems by Currer, Ellis and Acton Bell*.

77 I've dreamt in my life dreams that have stayed with me ever after, and changed my ideas; they've gone through and through me, like wine through water, and altered the colour of my mind.
1847 *Wuthering Heights*, ch.9.

78 As different as a moonbeam from lightning, or frost from fire.
1847 *Wuthering Heights*, ch.9.

79 My love for Linton is like the foliage in the woods. Time will change it, I'm well aware, as winter changes the trees. My Love for Heathcliff resembles the eternal rocks beneath—a source of little visible delight but necessary. Nelly, I *am* Heathcliff.
1847 *Wuthering Heights*, ch.9.

80 He might as well plant an oak in a flower-pot, and expect it to thrive, as imagine he can restore her to vigour in the soil of his shallow cares!
1847 *Wuthering Heights*, ch.14.

81 The more the worms writhe, the more I yearn to crush out their entrails!
1847 Heathcliff. *Wuthering Heights*, ch.14.

82 I lingered around them, under the benign sky; watched the moths fluttering among the heath and hare-bells; listened to the soft wind breathing through the grass; and wondered how anyone could ever imagine unquiet slumbers, for the sleepers in that quiet earth.
1847 *Wuthering Heights*, ch.34, closing words.

Brooke, Frances née Moore 1724–89

English writer. In Canada (1763–8) with her minister husband, she produced 'Canada's first novel', *The History of Emily Montague* (1769). She wrote other novels and plays, and edited a periodical, *The Old Maid*.

83 I no longer wonder the elegant arts are unknown here; the rigor of the climate suspends the very powers of the understanding; what then must become of those of the imagination?... Genius will never mount high, where the faculties of the mind are benumbed half the year.
1769 *The History of Emily Montague*, 'Letter 49'.

Brooke, Rupert Chawner 1887–1915

English poet, icon of the World War I 'lost generation'. His early verse was published in 1911, and his reputation was established by the posthumous publication of *1914 and Other Poems* (1915). He died of blood poisoning on Skyros.

84 Breathless, we flung us on the windy hill,
Laughed in the sun, and kissed the lovely grass.
1910 'Sonnet'.

85 But there's wisdom in women, of more than they have known,
And thoughts go blowing through them, are wiser than their own.
1913 'There's Wisdom in Women'.

86 Then, the cool kindliness of sheets, that soon
Smooth away trouble; and the rough male kiss
Of blankets.
1914 'The Great Lover'.

87 The benison of hot water; furs to touch;
The good smell of old clothes.
1914 'The Great Lover'.

88 If I should die, think only this of me:
That there's some corner of a foreign field
That is for ever England.
There shall be
In that rich dust a richer dust concealed;
A dust whom England bore, shaped, made aware,
Gave, once, her flowers to love, her ways to roam,
A body of England's, breathing English air,
Washed by the rivers, blest by suns of home.
1914 'The Soldier'.

89 In hearts at peace, under an English heaven.
1914 'The Soldier'.

90 Blow out, you bugles, over the rich Dead!
There's none of these so lonely and poor of old,
But, dying, has made us rarer gifts than gold.
1914 'The Dead'.

91 Naught broken save this body, lost but breath;
Nothing to shake the laughing heart's long peace there
But only agony, and that has ending;
And the worst friend and enemy is but Death.
1914 'Peace'.

92 Here tulips bloom as they are told;
Unkempt about those hedges blows
An English unofficial rose.
1915 'The Old Vicarage, Grantchester'.

93 And spectral dance, before the dawn,
A hundred Vicars down the lawn;
Curates, long dust, will come and go
On lissom, clerical, printless toe;
And oft between the boughs is seen
The sly shade of a Rural Dean.
1915 'The Old Vicarage, Grantchester'.

94 God! I will pack, and take a train,
And get me to England once again!
For England's the one land, I know,
Where men with Splendid Hearts may go.
1915 'The Old Vicarage, Grantchester'.

95 For Cambridge people rarely smile,
Being urban, squat, and packed with guile.
1915 'The Old Vicarage, Grantchester'.

96 They love the Good; they worship Truth;
They laugh uproariously in youth;
(And when they get to feeling old,
They up and shoot themselves, I'm told).
1915 'The Old Vicarage, Grantchester'.

97 Stands the Church clock at ten to three?
And is there honey still for tea?
1915 'The Old Vicarage, Grantchester'.

98 Fish (fly-replete, in depth of June,
   Dawdling away their wat'ry noon).
   1915 'Heaven'.

99 Fish say, they have their stream and pond;
   But is there anything beyond?
   1915 'Heaven'.

1 But somewhere, beyond Space and Time
  Is wetter water, slimier slime!
  1915 'Heaven'.

2 Unfading moths, immortal flies,
  And the worm that never dies.
  And in that heaven of all their wish,
  There shall be no more land, say fish.
  1915 'Heaven'.

Brookner, Anita 1928–

English novelist and art historian. A spare, elegant stylist, she won the Booker Prize in 1984 for her novel *Hôtel du Lac*.

3 It is best to marry for purely selfish reasons.
  1981 *A Start in Life*.

4 It is my contention that Aesop was writing for the tortoise market…hares have no time to read.
  1984 *Hôtel du Lac*, ch.2.

5 Good women always think it is their fault when someone else is being offensive. Bad women never take the blame for anything.
  1984 *Hôtel du Lac*, ch.7.

6 Blanche Vernon occupied her time most usefully in keeping feelings at bay.
  1986 *Misalliance*, ch.1.

7 I think you always feel braver in another language.
  1988 In the *Observer*, 7 Aug.

8 They were privileged children…they would always expect to be greeted with smiles.
  1989 *Lewis Percy*, ch.9.

9 Satire is dependent on strong beliefs, and on strong beliefs wounded.
  1989 In *The Spectator*, 23 Mar.

10 I reflected how easy it is for a man to reduce women of a certain age to imbecility. All he has to do is give an impersonation of desire, or better still, of secret knowledge, for a woman to feel herself a source of power.
   1993 *A Family Romance*, ch.7.

11 In youth Beatrice had been attractive, but what was attractive about her was not her appearance but her disposability.
   1998 *Falling Slowly*.

Brooks, Louise 1906–85

US film actress, embodiment of the flapper age, renowned for her innocent sexuality and natural screen presence.

12 Every actor has a natural animosity toward every other actor, present or absent, living or dead.
   1982 *Lulu in Hollywood*.

Brooks, Mel *pseudonym of* Melvin Kaminsky 1926–

US director, writer and actor. His successful comedies have included *The Producers* (1968), *Blazing Saddles* (1974) and *Young Frankenstein* (1974).

13 That's it baby. If you've got it, flaunt it.
   1968 *The Producers*.

14 Tragedy is if I cut my finger. Comedy is if I walk into an open sewer and die.
   Attributed.

Brooks, Van Wyck 1886–1963

US author and critic. He wrote biographical studies of Mark Twain (1920), Henry James (1925) and Emerson (1932). His works, which attacked materialism, also include *The Flowering of New England* (1936, Pulitzer Prize).

15 It is not that the French are not profound, but they all express themselves so well that we are led to take their geese for swans.
   1958 *From A Writer's Notebook*.

Brougham, Henry Peter, 1st Baron Brougham and Vaux 1778–1868

Scottish jurist and politician. He was called to the English bar in 1808 and entered parliament in 1810. Noted for his eloquence, he became Lord Chancellor in 1830 and promoted the passage of the Reform Bill.

16 A legal gentleman who rescues your estate from your enemies, and keeps it himself.
   His definition of a lawyer. Quoted in Richard Fountain *The Wit of the Wig* (1968).

Broun, (Matthew) Heywood Campbell 1888–1939

US journalist, humorist and novelist.

17 Except that right side is up is best, there is not much to learn about holding a baby. There are one hundred and fifty-two distinctly different ways—and all are right! At least, all will do.
   1921 *Seeing Things at Night*, 'Holding a Baby'.

18 The tragedy of life is not that man loses, but that he almost wins.
   1922 *Pieces of Hate, and Other Enthusiasms*, 'Sport for Art's Sake'.

19 Just as every conviction begins as a whim so does every emancipator serve his apprenticeship as a crank. A fanatic is a great leader who is just entering the room.
   1928 In *New York World*, 6 Feb.

20 The tradition of baseball always has been agreeably free of chivalry. The rule is 'Do anything you can get away with'.
   Quoted in Colin Jarman *The Guinness Dictionary of Sports Quotations* (1990).

21 Sports do not build character. They reveal it.
   Quoted in Colin Jarman *The Guinness Dictionary of Sports Quotations* (1990).

Brown, (James) Gordon 1951–

Scottish Labour politician, Chancellor of the Exchequer (1997–2007), succeeding Tony Blair as Prime Minister (2007–2010). He resigned on losing a general election after less than three years in office.

22 We have been prudent for a purpose: a stronger, fairer Britain.
   2000 Budget speech, 21 Mar.

23 It is about time we had an end to the old Britain, where all that matters is the privileges you were born with, rather than the potential you actually have.
   2000 Speech, 25 May.

24 I'm a father, that's what matters most. Nothing matters more.
2003 Following the birth of his son. Quoted in the Observer, *19 Oct.*

25 There are values far beyond those of contracts, markets and exchange.
2006 Moving Britain Forward: Selected Speeches, 1997–2006.

26 The Arctic Monkeys really wake you up in the morning.
2006 Claiming familiarity with the Sheffield rock band, in New Woman *magazine, summer issue.*

27 The calendar says we are half way from 2000 to 2015. But the reality is that we are we are a million miles away from success.
2007 Speech at UN headquarters, NewYork, Jul.

Brown, John 1800–59

US militant abolitionist. In 1859 he led an unsuccessful raid on the US Armory at Harper's Ferry, Virginia, and was convicted of treason and hanged. He was twice married and had 20 children.

28 I am as content to die for God's eternal truth on the scaffold as in any other way.
1859 Letter to his children on the eve of his execution, 2 Dec.

Brown, John Mason 1900–69

US theatre critic. He wrote long-running theatre columns in the *New York Post* and *Saturday Review* as well as publishing several books on the theatre.

29 Tallulah Bankhead barged down the Nile last night as Cleopatra—and sank.
1937 In the New York Post, *11 Nov.*

30 To many, dramatic criticism must seem like an attempt to tattoo soap bubbles.
1963 Stagebill.

31 He has ears he likes to bathe in sound.
1963 Of playwright Maxwell Anderson. Dramatis Personae.

Brown, Michael DeWayne 1954–

US lawyer and politician. In 2005 he resigned as director of the Federal Emergency Management Agency after criticism of his response to Hurricane Katrina, which devastated the Gulf Coast.

32 Considering the dire circumstances that we have in New Orleans, virtually a city that has been destroyed, things are going relatively well.
2005 Interview, 1 Sep.

Brown, Olympia 1835–1900

US religious leader, the first woman ordained in the US.

33 The more we learn of science, the more we see that its wonderful mysteries are all explained by a few simple laws so connected together and so dependent upon each other, that we see the same mind animating them all.
1895 Sermon in Wisconsin, c.13 Jan.

Brown, Pat (Edmund Gerald, Sr) 1905–96

US lawyer and politician, Governor of California (1959–66).

34 Why, this is the worst disaster since my election.
1965 Of the Watts riots. Recalled in the New York Times, *21 Aug 1994.*

Brown, Rita Mae 1944–

US writer and feminist, a campaigner for gay rights. She is the author of a number of popular novels.

35 No government has the right to tell its citizens when or whom to love. The only queer people are those who don't love anybody.
1982 Speech, 28 Aug, at the opening ceremony of the Gay Olympics, San Francisco.

36 If Michaelangelo were a heterosexual, the Sistine Chapel would have been painted basic white and with a roller.
1988 In the New York Times, *15 May.*

37 I think the reward for conformity is that everyone likes you except yourself.
1988 Bingo, *ch.35.*

38 I think you can judge the level of success for any group of people by the reaction against it.
2008 In Time, *18 Mar.*

39 Happiness is pretty simple: someone to love, something to do, something to look forward to.
2011 Hiss of Death.

Brown, Thomas 1663–1704

English satirical writer.

40 I do not love thee, Dr Fell.
   The reason why I cannot tell;
   But this I know, and know full well,
   I do not love thee, Dr Fell.
Composed while an undergraduate at Christ Church, Oxford, under the Deanship of Dr Fell.

Brown, Walter fl.15c

Scottish poet. *Letters of Gold* is his only known surviving poem.

41 Grit riches and prosperitie
   Upfosteris vyce.
15c Letters of Gold, *l.131–2.*

Browne, Sir Thomas 1605–82

English writer and physician. His meditative *Religio Medici* appeared in an authorized version in 1643. Other works include *Pseudodoxia Epidemica, or Enquiries into... Vulgar and Common Errors* (1646) and *Hydriotaphia* (Urn Burial) (1658).

42 For my religion, though there be several circumstances that might persuade the world I have none at all—as the general scandal of my profession, the natural course of my studies, the indifferency of my behaviour and discourse in matters of religion, neither violently defending one, nor with that common ardour and contention opposing another—yet in despite hereof I dare without usurpation assume the honourable style of a Christian.
1634–5 Religio Medici *(published 1643), pt.1, section 1.*

43 My common conversation I do acknowledge austere, my behaviour full of rigor, sometimes not without morosity; yet at my devotion I love to use the civility of my knee, my hat, and hand, with all those outward and sensible motions which may express or promote my invisible devotion.
1634–5 Religio Medici *(published 1643), pt.1, section 3.*

44 Those vulgar heads that look asquint on the face of truth.
1634–5 Religio Medici *(published 1643), pt.1, section 3.*

45 In brief, where the Scripture is silent, the church is my text; where that speaks, 'tis but my comment; where

there is a joint silence of both, I borrow not the rules of my religion from Rome or Geneva, but the dictates of my own reason.
1634–5 *Religio Medici* (published 1643), pt.1, section 5.

46 Where we desire to be informed, 'tis good to contest with men above ourselves; but to confirm and establish our opinions, 'tis best to argue with judgements below our own, that the frequent spoils and victories over their reasons may settle in ourselves an esteem and confirmed opinion of our own.
1634–5 *Religio Medici* (published 1643), pt.1, section 6.

47 Every man is not a proper champion for truth, nor fit to take up the gauntlet in the cause of verity.
1634–5 *Religio Medici* (published 1643), pt.1, section 6.

48 Every man's own reason is his best Oedipus.
1634–5 Oedipus here means riddle-solver. *Religio Medici* (published 1643), pt.1, section 6.

49 For indeed heresies perish not with their authors, but like the river Arethusa, though they lose their currents in one place, they rise up again in another.
1634–5 *Religio Medici* (published 1643), pt.1, section 6.

50 Men are lived over again; the world is now as it was in ages past.
1634–5 *Religio Medici* (published 1643), pt.1, section 6.

51 Methinks there be not impossibilities enough in religion for an active faith.
1634–5 *Religio Medici* (published 1643), pt.1, section 6.

52 I desire to exercise my faith in the difficultest points, for to credit ordinary and visible objects is not faith but persuasion.
1634–5 *Religio Medici* (published 1643), pt.1, section 6.

53 I love to lose myself in a mystery, to pursue my reason to an *O altitudo!*
1634–5 *Religio Medici* (published 1643), pt.1, section 9.

54 Who can speak of eternity without a solecism, or think thereof without an ecstasy? Time we may comprehend, 'tis but five days elder than ourselves.
1634–5 *Religio Medici* (published 1643), pt.1, section 11.

55 We carry with us the wonders we seek without us: there is all Africa and her prodigies in us.
1634–5 *Religio Medici* (published 1643), pt.1, section 15.

56 We are that bold and adventurous piece of nature which he that studies wisely learns in a compendium what others labour at in a divided piece and endless volume.
1634–5 *Religio Medici* (published 1643), pt.1, section 15.

57 Nature is not at variance with art nor art with nature, they both being the servants of his providence: art is the perfection of nature.
1634–5 *Religio Medici* (published 1643), pt.1, section 16.

58 All things are artificial, for nature is the art of God.
1634–5 *Religio Medici* (published 1643), pt.1, section 16.

59 Obstinacy in a bad cause, is but constancy in a good.
1634–5 *Religio Medici* (published 1643), pt.1, section 25.

60 Persecution is a bad and indirect way to plant religion.
1634–5 *Religio Medici* (published 1643), pt.1, section 25.

61 There are many…canonized on earth, that shall never be Saints in Heaven.
1634–5 *Religio Medici* (published 1643), pt.1, section 26.

62 I am not so much afraid of death, as ashamed thereof.
1634–5 *Religio Medici* (published 1643), pt.1, section 40.

63 Certainly there is no happiness within this circle of flesh, nor is it in the optics of these eyes to behold felicity; the first day of our Jubilee is death.
1634–5 *Religio Medici* (published 1643), pt.1, section 44.

64 I have tried if I could reach that great resolution…to be honest without a thought of Heaven or Hell.
1634–5 *Religio Medici* (published 1643), pt.1, section 47.

65 To believe only in possibilities, is not faith, but mere Philosophy.
1634–5 *Religio Medici* (published 1643), pt.1, section 48.

66 There is no road or ready way to virtue.
1634–5 *Religio Medici* (published 1643), pt.1, section 55.

67 The world was before the creation and at an end before it had a beginning; and thus was I dead before I was alive. Though my grave be England, my dying place was Paradise, and Eve miscarried of me before she conceived of Cain.
1634–5 *Religio Medici* (published 1643), pt.1, section 59.

68 All places, all airs make unto me one country; I am in England, everywhere, and under any meridian.
1634–5 *Religio Medici* (published 1643), pt.2, section 1.

69 It is the common wonder of all men, how among so many millions of faces, there should be none alike.
1634–5 *Religio Medici* (published 1643), pt.2, section 1.

70 I could be content that we might procreate like trees, without conjunction, or that there were any way to perpetuate the World without this trivial and vulgar way of coition: it is the foolishest act a wise man commits in all his life.
1634–5 *Religio Medici* (published 1643), pt.2, section 9.

71 We all labour against our own cure, for death is the cure of all diseases.
1634–5 *Religio Medici* (published 1643), pt.2, section 9.

72 Whilst I study to find how I am a microcosm of little world, I find myself something more than the great. There is surely a piece of divinity in us; something that was before the elements, and owes no homage unto the sun.
1634–5 *Religio Medici* (published 1643), pt.2, section 11.

73 Old mortality, the ruins of forgotten times.
1658 *Hydriotaphia* (Urn Burial), Epistle Dedicatory.

74 Were the happiness of the next world as closely apprehended as the felicities of this, it were a martyrdom to live.
1658 *Hydriotaphia* (Urn Burial), ch.4.

75 The long habit of living indisposeth us for dying.
1658 *Hydriotaphia* (Urn Burial), ch.5.

76 Adversity stretcheth our days.
1658 *Hydriotaphia* (Urn Burial), ch.5.

77 We cannot hope to live so long in our names as some have done in their persons.
1658 *Hydriotaphia* (Urn Burial), ch.5.

78 'Tis too late to be ambitious.
1658 *Hydriotaphia* (Urn Burial), ch.5.

79 There is no antidote against the opium of time.
1658 *Hydriotaphia* (Urn Burial), ch.5.

80 To be nameless in worthy deeds exceeds an infamous history… Who would not rather have been the good thief than Pilate?
1658 *Hydriotaphia* (Urn Burial), ch.5.

81 Man is a noble animal, splendid in ashes, and pompous in the grave.
   1658 *Hydriotaphia* (Urn Burial), ch.5.

82 Life is a pure flame, and we live by an invisible sun within us.
   1658 *Hydriotaphia* (Urn Burial), ch.5.

83 Life itself is but the shadow of death, and souls departed but the shadows of the living. All things fall under this name. The sun itself is but the dark *simulacrum*, and light but the shadow of God.
   1658 *The Garden of Cyrus*, ch.2.

84 The quincunx of heaven runs low, and 'tis time to close the five parts of knowledge.
   1658 *The Garden of Cyrus*, ch.5.

85 All things began in order, so shall they end, and so shall they begin again; according to the ordainer of order and mystical mathematics of the city of heaven.
   1658 *The Garden of Cyrus*, ch.5.

86 Nor will the sweetest delight of gardens afford much comfort in sleep; wherein the dullness of that sense shakes hands with delectable odours; and though in the bed of Cleopatra, can hardly with any delight raise up the ghost of a rose.
   1658 *The Garden of Cyrus*, ch.5.

Browne, William 1692–1774
English physician and poet.

87 The King to Oxford sent a troop of horse,
   For Tories own no argument but force;
   With equal skill to Cambridge books he sent,
   For Whigs admit no force but argument.
   Literary Anecdotes.

Browning, Elizabeth *née Barrett* 1806–61
English poet, who married Robert Browning (1846). Her early work includes her *Essay on Mind, and other Poems* which was published anonymously when she was 19. Her other writings include *Poems* (1884), translations of Aeschylus's *Prometheus Bound* (1833 and a new translation in her *Poems* of 1850), the long narrative poem *Aurora Leigh* (1856), *Sonnets from the Portuguese* (also published in *Poems*, 1850) which were not translations but express her own love, and *Casa Guidi Windows* (1851) on the theme of Italian Liberation. *Last Poems* was published posthumously in 1862.

88 Thou large-brained woman and large-hearted man.
   1844 *Poems*, 'To George Sand. A Desire', l.1.

89 And because I was a poet, and because the public praised me,
   With their critical deductions for the modern writer's fault;
   I could sit at rich men's tables,—though the courtesies that raise me,
   Still suggested clear between us, the pale spectrum of the salt.
   1844 *Poems*, 'Lady Geraldine's Courtship', stanza 9.

90 And the rolling anapaestic
   Curled, like vapour over shrines.
   1844 *Poems*, 'Wine of Cyprus', stanza 10.

91 I am floated along, as if I should die
   Of Liberty's exquisite pain.
   1849 'The Runaway Slave at Pilgrim's Point', stanza 36.

92 Straightway I was 'ware
   So weeping, how a mystic shape did move
   Behind me, and drew me backward by the hair
   And a voice said in mastery while I strove…
   'Guess now who holds thee!'—'*Death*', I said, but there
   The silver answer rang… 'Not Death, but Love.'
   1850 *Poems*, 'Sonnets from the Portuguese', sonnet 1.

93 If thou must love me, let it be for naught
   Except for love's sake only.
   1850 *Poems*, 'Sonnets from the Portuguese', sonnet 14.

94 When our two souls stand up erect and strong,
   Face to face, silent, drawing nigh and nigher,
   Until their lengthening wings break into fire
   At either curvèd point,…what bitter wrong,
   Can the earth do to us, that we should not long
   Be here contented?
   1850 *Poems*, 'Sonnets from the Portuguese', sonnet 22.

95 Let the world's sharpness like a clasping knife
   Shut in upon itself, and do no harm
   In this close hand of love.
   1850 *Poems*, 'Sonnets from the Portuguese', sonnet 24.

96 First time he kissed me, but only kissed
   The fingers of this hand wherewith I write,
   And ever since it grew more clean and white…
   1850 *Poems*, 'Sonnets from the Portuguese', sonnet 38.

97 How do I love thee? Let me count the ways!—
   I love thee to the depth and breadth and height
   My soul can reach, when feeling out of sight
   For the ends of Being and Ideal Grace.
   1850 *Poems*, 'Sonnets from the Portuguese', sonnet 43.

98 I love thee with the love I seemed to lose
   With my lost Saints,—I love thee with the breath
   Smiles, tears, of all my life!—and, if God choose,
   I shall but love thee better after death.
   1850 *Poems*, 'Sonnets from the Portuguese', sonnet 43.

99 God answers sharp and sudden on some prayers,
   And thrusts the thing we have prayed for in our face,
   A gauntlet with a gift in't.
   1856 *Aurora Leigh*, bk.2.

1 The music soars within the little lark,
   And the lark soars.
   1856 *Aurora Leigh*, bk.3.

2 Since when was genius found respectable?
   1856 *Aurora Leigh*, bk.6.

3 Earth's crammed with heaven,
   And every common bush afire with God.
   1856 *Aurora Leigh*, bk.7.

Browning, Guy 1964–
English writer and broadcaster.

4 A shoal of a million fish might not be able to write *Romeo and Juliet* but they can change direction as one in the blink of an eye. Using language a human team leader can giver an order to a team of six and have it interpreted in six completely different ways.
   1999 In *The Guardian*, 24 Jul.

5 Major cities are divided into two parts; the bits that are in the guidebook and the bits that aren't. If you don't take a guidebook, you'll see a different city.
   2002 In *The Guardian*, 21 May.

6 Maths is the purest science in that you don't need any test tubes or animal testing to do it. All the other sciences eventually boil down to maths, apart from biology, which boils down to soup.
   2004 In *The Guardian*, 19 Jun.

7 Men love women because they are the loveliest things on God's earth. Women love men because chocolate can't mow the lawn.
   2004 *Never Hit a Jellyfish with a Spade: How to Survive Life's Smaller Challenges.*

Browning, Robert 1812–89

English poet, who married Elizabeth Browning (1846). His poetry offers a wide range of characters, dramatic situations, and a rich variety of forms and rhythms. His work includes *Men and Women* (1855), *Dramatis Personae* (1864) and *The Ring and the Book* (1868–9).

8 God is the perfect poet,
   Who in his person acts his own creations.
   1835 *Paracelsus*, pt.2, l.648–9.

9 The year's at the spring,
   And days at the morn;
   Morning's at seven;
   The hill-side's dew-pearled;
   The lark's on the wing;
   The snail's on the thorn;
   God's in His heaven—
   All's right with the world.
   1841 *Pippa Passes*, pt.1.

10 Like a god going thro' his world there stands
   One mountain, for a moment in the dusk,
   Whole brotherhoods of cedars on its brow
   1841 *Pippa Passes*, pt.2.

11 There's a great text in Galatians,
   Once you trip on it, entails
   Twenty-nine distinct damnations,
   One sure, if another fails.
   1842 *Dramatic Lyrics*, 'Soliloquy of the Spanish Cloister'.

12 My scrofulous French novel
   On grey paper with blunt type!
   1842 *Dramatic Lyrics*, 'Soliloquy of the Spanish Cloister'.

13 The moth's kiss, first!
   Kiss me as if you made believe
   You were not sure, this eve,
   How my face, your flower, had pursed
   Its petals up.
   1842 *Dramatic Lyrics*, 'In a Gondola'.

14 What's become of Waring
   Since he gave us all the slip?
   1842 *Dramatic Lyrics*, 'Waring'. The first line was used as the title of a novel by Anthony Powell.

15 Hamelin Town's in Brunswick,
   By famous Hanover city;
   The river Weser, deep and wide,
   Washes its wall on the southern side;
   A pleasanter spot you never spied.
   1842 *Dramatic Lyrics*, 'The Pied Piper of Hamlin'.

16 Rats!
   They fought the dogs and killed the cats,
   And bit the babies in the cradles.
   And ate the cheeses out of the vats.
   1842 *Dramatic Lyrics*, 'The Pied Piper of Hamlin'.

17 I sprang to the stirrup, and Joris, and he;
   I galloped, Dirck galloped, we galloped all three.
   1845 *Dramatic Romances and Lyrics*, 'How they brought the Good News from Ghent to Aix'.

18 Just for a handful of silver he left us,
   Just for a riband to stick in his coat.
   1845 Of Wordsworth. *Dramatic Romances and Lyrics*, 'The Lost Leader'.

19 Never glad confident morning again!
   1845 *Dramatic Romances and Lyrics*, 'The Lost Leader'.

20 Oh, to be in England
   Now that April's there,
   And whoever wakes in England
   Sees, some morning, unaware,
   That the lowest boughs and the brushwood sheaf
   Round the elm-tree bole are in tiny leaf,
   While the chaffinch sings on the orchard bough
   In England—now!
   1845 *Dramatic Romances and Lyrics*, 'Home-Thoughts, from Abroad'.

21 That's the wise thrush; he sings each song twice over,
   Lest you think he never could recapture
   The first fine careless rapture!
   1845 *Dramatic Romances and Lyrics*, 'Home-Thoughts, from Abroad'.

22 'Here and here did England help me: how can I help England?'—say.
   1845 *Dramatic Romances and Lyrics*, 'Home-Thoughts, from the Sea'.

23 And then how I shall lie through centuries,
   And hear the blessed mutter of the mass,
   And see God made and eaten all day long,
   And feel the steady candle-flame, and taste
   Good strong thick stupefying incense-smoke!
   1845 *Dramatic Romances and Lyrics*, 'The Bishop Orders his Tomb'.

24 A tap at the pane, the quick sharp scratch
   And blue spurt of a lighted match,
   And a voice less loud, through its joys and fears,
   Than the two hearts beating each to each!
   1845 *Dramatic Romances and Lyrics*, 'Meeting at Night'.

25 There may be heaven; there must be hell.
   1845 *Dramatic Romances and Lyrics*, 'Time's Revenges'.

26 In the natural fog of the good man's mind.
   1850 'Christmas Eve'.

27 Where the quiet-coloured end of evening smiles,
   Miles and miles.
   1855 *Men and Women*, 'Love among the Ruins'.

28 If you get simple beauty and naught else,
   You get about the best thing God invents.
   1855 *Men and Women*, 'Fra Lippo Lippi'.

29 This world's no blot for us
   Nor blank; it means intensely, and means good:
   To find its meaning is my meat and drink.
   1855 *Men and Women*, 'Fra Lippo Lippi'.

30 Hark—the dominant's persistence till it must be answered to!
   1855 *Men and Women*, 'A Toccata of Galuppi's'.

31 What of soul was left, I wonder, when the kissing had to stop?
   1855 *Men and Women*, 'A Toccata of Galuppi's'.

32 Dear, dead woman, with such hair, too—what's become
ของ all the gold
Used to hang and brush their bosoms? I feel chilly and
grown old.
1855 *Men and Women*, 'A Toccata of Galuppi's'.

33 'Tis the Last Judgement's fire must cure this place,
Calcine its clods and set my prisoners free.
1855 *Men and Women*, 'Childe Roland to the Dark Tower Came'.

34 As for the grass, it grew as scant as hair in leprosy—thin
dried blades pricked the mud which underneath looked
kneaded up with blood.
One stiff blind horse, his every bone a-stare, stood stupefied.
1855 *Men and Women*, 'Childe Roland to the Dark Tower Came'.

35 I never saw a brute I hated so;
He must be wicked to deserve such pain.
1855 *Men and Women*, 'Childe Roland to the Dark Tower Came'.

36 It was roses, roses, all the way.
1855 *Men and Women*, 'The Patriot'.

37 And find a poor devil has ended his cares
At the foot of your rotten-runged rat-riddled stairs?
Do I carry the moon in my pocket?
1855 *Men and Women*, 'Master Hugues of Saxe-Gotha'.

38 Just when we are safest, there's a sunset-touch,
A fancy from a flower-bell, some one's death,
A chorus-ending from Euripides,—
And that's enough for fifty hopes and fears
As old and new at once as Nature's self,
To rap and knock and enter in our soul.
Take hands and dance there, a fantastic ring,
Round the ancient idol, on his base again,—
The grand Perhaps.
1855 *Men and Women*, 'Bishop Blougram's Apology'.

39 All we have gained then by our unbelief
Is a life of doubt diversified by faith,
For one of faith diversified by doubt:
We called the chess-board white,—we call it black.
1855 *Men and Women*, 'Bishop Blougram's Apology'.

40 You, for example, clever to a fault,
The rough and ready man who write apace,
Read somewhat seldomer, think perhaps even less.
1855 *Men and Women*, 'Bishop Blougram's Apology'.

41 No, when the fight begins within himself,
A man's worth something.
1855 *Men and Women*, 'Bishop Blougram's Apology'.

42 He said true things but called them by wrong names.
1855 *Men and Women*, 'Bishop Blougram's Apology'.

43 Ah, did you once see Shelley plain,
And did he stop to speak to you
And did you speak to him again?
How strange it seems, and new!
1855 *Men and Women*, 'Memorabilia'.

44 So free we seem, so fretted fast we are!
1855 *Men and Women*, 'Andrea del Sarto'.

45 Ah, but a man's reach should exceed his grasp,
Or what's a heaven for?
1855 *Men and Women*, 'Andrea del Sarto', l.97–8.

46 Your ghost will walk, you lover of trees,
(If love remains)
In an English lane.
1855 *Men and Women*, 'De Gustibus'.

47 Open your heart and you will see
graved inside of it, 'Italy.'
Such lovers old are I and she;
So it always was, so it still shall be!
1855 *Men and Women*, 'De Gustibus'.

48 Stand still, true poet that you are!
I know you; let me try and draw you.
Some night you'll fail us: when afar
You rise, remember one man saw you,
Knew you, and named a star!
1855 *Men and Women*, 'Popularity'.

49 I would that you were all to me,
You that are just so much, no more.
1855 *Men and Women*, 'Two in the Campagna'.

50 Only I discern—
Infinite passion, and the pain
Of finite hearts that yearn.
1855 *Men and Women*, 'Two in the Campagna'.

51 There they are, my fifty men and women
Naming me the fifty poems finished!
Take them, Love, the book and me together.
Where the heart lies, let the brain lie also.
1855 *Men and Women*, 'One Word More. To E.B.B.', stanza 1.

52 Suddenly, as rare things will, it vanished.
1855 *Men and Women*, 'One Word More. To E.B.B.', stanza 4.

53 Dante, who loved well because he hated,
Hated wickedness that hinders loving.
1855 *Men and Women*, 'One Word More. To E.B.B.', stanza 5.

54 Proves she like some portent of an iceberg
Swimming full upon the ship it founders
Hungry with huge teeth of splintered crystals?
1855 *Men and Women*, 'One Word More. To E.B.B.', stanza 17.

55 What's come to perfection perishes.
Things learned on earth, we shall practise in heaven.
Work done least rapidly, Art most cherishes.
1855 *Men and Women*, 'One Word More. To E.B.B.', stanza 17.

56 God be thanked, the meanest of his creatures
Boasts two soul-sides, one to face the world with,
One to show a woman when he loves her!
1855 *Men and Women*, 'One Word More. To E.B.B.', stanza 18.

57 Wrote one song—and in my brain I sing it,
Drew one angel—borne, see, on my bosom!
1855 *Men and Women*, 'One Word More. To E.B.B.', closing lines.

58 But God has a few of us to whom he whispers in the ear;
The rest may reason and welcome; 'tis we musicians
know.
1864 *Dramatis Personae*, 'Abt Vogler'.

59 Grow old along with me!
The best is yet to be,
The last of life, for which the first was made:
Our times are in His hand
Who saith, 'A whole I planned,
Youth shows but half; trust God:
See all nor be afraid!'
1864 *Dramatis Personae*, 'Rabbi ben Ezra', stanza 1.

60 Time's wheels runs back or stops: Potter and clay
endure.
1864 *Dramatis Personae*, 'Rabbi ben Ezra', stanza 27.

61 My times be in Thy hand!
Perfect the cup as planned!

Let age approve of youth, and
Death complete the same!
1864 *Dramatis Personae*, 'Rabbi ben Ezra', stanza 32.

62 Stung by the splendour of a sudden thought.
1864 *Dramatis Personae*, 'A Death in the Desert'.

63 For I say, this is death and the sole death,
When a man's loss comes to him from his gain,
Darkness from light, from knowledge ignorance,
And lack of love from love made manifest.
1864 *Dramatis Personae*, 'A Death in the Desert'.

64 Progress, man's distinctive mark alone,
Not God's, and not the beasts'; God is, they are,
Man partly is and wholly hopes to be.
1864 *Dramatis Personae*, 'A Death in the Desert'.

65 And it is good to cheat the pair, and gibe,
Letting the rank tongue blossom into speech.
Setebos, Setebos, and Setebos!
Thinketh, He dwelleth i' the cold o' the moon.
Thinketh He made it, with the sun to match,
But not the stars; the stars came otherwise.
1864 *Dramatis Personae*, 'Caliban upon Setebos', stanza 1.

66 Let twenty pass, and stone the twenty-first,
Loving not, hating not, just choosing so.
1864 *Dramatis Personae*, 'Caliban upon Setebos', stanza 1.

67 We loved, sir—used to meet:
How sad and bad and mad it was—
But then, how it was sweet!
1864 *Dramatis Personae*, 'Confessions', stanza 9.

68 There's more hateful form of foolery—
The social sage's, Solomon of saloons
And philosophic diner-out.
1864 *Dramatis Personae*, 'Mr Sludge, The Medium', stanza 1.

69 Well, British Public, ye who like me not,
(God love you!)
1868–9 *The Ring and the Book*, bk.1, l.410

70 'Go get you manned by Manning and new-manned
By Newman and, mayhap, wise-manned to boot
By Wiseman.'
1868–9 *The Ring and the Book*, bk.1, l.444–6.

71 Youth means love,
Vows can't change nature, priests are only men.
1868–9 *The Ring and the Book*, bk.1, l.1056–7.

72 O lyric love half angel and half bird
And all a wonder and a wild desire.
1868–9 *The Ring and the Book*, bk.1, l.1391–2.

73 In the great right of an excessive wrong.
1868–9 *The Ring and the Book*, bk.3, l.1055.

74 Faultless to a fault.
1868–9 *The Ring and the Book*, bk.9, l.1175.

75 Why comes temptation but for a man to meet
And master and make crouch beneath his foot,
And so be pedestalled in triumph?
1868–9 *The Ring and the Book*, bk.10, l.1184–6.

76 White shall not neutralize the black, nor good
Compensate bad in man, absolve him so:
Life's business being just the terrible choice.
1868–9 *The Ring and the Book*, bk.10, l.1235–7.

77 There's a new tribunal now
Higher than God's,—the educated man's!
1868–9 *The Ring and the Book*, bk.10, l.1975–6.

78 Into that sad obscure sequestered state
Where God unmakes but to remake the soul
He else made first in vain; which must not be.
1868–9 *The Ring and the Book*, bk.10, l.2129–31.

79 It is the glory and good of Art,
That Art remains the one way possible
Of speaking truth, to mouths like mine, at least.
1868–9 *The Ring and the Book*, bk.12, l.838–40.

80 But, thanks to wine-less and democracy,
We've still our stage where truth calls spade a spade!
1875 'Aristophanes' Apology', stanza 1.

81 Ignorance is not innocence but sin.
1875 *The Inn Album*, canto 5.

82 I want to know a butcher paints,
A baker rhymes for his pursuit,
Candlestick-maker much acquaints
His soul with song, or, haply mute,
Blows out his brains upon the flute.
1876 'Shop', stanza 21.

83 Good, to forgive;
Best, to forget!
Living, we fret;
Dying, we live.
1878 *La Saisiaz*, prologue.

84 At midnight in the silence of the sleep-time,
When you set your fancies free.
1889 *Asolando*, epilogue.

85 One who never turned his back but marched breast
   forward,
Never doubted clouds would break,
Never dreamed, though right were worsted, wrong
   would triumph,
Held we fall to rise, are baffled to fight better,
Sleep to wake.
1889 *Asolando*, epilogue.

86 Greet the unseen with a cheer!
1889 *Asolando*, epilogue.

Broyard, Anatole 1920–90
Literary critic, writer and editor at the *New York Times*.

87 She has always ridden the passions as if they were a
   magnificent horse.
1978 On Edna O'Brien. In the *New York Times*, 1 Jan.

88 Such a fatigue of adjectives, a drone of alliterations, a
   huffing of hyphenated words hurdling the meter like
   tired horses. Such a faded upholstery of tears, stars, bells,
   bones, flood and blood…a thud of consonants in
   tongue, night, dark, dust, seed, wound and wind.
1974 On Dylan Thomas's poetry. *Aroused by Books*.

89 I remember a table in *Barchester Towers* that had more
   character than the combined heroes of three recent
   novels I've read.
1974 *Aroused by Books*.

90 When Harriet goes to bed with a man, she always takes
   her wet blanket with her.
1974 On a character in Iris Owen's *After Claude* (1973). *Aroused by Books*.

91 Chic is a convent for unloved women.
1988 In the *New York Times*, 10 Jan.

Brummel, George Bryan called Beau Brummell
1778–1840

English dandy, a leader of 19c fashionable society. A close friend of the Prince Regent (later George IV), he quarrelled with him in 1813, and was later forced to flee to Calais with gambling debts. He died a pauper in a lunatic asylum.

92 Who's your fat friend?
> c.1813 Of the Prince Regent. Remark addressed to his companion, whom the Prince had acknowledged while studiously ignoring Brummell. Quoted in Jesse *Life of George Brummell* (1844), vol.1.

Brunet, Michel 1917–85
Canadian historian.

93 The thing which amazes me is that I know perfectly well, as a historian, that there is corruption in any government—there's always corruption. It's bad when it's more than fifteen percent.
> Interviewed by Ramsay Cook in Eleanor Cook (ed) *The Craft of History* (1973).

Brunner, John Kilian Houston 1934–95
English science-fiction writer, an important contributor to the more literary aspirations of the genre. *Stand On Zanzibar* (1969) is his best-known work.

94 POPULATION EXPLOSION Unique in human experience, an event which happened yesterday but which everyone swears won't happen until tomorrow.
> 1969 *Stand On Zanzibar*, 'The Hipcrime Vocab'.

Bruno, Frank(lin Roy) 1961–
English boxer. He won the European heavyweight title in 1985, and the World Championship in 1995.

95 Know what I mean, Harry?
> Catchphrase, addressed to sports commentator Harry Carpenter.

Bryan, Richard H(udson) 1937–
US politician, Governor of Nevada (1983–9) and Senator (1989–2001).

96 Being chairman of the Senate Ethics Committee is like jumping off a cliff. The thrill is very short.
> 1993 NPR broadcast, 2 Nov.

Bryan, William Jennings 1860–1925
US lawyer, Democratic politician and pacifist. Elected to Congress in 1890, he ran unsuccessfully in two presidential elections (1896, 1900). Appointed Secretary of State by Woodrow Wilson (1913), he resigned in 1915 over the USA's second *Lusitania* note to Germany.

97 There are two ideas of government. There are those who believe that, if you will only legislate to make the well-to-do prosperous, their prosperity will leak through on those below. The Democratic idea, however, has been that if you legislate to make the masses prosperous, their prosperity will find its way up through every class which rests upon them.
> 1896 Speech at the Democratic National Convention, 10 Jul.

98 What shall we say of the intelligence, not to say religion, of those who are so particular to distinguish between fishes and reptiles and birds, but put a man with an immortal soul in the same circle with the wolf, the hyena, and the skunk? What must be the impression made upon children by such a degradation of man?
> Statement issued in Dayton, Tennessee, 28 Jul 1925, by Mrs W J Bryan, shortly after the end of the Scopes trial and her husband's death.

Bryant, David 1931–
English bowls player. He was the World Singles Champion in 1966, 1980 and 1988.

99 I'm not an athlete, more a gymnast and golfer, soldered together.
> Quoted in Colin Jarman *The Guinness Dictionary of Sports Quotations* (1990).

1 Bowls is a young man's game which old men can play.
> Quoted in Colin Jarman *The Guinness Dictionary of Sports Quotations* (1990).

Bryant, William Cullen 1794–1878
US writer and journalist. Originally a lawyer, after the success of *Thanatopsis* (1817) he turned increasingly to prose and verse writing, becoming editor of the New York *Evening Post* (1829).

2 All that tread
The globe are but a handful to the tribes
That slumber in its bosom.
> 1817 'Thanatopsis', in the *North American Review*, Sep.

3 These are the gardens of the Desert, these
The unshorn fields, boundless and beautiful,
For which the speech of England has no name—
The Prairies.
> 1832 *Poems*, 'The Prairies'.

Bryson, Bill 1951–
US author, particularly known for his humorous travel memoirs.

4 My mother only ever said two things. She said, 'I don't know, dear.' And she said, 'Can I get you a sandwich, honey?'
> 1989 *The Lost Continent*, ch.1.

5 There are three things you just can't do in life. You can't beat the phone company, you can't make a waiter see you until he's ready to see you, and you can't go home again.
> 1989 *The Lost Continent*, ch.2.

6 It sometimes occurs to me that the British have more heritage than is good for them.
> 1995 *Notes from a Small Island*.

7 I have a small tattered clipping that I sometimes carry with me and pull out for purposes of private amusement. It's a weather forecast from the *Western Daily Mail* and it says, in toto: 'Outlook: Dry and warm, but cooler with some rain.'
> 1995 *Notes from a Small Island*.

8 Hunters will tell you that a moose is a wily and ferocious forest creature. In fact, a moose is a cow drawn by a three-year-old.
> 1998 *Notes from a Big Country*.

9 He was the only person in American history for whom attaining the White House was a bad career move.
> 1998 On Herbert Hoover. *Notes from a Big Country*.

10 In the first three months of this year the US edition of *Time* did not have a single report from France, Italy, Spain or Japan, to name just a few of the countries that seem to have escaped its notice.
> 1998 *Notes from a Big Country*.

11 According to an opinion poll, 13 per cent of women in the United States cannot say whether they wear their tights under their knickers or over them. That's something like a million women walking around in a state of chronic foundation garment uncertainty.
1998 *Notes from a Big Country.*

12 Not one of your pertinent ancestors was squashed, devoured, drowned, starved, stranded, stuck fast, untimely wounded, or otherwise deflected from its life's quest of delivering a tiny charge of genetic material to the right partner at the right moment in order to perpetuate the only possible sequence of hereditary combinations that could result—eventually, astoundingly, and all too briefly—in you.
2003 *A Short History of Nearly Everything.*

13 There are three stages in scientific discovery. First, people deny that it is true, then they deny that it is important; finally they credit the wrong person.
2003 *A Short History of Nearly Everything.*

14 Protons give an atom its identity, electrons its personality.
2003 *A Short History of Nearly Everything.*

15 Physics is really nothing more than a search for ultimate simplicity, but so far all we have is a kind of elegant messiness.
2003 *A Short History of Nearly Everything.*

16 There seemed to be a mystifying universal conspiracy among textbook authors to make certain the material they dealt with never strayed too near the realm of the mildly interesting and was always at least a long-distance phone call from the frankly interesting.
2003 *A Short History of Nearly Everything.*

17 Energy is liberated matter, matter is energy waiting to happen.
2003 *A Short History of Nearly Everything.*

18 Geologists are never at a loss for paperweights.
2003 *A Short History of Nearly Everything.*

19 Nearly a quarter of American men were in the Armed forces. The rest were in school, in prison, or were George W. Bush.
2006 Recalling 1968 in *The Life and Times of the Thunderbolt Kid.*

Buber, Martin 1878–1965

Austrian Jewish theologian and philosopher, founding editor of *Der Jude* (1916–24, 'The Jew'), known for his important studies in Hasidism and Existentialism. Professor at Frankfurt (1923–33), he fled Germany for Palestine in 1938, becoming Professor of the Sociology of Religion in Jerusalem.

20 Egos appear by setting themselves apart from other egos. Persons appear by entering into relation with other persons.
1923 *Ich und Du* (translated by R G Smith as *I and Thou*, 1936).

21 *Jedes geeinzelte Du ist ein Durchblick zu ihm. Durch jedes geeinzelte Du spricht das Grundwort das Ewige an.*
Every particular *Thou* is a glimpse through to the eternal *Thou*; by means of every particular *Thou* the primary word addresses the eternal *Thou.*
1923 *Ich und Du* (translated by R G Smith as *I and Thou*, 1936).

Buchan, John, 1st Baron Tweedsmuir 1875–1940

Scottish author and statesman, best known for his fast-moving adventure stories, particularly *The Thirty-Nine Steps* (1915). He was Governor-General of Canada from 1935 until his death.

22 You think that a wall as solid as the earth separates civilisation from barbarism. I tell you the division is a thread, a sheet of glass.
1916 *The Power-House,* ch.3, 'Tells of a Midsummer Night'.

23 Civilisation is a conspiracy.
1916 *The Power-House,* ch.3, 'Tells of a Midsummer Night'.

24 It's a great life if you don't weaken.
1919 *Mr Standfast,* ch.5.

25 Look at the Irish! They are the cleverest propagandists extant, and managed to persuade most people that they were a brave, generous, humorous, talented, warm-hearted race, cruelly yoked to a dull mercantile England, when, God knows, they were exactly the opposite.
1924 *The Three Hostages.*

26 To live for a time close to great minds is the best kind of education.
1940 *Memory Hold-the-Door,* ch.2.

27 An atheist is a man who has no invisible means of support.
1943 Quoted in H E Fosdick *On Being a Real Person,* ch.10.

Buchanan, James 1791–1868

US statesman and 15th President (1857–61). A Democrat, he tried to maintain a balance between pro-slavery and anti-slavery factions, but was unable to avert the Civil War (1861–5).

28 All the friends that I loved and wanted to reward are dead, and all the enemies that I hated and I had marked out for punishment are turned to my friends.
1857 On finally achieving his country's highest political office at the age of 65.

29 If you are as happy, my dear Sir, on entering this house as I am on leaving it and returning home, you are the happiest man in the country.
1861 Said on welcoming his successor, Abraham Lincoln, to the White House.

Buchman, Sidney 1902–75

US film writer and producer. His films include *Mr Smith Goes to Washington* (1939), *Here Comes Mr Jordan* (1941) and *The Group* (1966).

30 I wouldn't give you two cents for all your fancy rules if, behind them, they didn't have a little bit of plain, ordinary kindness—and a little looking out for the other fella, too.
1939 Line delivered by James Stewart in *Mr Smith Goes to Washington.*

Buchwald, Art 1925–2007

US writer and humorist. He won a Pulitzer Prize for outstanding commentary (1982).

31 This is not an easy time for humorists because the government is far funnier than we are.
1987 Speech to international meeting of satirists and cartoonists. Reported in the *New York Times,* 28 Jun.

Buck, Gene (Edward Eugene) 1885–1957

US songwriter.

32 That Shakespearian rag,—
Most intelligent, very elegant.
1912 'That Shakespearian Rag' (with Herman Ruby).
▶ See Eliot 318:1.

Buck, Pearl née Sydenstricker 1892–1973
US novelist, brought up in China and later a teacher and missionary there. Her works include *The Good Earth* (1931), set in China. She won the Nobel prize for literature in 1938.

33 Race prejudice is not only a shadow over the colored—it is a shadow over all of us, and the shadow is darkest over those who feel it least and allow its evil effects to go on.
   1943 *What America Means To Me*, ch.1.

34 None who have always been free can understand the terrible fascinating power of the hope of freedom to those who are not free.
   1943 *What America Means To Me*, ch.4.

35 Every great mistake has a halfway moment, a split second when it can be recalled and perhaps remedied.
   1943 *What America Means To Me*, ch.10.

36 Praise out of season, or tactlessly bestowed, can freeze the heart as much as blame.
   1967 *To My Daughters, With Love*, 'First Meeting'.

37 Nothing and no one can destroy the Chinese people. They are relentless survivors... They yield, they bend to the wind, but they never break.
   1972 *China, Past and Present*, ch.1.

Bucke, Richard Maurice 1837–1902
Canadian psychiatrist and author. His works include *Cosmic Consciousness: A Study in the Evolution of the Human Mind* (1901).

38 Cosmic consciousness.
   1894 Phrase first used in a paper read by Bucke to the American Medico-Psychological Association, Philadelphia, 18 May. He defined it as 'a higher form of consciousness than that possessed by the ordinary man'.

Buckingham, George Villiers, 2nd Duke of 1628–87
English statesman, exiled after the Royalist defeat in the Civil War. He became a member of Charles II's cabal after the Restoration, and was instrumental in Clarendon's downfall (1667), but lost power and was dismissed in 1674.

39 Ay, now the plot thickens very much upon us.
   1672 *The Rehearsal*, act 3, sc.1.

40 The world is made up for the most part of fools and knaves.
   'To Mr Clifford, on his *Humane Reason*', collected in *The Dramatic Works* (1715), vol.2.

Buechner, (Carl) Frederick 1926–
US clergyman, novelist, poet and essayist. His works include *Lion Country* (1971) and *Godric* (1980).

41 Glory is to God what style is to an artist... To behold God's glory, to sense his style, is the closest you can get this side of Paradise, just as to read King Lear is the closest you can get to Shakespeare.
   1973 *Wishful Thinking*.

42 There is no event so commonplace but that God is present in it, always hiddenly, always leaving you room to recognize him or not to recognize him... Listen to your life. See it for the fathomless mystery it is. In the boredom and pain of it no less than in the excitement and gladness: touch, taste, smell your way to the heavenly and hidden heart of it because in the last analysis all moments are key moments, and life itself is grace.
   1983 *Now and Then*.

43 Here is the world. Beautiful and terrible things will happen. Don't be afraid.
   2004 *Beyond Words: Daily Readings in the ABC's of Faith*.

Buffett, Warren Edward 1930–
US investment broker and corporate executive.

44 It is better to be approximately right than precisely wrong.
   1994 In *Fortune*, 4 Apr.

45 This is all happening because my father didn't buy me a train set as a kid.
   2009 Comment on purchasing the Burlington Northern Santa Fe railroad for $26 billion.

46 I made my first investment at age eleven. I was wasting my life up until then.
   2009 *The Tao of Warren Buffet*.

47 Rule No.1: Never lose money. Rule No.2: Never forget rule No.1.
   2009 *The Tao of Warren Buffet*.

48 My friends and I have been coddled long enough by a billionaire-friendly Congress.
   2011 Proposing a higher tax rate for the very wealthy.

49 I'm ready for another elephant. Please, if you see any walking by, just call me.
   2013 After bidding successfully for Heinz, CNBC interview.

Buford, Bill (William Holmes) 1954–
US-born editor and writer who has spent much of his career in Britain. He edited *Granta* (1979–95), then moved to the *New Yorker* as Fiction and Literary Editor (1995–2002) and became its European Correspondent in 2002.

50 I found myself growing increasingly irritated with the notion of a British novel, which was really an irritation with the word British, a grey, unsatisfactory, bad-weather kind of word, a piece of linguistic compromise.
   1994 Editorial, *Granta*, no.43.

51 You can't do traditional work at a modern pace. Traditional work has traditional rhythms. You need calm. You can be busy, but you must remain calm.
   2006 *Heat: An Amateur's Adventures as Kitchen Slave, Line Cook, Pasta-Maker, and Apprentice to a Dante-Quoting Butcher in Tuscany*.

52 The most important knowledge is understanding what you can't do.
   2006 *Heat: An Amateur's Adventures as Kitchen Slave, Line Cook, Pasta-Maker, and Apprentice to a Dante-Quoting Butcher in Tuscany*.

Bukowski, Charles 1920–94
German-born US poet and writer. His spare, sardonic writing evoked a seamy, low-life urban netherworld in poems, short stories and novels.

53 Show me a man who lives alone and has a perpetually clean kitchen, and 8 times out of 9 I'll show you a man with detestable spiritual qualities.
   1967 *Tales of Ordinary Madness*, 'Too Sensitive'.

54 You begin saving the world by saving one man at a time; all else is grandiose romanticism or politics.
  1967 *Tales of Ordinary Madness*, 'Too Sensitive'.

55 Erections, Ejaculations, Exhibitions and General Tales of Ordinary Madness.
  1972 Title of book.

56 Love is a Dog from Hell.
  1977 Title of book.

57 Play the Piano Drunk Like a Percussion Instrument Until the Fingers Begin to Bleed a Bit.
  1979 Title of book.

Buller, A(rthur) H(enry) Reginald 1874–1944

Canadian botanist, Professor of Botany at the University of Manitoba.

58 There was a young lady named Bright
  Whose speed was far faster than light;
  She set out one day
  In a relative way
  And returned on the previous night.
  1923 'Relativity', published anonymously in *Punch*, 19 Dec. Buller's claim to authorship is recorded in W S Baring-Gould *The Lure of the Limerick* (1968).

Bullock, Alan Louis Charles, Baron Bullock 1914–2004

British historian, notably of 20c Europe. He was Master of St Catherine's College, Oxford (1960–80).

59 Hitler showed surprising loyalty to Mussolini, but it never extended to trusting him.
  1952 *Hitler: A Study in Tyranny*.

60 The people Hitler never understood, and whose actions continued to exasperate him to the end of his life, were the British.
  1952 *Hitler: A Study in Tyranny*.

Bulmer-Thomas, Ivor 1905–93

British politician and writer. He joined *The Times* (1930–7) and was later deputy editor of the *Daily Telegraph* (1953–4). He entered parliament as a Labour MP in 1942, turning Conservative in 1949.

61 If he ever went to school without any boots, it was because he was too big for them.
  1949 At the Conservative Party conference, responding to remarks by Harold Wilson about his humble upbringing.
  ▶ See Wilson 948:58.

Bülow, Prince Bernhard Heinrich von 1849–1929

German statesman, Chancellor (1900–9), Foreign Secretary (1897), Count (1899) and Prince (1905). He wrote *Imperial Germany* (translated 1916) and *Memoirs* (translated 1931–2).

62 *Mit einem Worte: wir wollen niemand in den Schatten stellen aber wir verlangen auch unseren Platz an der Sonne.*
  In a word, we desire to throw no one into the shade, but we also demand our own place in the sun.
  1897 Speech to the Reichstag, 6 Dec.

Bulwer-Lytton, Edward George Lytton, 1st Baron Lytton 1803–73

English writer and politician, known for historical novels such as *The Last Days of Pompeii* (1834), poetry and several plays. A Reform MP (1831–41), he returned as a Conservative in 1852.

63 It was a dark and stormy night.
  1830 Opening words of *Paul Clifford*.

64 Beneath the rule of men entirely great, the pen is mightier than the sword.
  1839 *Richelieu*, act 2, sc.2.

Bunting, Basil 1900–85

English poet. He was encouraged by Pound and worked with Ford Madox Ford on *The Transatlantic Review*, but never found a wide audience. The long poem *Briggflatts* (1966) is his best-known work.

65 Our doom
  is, to be sifted by the wind,

  heaped up, smoothed down like silly sands.
  We are less permanent than thought.
  1925 *Villon*, pt.1.

66 Name and date
  split in soft slate
  a few months obliterate.
  1966 *Briggflatts*.

67 It looks well enough on the page, but never well enough.
  1966 *Briggflatts*.

68 Clear Cymric voices carry well this Autumn night,
  Aneurin and Taliesin, cruel owls
  for whom it is never altogether dark
  before the rules made poetry a pedant's game.
  1966 *Briggflatts*.

69 Who
  swinging his axe
  to fell kings,
  guesses
  where we go?
  1966 *Briggflatts*, coda.

Buñuel, Luis 1900–83

Spanish film director, who was successful with early surrealist experiments in collaboration with Dalí. *His work is characterized by a poetic, often erotic, use of imagery, black humour and a hatred of Catholicism.*

70 *Grâce à Dieu, je suis toujours athée.*
  Thanks be to God, I am still an atheist.
  1959 In *Le Monde*, 16 Dec.

71 *Le Charme discret de la bourgeoisie.*
  The Discreet Charm of the Bourgeoisie.
  1972 Title of film.

Bunyan, John 1628–88

English writer and preacher. His father was a tinker and he received little formal education. His works, including an autobiography *Grace Abounding to the Chief of Sinners* (1666) and probably most of *The Pilgrim's Progress* (1st part 1678, 2nd part 1684), were written while imprisoned for nonconformity.

72 Oh, the diligence of Satan! Oh, the desperateness of man's heart!
  1666 *Grace Abounding to the Chief of Sinners*.

73 This miry slough, is such a place as cannot be mended: It is the descent whither the scum and filth that attends

conviction for sin doth continually run, and therefore is it called the Slough of Despond.
1678 *The Pilgrim's Progress*, pt.1.

74 The valley of Humiliation.
1678 *The Pilgrim's Progress*, pt.1.

75 It beareth the name of Vanity-Fair, because the town where 'tis kept, is lighter than vanity.
1678 *The Pilgrim's Progress*, pt.1.

76 Hanging is too good for him, said Mr Cruelty.
1678 *The Pilgrim's Progress*, pt 1.

77 Now Giant Despair had a wife, and her name was Diffidence.
1678 *The Pilgrim's Progress*, pt.1.

78 Sleep is sweet to the labouring man.
1678 *The Pilgrim's Progress*, pt.1.

79 So I awoke, and behold it was a dream.
1678 *The Pilgrim's Progress*, pt.1.

80 A man that could look no way but downwards, with a muckrake in his hand.
1684 *The Pilgrim's Progress*, pt.2.

81 For though when he was here, he was Fool in every man's mouth, yet now he is gone he is highly commended of all.
1684 *The Pilgrim's Progress*, pt.2.

82 He that is down needs fear no fall,
He that is low no pride.
He that is humble ever shall
Have God to be his guide.
1684 *The Pilgrim's Progress*, pt.2.

83 My Sword, I give to him that shall succeed me in my Pilgrimage, and my Courage and Skill, to him that can get it. My Marks and Scars I carry with me, to be a witness for me, that I have fought his Battles, who now will be my Rewarder... As he went, he said, Death, where is thy Sting? And as he went down deeper, he said, Grave where is thy Victory? So he passed over, and the Trumpets sounded for him on the other side.
1684 Mr Valiant-for-Glory. *The Pilgrim's Progress*, pt.2.

84 He that lives in sin and looks for happiness hereafter is like him that soweth cockle and thinks to fill his barn with wheat or barley.
1684 *The Pilgrim's Progress*, pt.2.

Burbank, Luther 1849–1926
US plant breeder and natural scientist.

85 Science is knowledge arranged and classified according to truth, facts, and the general laws of nature.
1926 Interview in the *San Francisco Bulletin*, 22 Jan.

Burchard, Samuel Dickinson 1812–91
US Presbyterian minister and staunch Republican supporter.

86 The party whose antecedents are rum, Romanism, and rebellion.
1884 Of the Democratic party. Speech at the Fifth Avenue Hotel, NewYork City, 29 Oct.

Burgess, Anthony *real name* John Anthony Burgess Wilson 1917–94
English writer. He is widely regarded as among the most important novelists of his generation, notably for his controversial dystopian novel *A Clockwork Orange* (1962).

87 Who ever heard of a clockwork orange? Then I read a malenky bit out loud in a sort of very high type preaching goloss: 'The attempt to impose upon man, a creature of growth and capable of sweetness, to ooze juicily at the last round the bearded lips of God, to attempt to impose, I say, laws and conditions appropriate to a mechanical creation, against this I raise my sword-pen.'
1962 *A Clockwork Orange*.

88 He said it was artificial respiration, but now I find I am to have his child.
1963 *Inside Mr Enderby*, pt.1, ch.4.

89 Bath twice a day to be really clean, once a day to be passably clean, once a week to avoid being a public menace.
1963 *Inside Mr Enderby*, pt.2, ch.1.

90 Rome's just a city like anywhere else. A vastly overrated city, I'd say. It trades on belief just as Stratford trades on Shakespeare.
1963 *Inside Mr Enderby*, pt.2, ch.1.

91 *Pax Romana*. Where they made a desolation they called it a peace. What absolute nonsense! It was a nasty, vulgar sort of civilization, only dignified by being hidden under a lot of declensions.
1963 *Inside Mr Enderby*, pt.2, ch.2.

92 Keep away from physicians. It is all probing and guessing and pretending to them. They leave it to Nature to cure in her own time, but they take the credit. As well as very fat fees.
1964 *Nothing Like the Sun*.

93 The possession of a book becomes a substitute for reading it.
1966 In the *New York Times Book Review*, 4 Dec.

94 A sure sign of an amateur is too much detail to compensate for too little life.
1971 In the *Times Literary Supplement*, 18 Jun.

95 Death comes along like a gas bill one can't pay—and that's all one can say about it.
1974 Interview in *Playboy*.

96 There is usually something wrong with writers the young like.
1974 Interview in *Playboy*.

97 It was the afternoon of my eighty-first birthday, and I was in bed with my catamite when Ali announced that the archbishop had come to see me.
1980 *Earthly Powers*, opening lines.

98 Reality is what I see, not what you see.
1983 In the *Sunday Times Magazine*, 18 Dec.

99 God was good on the physical and emotional sides and a great one for hate. He generously spilled his own hate into his dearest creation.
1984 *Enderby's Dark Lady*.

1 If Freud had worn a kilt in the prescribed Highland manner he might have had a very different attitude to genitals.
1986 In the *Observer*, 24 Aug.

2 Death, like the quintessence of otherness, is for others.
1987 *Little Wilson and Big God*, ch.6.

3 Music says nothing to the reason: it is a kind of closely structured nonsense.
1989 In the *Observer*, 23 Jul.

4 I could see now that a literary education did not fit one for the popular novelist's trade. Once you had started using words like flavicomous or acroamatic, because you liked the sound of them, you were lost.
1990 *You've Had Your Time*, ch.1.

Burgon, John William 1813–88
English cleric, Dean of Chichester from 1876.

5 Match me such marvel, save in Eastern clime,—
A rose-red city—'half as old as Time'!
1845 *Petra*.

Burke, Edmund 1729–97
Anglo-Irish statesman and political philosopher. He became Secretary for Ireland (1759) and an MP (1765). His works include *Reflections on the French Revolution* (1790).

6 No passion so effectually robs the mind of all its powers of acting than fear.
1757 *On the Sublime and Beautiful*, pt.2, section 2.

7 Custom reconciles us to everything.
1757 *On the Sublime and Beautiful*, pt.4, section 18.

8 It is a general popular error to imagine the loudest complainers for the public to be the most anxious for its welfare.
1769 *Observations on a Late Publication on the Present State of the Nation*, 2nd edn.

9 To complain of the age we live in, to murmur at the present possessors of power, to lament the past, to conceive extravagant hopes of the future, are the common dispositions of the greatest part of mankind.
1770 *Thoughts on the Cause of the Present Discontents*.

10 When bad men combine, the good must associate; else they will fall, one by one, an unpitied sacrifice in a contemptible struggle.
1770 *Thoughts on the Cause of the Present Discontents*.

11 It is therefore our business carefully to cultivate in our minds, to rear to the most perfect vigour and maturity, every sort of generous and honest feeling that belongs to our nature. To bring the dispositions that are loved in private life into the service and conduct of the commonwealth; so to be patriots, as not to forget we are gentlemen.
1770 *Thoughts on the Cause of the Present Discontents*.

12 The greater the power, the more dangerous is the abuse.
1771 *Speech on the Middlesex Election, House of Commons*, 7 Feb.

13 Parliament is a deliberative assembly of one nation. You choose a Member indeed; but when you have chosen him, he is not the Member for Bristol, but he is a Member of Parliament.
1774 *Speech to Bristol voters*.

14 The concessions of the weak are the concessions of fear.
1775 *On Conciliation with America*.

15 The use of force alone is but temporary. It may subdue for a moment; but it does not remove the necessity of subduing again; and a nation is not governed, which is perpetually to be conquered.
1775 *On Conciliation with America*.

16 Nothing less will content me, than *whole America*.
1775 *On Conciliation with America*.

17 All Protestantism, even the most cold and passive, is a sort of dissent. But the religion most prevalent in our northern colonies is a refinement on the principle of resistance; it is the dissidence of dissent, and the Protestantism of the Protestant religion.
1775 *On Conciliation with America*.

18 It is not, what a lawyer tells me I may do; but what humanity, reason, and justice, tells me I ought to do.
1775 *On Conciliation with America*.

19 Freedom and not servitude is the cure of anarchy; as religion, and not atheism, is the true remedy for superstition.
1775 *On Conciliation with America*.

20 Slavery they can have anywhere. It is a weed that grows in every soil.
1775 *On Conciliation with America*.

21 It is the love of the people; it is their attachment to their government, from the sense of the deep stake they have in such a glorious institution, which gives you your army and your navy, and infuses into both that liberal obedience, without which your army would be a base rabble, and your navy nothing but rotten timber.
1775 *On Conciliation with America*.

22 A great empire and little minds go ill together.
1775 *On Conciliation with America*.

23 All government, indeed every human benefit and enjoyment, every virtue and every prudent act, is founded on compromise and barter.
1775 *On Conciliation with America*.

24 Between craft and credulity, the voice of reason is stifled.
1777 *Letter to the Sheriffs of Bristol*.

25 Liberty too must be limited in order to be possessed.
1777 *Letter to the Sheriffs of Bristol*.

26 Among a people generally corrupt, liberty cannot long exist.
1777 *Letter to the Sheriffs of Bristol*.

27 If any man ask me what a free government is, I answer that for any practical purpose, it is what the people think it so.
1777 *Letter to the Sheriffs of Bristol*.

28 People crushed by law have no hope but from power. If laws are their enemies, they will be enemies to laws; and those, who have much to hope and nothing to lose, will always be dangerous, more or less.
1777 Letter to Charles James Fox, 8 Oct.

29 Individuals pass like shadows, but the Commonwealth is fixed and stable.
1780 Speech, House of Commons, 11 Feb.

30 The people are the masters.
1780 Speech, House of Commons, 11 Feb.

31 Bad laws are the worst sort of tyranny.
1780 Speech, Bristol.

32 He was not merely a chip off the old block, but the old block itself.
1781 Commenting on William Pitt the Younger's maiden speech in the House of Commons, 26 Feb.

33 The people never give up their liberties but under some delusion.
1784 Speech, Buckinghamshire.

34 Whenever our neighbour's house is on fire, it cannot be amiss for the engines to play a little on our own.
1790 Reflections on the Revolution in France.

35 A state without the means of some change is without the means of its conservation.
1790 Reflections on the Revolution in France.

36 People will not look forward to posterity, who never look backward to their ancestors.
1790 Reflections on the Revolution in France.

37 Those who attempt to level never equalize.
1790 Reflections on the Revolution in France.

38 Whatever each man can separately do, without trespassing upon others, he has a right to do for himself; and he has a right to a fair portion of all which society, with all its combination of skill and force, can do in his favour.
1790 Reflections on the Revolution in France.

39 Government is a contrivance of human wisdom to provide for human wants.
1790 Reflections on the Revolution in France.

40 The age of chivalry is gone.—That of sophisters, economists, and calculators, has succeeded; and the glory of Europe is extinguished for ever.
1790 Reflections on the Revolution in France.

41 The unbought grace of life, the cheap defence of nations, the nurse of manly sentiment and heroic enterprise is gone! it is gone, that sensibility of
principle, that chastity of honour, which felt a stain like a wound, which ennobled whatever it touched, and under which vice itself lost half its evil, by losing all its grossness.
1790 Reflections on the Revolution in France.

42 In the groves of their academy, at the end of every vista, you see nothing but the gallows.
1790 Reflections on the Revolution in France.

43 Kings will be tyrants from policy when subjects are rebels from principle.
1790 Reflections on the Revolution in France.

44 Man is by his constitution a religious animal; atheism is against not only our reason, but our instincts.
1790 Reflections on the Revolution in France.

45 Society is indeed a contract...it becomes a partnership not only between those who are living, but between those who are living, those who are dead, and those who are to be born.
1790 Reflections on the Revolution in France.

46 Superstition is the religion of feeble minds.
1790 Reflections on the Revolution in France.

47 Our patience will achieve more than our force.
1790 Reflections on the Revolution in France.

48 By hating vices too much, they come to love men too little.
1790 Reflections on the Revolution in France.

49 We begin our public affection in our families. No cold relation is a zealous citizen.
1790 Reflections on the Revolution in France.

50 Good order is the foundation of all good things.
1790 Reflections on the Revolution in France.

51 The only infallible criterion of wisdom to vulgar judgements—success.
1791 Letter to a Member of the National Assembly.

52 Tyrants seldom want pretexts.
1791 Letter to a Member of the National Assembly.

53 Somebody has said, that a king may make a nobleman but he cannot make a gentleman.
1795 Letter to William Smith, 29 Jan.

54 And having looked to government for bread, on the very first scarcity they will turn and bite the hand that fed them. To avoid that evil, government will redouble the causes of it; and then it will become inveterate and incurable.
1795 Thoughts and Details on Scarcity, Nov (published 1800).

55 To innovate is not to reform.
1796 A Letter to a Noble Lord.

56 All men that are ruined are ruined on the side of their natural propensities.
1796 Two Letters on the Proposals for Peace with the Regicide Directory, 9th edn.

57 Example is the school of mankind, and they will learn at no other.
1796 Two Letters on the Proposals for Peace with the Regicide Directory, 9th edn.

58 It is necessary only for the good man to do nothing for evil to triumph.
Attributed.

Burke, Johnny 1908–64
US lyricist.

59 Every time it rains, it rains
Pennies from heaven.
1936 'Pennies from Heaven'.
▶ See also Thatcher 881:56.

60 Like Webster's dictionary, we're Morocco bound.
1942 Title song in *Road to Morocco,* sung by Bing Crosby and Bob Hope. Music by Jimmy Van Heusen.

61 Or would you like to swing on a star
Carry moonbeams home in a jar
And be better off than you are
Or would you rather be a fish?
1944 Swinging on a Star, sung by Bing Crosby in the film *Going My Way.* Music by Jimmy Van Heusen.

Burke, Kathy 1964–
English actress.

62 If they want rough, then I get the phone call.
1997 In the *Observer,* 5 Jan.

Burke, Kenneth 1897–1986
US music and literary critic. His theory of literature as 'symbolic action' was very influential.

63 Any performance is discussable from the standpoint of what it *attains* or what it *misses*. Comprehensiveness can be discussed as superficiality, intensiveness as stricture, tolerance as uncertainty—and the poor *pedestrian* abilities of a fish are clearly explainable in terms of his excellence as a *swimmer*. A way of seeing is also a way of not seeing.
1936 Permanence and Change.

Burke, Tim(othy) c.1942–
Canadian newspaper columnist.

64 There are no lapsed Catholics after a Christmas concert by Pavarotti.
1987 In *The Montreal Gazette*, 8 Dec.

Burns, Ken Lauren 1953–
US film-maker and historian. He has won numerous awards for documentary and historical films on aspects of American life.

65 We are a people starved for self-definition.
1991 On the success of his 11-hour television documentary *The Civil War*. In *People*, 7 Jan.

Burns, Robert 1759–96
Scottish poet and songwriter, the son of a farmer. The Kilmarnock edition (1786) of his poems made his name, and his skill at providing lyrics for old Scottish airs assured his place as one of the world's most popular poets and as his country's national bard. His influence in promoting Scots in literature was enormous.

66 Green grow the rashes, O;
Green grow the rashes, O;
The sweetest hours that e'er I spend,
Are spent amang the lasses, O.
1784 'Green grow the Rashes. A Fragment', chorus.

67 What signifies the life o' man,
An 'twere na for the lasses, O.
1784 'Green grow the Rashes. A Fragment', stanza 1.

68 If honest Nature made you *fools*,
What sairs your grammars.
1785 'Epistle to J. Lapraik, An Old Scotch Bard, 1 April 1785', stanza 11.

69 They *gang* in Stirks, and *come out* Asses,
Plain truth to speak;
An' syne they think to climb Parnassus
By dint o' Greek!
1785 'Epistle to J. Lapraik, An Old Scotch Bard, 1 April 1785', stanza 12.

70 Gie me ae spark o' Nature's fire,
That's a' the learning I desire.
1785 'Epistle to J. Lapraik, An Old Scotch Bard, 1 April 1785', stanza 13.

71 O Thou that in the heavens does dwell!
Wha, as it pleases best Thysel,
Sends ane to heaven, an' ten to hell,
A' for Thy glory,
And no for ony gude or ill
They've done before Thee!
1785 'Holy Willie's Prayer', stanza 1.

72 My curse upon your whunstane hearts,
Ye Enbrugh Gentry!
The tythe o' what ye waste at *cartes*
Wad stow'd his pantry!
1785 'To W. Simpson, Ochiltree', stanza 4, referring to the poet Robert Fergusson, who died a pauper in the Edinburgh bedlam in 1774 at the age of 24, and whom Burns considered 'my elder brother in misfortune, by far my elder brother in the muse'.

73 Some books are lies frae end to end,
And some great lies were never penn'd.
1785 'Death and Doctor Hornbook. A True Story', stanza 1.

74 I was na fou, but just had plenty.
1785 'Death and Doctor Hornbook. A True Story', stanza 3.

75 There's some are fou o' *love divine*;
There's some are fou o' *brandy*.
1785 'The Holy Fair', stanza 27.

76 From scenes like these, old SCOTIA's grandeur springs,
That makes her lov'd at home, rever'd abroad:
Princes and lords are but the breath of kings,
'An honest man's the noble work of GOD'.
1785 'The Cotter's Saturday Night', stanza 19. The last line is in fact a misquotation of Pope; 'noble' was corrected to 'noblest' in the 1794 edition of Burns's poems.
▶ See Pope 687:89.

77 Wee, sleeket, cowrin, tim'rous *beastie*,
O, what a panic's in thy breastie!
Thou need na start awa sae hasty
Wi' bickering brattle!
I wad be laith to rin an' chase thee,
Wi' murd'ring *pattle*!
1785 'To A Mouse, On turning her up in her Nest with the Plough, November, 1785', stanza 1.

78 The best-laid schemes o' *Mice* an' *Men*
Gang aft a-gley.
1785 'To A Mouse, On turning her up in her Nest with the Plough, November, 1785', stanza 7.

79 A fig for those by law protected!
Liberty's a glorious feast!
Courts for Cowards were erected,
Churches built to please the Priest.
c.1786 'The Jolly Beggars', or 'Love and Liberty, a Cantata', chorus to a song to the tune 'Jolly Mortals, fill your glasses'.

80 His lockèd, letter'd, braw brass-collar,
Show'd him the *gentleman* an' *scholar*.
1786 'The Twa Dogs'.

81 The tither was a *ploughman's collie*,
A rhyming, ranting, raving billie.
1786 'The Twa Dogs'.

82 FREEDOM and WHISKY gang thegither,
Tak aff your *dram!*
1786 'The Author's Earnest Cry and Prayer, to the Right Honorable and Honorable, the Scotch Representatives in the House of Commons', stanza 30.

83 O Thou, whatever title suit thee!
Auld Hornie, Satan, Nick, or Clootie.
1786 'Address to the Deil', stanza 1.

84 An' now, auld *Cloots*, I ken ye're thinkan,
A certain *Bardie's* rantin, drinkin,
Some luckless hour will send him linkan,
To your black pit;
But faith! he'll turn a corner jinkan,
An' cheat you yet.
1786 'Address to the Deil', stanza 20.

85 But *Facts* are cheels that winna ding,
And downa be disputed.
1786 'A Dream', stanza 4.

86 Man's inhumanity to Man
Makes countless thousands mourn!
1786 'Man was made to Mourn, A Dirge', stanza 7.

87 O wad some Pow'r the giftie gie us
To see oursels as ithers see us!
It wad frae monie a blunder free us
An' foolish notion.
1786 'To a Louse, On Seeing one on a Lady's Bonnet at Church', stanza 8.

88 It was upon a Lammas night,
When corn rigs are bonie,

Beneath the moon's unclouded light,
I held awa to Annie.
1786 'Song, The Rigs o' Barley', or 'Corn Rigs Are Bonie', stanza 1.

89 I hae been blythe wi' Comrades dear;
I hae been merry drinking.
1786 'Song, The Rigs o' Barley', or 'Corn Rigs Are Bonie', stanza 4.

90 Corn rigs, an' barley rigs,
An' corn rigs are bonie:
I'll ne'er forget that happy night,
Amang the rigs wi' Annie.
1786 'Song, The Rigs o' Barley', or 'Corn Rigs Are Bonie', chorus.

91 Now westlin winds, and slaught'rin guns
Bring Autumn's pleasant weather.
1786 'Song, composed in August', stanza 1.

92 O ye wha are sae guid yoursel,
Sae pious and sae holy,
Ye've nought to do but mark and tell
Your Neebours' fauts an folly!
1786 'Address to the Unco Guid, or the Rigidly Righteous', stanza 1.

93 Then gently scan your brother Man,
Still gentler sister Woman;
Tho' they may gang a kennin wrang,
To step aside is human.
1786 'Address to the Unco Guid, or the Rigidly Righteous', stanza 7.

94 Fair fa' your honest, sonsie face,
Great Chieftain o' the Puddin-race!
Aboon them a' ye tak your place,
Painch, tripe, or thairm:
Weel are ye wordy of a *grace*
As lang's my arm.
1786 'To a Haggis', stanza 1.

95 Auld Scotland wants nae skinking ware That jaups in luggies;
But, if ye wish her gratefu' prayer,
Gie her a *Haggis!*
1786 'To a Haggis', stanza 8.

96 Edina! *Scotia's* darling seat,
All hail thy palaces and tow'rs,
Where once beneath a monarch's feet
Sat Legislation's sov'reign pow'rs.
1786 'Address to Edinburgh', stanza 1.

97 There was a lad was born in Kyle,
But what na day o' what na style.
I doubt it's hardly worth the while
To be sae nice wi' Robin.
1787 'There was a lad', or 'Rantin Rovin' Robin', stanza 1.

98 Robin was a rovin' Boy,
Rantin' rovin', rantin', rovin',
Robin was a rovin' Boy,
Rantin' rovin' Robin.
1787 'There was a lad', or 'Rantin' Rovin' Robin', chorus.

99 There was three kings into the east,
Three kings both great and high,
And they hae sworn a solemn oath
John Barleycorn should die.
1787 'John Barleycorn. A Ballad', stanza 1.

1 Bony lassie will ye go
To the birks of Aberfeldey.
1787 'The Birks of Aberfeldey', chorus.

2 Sae rantingly, sae wantonly,
Sae dauntingly gae'd he:
He play'd a spring, and danc'd it round
Below the gallows-tree.
1788 'McPherson's Farewell', chorus.

3 O rattlin, roarin Willie,
O he held to the fair;
An' for to sell his fiddle
And buy some other ware.
1788 'Rattlin, roarin Willie', stanza 1.

4 Rattlin, roarin Willie,
Ye're welcome hame to me!
1788 'Rattlin, roarin Willie', stanza 3.

5 Should auld acquaintance be forgot
And never brought to mind?
Should auld acquaintance be forgot,
And auld lang syne!
1788 'Auld Lang Syne', stanza 1. This is the most familiar version of an older, traditional song, reworked by Burns.

6 For auld lang syne, my jo,
For auld lang syne,
We'll tak a cup o' kindness yet
For auld lang syne.
1788 'Auld Lang Syne', chorus. This is the most familiar version of an older, traditional song, reworked by Burns.

7 And there's a hand, my trusty fiere!
And gie's a hand o' thine!
1788 'Auld Lang Syne', stanza 5. This is the most familiar version of an older, traditional song, reworked by Burns.

8 Go fetch to me a pint o' wine,
And fill it in a silver tassie,
That I may drink, before I go,
A service to my bonie lassie.
1788 'My Bonie Mary', stanza 1.

9 Of a' the airts the wind can blaw,
I dearly like the West;
For there the bonie Lassie lives,
The Lassie I lo'e best.
1788 'Of a' the airts the wind can blaw', or 'I Love my Jean', stanza 1.

10 Flow gently, sweet Afton, among thy green braes,
Flow gently, I'll sing thee a song in thy praise.
1789 'Afton Water', stanza 1.

11 The golden Hours, on angel wings,
Flew o'er me and my Dearie;
For dear to me as light and life
Was my sweet Highland Mary.
1789 'Highland Mary', stanza 2.

12 We are na fou, we're nae that fou,
But just a drappie in our e'e;
The cock may craw, the day may daw,
And ay we'll taste the barley bree.
1789 'Willie brew'd a peck o' maut', chorus.

13 Ay waukin, O,
Waukin still and weary:
Sleep I can get nane,
For thinkin on my Dearie.
1790 'Ay waukin O', chorus.

14 My love she's but a lassie yet,
My love she's but a lassie yet;

We'll let her stand a year or twa,
She'll no be half sae saucy yet.
1790 'My love she's but a lassie yet', chorus.

15 My heart's in the Highlands, my heart is not here,
My heart's in the Highlands a chasing the deer;
Chasing the wild deer, and following the roe;
My heart's in the Highlands, wherever I go.
1790 'My heart's in the Highlands', chorus.

16 John Anderson my jo, John,
When we were first acquent;
Your locks were like the raven,
Your bonie brow was brent;
But now your brow is beld, John,
Your locks are like the snaw;
But blessings on your frosty pow,
John Anderson my jo.
1790 'John Anderson my Jo', stanza 1.

17 An ye had been whare I hae been,
Ye wad na been sae canty, O;
An ye had seen what I hae seen,
I' th' braes o' Killiecrankie, O.
1790 'Killiecrankie', chorus.

18 When chapman billies leave the street,
And drouthy neebors, neebors meet,
As market-days are wearing late,
An' folk begin to tak the gate.
1790 'Tam o' Shanter. A Tale'.

19 Whare sits our sulky sullen dame,
Gathering her brows like gathering storm,
Nursing her wrath to keep it warm.
1790 'Tam o' Shanter. A Tale'.

20 Auld Ayr, wham ne'er a town surpasses,
For honest men and bonny lasses.
1790 'Tam o' Shanter. A Tale'.

21 Ah! gentle dames! it gars me greet,
To think how mony counsels sweet,
How mony lengthen'd sage advices,
The husband frae the wife despises!
1790 'Tam o' Shanter. A Tale'.

22 Tam lo'ed him like a vera brither;
They had been fou for weeks thegither.
1790 'Tam o' Shanter. A Tale'.

23 The storm without might rair and rustle,
Tam did na mind the storm a whistle.
1790 'Tam o' Shanter. A Tale'.

24 Kings may be blest but Tam was glorious,
O'er a' the ills o' life victorious!
1790 'Tam o' Shanter. A Tale'.

25 But pleasures are like poppies spread,
You seize the flower, its bloom is shed;
Or like the snow falls in the river,
A moment white—then melts for ever.
1790 'Tam o' Shanter. A Tale'.

26 Nae man can tether time or tide;
The hour approaches Tam maun ride;
That hour, o' night's black arch the key-stane,
That dreary hour Tam mounts his beast in.
1790 'Tam o' Shanter. A Tale'.

27 Inspiring, bold John Barleycorn!
What dangers thou canst make us scorn!

Wi' tippenny, we fear nae evil;
Wi' usquabae, we'll face the devil!
1790 'Tam o' Shanter. A Tale'. 'Usquabae' = whisky.

28 Five tomahawks, wi' blude red-rusted;
Five scymitars, wi' murder crusted.
1790 'Tam o' Shanter. A Tale'.

29 As Tammie glowr'd, amaz'd, and curious,
The mirth and fun grew fast and furious:
The piper loud and louder blew;
The dancers quick and quicker flew.
1790 'Tam o' Shanter. A Tale'.

30 Ah, Tam! Ah, Tam! thou'll get thy fairin!
In hell they'll roast thee like a herrin!
1790 'Tam o' Shanter. A Tale'.

31 Whene'er to drink you are inclin'd,
Or cutty sarks run in your mind,
Think, ye may buy the joys o'er dear—
Remember Tam o' Shanter's mare.
1790 'Tam o' Shanter. A Tale'.

32 Ye banks and braes o' bonie Doon,
How can ye bloom sae fresh and fair;
How can ye chant, ye little birds,
And I sae weary fu' o' care!
1791 'The Banks o' Doon' (2nd version), stanza 1.

33 And my fause Luver staw my rose,
But, ah! he left the thorn wi' me.
1791 'The Banks o' Doon' (2nd version), stanza 2.

34 Ae fond kiss, and then we sever!
Ae fareweel, and then for ever!
Deep in heart-wrung tears I'll pledge thee,
Warring sighs and groans I'll wage thee.
1791 'Ae Fond Kiss', stanza 1.

35 Had we never lov'd sae kindly,
Had we never lov'd sae blindly!
Never met—or never parted,
We had ne'er been broken-hearted.
1791 'Ae Fond Kiss', stanza 4.

36 Fare-thee-weel, thou first and fairest!
Fare-thee-weel, thou best and dearest!
Thine be ilka joy and treasure,
Peace, Enjoyment, Love and Pleasure!
1791 'Ae Fond Kiss', stanza 5.

37 Ye Jacobites by name, give an ear, give an ear!
Ye Jacobites by name, give an ear.
1792 'Ye Jacobites by name', stanza 1.

38 Sic a wife as Willie's wife,
I wad na gie a button for her.
1792 'Willie Wastle', or 'Sic a wife as Willie's wife', stanza 1.

39 Willie Wastle dwalt on Tweed,
The spot they ca'd it Linkumdoddie.
1792 'Willie Wastle', or 'Sic a wife as Willie's wife', stanza 1.

40 Fareweel to a' our Scottish fame,
Fareweel our ancient glory.
1792 'Such a parcel of rogues in a nation', stanza 1.

41 Now Sark rins o'er the Solway sands,
An' Tweed rins to the ocean,
To mark where England's province stands,
Such a parcel of rogues in a nation!
1792 'Such a parcel of rogues in a nation', stanza 1.

42 We're bought and sold for English gold,
    Such a parcel of rogues in a nation!
    1792 'Such a parcel of rogues in a nation', stanza 3.

43 The deil cam fiddlin thro' the town,
    And danc'd awa wi' th' Exciseman;
    And ilka wife cries, auld Mahoun,
    I wish you luck o' the prize, man!
    1792 'The Deil's awa wi' th' Exciseman', stanza 1.

44 There's threesome reels, there's foursome reels,
    There's hornpipes and strathspeys, man,
    But the ae best dance e'er cam to the Land
    Was, the deil's awa wi' th' Exciseman.
    1792 'The Deil's awa wi' th' Exciseman', stanza 3.

45 When o'er the hill the eastern star
    Tells bughtin-time is near, my jo,
    And owsen frae the furrowed field
    Return sae dowf and weary O.
    1792 'My ain kind dearie', or 'The Lea-rig', stanza 1.

46 I'll meet thee on the lea-rig,
    My ain kind Dearie, O.
    1792 'My ain kind dearie', or 'The Lea-rig', stanza 1.

47 Scots, wha hae wi' Wallace bled,
    Scots, wham Bruce has aften led,
    Welcome to your gory bed,—
    Or to victorie!—
    Now's the day, and now's the hour;
    See the front o' battle lour;
    See approach proud Edward's power,
    Chains and Slaverie!
    1793 'Bruce's Address at Bannockburn', stanza 1.

48 Liberty's in every blow!
    Let us do or die!
    1793 'Bruce's Address at Bannockburn', stanza 3.

49 Though this was fair, and that was braw,
    And yon the toast of a' the town,
    I sigh'd, and said amang them a',
    'Ye are na Mary Morison.'
    1793 'Mary Morison', stanza 2.

50 O my Luve's like a red, red rose
    That's newly sprung in June;
    O my luve's like the melodie
    That's sweetly play'd in tune.
    As fair art thou, my bonie lass,
    So deep in luve am I;
    And I will luve thee still, my Dear,
    Till a' the seas gang dry.
    Till a' the seas gang dry, my Dear,
    And the rocks melt wi' the sun:
    O I will love thee still, my Dear,
    While the sands o' life shall run.
    1794 'A red, red rose'.

51 Ca' the yowes to the knowes,
    Ca' them whare the heather grows,
    Ca' them whare the burnie rowes,
    My bonie Dearie!
    1794 'Ca' the yowes to the knowes' (2nd version), chorus.

52 Is there for honest Poverty
    That hings his head, and a' that;
    The coward-slave, we pass him by,
    We dare be poor for a' that!
    For a' that, and a' that,
    Our toils obscure, and a' that,
    The rank is but the guinea's stamp,
    The man's the gowd for a' that.
    1795 'For a' that and a' that', stanza 1.

53 A man's a man for a' that.
    1795 'For a' that and a' that', stanza 2.

54 For a' that, and a' that,
    It's comin' yet for a' that,
    That Man to Man the warld o'er
    Shall brothers be, for a' that.
    1795 'For a' that and a' that', stanza 5.

55 Gin a body meet a body
    Comin thro' the rye,
    Gin a body kiss a body
    Need a body cry?
    1796 'Comin thro' the rye', stanza 2.

56 An' Charlie he's my darling, my darling, my darling,
    Charlie he's my darling, the young Chevalier.
    1796 'Charlie he's my darling', chorus.

57 It was a' for our rightfu' king,
    We left fair Scotland's strand.
    1796 'It was a' for our rightfu' king', stanza 1.

58 Now a' is done that men can do,
    And a' is done in vain.
    1796 'It was a' for our rightfu' king', stanza 2.

59 He turn'd him right and round about,
    Upon the Irish shore,
    And gae his bridle reins a shake,
    With, Adieu for evermore, my dear,
    And Adieu for evermore!
    1796 'It was a' for our rightfu' king', stanza 3.

60 Oh wert thou in the cauld blast,
    On yonder lea, on yonder lea;
    My plaidie to the angry airt,
    I'd shelter thee, I'd shelter thee.
    1796 'Oh wert thou in the cauld blast', stanza 1.

61 There's death in the cup—sae beware!
    Nay, more—there is danger in touching;
    But wha can avoid the fell snare?
    The man and his wine's sae bewitching!
    1796 'Inscription on a Goblet'.

Burroughs, Edgar Rice   1875–1950

US novelist. He was a hugely successful writer of popular fiction, much of it in the science-fiction and fantasy genres, and is best known as the creator of Tarzan. The much-quoted line 'Me Tarzan, you Jane', does not appear in any story, and is a misattribution by actor Johnny Weissmuller.

62 Tarzan of the Apes.
    1912 Title of story.

Burroughs, William S(eward)   1914–97

US writer. He wandered through the USA and Europe after graduating from Harvard, becoming a heroin addict in New York (1944). His novels draw on his experiences, establishing him as a spokesman of the 'beat' generation.

63 The face of 'evil' is always the face of total need.
    1959 *The Naked Lunch*, introduction.

64 I think there are innumerable gods. What we on earth call God is a little tribal God who has made an awful mess.
1965 In *Paris Review*, Fall.

65 After one look at this planet any visitor from outer space would say 'I WANT TO SEE THE MANAGER.'
1985 *The Adding Machine*, 'Women: A Biological Mistake'.

66 You can't fake quality any more than you can fake a good meal.
1987 *The Western Lands*, ch.2.

67 No problems can be solved, and all solutions lead to more problems.
Comment to Allen Ginsberg. Quoted in Barry Miles *Ginsberg* (1989), ch.17.

68 Nothing exists until or unless it is observed. An artist is making something exist by observing it.
1992 *Painting and Guns*, 'The Creative Observer'.

69 Virtue is simply happiness, and happiness is a by-product of function. You are happy when you are functioning.
1992 *Painting and Guns*, 'The Creative Observer'.

Burt, Benjamin Hapgood 1880–1950
US songwriter.

70 All Dressed Up and No Place to Go.
1913 Song title, *The Beauty Shop* (music by Silvio Hein).

71 One evening in October, when I was one-third sober,
An' taking home a 'load' with manly pride;
My poor feet began to stutter, so I lay down in the gutter,
And a pig came up an' lay down by my side.
Then we sang 'It's all fair weather when good fellows get together,'
Till a lady passing by was heard to say:
'You can tell a man who boozes by the company he chooses',
And the pig got up and slowly walked away.
1933 'The Pig Got Up and Slowly Walked Away'.

Burton, C(harles) L(uther) 1876–1961
Canadian businessman.

72 I hold no brief for private enterprise. But I have unshakeable faith in individual enterprise.
1952 *A Sense of Urgency: Memoirs of a Canadian Merchant*.

73 Life, if you have a bent for it, is a beautiful thing. It consists, I do believe, of having a sense of urgency.
1952 *A Sense of Urgency: Memoirs of a Canadian Merchant*.

Burton, Robert *pseudonym* Democritus Junior 1577–1640
English writer and clergyman. Educated at Oxford, he remained at Christ Church for life. His *Anatomy of Melancholy* (1621) is a vast, witty compendium of Jacobean knowledge and superstition about the 'disease' of melancholy; it went through several editions in his lifetime.

74 All my joys to this are folly,
Naught so sweet as melancholy.
1621 *Anatomy of Melancholy*, 'The Author's Abstract of Melancholy'.

75 A loose, plain, rude writer…I call a spade a spade.
1621 *Anatomy of Melancholy*, 'Democritus to the Reader'.

76 All poets are mad.
1621 *Anatomy of Melancholy*, 'Democritus to the Reader'.

77 I may not here omit those two main plagues, and common dotages of human kind, wine and women, which have infatuated and besotted myriads of people. They go commonly together.
1621 *Anatomy of Melancholy*, pt.1, section 2, member 3, subsection 13.

78 *Hinc quam sit calamus saevior ense patet.*
From this it is clear how much the pen is worse than the sword.
1621 *Anatomy of Melancholy*, pt.1, section 2, member 4, subsection 4.

79 See one promontory (said Socrates of old), one mountain, one sea, one river, and see all.
1621 *Anatomy of Melancholy*, pt.1, section 2, member 4, subsection 7.

80 One was never married, and that's his hell; another is, and that's his plague.
1621 *Anatomy of Melancholy*, pt.1, section 2, member 4, subsection 7.

81 Who cannot give good counsel? 'tis cheap, it costs them nothing.
1621 *Anatomy of Melancholy*, pt.2, section 3, member 1, subsection 1.

82 What is a ship but a prison?
1621 *Anatomy of Melancholy*, pt.2, section 3, member 4, subsection 1.

83 Tobacco, divine, rare, superexcellent tobacco, which goes far beyond all their panaceas, potable gold, and philosopher's stones, a sovereign remedy to all diseases… But, as it is commonly abused by most men, which take it as tinkers do ale, 'tis a plague, a mischief, a violent purger of goods, lands, health, hellish, devilish, and damned tobacco, the ruin and overthrow of body and soul.
1621 *Anatomy of Melancholy*, pt.2, section 4, member 2, subsection 1.

84 But this love of ours is immoderate, inordinate, and not to be comprehended in any bounds. It will not contain itself within the union of marriage or apply to one object, but is a wandering, extravagant, a domineering, a boundless, an irrefragable, a destructive passion.
1621 *Anatomy of Melancholy*, pt.3, section 2, member 1, subsection 2.

85 No cord nor cable can so forcibly draw, or hold so fast, as love can do with a twined thread. The scorching beams under the equinoctial or extremity of cold within the circle Arctic, where the very seas are frozen, cold or torrid zone cannot avoid or expel this heat, fury, and rage of mortal men.
1621 *Anatomy of Melancholy*, pt.3, section 2, member 1, subsection 2.

86 Of women's unnatural, unsatiable lust, what country, what village doth not complain?
1621 *Anatomy of Melancholy*, pt.3, section 2, member 1, subsection 2.

87 A passion of the brain, as all other melancholy, by reason of corrupt imagination.
1621 Of love. *Anatomy of Melancholy*, pt.3, section 2, member 1, subsection 2.

88 One religion is as true as another.
1621 *Anatomy of Melancholy*, pt.3, section 4, member 2, subsection 1.

89 Be not solitary, be not idle.
1621 *Anatomy of Melancholy*, closing words.

Buruma, Ian 1951–
Dutch writer. His works include *The Wages of Guilt* (1994).

90 Isherwood did not so much find himself in Berlin as reinvent himself; Isherwood became a fiction, a work of art.
1986 Of Christopher Isherwood. In the *New Republic*, 4 Nov.

91 A nation of people longing to be 12-year-olds or even younger.
1994 Of Japan. *The Wages of Guilt*.

92 German memory was like a massive tongue seeking out, over and over, a sore tooth.
1994 *The Wages of Guilt*.

Busby, Sir Matt(hew) 1909–94
Scottish football player and manager. He led Manchester United to glory in the 1950s, and successfully rebuilt the team after the Munich air crash in 1958 to win the European Cup in 1968.

93 The theory that the League and Cup double will never be done in modern times is nonsense. I realize no one has done it for sixty years, but there is a simple explanation for that. No club has been good enough.
1957 Attributed, four years before Tottenham Hotspur won both the League Championship and the FA Cup.

Bush, Barbara Pierce 1925–
Former US First Lady. The daughter of a wealthy New York publisher, she married George Bush (1945), who became President in 1989.

94 No other single building is so much a part of the American consciousness.
1992 At the 200th anniversary of the laying of the White House cornerstone. Reported in the *Washington Times*, 24 Jan.

95 I wrote in my diaries about…good meals that I have eaten and am wearing today.
1994 *Barbara Bush: A Memoir*.

96 I am advising the former President, the governor of Florida and the President of the United States—I guess you could say I rule the world.
2003 On her political power. Quoted in *Newsweek*, 31 Mar.

97 What I'm hearing, which is sort of scary, is that they all want to stay in Texas. Everyone is so overwhelmed by the hospitality. And so many of the people in the arena here, you know, were underprivileged anyway, so this is working very well for them.
2005 Referring to Hurricane Katrina refugees sheltering in the Astrodome in Houston.

Bush, George Herbert Walker 1924–
US Republican politician and 41st President. After losing to Reagan for the Republican candidacy in the 1980 elections, he became his Vice-President and later President (1989–92). He presided over the US-led UN coalition to defeat Iraq in the Gulf War.

98 The United States is the best and fairest and most decent nation on the face of the earth.
1988 Speech, May.

99 Read my lips: no new taxes.
1988 Accepting the Republican presidential nomination, 19 Aug.

1 It's amazing how many people beat you at golf now that you're no longer president.
1996 In the *Sunday Times*, 22 Dec.

2 I have opinions of my own—strong opinions, but I don't always agree with them.
2007 Attributed.

Bush, George W(alker) 1948–
US Republican politician and 43rd President. The son of George H W Bush, he was Governor of Texas (1995–2000) before becoming President (2001–9). A controversial figure, he launched the War on Terror following the 9/11 attacks, and became well known for his muddled delivery when speaking in public.

3 I've inherited 100 per cent of his enemies and only 50 per cent of his friends.
1994 Of the influence of his father, during his campaign for governor. In the *Washington Times*, 12 Oct.

4 I'm not going to talk about what I did as a child.
1999 On being asked if he ever used marijuana or cocaine. Quoted in *Time*, 22 Feb.

5 Keep good relations with the Grecians.
1999 Quoted in *The Economist*, 12 Jun.

6 New Hampshire has long been known as the bump in the road for front runners—and this year is no exception.
2000 After being defeated in the New Hampshire primary. In the *Sunday Times*, 6 Feb.

7 Reading is the basics for all learning.
2000 Announcing his 'Reading First' initiative in Virginia, 28 Mar.

8 It's no sign of weakness to talk to your dad.
2000 Denying that he is too much under his father's influence. In the *Sunday Telegraph*, 30 Jul.

9 Well, I think if you say you're going to do something and don't do it, that's trustworthiness.
2000 CNN online chat, 30 Aug.

10 I know the human being and fish can coexist peacefully.
2000 Speaking in Saginaw, Michigan, 29 Sep.

11 I am mindful not only of preserving executive powers for myself, but for my predecessors as well.
2001 Speaking in Washington, 29 Jan.

12 You teach a child to read, and he or her will be able to pass a literacy test.
2001 Speaking in Townsend, Tennessee, 21 Feb.

13 According to the *Oxford English Dictionary*, Mr Jefferson contributed more new words to the language than any other US President. I especially like his term for barbaric pirates: barbaresques. I'm also impressed by his words, debarrass and graffage. The other day I tried a new word for our press corps: misunderestimate. It's not quite in Jefferson's league, but I am giving it my best shot.
2001 Speaking in Washington, 12 Apr.

14 We spent a lot of time talking about Africa, as we should. Africa is a nation that suffers from incredible disease.
2001 Speaking in Gothenburg, Sweden, 14 Jun.

15 We cannot let terrorist and rogue nations hold this nation hostile or hold our allies hostile.
2001 Speaking in Des Moines, Iowa, 21 Aug.

16 Whether we bring our enemies to justice, or bring justice to our enemies, justice will be done.
2001 Address to a joint session of Congress, 20 Sep.

17 Every nation, in every region, now has a decision to make. Either you are with us, or you are with the terrorists. From this day forward, any nation that continues to harbor or support terrorism will be regarded by the United States as a hostile regime.
2001 Address to a joint session of Congress, 20 Sep.

18 States like these, and their terrorist allies, constitute an axis of evil, arming to threaten the peace of the world. By seeking weapons of mass destruction, these regimes pose a grave and growing danger.
2002 State of the Union Address, 29 Jan.

19 Our war on terror is well begun, but it is only begun. This campaign may not be finished on our watch—yet it must be and it will be waged on our watch.
2002 State of the Union Address, 29 Jan.

20 For a century and a half now, America and Japan have formed one of the great and enduring alliances of modern times.
2002 Speaking in Tokyo, Japan, 18 Feb.

21 If this is not evil, then evil has no meaning.
2003 On torture in Iraq. State of the Union Address, 28 Jan.

22 The Columbia is gone. There are no survivors.
2003 On the loss of the space shuttle. Quoted in *Newsweek*, 10 Feb.

23 You're free. And freedom is beautiful. And, you know, it'll take time to restore chaos and order—order out of chaos. But we will.
2003 Speaking in Washington, 13 Apr.

24 Our country puts $1 billion a year up to help feed the hungry. And we're by far the most generous nation in the world when it comes to that, and I'm proud to report that. This isn't a contest of who's the most generous. I'm just telling you as an aside. We're generous. We shouldn't be bragging about it. But we are. We're very generous.
2003 Speaking in Washington, 16 Jul.

25 The best way to get news is from objective sources. And the most objective sources I have are people on my staff who tell me what's happening in the world.
2003 On Fox News, 22 Sep.

26 See, free nations are peaceful nations. Free nations don't attack each other. Free nations don't develop weapons of mass destruction.
2003 Speaking in Milwaukee, Wisconsin, 3 Oct.

27 The illiteracy level of our children are appalling.
2004 Speaking in Washington, 23 Jan.

28 Iraqis are sick of foreign people coming in their country and trying to destabilize their country. And we will help them rid Iraq of these killers.
2004 Interview on Al Arabiya Television, 4 May.

29 When I speak about the blessings of liberty, coarse videos and crass commercialism are not what I have in mind.
2004 Speaking in Istanbul, 29 Jun.

30 See if Saddam did this. See if he's linked in any way.
In the wake of the 11 September 2001 attacks. Quoted in Richard A Clarke *Against All Enemies: Inside America's War on Terror* (2004).

31 Because he's hiding.
2005 His reply when asked aboard Air Force One why his administration had not yet located and arrested Osama Bin Laden, 14 Jan.

32 You work three jobs? ... Uniquely American, isn't it? I mean, that is fantastic that you're doing that.
2005 Speaking to a divorced mother of three in Omaha, Nebraska, 4 Feb.

33 See, in my line of work you got to keep repeating things over and over and over again for the truth to sink in, to kind of catapult the propaganda.
2005 Speech, Greece, New York, 24 May.

34 We do not create terrorism by fighting the terrorists. We invite terrorism by ignoring them.
2005 Speech, 18 Dec.

35 Brownie, you're doing a heck of a job.
2005 Congratulating FEMA director Michael Brown on his handling of the Hurricane Katrina relief effort, 2 Sep. Brown resigned ten days later after severe criticism of his role.

36 What didn't go right?
2005 His response to criticism of his government's efforts to aid those affected by Hurricane Katrina.

37 I think I've found my limitations.
2005 Attributed after injuring two fingers in a collision with a police officer while mountain biking in Scotland.

38 Before history is written down in books, it is written in courage.
2006 State of the Union address, 31 Jan.

39 I would say the best moment of all was when I caught a 7.5 pound largemouth bass in my lake.
2006 His answer when asked what was his best moment since he took office in 2001, *Bild am Sonntag*, 7 May.

40 A year ago my approval rating was in the thirties, my nominee for the Supreme Court had just withdrawn, and my vice president had shot someone. Ah, those were the good ol' days.
2007 Speech at Radio and Television Correspondents' Association dinner, 28 Mar.

41 Sometimes we must fight terror with tyranny.
2007 Press conference, 7 Nov.

42 Goodbye, from the world's biggest polluter.
2008 Parting statement at Tokyo G8 summit, 12 Jul.

43 If money isn't loosened up, this sucker could go down.
2008 Referring to the global economy, 26 Sep.

44 I think playing golf during a war just sends the wrong signal.
2008 Explaining why he gave up golf in 2003.

45 I suspected there would be a good-size crowd once the word got out about my hanging.
2008 Acknowledging the large crowd attending the unveiling of his portrait at the National Portrait Gallery, 19 Dec.

46 I'll be long gone before some smart person ever figures out what happened inside this Oval Office.
2008 Speaking at the White House, 12 May.

Bush, Laura Lane Welch 1946–

Former US First Lady. A teacher and librarian, she married George W. Bush (1977), who became President in 2001.

47 I'm proud of George. He's learned a lot about ranching since that first year when he tried to milk the horse. What's worse, it was a male horse.
2005 Speaking at the White House Correspondents' Dinner.

48 I said, 'George, if you really want to end tyranny in this world, you're going to have to stay up later.' Nine o'clock and Mr. Excitement here is sound asleep.'
2005 Speaking at the White House Correspondents' Dinner.

Bush, Vannevar 1890–1974

US electrical engineer and physicist, Dean of Engineering at the Massachusetts Institute of Technology. He later led the US Office of Scientific Research.

49 To pursue science is not to disparage things of the spirit.
   1953 Speech at the Massachusetts Institute of Technology, 5 Oct.

50 It was through the Second World War that most of us suddenly appreciated for the first time the power of man's concentrated efforts to understand and control the forces of nature. We were appalled by what we saw.
   1967 *Science is Not Enough*.

51 Knowledge for the sake of understanding, not merely to prevail, that is the essence of our being. None can define its limits, or set its ultimate boundaries.
   1967 *Science is Not Enough*.

Bushnell, Candace 1958–

US journalist and author.

52 Let's face it, the unmarried guys in New York suck.
   1996 *Sex in the City*.

53 Modelizers are a particular breed. They're a step beyond womanizers, who will sleep with just about anything in a skirt. Modelizers are obsessed not with women but with models. They love them for their beauty and hate them for everything else.
   1996 *Sex in the City*.

Busoni, Ferruccio Benvenuto 1866–1924

Italian pianist and composer. An infant prodigy, he taught and played throughout Europe and wrote four operas among other works, mainly for piano. His pupils included Kurt Weill.

54 Music is the art of sounds in the movement of time.
   1923 *The Essence of Music*.

Bussy-Rabutin, Comte de 1618–93

French soldier and poet.

55 *L'absence est à l'amour ce qu'est au feu le vent;*
   Il éteint le petit, il allume le grand.
   Absence is to love what wind is to fire;
   It extinguishes the small, it kindles the great.
   1665 *Histoire Amoureuse des Gaules. Maximes d'Amour*, pt.2.

56 *Comme vous savez, Dieu est d'ordinaire pour les gros escadrons contre les petits.*
   As you know, God is usually on the side of the big squadrons against the small.
   1677 Letter to the Comte de Limoges, 18 Oct.

Butler, Joseph 1692–1752

English moral philosopher, cleric and Christian apologist. Originally a dissenter, he joined the Church of England and became Bishop of Bristol, and later of Durham.

57 But to us, probability is the very guide of life.
   1736 *The Analogy of Religion*, introduction.

58 Sir, the pretending to extraordinary revelations and gifts of the Holy Ghost is a horrid thing, a very horrid thing.
   Comment to John Wesley. Quoted in John Wesley *Works*, pt.13.

Butler (of Saffron Walden), R(ichard) A(usten) Butler, Baron 1902–82

British Conservative politician. He became Chancellor of the Exchequer, Home Secretary and Deputy Prime Minister, and narrowly lost the premiership to Alec Douglas-Home, becoming Foreign Secretary (1963–4).

59 After all, it is not every man who nearly becomes Prime Minister of England.
   1957 On being passed over as Harold Macmillan's successor in favour of Alec Douglas-Home, Jan.

60 Politics is the art of the possible.
   1971 *The Art of the Possible*.
   ▶ See Galbraith 357:18.

61 The best Prime Minister we've got.
   Attributed comment on Harold Macmillan, made on a train going to the Party Conference in Brighton.

Butler, Samuel 1612–80

English satirist, who served in noble households and in government. His *Hudibras* (1663–78), a burlesque satire on Puritanism, was a special favourite of Charles II. Despite royal favour, he died in penury.

62 A client is fain to hire a lawyer to keep from the injury of other lawyers—as Christians that travel in Turkey are forced to hire Janissaries, to protect them from the insolencies of other Turks.
   1660 *Prose Observations*.

63 But here our authors make a doubt
   Whether he were more wise or stout.
   Some hold the one and some the other;
   But howsoe'er they make a pother,
   The difference was so small his brain
   Outweighed his rage but half a grain;
   Which made some take him for a tool
   That knaves do work with, called a fool.
   1663 *Hudibras*, pt.1, canto 1, l.29–36.

64 We grant, although he had much wit,
   He was very shy of using it;
   As being loath to wear it out,
   And therefore bore it not about,
   Unless on holidays, or so,
   As men their best apparel do.
   1663 *Hudibras*, pt.1, canto 1, l.45–50.

65 'Tis known he could speak Greek
   As naturally as pigs squeak.
   1663 *Hudibras*, pt.1, canto 1, l.51–2.

66 He was in logic a great critic,
   Profoundly skilled in analytic.
   He could distinguish and divide
   A hair 'twixt south and southwest side.
   1663 *Hudibras*, pt.1, canto 1, l.65–8.

67 For every *why* he had a *wherefore*.
   1663 *Hudibras*, pt.1, canto 1, l.132.

68 He knew what's what, and that's as high
   As metaphysic wit can fly.
   1663 *Hudibras*, pt.1, canto 1, l.149–50.

69 And with as delicate a hand
   Could twist as tough a rope of sand;
   And weave fine cobwebs, fit for skull
   That's empty when the moon is full;

Such as take lodgings in a head
That's to be let unfurnishèd.
1663 *Hudibras*, pt.1, canto 1, l.155–60.

70 And still be doing, never done:
As if Religion were intended
For nothing else but to be mended.
1663 *Hudibras*, pt.1, canto 1, l.202–4.

71 For rhyme the rudder is of verses,
With which like ships they steer their courses.
1663 *Hudibras*, pt.1, canto 1, l.457–8.

72 Great actions are not always true sons
Of great and mighty resolutions.
1663 *Hudibras*, pt.1, canto 1, l.877–8.

73 Ay me! what perils do environ
The man that meddles with cold iron!
1663 *Hudibras*, pt.1, canto 3, l.1–2.

74 I'll make the fur
Fly 'bout the ears of the old cur.
1663 *Hudibras*, pt.1, canto 3, l.277–8.

75 I am not now in fortune's power
He that is down can fall no lower.
1663 *Hudibras*, pt.1, canto 3, l.871–2.

76 Learning, that cobweb of the brain,
Profane, erroneous, and vain.
1663 *Hudibras*, pt.1, canto 3, l.1339–40.

77 She that with poetry is won
Is but a desk to write upon.
1664 *Hudibras*, pt.2, canto 1, l.591–2.

78 Love is a boy, by poets styled,
Then spare the rod, and spoil the child.
1664 *Hudibras*, pt.2, canto 1, l.843–4.

79 Oaths are but words, and words but wind.
1664 *Hudibras*, pt.2, canto 2, l.107.

80 For saints may do the same things by
The spirit, in sincerity,
Which other men are tempted to.
1664 *Hudibras*, pt.2, canto 2, l.235–7.

81 Doubtless the pleasure is as great
Of being cheated, as to cheat.
As lookers-on feel most delight,
That least perceive a juggler's sleight,
And still the less they understand,
The more th' admire his sleight of hand.
1664 *Hudibras*, pt.2, canto 3, l.1–6.

82 For in what stupid age or nation
Was marriage ever out of fashion?
1678 *Hudibras*, pt.3, canto 1, l.817–18.

83 What makes all doctrines plain and clear?
About two hundred pounds a year.
And that which was prov'd true before,
Prove false again? Two hundred more.
1678 *Hudibras*, pt.3, canto 1, l.1277–80.

84 For if it be but half denied,
'Tis half as good as justified.
1678 *Hudibras*, pt.3, canto 2, l.803–4.

85 For, those that fly, may fight again,
Which he can never do that's slain.
1678 *Hudibras*, pt.3, canto 3, l.243–4.

86 He that complies against his will
Is of his own opinion still.
1678 *Hudibras*, pt.3, canto 3, l.547.

87 Neither have the heart to stay,
Nor wit enough to run away.
1678 *Hudibras*, pt.3, canto 3, l.569–60.

88 For money has a power above
The stars and fate, to manage love.
1678 *Hudibras*, pt.3, canto 3, l.1279–80.

Butler, Samuel 1835–1902

English writer and parliamentary secretary. His Utopian satire *Erewhon* (1872) and its supplement *Erewhon Revisited* (1901) deal with the origins of religious belief. His autobiographical novel *The Way of All Flesh* was published posthumously (1903).

89 I am forgetting myself into admiring a mountain which is of no use for sheep. This is wrong. A mountain here is only beautiful if it has good grass on it.
1863 Of Mt Cook. *A First Year in Canterbury Settlement*.

90 The wish to spread those opinions that we hold conducive to our own welfare is so deeply rooted in the English character that few of us can escape its influence.
1872 *Erewhon*.

91 Exploring is delightful to look forward to and back upon, but it is not comfortable at the time, unless it be of such an easy nature as not to deserve the name.
1872 *Erewhon*.

92 A hen is only an egg's way of making another egg.
1877 *Life and Habit*, ch.8.

93 It was very good of God to let Carlyle and Mrs Carlyle marry one another and so make only two people miserable instead of four.
1884 Letter to Miss E M A Savage, 21 Nov.

94 Life is like playing a violin solo in public and learning the instrument as one goes on.
1895 Speech at the Somerville Club, 27 Feb.

95 It has been said that although God cannot alter the past, historians can; it is perhaps because they can be useful to Him in this respect that He tolerates their existence.
1901 *Erewhon Revisited*, ch.14.

96 All animals, except man, know that the principal business of life is to enjoy it.
1903 *The Way of All Flesh*, ch.19.

97 The advantage of doing one's praising for oneself is that one can lay it on so thick and exactly in the right places.
1903 *The Way of All Flesh*, ch.34.

98 Young as he was, his instinct told him that the best liar is he who makes the smallest amount of lying go the longest way.
1903 *The Way of All Flesh*, ch.39.

99 A man's friendships are, like his will, invalidated by marriage.
1903 *The Way of All Flesh*, ch.75.

1 'Getting into the key of C sharp,' he said, 'is like an unprotected female travelling on the Metropolitan Railway, and finding herself at Shepherd's Bush, without quite knowing where she wants to go to. How is she ever to get safe back to Clapham Junction?'
1903 *The Way of All Flesh*.

2 There's many a good tune played on an old fiddle.
1903 *The Way of All Flesh*.

3   As soon as any art is pursued with a view to money, then farewell, in ninety-nine cases out of a hundred, all hope of genuine good work.
    Collected in H F Jones (ed) *The Notebooks of Samuel Butler* (1912).

4   Justice is being allowed to do whatever I like. Injustice is whatever prevents my doing it.
    Collected in H F Jones (ed) *The Notebooks of Samuel Butler* (1912).

5   An apology for the Devil: It must be remembered that we have only heard one side of the case. God has written all the books.
    Collected in H F Jones (ed) *The Notebooks of Samuel Butler* (1912), ch.14.

6   Handel is so great and so simple that no one but a professional musician is unable to understand him.
    Collected in H F Jones (ed) *The Notebooks of Samuel Butler* (1912).

7   The healthy stomach is nothing if not conservative. Few radicals have good digestions.
    Collected in H F Jones (ed) *The Notebooks of Samuel Butler* (1912).

8   Science, after all, is only an expression for our ignorance of our own ignorance.
    Collected in H F Jones (ed) *The Notebooks of Samuel Butler* (1912).

9   To live is like to love—all reason is against it, and all healthy instinct for it.
    Collected in H F Jones (ed) *The Notebooks of Samuel Butler* (1912).

10 The three most important things a man has are, briefly, his private parts, his money, and his religious opinions.
    Collected in *Further Extracts from the Notebooks* (1934).

11 Jesus! with all thy faults I love thee still.
    Collected in *Further Extracts from the Notebooks* (1934).

12 A lawyer's dream of heaven: every man reclaimed his own property at the resurrection, and each tried to recover it from all his forefathers.
    Collected in *Further Extracts from the Notebooks* (1934).

Butler, William 1535–1618
English royal physician.

13 Doubtless God could have made a better berry, but doubtless God never did.
    Of the strawberry. Quoted in Izaak Walton *The Compleat Angler* (3rd edn, 1661), pt.1, ch.5.

Butterfield, Sir Herbert 1900–79
English historian, Professor of Modern History at Cambridge.

14 We can do worse than remember the principle which both gives us a firm Rock and leaves us the maximum elasticity for our minds—Hold to Christ, and for the rest be totally uncommitted.
    1949 *Christianity and History*.

15 In a profound sense we may say that the crucifixion, however else we may interpret it, accuses human nature, accuses all of us in the very things that we think are our righteousness.
    1951 *History and Human Relations*.

Byatt, Dame A(ntonia) S(usan) née Drabble 1936–
English writer and critic, sister of Margaret Drabble. Her works include critical studies, short stories and novels, such as *Possession* (Booker Prize, 1990), which explores the experience of women in 20c society, *The Biographer's Tale* (2000) and *The Children's Book* (2009).

16 There is something both gratifying and humiliating in watching a man who has taken you for a routinely silly woman begin to take you seriously.
    1985 *Still Life*, ch.18, 'Hic Ille Raphael'.

17 Autobiographies tell more lies than all but the most self-indulgent fiction.
    1987 'The Day That E.M. Forster Died'.

18 He's one of those men who argues by increments of noise—so that as you open your mouth he says another, cleverer, louder thing.
    1990 *Possession*, ch.15.

19 [J K] Rowling speaks to an adult generation that hasn't known and doesn't care about mystery. They are inhabitants of urban jungles, not of the real wild. They don't have the skills to tell ersatz magic from the real thing, for as children they daily invested the ersatz with what imagination they had.
    2003 In the *New York Times*, 8 Jul.

20 No man has a right to dictate another man's inner life—the furniture inside his skull.
    2009 *The Children's Book*.

Byrd, William 1543–1623
English composer and organist. A firm Catholic, prosecuted as a recusant, he wrote music for both Catholic and Anglican services, as well as madrigals, songs and music for strings.

21 The exercise of singing is delightful to nature and good to preserve the health of Man.
    1588 *Psalmes, Sonets and Songs*.

Byrne, David 1952–
Scottish rock singer and guitarist, member of Talking Heads.

22 Book learning, or intelligence of one sort, doesn't guarantee you intelligence of another sort. You can behave just as stupidly with a good college education.
    2004 In *Scotland on Sunday*, 29 Feb.

Byron, George Gordon, 6th Baron Byron of Rochdale 1788–1824
English Romantic poet. Lame from birth, he later dramatized himself as a gloomy, romantic man of mystery, the 'Byronic hero'. Suspected of an incestuous affair with his half-sister, he left for Venice, where he wrote *Beppo* (1818) and *Don Juan* (1819–24). He died fervently supporting the Greek war of independence against the Turks.

23 Yet, when confinement's lingering hour was done,
    Our sport, our studies, and our souls were one:
    Together we impell'd the flying ball;
    Together waited in our tutor's hall;
    Together join'd in cricket's manly toil.
    1807 *Hours of Idleness*, 'Childish Recollections'. Of his childhood days at Harrow public school.

24 I'll publish, right or wrong:
    Fools are my theme, let satire be my song.
    1809 *English Bards and Scotch Reviewers*, l.5–6.

25 A man must serve his time to every trade
    Save censure—critics all are ready made.

Take hackneyed jokes from Miller, got by rote,
With just enough of learning to misquote.
1809 *English Bards and Scotch Reviewers*, l.63–6.

26 Be warm, but pure; be amorous, but be chaste.
1809 *English Bards and Scotch Reviewers*, l.306.

27 The petrifactions of a plodding brain.
1809 *English Bards and Scotch Reviewers*, l.416.

28 Then let Ausonia, skilled in every art
To soften manners, but corrupt the heart,
Pour her exotic follies o'er the town,
To sanction Vice, and hunt Decorum down.
1809 *Engish Bards and Scotch Reviewers*, l.618–21.

29 Let simple Wordsworth chime his childish verse,
And brother Coleridge lull the babe at nurse.
1809 *English Bards and Scotch Reviewers*, l.917–18.

30 And glory, like the phoenix midst her fires,
Exhales her odours, blazes, and expires.
1809 *English Bards and Scotch Reviewers*, l.959–60.

31 Never under the most despotic of infidel Governments did I behold such squalid wretchedness as I have seen since my return, in the very heart of a Christian country. And what are your remedies? After months of inaction, and months of action worse than inactivity, at length comes forth the grand specific—the never-failing nostrum of all state physicians from the days of Draco to the present time; death. Is there not blood enough upon your penal code that more must be poured forth to ascend to Heaven and testify against you?
1812 Maiden speech, House of Lords, 27 Feb, against a proposal to introduce the death penalty for machine-wrecking.

32 A land of meanness, sophistry and mist.
1812 Of Scotland. 'The Curse of Minerva', l.138.

33 Each breeze from foggy mount and marshy plain
Dilutes with drivel every drizzly brain,
Till, burst at length, each wat'ry head o'er flows,
Foul as their soil, and frigid as their snows.
1812 Of Scotland and the Scots. 'The Curse of Minerva', l.139–42.

34 The laughing dames in who he did delight,
Whose large blue eyes, fair locks, and snowy hands,
Might shake the saintship of an anchorite.
1812–18 *Childe Harold's Pilgrimage*, canto 1, stanza 11.

35 Adieu, adieu! my native shore
Fades o'er the waters blue.
1812–18 *Childe Harold's Pilgrimage*, canto 1, stanza 13.

36 Here all were noble, save Nobility.
1812–18 *Childe Harold's Pilgrimage*, canto 1, stanza 85.

37 None are so desolate but something dear,
Dearer than self, possesses or possessed
A thought, and claims the homage of a tear.
1812–18 *Childe Harold's Pilgrimage*, canto 2, stanza 24.

38 Oh, lovely Spain! renown'd, romantic land!
1812–18 *Childe Harold's Pilgrimage*, canto 2, stanza 35.

39 Dark Sappho! could not verse immortal save
That beast imbued with such immortal fire?
Could she not live who life eternal gave?
1812–18 *Childe Harold's Pilgrimage*, canto 2, stanza 39.

40 Fair Greece! sad relic of departed worth!
Immortal, though no more! though fallen, great!
1812–18 *Childe Harold's Pilgrimage*, canto 2, stanza 73.

41 Hereditary bondsmen! know ye not
Who would be free themselves must strike the blow?
1812–18 *Childe Harold's Pilgrimage*, canto 2, stanza 76.

42 And yet how lovely in thine age of woe,
Land of lost gods and godlike men! art thou!
1812–18 Of Greece. *Childe Harold's Pilgrimage*, canto 2, stanza 85.

43 Art, Glory, Freedom fail, but Nature still is fair.
1812–18 *Childe Harold's Pilgrimage*, canto 2, stanza 87.

44 What is the worst of woes that wait on age?
What stamps the wrinkle deeper on the brow?
To view each loved one blotted from life's page,
And be alone on earth, as I am now.
1812–18 *Childe Harold's Pilgrimage*, canto 2, stanza 98.

45 Once more upon the waters! yet once more!
And the waves bound beneath me as a steed
That knows his rider.
1812–18 *Childe Harold's Pilgrimage*, canto 3, stanza 2.

46 The wandering outlaw of his own dark mind.
1812–18 *Childe Harold's Pilgrimage*, canto 3, stanza 3.

47 Years steal
Fire from the mind as vigour from the limb;
And life's enchanted cup but sparkles near the brim.
1812–18 *Childe Harold's Pilgrimage*, canto 3, stanza 8.

48 Where rose the mountains, there to him were friends;
Where rolled the ocean, thereon was his home;
Where a blue sky, and glowing clime, extends,
He had the passion and the power to roam.
1812–18 *Childe Harold's Pilgrimage*, canto 3, stanza 13.

49 The very knowledge that he lived in vain,
That all was over on this side the tomb,
Had made Despair a smilingness assume.
1812–18 *Childe Harold's Pilgrimage*, canto 3, stanza 16.

50 There was a sound of revelry by night,
And Belgium's capital had gathered then
Her beauty and her chivalry, and bright
The lamps that shone o'er fair women and brave men;
A thousand hearts beat happily; and when
Music arose with its voluptuous swell,
Soft eyes looked love to eyes which spake again,
And all went merry as a marriage bell;
But hush! hark! a deep sound strikes like a rising knell!
1812–18 *Childe Harold's Pilgrimage*, canto 3, stanza 21.

51 He rushed into the field, and, foremost fighting, fell.
1812–18 *Childe Harold's Pilgrimage*, canto 3, stanza 23.

52 Quiet to quick bosoms is a hell.
1812–18 *Childe Harold's Pilgrimage*, canto 3, stanza 42.

53 I live not in myself, but I become
Portion of that around me; and to me,
High mountains are a feeling, but the hum
Of human cities torture.
1812–18 *Childe Harold's Pilgrimage*, canto 3, stanza 72.

54 His love was passion's essence:—as a tree
On fire by lightning, with ethereal flame
Kindled he was, and blasted.
1812–18 *Childe Harold's Pilgrimage*, canto 3, stanza 78.

55 Sapping a solemn creed with solemn sneer.
1812–18 Of Edward Gibbon. *Childe Harold's Pilgrimage*, canto 3, stanza 107.

56 I have not loved the world, nor the world me.
1812–18 *Childe Harold's Pilgrimage*, canto 3, stanza 113.

57 I stood
Among them, but not of them; in a shroud
Of thoughts which were not their thoughts.
1812–18 Childe Harold's Pilgrimage, canto 3, stanza 113.

58 I stood in Venice, on the Bridge of Sighs;
A palace and a prison on each hand:
I saw from out the wave her structures rise
As from the stroke of the enchanter's wand:
A thousand years their cloudy wings expand
Around me, and a dying Glory smiles
O'er the far times, when many a subject land
Look'd to the winged Lion's marble piles,
Where Venice sate in state, thron'd on her hundred isles!
1812–18 Childe Harold's Pilgrimage, canto 4, stanza 1.

59 Fair Italy!
Thou art the garden of the world, the home
Of all Art yields, and Nature can decree;
Even in thy desert, what is like to thee?
1812–18 Childe Harold's Pilgrimage, canto 4, stanza 26.

60 The moon is up, and yet it is not night;
Sunset divides the sky with her—a sea
Of glory streams along the Alpine height
Of blue Friuli's mountains; Heaven is free
From clouds, but of all colours seems to be
Melted to one vast Iris of the West,
Where the day joins the past eternity.
1812–18 Childe Harold's Pilgrimage, canto 4, stanza 27.

61 Italia! oh Italia! thou who hast
The fatal gift of beauty.
1812–18 Childe Harold's Pilgrimage, canto 4, stanza 42.

62 Oh Rome! my country! city of the soul!
1812–18 Childe Harold's Pilgrimage, canto 4, stanza 78.

63 From mighty wrongs to petty perfidy
Have I not seen what human things could do?
From the loud roar of foaming calumny
To the small whisper of the asp paltry few,
And subtler venom of the reptile crew,
The Janus glance of whose significant eye,
Learning to lie with silence, would seem true,
And without utterance, save the shrug or sigh,
Deal round to happy fools its speechless obloquy.
1812–18 Childe Harold's Pilgrimage, canto 4, stanza 136.

64 But I have lived, and have not lived in vain:
My mind may loose its force, my blood its fire,
And my frame perish even in conquering pain;
But there is that within me which shall tire
Torture and Time, and breathe when I expire.
Something unearthly, which they deem not of,
Like the remembered tone of a mute lyre,
Shall on their softened spirits sink, and move
In hearts all rocky now the late remorse of love.
1812–18 Childe Harold's Pilgrimage, canto 4, stanza 137.

65 The seal is set.—Now welcome, thou dread power!
Nameless, yet thus omnipotent, which here
Walk'st in the shadow of the midnight hour
With a deep awe, yet all distinct from fear;
Thy haunts are ever where the dead walls rear
Their ivy mantles, and the solemn scene
Derives from thee a sense so deep and clear
That we become a part of what has been,
And grow unto the spot, all-seeing but unseen.
1812–18 Childe Harold's Pilgrimage, canto 4, stanza 138.

66 There were his young barbarians all at play,
There was their Dacian mother—he, their sire,
Butchered to make a Roman holiday.
1812–18 Childe Harold's Pilgrimage, canto 4, stanza 141.

67 A ruin—yet what ruin! from its mass
Walls, palaces, half-cities, have been reared.
1812–18 Childe Harold's Pilgrimage, canto 4, stanza 143.

68 While stands the Coliseum, Rome shall stand;
When falls the Coliseum, Rome shall fall;
And when Rome falls—the World.
1812–18 Childe Harold's Pilgrimage, canto 4, stanza 145.

69 Oh! that desert were my dwelling-place,
With one fair spirit for my minister,
That I might all forget the human race,
And, hating no one, love but only her!
1812–18 Childe Harold's Pilgrimage, canto 4, stanza 177.

70 There is a pleasure in the pathless woods,
There is a rapture on the lonely shore,
There is society, where none intrudes,
By the deep sea, and music in its roar:
I love not man less, but nature more.
1812–18 Childe Harold's Pilgrimage, canto 4, stanza 178.

71 Roll on, thou deep and dark blue Ocean—roll!
Ten thousand fleets sweep over thee in vain;
Man marks the earth with ruin—his control
Stops with the shore.
1812–18 Childe Harold's Pilgrimage, canto 4, stanza 179.

72 When for a moment, like a drop of rain,
He sinks into thy depths with bubbling groan,
Without a grave, unkindled, uncoffined, and unknown.
1812–18 Childe Harold's Pilgrimage, canto 4, stanza 179.

73 Dark-heaving;—boundless, endless, and sublime—
The image of eternity.
1812–18 Of the sea. *Childe Harold's Pilgrimage,* canto 4, stanza 183.

74 Such hath it been—shall be—beneath the sun
The many still must labour for the one.
1814 The Corsair, canto 1, stanza 8.

75 There was a laughing devil in sneer,
That raised emotions both of rage and fear;
And where his frown of hatred darkly fell,
Hope withering fled, and Mercy sighed farewell!
1814 The Corsair, canto 1, stanza 9.

76 Deep in my soul that tender secret dwells,
Lonely and lost to light for evermore,
Save when to thine my heart responsive swells,
Then trembles into silence as before.
1814 The Corsair, 'Medora's Song', canto 1, stanza 14.

77 The spirit burning but unbent
May writhe, rebel—the weak alone repent!
1814 The Corsair, canto 2, stanza 10.

78 Oh! too convincing—dangerously dear—
In woman's eye the unanswerable tear!
1814 The Corsair, canto 2, stanza 15.

79 Shakespeare's name, you may depend upon it, stands absurdly too high and will go down. He had no invention as to stories, none whatever. He took all his plots from old novels, and threw their stories into dramatic shape... That he threw over whatever he did

write some flashes of genius, nobody can deny; but this
was all.
1814 Letter to James Hogg, 24 Mar.

80 She walks in beauty like the night
Of cloudless climes and starry skies;
And all that's best of dark and bright
Meet in her aspect and her eyes:
Thus mellowed to that tender light
Which heaven to gaudy day denies.
1815 'She Walks in Beauty'.

81 There's not a joy the world can give like that it takes
away.
1816 'Stanzas for Music'.

82 The mind can make
Substance, and people planets of its own
With beings brighter than have been, and give
A breath to forms which can outlive all flesh.
1816 *The Dream*, stanza 1.

83 Sorrow is knowledge: they who know the most
Must mourn the deepest o'er the fatal truth,
The tree of knowledge is not that of Life.
1817 *Manfred*, act 1, sc.1.

84 How beautiful is all this visible world!
How glorious in its action and itself!
But we, who name ourselves its sovereigns, we,
Half dust, half deity, alike unfit
To sink or soar, with our mixed essence make
A conflict of its elements, and breathe
The breath of degradation and of pride.
1817 *Manfred*, act 1, sc.2.

85 In short he was a perfect cavaliero,
And to his very valet seemed a hero.
1818 *Beppo*, stanza 33.

86 His heart was one of those which most enamour us,
Wax to receive, and marble to retain.
1818 *Beppo*, stanza 34.

87 Our cloudy climate, and our chilly women.
1818 *Beppo*, stanza 49.

88 Old man! 'tis not so difficult to die.
1819 *Manfred* (2nd edn), act 3, sc.4.

89 And Coleridge, too, has lately taken wing,
But, like a hawk encumbered with his hood,
Explaining metaphysics to the nation—
I wished he would explain his explanation.
1819–24 *Don Juan*, canto 1, dedication, stanza 2.

90 But—Oh! ye lords of ladies intellectual,
Inform us truly, have they not hen-pecked you all?.
1819–24 *Don Juan*, canto 1, stanza 22.

91 Married, charming, chaste, and twenty-three.
1819–24 *Don Juan*, canto 1, stanza 59.

92 What men call gallantry, and gods adultery,
Is much more common where the climate's sultry.
1819–24 *Don Juan*, canto 1, stanza 63.

93 Christians have burnt each other, quite persuaded
That all the Apostles would have done as they did.
1819–24 *Don Juan*, canto 1, stanza 83.

94 He thought about himself, and the whole earth,
Of man the wonderful, and of the stars,
And how the deuce they ever could have birth;
And then he thought of earthquakes, and of wars,
How many miles the moon might have in girth,
Of air-balloons, and of the many bars
To perfect knowledge of the boundless skies;
And then he thought of Donna Julia's eyes.
1819–24 *Don Juan*, canto 1, stanza 92.

95 A little still she strove, and much repented,
And whispering 'I will ne'er consent'—consented.
1819–24 *Don Juan*, canto 1, stanza 117.

96 Sweet is revenge—especially to women.
1819–24 *Don Juan*, canto 1, stanza 124.

97 'Tis sweet to win, no matter how, one's laurels
By blood or ink; 'tis sweet to put an end
To strife; 'tis sometimes sweet to have our quarrels,
Particularly with a tiresome friend;
Sweet is old wine in bottles, ale in barrels;
Dear is the helpless creature we defend
Against the world; and dear the schoolboy spot
We ne'er forget, though there we are forgot.
1819–24 *Don Juan*, canto 1, stanza 126.

98 But sweeter still than this, than these, than all,
Is first and passionate love—it stands alone,
Like Adam's recollection of his fall;
The tree of knowledge hath been pluck'd—all's known
And life yields nothing further to recall
Worthy of this ambrosial sin, so shown,
No doubt in fable, as the unforgiven
Fire which Prometheus filch'd for us from heaven.
1819–24 *Don Juan*, canto 1, stanza 127.

99 Pleasure's a sin, and sometimes sin is a pleasure.
1819–24 *Don Juan*, canto 1, stanza 133.

1 Man's love is of man's life a thing apart,
'Tis woman's whole existence.
1819–24 *Don Juan*, canto 1, stanza 194.
▶ See Amis 16:31.

2 If ever I should condescend to prose,
I'll write poetical commandments, which
Shall supersede beyond all doubt all those
That went before; in these I shall enrich
My text with many things that no one knows,
And carry precept to the highest pitch:
I'll call the work 'Longinus o'er a Bottle,
Or, Every Poet his own Aristotle'.
1819–24 *Don Juan*, canto 1, stanza 204.

3 Thou shalt believe in Milton, Dryden, Pope;
Thou shalt not set up Wordsworth, Coleridge, Southey;
Because the first is crazed beyond all hope,
The second drunk, the third so quaint and mouthey:
With Crabbe it may be difficult to cope,
And Campbell's Hippocrene is somewhat drouthy:
Thou shalt not steal from Samuel Rogers, nor
Commit flirtation with the muse of Moore.
1819–24 *Don Juan*, canto 1, stanza 205.

4 So for a good old-gentlemanly vice,
I think I must take up with avarice.
1819–24 *Don Juan*, canto 1, stanza 216.

5 There's nought, no doubt, so much the spirit calms
As rum and true religion.
1819–24 *Don Juan*, canto 2, stanza 34.

6 It was a wild and breaker-beaten coast,
With cliffs above, and a broad sandy shore,
Guarded by shoals and rocks as by an host,

Byron

With here and there a creek, whose aspect wore
A better welcome to the tempest-tost;
And rarely ceased the haughty billow's roar,
Save on the dead long summer days, which make
The outstretch'd ocean glitter like a lake.
1819–24 *Don Juan*, canto 2, stanza 177.

7 Few things surpass old wine; and they may preach
Who please,—the more because they preach in vain,
Let us have wine and woman, mirth and laughter,
Sermons and soda water the day after.
1819–24 *Don Juan*, canto 2, stanza 178.

8 Man, being reasonable, must get drunk;
The best of Life is but intoxication.
Glory, the grape, love, gold, in these are sunk
The hopes of all men, and of every nation.
1819–24 *Don Juan*, canto 2, stanza 179.

9 They looked up to the sky, whose floating glow
Spread like a rosy ocean, vast and bright;
They gazed upon the glittering sea below,
Whence the broad moon rose circling into sight;
They heard the wave's splash, and the wind so low,
And saw each other's dark eyes darting light
Into each other—and, beholding this,
Their lips drew near, and clung to a kiss.
1819–24 *Don Juan*, canto 2, stanza 185.

10 In her first passion woman loves her lover,
In all the others all she loves is love.
1819–24 *Don Juan*, canto 3, stanza 3.

11 'Tis melancholy, and a fearful sign
Of human frailty, folly, also crime,
That love and marriage rarely can combine,
Although they both are born in the same clime;
Marriage from love, like vinegar from wine
A sad, sour, sober beverage—by time
Is sharpened from its high celestial flavour,
Down to a very homely household savour.
1819–24 *Don Juan*, canto 3, stanza 5.

12 Think you, if Laura had been Petrach's wife,
He would have written sonnets all his life?
1819–24 *Don Juan*, canto 3, stanza 8.

13 All tragedies are finished by a death,
All comedies are ended by a marriage;
The future states of both are left to faith.
1819–24 *Don Juan*, canto 3, stanza 9.

14 He was the mildest mannered man
That ever scuttled ship or cut a throat,
With such true breeding of a gentleman,
You never could divine his real thought.
1819–24 *Don Juan*, canto 3, stanza 41.

15 The mountains look on Marathon—
And Marathon looks on the sea;
And musing there an hour alone,
I dreamed that Greece might still be free.
1819–24 *Don Juan*, canto 3, stanza 86.

16 And if I laugh at any mortal thing
'Tis that I may not weep.
1819–24 *Don Juan*, canto 4, stanza 4.

17 But after being fired at once or twice,
The ear becomes more Irish, and less nice.
1819–24 *Don Juan*, canto 4, stanza 41.

18 I have a passion for the name of 'Mary,'
For once it was a magic sound to me;
And still it half calls up the realms of fairy,
Where I beheld what never was to be.
1819–24 *Don Juan*, canto 5, stanza 4.

19 There is a tide in the affairs of women,
Which taken at the flood, leads—God knows where.
1819–24 *Don Juan*, canto 6, stanza 2.

20 Gaunt Famine never shall approach the throne.
Though Ireland starve, great George weighs twenty stone.
1819–24 *Don Juan*, canto 8, stanza 126.

21 And, after all what is a lie? 'Tis but
The truth in masquerade.
1819–24 *Don Juan*, canto 11, stanza 37.

22 Now hatred is by far the longest pleasure;
Men love in haste, but they detest at leisure.
1819–24 *Don Juan*, canto 13, stanza 4.

23 The English winter—ending in July,
To recommence in August.
1819–24 *Don Juan*, canto 13, stanza 42.

24 Society is now one polished horde,
Formed of two mighty tribes, the Bores and Bored.
1819–24 *Don Juan*, canto 13, stanza 95.

25 'Tis strange but true; for truth is always stranger;
Stranger than fiction.
1819–24 *Don Juan*, canto 14, stanza 101.

26 All present life is but an interjection,
An 'Oh!' or 'Ah!' of joy or misery,
Or a 'Ha! ha!' or 'Bah!'—a yawn or 'Pooh!'
Of which perhaps the latter is most true.
1819–24 *Don Juan*, canto 15, stanza 1.

27 There's music in the sighing of a reed;
There's music in the gushing of a rill;
There's music in all things, if men had ears:
Their earth is but an echo of the spheres.
1819–24 *Don Juan*, canto 15, stanza 5.

28 Between two worlds life hovers like a star,
'Twixt night and morn, upon the horizon's verge.
How little do we know that which we are!
How less what we may be!
1819–24 *Don Juan*, canto 15, stanza 99.

29 Eat, drink, and love; the rest's not worth a fillip.
1821 *Sardanapalus*, act 1, sc.2.

30 Oh, talk not to me of a name great in story;
The days of our youth are the days of our glory;
And the myrtle and ivy of sweet two-and-twenty
Are worth all your laurels, though ever so plenty.
1821 'Stanzas Written on the Road between Florence and Pisa, November 1821'.

31 The angels all were singing out of tune,
And hoarse with having little else to do,
Excepting to wind up the sun and moon,
Or curb a runaway young star or two.
1822 *The Vision of Judgement*, stanza 2.

32 As he drew near, he gazed upon the gate
Ne'er to be entered more by him or Sin,
With such a glance of supernatural hate,
As made Saint Peter wish himself within;
He pattered with his keys at a great rate,
And sweated through his apostolic skin:

Of course his perspiration was but ichor,
Or some such other spiritual liquor.
1822 *The Vision of Judgement*, stanza 25.

33 And when the tumult dwindled to a calm,
I left him practising the hundredth psalm.
1822 *The Vision of Judgement*, stanza 106.

34 For what were all these country patriots born?
To hunt, and vote, and raise the price of corn?
1823 *The Age of Bronze*, stanza 14.

35 I awoke one morning and found myself famous.
Of the instant popularity of *Childe Harolde*. Quoted in Thomas Moore *Letters and Journals of Lord Byron* (1830), vol.1.

Byron, Henry James 1834–84

English playwright and actor. His most successful plays included *Our Boys* (1874) and the comedies *War to the Knife* (1865) and *A Hundred Thousand Pounds* (1866), as well as numerous burlesques and extravaganzas.

36 Life's too short for chess.
1874 *Our Boys*.

Byron, Robert 1905–41

English traveller, critic of art and architecture and historian, who travelled extensively in Europe and Asia. His best-known book is *The Road to Oxiana* (1937). He drowned in 1941 when his ship to the Mediterranean was torpedoed.

37 The existence of St Sophia is atmospheric; that of St Peter's, overpowering, imminently substantial. One is a church to God; the other a salon for his agents. One is consecrated to reality, the other to illusion. St Sophia, in fact, is large, and St Peter's is vilely, tragically small.
1929 *The Byzantine Achievement*.

38 *Herat, 8 December*. What a day it was! God save me from any more adventures on a drained stomach.
1937 *The Road to Oxiana*.

39 I shall have warmonger put on my passport.
c.1938 Comment in response to the rise of Nazism, opposing the policy of appeasement. Quoted in Bruce Chatwin's introduction to *The Road to Oxiana* (1980 edn).

C

Cabell, James Branch 1879–1958

US novelist and critic. *Jurgen* (1919) is the best known of a sequence of 18 novels, collectively known as *Biography of Michael*. His *Preface to the Past* (1936) is a book of criticism.

1 I am willing to taste any drink once.
1919 *Jurgen*, ch.1.

2 A man possesses nothing certainly save a brief loan of his own body.
1919 *Jurgen*, ch.20.

3 I shall marry in haste and repeat at leisure.
1919 *Jurgen*, ch.26.
▸ See Congreve 240:30.

4 Drunkenness is a joy reserved for the Gods: so do men partake of it impiously, and so are they very properly punished for their audacity.
1919 *Jurgen*, ch.28.

5 Poetry is man's rebellion against being what he is.
1919 *Jurgen*.

6 The optimist proclaims that we live in the best of all possible worlds; and the pessimist fears this is true.
1926 *The Silver Stallion*, bk.4, ch.26.

Cable, (John) Vince(nt) 1943–

English Liberal Democrat politician. Elected MP for Twickenham in 1997, he became the Liberal Democrat Deputy Leader (2006–10), and Secretary for Business, Innovation and Skills (2010–) under Conservative Prime Minister David Cameron.

7 The House has noticed the Prime Minister's remarkable transformation in the past few weeks from Stalin to Mr Bean, creating chaos out of order, rather than order out of chaos.
2007 Referring to Labour Prime Minister Gordon Brown in the House of Commons, 28 Nov.

Cabrera Infante, Guillermo 1929–2005

Cuban novelist, scriptwriter, film critic and diplomat. He supported Castro's revolutionary forces initially, but later left the country and settled in London (1965), becoming a British subject. *Tres tristes tigres* (1967, translated as *Three Trapped Tigers*, 1971) is full of puns, neologisms and humorous word play.

8 *Hablando siempre y siempre contando chismes y haciendo chistes y siempre y también filosofando o estetizando o moralizando, siempre: la cuestión era hacer ver como que no trabajábamos porque en La Habana, Cuba, esa es la única manera de ser gente bien.*
Talking all the time and telling jokes or gossiping all the time and always and also philosophizing or aestheticizing or moralizing, but always: the thing was to make it look like we didn't have to work because in Havana, Cuba, this is the only way to be high society . . .
1967 *Tres tristes tigres* (*Three Trapped Tigers*, 1971), 'Bachata'.

Cadoria, Brigadier General Sherian G(race) 1940–

US soldier. In 1985 she became the highest-ranking black woman in the US military. She retired in 1990.

9 By act of Congress, male officers are gentlemen, but by act of God, we are ladies.
1989 In *US News and World Report*, 13 Feb.

Caesar, Irving 1895–1996

US librettist and lyricist.

10 Tea for two, and two for tea.
1924 *No! No! Nanette*, 'Tea for Two' (with Otto Harbach. Music by Vincent Youmans).

Caesar, Gaius Julius 100/102–44 BC

Roman general and statesman. As consul (59 BC) and pro-consul (58–50 BC) he extended Roman power in Gaul and Britain. Refusing to disband his army, he came into conflict with the Senate, supported by Pompey, whom Caesar defeated in the civil war that followed. He became dictator for life, but was assassinated in 44 BC. His works include the *Commentarii* ('War

Commentaries'), *De Bello Gallico* ('On the Gallic War', 7 vols) and *De Bello Civili* ('On the Civil War', 3 vols).

11 *Gallia est omnis divisa in partes tres.*
Gaul as a whole is divided into three parts.
51 BC *De Bello Gallico*, bk.1, section 1, opening words.

12 *Fere libenter homines id quod volunt credunt.*
Men are nearly always willing to believe what they wish.
51 BC *De Bello Gallico*, bk.3, section 18.

13 *Iacta est alea.*
The die is cast.
49 BC Comment on crossing the river Rubicon (the border between his province and Italy) with his troops, thereby committing himself to civil war. Quoted in Suetonius *Lives of the Twelve Caesars*, 'Divus Iulius', section 32.

14 *Veni, vidi, vici.*
I came, I saw, I conquered.
46 BC Said to have been written on a *titulus* (placard) carried along in Caesar's triumph after a campaign in Pontus (Asia Minor) during the civil war (46 BC). Quoted in Suetonius *Lives of the Twelve Caesars*, 'Divus Iulius', section 37. Another source reports that Caesar used this expression in a letter to the Senate after the same campaign (cf Plutarch, *Caesar* 50, 3–4).

15 Caesar's wife must be above suspicion.
Attributed. Based on an episode in Plutarch *Caesar* 10.6, which tells that Caesar divorced his wife after accusations of impiety, although he defended her in court.

16 *Et tu, Brute?*
You too, Brutus?
Attributed last words, when struck by his murderers, Cassius and Brutus. The tradition is based on Suetonius *Lives of the Twelve Caesars*, 'Divus Iulius', section 82: 'Some say that when he saw Marcus Brutus about to deliver the second blow, he reproached him in Greek with: "You too, my son?" (the Greek is *kai su, teknon*).

Cage, John 1912–92

US ultra-modernist composer. His experiments included 'aleatory' music, in which the role of chance determines how a piece will develop. *Silence* (1961), *M* (1973), and *Empty Works* (1979) are among his books.

17 Which is more musical, a truck passing by a factory or a truck passing by a music school?
1961 *Silence*.

18 I have nothing to say and I am saying it and that is poetry.
1961 'Lecture on Nothing'.

Cagney, James 1899–1986

US film actor. A leading role in *Public Enemy* (1931) established him as the quintessential screen gangster. He won an Academy Award for his performance in *Yankee Doodle Dandy* (1942).

19 Look Ma—top of the world.
1949 Line delivered in *White Heat* (screenplay by Ivan Goff and Ben Roberts).

Cain, James M(allahan) 1892–1977

US crime writer.

20 The Postman Always Rings Twice.
1934 Title of novel.

21 Double Indemnity.
1943 Title of novel.

Calas, Nicolas 1907–88

Greek-born art critic and poet, who associated with the Surrealists in Paris in the 1930s. He moved to the United States in 1939.

22 Art is a form of communication that insinuates. We *expect* the artist to have more to say than what he communicated and *suspect* that what he said was a subterfuge for hiding something.
1968 *Art in the Age of Risk*.

Caldwell, Philip 1920–2013

US company executive, Chairman of the Ford Motor Co (1980–5).

23 We redesigned everything but the air in the tires.
1995 Of the development of the Taurus, which was to become America's best-selling car. In *Fortune*, 3 Apr.

Calhoun, John Caldwell 1782–1850

US statesman and orator, Vice-President under John Q Adams and then Andrew Jackson. His *Address to the People of South Carolina* (1831) set forth his theory of state rights.

24 The Government of the absolute majority, instead of the Government of the people, is but the Government of the strongest interests; and when not efficiently checked, it is the most tyrannical and oppressive that can be devised.
1833 Speech, US Senate, 15 Feb.

Caligiuri, Paul 1964–

US footballer.

25 The world knows the American athlete is superior. It's only a matter of time before we develop the world's best soccer teams.
2002 In *The Times*, 28 Dec.

Caligula properly Gaius Julius Caesar Germanicus AD 12–41

Roman Emperor (AD 37–41), nicknamed Caligula as a child from his little soldier's boots (*caligae*). His extravagant, autocratic, vicious and mentally unstable behaviour resulted in his assassination.

26 *Utinam populus Romanus unam cervicem haberet!*
Would that the Roman people had but one neck!
c.40 AD Quoted in Suetonius *Lives of the Twelve Caesars*, 'Gaius Caligula', section 30.

Callaghan (of Cardiff), (Leonard) James Callaghan, Baron 1912–2005

English Labour politician. As Chancellor of the Exchequer he introduced controversial corporation and selective employment taxes. He was Home Secretary (1967–70), Foreign Secretary (1974–6) and Prime Minister (1976–9).

27 Britain has lived for too long on borrowed time, borrowed money, and even borrowed ideas.
1976 Quoted in the *Observer*, 3 Oct.

28 There is no virtue in producing socially well adjusted members of society who are unemployed because they do not have the skills. Nor at the other extreme must they be technically efficient robots.
1976 Speech at Ruskin College, Oxford, reprinted in the *Times Higher Education Supplement*, 15 Oct. This speech began the so-called 'Great Debate' on education.

29 A lie can travel halfway round the world before the truth has got its boots on.

1976 Speech in the House of Commons, Nov.
▶ *See* Spurgeon 841:89.

30 Either back us or sack us.
1977 Speech, Labour Party Conference, 5 Oct.

31 Crisis? What crisis?
1979 Headline in *The Sun*, 11 Jan, alluding to his remark on returning from the Guadaloupe summit to be confronted by widespread strikes. His actual words were, 'I don't think that other people in the world would share the view that there is mounting chaos.'

Callanan, Jeremiah John 1795–1829

Irish poet. Born in Cork and sent by his parents to study for the priesthood, he developed instead his interest in lyrical poetry. He supported himself by teaching and writing. He gained general celebrity with 'Gougane Barra' (1826).

32 There grows the wild ash; and a time-stricken willow
Looks chidingly down on the mirth of the billow,
As, like some gay child that sad monitor scorning,
It lightly laughs back to the laugh of the morning.
1826 'Gougane Barra'.

Callow, Simon Phillip Hugh 1949–

English actor and director.

33 When he speaks, I hear Shakespeare think.
On Sir John Gielgud. Quoted in *The Guardian*, 14 Apr 2004.

Calonne, Charles Alexandre de 1734–1802

French politician. Appointed Controller-General in 1783, he was exiled in 1787 when he failed to provide a statement of accounts to explain the treasury deficit. Napoleon I permitted his return in 1802.

34 *Madame, si c'est possible, c'est fait; impossible? cela se fera.*
Madam, if a thing is possible, consider it done; the impossible? that will be done.
Quoted in J Michelet *Histoire de la Révolution Française* (1847), vol.1, pt.2. This has been adapted as the slogan of the US army: 'The difficult we do immediately; the impossible takes a little longer.'

Calvino, Italo 1923–85

Italian modernist writer and journalist, born in Cuba. A fascist under compulsion, he later joined the Resistance (1943) and wrote for the Communist *L'unità* in the 1940s. His novels combine fantasy with a hard satirical wit.

35 *Lo sguardo dei cani che non capiscono e non sanno che possono aver ragione a non capire.*
The gaze of dogs who don't understand and who don't know that they may be right not to understand.
1957 *Il Barone Rampante*, ch.10.

Cambronne, Pierre, Baron de 1770–1842

French general in the Napoleonic wars.

36 *La Garde meurt, mais ne se rend pas.*
The Guards die but do not surrender.
1815 Attributed, when called upon to surrender at the Battle of Waterloo, 18 Jun.

Cameron, David William Donald 1966–

English Conservative politician. He was elected as MP for Witney in 2001 and became leader of the Conservative Party in 2005. In 2010 he became the youngest Prime Minister in nearly 200 years, at the head of a Conservative-led coalition government with the Liberal Democrats.

37 I am the heir to Blair.
2005 Speaking to newspaper executives, 3 Oct.

38 There is such a thing as society. It's just not the same thing as the state.
2005 Speech upon winning the Conservative Party leadership contest, 6 Dec.

39 Too many twits make a twat.
2009 Referring to Twitter, Absolute Radio interview, 29 Jul.

40 Press freedom does not mean that the press should be above the law. While it's vital that a free press can tell truth to power, it is equally important that those in power can tell truth to the press.
2011 In the *New York Times*, 10 Jul.

41 Calm down, dear.
2011 Speaking to Angela Eagle MP during Prime Minister's Questions.

42 When people's love is divided by law, it is the law that needs to change.
2014 Referring to the legalisation of same-sex marriage in the UK, in *Pink News*, 28 Mar.

Cameron, James 1954–

Canadian film director. His film *Titanic* (1997) won eleven Academy Awards, equalling the record set by *Ben Hur* in 1959.

43 I'm king of the world.
1998 Accepting his Best Director Oscar for *Titanic* (1997), 23 Mar, an allusion to a line in *Titanic*.

Campbell, Donald Malcolm 1921–67

English speedboat racer. Son of Sir Malcolm Campbell, he broke all his father's land and water speed records, but was killed when his hydroplane *Bluebird* crashed on Lake Coniston at about 300mph.

44 There is no hope of bailing out of a speedboat. You hit the water and become so much pulp.
Quoted in Douglas Young-James *Donald Campbell: An Informal Biography* (1968).

Campbell, Kim *originally* Avril Phaedra Campbell 1947–

Canadian politician. She entered the Commons in 1988 as a Progressive Conservative, becoming Canada's first woman Prime Minister (Jun–Dec, 1993); she lost her parliamentary seat in the 1993 election.

45 Charisma without substance is a dangerous thing.
1986 Speech, while unsuccessfully contesting the leadership of the Social Credit Party of British Columbia, 22 Oct.

Campbell, Mrs Patrick *née* Beatrice Rose Stella Tanner 1865–1940

English actress. Famed for her stage presence and incisive wit, she made her debut in 1888. She corresponded with George Bernard Shaw, who wrote *Pygmalion* especially for her.

46 When you were quite a little boy somebody ought to have said 'hush' just once.
1912 Letter to George Bernard Shaw, 1 Nov.

47 The deep, deep peace of the double-bed after the hurly-burly of the chaise-longue.
Her definition of marriage, quoted in Alexander Woollcott *While Rome Burns* (1934), 'The First Mrs Tanqueray'.

48 It doesn't matter what you do in the bedroom
as long as you don't do it in the street and frighten
the horses.
Quoted in Daphne Fielding *The Duchess of Jermyn Street* (1964),
ch.2. Sometimes attributed to Edward VII.

49 Watching Tallulah Bankhead on the stage is like
watching somebody skating on very thin ice—and the
English want to be there when she falls through.
Quoted in *The Times*, 13 Dec 1968.

Campbell, (Ignatius) Roy Dunnachie 1901–57

South African poet, who spent much of his life in Britain.
He moved from an early liberalism to outspoken right-
wing Catholicism, and is best remembered for his early lyric
poems.

50 South Africa, renowned both far and wide
For politics and little else besides.
1928 'The Wayzgoose'.

51 You praise the firm restraint with which they write—
I'm with you there, of course:
They use the snaffle and the curb all right,
But where's the bloody horse?
1930 'On Some South African Novelists'.

52 Of all the clever people round me here
I most delight in Me—
Mine is the only voice I care to hear,
And mine the only face I like to see.
1930 'Home Thoughts in Bloomsbury'.

53 Write with your spade, and garden with your pen,
Shove your couplets to their long repose.
And type your turnips down the field in rows.
1931 'The Georgiad', pt.2.

54 Burn, with Athens and with Rome,
A sacred city of the mind.
1936 'Toledo, July 1936'.

55 I will go stark: and let my meanings show
Clear as a milk-white feather in a crow
Or a black stallion on a field of snow.
1936 'A Good Resolution'.

56 He shouldered high his voluntary Cross,
Wrestled his hardships into forms of beauty,
And taught his gorgon destinies to sing.
1943 'Luis de Camões'.

57 Giraffes!—a People
Who live between the earth and skies,
Each in his own religious steeple,
Keeping a light-house with his eyes.
1946 'Dreaming Spires'.

58 Translations, like wives, are seldom faithful if they are in
the least attractive.
1949 *The Poetry Review*, Jun/Jul.

59 I hate 'Humanity' and all such abstracts: but I love
people. Lovers of 'Humanity' generally hate *people and
children*, and keep parrots or puppy dogs.
1951 *Light On A Dark Horse*, ch.13.

Campbell, Thomas 1777–1844

Scottish poet and journalist. Editor from 1820 to 1830 of *The New
Monthly Magazine*, to which he contributed many poems. He is
buried in Westminster Abbey.

60 On the green banks of Shannon, when Sheelah was nigh,
No blithe Irish lad was so happy as I;
No harp like my own could so cheerily play,
And wherever I went was my poor dog Tray.
1799 'The Harper', stanza 1.

61 'Tis distance lends enchantment to the view,
And robes the mountain in its azure hue.
1799 *The Pleasures of Hope*, pt.1, l.7–8.

62 Hope, for a season, bade the world farewell,
And Freedom shrieked—as Kosciusko fell!
1799 *The Pleasures of Hope*, pt.1, l.381–2.

63 What millions died—that Caesar might be great!
1799 *The Pleasures of Hope*, pt.2, l.174.

64 What though my wingèd hours of bliss have been,
Like angel-visits, few and far between?
1799 *The Pleasures of Hope*, pt.2, l.375–6.

65 A chieftain to the Highlands bound
Cries 'Boatman, do not tarry!
And I'll give thee a silver pound
To row us o'er the ferry.'
1809 'Lord Ullin's Daughter', stanza 1.

66 And yet, amidst that joy and uproar,
Let us think of them that sleep,
Full many a fathom deep,
By thy wild and stormy steep,
Elsinore!
1809 'The Battle of the Baltic', stanza 8.

67 To-morrow let us do or die!
1809 'Gertrude of Wyoming', pt.3, stanza 37.

68 An original something, fair maid you would win me
To write—but how shall I begin?
For I fear I have nothing original in me—
Excepting Original Sin.
1843 'To a Young Lady, Who Asked Me to Write Something
Original for Her Album'.

69 Now Barabbas was a publisher.
Attributed. Quoted in Samuel Smiles *A Publisher and his Friends:
Memoir and Correspondence of the late John Murray* (1891), vol.1,
ch.14. The quote is sometimes attributed to Byron.

Campbell, Sir (Walter) Menzies 1941–

Scottish Liberal Democrat politician. A former sprinter at
international level, he worked as a lawyer before election as MP
for North East Fife in 1975. He served as leader of the Liberal
Democrats (2006–7).

70 It's like a soap opera. It's certainly an identity crisis.
Gordon wants to be like Maggie, but he doesn't want to
be like Tony. Tony also wanted to be like Maggie, but
Maggie only wanted to be like Ronnie. Now Dave, he
wants to be like Tony, but he doesn't want to be like
William, or Iain, or Michael, and certainly not like
Maggie either. Confused? You must be, but you can
be clear on this: I don't want to be like any of them.
2007 Speech to the Liberal Democrat conference, Brighton,
20 Sep 2007.

Campion, Jane 1954–

New Zealand film director and writer. She dramatized Janet Frame's
autobiography *An Angel at My Table* for television (1990) and won
an Academy Award for her screenplay for *The Piano* (1993), which
she also directed.

71 Remember your own childhood. That complete certainty you had, looking at the grown-ups, that you would never be like that. It was a lonely feeling, but euphoric, too.
1994 Interview with Sarah Gristwood in *The Times Magazine*, 'Jane Campion: A Childhood', 1 Jan.

Campion, Thomas 1567–1620

English physician, poet and composer. As well as poetry in Latin and English he wrote four *Books of Airs* for voice and lute (1601–17) and *Observations in the Art of English Poesie* (1602), defending classical structures.

72 My sweetest Lesbia, let us live and love,
And though the sager sort our deeds reprove,
Let us not weigh them. Heaven's great lamps do dive
Into their west, and straight again revive,
But soon as once set is our little light,
Then must we sleep one ever-during night.
1601 *A Book of Airs*, no.1, 'My Sweetest Lesbia', translation of a song by Catullus.
▶ See Catullus 209:6.

73 As her lute doth live or die,
Led by her passion, so must I:
For when of pleasure she doth sing,
My thoughts enjoy a sudden spring,
But if she doth of sorrow speak,
Ev'n from my heart the strings do break.
1601 *A Book of Airs*, no.6, 'When to Her Lute Corinna Sings'.

74 I care not for these ladies that must be wooed and prayed.
Give me kind Amaryllis, the wanton country maid.
1601 *A Book of Airs*, 'I Care Not for These Ladies'.

75 Rose-cheeked Laura, come,
Sing thou smoothly with thy beauty's
Silent music, either other
Sweetly gracing.
1602 *Second Book of Airs*, 'Rose-Cheeked Laura'.

76 There is a garden in her face,
Where roses and white lilies grow,
A heavenly paradise is that place,
Wherein all pleasant fruits do flow.
There cherries grow, which none may buy
Till 'Cherry ripe!' themselves do cry.
1617 *Fourth Book of Airs*, 'There is a Garden in her Face'.

77 Fain would I wed a fair young man that night and day could please me,
When my mind or body grieved that had the power to ease me.
Maids are full of longing thoughts that breed a bloodless sickness,
And that, oft I hear men say, is only cured by quickness.
1617 *Fourth Book of Airs*, 'Fain Would I Wed'.

78 Yet I would not die a maid, because I had a mother,
As I was by one brought forth, I would bring forth another.
1617 *Fourth Book of Airs*, 'Fain Would I Wed'.

Campo, Estanislao de 1834–80

Argentinian soldier, political journalist and *gaucho* (pampas cowboy) poet. *Fausto*, a long poetic dialogue in six episodes, relates a *gaucho's* impressions of a performance of Gounod's *Faust* in Buenos Aires.

79 *Por hembras yo no me pierdo.*
La que me empaca su amor
pasa por el cernidor
y…si te vi, no me acuerdo.
I make no fuss about females.
The one who gives me her love
Gets sifted in my private sieve
and…I don't think we ever met.
1866 *Fausto* (translated as *Faust*, 1943), pt.3.

Camus, Albert 1913–60

French writer. Active in the French Resistance, he found fame with his Existentialist novel *L'Étranger* (1942). Other works include *La Peste* (1947), *La Chute* (1956), plays and political writings. He was awarded a Nobel prize in 1957 and he died in a car accident.

80 *Intellectuel = celui qui se dédouble.*
Intellectual: someone whose mind watches itself.
Carnets, 1935–42 (published 1962).

81 *La politique et le sort des hommes sont formés par des hommes sans idéal et sans grandeur. Ceux qui ont une grandeur en eux ne font pas de politique.*
Politics and the fate of mankind are shaped by men without ideals and without greatness. Those who have greatness within them do not go in for politics.
Carnets, 1935–42 (published 1962).

82 *L'absurde est la notion essentielle et la première vérité.*
The absurd is the fundamental idea and the first truth.
1942 *Le Mythe de Sisyphe* (*The Myth of Sisyphus*, 1955).

83 *Il n'y a qu'un problème philosophique vraiment sérieux: c'est le suicide. Juger que la vie vaut ou ne vaut pas la peine d'être vécue, c'est répondre à la question fondamentale de la philosophie.*
There is but one truly serious philosophical problem, and that is suicide. Judging whether life is or is not worth living amounts to answering the fundamental question of philosophy.
1942 *Le Mythe de Sisyphe* (*The Myth of Sisyphus*, 1955), 'Absurdity and Suicide'.

84 *L'homme se trouve devant l'irrationnel. Il sent en lui son désir de bonheur et de raison. L'absurde naît de cette confrontation entre l'appel humain et le silence déraisonnable du monde.*
Man stands face to face with the irrational. He feels within him his longing for happiness and for reason. The absurd is born of this confrontation between the human need and the unreasonable silence of the world.
1942 *Le Mythe de Sisyphe* (*The Myth of Sisyphus*, 1955), 'The Absurd Walls'.

85 *Il n'est pas de destin que ne se surmonte par le mépris.*
There is no fate that cannot be surmounted by scorn.
1942 *Le Mythe de Sisyphe* (*The Myth of Sisyphus*, 1955).

86 *La lutte elle-même vers les sommets suffit à remplir un coeur d'homme. Il faut imaginer Sisyphe heureux.*
The struggle itself towards the heights is enough to fill a human heart. One must imagine that Sisyphus is happy.
1942 *Le Mythe de Sisyphe* (*The Myth of Sisyphus*, 1955).

87 *Aujourd'hui, maman est morte. Ou peut-être hier, je ne sais pas.*

Mother died today. Or perhaps it was yesterday, I don't know.
1942 *L'Etranger*.

88 *Peut-on être un saint sans Dieu: C'est le seul problème concret que je connaisse aujourd'hui.*
Can one become a saint without God? That is the only concrete problem I know of today.
1947 *La Peste*.

89 *Il y a dans les hommes plus de choses à admirer que de choses à mépriser.*
There are more things to admire in people than to despise.
1947 *La Peste*.

90 *Qu'est-ce qu'un homme révolté? Un homme qui dit non.*
What is a rebel? A man who says no.
1951 *L'Homme révolté*.

91 *Toutes les révolutions modernes ont abouti à un renforcement de l'Etat.*
All modern revolutions have ended in a reinforcement of the State.
1951 *L'Homme révolté*.

92 *Tout révolutionnaire finit en oppresseur ou en hérétique.*
Every revolutionary ends as an oppressor or a heretic.
1951 *L'Homme révolté*.

93 *Le style, comme la popeline, dissimule trop souvent de l'eczéma.*
Style, like sheer silk, too often hides eczema.
1956 *La Chute*, ch.1 (translated by Stuart Gilbert).

94 *Vous savez ce qu'est le charme: une manière de s'entendre répondre oui sans avoir posé aucune question claire.*
You know what charm is: a way of getting the answer yes without having asked any clear question.
1956 *La Chute* (translated by Stuart Gilbert).

95 *Chacun exige d'être innocent, à tout prix, même si, pour cela, il faut accuser le genre humain et le ciel.*
Everyone insists on his or her innocence, at all costs, even if it means accusing the rest of the human race and heaven.
1956 *La Chute* (translated by Stuart Gilbert).

96 *C'est si vrai que nous nous confions rarement à ceux qui sont meilleurs que nous.*
It is true that we seldom confide in those who are better than ourselves.
1956 *La Chute* (translated by Stuart Gilbert).

97 *N'attendez pas le jugement dernier. Il a lieu tous les jours.*
Do not wait for the last judgment. It happens every day.
1956 *La Chute* (translated by Stuart Gilbert).

98 *Combien de crimes commis simplement parce que leur auteur ne pouvait supporter d'être en faute!*
How many crimes are committed merely because their authors could not endure being wrong!
1956 *La Chute* (translated by Stuart Gilbert).

99 *La vérité, comme la lumière, aveugle. Le mensonge, au contraire, est un beau crépuscule qui met chaque objet en valeur.*
Truth, like light, blinds. A lie, on the contrary, is a beautiful twilight which shows the value of each object.
1956 *La Chute* (translated by Stuart Gilbert).

1 All that I know surely about morality and the obligations of man, I owe to football.
1957 'What I owe to Football', in *France Football*. In his youth, Camus kept goal for the Oran football club in Algiers.

2 A novel is never anything but a philosophy put into images.
Recalled on his death, 4 Jan 1960.

Canmore, Malcolm   d.1093

King of Scotland. The son of Duncan (who was killed by Macbeth), he spent his youth in Northumbria and returned in 1057 to take the throne after Macbeth's death.

3 *Excellentioris personæ semper casus in vitium, minoris lapsum, comparatione scandali multe longius antecedit.*
The scandal of an exalted person's fall into vice, when compared to the lapse of one lesser, always far exceeds it.
c.1057 Quoted in John Fordun's *Chronicle of Scotland* (c.1384), bk.5, ch.4.

Cannadine, Sir David   1950–

English historian and academic.

4 Prince Albert...discovered the impotence of being earnest.
1991 Of Queen Victoria's consort. *The Pleasure of the Past*.

5 Neville Chamberlain had greatness thrust upon him—and in trying to prove he could bear it, collapsed under the weight.
1991 *The Pleasure of the Past*.

Cannan, Edwin   1861–1935

English economist, Professor at the London School of Economics. He was editor of the standard edition of Adam Smith's *Wealth of Nations* in 1904.

6 It often happens that a man of considerable eminence in his own profession, but without the smallest acquaintance with the fundamentals of economics, will make a suggestion which is precisely on a level with the proposition that the locomotive would be much more efficient if its weight were taken off the driving wheels so that they could revolve more easily. The editor of an important magazine accepts with joy the contribution in which he develops his ideas, and the public feebly thinks that there may be something in it, and is confirmed in this view by the fact that professional economists are as disinclined to publish a refutation of it as the Astronomer Royal is to answer the theorists who declare that the world is flat.
1914 *Wealth*, ch.6.

Canning, George   1770–1827

English statesman. He became Foreign Secretary in 1822 on the death of his political opponent Castlereagh, and began a programme of liberalization. On Liverpool's resignation in 1827, he formed his own administration but died the same year.

7 Pitt is to Addington
As London is to Paddington.
c.1803 'The Oracle'. Henry Addington, 1st Viscount Sidmouth (1757–1844) was Prime Minister (1801–4) and a political rival of Pitt, who served in his administration.

8 And finds, with keen discriminating sight,
Black's not so black;—nor white so very white.
1821 'New Morality', l.199–200.

9 Give me the avowed, erect and manly foe;
Firm I can meet, perhaps return the blow;
But of all plagues, good Heaven, thy wrath can send,
Save me, oh, save me, from the candid friend.
1821 'New Morality', l.207–8.

10 In matters of commerce
The fault of the Dutch
Is offering too little
And asking too much.
1826 Dispatch enciphered to Sir Charles Bagehot, English ambassador at The Hague, 31 Jan.

11 I called the New World into existence, to redress the balance of the Old.
1826 Speech to the Commons, on Portugal, 12 Dec.

Cantillon, Richard c.1680–1734

Irish-born banker and economist who made a fortune in Paris after the collapse of the Mississippi Company. His single surviving work is *Essai sur la nature du Commerce en Général* ('Essay on the Nature of Trade', published 1755).

12 If all the Labourers in a Village breed up several Sons to the same work there will be too many Labourers to cultivate the Lands belonging to the Village, and the surplus Adults must go to seek a livelihood elsewhere, which they generally do in Cities.
1730–4 *Essay on the Nature of Trade.*

13 The Crafts which require the most Time in training or most Ingenuity and Industry must necessarily be the best paid.
1730–4 *Essay on the Nature of Trade.*

14 Men multiply like Mice in a barn if they have unlimited Means of Subsistence.
1730–4 *Essay on the Nature of Trade.*

Cantona, Eric 1966–

French footballer. He retired from football in 1997 to develop an acting career.

15 When the seagulls follow a trawler, it is because they think sardines will be thrown into the sea.
1995 At a press conference, 31 Mar.

16 I was always being creative. I could never have played a defensive role because I would have been forced to destroy the other player's creativity.
2003 In *The Guardian*, 26 Sep.

Capello, Fabio 1946–

Italian footballer and manager. Having won numerous titles as manager of several leading European clubs, he served as manager of England (2007–12).

17 Young players, young boys, rich boys—this is the problem.
2010 Defining the main problem faced by English football.

Capote, Truman 1924–84

US novelist. His best-known works include the semi-documentary novel *In Cold Blood* (1966), *Breakfast at Tiffany's* (1958) and *Music for Chameleons* (1980).

18 Other Voices, Other Rooms.
1948 Title of novel.

19 None of these people have anything interesting to say, and none of them can write, not even Mr Kerouac. What they do isn't writing at all—it's typing.
1959 On the Beat novelists. Television discussion, reported in the *New Republic*, 9 Feb.

20 Venice is like eating an entire box of chocolate liqueurs in one go.
1961 In the *Observer*, 26 Nov.

21 Even an attorney of modest talent can postpone doomsday year after year, for the system of appeals that pervades American jurisprudence amounts to a legalistic wheel of fortune, a game of chance, somewhat fixed in the favor of the criminal, that the participants play interminably.
1965 *In Cold Blood*, ch.4.

22 Buddy, it's fruitcake weather!
1966 Of December in Alabama. *A Christmas Memory*.

23 I don't care what anybody says about me as long as it isn't true.
Quoted in David Frost *The Americans* (1970), 'When Does A Writer Become A Star'.

24 Writing has laws of perspective, of light and shade, just as painting does, or music. If you are born knowing them, fine. If not, learn them. Then rearrange the rules to suit yourself.
1974 Interview in *Paris Review*, Summer.

25 When God hands you a gift, he also hands you a whip; and the whip is intended for self-flagellation solely.
1979 In *Vogue*, Dec. Collected in *Music for Chameleons* (1980), 'Music for Chameleons'.

26 Writing stopped being fun when I discovered the difference between good writing and bad, and then made an even more terrifying discovery—the difference between very good writing and true art: it is subtle, but savage.
1979 In *Vogue*, Dec.

27 Great fury, like great whisky, requires long fermentation.
1980 *Music for Chameleons*, 'Handcarved Coffins'.

28 Finishing a book is just like you took a child out in the yard and shot it.
Quoted in Linda Botts (ed) *Loose Talk* (1980).

29 The chic old blue-haired ladies…chew in mute chandeliered isolation.
Of elderly residents of the Ritz. *Answered Prayers* (1986).

30 The morals of a baboon and the guts of a butterfly.
Of Kenneth Tynan. Quoted in Gerald Clarke *Capote* (1988).

31 The better the actor the more stupid he is.
Attributed.

Capp, Al originally Alfred Gerald Caplin 1909–79

US cartoonist, best known for his strip 'L'il Abner' (1934–77), which satirized current affairs with a hillbilly cast of characters in Dogpatch.

32 A product of the untalented, sold by the unprincipled to the utterly bewildered.
1963 Of abstract art. In the *National Observer*, 1 Jul.

Capra, Frank 1897–1991

Italian-born US film director. He became renowned for his films celebrating the common man, such as *You Can't Take It With You* (1938).

33 There are no rules in filmmaking. Only sins. And the cardinal sin is dullness.
Recalled on his death in *People*, 16 Sep 1991.

Caraway, Hattie Wyatt 1878–1950

US politician. In 1932, she was the first woman to be elected to the US Senate.

34 The windows need washing.
1932 On arriving in the Senate. Recalled on her death, 21 Dec 1950.

35 I haven't the heart to take a minute from the men. The poor dears love it so.
Explaining why she never made a speech during 13 years as the first woman in the US Senate. Quoted in David Brinkley *Washington Goes to War* (1988).

Carballido, Emilio 1925–2008

Mexican short-story writer and dramatist. He is one of the most popular Latin American playwrights.

36 *Es usted un homo sapiens, mamífero vertebrado… Se encuentra en el periodo de domesticación, y sería colocado en una jaula al menor síntoma de ferocidad. En la escuela, en los laboratorios o en las oficinas de gobierno sabemos todo cuanto puede saberse de usted, de sus semejantes o de los otros seres en la escala zoológica.*
You are a homo sapiens, a vertebrate mammal… You are currently being tamed, and you would be put in a cage if you showed any sign of fierceness. At school, in the laboratories and in government offices we know as much as can be known about you, about your fellow beings and about the other beings in the zoological scale.
1960 *El día que se soltaron los leones* ('The Day When They Let the Lions Loose'), act 1.

Cardus, Sir Neville 1889–1975

English critic and journalist. He joined the *Manchester Guardian* as a music critic (1916), later becoming a cricket writer, and wrote several books on his two passions.

37 Pussycats.
1938 Of Bruch's violin concertos. In the *Manchester Guardian*.

38 Sawdust and spangles.
1938 Of Liszt's Second Piano Concerto. In the *Manchester Guardian*.

39 Like the British constitution, cricket was not made: it has 'grown'.
1945 *English Cricket*.

40 The opera…is the only one in existence that might conceivably have been composed by God.
1961 Of Mozart's *The Magic Flute*. In the *Manchester Guardian*.

41 The laws of cricket tell of the English love of compromise between a particular freedom and a general orderliness, or legality.
Quoted in Sir Rupert Hart-Davis *Cardus on Cricket* (1977).

42 Cricket more than any other game is inclined towards sentimentalism and cant.
Quoted in Sir Rupert Hart-Davis *Cardus on Cricket* (1977).

43 There ought to be some other means of reckoning quality in this the best and loveliest of games; the scoreboard is an ass.
1981 *A Fourth Innings with Cardus*.

44 It is far more than a game, this cricket.
1981 *A Fourth Innings with Cardus*.

45 The elements are cricket's presiding geniuses.
1981 *A Fourth Innings with Cardus*.

Carew, Thomas 1595–1639

English Cavalier poet, courtier and statesman. His most notable works include 'Rapture', 'To Ben Jonson' and an elegy for John Donne.

46 Why should the follies of this dull age
Draw from thy pen such an immodest rage
As seems to blast thy else-immortal bays,
When thine own tongue proclaims thy itch of praise?
Such thirst will argue drought.
1631 'To Ben Jonson, Upon occasion of his Ode of Defiance annexed to his play of *The New Inn*'.

47 The wiser world doth greater thee confess
Than all men else, than thy self only less.
1631 'To Ben Jonson, Upon occasion of his Ode of Defiance annexed to his play of *The New Inn*'.

48 Can we not force from widowed poetry,
Now thou art dead, great Donne, one elegy
To crown thy hearse?
1633 'An Elegy upon the Death of the Dean of Paul's, Dr. John Donne'.

49 Unkneaded dough-baked prose.
1633 'An Elegy upon the Death of the Dean of Paul's, Dr. John Donne'.

50 You committed holy rapes upon our will.
1633 'An Elegy upon the Death of the Dean of Paul's, Dr. John Donne'.

51 The Muses' garden, with pedantic weeds
O'erspread, was purged by thee; the lazy seeds
Of servile imitation thrown away,
And fresh invention planted.
1633 'An Elegy upon the Death of the Dean of Paul's, Dr. John Donne'.

52 Here lies a king, that ruled as he thought fit
The universal monarchy of wit.
1633 'An Elegy upon the Death of the Dean of Paul's, Dr. John Donne'.

53 And so our souls that cannot be embraced
Shall the embraces of our bodies taste.
1640 'A Rapture'.

54 I'll seize the rosebuds in their perfumed bed,
The violet knots, like curious mazes spread
O'er all the garden, taste the ripened cherry,
The warm, firm apple, tipped with coral berry.
Then will I visit with a wandering kiss
The vale of lilies and the bower of bliss,
And where the beauteous region doth divide
Into two milky ways, my lips shall slide
Down those smooth alleys, wearing as I go
A track for lovers on the printed snow.
1640 'A Rapture'.

55 All things are lawful there that may delight
Nature or unrestrainèd appetite.
1640 'A Rapture'.

56 Then tell me why
This goblin Honour which the world adores
Should make men atheists and not women whores.
1640 'A Rapture'.

57 Ask me no more whither dost haste
The nightingale when May is past;
For in your sweet dividing throat
She winters, and keeps warm her note.
1640 'A Song'.

58 Ask me no more if east or west
The Phoenix builds her spicy nest;
For unto you at last she flies,
And in your fragrant bosom dies.
1640 'A Song'.

59 Give me more love or more disdain;
The torrid or the frozen zone:
Bring equal ease unto my pain;
The temperate affords me none.
1640 'Mediocrity in Love Rejected'.

60 So though a virgin, yet a bride
To every Grace, she justified
A chaste polygamy, and died.
1640 'Inscription on the Tomb of Lady Mary Wentworth'.

Carey, John 1934–

English literary critic, Professor of English Literature at Oxford (1976–2001).

61 Given the state of the planet, humans, or some humans, must now be categorized as vermin.
1992 *The Intellectuals and the Masses*, postscript.

Carey, Peter 1943–

Australian novelist and short-story writer, twice winner of the Booker Prize for *Oscar and Lucinda* (1988) and *True History of the Kelly Gang* (2001).

62 Glass is a thing in disguise, an actor, is not solid at all, but a liquid…an old sheet of glass will not only take on a royal and purplish tinge but will reveal its true liquid nature by having grown fatter at the bottom and thinner at the top, and… It is invisible, solid, in short a joyous and paradoxical thing, as good a material as any to build a life from.
1988 *Oscar and Lucinda*, ch.32, 'Prince Rupert's Drops'.

63 The declared meaning of a spoken sentence is only its overcoat, and the real meaning lies underneath its scarves and buttons.
1988 *Oscar and Lucinda*, ch.43, 'Leviathan'.

64 Writers are always envious, mean-minded, filled with rage and envy at other's good fortune. There is nothing like the failure of a close friend to cheer us up.
2002 In the *Observer*, 18 Aug.

65 The big question for me is, What sort of person would do that thing—not just because it suits a story or suits something symbolically, but who would really, really do that? When I continue to ask myself that question and I don't take the easy answer, complicated characters are born.
2006 *The Paris Review*, summer issue.

66 I have travelled widely. I have seen this country in its infancy. I tell you what it will become. The public squares will be occupied by an uneducated class who will not be able to quote a line of Shakespeare.
2010 *Parrot and Olivier in America*.

Carleton, William 1794–1869

Irish writer, the youngest of 14 children born to peasant parents. His sketches were collected as *Traits and Stories of the Irish Peasantry* (1830, 2nd series 1833). Other works include *The Squanders of Castle Squander* (1852).

67 I remember on one occasion, when she was asked to sing the English version of the touching melody 'The Red-Haired Man's Wife', she replied, 'I will sing it for you; but the English words and the air are like a quarrelling man and wife; *the Irish melts into the tune*, but the English doesn't.'
1830 *Traits and Stories of the Irish Peasantry*, introduction.

Carlyle, Jane Baillie née *Jane Baillie Welsh* 1801–66

Wife of Thomas Carlyle. She married Carlyle in 1826, supporting him loyally through his depressions and ill-health, though resisting his suggestions that she write herself. After her death, Carlyle wrote a memoir of her in *Reminiscences* (1881) and edited her letters and diaries.

68 I am not at all the sort of person you and I took me for.
1822 Letter to Thomas Carlyle, 2 May.

69 Medical men all over the world having merely entered into a tacit agreement to call all sorts of maladies people are liable to, in cold weather, by one name; so that one sort of treatment may serve for all, and their practice thereby be greatly simplified.
1837 Letter to John Welsh, 4 Mar.

70 When I think of what I is
And what I used to was,
I gin to think I've sold myself
For very little cas.
1855 Journal entry, 5 Nov. Collected in James Anthony Froude (ed) *Letters and Memorials of Jane Welsh Carlyle* (1883), vol.2.

71 I scorched my intellect into a cinder of stolidity.
Quoted in Alexander Carlyle (ed) *New Letters and Memorials of Jane Welsh Carlyle* (1903), 'Mrs Carlyle's Notebook'.

72 If you hate a man, though only in secret, never trust him, because hate is hardly to be hidden.
Quoted in Alexander Carlyle (ed) *New Letters and Memorials of Jane Welsh Carlyle* (1903), 'Mrs Carlyle's Notebook'.

Carlyle, Thomas 1795–1881

Scottish historian and essayist. His best-known work, *Sartor Resartus*, on social philosophy, appeared in 1833–4. In 1834 he moved to London, where his major works included *The French Revolution* (3 vols, 1837) and *Frederick the Great* (6 vols, 1858–65).

73 His fellow creatures are still objects of reverence and love, though their basenesses are plainer to no eye than to his. To reconcile these contradictions is the task of all good men.
1824 *Goethe*, vol.4, 'Introduction to German Romance'.

74 A mind that has seen, and suffered, and done, speaks to us of what it has tried and conquered.
1824 *Goethe*, vol.4, 'Introduction to German Romance'.

75 The true Church of England, at this moment, lies in the Editors of the newspapers.
1829 *Signs of the Times*.

76 It is no very good symptom either of nations or individuals, that they deal much in vaticination.
1829 *Signs of the Times*.

77 Seldom can the unhappy be persuaded that the evil of the day is sufficient for it; and the ambitious will not be content with the present splendour, but paints yet more glorious triumphs, on the cloud curtain of the future.
   1829 *Signs of the Times.*

78 Meanwhile, we too admit that the present is an important time… We were wise indeed, could we discern truly the signs of our own time; and by knowledge of its wants and advantages, wisely adjust our own position in it.
   1829 *Signs of the Times.*

79 Were we required to characterise this age of ours by any single epithet, we should be tempted to call it, not an Heroical, Devotional, Philosophical, or Moral Age, but above all others, the Mechanical Age. It is the Age of Machinery, in every outward and inward sense of the word.
   1829 *Signs of the Times.*

80 We remove mountains, and make seas our smooth highway; nothing can resist us. We war with rude Nature; and, by our resistless engines, come off always victorious, and loaded with spoils.
   1829 *Signs of the Times.*

81 Wealth has more and more increased, and at the same time gathered itself more and more into masses, strangely altering the old relations, and increasing the distance between the rich and the poor.
   1829 *Signs of the Times.*

82 Men are grown mechanical in head and in the heart, as well as in the hand. They have lost faith in individual endeavour, and in natural force of any kind.
   1829 *Signs of the Times.*

83 By our skill in Mechanism, it has come to pass, that in the management of external things we excel all other ages; while in whatever respects the pure mortal nature, in true dignity of soul and character, we are perhaps inferior to most civilised ages.
   1829 *Signs of the Times.*

84 We are Giants in physical power: in a deeper than metaphorical sense, we are Titans, that strive, by heaping mountain on mountain, to conquer Heaven also.
   1829 *Signs of the Times.*

85 Philosophers…stand among us not to do, nor to create anything, but as a sort of Logic-mill to grind out the true causes and effects of all that is done and created.
   1829 *Signs of the Times.*

86 We have a faith in the imperishable dignity of man; in the high vocation to which, throughout this his earthly history, he has been appointed.
   1829 *Signs of the Times.*

87 To reform a world, to reform a nation no wise man will undertake; and all but foolish men know, that the only solid, though a far slower reformation, is what each begins and perfects on himself.
   1829 *Signs of the Times.*

88 No man who has once heartily and wholly laughed can be altogether irreclaimably bad.
   1833–4 *Sartor Resartus*, bk.1, ch.4.

89 He who first shortened the labour of copyists by device of *Movable Types* was disbanding hired armies, and cashiering most Kings and Senates, and creating a whole new democratic world: he had invented the art of printing.
   1833–4 *Sartor Resartus*, bk.1, ch.5.

90 Man is a tool-using animal… Without tools he is nothing, with tools he is all.
   1833–4 *Sartor Resartus*, bk.1, ch.5.

91 Whoso has sixpence is sovereign (to the length of sixpence) over all men; commands cooks to feed him, philosophers to teach him, kings to mount guard over him,—to the length of sixpence.
   1833–4 *Sartor Resartus*, bk.1, ch.5.

92 Man's earthly interests, 'are all hooked and buttoned together, and held up, by Clothes.'
   1833–4 *Sartor Resartus*, bk.1, ch.8.

93 Be not the slave of words.
   1833–4 *Sartor Resartus*, bk.1, ch.8.

94 Language is called the garment of thought: however, it should rather be, language is the flesh-garment, the body, of thought.
   1833–4 *Sartor Resartus*, bk.1, ch.11.

95 The end of man is an action and not a thought, though it were the noblest.
   1833–4 *Sartor Resartus*, bk.2, ch.6.

96 The everlasting No.
   1833–4 *Sartor Resartus*, bk.2, ch.7, title.

97 Most true it is, as a wise man teaches us, that 'doubt of any sort cannot be removed except by Action.' On which ground, too, let him who gropes painfully in darkness or in uncertain light, and prays vehemently that the dawn may ripen into day, lay this other precept well to heart, which to me was of invaluable service: '*Do the Duty which lies nearest thee*', which thou knowest to be a Duty! Thy second duty will already have become clearer.
   1833–4 *Sartor Resartus*, bk.2, ch.9.

98 Man's unhappiness, as I construe, comes of his greatness; it is because there is an Infinite in him, which with all his cunning he cannot quite bury under the Finite.
   1833–4 *Sartor Resartus*, bk.2, ch.9.

99 Be no longer a chaos, but a world, or even worldkin. Produce! Produce! Were it but the pitifullest infinitesimal fraction of a product, produce it in God's name! 'Tis the utmost thou hast in thee: out with it, then.
   1833–4 *Sartor Resartus*, bk.2, ch.9.

1 Friends! trust not the heart of that man for whom Old Clothes are not venerable.
   1833–4 *Sartor Resartus*, bk.3, ch.6.

2 How great a Possibility, how small a realized Result.
   1834 Of Samuel Taylor Coleridge. Letter to Emerson, 12 Aug.

3 The public is an old woman. Let her maunder and mumble.
   1835 Journal entry.

4 Hope ushers in a Revolution—as earthquakes are preceded by bright weather.
   1837 *History of the French Revolution*, vol.1, bk.2, ch.1.

5 A whiff of grapeshot.
   1837 *History of the French Revolution*, vol.1, bk.5, ch.3.

6 Under all the roofs of this distracted City is the nodus of a drama, not untragical, crowding towards solution.
   1837 *History of the French Revolution*, vol.1, bk.5, ch.6.

7 How true it is, that there is nothing dead in this Universe; that what we call dead is only changed, its forces working in inverse order! 'The leaf that lies rotting in moist winds,' says one, 'has still force; else how could it rot?'
1837 *History of the French Revolution*, vol.2, bk.3, ch.1.

8 The difference between Orthodoxy or My-doxy and Heterodoxy or Thy-doxy.
1837 *History of the French Revolution*, vol.2, bk.4, ch.2.

9 The seagreen Incorruptible.
1837 Of Robespierre. *History of the French Revolution*, vol.2, bk.4, ch.4.

10 Pity is lost in rage and fear.
1837 *History of the French Revolution*, vol.3, bk.2, ch.7.

11 France was long a despotism tempered by epigrams.
1837 *History of the French Revolution*, vol.3, bk.7, ch.7.

12 Aristocracy of the Moneybag.
1837 *History of the French Revolution*, vol.3, bk.7, ch.7.

13 The 'golden-calf of self-love'.
1838 *Critical and Miscellaneous Essays*, 'Burns'.

14 For, strictly considered, what is all knowledge too but recorded experience, and a product of history; of which, therefore, reasoning and belief, no less than action and passion are essential materials?
1838 *Critical and Miscellaneous Essays*, 'History'.

15 History is the essence of innumerable biographies.
1838 *Critical and Miscellaneous Essays*, 'History'.

16 When the oak-tree is fallen, the whole forest echoes with it; but a hundred acorns are planted silently by some unnoticed breeze.
1838 *Critical and Miscellaneous Essays*, 'History'.

17 Laws themselves, political Constitutions, are not our Life; but only the house wherein our Life is led.
1838 *Critical and Miscellaneous Essays*, 'History'.

18 History is philosophy teaching by experience.
1838 *Critical and Miscellaneous Essays*, 'History'.

19 A well-written life is almost as rare as a well-spent one.
1838 *Critical and Miscellaneous Essays*, 'Jean Paul Fredrich Richter'.

20 There is no life of a man, faithfully recorded, but is a heroic poem of its sort, rhymed or unrhymed.
1838 *Critical and Miscellaneous Essays*, 'Sir Walter Scott'.

21 Under all speech there lies a silence that is better. Silence is deep as Eternity; speech is shallow as Time.
1838 *Critical and Miscellaneous Essays*, 'Sir Walter Scott'.

22 A feeling generally exists that the condition and disposition of the Working Class is a rather ominous matter at present; that something ought to be said, something ought to be done, in regard to it.
1839 *Chartism*, ch.1.

23 A witty statesman said, you might prove anything by figures.
1839 *Chartism*, ch.2.

24 To believe practically that the poor and luckless are here only as a nusiance to be abraded and abated, and in some permissable manner made away with, and swept out of sight, is not an amiable faith.
1839 *Chartism*, ch.3.

25 A man willing to work, and unable to find work, is perhaps the saddest sight that fortune's inequality exhibits under the sun.
1839 *Chartism*, ch.4.

26 Surely of all 'rights of man', this right of the ignorant man to be guided by the wiser, to be, gently or forcibly, held in the true course by him, is the indisputablest.
1839 *Chartism*, ch.6.

27 In epochs when cash payment has become the sole nexus of man to man.
1839 *Chartism*, ch.6.

28 The English are used to suffrage; it is their panacea for all that goes wrong with them.
1839 *Chartism*, ch.9.

29 Books are written by martyr-men, not for rich men alone but for all men. If we consider it, every human being has, by the nature of the case, a *right* to hear what other wise human beings have spoken to him. It is one of the Rights of Men; a very cruel injustice if you deny it to a man!
1840 Letter to John Sterling, collected in *New Letters of Carlyle* (1904), vol.1.

30 It is well said, in every sense, that a man's religion is the chief fact with regard to him.
1841 *On Heroes, Hero-Worship, and the Heroic*, 'The Hero as Divinity' (published 1897).

31 Worship is transcendent wonder.
1841 *On Heroes, Hero-Worship, and the Heroic*, 'The Hero as King'.

32 I hope we English will long maintain our *grand talent pour le silence*.
1841 *On Heroes, Hero-Worship, and the Heroic*, 'The Hero as King'.

33 In books lies the soul of the whole Past Time; the articulate audible voice of the Past, when the body and material substance of it has altogether vanished like a dream.
1841 *On Heroes, Hero-Worship, and the Heroic*, 'The Hero as Man of Letters'.

34 The true University these days is a collection of books.
1841 *On Heroes, Hero-Worship, and the Heroic*, 'The Hero as Man of Letters'.

35 Adversity is sometimes hard upon a man; but for one man who can stand prosperity, there are a hundred that will stand adversity.
1841 *On Heroes, Hero-Worship, and the Heroic*, 'The Hero as Man of Letters'.

36 Heaven's splendour over his head, Hell's darkness under his feet.
1843 *Past and Present*, bk.2, ch.15.

37 Work earnestly at anything, you will by degrees learn to work at all things.
1843 *Past and Present*, bk.3, ch.2.

38 Captains of Industry.
1843 *Past and Present*, bk.4, ch.4, title.

39 Respectable Professors of the Dismal Science.
1850 *Latter-Day Pamphlets*, no.1, 'The Present Time'.

40 Nature admits no lie.
1850 *Latter-Day Pamphlets*, no.5.

41 A Parliament speaking through reporters to Buncombe and the twenty-seven millions mostly fools.
1850 *Latter-Day Pamphlets*, no.6, 'Parliaments'.

42 Transcendental moonshine.
1851 Of the romantic impulses that had led Sterling to the priesthood. *The Life of John Sterling*, pt.1, ch.15.

43 Maid-servants, I hear people complaining, are getting instructed in the 'ologies'.
1866 Inaugural address as Rector of Edinburgh University, 2 Apr.

44 All reform except a moral one will prove unavailing.
1872 *Critical and Miscellaneous Essays*, 'Corn Law Rhymes'.

45 If Jesus Christ were to come today, people would not even crucify him. They would ask him to dinner, and hear what he had to say, and make fun of it.
Quoted in D A Wilson *Carlyle at his Zenith* (1927).

Carman, (William) Bliss 1861–1929

Canadian poet. His vivid and optimistic poetry includes *Songs from Vagabondia* (with Richard Hovey, 1894, 1896 and 1901) and *Pipes of Pan* (1902–5).

46 Have little care that Life is brief,
   And less that art is long.
   Success is in the silences,
   Though fame is in the song.
1923 *Ballads and Lyrics*, 'Envoi'. These lines are reproduced on the plaque erected in his honour at the University of New Brunswick, Fredericton, Canada.

Carnegie, Andrew 1835–1919

Scottish-born US steel magnate and philanthropist. He emigrated with his family in 1848, investing his savings in oil lands as a youth and amassing a vast fortune, with which he endowed numerous institutions and good causes.

47 The man who dies rich...dies disgraced.
1889 'The Gospel of Wealth', in the *North American Review*, Jun.

48 While the law [of competition] may be sometimes hard for the individual, it is best for the race, because it insures the survival of the fittest in every department. We accept and welcome, therefore, as conditions to which we must accommodate ourselves, great inequality of environment, the concentration of business, industrial and commercial, in the hands of a few, and the law of competition between these, as being not only beneficial, but essential to the future progress of the race.
1889 'The Gospel of Wealth', in the *North American Review*, Jun.

Carnegie, Dale originally Dale Carnagey 1888–1955

US lecturer and writer, a pioneer of self-help psychology.

49 How to Win Friends and Influence People.
1930 Title of book.

Carpentier, Alejo 1904–80

Cuban novelist, musicologist and journalist, Ambassador to Europe for a considerable period of Castro's regime. His style has been called neo-Baroque.

50 *A tal punto me hunden mis palabras, como dichas por otro, por un juez que yo llevara dentro sin saberlo y se valiera de mis propios medios físicos para expresarse, que me aterro, al oírme, de lo difícil que es volver a ser hombre cuando se ha dejado de ser hombre.*
As though they were coming from the lips of another, from a judge I carried within me without knowing it, and who made use of my own faculties to express himself, my words took such hold upon me that it frightened me to realize, as I listened to myself, how hard it is to become a man when one has ceased to be a man.
1953 *Los pasos perdidos* (translated as *The Lost Steps*, 1956), ch.1, pt.2.

Carr, E(dward) H(allet) 1892–1982

English political scientist and historian. In the diplomatic service until 1936, he was Assistant Editor of *The Times* (1941–6) and wrote several important historical texts, including biographies of Marx (1934) and Bakunin (1937).

51 The unending dialogue between the present and the past.
Of biography. Quoted in James G Hershberg *James B Conant* (1993).

Carr, Emily 1871–1945

Canadian painter and writer, who recorded the lives of west-coast native Canadians in words and paintings. Her first book *Klee Wyck* (1941) won the Governor-General's Award.

52 The outstanding event was the *doing* which I am still at. Don't pickle me away as done.
c.1940 Quoted in Ira Dilworth's foreword to *Klee Wyck* (1951 edn).

53 There was neither horizon, cloud, nor sound; of that pink, spread silence even I had become part, belonging as much to sky as to earth.
1941 *Klee Wyck*, ch.17, 'Salt Water'.

Carr, J(ames) L(loyd) 1912–94

English novelist. His best-known work is *A Month in the Country* (1980), which was also filmed.

54 'I've never been spoken to like this before in all my thirty years' experience,' she wails. '*You* have not had thirty years' experience, Mrs Grindle-Jones,' he says witheringly. '*You* have had one year's experience 30 times.'
1972 *The Harpole Report*, ch.21.

55 In rural England, people live wrapped tight in a cocoon; only their eyes move to make sure that nobody gets more than themselves.
1975 *How Steeple Sinderby Wanderers Won the FA Cup*, pt.2.

56 You must understand, James, that their English God is not so dominant a business institution as ours.
1985 On the US version of God. *The Battle of Pollocks Crossing*.

Carrà, Carlo 1881–1966

Italian painter, involved first in *Pittura metafisica* and then in Futurism.

57 The painting of sounds, noises and smells calls for:
1. Reds, rrrrreds, the rrrrrreddest rrrrrrreds that shouuuuuuut.
2. Greens, that can never be greener, greeeeeeeeeeeens that screeeeeeam, yellows, as violent as can be: polenta yellows, saffron yellows, brass yellows.
1913 In the *Manifesto of Futurist Painting*, quoted in *Futurismo e Futurismi* (1986).

58 This is the truth! In order to achieve this *total painting*, which requires the active cooperation of all the senses, *a painting which is a plastic state of mind of the universal*, you must paint, as drunkards sing and vomit, sounds, noises and smells!
1913 In the *Manifesto of Futurist Painting*, quoted in *Futurismo e Futurismi* (1986).

Carracci, Annibale 1560–1609

Italian painter, one of a family of artists from Bologna.

59 Poets paint with words, painters speak with works.
Attributed rebuke to his brother Agostino. Quoted in G P Bellori *Vite* (1672).

Carrigan, Jim R(ichard) 1929–2014
US lawyer, judge at the US Court of Appeals.

60 It is all too rare today to hear the clear, clean ring of a really original insult.
1987 In *Time*, 28 Aug.

Carroll, Lewis *pseudonym of* Rev Charles Lutwidge Dodgson 1832–98
English poet, mathematician and logician. A shy man with a stammer, he was most comfortable in the company of children. He is best known for his children's books *Alice's Adventures in Wonderland* (1865) and *Through the Looking-Glass* (1871).

61 'And what is the use of a book,' thought Alice, 'without pictures or conversations?'
1865 *Alice's Adventures in Wonderland*, ch.1, 'Down the Rabbit-Hole'.

62 'Even if my head *would* go through,' thought poor Alice, 'it would be of very little use without my shoulders.'
1865 *Alice's Adventures in Wonderland*, ch.1, 'Down the Rabbit-Hole'.

63 'Curiouser and curiouser!' cried Alice (she was so much surprised, that for the moment she quite forgot how to speak good English).
1865 *Alice's Adventures in Wonderland*, ch.2, 'The Pool of Tears'.

64 How doth the little crocodile
Improve his shining tail,
And pour the waters of the Nile
On every golden scale!

How cheerfully he seems to grin,
How neatly spreads his claws,
And welcomes little fishes in,
With gently smiling jaws!
1865 *Alice's Adventures in Wonderland*, ch.2, 'The Pool of Tears'.

65 'I'll be judge, I'll be jury,' said cunning old Fury;
'I'll try the whole cause, and condemn you to death.'
1865 *Alice's Adventures in Wonderland*, ch.3, 'A Caucus-Race and a Long Tale', told by the Dormouse.

66 'You are old, Father William,' the young man said,
'And your hair has become very white;
And yet you incessantly stand on your head—
Do you think, at your age, it is right?'

'In my youth,' Father William replied to his son,
'I feared it might injure the brain;
But now that I'm perfectly sure I have none,
Why, I do it again and again.'
1865 *Alice's Adventures in Wonderland*, ch.5, 'Advice from a Caterpillar'.
▶ See Southey 835:43.

67 'If everybody minded their own business,' the Duchess said, in a hoarse growl, 'the world would go round a deal faster than it does.'
1865 *Alice's Adventures in Wonderland*, ch.6, 'Pig and Pepper'.

68 Speak roughly to your little boy,
And beat him when he sneezes:
He only does it to annoy,
Because he knows it teases.
1865 The Duchess's lullaby. *Alice's Adventures in Wonderland*, ch.6, 'Pig and Pepper'.

69 'All right,' said the Cat; and this time it vanished quite slowly, beginning with the end of the tail, and ending with the grin, which remained some time after the rest of it had gone.
1865 The disappearance of the Cheshire Cat. *Alice's Adventures in Wonderland*, ch.6, 'Pig and Pepper'.

70 'Then you should say what you mean,' the March Hare went on.
'I do,' Alice hastily replied; 'at least—at least I mean what I say—that's the same thing, you know.'
'Not the same thing a bit! ' said the Hatter. 'Why, you might just as well say that "I see what I eat" is the same thing as "I eat what I see!"'
1865 *Alice's Adventures in Wonderland*, ch.7, 'A Mad Tea-Party'.

71 Twinkle, twinkle, little bat!
How I wonder what you're at!
Up above the world you fly!
Like a teatray in the sky.
1865 *Alice's Adventures in Wonderland*, Ch. 7, 'A Mad Tea-Party'.

72 'Take some more tea,' the March Hare said to Alice, very earnestly.
'I've had nothing yet,' Alice replied in an offended tone, 'so I can't take more.'
'You mean you can't take *less*,' said the Hatter: 'It's very easy to take *more* than nothing.'
1865 *Alice's Adventures in Wonderland*, ch.7, 'A Mad Tea-Party'.

73 Off with her head!
1865 The Queen of Hearts. *Alice's Adventures in Wonderland*, ch.8, 'The Queen's Croquet Ground'.

74 Everything's got a moral, if only you can find it.
1865 The Duchess. *Alice's Adventures in Wonderland*, ch.9, 'The Mock Turtle's Story'.

75 Take care of the sense, and the sounds will take care of themselves.
1865 The Duchess. *Alice's Adventures in Wonderland*, ch.9, 'The Mock Turtle's Story'.

76 'Just about as much right,' said the Duchess, 'as pigs have to fly.'
1865 *Alice's Adventures in Wonderland*, ch.9, 'The Mock Turtle's Story'.

77 'That's the reason they're called lessons,' the Gryphon remarked: 'because they lessen from day to day.'
1865 *Alice's Adventures in Wonderland*, ch.9, 'The Mock Turtle's Story'.

78 'I only took the regular course.'
'What was that?' inquired Alice.
'Reeling and Writhing, of course, to begin with,' the Mock Turtle replied; 'and then the different branches of Arithmetic—Ambition, Distraction, Uglification, and Derision.'
1865 *Alice's Adventures in Wonderland*, ch.9, 'The Mock Turtle's Story'.

79 The Drawling-master was an old conger-eel, that used to come once a week: *he* taught us Drawling, Stretching, and Fainting in Coils.
1865 *Alice's Adventures in Wonderland*, ch.9, 'The Mock Turtle's Story'.

80 'Will you walk a little faster?' said a whiting to a snail, 'There's a porpoise close behind us and he's treading on my tail.'
1865 *Alice's Adventures in Wonderland*, ch.10, 'The Lobster-Quadrille'.

81 Will you, won't you, will you, won't you, will you join the dance?
   1865 *Alice's Adventures in Wonderland*, ch.10, 'The Lobster-Quadrille'.

82 Beautiful Soup, so rich and green,
   Waiting in a hot tureen!
   Who for such dainties would not stoop?
   Soup of the evening, beautiful Soup!
   1865 Song of the Mock Turtle. *Alice's Adventures in Wonderland*, ch.10.

83 'Tis the voice of the lobster; I heard him declare,
   'You have baked me too brown, I must sugar my hair.'
   1865 *Alice's Adventures in Wonderland*, ch.10, 'The Lobster-Quadrille'.

84 The Queen of Hearts, she made some tarts,
   All of a summer day:
   The Knave of Hearts, he stole those tarts
   And took them quite away!
   1865 *Alice's Adventures in Wonderland*, ch.11, 'Who Stole the Tarts?'.

85 'Where shall I begin, please your Majesty?' he asked.
   'Begin at the beginning,' the King said, gravely, 'and go on till you come to the end; then stop.'
   1865 *Alice's Adventures in Wonderland*, ch.12, 'Alice's Evidence'.

86 'That's not a regular rule: you invented it just now.'
   'It's the oldest rule in the book,' said the King.
   'Then it ought to be Number One,' said Alice.
   1865 *Alice's Adventures in Wonderland*, ch.12, 'Alice's Evidence'.

87 'No, no!' said the Queen. 'Sentence first—verdict afterwards.'
   1865 *Alice's Adventures in Wonderland*, ch.12, 'Alice's Evidence'.

88 'Why,' said the Dodo, 'the best way to explain it is to do it.'
   1865 *Alice's Adventures in Wonderland*, ch.3, 'A Caucus-Race and a Long Tale'.

89 'Twas brillig, and the slithy toves
   Did gyre and gimble in the wabe;
   All mimsy were the borogoves,
   And the mome raths outgrabe.

   'Beware the Jabberwock, my son!
   The jaws that bite, the claws that catch!
   Beware the Jubjub bird, and shun
   The frumious Bandersnatch!'
   1871 *Through the Looking-Glass*, ch.1, 'Looking-Glass House'.

90 And, as in uffish thought he stood,
   The Jabberwock, with eyes of flame,
   Came whiffling through the tulgey wood,
   And burbled as it came!

   One, two! One, two! And through and through
   The vorpal blade went snicker-snack!
   He left it dead and with its head
   He went galumphing back.

   'And hast thou slain the Jabberwock?
   Come to my arms, my beamish boy!
   Oh frabjous day! Callooh! Callay!'
   He chortled in his joy.
   1871 *Through the Looking-Glass*, ch.1, 'Looking-Glass House'.

91 Curtsey while you're thinking what to say. It saves time.
   1871 *Through the Looking-Glass*, ch.2, 'The Garden of Live Flowers'.

92 'When you say "hill",' the Queen interrupted, 'I could show you hills, in comparison with which you'd call that a valley.'
   'No, I shouldn't,' said Alice, surprised into contradicting her at last: 'a hill *can't* be a valley, you know. That would be nonsense—'
   The Red Queen shook her head. 'You may call it "nonsense" if you like,' she said, 'but *I've* heard nonsense, compared with which that would be as sensible as a dictionary!'
   1871 *Through the Looking-Glass*, ch.2, 'The Garden of Live Flowers'.

93 Now, *here*, you see, it takes all the running *you* can do, to keep in the same place. If you want to get somewhere else, you must run at least twice as fast as that!
   1871 *Through the Looking-Glass*, ch.2, 'The Garden of Live Flowers'.

94 Speak in French when you can't think of the English for a thing—turn out your toes as you walk—and remember who you are!
   1871 The Red Queen's advice to Alice as she begins the chess game. *Through the Looking-Glass*, ch.2, 'The Garden of Live Flowers'.

95 'You shouldn't make jokes,' Alice said, 'if it makes you so unhappy.'
   1871 Alice to the gnat. *Through the Looking-Glass*, ch.3, 'Looking-Glass Insects'.

96 Tweedledum and Tweedledee
   Agreed to have a battle;
   For Tweedledum said Tweedledee
   Had spoilt his nice new rattle.
   1871 *Through the Looking-Glass*, ch.4, 'Tweedledum and Tweedledee'.

97 'Contrariwise,' continued Tweedledee, 'if it was so, it might be; and if it were so, it would be: but as it isn't it ain't. That's logic.'
   1871 *Through the Looking-Glass*, ch.4, 'Tweedledum and Tweedledee'.

98 The sun was shining on the sea,
   Shining with all his might:
   He did his very best to make
   The billows smooth and bright—
   And this was odd, because it was
   The middle of the night.
   1871 Tweedledee. *Through the Looking-Glass*, ch.4, 'Tweedledum and Tweedledee'.

99 The Walrus and the Carpenter
   Were walking close at hand;
   They wept like anything to see
   Such quantities of sand:
   'If this were only cleared away,'
   They said, 'it would be grand!'
   1871 Tweedledee. *Through the Looking-Glass*, ch.4, 'Tweedledum and Tweedledee'.

1 'The time has come,' the Walrus said,
   'To talk of many things:
   Of shoes—and ships—and sealing-wax—
   Of cabbages—and kings—
   And why the sea is boiling hot—
   And whether pigs have wings.'
   1871 Tweedledee. *Through the Looking-Glass*, ch.4, 'Tweedledum and Tweedledee'.

2 'You know,' he said very gravely, 'it's one of the most serious things that can possibly happen to one in a battle—to get one's head cut off.'
1871 *Through the Looking-Glass*, ch.4, 'Tweedledum and Tweedledee'.

3 The rule is, jam to-morrow and jam yesterday—but never jam to-day.
1871 The White Queen. *Through the Looking-Glass*, ch.5, 'Wool and Water'.

4 'It's a poor sort of memory that only works backwards,' the Queen remarked.
1871 *Through the Looking-Glass*, ch.5, 'Wool and Water'.

5 Consider anything, only don't cry!
1871 *Through the Looking-Glass*, ch.5, 'Wool and Water'.

6 Alice laughed. 'There's no use trying,' she said: 'one can't believe impossible things.'
'I daresay you haven't had much practice,' said the Queen. 'When I was your age, I always did it for half-an-hour a day. Why, sometimes I've believed as many as six impossible things before breakfast.'
1871 *Through the Looking-Glass*, ch. 5, 'Wool and Water'.

7 'It's *very* provoking,' Humpty Dumpty said after a long silence, looking away from Alice as he spoke, 'to be called an egg—*very!*'
1871 *Through the Looking-Glass*, ch.6, 'Humpty Dumpty'.

8 With a name like yours you might be any shape, almost.
1871 *Through the Looking-Glass*, ch.6, 'Humpty Dumpty'.

9 'They gave it me,' Humpty Dumpty continued thoughtfully... 'for an un-birthday present.'
1871 *Through the Looking-Glass*, ch.6, 'Humpty Dumpty'.

10 'The question is,' said Humpty Dumpty, 'which is to be master—that's all.'
1871 *Through the Looking-Glass*, ch.6, 'Humpty Dumpty'.

11 'That's a great deal to make one word mean,' Alice said in a thoughtful tone.
'When I make a word do a lot of work like that,' said Humpty Dumpty, 'I always pay it extra.'
1871 *Through the Looking-Glass*, ch.6, 'Humpty Dumpty'.

12 'Slithy' means 'lithe and slimy'... You see it's like a portmanteau—there are two meanings packed up into one word.
1871 Humpty Dumpty explaining the *Jabberwock* poem. *Through the Looking-Glass*, ch.6, 'Humpty Dumpty'.

13 'I can repeat poetry as well as other folk if it comes to that—'
'Oh, it needn't come to that!' Alice hastily said.
1871 *Through the Looking-Glass*, ch.6, 'Humpty Dumpty'.

14 'There's glory for you!'
'I don't know what you mean by "glory",' Alice said.
'I meant, "there's a nice knock-down argument for you!"'
'But "glory" doesn't mean "a nice knock-down argument",' Alice objected.
'When I use a word,' Humpty Dumpty said in a rather scornful tone, 'it means just what I choose it to mean—neither more nor less.'
1871 *Through the Looking-Glass*, ch.6, 'Humpty Dumpty'.

15 The Lion and the Unicorn were fighting for the crown:
The Lion beat the Unicorn all round the town.
Some gave them white bread, some gave them brown;
Some gave them plum-cake and drummed them out of town.
1871 *Through the Looking-Glass*, ch.7, 'The Lion and the Unicorn'.

16 He's an Anglo-Saxon Messenger—and those are Anglo-Saxon attitudes.
1871 *Through the Looking-Glass*, ch.7, 'The Lion and the Unicorn'.

17 The Lion looked at Alice wearily. 'Are you animal—or vegetable—or mineral?' he said, yawning at every other word.
1871 *Through the Looking-Glass*, ch.7, 'The Lion and the Unicorn'.

18 I must have *two* you know—to come and go. One to come, and one to go.
1871 The King speaking of his messengers. *Through the Looking-Glass*, ch.7, 'The Lion and the Unicorn'.

19 It's as large as life and twice as natural!
1871 *Through the Looking-Glass*, ch.7, 'The Lion and the Unicorn'.

20 'It's long,' said the Knight, 'but it's very, *very* beautiful. Everybody that hears me sing it—either it brings the *tears* into their eyes, or else—'
'Or else what?' said Alice, for the Knight had made a sudden pause.
'Or else it doesn't, you know.'
1871 *Through the Looking-Glass*, ch.8, 'It's My Own Invention'.

21 I'll tell thee everything I can:
There's little to relate.
I saw an aged, aged man,
A-sitting on a gate.
1871 *Through the Looking-Glass*, ch.8, 'It's My Own Invention'.

22 Or madly squeeze a right-hand foot
Into a left-hand shoe.
1871 *Through the Looking-Glass*, ch.8, 'It's My Own Invention'.

23 Un-dish-cover the fish, or dishcover the riddle.
1871 *Through the Looking-Glass*, ch.9, 'Queen Alice'.

24 'Fan her head!' the Red Queen anxiously interrupted. 'She'll be feverish after so much thinking.'
1871 *Through the Looking-Glass*, ch.9, 'Queen Alice'.

25 'Do you know Languages? What's the French for fiddle-de-dee?'
'Fiddle-de-dee's not English,' Alice replied gravely.
'Who ever said it was?' said the Red Queen.
Alice thought she saw a way out of the difficulty this time. 'If you'll tell me what language "fiddle-de-dee" is, I'll tell you the French for it!' she exclaimed triumphantly.
But the Red Queen drew herself up rather stiffly, and said 'Queens never make bargains.'
1871 *Through the Looking-Glass*, ch.9, 'Queen Alice'.

26 What I tell you three times is true.
1876 *The Hunting of the Snark*, 'Fit the First: The Landing'.

27 He would answer to 'Hi!' or to any loud cry,
Such as 'Fry me!' or 'Fritter-my-wig!'
1876 *The Hunting of the Snark*, 'Fit the First: The Landing'.

28 His intimate friends called him 'Candle-ends',
And his enemies, 'Toasted-cheese'.
1876 *The Hunting of the Snark*, 'Fit the First: The Landing'.

29 'What's the good of Mercator's North Poles and Equators,
Tropics, Zones and Meridian lines?'
So the Bellman would cry: and the crew would reply,
'They are merely conventional signs!'

1876 *The Hunting of the Snark*, 'Fit the Second: The Bellman's Speech'.

30 But the principal failing occurred in the sailing,
And the Bellman, perplexed and distressed,
Said he *had* hoped, at least, when the wind blew due East,
That the ship would *not* travel due West!
1876 *The Hunting of the Snark*, 'Fit the Second: The Bellman's Speech'.

31 They sought it with thimbles, they sought it with care;
They pursued it with forks and hope;
They threatened its life with a railway-share;
They charmed it with smiles and soap.
1876 *The Hunting of the Snark*, 'Fit the Fifth: The Beaver's Lesson'.

32 He thought he saw an Elephant,
That practised on a fife:
He looked again, and found it was
A letter from his wife.
'At length I realize,' he said
'The bitterness of life!'
1889 *Sylvie and Bruno*, ch.5.

33 He thought he saw a Rattlesnake
That questioned him in Greek,
He looked again and found it was
The Middle of Next Week.
'The one thing I regret,' he said,
'Is that it cannot speak!'
1889 *Sylvie and Bruno*, ch.6.

Carson, Edward Henry, Baron 1854–1935

Irish Unionist politician, Solicitor General in the Conservative Government (1900–5). He successfully defended the Marquis of Queensberry against Oscar Wilde's libel suit in 1895. In 1912, he forced the Government to exclude Ulster from the Home Rule settlement. During World War I, he served as Attorney General (1915), First Lord of the Admiralty (1916–17) and a member of the war cabinet (1917–18).

34 A sentence of death with a stay of execution for six years.
1914 On the British Government's compromise terms by which Ireland was to be allowed to defer Home Rule for six years. Speech, Mar.

35 My only great qualification for being put at the head of the navy is that I am wholly at sea.
c.1916 Quoted in I Colvin *Life of Lord Carson* (1936), vol.3, ch.23.

Carter, Angela Olive 1940–92

English novelist and essayist, whose works combine fantasy and genre pastiche. They include *The Magic Toyshop* (1967) and *The Sadeian Woman* (1979).

36 Clothes are our weapons, our challenges, our visible insults.
1967 'Notes for a Theory of Sixties Style', in *New Society* (1967). Collected in *Nothing Sacred* (1982).

37 Solitude and melancholy, that is a woman's life.
1977 *The Passion of New Eve*, ch.9.

38 Myth deals in false universals, to dull the pain of particular circumstances.
1979 *The Sadeian Woman*, 'Polemical Preface'.

39 What is marriage but prostitution to one man instead of many?
1985 *Nights at the Circus*, 'London 2'.

40 I notice that I'm getting more sentimental as I get older; I feel I owe it to myself somehow.
Quoted in John Haffenden *Novelists in Interview* (1985).

41 He was a man with a great future behind him, already.
1991 *Wise Children*, ch.3.

42 She looked like a million dollars, I must admit, even if in well-used notes.
1991 *Wise Children*, ch.5.

Carter, Jimmy (James Earl) 1924–

US Democratic politician and 39th President (1977–81). He helped to effect the Egypt–Israel peace treaties (1979), but after the Iran hostage crisis and the Soviet invasion of Afghanistan he was defeated by Reagan in 1980. Latterly he has been a prolific human rights campaigner and negotiator. He won the Nobel peace prize in 2002.

43 Why not the best?
1976 Presidential campaign slogan.

44 I am convinced that UFOs exist, because I have seen one.
1976 TV interview, 16 Jun.

45 We become not a melting pot but a beautiful mosaic. Different people, different beliefs, different yearnings, different hopes, different dreams.
1976 Speech at Pittsburgh, 27 Oct.

46 I have looked on a lot of women with lust. I have committed adultery in my heart many times. God recognizes I will do that, and forgives me.
1976 *Playboy* interview, Nov.

47 The experience of democracy is like the experience of life itself—always changing, infinite in its variety, sometimes turbulent and all the more valuable for having been tested by adversity.
1978 Address to the Parliament of India, 2 Jun.

48 If you fear making anyone mad, then you ultimately probe for the lowest common denominator of human achievement.
1978 Address to the Future Farmers of America, Kansas City, 9 Nov.

49 All of you have met another Democratic President. I've never had that opportunity yet.
1991 On greeting former Presidents Bush, Reagan, Ford and Nixon at the dedication of the Reagan Library. Reported in the *New York Times*, 5 Nov.

50 My role is one of filling vacuums.
1994 On his work with 105 countries since leaving the White House. Broadcast on ABC TV, 13 Dec.

51 I feel truer to myself…more of a missionary than a politician.
1995 On the Carter Library as a centre for the study of international issues. In *Life*, Nov.

52 I can't deny I'm a better ex-president than I was a president.
2005 Interview quoted in *The Washington Times*, 3 Nov.

53 America does not at the moment have a functioning democracy.
2013 Referring to mass surveillance by the US government, quoted in *International Business Times*, 18 Jul.

Carter, Lillian 1898–1983

Mother of US President Jimmy Carter.

54 Sometimes when I look at my children, I say to myself, 'Lillian, you should have stayed a virgin.'
   1977 In *Woman* magazine, 9 Apr.

Cartier, Jacques 1491–1557
French navigator and explorer in North America, discoverer of the St Lawrence river.

55 In fine I am rather inclined to believe that this is the land God gave to Cain.
   1534 Of Canada, as he sailed past the bleak northern shore of the Gulf of St Lawrence. Journal entry, summer. Quoted in H P Biggar (ed) *The Voyages of Jacques Cartier* (1924).

Cartland, Dame (Mary) Barbara Hamilton
1901–2000

English romantic novelist. A prolific writer of popular romances, she became a media celebrity for her garish dress and well-honed sense of social status.

56 At fifty you have the choice of keeping your face or your figure and it's *much* better to keep your face.
   1981 In the *Daily Mail*, 10 Jul.

57 I answer 20,000 letters a year and so many couples are having problems because they are not getting the right proteins and vitamins.
   1986 Quoted in the *Observer*, 31 Aug.

Cartwright, John 1740–1824
English reformer, 'The Father of Reform', and political writer.

58 One man shall have one vote.
   1780 *The People's Barrier Against Undue Influence*, ch.1, 'Principles, maxims, and primary rules of politics'.

Caruso, Enrico 1873–1921
Italian operatic tenor renowned for the power and musical purity of his voice.

59 You know whatta you do when you shit? Singing, it's the same thing, only up!
   Quoted in H Brown *Whose Little Boy Are You?* (1983).

Cary, (Arthur) Joyce Lunel 1888–1957
English novelist. His best-known books are *Mister Johnston* (1939), set in Africa, and *The Horse's Mouth* (1944), the final work in a trilogy exploring the pretensions of the art world.

60 This is not to pretend that reading is a passive act. On the contrary, it is highly creative, or re-creative; itself an art.
   1939 *Mister Johnston*, preface.

61 I ain't complaining—it's a duty laid down upon us by God—but the Pax Britannia takes a bit of keeping up—with 'arf the world full of savages and 'arf the other 'arf just getting in the way.
   1939 *Mister Johnston*.

62 She had a mannish manner of mind and face, able to feel hot and think cold.
   1940 *Herself Surprised*, ch.7.

63 It is the misfortune of an old man that though he can put things out of his head he can't put them out of his feelings.
   1942 *To Be A Pilgrim*, ch.8.

64 Sara could commit adultery at one end and weep for her sins at the other, and enjoy both at once.
   1944 *The Horse's Mouth*, ch.8.

65 Remember I'm an artist. And you know what that means in a court of law. Next worse to an actress.
   1944 *The Horse's Mouth*, ch.14.

66 To a real anarchist a poke in the eye is better than a bunch of flowers. It makes him see stars.
   1944 *The Horse's Mouth*, ch.16.

67 The only good government…is a bad one in a hell of a fright.
   1944 *The Horse's Mouth*, ch.32.

68 It is the tragedy of the world that no one knows what he doesn't know; and the less a man knows, the more sure he is that he knows everything.
   1958 *Art and Reality*, introduction.

Casal, Julián del 1863–93
Cuban poet, forerunner of the *modernista* movement, influenced by Baudelaire and the Parnassian poets. He was a chronic invalid and frequently took a morbid view of life.

69 *Tengo el impuro amor de las ciudades,*
   y a este sol que ilumina las edades
   prefiero yo del gas las claridades.
   I have an impure love for cities,
   and I prefer the light coming from gaslamps
   rather than this sun that lights the ages.
   1893 *Bustos y rimas*, 'En el campo' ('In the Countryside').

Casals, Pablo 1876–1973
Spanish cellist, conductor and composer. In 1936 he emigrated because of the Civil War.

70 The most perfect technique is that which is not noticed at all.
   Quoted in Julian Lloyd Webber *The Song of the Birds* (1985).

Cassini, Oleg Lolewski 1913–2006
French-born US fashion designer, raised in Italy.

71 I imagined her as an ancient Egyptian princess.
   1987 On designing for Jacqueline Kennedy as First Lady. *In My Own Fashion*.

72 Fashion anticipates, and elegance is a state of mind.
   1987 *In My Own Fashion*.

Casson, Sir Hugh Maxwell 1910–99
English architect and artist, Director of Architecture for the Festival of Britain (1948–51). Among his works are *Homes by the Million* (1947) and a series, *Hugh Casson's London* (1983), *Oxford* (1988) and *Cambridge* (1992).

73 Architecture cannot be understood without some knowledge of the society it serves.
   1948 *An Introduction to Victorian Architecture*.

74 The Victorians expected every building, like every painting, to tell a story, and preferably to point to a moral as well.
   1948 *An Introduction to Victorian Architecture*.

Castle (of Blackburn), Barbara Anne Castle, Baroness 1910–2002
English Labour politician.

75 Dogs make you walk. Politics make you think. Only boredom makes you old.
   1997 In the *Daily Mail*, 11 Jan.

Castle (of Islington), Ted (Edward Cyril) Castle, Baron 1907–79
English journalist, Assistant Editor (1944–50) and Editor (1951–2) of *Picture Post*.

76 In Place of Strife.
   1969 Title of a White Paper on industrial relations, 17 Jan. Suggested by Castle to his wife Barbara Castle, Secretary of State for Employment and Productivity.

Castro (Ruz), Fidel 1927–
Cuban revolutionary. He landed in Cuba in 1956 with a small band of insurgents. In 1958 Batista was forced to flee and Castro became Prime Minister (1959–76) and President (1976–2006), instituting a Marxist–Leninist programme. In 2006 he transferred the presidency to his brother Ruiz because of failing health.

77 *La historia me absolverá*.
   History will absolve me.
   1953 Title of propaganda pamphlet.

78 We are not politicians. We made our revolution to get the politicians out.
   1961 Speech on assuming the presidency, two years after overthrowing the Batista regime.

79 A man who does not believe in human beings is not a revolutionary.
   1967 Speech, 29 Jan.

80 I was a man lucky enough to have discovered a political theory, a man who was caught up in the whirlpool of Cuba's political crisis long before becoming a fully-fledged communist. Discovering Marxism was like finding a map in a forest.
   1971 Speech, Chile, 18 Nov.

Caswall, Edward 1814–78
English hymnwriter and translator.

81 Jesu, the very thought of Thee
   With sweetness fills the breast.
   1849 *Hymns and Poems*, 'Jesu, the Very Thought of Thee' (a translation from 12c Latin, often attributed to St Bernard).

82 When morning gilds the skies.
   1854 Title and first line of hymn.

83 See amid the winter's snow,
   Born for us on earth below,
   See, the Lamb of God appears,
   Promised from eternal years!

   Hail thou ever-blessèd morn!
   Hail, redemption's happy dawn!
   Sing through all Jerusalem:
   Christ is born in Bethlehem!
   1858 'See Amid the Winter's Snow'.

Cather, Willa Sibert 1873–1947
US novelist, poet and journalist. Her best-known books are the trilogy on pioneering life, *O Pioneers!* (1913), *The Song of the Lark* (1915) and *My Antonia* (1918).

84 The history of every country begins in the heart of a man or a woman.
   1913 *O Pioneers!*, pt.1, ch.5.

85 Isn't it queer: there are only two or three human stories, and they go on repeating themselves as fiercely as if they had never happened before; like the larks in this country, that have been singing the same five notes over for thousands of years.
   1913 *O Pioneers!*, p.2, ch.4.

86 I like trees because they seem more resigned to the way they have to live than other things do.
   1913 *O Pioneers!*, pt.2, ch.8.

87 Artistic growth is, more than it is anything else, a refining of the sense of truthfulness.
   1915 *The Song of the Lark*, pt.6, ch.11.

88 Winter lies too long in country towns; hangs on until it is stale and shabby, old and sullen.
   1918 *My Antonia*, bk.2, ch.7.

89 The dead might as well speak to the living as the old to the young.
   1922 *One of Ours*, bk.2, ch.6.

90 When it has left a place where we have always found it, it is like shipwreck; we drop from security into something malevolent and bottomless.
   1926 Of kindness. *My Mortal Enemy*.

91 Oh, the Germans classify, but the French arrange.
   1927 *Death Comes to the Archbishop*, prologue.

92 The irregular and intimate quality of things made entirely by the human hand.
   1927 *Death Comes to the Archbishop*, bk.1, ch.3.

93 Most of the basic material a writer works with is acquired before the age of fifteen.
   Quoted in René Rapin *Willa Cather* (1930).

94 Only solitary men know the full joys of friendship. Others have their family—but to a solitary and an exile his friends are everything.
   1931 *Shadows On The Rock*, bk.3, ch.5.

95 Religion and art spring from the same root and are close kin. Economics and art are strangers.
   1936 In *Commonweal*, 17 Apr.

96 Every fine story must leave in the mind of the sensitive reader an intangible residuum of pleasure, a cadence, a quality of voice that is exclusively the writer's own, individual, unique.
   1936 *Not Under Forty*, 'Miss Jewett'.

Catiline *full name* Lucius Sergius Catilina c.108–62 BC
Roman conspirator, from an obscure senatorial family. In 63 BC, he plotted to murder Cicero and other hostile senators, and to seize power, but was arrested and executed.

97 *Idem velle atque idem nolle, ea demum firma amicitia est*.
   Agreements in likes and dislikes—this, and only this is what constitutes true friendship.
   Quoted in Sallust *De Catilinae coniuratione*, bk.20, pt.4 (translated by J C Rolfe).

Cato *full name* Marcus Porcius Cato *known as* 'the Elder' *or* 'the Censor' 234–149 BC
Roman statesman and orator, renowned for his strict morality and conservatism. Appointed censor in 184 BC, he discharged his duties rigorously. He was sent on a mission to Carthage in 175 BC.

98 All mankind rules its women, and we rule all mankind, but our women rule us.

Criticizing the prevalent domination of women. Quoted (in Greek) in Plutarch *Regum et imperatorum apophthegmata*, pt.198d (translated by F C Babbitt).

99 *Orator vir bonus dicendi peritus.*
An orator is a good man, skilled in speaking.
Quoted in Quintilian *Institutio Oratoria*, bk.12, pt.1, section 1 (translated by H E Butler).

1 *Rem tene, verba sequentur.*
Stick to your subject, and words will follow.
Attributed advice to orators. Quoted in Gaius Julius Victor *Ars Rhetorica*, 'De inventione'.

2 *Delenda est Carthago.*
Carthage must be destroyed.
Attributed. Quoted in Florus *Epitome*, bk.1, pt.31 (*Cato inexpiabili odio delendam esse Carthaginem, et cum de alio consuletur, pronuntiabat*, Cato bore an unquenchable hatred to Carthage and used to announce that Carthage had to be destroyed, even when he was consulted on a different subject) and Pliny *Naturalis Historia*, bk.15, ch.74.

Cattell, Raymond B(ernard) 1905–98

British psychologist, designer of intelligence and personality tests. Associated with the eugenics movement in the 1930s, he believed that the large size and low IQs of lower-class families would undermine the nation's intellect.

3 The Fight for our National Intelligence.
1937 Title of book.

Catto, Henry E(dward) 1930–2011

US government official, chief of protocol at the White House (1974–6), Ambassador to the UK (1989–91) and Director of the US Information Agency (1991–3).

4 Like being the captain of a mine-sweeper, if you do your job well, nobody notices. If you don't, there's a hell of an explosion.
1988 On his role as chief of protocol. In the *Washington Post*, 22 Mar.

Catullus full name Gaius Valerius Catullus c.84–c.54 BC

Latin poet, mainly known for his passionate love poems for Lesbia. Her true name was Clodia, and she was probably the sister of Cicero's enemy P Clodius Pulcher.

5 *Cui dono lepidum novum libellum*
arida modo pumice expolitum?
Corneli, tibi.
Who shall I give my nice new little book to,
my little book polished with dry pumice? To you, Cornelius.
Dedication to Cornelius Nepos, the biographer.
Carmina, no.1.

6 *Vivamus, mea Lesbia, atque amemus,*
rumoresque senum severiorum
omnes unius aestimemus assis.
Let us live, my Lesbia, and let us love!
Let us not give one penny if old men protest and disapprove.
Carmina, no.5.
▶ See Campion 195:72.

7 *Quaeris, quot mihi basiationes*
tuae, Lesbia, sint satis superque?
You ask me, Lesbia, how many kisses
it will take to make me fully satisfied?
Carmina, no.7.

8 *Nam risu inepto res ineptior nulla est.*
For there is nothing more ridiculous than a ridiculous laugh.
Carmina, no.39.

9 *Ille mi par esse Deo videtur,*
ille, si fas est, superare Divos,
qui sedens adversus identidem te
spectat et audit
dulce ridentem.
He seems to me to be like a god,
even superior to the Gods, if it is
permitted to say so, the man who sits
gazing on you all day and listens to
your sweet laughter.
Carmina, no.51.

10 *Otium et reges prius et beatas*
perdidit urbes.
Often has leisure ruined great kings and fine cities.
Carmina, no.51.

11 *Odi et amo. quare id faciam, fortasse requiris.*
nescio sed fieri sentio et excrucior.
I hate and I love. You ask me to explain, perhaps.
I don't know. But I feel it happen and the pain is dreadful.
Carmina, no.85.

Caulfield, Sir Bernard 1914–94

English high court judge.

12 Remembering Mary Archer in the witness box. Your vision of her probably will never disappear. Has she elegance? Has she fragrance? Would she have, without the strain of this trial, radiance?
Summing up in 1987 libel trial in which Jeffrey Archer contested a newspaper's claim that he had sex with a prostitute. Quoted in Michael Crick *Jeffrey Archer: Stranger than Fiction* (1996).

Causley, Charles 1917–2003

English poet of verse for adults and children, much of it set in his native Cornwall.

13 You must take off your clothes for the doctor
And stand as straight as a pin,
His hand of stone on your white breastbone
Where the bullets all go in.
1953 'Recruiting Drive'.

14 Timothy Winters comes to school
With eyes as wide as a football pool,
Ears like bombs and teeth like splinters:
A blitz of a boy is Timothy Winters.
1957 'Timothy Winters'.

15 Who is the smiling stranger
With hair as white as gin,
What is he doing with the children
And who could have let him in?
1961 'Innocent's Song'.

Cavafy, Constantine pseudonym of Konstantínos Pétron Kaváfis 1863–1933

Egyptian-born Greek poet who spent much of his life working as a civil servant in Alexandria. Most of his work was published posthumously, including in English translation *Poems* (1951) and *Complete Poems* (1961).

16 And now, what will become of us without any barbarians?
Those people were a kind of solution.
1904 'Waiting for the Barbarians' (translated by E Keeley and P Sherrard).

17 Have Ithaka always in your mind
Your arrival there is what you are destined for.
1911 'Ithaka' (translated by E Keeley and P Sherrard).

18 New places you will not find, you will not find another sea
The city will follow you.
1911 'The Town' (translated by E Keeley and P Sherrard).

Cavell, Edith Louisa 1865–1915

English nurse, matron of a Red Cross hospital in Brussels during World War I. She was arrested by the Germans in 1915, charged with helping Allied soldiers escape to Holland, and executed when she did not deny the charges.

19 Standing, as I do, in view of God and eternity, I realize that patriotism is not enough. I must have no hatred or bitterness towards anyone.
1915 On the eve of her execution. Reported in *The Times*, 23 Oct.

Cavendish, Margaret, Duchess of Newcastle 1624–74

English writer and playwright. She was a maid of honour at the court of Charles I, and married the Duke of Newcastle in 1645. They lived in exile in Europe during the Civil War.

20 Marriage is the grave or tomb of wit.
1662 *Plays*, 'Nature's Three Daughters', pt.2, act 5, sc.20.

21 If Nature had not befriended us with beauty, and other good graces, to help us to insinuate our selves into men's affections, we should have been more enslaved than any other of Nature's creatures she hath made.
1664 *Sociable Letters*.

Caxton, William c.1422–c.1491

English printer responsible for printing the first book in English.

22 I, according to my copy, have done set it in imprint, to the intent that noble men may see and learn the noble acts of chivalry, the gentle and virtuous deeds that some knights used in those days.
1485 Thomas Malory *Le Morte D'Arthur*, prologue.

Cecil, Lord (Edward Christian) David Gascoyne 1902–86

English literary critic and essayist, Professor of English Literature at Oxford (1948-70) and a respected literary biographer. His traditional approach to literary criticism earned him the scorn of F R Leavis.

23 It does not matter that Dickens's world is not life-like; it is alive.
1934 *Early Victorian Novelists*.

24 The primary object of a student of literature is to be delighted.
1949 *Reading as One of the Fine Arts*.

25 Funny you should ask. As a matter of fact I did have a light temperature when I set out.
Response to a Berlin nightclubber's ambiguous question, 'Sind Sie normal?'. Quoted in Jonathan Keates 'The Delightful Lord David', in the *Times Literary Supplement*, 1 Mar 1991. Keates also describes how Cecil had confessed that, had he visited Sodom and Gomorrah, he would probably only have noticed the cathedral.

Cecil, Robert Arthur James Gascoyne, 5th Marquis of Salisbury 1893–1972

English Conservative statesman. Opposition Leader in the Lords (1945–51), he became Secretary of State for Commonwealth Relations in Churchill's Government and Leader of the Lords (1951–7).

26 The Colonial Secretary [Iain Macleod] has been too clever by half. I believe that he is a very fine bridge player. It is not considered immoral, or even bad form, to outwit one's opponent at bridge. It almost seems to me as if the Colonial Secretary, when he abandoned the sphere of bridge for the sphere of politics, brought his bridge technique with him.
1961 Speech, House of Lords.

Cecil, Robert Arthur Talbot Gascoyne, 3rd Marquis of Salisbury 1830–1903

English Conservative statesman and three times Prime Minister (1885–6, 1886–92, 1895–1902), often serving as his own Foreign Secretary. He remained as head of government during the Boer War (1899–1902), and then retired.

27 Peace without honour is not only a disgrace, but, except as a temporary respite, it is a chimera.
1864 In the *Quarterly Review*, Apr.

28 Under a more heroic Minister, and in a less self-seeking age, it is probable that England would have preferred the risk, whatever its extent, to the infamy of betraying an ally whom she had enticed into peril. But our Ministry is not heroic; and our generation, though not indifferent to glory, prefers it when it is safe and cheap.
1864 On Palmerston's failure to defend Denmark against Prussia, in the *Quarterly Review*, Jul.

29 Horny-handed sons of toil.
1873 In the *Quarterly Review*, Oct.

30 English policy is to float lazily downstream, occasionally putting out a diplomatic boathook to avoid collisions.
1877 Letter to Lord Lytton, 9 Mar.

31 The commonest error in politics is sticking to the carcasses of old policies.
1877 Speech, Hatfield, 25 May.

32 Randolph and the Mahdi have occupied my thoughts about equally. The Mahdi pretends to be half mad, but is very sane in reality. Randolph occupies exactly the converse position.
1884 Of Lord Randolph Churchill. Letter to Lady John Manners, May.

33 We are part of the community of Europe, and we must do our duty as such.
1888 Speech, Caernarvon, 10 Apr.

34 It is a superstition of an antiquated diplomacy that there is any necessary antagonism between Russia and Great Britain.
1896 Speech, London Guildhall, 9 Nov.

Céline, Louis-Ferdinand *pseudonym of* Louis Ferdinand Destouches 1894–1961

French novelist, author of *Journey to the End of Night* (1932), and other misanthropic works. He wrote anti-Semitic tracts before World War II and collaborated with the Germans. He escaped to Denmark after the war, but returned to France in 1951.

35 *Entre le pénis et les mathématiques…il n'existe rien. Rien!*
Between the penis and mathematics…there's nothing. Nothing!
1932 *Voyage au bout de la nuit* (*Journey to the End of Night*, translated by John H P Marks, 1960).

36 *Voyager, c'est bien utile, ça fait travailler l'imagination. Tout le reste n'est que déceptions et fatigues. Notre voyage à nous est entièrement imaginaire. Voilà sa force.*
To travel is useful. It engages the imagination. Everything else is deceitful and boring. Our own voyage is entirely imaginary. And therein lies its force.
1932 *Voyage au bout de la nuit* (*Journey to the End of Night*, translated by John H P Marks, 1960).

37 *Quand on a pas d'imagination, mourir c'est peu de chose, quand on en a, mourir c'est trop.*
For those who have no imagination, death means little. For those who have one, death is often too much.
1932 *Voyage au bout de la nuit* (*Journey to the End of Night*, translated by John H P Marks, 1960).

38 *C'est l'actuel qui compte. Invoquer sa postérité, c'est faire un discours aux asticots.*
It is the present that counts. To invoke one's posterity is to make a speech to maggots.
1932 *Voyage au bout de la nuit* (*Journey to the End of Night*, translated by John H P Marks, 1960).

39 *La plupart des gens ne meurent qu'au dernier moment; d'autres commencent et s'y prennent vingt ans d'avance et parfois davantage. Ce sont les malheureux de la terre.*
Most people only die at the last moment; others begin early and take twenty years and sometimes more. These are the most miserable people on earth.
1932 *Voyage au bout de la nuit* (*Journey to the End of Night*, translated by John H P Marks, 1960).

40 *Des pauvres, c'est-à-dire des gens dont la mort n'intéresse personne.*
The poor—that is, the people whose death interests no one.
1932 *Voyage au bout de la nuit* (*Journey to the End of Night*, translated by John H P Marks, 1960).

41 *Les Anglais, c'est drôle quand même comme dégaine, c'est mi-curé, mi-garçonnet.*
The English are funny and peculiar, half-clergymen and half-little boys.
1936 *Mort à crédit*.

Cellini, Benvenuto 1500–71

Italian goldsmith and sculptor, known for his autobiography as much as for his art.

42 A painting is merely the image of a tree, a man, or any other object reflected in a fountain. The difference between a painting and sculpture is the difference between a shadow and the thing which casts it.
1547 Letter to Benedetto Varchi.

Cennini, Cennino c.1370–c.1440

Florentine painter and writer, best remembered for his *Il Libro dell'Arte*, a practical guide for the art student.

43 Do not fail, as you go on, to draw something every day, for no matter how little it is it will be well worth while, and it will do you a world of good.
c.1400 *Il Libro dell' Arte* ('The Craftsman's Handbook').

44 There is another cause which, if you indulge it, can make your hand so unsteady that it will waver more, and flutter far more, than leaves do in the wind, and this is indulging too much in the company of women.
c.1400 *Il Libro dell' Arte* ('The Craftsman's Handbook').

Cervantes, Miguel de 1547–1616

Spanish writer, best known for his novel *Don Quixote* (in two parts 1605, 1615), the first part of which is thought to have been written in prison in La Mancha. Other works include *La Galatea* (1585), a pastoral romance, and many plays, only two of which survive.

45 *La mejor salsa del mundo es el hambre.*
Hunger is the best sauce in the world.
1615 *Don Quixote*, pt.2, ch.5.

46 *El pan comido y la compañía deshecha.*
With the bread eaten, the company breaks up.
1615 *Don Quixote*, pt.2, ch.7.

47 *Para todo hay remedio, si no es para la muerte.*
There's a remedy for everything except death.
1615 *Don Quixote*, pt.2, ch.10.

48 *Dos linajes sólo hay en el mundo, como decía una abuela mía, que son el tener y el no tener.*
There are but two families in the world, as my grandmother used to say—the Haves and the Havenots.
1615 *Don Quixote*, pt.2, ch.20.

49 *Digo, paciencia y barajar.*
What I say is, patience, and shuffle the cards.
1615 *Don Quixote*, pt.2, ch.23.

Césaire, Aimé Fernand 1913–2008

Caribbean poet known for his visionary, surrealist style and as a Marxist and anti-colonialist.

50 *Ma bouche sera la bouche des malheurs qui n'ont point de bouche, ma voix, la liberté de celles qui s'affaissent au cachot du désespoir.*
My voice will be the voice of those who suffer and have no voice. My voice, the freedom of those weakened in the dungeon of despair.
1939 *Cahier d'un retour au pays natal*.

51 *Je vois l'Afrique multiple et une
verticale dans la tumultueuse péripétie
avec ses bourrelets, ses nodules,
un peu à part, mais à portée
du siècle, comme un coeur de réserve.*
I see several Africas and one
vertical in the tumultuous event
with its screens and nodules,
a little separated, but within
the century, like a heart in reserve.
1960 *Ferrements*, 'Pour saluer le Tiers-Monde'.

Cézanne, Paul 1839–1906

French Post-Impressionist painter, a friend of Zola who persuaded him to go to Paris to paint in 1862. His paintings foreshadow Cubism, emphasizing underlying forms with glowing colours.

52 May I repeat what I told you here: treat nature by the cylinder, the sphere, the cone, everything in perspective.
1904 Letter to Émile Bernard, 15 Apr.

53 The Louvre is the book in which we learn to read.
1905 Letter to Émile Bernard.

54 Monet is only an eye, but my God what an eye!
Attributed, in conversation with Ambroise Vollard. Quoted in Cooper *Claude Monet* (1957).

55 I wished to copy nature but I could not. But I was satisfied when I discovered that the sun could not be reproduced but that it must be represented by something else—colour.
Quoted in D Hooker (ed) *Art of the Western World* (1989).

Chalmers, Patrick Reginald 1872–1942
English writer and banker, an authority on field sports.

56 What's lost upon the roundabouts we pulls up on the swings!
1912 *Green Days and Blue Days*, 'Roundabouts and Swings'.

Chamberlain, Sir (Joseph) Austen 1863–1937
English Conservative politician, successively Chancellor of the Exchequer, Secretary for India, Unionist leader, Foreign Secretary and First Lord of the Admiralty. He received the 1925 Nobel peace prize for negotiating the Locarno Pact.

57 I yield to no one in my devotion to this great League of Nations, but not even for this will I destroy that smaller but older league of which my own country was the birthplace, and of which it remains the centre… Beware how you so draw tight the bonds, how you so pile obligation on obligation and sanction on sanction, lest at last you find that you are not living nations but dead states.
1927 Speech, League of Nations Assembly, Geneva, 9 Sep.

Chamberlain, Joseph 1836–1914
English Liberal politician. He was President of the Board of Trade, but resigned over Gladstone's Home Rule bill (1880). Leader of the Liberal Unionists from 1889, he was also Secretary of State for the Colonies (1895), and retired in 1903.

58 Lord Salisbury constitutes himself the spokesman of a class, of the class to which he himself belongs, who 'toil not neither do they spin'.
1883 Speech, 30 Mar.

59 Provided that the City of London remains, as it is at present, the clearing-house of the world, any other nation may be its workshop.
1904 Speech at the Guildhall, 19 Jan.

60 The day of small nations has passed away. The day of Empires has come.
1904 Speech at Birmingham, 12 May, advocating preferential trade within the British Empire as a means of ensuring Britain's security.

Chamberlain, (Arthur) Neville 1869–1940
English politician, who played a leading part in the formation of the National Government (1931). As Prime Minister (1937–40) he advocated appeasement of Italy and Germany. He resigned as a result of criticism of his war leadership.

61 In war, whichever side may call itself the victor, there are no winners, but all are losers.
1938 Speech at Kettering, 3 Jul.

62 How horrible, fantastic, incredible it is that we should be digging trenches and trying on gas-masks here because of a quarrel in a far away country between people of whom we know nothing.
1938 Radio broadcast, 27 Sep, referring to Germany's annexation of the Sudetenland.

63 This morning I had another talk with the German Chancellor, Herr Hitler, and here is the paper that bears his name upon it as well as mine: 'We regard the agreement signed last night and the Anglo-German naval agreement, as symbolic of the desire of our two people never to go to war with one another again.'
1938 Speech on the signing of the Munich Agreement, Heston airport, 30 Sep.

64 My good friends, this is the second time in our history that there has come back from Germany to Downing Street peace with honour. I believe it is peace for our time. Go home and have a nice, quiet sleep.
1938 Speech from the window of No. 10 Downing Street to the crowds outside, 30 Sep, having returned that day from signing the Munich Agreement. The earlier peace referred to was the Treaty of Berlin which Beaconsfield brought back in 1878.
▶ See also Disraeli 288:66.

65 We should seek by all means in our power to avoid war, by analysing possible causes, by trying to remove them, by discussion in a spirit of collaboration and good will. I cannot believe that such a programme would be rejected by the people of this country, even if it does mean the establishment of personal contact with the dictators.
1938 Speech in the House of Commons, 6 Oct.

66 This morning, the British ambassador in Berlin handed the German Government a final note stating that, unless we heard from them by 11 o'clock, that they were prepared at once to withdraw their troops from Poland, a state of war would exist between us. I have to tell you that no such undertaking has been received, and that consequently this country is at war with Germany.
1939 Radio broadcast, 3 Sep.

67 Whatever may be the reason—whether it was that Hitler thought he might get away with what he had got without fighting for it, or whether it was that after all the preparations were not sufficiently complete—however, one thing is certain—he missed the bus.
1940 Speech at Central Hall, Westminster, 4 Apr.

Chamberlain, Wilt(on Norman) 1936–99
US basketball player. Over seven feet tall, he set many individual scoring records.

68 Nobody roots for Goliath.
1967 Quoted in Colin Jarman *The Guinness Dictionary of Sports Quotations* (1990).

Chamfort, Sébastien-Roch Nicolas 1741–94
French writer. He joined the Jacobins at the outbreak of the French Revolution, but his remarks on the terror brought him into disfavour. Threatened with arrest, he attempted suicide, dying several days later.

69 *Guerre aux châteaux, paix aux chaumières.*
War to the castles, peace to the cottages.
1790 Motto for the Revolution.

70 Society is composed of two large classes; those who have more dinners than appetites, and those with more appetites than dinners.
Maximes et Pensées (1795), ch.1.

71 *Vivre est une maladie dont le sommeil nous soulage toutes les 16 heures. C'est un palliatif. La mort est le remède.*
Living is an illness to which sleep provides relief every 16 hours. It's a palliative. Death is the remedy.
Maximes et Pensées (1795), ch.2.

72 *Sois mon frère, ou je te tue.*
Be my brother, or I kill you.
His interpretation of the motto 'Fraternité ou la mort'. Quoted in P R Angus (ed) *Oeuvres Complètes* (1824), vol.1.

Chandler, Raymond 1888–1959

US crime writer, brought up in England. He returned to America and lived in California. He is best known for his creation of Philip Marlowe, a cynically philosophical, wise-cracking private detective whose career is closely involved with a series of beautiful and seductive *femmes fatales*.

73 I was neat, clean, shaved and sober, and I didn't care who knew it.
1939 Philip Marlowe. *The Big Sleep*, ch.1.

74 The General spoke again, slowly, using his strength as carefully as an out-of-work showgirl uses her last good pair of stockings.
1939 *The Big Sleep*, ch.2.

75 He looked about as inconspicuous as a tarantula on a slice of angel food.
1940 Of Moose Malloy. *Farewell, My Lovely*, ch.1.

76 It was a blonde. A blonde to make a bishop kick a hole in a stained glass window.
1940 *Farewell, My Lovely*, ch.13.

77 She gave me a smile I could feel in my hip pocket.
1940 *Farewell, My Lovely*, ch.18

78 Down these mean streets a man must go who is not himself mean, who is neither tarnished nor afraid.
1944 'The Simple Art of Murder'. In *Atlantic Monthly*, Dec.

79 The English may not always be the best writers in the world, but they are incomparably the best dull writers.
1944 'The Simple Art of Murder'. In *Atlantic Monthly*, Dec.

80 If my books had been any worse, I should not have been invited to Hollywood, and if they had been any better, I should not have come.
1945 Letter to Charles W Morton, 12 Dec.

81 Just don't get too complicated Eddie. When a guy gets too complicated he's unhappy. And when he's unhappy—his luck runs out.
1945 *The Blue Dahlia*.

82 Would you convey my compliments to the purist who reads your proofs and tell him or her that I write in a sort of broken-down patois which is something like the way a Swiss waiter talks, and that when I split an infinitive, God damn it, I split it so it will stay split.
1947 Letter to Edward Weeks at *Atlantic Monthly*, 18 Jan.

83 By the way, do you ever read the Bible? I suppose not very often, but I had occasion to the other night and believe me it is a lesson in how not to write for the movies. The worst kind of overwriting. Whole chapters that could have been said in one paragraph. And the dialogue!
1947 Letter to Edgar Carter, 28 Mar.

84 It wasn't exactly carelessness; her knowledge of literate English contained such vast areas of desert that she took it for granted that half of what she wrote would be meaningless to her.
1947 On the shortcomings of his ex-secretary. Letter to Erle Stanley Gardner, 1 Jul.

85 California, the department-store state. The most of everything and the best of nothing.
1949 *The Little Sister*, ch.13.

86 A big hard-boiled city with no more personality than a paper cup.
1949 Of Los Angeles. *The Little Sister*, ch.26.

87 It is pretty obvious that the debasement of the human mind caused by a constant flow of fraudulent advertising is no trivial thing. There is more than one way to conquer a country.
1951 Letter to Carl Barndt, 15 Nov.

88 Some people are better off dead—like your wife and my father for instance.
1951 Line delivered by Robert Walker as Bruno in the film *Strangers on a Train* (with Czenzi Ormonde), based on the novel by Patricia Highsmith.

89 A preoccupation with words for their own sake is fatal to good film-making. It's not what films are for.
1951 To Dale Warren, 7 Nov.

90 If people could deal with each other honestly, they would not need agents.
1952 'Ten Per Cent of Your Life', in *Atlantic Monthly*, Feb.

91 Alcohol is like love… The first kiss is magic, the second is intimate, the third is routine. After that you take the girl's clothes off.
1953 *The Long Good-Bye*, ch.4.

92 A dead man is the best fall guy in the world. He never talks back.
1953 *The Long Good-Bye*, ch.10.

93 By his standards anyone who noticed how many walls the room had would be observant.
1953 On an interviewer. Letter to Roger Machell, 15 Mar.

94 I suppose all writers are crazy, but if they are any good, I believe they have a terrible honesty.
1957 Letter to Edgar Carter, 3 Jun.

95 Dashiell Hammett took murder out of the Venetian vase and dropped it into the alley.
On the moving of murder mysteries from the English country house to more realistic areas. Quoted in *Contemporary Authors* (1979).

96 As elaborate a waste of human intelligence as you can find outside an advertising agency.
Of chess. Quoted in Colin Jarman *The Guinness Dictionary of Sports Quotations* (1990).

97 The streets were dark with something more than night.
Quoted in the *Smithsonian*, May 1994.

Chanel, Gabrielle known as *Coco* 1883–1971

French couturier. In the 1920s she came to prominence with designs notable for simple elegance and comfort, such as her 'chemise' dress and collarless cardigan jacket. She also developed a perfume, Chanel No.5.

98 Fashion is made to become unfashionable.
   1957 In *Life*, 19 Aug.

99 Youth is something very new: twenty years ago no one mentioned it.
   Quoted in Marcel Haedrich *Coco Chanel: Her Life, Her Secrets* (1972), ch.1 (translated by Charles Lam Markmann).

1 A fashion for the young? That is a pleonasm: there is no fashion for the old.
   Quoted in Marcel Haedrich *Coco Chanel: Her Life, Her Secrets* (1972), ch.1 (translated by Charles Lam Markmann).

2 Nature gives you the face you have when you are twenty. Life shapes the face you have at thirty. But it is up to you to earn the face you have at fifty.
   Quoted in Marcel Haedrich *Coco Chanel: Her Life, Her Secrets* (1972), ch.1 (translated by Charles Lam Markmann).
   ▸ See Orwell 655:80, Cartland 207:56.

3 Fashion is architecture: it is a matter of proportions.
   Quoted in Marcel Haedrich *Coco Chanel: Her Life, Her Secrets* (1972), ch.1 (translated by Charles Lam Markmann).

4 You ask if they were happy. This is not a characteristic of a European. To be contented—that's for the cows.
   Quoted in A Madsen *Coco Chanel* (1990), ch.35.

Channing, Carol Elaine 1921–

US comedienne. A star of US cabaret, she has made occasional appearances in films, notably in *Thoroughly Modern Millie* (1967).

5 Laughter is much more important than applause. Applause is almost a duty. Laughter is a reward. Laughter means they trust and like you.
   Attributed.

6 I am terribly shy, but of course no one believes me. Come to think of it, neither would I.
   Attributed.

Channon, Sir Henry 1897–1958

English Conservative politician. He became an MP in 1935, becoming a parliamentary private secretary in 1938. He kept a witty diary recording the political and society figures of the time.

7 This afternoon I slept for two hours in the Library of the House of Commons. A deep House of Commons sleep. There is no sleep to compare with it—rich, deep, and guilty.
   Attributed.

8 I love the House of Commons so passionately that were I to be offered a peerage, I should be tempted to refuse it. Only tempted, of course.
   Attributed.

Chao AD 168–89

Chinese poet. Little is known of him and only fragments of his poetry have survived.

9 Obsequiousness is glorified:
   While honest worth must wait outside.
   c.180 AD 'Poems of Disgust, no.1', collected in *A Golden Treasury of Chinese Poetry* (translated by John Turner, 1976).

Chaplin, Charlie (Sir Charles Spencer) 1889–1977

English film actor and director. He developed his skill in comedy under Fred Karno and moved to Hollywood in 1914. His early short comedies were extremely popular. His feature films included *Modern Times* (1936), *The Great Dictator* (1940) and *Limelight* (1952).

10 They are spoiling the oldest art in the world—the art of pantomime. They are ruining the great beauty of silence.
   1929 Of the advent of talking pictures. Interview in *Motion Picture Magazine*, May.

11 All I need to make a comedy is a park, a policeman and a pretty girl.
   1964 *My Autobiography*, ch.10.

Chapman, Arthur 1873–1935

US poet and author, best known for his long poem *Out Where The West Begins* (1916).

12 Out where the handclasp's a little stronger,
   Out where the smile dwells a little longer,
   That's where the West begins.
   1916 *Out Where the West Begins*, stanza 1.

Chapman, (Anthony) Colin Bruce 1928–82

English motor racing manager, founder of the Lotus racing team.

13 Money is how we keep the score in motor racing nowadays.
   1974 Quoted in Colin Jarman *The Guinness Dictionary of Sports Quotations* (1990).

Chapman, Dinos 1962–

English installation artist, who works with his brother Jake under the name the Chapman Brothers.

14 We will just make it again—it's only art.
   2004 After the installation *Hell* was destroyed in a fire in east London. Quoted in *The Scotsman*, 5 Jun.

Chapman, George c.1559–1634

English dramatist, poet and translator. His plays include *The Blind Beggar of Alexandria* (1595) and *Bussy d'Ambois* (1607). In 1598 he wrote a continuation of Marlowe's unfinished *Hero and Leander*, and he made important translations of Homer (1598–1624).

15 Man is a torch borne in the wind; a dream
   But of a shadow, summed with all his substance.
   1607 *Bussy d'Ambois*, act 1, sc.1.

16 Who to himself is law, no law doth need,
   Offends no law, and is a king indeed.
   1607 *Bussy d'Ambois*, act 1, sc.1.

17 Perfect happiness, by princes sought,
   Is not with birth born, nor exchequers bought.
   1611 *The Iliads of Homer Prince of Poets*, 'Epistle Dedicatory'.

18 Fate's such a shrewish thing.
   1611 *The Iliads of Homer Prince of Poets*, bk.4, l.21.

19 We have watered our houses in Helicon.
   1611 *May-Day*, act 3, sc.3. This is sometimes misquoted as 'We have watered our horses in Helicon'.

20 A poem, whose subject is not truth, but things like truth.
   1613 *The Revenge of Bussy d'Ambois*, dedication.

21 Danger, the spur of all great minds.
   1613 *The Revenge of Bussy d'Ambois*, act 5, sc.1.

22 I know an Englishman
   Being flattered, is a lamb; threatened, a lion.
   Alphonsus, Emperor of Germany (published posthumously, 1654), act 1. Although this is credited to Chapman, his authorship is doubtful.

23 I am ashamed the law is such an ass.
Revenge for Honour (published posthumously, 1654), act 3, sc.2. Although this is credited to Chapman, his authorship is doubtful.
▸ See Dickens 278:72.

Chapman, Jake 1966–
English installation artist, who works with his brother Dinos under the name the Chapman Brothers.

24 I hold God personally responsible.
2004 After the installation *Hell* was destroyed in a fire in east London. In the *London Evening Standard*, 26 May.

Chapman, John 1900–72
US theatre critic.

25 It is three and a half hours long, four characters wide, and a cesspool deep.
1962 In the *New York Daily News*, 15 Oct, reviewing Edward Albee's *Who's Afraid of Virginia Woolf?*

Chardin, Jean-Baptiste-Siméon 1699–1779
French painter of genre scenes and still-life.

26 The man who has not realized the difficulty of art never does anything worthwhile; the man who realizes it too soon does nothing at all.
1765 Quoted in Frank Elgar *Mondrian* (1968).

Chargaff, Erwin 1905–2002
Czech-born US biochemist. He settled at Columbia University in 1935, where his pioneering research on nucleic acids laid the foundations for modern molecular biology.

27 What counts…in science is to be not so much the first as the last.
1971 In *Science*, vol.172.

Charles, Elizabeth 1828–96
British writer.

28 To know how to say what others only know how to think is what makes men poets or sages; and to dare to say what others only dare to think makes men martyrs or reformers—or both.
Chronicle of the Schönberg-Cotta Family.

Charles I 1600–49
King of Scotland and England. His marriage to the Catholic French princess, Henrietta Maria, his expensive foreign wars and his high-handed treatment of Parliament (he dismissed three parliaments and ruled for 11 years without one) culminated in the Civil War and his execution.

29 A rule that may serve for a statesman, a courtier, or a lover—never make a defence or an apology before you be accused.
1636 Letter to Lord Wentworth, 3 Sep.

30 I see all the birds are flown.
1642 After his unsuccessful attempt to arrest the Five Members in the House of Commons, 4 Jan.

31 I tell you (and I pray God it be not laid to your charge) that I am the martyr of the people.
1649 Speech upon the scaffold.

Charles II 1630–85
King of Scotland and England. Exiled during the Civil War, on the execution of his father Charles I (1649) he was proclaimed king in Edinburgh but was not recalled as king to England until 1660. His childless marriage produced a succession crisis and contributed to much political and religious tension.

32 Whereas, women's parts in plays have hitherto been acted by men in the habits of women…we do permit and give leave for the time to come that all women's parts be acted by women.
1662 Royal licence, sanctioning the appearance of actresses on the English stage.

33 Better than a play.
1670 Commenting on the debates in the House of Lords over the Divorce Bill. Quoted in A Bryant *King Charles II* (1931).

34 This is very true—for my words are my own, and my actions are my Ministers'.
Riposte to 'The King's Epitaph'.
▸ See Rochester 720:27.

35 Let not poor Nelly starve.
c.**1685** Worrying on his deathbed about his mistress, Nell Gwynn. Quoted in Bishop Gilbert Burney *History of My Own Time* (1724), vol.1, bk.2.

Charles V 1500–58
Holy Roman Emperor (1519–58) and King of Spain (1516–56), founder of the Habsburg dynasty. His wars against France led to the formation of the Holy League against him. After numerous wars, he divided his Empire between his son and brother and retired to a monastery in Spain.

36 I came, I saw, God conquered.
1547 Attributed remark after the Battle of Muhlberg, 23 Apr.
▸ See also Caesar 192:14, John III Sobieski 456:76.

37 Remember, the prince is like a mirror exposed to the eyes of all his subjects who continually look to him as a pattern on which to model themselves, and who in consequence without much trouble discover his vices and virtues.
1555 *Instructions à Philippe II son Fils* (*Advice To His Son*, translated 1788). Quoted in G R Elton *Renaissance and Reformation, 1300–1648* (2nd edn, 1968), p.137.

38 To God I speak Spanish, to women Italian, to men French, and to my horse—German.
Attributed.

Charles, Prince of Wales 1948–
HRH The Prince of Wales, son of Elizabeth II.

39 Yes…whatever that may mean.
1981 On being asked whether he was in love, after the announcement of his engagement, 24 Feb.

40 What is proposed is like a monstrous carbuncle on the face of a much-loved and elegant friend.
1984 On the proposed extension to the National Gallery, London. Speech at the 150th anniversary of the Royal Institute of British Architects, 30 May.

41 I just come and talk to the plants, really—very important to talk to them, they respond I find.
1986 In a television interview, 21 Sep.

42 Both myself and the Respondent recognized there were irreconcilable differences and that accordingly we could no longer live together.

1996 On why he and Diana, Princess of Wales, were getting a divorce. Quoted in *The Times*, 16 Jul.

43 It's really the result of talking to trees too often.
2001 Explaining his appearance in public wearing an eyepatch.

44 I am not part of the PlayStation generation.
2011 Attributed.

45 I've been called a pommy bastard many times, but look what it has done for me. If you want to develop character, go to Australia.
2011 Speaking on Australia Day.

Charlton, Sir Bobby (Robert) 1937–
English footballer. He won 106 caps for England and played in the victorious World Cup team of 1966.

46 Some people tell me that we professional players are soccer slaves. Well, if this is slavery, give me a life sentence.
1960 Quoted in Peter Ball and Phil Shaw *The Book of Football Quotations* (1989).

47 They know on the Continent that European football without the English is like a hot dog without the mustard.
1988 Quoted in Peter Ball and Phil Shaw *The Book of Football Quotations* (1989). There was at the time a European ban in force against English clubs.

Charlton, Jack (John) 1935–
English footballer, brother of Sir Bobby Charlton. He played in the victorious World Cup team of 1966, and later managed the Republic of Ireland team (1986–95).

48 Soccer is a man's game; not an outing for mamby-pambies.
1967 *For Leeds and England*.

49 I have a little black book with two players in it, and if I get a chance to do them I will. I will make them suffer before I pack this game in. If I can kick them four years over the touch-line, I will.
1970 Remark to reporters, which led to severe trouble with the soccer authorities. Quoted in Colin Jarman *The Guinness Dictionary of Sports Quotations* (1990).

Charpak, Georges 1924–2010
French physicist, born in Poland. He was awarded the Nobel prize for physics in 1992.

50 I can buy a new pair of shoes this afternoon.
1992 On being awarded $1.2 million for his work on atom smashers. In the *Washington Post*, 15 Oct.

Chase, Edna Woolman 1877–1954
US fashion journalist, editor of *Vogue* (1914–52).

51 Fashion can be bought. Style one must possess.
1954 *Always in Vogue*, ch.12.

Chatwin, Bruce 1940–89
English travel writer and novelist. His travels in the Sudan, Patagonia and Australia converted him to nomadic asceticism. His prize-winning books are a mixture of documentary, fiction, anthropology and philosophy.

52 That will not bring back the things we love: the high, clear days and the blue icecaps on the mountains; the lines of white poplars fluttering in the wind, and the long white prayer flags… Nor shall we get back the smell of the beanfields; the sweet, resinous smell of deodar wood burning, or the whiff of a snow leopard at 14,000 feet. Never. Never. Never.
1980 Introduction to Robert Byron's *The Road to Oxiana*.

53 Being lost in Australia gives you a lovely feeling of security.
1987 *The Songlines*, ch.10.

54 Tyranny sets up its own echo-chamber.
1988 *Utz*.

55 Like all self-possessed people, he was prey to doubt.
1989 *What Am I Doing Here*, 'Heavenly Horses'.

Chaucer, Geoffrey c.1345–1400
English poet. He served in the King's household, travelling extensively on state business. Much influenced by Boccaccio, his spirited and often humorous poetry established the literary language of English. He lost his offices in 1386 and fell on hard times, but in 1399 was awarded a pension.

56 Ful craftier to pley she was
Than Athalus, that made the game
First of the ches, so was his name.
c.1370 *The Book of the Duchess*, l.662–4.

57 That lyf so short, the craft so long to lerne,
Th'assay so hard, so sharp the conquerynge.
c.1380 *The Parliament of Fowls*, l.1–2.

58 But love a womman that she woot it nought,
And she wol quyte it that thow shalt nat fele;
Unknowe, unkist, and lost, that is unsought.
c.1385 *Troilus and Criseyde*, bk.1, l.807–9.

59 So longe mote ye lyve, and alle proude,
Til crowes feet be growen under youre y'.
c.1385 *Troilus and Criseyde*, bk 2, l.402–3.

60 It is nought good a slepyng hound to wake.
c.1385 *Troilus and Criseyde*, bk.3, l.764.

61 For I have seyn of a ful misty morwe
Folowen ful ofte a myrie someris day.
c.1385 *Troilus and Criseyde*, bk.3, l.1060–1.

62 Right as an aspes leef she gan to quake.
c.1385 *Troilus and Criseyde*, bk.3, l.1200.

63 For of fortunes sharpe adversitee
The worst kynde of infortune is this,
A man to han ben in prosperitee,
And it remembren, whan it passed is.
c.1385 *Troilus and Criseyde*, bk.3, l.1625–8.

64 Oon ere it herde, at tother out it went.
c.1385 *Troilus and Criseyde*, bk.4, l.434.

65 For tyme ylost may nought recovered be.
c.1385 *Troilus and Criseyde*, bk.4, l.1283.

66 Ek gret effect men write in place lite;
Th'entente is al, and nat the lettres space.
c.1385 *Troilus and Criseyde*, bk.5, l.1629–30.

67 Go, litel bok, go, litel myn tragedye,
Ther God thi makere yet, er that he dye,
So sende myght to make in som comedye!
c.1385 *Troilus and Criseyde*, bk.5, l.1786–8.

68 And for ther is so gret diversite
In Englissh and in writing of oure tonge,
So prey I God that non myswrite the,
Ne the mysmetre for defaute of tonge.

And red wherso thow be, or elles songe,
That thow be understonde, God I bisechel
c.1385 *Troilus and Criseyde*, bk.5, 1.1793–8.

69 Whan that Aprill with his shoures soote
The droghte of March hath perced to the roote.
1387 *Canterbury Tales*, 'General Prologue', l.1–2.

70 And smale foweles maken melodye,
That slepen al the nyght with open ye
(So priketh hem nature in hir corages);
Thanne longen folk to goon on pilgrimages.
1387 *Canterbury Tales*, 'General Prologue', l.9–12.

71 He loved chivalrie,
Trouthe and honour, fredom and curteisie.
1387 *Canterbury Tales*, 'General Prologue', l.45–6.

72 He was a verray, parfit gentil knyght.
1387 *Canterbury Tales*, 'General Prologue', l.72.

73 Ful weel she soong the service dyvyne,
Entuned in hir nose ful semely,
And Frenssh she spak ful faire and fetisly,
After the scole of Stratford atte Bowe,
For Frenssh of Parys was to hire unknowe.
1387 *Canterbury Tales*, 'General Prologue', l.122–6.

74 A Clerk ther was of Oxenford also,
That unto logyk hadde longe ygo.
As leene was his hors as is a rake.
1387 *Canterbury Tales*, 'General Prologue', l.285–7.

75 But al be that he was a philosophre,
Yet hadde he but litel gold in cofre.
1387 *Canterbury Tales*, 'General Prologue', l.298–9.

76 Nowher so bisy a man as he ther nas,
And yet he semed bisier than he was.
1387 *Canterbury Tales*, 'General Prologue', l.321–2.

77 And thries hadde she been at Jerusalem;
She hadde passed many a straunge strem;
At Rome she hadde been, and at Boloigne,
In Galice at Seint-Jame, and at Coloigne.
1387 *Canterbury Tales*, 'General Prologue', l.463–6.

78 If gold ruste, what shall iren do?
1387 *Canterbury Tales*, 'General Prologue', l.500.

79 But Cristes lore, and his apostles twelve,
He taughte, but first he folwed it him-selve.
1387 *Canterbury Tales*, 'General Prologue', l.527–8.

80 And therefore, at the kynges court, my brother,
Ech man for hymself, ther is noon oother.
1387 *Canterbury Tales*, 'The Knight's Tale', l.1181–2.

81 Ther is no newe gyse that it nas old.
1387 *Canterbury Tales*, 'The Knight's Tale', l.1267.

82 The bisy larke, messager of day.
1387 *Canterbury Tales*, 'The Knight's Tale', l.1491.

83 Pitee renneth soone in gentil herte.
1387 *Canterbury Tales*, 'The Knight's Tale', l.1761.

84 The smylere with the knyf under the cloke.
1387 *Canterbury Tales*, 'The Knight's Tale', l.1999.

85 What is this world? what asketh men to have?
Now with his love, now in his colde grave.
1387 *Canterbury Tales*, 'The Knight's Tale', l.2777–8.

86 This world nys but a thurghfare ful of wo,
And we been pilgrymes, passynge to and fro.
1387 *Canterbury Tales*, 'The Knight's Tale', l. 2847–8.

87 'The gretteste clerkes been noght wisest men.'
1387 *Canterbury Tales*, 'The Reeve's Tale', l.4054.

88 Yblessed be god that I have wedded fyve!
Welcome the sixte, whan that evere he shal.
1387 *Canterbury Tales*, 'The Wife of Bath's Prologue', l.44–5.

89 Crist wole we claym of him oure gentilleesse,
Nat of oure eldres for hire old richesse.
1387 *Canterbury Tales*, 'The Wife of Bath's Tale', l.1117–8.

90 Love wol nat been constreyned by maistrye.
Whan maistrie comth, the God of Love anon
Beteth his wynges, and farewel he is gon!
1387 *Canterbury Tales*, 'The Franklin's Tale', l.764–6.

91 Wommen, of kynde, desiren libertee,
And nat to been constreyned as a thral;
And so doon men, if I sooth seyen shal.
1387 *Canterbury Tales*, 'The Franklin's Tale', l.768–70.

92 Til that the brighte sonne loste his hewe;
For th'orisonte hath reft the sonne his lyght;
This is as muche to seye as it was nyght!
1387 *Canterbury Tales*, 'The Franklin's Tale', l.1016–8.

93 Trouthe is the hyest thyng that man may kepe.
1387 *Canterbury Tales*, 'The Franklin's Tale', l.1479.

94 O wombe! O bely! O stynkyng cod
Fulfilled of dong and of corrupcioun!
1387 *Canterbury Tales*, 'The Pardoner's Tale', l.534–5.

95 'By God,' quod he, 'for pleynly, at a word,
Thy drasty rymyng is nat worth a toord!'
1387 *Canterbury Tales*, 'Sir Thopas', l.929–30.

96 What is bettre than gold? Jaspre. What is bettre than jaspre? Wisedoom.
1387 *Canterbury Tales*, 'The Tale of Melibee', l.1106–7.

97 And what is bettre than wisedoom? Womman. And what is bettre than a good womman? Nothyng.
1387 *Canterbury Tales*, 'The Tale of Melibee', l.1107–8.

98 His coomb was redder than the fyn coral,
And batailled as it were a castle wal;
His byle was blak, and as the jeet it shoon;
Lyk asure were his legges and his toon;
His nayles whitter than the lylye flour,
And lyk the burned gold was his colour.
1387 Of Chaunteleer. *Canterbury Tales*, 'The Nun's Priest's Tale', l.2859–64.

99 Mordre wol out, that see we day by day.
1387 *Canterbury Tales*, 'The Nun's Priest's Tale', l.3052.

1 Thou shalt make castels thanne in Spayne
And dreme of joye, all but in vayne.
The Romaunt of the Rose, l.2573–4. This translation of the *Roman de la Rose* has been attributed to Chaucer but it is thought now to be the work of several authors, including Chaucer.

Chávez (Frías), Hugo Rafael   1954–2013

Venezuelan politician. Leader of the leftist Fifth Republic Movement, he became President of Venezuela (1999–2013) and implemented radical social reforms, earning fanatical devotion at home but attracting criticism internationally for his outspoken Marxist views.

2 When imperialism feels weak, it resorts to brute force.
2005 Speech, 31 Jan.

3 Yesterday the Devil came here. Right here. This place still smells of sulphur.

2006 Speech from the rostrum at the UN General Assembly, one day after US President George W. Bush had addressed the Assembly.

Cheever, John William 1912–82

US short-story writer and novelist. He sold his first short story, 'Expelled', after being thrown out of school at the age of 17, and became a regular contributor to the *New Yorker*, writing lyrical tales of alcoholism, adultery and loss. His novels include *The Wapshot Chronicle* (1957) and *Falconer* (1977).

4 The city is old, out of step with the century, but age only seems to have quickened its elements... Relics from the past continually pierce the present. Some dream of love survives the sandstone apartment houses.
1934 Of Boston. Letter to Elizabeth Ames.

5 When the beginnings of self-destruction enter the heart it seems no bigger than a grain of sand.
1952 Collected in *The Journals*, 'The Late Forties and Fifties'.

6 Wisdom we know is the knowledge of good and evil—not the strength to choose between the two.
1956 Collected in *The Journals*, 'The Late Forties and Fifties'.

7 Neither you nor I nor anyone else can describe the volcanic landscapes a poor girl strays into when she marries a literary man.
1965 Letter to Frederick Exley, 16 Jun.

8 A lonely man is a lonesome thing, a stone, a bone, a stick, a receptacle for Gilbey's gin, a stooped figure sitting at the edge of a hotel bed, heaving copious sighs like the autumn wind.
1966 Collected in *The Journals*, 'The Sixties'.

9 We travel by plane, oftener than not, and yet the spirit of our country seems to have remained a country of railroads.
1969 On the US. *Bullet Park*, pt.1, ch.1.

10 My veins are filled once a week with a Neapolitan carpet cleaner distilled from the Adriatic and I am as bald as an egg. However I still get around and am mean to cats.
1982 On his cancer treatment. Letter to Philip Roth, 10 May.

11 Yevtushenko has...an ego that can crack crystal at a distance of 20 feet.
Recalled on Cheever's death, 18 Jun 1982.

12 Trust your editor, and you'll sleep on straw.
Favourite axiom, quoted in Susan Cheever *Home Before Dark* (1984).

Chekhov, Anton 1860–1904

Russian playwright and short-story writer. His first play, *The Seagull* (1896), failed initially but was revived in Moscow in 1898. Others include *Uncle Vanya* (1897), *The Three Sisters* (1901) and *The Cherry Orchard* (1904).

13 Brevity is the sister of talent.
1889 Letter to Alexander Chekhov, 11 Apr.

14 MEDVEDENKO: Why do you wear black all the time?
MASHA: I'm in mourning for my life.
1896 *The Seagull*, act 1.

15 Women can't forgive failure.
1896 *The Seagull*, act 2.

16 The chief thing, my dear fellows, is to play it simply, without any theatricality: just very simply. Remember that they are all ordinary people.
1896 Attributed advice to actors, during a rehearsal of *The Seagull*.

17 A woman can become a man's friend only in the following stages—first an acquaintance, next a mistress, and only then a friend.
1897 *Uncle Vanya*, act 2.

18 When a woman isn't beautiful, people always say, 'You have lovely eyes, you have lovely hair.'
1897 *Uncle Vanya*, act 3.

19 If a lot of cures are suggested for a disease, it means that the disease is incurable.
1904 *The Cherry Orchard*, act 1 (translated by Elisaveta Fen).

20 To begin to live in the present, we must first atone for our past and be finished with it, and we can only atone for it by suffering, by extraordinary, unceasing exertion.
1904 *The Cherry Orchard*, act 2 (translated by Elisaveta Fen).

Chelmsford, Frederick John Napier Thesiger, 1st Viscount 1868–1933

English colonial administrator, Governor of Queensland (1905–9) and of New South Wales (1909–13), Viceroy of India (1916–21) and First Lord of the Admiralty (1924).

21 We have here an educated class 95 per cent of whom hate us.
1918 Of the situation in India. Letter to George V.

Cheney, Dick (Richard Bruce) 1946–

US politician. He was Secretary of Defense under George Bush from 1989 to 1993 and served as Vice-President under George W Bush (2001–9).

22 Except for the occasional heart attack, I never felt better.
2003 In *Newsweek*, 16 Jun.

23 The days of looking the other way while despotic regimes trample human rights, rob their nations' wealth, and then excuse their failings by feeding their people a steady diet of anti-Western hatred are over.
2004 Speaking at the World Economic Forum in Davos, Switzerland, 24 Jan.

24 When diplomacy fails, we must be prepared to face our responsibilities and be willing to use force if necessary. Direct threats require decisive action.
2004 Speaking at the World Economic Forum in Davos, Switzerland, 24 Jan.

25 They're very well treated down there. They're living in the tropics. They're well fed.
2005 Referring to the prisoners detained in Guantanamo Bay.

26 If fine speech-making, appeals to reason, or pleas for compassion had the power to move them, the terrorists would long ago have abandoned the field.
2009 Speech at the American Enterprise Institute, 21 May.

Cher originally Cheryl Sarkisian La Pier 1946–

US pop singer and film actress.

27 Do I enjoy getting older? No. I'm thrilled and delighted for those people who enjoy the experience. I just don't happen to be one of them.
2004 In *The Scotsman*, 11 May.

28 Singing is like going to a party at someone else's house. Acting is like having the party at your house.
2010 In *Entertainment Weekly*.

Chereskin, Alvin 1928–
US advertising executive, founder and president of AC & R Advertising (later affiliated with Saatchi & Saatchi).

29 Sex! What is that but *life*, after all? We're all of us selling sex, because we're all selling life.
1986 In the *New Yorker*, 15 Sep.

Chernow, Ron 1949–
US journalist, a columnist with *The Wall Street Journal* (1990–).

30 Capitalism requires people to be pious souls in the workplace, wild pagans at the cash register.
1993 In *The Wall Street Journal*, 31 Aug.

Cherry-Garrard, Apsley 1886–1959
Polar explorer and a member of Scott's last expedition. His group found the bodies of Scott and his companions in 1912.

31 At once the cleanest and most isolated way of having a bad time which has ever been devised.
1952 Of polar exploration. Recalled in *The Worst Journey in the World*.

Chesnut, Mary Boykin Miller 1823–86
US diarist, daughter of a South Carolina senator and wife of the heir to a large plantation. Her diary of the Civil War, *A Diary from Dixie*, was published in 1905.

32 Mrs. Stowe did not hit the sorest spot. She makes Legree a bachelor.
1861 Diary entry, 26 Aug, recording the conversation of a group of southern white women on the subject of men and slavery. The reference is to the principal slaveholder in Harriet Beecher Stowe's *Uncle Tom's Cabin*.

Chesnutt, Charles Waddell 1858–1932
US writer, the first black fiction writer to gain national acclaim when his stories were published in the *Atlantic Monthly* in the 1880s. He also wrote a biography of Frederick Douglass (1899).

33 Those who set in motion the forces of evil cannot always control them afterwards.
1901 *The Marrow of Tradition*, ch.35.

Chesterfield, Philip Dormer Stanhope, 4th Earl of 1694–1773
English statesman and orator, a member of the Pelham ministry (1744), Irish Lord-Lieutenant (1745) and Secretary of State (1746–8). His *Letters to his Son* (published 1774) are a worldly guide to manners and success.

34 The difference in this case between a man of sense and a fop, is, that the fop values himself upon his dress; the man of sense laughs at it, at the same time that he knows he must not neglect it.
1745 Letter to his son, 19 Nov.

35 Whatever is worth doing at all is worth doing well.
1746 Letter to his son, 10 Mar.

36 An injury is much sooner forgotten than an insult.
1746 Letter to his son, 9 Oct.

37 I recommend you to take care of the minutes, for hours will take care of themselves.
1747 Letter to his son, 6 Nov.

38 Advice is seldom welcome; and those who want it the most always like it the least.
1748 Letter to his son, 29 Jan.

39 Wear your learning, like your watch in a private pocket: and do not merely pull it out and strike it, merely to show that you have one.
1748 Letter to his son, 22 Feb.

40 There is nothing so illiberal and so ill-bred, as audible laughter.
1748 Letter to his son, 9 Mar.

41 It must be owned, that the Graces do not seem to be natives of Great Britain; and I doubt, the best of us here have more of rough than polished diamond.
1748 Letter to his son, 11 Nov.

42 Style is the dress of thoughts.
1749 Letter to his son, 24 Nov.

43 Fashion is more tyrannical at Paris than in any other place in the world; it governs even more absolutely than their king, which is saying a great deal. The least revolt against it is punished by proscription. You must observe and conform to all the minutiae of it, if you will be in fashion there yourself; and if you are not in fashion, you are nobody.
1750 Letter to his son, 30 Apr.

44 The chapter of knowledge is very short, but the chapter of accidents is a very long one.
1753 Letter to Solomon Dayrolles, 16 Feb.

45 In matters of religion and matrimony I never give any advice; because I will not have anybody's torments in this world or the next laid to my charge.
1765 Letter to Arthur Charles Stanhope, 12 Oct.

46 In case my godson Philip Stanhope shall at anytime keep or be concerned in keeping any racehorse or pack of hounds, or reside one night at Newmarket, that infamous seminary of iniquity and ill-manners, during the course of the races there, or shall resort to the said races or shall lose in one day at any game or bet whatsoever the sum of £500 then in any of the cases aforesaid it is my express will that he, my said godson, shall forfeit and pay out of my estate the sum of £50,000 to and for the use of the Dean and Chapter of Westminster.
1773 Clause in his will.

47 David, you are an actor everywhere but upon the stage.
Attributed, in conversation with the actor David Garrick.

48 The pleasure is momentary, the position ridiculous, and the expense damnable.
Of sex. Attributed.

Chesterton, G(ilbert) K(eith) 1874–1936
English critic, novelist and poet, one of the most colourful and provocative writers of his day. His amiable detective-priest Father Brown first appeared in *The Innocence of Father Brown* (1911). Many of his essays and articles were published in his own *G.K.'s Weekly*.

49 I share all your antipathy to the noisy Plebeian excursionist. A visit to Ramsgate during the season and the vision of the crowded, howling sands has left in me feelings which all my Radicalism cannot allay. At the same time I think that the lower orders are seen unfavourably when enjoying themselves. In labour and trouble they are more dignified and less noisy.

1891 Letter to E C Bentley. Collected in Maisie Ward *Gilbert Keith Chesterton* (1943).

50 With monstrous head and sickening cry
And ears like errant wings,
The devil's walking parody
Of all four-footed things.
1900 'The Donkey'.

51 Fools! For I also had my hour;
One far fierce hour and sweet:
There was a shout about my ears,
And palms before my feet.
1900 'The Donkey'.

52 Literature is a luxury; fiction is a necessity.
1901 *The Defendant*, 'Defence of Penny Dreadfuls'.

53 All slang is metaphor, and all metaphor is poetry.
1901 *The Defendant*, 'Defence of Slang'.

54 'My country right or wrong', is a thing that no patriot would think of saying except in a desperate case. It is like saying, 'My mother, drunk or sober'.
1901 *The Defendant*, 'Defence of Patriotism'.
▶ See Decatur 268:64.

55 The human race, to which so many of my readers belong, has been playing at children's games from the beginning, and will probably do it till the end, which is a nuisance for the few people who grow up.
1904 *The Napoleon of Notting Hill*, ch.1.

56 The word 'orthodoxy' not only no longer means being right; it practically means being wrong.
1905 *Heretics*, ch.1.

57 There is no such thing on earth as an uninteresting subject; the only thing that can exist is an uninterested person.
1905 *Heretics*, ch.3.

58 In the case of Smith, the name is so poetical that it must be an arduous and heroic matter for the man to live up to it… The name shouts poetry at you.
1905 *Heretics*, ch.3.

59 Charity is the power of defending that which we know to be indefensible. Hope is the power of being cheerful in circumstances which we know to be desperate.
1905 *Heretics*, ch.12.

60 Science in the modern world has many uses; its chief use, however, is to provide long words to cover the errors of the rich.
1905 *Heretics*, ch.13.

61 A good novel tells us the truth about its hero; but a bad novel tells us the truth about its author.
1905 *Heretics*, ch.15.

62 The artistic temperament is a disease that afflicts amateurs. It is a disease which arises from men not having sufficient power of expression to utter and get rid of the element of art in their being.
1905 *Heretics*, ch.17.

63 Bigotry may be roughly defined as the anger of men who have no opinions.
1905 *Heretics*, ch.20.

64 There is a great man who makes every man feel small. But the real great man is the man who makes every man feel great.
1906 *Charles Dickens*, ch.1.

65 The madman is not the man who has lost his reason. The madman is the one who has lost everything except his reason.
1908 *Orthodoxy*, ch.2.

66 Poets do not go mad; but chess players do.
1908 *Orthodoxy*, ch.2.

67 The men who really believe in themselves are all in lunatic asylums.
1908 *Orthodoxy*, ch.2.

68 It is an act of faith to assert that our thoughts have any relation to reality at all.
1908 *Orthodoxy*, ch.3.

69 Tradition means giving votes to the most obscure of all classes, our ancestors. It is the democracy of the dead.
1908 *Orthodoxy*, ch.4.

70 All conservatism is based upon the idea that if you leave things alone you leave them as they are. But you do not. If you leave a thing alone you leave it to a torrent of change.
1908 *Orthodoxy*, ch.7.

71 Angels can fly because they take themselves lightly.
1908 *Orthodoxy*, ch.7.

72 Thieves respect property. They merely wish the property to become their property that they may more perfectly respect it.
1908 *The Man who was Thursday*, ch.4.

73 An adventure is only an inconvenience rightly considered. An inconvenience is only an adventure wrongly considered.
1908 *All Things Considered*, 'On Running After One's Hat'.

74 No animal ever invented anything so bad as drunkenness—or so good as drink.
1908 *All Things Considered*, 'Wine When It Is Red'.

75 Lying in bed would be an altogether perfect and supreme experience if only one had a coloured pencil long enough to draw on the ceiling.
1909 'On Lying In Bed'.

76 He desired all beautiful things—even God.
1909 Of Oscar Wilde. In the *Daily News*, 19 Oct.

77 The Christian ideal has not been tried and found wanting. It has been found difficult; and left untried.
1910 *What's Wrong with the World*, ch.1, 'The Unfinished Temple'.

78 Compromise used to mean that half a loaf was better than no bread. Among modern statesmen, it really seems to mean that half a loaf is better than a whole loaf.
1910 *What's Wrong with the World*, ch.3.

79 She was maintaining the prime truth of woman, the universal mother…that if a thing is worth doing, it is worth doing badly.
1910 *What's Wrong with the World*, pt.4, 'Folly and Female Education'.

80 I tell you naught for your comfort,
Yea, naught for your desire,
Save that the sky grows darker yet
And the sea rises higher.
1911 *Ballad of the White Horse*, bk.1.

81 For the great Gaels of Ireland
Are the men that God made mad,
For all their wars are merry,
And all their songs are sad.
1911 *Ballad of the White Horse*, bk.2.

82 There is always a forgotten thing,
    And love is not secure.
    1911 *Ballad of the White Horse*, bk.3.

83 When all philosophies shall fail,
    This word alone shall fit;
    That a sage feels too small for life,
    And a fool too large for it.
    1911 *Ballad of the White Horse*, bk.8.

84 He could not think up to the height of his own towering style.
    1912 Of Tennyson. *The Victorian Age in Literature*, ch.3.

85 And Noah he often said to his wife when he sat down to dine.
    'I don't care where the water goes if it doesn't get into the wine.'
    1914 *The Flying Inn*, ch.5, stanza 1. Collected as 'Wine and Water' in *Wine, Water and Song* (1915).

86 The rich are the scum of the earth in every country.
    1914 *The Flying Inn*, ch.15.

87 Tea is like the East he grows in,
    A great yellow Mandarin
    With urbanity of manner
    And unconsciousness of sin.
    1914 *The Flying Inn*, ch.18, stanza 2. Collected as 'The Song of Right and Wrong' in *Wine, Water and Song* (1915).

88 Tea, although an Oriental,
    Is a gentleman at least;
    Cocoa is a cad and coward,
    Cocoa is a vulgar beast.
    1914 *The Flying Inn*, ch.18, stanza 3. Collected as 'The Song of Right and Wrong' in *Wine, Water and Song* (1915).

89 When red wine had brought red ruin
    And the death-dance of our times,
    Heaven sent us Soda Water
    As a torment for our crimes.
    1914 *The Flying Inn*, ch.18, stanza 4. Collected as 'The Song of Right and Wrong' in *Wine, Water and Song* (1915).

90 The folk that live in Liverpool, their heart is in their boots;
    They go to hell like lambs, they do, because the hooter hoots.
    1914 'Me Heart'.

91 They haven't got no noses,
    The fallen sons of Eve.
    1914 'Song of Quoodle'.

92 And goodness only knowses
    The Noselessness of Man.
    1914 'Song of Quoodle'.

93 Before the Roman came to Rye or out to Severn strode,
    The rolling English drunkard made the rolling English road.
    1914 'The Rolling English Road'.

94 A merry road, a mazy road, and such as we did tread
    The night we went to Birmingham by way of Beachy Head.
    1914 'The Rolling English Road'.

95 For there is good news yet to hear and fine things to be seen,
    Before we go to Paradise by way of Kensal Green.
    1914 'The Rolling English Road'.

96 To be clever enough to get all that money, one must be stupid enough to want it.
    1914 *The Wisdom of Father Brown*, 'Paradise of Thieves'.

97 Journalism largely consists in saying 'Lord Jones Dead' to people who never knew Lord Jones was alive.
    1914 *The Wisdom of Father Brown*, 'The Purple Wig'.

98 We only know the last sad squires ride slowly towards the sea,
    And a new people takes the land: and still it is not we.
    1915 'The Secret People'.

99 The souls most fed with Shakespeare's flame
    Still sat unconquered in a ring,
    Remembering him like anything.
    1915 'Shakespeare Memorial'.

1   John Grubby, who was short and stout
    And troubled with religious doubt,
    Refused about the age of three
    To sit upon the curate's knee.
    1915 'The New Freethinker'.

2   And I dream of the days when work was scrappy,
    And rare in our pockets the mark of the mint,
    When we were angry and poor and happy,
    And proud of seeing our names in print.
    1915 'Song of Defeat'.

3   The gallows in my garden, people say,
    Is new and neat and adequately tall.
    1915 'Ballade of Suicide'.

4   The strangest whim has seized me... After all
    I think I will not hang myself today.
    1915 'Ballade of Suicide'.

5   They died to save their country and they only saved the world.
    1922 'English Graves'.

6   Democracy means government by the uneducated, while aristocracy means government by the badly educated.
    1931 In the *New York Times*, 1 Feb.

7   A great deal of contemporary criticism reads to me like a man saying: 'Of course I do not like green cheese: I am very fond of brown sherry'.
    1933 *All I Survey*, 'On Jonathan Swift'.

8   Why do you rush through the fields in trains,
    Guessing so much and so much.
    Why do you flash through the flowery meads,
    Fat-head poet that nobody reads;
    And why do you know such a frightful lot
    About people in gloves and such?
    1933 'The Fat White Woman Speaks', a response to Frances Cornford's poem.
    ▶ See Cornford 247:3.

9   It isn't that they can't see the solution. It is that they can't see the problem.
    1935 *The Scandal of Father Brown*, 'Point of a Pin'.

10 Am in Market Harborough. Where ought I to be?
    Attributed. Chesterton remarks in his *Autobiography* (1936), ch.16, 'I cannot remember whether this story is true; but it is not unlikely, or, I think, unreasonable.'

11 Music with dinner is an insult both to the cook and the violinist.
    Quoted in *The New York Times*, 16 Nov 1967.

12 I regard golf as an expensive way of playing marbles.
    Quoted in Colin Jarman *The Guinness Dictionary of Sports Quotations* (1990).

Chiang Kai-Shek 1887–1975
Chinese general and nationalist, defeated by Mao Zedong's forces. In 1948 he was forced to withdraw to Taiwan where he retained the office of President.

13 The sky cannot have two suns.
   c.1945 Quoted in Ross Merrill *Mao* (1993) ch.10.

Chilcott, Gareth 1956–
English rugby union player.

14 I thought I would have a quiet pint…and about 17 noisy ones.
   1993 On playing his last game of rugby for Bath.

Child, Julia McWilliams 1912–2004
US cookery expert.

15 Life itself is the proper binge.
   1980 In *Time*, 7 Jan.

16 The view of history that we get through the kitchen window is a more gentle view, not of war and politics, but of family and community and sharing.
   1993 On studying cookbooks dating back to the 1400s in the Library of Congress. In *Memory and Imagination*, PBS TV, 15 Aug.

Ch'in Chia c.150 BC
Chinese poet and civil servant about whom very little is known. He wrote a series of three poems on his separation from his wife, the result of a posting to Beijing.

17 I sent a carriage to bring you back
   But it went empty, and empty it returned.
   c.150 BC 'To My Wife 1', collected in *A Book of Chinese Verse* (translated by N L Smith and R H Kotewall).

18 Sorrow comes as in a circle
   And cannot be rolled up like a map.
   c.150 BC 'To My Wife 2', collected in *A Book of Chinese Verse* (translated by N L Smith and R H Kotewall).

19 One separation breeds ten thousand regrets.
   c.150 BC 'To My Wife 2', collected in *A Book of Chinese Verse* (translated by N L Smith and R H Kotewall).

Chirac, Jacques René 1932–
French Conservative politician, Prime Minister (1974–6, 1986–8) and President (1995–2007) of France.

20 What's it for?
   On being shown a scale model of the Millennium Dome. Quoted in *Servants of the People: The Inside Story of New Labour* (2000).

21 Tony Blair is very convincing, he will sway public opinion.
   2004 On the proposed British referendum on the EU Constitution, 9 May.

22 This cuisine here in America was certainly on a par with French cuisine.
   2004 At the G8 meeting on Sea Island, Georgia, 10 Jun.

Chirico, Giorgio de 1888–1978
Italian painter, born in Greece, the developer of 'metaphysical painting', based on semi-abstract geometric figures. In the 1930s he renounced his earlier work and returned to an academic style.

23 If a work of art is to be truly immortal, it must pass quite beyond the limits of the human world, without any sign of common sense and logic. In this way the work will draw nearer to dream and to the mind of a child.
   Quoted in Saranne Alexandrian *Surrealist Art* (1970).

Chisholm, Caroline née Jones 1808–77
English-born Australian social worker and philanthropist. She married an army officer and settled in New South Wales in 1838, where she worked with impoverished immigrant women and children. Her petition to Earl Grey helped persuade the British Government to grant free passage to the families of convicts.

24 If Her Majesty's Government be really desirous of seeing a well-conducted community spring up in these Colonies, the social wants of the people must be considered… For all the clergy you can despatch, all the schoolmasters you can appoint, all the churches you can build, and all the books you can export, will never do much good without what a gentleman in that Colony very appropriately called 'God's police'—wives and little children—good and virtuous women.
   1847 *Emigration and Transportation Relatively Considered; in a Letter, Dedicated, by Permission, to Earl Grey*, 17 Jun. The phrase 'God's police' was adopted by Australian feminist Anne Summers in her feminist critique of Australian culture, *Damned Whores and God's Police* (1975).
   ▶ See Clark 228:63.

Chocano, José Santos 1875–1934
Peruvian poet, teacher, editor and diplomat. He visited almost every Central and South American country, often being expelled for political intrigue. He was assassinated in Chile.

25 Soy el cantor de América autóctono y salvaje;
   mi lira tiene un alma, mi canto un ideal.
   Mi verso no se mece colgado de un ramaje
   con un vaivén pausado de hamaca tropical.
   I am the aboriginal and savage singer of America;
   my lyre has a soul, my song has an ideal.
   My poetry does not swing from the branches
   with the slow movement of a tropical hammock.
   1906 *Alma América*, 'Blas[4]n' (translated as 'Blazon', 1935).

Chomsky, (Avram) Noam 1928–
US linguist and social critic. His theories revolutionized the study of language and remain controversial. In the political arena, he has criticized many aspects of US foreign policy.

26 An obscenity, a depraved act by weak and miserable men, including all of us, who have allowed it to go on and on with endless fury.
   1969 Of US involvement in the war in Vietnam. *American Power and the New Mandarins*.

27 As soon as questions of will or decision arise, human science is at a loss.
   1978 Television interview, 30 Mar, reported in *The Listener*, 6 Apr.

28 The military system is, to a substantial extent, a method whereby the population provides a subsidy to the high technology industry.
   1988 Interview, Public Broadcasting System, 4 Nov.

29 Science talks about very simple things, and asks hard questions about them. As soon as things become too complex, science can't deal with them… But it's a complicated matter: Science studies what's at the edge

of understanding, and what's at the edge of understanding is usually fairly simple. And it rarely reaches human affairs. Human affairs are way too complicated. In fact even understanding insects is an extremely complicated problem in the sciences. So the actual sciences tell us virtually nothing about human affairs.
2006 Quoted in *Science in the Dock, Discussion with Noam Chomsky*, Lawrence Krauss and Sean M. Carroll (2011).

Chopin, Kate (Katherine) née O'Flaherty 1851–1904

US novelist and short-story writer. After the death of her husband she began to write sketches of Creole life, including *Bayou Folk* (1894). Her novel *The Awakening* (1899) was harshly condemned for its frank treatment of female sexuality.

30 The voice of the sea speaks to the soul. The touch of the sea is sensuous, enfolding the body in its soft, close embrace.
1899 *The Awakening*, ch.6.

31 The past was nothing to her… The future was a mystery which she never attempted to penetrate. The present alone was significant.
1899 *The Awakening*, ch.15.

32 She was becoming herself and daily casting aside that fictitious self which we assume like a garment with which to appear before the world.
1899 *The Awakening*, ch.19.

33 The artist must possess the courageous soul that dares and defies.
1899 *The Awakening*, ch.39.

34 I trust I will not be giving away professional secrets to say that many readers would be surprised, perhaps shocked, at the questions which some newspaper editors will put to a defenseless woman under the guise of flattery.
1899 'On Certain Brisk Days', in the *St Louis Post-Dispatch*, 26 Nov.

Christiansen, Arthur 1904–63

British journalist, Editor of the *Daily Express* (1933–58).

35 Whenever possible print a woman's age.
1957 Quoted in Francis Williams *Dangerous Estate*.

36 The people who lived behind those clean lace curtains in row after row of identical boxes were newspaper readers, and every word in at any rate *my* newspaper must be clear and comprehensible to them, must be interesting to them, must encourage them to break away from littleness, stimulate their ambition, help them to want to build a better land.
1961 *Headlines all my Life*, ch.1.

37 Remember the people in the back streets of Derby.
1961 *Headlines all my Life*, ch.1.

38 Show me a contented newspaper editor and I will show you a bad newspaper.
1961 *Headlines all my Life*, ch.15.

39 No matter how many media for the dissemination of news are created, there is one rule that should never be broken: TELL THE PEOPLE!
1961 *Headlines all my Life*, ch.18.

40 My approach to newspapers was based on the idea that when you looked at the front page you said: 'Good heavens', when you looked at the middle page you said: 'Holy smoke', and by the time you got to the back page—well, I'd have to utter a profanity to show how exciting it was.
1961 *Headlines all my Life*, ch.19.

Christie, Dame Agatha Mary Clarissa née Miller 1890–1976

English author, who wrote more than 70 classic detective novels including *The Mysterious Affair at Styles* (1920), *Murder on the Orient Express* (1934) and *Death on the Nile* (1937).

41 He tapped his forehead. 'These little grey cells. It is up to them—as you say over here.'
1920 *The Mysterious Affair at Styles*, ch.10.

42 Life nowadays is dominated and complicated by the remorseless Zip. Blouses zip up, skirts zip down, ski-ing suits zip everywhere… Why? Is there anything more deadly than a Zip that turns nasty on you?
1946 *Come, Tell Me How You Live*, ch.1.

43 Here, in the west of Ireland, the Romans had never marched, tramp, tramp, tramp: had never fortified a camp: had never built a well-ordered, sensible, useful road. It was a land where common sense and an orderly way of life were unknown.
Hercule Poirot looked down at the tips of his patent-leather shoes and sighed. He felt forlorn and very much alone. The standards by which he lived were here not appreciated.
1947 *The Labours of Hercules*.

44 War settles *nothing*…to *win* a war is as disastrous as to lose one.
1977 *An Autobiography*, ch.10.

Christie, Linford 1960–

English athlete who won an Olympic gold medal for the 100m at the 1992 games in Barcelona.

45 I could have been a god, but people only allow you to get so far in this country.
2002 In *The Independent*, 20 Dec.

Christine de Pisan 1364–1430

Italian-born French writer. Taken to the court of Charles V as a child, married at 15 and widowed at 25, she became the first professional woman poet and official biographer of Charles V. Other works include lyrics and essays on politics and the status of women in society.

46 *En la hauteur ou abaissement des gens ne gist mie es corps selonc le sexe, mais en la perfeccion des meurs et vertus.*
The dignity or baseness of a person lies not in their body according to the sex, but in the perfection of behaviour and virtues.
1405 *Le livre de la Cité des Dames*, bk.1, ch.9.

47 *De tant comme femmes ont le corps plus delie que les hommes, plus foible et moins habile a plusieurs choses faire, de tant ont elles l'entendement plus a delivre et plus agu ou elles s'appliquent.*
Just as women's bodies are more delicate than men's, weaker and less able for many things, so, where they apply themselves, their understanding is freer and sharper.
1405 *Le livre de la Cité des Dames*, bk.1, ch.27.

Christopher, Warren Minor 1925–2011
US lawyer and government official, Secretary of State (1993–6). In 1980 he negotiated for the release of US hostages in Iran.

48 I wish the meeting had been as good as the lunch.
1994 On beginning talks in Beijing with China's Prime Minister. In the *New York Times*, 13 Mar.

49 Sometimes you have to learn how to give the right answer to the wrong question.
1994 On Syrian President Hafez Assad's complaint that he had been put off by a hostile question in a news conference shared with President Clinton. In *US News and World Report*, 19 Dec.

Church, Richard 1893–1972
English author, known for his poems, novels, literary criticism, travel books and children's stories.

50 We have to accept the verbal portraits, as indeed we have to accept paintings and sculptures, as well as photographs, of the immortals whose influence on our lives is often greater than that of our own family members.
In praise of biography. Quoted in *Christian Science Monitor*, 30 Apr 1963.

51 He delights to expose the raw nerves of evil, showing it as a force in the world, a skeletonlike figure working visible mischief in the ordinary everyday affairs of men and women and children.
Of Graham Greene. Recalled on Greene's death in the *New York Times*, 4 Apr 1991.

Churchill, Charles 1731–64
English satirical poet. His works savagely attacked many well-known figures of his time, including Samuel Johnson, Tobias Smollett and William Hogarth. He is best known for *The Rosciad* (1761).

52 A pert, prim Prater of the northern race,
Guilt in his heart, and famine in his face.
1761 Of the Scottish-born judge Alexander Wedderburn, later Lord Loughborough. *The Rosciad*, l.75–6.

53 Fashion—a word which knaves and fools may use,
Their knavery and folly to excuse.
1761 *The Rosciad*, l.455–6.

54 So much they talked, so very little said.
1761 *The Rosciad*, l.550.

55 But, spite of all the criticizing elves,
Those who would make us feel, must feel themselves.
1761 *The Rosciad*, l.961–2.

56 Keep up appearances; there lies the test;
The world will give thee credit for the rest.
Outward be fair, however foul within;
Sin if thou wilt, but then in secret sin.
1762 *Night*, l.311–12.

57 Just to the windward of the law.
1763 *The Ghost*, bk.3, l.56.

58 A joke's a very serious thing.
1763 *The Ghost*, bk.3, l.1386.

59 Apt Alliteration's artful aid.
1763 *The Prophecy of Famine*, l.86.

60 The danger chiefly lies in acting well;
No crime's so great as daring to excel.
1763 *An Epistle to William Hogarth*, l.51–2.

61 Be England what she will,
With all her faults, she is my country still.
1764 *The Farewell*, l.27–8.

62 It can't be Nature, for it is not sense.
1764 *The Farewell*, l.200.

Churchill, Jeanette *née Jeanette Jerome* 1852–1921
US-born wife of Lord Randolph Henry Spencer Churchill, daughter of a prominent New York businessman.

63 There is no such thing as a moral dress… It's people who are moral or immoral.
1921 'That Moral Dress', in the *Daily Chronicle*, 16 Feb.

Churchill, Lord Randolph Henry Spencer 1849–95
English politician, the leader of a guerrilla band of Conservatives known as the 'Fourth Party' (from 1880) and father of Sir Winston Churchill. He was Chancellor of the Exchequer and leader of the House of Commons (1886).

64 Ulster will not be a consenting party. Ulster, at the proper time, will resort to the supreme arbitrament of force; Ulster will fight and Ulster will be right.
1886 Public letter, 7 May.

65 This monstrous mixture of imbecility, extravagance and political hysteria, better known as the Bill for the future government of Ireland—this farrago of superlative nonsense, is to be put in motion for this reason and no other: to gratify the ambition of an old man in a hurry.
1886 Pamphlet attacking Gladstone's Home Rule Bill, Jun.

66 I could never make out what those damned dots meant.
Of decimal points. Quoted in Winston Churchill *Lord Randolph Churchill* (1906).

67 The duty of an Opposition is to oppose.
Remark attributed by his son, Winston Churchill. The phrase was used earlier by Edward Stanley, 14th Earl of Derby, who attributed it to Mr Tierney (4 Jun 1841).

Churchill, Sir Winston Leonard Spencer 1874–1965
English statesman, Prime Minister (1940–5, 1951–2) and writer. He became a Conservative MP in 1900 but turned Liberal in 1904 and was made First Lord of the Admiralty (1911) and Chancellor of the Exchequer (1924–9). He returned to the Conservative Party in 1929 and on Chamberlain's defeat formed a coalition government to pursue the war with Germany.

68 Business carried on as usual during alterations on the map of Europe.
1914 Of the British people's view of World War I. Speech at the Guildhall, London, 9 Nov.

69 In war: resolution. In defeat: defiance. In victory: magnanimity. In peace: goodwill.
c.1918 *The Second World War* (1948), vol.1, epigraph. According to Sir Edward Marsh, in *A Number of People* (1939), the phrase occurred to Churchill shortly after the end of World War I. Some sources attribute it to Marsh himself.

70 Of all tyrannies in history, the Bolshevik tyranny is the worst, the most destructive, the most degrading. Every British and French soldier killed last year was really done to death by Lenin and Trotsky—not in fair war, but by the treacherous desertion of an ally without parallel in the history of the world.
1919 Speech, London, 11 Apr.

71 The community lacks goods and a million and a quarter people lack work. It is certainly one of the highest functions of national finance and credit to bridge the gap between the two.
1925 Letter to Otto Niemeyer, 22 Feb. Collected in D E Moggridge *Maynard Keynes* (1992).

72 The day must come when the nation's whole scale of living must be reduced. If that day comes, Parliament must lay the burden equally on all classes.
1925 Speech as Chancellor of the Exchequer, House of Commons, 7 Aug.

73 Jellicoe was the only man on either side who could lose the war in an afternoon.
1927 On Admiral Jellicoe, commander of the Grand Fleet in World War I. *The World Crisis*, pt.1, ch.5.

74 The loss of India would mark and consummate the downfall of the British Empire. That great organism would pass at a stroke out of life into history. From such a catastrophe there could be no recovery.
1930 Speech to the Indian Empire Society, London, 12 Dec.

75 Mr Gladstone read Homer for fun, which I thought served him right.
1930 *My Early Life*.

76 Those who can win a war well can rarely make a good peace, and those who could make a good peace would never have won the war.
1930 *My Early Life*.

77 The War was decided in the first twenty days of fighting, and all that happened afterwards consisted in battles which, however formidable and devastating, were but desperate and vain appeals against the decision of Fate.
1930 His preface to E L Spears *Liaison 1914*.

78 I remember, when I was a child, being taken to the celebrated Barnum's circus, which contained an exhibition of freaks and monstrosities, but the exhibit on the programme which I most desired to see was the one described as 'The Boneless Wonder'. My parents judged that the spectacle would be too revolting and demoralizing for my youthful eyes, and I have waited 50 years to see the boneless wonder sitting on the Treasury Bench.
1931 Alluding to Ramsay MacDonald. Speech in the House of Commons, 28 Jan.

79 It is alarming and odious to see Mr Gandhi, a seditious Middle Temple lawyer, now posing as a fakir of a type well-known in the East, striding half-naked up the steps of the vice-regal palace, while he is still conducting a defiant campaign of civil disobedience, to parley on equal terms with the representative of the King-Emperor.
1931 Speech, 23 Feb.

80 That long frontier from the Atlantic to the Pacific oceans, guarded only by neighbourly respect and honourable obligations, is an example to every country and a pattern for the future of the world.
1939 Address at the Canada Club, London, 20 Apr.

81 This is no war for domination or imperial aggrandisement or material gain... It is a war...to establish, on impregnable rocks, the rights of the individual and it is a war to establish and revive the stature of man.
1939 Speech in the House of Commons, 3 Sep, on the declaration of war against Germany by Britain and France.

82 I cannot forecast to you the action of Russia. It is a riddle wrapped inside a mystery inside an enigma. But perhaps there is a key; that key is Russian national interest.
1939 Radio broadcast, 1 Oct.

83 You ask what is our aim. I can answer in one word—victory. Victory at all costs, victory in spite of all terror, victory, however long and hard the road may be.
1939 Radio broadcast, 1 Oct.

84 I have nothing to offer but blood, toil, tears and sweat.
1940 Speech in the House of Commons on assuming the premiership, 13 May.

85 We shall not flag or fail. We shall go on to the end. We shall fight in France, we shall fight on the seas and oceans, we shall fight with growing confidence and growing strength in the air, we shall defend our island whatever the cost may be. We shall fight on the beaches, we shall fight on the landing grounds, we shall fight in the fields and in the streets, we shall fight in the hills. We shall never surrender.
1940 Speech in the House of Commons, 4 Jun, after the Dunkirk evacuation.

86 Let us therefore brace ourselves to our duties, and so bear ourselves that, if the British Empire and its Commonwealth last for a thousand years, men will still say: 'This was their finest hour.'
1940 Speech, 18 Jun. Quoted in A J P Taylor *English History 1914–45*, p.491.

87 Never in the field of human conflict has so much been owed by so many, to so few.
1940 On the Battle of Britain pilots. Speech, House of Commons, 20 Aug.

88 No one can guarantee success in war, but only deserve it.
1940 Letter to Lord Wavell, 26 Nov. Quoted in Winston Churchill *The Second World War*, vol.2 (1949), ch.27.

89 Here is the answer that I will give to President Roosevelt... Give us the tools, and we will finish the job.
1941 Radio broadcast, 9 Feb.

90 No one has been a more consistent opponent of Communism than I have for the last 25 years. I will unsay no word that I have spoken about it, but all that fades away before the spectacle that is now unfolding. The past, with its crimes, its follies, and its tragedies, flashes away. I see the Russian soldiers standing on the threshold of their native land, guarding the fields that their fathers have tilled from time immemorial. Any man or state who fights on against Nazidom will have our aid. Any man or state who marches with Hitler is our foe.
1941 Radio broadcast on the German invasion of Russia, 22 Jun.

91 When I warned the French that Britain would fight on alone, General Weygand told their Prime Minister and his divided Cabinet that in three weeks England will have her neck wrung like a chicken. Some chicken, some neck!
1941 Speech to the Canadian Parliament, 30 Dec.

92 What kind of people do they think we are?
1941 Of the Japanese. Speech to Congress, Dec.

93 Commanders and senior officers should die with troops. The honour of the British Empire and the British Army is at stake.
1942 Telegram to Wavell, the commander in chief of armed forces in Singapore, 10 Feb, after being told that a Japanese victory was inevitable. Recalled in *The Second World War*, vol.4 (1951).

94 The latest refinements of science are linked with the cruelties of the Stone Age.
1942 Speech, 26 Mar, in devastated war-time London.

95 Now this is not the end. It is not even the beginning of the end. But it is, perhaps, the end of the beginning.
1942 Speech at the Mansion House, London, 10 Nov, referring to the Battle of Egypt.

96 I have not become the King's First Minister in order to preside over the liquidation of the British Empire.
1942 Speech at the Mansion House, London, 10 Nov.

97 We make this wide encircling movement in the Mediterranean, having for its primary object the recovery of the command of that vital sea, but also having for its object the exposure of the under-belly of the Axis, especially Italy, to heavy attack.
1942 Speech in the House of Commons, 11 Nov.

98 There is no finer investment for any community than putting milk into babies. Healthy citizens are the greatest asset any country can have.
1943 Speech on BBC radio, 21 Mar.

99 The Bomb brought peace, but man alone can keep that peace.
1945 Speech in the House of Commons, 16 Aug.

1 If this is a blessing, it is certainly very well disguised.
1945 On his defeat in the first post-war general election, quoted in Richard Nixon *Memoirs* (1978).

2 From Stettin in the Baltic to Trieste in the Adriatic, an iron curtain has descended across the Continent.
1946 Speech at Fulton, Missouri, 5 Mar. He had used the phrase in a telegraph to President Truman, 12 May 1945, when he said of the Russian-held territories that 'An iron curtain is drawn down upon their front'.

3 Would a special relationship between the United States and the British Commonwealth be inconsistent with our overriding loyalty to the world organization?
1946 Speech at Fulton, Missouri, Mar.

4 No one pretends that democracy is perfect or all-wise. Indeed, it has been said that democracy is the worst form of Government except all those other forms that have been tried from time to time.
1947 Speech in the House of Commons, 11 Nov.

5 Science bestowed immense new powers on man, and, at the same time, created conditions which were largely beyond his comprehension and still more beyond his control.
1949 Speech, Massachusetts Institute of Technology, 31 Mar.

6 I am ready to meet my maker. Whether my maker is ready for the ordeal of meeting me is another matter.
1949 Speech, Nov.

7 I have only one purpose—the destruction of Hitler, and my life is much simplified thereby. If Hitler invaded Hell, I would at least make a favourable reference to the Devil in the House of Commons.
Recalled in *The Second World War*, vol.3 (1950), ch.20.

8 Perhaps it is better to be irresponsible and right than to be responsible and wrong.
1950 Radio broadcast, 26 Aug.

9 If you recognize anyone, it does not mean that you like him. We all, for instance, recognize the honourable Member for Ebbw Vale.

1952 Of Ernest Bevin, in a House of Commons debate on 1 Jul on British recognition of communist China.

10 I have lived 78 years without hearing of bloody places like Cambodia.
1953 Comment, 28 Apr. Quoted in Lord Moran *Winston Churchill, The Struggle for Survival* (1966).

11 Talking jaw is better than going to war.
1954 White House speech, 26 Jun. His comment is often rendered 'To jaw-jaw is always better than to war-war.'

12 I have never accepted what many people have kindly said—that I inspired the nation. It was the nation and the race living around the globe that had the lion heart. I had the luck to be called upon to give the roar.
1954 Speech to both Houses of Parliament in Westminster Hall, Nov, on the occasion of his 80th birthday.

13 An appeaser is someone who feeds a crocodile, hoping it will eat him last.
Attributed. Quoted in *Reader's Digest*, Dec 1954.

14 In defeat unbeatable: in victory unbearable.
Of Montgomery. Quoted in Sir Edward Howard Marsh *Ambrosia and Small Beer* (1964), ch.5.

15 Scientists should be on tap, but not on top.
Quoted in Randolph S Churchill *Twenty-One Years* (1965).

16 An empty taxi arrived at 10 Downing Street, and when the door was opened Attlee got out.
Attributed. Quoted in Kenneth Harris *Attlee* (1982), ch.16.

17 An ineffectual attempt to direct an uncontrollable sphere into an inaccessible hole with instruments ill-adapted for the purpose.
Quoted in Michael Hobbs *The Golf Quotations Book* (1992).

18 All I wanted was compliance with my wishes after reasonable discussion.
Attributed. Quoted in A J P Taylor *From the Boer War to the Cold War: Essays on Twentieth-Century Europe* (1995).

19 Do not criticize your Government when out of the country. Never cease to do so when at home.
Attributed.

20 There, but for the grace of God, goes God.
Of Sir Stafford Cripps. Attributed.

21 I am so bored with it all.
Attributed last words.

Ciardi, John 1916–85

US poet, critic and translator. His translation of Dante's *Inferno* is much admired.

22 This island rock in space turns flowering endlessly
To peaks of cloud still mounting where you took
Your last high passage and your faltering luck.
1947 'Elegy for Kurt Porjescz, Missing in Action, 1 April, 1945'.

23 At the next vacancy for God, if I am elected,
I shall forgive last the delicately wounded
who, having been slugged no harder than anyone else,
never got up again, neither to fight back,
nor to finger their jaws in painful admiration.
1959 'In Place of a Curse'.

24 You don't have to suffer to be a poet. Adolescence is enough.
1962 In the *Saturday Review*, Fall issue.

Cibber, Colley 1671–1757

English actor and dramatist. He worked for most of his career at the Theatre Royal in Drury Lane, and in 1696 established himself as both playwright and actor with his first comedy, *Love's Last Shift*. From 1730 he was Poet Laureate.

25 One had as good be out of the World, as out of the Fashion.
1696 *Love's Last Shift: or, The Fool in Fashion*, act 2, sc.1.

26 Perish the thought!
1700 *Richard III*, act 5 (his adaptation of Shakespeare's play).

27 Stolen sweets are best.
1709 *The Rival Fools*, act 1.

Cicero full name Marcus Tullius Cicero 106–43 BC

Roman orator and statesman, exiled after his unconstitutional execution of the Catiline conspirators. Although recalled by the people (57 BC) he lost the respect of both Caesar and Pompey by his vacillations. He wrote most of his major works on rhetoric and philosophy in retirement in Rome. His speeches against Mark Antony after Caesar's death (*The Philippics*) cost him his life.

28 *Quo usque tandem abutere, Catilina, patientia nostra?*
In heaven's name, Catiline, how long will you abuse our patience?
63 BC Opening line of the first of four speeches against the conspirator L Sergius Catilina, 8 Nov. *In Catilinam* 1.1.

29 *Salus populi suprema est lex.*
The good of the people is the chief law.
52 BC *De Legibus*, bk.3, ch.3.

30 *Silent enim leges inter arma.*
For laws are silent in time of war.
51 BC *Pro Milone*, ch.11.

31 *Cui bono?*
Who benefits?
51 BC *Pro Milone*, ch.12 (and elsewhere).

32 *Nervos belli, pecuniam infinitam.*
The sinews of war, unlimited money.
44 BC *Fifth Philippic*, ch.5.

33 *Nihil tam absurde dici potest quo non dicatur ab aliquo philosophorum.*
There is nothing so absurd that it has not been said by some philosopher.
c.44 BC *De Divinatione*, bk.2, section 58.

34 *Civis Romanus sum.*
I am a Roman citizen.
In Verrem 5.147. This is a reference to the tradition that Roman citizens in foreign courts could often expect preferential treatment. The Roman governor Verres, whom Cicero was prosecuting, had ignored this fact altogether, even executing Roman citizens.

35 *Cedant arma togae, concedant laurea laudi.*
Let war yield to peace, laurels to paeans.
De Officiis, bk.1, ch.77.

36 *Mens cuiusque is est quisque: non ea figura quae digito demonstrari potest.*
The mind is the true self, not the person that can be pointed to with the finger.
De Republica bk.6, ch.24.

37 *O fortunatam natam me consule Romam!*
O lucky Rome, born when I was consul!
Cicero was consul in 63 BC. His only extant line of poetry, quoted in Juvenal, *Satires* 10, l.122.

38 *O tempora, o mores!*
What times! what morals!
Favourite phrase, used on various occasions. See *In Catilinam* 1.1, *In Verrem* 4.25 and *Pro rege Deiotaro* 11.31.

Cisneros, Henry 1947–

US politician, Secretary of Housing and Urban Development (1993–7).

39 Like piles of dry wood with red-hot coals underneath.
1993 Of US cities, rife with racial tension. In *US News and World Report*, 19 Apr.

40 We have to be honest, we have to be truthful and speak to the one dirty secret in American life, and that is racism.
1993 In *US News and World Report*, 19 Apr.

Cixous, Hélène 1937–

French feminist author and critic who has argued that women write differently from men by virtue of their bodies.

41 *On dit que la vie et la mort sont au pouvoir de la langue.*
It is said that life and death are under the power of language.
1969 *Dedans*.

42 *La seule différence incontestable n'est pas celle des sexes ou des âges ou des forces, mais celle des vifs et des morts.*
The only incontestable difference is not that of sex or age or strength, but that of the living and the dead.
1969 *Dedans*.

43 *J'ai peu de mots. Mon père qui les avait tous, est parti si précipitamment, qu'il n'a pas eu le temps de me les donner.*
I have few words. My father, who had all of them, left so suddenly that he did not have the time to give them all to me.
1969 *Dedans*.

44 *Le temps et le monde et la personne ne se rencontrent qu'une seule fois.*
Time, the world and the person only encounter one another once.
1969 *Dedans*.

45 *Je me cherche à travers les siècles et je ne me vois nulle part.*
I have searched for myself across time and have not found myself anywhere.
1974 *Prénoms du soleil* (translated by Morag Shiach in *Hélène Cixous: A Politics of Writing*).

46 *Des mots sont arrachés vivants à la langue défunte.*
Words are taken alive from a defunct language.
1976 *La*.

47 *On ne s'éveille qu'au contact de l'amour. Et avant ce temps, on n'est que jardins sans douleurs, espaces fourmillant de corps érotiques, champs de mers poissonneuses, chairs sans soucis.*
One wakes only to the touch of love. Before then, we are only gardens without sorrows, spaces swarming with erotic bodies, landscapes of seas full of fish, flesh without cares.
1976 *La*.

48 *Quand je n'écris pas, c'est comme si j'étais morte.*
When I do not write, it's as though I'm dead.
Quoted in Jean-Louis Rambures *Comment travaillent les écrivains* (1978).

49 Je ne suis pas innocente. L'innocence est une science du sublime. Et je ne suis qu'au tout début de l'apprentissage.
I am not innocent. Innocence is a science of the sublime. And I am only at the very beginning of the apprenticeship.
1979 *Vivre l'orange/ To Live the Orange* (bilingual text, translated by Ann Liddle and Sarah Cornell).

50 Je voudrais tant être une femme sans y penser.
I would like so much to be a woman without thinking about it.
1983 *Le Livre de Promethea*.

Clare, John 1793–1864

English poet, whose work reflects the harsh rural world of the 19c. He became mentally unstable in 1823 and spent the last 23 years of his life in a lunatic asylum.

51 When badgers fight and everyone's a foe.
1836 'Badger'.

52 A quiet, pilfering, unprotected race.
1841 'The Gipsy Camp'.

53 The present is the funeral of the past,
And man the living sepulchre of life.
1845 'The Present is the Funeral of the Past'.

54 I am—yet what I am, none cares or knows;
My friends forsake me like a memory lost:
I am the self-consumer of my woes.
1848 'I Am'.

55 I long for scenes where man hath never trod
A place where woman never smiled or wept
There to abide with my Creator God
And sleep as I in childhood sweetly slept,
Untroubling and untroubled where I lie
The grass below, above, the vaulted sky.
1848 'I Am'.

56 He could not die when the trees were green,
For he loved the time too well.
'The Dying Child' (published 1873).

Clark, Alan Kenneth McKenzie 1928–99

English Conservative politician, noted for his diaries, which were published from 1993. He was the son of the art historian Kenneth Clark.

57 There are no true friends in politics. We are all sharks circling, and waiting, for traces of blood to appear in the water.
1990 Diary entry, 30 Nov.

58 Safe is spelled D-U-L-L. Politics has got to be a fun activity.
1997 On being selected as parliamentary candidate for Kensington and Chelsea, 24 Jan. In the *Daily Telegraph*, 25 Jan.

59 If I can comport myself with the dignity and competence of Ms Mo Mowlam, I shall be very satisfied.
1999 After surgery for a brain tumour. In the *Sunday Times*, 'Talking Heads', 6 Jun.

Clark, Eleanor 1913–96

US writer, wife of Robert Penn Warren. Her works include *Eyes, Etc.* (1977), on her experience of blindness. She won the National Book Award, 1965, for *The Oysters of Locmariaquer*.

60 If you don't love life you can't enjoy an oyster.
1964 *The Oysters of Locmariaquer*, ch.1.

Clark, Kenneth Mackenzie Clark, Baron 1903–83

English art historian, particularly remembered for his pioneering television series, *Civilisation* (1969).

61 All great civilisations, in their early stages, are based on success in war.
1969 *Civilisation*, ch.1.

62 Medieval marriages were entirely a matter of property, and, as everyone knows, marriage without love means love without marriage.
1969 *Civilisation*, ch.3.

Clark, Ralph c.1755–1794

British lieutenant of the First Fleet to Australia.

63 The damned whores the moment that they got below fell a fighting amongst one and another and Capt Meridith order the Sergt. not to part them but to let them fight it out.
c.1789 *The Journal and Letters of Lt Ralph Clark 1787–1792*. The phrase 'damned whores' was adopted by Australian feminist Anne Summers in her feminist critique of Australian culture, *Damned Whores and God's Police* (1975).
▶ See Chisholme 222:24.

Clark, Ramsey 1927–

US lawyer, appointed Attorney General (1967–9), known for his staunch defence of civil liberties and his opposition to the Vietnam War.

64 A right is not what someone gives you; it's what no one can take from you.
1977 In the *New York Times*, 2 Oct.

Clark, William R and Michael Grunstein

US scientists.

65 Why are human beings so different from one another?
2000 *Are We Hardwired? The Role of Genes in Human Behaviour*.

Clarke, Sir Arthur C(harles) 1917–2008

English author, a prolific and entertaining writer of works of science fiction, popular science, mysticism and speculative thought. His story 'The Sentinel' was the basis of Stanley Kubrick's film *2001: A Space Odyssey* (1968).

66 Overhead without any fuss the stars were going out.
1958 'The Nine Billion Names of God'.

67 Any sufficiently advanced technology is indistinguishable from magic.
1962 *Profiles of the Future*, introduction.

68 When a distinguished but elderly scientist states that something is possible he is almost certainly right. When he states that something is impossible, he is very probably wrong.
1962 *Profiles of the Future*.

69 For the radiance of eternity is not white: it is infra-red.
1993 *By Space Possessed*.

Clarke, Kenneth Harry 1940–

English Conservative politician.

70 I do not wear a bleeper. I can't speak in soundbites.
I refuse to repeat slogans... I hate focus groups.
I absolutely hate image consultants.
1999 In the *New Statesman*, 12 Feb.

Claudel, Paul 1868–1955
French dramatist, poet and diplomat, whose writing reflects his mystical Catholicism. He was ambassador to Japan (1921–7), the US (1927–33) and Belgium (1933–35). His works include the play *Tidings Brought to Mary* (1912) and *Five Great Odes* (1910).

71 You explain nothing, O poet, but thanks to you all things become explicable.
Recalled on his death, 23 Feb 1955.

72 A cocktail is to a glass of wine as rape is to love.
Quoted by William Grimes in 'The American Cocktail', *Americana*, Dec 1992.

Claudius Caecus, Appius 4c–3c BC
Roman statesman and lawgiver. He oversaw the construction of Rome's first aqueduct, the Aqua Appia. He later became blind, hence his surname, Caecus.

73 *Faber est suae quisque fortunae.*
Each man is the architect of his own fate.
Quoted in Sallust *Ad Caesarem Senem de Re Publica Oratio*, ch.1, section 2.

Clausewitz, Karl von 1780–1831
Prussian general, Director of the Prussian army school in Berlin (1818–30) and Gneisenau's Chief-of-Staff. His treatise *Vom Kriege* ('On War', 1833) had a major impact on strategic studies.

74 Battles decide everything.
1812 *Principles of War* (translated by J J Graham).

75 Only the study of military history is capable of giving those who have no experience of their own a clear picture of what I have just called the friction of the whole machine.
1812 *Principles of War* (translated by J J Graham).

76 *Der Krieg ist nichts als eine Fortsetzung des politischen Verkehrs mit Einmischung anderer Mittel.*
War is merely the continuation of policy with the admixture of other means.
1833 *Vom Kriege*, bk.8, ch.6, section b. The phrase is commonly rendered 'War is the continuation of politics by other means.'

Clavell, James du Maresq 1924–94
Australian-born US novelist. His first novel, *King Rat* (1962), is set in Singapore's Changi prison, where the Japanese kept prisoners of war (1942–5). Clavell was himself a prisoner of war in Java.

77 These men too were criminals. Their crime was vast. They had lost a war. And they had lived.
1962 *King Rat*.

Cleaver, Eldridge 1935–98
US political activist.

78 You're either part of the solution, or you're part of the problem.
1968 Speech, San Francisco.

Cleese, John 1939–
British actor, comedian and writer, best known for his contribution to the satirical television series, *Monty Python's Flying Circus* (1969–74).

79 I wish to complain about this parrot what I have purchased not half an hour ago from this very boutique.
1968 As Mr Praline in the 'Dead Parrot' sketch, *Monty Python's Flying Circus*.

80 Don't mention the war. I mentioned it once but I think I got away with it.
1975 As Basil Fawlty in *Fawlty Towers*, 'The Germans'.

81 Loving your neighbour as much as yourself is practically bloody impossible... You might as well have a commandment that states, 'Thou shalt fly'.
1993 In *The Times*.

82 You do realise as you grow older that almost nobody knows what they are talking about.
2009 Attributed.

Clegg, Nick (Nicholas William Peter) 1967–
English Liberal Democrat politician. A former Member of the European Parliament (1999–2004), he was elected MP for Sheffield Hallam in 2005 and became leader of the Liberal Democrats in 2007. In 2010 he became Deputy Prime Minister under Conservative Prime Minister David Cameron in the coalition government.

83 I need to say this—you shouldn't trust any government, actually including this one. You should not trust government—full stop. The natural inclination of government is to hoard power and information; to accrue power to itself in the name of the public good.
2011 Attributed.

Clemenceau, Georges 1841–1929
French statesman, leader of the extreme left, known as 'The Tiger'. He was Premier (1906–9, 1917–20) and presided at the 1919 Peace Conference.

84 *La guerre, c'est une chose trop grave pour la confier à des militaires.*
War is too serious a business to be left to generals.
Quoted in Hampden Jackson *Clemenceau and the Third Republic* (1946), but also attributed elsewhere to others.

85 He died as he had lived—like a second lieutenant.
1891 On the death of General Boulanger, who had shot himself on the grave of his mistress, who had died two months earlier. In *La Justice*. Quoted in Edgar Holt *The Tiger: The Life of Georges Clemenceau 1841–1929* (1976).

86 Your verdict, gentlemen, will be less upon us than upon yourselves. We appear before you. You appear before history.
1898 Addressing the jury as a member of the defence at Zola's trial, 22 Feb, following the publication of *J'Accuse*.

87 *Politique intérieure, je fais la guerre; politique extérieure, je fais toujours la guerre. Je fais toujours la guerre.*
My home policy? I wage war. My foreign policy? I wage war. Always, everywhere, I wage war.
1918 Speech to the Chamber of Deputies, 8 Mar.

88 *Il est plus facile de faire la guerre que la paix.*
It is far easier to make war than to make peace.
1919 Speech at Verdun, 20 Jul.

Cleveland

89 America is the only country in history that miraculously has gone directly from barbarism to decadence without the usual interval of civilization.
Attributed. This has also been attributed to George Bernard Shaw.

90 We have won the war. Now we have to win the peace—and that may be more difficult.
Quoted in David R Watson George Clemenceau: A Political Biography *(1974).*

Cleveland, (Stephen) Grover 1837–1908

22nd and 24th US President (1885–9, 1893–7). He supported civil service reform and lower tariffs, and in his second term he took a strong stance against Britain in its boundary dispute with Venezuela.

91 I have considered the pension list of the republic a roll of honour.
1888 Veto of the Dependent Pension Bill, 5 Jul.

Cleveland, John 1613–1658

English poet, a satirical propagandist for the Royalists in the Civil War, and for a time a political prisoner. Two collections of his poems were published during his lifetime, one in 1651 and the other in 1653.

92 Had Cain been Scot, God would have changed his doom
Nor forced him wander, but confined him home.
1647 'The Rebel Scot'.

93 Mystical grammar of amorous glances,
Feeling of pulses the physic of love,
Rhetorical courtings, and musical dances;
Numbering of kisses arithmetic prove.
1651 'Mark Antony'.

94 Virtue's no more in womankind
But the green sickness of the mind.
Philosophy, their new delight,
A kind of charcoal appetite.
1653 'The Antiplatonic'.

95 Give me a lover bold and free,
Not eunuched with formality.
1653 'The Antiplatonic'.

96 Like an ambassador that beds a queen
With the nice caution of a sword between.
1653 'The Antiplatonic'.

Clifford, Clark M(cAdams) 1906–98

US lawyer, adviser to Truman and Kennedy and later Secretary of Defense (1968–9) under Johnson.

97 The amiable dunce.
Of Ronald Reagan. Quoted in Haynes Johnson Sleep-Walking Through History *(1991).*

Clinton, Bill (William) 1946–

US Democratic politician and 42nd President. He became Governor of Arkansas in 1978 and served for five terms (1979–81, 1983–92). In 1992 he became the first Democrat President for twelve years and in 1996 the first Democrat to gain re-election since Roosevelt in 1936. In 1998 his initial denial of an affair with White House intern Monica Lewinsky was followed by charges of perjury and obstruction of justice, although he was subsequently acquitted by the Senate. He is married to Hillary Rodham Clinton.

98 Cash for trash.
1992 On tabloid payments to his alleged mistress Gennifer Flowers. On ABC TV, 23 Jan.

99 I experimented with marijuana a time or two. And I didn't like it, and I didn't inhale.
1992 In the Washington Post, *30 Mar.*

1 On this day with high hopes and brave hearts, in massive numbers, the American people have voted to make a new beginning.
1992 Accepting victory in the election, 3 Nov.

2 When somebody tells you it is not a money problem, they're talking about somebody else's money.
1992 In USA Today, *20 Dec.*

3 That hallowed piece of earth, that land of light and revelation, is the home to the memories and dreams of Jews, Muslims and Christians throughout the world.
1993 On the signing of Palestinian–Israeli peace accord at the White House, 13 Sep.

4 I have had a drill to the tooth of America for the last two years.
1994 Of painful political decisions. In the US News & World Report, *13 Feb.*

5 I can't stop being President.
1994 Comment after a suicide plane attack and two incidents of gunfire on the White House. Reported in the New York Times, *18 Dec.*

6 If something makes you cry, you have to do something about it. That's the difference between politics and guilt.
On what makes a liberal. Quoted in Meredith Oakley On the Make *(1994).*

7 Half the time when I see the evening news, I wouldn't be for me, either.
1995 Comment, 2 Jun.

8 Hillary was born 40, and she'll always be 40... I was born 16, and I'll always be 16.
Quoted in Gore Vidal Virgin Islands: Essays 1992–1997 *(1997).*

9 I did not have sexual relations with that woman.
1998 On Monica Lewinsky, in a television interview. Quoted in the Daily Telegraph, *27 Jan.*

10 I did have a relationship with Ms Lewinsky that was not appropriate. In fact, it was wrong.
1998 Television broadcast to America, 18 Aug. In The Times, *19 Aug.*

11 It depends on what the meaning of 'is' is.
1998 Evidence to the grand jury. Quoted in The Guardian, *2 Sep.*

12 I believe any person who asks for forgiveness has to be prepared to give it.
1999 Statement after being acquitted by the Senate, 12 Feb.

13 Golf is like life in a lot of ways. The most important competition is the one against yourself.
2000 Quoted in The Independent, *23 Dec.*

14 A terrible moral error.
2004 On his affair with Monica Lewinsky. In an interview on CBS television programme 60 Minutes, *20 Jun.*

15 I did something for the worst possible reason. Just because I could.
2004 On his affair with Monica Lewinsky. In an interview on CBS television programme 60 Minutes, *20 Jun.*

16 Don't ask, don't tell.
2004 The Clinton family motto. In My Life.

17 Do I have regrets? Sure, both private and public ones.
2004 My Life.

18 During the government shutdowns I was engaged in two titanic struggles: a public one with Congress over the future of our country, and a private one to hold the old

demons at bay. I had won the public fight and lost the private one.
2004 *My Life*.

19 Criticism is part of the lifeblood of democracy. No one is right all the time. But we should remember that there is a big difference between criticizing a policy or a politician and demonizing the government that guarantees our freedoms and the public servants who enforce our laws.
2010 Speech marking the fifteenth anniversary of the Oklahoma City bombing, *The New York Times*, 19 Apr.

20 A great democracy does not make it harder to vote than to buy an assault weapon.
2013 Speech at the Lincoln Memorial marking the fiftieth anniversary of the March on Washington, 28 Aug.

21 It's the most important battle of the twenty-first century, whether what we have in common is more important than their differences.
2013 Speech at the Clinton Global Initiative, New York City.

Clinton, Hillary Rodham 1947–

US politician and lawyer, wife of President Bill Clinton. As a lawyer she specialized in family issues and children's rights, and after her husband's election she served as chief presidential adviser. In 2001 she became Senator for New York, the first First Lady to be elected to public office. She was also Secretary of State (2009–2013) under Barack Obama.

22 I suppose I could have stayed home, baked cookies, and had teas.
1992 Rejecting charges of a conflict of interest between politics and her legal career. In the *New York Times*, 18 May.

23 I'd be a terrific governor…a terrific president.
1992 Statement during her husband's presidential campaign. Reported in the *Washington Post*, 22 Feb 1995.

24 It is time for us to say here in Beijing, and the world to hear, that it is no longer acceptable to discuss women's rights as separate from human rights.
1995 Addressing the 4th World Conference on Women. Reported in the *New York Times*, 6 Sep.

25 I was talking to one of the Secret Service men about security the other day, and he said that as far as they were concerned, they'd be happier if we lived in a bunker and travelled the streets in a tank.
Quoted in Gore Vidal *Virgin Islands: Essays 1992–1997* (1997).

26 The great story here…is this vast right-wing conspiracy that has been conspiring against my husband since the day he announced for president.
1998 Interview on NBC television's *Today*, 27 Jan.

27 A hard dog to keep on the porch.
1999 On her husband. In *The Guardian*, 2 Aug.

28 Freedom is never granted. It is earned by each generation.
2007 Speaking to Veterans of Foreign Wars, Kansas City, Missouri, 20 Aug.

29 Rich people, God bless us. We deserve all the opportunities to make sure our country and our blessings continue to the next generation.
2008 Interview on Fox News, 30 Apr.

30 We used to say in the White House that if a place is too dangerous, too small or too poor, send the First Lady.
2008 Campaign speech, Iowa.

31 Although we weren't able to shatter this highest, hardest glass ceiling this time, thanks to you, it's got about eighteen million cracks in it, and the light is shining through like never before.
2008 Acknowledging her failure to secure the Democratic nomination for President.

32 When it comes to foreign policy, it is important to remember that politics stops at the water's edge.
2010 Quoted by Politico, 3 Nov.

33 No society can thrive when half its people are left behind.
2011 In *Newsweek*, 26 Sep.

34 We came, we saw, he died.
2011 On the death of Libyan leader Muammar Gaddafi, CBS News interview, 20 Oct.

35 When women participate in politics, it ripples out to the entire society… Women are the world's most underused resource.
2013 Interview, *New York Magazine*, 22 Sep.

36 While there are few problems in today's world that the United States can solve alone, there are even fewer that can be solved without the United States.
2014 *Hard Choices*.

37 Great nations need organizing principles, and 'Don't do stupid stuff' is not an organizing principle.
2014 Interview, *Atlantic Online*, 10 Aug.

Clive, Kitty 1711–85

English comic actress. Though she longed to be a tragic actress, she excelled in light comedy under the management of David Garrick at Drury Lane. She retired in 1769.

38 Damn him, he could act a gridiron.
On watching a performance by David Garrick. Quoted in William Archer's introduction to *Dramatic Essays of Leigh Hunt* (1894).

Clive, Robert, 1st Baron of Plassey 1725–74

English soldier and administrator in India, who defeated a large Indian–French force at Plassey (1757). After a spell in Parliament in Britain he returned to Calcutta (1765) to reform the civil service and the military, but was criticized for his drastic measures.

39 It is scarcely hyperbole to say that tomorrow the whole Moghul Empire is in our power.
1757 Letter, 24 Jun, following victory at Plassey the previous day.

40 By God, Mr Chairman—at this moment I stand astonished at my own moderation!
1773 At a parliamentary inquiry into his rapacious policies on India.

Clooney, George Timothy 1961–

US film and television actor. His films, which include *Three Kings* (1999), *Ocean's Eleven* (2001), and *The Monuments Men* (2014), have won him numerous awards, including two Academy Awards as an actor and producer.

41 Theatre actors look down on film actors, who look down on TV actors. Thank God for reality shows or we wouldn't have anybody to look down on.
2008 Attributed.

42 I cut tobacco for a living in Kentucky… I sold insurance door to door. That's hard work. Acting is not hard work.
2011 Attributed.

43 As for me running for president, look, there's a guy in office who is smarter than anyone you know, and nicer,

and he's having an almost impossible time governing. Why would anyone volunteer for that job? I have a very good job, so I have no interest.
2011 His response when asked if he would consider running for president, 6 Sep.

Clough, Arthur Hugh 1819–61

English poet. A friend of Ruskin, Arnold and Carlyle, he experienced a religious crisis in Oxford which pervades much of his writing.

44 Sesquipedalian blackguard.
   1848 *The Bothie of Tober-na-Vuolich*, pt.2, l.223.

45 Grace is given of God, but knowledge is bought in the market.
   1848 *The Bothie of Tober-na-Vuolich*, pt.4, l.159.

46 What shall we do without you? Think where we are. Carlyle has led us all out into the desert, and he has left us there.
   1848 Parting words to Ralph Waldo Emerson, 15 Jul. Quoted in E E Hale *James Russell Lowell and His Friends* (1898), ch.9.

47 Say not the struggle naught availeth
The labour and the wounds are vain,
The enemy faints not, nor faileth,
And as things have been, things remain.
   1849 'Say Not the Struggle Naught Availeth'.

48 If hopes were dupes, fears may be liars.
   1849 'Say Not the Struggle Naught Availeth'.

49 And not by eastern windows only,
When daylight comes, comes in the light,
In front the sun climbs slow, how slowly,
But westward, look, the land is bright.
   1849 'Say Not the Struggle Naught Availeth'.

50 Afloat. We move: Delicious! Ah,
What else is like the gondola?
   1850 *Dipsychus* (published 1865), sc.5.

51 This world is bad enough maybe;
We do not comprehend it;
But in one fact can all agree
God won't, and we can't mend it.
   1850 *Dipsychus* (published 1865), sc.5.

52 'There is no God', the wicked saith,
'And truly it's a blessing,
For what he might have done with us
It's better only guessing.'
   1850 *Dipsychus* (published 1865), sc.6.

53 And almost every one when age,
Disease, or sorrow strike him,
Inclines to think there is a God,
Or something very like him.
   1850 *Dipsychus* (published 1865), sc.6.

54 'Tis better to have fought and lost,
Than never to have fought at all.
   1854 'Peschiera'.
   ▶ See Tennyson 874:69.

55 Rome, believe me, my friend, is like its own Monte Testaceo,
Merely a marvellous mass of broken and castaway wine-pots.
   1858 *Amours de Voyage*, canto 1, pt.2.

56 The horrible pleasure of pleasing inferior people.
   1858 *Amours de Voyage*, canto 1, pt.11.

57 Am I prepared to lay down my life for the British female? Really, who knows?...
Ah, for a child in the street I could strike; for the full-blown lady—
Somehow, Eustace, alas! I have not felt the vocation.
   1858 *Amours de Voyage*, canto 2, pt.4.

58 I do not like being moved: for the will is excited; and action
Is a most dangerous thing: I tremble for something factitious,
Some malpractice of heart and illegitimate process;
We are so prone to these things with our terrible notions of duty.
   1858 *Amours de Voyage*, canto 2, pt.11.

59 But for his funeral train which the bridegroom sees in the distance,
Would he so joyfully, think you, fall in with the marriage-procession?
   1858 *Amours de Voyage*, canto 3, pt.6.

60 Allah is great, no doubt, and Juxtaposition his prophet.
   1858 *Amours de Voyage*, canto 3, pt.6.

61 Mild monastic faces in quiet collegiate cloisters.
   1858 *Amours de Voyage*, canto 3, pt.9.

62 Whither depart the souls of the brave that die in the battle,
Die in the lost, lost fight, for the cause that perishes with them?
   1858 *Amours de Voyage*, canto 5, pt.6.

63 Thou shalt have one God only: who
Would be at the expense of two?
   1862 *The Latest Decalogue*.

64 Thou shalt not kill; but need'st not strive
Officiously to keep alive.
   1862 *The Latest Decalogue*.

65 Do not adultery commit;
Advantage rarely comes of it.
   1862 *The Latest Decalogue*.

66 Thou shalt not steal; an empty feat,
When it's so lucrative to cheat.
   1862 *The Latest Decalogue*.

67 Thou shalt not covet; but tradition
Approves all forms of competition.
   1862 *The Latest Decalogue*.

Clough, Brian 1935–2004

English football player and manager. As a player, he set a postwar goal-scoring record of 254 goals, and also won two England caps. He went on to become a controversial and outspoken but successful manager.

68 Football hooligans? Well, there are 92 club chairmen for a start.
   Quoted in Colin Jarman *The Guinness Dictionary of Sports Quotations* (1990).

69 Say nowt, win it, then—talk your head off.
   Quoted in Colin Jarman *The Guinness Dictionary of Sports Quotations* (1990).

70 My wife says OBE stands for Old Big 'Ead.
   Quoted in Phil Shaw *The Book of Football Quotations* (2003).

71 Resignations are for Prime Ministers and those caught with their trousers down, not for me.
   Quoted in Phil Shaw *The Book of Football Quotations* (2003).

Cobain, Kurt (Donald) 1967–94

US singer and guitarist, founder member of the band Nirvana.

72 Here we are now, entertain us.
1991 'Smells Like Teen Spirit'.

73 Here's the one who likes all our pretty songs
And he likes to sing along
And he likes to shoot his gun
But he don't know what it means.
1991 'In Bloom'.

Cobbett, William 1762–1835

English radical politician and journalist. His pioneering essays on the the conditions of the rural poor were collected in his best-known work, *Rural Rides* (1830).

74 Protestations of impartiality I shall make none. They are always useless and are besides perfect nonsense, when used by a news-monger.
1797 In the first issue of *Porcupine's Gazette*, 4 Mar, 'Address to the public'.

75 All Middlesex is *ugly*, notwithstanding the millions upon millions which it is continually sucking up from the rest of the kingdom.
1822 *Rural Rides* (published 1830), entry for 25 Sep.

76 DEAL is a most villainous place. It is full of filthy-looking people. Great desolation of abomination has been going on here.
1823 On Deal, Kent. *Rural Rides* (published 1830), entry for 3 Sep.

77 The town of GUILDFORD, which (taken with its environs) I, who have seen so many, many towns, think the prettiest, and, taken all together, the most agreeable and most happy-looking, that I ever saw in my life.
1825 On Guildford, Surrey. *Rural Rides* (published 1830), entry for 23 Oct.

78 WESTBURY, a nasty odious *rotten-borough*, a really *rotten* place.
1826 On Westbury, Wiltshire. *Rural Rides* (published 1830), entry for 3 Sep.

79 From a very early age, I had imbibed the opinion, that it was every man's duty to do all that lay in his power to leave his country as good as he had found it.
1832 *Political Register*, 22 Dec.

Cobden, Richard 1804–65

English economist and politician, known as 'The Apostle of Free Trade'. In 1838 he co-founded the Anti-Corn League, and as MP from 1841 he spoke in support of the cause, bringing about the repeal of the Corn Laws in 1846.

80 Are we to be the Don Quixotes of Europe—to go about fighting for every cause where we find that someone has been wronged?
1854 Referring to the Crimean War, House of Commons, 22 Dec.

Cockburn, Alison *née Rutherford* 1713–94

Scottish poet, whose best-known lyric 'The Flowers of the Forest' commemorates a calamity in Ettrick Forest. Walter Scott was her protégé.

81 I've seen the smiling of Fortune beguiling,
I've felt all its favours and found its decay;
Sweet was its blessing, kind its caressing,
But now it is fled, fled far, far away.
1765 'The Flowers of the Forest'.

82 O fickle Fortune, why this cruel sporting?
Why thus torment us poor sons of day?
Nae mair your smiles can cheer me, nae mair your frowns can fear me,
For the flowers of the forest are a' wade away.
1765 'The Flowers of the Forest'. wade = weeded. The last line is often rendered 'For the flowers of the forest are withered away'.

Cocker, Jarvis 1963–

English singer, member of the band Pulp.

83 Let's all meet up in the year 2000
Won't it be strange when we're all fully grown?
1995 'Disco 2000'.

Cocteau, Jean 1889–1963

French poet, playwright and film director, a key figure in Surrealism and Dadaism, elected to the French Academy in 1955. His works explore the problems of adolescence and family relationships.

84 *Le tact dans l'audace c'est de savoir jusqu'où on peut aller trop loin.*
Being tactful in audacity is knowing how far one can go too far.
1918 *Le Coq et l' Arlequin*.

85 *Le pire drame pour un poète, c'est d'être admiré par malentendu.*
The worst tragedy for a poet is to be admired through being misunderstood.
1918 *Le Coq et l' Arlequin*.

86 *S'il faut choisir un crucifié, la foule sauve toujours Barabbas.*
If it has to choose who is to be crucified, the crowd will always save Barabbas.
1918 *Le Coq et l' Arlequin*.

87 *Vivre est une chute horizontale.*
Life is a horizontal fall.
1930 *Opium*.

88 Art produces ugly things which frequently become beautiful with time. Fashion, on the other hand, produces beautiful things which always become ugly with time.
1960 In the *New York World-Telegram and Sun*, 21 Aug.

Coen, Joel 1954–

US film director and screenwriter who often works in collaboration with his brother Ethan Coen.

89 We'll gladly enter the mainstream any time the mainstream will have us.
2004 In *The Guardian*, 15 Jun.

Coetzee, J(ohn) M(axwell) 1940–

South African novelist, an Australian citizen since 2006. Notable works include the novels *Life & Times of Michael K* (1983) and *Disgrace* (1999) and the fictionalized autobiography *Summertime* (2009). He received the Nobel Prize in Literature in 2003.

90 Our lies reveal as much about us as our truths.
2005 *Slow Man*.

Coffee, Lenore 1900–84
US screenwriter, Oscar-nominated for *Four Daughters* (1938).

91 What a dump!
   1949 Spoken by Bette Davis in *Beyond the Forest*.

Coffinhal, Jean Baptiste 1754–94
Presiding judge at the trial of chemist Antoine Lavoisier.

92 The Republic has no need for scientists.
   1794 Quoted in the *Encyclopedia Britannica* (1911), vol.16.

Cohan, George M(ichael) 1878–1942
US actor-manager and playwright. Having started out in vaudeville, he became one of the great Broadway personalities, appearing in plays by himself and others at his own George M Cohan Theatre from 1911.

93 I'm a Yankee Doodle Dandy
   A Yankee Doodle, do or die;
   A real live nephew of my Uncle Sam's,
   Born on the fourth of July.
   1904 'Yankee Doodle Boy'.

94 I don't care what you say about me, as long as you say *something* about me, and as long as you spell my name right.
   Quoted in John McCabe *George M Cohan, The Man Who Owned Broadway* (1973), ch.13.

Coke, Sir Edward 1552–1634
English jurist, prosecutor of Essex, Raleigh and the Gunpowder conspirators. After 1606 he vindicated national liberties against the royal prerogative. Dismissed in 1617, he led the popular party in Parliament from 1620 and instigated the Petition of Right (1628).

95 How long soever it hath continued, if it be against reason, it is of no force in law.
   1628 *The First Part of the Institutes of the Laws of England*, bk.1, ch.10, section 80.

96 We have a saying in the House of Commons; that old ways are the safest and surest ways.
   1628 Speech, London, 8 May.

97 A man's house is his castle.
   1628 *The Third Part of the Institutes of the Laws of England*, ch.73.

Coke, F T Desmond 1879–1931
English novelist. A schoolmaster, he wrote several popular novels set in English public schools and universities, notably *The Bending of a Twig* (1906) and *Sandford of Merton* (1908).

98 His blade struck the water a full second before any other…until, as the boats began to near the winning post his own was dipping in the water twice as fast as any other.
   1908 *Sandford of Merton*, ch.12. Often misquoted as 'All rowed fast but none so fast as stroke'.

Cole, Mac
Founder, Cole Carnival Shows.

99 The first carnival person was Christopher Columbus. When he sailed, he didn't know where he was going. When he got there, he didn't know where he was. And when he got back, he didn't know where he'd been.
   1989 In the *Washington Times*, 18 Aug.

Cole, W Sterling 1904–88
Chair, Joint Committee on Atomic Energy.

1 It is more sinful to conceal the power of the atom than it is to reveal it.
   1954 Statement, 9 Mar, endorsed by Winston Churchill in a letter to President Eisenhower. Quoted in Peter G Boyle (ed) *The Churchill–Eisenhower Correspondence 1953–55*.

Cole, William 1919–2000
US children's writer. His output consisted chiefly of humorous verse, such as *A Boy Named Mary Jane* (1975). He also edited many poetry and verse collections.

2 Said Jerome K. Jerome to Ford Madox Ford,
   'There's something, old boy, that I've always abhorred:
   When people address me and call me 'Jerome',
   Are they being standoffish, or too much at home?'
   Said Ford, 'I agree;
   It's the same thing with me.'
   'Mutual Problem', collected in *The Oxford Book of American Light Verse* (1979).

Coleman, Ornette 1930–
US jazz saxophonist and composer. A controversial figure when he first appeared in New York in the late 1950s, he went on to become a key figure in the development of Free Jazz, and beyond.

3 The creation of music is just as natural as the air we breathe. I believe music is really a free thing, and any way you can enjoy it, you should.
   1958 Sleeve-note, *Something Else!*

4 Many people apparently don't trust their reactions to art or to music unless there is a verbal *explanation* for it. In music the only thing that matters is whether you *feel* it or not.
   1959 Sleeve-note, *Change of the Century*.

5 When I have them working together, it's like a beautiful kaleidoscope.
   1981 On the music of his band Prime Time. Quoted in John Litweiler *The Freedom Principle* (1984).

Coleridge, Samuel Taylor 1772–1834
English poet, with Wordsworth one of the founders of the Romantic movement. Among his best-known poems are 'The Rime of the Ancient Mariner' (1798), 'Christabel' (1816) and 'Kubla Khan' (1816).

6 So for the mother's sake the child was dear,
   And dearer was the mother for the child.
   1797 'Sonnet to a Friend Who Asked Me How I Felt When the Nurse First Presented My Infant to Me'.

7 No sound is dissonant which tells of life.
   1797 'This Lime-Tree Bower my Prison'.

8 It is an ancient Mariner,
   And he stoppeth one of three.
   'By thy long grey beard and glittering eye,
   Now wherefore stopp'st thou me?'
   1798 'The Rime of the Ancient Mariner', pt.1.

9 He holds him with his glittering eye—
   The Wedding-Guest stood still,
   And listens like a three years' child:
   The Mariner hath his will.

The Wedding-Guest sat on a stone:
He cannot choose but hear;
And thus spake on that ancient man,
The bright-eyed Mariner.
1798 'The Rime of the Ancient Mariner', pt.1.

10 'God save thee, ancient Mariner!
From the fiends that plague thee thus!
Why look'st thou so?'—With my cross-bow
I shot the Albatross.
1798 'The Rime of the Ancient Mariner', pt.1.

11 We were the first that ever burst
Into that silent sea.
1798 'The Rime of the Ancient Mariner', pt.2.

12 As idle as a painted ship
Upon a painted ocean.
1798 'The Rime of the Ancient Mariner', pt.2.

13 Water, water, everywhere,
Nor any drop to drink.
The very deep did rot: O Christ!
That ever this should be!
Yes, slimy things did crawl with legs
Upon the slimy sea.
1798 'The Rime of the Ancient Mariner', pt.2.

14 I fear thee ancient Mariner!
I fear thy skinny hand!
And thou art long, and lank, and brown,
As is the ribbed sea-sand.
1798 'The Rime of the Ancient Mariner', pt.4.

15 And a thousand thousand slimy things
Lived on; and so did I.
1798 'The Rime of the Ancient Mariner', pt.4.

16 A spring of love gushed from my heart,
And I blessed them unaware.
1798 'The Rime of the Ancient Mariner', pt.4.

17 We were a ghastly crew.
1798 'The Rime of the Ancient Mariner', pt.5.

18 Like one, that on a lonesome road
Doth walk in fear and dread,
And having once turned round walks on,
And turns no more his head;
Because he knows, a frightful fiend
Doth close behind him tread.
1798 'The Rime of the Ancient Mariner', pt.6.

19 No voice, but oh! the silence sank
Like music on my heart.
1798 'The Rime of the Ancient Mariner', pt.6.

20 He prayeth well, who loveth well
Both man and bird and beast.
He prayeth best, who loveth best
All things both great and small.
1798 'The Rime of the Ancient Mariner', pt.7.

21 He went like one that hath been stunned,
And is of sense forlorn:
A sadder and wiser man,
He rose the morrow morn.
1798 'The Rime of the Ancient Mariner', pt.7.

22 O let me be awake, my God!
Or let me sleep alway.
1798 'The Rime of the Ancient Mariner', pt.7.

23 The frost performs its secret ministry,
Unhelped by any wind.
1798 'Frost at Midnight'.

24 Bells, the poor man's only music.
1798 'Frost at Midnight'.

25 And hark! the Nightingale begins its song,
'Most musical, most melancholy' bird!
A melancholy bird?…his song
Should make all Nature lovelier, and itself
Be loved like Nature!
1798 'The Nightingale'.

26 Belovèd, what are names but air?
Choose thou whatever suits the line;
Call me Sappho, call me Chloris,
Call me Lalage or Doris,
Only, only call me Thine.
1799 'Names', a translation from G E Lessing's German original
(first published in the *Morning Post*, 1803).

27 All thoughts, all passions, all delights
Whatever stirs this mortal frame,
All are but ministers of Love,
And feed his sacred flame.
1799 'Love'.

28 Those sounds which oft have raised me, whilst they awed,
And sent my soul abroad,
Might now perhaps their wonted impulse give,
Might startle this dull pain, and make it move and live!
1802 'Dejection: An Ode', stanza 1.

29 I may not hope from outward forms to win
The passion and the life, whose fountains are within.
1802 'Dejection: An Ode', stanza 3.

30 Ah! from the soul itself must issue forth
A light, a glory, a fair luminous cloud
Enveloping the Earth—
And from the soul itself must there be sent
A sweet and potent voice, of its own birth
Of all sweet sounds the life and element!
1802 'Dejection: An Ode', stanza 4.

31 O pure of heart! thou need'st not ask of me
What this strong music in the soul may be!
What, and wherein it doth exist,
This light, this glory, this fair luminous mist,
This beautiful and beauty-making power.
1802 'Dejection: An Ode', stanza 5.

32 'Alas!' said she, 'we ne'er can be
Made happy by compulsion!'
1809 'The Three Graves', pt.4, stanza 12.

33 What is an Epigram? a dwarfish whole,
Its body brevity, and wit its soul.
1809 'Epigram'.

34 Alas! they had been friends in youth;
But whispering tongues can poison truth;
And constancy lives in realms above;
And life is thorny; and youth is vain;
And to be wroth with one we love
Doth work like madness on the brain.
1816 'Christabel', pt.2.

35 On awaking he…instantly and eagerly wrote down the
lines that are here preserved. At this moment he was
unfortunately called out by a person on business from
Porlock.

36 In Xanadu did Kubla Khan
A stately pleasure-dome decree:
Where Alph, the sacred river, ran
Through caverns measureless to man
Down to a sunless sea.
1816 'Kubla Khan', opening lines.

Preliminary note to 'Kubla Khan', explaining the reasons for the fragmented end of the poem.
1816

37 A savage place! as holy and enchanted
As e'er beneath a waning moon was haunted
By woman wailing for her demon-lover!
1816 'Kubla Khan'.

38 And from this chasm, with ceaseless turmoil seething,
As if this earth in fast thick pants were breathing,
A mighty fountain momently was forced.
1816 'Kubla Khan'.

39 It was a miracle of rare device,
A sunny pleasure-dome with caves of ice!
1816 'Kubla Khan'.

40 Through wood and dale the sacred river ran,
Then reached the caverns measureless to man,
And sank in tumult to a lifeless ocean:
And 'mid this tumult Kubla heard from far
Ancestral voices prophesying war!
1816 'Kubla Khan'.

41 A damsel with a dulcimer
In a vision once I saw:
It was an Abyssinian maid,
And on her dulcimer she played,
Singing of Mount Abora.
1816 'Kubla Khan'.

42 And all who heard should see them there,
And all should cry, Beware! Beware!
His flashing eyes, his floating hair!
Weave a circle round him thrice,
And close your eyes with holy dread,
For he on honey-dew hath fed,
And drunk the milk of Paradise.
1816 'Kubla Khan'.

43 Until you understand a writer's ignorance, presume yourself ignorant of his understanding.
1817 *Biographia Literaria*, ch.12.

44 That willing suspension of disbelief for the moment, which constitutes poetic faith.
1817 *Biographia Literaria*, ch.14.

45 Kean is original; but he copies from himself. His rapid descents from the hyper-tragic to the infra-colloquial, though sometimes productive of great effect, are often unreasonable. To see him act, is like reading Shakespeare by flashes of lightning.
1823 Of Edmund Kean. *Table Talk* (published 1835), entry for 27 Apr.

46 He who begins by loving Christianity better than Truth will proceed by loving his own sect or church better than Christianity, and end by loving himself better than all.
1825 *Aids to Reflection: Moral and Religious Aphorisms*.

47 Summer has set in with its usual severity.
1826 Letter to Vincent Novello, 9 May.

48 Prose = words in their best order;—poetry = the *best* words in the best order.
1827 *Table Talk* (published 1835), entry for 12 Jul.

49 The man's desire is for the woman; but the woman's desire is rarely other than for the desire of the man.
1827 *Table Talk* (published 1835), entry for 23 Jul.

50 In Köhln, a town of monks and bones,
And pavements fang'd with murderous stones
And rags, and hags, and hideous wenches;
I counted two and seventy stenches,
All well defined, and several stinks!
Ye Nymphs that reign o'er sewers and sinks,
The river Rhine, it is well known,
Doth wash your city of Cologne;
But tell me, Nymphs, what power divine
Shall henceforth wash the river Rhine?
1828 'Cologne', first published in *Friendship's Offering* (1834), as 'Lightheartedness in Rhyme', no.4.

51 If men could learn from history, what lessons it might teach us! But passion and party blind our eyes, and the light which experience gives is a lantern on the stern, which shines only on the waves behind us!
1831 *Table Talk* (published 1835), entry for 18 Dec.

52 Farce is nearer tragedy in its essence than comedy is.
1833 *Table Talk* (published 1835), entry for 25 Aug.

53 Of no age—nor of any religion, or party or profession. The body and substance of his works came out of the unfathomable depths of his own oceanic mind.
1834 Of Shakespeare. *Table Talk* (published 1835), entry for 15 Mar.

54 Iago's soliloquy—the motive-hunting of motiveless malignity.
The Literary Remains of Samuel Taylor Coleridge (published 1836), bk.2, 'Notes on the Tragedies of Shakespeare: Othello'.

Colette full name Sidonie Gabrielle Colette 1873–1954

French writer. Her first husband, Henri Gauthier-Villars, published her early *Claudine* series under his pen-name 'Willy'. Her writing is marked by its exploration of the sensual. Later works include *Chéri* (1920) and *Gigi* (1944).

55 *Quand elle lève ses paupières, on dirait qu'elle se déshabille.*
When she raises her eyelids it's as if she were taking off all her clothes.
1903 *Claudine et Annie*, ch.3 (translated by Antonia White).

56 *Il découvrait...le monde des émotions qu'on nomme, à la légère, physiques.*
He was discovering...the world of the emotions that are so lightly called physical.
1923 *Le Blé en herbe*.

57 *Ne porte jamais de bijoux artistiques, ça déconsidère complètement une femme.*
Don't ever wear artistic jewellery; it wrecks a woman's reputation.
1944 *Gigi*.

Collingwood, Cuthbert, Baron 1748–1810

English admiral. He rose from midshipman to become second-in-command to Nelson at Trafalgar, on board the *Royal Sovereign*.

58 Now, gentlemen, let us do something today which the world may talk of hereafter.
1805 Remark to troops before the Battle of Trafalgar, 21 Oct. Quoted in G L Newnham Collingwood (ed) *A Selection from the Correspondence of Lord Collingwood* (1828), vol.1.

Collingwood, R(obin) G(eorge) 1889–1943

English philosopher and historian, with a strong archaeo-logical interest. He wrote widely on the philosophy of history although his work was not well known until well after his death.

59 Perfect freedom is reserved for the man who lives by his own work and in that work does what he wants to do.
   1924 *Speculum Mentis*.

60 A man ceases to be a beginner in any given science and becomes a master in that science when he has learned that…he is going to be a beginner all his life.
   1942 *New Leviathan*, pt.1 ch.1.

Collins, Billy 1941–

US poet.

61 The name of the author is the first to go
   followed obediently by the title, the plot,
   the heartbreaking conclusion, the entire novel
   which suddenly becomes one you have never read,
   never even heard of.
   2000 *Taking off Emily Dickinson's Clothes: Selected Poems*, 'Forgetfulness'.

62 While the novelist is banging on his typewriter, the poet is watching a fly in the windowpane.
   Attributed.

Collins, Charles 1874–1926

English songwriter. He wrote rapid patter songs for use by music-hall stars of the day such as Harry Champion.

63 Any old iron, any old iron,
   Any any old old iron?
   You look neat
   Talk about a treat,
   You look dapper from your napper to your feet.
   Dressed in style, brand new tile,
   And your father's old green tie on,
   But I wouldn't give you tuppence for your old watch chain;
   Old iron, old iron?
   1911 'Any Old Iron' (with E A Sheppard and Fred Terry). The second line is commonly rendered 'Any any any old iron?'.

64 My old man said, 'Follow the van,
   Don't dilly-dally on the way!'
   Off went the cart with the home packed in it,
   I walked behind with my old cock linnet.
   But I dillied and dallied, dallied and dillied,
   Lost the van and don't know where to roam.
   You can't trust the 'specials' like the old time 'coppers'
   When you can't find your way home.
   1919 'Don't Dilly-Dally on the Way' (with Fred Leigh).

Collins, Michael 1890–1922

Irish patriot and leader of the IRA. He signed the treaty of 1921 giving Ireland dominion status, believing it the best possible at the time, and after attempting to form a government under the terms of the treaty was killed in an ambush by hardline republicans.

65 Think—what I have got for Ireland? Something which she has wanted these past seven hundred years. Will anyone be satisfied with the bargain? Will anyone? I tell you this—early this morning I signed my death warrant. I thought at the time how odd, how ridiculous—a bullet may just as well have done the job five years ago.
   1921 Letter, written after signing the peace treaty with Great Britain, 6 Dec.

Collins, Michael 1930–

Italian-born US astronaut who as a crew member of Apollo 11 piloted the spacecraft during its historic mission to the moon (1969). He orbited the moon alone in the command unit while Neil Armstrong and Buzz Aldrin made the first manned lunar landing.

66 I knew I was alone in a way that no earthling has ever been before.
   1972 In *Time*, Dec 11.

Collins, Phil 1951–

English singer, drummer and songwriter. He joined Genesis as drummer in 1970, and took over as lead vocalist when Peter Gabriel left the group (1985). He has also had a successful solo career.

67 I suppose Phil Collins offers something for everybody, and in hipdom that's not cool. But in the real world, there's no shame in that at all.
   Quoted in *Guinness Rockopedia* (1998).

Collins, Suzanne Marie 1962–

US novelist. Her works include the best-selling *Hunger Games* trilogy.

68 May the odds be ever in your favour.
   2008 *The Hunger Games*.

Collins, William 1721–59

English poet, first published at the age of 17. His poetry, which is original and even experimental for the day, includes the 'Ode to Simplicity', 'Dirge in Cymbeline', 'Ode to Evening' and 'How Sleep the Brave'.

69 Too nicely Jonson knew the critic's part,
   Nature in him was almost lost in Art.
   1743 'Verses addressed to Sir Thomas Hanmer'.

70 To fair Fidele's grassy tomb
   Soft maids and village hinds shall bring
   Each opening sweet of earliest bloom,
   And rifle all the breathing spring.
   1744 'Dirge in Cymbeline'.

71 How sleep the brave, who sink to rest,
   By all their country's wishes blest!
   1746 'How Sleep the Brave' (published 1748), no.1.

72 By fairy hands their knell is rung,
   By forms unseen their dirge is sung.
   1746 'How Sleep the Brave' (published 1748), no.2.

73 O thou, the friend of man assigned,
   With balmy hands his wounds to bind,
   And charm his frantic woe:
   When first Distress with dagger keen
   Broke forth to waste his destined scene,
   His wild unsated foe!
   1747 *Odes on Several Descriptive and Allegoric Subjects*, 'Ode to Pity', no.1.

74 Ah Fear! Ah frantic Fear!
   I see, I see thee near.
   1747 *Odes on Several Descriptive and Allegoric Subjects*, 'Ode to Fear', l.5–6.

75 Though taste, though genius bless
To some divine excess,
Faints the cold work till thou inspire the
  whole;
What each, what all supply
May court, may charm our eye,
Thou, only thou can'st raise the meeting soul!
1747 *Odes on Several Descriptive and Allegoric Subjects*, 'Ode to Simplicity', no.8.

76 Now air is hushed, save where the weak-eyed bat
With short shrill shriek flits by on leathern wing,
Or where the beetle winds
His small but sullen horn,
As oft he rises midst the twilight path,
Against the pilgrim borne in heedless hum.
1747 *Odes on Several Descriptive and Allegoric Subjects*, 'Ode to Evening', l.9–14.

77 While Spring shall pour his showers, as oft he wont,
And bathe thy breathing tresses, meekest Eve!
While Summer loves to sport
Beneath thy lingering light;
While sallow Autumn fills thy lap with leaves,
Or Winter, yelling through the troublous air,
Affrights thy shrinking train,
And rudely rends thy robes.
1747 *Odes on Several Descriptive and Allegoric Subjects*, 'Ode to Evening', l.41–8.

78 With eyes up-raised, as one inspired,
Pale Melancholy sate retired,
And from her wild sequestered seat,
In notes by distance made more sweet,
Poured thro' the mellow horn her pensive soul.
1747 'The Passions, An Ode for Music', l.57–61.

79 Love of peace, and lonely musing,
In hollow murmurs died away.
1747 'The Passions, An Ode for Music', l.67–8.

Colombo, John Robert 1936–
Canadian editor and poet.

80 Canada could have enjoyed:
English government,
French culture,
And American know-how.
Instead it ended up with:
English know-how,
French government,
And American culture.
1965 'O Canada', collected in Al Purdy (ed) *The New Romans* (1968).

Colton, Charles Caleb 1780–1832
British clergyman and writer. He was also a successful sportsman and was known for his gambling, which eventually led to his financial ruin and suicide.

81 Men will wrangle for religion; write for it; fight for it—anything but live for it.
1820 *Lacon*, vol.1, no.25.

82 When you have nothing to say, say nothing.
1820 *Lacon*, vol.1, no.183.

83 Imitation is the sincerest form of flattery.
1820 *Lacon*, vol.1, no.217.

84 Examinations are formidable even to the best prepared, for the greatest fool may ask more than the wisest man can answer.
1820 *Lacon*, vol.1, no.322.

85 If you would be known, and not know, vegetate in a village; if you would know, and not be known, live in a city.
1820 *Lacon*, vol.1, no.334.

Coltrane, John 1926–67
US jazz saxophonist. He was the most influential tenor and soprano saxophonist of the postwar era.

86 The main thing a musician would like to do is to give a picture to the listener of the many wonderful things he knows and senses in the universe.
1966 Quoted in sleeve-note to the re-issue of *Coltrane's Sound* (originally published 1961).

Colum, Padraic 1881–1972
Irish poet, playwright, novelist, biographer, critic and children's writer, a central figure in the Irish Literary Renaissance. Reflecting a peasant background, his work was realistic rather than romantic. His collections include *Wild Earth* (1907).

87 Sunset and silence! A man: around him earth savage, earth broken;
Beside him two horses—a plough!

Earth savage, earth broken, the brutes, the dawn-man there in the sunset,
And the Plough that is twin to the Sword, that is founder of cities!
1907 *Wild Earth*, 'The Plougher'.

88 My young love said to me, 'My brothers won't mind,
And my parents won't slight you for your lack of kind.'
Then she stepped away from me, and this she did say,
'It will not be long, love, till our wedding day.'
1907 *Wild Earth*, 'She Moved through the Fair'.

89 Then the wet, winding roads,
Brown bogs with black water;
And my thoughts on white ships
And the King o' Spain's daughter.
1907 'A Drover'.

90 Oh, to have a little house!
To own the hearth and stool and all!
The heaped-up sods upon the fire,
The pile of turf against the wall!
To have a clock with weights and chains
And pendulum swinging up and down,
A dresser filled with shining delph,
Speckled and white and blue and brown!
c.1907 'An Old Woman of the Roads'.

Columbus, Christopher Spanish name Cristóbal Colón 1451–1506
Genoese explorer, and discoverer of the New World (1492). His *Carta del descubrimiento* (1493) is the first European historical document about America.

91 Toda la cristiandad debe tomar alegría y hacer grandes fiestas, y dar gracias solemnes a la Santa Trinidad, con muchas oraciones solemnes por el tanto ensalzamiento que habrán, en tornándose tantos *pueblos a nuestra Santa Fe, y después por los bienes temporales que no solamente a la España, mas a todos los cristianos tendrán aquí refigerio y ganancia.* All Christendom ought to feel joyful and make great celebrations and give solemn thanks to the Holy Trinity with many solemn prayers for the great exaltation which it will have, in the turning of so many people to our holy faith, and afterwards for material benefits, since not only Spain but all Christians will hence have refreshment and profit.

1493 *Carta del descubrimiento* (translated as *The Letter in Spanish of Christopher Columbus*, 1889).

Comden, Betty *pseudonym of* Elizabeth Cohen 1919–2006

US screenwriter and lyricist, who worked with Adolph Green on a number of musicals. Her scripts include *On the Town* (1949), *Singin' in the Rain* (1952) and *Bells are Ringing* (1960).

92 I can stand anything but failure.
   1953 Line delivered by Oscar Levant in *The Band Wagon*.

93 The party's over, it's time to call it a day.
   1956 'The Party's Over' (with Adolphe Green, music by Jule Styne).

Commoner, Barry 1917–2012

US biologist closely associated with issues of ecology, public health and environmental policy.

94 Science is triumphant with far-ranging success, but its triumph is somehow clouded by growing difficulties in providing for the simple necessities of human life on earth.
   1966 *Science and Survival*.

95 The gap between brute power and human need continues to grow, as the power fattens on the same faulty technology that intensifies the need.
   1972 'The Closing Circle', in *Technology*.

Comnena, Anna 1083–1153

Byzantine princess and historian, daughter of Emperor Alexius I. She retired to a convent to write an account of her father's reign after failing to secure the imperial throne for her husband, Nicephorus Bryennius.

96 A mounted Kelt is irresistible; he would bore his way through the walls of Babylon.
   c.1148 Her description of the Frankish knights who passed through Constantinople on the First Crusade, 1097. *The Alexiad of Anna Comnena*, bk.13, ch.8 (translated by E R A Sewter).

Compton-Burnett, Dame Ivy 1892–1969

English novelist. Her novels, which explore the nuances of human relationships, include *Pastors and Masters* (1925), *Brothers and Sisters* (1929), *More Women than Men* (1933) and *Mother and Son* (1955).

97 'Well, of course, people are only human,' said Dudley to his brother, as they walked to the house behind the women. 'But it really does not seem much for them to be.'
   1939 *A Family and a Fortune*, ch.2.

98 People don't resent having nothing nearly as much as too little.
   1939 *A Family and a Fortune*, ch.4.

99 It will be a beautiful family talk, mean and worried and full of sorrow and spite and excitement. I cannot be asked to miss it in my weak state. I should only fret.
   1939 *A Family and a Fortune*, ch.10.

1 As regards plots I find real life no help at all. Real life seems to have no plots.
   1945 *Orion*, no.1, 'A Conversation'.

2 And people in life hardly seem definite enough to appear in print. They are not good or bad enough, or clever or stupid enough, or comic or pitiful enough.
   1945 *Orion*, no.1, 'A Conversation'.

3 We must use words as they are used, or stand aside from life.
   1955 *Mother and Son*, ch.9.

4 There is more difference within the sexes than between them.
   1955 *Mother and Son*, ch.10.

5 When I die people will say it is the best thing for me. It is because they know it is the worst. They want to avoid the feeling of pity.
   1961 *The Mighty and Their Fall*, ch.4.

6 There are different kinds of wrong. The people sinned against are not always the best.
   1961 *The Mighty and Their Fall*, ch.7.

7 There's not much to say. I haven't been at all deedy.
   1969 When asked about her life. In *The Times*, 30 Aug.

Comte, Auguste Isidore Marie Françoise 1798–1857

French social scientist, mathematician and philosopher of social science, whose work in logical positivism laid the foundations for contemporary social science.

8 To understand a science it is necessary to know its history.
   1851–4 *Système de politique positive* (*Positive Philosophy*).

Conant, James Bryant 1893–1978

US educator, President of Harvard University (1933–53).

9 There is only one proved method of assisting the advancement of pure science—that of picking men of genius, backing them heavily, and leaving them to direct themselves.
   1945 Letter to the *New York Times*, 13 Aug.

10 It seems as though I were in a lunatic asylum, but I am never sure who is the attendant and who the inmate.
   1950 Of Washington. Letter to Bernard Baruch, Feb. Quoted in James G Hershberg *James B Conant* (1993).

11 A Harvard education consists of what you learn at Harvard while you are not studying.
   Quoted in *Time*, 29 Sep 1986.

Condon, Richard 1915–96

US writer. He made his reputation with his successful novel of political intrigue, *The Manchurian Candidate* (1959).

12 In Mexico the gods ruled, the priests interpreted and interposed, and the people obeyed. In Spain, the priests ruled, the king interpreted and interposed, and the gods obeyed. A nuance in an ideological difference is a wide chasm.
   1961 *A Talent for Loving*, bk.1, ch.6.

13 He was an unzipped fly caught in forever amber.
   1967 *The Ecstasy Business*, ch.1.

14 What is art is not likely to be decided for decades or longer after the work has been produced—and then is often redecided—so we must not think badly if we regard literature as entertainment rather than as transcendent enlightenment.
1976 Comment in D L Fitzpatrick (ed) *Contemporary Novelists*.

15 She felt sexual urgings towards Yvonne in the manner that politicians feel an enormous sexual pull towards mirrors.
1978 *Bandicoot*, ch.21.

Confucius or K'ung Fu–tse, 'The Master K'ung' 551–479 BC

Chinese philosopher. He was Governor of Chung-tu, Minister of Works and later Minister of Justice. Although his social reform measures were popular, his enemies forced him into exile. His sayings are collected in the *Confucian Analects*, compiled by his pupils after his death.

16 Man has three ways of acting wisely. First, on meditation; that is the noblest. Secondly, on imitation; that is the easiest. Thirdly, on experience; that is the bitterest.
c.479 BC *The Analects*.

17 The people may be made to follow a course of action, but they may not be made to understand it.
c.479 BC *The Analects*.

18 When you meet someone better than yourself, turn your thoughts to becoming his equal. When you meet someone not as good as you are, look within and examine your own self.
c.479 BC *The Analects*.

19 When I have pointed out one corner of a square to anyone and he does not come back with the other three, I will not point it out to him a second time.
c.479 BC *The Analects*.

20 You can rob an army of its commander-in-chief, but you cannot deprive the humblest man of his free will.
c.479 BC *The Analects*.

21 But without the trust of the people, no government can stand.
c.479 BC *The Analects*.

22 He that in his studies wholly applies himself to labour and exercise, and neglects meditation, loses his time, and he that only applies himself to meditation, and neglects labour and exercise, only wanders and loses himself.
Quoted in Colin Jarman *The Guinness Dictionary of Sports Quotations* (1990).

Congreve, William 1670–1729

English dramatist and poet. His first publication was the novel *Incognita* (1692), and he translated Juvenal and wrote original verse. He is best remembered for his witty plays, including *Love for Love* (1695) and *The Way of the World* (1700).

23 I am always of the opinion with the learned, if they speak first.
1692 *Incognita*.

24 In my conscience I believe the baggage loves me, for she never speaks well of me herself, nor suffers any body else to rail at me.
1693 Bellemore to Sharper. *The Old Bachelor*, act 1, sc.3.

25 Man was by Nature Woman's cully made:
We never are, but by ourselves, betrayed.
1693 Lucy to Silvia. *The Old Bachelor*, act 3, sc.1.

26 Bilbo's the word, and slaughter will ensue.
1693 Bluffe to Sir Joseph. *The Old Bachelor*, act 3, sc.7.

27 If this be not love, it is madness, and then it is pardonable.
1693 Heartwell to Sylvia. *The Old Bachelor*, act 3, sc.10.

28 Eternity was in that moment.
1693 Bellmore to Laetitia. *The Old Bachelor*, act 4, sc.7.

29 Now am I slap-dash down in the mouth.
1693 Sir Joseph to Bluffe. *The Old Bachelor*, act 4, sc.9.

30 Thus grief still treads upon the heels of pleasure:
Married in haste, we may repent at leisure.
1693 Sharper to Setter. *The Old Bachelor*, act 5, sc.1.

31 Some by experience find those words mis-placed:
At leisure married, they repent in haste.
1693 Setter to Sharper. *The Old Bachelor*, act 5, sc.1.

32 I could find it in my heart to marry thee, purely to be rid of thee.
1693 Belinda to Bellmore. *The Old Bachelor*, act 5, sc.10.

33 Courtship to marriage, as a very witty prologue to a very dull play.
1693 Bellmore to Belinda. *The Old Bachelor*, act 5, sc.10.

34 It is the business of a comic poet to paint the vices and follies of human kind.
1693 *The Double Dealer*, epistle dedicatory.

35 Retired to their tea and scandal, according to their ancient custom.
1693 Mellefont to Charles. *The Double Dealer*, act 1, sc.1.

36 There is nothing more unbecoming a man of quality than to laugh; Jesu, 'tis such a vulgar expression of the passion!
1693 Lord Froth to Brisk. *The Double Dealer*, act 1, sc.4.

37 Tho' marriage makes man and wife one flesh, it leaves 'em still two fools.
1693 Cynthia to Mellefont. *The Double Dealer*, act 2, sc.3.

38 She lays it on with a trowel.
1693 Brisk to Lord Froth. *The Double Dealer*, act 3, sc.10.

39 See how love and murder will out.
1693 *The Double Dealer*, act 4, sc.6.

40 No mask like open truth to cover lies,
As to go naked is the best disguise.
1693 *The Double Dealer*, act 5, sc.6.

41 Has he not a rogue's face?…a haunting-look to me…has a damned Tyburn-face, without the benefit o' the Clergy.
1695 Of Sir Sampson. *Love for Love*, act 2, sc.7.

42 I came upstairs into the world; for I was born in a cellar.
1695 Jeremy. *Love for Love*, act 2, sc.7.

43 I know that's a secret, for it's whispered every where.
1695 Tattle to Scandal. *Love for Love*, act 3, sc.3.

44 He that first cries out stop thief, is often he that has stolen the treasure.
1695 Scandal to Mrs Foresight. *Love for Love*, act 3, sc.14.

45 Women are like tricks by sleight of hand, which, to admire, we should not understand.
1695 Valentine. *Love for Love*, act 4, sc.21.

46 A branch of one of your antediluvian families, fellows that the flood could not wash away.
1695 Sir Sampson to Angelica. *Love for Love*, act 5, sc.2.

47 To find a young fellow that is neither a wit in his own eye, nor a fool in the eye of the world, is a very hard task.
1695 Sir Sampson to Angelica. *Love for Love*, act 5, sc.2.

48 Aye, 'tis well enough for a servant to be bred at an University. But the education is a little too pedantic for a gentleman.
1695 Tattle to Jeremy. *Love for Love*, act 5, sc.3.

49 Nay, for my part I always despised Mr Tattle of all things; nothing but his being my husband could have made me like him less.
1695 Mrs Frail to Mrs Foresight. *Love for Love*, act 5, sc.11.

50 I confess freely to you, I could never look long upon a Monkey, without very Mortifying Reflections.
1695 Letter to John Dennis, 10 Jul.

51 Music hath charms to soothe a savage breast,
To soften rocks, or bend a knotted oak.
1697 Almeria to Leonora. *The Mourning Bride*, act 1, sc.1.

52 Heaven has no rage, like love to hatred turned,
Nor Hell a fury, like a woman scorned.
1697 Zara. *The Mourning Bride*, act 3, sc.8.

53 Is he then dead?
What, dead at last, quite, quite for ever dead!
1697 Almeria to Leonora. *The Mourning Bride*, act 5, sc.11.

54 They come together like the Coroner's Inquest, to sit upon the murdered reputations of the week.
1700 Fainall to Mirabell. *The Way of the World*, act 1, sc.1.

55 She once used me with that insolence that in revenge I took her to pieces; sifted her, and separated her failings; I studied 'em, and got 'em by rote. The catalogue was so large that I was not without hopes, one day or other, to hate her heartily.
1700 *The Way of the World*, act 1, sc.3.

56 Ay, ay, I have experience: I have a wife, and so forth.
1700 Fainall to Mirabell. *The Way of the World*, act 1, sc.3.

57 FAINALL: 'Tis for the honour of England that all Europe should know that we have blockheads of all ages.
MIRABELL: I wonder there is not an Act of Parliament to save the credit of the nation, and prohibit the exportation of fools.
1700 *The Way of the World*, act 1, sc.5.

58 A wit should no more be sincere than a woman constant; one argues a decay of parts, as t'other of beauty.
1700 *The Way of the World*, act 1, sc.6.

59 What, he speaks unseasonable truths sometimes, because he has not wit enough to invent an evasion.
1700 *The Way of the World*, act 1, sc.6.

60 I always take blushing either for a sign of guilt, or of ill breeding.
1700 Petulant to Mirabell. *The Way of the World*, act 1, sc.9.

61 To pass over youth in dull indifference, to refuse the sweets of life because they once must leave us, is as preposterous as to wish to have been born old, because we one day may be old. For my part, my youth may wear and waste, but it shall never rust in my possession.
1700 *The Way of the World*, act 2, sc.1.

62 Say what you will, 'tis better to be left than never to have been loved.
1700 Mrs Warwood to Mrs Fainall. *The Way of the World*, act 2, sc.1.

63 Beauty is the lover's gift.
1700 Mirabell. *The Way of the World*, act 2, sc.4.

64 Here she comes i' faith full sail, with her fan spread and streamers out, and a shoal of fools for tenders.
1700 Of Mirabell. *The Way of the World*, act 2, sc.5.

65 Nobody knows how to write letters; and yet one has 'em, one does not know why.—They serve one to pin up one's hair.
1700 *The Way of the World*, act 2, sc.5.

66 WITWOUD: Madam, do you pin up your hair with all your letters?
MILLAMANT: Only with those in verse, Mr Witwoud. I never pin up my hair with prose.
1700 *The Way of the World*, act 2, sc.5.

67 To please a fool is some degree of folly.
1700 *The Way of the World*, act 2, sc.6.

68 A fellow that lives in a windmill has not a more whimsical dwelling than the heart of a man that is lodged in a woman.
1700 *The Way of the World*, act 2, sc.7.

69 A little disdain is not amiss; a little scorn is alluring.
1700 Lady Wishfort to Foible. *The Way of the World*, act 3, sc.5.

70 Love's but the frailty of the mind,
When 'tis not with ambition joined;
A sickly flame, which if not fed expires;
And feeding, wastes in self-consuming fires.
1700 *The Way of the World*, act 3, sc.12.

71 Marriage is honourable, as you say; and if so, wherefore should cuckoldom be a discredit, being derived from so honourable a root?
1700 *The Way of the World*, act 3, sc.12.

72 I confess I have deserted the high place I once held of sighing at your feet.
1700 *The Way of the World*, act 3, sc.12.

73 O, nothing is more alluring than a levee from a couch in some confusion.
1700 Lady Wishfort to Foible. *The Way of the World*, act 4, sc.1.

74 Don't let us be familiar or fond, nor kiss before folks, like my Lady Fadler and Sir Francis: nor go to Hyde-Park together the first Sunday in a new chariot, to provoke eyes and whispers, and then never be seen there together again; as if we were proud of one another the first week, and ashamed of one another ever after... Let us be very strange and well-bred: Let us be as strange as if we had been married a great while, and as well-bred as if we were not married at all.
1700 Millamant to Mirabell. *The Way of the World*, act 4, sc.5.

75 These articles subscribed, if I continue to endure you a little longer, I may by degrees dwindle into wife.
1700 Millamant to Mirabell. *The Way of the World*, act 4, sc.5.

76 I hope you do not think me prone to any iteration of nuptials.
1700 Lady Wishfort to Whitwell disguised as Sir Roland. *The Way of the World*, act 4, sc.12.

77 Music alone with sudden charms can bind
The wand'ring sense, and calm the troubled mind.
c.1701 'Hymn to Harmony'.

78 Would I were free from this restraint,
Or else had hopes to win her;
Would she could make of me a saint,
Or I of her a sinner.
'Pious Selinda Goes to Prayers'.

Conklin, Edwin G(rant) 1863–1952

Professor of Embryology at Princeton. He was a specialist in the embryology of marine organisms.

79 Wooden legs are not inherited but wooden heads may be.
Recalled on his death, 21 Nov 1952.

Connally, John Bowden 1917–93
US politician and lawyer. He was Governor of Texas (1963–9).

80 A chess tournament disguised as a circus.
1964 Of US political conventions. In the *National Observer*. Quoted in Edwin A Roberts Jr *Elections 1964* (1964).

81 It's not a sin to be rich anymore—it's a miracle.
1988 In *Time*, 18 Jan.

82 All hat and no cattle.
1989 Responding to George Bush's claim to be a Texan. In the *New York Times*, 14 Feb.

Connally, Tom (Thomas Terry) 1877–1963
US Congressman and lawyer. He was Representative for Texas (1917–29) and a Senator (1929–53). A Democrat, he supported southern business interests and opposed anti-lynching legislation. He was a strong supporter of the UN and NATO.

83 Don't you ever shake that lanky Yankee finger at me.
1963 To Senator Charles Tobey. Reported in *Time*, 8 Nov.

Connell, James 1852–1929
Irish socialist and songwriter.

84 The people's flag is deepest red;
It shrouded oft our martyred dead.
And ere their limbs grew stiff and cold,
Their heart's blood dyed its every fold.
Then raise the scarlet standard high!
Within its shade we'll live or die.
Tho' cowards flinch and traitors sneer,
We'll keep the red flag flying here.
1889 'The Red Flag', official anthem of the Labour Party.

Connery, Sir Sean 1930–
Scottish actor who became an international film star in the role of secret agent James Bond.

85 It is Scotland's rightful heritage that its people should create a modern Parliament… This entire issue is above and beyond any political party.
1997 Speech in Edinburgh. In the *Daily Record*, 8 Sep.

86 We have waited nearly 300 years. My hope is that it will evolve with dignity and integrity and it will truly reflect the new voice of Scotland. My position on Scotland has never changed in 30-odd years. Scotland should be nothing less than an equal of other nations in the world.
1999 On the Scottish Parliament. In the *Daily Telegraph*, 27 Apr.

Connolly, Billy 1942–
Scottish comedian and actor.

87 Marriage is a wonderful invention; but then again so is a bicycle repair kit.
Duncan Campbell *Billy Connolly* (1976).

88 I spent the whole time battering people I liked and singing with my arm round people I loathed.
Talking about his drinking days. Quoted in Pamela Stephenson *Billy* (2001).

89 I decided to stop drinking while it was still my idea.
Quoted in Pamela Stephenson *Billy* (2001).

90 For me, it's about the desire to win. My audience becomes a crowd of wild animals and I have to be the lion-tamer or be eaten.
Quoted in Pamela Stephenson *Billy* (2001).

91 Life is a waste of time. Time is a waste of life. Get wasted all the time and you'll have the time of your life.
2005 *'Too Old To Die Young' Live in New York*.

Connolly, Cyril Vernon 1903–74
English author and journalist. He founded and edited the influential cultural journal *Horizon* (1939–50). His best-known books are *Enemies of Promise* (1938) and *The Unquiet Grave* (1944).

92 Better to write for yourself and have no public, than to write for the public and have no self.
1933 In the *New Statesman*, 25 Feb.

93 Destroy him as you will, the bourgeois always bounces up—execute him, expropriate him, starve him out *en masse*, and he reappears in your children.
1937 In the *Observer*, 7 Mar.

94 A great writer creates a world of his own and his readers are proud to live in it. A lesser writer may entice them in for a moment, but soon he will watch them filing out.
1938 *Enemies of Promise*, ch.1.

95 Literature is the art of writing something that will be read twice; journalism what will be read once.
1938 *Enemies of Promise*, ch.3.

96 As repressed sadists are supposed to become policemen or butchers, so those with an irrational fear of life become publishers.
1938 *Enemies of Promise*, ch.10.

97 I should like to see the custom introduced of readers who are pleased with a book sending the author some small cash token… Not more than a hundred pounds—that would be bad for my character—not less than half a crown—that would do no good to yours.
1938 *Enemies of Promise*, ch.13.

98 Whom the gods wish to destroy they first call promising.
1938 *Enemies of Promise*, ch.13.

99 There is no more sombre enemy of good art than the pram in the hall.
1938 *Enemies of Promise*, ch.14.

1 All charming people have something to conceal, usually their total dependence on the appreciation of others.
1938 *Enemies of Promise*, ch.16.

2 Humorists are not happy men. Like Beachcomber or Saki or Thurber they burn while Rome fiddles.
1938 *Enemies of Promise*, ch.16.

3 A private school has all the faults of a public school without any of its compensations.
1938 *Enemies of Promise*, ch.19.

4 I have called this style the Mandarin style… It is the style of those writers whose tendency is to make their language convey more than they mean or more than they feel, it is the style of most artists and all humbugs.
1938 *Enemies of Promise*, ch.20.

5 Were I to deduce any system from my feelings on leaving Eton, it might be called *The Theory of Permanent Adolescence*.
1938 *Enemies of Promise*, ch.24.

6 The more books we read, the sooner we perceive that the only function of a writer is to produce a masterpiece. No other task is of any consequence.
1944 *The Unquiet Grave*, pt.1.

7 There is no fury like an ex-wife looking for a new lover.
1944 *The Unquiet Grave*, pt.1.

8 In the sex war thoughtlessness is the weapon of the male, vindictiveness of the female.
1944 *The Unquiet Grave*, pt.1.

9 Life is a maze in which we take the wrong turning before we have learnt to walk.
1944 *The Unquiet Grave*, pt.1.

10 Everything is a dangerous drug to me except reality, which is unendurable.
1944 *The Unquiet Grave*, pt.1.

11 The civilization of one epoch becomes the manure of the next.
1944 *The Unquiet Grave*, pt.2.

12 The disasters of the world are due to its inhabitants not being able to grow old simultaneously.
1944 *The Unquiet Grave*, pt.2.

13 Imprisoned in every fat man a thin one is wildly signalling to be let out.
1944 *The Unquiet Grave*, pt.2.

14 The true index of a man's character is the health of his wife.
1944 *The Unquiet Grave*, pt.2.

15 We are all serving a life-sentence in the dungeon of self.
1944 *The Unquiet Grave*, pt.2.

16 Our memories are card-indexes consulted, and then put back in disorder by authorities whom we do not control.
1944 *The Unquiet Grave*, pt.2.

17 It is closing time in the gardens of the West and from now on an artist will be judged only by the resonance of his solitude or the quality of his despair.
1949 *Horizon*, no.120–1, Dec 1949– Jan 1950 (double issue, the final issue of the journal).

18 A romantic interest in our own sex, not necessarily carried as far as physical experiments, was the intellectual fashion.
Of Oxford during his student days. Quoted in Peter Quennell *The Marble Foot* (1977).

Connolly, James 1868–1916

Irish Labour leader and insurgent. He organized the Irish Socialist Republican party and founded *The Workers' Republic*, the first Irish socialist paper. He lectured in the US and organized strikes in Ireland, and was executed for his part in the 1916 Easter rebellion.

19 It is an axiom enforced by all the experience of the ages, that they who rule industrially will rule politically.
1909 *Socialism Made Easy*.

20 Don't be 'practical' in politics. To be practical in that sense means that you have schooled yourself to think along the lines, and in the grooves that those who rob you would desire you to think.
1909 *Socialism Made Easy*.

21 The day has passed for patching up the capitalist system; it must go. And in the work of abolishing it the Catholic and the Protestant, the Catholic and the Jew, the Catholic and the Freethinker, the Catholic and the Buddhist, the Catholic and the Mahometan will co-operate together… For, as we have said elsewhere, Socialism is neither Protestant nor Catholic, Christian nor Freethinker, Buddhist, Mahometan, nor Jew; it is only HUMAN.
1910 *Labour, Nationality, and Religion*.

22 The worker is the slave of capitalist society, the female worker is the slave of that slave.
1915 *The Re-conquest of Ireland*.

Connor, Sir William Neil *pseudonym* Cassandra 1909–67

English journalist, a columnist with the *Daily Mirror* from 1935 until his death.

23 As I was saying when I was interrupted, it is a powerful hard thing to please all of the people all of the time.
1946 On resuming his Cassandra column in the *Daily Mirror*, Sep, after the end of World War II.

Conrad, Joseph *originally* Jozef Teodor Konrad Nalecz Korzeniowski 1857–1924

Polish-born British novelist who joined an English merchant ship in 1878, and was naturalized in 1884 as a master mariner. The sea provided the background for much of his work, notably *Heart of Darkness* (1899) and *Lord Jim* (1900).

24 It is only those who do nothing that make no mistakes, I suppose.
1896 *An Outcast of the Islands*, pt.3, ch.2.

25 Any work that aspires, however humbly, to the condition of art should carry its justification in every line.
1897 *The Nigger of the Narcissus*, preface.

26 My task which I am trying to achieve is, by the power of the written word to make you hear, to make you feel—it is, before all, to make you *see*. That—and no more, and it is everything.
1897 *The Nigger of the Narcissus*, preface.

27 The conquest of the earth, which mostly means the taking it away from those who have a different complexion or slightly flatter noses than ourselves, is not a pretty thing when you look into it too much. What redeems it is an idea only.
1899 *Heart of Darkness*, pt.1 (first published in *Blackwood's Magazine*, collected in *Youth: A Narrative, and Two Other Stories*, 1902).

28 We live, as we dream—alone.
1899 *Heart of Darkness*, pt.1 (first published in *Blackwood's Magazine*, collected in *Youth: A Narrative, and Two Other Stories*, 1902).

29 Exterminate all the brutes!
1899 *Heart of Darkness*, pt.2 (first published in *Blackwood's Magazine*, collected in *Youth: A Narrative, and Two Other Stories*, 1902).

30 He cried in a whisper at some image, at some vision—he cried out twice, a cry that was no more than a breath: 'The horror! The horror!'
1899 Kurtz's final words. *Heart of Darkness*, pt.3 (first published in *Blackwood's Magazine*, collected in *Youth: A Narrative, and Two Other Stories*, 1902).

31 Mistah Kurtz—he dead.
1899 *Heart of Darkness*, pt.3 (first published in *Blackwood's Magazine*, collected in *Youth: A Narrative, and Two Other Stories*, 1902).

32 A man that is born falls into a dream like a man who falls into the sea... The way is to the destructive element submit yourself, and with the exertions of your hands and feet in the water make the deep, deep sea keep you up.
   1900 *Lord Jim*, ch.20.

33 You shall judge a man by his foes as well as by his friends.
   1900 *Lord Jim*, ch.34.

34 Suddenly a puff of wind, a puff faint and tepid and laden with strange odours of blossoms, of aromatic wood, comes out of the still night—the first sigh of the east on my face.
   1902 'Youth'.

35 The mysterious East, perfumed like a flower, silent like death, dark like a grave.
   1902 'Youth'.

36 I remember my youth and the feeling that it will never come back any more—the feeling that I could last for ever, outlast the sea, the earth, and all men; the deceitful feeling that lures us on to joys, to perils, to love, to vain effort—to death; the triumphant conviction of strength, the heat of life in the handful of dust, the glow in the heart that with every year grows dim, grows cold, grows small, and expires—and expires, too soon, too soon—before life itself.
   1902 'Youth'.

37 Action is consolatory. It is the enemy of thought and the friend of flattering illusions.
   1904 *Nostromo*, pt.1, ch.6.

38 Liberty of the imagination should be the most precious possession of a novelist.
   1905 'Books'.

39 To be hopeful in an artistic sense it is not necessary to think that the world is good. It is enough to believe that there is no impossibility of it being made so.
   1905 'Books'.

40 Of all the inanimate objects, of all men's creations, books are the nearest to us, for they contain our very thoughts, our ambitions, our indignations, our illusions, our fidelity to truth, and our persistent leaning towards error. But most of all they resemble us in their precarious hold on life.
   1905 'Books'.

41 The terrorist and the policeman both come from the same basket.
   1907 *The Secret Agent*, ch.4.

42 Some kind of moral discovery should be the object of every tale.
   1911 *Under Western Eyes*, prologue.

43 Words, as is well known, are the great foes of reality.
   1911 *Under Western Eyes*, prologue.

44 The scrupulous and the just, the noble, humane, and devoted natures; the unselfish and the intelligent may begin a movement—but it passes away from them. They are not the leaders of a revolution. They are its victims.
   1911 *Under Western Eyes*, pt.2, ch.3.

45 A belief in a supernatural source of evil is not necessary; men alone are quite capable of every wickedness.
   1911 *Under Western Eyes*, pt.2, ch.4.

46 All ambitions are lawful except those which climb upwards on the miseries or credulities of mankind.
   1912 *Some Reminiscences*, preface.

47 On the contrary, the mere fact of dealing with matters outside the general run of everyday experience laid me under the obligation of a more scrupulous fidelity to the truth of my own sensations. The problem was to make unfamiliar things credible.
   1915 *Within the Tides*, preface.

48 Thinking is the great enemy of perfection. The habit of profound reflection, I am compelled to say, is the most pernicious of all the habits formed by civilized man.
   1915 *Victory*, author's note.

49 It is not the clear-sighted who rule the world. Great achievements are accomplished in a blessed, warm fog.
   1915 *Victory*, author's note.

50 It was amazing to think that in those miles of human habitations there was not probably half a dozen pounds of nails.
   1917 Of Bangkok. *The Shadow-Line*.

51 In plucking the fruit of memory one runs the risk of spoiling its bloom.
   1920 *The Arrow of Gold*, author's note.

Conran, Shirley Ida *née Pearce* 1932–
English designer, fashion editor and author, first wife of the designer and businessman Sir Terence Conran. Her books include *Superwoman* (1975) and *Lace* (1982).

52 Our motto: Life is too short to stuff a mushroom.
   1975 *Superwoman*, epigraph.

Conroy, (Donald) Pat(rick) 1945–
US writer. His works include *The Prince of Tides* (1986) and *Beach Music* (1997).

53 It was like walking down the street with the Statue of Liberty.
   1995 On walking in Manhattan with the instantly recognizable Barbra Streisand. In *WAMU*, 4 Sep.

54 Humanity is best described as inhumanity.
   2009 *South of Broad*.

55 He treated the stars as though they were love songs written to him by God.
   2009 *South of Broad*.

56 The most powerful words in English are, 'Tell me a story.'
   2010 *My Reading Life*.

Constable, John 1776–1837
English landscape painter. With Turner, one of Britain's most important and best-loved landscape painters.

57 A gentleman's park is my aversion. It is not beauty because it is not nature.
   1822 In R B Beckett (ed) *Constable's Correspondence*, Suffolk Records Society (1962–70).

58 In Claude's landscape all is lovely—all amiable—all is amenity and repose;—the calm sunshine of the heart.
   1836 Lecture, 2 Jun. Quoted in C R Leslie *Memoirs of the Life of John Constable* (1843).

59 When I set down to make a sketch from nature, the first thing I try to do is to forget that I have ever seen a picture.
   Quoted in C R Leslie *Memoirs of the Life of John Constable* (1843).

60 There is nothing ugly; *I never saw an ugly thing in my life*: for let the form of an object be what it may—light, shade and perspective will always make it beautiful.
Quoted in C R Leslie *Memoirs of the Life of John Constable* (1843).

61 He seems to paint with tinted steam.
Of Turner. Quoted in *Treasures of the Fitzwilliam Museum* (1982).

Constant (de Rebecque), (Henri) Benjamin 1767–1830

French novelist and politician. He supported the Revolution in Paris (1795) and was banished (1802) for opposing Napoleon. On his return in 1814 he became leader of the liberal opposition. His best-known novel *Adolphe* (1816) is based on his relationship with Mme de Staël.

62 *L'art pour l'art, sans but, car tout but dénature l'art. Mais l'art atteint au but qu'il n'a pas.*
Art for art's sake, with no purpose, for any purpose perverts art. But art achieves a purpose which is not its own.
1804 *Journal intime*, 11 Feb, quoted in the *Revue Internationale*, 10 Jan 1887.

Constantine full name Flavius Valerius Aurelius Constantinus c.274–337 AD

Roman Emperor, who adopted Christianity c.312 AD. He founded a royal residence at Byzantium (Constantinople), an act of great historical importance.

63 *In hoc signo vinces.*
In this sign thou shalt conquer.
AD 312 'Constantine's Vision', quoted in Eusebius *Life of Constantine*.

Cook, Arthur James 1883–1931

Welsh miners' leader, General Secretary of the national union and a key figure in the General Strike of 1926.

64 Not a penny off the pay; not a second on the day.
1926 Miners' strike slogan, coined in a speech, 3 Apr. It is often rendered 'not a minute on the day'.

Cook, Captain James 1728–79

English navigator. He undertook expeditions to the Pacific, the Antarctic and the west coast of North America, charting all these regions. He was killed in Hawaii by local people as he landed to recover a stolen boat.

65 As to a Southern Continent, I do not believe any such thing exists, unless in a high altitude.
1768–71 *Captain Cook's Journal during his First Voyage Round the World made in H. M. Bark 'Endeavour'*.

66 Curse the scientists, and all science into the bargain.
Quoted in J C Beaglehole (ed) *The Voyage of the Resolution* (1961).

Cook, Peter 1937–94

English comedian. He appeared in revue at Cambridge University and went on to write and star in the revue *Beyond the Fringe* (1960).

67 We exchanged many frank words in our respective languages.
1961 Impersonation of Harold Macmillan. *Beyond the Fringe*.

68 I go to the theatre to be entertained. I don't want to see plays about rape, sodomy and drug addiction—I can get all that at home.
Comedy routine. Also used as a cartoon caption in the *Observer*, 8 Jul 1962.

Cook, Robin originally Robert Finlayson Cook 1946–2005

Scottish Labour politician. In 2001 he became Leader of the House of Commons, a position he resigned in 2003 over the war with Iraq.

69 Chicken masala is now Britain's true national dish, not only because it is the most popular, but because it is a perfect illustration of the way Britain absorbs and adapts external influences.
2001 Speech to the Social Market Foundation, London, 19 Apr.

70 Iraq probably has no weapons of mass destruction in the commonly understood sense of the term—namely a credible device capable of being delivered against a strategic city target.
2003 Speech to the House of Commons, following his resignation as Leader of the House, 17 Mar.

71 What has come to trouble me most over past weeks is the suspicion that if the hanging chads in Florida had gone the other way and Al Gore had been elected, we would not now be about to commit British troops.
2003 Speech to the House of Commons, following his resignation as Leader of the House, 17 Mar.

Cooke, (Alfred) Alistair 1908–2004

English-born US journalist and broadcaster, best known for his 'Letter from America', first broadcast by the BBC in 1946, which became the world's longest-running radio series with the same presenter. He retired shortly before his death.

72 All Presidents start out pretending to run a crusade, but after a couple of years they find they are running something much less heroic, much more intractable: namely, the Presidency.
1963 In *The Listener*.

73 An episode out of George Orwell rewritten by Charles Dickens.
1979 Of Gerald R Ford's succession to the US presidency on Richard M Nixon's resignation. *The Americans*.

74 Like a christening, a wedding, a graduation ceremony, a holy war, a revolution even…a fireworks display, a gaudy promise of what life ought to be, not life itself.
1979 Of elections. *The Americans*.

75 But after all it's not the winning that matters, is it? Or is it? It's—to coin a word—the amenities that count: the smell of the dandelions, the puff of the pipe, the click of the bat, the rain on the neck, the chill down the spine, the slow, exquisite coming on of sunset and dinner and rheumatism.
Quoted in Helen Exley *Cricket Quotations* (1992).

76 Canned music is like audible wallpaper.
Quoted in David Pickering *Brewer's Twentieth Century Music* (1994).

Coolidge, (John) Calvin 1872–1933

US Republican politician and 30th President (1923–9). A strong supporter of US business interests, he was re-elected in 1924 but refused renomination in 1928.

77 Civilization and profits go hand in hand.
1920 Speech, New York, 27 Nov.

78 There is no right to strike against the public safety by anybody, anywhere, at any time.

1919 Telegram to the President of the American Federation of Labor, while Coolidge was Governor of Massachusetts during the Boston police strike.

79 The chief business of the American people is business.
1925 Speech to the Society of Newspaper Editors, Washington, 17 Jan.

80 Prosperity is only an instrument to be used, not a deity to be worshipped.
1928 Speech, Boston, 11 Jun.

81 Perhaps one of the most important accomplishments of my Administration has been minding my own business.
1929 Press conference, Mar.

82 Patriotism is easy to understand in America. It means looking out for yourself while looking out for your country.
Attributed.

Cooper, Dame Gladys 1888–1971

English actress. She made her stage debut in 1905 and subsequently achieved stardom with her performance in Pinero's *The Second Mrs Tanqueray* (1922).

83 If this is what virus pneumonia does to one, I really don't think I shall bother to have it again.
1971 Last words.

Cooper, James Fenimore 1789–1851

US writer, a prolific novelist and essayist. He is now chiefly remembered for his 5-volume *Leatherstocking Tales*, which includes *The Last of the Mohicans* (1826).

84 The tendency of democracies is, in all things, to mediocrity.
1838 *The American Democrat*, 'On the Disadvantages of Democracy'.

85 Equality of condition is incompatible with civilization, and is found only to exist in those communities that are but slightly removed from the savage state. In practice, it can only mean a common misery.
1838 *The American Democrat*, 'On the Disadvantages of a Monarchy'.

86 Individuality is the aim of political liberty.
1838 *The American Democrat*, 'Individuality'.

87 It is a misfortune that necessity has induced men to accord greater license to this formidable engine, in order to obtain liberty, than can be borne with less important objects in view; for the press, like fire, is an excellent servant, but a terrible master.
1838 *The American Democrat*, 'On the Press'.

Cooper, William *pseudonym of* Harry Summerfield Hoff 1910–2002

English novelist. A barbed and witty satirist, he was a forerunner of the 'angry young man' school of the 1950s.

88 I would gladly have thrashed her for it. Unfortunately, thrashing your young woman doesn't make her admire you more as a novelist.
1950 *Scenes from Provincial Life*, pt.3, ch.1.

89 If girls aren't ignorant, they're cultured… You can't avoid suffering.
1950 *Scenes from Provincial Life*, pt.3, ch.2.

90 The trouble about finding a husband for one's mistress, is that no other man seems quite good enough.
1950 *Scenes from Provincial Life*, pt.3, ch.5.

Coover, Robert Lowell 1932–

US novelist, short-story writer and playwright, best known for his experimental stories.

91 The narrative impulse is always with us; we couldn't imagine ourselves through a day without it.
1986 In *Time Out*, 7 May.

Cope, Wendy 1945–

English poet. Her collections include *Making Cocoa for Kingsley Amis* (1986) and *If I Don't Know* (2001).

92 I used to think all poets were Byronic—
Mad, bad and dangerous to know.
And then I met a few.
1986 'Triolet'.
▶ See Lamb 504:75.

93 There are so many kinds of awful men—
One can't avoid them all. She often said
She'd never make the same mistake again:
She always made a new mistake instead.
1986 'Rondeau Redoublé'.

94 Bloody men are like bloody buses—
You wait for about a year
And as soon as one approaches your stop
Two or three others appear.
1992 *Serious Concerns*, 'Bloody Men', stanza 1.

95 My heart has made its mind up
And I'm afraid it's you.
1992 *Serious Concerns*, 'Valentine'.

96 Some socks are loners
They can't live in pairs.
2001 *If I Don't Know*, 'The Sorrow of Socks'.

97 Never trust a journalist.
2001 *If I Don't Know*, 'How to Deal with the Press'.

Copland, Aaron 1900–90

US composer. His early works employed jazz idioms, and he later drew on US folk tradition, as in the ballets *Billy the Kid* (1938) and *Appalachian Spring* (1944). He also composed film scores, operas and symphonies.

98 The whole problem can be stated quite simply by asking, 'Is there a meaning to music?' My answer would be, 'Yes'. And 'Can you state in so many words what the meaning is?' My answer to that would be 'No'.
1939 *What to Listen for in Music*.

99 The difference between Beethoven and Mahler is the difference between watching a great man walk down the street and watching a great actor act the part of a great man walking down the street.
Quoted in the *Wall Street Journal*, 9 Jun 1995.

Coppola, Francis Ford 1939–

US film director, screenwriter and producer. Among his films are *The Godfather* (1972; Part II 1974; Part III, 1990) and his controversial study of the Vietnam War, *Apocalypse Now* (1979).

1 When you start you want to make the greatest film in the world, but when you get into it, you just want to get it done, let it be passable and not embarrassing.
Quoted in Michael Schumacher *Francis Ford Coppola: A Film-Maker's Life* (1999).

Cornford, Frances née Darwin 1886–1960

English poet, the granddaughter of Charles Darwin. She lived most of her life in Cambridge, and her poetry deals with the minute details of emotion.

2 A young Apollo, golden-haired,
Stands dreaming on the verge of strife,
Magnificently unprepared
For the long littleness of life.
1910 Of Rupert Brooke.'Youth'.

3 O fat white woman whom nobody loves,
Why do you walk through the fields in gloves,
When the grass is soft as the breast of doves
And shivering-sweet to the touch?
Oh why do you walk through the fields in gloves,
Missing so much and so much?
1910 'To a Fat Lady Seen from a Train'.
▶ See Chesterton 221:8.

4 Now we know nothing, nothing is richer now
Because of all he was. O friend we have loved
Must it be thus with you?—and if it must be
How can men bear laboriously to live?
1915 'Rupert Brooke'.

5 I hope to meet my Maker brow to brow
And find my own the higher.
1954 'Epitaph for a Reviewer'.

Cornforth, Sir John Warcup 1917–2013

Australian organic chemist. Despite being totally deaf from childhood, he pioneered the study of enzyme stereochemistry and was awarded the Nobel prize for chemistry in 1975.

6 In a world where it is so easy to neglect, deny, pervert and suppress the truth, the scientist may find his discipline severe. For him, truth is so seldom the sudden light that shows new order and beauty; more often, truth is the uncharted rock that sinks his ship in the dark.
1975 Nobel prize speech.

Corwin, Thomas 1794–1865

US politician, Governor of Ohio (1840–2), Senator (1845–50) and Secretary of the Treasury (1850–3) under President Fillmore.

7 If I were a Mexican, I would tell you, 'Have you not enough room in your own country to bury your dead men? If you come into mine, we will greet you with bloody hands and hospitable graves.'
1846 Speech to the Senate against the American–Mexican War, 11 Feb.

Cory, William originally William Johnson 1823–92

English academic, translator and poet. He was assistant master at Eton (1845–72), when he wrote the 'Eton Boat Song', but he resigned over controversy about his friendships with pupils. He also tutored Mary Coleridge (1861–1907).

8 They told me, Heraclitus, they told me you were dead,
They brought bitter news to hear, and bitter tears to shed.
I wept as I remembered how often you and I
Had tired the sun with talking and sent him down the sky.
1858 *Ionica, Poems*, 'Heraclitus', his translation of an epigram by Callimachus.

9 A handful of grey ashes, long long ago at rest.
1858 *Ionica, Poems*, 'Heraclitus', his translation of an epigram by Callimachus.

10 You promise heavens free from strife,
Pure truth, and perfect change of will;
But sweet, sweet is this human life,
So sweet, I fain would breathe it still;
Your chilly stars I can forgo,
This warm kind world is all I know.
1858 *Ionica, Poems*, 'Mimnermus in Church'.

11 All beauteous things for which we live
By laws of space and time decay.
But Oh, the very reason why
I clasp them, is because they die.
1858 *Ionica, Poems*, 'Mimnermus in Church'.

12 Jolly boating weather
And a hay-harvest breeze,
Blade on the feather,
Shade off the trees;
Swing, swing together,
With your body between your knees.
1865 'Eton Boat Song'.

Coryate, Thomas c.1577–1617

English traveller and wit. In 1608 he set out on a journey on foot through central Europe, later travelling east as far as India. In 1611 he published *Coryat's Crudities Hastily Gobled Up in Five Moneths' Travells*.

13 Of all the pleasures in the world, travel is (in my opinion) the sweetest and most delightful.
1611 *Coryat's Crudities Hastily Gobled Up in Five Moneths' Travells*.

Costello, Elvis real name Declan Patrick McManus 1954–

English singer-songwriter and composer.

14 It would be like comparing blancmange and mustard gas.
2002 Asked how he would compare Tony Blair and Margaret Thatcher. Quoted on www.independent.co.uk.

15 There is something kind of absurd about people who live in such a comfortable, cushioned, spoiled society tattooing themselves and piercing themselves to make them appear tribal.
2002 In *Interview Magazine*, May.

16 Some music that I don't take to in modern orchestral stuff just seems to be trying to do something with an orchestra that Jimi Hendrix could do so much better with an electric guitar and a fuzzbox. Why create a hideous sound with violas when they were made to sound melodious and agreeable?
2002 In *The Irish Times*, 23 Mar.

17 The songs weren't theirs any more. They were everybody's.
2004 On why the Beatles stopped performing. *Rolling Stone*, 15 Apr.

Cotman, John Sell 1782–1842

English landscape painter and etcher, best known for his work in watercolour.

18 Three quarters of mankind, you know, mind more what is represented than how it is done.
Quoted in William Vaughn *Romantic Art* (1978).

Coubertin, Pierre de, Baron 1863–1937
French educationalist. He revived the Olympic Games at Athens in 1896, in the hope that they would foster national and international understanding through sport.

19 Women have but one task, that of crowning the winner with garlands.
1902 Quoted in Colin Jarman *The Guinness Dictionary of Sports Quotations* (1990).

20 The most important thing in the Olympic games is not winning but taking part—just as the most important thing in life is not the triumph but the struggle. The essential thing in life is not conquering but fighting well.
1908 Speech to Olympic Games officials, London, 24 Jul.

Coué, Émile 1857–1926
French pharmacist, pioneer of 'auto-suggestion'. He opened a free clinic in Nancy in 1910 and 'Couéism' subsequently attracted followers all round the world.

21 *Tous les jours, à tous points de vue, je vais de mieux en mieux.*
Every day, in every way, I am getting better and better.
1915 *De la suggestion et de ses applications*. Maxim recommended by Coué to his patients, to be repeated several times over on rising and on going to bed.

Coulter, Ann Hart 1961–
US political commentator.

22 It is a law of nature that everything run by the government will get more expensive and worse over time. Everything run by the private sector will get better and cheaper over time.
2013 Fox News, 21 Oct.

Coupland, Douglas 1961–
Canadian novelist. His *Generation X: Tales for an Accelerated Culture* (1991) was a cult novel defining the angst of the children of the baby boomers.

23 Generation X.
1991 From the title of his satiric novel *Generation X: Tales for an Accelerated Culture*. The phrase refers to young people born in the mid-1960s who are in no hurry to 'find themselves'.

24 MCJOB: A low-pay, low-prestige, low-dignity, no-future job in the service sector. Frequently considered a satisfying career choice for people who have never held one.
1991 *Generation X*, 'The Sun Is Your Enemy'.

25 HISTORICAL OVERDOSING: To live in a period of time when too much seems to happen.
1991 *Generation X*, 'The Sun Is Your Enemy'.

26 HISTORICAL SLUMMING: the act of visiting locations such as diners, smokestack industrial sites, rural villages—locations where time appears to have been frozen many years back—so as to experience relief when one returns back to 'the present'.
1991 *Generation X*, 'Our Parents Had More'.

27 BRAZILIFICATION: The widening gulf between the rich and the poor and the accompanying disappearance of the middle classes.
1991 *Generation X*, 'Our Parents Had More'.

28 CONSENSUS TERRORISM: The process that decides in-office attitudes and behavior.
1991 *Generation X*, 'Quit Recycling the Past'.

29 Marketing is essentially about feeding the poop back to diners fast enough to make them think they're still getting real food.
1991 *Generation X*, 'Quit Your Job'.

30 Shopping is Not Creating.
1991 *Generation X*, chapter heading.

31 Their talk was endless, compulsive, and indulgent, sometimes sounding like the remains of the English language after having been hashed over by nuclear war survivors for a few hundred years.
1991 *Generation X*, 'It Can't Last'.

32 I want to tell them that I envy their upbringings that were so clean, so free of *futurelessness*. And I want to throttle them for blithely handing over the world to us like so much skid-marked underwear.
1991 Claire speaking of her parents. *Generation X*, 'Eat Your Parents'.

33 BRADYISM: A multisibling sensibility derived from having grown up in large families...symptoms of *Bradyism* include a facility for mind games, emotional withdrawal in situations of overcrowding, and a deeply felt need for a well-defined personal space.
1991 *Generation X*, 'Define Normal'.

34 STRANGELOVE REPRODUCTION: Having children to make up for the fact that one no longer believes in the future.
1991 *Generation X*, 'Define Normal'.

35 PERSONALITY TITHE: A price paid for becoming a couple; previously amusing human beings become boring: *'Thanks for inviting us, but Noreen and I are going to look at flatware catalogs tonight. Afterward we're going to watch the shopping channel.'*
1991 *Generation X*, 'M T V Not Bullets'.

36 NOSTALGIA IS A WEAPON
1991 *Generation X*, 'Welcome Home from Vietnam, Son'.

37 TV and the Internet are good because they keep stupid people from spending too much time out in public.
2006 *JPod*.

38 Life always kills you in the end, but first it prevents you from getting what you want.
2007 *The Gum Thief*.

39 Fame without the money to insulate you from it is one of the most wretched human conditions possible.
2009 *Generation A*.

Cousins, Norman 1915–90
US editor and activist. As director of the *Saturday Review* (1942–71, 1973–7), he broadened its scope and circulation, campaigning on issues such as nuclear disarmament. His works include *Who Speaks for Man?* (1953).

40 The poet reminds men of their uniqueness and it is not necessary to possess the ultimate definition of this uniqueness. Even to speculate is a gain.
1978 In the *Saturday Review*, 15 Apr.

41 President Nixon's motto was, if two wrongs don't make a right, try three.
1979 In the *Daily Telegraph*, 17 Jul.

Cousteau, Jacques Yves 1910–97
French underwater explorer, who helped develop the Aqua-Lung (1943) and later became famous for a series of documentaries about the world's oceans.

42 The sea is the universal sewer.
   1971 Testimony before the House Committee on Science and Astronautics, 28 Jan.

Coventry, Thomas, 1st Baron 1578–1640
English judge.

43 The dominion of the sea, as it is an ancient and undoubted right of the crown of England, so it is the best security of the land… The wooden walls are the best walls of this kingdom.
   1635 Speech to the Star Chamber, 17 Jun. 'Wooden walls' refers to ships.

Coward, Sir Noël Peirce 1899–1973
English playwright, actor, director, composer and singer. His witty, stylish and sometimes biting plays include *Hay Fever* (1925), *Private Lives* (1930), *Blithe Spirit* (1941) and *Present Laughter* (1943). His films include the Academy Award-winning *In Which We Serve* (1941).

44 Poor Little Rich Girl.
   1925 Title of song.

45 There's sand in the porridge and sand in the bed,
   And if this is pleasure we'd rather be dead.
   1928 'The English Lido' (song).

46 I believe that since my life began
   The most I've had is just
   A talent to amuse.
   Heigho, if love were all!
   1929 'If Love Were All'.

47 Very flat, Norfolk.
   1930 *Private Lives*, act 1.

48 Extraordinary how potent cheap music is.
   1930 *Private Lives*, act 1.

49 Certain women should be struck regularly, like gongs.
   1930 *Private Lives*, act 3.

50 Mad dogs and Englishmen
   Go out in the midday sun.
   1931 'Mad Dogs and Englishmen' (song).

51 In the Philippines, there are lovely screens
   To protect you from the glare.
   1931 'Mad Dogs and Englishmen' (song).

52 Mad about the boy,
   It's pretty funny but I'm mad about the boy.
   He has a gay appeal
   That makes me feel
   There may be something sad about the boy.
   1932 'Mad About the Boy' (song).

53 People are wrong when they say the opera isn't what it used to be. It is what it used to be. That's what's wrong with it.
   1933 *Design for Living*.

54 Don't put your daughter on the stage, Mrs Worthington,
   Don't put your daughter on the stage.
   1935 'Mrs Worthington' (song).

55 The stately homes of England,
   How beautiful they stand,
   To prove the upper classes
   Have still the upper hand.
   1938 'The Stately Homes of England' (song).

56 Dear Mrs A,
   Hooray, hooray,
   At last you are deflowered.
   On this as every other day
   I love you—Noël Coward.
   1940 Telegram sent to Gertrude Lawrence the day after her marriage, quoted in Gertrude Lawrence *A Star Danced* (1945).

57 It's discouraging to think how many people are shocked by honesty and how few by deceit.
   1941 *Blithe Spirit*.

58 Don't Let's Be Beastly to the Germans.
   1943 Song title.

59 Speak clearly, don't bump into people, and if you must have motivation think of your pay packet on Friday.
   1962 Speech, Gallery First-Nighters' Club, sharing his advice to young actors. On other occasions he repeated it in the form 'Just say your lines and don't trip over the furniture'.

60 I never realised before that Albert married beneath him.
   c.1964 Quoted in Kenneth Tynan *Tynan on Theatre* (1964), alluding to the performance of a particular actress in the role of Queen Victoria.

61 Squash—that's not exercise, it's flagellation.
   Quoted in Colin Jarman *The Guinness Dictionary of Sports Quotations* (1990).

62 I love criticism just so long as it's unqualified praise.
   Attributed.

63 Two things should have been cut. The second act and that youngster's throat.
   After watching a play featuring a 14-year-old child star (sometimes identified as Bonnie Langford). Attributed.

64 He must have been a marvellously good shot.
   On hearing that an impresario he disliked had blown his brains out. Attributed.

65 I'm not very keen on Hollywood. I'd rather have a nice cup of cocoa really.
   Attributed.

Cowell, Simon (Phillip) 1959–
English television producer and celebrity presenter. Notorious for his acerbic responses to the acts performing in front of him, he has appeared as a talent judge on such popular television shows as *Pop Idol*, *The X Factor* and *Britain's Got Talent*.

66 Let me throw a mathematical dilemma at you—there's 500 left, well, how come the odds of you winning are a million to one?
   2001 *Pop Idol*.

67 If your lifeguard duties were as good as your singing, a lot of people would be drowning.
   2003 *American Idol*.

68 It was like ordering a hamburger and getting only the bun.
   2008 *American Idol*.

69 You have the showmanship of a peanut.
   2011 *Britain's Got Talent*.

70 I need a bath. And possibly an exorcism.
   2012 *Britain's Got Talent*.

Cowley, Abraham 1618–67

English poet, essayist and Royalist. He served Queen Henrietta Maria in exile during the Civil War, and only returned to England permanently at the Restoration. His works include a lyric collection, *Poetical Blossomes* (1633), and the epic *Davideis* (1656).

71 The world's a scene of changes, and to be
Constant, in Nature were inconstancy.
1647 *The Mistress*, 'Inconstancy'.

72 Such were the numbers which could call
The stones into the Theban wall.
Such miracles are ceased, and now we see
No towns or houses raised by poetry.
1656 *Poems*, 'Ode: Of Wit'.

73 Ye fields of Cambridge, our dear Cambridge, say,
Have ye not seen us walking every day?
Was there a tree about which did not know
The love betwixt us two?
1656 'On the Death of Mr William Harvey'.

74 Life is an incurable disease.
1656 'To Dr Scarborough', stanza 6.

75 Fill all the glasses there, for why
Should every creature drink but I,
Why, man of morals, tell me why?
1656 'Drinking'.

76 God the first garden made, and the first city Cain.
1668 *Essays, in Verse and Prose*, 'The Garden'.

77 This only grant me, that my means may lie
Too low for envy, for contempt too high.
1668 *Essays, in Verse and Prose*, 'Of Myself'.

Cowley, Hannah 1743–1809

English playwright and poet, an early exponent of the comedy of manners. She also wrote long narrative verses (1780–94).

78 But what is woman?—only one of Nature's agreeable blunders.
1779 *Who's the Dupe?*, act 2.

79 Five minutes! Zounds! I have been five minutes too late all my life-time!
1780 *The Belle's Stratagem*, act 1, sc.1.

Cowley, Malcolm 1898–1989

US writer and critic, known for his studies of US expatriate writers in the 1920s and for his works on William Faulkner.

80 A new generation does not appear every 30 years. It appears when writers of the same age join in a common revolt against the fathers and when, in the process of adopting a new life style, they find their own models and spokesmen.
Quoted in the *New York Times*, 29 Mar 1989.

81 I...chopped the manuscript down to size, or sawed it into fireplace lengths.
Quoted in the *New York Times*, 29 Mar 1989.

82 Going back to Hemingway's work after several years is like going back to a brook where you had often fished and finding the woods as deep and cool as they used to be.
Quoted in Pete Hamill *A Drinking Life* (1994).

Cowper, William 1731–1800

English poet, whose work reflects the evangelical revival. Regarded as a precursor of Wordsworth, he wrote *The Task* (1785), a long rural poem, and a collection of moral satires, *Poems* (1782).

83 Damned below Judas; more abhorred than he was.
c.1774 Of himself. 'Hatred and Vengeance, my eternal portion'.

84 O make this heart rejoice or ache;
Decide this doubt for me;
And if it be not broken, break—
And heal it if it be.
1779 *Olney Hymns*, 'The Contrite Heart'.

85 God moves in a mysterious way
His wonders to perform;
He plants his footsteps in the sea,
And rides upon the storm.
1779 *Olney Hymns*, 'Light Shining out of Darkness'.

86 Blind unbelief is sure to err,
And scan his work in vain;
God is his own interpreter,
And he will make it plain.
1779 *Olney Hymns*, 'Light Shining out of Darkness'.

87 Behind a frowning providence
He hides a smiling face.
1779 *Olney Hymns*, 'Light Shining out of Darkness'.

88 Oh! for a closer walk with God,
A calm and heav'nly frame;
A light to shine upon the road
That leads me to the Lamb!
1779 *Olney Hymns*, 'Walking with God'.

89 A tale should be judicious, clear, succinct;
The language plain, and incidents well linked;
Tell not as new what ev'ry body knows,
And new or old, still hasten to a close.
1782 *Poems*, 'Conversation', l.235–8.

90 The pipe with solemn interposing puff,
Makes half a sentence at a time enough;
The dozing sages drop the drowsy strain,
Then pause, and puff—and speak, and pause again.
1782 *Poems*, 'Conversation', l.245–8.

91 His wit invites you by his looks to come,
But when you knock it never is at home.
1782 *Poems* 'Conversation', l.303–4.

92 The discumbered Atlas of the state.
1782 *Poems*, 'Retirement'.

93 He likes the country, but in truth must own,
Most likes it, when he studies it in town.
1782 *Poems*, 'Retirement'.

94 Religion Caesar never knew
Thy posterity shall sway,
Where his eagles never flew,
None as invincible as they.
1782 *Poems*, 'Boadicea: an Ode'.

95 Rome shall perish—write that word
In the blood that she has spilt.
1782 *Poems*, 'Boadicea: an Ode'.

96 I am monarch of all I survey,
My right there is none to dispute;
From the centre all round to the sea,
I am lord of the fowl and the brute.
O Solitude! where are the charms
That sages have seen in thy face?
Better dwell in the midst of alarms,
Than reign in this horrible place.
1782 *Poems*, 'Verses Supposed to be Written by Alexander Selkirk, During His Solitary Abode in the Island of Juan Fernandez'.

97 I am out of humanity's reach.
   1782 *Poems*, 'Verses Supposed to be Written by Alexander Selkirk, During His Solitary Abode in the Island of Juan Fernandez'.

98 When I think of my own native land,
   In a moment I seem to be there;
   But alas! recollection at hand
   Soon hurries me back to despair.
   1782 *Poems*, 'Verses Supposed to be Written by Alexander Selkirk, During His Solitary Abode in the Island of Juan Fernandez'.

99 Grief is itself a med'cine.
   1782 *Poems*, 'Charity', l.159.

1 He found it inconvenient to be poor.
   1782 *Poems*, 'Charity', l.189.

2 Spare the poet for his subject's sake.
   1782 *Poems*, 'Charity', l.636.

3 The man that hails you Tom or Jack,
   And proves by thumps upon your back
   How he esteems your merit,
   Is such a friend, that one had need
   Be very much his friend indeed
   To pardon or to bear it.
   1782 *Poems*, 'Friendship', l.169–74.

4 Remorse, the fatal egg by pleasure laid.
   1782 *Poems*, 'The Progress of Error', l.239.

5 As creeping ivy clings to wood or stone,
   And hides the ruin that it feeds upon,
   So sophistry, cleaves close to, and protects
   Sin's rotten trunk, concealing its defects.
   1782 *Poems*, 'The Progress of Error', l.285–8.

6 How much a dunce that has been sent to roam
   Excels a dunce that has been kept at home.
   1782 *Poems*, 'The Progress of Error', l.415–6.

7 Laugh at all you trembled at before.
   1782 *Poems*, 'The Progress of Error', l.592.

8 Our severest winter, commonly called the spring.
   1783 Letter to Rev William Unwin, 8 Jun.

9 There is a mixture of evil in everything we do; indulgence encourages us to encroach, while we exercise the rights of children, we become childish.
   1783 Letter to Rev William Unwin, 7 Sep.

10 Thus first necessity invented stools,
   Convenience next suggested elbow-chairs,
   And luxury the accomplished sofa last.
   1785 *The Task*, bk.1, 'The Sofa', l.86–8.

11 God made the country, and man made the town.
   1785 *The Task*, bk.1, 'The Sofa', l.749.

12 At eve
   The moonbeam, sliding softly in between
   The sleeping leaves, is all the light they wish,
   Birds warbling all the music.
   1785 *The Task*, bk.1, 'The Sofa'.

13 England, with all thy faults I love thee still—
   My country!
   1785 *The Task*, bk.2, 'The Timepiece', l.206–7.

14 There is a pleasure in poetic pains
   Which only poets know.
   1785 *The Task*, bk.2, 'The Timepiece', l.285–6.

15 Variety's the spice of life,
   That gives it all its flavour.
   1785 *The Task*, bk.2, 'The Timepiece', l.606–7.

16 Defend me, therefore, common sense, say I,
   From reveries so airy, from the toil
   Of dropping buckets into empty wells,
   And growing old in drawing nothing up!
   1785 *The Task*, bk.3, 'The Garden', l.187–90.

17 Detested sport,
   That owes its pleasure to another's pain.
   1785 Of hunting. *The Task*, bk.3, 'The Garden', l.326–7.

18 Studious of laborious ease.
   1785 *The Task*, bk.3, 'The Garden', l.361.

19 Now stir the fire, and close the shutters fast,
   Let fall the curtains, wheel the sofa round,
   And, while the bubbling and loud-hissing urn
   Throws up a steamy column, and the cups,
   That cheer but not inebriate, wait on each,
   So let us welcome peaceful evening in.
   1785 *The Task*, bk.4, 'The Winter Evening', l.34–9.

20 But war's a game, which, were their subjects wise,
   Kings should not play at. Nations would do well
   To extort their truncheons from the puny hands
   Of heroes, whose infirm and baby minds
   Are gratified with mischief, and who spoil,
   Because men suffer it, their toy the world.
   1785 *The Task*, bk.5, 'The Winter Morning Walk', l.187–92.

21 Knowledge dwells
   In heads replete with thoughts of other men;
   Wisdom in minds attentive to their own.
   1785 *The Task*, bk.6, 'The Winter Walk at Noon', l.89–91.

22 Knowledge is proud that he has learned so much;
   Wisdom is humble that he knows no more.
   1785 *The Task*, bk.6, 'The Winter Walk at Noon', l.96–7.

23 Nature is but a name for an effect,
   Whose cause is God.
   1785 *The Task*, bk.6, 'The Winter Walk at Noon', l.223.

Crabbe, George 1754–1832

English poet and clergyman, whose early career was spent in poverty until Edmund Burke befriended him. His best-known poem, *The Village* (1783), is a bleak account of rural life.

24 Lo! the poor toper whose untutored sense,
   Sees bliss in ale, and can with wine dispense;
   Whose head proud fancy never taught to steer,
   Beyond the muddy ecstasies of beer.
   1775 *Inebriety, a Poem*, pt.1, l.132–5.

25 With awe, around these silent walks I tread;
   These are the lasting mansions of the dead.
   1781 *The Library* (published 1808), l.105–6.

26 Lo! all in silence, all in order stand,
   And mighty folios first, a lordly band:
   Then quartos their well-ordered ranks maintain,
   And light octavos fill a spacious plain;
   See yonder, ranged in more frequented rows,
   A humbler band of duodecimos.
   1781 *The Library* (published 1808), l.128–33.

27 Fashion, though Folly's child, and guide of fools,
   Rules e'en the wisest, and in learning rules.
   1781 *The Library* (published 1808), l.167–8.

28 Coldly profane and impiously gay.
   1781 *The Library* (published 1808), l.265.

29 Yes, thus the Muses sing of happy swains,
   Because the Muses never knew their pains:
   They boast their peasants' pipes, but peasants now
   Resign their pipes and plod behind the plough.
   1783 *The Village*, bk.1, 1.21–4.

30 I grant indeed that fields and flocks have charms,
   For him that gazes or for him that farms.
   1783 *The Village*, bk.1, 1.39–40.

31 I paint the cot,
   As truth will paint it, and as bards will not.
   1783 *The Village*, bk.1, 1.53–4.

32 Where Plenty smiles—alas! she smiles for few,
   And those who taste not, yet behold her store,
   Are as the slaves that dig the golden ore,
   The wealth around them makes them doubly
     poor.
   1783 *The Village*, bk.1, 1.136–9.

33 The cold charities of man to man.
   1783 *The Village*, bk.1, 1.245.

34 A potent quack, long versed in human ills,
   Who first insults the victim whom he kills;
   Whose murd'rous hand a drowsy bench protect,
   And whose most tender mercy is neglect.
   1783 *The Village*, bk.1, 1.282.

35 The murmuring poor, who will not fast in peace.
   1785 *The Newspaper*, 1.158.

36 A master passion is the love of news.
   1785 *The Newspaper*, 1.279.

37 Our farmers round, well pleased with constant gain,
   Like other farmers, flourish and complain.
   1807 *Poems*, 'The Parish Register', pt.1, 1.273–4.

38 'What is a church?'—Our honest sexton tells,
   "Tis a tall building, with a tower and bells.'
   1810 *The Borough*, letter 2, 'The Church', 1.11–12.

39 Virtues neglected then, adored become,
   And graces slighted, blossom on the tomb.
   1810 *The Borough*, letter 2, 'The Church', 1.133–4.

40 Ye Lilies male! think (as your tea you sip,
   While the Town small-talk flows from lip to lip;
   Intrigues half-gathered, conversation-scraps,
   Kitchen-cabals, and nursery-mishaps),
   If the vast world may not some scene produce,
   Some state where your small talents might
     have use.
   1810 *The Borough*, letter 3, 'The Vicar', 1.69–74.

41 Habit with him was all the test of truth,
   'It must be right: I've done it from my youth.'
   1810 *The Borough*, letter 3, 'The Vicar', 1.138–9.

42 There anchoring, Peter chose from man to hide,
   There hang his head, and view the lazy tide
   In its hot slimy channel slowly glide;
   Where the small eels that left the deeper way
   For the warm shore, within the shallows play;
   Where gaping mussels, left upon the mud,
   Slope their slow passage to the fallen flood.
   1810 *The Borough*, letter 22, 'Peter Grimes', 1.185–91.

43 He nursed the feelings these dull scenes produce,
   And loved to stop beside the opening sluice;
   Where the small stream, confined in narrow
     bound,
   Ran with a dull, unvaried, sad'ning sound;
   Where all presented to the eye or ear,
   Oppressed the soul! with misery, grief, and fear.
   1810 *The Borough*, letter 22, 'Peter Grimes', 1.194–9.

44 That all was wrong because not all was right.
   1812 *Tales*, 'The Convert', 1.313.

45 He tried the luxury of doing good.
   1819 *Tales of the Hall*, 'Boys at School', 1.139.

46 'The game,' said he, 'is never lost till won.'
   1819 *Tales of the Hall*, 'Gretna Green', 1.334.

47 The face the index of a feeling mind.
   1819 *Tales of the Hall*, 'Lady Barbara', 1.124.

48 Secrets with girls, like loaded guns with boys,
   Are never valued till they make a noise.
   1819 *Tales of the Hall*, 'The Maid's Story', 1.84–5.

Craig, Daniel Wroughton 1968–

English actor. He is best known as James Bond, a part he first played in the 2006 movie *Casino Royale*.

49 Why is it that people who can't take advice always insist
     on giving it?
   2006 As James Bond in *Casino Royale* (screenplay by Neal Purvis, Robert Wade, and Paul Haggis).

50 Do I look like I give a damn?
   2006 As James Bond in *Casino Royale*, when asked if he wanted his martini shaken or stirred.

Craik, Dinah Maria née Mulock 1826–87

English novelist, essayist and poet. She published over 20 novels, the best known being *John Halifax, Gentleman* (1858). Although sentimental, her work emphasizes the self-reliance of women.

51 Leonora, Leonora,
   How the word rolls—*Leonora*—
   Lion-like, in full-mouthed sound,
   Marching o'er the metric ground
   With a tawny tread sublime;
   So your name moves, Leonora,
   Down my desert rhyme.
   1881 *Collected Poems*, 'Leonora'.

Crane, (Harold) Hart 1899–1932

US poet. He was an alcoholic who led a troubled life which ended in suicide. He has come to be regarded as one of the most important US poets of the 20c.

52 The Cross alone has flown the wave.
   But since the Cross sank, much that's warped and
     cracked
   Has followed in its name, has heaped its grave.
   1920 'The Mermen', in *The Dial*, no.85, Jul.

53 The bottom of the sea is cruel.
   1926 *White Buildings*, 'Voyages', pt.1.

54 And onwards, as bells off San Salvador
   Salute the crocus lustres of the stars,
   In these poinsettia meadows of her tides.
   1926 *White Buildings*, 'Voyages', pt.2.

55 Bequeath us no earthly shore until
   Is answered in the vortex of our grave
   The seal's wide spindrift gaze toward paradise.
   1926 *White Buildings*, 'Voyages', pt.2.

56 Light wrestling there incessantly with light,
    Star kissing star through wave on wave unto
    Your body rocking!
    1926 *White Buildings*, 'Voyages', pt.3.

57 Slow tyranny of moonlight, moonlight loved
    And changed.
    1926 *White Buildings*, 'Voyages', pt.5.

58 O Sleepless as the river under thee,
    Vaulting the sea, the prairies' dreaming sod,
    Unto us lowliest sometime sweep, descend
    And of the curveship lend a myth to God.
    1927 'To Brooklyn Bridge', in *The Dial*, Jun.

59 You who desired so much—in vain to ask—
    Yet fed your hunger like an endless task,
    Dared dignify the labor, bless the quest—
    Achieved that stillness ultimately best,
    Being, of all, least sought for: Emily, hear!
    1929 'To Emily Dickinson', in *The Nation*, 29 Jun.

60 The last bear, shot drinking in the Dakotas
    Loped under wires that span the mountain stream.
    Keen instruments, strung to a vast precision
    Bind town to town and dream to ticking dream.
    1930 *The Bridge*, 'The River'.

61 Hobo-trekkers that forever search
    An empire wilderness of freight and rails.
    1930 *The Bridge*, 'The River'.

62 Dead echoes! But I knew her body there,
    Time like a serpent down her shoulder, dark,
    And space, an eaglet's wing, laid on her hair.
    1930 *The Bridge*, 'The River'.

63 Few evade full measure of their fate.
    1930 *The Bridge*, 'The River'.

64 Thin squeaks of radio static,
    The captured fume of space foams in our ears.
    1930 *The Bridge*, 'Cape Hatteras'.

65 Stars scribble on our eyes the frosty sagas,
    The gleaming cantos of unvanquished space.
    1930 *The Bridge*, 'Cape Hatteras'.

66 Cowslip and shad-blow, flaked like tethered foam
    Around bared teeth of stallions, bloomed that spring
    When first I read thy lines, rife as the loam
    Of prairies, yet like breakers cliffward leaping!
    1930 Of Walt Whitman. *The Bridge*, 'Cape Hatteras'.

67 Our Meistersinger, thou set breath in steel;
    And it was thou who on the boldest heel
    Stood up and flung the span on even wing
    Of that great Bridge, our Myth, whereof I sing.
    1930 On Whitman and Brooklyn Bridge. *The Bridge*, 'Cape Hatteras'.

68 Our tongues recant like beaten weather vanes.
    1930 *The Bridge*, 'The Tunnel'.

69 The phonographs of hades in the brain
    Are tunnels that re-wind themselves, and love
    A burnt match skating in a urinal.
    1930 *The Bridge*, 'The Tunnel'.

70 The bell-rope that gathers God at dawn
    Dispatches me as though I dropped down the knell
    Of a spent day.
    1932 'The Broken Tower', in the *New Republic*, 8 Jun.

Crane, Stephen 1871–1900

US writer. His reputation rests on *The Red Badge of Courage* (1895), which relates the experience of a soldier in the Civil War. His well-known short stories include *The Open Boat* (1898). He died of tuberculosis in Baden Baden.

71 The Red Badge of Courage.
    1895 Title of novel.

72 'It is bitter—bitter,' he answered;
    'But I like it
    Because it is bitter,
    And because it is my heart.'
    1895 *The Black Riders*, 'The Heart'. The speaker is a 'naked, bestial' creature which the narrator sees eating its heart in the desert.

73 None of them knew the color of the sky.
    1898 *The Open Boat*.

74 A man said to the universe:
    'Sir, I exist!'
    'However,' replied the universe,
    'The fact has not created in me
    A sense of obligation.'
    1899 *A Man Said to the Universe*.

Cranfield, Ingrid 1945–

Australian-born writer and journalist. Her books on adventurers and travellers include *The Challengers* (1976) and *Skiing down Everest and Other Crazy Adventures* (1983).

75 To Hunt an 'assault' on the mountain merely meant a concerted, military-style operation; whereas to Shipton 'assault' sounded more like a criminal offence.
    1978 Of the contrast in approach to the climbing of Mt Everest between Eric Shipton, originally appointed as leader of the 1953 expedition, and John Hunt, who replaced him. In *Expedition*, vol.8, no.4, Jul.

Cranmer, Thomas 1489–1556

English Protestant prelate, Archbishop of Canterbury (1533–53), largely responsible for the Book of Common Prayer (1549, 1552). He was convicted of treason for his part in the plan to divert the succession of the English Crown to Lady Jane Grey, and was burned at the stake.

76 This hath offended! Oh this unworthy hand!
    1556 Last words at the stake, referring to the hand which had signed several recantations, later withdrawn.

Crashaw, Richard c.1613–1649

English metaphysical poet. He abandoned Puritanism for Catholicism, but lost his fellowship at Cambridge in 1643 and went to the Continent. His works include *Steps to the Temple* (1646) and *The Delights of the Muses* (1646).

77 *Nympha pudica Deum vidit, et erubuit.*
    The conscious water saw its God, and blushed.
    1634 Of the water which Jesus turned into wine at Cana. *Epigrammata Sacra*, 'Aquae in Vinum Versae' (translated by Dryden).

78 Wellcome, all Wonders in one sight!
    Eternity shut in a span.
    Summer in Winter, Day in Night.
    Heaven in Earth and God in Man.
    1646 'Hymn of the Nativity' (published 1652), l.79.

79 I would be married, but I'd have no wife,
    I would be married to a single life.
    1646 'On Marriage'.

80 Th' have left thee naked, Lord, O that they had!
This garment too I would they had denied.
Thee with thyself they have too richly clad,
Opening the purple wardrobe of thy side.
O never could be found garments too good
For thee to wear, but these, of thine own blood.
1646 'On Our Crucified Lord, Naked and Bloody'.

81 And now where'er he strays
Among the Galilean mountains
Or more unwelcome ways,
He's followed by two faithful fountains;
Two walking baths; two weeping motions;
Portable and compendious oceans.
1646 'Saint Mary Magdalene, or The Weeper'.

82 What heaven-entreated heart is this,
Stands trembling at the gate of bliss,
Holds fast the door, yet dares not venture
Fairly to open it, and enter?
1646 'To the Noblest and Best of Ladies, the Countess of Denbigh'.

83 Say, lingering fair! why comes the birth
Of your brave soul so slowly forth?
1646 'To the Noblest and Best of Ladies, the Countess of Denbigh'.

84 What yet fantastic bands
Keep the free heart from its own hands!
1646 'To the Noblest and Best of Ladies, the Countess of Denbigh'.

85 Yield, then, O yield, that love may win
The fort at last, and let life in.
1646 'To the Noblest and Best of Ladies, the Countess of Denbigh'.

86 In love's field was never found
A nobler weapon than a wound.
'The Flaming Heart Upon the Book and Picture of Saint Teresa', collected in *Carmen Deo Nostro* (published posthumously, 1652).

87 All thy brim-filled bowls of fierce desire
'The Flaming Heart Upon the Book and Picture of Saint Teresa', collected in *Carmen Deo Nostro* (published posthumously, 1652).

Craster, Mrs Edmund d.1874

88 The centipede was happy quite,
Until the toad in fun
Asked him which leg went after which,
Which drove him into such a pitch
He lay distracted in a ditch,
Considering how to run.
Attributed.

Crawford, Joan *originally* Lucille Fay le Sueur 1904–77

US film actress. Originally a nightclub dancer, she began in silent films in 1925 and found fame in the 1930s and 1940s.

89 I found that incredible thing, a public.
Quoted in Alexander Walker *Joan Crawford* (1983).

Crichton, Michael 1942–2008

US writer and film-maker. His many scientific and medical thrillers include *The Andromeda Strain* (1969), *Jurassic Park* (1990) and *Timeline* (1999).

90 Physics was the first of the natural sciences to become fully modern and highly mathematical. Chemistry followed in the wake of physics, but biology, the retarded child, lagged far behind.
1969 *The Andromeda Strain*.

91 There is always a cause for fear. The cause may change over time, but the fear is always with us.
2004 *State of Fear*.

92 Do you know what we call opinion in the absence of evidence? We call it prejudice.
2004 *State of Fear*.

93 Nobody wants to feel they're *not* a rebel.
2006 *Next*.

Crick, Francis Harry Compton 1916–2004

English molecular biologist, winner (with James Watson and Maurice Wilkins) of the Nobel prize for physiology or medicine in 1962 for work on the structure of DNA.

94 We have discovered the secret of life!
1953 Announcement, with James Watson, to the patrons of The Eagle public house in Cambridge on solving the structure of DNA.
▶ See Watson 922:40.

95 Almost all aspects of life are engineered at the molecular level, and without understanding molecules we can only have a very sketchy understanding of life itself.
1988 *What Mad Pursuit*, ch.5.

Cripps, Arthur S(hearly) 1869–1952

English clergyman. He was the writer of occasional verse, mainly on rural or religious themes.

96 England has greater counties—
Their peace to hers is small;
Low hills, rich fields, calm rivers,
In Essex seek them all.
Quoted in S P B Mais and Tom Stephenson (eds) *Lovely Britain* (c.1930).

Cripps, Sir (Richard) Stafford 1889–1952

English Labour politician and economist, expelled from the Party for his opposition to appeasement (1939). In 1945 he was readmitted and subsequently became Chancellor of the Exchequer, with a successful austerity policy.

97 There is only a certain sized cake to be divided up, and if a lot of people want a larger slice they can only take it from others who would, in terms of real income, have a smaller one.
1948 Speech, Trades Union Congress, 7 Sep.

Crisp, Quentin 1908–99

English writer. He achieved notoriety with the publication of *The Naked Civil Servant* (1968), an account of his experiences growing up as a flamboyant gay young man in England.

98 Keeping up with the Joneses was a full-time job with my mother and father. It was not until many years later when I lived alone that I realized how much cheaper it was to drag the Joneses down to my level.
1968 *The Naked Civil Servant*, ch.1.

99 As soon as I stepped out of my mother's womb on to dry land, I realized that I had made a mistake…but the trouble with children is that they are not returnable.
1968 *The Naked Civil Servant*, ch.2.

1 This woman did not fly to extremes, she lived there.
1968 *The Naked Civil Servant*, ch.3.

2 I don't hold with abroad and think that foreigners speak English when our backs are turned.
1968 *The Naked Civil Servant*, ch.4.

3 If one is not going to take the necessary precautions to avoid having parents, one must undertake to bring them up.
1968 *The Naked Civil Servant*, ch.5.

4 There was no need to do any housework after all. After the first four years the dirt doesn't get any worse.
1968 *The Naked Civil Servant*, ch.15.

5 Life was a funny thing that happened to me on the way to the grave.
1968 *The Naked Civil Servant*, ch.18.

6 I became one of the stately homos of England.
1968 *The Naked Civil Servant*, ch.24.

7 An autobiography is an obituary in serial form with the last instalment missing.
1968 *The Naked Civil Servant*, ch.29.

8 In England, the system is benign and the people are hostile. In America, the people are friendly—and the system is brutal!
1985 In *The Guardian*, 23 Oct.

Critchfield, Richard Patrick 1931–94

US journalist. His books include *The Long Charade: Political Subversion in the Vietnam War* (1968) and *An American Looks at Britain* (1990).

9 What people read most of the time should be as worth mentioning as what they read almost none of the time.
1990 *An American Looks at Britain*.

Critchley, Sir Julian Michael Gordon 1930–2000

English Conservative MP, writer and broadcaster, known for his acerbic and witty comments on Westminster life.

10 I was told when a young man that the two occupational hazards of the Palace of Varieties were alcohol and adultery. The hurroosh that follows the intermittent revelation of the sexual goings-on of an unlucky MP has convinced me that the only safe pleasure for a parliamentarian is a bag of boiled sweets.
1982 In *The Listener*, 10 Jun.

11 She has been beastly to the Bank of England, has demanded that the BBC 'set its house in order' and tends to believe the worst of the Foreign and Commonwealth Office. She cannot see an institution without hitting it with her handbag.
1982 Profile of Margaret Thatcher in *The Times*, 21 Jun.

Critias c.460–403 BC

Athenian aristocrat and politician, one of the 30 tyrants who ruled Athens after the Peloponnesian war (404 BC). He was killed in the democratic revolution of 404/3. Only fragments of his poetry and tragedies survive.

12 Is not living at all not better than living badly?
Fragment, quoted in H Diels and W Kranz (eds) *Die Fragmente der Vorsokratiker* (1952), vol.2, 385, no.23.

Croker, John Wilson 1780–1857

Irish politician and essayist, known for his satires on the Irish stage and Dublin society. He became an MP (1807) and helped found the *Quarterly Review* (1809).

13 We are now, as we have always been, decidedly and conscientiously attached to what is called the Tory, and which might with more propriety be called the Conservative party.
1830 *Quarterly Review*, Jan.

Cromer, Evelyn Baring, Earl 1841–1917

English colonial administrator.

14 It is well that Gordon should be under my orders, but a man who habitually consults the prophet Isaiah when he is in difficulty is not apt to obey the orders of anyone.
Of General Charles George Gordon. Quoted in Charles Chevenix Trench *Charley Gordon* (1978).

Crompton, Richmal *originally* Richmal Samuel Lamburn 1890–1969

English writer, a classics teacher until she contracted polio in 1923. Her best-known children's books are those in the 'William' series, beginning with *Just William* (1922).

15 I'll thcream and thcream and thcream until I'm thick.
1925 Violet Elizabeth. *Still William*, ch.8.

Cromwell, Oliver 1599–1658

English soldier and Puritan statesman. In the Civil War he led his New Model Army to victory at Naseby (1645). After the execution of Charles I, he established a Commonwealth, and later, on dissolving the Rump Parliament (1653) and refusing the crown, a Protectorate.

16 A few honest men are better than numbers.
1643 Letter to Sir William Spring, Sep. Quoted in Thomas Carlyle *Letters and Speeches of Oliver Cromwell* (1845).

17 I had rather have a plain, russet-coated Captain, that knows what he fights for, and loves what he knows, than that which you call a Gentle-man and is nothing else.
1643 Letter to Sir William Spring, Sep. Quoted in Thomas Carlyle *Letters and Speeches of Oliver Cromwell* (1845).

18 The state, in choosing men to serve it, takes no notice of their opinions. If they be willing faithfully to serve it, that satisfies.
1644 Said before the Battle of Marston Moor, 2 Jul.

19 EARL OF MANCHESTER: If we beat the King ninety-nine times, yet he is King still so will his posterity be after him; but if the King beat us once we shall be hanged, and our posterity made slaves.
OLIVER CROMWELL: My Lord, if this be so, why did we take up arms at first? This is against fighting hereafter. If so, let us make peace, be it never so base.
1644 Recorded in *The Calendar of State Papers*, 10 Nov.

20 I beseech you, in the bowels of Christ, think it possible you may be mistaken.
1650 Letter to the General Assembly of the Church of Scotland, 3 Aug.

21 Mr Lely, I desire you would use all your skill to paint my picture truly like me, and not flatter me at all; but remark all these roughnesses, pimples, warts, and everything as you see me, otherwise I will never pay a farthing for it.
1650 Remark to Sir Peter Lely, who was about to paint his portrait. Quoted in H Walpole *Anecdotes of Painting in England*, vol.3 (1763).

22 You have sat too long here for any good you have been doing. Depart, I say, and let us have done with you. In the name of God, go!
1653 On dismissing the Rump Parliament, 20 Apr.

23 Take away that fool's bauble—the Mace.
   1653 On dismissing the Rump Parliament, 20 Apr.

24 My desire is to make what haste I can to be gone.
   1658 Last words. Quoted in John Morley *Oliver Cromwell* (1900), bk.5, ch.10.

Cronenberg, David 1943–

Canadian sci-fi and horror film director. His films include *The Fly* (1986), *Crash* (1996) and *A History of Violence* (2005).

25 More blood! More blood!
   Characteristic on-set declaration. Quoted in Neil Gaiman and Kim Newman *Ghastly Beyond Belief* (1985).

26 I don't have a moral plan. I'm a Canadian.
   Quoted in Leslie Halliwell *Halliwell's Filmgoer's and Video Viewer's Companion* (9th edn, 1988).

27 All stereotypes turn out to be true. This is a horrifying thing about life. All those things you fought against as a youth: you begin to realize they're stereotypes because they're true.
   2011 Quoted in *InFuze Magazine*, 14 Dec.

28 The only authentic literature of the modern era is the owner's manual.
   2014 *Consumed*.

29 Why do I concern myself so much with sex and death? It's simple. Sex is the only way we have of keeping death at bay.
   2014 Quoted on thestar.com, 26 Dec.

Cronkite, Walter 1916–2009

US journalist.

30 And that's the way it is.
   Catchphrase, used at the end of the CBS *Evening News* (1962–81).

Cronyn, Hume 1911–2003

Canadian-born actor, writer and director. He was married to Jessica Tandy, with whom he acted many times.

31 The most magical moment in the theater is a silence so complete that you can't even hear people breathe. It means that you've got them.
   1990 In *Time*, 2 Apr.

Crosby, Bing originally Harry Lillis Crosby 1904–77

US film actor and singer. His many successful films include the *Road to* series with Bob Hope and Dorothy Lamour.

32 That was a great game of golf.
   1977 Last words, as he finished play at the 18th hole before suffering a heart attack.

33 He was an average guy who could carry a tune.
   Suggesting his own epitaph. Quoted in David Pickering *Brewer's Twentieth Century Music* (1994).

Cross, Henry Douglass 1920–75

US songwriter.

34 I Left My Heart in San Francisco.
   1954 Title of song.

Crossman, Richard Howard Stafford 1907–74

British Labour politician. He chronicled his ministerial career and the workings of government in a series of diaries, begun in 1952, which were published in four volumes (1975–81), despite attempts to suppress them.

35 My Minister's room is like a padded cell, and in certain ways I am like a person who is suddenly certified a lunatic and put safely into this great, vast room, cut off from real life. Of course they don't behave *quite* like nurses, because the Civil Service is profoundly deferential—'Yes, Minister! No, Minister! If you wish it, Minister!'
   1964 *The Diaries of a Cabinet Minister*, vol.1 (1975), 22 Oct.

Crowley, (Edward) Aleister 1875–1947

English writer and occultist. He founded his own order and became notorious for rumours of orgies, drugs and the sacrifice of babies in the course of black magic ceremonies.

36 Do what thou wilt shall be the whole of the Law.
   1909 *Book of the Law*.

Cruyff, Johan 1947–

Dutch footballer, European Footballer of the Year (1971, 1973, 1974).

37 I am no longer a footballer. I am an industry.
   1973 On being transferred from Ajax to Barcelona for a record £922,000. Quoted in Peter Ball and Phil Shaw *The Book of Football Quotations* (1989).

Cruz, Sor Juana Inés de la 1651–95

Mexican intellectual, nun and poet. After she took her vows at the age of 16, attempts were made to stop her writing. Two years after writing her defence, *Respuesta a sor Filotea* (1691), she sold her books and devoted herself to religion.

38 *En perseguirme, Mundo, Qué interesas?*
   En qué te ofendo, cuando sólo intento
   poner bellezas en mi entendimiento
   y no mi entendimiento en las bellezas?
   World, in hounding me, what do you gain?
   How can it harm you if I choose, astutely,
   rather to stock my mind with things of beauty,
   than waste its stock on every beauty's claim?
   1688 *Poesía, teatro y prosa*, 'Quéjase de la suerte' (translated as 'She Complains about Her Fate', 1985).

39 *Aprendamos a ignorar,*
   pensamiento, pues hallamos
   que cuanto añado al discurso,
   tanto le usurpo a los años.
   Thought, let's learn not to know,
   since so plainly it appears
   that whatever we add to our minds
   we take away from our years.
   1688 *A Sor Juana Anthology*, 'Acusa la hidropesía de mucha ciencia' (translated as 'She Condemns the Bloatedness of Much Learning', 1985).

40 *Este natural impulso que Dios puso en mí...su Majestad sabe por qué y para qué; y sabe que le he pedido que apague la luz de mi entendimiento dejando sólo lo que baste para guardar su Ley, pues lo demás sobra, (según algunos) en una mujer; y aun hay quien dice que daña.*
   This natural impulse which God has implanted in me...only His Majesty knows why and wherefore and His Majesty also knows that I have prayed to Him to extinguish the light of my mind, only leaving sufficient to keep His Law, since any more is overmuch, so some say, in a woman, and there are even those who say it is harmful.

1691 *Poesía, teatro y prosa*, '*Respuesta sor Filoted* ('An Answer to Sister Filotea', 1982).

Cuarón, Alfonso 1961–
Mexican film director.

41 You speed up and up then you realise that your scarf has got caught in the machinery and if you don't keep up you're going to be strangled.
2004 On the pace of work involved in directing *Harry Potter and the Prisoner of Azkaban*. Quoted in the *Sunday Herald*, 23 May.

Cullen, Countee 1903–46
Black US poet and novelist, an important figure in the Harlem Renaissance of the 1920s.

42 She even thinks that up in heaven
Her class lies late and snores,
While poor black cherubs rise at seven
To do celestial chores.
1925 *On These I Stand*, 'For a Lady I Know'.

43 What is Africa to me:
Copper sun or scarlet sea,
Jungle star or jungle track,
Strong bronzed men, or regal black
Women from whose loins I sprang
When the birds of Eden sang?
1925 *On These I Stand*, 'Heritage'.

44 One three centuries removed
From the scenes his fathers loved,
Spicy grove, cinnamon tree,
What is Africa to me?
1925 *On These I Stand*, 'Heritage'.

45 So I lie, whose fount of pride,
Dear distress, and joy allied,
Is my somber flesh and skin,
With the dark blood dammed within.
1925 *On These I Stand*, 'Heritage'.

46 Ever at Thy glowing altar
Must my heart grow sick and falter,
Wishing He I served were black.
1925 *On These I Stand*, 'Heritage'.

47 Lord, forgive me if my need
Sometimes shapes a human creed.
1925 *On These I Stand*, 'Heritage'.

cummings, e e *pen name of* Edward Estlin Cummings 1894–1962
US writer and painter, best known as an eccentric innovator in lyrical poetry, using idiosyncratic typography. He also wrote a novel, plays and essays.

48 He had no nose, properly speaking, but a large beak of preposterous widthlessness, which gave his whole face the expression of falling gravely downstairs, and quite obliterated the unimportant chin.
1922 *The Enormous Room*, ch.3.

49 Subconsciously every one was, of course, fearful that he himself would go nuts—everyone with the exception of those who had already gone nuts, who were in the wholly pleasant situation of having no fear.
1922 *The Enormous Room*, ch.5.

50 To create is first of all to destroy…there is and can be no such thing as authentic art until the *bons trucs* (whereby we are taught to see and imitate on canvas and in stone and by words this so-called world) are entirely and thoroughly and perfectly annihilated by that vast and painful process of Unthinking which may result in a minute bit of purely personal Feeling. Which minute bit is Art.
1922 *The Enormous Room*, ch.12.

51 The tall, impossibly tall, incomparably tall, city shoulderingly upwards into hard sunlight leaned a little through the octaves of its parallel edges, leaningly strode upwards into firm, hard, snowy sunlight; the noises of America nearingly throbbed with smokes and hurrying dots which are men and which are women and which are things new and curious and hard and strange and vibrant and immense, lifting with a great ondulous stride firmly into immortal sunlight…
1922 *The Enormous Room*, ch.13, closing words.

52 spring
when the world is puddle wonderful
1923 *Tulips and Chimneys*, 'Chanson Innocente'.

53 the Cambridge ladies who live in furnished souls
are unbeautiful and have comfortable minds
1923 *Tulips and Chimneys*, 'Sonnets-Realities', no.1.

54 Buffalo Bill's
defunct
—who used to
—ride a watersmooth-silver
——stallion
and break onetwothreefourfive pigeonsjustlikethat
1923 *Tulips and Chimneys*, 'Portraits', no.8.

55 Humanity i love you because you
are perpetually putting the secret of
life in your pants and forgetting
it's there and sitting down
on it.
1925 *XLI Poems*, no.2, 'La Guerre'.

56 who knows if the moon's
a balloon, coming out of a keen city
in the sky—filled with pretty people?
1925 'Seven Poems, VII'. David Niven used the phrase for his autobiography, *The Moon's a Balloon* (1975).

57 If a poet is anybody, he is somebody to whom things made matter very little—somebody who is obsessed by Making.
1926 *is 5*, foreword.

58 'next to of course god america i
love you land of the pilgrims' and so forth oh
say can you see by the dawn's early my
country 'tis of centuries come and go
and are no more what of it we should worry
in every language even deafanddumb
they sons acclaim you glorious name by gorry
by jingo by gee by gosh by gum
1926 *is 5*, 'Two, III'.

59 why talk of beauty what could be more beautiful than these heroic happy dead
who rushed like lions to the roaring slaughter
they did not stop to think they died instead
then shall the voices of liberty be mute?
He spoke. And drank rapidly a glass of water.
1926 *is 5*, 'Two, III'.

60 America makes prodigious mistakes, America has colossal faults, but one thing cannot be denied: America is always on the move. She may be going to Hell, of course, but at least she isn't standing still.
  1927 'Why I Like America', in *Vanity Fair*, May.

61 nobody, not even the rain, has such small hands
  1931 *w*, 'somewhere I have never travelled'.

62 unless statistics lie he was
  more brave than me: more blond than you
  1931 *w*, 'i sing of Olaf glad and big'.

63 What about the world, Mr Cummings? I live in so many: which one do you mean?
  1934 Introduction to revised edition of *The Enormous Room*.

64 my father moved through dooms of love
  through sames of am through haves of give,
  singing each morning out of each night
  my father moved through depths of height
  1940 *50 poems*, 'my father moved through dooms of love'.

65 because my father lived his soul
  love is the whole and more than all
  1940 *50 poems*, 'my father moved through dooms of love'.

66 a politician is an arse upon
  which everyone has sat except a man
  1944 *1x1*, no.10.

67 pity this busy monster, manunkind,
  not. Progress is a comfortable disease.
  1944 *1x1*, no.14.

68 We doctors know
  a hopeless case if—listen: there's a hell
  of a good universe next door; let's go
  1944 *1x1*, no.14.

69 anyone lived in a pretty how town
  (with up so floating many bells down)
  spring summer autumn winter
  he sang his didn't he danced his did
  1949 *50 poems*, no.29.

70 Knowledge is a polite word for dead but not buried imagination.
  1951 'Jottings', in *Wake*, no.10.

71 for whatever we lose (like a you or a me)
  it's always ourselves we find in the sea
  'maggie and milly and molly and may'.

72 Humane, but not human.
  On Ezra Pound. Recalled on Cummings's death, 3 Sep 1962.

73 A draftsman of words.
  Self-description. Quoted in the *New York Times*, 30 Oct 1963.

Cunningham, Allan 1784–1842

Scottish poet, friend and acquaintance of James Hogg and Walter Scott.

74 A wet sheet and a flowing sea,
  A wind that follows fast,
  And fills the white and rustling sail,
  And bends the gallant mast
  1825 'A Wet Sheet and a Flowing Sea', stanza 1.

75 Wha the deil hae we got for a King,
  But a wee, wee German lairdie!
  1847 *Poems and Songs*, 'The Wee, Wee German Lairdie', stanza 1.

Cunningham, Roseanna 1951–

Scottish advocate and politician. She was an MP (1995–2001) before becoming an MSP in 1999 and Deputy Leader of the Scottish National Party (2000–4).

76 Until a woman is free to be as incompetent as the average male then she will never be completely equal.
  1995 By-election campaign speech, May.

Cuomo, Mario Matthew 1932–2015

US lawyer and Democratic politician, Governor of New York (1983–95).

77 You campaign in poetry, you govern in prose.
  1985 In *The New Republic*, 4 Apr.

78 We propose it, we massage it, and we often have to ram it.
  1988 Of legislation. In the *US News and World Report*, 25 Jan.

79 If there's a plastic surgeon who claims to be responsible for this face, then New York State will decertify him immediately.
  1991 On reports that he had undergone plastic surgery. In *Newsweek*, 11 Nov.

80 President Bush…seems to think that the ship [of state] will be saved by imperceptible undercurrents, directed by the invisible hand of some cyclical economic god, that will gradually move the ship so that at the last moment it will miraculously glide past the rocks to safer shores.
  1992 Address nominating Bill Clinton as Democratic presidential candidate, 15 Jul.

81 It is as if Homer not only chronicled the siege of Troy, but conducted the siege as well. As if Shakespeare set his play writing aside to lead the English against the Armada.
  1992 Tribute to Lincoln's literary and political genius. In the *New York Times*, 18 Nov.

82 Commitment seems to live more in the poetry of our aspirations than in the prose of the realities we have created.
  1992 In the *New York Times*, 18 Nov.

83 Ever since the Republican landslide on Nov 8, it's been getting dark outside a little earlier every day. You notice that?
  1994 In the *New York Times*, 17 Dec.

84 Dog eat dog produces, inevitably, just one dog.
  1994 In the *New York Times*, 31 Dec.

Cupitt, Rev Don 1934–

English radical theologian, Dean of Emmanuel College, Cambridge (1966–91).

85 A belief is made religious, not so much by its content, as rather by the way it is held.
  1984 *The Sea of Faith*.

86 It is hardest of all to give up the last slivers and shreds of objectivity, but only by doing so can faith finally free itself from all that is outworn and become as fully voluntary, creative and courageous as it is required to be today.
  1984 *The Sea of Faith*.

Curie, Marie originally Marya Sklodowska 1867–1934

Polish-born French chemist, who shared a 1903 Nobel prize with her husband Pierre and with Henri Becquerel for research on radioactivity. In 1911 she again won the Nobel prize for the discovery of radium and polonium.

87 In science, we must be interested in things, not in persons.
Quoted in Eve Curie *Madame Curie* (1937), ch.16 (translated by Vincent Sheean, 1943).

Curnow, (Thomas) Allen Munro 1911–2001

New Zealand poet and critic, whose works focus on his country's past and its quest for national identity.

88 Fluent in all the languages dead or living,
the sun comes up with a word of worlds all spinning in a world of words.
1979 *An Incorrigible Music*, 'A Balanced Bait in Handy Pellet Form'.

Curran, Charles

US journalist.

89 One of nature's Balkans.
Of his friend and fellow journalist, Rebecca West. Quoted by V S Pritchett in the *New Yorker*, 21 Dec 1987.

90 [She] has several skins fewer than any other human being…a kind of psychological haemophilia, which is one reason why she writes so well, and why she is so vulnerable.
Of his friend and fellow journalist, Rebecca West. Quoted by V S Pritchett in the *New Yorker*, 21 Dec 1987.

Curran, John Philpot 1750–1817

Irish judge and orator, called to the Irish bar in 1775. He entered Parliament in 1783, and although a staunch Protestant strongly opposed the Union.

91 But as in wailing there's nought availing,
And Death unfailing will strike the blow,
Then for that reason, and for a season,
Let us be merry before we go.
?1773 'Let Us Be Merry Before We Go'.

92 The condition upon which God hath given liberty to man is eternal vigilance; which condition if he break, servitude is at once the consequence of his crime, and the punishment of his guilt.
1790 Speech, Dublin, 10 Jul.

93 Like the silver plate on a coffin.
Of Sir Robert Peel's smile. Quoted by Daniel O'Connell in the House of Commons, 26 Feb 1835.

Currie, Edwina 1946–

English Conservative politician and novelist. She was appointed Health Minister (1986–8), and attracted notoriety for her outspoken comments on various health issues.

94 My message to the businessmen of this country when they go abroad on business is that there is one good thing above all they can take with them to stop them catching AIDS—and that is the wife.
1987 Speech as Health Minister, 12 Feb.

95 The strongest possible piece of advice that I could give to any young woman is: Don't screw around and don't smoke.
1988 In the *Observer*, 3 Apr.

96 Most of the egg production in this country, sadly, is now infected with salmonella.
1988 Radio interview as junior Health Minister, 3 Dec, which outraged both the domestic poultry industry and those of her own back-benchers who represented agricultural constituencies, forcing her resignation two weeks later.

Curtis, Charles P

97 Literature is a power line and the motor, mark you, is the reader.
1957 *A Commonplace Book*.

Curtis, Lionel 1872–1955

British writer on international affairs.

98 In private conversation he tries on speeches like a man trying on ties in his bedroom, to see how he would look in them.
1912 Of Winston Churchill. Letter to Nancy Astor.

Curtis, Richard Whalley Anthony 1956–

British writer for film and television, best known for the TV series *Not the Nine O'Clock News* (1979–83) and *Blackadder* (1984–9), and for films including *Four Weddings and a Funeral* (1994), *Notting Hill* (1999) and *Love Actually* (2003).

99 Whatever your script is like, no matter how much stewing and rewriting—if the punters don't want to sleep with the star, you may never be asked to write another one.
1994 Introduction to the published script of *Four Weddings and a Funeral*.

Curtis, Tony *pseudonym of* Bernie Schwartz 1925–2010

US film actor.

1 Like kissing Hitler.
Of working with Marilyn Monroe on *Some Like It Hot*. Attributed.

Curtiz, Michael *originally* Mihaly Kertesz 1888–1962

Hungarian-born film director.

2 Bring on the empty horses!
1936 Instructions during the filming of *The Charge of the Light Brigade*, subsequently used by David Niven for the title of one of his books. Curtiz's less-than-perfect English was renowned for producing such felicitous phrases.

Curzon (of Kedleston), Lord George Nathaniel 1859–1925

English statesman. As Viceroy of India from 1898 he introduced many social and political reforms and partitioned Bengal. He resigned after a disagreement with Kitchener (1905), but returned to politics as Lord Privy Seal (1915) and Foreign Secretary (1919–24).

3 It is only when you get to see and realize what India is—that she is the strength and the greatness of England—that you feel that every nerve a man may strain, every energy he may put forward, cannot be devoted to a nobler purpose than keeping tight the cords that hold India to ourselves.
1893 Speech at Southport, 15 May.

4 I hesitate to say what the functions of the modern journalist may be, but I imagine that they do not exclude the intelligent anticipation of the facts even before they occur.
1898 House of Commons, 29 Mar.

5   To fight for the right, to abhor the imperfect, the unjust, or the mean, to swerve neither to the right hand nor the left, to care nothing for flattery or applause or odium or abuse—it is so easy to have any of them in India—never to let your enthusiasm be soured or your courage grow dim but to remember that the Almighty has placed your hand on the greatest of his ploughs, in whose furrow the nations of the future are germinating and taking shape, to drive the blade a little forward in your time and to feel that somewhere among those millions you have left, a little justice, or happiness or prosperity, a sense of manliness or moral dignity, a spring of patriotism, a dawn of intellectual enlightenment or a stirring of duty where it did not exist before—that is enough, that is the Englishman's justification in India.
1906 Farewell speech on departing from Bombay as Viceroy of India.

6   I never knew that the lower classes had such white skins.
c.1915 Remark made during a visit of front-line British troops in World War I, after observing some of them bathing in old beer barrels.

7   Gentlemen do not take soup at luncheon.
Attributed. Quoted in E L Woodward *Short Journey* (1942), ch.7.

St Cyprian *full name* Thascius Caecilius Cyprianus   c.200–258 AD

Christian martyr and Father of the Church. Probably born in Carthage, he became a bishop and theologian. He was excommmunicated for his views on baptism and beheaded in Valerian's reign.

8   *Habere non potest Deum patrem qui ecclesiam non habet matrem.*
He cannot have God for his father who has not the church for his mother.
AD 251 *De Ecclesiae Catholicae Unitate*, ch 6.

9   *Salus extra ecclesiam non est.*
There is no salvation outside the church.
AD 256 *Letters*, no.73.

Cyrano de Bergerac, Savinien de   1619–55

French poet and soldier, famous as a duellist. He was a student of Gassendi, who influenced him in the philosophy of free-thinking.

10 *Peut-on être innocent, lorsqu'on aime un coupable?*
Can one be innocent when one loves a guilty person?
1653 *La Mort d'Agrippine*, act 5, sc.5.

11 *Un Philosophe doit juger le vulgaire, et non pas juger comme le vulgaire.*
A philosopher should judge the masses and should not judge like the masses.
1654 *Lettres diverses, Contre les sorciers* (later published as *Voyage dans la lune*).

12 *Non, non, si ce Dieu visible éclaire l'homme, c'est par accident, comme le flambeau du roi éclaire par accident au crocheteur qui passe par la rue.*
No, no, if this manifest God enlightens men, it is purely by accident, just as the king's torch throws its light upon a labourer who passes him in the street.
1656 *L'Autre Monde; ou, Les Estats et empires de la lune* (later published as *Voyage dans la lune*).

d

Daché, Lilly   1904–89

French-born US milliner. Her autobiography, *Talking Through My Hats*, was published in 1946.

1   Glamour is what makes a man ask for your telephone number. But it also is what makes a woman ask for the name of your dressmaker.
1955 'Lilly Daché's Secrets of Lifelong Glamour Book', in *Woman's Home Companion*, vol.82, Jul.

Dafoe, John W   1866–1944

Canadian publisher and editor.

2   A journalist is hardly an authority upon anything—unless perhaps upon the appraisal of the drift of public opinion.
1923 Convocation address at the University of Manitoba, Winnipeg, May. Quoted in Murray Donnelly *Dafoe of the Free Press* (1968).

3   There are only two kinds of government, the scarcely tolerable and the absolutely unbearable.
Characteristic remark, quoted in Murray Donnelly *Dafoe of the Free Press* (1968).

Daily Express

British tabloid newspaper.

4   Britain will not be involved in a European war this year, or next year either.
1938 Headline, 30 Sep. The newspaper used similar phrases frequently, up to 11 Aug 1939, three weeks before the outbreak of World War II.

Daily Mail

British tabloid newspaper.

5   Nobel Prize for British Wife.
1964 Headline announcing that the Nobel prize for chemistry had been awarded to Professor Dorothy Hodgkin.

Daily Mirror

British tabloid newspaper.

6   Whose finger do you want on the trigger?
1951 Headline, 21 Sep, referring to the atom bomb.

Dalai Lama *originally* Tenzin Gyatso   1935–

Spiritual and temporal leader of Tibet since 1940. He negotiated an autonomy agreement for Tibet with the Chinese in 1951 but went into exile after the suppressed nationalist uprising in 1959. Now living in India, he continues to move for Tibetan independence. He was awarded the Nobel peace prize in 1989.

7   Frankly speaking, it is difficult to trust the Chinese. Once bitten by a snake, you feel suspicious even when you see a piece of rope.
1981 Quoted in the *Observer Colour Magazine*, 5 Apr.

8   Media people should have long noses like an elephant to smell out politicians, mayors, prime ministers and

businessmen. We need to know the reality, the good and the bad, not just the appearance.
2006 News conference, Vancouver, B.C., quoted in *The Globe and Mail*, 8 Sep.

9 Westerners are too self-absorbed.
2006 Quoted in *The Daily Telegraph*, 1 Mar.

10 Fundamentalism is terrifying because it is based purely on emotion, rather than intelligence. It prevents followers from thinking as individuals and about the good of the world.
2006 Quoted in *The Daily Telegraph*, 1 Mar.

Dalglish, Kenny 1951–
Scottish footballer and manager. As manager of Liverpool, he won the League and Cup double in 1986.

11 The saddest and most beautiful sight I have ever seen.
1989 Of the display of flowers and club scarfs that were piled on Liverpool's Anfield pitch in memory of those who died in the Hillsborough football disaster. Quoted in Peter Ball and Phil Shaw *The Book of Football Quotations* (1989).

Dalí, Salvador 1904–89
Spanish painter, graphic artist and sculptor, the most flamboyant of the Surrealist artists. His work draws on the symbolism of dreams and, later, religion.

12 At the age of six I wanted to be a cook. At seven I wanted to be Napoleon. And my ambition has been growing steadily ever since.
1942 *The Secret Life of Salvador Dalí*, prologue.

13 I do not paint a portrait to look like the subject, rather does the person grow to look like his portrait.
Quoted in Esar *A Treasury of Humorous Quotations* (1951).

14 The first man to compare the cheeks of a young woman to a rose was obviously a poet; the first to repeat it was possibly an idiot.
1968 *Dialogues with Marcel Duchamp*, preface.

15 The famous soft watches are nothing else than the tender, extravagant, solitary, paranoiac-critical camembert of time and space.
1969 *Conquest of the Irrational*.

16 Every good painter who aspires to the creation of genuine masterpieces should first of all marry my wife.
Quoted in Saranne Alexandrian *Surrealist Art* (1970).

17 *Le surréalisme, c'est moi.*
I am surrealism.
Quoted in Saranne Alexandrian *Surrealist Art* (1970), ch.5.
▸ See Louis XIV 537:66.

Dallek, Robert 1934–
US historian.

18 What makes war interesting for Americans is that we don't fight war on our soil, we don't have direct experience of it, so there's an openness about the meanings we give it.
1991 In the *New York Times*, 24 Feb.

Daly, Daniel 1874–1937
US gunnery sergeant in World War I.

19 Come on you sons of bitches! Do you want to live forever?
1918 Attributed, to his troops at Belleau Wood, 4 Jun.
▸ See Frederick the Great 349:38.

Daly, John 1966–
US golfer.

20 I spent $3m on drink and $3m on gambling, but I wasted the rest.
2000 On spending his winnings. Quoted in *The Independent*, 23 Dec.

Daly, Mary 1928–2010
US feminist theorist and theologian. She advocated a feminist spirituality in *Beyond God the Father* (1973) and *Gyn/Ecology: the Metaethics of Radical Feminism* (1978).

21 Mister-ectomy n.: guaranteed solution to The Contraceptive Problem, tried and true and therefore taboo birth control method, recommended by Gyn/Ecologists, insisted upon by spinsters.
1987 *Webster's First New Intergalactic Wickedary of the English Language* (with Jane Caputi), Word Web 2.

St Peter Damian or Pietro Damiani 1007–72
Italian cleric and saint. A swineherd in his youth, he rose to become Bishop of Ostia and a Cardinal. He was active in attempts to reform the clergy in order to correct immorality.

22 *Sanctum Satanum meum.*
My holy Satan.
c.1070 Of Hildebrand, later Pope Gregory VII. Letter to Pope Alexander II and Cardinal Archdeacon Hildebrand.

Damrosch, Walter Johannes 1862–1950
German-born US conductor and composer. Having established a reputation as a conductor of Wagner, he became a champion of works by contemporary composers.

23 If a young man at the age of twenty-three can write a symphony like that, in five years he will be ready to commit murder.
1925 After conducting Aaron Copland's *Symphony for Organ and Orchestra*. Quoted in Machlis *Introduction to Contemporary Music* (1963).

Dana, Charles Anderson 1819–97
US newspaper editor. From 1848 to 1862 he edited the New York *Tribune*. From 1863 to the end of the Civil War he was Assistant-Secretary of War. In 1867 he purchased the New York *Sun*.

24 I have always felt that whatever Divine Providence permitted to occur I was not too proud to report.
1888 *The Art of Newspaper Making*, 'The Modern American Newspaper'.

25 Get the news, get all the news, and nothing but the news.
1888 *The Art of Newspaper Making*, 'The Modern American Newspaper'.

26 The invariable law of the newspaper is to be interesting.
1888 *The Art of Newspaper Making*, 'The Making of a Newspaper Man'.

Danforth, John Claggett 1936–
US lawyer and politician, Senator of Missouri (1976–95).

27 It has locked candidates into ridiculous positions because only ridiculous positions can be compacted into 30-second commercials.
1990 Of television in politics. In the *New York Times*, 18 Mar.

Dangarembga, Tsitsi 1959–

Zimbabwean writer. Her novel *Nervous Conditions* (1988) portrays the effect of white values on black African society, especially women.

28 This business of womanhood is a heavy burden... And these days it is worse, with the poverty of blackness on one side and the weight of womanhood on the other.
1988 *Nervous Conditions*, ch.1.

Dangerfield, George 1904–86

English-born writer and historian who moved to the US in 1930.

29 Ireland is one of the few countries—perhaps the last—where the boundaries between politics and art have never been fixed.
1935 *The Strange Death of Liberal England*.

Daniel, Samuel 1562–1619

English poet and dramatist. A private tutor and courtier, he wrote masques, plays and epistles. His poetic works include the sonnet sequence *Delia* (1592) and the epic *Civil Wars Between the Two Houses of Lancaster and York* (1594–1609).

30 I that have loved thee thus before thou fadest,
My faith shall wax, when thou art in thy waning.
The world shall find this miracle in me,
That fire can burn when all the matter's spent.
1592 *Delia*, sonnet 33.

31 Care-charmer Sleep, son of the sable Night,
Brother to Death, in silent darkness born,
Relieve my languish and restore the light;
With dark forgetting of my care return.
And let the day be time enough to mourn
The shipwreck of my ill adventured youth:
Let waking eyes suffice to wail their scorn
Without the torment of the night's untruth.
1592 *Delia*, sonnet 54.

32 O thou whom envy ev'n is force t'admire!
1594 'To the Right Honourable, the Lady Mary, Countess of Pembroke'. Daniel was part of the group of writers who met at Wilton, which also included Jonson and Drayton, and he tutored Pembroke's son.

33 Unless above himself he can
Erect himself, how poor a thing is man!
1594 'To the Lady Margaret, Countess of Cumberland'.

34 Custom that is before all law, Nature that is above all art.
1603 *A Defence of Rhyme*.

35 But years hath done this wrong,
To make me write too much, and live too long.
1605 *Philotas*, 'To the Prince', dedication.

Dante Alighieri *originally* Durante 1265–1321

Italian poet and scholar, author of *The Divine Comedy* (a poet's journey through hell, purgatory and paradise, begun c.1307). A White Guelf, he was exiled from his native Florence when the Black Guelfs triumphed in 1309. He died in Ravenna.

36 *Nel mezzo del cammin di nostra vita
mi ritrovai per una selva oscura
ché la diritta via era smarrita.*
In the middle of the journey of our life
I found myself in a dark wood
where the straight path was lost.
c.1320 *Divina Commedia*, 'Inferno', canto 1, l.1–3.

37 *Lasciate ogni speranza voi ch'entrate.*
Abandon all hope ye who enter here.
c.1320 Inscription above the gates of Hell. *Divina Commedia*, 'Inferno', canto 3, l.9.

38 *Nessun maggior dolore,
Che ricordarsi del tempo felice
Nella miseria.*
There is no greater pain than to remember a happy time when one is in misery.
c.1320 *Divina Commedia*, 'Inferno', canto 5, l.121–3.

39 *E quindi uscimmo a riveder le stelle.*
Thence we came forth to see the stars again.
c.1320 *Divina Commedia*, 'Inferno', canto 34, l.139.

40 *Lì si vedrà la superbia ch'asseta,
che fa lo Scotto e l'Inghilese folle,
sì che non può soffrir dentro a sua meta.*
There shall you see the pride which causes thirst, which makes the Scots and the English mad, so that they cannot remain within their boundaries.
c.1320 *Divina Commedia*, 'Paradiso', canto 1, l.121–3.

41 *E'n la sua voluntade è nostra pace.*
In His will is our peace.
c.1320 *Divina Commedia*, 'Paradiso', canto 3, l.85.

42 *L'amor che move il sole e l'altre stelle.*
The love that moves the sun and the other stars.
c.1320 *Divina Commedia*, 'Paradiso', canto 33, l.145.

Danton, Georges Jacques 1759–94

French revolutionary leader. As Minister of Justice (1792) he voted for the king's death. He tried to moderate the severity of the Revolutionary Tribunal, but lost the leadership to Robespierre and was executed for conspiracy.

43 *De l'audace, et encore de l'audace, et toujours de l'audace!*
Boldness, and again boldness, and always boldness!
1792 Speech to the Legislative Committee of General Defence, 2 Sep.

Darío, Rubén *pseudonym of* Félix Rubén García Sarmiento 1867–1916

Nicaraguan poet, journalist and diplomat. From 1886 he travelled extensively throughout Latin America and Europe. A key figure of Spanish-American Modernism, he experimented with rhythm, metre and imagery.

44 *Si hay poesía en nuestra América, ella está en las cosas viejas: en Palenke y Uatlán, en el indio legendario y el inca sensual y fino y en el gran Moctezuma de la silla de oro. Lo demás es tuyo, demócrata Walt Whitman.*
If there is poetry in our America, it is in ancient items: in Palenke and Uatlán, in the legendary Indian and in the sensuous and elegant Inca and the great Moctezuma. The rest is yours, democratic Walt Whitman.
1896 *Prosas profanas*, 'Palabras liminares'.

45 *Yo persigo una forma que no encuentra mi estilo,
botón de pensamiento que busca ser la rosa;
se anuncia con un beso que en mis labios se posa
al abrazo imposible de la Venus de Milo.*

I seek a form that my style cannot discover,
a bud of thought that wants to be a rose;
it is heralded by a kiss that is placed on my lips
in the impossible embrace of the Venus de Milo.
1896 *Prosas profanas*, 'Yo persigo una forma...' (translated as 'I seek a form...', 1922).

46 Dichoso el árbol que es apenas sensitivo,
y más la piedra dura porque ésa ya no siente,
pues no hay dolor más grande que el dolor de ser vivo,
ni mayor pesadumbre que la vida consciente.
Blessed is the almost insensitive tree,
more blessed is the hard stone that doesn't feel,
for no pain is greater than the pain of being alive,
and no sorrow more intense than conscious life.
1901 *Cantos de vida y esperanza*, 'Lo fatal' ('Fatalism').

Dark, Eleanor née O'Reilly pseudonym Patricia O'Rane 1901–85

Australian novelist and poet. Her works include the historical trilogy *The Timeless Land* (1941), *Storm of Time* (1948) and *No Barrier* (1953).

47 Silence ruled this land. Out of silence mystery comes, and magic, and the delicate awareness of unreasoning things.
1941 *The Timeless Land*, pt.1, '1788'.

Darman, Richard G(ordon) 1943–2008

US government official and businessman, Director of the Office of Management and the Budget in President Bush's Cabinet (1988–93).

48 I am now celebrating the 20th anniversary of the first request for my resignation. I look forward to many more.
Address to the White House press room. Quoted in Brian Kelly *Adventures in Porkland* (1992).

Darnell, Bill c.1940–

Canadian ecologist and activist, one of the original founders of the Greenpeace Foundation in Vancouver, British Columbia.

49 Make it a *green* peace.
1970 Quoted in Robert Hunter *Warriors of the Rainbow* (1979).

Darrow, Clarence Seward 1857–1938

US lawyer. He undertook the defence of John T Scopes (1925) for the teaching of Darwinism in school.

50 I do not consider it an insult but rather a compliment to be called an agnostic. I do not pretend to know where many ignorant men are sure—that is all that agnosticism means.
1925 Speech in defence of John T Scopes, 15 Jul.

Darwin, Charles Robert 1809–82

English naturalist. He joined the HMS *Beagle* scientific survey (1831–6) to South America and Australasia, which led eventually to his theory of evolution and the publication of many scientific works, including *The Origin of Species by Means of Natural Selection* (1859).

51 The naturalist in England, in his walks, enjoys a great advantage over others in frequently meeting with something worthy of attention; here he suffers a pleasant nuisance in not being able to walk a hundred yards without being fairly tied to the spot by some new and wondrous creature.
1832 In Brazil. *Journey of Researches into the Geology and Natural History of the Various Countries Visited during the Voyage of HMS 'Beagle' Round the World* (published 1839).

52 I have called this principle, by which each slight variation, if useful, is preserved, by the term of Natural Selection, in order to mark its relation to man's power of selection.
1859 *The Origin of Species by Means of Natural Selection*, ch.3.

53 From the war of nature, from famine and death, the most exalted object which we are capable of conceiving, namely, the production of the higher animals, directly follows. There is grandeur in this view of life.
1859 *The Origin of Species by Means of Natural Selection*, ch.14.

54 Great is the power of steady misrepresentation—but the history of science shows how, fortunately, this power does not long endure.
1859 *The Origin of Species by Means of Natural Selection*.

55 I have tried lately to read Shakespeare, and found it so intolerably dull that it nauseated me.
1860 *The Life and Letters of Charles Darwin*, vol.1.

56 False facts are highly injurious to the progress of science, for they often long endure; but false views, if supported by some evidence, do little harm, as every one takes a salutary pleasure in proving their falseness.
1871 *The Descent of Man and Selection in Relation to Sex*, ch.13.

57 The chief distinction in the intellectual powers of the two sexes is shewn by man's attaining to a higher eminence in whatever he takes up, than can woman—whether requiring deep thought, reason, or imagination, or merely the use of the senses and hands.
1871 *The Descent of Man and Selection in Relation to Sex*, ch.19.

58 We must however acknowledge, as it seems to me, that man with all his noble qualities...still bears in his bodily frame the indelible stamp of his lowly origin.
1871 *The Descent of Man and Selection in Relation to Sex*, ch.21.

59 I must begin with a good body of facts and not from a principle (in which I always suspect some fallacy) and then as much deduction as you please.
1874 Letter to J Fiske, 8 Dec.

60 A mathematician is a blind man in a dark room looking for a black cat which isn't there.
Quoted in John D Barrow *Pie in the Sky, Counting, Thinking and Being* (1992).

Darwin, Sir Francis 1848–1925

English botanist, son of Charles Darwin. He became a Reader in Botany at Oxford (1888) and produced his father's *Life and Letters* (1887–1903).

61 In science the credit goes to the man who convinces the world, not to the man to whom the idea first occurs.
1914 'Francis Galton', in *Eugenics Review*, vol.6, issue 1, Apr.

Daugherty, Harry Micajah 1860–1941

US politician, manager of Warren G Harding's political career from 1902. He was tried and acquitted (1927) on fraud charges.

62 A group of senators, bleary eyed for lack of sleep, will have to sit down at about two o'clock in the morning

1920 On the Republicans' failure to choose a presidential candidate at their convention.

David, Hal 1921–2012
US lyricist. He frequently worked with Burt Bacharach. His lyrics include *What the World Needs Now Is Love* and *Do You Know the Way to San Jose*.

63 Raindrops Keep Fallin' on My Head.
 1969 Title of song. (Music by Burt Bacharach.)

Davidson, John 1857–1909
Scottish poet and writer. He moved to London in 1885, publishing *Fleet Street Eclogues* (1893) and *Ballads and Songs* (1894). He committed suicide by drowning himself at Penzance.

64 The difficultest job a man can do,
 is to come it brave and meek with thirty bob a week,
 and feel that that's the proper thing for you.
 1894 *Ballads and Songs*, 'Thirty Bob a Week', stanza 15.

65 It's naked child against hungry wolf;
 it's playing bowls upon a splitting wreck;
 it's walking on a string across a gulf
 with millstones fore-and-aft about your neck;
 but the thing is daily done by many and many a one;
 and we fall, face forward, fighting, on the deck.
 1894 *Ballads and Songs*, 'Thirty Bob a Week', stanza 16.

66 In anguish we uplift
 A new unhallowed song:
 The race is to the swift,
 The battle to the strong.
 1899 'War Song', stanza 1.
 ▶ See Bible 106:29.

67 And blood in torrents pour
 In vain—always in vain,
 For war breeds war again.
 1899 'War Song', stanza 7.

68 When the pods went pop on the broom, green broom,
 And apples began to be golden-skinned,
 We harboured a stag in the Priory coomb.
 1906 *Holiday and Other Poems*, 'A Runnable Stag', stanza 1.

69 A stag of warrant, a stag, a stag,
 A runnable stag, a kingly crop,
 Brow, bay and tray and three on top,
 A stag, a runnable stag.
 1906 *Holiday and Other Poems*, 'A Runnable Stag', stanza 1.

Davie, George Elder 1912–2007
Scottish philosopher, a pioneer in studies of the Scottish Enlightenment.

70 The Democratic Intellect.
 1961 Title of book.

Davies, (Sarah) Emily 1830–1921
English feminist and educational reformer who campaigned vigorously for equal opportunities for women in education.

71 If neither governesses or mothers *know*, how can they teach? So long as education is not provided *for* them, how can it be provided *by* them?
 1868 Paper read at the Annual Meeting of the National Association for the Promotion of Social Sciences, published in *Thoughts on Some Questions Relating to Women 1860–1908*.

72 We have persuaded ourselves that Englishmen of the present day are such a nervously excitable race, that the only chance for their descendants is to keep the mothers in a state of coma. The fathers, we think are incurable.
 1868 Paper read at the Annual Meeting of the National Association for the Promotion of Social Sciences, published in *Thoughts on Some Questions Relating to Women 1860–1908*.

Davies, Sir John 1569–1626
English poet and civil servant. He held high office in Ireland where he supported severe repressive measures and was nominated Chief Justice (1626). His poems include *Orchestra, or a Poem of Dancing* (1596) and *Hymns to Astraea* (1599).

73 Dancing is a frenzy and a rage.
 1596 *Orchestra, or a Poem of Dancing*, stanza 16.

74 This wondrous miracle did Love devise,
 For dancing is love's proper exercise.
 1596 *Orchestra, or a Poem of Dancing*, stanza 18.

75 Learn then to dance, you that are princes born,
 And lawful lords of earthly creatures all;
 Imitate them, and thereof take no scorn,
 (For this new art to them is natural)
 And imitate the stars celestial.
 For when pale death your vital twist shall sever,
 Your better parts must dance with them forever.
 1596 *Orchestra, or a Poem of Dancing*, stanza 60.

76 Skill comes so slow, and life so fast doth fly,
 We learn so little and forget so much.
 1599 *Nosce Teipsum*, stanza 19.

77 I know my life's a pain and but a span,
 I know my sense is mocked in every thing;
 And to conclude, I know myself a man,
 Which is a proud and yet a wretched thing.
 1599 *Nosce Teipsum*, stanza 45.

78 Wedlock, indeed, hath oft compared been
 To public feasts where meet a public rout,
 Where they that are without would fain go in
 And they that are within would fain go out.
 1608 'A Contention Betwixt a Wife, a Widow, and a Maid for Precedence', l.193–6.

Davies, Nigel 1960–
English chess player.

79 One very important aspect of actually achieving something is, I believe, the ability to avoid making excuses, in all their guises.
 Quoted on www.chessville.com.

Davies, Ray(mond Douglas) 1944–
British songwriter and rock musician, founder of The Kinks (1963). His lyrics are noted for their lightly satirical commentary.

80 One week he's in polka-dots, the next week he's in stripes
 'Cos he's a dedicated follower of fashion.
 1966 'Dedicated Follower of Fashion'.

Davies, Robertson 1913–95
Canadian novelist, playwright, critic and essayist. After the Deptford trilogy (1970–5) he wrote another trilogy, including

What's Bred in the Bone (1985), shortlisted for the Booker Prize.

81 There is more to marriage than four bare legs under a blanket.
1957 Love and Libel.

82 'Mary, what made you do it?'
She looked him honestly in the face and gave the answer that became famous in Deptford: 'He was very civil, 'Masa. And he wanted it so badly.'
1970 Mrs. Dempster explains to her parson husband why she had sex with a tramp. *Fifth Business*, pt.1, ch.10.

83 I saw corpses, and grew used to their unimportant look, for a dead man without any of the panoply of death is a desperately insignificant object.
1970 Of World War I. *Fifth Business*, pt.2, ch.1.

84 When a man is down on his luck he seems to consume all he can get of coffee and doughnuts.
1970 Fifth Business, pt.4, ch.1.

85 He was killed by the usual cabal: by himself, first of all; by the woman he knew; by the woman he did not know; by the man who granted his inmost wish; and by the inevitable fifth, who was keeper of his conscience and keeper of the stone.
1970 Fifth Business, pt.6, ch.8.

86 Canada is not really a place where you are encouraged to have large spiritual adventures.
1972 Interviewed by Peter C Newman, 'The Master's Voice', in *Maclean's*, Sep.

87 The ideal companion in bed is a good book.
Interviewed by Terence M Green, recorded in J Madison Davis (ed) *Conversations with Robertson Davies* (1989).

Davies, Ron(ald) 1946–
Welsh Labour politician, Secretary of State for Wales (1997–8).

88 It was a moment of madness for which I have subsequently paid a very, very heavy price.
1998 Talking about the episode on Clapham common which led to his resignation as Welsh Secretary. Television interview, 30 Oct.

Davies, W(illiam) H(enry) 1871–1940
Welsh poet, who emigrated to the US at the age of 22. He lost a leg there while jumping a train and returned to England, where he lived as a tramp until his poetry found a public. He also wrote novels and autobiographical works.

89 It was the Rainbow gave thee birth,
And left thee all her lovely hues.
1910 'The Kingfisher'.

90 What is this life if, full of care,
We have no time to stand and stare?
1911 'Leisure'.

91 A rainbow and a cuckoo's song
May never come together again;
May never come
This side the tomb.
1914 'A Great Time'.

92 And hear the pleasant cuckoo, loud and long—
The simple bird that thinks two notes a song.
1916 'April's Charms'.

da Vinci, Leonardo
▸ *See Leonardo da Vinci*

Davis, Adelle 1904–74
US nutritionist.

93 People in nutrition do get the idea that they are going to live to be 150. And they never do.
1973 Quoted in Daniel Yergin's 'Supernutritionist', *New York Times* magazine, 20 May.

Davis, Bette *originally* Ruth Elizabeth Davis 1908–89
US film actress. She made her screen debut in 1931 and in the late 1930s and 1940s starred in a string of romantic melodramas such as *The Old Maid* (1939) and *Now Voyager* (1942).

94 Mother of three; divorcee; American. Twenty years experience as an actress in motion pictures. Mobile still and more affable than rumour would have it. Wants steady employment in Hollywood. (Has had Broadway). References upon request.
1962 Advertisement placed in the Hollywood trade papers.

95 Evil people…you never forget them. And that's the aim of any actress—never to be forgotten.
1966 On her favourite character roles. In the New York State Theater programme, Jun.

96 The best time I ever had with Joan Crawford was when I pushed her down the stairs in *Whatever Happened to Baby Jane*?
Quoted in Doug McClelland *Star Speak* (1987).

97 I have eyes like a bullfrog, a neck like an ostrich and long, limp hair. You just have to be good to survive with that equipment.
Attributed.

98 She's the original good time who was had by all.
On an anonymous starlet. Attributed.

Davis, Jefferson 1808–89
US statesman. He led the Senate's extreme State Rights Party, supported slavery, and was President of the rebel Confederate States during the Civil War (1861–5). Later imprisoned, he was never brought to trial.

99 All we ask is to be let alone.
1861 Inaugural address, 18 Feb.

Davis, Miles Dewey, III 1926–91
US jazz trumpeter and composer. A leading figure in postwar jazz, he also won wide acceptance with rock audiences in the 1970s and 1980s.

1 An artist's first responsibility is to himself.
1961 Ebony, Jan.

2 You could be a great musician, an innovative and important artist, but nobody cared if you didn't make the white people who were in control some money.
1989 Autobiography, ch.10.

Davis, Sammy, Jnr 1925–90
US jazz musician, actor, dancer and comedian.

3 Being a star has made it possible for me to get insulted in places where the average Negro could never hope to go and get insulted.
1965 Yes I Can, pt.3, ch.23.

Davis, Steve 1957–
English snooker player. He won the world championships six times.

4 Billiards is very similar to snooker, except there are only three balls and no one watches it.
1988 Quoted in Colin Jarman *The Guinness Dictionary of Sports Quotations* (1990).

Davis, Stuart 1894–1964
US Cubist painter.

5 An artist who has travelled on a steam train, driven an automobile, or flown in an airplane doesn't feel the same way about form and space as one who has not.
1940 'Is There a Revolution in the Arts?', in *Bulletin of America's Town Meeting of the Air*, vol.5, no.19 (19 Feb).

6 It has been often said, even by proponents of those pictures known in aesthetic slang as Cubist and Abstract, that they have no subject matter. Such a statement is equivalent to saying that life has no subject matter.
1943 'The Cube Root', in *Art News*, vol.41, 1 Feb.

Davis, Thomas Osborne 1814–45
Irish poet and politician, head of the Young Ireland Movement. He cofounded the weekly *Nation* in 1842, and wrote patriotic verses which became anthems of the Sinn Féin movement.

7 'Did they dare, did they dare, to slay Owen Roe O'Neil?'
'Yes, they slew with poison him they feared to meet with steel.'
'May God wither up their hearts! May their blood cease to flow!
May they walk in living death, who poisoned Owen Roe!'
1842 'Lament for the Death of Owen Roe O'Neil'.

8 Sagest in the council was he, kindest in the hall:
Sure we never won a battle—'twas Owen won them all.
Had he lived, had he lived, our dear country had been free;
But he's dead, but he's dead, and 'tis slaves we'll ever be.
1842 'Lament for the Death of Owen Roe O'Neil'.

9 They fought as they revelled, fast, fiery, and true,
And, though victors, they left on the field not a few;
And they who survived fought and drank as of yore,
But the land of their heart's hope they never saw more,
For in far, foreign fields, from Dunkirk to Belgrade
Lie the soldiers and chiefs of the Irish Brigade.
1845 *The Spirit of the Nation*, 'The Battle-Eve of the Brigade'.

10 Our colonel comes from Brian's race,
His wounds are in his breast and face.
1845 *The Spirit of the Nation*, 'Clare's Dragoons'.

11 Viva la the New Brigade!
Viva la the Old One, too!
Viva la, the Rose shall fade,
And the Shamrock shine for ever new!
1845 *The Spirit of the Nation*, 'Clare's Dragoons'.

12 Come in the evening, or come in the morning,
Come when you're looked for, or come without warning.
1846 'The Welcome'.

Davison, Emily Wilding 1872–1913
English militant suffragette, who campaigned fiercely for women's emancipation. She was frequently imprisoned, and died after running in front of the King's horse at the 1913 Derby.

13 As I am a woman and women do not count in the State, I refuse to be counted. Rebellion against tyrants is obedience to God.
1911 Comment on uncompleted Census paper, quoted in Gertrude Colmore *The Life of Emily Wilding Davison* (1913).

Dawkins, Richard 1941–
British ethologist, Professor at Oxford (1995–2008). He has done much to popularize the theories of Charles Darwin, most notably in his work *The Selfish Gene* (1976). His other books include *The God Delusion* (2006).

14 There is a better reason for studying zoology than its possible 'usefulness', and the general likeableness of animals. This reason is that we animals are the most complicated and perfectly designed pieces of machinery in the known universe. Put it like that, and it is hard to see why anybody studies anything else!
1976 *The Selfish Gene*, preface.

15 We are survival machines—robot vehicles blindly programmed to preserve the selfish molecules known as genes. This is a truth which still fills me with astonishment.
1976 *The Selfish Gene*, ch.2.

16 It has no vision, no foresight, no sight at all. If it can be said to play the role of watchmaker in nature, it is the *blind* watchmaker.
1986 Of natural selection. *The Blind Watchmaker*, ch.1.
▶ See Paley 661:57.

17 However many ways there may be of being alive, it is certain that there are vastly more ways of being dead.
1986 *The Blind Watchmaker*, ch.1.

18 The fact that life evolved out of nearly nothing, some ten billion years after the universe evolved out of literally nothing, is a fact so staggering that I would be mad to attempt words to do it justice.
2005 In *The Scotsman*, 9 Apr.

19 The God of the Old Testament is arguably the most unpleasant character in all fiction: jealous and proud of it; a petty, unjust, unforgiving control-freak; a vindictive, bloodthirsty ethnic cleanser; a misogynistic, homophobic, racist, infanticidal, genocidal, filicidal, pestilential, megalomaniacal, sadomasochistic, capriciously malevolent bully.
2006 *The God Delusion*.

20 You could almost define a philosopher as someone who won't take common sense for an answer.
2006 *The God Delusion*.

21 One of the truly bad effects of religion is that it teaches us that it is a virtue to be satisfied with not understanding.
2006 *The God Delusion*.

22 There is something infantile in the presumption that somebody else (parents in the case of children, God in the case of adults) has a responsibility to give your life meaning and point.
2006 *The God Delusion*.

23 I am thrilled to be alive at a time when humanity is pushing against the limits of understanding. Even better, we may eventually discover that there are no limits.
2006 *The God Delusion*.

24 We should be open-minded, but not so open-minded that our brain falls out.
2007 'The Enemies of Reason'.

25 Such delusions of grandeur to think that a God with a hundred billion galaxies on his mind would give a tuppenny damn who you sleep with, or indeed whether you believe in him.
2013 In public debate with Archbishop Rowan Williams.

26 The chicken is only an egg's way for making another egg.
Attributed.

Day, Clarence Shepard 1874–1935

US humorist, best known for his writings in the *New Yorker* and for his autobiographical sketches in *Life With Father* (1935).

27 The poets of each generation seldom sing a new song. They turn themes men always have loved, and sing them in the mode of their times.
1921 *The Crow's Nest*, 'Humpty-Dumpty and Adam'.

28 The real world is not easy to live in. It is rough; it is slippery. Without the most clear-eyed adjustments we fall and get crushed. A man must stay sober: not always, but most of the time.
1921 *The Crow's Nest*, 'In His Baby Blue Ship'.

29 I meant to be prompt, but it never occurred to me that I had better try to be early.
1935 *Life With Father*, 'Father teaches me to be prompt'.

30 Imagine the Lord talking French! Aside from a few odd words in Hebrew, I took it for granted that God had never spoken anything but the most dignified English.
1935 *Life With Father*, 'Father interferes'.

31 'If you don't go to other men's funerals,' he told Father stiffly, 'they won't go to yours.'
1935 *Life With Father*, 'Father interferes'.

32 Father declared he was going to buy a new plot in the cemetery, a plot all for himself. 'And I'll buy one on a corner,' he added triumphantly, 'where I can get out.'
1935 *Life With Father*, penultimate paragraph.

Day, Doris originally Doris Kappelhoff 1924–

US singer and film actress, whose sunny personality and girl-next-door image made her a star of 1950s musicals.

33 The really frightening thing about middle age is the knowledge that you'll grow out of it.
Quoted in A E Hotchner *Doris Day* (1978).

Dayan, Moshe 1915–81

Israeli soldier and politician. He left the Labour Party in 1966 to set up the Rafi Party with Ben Gurion. His heavily outnumbered forces were successful in the Six-Day War (1967), and as Foreign Minister he helped secure peace with Egypt (1977).

34 Whenever you accept our views, we shall be in full agreement with you.
Remark to US envoy Cyrus Vance during the Arab–Israeli negotiations, quoted in the *Observer*, 14 Aug 1977.

Day-Lewis, Cecil 1904–72

Irish poet and critic. Professor at Oxford (1951–6) and Harvard (1964–5), he became Poet Laureate in 1968. As well as poetry he wrote criticism, translation and, under the pseudonym Nicholas Blake, detective novels.

35 Tempt me no more; for I
Have known the lightning's hour,
The poet's inward pride,
The certainty of power.
1933 *The Magnetic Mountain*, pt.3, no.24.

36 You that love England, who have an ear for her music,
The slow movement of clouds in benediction,
Clear arias of light thrilling over her uplands,
Over the chords of summer sustained peacefully.
1933 *The Magnetic Mountain*, pt.4, no.32.

37 Do not expect again a phoenix hour,
The triple-towered sky, the dove complaining,
Sudden the rain of gold and heart's first ease
Traced under trees by the eldritch light of sundown.
1935 'From Feathers to Iron'.

38 Now we lament one
Who danced on a plume of words,
Sang with a fountain's panache,
Dazzled like slate roofs in sun
After rain, was flighty as birds
And alone as a mountain ash.
The ribald, inspired urchin
Leaning over the lip
Of his world, as over a rock pool
Or a lucky dip,
Found everything brilliant and virgin.
1953 'In Memory of Dylan Thomas'.

Dean, John 1938–

US lawyer and author. As White House adviser to President Nixon, he was implicated in the Watergate scandal.

39 I am convinced that we are going to make the whole road and put this thing in the funny pages of the history books.
1973 Taped conversation with the President, Feb.

40 We have a cancer within, close to the presidency, that is growing. It is growing daily.
1973 Taped conversation with the President, Mar.

41 Doing time is like climbing a mountain wearing roller skates.
1977 On conviction after the Watergate scandal. In *Newsweek*, 4 Jul.

42 History never exactly repeats itself, but it does some rather good impressions.
Comparing the presidential styles of Richard Nixon and George W Bush. Quoted in *Worse than Watergate* (2004).

de Beauvoir, Simone 1906–86

French philosopher, feminist and writer, who maintained a lifelong association with fellow-existentialist Jean-Paul Sartre. Her *Le Deuxième Sexe* (*The Second Sex*, 1949–50) is a pioneering feminist text.

43 There is a good case for showing that airplanes, machines, the telephone and the radio do not make men of today happier than those of former times.
1948 *Ethics of Ambiguity*.

44 *On ne naît pas femme: on le devient.*
One is not born a woman: one becomes a woman.
1949 *Le Deuxième Sexe (The Second Sex)*, bk.2, pt.1, ch.1.

45 *Ce n'est guère que dans les asiles que les coquettes gardent avec entêtement une foi entière en des regards absents; normalement, elles réclament des témoins.*
Women fond of dress are hardly ever entirely satisfied not to be seen, except among the insane; usually they want witnesses.
1949 *Le Deuxième Sexe (The Second Sex)*, bk.2, pt.5, ch.18 (translated by H M Parshley, 1952).

46 *La femme...sait que quand on la regarde on ne la distingue pas de son apparence: elle est jugée, respectée, désirée à travers sa toilette.*
Woman...knows that when she is looked at she is not considered apart from her appearance: she is judged, respected, desired, by and through her toilette.
1949 *Le Deuxième Sexe (The Second Sex)*, bk.2, pt.7, ch.25 (translated by H M Parshley, 1952).

47 *Si l'on vit assez longtemps, on voit que toute victoire se change un jour en défaite.*
If you live long enough, you'll find that every victory turns into a defeat.
1955 *Tous les hommes sont mortels (All Men Are Mortal)*.

de Bernières, Louis 1954–
English author who achieved international fame with *Captain Corelli's Mandolin* (1994), a love story set on a small island in Greece during World War II.

48 Writing today is like being stood stark naked in Trafalgar Square and being told to get an erection.
2001 On being asked how he was making progress on a successor to *Captain Corelli's Mandolin* (1994), Apr.

de Botton, Alain 1969–
British author, born in Switzerland.

49 How generous was it to offer gifts to people one knew would never accept them?
1994 *The Romantic Movement*, 'Martyrdom'.

50 How Proust Can Change Your Life.
1997 Book title.

51 It is perhaps when our lives are at their most problematic that we are likely to be most receptive to beautiful things.
2006 *The Architecture of Happiness*.

52 It is in dialogue with pain that many beautiful things acquire their value. Acquaintance with grief turns out to be one of the more unusual prerequisites of architectural appreciation. We might, quite aside from all other requirements, need to be a little sad before buildings can properly touch us.
2006 *The Architecture of Happiness*.

53 The origins and travels of our purchases remain matters of indifference, although—to the more imaginative at least—a slight dampness at the bottom of a carton, or an obscure code printed along a computer cable, may hint at processes of manufacture and transport nobler and more mysterious, more worthy of wonder and study, than the very goods themselves.
2009 *The Pleasures and Sorrows of Work*.

54 To look at the paper is to raise a seashell to one's ear and to be overwhelmed by the roar of humanity.
2009 *The Pleasures and Sorrows of Work*.

55 Travel agents would be wiser to ask us what we hope to change about our lives rather than simply where we wish to go.
2009 *A Week at the Airport: A Heathrow Diary*.

Debray, Regis 1941–
French Marxist theorist. He gained international fame through his association with Che Guevara in Latin America.

56 Since the Cuban Revolution and since the invasion of Santo Domingo *a state of emergency* has existed in Latin America. The Marines shoot at anything that moves, regardless of party affiliation.
1967 *Révolution dans la Révolution?*

57 *Vedi Napoli, e poi muori? Oui, mais pour voir Venise, mourez d'abord.*
See Naples and die? Yes, but to see Venice, die first.
1995 *Contre Venise*.

58 *À Naples, personne ne vous demande dans quel hôtel ou chez qui vous êtes descendu: c'est indifférent. À Venise, impossible d'échapper la question: Gritti? Danieli? Palazzo du duc de C.? Appartement de M.? (Consternation si vous répondez: auberge de jeunesse, ou dortoir de l'institut universitaire.)*
In Naples, no one asks you which hotel you're in or who you're staying with: it doesn't matter. In Venice, you can't avoid the question: the Gritti? the Danieli? the Duke of C.'s palazzo? M.'s apartment? (Dismay if you reply: the youth hostel, or the university halls of residence.)
1995 *Contre Venise*.

Debussy, Claude Achille 1862–1918
French composer. His writing for piano was described as 'musical Impressionism'. He translated it to the orchestra in *La Mer* (1905), to his opera, *Pelléas et Mélisande*, and to other works.

59 The colour of my soul is iron-grey and sad bats wheel about the steeple of my dreams.
1894 Letter.

60 That old poisoner.
1896 Letter, alluding to Wagner.

61 People don't very much like things that are beautiful—they are so far from their nasty little minds.
1900 Letter.

62 A pink bonbon stuffed with snow.
1903 Of the music of Edvard Grieg. *Gil Blas*.

63 A century of aeroplanes deserves its own music. As there are no precedents, I must create anew.
1913 Quoted in *La Revue S.I.M.*

Decatur, Stephen 1779–1820
US naval officer, who distinguished himself in the war with Tripoli (1801–5) and fought against Britain, capturing the frigate *Macedonian* (1812), but surrendering in 1814.

64 Our country! In her intercourse with foreign nations, may she always be in the right; but our country, right or wrong.

1816 Speech made in Norfolk, Virginia, Apr.
▶ See Adams 5:4, Chesterton 220:54.

Deedes, William Francis Deedes, Baron 1913–2007

English Conservative politician and journalist. He was an MP (1950–1974), and later pursued a career in journalism, becoming Editor of the *Daily Telegraph* (1974–86).

65 One golden rule for people who want to get on in politics is to keep their traps shut in August.
1999 In *The Mail on Sunday*, 22 Aug.

Deffand, Marquise du 1697–1780

French noblewoman, famous for her wit and beauty. Her salon was frequented by leading figures in Paris literary society, including Voltaire, Montesquieu and D'Alembert.

66 The distance does not matter; it is only the first step that counts.
1763 Commenting on the legend of St Denis, said to have carried his severed head for six miles following his execution. Letter, 7 Jul.

Defoe, Daniel 1660–1731

English writer, best known for his novels *Robinson Crusoe* (1719) and *Moll Flanders* (1722), and for his partly factual *Journal of the Plague Year* (1724). He also wrote a travel book, *A Tour Through the Whole Island of Great Britain* (1724–7).

67 The soul is placed in the body like a rough diamond, and must be polished, or the lustre of it will never appear.
1697 *An Essay upon Projects*,'Of Academies: An Academy for Women'.

68 The best of men cannot suspend their fate:
The good die early, and the bad die late.
1697 'Character of the Late Dr Annesley'.

69 Wherever God erects a house of prayer,
The Devil always builds a chapel there;
And 'twill be found, upon examination,
The latter hast the largest congregation.
1701 *The True-Born Englishman*, pt.1, l.1–4.

70 From this amphibious ill-born mob began
That vain, ill-natured thing, an Englishman.
1701 *The True-Born Englishman*, pt.1, l.132–3.

71 Your Roman-Saxon-Danish-Norman English.
1701 *The True-Born Englishman*, pt.1, l.139.

72 His lazy, long, lascivious reign.
1701 Of Charles II. *The True-Born Englishman*, pt.1, l.236.

73 Actions receive their tincture from the times,
And as they change are virtues made or crimes.
1703 *A Hymn to the Pillory*, l.29–30.

74 It happened one day, about noon, going towards my boat, I was exceedingly surprised with the print of a man's naked foot on the shore, which was very plain to be seen in the sand. I stood like one thunderstruck, or as if I had seen an apparition.
1719 *Robinson Crusoe*.

75 My man Friday.
1719 *Robinson Crusoe*.

76 Vice came in always at the door of necessity, not at the door of inclination.
1722 *Moll Flanders*.

77 Manchester, one of the greatest, if not really the greatest mere village in England.
1724–7 *A Tour Through the Whole Island of Great Britain*, letter 10.

78 Here is a pleasant situation, and yet nothing pleasant to be seen. Here is a harbour without ships, a port without trade, a fishery without nets, a people without business; and, that which is worse than all, they do not seem to desire business, much less do they understand it.
1724–7 Of Kirkcudbright, Scotland. *A Tour Through the Whole Island of Great Britain*, letter 12.

79 A very fine city; the four principal streets are the fairest for breadth, and the finest built that I have ever seen in one city together... In a word, 'tis the cleanest and beautifullest, and best built city in Britain, London excepted.
1724–7 Of Glasgow. *A Tour Through the Whole Island of Great Britain*, letter 12.

80 Pleasure is a *thief* to business.
1725 *The Complete English Tradesman*, vol.1, ch.9.

81 Things as certain as death and taxes, can be more firmly believed.
1726 *History of the Devil*, bk.2, ch.6.
▶ See also Franklin 348:19.

De Forest, Lee 1873–1961

US inventor, pioneer in the development of wireless telegraphy and radio.

82 While theoretically and technically television may be feasible, commercially and financially I consider it an impossibility, a development of which we need waste little time dreaming.
1926 In the *New York Times*.

Degas, (Hilaire Germain) Edgar 1834–1917

French artist. After a trip to Italy, where he was influenced by Renaissance painters, he returned to Paris and exhibited with the Impressionists (1874–86).

83 Art does not expand, it repeats itself.
1872 Letter to Paul Frölich, 27 Nov.

84 It is essential to do the same subject over again, ten times, a hundred times.
1886 Letter to Bartholomé, 17 Jan.

85 Aren't all beautiful things made by renunciation?
Quoted in P Lafond *Degas* (1918–9).

86 Drawing is not the form; it is the way of seeing the form.
Quoted in P Valéry *Degas, danse, dessin* (1938).

87 Art cannot be made with an intent to please.
Quoted in R H Ives Gammell *The Shop-Talk of Edgar Degas* (1961).

88 It is all very well to copy what you see; it is much better to draw what you see only in memory.
Quoted in R H Ives Gammell *The Shop-Talk of Edgar Degas* (1961).

89 Everybody has talent at twenty-five. The difficult thing is to have it at fifty.
Quoted in R H Ives Gammell *The Shop-Talk of Edgar Degas* (1961).

de Gaulle, Charles 1890–1970

French general. Leader of the Free French during World War II, he became head of the provisional government, and later Prime Minister (1958). As President of the Fifth Republic, he implemented an assertive foreign policy, but in 1969 resigned after the defeat of his referendum proposals for senate and regional reforms.

DeGeneres

90 Nothing great will ever be achieved without great men—and men only become great if they are determined to be so.
1934 Le Fil de l'épée.

91 La France a perdu une bataille! Mais la France n'a pas perdu la guerre!
France has lost a battle! But France has not lost the war!
1940 Proclamation, 18 Jun. Collected in *Discours, messages et déclarations du Général de Gaulle* (1941).

92 Puisque ceux qui avaient le devoir de manier l'épée de la France l'ont laissée tomber brisée, moi, j'ai ramassé le tronçon du glaive.
Since those whose duty it was to wield the sword of France have let it fall shattered to the ground, I have taken up the broken blade.
1940 Speech, 13 Jul.

93 The French will only be united under the threat of danger. How else can one govern a country that produces 246 different types of cheese?
1951 Speech. Quoted in *Les Mots du Général* (1962).

94 Les traités, voyez-vous, sont comme les jeunes filles et comme les roses: ça dure ce que ça dure.
Treaties are like girls and roses—they last while they last.
1963 Speech at the Elysée Palace, 2 Jul. Quoted in Brian Crozier *De Gaulle the Statesman* (1973).

95 I myself have become a Gaullist only little by little.
1963 In the *Observer*, 29 Dec.

96 I respect only those who resist me, but I cannot tolerate them.
1966 In the *New York Times*, 12 May.

97 Vive le Québec! Vive le Québec libre! Vive le Canada français! Vive la France!
1967 Address to the crowd before Montreal's City Hall, 24 Jul. The slogan 'Québec libre' was identified with the separatist cause.

98 When I want to know what France thinks, I ask myself.
Sons of France.

99 In order to become the master, the politician poses as the servant.
Attributed.

1 Politics is too important to be left to the politicians.
Attributed.

DeGeneres, Ellen (Lee) 1958–

US comedian and television host.

2 There's no one way to dance. And that's kind of my philosophy about everything.
Quoted in *People* (2005).

3 Never follow anyone else's path, unless you're in the woods and you're lost and you can see a path; then, by all means, you should follow that path.
Quoted in Katie Couric, *The Best Advice I Ever Got* (2011).

4 Accept who you are. Unless you're a serial killer.
2011 Seriously... I'm Kidding.

5 It's failure that gives you the proper perspective on success.
2011 Seriously... I'm Kidding.

6 I've always said, I like my coffee like I like my men... I don't drink coffee.
2014 The Ellen DeGeneres Show, 13 Mar.

Dekanahwideh fl.c.1450

Native American leader, traditional founder of the Six Nations Confederacy.

7 I, Dekanahwideh, and the Confederated Chiefs, now uproot the tallest pine tree, and into the cavity thereby made we cast all weapons of war... Thus shall the Great Peace be established.
Traditional words from the Six Nations Confederacy (present-day Ontario and the Northeastern United States), one of the world's oldest constitutions, quoted in Paul A W Wallace *The White Roots of Peace* (1946).

Dekker, Thomas c.1570–c.1641

English dramatist. He wrote dramas for both public and private stages, masques, pageants and topical pamphlets, and was imprisoned for debt for three years. He frequently collaborated with other dramatists.

8 Ill is the weather that bringeth no gain.
1600 The Shoemaker's Holiday, 'The First Three-men's Song'.

9 Dost thou not know that love respects no blood,
Cares not for difference of birth or state?
1600 The Shoemaker's Holiday, act 5, sc.5.

10 Golden slumbers kiss your eyes,
Smiles awake you when you rise;
Sleep, pretty wantons, do not cry,
And I will sing a lullaby,
Rock them, rock them, lullaby.
1603 The Pleasant Comedy of Patient Grisill, act 4, sc.2.

11 That great fishpond.
1604 Of the seas. The Honest Whore, pt.1, act 1, sc.2.

12 This wench we speak of strays so from her kind,
Nature repents she made her; 'tis a mermaid
Has tolled my son to shipwreck
1611 The Roaring Girl (with Thomas Middleton), act 1, sc.2.

13 'Tis the maddest fantasticalest girl. I never knew so much flesh and so much nimbleness put together.
1611 The Roaring Girl (with Thomas Middleton), act 2, sc.2.

14 I have no humour to marry; I love to lie o' both sides of the bed myself; and again, o' th' other side.
1611 The Roaring Girl (with Thomas Middleton), act 2, sc.2.

15 I have the head now of myself, and am man enough for a woman.
1611 The Roaring Girl (with Thomas Middleton), act 2, sc.2.

16 Thou'rt one of those
That thinks each woman thy fond flexible whore.
1611 The Roaring Girl (with Thomas Middleton), act 3, sc.1.

de Klerk, F(rederik) W(illem) 1936–

South African politician. He was President of South Africa (1989–94) and in 1993 was jointly awarded the Nobel peace prize with Nelson Mandela.

17 Today we have closed the book on apartheid.
1992 On the endorsement of his government's reform programme following a referendum of white South Africans. In *The Independent*, 19 Mar.

de Kooning, Willem 1904–97

Dutch-born US painter, who emigrated to the US in 1926 and became a leader of Abstract Expressionism, especially in action painting. His works, which focus on the human form, include the controversial series *Woman I–V* (1952–3).

18 Style is a fraud. I always felt the Greeks were hiding behind their columns.
1949 'A Desperate View', lecture given in New York.

19 Flesh was the reason why oil painting was invented.
1980 In *Bulletin*, Pittsburgh International Museum.

Delacroix, (Ferdinand Victor) Eugène 1798–1863
French Romantic painter, whose loose drawing and vivid colour aroused controversy. He continued to experiment with non-classical techniques and the use of colour.

20 What makes men of genius, or rather, what they make, is not new ideas, it is that idea—possessing them—that what has been said has still not been said enough.
1824 *The Journal of Eugène Delacroix* (translated by W Pach, 1948), entry for 15 May.

21 I live in company with a body, a silent companion, exacting and eternal. He it is who notes that individuality which is the seal of the weakness of our race. My soul has wings, but the brutal jailer is strict.
1824 *The Journal of Eugène Delacroix* (translated by W Pach, 1948), entry for 4 Jun.

22 A taste for simplicity cannot endure for long.
1847 *The Journal of Eugène Delacroix* (translated by W Pach, 1948).

23 Painters who are not colourists produce illumination and not painting.
1852 *The Journal of Eugène Delacroix* (translated by W Pach, 1948).

de la Mare, Walter 1873–1956
English poet and novelist. He worked for an oil company until 1908, when he became a full-time writer. His work included volumes of verse, novels, prose fantasy and short stories for both children and adults.

24 Oh, no man knows
Through what wild centuries
Roves back the rose.
1912 'All That's Past'.

25 'Is there anybody there?' said the Traveller,
Knocking on the moonlit door;
And his horse in the silence champed the grasses
Of the forest's ferny floor.
1912 'The Listeners'.

26 'Tell them I came, and no one answered,
That I kept my word,' he said.
1912 'The Listeners'.

27 Aye, they heard his foot upon the stirrup,
And the sound of iron on stone,
And how the silence surged softly backward,
When the plunging hoofs were gone.
1912 'The Listeners'.

28 He is crazed with the spell of far Arabia,
They have stolen his wits away.
1912 'Arabia'.

29 But beauty vanishes; beauty passes;
However rare—rare it be;
And when I crumble, who will remember
This lady of the West Country?
1912 'Epitaph'.

30 Ann, Ann!
Come! quick as you can!

There's a fish that *talks*
In the frying pan.
1913 'Alas, Alack'.

31 Slowly, silently, now the moon
Walks the night in her silver shoon.
1913 'Silver'.

32 A face peered. All the grey night
In chaos of vacancy shone;
Nought but vast Sorrow was there—
The sweet cheat gone.
1918 'The Ghost'.

33 When I lie where shades of darkness
Shall no more assail mine eyes.
1918 'Fare Well'.

34 Look thy last on all things lovely,
Every hour. Let no night
Seal thy sense in deathly slumber
Till to delight
Thou have paid thy utmost blessing.
1918 'Fare Well'.

35 Too late for fruit, too soon for flowers.
Attributed, when asked, while ill, if he would prefer fruit or flowers. Quoted in Clifton Fadiman *The Faber Book of Anecdotes* (1985).

Delaney, Shelagh 1939–2011
English playwright and screenwriter, whose best-known play, *A Taste of Honey* (produced 1958), was written when she was 17.

36 Women never have young minds. They are born three thousand years old.
1958 *A Taste of Honey*, act 1, sc.2.

DeLillo, Don 1936–
US novelist. His ambitious dissections of modern cultural codes in such novels as *White Noise* (1985), *Libra* (1988) and *Underworld* (1998) have made him an important voice in contemporary fiction.

37 I've come to think of Europe as a hardcover book, America as the paperback version.
1982 Owen Brademas. *The Names*, ch.1.

38 Tourism is the march of stupidity.
1982 James Axton. *The Names*, ch.3.

39 If I were a writer, how I would enjoy being told the novel is dead. How liberating to work in the margins, outside a central perception. You are the ghoul of literature. Lovely.
1982 Owen Brademas. *The Names*, ch.4.

40 To a writer, madness is a final distillation of self, a final editing down. It's the drowning out of false voices.
1982 Owen Brademas. *The Names*, ch.5.

41 Men with secrets tend to be drawn to each other, not because they want to share what they know but because they need the company of the like-minded, the fellow-afflicted.
1988 Walter Everett, Jr. *Libra*, pt.1, '17 April'.

42 A conspiracy is everything that ordinary life is not. It's the inside game, cold, sure, undistracted, forever closed off to us. We are the flawed ones, the innocents, trying to make some rough sense of the daily jostle. Conspirators have a logic and a daring beyond our reach.
1988 *Libra*, pt.2, 'In Dallas'.

43 The dead have come to take the living. The dead in winding-sheets, the regimented dead on horseback, the skeleton that plays a hurdy-gurdy.
   1998 *Underworld*.

44 It's what no one knows about you that allows you to know yourself.
   2010 *Point Omega*.

45 The less there was to see, the harder he looked, the more he saw.
   2010 *Point Omega*.

Delius, Frederick 1862–1934
English composer of German-Scandinavian descent. He settled in France in 1890, establishing himself as a prolific and highly original composer. In 1924 he became paralysed and blind, but continued to work with the help of his amanuensis Eric Fenby.

46 It is only that which cannot be expressed otherwise that is worth expressing in music.
   1920 'At the Crossroads'.

Deming, W(illiam) Edwards 1900–93
US statistician, inventor of modern quality control.

47 What's the aim of the school of business, for example? They teach students how business is conducted today and how to perpetuate it. Any wonder we're in trouble? They ought to be preparing students for the future, not for the past.
   1990 Interview in the *Wall Street Journal*, 4 Jun.

Democritus c.460–c.370 BC
Greek philosopher. Only fragments of his extensive work on ethics have survived.

48 Nothing exists except atoms and empty space; everything else is opinion.
   Diogenes Laertius, vol.9.

49 Strength and beauty are the blessings of youth; temperance, however, is the flower of old age.
   Fragment quoted in H Diels and W Kranz (eds) *Die Fragmente der Vorsokratiker*, vol.2 (1952), no.294.

Dempsey, (William Harrison) Jack 1895–1983
US boxer. He won the world heavyweight title in 1919 and lost it to Gene Tunney in 1926. He retired in 1940 and became a successful restaurateur.

50 Honey, I forgot to duck.
   1926 Attributed, to his wife after he was knocked out by Gene Tunney. US President Ronald Reagan repeated the phrase to his wife when wounded in an attempted assassination, 1981.

51 When you're fighting, you're fighting for one thing—money.
   Quoted in Colin Jarman *The Guinness Dictionary of Sports Quotations* (1990).

Deneuve, Catherine 1943–
French film actress. She has appeared in over 100 films and won many awards under the direction of such notable directors as Roman Polanski and Luis Buñuel.

52 Actresses have to be able to frown.
   2007 When asked why she opposed cosmetic surgery.

Dench, Dame Judi(th Olivia) 1934–
English actress. Acclaimed as one of the greatest classical stage actors of her generation, she has also won numerous awards for her sensitive performances in such films as *Mrs Brown* (1997), *Shakespeare in Love* (1998), *Chocolat* (2000), *Iris* (2001) and *Philomena* (2013).

53 We get up in the morning. We do our best. Nothing else matters.
   2012 As Evelyn Greenslade in *The Best Exotic Marigold Hotel* (screenplay by Ol Parker).

54 Just because you're in First Class doesn't make you a first-class person.
   2013 As Philomena Lee in *Philomena* (screenplay by Steve Coogan and Jeff Pope).

55 I get sillier as I get older, so I don't know what wisdom means. I can only pass on something that I've been acquainted with and let whomever it is pick the bones out of it.
   Attributed.

Deng Xiaoping 1904–97
Chinese political leader who rose to power (1978) after disgrace during the Cultural Revolution. His international esteem suffered after he sanctioned the Tiananmen Square massacre of pro-democracy supporters, Jun 1989.

56 It doesn't matter whether the cat is black or white, as long as it catches mice.
   1962 Speech at Communist Youth League conference, Jul.

57 A fundamental contradiction does not exist between socialism and a market economy.
   1985 Address to US businessmen organized by *Time* magazine, 18 Dec.

58 Even if they're functioning out of ignorance, they are still participating and must be suppressed. In China, even one million people can be considered a small sum.
   1989 Of pro-democracy demonstrators. In *The Times*, 5 Jun.

Denham, Sir John 1615–69
Irish poet and Royalist, who undertook secret missions for Charles I and Charles II during the Civil War and Protectorate, and was knighted in 1661. He is credited with introducing to English verse the couplet form which later dominated 18c poetry.

59 Can knowledge have no bound, but must advance
   So far, to make us wish for ignorance?
   1642 *Cooper's Hill*, l.145–6.

60 O could I flow like thee, and make thy stream
   My great example, as it is my theme!
   Though deep, yet clear, though gentle, yet not dull,
   Strong without rage, without o'erflowing full.
   1642 Of the Thames. *Cooper's Hill*, l.189–92.

61 Such is our pride, our folly, or our fate,
   That few, but such as cannot write, translate.
   1648 'To Richard Fanshaw'.

62 Old Mother Wit, and Nature gave
   Shakespeare and Fletcher all they have;
   In Spenser, and in Jonson, Art
   Of slower Nature got the start.
   1667 'On Mr Abraham Cowley'.

63 Youth, what man's age is like to be doth show;
   We may our ends by our beginnings know.
   1668 'Of Prudence', l.225–6.

Deniehy, Daniel Henry 1828–65
Australian lawyer, politician, orator and writer, who formed his own famous library.

64 A Bunyip Aristocracy.
  1853 Quoted in *The Australian Dictionary of Biography*, vol 4. The bunyip is a mythical, chimerical animal of Australian folklore.

De Niro, Robert 1943–
US actor and film producer. Widely recognised as one of the leading actors of his generation, he has won numerous awards for his performances in such films as *Mean Streets* (1973), *The Godfather Part II* (1974), *Taxi Driver* (1976), *The Deer Hunter* (1978), *Raging Bull* (1980), *Goodfellas* (1990), *Cape Fear* (1991), and *Silver Linings Playbook* (2012).

65 You talking to me? Well, I'm the only one here. Who the fuck do you think you're talking to?
  1976 As Travis Bickle in *Taxi Driver* (screenplay by Paul Schrader).

66 Someday a real rain will come and wash all this scum off the streets.
  1976 As Travis Bickle in *Taxi Driver* (screenplay by Paul Schrader).

67 Better to be king for a night than schmuck for a lifetime.
  1983 As Rupert Pupkin in *The King of Comedy* (screenplay by Paul D. Zimmerman).

68 Never rat on your friends and always keep your mouth shut.
  1990 As James Conway in *Goodfellas* (screenplay by Nicholas Pileggi and Martin Scorsese).

69 You're gonna learn about loss.
  1991 As Max Cady in *Cape Fear* (screenplay by Wesley Strick).

70 There are three ways of doing things around here: the right way, the wrong way and the way that I do it.
  1995 As Sam Rothstein in *Casino* (screenplay by Nicholas Pileggi and Martin Scorsese).

Denis, Maurice 1870–1943
French painter and art theorist, associated with the Nabis group ('prophets' influenced by Gauguin), and Symbolism.

71 Remember that a painting—before it is a battlehorse, a nude woman, or some anecdote—is essentially a flat surface covered with colours assembled in a certain order.
  1912 *Théories: 1890–1910*.

Denman, Thomas, 1st Baron 1779–1854
English jurist. A Whig MP (1818–26), he was Attorney-General in Earl Grey's administration (1830–2) and Lord Chief Justice (1832–50).

72 Trial by jury itself, instead of being a security to persons who are accused, will be a delusion, a mockery, and a snare.
  1844 Judgement in *O'Connell v The Queen*, 4 Sep.

Denning, Alfred Thompson, Lord 1899–1999
English judge. As Master of the Rolls (1962–82) he earned a reputation for his outspoken opinions.

73 A wrong decision can make me very miserable. But I have trust in God. If you have this trust you don't have to worry, as you don't have the sole responsibility.
  1982 Speech on his retirement.

Dennis, C(larence Michael) J(ames) 1876–1938
Australian poet and journalist. His poems have been popular for their vernacular humour.

74 Me pal 'e trots 'er up an' does the toff—
  'E allus wus a bloke fer showin' off.
  'This 'ere's Doreen,' 'e sez. 'This 'ere's the Kid.'
  I dips me lid.
  1915 *Songs of a Sentimental Bloke*, 'The Intro'. Bill persuades his friend to introduce him to a girl.

Dennis, John 1657–1734
English playwright and critic. He was among the most famous critics of his day, but his own plays met with little success and he was one of the targets of Alexander Pope's satire in *The Dunciad*.

75 Damn them, see how the rascals use me! They will not let my play run, and yet they steal my thunder!
  1709 Attributed, when watching a production of *Macbeth* that featured a thunder machine he had designed for use in his own play *Appius and Virginia*, which had been denied a long run. Said to be the origin of the phrase 'to steal one's thunder'.

76 A man who could make so vile a pun would not scruple to pick a pocket.
  Of Dennis. In the *Gentleman's Magazine* 1781, editorial note.

Depp, Johnny (John Christopher) 1963–
US actor.

77 If you were waiting for the opportune moment, that was it.
  2003 As Captain Jack Sparrow in *Pirates of the Caribbean* (screenplay by Ted Elliott and Terry Rossio).

78 I'm not swimming in the soup bowl. I'm not getting overcooked in that big stew pot.
  2004 On why he lives in France rather than in Los Angeles. Quoted in *Scotland on Sunday*, 2 May.

79 Mate, if you choose to lock your heart away, you lose it forever.
  2007 As Captain Jack Sparrow in *Pirates of the Caribbean: At World's End* (screenplay by Ted Elliott and Terry Rossio).

80 Acting is reacting.
  2011 As the voice of Rango in *Rango* (screenplay by John Logan).

De Quincey, Thomas 1785–1859
English writer. He ran away from school in 1802, lived with a prostitute in London, became an opium addict at Oxford, lived for a time in the Lake District and moved to Edinburgh in 1828.

81 A duller spectacle this earth of ours has not to show than a rainy Sunday in London.
  1821 *Confessions of an English Opium Eater* (originally serialized in the *London Magazine*, published 1822).

82 Thou hast the keys of Paradise, oh just, subtle, and mighty opium!
  1821 *Confessions of an English Opium Eater* (originally serialized in the *London Magazine*, published 1822).

83 Books, we are told, propose to *instruct* or to *amuse*. Indeed!… The true antithesis to knowledge, in this case, is not *pleasure*, but *power*. All that is literature seeks to communicate power; all that is not literature, to communicate knowledge.
  1823 *Letters to a Young Man whose Education has been Neglected*, no.3, in the London Magazine, Jan–Jul.

84 Murder Considered as One of the Fine Arts.
  1827 Title of essay, in *Blackwood's Magazine*, Feb.

85 If once a man indulges himself in murder, very soon he comes to think little of robbing; and from robbing he comes next to drinking and sabbath-breaking, and from that to incivility and procrastination.
1839 'On Murder Considered as One of the Fine Arts' (supplementary paper), in *Blackwood's Magazine*, Nov.

Derby, Edward Geoffrey Smith Stanley, 14th Earl of 1799–1869

English statesman and Conservative Prime Minister (1852, 1858–9, 1866–8), formerly a Whig. He entered the Lords in 1844 and headed the Protectionists from 1846, the year he became Party leader.

86 The foreign policy of the noble Earl, Lord Russell, may be summed up in two truly expressive words: meddle and muddle.
1864 Speech in the House of Lords, Feb, referring to the Prime Minister's policy on the American Civil War.

Desai, Anita *née Mazumbar* 1937–

Indian novelist, who writes for children and adults. Her novels *The Clear Light of Day* (1980), *In Custody* (1984) and *Fasting, Feasting* (1999) were all shortlisted for the Booker Prize.

87 Do you know anyone who would—secretly, sincerely, in his innermost self—*really* prefer to return to childhood?
1980 *The Clear Light of Day*, ch.1.

Desbiens, Jean-Paul 1927–2006

Canadian writer and educator.

88 Education is impossible without love, without loving a few of the great men of the past.
1965 *For Pity's Sake* (translated by Frédéric Côte).

Desbordes-Valmore, Marceline 1786–1859

French poet. She worked in the theatre and published children's stories before turning to poetry. Her poems are written in an open, informal style, often as dialogues.

89 *Par toi tout le bonheur que m'offre l'avenir*
Est dans mon souvenir.
Through you, all the happiness that the future offers
Is in my memory.
1819 *Élegies, Marie et romances*, 'Le Souvenir'.

90 *Ce qu'on donne à l'amour est à jamais perdu.*
What one gives in love is forever lost.
1830 *Poésies*, 'L'Isolement'.

91 *J'ai vécu d'aimer, j'ai donc vécu de larmes.*
I lived to love. I lived, therefore, in tears.
1860 *Poésies posthumes*, 'Rêve intermittent d'une nuit triste'.

Descartes, René 1596–1650

French philosopher and mathematician. He travelled widely before settling in Holland and writing his major works (both popular, in French, and scholarly, in Latin): the *Discours de la méthode* (1637), *Meditationes de prima philosophia* (1641), and *Principia philosophiae* (1644).

92 *La lecture de tous les bons livres est comme une conversation avec les plus honnêtes gens des siècles passés, qui en ont été les auteurs, et même une conversation étudiée en laquelle ils ne nous découvrent que les meilleures de leurs pensées.*
The reading of good books is like a conversation with the best men of past centuries—in fact like a prepared conversation, in which they reveal their best thoughts.
1637 *Discours de la méthode* (*Discourse on Method*), 1st discourse (translated by G E M Anscombe and Peter Geach).

93 *Le bon sens est la chose du monde la mieux partagée: car chacun pense en être si bien pourvu, que ceux même qui sont les plus difficiles à contenter en toute autre chose n'ont point coutume d'en désirer plus qu'ils ont. En quoi il n'est pas vraisemblable que tous se trompent; mais plutôt cela témoigne que la puissance de bien juger et distinguer le vrai d'avec le faux, qui est proprement ce qu'on nomme le bon sens ou la raison, est naturellement égale en tous les hommes.*
Good sense is the most fairly distributed thing in the world; for everyone thinks himself so well supplied with it, that even those who are hardest to satisfy in every other way do not usually desire more of it than they already have. In this matter it is not likely that everybody is mistaken; it rather goes to show that the power of judging well and distinguishing truth from falsehood, which is what we properly mean by good sense or reason, is naturally equal in all men.
1637 *Discours de la méthode* (*Discourse on Method*), 1st discourse (translated by G E M Anscombe and Peter Geach).

94 *Pour ce qu'alors je désirais vaquer seulement à la recherche de la vérité, je pensai qu'il fallait que je…rejetasse comme absolument faux tout ce en quoi je pourrais imaginer le moindre doute, afin de voir s'il ne resterait point, après cela, quelque chose en ma créance qui fût entièrement indubitable.*
Since my present aim was to give myself up to the pursuit of truth alone, I thought I must…reject as if absolutely false anything as to which I could imagine the least doubt, in order to see if I should not be left at the end believing something that was absolutely indubitable.
1637 *Discours de la méthode* (*Discourse on Method*), 4th discourse (translated by G E M Anscombe and Peter Geach).

95 *Je pris garde que, pendant que je voulais ainsi penser que tout était faux, il fallait nécessairement que moi, qui le pensais, fusse quelque chose.*
I noticed that while I was trying to think everything false, it must needs be that I, who was thinking this, was something.
1637 *Discours de la méthode* (*Discourse on Method*), 4th discourse (translated by G E M Anscombe and Peter Geach).

96 *Je pense, donc je suis.*
I think, therefore I am.
1637 *Discours de la méthode* (*Discourse on Method*), 4th discourse (translated by G E M Anscombe and Peter Geach). Often quoted as 'Cogito, ergo sum', but Descartes wrote the French version before the Latin.

97 *Je pouvais prendre pour règle générale, que les choses que nous concevons fort clairement et fort distinctement sont toutes vraies.*
I could take it as a general rule that whatever we conceive very clearly and very distinctly is true.
1637 *Discours de la méthode* (*Discourse on Method*), 4th discourse (translated by G E M Anscombe and Peter Geach).

98 *Animadverti jam ante aliquot annos quam multa, ineunte aetate, falsa pro veris admiserim, et quam*

dubia sint quaecunque istis postea superextruxi, ac proinde funditus omnia semel in vita esse evertenda, atque a primis fundamentis denno inchoandum, si quid aliquando firmum et mansurum cupiam in scientiis stabilire.
Some years ago now I observed the multitude of errors that I had accepted as true in my earliest years, and the dubiousness of the whole superstructure I had since then reared on them; and the consequent need of making a clean sweep for once in my life, and beginning again from the very foundations, if I would establish some secure and lasting result in science.
1641 *Meditationes*, 1st meditation (translated by G E M Anscombe and Peter Geach).

99 *Supponam igitur non optimum Deum, fontem veritatis, sed genium aliquum malignum, eundemque summe potentem et callidum, omnem suam industriam in eo posuisse, ut me falleret.*
I will suppose then, not that there is a supremely good God, the source of truth; but that there is an evil spirit, who is supremely powerful and intelligent, and does his utmost to deceive me.
1641 *Meditationes*, 1st meditation (translated by G E M Anscombe and Peter Geach).

1 *Agnoscam fieri non posse ut existam talis naturae qualis sum, nempe ideam Dei in me habens, nisi revera Deus etiam existeret, Deus, inquam, ille idem cujus idea in me est.*
I could not possibly exist with the nature I actually have, that is, one endowed with the idea of God, unless there really is a God; the very God, I mean, of whom I have an idea.
1641 *Meditationes*, 3rd meditation (translated by G E M Anscombe and Peter Geach)

Deschamps, Eustache c.1345–1406

French poet, soldier and courtier.

2 *Rien ne se peut comparer à Paris.*
Nothing can compare to Paris.
c.1370 'Ballade de Paris', refrain.

Deschamps, Yvon 1935–

Canadian entertainer, known for his separatist allegiances.

3 All we want is an independent Quebec within a strong and united Canada.
Quoted by Peter C Newman in *Maclean's*, 13 Nov 1978. This has become the classic formulation of Quebec's national and political aspirations.

Destouches, Philippe originally Néricault 1680–1754

French playwright, a diplomat in England (1717–23). His early comedies are undistinguished, but his masterpiece is *Le Glorieux* (1732, 'The Boaster').

4 *Les absents ont toujours tort.*
The absent are always in the wrong.
1717 *L'Obstacle imprévu*, act 1, sc.6.

Dettori, Frankie (Lanfranco) 1970–

Italian jockey. He was Champion Jockey (1994, 1995, 2004) and in 1996 achieved the unparalleled feat of winning all seven races on the card at Ascot.

5 When I'm good, I can be really good—I can do things even I didn't think I could do. I would say my worst is still not so bad, either.
2003 Quoted in *The Times*, 27 Sep.

De Valera, Éamon 1882–1975

Irish statesman, born in the US. He narrowly escaped execution for his part in the 1916 Easter Rebellion, and became leader of Sinn Féin (1917–26). He was Prime Minister (1932–48, 1951–4, 1957–9) and President (1959–73).

6 Why doesn't he use a spoon?
1921 On being told that David Lloyd George had said talking to him was like trying to pick up mercury with a fork.

7 Whenever I wanted to know what the Irish people wanted, I had only to examine my own heart and it told me straight off what the Irish people wanted.
1922 Speech to the Irish Parliament, 6 Jan.

Devlin, Denis 1908–59

Irish poet and diplomat, born in Scotland. His poetry, which assimilates Christian iconography into cosmopolitan settings, was not appreciated until after his death.

8 And sad, Oh sad, that glen with one thin stream
He met his death in; and a farmer told me
There was but one small bird to shoot: it sang
'Better Beast and know your end, and die
Than Man with murderous angels in his head.'
c.1956 'The Tomb of Michael Collins'.

De Voto, Bernard 1897–1955

US historian and writer, known for 'The Easy Chair' in *Harper's Magazine* from 1935. His works include the historical trilogy beginning with *The Year of Decision: 1846* (1943) and he edited Twain's work.

9 The proper union of gin and vermouth is a great and sudden glory; it is one of the happiest marriages on earth, and one of the shortest lived.
1949 In *Harper's Magazine*, Dec.

10 Novelists, whatever else they may be besides, are also children talking to children—in the dark.
1950 *The World of Fiction*.

11 When evening quickens in the street, comes a pause in the day's occupation that is known as the cocktail hour.
1951 *The Hour*.

12 You can no more keep a martini in the refrigerator than you can keep a kiss there.
1951 *The Hour*.

De Vries, Peter 1910–93

US novelist and humorist, best known for *The Tunnel of Love* (1954).

13 It is the final proof of God's omnipotence that he need not exist in order to save us.
1958 *The Mackerel Plaza*, ch.1.

14 Look at it this way: Psychoanalysis is a permanent fad.
1973 *Forever Panting*.

Dewar, Donald Campbell 1937–2000

Scottish Labour politician. He was Secretary of State for Scotland (1997–9) and the first First Minister of the new Scottish Parliament (1999–2000).

15 He could start a party in an empty room—and often did—filling it with good cheer, Gaelic songs, and argument.
  1994 Of John Smith, leader of the Labour Party, at his funeral, 19 May.

16 'There shall be a Scottish Parliament.' Through long years, those words were first a hope, then a belief, then a promise. Now they are a reality.
  1999 Speech at the official opening of the Scottish Parliament, 1 Jul.

17 We look forward to the time when this moment will be seen as a turning point: the day when democracy was renewed in Scotland, when we revitalized our place in this our United Kingdom.
  1999 Speech at the official opening of the Scottish Parliament, 1 Jul.

18 This is about more than our politics and our laws. This is about who we are, how we carry ourselves.
  1999 Speech at the official opening of the Scottish Parliament, 1 Jul.

Dewey, John 1859–1952

US philosopher and educator. A leading pragmatist, he developed an influential philosophy of education which stressed learning through experience. His writings include *The Quest for Certainty* (1929) and *The Child and the Curriculum* (1902).

19 When physics, chemistry, biology, medicine, contribute to the detection of concrete human woes and to the development of plans for remedying them and relieving the human estate, they become moral; they become part of the apparatus of moral inquiry or science... When the consciousness of science is fully impregnated with the consciousness of human value, the greatest dualism which now weighs humanity down, the split between the material, the mechanical and the scientific and the moral and ideal will be destroyed.
  1920 *Reconstruction in Philosophy.*

20 The function of criticism is the reeducation of perception of works of art... The conception that its business is to appraise, to judge in the legal and moral sense, arrests the perception of those who are influenced by the criticism that assumes this task.
  1934 *Art as Experience.*

De Wolfe, Elsie 1865–1950

English actress, interior decorator and hostess, the wife of the British diplomat Sir Charles Mendl.

21 Beige! Just my color.
  On seeing the Acropolis for the first time. Quoted in Nina Campbell and Caroline Seebohm *Elsie de Wolfe: A Decorative Life* (1992), ch.1.

Diaghilev, Sergei 1872–1929

Russian impresario. His Ballets Russes company, formed in 1911, created a sensation throughout Europe and launched the careers of such dancers as Balanchine, Fokine, Nijinsky and Pavlova.

22 *Étonne-moi!*
  Astonish me!
  1912 Attributed, when Jean Cocteau complained that he was getting insufficient direction when designing the scenario for a new ballet. Quoted in Wallace Fowlie (ed) *Journals of Jean Cocteau* (1956), ch.1.

Diana, Princess of Wales 1961–97

British princess. She married Charles, Prince of Wales, in 1981 and they were divorced in 1996.

23 I'm as thick as a plank.
  Remark quoted in *Sunday Today*, 25 Jan 1987.

24 There were three of us in this marriage, so it was a bit crowded.
  1995 Of her marriage to Charles, Prince of Wales, and his relationship with Camilla Parker-Bowles. Television interview on BBC1's *Panorama*, 20 Nov.

25 I'd like to be a queen in people's hearts but I don't see myself being Queen of this country.
  1995 Television interview on BBC1's *Panorama*, 20 Nov.

Díaz, Jorge 1930–2007

Chilean dramatist, born in Argentina. He lived in Spain after 1965. His plays are influenced by the theatre of the absurd and other avant-garde experimental movements.

26 ¡Pero la verdad es que estoy cansada, horriblemente cansada de ser la esposa femenina de ese animal masculino que se rasca, pierde el pelo sistemáticamente y canta tangos pasados de moda!... Quisiera...quisiera engordar, fumar un puro y enviudar de una manera indolora y elegante.
  The truth is, I'm tired, frightfully tired of being the feminine spouse to the masculine animal who scratches himself, systematically loses his hair and sings outdated tangos!... I'd like... I'd like to get fat, to smoke cigars and to become a widow in a painless and elegant fashion.
  1961 *El cepillo de dientes* (*The Toothbrush*), act 1.

Díaz, Porfirio 1830–1915

President of Mexico. He supported Juarez in the War of Reform and gained the presidency through rebellion in 1877.

27 Poor Mexico, so far from God and so close to the United States.
  1846 Attributed, at the beginning of the American–Mexican War (1846–8).

Dibdin, Charles 1745–1814

English songwriter, who wrote his first operetta (*The Shepherd's Artifice*, performed at Covent Garden 1762) as a boy. He wrote nearly 100 sea songs and 70 dramatic pieces.

28 For a soldier I listed, to grow great in fame,
  And be shot at for sixpence a day.
  1791 'Charity'.

29 Did you ever hear of Captain Wattle?
  He was all for love, and a little for the bottle.
  1797 'Captain Wattle and Miss Roe'.

30 Then trust me, there's nothing like drinking
  So pleasant this side of the grave;
  It keeps the unhappy from thinking,
  And makes e'en the valiant more brave.
  'Nothing Like Grog'. First published 1803.

31 What argufies pride and ambition?
  Soon or late death will take us in tow:
  Each bullet has got its commission,
  And when our time's come we must go.
  'Each Bullet Has Got Its Commission'. First published 1803.

Dick, Philip K(indred) 1928–82
US science-fiction writer. His output was prolific, marked by a strong literary sensibility as well as a powerful, often chilling imagination and humour.

32 Dr Bloodmoney, Or How We Got Along After The Bomb.
1965 Title of novel.

33 I mean, after all; you have to consider that we're only made out of dust. That's admittedly not much to go on and we shouldn't forget that. But even considering, I mean, it's sort of a bad beginning, we're not doing too bad. So I personally have faith that even in this lousy situation we're faced with we can make it. You get me?
1966 *The Three Stigmata of Palmer Eldritch*, closing words.

34 Do Androids Dream Of Electric Sheep?
1968 Title of novel, later the basis for the film *Blade Runner*.

35 Reality is that which, when you stop believing in it, doesn't go away.
1972 Quoted in introduction to *I Hope I Shall Arrive Soon* (1986).

36 Drug misuse is not a disease, it is a decision, like the decision to step out in front of a moving car. You would call that not a disease but an error of judgement.
1977 *A Scanner Darkly*, author's note.

37 The basic tool for the manipulation of reality is the manipulation of words. If you can control the meaning of words, you can control the people who must use the words.
1986 *I Hope I Shall Arrive Soon*, 'How To Build A Universe That Doesn't Fall Apart Two Days Later'.

Dickens, Charles John Huffam 1812–70
English novelist. After a childhood of poverty and hardship, during which his father was sent to a debtors' prison, he became one of England's most popular and prolific novelists, exposing the inhumanities of the 19c with an idiosyncratic blend of wit, satire, sentiment and seriousness and a gallery of memorable characters.

38 Grief never mended no broken bones, and as good people's wery scarce, what I says is, make the most on 'em.
1836–7 *Sketches by Boz*, 'Gin Shops'.

39 We shall never forget the mingled feelings of awe and respect with which we used to gaze on the exterior of Newgate in our schoolboy days…[the doors] looking as if they were made for the express purpose of letting people in, and never letting them out again.
1836–7 *Sketches by Boz*, 'Criminal Courts'.

40 A smattering of everything, and a knowledge of nothing.
1836–7 *Sketches by Boz*, 'Sentiment'.

41 He had used the word in its Pickwickian sense.
1836–7 Of Mr Blotton, a member of the Pickwick Club. *Pickwick Papers*, ch.1.

42 'Heads, heads—take care of your heads!' cried the loquacious stranger, as they came out under the low archway, which in those days formed the entrance to the coachyard. 'Terrible place—dangerous work—five children—mother—tall lady, eating sandwiches—forgot the arch—crash—knock—children look round—mother's head off—sandwich in her hand—no mouth to put it in—head of a family off—shocking, shocking!
1836–7 Jingle. *Pickwick Papers*, ch.2.

43 'I was ruminating,' said Mr Pickwick, 'on the strange mutability of human affairs.' 'Ah! I see—in at the palace door one day, out at the window the next. Philosopher, Sir?' 'An observer of human nature, sir,' said Mr Pickwick.
1836–7 *Pickwick Papers*, ch.2.

44 'Ah! You should keep dogs—fine animals—sagacious creatures—dog of my own once—Pointer—surprising instinct—out shooting one day—entering enclosure—whistled—dog stopped—whistled again—Ponto—no go; stock still—called him—Ponto, Ponto—wouldn't move— dog transfixed—staring at a board—looked up, saw an inscription—"Gamekeeper has orders to shoot all dogs found in this enclosure"— wouldn't pass it—wonderful dog—valuable dog that—very.'
1836–7 Jingle. *Pickwick Papers*, ch.2.

45 Kent, sir—everyone knows Kent—apples, cherries, hops and women.
1836–7 Jingle. *Pickwick Papers*, ch.2.

46 There are very few moments in a man's existence when he experiences so much ludicrous distress, or meets with so little charitable commiseration, as when he is in pursuit of his own hat.
1836–7 *Pickwick Papers*, ch.4.

47 There was a fine gentle wind, and Mr Pickwick's hat rolled sportively before it. The wind puffed, and Mr Pickwick puffed, and the hat rolled over and over as merrily as a lively porpoise in a strong tide.
1836–7 *Pickwick Papers*, ch.4.

48 I wants to make your flesh creep.
1836–7 The Fat Boy. *Pickwick Papers*, ch.8.

49 'It's always best on these occasions to do what the mob do.' 'But suppose there are two mobs?' suggested Mr Snodgrass. 'Shout with the largest,' replied Mr Pickwick.
1836–7 *Pickwick Papers*, ch.13.

50 And a wery good name it is—only one I know, that ain't got a nickname to it.
1836–7 Sam Weller comments on Job Trotter's Christian name. *Pickwick Papers*, ch.16.

51 Tongue; well, that's a wery good thing when it an't a woman's.
1836–7 Sam Weller's father. *Pickwick Papers*, ch.19.

52 Poverty and oysters always seem to go together.
1836–7 Sam Weller. *Pickwick Papers*, ch.22.

53 Dumb as a drum vith a hole in it, sir.
1836–7 Sam Weller. *Pickwick Papers*, ch.25.

54 Our noble society for providing the infant negroes in the West Indies with flannel waistcoats and moral pocket handkerchiefs.
1836–7 Rev Mr Stiggins. *Pickwick Papers*, ch.27.

55 Poetry's unnat'ral; no man ever talked poetry 'cept a beadle on boxin' day, or Warren's blackin', or Rowland's oil, or some o' them low fellows; never you let yourself down to talk poetry, my boy.
1836–7 Sam Weller's father. *Pickwick Papers*, ch.33.

56 It's my opinion, sir, that this meeting is drunk, sir!
1836–7 Rev Mr Stiggins. *Pickwick Papers*, ch.33.

57 'Yes, I have a pair of eyes,' replied Sam, 'and that's just it. If they wos a pair o' patent double million magnifyin'

gas microscopes of hextra power, p'raps I might be able to see through a flight o' stairs and a deal door; but bein' only eyes, you see, my wision's limited.'
1836–7 *Pickwick Papers*, ch.34.

58 Miss Bolo rose from the table considerably agitated, and went straight home, in a flood of tears, and a sedan chair.
1836–7 *Pickwick Papers*, ch.35.

59 We know, Mr. Weller—we, who are men of the world —that a good uniform must work its way with the women, sooner or later.
1836–7 The Gentleman in Blue. *Pickwick Papers*, ch.37.

60 You're a amiably-disposed young man, sir, I don't think.
1836–7 Sam Weller's father. *Pickwick Papers*, ch.38.

61 It's a regular holiday to them—all porter and skittles.
1836–7 *Pickwick Papers*, ch.41.

62 Anythin' for a quiet life, as the man said wen he took the sitivation at the lighthouse.
1836–7 Sam Weller. *Pickwick Papers*, ch.43.

63 The fact is, that there was considerable difficulty in inducing Oliver to take upon himself the office of respiration—a troublesome practice, but one which custom has rendered necessary to our easy existence; and for some time he lay gasping on a little flock mattress, rather unequally poised between this world and the next: the balance being decidedly in favour of the latter. Now, if during this brief period, Oliver had been surrounded by careful grandmothers, anxious aunts, experienced nurses, and doctors of profound wisdom, he would most inevitably and indubitably have been killed in no time.
1837–9 *Oliver Twist*, ch.1.

64 Please, sir, I want some more.
1837–9 Oliver. *Oliver Twist*, ch.2.

65 It was a nice sickly season just at this time. In commercial phrase, coffins were looking up.
1837–9 *Oliver Twist*, ch.6.

66 What a fine thing capital punishment is! Dead men never repent; dead men never bring awkward stories to light. Ah, it's a fine thing for the trade! Five of 'em strung up in a row; and none left to play booty, or turn white-livered!
1837–9 Fagin. *Oliver Twist*, ch.9.

67 'Hard,' replied the Dodger. 'As nails,' added Charley Bates.
1837–9 *Oliver Twist*, ch.9.

68 There is a passion for hunting something deeply implanted in the human breast.
1837–9 *Oliver Twist*, ch.10.

69 I'll eat my head.
1837–9 Mr Grimwig. *Oliver Twist*, ch.14.

70 I only know two sorts of boys. Mealy boys, and beef-faced boys.
1837–9 Mr Grimwig. *Oliver Twist*, ch.14.

71 This ain't the shop for justice.
1837–9 The Artful Dodger. *Oliver Twist*, ch.43.

72 'If the law supposes that,' said Mr Bumble...'the law is a ass—a idiot.'
1837–9 *Oliver Twist*, ch.51.

73 The delights—the ten thousand million delights of a pantomime.
1838 *Memoirs of Joseph Grimaldi*, ed Dickens.

74 United Metropolitan Improved Hot Muffin and Crumpet Baking and Punctual Delivery Company.
1838–9 *Nicholas Nickleby*, ch.2.

75 EDUCATION.—At Mr Wackford Squeers's Academy, Dotheboys Hall, at the delightful village of Dotheboys, near Greta Bridge in Yorkshire. Youth are boarded, clothed, booked, furnished with pocket-money, provided with all necessaries, instructed in all languages, living and dead, mathematics, orthography, geometry, astronomy, trigonometry, the use of the globes, algebra, single stick (if required), writing, arithmetic, fortification, and every other branch of classical literature. Terms, twenty guineas per annum. No extras, no vacations, and diet unparalleled.
1838–9 *Nicholas Nickleby*, ch.3.

76 Mr Squeers's appearance was not prepossessing. He had but one eye, and the popular prejudice runs in favour of two.
1838–9 *Nicholas Nickleby*, ch.4.

77 Subdue your appetites, my dears, and you've conquered human nature.
1838–9 *Nicholas Nickleby*, ch.5.

78 There are only two styles of portrait painting, the serious and the smirk.
1838–9 Miss LaCreevy. *Nicholas Nickleby*, ch.10.

79 Oh! They're too beautiful to live, much too beautiful!
1938–9 Mrs Kenwigs, of her four daughters. *Nicholas Nickleby*, ch. 14.

80 Sir, My pa requests me to write to you. The doctors considering it doubtful whether he will ever recuvver the use of his legs which prevents his holding a pen.
1838–9 Fanny Squeers. *Nicholas Nickleby*, ch.15.

81 'What's the water in French, sir?' 'L'eau,' replied Nicholas. 'Ah!' said Mr Lillyvick, shaking his head mournfully, 'I thought as much. Lo, eh? I don't think anything of that language—nothing at all.'
1838–9 *Nicholas Nickleby*, ch.16.

82 'It's very easy to talk,' said Mrs Mantalini. 'Not so easy when one is eating a demnition egg,' replied Mr Mantalini; 'for the yolk runs down the waistcoat, and yolk of egg does not match any waistcoat but a yellow waistcoat, demmit.'
1838–9 *Nicholas Nickleby*, ch.17.

83 Language was not powerful enough to describe the infant phenomenon.
1838–9 *Nicholas Nickleby*, ch.23.

84 'I'm always ill after Shakespeare,' said Mrs Wititterly. 'I scarcely exist the next day; I find the re-action so very great after a tragedy...and Shakespeare is such a delicious creature.'
1838–9 *Nicholas Nickleby*, ch.27.

85 Every baby born into the world is a finer one than the last.
1838–9 *Nicholas Nickleby*, ch.36.

86 Bring in the bottled lightning, a clean tumbler, and a corkscrew.
1838–9 The Gentleman in the Small-Clothes. *Nicholas Nickleby*, ch.49.

87 All is gas and gaiters.
  1838–9 The Gentleman in the Small-Clothes. *Nicholas Nickleby*, ch.49.

88 My life is one demd horrid grind!
  1838–9 Mr Mantalini. *Nicholas Nickleby*, ch.64.

89 What is the odds so long as the fire of soul is kindled at the taper of conviviality, and the wing of friendship never moults a feather!
  1840–1 Dick Swiveller. *The Old Curiosity Shop*, ch.2.

90 Fan the sinking flame of hilarity with the wing of friendship; and pass the rosy wine.
  1840–1 Dick Swiveller. *The Old Curiosity Shop*, ch.7.

91 She's all my fancy painted her, Sir, that's what she is.
  1840–1 Dick Swiveller. *The Old Curiosity Shop*, ch.7.

92 Codlin's the friend, not Short.
  1840–1 Codlin. *The Old Curiosity Shop*, ch.19.

93 And don't you think you must be a very wicked little child…to be a wax-work child at all?
  1840–1 Miss Monflathers to Nell. *The Old Curiosity Shop*, ch.31.

94 'Did you ever taste beer?'
  'I had a sip of it once,' said the small servant.
  'Here's a state of things!' cried Mr. Swiveller, raising his eyes to the ceiling. 'She *never* tasted it—it can't be tasted in a sip!'
  1840–1 *The Old Curiosity Shop*, ch.57.

95 They moved so gently, that their footsteps made no noise; but there were sobs from among the group, and sounds of grief and mourning.
  1840–1 The death of little Nell. *The Old Curiosity Shop*, ch.71.

96 Something will come of this. I hope it mayn't be human gore!
  1841 Simon Tappertit. *Barnaby Rudge*, ch.4.

97 Polly put the kettle on, we'll all have tea.
  1841 Grip, the raven. *Barnaby Rudge*, ch.17.

98 'There are strings,' said Mr Tappertit…'in the human heart that had better not be wibrated.'
  1841 Mr Tappertit. *Barnaby Rudge*, ch.22.

99 Oh gracious, why wasn't I born old and ugly?
  1841 Miss Miggs. *Barnaby Rudge*, ch.70.

1 Was there ever such a sunny street as this Broadway! The pavement stones are polished with the tread of feet until they shine again… Heaven save the ladies, how they dress! We have seen more colours in these ten minutes, than we should have seen elsewhere, in as many days. What various parasols! what rainbow silks and satins! what pinking of thin stockings and pinching of thin shoes, and fluttering of ribbons and silk tassels, and display of rich cloaks with gaudy hoods and linings!
  1842 *American Notes*.

2 Politics are much discussed, so are banks, so is cotton. Quiet people avoid the question of the Presidency…the great constitutional feature of this institution being, that directly the acrimony of the last election is over, the next one begins.
  1842 *American Notes*.

3 'Bah!' said Scrooge, 'Humbug!'
  1843 *A Christmas Carol*, stave 1.

4 'You are fettered,' said Scrooge, trembling. 'Tell me why?'
  'I wear the chain I forged in life,' replied the Ghost. 'I made it link by link, and yard by yard; I girded it on of my own free will, and of my own free will I wore it.'
  1843 *A Christmas Carol*, stave 1.

5 'God bless us every one!' said Tiny Tim, the last of all.
  1843 *A Christmas Carol*, stave 3.

6 But however and whenever we part from one another, I am sure we shall none of us forget poor Tiny Tim.
  1843 *A Christmas Carol*, stave 4.

7 It *was* a turkey! He could never have stood upon his legs, that bird. He would have snapped 'em off short in a minute, like sticks of sealing-wax.
  1843 *A Christmas Carol*, stave 5.

8 The Lord No Zoo.
  1843–4 Toby Chuzzlewit. *Martin Chuzzlewit*, ch.1.

9 'The name of those fabulous animals (pagan, I regret to say) who used to sing in the water, has quite escaped me.' Mr George Chuzzlewit suggested 'Swans'. 'No,' said Mr Pecksniff. 'Not swans. Very like swans, too. Thank you.' The nephew…propounded 'Oysters'. 'No,' said Mr Picksniff…'nor oysters. But by no means unlike oysters… Wait! Sirens. Dear me! sirens, of course.'
  1843–4 *Martin Chuzzlewit*, ch.4.

10 Any man may be in good spirits and good temper when he's well dressed. There an't much credit in that. If I was very ragged and very jolly, then I should begin to feel I had gained a point, Mr. Pinch.
  1843–4 Mark Tapley. *Martin Chuzzlewit*, ch.5.

11 His moral character…was full of promise, but of no performance.
  1843–4 Of Mr Pecksniff. *Martin Chuzzlewit*, ch.5.

12 Affection beaming in one eye, and calculation shining out of the other.
  1843–4 Of Mrs Todgers. *Martin Chuzzlewit*, ch.8.

13 Let us be moral. Let us contemplate existence.
  1843–4 Mr Pecksniff. *Martin Chuzzlewit*, ch.9.

14 Here's the rule for bargains: 'Do other men, for they would do you.' That's the true business precept.
  1843–4 Jonas Chuzzlewit. *Martin Chuzzlewit*, ch.11.

15 Buy an annuity cheap, and make your life interesting to yourself and everybody else that watches the speculation.
  1843–4 Jonas Chuzzlewit. *Martin Chuzzlewit*, ch.18.

16 'Mrs Harris,' I says, 'leave the bottle on the chimley-piece, and don't ask me to take none, but let me put my lips to it when I am so dispoged.'
  1843–4 Mrs Gamp. *Martin Chuzzlewit*, ch.19.

17 Features are an index to the heart.
  1843–4 *Martin Chuzzlewit*, ch.24.

18 At the same moment a peculiar fragrance was borne upon the breeze, as if a passing fairy had hiccuped, and had previously been to a wine vaults.
  1843–4 On Mrs Gamp's entering a room. *Martin Chuzzlewit*, ch.25.

19 Gamp would certainly have drunk its little shoes right off its feet, as with our precious boy he did, and arterwards send the child a errand to sell his wooden leg for any money it 'ud fetch as matches in the rough, and bring it home in liquor.
  1843–4 Mrs Gamp. *Martin Chuzzlewit*, ch.25.

20 She's the sort of woman...one would almost feel disposed to bury for nothing: and do it neatly, too!
1843–4 Mould speaking about Mrs Gamp. *Martin Chuzzlewit*, ch.25.

21 He'd make a lovely corpse.
1843–4 Mrs Gamp speaking of Jonas Chuzzlewit. *Martin Chuzzlewit*, ch.25.

22 We never knows wot's hidden in each other's hearts; and if we had glass winders there, we'd need keep the shutters up, some on us, I do assure you!
1843–4 Mrs Gamp. *Martin Chuzzlewit*, ch.29.

23 A lane was made; and Mrs Hominy...came slowly up it, in a procession of one.
1843–4 *Martin Chuzzlewit*, ch.34.

24 'Mind and matter,' said the lady in the wig, 'glide swift into the vortex of immensity. Howls the sublime, and softly sleeps the calm Ideal, in the whispering chambers of Imagination.'
1843–4 A Transcendental literary lady. *Martin Chuzzlewit*, ch.34.

25 Farewell! Be the proud bride of a ducal coronet, and forget me!... Unalterably, never yours, Augustus.
1843–4 Augustus Moddle. *Martin Chuzzlewit*, ch.54.

26 Oh let us love our occupations,
Bless the squire and his relations,
Live upon our daily rations,
And always know our proper stations.
1844 Lady Bowley. *The Chimes*, second quarter.

27 The earth was made for Dombey and Son to trade in, and the sun and moon were made to give them light. Rivers and seas were formed to float their ships; rainbows gave them promise of fair weather; winds blew for or against their enterprises; stars and planets circled in their orbits, to preserve inviolate a system of which they were the centre.
1846–8 *Dombey and Son*, ch.1.

28 Dombey and Son had often dealt in hides, but never in hearts. They left that fancy ware to boys and girls, and boarding-schools and books.
1846–8 *Dombey and Son*, ch.1.

29 'The sea, Floy, what is it that it keeps on saying?'
She told him that it was only the noise of the rolling waves.
'Yes, yes,' he said. 'But I know that they are always saying something. Always the same thing. What place is over there?'...
She told him there was another country opposite, but he said he didn't mean that; he meant farther away—farther away!
Very often afterwards, in the midst of their talk, he would break off, to try to understand what it was that the waves were always saying; and would rise up in his couch to look towards that invisible region, far away.
1846–8 Of little Paul Dombey. *Dombey and Son*, ch.8.

30 She was dry and sandy with working in the graves of deceased languages. None of your live languages for Miss Blimber. They must be dead—stone dead—and then Miss Blimber dug them up like a Ghoul.
1846–8 *Dombey and Son*, ch.11.

31 As to Mr Feeder, B.A., Doctor Blimber's assistant, he was a kind of human barrel-organ, with a little list of tunes at which he was continually working, over and over again, without any variation.
1846–8 *Dombey and Son*, ch.11.

32 When found, make a note of.
1846–8 Captain Cuttle. *Dombey and Son*, ch.15.

33 Train up a fig-tree in the way it should go, and when you are old sit under the shade of it.
1846–8 Captain Cuttle. *Dombey and Son*, ch.19.

34 The bearings of this observation lays in the application on it.
1846–8 Captain Bunsby. *Dombey and Son*, ch.23.

35 Say, like those wicked Turks, there is no What's-his-name but Thingummy, and What-you-may-call-it is his prophet!
1846–8 Mrs Skewton. *Dombey and Son*, ch.27.

36 If you could see my legs when I take my boots off, you'd form some idea of what unrequited affection is.
1846–8 Mr Toots. *Dombey and Son*, ch.48.

37 I am a lone lorn creetur...and everythink goes contrairy with me.
1849–50 Mrs Gummidge. *David Copperfield*, ch.3.

38 'I feel it more than other people,' said Mrs Gummidge.
1849–50 *David Copperfield*, ch.3.

39 I'd better go into the house, and die and be a riddance!
1849–50 Mrs Gummidge. *David Copperfield*, ch.3.

40 Barkis is willin'.
1849–50 Barkis's proposal of marriage to Peggotty. *David Copperfield*, ch.5.

41 Experientia does it—as papa used to say.
1849–50 Mrs Micawber. *David Copperfield*, ch.11.

42 I never will desert Mr Micawber.
1849–50 Mrs Micawber. *David Copperfield*, ch.12.

43 Annual income twenty pounds, annual expenditure nineteen nineteen six, result happiness. Annual income twenty pounds, annual expenditure twenty pounds ought and six, result misery.
1849–50 Mr Micawber. *David Copperfield*, ch.12.

44 I am well aware that I am the umblest person going... My mother is likewise a very umble person. We live in a numble abode.
1849–50 Uriah Heep. *David Copperfield*, ch.16.

45 We are so very umble.
1849–50 Uriah Heep. *David Copperfield*, ch.17.

46 The mistake was made of putting some of the trouble out of King Charles's head into my head.
1849–50 Mr Dick. *David Copperfield*, ch.17.

47 'Orses and dorgs is some men's fancy. They're wittles and drink to me—lodging, wife, and children—reading, writing and 'rithmetic—snuff, tobacker, and sleep.
1849–50 Man on the Canterbury coach. *David Copperfield*, ch.19.

48 I only ask for information.
1849–50 Rosa Dartle. *David Copperfield*, ch.20.

49 'It was as true,' said Mr Barkis, '...as taxes is. And nothing's truer than them.'
1849–50 *David Copperfield*, ch.21.

50 What a world of gammon and spinnage it is, though, ain't it?
1849–50 Miss Mowcher. *David Copperfield*, ch.22.

51 Accidents will occur in the best-regulated families.
1849–50 Mr Micawber. *David Copperfield*, ch.28.

52 'People can't die, along the coast,' said Mr Peggotty, 'except when the tide's pretty nigh out. They can't be

born, unless it's pretty nigh in—not properly born, till flood. He's a going out with the tide.'
1849–50 On the death of Barkis. *David Copperfield*, ch.30.

53 Mrs Crupp had indignantly assured him that there wasn't room to swing a cat there; but, as Mr Dick justly observed to me… 'You know, Trotwood, I don't want to swing a cat. I never do swing a cat. Therefore, what does that signify to me!'
1849–50 *David Copperfield*, ch.35.

54 'No better opening anywhere,' said my aunt, 'for a man who conducts himself well, and is industrious.'
1849–50 Of Mr Micawber's prospects in Australia. *David Copperfield*, ch.52.

55 Fog everywhere. Fog up the river, where it flows among green aits and meadows; fog down the river, where it rolls defiled among the tiers of shipping, and the waterside pollutions of a great (and dirty) city. Fog on the Essex marshes, fog on the Kentish heights. Fog creeping into the cabooses of collier-brigs; fog lying out on the yards, and hovering in the rigging of great ships… And hard by Temple Bar, in Lincoln's Inn Hall, at the very heart of the fog, sits the Lord High Chancellor in his High Court of Chancery.
1852–3 *Bleak House*, ch.1.

56 But Jarndyce and Jarndyce still drags its dreary length before the court, perennially hopeless.
1852–3 *Bleak House*, ch.1.

57 The evil of it is, that it is a world wrapped up in too much jeweller's cotton and fine wool, and cannot hear the rushing of the larger worlds, and cannot see them as they circle round the sun. It is a deadened world, and its growth is sometimes unhealthy for want of air.
1852–3 Of the world of fashion. *Bleak House*, ch.2.

58 This is a London particular… A fog, miss.
1852–3 Mr Guppy to Esther. *Bleak House*, ch.3.

59 I expect a judgement. Shortly.
1852–3 Miss Flyte. *Bleak House*, ch.3. The judgement predicted, in the case of *Jarndyce* v *Jarndyce*, fails to materialize for many decades.

60 The wind's in the east… I am always conscious of an uncomfortable sensation now and then when the wind is blowing in the east.
1852–3 Mr Jarndyce. *Bleak House*, ch.6.

61 It is said that the children of the poor are not brought up, but dragged up.
1852–3 Mr Jarndyce. *Bleak House*, ch.6.

62 I don't feel any vulgar gratitude to you. I almost feel as if *you* ought to be grateful to *me*, for giving you the opportunity of enjoying the luxury of generosity… For anything I can tell, I may have come into the world expressly for the purpose of increasing your stock of happiness.
1852–3 Harold Skimpole. *Bleak House*, ch.6.

63 An oyster of the old school whom nobody can open.
1852–3 Of Mr Tulkinghorn. *Bleak House*, ch.10.

64 He wos wery good to me, he wos!
1852–3 Jo speaking of Nemo. *Bleak House*, ch.11.

65 'For I don't,' says Jo, 'I don't know nothink.'
1852–3 *Bleak House*, ch.16.

66 You are a human boy, my young friend. A human boy. O glorious to be a human boy!…

O running stream of sparkling joy
To be a soaring human boy!
1852–3 Rev Mr Chadband. *Bleak House*, ch.19.

67 Jobling, there *are* chords in the human mind.
1852–3 Mr Guppy. *Bleak House*, ch.20.

68 'It is,' says Chadband, 'the ray of rays, the sun of suns, the moon of moons, the star of stars. It is the light of Terewth.'
1852–3 *Bleak House*, ch.25.

69 'Old girl,' said Mr Bagnet, 'give him my opinion. You know it.'
1852–3 *Bleak House*, ch.27.

70 It is a melancholy truth that even great men have their poor relations.
1852–3 *Bleak House*, ch.28.

71 Never have a mission.
1852–3 Mr Jellyby. *Bleak House*, ch.30.

72 The one great principle of the English law is, to make business for itself. There is no other principle distinctly, certainly, and consistently maintained through all its narrow turnings.
1852–3 *Bleak House*, ch.39.

73 He is not a genuine foreign-grown savage; he is the ordinary home-made article. Dirty, ugly, disagreeable to all the senses, in body a common creature of the common streets, only in soul a Heathen. Homely filth begrimes him, homely parasites devour him, homely sores are in him, homely rags are on him: native ignorance, the growth of English soil and climate, sinks his immortal nature lower than the beasts that perish.
1852–3 Of Jo. *Bleak House*, ch.47.

74 Dead, your Majesty. Dead, my lords and gentlemen. Dead, Right Reverends and Wrong Reverends of every order. Dead, men and women, born with Heavenly compassion in your hearts. And dying thus around us every day.
1852–3 On the death of Jo. *Bleak House*, ch.47.

75 Now, what I want is, Facts. Teach these boys and girls nothing but Facts. Facts alone are wanted in life.
1854 Mr Gradgrind. *Hard Times*, bk.1, ch.1.

76 The speaker, and the schoolmaster, and the third grown person present, all backed a little, and swept with their eyes the inclined plane of little vessels then and there arranged in order, ready to have imperial gallons of facts poured into them until they were full to the brim.
1854 *Hard Times*, bk.1, ch.1.

77 'Girl number twenty unable to define a horse!' said Mr Gradgrind… 'Girl number twenty possessed of no facts, in reference to one of the commonest of animals!'…
'Bitzer' said Thomas Gradgrind. 'Your definition of a horse.'
'Quadruped. Graminivorous. Forty teeth, namely twenty-four grinders, four eye-teeth, and twelve incisive. Sheds coat in the spring; in marshy countries, sheds hoofs, too. Hoofs hard, but requiring to be shod with iron. Age known by marks in mouth.' Thus (and much more) Bitzer.
'Now girl number twenty,' said Mr Gradgrind. 'You know what a horse is.'
1854 *Hard Times*, bk.1, ch.2.

78 It was a town of red brick, or of brick that would have been red if the smoke and ashes had allowed it; but, as matters stood it was a town of unnatural red and black as the painted face of a savage.
1854 Of Coketown. *Hard Times*, bk.1, ch.5.

79 Coketown...ugly citadel, where Nature was as strongly bricked out as killing airs and gases were bricked in.
1854 *Hard Times*, bk.1, ch.10.

80 I see traces of the turtle soup, and venison, and gold spoon in this.
1854 Mr Bounderby. *Hard Times*, bk.1, ch.11.

81 Ah, Rachel, aw a muddle! Fro' first to last, a muddle!
1854 Stephen Blackpool. *Hard Times*, bk.3, ch.6.

82 People mutht be amuthed. They can't be alwayth a learning, nor yet they can't be alwayth a working, they an't made for it.
1854 Mr Sleary. *Hard Times*, bk.3, ch.8.

83 Whatever was required to be done, the Circumlocution Office was beforehand with all the public departments in the art of perceiving—HOW NOT TO DO IT.
1855–7 *Little Dorrit*, bk.1, ch.10.

84 Take a little time—count five-and-twenty, Tattycoram.
1855–7 Mr Meagles. *Little Dorrit*, bk.1, ch.16.

85 In company with several other old ladies of both sexes.
1855–7 *Little Dorrit*, bk.1, ch.17.

86 It was not a bosom to repose upon, but it was a capital bosom to hang jewels upon.
1855–7 Of Mrs Merdle. *Little Dorrit*, bk.1, ch.21.

87 There's milestones on the Dover Road!
1855–7 Mr F's Aunt. *Little Dorrit*, bk.1, ch.23.

88 I revere the memory of Mr F. as an estimable man and most indulgent husband, only necessary to mention Asparagus and it appeared or to hint at any little delicate thing to drink and it came like magic in a pint bottle it was not ecstasy but it was comfort.
1855–7 Flora Finching. *Little Dorrit*, bk.1, ch.24.

89 As to marriage on the part of a man, my dear, Society requires that he should retrieve his fortunes by marriage. Society requires that he should gain by marriage. Society requires that he should found a handsome establishment by marriage. Society does not see, otherwise, what he has to do with marriage.
1855–7 Mrs Merdle. *Little Dorrit*, bk.1, ch.33.

90 Mrs General had no opinions. Her way of forming a mind was to prevent it from forming opinions...Mrs General was not to be told of anything shocking. Accidents, miseries, and offences, were never to be mentioned before her. Passion was to go to sleep in the presence of Mrs General, and blood was to change to milk and water. The little that was left in the world, when all these deductions were made, it was Mrs General's province to varnish.
1855–7 *Little Dorrit*, bk.2, ch.2.

91 Father is rather vulgar, my dear. The word Papa, besides, gives a pretty form to the lips. Papa, potatoes, poultry, prunes, and prism, are all very good words for the lips: especially prunes and prism.
1855–7 Mrs General. *Little Dorrit*, bk.2, ch.5.

92 That it is at least as difficult to stay a moral infection as a physical one; that such a disease will spread with the malignity and rapidity of the Plague; that the contagion, when it has once made head, will spare no pursuit or condition, but will lay hold on people in the soundest health, and become developed in the most unlikely constitutions; is a fact as firmly established by experience as that we human creatures breathe an atmosphere.
1855–7 *Little Dorrit*, bk.2, ch.13.

93 Once a gentleman, and always a gentleman.
1855–7 Rigaud. *Little Dorrit*, bk.2, ch.28.

94 It was the best of times, it was the worst of times, it was the age of wisdom, it was the age of foolishness, it was the epoch of belief, it was the epoch of incredulity, it was the season of Light, it was the season of Darkness, it was the spring of hope, it was the winter of despair, we had everything before us, we had nothing before us, we were all going direct to Heaven, we were all going direct the other way.
1859 *A Tale of Two Cities*, bk.1, ch.1.

95 I pass my whole life, miss, in turning an immense pecuniary Mangle.
1859 Mr Lorry. *A Tale of Two Cities*, bk.1, ch.4.

96 If it was ever intended that I should go across salt water, do you suppose Providence would have cast my lot in an island?
1859 Miss Pross. *A Tale of Two Cities*, bk.1, ch.4.

97 If you must go flopping yourself down, flop in favour of your husband and child, and not in opposition to 'em.
1859 Jerry Cruncher. *A Tale of Two Cities*, bk.2, ch.1.

98 I care for no man on earth, and no man on earth cares for me.
1859 Sydney Carton. *A Tale of Two Cities*, bk.2, ch.4.

99 Although it's a long time on the road, it is on the road and coming. I tell thee it never retreats, and never stops.
1859 Madame Defarge. *A Tale of Two Cities*, bk.2, ch.16.

1 It is a far, far better thing that I do, than I have ever done; it is a far, far better rest that I go to than I have ever known.
1859 Sydney Carton. *A Tale of Two Cities*, bk.3, ch.15.

2 Cleanliness is next to Godliness, and some people do the same by their religion.
1860–1 *Great Expectations*, ch.4.

3 I was always treated as if I had insisted on being born in opposition to the dictates of reason, religion, and morality.
1860–1 Pip. *Great Expectations*, ch.4.

4 Your sister is given to government.
1860–1 Joe Gargery. *Great Expectations*, ch.7.

5 In the little world in which children have their existence, whosoever brings them up, there is nothing so finely perceived and so finely felt, as injustice.
1860–1 *Great Expectations*, ch.8.

6 I had cherished a profound conviction that her bringing me up by hand, gave her no right to bring me up by jerks.
1860–1 *Great Expectations*, ch.8.

7 It is a most miserable thing to feel ashamed of home.
1860–1 *Great Expectations*, ch.14.

8 Probably every new and eagerly expected garment ever put on since clothes came in, fell a trifle short of the wearer's expectation.
1860–1 *Great Expectations*, ch.19.

9 You wouldn't mind being at once introduced to the Aged, would you?
1860–1 Wemmick introduces Pip to his father. *Great Expectations*, ch.25.

10 I loved Estella... I loved her against reason, against promise, against peace, against hope, against happiness, against all discouragement that could be.
1860–1 *Great Expectations*, ch.29.

11 Words cannot state the amount of aggravation and injury wreaked upon me by Trabb's boy, when passing abreast of me, he pulled up his shirt-collar, twined his side-hair, stuck an arm akimbo, and smirked extravagantly by, wriggling his elbows and body, and drawling to his attendants, 'Don't know yah, don't know yah, 'pon my soul don't know yah!'
1860–1 *Great Expectations*, ch.30.

12 'Halloa! Here's a church!... Let's go in!... Here's Miss Skiffins! Let's have a wedding.'
1860–1 *Great Expectations*, ch.55.

13 I listened with hadmiration amounting to haw.
1864–5 Mr Boffin. *Our Mutual Friend*, bk.1, ch.5.

14 A literary man—*with* a wooden leg—and all Print is open to him.
1864–5 Mr Boffin speaking of Silas Wegg. *Our Mutual Friend*, bk.1, ch.5.

15 Mrs Boffin...is a highflyer at Fashion.
1864–5 *Our Mutual Friend*, bk.1, ch.5.

16 'Was you thinking at all of poetry?' Mr Wegg inquired, musing.
'Would it come dearer?' Mr Boffin asked.
'It would come dearer,' Mr Wegg returned. 'For when a person comes to grind off poetry night after night, it is but right he should expect to be paid for its weakening effect on his mind.'
1864–5 *Our Mutual Friend*, bk.1, ch.5.

17 These two ignorant and unpolished people had guided themselves so far on in their journey of life, by a religious sense of duty and desire to do right.
1864–5 Of Mr and Mrs Boffin. *Our Mutual Friend*, bk.1, ch.9.

18 Mr Podsnap was well to do, and stood very high in Mr Podsnap's opinion.
1864–5 *Our Mutual Friend*, bk.1, ch.11.

19 A certain institution in Mr Podsnap's mind which he called 'the young person' may be considered to have been embodied in Miss Podsnap, his daughter...The question about everything was, would it bring a blush into the cheek of the young person?
1864–5 *Our Mutual Friend*, bk.1, ch.11.

20 'Our Language,' said Mr Podsnap, with a gracious consciousness of being always right, 'is Difficult. Ours is a Copious Language, and Trying to Strangers. I will not Pursue my Question... It merely referred,' Mr Podsnap explained, with a sense of meritorious proprietorship, 'to our Constitution, Sir. We Englishmen are Very Proud of our Constitution, Sir. It Was Bestowed Upon Us By Providence. No Other Country is so Favoured as This Country.'
1864–5 *Our Mutual Friend*, bk.1, ch.11.

21 Mr Podsnap settled that whatever he put behind him he put out of existence... 'I don't want to know about it; I don't choose to discuss it; I don't admit it!'
1864–5 *Our Mutual Friend*, bk.1, ch.11.

22 I think...that it is the best club in London.
1864–5 Mr Twemlow's description of the House of Commons. *Our Mutual Friend*, bk.2, ch.3.

23 Come up and be dead! Come up and be dead!
1864–5 Jenny Wren. *Our Mutual Friend*, bk.2, ch.5.

24 A slap-up gal in a bang-up chariot.
1864–5 The scout's description of Bella. *Our Mutual Friend*, bk.2, ch.8.

25 I want to be something so much worthier than the doll in the doll's house.
1864–5 Bella. *Our Mutual Friend*, bk.4, ch.5.

26 Stranger, pause and ask thyself the question, Canst thou do likewise? If not, with a blush retire.
1870 Mr Sapsea's epitaph for his wife. *Edwin Drood*, ch.4.

Dickinson, Emily Elizabeth 1830–86

US poet who spent her life in seclusion in Massachusetts, writing over 1000 intensely lyrical and personal poems, few of which were published during her lifetime.

27 Success is counted sweetest
By those who ne'er succeed.
c.1859 *Complete Poems*, no.67 (first published 1890).

28 Can I expound the skies?
How still the Riddle lies!
c.1859 *Complete Poems*, no.89 (first published 1890).

29 Surgeons must be very careful
When they take the knife!
Underneath their fine incisions
Stirs the culprit—*Life!*
c.1859 *Complete Poems*, no.108 (first published 1891).

30 To fight aloud, is very brave,
But gallanter, I know,
Who charge within the bosom
The Cavalry of Woe.
c.1859 *Complete Poems*, no.126 (first published 1890).

31 Musicians wrestle everywhere—
All day—among the crowded air
I hear the silver strife—
And—waking—long before the morn—
Such transport breaks upon the town
I think it that 'New Life!'
c.1860 *Complete Poems*, no.157 (first published 1891).

32 'Faith' is a fine invention
When Gentlemen can *see*—
But *Microscopes* are prudent
In an Emergency.
c.1860 *Complete Poems*, no.185 (first published 1891).

33 Inebriate of Air—am I—
And Debauchee of Dew—
Reeling—thro endless summer days—
From inns of Molten Blue—
c.1860 *Complete Poems*, no.214 (first published 1861).

34 'Hope' is the thing with feathers—
That perches in the soul—
And sings the tune without the words—
And never stops—at all—
c.1860 *Complete Poems*, no.254 (first published 1891).

35 Some keep the Sabbath going to Church—
I keep it, staying at Home—
With a Bobolink for a Chorister—

And an Orchard, for a Dome—
c.1860 *Complete Poems*, no.324 (first published 1864).

36 After great pain, a formal feeling comes—
The Nerves sit ceremonious, like Tombs.
c.1862 *Complete Poems*, no.341 (first published 1929).

37 Much Madness is divinest Sense—
To a discerning Eye—
Much Sense—the starkest Madness—
c.1862 *Complete Poems*, no.435 (first published 1890).

38 They shut me up in Prose—
As when a little girl
They put me in the Closet—
Because they liked me 'still'.
c.1862 *Complete Poems*, no.613 (first published 1935).

39 The Brain—is wider than the Sky.
c.1862 *Complete Poems*, no.632 (first published 1896).

40 I cannot live with You—
It would be Life—
And Life is over there—
Behind the Shelf.
c.1862 *Complete Poems*, no.640 (first published 1890).

41 One need not be a Chamber—to be Haunted—
One need not be a House—
The brain has Corridors—surpassing
Material Place—
c.1863 *Complete Poems*, no.670 (first published 1891).

42 Because I could not stop for Death—
He kindly stopped for me—
The carriage held but just Ourselves—
And Immortality.
c.1863 *Complete Poems*, no.712 (first published 1890).

43 Ample make this Bed—
Make this Bed with Awe—
In it wait till Judgement break
Excellent and Fair.
c.1864 *Complete Poems*, no.829 (first published 1891).

44 Of Consciousness, her awful Mate
The soul cannot be rid—
As easy the secreting her
Behind the Eyes of God.
c.1864 *Complete Poems*, no.894 (first published 1945).

45 Faith—is the Pierless Bridge
Supporting what We see
Unto the Scene that We do not.
c.1864 *Complete Poems*, no.915 (first published 1929).

46 Death is a dialogue between
The Spirit and the Dust.
c.1864 *Complete Poems*, no.976 (first published 1890).

47 Tell all the Truth but tell it slant—
Success in Circuit lies
Too bright for our infirm Delight
The Truth's superb surprise.
c.1868 *Complete Poems*, no.1129 (first published 1945).

48 A word is dead
When it is said,
Some say.
I say it just
Begins to live
That day.
?1872 *Complete Poems*, no.1212 (first published 1894).

49 The abdication of Belief
Makes the Behavior small—
Better an ignis fatuus
Than no illume at all.
c.1882 *Complete Poems*, no.1551 (first published 1945).

50 He ate and drank the precious Words,
His Spirit grew robust;
He knew no more that he was poor,
Nor that his frame was Dust.
c.1883 *Complete Poems*, no.1587 (first published 1890).

51 The Pedigree of Honey
Does not concern the Bee—
A Clover, any time, to him,
Is Aristocracy—
c.1884 *Complete Poems*, no.1627 (first published 1890).

52 'Eternity' is there,
We say, as of a station.
Meanwhile, he is so near,
He joins me in my Ramble—
Divides abode with me—
No Friend have I that so persists
As this Eternity.
Complete Poems, no.1684 (first published 1914).

53 Parting is all we know of heaven,
And all we need of hell.
Complete Poems, no.1732 (first published 1896).

54 Rearrange a 'Wife's' affection!
When they dislocate my Brain!
Amputate my freckled Bosom!
Make me bearded like a man!
Complete Poems, no.1737 (first published 1891).

55 The distance that the dead have gone
Does not at first appear—
Their coming back seems possible
For many an ardent year.
Complete Poems, no.1742 (first published 1896).

56 Let us go in; the fog is rising.
Last words, attributed.

Dickinson, John 1732–1808

US revolutionary statesman, leader of conservative opposition to the British. His draft formed the basis of the Articles of Confederation.

57 Then join hand in hand, brave Americans all—
By uniting we stand, by dividing we fall.
1768 'The Liberty Song'.

58 We have counted the cost of this contest, and find nothing so dreadful as voluntary slavery... Our cause is just, our union is perfect.
1775 Declaration of reasons for taking up arms against Britain, 8 Jul, presented to Congress. Quoted in C J Stille *The Life and Times of John Dickinson* (1891), ch.5.

Diderot, Denis 1713–84

French philosopher, novelist, essayist, playwright and critic. A leading figure in the Enlightenment, he is best remembered for his ambitious *Encyclopédie* (1751–72). Other writings include sentimental dramas and theoretical studies of the theatre.

59 *Il ne faut point donner d'esprit à ses personnages; mais savoir les placer dans des circonstances qui leur en donnent.*

You should not give wit to your characters, but know instead how to put them in situations which will make them witty.
1757 *Entretiens sur le fils naturel*, pt.2.

60 *Les passions détruisent plus de préjugés que la philosophie. Et comment le mensonge leur résisterait-il? Elles ébranlent quelquefois la vérité.*
Passions destroy more prejudices than philosophy. And how would lies resist passions? Passions sometimes weaken the truth.
1757 *Entretiens sur le fils naturel*, pt.2.

61 *Les beautés ont, dans les arts, le même fondement que les vérités dans la philosophie. Qu'est-ce que la vérité? La conformité de nos jugements avec les êtres. Qu'est-ce que la beauté d'imitation? La conformité de l'image avec la chose.*
Beauty has in art the same foundation as does truth in philosophy. What is the truth? The conformity of our judgements with beings. What is the beauty of imitation? The conformity of the image with the thing.
1757 *Entretiens sur le fils naturel*, pt.3.

62 *Une danse est un poème.*
A dance is a poem.
1757 *Entretiens sur le fils naturel*, pt.3.

63 *Soit donc que vous composiez, soit donc que vous jouiez, ne pensez non plus au spectateur que s'il n'existait pas. Imaginez sur le bord du théâtre, un grand mur qui vous sépare du parterre; jouez comme si la toile ne se levait pas.*
Whether you compose or act, think no more of the spectator than if he did not exist. Imagine at the edge of the stage a large wall which separates you from the orchestra; act as if the curtain never rose.
1758 *Discours sur la poésie dramatique*, introducing the theatrical concept of the 'fourth wall'.

64 *Le génie se sent; mais il ne s'imite point.*
Genius is felt, but it is not imitated.
1758 *Discours sur la poésie dramatique*.

65 *En général, plus un peuple est civilisé, poli, moins ses moeurs sont poétiques; tout s'affaiblit en s'adoucissant.*
In general, the more civilized and refined the people, the less poetic are its morals; everything weakens as it mellows.
1758 *Discours sur la poésie dramatique*.

66 *La poésie veut quelque chose d'énorme, de barbare et de sauvage.*
Poetry needs something on the scale of the grand, the barbarous, the savage.
1758 *Discours sur la poésie dramatique*.

67 *Le public ne sait pas toujours désirer le vrai.*
The public does not always know how to desire the truth.
1758 *Discours sur la poésie dramatique*.

68 *Le rôle d'un auteur est un rôle assez vain; c'est celui d'un homme qui se croit en état de donner des leçons au public. Et le rôle du critique? Il est bien plus vain encore; c'est celui d'un homme qui se croit en état de donner des leçons à celui qui se croit en état d'en donner au public.*
The role of the author is vain enough; it is that of a person who considers himself able to give lessons to the public. And the role of the critic? It is vainer still; it is that of a person who considers himself able to give lessons to he who considers himself able to give them to the public.
1758 *Discours sur la poésie dramatique*.

69 *Ce n'est que par la mémoire que nous sommes un même individu pour les autres et pour nous-mêmes. Il ne me reste peut-être pas, à l'âge que j'ai, une seule molécule du corps que j'apportai en naissant.*
It is only in memory that we are the same person for others and for ourselves. At the age I am now, there is probably not a single molecule of my body that I had when born.
1758 *Discours sur la poésie dramatique*.

70 *Mes pensées sont mes catins.*
My thoughts are my prostitutes.
1761–74 *Le Neveu de Rameau*.

71 *Rien ne dissemble plus de lui que lui-même.*
Nothing resembles him less than himself.
1761–74 *Le Neveu de Rameau*.

72 *Voyez-vous cet oeuf. C'est avec cela qu'on renverse toutes les écoles de théologie, et tous les temples de la terre.*
See this egg. It is with this that all the schools of theology and all the temples of the earth are to be overturned.
1769 *Le Rêve de d'Alembert* (published 1830), pt.1.

73 *Tous les jours on couche avec des femmes qu'on n'aime pas, et l'on ne couche pas avec des femmes qu'on aime.*
Every day we sleep with women we do not love and don't sleep with the women we do love.
c.1773 *Jacques le fataliste et son maître* (published 1796).

74 *L'esprit de l'escalier.*
Staircase wit.
1773–8 That is, the witty reply that comes to mind after leaving the company, while descending the stairs. *Paradoxe sur le comédien* (published 1830).

75 Two qualities essential for the artist: morality and perspective.
1776–81 *Pensées détachées sur la peinture*.

76 One composition is meagre, though it has many figures; another is rich, though it has few.
1776–81 *Pensées détachées sur la peinture*.

77 Paint as they spoke in Sparta.
1776–81 *Pensées détachées sur la peinture*.

78 *L'homme est né pour la société; séparez-le, isolez-le, ses idées se désuniront, son caractère se tournera, mille affections ridicules s'élèveront dans son coeur; des pensées extravagantes germeront dans son esprit, comme les ronces dans une terre sauvage.*
Man is born to live in society: separate him, isolate him, and his ideas disintegrate, his character changes, a thousand ridiculous affectations rise up in his heart; extreme thoughts take hold in his mind, like the brambles in a wild field.
1796 *La Religieuse*.

Didion, Joan 1934–

US writer, a respected essayist on US life and culture. Her works include the novel *A Book of Common Prayer* (1977) and the non-fiction titles *The White Album* (1979), *Political Fictions* (2001) and *The Year of Magical Thinking* (2005).

79 Innocence ends when one is stripped of the delusion that one likes oneself.
   1961 'On Self Respect', collected in *Slouching Towards Bethlehem* (1968).

80 Was there ever in anyone's life span a point free in time, devoid of memory, a night when choice was any more than the sum of all the choices gone before?
   1963 *Run River*, ch.4.

81 New York was no mere city. It was instead an infinitely romantic notion, the mysterious nexus of all love and money and power, the shining and perishable dream itself. To think of 'living' there was to reduce the miraculous to the mundane; one does not 'live' at Xanadu.
   1967 'Goodbye To All That', collected in *Slouching Towards Bethlehem* (1968).

82 We tell ourselves stories in order to live.
   1979 *The White Album*, 'The White Album, 1'.

83 Everything was unmentionable but nothing was unimaginable.
   1979 Of Los Angeles in 1968–9. *The White Album*, 'The White Album, 10'.

84 To believe in 'the greater good' is to operate, necessarily, in a certain ethical suspension.
   1979 *The White Album*, 'The Woman's Movement'.

85 Grief turns out to be a place none of us know until we reach it.
   2005 *The Year of Magical Thinking*.

86 Life changes in the instant. The ordinary instant.
   2005 *The Year of Magical Thinking*.

87 Novels are like paintings, specifically watercolours. Every stroke you put down you have to go with. Of course you can rewrite, but the original strokes are still there in the texture of the thing.
   2006 Quoted in *The Paris Review*, spring issue.

88 In the early years, you fight because you don't understand each other. In later years, you fight because you do.
   Quoted in Sara Davidson, *Joan: Forty Years of Life, Loss, and Friendship with Joan Didion* (2011).

Dietz, Howard 1896–1983
US writer and lyricist.

89 That's Entertainment.
   1953 Title of song reputedly written by Dietz and Arthur Schwartz for the film *The Band Wagon* in less than an hour.

90 More stars than there are in heaven.
   MGM slogan.

Dillard, Annie 1945–
US writer. She is best known for her essay collection *Pilgrim at Tinker Creek* (1974), and has also written poetry and fiction.

91 It was a bitter birthday present from evolution.
   1974 Of self-consciousness. *Pilgrim at Tinker Creek*, ch.6.

92 I don't know what it is about fecundity that so appals. I suppose it is the teeming evidence that birth and growth, which we value, are ubiquitous and blind, that life itself is so astonishingly cheap, that nature is as careless as it is bountiful, and that with extravagance goes a crushing waste that will one day include our own cheap lives.
   1974 *Pilgrim at Tinker Creek*, ch.10.

93 I think the dying pray at the last not please but thank you as a guest thanks his host at the door.
   1974 *Pilgrim at Tinker Creek*, ch.15.

Dillingham, Charles 1868–1934
US theatre producer.

94 I bet you, Ziggie, a hundred bucks that he ain't in here.
   1926 Attributed whisper to Florenz Ziegfeld as they acted as pall-bearers at the funeral of escapologist Harry Houdini.

Dillon, Wentworth c.1633–1685
Irish poet and critic.

95 Choose an author as you choose a friend.
   1684 *Essay on Translated Verse*, l.96.

96 Immodest words admit of no defence,
   For want of decency is want of sense.
   1684 *Essay on Translated Verse*, l.113.

DiMaggio, Joe (Joseph Paul) 1914–99
US baseball player. A powerful and elegant centre fielder and hitter, he played for 15 seasons with the New York Yankees, voted Most Valuable Player three times. In 1954 he married (briefly) Marilyn Monroe.

97 There's no skill involved. Just go up there and swing at the ball.
   Of baseball. Quoted in Colin Jarman *The Guinness Dictionary of Sports Quotations* (1990).

98 It's no fun being married to an electric light.
   Of his marriage to Marilyn Monroe. Quoted in Colin Jarman *The Guinness Dictionary of Sports Quotations* (1990).

Dimbleby, Richard 1913–65
English broadcaster, best known for his commentaries on state occasions. He joined the BBC's news team in 1936, becoming its first war correspondent (1939).

99 The moment of the Queen's crowning is come.
   1953 Commentary on the coronation at Westminster Abbey, 2 Jun.

Dinesen, Isak
▶ See Blixen, Karen, Baroness

Diogenes of Sinope c.410–c.320 BC
Greek Cynic philosopher and moralist, student of Antisthenes.

1 Yes…stand out of my sun a little.
   His reply when asked by Alexander the Great if he lacked anything. Quoted in Plutarch *Parallel Lives*, 'Alexander'.
   ▶ See Alexander the Great 12:57.

2 I am looking for an honest man.
   His reply when asked why he was wandering the streets of Athens during the day with a lantern.

Dior, Christian 1905–57
French couturier who founded his own Paris house in 1947 and achieved worldwide fame with his 'New Look' in the same year.

3 Women are most fascinating between the ages of thirty-five and forty, after they have won a few races and know how to pace themselves. Since few women ever pass forty, maximum fascination can continue indefinitely.
   1955 In *Collier's Magazine*, 10 Jun.

4 In the world today *haute couture* is one of the last repositories of the marvellous, and the *couturiers* the last possessors of the wand of Cinderella's Fairy Godmother.
Dior by Dior (translated by Antonia Fraser, 1957).

Dirksen, Everett McKinley 1896–1969
US Republican politician.

5 The oil can is mightier than the sword.
1964 In *Life*, 5 Jun.

6 I am a man of fixed and unbending principles, the first of which is to be flexible at all times.
Recalled on his death, 7 Sep 1969.

7 A billion here, a billion there. Pretty soon it runs into real money.
Quoted in 'Half a Trillion in Real Money', editorial in the *New York Times*, 2 Dec 1979.

Disch, Thomas M(ichael) 1940–2008
US writer and critic, best known for his sophisticated, politically conscious science fiction, such as *Camp Concentration* (1968). He has also written several volumes of poetry.

8 Mankind Under The Leash.
1966 Title of novel.

9 A predilection for genre fiction is symptomatic of a kind of arrested development.
1986 In *The Face*, Mar.

10 Science fiction, like Brazil, is where the nuts come from.
1987 In the *Observer*, 23 Aug.
▶ See Thomas 883:98.

Diski, Jenny 1947–
English author and journalist.

11 Statistics are designed to keep you safe.
1997 *Skating to Antarctica*.

12 For the most part, quantum theory has been of little practical value in my life.
1997 *Skating to Antarctica*.

13 There's a cultural conviction that any 'artist' must have personal suffering to back up their work, otherwise there's something undeserved and therefore inauthentic about it, perhaps even some sort of cheating.
2009 In the *London Review of Books*.

Disney, Walt(er Elias) 1901–66
US artist and film producer. His animated characters such as Mickey Mouse (1928) featured in *Silly Symphonies* (from 1929) and later full-length animated films.

14 Fancy being remembered around the world for the invention of a mouse!
c.1966 Comment to his wife during his last illness. Quoted in Leonard Mosley *Disney's World* (1985).

Disraeli, Benjamin, 1st Earl of Beaconsfield 1804–81
British statesman, first known for his political novels *Coningsby* (1844) and *Sybil* (1845). He became a Tory MP in 1837, Chancellor of the Exchequer (1852, 1858–9 and 1866), and Prime Minister (1868, 1874–80). His second administration (1874–80) was notable both for diplomacy and social reform.

15 Experience is the child of Thought, and Thought is the child of Action. We cannot learn men from books.
1826–7 *Vivian Grey*, bk.5, ch.1.

16 I repeat…that all power is a trust—that we are accountable for its exercise—that, from the people, and for the people, all springs, and all must exist.
1826–7 *Vivian Grey*, bk.6, ch.10.

17 A good eater must be a good man; for a good eater must have a good digestion, and a good digestion depends upon a good conscience.
1831 *The Young Duke*, bk.1, ch.14.

18 'The age of chivalry is past,' said May Dacre. 'Bores have succeeded to dragons.'
1831 *The Young Duke*, bk.2, ch.5.

19 Read no history: nothing but biography, for that is life without theory.
1832 *Contarini Fleming*, pt.1, ch.23.

20 The practice of politics in the East may be defined by one word—dissimulation.
1832 *Contarini Fleming*, pt.5, ch.10.

21 Time is the great physician.
1837 *Henrietta Temple*, bk.6, ch.9.

22 Though I sit down now, the time will come when you will hear me.
1837 On being barracked during his overly ornate maiden speech in the House of Commons, 7 Dec.

23 The Continent will not suffer England to be the workshop of the world.
1838 House of Commons, 15 Mar.

24 No Government can be long secure without a formidable Opposition.
1844 *Coningsby*, bk.2, ch.1.

25 Conservatism discards Prescription, shrinks from Principle, disavows Progress; having rejected all respect for antiquity, it offers no redress for the present, and makes no preparation for the future.
1844 *Coningsby*, bk.2, ch.5.

26 Youth is a blunder; Manhood a struggle; Old Age a regret.
1844 *Coningsby*, bk.3, ch.1.

27 It seems to me a barren thing this Conservatism—an unhappy cross-breed, the mule of politics that engenders nothing.
1844 *Coningsby*, bk.3, ch.5.

28 What Art was to the ancient world, Science is to the modern.
1844 *Coningsby*, bk.4, ch.1.

29 The depository of power is always unpopular.
1844 *Coningsby*, bk.4, ch.13.

30 Man is only truly great when he acts from the passions.
1844 *Coningsby*, bk.4, ch.13.

31 Consider Ireland. Thus you have a starving population, an absentee aristocracy, and an alien Church—and in addition, the weakest executive in the world. That is the Irish Question.
1844 Speech, House of Commons, 16 Feb.

32 I am neither a Whig nor a Tory. My politics are described in one word, and that word is England.
1844 Speech, House of Commons.

33 To do nothing and get something, formed a boy's ideal of a manly career.
1845 *Sybil*, bk.1, ch.5.

34 'Two nations; between whom there is no intercourse and no sympathy; who are as ignorant of each other's habits, thoughts and feelings, as if they were dwellers in different zones, or inhabitants of different planets; who are formed by a different breeding, are fed by a different food, are ordered by different manners, and are not governed by the same laws.' 'You speak of—' said Egremont, hesitatingly. 'THE RICH AND THE POOR.'
1845 *Sybil*, bk.2, ch.5.

35 Little things affect little minds.
1845 *Sybil*, bk.3, ch.2.

36 The Youth of a Nation are the trustees of Posterity.
1845 *Sybil*, bk.6, ch.13

37 The right honourable gentleman caught the Whigs bathing and walked away with their clothes.
1845 House of Commons speech, 28 Feb, attacking Prime Minister Sir Robert Peel for bullying his back-benchers into supporting the Government's action in intercepting the private mail of radical MPs.

38 A Conservative government is an organized hypocrisy.
1845 Speech, House of Commons, 17 Mar.

39 A majority is always the best repartee.
1847 *Tancred*, bk.2, ch.14.

40 London is a modern Babylon.
1847 *Tancred*, bk.5, ch.5.

41 Justice is truth in action.
1851 Speech, House of Commons, 11 Feb.

42 He has to learn that petulance is not sarcasm, and that insolence is not invective.
1852 Of Sir Charles Wood. Speech, House of Commons, 16 Dec.

43 England does not love coalitions.
1852 Speech, House of Commons, 17 Dec.

44 The blue ribbon of the turf.
1852 Of the Derby race. *Life of Lord George Bentinck*, ch.26.

45 If a traveller were informed that such a man was Leader of the House of Commons, he may well begin to comprehend how the Egyptians came to worship an insect.
1852 Of Lord John Russell. Attributed.

46 His temper, naturally morose, has become licentiously peevish. Crossed in his Cabinet, he insults the House of Lords and plagues the most eminent of his colleagues with the crabbed malice of a maundering witch.
1855 Of Lord Aberdeen, whose disagreements with his Whig–Peelite coalition over the Crimean War eventually forced his resignation.

47 Finality is not the language of politics.
1859 Speech, House of Commons, 28 Feb.

48 I hold that the characteristic of the present age is craving credulity.
1864 Speech, Oxford, 25 Nov.

49 Party is organized opinion.
1864 Speech, Oxford, 25 Nov.

50 The question is this: is man an ape or an angel? I am on the side of the angels.
1864 Speech, Oxford, 25 Nov.

51 Assassination has never changed the history of the world.
1865 Speech, House of Commons, 1 May, paying tribute to US President Abraham Lincoln who had been assassinated in Washington, 14 Apr.

52 I have climbed to the top of the greasy pole.
1868 On becoming Prime Minister.

53 The pursuit of science leads only to the insoluble.
1870 *Lothair*, ch.17.

54 A Protestant, if he wants aid or advice on any matter, can only go to his solicitor.
1870 *Lothair*, ch.27.

55 When a man fell into his anecdotage it was a sign for him to retire from the world.
1870 *Lothair*, ch.28.

56 Every woman should marry—and no man.
1870 *Lothair*, ch.30.

57 You know who the critics are? The men who have failed in literature and art.
1870 *Lothair*, ch.35.

58 'My idea of an agreeable person,' said Hugo Bohun, 'is a person who agrees with me.'
1870 *Lothair*, ch.35.

59 Increased means and increased leisure are the two civilizers of man.
1872 Speech at Manchester, 3 Apr.

60 A University should be a place of light, of liberty, and of learning.
1873 Speech, House of Commons, 11 Mar.

61 An author who speaks about his own books is almost as bad as a mother who talks about her own children.
1873 Rectorial address, Glasgow, 19 Nov.

62 Upon the education of the people of this country the fate of this country depends.
1874 Speech, House of Commons, 15 Jun.

63 Posterity will do justice to that unprincipled maniac Gladstone—an extraordinary mixture of envy, vindictiveness, hypocrisy and superstition and with one commanding characteristic. Whether Prime Minister or Leader of the Opposition, whether preaching, praying, speechifying, or scribbling—never a gentleman. He is so vain that he wants to figure in history as the settler of all the great questions; but a parliamentary Constitution is not favourable to such ambitions. Things must be done by parties, not by persons using parties as tools.
c.1874 Letter.

64 I am dead: dead, but in the Elysian fields.
1876 On his elevation to the House of Lords.

65 Gladstone, like Richelieu, cannot write. Nothing can be more unmusical, more involved, or more uncouth than all his scribblement.
1877 Letter, 3 Oct.

66 Lord Salisbury and myself have brought you peace—but a peace, I hope, with honour.
1878 Declaration, 16 Jul, on returning from the Berlin Congress with the guarantees it had produced of continuing peace in Europe.
▸ See also Chamberlain 212:64.

67 A sophistical rhetorician inebriated with the exuberance of his own verbosity.
1878 Of Gladstone. Speech reported in *The Times*, 29 Jul.

68 His Christianity was muscular.
1880 *Endymion*, ch.14.

69 You must dress according to your age, your pursuits, your object in life.
1880 *Endymion*, ch.23.

70 What all men should avoid is the 'shabby genteel'. No man ever gets over it... You had better be in rags.
1880 *Endymion*, ch.23.

71 'Sensible men are all the same religion.' 'And pray what is that?' inquired the prince. 'Sensible men never tell.'
1880 Waldershire. *Endymion*, ch.81.

72 I believe they went out, like all good things, with the Stuarts.
1880 *Endymion*, ch.99.

73 I will not go down to posterity talking bad grammar.
1881 On correcting proofs of his last parliamentary speech, 31 Mar. Quoted in Robert Blake *Disraeli*, ch.32.

74 There are three kinds of lies: lies, damned lies and statistics.
Attributed. Quoted in Mark Twain *Autobiography*, vol.1 (published 1924).

75 Millstones around our neck.
Of the colonies. Quoted in Robert Blake *The Conservative Party from Peel to Churchill* (1970).

76 England is unrivalled for two things—sport and politics.
Quoted in Colin Jarman *The Guinness Dictionary of Sports Quotations* (1990).

Dobson, (Henry) Austin   1840–1921

English poet. He published several volumes of carefully crafted, often humorous verse, and prose studies of famous writers.

77 Time goes, you say? Ah no!
   Alas, Time stays, we go.
1877 'Paradox of Time'.

78 Fame is a food that dead men eat,
   I have no stomach for such meat.
1906 'Fame is a Food'.

Dobzhansky, Theodosius G   1900–75

Russian-born US geneticist, Professor at Columbia University and the University of California at Davis.

79 Nature's stern discipline enjoins mutual help at least as often as warfare. The fittest may also be the gentlest.
1962 *Mankind Evolving*.

Docherty, Tommy (Thomas Henderson)   1928–

Scottish footballer and manager. In a tempestuous career he played for Scotland and managed ten clubs, including Manchester United and Queen's Park Rangers, and was briefly manager of Scotland (1971–2).

80 The ideal board of directors should be made up of three men—two dead and the other dying.
1977 Quoted in Colin Jarman *The Guinness Dictionary of Sports Quotations* (1990).

81 Our strikers couldn't score in a brothel.
1985 Of the forwards at Wolverhampton Wanderers. Quoted in Peter Ball and Phil Shaw *The Book of Football Quotations* (1989).

Doctorow, E(dgar) L(awrence)   1931–

US novelist, best known for *Ragtime* (1975), *Billy Bathgate* (1989) and *The March* (2005).

82 A few professional alienists understood his importance, but to most of the public he appeared as some kind of German sexologist, an exponent of free love who used big words to talk about dirty things. At least a decade would have to pass before Freud would have his revenge and see his ideas begin to destroy sex in America forever.
1975 *Ragtime*, ch.5.

83 There is no longer any such thing as fiction or non-fiction; there's only narrative.
1988 In the *New York Times Book Review*, 27 Jan.

84 Like art and politics, gangsterism is a very important avenue of assimilation into society.
1990 In the *International Herald Tribune*, 1 Oct.

85 It is the immigrant hordes who keep this country alive, the waves of them arriving year after year... Who believes in America more than the people who run down the gangplank and kiss the ground?
2009 *Homer & Langley*.

86 Someone dying asks if there is life after death. Yes, comes the answer, only not yours.
2009 *Homer & Langley*.

Dodd, Christopher J   1944–

US Democratic politician.

87 Time is the 101st Senator...the ally of the people who want to do nothing.
1994 On the difficulty of passing President Clinton's health programme when legislators were longing for the holidays. In the *New York Times*, 26 Aug.

Dodd, Ken(neth)   1927–

English stand-up comedian, singer and actor.

88 The trouble with Freud is that he never had to play the old Glasgow Empire on a Saturday night after Rangers and Celtic had both lost.
1965 Television interview, discussing Freud's theory of catharsis through laughter, whereby jokes produce a feeling of elation.

89 Comedy should never be over-analysed. It's either funny or it isn't. There's a subtle difference between those who say funny things and those who say things funny.
2008 Quoted in the *Manchester Evening News*, 28 Apr.

Doddridge, Philip   1702–51

English nonconformist minister and hymn-writer.

90 Hark, the glad sound! The Saviour comes,
   The Saviour promised long;
   Let every heart exult with joy,
   And every voice be song!
Hymns, 'Hark, the Glad Sound' (published 1755).

91 O God of Bethel! by whose hand
   Thy people still are fed,
   Who through this weary pilgrimage
   Hast all our fathers led.
Hymns, 'O God of Bethel' (published 1755).

92 Ye servants of the Lord,
   Each in his office wait,
   Observant of the heavenly word,
   And watchful at his gate.
Hymns, 'Ye Servants of the Lord' (published 1755).

93 Father of Peace, and God of love!
   We own Thy power to save,
   That power by which our Shepherd rose
   Victorious o'er the grave.
Hymns, 'Father of Peace' (published 1755).

Dole, Bob (Robert Joseph) 1923–

US Republican politician. Having run unsuccessfully for presidential nomination in 1980 and 1988, he became a presidential candidate in 1996, but lost the election to Bill Clinton.

94 George Meany could run for President, but then why should he step down?
1976 On Meany's status as president of the American Federation of Labor. In the *Wall Street Journal*, 7 Sep.

95 It is inside work with no heavy lifting.
1988 On the vice presidency. ABC TV broadcast, 24 Jul.

96 Contrary to reports that I took the loss badly, I slept like a baby—every two hours I woke up and cried.
1988 On losing the presidential nomination. ABC TV broadcast, 14 Aug.

97 Putting a majority together is like a one-armed man wrapping cranberries.
Quoted in Hedrick Smith *The Power Game* (1988).

98 This President will go down in history as the only President who raised taxes before he took office and cut spending after he left office.
1993 On Bill Clinton's retroactive tax increases and promises of future spending cuts. In the *Los Angeles Times*, 16 Feb.

99 I thought about it a lot and I think every country ought to have a President.
1995 To television host David Letterman on his decision to seek high office. Reported in *Time*, 13 Feb.

1 We really win if we win. But we may even win if we lose.
1995 On the prospect of gaining popularity by reintroducing a balanced budget amendment. In the *New York Times*, 2 Mar.

Dole, Elizabeth Hanford 1936–

US lawyer and Republican politician, former President of the American Red Cross. She is married to Bob Dole.

2 Sometimes I think we're the only two lawyers in Washington who trust each other.
1987 On her marriage to Senator Bob Dole. In *Newsweek*, 3 Aug.

Domínguez Camargo, Hernando 1606–59

Colombian epic poet. A Jesuit, he probably abandoned this calling at the end of his life. His major work, the unfinished *Poema heroyco*, is a long, ambitious narrative in a highly Baroque style.

3 ¡En tantas de la muerte librerías,
los cuerpos de esos huesos, mal seguro,
estudia, Julio; y en su letra advierte,
que son abecedarios de la muerte!
Julio, in those libraries of death
study the bodies of those bones—an assured evil;
and learn from those characters
that they form the abecedary of death!
1666 *San Ignacio de Loyola, Poema heroyco* ('Heroic Poem of Saint Ignatius of Loyola'), bk.4, canto 6.

Donaghy, Siobhan 1984–

English pop singer, former member of the band the Sugababes.

4 Everyone else gets themselves dressed in the morning so why can't I?
2003 When asked why, unlike other pop stars, she had no stylist. Quoted in the *Sunday Times*, 21 Sep.

Donahue, Phil 1935–

US broadcaster, host of the daytime talk show *Donahue* (1967–96) and credited with inventing the genre. His political talk show was axed after six months in 2003.

5 The breasts, the hallmark of our culture. You cannot sell anything in America without the breasts.
1990 On NBC TV, Aug.

Donald, David Herbert 1920–2009

US historian and writer, Professor at Harvard (1973–91, emeritus from 1991). His many works include *Charles Sumner and the Coming of the Civil War* (1960, Pulitzer Prize) and *Lincoln* (1995).

6 Their correspondence was something like a duet between a tuba and a piccolo.
1987 On letters of Thomas Wolfe and Aline Bernstein. *Look Homeward: A Life of Thomas Wolfe*.

Donleavy, J(ames) P(atrick) 1926–

US-born Irish writer, best known for his picaresque novel *The Ginger Man* (1955).

7 To marry the Irish is to look for poverty.
1955 *The Ginger Man*, ch.2.

8 But Jesus, when you don't have any money the problem is food. When you have money, it's sex. When you have both it's health, you worry about getting ruptured or something. If everything is simply jake then you're frightened of death.
1955 *The Ginger Man*, ch.5.

9 When I die I want to decompose in a barrel of porter and have it served in all the pubs in Dublin. I wonder would they all know it was me?
1955 *The Ginger Man*, ch.31.

10 I got disappointed in human nature as well and gave it up because I found it too much like my own.
1973 *A Fairy Tale of New York*, ch.18.

11 Writing is turning one's worst moments into money.
1979 In *Playboy*, May.

Donne, John c.1572–1631

English priest and poet. He converted from Catholicism to Anglicanism, becoming Dean of St Paul's.

12 Shall I leave all this constant company,
And follow headlong, wild uncertain thee?
1594–5 *Satires*, no.1.

13 For if one eat my meat, though it be known
The meat was mine, the excrement is his own.
1594–5 *Satires*, no.2.

14 Kind pity chokes my spleen.
1594–5 *Satires*, no.3.

15 On a huge hill,
Cragged, and steep, Truth stands, and he that will
Reach her, about must, and about must go.
1594–5 *Satires*, no.3.

16 Are not your kisses then as filthy, and more,
As a worm sucking an envenomed sore?
Doth not thy fearful hand in felling quake,
As one which gathering flowers, still fears a snake?
Is not your last act harsh, and violent,
As when a plough a stony ground doth rent?
c.1595 *Elegies*, no.8, 'The Comparison'.

17 Filled with her love, may I be rather grown
Mad with much heart than idiot with none.
c.1595 *Elegies*, no.10, 'The Bracelet'.

18 I will not look upon the quickening sun,
But straight her beauty to my sense shall run;
The air shall note her soft, the fire most pure;
Water suggest her clear, and the earth sure;
Time shall not lose our passages.
c.1595 *Elegies*, no.12, 'His Parting from Her'.

19 Come, madam, come, all rest my powers defy,
Until I labour, I in labour lie.
The foe oft-times having the foe in sight,
Is tired with standing though he never fight.
Off with that girdle, like heaven's zone glistering,
But a far fairer world encompassing.
Unpin that spangled breastplate which you wear,
That busy fools may be stopped there.
Unlace yourself, for that harmonious chime
Tells me from you that now 'tis your bed time.
c.1595 *Elegies*, no.19, 'To His Mistress Going to Bed'.

20 License my roving hands, and let them go
Before, behind, between, above, below.
O my America! my new-found-land,
My kingdom, safeliest when with one man manned.
c.1595 *Elegies*, no.19, 'To His Mistress Going to Bed'.

21 I wonder, by my troth, what thou and I
Did, till we loved? were we not weaned till then?
But sucked on country pleasures, childishly?
c.1595–1605 'The Good Morrow', collected in *Songs and Sonnets* (1633).

22 Now thou hast loved me one whole day,
Tomorrow when thou leav'st, what wilt thou say?
c.1595–1605 'Woman's Constancy', collected in *Songs and Sonnets* (1633).

23 Go, and catch a falling star,
Get with child a mandrake root,
Tell me, where all past years are,
Or who cleft the Devil's foot.
c.1595–1605 'Song: Go and catch a falling star', collected in *Songs and Sonnets* (1633).

24 Sweetest love I do not go,
For weariness of thee,
Nor in hope the world can show
A fitter Love for me;
But since that I
Must die at last, 'tis best,
To use myself in jest
Thus by feigned deaths to die.
c.1595–1605 'Song: Sweetest love I do not go', collected in *Songs and Sonnets* (1633).

25 Busy old fool, unruly sun,
Why dost thou thus,
Through windows, and through curtains, call on us?
Must to thy motions lovers' seasons run?
Saucy pedantic wretch, go chide
Late schoolboys, and sour prentices,
Go tell court-huntsmen that the King will ride,
Call country ants to harvest offices;
Love, all alike, no season knows, nor clime,
Nor hours, days, months, which are the rags of time.
c.1595–1605 'The Sun Rising', collected in *Songs and Sonnets* (1633).

26 She's all states, and all princes I,
Nothing else is.
Princes do but play us; compared to this,
All honour's mimic, all wealth alchemy.
c.1595–1605 'The Sun Rising', collected in *Songs and Sonnets* (1633).

27 For God's sake, hold your tongue, and let me love,
Or chide my palsy, or my gout,
My five grey hairs, or ruined fortune flout,
With wealth your state, your mind with arts improve,
Take you a course, get you a place,
Observe his honour, or his grace,
Or the King's real, or his stamped face
Contemplate; what you will, approve,
So you will let me love.
c.1595–1605 'The Canonization', collected in *Songs and Sonnets* (1633).

28 Alas, alas, who's injured by my love?
What merchant's ships have my sighs drowned?
Who says my tears have overflowed his ground?
When did my colds a forward spring remove?
When did the heats which my veins fill
Add one more to the plaguey bill?
Soldiers find wars, and lawyers find out still
Litigious men, which quarrels move,
Though she and I do love.
c.1595–1605 'The Canonization', collected in *Songs and Sonnets* (1633).

29 'Tis the year's midnight, and it is the day's.
c.1595–1605 'Nocturnal upon St Lucy's Day', collected in *Songs and Sonnets* (1633).

30 I sing the progress of a deathless soul.
c.1595–1605 'The Progress of the Soul', stanza 1, collected in *Songs and Sonnets* (1633).

31 Nature's great masterpiece, an Elephant.
c.1595–1605 'The Progress of the Soul', stanza 39, collected in *Songs and Sonnets* (1633).

32 I am two fools, I know,
For loving, and for saying so
In whining poetry.
c.1595–1605 'The Triple Fool', collected in *Songs and Sonnets* (1633).

33 Twice or thrice had I loved thee,
Before I knew thy face or name;
So in a voice, so in a shapeless flame
Angels affect us oft, and worshipped be;
Still when, to where thou wert, I came,
Some lovely glorious nothing did I see.
c.1595–1605 'Air and Angels', collected in *Songs and Sonnets* (1633).

34 He which hath business, and makes love, doth do
Such wrong, as when a married man doth woo.
c.1595–1605 'Break of Day', collected in *Songs and Sonnets* (1633).

35 O more than moon,
Draw not up seas to drown me in thy sphere,
Weep me not dead, in thine arms, but forbear
To teach the sea what it may do too soon.
c.1595–1605 'A Valediction: Of Weeping', collected in *Songs and Sonnets* (1633).

36 Mark but this flea, and mark in this
How little that which thou deny'st me is;
It sucked me first, and now sucks thee,
And in this flea our two bloods mingled be.
c.1595–1605 'The Flea', collected in *Songs and Sonnets* (1633).

37 Come live with me, and be my love,
   And we will some new pleasures prove
   Of golden sands, and crystal brooks:
   With silken lines, and silver hooks.
   c.1595–1605 'The Bait', collected in *Songs and Sonnets* (1633).
   ▶ See Marlowe 574:41, Raleigh 705:43.

38 As virtuous men pass mildly away,
   And whisper to their souls, to go,
   Whilst some of their sad friends do say,
   The breath goes now, and some say, no:

   So let us melt, and make no noise,
   No tear-floods, nor sigh-tempests move;
   'Twere profanation of our joys
   To tell the laity of our love.
   c.1595–1605 'A Valediction: Forbidding Mourning', collected in *Songs and Sonnets* (1633).

39 Our two souls therefore, which are one,
   Though I must go, endure not yet
   A breach, but an expansion,
   Like gold to airy thinness beat.
   c.1595–1605 'A Valediction: Forbidding Mourning', collected in *Songs and Sonnets* (1633).

40 Thy firmness makes my circle just,
   And makes me end, where I begun.
   c.1595–1605 'A Valediction: Forbidding Mourning', collected in *Songs and Sonnets* (1633).

41 Where, like a pillow on a bed,
   A pregnant bank swelled up, to rest
   The violet's reclining head,
   Sat we two, one another's best.
   c.1595–1605 'The Ecstasy', collected in *Songs and Sonnets* (1633).

42 Our eye-beams twisted, and did thread
   Our eyes, upon one double string.
   c.1595–1605 'The Ecstasy', collected in *Songs and Sonnets* (1633).

43 So to engraft our hands, as yet
   Was all the means to make us one,
   And pictures in our eyes to get
   Was all our propagation.

   And whilst our souls negotiate there,
   We like sepulchral statues lay;
   All day, the same our postures were,
   And we said nothing all the day.
   c.1595–1605 'The Ecstasy', collected in *Songs and Sonnets* (1633).

44 I had rather owner be
   Of thee one hour, than all else ever.
   c.1595–1605 'A Fever', collected in *Songs and Sonnets* (1633).

45 To what a cumbersome unwieldiness
   And burdenous corpulence my love had grown,
   But that I did, to make it less,
   And keep it in proportion,
   Give it a diet, made it feed upon
   That which love worst endures, *discretion*.
   ?1595–1605 'Love's Diet', collected in *Songs and Sonnets* (1633).

46 And seeing the snail, which everywhere doth roam,
   Carrying his own house still, still is at home,
   Follow (for he is easy paced) this snail,
   Be thine own palace, or the world's thy gaol.
   1597–8 'To Sir Henry Wotton'.

47 More than kisses, letters mingle souls.
   1597–8 'To Sir Henry Wotton'.

48 John Donne, Anne Donne, Un-done.
   1602 Letter to his wife from prison. Quoted in Izaak Walton *The Life of Doctor Donne* (1640).

49 Immensity cloistered in thy dear womb.
   1609 *La Corona*, 'Nativity'.

50 At the round earth's imagined corners, blow
   Your trumpets, angels, and arise, arise
   From death, you numberless infinities
   Of souls, and to your scattered bodies go.
   c.1610–1615 *Holy Sonnets*, no.7.

51 Death be not proud, though some have called thee
   Mighty and dreadful, for thou art not so,
   For those, whom thou think'st thou dost overthrow,
   Die not, poor death, nor yet canst thou kill me.
   From rest and sleep, which but thy pictures be,
   Much pleasure, then from thee much more must flow,
   And soonest our best men with thee do go,
   Rest of their bones and soul's delivery.
   c.1610–1615 *Holy Sonnets*, no.10.

52 One short sleep past, we wake eternally,
   And Death shall be no more: Death, thou shalt die!
   c.1610–1615 *Holy Sonnets*, no.10.

53 Oh let me then His strange love still admire.
   c.1610–1615 *Holy Sonnets*, no.11.

54 Batter my heart, three-personed God; for You
   As yet but knock, breathe, shine, and seek to mend.
   c.1610–1615 *Holy Sonnets*, no.14.

55 Take me to You, imprison me, for I,
   Except You enthrall me, never shall be free,
   Nor ever chaste, except You ravish me.
   c.1610–1615 *Holy Sonnets*, no.14.

56 I am a little world made cunningly
   Of elements and an angelic sprite.
   c.1610–1615 *Holy Sonnets*, no.15.

57 What if this present were the world's last night?
   c.1610–1615 *Holy Sonnets*, no.19.

58 And new philosophy calls all in doubt,
   The element of fire is quite put out;
   The sun is lost, and th'earth, and no man's wit
   Can well direct him, where to look for it.
   1611 'An Anatomy of the World: The First Anniversary'.

59 If man were anything, he's nothing now.
   1611 'An Anatomy of the World: The First Anniversary'.

60 'Tis all in pieces, all coherence gone.
   1611 'An Anatomy of the World: The First Anniversary'.

61 She, she is dead; she's dead; when thou know'st this,
   Thou know'st how dry a cinder this world is.
   1611 'An Anatomy of the World: The First Anniversary'.

62 Verse hath a middle nature: heaven keeps souls,
   The grave keeps bodies, verse the fame enrols.
   1611 'An Anatomy of the World: The First Anniversary'.

63 It comes equally to us all, and makes us all equal when it comes. The ashes of an oak in the chimney are no epitaph of that oak, to tell me how high or how large that was; it tells me not what flocks it sheltered while it stood, nor what men it hurt when it fell...and when a whirlwind hath blown the dust of the churchyard into the church, and the man sweeps out the dust of the

church into the churchyard, who will undertake to sift those dusts again, and to pronounce, This is the Patrician, this the noble flower, and this the yeomanly, this the Plebeian bran.
c.1621 Of death. Sermon, 8 Mar.

64 Since I am coming to that holy room
Where, with Thy choir of saints forevermore,
I shall be made Thy Music, as I come
I tune the instrument here at the door,
And what I must do then, think now before.
c.1623 'Hymn to God My God, in My Sickness'.

65 Wilt thou forgive that sin, where I begun,
Which is my sin, though it was done before?
Wilt thou forgive those sins through which I run
And do them still, though still I do deplore?
When thou hast done, thou hast not done,
For I have more.
c.1623 'Hymn to God the Father'.

66 It is too little to call man a little world; except God, man is a diminutive to nothing.
1624 *Devotions upon Emergent Occasions*, Meditation no.4.

67 But I do nothing upon my self, and yet I am mine own executioner.
1624 *Devotions upon Emergent Occasions*, Meditation no.12.

68 No man is an island, entire of itself; every man is a piece of the continent, a part of the main.
1624 *Devotions upon Emergent Occasions*, Meditation no.17.

69 Any man's death diminishes me, because I am involved in mankind; and therefore never send to know for whom the bell tolls; it tolls for thee.
1624 *Devotions upon Emergent Occasions*, Meditation no.17.

70 My God, my God, thou art a direct God, may I not say a literal God... But thou art also...a figurative, a metaphorical God too.
1624 *Devotions upon Emergent Occasions*, Expostulation 19, 'The Language of God'.

71 The air is not so full of motes, of atoms, as the church is of mercies.
1624 *Sermons*, 'Christmas Day, 1624'.

72 He brought light out of darkness, not out of a lesser light; he can bring thy summer out of winter, though thou have no spring... God comes to thee, not as in the dawning of the day, not as in the bud of the spring, but as the sun at noon to illustrate all shadows, as the sheaves in harvest to fill all penuries. All occasions invite his mercies, and all times are his seasons.
1624 *Sermons*, 'Christmas Day, 1624'.

73 All the four Monarchies, with all their thousands of years, and all the powerful Kings and all the beautiful Queens of this world, were but as a bed of flowers, some gathered at six, some at seven, some at eight, all in one morning, in respect to this day.
1626 On eternity. Sermon, 30 Apr.

74 I throw myself down in my Chamber, and I call in, and invite God, and his Angels thither, and when they are there, I neglect God and his Angels, for the noise of a fly, for the rattling of a coach, for the whining of a door.
1626 Sermon preached at the funeral of Sir William Cockayne, 12 Dec.

75 How imperfect is all our knowledge!
1626 Sermon preached at the funeral of Sir William Cockayne, 12 Dec.

76 Young men mend not their sight by using old men's spectacles.
1626 Sermon preached at the funeral of Sir William Cockayne, 12 Dec.

77 And if there be any addition to knowledge, it is rather a new knowledge than a greater knowledge; rather a singularity in a desire of proposing something that was not known at all before than an improving, an advancing, a multiplying of former inceptions; and by that means, no knowledge comes to be perfect.
1626 Sermon preached at the funeral of Sir William Cockayne, 12 Dec.

78 He that purchases a manor will think to have an exact survey of the land, but who thinks of taking so exact a survey of his conscience, how that money was got that purchased that manor? We call that a man's means, which he hath; but that is truly his means, what way he came by it.
1626 Sermon preached at the funeral of Sir William Cockayne, 12 Dec.

79 The world is a great volume, and man the index of that book.
1626 'Sermon preached at the Funeral of Sir William Cockayne', 12 Dec.

80 Let man's soul be a sphere, and then, in this,
The intelligence that moves, devotion is.
'Good Friday, 1613. Riding Westward', published 1635.

Donoghue, Denis 1928–
Irish literary critic, Professor at New York University.

81 If there is a distinctive Irish experience, it is one of division, exacerbated by the fact that division in a country so small seems perverse. But the scale doesn't matter.
1986 *We Irish*.

Donoso, José 1924–96
Chilean novelist. After teaching at several universities in Chile and the US, he lived in Europe for 15 years before returning to Chile. *El obsceno pájaro de la noche* (1970), his masterpiece, presents a hallucinatory and grotesque vision of Chilean society.

82 *Los servidores acumulan los privilegios de la miseria...conservan los instrumentos de la venganza porque van acumulando en sus manos ásperas y verrugosas esa otra mitad de sus patrones, la mitad inútil, descartada, lo sucio y lo feo que ellos...les han ido entregando con el insulto de cada enagua gastada que les regalan.*
Servants accumulate the privileges of misery... They save up the instruments of vengeance because their coarse warty hands collect, bit by bit, that other side of their employers—the useless, discarded side, the filth and the sordidness that...they've been putting into their servants' hands with the insult of each shabby skirt they gave them.
1970 *El obsceno pájaro de la noche*, ch.4 (translated as *The Obscene Bird of Night*, 1973).

Doolittle, James Harold 1896–1993
US air force officer. He was the Commanding General, US 8th Air Force, in the ETO (European Theatre of Operations) in 1944.

83 Next to a letter from home, Captain Miller, your organization is the greatest morale builder in the ETO.
1944 Of Glenn Miller's wartime band. Comment on stage after a concert for the troops at Wycombe Abbey, 29 Jul. The words were later attributed to General Eisenhower in the publicity for the film *The Glenn Miller Story* (1954).

Doram-Smith, Sir Reginald Hugh 1899–1977

Irish-born British politician, a former army colonel who became an MP in 1935, Minister of Agriculture and Fisheries (1939–40) and Governor of Burma (1941–6).

84 Let 'Dig for Victory' be the motto of everyone with a garden and of every able-bodied man and woman capable of digging an allotment in their spare time.
1939 Radio broadcast, 3 Oct.

Dorgan, Tad (Thomas Aloysius) 1877–1929

US cartoonist and sportswriter. He was known for his satiric cartoons and colourful use of slang.

85 Yes, We Have No Bananas.
1922 Cartoon caption, later used as the title of a song by Irving Conn and Frank Silver (1923) and as an advertising slogan for Elders and Fyffes, British banana importers.

Dos Passos, John Roderigo 1896–1970

US novelist, playwright, travel writer and poet. He is best known for his novels such as *Manhattan Transfer* (1925) and the massive, formally experimental epic trilogy *U.S.A.* (1930–6).

86 U.S.A. is the slice of a continent. U.S.A. is a group of holding companies, some aggregations of trade unions, a set of laws bound in calf, a radio network, a chain of moving picture theatres, a column of stock quotations rubbed out and written in by a Western Union boy on a black-board, a publiclibrary full of old newspapers and dogeared historybooks with protests scrawled in the margins in pencil. U.S.A. is the world's greatest rivervalley fringed with mountains and hills. U.S.A. is a set of bigmouthed officials with too many bankaccounts. U.S.A. is a lot of men buried in their uniforms in Arlington Cemetery. U.S.A. is the letters at the end of an address when you are away from home. But mostly U.S.A. is the speech of the people
1938 *U.S.A.*, 'U.S.A.' (new prologue to collected trilogy).

87 People don't choose their careers. They are engulfed by them.
1959 In the *New York Times*, 25 Oct.

Dostoevsky, Fyodor Mikhailovich 1821–81

Russian novelist. He was condemned to death in 1849 for his revolutionary connections, but was instead sent to hard labour in Siberia until 1859.

88 The formula 'Two and two is five' is not without its attractions.
1864 *Notes from Underground*.

89 All people seem to be divided into 'ordinary' and 'extraordinary'. The ordinary people must lead a life of strict obedience and have no right to transgress the law because...they are ordinary. Whereas the extraordinary people have the right to commit any crime they like and transgress the law in any way just because they happen to be extraordinary.

1866 *Crime and Punishment*, pt.3, ch.5 (translated by David Magarshak).

90 Power is given only to him who dares to stoop and take it...one must have the courage to dare.
1866 *Crime and Punishment*, pt.5, ch.4 (translated by David Magarshak).

91 If you were to destroy in mankind the belief in immortality, not only love but every living force maintaining the life of the world would at once be dried up.
1879–80 *The Brothers Karamazov*, bk.2, ch.6.

92 If the devil doesn't exist, but man has created him, he has created him in his own image and likeness.
1879–80 *The Brothers Karamazov*, bk.5, ch.4.

93 So long as man remains free he strives for nothing so incessantly and so painfully as to find someone to worship.
1879–80 *The Brothers Karamazov*, bk.5, ch.5.

94 Love all God's creation, the whole of it and every grain of sand in it. Love every leaf, every ray of God's lights. Love the animals, love the plants, love everything. If you love everything, you will perceive the divine mystery in things.
1879–80 *The Brothers Karamazov*, bk.6, ch.3.

Douglas, Lord Alfred Bruce 1870–1945

English poet. He is remembered chiefly for his relationship with Oscar Wilde, which precipitated Wilde's downfall.

95 I am the love that dare not speak its name.
1894 'Two Loves'.

96 All good poetry is forged slowly and patiently, link by link, with sweat and blood and tears.
1919 *Collected Poems*, introduction.

Douglas, Charles 1840–74

New Zealand explorer, who travelled over much uncharted territory in the South Island of New Zealand.

97 I am perfectly aware that the mosquito and sandfly have a purpose in this world, but why don't they attend to it? Their destiny is to keep down microscopic insects...but their sphere of use is when they are in the grub state. Why don't they stick at that and not trouble innocent unoffending prospectors who can't carry a curtain?
1891 Quoted in J Pascoe (ed) *Mr Explorer Douglas* (1957).

98 I believe the reason I escaped, both this time and on other occasions, was the idea of perishing never entered my head. Nothing is so bad as terror for lowering a man's stamina.
1891 Quoted in J Pascoe (ed) *Mr Explorer Douglas* (1957).

Douglas, Gavin c.1474–1522

Scottish poet and, from 1515, Bishop of Dunkeld. His translation of Virgil's *Aeneid* is considered to be one of the greatest achievements of Scots vernacular literature.

99 First I protest, beau schiris, by your leif
Beis weill adivisit my werk or ye repreif;
Consider it warely, read ofter than anis,
Weill, at ane blenk, slee poetry nocht ta'en is.
c.1513 *Eneados*, bk.1, prologue.

1 Riveris ran reid on spate with water broun,
And burnis hurlis all their bankis doun.
c.1513 *Eneados*, bk.7, prologue.

2 And all small fowlys singis on the spray:
 Welcum the lord of lycht and lamp of day.
 c.1513 *Eneados*, bk.12, prologue.

Douglas, Keith Castellain 1920–44

English poet. Only one volume of his poems was published in his lifetime, and he was killed in action shortly after the D-Day landings in Normandy.

3 Remember me when I am dead
 and simplify me when I'm dead.
 1941 'Simplify Me When I'm Dead'.

4 For here the lover and killer are mingled
 who had one body and one heart.
 And death, who had the soldier singled
 has done the lover mortal hurt.
 1943 'Vergissmeinnicht'.

5 If at times my eyes are lenses
 through which the brain explores
 constellations of feeling
 my ears yielding like swinging doors
 admit princes to the corridors
 into the mind, do not envy me.
 I have a beast on my back.
 1944 'Bête Noire'.

6 And all my endeavours are unlucky explorers
 come back, abandoning the expedition;
 the specimens, the lilies of ambition
 still spring in their climate, still unpicked;
 but time, time is all I lacked
 to find them, as the great collectors before me.
 1944 'On a Return from Egypt, 1943–44' (published 1946).

Douglas, (George) Norman 1868–1952

Scottish novelist, travel writer and essayist. His works include *Siren Land* (1911), an account of his travels in Italy, and the novel *South Wind* (1917).

7 Bouillabaisse is only good because cooked by the French, who, if they cared to try, could produce an excellent and nutritious substitute out of cigar stumps and empty matchboxes.
 1911 *Siren Land*, 'Rain on the Hills'.

8 Don Francesco was a fisher of men, and of women. He fished *ad maiorem Dei gloriam*, and for the fun of the thing. It was his way of taking exercise.
 1917 *South Wind*, ch.2.

9 You can tell the ideals of a nation by its advertisements.
 1917 *South Wind*, ch.6.

10 Many a man who thinks to found a home discovers that he has merely opened a tavern for his friends.
 1917 *South Wind*, ch.20.

11 It is the drawback of all sea-side places that half the landscape is unavailable for purposes of human locomotion, being covered by useless water.
 1921 *Alone*, 'Mentone'.

12 As to abuse—I thrive on it. Abuse, hearty abuse, is a tonic to all save men of indifferent health.
 1928 *Some Limericks*.

13 Education is a state-controlled manufactory of echoes.
 1929 *How About Europe?*

14 To find a friend one must close one eye. To keep him—two.
 1941 *Almanac*.

15 A child of eight is many-sided. By eighteen most of his auspicious angles have been polished away; he is standardised; transformed, perhaps into the perfect citizen. Your perfect citizen may be a fine fellow, but he is not the perfect man.
 1946 *Late Harvest*.

Douglas, Michael Kirk 1944–

US actor, the son of Kirk Douglas. In 1987 he won an Academy Award for Best Actor in *Wall Street*; his other notable films include *Fatal Attraction* (1987), *The War of the Roses* (1989), *Basic Instinct* (1992), *Falling Down* (1993), *Traffic* (2000) and *Behind the Candelabra* (2013).

16 The point is, ladies and gentlemen, that greed, for lack of a better word, is good.
 1987 As Gordon Gekko in *Wall Street* (screenplay by Stanley Weiser and Oliver Stone).

17 Money never sleeps, pal.
 1987 As Gordon Gekko in *Wall Street* (screenplay by Stanley Weiser and Oliver Stone).

18 Lunch? You gotta be kidding. Lunch is for wimps.
 1987 As Gordon Gekko in *Wall Street* (screenplay by Stanley Weiser and Oliver Stone).

19 Parents are the bones on which children sharpen their teeth.
 2010 As Gordon Gekko in *Wall Street: Money Never Sleeps* (screenplay by Allan Loeb, Stephen Schiff, Stanley Weiser, and Oliver Stone).

20 It's not about the money. It's about the game.
 2010 As Gordon Gekko in *Wall Street: Money Never Sleeps* (screenplay by Allan Loeb, Stephen Schiff, Stanley Weiser, and Oliver Stone).

Douglas, William Orville 1898–1980

US lawyer, Associate Justice of the US Supreme Court (1939–80). His consistently liberal decisions were occasionally controversial, such as the stay of execution granted to the Rosenbergs, convicted spies, in 1953.

21 It is procedure that spells much of the difference between rule by law and rule by whim or caprice.
 1951 Ruling to strike the Joint Anti-Fascist Refugee Committee and two other organizations from the Attorney General's list of subversive groups until final adjudication, 30 Apr.

22 We are a religious people whose institutions presuppose a Supreme Being.
 1952 Ruling to allow the release of public school students for religious instruction, 28 Apr.

23 If the individual is no longer to be sovereign, if the police can pick him up whenever they do not like the cut of his jib…we enter a new regime.
 1968 Dissenting opinion in ruling to uphold the police right 'to stop and frisk', 10 Jun.

Douglass, Frederick *originally* Frederick Augustus Washington Bailey 1817–95

US abolitionist. Born a slave, in 1838 he escaped and changed his name. He lectured on slavery in Great Britain (1845–47) and £150 was collected so that he could purchase his freedom.

24 The white man's happiness cannot be purchased by the black man's misery.
1849 'The Destiny of Colored Americans' in *The North Star*, 16 Nov.

25 To imagine that we shall ever be eradicated is absurd and ridiculous. We can be remodified, changed, and assimilated, but never extinguished.
1849 'The Destiny of Colored Americans' in *The North Star*, 16 Nov.

26 Where justice is denied, where poverty is enforced, where ignorance prevails, and where one class is made to feel that society is an organized conspiracy to oppress, rob, and degrade them, neither persons nor property will be safe.
1886 Speech in Washington DC, commemorating the 24th anniversary of emancipation.

27 No man can point to any law in the U.S. by which slavery was originally established. Men first make slaves and then make laws.
1889 Speech, Bethel Literary and Historical Association, Washington DC, Apr.

Dove, Rita Frances 1952–

US poet. Her poetry collections include *Thomas and Beulah* (1986, Pulitzer Prize), *On the Bus with Rosa Parks* (1999) and *American Smooth* (2004). From 1993 to 1995 she was US Poet Laureate.

28 A good poem is like a bouillon cube. It's concentrated and it nourishes you when you need it.
1989 In *Time*, 18 Oct.

Dowd, Maureen 1952–

US newspaper columnist, winner of the 1999 Pulitzer Prize for distinguished commentary.

29 President Clinton returned today…to the university where he didn't inhale, didn't get drafted, and didn't get a degree.
1994 On President Clinton's visit to Oxford where as a Rhodes Scholar he had tried marijuana, avoided conscription, and left to attend Yale Law School. In the *New York Times*, 9 Jun.

30 Don't write anything down, but save everything that anyone else writes down.
1995 Advice for political survival in Washington. In the *US News and World Report*, 9 Jan.

31 We no longer have natural selection. We have unnatural selection. Survival of the fittest has been replaced by survival of the fakest.
2005 *Are Men Necessary? When Sexes Collide*.

32 The sounds of silence are a dim recollection now, like mystery, privacy and paying attention to one thing—or one person—at a time.
2011 In the *New York Times*, 6 Dec.

33 Just because digital technology makes connecting possible doesn't mean you're actually reaching people.
2013 In the *New York Times*.

Dowland, John 1563–1626

English lutenist and songwriter. Having failed, as a Catholic, to win a place at the court of Elizabeth I, he made his name in Europe before returning home. His *First Book of Songes* appeared in 1597 and ran to five editions by 1613.

34 Who loves not music and the heavenly muse,
That man God hates.
1614 Commendatory poem to William Leighton's *Teares or Lamentations of a Sorrowfull Soule*.

Downey, Dr Richard 1881–1953

English prelate, Bishop of Liverpool.

35 If Stalin had learned to play cricket, the world might now be a better place.
1948 Quoted in Colin Jarman *The Guinness Dictionary of Sports Quotations* (1990).

Dowson, Ernest 1867–1900

English poet. A member of the 'decadent' school, he studied at Oxford and became part of the Rhymers' Club. He developed friendships with W B Yeats and Arthur Symons and lived in France, where he died of alcoholism.

36 I have forgot much, Cynara! Gone with the wind,
Flung roses, roses, riotously with the throng,
Dancing, to put thy pale, lost lilies out of mind;
But I was desolate and sick of an old passion,
Yea, all the time, because the dance was long:
I have been faithful to thee, Cynara! in my fashion.
1896 *Verses*, 'Non Sum Qualis Eram Bonae Sub Regno Cynarae'.

37 They are not long, the days of wine and roses:
Out of a misty dream
Our path emerges for a while, then closes
Within a dream.
1896 'Vitae Summa Brevis'.

Doyle, Sir Arthur Conan 1859–1930

Scottish physician and writer. His stories of the brilliant and resourceful detective Sherlock Holmes and his assistant, Dr Watson, are among the most enduringly popular works of crime fiction ever written. He also wrote historical romances and other novels.

38 London, that great cesspool into which all the loungers and idlers of the Empire are irresistibly drained.
1887 *A Study in Scarlet*, ch.1.

39 It is a capital mistake to theorize before one has all the evidence. It biases the judgement.
1887 *A Study in Scarlet*, ch.3.

40 Where there is no imagination there is no horror.
1887 *A Study in Scarlet*, ch.5.

41 It is a mistake to confound strangeness with mystery.
1887 *A Study in Scarlet*, ch.7.

42 Our ideas must be as broad as Nature if they are to interpret Nature.
1887 *A Study in Scarlet*, ch.7.

43 Detection is, or ought to be, an exact science, and should be treated in the same cold and unemotional manner. You have attempted to tinge it with romanticism, which produces much the same effect as if you worked a love-story or an elopement into the fifth proposition of Euclid.
1890 *The Sign of Four*, ch.1.

44 The most winning woman I ever knew was hanged for poisoning three little children for their insurance money.
1890 *The Sign of Four*, ch.2.

45 I never make exceptions. An exception disproves the rule.
1890 *The Sign of Four*, ch.2.

46 How often have I said to you that when you have eliminated the impossible, whatever remains, *however improbable*, must be the truth?
1890 The Sign of Four, ch.6.

47 You know my methods. Apply them.
1890 The Sign of Four, ch.6.

48 'It is the unofficial force—the Baker Street irregulars.' As he spoke, there came a swift pattering of naked feet upon the stairs, a clatter of high voices, and in rushed a dozen dirty and ragged little street Arabs.
1890 The Sign of Four, ch.8.

49 The bow was made in England,
Of true wood, of yew wood,
The wood of English bows.
1891 The White Company, 'Song of the Bow'.

50 Singularity is almost invariably a clue. The more featureless and commonplace a crime is, the more difficult it is to bring it home.
1892 The Adventures of Sherlock Holmes, 'The Boscombe Valley Mystery'.

51 You know my method. It is founded upon the observance of trifles.
1892 The Adventures of Sherlock Holmes, 'The Boscombe Valley Mystery'.

52 It has long been an axiom of mine that the little things are infinitely the most important.
1892 The Adventures of Sherlock Holmes, 'A Case of Identity'.

53 Depend upon it, there is nothing so unnatural as the commonplace.
1892 The Adventures of Sherlock Holmes, 'A Case of Identity'.

54 The case has, in some respects, been not entirely devoid of interest.
1892 The Adventures of Sherlock Holmes, 'A Case of Identity'.

55 It is quite a three-pipe problem, and I beg that you won't speak to me for fifty minutes.
1892 The Adventures of Sherlock Holmes, 'The Red-Headed League'.

56 To Sherlock Holmes she is always *the* woman. I have seldom heard him mention her under any other name. In his eyes she eclipses and predominates the whole of her sex.
1892 Of Irene Adler. *The Adventures of Sherlock Holmes*, 'Scandal in Bohemia'.

57 You see, but you do not observe.
1892 The Adventures of Sherlock Holmes, 'Scandal in Bohemia'.

58 A man should keep his little brain attic stocked with all the furniture that he is likely to use, and the rest he can put away in the lumber room of his library, where he can get it if he wants it.
1892 The Adventures of Sherlock Holmes, 'The Five Orange Pips'.

59 It is my belief, Watson, founded upon my experience, that the lowest and vilest alleys in London do not present a more dreadful record of sin than does the smiling and beautiful countryside.
1892 The Adventures of Sherlock Holmes, 'The Copper Beeches'.

60 Crime is common. Logic is rare. Therefore it is upon the logic rather than upon the crime that you should dwell.
1892 The Adventures of Sherlock Holmes, 'The Copper Beeches'.

61 A long shot, Watson; a very long shot!
1894 The Memoirs of Sherlock Holmes, 'Silver Blaze'.

62 Ex-Professor Moriarty of mathematical celebrity…is the Napoleon of crime, Watson.
1894 The Memoirs of Sherlock Holmes, 'The Final Problem'.

63 'Excellent!', I cried.
'Elementary', said he.
1894 The Memoirs of Sherlock Holmes, 'The Crooked Man'. The famous phrase 'Elementary, my dear Watson' does not in fact appear in any of the Conan Doyle books. It may have originated with a review of the film *The Return of Sherlock Holmes* in the *New York Times*, 19 Oct 1929.

64 They were the footprints of a gigantic hound!
1902 The Hound of the Baskervilles, ch.2.

65 A study of family portraits is enough to convert a man to the doctrine of reincarnation.
1902 The Hound of the Baskervilles, ch.13.

66 You mentioned your name as if I should recognise it, but I assure you that, beyond the obvious facts that you are a bachelor, a solicitor, a Freemason, and an asthmatic, I know nothing whatever about you.
1905 The Return of Sherlock Holmes, 'The Norwood Builder'.

67 Now, Watson, the fair sex is your department.
1905 The Return of Sherlock Holmes, 'The Second Stain'.

68 It is horrible, yet fascinating, this struggle between a set purpose and an utterly exhausted frame.
1908 Of the final moments of the 1908 Olympic marathon, in which the Italian runner Dorando Pietri had to be helped over the finishing line and was thus disqualified. Quoted in Colin Jarman *The Guinness Dictionary of Sports Quotations* (1990).

69 'I am inclined to think—' said I.
'I should do so,' Sherlock Holmes remarked, impatiently.
1915 The Valley of Fear, ch.1.

70 Mediocrity knows nothing higher than itself, but talent instantly recognises genius.
1915 The Valley of Fear, ch.1.

71 All other men are specialists, but his specialism is omniscience.
1917 His Last Bow, 'Bruce-Partington Plans'.

72 Good old Watson! You are the one fixed point in a changing age.
1917 His Last Bow, title story.

73 There is but one step from the grotesque to the horrible.
1917 His Last Bow, 'Wisteria Lodge'.

74 Matilda Briggs…was a ship which is associated with the giant rat of Sumatra, a story for which the world is not yet prepared.
1927 The Case-Book of Sherlock Holmes, 'The Sussex Vampire'.

Doyle, Charles (Mike) 1928–

British-born Canadian poet, primarily of the city and suburbs. His collections include *A Splinter of Glass* (1956), *Messages for Herod* (1965) and *The Watchman's Dance* (2009).

75 If only to be born were being invented
Merely, or, better still, to concoct oneself
From an antique alembic, a receipt. How splendid
To take the phial cleanly from its shelf;

Powders and liquids, all one's favourite hues
Making the being one would be, the looker at stars
Or storks on the spires of Denmark, drinker of dews,
Or an eye simply.
'Phials', collected in *Quadrant*, 1964.

Doyle, Roddy 1958–
Irish novelist. His works include the 'Barrytown trilogy'—*The Commitments* (1987), *The Snapper* (1990) and *The Van* (1991) and the sequel *The Guts* (2013)—and the Booker Prize-winning *Paddy Clarke Ha Ha Ha* (1993).

76 The Irish are the niggers of Europe...An' Dubliners are the niggers of Ireland...An' the northside Dubliners are the niggers o' Dublin—Say it loud. I'm black and I'm proud.
   1987 *The Commitments.*

77 'A song belongs to no man,' said Joey The Lips. 'The Lord holds copyright on all songs.'
   'Me arse,' said Outspan.
   1987 *The Commitments.*

78 I said one Hail Mary and four Our Fathers, because I preferred the Our Father to the Hail Mary and it was longer and better.
   1993 *Paddy Clarke Ha Ha Ha.*

Drabble, Margaret 1939–
English novelist, critic and editor. Her novels often deal with the experiences and difficulties of educated young women.

79 Sometimes it seems the only accomplishment my education ever bestowed on me was the ability to think in quotations.
   1963 *A Summer Birdcage,* ch.1.

80 Perhaps the rare and simple pleasure of being seen for what one is compensates for the misery of being it.
   1963 *A Summer Birdcage,* ch.7.

81 What fools middle-class girls are to expect other people to respect the same gods as themselves and E M Forster.
   1963 *A Summer Birdcage,* ch.11.

82 Lord knows what incommunicable small terrors infants go through, unknown to all.
   1965 *The Millstone.*

83 England's not a bad country... It's just a mean, cold, ugly, divided, tired, clapped-out, post-imperial, post-industrial slag-heap covered in polystyrene hamburger cartons.
   1989 *A Natural Curiosity.*

84 Some make a point of boasting that they are never bored. 'Oh, I've always known how to occupy myself, I've never known a day's boredom in my life!' are lines often spoken by those bores who do not fear boring others.
   2009 *The Pattern in the Carpet: A Personal History with Jigsaws.*

85 Our capacity for disapproving of and moralising about one another's amusements, as of one another's artistic tastes, is almost limitless.
   2009 *The Pattern in the Carpet: A Personal History with Jigsaws.*

Drake, Sir Francis c.1540–1596
Elizabethan seaman, the first Englishman to circumnavigate the world. In 1585 he sailed on a successful expedition to the Spanish Indies. He commanded the fleet that defended England against the Spanish Armada in 1588.

86 The singeing of the King of Spain's beard.
   1587 His description of an expedition to Cadiz, quoted in Francis Bacon *Considerations Touching a War with Spain* (1629).

87 The advantage of time and place in practical actions is half the victory; which being lost is irrecoverable.
   1588 Letter to Elizabeth I, 13 Apr.

88 There is plenty of time to win this game, and to thrash the Spaniards too.
   1588 Attributed, while finishing a game of bowls at Plymouth Hoe, 20 Jul, before sailing to meet the Armada. Quoted in the *Dictionary of National Biography* (1917–), vol.5, p.1342.

Drapeau, Jean 1916–99
Canadian politician, Mayor of Montreal (1954–57, 1960–86).

89 The Montreal Olympics can no more have a deficit than a man can have a baby.
   1973 Comment at press conference, Montreal, 29 Jan. The games went well over budget.

Drayton, Michael 1563–1631
English poet and dramatist. After his first work *The Harmony of the Church* (1591) was condemned by the Church, he turned to pastoral and historical themes. *Polyolbion* (1616–22) is a topographical survey of Britain. Only one play survives, *The First Part of Sir John Oldcastle* (1600).

90 She wore a frock of frolic green.
   1593 *Idea, the Shepherd's Garland,* 'The Eighth Eclogue'.

91 So in all humours sportively I range;
   My muse is rightly of the English strain,
   That cannot long one fashion entertain.
   1594 *Ideas Mirrour,* 'To the Reader of These Sonnets'.

92 Dear, why should you command me to my rest,
   When now the night doth summon all to sleep?
   Methinks this time becometh lovers best;
   Night was ordained together friends to keep.
   1594 *Ideas Mirrour,* sonnet 37.

93 When Time shall turn those amber locks to grey,
   My verse again shall gild and make them gay.
   1597 *England's Heroic Epistles,* 'Henry Howard, Earl of Surrey, to the Lady Geraldine'.

94 Fair stood the wind for France
   When we our sails advance,
   Nor now to prove our chance
   Longer will tarry.
   1606 *Poems Lyrick and Pastorall,* 'To the Cambro-Britons and Their Harp, His Ballad of Agincourt', describing Henry V's expedition to France, 1415.

95 Upon Saint Crispin's day
   Fought was this noble fray,
   Which fame did not delay
   To England to carry;
   Oh, when shall English men
   With such acts fill a pen,
   Or England breed again
   Such a King Harry?
   1606 Of the Battle of Agincourt. *Poems Lyrick and Pastorall,* 'To the Cambro-Britons and Their Harp, His Ballad of Agincourt'.

96 But she, good sir,
   Did not prefer
   You, for that I was ranging;
   But for that she
   Found faith in me
   And she loved to be changing.
   1606 *Poems Lyrick and Pastorall,* 'To His Rival'.

97 That shire which we the Heart of England well may call.
   1612–22 Of Warwickshire. *Polyolbion,* song 13, l.2.

98   Neat Marlowe, bathed in the Thespian springs,
     Had in him those brave translunary things
     That the first poets had; his raptures were
     All air and fire, which made his verses clear,
     For that fine madness still he did retain
     Which rightly should possess a poet's brain.
     1619 'To My Most Dearly Loved Henry Reynolds, Esquire, of Poets and Poesie'.

99   Since there's no help, come let us kiss and part;
     Nay, I have done, you get no more of me,
     And I am glad, yea glad with all my heart
     That thus so cleanly I myself can free;
     Shake hands forever, cancel all our vows,
     And when we meet at any time again,
     Be it not seen in either of our brows
     That we one jot of former love retain.
     1619 *Idea*, sonnet 61.

1   The walls of spiders' legs are made,
     Well mortised and finely laid;
     He was the master of his trade
     It curiously builded;
     The windows of the eyes of cats,
     And for the roof, instead of slats,
     Is covered with the skins of bats,
     With moonshine that are gilded.
     1627 *Nymphidia, the Court of Fairy*.

Drennan, William 1754–1820
Irish patriot and poet.

2   Nor one feeling of vengeance presumed to defile
     The cause, or the men, or the Emerald Isle.
     1795 *Erin*, stanza 3.

Drescher, Fran(cine Joy) 1957–
US comedian and actress.

3   Cancer is a membership to a club nobody wanted to join. But when you get to the other side, your life has changed for the better. Sometimes the best gifts come in the ugliest packages.
     2014 Quoted on thestar.com, 26 Dec.

Drexler, Arthur 1925–87
US art administrator, Director of Architecture and Design at the Metropolitan Museum of Art, New York (1956–87).

4   History is written for the victors and what they leave out is the losers.
     1975 In the *New York Review*, 27 Nov.

Driberg, Tom (Thomas Edward Neil), Baron of Bradwell 1905–76
English journalist, broadcaster and politician. On the editorial staff of the *Daily Express* (1928–43), he became an independent (1942) then Labour (1945) MP and was created a life peer in 1975.

5   Sincerity is all that counts is a widespread modern heresy. Think again. Bolsheviks are sincere. Fascists are sincere. Lunatics are sincere. People who believe that the earth is flat are sincere. They can't all be right. Better make certain first that you have something to be sincere about, and with.
     1937 In the *Daily Express*.

Drucker, Peter Ferdinand 1909–2005
Austrian-born US management consultant, Professor of Social Science and Management at Claremont Graduate University, California.

6   Entrepreneurship can be learned, but it can't be taught, so schools are not much good.
     1988 Interviewed in 'Adam Smith' *The Roaring '80s* (1988), ch.2.

7   If you ever run into an industry that says it needs better people, sell its shares. There *are* no better people. You have to use ordinary, every-day people and make them capable of doing the work.
     1991 In the *Los Angeles Times*, 17 Sep.

Drummond, Thomas 1797–1840
Scottish engineer and statesman, developer of the Drummond Light (limelight). He was appointed Under-Secretary for Ireland in 1835.

8   Property has its duties as well as its rights.
     1838 Letter to the Earl of Donoughmore, 22 May.

Dryden, John 1631–1700
English poet, critic and playwright. He was made Poet Laureate in 1668 and his satirical verses such as *Absalom and Achitophel* (1681) were highly regarded. Among his best plays are *Marriage-à-la-Mode* (1672) and *All for Love* (1678); his works were prefaced with critical essays, including the seminal *Essay of Dramatic Poesy* (1668). He became a Catholic in 1685 and on refusing to swear allegiance to William and Mary was deprived of his laureateship.

9   An horrid stillness first invades the ear,
     And in that silence we the tempest fear.
     1660 *Astraea Redux*, l.7–8.

10   His colours laid so thick on every place,
     As only showed the paint, but hid the face.
     1660 Epistle 'To my honoured friend Sir Robert Howard', l.75–6.

11   I strongly wish for what I faintly hope:
     Like the day-dreams of melancholy men,
     I think and think on things impossible,
     Yet love to wander in that golden maze.
     1664 *The Rival Ladies*, act 3, sc.1.

12   And love's the noblest frailty of the mind.
     1665 *The Indian Emperor*, act 2, sc.2.

13   Repentance is the virtue of weak minds.
     1665 *The Indian Emperor*, act 3, sc.1.

14   For all the happiness mankind can gain
     Is not in pleasure, but in rest from pain.
     1665 *The Indian Emperor*, act 4, sc.1.

15   By viewing nature, nature's handmaid art,
     Makes mighty things from small beginnings grow:
     Thus fishes first to shipping did impart,
     Their tail the rudder, and their head the prow.
     1667 *Annus Mirabilis*, stanza 155.

16   For secrets are edged tools,
     And must be kept from children, and from fools.
     1667 *Sir Martin Mar-All*, act 2, sc.2.

17   I am resolved to grow fat and look young till forty, and then slip out of the world with the first wrinkle and the reputation of five-and-twenty.
     1668 *The Maiden Queen*, act 3, sc.1.

18 Every age has a kind of universal genius, which inclines those that live in it to some particular studies.
1668 An Essay of Dramatic Poesy, 'Shakespeare and Ben Jonson Compared'.

19 A thing well said will be wit in all languages...though it may lose something in the translation.
1668 An Essay of Dramatic Poesy, 'The Wit of the Ancients: The Universal'.

20 Shakespeare...was the man who of all modern, and perhaps ancient poets, had the largest and most comprehensive soul. All images of Nature were still present to him, and he drew them, not laboriously, but luckily; when he describes anything, you more than see it, you feel it too. Those who accuse him to have wanted learning, give him the greater commendation: he was naturally learned; he needed not the spectacles of books to read Nature; he looked inwards, and found her there... He is many times flat, insipid; his comic wit degenerating into clenches, his serious swelling into bombast. But he is always great.
1668 An Essay of Dramatic Poesy, 'Shakespeare and Ben Jonson Compared'.

21 He invades authors like a monarch; and what would be theft in other poets, is only victory in him.
1668 Of Ben Jonson. An Essay of Dramatic Poesy, 'Shakespeare and Ben Jonson Compared'.

22 If by the people you understand the multitude, the *hoi polloi*, 'tis no matter what they think; they are sometimes in the right, sometimes in the wrong: their judgement is a mere lottery.
1668 An Essay of Dramatic Poesy, 'Shakespeare and Ben Jonson Compared'.

23 One cannot say he wanted wit, but rather that he was frugal of it.
1668 Of Ben Jonson. An Essay of Dramatic Poesy, 'Shakespeare and Ben Jonson Compared'.

24 You seldom find him making love in any of his scenes or endeavouring to move the passions; his genius was too sullen and saturnine to do it gracefully, especially when he knew he came after those who had performed both to such an height.
1668 Of Ben Jonson. An Essay of Dramatic Poesy, 'Shakespeare and Ben Jonson Compared'.

25 If I would compare [Jonson] with Shakespeare, I must acknowledge him the more correct poet, but Shakespeare the greater wit.
1668 An Essay of Dramatic Poesy, 'Shakespeare and Ben Jonson Compared'.

26 Shakespeare was the Homer, or father of our dramatic poets; Jonson was the Virgil, the pattern of elaborate writing; I admire him, but I love Shakespeare.
1668 An Essay of Dramatic Poesy, 'Shakespeare and Ben Jonson Compared'.

27 And he, who servilely creeps after sense,
Is safe, but ne'er will reach an excellence.
1669 Tyrannic Love, prologue.

28 All delays are dangerous in war.
1669 Tyrannic Love, act 1, sc.1.

29 Pains of love be sweeter far
Than all other pleasures are.
1669 Tyrannic Love, act 4, sc.1.

30 I am as free as nature first made man,
Ere the base laws of servitude began,
When wild in woods the noble savage ran.
1670 The Conquest of Granada, pt.1, act 1, sc.1.

31 Forgiveness to the injured does belong;
But they ne'er pardon, who have done the wrong.
1670 The Conquest of Granada, pt.2, act 1, sc.2.

32 Thou strong seducer, opportunity!
1670 The Conquest of Granada, pt.2, act 4, sc.3.

33 I am to be married within these three days; married past redemption.
1672 Marriage-à-la-Mode, act 1, sc.1.

34 The very Janus of poets; he wears almost everywhere two faces; and you have scarce begun to admire the one, ere you despise the other.
1672 Of Shakespeare. *Essay on the Dramatic Poetry of the Last Age.*

35 So poetry, which is in Oxford made
An art, in London only is a trade.
1673 'Prologue to the University of Oxon...at the Acting of *The Silent Woman*'.

36 Sure the poet...spewed up a good lump of clotted nonsense at once.
1674 Notes and Observations on the Empress of Morocco, 'The First Act'.

37 Death, in itself, is nothing; but we fear,
To be we know not what, we know not where.
1675 Aureng-Zebe, act 4, sc.1.

38 None would live past years again,
Yet all hope pleasure in what yet remain;
And, from the dregs of life, think to receive,
What the first sprightly running could not give.
1675 Aureng-Zebe, act 4, sc.1.

39 They, who would combat general authority with particular opinion, must first establish themselves a reputation of understanding better than other men.
1677 'The Author's Apology for Heroic Poetry and Heroic Licence', an essay prefacing *State of Innocence,* a libretto based on *Paradise Lost.*

40 Virgil and Horace [were] the severest writers of the severest age.
1677 'The Author's Apology for Heroic Poetry and Heroic Licence', an essay prefacing *State of Innocence,* a libretto based on *Paradise Lost.*

41 A propriety of thoughts and words; or, in other terms, thought and words elegantly adapted to the subject.
1677 Definition of wit. 'The Author's Apology for Heroic Poetry and Heroic Licence', an essay prefacing *State of Innocence,* a libretto based on *Paradise Lost.*

42 All human things are subject to decay,
And, when fate summons, monarchs must obey.
1678 MacFlecknoe (published 1682), l.1-2.

43 Shadwell alone, of all my sons, is he
Who stands confirmed in full stupidity.
1678 Richard Flecknoe selects Shadwell as heir to the kingdom of dullness. *MacFlecknoe* (published 1682), l.17-18.

44 The rest to some faint meaning make pretence,
But Shadwell never deviates into sense.
Some beams of wit on other souls may fall,
Strike through and make a lucid interval;
But Shadwell's genuine night admits no ray,

His rising fogs prevail upon the day.
1678 *MacFlecknoe* (published 1682), l.19–24.

45 Thy genius calls thee not to purchase fame
In keen iambics, but mild anagram:
Leave writing plays, and choose for thy command
Some peaceful province in Acrostic Land.
There thou mayest wings display and altars raise,
And torture one poor word ten thousand ways.
1678 *MacFlecknoe* (published 1682), l.203–8.

46 Errors, like straws, upon the surface flow;
He who would search for pearls must dive below.
1678 *All for Love, or The World Well Lost*, prologue.

47 Then he defies the world and bids it pass.
1678 Of Antony. *All for Love, or The World Well Lost*, act 1.

48 Virtue's his path; but sometimes 'tis too narrow
For his vast soul; and then he starts out wide,
And bounds into a vice.
1678 Of Antony. *All for Love, or The World Well Lost*, act 1.

49 Sure there's contagion in the tears of friends.
1678 *All for Love, or The World Well Lost*, act 1.

50 My love's a noble madness.
1678 Cleopatra to Iris. *All for Love, or The World Well Lost*, act 2, sc.1.

51 Give, you gods,
Give to your boy, your Caesar,
The rattle of a globe to play withal,
This gewgaw world, and put him cheaply off:
I'll not be pleased with less than Cleopatra.
1678 Anthony. *All for Love, or The World Well Lost*, act 2, sc.1.

52 Moderate sorrow
Fits vulgar love, and for a vulgar man:
But I have lov'd with such transcendent passion,
I soar'd, at first, quite out of reason's view,
And now am lost above it.
1678 *All for Love, or The World Well Lost*, act 2.

53 O that faint word, *respect*! how I disdain it!
1678 *All for Love, or The World Well Lost*, act 2.

54 My heart's so full of joy,
That I shall do some wild extravagance
Of love in public; and the foolish world,
Which knows not tenderness, will think me mad.
1678 *All for Love, or The World Well Lost*, act 2.

55 We were so clos'd within each other's breasts
The rivets were not found that join'd us first.
That does not reach us yet: we were so mix'd,
As meeting streams, both to ourselves were lost;
We were one mass; we could not give or take,
But from the same; for he was I, I he!
1678 Antony speaking of his friendship with Dollabella. *All for Love, or The World Well Lost*, act 3.

56 What I have left is from my native spring;
I've still a heart that swells, in scorn of fate,
And lifts me to my banks.
1678 *All for Love, or The World Well Lost*, act 3.

57 The worst your malice can,
Is but to say the greatest of mankind
Has been my slave. The next, but far above him
In my esteem, is he whom law calls yours,
But whom his love made mine.
1678 Cleopatra boasts to Octavia of her conquest of Caesar and Antony. *All for Love, or The World Well Lost*, act 3.

58 Men are but children of a larger growth;
Our appetites as apt to change as theirs,
And full as craving too, and full as vain.
1678 Dollabella. *All for Love, or The World Well Lost*, act 4, sc.1.

59 Nature meant me
A wife, a silly, harmless, household dove,
Fond without art, and kind without deceit;
But Fortune, that has made a mistress of me,
Has thrust me out to the wide world, unfurnish'd
Of falsehood to be happy.
1678 Cleopatra. *All for Love, or The World Well Lost*, act 4.

60 Welcome, thou kind deceiver!
Thou best of thieves; who with an easy key,
Dost open life, and, unperceived by us,
Even steal us from ourselves.
1678 Cleopatra speaking of love. *All for Love, or The World Well Lost*, act 5, sc.1.

61 My whole life
Has been a golden dream of love and friendship.
1678 *All for Love, or The World Well Lost*, act 5.

62 All the learn'd are cowards by profession.
1678 *All for Love, or The World Well Lost*, act 5.

63 In pious times, ere priestcraft did begin,
Before polygamy was made a sin.
1681 *Absalom and Achitophel*, pt.1, l.1–2.

64 Then Israel's monarch, after Heaven's own heart,
His vigorous warmth did, variously, impart
To wives and slaves: and, wide as his command,
Scattered his Maker's image through the land.
1681 *Absalom and Achitophel*, pt.1, l.7–10. An oblique reference to Charles II, who had no legitimate, but many illegitimate, children.

65 Whate'er he did was done with so much ease,
In him alone, 'twas natural to please.
1681 *Absalom and Achitophel*, pt.1, l.27–8.

66 His motions all accompanied with grace;
And paradise was opened in his face.
1681 *Absalom and Achitophel*, pt.1, l.29–30.

67 The Jews, a headstrong, moody, murmuring race.
1681 *Absalom and Achitophel*, pt.1, l.45.

68 But when to sin our biased nature leans,
The careful Devil is still at hand with means;
And providently pimps for ill desires.
1681 *Absalom and Achitophel*, pt.1, l.79–81.

69 Plots, true or false, are necessary things,
To raise up commonwealths and ruin kings.
1681 Alluding to the alleged Popish plot to murder the King, which brought about the Exclusion crisis. *Absalom and Achitophel*, pt.1, l.83–4.

70 Some truth there was, but dashed and brewed with lies,
To please the fools, and puzzle all the wise.
1681 *Absalom and Achitophel*, pt.1, l.114–15.

71 Pleased with the danger, when the waves went high
He sought the storms; but for a calm unfit,
Would steer too nigh the sands to boast his wit.
1681 Alluding to Anthony Ashley Cooper, first Earl of Shaftesbury, leader of the Exclusion forces. *Absalom and Achitophel*, pt.1, l.160–2.

72 Great wits are sure to madness near allied,
And thin partitions do their bands divide.
1681 *Absalom and Achitophel*, pt.1, l.163–4.

Dryden

73 Why should he, with wealth and honour blest,
Refuse his age the needful hours of rest?
Punish a body which he could not please;
Bankrupt of life, yet prodigal of ease?
And all to leave what with his toil he won
To that unfeathered two-legged thing, a son.
1681 *Absalom and Achitophel*, pt.1, l.165–70.

74 In friendship false, implacable in hate:
Resolved to ruin or to rule the state.
1681 *Absalom and Achitophel*, pt.1, l.173–4.

75 He stood at bold defiance with his prince;
Held up the buckler of the people's cause
Against the crown, and skulked behind the laws.
1681 *Absalom and Achitophel*, pt.1, l.205–7.

76 Politicians neither love nor hate.
1681 *Absalom and Achitophel*, pt.1, l.223.

77 The people's prayer, the glad diviner's theme,
The young men's vision and the old men's dream!
1681 *Absalom and Achitophel*, pt.1, l.238–9.
▶ See Bible 111:48.

78 What cannot praise effect in mighty minds,
When flattery soothes, and when ambition blinds!
1681 *Absalom and Achitophel*, pt.1, l.303–4.

79 Desire of power, on earth a vicious weed,
Yet, sprung from high, is of celestial seed:
In God 'tis glory; and when men aspire,
'Tis but a spark too much of heavenly fire.
1681 *Absalom and Achitophel*, pt.1, l.305–9.

80 All empire is no more than power in trust.
1681 *Absalom and Achitophel*, pt.1, l.411.

81 Better one suffer, than a nation grieve.
1681 *Absalom and Achitophel*, pt.1, l.416.

82 But far more numerous was the herd of such
Who think too little and who talk too much.
1681 *Absalom and Achitophel*, pt.1, l.533–4.

83 A man so various that he seemed to be
Not one, but all mankind's epitome.
Stiff in opinions, always in the wrong;
Was everything by starts, and nothing long:
But, in the course of one revolving moon,
Was chemist, fiddler, statesman, and buffoon.
1681 *Absalom and Achitophel*, pt.1, l.545–60.

84 In squandering wealth was his peculiar art:
Nothing went unrewarded, but desert.
Beggared by fools, whom still he found too late:
He had his jest, and they had his estate.
1681 *Absalom and Achitophel*, pt.1, l.559–62.

85 Youth, beauty, graceful action seldom fail:
But common interest always will prevail:
And pity never ceases to be shown
To him, who makes the people's wrongs his own.
1681 *Absalom and Achitophel*, pt.1, l.723–6.

86 For who can be secure of private right,
If sovereign sway may be dissolved by might?
Nor is the people's judgement always true:
The most may err as grossly as the few.
1681 *Absalom and Achitophel*, pt.1, l.779–82.

87 Government itself at length must fall
To nature's state, where all have right to all.
1681 *Absalom and Achitophel*, pt.1, l.793–4.

88 The court he practised, not the courtier's art:
Large was his wealth, but larger was his heart.
1681 Of the loyalist James Butler, Duke of Ormond. *Absalom and Achitophel*, pt.1, l.825–6.

89 Swift was the race, but short the time to run.
1681 *Absalom and Achitophel*, pt.1, l.837.

90 Never was patriot yet, but was a fool.
1681 *Absalom and Achitophel*, pt.1, l.968.

91 From plots and treasons Heaven preserve my years,
But save me most from my petitioners.
Unsatiate as the barren womb or grave;
God cannot grant so much as they can crave.
1681 *Absalom and Achitophel*, pt.1, l.985–8.

92 Beware the fury of a patient man.
1681 *Absalom and Achitophel*, pt.1, l.1005.

93 For lawful power is still superior found,
When long driven back, at length it stands the ground.
1681 *Absalom and Achitophel*, pt.1, l.1024–5.

94 Doeg, though without knowing how or why,
Made still a blund'ring kind of melody;
Spurred boldly on, and dashed through thick and thin,
Through sense and nonsense, never out nor in;
Free from all meaning, whether good or bad,
And in one word, heroically mad.
1681 *Absalom and Achitophel*, pt.2, l.412–17.

95 Rhyme is the rock on which thou art to wreck.
1681 *Absalom and Achitophel*, pt.2, l.486.

96 But 'tis the talent of our English nation,
Still to be plotting some new reformation.
1681 *Sophonisba* (2nd edn).

97 There is a pleasure sure,
In being mad, that none but madmen know!
1681 *The Spanish Friar*, act 1, sc.1.

98 And, dying, bless the hand that gave the blow.
1681 *The Spanish Friar*, act 2, sc.2.

99 We loathe our manna, and we long for quails.
1682 *The Medal*, l.131.

1 But treason is not owned when 'tis descried;
Successful crimes alone are justified.
1682 *The Medal*, l.207–8.

2 And this unpolished rugged verse I chose
As fittest for discourse and nearest prose.
1682 *Religio Laici*, l.453–4.

3 Farewell, too little, and too lately known,
Whom I began to think and call my own.
1684 'To the Memory of Mr Oldham'. John Oldham was the author of *Satires upon the Jesuits* (1681).

4 Bold knaves thrive without one grain of sense,
But good men starve for want of impudence.
1684 *Constantine the Great*, epilogue.

5 Mute and magnificent, without a tear.
1685 *Threnodia Augustalis*, stanza 2.

6 Freedom which in no other land will thrive,
Freedom an English subject's sole prerogative.
1685 *Threnodia Augustalis*, stanza 10.

7 Her pencil drew whate'er her soul designed,
And oft the happy draft surpassed the image in her mind.
1686 'To the Pious Memory of the Accomplished Young Lady Mrs Anne Killigrew'.

8 O double sacrilege on things divine,
To rob the relic, and deface the shrine!
1686 'To the Pious Memory of the Accomplished Young Lady Mrs Anne Killigrew'. Killigrew had died of smallpox.

9 And doomed to death, though fated not to die.
1687 *The Hind and the Panther*, pt.1, l.8.

10 For truth has such a face and such a mien
As to be loved needs only to be seen.
1687 *The Hind and the Panther*, pt.1, l.33–4.

11 My thoughtless youth was winged with vain desires,
My manhood, long misled by wandering fires,
Followed false lights; and when their glimpse was gone
My pride struck out new sparkles of her own...
Good life be now my task: my doubts are done;
(What more could fright my faith than Three in One?)
1687 *The Hind and the Panther*, pt.1, l.71–6.

12 Reason to rule, but mercy to forgive:
The first is law, the last prerogative.
1687 *The Hind and the Panther*, pt.1, l.261–2.

13 Either be wholly slaves or wholly free.
1687 *The Hind and the Panther*, pt.2, l.285.

14 Much malice mingled with a little wit
Perhaps may censure this mysterious writ.
1687 *The Hind and the Panther*, pt.3, l.1–2.

15 For present joys are more to flesh and blood
Than a dull prospect of a distant good.
1687 *The Hind and the Panther*, pt.3, l.364–5.

16 By education most have been misled;
So they believe, because they so were bred.
The priest continues what the nurse began,
And thus the child imposes on the man.
1687 *The Hind and the Panther*, pt.3, l.389–92.

17 T'abhor the makers, and their laws approve,
Is to hate traitors and the treason love.
1687 *The Hind and the Panther*, pt.3, l.706–7.

18 For those whom God to ruin has designed,
He fits for fate, and first destroys their mind.
1687 *The Hind and the Panther*, pt.3, l.1093–4.

19 Three poets, in three distant ages born,
Greece, Italy, and England did adorn.
The first in loftiness of thought surpassed,
The next in majesty, in both the last:
The force of Nature could no farther go;
To make a third, she joined the former two.
1688 'Epigram on Milton', engraved on the frontispiece to the 1688 edition of *Paradise Lost*. The three poets are Homer, Virgil and Milton.

20 That fairy kind of writing which depends only upon the force of imagination.
1691 *King Arthur*, dedication.

21 War is the trade of kings.
1691 *King Arthur*, act 2, sc.2.

22 Fairest Isle, all isles excelling,
Seat of pleasures, and of loves;
Venus here will choose her dwelling,
And forsake her Cyprian groves.
1691 *King Arthur*, act 5, 'Song of Venus'.

23 Music, Music for a while
Shall all your cares beguile.
1692 *Oedipus* (with Nathaniel Lee).

24 How easy it is to call rogue and villain, and that wittily! But how hard to make a man appear a fool, a blockhead, or a knave, without using any of those opprobrious terms! To spare the grossness of the names, and to do the thing yet more severely, is to draw a full face, and to make the nose and cheeks stand out, and yet not to employ any depth of shadowing.
1693 *A Discourse Concerning the Original and Progress of Satire*, 'The Art of Satire'.

25 A man may be capable, as Jack Ketch's wife said of his servant, of a plain piece of work, a bare hanging; but to make a malefactor die sweetly was only belonging to her husband.
1693 *A Discourse Concerning the Original and Progress of Satire*, 'The Art of Satire'.

26 Ovid, the soft philosopher of love.
1694 *Love Triumphant*, act 2, sc.1.

27 Thou tyrant, tyrant Jealousy,
Thou tyrant of the mind!
1694 *Love Triumphant*, act 3, sc.1, 'Song of Jealousy'.

28 Happy, happy, happy, pair!
None but the brave,
None but the brave,
None but the brave deserves the fair.
1697 *Alexander's Feast*, l.4–7.

29 With ravished ears
The monarch hears,
Assumes the god,
Affects to nod,
And seems to shake the spheres.
1697 *Alexander's Feast*, l.42–6.

30 Drinking is the soldier's pleasure;
Rich the treasure;
Sweet the pleasure;
Sweet is pleasure after pain.
1697 *Alexander's Feast*, l.57–60.

31 Fallen from his high estate,
And welt'ring in his blood:
Deserted at his utmost need
By those his former bounty fed;
On the bare earth expos'd he lies,
With not a friend to close his eyes.
1697 *Alexander's Feast*, l.78–83.

32 Revolving in his altered soul
The various turns of chance below.
1697 *Alexander's Feast*, l.85–6.

33 War, he sung, is toil and trouble;
Honour but an empty bubble.
Never ending, still beginning,
Fighting still, and still destroying,
If the world be worth thy winning,
Think, oh think, it worth enjoying.
1697 *Alexander's Feast*, l.97–102.

34 Sighed and looked, and sighed again.
1697 *Alexander's Feast*, l.120.

35 Let old Timotheus yield the prize,
Or both divide the crown:
He raised a mortal to the skies;
She drew an angel down.
1697 Of 'Divine Cecilia'. *Alexander's Feast*, l.177–80.

36 We must beat the iron while it is hot, but we may polish it at leisure.
  1697 *Aeneis* (his translation of Virgil's *Aeneid*), dedication.

37 Arms, and the man I sing, who, forced by fate,
  And haughty Juno's unrelenting hate,
  Expelled and exiled, left the Trojan shore.
  1697 *Aeneis* (his translation of Virgil's *Aeneid*), bk.1, l.1–3.

38 What judgement I had increases rather than diminishes; and thoughts, such as they are, come crowding in so fast upon me, that my only difficulty is to choose or reject; to run them into verse or give them the other harmony of prose.
  1700 *Fables Ancient and Modern*, preface.

39 We can only say that he lived in the infancy of our poetry, and that nothing is brought to perfection at the first.
  1700 *Fables Ancient and Modern*, preface, 'In Praise of Chaucer'.

40 [Chaucer] must have been a man of a most wonderful comprehensive nature, because, as it has been truly observed of him, he has taken into the compass of his *Canterbury Tales* the various manners and humours of the whole English nation in his age.
  1700 *Fables Ancient and Modern*, preface, 'In Praise of Chaucer'.

41 A perpetual fountain of good sense.
  1700 Of Chaucer. *Fables Ancient and Modern*, preface.

42 'Tis sufficient to say, according to the proverb, that here is God's plenty.
  1700 Of the *Canterbury Tales*. *Fables Ancient and Modern*, preface, 'In Praise of Chaucer'.

43 One of our great poets is sunk in his reputation, because he could never forgive any conceit which came in his way; but swept like a drag-net, great and small. There was plenty enough, but the dishes were ill-sorted; whole pyramids of sweetmeats, for boys and women; but little of solid meat for men.
  1700 Of Abraham Cowley. *Fables Ancient and Modern*, preface.

44 Refined himself to soul, to curb the sense
  And made almost a sin of abstinence.
  1700 'The Character of a Good Parson', l.10–11.

45 He trudged along unknowing what he sought,
  And whistled as he went, for want of thought.
  1700 *Cymon and Iphigenia*, l.84–5.

46 She hugged the offender, and forgave the offence.
  1700 *Cymon and Iphigenia*, l.367.

47 Of seeming arms to make a short essay,
  Then hasten to be drunk, the business of the day.
  1700 *Cymon and Iphigenia*, l.407–8.

48 Better to hunt in fields, for health unbought,
  Than fee the doctor for a nauseous draught.
  The wise, for cure, on exercise depend;
  God never made his work, for man to mend.
  1700 Epistle, 'To my honoured kinsman John Driden', l.92–5.

49 Even victors are by victories undone.
  1700 Epistle, 'To my honoured kinsman John Driden', l.164.

50 But love's a malady without a cure.
  1700 *Palamon and Arcite*, bk.2, l.110.

51 Fool, not to know that love endures no tie,
  And Jove but laughs at lovers' perjury.
  1700 *Palamon and Arcite*, bk.2, l.148–9.

52 And Antony, who lost the world for love.
  1700 *Palamon and Arcite*, bk.2, l.607.

53 Repentance is but want of power to sin.
  1700 *Palamon and Arcite*, bk.3, l.813.

54 Since every man who lives is born to die,
  And none can boast sincere felicity,
  With equal mind, what happens, let us bear,
  Nor joy nor grieve too much for things beyond our care.
  Like pilgrims to th'appointed place we tend;
  The world's an inn, and death the journey's end.
  1700 *Palamon and Arcite*, bk.3, l.883–8.

55 A virgin-widow, and a mourning bride.
  1700 *Palamon and Arcite*, bk.3, l.927.

56 A very merry, dancing, drinking,
  Laughing, quaffing, and unthinking time.
  1700 *The Secular Masque*, l.39–40.

57 Joy ruled the day, and Love the night.
  1700 *The Secular Masque*, l.81.

58 All, all of a piece throughout;
  Thy chase had a beast in view;
  Thy wars brought nothing about;
  Thy lovers were all untrue.
  'Tis well an old age is out,
  And time to begin a new.
  1700 *The Secular Masque*, l.92–7.

Dubin, Al 1891–1945
Swiss-born US lyricist.

59 Come and meet those dancing feet
  On the avenue I'm taking you to
  Forty-Second Street.
  1932 From the title song, *Forty-Second Street*. Music by Harry Warren.

60 You're Getting to be a Habit with Me.
  1932 Title of song in *Forty-Second Street*. Music by Harry Warren.

61 We're in the money, we're in the money
  We've got a lot of what it takes to get along.
  1933 From the song 'We're in the Money' featured in *Gold Diggers of 1933*. Music by Harry Warren.

62 I Only Have Eyes For You.
  1934 Title of song from the film *Dames*. Music by Harry Warren.

63 You may not be an angel
  Cause angels are so few
  But until the day that one comes along
  I'll string along with you.
  1934 From the song 'I'll String Along With You' in *Twenty Million Sweethearts*. Music by Harry Warren.

64 Come on along and listen to
  The Lullaby of Broadway
  The hip hooray and bally hoo
  The Lullaby of Broadway.
  1935 From the song 'Lullaby of Broadway' in *Gold Diggers of 1935*. Music by Harry Warren.

Du Bois, W(illiam) E(dward) B(urghardt) 1868–1963
US writer. He became a leading figure in and spokesman for the black community, and wrote a number of pioneering books on black life and social reform.

65 The problem of the twentieth century is the problem of the colour line.
  1900 Address to the Pan-African Conference, London.

66 To be a poor man is hard, but to be a poor race in a land of dollars is the very bottom of hardships.
1903 The Souls of Black Folk, ch.1.

67 Herein lies the tragedy of the age: not that men are poor…not that men are wicked…but that men know so little of men.
1903 The Souls of Black Folk, ch.12.

68 If there is anybody in this land who thoroughly believes that the meek shall inherit the earth they have not often let their presence be known.
1924 The Gift of Black Folk, ch.9.

69 One thing alone I charge you. As you live, believe in life! Always human beings will live and progress to a greater, broader and fuller life. The only possible death is to lose belief in this truth simply because the great end comes slowly, because time is long.
1957 Written 26 Jun, and read as an oration at his funeral.

70 Today I see more clearly than yesterday that back of the problem of race and color, lies a greater problem which both obscures and implements it: and that is the fact that so many civilized persons are willing to live in comfort even if the price of this is poverty, ignorance and disease of the majority of their fellowmen; that to maintain this privilege men have waged war until today war tends to become universal and continuous, and the excuse for this war continues largely to be color and race.
Preface to reprint of *The Souls of Black Folk* (1969).

Du Bos, Jean-Baptiste 1670–1742
French critic, whose work influenced aesthetic theory.

71 *Les larmes d'un inconnu nous émeuvent même avant que nous sachions le sujet qui le fait pleurer.*
The tears of someone we do not know move us even before we know the reason why he weeps.
1719 Réflexions critiques sur la poésie et la peinture.

72 *Le sentiment enseigne bien mieux si l'ouvrage touche que toutes les dissertations composées par les critiques.*
Feeling teaches much more than all the writing of critics if the work touches us.
1719 Réflexions critiques sur la poésie et la peinture.

Dudek, Louis 1918–2001
Canadian poet, critic, teacher and aphorist, whose works attempt to liberate Candian poetry from its British influences. His early lyric poetry was followed by longer poems such as *En México* (1958).

73 Aphorisms give you more for your time and money than any other literary form. Only the poem comes near to it, but then most good poems either start off from an aphorism or arrive at one… Aphorisms and epigrams are the corner-stones of literary art.
Collected in *Notebooks 1960–1994* (1994).

74 Fame is based on what people say about you, reputation on what they think of you.
Collected in *Notebooks 1960–1994* (1994).

75 If there is a heaven it's no doubt already filled—with horses, chickens, lambs, and other poor creatures. People will simply not get in.
Collected in *Notebooks 1960–1994* (1994).

76 All the ills of mankind spring from belonging to a race, a nation, a city, a group of some kind. The ideal would be to belong to none, and to care for all—but who is capable of that?
Collected in *Notebooks 1960–1994* (1994).

77 Intellectually, most people never wash. They never free their minds of the accumulated rubbish of centuries.
Collected in *Notebooks 1960–1994* (1994).

78 Imagination should be integrated with life, not turned into a separate activity, art, that monopolizes one's whole existence.
Collected in *Notebooks 1960–1994* (1994).

79 Hatred is generalized, but love is for the particular.
Collected in *Notebooks 1960–1994* (1994).

80 The twentieth century had a wonderful capacity for seeing nothing as the sum of everything.
Collected in *Notebooks 1960–1994* (1994).

Duell, Charles H 1850–1920
US government official, Commissioner of the Office of Patents.

81 Everything that can be invented has been invented.
1899 Letter to President William McKinley, suggesting that an Office of Patents was no longer necessary.

Duesenberry, James Stemble 1918–2009
US economist, Emeritus Professor at Harvard.

82 Economics is all about how people make choices. Sociology is all about why they don't have any choices to make.
1960 In the National Bureau of Economic Research's *Demographic and Economic Change in the Developed World*.

Duffield, George 1818–88
US Presbyterian minister and hymnwriter.

83 Stand Up! Stand Up For Jesus!
1858 The *Psalmist*, title of hymn. Duffield's inspiration for the hymn came from the dying words of the evangelist Dudley Atkins Tyng to him: 'Tell them to stand up for Jesus.'

Duffy, Dame Carol Ann 1955–
Scottish poet and playwright. Her collections of poetry include *Standing Female Nude* (1985), *Mean Time* (1993) and *Rapture* (2005). In 2009 she became the first woman to be appointed Poet Laureate.

84 I like to use simple words, but in a complicated way.
2002 In *The Guardian*.

85 When you have a child, your previous life seems like someone else's. It's like living in a house and suddenly finding a room you didn't know was there, full of treasure and light.
2005 In *The Guardian*, 4 Dec.

Dugommier, General Jean François Coquille 1736–94
General of the French Republic.

86 *Récompensez, avancez ce jeune homme; car, si l'on était ingrat envers lui, il s'avancerait de lui-même.*
Reward that young man, promote him; for if his services are not recognised, he will promote himself.
1794 Comment to the Minister for War, speaking of the 24-year-old

Dulles, John Foster 1888–1959

US Republican politician, Secretary of State from 1953 until his resignation just a week before his death. His vigorous diplomacy led to many personal conferences with statesmen in other countries.

87 You have to take chances for peace, just as you must take chances in war... The ability to get to the verge without getting into the war is the necessary art. If you try to run away from it, if you are scared to go to the brink, you are lost.
1956 Quoted in 'How Dulles Averted War', in *Life* magazine, 16 Jan. His biographer Peter Grose in *Gentleman Spy* (1994) claims Dulles 'never actually used the word '*brinkmanship*', but the label stuck to him as the legacy of a diplomatic strategy that was reckless for the nuclear age'.

88 The Soviets sought not a place in the sun, but the sun itself. Their objective was the world. They would not tolerate compromise on goals, only on tactics.
Comment to his brother Allen. Quoted in Peter Grose *Gentleman Spy* (1994).

Dumas, Alexandre, père 1802–70

French novelist and playwright. He began writing plays, but turned to travelogues and historical novels, including *Le Comte de Monte Cristo* (*The Count of Monte Cristo*, 1844–5).

89 *Tous pour un, un pour tous.*
All for one, one for all.
1844 *Les Trois Mousquetaires*, ch.9.

90 *Cherchons la femme.*
Let us look for the woman.
1854–5 *Les Mohicans de Paris*.

Dumas, Alexandre, fils 1824–95

French writer, illegitimate son of Dumas père. In addition to his novel *La Dame aux camélias* (1848), he produced many brilliant dramas, essays, letters and speeches, and may have aided George Sand with her work for the stage.

91 The demi-monde does not represent the crowd of courtesans, but the class of declassed women... It is divided from that of honest women by public scandal, and divided from that of the courtesans by money.
1855 On the first performance of his play *La Dame aux camélias*, 20 Mar, the first recorded use of the phrase. Quoted in Joanna Richardson *The Courtesans* (1967), p.227.

92 All generalizations are dangerous, even this one.
Attributed.

du Maurier, Dame Daphne 1907–89

English novelist and short-story writer.

93 Last night I dreamt I went to Manderley again.
1938 *Rebecca*, opening words.

94 Every book is like a purge; at the end of it one is empty...like a dry shell on the beach, waiting for the tide to come in again.
1956 In the *Ladies Home Journal*, Nov.

Dunbar, Paul Laurence 1872–1906

US poet, the son of escaped slaves. He wrote several volumes of poetry in dialect, including *Lyrics of Lowly Life* (1896).

95 We wear the mask that grins and lies,
It hides our cheeks and shades our eyes.
1895 'We Wear the Mask', stanza 1.

96 I know why the caged bird sings!
1895 'Sympathy', stanza 3. This was used by Maya Angelou as the title of her autobiography in 1970.

Dunbar, William c.1460–c.1520

Scottish poet, thought to have graduated from St Andrew's University in 1479. He was a courtier of James IV, and wrote many short poems, remarkable for their range of style and subject.

97 He that may be but sturt or stryfe,
And leif ane lusty plesand lyfe,
And syne with mariege dois him mell,
And bindis him with ane wicket wyfe,
He wirkis sorrow to him sell.
early 16c 'Ane His Awin Ennemy', l.6–10.

98 Now of wemen this I say for me,
Off erthly thingis nane may bettir be;
Thay suld haif wirschep and great honoring
Off men, aboif all uthir erthly thing.
early 16c 'In Prais of Wemen', l.1–4.

99 Be riche in patience, gif thow in gudis be pure;
Quho levis mirry, he levis michtely:
Without glaidnes availis no tresour.
early 16c 'No Tressour Availis without Glaidnes', l.22–4.

1 Be courtly ay in clething and costly arrayit,
That hurtis yow nought worth a hen; yowr husband pays for all.
early 16c *The Tua Mariit Wemen and the Wedo*, l.268–9.

2 London, thou art of townes *A per se*.
Soveraign of cities, someliest in sight,
Of high renoun, riches, and royaltie;
Of lordis, barons, and many goodly knyght;
Of most delectable lusty ladies bright;
Of famous prelatis in habitis clericall;
Of merchauntis full of sybstaunce and myght;
London, thou art the flour of Cities all.
c.1501 'To the City of London', attributed to 'A Rhymer of Scotland'. Dunbar was a member of the Scots party negotiating the marriage of James I V to Margaret Tudor, and is popularly credited with the verse.

3 I that in heill wes and gladnes
Am trublit now with gret seiknes
And feblit with infermite:
Timor mortis conturbat me.
c.1505 'Lament for the Makaris', stanza 1. The Latin is from the Office for the Dead: 'The fear of death disturbs me'.

4 Sen for the deid remeid is none,
Best is that we for dede dispone
Eftir our deid that lif may we:
Timor mortis conturbat me.
c.1505 'Lament for the Makaris', stanza 25.

5 In to thir dirk and drublie dayis,
Quhone sabill all the hevin arrayis
With mystie vapouris, cluddis and skyis,
Nature all curage me denyis
Off sangis, ballattis, and of playis.
'Meditatioun in Wyntir', stanza 1.

Duncan, Isadora *originally* **Angela Duncan** 1878–1927
US dancer. She was hailed as one of the most innovative dancers of her day, espousing a free-flowing interpretative style of dance that was quite distinct from conventional ballet.

6 *Adieu, mes amis. Je vais à la gloire!*
Farewell, my friends. I am going to glory!
1927 Last words, shortly before she broke her neck when her long scarf caught in the wheels of her open-topped Bugatti sportscar. Quoted in Mary Desti *Isadora Duncan's End* (1929), ch.25.

Duncan, Robert Edwards *originally* **Edward Howard Duncan** 1919–88
US poet. He was associated with the Black Mountain Poets including Charles Olsen and Robert Creeley.

7 Among my friends love is a payment.
It is an old debt for a borrowing foolishly spent.
1946 *Early Poems 1939–46*, 'Among My Friends Love Is a Great Sorrow'.

8 Neither our vices nor our virtues
further the poem.
1960 *The Opening of the Field*, 'Poetry, a Natural Thing'.

9 Noble men in the quiet of morning hear
Indians singing the continent's violent requiem.
1960 *The Opening of the Field*, 'A Poem Beginning with a Line by Pindar'.

10 Desire paces Eternity as if it had bounds, craving death.
The Word climbs upward into Its crown.
1964 *Roots and Branches*, 'Structure of Rime X VII'.

11 I would be a falcon and go free.
I tread her wrist and wear the hood,
Talking to myself, and would draw blood.
1968 *Bending the Bow*, 'My Mother Would Be a Falconress'.

12 The great house of our humanity
No longer stands.
1984 *Ground Work: Before the War*, 'Bring It Up from the Dark'.

Dunlop, Ian 1925–
English art historian.

13 *The Shock of the New: seven historic exhibitions of modern art.*
1972 Title of book.

Dunn, Douglas Eaglesham 1942–
Scottish poet, essayist and anthologizer. A librarian at Hull University, he was encouraged by Philip Larkin. He is one of Scotland's most respected contemporary poets.

14 This masculine invisibility makes gods of them,
A pantheon of boots and overalls.
1969 'Men of Terry Street'.

15 And all their lives, like that, they'll have to rush
Forwards in reverse, always holding their caps.
1979 'Glasgow Schoolboys, Running Backwards'.

16 Snow has begun to fall on the guilty secrets of Europe.
1981 'The Deserter'.

17 Nationalism, and its chum, patriotism, encourage unedifying hyperbole.
1992 'Language and Liberty', introduction to the *Faber Book of Twentieth Century Scottish Poetry*.

18 What I tell my students is there are three places where poems must happen and a poem must happen in these three places simultaneously for it to be a good poem. It happens between the ears, that's intelligence; behind the left nipple, heart and feeling; between the tongue and teeth, the noise it makes.
1999 Interview in *The Dark Horse*, Autumn.

Dunne, Finley Peter 1867–1936
US humorist, editor of the *Chicago Journal* (1897–1900). His philosopher-bartender Mr Dooley became the exponent of Irish-American topical satire.

19 Glory Be, whin Business gets above sellin' tinpinny nails in a brown paper cornucopy, 'tis hard to tell it fr'm murther.
1901 *Mr Dooley's Opinions*, 'On Wall Street'.

20 Even an Englishman was niver improved by bein' blown up.
'Revolution'. Collected in Louis Filler (ed) *The World of Mr Dooley* (1962).

Dunne, Philip 1908–92
US screenwriter. His films include *Suez* (1938), *How Green Was My Valley* (1941), *Forever Amber* (1947) and *The Robe* (1953).

21 A perfumed parlor snake.
1947 Daniel Gregg's description of Miles Fairley in *The Ghost and Mrs Muir*.

Dunning, John 1731–1820
British lawyer and politician.

22 The influence of the Crown has increased, is increasing, and ought to be diminished.
1780 Motion passed by the House of Commons.

Duplessis, Maurice 1890–1959
Canadian statesman, Premier of Quebec (1936–9, 1944–59).

23 The bishops eat from my hand.
Characteristic remark, recalled in Conrad Black *Duplessis* (1977).

Durant, William James 1885–1981
US historian and essayist. He wrote a series of popular works culminating in the massive *Story of Civilization* (11 vol, 1935–67), written with his wife.

24 There is nothing in Socialism that a little age or a little money will not cure.
Attributed.

Dürer, Albrecht 1471–1528
German painter and engraver. He travelled widely (1490–4) and in 1498 published his first major series of woodcuts, illustrations of the Apocalypse. He was employed by Emperor Maximilian I and later Charles V.

25 The art of painting cannot be truly judged save by such as are themselves good painters; from others verily it is hidden even as a strange tongue.
c.1512 Quoted in William Martin Conway *Literary Remains of Albrecht Dürer* (1889).

26 He that would be a painter must have a natural turn thereto. Love and delight are better teachers of the Art of Painting than compulsion is.
c.1512 *On Painting*. Quoted in William Martin Conway *Literary Remains of Albrecht Dürer* (1889).

Durkheim, Émile 1858–1917

French sociologist, appointed to the first chair of sociology in France in 1913.

27 The economic services that it can render are picayune compared to the moral effect that it produces, and its true function is to create in two or more persons a feeling of solidarity.
 1893 Of labour. *The Division of Labor in Society* (translated by George Simpson, 1933).

28 The division of labor does not present individuals to one another, but social functions.
 1893 *The Division of Labor in Society* (translated by George Simpson, 1933).

29 Our excessive tolerance of suicide is due to the fact that, since the state of mind from which it springs is a general one, we cannot condemn it without condemning ourselves; we are too saturated with it not partly to excuse it.
 1897 *Suicide: a Study in Sociology* (translated by John A Spaulding and George Simpson, 1952).

30 All known religious beliefs, whether simple or complex, present one common characteristic: they presuppose a classification of all things, real and ideal, of which men think, into two classes or opposed groups, generally designated…*profane* and *sacred*.
 1912 *The Elementary Forms of the Religious Life* (translated by Joseph Ward Swain, 1965).

31 If the idea of society were extinguished in individual minds and the beliefs, traditions and aspirations of the group were no longer felt and shared by individuals, society would die. We can say of it what we just said of divinity: it is real only in so far as it has a place in the human consciousness, and this place is whatever we may give it.
 1912 *The Elementary Forms of the Religious Life* (translated by Joseph Ward Swain, 1965).

Durocher, Leo 1906–91

US baseball manager, noted for his toughness.

32 Nice guys finish last.
 1946 When asked if he regretted beating the New York Giants, who had been described as a 'nice bunch of guys'. He later used this as a book title, 1975.

33 Show me a good loser and I'll show you an idiot.
 1950 Attributed.

Durranc, Edouard

34 How beautiful the Republic was—under the Empire.
 Quoted in Edgar Holt *The Tiger: The Life of Georges Clemenceau 1841–1929* (1976).

Durrell, Lawrence George 1912–90

English novelist, poet, travel writer and playwright, born in India. His best-known works are the novel sequences *The Alexandria Quartet* (1957–60) and *The Avignon Quincunx* (1974–85).

35 I love to feel events overlapping each other, crawling over one another like wet crabs in a basket.
 1958 *Balthazar*, pt.1.

36 No one can go on being a rebel too long without turning into an autocrat.
 1958 *Balthazar*, pt.2.

37 Poggio's, where people go to watch each other watch each other.
 1968 *Tunc*, ch.1.

38 History is the endless repetition of the wrong way of living, and it'll start again tomorrow, if it's moved from here today.
 1978 In *The Listener*, 20 Apr.

Dürrenmatt, Friedrich 1921–90

Swiss writer. After several novels he established an international reputation as a playwright with works such as *The Physicists* (1962) and *Play Strindberg* (1969).

39 What was once thought can never be unthought.
 1962 *The Physicists*.

Dury, Ian 1942–2000

British rock singer, associated with the punk era of the late 1970s.

40 Sex 'n' drugs 'n' rock 'n' roll.
 1977 Title of song.

Duvall, Robert 1931–

US actor.

41 The English have Shakespeare, the Russians have Chekhov, the French Molière but we have the western.
 2004 In the *Sunday Times*, 21 Mar.

Dvořák, Antonín 1841–1904

Czech composer and organist. His work, basically classical but with colourful Slavonic motifs, became increasingly popular throughout Europe.

42 I have composed too much.
 Letter to Sibelius.

Dworkin, Andrea 1946–2005

US radical feminist, civil-rights activist and writer, whose work examines the relationship between male power and pornography. In 1983 she made an unsuccessful attempt to define pornography as sexual discrimination under law.

43 A man wants what a woman has—sex. He can steal it (rape), persuade her to give it away (seduction), rent it (prostitution), lease it over the long term (marriage in the United States), or own it outright (marriage in most societies).
 1976 In *Ms*, vol.5, no.6, Dec. Collected as 'Phallic Imperialism: why economic recovery will not work for us' in *Letters from a War Zone* (1988).

44 The power of money is a distinctly male power. Money speaks, but it speaks with a male voice. In the hands of women, money stays literal, count it out, it buys what it is worth or less. In the hands of men, money buys women, sex, status, dignity, esteem, recognition, loyalty, all manner of possibility.
 1981 *Pornography: Men Possessing Women*.

45 One of the differences between marriage and prostitution is that in marriage you only have to make a deal with one man.
 1984 In *The A.B.C.s of Reading*, winter issue. Collected as 'Feminism: An Agenda' in *Letters from a War Zone* (1988).

46 Violation is a synonym for intercourse.
 1987 *Intercourse*, 'Occupation/Collaboration'.

Dyer, Sir Edward c.1545–1607

English poet, diplomat and courtier, a friend of Sir Philip Sidney. Only a few of his poems survive.

47 My mind to me a kingdom is;
Such perfect joy therein I find
That it excels all other bliss
That world affords or grows by kind.
Though much I want which most men have,
Yet still my mind forbids to crave.
1588 'In Praise of a Contented Mind'.

48 No princely pomp, no wealthy store,
No force to win the victory,
No wily wit to salve a sore,
No shape to feed each gazing eye;
To none of these I yield as thrall.
For why my mind doth serve for all.
1588 'In Praise of a Contented Mind'.

49 Some weigh their pleasure by their lust,
Their wisdom by their rage of will,
Their treasure is their only trust;
And cloakèd craft their store of skill.
But all the pleasure that I find
Is to maintain a quiet mind.
1588 'In Praise of a Contented Mind'.

50 My wealth is health and perfect ease;
My conscience clear my chief defence;
I neither seek by bribes to please,
Nor by deceit to breed offence.
Thus do I live; thus will I die.
Would all did so well as I!
1588 'In Praise of a Contented Mind'.

Dylan, Bob *pseudonym of Robert Allen Zimmerman* 1941–

US singer and song-writer. His early acoustic, folk-influenced songs such as 'Blowin' in the Wind' were succeeded in 1965 by rock 'n' roll, with 'Mr Tambourine Man' and 'Like a Rolling Stone'.

51 How many roads must a man walk down
Before you can call him a man?…
The answer, my friend, is blowin' in the wind,
The answer is blowin' in the wind.
1962 'Blowin' in the Wind'.

52 But I can't think for you,
You'll have to decide,
Whether Judas Iscariot
Had God on his side.
1963 'With God on Our Side'.

53 Ah, but I was so much older then,
I'm younger than that now.
1964 'My Back Pages'.

54 The Times They Are A' Changing.
1964 Title of song.

55 The motorcycle black madonna
Two-wheeled gypsy queen.
1965 'Gates of Eden'.

56 Money doesn't talk, it swears.
1965 'It's Alright, Ma (I'm Only Bleeding)'.

57 Hey! Mr Tambourine Man, play a song for me.
I'm not sleepy and there is no place I'm going to.
1965 'Mr Tambourine Man'.

58 Folk music is a bunch of fat people.
Quoted in David Pickering *Brewer's Twentieth Century Music* (1994).

Dyson, Freeman J(ohn) 1923–

English-born US theoretical physicist, a nuclear weapons designer who has subsequently undertaken major work in arms control and disarmament. His works include *Weapons and Hope* (1984) and *The Sun, the Genome, and the Internet* (1999).

59 For insight into human affairs I turn to stories and poems rather than to sociology. This is the result of my upbringing and background. I am not able to make use of the wisdom of the sociologists because I do not speak their language.
1979 *Disturbing the Universe*, ch.1.

60 Science and technology, like all original creations of the human spirit, are unpredictable. If we had a reliable way to label our toys good and bad, it would be easy to regulate technology wisely. But we can rarely see far enough ahead to know which road leads to damnation. Whoever concerns himself with big technology, either to push it forward or to stop it, is gambling in human lives.
1979 *Disturbing the Universe*, ch.1.

Dyson, Will(iam Henry) 1880–1938

Australian-born radical cartoonist of the London *Daily Herald*.

61 Curious! I seem to hear a child weeping.
1919 Cartoon caption in the *Daily Herald*, 17 May. French minister Clemenceau is shown leaving the Palais de Versailles with Woodrow Wilson and Lloyd George after signing the peace treaty with Germany. The 'child' is the generation of 1940.

Eagleton, Terry 1943–

English literary critic and Professor of English Literature and Cultural Theory Literature at Oxford, Manchester, Lancaster and other universities.

1 Homosexuality was the badge of the upper class and the sign of a revolt against it; and it is small wonder that someone locked for a lifetime in this impossible contradiction should end up with cirrhosis of the liver.
1993 Review of Sean French's *Patrick Hamilton: a Life* (1993). In the *London Review of Books*, 2 Dec.

2 If there are indeed any iron laws of history, one of them is surely that in any major crisis of the capitalist system, a sector of the liberal middle class will shift to the left, and then shift smartly back again once the crisis has blown over.
1993 In the *London Review of Books*, 2 Dec.

3 After all, if you do not resist the apparently inevitable, you will never know how inevitable the inevitable was.
2011 *Why Marx Was Right*, ch.1.

4 Socialism is the completion of democracy, not the negation of it.
2011 *Why Marx Was Right*, ch.9.

Earhart, Amelia 1897–1937
US aviator. In 1932 she was the first woman to fly solo across the Atlantic and in 1935 she was the first person to fly alone from Hawaii to California.

5 Of course I realized there was a measure of danger. Obviously I faced the possibility of not returning when first I considered going. Once faced and settled there really wasn't any good reason to refer to it.
1928 *20 Hours: 40 MinutesOur Flight in the Friendship*, ch.5.

Eastwood, Clint 1930–
US actor and director. He achieved fame initially for his roles in westerns, but more recently has directed several well-respected films, including *Unforgiven* (1992) and *Mystic River* (2003).

6 You've got to ask yourself a question. Do I feel lucky. Well do I punk?
1971 As Harry Callahan in *Dirty Harry* (screenplay by Harry Julian Fink, Rita M Fink and Dean Riesner).

7 Nothing wrong with shooting so long as the right people get shot.
1973 As Harry Callahan in *Magnum Force* (screenplay by John Milius and Michael Cimino).

Eban, Abba *originally* Aubrey Solomon 1915–2002
Israeli diplomat and politician, born in South Africa. He was Israeli UN representative (1948), Ambassador to Washington (1950–9) and Foreign Minister (1966–74), but was unexpectedly defeated in the 1989 general election.

8 History teaches us that men and nations behave wisely once they have exhausted all other alternatives.
1970 Speech, London, 16 Dec.

Ebbinghaus, Hermann 1850–1909
German experimental psychologist. He carried out pioneering research on memory to investigate higher mental processes, and published his findings in *Über das Gedächtnis* (1885).

9 Psychology has a long past, but only a short history.
1885 *Summary of Psychology*.

Eberhart, Richard Ghormley 1904–2005
US poet and academic.

10 If I could only live at the pitch that is near madness
When everything is as it was in my childhood
Violent, vivid and of infinite possibility.
1947 'If I Could Only Live at the Pitch That Is Near Madness'.

11 You would think the fury of aerial bombardment
Would rouse God to relent; the infinite spaces
Are still silent. He looks on shock-pried faces.
History, even, does not know what is meant.
1951 'The Fury of Aerial Bombardment'.

12 Was man made stupid to see his own stupidity?
Is God by definition indifferent, beyond us all?
Is the eternal truth man's fighting soul
Wherein the Beast ravens in its own avidity?
1951 'The Fury of Aerial Bombardment'.

Eberts, Jake 1941–2012
Canadian-born film producer. In 1977 he founded Goldcrest Films which made *Chariots of Fire* (1981) and *Local Hero* (1983).

13 My Indecision Is Final.
1990 Title of his book on Goldcrest Films.

Echeverría, Esteban 1805–51
Argentinian poet and fiction writer. An opponent of the dictator Rosas, he was exiled in 1839 and lived in Uruguay until his death. He was the innovator of the Romantic school in Spanish American literature.

14 *A pesar de que la mía es historia, no la empezaré por el arca de Noé y la genealogía de sus ascendientes como acostumbraban hacerlo los antiguos historiadores españoles de América, que deben ser nuestros prototipos.*
I'm going to tell a true story, but I won't start with Noah's Ark and the genealogy of his forefathers, as is usual among the ancient Spanish historians of America, who we consider our prototypes.
1838 *El matadero* (*The Slaughter-House*, 1959).

Eco, Umberto 1932–
Italian novelist and semiotician. He is, perhaps, best known for *The Name of the Rose* (1980), a suspense story set in a medieval monastery.

15 In the United States there's a Puritan ethic and a mythology of success. He who is successful is good. In Latin countries, in Catholic countries, a successful person is a sinner.
1988 In the *International Herald Tribune*, 14 Dec.

16 I enjoyed your article, but I preferred my own.
Speaking to Jeremy Treglown, editor of the *Times Literary Supplement*. Quoted in Derwent May *Critical Times: The History of the Times Literary Supplement* (2001).

17 When you are on the dance floor, there is nothing to do but dance.
2005 *The Mysterious Flame of Queen Loana*.

18 I always assume that a good book is more intelligent than its author. It can say things that the writer is not aware of.
2008 In *The Paris Review*, summer issue.

19 People are never so completely and enthusiastically evil as when they act out of religious conviction.
2010 *The Prague Cemetery*.

The Economist
British journal, founded in 1843.

20 Michael Harrington…was America's leading socialist; a position, one might have thought, that almost epitomized marginality.
1989 *The Economist*, 12 Aug.

21 Corruption is more than a poison afflicting Chinese business life. It *is* Chinese business life.
1994 *The Economist*, 29 Jan.

22 One of the saddest features of the real world is that goods do not spontaneously present themselves for distribution.
1994 *The Economist*, 5 Nov.

23 Why Silvio Berlusconi is unfit to lead Italy.
2001 Front cover headline. In *The Economist*, 28 Apr.

Eddington, Sir Arthur Stanley 1882–1944
English astronomer and physicist, Professor of Astronomy (from 1913) and Director of the Observatory (from 1914) at Cambridge University.

24 Let us draw an arrow arbitrarily. If as we follow the arrow we find more and more of the random element in the world, then the arrow is pointing towards the future; if the random element decreases the arrow points towards the past... I shall use the phrase 'time's arrow' to express this one-way property of time which has no analogue in space.
1928 The Nature of the Physical World, ch.4. Martin Amis used the phrase 'Time's Arrow' for the title of his 1991 novel.

25 I ask you to look both ways. For the road to a knowledge of the stars leads through the atom; and important knowledge of the atom has been reached through the stars.
1928 Stars and Atoms, lecture 1.

26 I think it is something of the same sort of security we should seek in our relationship with God. The most flawless proof of the existence of God is no substitute for it; and if we have that relationship, the most convincing disproof is turned aimlessly aside. If I may say it with reverence, the soul and God laugh together over so odd a conclusion.
1929 Science and the Unseen World.

27 I believe that there are 15,747,724,136,275,002,577, 605,653,961,181,555,468,044,717,914,527,116,709, 366,231,425,076,185,631,031,296 protons in the universe, and the same number of electrons.
1938 Tarner Lecture.

Eddy, Mary Baker 1821–1910
US founder of the Christian Science Church.

28 Christian Science explains all cause and effect as mental, not physical.
1875 Science and Health with Key to the Scriptures.

29 Jesus of Nazareth was the most scientific man that ever trod the globe. He plunged beneath the material surface of things, and found the spiritual cause.
1875 Science and Health with Key to the Scriptures.

Eden, Sir (Robert) Anthony, 1st Earl of Avon 1897–1977
Anglo-Irish politician and Conservative Prime Minister (1955–7). He ordered British forces to occupy the Suez Canal Zone (1956), an action which caused widespread condemnation.

30 Everybody is always in favour of general economy and particular expenditure.
1956 In the Observer, 17 Jun.

31 We best avoid wars by taking even physical action to stop small ones. Everybody knows that the United Nations is not in a position to do that... We must face the fact that the United Nations is not yet the internal equivalent of our own legal system and rule of law. Police action must be to separate the belligerents and to prevent a resumption of hostilities.
1956 House of Commons, 1 Nov.

32 We are not at war with Egypt. We are in armed conflict.
1956 On the Suez crisis, House of Commons, 4 Nov.

Eden, Lady Clarissa 1920–
Wife of Sir Anthony Eden.

33 During the past few weeks, I felt sometimes that the Suez canal was flowing through my drawing room.
1956 Speech, Nov.

Edgeworth, Maria 1767–1849
Anglo-Irish novelist, whose novels reflect the rhythms of Irish country speech in their wry observation and humour. She is best remembered for *Castle Rackrent* (1800) and *The Absentee* (1812).

34 Possessed, as are all the fair daughters of Eve, of an hereditary propensity, transmitted to them undiminished through succeeding generations, to be 'soon moved with the slightest touch of blame'; very little precept and practice will confirm them in the habit, and instruct them all the maxims, of self-justification.
1795 Letters for Literary Ladies, 'An Essay on the Noble Science of Self-Justification'.

35 Man is to be held only by the *slightest* chains; with the idea that he can break them at pleasure, he submits to them in sport.
1795 Letters for Literary Ladies, 'Letters of Julia and Caroline', no.1.

36 Sir Patrick died that night—just as the company rose to drink his health with three cheers, he fell down in a sort of fit, and was carried off—they sat it out, and were surprised, on enquiry, in the morning, to find it was all over with poor Sir Patrick.
1800 Castle Rackrent, 'An Hibernian Tale'.

37 Sir Patrick Rackrent lived and died a monument of old Irish hospitality.
1800 Castle Rackrent, 'An Hibernian Tale'.

38 I've a great fancy to see my funeral before I die.
1800 Sir Cody to Thady. Castle Rackrent, 'History of Sir Conolly Rackrent'.

39 Did the Warwickshire militia, who were chiefly artisans, teach the Irish to drink beer, or did they learn from the Irish how to drink whiskey?
1800 Castle Rackrent, 'History of Sir Conolly Rackrent'.

40 Come when you're called;
And do as you're bid;
Shut the door after you;
And you'll never be chid.
1804 The Contrast, ch.1.

41 What a misfortune it is to be born a woman!... Why seek for knowledge, which can prove only that our wretchedness is irremediable? If a ray of light break in upon us, it is but to make darkness more visible; to show us the new limits, the Gothic structure, the impenetrable barriers of our prison.
1806 Leonora, letter 1.

42 There need, at all events, be none of this, if people would but live upon their own estates, and kill their own mutton.
1812 Sir Terence O'Fay. The Absentee, ch.5.

43 Those enemies to Ireland—those cruel absentees!
1812 Count O'Halloran. The Absentee, ch.8.

44 Deeds, not words.
1812 Sir James Brooke's motto. The Absentee, ch.9.

45 Let me not, even in my own mind, commit the injustice of taking a speck for the whole.
1812 The Absentee, ch.11.

46 Her son saw that the *Londonmania* was now stronger than ever upon her.
1812 The Absentee, ch.14.

47 In marrying, a man does not, to be sure, marry his wife's mother; and yet a prudent man, when he begins to think

Edinburgh

of the daughter, would look sharp at the mother; ay, and back to the grandmother too, and along the whole female line of ancestry.
1812 Count O'Halloran's advice to Lord Colambare. *The Absentee*, ch.15.

Edinburgh, Prince Philip, Duke of 1921–

Consort of Elizabeth II, son of Prince Andrew of Greece and Princess Alice of Battenberg. He entered the Royal Navy in 1939, became a naturalized British subject in 1947, and was created Duke of Edinburgh on the eve of his marriage (20 Nov). In 1956 he began the Duke of Edinburgh Award Scheme to foster the leisure activities of young people.

48 I have very little experience of self-government. In fact, I am one of the most governed people in the world.
1959 In the *New York Times*, 30 Dec.

49 We are suffering a national defeat comparable to any lost military campaign, and what is more, it is self-inflicted… It is about time that we pulled our fingers out… The rest of the world most certainly does not owe us a living.
1961 Speech to British industrialists, London, 17 Oct.

50 There is a widely held and quite erroneously held belief that cricket is just another game.
1975 In *Wisden: Cricketers' Almanack*, 'The Pleasures of Cricket'.

51 The grouse are in no danger at all from people who shoot grouse.
1988 Quoted in *Private Eye*, no.693, 8 Jul.

52 Constitutionally I don't exist.
2011 Quoted on *BBC News*, 27 Jan.

Edison, Thomas Alva 1847–1931

US inventor, one of the most productive of his time. Among his inventions were the gramophone and the motion picture.

53 The phonograph…is not of any commercial value.
c.1860 Comment to his assistant, Samuel Insull. Edison hoped that his invention would find a place in businesses and offices, rather than in the entertainment world. Quoted in Robert A Conot *A Streak of Luck: The Life and Legend of Thomas Edison* (1979).

54 Genius is one per cent inspiration, ninety-nine per cent perspiration.
c.1903 Quoted in *Harper's Monthly Magazine*, Sep 1932.

Edmeston, John 1721–1867

English architect and hymnwriter.

55 Lead us, Heavenly Father, lead us
O'er the world's tempestuous sea.
1821 *Sacred Lyrics*, Set 2, 'Lead us, Heavenly Father'.

Edward II 1284–1327

King of England (from 1307). His invasion of Scotland resulted in defeat by Robert the Bruce at Bannockburn (1314). He was eventually murdered.

56 Forasmuch as there is great noise in the city caused by hustling over large balls, from which many evils may arise, which God forbid, we command and forbid on behalf of the King, on pain of imprisonment, such game to be used in the city in future.
1314 Royal proclamation, banning football from the streets of London.

Edward III 1312–77

King of England (from 1327). He started hostilities against France in 1337 and assumed the title of King of France in 1340. Victories at Crecy (1346) and Poitiers (1356) led to a large concession of territory by the French. He also invaded Scotland.

57 Also say to them, that they suffre hym this day to wynne his spurres, for if god be pleased, I well this journey be his, and the honoure thereof.
1346 Of his 16-year-old son, Edward the Black Prince. Quoted in the *Chronicle of Froissart* (translated by Sir John Bourchier, Lord Berners, 1523–5), ch.130.

58 *Honi soit qui mal y pense.*
Evil be to him that evil thinks.
c.1348 Motto of the Order of the Garter. Said to have been uttered by Edward when adjusting the Countess of Salisbury's garter, which had slipped down.

Edward VII 1841–1910

King of the UK (from 1901), son of Queen Victoria. In 1863 he married Alexandra of Denmark. His scandalous behaviour as Prince of Wales led to his exclusion from affairs of state, but as King he made several visits to improve international relations.

59 Because a man has a black face and a different religion from ours, there is no reason why he should be treated as a brute.
1875 Letter from India to Lord Granville, 30 Nov.

Edward VIII 1894–1972

King of the UK (1936). He succeeded his father George V in 1936, but abdicated (11 Dec) because of his proposed marriage to divorcee Mrs Wallis Simpson. As Duke of Windsor, he lived in Paris except during his governorship of the Bahamas (1940–5).

60 These works brought all these people here. Something should be done to get them at work again.
1936 Comment while viewing the derelict Dowlais Iron and Steel Works, 18 Nov. It is often rendered 'Something must be done'.

61 I have found it impossible to carry the heavy burden of responsibility, and to discharge my duties as King as I would wish, without the help and support of the woman I love.
1936 Radio broadcast to the nation, 11 Dec, following his abdication to marry Wallis Simpson.

Edwards, Bob (Robert Chambers) 1864–1922

Canadian publisher and writer.

62 One can always tell when one is getting old and serious by the way that holidays seem to interfere with one's work.
1913 In *Eye Opener*, 20 Dec.

Edwards, Oliver 1711–91

English lawyer, an acquaintance of Samuel Johnson.

63 You are a philosopher, Dr Johnson. I have tried too in my time to be a philosopher; but, I don't know how, cheerfulness was always breaking in.
1778 In conversation with Dr Johnson, 17 Apr. Quoted in James Boswell *Life of Samuel Johnson* (1791).

Edwards, Otis C(arl), Jr 1928–

US theologian and educator, ordained into the Episcopal Church in 1954. After serving in several churches as curate and rector, he taught at Nashotah House (1969–74) before being appointed Dean of Seabury-Western Theological Seminary (1974–83).

64 To be loose with grammar is to be loose with the worst woman in the world.
1966 New Testament lecture, Nashotah House, 10 Jan.

Egan, Pierce 1772–1849

English sporting writer. A London journalist, he wrote *Boxiana: or Sketches of Ancient and Modern Pugilism* (1812–13), and is best remembered for *Life in London* (1821), a description of the life of a 'man about town'.

65 Here lies, bowl'd out by Death's unerring ball,
A cricketer renowned, by name John Small;
But though his name was small, yet great was his fame,
For nobly did he play the 'noble game'.
His life was like his innings—long and good;
Full ninety summers had Death withstood,
At length the ninetieth winter came—when (Fate
Not leaving him one solitary mate)
This last of Hambledonians, old John Small,
Gave up his bat and ball—his leather, wax and all.
1832 Epitaph on cricketer John Small. *Pierce Egan's Book of Sports.*

Eggers, Dave 1970–

US magazine editor and novelist.

66 A Heartbreaking Work of Staggering Genius.
2000 Book title.

67 When there is pleasure, there is often abandon, and mistakes are made.
2006 What is the What.

68 Better to be at the bottom of a ladder you want to climb than in the middle of some ladder you don't, right?
2013 The Circle.

Ehrlich, Paul Ralph 1932–

US biologist, Professor at Stanford University.

69 The first rule of intelligent tinkering is to save all the parts.
1971 In the *Saturday Review*, 5 Jun.

Ehrlichman, John 1925–99

US government official, Special Counsel to the Nixon White House, implicated in the Watergate scandal.

70 He's the Big Enchilada.
1973 On the possibility of pinning the blame for Watergate on Attorney General John Mitchell. Taped conversation, 27 Mar.

71 I think we ought to let him hang there. Let him twist slowly, slowly in the wind.
1973 Of Patrick Gray, regarding his nomination as Director of the FBI. Taped conversation with John Dean, reported in the *Washington Post*, 27 Jul.

Eichelbaum, Samuel 1894–1969

Argentinian playwright and fiction writer. He began writing in a naturalistic style, but later adopted an emotional realism to show the effect of social environment on the individual. ¡

72 ¡No hay políticos malos! Y buenos, tampoco, ¡qué caray! Los políticos no son ni buenos ni malos. Son hombres de oficio. Como los carpinterios y los albañiles.
There are no bad politicians! There aren't any good ones either, damn it! Politicians are neither bad nor good. They are professionals, like carpenters or masons.
1940 Un guapo del 900 ('A Handsome Man from the Nineteen Hundreds'), act 1.

Einstein, Albert 1879–1955

German-born theoretical physicist, who took Swiss (1901) and US (1940) citizenship. His early work on the photoelectric effect pioneered quantum theory and won him the 1921 Nobel prize. He is best known for his special (1905) and general (1916) theories of relativity. After Hitler's rise to power he lectured in the US, and later urged international control of atomic weapons.

73 E = mc^2
1905 Zur Elektrodynamik bewegter Körper ('The Electrodynamics of Moving Bodies').

74 *Raffiniert ist der Herrgott, aber boshaft ist er nicht.*
God is subtle, but he is not malicious.
1921 Said on a visit to Princeton University, May, and later carved above a fireplace there.

75 *Jedenfalls bin ich überzeugt, dass der nicht würfelt.*
Anyway, I am sure that he [God] does not play dice.
1926 Letter to Max Born, 4 Dec.
▶ See Hawking 401:87.

76 One of the strongest motives that lead people to give their lives to art and science is the urge to flee from everyday life, with its drab and deadly dullness and thus to unshackle the chains of one's own transient desires, which supplant one another in an interminable succession so long as the mind is fixed on the horizon of daily environment.
1933 Prologue to Max Planck *Where is Science Going?* (1933).

77 I think and think for months and years. Ninety-nine times, the conclusion is false. The hundredth time I am right.
1934 The World as I See It.

78 It may be possible to set up a nuclear reaction in uranium by which vast amounts of power could be released… This new phenomenon would also lead to the construction of…extremely powerful bombs of a new type.
1939 Letter to President Franklin D Roosevelt.

79 Science without religion is lame, religion without science is blind.
1941 Science, Philosophy and Religion: A Symposium, ch.13.

80 The most beautiful emotion we can experience is the mystical. It is the power of all true art and science. He to whom this emotion is a stranger, who can no longer wonder and stand rapt in awe, is as good as dead. To know that what is impenetrable to us really exists, manifesting itself as the highest wisdom and the most radiant beauty, which our dull faculties can comprehend only in their most primitive forms—this knowledge, this feeling, is at the center of true religiousness. In this sense, and in this sense only, I belong to the rank of devoutly religious men.
Quoted in Philipp Frank *Einstein: His Life and Times* (1947), ch.12, section 5.

81 Science can only state what is, not what should be.
1950 Out of My Later Years.

82 Perfections of means and confusion of goals seem—in my opinion—to characterize our age.
1950 Out of My Later Years.

83 The man of science is a poor philosopher.
   1950 *Out of My Later Years.*

84 The whole of science is nothing more than a refinement of everyday thinking.
   1950 *Out of My Later Years.*

85 Education is what remains, if one has forgotten everything one learned in school.
   1950 *Out of My Later Years.*

86 If A is success in life, then A equals x plus y plus z. Work is x; y is play; and z is keeping your mouth shut.
   1950 In the *Observer*, 15 Jan.

87 The most incomprehensible thing about the world is that it is comprehensible.
   1950 In *Life Magazine*.

88 If only I had known, I would have become a watchmaker.
   1955 On his part in developing the atom bomb. In the *New Statesman*, 16 Apr.

89 The grand aim of all science is to cover the greatest number of empirical facts by logical deduction from the smallest number of hypotheses or axioms.
   1970 Quoted in *Life Magazine*, 9 Jan.

90 As far as the laws of mathematics refer to reality, they are not certain, and as far as they are certain, they do not refer to reality.
   Quoted in Fritjof Capra *The Tao of Physics* (1975), ch.2.

91 Everything should be made as simple as possible, but not simpler.
   Quoted in *Newsweek*, 16 Apr 1979.

Eisenhower, Dwight D(avid) 1890–1969

US soldier and Republican politician, whose success as Supreme Commander of Allied forces during World War II and later of NATO swept him to victory as 34th US President (1953–61). His main concerns were foreign policy and anti-communism.

92 The eyes of the world are upon you. The hopes and prayers of liberty-loving people everywhere march with you.
   1944 Despatch to US forces on D-Day, 6 Jun.

93 Neither a wise man nor a brave man lies down on the tracks of history to wait for the train of the future to run over him.
   1952 In *Time*, 6 Oct.

94 I shall go to Korea, to try to end the war.
   1952 Presidential campaign pledge, Oct.

95 A soldier's pack is not so heavy a burden as a prisoner's chains.
   1953 Inaugural address, 20 Jan.

96 History does not long entrust the care of freedom to the weak or the timid.
   1953 Inaugural address, 20 Jan.

97 I just won't get into a pissing contest with that skunk.
   1953 Comment to his brother Milton, refusing to publicly contend with Senator Joseph R McCarthy. Quoted in Piers Brandon *Ike* (1986).

98 You have a row of dominoes set up. You knock over the first one, and what will happen to the last is that it will go over very quickly.
   1954 Explaining the domino theory in relation to SE Asia, 7 Apr.

99 There can be no law if we were to invoke one code of international conduct for those who oppose us and another for our friends.
   1956 Speech on the Suez crisis, 31 Oct.

1 If the United Nations once admits that international disputes can be settled by using force, we will have destroyed the foundation of the organization and our best hope of establishing a world order.
   1957 Address to the nation on Israel's invasion of Egypt, 20 Feb.

2 In the councils of government, we must guard against the acquisition of unwarranted influence, whether sought or unsought, by the military-industrial complex. The potential for the disastrous rise of misplaced powers exists and will persist.
   1961 Farewell address to the nation, 17 Jan.

3 Now, on Friday noon, I am to become a private citizen. I am proud to do so. I look forward to it.
   1961 Concluding his farewell address to the nation, 17 Jan.

4 I want...the $60 GI job and no medals on my chest.
   1963 To President Truman, 25 Nov. Quoted in Michael R Beschloss *Eisenhower* (1990).

5 There's one thing to be said about being President—nobody can tell you when to sit down.
   1964 Speech.

6 A fine man who, in the middle of a stormy lake, knows nothing of swimming.
   His initial impression of President Harry S Truman while he was military chief of staff. Quoted in Michael R Beschloss *Eisenhower* (1990).

7 Just what does he think the Presidency *is*?
   On being warned by a doctor to avoid 'irritation, frustration, anxiety, fear, and above all else, anger'. Quoted in Michael R Beschloss *Eisenhower* (1990).

8 This embattled shore, portal of freedom, is forever hallowed by the ideals, the valor and the sacrifices of our fellow countrymen.
   Inscription at US cemetery near St-Laurent. Quoted in the *New York Times*, 5 Jun 1994.

Eisenstaedt, Alfred 1898–1995

German-born US photographer and photojournalist, renowned for his candid pictures of both everyday life and historic occasions.

9 The most important thing about photographing people is not clicking the shutter...it is clicking with the subject.
   1966 *Witness to Our Time.*

10 I want to be a mouse in a mousehole.
   1995 On the unobtrusiveness of the photographer. In NPR broadcast, 24 Aug.

Elgar, Sir Edward 1857–1934

English composer. His *Enigma Variations* (1899) and the oratorio *The Dream of Gerontius* (1900) established his reputation as the leading English composer of his generation. He was Master of the King's Musick from 1924.

11 To my friends pictured within.
   1899 Dedication to the *Enigma Variations*.

12 My idea is that there is music in the air, music all around us, the world is full of it and you simply take as much as you require.
   Quoted in R J Buckley *Sir Edward Elgar* (1905), ch.4.

Elgin, James Bruce 1811–63
English government official. In 1860 he was in China, enforcing the treaty of Tientsin (1858), and his actions included the burning of the Summer Palace in Beijing.

13 You can scarcely imagine the beauty and magnificence of the buildings we burnt.
1860 Letter, 18 Aug. Quoted in Nigel Cameron *Barbarians and Mandarins* (1989), ch.16.

Eliot, George *pseudonym of* Mary Ann Evans 1819–80
English novelist, renowned for her powers of observation and characterization. Her novels include *Adam Bede* (1859), *The Mill on the Floss* (1860), *Silas Marner* (1861) and her masterpiece, *Middlemarch* (1871–2).

14 Life is too precious to be spent in this weaving and unweaving of false impressions, and it is better to live quietly under some degree of misrepresentation than to attempt to remove it by the uncertain process of letter-writing.
1856 Letter to Mrs Peter Taylor, 8 Jun. Collected in G S Haight (ed) *The George Eliot Letters* (1954), vol.2.

15 In every parting there is an image of death.
1858 *Scenes of Clerical Life*, ch.10.

16 Errors look so very ugly in persons of small means—one feels they are taking quite a liberty in going astray; whereas people of fortune may naturally indulge in a few delinquencies.
1858 *Scenes of Clerical Life*, ch.25.

17 He knew two kinds of Methodists—the ecstatic and the bilious.
1859 *Adam Bede*, ch.2.

18 We are apt to be kinder to the brutes that love us than to the women that love us. Is it because the brutes are dumb?
1859 *Adam Bede*, ch.4.

19 Young souls, in such pleasant delirium as hers, are as unsympathetic as butterflies sipping nectar.
1859 Of Hetty. *Adam Bede*, ch.9.

20 I aspire to give no more than a faithful account of men and things as they have mirrored themselves in my mind.
1859 *Adam Bede*, ch.17.

21 Our deeds determine us, as much as we determine our deeds; and until we know what has been or will be the peculiar combination of outward with inward facts, which constitute a man's critical actions, it will be better not to think ourselves wise about his character.
1859 *Adam Bede*, ch.29.

22 A maggot must be born i' the rotten cheese to like it.
1859 *Adam Bede*, ch.32.

23 There's no pleasure i' living, if you're to be corked up for iver, and only dribble your mind out by the sly, like a leaky barrel.
1859 Mrs Poyser. *Adam Bede*, ch.32.

24 He was like a cock who thought the sun had risen to hear him crow.
1859 *Adam Bede*, ch.33.

25 Deep, unspeakable suffering may well be called a baptism, a regeneration, the initiation into a new state.
1859 *Adam Bede*, ch.42.

26 We hand folks over to God's mercy, and show none ourselves.
1859 *Adam Bede*, ch.42.

27 The mother's yearning, that completest type of the life in another life which is the essence of real human love, feels the presence of the cherished child even in the debased, degraded man.
1859 *Adam Bede*, ch.43.

28 If art does not enlarge men's sympathies, it does nothing morally.
1859 Letter to Charles Bray, 5 Jul.

29 He would punish everyone who deserved it: why, he wouldn't have minded being punished himself if he deserved it; but, then, he never did deserve it.
1860 Of Tom Tulliver. *The Mill on the Floss*, bk.1. ch.5.

30 Anger and jealousy can no more bear to lose sight of their objects than love.
1860 *The Mill on the Floss*, bk.1, ch.10.

31 The Catholics, bad harvests, and the mysterious fluctuations of trade—three evils mankind had to fear.
1860 *The Mill on the Floss*, bk.1, ch.12.

32 In a mind charged with an eager purpose and an unfinished vindictiveness, there is no room for new feelings.
1860 *The Mill on the Floss*, bk.4, ch.3.

33 Our life is determined for us—and it makes the mind very free when we give up wishing and only think of bearing what is laid upon us and doing what is given us to do.
1860 *The Mill on the Floss*, bk.5, ch.1.

34 The dead level of provincial existence.
1860 *The Mill on the Floss*, bk.5, ch.3.

35 The happiest women, like the happiest nations, have no history.
1860 *The Mill on the Floss*, bk.6, ch.3.

36 I should like to know what is the proper function of women, if it is not to make reasons for husbands to stay at home, and still stronger reasons for bachelors to go out.
1860 *The Mill on the Floss*, bk.6, ch.6.

37 'Character' says Novalis, in one of his questionable aphorisms, 'character is destiny.'
1860 *The Mill on the Floss*, bk.6, ch.6.

38 Half the sorrows of women would be averted if they could repress the speech they know to be useless; nay, the speech they have resolved not to make.
1866 *Felix Holt*, ch.2.

39 There is no private life which has not been determined by a wider public life.
1866 *Felix Holt*, ch.3.

40 An election is coming. Universal peace is declared, and the foxes have a sincere interest in prolonging the lives of the poultry.
1866 *Felix Holt*, ch.5.

41 Speech is often barren; but silence also does not necessarily brood over a full nest. Your still fowl, blinking at you without remark, may all the while be sitting on one addled egg; and when it takes to cackling will have nothing to announce but that addled delusion.
1866 *Felix Holt*, ch.15.

42 A woman can hardly ever choose...she is dependent on what happens to her. She must take meaner things, because only meaner things are within her reach.
1866 *Felix Holt*, ch.27.

43 There's many a one who would be idle if hunger didn't pinch him; but the stomach sets us to work.
1866 *Felix Holt*, ch.30.

44 Women were expected to have weak opinions; but the great safeguard of society and of domestic life was, that opinions were not acted on. Sane people did what their neighbours did, so that if any lunatics were at large, one might know and avoid them.
1871-2 *Middlemarch*, bk.1, ch.1.

45 A woman dictates before marriage in order that she may have an appetite for submission afterwards.
1871-2 *Middlemarch*, bk.1, ch.9.

46 He said he should prefer not to know the sources of the Nile, and that there should be some unknown regions preserved as hunting-grounds for the poetic imagination.
1871-2 *Middlemarch*, bk.1, ch.9.

47 Among all forms of mistake, prophecy is the most gratuitous.
1871-2 *Middlemarch*, bk.1, ch.10.

48 Plain women he regarded as he did the other severe facts of life, to be faced with philosophy and investigated by science.
1871-2 *Middlemarch*, bk.1, ch.11.

49 Any one watching keenly the stealthy convergence of human lots, sees a slow preparation of effects from one life on another, which tells like a calculated irony on the indifference or the frozen stare with which we look at our unintroduced neighbour.
1871-2 *Middlemarch*, bk.1, ch.11.

50 To point out other people's errors was a duty that Mr Bulstrode rarely shrank from.
1871-2 *Middlemarch*, bk.2, ch.13.

51 If we had a keen vision and feeling of all ordinary human life, it would be like hearing the grass grow and the squirrel's heart beat, and we should die of that roar which lies on the other side of silence.
1871-2 *Middlemarch*, bk.2, ch.20.

52 We do not expect people to be deeply moved by what is not unusual. That element of tragedy which lies in the very fact of frequency, has not yet wrought itself into the coarse emotion of mankind.
1871-2 *Middlemarch*, bk.2, ch.20.

53 A woman, let her be as good as she may, has got to put up with the life her husband makes for her.
1871-2 *Middlemarch*, bk.3, ch.25.

54 It is an uneasy lot at best, to be what we call highly taught and yet not to enjoy: to be present at this great spectacle of life and never to be liberated from a small hungry shivering self.
1871-2 *Middlemarch*, bk.3, ch.29.

55 A man is seldom ashamed of feeling that he cannot love a woman so well when he sees a certain greatness in her; nature having intended greatness for men.
1871-2 *Middlemarch*, bk.4, ch.39.

56 Gossip is a sort of smoke that comes from the dirty tobacco-pipes of those who diffuse it: it proves nothing but the bad taste of the smoker.
1876 *Daniel Deronda*, bk.2, ch.13.

57 A difference of taste in jokes is a great strain on the affections.
1876 *Daniel Deronda*, bk.2, ch.15.

58 There is a great deal of unmapped country within us which would have to be taken into account in an explanation of our gusts and storms.
1876 *Daniel Deronda*, bk.3, ch.24.

59 Friendships begin with liking or gratitude—roots that can be pulled up.
1876 *Daniel Deronda*, bk.4, ch.32.

Eliot, T(homas) S(tearns) 1888–1965

US-born English poet, dramatist and critic, whose work enshrined the disillusionment of the post-World War I generation and the advance of modernism. His most significant poetic works are *The Waste Land* (1922) and *Four Quartets* (1935–42). In 1948 he was awarded the Nobel prize for literature.

60 Let us go then, you and I,
When the evening is spread out against the sky
Like a patient etherized upon a table.
1915 'The Love Song of J Alfred Prufrock' (first published in *Poetry* magazine, collected in *Prufrock and Other Observations*, 1917), opening lines.

61 In the room the women come and go
Talking of Michelangelo.
1915 'The Love Song of J Alfred Prufrock' (first published in *Poetry* magazine, collected in *Prufrock and Other Observations*, 1917).

62 Should I, after tea and cakes and ices,
Have the strength to force the moment to its crisis?
1915 'The Love Song of J Alfred Prufrock' (first published in *Poetry* magazine, collected in *Prufrock and Other Observations*, 1917).

63 For I have known them all already, known them all—
Have known the evenings, mornings, afternoons,
I have measured out my life with coffee spoons;
I know the voices dying with a dying fall
Beneath the music from a farther room.
1915 'The Love Song of J Alfred Prufrock' (first published in *Poetry* magazine, collected in *Prufrock and Other Observations*, 1917).

64 I should have been a pair of ragged claws
Scuttling across the floors of silent seas.
1915 'The Love Song of J Alfred Prufrock' (first published in *Poetry* magazine, collected in *Prufrock and Other Observations*, 1917).

65 I am no prophet—and here's no great matter;
I have seen the moment of my greatness flicker,
And I have seen the eternal Footman hold my coat, and snicker,
And in short, I was afraid.
1915 'The Love Song of J Alfred Prufrock' (first published in *Poetry* magazine, collected in *Prufrock and Other Observations*, 1917).

66 No! I am not Prince Hamlet, nor was meant to be;
Am an attendant lord, one that will do
To swell a progress, start a scene or two,
Advise the prince.
1915 'The Love Song of J Alfred Prufrock' (first published in *Poetry* magazine, collected in *Prufrock and Other Observations*, 1917).

67 I grow old...I grow old...
I shall wear the bottoms of my trousers rolled.
1915 'The Love Song of J Alfred Prufrock' (first published in *Poetry* magazine, collected in *Prufrock and Other Observations*, 1917).

68 Do I dare to eat a peach?
   1915 'The Love Song of J Alfred Prufrock' (first published in *Poetry* magazine, collected in *Prufrock and Other Observations*, 1917).

69 I have heard the mermaids singing, each to each.
   I do not think that they will sing to me.
   1915 'The Love Song of J Alfred Prufrock' (first published in *Poetry* magazine, collected in *Prufrock and Other Observations*, 1917).

70 The winter evening settles down
   With smell of steaks in passageways
   Six o'clock.
   The burnt-out ends of smoky days.
   1917 *Prufrock and Other Observations*, 'Preludes', pt.1.

71 The morning comes to consciousness
   Of faint stale smells of beer
   From the sawdust-trampled street.
   1917 *Prufrock and Other Observations*, 'Preludes', pt.2.

72 Held in a lunar synthesis,
   Whispering lunar incantations
   Dissolve the floors of memory
   And all its clear relations
   Its divisions and precisions.
   1917 *Prufrock and Other Observations*, 'Rhapsody on a Windy Night'.

73 Midnight shakes the memory
   As a madman shakes a dead geranium.
   1917 *Prufrock and Other Observations*, 'Rhapsody on a Windy Night'.

74 Stand on the highest pavement of the stair—
   Lean on a garden urn—
   Weave, weave the sunlight in your hair.
   1917 *Prufrock and Other Observations*, 'La Figlia Che Piange'.

75 Sometimes these cogitations still amaze
   The troubled midnight and the noon's repose.
   1917 *Prufrock and Other Observations*, 'La Figlia Che Piange'.

76 I am aware of the damp souls of housemaids
   Sprouting despondently at area gates.
   1917 *Prufrock and Other Observations*, 'Morning at The Window'.

77 Webster was much possessed by death
   And saw the skull beneath the skin;
   And breastless creatures under ground
   Leaned backward with a lipless grin.
   1919 'Whispers of Immortality'.

78 Uncorseted, her friendly bust
   Gives promise of pneumatic bliss.
   1919 'Whispers of Immortality'.

79 Polyphiloprogenitive
   The sapient sutlers of the Lord
   Drift across the window-panes
   In the beginning was the Word.
   1919 'Mr Eliot's Sunday Morning Service'.

80 Apeneck Sweeney spreads his knees
   Letting his arms hang down to laugh,
   The zebra stripes along his jaw
   Swelling to maculate giraffe.
   1919 'Sweeney among the Nightingales'.

81 And let their liquid siftings fall
   To stain the stiff dishonoured shroud.
   1919 'Sweeney among the Nightingales'.

82 Here I am, an old man in a dry month,
   Being read to by a boy, waiting for rain.
   1919 'Gerontion'.

83 Signs are taken for wonders. 'We would see a sign!'
   The word within the word, unable to speak a word,
   Swaddled with darkness. In the juvescence of the year
   Came Christ the tiger.
   1919 'Gerontion'.

84 After such knowledge, what forgiveness? Think now
   History has many cunning passages, contrived corridors
   And issues, deceives with whispering ambitions,
   Guides us by vanities.
   1919 'Gerontion'.

85 Neither fear nor courage saves us. Unnatural vices
   Are fathered by our heroism. Virtues
   Are forced upon us by our impudent crimes.
   1919 'Gerontion'.

86 Tenants of the house,
   Thoughts of a dry brain in a dry season.
   1919 'Gerontion'.

87 Where are the eagles and the trumpets?
   Buried beneath some snow-deep Alps.
   Over buttered scones and crumpets
   Weeping, weeping multitudes
   Droop in a hundred A.B.C.'s.
   1920 'Cooking Egg'.

88 The emotion of art is impersonal.
   1920 *The Sacred Wood*, 'Tradition and Individual Talent'.

89 Poetry is not a turning loose of emotion, but an escape from emotion; it is not the expression of personality but an escape from personality.
   1920 *The Sacred Wood*, 'Tradition and Individual Talent'.

90 The only way of expressing emotion in the form of art is by finding an 'objective correlative'…such that when the external facts, which must terminate in sensory experience, are given, the emotion is immediately evoked.
   1920 *The Sacred Wood*, 'Hamlet and His Problems'.

91 The bad poet dwells partly in a world of objects and partly in a world of words, and he never can get them to fit.
   1920 *The Sacred Wood*, 'Swinburne as a Poet'.

92 Immature poets imitate; mature poets steal; bad poets deface what they take, and good poets make it into something better, or at least something different.
   1920 *The Sacred Wood*, 'Philip Massinger'.

93 In the seventeenth century a dissociation of sensibility set in from which we have never recovered; and this dissociation, as is natural, was due to the influence of the two most powerful poets of the century, Milton and Dryden.
   1921 *Selected Essays* (1932), 'The Metaphysical Poets'.

94 When a poet's mind is perfectly equipped for its work, it is constantly amalgamating disparate experience…in the mind of the poet these experiences are always forming new wholes.
   1921 *Selected Essays* (1932), 'The Metaphysical Poets'.

95 April is the cruellest month, breeding
   Lilacs out of the dead land, mixing
   Memory and desire, stirring
   Dull roots with spring rain.
   1922 *The Waste Land*, pt.1, 'The Burial of the Dead'.

96 And I will show you something different from either
   Your shadow at morning striding behind you

Eliot

Or your shadow at evening rising to meet you;
I will show you fear in a handful of dust.
1922 *The Waste Land*, pt.1, 'The Burial of the Dead'.

97 Unreal City,
Under the brown fog of a winter dawn,
A crowd flowed over London Bridge, so many,
I had not thought death had undone so many.
1922 *The Waste Land*, pt.1, 'The Burial of the Dead'.

98 'You! hypocrite lecteur!—mon semblable,—mon frère!'
1922 *The Waste Land*, pt.1, 'The Burial of the Dead'.
▶ See Baudelaire 68:57.

99 The Chair she sat in, like a burnished throne,
Glowed on the marble.
1922 *The Waste Land*, pt.2, 'A Game of Chess'.
▶ See Shakespeare 794:55.

1 O O O O that Shakespeherian Rag—
It's so elegant
So intelligent.
1922 *The Waste Land*, pt.2, 'A Game of Chess'.

2 Hurry up please it's time.
1922 *The Waste Land*, pt.2, 'A Game of Chess'.

3 Sweet Thames, run softly till I end my song,
Sweet Thames, run softly, for I speak not loud or long.
But at my back in a cold blast I hear
The rattle of the bones, and chuckle spread from ear
  to ear.
1922 *The Waste Land*, pt.3, 'The Fire Sermon'.
▶ See Marvell 577:91.

4 I Tiresias, old man with wrinkled dugs
Perceived the scene, and foretold the rest—
I too awaited the expected guest.
He, the young man carbuncular, arrives,
A small house agent's clerk, with one bold stare,
One of the low on whom assurance sits
As a silk hat on a Bradford millionaire.
1922 *The Waste Land*, pt.3, 'The Fire Sermon'.

5 When lovely woman stoops to folly and
Paces about her room again, alone,
She smoothes her hair with automatic hand,
And puts a record on the gramophone.
1922 *The Waste Land*, pt.3, 'The Fire Sermon'.
▶ See Goldsmith 376:93.

6 A current under sea
Picked his bones in whispers.
1922 *The Waste Land*, pt.4, 'Death by Water'.

7 O you who turn the wheel and look to windward,
Consider Phlebas, who was once handsome and tall
  as you.
1922 *The Waste Land*, pt.4, 'Death by Water'.

8 He who was living is now dead
We who were living are now dying
With a little patience.
1922 *The Waste Land*, pt.5, 'What the Thunder Said'.

9 Who is the third who walks always beside you?
When I count, there are only you and I together
But when I look ahead up the white road
There is always another one walking beside you.
1922 *The Waste Land*, pt.5, 'What the Thunder Said'.

10 In this decayed hole among the mountains
In the faint moonlight, the grass is singing

Over the tumbled graves.
1922 *The Waste Land*, pt.5, 'What the Thunder Said'.

11 The awful daring of a moment's surrender
Which an age of prudence can never retract.
1922 *The Waste Land*, pt.5, 'What the Thunder Said'.

12 These fragments I have shored against my ruins.
1922 *The Waste Land*, pt.5, 'What the Thunder Said'.

13 We are the hollow men
We are the stuffed men
Leaning together
Headpiece filled with straw. Alas!
1925 'The Hollow Men'.

14 This is the dead land
This is cactus land
Here the stone images
Are raised, here they receive
The supplication of a dead man's hand
Under the twinkle of a fading star.
1925 'The Hollow Men'.

15 Between the idea
And the reality
Between the motion
And the act
Falls the shadow.
1925 'The Hollow Men'.

16 This is the way the world ends
Not with a bang but a whimper.
1925 'The Hollow Men', closing lines.

17 A cold coming we had of it,
Just the worst time of the year
For a journey, and such a long journey:
The ways deep and the weather sharp,
The very dead of winter.
1927 'The Journey of the Magi'.

18 But set down
This, set down
This: were we led all that way for
Birth or Death? There was a Birth, certainly,
We had evidence and no doubt. I had seen birth and
  death
But had thought they were different; this Birth was
Hard and bitter agony for us, like Death, our death.
We returned to our places, these Kingdoms,
But no longer at ease here, in the old dispensation,
With an alien people clutching their gods.
I should be glad of another death.
1927 'The Journey of the Magi'.

19 All great poetry gives the illusion of a view of life.
1927 'Shakespeare and the Stoicism of Seneca'.

20 We know too much and are convinced of too little. Our literature is a substitute for religion, and so is our religion.
1928 'A Dialogue on Dramatic Poetry', collected in *Selected Essays* (1932).

21 Genuine poetry can communicate before it is understood.
1929 *Dante*.

22 Because I do not hope to turn again
Because I do not hope
Because I do not hope to turn.
1930 'Ash Wednesday'.

23 Because these wings are no longer wings to fly
But merely vans to beat the air
The air which is now thoroughly small and dry
Smaller and dryer than the will.
1930 'Ash Wednesday'.

24 Teach us to care and not to care
Teach us to sit still.
1930 'Ash Wednesday'.

25 Lady, three white leopards sat under a juniper-tree
In the cool of the day.
1930 'Ash Wednesday'.

26 Birth, and copulation, and death.
That's all the facts when you come to brass tacks:
Birth, and copulation, and death.
I've been born, and once is enough.
1932 *Sweeney Agonistes*, 'Fragment of an Agon'.

27 Any man has to, needs to, wants to
Once in a lifetime, do a girl in.
1932 *Sweeney Agonistes*, 'Fragment of an Agon'.

28 The people which ceases to care for its literary inheritance becomes barbaric; the people which ceases to produce literature ceases to move in thought and sensibility.
1933 *The Use of Poetry and the Use of Criticism*.

29 Poetry is not a career, but a mug's game.
1933 *The Use of Poetry and the Use of Criticism*.

30 But the essential advantage for a poet...is to be able to see beneath both beauty and ugliness; to see the boredom, and the horror, and the glory.
1933 *The Use of Poetry and the Use of Criticism*.

31 Where is the Life we have lost in living?
Where is the wisdom we have lost in knowledge?
Where is the knowledge we have lost in information?
1934 *The Rock*, pt.1.

32 And the wind shall say: 'Here were decent godless people:
Their only monument the asphalt road
And a thousand lost golf balls.'
1934 *The Rock*, pt.1.

33 What life have you if you have not life together?
There is not life that is not in community,
And no community not lived in praise of God.
1934 Choruses from *The Rock*.

34 A book is not harmless merely because no one is consciously offended by it.
1935 *Religion and Literature*.

35 Those who talk of the Bible as a 'monument of English prose' are merely admiring it as a monument over the grave of Christianity.
1935 *Religion and Literature*.

36 Time present and time past
Are both perhaps present in time future,
And time future contained in time past.
1935 *Four Quartets*, 'Burnt Norton', pt.1.

37 Footfalls echo in the memory
Down the passage which we did not take
Towards the door we never opened
Into the rose-garden. My words echo
Thus, in your mind.
1935 *Four Quartets*, 'Burnt Norton', pt.1.

38 Go, go, go, said the bird: human kind
Cannot bear very much reality.
1935 *Four Quartets*, 'Burnt Norton', pt.1.

39 At the still point of the turning world. Neither flesh nor fleshless;
Neither from nor towards; at the still point, there the dance is,
But neither arrest nor movement.
1935 *Four Quartets*, 'Burnt Norton', pt.2.

40 Time past and time future
Allow but a little consciousness.
1935 *Four Quartets*, 'Burnt Norton', pt.2.

41 Only through time time is conquered.
1935 *Four Quartets*, 'Burnt Norton', pt.2.

42 Time and the bell have buried the day,
The black cloud carries the sun away.
1935 *Four Quartets*, 'Burnt Norton', pt.4.

43 After the kingfisher's wing
Has answered light to light, and is silent, the light is still
At the still point of the turning world.
1935 *Four Quartets*, 'Burnt Norton', pt.5.

44 Or say that the end precedes the beginning,
And the end and the beginning were always there before the beginning and after the end.
And all is always now.
1935 *Four Quartets*, 'Burnt Norton', pt.5.

45 Words strain,
Crack and sometimes break, under the burden,
Under the tension, slip, slide, perish,
Decay with imprecision, will not stay in place,
Will not stay still.
1935 *Four Quartets*, 'Burnt Norton', pt.5.

46 Yet we have gone on living,
Living and partly living.
1935 *Murder in the Cathedral*, pt.1.

47 The last temptation is the greatest treason:
To do the right deed for the wrong reason.
1935 *Murder in the Cathedral*, pt.1.

48 Clear the air! clean the sky! wash the wind! take the stone from the stone, take the skin from the arm, take the muscle from bone, and wash them.
1935 *Murder in the Cathedral*, pt.2.

49 How unpleasant to meet Mr Eliot!
With his features of clerical cut,
And his brow so grim
And his mouth so prim.
1936 'Five-Finger Exercises'.

50 Success is relative:
It is what we can make of the mess we have made of things.
1939 *The Family Reunion*, pt.2, sc.3.

51 Round and round the circle
Completing the charm
So the knot be unknotted
The cross be uncrossed
The crooked be made straight
And the curse be ended.
1939 *The Family Reunion*, pt.2, sc.3.

52 At first you may think I'm as mad as a hatter
When I tell you a cat must have THREE DIFFERENT NAMES.
1939 *Old Possum's Book of Practical Cats*, 'The Naming of Cats'.

53 When you notice a cat in profound meditation
　 The reason, I tell you, is always the same:
　 His mind is engaged in a rapt contemplation
　 Of the thought, of the thought, of the thought of
　　 his name:
　 His ineffable effable
　 Effanineffable
　 Deep and inscrutable singular name.
　 1939 *Old Possum's Book of Practical Cats*, 'The Naming of Cats'.

54 Macavity, Macavity, there's no one like Macavity,
　 There never was a Cat of such deceitfulness and suavity.
　 He always has an alibi, and one or two to spare:
　 At whatever time the deed took place—MACAVITY WASN'T
　　 THERE!
　 1939 *Old Possum's Book of Practical Cats*, 'Macavity: The Mystery Cat'.

55 No *vers* is *libre* for the man who wants to do a good job.
　 1940 Introduction to Ezra Pound *Poems*.

56 In my beginning is my end.
　 1940 *Four Quartets*, 'East Coker', pt.1.

57 I said to my soul, be still, and wait without hope
　 For hope would be hope for the wrong thing; wait
　　 without love
　 For love would be love of the wrong thing; there is
　　 yet faith
　 But the faith and the hope and the love are all in the
　　 waiting.
　 Wait without thought, for you are not ready for thought,
　 So the darkness shall be the light and the stillness the
　　 dancing.
　 1940 *Four Quartets*, 'East Coker', pt.1.

58 A periphrastic study in a worn-out poetical fashion,
　 Leaving one still with the intolerable wrestle
　 With words and meanings.
　 1940 *Four Quartets*, 'East Coker', pt.1.

59 There is, it seems to us,
　 At best, only a limited value
　 In the knowledge derived from experience.
　 1940 *Four Quartets*, 'East Coker', pt.2.

60 Do not let me hear
　 Of the wisdom of old men, but rather of their folly.
　 1940 *Four Quartets*, 'East Coker', pt.2.

61 The only wisdom we can hope to acquire
　 Is the wisdom of humility: humility is endless.
　 1940 *Four Quartets*, 'East Coker', pt.2.

62 O dark dark dark. They all go into the dark,
　 The vacant interstellar spaces, the vacant into the
　　 vacant.
　 1940 *Four Quartets*, 'East Coker', pt.3.

63 And what you do not know is the only thing you know
　 And what you own is what you do not own
　 And where you are is where you are not.
　 1940 *Four Quartets*, 'East Coker', pt.3.

64 The wounded surgeon plies the steel
　 That questions the distempered part;
　 Beneath the bleeding hands we feel
　 The sharp compassion of the healer's art
　 Resolving the enigma of the fever chart.
　 1940 *Four Quartets*, 'East Coker', pt.4.

65 The dripping blood our only drink,
　 The bloody flesh our only food:
　 In spite of which we like to think
　 That we are sound, substantial flesh and blood—
　 Again, in spite of that, we call this Friday good.
　 1940 *Four Quartets*, 'East Coker', pt.4.

66 And so each venture
　 Is a new beginning, a raid on the inarticulate
　 With shabby equipment always deteriorating
　 In the general mess of imprecision of feeling,
　 Undisciplined squads of emotion.
　 1940 *Four Quartets*, 'East Coker', pt.5.

67 There is only the fight to recover what has been lost
　 And found and lost again and again: and now, under
　　 conditions
　 That seem unpropitious. But perhaps neither gain
　　 nor loss.
　 For us, there is only the trying. The rest is not our
　　 business.
　 1940 *Four Quartets*, 'East Coker', pt.5.

68 Home is where one starts from. As we grow older
　 The world becomes stranger, the pattern more
　　 complicated
　 Of dead and living.
　 1940 *Four Quartets*, 'East Coker', pt.5.

69 Love is most nearly itself
　 When here and now cease to matter.
　 1940 *Four Quartets*, 'East Coker', pt.5.

70 I do not know much about gods; but I think that the river
　 Is a strong brown god—sullen, untamed and intractable,
　 1941 *Four Quartets*, 'The Dry Salvages', pt.1.

71 The river is within us, the sea is all about us.
　 1941 *Four Quartets*, 'The Dry Salvages', pt.1.

72 The tolling bell
　 Measures time not our time, rung by the unhurried
　 Ground swell, a time
　 Older than the time of chronometers.
　 1941 *Four Quartets*, 'The Dry Salvages', pt.1.

73 We had the experience but missed the meaning,
　 And approach to the meaning restores the experience
　 In a different form, beyond any meaning
　 We can assign to happiness.
　 1941 *Four Quartets*, 'The Dry Salvages', pt.2.

74 Time the destroyer is time the preserver.
　 1941 *Four Quartets*, 'The Dry Salvages', pt.2.

75 You cannot face it steadily, but this thing is sure,
　 That time is no healer: the patient is no longer here.
　 1941 *Four Quartets*, 'The Dry Salvages', pt.3.

76 And right action is freedom
　 From past and future also.
　 1941 *Four Quartets*, 'The Dry Salvages', pt.5.

77 For most of us, there is only the unattended
　 Moment, the moment in and out of time.
　 1941 *Four Quartets*, 'The Dry Salvages', pt.5.

78 These are only hints and guesses,
　 Hints followed by guesses; and the rest
　 Is prayer, observance, discipline, thought and action.
　 The hint half guessed, the gift half understood, is
　 Incarnation.
　 1941 *Four Quartets*, 'The Dry Salvages', pt.5.

79 Here the impossible union
　 Of spheres of existence is actual,

Here the past and future
Are conquered, and reconciled.
1941 *Four Quartets*, 'The Dry Salvages', pt.5.

80 Midwinter Spring is its own season
Sempiternal though sodden towards sundown,
Suspended in time, between pole and tropic.
1942 *Four Quartets*, 'Little Gidding', pt.1.

81 And glow more intense than blaze of branch, or brazier,
Stirs the dumb spirit: no wind, but pentecostal fire
In the dark time of the year. Between melting and freezing
The soul's sap quivers.
1942 *Four Quartets*, 'Little Gidding', pt.1.

82 And what you thought you came for
Is only a shell, a husk of meaning
From which the purpose breaks only when it is fulfilled
If at all. Either you had no purpose
Or the purpose is beyond the end you figured
And is altered in fulfilment.
1942 *Four Quartets*, 'Little Gidding', pt.1.

83 And what the dead had no speech for, when living,
They can tell you, being dead: the communication
Of the dead is tongued with fire beyond the language of the living.
1942 *Four Quartets*, 'Little Gidding', pt.1.

84 Dust in the air suspended
Marks the place where a story ended.
1942 *Four Quartets*, 'Little Gidding', pt.2.

85 In the uncertain hour before the morning
Near the ending of interminable night
At the recurrent end of the unending.
1942 *Four Quartets*, 'Little Gidding', pt.2.

86 Since our concern was speech, and speech impelled us
To purify the dialect of the tribe
And urge the mind to aftersight and foresight.
1942 *Four Quartets*, 'Little Gidding', pt.2.

87 From wrong to wrong the exasperated spirit
Proceeds, unless restored by that refining fire
Where you must move in measure, like a dancer.
1942 *Four Quartets*, 'Little Gidding', pt.2.

88 History may be servitude,
History may be freedom.
1942 *Four Quartets*, 'Little Gidding', pt.3.

89 This is the use of memory:
For liberation—not less of love but expanding
Of love beyond desire, and so liberation
From the future as well as the past.
1942 *Four Quartets*, 'Little Gidding', pt.3.

90 The dove descending breaks the air
With flame of incandescent terror
Of which the tongues declare
The one discharge from sin and error.
1942 *Four Quartets*, 'Little Gidding', pt.4.

91 We shall not cease from exploration
And the end of all our exploring
Will be to arrive where we started
And know the place for the first time.
1942 *Four Quartets*, 'Little Gidding', pt.4.

92 What we call the beginning is often the end
And to make an end is to make a beginning.
The end is where we start from.
1942 *Four Quartets*, 'Little Gidding', pt.5.

93 A people without history
Is not redeemed from time, for history is a pattern
Of timeless moments.
1942 *Four Quartets*, 'Little Gidding', pt.5.

94 And all shall be well and
All manner of thing shall be well
When the tongues of flame are in-folded
Into a crowned knot of fire
And the fire and the rose are one.
1942 *Four Quartets*, 'Little Gidding', pt.5.

95 Culture may even be described simply as that which makes life worth living.
1948 *Notes towards a Definition of Culture*, ch.1.

96 You've missed the point completely, Julia:
There *were* no tigers. *That* was the point.
1950 *The Cocktail Party*, act 1, sc.1, opening lines.

97 What is hell?
Hell is oneself,
Hell is alone, the other figures in it
Merely projections. There is nothing to escape from
And nothing to escape to. One is always alone.
1950 *The Cocktail Party*, act 1, sc.3.

Elizabeth I   1533–1603

Queen of England (from 1558), daughter of Henry VIII and Anne Boleyn. Imprisoned by her Catholic half-sister Mary (later Mary I), she ascended the throne as a Protestant ruler on Mary's death. After several conspiracies she had Mary, Queen of Scots executed (1587) and her subsequent persecution of Catholics led Philip of Spain to send an Armada, which was defeated (1588). Elizabeth never married.

98 If I am to disclose to you what I should prefer if I follow the inclination of my nature, it is this: beggar-woman and single, far rather than queen and married!
1563 Attributed reply to an imperial envoy. Quoted in J E Neale *Queen Elizabeth I* (1979).

99 Though I be a woman yet I have as good a courage answerable to my place as ever my father had. I am your anointed queen. I will never be by violence constrained to do anything. I thank God I am indeed endued with such qualities that if I were turned out of the realm in my petticoat I were able to live in any place of Christendom.
1566 Speech to a parliamentary delegation, 5 Nov. Quoted in Christopher Haigh *Elizabeth I* (1988).

1 The doubt of future foes exiles my present joy.
c.1568 'The Doubt of Future Foes'.

2 No foteball player be used or suffered within the City of London and the liberties thereof upon pain of imprisonment.
1572 Royal proclamation, banning football from the streets of London.

3 My care is like my shadow in the sun,
Follows me flying, flies when I pursue it,
Stands and lies by me, doth what I have done.
c.1582 'On Monsieur's Departure'.

4 I know that I have the body of a weak and feeble woman, but I have the heart and stomach of a king—and a king of England too; and think foul scorn that Parma or

Elizabeth II

Spain, or any Prince of Europe, should dare to invade the borders of my realm.
1588 Address at Tilbury on the approach of the Spanish Armada.

5 My lord, we make use of you, not for your bad legs, but for your good head.
c.1590 To her gout-stricken courtier William Cecil. Quoted in F Chamberlain *Sayings of Queen Elizabeth* (1923).

6 To be a King and to wear a crown is a thing more glorious to them that see it than it is pleasant to them that bear it.
1601 Address to parliament. Quoted in G R Elton *Renaissance and Reformation 1300–1648* (2nd edn, 1968), p.134.

7 Little man, little man! The word 'must' is not to be used to princes!
1603 To Robert Cecil when, during her last illness, he told her that she must go to bed. Quoted in Christopher Haigh *Elizabeth I* (1988), p.24.

8 Like strawberry wives, that laid two or three great strawberries at the mouth of their pot, and all the rest were little ones.
Of the Commission of Sales. Quoted in Francis Bacon *Apophthegms New and Old* (1625), no.54.

Elizabeth II 1926–

Queen of the UK and Head of the Commonwealth, daughter of George VI. She was proclaimed Queen on 6 February 1952, and crowned on 2 June 1953. She married Philip, Duke of Edinburgh, in 1947.

9 I think that people will concede that, on this of all days, I should begin my speech with the words, 'My husband and I'.
1972 Speech at a banquet to celebrate her silver wedding anniversary, 20 Nov.

10 Experience shows that great enterprises seldom end with a tidy and satisfactory flourish. Together, we are doing our best to re-establish peace and civil order in the Gulf region, and to help those members of civil and ethnic minorities who continue to suffer through no fault of their own. If we succeed, our military success will have achieved its true objective.
1991 Commenting on the aftermath of the Gulf War in the first address by a British monarch to Congress, 16 May.

11 1992 is not a year I shall look back on with undiluted pleasure. In the words of one of my more sympathetic correspondents, it has turned out to be an *annus horribilis*.
1992 Speech at the Guildhall, 24 Nov.

12 It has perhaps always been the case that the waging of peace is the hardest form of leadership of all.
2010 Quoted in *Newsweek*.

13 We all need to get the balance right between action and reflection. With so many distractions, it is easy to forget to pause and take stock.
2013 Christmas broadcast, 25 Dec.

14 The true measure of all our actions is how long the good in them lasts... everything we do, we do for the young.
2014 Speech commemorating D-Day, 6 Jun.

Elizabeth, Queen, the Queen Mother 1900–2002

Queen Consort of King George VI, mother of Elizabeth II. Until her marriage to the King in 1923, she was Lady Elizabeth Bowes-Lyon.

15 I'm glad we've been bombed. It makes me feel I can look the East End in the face.
1940 Comment to a London policeman, 13 Sep. Quoted in John Wheeler-Bennet *King George VI* (1948), pt.3, ch.6.

Elkin, Stanley Lawrence 1930–95

US novelist and short-story writer. His novels include *Boswell* (1964), *The Magic Kingdom* (1985) and *The MacGuffin* (1991).

16 All books *are* the Book of Job, high moral tests and tasks set in fairy tales, landmined and unforgiving as golf greens, as steeplechase and gameboard and obstacle course.
1991 'The Future of the Novel', in the *New York Times*, 17 Feb.

17 Story is just just deserts…man in the crucible like jack in the box.
1991 'The Future of the Novel', in the *New York Times*, 17 Feb.

Ellerton, John 1826–93

English cleric, hymnologist, hymnwriter and translator.

18 God the Omnipotent! King, who ordainest
Great winds Thy clarions, lightnings Thy sword.
1866 Hymn (with Henry Fothergill Chorley, 1808–72).

19 The day Thou gavest, Lord, is ended,
The darkness falls at Thy behest.
1870 *A Liturgy for Missionary Meetings*, 'The Day Thou Gavest'.

Ellington, Duke (Edward Kennedy) 1899–1974

US composer, bandleader and pianist. He founded his first regular group in New York in 1924 and became a key figure in orchestral jazz. He composed about 2,000 works, including 'Mood Indigo' and 'Sophisticated Lady'.

20 Playing bop is like playing Scrabble with all the vowels missing.
1954 In *Look*, 10 Aug.

21 When it sounds good, it *is* good.
1957 *Such Sweet Thunder*, programme note.

22 Bubber was the first man I heard use the expression, 'it don't mean a thing if it ain't got that swing.' Everything, and I repeat, everything had to swing.
1965 Of trumpeter Bubber Miley. 'The Most Essential Instrument', in *Jazz Journal*, Dec.

23 New music? Hell, there's been no new music since Stravinsky.
1970 Quoted in D Jewell *Duke* (1977).

24 Music is my mistress, and she plays second fiddle to none.
1973 *Music Is My Mistress*.

Elliot, Jean *also known as* Jane Elliot 1727–1805

Scottish poet and songwriter, whose only surviving work, based on traditional versions, was written as a lament for the Battle of Flodden.

25 I've heard the lilting at our yowe-milking,
Lasses a-lilting before the dawn o' day;
But now they are moaning on ilka green loaning:
'The Flowers of the Forest are a' wede away'.
1769 'The Flowers of the Forest', stanza 1.
▶ *See Cockburn 233:82.*

Elliott, Charlotte 1789–1871

English religious poet and hymnwriter.

26 Just as I am, without one plea
  But that Thy blood was shed for me,
  And that Thou bid'st me come to Thee,
  O Lamb of God, I come!
  1834 *Invalid's Hymn Book*, 'Just As I Am'.

Elliott, Sir Claude Aurelius 1888–1973
English schoolmaster, head and Provost of Eton College.

27 I've often thought I should like to have a set of postcards printed: 'Dear Sir or Madam, Thank you for your communication. Go to hell. Yours sincerely.'
  Quoted in the *Times Literary Supplement*, 22 Jan 1988.

Ellis, George 1753–1815
British poet, born in the West Indies. He co-founded the Tory *Anti-Jacobin* (1797) and made important translations of Middle English verse.

28 Snowy, Flowy, Blowy,
  Showery, Flowery, Bowery,
  Hoppy, Croppy, Droppy,
  Breezy, Sneezy, Freezy.
  'The Twelve Months'.

Ellis, Havelock 1859–1939
English physician and writer. His seven-volume *Studies in the Psychology of Sex* (1897–1928, rev edn 1936), caused tremendous controversy, and was banned in Great Britain.

29 All civilization has from time to time become a thin crust over a volcano of revolution.
  1922 *Little Essays of Love and Virtue*.

30 What we call morals is simply blind obedience to words of command.
  1923 *The Dance of Life*.

Ellison, Harlan Jay 1934–
US novelist, essayist, critic and editor. He has written mainly in the genres of science fiction and fantasy, where he has been a radical and outspoken contributor.

31 I Have No Mouth And I Must Scream.
  1967 Title of story collection.

32 The reason men are greater than animals isn't because we can dream of the stars...it's because we have something they haven't. Greed.
  1970 *The Glass Teat*, introduction.

33 Our childhoods are sowing the wind, our adulthoods are reaping the whirlwind.
  1974 *Approaching Oblivion*, introduction.

34 All The Lies That Are My Life.
  1989 Title of autobiography.

Ellison, Ralph Waldo 1914–94
US novelist, best known for his classic account of black urban existence, *Invisible Man* (1952), his only completed novel. He also wrote essays on music and culture.

35 I am an invisible man. No, I am not a spook like those who haunted Edgar Allen Poe; nor am I one of your Hollywood-movie ectoplasms. I am a man of substance, of flesh and bone, fibre and liquids—and I might even be said to possess a mind. I am invisible, understand, simply because people refuse to see me... When they approach me they see only my surroundings, themselves, or figments of their imagination—indeed, everything and anything except me.
  1952 *Invisible Man*, prologue.

36 I was never more hated than when I tried to be honest... On the other hand, I've never been more loved and appreciated than when I tried to 'justify' and affirm someone's mistaken beliefs; or when I've tried to give my friends the incorrect, absurd answers they wished to hear.
  1952 *Invisible Man*, epilogue.

37 All novels are about certain minorities: the individual is a minority.
  1955 Interview in *Paris Review*, Spring.

38 Part of the problem for the invisible man was that he was invisible to himself, that he didn't grasp his own complexity.
  1992 Quoted by Keith Botsford in Ellison's obituary, 18 Apr 1994, in *The Independent*.

Ellwood, David T 1953–
US economist, Dean and Professor at John F Kennedy School of Government, Harvard University.

39 The chief source of economic insecurity in America used to be growing old; now it's being born into or raised in a single-parent family.
  1991 In the *Washington Post*, 22 Feb.

Eltit, Diamela 1949–
Chilean novelist. Her novels are complex and experimental, but she has found a devoted readership among intellectuals and feminist circles.

40 *Para decirlo de otra manera, no es la herida la que causó el grito, sino exactamente a la inversa; para herirse es preciso el grito, todo lo demás es un pretexto.*
  In other words, it was not the wound that caused the scream, but precisely the opposite: to get wounded one needs the scream; the rest is only a pretext.
  1983 *Lumpérica*, 1.

Elton, Ben 1959–
English comedian and writer.

41 I did not vote Labour because they've heard of Oasis and nobody is going to vote Tory because William Hague has got a baseball cap.
  1998 In *The Radio Times*, 18 Apr.

Elton, Sir Geoffrey Rudolph 1921–94
British historian, Professor at Cambridge University.

42 When I meet a historian who cannot think that there have been great men, great men moreover in politics, I feel myself in the presence of a bad historian; and there are times when I incline to judge all historians by their opinion of Winston Churchill—whether they can see that, no matter how much better the details, often damaging, of man and career become known, he still remains, quite simply, a great man.
  1970 *Political History*, ch.2.

Éluard

Éluard, Paul *pseudonym of* **Eugène Grindel** 1895–1952
French poet, a founder of the Surrealist movement with which he later parted (1938). He was active in political affairs, in the Resistance and the Communist Party.

43 *Le poète est celui qui inspire bien plus que celui qui est inspiré.*
The poet is more the inspirer than the one who is inspired.
1936 *L'Evidence poétique.*

44 *Je suis né pour te connaître*
Pour te nommer
Liberté.
I was born to know you
To give you your name:
Freedom.
1942 *Poésie et vérité*, 'Liberté'.

45 *Adieu tristesse*
Bonjour tristesse.
Farewell sadness
Hello sadness.
1942 *Poésie et vérité*, 'La Vie immédiate'.

Emecheta, Buchi 1944–
Nigerian-born British writer.

46 Sometimes it seemed that matrimony, apart from being a way of getting free sex when men felt like it, was also a legalized way of committing assault and getting away with it.
1972 *In the Ditch.*

47 I am a woman and a woman of Africa. I am a daughter of Nigeria and if she is in shame, I shall stay and mourn with her in shame.
1982 *Destination Biafra.*

Emerson, Ralph Waldo 1803–82
US philosopher and poet, a central figure of the transcendentalist movement. He was a minister in the Unitarian church, but resigned after a controversy over his belief in spiritual independence.

48 By the rude bridge that arched the flood,
Their flag to April's breeze unfurled,
Here once the embattled farmers stood
And fired the shot heard around the world.
1837 'Concord Hymn', opening lines. This poem was sung on 4 Jul 1837 at the dedication of the monument commemorating the battle of 19 Apr 1775.

49 This time, like all times, is a very good one, if we but know what to do with it.
1837 'The American Scholar', lecture at Harvard University.

50 All are needed by each one;
Nothing is fair or good alone.
1839 'Each and All', l.11–12.

51 In every work of genius we recognize our own rejected thoughts: they come back to us with a certain alienated majesty.
1841 *Essays: First Series*, 'Self-Reliance'.

52 Every Stoic was a Stoic; but in Christendom where is the Christian?
1841 *Essays: First Series*, 'Self-Reliance'.

53 Whoso would be a man must be a nonconformist.
1841 *Essays: First Series*, 'Self-Reliance'.

54 A foolish consistency is the hobgoblin of little minds, adored by little statesmen and philosophers and divines. With consistency a great soul has simply nothing to do.
1841 *Essays: First Series*, 'Self-Reliance'.

55 To be great is to be misunderstood.
1841 *Essays: First Series*, 'Self-Reliance'.

56 Nothing can bring you peace but yourself.
1841 *Essays: First Series*, 'Self-Reliance'.

57 The dice of God are always loaded.
1841 *Essays: First Series*, 'Compensation'.

58 There is properly no history; only biography.
1841 *Essays: First Series*, 'History'.

59 All mankind love a lover.
1841 *Essays: First Series*, 'Love'.

60 A friend may well be reckoned the masterpiece of nature.
1841 *Essays: First Series*, 'Friendship'.

61 The only reward of virtue is virtue; the only way to have a friend is to be one.
1841 *Essays: First Series*, 'Friendship'.

62 In skating over thin ice, our safety is in our speed.
1841 *Essays: First Series*, 'Prudence'.

63 People wish to be settled: only as far as they are unsettled is there any hope for them.
1841 *Essays: First Series*, 'Circles'.

64 Nothing great was ever achieved without enthusiasm.
1841 *Essays: First Series*, 'Circles'.

65 Though we travel the world over to find the beautiful, we must carry it with us, or we find it not.
1841 *Essays: First Series*, 'Art'.

66 In sculpture, did ever anybody call the Apollo a fancy piece? Or say of the Laocoön how it might be made different? A masterpiece of art has in the mind a fixed place in the chain of being, as much as a plant or a crystal.
1841 'Thoughts on Art', in *The Dial*, vol.1, no.3, Jan.

67 Have I a lover
Who is noble and free?
I would he were nobler
Than to love me.
1841 'The Sphinx', stanza 12.

68 The reward of a thing well done is to have done it.
1844 'New England Reformers', lecture to the Society, 3 Mar.

69 It is not metres, but a metre-making argument, that makes a poem.
1844 *Essays: Second Series*, 'The Poet'.

70 Let the Stoics say what they please, we do not eat for the good of living, but because the meat is savory and the appetite is keen.
1844 *Essays: Second Series*, 'Nature'.

71 The only gift is a portion of thyself.
1844 *Essays: Second Series*, 'Gifts'.

72 Every man is wanted, and no man is wanted much.
1844 *Essays: Second Series*, 'Nominalist and Realist'.

73 Things are in the saddle,
And ride mankind.
1847 *Poems*, 'Ode', dedicated to W H Channing.

74 Belief consists in affirming the affirmations of the soul; unbelief, in denying them.
1850 *Representative Men*, 'Montaigne; or, The Skeptic'.

75 Is not marriage an open question, when it is alleged, from the beginning of the world, that such as are in the institution wish to get out; and such as are out wish to get in.
1850 *Representative Men*, 'Montaigne; or, The Skeptic'.

76 Keep cool: it will be all one a hundred years hence.
1850 *Representative Men*, 'Montaigne; or, The Skeptic'.

77 I can reason down or deny everything, except this perpetual Belly: feed he must and will, and I cannot make him respectable.
1850 *Representative Men*, 'Montaigne; or, The Skeptic'.

78 The world is upheld by the veracity of good men: they make the earth wholesome.
1850 *Representative Men*, 'Uses of Great Men'.

79 Every hero becomes a bore at last.
1850 *Representative Men*, 'Uses of Great Men'.

80 Perpetual modernness is the measure of merit in every work of art.
1850 *Representative Men*, 'Plato'.

81 Men's actions are too strong for them. Show me a man who has acted, and who has not been the victim and slave of his action.
1850 *Representative Men*, 'Goethe'.

82 The aristocrat is the democrat ripe, and gone to seed.
1850 *Representative Men*, 'Napoleon, the Man of the World'.

83 As long as our civilization is essentially one of property, of fences, of exclusiveness, it will be mocked by delusions. Our riches will leave us sick; there will be bitterness in our laughter; and our wine will burn our mouth.
1850 *Representative Men*, 'Napoleon, the Man of the World'.

84 They have in themselves what they value in their horses, mettle and bottom.
1856 Of Englishmen. *English Traits*, 'Manners'.

85 If the red slayer think he slays,
Or if the slain think he is slain,
They know not well the subtle ways
I keep, and pass, and turn again.
1857 'Brahma'. Collected in *May Day* (1867).
▶ See Lang 507:41.

86 A person seldom falls sick, but the bystanders are animated with a faint hope that he will die.
1860 *The Conduct of Life*, 'Considerations by the Way'.

87 Art is a jealous mistress, and if a man have a genius for painting, poetry, music, architecture, or philosophy, he makes a bad husband and an ill provider.
1860 *The Conduct of Life*, 'Wealth'.

88 We are born believing. A man bears beliefs as a tree bears apples.
1860 *The Conduct of Life*, 'Worship'.

89 Immortality will come to such as are fit for it, and he who would be a great soul in future must be a great soul now.
1860 *The Conduct of Life*, 'Worship'.

90 The louder he talked of his honour, the faster we counted our spoons.
1860 *The Conduct of Life*, 'Worship'.

91 The revelation of Thought takes men out of servitude into freedom.
1860 *The Conduct of Life*, 'Fate'.

92 He has not learned the lesson of life who does not every day surmount a fear.
1870 *Society and Solitude*, 'Courage'.

93 Raphael paints wisdom; Handel sings it, Phidias carves it, Shakespeare writes it, Wren builds it, Columbus sails it, Luther preaches it, Washington arms it, Watt mechanizes it.
1870 *Society and Solitude*, 'Art'.

94 Hitch your wagon to a star.
1870 *Society and Solitude*, 'Civilization'.

95 We boil at different degrees.
1870 *Society and Solitude*, 'Eloquence'.

96 Can anybody remember when the times were not hard, and money was not scarce?
1870 *Society and Solitude*, 'Works and Days'.

97 We do not count a man's years, until he has nothing else to count.
1870 *Society and Solitude*, 'Old Age'.

98 America is a country of young men.
1870 *Society and Solitude*, 'Old Age'.

99 A rogue alive to the ludicrous is still convertible. If that sense is lost, his fellow-men can do little for him.
1876 *Letters and Social Aims*, 'The Comic'.

1 Music is the poor man's Parnassus.
1876 *Letters and Social Aims*, 'Poetry and Imagination'.

Emery, Jane c.1918–
US biographer and academic.

2 As thin and neat as a furled umbrella.
1992 On Rose Macaulay. *Rose Macaulay*.

Emin, Tracey 1964–
English artist. She gained widespread public attention with various 'confessional' installation works such as *Everyone I Have Ever Slept With, from 1963 to 1995* (1995), which was later destroyed in a fire.

3 The wheel that squeaks gets the oil.
2001 In the *Observer*, 22 Apr.

4 The majority of the British public have no regard or no respect for what me and my peers do to the point where they actually laugh at a disaster like a fire.
2004 After some of her work (and the work of other contemporary artists) was destroyed in a fire in London. Quoted in *The Scotsman*, 31 May.

5 Just love me.
2004 Words spelled out in a neon light installation she created.

Emmet, Robert 1778–1803
Irish patriot, member of the United Irishmen. In 1803 he plotted an insurrection against the English, and was hanged after returning from the Wicklow Mountains for a last meeting with his sweetheart.

6 I have but one request to make at my departure from this world, it is—the charity of its silence. Let no man write my epitaph; for as no man who knows my motives, dare now vindicate them, let no prejudice or ignorance asperse them. Let them rest in obscurity and peace! Let my memory be left in oblivion, and my tomb remain uninscribed, until other times and other men can do justice to my character. When my country takes her

place among the nations of the earth, *then*, and *not till then*, let my epitaph be written.
1803 Speech before being sentenced.

Empson, Sir William 1906–84
English critic and poet. He established his reputation with his first book on textual criticism, *Seven Types of Ambiguity* (1930, revised 1947). An edition of *Collected Poems* was published in 1955.

7 Seven Types of Ambiguity.
1930 Title of book.

8 Slowly the poison the whole blood stream fills.
It is not the effort or the failure tires.
The waste remains, the waste remains and kills.
1935 'Missing Dates'.

9 Ripeness is all; her in her cooling planet
Revere; do not presume to think her wasted.
1935 'To an Old Lady'.

10 But as to risings, I can tell you why.
It is on contradiction that they grow.
It seemed the best thing to be up and go.
Up was the heartening and the strong reply.
The heart of standing is we cannot fly.
1935 'Aubade'.

11 Waiting for the end, boys, waiting for the end.
What is there to be or do?
What's become of me or you?
1940 'Just a Smack at Auden'.

Engels, Friedrich 1820–95
German socialist philosopher, founder of 'scientific socialism'. He first met Karl Marx in Brussels in 1844, collaborated with him on the *Communist Manifesto* (1848), and later edited and translated Marx's writings.

12 [The] English proletariat is becoming more and more bourgeois, so that this most bourgeois of all nations is apparently aiming ultimately at the possession of a bourgeois aristocracy and a bourgeois proletariat *as well as* a bourgeoisie. For a nation which exploits the whole world this is of course to a certain extent justifiable.
1858 Letter to Karl Marx, 7 Oct.

13 *Der Staat wird nicht 'abgeschafft', er stirbt ab.*
The state is not 'abolished'; it withers away.
1878 *Anti-Dühring*, pt.3, ch.2.

14 The British Labour movement is today, and for many years has been, working in a narrow circle of strikes that are looked upon, not as an expedient, and not as a means of propaganda, but as an ultimate aim.
1878 Letter to Eduard Bernstein, 17 Jul.

15 The society that will organize production on the basis of a free and equal association of the producers will put the whole machinery of the state where it will then belong: into the museum of antiquities, by the side of the spinning wheel and the bronze axe.
1884 *The Origin of the Family, Private Property, and the State*.

Engle, Paul Hamilton 1908–91
US poet, novelist and critic, whose writing is formal, elegant and accessible. He ran courses in literature and writing in his native Iowa.

16 Poetry—tries to tell you about a vision in the unvisionary language of farm, city and love.
1956 In *Life*, 28 May.

Ennius, Quintus Ennius c.239–169 BC
Roman poet, probably of Greek extraction. He was a friend of Scipio Africanus the Elder, and he introduced the hexameter into Latin. Only fragments have survived of his work.

17 *Quod est ante pedes nemo spectat, caeli scrutantur plagas.*
No one regards the things before his feet, but views with care the regions of the sky.
Fragment of *Iphigeneia*, quoted in Cicero *De Divinatione*, bk.2 (translated by W A Falconer, 1979).

18 How like us is that ugly brute, the ape!
Quoted in Cicero *De Divinatione*, bk.50 (translated by H Rackham, 1942).

Enright, Anne Teresa 1962–
Irish novelist. Her acclaimed books include *The Gathering*, which won the 2007 Man Booker Prize.

19 There is nothing as tentative as an old woman's touch; as loving or as horrible.
2007 *The Gathering*.

20 People do not change, they are merely revealed.
2007 *The Gathering*.

Enright, D(ennis) J(oseph) 1920–2002
English poet, critic and literary journalist. He held posts in universities around the world (1947–60), although his humanistic work rejects academic politics.

21 Metaphysical lederhosen.
On the murky philosophizing and cumbrous symbolism of German novels. Quoted by John Gross in the *New York Times*, 20 Jan 1987.

Ephorus of Cumæ c.400–330 BC
Greek historian.

22 Music was invented to deceive and delude mankind.
History, preface.

Ephron, Nora 1941–2012
US screenwriter and director.

23 I always say that a successful parent is one who raises a child so that they can pay for their own psychoanalysis.
1995 In *The Guardian*, 26 Jun.

24 Never marry a man you wouldn't want to be divorced from.
2006 *I Feel Bad About My Neck: And Other Thoughts on Being a Woman*.

Epstein, Jacob 1880–1959
US-born British sculptor.

25 Why don't they stick to murder and leave art to us?
Attributed. On hearing that his statue, Lazarus, in New College chapel, Oxford, kept Nikita Khrushchev awake at night.

Epstein, Julius J 1909–2000
US screenwriter, twin brother of Philip G Epstein. The two worked as a screenwriting team for many years on films such as *Casablanca* (1942) and *My Foolish Heart* (1949).

26 Of all the gin joints in all the towns in all the world, she walks into mine.
1942 Humphrey Bogart as Rick in *Casablanca* (with Philip G Epstein and Howard Koch).

27 If she can stand it, I can. Play it!
1942 Humphrey Bogart as Rick in *Casablanca* (with Philip G Epstein and Howard Koch). The line is commonly rendered 'Play it again, Sam', a conflation with an earlier line of Ingrid Bergman, 'Play it, Sam. Play *As Time Goes By*.'

28 Here's looking at you, kid.
1942 Humphrey Bogart as Rick in *Casablanca* (with Philip G Epstein and Howard Koch).

29 I'm no good at being noble, but it doesn't take much to see that the problems of three little people don't amount to a hill of beans in this crazy world.
1942 Humphrey Bogart as Rick in *Casablanca* (with Philip G Epstein and Howard Koch).

30 If that plane leaves the ground and you're not with him, you'll regret it. Maybe not today, maybe not tomorrow, but soon and for the rest of your life.
1942 Humphrey Bogart as Rick in *Casablanca* (with Philip G Epstein and Howard Koch).

31 Major Strasser has been shot. Round up the usual suspects.
1942 Claude Rains as Captain Louis Renault in *Casablanca* (with Philip G Epstein and Howard Koch).

32 A woman is beautiful only when she is loved.
1944 Mr Skeffington (with Philip Epstein).

33 Honeymoon's over—time to get married.
1972 Pete 'n Tillie.

34 When you've reached my age, and your friends are beginning to worry about you, blind dates are a way of life.
1972 Pete 'n Tillie.

35 Dear J W, have the bank president finish the script.
Response to a note from Jack Warner which had read 'Railroad presidents get in at nine o'clock, bank presidents get in at nine o'clock, read your contract, you're coming in at nine o'clock.'
Quoted in Aljean Harmetz *Round Up the Usual Suspects* (1993).

Erasmus, Desiderius *originally* Gerrit Gerritszoon
1466–1536

Dutch humanist and scholar, author of the satire *Encomium Moriae* (*Praise of Folly*, 1509) and *Colloquia familiaria* (1519), an audacious treatment of Church abuses. Other works include the first translation of the Greek New Testament.

36 *In regione caecorum rex est luscus.*
In the country of the blind the one-eyed man is king.
c.1500 Adages, bk.3, century 4, no.96.

37 Let a king recall that it is better to improve his realm than to increase his territory.
1517 Querela Pacis.

Eriksson, Sven Goran 1948–

Swedish football coach, manager of the England football team (2001–6).

38 There is more politics in football than in politics.
2004 In *Varsity*, 23 Jan.

Ernst, Max 1891–1976

German-born artist, a founder of the Dada group and later a key figure of Surrealism. He settled in the US in 1941 but returned to France in 1953.

39 The artist is a spectator, indifferent or impassioned, at the birth of his work, and observes the phases of its development.
Quoted in Saranne Alexandrian *Surrealist Art* (1970).

40 Collage is a supersensitive and scrupulously accurate instrument, similar to a seismograph, which is able to record the exact amount of the possibility of human happiness at any period.
Quoted in Saranne Alexandrian *Surrealist Art* (1970).

Ertz, Susan *pseudonym of* Mrs Ronald McCrindle
c.1894–1985

US novelist, born in England. She was the author of a great many popular novels.

41 Someone has somewhere commented on the fact that millions long for immortality who don't know what to do with themselves on a rainy Sunday afternoon.
1943 Anger in the Sky, ch.5.

Etherege, Sir George c.1635–1691

English dramatist, who spent most of his life in royal service abroad. Inspired by Molière, he founded the comedy of intrigue in English literature.

42 Like dancers on the ropes poor poets fare,
Most perish young, the rest in danger are.
1676 The Man of Mode or, Sir Fopling Flutter, prologue.

43 What a dull, insipid thing is a billet-doux written in cold blood, after the heat of the business is over!
1676 The Man of Mode or, Sir Fopling Flutter, act 1, sc.1.

44 Next to the coming to a good understanding with a new mistress, I love a quarrel with an old one.
1676 The Man of Mode or, Sir Fopling Flutter, act 1, sc.1.

45 I know he is a devil, but he has something of the angel yet undefaced in him, which makes him so charming and agreeable that I must love him, be he never so wicked.
1676 The Man of Mode or, Sir Fopling Flutter, act 2, sc.2.

46 We are not masters of our own affections; our inclinations daily alter: now we love pleasure, and anon we shall dote on business. Human frailty will have it so, and who can help it?
1676 The Man of Mode or, Sir Fopling Flutter, act 2, sc.2.

47 When love grows diseased, the best thing we can do is to put it to a violent death. I cannot endure the torture of a lingering and consumptive passion.
1676 The Man of Mode or, Sir Fopling Flutter, act 2, sc.2.

48 I must confess I am a fop in my heart; ill customs influence my very senses, and I have been so used to affectation that without the help of the air of the court what is natural cannot touch me.
1688 Letter to Mr Poley, 12 Jan.

Eubank, Chris 1966–

English boxer.

49 All the rudiments of life are to be found ironing trousers.
2003 Quoted in *The Independent,* 29 Dec.

Euclid 4c BC

Greek mathematician, best known for his 13-volume work *The Elements,* dealing with plane and solid geometry and arithmetic.

50 That which was to be proved.
   c.300 BC *Elementa*, bk.1, proposition 5. Although originally written in Greek, this phrase is usually quoted in its Latin form, 'Quod erat demonstrandum', sometimes abbreviated to 'QED'.

51 There is no 'royal road' to geometry.
   c.300 BC Response to Ptolemy I, when asked if there were an easier way to solve theorems. Quoted in Proclus *Commentary on the First Book of Euclid's Elementa*, prologue.

Eudamidas 4c BC

King of Sparta, the brother of Agis I whom he succeeded in 331/330 BC.

52 The speech is admirable, but the speaker is not to be trusted; for he has never been amid the blare of trumpets.
   Of a philosopher who had claimed that philosophers were the only good generals. Quoted in Plutarch *Apophthegmata Laconica*, 220E (translated by F C Babbitt, 1931).

Euripides 480 or 484–406 BC

Greek dramatist. Of more than 80 plays only 18 survive complete. He won the tragic prize only five times, but his plays gained popularity after his death.

53 Regard this day's life as yours, but all else as Fortune's.
   Alcestis, l.788–9 (translated by D Kovacs, 1994).

54 I have found nothing stronger than Necessity.
   Alcestis, l.965 (translated by D Kovacs, 1994).

55 Nothing else that a wife may suffer, equals this: if she loses her husband, she loses her life.
   Andromacha, l.375–6.

56 Women's love is for their men, not for their children.
   Electra, l.265.

57 None wise dares hopeless venture.
   Helena, l.811 (translated by A S Way, 1959).

58 The life of men is painful.
   Hippolytus, l.190.

59 It is necessary for mortals to be worn with toil.
   Hippolytus, l.207.

60 Your very silence is your confession.
   Clytemnestra to Agamemnon, realizing that he plans to sacrifice their daughter, Iphigenia, to secure favourable winds during the Greek expedition against Troy. *Iphigenia Aulidensis*, l.1142.

61 The meanest life is better than the most glorious death.
   Iphigenia Aulidensis, l.1252 (translated by W S Merwin and G E Dimock Jr, 1978).

62 Wrath brings mortal men their gravest hurt.
   Medea, l.1080 (translated by D Kovacs, 1994).

63 A change is always nice.
   Orestes, l.234 (translated by M L West, 1987).

64 Lucky is the man who has been successful with his children and not got ones who are notorious disasters.
   Orestes, l.542–3 (translated by M L West, 1987).

65 And wealth abides not, it is but for a day.
   Phoenissae, l.558.

Evans, Bergen 1904–78

US scholar and literary critic, Professor of English at Indiana University.

66 It was said of Metternich that he was so conservative that had *he* been present at the Creation, he would have begged God to have retained Chaos.
   1968 Note in his *Dictionary of Quotations*.

Evans, Dame Edith 1888–1976

English actress, best remembered for her starchy Lady Bracknell in Oscar Wilde's *The Importance of Being Earnest* (1939), which she also played on film.

67 People always ask me the most ridiculous questions. They want to know, 'How do you approach a role?' Well, I don't know. I approach it by first saying yes, then getting on with the bloody thing.
   Attributed.

Evans, George Essex 1863–1909

Australian poet, born in England. A journalist and literary editor, he is best known for his patriotic ceremonial verse.

68 Not as the songs of other lands
   Her song shall be.
   'An Australian Symphony', in *Collected Verse* (1920).

Evans, Walker 1903–75

US photographer, chronicler of the harsh life in the rural South during the Great Depression of the 1930s. His photographs appear in James Agee's *Let Us Now Praise Famous Men* (1941).

69 People out of work are not given to talking much about the one thing on their minds. You only sense by indirection, degrees of anger, shades of humiliation and echoes of fear.
   Quoted in *Fortune*, 11 Feb 1980.

Evelyn, John 1620–1706

English diarist. His *Diary*, which covers the years 1641–1706, offers an insight into life in post-Restoration England.

70 This knight was indeed a valiant Gent: but not a little given to romance, when he spake of himself.
   1651 Diary entry, 6 Sep.

71 I saw *Hamlet Prince of Denmark* played, but now the old plays begin to disgust this refined age.
   1661 Diary entry, 26 Nov.

Ewart, Gavin Buchanan 1916–95

Scottish-born poet. His poems are often humorous or scatological in nature, and frequently mimic comic popular forms like the limerick. He published his first book of poems in 1939.

72 Miss Twye was soaping her breasts in the bath
   When she heard behind her a meaning laugh
   And to her amazement she discovered
   A wicked man in the bathroom cupboard.
   1939 'Miss Twye'.

73 Sex suppressed will go berserk,
   But it keeps us all alive.
   It's a wonderful change from wives and work
   And it ends at half past five.
   1966 'Office Friendships'.

74 Would you rather live in lively London
   or where a young penguin lies screaming?
   1977 *Where a Young Penguin Lies Screaming*, epigraph.

75 He's very popular among his mates.
   I think I'm Auden, he thinks he's Yeats.
   1986 'Seamus Heaney'.

76 On the Last Day the wrecks will surface over the sea.
   1986 'Resurrection'.

Ewer, William Norman 1885–1976
British writer.

77 How odd
Of God
To choose
The Jews.
1924 In *The Week-End Book*.

Ewing, Winnie 1929–
Scottish Nationalist politician.

78 The Scottish Parliament which adjourned on 25 March in the year 1707 is hereby reconvened.
1999 Speech at the opening of the new Scottish Parliament, 12 May.

79 Time after time, on matters great and small, we are still standing on the sidelines, mutely accepting what is decided elsewhere instead of raising our voices and making our own choices. Scotland's much vaunted partnership of Jonah and the whale.
Quoted in Michael Russell (ed) *Stop the World: The Autobiography of Winnie Ewing* (2004).

Fackenheim, Emil L 1916–2003
Jewish rabbi and philosopher. He was Professor at the University of Toronto until 1984, when he moved to Jerusalem, where he continued to teach and write.

1 Had every Christian in Hitler's Europe followed the example of the king of Denmark and decided to put on the yellow star, there would be today neither despair in the church nor talk of the death of God.
1968 Quest for Past and Future.

Fadiman, Anne 1953–
US writer.

2 Sharing a bed and a future was child's play compared to sharing my copy of The Complete Poems of W B Yeats.
1998 On the joys and pain of combining libraries when couples move in together. In *Ex Libris: Confessions of a Common Reader*.

3 If my father were still writing essays, every full-grown 'girl' would probably be transformed into a 'woman'.
1998 On her father, Clifton Fadiman, a renowned man-of-letters. In *Ex Libris: Confessions of a Common Reader*.

Fadiman, Clifton 1904–99
US writer, literary critic and lecturer. He worked as a book reviewer for the *New Yorker*.

4 Liquor is not a necessity. It is a means of momentarily sidestepping necessity.
1955 Party of One, 'From My Notebooks'.

5 The mama of dada.
1955 Of Gertrude Stein. *Party of One*.

6 Cheese, milk's leap toward immortality.
1957 Any Number Can Play, 'The Cheese Stands Alone'.

7 The police dog of American fiction, except that his hatred is not the result of mere crabbedness but of an eye that sees too deep for comfort.
Of US writer Ring Lardner. Quoted in Scott Meredith *George S Kaufman and His Friends* (1974).

8 Poetry in a bottle.
1985 Of wine. In *Manhattan Inc*, Jul.

Falkland, Lucius Cary, Viscount 1610–43
English statesman and writer, whose house at Tew attracted the brightest intellects of Oxford and London. A Royalist during the Civil War, he was Secretary of State in 1642 and was killed at the first Battle of Newbury.

9 When it is not necessary to change, it is necessary not to change.
1641 Speech, House of Commons, 22 Nov. Collected as 'A Speech concerning Episcopacy' in *Discourses of Infallibility* (1660).

Faludi, Susan 1960–
US journalist and writer. She has written *Backlash: The Undeclared War Against American Women* (1991), a controversial and award-winning study of feminism, and *Stiffed: The Betrayal of Modern Man* (2000).

10 The more women are paid, the less eager they are to marry.
1992 Backlash (UK edn), ch.2, 'Man Shortages and Barren Wombs'.

11 Social scientists *could* supply plenty of research to show that one member of the family, at least, is happier and more well adjusted when mum stays home and looks after the children. But that person is dad—a finding of limited use to backlash publicists.
1992 Backlash (UK edn), ch.2, 'Man Shortages and Barren Wombs'.

12 A backlash against women's rights is nothing new. Indeed, it's a recurring phenomenon: it returns every time women begin to make some headway towards equality, a seemingly inevitable early frost to the brief flowerings of feminism.
1992 Backlash (UK edn), ch.3, 'Backlashes Then and Now'.

Fanon, Frantz Omar 1925–61
French West Indian psychoanalyst and social philosopher, editor of *El Moudjahid* in Tunis and Ambassador to Ghana. He is best remembered for his critiques of colonialism.

13 *Aux colonies, l'infrastructure économique est également une superstructure. La cause est conséquence: on*
est riche parce que blanc, on est blanc parce que riche.
In the colonies the economic substructure is also a superstructure. The cause is the consequence; you are rich because you are white, you are white because you are rich.
1961 Les Damnés de la terre (*The Wretched of the Earth*, translated by Constance Farrington, 1965), ch.1, 'Concerning Violence'.

14 *Le colonialisme ne se satisfait pas d'enserrer le peuple dans ses mailles, de vider le cerveau colonisé de toute forme et de tout contenu. Par une sorte de perversion de la logique, il s'oriente vers le passé du*

peuple opprimé, le distort, le défigure, l'anéantit.
Colonialism is not satisfied merely with holding a people in its grip and emptying the native's brain of all form and content. By a kind of perverted logic, it turns to the past of the oppressed people, and distorts, disfigures and destroys it.
1961 *Les Damnés de la terre* (*The Wretched of the Earth*, translated by Constance Farrington, 1965), ch.4, 'On National Culture'.

15 *Le colonialisme accule le peuple dominé à se poser constamment la question: 'Qui suis-je en réalité?'*
Colonialism forces the people it dominates to ask themselves the question constantly: 'In reality, who am I?'
1961 *Les Damnés de la terre* (*The Wretched of the Earth*, translated by Constance Farrington, 1965), ch.5, 'Colonial War and Mental Disorders'.

Fanthorpe, U(rsula) A(skham) 1929–2009
English poet.

16 I wasn't good
   At growing up. Never learned
   The natives' art of life.
   1984 'Growing Up'.

Farage, Nigel Paul 1964–
English politician, leader of the UK Independence Party (2010–).

17 You have the charisma of a damp rag, and the appearance of a low-grade bank clerk.
   2010 Addressing Herman Van Rompuy, President of the EU, at the European Parliament, 24 Feb.

18 She is incredibly cold. I always say—I agree this is a bit rude—but whatever you think of the public image of Merkel, in private she is even more miserable.
   2014 Describing German leader Angela Merkel in *GQ* magazine, May issue.

Farjeon, Eleanor 1881–1965
English children's writer. Her copious output comprises stories, poems, recountings, fables, saints' lives and prayers, and includes *Nursery Rhymes of London Town* (1916) and 'A Morning Song' (1957).

19 Morning has broken
   Like the first morning,
   Blackbird has spoken
   Like the first bird.
   Praise for the singing!
   Praise for the morning!
   Praise for them springing
   Fresh from the Word!
   1957 *Children's Bells*, 'A Morning Song'.

20 There's Carol like a rolling car,
   And Martin like a flying bird,
   And Adam like the Lord's First Word,
   And Raymond like the Harvest Moon,
   And Peter like a piper's tune,
   And Alan like the flowing on
   Of water. And there's John, like John.
   1958 *Then There Were Three*, 'Boys' Names'.

Farjeon, Herbert 1887–1945
English actor, theatre manager and critic.

21 I've danced with a man, who's danced with a girl, who's danced with the Prince of Wales.
   1927 *The Picnic*.

Farquhar, George c.1677–1707
Irish playwright, who turned to soldiering after an early career as an actor. His comic plays include *Love and a Bottle* (1698), *The Recruiting Officer* (1706) and, most famously, *The Beaux' Stratagem* (1707).

22 Poetry's a mere drug, Sir.
   1698 *Love and a Bottle*, act 3, sc.2.

23 I hate all that don't love me, and slight all that do.
   1699 *The Constant Couple*, act 1, sc.2.

24 Crimes, like virtues, are their own reward.
   1702 *The Inconstant*, act 4, sc.2.

25 Hanging and marriage, you know, go by destiny.
   1706 *The Recruiting Officer*, act 3, sc.2.

26 Sir, you shall taste my Anno Domini.
   1707 *The Beaux' Stratagem*, act 1, sc.1.

27 I have fed purely upon ale; I have eat my ale, drank my ale, and I always sleep upon ale.
   1707 *The Beaux' Stratagem*, act 1, sc.1.

28 There is no scandal like rags, nor any crime so shameful as poverty.
   1707 *The Beaux' Stratagem*, act 1, sc.1.

29 Since a woman must wear chains, I would have the pleasure of hearing 'em rattle a little.
   1707 *The Beaux' Stratagem*, act 2, sc.2.

30 No woman can be a beauty without a fortune.
   1707 *The Beaux' Stratagem*, act 2, sc.2.

Farragut, David Glasgow 1801–70
US admiral. He served in the War of 1812 and had minor commands in the American–Mexican War before leading a Union fleet in the Civil War. He was the US navy's first vice-admiral (1864) and admiral (1866).

31 Damn the torpedoes! Full speed ahead.
   1864 At the Battle of Mobile Bay, 5 Aug. Quoted in A T Mahan *Great Commanders: Admiral Farragut* (1892), ch.10.

Fassbinder, Rainer Werner 1946–82
German film director, who made over 40 films.

32 I hope to build a house with my films. Some of them are the cellar, some are the walls, and some are the windows. But I hope in time there will be a house.
   Quoted in Leslie Halliwell *Halliwell's Filmgoer's Companion* (1993).

Faulkner, William Harrison 1897–1962
US novelist, known for his experiments in literary form and style and for his treatment of social and racial problems in the US South in a series of novels beginning with *Sartoris* (1929). He was awarded the Nobel prize for literature in 1949.

33 Yes, he thought, *between grief and nothing I will take grief.*
   1939 Wilborne. *The Wild Palms*, 'Wild Palms', no.5.

34 No man can cause more grief than that one clinging blindly to the vices of his ancestors.
   1948 *Intruder in the Dust*, ch.3.

35 He must teach himself that the basest of all things is to be afraid and, teaching himself that, forget it forever, leaving no room in his workshop for anything but the old verities and truths of the heart, the old universal truths lacking which any story is ephemeral and doomed—love and honour and pity and compassion and sacrifice.
1950 Nobel prize acceptance speech.

36 I believe man will not merely endure, he will prevail. He is immortal, not because he, alone among creatures, has an inexhaustible voice but because he has a soul, a spirit capable of compassion and sacrifice and endurance.
1950 Nobel prize acceptance speech.

37 Maybe the only thing worse than having to give gratitude constantly all the time, is having to accept it.
1951 *Requiem for a Nun*, act 2, sc.1.

38 Since his capacity to do is forced into channels of evil through environment and pressures, man is strong before he is moral. The world's anguish is caused by people between twenty and forty.
1956 Interview in *Paris Review*, Spring.

39 An artist is a creature driven by demons.
1956 Interview in *Paris Review*, Spring.

40 The writer's only responsibility is to his art. He will be completely ruthless if he is a good one.
1956 Interview in *Paris Review*, Spring.

41 If a writer has to rob his mother, he will not hesitate; the *Ode on a Grecian Urn* is worth any number of old ladies.
1956 Interview in *Paris Review*, Spring.

42 The aim of every artist is to arrest motion, which is life, by artificial means and hold it fixed so that a hundred years later, when a stranger looks at it, it moves again since it is life.
1956 Interview in *Paris Review*, Spring.

43 All of us failed to match our dreams of perfection. So I rate us on the basis of our splendid failure to do the impossible.
1956 On his generation of writers. Interview in *Paris Review*, Spring.

44 If I were reincarnated, I'd want to come back as a buzzard. Nothing hates him or envies him or wants him or needs him. He is never bothered or in danger, and he can eat anything.
1956 Interview in *Paris Review*, Spring.

45 Success is feminine and like a woman; if you cringe before her she will override you. So the way to treat her is to show her the back of your hand. Then maybe she will do the crawling.
1956 Interview in *Paris Review*, Spring.

46 No man can write who is not first a humanitarian.
1957 In *Time*, 25 Feb.

47 The last sound on the worthless earth will be two human beings trying to launch a homemade spaceship and already quarreling about where they are going next.
1959 Speech to UNESCO Commission, in the *New York Times*, 3 Oct.

48 But a man shouldn't fool with booze until he's fifty; then he's a damn fool if he doesn't.
Quoted in Webb and Wigfall Green *William Faulkner of Oxford* (1965).

Fauré, Gabriel Urbain 1845–1924

French composer. Director of the Conservatoire (1905–20), he is remembered chiefly for his songs and instrumental music, and for his *Requiem* (1887–90).

49 If that was music, I have never understood what music was.
1902 After attending the première of Debussy's *Pelléas et Mélisande*. Quoted in R Orledge *Gabriel Fauré* (1979).

Favre, Jules Claude Gabriel 1809–80

French lawyer and politician. He took part in the July Revolution (1830), becoming a Republican leader and, after the fall of Napoleon III, Foreign Minister. He negotiated the Treaty of Frankfurt (1871).

50 Not an inch of our territory or a stone of our fortresses.
1870 Reply to Bismarck's demands for concessions, 18 Sep, following France's defeat in the Franco-Prussian War. Quoted in A J P Taylor *The Struggle for Mastery in Europe 1848–1918* (1954), p.212.

Fawcett, Percy Harrison 1867–c.1925

English explorer. After military service he made several expeditions to Brazil (1906–25) in search of traces of ancient civilizations, disappearing with his son and a companion in the Mato Grosso region. Their fate is a mystery.

51 There, I believed, lay the greatest secrets of the past yet preserved in our world of today. I had come to the turn of the road; and for better or worse I chose the forest path.
1911 Of South America. Collected in Brian Fawcett (ed) *Exploration Fawcett* (1953).

52 You need have no fear of any failure.
1925 Last words written to his wife. Collected in Brian Fawcett (ed) *Exploration Fawcett* (1953).

Fawkes, Guy 1570–1606

English conspirator. He converted to Catholicism at an early age, and served in the Spanish army in the Netherlands (1593–1604). He was involved in the Gunpowder Plot, and was caught red-handed and hanged.

53 A desperate disease requires a dangerous remedy.
1605 When questioned after his arrest on 5 Nov.

Feibleman, Peter 1930–

US novelist, playwright and literary executor of Lillian Hellman. His novels include *A Place Without Twilight* (1958) and *The Daughters of Necessity* (1959). With Lillian Hellman he wrote *Eating Together* (1985).

54 The biggest difference between Lillian as a grown-up and Lillian as a child was that she was taller.
1988 On Lillian Hellman. *Lily*.

Feiffer, Jules 1929–

US cartoonist and writer. His early cartoons in *Village Voice* (1956) were followed by *Little Murders* (a black comedy, 1965), novels and screenplays, including *Carnal Knowledge* (1971). He currently writes and illustrates children's books.

55 I used to think I was poor. Then they told me I wasn't poor, I was needy. They told me it was self-defeating to think of myself as needy, I was deprived. Then they told me underprivileged was overused. I was disadvantaged. I still don't have a dime. But I have a great vocabulary.
1956 Cartoon caption.

56 As a matter of racial pride we want to be called *blacks*. Which has replaced the term *Afro-American*. Which replaced *Negroes*. Which replaced *colored people*. Which replaced *darkies*. Which replaced *blacks*.
Quoted in William Safire *Language Maven Strikes Again* (1990).

Feininger, Lyonel 1871–1956
US Cubist painter, also associated with the German painters of the Blaue Reiter.

57 Each individual work serves as an expression of our most personal state of mind at that particular moment and of the inescapable, imperative need for release by means of an appropriate act of creation: in the rhythm, form, colour and mood of a picture.
1917 Letter to Paul Westheim, quoted in Wolf-Dieter Dube *The Expressionists* (1972).

Fellini, Federico 1920–93
Italian film director. His most famous and controversial work, *La Dolce Vita* (1960, 'The Sweet Life'), was a cynical evocation of modern Roman high life.

58 I always direct the same film. I can't distinguish one from the other.
Quoted in Leslie Halliwell *Halliwell's Filmgoer's Companion* (1993).

Fenton, James 1949–
English satirical poet and critic, formerly a foreign correspondent. He was Professor of Poetry at Oxford (1994–9).

59 It is not what they built. It is what they knocked down.
It is not the houses. It is the spaces between the houses.
It is not the streets that exist. It is the streets that no longer exist.
It is not your memories which haunt you.
It is not what you have written down.
It is what you have forgotten, what you must forget.
What you must go on forgetting all your life.
1981 'A German Requiem'.

60 And I'm afraid, reading this passage now,
That everything I knew has been destroyed
By those whom I admired but never knew;
The laughing soldiers fought to their defeat
And I'm afraid most of my friends are dead.
1982 'In a Notebook'.

61 Oh let us not be condemned for what we are.
It is enough to account for what we do.
1983 'Children in Exile'.

62 English poetry begins whenever we decide to say the modern English language begins, and it extends as far as we decide to say that the English language extends.
2002 *An Introduction to English Poetry*.

63 A properly written poem should have, implicit in its writing, the best indications as to how it should be read—how it should be interpreted is another matter, but the plainest pointer to how it should be read, built into the text, is what makes a poem a poem.
2007 *The Guardian*, 31 Mar.

Fenwick, Millicent Hammond 1910–93
US politician and diplomat, congresswoman from New Jersey (1975–83). She compiled the *Vogue Book of Etiquette* (1948).

64 The gentle and respectful ways of saying 'To hell with you' are being abandoned.
Recalled on her death, 16 Sep 1993.

Ferber, Edna 1887–1968
US writer. She wrote a number of novels and short stories, and is remembered as the writer of *Show Boat* (1926), which inspired the successful musical.

65 Mother Knows Best.
1923 Title of story.

66 I am not belittling the brave pioneer men but the sunbonnet as well as the sombrero has helped to settle this glorious land of ours.
1929 *Cimarron*, ch.23.

67 America—rather, the United States—seems to me to be the Jew among the nations. It is resourceful, adaptable, maligned, envied, feared, imposed upon. It is warm-hearted, overfriendly; quick-witted, lavish, colorful; given to extravagant speech and gestures; its people are travellers and wanderers by nature, moving, shifting, restless; swarming in Fords, in ocean liners; craving entertainment; volatile.
1939 *A Peculiar Treasure*, ch.1.

68 It was part of the Texas ritual… We know about champagne and caviar but we talk hog and hominy.
1952 *Giant*, ch.2.

69 A woman can look both moral and exciting—if she also looks as if it was quite a struggle.
1954 In *Reader's Digest*, Dec.

70 Science had married the wilderness and was taming the savage shrew.
1958 Of Alaska. *Ice Palace*.

71 Being an old maid is like death by drowning, a really delightful sensation after you cease to struggle.
Quoted in 'Completing the Circle', in R E Drennan *Wit's End* (1973).

72 Dinner parties are for eating, not mating.
Reminder to hostesses who only invite people in pairs. In the *New York Times*, 25 Sep 1984.

Ferdinand I 1503–64
Holy Roman Emperor from 1558, heir to his elder brother, Charles V, whom he joined in battling against Ottoman incursions. He was mainly responsible for the compromise at Augsburg (1555) which ended the religious wars.

73 *Fiat justitia et pereat mundus.*
Let justice be done, though the world may perish.
Motto.
▶ See Watson 922:44.

Ferguson, Sir Alex 1941–
Scottish football manager. He managed Manchester United from 1986 to 2013, winning many titles, including the treble (the League Championship, FA Cup and European Championship) in 1999.

74 Never use sarcasm on players. It doesn't work.
2002 In the *Observer*, 19 May.

75 Control is very, very important because if I lose control of all these multi-millionaires in my dressing room, I'm dead. So, if anyone steps out of my control, that's them dead.
2010 Lecture in Dublin, quoted in the *Daily Mail*, 22 Jan.

76 Sometimes you look in a field and you see a cow and you think it's a better cow than the one you've got in your own field. It's a fact. Right? And it never really works out that way.
2010 Referring to a transfer request from his star player Wayne Rooney. Quoted on Goal.com, 20 Oct.

Ferguson, Niall 1964–
Scottish historian.

77 It is of course a truth universally acknowledged that large overseas military commitments cannot be sustained without even larger economic resources.
2004 *Colossus: The Rise and Fall of the American Empire.*

78 The United States today is an empire—but a peculiar kind of empire. It is vastly wealthy. It is militarily peerless. It has astonishing cultural reach. Yet by comparison with other empires it often struggles to impose its will beyond its shores.
2004 *Colossus: The Rise and Fall of the American Empire.*

79 The ascent of money has been essential to the ascent of man.
2008 *The Ascent of Money: A Financial History of the World.*

80 History is not politically correct. Many on the left therefore struggle with its findings.
2011 *The Spectator*, 17 Dec.

81 The law of unintended consequences is the only real law of history.
2012 In *Newsweek*, 18 Jun.

82 I refuse to accept that Western civilization is like some hopeless old version of Microsoft DOS, doomed to freeze, then crash. I still cling to the hope that the United States is the Mac to Europe's PC, and that if one part of the West can successfully update and reboot itself, it's America.
2012 In *Newsweek*, 6 Dec.

Ferguson, Sir Samuel 1810–86
Irish poet and Celtic scholar, president of the Royal Irish Academy and a key figure in the study of early Irish art. His spirited poetry draws on Irish myth.

83 Wider comprehensions, deeper insights to the dead belong:—
Since for Love thou wakest not, sleeper, yet awake for sake of Song!
c.1864 'The Tain-Quest'.

Fergusson, Robert 1750–74
Scottish poet, much admired by Burns. He wrote primarily of Edinburgh life and died in its lunatic asylum aged 24.

84 For thof ye had as wise a snout on
As Shakespeare or Sir Isaac Newton,
Your judgement fouk wou'd hae a doubt on,
I'll tak my aith,
Till they cou'd see ye wi' a suit on
O' gude Braid Claith.
1772 'Braid Claith', stanza 9.

85 Wanwordy, crazy, dinsome thing,
As e'er was fram'd to jow or ring,
What gar'd them sic in steeple hing
They ken themsel',
But weel wat I they coudna bring
Waur sounds frae hell.
1772 'To the Tron-Kirk Bell', stanza 1.

86 Auld Reikie! wale o' ilka town
That Scotland kens beneath the moon;
Whare couthy chiels at e'ening meet
Their bizzing craigs and mous to weet.
1773 'Auld Reikie, A Poem'.

87 Now gae your wa's—Tho' anes as gude
As ever happit flesh and blude,
Yet part we maun—the case sae hard is,
Amang the writers and the bardies
That lang they'll brook the auld I trow,
Or neibours cry, 'Weel brook the new'.
1773 'To My Auld Breeks'.

Ferlinghetti, Lawrence 1919–
US poet and publisher. A member of the Beat Generation of poets, he founded the important radical bookstore and publishing house, City Lights, in San Francisco.

88 A Coney Island of the Mind.
1958 Title of book.

89 the poet like an acrobat
climbs on rime
to a high wire of his own making.
1958 'A Coney Island of the Mind', section 15.

90 I have a feeling I'm falling
on rare occasions
but most of the time I have my feet on the ground
I can't help it if the ground itself is falling.
1973 'Mock Confessional'.

91 For even bad poetry has relevance
for what it does not say
for what it leaves out.
1988 'Uses of Poetry'.

92 As I get older I perceive
Life has its tail in its mouth.
1988 'Poet as Fisherman'.

93 Poetry is a naked woman, a naked man, and the distance between them.
2007 *Poetry as Insurgent Art.*

Fermat, Pierre de 1601–65
French lawyer, mathematician and founder of number theory. A great deal of his fame stems from Fermat's Last Theorem.

94 To divide a cube into two other cubes, a fourth power or in general any power whatever into two powers of the same denomination above the second is impossible, and I have assuredly found an admirable proof of this, but the margin is too narrow to contain it.
Scribbled note in the margins of his copy of Diophantus's *Arithmetica*. He did not live to provide the promised proof, and the conjecture became famous as Fermat's Last Theorem. In 1993 Andrew Wiles, a British mathematician, claimed to have discovered the proof.

Fermi, Enrico 1901–54
Italian-born US physicist, discoverer of the element neptunium and winner of the 1938 Nobel prize. In 1942 he created the first self-sustaining chain reaction in uranium, which led to the atomic bomb.

Fern, Fanny née Willis 1811–72

US writer, whose witty sketches were collected in *Fern Leaves from Fanny's Portfolio* (1853). When he made his famous attack on women writers, Nathaniel Hawthorne was careful to exempt her.

96 Well, it is a humiliating reflection, that the straightest road to a man's heart is through his palate.
1854 *Fern Leaves from Fanny's Portfolio, Second Series*, 'Hungry Husbands'. Often quoted as 'The way to a man's heart is through his stomach'.

Fernández, Macedonio 1874–1952

Argentinian philosopher, poet and novelist. He lived a secluded life, reluctant to publish his manuscripts. His philosophical postulates anticipate the work of later writers such as Borges and Bioy Casares.

97 *Todo se ha escrito, todo se ha dicho, todo se ha hecho, oyó Dios que le decían y aún no había creado el mundo, todavía no había nada. También eso ya me lo han dicho, repuso quizá desde la vieja, hendida Nada. Y comenzó.*
Everything has been written, everything has been said, everything has been made: that's what God heard before creating the world, when there was nothing yet. I have also heard that one, he may have answered from the old, split Nothingness. And then he began.
1967 *Museo de la novela de la Eterna* ('The Museum of Eternity's Novel'), 'Prólogo a la eternidad'.

Ferré, Rosario 1943–

Puerto Rican novelist and critic, who has lived and taught in both Puerto Rico and the US.

98 *Dios sólo nos tiene aquí prestados, en este valle de lágrimas no estamos más que de paso. Si llegara algún día a pensar que ha perdido a su hija para el mundo de los hombres, la habrá ganado para el de los ángeles.*
God has us here only on loan, we are transitory in this vale of tears. If you ever come to think that you have lost your daughter to the world of men, think also that you have given her to that of the angels.
1976 *La Bella Durmiente* ('Sleeping Beauty').

Ferrier, Kathleen 1912–53

English contralto. The range and richness of her voice, together with her remarkable technical control, rapidly won her a great reputation until her early death from cancer.

99 Now I'll have eine kleine pause.
1953 Last words. Quoted in Gerald Moore *Am I Too Loud?* (1962).

Feuerbach, Ludwig 1804–72

German philosopher, famous for his interpretation of Christian doctrine in secular terms and for its adaptation by Karl Marx.

1 While Socrates empties the cup of poison with unshaken soul, Christ exclaims, 'If it is possible, let this cup pass from me'. Christ in this respect is the self-confession of human sensibility.
1841 *Das Wesen des Christentums* (translated by MaryAnn Evans (George Eliot) as *The Essence of Christianity*, 1854).

2 The power of miracle is the power of imagination.
1841 *Das Wesen des Christentums* (translated by MaryAnn Evans (George Eliot) as *The Essence of Christianity*, 1854).

3 *Der Mensch ist, was er isst.*
Man is what he eats.
Quoted in Jacob Moleschott *Lehre der Nahrungsmittel: Für das Volk* (1850).

Fey, Tina (Elizabeth Stamatina) 1970–

US actress and comedian.

4 I can see Russia from my house!
2008 Parodying Republican politician Sarah Palin on *Saturday Night Live*.

Feynman, Richard P(hillips) 1918–88

US physicist who shared (1965) the Nobel prize in physics for his work on quantum electrodynamics.

5 We have a habit in writing articles published in scientific journals to make the work as finished as possible, to cover up all the tracks, to not worry about the blind alleys or describe how you had the wrong idea first, and so on. So there isn't any place to publish, in a dignified manner, what you actually did in order to do the work.
1966 Nobel lecture.

6 You know how it always is, every new idea, it takes a generation or two until it becomes obvious that there's no real problem. I cannot define the real problem, therefore I suspect there's no real problem, but I'm not sure there's no real problem.
1982 Explaining his feelings on quantum mechanics. In the *International Journal of Theoretical Physics*, vol.21.

7 If I could explain it to the average person, I wouldn't have been worth the Nobel prize.
1985 In *People Magazine*, 22 Jul.

8 For a successful technology, reality must take precedence over public relations, for nature cannot be fooled.
1988 *What Do YOU Care What Other People Think?*

Fiedler, Leslie A(aron) 1917–92

US critic and novelist. His reputation rests on his influential and often controversial books on US 'literary anthropology', of which *Love and Death in the American Novel* (1960) is the best known.

9 Come Back To The Raft Again, Huck Honey!
1955 Title of essay on the repressed homoerotic undercurrent in US writing.

10 To be an American (unlike being English or French or whatever) is precisely to *imagine* a destiny rather than to inherit one; since we have always been, insofar as we are Americans at all, inhabitants of myth rather than history.
1969 'Cross the Border—Close the Gap', in *Playboy*, Dec.

Field, Barron 1786–1846

Australian jurist, born in London. He went to Sydney in 1817 as Judge of the New South Wales Supreme Court and published the first collection of Australian verse, *First Fruits of Australian Poetry* (1819).

---

95 Whatever Nature has in store for mankind, unpleasant as it may be, men must accept, for ignorance is never better than knowledge.
Quoted in Laura Fermi *Atoms in the Family* (1954).

11 Kangaroo, Kangaroo!
    Thou Spirit of Australia,
    That redeems from utter failure,
    From perfect desolation,
    And warrants the creation
    Of this fifth part of the Earth.
    1819 *First Fruits of Australian Poetry*, 'The Kangaroo'.

Field, Eugene 1850–95
US writer and theatre critic. A columnist for the *Chicago Morning News*, he achieved a reputation as a humorist and poet with his column 'Sharps and Flats'. He also published several books of children's verse.

12 Mr Creston Clarke played King Lear at the Tabor Grand last night. All through five acts of Shakespeare's tragedy he played the king as though under momentary apprehension that someone else was about to play the ace.
    c.1880 Attributed review in the *Denver Post*.

13 Wynken, Blynken, and Nod one night
    Sailed off in a wooden shoe—
    Sailed on a river of crystal light,
    Into a sea of dew.
    1889 'Wynken, Blynken, and Nod'.

14 I never lost a little fish. Yes, I am free to say.
    It always was the biggest fish I caught that got away.
    Attributed.

Field, Frank 1942–
English Labour politician. Director of the Child Poverty Action Group (1969–79) and the Low Pay Unit (1974–80), he became an MP in 1979 and has campaigned strenuously for social justice.

15 The House of Lords is a model of how to care for the elderly.
    1981 In the *Observer*, 24 May.

Field, Sally Margaret 1946–
US film actress.

16 If mothers ruled the world, there wouldn't be any goddamn wars in the first place.
    2007 Acceptance speech at the Emmy Awards.

Fielding, Henry 1707–54
English novelist and playwright. After the introduction of the Theatrical Licensing Act in 1737 he turned to fiction, with works such as *The Adventures of Joseph Andrews* (1742), *Tom Jones* (1749) and *Amelia* (1751). He died in Lisbon.

17 Love and scandal are the best sweeteners of tea.
    1728 *Love in Several Masques*, act 4, sc.11.

18 Map me no maps, sir, my head is a map, a map of the whole world.
    1730 *Rape upon Rape*, act 2, sc.5.

19 Oh! The roast beef of England,
    And old England's roast beef!
    1731 *Grub Street Opera*, act 3, sc.3.

20 All Nature wears one universal grin.
    1731 *Tom Thumb the Great*, act 1, sc.1.

21 I am as sober as a Judge.
    1734 *Don Quixote in England*, act 3, sc.14.

22 He in a few minutes ravished this fair creature, or at least would have ravished her, if she had not, by a timely compliance, prevented him.
    1743 *Jonathan Wild*, bk.3, ch.7.

23 Thwackum was for doing justice, and leaving mercy to heaven.
    1749 *Tom Jones*, bk.3, ch.10.

24 What is commonly called love, namely the desire of satisfying a voracious appetite with a certain quantity of delicate white human flesh.
    1749 *Tom Jones*, bk.6, ch.1.

25 His designs were strictly honourable, as the phrase is; that is, to rob a lady of her fortune by way of marriage.
    1749 *Tom Jones*, bk.11, ch.4.

26 It hath been often said, that it is not death, but dying, which is terrible.
    1751 *Amelia*, bk.3, ch.4.

27 One fool at least in every married couple.
    1751 *Amelia*, bk.9, ch.4.

Fields, Dorothy 1905–74
US author and lyricist, daughter of comedian Lew Fields. She wrote the books and lyrics for many Broadway shows and films, often with Jimmy McHugh or Jerome Kern.

28 Grab your coat, and get your hat,
    Leave your worry on the doorstep,
    Just direct your feet
    To the sunny side of the street.
    1930 'On the Sunny Side of the Street'.

29 I might as well play bridge with my old maid aunts
    I haven't got a chance
    This is a fine romance.
    1934 'A Fine Romance', song featured in the film *Swing Time* (music by Jerome Kern).

Fields, W C originally William Claude Dukenfield 1880–1946
US comedian. He wrote and performed in several classic comedies including *The Bank Dick* (1940), *My Little Chickadee* (1940) and *Never Give a Sucker an Even Break* (1940).

30 It ain't a fit night out for man or beast.
    1932 *The Fatal Glass of Beer*.

31 Women are like elephants to me. I like to look at them, but I wouldn't want to own one.
    1935 *Mississippi*.

32 Egbert, is it true that married people live longer?
    No, it just seems longer.
    1940 *The Bank Dick*.

33 Never Give a Sucker an Even Break.
    1941 Title of film, but an earlier catchphrase of Fields's that may have originated in the 1923 film *Poppy*.

34 I was in love with a beautiful blonde once, dear. She drove me to drink. That's the one thing I'm indebted to her for.
    1941 *Never Give a Sucker an Even Break*.

35 Anybody who hates children and dogs can't be all bad.
    Attributed.

36 Fish fuck in it.
    Attributed, his reason for not drinking water.

Fiennes, Ralph Nathaniel 1962–
English actor.

37 We're in a world of truncated sentences, soundbites and Twitter... our expressiveness and our ease with some words is being diluted so that the sentence with more than one clause is a problem for us, and the word of more than two syllables is a problem for us.
  2011 In *The Daily Mail*, 28 Oct.

Fiennes, Sir Ranulph 1944–
English explorer.

38 To write about hell it helps if you have been there.
  2004 *Captain Scott*.

39 There is no bad weather, only inappropriate clothing.
  Attributed.

Fierstein, Harvey Forbes 1954–
US playwright and actor. He began as a female impersonator and acts on stage and screen. He has won awards for *Torch Song Trilogy* (produced 1982) and for the books of the Broadway musicals *La Cage Aux Folles* (1983) and *Kinky Boots* (2013).

40 I assume everyone is gay, unless told otherwise.
  1994 In *Life*, Jan.

50 Cent originally Curtis Jackson 1976–
US rapper.

41 Where I grew up if you have two parents you're spoilt.
  2003 In the *Sunday Times*, 15 Jun.

42 If you die in an elevator make sure you press the up button.
  Attributed.

Findley, Timothy 1931–2002
Canadian writer and actor. His novels include *The Wars* (1977), *The Piano Man's Daughter* (1995) and *Pilgrim* (1999).

43 He did the thing that no one else would even dare to think of doing. And that to me's as good a definition of a 'hero' as you'll get. Even when the thing that's done is something of which you disapprove.
  1977 Juliet D'Orsey. *The Wars*, pt.1, section 3.

44 Dead men are serious.
  1977 *The Wars*, pt.1, section 20.

45 Any man whose love of horses is stronger than his fear of being an absurdity is all right with me.
  1977 Rodwell. *The Wars*, pt.2, section 8.

Firbank, (Arthur Annesley) Ronald 1886–1926
English novelist. Solitary and somewhat eccentric, he wrote slight but witty and innovative novels. His works include *Valmouth* (1919) and *Prancing Nigger* (1924).

46 There was a pause—just long enough for an angel to pass, flying slowly.
  1915 *Vainglory*, ch.6.

47 The world is disgracefully managed, one hardly knows to whom to complain.
  1915 *Vainglory*, ch.10.

48 All millionaires love a baked apple.
  1915 *Vainglory*, ch.13.

49 She stands, I fear, poor thing, now, for something younger than she looks.
  1919 *Valmouth*, ch.1.

50 'I know of no joy,' she airily began, 'greater than a cool white dress after the sweetness of confession.'
  1919 *Valmouth*, ch.4.

51 There was really no joy in pouring out one's sins while he sat assiduously picking his nose.
  1919 *Valmouth*, ch.6.

52 His Weariness the Prince entered the room in all his tinted orders.
  1923 *The Flower Beneath the Foot*, ch.1.

53 'O! help me heaven,' she prayed, 'to be decorative and to do right!'
  1923 *The Flower Beneath the Foot*, ch.2.

54 Beneath the strain of expectation even the little iced sugar cakes upon the tea-table looked green with worry.
  1923 *The Flower Beneath the Foot*, ch.3.

55 Looking back, I remember the average curate at home as something between a eunuch and a snigger.
  1923 *The Flower Beneath the Foot*, ch.4.

56 'Basta!' his master replied with all the brilliant glibness of the Berlitz-school.
  1923 *The Flower Beneath the Foot*, ch.5.

57 She looks at other women as if she would inhale them.
  1923 *The Flower Beneath the Foot*, ch.5.

58 'I've never travelled,' Dona Consolation blandly confessed, 'but I dare say, dear, you can't judge Egypt by Aïda.'
  1926 *Concerning the Eccentricities of Cardinal Pirelli*, ch.9.

Firth, Colin 1960–
English actor. His most notable roles have included that of George VI in *The King's Speech* (2010), for which he won an Oscar.

59 I have a feeling my career has just peaked.
  2011 Acceptance speech at the Academy Awards.

Fish, Michael 1944–
English weather forecaster.

60 A woman rang to say she heard there was a hurricane on the way. Well don't worry, there isn't.
  1987 Television weather forecast prior to severe gales in southern England, 15 Oct.

Fisher (of Lambeth), Geoffrey Francis Fisher, Baron 1887–1972
English prelate and Archbishop of Canterbury (1945–61). He officiated at the coronation of Elizabeth II in Westminster Abbey (1953).

61 The long and distressing controversy over capital punishment is very unfair to anyone meditating murder.
  1957 In the *Sunday Times*, 24 Feb.

Fisher, H(erbert) A(lbert) L(aurens) 1865–1940
English historian. As Education Minister (1916–22) he sponsored the Fisher Act (1918). He wrote on Napoleon, and is best known for his *History of Europe* (1936).

62 Men wiser and more learned than I have discerned in history a plot, a rhythm, a predetermined pattern. Those harmonies are concealed from me. I can see only one emergency following upon another, as wave follows upon wave; only one real fact with respect to which, since it is unique, there can be no generalizations. Only one safe rule for the historian: that he should recognize in the development of human destinies the play of the contingent and the unforeseen.
1936 History of Europe, introduction.

63 Purity of race does not exist. Europe is a continent of energetic mongrels.
1936 History of Europe, ch.1.

Fisher, M(ary) F(rances) K(ennedy) 1908–92
US cookery writer.

64 Sharing food with another human being is an intimate act that should not be indulged in lightly.
1949 An Alphabet for Gourmets, 'A Is for Dining Alone'.

65 In America we eat, collectively, with a glum urge for food to fill us. We are ignorant of flavor. We are as a nation taste-blind.
1976 The Art of Eating.

Fiske, John 1842–1901
US historian, tutor and librarian at Harvard. He wrote many popular books on US history, Spencerian philosophy and Darwinism.

66 The element of chance…is expelled. Nobody would now waste his time in theorizing about a fortuitous concourse of atoms. We have so far spelled out the history of creation as to see that all has been done in strict accordance with law. The method has been the method of evolution, and the more we study it the more do we discern in it intelligible coherence.
1900 Through Nature to God.

Fitt, Gerry (Gerard) Fitt, Baron 1926–2005
Northern Ireland politician.

67 The people have spoken and the politicians have had to listen.
1998 In the Sunday Telegraph, 24 May.

Fitzgerald, Edward 1809–83
English scholar, poet and translator, a friend of Thackeray, Carlisle and Tennyson. His translation of the *Rubáiyát of Omar Khayyám* was first published anonymously in 1859.

68 Awake! for Morning in the bowl of night
Has flung the stone that puts the stars to flight:
And Lo! the Hunter of the East has caught
The Sultan's turret in a noose of light.
1859 The Rubáiyát of Omar Khayyám of Naishapur, stanza 1.

69 Here with a loaf of bread beneath the bough,
A flask of wine, a book of verse—and Thou
Beside me singing in the wilderness—
And wilderness is paradise enow.
1859 The Rubáiyát of Omar Khayyám of Naishapur, stanza 12. In the 1879 edn this was changed to 'A Book of Verses underneath the Bough, / A Jug of Wine, a loaf of Bread—and Thou / Beside me singing in the Wilderness— / Oh, Wilderness were Paradise enow!'

70 The moving finger writes; and, having writ,
Moves on: nor all thy piety nor wit
Shall lure it back to cancel half a line,
Nor all thy tears wash out a word of it.
1859 The Rubáiyát of Omar Khayyám of Naishapur, stanza 51.

71 Drink! for you know not whence you came, nor why:
Drink! for you know not why you go nor where.
1859 The Rubáiyát of Omar Khayyám of Naishapur, stanza 74.

72 And when Thyself with shining foot shall pass
Among the guests star-scattered on the grass,
And in thy joyous errand reach the spot
Where I made one—turn down an empty glass!
1859 The Rubáiyát of Omar Khayyám of Naishapur, stanza 75. In the 1879 edition this was changed to 'And when like her, O Saki, you shall pass…'.

Fitzgerald, F(rancis) Scott Key 1896–1940
US novelist who epitomized the Jazz Age in his best-known book, *The Great Gatsby* (1925). He wrote about US expatriates in *Tender is the Night* (1934).

73 At eighteen our convictions are hills from which we look; at forty-five they are caves in which we hide.
1920 'Bernice Bobs Her Hair', in the Saturday Evening Post, 1 May.

74 The wise writer, I think, writes for the youth of his own generation, the critics of the next, and the schoolmasters of ever afterward.
1920 Interview in the New York Tribune, 7 May.

75 She had once been a Catholic, but discovering that priests were infinitely more attentive when she was in process of losing or regaining faith in Mother Church, she maintained an enchantingly wavering attitude.
1921 Of Beatrice Blaine. This Side of Paradise, bk.1, ch.1.

76 If I start to hold somebody's hand they laugh at me, and *let* me, just as if it wasn't part of them. As soon as I get hold of a hand they sort of disconnect it from the rest of them.
1921 This Side of Paradise, bk.1, ch.1.

77 The Beautiful and the Damned.
1922 Title of novel.

78 Personality is an unbroken series of successful gestures.
1925 The Great Gatsby, ch.1.

79 One of those men who reach such an acute limited excellence at twenty-one that everything afterward savors of anti-climax.
1925 Of Tom Buchanan. The Great Gatsby, ch.1.

80 In his blue gardens, men and girls came and went like moths among the whisperings and the champagne and the stars.
1925 The Great Gatsby, ch.3.

81 Everyone suspects himself of at least one of the cardinal virtues, and this is mine: I am one of the few honest people that I have ever known.
1925 Nick Carraway, the narrator. The Great Gatsby, ch.3.

82 There are only the pursued, the pursuing, the busy, and the tired.
1925 The Great Gatsby, ch.4.

83 Reach me a rose, honey, and pour me a last drop into that there crystal glass.
1925 The Great Gatsby, ch.4.

84 Her voice is full of money.
1925 The Great Gatsby, ch.7.

85 They were careless people, Tom and Daisy—they smashed up things and creatures and then retreated back into their money or their vast carelessness, or whatever it was that kept them together, and let other people clean up the mess they had made.
1925 *The Great Gatsby*, ch.9.

86 And as the moon rose higher the unessential houses began to melt away until gradually I became aware of the old island here that flowered once for Dutch sailors' eyes—a fresh, green breast of the new world... For a transitory enchanted moment man must have held his breath in the presence of this continent, compelled into an aesthetic contemplation he neither understood nor desired, face to face for the last time in history with something commensurate to his capacity for wonder.
1925 *The Great Gatsby*, ch.9.

87 Gatsby believed in the green light, the orgiastic future that year by year recedes before us. It eluded us then, but that's no matter—to-morrow we will run faster, stretch out our arms further... And one fine morning... So we beat on, boats against the current, borne back ceaselessly into the past.
1925 *The Great Gatsby*, ch.9.

88 Let me tell you about the very rich. They are different from you and me.
1926 *All the Sad Young Men*, 'The Rich Boy'. Hemingway published an ironic rejoinder in 'The Snows of Kilimanjaro': 'Yes, they have more money'.
▶ See Hemingway 410:78.

89 Though the Jazz Age continued, it became less and less of an affair of youth. The sequel was like a children's party taken over by the elders.
1931 'Echoes of the Jazz Age', *Scribner's Magazine*, Nov.

90 Mostly, we authors repeat ourselves—that's the truth.
1933 'One Hundred False Starts', in the *Saturday Evening Post*, 4 Mar.

91 Tender is the Night.
1934 Title of novel.

92 When people are taken out of their depths they lose their heads, no matter how charming a bluff they may put up.
1934 *Tender is the Night*, bk.3, ch.12.

93 The test of a first-rate intelligence is the ability to hold two opposed ideas in the mind at the same time, and still retain the ability to function.
1936 'The Crack-Up', in *Esquire*, Feb.

94 In a real dark night of the soul, it is always three o'clock in the morning, day after day.
1936 'Handle With Care', in *Esquire*, Mar.

95 Often I think writing is a sheer paring away of oneself leaving always something thinner, barer, more meagre.
1940 Letter, 27 Apr.

96 The faces of most American women over thirty are relief maps of petulant and bewildered unhappiness.
1940 Letter, 5 Oct.

97 It's not a slam at *you* when people are rude—it's a slam at the people they've met before.
1941 *The Last Tycoon*, ch.1.

98 No grand idea was ever born in a conference, but a lot of foolish ideas have died there.
Note Books, E, in Edmund Wilson (ed) *The Crack-Up* (1945).

99 Show me a hero and I will write you a tragedy.
Note Books, E, in Edmund Wilson (ed) *The Crack-Up* (1945).

1 Great art is the contempt of a great man for small art.
Note Books, L, in Edmund Wilson (ed) *The Crack-Up* (1945).

2 When the first-rate author wants an exquisite heroine or a lovely morning, he finds that all the superlatives have been worn shoddy by his inferiors. It should be a rule that bad writers must start with plain heroines and ordinary mornings, and, if they are able, work up to something better.
Note Books, L, in Edmund Wilson (ed) *The Crack-Up* (1945).

Fitzgerald, Penelope Mary   1916–2000

English novelist and biographer. She won the Booker Prize in 1979 for *Offshore*.

3 Patience is passive, resignation is active.
1986 *Innocence*.

4 A human being is old when he has survived long enough to name, with absolute confidence, a year, one of the next thirty, which he won't be there to see.
A House of Air—Selected Writings, 'Last Words' (2003).

5 Twice in your life you know that you are approved of by everyone: when you learn to walk, and when you learn to read.
A House of Air—Selected Writings, 'Schooldays' (2003).

Flanagan, Bud *stage name of* Robert Winthrop   1896–1968

English comedian. He was immensely popular both as one of the Crazy Gang of comedians and in a duo with Chesney Allen.

6 Underneath the Arches,
I dream my dreams away,
Underneath the Arches,
On cobble-stones I lay.
1932 'Underneath the Arches' (song).

7 No dog can go as fast as the money you bet on him.
Quoted in Colin Jarman *The Guinness Dictionary of Sports Quotations* (1990).

Flanders, Michael and Swann, Donald   1922–75, 1923–94

English songwriting team, who made their name with *At the Drop of a Hat* (1956).

8 Mud! Mud! Glorious mud!
Nothing quite like it for cooling the blood.
So follow me, follow,
Down to the hollow,
And there let us wallow
In glorious mud.
1952 'The Hippopotamus'.

9 Eating people is wrong!
1956 'The Reluctant Cannibal'. Malcolm Bradbury took the phrase as the title of his 1959 novel.

10 Ma's out, Pa's out—let's talk rude:
Pee, po, belly, bum, drawers.
c.1956 'P, P, B, B, D'.

11 The English, the English, the English are best!
I wouldn't give tuppence for all of the rest!
1963 'Song of Patriotic Prejudice'.

Flaubert, Anne Justine Caroline 1793–1872
Mother of Gustave Flaubert.

12 Your mania for sentences has dried up your heart.
To her son. Quoted in D J Enright *A Mania for Sentences* (1983), p.101.

Flaubert, Gustave 1821–80
French novelist, master of the realistic novel. He studied law at Paris before turning to writing. His works include *Madame Bovary* (1857) and *Trois contes* (1877). He intended to include a *Dictionnaire des idées reçues* in the second volume of *Bouvard et Pécuchet*.

13 *Je suis autant Chinois que Français.*
I am as much Chinese as French.
1846 Letter to Mme Louise Colet, 8 Aug.

14 *L'Idée seule est éternelle et nécessaire.*
The idea alone is eternal and necessary.
1846 Letter to Mme Louise Colet, 9 Aug.

15 *Il ne faut pas toujours croire que le sentiment soit tout. Dans les arts, il n'est rien sans la forme.*
You must not think that feeling is everything. Art is nothing without form.
1846 Letter to Mme Louise Colet, 12 Aug.

16 *On fait de la critique quand on ne peut pas faire de l'art, de même qu'on se met mouchard quand on ne peut pas être soldat.*
Someone is a critic when he cannot be an artist in the same way that a man becomes an informer when he cannot be a soldier.
1846 Letter to Mme Louise Colet, 22 Oct.

17 *Les oeuvres les plus belles sont celles où il y a le moins de matière; plus l'expression se rapproche de la pensée, plus le mot colle dessus et disparaît, plus c'est beau. Je crois que l'avenir de l'art est dans ces voies.*
The most beautiful works are those that have the least content; the closer the expression is to the thought, the more indistinguishable the word from the content, the more beautiful is the work. I believe that the future of art lies in this direction.
1852 Letter to Mme Louise Colet, 16 Jan.

18 *La courtisane est un mythe. Jamais une femme n'a inventé une débauche.*
The courtesan is a myth. No woman has ever invented any new sensual pleasure.
1852 Letter to Mme Louise Colet, Aug.

19 *L'amour, croyait-elle, devait arriver tout à coup, avec de grands éclats et des fulgurations.*
She believed that love should appear instantaneously, with the brilliance of a lightning storm.
1857 *Madame Bovary*, pt.1, ch.8.

20 *La parole humaine est comme un chaudron fêlé où nous battons des mélodies à faire danser les ours, quand on voudrait attendrir les étoiles.*
Human speech is like a cracked kettle on which we beat out tunes for bears to dance to, when all the time we are longing to move the stars to pity.
1857 *Madame Bovary*, pt.1, ch.12.

21 *Le charme de la nouveauté, peu à peu tombant comme un vêtement, laissait voir à nu l'éternelle monotonie de la passion, qui a toujours les mêmes formes et le même langage.*
The charm of novelty, falling little by little like a robe, revealed the eternal monotony of passion, which has always the same forms and the same language.
1857 *Madame Bovary*, pt.2, ch.12.

22 *Il faut écrire pour soi, avant tout. C'est la seule chance de faire beau.*
It is necessary to write for oneself, above all. It is the only hope of creating something beautiful.
1858 Letter to Mlle Leroyer de Chantepie, 11 Jul.

23 *Un romancier, selon moi, n'a pas le droit de dire son avis sur les choses de ce monde. Il doit, dans sa vocation, imiter Dieu dans la sienne, c'est-à-dire faire et se taire.*
A novelist, in my opinion, does not have the right to give advice on the affairs of the world. He must, in his occupation, imitate God in His; that is to say, create and keep quiet.
1866 Letter to Mlle Bosquet.

24 *Axiome: la haine du bourgeois est le commencement de la vertu.*
Axiom: Hatred of the bourgeois is the beginning of wisdom.
1867 Letter to George Sand, 10 May.

25 *Il tournait dans son désir, comme un prisonnier dans son cachot.*
He was circling in his desire, like a prisoner in his dungeon.
1869 *L'Education sentimentale*, pt.1, ch.5.

26 My kingdom is as wide as the universe and my wants have no limits. I go forward always, freeing spirits and weighing words, without fear, without compassion, without love, without God. I am called science.
1874 *The Temptation of St Antony*.

27 *Antiquité. —en tout ce qui s'y rapporte: Est poncif, embêtant! etc.*
Antiquity. And everything to do with it, clichéd and boring.
Bouvard et Pécuchet avec un choix des scénarios, du Sottisier, L'Album de la Marquise et Le Dictionnaire des idées reçues. (published 1881, translated by Geoffrey Wall, 1994).

28 *Homère. Célèbre par sa façon de rire: rire homérique. N'a jamais existé.*
Homer. Famous for his laugh. 'Homeric laughter'. Never existed.
Bouvard et Pécuchet avec un choix des scénarios, du Sottisier, L'Album de la Marquise et Le Dictionnaire des idées reçues. (published 1881, translated by Geoffrey Wall, 1994).

29 *Latin. Langage naturel de l'homme. Gâte l'écriture. Est seulement utile pour comprendre les inscriptions des fontaines publiques. Il faut se méfier des citations en Latin; elles cachent toujours quelque chose de leste.*
Latin. Man's natural language. Spoils your style. Useful only for reading the inscriptions on public fountains. Beware of quotations in Latin: they always conceal something improper.
Bouvard et Pécuchet avec un choix des scénarios, du Sottisier, L'Album de la Marquise et Le Dictionnaire des idées reçues. (published 1881, translated by Geoffrey Wall, 1994).

Flecker, James Elroy 1884–1915
English poet. He studied Oriental languages and joined the consular service, symptoms of a fascination with the East which is reflected in much of his verse.

30 O friend unseen, unborn, unknown,
   Student of our sweet English tongue,
   Read out my words at night, alone:
   I was a poet, I was young.
   1910 'To a Poet a Thousand Years Hence'.

31 We who with songs beguile your pilgrimage
   And swear that Beauty lives though lilies die,
   We Poets of the proud old lineage
   Who sing to find your hearts, we know not why—
   What shall we tell you? Tales, marvellous tales
   Of ships and stars and isles where good men rest.
   1913 'The Golden Journey to Samarkand', epilogue.

32 For lust of knowing what should not be known,
   We take the Golden Road to Samarkand.
   1913 'The Golden Journey to Samarkand', epilogue.

33 How splendid in the morning glows the lily; with what grace he throws
   His supplication to the rose.
   1913 'Yasmin'.

34 The dragon-green, the luminous, the dark, the serpent-haunted sea.
   1913 'The Gates of Damascus'.

35 For pines are gossip pines the wide world through
   And full of runic tales to sigh or sing.
   1913 'Brumana'.

36 Half to forget the wandering and pain,
   Half to remember days that have gone by,
   And dream and dream that I am home again!
   1913 'Brumana'.

37 West of these out to seas colder than the Hebrides
   I must go
   Where the fleet of stars is anchored and the young
   Star captains glow.
   1913 'The Dying Patriot'.

38 A ship, an isle, a sickle moon—
   With few but with how splendid stars
   The mirrors of the sea are strewn
   Between their silver bars!
   1913 'A Ship, an Isle, a Sickle Moon'.

39 I have seen old ships sail like swans asleep.
   1915 'The Old Ships'.

Fleming, Ian Lancaster 1908–64
English novelist. He is best known for his creation of the hugely popular secret service agent, James Bond.

40 Live and Let Die.
   1954 Title of novel.

41 From Russia with Love.
   1957 Title of novel.

42 I would like a medium Vodka dry Martini—with a slice of lemon peel. Shaken and not stirred, please. I would prefer Russian or Polish vodka.
   1958 *Dr No*, ch.14.

Fleming, Marjory 1803–11
Scottish child writer, the subject of an essay by Dr John Brown which popularized her image as 'Pet Marjorie' and invented an affectionate relationship with her distant relative Walter Scott.

43 The most Devilish thing is 8 times 8 and 7 times 7 it is what nature itselfe cant endure.
   1810 'Journal 2' in F Sidgwick (ed) *The Complete Marjory Fleming* (1934).

44 Many girls have not the advantage I have and I [am] very very glad that satan has not geven me boils and many other Misfortunes.
   1810 'Journal 2' in F Sidgwick (ed) *The Complete Marjory Fleming* (1934).

45 To Day I pronounced a word which should never come out of a ladys lips it was that I called John a Impudent Bitch.
   1810 'Journal 2' in F Sidgwick (ed) *The Complete Marjory Fleming* (1934).

46 I would rather have a man dog then a women dog because they do not bear like women dogs, it is a hard case it is shoking.
   1810 'Journal 2' in F Sidgwick (ed) *The Complete Marjory Fleming* (1934).

47 I hope I will be religious again but as for reganing my charecter I despare for it.
   1810 'Journal 2' in F Sidgwick (ed) *The Complete Marjory Fleming* (1934).

48 An annibaptist is a thing I am not a member of:—I am a Pisplikan just now & a Prisbeteren at Kercaldy my native town which thugh dirty is clein in the country.
   1811 'Journal 3' in F Sidgwick (ed) *The Complete Marjory Fleming* (1934).

49 Love is a very papithatick thing as well as troublesom & tiresome but O Isabella forbid me to speak about it.
   1811 'Journal 3' in F Sidgwick (ed) *The Complete Marjory Fleming* (1934).

Fletcher (of Saltoun), Andrew 1655–1716
Scottish patriot, fierce opponent of Stuart policy and of union with England. After the Union he retired in disgust and devoted himself to agriculture.

50 This will be the issue of that darling Plea, of being one and not two; it will be turned upon the Scots with a Vengeance; and their 45 Scots Members may dance round to all Eternity, in this Trap of their own making.
   1706 *State of the Controversy betwixt United and Separate Parliaments*, a critique of the proposed Union.

51 It is only fit for the slaves who sold it.
   1707 Of Scotland, on leaving it after the signing of the Treaty of Union. Quoted in G W T Ormond *Fletcher of Saltoun* (1897).

Fletcher, John 1579–1625
English dramatist, who collaborated with Beaumont until the latter's marriage in 1613, and also with Shakespeare, Jonson, Middleton, Massinger and Rowley, as well as writing on his own. He died of plague.

52 Care-charming Sleep, thou easer of all woes,
   Brother to Death.
   c.1610–1614 *Valentinian*, act 5, sc.7.

53 Best while you have it use your breath,
   There is no drinking after death.

54 And he that will go to bed sober,
Falls with the leaf still in October.
1616 The Bloody Brother, act 2, sc.2, song (with Ben Jonson, George Chapman and Philip Massinger).

55 We are stark naught all, bad's the best of us.
1616 The Bloody Brother, act 4, sc.2 (with Ben Jonson, George Chapman and Philip Massinger).

56 We are beasts now, and the beasts are our masters.
c.1621 The Wild-Goose Chase, act 1, sc.1.

57 Blush at your faults.
c.1621 The Wild-Goose Chase, act 1, sc.1.

58 Give me the plump Venetian, fat, and lusty,
That meets me soft and supple, smiles upon me
As if a cup of full wine leaped to kiss me.
c.1621 The Wild-Goose Chase, act 1, sc.2.

59 Health and an able body are two jewels.
c. 1621 The Wild-Goose Chase, act 2, sc.1.

60 Nothing is thought rare
Which is not new and follow'd, yet we know
That what was worne some twenty yeare agoe,
Comes into grace againe.
c.1623 The Noble Gentleman, prologue.

61 Are you at ease now? Is your heart at rest?
Now you have got a shadow, an umbrella
To keep the scorching world's opinion
From your fair credit.
1624 Rule a Wife and Have a Wife, act 3, sc.1.

Florio, John c.1553–1625

English scholar, writer and translator, born of Italian Protestant family in London. His most famous work is his translation of Montaigne's *Essays* (1603); he also published an Italian–English dictionary, *A World of Words* (1598), and two compendiums of Italian proverbs.

62 England is the paradise of women, the purgatory of men, and the hell of horses.
1591 Second Frutes, ch.12.

Flynn, Errol 1909–59

Hollywood actor born in Tasmania. He starred in historical swashbucklers such as *Captain Blood* (1935), *The Adventures of Robin Hood* (1938) and *The Sea Hawk* (1940). His off-screen reputation for drinking, drug-taking and womanizing became legendary and eventually affected his career.

63 The public has always expected me to be a playboy and a decent chap never lets his public down.
Quoted in Gary Herman *The Book of Hollywood Quotes* (1979).

64 Inside this Hollywood playboy is a someway decent actor waiting for a chance to prove it. But, since Hollywood will never give me that chance, I drink to obliviate that decent actor.
Quoted in Michael Wilding and Pamela Wilcox *Apple Sauce* (1982).

Flynt, Larry Claxton 1942–

US publisher.

65 No one understands that the First Amendment is only important if you are going to offend somebody. If you're not going to offend somebody, you don't need protection of the First Amendment.
2014 On *Sunday Morning*, CBS, 19 Jan.

Fo, Dario 1926–

Italian playwright and actor-manager, whose often controversial plays and revues deal with political themes. His plays include *Accidental Death of an Anarchist* (1970) and *Trumpets and Raspberries* (1984). He was awarded the Nobel prize for literature in 1997.

66 *Non si paga, non si paga.*
We won't pay, we won't pay.
1974 Play title, translated into English in 1981 as *Can't pay? Won't pay!*

Foch, Ferdinand 1851–1929

French marshal, born in Tarbes. He taught at the École de Guerre, and proved himself a great strategist at the Battles of the Marne and Ypres. He commanded the Allied armies in 1918.

67 *Mon centre cède, ma droite recule, situation excellente, j'attaque.*
My centre is giving way, my right is retreating, situation excellent, I am attacking.
1914 Message sent during the first Battle of the Marne, Sep. Quoted in R Recouly *Foch* (1919), ch.6.

68 *Ce n'est pas un traité de paix, c'est un armistice de vingt ans.*
This is not a peace treaty, it is an armistice for twenty years.
1919 At the signing of the Treaty of Versailles. Quoted in Paul Reynaud *Memoires* (1963), vol.2.

Follett, Ken 1949–

Welsh novelist.

69 They are the rent boys of politics.
2000 Of those who give off-the-record briefings against ministers. In the *Observer*, 2 Jul.

70 The polite fiction that the Prime Minister's advisers are responsible is absurd. Control-freak Tony doesn't let Alastair Campbell and Peter Mandelson go around saying anything they like… Peter isn't the Prince of Darkness, though he may be Lady Macbeth.
2000 In the *Observer*, 2 Jul.

71 You never get cheered for telling people the situation is not as simple as they think.
2010 Fall of Giants.

72 A white American can orbit the earth, but a black American can't enter a restroom.
2014 Edge of Eternity.

Fontenelle, Bernard le Bovier de 1657–1757

French writer, the nephew of Corneille. He introduced mathematics and the natural sciences into the conversation of the salons, and expressed scientific ideas through literature. He was secretary of the Académie des Sciences (1699–1741).

73 *Ah! si l'on ôtait les chimères aux hommes, quel plaisir leur resterait?*
Oh! If man were robbed of his fantasies, what pleasure would be left him?
1683 Dialogue des morts.

74 *L'univers…je l'en estime plus depuis que je sais qu'il ressemble à une montre; il est surprenant que l'ordre* *de la nature, tout admirable qu'il est, ne roule que sur des choses si simples.*

I have come to esteem the universe more now that I know it resembles a watch; it is surprising that the order of nature, as admirable as it is, only runs on such simple things.
1686 *Entretiens sur la pluralité des mondes.*

75 *Les mouvements les plus naturels, et les plus ordinaires, sont ceux qui se font le moins sentir; cela est vrai jusque dans la morale. Le mouvement de l'amour-propre nous est si naturel que, le plus souvent, nous ne le sentons pas.*

The most natural and ordinary movements are those which are the least felt; this is also true in morals. Pride is so natural to us that, most often, we never feel it.
1686 *Entretiens sur la pluralité des mondes, Premier soir.*

76 *Les vrais philosophes sont comme les éléphants, qui en marchant ne posent jamais le second pied à terre que le premier ne soit bien affermi.*

True philosophers are like elephants, who when walking never place their second foot on the ground until the first is steady.
1686 *Entretiens sur la pluralité des mondes, Sixième soir.*

77 *Un grand obstacle au bonheur, c'est de s'attendre à un trop grand bonheur.*

The greatest obstacle to happiness is the expectation of too great a happiness.
1724 *Du bonheur.*

78 *Leibniz n'était point marié; il y avait pensé à l'âge de cinquante ans; mais la personne qu'il avait en vue voulut avoir le temps de faire ses réflexions. Cela donne à Leibniz le loisir de faire aussi les siennes, et il ne se maria point.*

Leibniz never married; he had considered it at the age of fifty, but the person he had in mind desired time to think about it. This gave Leibniz time to reflect, also, and he didn't marry.
Éloge des académiciens, Leibniz.

Foot, Michael Mackintosh 1913–2010

English Labour politician. He resigned the leadership of the Labour Party in 1983, after a heavy defeat in the general election. A pacifist and CND supporter, his prolific writings include a two-volume biography of Aneurin Bevan.

79 The only man I knew who could make a curse sound like a caress.
1962 Of Aneurin Bevan. *Aneurin Bevan 1897–1945*, vol.1.

80 The members of our secret service have apparently spent so much time looking under the bed for Communists that they haven't had time to look in the bed.
1963 Attributed comment on the Profumo scandal.

81 A Royal Commission is a broody hen sitting on a china egg.
1964 Speech, House of Commons.

82 Men of power have not time to read; yet men who do not read are unfit for power.
1980 *Debts of Honour.*

Foote, Samuel 1720–77

English actor-manager and playwright. Dubbed the 'English Aristophanes', he excelled in satirical comedy at the Haymarket Theatre, which he managed. He won a limited theatrical patent as compensation when he lost a leg in a practical joke involving the Duke of York. His plays include *The Englishman in Paris* (1753) and *The Minor* (1760).

83 So she went into the garden to cut a cabbage-leaf, to make an apple-pie; and at the same time a great she-bear coming up the street, pops its head into the shop. 'What! no soap?' So he died and she very imprudently married the barber; and there were present the Picninnies, and the Joblillies, and the Garyulies, and the Grand Panjandrum himself, with the little round button at top; and they all fell to playing the game of catch-as-catch-can till the gunpowder ran out of the heels of their boots.
Responding to a challenge from the actor Charles Macklin that there was no speech he could not repeat from memory after just one hearing. Macklin had to acknowledge defeat. Foote's phrases 'no soap' and 'the grand Panjandrum' became widely adopted.
Quoted in Maria Edgeworth *Harry and Lucy* (1825), vol.2.

Forbes, (Malcolm Stevenson) 'Steve', Jr 1947–

US publisher. He is President and Chief Executive Officer of Forbes and Editor-in-Chief of *Forbes* magazine and ran for the Republican presidential nomination in 1996 and 2000.

84 People who never get carried away, should be.
1976 In *Town and Country*, Nov.

85 It is unfortunate we can't buy many business executives for what they are worth and sell them for what they think they are worth.
Quoted in David Mahoney *Confessions of a Street-Smart Manager* (1988).

Ford, Anna 1943–

English television news presenter.

86 Let's face it, there are no plain women on television.
1979 In the *Observer*, 23 Sep.

Ford, Ford Madox originally Ford Hermann Hueffer 1873–1939

English writer and editor. He was associated with the modernist movement, and launched the *English Review* and later the *Transatlantic Review*. His best-known novels are *The Good Soldier* (1915) and the *Parade's End* (1924–8) tetralogy.

87 God knows that the lesson we learn from life is that our very existence in the nature of things is a perpetual harming of somebody else—if only because every mouthful of food that we eat is a mouthful taken from somebody else.
1911 *Ancient Lights*, dedication.

88 I should say that Rossetti was a man without principles at all, who earnestly desired to find salvation along the lines of least resistance.
1911 Of Dante Gabriel Rossetti. *Memories and Impressions.*

89 You cannot be absolutely dumb when you live with a person unless you are an inhabitant of the North of England or the State of Maine.
1915 *The Good Soldier*, pt.3, ch.4.

90 Alas, it does indeed seem a monstrous thing, but after all, what is chaste in Constantinople may have the aspect of lewdness in Liverpool, and what in Liverpool may pass for virtue in Constantinople is frequently regarded as vice.
1915 Letter to John Lane, 17 Dec.

91 Only two classes of books are of universal appeal. The very best and the very worst.
   1924 *Joseph Conrad, a Personal Remembrance*, pt.1.

92 We used to say that a passage of good style began with a fresh, usual word, and continued with fresh, usual words to the end; there was nothing more to it.
   1924 *Joseph Conrad, a Personal Remembrance*, pt.3.

93 We agreed that the novel is absolutely the only vehicle for the thought of our day.
   1924 *Joseph Conrad, a Personal Remembrance*, pt.3.

94 I have always had the greatest contempt for novels written with a purpose. Fiction should render, not draw morals. But…I sinned against my gods to the extent of saying that I was going—to the level of the light vouchsafed me—to write a work that should have for its purpose the obviating of all future wars.
   1934 On *Parade's End*.

Ford, Henry 1863–1947
US automobile engineer and manufacturer. In 1903 he started the Ford Motor Company, pioneering 'assembly line' mass-production techniques for his famous Model T (1908–9), 15 million of which were produced up to 1928.

95 History is more or less bunk. It's tradition.
   1916 Interview, *Chicago Tribune*, May.

96 Any color—so long as it's black.
   Of the Model T Ford. Quoted in Allan Nevins *Ford* (1957), vol.2.

97 Exercise is bunk. If you are healthy, you don't need it: if you are sick, you shouldn't take it.
   Attributed.

Ford, Henry 1917–87
US businessman, grandson of Henry Ford, president of the Ford Motor Co from 1945 and chairman from 1960. He introduced many modernizing measures.

98 My name is on the building.
   His habitual justification for having the last word. Recalled on his death, 29 Sep 1987.

Ford, John c.1586–c.1640
English dramatist, who collaborated with Dekker, Fletcher, Rowley and Webster. His works include *The Broken Heart* (1633), *'Tis Pity She's a Whore* (1633) and *Perkin Warbeck* (1634), a historical play.

99 I am…a mushroom
   On whom the dew of heaven drops now and then.
   1633 *The Broken Heart*, act 1, sc.3.

1 The joys of marriage are the heaven on earth,
   Life's paradise, great princess, the soul's quiet,
   Sinews of concord, earthly immortality,
   Eternity of pleasures; no restoratives
   Like to a constant woman.
   1633 *The Broken Heart*, act 2, sc.2.

2 He hath shook hands with time.
   1633 *The Broken Heart*, act 5, sc.2.

3 Nice philosophy
   May tolerate unlikely arguments,
   But heaven admits no jest.
   1633 *'Tis Pity She's a Whore*, act 1, sc.1.

4 'Tis my destiny
   That you must either love, or I must die.
   1633 *'Tis Pity She's a Whore*, act 1, sc.2.

5 Busy opinion is an idle fool.
   1633 *'Tis Pity She's a Whore*, act 5, sc.3.

6 Why, I hold fate
   Clasped in my fist, and could command
      the course
   Of time's eternal motion, hadst thou been
   One thought more steady than an ebbing sea.
   1633 *'Tis Pity She's a Whore*, act 5, sc.4.

7 Of one so young, so rich in nature's store,
   Who could not say, 'tis pity she's a whore?
   1633 *'Tis Pity She's a Whore*, act 5, sc.6.

8 Tell us, pray, what devil
   This melancholy is, which can transform
   Men into monsters.
   1638 *The Lady's Trial*, act 3, sc.1.

Ford, Lena Guilbert 1870–1916
English songwriter.

9 Keep the Home-fires burning,
   While your hearts are yearning,
   Though your lads are far away
   They dream of Home.
   There's a silver lining
   Through the dark clouds shining;
   Turn the dark cloud inside out,
   Till the boys come Home.
   1914 'Till the Boys Come Home', a wartime anthem (music by Ivor Novello).

Ford, Richard 1944–
US writer. He has edited anthologies and written short stories and novels, including *The Sportswriter* (1986) and *Independence Day* (1996, Pulitzer Prize).

10 If there's another thing that sportswriting teaches you, it is that there are no transcendent themes in life. In all cases things are here and they're over, and that has to be enough.
   1986 *The Sportswriter*, ch.1.

11 Married life requires shared mystery even when all the facts are known.
   1986 *The Sportswriter*, ch.5.

12 Leaving reminds us what we can part with and what we can't, then offers us something new to look forward to, to dream about.
   1992 'An Urge for Going', in *Harper's*, Feb.

13 Humans generally get out the gist of what they need to say right at the beginning, then spend forever qualifying, contradicting, burnishing or taking important things back. You rarely miss anything by cutting most people off after two sentences.
   2006 *The Lay of the Land*.

14 You're only good if you can do bad and decide not to.
   2012 *Canada*.

15 Most things don't stay the way they are very long.
   2012 *Canada*.

Ford, Rob(ert Bruce) 1969–
Canadian politician and businessman. He attracted controversy as Mayor of Toronto (2010–14) for his flamboyant behaviour and after admitting to drunkenness and taking illegal drugs.

16 What I compare bike lanes to is swimming with the sharks. Sooner or later you're going to get bitten. And every year we have dozens of people that get hit by cars or trucks. Well, no wonder: roads are built for buses, cars, and trucks, not for people on bikes. My heart bleeds for them when I hear someone gets killed, but it's their own fault at the end of the day.
2007 Speaking as a Toronto city councillor, 7 Mar.

17 Yes, I have smoked crack cocaine. But do I? Am I an addict? No. Have I tried it? Probably in one of my drunken stupors, probably approximately about a year ago.
2013 Press conference, 5 Nov.

Foreman, George 1949–
US boxer, world heavyweight champion (1973–4, 1994–5).

18 A boxer never sees the big one that hits him.
Quoted in Colin Jarman *The Guinness Dictionary of Sports Quotations* (1990).

Forgy, Howell Maurice 1908–83
US naval chaplain.

19 Praise the Lord and pass the ammunition.
1941 At Pearl Harbor, 7 Dec. Reported in the *New York Times*, 1 Nov 1942, and used as a song title by Frank Loesser, 1942.
▶ See Blacker 137:42.

Formby, George 1904–61
English entertainer. He developed a music-hall act featuring a ukulele and comic songs which translated well to film, and became one of Britain's most popular pre-war stars.

20 When I'm Cleaning Windows.
1936 Title of song (with Harry Gifford and Fred E Cliffe), first featured in the film *Keep Your Seats Please*.

21 It's me Auntie Maggie's home-made remedy
Guaranteed never to fail
Now that's the stuff that will do the trick
It's sold at ev'ry chemist for 'one and a kick'.
1941 'Auntie Maggie's Remedy' (with Eddie Latta), song featured in the film *Turned Out Nice Again*.

Forster, E(dward) M(organ) 1879–1970
English novelist and critic, a member of the Bloomsbury circle. His novels include *Howards End* (1910) and *A Passage to India* (1924). *Maurice* (written 1913–14), on homosexuality, was published posthumously in 1971. He was a prolific essayist and critic.

22 Here is the heart of our island: the Chilterns, the North Downs, the South Downs radiate hence. The fibres of England unite in Wiltshire, and did we condescend to worship her, here should we erect our national shrine.
1907 *The Longest Journey*, ch.13.

23 A Room with a View.
1908 Title of novel.

24 They are our gates to the glorious and the unknown. Through them we pass out into adventure and sunshine, to them, alas! we return.
1910 On railway termini. *Howards End*, ch.2.

25 It will be generally admitted that Beethoven's Fifth Symphony is the most sublime noise that has ever penetrated into the ear of man.
1910 *Howards End*, ch.5.

26 He believed in sudden conversion, a belief which may be right, but which is peculiarly attractive to the half-baked mind.
1910 *Howards End*, ch.6.

27 She felt that those who prepared for all the emergencies of life beforehand may equip themselves at the expense of joy.
1910 *Howards End*, ch.7.

28 The poor cannot always reach those whom they want to love, and they can hardly ever escape from those whom they no longer love.
1910 *Howards End*, ch.7.

29 Personal relations are the important thing for ever and ever, and not this outer life of telegrams and anger.
1910 *Howards End*, ch.19.

30 Only connect! That was the whole of her sermon. Only connect the prose and the passion, and both will be exalted, and human love will be seen at its height. Live in fragments no longer.
1910 *Howards End*, ch.22.

31 Death destroys a man: the idea of death saves him.
1910 *Howards End*, ch.27.

32 There is much to be said for apathy in education.
1913–14 *Maurice* (published 1971), ch.1.

33 Religion is far more acute than science, and if it only added judgement to insight, would be the greatest thing in the world.
1913–14 *Maurice* (published 1971), ch.44.

34 'I don't think I understand people very well. I only know whether I like or dislike them.' 'Then you are an Oriental.'
1924 *A Passage to India*, ch.2.

35 The so-called white races are really pinko-grey.
1924 *A Passage to India*, ch.7.

36 Nothing in India is identifiable, the mere asking of a question causes it to disappear or to merge in something else.
1924 *A Passage to India*, ch.8.

37 The echo began in some indescribable way to undermine her hold on life. Coming at a moment when she chanced to be fatigued, it had managed to murmur, 'Pathos, piety, courage—they exist, but are identical, and so is filth. Everything exists, nothing has value.'
1924 *A Passage to India*, ch.14.

38 Yes—oh dear yes—the novel tells a story.
1927 *Aspects of the Novel*, ch.2.

39 *Ulysses*…is a dogged attempt to cover the universe with mud, an inverted Victorianism, an attempt to make crossness and dirt succeed where sweetness and light failed, a simplification of the human character in the interests of Hell.
1927 Of James Joyce's 1922 novel. *Aspects of the Novel*, ch.6.

40 They go forth into a world…of men who are as various as the sands of the sea; into a world of whose richness and subtlety they have no conception. They go forth into it with well-developed bodies, fairly developed minds, and undeveloped hearts.

1936 On public schoolboys. *Abinger Harvest*, 'Notes on English Character'.

41 It is not that the Englishman can't feel—it is that he is afraid to feel.
1936 *Abinger Harvest*, 'Notes on English Character'.

42 It is frivolous stuff, and how rare, how precious is frivolity! How few writers can prostitute all their powers! They are always implying 'I am capable of higher things.'
1936 *Abinger Harvest*, 'Ronald Firbank'.

43 The historian must have a third quality as well: some conception of how men who are not historians behave. Otherwise he will move in a world of the dead.
1936 *Abinger Harvest*, 'Captain Edward Gibbon'.

44 Works of art, in my opinion, are the only objects in the material universe to possess internal order, and that is why, though I don't believe that only art matters, I do believe in Art for Art's sake.
1951 *Two Cheers for Democracy*, 'Art for Art's Sake'.

45 I do not believe in Belief... Lord I disbelieve—help thou my unbelief.
1951 *Two Cheers for Democracy*, 'What I Believe'.

46 I hate the idea of causes, and if I had to choose between betraying my country and betraying my friend, I hope I should have the guts to betray my country.
1951 *Two Cheers for Democracy*, 'What I Believe'.

47 So two cheers for democracy: one because it admits variety and two because it permits criticism. Two cheers are quite enough: there is no occasion to give three. Only Love the Beloved Republic deserves that.
1951 *Two Cheers for Democracy*, 'What I Believe'. The phrase 'Love the Beloved Republic' is taken from Swinburne's poem 'Hertha'.

48 Think before you speak is criticism's motto; speak before you think creation's.
1951 *Two Cheers for Democracy*, 'Raison d'être of Criticism'.

49 Creative writers are always greater than the causes that they represent.
1951 *Two Cheers for Democracy*, 'Gide and George'.

50 I would suggest that the only books that influence us are those for which we are ready, and which have gone a little farther down our particular path than we have yet got ourselves.
1951 *Two Cheers for Democracy*, 'Books That Influenced Me'.

51 One was left, too, with a gap in Christianity: the canonical gospels do not record that Christ laughed or played. Can a man be perfect if he never laughs or plays? Krishna's jokes may be vapid, but they bridge a gap.
1953 *The Hill of Devi*, 'Gokul Ashtami'.

Foster, Sir George 1847–1931

Canadian politician.

52 These somewhat troublesome days when the great Mother Empire stands splendidly isolated in Europe.
1896 Speech in the House of Commons, 16 Jan. *The Times* reported the speech under the heading of 'Splendid Isolation', 22 Jan.

Foster, Stephen Collins 1826–64

US songwriter. His 125 compositions include 'The Old Folks at Home', 'Camptown Races' and 'Jeannie with the Light Brown Hair', but despite their success, he died in poverty and obscurity.

53 Gwine to run all night,
Gwine to run all day,
I'll bet my money on de bob-tail nag,
Somebody bet on de bay.
1850 'Camptown Races', chorus.

54 Way down upon the Swanee River,
Far, far away,
There's where my heart is turning ever;
There's where the old folks stay.
1851 'The Old Folks at Home'.

55 I dream of Jeannie with the light brown hair,
Floating, like a vapour, on the soft summer air.
1854 'Jeannie with the Light Brown Hair'.

56 Beautiful dreamer, wake unto me,
Starlight and dewdrop are waiting for thee.
1864 'Beautiful Dreamer'.

Foster, Vince(nt W, Jr) 1945–93

US lawyer. Deputy Counsel in the Clinton White House.

57 I was not meant for the spotlight of public life in Washington. Here running people down is considered sport.
1993 Note found after his suicide. Reported in the *New York Times*, 13 Aug.

Foucault, Michel 1926–84

French philosopher and historian of ideas.

58 For the nineteenth century, the initial model of madness would be to believe oneself to be God, while for the preceding centuries it had been to deny God.
1967 *Madness and Civilization*.

Fowles, John Robert 1926–2005

English novelist. He scored a cult success with *The Magus* (1965, revised 1977), and consolidated his reputation as an ambitious experimental writer with *The French Lieutenant's Woman* (1969, filmed 1981).

59 All perfect republics are a perfect nonsense. The craving to risk death is our last great perversion. We come from night, we go into night. Why live in night?
1965 *The Magus*, ch.19.

60 And if you are wise you will never pity the past for what it did not know, but pity yourself for what it did.
1965 *The Magus*, ch.24.

61 That is the great distinction between the sexes. Men see objects, women see the relationship between objects... It is an extra dimension of feeling which we men are without and one that makes war abhorrent to all real women—and absurd.
1965 *The Magus*, ch.52.

62 In essence the Renaissance was simply the green end of one of civilization's hardest winters.
1969 *The French Lieutenant's Woman*, ch.10.

63 We all write poems; it is simply that poets are the ones who write in words.
1969 *The French Lieutenant's Woman*, ch.19.

64 The more abhorrent a news item the more comforting it was to be the recipient since the fact that it had happened elsewhere proved that it had not happened

here, was not happening here, and would therefore never happen here.
1974 *The Ebony Tower*, 'Poor Koko'.

65 Cricket remains for me the game of games, the sanspareil, the great metaphor, the best marriage ever devised of mind and body... For me it remains the Proust of pastimes, the subtlest and most poetic, the most past-and-present; whose beauty can lie equally in days, in a whole, or in one tiny phrase, a blinding split second.
Quick Singles, 'Vain Memories'. Quoted in Helen Exley *Cricket Quotations* (1992).

66 The diary will really try and tell people who you are and what you were. The alternative is writing nothing, or creating a totally lifeless, as it is leafless, garden.
2003 *The Journals: Volume 1*.

67 One degrades oneself sometimes in the effort not to be lonely.
2003 After a late night socializing. In *The Journals: Volume 1*, 24 Dec 1950.

Fox, Charles James 1749–1806

English Liberal statesman. He formed an administration with Lord North in 1783, and on its failure became Pitt's leading parliamentary adversary. He was a strong opponent of the war with France, and an advocate of non-intervention.

68 How much the greatest event it is that ever happened in the world—and how much the best.
1779 On the fall of the Bastille. Letter to Richard Fitzpatrick, 30 Jul.

69 The worst of a revolution is a restoration.
1785 House of Commons, 10 Dec.

70 I die happy.
1806 Last words. Quoted in Lord John Russell *Life and Times of C J Fox*, vol.3 (1860), ch.9.

Fox, George 1624–91

English itinerant Puritan preacher and writer, who was imprisoned for dissent. He was the founder of Society of Friends (known as 'Quakers').

71 One morning, as I was sitting by the fire, a great cloud came over me, and a temptation beset me, and I sate still... And as I sate still under it and let it alone, a living hope rose in me, and a true voice arose in me which cried: There is a living God who made all things. And immediately the cloud and temptation vanished away, and the life rose over it all, and my heart was glad, and I praised the living God.
1648 *Journal of George Fox*.

72 Walk cheerfully over the world, answering that of God in everyone.
1656 *Journal of George Fox*.

Fox, Michael J. originally Michael Andrew Fox 1961–

US film actor. The star of such popular films as *Back to the Future* (1985) and *Bright Lights, Big City* (1988), his film career was cut short in the late 1990s by Parkinson's disease although he has continued to make guest appearances in popular television series and to work as a voice-over artist.

73 Do the right thing, and then do the next right thing, and that will lead you to the next right thing after that.
2012 Quoted in *Huff Post*, 5 Apr.

74 With Parkinson's, it's like you're in the middle of the street and you're stuck there in cement shoes and you know a bus is coming at you, but you don't know when. You think you can hear it rumbling, but you have a lot of time to think. And so you just don't live that moment of the bus hitting you until it happens. There's all kinds of room in that space.
2011 In *Good Housekeeping*, June issue.

Frame, Janet Paterson also known as Jean Paterson Frame 1924–2004

New Zealand poet and writer. She was misdiagnosed as schizophrenic, and spent eight years in psychiatric hospitals. Her autobiographical trilogy *To the Is-land* (1982), *An Angel at My Table* (1984) and *The Envoy from Mirror City* (1985) was made into an award-winning film by Jane Campion.

75 What use the green river, the gold place, if time and death pinned human in the pocket of my land not rest from taking underground the green all-willowed and white rose and bean flower and morning-mist picnic of song in pepper-pot breast of thrush?
1961 *Owls Do Cry*, pt.1, ch.4.

76 From the first place of liquid darkness, within the second place of air and light, I set down the following record with its mixture of fact and truths and memories of truths and its direction always toward the Third Place, where the starting point is myth.
1982 *To the Is-land*, ch.1, 'In the Second Place'.

77 I was born...with ready-made parents and a sister and brother who had already begun their store of experience, inaccessible to me except through their language and the record, always slightly different, of our mother and father, and as each member of the family was born, each, in a sense with memories on loan, began to supply the individual furnishings of each Was-land, each Is-land, and the hopes and dreams of the Future.
1982 *To the Is-land*, ch.1, 'In the Second Place'.

78 The word *permanent*...had its own kind of revenge on those who misused it, for the Bible said that nothing was permanent and everything came and went.
1982 *To the Is-land*, ch.2, 'Toward the Is-Land'.

France, Anatole pseudonym of Jacques Anatole François Thibault 1844–1924

French novelist, poet and essayist, who won the Nobel prize for literature in 1921. Along with Émile Zola, he championed the cause of Dreyfus.

79 *Le bon critique est celui qui raconte les aventures de son âme au milieu des chefs-d'oeuvres.*
The good critic is one who recognizes the adventures of his own soul in great works of art.
1892 *La Vie littéraire*, préface.

80 *Le livre est l'opium de l'Occident.*
Books are the opium of the West.
1892 *La Vie littéraire*, préface.
▶ See Marx 578:24.

81 *La faim et l'amour sont les deux axes du monde.*
Hunger and love are the two axes of the world.
1892 *La Vie littéraire*, pt.3.

82 *L'histoire est condamnée, par un vice de nature, au mensonge.*

History is condemned, by a defect of nature, to lies.
1892 *La Vie littéraire*, pt.17.

83 *Les vérités découvertes par l'intelligence demeurent stériles.*
Truths discovered by intelligence are sterile.
1892 *La Vie littéraire*, pt.21.

84 *Je tiens à mon imperfection comme à ma raison d'être.*
I hold on to my imperfection as tightly as my reason for being.
1894 *Le Jardin d'Epicure*.

85 *Il y a toujours un moment où la curiosité devient un péché, et le diable s'est toujours mis du côté des savants.*
There is always a moment when curiosity becomes a sin and the devil is always on the side of the learned.
1894 *Le Jardin d'Epicure*.

86 *L'histoire n'est pas une science, c'est un art. On n'y réussit que par l'imagination.*
History is not a science. It is an art. One can succeed in it only through the imagination.
1894 *Le Jardin d'Epicure*.

87 To disarm the strong and arm the weak would be to change the social order which it's my job to preserve. Justice is the means by which established injustices are sanctioned.
1901 *Crainquebille*.

88 *Le poireau, c'est l'asperge du pauvre.*
The leek is the asparagus of the poor.
1906 *Crainquebille*.

89 *La majestueuse égalité des lois, qui interdit au riche comme au pauvre de coucher sous les ponts, de mendier dans les rues et de voler du pain.*
The majestic equality of laws forbids the rich as well as the poor to sleep under bridges, to beg in the streets and to steal bread.
1910 *Le Lys rouge*.

Pope Francis originally Jorge Mario Bergoglio 1936–

Argentinian priest. Born in Buenos Aires, of Italian parents, he was ordained a priest in 1969. He served as Provincial Superior of the Society of Jesus (1973–9) before becoming Archbishop of Buenos Aires (1998–2013) and a Cardinal (2001). He succeeded Benedict XVI as Pope in 2013.

90 This is what I want, a poor Church for the poor.
2013 First audience at the Vatican, *NBC News*, 16 Mar.

91 Throwing away food is like stealing from the table of those who are poor and hungry.
2013 Papal audience, 5 Jun.

92 Inconsistency on the part of pastors and the faithful between what they say and what they do, between word and manner of life, is undermining the Church's credibility.
2014 Quoted in *AWAKE!*, Feb.

93 Depicting the Pope as a sort of Superman, a star, is offensive to me… the Pope is a man who laughs, cries, sleeps calmly, and has friends like everyone else. A normal person.
2014 In *Corriere della Serra*, 5 Mar.

94 The Internet, in particular, offers immense possibilities for encounter and solidarity; this is something truly good, a gift from God.
2014 Quoted on CNN, 23 Jan.

Francis I 1494–1547

King of France (1515–47) after his father-in-law Louis XII. The chief feature of his reign was his military conflict with Emperor Charles V.

95 *De toutes choses ne m'est demeuré que l'honneur et la vie qui est saulve.*
Of all I had, only honour and life have been spared.
1525 Letter to his mother, Louise of Savoy, after his defeat and capture by Charles V at Pavia, 24 Feb. Collected in *Collection des documents inédits sur l'histoire de France* (1847), vol.1.

96 *Souvent femme varie,*
Mal habil qui s'y fie
Woman is often fickle,
Foolish the man who trusts her.
Couplet scratched by the King on the glass of a window at Chambord. Quoted in Vincent Cronin *Louis XI V* (1964), p.175.

97 But is he a patriot for me?
On being assured of the loyalty of a candidate for high office. The phrase was later used as a title by John Osborne for his 1965 play.

St Francis of Assisi c.1181–1226

Italian monk and saint, founder of the Franciscan order. The son of a wealthy merchant, in 1206 he renounced his patrimony and became a hermit, attracting followers who rejected all forms of property. His works include sermons, ascetic treatises and hymns.

98 *Bene veniat soror mea mors.*
Welcome, my sister Death.
1226 Last words. Quoted in Thomas of Celano *Life of St Francis* (c.1245), bk.2, ch.163.

99 Lord, make me an instrument of Your peace.
Where there is hatred, let me sow love;
Where there is injury, pardon;
Where there is doubt, faith;
Where there is despair, hope;
Where there is darkness, light;
Where there is sadness, joy.

O divine Master, grant that I may not so much seek
To be consoled as to console;
To be understood as to understand;
To be loved as to love.
For it is in giving that we receive;
It is in pardoning that we are pardoned;
And it is in dying that we are born to eternal life.
Attributed prayer, traditionally known as the 'Prayer of St Francis'.

Francis, Dick (Richard Stanley) 1920–2010

English jockey and writer. In the Grand National of 1956 he was on the point of winning when his horse collapsed. Subsequently he became a writer of popular thrillers with a racing background.

1 I approach chapter one each year with a deeper foreboding than I ever felt facing Becher's.
Quoted in Colin Jarman *The Guinness Dictionary of Sports Quotations* (1990).

Frank, Anne 1929–45

German Jewish diarist, whose diary covers her time in hiding in Amsterdam. She died in Bergen–Belsen concentration camp.

2 It was a terrible time through which I was living. The war raged about us, and nobody knew whether or not he would be alive the next week.
1944 Diary entry, 25 Mar.

3 I want to go on living even after death!
   1944 Diary entry, 4 Apr.

4 We all live with the objective of being happy; our lives are all different and yet the same.
   1944 Diary entry, 6 Jul.

Frankenthaler, Helen 1928–2011

US artist, a key figure in the Abstract Expressionism school. Her innovative, colourful works include *The Human Edge* (1967). The Museum of Modern Art in New York presented her retrospective in 1989.

5 A picture that is beautiful, or that comes off, or that works, looks as if it was all made at one stroke.
   1972 Quoted in Ian Crofton (ed) *A Dictionary of Art Quotations* (1988).

6 I follow the rules until I go against them all.
   1993 On translating her large, lyrical abstracts from paintings to prints. In the *Washington Times*, 16 Apr.

Franklin, Benjamin 1706–90

US statesman, author and scientist, whose popular *Poor Richard's Almanack* first appeared in 1732. He proved that lightning and electricity are identical and suggested that buildings should be protected by lightning conductors. He was involved in the Declaration of Independence (1775), and helped secure British recognition (1783).

7 The body of
   Benjamin Franklin, printer,
   (Like the cover of an old book,
   Its contents worn out,
   And stripped of its lettering and gilding)
   Lies here, food for worms!
   Yet the work itself shall not be lost,
   For it will, as he believed, appear once more
   In a new
   And more beautiful edition,
   Corrected and amended
   By its Author!
   1728 Proposed epitaph for himself.

8 To lengthen thy Life, lessen thy Meals.
   1733 *Poor Richard's Almanack*, Jun.

9 He that drinks fast, pays slow.
   1733 *Poor Richard's Almanack*, Aug.

10 Necessity never made a good bargain.
   1735 *Poor Richard's Almanack*, Apr.

11 Nothing but Money,
   Is sweeter than Honey.
   1735 *Poor Richard's Almanack*, Jun.

12 Time is money.
   1748 *Advice to a Young Tradesman*.

13 Fond Pride of Dress is sure an Empty Curse;
   E'er Fancy you consult, consult your Purse.
   1751 *Poor Richard Improved*, May.

14 A little neglect may breed mischief…for want of a nail, the shoe was lost; for want of a shoe, the horse was lost; and for want of a horse the rider was lost.
   1758 *Poor Richard's Almanack*, preface.

15 Some punishment seems preparing for a people who are so ungratefully abusing the best Constitution and the best king that any nation was ever blessed with.
   1768 Speech in London during the Wilkes riots, May.

16 There never was a good war or a bad peace.
   1773 Letter, 11 Sep.

17 We must indeed all hang together or, most assuredly, we shall all hang separately.
   1776 On signing the Declaration of Independence, 4 Jul.

18 Furnished as all Europe is with Academies of Science, with nice instruments and the spirit of experimentation, the progress of human knowledge will be rapid and discoveries made of which we have at present no conception. I begin to be almost sorry I was born since I cannot have the happiness of knowing what will be known a hundred years hence.
   1783 Letter to Sir Joseph Banks, President of the Royal Society, 27 Jul.

19 In this world nothing can be said to be certain, except death and taxes.
   1789 Letter to Jean Baptiste Le Roy, 13 Nov.
   ▶ See Defoe 269:81.

20 What is the use of a new-born child?
   Reply when questioned as to the use of a new invention. Quoted in J Parton *Life and Times of Benjamin Franklin* (1864), pt.4, ch.17.

Franklin, (Stella Marian Sarah) Miles *pseudonym* Brent of Bin Bin 1879–1954

Australian novelist, journalist and feminist. After writing *My Brilliant Career* (1901), she moved to the US (1906) then England (1915), returning to Australia in 1927. Other work includes the *Brent of Bin* series (1928), the autobiographical *My Career Goes Bung* (1946) and critical essays.

21 This was life—my life—my career, my brilliant career!
   1901 *My Brilliant Career*, ch.5.

22 Grannie remarked that I might have the spirit of an Australian but I had by no means the manners of a lady.
   1901 *My Brilliant Career*, ch.19.

23 I am proud that I am an Australian, a daughter of the Southern Cross, a child of the mighty bush. I am thankful I am a peasant, a part of the bone and muscle of my nation, and earn my bread by the sweat of my brow, as man was meant to do. I rejoice I was not born a parasite, one of the blood-suckers who loll on velvet and satin, crushed from the proceeds of human sweat and blood and souls.
   1901 *My Brilliant Career*, ch.38.

Franz Josef I 1830–1916

Emperor of Austria (1848) and King of Hungary (1867).

24 Farewell youth!
   1848 On signing the document that made him Emperor, following the abdication of Ferdinand. Attributed, quoted in A J P Taylor *From Napoleon to the Second International* (1993).

Franzen, Jonathan 1959–

US novelist. *The Corrections* (2001) won the National Book Award.

25 It's the fate of most Ping-Pong tables in home basements eventually to serve the ends of other, more desperate games.
   2001 *The Corrections*.

26 Just as the camera draws a stake through the heart of serious portraiture, television has killed the novel of social reportage.
   2002 *How to Be Alone*.

27 Nice people don't necessarily fall in love with nice people.
   2010 *Freedom.*

28 Integrity's a neutral value. Hyenas have integrity, too. They're pure hyena.
   2010 *Freedom.*

29 Seriously, the world is changing so quickly that if you had any more than eighty years of change I don't see how you could stand it psychologically.
   2012 In *The Guardian*, 30 Jan.

Fraser, Lady Antonia 1932–
English writer, best known for her historical biographies.

30 As with all forms of liberation, of which the liberation of women is only one example, it is easy to suppose in a time of freedom that the darker days of repression can never come again.
   1984 *The Weaker Vessel*, epilogue.

31 I love hearing details of writers' craft, as cannibals eat the brains of clever men to get cleverer.
   2011 *Must You Go?: My Life With Harold Pinter.*

Fraser, George MacDonald 1925–2008
English writer of historical fiction.

32 I have observed, in the course of a dishonest life, that when a rogue is outlining a treacherous plan, he works harder to convince himself than to move his hearers.
   1969 *Flashman.*

Fraser, Major Sir Keith Alexander 1867–1935
British politician. After his army career he became MP for Leicestershire (1918–23) and a Justice of the Peace for Ross and Cromarty.

33 I never met anyone in Ireland who understood the Irish question, except one Englishman who had been there only a week.
   1919 House of Commons, May.

Fraser, (John) Malcolm 1930–2015
Australian politician. He became an MP in 1955 and leader of the Liberals in 1975. He formed a caretaker government until becoming Prime Minister. Defeated in the 1983 elections, he retired soon afterwards.

34 Life is not meant to be easy.
   1971 The Deakin Lecture, Melbourne, 20 Jul.

Frayne, Trent 1918–2012
Canadian sportswriter.

35 It is an axiom of sports that the legs go first. For sportswriters, it's the enthusiasm.
   1990 *The Tales of an Athletic Supporter.*

Frederick II 1194–1250
Holy Roman Emperor, last of the Hohenstaufen line. His plans to consolidate his power in Italy were frustrated by the Lombard cities and the popes. During the Fifth Crusade in 1228 he took possession of Jerusalem, and crowned himself king there (1229).

36 Our work is to present things that are as they are.
   De Ate Venandi cum Avibus.

Frederick II, the Great 1712–86
King of Prussia from 1740. He fought against the Austrians in the War of the Austrian Succession (1740–8) and seized Silesia in 1741. In 1772 he shared in the first partition of Poland. By the time of his death, Prussia had become a world power.

37 Troops always ready to act, my well-filled treasury, and the liveliness of my disposition—these were my reasons for making war on Maria Theresa.
   1741 Letter to Voltaire.

38 Rascals, would you live for ever?
   1757 Attributed, to hesitant guards at the Battle of Kolin, 18 Jun.
   ▶ See Daly 261:19.

39 *Chassez les préjugés par la porte, ils rentreront par la fenêtre.*
   Drive out prejudices through the door, and they will return through the window.
   1771 Letter to Voltaire, 19 Mar.

40 *Vanité des Vanités; Vanité de la géométrie.*
   Vanity of vanities! Vanity of mathematics!
   1778 Letter to Voltaire, 25 Jan, protesting against the increasing use of mathematical calculation in engineering projects, which he saw as theory triumphing over practical experience.

41 My people and I have come to an agreement that satisfies us both. They are to say what they please, and I am to do what I please.
   Attributed.

Freed, Arthur *pseudonym of* Arthur Grossman 1894–1973
US producer and lyricist. He came to Hollywood in 1929 and worked for MGM, producing many well-known musicals. As a lyricist he frequently worked with composer Nacio Herb Brown.

42 I'll walk down the lane with a happy refrain
   And singin' just singin' in the rain.
   1929 'Singin' in the Rain' featured in *Hollywood Revue of 1929* and other films, including the famous musical of the same title (music by Nacio Herb Brown).

43 You Are My Lucky Star.
   1935 Title of song featured in *Broadway Melody of 1936* (music by Nacio Herb Brown).

Freeman, Bud (Lawrence) 1906–91
US jazz saxophonist. He was a leading figure in the evolution of the Chicago style in the 1920s and 1930s.

44 I think audiences come to hear older musicians like me just to see if we can pick up a horn without falling over.
   1989 *Crazeology: The Autobiography of a Chicago Jazzman* (as told to Robert Wolf), ch.9.

Freeman, Edward Augustus 1823–92
English historian, Regius Professor of Modern History at Oxford. Among his prolific output were his *History of Federal Government* (1863) and *History of the Norman Conquest* (1867–76).

45 This would be a grand land if only every Irishman would kill a negro, and be hanged for it.
   1881 Of America. Letter to F H Dickinson from New Haven, 4 Dec.

46 Nobody can't do nothing never at all for Ireland—you can't help people against their will; that's what it comes to—let it go, let it go.
   1882 Letter to Edith Thompson, 29 Jan.

47 History is past politics, and politics is present history.
  1886 *Methods of Historical Study*.

Freeman, John 1880–1929
English poet.

48 In that sharp light the fields did lie
  Naked and stone-like; each tree stood
  Like a tranced woman, bound and stark,
  Far off the wood
  With darkness ridged the riven dark.
  1916 'Stone Trees'.

49 Than these November skies
  Is no sky lovelier. The clouds are deep;
  Into their grey the subtle spies
  Of colour creep,
  Changing their high austerity to delight,
  Till ev'n the leaden interfolds are bright.
  1916 'November Skies'.

50 It was the lovely moon—she lifted
  Slowly her white brow among
  Bronze cloud-waves that ebbed and drifted
  Faintly, faintlier afar.
  1916 'It Was the Lovely Moon'.

Freleng, Friz born Isadore Freleng 1905–95
US cartoon director.

51 That's all folks!
  Porky Pig's stammered trademark, sign-off line for Warner Brothers' *Looney Tunes*.

French, Marilyn 1929–2009
US writer and feminist scholar. She enjoyed a huge success with her bestselling first novel, *The Women's Room* (1977), and has written further novels and feminist studies.

52 'I hate discussions of feminism that end up with who does the dishes,' she said. So do I. But at the end, there are always those damned dishes.
  1977 *The Women's Room*, bk.1, ch.21.

53 Whatever they may be in public life, whatever their relations with men, in their relations with women, all men are rapists, and that's all they are. They rape us with their eyes, their laws, and their codes.
  1977 *The Women's Room*, bk.5, ch.19.

Freud, Sir Clement 1924–2009
English writer and broadcaster.

54 If you resolve to give up smoking, drinking and loving, you don't actually live longer; it just seems longer.
  1964 In the *Observer*, 27 Dec.

Freud, Sigmund 1856–1939
Austrian neurologist, founder of psychoanalysis. He published his controversial but influential ideas in such works as *The Interpretation of Dreams* (1900), *The Psychopathology of Everyday Life* (1904) and *Ego and Id* (1923).

55 I am actually not at all a man of science… I am by temperament nothing but a conquistador, an adventurer.
  1900 Letter to Wilhelm Fliess, Feb.

56 Congratulations and bouquets keep pouring in, as if the role of sexuality had been suddenly recognised by His Majesty, the interpretation of dreams confirmed by the Council of Ministers, and the necessity of the psychoanalytic therapy of hysteria carried by a two-thirds majority in Parliament.
  1902 Letter to Wilhelm Fliess, 11 Mar, describing the public enthusiasm in Vienna that greeted his appointment to an associate professorship at the age of 45.

57 The principal task of civilisation, its actual raison d'être, is to defend us against nature.
  1903 *Introductory Lectures*.

58 A woman who is very anxious to get children always reads 'storks' for 'stocks'.
  1904 *The Psychopathology of Everyday Life*.

59 *Die Anatomie ist das Schicksal.*
  Anatomy is destiny.
  1924 *Collected Works*, vol.5.

60 At bottom God is nothing more than an exalted father.
  1927 *The Future of an Illusion*.

61 The more the fruits of knowledge become accessible to men, the more widespread is the decline of religious belief.
  1927 *The Future of an Illusion*.

Friday, Nancy 1937–
US feminist and writer, whose works include *My Secret Garden* (1973), *My Mother, My Self* (1977) and *Women on Top* (1991).

62 If you believe in the maternal instinct and fail at mother love, you fail as a woman. It is a controlling idea that holds us in an iron grip.
  1977 *My Mother, My Self*, ch.1.

63 The older I get, the more of my mother I see in myself.
  1977 *My Mother, My Self*, ch.1.

Friedan, Betty (Elizabeth) Naomi née Goldstein 1921–2006
US feminist and writer, founder of the National Organization for Women (1966) and author of the seminal feminist text *The Feminine Mystique* (1963).

64 The problem lay buried, unspoken, for many years in the minds of American women. It was a strange stirring, a sense of dissatisfaction, a yearning that women suffered in the middle of the twentieth century in the United States. Each suburban wife struggled with it alone. As she made the beds, shopped for groceries, matched slipcover material, ate peanut butter sandwiches with her children, chauffeured Cub Scouts and Brownies, lay beside her husband at night—she was afraid to ask even of herself the silent question—'Is this all?'
  1963 *The Feminine Mystique*, ch.1, 'The Problem that has No Name'.

65 Women, even though they are almost too visible as sex objects in this country, are invisible people.
  1969 Speech at First National Conference for Repeal of Abortion Laws, Chicago.

66 Motherhood will only be a joyous and responsible human act when women are free to make, with full conscious choice and full human responsibility, the decisions to become mothers.
  1969 Speech at First National Conference for Repeal of Abortion Laws, Chicago.

Friedman, Kinky (Richard Samet) 1944–
US country singer and humorist.

67 I'm flattered at the possibility of being the Democratic pallbearer, I mean standard-bearer.
2005 His response when invited to join the Democrats while running as an independent gubernatorial candidate, in the *Austin American-Statesman*, 12 Aug.

Friedman, Milton 1912–2006
US economist. A leading monetarist, his work includes the permanent income theory of consumption, and the role of money in determining events, particularly the US Great Depression. He was awarded the Nobel prize for economics in 1976.

68 Economics as a positive science is a body of tentatively accepted generalizations about economic phenomena that can be used to predict the consequences of changes in circumstances.
1953 'The Methodology of Positive Economics' in *Essays in Positive Economics*.

69 There is no such thing as a free lunch.
1973 Lecture. The phrase is thought to have been coined anonymously, perhaps referring to the 19c US tradition of supplying food in bars to patrons buying drinks.

70 The price that the market sets on the services of our resources is similarly affected by a bewildering mixture of chance and choice. Frank Sinatra's voice was highly valued in twentieth-century United States. Would it have been highly valued in twentieth-century India, if he had happened to be born and to live there?
1981 *Free to Choose* (with Rose Friedman).

71 No major institution in the US has so poor a record of performance over so long a period as the Federal Reserve, yet so high a public reputation.
1988 'The Fed Has No Clothes', in *The Wall Street Journal*, 15 Apr.

Friedrich, Carl J(oachim) 1901–84
German political theorist. He taught at the universities of Harvard and Heidelberg.

72 To be an American is an ideal, while to be a Frenchman is a fact.
1987 In *Time*, 9 Nov.

Friedrich, Caspar David 1774–1840
German painter, who depicted landscape as vast and desolate expanses in which man is a melancholy spectator.

73 Just as the pious man prays without speaking a word and the Almighty hearkens unto him, so the artist with true feelings *paints* and the sensitive man understands and recognizes it.
Quoted in S Hinz *Caspar David Friedrich in Briefen und Bekenntnissen* (1968).

74 The Divine is everywhere, even in a grain of sand, here I have represented it in bull-rushes.
Remark to the German artist Peter Cornelius, quoted in S Hinz *Caspar David Friedrich in Briefen und Bekenntnissen* (1968).

75 Close your bodily eye, so that you may see your picture first with the spiritual eye. Then bring to the light of day that which you have seen in the darkness so that it may react on others from the outside inwards.
Quoted in *Caspar David Friedrich 1774–1840*, Tate Gallery (1972).

76 Despite what even many artists appear to believe, art is not and should not be merely a skill. It should actually be completely and utterly the language of our feelings, our frame of mind; indeed, even of our devotion and our prayers.
Quoted in *Caspar David Friedrich 1774–1840*, Tate Gallery (1972).

77 The artist should not only paint what he sees before him, but also what he sees within him. If, however, he sees nothing within him, then he should also omit to paint that which he sees before him.
Quoted in *Caspar David Friedrich 1774–1840*, Tate Gallery (1972).

78 Every true work of art must express a distinct feeling.
Quoted in William Vaughn *Romantic Art* (1978).

Friel, Brian 1929–
Northern Irish playwright and short-story writer.

79 Two such wonderful phrases—'I understand perfectly' and 'That is a lie'—a précis of life, aren't they?
1983 *The Communication Cord*.

80 Do you want the whole countryside to be laughing at us?—women of our years?—mature women, *dancing?*
1990 *Dancing at Lughnasa*.

Frisch, Max Rudolph 1911–91
Swiss writer, novelist and playwright. His novels include *I'm Not Stiller* (1954), *Homo Faber* (1957), and *A Wilderness of Mirrors* (1964). His plays include *The Firebugs* (1953) and *Andorra* (1961, translated 1962).

81 *Ich kann nur berichten, was ich weiß.*
I can only report on what I know.
1957 *Homo Faber*, pt.1.

82 *Technik…Kniff, die Welt so einzurichten, dass wir sie nicht erleben müssen.*
Technology…the knack of so arranging the world that we don't have to experience it.
1957 *Homo Faber*, pt.2.

83 *Kein Mensch, wenn er die Welt sieht, die sie ihm hinterlassen, versteht seine Eltern.*
No one understands their parents when we look at the world that they have bequeathed us.
1961 *Andorra*, sc.9.

84 *Ich habe kein Gemüt, sondern Angst.*
I have no comfort, only anxiety.
1961 *Andorra*, sc.9.

85 *Man kann sich seinen Vater nicht wählen.*
A person cannot choose his father.
1961 *Andorra*, 10.

86 *Ich gehe ins Theater ja auch nicht als Voyeur.*
I do not go into the theatre as a voyeur.
1967 *Biographie*.

Frohman, Charles 1860–1915
US theatre manager. Among his many successful productions were several plays by J M Barrie.

87 Why fear death? It's the most beautiful adventure in life.
1915 Last words, paraphrasing a line in J M Barrie's *Peter Pan*, said to the actress Rita Jolivet as the *Lusitania* went down after being torpedoed by a German submarine, 7 May.

Fromm, Erich 1900–80

German-born US psychoanalyst and author, who emigrated in 1934 to the US, where he practised psychoanalysis and lectured at various institutions.

88 The pace of science forces the pace of technique. Theoretical physics forces atomic energy on us; the successful production of the fission bomb forces upon us the manufacture of the hydrogen bomb. We do not choose our problems, we do not choose our products; we are pushed, we are forced—by what? By a system which has no purpose and goal transcending it, and which makes man its appendix.
1955 *The Sane Society*.

Frost, Robert Lee 1874–1963

US poet, whose work is rooted in New England. He established his reputation with *A Boy's World* (1913) and *North of Boston* (1914) and won Pulitzer Prizes in 1924, 1931, 1937 and 1943.

89 Most of the change we think we see in life
Is due to truths being in and out of favour.
1914 *North of Boston*, 'The Black Cottage'.

90 Something there is that doesn't love a wall,
That sends the frozen-ground-swell under it,
And spills the upper boulders in the sun;
And makes gaps even two can pass abreast.
1914 *North of Boston*, 'Mending Wall'.

91 Before I built a wall I'd ask to know
What I was walling in or walling out,
And to whom I was like to give offence.
1914 *North of Boston*, 'Mending Wall'.

92 Part of a moon was falling down the west,
Dragging the whole sky with it to the hills.
1914 *North of Boston*, 'The Death of the Hired Man'.

93 'Home is the place where, when you have to go there,
They have to take you in.'
'I should have called it
Something you somehow haven't to deserve.'
1914 *North of Boston*, 'The Death of the Hired Man'.

94 A sentence is a sound in itself on which sounds called words may be strung.
1914 Letter to John Bartlett, 22 Feb.

95 I shall be telling this with a sigh
Somewhere ages and ages hence:
Two roads diverged in a wood, and I—
I took the one less traveled by,
And that has made all the difference.
1916 'The Road Not Taken'.

96 We love the things we love for what they are.
1916 'Hyla Brook'.

97 The question that he frames in all but words
Is what to make of a diminished thing.
1916 'The Oven Bird'.

98 I'd like to go by climbing a birch tree
And climb black branches up a snow-white trunk
Toward heaven, till the tree could bear no more,
But dipped its top and set me down again.
That would be good both going and coming back.
One could do worse than be a swinger of birches.
1916 'Birches'.

99 They listened at his heart.
Little—less—nothing!—and that ended it.
No more to build on there. And they, since they
Were not the one dead, turned to their affairs.
1916 'Out, Out—'.

1 No wonder poets sometimes have to *seem*
So much more businesslike than businessmen.
Their wares are so much harder to get rid of.
1923 'New Hampshire'.

2 He knew too well for any earthly use
The line where man leaves off and nature starts,
And never overstepped it save in dreams.
1923 'New Hampshire'.

3 Never tell me that not one star of all
That slip from heaven at night and softly fall
Has been picked up with stones to build a wall.
1923 'A Star in a Stoneboat'.

4 Some say the world will end in fire,
Some say in ice.
From what I've tasted of desire
I hold with those who favour fire.
But if I had to perish twice,
I think I know enough of hate
To say that for destruction ice
Is also great
And would suffice.
1923 'Fire and Ice', complete poem.

5 The woods are lovely, dark and deep.
But I have promises to keep,
And miles to go before I sleep,
And miles to go before I sleep.
1923 'Stopping by Woods on a Snowy Evening'.

6 I have been one acquainted with the night.
1928 'Acquainted with the Night'.

7 It is this backward motion toward the source,
Against the stream, that most we see ourselves in.
The tribute of the current to the source.
1928 'West-Running Brook'.

8 The land may vary more;
But wherever the truth may be—
The water comes ashore,
And the people look at the sea.
1928 'Neither Far Out Nor in Deep'.

9 A poet is a person who thinks there is something special about a poet and about his loving one unattainable woman. You'll usually find he takes the physical out on whores. I am defining a romantic poet—and there is no other kind. An unromantic poet is a self-contradiction.
1930 Letter to Louis Untermeyer, 6 Jun.

10 Writing free verse is like playing tennis with the net down.
1935 Address at Milton Academy, Mass, 17 May.

11 What brought the kindred spider to that height,
Then steered the white moth thither in the night?
What but design of darkness to appall?—
If design govern in a thing so small.
1936 'Design'.

12 I never dared be radical when young
For fear it would make me conservative when old.
1936 'Ten Mills, 1. Precaution'.

13 Like a piece of ice on a hot stove the poem must ride on its own melting. A poem may be worked over once it is in being, but may not be worried into being.
1939 'The Figure a Poem Makes', preface to *Collected Poems*.

14 Happiness Makes Up in Height for What It Lacks in Length.
1942 Title of poem.

15 The land was ours before we were the land's.
She was our land more than a hundred years
Before we were her people.
1942 'The Gift Outright'.

16 And were an epitaph to be my story
I'd have a short one ready for my own.
I would have written of me on my stone:
I had a lover's quarrel with the world.
1942 'The Lesson for Today'.

17 We dance round in a ring and suppose,
But the Secret sits in the middle and knows.
1942 'The Secret Sits', complete poem.

18 I have never started a poem yet whose end I knew. Writing a poem is discovering.
1955 In the *New York Times*, 7 Nov.

19 Forgive, O Lord, my little jokes on Thee
And I'll forgive Thy great big one on me.
1959 'The Preacher', complete poem.

20 Poetry is a way of taking life by the throat.
Quoted in Elizabeth S Sergeant *Robert Frost: The Trial By Existence* (1960).

21 Summoning artists to participate
In the august occasions of the state
Seems something artists ought to celebrate.
1961 'For John F Kennedy: His Inauguration', 20 Jan. Snow-blindness prevented the aged poet from reading beyond the first three lines on the occasion.

22 Courage is in the air in bracing whiffs.
1961 'For John F Kennedy: His Inauguration', 20 Jan.

23 Education is… hanging around until you've caught on.
Recalled on his death, 29 Jan 1963.

24 The mind skating circles around itself as it moves forward.
His definition of style. Recalled on his death, 29 Jan 1963.

25 The right reader of a good poem can tell the moment it strikes him that he has taken an immortal wound—that he will never get over it.
Recalled on his death, 29 Jan 1963.

26 Poetry is what is lost in translation. It is also what is lost in interpretation.
Quoted in Louis Untermeyer *Robert Frost: A Backward Look* (1964).

Froude, James Anthony 1818–94

English writer and historian, who resigned his Oxford fellowship after controversy over his early novels. He wrote a *History of England from the Fall of Wolsey to the Spanish Armada* (12 vols, 1856–69).

27 Wild animals never kill for sport. Man is the only one to whom the torture and death of his fellow-creatures is amusing in itself.
1886 *Oceana*.

Fry, C(harles) B(urgess) 1872–1956

English all-round sportsman, who represented his country in athletics, cricket and soccer. As a cricketer, he played 26 Tests for England, some as captain. After World War II he served as India's delegate to the League of Nations and declined an offer of the throne of Albania.

28 It is a standing insult to sportsmen to have to play under a rule which assumes that players intend to trip, hack and push their opponents, and to behave like cads of the most unscrupulous kidney. The lines marking a penalty area are a disgrace to the playing fields of a public school.
1907 Quoted in Colin Jarman *The Guinness Dictionary of Sports Quotations* (1990).

29 In football it is widely acknowledged that if both sides agree to cheat, cheating is fair.
1911 Quoted in Colin Jarman *The Guinness Dictionary of Sports Quotations* (1990).

30 The game is so full of plot-interest and drama.
Of rugby union. Quoted in E H D Sewell *Rugger: The Man's Game* (1950).

Fry, Christopher *pseudonym of* Christopher Harris 1907–2005

English playwright. His early poetic drama was succeeded by comedies and tragi-comedies such as *A Phoenix Too Frequent* (1946) and *Venus Observed* (1950).

31 The Lady's Not for Burning.
1949 Play title, subsequently reworked by Margaret Thatcher in the form 'The lady's not for turning' at the Conservative Party Conference, 1980.

32 What after all
Is a halo? It's only one more thing to keep clean.
1949 *The Lady's Not for Burning*, act 1.

33 Where in this small-talking world can I find
A longitude with no platitude?
1949 *The Lady's Not for Burning*, act 3.

34 I hope
I've done nothing so monosyllabic as to cheat.
A spade is never so merely a spade as the word
Spade would imply.
1950 *Venus Observed*, act 1.

35 The Dark Is Light Enough.
1954 Title of play.

Fry, Elizabeth 1780–1845

English Quaker prison reformer who devoted her life to prison and asylum reform at home and abroad.

36 Does capital punishment tend to the security of the people? By no means. It hardens the hearts of men, and makes the loss of life appear light to them; and it renders life insecure, inasmuch as the law holds out that property is of greater value than life.
Quoted in Rachel E Cresswell and Katharine Fry *Memoir of the Life of Elizabeth Fry* (1848).

37 Punishment is not for revenge, but to lessen crime and reform the criminal.
Quoted in Rachel E Cresswell and Katharine Fry *Memoir of the Life of Elizabeth Fry* (1848).

Fry, Roger Eliot 1866–1934

English artist and art critic, who championed modern artists such as Cézanne, organizing the first London exhibition of Post-Impressionists in 1910. He devised an aesthetic theory of 'significant form'.

38 The trouble with Moore is that he knows what a work of art is, and is trying to make one.
  c.1930 Of Henry Moore. Quoted in Robert Medley *Drawn from the Life: a Memoir* (1983).

39 Art is significant deformity.
  Quoted in Virginia Woolf *Roger Fry* (1940), ch.8.

Fry, Stephen John 1957–
English comedian, actor, writer and television presenter.

40 Cynical is the name we give those we fear may be laughing at us.
  1994 *The Hippopotamus*.

41 I was also absolutely convinced, if I want to put it more petulantly, that if there was a God his caprice, malice, arbitrariness and sheer lack of taste made him repulsive to me.
  1997 *Moab Is My Washpot*.

42 No adolescent ever wants to be understood, which is why they complain about being misunderstood all the time.
  1997 *Moab Is My Washpot*.

43 It is a cliché that most clichés are true, but then like most clichés, that cliché is untrue.
  1997 *Moab Is My Washpot*.

44 Sex without smiling is as sickly and as base as vodka and tonic without ice.
  1997 *Moab Is My Washpot*.

45 Only my tongue, sir.
  2004 When asked by a security guard at Heathrow Airport whether he had any sharp objects on him. Quoted in the *Observer*, 6 Jun.

46 This is the point. One technology doesn't replace another, it complements. Books are no more threatened by Kindle than stairs by elevators.
  2009 On Twitter, 11 Mar.

47 God once had Bach and Michelangelo on his side, he had Mozart, and now who does he have? People with ginger whiskers and tinted spectacles who reduce the glories of theology to a kind of sharing, you know?
  2009 *The Blasphemy Debate*, quoted in *The Guardian*.

48 Nature admits no hierarchy of beauty or usefulness or importance.
  2009 *Last Chance to See: In the Footsteps of Douglas Adams*.

49 Wine can be a better teacher than ink, and banter is often better than books.
  2010 *The Fry Chronicles: An Autobiography*.

50 I feel sorry for straight men. The only reason women will have sex with them is that sex is the price they are willing to pay for a relationship with a man, which is what they want.
  2010 *Attitude*, October issue.

51 We are not nouns, we are verbs. I am not a thing—an actor, a writer—I am a person who does things—I write, I act—and I never know what I'm going to do next. I think you can be imprisoned if you think of yourself as a noun.
  Attributed.

52 Compromise is a stalling between two fools.
  Attributed.

Frye, Northrop 1912–91
Canadian literary critic and Episcopalian priest. His influential *Anatomy of Criticism* (1957) explores the common motifs and myths underlying literature.

53 Literature is a human apocalypse, man's revelation to man, and criticism is not a body of adjudications, but the awareness of that revelation, the last judgment of mankind.
  1963 *The Educated Imagination*, 'The Keys of Dreamland'.

54 Literature is conscious mythology: as society develops, its mythical stories become structural principles of storytelling, its mythical concepts, sun-gods and the like, become habits of metaphoric thought. In a fully mature literary tradition the writer enters into a structure of traditional stories and images.
  1971 *The Bush Garden*, 'Conclusion'.

55 Where is here?
  'Haunted by Lack of Ghosts', in David Staines (ed) *The Canadian Imagination* (1977).

56 Most of my writing consists of an attempt to translate aphorisms into continuous prose.
  Quoted in Richard Kostelanetz, 'The Literature Professors' Literature Professor', in *The Michigan Quarterly Review*, Fall 1978.

57 The knowledge that you can have is inexhaustible, and what is inexhaustible is benevolent. The knowledge that you cannot have is of the riddles of birth and death, of our future destiny and the purposes of God. Here there is no knowledge, but illusions that restrict freedom and limit hope. Accept the mystery behind knowledge: It is not darkness but shadow.
  1988 Address, Metropolitan United Church, Toronto, 10 Apr, quoted by Alexandra Johnston in *Vic Report*, spring 1991.

58 Even the human heart is slightly left of centre.
  Quoted by Paul Wilson in 'Growing Up with Orwell', in *The Idler*, Jul–Aug 1989.

Fuentes, Carlos 1928–2012
Mexican novelist and playwright, press secretary with the UN and Ambassador to France (1975–7). His works include short stories, and novels such as *Terra nostra* (1975), *The Old Gringo* (1985) and *The Years with Laura Diaz* (1999).

59 Yo soy un artista. El placer de la carne le resta fuerzas a mi vocación pictórica, prefiero sentir que los jugos de mi sexo fluyen hacia un cuadro, lo irrigan, lo fertilizan, lo realzan; cástrame el goce de la carne, satisfáceme el goce del arte.
  I am an artist. The pleasure of the flesh robs strength from my artistic vocation, I prefer to feel my sexual juices flow toward a painting, wash over it, fertilize it, realize it; the delights of the flesh castrate me, the delights of art satisfy me.
  1975 *Terra nostra*, 'El cronista'.

60 What America does best is to understand itself. What it does worst is to understand others.
  1986 In *Time*, 16 Jun.

Fulbright, J(ames) William 1905–95
US Democratic politician, lawyer and author. As Chairman of the Senate Committee on Foreign Relations, he became a major critic of the Vietnam War (1964–75).

61 We have the power to do any damn fool thing we want to do, and we seem to do it every 10 minutes.
1952 In *Time*, 4 Feb.

62 In a democracy dissent is an act of faith. Like medicine, the test of its value is not in its taste, but its effects.
1966 Speech to the US Senate, 21 Apr.

63 Fearful and hostile behavior is not rational but neither is it uncommon, either to individuals or to nations, including our own.
1995 On the 'arrogance of power' of US policy on Vietnam. In the *New Yorker*, 6 Mar.

Fulford, Robert 1932–
Canadian cultural commentator.

64 My generation of Canadians grew up believing that, if we were very good or very smart, or both, we would someday *graduate* from Canada.
1970 'Notebook', in *Saturday Night*, Oct.

Fuller, (Sarah) Margaret, Marchioness Ossoli 1810–50
US feminist and literary critic. She edited *Dial* (a transcendentalist journal, 1840–2) and moved to New York (1844) then Italy (1847), where she married Marquis Ossoli and was involved in the Revolution. She was shipwrecked returning to New York.

65 Beware of over-great pleasure in being popular or even beloved.
1840 Letter to her brother, 20 Dec. Collected in Alice Rossi *The Feminist Papers* (1973).

66 As the friend of the negro assumes that one man cannot, by right, hold another in bondage, should the friend of woman assume that man cannot, by right, lay even well-meant restrictions on woman.
1843 'The Great Lawsuit', in *Dial*, vol.4, Jul.

67 It is well known that of every strong woman they say she has a masculine mind.
1843 'The Great Lawsuit', in *Dial*, vol.4, Jul.

Fuller, Peter 1947–90
English art critic, writer and founder of the magazine *Modern Painters*.

68 It is only a mild exaggeration to say that now no one wants Fine Artists, except Fine Artists, and that neither they nor anyone else have the slightest idea what they should be doing, or for whom they should be doing it.
1981 *Beyond the Crisis in Art*.

Fuller, R(ichard) Buckminster 1895–1983
US architect, inventor, engineer and philosopher, whose revolutionary technological designs reflect his personal vision of a better-designed and more efficient future. In 1962 he became Norton Professor of Poetry at Harvard.

69 God, to me, it seems,
is a verb
not a noun
proper or improper.
1940 Poem, published in *No More Secondhand God* (1963).
▶ See Hugo 437:45.

70 I just invent, then wait until man comes around to needing what I've invented.
1964 On his innovative geodesic domes. In *Time*, 10 Jun.

71 Either war is obsolete or men are.
1966 In the *New Yorker*, 8 Jan.

72 I am a passenger on the spaceship, Earth.
1969 *Operating Manual for Spaceship Earth*, ch.1.

73 Now there is one outstandingly important fact regarding Spaceship Earth, and that is that no instruction book came with it.
1969 *Operating Manual for Spaceship Earth*, ch.4.

74 If we do more with less, our response will be adequate to take care of everybody.
1972 In *Playboy*.

Fuller, Roy Broadbent 1912–91
English poet and novelist. His work is marked by careful construction and acute observation.

75 As horrible thoughts,
Loud fluttering aircraft slope above his head
At dusk.
The ridiculous empires break like biscuits.
1942 'The Middle of a War'.

76 The poets get a quizzical ahem.
They reflect time, I am the very ticking.
1944 'A Wry Smile'.

77 Anyone happy in this age and place
Is daft or corrupt. Better to abdicate
From a material and spiritual terrain
Fit only for barbarians.
1954 'Translation'.

Fuller, Thomas 1608–61
English antiquarian and divine. His 11-volume *Church History of Britain* (1655) was attacked as a 'rhapsody'. The unfinished *Great Worthies of England*, a biographical miscellany, was published by his son in 1661.

78 Know most of the rooms of thy native country before thou goest over the threshold thereof.
1642 *The Holy and Profane State*, bk.2, ch.4, 'Of Travelling'.

79 *Mon Mam Cymbry*. That is, Anglesea is the Mother of Wales.
1662 *History of the Worthies of England*, 'Anglesea'. The saying is an old one, meaning that Anglesey's corn is enough to sustain all Wales.

Fuller, Thomas 1654–1734
English physician and writer.

80 Bacchus hath drowned more men than Neptune.
1732 *Gnomologia*, no.830.

81 Borrowed garments never fit well.
1732 *Gnomologia*, no.1008.

82 Eat-well is drink-well's brother.
1732 *Gnomologia*, no.1357.

83 Fine cloth is never out of fashion.
1732 *Gnomologia*, no.1537.

84 God sends meat, and the devil sends cooks.
1732 *Gnomologia*, no.1687.

85 Good clothes open all doors.
1732 *Gnomologia*, no.1705.

86 It is in vain to mislike the current fashion.
1732 *Gnomologia*, no.2968.

87 The present fashion is always handsome.
   1732 *Gnomologia*, no.4718.

88 Often drunk, and seldom sober
   Falls like the leaves in October.
   1732 *Gnomologia*, no.6219.

89 It signifies nothing to play well and lose.
   1732 Quoted in Colin Jarman *The Guinness Dictionary of Sports Quotations* (1990).

Furthman, Jules 1888–1966

US screenwriter. His credits include *Shanghai Express* (1932), *Mutiny on the Bounty* (1935), *To Have and Have Not* (1945) and *The Big Sleep* (1946).

90 You know you don't have to act with me, Steve. You don't have to say anything and you don't have to do anything. Not a thing. Oh, maybe just whistle. You know how to whistle, don't you, Steve? You just put your lips together—and blow.
   1945 Lauren Bacall as Slim to Humphrey Bogart (Steve) in *To Have and Have Not* (with William Faulkner).

Fuseli, Henry 1741–1825

Swiss-born British painter and art critic. He was a key figure of the Romantic movement.

91 Art, like love, excludes all competition and absorbs the man.
   1789 *Aphorisms on Art*, no.3 (published 1831).

92 The superiority of the Greeks seems not so much the result of climate and society, as of the simplicity of their end and the uniformity of their means.
   1789 *Aphorisms on Art*, no.148 (published 1831).

93 Art among a religious race produces reliques; among a military one, trophies, among a commercial one, articles of trade.
   1789 *Aphorisms on Art*, no.149 (published 1831).

94 The forms of virtue are erect, the forms of pleasure undulate.
   1789 *Aphorisms on Art*, no.194 (published 1831).

95 Selection is the invention of the landscape painter.
   1789 *Aphorisms on Art*, no.237, (published 1831).

Fyffe, Will 1885–1947

Scottish comedian, singer and actor. He wrote several sketches for Harry Lauder and when they were rejected performed them himself, thereby launching a long and successful career on stage and in film.

96 I belong to Glasgow
   Dear old Glasgow town!
   But what's the matter with Glasgow?
   For it's going round and round.
   I'm only a common old working chap,
   As anyone can see,
   But when I get a couple of drinks on a Saturday,
   Glasgow belongs to me.
   1921 'I Belong to Glasgow', chorus.

Fyleman, Rose 1877–1957

English children's writer.

97 There are fairies at the bottom of our garden.
   1918 *Fairies and Chimneys*, 'The Fairies'.

g

Gabor, Dennis 1900–79

Hungarian-born British physicist. Gabor studied and worked in Germany but left in 1933 to become professor of electronics at Imperial College, London. He did important work on the electronic microscope and is generally recognized as the main contributor to the discovery of holography.

1 Till now man has been up against Nature: from now on he will be up against his own nature.
   1964 *Inventing the Future*.

2 The most important and urgent problems of the technology of today are no longer the satisfactions of the primary needs or of archetypal wishes, but the reparation of the evils and damages wrought by the technology of yesterday.
   1970 *Innovations*.

Gabor, Zsa Zsa 1919–

Hungarian-born US actress, sister of Eva Gabor. Her films include *Moulin Rouge* (1953), *Touch of Evil* (1958) and *Arrivederci Baby* (1966).

3 I never hated a man enough to give him diamonds back.
   Quoted in the *Observer*, 28 Aug 1957.

4 A girl must marry for love and keep on marrying until she finds it.
   Attributed.

Gaga, Lady *pseudonym of* Stefani Joanne Angelina Germanotta 1986–

US singer-songwriter.

5 Some women choose to follow men, and some women choose to follow their dreams. If you're wondering which way to go, remember that your career will never wake up and tell you that it doesn't love you anymore.
   2010 In *Cosmopolitan*, April issue.

6 Just when I get into it, it stops. It's like a really bad orgasm.
   2011 Referring to Bing Crosby's 'White Christmas'.

7 People will always talk, so let's give them something to talk about.
   Attributed.

Gagarin, Yuri A(lekseyevich) 1934–68

Soviet cosmonaut, the first person to achieve orbital space flight, on 12 Apr 1961.

8 I could have gone on flying through space forever.
   1961 In the *New York Times*, 14 Apr.

Gainsborough, Thomas 1727–88

English portrait and landscape painter.

9 I wish you would recollect that Painting and Punctuality mix like Oil and Vinegar, and that Genius and regularity are utter Enemies and must be to the end of time.

1772 Letter to Edward Stratford, 1 May, excusing himself for not yet finishing the portrait of him and his wife.

10 We are all going to heaven, and Vandyke is of the company.
1788 Last words (attributed), quoted in William B Boulton *Thomas Gainsborough* (1905), ch.9.

Gaitskell, Hugh 1906–63

English Labour politician, Leader of the Opposition (1955–63). He opposed Eden's Suez action (1956), and refused to accept a narrow conference vote for unilateral disarmament (1960), surviving the subsequent leadership challenge.

11 Some of us will fight and fight again to save the party we love. We will fight and fight again to bring back sanity and honesty and dignity, so that our party, with its great past, may retain its glory and its greatness.
1960 Denouncing unilateralists trying to gain control of the party. Labour Party conference speech, Oct.

12 Let us not forget that we can never go farther than we can persuade at least half the people to go.
1961 Labour Party conference speech, Oct.

13 It does mean the end of Britain as an independent European state. It means the end of a thousand years of history.
1962 On Britain joining the European Community. Labour Party conference speech, Oct.

Galbraith, John Kenneth 1908–2006

Canadian-born US economist and diplomat, Professor at Harvard (1949–75), Ambassador to India (1961–3) and adviser to Presidents Kennedy and Johnson.

14 The charge that an idea is radical, impractical, or long-haired is met by showing that a prominent businessman has favored it…an additional tactic in this strategy of defense…is to assert that Winston Churchill once sponsored the particular idea. If one is challenged, a sufficiently careful investigation will show that he did.
1955 *Economics and the Art of Controversy.*

15 Few things are as immutable as the addiction of political groups to the ideas by which they have once won office.
1958 *The Affluent Society.*

16 In the affluent society, no useful distinction can be made between luxuries and necessities.
1958 *The Affluent Society.*

17 It takes a certain brashness to attack the accepted economic legends but none at all to perpetuate them. So they are perpetuated.
1960 *The Liberal Hour.*

18 Politics is not the art of the possible. It consists in choosing between the disastrous and the unpalatable.
1962 Letter to John F Kennedy, 2 Mar.
▶ See Butler 184:60.

19 The line dividing the state from what is called private enterprise, or at least from the highly organized part of it, is a traditional fiction.
1967 *The New Industrial State.*

20 The real accomplishment of modern science and technology consists in taking ordinary men, informing them narrowly and deeply and then, through appropriate organization, arranging to have their knowledge combined with that of other specialized but equally ordinary men. This dispenses with the need for genius. The resulting performance, though less inspiring, is far more predictable.
1967 *The New Industrial State.*

21 There are times in politics when you must be on the right side and lose.
1968 In the *Observer*, 11 Feb.

22 It is the good fortune of the affluent country that the opportunity cost of economic discussion is low and hence it can afford all kinds.
1971 *Economics, Peace, and Laughter.*

23 In a world where for pedagogic and other purposes a very large number of economists is required, an arrangement which discourages many of them from rendering public advice would seem to be well conceived.
1971 *Economics, Peace, and Laughter.*

24 Much discussion of money involves a heavy overlay of priestly incantation.
1975 *Money*, p.4.

25 Much of the world's work, it has been said, is done by men who do not feel quite well. Marx is a case in point.
1977 *The Age of Uncertainty*, ch.3.

26 We have escapist fiction…why not escapist biography?
1980 In the *New York Times*, 27 Jul.

27 Speeches in our culture are the vacuum that fills a vacuum.
1984 Speech at the American University, Washington DC. Quoted in *Time* magazine, 18 Jun.

Galeano, Eduardo 1940–

Uruguayan writer and journalist. His books include *Days and Nights of Love and War* (1978) and the trilogy *Memory of Fire* (1985–8).

28 In the house of words was a table of colors. They offered themselves in great fountains and each poet took the color he needed: lemon yellow or sun yellow, ocean blue or smoke blue, crimson red, blood red, wine red.
1991 *The Book of Embraces.*

Galen or *Claudius Galenus* c.130–c.201AD

Greek physician, imperial physician to Marcus Aurelius, Commodus and Severus. He wrote extensively on medical and philosophical matters, and his theories have been highly influential.

29 Much music marreth men's manners.
Quoted in Roger Ascham *Toxophilus* (1545).

Galilei, Galileo 1564–1642

Italian astronomer, mathematician and physicist, credited with anticipating Newton's laws of motion. He constructed the first astronomical telescope, and controversially argued that the earth revolved around the sun.

30 *Eppur si muove.*
Nevertheless, it moves.
1632 Attributed muttered remark, after being compelled to publicly renounce his arguments against a geocentric universe. This famous quotation is almost certainly an invention.

31 Light held together by moisture.
Attributed, a description of wine.

Gallagher, Noel 1967–
English rock star, founder member of the band Oasis.

32 Some might say they don't believe in heaven
Go and tell it to the man who lives in hell.
1995 'Some Might Say'.

33 I would hope we mean more to people than putting money in a church basket and saying ten Hail Marys on a Sunday. Has God played Knebworth recently?
1997 On the attraction of Oasis. In the *New Musical Express*, 12 Jul.

34 The funny thing is, that mouthing off three years ago about how we were going to be the biggest band in the world, we actually went and done it. And it was a piece of piss.
1998 Quoted in the *Guinness Rockopedia*.

35 He's like a man with a fork, in a world of soup.
2009 Referring to his brother Liam Gallagher.

36 We were working class, and we were the lowest. There's a level underneath that now: the can't-be-bothered working class.
2011 On BBC *Newsnight*, 11 Oct.

Gallico, Paul William 1897–1976
US journalist, novelist and short-story writer. His works include *The Snow Goose* (1941) and *The Poseidon Adventure* (1969).

37 College football today is one of the last great strongholds of genuine old-fashioned American hypocrisy.
1938 Farewell to Sport.

38 When in Doubt—Wash.
1950 Jennie, ch.5, chapter title. Peter, having turned into a cat, is taught the proper etiquette.

39 I have covered boxing, promoted boxing, watched it, thought about it, and after long reflection I cannot find a single thing that is good about it either from the point of view of participant or spectator.
Quoted in Edith Summerskill *The Ignoble Art* (1956).

40 No one can be as calculatedly rude as the British, which amazes Americans, who do not understand studied insult and can only offer abuse as a substitute.
1962 In the *New York Times*, 14 Jan.

Galloway, George 1954–
Scottish politician, MP for Labour (1987–2005) and later, having been expelled from the party, Respect (2005–10, 2012–).

41 I saw 'New Labour' conceived, watched it gestate, witnessed its birth and growth. Now I fervently hope I will be present at its death.
2004 I'm Not the Only One.

Galloway, Janice 1955–
Scottish writer. She worked as a teacher, but became a full-time writer after the success of her first novel *The Trick Is to Keep Breathing* (1989), chronicling a mental breakdown. Other works include the short-story collection *Blood* (1991) and the novel *Clara* (2002).

42 The Trick Is to Keep Breathing.
1989 Title of first novel.

43 I write because I hate being told HOW IT IS. I didn't realise that for a long while. I thought it was LIFE I hated: that the unfairnesses that were explained as JUST HOW IT IS were JUST HOW IT IS. BUT HOW IT IS wasn't.
1993 'Objective Truth and the Grinding Machine'. In Brown and Munro (eds) *Writers Writing* (1993).

44 Quiet book-learning in monasteries and ethereal music, sonnets and courtly love—that stuff is all fantasy and veneer… You couldn't afford to let the beauty of the thing seduce you too far or you forgot the truth and the truth was always hard as iron bloody bars.
1994 Foreign Parts, ch.7.

Gallup, George Horace 1901–84
US statistician and public opinion expert. He developed the Gallup polls for testing public opinion, which proved their worth by correctly predicting Franklin Roosevelt's 1936 election victory.

45 Polling is merely an instrument for gauging public opinion. When a president or any other leader pays attention to poll results, he is, in effect, paying attention to the views of the people. Any other interpretation is nonsense.
1979 NBC news, 1 Dec.

46 I could prove God statistically.
Attributed.

Galsworthy, John 1867–1933
English novelist and playwright, best known for his series of novels *The Forsyte Saga* (1906–28). His plays, including *Strife* (1909), illustrate his interest in social and ethical issues. He was awarded the Nobel prize in 1932.

47 From all *I* can learn, he's got no business, no income, and no connection worth speaking of; but then, I know nothing—nobody tells me anything.
1906 The Man of Property, pt.1, ch.1.

48 When a Forsyte was engaged, married, or born, the Forsytes were present; when a Forsyte died—but no Forsyte had as yet died; they did not die; death being contrary to their principles, they took precautions against it, the instinctive precautions of highly vitalised persons who resent encroachments on their property.
1906 The Man of Property, pt.1, ch.1.

49 It is not good enough to spend time and ink in describing the penultimate sensations and physical movements of people getting into a state of rut, we all know them so well.
1914 On D H Lawrence's *Sons and Lovers*, in a letter to Edward Garnett, 13 Apr.

50 He was afflicted by the thought that where Beauty was, nothing ever ran quite straight, which, no doubt, was why so many people looked on it as immoral.
1920 In Chancery, pt.1, ch.13.

51 When we began this fight, we had clean hands—are they clean now? What's gentility worth if it can't stand fire?
1920 The Skin Game, act 3.

52 Slang is vigorous and apt. Probably most of our vital words were once slang.
1927 Castles in Spain and Other Screeds.

Galt, John 1779–1839
Scottish novelist and Canadian pioneer. After a failed business venture in London he travelled in the Levant (1809–11) and later turned to writing.

53 In a word, man in London is not quite so good a creature as he is out of it.
1821 The Ayrshire Legatees, ch.7, 'Discoveries and Rebellions', letter 22.

54 From the lone shieling of the misty island
Mountains divide us, and the waste of seas—
Yet still the blood is strong, the heart is Highland,
And we in dreams behold the Hebrides!
Fair these broad meads, these hoary woods are grand;
But we are exiles from our fathers' land.
1829 'Canadian Boat Song', a translation from the Gaelic attributed to Galt, published in *Blackwood's Magazine*, Sep. It has also been attributed to Walter Scott.

Galtieri, Leopoldo Fortunato 1926–2003
Argentinian soldier and politician, President of Argentina (1981–3). In 1982, he ordered the invasion of the disputed Malvinas (Falkland) Islands; their recovery by Britain led to his downfall.

55 Why are you telling me this? The British won't fight.
1982 Responding to a warning from US Secretary of State Alexander Haig about the consequence of the invasion.

Galton, Sir Francis 1822–1911
English scientist. He travelled widely in Africa and wrote *The Art of Travel* (1855), which became the explorer's standard handbook.

56 There are even times when any assumption of dignity becomes ludicrous, and the traveller must, as Mungo Park once had to do, 'lay down as a rule to make himself as useless and as insignificant as possible, as the only means of recovering his liberty'.
1855 The Art of Travel.

Gandhi, Indira Priyad Arshini 1917–84
Indian politician and Prime Minister (1966–77, 1980–4). Although a leader of the developing nations, she failed to suppress sectarian violence at home and was assassinated by Sikh extremists, members of her bodyguard.

57 Even if I die in the service of this nation, I would be proud of it. Every drop of my blood, I am sure, will contribute to the growth of this nation and make it strong and dynamic.
1984 Speech at Orissa, 31 Oct, the day before her assassination.

Gandhi, Mohandas Karamchand known as Mahatma [great soul] 1869–1948
Indian nationalist leader, who advocated peaceful non-cooperation to achieve independence, but was jailed for conspiracy (1922–4) following his civil disobedience campaign. After independence (1947), his attempts to stop the Hindu–Muslim conflict in Bengal led to his assassination by a Hindu fanatic.

58 I claim that in losing the spinning wheel we lost our left lung. We are, therefore, suffering from galloping consumption. The restoration of the wheel arrests the progress of the...disease.
1921 Speech, 13 Oct.

59 Non-violence is the first article of my faith. It is also the last article of my creed.
1922 Speech at Shahi Bag, 18 Mar.

60 Non-violence is not a garment to be put on and off at will. Its seat is in the heart, and it must be an inseparable part of our very being.
1926 War or Peace, 'Young India'.

61 What do I think of Western civilization? I think that it would be a good idea.
Attributed.

Gandhi, Sonia 1946–
Italian-born Indian politician, widow of Rajiv Gandhi and daughter-in-law of Indira Gandhi.

62 There is no question. It is my inner voice, it is my conscience.
2004 On turning down the office of Indian prime minister, 18 May.

Garbo, Greta *pseudonym of* Greta Lovisa Gustafsson 1905–90
Swedish-born actress who went to the US in 1925 with director Mauritz Stiller. Her films at MGM during the 1930s include *Queen Christina* (1933), *Anna Karenina* (1936) and *Ninotchka* (1939). She retired in 1941.

63 I want to be alone.
1932 The media have famously attributed these words to Garbo although she always denied she said them. In the film *Grand Hotel* (1932) Grusinskaya (played by Garbo) says 'I want to be left alone'.

64 One day, there's a hand that goes over the face and changes it. You look like an apple that isn't young anymore.
Quoted in *Vanity Fair*, Feb 1994.

García Márquez, Gabriel 1927–2014
Colombian novelist and journalist, awarded the Nobel prize for literature (1982). His fiction, typically set in the imaginary village of Macondo, tended to magic realism.

65 *No se le había ocurrido pensar hasta entonces que la literatura fuera el mejor juguete que se había inventado para burlarse de la gente.*
It had never occurred to him until then to think that literature was the best plaything that had ever been invented to make fun of people.
1967 Cien años de soledad (translated as *One Hundred Years of Solitude*, 1970).

66 The last optimist left in Colombia.
Attributed.

Garcilaso de la Vega, Inca 1539–1616
Peruvian soldier, translator and historian, son of a Spanish father and an Inca princess. He went to Spain in 1560 and became a soldier. His historical compositions draw on both indigenous sources and imagination.

67 *Porque allá los españoles y las otras naciones...como tienen historias divinas y humanas, saben por ellas cuándo empezaron a reinar sus Reyes y los ajenos...todo esto y mucho más saben por sus libros. Empero vosotros, que carecéis de ellos, Qué memoria tenéis de vuestras antiguallas?, Quién fue el primero de nuestros Incas?*
Over there Spaniards and other nations know from their divine and human history when their Kings and other

peoples' Kings began their reigns... Their books teach them all of this, and much more. But you, who have no books, what memories do you have of your ancient past? Who was our first Inca?
1609 *Comentarios reales* (*The Royal Commentaries of Peru*, 1688), bk.1, ch.15.

Gardner, Ava originally Lucy Johnson 1922–90

US film actress. Signed for MGM as a teenager, she achieved fame in *The Killers* (1946) and later *The Barefoot Contessa* (1954) and *Night of the Iguana* (1964). She was married to Mickey Rooney, Artie Shaw and Frank Sinatra.

68 *On the Beach* is a story about the end of the world, and Melbourne sure is the right place to film it.
1959 Alleged comment to Australian journalist Neil Jillett of the Melbourne *Age* at the shooting of a film based on the book by British–Australian novelist Nevil Shute.

69 What I'd really like to say about stardom is that it gave me everything I never wanted.
1990 *Ava: My Story*.

Gardner, John William 1912–77

US public official, Secretary of Health, Education and Welfare (1965–8). In 1970 he founded the citizens' lobby Common Force, which he chaired until his death.

70 We are all faced with a series of great opportunities—brilliantly disguised as insoluble problems.
Quoted in *Reader's Digest*, Mar 1966.

71 We get richer and richer in filthier and filthier communities until we reach a final stage of affluent misery—a crocus on a garbage heap.
1969 In the *New York Times*, 9 Oct.

Garibaldi, Giuseppe 1807–82

Italian patriot, twice forced to flee the country for his revolutionary activities. He returned in 1859 for Italy's war of liberation, leading his thousand 'Red Shirts', conquering Sicily and Naples for the unified kingdom of Italy.

72 England is a great and powerful nation, foremost in human progress, enemy to despotism, the only safe refuge for the exile, friend of the oppressed. If ever England should be so circumstanced as to require the help of any ally, cursed be the Italian who would not step forward with me in her defence.
1854 Letter, 12 Apr.

73 *Soldati, io esco da Roma. Chi vuole continuare la guerra contro lo straniero venga con me. Non posso offrigli né onori né stipendi; gli offro fame, sete, marce forzate, battaglie e morte. Chi ama la Patria me segua.*
Soldiers, I'm getting out of Rome. Anyone who wants to carry on the war against the outsiders, follow me. I can offer you neither honours nor wages, I offer you hunger, thirst, forced marches, battles and death. Anyone who loves his country, follow me.
Quoted in Giuseppe Guerzoni *Garibaldi* (1882), vol.1.

Garland, (Hannibal) Hamlin 1860–1940

US writer. He is remembered chiefly for his stories of Midwest farm life in books including *Main-Travelled Roads* (1891) and *Prairie Folks* (1892), but also wrote novels, essays and memoirs.

74 Like the main-travelled road of life it is traversed by many classes of people, but the poor and the weary predominate.
1891 *Main-Travelled Roads*, 'The Main-Travelled Road of the West'.

75 There is no gilding of setting sun or glamor of poetry to light up the ferocious and endless toil of the farmers' wives.
1899 *Boy Life on the Prairie*, 'Melons and Early Frost'.

Garner, Eric (1970–2014)

US citizen whose death when being physically restrained by NYPD officers sparked nationwide protests after a grand jury decided not to indict the men concerned.

76 I can't breathe.
2014 His protest when put in a chokehold by arresting officers, 17 Jul. Garner's last words were subsequently widely adopted by protesters criticizing the court's failure to take action in the case.

Garner, John Nance 1868–1967

US lawyer and politician, Speaker of the House (1931–3) and Vice-President under President Roosevelt (1933–41). He opposed Roosevelt's third-term candidacy and retired in 1941.

77 Worst damnfool mistake I ever made was letting myself be elected Vice-President of the United States. Should have stuck...as Speaker of the House... Gave up the second most important job in Government for eight long years as Roosevelt's spare tire.
1963 In the *Saturday Evening Post*, 2 Nov.

78 The vice-presidency isn't worth a pitcher of warm piss. It doesn't amount to a hill of beans.
Quoted in O C Fisher *Cactus Jack* (1978), ch.11.

Garrick, David 1717–79

English actor and theatre manager. He revolutionized acting with his naturalistic Shakespearean heroes and in 1747 became manager of the Drury Lane theatre, introducing many theatrical reforms.

79 Here lies Nolly Goldsmith, for shortness called Noll, Who wrote like an angel, but talked like poor Poll.
1773 Of Oliver Goldsmith. 'Impromptu Epitaph'.

80 Are these the choice dishes the Doctor has sent us? Is this the great poet whose works so content us? This Goldsmith's fine feast, who has written fine books? Heaven sends us fine meat, but the Devil sends cooks.
1777 'On Doctor Goldsmith's Characteristical Cookery'.

81 Comedy is a very serious thing.
Attributed, in conversation with the actor Jack Bannister.

Garvey, Marcus 1887–1940

Jamaican activist and advocate of black nationalism. In 1914 he founded the Universal Negro Improvement Association (UNIA). Rejecting integration, he called for a 'back to Africa' movement.

82 We are not engaged in domestic politics, in church building or in social uplift work, but we are engaged in nation building.
1922 Speech to the Principles of the Universal Negro Improvement Association, New York, 25 Nov.

83 There is no humanity before that which starts with yourself.
1923 'African Fundamentalism, a Racial Hierarchy and Empire for Negroes'.

Gaskell, Mrs Elizabeth Cleghorn née Stevenson
1810–65

English novelist. She is best known for her novels of social realism, including *North and South* (1855), in which she criticized the conditions in English factories, and *Cranford* (1851–3).

84 Their dress is very independent of fashion; as they observe, 'What does it signify how we dress here at Cranford, where everybody knows us?' And if they go from home, their reason is equally cogent, 'What does it signify how we dress here, where nobody knows us?'
1851–3 Of the Cranford ladies. *Cranford*, ch.1.

85 A man…is *so* in the way in the house!
1851–3 *Cranford*, ch.1.

Gass, William H(oward) 1924–

US novelist, literary theorist and philosopher, best known for his experimental story collection *In the Heart of the Heart of the Country* (1968). His massive autobiographical novel, *The Tunnel* (1995), was in progress for more than 20 years.

86 I love metaphor the way some people love junk food.
1977 Interview in *Paris Review*, Summer.

87 One's complete sentences are attempts, as often as not, to complete an incomplete self with words.
1977 Interview in *Paris Review*, Summer.

88 The true alchemists do not change lead into gold; they change the world into words.
2006 *A Temple of Texts*.

89 A cause is a lie with a fan club.
Attributed.

Gates, Bill (William Henry III) 1955–

US businessman and philanthropist, who founded the Microsoft Corporation with Paul Allen in 1974. In 1980 the company bought an operating system and adapted it for the IBM personal computer; the company is now the world's chief software producer for personal computers. He stepped down as chairman in 2014.

90 I think business is very simple. Profit. Loss. Take the sales, subtract the costs, you get this big positive number. The math is quite straightforward.
1993 Quoted in the *US News and World Report*, 15 Feb.

91 Technology is just a tool. In terms of getting the kids working together and motivating them, the teacher is the most important.
1997 In the *Independent on Sunday*, 12 Oct.

92 A fundamental new rule for business is that the Internet changes everything.
1999 *Business@the Speed of Thought* (co-written with Collins Hemingway).

93 The Internet is becoming the town square for the global village of tomorrow.
1999 *Business@the Speed of Thought* (co-written with Collins Hemingway).

94 If you show people the problems and you show people the solutions they will be moved to act.
2005 Speaking at Live 8 concert, quoted on BBC News, 2 Jul.

95 If geek means you're willing to study things, and if you think science and engineering matter, I plead guilty. If your culture doesn't like geeks, you are in real trouble.
2010 In *The Daily Telegraph*, 20 Oct.

96 Rich people spend a lot more money on their own problems, like baldness, than they do to fight malaria.
2010 Criticizing Italian Prime Minister Silvio Berlusconi, who was rumoured to have paid for hair transplants at a time when Italy's foreign aid contributions were deemed very low. In *The Guardian*, 28 Jan.

97 If you can't make it good, at least make it look good.
Attributed.

Gates, Robert Michael 1943–

US politician. After 26 years with the Central Intelligence Agency, he served as Secretary of Defense (2006–11).

98 Every time we have come to the end of a conflict, somehow we have persuaded ourselves that the nature of mankind and the nature of the world have changed on an enduring basis and so we have dismantled our military and intelligence capabilities. My hope is that as we wind down in Iraq and whatever the level of our commitment in Afghanistan, that we not forget the basic nature of humankind has not changed.
2009 In the *National Journal*, 22 Jan.

99 Most governments lie to each other. That's the way business gets done.
2011 CNN interview, 19 Jun.

Gauguin, Paul 1848–1903

French Post-Impressionist painter, printmaker and sculptor.

1 There are noble tones, ordinary ones, tranquil harmonies, consoling ones, others which excite by their vigour.
1885 Letter to Emile Schuffenecker.

2 Some advice: do not paint too much after nature. Art is an abstraction; derive this abstraction from nature while dreaming before it, and think more of the creation which will result than of nature.
1888 Letter to Emile Schuffenecker.

3 You may dream freely when you listen to music as well as when you look at painting. When you read a book you are the slave of the author's mind.
c.1888 *Notes Synthétiques*, quoted in J Rewald *Gauguin* (1938).

Gautier, Théophile 1811–72

French poet, novelist and critic. He propounded the theory of 'art for art's sake', and was honoured by Baudelaire. His many novels include the celebrated *Mademoiselle de Maupin* (1835).

4 *Virginité, mysticisme, mélancolie! Trois mots inconnus, trois maladies nouvelles apportées par le Christ.*
Virginity, mysticism, melancholy! Three unknown words, three new illnesses brought by Christ.
1835 *Mademoiselle de Maupin*.

5 *Hélas! Les femmes n'ont lu que le roman de l'homme et jamais son histoire.*
Alas, women have read only the novel of mankind, not the history.
1835 *Mademoiselle de Maupin*.

6 *L'orgueil sort du coeur le jour où l'amour y entre.*
Pride leaves the heart the moment love enters it.
1835 *Mademoiselle de Maupin*.

7 The religion of money is today the only one which has no unbelievers.

1860s On the France of the Second Republic. Quoted in Joanna Richardson *The Courtesans* (1967), p.2.

Gavarni *real name* Guillaume Sulpice Chevalier 1804–88
French lithographer.

8 *Les Enfants Terribles*.
The Little Terrors.
1842 Title of a series of prints.

Gay, James 1810–91
Canadian poet, the self-styled 'Poet Laureate of Canada'.

9 Hail our Great Queen in her regalia;
One foot in Canada, the other in Australia.
Attributed to Gay by William Arthur Deacon in *The Four Jameses* (1927).

Gay, John 1685–1732
English poet, best known for his extraordinarily popular *The Beggar's Opera* (1728), set to music by Pepusch. In his final years he lived chiefly with his patrons, the Duke and Duchess of Queensberry.

10 Praising all alike, is praising none.
1714 'A Letter to a Lady', l.114.

11 Life is a jest; and all things show it.
I thought so once; but now I know it.
1720 'My Own Epitaph'.

12 A woman's friendship ever ends in love.
1720 *Dione*, act 4, sc.6.

13 And when a lady's in the case,
You know, all other things give place.
1727 *Fables*, 'The Hare and Many Friends', l.41.

14 She who trifles with all
Is less likely to fall
Than she who but trifles with one.
1727 'The Coquet Mother and the Coquet Daughter'.

15 How, like a moth, the simple maid
Still plays around the flame!
1728 *The Beggar's Opera*, act 1, sc.4, air 4.

16 Do you think your mother and I should have lived comfortably so long together, if ever we had been married?
1728 *The Beggar's Opera*, act 1, sc.8.

17 Money, wife, is the true fuller's earth for reputations, there is not a spot or a stain but what it can take out.
1728 *The Beggar's Opera*, act 1, sc.9.

18 The comfortable estate of widowhood, is the only hope that keeps up a wife's spirits.
1728 *The Beggar's Opera*, act 1, sc.10.

19 If with me you'd fondly stray
Over the hills and far away.
1728 *The Beggar's Opera*, act 1, sc.13, air 16.

20 I must have women. There is nothing unbends the mind like them.
1728 *The Beggar's Opera*, act 2, sc.3.

21 To cheat a man is nothing; but the woman must have fine parts indeed who cheats a woman!
1728 *The Beggar's Opera*, act 2, sc.4.

22 How happy I could be with either,
Were t'other dear charmer away!
1728 *The Beggar's Opera*, act 2, sc.13.

23 Music might tame and civilize wild beasts, but 'tis evident it never yet could tame and civilize musicians.
1729 *Polly*.

24 From wine what sudden friendship springs!
1738 *Fables*, 'The Squire and His Cur', l.4.

Gay, Noel *pseudonym of* Richard Moxon Armitage 1898–1954
British songwriter who wrote for stage and screen. His song 'Leaning on a Lamp-Post' became one of George Formby's greatest successes.

25 I'm leaning on a lamp-post at the corner of the street
In case a certain little lady comes by.
1937 Song sung by George Formby, featured in the film *Feather Your Nest*.

Geddes, Sir Eric Campbell 1875–1937
British politician, a member of the War Cabinet in 1918. He presided over the 'Geddes Axe' committee on national expenditure in 1922.

26 The Germans, if this Government is returned, are going to pay every penny. They are going to be squeezed as a lemon is squeezed—until the pips squeak. My only doubt is not whether we can squeeze hard enough, but whether there is enough juice.
1918 Speech at Cambridge Guildhall, 10 Dec.

Gee, Maggie 1948–
English novelist. She has written a number of highly regarded literary novels.

27 There are people not spoken about, people not written about, people whose name is a way of saying they are not there. *Hibakusha*, atomic victims—the scarred who carry our scars.
1983 Of the victims of the bombing of Hiroshima and Nagasaki. *The Burning Book*, ch.1.

28 The alcohol made the present enough, it held her in its golden hand, where past and future were comprehended, where nothing mattered, nothing was lost, where everything could be known and forgiven, where she herself could be whole at last.
1994 *Lost Children*, ch.35.

Geldof, Bob 1954–
Irish rock musician and philanthropist, founder of the Boomtown Rats (1975–86). He established the pop charity Bandaid in 1984 for African famine relief, and organized simultaneous Live Aid concerts in Philadelphia and London in 1985. He was awarded an honorary KBE in 1986.

29 Most people get into bands for three very simple rock and roll reasons: to get laid, to get fame, and to get rich.
1977 In *Melody Maker*, 27 Aug.

30 Irish Americans are about as Irish as Black Americans are African.
1986 In the *Observer*, 22 Jun.

31 Rock 'n' roll is instant coffee.
Quoted in David Pickering *Brewer's Twentieth Century Music* (1994).

Gellhorn, Martha Ellis 1908–98
US journalist and novelist. She covered numerous wars throughout the world between 1936 and 1985 and also wrote essays and fiction. Her first husband (1940–5) was Ernest Hemingway.

32 I see mysteries and complications wherever I look, and I have never met a steadily logical person.
1959 *The Face of War*, introduction.

33 It would be a bitter cosmic joke if we destroy ourselves due to atrophy of the imagination.
1959 *The Face of War*, introduction.

34 Gradually I came to realize that people will more readily swallow lies than truth, as if the taste of lies was homey, appetizing: a habit.
1959 *The Face of War*, introduction.

35 You define your own horror journey, according to your taste. My definition of what makes a journey wholly or partially horrible is boredom. Add discomfort, fatigue, strain in large amounts to get the purest-quality horror, but the kernel is boredom. I offer that as a universal test of travel; boredom, called by any other name, is why you yearn for the first available transport out. But what bores whom?... The threshold of boredom must be like the threshold of pain, different in all of us.
1979 *Travels with Myself and Another*.

36 We savaged them, though they had never hurt us, and we cannot find it in our hearts, our honor, to give them help—because the government of Vietnam is Communist. And perhaps because they won.
1986 On the Vietnamese. *The Face of War* (rev edn), 'The War in Vietnam—Vietnam Again, 1986'.

Gell-Mann, Murray 1929–

US physicist. He received the 1969 Nobel Prize in Physics for his work on the theory of elementary particles.

37 If I have seen further than others, it is because I am surrounded by dwarfs.
2009 Parodying Isaac Newton's 'If I have seen further it is only by standing on the shoulders of giants'. Quoted in *New Scientist*, 19 Sep.

Genet, Jean 1910–86

French playwright, author and poet who spent much of his youth in jail. Once his literary talent was discovered, many, including Sartre, came to champion his cause, even dubbing him 'Saint Genet'.

38 *Jean Cocteau me croit un mauvais voleur. C'est parce qu'auprès de lui je suis d'abord un écrivain. Les voleurs me croient un mauvais écrivain.*
Jean Cocteau thinks that I am a poor thief. That's because next to him I am primarily a writer. Thieves think that I am a poor writer.
1949 *Journal du voleur*.

39 *L'artiste n'a pas—ou le poète—pour fonction de trouver la solution pratique des problèmes du mal.*
It is not up to the artist or to the poet to find practical solutions to the problems of evil.
1956 *Le Balcon*, 'Avertissement'.

40 *Prisons, cachots, lieux bénis où le mal est impossible, puisqu'ils sont le carrefour de toute la malédiction du monde. On ne peut pas commettre le mal dans le mal.*
Prison, dungeons, blessed places where evil is impossible because they are the crossroads of all the evil in the world. One cannot commit evil in hell.
1956 *Le Balcon*, 'Deuxième tableau'.

41 *Ce qu'il nous faut, c'est la haine. D'elle naîtront nos idées.*
Hatred is what we need. Ideas are born from hatred.
1958 *Les Nègres*, épigraphe.

42 *Dans les villes actuelles, le seul lieu,—hélas encore vers la périphérie—où un théâtre pourrait être construit, c'est le cimetière.*
In today's cities, the only place—unfortunately on the outskirts—to construct a theatre is a cemetery.
1959 *L'Étrange Mort d'...*

Genghis Khan originally Temujin c.1167–1227

Mongol conqueror. Leader of the Mongols from 1206, he conquered widely throughout Asia, penetrating Persia and Eastern Europe as far as the Dnieper River. His empire was divided between his sons and grandsons on his death.

43 Happiness lies in conquering one's enemies, in driving them in front of oneself, in taking their property, in savouring their despair, in outraging their wives and daughters.
c.1210 Quoted in Witold Rodzinski *The Walled Kingdom: A History of China* (1979).

Geoffrey de Breteuil fl.12c

French ecclesiastic.

44 *Claustrum sine armario quasi castrum sine armamentario. Ipsum armarium nostrum est armamenturium.*
A cloister without a library is like a castle without an armoury. For the library is our armoury.
c.1165 Letter to Peter Mangot.

George I 1660–1727

King of Great Britain and Ireland and Elector of Hanover. He succeeded to the British throne in 1714 on the death of Queen Anne in accordance with the Act of Settlement (1701) and was the first Hanoverian King of Great Britain and Ireland. He never mastered English.

45 I hate all Boets and Bainters.
In John Campbell *Lives of the Chief Justices*, 'Lord Mansfield' (1849).

George II 1683–1760

King of Great Britain and Ireland (1727–60) and Elector of Hanover, last British king to command in the field, at Dettingen, 1743. His reign saw the Jacobite defeat at Culloden (1746), British involvement in India after Plassey (1757) and the onset of the Seven Years War.

46 Oh! he is mad is he? Then I hope he will *bite* some of my other generals.
c.1759 Replying to remarks made about General James Wolfe by the Duke of Newcastle. Quoted in Henry Beckles Wilson *Life and Letters of James Wolfe* (1909), ch.17.

George III 1738–1820

King of Great Britain and Ireland (1760–1820). In the 1770s he was blamed with North for the loss of the American colonies. In 1783 he called Pitt (the Younger) to office, ending the supremacy of the old Whig families. As a result of his supposed insanity (now believed to have been porphyria), his son George was made Regent.

47 I can never suppose this country so far lost to all ideas of self-importance as to be willing to grant America

George V

independence; if that could ever be adopted, I shall despair of this country being ever preserved from a state of inferiority, and consequently falling into a very low class among the European states.
1780 Letter to Lord North, 7 Mar.

48 I was the last to consent to the separation, but the separation having been made, and having become inevitable, I have always said that I would be the first to meet the friendship of the United States as an independent power.
1785 Letter to John Adams, first US Ambassador to England, 1 Jun.

George V 1865–1936

King of Great Britain and Northern Ireland (1910–36). He served in the navy and travelled widely in the Empire. His reign saw the Union of South Africa (1910), World War I (1914–18), the Irish Free State Settlement (1922) and the General Strike (1926).

49 I have many times asked myself whether there can be more potent advocates of peace on earth through the years to come than this massed multitude of silent witnesses to the desolation of war.
1922 Message read at the Terlincthun Cemetery, Boulogne, 13 May.

50 Today 23 years ago, dear Grandmama died. I wonder what she would have thought of a Labour government.
1924 Of Queen Victoria. Diary entry, 22 Jan, on having invited Ramsay Macdonald to form the first Labour administration.

51 Bugger Bognor.
1929 or 1936 Reply to a courtier who had remarked 'Cheer up, your Majesty, you will soon be at Bognor again', either during his convalescence or on his deathbed. Quoted in Kenneth Rose *King George V* (1983), ch.9.

52 I will not have another war. If there is another and we are threatened with being brought into it, I will go to Trafalgar Square and wave a red flag myself sooner than allow this country to be brought in.
1935 To David Lloyd George, 10 May.

53 Golf always makes me so damned angry.
Quoted in Colin Jarman *The Guinness Dictionary of Sports Quotations* (1990).

George VI 1895–1952

King of Great Britain and Northern Ireland (1936–52). After ascending the throne (on the abdication of his elder brother, Edward VIII), he remained in bomb-damaged Buckingham Palace during World War II and delivered many broadcasts, mastering a speech impediment.

54 The British Empire has advanced to a new conception of autonomy and freedom, to the idea of a system of British nations, each freely ordering its own individual life, but bound together in unity by allegiance to one Crown, and co-operating in all that concerns the common weal.
1927 Opening, as Duke of York, the first Australian Parliament to assemble in Canberra, 9 May.

55 Abroad is bloody.
Quoted in W H Auden *A Certain World* (1970), 'Royalty'.

George, Chief Dan 1899–1981

Canadian native spokesperson.

56 The heart never knows the colour of the skin.
1974 *My Heart Soars*.

George, Daniel *pseudonym of* Daniel George Bunting 1890–1967

English author and critic.

57 O Freedom, what liberties are taken in thy name!
1963 *The Perpetual Pessimist*.

George-Brown, George (Alfred) Brown, Baron 1914–85

English Labour politician. He was Vice-Chairman and Deputy Leader of the party (1960–70), and unsuccessfully contested Harold Wilson for party leadership in 1963.

58 Most British statesmen have either drunk too much or womanised too much. I never fell into the second category.
1974 In the *Observer*, Nov.

59 Lovely creature in scarlet, dance with me!
Drunken invitation to a red-robed apostolic delegate. Attributed.

Geracimos, Ann

US journalist and feature writer.

60 Washington is a town where more people probably contemplate writing a book than finish reading one.
1989 In the *Washington Times*, 29 Mar.

Gerald of Wales *also called* Giraldus Cambrensis c.1146–c.1223

Welsh bishop and historian. He wrote 17 books and planned several others, all in Latin. His best-known works are *The History and Topography of Ireland* (1185) and *Journey through Wales* (1191).

61 Among the smaller islands there is one of fair size that is now called the Isle of Man… There was a great controversy in antiquity concerning the question: to which of the two countries should the island properly belong? Eventually, however, the matter was settled. All agreed that since it allowed poisonous reptiles to live in it, it should belong to Britain.
1185 *The History and Topography of Ireland*, pt.2 (translated by John J O'Meara, 1951).

Gerbert *later* Pope Sylvester II 940–1003

French divine and scholar, whose chemical, mathematical and philosophical expertise led to claims that he was in league with the devil. In 982 he became Abbot of Bobbio, and was appointed Archbishop of Ravenna in 988. He was elected Pope in 999. He opposed the separatist tendencies of the French Church.

62 *Cum studio bene vivendi semper conjunxi studium bene dicendi.*
I have always combined the study of how to live well with the study of how to speak well.
985 Letter to Ebrard, Abbot of Tours.

63 *An quicquam melius amicas divinitas mortalibus concesserit nescio.*
I do not know if the divinity has provided mortals with anything better than friends.
985 Letter to Abbot Gerald of Aurillac.

64 *Delegimus certum otium studiorum, quam incertum negotium bellorum.*

We have opted for the certain leisure of study, rather than the uncertain business of war.
985 Letter to Monk Raymond.

Gergen, David Richmond 1942–

US government official, an assistant and later adviser to Presidents Nixon, Ford, Reagan and Clinton. He is editor-at-large at *US News & World Report*.

65 About the time you are writing a line that you have written so often that you want to throw up, that is the first time the American people will hear it.
1993 On working as a speech-writer in the Nixon White House. In the *New York Times*, 31 Oct.

66 A naked moment in politics.
1993 On the vulnerability of the President. In the *New York Times*, 31 Oct.

67 We are making politics a spectator sport in which our only duty is to vote somebody into office and then retire to the grandstands.
1993 In *US News & World Report*, 10 May.

Gerhardie, William Alexander 1895–1977

English novelist, born and educated in St Petersburg. His best-known books are the novels *Futility* (1922) and *Polyglots* (1925).

68 She even sighed offensively...as if she meant to charge me with the necessity of doing so.
1922 *Futility*, pt.3, ch.3.

69 There are as many fools at a university as anywhere... But their folly, I admit, has a certain stamp—the stamp of university training, if you like. It is trained folly.
1925 *Polyglots*, ch.7.

70 We are like icebergs in the ocean: one-eighth part consciousness and the rest submerged beneath the surface of articulate apprehension.
1925 *Polyglots*, ch.14.

Gershwin, George 1898–1937

US composer. His early works are Broadway musicals, such as *Lady Be Good* (1924), written with his brother Ira. Other works include *Rhapsody in Blue* (1924, a concert piece in the jazz idiom), *An American in Paris* (1928) and the opera *Porgy and Bess* (1935).

71 Not many composers have ideas. Far more of them know how to use strange instruments which do not require ideas.
1930 'The Composer in the Machine Age'.

72 Jazz is the result of the energy stored up in America.
Quoted in D Morgenstern *Composers on Music* (1958).

Gershwin, Ira originally Israel Gershowitz 1896–1983

US lyricist. He worked exclusively with his brother George Gershwin until George died, and then with other composers including Kurt Weill and Jerome Kern.

73 I got rhythm,
I got music,
I got my man—
Who could ask for anything more.
1930 'I Got Music', featured in the film *Girl Crazy* (music by George Gershwin).

74 Away with the music of Broadway!
Be off with your Irving Berlin!
Oh, I'd give no quarter
to Kern or Cole Porter
and Gershwin keeps pounding on tin.
How can I be civil
when hearing this drivel?
It's only for night-clubbing souses.
Oh, give me the free 'n' easy
waltz that is Viennesey
And go tell the band
if they want a hand
the waltz must be Strauss's!
1936 'By Strauss'.

75 The way you wear your hat,
The way you sip your tea,
The mem'ry of all that—
No, no! They can't take that away from me!
1937 'They Can't Take That Away from Me', song from the film musical *Shall We Dance?* (music by George Gershwin).

76 The way your smile just beams
The way you sing off key
The way you haunt my dreams
No, no! They can't take that away from me!
1937 'They Can't Take That Away from Me', song from the film musical *Shall We Dance?* (music by George Gershwin).

77 You say potato and I say po-tah-to
You say tomato and I say to-mah-to...
Let's call the whole thing off!
1937 'Let's Call the Whole Thing Off', song from the film musical *Shall We Dance?* (music by George Gershwin).

78 A foggy day in London Town
Had me low and had me down.
1937 'A Foggy Day', song from the musical *Damsel in Distress* (music by George Gershwin).

79 Holding hands at midnight
'Neath a starry sky,
Nice work if you can get it,
And you can get it if you try.
1937 'Nice Work If You Can Get It', song from the musical *Damsel in Distress* (music by George Gershwin).

80 In time the Rockies may crumble
Gibraltar may tumble
They're only made of clay,
But our love is here to stay.
1938 'Love Is Here to Stay', sung by Kenny Baker in *The Goldwyn Follies* (music by George Gershwin).

Gervais, Ricky 1961–

English comic writer and performer, creator of such award-winning comedy series as *The Office* (2001–3), *Extras* (2005–7) and *Derek* (2011–14).

81 If you work for Nasa or the Cosa Nostra, I bet it's all the same. Why's his chair bigger than my chair? I've been an assassin longer than him and he gets to sit nearest the water cooler.
2002 In *The Guardian*, 7 Sep.

82 Fact is stranger than fiction. You see people walking down the street that would never be allowed on television. You have to tone it down.
2002 On the Jo Whiley show, BBC Radio 1, 30 Sep.

83 If David Brent is the best thing that I ever come up with, then so be it. What are you supposed to do—time the best thing you do for just before you die?

2003 On his character in the television series *The Office*. Quoted in the *Observer*, 14 Dec.

84 Just because you're offended, doesn't mean you're right.
2011 Quoted on CNN *Tonight* Show, 20 Jan.

85 It's a strange myth that atheists have nothing to live for. It's the opposite. We have nothing to die for. We have everything to live for.
2013 On CNN, 6 Sep.

86 The best advice I've ever received is, 'No one else knows what they're doing either.'
Attributed.

Getty, Jean Paul 1892-1976

US oil executive, multimillionaire and art collector. He entered the oil business in his early 20s, and merged his father's fortune with his own in 1930. Despite his legendary wealth, he acquired a reputation for miserliness.

87 If you can actually count your money, then you are not really a rich man.
1957 In the *Observer*, 3 Nov.

88 Some people find oil, some don't.
His entire submission when asked by a magazine editor to submit an article entitled 'The Secret of My Success'. Quoted by L M Boyd in the *San Francisco Chronicle*, 2 Mar 1991.

Giacosa, Giuseppe 1847-1906

Italian librettist.

89 Che gelida manina.
Your tiny hand is frozen.
1896 Rodolpho to Mimi. *La Bohème* (with Luigi Illica, music by Puccini).

Gibbon, Edward 1737-94

English historian. After a visit to Rome (1764) he embarked on a history of the Roman Empire. He became an MP in 1774, and the first volume of *The Decline and Fall of the Roman Empire* appeared in 1776. Lord Sheffield published his *Miscellaneous Works* (1796), including his autobiography.

90 If a man were called to fix the period in the history of the world during which the condition of the human race was most happy and prosperous, he would, without hesitation, name that which elapsed from the death of Domitian to the accession of Commodus.
1776-88 *The Decline and Fall of the Roman Empire*, ch.3.

91 The principles of a free constitution are irrevocably lost when the legislative power is nominated by the executive.
1776-88 *The Decline and Fall of the Roman Empire*, ch.3.

92 In every age and country, the wiser, or at least the stronger, of the two sexes, has usurped the powers of the state, and confined the other to the cares and pleasures of domestic life.
1776-88 *The Decline and Fall of the Roman Empire*, ch.6.

93 Corruption, the most infallible symptom of constitutional liberty.
1776-88 *The Decline and Fall of the Roman Empire*, ch.21.

94 The Huns...chanted a funeral song to the memory of a hero, glorious in his life, invincible in his death, the father of his people, the scourge of his enemies, and the terror of the world.
1776-88 Description of the funeral of Attila the Hun. *The Decline and Fall of the Roman Empire*, ch.35.

95 The Rhine is not more impassable than the Nile or Euphrates, and the Arabian fleet might have sailed without a naval combat into the mouth of the Thames. Perhaps the interpretation of the Koran would now be taught in the schools of Oxford, and her pupils might demonstrate to a circumcised people the sanctity and truth of the revelation of Mahomet.
1776-88 *The Decline and Fall of the Roman Empire*, ch.52.

96 Persuasion is the resource of the feeble; and the feeble can seldom persuade.
1776-88 *The Decline and Fall of the Roman Empire*, ch.68.

97 All that is human must retrograde if it does not advance.
1776-88 *The Decline and Fall of the Roman Empire*, ch.71.

98 To the University of Oxford I acknowledge no obligation; and she will as cheerfully renounce me for a son, as I am willing to disclaim her for a mother. I spent fourteen months at Magdalen College: they proved the fourteen months the most idle and unprofitable of my whole life.
Memoirs of My Life (published 1796), ch.3.

99 It was here that I suspended my religious inquiries (aged 17).
Memoirs of My Life (published 1796), ch.4.

1 I sighed as a lover, I obeyed as a son.
On his enforced visit to Lausanne, leaving behind Suzanne Curchod. *Memoirs of My Life* (published 1796), ch.4. This passage was inserted (from a draft) by Lord Sheffield.

2 It was at Rome, on the fifteenth of October 1764, as I sat musing amidst the ruins of the Capitol, while the barefooted friars were singing vespers in the temple of Jupiter, that the idea of writing the decline and fall of the City first started to my mind.
Memoirs of My Life (published 1796), ch.6, note. Variations of the lines can be found in the various drafts of Gibbon's autobiography and in the last lines of the *Decline and Fall*: 'It was among the ruins of the Capitol that I first conceived the idea of a work which has amused and exercised near twenty years of my life, and which, however inadequate to my own wishes, I finally deliver to the curiosity and candour of the public' (vol.6, ch.71).

3 My English text is chaste, and all licentious passages are left in the obscurity of a learned language.
Memoirs of My Life (published 1796), ch.8.

Gibbon, Lewis Grassic 1901-35

Scottish novelist.

4 So that was Chris and her reading and schooling, two Chrisses there were that fought for her heart and tormented her. You hated the land and the coarse speak of the folk and learning was brave and fine one day and the next you'd waken with the peewits crying across the hills, deep and deep, crying in the heart of you, and the smell of the earth in your face, almost you'd cry for that, the beauty of it and the sweetness of the Scottish land and skies.
1932 *Sunset Song*.

5 For the cleansing of that horror, if cleanse it they could, I would welcome the English in suzerainty over Scotland till the end of time. I would welcome the end of Braid Scots and Gaelic, our culture, our history, our nationhood under the heels of a Chinese army of occupation if it could cleanse the Glasgow slums, give a

surety of food and play—the elementary right of every human being—to those people of the abyss…
1934 *Scottish Scene*, 'Glasgow' (with Hugh MacDiarmid).

Gibbons, Kaye 1960–
US novelist. Her first novel, *Ellen Foster* (1986), was widely acclaimed. Other works include *A Virtuous Woman* (1989) and *Divining Women* (2004).

6 I read about writers' lives with the fascination of one slowing down to get a good look at an automobile accident.
1990 In the *New York Times*, 7 Jan.

Gibbons, Orlando 1583–1625
English composer and organist of Westminster Abbey (from 1623). He wrote little, but some of his anthems, services and madrigals are regarded as masterpieces.

7 The silver swan, who living had no note,
When death approached, unlocked her silent throat;
Leaning her breast against the reedy shore,
Thus sung her first and last, and sung no more:
'Farewell, all joys; Oh death, come close mine eyes;
More geese than swans now live, more fools than wise.'
1612 *The First Set of Madrigals and Motets of Five Parts*, 'The Silver Swan'.

Gibbons, Stella Dorothea 1902–89
English writer. She worked as a journalist, and wrote novels, poetry and short stories. Her reputation rests on her famous parody of rural fiction, *Cold Comfort Farm* (1932).

8 The life of the journalist is poor, nasty, brutish and short. So is his style.
1932 *Cold Comfort Farm*, foreword.

9 And when the spring comes her hour is upon her again. 'Tes the hand of Nature and we women cannot escape it.
1932 Judith Starkadder, of Meriam. *Cold Comfort Farm*, ch.5.

10 Something nasty in the woodshed.
1932 Aunt Ada Doom. *Cold Comfort Farm*, ch.10.

11 He said that, by god, D. H. Lawrence was right when he had said there must be a dumb, dark, dull, bitter belly-tension between a man and a woman, and how else could this be achieved save in the long monotony of marriage?
1932 Mr Mybug, proposing to Rennet. *Cold Comfort Farm*, ch.20.

Gibbs, Wolcott 1902–58
US journalist and critic.

12 Backward ran sentences until reeled the mind.
1936 Parody of *Time* magazine's literary style. 'Time…Fortune…Life…Luce', in the *New Yorker*, 28 Nov.

Gibran, Kahlil 1883–1931
Syrian mystic, author and artist, whose most famous work is *The Prophet* (1923).

13 Your children are not your children.
They are the sons and daughters of Life's longing for itself.
They came through you but not from you
And though they are with you yet they belong not to you.
You may give them your love but not your thoughts,
For they have their own thoughts.
You may house their bodies, but not their souls.
1923 *The Prophet*, 'On Children'.

Gibson, Wilfred Wilson 1878–1962
English poet. He was a prolific writer of both poetry and plays, rooted in the reality of everyday life.

14 But we, how shall we turn to little things
And listen to the birds and winds and streams
Made holy by their dreams,
Nor feel the heart-break in the heart of things?
1918 'Lament'.

Gibson, William Ford 1948–
US science-fiction writer, best known as the author of *Neuromancer* (1984), which spawned the genre of cyberpunk fiction.

15 Cyberspace. A consensual hallucination experienced daily by billions of legitimate operators, in every nation, by children being taught mathematical concepts… A graphical representation of data abstracted from the banks of every computer in the human system. Unthinkable complexity. Lines of light ranged in the non-space of the mind, clusters and constellations of data. Like city lights, receding.
1984 *Neuromancer*. This is the first recorded use of the term 'cyberspace'.

16 Cyberspace is where you are when you're on the telephone.
1994 In the *US News & World Report*, 21 Jun.

17 When you want to know how things really work, study them when they're coming apart.
2010 *Zero History*.

Gide, André Paul Guillaume 1869–1951
French writer of fiction, poetry, plays, criticism, biography and translations. His novels focus on the conflict between the spiritual and the physical. He won the Nobel prize for literature in 1947.

18 *Nous avons bâti sur le sable*
Des cathédrales impérissables.
We have built immovable cathedrals
In the sand.
1895 *Paludes*.

19 *Que mon livre t'enseigne à t'intéresser plus à toi qu'à lui-même — puis à tout le reste plus qu'à toi.*
May my book teach you to be more interested in yourself than in it—then, in everyone else more than yourself.
1897 *Les Nourritures terrestres*, pt.1.

20 *La sagesse n'est pas dans la raison, mais dans l'amour.*
Wisdom comes not from reason but from love.
1897 *Les Nourritures terrestres*, pt.1.

21 *Familles! je vous hais! Foyers clos; portes refermées; possessions jalouses du bonheur.*
Families! I hate you! Enclosed hallways, shut doors, jealous possessions of happiness.
1897 *Les Nourritures terrestres*, pt.4.

22 *Chaque instant de notre Vie est essentiellement irremplaçable: sache parfois t'y concentrer uniquement.*

Every instant of Life is essentially irreplaceable:
concentrate on it fully from time to time.
1897 *Les Nourritures terrestres*, pt.4.

23 C'est avec de beaux sentiments qu'on fait de la
mauvaise littérature.
Bad literature is written with beautiful sentiments.
1928 Letter to François Mauriac.

24 Le bonheur de l'homme n'est pas dans la liberté, mais
dans l'acceptation d'un devoir.
Man's happiness does not come from freedom but in the
acceptance of a task.
1932 Journal entry, 8 Feb.

Gielgud, Sir (Arthur) John 1904–2000
English actor and producer. A leading Shakespearean actor, he appeared in many films, notably as Cassius in *Julius Caesar* (1952) and in *Prospero's Books* (1991).

25 When you're my age, you just never risk being ill—
because then everyone says: Oh, he's done for.
1988 In the *Sunday Express*, 17 Jul.

26 Daniel Day Lewis has what every actor in Hollywood
wants: talent. And what every actor in England wants:
looks.
1995 In *The Independent*, 13 May.

27 Being another character is more interesting than being
yourself.
Attributed.

Gilbert, Sir Humphrey 1537–83
English navigator and explorer. He took Newfoundland for the crown in 1583, establishing a colony at St John's. He was drowned on the journey home.

28 We are as near to heaven by sea as by land!
1583 Dying words as his frigate *Squirrel* sank in the Atlantic Ocean near the Azores, 5 Aug. Quoted in Richard Hakluyt *Third and Last Volume of the Voyages…of the English Nation* (1600).

Gilbert, Sir W(illiam) S(chwenck) 1836–1911
English parodist and librettist. His humorous verse was collected in 1869 as the *Bab Ballads*. His partnership with Sir Arthur Sullivan, from 1871, produced a succession of light operas, from *Trial by Jury* (1875) to *The Grand Duke* (1896).

29 So I fell in love with a rich attorney's
Elderly, ugly daughter.
1875 *Trial by Jury*.

30 She may very well pass for forty-three
In the dusk with a light behind her!
1875 *Trial by Jury*.

31 I'm called little Buttercup—dear Little Buttercup,
Though I could never tell why.
1878 *HMS Pinafore*, act 1.

32 CAPT: Bad language or abuse,
I never, never use,
Whatever the emergency;
Though 'Bother it' I may
Occasionally say,
I never use a big, big D—
ALL: What, never?
CAPT: No, never!
ALL: What *never*?
CAPT: Well, hardly ever!
ALL: Hardly ever swears a big, big D—
Then give three cheers, and one cheer more,
For the well-bred Captain of the *Pinafore*!
1878 *HMS Pinafore*, act 1.

33 I am the monarch of the sea,
The Ruler of the Queen's Navee,
Whose praise Great Britain loudly chants
And we are his sisters, and his cousins, and his aunts!
1878 *HMS Pinafore*, act 1.

34 When I was a lad I served a term
As office boy to an attorney's firm.
I cleaned the windows and I swept the floor,
And I polished up the handle of the big front door.
I polished up that handle so carefullee
That now I am the Ruler of the Queen's Navee!
1878 *HMS Pinafore*, act 2.

35 In spite of all temptations
To belong to other nations,
He remains an Englishman!
1878 *HMS Pinafore*, act 2.

36 Climbing over rocky mountain,
Skipping rivulet and fountain.
1879 Girls' chorus, *The Pirates of Penzance*, act 1.

37 It is, it is a glorious thing
To be a Pirate King.
1879 Pirate King's song, *The Pirates of Penzance*, act 1.

38 Oh, is there not one maiden here
Whose homely face and bad complexion
Have caused all hopes to disappear
Of ever winning man's affection?
1879 Frederic's song, *The Pirates of Penzance*, act 1.

39 I am the very model of a modern Major-General,
I've information vegetable, animal and mineral,
I know the kings of England, and I quote the fights
historical,
From Marathon to Waterloo, in order categorical.
1879 The Major-General's song, *The Pirates of Penzance*, act 1.

40 I can hum a fugue of which I've heard the music's din
afore,
And whistle all the airs from that infernal nonsense
Pinafore.
1879 The Major-General's song, *The Pirates of Penzance*, act 1.

41 Stay, Frederic, stay!
Nay, Mabel, nay!
1879 Mabel and Frederic's duet, *The Pirates of Penzance*, act 2.

42 When a felon's not engaged in his employment
Or maturing his felonious little plans
His capacity for innocent enjoyment
Is just as great as any honest man's—
Ah! When constabulary duty's to be done
A policeman's lot is not a happy one.
1879 Sergeant's song, *The Pirates of Penzance*, act 2.

43 And everyone will say,
As you walk your mystic way,
'If this young man expresses himself in terms too deep
for me,
Why, what a very singularly deep young man this deep
young man must be!'
1881 Bunthorne's song, *Patience*, act 1.

44 Sing 'Booh to you—
   Pooh, pooh to you'—
   And that's what I shall say!
   1881 Jane and Bunthorne's duet, *Patience*, act 2.

45 A commonplace young man,
   A matter-of-fact young man,
   A steady and stolid-y, jolly Bank-Holiday
   Every-day young man!
   1881 Bunthorne and Grosvenor's duet, *Patience*, act 2.

46 A Japanese young man,
   A blue and white young man,
   Francesca di Rimini, miminy, piminy,
   Je-ne-sais-quoi young man.
   1881 Bunthorne and Grosvenor's duet, *Patience*, act 2.

47 A Chancery Lane young man,
   A Somerset House young man,
   A very delectable, highly respectable,
   Threepenny-bus young man!
   1881 Bunthorne and Grosvenor's duet, *Patience*, act 2.

48 A pallid and thin young man,
   A haggard and lank young man,
   A greenery-yallery, Grosvenor Gallery,
   Foot-in-the-grave young man!
   A Sewell & Cross young man,
   A Howell & James young man,
   A push-ing young par-ti-cle—
   'What's the next ar-ti-cle?'—
   Wa-ter-loo House young man!
   1881 Bunthorne and Grosvenor's duet, *Patience*, act 2.

49 Bow, bow, ye lower middle classes!
   Bow, bow, ye tradesmen, bow ye masses!
   1882 Chorus, *Iolanthe*, act 1 (first performed 25 Nov, simultaneously in London and New York).

50 The Law is the true embodiment
   Of everything that's excellent.
   It has no kind of fault or flaw,
   And I, my Lords, embody the Law.
   1882 *Iolanthe*, act 1.

51 When I went to the Bar as a very young man,
   (Said I to myself—said I),
   I'll work on a new and original plan,
   (Said I to myself—said I).
   1882 *Iolanthe*, act 1.

52 I often think it's comical
   How Nature always does contrive
   That every boy and every gal
   That's born into the world alive
   Is either a little Liberal
   Or else a little Conservative!
   1882 Private Willis's song, *Iolanthe*, act 2.

53 The House of Peers, throughout the war,
   Did nothing in particular,
   And did it very well:
   Yet Britain set the world ablaze
   In good King George's glorious days!
   1882 Lord Mountarat's song, *Iolanthe*, act 2.

54 When you're lying awake with a dismal headache, and repose is taboo'd by anxiety,
   I conceive you may use any language you choose to indulge in, without impropriety.
   1882 Lord Chancellor's nightmare song, *Iolanthe*, act 2.

55 Expressive glances
   Shall be our lances
   And pops of Sillery
   Our light artillery.
   1884 Trio, *Princess Ida*, act 1.

56 I've an irritating chuckle, I've a celebrated sneer,
   I've an entertaining snigger, I've a fascinating leer.
   To everybody's prejudice I know a thing or two;
   I can tell a woman's age in half a minute—and I do.
   But although I try to make myself as pleasant as I can,
   Yet everybody says I'm such a disagreeable man!
   1884 Gama's song, *Princess Ida*, act 1.

57 Oh, doughty sons of Hungary!
   May all success
   Attend and bless
   Your warlike ironmongery!
   1884 Chorus, *Princess Ida*, act 3.

58 A wandering minstrel I—
   A thing of shreds and patches
   Of ballads, songs and snatches
   And dreamy lullaby!
   1885 Nanki-Poo's song, *The Mikado*, act 1.

59 As in a month you've got to die
   If Ko-Ko tells us true,
   'Twere empty compliment to cry
   'Long life to Nanki-Poo!'
   But as one month you have to live
   As fellow-citizen,
   This toast with three times three we'll give—
   'Long life to you—till then!'
   1885 Pooh-Bah's solo, *The Mikado*, act 1.

60 As some day it may happen that a victim must be found,
   I've got a little list—I've got a little list
   Of society offenders who might well be underground,
   And who never would be missed— who never would be missed!
   There's the pestilential nuisances who write for autographs—
   All people who have flabby hands and irritating laughs.
   1885 Ko-Ko's song, *The Mikado*, act 1.

61 The idiot who praises, with enthusiastic tone,
   All centuries but this, and every country but his own;
   And the lady from the provinces, who dresses like a guy,
   And who 'doesn't think she dances, but would rather like to try';
   And that singular anomaly, the lady novelist—
   I don't think she'd be missed—I'm *sure* she'd not be missed!
   1885 Ko-Ko's song, *The Mikado*, act 1.

62 Defer, defer,
   To the Lord High Executioner!
   1885 Chorus, *The Mikado*, act 1.

63 Three little maids from school are we,
   Pert as a school-girl well can be
   Filled to the brim with girlish glee.
   1885 Trio for Yum-yum, Peep-Bo and Pitti Sing, with Chorus of Girls, *The Mikado*, act 1.

64 To sit in solemn silence in a dull, dark dock,
   In a pestilential prison, with a life-long lock,
   Awaiting the sensation of a short, sharp shock,
   From a cheap and chippy chopper on a big black block!
   1885 Trio, *The Mikado*, act 1.

65 Here's a how-de-do!
   1885 Trio, *The Mikado*, act 2.

66 My object all sublime
   I shall achieve in time—
   To let the punishment fit the crime.
   1885 The Mikado's song, *The Mikado*, act 2.

67 And there he plays extravagant matches
   In fitless finger-stalls
   On a cloth untrue
   With a twisted cue
   And elliptical billiard balls.
   1885 The doom of the billiard sharp. *The Mikado*, act 2.

68 On a tree by a river a little tom-tit
   Sang 'Willow, titwillow, titwillow!'
   1885 Ko-Ko's song, *The Mikado*, act 2.

69 This particularly rapid unintelligible patter
   Isn't generally heard, and if it is it doesn't matter!
   1887 *Ruddigore*, act 2.

70 For I have a song to sing, O!...
   It is sung to the moon
   By a love-lorn loon,
   Who fled from the mocking throng, O!
   It's the song of a merryman moping mum,
   Whose soul was sad and whose glance was glum
   Who sipped no sup and who craved no crumb,
   As he sighed for the love of a ladye!
   1888 Jack Point's song, *The Yeomen of the Guard*.

71 In enterprise of martial kind,
   When there was any fighting,
   He led his regiment from behind—
   He found it less exciting.
   But when away his regiment ran,
   His place was at the fore, O—
   That celebrated,
   Cultivated
   Underrated
   Nobleman,
   The Duke of Plaza-Toro!
   1889 Duke's song, *The Gondoliers*, act 1.

72 I am a courtier grave and serious
   Who is about to kiss your hand:
   Try to combine a pose imperious
   With a demeanour nobly bland.
   1889 *The Gondoliers*, act 2.

73 Take a pair of sparkling eyes.
   1889 Marco's song, *The Gondoliers*, act 2.

74 Funny without being vulgar.
   1893 Of Sir Henry Beerbohm Tree's performance as Hamlet. Attributed.

75 Do you know how they are going to decide the Shakespeare–Bacon dispute? They are going to dig up Shakespeare and dig up Bacon; they are going to get Tree to recite *Hamlet* to them. And the one who turns in his coffin will be the author of the play.
   Letter.

76 My dear chap! Good isn't the word!
   To an actor who had just given a very weak performance. Attributed.

Gill, Brendan 1914–97

US writer and critic of film, theatre and architecture. His works include *The Day the Money Stopped* (1957) and *A New York Life: of friends and others* (1990). He received the national Book Award for *The Trouble of One House* (1951).

77 In the later nineteenth century, the tops of skyscrapers often took the shape of domes, surmounted by jaunty gilded lanterns; later came ziggurats, mausoleums, Alexandrian lighthouses, miniature Parthenons. These charming follies contained neither royal corpses nor effigies of gods and goddesses; rather they contained large wooden tanks filled with water.
   1982 Quoted in Laura Rosen *Top of the City: New York's hidden rooftop world* (1990), foreword.

78 He stared the assorted meannesses and failed promises of American life straight in the face, and they stared back.
   1990 On Walker Evans's photographs for James Agee's book on the destitute South. *A New York Life*.

79 The big houses sat in self-congratulatory propinquity on their level green lawns...stout matrons seated elbow to elbow, implacably chaperoning a ball.
   1990 On a residential boulevard of Rochester, NewYork. *A New York Life*.

80 A vain attempt to subdue that unsubduable country.
   1990 Of Cromwell's settlement of Scots in the north of Ireland. *A New York Life*.

Gill, (Arthur) Eric Rowton 1882–1940

English artist, type designer and writer.

81 That state is a state of Slavery in which a man does what he likes to do in his spare time and in his working time that which is required of him.
   1929 *Art-nonsense and Other Essays*, 'Slavery and Freedom'.

82 The artist is not a special kind of man but every man a special kind of artist.
   1934 *Art*, introduction.

83 Man cannot live on the human plane, he must be either above or below it.
   1940 *Autobiography*, closing words.

84 Science is analytical, descriptive, informative. Man does not live by bread alone, but by science he attempts to do so. Hence the deadliness of all that is purely scientific.
   'Art'. Collected in *Essays* (1948).

Gillespie, Dizzy (John Birks) 1917–93

US jazz trumpeter, composer and bandleader. A leading exponent of bebop in the 1940s, he formed several big bands and led an international touring orchestra (1956).

85 It's taken me all my life to learn what not to play.
   Quoted in N Hentoff *Jazz Is* (1978).

86 When I first heard Charlie Parker, I said, 'That's how our music should be played.'... After we got it together, yeah, I knew we were making something new. It was magic. Nobody on the planet was playing like that but us.
   1991 On bebop. In the *San Francisco Chronicle*, 25 May.

87 Now, our music is universal. It shares the rhythmic content of African music, music of the Western Hemisphere and various lands of the East, and has merged this rhythm with European harmonies, the soul of the slaves, the blues, and the spirituals to create jazz.
   1979 *Dizzy– To Be Or Not To Bop* (with Al Fraser), 'Evolutions'.

Gillette, King Camp 1855–1932
US inventor of the safety razor (c.1895), founder of the Gillette Safety Razor Company (1901).

88 To be successful in business, you should produce something cheap, habit-forming, and consumed by use.
Attributed.

Gilliam, Terry (Terence Vance) 1940–
US-born British screenwriter and film director.

89 Film-making is just a cheap version of being God. And you've got to do it in six days. It's never enough time, just like there wasn't for Him.
2009 Quoted in *New Statesman*, 16 Oct.

Gilligan, Andrew 1968–
English journalist.

90 I have spoken to a British official who was involved in the preparation of the dossier… He said: 'It was transformed in the week before it was published, to make it sexier.'
2003 Referring to the Government's dossier on weapons of mass destruction in Iraq. On BBC Radio 4's *Today* programme, 29 May.

Gilman, Charlotte Anna *pen names* Charlotte Perkins Gilman *and* Charlotte Perkins Stetson 1860–1935
US feminist and writer. She lectured on women's and other social issues, and her *Women and Economics* (1898) is regarded as a feminist landmark. Her fiction includes the story 'The Yellow Wall-Paper' (1892), a feminist study of madness.

91 The economic status of women generally depends on that of men generally, and…the economic status of women individually depends upon that of men individually, those men to whom they are related.
1898 *Women and Economics: A Study of the Economic Relation between Men and Women as a Factor in Social Evolution*, ch.1.

92 The labor of women in the house, certainly, enables men to produce more wealth than they otherwise could; and in this way [they] are economic factors in society. But so are horses.
1898 *Women and Economics: A Study of the Economic Relation between Men and Women as a Factor in Social Evolution*, ch.1.

93 Whatever the economic value of the domestic industry of women is, they do not get it. The women who do the most work get the least money, and the women who have the most money do the least work.
1898 *Women and Economics: A Study of the Economic Relation between Men and Women as a Factor in Social Evolution*, ch.1.

94 His dominance is not that of one chosen as best fitted to rule…but it is sovereignty based on the accident of sex.
1898 *Women and Economics: A Study of the Economic Relation between Men and Women as a Factor in Social Evolution*, ch.1.

Gilmore, Dame Mary Jean *née* Mary Jean Cameron 1865–1962
Australian writer and poet. She sailed to Paraguay in 1893 to help establish the New Australia Movement Utopian community, and when this failed returned to Australia (1902), becoming a journalist. A lifelong supporter of aboriginal rights, in 1936 she was awarded the DBE.

95 I span and Eve span
A thread to bind the heart of man!
1918 *The Passionate Heart and Other Poems*, 'Eve-song'.

96 Lone, lone, and lone I stand,
With none to hear my cry,
As the black feet of the night
Go walking down the sky.
1932 *Under the Wilgas*, 'The Myall in Prison'.

Gilmour of Craigmillar, Ian Gilmour, Baron 1926–2007
English Conservative politician, Secretary of State for Defence (1970–4) and Lord Privy Seal (1979–81). He published several books on politics.

97 It does no harm to throw the occasional man overboard, but it does not do much good if you are steering full speed ahead for the rocks.
1981 In *The Times*, after he was sacked by Margaret Thatcher for publicly criticizing her anti-European stance.

Gingold, Hermione 1897–1987
English actress. A star of intimate revue, she also appeared with success in plays by Noël Coward and in musicals by Stephen Sondheim.

98 I got all the schooling any actress needs. That is, I learned to write enough to sign contracts.
Attributed.

Gingrich, Newt(on Leroy) 1943–
US politician. Originally a history professor, he became representative from Georgia in 1978 and subsequently leader of conservative Republicans in the House. He was Speaker of the House (1995–99).

99 One reason I try to get people to call me Newt is to break down barriers. It's a whole lot easier for someone to say, 'Newt, you've got a spot on your tie,' than it is to say 'Congressman'.
1979 Attributed comment.

1 The secular socialist machine represents as great a threat to America as Nazi Germany or the Soviet Union once did.
2010 *To Save America: Stopping Obama's Secular-Socialist Machine*.

2 If Thomas Edison invented electric light today, Dan Rather would report it on CBS News as, 'Candle-making industry threatened'.
Attributed.

3 Perseverance is the hard work you do after you get tired of doing the hard work you already did.
Attributed.

Ginsberg, Allen 1926–97
US poet, a key member of the Beat movement with Jack Kerouac and William Burroughs. Despite his anti-establishment views, he was a popular poet and performer. His works include *Kaddish and Other Poems* (1961).

4 A naked lunch is natural to us,
we eat reality sandwiches.
But allegories are so much lettuce.
Don't hide the madness.
1954 'On Burroughs' Work'.

Giovanni

5 The madman bum and angel beat in Time, unknown, yet putting down here what might be left to say in time come after death.
   1956 *Howl and Other Poems*, 'Howl, I'.

6 Moloch whose mind is pure machinery! Moloch whose blood is running money! Moloch whose fingers are ten armies! Moloch whose breast is a cannibal dynamo! Moloch whose ear is a smoking tomb!
   1956 *Howl and Other Poems*, 'Howl, II'.

7 You were never no locomotive, Sunflower, you were a sunflower!
   And you Locomotive, you are a locomotive, forget me not!
   1956 *Howl and Other Poems*, 'Sunflower Sutra'.

8 America I've given you all and now I'm nothing.
   1956 *Howl and Other Poems*, 'America'.

9 America I'm putting my queer shoulder to the wheel.
   1956 *Howl and Other Poems*, 'America'.

10 Democracy! Bah! When I hear that word I reach for my feather Boa!
   1960 Journal entry, Oct. Collected in *Journals: Early Fifties Early Sixties*, 'New York City'.

11 and poets should stay out of politics or become monsters
   I have become monstrous with politics.
   1961 *Kaddish and Other Poems*, 'Death to Van Gogh's Ear!'.

12 A very unique cat…a French Canadian Hinayana Buddhist Beat Catholic savant.
   1970 Of Jack Kerouac. *This Fabulous Century 1950–1960*.

13 What if someone gave a war & Nobody came?
   Life would ring the bells of Ecstasy and Forever be Itself again.
   1973 *The Fall of America*, 'Graffiti 12th Cubicle Men's Room Syracuse Airport'.
   ▶ See Sandburg 742:27.

14 All this time [San Francisco, from 1955] I realized we were involved as a community with a historical change of consciousness and some kind of cultural revolution… I thought it was really in some respects a contest between further liberation or 1984 authoritarianism, police state; that it was creeping police state or creeping socialism-libertarianism.
   1984 Quoted in Gordon Ball (ed) *Allen Ginsberg: Journals Mid-Fifties* (1995), 'Meditations on Record Keeping by Poet, Transcribed by Editor'.

15 Poetry is not an expression of the party line. It's that time of night, lying in bed, thinking what you really think, making the private world public, that's what the poet does.
   Quoted in Barry Miles *Ginsberg* (1989), ch.5.

Giovanni, Nikki in full Yolande Cornelia Giovanni, Jr 1943–

US poet, a significant voice in the development of black consciousness. Her early work was more radical in tone than subsequent more introspective volumes.

16 Mistakes are a fact of life
   It is the response to error that counts.
   1968 *Black Judgement*, 'Of Liberation', stanza 16.

17 and I really hope no white person ever has cause to write about me
because they never understand Black love is Black wealth and they'll
probably talk about my hard childhood and never understand that
all the while I was quite happy
   1968 *Black Judgement*, 'Nikki–Rosa'.

18 it's a sex object if you're pretty
and no love
or love and no sex if you're fat
   1968 *Black Judgement*, 'Woman Poem'.

19 White people really deal more with God and black people with Jesus.
   1971 Conversation with James Baldwin, London, 4 Nov. Collected in *A Dialogue* (1973).

20 A white face goes with a white mind. Occasionally a black face goes with a white mind. Very seldom a white face will have a black mind.
   1971 Conversation with James Baldwin, London, 4 Nov. Collected in *A Dialogue* (1973).

Gipp, George 1895–1920

US American football player. His success on the field inspired Notre Dame to two unbeaten seasons (1919 and 1920), though his career was cut short by his death from pneumonia.

21 Some time, Rock, when the team's up against it, when things are wrong and the breaks are beating the boys–tell them to go in there with all they've got and win just one for the Gipper.
   1920 Last words, to coach Knute Rockne. Rockne told the team about Gipp's request in 1928, when their fortunes were low, and inspired the squad to new efforts. 'Win one for the Gipper' subsequently became a catchphrase throughout US sport.

Giraudoux, (Hippolyte) Jean 1882–1944

French writer, head of propaganda in World War II. He is best known for his poetic plays, including *La Guerre de Troie n'aura pas lieu* (1935, translated as *The Tiger at the Gates*, 1955) and *Pour Lucrèce* (1953, translated as *Duel of Angels*, 1958).

22 Le plagiat est la base de toutes les littératures, excepté de la première, qui d'ailleurs est inconnue.
   Plagiarism is the base of all literature except the first text which, however, is unknown.
   1922 *Siegfried et le Limousin*.

23 L'humanité est…une entreprise surhumaine.
   Humanity is…a superhuman undertaking.
   1933 *Intermezzo*, act 1, sc.6.

24 A golf course is the epitome of all that is purely transitory in the universe, a space not to dwell in, but to get over as quickly as possible.
   1933 Quoted in Colin Jarman *The Guinness Dictionary of Sports Quotations* (1990).

25 Nous savons tous ici que le droit est la plus puissante des écoles de l'imagination. Jamais poète n'a interprété la nature aussi librement qu'un juriste la réalité.
   We all know here that the law is the most powerful of schools for the imagination. No poet ever interpreted nature as freely as a lawyer interprets the truth.
   1935 *La Guerre de Troie n'aura pas lieu*, act 2, sc.5.

26 Il n'est pas très prudent d'avoir des dieux et des légumes trop dorés.

It is not wise to have either your gods or your vegetables too gilded.
1935 *La Guerre de Troie n'aura pas lieu*, act 2, sc.13.

27 C'est de là que vient tout le mal: Dieu est un homme.
All evil comes from this fact: God is a man.
1937 *Sodome et Gomorrhe*, act 1, sc.2.

Girondo, Oliverio 1891–1967

Argentinian poet, who travelled extensively in Europe and Africa and had close contact with the French avant garde. He edited the Ultraist manifesto in the avant-garde magazine *Martín Fierro* (1924).

28 Cansado,
sobre todo,
de estar siempre conmigo,
de hallarme cada día,
cuando termina el sueño,
allí, donde me encuentre,
con las mismas narices
y con las mismas piernas.
Tired,
above all,
of being always with myself,
of finding myself everyday,
when the dream comes to an end,
wherever I am,
with the same old nose
and with the same old legs.
1942 *Persuasión de los días*, 'Cansancio' ('Fatigue').

Giscard d'Estaing, Valéry 1926–

French politician, born in Germany. A Resistance worker during World War II, he was Finance Minister (1962–6) before launching the National Federation of Independent Republicans. He was President of France (1974–81) and in 1989 he resigned from the French National Assembly to play, instead, a leading role in the EU.

29 During my seven years in office, I was in love with seventeen million French women... I know this declaration will inspire irony and that English language readers will find it very French.
1988 *Le Pouvoir et la vie*.

30 Europe without Greece is like a child without a birth certificate.
Attributed.

Gitlin, Todd 1943–

US academic and columnist. He is Professor of Journalism and Sociology at Columbia University. He has written on culture, politics and the media and is also a published poet.

31 There is a misunderstanding by marketers in our culture about what freedom of choice is. In the market, it is equated with multiplying choice. This is a misconception. If you have infinite choice, people are reduced to passivity.
1990 In the *New York Times*, 14 Feb.

Giuliani, Rudy (Rudolph William) 1944–

US lawyer and politician. He was mayor of New York City at the time of the 11 September terrorist attacks on the World Trade Center.

32 Show your confidence. Show you're not afraid. Go to restaurants. Go shopping.
2001 Encouraging the people of New York to resume their normal lives after the terrorist attack of 11 Sep. Press conference, 12 Sep.

33 Our hearts are broken, but they continue to beat, and the spirit of our City has never been stronger.
2001 *One Nation: America Remembers September 11, 2001*, introduction.

34 When you confront a problem, you begin to solve it.
2005 In *RFID Journal*, 28 Feb.

35 Change is not a destination as hope is not a strategy.
2008 Speaking at the Republican National Convention.

Gladstone, W(illiam) E(wart) 1809–98

English Liberal statesman. He entered Parliament as a Conservative (1832), and in 1867 became leader of the Liberal Party. As Prime Minister (1868–74, 1880–5, 1886, 1892–4) he established a system of national education (1870), introduced parliamentary reforms aimed at universal male suffrage and argued for Irish Home Rule.

36 It is upon those who say that it is necessary to exclude forty-nine fiftieths of the working classes [from the vote] to show cause, and I venture to say that every man who is not presumably incapacitated by some consideration of personal unfitness or of political danger, is morally entitled to come within the pale of the Constitution.
1864 House of Commons, 11 May.

37 One cannot fight against the future. Time is on our side.
1866 Speech on the Reform Bill, House of Commons, 27 Apr.

38 Remember the rights of the savage, as we call him. Remember that the happiness of his humble home, remember that the sanctity of life in the hill villages of Afghanistan, among the winter snows, is as inviolable in the eye of Almighty God as can be your own.
1879 Speech at Edinburgh Foresters' Hall, during the Midlothian Campaign, 26 Nov.

39 England's foreign policy should always be inspired by the love of freedom. There should be a sympathy with freedom, a desire to give it scope, founded not upon visionary ideas but upon the long experience of many generations within the shores of this happy isle, that in freedom one lays the firmest foundations both of loyalty and order.
1879 Speech, West Calder, 27 Nov.

40 All the world over, I will back the masses against the classes.
1886 Speech, Liverpool, 28 Jun.

41 We are part of the community of Europe, and we must do our duty as such.
1888 Speech, 10 Apr.

42 What that Sicilian mule was to me, I have been to the Queen.
1894 Memorandum on his relationship with Queen Victoria, 20 Mar.

43 It is not a Life at all. It is a Reticence, in three volumes.
Of J W Cross's *Life of George Eliot*. Quoted in E F Benson *As We Were* (1930), ch.6.

Glasgow, Ellen Anderson Gholson 1874–1945

US novelist. Much of her fiction was set in the South. She won a Pulitzer Prize in 1941 for *In This Our Life*.

44 It was not the matter of the work, but the mind that went into, that counted—and the man who was not content to do small things well would leave great things undone.
1900 *The Voice of the People*, bk.2, ch.4.

45 Women like to sit down with trouble as if it were knitting.
1932 *The Sheltered Life*, pt.3, section 3.

46 No matter how vital experience might be while you lived it, no sooner was it ended and dead than it became as lifeless as the piles of dry dust in a school history book.
1941 *In This Our Life*, pt.3, ch.9.

Gleick, James 1954–

US software designer and science writer. His books include *Faster: The Acceleration of Just About Everything* (1999), *Isaac Newton* (2003) and *The Information* (2011).

47 To some physicists chaos is a science of process rather than state, of becoming rather than being.
1987 *Chaos*.

48 The Internet has taken shape with startlingly little planning… The most universal and indispensable network on the planet somehow burgeoned without so much as a board of directors, never mind a mergers-and-acquisitions department. There is a paradoxical lesson here for strategists. In economic terms, the great corporations are acting like socialist planners, while old-fashioned free-market capitalism blossoms at their feet.
1994 In the *New York Times Magazine*, 1 May.

Glen, Iain 1961–

Scottish actor.

49 I used to have this terrible wish. I didn't mind dying as long as the rest of the world ground to a halt when I did.
2001 In *The Herald*, 8 Jul.

Glennie, Dame Evelyn 1965–

Scottish percussion player. Judged to be a percussionist of outstanding abilities, she is additionally remarkable in her achievements as she experienced a gradual but total loss of hearing in her early teens.

50 If we cannot spare some patience towards a piece of music or art, what hope do we have for showing it to another human being?
2004 In *Scotland on Sunday*, 30 May.

Gloucester, William Henry, 1st Duke of 1743–1805

British nobleman and military officer. He was the son of Frederick Louis, Prince of Wales and Augusta of Saxe-Gotha.

51 Another damned, thick, square book! Always scribble, scribble, scribble! Eh! Mr Gibbon?
1781 Attributed, when presented with the second volume of *The Decline and Fall of the Roman Empire*. These words have also been attributed to George III and the Duke of Cumberland.

Godard, Jean-Luc 1930–

French film critic and director. His first feature *À bout de souffle* (1959) established him as one of the leading members of the 'New Wave'. Other notable films include *Pierrot Le Fou* (1965), *Alphaville* (1965) and *Week-end* (1967).

52 *La photographie, c'est la vérité. Le cinéma: la vérité vingt-quatre fois par seconde.*
Photography is truth. And cinema is truth twenty-four times a second.
1960 *Le Petit Soldat*.

Goebbels, (Paul) Joseph 1897–1945

German Nazi official. In 1926 Hitler appointed him district party leader for Berlin and in 1928 he entered the Reichstag. As Minister for Propaganda from 1933 he was a vociferous and virulent anti-Semite. He killed his family and committed suicide as Berlin fell in 1945.

53 *Ohne Butter werden wir fertig, aber nicht beispielsweise ohne Kanonen. Wenn wir einmal überfallen werden, dann können wir uns nicht mit Butter, sondern nur mit Kanonen verteidigen.*
We can manage without butter but not, for example, without guns. If we are attacked, we can only defend ourselves with guns not butter.
1936 Speech in Berlin, 17 Jan.

54 *Wenn das deutsche Volk die Waffen niederlegte, würden die Sowjets…ganz Ost- und Südosteuropa zuzüglich des größten Teiles des Reiches besetzen. Vor diesem einschließlich der Sowjetunion riesigen Territorium würde sich sofort ein eiserner Vorhang heruntersenken.*
Should the German people lay down their arms, the Soviets…would occupy all eastern and south-eastern Europe together with the greater part of the Reich. Over all this territory, which with the Soviet Union would be of enormous extent, an iron curtain would at once descend.
1945 In *Das Reich*, a Nazi propaganda weekly, quoted in *The Times* and the *Manchester Guardian* on 23 Feb.
▶ See also Churchill 226:2.

Goering, Hermann Wilhelm 1893–1946

German soldier and Nazi leader, commander of the Hitler storm troopers and head of the Gestapo. He was sentenced to death at the Nuremberg Trials, but committed suicide.

55 Our movement took a grip on cowardly Marxism, and from it, extracted the meaning of socialism. It also took from the cowardly, middle-class parties their nationalism. Throwing both into the cauldron of our way of life there emerged, as clear as crystal, the synthesis —German National Socialism.
1933 Speech, Berlin, 9 Apr.

56 Would you rather have butter or guns? …preparedness makes us powerful. Butter merely makes us fat.
1936 Speech, Hamburg.
▶ See Goebbels 374:53.

57 I hereby commission you to carry out all the preparations with regard to…a total solution of the Jewish question, in those territories of Europe that are under German influence.
1941 Directive to the Nazi High Command, 31 Jul, quoted in William Shirer *The Rise and Fall of the Third Reich* (1962).

Goethe, Johann Wolfgang von 1749–1832

German poet, dramatist and scientist. His early nationalistic, 'Sturm und Drang' dramas were followed by lyric poetry and poetical drama. His masterpiece was *Faust* (1808), on which he worked for most of his life.

58 English plays,
Atrocious in content,
Absurd in form,
Objectionable in action,
Execrable English Theatre!
1749 Attributed.

59 For a woman, she has extraordinary talent. One must look for what she does, not what she fails to do.
1786–8 Of the painter Angelica Kauffman. *Italienische Reise* (published 1816–17, translated by W H Auden and Elizabeth Mayer as *Italian Journey*, 1962).

60 *Wenn es eine Freude ist das Gute zu genießen, so ist es eine größere das Bessere zu empfinden, und in der Kunst ist das Beste gut genug.*
As it is a joy to enjoy what is good, so it is a greater joy to experience what is better, and in art the best is good enough.
1787 *Italienische Reise* 3 Mar (published 1816–17, translated by W H Auden and Elizabeth Mayer as *Italian Journey*, 1962).

61 *Wer nie sein Brot mit Tränen aß,*
Wer nie die kummervollen Nächte,
Auf seinem Bette weinen saß,
Der kennt euch nicht, ihr himmlischen Mächte.
Who never ate his bread in sorrow,
Who never spent the darksome hours
Weeping and watching for the morrow
He knows ye not, ye heavenly powers.
1795–6 *Wilhelm Meisters Lehrjahre* (translated by Carlyle in 1824 as *Wilhelm Meister's Apprenticeship*).

62 *Es irrt der Mensch, so lang er strebt.*
Man will err while yet he strives.
1808 *Faust*, pt.1, 'Prolog im Himmel'.

63 *Grau, teurer Freund, ist alle Theorie.*
Und grün des Lebens goldner Baum.
All theory, dear friend, is grey, but the golden tree of actual life springs ever green.
1808 *Faust*, pt.1, 'Studierzimmer'.

64 *Alles Gescheite ist schon gedacht worden; man muss nur versuchen, es noch einmal zu denken.*
Everything clever has been thought of before. We must try to think it again.
1819 *Sprüche in Prosa, Maximen und Reflexionen*, pt.1.

65 *Der Aberglaube ist die Poesie des Lebens.*
Superstition is the poetry of life.
1819 *Sprüche in Prosa, Maximen und Reflexionen*, pt.3.

66 *Neuere Poeten tun viel Wasser in die Tinte.*
Modern poets mix a lot of water with their ink.
1819 *Sprüche in Prosa, Maximen und Reflexionen*, pt.6.

67 *Das Erste und Letzte, was vom Genie gefordert wird, ist Wahrheitsliebe.*
The first and the last thing demanded of genius is the love of truth.
1819 *Sprüche in Prosa, Maximen und Reflexionen*, pt.6.

68 *Klassisch ist das Gesunde, romantisch das Kranke.*
The classical period was healthy; the romantic diseased.
1819 *Sprüche in Prosa, Maximen und Reflexionen*, pt.7.

69 Lord Byron is only great as a poet; as soon as he reflects he is a child.
1825 Eckermann's *Conversations with Goethe*, 18 Jan.

70 *Ich kenne mich auch nicht und Gott soll mich auch davor behuten.*
I do not know myself, and God forbid that I should.
1829 Eckermann's *Conversations with Goethe*, 10 Apr.

71 *Mehr Licht!*
More light!
1832 Last words.

72 *Ach da ich irrte, hatt' ich viel Gespielen,*
Da ich dich kenne, bin ich fast allein.
Ah! while I erred I had many friends.
Now that I know you, I am alone.
Gedichte, Zuneigung (published 1910).

Goheen, Robert F(rancis) 1919–2008

US classical scholar and educator, born in India. He joined Princeton University in 1948, and became President there (1957–72). He was Ambassador to India (1977–80).

73 If you feel that you have both feet planted on level ground, then the university has failed you.
1961 Baccalaureate address. Reported in *Time* magazine, 23 Jun.

Golding, Sir William (Gerald) 1911–93

English novelist. He achieved fame with his first novel *Lord of the Flies* (1954), and was awarded the Nobel prize for literature in 1983.

74 Ralph wept for the end of innocence, the darkness of man's heart, and the fall through the air of a true, wise friend called Piggy.
1954 *Lord of the Flies*, ch.12.

75 Sleep is when all the unsorted stuff comes flying out as from a dustbin upset in a high wind.
1956 *Pincher Martin*, ch.6.

76 Philip is a living example of natural selection. He was as fitted to survive in this modern world as a tapeworm in an intestine.
1959 *Free Fall*, ch.2.

77 Eighteen is a good time for suffering. One has all the necessary strength, and no defences.
1967 *The Pyramid*.

78 With lack of sleep and too much understanding I grow a little crazy, I think, like all men at sea who live too close to each other and too close thereby to all that is monstrous under the sun and moon.
1980 *Rites of Passage*, closing words.

79 The theme defeats structuralism, for it is an emotion. The theme of *Lord of the Flies* is grief, sheer grief, grief, grief, grief.
1982 'Moving Target'.

80 It really means nothing in this country whatsoever—but then being a writer here means nothing either.
1983 On winning the Nobel prize. Quoted in the *Observer*, 31 May.

81 Life should serve up its feast of experience in a series of courses.
1987 *Close Quarters*.

Goldman, William 1931–

US screenwriter, who has written the scripts for films such as *Butch Cassidy and the Sundance Kid* (1969, Academy Award), *All the President's Men* (1976, Academy Award) and *Misery* (1990).

82 Boy, I got vision. The rest of the world wears bifocals.
1969 Anachronistic line delivered by Paul Newman in *Butch Cassidy and the Sundance Kid*.

Goldmark, Peter Carl, Jr 1940–
US government official, President of the Rockefeller Foundation (1988–97) and Director of the Global and Regional Air Program at Environmental Defense (2003–10).

83 Welfare is hated by those who administer it; mistrusted by those who pay for it; and held in contempt by those who receive it.
   1977 In the *New York Times*, 24 May.

Goldsmith, Oliver 1728–74
Irish novelist, poet, and playwright. After studying medicine and attempting to join the Church, he began a literary career. He is best known for the novel *The Vicar of Wakefield* (1766), the poem *The Deserted Village* (1770) and the play *She Stoops to Conquer* (1773).

84 The doctor found, when she was dead,
   Her last disorder mortal.
   1759 'Elegy on Mrs Mary Blaize'.

85 Where'er I roam, whatever realms to see,
   My heart untravelled fondly turns to thee;
   Still to my brother turns with ceaseless pain,
   And drags at each remove a lengthening chain.
   1764 *The Traveller*, l.7–10.

86 Such is the patriot's boast, where'er we roam,
   His first, best country ever is, at home.
   1764 *The Traveller*, l.73–4.

87 Laws grind the poor, and rich men rule the law.
   1764 *The Traveller*, l.386.

88 How small, of all that human hearts endure,
   That part which laws or kings can cause or cure!
   1764 *The Traveller*, l.429–30.

89 I was ever of the opinion, that the honest man who married and brought up a large family, did more service than he who continued single and only talked of population.
   1766 *The Vicar of Wakefield*, ch.1.

90 Let us draw upon content for the deficiencies of fortune.
   1766 *The Vicar of Wakefield*, ch.3.

91 Conscience is a coward, and those faults it has not strength enough to prevent it seldom has justice enough to accuse.
   1766 *The Vicar of Wakefield*, ch.13.

92 It seemed to me pretty plain, that they had more of love than of matrimony in them.
   1766 *The Vicar of Wakefield*, ch.16.

93 When lovely woman stoops to folly
   And finds too late that men betray,
   What charm can soothe her melancholy,
   What art can wash her guilt away?
   1766 *The Vicar of Wakefield*, ch.29.

94 Friendship is a disinterested commerce between equals; love, an abject intercourse between tyrants and slaves.
   1768 *The Good-Natured Man*, act 1.

95 Silence is become his mother tongue.
   1768 *The Good-Natured Man*, act 2.

96 Sweet Auburn, loveliest village of the plain,
   Where health and plenty cheered the labouring swain.
   1770 *The Deserted Village*, l.1–2.

97 How often have I paused on every charm,
   The sheltered cot, the cultivated farm,
   The never-failing brook, the busy mill,
   The decent church that topped the neighbouring hill.
   1770 *The Deserted Village*, l.9–12.

98 Ill fares the land, to hastening ills a prey
   Where wealth accumulates and men decay:
   Princes and lords may flourish or may fade;
   A breath can make them, as a breath has made;
   But a bold peasantry, their country's pride,
   When once destroyed, can never be supplied.
   1770 *The Deserted Village*, l.51–6.

99 The village preacher's modest mansion rose.
   A man he was to all the country dear,
   And passing rich with forty pounds a year.
   1770 *The Deserted Village*, l.140–2.

1 The village master taught his little school;
   A man severe he was and stern to view;
   I knew him well, and every truant knew;
   Well had the boding tremblers learned to trace
   The day's disasters in his morning face;
   Full well they laughed, with counterfeited glee,
   At all his jokes, for many a joke had he.
   1770 *The Deserted Village*, l.196–202.

2 In arguing too, the parson owned his skill,
   For e'en though vanquished, he could argue still;
   While words of learned length, and thund'ring sound
   Amazed the gazing rustics ranged around,
   And still they gazed, and still the wonder grew,
   That one small head could carry all he knew.
   1770 *The Deserted Village*, l.211–16.

3 And, even while fashion's brightest arts decoy,
   The heart distrusting asks, if this be joy.
   1770 *The Deserted Village*, l.263–4.

4 The rich man's joys increase, the poor's decay,
   'Tis yours to judge how wide the limits stand
   Between a splendid and a happy land.
   1770 *The Deserted Village*, l.266–8.

5 Thus fares the land, by luxury betrayed.
   1770 *The Deserted Village*, l.295.

6 In all the silent manliness of grief.
   1770 *The Deserted Village*, l.384.

7 I see the rural virtues leave the land.
   1770 *The Deserted Village*, l.398.

8 Though very poor, may still be very blest.
   1770 *The Deserted Village*, l.426.

9 I love everything that's old: old friends, old times, old manners, old books, old wine.
   1773 *She Stoops to Conquer*, act 1, sc.1.

10 Is it one of my well-looking days, child? Am I in face to-day?
    1773 *She Stoops to Conquer*, act 1, sc.1.

11 Let school-masters puzzle their brain,
    With grammar, and nonsense, and learning;
    Good liquor, I stoutly maintain,
    Gives genius a better discerning.
    1773 *She Stoops to Conquer*, act 1, sc.2.

12 I'll be with you in a squeezing of a lemon.
    1773 *She Stoops to Conquer*, act 1, sc.2.

13 It's a damned long, dark, boggy, dirty, dangerous way.
    1773 *She Stoops to Conquer*, act 1, sc.2.

14 The first blow is half the battle.
1773 *She Stoops to Conquer*, act 2, sc.1.

15 But there's no love lost between us.
1773 *She Stoops to Conquer*, act 4, sc.1.

16 Our Garrick's a salad; for in him we see
Oil, vinegar, sugar, and saltness agree.
1774 *Retaliation*, 1.11–12.

17 Who, too deep for his hearers, still went on refining,
And thought of convincing, while they thought of dining;
Though equal to all things, for all things unfit,
Too nice for a statesman, too proud for a wit.
1774 Of Edmund Burke. *Retaliation*, l.29–32.

18 On the stage he was natural, simple, affecting;
'Twas only that when he was off he was acting.
1774 Of Garrick. *Retaliation*, l.101–2.

19 When they talked of their Raphaels, Correggios, and stuff,
He shifted his trumpet, and only took snuff.
1774 Of Reynolds. *Retaliation*, l.145–6.

Goldwater, Barry M(orris) 1909–98

US politician, Senator from Arizona (1952–64, 1969–87) and leader of the extreme right Republican wing. He was defeated in the 1964 presidential election by Lyndon B Johnson.

20 Extremism in the defence of liberty is no vice, and moderation in the pursuit of justice is no virtue.
1964 Speech to the Republican convention, 16 Jul.

21 In your heart, you know I'm right.
1964 Presidential campaign slogan.

22 He had probably been vaccinated with a phonograph needle.
1979 On the windy presidential candidate Hubert Humphrey. *With No Apologies*.

23 You don't need to be 'straight' to fight and die for your country. You just need to shoot straight.
1993 On homosexuals in the military. In *Life*, Dec.

Goldwyn, Sam(uel) *originally* Schmuel Gelbfisz
1882–1974

Polish-born US film producer. In 1917 he founded Goldwyn Pictures Corporation and in 1925 the Metro-Goldwyn-Mayer Company. His films include *Wuthering Heights* (1939), *The Little Foxes* (1941) and *Guys and Dolls* (1955). He is credited with many artless Goldwynisms, most probably apocryphal.

24 I'll cable Hitler and ask him to shoot around you.
1939 Remark to David Niven, Sep, when Niven left Hollywood to return to England. Quoted in David Niven *Bring on the Empty Horses* (1975).

25 I don't care if it doesn't make a nickel. I just want every man, woman and child in America to see it!
1946 Of *The Best Years of Our Lives*. Quoted in Leslie Halliwell *Halliwell's Filmgoer's and Video Viewer's Companion* (9th edn, 1989).

26 Any man who goes to a psychiatrist should have his head examined.
Quoted in Norman Zierold *Moguls* (1969), ch.3.

27 Please write music like Wagner, only louder.
Note to a composer of a forthcoming film soundtrack. Recalled on his death, 31 Jan 1974.

28 You ought to take the bull between the teeth.
Recalled on his death, 31 Jan 1974.

29 Now why did you name your baby 'John'? Every Tom, Dick and Harry is named 'John'.
Attributed. Quoted in Fred Metcalf (ed) *The Penguin Dictionary of Humorous Quotations* (1986).

30 I seriously object to seeing on the screen what belongs in the bedroom.
Attributed maxim. Quoted in Leslie Halliwell *Halliwell's Filmgoer's and Video Viewer's Companion* (9th edn, 1989).

31 What we want is a story that starts with an earthquake and works its way up to a climax.
Quoted in Leslie Halliwell *Halliwell's Filmgoer's and Video Viewer's Companion* (9th edn, 1989).

32 A verbal contract isn't worth the paper it's written on.
Attributed. Quoted in A Scott Berg *Goldwyn* (1989).

33 I'll give you a definite maybe.
Attributed. Quoted in A Scott Berg *Goldwyn* (1989).

34 Include me out.
Attributed. Quoted in A Scott Berg *Goldwyn* (1989).

35 We are dealing in facts, not realities.
Attributed. Quoted in A Scott Berg *Goldwyn* (1989).

36 You gotta take the sour with the bitter.
Remark allegedly said to Billy Wilder when one of his films flopped. Quoted in A Scott Berg *Goldwyn* (1989).

37 The most important thing in acting is honesty. Once you've learned to fake that, you're in.
Attributed.

38 The only reason so many people showed up at his funeral was because they wanted to make sure he was dead.
Of Louis B Mayer. Attributed.

Gomez, Vernon Louis *known as* 'Lefty' 1908–89

US baseball player, pitcher for the New York Yankees in the 1930s.

39 Tell you what, you keep the salary and pay me the cut.
When asked to take a cut in salary from $20,000 to $7,500 following a poor season. Quoted in Colin Jarman *The Guinness Dictionary of Sports Quotations* (1990).

Goncharov, Ivan Alexandrovich 1812–91

Russian novelist. He led an uneventful life in the civil service and produced *Oblomov* (1857, translated 1915), one of the greatest works of Russian realism.

40 The trouble is that no devastating or redeeming fires have ever burnt in my life... My life began by flickering out.
1859 *Oblomov*, pt.2, ch.4 (translated by David Magarshak).

41 You lost your ability for doing things in childhood... It all began with your inability to put on your socks and ended by your inability to live.
1859 *Oblomov*, pt.4, ch.2 (translated by David Magarshak).

Gonne, Maud 1865–1953

Irish nationalist and actress. She met W B Yeats in the early 1890s and, though Yeats wished to marry her, she ultimately rejected him and married Major John MacBride.

42 Poets should never marry. The world should thank me for not marrying you.
Attributed. Said to W B Yeats.

González Prada, Manuel 1848–1918

Peruvian reformer, journalist and poet. Nationalistic, pro-Indian, anti-Spanish and anti-clerical, he was a virtuoso in the vocabulary of invective, combining intensity of emotion with a pervasive sense of form.

43 *Aunque chillen los pedantes*
   y arruguen todos el ceño,
   lo declaro yo: Cervantes
   suele producirme sueño
   Pedants may cry out loud
   or frown at me,
   but I must say it: Cervantes
   usually puts me to sleep.
   1937 *Grafitos*, 'Hombres y libros' ('Men and Books').

Gooch, George Peabody 1873–1968
English historian and politician. He wrote several works on political and diplomatic history.

44 We can now look forward with something like confidence to the time when war between civilised nations will be considered as antiquated as a duel.
   1911 *History of Our Time 1855–1911*.

Goodall, John 1863–1942
English footballer, captain of Preston North End. He also captained England, winning a total of 14 caps. He subsequently played cricket at county level for Derbyshire.

45 The one passion of my life has been football—the most exhilarating game I know, and the strongest protest against selfishness, without sermonizing, that was ever put before a thoughtful people.
   Quoted in Andrew Ward and Anton Rippon *The Derby County Story* (1983).

Gorbachev, Mikhail Sergeyevich 1931–
Russian politician, President of the Supreme Soviet of the USSR (1988–90) and first executive President of the USSR. Despite his historic achievements as the father of *glasnost* (openness of information) and *perestroika* (a radical reform programme), which ended the Cold War, he was forced to resign on 25 Dec 1991. He was awarded the Nobel peace prize in 1990.

46 Some comrades apparently find it hard to understand that democracy is just a slogan.
   1987 In the *Observer*, 1 Feb.

47 If the Russian word 'perestroika' has easily entered the international lexicon, it is due to more than just interest in what is going on in the Soviet Union. Now the whole world needs restructuring; that is, progressive development, a fundamental change.
   1987 *Perestroika: New Thinking for Our Country and the World*.

48 The Soviet people want full-blooded and unconditional democracy.
   1988 Speech, Jul.

49 Life is making us abandon established stereotypes and outdated views; it is making us discard illusions.
   1988 Speech, United Nations, 7 Dec.

50 Mitterrand has 100 lovers. One has AIDS, but he doesn't know which one. Bush has 100 bodyguards. One is a terrorist, but he doesn't know which one. Gorbachev has 100 economic advisers. One is smart, but he doesn't know which one.
   1990 In the *Sunday Times*, 9 Dec.

51 We had ten years after the Cold War to build a new world order and yet we squandered them. The United States cannot tolerate anyone acting independently. Every US president has to have a war.
   2009 In *The Daily Telegraph*, 7 May.

Gordon, Adam Lindsay 1833–70
Australian poet, born in the Azores. A series of personal tragedies led to a mental breakdown, and he committed suicide.

52 Question not, but live and labour
   Till yon goal be won,
   Helping every feeble neighbour,
   Seeking help from none;
   Life is mostly froth and bubble,
   Two things stand like stone:
   KINDNESS in another's trouble,
   COURAGE in your own.
   1866 'Ye Wearie Wayfarer: Hys Ballad. In Eight Fyttes', in *Bell's Life in Victoria*, Nov 1866, collected in *Sea Spray and Smoke Drift* (1867).

53 I would that with sleepy, soft embraces
   The sea would fold me—would find me rest
   In luminous shades of her secret places,
   In depths where her marvels are manifest;
   So the earth beneath her should not discover
   My hidden couch—nor the heaven above her—
   As a strong love shielding a weary lover,
   I would have her shield me with shining breast.
   'The Swimmer', stanza 5, collected in *Bush Ballads and Galloping Rhymes* (1870).

54 A little season of love and laughter,
   Of light and life, and pleasure and pain,
   And horror of outer darkness after,
   And dust returneth to dust again.
   Then the lesser life shall be as the greater,
   And the lover of life shall join the hater,
   And the one thing cometh sooner or later,
   And no one knoweth the loss or gain.
   'The Swimmer', stanza 10, collected in *Bush Ballads and Galloping Rhymes* (1870).

Gordon, Mack 1904–59
Polish-born US lyricist.

55 Pardon me boy is that the Chattanooga Choo-choo,
   Track twenty nine,
   Boy you can give me a shine.
   1941 Song 'Chattanooga Choo Choo', featured in *Sun Valley Serenade* (music by Harry Warren).

56 Dinner in the diner
   nothing could be finer
   than to have your ham'n' eggs in Carolina.
   1941 Song 'Chattanooga Choo Choo', featured in *Sun Valley Serenade* (music by Harry Warren).

Gordon, Ruth 1896–1985
US actress and playwright, best known for the screenplays she wrote with her husband Garson Kanin, *Adam's Rib* (1949) and *Pat and Mike* (1952). She won an Oscar for her performance in *Rosemary's Baby* (1968).

57 MAX: Say, is it too early for a drink?
   POLLY: What's early about it? It's tomorrow in Europe and yesterday in China.
   1943 *Over Twenty-One*, act 3.

Gore, Al(bert, Jr) 1948–

US Vice-President under Bill Clinton (1992–2000). In 2000 he ran for President in what turned out to be the closest contest in over 100 years, losing to Republican George W Bush. In 2007 he shared the Nobel peace prize for his role in climate change activism.

58 You get all the French-fries the President can't get to.
1994 On being Vice-President. In the *New York Times*, 8 Apr.

59 It makes no more sense to launch an assault on our civil liberties as the best way to get at terrorists than it did to launch an invasion on Iraq as the best way to get at Osama Bin Laden.
2003 Speech calling for the repeal of the US Patriot Act, 9 Nov.

60 You can't make somebody understand something if their salary depends upon them not understanding it.
2006 An Inconvenient Truth.

61 The planet has a fever. If your baby has a fever, you go to the doctor. If the doctor says you need to intervene here, you don't say, 'Well, I read a science fiction novel that told me it's not a problem.' If the crib's on fire, you don't speculate that the baby is flame retardant. You take action.
2007 Testimony before Congress, CBS *Evening News*, 21 Mar.

62 The planet is in distress and all of the attention is on Paris Hilton.
2007 In *The Sun*, 18 Jun.

63 Here is the truth: The Earth is round; Saddam Hussein did not attack us on 9/11; Elvis is dead; Obama was born in the United States; and the climate crisis is real.
2011 In *Rolling Stone* magazine, 22 Jun.

64 Air travel is nature's way of making you look like your passport photo.
Attributed.

Gorman, Dave 1971–

English comedian.

65 Fictional comedy tells us that the writer is remarkable. Factual comedy tells us that the world is remarkable. I suppose I prefer to live in a remarkable world.
2004 In *Varsity*, 23 Jan.

Gorostiza, José 1901–73

Mexican poet and diplomat. The most famous member of the avant-garde *Contemporáneos* group, his published poems are few but complex.

66 ¡Oh inteligencia, soledad en llamas,
que todo lo concibe sin crearlo!
Oh intelligence, flaming solitude,
envisioning all without creating!
1939 *Muerte sin fin*, pt.1 (translated as *Death without End*, 1969).

Gorostiza, Manuel Eduardo de 1789–1851

Mexican dramatist and diplomat. He spent his youth in Spain, returning to Mexico in 1833 where he fought in the US invasion. He was a key figure in Latin American neoclassical theatre.

67 Yo no digo por eso que el té no sea saludable…cuando duelen las tripas…pero al cabo no pasa de ser agua caliente; sólo podía habernos venido de Inglaterra, que como allí son herejes, ni tendrán vino, ni bueyes cebones.
I'm not saying that tea is not healthy…when you have a stomach ache…but, all in all, it is only hot water; it could only come from the English, who, being heretics as they are, probably have no wine or good beer.
1833 *Contigo pan y cebolla*, act 1.

Gosse, Sir Edmund 1849–1928

English critic and translator. He wrote biographies of many notable literary figures, and translated the plays of Henrik Ibsen.

68 A sheep in sheep's clothing.
Of Sturge Moore, a poet. Quoted in F Greenslet *Under the Bridge* (1943), ch.10.

69 We were as nearly bored as enthusiasm would permit.
Of a play by Algernon Swinburne. Quoted in C Hassall *Biography of Edward Marsh*.

Gottfried von Strassburg fl.c.1200

German poet. His major work is a version of the Tristan and Isolde legend, *Tristan* (c.1210), but his appraisals of the works of other writers are a striking early example of literary criticism.

70 *Wan swelh wîp tugendet wider ir art,
diu gerne wider ir art bewart
ir lop, ir êre unde ire lîp,
diu ist niwan mit namen ein wîp
und ist ein man mit muote.*
When a woman grows in virtue despite her nature and gladly preserves the integrity of her honour, her reputation, and her person, she is only a woman in name: in spirit she is a man.
c.1210 *Tristan*, l.17971–3.

Gottlieb, Adolph 1903–74

US painter, one of the leaders of Abstract Expressionism.

71 Certain people always say we should go back to nature. I notice they never say we should go forward to nature. It seems to me they are more concerned that we should go back, than about nature.
1947 In *Tiger's Eye*, vol.1, no.2, Dec, quoted in C Harrison and Paul Wood (eds) *Art in Theory 1900–1990* (1992).

Gould, Glenn 1932–82

Canadian pianist and musical theorist. He performed his last live concert in 1964, thereafter confining himself to recording.

72 The concert is dead.
Quoted in Richard Kostelanetz *Master Minds* (1969).

73 The purpose of art is the lifelong construction of a state of wonder.
Quoted by Lorraine Monk at the Commencement Address, York University, Toronto, 6 Nov 1982.

Gould of Brookwood, Philip Gould, Baron 1950–2011

English political strategist and senior adviser to Tony Blair.

74 The New Labour brand has been badly contaminated. It is the object of constant criticism and, even worse, ridicule.
2000 Internal memo, May, later leaked to the press. In *The Guardian*, 20 Jul.

Gould, Stephen Jay 1941–2002

US palaeontologist, evolutionary biologist and science writer, Professor at Harvard University (1967–2002).

75 A man does not attain the status of Galileo merely because he is persecuted, he must also be right.
1977 *Ever Since Darwin.*

76 Science must be understood as a social phenomenon, a gutsy, human enterprise, not the work of robots programmed to collect pure information.
1981 *The Mismeasure of Man.*

77 Science is an integral part of culture. It's not this foreign thing, done by an arcane priesthood. It's one of the glories of the human intellectual tradition.
1990 In *The Independent,* 24 Jan.

Gounod, Charles François 1818–93

French composer. His works include operas, masses, hymns and oratorios, and he was popular as a songwriter. He fled to England in the Franco-Prussian War (1870), becoming a commander of the Legion of Honour in 1877.

78 God grant me a failure like that!
1861 Of Wagner's opera *Tannhäuser,* after the disastrous première of its revised version at the *Opéra,* 13 Mar, when it was withdrawn after only three performances. Quoted in Joanna Richardson *La Vie Parisienne* (1971).
▶ See Mérimée 588:42.

Gourmont, Rémy de 1858–1915

French writer and critic, leader of the Symbolist movement. He founded the periodical *Le Mercure de France,* and wrote essays, literary criticism and novels.

79 Science is the only truth and it is the great lie. It knows nothing, and people think it knows everything. It is misrepresented. People think that science is electricity, automobilism, and dirigible balloons. It is something very different. It is life devouring itself. It is the sensibility transformed into intelligence. It is the need to know stifling the need to live. It is the genius of knowledge vivisecting the vital genius.
1905 *Promenades philosophiques* (translated by Glen S Burne, 1966).

Gowers, Sir Ernest Arthur 1880–1966

English civil servant, called to the bar in 1906. His *Plain Words* (1948) and *ABC of Plain Words* (1951) are guides for officials in writing clear English. He revised Fowler's *Dictionary of Modern English Usage* (1965).

80 It is not easy nowadays to remember anything so contrary to all appearances as that officials are the servants of the public; and the official must try not to foster the illusion that it is the other way round.
1948 *Plain Words,* ch.3.

81 Sociology is a new science concerning itself not with esoteric matters outside the comprehension of the layman, as the older sciences do, but with the ordinary affairs of ordinary people. This seems to engender in those who write about it a feeling that the lack of any abstruseness in their subject matter demands a compensatory abstruseness in their language.
1965 'Sociologese', in H F Fowler *A Dictionary of Modern English Usage* (2nd rev edn).

Goya, Francisco de 1746–1828

Spanish painter and graphic artist, perhaps best known for his series of etchings *The Disasters of War.*

82 But where do they find these lines in nature? Personally I only see forms that are lit up and forms that are not, planes which advance and planes which recede, relief and depth. My eye never sees outlines or particular features or details. I do not count the hairs in the beard of the man who passes by any more than the buttonholes on his jacket attract my notice. My brush should not see better than I do.
Quoted in Enriqueta Harris *Goya* (1969).

Grace, W(illiam) G(ilbert) 1848–1915

English cricketer and physician. He made his debut in first-class cricket in 1864; by the time he retired in 1908 he had scored 126 first-class centuries and 54,896 runs, and taken 2,864 wickets.

83 Let's be getting at them before they get at us.
His reason for always choosing to bat first if his team won the toss. Quoted in Colin Jarman *The Guinness Dictionary of Sports Quotations* (1990).

84 They haven't come to see you umpiring, they have come to see me bat.
On refusing to leave the crease after an umpire gave him out before he had scored, attributed. Other versions of the story have the umpire refusing to call out on the first ball, explaining to the outraged bowler that the crowd had paid not to see him bowl, but to see Grace bat.

Graham, Harry 1874–1936

English writer of light verse. His blackly comic rhymes in *Ruthless Rhymes for Heartless Homes* (1899) and the later *More Ruthless Rhymes* (1930) won widespread popularity.

85 Aunt Jane observed, the second time
She tumbled off a bus,
'The step is short from the Sublime
To the Ridiculous.'
1899 *Ruthless Rhymes for Heartless Homes,* 'Equanimity'.

86 O'er the rugged mountain's brow
Clara threw the twins she nursed,
And remarked, 'I wonder now
Which will reach the bottom first?'
1899 *Ruthless Rhymes for Heartless Homes,* 'Calculating Clara'.

87 Billy, in one of his nice new sashes,
Fell in the fire and was burnt to ashes;
Now, although the room grows chilly,
I haven't the heart to poke poor Billy.
1899 *Ruthless Rhymes for Heartless Homes,* 'Tender-Heartedness'.

88 Weep not for little Léonie
Abducted by a French *Marquis*!
Though loss of honour was a wrench
Just think how it's improved her French.
1930 *More Ruthless Rhymes for Heartless Homes,* 'Compensation'.

Grahame, Kenneth 1859–1932

Scottish children's writer and Secretary of the Bank of England (1898–1908). He wrote essays and country tales but is best remembered for *The Wind in the Willows* (1908).

89 Believe me, my young friend, there is *nothing*—absolutely nothing—half so much worth doing as simply messing about in boats.
1908 *The Wind in the Willows,* ch.1.

90 The poetry of motion! The *real* way to travel! The *only* way to travel! Here today—in next week tomorrow!

Villages skipped, towns and cities jumped—always somebody else's horizon!
1908 Toad rhapsodizes about the motor car. *The Wind in the Willows*, ch.2.

91 The smell of buttered toast simply talked to Toad, and with no uncertain voice; talked of warm kitchens, of breakfasts on bright frosty mornings, of cosy parlour firesides on winter evenings, when one's ramble was over and slippered feet were propped on the fender; of the purring of contented cats, and the twitter of sleepy canaries.
1908 *The Wind in the Willows*, ch.8.

92 The clever men at Oxford
Know all that there is to be knowed.
But they none of them know one half as much
As intelligent Mr Toad.
1908 *The Wind in the Willows*, ch.10.

Gramm, Phil (William Philip) 1942–
US Senator (1985–2002) and economist.

93 If I had to decide today, I would run. But I may come to my senses.
1994 On seeking presidential nomination. In *Time*, 26 Sep.

94 I didn't come to Washington to be loved and I haven't been disappointed.
1995 In NPR broadcast, 24 Feb.

95 Sophia Loren is not a citizen.
1995 On being asked if he would choose a woman as a running mate. In *Newsweek*, 13 Mar.

96 I have the most reliable friend that you can have in American politics—ready money.
1995 On seeking presidential nomination. In the *New York Times*, 23 Apr.

Grand, Sarah *pseudonym of* Frances Elizabeth McFall *née* Clarke 1854–1943
British novelist and feminist, born in Ireland. She was Mayoress of Bath (1923, 1925–9), and is best known for her novels which explore sexual double standards.

97 Both the cow-woman and the scum-woman are well within range of the comprehension of the Bawling Brotherhood, but the new woman is a little above him, and he never thought of looking up to where she has been sitting apart in silent contemplation all these years.
1894 *North American Review*, 'The New Aspect of the Woman Question', Mar.

Grant, Cary *pseudonym of* Archibald Leach 1904–86
English-born US film star. He made his film debut in 1932 and developed a reputation as a suave, debonair performer in sophisticated light comedy. His films include *Bringing up Baby* (1938), *His Girl Friday* (1940), *An Affair to Remember* (1957) and *North by Northwest* (1959).

98 Not only will I not play it, but if Rex Harrison doesn't do it, I won't even go to see it.
c.1963 Response when offered the role of Professor Henry Higgins in the film of *My Fair Lady*. Attributed.

99 Old Cary Grant fine. How you?
His response to a journalist's terse cable to his press agent, 'How old Cary Grant?' Attributed.

Grant, George P 1918–88
Canadian philosopher and teacher.

1 We listen to others to discover what we ourselves believe.
Quoted in *CBC Times*, 18 Feb 1959.

Grant, Hugh 1960–
English actor, who became an international star after starring in *Four Weddings and a Funeral* (1994). Subsequent films include *Notting Hill* (1999) and *Bridget Jones's Diary* (2001).

2 I play the sort of character who would sell his grandmother for career advancement, something I've come across a lot with actors.
1994 On his role in *Restoration*. In *Screen International*, 2 Sep.

3 If *Pulp Fiction* had been set in the Sussex countryside—and I'm sure it could have worked—then things might have turned out very differently.
1995 Contrasting *Four Weddings and a Funeral* with a notoriously violent urban US drama. Speech at the British Academy of Film and Television Arts award ceremony, reported in *Screen International*, 28 Apr.

4 I just don't believe in love at first sight any more, even though I've based my whole career on the concept.
Quoted in the *Daily Telegraph*, 1 Jan 2004.

Grant, Sir Robert 1779–1838
English lawyer and politician, Advocate-General and Governor of Bombay.

5 O worship the King, all glorious above;
O gratefully sing his power and his love:
Our Shield and Defender, the Ancient of Days,
Pavilioned in splendour, and girded with praise.
1833 'O worship the King, all glorious above', collected in *Sacred Poems* (1839).

6 O tell of his might, O sing of his grace,
Whose robe is the light, whose canopy space.
His chariots of wrath the deep thunder-clouds form,
And dark is his path on the wings of the storm.
1833 'O worship the King, all glorious above', collected in *Sacred Poems* (1839).

Grant, Ulysses S(impson) 1822–85
US soldier and 18th President (1869–77), Union general in the Civil War, who accepted the Confederate surrender at Appomattox Court House (1865). He presided over the reconstruction of the South, but his administration was marred by scandal and corruption.

7 No terms except unconditional and immediate surrender can be accepted. I propose to move immediately upon your works.
1862 Message to Simon Bolivar Buckner, besieged at Fort Donelson, 16 Feb. Quoted in P C Headley *The Life and Campaigns of General U. S. Grant* (1869), ch.6.

8 I purpose to fight it out on this line, if it takes all summer.
1864 Despatch to Washington from Spottsylvania, 11 May. Quoted in P C Headley *The Life and Campaigns of General U. S. Grant* (1869), ch.23.

9 I know no method to secure the repeal of bad or obnoxious laws so effective as their stringent execution.
1869 Inaugural address, 4 Mar.

10 I only know two tunes. One of them is 'Yankee Doodle', and the other isn't.
    Attributed. Quoted in Derek Watson *Music Quotations* (1991).

Grass, Günter Wilhelm 1927–

German novelist, poet and playwright. Intellectual and experimental in form, theme and language, his books consistently challenge the status quo and question our reading of the past. He was awarded the Nobel prize for literature in 1999.

11 *Ich bin Schriftsteller von Beruf. Ich versuche, gegen die vergehende Zeit anzuschreiben, damit das Vergangene nicht unbekannt bleibt.*
    I am a writer by profession. I seek in my writing to hold back time so that the past is not forgotten.
    1978 *Denkzettel: Politische Reden und Aufsätze.*

12 *Ich sei nicht nur als Autor, sondern auch als Mann betroffen. Und zwar irgendwie schuldhaft.*
    I am moved, not only as an author, but as a person. And feel somehow guilty.
    1977 *Der Butt* (translated as *The Flounder*, 1978).

13 We of the long tails! We of the presentient whiskers! We of the perpetually growing teeth! We, the serried footnotes to man, his proliferating commentary. We, indestructible!
    1987 *Die Ratten* (translated as *The Rat*, 1987).

Grattan, Henry 1746–1820

Irish statesman. He abandoned law for politics in 1775, leading the fight for independence. Unable to prevent the Act of Union, he sat at Westminster until his death.

14 She hears the ocean protesting against separation, but she hears the sea protesting against union. She follows therefore her physical destination when she protests against the two situations, both equally unnatural—separation and union.
    Of Ireland. Quoted in Conor Cruise O'Brien *Parnell and His Party* (1957).

Graves, Robert von Ranke 1895–1985

English writer. He lived abroad for much of his adult life. His works include novels, poems, essays, studies of mythology, criticism, and his autobiography, *Goodbye to All That* (1929).

15 His eyes are quickened so with grief,
    He can watch a grass or a leaf
    Every instant grow.
    1921 'Lost Love'.

16 Love shall come at your command
    Yet will not stay.
    1923 'Song of Contrariety'.

17 Children are dumb to say how hot the day is,
    How hot the scent is of the summer rose.
    1927 'The Cool Web'.

18 Goodbye to All That.
    1929 Title of autobiography.

19 Take your delight in momentariness,
    Walk between dark and dark—a shining space
    With the grave's narrowness, though not its peace.
    1938 'Sick Love'.

20 In fear begotten, I begot in fear.
    Would you have had me cast fear out
    So that you should not be?
    1938 'Parents to Child'.

21 What, then, was war?
    No mere discord of flags
    But an infection of the common sky
    That sagged ominously upon the earth
    Even when the season was the airiest May?
    1938 'Recalling War'.

22 To evoke posterity
    Is to weep on your own grave,
    Ventriloquizing for the unborn.
    1938 'To Evoke Posterity'.

23 To bring the dead to life
    Is no great magic.
    Few are wholly dead:
    Blow on a dead man's embers
    And a live flame will start.
    1938 'To Bring the Dead to Life'.

24 Truth-loving Persians do not dwell upon
    The trivial skirmish fought near Marathon.
    1945 'The Persian Version'.

25 Stirring suddenly from long hibernation,
    I knew myself once more a poet
    Guarded by timeless principalities
    Against the worm of death.
    1945 'Mid-Winter Waking'.

26 To be a poet is a condition rather than a profession.
    1946 Response to a questionnaire from the editor of *Horizon*.

27 The function of poetry is religious invocation of the Muse; its use is the experience of mixed exaltation and horror that her presence excites.
    1948 *The White Goddess*, foreword.

28 For a woman to have a *liaison* is almost always pardonable, and occasionally, when the lover chosen is sufficiently distinguished, even admirable.
    1950 *Occupation: Writer*, 'Lars Porsena'.

29 In love as in sport, the amateur status must be strictly maintained.
    1950 *Occupation: Writer*, 'Lars Porsena'.

30 Counting the slow heart beats,
    The bleeding to death of time in slow heart beats,
    Wakeful they lie.
    1951 'Counting the Beats'.

31 Prose books are the show dogs I breed and sell to support my cat.
    1958 On writing novels to support his love of writing poetry. In the *New York Times*, 13 Jul.

32 Why have such scores of lovely, gifted girls
    Married impossible men?
    1958 'A Slice of Wedding Cake'.

33 Julia: how Irishly you sacrifice
    Love to pity, pity to ill-humour,
    Yourself to love, still haggling at the price.
    'Reproach to Julia', collected in *Collected Poems* (1959).

34 Love is a universal migraine
    A bright stain on the vision
    Blotting out reason.
    1961 'Symptoms of Love'.

35 A well-chosen anthology is a complete dispensary of medicine for the more common mental disorders, and may be used as much for prevention as cure.
    1962 *On English Poetry*, 'Definitions'.

36 Nine-tenths of English poetic literature is the result either of vulgar careerism, or of a poet trying to keep his hand in. Most poets are dead by their late twenties.
1962 In the *Observer*, 11 Nov.

37 If there's no money in poetry, neither is there poetry in money.
1963 Speech at London School of Economics, 6 Dec.

38 The remarkable thing about Shakespeare is that he is really very good—in spite of all the people who say he is very good.
1964 Attributed.

39 The poet is the unsatisfied child who dares to ask the difficult question which arises from the schoolmaster's answer to his simple question, and then the still more difficult question which arises from that.
Recalled on his death, 7 Dec 1985.

40 Love without hope, as when the young bird-catcher
Swept off his tall hat to the Squire's own daughter,
So let the imprisoned larks escape and fly
Singing about her head, as she rode by.
'Love without Hope'.

Gray, Alasdair James 1934–

Scottish novelist, painter and playwright. His novel *Lanark* (1981) is an inventive semi-fantasy based in Glasgow. He has subsequently written and illustrated several equally unconventional novels.

41 Of course in nature the only ending is death, but death hardly ever happens when people are at their best. That is why we like tragedies. They show men energetically with their wits about them and deserving to do it.
1981 *Lanark*, bk.1, interlude.

42 Art is the only work open to people who can't get along with others and still want to be special.
1981 *Lanark*, bk.3, ch.1.

43 Glasgow, the sort of industrial city where most people live nowadays but nobody imagines living.
1981 *Lanark*, bk.3, ch.11.

Gray, Alexander 1882–1968

Scottish economist, Professor at Aberdeen and Edinburgh Universities.

44 The services of a menial servant, taking him as an example of unproductive labour, 'generally perish in the very instant of their performance'—and forthwith into this galley, along with the menial servant, goes the sovereign, accompanied by all the army, the navy, and the civil service, followed by churchmen, lawyers, buffoons and opera dancers. All these—and it is a hard saying—render services which perish in the very instant of their performance.
1931 *The Development of Economic Doctrine*.

Gray, Thomas 1716–71

English poet. In 1742 he wrote his *Ode on a Distant Prospect of Eton College* (1747) and began the famous *Elegy Written in a Country Churchyard* (1751). He declined the Laureateship (1757), and became Professor of History and Modern Languages at Cambridge (1768).

45 Ye distant spires, ye antique towers,
That crown the wat'ry glade.
1742 *Ode on a Distant Prospect of Eton College* (published 1747), l.1–2.

46 Still as they run they look behind,
They hear a voice in every wind,
And snatch a fearful joy.
1742 *Ode on a Distant Prospect of Eton College* (published 1747), l.38–40.

47 Alas, regardless of their doom,
The little victims play!
No sense have they of ills to come,
Nor care beyond to-day.
1742 *Ode on a Distant Prospect of Eton College* (published 1747), l.51–4.

48 To each his suff'rings, all are men,
Condemned alike to groan;
The tender for another's pain,
Th' unfeeling for his own.

Yet ah! why should they know their fate?
Since sorrow never comes too late,
And happiness too swiftly flies.
Thought would destroy their paradise.
No more; where ignorance is bliss,
'Tis folly to be wise.
1742 *Ode on a Distant Prospect of Eton College* (published 1747), l.91–100.

49 The language of the age is never the language of poetry, except among the French, whose verse, where the thought or image does not support it, differs in nothing from prose.
1742 Letter to Richard West, 8 Apr. Collected in H W Starr (ed) *Correspondence of Thomas Gray* (1971).

50 Demurest of the tabby kind,
The pensive Selima reclined,
Gazed on the lake below.
1747 *Ode on the Death of a Favourite Cat, Drowned in a Tub of Gold Fishes*, l.4–6.

51 The velvet of her paws,
Her coat that with the tortoise vies,
Her ears of jet and emerald eyes,
She saw; and purred applause.
1747 *Ode on the Death of a Favourite Cat, Drowned in a Tub of Gold Fishes*, l.9–12.

52 What female heart can gold despise?
What cat's averse to fish?
1747 *Ode on the Death of a Favourite Cat, Drowned in a Tub of Gold Fishes*, l.23–4.

53 A favourite has no friend!
1747 *Ode on the Death of a Favourite Cat, Drowned in a Tub of Gold Fishes*, l.36.

54 Not all that tempts your wandering eyes
And heedless hearts, is lawful prize;
Nor all that glisters gold.
1747 *Ode on the Death of a Favourite Cat, Drowned in a Tub of Gold Fishes*, l.40–3. Derived from 'All that glitters is not gold', *The Merchant of Venice*, act 2, scene 7.

55 The Attic warbler pours her throat,
Responsive to the cuckoo's note,
The untaught harmony of spring.
1748 *Ode on the Spring*, l.5–7.

56 Where'er the oak's thick branches stretch
A broader browner shade;

Where'er the rude and moss-grown beech
O'er-canopies the glade,
Beside some water's rushy brink
With me the Muse shall sit, and think.
1748 *Ode on the Spring*, l.11–16.

57 How low, how little are the proud,
How indigent the great!
1748 *Ode on the Spring*, l.19–20.

58 The insect youth are on the wing,
Eager to taste the honeyed spring,
And float amid the liquid noon:
Some lightly o'er the current skim,
Some show their gaily-gilded trim
Quick-glancing to the sun.
1748 *Ode on the Spring*, l.25–30.

59 Methinks I hear in accents low
The sportive kind reply:
Poor moralist! and what art thou?
A solitary fly!
1748 *Ode on the Spring*, l.41–4.

60 Shame of the versifying tribe!
Your history whither are you spinning?
Can you do nothing but describe?
1750 *A Long Story*, l.17–20.

61 To celebrate her eyes, her air—
Coarse panegyrics would but tease her.
Melissa is her nom de guerre.
Alas, who would not wish to please her!
1750 *A Long Story*, l.33–6.

62 The curfew tolls the knell of parting day,
The lowing herd wind slowly o'er the lea,
The ploughman homeward plods his weary way,
And leaves the world to darkness and to me.

Now fades the glimmering landscapes on the sight,
And all the air a solemn stillness holds,
Save where the beetle wheels his droning flight,
And drowsy tinklings lull the distant folds.
1751 *Elegy Written in a Country Churchyard*, l.1–8.

63 Save that from yonder ivy-mantled tower
The moping owl does to the moon complain.
1751 *Elegy Written in a Country Churchyard*, l.9–10.

64 Beneath those rugged elms, that yew-tree's shade,
Where heaves the turf in many a mouldering heap,
Each in his narrow cell for ever laid,
The rude forefathers of the hamlet sleep.

The breezy call of incense-breathing Morn,
The swallow twitt'ring from the straw-built shed,
The cock's shrill clarion, or the echoing horn,
No more shall rouse them from their lowly bed.
1751 *Elegy Written in a Country Churchyard*, l.13–20.

65 For them no more the blazing hearth shall burn,
Or busy housewife ply her evening care:
No children run to lisp their sire's return,
Or climb upon his knees the envied kiss to share.
1751 *Elegy Written in a Country Churchyard*, l.21–4.

66 Let not Ambition mock their useful toil,
Their homely joys and destiny obscure;
Nor Grandeur hear, with a disdainful smile,
The short and simple annals of the poor.

The boast of heraldry, the pomp of power,
And all that beauty, all that wealth e'er gave,
Awaits alike th' inevitable hour,
The paths of glory lead but to the grave.
1751 *Elegy Written in a Country Churchyard*, l.29–36.

67 Can storied urn or animated bust
Back to its mansion call the fleeting breath?
Can Honour's voice provoke the silent dust,
Or Flattery soothe the dull cold ear of Death?
1751 *Elegy Written in a Country Churchyard*, l.41–4.

68 But knowledge to their eyes her ample page
Rich with the spoils of time did ne'er unroll;
Chill Penury repressed their noble rage,
And froze the genial current of the soul.
1751 *Elegy Written in a Country Churchyard*, l.49–52.

69 Full many a gem of purest ray serene
The dark unfathomed caves of ocean bear:
Full many a flower is born to blush unseen
And waste its sweetness on the desert air.
1751 *Elegy Written in a Country Churchyard*, l.52–6.

70 Some mute inglorious Milton here may rest,
Some Cromwell guiltless of his country's blood.
1751 *Elegy Written in a Country Churchyard*, l.59–60.

71 Their lot forbad: nor circumscribed alone
Their growing virtues, but their crimes confined:
Forbad to wade through slaughter to a throne,
And shut the gates of mercy on mankind.
1751 *Elegy Written in a Country Churchyard*, l.65–8.

72 Far from the madding crowd's ignoble strife
Their sober wishes never learned to stray;
Along the cool sequestered vale of life
They kept the noiseless tenor of their way.
1751 *Elegy Written in a Country Churchyard*, l.73–6. Thomas Hardy popularized the phrase as the title of his novel *Far From the Madding Crowd* (1874).

73 Their name, their years, spelt by the unlettered muse,
The place of fame and elegy supply:
And many a holy text around she strews,
That teach the rustic moralist to die.
1751 *Elegy Written in a Country Churchyard*, l.81–4.

74 For who to dumb Forgetfulness a prey,
This pleasing anxious being e'er resigned,
Left the warm precincts of the cheerful day,
Nor cast one longing ling'ring look behind?
1751 *Elegy Written in a Country Churchyard*, l.85–8.

75 Mindful of the unhonoured dead.
1751 *Elegy Written in a Country Churchyard*, l.93.

76 Oft have we seen him at the peep of dawn
Brushing with hasty steps the dews away
To meet the sun upon the upland lawn.
1751 *Elegy Written in a Country Churchyard*, l.98–100.

77 Here rest his head upon the lap of earth
A youth to fortune and to fame unknown.
Fair Science frowned not on his humble birth,
And Melancholy marked him for her own.
1751 *Elegy Written in a Country Churchyard*, l.117–20, 'The Epitaph'.

78 No farther seek his merits to disclose,
Or draw his frailties from their dread abode,
(There they alike in trembling hope repose)
The bosom of his Father and his God.
1751 *Elegy Written in a Country Churchyard*, l.125–8, 'The Epitaph'.

79 Ruin seize thee, ruthless King!
Confusion on thy banners wait,
Tho' fanned by Conquest's crimson wing
They mock the air with idle state.
1757 *The Bard. A Pindaric Ode*, l.1–4.

80 To save thy secret soul from nightly fears.
1757 *The Bard. A Pindaric Ode*, l.6.

81 Loose his beard, and hoary hair
Streamed, like a meteor, to the troubled air.
1757 *The Bard. A Pindaric Ode*, l.19–20.

82 Cold is Cadwallon's tongue,
That hushed the stormy main.
1757 *The Bard. A Pindaric Ode*, l.29–30.

83 Dear as the light that visits these sad eyes,
Dear as the ruddy drops that warm my heart,
Ye died amidst your dying country's cries.
1757 *The Bard. A Pindaric Ode*, l.40–2.

84 Weave the warp, and weave the woof,
The winding-sheet of Edward's race.
Give ample room, and verge enough
The characters of hell to trace.
1757 *The Bard. A Pindaric Ode*, l.49–52.

85 Mighty victor, mighty lord,
Low on his funeral couch he lies!
No pitying heart, no eye, afford
A tear to grace his obsequies.
1757 *The Bard. A Pindaric Ode*, l.63–6.

86 Fair laughs the morn and soft the zephyr blows,
While proudly riding o'er the azure realm
In gallant trim the gilded vessel goes;
Youth on the prow, and Pleasure at the helm;
Regardless of the sweeping whirlwind's sway,
That, hushed in grim repose, expects his evening prey.
1757 *The Bard. A Pindaric Ode*, l.71–6.

87 In buskined measures move
Pale Grief and pleasing Pain,
With Horror, tyrant of the throbbing breast.
1757 *The Bard. A Pindaric Ode*, l.128–30.

88 'Be thine despair and sceptred care;
To triumph, and to die, are mine.'
He spoke, and headlong from the mountain's height
Deep in the roaring tide he plunged to endless night.
1757 *The Bard. A Pindaric Ode*, l.141–4.

89 Far from the sun and summer-gale,
In thy green lap was Nature's darling laid.
1757 *Of William Shakespeare. The Progress of Poesy*, l.83–4.

90 Nor second he, that rode sublime
Upon the seraph-wings of ecstasy,
The secrets of th' abyss to spy.
He passed the flaming bounds of place and time:
The living throne, the sapphire-blaze,
Where angels tremble, while they gaze,
He saw; but blasted with excess of light,
Closed his eyes in endless night.
1757 *Of Milton. The Progress of Poesy*, l.95–102.

91 Thoughts, that breathe, and words, that burn.
1757 *The Progress of Poesy*, l.110.

92 Beyond the limits of a vulgar fate,
Beneath the good how far—but far above the great.
1757 *The Progress of Poesy*, l.122–3.

93 It has been usual to catch a mouse or two (for form's sake) in public once a year.
1757 On refusing the Laureateship. Letter to William Mason, 19 Dec.

94 Too poor for a bribe, and too proud to importune,
He had not the method of making a fortune.
1761 'Sketch of His Own Character'.

95 I shall be but a shrimp of an author.
1768 Letter to Horace Walpole, 25 Feb.

96 Any fool may write a most valuable book by chance, if he will only tell us what he heard and saw with veracity.
1768 Letter to Horace Walpole, 25 Feb.

Greeley, Horace 1811–72
US journalist, founding editor of the *New York Tribune*.

97 Go West, young man, and grow up with the country.
1850 *Hints toward Reforms*.

Greenaway, Peter 1942–
English film-maker and painter. His films include *The Cook, the Thief, His Wife and Her Lover* (1989) and *Prospero's Books* (1991).

98 Most cinema is built along 19th-century models. You would hardly think that the cinema had discovered James Joyce sometimes. Most of the cinema we've got is modelled on Dickens and Balzac and Jane Austen.
2004 In *The Guardian*, 10 May.

Greenberg, Clement 1909–94
US art critic.

99 When you don't like something the words come more readily.
1991 Aged 82, on the relative ease of negative criticism over positive. In the *New York Times*, 3 Oct.

1 For every good art critic there may be ten great artists.
1991 In the *New York Times*, 3 Oct.

Greene, (Henry) Graham 1904–91
English writer. His writings included novels (which he divided into 'entertainments' and more serious works), short stories, essays, plays, biography, criticism, travel books and two volumes of autobiography.

2 At one with the One, it didn't mean a thing beside a glass of Guinness on a sunny day.
1938 *Brighton Rock*, pt.1, ch.1.

3 He trailed the clouds of his own glory after him; hell lay about him in his infancy. He was ready for more deaths.
1938 *Brighton Rock*, pt.2, ch.2.
▶ See Wordsworth 959:8.

4 I couldn't eat, just went on drinking coffee, and sweating it out again. Liquid had no time to be digested; it came through the pores long before it reached the stomach. I lay wet through with sweat for four hours—it was very nearly like happiness.
1939 In Mexico. *The Lawless Roads* (published in the US as *Another Mexico*).

5 There is always one moment in childhood when the door opens and lets the future in.
1940 *The Power and the Glory*, pt.1, ch.1.

6 A virtuous man can almost cease to believe in Hell, but he carried Hell about with him. Sometimes at night

he dreamed of it... Evil ran like malaria in his veins.
1940 *The Power and the Glory*, pt.3, ch.1.

7 They had been corrupted by money, and he had been corrupted by sentiment. Sentiment was the more dangerous, because you couldn't name its price.
1948 *The Heart of the Matter*, bk.1, pt.1, ch.2, iii.

8 He felt the loyalty we all feel to unhappiness—the sense that that is where we really belong.
1948 *The Heart of the Matter*, bk.2, pt.2, ch.1, i.

9 His hilarity was like a scream from a crevasse.
1948 *The Heart of the Matter*, bk.3, pt.1, ch.1, i.

10 Of those four winters which I passed in Indo-China opium has left the happiest memory.
1955 *The Quiet American*, introduction.

11 That feeling of exhilaration which a measure of danger brings to the visitor with a return ticket.
1955 *The Quiet American*, introduction.

12 Death was the only absolute value in my world. Lose life and one would lose nothing again for ever... Death was far more certain than God, and with death there would no longer be the daily possibility of love dying.
1955 *The Quiet American*, pt.1, ch.3.

13 Our Man in Havana.
1958 Title of novel.

14 Hail Mary, quite contrary!
1958 *Our Man in Havana*, pt.1, ch.2.

15 Those who marry God...can become domesticated too—it's just as humdrum a marriage as all the others.
1961 *A Burnt-Out Case*, ch.1.

16 Fame is a powerful aphrodisiac.
1964 In the *Radio Times*, 10 Sep.

17 His slang...was always a little out of date, as though he had studied in a dictionary of popular usage, but not in the latest edition.
1966 *The Comedians*, pt.1, ch.1.

18 The man who offers a bribe gives away a little of his own importance; the bribe once accepted, he becomes the inferior, like a man who has just paid for a woman.
1966 *The Comedians*, pt.1, ch.4.

19 We mustn't complain too much of being comedians—it's an honourable profession. If only we could be good ones the world might gain at least a sense of style.
1966 *The Comedians*, pt.2, ch.5.

20 An autobiography is only 'a sort of life'—it may contain less errors of fact than a biography, but it is of necessity even more selective: it begins later and it ends prematurely.
1971 *A Sort of Life*, preface.

21 And the motive for recording these scraps of the past? It is much the same motive that has made me a novelist: a desire to reduce a chaos of experience to some sort of order, and a hungry curiosity.
1971 *A Sort of Life*, preface.

22 I put the muzzle of the revolver into my right ear and pulled the trigger... I was out by one. I remember an extraordinary sense of jubilation, as if carnival lights had been switched on in a drab street. My heart knocked in its cage, and life contained an infinite number of possibilities.

1971 Recalling a game of Russian roulette with his brother's revolver in 1923. *A Sort of Life*, ch.6, pt.2.

23 He would certainly have despised Christ for being the son of a carpenter, if the New Testament had not proved in time to be such a howling commercial success.
1980 *Dr Fischer of Geneva*, ch.7.

24 Writing a novel does not become easier with practice.
1980 *Ways of Escape*, ch.5.

25 Writing is a form of therapy; sometimes I wonder how all these people who do not write, compose or paint can manage to escape the madness, the melancholia, the panic fear which is inherent in the human situation.
1980 *Ways of Escape*, ch.9.

26 Perhaps we are all fictions, father, in the minds of God.
1982 *Monsignor Quixote*, pt.1, ch.1.

27 The believer will fight another believer over a shade of difference: the doubter fights only with himself.
1982 *Monsignor Quixote*, pt.1, ch.4.

28 A solitary laugh is often a laugh of superiority.
1982 *Monsignor Quixote*, pt.1, ch.9.

29 The world is not black and white. More like black and grey.
1982 Quoted in 'Sayings of the Year', the *Observer*, Dec.

30 What's the good of a lie if it's seen through? When I tell a lie no-one can tell it from the gospel truth. Sometimes I can't even tell it myself.
1988 The Captain. *The Captain and the Enemy*, pt.1, ch.1.

Greene, Robert 1558–92

English dramatist. His many plays and romances include the prose romance *Pandosto* (1588) and the comedy *Friar Bacon and Friar Bungay* (c.1589). He laid the foundations of English drama.

31 Love taught me that your honour did but jest.
c.1589 *Friar Bacon and Friar Bungay* (published 1594), sc.8.

32 Only your hearts be frolic, for the time
Craves that we taste of naught but jouissance.
c.1589 *Friar Bacon and Friar Bungay* (published 1594), sc.16.

33 For there is an upstart crow, beautified with our feathers, that with his tiger's heart wrapped in a player's hide, supposes he is as well able to bombast out a blank verse as the best of you; and being an absolute *Iohannes fac totum*, is in his own conceit the only Shake-scene in a country.
1592 Of Shakespeare. *The Groatsworth of Wit, Bought with a Million of Repentance. Iohannes fac totum* = 'Jack-of-all-trades'.

Greenspan, Alan 1926–

US financier and economist, chairman of the board of governors of the Federal Reserve System.

34 Since I've become a central banker, I've learned to mumble with great coherence... If I seem unduly clear to you, you must have misunderstood what I said.
1987 Address to Congress, Sep. Quoted by Jonathan Marshall in the *San Francisco Chronicle*, 9 Jun 1995.

35 The buck starts here.
Sign on his desk. Quoted in Bob Woodward *The Agenda* (1994). ▶ See Truman 900:93.

36 The gut-feel of the 55-year old trader is more important than the mathematical elegance of the 25-year old genius.

1995 In the *New York Times*, 6 Mar, shortly after the collapse of Barings in Singapore brought about by a young derivatives trader.

37 I worry incessantly that I might be too clear.
1995 In the *New York Times*, 25 Jun.

38 The free lunch has still to be invented.
2004 On the US budget deficit, 6 May.

39 Government regulation cannot substitute for individual integrity.
2007 *The Age of Turbulence: Adventures in a New World*.

Greer, Germaine 1939–

Australian feminist, author and lecturer. Her first book *The Female Eunuch* (1970) challenges male dominance and the misrepresentation of female sexuality, which she attributes to Freud.

40 A full bosom is actually a millstone around a woman's neck.
1970 *The Female Eunuch*, 'Body: Curves'.

41 Freud is the father of psychoanalysis. It had no mother.
1970 *The Female Eunuch*, 'Soul: The Psychological Sell'.

42 If women understand by emancipation the adoption of the masculine role then we are lost indeed.
1970 *The Female Eunuch*, 'Soul: Womanpower'.

43 English children have lost their innocence, for their first lessons have been in the exploitation of their adult slave.
1970 Of the mother's subjugation to her family's demands. *The Female Eunuch*, 'Love: Family'.

44 Many a housewife staring at the back of her husband's newspaper, or listening to his breathing in bed is lonelier than any spinster in a rented room.
1970 *The Female Eunuch*, 'Love: Security'.

45 Libraries are reservoirs of strength, grace and wit, reminders of order, calm and continuity, lakes of mental energy, neither warm nor cold, light nor dark.
1991 In the *New York Times*, 24 Mar.

46 Football is an art more central to our culture than anything the Arts Council deigns to recognize.
1996 In *The Independent*, 28 Jun.

47 Diana was never a fashion icon. She dressed to the same demotic standard of elegance as TV anchorwomen do, plus the inevitable hat. This was a desperate woman seeking applause. In death she has it, doled out in huge amounts.
2007 Referring to Princess Diana. Quoted in the *Sydney Morning Herald*, 26 Aug.

48 If you love your bluebells, kill your dog.
2011 Recommending, at the Hay on Wye literary festival, the best way to protect woodland flowers. Quoted in the *Daily Mail*, 11 Jun.

Pope Gregory I known as 'the Great' 540–604

Italian divine. He resigned as Praetor of Rome in 575, distributing his wealth to the poor, and entered a monastery. Reluctantly elected Pope in 590, he carried out many reforms. He wrote numerous biblical commentaries and homilies.

49 *Non Angli, sed angeli.*
Not Angles, but angels.
c.580 Reference to Angle slave children seen by Gregory in Rome, which inspired him with the desire to convert Britain to Christianity. Quoted in Bede *Historia Ecclesiastica gentis Anglorum* (c.731), bk.2, ch.1. His exact words according to Bede were 'Nam et angelicam habent faciem, et tales angelorum in caelis decet esse coheredes' ('Since they have the faces of angels, they should be the co-heirs of the angels in heaven').

50 *Scriptura sacra mentis oculis quasi quoddam speculum opponitur, ut interna nostra facies in ipsa videatur.*
Holy scripture is placed before the eyes of our mind like a mirror, so that we may view our inner face therein.
c.582 *Moralia in Job*, bk.2, ch.1, section 1.

Pope Gregory VII also known as Hildebrand c.1020–1085

Italian cleric. He was appointed Cardinal by Leo IX and as Pope from 1073 instituted many reforms to the clergy. He asserted the right of the Pope to direct temporal authorities, and conflicted violently with Emperor Henry IV, who appointed an anti-Pope (Clement III) and seized Rome (1084).

51 *Dilexi iustitiam et odi iniquitatem, propterea morior in exilio.*
I have loved righteousness and hated iniquity, and therefore I die in exile.
1085 Last words. Quoted in Christopher Brooke *Europe in the Central Middle Ages 962–1154* (1964), ch.15.

Gregory, Lady Isabella Augusta née Persse 1852–1932

Irish playwright. After marrying Sir William Gregory, Governor of Ceylon (1880), she founded with W B Yeats Dublin's Abbey Theatre. Her plays include *Spreading the News* (1904), and she also wrote Irish legends and translated Molière.

52 His eyesight has always been weak, a sort of film over the eyes. A doctor advised him not to read, but he said, 'Then I should be ignorant', and he refused an operation because there was a thousandth chance he might go blind and so remain ignorant.
1924 Of Sean O'Casey. Journal entry, 8 Jun.

Gregory, John Walter 1864–1932

English geologist, geographer and explorer, Professor of Geology at Melbourne University (1900–4), and then at Glasgow. In 1932 he joined an expedition to Peru, where he was drowned on a canoeing trip.

53 The Dead Heart of Australia.
1906 Title of book, dealing with the central deserts of Australia.

Grellet, Stephen 1773–1855

French-born missionary to America.

54 I expect to pass through this world but once. Any good thing, therefore, that I can do, or any kindness that I can show to any fellow-creature, let me do it now…for I shall not pass this way again.
Attributed.

Grenfell, Joyce née Phipps 1910–79

English comedienne. She starred in intimate revue in the 1940s and developed a fine line in the art of comic monologues; occasional film appearances included parts in such comedies as *Laughter in Paradise* (1951) and *The Belles of St Trinian's* (1954).

55 George—don't do that.
Catchphrase from one of her comic monologues, also the title of her autobiography, 1977.

56 Stately as a galleon, I sail across the floor,
Doing the Military Two-step, as in the days of yore.
1978 'Stately as a Galleon' (song).

Grenfell, Julian Henry Francis 1888–1915

English poet, killed in action during World War I. He is largely remembered for his patriotic poem 'Into Battle'.

57 And life is colour and warmth and light
And a striving evermore for these;
And he is dead, who will not fight;
And who dies fighting has increase.
1915 'Into Battle', in *The Times*, 27 May.

Grenfell, Sir Wilfred 1865–1940

English medical missionary and writer.

58 The service we render to others is really the rent we pay for our room on this earth.
1938 *A Labrador Logbook*.

Grenville, George 1712–70

English statesman. He became Prime Minister in 1763, and his period of office was marked by the prosecution of John Wilkes and the passing of the American Stamp Act before his resignation in 1765.

59 It is clear that both England and America are now to be governed by the mob.
1765 On the repeal of the Stamp Act, Jul.

Grey of Fallodon, Edward Grey, 1st Viscount 1862–1933

British statesman. He was Liberal MP for Berwick-on-Tweed (1885–1916), and Secretary for Foreign Affairs (1905–16), distinguishing himself in the Balkans peace negotiations (1913) and on the outbreak of World War I in 1914. He was subsequently Ambassador to Washington (1919–20) and Chancellor of Oxford University from 1928.

60 It is the lees left by Bismarck that still foul the cup.
1906 On the duplicity of international diplomacy as practised in the early 20c. Letter to President Roosevelt, Dec. Quoted in G M Trevelyan *Grey of Fallodon* (1937).

61 If there is war, there will be Labour governments in every country—and quite right too.
1914 In conversation with the Italian Ambassador, Jul.

62 The lamps are going out all over Europe. We shall not see them lit again in our lifetime.
1914 Remark made on the eve of World War I, 3 Aug, in his room at the Foreign Office, recounted in *Twenty-Five Years* (1925), vol.2, ch.18.

63 In 1914, Europe had arrived at a point at which every country except Germany was afraid of the present, and Germany was afraid of the future.
1924 House of Lords, 24 Jul.

Greyser, Stephen A

US marketing expert, Professor of Business Administration (Marketing/ Communications) Emeritus at Harvard Business School.

64 The poets of commerce.
1987 Of advertising copywriters. In the *New York Times*, 28 Apr.

Grieg, Edvard Hagerup 1843–1907

Norwegian composer, whose works, much influenced by folk heritage, include orchestral suites, incidental music for Ibsen's *Peer Gynt*, choral music and piano pieces.

65 I am sure my music has a taste of codfish in it.
1903 Speech. Quoted in Ian Crofton and Donald Fraser *A Dictionary of Musical Quotations* (1985).

Griffith, D(avid Lewelyn) W(ark) 1874–1948

US film director. He began as an actor and short-story writer before entering the infant film industry, learning his trade in hundreds of short films. He is best known for *The Birth of a Nation* (1915) and *Intolerance* (1916).

66 Viewed as a drama, the war is somewhat disappointing.
c.1915 Comment on World War I. Quoted in Leslie Halliwell *Halliwell's Filmgoer's Companion* (1984).

67 Out of the cradle, endlessly rocking.
1916 *Intolerance*.

Griffiths, Richard 1947–2013

English actor. He won numerous awards for his performance in Alan Bennett's *The History Boys*, among other notable roles.

68 Everyone over fifty, as part of the NHS, should be issued every week with a wet fish in a plastic bag by the Post Office so that whenever you see someone young and happy you can hit them as hard as you can across the face.
2008 In the *Daily Express*, 20 Nov.

Grillparzer, Franz 1791–1872

Austrian politician, poet and playwright. He was prone to hypochondria and depression.

69 *Es binden Sklavenfesseln nur die Hände,*
Der Sinn, er macht den Freien und den Knecht.
The chains of slavery can only bind the hands.
The mind makes us either free or enslaved.
1818 *Sappho*, act 2, sc.4.

70 *Gold schenkt die Eitelkeit, der rauhe Stolz,*
Die Freundschaft und die Liebe schenken Blumen.
Gold is the gift of vanity and pride,
Friendship and love offer flowers.
1818 *Sappho*, act 2, sc.4.

71 *Ich suchte dich und habe mich gefunden.*
I sought you and I found myself.
1818 *Sappho*, act 5, sc.6.

Grimaldi, Joseph 1779–1837

English comedian, of Italian descent. His Clown figure transformed English pantomime, though his career was virtually over by 1824 as a result of the injuries he suffered in slapstick routines on stage.

72 Here we are again!
c.1800 His customary greeting to the audience on making his entrance as Clown, later adopted as a catchphrase by clowns everywhere.

Grisham, John 1955–

US author, known for his suspenseful courtroom dramas.

73 I cannot write as well as some people; my talent is in coming up with good stories about lawyers. That is what I am good at.
1994 In the *Independent on Sunday*, 5 Jun.

Griswold, Alfred Whitney 1906–63

US educator, President of Yale University (1950–63).

74 A Socrates in every classroom.
   1951 On his hopes for the Yale faculty. In *Time*, 11 Jun.

75 Could Hamlet have been written by a committee, or the *Mona Lisa* painted by a club? Could the New Testament have been composed as a conference report?
   1957 Baccalaureate address, 9 Jun.

76 Self-respect...comes to us when we are alone, in quiet moments in quiet places when we suddenly realize that, knowing the good, we have done it; knowing the beautiful, we have served it; knowing the truth, we have spoken it.
   1957 Baccalaureate address, 9 Jun.

Gromyko, Andrei Andreyevich 1909–89

Soviet politician, notorious for his austere and humourless demeanour. As Foreign Minister (1957–85) he influenced Soviet relations with the West during the Cold War. President in 1985, he was replaced by Gorbachev.

77 Every night, whisper 'Peace' in your husband's ear.
   1984 Said to Nancy Reagan at a White House reception, 28 Sep.

78 This man, Comrades, has a nice smile, but he has iron teeth.
   1985 Speech to the Supreme Soviet on proposing Mikhail Gorbachev as the new party leader.

Grossmith, George 1847–1912

English comedian and entertainer. He took leading parts in Gilbert and Sullivan operettas (1877–89) and with his brother, Weedon, wrote *The Diary of a Nobody*, first serialized in *Punch* (published 1892).

79 What's the good of a home if you are never in it?
   1892 *The Diary of a Nobody* (with Weedon Grossmith), ch.1.

80 I left the room with silent dignity, but caught my foot in the mat.
   1892 *The Diary of a Nobody* (with Weedon Grossmith), ch.7.

Grosvenor, Gilbert M 1875–1966

US geographer and editor, Director then President of the National Geographic Society (1899–1954) and editor of its magazine. He pioneered the use of colour photography, and encouraged conservation and wildlife protection.

81 If you don't know where you are, you're nowhere.
   On the NGS's establishment of a $20-million foundation to fight ignorance of geography. Quoted in the *Washington Post*, 14 Jan 1988.

Guare, John 1938–

US dramatist.

82 Everybody on this planet is separated by only six other people. Six degrees of separation. Between us and everybody else on this planet.
   1990 *Six Degrees of Separation*.

Guedalla, Philip 1889–1944

English historian and biographer, known for his irreverent wit. His books include *Supers and Supermen* (1920), *Palmerston* (1926), a biography of Wellington, *The Duke* (1931), and *Mr Churchill* (1941).

83 The work of Henry James has always seemed divisible by a simple dynastic arrangement into three reigns: James I, James II, and the Old Pretender.
   1920 *Supers and Supermen*, 'Some Critics'.

84 History repeats itself. Historians repeat each other.
   1920 *Supers and Supermen*, 'Some Historians'.

85 The Crimean War is one of the bad jokes of history.
   1943 *The Two Marshals*.

Guibert of Nogent fl.c.1097

Medieval historian.

86 God has instituted in our time holy wars, so that the order of knights and the crowd running in their wake, who following the example of the ancient pagans have been engaged in slaughtering one another, might find a new way of gaining salvation.
   c.1097 *Gesta Dei per Francos*, in *Recueil des historiens de croisades occidentaux*, edited by L'Académie des Inscriptions et Belles-Lettres (1847–95), vol.4, p.124.

Guillén, Nicolás 1902–89

Cuban poet, of mixed African and European descent, a leader of the Afro-Cuban movement. An outspoken member of the Communist Party, he was active in Castro's regime.

87 *Según un yanqui que debe*
   ser todo un derrochador,
   es Cuba donde mejor
   se come siempre y se bebe.
   According to a gringo who must
   be a true spendthrift,
   Cuba is always the best place
   to eat and to drink.
   1953 *Sátira política*, 'Depende' ('It Depends').

Guimarães Rosa, João 1908–67

Brazilian novelist. He practised medicine, then joined the foreign service. *Grande Sertão* (1956) is derived from the oral tradition of the hinterland of Brazil.

88 *Um está sempre no escuro, só no último derradeiro é*
   que clareiam a sala.
   One is always in the dark, and it is only at the last moment that they turn on the lights in the room.
   1956 *Grande Sertão: Verédas* (translated as *The Devil to Pay in the Backlands*, 1963).

Guiraldes, Ricardo 1886–1927

Argentinian poet and novelist, renowned for his masterful blending of the gaucho (cowboy) tale with modernist techniques.

89 *Si sos gaucho en de veras, no has de mudar, porque*
   andequiera que vayas irás con tu alma por delante.
   If you're really a gaucho, you can't change, because wherever you go, you'll go with your soul leading the way.
   1926 *Don Segundo Sombra* (translated 1935), ch.26.

Guitry, Sacha 1885–1957

French actor and playwright. Born in Russia, he established himself as a popular light comedian as well as writing a number of screenplays and directing several films.

90 The others were only my wives. But you, my dear, will be my widow.
   Attributed reply to his fifth wife, when she expressed jealousy of her predecessors.

Gulbenkian, Nubar Sarkis 1896–1972
British industrialist and philanthropist. He worked with his father in the oil business, advising on Middle East oil negotiations (1926–8, 1948–54), and was honorary counsellor at the Turkish embassy (1966–72).

91 The best number for a dinner party is two—myself and a damn good head waiter.
1965 In the *Daily Telegraph*, 14 Jan.

Gullit, Ruud 1962–
Dutch footballer and manager. He transferred to the Italian club AC Milan for a record £6 million in 1987.

92 If I'd wanted to be an individual, I'd have taken up tennis.
Quoted in Colin Jarman *The Guinness Dictionary of Sports Quotations* (1990).

93 I'm looking forward to seeing some sexy football.
1996 Comment as BBC TV pundit at Euro 96.

Gunn, Jeannie known as Mrs Aeneas Gunn 1870–1961
Australian writer. In 1901 she married Aeneas James Gunn and went with him to Elsey Station, Northern Territory. When her husband died in 1903 she returned to Melbourne and wrote of her experiences in the outback.

94 There's time enough for everything in the Never-Never.
1908 *We of the Never-Never*, ch.5.

Gunn, Thom(son William) 1929–2004
English poet. He lived in the US from 1954 until his death. He is recognized as one of the major poets of his generation.

95 I saw that lack of love contaminates,
You know I know you know I know you know.
1954 'Carnal Knowledge'.

96 At worst, one is in motion; and at best,
Reaching no absolute, in which to rest,
One is always nearer by not keeping still.
1957 'On the Move'.

Gunther, John 1901–70
US author and journalist. He established his reputation with the best-selling *Inside Europe* (1939), and followed it with a series of *Inside* books.

97 Bright grayness. Both the clothes and hair were neat and gray. The gray-framed spectacles magnified the gray hazel eyes, but there was no grayness in the mind.
Of Harry S Truman. Quoted in David McCullough *Truman* (1992).

Gurney, Dorothy Frances 1858–1932
English poet and hymnwriter.

98 The kiss of the sun for pardon,
The song of the birds for mirth,
One is nearer God's Heart in a garden
Than anywhere else on earth.
1913 'God's Garden'.

Gurney, Ivor 1890–1937
English poet and composer, especially renowned for his war poems.

99 The songs I had are withered
Or vanished clean,
Yet there are bright tracks
Where I have been.
1922 'The Songs I Had'.

1 I paid the prices of life
Standing where Rome immortal heard October's strife,
A war poet whose right of honour cuts falsehood like a knife.
c.1922 'Poem for End'.

Gurney, John Hampden 1802–62
English clergyman and hymnwriter.

2 Ye holy angels bright,
Who wait at God's right hand,
Or through the realms of light
Fly at your Lord's command,
Assist our song,
Or else the theme too high doth seem
For mortal tongue.
1838 'Ye Holy Angels Bright', based on a poem by Richard Baxter (1615–91).

Gustavus II (Adolphus) 1594–1632
King of Sweden (1611), who entered the Thirty Years War by invading Poland in 1621. His armies conquered much of Germany in 1631, and he was killed at the Battle of Lützen, 1632.

3 All the wars that are now afoot in Europe have been fused together, and have become a single war.
1630 Letter to Axel Oxenstierna, referring to the Thirty Years War, 1618–48.

Guston, Philip 1913–80
Canadian-born painter. He moved with his family to California in 1916. His early paintings combine realism with surrealism and his later work is characterized by its cartoon-like style.

4 I go to my studio every day, because one day I may go and the angel will be there. What if I don't go and the angel came?
1991 Quoted by Gail Godwin in the *Washington Post*, 7 Mar.

Guthrie, Woody (Woodrow Wilson) 1912–67
US folk-singer, songwriter and author. His songs draw on traditional country music and blues themes and reflect his social and political concerns.

5 This land is your land, this land is my land,
From California to the New York Island.
From the redwood forest to the Gulf Stream waters
This land was made for you and me.
1956 'This Land is Your Land'.

6 You can't write a good song about a whore-house unless you been in one.
1964 Quoted in *Broadside*.

Guy, Ray 1939–2013
Canadian columnist.

7 Pity the poor creatures in warmer countries where the seasons never change. Where summer is eternal and they never know the pain of waiting and the joy at last when summer comes.
1976 *That Far Greater Bay*, 'Catching Conners'.

Gwyn, Nell 1650–87

English actress. Originally an orange-seller at Drury Lane, she became a popular performer in comedies; her admirers included Charles II, whose mistress she became in about 1669. She retired from the stage in 1670.

8 Pray, good people, be civil; I am the Protestant whore.
   1675 Attributed, when angry crowds pressed round her carriage in the belief that she was Charles II's unpopular Catholic mistress Louise de Kérouaille.

Haas, Ernst 1921–86

Austrian photographer and author. Known for his early black and white photojournalism (particularly his 'Returning Prisoners of War' story in 1949), he was a pioneer of early colour, and his work on colour-blur made his fame. His film assignments included *Moby Dick* (1956), *The Misfits* (1961), *West Side Story* (1961) and *Heaven's Gate* (1980).

1 Beauty pains, and when it pained most, I shot.
   1955 In *Life*, 1 Aug. 'The Glow of Paris'.

Habington, William 1605–54

English writer, one of the metaphysical followers of Donne. He published a book of lyrics, *Castara* (1634), a play, *The Queen of Aragon* (1640) and *The History of Edward the Fourth* (1640).

2 O empty boast of flesh.
   1634 *Castara*, 'Upon Beauty'.

3 'Cause some make forfeit of their name,
   And slave themselves to man's desire;
   Shall the sex free
   From guilt, damn'd to the bondage be?
   1634 *Castara*, 'Against Them Who Lay Unchastity to the Sex of Women'.

Haeckel, Ernst Heinrich 1834–1919

German biologist and philosopher, who popularized Darwinism in the German-speaking world. He became Professor of Comparative Anatomy at the University of Jena.

4 God…a gaseous vertebrate.
   1899 *Welträtsel* ('The Riddle of the Universe').

Hagen, Walter 1892–1969

US golfer. The first great professional US golfer, he won the US Open twice and the British Open four times.

5 Give me a man with big hands and big feet and no brains and I'll make a golfer out of him.
   Quoted in Michael Hobbs *The Golf Quotation Book* (1992).

Haggai, Thomas 1939–

US businessman.

6 Cast your bread upon the waters, but wait until the tide is coming in to do it.
   1988 In *Fortune*, 7 Nov.

Haggard, Sir (Henry) Rider 1856–1925

English novelist. He travelled to Natal and the Transvaal (1875–9) before embarking on a literary life. His first successful novel was *King Solomon's Mines* (1885), followed by *She* (1887) and *Ayesha* (1905), among others.

7 A little while and I will be gone from among you, whither I cannot tell. From nowhere we came, into nowhere we go. What is Life? It is a flash of a firefly in the night. It is a breath of a buffalo in the winter time. It is as the little shadow that runs across the grass and loses itself in the sunset.
   1885 Dying words of the African chief Umbopa in *King Solomon's Mines*. John Peter Turner in *The North-West Mounted Police* (1950) credited them to Crowfoot (c.1830–1890), chief of the Blackfoot Indians, who died in his teepee overlooking the Bow River, Alberta, 25 Apr 1890, and this attribution gained popular acceptance.

8 She who must be obeyed.
   1887 *She*, ch.6, and passim.

9 What a terrifying reflection it is, by the way, that nearly all our deep love for women who are not our kindred depends—at any rate, in the first instance—upon their personal appearances. If we lost them, and found them again dreadful to look on, though otherwise they were the very same, should we still love them?
   1887 *She*, ch.26 'What We Saw', narrator's note.

Hague, William 1961–

English Conservative politician, Leader of the Conservative Party (1997–2001), Foreign Secretary (2010–14) and Leader of the House of Commons (2014–).

10 It was inevitable the Titanic was going to set sail, but that doesn't mean it was a good idea to be on it.
    1998 In *The Mail on Sunday*, 'Quotes of the Week', 11 Jan.

11 This is a candidate of probity and integrity—I am going to back him to the full.
    1999 On Jeffrey Archer as a London mayoral candidate, at the Conservative Party conference, Oct.

12 People work hard and save hard to own a car. They do not want to be told that they cannot drive it by a Deputy Prime Minister whose idea of a park and ride scheme is to park one Jaguar and drive away in another.
    1999 Of John Prescott. In the House of Commons, 17 Nov.

Haig, Alexander Meigs, Jr 1924–2010

US soldier and Republican politician, White House Chief of Staff at the end of Nixon's presidency and Supreme NATO Commander. He was Secretary of State under Reagan (1981–2), and unsuccessfully sought presidential nomination in 1988.

13 As of now, I am in control here in the White House.
    1981 Said immediately after the attempted assassination of President Reagan, 30 Mar, in Vice-President George Bush's absence from Washington DC.

14 I take it as a compliment when an agent of the largest and most heinous bully of the century, the Soviet Union, accuses me of being a bully.
    1995 On how he was seen as US Secretary of State by former Soviet Ambassador Anatoly Dobrynin. In the *Washington Post*, 27 Oct.

Haig (of Bemersyde), Douglas Haig, 1st Earl 1861–1928

Scottish field marshal. He became Commander of the British Expeditionary Force in 1915. His war of attrition was costly and widely criticized; he led the final successful offensive of World War I in Aug 1918.

15 Every position must be held to the last man: there must be no retirement. With our backs to the wall, and believing in the justice of our cause, each one of us must fight on until the end.
1918 Order to British troops facing the German offensive across the Somme battlefields, 12 Apr. Quoted in A Duff Cooper *Haig* (1936), vol.2, ch.23.

Haile Selassie *originally* Prince Ras Tafari Makonnen
1891–1975

Emperor of Ethiopia (1930–6, 1941–74), leader of the revolution against Lij Yasu (1916). He was exiled after the Italian conquest of Abyssinia (1935–6), and restored after British liberation. Although deposed after the famine of 1973, he is still much revered, notably by Rastafarians.

16 Throughout history it has been the inaction of those who could have acted, the indifference of those who should have known better, the silence of the voice of justice when it mattered most, that has made it possible for evil to triumph.
1963 Address to a special session of the UN General Assembly, 4 Oct, making him the first head of state to address both that organization and the League of Nations.

Hailsham, Quintin (McGarel) Hogg, 2nd Viscount
1907–2001

English Conservative politician. After succeeding to his title (1950), he held a number of senior state posts. In 1963 he renounced his peerage in an unsuccessful bid to become Leader of the Conservative Party. He was later Lord Chancellor.

17 Conservatives do not believe that the political struggle is the most important thing in life… The simplest of them prefer fox-hunting, the wisest religion.
1947 *The Case for Conservatism*, pt.1.

18 A great party ought not to be brought down because of a squalid affair between a woman of easy virtue and a proved liar.
1963 On the Profumo affair, BBC TV, 13 Jun.

19 If the British public falls for this, I say that it will be stark, staring bonkers.
1964 Press conference on the Labour election manifesto, 12 Oct.

20 I've known every prime minister to a greater or lesser extent since Balfour, and most of them have died unhappy.
Attributed.

Halberstam, David 1934–2007

US journalist and author, staff writer and correspondent for the *New York Times* (1960–7). His books include *The Powers That Be* (1979) and *Firehouse* (2002).

21 He has seen the future and it is hamburgers.
1993 On Ray Kroc's decision to buy and expand the original McDonald's. *The Fifties*.
▶ See Steffens 844:55.

Haldane, J(ohn) B(urdon) S(anderson) 1892–1964

Anglo-Indian biologist. He wrote many popular books on biology and genetics, and was Chairman of the *Daily Worker* (1940–9), but left the Communist Party in 1956.

22 Bad as our urban conditions often are, there is not a slum in the country which has a third of the infantile death-rate of the royal family in the middle ages.
1924 *Daedalus, or Science and the Future*.

23 Now, my own suspicion is that the universe is not only queerer than we suppose, but queerer than we *can* suppose.
1927 *Possible Worlds and Other Essays*, 'Possible Worlds'.

24 You can drop a mouse down a thousand-yard mine shaft; and, on arriving at the bottom, it gets a slight shock and walks away. A rat is killed, a man is broken, a horse splashes.
1927 *Possible Worlds and Other Essays*, 'On Being the Right Size'.

25 I believe that the scientist is trying to expand absolute truth and the artist absolute beauty, so that I find in art and science, and in an attempt to live a good life, all the religion I want.
1931 *Living Philosophies*.

26 My final word, before I'm done,
Is 'Cancer can be rather fun'.
Thanks to the nurses and Nye Bevan
The NHS is quite like heaven
Provided one confronts the tumour
With a sufficient sense of humour.
I know that cancer often kills,
But so do cars and sleeping pills;
And it can hurt one till one sweats,
So can bad teeth and unpaid debts.
1964 'Cancer's a Funny Thing'.

Hale, Nathan 1755–76

American revolutionary soldier. In 1776 he volunteered to penetrate British lines on Long Island and procure intelligence for Washington, but was detected and hanged as a spy.

27 I only regret that I have but one life to lose for my country.
1776 At his execution, 22 Sep.

Hale, Robert Beverly 1901–85

US artist, teacher and curator. He has works in the Whitney, the Metropolitan Museum of Art, New York City, and in many private collections. He was curator at the Metropolitan (1949–85) and lectured at Pennsylvania Academy of Fine Arts (1968–85) and Columbia University. He wrote, edited and translated books on art.

28 New artists must break a hole in the subconscious and go fishing there.
1960 In *Time*, 11 Apr.

Hale, Sarah Josepha *née* Buell 1788–1879

US writer. In 1828 she became editor of the *Ladies' Magazine* in Boston. She wrote a novel, *Northwood* (1827), and *Poems for Our Children* (1830).

29 Mary had a little lamb,
Its fleece was white as snow,
And everywhere that Mary went
The lamb was sure to go.
1830 *Poems for Our Children*, 'Mary's Little Lamb'.

Hales, Stephen 1677–1761

English clergyman and physiologist, considered the founder of plant physiology. His investigations are reported in his work

Statickal Essays, the first of which, *Vegetable Staticks*, was published in 1727.

30 Since we are assured that the all-wise Creator has observed the most exact proportions of number, weight and measure in the make of all things, the most likely way therefore to get any insight into the nature of those parts of the Creation which come within our observation must in all reason be to number, weigh and measure.
1727 *Vegetable Staticks*.

Haliburton, Thomas Chandler 1796–1865

Canadian lawyer and satirist. In 1835 he began a series of satiric sketches later enlarged as *The Clockmaker; or The Sayings and Doings of Samuel Slick* (1836). *The Old Judge; or Life in a Colony* (1849) combines social history and satire.

31 I was always well mounted. I am fond of a horse, and always piqued myself on having the fastest trotter in the Province. I have made no great progress in the world. I feel doubly, therefore, the pleasure of not being surpassed on the road.
1836 *The Clockmaker* (first series), 'The Trotting Horse'.

32 If a chap seems bent on cheatin' himself, I like to be neighbourly and help him to do it.
1838 *The Clockmaker* (second series), 'A Cure for Smuggling'.

Halifax, Edward Frederick Lindley Wood, 1st Earl of 1881–1959

English Conservative politician, Viceroy of India (1926–31). He was Foreign Secretary (1938–40) under Neville Chamberlain, whose 'appeasement' policy he implemented, and Ambassador to the US (1941–6).

33 I often think how much easier the world would have been to manage if Herr Hitler and Signor Mussolini had been at Oxford.
1937 Speech, York, 4 Nov.

Halifax, George Savile, 1st Marquis of 1633–95

English statesman, created viscount (1668) at the Restoration. Under James II, he was dismissed as President of the Council for opposing the repeal of the Test and Habeas Corpus Acts. He gave allegiance to William of Orange, but joined the Opposition in 1689.

34 Men are not hanged for stealing horses, but that horses may not be stolen.
c.1687 *Political Thoughts and Reflections*, 'Of Punishment'.

35 Anger is never without an argument, but seldom with a good one.
c.1687 *Political Thoughts and Reflections*, 'Of Anger'.

36 Malice is of a low stature, but it hath very long arms.
c.1687 *Political Thoughts and Reflections*, 'Of Malice and Envy'.

37 The best way to suppose what may come, is to remember what is past.
c.1687 *Political Thoughts and Reflections*, 'Miscellaneous Experience'.

38 When the people contend for their liberty, they seldom get anything by their victory but new masters.
c.1687 *Political Thoughts and Reflections*, 'Of Prerogative, Power and Liberty'.

39 Most men's anger about religion is as if two men should quarrel for a lady they neither of them care for.
Collected in *Complete Works* (published 1912).

Hall, Charles 1745–1825

English physician educated in Holland, best known for his socialist work *The Effects of Civilization on the People in European States* (1805). In 1805 he was impoverished by a lawsuit and, refusing aid, later died in prison determined to show that he had been unjustly treated.

40 The effect of trade and commerce with respect to most civilized states is to send out of their countries what the poor, that is, the great mass of mankind, have occasion for, and to bring back, in return, what is consumed almost wholly by a small part of those nations, viz. the rich. Hence it appears that the greater part of manufactures, trade and commerce is highly injurious to the poor as being the chief means of depriving them of the necessaries of life.
1805 *The Effects of Civilization on the People in European States*.

Hall, J(oyce) C(lyde) 1891–1982

US businessman, founder of Hallmark Cards Inc.

41 The art of the masses.
Of illustrated greetings cards. Recalled on his death, quoted in *The Annual Obituary 82* (1983).

Halliwell, Geri 1972–

English pop star, former member of The Spice Girls.

42 The Ginger character was my own invention, of course. It was like putting on a uniform. You don't have to think. You don't have to deal with being a human being.
2002 *Geri Just For The Record*.

Halsey, W(illiam) F(rederick) known as 'Bull' Halsey 1882–1959

US naval officer, commander at the Battle of Leyte Gulf (1944) and others. He received the formal Japanese surrender on his flagship, the USS *Missouri*, on 2 Sep 1945.

43 The Third Fleet's sunken and damaged ships have been salvaged and are retiring at high speed toward the enemy.
1944 Comment, 14 Oct, on hearing claims that the Japanese had virtually annihilated the US fleet. Quoted in E B Potter *Bull Halsey* (1985), ch.17.

Hamer, Robert 1911–63

British film director and screenwriter. He is best known for *It Always Rains on Sunday* (1947), *Kind Hearts and Coronets* (1949, with John Dighton) and *School for Scoundrels* (1960).

44 I shot an arrow in the air. She fell to earth in Berkeley Square.
1949 *Kind Hearts and Coronets* (with John Dighton).

45 Every lunch time I went to see how my inheritance was proceeding. Sometimes the deaths column brought good news. Sometimes the births column brought bad. The advent of twin sons to the Duke was a terrible blow. Fortunately an epidemic of diphtheria restored the status quo almost immediately.
1949 *Kind Hearts and Coronets* (with John Dighton).

46 I always say that my west window has all the exuberance of Chaucer without, happily, any of the concomitant crudities of his period.
1949 *Kind Hearts and Coronets* (with John Dighton).

Hamilton, Alexander c.1755–1804

US statesman, Washington's aide-de-camp in the American Revolution and later a congressman. As Secretary of the Treasury (1789–95) he restored the country's finances, but he was killed in a duel with a rival.

47 A national debt, if it is not excessive, will be to us a national blessing.
1781 Letter to Robert Morris, 30 Apr.

48 To model our political systems upon speculations of lasting tranquillity is to calculate on the weaker springs of the human character.
1787–8 The Federalist Papers.

Hamilton, Edith 1867–1963

German-born US classicist, whose popular works include *The Greek Way* (1930).

49 To be able to be caught up into the world of thought—that is educated.
Quoted in the Saturday Evening Post, 27 Sep 1958.

Hamilton, (Robert) Ian 1938–2001

English poet. He was editor of *Review* (1962–72) and poetry and fiction editor of the *Times Literary Supplement* (1965–73).

50 If my life were like hers, I'd rather be dead. Come to think of it, if my life were like mine, I'd rather be dead.
Quoted by Al Alvarez in D Harsent (ed) Another Road at the Pillars: Essays, Poems and Reflections on Ian Hamilton (1972).

51 Back in the early Sixties, when I first started out, insolvency spelt glamour.
1998 The Trouble with Money and Other Essays.

52 Show me an enemy of literature, and I will show him my accounts.
1998 The Trouble with Money and Other Essays.

Hammarskjöld, Dag Hjalmar Agne Carl 1905–61

Swedish statesman. As Secretary-General of the United Nations from 1953 he took part in conciliation moves in the Middle East. He was awarded the Nobel peace prize posthumously, after he was killed in an air crash while involved in the Congo crisis.

53 For what has been—thanks!
For what shall be—yes!
1950 Vägmarken (translated by L Sjsÿberg and W H Auden as Markings, 1964).

54 God does not die on the day when we cease to believe in a personal deity, but we die on the day when our lives cease to be illumined by the steady radiance, renewed daily, of a wonder, the source of which is beyond all reason.
1950 Vägmarken (translated by L Sjsÿberg and W H Auden as Markings, 1964).

55 Before Thee in humility, with Thee in faith, in Thee in peace.
1955 Vägmarken (translated by L Sjsÿberg and W H Auden as Markings, 1964).

56 The 'men of the hour', the self-assured who strut among us in the jingling harness of their success and importance, how can you let yourself be irritated by them. Let them enjoy their triumph—on the level to which it belongs.
1956 Vägmarken (translated by L Sjsÿberg and W H Auden as Markings, 1964).

57 I didn't know Who—or what—put the question, I don't know when it was put. I don't even remember answering. But at some moment I did answer Yes to Someone—or Something—and from that hour I was certain that existence is meaningful and that, therefore, my life, in self-surrender, had a goal.
1961 Vägmarken (translated by L Sjsÿberg and W H Auden as Markings, 1964).

58 Weep
If you can,
Weep,
But do not complain—
And you must be thankful.
1961 Vägmarken (translated by L Sjsÿberg and W H Auden as Markings, 1964).

59 Never let success hide its emptiness from you; achievement its nothingness; toil its desolation. Keep alive the incentive to push on further, that pain in the soul that drives us beyond ourselves. Do not look back, and do not dream about the future either. It will neither give you back the past, nor satisfy your other daydreams. Your duty, your reward, your destiny are here and now.
1961 Vägmarken (translated by L Sjsÿberg and W H Auden as Markings, 1964).

Hammer, Armand 1898–1990

US business executive and art collector.

60 The art world is a jungle echoing to the calls of vicious jealousies and ruthless combat between dealers and collectors; but I have been walking in the jungles of business all my life, and fighting tooth and nail for pictures comes as a form of relaxation to me.
1987 Hammer, Witness to History, his autobiography.

61 My Van Gogh is better than *Irises*. I have the whole garden.
On ranking his own Van Gogh, Hospital at Saint-Rémy, over the Irises that brought £53.9 million at auction. In Connoisseur, Jan 1991.

Hammerstein, Oscar, II 1895–1960

US lyricist–librettist. In collaboration with composer Richard Rodgers he wrote such hit musicals as *Oklahoma!* (1943), *South Pacific* (1949) and *The Sound of Music* (1959).

62 Fish got to swim and birds got to fly
I got to love one man till I die
Can't help lovin' dat man of mine.
1927 Song from Show Boat (music by Jerome Kern).

63 Ol' Man River.
1927 Title of song from Show Boat (music by Jerome Kern).

64 When I grow too old to dream
Your love will live in my heart.
1935 Song from The Night is Young (music by Sigmund Romberg).

65 As you walk through the storm,
Hold your head up high,
And don't be afraid of the dark,
At the end of the storm,
Is a golden sky,
And the sweet silver song of the lark,
Walk on through the wind,
Walk on through the rain,
Though your dreams be tossed and blown.

Walk on, walk on,
With hope in your hearts,
And you'll never walk alone,
You'll never walk alone.
1945 *Carousel*, 'You'll Never Walk Alone' (music by Richard Rodgers). The song was subsequently released in a pop version by Gerry and the Pacemakers in 1963 and adopted as a club song by Liverpool football club.

66 I'm Gonna Wash That Man Right Outa My Hair.
1949 Title of song sung by Mitzi Gaynor in *South Pacific* (music by Richard Rodgers).

67 You've got to be taught to be afraid
Of people whose eyes are oddly made,
Of people whose skin is a different shade.
You've got to be carefully taught.

You've got to be taught before it's too late,
Before you are six or seven or eight,
To hate all the people your relatives hate.
You've got to be carefully taught.
1949 'You've Got to Be Carefully Taught', song from *South Pacific* (music by Richard Rodgers).

68 The hills are alive with the sound of music
With the songs they have sung
For a thousand years.
1959 *The Sound of Music*, title song (music by Richard Rodgers).

Hammett, (Samuel) Dashiell 1894–1961

US crime writer. He joined the Pinkerton Detective Agency as an operator, and later translated his experiences into literature. He suffered from alcohol abuse, which broke his health, and like his partner Lillian Hellman, came into conflict with McCarthy in the anti-Communist trials.

69 He looked rather pleasantly like a blond satan.
1930 Of Sam Spade. *The Maltese Falcon*, 'Spade and Archer'.

70 'I mean that you paid us more than if you'd been telling the truth,' he explained blandly, 'and enough more to make it all right.'
1930 *The Maltese Falcon*, 'The Black Bird'.

71 I distrust a man that says when. If he's got to be careful not to drink too much it's because he's not to be trusted when he does.
1930 *The Maltese Falcon*, 'The Fat Man'.

72 Murder doesn't round out anybody's life except the murdered's and sometimes the murderer's.
1932 *The Thin Man*, ch.31.

Hampton, Christopher James 1946–

English playwright and screenwriter. He is known for such plays as *The Philanthropist* (1970). He adapted *Les Liaisons Dangereuses* (1986) from the novel by Laclos, Graham Greene's *The Quiet American* (2002) and Ian McEwan's *Atonement* (2007) for the screen.

73 Masturbation is the thinking man's television.
1970 *The Philanthropist*.

74 I always divide people into two groups. Those who live by what they know to be a lie, and those who live by what they believe, falsely, to be the truth.
1970 *The Philanthropist*.

75 If I had to give a definition of capitalism, I would say: the process whereby American girls turn into American women.
1974 *Savages*, sc.16.

76 Asking a working writer what he thinks about critics is like asking a lamp-post how it feels about dogs.
Attributed.

Hancock, Lang(ley George) 1909–92

Australian mining industrialist, who discovered iron ore in the Pilbara region with his light aircraft. His various claims, including Rhodes Ridge, made him one of Australia's richest men.

77 The best way to help the poor is not to become one of them.
Quoted in R W Kent (ed) *Money Talks* (1985).

Hand, (Billings) Learned 1872–1961

US jurist, senior judge at the US Court of Appeals for the Second Circuit (1924–51). His legal judgements had enormous influence on the Supreme Court.

78 The spirit of liberty is the spirit which is not too sure that it is right.
1944 Address at 'I Am An American Day' in New York's Central Park, recalled on his death, 18 Aug 1961.

Handel, George Frideric 1685–1759

German-born English composer. He settled in England in 1712, becoming first Director of the Royal Academy of Music (1720). He turned from opera to oratorio in 1739, most notably with *Messiah* (1742). Other works include *Water Music* (1717) and *Music for the Royal Fireworks* (1749).

79 Whether I was in my body or out of my body as I wrote it I know not. God knows.
Of the 'Hallelujah Chorus' in his *Messiah*. Quoted in Romain Rolland *Essays on Music* (1948).

Handy, Charles Brian 1932–

Irish writer and management theorist. His works include *The Making of Managers* (1988) and *The New Alchemists* (1999).

80 Words are the bugles of social change.
1991 *The Age of Unreason*.

Hankey, Katherine 1834–1911

English evangelist and hymnwriter.

81 Tell me the old, old story,
Of unseen things above.
1866 *The Story Wanted*, 'Tell Me the Old, Old Story'.

Hanks, Tom (Thomas Jeffrey) 1956–

US film actor. He became one of the most popular leading men of his generation, winning numerous awards for his performances in such films as *Forrest Gump* (1994), *Apollo 13* (1995), *Saving Private Ryan* (1998), *Cast Away* (2000), *Captain Phillips* (2013) and *Saving Mr Banks* (2013).

82 It's supposed to be hard. If it were easy, everyone would do it.
1992 As Jimmy Dugan in *A League of Their Own* (screenplay by Lowell Ganz and Babaloo Mandel).

83 Mama always said life was like a box of chocolates. You never know what you're gonna get.
1994 In the title role in *Forrest Gump* (screenplay by Eric Roth).

84 Every day the sun will rise and you never know what the tide will bring in.
2000 In *Cast Away* (screenplay by William Broyles Jr).

85 Only something fake could work one hundred per cent of the time.
   2008 As Mr Gable in *The Great Buck Howard* (screenplay by Sean McGinly).

Hansberry, Lorraine Vivian 1930–65
US playwright. Her semi-autobiographical *A Raisin in the Sun* (1959), the first Broadway play written by a black woman, dealt with the problems facing a black family in a white neighbourhood.

86 Though it be a thrilling and marvelous thing to be merely young and gifted in such times, it is doubly so—doubly dynamic—to be young, gifted and black.
   Speech to entrants in the United Negro College Fund writers competition. The phrase was later used as the title of her biography *Young, Gifted and Black* (1969).

Harburg, E(dgar) Y(ip) 1898–1981
US lyricist–librettist, born in New York, who contributed to many Broadway shows. He is best known for the songs in *The Wizard of Oz* (1939).

87 Brother can you spare a dime?
   1932 Title of song.

88 Say, it's only a paper moon,
   Sailing over a cardboard sea.
   1933 'It's Only a Paper Moon' (with Billy Rose, music by Harold Arlen).

89 Lydia the Tattooed Lady.
   1939 Title of song featured in the Marx Brothers film *At the Circus* (music by Harold Arlen).

90 Somewhere over the rainbow
   Way up high,
   There's a land that I heard of
   Once in a lullaby.
   1939 'Over the Rainbow', sung by Judy Garland in *The Wizard of Oz* (music by Harold Arlen).

Hardie, (James) Keir 1856–1915
Scottish Labour politician, a former miner. He founded and edited the *Labour Leader*, and was Chairman of the Independent Labour Party and of the Labour Party (1906–8), which he helped to found. He was a strong pacifist, and lost his seat opposing the Boer War.

91 From his childhood onward this boy will be surrounded by sycophants and flatterers by the score, and will be taught to believe himself as of a superior creation. A line will be drawn between him and the people whom he is to be called upon some day to reign over. In due course, following the precedent which has already been set, he will be sent on a tour round the world, and probably rumours of a morganatic alliance will follow, and the end of it all will be that the Country will be called upon to pay the bill.
   1894 Speech in the House of Commons, 28 Jun, opposing an Address of Congratulation to the Queen being passed in the House of Commons, on the birth of a son (the future Edward VIII) to the Duke and Duchess of York.

92 Can a Man be a Christian on a Pound a Week?
   1901 Title of pamphlet.

Hardie, Robert 1904–73
Scottish doctor who, when Singapore fell in 1942, became one of the 61,000 Allied prisoners of war forced by the Japanese to work on the Burma–Siam railway. He kept a secret diary while a prisoner.

93 This is the last day of 1943, a year to be said goodbye to without regret, holding as it did nothing beyond captivity and depression, weary waiting, and above all the sight of immeasurable human misery, suffering and death.
   1943 Diary entry, 31 Dec.

Harding, Warren G(amaliel) 1865–1923
US politician and 29th President. A successful journalist, he emerged as a power in the Republican Party, won its nomination and became President (1920–3) when he campaigned against US membership of the League of Nations.

94 America's present need is not heroics but healing; not nostrums but normalcy; not revolution but restoration.
   1920 Speech, Boston, Jun.

Hardwicke, Sir Cedric 1893–1964
English actor and director. He made his stage debut in 1912 and appeared in plays by George Bernard Shaw, Emlyn Williams and Shakespeare among others, receiving acclaim on both sides of the Atlantic.

95 I can't act. I have never acted. And I shall never act. What I do is suspend my audience's power of judgement till I've finished.
   1945 Attributed.

96 When in doubt, shout—that's the motto.
   Attributed, repeating advice that was given to him as a young actor.

Hardy, Godfrey Harold 1877–1947
English mathematician, a professor at Oxford and Cambridge. With Srinivasa Ramanujan, he found an exact formula for the partition function, which expresses the number of ways a number can be written as a sum of smaller numbers.

97 Beauty is the first test: there is no permanent place in the world for ugly mathematics.
   1941 *A Mathematician's Apology*.

98 A science is said to be useful if its development tends to accentuate the existing inequities in the distribution of wealth, or more directly promotes the destruction of human life.
   1941 *A Mathematician's Apology*.

Hardy, Oliver originally Norvell Hardy Jr 1892–1957
US comic actor. He is best known for his partnership with Stan Laurel, and together they produced more than 100 films.

99 Here's another fine mess you've gotten me into.
   Of Laurel. Line delivered in *Another Fine Mess* (1930) and other films.

Hardy, Thomas 1840–1928
English novelist and poet. His novels include *The Mayor of Casterbridge* (1886), *Tess of the D'Urbervilles* (1891) and *Jude the Obscure* (1896). His poetry was collected in *Wessex Poems* (1898), and he also wrote a drama, *The Dynasts* (1903–8).

1 Good, but not religious-good.
   1872 *Under the Greenwood Tree*, ch.2.

2 That man's silence is wonderful to listen to.
   1872 *Under the Greenwood Tree*, ch.14.

3 No man likes to see his emotions the sport of a merry-go-round of skittishness.
   1874 *Far from the Madding Crowd*, ch.4.

4 Men thin away to insignificance and oblivion quite as often by not making the most of good spirits when they have them as by lacking good spirits when they are indispensable.
1874 *Far from the Madding Crowd*, ch.22.

5 He was moderately truthful towards men, but to women lied like a Cretan.
1874 Of Sergeant Troy. *Far from the Madding Crowd*, ch.25.

6 It is hard for a woman to define her feelings in language which is chiefly made by men to express theirs.
1874 *Far from the Madding Crowd*, ch.81.

7 Human beings, in their generous endeavour to construct a hypothesis that shall not degrade a First Cause, have always hesitated to conceive a dominant power of a lower moral quality than their own.
1878 *The Return of the Native*, bk.6, ch.1.

8 There was a natural instinct to abjure man as the blot on an otherwise kindly universe.
1886 *The Mayor of Casterbridge*, ch.1.

9 Her bygone simplicity was the art that conceals art.
1886 *The Mayor of Casterbridge*, ch.15.

10 Sex had never before asserted itself in her so strongly, for in former days she had perhaps been too impersonally human to be distinctively feminine.
1886 Of Miss Newson. *The Mayor of Casterbridge*, ch.15.

11 Her occasional pretty and picturesque use of dialect words—those terrible marks of the beast to the truly genteel.
1886 *The Mayor of Casterbridge*, ch.20.

12 It is not by what is, in this life, but by what appears, that you are judged.
1886 *The Mayor of Casterbridge*, ch.25.

13 She whose youth had seemed to teach that happiness was but the occasional episode in a general drama of pain.
1886 *The Mayor of Casterbridge*, ch.45.

14 It was one of those sequestered spots outside the gates of the world.
1887 *The Woodlanders*, ch.1.

15 Why it was that upon this beautiful feminine tissue, sensitive as gossamer, and practically blank as snow as yet, there should have been traced such a coarse pattern as it was doomed to receive; why so often the coarse appropriates the finer thus, the wrong man the woman, the wrong woman the man, many thousand years of analytical philosophy have failed to explain to our sense of order.
1891 *Tess of the D'Urbervilles*, ch.11.

16 'Justice' was done, and the President of the Immortals (in Aeschylean phrase) had ended his sport with Tess.
1891 *Tess of the D'Urbervilles*, ch.59.

17 A novel is an impression, not an argument.
1892 *Tess of the D'Urbervilles*, preface to 5th edn.

18 His face wearing the fixity of a thoughtful child's who has felt the pricks of life somewhat before his time.
1896 *Jude the Obscure*, pt.1, ch.1.

19 What was good for God's birds was bad for God's gardener.
1896 *Jude the Obscure*, pt.1, ch.2.

20 It was better to love a woman than to be a graduate, or a parson; ay, or a pope!
1896 *Jude the Obscure*, pt.1, ch.7.

21 Cruelty is the law pervading all nature and society; and we can't get out of it if we would!
1896 *Jude the Obscure*, pt.5, ch.8.

22 Done because we are too menny.
1896 The note left by Jude's young son, who had hanged his siblings and himself. *Jude the Obscure*, pt.6, ch.2.

23 An aged thrush, frail, gaunt and small,
In blast-beruffled plume,
Had chosen thus to fling his sail
Upon the growing gloom.

So little cause for carollings
Of such ecstatic sound
Was written on terrestrial things
Afar or nigh around,
That I could think there trembled through
His happy good-night air
Some blessed Hope, whereof he knew
And I was unaware.
1902 'The Darkling Thrush'.

24 If way to the Better there be, it exacts a full look at the worst.
1902 'De Profundis'.

25 What we gain by science is, after all, sadness, as the Preacher saith. The more we know of the laws and nature of the Universe the more ghastly a business we perceive it all to be—and the non-necessity of it.
1902 Letter to Edward Clodd, 27 Feb.

26 A local thing called Christianity.
1904 *The Dynasts*, pt.1, act 1, sc.6.

27 War makes rattling good history; but Peace is poor reading.
1904 *The Dynasts*, pt.1, act 2, sc.5.

28 Woman much missed, how you call to me, call to me,
Saying that now you are not as you were
When you had changed from the one who was all to me,
But as at first, when our day was fair.
1914 'The Voice'.

29 This is the weather the cuckoo likes,
And so do I;
When showers betumble the chestnut spikes,
And nestlings fly:
And the little brown nightingale bills his best,
And they sit outside at 'The Travellers' Rest',
And maids come forth sprig-muslin drest,
And citizens dream of the south and west,
And so do I.
1922 *Late Lyrics and Earlier*, 'Weathers'.

30 Well, World, you have kept faith with me,
Kept faith with me;
Upon the whole you have proved to be
Much as you said you were.
1928 *Winter Words*, 'He Never Expected Much'.

Hargreaves, W F 1846–1919

English songwriter. Married to US singer Ella Shields, he wrote such music-hall standards as 'I Must Go Home Tonight'.

31 I acted so tragic the house rose like magic,
The audience yelled, 'You're sublime'.
They made me a present of Mornington Crescent,
They threw it a brick at a time.
'The Night I Appeared as Macbeth' (song).

Harington, Sir John 1561–1612

English courtier and writer, godson of Elizabeth I. He translated Ariosto's *Orlando Furioso* (1591) and published the satiric *The Metamorphosis of Ajax* (1596), which contained the first design of a flushing toilet. His government work in Ireland inspired *A Short View of the State of Ireland* (1605).

32 When I would make a feast
I would my guests should praise it, not the cooks.
1618 *Epigrams*, bk.1, no.5, 'Against Writers That Carp at Other Men's Books'.

33 Treason doth never prosper, what's the reason?
For if it prosper, none dare call it treason.
1618 *Epigrams*, bk.4, no.5.

Harkin, Tom (Thomas) 1939–

US politician, Democratic Senator from Iowa.

34 The Gulf War was like teenage sex. We got in too soon and we got out too soon.
1991 Quoted in the *Independent on Sunday*, 29 Sep.

Harkness, Richard Long 1907–77

US radio and television news commentator. He was also a journalist and government official. As the Washington correspondent for NBC (1943–72) he covered the Roosevelt–Churchill war conferences, as well as UN sessions, NATO and domestic political campaigns.

35 A group of the unwilling, picked from the unfit, to do the unnecessary.
1960 Definition of a committee. In the *New York Herald Tribune*, 15 Jun.

Harlech, William David Ormsby Gore, 5th Baron 1918–85

English Conservative politician and businessman, British Ambassador in Washington (1961–5). On his return he obtained the franchise for Harlech Television (1967). He was President of the British Board of Film Censors at a time of increasing permissiveness.

36 It would indeed be the ultimate tragedy if the history of the human race proved to be nothing more noble than the story of an ape playing with a box of matches on a petrol dump.
1960 In the *Christian Science Monitor*, 25 Oct.

Harlow, Jean *pseudonym of* Harlean Carpentier 1911–37

US actress, best known for her roles as a fast-talking wisecracking blonde in *Hell's Angels* (1930), *Red Dust* (1932) and *Libelled Lady* (1936). She died young from cerebral oedema.

37 Excuse me while I slip into something more comfortable.
1930 Line delivered in *Hell's Angels* (screenplay by Howard Estabrook and Harry Behn).

Harman, Harriet Ruth 1950–

English politician. She became MP for Camberwell and Peckham in 1982 and Deputy Leader of the Labour Party in 2007.

38 It wouldn't be possible because there aren't enough airports for all the men who'd want to flee the country.
2008 Responding to speculation that she might become Prime Minister, Prime Minister's Questions, quoted in *The Telegraph*, 9 Jul.

39 For many young people, social mobility now means a bus down to the job centre.
2011 During House of Commons debate, 5 Apr.

Harold II c.1019–1066

Earl of Wessex and King of England (1066). Shipwrecked in Normandy, he swore an oath to support Duke William's claim to the English throne. When he was elected king, William invaded, and Harold was killed at Hastings.

40 He will give him seven feet of English ground, or as much more as he may be taller than other men.
1066 His offer to the invading Norse King Harald Hardrada, quoted in Snorri Sturluson *Heimskringla* (c.1260), 'King Harald's Saga', section 91 (translated by Samuel Laing as *History of the Norse Kings*, 1844).

Harpur, Charles 1813–68

Australian poet. He used traditional, ornate 18c English verse patterns, overlaid with pastoral Australian imagery, in an attempt to create an appropriate colonial style.

41 Stale is their gladness who were never sad.
'Sonnet XIII', collected in C W Salier (ed) *Rosa: Love Sonnets to Mary Doyle* (1949).

Harrington, James 1611–77

English political theorist. Although a republican, he was an attendant of Charles I and was with him at the scaffold. His semi-romance *The Commonwealth of Oceana* (1656) proposed a commonwealth based on property. He was arrested and imprisoned in 1661.

42 No man can be a politician except he first be an historian or a traveller; for except he can see what must be, or what may be, he is no politician.
1656 *The Commonwealth of Oceana*.

Harrington, Michael 1928–89

US political activist and writer. In 1973 he set up the Democratic Socialist Organizing Committee. *The Other America: Poverty in the United States* (1962) is an indictment of poverty in the US.

43 If there is technological advance without social advance, there is, almost automatically, an increase in human misery, in impoverishment.
1962 *The Other America: Poverty in the United States*, ch.1.

44 Clothes make the poor invisible too: America has the best-dressed poverty the world has ever known.
1962 *The Other America: Poverty in the United States*, ch.1.

Harris, Joel Chandler 1848–1908

US author, who worked for the Atlanta *Constitution* (1876–1900). His reputation rests on his Uncle Remus stories, told in dialect. They include *Uncle Remus: His Songs and His Sayings* (1880) and *Nights with Uncle Remus* (1883).

45 Tar-Baby, she stay still, en Brer Fox, he lay low.
1880 *Uncle Remus: His Songs and His Sayings*, 'The Wonderful Tar-Baby Story'.

46 Bred en bawn in a brier-patch!
1880 *Uncle Remus: His Songs and His Sayings*, 'How Mr. Rabbit Was Too Sharp for Mr. Fox'.

47 Licker talks mighty loud w'en it git loose fum de jug.
1880 *Uncle Remus: His Songs and His Sayings,* 'Plantation Proverbs'.

48 Hongry rooster don't cackle w'en he fine a wum.
1880 *Uncle Remus: His Songs and His Sayings,* 'Plantation Proverbs'.

49 Watch out w'en you'er gittin all you want. Fattenin' hogs ain't in luck.
1880 *Uncle Remus: His Songs and His Sayings,* 'Plantation Proverbs'.

50 When folks git ole en strucken wid de palsy, dey mus' speck ter be laff'd at.
1883 *Nights with Uncle Remus,* 'Mr. Man Has Some Meat'.

51 All by my own-alone self.
1883 *Nights with Uncle Remus,* 'Brother Wolf Falls a Victim'.

Harris, Robert 1957–
English writer. He has worked as a news reporter and journalist and has also published novels.

52 The only leaders Labour loves are dead ones.
1996 In the *Sunday Times,* 11 Aug.

53 A book unwritten is a delightful universe of infinite possibilities. Set down one word, however, and it immediately becomes earthbound. Set down one sentence and it's halfway to being just like every other bloody book that's ever been written.
2007 *The Ghost.*

54 The Greek philosopher Epictetus recognised this two thousand years ago when he wrote: 'What disturbs and alarms man are not the things but his opinions and fancies about the things.'
2011 *The Fear Index.*

Harris, Sir (Theodore) Wilson *pseudonym of* Kona Waruk 1921–
British novelist, born in Guyana. His best-known work is *The Guyana Quartet* (1960–3).

55 The dark notes rose everywhere, so dark, so sombre, they broke into a fountain—light as the rainbow—sparkling and immaterial as invisible sources and echoes. The savannahs grew lonely as the sea and broke again into a wave and forest. Tall trees with black marching boots and feet were clad in the spurs and sharp wings of a butterfly.
1960 *The Palace of the Peacock,* ch.11.

Harrison, Tony 1937–
English poet. His work has focused on giving voice to working class culture. His best-known work is the inflammatory poem *V* (1985), a denunciation of contemporary British life.

56 Articulation is the tongue-tied's fighting.
1978 'On Not Being Milton'.

57 This pen's all I have of magic wand.
1985 *V.*

58 I have always disliked the idea of an arts ghetto in which poetry is kept on a life-support system.
1989 In the *Observer,* 23 Jul.

Harrison, Wallace K(irkman) 1895–1981
US architect, whose best-known designs include the UN Secretariat building and the Metropolitan Opera House, both in New York. He married into the Rockefeller dynasty.

59 When we started the UN we were not trying to make a monument. We were building a workshop—a workshop for world peace. And we tried to make it the best damn workshop we could.
1952 In *Time,* 22 Sep.

Harrod, Sir Roy 1900–78
English economist, Professor at Oxford (1922–67), noted for his work on international economics and economic growth.

60 The most basic law of economics…that one cannot get something for nothing.
1948 *Towards a Dynamic Economics.*

61 No economy ever stands still.
1963 *The British Economy.*

Harry (Henry Charles Albert David), Prince of Wales 1984–
Member of the English royal family, the younger son of Charles, Prince of Wales and Diana, Princess of Wales.

62 I don't know what normal is any more and I never really have done. There are three parts of me; one wearing a uniform, one being Prince Harry and the other one which is the private behind closed doors stuff.
2013 On returning from military service in Afghanistan, quoted in the *Daily Mirror,* 14 Sep. 2014.

Hart, Gary *originally* Gary Hartpence 1936–
US lawyer and Democrat politician. He entered the Senate in 1974, and was narrowly defeated for the presidential nomination by Walter Mondale in 1984. He made a further unsuccessful bid for the presidency in 1988.

63 You can get awful famous in this country in seven days.
1984 Rueful comment after reports of his marital infidelity ended his presidential campaign. In the *New York Times,* 7 Oct.

64 This is one Hart that you will not leave in San Francisco.
1984 Said after his failed bid for the presidential nomination at the Democratic National Convention in San Francisco.

Hart, Ian 1964–
English actor.

65 There's a statistical theory that if you gave a million monkeys typewriters and set them to work, they'd eventually come up with the entire works of Shakespeare. Thanks to the internet, we now know this isn't true.
2001 In the *Sunday Herald,* 30 Dec.

Hart, Lorenz 1895–1943
US songwriter.

66 When love congeals
It soon reveals
The faint aroma of performing seals,
The double-crossing of a pair of heels.
I wish I were in love again!
1937 'I Wish I Were in Love Again' (music by Richard Rodgers), from *Babes in Arms.*

67 I get too hungry for dinner at eight.
    I like the theater, but never come late.
    I never bother with people I hate.
    That's why the lady is a tramp.
    1937 'The Lady Is a Tramp' (music by Richard Rodgers), from *Babes in Arms*.

68 I'm wild again
    Beguiled again
    A simpering, whimpering child again,
    Bewitched, bothered and bewildered am I.
    1941 'Bewitched' (music by Richard Rodgers), from *Pal Joey*.

Hart, Moss 1904–61
US playwright and author. He won a Pulitzer Prize for *You Can't Take It With You* (1937) and a Perry award for directing his own play *My Fair Lady* (1957). He also wrote *Once in a Lifetime* (1930).

69 A play for me never really takes on an aspect of reality until it has left the dry air of the study and begins to sniff the musty breezes of a bare stage.
    1959 *Act One*.

70 The four most dramatic words in the English language: 'Act One, Scene One.'
    1959 *Act One*.

Harte, (Francis) Bret 1836–1902
US writer, who wrote sketches of California miners in works such as 'The Luck of Roaring Camp' (1868). Secretary of the US Mint in San Francisco (1864–70), he became US consul at Krefeld (1878–80) and Glasgow (1880–5).

71 I reside at Table Mountain, and my name is Truthful James;
    I am not up to small deceit or any sinful games.
    1868 'The Society upon the Stanislaus', stanza 1.

72 Which I wish to remark—
    And my language is plain—
    That for ways that are dark
    And for tricks that are vain,
    The heathen Chinee is peculiar,
    Which the same I would rise to explain.
    1870 'Plain Language from Truthful James', stanza 1. The poem became popularly known as 'That Heathen Chinee'.

73 We are ruined by Chinese cheap labour.
    1870 'Plain Language from Truthful James', stanza 7.

74 And on that grave where English oak and holly
    And laurel wreaths entwine,
    Deem it not all a too presumptuous folly,
    This spray of Western pine!
    1870 On the death of Charles Dickens. 'Dickens in Camp', stanza 10.

75 If, of all words of tongue and pen,
    The saddest are, 'It might have been,'

    More sad are these we daily see:
    'It is, but hadn't ought to be.'
    1871 'Mrs. Judge Jenkins'.

Hartley, L(eslie) P(oles) 1895–1972
English writer. His early published works were short stories of a macabre turn. He went on to write successful novels of considerable psychological acuity.

76 The past is a foreign country: they do things differently there.
    1953 *The Go-Between*, prologue.

Harvey, P(olly) J(ean) 1969–
English singer and songwriter.

77 There would be more women in the rock scene if they were any good. But there are so few who are.
    2004 In *Scotland on Sunday*, 30 May.

Harvey, William 1578–1657
English physician and scientist, who established the foundations of modern medicine. He was the first to demonstrate the function of the heart and the complete circulation of the blood.

78 Nature is nowhere accustomed more openly to display her secret mysteries than in cases where she shows tracings of her workings apart from the beaten paths; nor is there any better way to advance the proper practice of medicine than to give our minds to the discovery of the usual law of nature, by careful investigation of cases of rarer forms of disease.
    1657 Letter to John Vlackveld, 24 Apr.

Harvey-Jones, Sir John 1924–2008
English industrial executive.

79 All in all, if one sought to design a life style which was destructive of the individual, the way that business has structured itself would seem to be almost ideal.
    1987 *Making It Happen: Reflections on Leadership*.

Haskell, Molly 1939–
US author and film critic.

80 The propaganda arm of the American Dream machine.
    1973 Of Hollywood. *From Reverence to Rape: the treatment of women in the movies*.

Haskins, Minnie Louise 1875–1951
English author and educationist.

81 And I said to the man who stood at the gate of the year: 'Give me a light that I may tread safely into the unknown.' And he replied: 'Go out into the darkness and put your hand into the hand of God. That shall be to you better than light and safer than a known way.'
    1908 *Desert*, 'God Knows'. Quoted by King George VI, Christmas address, 25 Dec 1939.

Hattersley, Roy Sydney George Hattersley, Baron 1932–
English Labour politician and writer. He was an MP from 1964 to 1997 and served in the Callaghan government.

82 As a boy I genuinely believed in the man who never ate bacon because its red and white stripes reminded him of Sheffield United—indeed in my blue and white Wednesday heart I applauded and supported his loyalty.
    1976 *Goodbye to Yorkshire*.

83 Politicians are entitled to change their minds. But when they adjust their principles some explanation is necessary.
    1999 In the *Observer*, 21 Mar.

Haughey, Charles James 1925–2006
Irish politician and Prime Minister (1979–81, 1982, 1987–92). He became a Fianna Fáil MP (1957), but was dismissed from the

Cabinet in 1970 after a quarrel with the Prime Minister, Jack Lynch. His career was controversial and scandalous allegations about his political, financial and personal affairs continued until his death.

84 It seems that the historic inability in Britain to comprehend Irish feelings and sensitivities still remains.
1988 In the *Observer*, Feb.

Havel, Václav 1936–2011

Czech playwright and politician. He was a co-founder of Charter '77, President of Czechoslovakia (1989–1992) and first President of the Czech Republic (1993–2003).

85 The worst thing is that we live in a contaminated moral environment. We fell morally ill because we became used to saying something different from what we thought.
1990 Speech, 1 Jan.

Hawes, Hampton 1928–77

US jazz pianist. He was an important (but often undervalued) figure in West Coast jazz.

86 The worst thing that can happen to old good music is that it might become dated for a while, but watch out, in twenty years it will come drifting back like bell-bottoms and W. C. Fields movies.
1974 *Raise Up Off Me* (with Don Asher), ch.22.

Hawking, Stephen William 1942–

English theoretical physicist, theorist of the astronomical bodies known as black holes. He has written several bestselling popular science books including *A Brief History of Time* (1988) and *The Universe in a Nutshell* (2001). From the 1960s he has suffered from progressive motor neurone disease.

87 God not only plays dice. He also sometimes throws the dice where they cannot be seen.
1975 In *Nature*, vol.257.
▸ See Einstein 313:75.

88 If we find the answer to that, it would be the ultimate triumph of human reason—for then we would know the mind of God.
1988 Referring to the question of why we and the universe exist. *A Brief History of Time*, ch.11.

89 What is it that breathes fire into the equations and makes a universe for them to describe... Why does the universe go to all the bother of existing?
1988 *A Brief History of Time*, ch.11.

90 I'm sorry to disappoint science fiction fans, but if information is preserved, there is no possibility of using black holes to travel to other universes. If you jump into a black hole, your mass energy will be returned to our universe but in a mangled form which contains the information about what you were like but in a state where it cannot be easily recognized. It is like burning an encyclopedia. Information is not lost, if one keeps the smoke and the ashes. But it is difficult to read.
2005 'Information Loss in Black Holes', *Physical Review*, Jul.

91 I have noticed even people who claim everything is predestined, and that we can do nothing to change it, look before they cross the road.
2006 Attributed in Rosemarie Jarski, *Words from the Wise*.

92 To confine our attention to terrestrial matters would be to limit the human spirit.
2007 Foreword to Lawrence Krauss, *The Physics of Star Trek*.

93 I thought I'd host an end of the world party, but the media might take it seriously.
2008 Joking upon the launch of the Large Hadron Collider, 16 Sep.

94 Because there is a law such as gravity, the universe can and will create itself from nothing. Spontaneous creation is the reason there is something rather than nothing, why the universe exists, why we exist. It is not necessary to invoke God to light the blue touch paper and set the universe going.
2010 *The Grand Design*.

95 If aliens visit us, the outcome would be much as when Columbus landed in America, which didn't turn out well for the Native Americans... We only have to look at ourselves to see how intelligent life might develop into something we wouldn't want to meet.
2010 *Into the Universe with Stephen Hawking*, film.

96 Women. They are a complete mystery.
2012 His response when asked what he thinks about most during the day, 'Stephen Hawking at 70', *New Scientist*, 4 Jan.

97 Remember to look up at the stars and not down to your feet. Try to make sense of what you see and wonder about what makes the universe exist. Be curious. And however difficult life may seem, there is always something you can do and succeed at. It matters that you don't just give up.
2012 Speaking on his seventieth birthday.

Hawthorn, Mike 1929–59

English racing driver. Driving for Ferrari, he won the Formula One World Championship in 1958 but then retired from the sport, only to be killed in a road accident a few months later.

98 Motor racing is dangerous; but what is danger? It is dangerous to climb a mountain. It is dangerous to cross main roads. It is dangerous to explore a jungle. One cannot frame regulations to make everything safe.
1959 Shortly before his death. Quoted in Colin Jarman *The Guinness Dictionary of Sports Quotations* (1990).

Hawthorne, Nathaniel 1804–64

US novelist, who worked in the Salem custom house and was Consul at Liverpool (1853–7). Between 1850 and 1852 he lived in Lenox near Herman Melville, where he wrote *The Scarlet Letter* (1850) and *The House of the Seven Gables* (1851).

99 We sometimes congratulate ourselves at the moment of waking from a troubled dream: it may be so the moment after death.
c.1836 *The American Notebooks*, ch.1.

1 The love of posterity is a consequence of the necessity of death. If a man were sure of living forever here, he would not care about his offspring.
1840 *The American Notebooks* (published 1868), ch.3.

2 Bees are sometimes drowned in the honey which they collect—so some writers are lost in their collected learning.
1842 *The American Notebooks* (published 1868), ch.5.

3 Human nature will not flourish, any more than a potato, if it be planted and replanted, for too long a series of generations, in the same worn-out soil.
1850 *The Scarlet Letter*, 'The Custom-House'.

4 The founders of a new colony, whatever Utopia of human virtue and happiness they might originally project, have invariably recognized it among their earliest practical necessities to allot a portion of the virgin soil as a cemetery, and another portion as the site of a prison.
   1850 *The Scarlet Letter*, ch.1.

5 Let men tremble to win the hand of woman, unless they win along with it the utmost passion of her heart!
   1850 *The Scarlet Letter*, ch.15.

6 No man, for any considerable period, can wear one face to himself, and another to the multitude, without finally getting bewildered as to which may be the true.
   1850 *The Scarlet Letter*, ch.20.

7 When a writer calls his work a Romance, it need hardly be observed that he wishes to claim a certain latitude, both as to its fashion and material, which he would not have felt himself entitled to assume had he professed to be writing a Novel.
   1851 *The House of the Seven Gables*, preface.

8 Life is made up of marble and mud.
   1851 *The House of the Seven Gables*, ch.2.

9 Life, within doors, has few pleasanter prospects than a neatly arranged and well-provisioned breakfast-table.
   1851 *The House of the Seven Gables*, ch.7.

10 The world, that grey-bearded and wrinkled profligate, decrepit, without being venerable.
   1851 *The House of the Seven Gables*, ch.12.

11 The world owes all its onward impulse to men ill at ease. The happy man inevitably confines himself within ancient limits.
   1851 *The House of the Seven Gables*, ch.20.

12 In the depths of every heart, there is a tomb and a dungeon, though the lights, the music, and revelry above may cause us to forget their existence, and the buried ones, or prisoners whom they hide.
   1851 *Twice-Told Tales*, 'The Haunted Mind'.

13 The greatest obstacle to being heroic is the doubt whether one may not be going to prove one's self a fool; the truest heroism is to resist the doubt; and the profoundest wisdom, to know when it ought to be resisted and when to be obeyed.
   1852 *The Blithedale Romance*, ch.2.

14 America is now wholly given over to a d—d mob of scribbling women.
   1855 Quoted in Caroline Ticknor *Hawthorne and His Publisher* (1913).

15 The present is burthened too much with the past.
   1856 Entry for 27 Mar at the British Museum, collected in *The English Notebooks* (1870).

16 Nobody has any conscience about adding to the improbabilities of a marvelous tale.
   1860 *The Marble Faun*, ch.4.

17 How is it possible to say an unkind or irreverential word of Rome? The city of all time, and of all the world!
   1860 *The Marble Faun*, ch.12.

18 Dr Johnson's morality was as English an article as a beefsteak.
   1863 *Our Old Home*.

Hay, Ian *pseudonym of* Major-General John Hay Beith 1876–1952

Scottish novelist and dramatist. His light popular novels (eg *Pip*, 1907) were followed by war books, including *The First Hundred Thousand* (1915). His best-known comedies are *Tilly of Bloomsbury* (1919) and *The Housemaster* (1936).

19 What do you mean, funny? Funny peculiar, or funny ha-ha?
   1936 *The Housemaster*, act 3.

Hayakawa, S(amuel) I(chiye) 1906–92

Canadian-born US philologist and politician. His semantics works include *Language in Action* (1941, later retitled *Language in Thought and Action*). He was president of San Francisco State College (1968–73) and entered the House as Senator for California (1977–83).

20 In a real sense, people who have read good literature have lived more than people who cannot or will not read.
   1941 *Language in Action*.

21 It's ours. We stole it fair and square.
   Of the Panama Canal Zone. Attributed.

Haydn, Franz Joseph 1732–1809

Austrian composer. Kapellmeister to the Esterházy family from 1761, he twice visited England and several works were first performed in London. His works include piano music, string quartets, concertos, symphonies, masses and choral works such as the oratorio *The Creation* (1798).

22 But all the world understands my language.
   1790 Reply to Mozart, who had advised him against visiting England because he could not speak the language. Quoted in Ian Crofton and Donald Fraser *A Dictionary of Musical Quotations* (1985).

Haydon, Benjamin Robert 1786–1846

English historical painter. He was twice imprisoned for debt, and, after a number of bitter disappointments, shot himself.

23 The French had a more martial air than the English. There seemed to be a species of military instinct in all classes. No young man appeared to have finished his education till after a bloody campaign... They were at this singular period, without the least exaggeration, a century behind us in notions of legal and moral responsibility.
   Autobiography (published 1847).

Hayek, Friedrich August von 1899–1992

Austrian-born British political economist and libertarian moral philosopher. Professor at the London School of Economics (1932–50), Chicago (1950–72) and Freiburg (1962–5) and a guru of the New Right, in 1974 he was awarded the Nobel prize for economics with Gunnar Myrdal.

24 The more the state 'plans' the more difficult planning becomes for the individual.
   1944 *The Road to Serfdom*.

25 We are only beginning to understand on how subtle a communication system the functioning of an advanced industrial society is based—a communications system which we call the market and which turns out to be a more efficient mechanism for digesting dispersed information than any that man has deliberately designed.
   1978 *New Studies in Philosophy, Politics, Economics and the History of Ideas*, 'The Pretence of Knowledge'.

26 [There is] a delusion that macro-economics is both viable and useful (a delusion encouraged by its extensive

Hayes, J Milton 1884–1940
British author.

27 There's a one-eyed yellow idol to the north of Khatmandu,
There's a little marble cross below the town,
There's a broken-hearted woman tends the grave of Mad Carew,
And the Yellow God forever gazes down.
1911 *The Green Eye of the Yellow God*.

Hayes, Rutherford B(irchard) 1822–93
US Republican statesman and 19th President (1877–81). Under his presidency, the country recovered commercial prosperity, and his policy included the reform of the civil service and the conciliation of the Southern states.

28 He serves his party best who serves his country best.
1877 Inaugural address, 5 Mar.

Hayward, Thomas Bibb 1924–
US admiral, Chief of Operations in the US Navy (1978–83). He served in both Korea and Vietnam.

29 We are…a one-and-a-half ocean navy with a three-ocean commitment.
1982 Congressional testimony, reported in the *New York Times*, 11 Apr.

Hazlitt, William 1778–1830
English essayist, whose controversial and witty work ranges from theatre and literature to politics and even sports. His various collections of essays include *Table Talk* (1821) and *Spirit of the Age, or Contemporary Portraits* (1825).

30 There is in Kean, an infinite variety of talent, with a certain monotony of genius.
1815 Of the actor Edmund Kean. In *The Examiner*, 10 Dec.

31 Mr Kemble sacrifices too much to decorum. He is chiefly afraid of being contaminated by too close an identity with the character he represents. This is the greatest vice in an actor, who ought never to *bilk* his part.
1816 Of John Philip Kemble's performance as Sir Giles Overreach in Massinger's *A New Way to Pay Old Debts*. In *The Examiner*, 5 May.

32 There is nothing good to be had in the country, or if there is, they will not let you have it.
1817 *The Round Table*, 'Observation on Mr Wordsworth's Poem *The Excursion*'.

33 The art of pleasing consists in being pleased.
1817 *The Round Table*, 'On Manner'.

34 He talked on for ever; and you wished him to talk on for ever.
1818 Of Coleridge. *Lectures on the English Poets*, 'On the Living Poets'.

35 Fashion constantly begins and ends in the two things it abhors most, singularity and vulgarity.
1818 'On Fashion', in the *Scots Magazine*.

36 The love of liberty is the love of others; the love of power is the love of ourselves.
1819 *Political Essays*, 'The Times Newspaper'.

37 Those who make their dress a principal part of themselves, will, in general, become of no more value than their dress.
1819 *Political Essays*, 'On the Clerical Character'.

38 You will hear more good things on the outside of a stagecoach from London to Oxford than if you were to pass a twelvemonth with the undergraduates, or heads of colleges, of that famous university.
1821 *Table Talk*, vol.1, 'The Ignorance of the Learned'.

39 We can scarcely hate any one that we know.
1822 *Table Talk*, vol.2, 'On Criticism'.

40 Give me the clear blue sky over my head, and the green turf beneath my feet, a winding road before me, and a three hours' march to dinner—and then to thinking! It is hard if I cannot start some game on these lone heaths.
1822 *Table Talk*, vol.2, 'On Going a Journey'.

41 *The Times* is, we suppose, entitled to the character it gives of itself, of being the 'leading journal of Europe', and is perhaps the greatest engine of temporary opinion in the world.
1823 In the *Edinburgh Review*, May.

42 It is a commercial paper, a paper of business, and it is conducted on principles of trade and business. It floats with the tide: it sails with the stream. It has no other principle.
1823 Of *The Times*. In the *Edinburgh Review*, May.

43 It takes up no falling cause; fights no uphill battle; advocates no great principle; holds out a helping hand to no oppressed or obscure individual. It is 'ever strong upon the stronger side'.
1823 Of *The Times*. In the *Edinburgh Review*, May.

44 Paris is a beast of a city to be in—to those who cannot get out of it. Rousseau said well, that all the time he was in it, he was only trying how he should leave it… The continual panic in which the passenger is kept, the alarm and the escape from it, the anger and the laughter at it, must have an effect on the Parisian character, and tend to make it the whiffling, skittish, snappish, volatile, inconsequential, unmeaning thing it is.
1824 *Notes on a Journey through France and Italy* (published 1856).

45 He is a kind of *fourth estate* in the politics of the country.
1825 Of the journalist and reformer William Cobbett. *Spirit of the Age*, 'Mr Cobbett'.

46 Death cancels everything but truth; and strips a man of everything but genius and virtue. It is a sort of natural canonization.
1825 *Spirit of the Age*, 'Lord Byron'.

47 The present is an age of talkers, and not of doers; and the reason is, that the world is growing old. We are so far advanced in the Arts and Sciences, that we live in retrospect, and dote on past achievement.
1825 *Spirit of the Age*, 'Mr Coleridge'.

48 He writes as fast as they can read, and he does not write himself down… His worst is better than any other person's best… His works (taken together) are almost like a new edition of human nature. This is indeed to be an author!
1825 *Spirit of the Age*, 'Sir Walter Scott'.

49 Mr Wordsworth's genius is a pure emanation of the Spirit of the Age. Had he lived in any other period of the world, he would never have been heard of.
   1825 *Spirit of the Age*, 'Mr Wordsworth'.

50 The dupe of friendship, and the fool of love; have I not reason to hate and to despise myself? Indeed I do; and chiefly for not having hated and despised the world enough.
   1826 *The Plain Speaker*, 'On the Pleasure of Hating'.

51 His sayings are generally like women's letters; all the pith is in the postscript.
   1826-7 Of Charles Lamb. *Conversations of James Northcote*.

52 The origin of all science is in the desire to know causes; and the origin of all false science and imposture is in the desire to accept false causes rather than none; or, which is the same thing, in the unwillingness to acknowledge our own ignorance.
   1829 In *The Atlas*, 15 Feb.

53 Well, I've had a happy life.
   1830 Last words. Quoted in W C Hazlitt *Memoirs of William Hazlitt* (1867).

54 So have I loitered my life away, reading books, looking at pictures, going to plays, hearing, thinking, writing on what pleased me best. I have wanted only one thing to make me happy, but wanting that have wanted everything.
   Literary Remains (published 1836), 'My First Acquaintance with Poets'.

55 But of all footmen the lowest class is *literary footmen*.
   Sketches and Essays (published 1839), 'Footmen'.

56 A nickname is the heaviest stone that the devil can throw at a man.
   Sketches and Essays (published 1839), 'Nicknames'.

57 The greatest offence against virtue is to speak ill of it.
   Sketches and Essays (published 1839), 'On Cant and Hypocrisy'.

58 There is an unseemly exposure of mind, as well as of the body.
   Sketches and Essays (published 1839), 'On Disagreeable People'.

59 Rules and models destroy genius and art.
   Sketches and Essays (published 1839), 'On Taste'.

60 All is without form and void. Someone said of his landscapes that they were pictures of nothing and very like.
   Of Turner's painting, quoted in J Lindsay *Turner: The Man and his Art* (1985).

Hazzard, Shirley 1931-
Australian-born US novelist. Her works include short stories, the satirical *People in Glass Houses* (1967) and novels including *The Transit of Venus* (1980) and *The Great Fire* (2003).

61 Nothing...makes a more fanatical official than a Latin. Organization is alien to their natures, but once they get the taste for it they take to it like drink.
   1967 *People in Glass Houses*, 'Official Life'.

Head, Bessie 1937-86
South African novelist.

62 Love is mutually feeding each other, not one living on another like a ghoul.
   1973 *A Question of Power*.

63 Poverty has a home in Africa—like a quiet second skin. It may be the only place on earth where it is worn with unconscious dignity.
   1989 *Tales of Tenderness and Power*.

Healey, Denis Winston Healey, Baron 1917-
English Labour politician, Secretary of State for Defence (1964-70) and Chancellor of the Exchequer (1974-9). Unsuccessful in the Labour leadership contests of 1976 and 1980, he became Deputy Leader (1980-3) and shadow Foreign Secretary (1980-7).

64 That part of his speech was rather like being savaged by a dead sheep.
   1978 Responding to a speech by Chancellor of the Exchequer Sir Geoffrey Howe, House of Commons, Jun.

65 For the past few months, [Margaret Thatcher] has been charging around like some bargain-basement Boadicea.
   1982 In the *Observer*, 7 Nov.

66 The great She-elephant, the great She-who-must-be-obeyed, the Catherine the Great of Finchley.
   1985 Of Margaret Thatcher. Comment when Trade Union recognition was withdrawn for employees working in GCHQ.

Heaney, Seamus Justin 1939-2013
Irish poet and critic, born in Northern Ireland. He moved to Dublin in 1976, was Professor of Poetry at Oxford (1989-94) and also taught at Harvard (1981-97). His works include *Death of a Naturalist* (1966) and *The Spirit Level* (1997) as well as translations. He won the Nobel prize for literature in 1995.

67 Between my finger and my thumb
   The squat pen rests.
   I'll dig with it.
   1966 *Death of a Naturalist*, 'Digging'.

68 My father worked with a horse-plough,
   His shoulders globed like a full sail strung
   Between the shafts and the furrow.
   1966 *Death of a Naturalist*, 'Follower'.

69 Love, you shall perfect for me this child
   Whose small imperfect limits would keep breaking:
   Within new limits now, arrange the world
   And square the circle: four walls and a ring.
   1966 *Death of a Naturalist*, 'Poem: For Marie'.

70 My poor scapegoat,

   I almost love you
   but would have cast, I know,
   the stones of silence.
   1975 *North*, 'Punishment'.

71 I hold my lady's head
   like a crystal

   and ossify myself
   by gazing: I am screes
   on her escarpments,
   a chalk giant

   carved upon her downs.
   Soon my hands, on the sunken
   fosse of her spine
   move towards the passes.
   1975 *North*, 'Bone Dreams', no.4.

72 He had gone miles away
    For he drank like a fish
    Nightly, naturally
    Swimming towards the lure
    Of warm lit-up places.
    1979 *Field Work*, 'Casualty'.

73 How culpable was he
    That last night when he broke
    Our tribe's complicity?
    'Now you're supposed to be
    An educated man,'
    I hear him say. 'Puzzle me
    The right answer to that one.'
    1979 *Field Work*, 'Casualty'. On a man killed breaking the curfew.

74 Don't be surprised,
    If I demur, for, be advised,
    My passport's green.
    No glass of ours was ever raised
    To toast The Queen.
    1983 'An Open Letter to Blake and Andrew, Editors, Contemporary British Verse, Penguin Books, Middlesex'. Heaney was complaining at his inclusion in the book edited by Blake Morrison and Andrew Motion on the grounds of his Irish nationality.

75 Need I go on? I hate to bite
    Hands that led me to the limelight
    In the Penguin book, I regret
    The awkwardness.
    But British, no, the name's not right.
    Yours truly, Seamus.
    1983 'An Open Letter to Blake and Andrew, Editors, Contemporary British Verse, Penguin Books, Middlesex'. Heaney was complaining at his inclusion in the book edited by Blake Morrison and Andrew Motion on the grounds of his Irish nationality.

76 The riverbed, dried-up, half full of leaves.
    Us, listening to a river in the trees.
    1987 *The Haw Lantern*, 'For Bernard and Jane McCabe', complete poem.

77 When I landed in the republic of conscience
    it was so noiseless when the engines stopped
    I could hear a curlew high above the runway.
    1987 *The Haw Lantern*, 'From the Republic of Conscience', pt.1, stanza 1.

78 Their embassies, he said, were everywhere
    but operated independently
    and no ambassador would ever be relieved.
    1987 *The Haw Lantern*, 'From the Republic of Conscience', pt.3, stanza 4.

79 She taught me what her uncle once taught her:
    How easily the biggest coal block split
    If you got the grain and hammer angled right.

    The sound of that relaxed alluring blow,
    Its co-opted and obliterated echo,
    Taught me to hit, taught me to loosen,

    Taught me between the hammer and the block
    To face the music. Teach me now to listen,
    To strike it rich behind the linear black.
    1987 *The Haw Lantern*, 'Clearances: In Memoriam M.K.H., 1911–1984'.

80 The Nobel is just another prize; it changes something but it doesn't change your being the way your first writing does.
    Quoted in Annalena McAfee (ed) *Lives and Works: Profiles of Leading Novelists, Poets and Playwrights* (2002).

81 If you have the words, there's always a chance that you'll find the way.
    2008 'Stepping Stones: Interviews with Seamus Heaney', *The Times*, 14 Nov.

82 *Noli timere.* Don't be afraid.
    2013 Last words, in a text message to his wife, quoted in *The Atlantic*, 4 Sep.

Hearst, William Randolph 1863–1951

US newspaper proprietor. He revolutionized journalism with innovations such as the banner headline, in papers such as the *Chicago Examiner, Boston American, Cosmopolitan* and *Harper's Bazaar*.

83 You furnish the pictures and I'll furnish the war.
    1898 Telegram to the artist Frederic Remington at the beginning of the Spanish–American War in Cuba, Mar. This may be apocryphal, but it inspired a famous line of dialogue in Orson Welles's film *Citizen Kane*.

Heath, Sir Edward Richard George also called Ted 1916–2005

English Conservative politician, chief negotiator for Britain's entry into the European Common Market, and Prime Minister (1970–4). He was replaced as leader by Margaret Thatcher, whose policies he openly criticized.

84 We are the trade union for pensioners and children; the trade union for the disabled and the sick; the trade union for the nation as a whole.
    1970 Election campaign speech, 20 Feb.

85 This would, at a stroke, reduce the rise in prices, increase productivity, and reduce unemployment.
    1970 Statement on proposed tax cuts and a price freeze by nationalized industries, 16 Jun. These words were contained in a press release, and were never actually spoken by Heath.

86 It is the unpleasant and unacceptable face of capitalism, but one should not suggest that the whole of British industry consists of practices of this kind.
    1973 House of Commons, 15 May, referring to the Lonrho tax-avoidance scandal involving 'Tiny' Rowland, owner of Harrods and the London and Rhodesia company.

87 If you want to see the acceptable face of capitalism, go out to an oil rig in the North Sea.
    1974 Election campaign speech, 18 Feb.

88 Rejoice! Rejoice! Rejoice!
    1990 On hearing of Margaret Thatcher's resignation, Nov.

89 British Conservatives base their entire approach to politics on the rule of law, and rightly so.
    1998 *The Course of My Life: My Autobiography*.

90 It was not totally inconceivable that she could have joined me as my wife at No.10.
    2000 Of the film star Jayne Mansfield. In the *Sunday Times*, 'Talking Heads', 6 Feb.

91 Ocean racing is like standing under a cold shower tearing up £5 notes.
    Quoted in Colin Jarman *The Guinness Dictionary of Sports Quotations* (1990).

Heat-Moon, William Least originally William Trogdon 1939–

US writer. He made his name with *Blue Highways: A Journey Into America* (1983), a travelogue of America which, like *Prairyerth* (1991), also explored his Native American heritage.

92 Beware thoughts that come in the night. They aren't turned properly; they come in askew, free of sense and restriction, deriving from the most remote of sources.
 1983 *Blue Highways: A Journey Into America*, opening words.

93 There are two kinds of adventurers: those who go truly hoping to find adventure and those who go secretly hoping they won't.
 1983 *Blue Highways: A Journey Into America*.

94 To say nothing is out here is incorrect; to say the desert is stingy with everything except space and light, stone and earth is closer to the truth.
 1983 *Blue Highways: A Journey Into America*.

95 Motels can be big, but never grand.
 1983 *Blue Highways: A Journey Into America*.

96 Whoever the last true cowboy in America turns out to be, he's likely to be an Indian.
 1983 *Blue Highways: A Journey Into America*.

Hebbel, Friedrich 1813–63
German dramatist, whose plays typically have a legendary or historical setting, exploring the conflict between the individual and humanity as a whole.

97 *Dies Österreich ist eine kleine Welt,*
 In der die große ihre Probe hält.
 Austria is a little world in which the big one holds its tryouts.
 On the social and political disintegration affecting the Austro-Hungarian Empire in the late 1890s. Quoted in Heinrich Benedikt (ed) *Geschichte der Republik Oesterreich* (1954).

Heber, Reginald 1783–1826
English divine and hymnwriter, Bishop of Calcutta from 1823.

98 Brightest and best of the sons of the morning!
 Dawn on our darkness and lend us Thine aid!
 1811 In the *Christian Observer*, Nov.

99 By cool Siloam's shady rill
 How sweet the lily grows!
 1812 In the *Christian Observer*, Apr.

1 From Greenland's icy mountains,
 From India's coral strand,
 Where Afric's sunny fountains
 Roll down their coral strand.
 1819 Quoted in the *Christian Observer*, Feb 1823.

2 Holy, Holy, Holy! Lord God Almighty!
 Early in the morning our song shall rise to Thee:
 Holy, Holy, Holy! merciful and mighty!
 God in Three Persons, blessèd Trinity.
 1826 'Holy, Holy, Holy!'.

Hecht, Ben 1894–1964
US writer. A journalist in Chicago, he began to write novels, plays and filmscripts. From 1946 he was dedicated to the Zionist cause.

3 The movie-makers are able to put more reality into a picture about the terrors of life at the ocean bottom than into a tale of two Milwaukeeans in love.
 1954 In news reports, 13 Jun.

Hedin, Sven Anders 1865–1952
Swedish explorer and geographer, who travelled in unexplored regions of central Asia, where he made the first detailed map (1908). He was outspoken in his political beliefs, including sympathy for Nazi Germany.

4 But the adventure, the conquest of an unknown country, the struggle against the impossible, all have a fascination which draws me with an irresistible force.
 1926 *My Life as an Explorer*.

Heffer, Simon 1960–
English journalist and writer.

5 If there is writing on Hadrian's Wall, it reads that the English should leave Scotland to its own devices.
 1999 *Nor Shall My Sword: The Reinventing of England*.

6 The more a climate can be created in which neither the English nor the Scots are given cause to resent each other, the better.
 1999 *Nor Shall My Sword: The Reinventing of England*.

Hegel, Georg Wilhelm Friedrich 1770–1831
German idealist philosopher. His first major work *Phänomenologie des Geistes* (1807, 'The Phenomenology of the Mind') attacked romantic intuitionism. Other works include *Enzyklopädie der philosophischen Wissenschaften* (1817, 'Encyclopedia of the Philosophical Sciences'), in which he set out his tripartite system of logic, philosophy of nature and of mind.

7 In England, even the poorest of people believe that they have rights; that is very different from what satisfies the poor in other lands.
 1821 *The Philosophy of Right*.

8 Experience and history teach…that nations and governments have never learned anything from history, or acted upon any lessons they might have drawn from it.
 1830 *Lectures on the Philosophy of World History*, introduction.

9 Political genius consists in identifying oneself with a principle.
 Constitution of Germany.

Heidegger, Martin 1889–1976
German philosopher, student of Husserl and Professor of Philosophy at Freiburg. He was an important theoretician of phenomenology. His major work is *Being and Time* (1927).

10 The essence of technology is by no means anything technological.
 1949 'The Question Concerning Technology', collected in *Basic Writings* (1977).

11 The mathematical is that evident aspect of things within which we are always already moving and according to which we experience them as things at all, and as such things. The mathematical is this fundamental position we take toward things by which we take up things as already given to us, and as they must and should be given. Therefore, the mathematical is the fundamental presupposition of the knowledge of things.
 'Modern Science, Metaphysics and Mathematics', collected in *Basic Writings* (1977).

Heifetz, Jascha 1901–87
US violinist of Russo-Polish birth. A child prodigy, he settled in the US after the Russian Revolution, becoming a citizen in 1924. He first appeared in Britain in 1920.

12 I occasionally play works by contemporary composers and for two reasons. First, to discourage the composer from writing any more, and secondly to remind myself how much I appreciate Beethoven.
1961 In *Life*.

Heine, Heinrich 1797–1856

German poet and critic, who lived most of his life in Paris. An incurable spinal disease left him bedridden from 1848. He became a prominent radical political journalist, writing essays on French and German culture and composing satirical verse.

13 Alle kräftige Menschen lieben das Leben
All great, powerful souls love life.
1835 *Idéen, Das Buch Le Grand*, pt.3.

14 Das Leben ist der Güter höchstes, und das schlimmste Übel ist der Tod.
Life is the greatest of blessings, and death the worst of evils.
1835 *Idéen, Das Buch Le Grand*, pt.3.

15 Ich glaube sogar, durch Leidenskämpfe könnten die Tiere zu Menschen werden.
I believe that by suffering even animals could be made human.
1836 *Französische Zustände*.

16 Nothing is more futile than theorizing about music. No doubt there are laws, mathematically strict laws, but these laws are not music; they are only its conditions… The essence of music is revelation.
1837 *Letters on the French Stage*.

17 Ich kenn es wohl, dein Missgeschick:
Verfehltes Leben, verfehlte Liebe!
I know it well, your mishap:
A missed life, a missed love!
1840–4 *Neue Gedichte, Unterwelt*, pt.5.

18 Dieu me pardonnera. C'est son métier.
God will forgive me. It is His trade.
1856 Attributed, on his deathbed.

Heinse, Wilhelm 1746–1803

German novelist and art critic, whose work influenced the writers and artists of the Romantic movement.

19 Drawing is only a necessary evil, proportions are easily determined: colour is the goal, the beginning and end of art.
1787 *Ardinghello*.

20 The best subjects for artists, surely, are animals and plants, grasses and trees; these they can represent, but human beings they ought to leave to poets.
1787 *Ardinghello*.

21 Every form is individual, there exists none which is abstract.
Quoted in J J W Heinse *Sämmtliche Werke* (1903–25).

Heisenberg, Werner 1901–76

German physicist, a founder of quantum theory. His 'uncertainty principle' states that it is impossible to determine both the position and momentum of a subatomic particle. He received the 1932 Nobel prize for physics.

22 Natural science does not simply describe and explain nature; it is part of the interplay between nature and ourselves; it describes nature as exposed to our method of questioning.
1959 *Physics and Philosophy*.

23 Unless you stake your life, life will not be won.
1969 *Der Teil und das Ganze*, translated by A J Pomerans as *Physics and Beyond* (1971).

24 An expert is someone who knows some of the worst mistakes that can be made in his subject and who manages to avoid them.
1969 *Der Teil und das Ganze*, translated by A J Pomerans as *Physics and Beyond* (1971).

Heller, Joseph 1923–99

US novelist. He drew on his wartime experience for his black comedy *Catch-22* (1961), which became an international bestseller. Later books include *Something Happened* (1974), *God Knows* (1984) and *Picture This* (1988).

25 He was a self-made man who owed his lack of success to nobody.
1961 Of Colonel Cargill. *Catch-22*, ch.3.

26 He had decided to live forever or die in the attempt, and his only mission each time he went up was to come down alive.
1961 Of Yossarian. *Catch-22*, ch.3.

27 There was only one catch and that was Catch-22, which specified that a concern for one's safety in the face of dangers that were real and immediate was the process of a rational mind. Orr was crazy and could be grounded. All he had to do was ask; and as soon as he did, he would no longer be crazy and would have to fly more missions. Orr would be crazy to fly more missions and sane if he didn't, but if he was sane he had to fly them. If he flew them he was crazy and didn't have to; but if he didn't want to he was sane and had to. Yossarian was moved very deeply by the absolute simplicity of this clause of Catch-22, and let out a respectful whistle. 'That's some catch, that Catch-22,' he observed. 'It's the best there is,' Doc Daneeka agreed.
1961 *Catch-22*, ch.5.

28 'Yossarian? Is that his name? Yossarian? What the hell kind of a name is Yossarian?' Lieutenant Scheisskopf had the facts at his finger tips. 'It's Yossarian's name, sir,' he explained.
1961 *Catch-22*, ch.8.

29 Hungry Joe collected lists of fatal diseases and arranged them in alphabetical order so that he could put his finger without delay on any one he wanted to worry about.
1961 *Catch-22*, ch.17.

30 Frankly, I'd like to see the government get out of the war altogether and leave the whole field to private industry.
1961 Milo Minderbinder. *Catch-22*, ch.24.

31 Success and failure are both difficult to endure. Along with success come drugs, divorce, fornication, bullying, travel, meditation, medication, depression, neurosis and suicide. With failure comes failure.
1975 Interview in *Playboy*, Jun.

32 If Richard Nixon was second-rate, what in the world *is* third-rate?
1979 *Good as Gold*, ch.6.

33 And a man who lay with a beast, said the Lord, would surely die. And if he doesn't lie with a beast, I would have countered, he won't die?
   1984 King David. *God Knows*, ch.2.

34 Mankind is resilient: the atrocities that horrified us a week ago become acceptable tomorrow.
   1988 *Picture This*, ch.37.

35 I used to joke—and it wasn't much of an exaggeration—that a story I would mail to the *New Yorker* in the morning would be back with its concise, slighting rejection slip in the afternoon mail that same day.
   1998 *Now and Then: A Memoir*.

36 There were reviews that were good, a good many that were mixed, and there were reviews that were bad, very bad, almost venomously spiteful, one might be tempted to say (and I am the one that might say it).
   1998 Recalling the critical reception to *Catch-22*. In *Now and Then: A Memoir*.

37 Who has?
   On being asked why he hadn't written another novel as good as *Catch-22*. Quoted by Peter Guttridge in the postscript of *Now and Then: A Memoir* (1998).

Heller, Walter Wolfgang 1915–87

Chairman of the US Council of Economic Advisers to the President under Kennedy and Johnson (1961–64).

38 An economist is someone who, when he finds something which works in practice, wonders if it will work in theory.
   1992 Attributed.

Hellman, Lillian Florence 1907–84

US playwright, whose plays include *The Children's Hour* (1934) and *The Little Foxes* (1939). In 1952 she came before McCarthy's House Un-American Activities Committee. She lived for many years with Dashiell Hammett.

39 That's cynical. [Smiles.] Cynicism is an unpleasant way of saying the truth.
   1939 Ben. *The Little Foxes*, act 1.

40 It's an indulgence to sit in a room and discuss your beliefs as if they were a juicy piece of gossip.
   1941 Sara. *Watch on the Rhine*, act 2.

41 I do not like subversion or disloyalty in any form and if I had ever seen any I would have considered it my duty to have reported it to the proper authorities. But to hurt innocent people whom I knew many years ago in order to save myself is to me inhuman and indecent and dishonorable.
   1952 Letter to John S Wood, 19 May, on being asked to give information for the McCarthy trials. Collected in *US Congress Committee Hearing on Un-American Activities* (1952), pt.8.

42 I cannot and will not cut my conscience to fit this year's fashions, even though I long ago came to the conclusion that I was not a political person and could have no comfortable place in any political group.
   1952 Letter to John S Wood, 19 May, on being asked to give information for the McCarthy trials. Collected in *US Congress Committee Hearing on Un-American Activities* (1952), pt.8.

43 That's what you always said, success isn't everything but it makes a man stand straight, and you were right.
   1960 Julian. *Toys in the Attic*, act 1.

44 Well, people change and forget to tell each other. Too bad—causes so many mistakes.
   1960 Anna. *Toys in the Attic*, act 3.

45 If I had to give young writers advice, I would say don't listen to writers talking about writing or themselves.
   1960 In the *New York Times*, 21 Feb.

46 Intellectuals can tell themselves anything, sell themselves any bill of goods, which is why they were so often patsies for the ruling classes in nineteenth-century France and England, or twentieth-century Russia and America.
   1967 Journal entry, 30 Apr. Collected in *An Unfinished Woman* (1969), ch.13.

47 It is a mark of many famous people that they cannot part with their brightest hour.
   1973 *Pentimento*, 'Theatre'.

48 The English don't raise their voices, Arthur, although they may have other vulgarities.
   1973 *Pentimento*, 'Arthur W. A. Cowan'.

49 I am suspicious of guilt in myself and in other people: it is usually a way of not thinking, or of announcing one's own fine sensibilities the better to be rid of them.
   1976 *Scoundrel Time*.

50 He was getting over a four-day drunk, and I was getting over a 4-year marriage.
   1985 On meeting Dashiell Hammett. In the *Christian Science Monitor*, 13 Oct.

Helmholtz, Hermann Ludwig Ferdinand von 1821–94

German scientist and investigator of thermodynamics and electrodynamics. He was Professor of Physics at the University of Berlin.

51 Whoever, in the pursuit of science, seeks after immediate practical utility may rest assured that he seeks in vain.
   1862 Lecture at Heidelberg, collected in *Popular Lectures on Scientific Subjects* (1873).

Helmsley, Leona (Mindy) née Rosenthal 1920–2007

US businesswoman. Convicted of tax evasion in 1989, she received a four-year jail sentence, but avoided jail until 1992. She was released in 1994.

52 We don't pay taxes. Only the little people pay taxes.
   1989 Remark to a former hotel housekeeper which became a byword of her trial and conviction for tax fraud. Reported in the *New York Times*, 13 Jul.

Héloïse 1101–64

French abbess. At 17 she had a child by her tutor, Peter Abelard. After Abelard was castrated by her family, she entered the convent of Argenteuil, becoming prioress there, and later became abbess at the Paraclete, founded by Abelard.

53 *Et si uxoris nomen sanctius ac validius videtur, dulcius mihi semper exstitit amicæ vocabulum; aut si non indigneris, concubinæ vel scorti.*
   If the name of wife seems more blessed or more binding, always sweeter to me will be the word lover, or if I may, concubine or whore.
   c.1135 First letter to Peter Abelard.

54 *Non enim quo quisque ditior sive potentior, ideo et melior: fortunae illud est, hoc virtutis.*

To be wealthier or more powerful is not necessarily to be worthier: the former are products of fortune, the latter stems from virtue.
c.1135 First letter to Peter Abelard.

55 *Non enim rei effectus, sed efficientis affectus in crimine est. Nec quæ fiunt, sed quo animo fiunt, æquitus pensat.*
Crime lies not in the deed, but in the doer's intention: it is not what was done, but the spirit in which it was done that justice should consider.
c.1135 First letter to Peter Abelard.

Helpmann, Sir Robert Murray 1909-86

Australian dancer, actor and choreographer. He debuted in Adelaide (1923), studied with Pavlova and in 1931 went to Britain. Star of the new Sadler's Wells Ballet (1933-50), he danced in many films and also acted with the Royal Shakespeare Company. His choreographic work includes *Hamlet* (1942) and *Miracle in the Gorbals* (1944).

56 You see there are portions of the human anatomy which would keep swinging after the music had finished.
c.1968 Disagreeing with the suggestion that there might be a future for nudity in dance. Quoted in Elizabeth Salter *Helpmann* (1978), ch.21. It is sometimes quoted as a comment on the opening night of the musical *Oh, Calcutta!*, as 'The trouble with nude dancing is that not everything stops when the music stops.'

Hemans, Felicia *née Browne* 1793-1835

English poet.

57 The stately homes of England,
How beautiful they stand!
Amid their tall ancestral trees,
O'er all the pleasant land.
1849 'The Homes of England'.
▶ See Coward 249:55.

58 The boy stood on the burning deck
Whence all but he had fled;
The flame that lit the battle's wreck
Shone round him o'er the dead.
1849 'Casabianca'.

Hemingway, Ernest Millar 1899-1961

US novelist, short-story writer and journalist, whose terse prose style was much imitated. He was a legendary figure known for his drinking, big-game hunting, and deep-sea fishing. He won the Nobel prize for literature in 1954. Depressed by his failing powers, he later committed suicide.

59 Switzerland is a small, steep country, much more up and down than sideways, and is all stuck over with large brown hotels built on the cuckoo clock style of architecture.
1922 In the *Toronto Star Weekly*, 4 Mar.

60 A man's got to take a lot of punishment to write a really funny book.
1924 Letter, 6 Dec.

61 God knows people who are paid to have attitudes toward things, professional critics, make me sick: camp-following eunuchs of literature.
1925 Letter to Sherwood Anderson, 23 May.

62 Don't you like to write letters? I do because it's such a swell way to keep from working and yet feel you've done something.
1925 Letter to F Scott Fitzgerald, 1 Jul.

63 Soon I was alone and began cursing the bloody bible because there were no titles in it—although I found the source of practically every good title you ever heard of. But the boys, principally Kipling, had been there before me and swiped all the good ones so I called the book Men Without Women hoping it would have a large sale among the fairies and old Vassar Girls.
1927 Letter to F Scott Fitzgerald, 15 Sep.

64 I did not say anything. I was always embarrassed by the words sacred, glorious and sacrifice and the expression in vain. We had heard them, sometimes standing in the rain almost out of earshot, so that only the shouted words came through, and had read them, on proclamations that were slapped up by billposters over other proclamations, now for a long time, and I had seen nothing sacred, and the things that were glorious had no glory and the sacrifices were like the stock-yards at Chicago if nothing was done with the meat except to bury it.
1929 Frederic Henry. *A Farewell to Arms*, ch.27.

65 I had the paper but I did not read it because I did not want to read about the war. I was going to forget the war. I had made a separate peace.
1929 Frederic Henry. *A Farewell to Arms*, ch.34.

66 The world breaks everyone and afterwards many are strong at the broken places. But those that will not break it kills. It kills the very good and the very gentle and the very brave impartially. If you are none of these you can be sure it will kill you too but there will be no special hurry.
1929 Frederic Henry. *A Farewell to Arms*, ch.34.

67 I mean grace under pressure.
1929 His definition of 'guts'. Interview with Dorothy Parker in the *New Yorker*, 30 Nov.

68 Hail nothing full of nothing, nothing is with thee.
1932 End of the older waiter's 'nada' prayer. *Winner Take Nothing*, 'A Clean, Well-Lighted Place'.

69 When you have shot one bird flying you have shot all birds flying. They are all different and they fly in different ways but the sensation is the same and the last one is as good as the first.
1932 *Winner Take Nothing*, 'Fathers and Sons'.

70 About morals, I know only that what is moral is what you feel good after and what is immoral is what you feel bad after.
1932 *Death in the Afternoon*, ch.1.

71 Bullfighting is the only art in which the artist is in danger of death and in which the degree of brilliance in the performance is left to the fighter's honor.
1932 *Death in the Afternoon*, ch.9.

72 There is no lonelier man in death, except the suicide, than the man who has lived many years with a good wife and then outlived her. If two people love each other there can be no happy end to it.
1932 *Death in the Afternoon*, ch.11.

73 Madame, all stories, if continued far enough, end in death, and he is no true story-teller who would keep that from you.
1932 *Death in the Afternoon*, ch.11.

74 The great thing is to last and get your work done, and see and hear and understand and write when there is something that you know and not before and not too damn much after.
1932 Death in the Afternoon, ch.16.

75 The hardest thing to do is to write straight honest prose on human beings.
1934 'Old Newsman Writes', in *Esquire*, Dec.

76 All modern American literature comes from one book by Mark Twain called *Huckleberry Finn*. American writing comes from that. There was nothing before. There has been nothing good since.
1935 The Green Hills of Africa, ch.1.

77 The only time it isn't good for you is when you write or when you fight. You have to do that cold. But it always helps my shooting. Modern life, too, is often a mechanical oppression and liquor is the only mechanical relief.
1935 Of whisky. Letter to Ivan Kashkin, 19 Aug.

78 He remembered poor Julian and his romantic awe of them and how he had started a story once that began, 'The very rich are different from you and me.' And somebody had said to Julian, 'Yes, they have more money.'
1936 'The Snows of Kilimanjaro', in *Esquire*, Aug. In the original version 'Julian' was named as F Scott Fitzgerald, but the pseudonym was used for book publication in *The Fifth Column and Other Stories* (1938).
▸ See Fitzgerald 338:88.

79 'A man...ain't got no hasn't got any can't really isn't any way out... One man alone ain't got...no chance.
1937 Harry Morgan's dying words. *To Have and Have Not*.

80 'Oh,' she said, 'I die each time. Do you not die?' 'No. Almost. But did thee feel the earth move?' 'Yes. As I died. Put thy arm around me, please.'
1940 For Whom the Bell Tolls, ch.7.

81 He was just a coward and that was the worst luck any man could have.
1940 For Whom the Bell Tolls, ch.30.

82 Cowardice, as distinguished from panic, is almost always simply a lack of ability to suspend the functioning of the imagination.
1942 Introduction to *Men At War*.

83 It wasn't by accident that the Gettysburg address was so short. The laws of prose writing are as immutable as those of flight, of mathematics, of physics.
1945 Letter, 23 Jul.

84 I started out very quiet and I beat Mr Turgenev. Then I trained hard and I beat Mr De Maupassant. I've fought two draws with Stendhal, and I think I had an edge in the last one. But nobody's going to get me in any ring with Mr Tolstoy unless I'm crazy or I keep getting better.
1950 In the *New Yorker*, 13 May.

85 Writing and travel broaden your ass if not your mind and I like to write standing up.
1950 Letter, 9 Jul.

86 All the contact I have had with politics has left me feeling as though I had been drinking out of spittoons.
1950 In the *New York Times*, 17 Sep.

87 A man can be destroyed but not defeated.
1952 The Old Man and the Sea.

88 It is because we have had such great writers in the past that a writer is driven out far past where he can go, out to where no one can help him.
1954 Nobel prize acceptance speech, 10 Dec.

89 No classic resembles any previous classic, so do not be discouraged.
1956 Advice to young writers, in *McCall's*, May.

90 Once writing has become your major vice and greatest pleasure only death can stop it.
1958 Interview in the *Paris Review*, Spring.

91 Under the black hat, when I had first seen them, the eyes had been those of an unsuccessful rapist.
1964 Of Percy Wyndham-Lewis. *A Moveable Feast*, ch.12 (published posthumously).

92 I always try to write as good as the best picture that was ever painted.
Quoted in the *Saturday Review*, 9 May 1964.

93 Never confuse movement with action.
Quoted in A E Hotchner *Papa Hemingway* (1966), pt.1, ch.1.

94 Hesitation increases in relation to risk in equal proportion to age.
Quoted in A E Hotchner *Papa Hemingway* (1966), pt.1, ch.3.

95 To be a successful father, there's one absolute rule: when you have a kid, don't look at it for the first two years.
Quoted in A E Hotchner *Papa Hemingway* (1966), pt.2, ch.5.

96 Wearing underwear is as formal as I ever hope I get.
Quoted in A E Hotchner *Papa Hemingway* (1966).

97 My writing is nothing, my boxing is everything.
Quoted in Colin Jarman *The Guinness Dictionary of Sports Quotations* (1990).

Hempstone, Smith 1929–2006

US journalist, writer and diplomat, Ambassador to Kenya (1989–93). His works include *Africa*, *Angry Young Giant* (1961) and *Rogue Ambassador: An African Memoir* (1997).

98 If you liked Beirut, you'll love Mogadishu.
1992 To US Marines in Somalia some years after the Corps' losing battle against Kenyan terrorists. Reported in the *Guardian Weekly*, 19 Dec.

99 It will take five years to get Somalia not on its feet but just on its knees.
1992 Reported in the *Guardian Weekly*, 19 Dec.

Henderson, Leon 1895–1986

US economist.

1 Having a little inflation is like being a little pregnant.
Attributed.

Henderson, Sir Nevile Meyrick 1882–1942

English diplomat. He served as Minister to Yugoslavia (1929–35) and as Ambassador to Argentina (1935–7) and to Germany until the outbreak of World War II.

2 When I go to see Herr Hitler I give him the Nazi salute because that is the normal thing. It carries no hint of approval of anything he or his regime may do. And, if I do it, why should you or your team object?
1938 When asked for advice by the England football team in 1938 about giving the Nazi salute before a match in Berlin against Germany. The England team gave the salute, and thereby attracted considerable notoriety at home.

Hendrix, Jimi (James Marshall) 1942–70
US rock guitarist and singer, based in Britain from 1966. Born into poverty, he taught himself guitar and became one of rock music's most innovative and influential instrumentalists before drugs and alcohol caused his death.

3 Purple haze is in my brain
Lately things don't seem the same.
1967 'Purple Haze'.

4 You can't mess with people's heads, that's for sure. But that's what music's all about, messing with people's heads.
Quoted in Nat Shapiro *An Encyclopedia of Quotations about Music* (1978).

Henley, W(illiam) E(rnest) 1849–1903
English poet, playwright, critic and editor. He collaborated with his friend R L Stevenson in four plays. He edited the *Scots Observer* (1889), renaming it *The National Observer*. The best known of his poetry collections is *In Hospital* (1903).

5 In the fell clutch of circumstance,
I have not winced nor cried aloud:
Under the bludgeonings of chance
My head is bloody but unbowed.
1888 'Invictus', collected in *In Hospital* (1903).

6 It matters not how strait the gate,
How charged with punishments the scroll,
I am the master of my fate:
I am the captain of my soul.
1888 'Invictus', collected in *In Hospital* (1903).

7 What have I done for you,
England, my England?
1900 'Pro Rege Nostro'.

Henri, Adrian Maurice 1932–2000
English poet, associated with the Mersey poets of the 1960s.

8 Beautiful boys with bright red guitars
In the spaces between the stars.
1967 'Mrs Albion You've Got a Lovely Daughter'.

9 Love is a fanclub with only two fans.
1967 'Love Is…'.

10 I wanted your soft verges
But you gave me the hard shoulder.
1967 'Song of a Beautiful Girl Petrol-pump Attendant'.

Henry II 1133–89
King of England from 1154. He instituted numerous political reforms aimed at diminishing the power of the barons and of the Church.

11 Will no one rid me of this turbulent priest?
1170 Of Thomas à Becket. Quoted in W L Warren *Henry II*, p508. Four of Henry's soldiers took his words to heart and proceeded to Canterbury, where they murdered Becket in the cathedral.

Henry V 1387–1422
King of England from 1413. He won a famous victory against the French at Agincourt in 1415, despite numerical disadvantage.

12 War has three handmaidens ever waiting on her, Fire, Blood, and Famine, and I have chosen the meekest maid of the three.

1418 Comment during the English army's siege of Rouen. Quoted in J R Green *A Short History of the English People*, vol.1 (1915), ch.5, section 6.

Henry VIII 1491–1547
King of England (1509–47). His desire to divorce his first wife, Catherine of Aragon, against papal decree led to ecclesiastical revolution, with Henry as sole head of the Church of England. In all he married six wives. His reign also saw the judicial murder of Sir Thomas More and others who dared to oppose him.

13 We at no time stand so highly in our estate royal as in the time of Parliament, wherein we as head, and you as members, are conjoined and knit together into one body politic, so as whatsoever offence or injury is offered to the meanest member of the House is to be judged as done against our person and the whole Court of Parliament.
1543 Address to a deputation from the House of Commons, 31 Mar.

Henry, Philip 1631–96
English clergyman.

14 All this, and heaven too!
Quoted in Matthew Henry *Life of Mr Philip Henry* (1698), ch.5.

Henry, Thierry 1977–
French footballer.

15 When you look at other sports, like golf, the players earn a lot more money without running around.
2003 In *The Times*, 31 Dec.

Henryson, Robert c.1425–c.1508
Scottish poet, usually designated 'schoolmaster of Dunfermline', whose surviving poems include *The Testament of Cresseid* (c.1470) and metrical versions of Aesop's fables.

16 For to be yong I wald not, for my wis,
Off all this warld to mak me lord and king:
The more of age, the nerar hevynnis blis.
c.1460 'The Praise of Age', l.5–9.

17 The man that will nocht quhen he may
Sall haif nocht quhen he wald.
c.1460 'Robene and Makeyne', l.91–2.

18 The nuttis schell, thocht it be hard and teuch,
Haldis the kirnell, sueit and delectabill;
Sa lyis thair ane doctrine wyse aneuch
And full of frute vnder ane fenyeit fabill.
c.1470 *Moral Fables*, prologue, l.15–19.

19 Ane bow that is ay bent
Worthis ay unsmart and dullis on the string;
Sa dois the mynd that is ay diligent
In ernistfull thochtis and in studying.
c.1470 *Moral Fables*, prologue, l.21–5.

20 Best thing in eird, I say for me,
Is merry hart with small possessioun.
c.1470 *Moral Fables*, 'The Two Mice', l.387–8.

21 Louers be war and tak gude heid about
Quhome that ye lufe, for quhome ye suffer paine.
I lat yow wit, thair is richt few thairout
Quhome ye may traist to haue trew lufe agane.
c.1470 *The Testament of Cresseid*, l.561–4.

22 Nocht is your fairnes bot ane faiding flour,
    Nocht is your famous laud and hie honour
    Bot wind inflat in uther mennis eiris.
    c.1470 *The Testament of Cresseid*, stanza 65.

Henze, Hans Werner 1926–2012
German composer. His stage works, often reflecting his socialist commitment, include the operas *Der Junge Lord* (1965) and *The English Cat* (1983). He also composed orchestral, chamber, vocal and piano music.

23 There is no such thing as an unmusical person.
    1969 'Does Music Have to Be Political?'

24 My profession...consists of bringing truths nearer to the point where they explode.
    1982 *Music and Politics*.

Hepburn, Katharine 1907–2003
US film and stage actress. She made her professional stage debut in *The Czarina* (1928). Her films included *Bringing up Baby* (1938) and *The African Queen* (1951). *The Lion in Winter* (1968) and *On Golden Pond* (1981) both won her Academy Awards. She was the professional and personal partner of Spencer Tracy.

25 The average Hollywood film star's ambition is to be admired by an American, courted by an Italian, married to an Englishman and have a French boyfriend.
    1954 In the *Journal American*, 22 Feb.

26 When a man says he likes a woman in a skirt, I tell him to try one.
    1994 WETA TV broadcast, Washington, 27 Jun.

27 She gave him sex and he gave her class.
    Explaining the success of the Fred Astaire and Ginger Rogers partnership. Attributed.

Hepworth, Dame Barbara 1903–75
English sculptor. She was an important figure in the development of British abstract art.

28 Carving is interrelated masses conveying an emotion: a perfect relationship between the mind and the colour, light and weight which is the stone, made by the hand which feels.
    1934 *Unit One*.

29 There is an inside and an outside to every form.
    1970 *A Pictorial Autobiography*.

30 My left hand is my thinking hand. The right is only a motor hand.
    1970 *A Pictorial Autobiography*.

Heraclitus fl.500 BC
Greek philosopher, born in Ephesus. Only fragments survive of his book 'On Nature', which was written in an aphoristic style.

31 All is flux, nothing is stationary.
    c.500 BC Quoted in Aristotle *De caelo*, bk.3, pt.1.18.

32 The path up and down is one and the same.
    c.500 BC Quoted in Kirk, Raven and Schofield (eds) *The Presocratic Philosophers* (1957), ch.6.

33 Upon those that step into the same rivers different and different waters flow. They scatter and gather, come together and flow away, approach and depart.
    c.500 BC Quoted in Kirk, Raven and Schofield (eds) *The Presocratic Philosophers* (1957), ch.6. Often quoted as 'It is not possible to step into the same river twice', from Plato, *Cratylus* 402a.

34 The world is an ever-living fire.
    c.500 BC Quoted in Kirk, Raven and Schofield (eds) *The Presocratic Philosophers* (1957), ch.6.

35 You would not find out the boundaries of the soul, even by travelling along every path: so deep a measure does it have.
    c.500 BC Quoted in Kirk, Raven and Schofield (eds) *The Presocratic Philosophers* (1957), ch.6.

36 Education is another sun to the educated.
    Fragment quoted in H Diels and W Kranz (eds) *Die Fragmente der Vorsokratiker*, vol.1 (1951), 181, no.134.

37 If you do not expect the unexpected, you will not find it; for it is hard to be sought out, and difficult.
    Collected in Charles H Kahn *The Art and Thought of Heraclitus* (1979).

38 The fairest order in the world is a heap of random sweepings.
    Collected in Charles H Kahn *The Art and Thought of Heraclitus* (1979).

Herbert, Sir A(lan) P(atrick) 1890–1971
English writer and politician. He was called to the bar but never practised, having established himself as a humorist. His 'Misleading Cases' were accounts of unusual trials, in such collections as *Uncommon Law* (1935). He was an MP (1935–50).

39 Don't tell my mother I'm living in sin,
    Don't let the old folks know.
    1925 'Don't Tell My Mother I'm Living in Sin'.

40 Don't let's go to the dogs tonight
    For mother will be there.
    1926 'Don't Let's Go to the Dogs Tonight'.

41 Not huffy, or stuffy, not tiny or tall,
    But fluffy, just fluffy, with no brains at all.
    1927 Of women. 'I Like Them Fluffy'.

42 Let's find out what everyone is doing
    And then stop everyone from doing it.
    1930 'Let's Stop Somebody from Doing Something'.

43 As my poor father used to say
    In 1863,
    Once people start on all this Art
    Goodbye, moralitee!
    1930 'Lines for a Worthy Person'.

44 Other people's babies—
    That's my life!
    Mother to dozens,
    And nobody's wife.
    1930 'Other People's Babies'.

45 Well, fancy giving money to the Government!
    Might as well have put it down the drain.
    Fancy giving money to the Government!
    Nobody will see the stuff again.
    1931 'Too Much!'.

46 For Kings and Governments may err
    But never Mr Baedeker.
    1931 'Mr Baedeker, or Britons Abroad'.

47 Holy Deadlock.
    1934 Title of novel.

48 Milord, in that case an Act of God was defined as 'something which no reasonable man could have expected'.
    1935 *Uncommon Law*, 'Act of God'.

49 People must not do things for fun. We are not here for fun. There is no reference to fun in any Act of Parliament.
   1935 *Uncommon Law*, 'Is it a Free Country?'.

50 The Common Law of England has been laboriously built about a mythical figure—the figure of 'The Reasonable Man'.
   1935 *Uncommon Law*, 'The Reasonable Man'.

51 The critical period in matrimony is breakfast-time.
   1935 *Uncommon Law*, 'Is Marriage Lawful?'.

52 The Englishman never enjoys himself except for a noble purpose.
   1935 *Uncommon Law*, 'Fox-Hunting Fun'.

53 It may be life, but ain't it slow?
   1941 'It May be Life'.

54 Nothing is wasted, nothing is in vain:
   The seas roll over but the rocks remain.
   c.1949 From an operetta, *Tough at the Top*, published in *My Life and Times* (1970), ch.7.

Herbert, George   1593–1633

English metaphysical poet and clergyman. His religious lyrics are collected in *The Temple, Sacred Poems and Private Ejaculations*, published posthumously in 1633.

55 Drink not the third glass, which thou canst not tame,
   When once it is within thee.
   'The Church-porch', collected in *The Temple, Sacred Poems and Private Ejaculations* (published posthumously, 1633).

56 A broken Altar, Lord, thy servant rears,
   Made of a heart, and cemented with tears.
   'The Altar', collected in *The Temple, Sacred Poems and Private Ejaculations* (published posthumously, 1633).

57 Avoid, Profaneness; come not here:
   Nothing but holy, pure, and clear,
   Or that which groaneth to be so,
   May at his peril further go.
   'Superliminare', collected in *The Temple, Sacred Poems and Private Ejaculations* (published posthumously, 1633).

58 Let all the world in ev'ry corner sing
   My God and King.
   'Antiphon', collected in *The Temple, Sacred Poems and Private Ejaculations* (published posthumously, 1633).

59 I got me flowers to strew Thy way,
   I got me boughs off many a tree;
   But Thou wast up by break of day,
   And brought'st Thy sweets along with Thee.
   'Easter Song', collected in *The Temple, Sacred Poems and Private Ejaculations* (published posthumously, 1633).

60 A servant with this clause
   Makes drudgery divine;
   Who sweeps a room as for Thy laws
   Makes it and th' action fine.
   'The Elixir', collected in *The Temple, Sacred Poems and Private Ejaculations* (published posthumously, 1633).

61 Teach me, my God and King,
   In all things Thee to see,
   And what I do in any thing
   To do it as for Thee.
   'The Elixir', collected in *The Temple, Sacred Poems and Private Ejaculations* (published posthumously, 1633).

62 Whereas my birth and spirit rather took
   The way that takes the town;
   Thou didst betray me to a lingering book,
   And wrap me in a gown.
   'Affliction (1)', collected in *The Temple, Sacred Poems and Private Ejaculations* (published posthumously, 1633).

63 Sorrow was all my soul; I scarce believed,
   Till grief did tell me roundly, that I lived.
   'Affliction (1)', collected in *The Temple, Sacred Poems and Private Ejaculations* (published posthumously, 1633).

64 I read, and sigh, and wish I were a tree;
   For sure then I should grow
   To fruit or shade: at least some bird would trust
   Her household to me, and I should be just.
   'Affliction (1)', collected in *The Temple, Sacred Poems and Private Ejaculations* (published posthumously, 1633).

65 Love bade me welcome: yet my soul drew back;
   Guilty of dust and sin.
   But quick-ey'd Love, observing me grow slack
   From my first entrance in,
   Drew nearer to me, sweetly questioning
   If I lacked any thing.
   'Love', collected in *The Temple, Sacred Poems and Private Ejaculations* (published posthumously, 1633).

66 'You must sit down,' says Love, 'and taste my meat,'
   So I did sit and eat.
   'Love', collected in *The Temple, Sacred Poems and Private Ejaculations* (published posthumously, 1633).

67 I know the ways of Pleasure, the sweet strains,
   The lullings and the relishes of it.
   'The Pearl', collected in *The Temple, Sacred Poems and Private Ejaculations* (published posthumously, 1633).

68 King of glory, King of peace
   I will love Thee
   And that love may never cease,
   I will move Thee.
   'Praise', collected in *The Temple, Sacred Poems and Private Ejaculations* (published posthumously, 1633).

69 My God, I heard this day,
   That none doth build a stately habitation,
   But that he means to dwell therein.
   What house more stately hath there been,
   Or can be, than is Man? to whose creation
   All things are in decay.
   'Man', collected in *The Temple, Sacred Poems and Private Ejaculations* (published posthumously, 1633).

70 Man is all symmetry,
   Full of proportions, one limb to another.
   'Man', collected in *The Temple, Sacred Poems and Private Ejaculations* (published posthumously, 1633).

71 O mighty love! Man is one world, and hath
   Another to attend him.
   'Man', collected in *The Temple, Sacred Poems and Private Ejaculations* (published posthumously, 1633).

72 Who says that fictions only and false hair
   Become a verse? Is there in truth no beauty?
   Is all good structure in a winding stair?
   'Jordan (1)', collected in *The Temple, Sacred Poems and Private Ejaculations* (published posthumously, 1633).

73 I sought out quaint words, and trim invention;
   My thoughts began to burnish, sprout, and swell,
   Curling with metaphors a plain intention,
   Decking the sense, as if it were to sell.
   'Jordan (2)', collected in *The Temple, Sacred Poems and Private Ejaculations* (published posthumously, 1633).

74 So did I weave my self into the sense.
'Jordan (2)', collected in *The Temple, Sacred Poems and Private Ejaculations* (published posthumously, 1633).

75 I struck the board, and cried, 'No more.
I will abroad.'
What? shall I ever sigh and pine?
My lines and life are free; free as the road,
Loose as the wind, as large as store.
'The Collar', collected in *The Temple, Sacred Poems and Private Ejaculations* (published posthumously, 1633).

76 Sure there was wine
Before my sighs did dry it; there was corn
Before my tears did drown it.
'The Collar', collected in *The Temple, Sacred Poems and Private Ejaculations* (published posthumously, 1633).

77 My crooked winding ways, wherein I live.
'A Wreath', collected in *The Temple, Sacred Poems and Private Ejaculations* (published posthumously, 1633).

78 The soul in paraphrase.
'Prayer (1)', collected in *The Temple, Sacred Poems and Private Ejaculations* (published posthumously, 1633).

79 O that thou shouldst give dust a tongue
To cry to thee,
And then not hear it crying!
'Denial', collected in *The Temple, Sacred Poems and Private Ejaculations* (published posthumously, 1633).

80 Sweet day, so cool, so calm, so bright,
The bridal of the earth and sky:
The dew shall weep thy fall tonight,
For thou must die.
'Virtue', collected in *The Temple, Sacred Poems and Private Ejaculations* (published posthumously, 1633).

81 Joy, I did lock thee up; but some bad man
Hath let thee out again.
'The Bunch of Grapes', collected in *The Temple, Sacred Poems and Private Ejaculations* (published posthumously, 1633).

82 When God at first made man,
Having a glass of blessings standing by,
'Let us,' said he, 'pour on him all we can:
Let the world's riches, which dispersèd lie,
Contract into a span'.
'The Pulley', collected in *The Temple, Sacred Poems and Private Ejaculations* (published posthumously, 1633).

83 Let him be rich and weary, that at least,
If goodness lead him not, yet weariness
May toss him to My breast.
'The Pulley', collected in *The Temple, Sacred Poems and Private Ejaculations* (published posthumously, 1633).

84 Farewell, sweet phrases, lovely metaphors:
But will ye leave me thus? when ye before
Of stews and brothels only knew the doors,
Then did I wash you with my tears, and more,
Brought you to church well-dressed and clad:
My God must have my best, even all I had.
'The Forerunners', collected in *The Temple, Sacred Poems and Private Ejaculations* (published posthumously, 1633).

85 Throw away thy rod,
Throw away thy wrath:
O my God,
Take the gentle path.
'Discipline', collected in *The Temple, Sacred Poems and Private Ejaculations* (published posthumously, 1633).

86 He that makes a good war makes a good peace.
Outlandish Proverbs (published posthumously, 1640), no.420.

87 Music helps not the toothache.
Jacula Prudentum (published posthumously, 1651). This is probably an older proverb.

88 God's mill grinds slow, but sure.
Jacula Prudentum (published posthumously, 1651).

89 He that will learn to pray, let him go to sea.
Jacula Prudentum (published posthumously, 1651).

Herbert, Xavier 1901–84

Australian writer. His novel *Capricornia* won the Sesquicentennial Literary Prize (1938) and the 1939 Australian Literary Society Gold Medal.

90 Since no normal humble man can help but feel magnificent in a brand-new suit of clothes, it is not surprising that those who don a fresh suit of bright white linen every day should feel magnificent always. Nor is it surprising that a normal humble head should swell beneath a solar topee, since a topee is more a badge of authority than a hat, as is the hat of a soldier.
1938 *Capricornia,* 'Psychological Effect of a Solar Topee'.

Herfindahl, Orris C 1918–72

US economist.

91 Conservation of one resource may entail the sacrifice of another resource which others want to conserve.
1974 *Resource Economics: Selected Writings*, p.6.

Hernández, Felisberto 1902–64

Uruguayan novelist and pianist. He led an obscure life and wrote stories describing banal events with fantastic resolutions. His surrealistic sense of humour paved the way for literary experiments in Latin America and beyond.

92 *Se ha hecho para los vivos y no para los muertos el porqué metafísico y las reflexiones sobre la vida y la muerte, pero no les hace falta aclarar todo el misterio, les hace falta distraerse y soñar en aclararlo.*
Metaphysical questions and reflections on life and death were created for people alive and not for the dead. However, they do not have to solve all mystery; it is enough for them to create some distraction and to dream that they clarify.
1929 *Libro sin tapas,* 'La piedra filosofal' ('The Philosopher's Stone').

Hernández, José 1834–86

Argentinian poet. He had little formal education and was a gaucho (pampas cowboy) in his youth, later becoming a soldier in the civil wars, a newspaper editor and a minor government official.

93 *Yo he conocido cantores
que era un gusto el escuchar;
mas no quieren opinar
y se divierten cantando;
pero yo canto opinando,
que es mi modo de cantar.*
I have known singers
it was a pleasure to listen to;
they amuse themselves singing
and don't care to give opinions;

but I sing giving opinions
and that's my kind of song.
1879 *La vuelta de Martín Fierro*, pt.1 (translated as *Martín Fierro*, 1923).

94 Hay hombres que de su ciencia
tienen la cabeza llena;
hay sabios de todas menas,
mas digo, sin ser muy ducho:
es mejor que aprender mucho
el aprender cosas buenas.
There are some men who have their heads
full up with the things they know.
Wise men come in all sizes,
but I don't need so much sense to say
that better than learning a lot of things
is learning things that are good.
1879 *La vuelta de Martín Fierro*, pt.32 (translated as *Martín Fierro*, 1923).

Herodotus c.485 BC–c.425 BC

Greek historian. His *Histories* deal with the wars between the Persians and the Greeks. He is often called 'The Father of History'.

95 In peace, children inter their parents; war violates the order of nature and causes parents to inter their children.
c.440 BC *The Histories of Herodotus*, bk.1, ch.87 (translated by Aubrey de Selincourt).

Herr, Michael 1940–

US journalist and war correspondent. He collaborated on the screenplays of *Apocalypse Now* (1979) and *Full Metal Jacket* (1987).

96 Vietnam was what we had instead of happy childhoods.
1977 *Dispatches*, 'Colleagues', section 3.

97 All the wrong people remember Vietnam. I think all the people who remember it should forget it, and all the people who forgot it should remember it.
1989 In the *Observer*, 15 Jan.

Herrick, Robert 1591–1674

English poet and clergyman, a Royalist who lost his living during the Civil War. His writing, both secular and religious, is collected in *Hesperides* and *Noble Numbers* (both 1648).

98 I write of *Hell*; I sing (and ever shall)
Of *Heaven*, and hope to have it after all.
1648 *Hesperides*, 'The Argument of His Book'.

99 I sing of brooks, of blossoms, birds, and bowers:
Of April, May, of June, and July-flowers.
I sing of May-poles, Hock-carts, wassails, wakes,
Of bride-grooms, brides, and of their bridal-cakes.
1648 *Hesperides*, 'The Argument of His Book'.

1 Is there no way to beget
In my limbs their former heat?
Aeson had (as *Poets* fain)
Baths that made him young again:
Find that *Medicine* (if you can)
For your dry-decrepit man:
Who would but fain his strength renew,
Were it but to pleasure you.
1648 'To His Mistress'.

2 But ah! if empty dreams so please,
Love give me more such nights as these.
1648 'The Vision to *Electra*'.

3 But thou liv'st fearless; and thy face ne'er shows
Fortune when she comes, or goes.
1648 'A Country Life: To His Brother, *M. Tho. Herrick*'.

4 Wealth cannot make a life, but Love.
1648 'A Country Life: To His Brother, *M. Tho. Herrick*'.

5 Soul of my lie, and fame!
Eternal lamp of love! whose radiant flame
Out-glares the Heav'ns *Osiris*; and thy gleams
Out-shine the splendour of his mid-day beams.
1648 'The Welcome to Sack'.

6 'Tis thou, alone, who with thy mystic fan,
Work'st more than Wisdom, Art, or Nature can,
To rouse the sacred madness; and awake
The frost-bound-blood, and spirits; and to make
Them frantic with thy raptures, flashing through
The soul, like lightning, and as active too.
1648 'His Fare-well to Sack'.

7 Let others drink thee freely; and desire
Thee and their lips espous'd; while I admire,
And love thee; but not taste thee. Let my Muse
Fail of thy former helps; and only use
Her inadult'rate strength: what's done by me
Hereafter, shall smell of the lamp, not thee.
1648 'His Fare-well to Sack'.

8 Her legs were such *Diana* shows,
When tuckt up she a hunting goes;
With buskins shortened to descry
The happy dawning of her thigh.
1648 'The Vision'.

9 Get up, get up for shame, the blooming morn
Upon her wings presents the god unshorn.
1648 'Corinna's Going a Maying'.

10 See how *Aurora* throws her fair
Fresh-quilted colours through the air:
Get up, sweet-slug-a-bed, and see
The dew-bespangling herb and tree.
1648 'Corinna's Going a Maying'.

11 So when or you or I are made
A fable, song, or fleeting shade;
All love, all liking, all delight
Lies drowned with us in endless night.
Then while time serves, and we are but decaying;
Come, my *Corinna*, come, let's go a Maying.
1648 'Corinna's Going a Maying'.

12 Gather ye rose-buds while ye may,
Old Time is still a flying:
And this same flower that smiles to day,
Tomorrow will be dying.
1648 'To the Virgins, to Make Much of Time'.

13 Go happy rose, and interwove
With other flowers, bind my love.
Tell her too, she must not be,
Longer flowing, longer free,
That so oft has fetter'd me.
1648 'To the Rose: Song'.

14 Then come on, come on, and yield
A savour like unto a blessed field,
When the bedabbled morn
Washes the golden ears of corn.
1648 'A Nuptial Song, or Epithalamion, on Sir Clipseby Crew and His Lady'.

15 Her eyes, the glow-worm lend thee,
    The shooting stars attend thee;
    And the elves also,
    Whose little eyes glow,
    Like the sparks of fire, befriend thee.
    1648 'The Night-piece, to Julia', written for his young daughter.

16 When as in silks my *Julia* goes,
    Then, then (me thinks) how sweetly flows
    That liquefaction of her clothes.
    1648 'Upon Julia's Clothes'.

17 A sweet disorder in the dress
    Kindles in clothes a wantonness:
    A lawn about the shoulders thrown
    Into a fine distraction...
    A careless shoe-string, in whose tie
    I see a wild civility:
    Do more bewitch me, than when Art
    Is too precise in every part.
    1648 'Delight in Disorder'.

18 Where we such clusters had,
    As made us nobly wild, not mad;
    And yet each verse of thine
    Out-did the meat, out-did the frolic wine.
    1648 'An Ode for [Ben Jonson]'.

Herriot, James *pseudonym of* James Alfred Wight 1916–95

Scottish-born veterinary surgeon and writer of a series of highly popular novels on the adventures of a country vet.

19 I have long held the notion that if a vet can't catch his patient there's nothing much to worry about.
    1976 *Vet in Harness*.

Hersey, John Richard 1914–93

US author, born in China. As Far East correspondent for *Time* magazine, his most famous piece was his eye-witness report in the *New Yorker* (31 Aug 1946) of the bombing of Hiroshima. His novels include *A Bell for Adano* (1944) and *The Walnut Door* (1977).

20 A gifted glassblower of language.
    1988 On the British poet and critic I A Richards. In the *New Yorker*, 18 Jul.

Herzen, Alexander Ivanovich 1812–70

Russian political thinker and writer, a revolutionary socialist active in the Paris revolution of 1848. He settled in London (1851), producing propagandist novels and treatises, and smuggling into Russia his journal *Kolokol* (1857–67, 'The Bell').

21 Science, which cuts its way through the muddy pond of daily life without mingling with it, casts its wealth to right and left, but the puny boatmen do not know how to fish for it.
    1855 Notebook entry, collected in *Byloe i dumy* (*My Past and Thoughts*), vol.3 (published 1861–7, translated by Constance Garnett, 1924).

22 There are those who prefer to get away *inwardly*, some with the help of a powerful imagination and an ability to abstract themselves from their surroundings...some with the help of opium or alcohol... I prefer shifting my whole body to shifting my brain, and going round the world to letting my head go round.
    1861–7 *Byloe i dumy* (*My Past and Thoughts*, translated by Constance Garnett, 1924).

23 There is a certain basis of truth in the fear that the Russian government is beginning to have of communism, for communism is Tsarist autocracy turned upside down.
    1861–7 *Byloe i dumy* (*My Past and Thoughts*, translated by Constance Garnett, 1924).

Herzl, Theodor 1860–1904

Hungarian Zionist leader. He graduated in law but wrote essays and plays until the anti-Semitism aroused by the Dreyfus trial (1894) roused him to political action and he convened the First Zionist Congress (1897).

24 Do you know out of what the German Empire arose? Out of dreams, songs, fantasies and black-red-gold ribbons... Bismarck merely shook the tree that fantasies had planted.
    Quoted in Carl E Schorske *Fin-de-Siècle Vienna* (1961), p.165.

Herzog, Maurice 1919–2012

French engineer and mountaineer. He led the French Himalayan Expedition of 1950, which made the first ascent of Annapurna, losing several fingers and toes through frostbite. *Annapurna* was dictated during his subsequent three-year period in hospital.

25 The mountains were there and so was I.
    1952 His reason for becoming a mountain climber. Quoted in *Annapurna: Conquest of the First 8000-metre Peak* (1952, translated by Nea Morin and Janet Adam Smith).

26 Annapurna, to which we had gone empty-handed, was a treasure on which we should live the rest of our lives. With this realization we turn the page: a new life begins. There are other Annapurnas in the lives of men.
    1952 Quoted in *Annapurna: Conquest of the First 8000-metre Peak* (translated by Nea Morin and Janet Adam Smith).

Heseltine, Michael Ray Dibdin Heseltine, Baron 1933–

British Conservative politician. He was Defence Secretary under Margaret Thatcher, and resigned on the issue of the takeover of Westland Helicopters (1986). Defeated by John Major in the 1990 leadership contest, he became Secretary of State for the Environment (1990–2) and for Trade and Industry (1992–5). He was Deputy Prime Minister from 1995 to 1997 and MP until 2001.

27 It is the only time that I can ever remember the Prime Minister reading out the conclusions of a meeting that did not take place. They were already written before it started.
    1986 Of the Cabinet meeting, Jan, on the Westland affair at which he resigned as Defence Minister.

28 I can foresee no circumstance in which I would allow my name to be put forward for the leadership of the Conservative Party.
    1990 Said on numerous occasions in the autumn.

29 I am persuaded now that I have a better prospect than Mrs Thatcher of leading the Conservatives to a fourth electoral victory and preventing the ultimate calamity of a Labour government.
    1990 On announcing his decision to stand for the leadership, Nov.

30 You can't wield a handbag from an empty chair.
    1999 At the launch of 'Britain in Europe', London, 14 Oct.

Hesiod c.8c BC

One of the earliest Greek poets, best known for *Opera et dies* (*Works and Days*), which depicts rural life in archaic Greece, and *Theogony*.

31 Potter is piqued with potter, joiner with joiner, beggar begrudges beggar, and singer singer.
Of a quarrel within a village. *Opera et dies*, 25 (translated by M L West, 1988).

32 The ill design is most ill for the designer.
Opera et dies, 266 (translated by M L West, 1988).

33 Inhibition is no good provider for a needy man, inhibition, which does men great harm and great good, inhibition attaches to poverty, boldness to wealth.
Opera et dies, 317–9 (translated by M L West, 1988).

Hess, Moses 1812–75
German political writer, and an early friend of Marx.

34 Imagine Rousseau, Voltaire, Holbach, Lessing, Heine, and Hegel united in one person—I say united, not lumped together—and you have Dr Marx.
Quoted in A J P Taylor's introduction to the Penguin edition of *The Communist Manifesto* (1967).

Heston, Charlton 1923–2008
US actor. His major early successes were the Cecil B De Mille films *The Greatest Show on Earth* (1952) and *The Ten Commandments* (1956). He is also remembered for larger-than-life roles in *Ben Hur* (1959, Academy Award) and *El Cid* (1961).

35 I'll give up my gun when you take it from my cold, dead hands.
2000 In his capacity as President of the National Rifle Association, in *The Guardian*, 31 Dec.

Hewart, Gordon Hewart, 1st Viscount 1870–1943
British barrister. He was called to the Bar in 1902 and attended the Paris Peace Conference in 1919 as Attorney-General. He was Lord Chief Justice of England (1922–40).

36 Justice should not only be done, but should manifestly and undoubtedly be seen to be done.
1923 Case of *Rex v. Sussex Justices*, 9 Nov.

Hewett, Dorothy Coade later Davies and Lilley 1923–2002
Australian playwright and poet. Her poetic works include *Windmill Country* (1965) and *Halfway up the Mountain* (2001), and her plays include *The Chapel Perilous* (1971) and *This Old Man Comes Rolling Home* (1976).

37 I had a tremendous world in my head and more than three-quarters of it will be buried with me.
1971 Sally Banner. *The Chapel Perilous*, act 2.

Hewlett, Sylvia Ann 1946–
US economist and writer.

38 What we've done in this country in the past few decades is socialize the cost of growing old and privatize the cost of childhood.
1991 In the *Washington Post*, 22 Feb.

Heyerdahl, Thor 1914–2002
Norwegian anthropologist and adventurer, best known for his voyages and journeys, particularly the *Kon-Tiki* and *Ra* expeditions, which reproduced the methods and materials used by early peoples.

39 Just occasionally you find yourself in an odd situation. You get into it by degrees and in the most natural way, but when you are right in the midst of it you are suddenly astonished and ask yourself how in the world it all came about. If, for example, you put to sea on a wooden raft with a parrot and five companions, it is inevitable that sooner or later you will wake up one morning out at sea, perhaps a little better rested than ordinarily, and begin to think about it.
1948 *The Kon-Tiki Expedition: By Raft across the South Seas* (translated by F H Lyon).

Heyward, Du Bose 1885–1940
US lyricist.

40 Summer time an' the livin' is easy,
Fish are jumpin' an' the cotton is high.
Oh, yo' daddy's rich, and yo' ma is good-lookin',
So hush, little baby, don' yo' cry.
1935 'Summertime' from *Porgy and Bess* (with Ira Gershwin, music by George Gershwin).

41 It ain't necessarily so,
De t'ings dat yo' li'ble
To read in the Bible
It ain't necessarily so.
1935 'It Ain't Necessarily So' from *Porgy and Bess* (with Ira Gershwin, music by George Gershwin).

Heywood, Thomas c.1574–1641
English dramatist, poet and actor. He claimed to have contributed to 220 plays, but much of his work has been lost, including his unpublished 'Lives of All the Poets…'.

42 Content's a kingdom, and I wear that crown.
c.1607 *A Woman Killed with Kindness*, sc.7.

43 That Time could turn up his swift sandy glass,
To untell the days.
c.1607 *A Woman Killed with Kindness*, sc.13.

44 With this kiss I wed thee once again.
c.1607 *A Woman Killed with Kindness*, sc.16.

Hicks, Sir Edward Seymour 1871–1949
English actor-manager and author. A popular light comedian, he appeared in many successful plays written by himself.

45 You will recognize, my boy, the first sign of old age: it is when you go out into the streets of London and realize for the first time how young the policemen look.
Quoted in C R D Pulling *They Were Singing* (1952), ch.7.

Hicks, Sir John Richard 1904–89
English economist, Professor of Political Economy at Manchester (1938–46) and Oxford (1952–65). He laid the foundation of modern welfare economics, and was awarded the Nobel prize for economics in 1972 with Kenneth Arrow.

46 The best of all monopoly profits is a quiet life.
1935 *Econometrica*, 'The Theory of Monopoly'.

47 We ought to define a man's income as the maximum value which he can consume during a week, and still expect to be as well off at the end of the week as he was at the beginning.
1946 *Value and Capital* (2nd edn).

48 Weapons grow rusty if unused, and a Union which never strikes may lose the ability to organise a formidable strike, so that its threats become less effective.
1963 *The Theory of Wages* (2nd edn).

49 There is much of economic theory which is pursued for no better reason than its intellectual attraction; it is a good game.
1979 *Causality in Economics.*

Hickson, William Eward 1803–70
British educator and writer on singing.

50 If at first you don't succeed,
Try, try again.
'Try and Try Again'.

Highfield, Roger 1958–
English chemist, science editor of the *Daily Telegraph*.

51 Can Reindeer Fly? The Science of Christmas.
1998 Book title.

52 There is now evidence to suggest that Santa's grotto lies not in icy Lapland, but among Mediterranean olive groves on Gemiler, a tiny island off Turkey.
1998 *Can Reindeer Fly? The Science of Christmas.*

53 If Newton had not, as Wordsworth put it, voyaged through strange seas of thought alone, someone else would have. If Marie Curie had not lived, we still would have discovered the radioactive elements polonium and radium. But if J. K. Rowling had not been born, we would never have known about Harry Potter. That is why Master Potter means so much to me. Science may be special but Harry, as a work of art, is more so. Harry Potter is unique.
2002 *The Science of Harry Potter: How Magic Really Works.*

Higley, Brewster Martin 1823–1911
US songwriter.

54 Oh give me a home where the buffalo roam,
Where the deer and the antelope play,
Where seldom is heard a discouraging word
And the skies are not cloudy all day.
c.1873 'Home on the Range'.

Hill, (Norman) Graham 1929–75
English racing driver. He won the Formula One World Championship in 1962 in a BRM. In 1967 he rejoined Lotus and won the world title for a second time (1968). He retired in 1975 and was killed in an air crash a few months later.

55 It is like balancing an egg on a spoon while shooting the rapids.
On motor racing. Quoted in Colin Jarman *The Guinness Dictionary of Sports Quotations* (1990).

Hill, Joe originally Joel Hägglund 1879–1915
US labour leader and songwriter.

56 You will eat, by and by,
In that glorious land above the sky;
Work and pray, live on hay,
You'll get pie in the sky when you die.
1911 *Songs of the Workers,* 'The Preacher and the Slave'.

Hill, Rowland 1744–1833
English popular preacher. He helped to found the Religious Tract Society and the London Missionary Society, and in 1801 published the popular *Village Dialogues*.

57 I do not see any reason why the devil should have all the good tunes.
Quoted in E. W Broome *The Rev. Rowland Hill* (1881), ch.7.

Hillaby, John 1917–96
English writer, naturalist and prodigious walker. He journeyed on foot, usually alone, through Africa, across Europe and across the length of Britain.

58 Walking is a way of being somewhere, rather than striving to arrive.
1964 *Journey to the Jade Sea.*

59 Fortunately for poets and those who like to walk about in the open air, the beauty of landscape is not something that can be reduced easily to basic geology or a few ready-wrapped phrases about what places are used for. Preference and prejudice creep in.
1968 *Journey through Britain.*

Hillary, Sir Edmund Percival 1919–2008
New Zealand mountaineer and explorer. He was a member of John Hunt's Everest expedition, and reached the summit with Sherpa Tenzing Norgay on 29 May 1953. He was New Zealand High Commissioner to India (1984–89) and raised funds to provide hospitals and schools in the Himalayan region.

60 We knocked the bastard off!
1953 On returning from the summit of Everest, Jun. Quoted in his autobiography *Nothing Venture, Nothing Win* (1975), ch.10.

61 Better if he had said something natural like, 'Jesus, here we are.'
1974 Criticizing Neil Armstrong's premeditated words on first stepping onto the moon. Quoted in the *Sunday Times*.
▶ See Armstrong 33:51.

62 It's not the mountain we conquer but ourselves.
2007 *O Magazine*, Apr. issue.

Hillebrand, Fred 1893–1963
US musical comedy actor and songwriter. He wrote *Ghosts of Broadway* for television and *Southlands*, an American opera.

63 Home James, and Don't Spare the Horses.
1934 Title of song.

Hillingdon, Lady Alice 1857–1940

64 I am happy now that Charles calls on my bedchamber less frequently than of old. As it is, I now endure but two calls a week and when I hear his steps outside my door I lie down on my bed, close my eyes, open my legs, and think of England.
1912 Journal entry. Quoted in J Gathorne-Hardy *The Rise and Fall of the British Nanny* (1972), ch.3. The phrase is often rendered 'Lie back and think of England'.

Hilton, James 1900–54
English novelist. Several of his books have been filmed, including *Lost Horizon* (1933), *Goodbye, Mr Chips* (1934) and *Random Harvest* (1941).

65 Nothing really wrong with him—only anno domini, but that's the most fatal complaint of all, in the end.
1934 *Goodbye, Mr Chips,* ch.1.

Hindemith, Paul 1895–1963
German composer. His early neo-classical compositions gave way to chromatic works such as *Konzertmusik* (1930–3). His symphony

Mathis der Maler (1934) was banned by the Nazis and he emigrated to Turkey then Britain, where he continued composing.

66 Tonality is a natural force, like gravity.
1937 *The Craft of Musical Composition.*

67 There are only two things worth aiming for: good music and a clean conscience.
1938 Letter to Willy Strecker.

68 There are only twelve notes. You must treat them carefully.
Quoted in Derek Watson *Music Quotations* (1991).

Hippocrates   c.460 BC–c.370 BC

Greek physician, the 'father of medicine', associated with the profession's 'Hippocratic oath'. He practised on Cos. The 'Hippocratic Corpus' is a collection of 72 medical and surgical treatises, but probably not written by him.

69 *Ars longa vita brevis.*
The craft so long [to learn], the life so short.
Quoted in Seneca *De brevitate vitae*, 1. The original was in Greek.

70 Science is the father of knowledge, but opinion breeds ignorance.
The Canon, vol. 4 (translated by John Chadwick).

Hirohito   1901–89

Emperor of Japan during World War II. In 1945 he announced the Japanese surrender in a broadcast to his people and called for their support.

71 We declared war on America and Britain out of Our sincere desire to ensure Japan's self-preservation and the stabilisation of East Asia.
1945 Declaration, 15 Aug. Quoted in Edward Behr *Hirohito* (1989).

72 Endure what is difficult to endure and to suffer what is difficult to suffer.
1945 Declaration, 15 Aug. Quoted in Hugh Cortazzi *The Japanese Achievement* (1990).

73 It was not clear to me that our course was unjustified. Even now I am not sure how historians will allocate the responsibility for the war.
1945 Remark to General Mac Arthur, quoted in Edward Behr *Hirohito* (1989), introduction.

Hirsch, E(ric) D(onald), Jr   1928–

US educational reformer, Professor Emeritus of Education and Humanities at the University of Virginia. His works include *Cultural Literacy: What Every American Needs to Know* (1987) and *The Schools We Need and Why We Don't Have Them* (1996).

74 Cultural literacy is the oxygen of social intercourse.
1987 *Cultural Literacy: What Every American Needs to Know*, introduction.

Hirschfeld, Al(bert)   1903–2003

US artist, theatrical caricaturist for the *New York Times* for over 70 years.

75 I was a sculptor. But that's really drawing—a drawing you fall over in the dark, a three-dimensional drawing.
1988 In the *New York Times*, 21 Jun. 85th birthday interview.

76 The opening-night audience is mostly friends of the cast and backers of the show, and they come to applaud their money.
1988 In the *New York Times*, 21 Jun.

77 Writers who drew, they all seemed to draw the same way. They managed to keep that childlike creativity in their line.
Of Edward Lear and James Thurber. Quoted in Neil A Grauer *Remember Laughter* (1994).

Hirst, Damien   1965–

English painter and installation artist. In 1993 he caused a sensation at the Venice Biennale with his *Mother and Child, Divided*, where a cow and a calf, both sliced in half, expressed the severing of the closest of bonds. He was awarded the 1995 Turner Prize.

78 What I really like is minimum effort for maximum effect. Like with Picasso's *Bull's Head*—a bike seat and handlebars.
1995 In the *Idler*, 10 Jul.

79 You have to step over the boundaries sometimes just to find out where they are.
2002 Quoted on www.bbc.co.uk, 20 Sep.

80 Sometimes I have nothing to say. I often want to communicate this.
Quoted on www.bbc.co.uk.

81 I love art and this proves I'm not alone.
2008 Commenting after 54 pieces of his work sold for $127 million.

82 Great art—or good art—is when you look at it, experience it and it stays in your mind. I don't think conceptual art and traditional art are all that different. There's boring conceptual art and there's boring traditional art. Great art is if you can't stop thinking about it, then it becomes a memory.
2010 In 'Damien Hirst: "Art is childish and childlike"', *The Guardian*, 26 Sep.

Hitchcock, Sir Alfred Joseph   1899–1980

English film director, a master of suspense thrillers. His films include (in Britain) *The Thirty Nine Steps* (1935) and *The Lady Vanishes* (1938), (in Hollywood) *Rebecca* (1940), *Psycho* (1960) and many others.

83 If I made *Cinderella*, the audience would immediately be looking for a body in the coach.
1956 In *Newsweek*, 11 Jun.

84 Television has brought back murder into the home— where it belongs.
1965 In the *Observer*, 19 Dec.

85 The more successful the villain, the more successful the picture.
Quoted in François Truffaut *Hitchcock* (1968).

86 Actors are cattle. Disney probably has the right idea. He draws them and if he doesn't like them he tears them up.
Quoted in Doug McClelland *Star Speak* (1987).

Hitchens, Christopher Eric   1949–2011

English-born US writer and journalist.

87 A bit of a stomach gives a chap a position in society.
2007 In *Vanity Fair*, Oct. issue.

88 My own view is that this planet is used as a penal colony, lunatic asylum and dumping ground by a superior civilization, to get rid of the undesirable and unfit. I can't prove it, but you can't disprove it either.
2007 *God Is Not Great.*

89 I became a journalist partly so that I wouldn't ever have to rely on the press for my information.
2010 *Hitch-22*.

Hitchens, Peter Jonathan 1951–
English writer and journalist, younger brother of Christopher Hitchens.

90 Frankly, I could carve a better opposition party out of a banana than the Tories.
2009 'QuestionTime', *The Guardian*, 14 May.

Hitler, Adolf 1889–1945
German dictator, Leader of the Third Reich for 12 years. He was defeated by the Allies in World War II, during which over six million people were killed by the Nazis in concentration camps. He died in a Berlin bunker in 1945.

91 *Die breite Masse eines Volkes...einer großen Lüge leichter zum Opfer fällt als einer kleinen.*
The broad mass of a nation...will more easily fall victim to a big lie than to a small one.
1925 *Mein Kampf* (*My Struggle*, 1939), ch.10.

92 *Wer in Europa die Brandfackel des Krieges erhebt, kann nur das Chaos wünschen.*
Whoever lights the torch of war in Europe can wish for nothing but chaos.
1935 Speech in the Reichstag, Berlin, 21 May.

93 *Ich gehe mit traumwandlerischer Sicherheit den Weg, den mich die Vorsehung gehen heißt.*
I go the way that Providence dictates with the assurance of a sleepwalker.
1936 Speech in Munich, 14 Mar, in Max Domarus (ed) *Hitler: Reden und Proklamationen 1932–1945* (1962), p.606.

94 *Es ist die letzte territoriale Forderung, die ich Europa zu stellen habe, aber es ist die Forderung, von der ich nicht abgehe, und die ich, so Gott will, erfüllen werde.*
It is the last territorial claim which I have to make in Europe, but it is the claim from which I will not recede and which, God-willing, I will make good.
1938 On the Sudetenland. Speech in Berlin, 26 Sep. In Max Domarus (ed) *Hitler: Reden und Proklamationen 1932–1945* (1962), p.927.

95 *In Bezug auf das sudetendeutsche Problem meine Geduld jetzt zu Ende ist!*
With regard to the problem of the Sudeten Germans, my patience is now at an end!
1938 Speech in Berlin, 26 Sep, in Max Domarus (ed) *Hitler: Reden und Proklamationen 1932–1945* (1962), p.932.

Hobbes, Thomas 1588–1679
English political philosopher. He wrote several works on government, and at the exiled English court in Paris wrote his major work, *Leviathan* (1651), combining metaphysics, psychology and political philosophy. In 1652 he returned to England and submitted to Cromwell.

96 Science [is] knowledge of the truth of Propositions and how things are called.
1650 *Human Nature*, ch.6.

97 In Geometry (which is the only science that it hath pleased God hitherto to bestow on mankind) men begin at settling the significations of their words; which...they call Definitions.
1651 *Leviathan*, pt.1, ch.4.

98 Science is the knowledge of consequences and the dependence of one fact upon another.
1651 *Leviathan*, pt.1, ch.5.

99 The value, or worth of a man, is as of all other things, his price; that is to say, so much as would be given for the use of his power.
1651 *Leviathan*, pt.1, ch.10.

1 I put for a general inclination of all mankind, a perpetual and restless desire of power after power, that ceaseth only in death.
1651 *Leviathan*, pt.1, ch.11.

2 Whatsoever therefore is consequent to a time of war, where every man is enemy to every man; the same is consequent to the time wherein men live without other security than what their own strength, and their own invention shall furnish them withall. In such condition, there is no place for industry; because the fruit thereof is uncertain: and consequently no culture of the earth; no navigation, nor use of the commodities that may be imported by sea; no commodious building; no instruments of moving, and removing such things as require much force; no knowledge of the face of the Earth; no account of Time; no Arts; no Letters; no Society; and which is worst of all, continual fear, and danger of violent death; and the life of man, solitary, poor, nasty, brutish, and short.
1651 *Leviathan*, pt.1, ch.13.

3 They that are discontented under monarchy call it tyranny; and they that are displeased with aristocracy call it oligarchy; so also, they which find themselves grieved under a democracy call it anarchy, which signifies the want of government; and yet I think no man believes that want of government is any new kind of government.
1651 *Leviathan*, pt.2, ch.19.

4 A Free Man is he, that in those things, which by his strength and wit he is able to do, is not hindered to do what he has a will to.
1651 *Leviathan*, pt.2, ch.21.

5 The Enemy has been here in the night of our natural ignorance, and sown the tares of spiritual errors.
1651 *Leviathan*, pt.4, ch.44.

Hobhouse, John Cam, 1st Baron Broughton 1786–1869
English statesman. He wrote *Journey through Albania* with Lord Byron (1813), entered Parliament as a radical in 1820, and after succeeding to his baronetcy held several Cabinet posts.

6 It is said to be hard on His Majesty's Ministers to raise objections to this proposition. For my part, I think it no more hard on His Majesty's Opposition to compel them to take this course.
1826 House of Commons, 27 Apr. This is the first recorded use of the term 'His Majesty's Opposition'.

Hobsbawm, Eric (John Ernest) 1917–2012
English historian, Professor Emeritus at Birkbeck College, London University. He was the author of numerous works of history including *Bandits* (1969) and *The Age of Extremes* (1994).

7 There is not much that even the most socially responsible scientists can do as individuals, or even

as a group, about the social consequences of their activities.
1970 In the *New York Review of Books*, 18 Nov.

8 Megalomania is the occupational disease of global victors, unless controlled by fear.
2002 *Interesting Times: A Twentieth-Century Life.*

9 History may judge my politics...readers may judge my books.
2002 *Interesting Times: A Twentieth-Century Life.*

Hobson, John Atkinson 1858–1940

English economist. An unorthodox figure, he believed 'underconsumption' to be the cause of unemployment. His works include an autobiography, *Confessions of an Economic Heretic* (1938).

10 Organised outdoor sports for the old ruling classes.
1902 On militarism and colonialism. *Imperialism.*

Hoby, Sir Edward 1560–1617

English politician.

11 On the 5th November we began our Parliament, to which the King should have come in person but refrained, through a practice but that morning discovered. The plot was to have blown up the King...at one instant to have ruined the whole estate and kingdom of England.
1605 Letter to the British Ambassador to Brussels, describing the Gunpowder Plot, 19 Nov.

Ho Chi Minh *originally* Nguyen That Thanh 1892–1969

Vietnamese political leader, who became President of North Vietnam in 1954. He led his country, first in the independence movement against the French (1946–54) and later in the war against US-backed South Vietnam in the 1960s.

12 Let him who has a rifle use his rifle, let him who has a sword use his sword! And let those who have no sword take up pick-axes and sticks.
1946 Rallying call, Dec. Quoted in J Facouture *Ho Chi-Minh.*

13 It is better to sniff France's dung for a while than eat China's all our lives.
1946 Attributed. Quoted in J Facouture *Ho Chi-Minh.*

Hockney, David 1937–

English painter, photographer, set designer and printmaker.

14 It's a myth that if you're liked by only four people it must be good. It might also be very bad: they might be your mother, your brother, your uncle and your aunt.
1978 *David Hockney.*

15 Art has to move you and design does not, unless it's a good design for a bus.
1988 In *The Guardian*, 26 Oct.

16 Teaching people to draw is teaching people to look.
2005 In 'Taking the fight to the dreary people', *The Sunday Times*, 2 Oct.

17 Most people feel that the world looks like the photograph. I've always assumed that the photograph is nearly right, but that little bit by which it misses makes it miss by a mile. This is what I grope at.
2011 In Martin Gayford, *A Bigger Message: Conversations with David Hockney.*

Hodges, Andrew 1949–

British mathematician.

18 When the history of science reaches Alan Turing, it hardly feels like history at all.
1987 *Man Masters Nature.*

Hodgson, Ralph 1871–1962

English poet. He published three volumes of Georgian poems, on the themes of nature and England (1907–17). After lecturing in Japan, he settled in the US.

19 Time, you old gipsy man,
   Will you not stay,
   Put up your caravan
   Just for one day?
1917 'Time, You Old Gipsy Man'.

20 I climbed a hill as light fell short,
   And rooks came home in scramble sort,
   And filled the trees and flapped and fought
   And sang themselves to sleep.
1917 'Song of Honour'.

21 I stood upon that silent hill
   And stared into the sky until
   My eyes were blind with stars and still
   I stared into the sky.
1917 'Song of Honour'.

22 When stately ships are twirled and spun
   Like whipping tops and help there's none
   And mighty ships ten thousand ton
   Go down like lumps of lead.
1917 'Song of Honour'.

23 'Twould ring the bells of heaven
   The widest peal for years,
   If Parson lost his senses
   And people came to theirs,
   And he and they together
   Knelt down with angry prayers
   For tamed and shabby tigers
   And dancing dogs and bears,
   And wretched, blind, pit ponies,
   And little hunted hares.
1917 'Bells of Heaven'.

Hoffer, Eric 1902–83

Migratory farm labourer, box factory worker and later longshoreman in San Francisco, who turned to writing social philosophy. His most influential work was *The True Believer* (1951), on mass movements in politics.

24 Where there is the necessary technical skill to move mountains, there is no need for the faith that moves mountains.
1955 *The Passionate State of Mind.*

Hoffman, Abbie 1936–89

US radical activist and writer. In 1968 he helped organize violent anti-Vietnam war demonstrations in Chicago, and was prominent in the 'Chicago Seven' trial in 1969. He was active in public demonstrations until 1986.

25 I always held my flower in a clenched fist.
1980 On his social activism as a 1960s flower child. *Soon to Be a Major Motion Picture.*

Hoffman, Dustin 1937–

US actor. He made his Broadway debut in 1961 and after a modest start achieved fame in the cinema with *The Graduate* (1967). He subsequently won Oscars for *Kramer vs Kramer* (1979) and *Rain Man* (1988).

26 If I'd seen me at a party, I'd never have gone up and met me.
   1995 In *Dateline*, NBC TV broadcast, 8 Mar.

27 It's three words that we usually use as one: woulda, shoulda, coulda. That hurts more than anything, I think. All of us.
   2006 When asked what is his least favourite word, *Inside the Actors Studio*, 18 Jun.

28 What would you feel like if you go in for brain surgery and the brain surgeon leans over and says 'I just want you to know that I am not a perfectionist. But don't worry, I'm a nice guy.'
   2007 Justifying his reputation for perfectionism.

29 Accountant—according to the word, it must be a cross between a 'counter' and a 'mutant'.
   2007 As Mr Edward Magorium in *Mr Magorium's Wonder Emporium* (screenplay by Zack Helm).

30 Unlikely adventures require unlikely tools.
   2007 As Mr Edward Magorium in *Mr Magorium's Wonder Emporium* (screenplay by Zack Helm).

Hoffman, Hans 1880–1966

German-born US painter, who emigrated to the US in 1930. His work is characterized by bold, clashing colours.

31 The ability to simplify means to eliminate the unnecessary so that the necessary may speak.
   1967 *Search for the Real*.

Hoffmann, Heinrich 1809–94

German physician and children's writer. His character Struwwelpeter is a slovenly, naughty boy who features in a book of cautionary tales written for his four-year-old son. He also wrote poetry, satire and medical works.

32 Augustus was a chubby lad;
   Fat, ruddy cheeks Augustus had:
   And everybody saw with joy
   The plump and hearty, healthy boy.
   He ate and drank as he was told,
   And never let his soup get cold.
   But one day, one cold winter's day,
   He screamed out, 'Take the soup away!
   O take the nasty soup away!
   I won't have any soup today.'
   1845 *Struwwelpeter*, 'Augustus'.

33 Look at little Johnny there,
   Little Johnny Head-in-Air!
   1845 *Struwwelpeter*, 'Johnny Head-in-Air'.

34 The door flew open, in he ran,
   The great, long, red-legged scissor-man.
   1845 *Struwwelpeter*, 'The Little Suck-a-Thumb'.

Hofstadter, Douglas R(ichard) 1945–

US cognitive scientist and writer, Professor of Cognitive Science and Computer Science at the University of Indiana. His *Gödel, Escher, Bach: An Eternal Golden Braid* (1979, Pulitzer Prize) is a series of ruminations on computers and cognition.

35 Hofstadter's Law: It always takes longer than you expect, even when you take into account Hofstadter's Law.
   1979 *Gödel, Escher, Bach: An Eternal Golden Braid*.

36 In the end, we self-perceiving, self-inventing, locked-in mirages are little miracles of self-reference.
   2007 *I Am a Strange Loop*.

37 Some of us, perhaps all of us, believe that it is legitimate to kill enemy soldiers in a war, as if war were a special circumstance that shrinks the sizes of enemy souls.
   2007 *I Am a Strange Loop*.

Hofstadter, Richard 1916–70

US historian, Professor at Columbia University (1946–70). He applied theories of natural selection and ideology to the study of US capitalism and politics in works such as *The Age of Reform* (1955).

38 The nation seems to slouch onward into its uncertain future like some huge inarticulate beast, too much attainted by wounds and ailments to be robust, but too strong and resourceful to succumb.
   Quoted in Hedrick Smith *The Power Game* (1988).

39 It has been our fate as a nation not to have ideologies but to be one.
   Quoted in the *New York Times*, 2 Jul 1989.

Hogarth, William 1697–1764

English painter and engraver. He is known for his moral paintings and prints of low life (such as the *Industry and Idleness* series, 1747).

40 Simplicity, without variety, is wholly insipid.
   1753 *The Analysis of Beauty*.

Hogg, James 1770–1835

Scottish poet and novelist. The self-taught 'Ettrick Shepherd' divided his time between literary Edinburgh and his native Borders countryside. His best-known work is the psychological novel *The Private Memoirs and Confessions of a Justified Sinner* (1824).

41 Lock the door, Lariston, lion of Liddesdale;
   Lock the door, Lariston, Lowther comes on;
   The Armstrongs are flying,
   The widows are crying,
   The Castletown's burning, and Oliver's gone!
   c.1810 'Lock the Door, Lariston', stanza 1.

42 'What a wonderful boy he is!' said my mother.
   'I'm feared he turn out to be a conceited gowk,' said old Barnet, the minister's man.
   1824 *The Private Memoirs and Confessions of a Justified Sinner*.

43 Where the pools are bright and deep,
   Where the grey trout lies asleep,
   Up the river and o'er the lea,
   That's the way for Billy and me.
   1831 'A Boy's Song', stanza 1. From *A Poetic Mirror* 1829–31.

Hoggart, Simon David 1946–2014

English political commentator and broadcaster, political columnist with *Punch* (1979–85) and parliamentary reporter with *The Guardian* (from 1993).

44 The nanny seemed to be extinct until 1975, when, like the coelacanth, she suddenly and unexpectedly reappeared in the shape of Margaret Thatcher.
1983 In *Vanity Fair*, Aug.

45 Everything we hear from Buckingham Palace suggests that [the Queen] is surrounded by stupid, blind, stuffy, self-promoting, rivalrous, gin-drinking courtiers, who haven't realised that a modern constitutional Monarch exists no longer by right but by consent and free will.
1997 Following the death of Diana, Princess of Wales. In *The Guardian*, 5 Sep.

46 Peter Mandelson is someone who can skulk in broad daylight.
1998 In *The Guardian*, 10 Jul.

Holiday, Billie 1915–59

US jazz singer. She was one of the most influential singers in jazz, and during the 1940s appeared in several films, although by the end of that decade she was falling victim to drug addiction.

47 Mama may have, papa may have,
But God bless the child that's got his own!
That's got his own.
1941 'God Bless the Child', with Arthur Herzog Jr.

48 People don't understand the sort of fight it takes to record what you want, to record the way you want to record it.
1956 *Lady Sings the Blues*, with William Duffy.

49 You can be up to your boobies in white satin, with gardenias in your hair and no sugar cane for miles, but you can still be working on a plantation.
1956 *Lady Sings the Blues*, with William Duffy.

Holland, Henry Scott 1847–1918

English clergyman and theologian, renowned for his eloquent preaching.

50 Death is nothing at all; it does not count. I have only slipped away into the next room.
1910 Sermon, Whit Sunday.

Hollander, Anne 1930–2014

US art historian. She explored the connections between fashion and art in *Seeing Through Clothes* (1975) and *Fabric of Vision: Dress and Drapery in Painting* (2002).

51 Dress is a form of visual art, a creation of images with the visible self as its medium.
1975 *Seeing Through Clothes*, ch.5.

Hollinghurst, Alan 1954–

English novelist. His novels include *The Swimming Pool Library* (1988), a highly acclaimed account of gay life; *The Folding Star* (1994); and Man-Booker prize winning *The Line of Beauty* (2004).

52 My life was a strange one that summer, the last summer of its kind there was ever to be. I was riding high on sex and self-esteem—it was my time, my *belle époque*—but all the while with a faint flicker of calamity, like flames around a photograph, something seen out of the corner of the eye.
1988 *The Swimming Pool Library*, ch.1.

53 All families are silly in their own way.
2004 *The Line of Beauty*.

54 There was the noise itself, which he thought of vaguely as the noise of classical music, sameish and rhetorical, full of feelings people surely never had.
2011 *The Stranger's Child*.

Holman, James 1786–1857

English naval officer. Although blind from the age of 25 he continued travelling, firstly to the Continent (1819–22), then to the Russian Empire and later to Brazil, South Africa, South Asia, Tasmania, New South Wales and New Zealand.

55 On the summit of the precipice and in the deep green woods emotions as palpable and as true have agitated me as if I were surveying them with the blessing of sight. There was an intelligence in the winds of the hills and in the solemn stillness of the buried foliage that could not be misleading. It entered into my heart and I could have wept, not that I did not see, but that I could not portray all I felt.
1834 *A Voyage round the World*.

Holme (of Cheltenham), Richard Holme, Baron 1936–2008

British electoral reformer and writer. He represented the Liberal Democrat Party in the House of Lords and was appointed to the Privy Council in 2000.

56 She is the Enid Blyton of economics. Nothing must be allowed to spoil her simple plots.
1980 Of Margaret Thatcher. Speech at the Liberal Party conference, 10 Sep.

Holmes, John Clellon 1926–88

US writer. He is credited with first use of the phrase 'The Beat Generation'. His own novels include *Go* (1952) and *The Horn* (1958).

57 To Walden the saxophone was, at once, his key to the world in which he found himself, and the way by which that world was rendered impotent to brand him either a failure or madman or Negro or saint.
1958 *The Horn*, 'Chorus: Walden'.

58 Jazz music has haunted America for seventy years. It has tempted us out of our lily-white reserve with its black promise of untrammeled joy.
1979 Preface to reprint of *The Horn*.

59 Some books accrete things to themselves like a magnet. The writer risks sterility by subjecting the mysterious power of imagination to the devices of mere comprehension.
1979 Preface to reprint of *The Horn*.

Holmes, Oliver Wendell 1809–94

US physician and writer, who in 1842 discovered that puerperal fever was contagious. His essays in the *Atlantic Monthly* were collected in four volumes, including *The Autocrat of the Breakfast Table* (1857–8) and *The Professor at the Breakfast Table* (1858–9). He also published three novels and several volumes of poetry.

60 Man wants but little drink below,
But wants that little strong.
1848 'A Song of Other Days'.

61 And, when you stick on conversation's burrs,
Don't strew your pathway with those dreadful *urs*.
1848 'A Rhymed Lesson'.

62 They are the brute beasts of the intellectual domain.
   1857-8 Of facts. *The Autocrat of the Breakfast Table*, ch.1.

63 A thought is often original, though you have uttered it a hundred times.
   1857-8 *The Autocrat of the Breakfast Table*, ch.1.

64 When one has had *all* his conceit taken out of him, when he has lost *all* his illusions, his feathers will soon soak through, and he will fly no more.
   1857-8 *The Autocrat of the Breakfast Table*, ch.1.

65 Some of the sharpest men in argument are notoriously unsound in judgment.
   1857-8 *The Autocrat of the Breakfast Table*, ch.1.

66 Put not your trust in money, but put your money in trust.
   1857-8 *The Autocrat of the Breakfast Table*, ch.2.

67 Build thee more stately mansions, O my soul,
   As the swift seasons roll!
   Leave thy low-vaulted past!
   1857-8 *The Autocrat of the Breakfast Table*, ch.4.

68 Truth is tough. It will not break, like a bubble, at a touch; nay, you may kick it about all day like a football, and it will be round and full at evening.
   1857-8 *The Autocrat of the Breakfast Table*, ch.5.

69 Sin has many tools, but a lie is the handle which fits them all.
   1857-8 *The Autocrat of the Breakfast Table*, ch.6.

70 Boston State-House is the hub of the solar system. You couldn't pry that out of a Boston man, if you had the tire of all creation straightened out for a crowbar.
   1857-8 *The Autocrat of the Breakfast Table*, ch.6.

71 The world's great men have not commonly been great scholars, nor its great scholars great men.
   1857-8 *The Autocrat of the Breakfast Table*, ch.6.

72 Talk about those subjects you have had long in your mind, and listen to what others say about subjects you have studied but recently. Knowledge and timber shouldn't be much used till they are seasoned.
   1857-8 *The Autocrat of the Breakfast Table*, ch.6.

73 Shabby gentility has nothing so characteristic as its hat.
   1857-8 *The Autocrat of the Breakfast Table*, ch.8.

74 Have you heard of the wonderful one-hoss shay
   That was built in such a logical way,
   It ran a hundred years to a day.
   1857-8 *The Autocrat of the Breakfast Table*, ch.11.

75 Nothing is so common-place as to wish to be remarkable.
   1857-8 *The Autocrat of the Breakfast Table*, ch.12.

76 Fate tried to conceal him by calling him Smith.
   1858 Of Samuel Francis Smith. 'The Boys'.

77 Depart,—be off,—excede,—evade,—erump!
   1858 'Aestivation'.

78 We must have a weak spot or two in a character before we can love it much.
   1858-9 *The Professor at the Breakfast Table*, ch.3.

79 Apology is only egotism wrong side out.
   1858-9 *The Professor at the Breakfast Table*, ch.6.

80 Fashion is only the attempt to realize Art in living forms and social intercourse.
   1858-9 *The Professor at the Breakfast Table*, ch.6.

81 A moment's insight is sometimes worth a life's experience.
   1857-8 *The Professor at the Breakfast Table*, ch.10.

82 Lord of all being, throned afar,
   Thy glory flames from sun and star;
   Centre and soul of every sphere,
   Yet to each loving heart how near!
   1858-9 *The Professor at the Breakfast Table*, 'A Sun-Day Hymn'.

83 It is the province of knowledge to speak, and it is the privilege of wisdom to listen.
   1872 *The Poet at the Breakfast Table*, ch.10.

84 To be seventy years young is sometimes far more cheerful and hopeful than to be forty years old.
   1879 Letter to Julia Ward Howe, 27 May.

85 The morning cup of coffee has an exhilaration about it which the cheering influence of the afternoon or evening cup of tea cannot be expected to reproduce.
   1891 *Over the Teacups*, ch.1.

Holmes, Oliver Wendell, Jr 1841–1935

US lawyer, Professor at Harvard Law School, Justice of the US Supreme Court for 30 years.

86 For the rational study of the law the blackletter man may be the man of the present, but the man of the future is the man of statistics and the master of economics.
   1897 'The Path of the Law', in the *Harvard Law Review*, 10:469.

Holroyd, Sir Michael de Courcy Fraser 1935–

English biographer. He is married to the novelist Margaret Drabble.

87 Between history and the novel stands biography, their unwanted offspring, which has brought a great embarrassment to them both.
   2002 *Works on Paper: The Craft of Biography & Autobiography*, 'The Case against Biography'.

88 In the historian's view biography is a kind of frogspawn—
   it takes ten thousand biographies to make one small history.
   2002 *Works on Paper: The Craft of Biography & Autobiography*, 'The Case against Biography'.

Holst, Gustav Theodore 1874–1934

British composer, of Swedish origin. Prevented by neuritis in his hand from becoming a concert pianist, he learned the trombone and taught music before establishing himself as a composer.

89 Never compose anything unless the not composing of it becomes a positive nuisance to you.
   1921 Letter to W G Whittaker.

Holt, Harold Edward 1908–67

Australian politician. He succeeded Robert Menzies as Prime Minister in 1966 but disappeared while swimming in the sea off Victoria the following year. He was a supporter of US policy in Vietnam.

90 All the way with LBJ.
   1966 Speech, Washington DC, Jun.

Holub, Miroslav 1923–98

Czech poet and immunologist.

91 Humankind can generally be divided into hunters and people who cope with consequences.
1990 *The Dimensions of the Present Moment and Other Essays.*

Homans, George C 1910–89
US sociologist, Professor at Harvard University.

92 It is really intolerable that we can say only one thing at a time; for social behavior displays many features at the same time, and so in taking them up one by one we necessarily do outrage to its rich, dark, organic unity.
1961 *Social Behavior: Its Elementary Forms.*

93 The rule of distributive justice is a statement of what ought to be, and what people say ought to be is determined in the long run and with some lag by what they find in fact to be the case.
1974 *Social Behavior: Its Elementary Forms* (rev edn).

Home of the Hirsel, Alec (Alexander Frederick) Douglas-Home, Baron 1903–95
Scottish Conservative statesman. An MP from 1931, he was Chamberlain's secretary during negotiations with Hitler and Mussolini (1937–9). He succeeded as 14th Earl of Home (1951), but after Macmillan's resignation he renounced his peerage and became Prime Minister (1963–4).

94 As far as the fourteenth earl is concerned, I suppose Mr Wilson, when you come to think of it, is the fourteenth Mr Wilson.
1963 Response to Harold Wilson's claim that the democratic process had 'ground to a halt with a fourteenth earl' when Home won the premiership. Reported in the *Daily Telegraph*, 22 Oct.

95 There are two problems in my life. The political ones are insoluble, and the economic ones are incomprehensible.
1964 Speech, Jan.

96 When I read economic documents, I have to have a box of matches and start moving them into position, to illustrate and simplify the points to myself.
1965 *The Making of the Prime Minister.*

97 Fishing is undoubtedly a form of madness but, happily for the once-bitten, there is no cure.
1976 Quoted in Colin Jarman *The Guinness Dictionary of Sports Quotations* (1990).

98 My wife had an uncle who could never walk down the nave of his abbey without wondering whether it would take spin.
In *The Twentieth Century Revisited*, BBC TV programme, 1982.

99 Oh God, if there be cricket in heaven, let there also be rain.
Quoted in Helen Exley *Cricket Quotations* (1992).

Homer 8c BC
Greek epic poet, in antiquity said to have been blind, to whom are attributed the *Iliad* (dealing with episodes in the Trojan War) and the *Odyssey* (dealing with the subsequent wanderings of Odysseus). Scholars now date the poems to the 8c BC, as the culmination of an oral tradition dating back to the Bronze Age.

1 He who battles with the immortals does not live long, nor do his children prattle about his knees when he has returned from battle.
c.700 BC *Iliad*, bk.5, l.407 (translated by Martin Hammond).

2 Like that of leaves is a generation of men.
c.700 BC *Iliad*, bk.6, l.146 (translated by Martin Hammond).

3 Always to be best, and to be distinguished above the rest.
c.700 BC Motto of the hero Glaucus. *Iliad*, bk.6, l.208 (translated by Martin Hammond).

4 Victory switches from man to man.
c.700 BC *Iliad*, bk.6, l.339 (translated by Martin Hammond).

5 One omen is best of all—to fight for your country.
c.700 BC *Iliad*, bk.7, l.243 (translated by Martin Hammond).

6 Tribeless, lawless, homeless is he who loves the horror of civil war.
c.700 BC *Iliad*, bk.9, l.63–4 (translated by Martin Hammond).

7 This is the best portent, to fight in defence of one's country.
c.700 BC *Iliad*, bk.12, l.243 (translated by Martin Hammond).

8 It is no shame for a man to die fighting for his country.
c.700 BC *Iliad*, bk.15, l.496 (translated by Martin Hammond).

9 Tell me, Muse, of the man of many ways, who was driven
far journeys, after he had sacked Troy's sacred citadel.
Many were they whose cities he saw, whose minds he learned of,
many the pains he suffered in his spirit on the wide sea,
struggling for his own life and the homecoming of his companions.
c.700 BC *Odyssey*, bk.1, l.1–5 (translated by Richmond Lattimore).

Homer, Winslow 1836–1910
US painter, known for his watercolours of rural and domestic scenes and especially for his seascapes after 1881.

10 The life that I have chosen gives me my full hours of enjoyment for the balance of my life. The sun will not rise, or set, without my notice, and thanks.
1895 Letter to his brother, Charles, 23 Feb.

11 I regret very much that I have painted a picture that requires any description.
On being asked about the meaning of a painting by a dealer. Quoted by Andrea Bennett in the *New York Times Book Review*, 15 Sep 1991.

Honegger, Arthur 1892–1955
French composer of Swiss descent. One of the group of Parisian composers known as *Les Six*, he established his reputation with the oratorio *King David* (1921). Subsequent works include the dramatic oratorio *Joan of Arc at the Stake* (1936).

12 The modern composer is a madman who persists in manufacturing an article which nobody wants.
1951 *I Am a Composer.*

13 Composing is not a profession. It is a mania—a harmless madness.
1951 *I Am a Composer.*

14 To write music is to raise a ladder without a wall to lean it against. There is no scaffolding: the building under construction is held in balance only by the miracle of a kind of internal logic, an innate sense of proportion.
1951 *I Am a Composer.*

15 The public doesn't want new music: the main thing it demands of a composer is that he be dead.
1951 *I Am a Composer.*

Honorius of Autun fl.1106–35

French ecclesiastic, and the author of numerous philosophical, theological and devotional works.

16 *Universitas in modo citharae sit disposita, in qua diversa genera in modo chordarum sit consonantia.*
The universe is arranged like a cithera, in which different kinds of things sound together harmoniously, just as they do in a chord.
c.1120 *Liber Duodecem Questionum*, ch.2.

17 *Quid confert animae pugna Hectoris, vel disputatio Platonis, aut carmina Maronis, vel neniae Nasonis?*
Of what benefit to the soul are the struggles of Hector, the disputations of Plato, the songs of Virgil, or the dirges of Ovid?
c.1130 *Gemma Animae*, prologue.

Hood, Thomas 1799–1845

English poet and journalist. His collection *Odes and Addresses* (1825) was followed by several volumes of humorous verse and political poems such as 'The Song of the Shirt' (1843).

18 I saw old Autumn in the misty morn
Stand shadowless like Silence, listening
To silence.
1823 'Ode: Autumn'.

19 Ben Battle was a soldier bold,
And used to war's alarms:
But a cannon-ball took off his legs,
So he laid down his arms!
1826 'Faithless Nelly Gray'.

20 For here I leave my second leg,
And the Forty-second Foot!
1826 'Faithless Nelly Gray'.

21 The love that loves a scarlet coat
Should be more uniform.
1826 'Faithless Nelly Gray'.

22 I remember, I remember,
The house where I was born,
The little window where the sun
Came peeping in at morn;
He never came a wink too soon,
Nor brought too long a day,
But now, I often wish the night
Had borne my breath away!
1826 'I Remember'.

23 I remember, I remember,
The fir trees dark and high;
I used to think their slender tops
Were close against the sky:
It was a childish ignorance,
But now 'tis little joy
To know I'm farther off from heav'n
Than when I was a boy.
1826 'I Remember'.

24 She stood breast high amid the corn,
Clasped by the golden light of morn,
Like the sweetheart of the sun,
Who many a glowing kiss had won.
1827 'Ruth'.

25 The sedate, sober, silent, serious, sad-coloured sect.
1839 Of the Quakers. *Comic Annual*, 'The Doves and the Crows'.

26 'Extremes meet', as the whiting said with its tail in its mouth.
1839 *Comic Annual*, 'The Doves and the Crows'.

27 Holland…lies so low they're only saved by being dammed.
1840 *Up the Rhine*, 'Letter from Martha Penny to Rebecca Page'.

28 Home-made dishes that drive one from home.
1841–3 *Miss Kilmansegg and her Precious Leg*, 'Her Misery'.

29 When Eve upon the first of Men
The apple pressed with specious cant,
Oh! what a thousand pities then
That Adam was not Adamant!
1842 'A Reflection'.

30 With fingers weary and worn,
With eyelids heavy and red,
A woman sat, in unwomanly rags
Plying her needle and thread—
Stitch! stitch! stitch!
In poverty, hunger, and dirt.
And still with a voice of dolorous pitch
She sang the 'Song of the Shirt'.
1843 'The Song of the Shirt'.

31 O! men with sisters dear,
O! men with mothers and wives!
It is not linen you're wearing out,
But human creatures' lives!
1843 'The Song of the Shirt'.

32 Oh! God! that bread should be so dear,
And flesh and blood so cheap!
1843 'The Song of the Shirt'.

33 Take her up tenderly,
Lift her with care;
Fashioned so slenderly,
Young, and so fair!
1844 'The Bridge of Sighs'.

34 Mad from life's history,
Glad to death's mystery,
Swift to be hurled—
Anywhere, anywhere,
Out of the world!
1844 'The Bridge of Sighs'.

35 But evil is wrought by want of thought,
As well as want of heart!
1844 'The Lady's Dream'.

36 No sun—no moon!
No morn—no noon
No dawn—no dusk—no proper time of day.
1844 'No'.

37 No warmth, no cheerfulness, no healthful ease,
No comfortable feel in any member—
No shade, no shine, no butterflies, no bees,
No fruits, no flowers, no leaves, no birds,—
November!
1844 'No'.

38 What is a modern poet's fate?
To write his thoughts upon a slate;
The critic spits on what is done,
Gives it a wipe—and all is gone.
'A Joke'. Collected in Hallam Tennyson *Alfred Lord Tennyson* (1897), vol.2, ch.3.

Hooker, Richard 1554–1600

English theologian, writer of an extensive treatise on the basis of Church government, which had a powerful influence on Anglican doctrine.

39 See we not plainly that obedience of creatures unto the law of nature is the stay of the whole world?
1594 *Laws of Ecclesiastical Polity.*

40 Man doth seek a triple perfection: first a sensual, consisting in those things which very life itself requireth either as necessary supplements, or as beauties and ornaments thereof; then an intellectual, consisting in those things which none underneath man is either capable of or acquainted with; lastly a spiritual and divine, consisting in those things whereunto we tend by supernatural means here, but cannot here attain unto them.
1594 *Laws of Ecclesiastical Polity.*

41 They must have hearts very dry and tough, from whom the melody of psalms doth not sometime draw that wherein a mind religiously affected delighteth.
1594 *Laws of Ecclesiastical Polity.*

Hoover, Herbert Clark 1874–1964

US Republican politician. As 31st President (1929–33), his opposition to direct assistance for the unemployed in the recession led to defeat by Roosevelt in 1932. He assisted with various US–European economic relief programmes after World War II.

42 The grass will grow in the streets of a hundred cities, a thousand towns; the weeds will overrun the fields of millions of farms if [tariff protection] is taken away.
1923 Presidential campaign speech, 22 Oct.

43 We are nearer today to the ideal of the abolition of poverty and fear from the lives of men and women than ever before in any land.
1923 Presidential campaign speech, 22 Oct.

44 The American system of rugged individualism.
1928 Speech, New York City, 22 Oct.

45 People moved in hushed and anxious hours while his life lingered on. It was thus I learned that some great man was at the helm of our country.
1951 On President Garfield's assassination, 2 Jul 1881. *The Memoirs of Herbert Hoover*, vol 1.

46 I should have been glad to have humanity forget all about stray alcoholic drinks…but in the present stage of human progress, this vehicle of joy could not be generally suppressed by federal law.
1951 On prohibition. *The Memoirs of Herbert Hoover*, vol.1.

47 All men are equal before a fish.
1951 Quoted in Colin Jarman *The Guinness Dictionary of Sports Quotations* (1990).

48 Democracy is not a polite employer… The only way out of elective office is to get sick or die or get kicked out.
1952 *The Memoirs of Herbert Hoover*, vol.2.

49 The White House…a palace more comfortable than that of most kings.
1952 *The Memoirs of Herbert Hoover*, vol.2.

50 A chameleon on plaid.
On his opponent Franklin D Roosevelt. Quoted in James MacGregor Burns *The Lion and the Fox* (1956).

51 Honour is not the exclusive property of any political party.
1964 In *Christian Science Monitor*, 21 May.

52 Sportsmanship, next to the Church, is the greatest teacher of morals.
Quoted in John Rickards Betts *America's Sporting Heritage: 1850–1950* (1974).

53 Dewey has no inner reserve of knowledge on which to draw for his thinking. A man couldn't wear a moustache like that without having it affect his mind.
Quoted in Richard Norton Smith *An Uncommon Man* (1984).

Hoover, J(ohn) Edgar 1895–1972

US public servant, director of the Federal Bureau of Investigation (1924–72). He remodelled it, making it more efficient, but his vendettas against liberal activists in later years were criticized.

54 We of the FBI are powerless to act in cases of oral–genital intimacy, unless it has in some way obstructed interstate commerce.
Quoted in the *New York Times*, 6 Oct 1980.

55 You are honored by your friends…distinguished by your enemies. I have been very distinguished.
Address to the House Sub-Committee on Appropriations. Quoted in Curt Gentry *J Edgar Hoover* (1991).

Hope, A(lec) D(erwent) 1907–2000

Australian poet and critic. He retired from academic life in 1972 to concentrate on poetry. Works include *The Wandering Isles* (1955), *The Drifting Continent* (1979) and *Orpheus* (1991).

56 Historians spend their lives and lavish ink
Explaining how great commonwealths collapse
From great defects of policy—perhaps
The cause is sometimes simpler than they think.
… Have more states perished, then,
For having shackled the enquiring mind,
Than those who, in their folly not less blind,
Trusted the servile womb to breed free men?
1965 'Advice to Young Ladies', in *Collected Poems 1930–1970* (1972).

57 They call her a young country, but they lie:
She is the last of lands, the emptiest,
A woman beyond her change of life, a breast
Still tender but within the womb is dry.
'Australia', in *Collected Poems 1930–1970* (1972).

Hope, Anthony *pseudonym of* Sir Anthony Hope Hawkins 1863–1933

English novelist. His novel *The Prisoner of Zenda* (1894), a romantic adventure set in fictitious Ruritania, established him as one of the most popular of all Victorian writers.

58 Oh, for an hour of Herod!
1904 On witnessing the first performance of J M Barrie's children's play *Peter Pan*. Quoted in Denis Mackail *Story of JMB* (1941), ch.17. Records exist of something similar having been said by the English actress Dorothea Jordan when watching the child actor William Betty and his imitators in the early 19c.

Hope, Bob *originally* Leslie Townes Hope 1903–2003

English-born US actor and humorist. With Bing Crosby and Dorothy Lamour he appeared in the successful *Road to…* comedies (1940–52). An entertainer of troops in World War II and a noted golfer and humanitarian, he became a show-business institution.

59 If you watch a game, it's fun. If you play it, it's recreation. If you work at it, it's golf.
Quoted in the *Reader's Digest*, Oct 1958.

60 I don't know what people have got against Jimmy Carter. He's done nothing.
1980 Campaign speech for Ronald Reagan, 2 Nov.

61 Fish don't applaud.
1989 When asked why he didn't retire and go fishing, in the *New York Times*, 28 Sep.

Hopkins, Sir Anthony 1937–
Welsh-born US film and stage actor.

62 I always check the last page of the script to see if I'm on it. I have a bit of an ego, you know.
1997 In the *Toronto Sun*, 24 Sep.

63 If you don't go when you want to go, when you do go, you'll find you've gone.
2005 As Burt Munro in *The World's Fastest Indian* (screenplay by Roger Donaldson).

64 I once asked a Jesuit priest what was the best short prayer he knew. He said '"Fuck it", as in "Fuck it, it's in God's hands."'
2007 *Inside the Actors Studio*, 15 Oct.

Hopkins, Gerard Manley 1844–89
English poet and Jesuit priest. His work is characterized by religious subjects and the use of natural imagery. His poems include 'The Wreck of the Deutschland' (1876), 'Pied Beauty' (1877) and 'The Windhover' (1877). His poetry was written in secret, only published 30 years after his death.

65 I have desired to go
Where springs not fail,
To fields where flies no sharp and sided hail
And a few lilies blow
And I have asked to be
Where no storms come,
Where the green swell is in the havens dumb,
And out of the swing of the sea.
1864 'Heaven-Haven'.

66 Crystal sincerity hath found no shelter but in a fool's cap.
1864 'Floris in Italy'. Collected in H House and G Storey (eds) *The Journals and Papers of Gerard Manley Hopkins* (1959), p.42.

67 Elected Silence, sing to me
And beat upon my whorled ear,
Pipe me to pastures still and be
The music that I care to hear.
1866 'The Habit of Perfection'.

68 Palate, the hutch of tasty lust,
Desire not to be rinsed with wine:
The can must be so sweet, the crust
So fresh that come in fasts divine!
1866 'The Habit of Perfection'.

69 I did say yes
O at lightning and lashed rod;
Thou heardst me truer than tongue confess
Thy terror, O Christ, O God.
1876 'The Wreck of the Deutschland', pt.1, stanza 2.

70 The world is charged with the grandeur of God.
It will flame out like shining from shook foil...
Generations have trod, have trod, have trod;
And all is seared with trade; bleared, smeared with toil;
And wears man's smudge and shares man's smell: the soil
Is bare now, nor can foot feel, being shod.
1877 'God's Grandeur'.

71 Because the Holy Ghost over the bent
World broods with warm breast and with ah! bright wings.
1877 'God's Grandeur'.

72 Glory be to God for dappled things.
1877 'Pied Beauty'.

73 All things counter, original, spare, strange;
Whatever is fickle, freckled (who knows how?)
With swift, slow; sweet, sour; adazzle, dim;
He fathers-forth whose beauty is past change:
Praise him.
1877 'Pied Beauty'.

74 The glassy peartree leaves and blooms, they brush
The descending blue; that blue is all in a rush
With richness.
1877 'Spring'.

75 Look at the stars! look, look up at the skies!
O look at all the fire-folk sitting in the air!
The bright boroughs, the circle-citadels there!
1877 'The Starlight Night'.

76 I caught this morning morning's minion, kingdom of Daylight's dauphin, dapple-dawn-drawn Falcon.
1877 'The Windhover'.

77 My heart in hiding
Stirred for a bird,—the achieve of, the mastery of the thing!
1877 'The Windhover'.

78 Towery city and branchy between towers;
Cuckoo-echoing, bell-swarmèd, lark-charmèd, rook-racked, river-rounded.
1879 Of Oxford. 'Duns Scotus's Oxford', published 1918.

79 Ten or twelve, only ten or twelve
Strokes of havoc unselve
The sweet especial scene
Rural scene, a rural scene
Sweet especial rural scene.
1879 'Binsey Poplars'.

80 Margaret, are you grieving
Over Goldengrove unleaving?
1880 'Spring and Fall: to a young child'.

81 Ah! as the heart grows older
It will come to such sights colder
By and by, not spare a sigh
Though worlds of wanwood leafmeal lie;
And yet you *will* weep and know why.
1880 'Spring and Fall: to a young child'.

82 It is the blight man was born for,
It is Margaret you mourn for.
1880 'Spring and Fall: to a young child'.

83 I can scarcely fancy myself to ask a superior to publish a volume of my verse and I own that humanly there is very little likelihood of that ever coming to pass. And to be sure if I chose to look at things on one side and not the other I could of course regret this bitterly. But there is more peace and it is the holier lot to be unknown than to be known.

1881 Letter to Richard Watson Dixon, 29 Oct. Collected in C C Abbott (ed) *The Correspondence of Gerard Manley Hopkins and Richard Watson Dixon* (1935).

84 What would the world be, once bereft
Of wet and wildness? Let them be left,
O let them be left, wildness and wet;
Long live the weeds and the wilderness yet.
1881 'Inversnaid'.

85 Time has three dimensions and one positive pitch or direction. It is therefore not so much like any river or any sea as like the Sea of Galilee, which has the Jordan running through it and giving a current to the whole.
1881 'Creation and Redemption: The Great Sacrifice'. Collected in C Devlin (ed) *The Sermons and Devotional Writings of Gerard Manley Hopkins* (1959), ch.8.

86 God…is so great that all things give him glory if you mean they should.
1882 'The Principle or Foundation', closing words. Collected in G Roberts (ed) *Gerard Manley Hopkins. Selected Prose* (1980).

87 Wild air, world-mothering air,
Nestling me everywhere.
1883 'The Blessed Virgin Compared to the Air We Breathe'.

88 Not, I'll not, carrion comfort, Despair, not feast on thee;
Not untwist—slack they may be—these last strands of man
In me or, most weary, cry *I can no more*. I can;
Can something, hope, wish day come, not choose not to be.
1885 'Carrion Comfort'.

89 That night, that year
Of now done darkness I wretch lay wrestling with (my God!) my God.
1885 'Carrion Comfort'.

90 No worst, there is none. Pitched past pitch of grief,
More pangs will, schooled at forepangs, wilder wring.
Comforter, where, where is your comforting?
1885 'No worst, there is none'.

91 O the mind, mind has mountains; cliffs of fall
Frightful, sheer, no-man-fathomed. Hold them cheap
May who ne'er hung there.
1885 'No worst, there is none'.

92 Here! creep,
Wretch, under a comfort serves in a whirlwind: all
Life death does end and each day dies with sleep.
1885 'No worst, there is none'.

93 The fine pleasure is not to do a thing but to feel that you could… If I could but get on, if I could but produce a work I should not mind its being buried, silenced, and going no further; but it kills me to be time's eunuch and never to beget.
1885 Letter to Robert Bridges, 1 Sep. Collected in C C Abbott (ed) *The Correspondence of Gerard Manley Hopkins and Robert Bridges* (1935).

94 I am all at once what Christ is, since he was what I am, and
This Jack, joke, poor potsherd, patch, matchwood, immortal diamond,
Is immortal diamond.
1888 'That Nature is a Heraclitean Fire'.

95 Thou art indeed just, Lord, if I contend
With thee; but, sir, so what I plead is just.
Why do sinners' ways prosper? and why must
Disappointment all I endeavour end?
1889 'Thou art indeed just, Lord'.

96 Birds build—but not I build; no, but strain,
Time's eunuch, and not breed one work that wakes.
Mine, O thou lord of life, send my roots rain.
1889 'Thou art indeed just, Lord'.

97 The male quality is the creative gift.
Quoted in C C Abbott (ed) *Correspondence of Gerard Manley Hopkins and Richard Watson Dixon* (1935).

98 I always knew in my heart Walt Whitman's mind to be more like my own than any other man's living.
Quoted in Denis Donoghue *England, Their England* (1988).

Hopkins, J Castell 1864–1923

Canadian editor and writer.

99 Canada only needs to be known in order to be great.
1901 *The Story of the Dominion*, preface.

Hopper, Edward 1882–1967

US painter, known for his haunting, atmospheric paintings of empty streets and houses. His works include *Early Sunday Morning* (1930).

1 A nation's art is greatest when it most reflects the character of its people.
Quoted in Anatole Broyard *Aroused by Books* (1974).

2 It's probably a reflection of my own, if I may say, loneliness. I don't know. It could be the whole human condition.
On the mood and content of his paintings. Quoted in the *Washington Post*, 25 Jun 1995.

Hopper, Grace Murray 1906–92

US computer scientist and naval officer, developer of the Cobol computer language.

3 Life was simple before World War II. After that, we had systems.
Quoted in the OCLC Newsletter, no.167, Mar/Apr 1987.

4 We've tended to forget that no computer will ever ask a new question.
Quoted in the OCLC Newsletter, no.167, Mar/Apr 1987.

5 A ship in port is safe but that's not what ships are built for.
1987 Address at Trinity College, Washington. Reported in *Time*, 22 Jun.

Horace full name Quintus Horatius Flaccus 65 BC–8 BC

Roman poet of the Augustan age. His works, which survive in their entirety, include the *Satires* (c.35 BC), *Odes* (c.23–13 BC), *Epistles* (c.19 BC) and the *Ars Poetica* (c.19 BC). His poetry is characterized by an urbane sociability and a love of the country.

6 *Carpe diem.*
Seize the day.
Odes, bk.1, no.11, l.8.

7 *Nunc est bibendum!*
Now is the time to drink!
Odes, bk.1, no.37, l.1.

8 *Eheu fugaces, Postume, Postume,
labuntur anni.*

Oh, my Postumus, Postumus, the fleeting years are slipping by.
Odes, bk.2, no.14, l.1–2.

9 *Odi profanum vulgus et arceo;*
Favete linguis; carmina non prius
Audita Musarum sacerdos
Virginibus puerisque canto.
I despise the uninitiated mob and I warn them off: keep your tongues well-omened; I, priest of the Muses, am singing songs, never heard before, to girls and boys.
Odes, bk.3, no.1, l.1–4 (translated by G Williams).

10 *Dulce et decorum est pro patria mori.*
It is a sweet and seemly thing to die for one's country.
Odes, bk.3, no.2, l.13.
▶ See Owen 657:31.

11 *Exegi monumentum, aere perennius.*
I have completed a memorial more lasting than bronze.
Odes, bk.3, no.30, l.1.

12 *Vixere fortes ante Agamemnona*
Multi; sed omnes illacrimabiles
Urgentur ignotique longa
Nocte, carent quia vate sacro.
Many brave men lived before Agamemnon's time; but they are all unmourned and unknown, covered by the long night, because they lack their sacred poet.
Odes, bk.4, no.9, l.25–8.

13 *Dulce est desipere in loco.*
Frivolity is sweet, at the right time.
Odes, bk.4, no.12, l.28.

14 *Quo semel est imbuta recens servabit odorem testa diu.*
The first scent you pour in a jar lasts for years.
Epistulae, bk.1, no.2, l.69.

15 *Concordia discors.*
Harmony in discord.
Epistulae, bk.1, no.12, l.7.

16 *Graecia capta ferum victorem cepit et artes*
Intulit agresti Latio.
Captive Greece overcame her savage conqueror and brought the arts into rustic Latium.
Epistulae, bk.2, no.1, l.156–7.

17 *Brevis esse laboro, Obscurus fio.*
I try hard to be succinct, and am merely obscure.
Ars Poetica, l.25–6.

18 *Si vis me flere, dolendum est Primum ipse tibi.*
If you wish me to shed tears you must first feel pain yourself.
Ars Poetica, l.102–3.

19 *Parturiunt montes; nascetur ridiculus mus.*
The mountains are in labour, and there will be born an absurd little mouse.
Ars Poetica, l.139.

20 *Omne tulit punctum, qui miscuit utile dulci.*
The man who has mixed profit with pleasure wins everyone's approval.
Ars Poetica, l.343.

21 *Indignor quandoque bonus dormitat Homerus.*
I am vexed when the worthy Homer nods.
Ars Poetica, l.359.

22 *Est modus in rebus.*
There is a measure in things.
Satirae, bk.1, no.1, l.106.

Horner, Jack (John R) 1946–

Curator of Palaeontology, Museum of the Rockies.

23 In the lifetime of one person, we went from figuring out where we came from to figuring out how to get rid of ourselves.
1993 On the 80-year period from Darwin's *Origin of Species* to the first nuclear bomb. In *Time*, 26 Apr.

24 The worse the country, the more tortured it is by water and wind, the more broken and carved, the more it attracts fossil hunters, who depend on the planet to open itself to us. We can only scratch away at what natural forces have brought to the surface.
2009 *How to Build a Dinosaur: Extinction Doesn't Have to Be Forever.*

Hornung, E(rnest) W(illiam) 1866–1921

English novelist. Brother-in-law of Arthur Conan Doyle, he created Raffles the gentleman burglar, hero of *The Amateur Cracksman* (1899), *Mr Justice Raffles* (1909) and many other adventure stories.

25 'Cricket,' said Raffles, 'like everything else, is a good enough sport until you discover a better. As a source of excitement it isn't in it with other things you wot of Bunny, and the involuntary comparison becomes a bore. What's the satisfaction of taking a man's wicket when you want his spoons?'
1899 *The Amateur Cracksman.*

Horsley, Samuel 1733–1806

English prelate, most famous for his theological controversy (1783–9) with Joseph Priestley over the uncreated divinity of Christ. He published several scientific works.

26 In *this* country, my Lords…the individual subject…has nothing to do with the laws but to obey them.
1795 Speech in the House of Lords, 13 Nov.

Hoskins, Bob 1942–2014

English actor.

27 It's good to talk.
1996 Advertising slogan for British Telecom.

Hosseini, Khaled 1965–

Afghan-born US novelist and physician. His debut novel *The Kite Runner* (2003) has been filmed and remains his best-known work.

28 There are a lot of children in Afghanistan, but little childhood.
2003 *The Kite Runner.*

29 When you tell a lie, you steal someone's right to the truth.
2003 *The Kite Runner.*

30 And that's the thing about people who mean everything they say. They think everyone else does too.
2003 *The Kite Runner.*

31 Marriage can wait, education cannot.
2007 *A Thousand Splendid Suns.*

Houllier, Gerard 1947–

French football manager. He was appointed joint manager at Liverpool in 1998, later becoming sole manager (1999–2004).

32 It used to be the rat race. Now it's the sack race.
   2004 On being a football manager. In *The Guardian*, 1 Mar.

Housman, A(lfred) E(dward) 1859–1936
English scholar and poet. He was a distinguished classical scholar, and is known primarily for his poetry, particularly *A Shropshire Lad* (1896), an anti-pastoral view of country life which was widely popular after an initially cool reception.

33 Loveliest of trees, the cherry now
   Is hung with bloom along the bough,
   And stands about the woodland ride
   Wearing white for Eastertide.
   1896 *A Shropshire Lad*, no.2.

34 Now, of my threescore years and ten,
   Twenty will not come again,
   And take from seventy springs a score,
   It only leaves me fifty more.
   1896 *A Shropshire Lad*, no.2.

35 And since to look at things in bloom
   Fifty springs are little room,
   About the woodlands I will go
   To see the cherry hung with snow.
   1896 *A Shropshire Lad*, no.2.

36 Clay lies still, but blood's a rover;
   Breath's a ware that will not keep.
   Up, lad: when the journey's over
   There'll be time enough to sleep.
   1896 *A Shropshire Lad*, no.4.

37 And naked to the hangman's noose
   The morning clocks will ring
   A neck God made for other use
   Than strangling in a string.
   1896 *A Shropshire Lad*, no.9.

38 When I was one-and-twenty
   I heard a wise man say,
   'Give crowns and pounds and guineas
   But not your heart away;
   Give pearls away and rubies,
   But keep your fancy free.'
   But I was one-and-twenty
   No use to talk to me.
   1896 *A Shropshire Lad*, no.13.

39 Oh, when I was in love with you,
   Then I was clean and brave,
   And miles around the wonder grew
   How well I did behave.
   1896 *A Shropshire Lad*, no.18.

40 And now the fancy passes by,
   And nothing will remain,
   And miles around they'll say that I
   Am quite myself again.
   1896 *A Shropshire Lad*, no.18.

41 And silence sounds no worse than cheers
   After dying has stopped the ears.
   1896 *A Shropshire Lad*, no.19.

42 Twice a week the winter through
   Here I stood to keep the goal:
   Football then was fighting sorrow
   For the young man's soul.
   1896 *A Shropshire Lad*, no.21.

43 In summertime in Bredon
   The bells they sound so clear;
   Round both the shires they ring them
   In steeples far and near,
   A happy noise to hear.
   1896 *A Shropshire Lad*, no.21.

44 Here of a Sunday morning
   My love and I would lie,
   And see the coloured counties,
   And hear the larks so high
   About us in the sky.
   1896 *A Shropshire Lad*, no.21.

45 'Come all to church, good people,'—
   Oh, noisy bells, be dumb;
   I hear you, I will come.
   1896 *A Shropshire Lad*, no.21.

46 The lads in their hundreds to Ludlow come in for
      the fair,
   There's men from the barn and the forge and the mill and
      the fold,
   The lads for the girls and the lads for the liquor are
      there,
   And there with the rest are lads that will never be old.
   1896 *A Shropshire Lad*, no.23.

47 On Wenlock Edge the wood's in trouble;
   His forest fleece the Wrekin heaves;
   The wind it plies the saplings double,
   And thick on Severn snow the leaves.
   1896 *A Shropshire Lad*, no.31.

48 The gale, it plies the saplings double,
   It blows so hard, 'twill soon be gone:
   To-day the Roman and his trouble
   Are ashes under Uricon.
   1896 *A Shropshire Lad*, no.31.

49 From far, from eve and morning
   And yon twelve-winded sky,
   The stuff of life to knit me
   Blew hither: here am I.
   1896 *A Shropshire Lad*, no.32.

50 Speak now, and I will answer;
   How shall I help you, say;
   Ere to the wind's twelve quarters
   I take my endless way.
   1896 *A Shropshire Lad*, no.32.

51 Into my heart an air that kills
   From yon far country blows:
   What are those blue remembered hills,
   What spires, what farms are those?
   1896 *A Shropshire Lad*, no.40.

52 That is the land of lost content,
   I see it shining plain,
   The happy highways where I went
   And cannot come again.
   1896 *A Shropshire Lad*, no.40.

53 And bound for the same bourn as I,
   On every road I wandered by,
   Trod beside me, close and dear,
   The beautiful and death-struck year.
   1896 *A Shropshire Lad*, no.41.

54 Clunton and Clunbury,
   Clungunford and Clun,

Are the quietest places
Under the sun.
1896 *A Shropshire Lad*, no.50, epigraph.

55 With rue my heart is laden
For golden friends I had,
For many a rose-lipt maiden
And many a lightfoot lad.
1896 *A Shropshire Lad*, no.54.

56 By brooks too broad for leaping
The lightfoot boys are laid;
The rose-lipt girls are sleeping
In fields where roses fade.
1896 *A Shropshire Lad*, no.54.

57 Say, for what were hop-yards meant,
Or why was Burton built on Trent?
Oh many a peer of England brews
Livelier liquor than the Muse,
And malt does more than Milton can
To justify God's ways to man.
Ale, man, ale's the stuff to drink
For fellows whom it hurts to think.
1896 *A Shropshire Lad*, no.62.

58 Oh I have been to Ludlow fair
And left my necktie God knows where,
And carried half-way home, or near,
Pints and quarts of Ludlow beer.
1896 *A Shropshire Lad*, no.62.

59 Then the world seemed none so bad,
And I myself a sterling lad;
And down in lovely muck I've lain,
Happy till I woke again.
1896 *A Shropshire Lad*, no.62.

60 I tell the tale that I heard told.
Mithridates, he died old.
1896 *A Shropshire Lad*, no.62.

61 This great College, of this ancient University, has seen some strange sights. It has seen Wordsworth drunk and Porson sober. And here am I, a better poet than Porson, and a better scholar than Wordsworth, betwixt and between.
1911 Speech on taking up the Chair of Latin at Trinity College, Cambridge.

62 Pass me the can, lad; there's an end of May.
1922 *Last Poems*, no.9.

63 May will be fine next year as like as not:
Oh, ay, but then we shall be twenty-four.
1922 *Last Poems*, no.9.

64 We for a certainty are not the first
Have sat in taverns while the tempest hurled
Their hopeful plans to emptiness, and cursed
Whatever brute and blackguard made the world.
1922 *Last Poems*, no.9.

65 The troubles of our proud and angry dust
Are from eternity, and shall not fail.
Bear them we can, and if we can we must.
Shoulder the sky, my lad, and drink your ale.
1922 *Last Poems*, no.9.

66 But men at whiles are sober
And think by fits and starts,
And if they think, they fasten
Their hands upon their hearts.
1922 *Last Poems*, no.10.

67 The laws of God, the laws of man,
He may keep that will and can;
Not I: let God and man decree
Laws for themselves and not for me;
And if my ways are not as theirs
Let them mind their own affairs.
1922 *Last Poems*, no.12.

68 And how am I to face the odds
Of man's bedevilment and God's?
I, a stranger and afraid
In a world I never made.
1922 *Last Poems*, no.12.

69 The candles burn their sockets,
The blinds let through the day,
The young man feels his pockets
And wonders what's to pay.
1922 *Last Poems*, no.21.

70 To think that two and two are four
And neither five nor three
The heart of man has long been sore
And long 'tis like to be.
1922 *Last Poems*, no.35.

71 These, in the day when heaven was falling,
The hour when earth's foundations fled,
Followed their mercenary calling
And took their wages and are dead.
1922 *Last Poems*, no.37, 'Epitaph on an Army of Mercenaries'.

72 Their shoulders held the sky suspended;
They stood, and earth's foundations stay;
What God abandoned, these defended,
And saved the sum of things for pay.
1922 *Last Poems*, no.37, 'Epitaph on an Army of Mercenaries'.

73 For nature, heartless, witless nature,
Will neither care nor know
What stranger's feet may find the meadow
And trespass there and go,
Nor ask amid the dews of morning
If they are mine or no.
1922 *Last Poems*, no.40.

74 Experience has taught me, when I am shaving of a morning, to keep watch over my thoughts, because, if a line of poetry strays into my memory, my skin bristles so that the razor ceases to act.
1933 'The Name and Nature of Poetry', Lecture at Cambridge, 9 May.

75 The seat of this sensation is the pit of the stomach.
1933 'The Name and Nature of Poetry', Lecture at Cambridge, 9 May.

76 The stroke of midnight ceases,
And I lie down alone.
1936 *More Poems*, no.11.

77 Life, to be sure, is nothing much to lose;
But young men think it is, and we were young.
1936 *More Poems*, no.36.

78 Good-night. Ensured release
Imperishable peace,
Have these for yours,
While earth's foundations stand
And sky and sea and land
And heaven endures.
1936 *More Poems*, no.48.

79 That is indeed very good. I shall have to repeat that on the Golden Floor!
1936 Remark made to his doctor after the latter had told him a risqué story on his deathbed.

80 The Grizzly bear is huge and wild;
He has devoured the infant child.
The infant child is not aware
He has been eaten by the bear.
'Infant Innocence', collected *The Oxford Book of Light Verse* (1938).

81 Oh who is that young sinner with the handcuffs on his wrist?
And what has he been after that they groan and shake their fists?
And wherefore is he wearing such a conscience-stricken air?
Oh they're taking him to prison for the colour of his hair.
'Additional Poems', no.18, in *Collected Poems* (1939).

82 'Tis a shame to human nature, such a head of hair as his;
In the good old time 'twas hanging for the colour that it is;
Though hanging isn't bad enough and flaying would be fair
For the nameless and abominable colour of his hair.
'Additional Poems', no.18, in *Collected Poems* (1939).

83 Now hollow fires burn out to black
And lamps are guttering low.
Square your shoulders, lift your pack,
And leave your friends and go.

Oh, never fear, man, nought's to dread
Look not left nor right.
In all the endless road you tread,
There's nothing but the night.
Quoted in Bernard Levin *Hannibal's Footsteps* (1985).

How, William Walsham 1823–97
English churchman and religious writer, the first Bishop of Wakefield.

84 For all the Saints who from their labours rest,
Who Thee by faith before the world confess'd,
Thy name, O Jesu, be for ever blest,
Alleluia!
1864 'For All the Saints', in Earl Nelson *Hymns for Saints' Days*.

85 From earth's wide bounds, from ocean's farthest coast,
Through gates of pearl streams in the countless host,
Singing to Father, Son, and Holy Ghost,
Alleluia!
1864 'For All the Saints', in Earl Nelson *Hymns for Saints' Days*.

Howard, Thomas, Earl of Surrey and 2nd Duke of Norfolk 1443–1524
English nobleman and soldier. He fought for Richard III at Bosworth (1485) and was imprisoned by Henry VII, but regained his estates and led successful campaigns against the Scots, including Flodden (1513).

86 He was my crowned King, and if the Parliamentary authority of England set the crown upon a stock, I will fight for that stock: And as I fought then for him, I will fight for you, when you are established by the said authority.
1485 Explaining before the future Henry VII his reasons for siding with Richard III at Bosworth, 22 Aug. Quoted in William Camden *Remains Concerning Britain* (1605).

Howe (of Aberavon), (Richard Edward) Geoffrey Howe, Baron 1926–
English Conservative politician. In 1989 he became Deputy Prime Minister, Lord President of the Council and Leader of the House of Commons. His resignation from Margaret Thatcher's government in Nov 1990, and his subsequent resignation speech, were instrumental in her downfall.

87 Megaphone diplomacy leads to a dialogue of the deaf.
1985 Quoted in the *Observer*, 29 Sep.

88 How on earth are the Chancellor of the Exchequer and the Governor of the Bank of England...to be taken seriously against that kind of background noise? It is rather like sending your opening batsmen to the crease, only for them to find, the moment the first balls are bowled, that their bats have been broken before the game by the team captain.
1990 Personal statement on his resignation, House of Commons, 13 Nov.

89 If some of my former colleagues are to be believed, I must be the first minister in history to have resigned because he was in full agreement with government policy.
1990 Personal statement on his resignation, House of Commons, 13 Nov.

Howe, Gordie (Gordon) 1928–
Canadian hockey player.

90 All pro athletes are bilingual. They speak English and profanity.
Dismissing Canadian bilingualism. Quoted by George Gamester in the *Toronto Star*, 27 May 1975.

Howe, Joseph 1804–73
Anglo-Canadian journalist and statesman.

91 A wise nation preserves its records, gathers up its muniments, decorates the tombs of its illustrious dead, repairs its great public structures, and fosters national pride and love of country, by perpetual references to the sacrifices and glories of the past.
1871 Address at Framingham, Massachusetts, 31 Aug. Collected in *Poems and Essays* (1874).

Howe, Julia Ward 1819–1910
US feminist and writer, influential in suffragette and Unitarian causes. Her poetry collections include *Passion Flowers* (1854). She made history as the first woman member of the American Academy.

92 Mine eyes have seen the glory of the coming of the Lord:
He is trampling out the vintage where the grapes of wrath are stored.
He hath loosed the fatal lightning of his terrible swift sword:
His truth is marching on.
1862 'Battle Hymn of the Republic'.

Howe, Louis McHenry 1871–1936
US diplomat.

93 You can't adopt politics as a profession and hope to remain honest.
   1933 Speech, Columbia University, 17 Jan.

Hoyle, Edmond 1672–1769

English authority on card games. He published manuals on whist, backgammon, brag, quadrille, piquet and chess.

94 When in doubt, win the trick.
   A Short Treatise on the Game of Whist (first published 1742, this edn edited by Charles Jones, 1790). This may be an addition by Jones.

Hoyle, Sir Fred 1915–2001

English astronomer and mathematician, one of the first to apply modern physics to cosmology. He was knighted in 1972.

95 To take an almost religious view, this earth is nothing very special. There have probably been millions of earths just like ours each producing a particular intelligent species. That is not to say that they all developed well, that they all achieved some sort of perfection. And if the planner made lots of them and some of them chose to destroy themselves, then we can only suppose that the planner is a hard and practical man.
   1974 In the *Daily Mail*.

96 Space isn't remote at all. It's only an hour's drive away if your car could go straight upwards.
   1979 Quoted in the *Observer*, 'Sayings of the Week', 9 Sep.

Hubbard, Elbert Green 1856–1915

US writer, editor and printer.

97 Life is just one damned thing after another.
   1909 In *The Philistine*, Dec.

98 Little minds are interested in the extraordinary; great minds in the commonplace.
   1911 *Thousand and One Epigrams*.

99 One machine can do the work of fifty ordinary men. No machine can do the work of one extraordinary man.
   1911 *Thousand and One Epigrams*.

1 Editor: a person employed by a newspaper, whose business it is to separate the wheat from the chaff, and to see that the chaff is printed.
   1914 *The Roycroft Dictionary*.

2 College football is a sport that bears the same relation to education that bullfighting does to agriculture.
   Quoted in Colin Jarman *The Guinness Dictionary of Sports Quotations* (1990).

Hubble, Edwin Powell 1889–1953

US astronomer. In 1929 he formulated Hubble's law: galaxies recede with speeds directly proportionate to their distance from us, confirming that the universe is expanding. The space telescope launched in 1990 was named in his honour.

3 We measure shadows, and we search among ghostly errors of measurement for landmarks that are scarcely more substantial.
   Quoted in Dennis Overbye *Lonely Hearts of the Cosmos* (1991).

Hügel, Friedrich von, Baron 1852–1925

Austrian-born British theologian and Bible critic, son of the Austrian Ambassador in Italy. He settled in England in 1871. His works include *The Mystical Element in Religion* (1908–9) and *The Reality of God* (published 1931).

4 I take these to be the seven great facts and doctrines concerning God—his richness; his double action, natural and supernatural; his perfect freedom; his delightfulness; his otherness; his adorableness and his prevenience.
   The Life of Prayer (published 1927).

5 Christianity has taught us to care. Caring is the greatest thing, caring matters most.
   Letter to his niece.

Hugh of St Victor c.1096–1141

German divine and scholar, who entered the Augustinian order despite his parents' objections. In 1115 he was sent to the Abbey of St Victor in Paris, where he completed his vows, later becoming master of the school. He composed many treatises on theological, philosophical and devotional subjects.

6 *Delicatus ille est adhuc cui patria dulcis est. Fortis autem jam cui omne solum patria est, perfectus vero cui mundus totus exsilium est.*
   He whose own homeland is sweet to him is a mere beginner. He to whom every soil is as his native land is strong. But he to whom the whole world is a place of exile has achieved perfection.
   c.1127 *Didascalicon*, bk.3, ch.20.

Hughes, Howard Robard 1905–76

US millionaire businessman, film producer and aviator. Known as an eccentric, he left Hollywood in 1932 to design, build and fly aircraft before returning to film production. After 1966 he lived in complete seclusion.

7 That man's ears make him look like a taxi-cab with both doors open.
   Of Clark Gable. Quoted in Charles Higham and Joel Greenbert *Celluloid Muse* (1969).

Hughes, (James Mercer) Langston 1902–67

US poet, a leading figure of the Harlem Renaissance, whose poetry and sketches reflect folk culture, jazz, blues and colloquial speech. His works include *Weary Blues* (1926) and the autobiographical *The Big Sea* (1940).

8 I, too, sing America.

   I am the darker brother.
   They send me to eat in the kitchen
   When company comes.
   But I laugh
   And eat well,
   And grow strong.
   1925 'I, Too', in *Survey Graphic*, Mar.

9 Tomorrow
   I'll sit at the table
   When company comes
   Nobody'll dare
   Say to me,
   'Eat in the kitchen'
   Then.
   1925 'I, Too', in *Survey Graphic*, Mar.

10 Swaying to and fro on his rickety stool
   He played that sad raggy tune like a musical fool.
   Sweet blues!
   1926 'The Weary Blues'.

11 I swear to the Lord,
    I still can't see,
    Why Democracy means,
    Everybody but me.
    1943 'The Black Man Speaks'.

12 What happens to a dream deferred?

    Does it dry up
    like a raisin in the sun?
    1951 'Dream Deferred'. Lorraine Hansberry used the phrase for the title of her play *A Raisin in the Sun* (1959).

13 Maybe it just sags
    like a heavy load.

    Or does it explode?
    1951 'Dream Deferred'.

14 You are white—
    yet a part of me, as I am a part of you.
    That's American.
    1951 'Theme for English B'.

15 A wonderful time—the War:
    when money rolled in
    and blood rolled out.
    1951 'Green Memory'.

16 'It's powerful,' he said.
    'What?'
    'That one drop of Negro blood—because just *one* drop of black blood makes a man coloured. *One* drop—you are a Negro!'
    1953 *Simple Takes a Wife*.

Hughes, Richard Arthur Warren 1900–76

English novelist. He is best known for his adventure tale *A High Wind in Jamaica* (1929, entitled *The Innocent Voyage* in the US). Other works include *Hazard: A Sea Story* (1938), *The Fox in the Attic* (1961) and *The Wooden Shepherdess* (1972).

17 Nature is as wasteful of promising young men as she is of fish-spawn. It's not just getting them killed in wars: mere middle age snuffs out ten times more talent than ever wars and sudden death do.
    1961 *The Fox in the Attic*, bk.1, ch.18.

18 For a politician rises on the backs of his friends (that's probably all they're good for), but it's through his enemies he'll have to govern afterwards.
    1961 *The Fox in the Attic*, bk.2, ch.20.

19 Do your bit to save humanity from lapsing back into barbarity by reading all the novels you can.
    1975 Speech at Foyle's Literary Luncheon, London, in honour of his 75th birthday.

Hughes, Robert Studley Forrest 1938–2012

Australian-born US art critic, writer with *Time* magazine (1970–2008). His books include *The Fatal Shore* (1987) and *Goya* (2003). He also wrote and narrated art documentaries for television including the series *American Visions* (1997).

20 Lentil-soup colors.
    1981 Of the paints used by French realists. In *Time*, 13 Apr.

21 The protein of our cultural imagination.
    1984 Of the US Museum of Modern Art. In *Time*, 14 May.

22 Close by the Hudson, in MANHATTAN'S TOWN,
    The iron palaces of Art glare down
    On such as, wandering in the streets below,
    Perambulate in glamorous SoHo,
    A spot acclaimed by savant and by bard
    As forcing chamber of the Avant-Garde.
    1984 'The SoHoiad', in the *New York Review of Books*.

23 Popular in our time, unpopular in his. So runs the stereotype of rejected genius.
    1985 On a Caravaggio exhibition. In *Time*, 11 Mar.

24 Landscape is to American painting what sex and psychoanalysis are to the American novel.
    1985 In *Time*, 30 Dec.

25 [A Gustave Courbet] portrait of a trout...has more death in it than Rubens could get in a whole Crucifixion.
    1986 In *Time*, 15 Sep.

26 Its clones have hung on so many suburban walls over the decades that it has become the *Mona Lisa* of the vegetable world.
    1987 On Vincent Van Gogh's *Sunflowers*. In *Time*, 13 Apr.

27 The self is now the sacred cow of American culture, self-esteem is sacrosanct, and so we labour to turn arts education into a system in which no one can fail. In the same spirit, tennis could be shorn of its elitist overtones: you just get rid of the net.
    1994 *Culture of Complaint: The Fraying of America*.

28 America came up with the idea of therapeutic avant-gardism, and built museums in its name. These temples stood on two pillars. The first was aestheticism... The second was the familiar one of social benefit.
    1994 *Culture of Complaint: The Fraying of America*.

29 My idea of a contact sport was chess.
    1999 *A Jerk on One End: Reflections of a Mediocre Fisherman*.

Hughes, Ted (Edward James) 1930–98

English poet. His elemental, highly symbolic works include *The Hawk in the Rain* (1957) and *Crow* (1970). Other works include *Birthday Letters* (1998) and books for children. He was Poet Laureate (1984–98).

30 The world rolls under the long thrust of his heel.
    Over the cage floor the horizons come.
    1957 'The Jaguar'.

31 It took the whole of Creation
    To produce my foot, my each feather:
    Now I hold Creation in my foot.
    1960 'Hawk Roosting'.

32 Nothing has changed since I began.
    My eye has permitted no change.
    I am going to keep things like this.
    1960 'Hawk Roosting'.

33 Pike, three inches long, perfect
    Pike in all parts, green tigering the gold.
    Killers from the egg: the malevolent aged grin.
    1960 'Pike'.

34 The gash in its throat was shocking, but not pathetic.
    1960 'View of a Pig'.

35 The deeps are cold:
    In that darkness camaraderie does not hold:
    Nothing touches but, clutching, devours.
    1960 'Relic'.

36 The brassy wood-pigeons
    Bubble their colourful voices, and the sun

Rises upon a world well-tried and old.
1967 'Stealing Trout on a May Morning'.

37 No, the serpent did not
Seduce Eve to the apple.
All that's simply
Corruption of the facts.

Adam ate the apple.
Eve ate Adam.
The serpent ate Eve.
This is the dark intestine.

The serpent, meanwhile,
Sleeps his meal off in Paradise—
Smiling to hear
God's querulous calling.
1967 'Theology'.

38 Who owns the whole rainy, stony earth? *Death.*
Who owns all of space? *Death.*
1970 'Examination at the Womb-door'.

39 But who is stronger than death?
Me, evidently.
1970 'Examination at the Womb-door'.

40 And he shivered with the horror of Creation.
1970 'Crow Alights'.

41 But Oedipus he had the luck
For when he hit the ground
He bounced up like a jackinabox
And knocked his Daddy down.
1970 'Song for a Phallus'.

42 And the elephant sings deep in the forest-maze
About a star of deathless and painless peace
But no astronomer can find where it is.
1972 'Crow's Elephant Totem Song'.

43 Black village of gravestones.
1979 'Heptonstall'.

44 Only the rain never tires.
1979 'Heptonstall'.

45 You were the jailer of your murderer—
Which imprisoned you.
And since I was your nurse and your protector
Your sentence was mine too.
1998 In Birthday Letters, *a collection of poems addressed to Sylvia Plath, his first wife.*

Hughes, Thomas 1822–96
English reformer and novelist. Called to the Bar in 1848, a Liberal MP (1865–74) and a county court judge (1882), he is best remembered for his semi-autobiographical classic, *Tom Brown's Schooldays* (1856).

46 Life isn't all beer and skittles—but beer and skittles, or something better of the same sort, must form a good part of every Englishman's education.
1856 Tom Brown's Schooldays, *pt.1, ch.2.*

47 He never wants anything but what's right and fair, only when you come to settle what's right and fair, it's everything that he wants and nothing that you want. And that's his idea of a compromise. Give me the Brown compromise when I'm on his side.
1856 Tom Brown's Schooldays, *pt.2, ch.2.*

48 It's more than a game. It's an institution.
1856 Of cricket. Tom Brown's Schooldays, *pt.2, ch.7.*

Hughes, William Morris 1864–1952
Welsh-born Australian statesman. He emigrated in 1884 and became Minister for External Affairs (1904) in the first Labour government and subsequently Prime Minister (1915–23). He founded the United Australian Party.

49 Mr President, I speak for sixty thousand dead!
1919 Reply to Woodrow Wilson at the Versailles Peace Conference, Jan, referring to the ANZAC fatalities in World War I. Wilson had asked 'Mr Hughes, I speak for very many millions of people. For whom do you speak?'.

50 Without the Empire we should be tossed like a cork in the cross current of world politics. It is at once our sword and our shield.
1926 Speech, Melbourne.

Hugo, Victor Marie 1802–85
French poet, dramatist and novelist. His great epics are *Notre-Dame de Paris* (1831, *The Hunchback of Notre Dame*) and *Les Misérables* (1862). His writings and theories were enormously influential.

51 *Le beau n'a qu'un type; le laid en a mille.*
Beauty has only one form; ugliness has a thousand.
1827 Cromwell, préface.

52 *Les temps primitifs sont lyriques, les temps antiques sont épiques, les temps modernes sont dramatiques.*
The primitive era was lyrical, the classical era was epic and the modern era is dramatic.
1827 Cromwell, préface.

53 *Il n'y a ni règles ni modèles; ou plutôt il n'y a d'autres règles que les lois générales de la nature qui planent sur l'art tout entier, et les lois spéciales qui, pour chaque composition, résultent des conditions d'existence propres à chaque sujet.*
There are no rules or models; that is, there are no rules except general laws of nature which hover over art and special laws which apply to specific subjects.
1827 Cromwell, préface.

54 *La vérité de l'art ne saurait jamais être…la réalité absolue. L'art ne peut donner la chose même.*
The truth of art should never be…*absolute reality*. Art cannot show the thing itself.
1827 Cromwell, préface.

55 *Le but de l'art est presque divin: ressusciter, s'il fait de l'histoire; créer, s'il fait de la poésie.*
The goal of art is almost divine: to resuscitate, if it concerns history; to create, if it concerns poetry.
1827 Cromwell, préface.

56 *Le vers est la forme optique de la pensée. Voilà pourquoi il convient surtout à la perspective scénique.*
Verse is the optical form of thought. That is the reason a scenic perspective suits it.
1827 Cromwell, préface.

57 *La langue française n'est point fixée et ne se fixera point.*
French is not a *static* language and will never become static.
1827 Cromwell, préface.

58 *Sois donc ami sincère ou sincère ennemi,*
Et ne reste pas traître et fidèle à demi.
Be either a sincere friend or a sincere enemy,
And never be half-traitor and half-faithful.
1827 *Cromwell*, act 1, sc.1.

59 *L'Angleterre toujours sera sïur de la France.*
England will always be the sister of France.
1827 *Cromwell*, act 2, sc.2.

60 *Vous me manquez, je suis absente de moi-même.*
I miss you, I am estranged from myself.
1830 *Hernani*, act 1, sc.2.

61 *Nos pères avaient un Paris de pierre, nos fils auront un Paris de plâtre.*
Our fathers had a Paris made of stone; our sons will have a Paris made of plaster.
1831 *Notre-Dame de Paris*, pt.3, ch.2.

62 *Rêver, c'est le bonheur; attendre, c'est la vie.*
To dream is happiness; to wait is life.
1831 *Les Feuilles d'automne*, no.27,'À mes amis L.B. et S.-B.'

63 *Au banquet du bonheur bien peu sont conviés.*
Few are invited to the banquet of happiness.
1831 *Les Feuilles d'automne*, no.32,'Pour les pauvres'.

64 *Mêlez toute votre âme à la création!*
Involve all of your soul in creation!
1831 *Les Feuilles d'automne*, no.38,'Pan'.

65 *O Virgile! ô poète! ô mon maître divin!*
Oh Virgil! Oh poet! Oh my divine master!
1837 *Les Voix intérieures*, no.7,'À Virgile'.

66 *Le drame tient de la tragédie par la peinture des passions et de la comédie par la peinture des caractères. Le drame est la troisième grande forme de l'art.*
In drama, tragedy paints the passions and comedy paints characters. Drama is the third great form of art.
1838 *Ruy Blas*, préface.

67 *Je ne veux pas tomber, non, je veux disparaître.*
I do not want to fall; I want to disappear.
1838 *Ruy Blas*, act 1, sc.1.

68 *Visage de traître!*
Quand la bouche dit oui, le regard dit peut-être.
Face of a traitor!
When the mouth says yes, the look says maybe.
1838 *Ruy Blas*, act 1, sc.2.

69 *Sous l'habit d'un valet, les passions d'un roi.*
Beneath the clothing of a manservant, the passions of a king.
1838 *Ruy Blas*, act 1, sc.3.

70 *Les femmes aiment fort à sauver qui les perd.*
Women love to save those who damn them.
1838 *Ruy Blas*, act 1, sc.4.

71 *Dieu s'est fait homme; Soit! Le diable s'est fait femme.*
God made himself a man. So be it! The devil made himself a woman.
1838 *Ruy Blas*, act 2, sc.5.

72 *Tout se fait par intrigue et rien par loyauté.*
Everything is done by intrigue, not by loyalty.
1838 *Ruy Blas*, act 3, sc.2.

73 *Ah! toute nation bénit qui la délie.*
Ah! every nation blesses what undoes it.
1838 *Ruy Blas*, act 3, sc.5.

74 *La popularité? c'est la gloire en gros sous.*
Popularity? It is glory in large coins.
1838 *Ruy Blas*, act 3, sc.5.

75 *Le mot, c'est le Verbe, et le Verbe, c'est Dieu.*
The word is the Verb, and the Verb is God.
1856 *Contemplations*, bk.1, no.8.

76 *Cette cloison qui nous sépare du mystère des choses et que nous appelons la vie.*
Life is a screen which separates us from the mystery of things.
1862 *Les Misérables*, vol.1, bk.1, ch.2.

77 *Ce génie particulier de la femme qui comprend l'homme mieux que l'homme ne se comprend.*
A woman's particular talent is to understand a man better than he understands himself.
1862 *Les Misérables*, vol.1, bk.1, ch.9.

78 *Les livres sont des amis froids et sûrs.*
Books are cold and certain friends.
1862 *Les Misérables*, vol.1, bk.5, ch.3.

79 *Conscience déchirée entraîne vie décousue.*
A torn conscience brings about a disconnected life.
1862.

80 *La symétrie, c'est l'ennui, et l'ennui est le fond même du deuil. Le désespoir bâille.*
Symmetry is boredom and boredom is the foundation of grief. Despair yawns.
1862 *Les Misérables*, vol.2, bk.4, ch.1.

81 *Personne ne garde un secret comme un enfant.*
No one keeps a secret like a child.
1862 *Les Misérables*, vol.2, bk.7, ch.8.

82 *Respirer Paris, cela conserve l'âme.*
To inhale Paris preserves the soul.
1862 *Les Misérables*, vol.3, bk.1, ch.6.

83 *On jugerait bien plus sûrement un homme d'après ce qu'il rêve que d'après ce qu'il pense.*
We would judge a man more certainly according to his dreams than to his thoughts.
1862 *Les Misérables*, vol.3, bk.5, ch.5.

84 *On a voulu, à tort, faire de la bourgeoisie une classe. La bourgeoisie est tout simplement la portion contentée du peuple. Le bourgeois, c'est l'homme qui a maintenant le temps de s'asseoir. Une chaise n'est pas une caste.*
Wrongly, one wanted to make the bourgeoisie a class. The bourgeoisie is simply a contented section of the public. A bourgeois is a man who now has the time to sit down. A chair is not a caste.
1862 *Les Misérables*, vol.4, bk.1, ch.2.

85 *La première égalité, c'est l'équité.*
The first equality is equity.
1862 *Les Misérables*, vol.4, bk.1, ch.4.

86 *Le premier symptôme de l'amour vrai chez un jeune homme, c'est la timidité, chez une jeune fille, c'est la hardiesse.*
The first symptom of true love in a young man is timidity; in a young woman, it is boldness.
1862 *Les Misérables*, vol.4, bk.3, ch.6.

87 *Le dix-neuvième siècle est grand, mais le vingtième sera heureux.*

The nineteenth century is great, but the twentieth will be happy.
1862 *Les Misérables*, vol.5, bk.1, ch.4.

88 Le suicide, cette mystérieuse voie de fait sur l'inconnu.
Suicide: that mysterious route towards the unknown.
1862 *Les Misérables*, vol.5, bk.3, ch.10.

89 Jésus a pleuré, Voltaire a souri; c'est de cette larme divine et de ce sourire humain qu'est faite la douceur de la civilisation actuelle.
Jesus wept; Voltaire smiled. Of that divine tear and of that human smile the sweetness of present civilization is composed.
1878 Speech on Voltaire's centenary, 30 May.

90 Science says the first word on everything and the last word on nothing.
Attributed.

Huidobro, Vicente 1893–1948
Chilean poet, who wrote in French as well as Spanish. He created the movement known as *creacionismo*, which abandons traditional descriptive poetry.

91 Que se rompa el andamio de los huesos
Que se derrumben las vigas del cerebro
Y arrastre el huracán los trozos a la nada al otro lado
En donde el viento azota a Dios
Smash the scaffold of the bones
Pull down the rafters of the brain
Let the hurricane drag the pieces to the nothing on the other side
Where the wind thrashes God
1931 *Altazor o el viaje en paracaídas*, canto 1 (translated as *Altazor, or, A Voyage in a Parachute*, 1988).

Humboldt, Alexander, Baron von 1769–1859
German naturalist and traveller. He travelled through Central and South America (1799–1804), and his observations laid the foundations for the sciences of physical geography and meteorology.

92 In the sphere of natural investigation, as in poetry and painting, the delineation of that which appeals most strongly to the imagination, derives its collective interest from the vivid truthfulness with which the individual features are portrayed.
1845–62 *Kosmos* (translated as *Cosmos*, 1897).

93 The great and solemn spirit that pervades the intellectual labour (of science) arises from the sublime consciousness of striving toward the infinite, and of grasping all that is revealed to us amid the boundless and inexhaustible fullness of creation, development and being.
1845–62 *Kosmos* (translated as *Cosmos*, 1897).

Hume, David 1711–76
Scottish philosopher and historian. His most important work, the empiricist *A Treatise of Human Nature*, was published anonymously (1739–40). He published a five-volume *History of England* (1754–62) and was secretary to the British Ambassador in Paris (1763–5).

94 Let us fix our attention out of ourselves as much as possible; let us chase our imagination to the heavens, or to the utmost limits of the universe; we never really advance a step beyond ourselves, nor can conceive any kind of existence, but those perceptions, which have appeared in that narrow compass.
1739 *A Treatise of Human Nature*, bk.1, pt.2, section 6.

95 We have no other notion of cause and effect, but that of certain objects, which have been *always conjoined* together, and which in all past instances have been found inseparable.
1739 *A Treatise of Human Nature*, bk.1, pt.3, section 6.

96 For my part, when I enter most intimately into what I call *myself*, I always stumble on some particular perception or other, of heat or cold, light or shade, pain or pleasure. I never can catch *myself* at any time without a perception, and never can observe anything but the perception.
1739 *A Treatise of Human Nature*, bk.1, pt.4, section 6.

97 In all the events of life, we ought still to preserve our scepticism. If we believe that fire warms, or water refreshes, it is only because it costs us too much pains to think otherwise.
1739 *A Treatise of Human Nature*, bk.1, pt.4, section 7.

98 Reason is, and ought only to be the slave of the passions, and can never pretend to any other office than to serve and obey them.
1739 *A Treatise of Human Nature*, bk.2, pt.3, section 3.

99 It is not contrary to reason to prefer the destruction of the whole world to the scratching of my finger.
1739 *A Treatise of Human Nature*, bk.2, pt.3, section 3.

1 It is not, therefore, reason, which is the guide of life, but custom.
1739 *A Treatise of Human Nature*, abstract.

2 Art may make a suit of clothes; But nature must produce a man.
1741–2 *Essays Moral, Political and Literary*, 'The Epicurean'.

3 It cannot reasonably be doubted, but a little miss, dressed in a new gown for a dancing-school ball, receives as complete enjoyment as the greatest orator, who triumphs in the splendour of his eloquence, while he governs the passions and resolutions of a numerous assembly.
1741–2 *Essays Moral, Political and Literary*, 'The Sceptic'.

4 The increase of riches and commerce in any one nation, instead of hurting, commonly promotes the riches and commerce of all its neighbours.
1741–2 *Essays Moral, Political and Literary*, 'Of the Jealousy of Trade'.

5 All the objects of human reason or enquiry may naturally be divided into two kinds, to wit, *Relations of Ideas*, and *Matters of Fact*.
1748 *An Enquiry Concerning Human Understanding*, section 4, pt.1.

6 A wise man proportions his belief to the evidence.
1748 *An Enquiry Concerning Human Understanding*, section 10, pt.1.

7 When we run over libraries, persuaded of these principles, what havoc must we make? If we take in our hand any volume; of divinity or school metaphysics, for instance; let us ask, *Does it contain any abstract reasoning concerning quantity or number?* No. *Does it contain any experimental reasoning concerning matter*

of fact or existence? No. Commit it then to the flames: for it can contain nothing but sophistry and illusion.
1748 *An Enquiry Concerning Human Understanding*, section 12, pt.3.

8 Never literary attempt was more unfortunate than my Treatise of Human Nature. It fell *dead-born from the press*, without reaching such distinction, as even to excite a murmur among the zealots.
1777 *My Own Life*, ch.1.

Humphrey, Hubert Horatio 1911–78

US politician. He served as Vice-President under Lyndon B Johnson but failed to win the Democratic candidature in 1968.

9 There are not enough jails, not enough policemen, not enough courts to enforce a law not supported by the people.
1965 Speech, 1 May.

Humphries, (John) Barry 1934–

Australian comedian and writer, best known for such comic creations as Dame Edna Everage and Sir Les Patterson.

10 When I became a big star I sacrificed my family, and nothing gave me more pleasure. My advice to women is to put your family last.
2007 As Dame Edna Everage.

11 The best jokes are often only understood by one other person.
2011 Quoted in *The Telegraph*, 20 Jun.

12 I am a lucky woman because I was born with a priceless gift: the ability to laugh at the misfortunes of others.
2012 As Dame Edna Everage, announcing his retirement.

Humphry, Derek 1930–

British journalist and co-founder of the Hemlock Society, which supports euthanasia for the terminally ill.

13 We're not lawbreakers, we're law reformers.
1992 In *Time*, 28 Dec.

Humphrys, John 1943–

Welsh broadcaster, particularly known as a tenacious presenter on BBC Radio 4's *Today* programme (since 1987).

14 It is largely on television and radio that real probing of what politicians are up to has to happen.
2000 *The Devil's Advocate*.

15 It is no good saying we [journalists] must report only what is true because what is true cannot always be proven.
2004 In the *Sunday Times*, 8 Feb.

Hunt, G W 1829–1904

English composer, lyricist and painter.

16 We don't want to fight, but by jingo if we do,
We've got the ships, we've got the men, we've got the money too!
1878 Music-hall song, inspired by Disraeli's speech of 9 Nov 1876 threatening Russia with war if it sent volunteers into Serbia and Montenegro. This is the origin of 'jingoism'.

Hunt, Johnnie B(ryan) 1927–2006

US businessman of poor origins.

17 I was hungry once and once you're hungry, you're different.
1992 In *Forbes*, 19 Oct.

Hunt, Lamar 1932–2006

US founder of the Kansas City Chiefs American football club.

18 My definition of utter waste is a coachload of lawyers going over a cliff, with three empty seats.
Quoted in Colin Jarman *The Guinness Dictionary of Sports Quotations* (1990).

Hunt, (James Henry) Leigh 1784–1859

English poet, critic and essayist. With his brother he edited *The Examiner* (1808–21) and popularized Keats and Shelley. His house in Hampstead was a literary meeting-place, and he was caricatured by Dickens as Harold Skimpole in *Bleak House*.

19 Never lay yourself open to what is called conviction: you might as well open your waist-coat to receive a knock-down blow.
1808 'Rules for the Conduct of Newspaper Editors', in *The Examiner*, 6 Mar.

20 A playful moderation in politics is just as absurd as a remonstrative whisper to a mob.
1808 'Rules for the Conduct of Newspaper Editors', in *The Examiner*, 6 Mar.

21 She can overpower, astonish, afflict, but she cannot win; her majestic presence and commanding features seem to disclaim love, as a trifle to which they cannot descend.
1808 Of Sarah Siddons. *Critical Essays on the Performers of the London Theatres*.

22 The two divinest things this world has got,
A lovely woman in a rural spot!
1816 'The Story of Rimini', canto 3, l.257–8.

23 The laughing queen that caught the world's great hands.
1818 Of Cleopatra. 'The Nile'.

24 Stolen sweets are always sweeter,
Stolen kisses much completer,
Stolen looks are nice in chapels,
Stolen, stolen, be your apples.
1830 'Song of Fairies Robbing an Orchard'.

25 Poetry, in the most comprehensive application of the term, I take to be the flower of any kind of experience, rooted in truth, and issuing forth into beauty.
1832 *The Story of Rimini*, preface to rev edn.

26 The pretension is nothing; the performance everything. A good apple is better than an insipid peach.
1832 *The Story of Rimini*, preface to rev edn.

27 'No love,' quoth he, 'but vanity, sets love a task like that.'
1836 'The Glove and the Lions'.

28 Abou Ben Adhem (may his tribe increase!)
Awoke one night from a deep dream of peace.
1838 'Abou Ben Adhem'.

29 I pray thee then,
Write me as one that loves his fellow-men.
1838 'Abou Ben Adhem'.

30 Jenny kissed me when we met,
Jumping from the chair she sat in;
Time, you thief, who love to get
Sweets into your list, put that in:

Say I'm weary, say I'm sad,
Say that health and wealth have missed me,
Say I'm growing old, but add,
Jenny kissed me.
1838 'Rondeau'.

31 That man must be very much absorbed in reflection, or stupid, or sulky, or unhappy, or a mere hog at his trough, who is not moved to say something when he dines.
1851 *Table-Talk*, 'Table-Talk'.

32 If you are ever at a loss to support a flagging conversation, introduce the subject of eating.
1851 *Table-Talk*, 'Eating'.

Hunt, Sir Rex 1926–2012

Governor of the Falkland Islands at the time of the Argentine invasion of 1982.

33 It is very uncivilised to invade British territory. You are here illegally.
1982 Attributed remark to an Argentinian general. Quoted in *Life*, Jan 1983.

Hunter, William 1718–83

Scottish anatomist and obstetrician, appointed physician-extraordinary to Queen Charlotte Sophia (1764) and first Professor of Anatomy to the Royal Academy (1768). His Hunterian Museum was bequeathed to Glasgow University.

34 Some physiologists will have it that the stomach is a mill;—others, that it is a fermenting vat;—others again that it is a stew-pan;—but in my view of the matter, it is neither a mill, a fermenting vat, nor a stew-pan—but a *stomach*, gentlemen, a *stomach*.
Quoted in J A Paris *A Treatise on Diet* (1824), epigraph, from a note made by Hunter on one of his lectures.

Hupfeld, Herman 1894–1951

US composer of popular songs, best known for 'Sing Something Simple' and 'As Time Goes By'.

35 You must remember this, a kiss is still a kiss,
    A sigh is just a sigh;
    The fundamental things apply,
    As time goes by.
1931 'As Time Goes By', sung by Dooley Wilson in the film *Casablanca* (1943).

Hurt, Sir John Vincent 1940–

English actor. As well as performing many roles in Shakespeare, he has made numerous film appearances over a long career, in such films as *10 Rillington Place* (1971), *Midnight Express* (1978), *Alien* (1979), *The Elephant Man* (1980), *Nineteen Eighty-Four* (1984), *The Field* (1990), *Captain Corelli's Mandolin* (2001) and *Tinker Tailor Soldier Spy* (2011).

36 The clergy is in the same business as actors, just a different department.
2007 In *The Guardian*, 20 Mar.

Hussein, ibn Talal 1935–99

King of Jordan (1952–99), four times married. The longest-serving Arab leader, pro-Western in attitude, he moved towards democracy in Jordan.

37 After all the doors were shut, our region is facing a deep abyss after the turning of the Gulf crisis into an imminent catastrophe. We have not left a door that we did not knock on, or a road that we did not take to find a political settlement of this crisis.
1991 On his attempts to intercede for peace in the Gulf War, Jan.

Hussein, Saddam 1937–2006

Iraqi politician, a key figure in Iraq's 1968 revolution and later President (1979–2003). He engaged in the Iran–Iraq War (1980–8) and in 1990 invaded Kuwait and was repulsed by a coalition of Western and Arab forces. He made further raids on Iran in 1993, defying UN ceasefire resolutions. He was captured by US forces in Iraq in 2003, then tried, convicted and hanged in 2006.

38 The devil Bush and his treacherous gang, with criminal Zionism, have begun the great showdown, the mother of all battles between good and evil.
1991 Speech in Baghdad, 6 Jan, describing Operation Desert Storm. Quoted in the *Sunday Times*, 27 Jan.

39 There is no other course but the one we have chosen, except the course of humiliation and darkness, after which there will be no bright sign in the sky or brilliant light on earth... All this will make us more patient and steadfast, and better prepared for the battle which God blesses and which good men support. Then there will only be a glorious conclusion, where a brilliant sun will clear the dust of battle, and where the clouds of battles will be dispelled.
1991 Baghdad radio broadcast, 21 Feb.

40 Baghdad is determined to force the Mongols of our age to commit suicide at its gates.
2003 Speech on the anniversary of the Gulf War, 17 Jan.

41 At dawn prayers today on March 20 2003 (17 Muharram 1424), the criminal, reckless little Bush and his aides committed this crime that he was threatening to commit against Iraq and humanity.
2003 Address to the nation of Iraq, broadcast on state television, after a US strike on Baghdad. Quoted in *The Guardian*, 20 Mar.

42 We do not have weapons of mass destruction.
Quoted in George Galloway *I'm Not the Only One* (2004).

43 If they come we are ready. We will fight them on the streets, from the rooftops, from house to house. We will never surrender our independence no matter what happens in any invasion.
Quoted in George Galloway *I'm Not the Only One* (2004).

44 I have saved you from destitution and misery and destroyed your enemies, the Persian and Americans.
2006 Responding to Iraqi soldiers who taunted him at his execution, 30 Dec.

Huston, John 1906–87

US actor, screenwriter and director, son of Walter Huston. He made his directorial debut with *The Maltese Falcon* (1941). Other successes include *Key Largo* (1948), *The African Queen* (1951), *Moulin Rouge* (1952) and *The Man Who Would Be King* (1975).

45 You're good, you're real good.
1941 Line delivered by Humphrey Bogart in *The Maltese Falcon*.

46 A work of art doesn't dare you to realize it. It germinates and gestates by itself.
1982 Reply to a tribute from the Directors Guild of America. Reported in *Variety*, 26 Apr.

Hutchens, John Kennedy 1905–95

US journalist and editor. He was theatre critic with the *New York Times* (1929–32, 1934–8), editor of the *New York Times Book Review* (1946–8), and was on the editorial board of the Book-of-the-Month Club (1963–88).

47 A writer and nothing else: a man alone in a room with the English language, trying to get human feelings right.
   1961 On Stephen Crane. In the *New York Herald Tribune*, 10 Sep.

Hutcheson, Francis 1694–1746

Scottish philosopher, born in Ulster, a Professor of Moral Philosophy at Glasgow (1729–46) and exponent of the theory of moral sense. His ideas were later expanded by David Hume and taken up by the Utilitarians.

48 Wisdom denotes the pursuing of the best ends by the best means.
   1725 *An Inquiry into the Original of Our Ideas of Beauty and Virtue*, treatise 1, sect.5.

49 That action is best, which procures the greatest happiness for the greatest numbers.
   1725 *An Inquiry into the Original of Our Ideas of Beauty and Virtue*, treatise 2, sect.3. This is the classic exposition of pragmatism.
   ▶ See Bentham 82:88.

Hutchins, Robert M 1899–1977

US educationalist, Chancellor of the University of Chicago.

50 On the principle laid down by Gilbert and Sullivan that when everybody is somebody, nobody is anybody; if everybody is abnormal, we don't need to worry about anybody.
   1951 Farewell address to students at the University of Chicago.

51 Whenever I feel like exercise, I lie down until the feeling passes.
   Quoted in Colin Jarman *The Guinness Dictionary of Sports Quotations* (1990).

Huxley, Aldous Leonard 1894–1963

English novelist and essayist. His satirical novels *Crome Yellow* (1921) and *Antic Hay* (1923) established his reputation, and his best-known work is the dystopian novel *Brave New World* (1932). Other works include *Eyeless in Gaza* (1936) and *Time Must Have a Stop* (1944).

52 I can sympathize with people's pains, but not with their pleasures. There is something curiously boring about somebody else's happiness.
   1920 *Limbo*, 'Cynthia'.

53 The proper study of mankind is books.
   1921 *Crome Yellow*, ch.28.
   ▶ See Pope 687:80.

54 There are few who would not rather be taken in adultery than in provincialism.
   1923 *Antic Hay*, ch.10.

55 Mr Mercaptan went on to preach a brilliant sermon on that melancholy sexual perversion known as continence.
   1923 *Antic Hay*, ch.18.

56 Lady Capricorn, he understood, was still keeping open bed.
   1923 *Antic Hay*, ch.21.

57 I'm afraid of losing my obscurity. Genuineness only thrives in the dark. Like celery.
   1925 *Those Barren Leaves*, pt.1, ch.1.

58 Science has 'explained' nothing: the more we know the more fantastic the world becomes and the profounder the surrounding darkness.
   1925 *Views of Holland*.

59 Facts do not cease to exist because they are ignored.
   1927 *Proper Studies*, 'Note on Dogma'.

60 Those who believe that they are exclusively in the right are generally those who achieve something.
   1927 *Proper Studies*, 'Note on Dogma'.

61 That all men are equal is a proposition to which, at ordinary times, no sane human being has ever given his assent.
   1927 *Proper Studies*, 'The Idea of Equality'.

62 Several excuses are always less convincing than one.
   1928 *Point Counter Point*, ch.1.

63 A bad book is as much of a labour to write as a good one; it comes as sincerely from the author's soul.
   1928 *Point Counter Point*, ch.13.

64 There is no substitute for talent. Industry and all the virtues are of no avail.
   1928 *Point Counter Point*, ch.13.

65 Brought up in an age when ladies apparently rolled along on wheels, Mr Quarles was peculiarly susceptible to calves.
   1928 *Point Counter Point*, ch.20.

66 Parodies and caricatures are the most penetrating of criticisms.
   1928 *Point Counter Point*, ch.28.

67 Happiness is like coke—something you get as a by-product in the process of making something else.
   1928 *Point Counter Point*, ch.30.

68 Too much consistency is as bad for the mind as it is for the body. Consistency is contrary to nature, contrary to life.
   1929 *Do What You Will*, 'Wordsworth in the Tropics'.

69 After silence, that which comes nearest to expressing the inexpressible is music.
   1931 *Music at Night*.

70 Experience is not what happens to a man; it is what a man does with what happens to him.
   1932 *Texts and Pretexts*, introduction.

71 Only man behaves with such gratuitous folly. It is the price he has to pay for being intelligent but not, as yet, quite intelligent enough.
   1932 *Texts and Pretexts*, 'Amor Fati'.

72 The escalator from the Social Predestination Room… One circuit of the cellar at ground level, one on the first gallery, half on the second, and on the two hundred and sixty-seventh morning, daylight in the Decanting Room. Independent existence—so called.
   1932 *Brave New World*, ch.1.

73 Our Ford…had been the first to reveal the appalling dangers of family life.
   1932 *Brave New World*, ch.3.

74 Oh, she's a splendid girl. Wonderfully pneumatic.
   1932 *Brave New World*, ch.3.

75 The sexophones wailed like melodious cats under the moon.
   1932 *Brave New World*, ch.5.

76 The real pitch lake is simply about two hundred asphalt tennis courts, in very bad condition, set in the midst of some gently undulating green meadows. I am inclined to ask for my money back.
   1934 On the Trinidad Pitch Lake. *Beyond the Mexique Bay*.

77 Official dignity tends to increase in inverse ratio to the importance of the country in which the office is held.
   1934 *Beyond the Mexique Bay*.

78 'Death,' said Mark Staithes. 'It's the only thing we haven't succeeded in completely vulgarizing.'
   1936 *Eyeless in Gaza*, ch.31.

79 The end cannot justify the means, for the simple and obvious reason that the means employed determine the nature of the ends produced.
   1937 *Ends and Means*, ch.1.

80 We are living now, not in the delicious intoxication induced by the early successes of science, but in a rather grisly morning-after, when it has become apparent that what triumphant science has done hitherto is to improve the means for achieving unimproved or actually deteriorated ends.
   1937 *Ends and Means*, ch.1.

81 So long as men worship the Caesars and Napoleons, Caesars and Napoleons will duly arise and make them miserable.
   1937 *Ends and Means*, ch.8.

82 The propagandist's purpose is to make one set of people forget that certain other sets of people are human.
   1937 *The Olive Tree*.

83 What is science? Science is angling in the mud—angling for immortality and for anything else that may happen to turn up.
   1939 *After Many a Summer Dies the Swan*.

84 The quality of moral behaviour varies in inverse ratio to the number of human beings involved.
   1941 *Grey Eminence*, ch.10.

85 There's only one corner of the universe you can be certain of improving, and that's your own self.
   1944 *Time Must Have a Stop*.

86 You learn to love by loving—by paying attention and doing what one thereby discovers has to be done.
   1944 *Time Must Have a Stop*.

87 Facts are ventriloquist's dummies. Sitting on a wise man's knee they may be made to utter words of wisdom; elsewhere they say nothing, or talk nonsense.
   1944 *Time Must Have a Stop*.

88 Most human beings have an infinite capacity for taking things for granted.
   1950 'Variations on a Philosopher'.

89 We participate in a tragedy; at a comedy we only look.
   1952 *The Devils of Loudun*, ch.11.

90 I was seeing what Adam had seen on the morning of his creation—the miracle, moment by moment, of naked existence.
   1954 *The Doors of Perception*.

91 I have spoken so far only of the blissful visionary experience... But visionary experience is not always blissful. It's sometimes terrible. There is hell as well as heaven.
   1956 *Heaven and Hell*.

92 'Bed,' as the Italian proverb succinctly puts it, 'is the poor man's opera.'
   1956 *Heaven and Hell*.

93 The most distressing thing that can happen to a prophet is to be proved wrong. The next most distressing thing is to be proved right.
   1956 'Brave New World Revisited', in *Esquire*.

94 But liberty, as we all know, cannot flourish in a country that is permanently on a war footing, or even a near-war footing. Permanent crisis justifies permanent control of everybody and everything by the agencies of central government.
   1956 'Brave New World Revisited', in *Esquire*.

95 But some of us still believe that, without freedom, human beings cannot become fully human and that freedom is therefore supremely valuable.
   1956 'Brave New World Revisited', in *Esquire*.

96 That men do not learn very much from the lessons of history is the most important of all the lessons that history has to teach.
   1959 'A Case of Voluntary Ignorance'.

97 Science is the reduction of the bewildering diversity of unique events to manageable uniformity within one of a number of symbol systems, and technology is the art of using these symbol systems so as to control and organize unique events. Scientific observation is always a viewing of things through the refracting medium of a symbol system, and technological praxis is always handling of things in ways that some symbol system has dictated. Education in science and technology is essentially education on the symbol level.
   1962 In *Daedalus*, spring issue.

98 Idealism is the noble toga that political gentlemen drape over their will to power.
   Quoted in his *New York Herald Tribune* obituary, 24 Nov 1963.

Huxley, Sir Julian Sorell   1887–1975

English biologist and humanist, grandson of T H Huxley. He was the first Director-General of UNESCO, and formulated a pragmatic ethical theory of 'evolutionary humanism'.

99 We all know how the size of sums of money appears to vary in a remarkable way according as they are being paid in or paid out.
   1923 *Essays of a Biologist*, ch.5.

1 Operationally, God is beginning to resemble not a ruler but the last fading smile of a cosmic Cheshire cat.
   1957 *Religion without Revelation* (rev edn), ch.3.

Huxley, T(homas) H(enry)   1825–95

English biologist, who made significant contributions to palaeontology and comparative anatomy. He famously supported Darwin's controversial theory of evolution by natural selection, and the term 'agnostic' has been attributed to him.

2 The generalizations of science sweep in ever-widening circles, and more aspiring flights, through a limitless creation.
   1859 Letter to *The Times*, 26 Dec.

3   Sit down before fact as a little child, be prepared to give up every preconceived notion, follow humbly wherever and to whatsoever abysses Nature leads, or you shall learn nothing.
    1860 Letter to Charles Kingsley.

4   Most of my colleagues were *-ists* of one sort or another; and however kind and friendly they might be, I, the man without a rag of a label to cover himself with, could not fail to have some of the uneasy feelings which must have beset the historical fox when, after leaving the trap in which his tail remained, he presented himself to his normally elongated companions. So I took thought, and invented what I conceived to be the appropriate title of 'agnostic'.
    1869 *Science and Christian Tradition*.

5   The central propositions [of Descartes]...are these: There is a path that leads to the truth so surely that any one who will follow it must needs reach the goal... And there is one guiding rule by which a man may always find this path...give unqualified assent to no propositions but those the truth of which is so clear and distinct that they cannot be doubted.
    1870 *Lay Sermons, Addresses, and Reviews*.

6   The great tragedy of Science—the slaying of a beautiful hypothesis by an ugly fact.
    1870 'Biogenesis and Abiogenesis', in the *British Association Annual Report*.

7   Our reverence for the nobility of manhood will not be lessened by the knowledge that man is in substance and in structure, one with the brutes; for he alone possesses the marvellous endowment of intelligible and rational speech whereby...he has slowly accumulated and organized the experience which is almost wholly lost with the cessation of individual life in other animals; so that he now stands raised above it as on a mountain-top, far above the level of his humble fellows, and transfigured from his grosser nature by reflecting, here and there, a ray from the infinite source of truth.
    1880 *Man's Place in Nature*.

8   It is the customary fate of new truths to begin as heresies and to end as superstitions.
    1880 *Science and Culture and Other Essays*, 'The Coming of Age of the Origin of the Species'.

9   Irrationally held truths may be more harmful than reasoned errors.
    1880 *Science and Culture and Other Essays*, 'The Coming of Age of the Origin of the Species'.

10 Science is nothing but trained and organized common sense, differing from the latter only as a veteran may differ from a raw recruit: and its methods differ from those of common sense only as far as the guardsman's cut and thrust differ from the manner in which a savage wields his club.
    1893–4 *Collected Essays*, no.4, 'The Method of Zadig'.

11 Some experience of popular lecturing had convinced me that the necessity of making things plain to uninstructed people was one of the very best means of clearing up the obscure corners in one's own mind.
    1894 *Man's Place in Nature* (rev edn), preface.

12 Next to being right in this world, the best of all things is to be clearly and definitely wrong. If you go buzzing about between right and wrong, vibrating and fluctuating, you come out nowhere; but if you are absolutely and thoroughly and persistently wrong you must, some of these days, have the extreme good fortune of knocking your head against a fact, and that sets you all straight again.
    Attributed.

Huxtable, Ada Louise *née Landman*   c.1921–2013

US architectural critic. In her columns for the *New York Times* (1963–82), she denounced new buildings and property speculation which spoiled American cities. Her work helped promote the preservation of historic buildings. She won the first Pulitzer Prize for criticism in 1970.

13 I got a terrible case of the Fountainblues.
    1970 On Miami Beach. In the *New York Times*, 15 Oct.

14 America the beautiful,
    Let me sing of thee;
    Burger King and Dairy Queen
    From sea to shining sea.
    1971 'Goodbye History, Hello Hamburger', in the *New York Times*, 21 Mar.

15 New York, thy name is irreverence and hyperbole. And grandeur.
    1975 In the *New York Times*, 20 Jul.

16 Good architecture is still the difficult, conscientious, creative, expressive planning for that elusive synthesis that is a near-contradiction in terms: efficiency and beauty.
    2008 *On Architecture*.

Hyde, Robin *pseudonym of* Iris Guiver Wilkinson   1906–39

New Zealand novelist, poet and journalist, born in South Africa. She was one of the few women career journalists of the 1930s. Brief affairs led to the births of two sons; the first, whose name she adopted, was stillborn. Her works include the autobiographical novel *The Godwits Fly* (1938).

17 Something there had been, something delicate, wild and far away. But it was shut out behind the doors of yesterday, lost beyond the hills.
    1938 *The Godwits Fly*, ch.3.

18 You were English and not English. It took time to realize that England was far away.
    1938 *The Godwits Fly*, ch.3.

19 We live half our lives in England...there can't have been anything quite like this since the Roman colonists settled in Britain: not the hanging on with one hand, and the other hand full of seas.
    1938 *The Godwits Fly*, ch.8.

20 Having a lover isn't much to write home about.
    1938 *The Godwits Fly*, ch.17.

21 She stands an instant in the sun
    Athwart her harsh land's red and green—
    Hands of a serf, and warrior eyes
    Of some flame-sceptred Irish queen.
    ... As if she does not care that life
    Has reft the jewels from her hair—
    But grieves that menial needs and base
    Were those that left her palace bare.
    1938 *The Godwits Fly*, ch.23. This poem is an adaptation of 'The Farmer's Wife', first published in *The Desolate Star* (1929).

Hyde-White, Wilfred 1903–91
English film actor.

22 The suaveness isn't born of confidence; it's born of fright.
Quoted in his obituary, in the *San Francisco Chronicle*, 7 May 1991.

Hynde, Chrissie 1951–
US singer, member of The Pretenders.

23 I feel displaced when I'm back in America, like a visitor. I feel like if I don't get a cup of tea I'm going to lose my mind.
2003 In the *Daily Telegraph*, 19 Apr.

24 There's the meat eaters and there's us. And that's the way I look at the world.
2003 In *The Independent*, 13 Sep.

Hytner, Sir Nicholas 1956–
English film and theatre director. He was artistic director at the National Theatre (2003–15).

25 The theatre on its own can't and doesn't change society, but plays can define a moment. *The Marriage of Figaro* did seem to predict a revolution, but I doubt it sent anybody onto the streets.
2004 In *Varsity*, 6 Feb.

Iacocca, Lee (Lido Anthony) 1924–
US businessman, president of the Ford Motor Company and later head of Chrysler Corporation (1979–1992).

1 People want economy and they will pay any price to get it.
1974 In the *New York Times*, 13 Oct.

2 Everybody in an organization has to believe their livelihood is based on the quality of the product they deliver.
1988 *Talking Straight*.

3 If you want to continue being leaders in the world, start by getting some of that [Federal] debt off your backs. Debtors can't be leaders. It's the guy holding the IOUs who can call the shots; the other guy is called a hostage.
1992 Quoted in the *New York Times*, 26 May.

4 Let's face it, if your car breaks down, you're not going to take it to the White House to get it fixed. But, if your company breaks down, you've got to go to the experts on the ground, not the bureaucrats.
2009 *Newsweek*, Apr.

Ibarruri Gomez, Dolores known as La Pasionaria 1895–1989
Spanish writer and politician, a founder of the Spanish Communist Party (1920). She urged the fight against the Fascist forces, and left for the USSR when Franco came to power. On returning to Spain in 1977, she was re-elected to the National Assembly.

5 It is better to die on your feet than live on your knees. *No pasarán*!
1936 Speech in Paris, 3 Sep, at the onset of the Spanish Civil War, imploring the people to defend the Republic against the Fascist uprising. 'No pasarán', meaning 'they will not pass' and associated with the World War I Battle of Verdun, was to become the battle-cry of the Republican cause.
▶ See Pétain 675:35.

Ibn Battutah 1304–68
Arab traveller and geographer, who spent 30 years visiting parts of Africa, Asia and southern Europe. He then settled in Fez and wrote the history of his journeys.

6 Never to travel any road a second time.
His guiding principle. *Travels in Asia and Africa 1325–1354* (translated by H A R Gibb, 1929).

Ibsen, Henrik Johan 1828–1906
Norwegian playwright, the founder of modern prose drama. His realistic plays on sensitive social issues revolutionized modern European drama. They include *En dukkehjem* (*A Doll's House*, 1879), *Vildanden* (*The Wild Duck*, 1884) and *Hedda Gabler* (1890).

7 Flertallet har aldrig retten på sin side. Aldrig, siger jeg! Det er en af disse samfundsløgner, som en fri, tinkende mand må gøre oprør imod. Hvem er det, som udgør flertallet af beboerne i et land? Er det de kloge folk, eller er det dè dumme? Jeg tinker, vi får vaere enige om, at dumme mennesker er tilstede i en ganske forskrækkelig overvildende majoritet rundt omkring på den hele vide jord.
The majority never has right on its side. Never, I say! That is one of the social lies that a free, thinking man is bound to rebel against. Who makes up the majority in any given country? Is it the wise men or the fools? I think we must agree that the fools are in a terrible overwhelming majority, all the wide world over.
1882 *En folkefiende* (*An Enemy of the People*), act 4.

8 En skulde aldrig ha' sine bedste buxer på, nå r en er ude og strider for frihed og sandhed.
You should never have your best trousers on when you turn out to fight for freedom and truth.
1882 *En folkefiende* (*An Enemy of the People*), act 5.

9 Luftslotter,—de er så nemme at ty ôûnd i, de. Og nemme at bygge også.
Castles in the air—they are so easy to take refuge in. And so easy to build, too.
1892 *Bygmester Solness* (*The Master Builder*), act 3.

10 On the contrary!
1906 Last words, refuting a nurse's suggestion that he was feeling better.

I Ching c.2000 BC
I Ching (*The Book of Changes*) is reputed to have been composed by a Chinese king and his son under guidance from a Taoist sage. It is a compendium of observations and advice regarding the rise and fall of individuals and their power groups and was later annotated by Confucius.

11 It is unlucky to sound off about happiness.
c.2000 BC *I Ching*, no.16 (translated by Thomas Cleary).

12 Change proves true on the day it is finished.
c.2000 BC *I Ching*, no.49 (translated by Thomas Cleary).

13 Cultured people practise self-examination with trepidation and fear.
c.2000 BC *I Ching*, no.51 (translated by Thomas Cleary).

Ignatieff, Michael 1947–
Canadian author, broadcaster and academic.

14 The medium's gaze is brief, intense, and promiscuous. The shelf life of the moral causes it makes its own is brutally short.
1988 'Is Nothing Sacred? The Ethics of Television', in *Daedalus: Journal of the American Academy of Arts and Sciences*, Fall.

15 Living fearlessly is not the same thing as never being afraid. It's good to be afraid occasionally. Fear is a great teacher.
2007 *O Magazine*, Apr.

16 Family traditions are more than arguments with the dead, more than collections of family letters you try to decipher. A tradition is also a channel of memory through which fierce and unrequited longings surge, longings that define and shape a whole life.
2009 *True Patriot Love: Four Generations in Search of Canada*.

Ignatow, David 1914–97
US poet and academic. He published several volumes of poetry, much of it highly autobiographical in content.

17 Faster and faster it rolled,
with me running after it
bent low, gritting my teeth,
and I found myself doubled over
and rolling down the street
head over heels, one complete somersault
after another like a bagel
and strangely happy with myself.
1968 *Rescue the Dead*, 'The Bagel'.

18 To love is to be a fish.
My boat wallows in the sea.
You who are free,
rescue the dead.
1968 *Rescue the Dead*, 'Rescue the Dead'.

Ihimaera, Witi Tame 1944–
New Zealand writer and diplomat. His novel *Tangi* (1973), about a son's return home to his father's funeral and to his Maori roots, was the first written by a Maori to have been published. Other works include *The Matriarch* (1986), *The Whale Rider* (1987) and *Sky Dancer* (2003).

19 The sunlight falls across the country, lighting up the greenstone years of a boy with his father.
1973 *Tangi*, ch.14.

20 *Titiro ki te rangi tahuri rawa ake, Kahore he whenua e…Kua riro*: We looked up to heaven and before we knew where we were there was no land left…gone.
1986 *The Matriarch*, ch.3.

Illich, Ivan 1926–2002
Austrian-born social critic, former priest and polymath. His works include *Deschooling Society* (1971) and *In the Vineyard of the Text* (1993).

21 Current nationalism is merely the affirmation of the right of colonial elites to repeat history and follow the road travelled by the rich toward the universal consumption of internationally marketed packages, a road which can ultimately lead only to universal pollution and universal frustration.
1970 *Celebration of Awareness*, ch.12.

22 In both rich and poor nations consumption is polarized while expectation is equalized.
1970 *Celebration of Awareness*, ch.12.

23 In a consumer society there are inevitably two kinds of slaves: the prisoners of addiction and the prisoners of envy.
1973 *Tools for Conviviality*, ch.3.

Independent on Sunday

24 Floral fascism and an explosion of almost medieval irrationality.
1997 Editorial reflecting on the response to the death of Diana, Princess of Wales, 9 Nov.

Inge, William Ralph 1860–1954
English prelate and theologian, known as 'The Gloomy Dean' for his pessimistic sermons as Dean of St Paul's (1911–34). His books include *Outspoken Essays* (1919, 1922), *Lay Thoughts of a Dean* (1926, 1931) and more serious theological works.

25 It takes in reality only one to make a quarrel. It is useless for the sheep to pass resolutions in favour of vegetarianism, while the wolf remains of a different opinion.
1919 *Outspoken Essays* (first series), 'Patriotism'.

26 A man may build himself a throne of bayonets, but he cannot sit on it.
1923 *Philosophy of Plotinus*, vol.2, lecture 22.

27 Many people believe that they are attracted by God, or by Nature, when they are only repelled by man.
1931 *More Thoughts of a Lay Dean*, pt.4, ch.1.

28 The enemies of freedom do not argue; they shout and they shoot.
1948 *The End of an Age*, ch.4.

29 The effect of boredom on a large scale in history is underestimated. It is a main cause of revolutions, and would soon bring to an end all the static Utopias and the farmyard civilization of the Fabians.
1948 *The End of an Age*, ch.6.

30 A nation is a society united by a delusion about its ancestry and by a common hatred of its neighbours.
Sagittarius and George.

Ingersoll, Robert 1833–99
US lawyer, orator and freethinker, called 'The Great Agnostic' for his anti-religious views.

31 The hope of science is the perfection of the human race. The hope of theology is the salvation of a few and the damnation of almost everybody.
1867 *The Age of Reason*, Mar.

32 An honest God is the noblest work of man.
1876 *The Gods*, pt.1.
▶ See Pope 687:89.

33 In nature there are neither rewards nor punishments —there are consequences.
1881 *Some Reasons Why*, pt.8, 'The New Testament'.

Ingham, Sir Bernard 1932–
English journalist and businessman, particularly known as Margaret Thatcher's chief press secretary (1979–90).

34 Blood sport is brought to its ultimate refinement in the gossip columns.
1986 Speech, 5 Feb.

35 It is utter hypocrisy of this nation, which breeds illegitimate children like flies and has relegated marriage to an eccentric arrangement, to take a lofty view of Prince Charles's right to marry Camilla.
2005 In *The Yorkshire Post*, 1 Mar.

Ingram, John Kells 1823–1907
Irish economist and poet, Professor of Oratory then of Greek at Trinity College, Dublin. In 1847 he co-founded the Dublin Statistical Society, attempting in his works to formulate a social rather than purely mathematical science of economics.

36 Who fears to speak of Ninety-Eight?
Who blushes at the name?
When cowards mock the patriot's fate,
Who hangs his head for shame?
He's all a knave or half a slave
Who slights his country thus:
But a *true* man, like you, man,
Will fill your glass with us.
1845 *The Spirit of the Nation*, 'The Memory of the Dead'.

Ingrams, Richard Reid 1937–
English writer, former editor of the satirical magazine *Private Eye*.

37 I have come to regard the law courts not as a cathedral but rather as a casino.
1977 Referring to libel suits against him. Quoted in *The Guardian*, 30 Jul.

Ingres, Jean Auguste Dominique 1780–1867
French painter, leading exponent of the Classical tradition in 19c France. He painted many of his famous nudes while living in Rome (1806–20).

38 Is there anyone among the great men who has not imitated? Nothing is made with nothing.
1821 Quoted in Henri Delaborde *Ingres, sa vie, ses travaux, sa doctrine* (1870).

39 What do these so-called artists mean when they preach the discovery of the 'new'? Is there anything new? Everything has been done, everything has been discovered.
1821 Quoted in Henri Delaborde *Ingres, sa vie, ses travaux, sa doctrine* (1870).

40 Anti-classic art, if it may even be called an art, is merely the art of the idle. It is the doctrine of those who desire to produce without working, to know without learning.
1821 Quoted in Henri Delaborde *Ingres, sa vie, ses travaux, sa doctrine* (1870).

41 Make copies, young man, many copies. You can only become a good artist by copying the masters.
1855 Attributed comment to Degas. Quoted in A Vollard *Souvenirs d'un marchand de tableaux* (1937).

42 They have let the wolf into the sheepfold!
1859 Attributed remark on hearing that Delacroix had been elected to the Academy. Quoted in P Amaury-Duval *L'Atelier d'Ingres* (1878).

43 One must go after the modelling like a fly crawling over a piece of paper.
Attributed aphorism. Quoted in P Valéry *Degas, Danse, Dessin* (1938).

Innis, Harold Adams 1894–1952
Canadian political economist.

44 Canadian nationalism was systematically encouraged and exploited by American capital. Canada moved from colony to nation to colony.
1948 'Great Britain, the United States and Canada', collected in Mary Quayle Innis (ed) *Essays in Canadian Economic History* (1956).

45 Property like incest holds the family together.
Quoted in William Christian (ed) *The Idea File of Harold Adams Innis* (1980).

Pope Innocent III originally Lotario de' Conti di Segni 1160–1216
Italian prelate and scholar, elected Pope in 1198. He asserted the authority of the papacy over secular princes, and strongly promoted the Fourth Crusade.

46 *Omnis cupidus at avarus contra naturam nititur et molitur. Natura namque pauperem adducit in mundum; natura pauperem reducit a mundo.*
Every covetous and avaricious man struggles and strives against nature. For nature brings him into the world poor, and takes him out of it poor.
1195 *De Miseraria Condicionis Humanae*, bk.2, ch.12.

47 *Gula carum tributem exigit, sed vilissimum reddit, quia quanto sunt delicaciora cibavia, tanto fetidiora sunt stercora.*
Gluttony demands a heavy tribute but gives the basest returns: the more delicate the food, the more reeking the dung.
1195 *De Miseraria Condicionis Humanae*, bk.2, ch.20.

48 This [Magna Carta] has been forced from the King. It constitutes an insult to the Holy See, a serious weakening of the royal power, a disgrace to the English nation, a danger to all Christendom, since this civil war obstructs the crusade. Therefore…we condemn the charter and forbid the King to keep it, or the barons and their supporters to make him do so, on pain of excommunication.
1215 Papal Bull, 24 Aug.

Inouye, Daniel Ken 1924–2012
US politician, Democratic senator from Hawaii (1962–2012). He served on the committees investigating Watergate (1973–4) and (as chairman) the Iran-Contra affair (1987).

49 No times were more dangerous than when our country was born, when revolution was our midwife.
1987 Response to Adm John M Poindexter and Lt Col Oliver L North's contention that their actions were greatly influenced by 'a dangerous world'. In the *New York Times*, 24 Jul.

50 These hearings will be remembered longest not for the facts they elicited, but for the extraordinary and extraordinarily frightening views of government they exposed.
1987 On the Iran-Contra hearings. In the *New York Times*, 24 Jul.

51 A great nation betrayed the principles which have made it great, and thereby became hostage to hostage-takers.
1987 Of the Iran-Contra scandal. In the *New York Times*, 24 Jul.

Ionesco, Eugène 1912–94

French playwright. He pioneered a new style of drama that came to be called the Theatre of the Absurd.

52 *Un fonctionnaire ne plaisante pas.*
   A civil servant doesn't make jokes.
   1958 *Tueur sans gages*, act 1.

53 *C'est une chose anormale de vivre.*
   Living is abnormal.
   1959 *Rhinocéros*, act 1.

Irigaray, Luce 1930–

Belgian-born French feminist literary critic and philosopher who has applied Lacan's psychoanalytic writings to the question of the difference between women's and men's writing.

54 *Il faut renouveler le langage.*
   We must re-invent language.
   1981 *Corps-à-corps avec la mère*.

Irving, Washington 1783–1859

US essayist. Under the pseudonym 'Geoffrey Crayon' he wrote *The Sketch Book* (1819–20) which included 'Rip Van Winkle' and 'The Legend of Sleepy Hollow'. Several collections are devoted to his European travels, including *Tales of a Traveller* (1824). He was US Ambassador to Spain (1842–6).

55 What is history, in fact, but a kind of Newgate calendar, a register of the crimes and miseries that man has inflicted on his fellow-man?
   1809 *A History of New York*, bk.4, ch.1.

56 My native country was full of youthful promise; Europe was rich in the accumulated treasures of age.
   1819–20 *The Sketch Book*, 'The Author's Account of Himself'.

57 A tart temper never mellows with age, and a sharp tongue is the only edged tool that grows keener with constant use.
   1819–20 *The Sketch Book*, 'Rip Van Winkle'.

58 A woman's whole life is a history of the affections.
   1819–20 *The Sketch Book*, 'The Broken Heart'.

59 Whenever a man's friends begin to compliment him about looking young, he may be sure that they think he is growing old.
   1822 *Bracebridge Hall*, 'Bachelors'.

60 I am always at a loss to know how much to believe of my own stories.
   1824 *Tales of a Traveller*, 'To the Reader'.

61 There is a certain relief in change, even though it be from bad to worse... I have often found in travelling in a stage-coach, that it is often a comfort to shift one's position, and be bruised in a new place.
   1824 *Tales of a Traveller*, 'To the Reader'.

62 The almighty dollar, that great object of universal devotion throughout our land.
   1855 *Wolfert's Roost*, 'The Creole Village'.

Isaacs, Jorge 1837–95

Colombian novelist. He worked variously as a journalist, businessman, government official and consul to Chile. His much-imitated romantic novel *María* (1867) is notable for its idyllic descriptions of nature.

63 *Las grandes bellezas de la creación no pueden a un tiempo ser vistas y cantadas: es necesario que vuelvan al alma empalidecidas por la memoria infiel.*
   The most beautiful things on earth cannot be seen and sung at the same time: they must return to the soul weakened by unfaithful memory.
   1867 *María*, ch.2 (translated as *María: A South American Romance*, 1977).

Isaacson, Walter Seff 1952–

US journalist and writer. He has been the managing editor of *Time* magazine (1996–2001) and chairman and chief executive officer of CNN. His books include *Kissinger: A Biography* (1992), *Benjamin Franklin: An American Life* (2003) and *Steve Jobs* (2011).

64 He was something between an epitome and a parody.
   1992 On Harvard Professor William Elliott, Kissinger's mentor. *Kissinger: A Biography*.

65 No one could shine his shoes, much less fill them.
   1992 On President Nixon's self-image at the time of his resignation. *Kissinger: A Biography*.

66 The people who are crazy enough to think they can change the world are the ones who do.
   2011 *Steve Jobs*.

67 On the day he unveiled the Macintosh, a reporter from *Popular Science* asked Jobs what type of market research he had done. Jobs responded by scoffing, 'Did Alexander Graham Bell do any market research before he invented the telephone?'
   2011 *Steve Jobs*.

Isherwood, Christopher William Bradshaw 1904–86

English novelist. He collaborated with Auden in the 1930s. He moved to California in 1939, and became a US citizen in 1946.

68 I am a camera with its shutter open, quite passive, recording, not thinking... Some day, all this will have to be developed, carefully printed, fixed.
   1930 'A Berlin Diary', in *Goodbye to Berlin* (1939).

69 Like Shelley and like Baudelaire it may be said of him that he suffered, in his own person, the neurotic ills of an entire generation.
   1937 Of T E Lawrence, 'Lawrence of Arabia'. Collected in *Exhumations* (1966).

70 They share the insult of each other's presence.
   1962 On characters in his novels. *Down There on a Visit*.

Ishiguro, Kazuo 1954–

British novelist, born in Japan. His first book, *A Pale View of Hills* (1982), was set in Japan, but later works have been English in tone and subject, notably *The Remains of the Day* (1989, Booker Prize).

71 *An Artist of the Floating World.*
   1988 Title of novel.

72 A 'great' butler can only be, surely, one who can point to his years of service and say that he has applied his talents to serving a great gentleman—and through the latter, to serving humanity.
   1989 *The Remains of the Day*, 'Day Two— Afternoon'.

73 Perhaps it is indeed time that I began to look at this whole matter of bantering more enthusiastically. After all, when we think about it, it is not such a foolish thing

to indulge in—particularly if it is the case that in bantering lies the key to human warmth.
1989 *The Remains of the Day*, 'Day Six—Evening'.

74 It was like when you make a move in chess and just as you take your finger off the piece, you see the mistake you've made, and there's this panic because you don't know yet the scale of disaster you've left yourself open to.
2005 *Never Let Me Go*.

75 All children have to be deceived if they are to grow up without trauma.
2005 *Never Let Me Go*.

Issigonis, Sir Alec (Alexander Arnold Constantine) 1906–88

Turkish-born British car designer. He came to the English Midlands where he designed some of Britain's most popular and influential cars, including the Morris Minor and the Mini.

76 All creative people hate mathematics. It's the most uncreative subject you can study.
Recalled on his death. Quoted in *The Australian*, 5 Oct 1988.

77 Styling is designing for obsolescence.
Recalled on his death. Quoted in *The Australian*, 5 Oct 1988.

78 A camel is a horse designed by a committee.
Attributed to him in *The Guardian*, 14 Jan 1991.

Ito, Lance Allan 1950–

US jurist, presiding judge at the Los Angeles Superior Court (1989–). His most famous case is the O J Simpson murder trial (1994–5).

79 Rule 1: Be cautious, careful and when in doubt, keep your mouth shut. Rule 2: When tempted to say something, take a deep breath and refer to Rule 1.
1994 In the *New York Times*, 23 Jul.

Ivan IV known as Ivan the Terrible 1530–84

Grand Prince of Moscow (1533–84), the first to assume the title of 'tsar' (Latin *Caesar*). In 1564 he began a reign of terror, directed mainly at the aristocracy.

80 To shave the beard is a sin that the blood of all the martyrs cannot cleanse. It is to deface the image of man created by God.
Quoted in David Maland *Europe in the Seventeenth Century* (1968).

Iverson, Allen 1975–

US basketball player.

81 The basket looked like an ocean, and I was just throwing rocks in.
2003 After scoring 55 points for the Philadelphia 76ers against the New Orleans Hornets. Quoted on SI.com, 20 Apr.

Ives, Charles Edward 1874–1954

US composer. His innovative, experimental works were unappreciated for most of his life, but in 1947 he was awarded a Pulitzer Prize for his 3rd symphony (composed 1911).

82 Please don't try to make things nice! All the wrong notes are *right*... I want it that way.
c.1914 Note to the copyist of *The Fourth of July*.

Izzard, Eddie 1962–

British comedian and actor.

83 It's my manifest destiny to wear a skirt in all countries.
2001 Quoted on www.theonionavclub.com, 31 Jan.

84 Drama is a complete meal, vitamins, proteins, carbohydrates. It's a slow burn thing. It's got an arc. Comedy is more like coke.
2004 In *The Guardian*, 17 May.

Jackson, Jesse Louis 1941–

US clergyman and Democratic politician, founder and President of the Rainbow/PUSH (People United to Save Humanity) coalition. In 1984 and 1988 he sought nomination for the presidency, the first black American to be a serious candidate for the office.

1 I cast my bread on the waters long ago. Now it's time for you to send it back to me—toasted, and buttered on both sides.
1984 Addressing black voters, New York, 30 Jan.

2 My constituency is the desperate, the damned, the disinherited, the disrespected, and the despised.
1984 Speech at the Democratic National Convention, San Francisco, 17 Jul.

3 Our flag is red, white and blue, but our nation is a rainbow—red, yellow, brown, black and white—and we are all precious in God's sight... America is not like a blanket—one piece of unbroken cloth, the same color, the same texture, the same size. America is more like a quilt—many patches, many pieces, many colors, many sizes; all woven and held together by a common thread.
1984 Launching his 'rainbow coalition' at the Democratic National Convention, San Francisco, 17 Jul.

4 If I can conceive it and believe it, I can achieve it. It's not my *aptitude* but my *attitude* that will determine my *altitude*—with a little intestinal fortitude!
1988 *Ebony*, Aug.

5 He was born with little, inherited nothing and left a lot.
2007 Eulogy at the burial of soul singer James Brown in Augusta, Georgia.

Jackson, Peter 1961–

New Zealand film director, best known for directing the *Lord of the Rings* trilogy (2001–3) and *The Hobbit* trilogy (2012–14).

6 I read the book when I was 18 years old and thought 'I can't wait till the movie comes out'. Twenty years later no one had done it—so I got impatient.
2003 On how he came to direct the *Lord of the Rings*. Quoted in the *Observer*, 30 Nov.

Jackson, Robert Houghwout 1892–1954

US jurist, Associate Justice of the US Supreme Court (1941–54). He took leave to be US Chief Counsel at the Nuremberg war trials (1945–6). His decisions upheld freedom of speech and religion.

7 We are not final because we are infallible, but we are infallible only because we are final.
   1953 Ruling to uphold the Supreme Court as the bench of last appeal, 9 Feb.

8 He who must search a haystack for a needle is likely to end up with the attitude that the needle is not worth the search.
   1953 Ruling to uphold the Supreme Court as the bench of last appeal, 9 Feb.

Jacobs, Andrew, Jr 1932–2013
US lawyer and Democratic politician. He retired from Congress in 1997.

9 It's like saying that the patient died but the good news is that he's eating less.
   1982 Of the Reagan administration's claim to have reduced inflation. In the *Washington Post*, 6 Jun.

Jacobs, Herman
Pharmaceutical store supplier.

10 It is not the mouse who is the thief, it is the hole that allows the mouse in.
   1994 His interpretation of Talmudic principles applied in business. In *Forbes*, 21 Nov.

Jacobs, Joe 1896–1940
US boxing manager. He was manager of boxer Max Schmeling.

11 We wuz robbed!
   1932 After Schmeling's unexpected defeat by Jack Sharkey, 21 Jun. Quoted in Peter Heller *In This Corner* (1975). Jack Dempsey in 1927 claimed 'I was robbed of the championship' when he lost to Gene Tunney. The cry was subsequently widely adopted by aggrieved losers.

Jacobs, W(illiam) W(ymark) 1863–1943
English short-story writer. He specialized in colourful yarns about the watermen on the Thames, and macabre stories.

12 'Dealing with a man,' said the night-watchman, 'is as easy as a teetotaller walking along a nice wide pavement; dealing with a woman is like the same teetotaller, after four or five whiskies, trying to get up a step that ain't there.'
   1919 *Deep Waters*, 'Husbandry'.

Jagger, Sir Mick and Richards, Keith 1943–, 1943–
English rock musicians, who with Bill Wyman, Charlie Watts and Brian Jones formed The Rolling Stones (1961). Their rebellious image and controversial lifestyles added to the extraordinary success of their music.

13 I can't get no satisfaction
   I can't get no girl reaction.
   1966 '(I Can't Get No) Satisfaction'.

14 Mother needs something today to calm her down,
   And though she's not really ill,
   There's a little yellow pill:
   She goes running for the shelter
   Of a mother's little helper,
   And it helps her on her way,
   Gets her through her busy day.
   1966 'Mother's Little Helper'.

15 Please allow me to introduce myself
   I'm a man of wealth and taste.

I've been around for a long, long year
Stole many a man's soul and faith.
And I was around when Jesus Christ
Had his moments of doubt and pain,
Made damn sure that Pilate
Washed his hands and sealed his fate.
Pleased to meet you, hope you guess my name
But what's puzzling you
Is the nature of my game.
   1968 'Sympathy for the Devil'.

16 I shouted out, 'Who killed the Kennedys?'
   When after all it was you and me.
   1968 'Sympathy for the Devil'.

17 It's Only Rock and Roll.
   1974 Title of song.

James I 1394–1437
King of Scotland (from 1424). He was imprisoned by the English for 18 years before returning to Scotland to take the throne. His measures to curb the nobles' power led to his murder. *The Kingis Quair* (c.1435), his only surviving work, is thought to have introduced Chaucerian style to Scotland.

18 The bird, the beste, the fisch eke in the see,
   They lyve in fredome, euerich in his kynd,
   And I, a man, and lakkith libertee!
   c.1435 *The Kingis Quair*, stanza 27.

James IV 1473–1513
King of Scotland (from 1488). His marriage to Margaret Tudor, daughter of Henry VII of England, led ultimately to the union of the crowns. He was defeated and killed at Flodden.

19 It is statute and ordained that in na place of the Realme there be used Fute-ball, Golfe, or uther sik unproffitable sportes.
   1491 Royal decree.

James V 1512–42
King of Scotland (from 1513). He succeeded to the throne as an infant, amid quarrelling pro-French and pro-English factions. As an adult he ruled with a mixture of good judgement and vindictiveness, strengthening the Crown's power and revenues.

20 Adieu, Farewell, it came with a lass, it will pass with a lass.
   1542 Said on his deathbed, 14 Dec, on hearing of the birth of his daughter Mary, referring to the Crown of Scotland passing from the Stewarts. Quoted in Robert Lindsay of Pitscottie (c.1532–1580) *The Historie and Cronicles of Scotland* (published 1728), vol.1.

James, Alice 1848–92
US diarist, sister of Henry and William James. She spent her childhood travelling with her family in Europe. A semi-invalid for much of her life, she lived in England to be near her brother Henry. Her diary was published posthumously.

21 How heroic to be able to suppress one's vanity to the extent of confessing that the game is too hard.
   1889 On suicide. Diary entry, 5 Aug.

22 When will women begin to have the first glimmer that above all other loyalties is the loyalty to Truth, i.e., to yourself, that husband, children, friends and country are as nothing to that.
   1889 Diary entry, 19 Nov.

23 How sick one gets of being 'good', how much I should respect myself if I could burst out and make every one wretched for 24 hours.
1889 Diary entry, 11 Dec.

24 I suppose one has a greater sense of intellectual degradation after an interview with a doctor than from any human experience.
1890 Diary entry, 27 Sep.

James, Clive Vivian Leopold 1939–

Australian journalist, writer and broadcaster, famous as a witty and perceptive cultural commentator.

25 A country so precipitously convoluted that the rivers flowing through it look like the silver trails of inebriated slugs.
1978 'Postcard from Japan', in the *Observer* magazine, 4 Jun.

26 She sounded like the book of Revelations read out over a railway station public-address system by a headmistress of a certain age wearing calico knickers.
1979 Of Margaret Thatcher. In the *Observer*.

27 I feared for her as I loved her, and the fear intensified the love.
1997 On the death of Diana, Princess of Wales. In the *New Yorker*, 15 Sep.

28 When you say a man writes badly, you are trying to hurt him. When you say it in words better than his, you have succeeded.
2003 In the *New York Times*, 7 Sep.

29 A painter can leave you with nothing left to say. A writer leaves you with everything to say.
2007 *Cultural Amnesia: Necessary Memories from History and the Arts*.

30 Fiction is life with the dull bits left out.
Attributed.

31 A sense of humour is just common sense, dancing.
Attributed.

James, C(yril) L(ionel) R(obert) 1901–89

Trinidadian writer, lecturer and political activist. Arguing for the freedom of blacks through Marxism and revolution, he was deported from the US and placed under house arrest in Trinidad.

32 Body-line was not an incident, it was not an accident, it was not a temporary aberration. It was the violence and ferocity of our age expressing itself in cricket.
1963 *Beyond the Boundary*.

James, E. L. *pseudonym of* Erika Leonard 1963–

English novelist. Her erotic novel *Fifty Shades of Grey* (2011) became the UK's fastest selling paperback ever published and spawned two equally successful sequels.

33 At the end of the day, we want someone who is going to do the bloody dishes.
2012 Explaining what women really want in a man.

James, Henry 1843–1916

US-born British novelist, brother of William and Alice James. He took British citizenship in 1915. Many of his novels explore his 'international theme', including *The Ambassadors* (1903) and *The Golden Bowl* (1904). His critical theory is defined in 'The Art of Fiction' (1884).

34 It's a complex fate, being an American, and one of the responsibilities it entails is fighting against a superstitious valuation of Europe.
1872 Letter to Charles Eliot Norton, 4 Feb.

35 It takes a great deal of history to produce a little literature.
1879 *Hawthorne*, ch.1.

36 It is, I think, an indisputable fact that Americans are, as Americans, the most self-conscious people in the world, and the most addicted to the belief that the other nations of the earth are in a conspiracy to under value them.
1879 *Hawthorne*, ch.6.

37 Cats and monkeys—monkeys and cats—all human life is there!
1879 *The Madonna of the Future*, vol.1. The *News of the World* took 'All human life is there' as its slogan from the late 1950s.

38 There are few hours in life more agreeable than the hour dedicated to the ceremony known as afternoon tea.
1881 *The Portrait of a Lady*, ch.1.

39 An Englishman's never so natural as when he's holding his tongue.
1881 Isabel Archer. *The Portrait of a Lady*, ch.10.

40 Money's a horrid thing to follow, but a charming thing to meet.
1881 Gilbert Osmond. *The Portrait of a Lady*, ch.35.

41 Art derives a considerable part of its beneficial exercise from flying in the face of presumptions.
1884 'The Art of Fiction', collected in *Partial Portraits* (1988).

42 The only obligation to which in advance we may hold a novel, without incurring the accusation of being arbitrary, is that it be interesting.
1884 'The Art of Fiction', collected in *Partial Portraits* (1888).

43 Experience is never limited, and it is never complete; it is an immense sensibility, a kind of huge spider-web of the finest silken threads suspended in the chamber of consciousness, and catching every air-borne particle in its tissue.
1884 'The Art of Fiction', collected in *Partial Portraits* (1888).

44 Try to be one of the people on whom nothing is lost!
1884 'The Art of Fiction', collected in *Partial Portraits* (1888).

45 What is character but the determination of incident? What is incident but the illustration of character?
1884 'The Art of Fiction', collected in *Partial Portraits* (1888).

46 The superiority of one man's opinion over another's is never so great as when the opinion is about a woman.
1890 *The Tragic Muse*, ch.9.

47 We work in the dark—we do what we can—we give what we have. Our doubt is in our passion and our passion is our task. The rest is madness.
1893 Dencombe speaking of the artist. 'The Middle Years', in *Scribner's Magazine*, May.

48 The time-honored bread-sauce of the happy ending.
1894–5 *Theatricals, Second Series*, preface.

49 Most English talk is a quadrille in a sentry box.
1899 The Duchess. *The Awkward Age*, bk.5, ch.4.

50 People talk about the conscience, but it seems to me one must just bring it up to a certain point and leave it there. You can let your conscience alone if you're nice to the second housemaid.
1899 Nanda Brookenham. *The Awkward Age*, bk.6, ch.3.

51 Live all you can; it's a mistake not to. It doesn't so much matter what you do in particular, so long as you have your life. If you haven't had that what *have* you had?
   1903 Lambert Strether. *The Ambassadors*, bk.5, ch.11.

52 In art economy is always beauty.
   1909 Preface for revised NewYork edn of *The Altar of the Dead* (first published 1895).

53 The terrible *fluidity* of self-revelation.
   1909 Preface for revised NewYork edn of *The Ambassadors* (first published 1903).

54 I'm glad you like adverbs—I adore them; they are the only qualifications I really much respect.
   1912 Letter to Miss M Bentham Edwards, 5 Jan, quoted in Percy Lubbock (ed) *The Letters of Henry James* (1920).

55 Summer afternoon—summer afternoon; to me those have always been the two most beautiful words in the English language.
   Quoted in Edith Wharton *A Backward Glance* (1934), ch.10, section 6.

56 So here it is at last, the distinguished thing!
   Quoted in Edith Wharton *A Backward Glance* (1934), ch.14, section 3. According to Wharton, these were James's last words.

57 I hate American simplicity. I glory in the piling up of complications of every sort.
   Remark to his niece. Quoted in Leon Edel *The Letters of Henry James* (1953–72), vol.4, introduction.

James (of Holland Park), P(hyllis) D(orothy) James, Baroness 1920–2014

English writer. She specialized in carefully detailed crime fiction.

58 I thought that writing a detective story would be a wonderful apprenticeship because, whatever people tell you, a crime novel is not easy to write well. As I continued with my craft I became increasingly fascinated by the form and realized that you can use the formula to say something true about men and women and the society in which they live.
   1991 'Series Detectives', collected in Brown and Munro (eds) *Writers Writing* (1993).

59 Murder is a unique crime for which we can never make reparation.
   1991 'Series Detectives', collected in Brown and Munro (eds) *Writers Writing* (1993).

60 How odd that sex should be so simple and love such a complication.
   2005 *The Lighthouse*.

61 I don't think writers choose the genre, the genre chooses us. I wrote out of the wish to create order out of disorder, the liking of a pattern.
   2009 In *The Telegraph*, 26 Sep.

James, William 1842–1910

US philosopher and psychologist, brother of Henry and Alice James. A 'radical empiricist', he is often considered the founder of pragmatism. *The Principles of Psychology* (1890) places psychology on a physiological basis. Other works include *The Will to Believe* (1897) and *Pragmatism* (1907).

62 Man lives by science as well as bread.
   1875 *Vivisection*.

63 Metaphysics means nothing but an unusually obstinate effort to think clearly.
   1890 *The Principles of Psychology*, ch.6.

64 But facts are facts, and if we only get enough of them they are sure to combine.
   1890 *The Principles of Psychology*, ch.7.

65 The aim of science is always to reduce complexity to simplicity.
   1890 *The Principles of Psychology*, ch.9.

66 Consciousness, then, does not appear to itself chopped up in bits. Such words as 'chain' or 'train' do not describe it fitly as it presents itself in the first instance. It is nothing jointed; it flows. A 'river' or a 'stream' are the metaphors by which it is most naturally described. *In talking of it hereafter, let us call it the stream of thought, of consciousness, or of subjective life.*
   1890 *The Principles of Psychology*, ch.9. This is the coining of the phrase 'stream of consciousness', later applied to the narrative technique used by Joyce and others.

67 The baby, assailed by eyes, ears, nose, skin, and entrails at once, feels it all as one great blooming, buzzing confusion.
   1890 *The Principles of Psychology*, ch.13.

68 As the art of reading (after a certain stage in one's education) is the art of skipping, so the art of being wise is the art of knowing what to overlook.
   1890 *The Principles of Psychology*, ch.22.

69 Man is essentially *the* imitative animal. His whole educability and in fact the whole history of civilization depend on this trait, which his strong tendencies to rivalry, jealousy, and acquisitiveness reinforce.
   1890 *The Principles of Psychology*, ch.24.

70 If this life be not a real fight, in which something is eternally gained for the universe by success, it is no better than a game of private theatricals from which one may withdraw at will.
   1897 *The Will to Believe*.

71 Sobriety diminishes, discriminates, and says no; drunkenness expands, unites, and says yes.
   1902 *The Varieties of Religious Experience*, 'Mysticism'.

72 The philosophy which is so important in each of us is not a technical matter; it is our more or less dumb sense of what life honestly and deeply means… it is our individual way of just seeing and feeling the total push and pressure of the cosmos.
   1907 *Pragmatism*, lecture 1.

73 Tender-minded and tough-minded.
   1907 His terms for two kinds of philosophical temperament. *Pragmatism*, lecture 1.

74 You must bring out of each word its practical cash-value, set it at work within the stream of your experience.
   1907 *Pragmatism*, lecture 2.

75 First, you know, a new theory is attacked as absurd; then it is admitted to be true, but obvious and insignificant; finally it is seen to be so important that its adversaries claim that they themselves discovered it.
   1907 *Pragmatism*, lecture 6.

76 'The true' to put it very briefly, is only the expedient in the way of our thinking, just as 'the right' is only the expedient in the way of our behaving.
   1907 *Pragmatism*, lecture 6.

77 Many persons nowadays seem to think that any conclusion must be very scientific if the arguments in favor of it are derived from twitching of frogs' legs—especially if the frogs are decapitated—and that—on the other hand—any doctrine chiefly vouched for by the feelings of human beings–with heads on their shoulders—must be benighted and superstitious.
1907 *Pragmatism*.

78 Hogamus, higamous
Man is polygamous
Higamus, hogamous
Woman monogamous.
Quoted in the *Oxford Book of Marriage* (1990).

Janeway, Elizabeth Hall 1913–2005
US author and critic.

79 As long as mixed grills and combination salads are popular, anthologies will undoubtedly continue in favor.
Quoted in Helen Hull (ed) *The Writer's Book* (1950), ch.32.

Janowitz, Tama 1957–
US writer. She has written novels and short stories, and scored a cult success with the story collection *Slaves of New York* (1986).

80 Long after the bomb falls and you and your good deeds are gone, cockroaches will still be here, prowling the streets like armoured cars.
1986 *Slaves of New York*, 'Modern Saint 271'.

81 With publicity comes humiliation.
1992 In the *International Herald Tribune*, 8 Sep.

Jarrell, Randall 1914–65
US poet and critic. A passionate poet and incisive critic, he also wrote one satirical novel, *Pictures from an Institution* (1954), and children's books. He committed suicide.

82 I felt quite funny when Freud died. It was like having a continent disappear.
1939 Letter to Allen Tate, Sep.

83 Six miles from earth, loosed from its dream of life,
I woke to black flak and the nightmare fighters.
When I died they washed me out of the turret with a hose.
1945 'The Death of the Ball Turret Gunner'.

84 A good poet is someone who manages, in a lifetime of standing out in thunderstorms, to be struck by lightning five or six times; a dozen or two dozen times and he is great.
1953 *Poetry and the Age*, 'The Obscurity of the Poet'.

85 President Robbins was so well adjusted to his environment that sometimes you could not tell which was the environment and which was President Robbins.
1954 *Pictures from an Institution*, pt.1, ch.4.

86 To Americans, English manners are far more frightening than none at all.
1954 *Pictures from an Institution*, pt.1, ch.4.

87 She looked at me the way you'd look at a chessman if it made its own move.
1954 *Pictures from an Institution*, pt.2, ch.1.

88 It's better to entertain an idea than to take it home to live with you for the rest of your life.
1954 *Pictures from an Institution*, pt.4, ch.9.

89 You Americans do not rear children, you *incite* them; you give them food and shelter and applause.
1954 *Pictures from an Institution*, pt.4, ch.10.

90 Is an institution always a man's shadow shortened in the sun, the lowest common denominator of everybody in it?
1954 *Pictures from an Institution*, pt.5, ch.9.

91 One of the most obvious facts about grown-ups, to a child, is that they have forgotten what it is like to be a child.
Introduction to Christina Stead *The Man Who Loved Children* (1965).

Jarry, Alfred 1873–1907
French playwright and humorist, best known for the creation of the petty tyrant in *Ubu Roi* (1896), a play first written when he was only 15.

92 Quant à l'action, elle se passe en Pologne, c'est à dire, nulle part.
The action takes place in Poland; in other words, nowhere.
1896 *Ubu Roi*, introduction.

93 Mère Ubu, tu es bien laide aujourd'hui. Est-ce parce que nous avons du monde?
Mother Ubu, you are very ugly today. Is it because we have company?
1896 *Ubu Roi*, act 1, sc.1.

94 La mort n'est que pour les médiocres.
Death is only for the mediocre.
1898 *Gestes et opinions du Docteur Faustroll Pataphysicien*, vol.8, pt.37.

95 Dieu est le point tangent de zéro et de l'infini.
God is the tangential point of zero and the infinite.
1898 *Gestes et opinions du Docteur Faustroll Pataphysicien*, vol.8, pt.41.

96 S'apercevoir que sa mère est vierge.—Les 36 situations dramatiques; trente-septième situation.
The thirty-seventh dramatic situation out of 36: To become aware that one's mother is a virgin.
1899 *L'Amour absolu*, pt.3, épigraphe.

Jason, Sir David 1940–
English actor, known for a variety of television roles.

97 Why do they call me David 'Del Boy' Jason? You never hear anyone talking about Alec 'Bridge Over the River Kwai' Guinness.
On his ongoing association with his character in *Only Fools and Horses*. Quoted in Stafford Hildred and Tim Ewbank *Arise Sir David Jason* (2003).

Jaurès, (Auguste Marie Joseph) Jean 1859–1914
French socialist leader, writer and orator. He co-founded the socialist paper *L'Humanité* (1904), and was central in the founding of the French Socialist Party. He was assassinated in Paris.

98 There is, then, over the affairs of the army a universal conspiracy of silence, of childlike mysteries, of clannishness, routine and intrigue.
1910 *L'Armée nouvelle*.

Jay, Sir Antony Rupert 1930–
English writer and television producer. He joined the BBC in 1955, editing *Tonight* (1962–3) and co-writing the successful *Yes, Minister* and *Yes, Prime Minister* (1980–8). He was knighted in 1988.

99 From now on you can keep the lot.
Take every single thing you've got,
Your land, your wealth, your men, your dames,
Your dream of independent power,
And dear old Konrad Adenauer,
And stick them up your Eiffel Tower.
1963 On France's rejection of British membership of the Common Market, in *Time*, 8 Feb.

1 The great modern corporations are so similar to independent or semi-independent states of the past that they can only be fully understood in terms of political or constitutional history, and management can only be properly studied as a branch of government.
1967 *Management and Machiavelli*.

2 Efficiency…is measured at the extremities. You do not find the efficiency of an army at headquarters, nor of a firm in head office. It is at the remotest point—the private soldier or humble legionary on the distant frontier, the girl at the counter or the branch-office junior salesman —that the really decisive test of an army or a firm is made. It is there that all the instruction and knowledge of relevant facts and procedural disciplines bear fruit—or wither on the tree.
1967 *Management and Machiavelli*.

3 The bigger the organization, the fewer the jobs worth doing.
1967 *Management and Machiavelli*.

Jay (of Paddington), Margaret Jay, Baroness 1939–
English Labour peer, Leader of the House of Lords (1998–2001).

4 I never aim to be unpredictable.
2000 In the *Observer*, 'They Said What…?', 20 Feb.

Jay, Peter 1937–
English economist, broadcaster and diplomat, Ambassador to the US (1977–9), later economics editor at the BBC (1990–2001).

5 [Prince Charles] is entitled to be as underwhelmed by the prospect of reigning over a fourth-class nation as the rest of us are by the prospect of living in it.
1986 Of Prince Charles. In the *London Illustrated News*, Apr.

Jay-Z *pseudonym of* Shawn Corey Carter 1969–
US rap artist and record producer.

6 Rosa Parks sat so Martin Luther King could walk. Martin Luther King walked so Obama could run. Obama's running so we all can fly.
2008 T-shirt slogan attributed to Jay-Z in support of Barack Obama's bid for president.

7 Hip-hop is a perfect mix between poetry and boxing.
2010 *Decoded*.

8 We change people through conversation, not through censorship.
2010 *Decoded*.

9 I'm not a businessman, I'm a business, man!
Attributed.

Jeffers, (John) Robinson 1887–1962
US poet and dramatist. A number of his works drew on themes from biblical stories and Greek drama. His veneration of nature often went hand in hand with a contempt for the works of humanity.

10 While this America settles in the mould of its vulgarity, heavily
thickening to empire.
1924 *Tamar and Other Poems*, 'Shine, Perishing Republic'.

11 And boys, be in nothing so moderate as in love of man, a clever servant,
insufferable master.
1924 *Tamar and Other Poems*, 'Shine, Perishing Republic'.

12 The poet as well
Builds his monument mockingly;
For man will be blotted out, the blithe earth die, the brave sun
Die blind, his heart blackening:
Yet stones have stood for a thousand years, and pained thoughts found
The honey peace in old poems.
1924 *Tamar and Other Poems*, 'To the Stone-Cutters'.

13 The wing trails like a banner in defeat,
No more to use the sky forever but live with famine
And pain a few days.
1928 *Cawdor*, 'Hurt Hawks'.

14 He is strong and pain is worse to the strong, incapacity is worse.
1928 *Cawdor*, 'Hurt Hawks'.

15 The wild God of the world is sometimes merciful to those
That ask mercy, not often to the arrogant.
You do not know him, you communal people, or you have forgotten him;
Intemperate and savage, the hawk remembers him;
Beautiful and wild, the hawks, and men that are dying, remember him.
1928 *Cawdor*, 'Hurt Hawks'.

16 I'd sooner, except the penalties, kill a man than a hawk.
1928 *Cawdor*, 'Hurt Hawks'.

17 This wild swan of a world is no hunter's game.
Better bullets than yours would miss the white breast,
Better mirrors than yours would crack in the flame.
1935 *Solstice*, 'Love the Wild Swan'.

18 Praise life, it deserves praise, but the praise of life
That forgets the pain is a pebble
Ruttled in dry ground.
1948 *The Double Axe and Other Poems*.

Jefferson, Thomas 1743–1826
US statesman, third President (1801–9). Prominent in the first Continental Congress (1774), he drafted the Declaration of Independence. His administration saw war with Tripoli, the Louisiana Purchase (1803) and the prohibition of the slave trade.

19 We hold these truths to be sacred and undeniable; that all men are created equal and independent; that from that equal creation they derive rights inherent and inalienable, among which are the preservation of life, and liberty, and the pursuit of happiness.
c.1776 Draft of the American Declaration of Independence. Collected in J P Boyd et al *Papers of Thomas Jefferson* (1950), vol.1.

20 Were it left to me to decide whether we should have a government without newspapers, or newspapers without

a government, I should not hesitate a moment to prefer the latter.
1787 Letter to Col Edward Carrington, 16 Jan.

21 A little rebellion now and then is a good thing.
1787 Letter to James Madison, 30 Jan.

22 The tree of liberty must be refreshed from time to time with the blood of patriots and tyrants. It is its natural manure.
1787 Letter to W S Smith, 13 Nov.

23 A bill of rights is what the people are entitled to against every government on earth, general or particular, and what no just government should refuse or rest on inference.
1787 Letter to James Madison, 20 Dec.

24 I have seen enough of one war never to wish to see another.
1794 Letter to John Adams, 25 Apr.

25 I am for encouraging the progress of science in all its branches; and not for…awing the human mind by stories of raw-head and bloody bones to a distrust of its own vision and to repose implicitly on that of others.
1799 Letter, 26 Jan.

26 Equal and exact justice to all men…freedom of religion, freedom of the press, freedom of the person under the protection of the habeas corpus; and trial by juries impartially selected—these principles form the bright constellation that has gone before us.
1801 Inaugural address, 4 Mar.

27 When a man assumes a public trust, he should consider himself as public property.
1807 Letter to Baron von Humboldt.

28 Some men look at Constitutions with sanctimonious reverence and deem them like the Ark of the Covenant—too sacred to be touched.
1816 Letter to Samuel Kercheval, 12 Jul.

29 Games played with the ball, and others of that nature, are too violent for the body, and stamp no character on the mind.
Quoted in Colin Jarman *The Guinness Dictionary of Sports Quotations* (1990).

Jeffrey, Lord Francis 1773–1850
Scottish critic, lawyer and judge, founder of the *Edinburgh Review*.

30 This will never do.
1814 Of Wordsworth's *The Excursion* (1814). In the *Edinburgh Review*, Nov.

Jenkins, David Edward 1925–
English churchman, Bishop of Durham (1984–94). He became notorious for his radical and often controversial views.

31 A conjuring trick with bones only proves that it is as clever as a conjuring trick with bones… A resuscitated corpse might be a resuscitated corpse and might be the sign of something, but there is still the question of what it is the symbol of.
1984 Of the Christian doctrine of Christ's physical resurrection. 'Poles Apart', BBC radio broadcast, 4 Oct.

32 Christians are not called to win battles, but to find ways of being in battles.
1988 *Spirituality for Conflict*.

Jenkins (of Hillhead), Roy Harris Jenkins, Baron 1920–2003
Welsh Labour politician and author.

33 I have become increasingly convinced that great men have strong elements of comicality in them.
2001 *Churchill*.

Jensen, Albert D
US soldier, colonel in the air force.

34 We're going faster and lower than anything out there. And we can bomb the knot off a tree.
1987 On the capabilities of the B-1 bomber 10 years after its initial development. In the *New York Times*, 4 Jul.

Jerome, Jerome K(lapka) 1859–1927
English humorous novelist and playwright. He became joint editor of *The Idler* (1892) and started his own weekly, *To-Day*. He is best known for his classic *Three Men in a Boat* (1889).

35 It is impossible to enjoy idling thoroughly unless one has plenty of work to do.
1886 *Idle Thoughts of an Idle Fellow*, 'On Being Idle'.

36 Love is like the measles; we all have to go through it.
1886 *Idle Thoughts of an Idle Fellow*, 'On Being in Love'.

37 We drink one another's healths, and spoil our own.
1886 *Idle Thoughts of an Idle Fellow*, 'On Eating and Drinking'.

38 It is a most extraordinary thing, but I never read a patent medicine advertisement without being impelled to the conclusion that I am suffering from the particular disease therein dealt with in its most virulent form.
1889 *Three Men in a Boat*, ch.1.

39 But there, everything has its drawbacks, as the man said when his mother-in-law died, and they came down upon him for the funeral expenses.
1889 *Three Men in a Boat*, ch.3.

40 I like work: it fascinates me. I can sit and look at it for hours. I love to keep it by me: the idea of getting rid of it nearly breaks my heart.
1889 *Three Men in a Boat*, ch.15.

41 It is always the best policy to speak the truth—unless, of course, you are an exceptionally good liar.
1892 In *The Idler* (edited by Robert Barr and Jerome), Feb.

42 I want a house that has got over all its troubles; I don't want to spend the rest of my life bringing up a young and inexperienced house.
1909 *They and I*, ch.11.

43 I did not know I was a humorist. I have never been sure about it. In the middle ages, I should probably have gone about preaching and got myself burned or hanged.
1926 *My Life and Times*, ch.6.

Jerome, William 1865–1932
US songwriter.

44 Any Old Place I Can Hang My Hat Is Home Sweet Home to Me.
1901 Title of song.

Jerrold, Douglas William 1803–57
English author, dramatist and wit. His works include the play *Black-ey'd Susan* (1829), various comedies and a series of novels.

He wrote for *Punch* under the pseudonym 'Q' and edited several magazines.

45 Religion's in the heart, not in the knees.
1830 *The Devil's Ducat*, act 1, sc.2.

46 Earth is here so kind, that just tickle her with a hoe and she laughs with a harvest.
Of Australia. *The Wit and Opinions of Douglas Jerrold* (published 1859), 'A Land of Plenty'.

47 Love's like the measles—all the worse when it comes late in life.
The Wit and Opinions of Douglas Jerrold (published 1859), 'Love'.

48 The best thing I know between France and England is—the sea.
The Wit and Opinions of Douglas Jerrold (published 1859), 'The Anglo-French Alliance'.

49 If an earthquake were to engulf England tomorrow, the English would manage to meet and dine somewhere among the rubbish, just to celebrate the event.
Quoted in Blanchard Jerrold *The Life and Remains of Douglas Jerrold* (1859), ch.14.

50 The only athletic sport I mastered was backgammon.
Quoted in W Jerrold *Douglas Jerrold* (1914), vol.1, ch.1.

Jevons, William Stanley 1835–82

English economist, Professor of Political Economy at University College London (1876–81).

51 Economics, if it is to be a science at all, must be a mathematical science.
1871 *The Theory of Political Economy*.

52 The point of equilibrium will be known by the criterion that an infinitely small amount of commodity exchanged in addition, at the same rate, will bring neither gain nor loss of utility.
1871 *The Theory of Political Economy*.

53 Labour once spent has no influence on the future value of any article; it is gone and lost for ever. In commerce bygones are for ever bygones; and we are always starting clear at each moment, judging the values of things with a view to future utility.
1871 *The Theory of Political Economy*.

54 All classes of society are trade unionists at heart, and differ chiefly in the boldness, ability, and secrecy with which they pursue their respective interests.
1882 *The State in Relation to Labour*, introduction.

55 It is requisite from time to time to remind one generation of the experience which led a former generation to important legislative actions.
1882 *The State in Relation to Labour*.

Jiang Qing or Chiang Ch'ing 1914–91

Chinese politician, third wife of Mao Zedong. After Mao's death in 1976 she was arrested—as one of the 'gang of four'—and sentenced to death in 1980, later commuted to life imprisonment. She committed suicide.

56 Sex is engaging in the first rounds but what sustains interest in the long run is power.
c.1970 Quoted in Ross Merrill *Mao* (1993), ch.10.

57 Man's contribution to human history is nothing more than a drop of sperm.
1984 In *Newsweek*, 20 Feb.

58 Today the revolution has been stolen by the revisionist clique of Deng.
1991 Remark, May. Quoted in Ross Merrill *Mao* (1993), introduction.

St Joan of Arc 1412–31

French patriot and saint. As a 13-year-old peasant she heard saintly voices bidding her to free Paris from the English, and in 1429 she led troops into Orleans and successfully raised the siege. She was later sold to the English, who burned her as a witch.

59 And as for you, archers, soldiers, gentlemen, and all others who are besieging Orleans, depart in God's name to your own country… I assure you that wherever I find your people in France I shall fight them, and pursue them, and expel them from here, whether they will or not.
1429 Letter to the English at Poitiers, 22 Mar. Quoted in *Les Procès de Jeanne d' Arc* (translated by C Larrington), p.33.

60 *Si je n'y suis, Dieu m'y veuille mettre; et si j'y suis, Dieu m'y veuille tenir.*
If I am not in grace, may God set me there; and if I am, may God keep me there.
1431 Quoted in the record of her trial at Rouen, 24 Feb.

Jobs, Steve (Steven Paul) 1955–2011

US businessman and innovator, who co-founded Apple Inc. with Steve Wozniak in 1976. A leading pioneer in the development of personal computers, he introduced the influential Macintosh computer in 1984 and went on to bring to the market such immensely successful products as the iPod and iPad before his premature death from cancer.

61 It's more fun to be a pirate than to join the navy.
1982 Quoted in John A. Bryne, *Odyssey: Pepsi to Apple*, 1987.

62 But it's a disservice to constantly put things in this radical new light—that it's going to change everything. Things don't have to change the world to be important.
1996 In *Wired*, Feb.

63 We made the buttons on the screen look so good you'll want to lick them.
2000 Referring to the Mac OS X, in *Fortune*, 24 Jan.

64 Your work is going to fill a large part of your life, and the only way to be truly satisfied is to do what you believe is great work. And the only way to do great work is to love what you do. If you haven't found it yet, keep looking. Don't settle. As with all matters of the heart, you'll know when you find it. And, like any great relationship, it just gets better and better as the years roll on. So keep looking until you find it. Don't settle.
2005 Address to staff of Pixar Animation Studios, 12 Jun.

65 Your time is limited, so don't waste it living someone else's life.
2005 Address to graduating students at Stanford University, 12 Jun.

66 People laughed at us for using the word 'magical'. But you know what? It turned out to be magical.
2011 Referring to the newly introduced iPad, Mar.

67 Oh wow, oh wow, oh wow.
2011 Last words, 5 Oct.

Joel, Billy 1949–

US singer, pianist and songwriter.

68 The piano is a percussion instrument, like a drum. You don't strum a piano. You don't bow a piano. You

bang and strike a piano. You beat the shit out of a piano.
2004 *Rolling Stone*, 15 Apr.

Johansson, Scarlett 1984–
US film actress.

69 You work hard making independent films for fourteen years and you get voted best breasts.
2006 In *Esquire* magazine, Nov.

70 The secret to talking is listening.
2011 As Kelly Foster in *We Bought a Zoo* (screenplay by Aline Brosh McKenna and Cameron Crowe).

71 The first rule when going on the run is, 'Don't run, walk'.
2014 As Natasha Romanoff/Black Widow in *Captain America: The Winter Soldier* (screenplay by Christopher Markus and Stephen McFeely).

Pope John XXIII originally Angelo Giuseppe Roncalli 1881–1963
Italian prelate, Pope (1958–63). He convened the 21st Ecumenical Council and in 1963 issued the encyclical *Pacem in Terris* ('Peace on Earth'), advocating reconciliation between East and West.

72 In order to imbue civilization with sound principles and enliven it with the spirit of the gospel, it is not enough to be illumined with the gift of faith and enkindled with the desire of forwarding a good cause. For this end it is necessary to take an active part in the various organizations and influence them from within. And since our present age is one of outstanding scientific and technical progress and excellence, one will not be able to enter these organizations and work effectively from within unless he is scientifically competent, technically capable and skilled in the practice of his own profession.
1963 *Pacem in Terris*, 10 Apr.

73 If civil authorities legislate for or allow anything that is contrary to that order and therefore contrary to the will of God, neither the laws made or the authorizations granted can be binding on the consciences of the citizens, since God has more right to be obeyed than man.
1963 *Pacem in Terris*, 10 Apr.

74 The social progress, order, security and peace of each country are necessarily connected with the social progress, order, security and peace of all other countries.
1963 *Pacem in Terris*, 10 Apr.

St John of the Cross originally Juan de Yepes y Álvarez 1542–91
Spanish Christian mystic, founder of the Order of Discalced Carmelites.

75 God passes through the thicket of the world, and wherever his glance falls he turns all things to beauty.
Cántico espiritual (translated by K Kavanaugh and O Rodriguez as *The Spiritual Canticle*).

John III Sobieski of Poland 1624–96
King of Poland (from 1674), elected after a distinguished military career. He formed the Holy League alliance with Pope Innocent XI and the Holy Roman Emperor, Leopold I, in 1688, campaigning against the Turks.

76 I came, I saw, God conquered.
1683 Message sent to the Pope after the defeat of the Turks at the Battle of Vienna, 12 Sep.
▶ See Caesar 192:14, Charles V 215:36.

Pope John Paul II originally Karol Jozef Wojtyła 1920–2005
Polish priest and theologian. He became Archbishop and Metropolitan of Cracow in 1964, was elected Cardinal (1967) and then Pope (1978), the first non-Italian pope in 456 years.

77 It is unbecoming for a cardinal to ski badly.
c.1968 Attributed, responding to criticism that it was unbecoming for him, then a cardinal, to be seen skiing.

78 The command 'Thou shalt not kill' must be binding on the conscience of humanity if the terrible tragedy and destiny of Cain is not to be repeated.
1979 Speech at Drogheda, Ireland, 29 Sep.

79 Violence is a lie, for it goes against the truth of our faith, the truth of our humanity… Violence is a crime against humanity, for it destroys the very fabric of society. On my knees I beg you to turn away from the paths of violence.
1979 Speech at Drogheda, Ireland, 29 Sep.

80 Commitment to the poor is based on the Gospel: it does not have to rely on some political manifesto.
1979 Speech at the Third Conference of Latin American Bishops, Puebla.

81 A process of genocide is being carried out before the eyes of the world.
1989 Of the situation in Beirut. In *The Independent*, 16 Aug.

John, Sir Elton Hercules originally Reginald Kenneth Dwight 1947–
English pop singer, songwriter and pianist. In a prolific career his albums have included *Tumbleweed Connection* (1970), *Don't Shoot Me I'm Only the Piano Player* (1973), *A Single Man* (1978), *Too Low for Zero* (1983), *Sleeping with the Past* (1989) and *Made in England* (1995).

82 Goodbye England's Rose;
May you ever grow in our hearts.
1997 From 'Candle in the Wind', sung at the funeral of Diana, Princess of Wales, co-written with Bernie Taupin. The song was a reworking of an earlier song to Marilyn Monroe.

83 I'm not a nest-egg person.
2000 On how he manages to spend £2m a month. In *The Guardian*, 31 Dec.

84 I think Jesus was a compassionate, super-intelligent gay man who understood human problems.
2010 In *Parade* magazine, 21 Feb.

John, Gwen 1876–1939
Welsh painter, sister of Augustus John. From 1904 she worked in Paris as an artist's model, becoming Rodin's mistress. She converted to Roman Catholicism in 1913 and became increasingly reclusive.

85 My religion and my art—they are all my life.
Quoted in K Petersen and J J Wilson *Women Artists* (1979).

Johns, Jasper 1930–
US painter and sculptor, a pioneer of Pop Art in the US. He challenged the relationship between art and reality, painting ordinary objects in a deliberately banal style (eg *Flag*, 1954).

86 Things that are seen but not looked at.
1988 Defining the subject of his art. Quoted by Deborah Solomon in 'The Unflagging Artistry of Jasper Johns', in the *New York Times*, 19 Jun.

87 To be an artist you have to give up everything, including the desire to be a good artist.
2008 Quoted in photographic exhibition 'Cy Twombley', Huis Marseille Museum for Photography, Amsterdam.

Johnson, Ben 1961–
Jamaican-born Canadian sprinter.

88 I have never, ever knowingly taken illegal drugs, and I would never embarrass my family, my friends, my country, and the kids who love me.
1988 Statement at press conference, Toronto, 4 Oct. Johnson tested positive to the use of banned substances, was stripped of his Olympic gold medal, and subsequently admitted using anabolic steroids.

Johnson, Boris 1964–
English journalist and Conservative politician. He was editor of *The Spectator* (1999–2005), MP for Henley (2001–08) and Mayor of London (2008–). He is noted for his flamboyant public persona.

89 The Lib Dems are not just empty. They are a void within a vacuum surrounded by a vast inanition.
2003 Describing the Liberal Democrats party.

90 My chances of being PM are about as good as the chances of finding Elvis on Mars, or my being reincarnated as an olive.
2004 In the *Observer*, 20 Jun.

91 Voting Tory will cause your wife to have bigger breasts and increase your chances of owning a BMW M3.
2005 Speaking during the general election, Apr.

92 Life isn't like coursework, baby. It's one damn essay crisis after another.
2005 In *The Daily Telegraph*, 12 May.

93 I think I was once offered cocaine but I sneezed so it didn't go up my nose. In fact, it may have been icing sugar.
2005 In the *Evening Standard*, 17 Oct.

94 All politicians are like crazed wasps in a jam jar, each individually convinced that they are going to make it.
2005 On *Desert Island Discs*, BBC radio, 30 Oct.

95 I'm down with the ethnics. You can't out-ethnic me. My children are a quarter Indian, so put that in your pipe and smoke it.
2008 On BBC radio's Asian Network, 17 Apr.

96 Unlike the current occupant of the White House, he has no difficulty in orally extemporising a series of grammatical English sentences, each containing a main verb.
2008 Speaking in support of Barack Obama, in *The Daily Telegraph*, 21 Oct 21.

97 He is like some sherry-crazed old dowager who has lost the family silver at roulette, and who now decides to double up by betting the house as well.
2008 Describing Prime Minister Gordon Brown, quoted on *Mail Online*, 25 Nov.

98 In 1904, twenty per cent of journeys were made by bicycle in London. I want to see a figure like that again. If you can't turn the clock back to 1904, what's the point of being a Conservative?
2010 Speaking at the launch of Barclays Cycle Hire, 30 Jul.

99 There are semi-naked women playing beach volleyball in the middle of the Horse Guards Parade immortalised by Canaletto. They are glistening like wet otters and the water is plashing off the brims of the spectators' sou'westers.
2012 Describing the beach volleyball event during the London Olympic Games, in *The Telegraph*, 30 Jul.

Johnson, Claudia Alta Taylor known as Lady Bird 1912–2007
US First Lady (1963–9), the widow of President Lyndon B Johnson. She was active in conservation and improvement programmes. After the presidency she published *A White House Diary* (1970).

1 We had a delicious dinner of too much.
1970 On dining at Manhattan's Plaza Hotel. *A White House Diary*.

2 Somehow that was one of the most poignant sights —that immaculate woman, exquisitely dressed, and caked in blood.
1970 On Jacqueline Kennedy after her husband's assassination. *A White House Diary*.

3 I face the prospect of another campaign like an open-ended stay in a concentration camp.
1970 *A White House Diary*.

4 Mrs Kennedy is going to marry Aristotle Socrates Onassis!… I feel strangely freer! No shadow walks behind me down the halls of the White House.
1970 *A White House Diary*.

5 We were distant. But that suited both of us.
1995 On her relationship with Jacqueline Kennedy Onassis. In the *Washington Post*, 23 Mar.

6 This country needs to be united. And sadly, sadly, he wasn't the man who could do it.
1995 On Lyndon B Johnson's decision not to seek a second term during the Vietnam War. In the *Washington Post*, 23 Mar.

Johnson, Earvin ('Magic') 1959–
US basketball player. He played with the Los Angeles Lakers (1979–91, 1996) and was a member of the gold medal-winning US Olympic basketball team ('Dream Team') in 1992.

7 We've dominated sports and we've dominated entertainment, but our problem has been we've never been able to dominate money. We still don't own our share of business, and it's killing us. It's killing our communities.
2003 On African Americans. Quoted in *Los Angeles Magazine*, Oct.

Johnson, Hiram Warren 1866–1945
US politician. He entered the Senate from California (1917–45) and as a founder of the Progressive Party was Theodore Roosevelt's running mate in his unsuccessful 1912 campaign. He outspokenly opposed the League of Nations.

8 The first casualty when war comes is truth.
1917 Speech, US Senate.

Johnson, Lindley
US scientist, a member of NASA's Near Earth Object Observation Program.

9 It is as likely to happen next week as in a randomly selected week a thousand years from now.
2004 Report to the US Senate on the probability of an object hitting the earth.

Johnson, Lyndon B(aines) *also called LBJ* 1908–73

US politician, 36th President (1963–9). He came to power after Kennedy's assassination, and was returned with a huge majority in 1964. He presided over the Civil Rights Act (1964) and the Voting Rights Act (1965), but the Vietnam War made him unpopular.

10 I am a free man, an American, a United States Senator, and a Democrat, in that order.
1958 *Texas Quarterly*, winter issue.

11 I want to be progressive without getting both feet off the ground at the same time...a progressive who is prudent.
1964 Interview, 16 Mar.

12 You let a bully come into your front yard, and the next day he'll be on your porch.
1964 In *Time*, Apr.

13 We are not about to send American boys 9,000 or 10,000 miles away from home to do what Asian boys ought to be doing for themselves.
1964 On the war in Vietnam. Speech at Akron University, 21 Oct.

14 Better to have him inside the tent pissing out, than outside pissing in.
Of J Edgar Hoover. Quoted in David Halberstam *The Best and the Brightest* (1971), ch.20.

15 I want loyalty. I want him to kiss my ass in Macy's window at high noon and tell me it smells like roses. I want his pecker in my pocket.
Of a potential assistant. Quoted in David Halberstam *The Best and the Brightest* (1971), ch.20.

16 So dumb he can't fart and chew gum at the same time.
Of Gerald Ford. Quoted in Richard Reeves *A Ford, Not a Lincoln*. (1975), ch.2.

17 Let's press the flesh.
Of shaking voters' hands. Quoted in Alistair Cooke *The Americans* (1980).

18 I want every family in America to have a carpet on the floor and a picture on the wall. After bread, you've got to have a picture on the wall.
On visiting Pittsburgh's Polish–Czech area. Quoted in Alistair Cooke *The Americans* (1980).

19 I don't believe I'll ever get credit for anything I do in foreign affairs, no matter how successful it is, because I didn't go to Harvard.
To columnist Hugh Sidey. Quoted in Alistair Cooke *The Americans* (1980).

20 I can teach it round or flat.
When asked by a school board about the shape of the earth. Quoted in Tom Wicker *One of Us* (1991).

Johnson, Michael 1967–

US track athlete. At the 1996 Olympics in Atlanta he won gold medals in both the 200-metre and 400-metre events, the first man ever to do so.

21 Pressure is nothing more than the shadow of great opportunity.
Attributed.

Johnson, Paul 1928–

English author.

22 Hell is being trapped in a night-club with the 'beautiful people' and forced to live in a 'luxury penthouse flat'.
1996 *To Hell With Picasso, and Other Essays*.

23 If we want foxes, to observe and delight in, we must have hunting.
1996 *To Hell With Picasso, and Other Essays*.

Johnson, Pauline 1861–1913

Native Canadian poet and patriot.

24 The Dutch may have their Holland, the Spaniard have his Spain,
The Yankee to the south of us must south of us remain;
For not a man dare lift a hand against the men who brag
That they were born in Canada beneath the British flag.
1903 'Canadian Born', collected in *Flint and Feather* (1912).

Johnson, Philander Chase 1866–1939

US journalist.

25 Cheer up—the worst is yet to come.
1920 In *Everybody's Magazine*, May.

Johnson, Philip Cortelyou 1906–2005

US architect, best known for his book *The International Style* (1932). His designs include the Lincoln Center (1964) and the American Telephone and Telegraph Headquarters Building (1978) in New York City.

26 American megalomania is largely responsible for the growth of the Skyscraper School.
1931 'The Skyscraper School of Modern Architecture', in *Arts*, X VII (May). Collected in *Writings* (1979).

27 They say a building is good architecture if it works. Of course, this is poppycock. All buildings work... You expect any architect, a graduate of Harvard or not, to be able to put the kitchen in the right place.
1954 'The Seven Crutches of Architecture', informal talk to students, School of Architectural Design, Harvard University, 7 Dec. Published in *Perspecta 3* (1955).

28 It's got to be clear, back in your own mind, that serving the client is one thing and the art of architecture another.
1954 'The Seven Crutches of Architecture', informal talk to students, School of Architectural Design, Harvard University, 7 Dec. Published in *Perspecta 3* (1955).

29 Surely architecture is the organization for pleasure of enclosed space. And what more magnificent enclosure than a town, a *place*, a place where the spirit is cuddled, made serene, made proud, happy, or excited depending on the ceremony, the day, the hour.
1954 'The Seven Crutches of Architecture', informal talk to students, School of Architectural Design, Harvard University, 7 Dec. Published in *Perspecta 3* (1955).

30 You can't learn architecture any more than you can learn a sense of music or of painting. You shouldn't talk about art, you should do it.
1954 'The Seven Crutches of Architecture', informal talk to students, School of Architectural Design, Harvard University, 7 Dec. Published in *Perspecta 3* (1955).

31 The automobile is the greatest catastrophe in the entire history of City architecture.
1955 'The Town and the Automobile or the Pride of Elm Street', published in *Writings* (1979).

32 The delicate operation of separating an American from the four-wheeled part of him has to be performed with tact.
1955 'The Town and the Automobile or the Pride of Elm Street', published in *Writings* (1979).

33 Some of the opera houses in Italy had to be burnt down because people could *neither* see nor hear. They gave up seeing years ago, but they did enjoy the music.
   1960 Informal talk, Architectural Association School of Architecture, 28 Nov. Collected in *Writings* (1979).

34 Architecture is the art of how to waste space.
   1964 In the *New York Times*, 27 Dec.

35 I'm about four skyscrapers behind.
   Excusing himself from a dinner party. Quoted in the *Wall Street Journal*, 20 Jun 1984.

Johnson, Samuel known as Dr Johnson 1709–84

English lexicographer, critic, poet and conversationalist, best known for his *A Dictionary of the English Language* (1755) and an edition of Shakespeare (1765). In 1773 he toured Scotland with James Boswell, and wrote *A Journey to the Western Isles of Scotland* (1775). Other works include *Rasselas* (1759) and *Lives of the English Poets* (1779–81).

36 Sir, we are a nest of singing birds.
   1730 Of Pembroke College, Oxford. Quoted in James Boswell *The Life of Samuel Johnson* (1791), vol.1.

37 It is incident to physicians, I am afraid, beyond all other men, to mistake subsequence for consequence.
   1734 Review of Dr Lucas's *Essay on Waters*, 25 Nov.

38 It is not easy to forbear reflecting with how little reason these men profess themselves the followers of Jesus, who left this great characteristic to his disciples, that they should be known by loving one another, by universal and unbounded charity and benevolence.
   1735 Of the Jesuit missionaries in Abyssinia. Johnson's preface to Fr J de Lobo's *Voyage to Abyssinia*.

39 Unmoved though witlings sneer and rivals rail;
   Studious to please, yet not ashamed to fail.
   c.1737 *Irene*, prologue (first produced 1749).

40 A thousand horrid Prodigies foretold it.
   A feeble government, eluded Laws,
   A factious Populace, luxurious Nobles,
   And all the maladies of stinking states.
   c.1737 *Irene*, act 1, sc.1 (first produced 1749).

41 There Poetry shall tune her sacred voice,
   And wake from ignorance the Western World.
   c.1737 *Irene*, act 4, sc.1 (first produced 1749).

42 For who would leave, unbrib'd, *Hibernia's* Land,
   Or change the rocks of *Scotland* for the *Strand*?
   1738 *London: a Poem*, l.9–10.

43 By numbers here from shame or censure free,
   All crimes are safe, but hated poverty.
   This, only this, the rigid law pursues,
   This, only this, provokes the snarling muse.
   1738 *London: a Poem*, l.158–61.

44 The stage but echoes back the public voice.
   The drama's laws the drama's patrons give,
   For we, who live to please, must please to live.
   1747 Prologue, written for David Garrick on the occasion of the opening of his management of the Theatre Royal, Drury Lane.

45 Let observation with extensive view,
   Survey mankind, from China to Peru.
   1749 *The Vanity of Human Wishes*, l.1–2.

46 Yet hope not life from grief or danger free,
   Nor think the doom of man reversed for thee:
   Deign on the passing world to turn thine eyes,
   And pause awhile from letters, to be wise;
   There mark what ills the scholar's life assail,
   Toil, envy, want, the patron and the jail.
   1749 *The Vanity of Human Wishes*, l.155–60.

47 Enlarge my life with multitude of days,
   In health, in sickness, thus the suppliant prays;
   Hides from himself his state, and shuns to know,
   That life protracted is protracted woe.
   Time hovers o'er, impatient to destroy,
   And shuts up all the passages of joy.
   1749 *The Vanity of Human Wishes*, l.255–60.

48 Must helpless man, in ignorance sedate,
   Roll darkling down the torrent of his fate?
   1749 *The Vanity of Human Wishes*, l.345–6.

49 Still raise for good the supplicating voice,
   But leave to heaven the measure and the choice.
   1749 *The Vanity of Human Wishes*, l.351–2.

50 A man may write at any time, if he will set himself doggedly to it.
   1750 Comment, Mar. Quoted in James Boswell *The Life of Samuel Johnson* (1791), vol.1.

51 I'll come no more behind your scenes, David: for the silk stockings and white bosoms of your actresses excite my amorous propensities.
   1750 In conversation with the actor-manager David Garrick. Quoted in James Boswell *The Life of Samuel Johnson* (1791), vol.1.

52 There are minds so impatient of inferiority, that their gratitude is a species of revenge, and they return benefits, not because recompense is a pleasure, but because obligation is a pain.
   1750–2 In *The Rambler*.

53 No place affords a more striking conviction of the vanity of human hopes, than a public library.
   1750–2 In *The Rambler*.

54 Wit, you know, is the unexpected copulation of ideas, the discovery of some occult relation between images in appearance remote from each other.
   1750–2 In *The Rambler*.

55 Almost every man wastes part of his life in attempts to display qualities which he does not possess, and to gain applause which he cannot keep.
   1750–2 In *The Rambler*.

56 The love of life is necessary to the vigorous prosecution of any undertaking.
   1750–2 In *The Rambler*.

57 I have laboured to refine our language to grammatical purity, and to clear it from colloquial barbarisms, licentious idioms, and irregular combinations.
   1750–2 In *The Rambler*.

58 A fly, Sir, may sting a stately horse and make him wince; but one is but an insect, and the other is a horse still.
   1754 Of Edwards's criticism of Thomas Warburton. Quoted in James Boswell *The Life of Samuel Johnson* (1791), vol.1.

59 They teach the morals of a whore, and the manners of a dancing master.
   1754 Of Lord Chesterfield's letters. Quoted in James Boswell *The Life of Samuel Johnson* (1791), vol.1.

60 This man I thought had been a Lord among wits; but, I find, he is only a wit among Lords.
   1754 Of Lord Chesterfield. Quoted in James Boswell *The Life of Samuel Johnson* (1791), vol.1.

61 Ignorance, madam, pure ignorance.
1755 Reply to a lady who had asked why he had defined *pastern* as the 'knee' of a horse. Quoted in James Boswell *The Life of Samuel Johnson* (1791), vol.1.

62 I had done all I could; and no man is well pleased to have his all neglected, be it ever so little.
1755 Letter to Lord Chesterfield, 7 Feb. Quoted in James Boswell *The Life of Samuel Johnson* (1791), vol.1.

63 Is not a Patron, my lord, one who looks with unconcern on a man struggling for life in the water, and, when he has reached ground, encumbers him with help? The notice which you have been pleased to take of my labours, had it been early, had been kind; but it has been delayed till I am indifferent, and cannot enjoy it; till I am solitary, and cannot impart it; till I am known, and do not want it.
1755 Letter to Lord Chesterfield, 7 Feb. Quoted in James Boswell *The Life of Samuel Johnson* (1791), vol.1.

64 There are two things which I am confident I can do very well: one is an introduction to a literary work, stating what it is to contain, and how it should be executed in the most perfect manner; the other is a conclusion, shewing from various causes why the execution has not been equal to what the author promised to himself and to the public.
1755 Quoted in James Boswell *The Life of Samuel Johnson* (1791), vol.1.

65 If a man does not make new acquaintance as he advances through life, he will soon find himself left alone. A man, Sir, should keep his friendship in constant repair.
1755 Quoted in James Boswell *The Life of Samuel Johnson* (1791), vol.1.

66 Change is not made without inconvenience, even from worse to better.
1755 A Dictionary of the English Language, preface.

67 It is the fate of those who toil at the lower employments of life...to be exposed to censure, without hope of praise; to be disgraced by miscarriage or punished for neglect... Among these unhappy mortals is the writer of dictionaries... Every other author may aspire to praise; the lexicographer can only hope to escape reproach.
1755 A Dictionary of the English Language, preface.

68 I am not yet so lost in lexicography as to forget that words are the daughters of earth, and that things are the sons of heaven. Language is only the instrument of science, and words are but the signs of ideas: I wish, however, that the instrument might be less apt to decay, and that signs might be permanent, like the things which they denote.
1755 A Dictionary of the English Language, preface.

69 I have protracted my work till most of those whom I wished to please have sunk into the grave; and success and miscarriage are empty sounds.
1755 A Dictionary of the English Language, preface.

70 Every quotation contributes something to the stability or enlargement of the language.
1755 A Dictionary of the English Language, preface.

71 But these were the dreams of a poet doomed at last to wake a lexicographer.
1755 A Dictionary of the English Language, preface.

72 If the changes we fear be thus irresistible, what remains but to acquiesce with silence, as in the other insurmountable distresses of humanity? It remains that we retard what we cannot repel, that we palliate what we cannot cure.
1755 A Dictionary of the English Language, preface.

73 *Dull*. To make dictionaries is dull work.
1755 A Dictionary of the English Language.

74 *Excise*. A hateful tax levied upon commodities.
1755 A Dictionary of the English Language.

75 *Lexicographer*. A writer of dictionaries, a harmless drudge.
1755 A Dictionary of the English Language.

76 *Net*. Anything reticulated or decussated at equal distances, with interstices between the intersections.
1755 A Dictionary of the English Language.

77 *Oats*. A grain, which in England is generally given to horses, but in Scotland supports the people.
1755 A Dictionary of the English Language.

78 *Patron*. Commonly a wretch who supports with insolence, and is paid with flattery.
1755 A Dictionary of the English Language.

79 *Pension*. Pay given to state hireling for treason to his country.
1755 A Dictionary of the English Language.

80 The only end of writing is to enable the readers better to enjoy life, or better to endure it.
1757 Reviewing Soame Jenyns *A Free Inquiry into the Nature and Origin of Evil*, in the *Literary Magazine*, Apr–Jul.

81 To us, who are regaled every morning and evening with intelligence, and are supplied from day to day with materials for conversation, it is difficult to conceive how man can subsist without a newspaper.
1758 In *The Idler*, no.7, 27 May.

82 When two Englishmen meet, their first talk is of the weather.
1758 In *The Idler*, no.11, 24 Jun.

83 To these compositions is required neither genius nor knowledge, neither industry nor spriteliness, but contempt of shame, and indifference to truth are absolutely necessary.
1758 Of journalistic reporting. In *The Idler*, no.31, 11 Nov.

84 Among the calamities of War may be justly numbered the diminution of the love of truth, by the falsehoods which interest dictates and credulity encourages.
1758 In *The Idler*, no.31, 11 Nov.

85 Nothing is more hopeless than a scheme of merriment.
1759 In *The Idler*, no.58, 26 May.

86 The Europeans have scarcely visited any coast, but to gratify avarice, and extend corruption; to arrogate dominion without right, and practice cruelty without incentive... But there is reason to hope...that the light of the gospel will at last illuminate the sands of Africa, and the deserts of America, though its progress cannot but be slow when it is so much obstructed by the lives of Christians.
1759 Introduction to *The World Displayed*.

87 Marriage has many pains, but celibacy has no pleasures.
1759 Rasselas, ch.26.

88 No man will be a sailor who has contrivance enough to get himself into jail; for being in a ship is being in a jail, with the chance of being drowned... A man in a jail has

more room, better food, and commonly better company.
1759 Remark, 16 Mar. Quoted in James Boswell *The Life of Samuel Johnson* (1791), vol.1.

89 Liberty is, to the lowest rank of every nation, little more than the choice of working or starving.
1760 'The Bravery of the English Common Soldier', in *The British Magazine*, Jan.

90 The notion of liberty amuses the people of England, and helps to keep off the taedium vitae. When a butcher tells you that his heart bleeds for his country he has, in fact, no uneasy feeling.
1763 Remark, 16 May. Quoted in James Boswell *The Life of Samuel Johnson* (1791), vol.1.

91 Yes, Sir, many men, many women, and many children.
1763 Remark, 16 May, on being asked if any man of a modern age could have written *Ossian*. Quoted in James Boswell *The Life of Samuel Johnson* (1791), vol.1.

92 The noblest prospect which a Scotchman ever sees, is the high road that leads him to England!
1763 Remark, 6 Jul. Quoted in James Boswell *The Life of Samuel Johnson* (1791), vol.1.

93 A man ought to read just as inclination leads him; for what he reads as a task will do him little good.
1763 Remark, 14 Jul. Quoted in James Boswell *The Life of Samuel Johnson* (1791), vol.1.

94 But if he does really think that there is no distinction between virtue and vice, why, Sir, when he leaves our houses, let us count our spoons.
1763 Remark, 14 Jul. Quoted in James Boswell *The Life of Samuel Johnson* (1791), vol.1.

95 A man with a good coat upon his back meets with a better reception than he who has a bad one.
1763 Remark, 20 Jul. Quoted in James Boswell *The Life of Samuel Johnson* (1791), vol.1.

96 All the arguments which are brought to represent poverty as no evil, show it to be evidently a great evil. You never find people labouring to convince you that you may live very happily upon a plentiful fortune.
1763 Remark, 20 Jul. Quoted in James Boswell *The Life of Samuel Johnson* (1791), vol.1.

97 Truth, Sir, is a cow, that will yield such people no more milk, and so they are gone to milk the bull.
1763 Of sceptics. Remark, 21 Jul. Quoted in James Boswell *The Life of Samuel Johnson* (1791), vol.1.

98 Young men have more virtue than old men; they have more generous sentiments in every respect.
1763 Remark, 21 Jul. Quoted in James Boswell *The Life of Samuel Johnson* (1791), vol.1.

99 In my early years I read very hard. It is a sad reflection, but a true one, that I knew almost as much at eighteen as I do now.
1763 Remark, 21 Jul. Quoted in James Boswell *The Life of Samuel Johnson* (1791), vol.1.

1 Your levellers wish to level down as far as themselves; but they cannot bear levelling up to themselves.
1763 Remark, 21 Jul. Quoted in James Boswell *The Life of Samuel Johnson* (1791), vol.1.

2 It is burning a farthing candle at Dover, to shew light at Calais.
1763 Summarizing the influence of the plays of Thomas Sheridan upon English literature, 28 Jul. Quoted in James Boswell *The Life of Samuel Johnson* (1791), vol.1.

3 Sir, a woman's preaching is like a dog walking on its hinder legs. It is not done well; but you are surprised to find it done at all.
1763 Remark, 31 Jul. Quoted in James Boswell *The Life of Samuel Johnson* (1791), vol.1.

4 He who does not mind his belly will hardly mind any thing else.
1763 Remark, 5 Aug. Quoted in James Boswell *The Life of Samuel Johnson* (1791), vol.1.

5 'I refute it *thus*.'
1763 Johnson refutes Bishop Berkeley's theory of the non-existence of matter by kicking a large stone, 6 Aug. Quoted in James Boswell *The Life of Samuel Johnson* (1791), vol.1.

6 Nature has given women so much power that the law has very wisely given them little.
1763 Letter to John Taylor, 18 Aug.

7 A very unclubbable man.
1764 Of Sir John Hawkins. Remark quoted in James Boswell *The Life of Samuel Johnson* (1791), vol.1.

8 Nothing can please many, and please long, but just representations of general nature.
1765 *Plays of William Shakespeare*, preface.

9 He that tries to recommend him by select quotations, will succeed like the pedant in Hierocles, who, when he offered his house to sale, carried a brick in his pocket as a specimen.
1765 Of Shakespeare. *Plays of William Shakespeare*, preface.

10 Love is only one of many passions.
1765 *Plays of William Shakespeare*, preface.

11 Notes are often necessary, but they are necessary evils.
1765 *Plays of William Shakespeare*, preface.

12 That all who are happy, are equally happy, is not true. A peasant and a philosopher may be equally satisfied, but not equally happy. Happiness consists in the multiplicity of agreeable consciousness.
1766 Remark, Feb. Quoted in James Boswell *The Life of Samuel Johnson* (1791), vol.2.

13 It is our first duty to serve society, and, after we have done that, we may attend wholly to the salvation of our own souls. A youthful passion for abstracted devotion should not be encouraged.
1766 Remark, Feb. Quoted in James Boswell *The Life of Samuel Johnson* (1791), vol.2.

14 Our tastes greatly alter. The lad does not care for the child's rattle, and the old man does not care for the young man's whore.
1766 Quoted in James Boswell *The Life of Samuel Johnson* (1791), vol.2.

15 It was not for me to bandy civilities with my sovereign.
1767 Remark, Feb. Quoted in James Boswell *The Life of Samuel Johnson* (1791), vol.2.

16 Now, sir, there is the liberty of the press, which you know is a constant topic. Suppose you and I and two hundred more were restrained from printing our thoughts: what then? What proportion would that restraint upon us bear to the private happiness of the nation?
1768 Remark, May. Quoted in James Boswell *The Life of Samuel Johnson* (1791), vol.2.

17 Sir, if a man has a mind to *prance*, he must study at Christ-Church and All-Souls.

1769 Remark, Autumn. Quoted in James Boswell *The Life of Samuel Johnson* (1791), vol.2.

18 We know our will is free, and there's an end on't.
1769 Remark, 16 Oct. Quoted in James Boswell *The Life of Samuel Johnson* (1791), vol.2.

19 It matters not how a man dies, but how he lives. The act of dying is not of importance, it lasts so short a time.
1769 Remark, 26 Oct. Quoted in James Boswell *The Life of Samuel Johnson* (1791), vol.2.

20 That fellow seems to me to possess but one idea, and that is a wrong one.
1770 Quoted in James Boswell *The Life of Samuel Johnson* (1791), vol.2.

21 The triumph of hope over experience.
1770 On a friend's second marriage shortly after the death of his first, troublesome, wife. Quoted in James Boswell *The Life of Samuel Johnson* (1791), vol.2.

22 I do not care to speak ill of any man behind his back, but I believe the gentleman is an *attorney*.
1770 Quoted in James Boswell *The Life of Samuel Johnson* (1791), vol.2.

23 Every man has a lurking wish to appear considerable in his native place.
1771 Letter to Sir Joshua Reynolds, 17 Jul. Quoted in James Boswell *The Life of Samuel Johnson* (1791), vol.2.

24 I would not give half a guinea to live under one form of government rather than another. It is of no moment to the happiness of an individual.
1772 Remark, 31 Mar. Quoted in James Boswell *The Life of Samuel Johnson* (1791), vol.2.

25 There is more knowledge of the heart in one letter of Richardson's, than in all *Tom Jones*.
1772 Remark, 6 Apr. Quoted in James Boswell *The Life of Samuel Johnson* (1791), vol.2.

26 Grief is a species of idleness.
1773 Letter to Mrs Thrale, whose son had just died, 17 Mar.

27 He has, indeed, done it very well; but it is a foolish thing well done.
1773 Of Oliver Goldsmith, who had responded to Thomas Evans's uncomplimentary open letter with a physical assault, and then published an apology in the *London Chronicle*. Remark, 3 Apr. Collected in James Boswell *The Life of Samuel Johnson* (1791), vol.2.

28 Read over your compositions, and where ever you meet with a passage which you think is particularly fine, strike it out.
1773 Remark, 30 Apr, quoting an old college tutor. Collected in James Boswell *The Life of Samuel Johnson* (1791), vol.2.

29 A lawyer has no business with the justice or injustice of the cause which he undertakes, unless his client asks his opinion, and then he is bound to give it honestly. The justice or unjustice of the cause is to be decided by the judge.
1773 Remark, 15 Aug. Quoted in James Boswell *The Journal of a Tour to the Hebrides* (1785).

30 I inherited a vile melancholy from my father, which has made me mad all my life, at least not sober.
1773 Remark, 16 Sep. Quoted in James Boswell *The Journal of a Tour to the Hebrides* (1785).

31 I am always sorry when any language is lost, because languages are the pedigrees of nations.
1773 Remark, 18 Sep. Quoted in James Boswell *The Journal of a Tour to the Hebrides* (1785).

32 A cucumber should be well sliced, and dressed with pepper and vinegar, and then thrown out, as good for nothing.
1773 Remark, 5 Oct. Quoted in James Boswell *The Journal of a Tour to the Hebrides* (1785).

33 At seventy-seven it is time to be in earnest.
1775 *A Journey to the Western Isles of Scotland*, 'Col'.

34 There are few ways in which a man can be so innocently employed than in getting money.
1775 Remark, 27 Mar. Collected in James Boswell *The Life of Samuel Johnson* (1791), vol.2. This is sometimes rendered 'A man is seldom so innocently occupied as when he is making money.'

35 It is wonderful, when a calculation is made, how little the mind is actually employed in the discharge of any profession.
1775 Remark, 6 Apr. Collected in James Boswell *The Life of Samuel Johnson* (1791), vol.2.

36 The greatest part of a writer's time is spent in reading, in order to write: a man will turn over half a library to make one book.
1775 Remark, 6 Apr. Collected in James Boswell *The Life of Samuel Johnson* (1791), vol.2.

37 Patriotism is the last refuge of a scoundrel.
1775 Remark, 7 Apr. Collected in James Boswell *The Life of Samuel Johnson* (1791), vol.2.

38 Knowledge is of two kinds. We know a subject ourselves, or we know where we can find information upon it.
1775 Remark, 18 Apr. Quoted in James Boswell *The Life of Samuel Johnson* (1791), vol.2.

39 Politics are now nothing more than means of rising in the world.
1775 Remark, 18 Apr. Quoted in James Boswell *The Life of Samuel Johnson* (1791), vol.2.

40 Players, Sir! I look upon them as no better than creatures set upon tables and joint stools to make faces and produce laughter, like dancing dogs.
1775 Letter to James Macpherson.

41 How is it that we hear the loudest yelps for liberty among the drivers of negroes?
1775 *Taxation No Tyranny*.

42 In lapidary inscriptions a man is not upon oath.
1775 Quoted in James Boswell *The Life of Samuel Johnson* (1791), vol.2.

43 There is nothing which has yet been contrived by man, by which so much happiness is produced as by a good tavern or inn.
1776 Remark, 21 Mar. Quoted in James Boswell *The Life of Samuel Johnson* (1791), vol.2.

44 Marriages would in general be as happy, and often more so, if they were all made by the Lord Chancellor, upon a due consideration of characters and circumstances, without the parties having any choice in the matter.
1776 Remark, 22 Mar. Quoted in James Boswell *The Life of Samuel Johnson* (1791), vol.2.

45 I had often wondered why young women should marry, as they have so much more freedom, and so much more attention paid to them while unmarried, than when married.
1776 Remark, 25 Mar. Quoted in James Boswell *The Life of Samuel Johnson* (1791), vol.2.

46 Fine clothes are good only as they supply the want of other means of procuring respect.
1776 Remark, 27 Mar. Quoted in James Boswell *The Life of Samuel Johnson* (1791), vol.2.

47 Consider, Sir, how should you like, though conscious of your innocence, to be tried before a jury for a capital crime, once a week.
1776 Remark, 3 Apr. Quoted in James Boswell *The Life of Samuel Johnson* (1791), vol.3.

48 We would all be idle if we could.
1776 Remark, 3 Apr. Quoted in James Boswell *The Life of Samuel Johnson* (1791), vol.3.

49 No man but a blockhead ever wrote, except for money.
1776 Remark, 5 Apr. Quoted in James Boswell *The Life of Samuel Johnson* (1791), vol.3.

50 It is better that some should be unhappy than that none should be happy, which would be the case in a general state of equality.
1776 Remark, 7 Apr. Quoted in James Boswell *The Life of Samuel Johnson* (1791), vol.3.

51 A man who has not been in Italy, is always conscious of an inferiority, from his not having seen what it is expected a man should see.
1776 Remark, 11 Apr. Quoted in James Boswell *The Life of Samuel Johnson* (1791), vol.3.

52 Every man of any education would rather be called a rascal, than accused of deficiency in the graces.
1776 Remark, May. Quoted in James Boswell *The Life of Samuel Johnson* (1791), vol.3.

53 Sir, you have but two topics, yourself and me. I am sick of both.
1776 Remark, May. Quoted in James Boswell *The Life of Samuel Johnson* (1791), vol.3.

54 If I had no duties, and no reference to futurity, I would spend my life in driving briskly in a post-chaise with a pretty woman.
1777 Remark, 19 Sep. Quoted in James Boswell *The Life of Samuel Johnson* (1791), vol.3.

55 Depend upon it, Sir, when a man knows he is to be hanged in a fortnight, it concentrates his mind wonderfully.
1777 Remark, 19 Sep, alluding to the forthcoming execution of Dr Dodd. Quoted in James Boswell *The Life of Samuel Johnson* (1791), vol.3.

56 When a man is tired of London, he is tired of life; for there is in London all that life can afford.
1777 Remark, 20 Sep. Quoted in James Boswell *The Life of Samuel Johnson* (1791), vol.3.

57 All argument is against it; but all belief is for it.
1778 Remark, 31 Mar, on the existence of ghosts. Quoted in James Boswell *The Life of Samuel Johnson* (1791), vol.3.

58 Seeing Scotland, Madam, is only seeing a worse England.
1778 Remark quoted in a letter to Boswell, 7 Apr. Quoted in James Boswell *The Life of Samuel Johnson* (1791), vol.3.

59 The more contracted that power is, the more easily it is destroyed. A country governed by a despot is an inverted cone.
1778 Remark, 14 Apr. Quoted in James Boswell *The Life of Samuel Johnson* (1791), vol.3.

60 As the Spanish proverb says, 'He, who would bring home the wealth of the Indies, must carry the wealth of the Indies with him.' So it is in travelling; a man must carry knowledge with him, if he would bring home knowledge.
1778 Remark, 17 Apr. Quoted in James Boswell *The Life of Samuel Johnson* (1791), vol.3.

61 Sir, the insolence of wealth will creep out.
1778 Remark, 18 Apr. Quoted in James Boswell *The Life of Samuel Johnson* (1791), vol.3.

62 Wine makes a man better pleased with himself. I do not say that it makes him more pleasing to others.
1778 Remark, 28 Apr. Quoted in James Boswell *The Life of Samuel Johnson* (1791), vol.3.

63 BOSWELL: There is more learning in their [Chinese] language than in any other, from the immense number of their characters.
JOHNSON: It is only more difficult from its rudeness, as there is more labour in hewing down a tree with a stone than with an axe.
1778 Conversation, 8 May. Quoted in James Boswell *The Life of Samuel Johnson* (1791), vol.3.

64 Were it not for imagination, Sir, a man would be as happy in the arms of a chambermaid as of a Duchess.
1778 Remark, 9 May. Quoted in James Boswell *The Life of Samuel Johnson* (1791), vol.3.

65 A man who exposes himself when he is intoxicated, has not the art of getting drunk.
1779 Remark, 24 Apr. Quoted in James Boswell *The Life of Samuel Johnson* (1791), vol.3.

66 Claret is the liquor for boys; port, for men; but he who aspires to be a hero [smiling] must drink brandy.
1779 Remark, 7 Aug. Quoted in James Boswell *The Life of Samuel Johnson* (1791), vol.3.

67 Remember that all tricks are either knavish or childish.
1779 Letter to Boswell, 9 Sep. Quoted in James Boswell *The Life of Samuel Johnson* (1791), vol.3.

68 BOSWELL: Is not the Giant's Causeway worth seeing?
JOHNSON: Worth seeing? Yes, but not worth going to see.
1779 Conversation, 12 Oct. Quoted in James Boswell *The Life of Samuel Johnson* (1791), vol.3.

69 If you are idle, be not solitary; if you are solitary, be not idle.
1779 Letter to Boswell, 27 Oct. Quoted in James Boswell *The Life of Samuel Johnson* (1791), vol.3.

70 Trade could not be managed by those who manage it, if it had much difficulty.
1779 Letter to Hester Thrale, 16 Nov.

71 The true genius is a mind of large general powers, accidentally determined to some particular direction.
1779–81 *Lives of the English Poets*, 'Cowley'.

72 The father of English criticism.
1779–81 Of Dryden. *Lives of the English Poets*, 'Dryden'.

73 To charge all unmerited praise with the guilt of flattery, and to suppose that the encomiast always knows and feels the falsehood of his assertions, is surely to discover great ignorance of human nature and human life. In determinations depending not on rules, but on experience and comparison, judgement is always to some degree subject to affection. Very near to admiration is the wish to admire.
1779–81 *Lives of the English Poets*, 'Halifax'.

74 It…had the effect, as was ludicrously said, of making Gay *rich*, and Rich *gay*.
1779–81 Of the *Beggar's Opera*, written by Gay and produced by Rich. *Lives of the English Poets*, 'John Gay'.

Johnson

75 An exotic and irrational entertainment.
1779–81 Of Italian opera. *Lives of the English Poets*, 'Hughes'.

76 I am disappointed by that stroke of death, which has eclipsed the gaiety of nations, and impoverished the public stock of harmless pleasure.
1779–81 His tribute to the recently deceased actor David Garrick. *Lives of the English Poets*, 'Edmund Smith'.

77 Every man has a right to utter what he thinks truth, and every other man has a right to knock him down for it. Martyrdom is the test.
1780 Quoted in James Boswell *The Life of Samuel Johnson* (1791), vol.4.

78 Depend upon it, said he, that if a man talks of his misfortunes there is something in them that is not disagreeable to him; for where there is nothing but pure misery, there never is any recourse to the mention of it.
1780 Quoted in James Boswell *The Life of Samuel Johnson* (1791), vol.4.

79 A wise Tory and a wise Whig, I believe, will agree. Their principles are the same, though their modes of thinking are different.
1781 Written note given to Boswell, May. Quoted in James Boswell *The Life of Samuel Johnson* (1791), vol.4.

80 Classical quotations is the parole of literary men all over the world.
1781 Remark, 8 May. Quoted in James Boswell *The Life of Samuel Johnson* (1791), vol.4.

81 Sir, I have two very cogent reasons for not printing any list of subscribers;—one, that I have lost all the names,—the other, that I have spent all the money.
1781 Remark, May. Quoted in James Boswell *The Life of Samuel Johnson* (1791), vol.4.

82 Why, that is, because, dearest, you're a dunce.
1781 To Lady Corke, who had said that she was affected by Sterne's writings. Quoted in James Boswell *The Life of Samuel Johnson* (1791), vol.4.

83 Always, Sir, set a high value on spontaneous kindness. He whose inclination prompts him to cultivate your friendship of his own accord, will love you more than one whom you have been at pains to attract to you.
1781 Remark, May. Quoted in James Boswell *The Life of Samuel Johnson* (1791), vol.4.

84 I hate a fellow whom pride, or cowardice, or laziness drives into a corner, and who does nothing when he is there but sit and growl; let him come out as I do, and bark.
1782 Remark, 10 Oct, alluding to Jeremiah Markland. Quoted in James Boswell *The Life of Samuel Johnson* (1791), vol.4.

85 Resolve not to be poor; whatever you have, spend less. Poverty is a great enemy to human happiness; it certainly destroys liberty, and it makes some virtues impracticable, and others extremely difficult.
1782 Letter to Boswell, 7 Dec. Quoted in James Boswell *The Life of Samuel Johnson* (1791), vol.4.

86 How few of his friends' houses would a man choose to be at when he is sick.
1783 Quoted in James Boswell *The Life of Samuel Johnson* (1791), vol.4.

87 There is a wicked inclination in most people to suppose an old man decayed in his intellects. If a young or middle-aged man, when leaving a company, does not recollect where he laid his hat, it is nothing; but if the same inattention is discovered in an old man, people will shrug up their shoulders, and say, 'His memory is going.'
1783 Quoted in James Boswell *The Life of Samuel Johnson* (1791), vol.4.

88 Sir, there is no settling the point of precedency between a louse and a flea.
1783 On the relative merits of two minor poets. Quoted in James Boswell *The Life of Samuel Johnson* (1791), vol.4.

89 My dear friend, clear your mind of cant… You may talk in this manner; it is a mode of talking in Society: but don't think foolishly.
1783 Remark, 15 May. Quoted in James Boswell *The Life of Samuel Johnson* (1791), vol.4.

90 It is as bad as bad can be: it is ill-fed, ill-killed, ill-kept, and ill-drest.
1783 Of the roast mutton he was served at an inn, 3 Jun. Quoted in James Boswell *The Life of Samuel Johnson* (1791), vol.4.

91 As I know more of mankind I expect less of them, and am ready now to call a man a good man, upon easier terms than I was formerly.
1783 Remark, Sep. Quoted in James Boswell *The Life of Samuel Johnson* (1791), vol.4.

92 Milton, Madam, was a genius that could cut a Colossus from a rock; but could not carve heads upon cherry-stones.
1784 Remark to Hannah More, 13 Jun, who had commented with surprise that Milton's sonnets failed to compare with his epic *Paradise Lost*. Quoted in James Boswell *The Life of Samuel Johnson* (1791), vol.4.

93 Talking of the Comedy of 'The Rehearsal', he said 'It has not enough wit to keep it sweet.' This was easy;—he therefore caught himself, and pronounced a more rounded sentence; 'It has not vitality enough to preserve it from putrefaction.'
1784 Remark, Jun. Quoted in James Boswell *The Life of Samuel Johnson* (1791), vol.4.

94 Sir, I have found you an argument; but I am not obliged to find you an understanding.
1784 Remark, Jun. Quoted in James Boswell *The Life of Samuel Johnson* (1791), vol.4.

95 No man is a hypocrite in his pleasures.
1784 Remark, Jun. Quoted in James Boswell *The Life of Samuel Johnson* (1791), vol.4.

96 Dictionaries are like watches, the worst is better than none, and the best cannot be expected to go quite true.
1784 Letter to Francesco Sastres, 21 Aug. Quoted in James Boswell *The Life of Samuel Johnson* (1791), vol.4.

97 Sir, I look upon every day to be lost, in which I do not make a new acquaintance.
1784 Remark, Nov. Quoted in James Boswell *The Life of Samuel Johnson* (1791), vol.4.

98 I will be conquered; I will not capitulate.
1784 Of his increasing ill health, Nov. Quoted in James Boswell *The Life of Samuel Johnson* (1791), vol.4.

99 An odd thought strikes me:—we shall receive no letters in the grave.
1784 Remark, Dec. Quoted in James Boswell *The Life of Samuel Johnson* (1791), vol.4.

1 Difficult do you call it, Sir? I wish it were impossible.
Of the playing of a famous violinist. Quoted in G B Hill *Johnsonian Miscellanies*, vol.2 (1784).

2 It is the only sensual pleasure without vice.
  1784 Of music. Quoted in Sir John Hawkins *Johnsoniana* (1787).

3 I would rather see the portrait of a dog that I know, than all the allegorical paintings they can show me in the world.
  Quoted in Mrs Piozzi *Anecdotes of the Late Samuel Johnson* (1786).

4 Corneille is to Shakespeare…as a clipped hedge is to a forest.
  Quoted in Mrs Piozzi *Anecdotes of the Late Samuel Johnson* (1786).

5 It is very strange, and very melancholy, that the paucity of human pleasures should persuade us ever to call hunting one of them.
  Quoted in Mrs Piozzi *Anecdotes of the Late Samuel Johnson* (1786).

6 Of all noises I think music the least disagreeable.
  Quoted in *The Morning Chronicle*, 1816.

7 Fly fishing may be a very pleasant amusement; but angling or float fishing I can only compare to a stick and a string, with a worm at one end and a fool at the other.
  Quoted in Hawker *Instructions to Young Sportsmen* (1859). The attribution is doubtful, and Swift has also been credited with the remark.

8 The use of travelling is to regulate imagination by reality, and instead of thinking how things may be, to see them as they are.
  Attributed.

Johnston, Brian 1912–94
English cricket commentator.

9 The bowler's Holding, the batsman's Willey.
  1976 Radio commentary, during a Test match between England and the West Indies.

10 Turner looks a bit shaky and unsteady, but I think he's going to bat on—one ball left!
  Radio commentary, during an England Test match after batsman Glenn Turner was hit on the box by a cricket ball on the fifth ball of the over.

Johst, Hanns 1890–1978
German dramatist.

11 *Wenn ich Kultur höre…entsichere ich meinen Browning!*
  When I hear anyone talk of culture…I take off the safety catch on my Browning!
  1933 *Schlageter*, act 1, sc.1. The phrase is often attributed to Hermann Goering, in the form 'Whenever I hear the word culture, I reach for my gun!'.

Jolie, Angelina *born* Angelina Jolie Voight 1975–
US film actress.

12 *Quod me nutrit me destruit.*
  What nourishes me destroys me.
  Tattoo.

Jolson, Al *pseudonym of* Asa Yoelson 1886–1950
Russian-born US actor and singer. He emigrated to the US in 1893 and made his stage debut in *The Children of the Ghetto* (1899). He was the star of the first talking picture *The Jazz Singer* in 1927.

13 You Ain't Heard Nothin' Yet.
  1919 Title of a song, allegedly taken from an earlier impromptu remark in a café in which Jolson was performing. It is popularly recognized as a line from *The Jazz Singer* (screenplay by Alfred Cohn), the first major film with sound.

Jonas, George 1935–
Hungarian-born Canadian author and journalist.

14 There are many wrongs in the world, but none that could be righted by the terrorist's program.
  1987 *Crocodiles in the Bathtub and Other Perils.*

15 Maybe that's what is crazy: to want to be free. A lot of people wouldn't cross the street for it.
  1989 *A Passion Observed: The Story of a Motorcycle Racer.*

Jones, Bobby (Robert Tyre) 1902–71
US golfer. He won the US Open four times, the British Open three times, the US Amateur Championship five times and the British Amateur Championship once. In 1930 he won the 'Grand Slam', and retired from competitive golf.

16 Golf is a game that is played on a five inch course—the distance between your ears.
  Quoted in Colin Jarman *The Guinness Dictionary of Sports Quotations* (1990).

Jones, Henry Arthur 1851–1929
English playwright. His early melodramas were followed by more realistic plays and social comedies.

17 O God! Put back Thy universe and give me yesterday.
  1907 *The Silver King* (with Henry Herman), act 2, sc.4.

Jones, James 1921–77
US writer. He is best known for his novel set in the run-up to the bombing of Pearl Harbor, *From Here to Eternity* (1951), and its sequel, *The Thin Red Line* (1962).

18 From Here to Eternity.
  1951 Title of novel.

19 I therefore solemnly declare to all young men trying to be writers that they do not actually have to become drunkards first.
  1959 Interview in the *Paris Review*, Winter.

20 To me politics is like one of those annoying and potentially dangerous, but generally just painful, chronic diseases that you just have to put up with all your life if you happen to have contracted it. Politics is like having diabetes.
  1959 Interview in the *Paris Review*, Winter.

21 Conversation is more often likely to be an attempt at deliberate evasion, deliberate confusion, rather than communication. We're all cheats and liars, really.
  1959 Interview in the *Paris Review*, Winter.

Jones, John Paul 1747–92
US admiral. He fought the English fleet in the American Revolution, and later became rear-admiral in the Russian navy.

22 Sir, I have not yet begun to fight.
  1779 His reply to a request for surrender when his ship was sinking, 23 Sep. He lashed his ship to his enemy's and boarded it, accepting the enemy captain's surrender. Quoted in Anna de Koven *Life and Letters of John Paul Jones* (1913).

Jones, Quincy Delight 1933–
US jazz trumpeter, songwriter and record producer. His many albums include *Body Heat* (1974) and *The Dude* (1981).

As Vice-President of Mercury Records he promoted Frank Sinatra and Michael Jackson among others.

23 Jazz has always been a man telling the truth about himself.
Quoted in Alan Kendall *The Tender Tyrant: Nadia Boulanger* (1976).

24 To try to talk to the young people who will run the future—in ten minutes—is a little like trying to put a cantaloupe in a coke bottle.
1995 At Claremont College commencement. Reported in the *New York Times*, 29 May.

Jones, Rev. Tim 1967–
English priest.

25 My advice, as a Christian priest, is to shoplift.
2009 Advice to poor and needy parishioners at St Lawrence's Church, York, quoted in *The Telegraph*, 23 Dec.

Jones, Tom 1940–
Welsh pop singer.

26 My pants are not as tight any more, I don't open my shirt so far and I don't pick up the underwear.
2004 On getting older. Quoted in *Mojo*, May.

Jones, Tommy Lee 1946–
US film actor.

27 Age will flatten a man.
2007 As Ed Tom Bell in *No Country for Old Men* (screenplay by Joel Coen and Ethan Coen).

28 You know what the most destructive force in the universe is? Regret.
2012 As Kevin Brown/Agent K in *Men in Black 3* (screenplay by Ethan Cohen).

Jong, Erica *née* Mann 1942–
US novelist and poet. She achieved notoriety with her controversial first novel, *Fear of Flying* (1973).

29 Everyone has talent. What is rare is the courage to follow the talent to the dark place where it leads.
1972 'The Artist as Housewife', in *The First Ms. Reader*.

30 If sex and creativity are often seen by dictators as subversive activities, it's because they lead to the knowledge that you own your own body (and with it your own voice), and that's the most revolutionary insight of all.
1972 'The Artist as Housewife', in *The First Ms. Reader*.

31 The zipless fuck is absolutely pure. It is free of ulterior motives. There is no power game. The man is not 'taking' and the woman is not 'giving'. No one is attempting to cuckold a husband or humiliate a wife. No one is trying to prove anything or get anything out of anyone. The zipless fuck is the purest thing there is. And it is rarer than the unicorn. And I have never had one.
1973 *Fear of Flying*, ch.1.

32 Solitude is un-American.
1973 *Fear of Flying*, ch.1.

33 Gossip is the opiate of the oppressed.
1973 *Fear of Flying*, ch.6.

34 Horrible as successful artists often are, there is nothing crueller or more vain than a failed artist.
1973 *Fear of Flying*, ch.9.

35 Jealousy is all the fun you *think* they had.
1977 *How To Save Your Own Life*.

36 Advice is what we ask for when we already know the answer but wish we didn't.
1977 *How To Save Your Own Life*.

37 Friends *love* misery, in fact. Sometimes, especially if we are too lucky or too successful or too pretty, our misery is the only thing that endears us to our friends.
1977 *How To Save Your Own Life*.

38 Every country gets the circus it deserves. Spain gets bullfights. Italy gets the Catholic Church. America gets Hollywood.
1977 *How To Save Your Own Life*.

39 Women are the only exploited group in the world who have been idealized into powerlessness.
1978 In *Time*.

40 Fear of Fifty.
1994 Title of memoir.

41 Murky language means someone wants to pick your pocket.
2006 *Seducing the Demon: Writing for My Life*.

42 Isn't it our job to be appalled by our parents? Isn't it every generation's duty to be dismayed by the previous generation? And to assert that we are different—only to discover later that we are distressingly the same?
2011 *Sugar in My Bowl*.

Jonson, Ben 1572–1637
English dramatist. Imprisoned for killing a man in a duel, he became a Catholic but later recanted. His plays reject romantic comedy for a more realistic mode and include *Volpone* (1606), *The Silent Woman* (1609) and *The Alchemist* (1610). He was regarded as superior to Shakespeare in his day.

43 Well, I will scourge those apes,
And to these courteous eyes oppose a mirror,
As large as is the stage whereon we act;
Where they shall see the time's deformity
Anatomised in every nerve, and sinew,
With constant courage, and contempt of fear.
1600 *Every Man out of His Humour*, Induction.

44 GENT: He hath been beyond-sea, once, or twice.
CARL: As far as *Paris*, to fetch over a fashion, and come back again.
1600 *Every Man out of His Humour*, act 2, sc.2.

45 Good morning to the day; and next, my gold!
1609 *Volpone*, act 1, sc.1.

46 Yet I glory
More in the cunning purchase of my wealth
Than in the glad possession.
1609 *Volpone*, act 1, sc.1.

47 What should I do,
But cocker up my genius, and live free
To all delights my fortune calls me to?
1609 *Volpone*, act 1, sc.2.

48 Hood an ass with reverend purple,
So you can hide his two ambitious ears,
And he shall pass for a cathedral doctor.
1609 *Volpone*, act 1, sc.3.

49 Give 'em words;
Pour oil into their ears, and send them hence.
1609 *Volpone*, act 1, sc.4.

50 He has no faith in physic. He does think
   Most of your doctors are the greater danger,
   And worse disease, t'escape.
   1609 *Volpone*, act 1, sc.4.

51 'Fore heaven, I wonder at the desperate valour
   Of the bold English, that they dare let loose
   Their wives to all encounters!
   1609 *Volpone*, act 1, sc.5.

52 Calumnies are answered best with silence.
   1609 *Volpone*, act 2, sc. 2.

53 Ay, a plague on't,
   My conscience fools my wit!
   1609 *Volpone*, act 2, sc.7.

54 Success hath made me wanton.
   1609 *Volpone*, act 3, sc.1.

55 All my house,
   But now, steamed like a bath with her thick breath.
   A lawyer could not have been heard; nor scarce
   Another woman, such a hail of words
   She has let fall.
   1609 Of Lady Politic Would-be. *Volpone*, act 3, sc.5.

56 Come, my Celia, let us prove,
   While we can, the sports of love,
   Time will not be ours for ever,
   He, at length, our good will sever;
   Spend not then his gifts in vain:
   Suns that set may rise again;
   But if once we lose this light,
   'Tis with us perpetual night.
   Why should we defer our joys?
   Fame and rumour are but toys.
   1609 *Volpone*, 'Song', act 3, sc.7.

57 His soul moves in his fee.
   1609 Of the lawyer. *Volpone*, act 4, sc.5.

58 I'd have your tongue, sir, tipped with gold for this.
   1609 *Volpone*, act 4, sc.6.

59 A pox of her autumnal face, her pieced beauty!
   1609–10 *Epicoene*, act 1, sc.1.

60 Still to be neat, still to be drest,
   As you were going to a feast;
   Still to be powdered, still perfumed,
   Lady, it is to be presumed,
   Though art's hid causes are not found,
   All is not sweet, all is not sound.

   Give me a look, give me a face,
   That makes simplicity a grace;
   Robes loosely flowing, hair as free:
   Such sweet neglect more taketh me,
   Than all the adulteries of art;
   They strike mine eyes, but not my heart.
   1609–10 *Epicoene*, act 1, sc.1.

61 Let me see: all discourses but mine own afflict me; they
   seem harsh, impertinent, and irksome.
   1609–10 *Epicoene*, act 2, sc.1.

62 A man of your head and hair should owe more to that
   reverend ceremony, and not mount the marriage bed
   like a town-bull, or a mountain-goat; but stay the due
   season and ascend it then with religion and fear.
   1609–10 *Epicoene*, act 3, sc.5.

63 Fortune, that favours fools.
   1610 *The Alchemist*, act 1, sc.4.

64 [The play] is like to be a very conceited scurvy one, in
   plain English.
   1614 *Bartholomew Fair*, Induction.

65 WIN LITTLEWIT: Come, indeed, la, you are such a fool, still!
   LITTLEWIT: No, but half a one, Win; you are the t'other half:
   man and wife make one fool, Win.
   1614 *Bartholomew Fair*, act 1, sc.1.

66 He is a fellow of a most arrogant and invincible dullness,
   I assure you.
   1614 *Bartholomew Fair*, act 1, sc.1.

67 There is a doing of right out of wrong, if the ways be
   found.
   1614 *Bartholomew Fair*, act 2, sc.2.

68 I see compassion may become a justice, though it be a
   weakness, I confess, and nearer a vice than a virtue.
   1614 *Bartholomew Fair*, act 4, sc.2.

69 There's reason good, that you good laws should make:
   Men's manners ne'er were viler, for your sake.
   1616 *Epigrams*, 'To the Parliament'.

70 Nor shall our cups make any guilty men:
   But, at our parting, we will be, as when
   We innocently met. No simple word,
   That shall be utter'd at our mirthful board,
   Shall make us sad next morning: or affright
   The liberty, that we'll enjoy tonight.
   1616 *Epigrams*, 'On Inviting a Friend to Supper'.

71 Thou art not, Penshurst, built to envious show
   Of touch or marble, nor canst boast a row
   Of polished pillars, or a roof of gold;
   Thou hast no lantern whereof tales are told,
   Or stair, or courts; but standst an ancient pile,
   And these grudged at, art reverenced the while.
   1616 *The Forest*, 'To Penshurst'.

72 Then hath thy orchard fruit, thy garden flowers,
   Fresh as the air, and new as are the hours.
   The early cherry, with the later plum,
   Fig, grape, and quince, each in his time doth come:
   The blushing apricot, and woolly peach
   Hang on thy walls, that every child may reach.
   1616 *The Forest*, 'To Penshurst'.

73 Freedom doth with degree dispense.
   1616 *The Forest*, 'To Sir Robert Wroth'.

74 Nor for my peace will I go far,
   As wanderers do, that still do roam,
   But make my strengths, such as they are,
   Here in my bosom, and at home.
   1616 *The Forest*, 'To the World'.

75 Drink to me, only, with thine eyes,
   And I will pledge with mine;
   Or leave a kiss but in the cup,
   And I'll not look for wine.
   1616 *The Forest*, 'To Celia'.

76 'Tis grown almost a danger to speak true
   Of any good mind, now: There are so few.
   1616 *The Forest*, 'Epistle to Katherine, Lady Aubigny'.

77 Rest in soft peace, and, asked, say here doth lie
   Ben Jonson his best piece of poetry.
   1616 'On My First Son'.

78 Soul of the Age!
The applause, delight, the wonder of our stage!
1623 'To the Memory of My Beloved, the Author, Mr. William Shakespeare, and What He Hath Left Us'.

79 Thou hadst small Latin, and less Greek.
1623 'To the Memory of My Beloved, the Author, Mr. William Shakespeare, and What He Hath Left Us', prefatory dedication to the first folio of Shakespeare's plays.

80 He was not of an age, but for all time!
1623 'To the Memory of My Beloved, the Author, Mr. William Shakespeare, and What He Hath Left Us', prefatory dedication to the first folio of Shakespeare's plays.

81 Sweet Swan of Avon! What a sight it were
To see thee in our waters yet appear,
And make those flights upon the banks of Thames
That so did take Eliza, and our James!
1623 'To the Memory of My Beloved, the Author, Mr. William Shakespeare, and What He Hath Left Us', prefatory dedication to the first folio of Shakespeare's plays.

82 O rare Ben Jonson.
1637 His epitaph in Westminster Abbey. It is thought that the words were inscribed on his gravestone at the order of a certain Sir John Young, possibly in error for 'Orare Ben Jonson' ('Pray for Ben Jonson').

83 For Love's sake, kiss me once again,
I long, and should not beg in vain,
Here's none to spy, or see;
Why do you doubt, or stay?
I'll taste as lightly as the Bee,
That doth but touch his flower, and flies away.
Once more, and (faith) I will be gone:
Can he that loves, ask less than one?
The Underwood, 'A Celebration of Charis', no.7 (published 1640).

84 Minds that are great and free,
Should not on fortune pause,
'Tis crown enough to virtue still, her own applause.
The Underwood, 'An Ode to Himself' (published 1640).

85 Helen, did Homer never see
Thy beauties, yet could write of thee?
The Underwood, 'An Ode' (published 1640).

86 Come, let us here enjoy the shade;
For love in shadow best is made.
Though envy oft his shadow be,
None brooks the sunlight worse than he.
The Underwood, 'A Song' (published 1640).

87 'Tis true, I'm broke! Vows, oaths, and all I had
Of credit lost. And I am now run mad,
Or do upon my self some desperate ill;
This sadness makes no approaches, but to kill.
The Underwood, 'An Elegy', no.40 (published 1640).

88 Wisdom without honesty is mere craft and cozenage. And therefore the reputation for honesty must first be gotten; which cannot be but by living well. A good life is a main argument.
Timber: or Discoveries made upon Men and Matter (published 1640).

89 Poetry in this latter age hath proved but a mean mistress to such as have wholly addicted themselves to her, or given their names up to her family. They who have but saluted her on the by, and now and then tendered their visits, she hath done much for, and advanced in the way of their own professions (both the law and the gospel) beyond all they could have hoped, or done for themselves without her favour.
Timber: or Discoveries made upon Men and Matter (published 1640).

90 I remember that the players have often mentioned it as an honour to Shakespeare that in his writing, whatsoever he penned, he never blotted out a line. My answer hath been, Would he had blotted a thousand: which they thought a malevolent speech...[but] I loved the man and do honour his memory, on this side idolatry, as much as any.
Timber: or Discoveries made upon Men and Matter (published 1640).

91 There was ever more in him to be praised than to be pardoned.
Of Shakespeare. *Timber: or Discoveries made upon Men and Matter* (published 1640).

92 The fear of every man that heard him was, lest he should make an end.
Of Francis Bacon. *Timber: or Discoveries made upon Men and Matter* (published 1640).

93 For a man to write well, there are required three necessaries: to read the best authors, observe the best speakers, and much exercise of his own style.
Timber: or Discoveries made upon Men and Matter (published 1640).

94 Ready writing makes not good writing, but good writing brings on ready writing.
Timber: or Discoveries made upon Men and Matter (published 1640).

95 Custom is the most certain mistress of language, as the public stamp makes the current money.
Timber: or Discoveries made upon Men and Matter (published 1640).

96 Our composition must be more accurate in the beginning and end than in the midst, and in the end more than in the beginning; for through the midst the stream bears us.
Timber: or Discoveries made upon Men and Matter (published 1640).

97 Our style should be as a skein of silk, to be carried and found by the right thread, not ravelled and perplexed; then all is a knot, a heap.
Timber: or Discoveries made upon Men and Matter (published 1640).

Joplin, Janis 1943-70

US rhythm and blues singer.

98 Lord, won't you buy me a Mercedes-Benz,
My friends all drive Porsches,
I must make amends.
1970 'Mercedes-Benz', co-written with Michael McClure and Bob Neuwirth.

Jordan, June 1936-2002

US poet, essayist, political activist and writer for children. Her work was marked by a strong commitment to black consciousness.

99 Body and soul, Black America reveals the extreme questions of contemporary life, questions of freedom and identity: *How can I be who I am?*
1969 'Black Studies: Bringing Back the Person', in the *Evergreen Review*, Oct.

1 We do not deride the fears of prospering white America. A nation of violence and private property has every reason to dread the violated and the deprived.
  1969 'Black Studies: Bringing Back the Person', in the *Evergreen Review*, Oct.

2 To rescue our children we will have to let them save us from the power we embody: we will have to trust the very difference that they forever personify.
  1978 Keynote address for Child Welfare League of America. Collected as 'Old Stories: New Lives' in *Moving Towards Home* (1989).

3 I am a feminist, and what that means to me is much the same as the meaning of the fact that I am Black: it means that I must undertake to love myself as though my very life depends upon self-love and self-respect.
  1978 Address to Black Writers Conference, Howard University. Collected as 'Where Is the Love?' in *Moving Towards Home* (1989).

Jordan, Michael 1963–

US basketball player. He played with the Chicago Bulls (1984–93, 1995–8), set numerous records, and was a member of the US Olympic gold medal-winning basketball teams in 1984 and 1992.

4 Talent wins games, but teamwork wins championships.
  Attributed.

5 Limits, like fears, are often just an illusion.
  2009 Speaking on the occasion of his induction into the Basketball Hall of Fame.

Jordan, Neil 1950–

Irish film-maker and writer. His films include *The Crying Game* (1992), *Interview with the Vampire* (1994), *The Butcher Boy* (1997) and *The End of the Affair* (1999).

6 The action movie in the 1980s became like what the silent movie used to be. The same movie could be seen in Los Angeles and Taiwan and Hong Kong and you didn't need subtitles because everybody understands Bruce Willis blowing things up in a torn vest.
  2004 In *The Scotsman*, 22 May.

Joseph II 1741–90

Holy Roman Emperor (1756–90), known as 'the revolutionary emperor' for his programme of modernization. He suppressed papal power and in 1781 published an Edict of Toleration for Protestants and Greeks.

7 As I have just come from making my Easter confession on Good Friday and have forgiven all those who trespass against me, I cannot harbour any thoughts of revenge, only contempt for an arrant shit who is bursting with pride, although he is simply being taken for a ride by his women.
  1786 Of the senior dignitary of the Holy Roman Empire, the Elector-Archbishop of Mainz. Letter to Trauttmansdorff (his representative at Mainz), 14 Apr. Quoted in T C W Blanning *Joseph II* (1994), p.148.

8 Here lies a prince whose intentions were pure, but who had the misfortune to see all his plans collapse.
  Epitaph for himself. Quoted in T C W Blanning *Joseph II* (1994), p.1.

Joseph of Exeter fl.12c

English poet.

9 The youths at cricks did play
  Throughout the merry day.
  1180 Quoted in Ivor Brown *A Book of England* (1958). This is thought to be the first mention of the game of cricket in English literature.

Josephus, Flavius AD 37–100

Jewish historian and soldier, commander of Galilee. He surrendered to the Romans rather than commit suicide, and later won imperial patronage and lived in Rome. His works include *The Antiquities of the Jews*.

10 Their exercises are unbloody battles, and their battles bloody exercises.
  c.75–79 AD Of the Romans. *A History of the Jewish War*, bk.3, ch.5, section 1 (translated by William Whiston).

Jourdan, Louis *originally* Louis Gendre 1921–2015

French-born actor. He appeared in French films (1940–6), then moved to the US. His many American and European film credits include *Gigi* (1958), *Can Can* (1960) and *Octopussy* (1983).

11 In New York people don't go to the theater—they go to see hits.
  1950 In the *New York Herald Tribune*, 1 Jan.

Jouvet, Louis 1887–1951

French actor and director. Appointed director of the Comédie des Champs-Élysées in 1922, he had a profound impact on the development of French theatre between the wars, making many reforms.

12 The one thing constant in a changing world is the avant-garde.
  Attributed.

Jovanovich, William 1920–2001

US publisher. He joined Harcourt Brace Jovanovich Inc in 1947, eventually becoming president and director.

13 The most important single thing in publishing is the English sentence, and the editor who cannot contemplate it again and again with a sense of wonder has not yet gained respect for the complexity of learning.
  1964 *Now, Barabbas*.

Jowell, Dame Tessa 1947–

English Labour politician, Secretary of State for Culture, Media and Sport (2001–7).

14 In the last Parliament, the House of Commons had more MPs called John than all the women MPs put together.
  1999 In the *Independent on Sunday*, 'Quotes', 14 Mar.

Jowett, Benjamin 1817–93

English classical scholar, Professor of Greek at Oxford (1855–93), ordained as an Anglican priest in 1845.

15 One man is as good as another until he has written a book.
  Quoted in Evelyn Abbott and Lewis Campbell (eds) *Life and Letters of Benjamin Jowett* (1897), vol.1.

16 Nowhere probably is there more true feeling, and nowhere worse taste, than in a churchyard.
  Quoted in Evelyn Abbott and Lewis Campbell (eds) *Letters of Benjamin Jowett* (1899), ch.6.

Joyce, James Augustine Aloysius 1882–1941

Irish writer who lived in exile on the Continent and was plagued for most of his life with deteriorating eyesight. His fiction includes *Dubliners* (1914), *Ulysses* (1922), one of the most influential works of 20c fiction, and *Finnegans Wake* (1939).

17 'O, pa!' he cried. 'Don't beat me, pa! And I'll...I'll say a *Hail Mary* for you... I'll say a *Hail Mary* for you, pa, if you don't beat me.'
 1914 *Dubliners*, 'Counterparts'.

18 His soul swooned slowly as he heard the snow falling faintly through the universe and faintly falling, like the descent of their last end, upon all the living and the dead.
 1914 *Dubliners*, 'The Dead'.

19 The fellows were practising long shies and bowling lobs and slow twisters. In the soft grey silence he could hear the bump of the balls: and from here and from there through the quiet air the sound of the cricket bats: pick, pack, pock, puck: like drops of water in a fountain falling softly in the brimming bowl.
 1916 *A Portrait of the Artist as a Young Man*.

20 At the door Dante turned round violently and shouted down the room, her cheeks flushed and quivering with rage:
 —Devil out of hell! We won! We crushed him to death! Fiend!
 The door slammed behind her. Mr Casey, freeing his arms from his holders, suddenly bowed his head on his hands with a sob of pain.
 —Poor Parnell! he cried loudly. My dead king!
 1916 *A Portrait of the Artist as a Young Man*.

21 The snotgreen sea. The scrotumtightening sea.
 1922 *Ulysses*.

22 It is a symbol of Irish art. The cracked looking-glass of a servant.
 1922 *Ulysses*.

23 When I makes tea I makes tea, as old mother Grogan said. And when I makes water I makes water...*Begob, ma'am*, says Mrs. Cahill, *God send you don't make them in the one pot.*
 1922 *Ulysses*.

24 History, Stephen said, is a nightmare from which I am trying to awake.
 1922 *Ulysses*.

25 Lawn Tennyson, gentleman poet.
 1922 *Ulysses*.

26 Come forth, Lazarus! And he came fifth and lost the job.
 1922 *Ulysses*.

27 A man of genius makes no mistakes. His errors are volitional and are the portals of discovery.
 1922 *Ulysses*.

28 Greater love than this, he said, no man hath that a man lay down his wife for his friend. Go thou and do likewise. Thus, or words to that effect, saith Zarathustra, sometime regius professor of French letters to the university of Oxtail.
 1922 *Ulysses*.

29 Mr. Leopold Bloom ate with relish the inner organs of beasts and fowls. He liked thick giblet soup, nutty gizzards, a stuffed roast heart; liver slices fried with crustcrumbs, fried hencod's roes. Most of all he liked grilled mutton kidneys which gave to his palate a fine tang of faintly scented urine.
 1922 *Ulysses*.

30 A woman loses a charm with every pin she takes out.
 1922 *Ulysses*.

31 Heavenly weather. If life was always like that. Cricket weather. Sit around under sunshades. Over after over. Out. They can't play it here. Still, Captain Buller broke a window in Kildare Street Club with a slog to square leg.
 1922 *Ulysses*. Legend has it that W G Grace performed the feat of breaking the Kildare Street Club window while playing at the distant College Park in the 1870s.

32 Her crocus dress she wore, lowcut, belongings on show.
 1922 *Ulysses*.

33 yes and how he kissed me under the Moorish wall and I thought well as well him as another and then I asked him with my eyes to ask again yes and then he asked me would I yes to say yes my mountain flower and first I put my arms around him yes and drew him down to me so he could feel my breasts all perfume yes and his heart was going like mad and yes I said yes I will Yes.
 1922 *Ulysses*, last words.

34 I read the first 2 pages of the usual sloppy English and [Stuart Gilbert] read me a lyrical bit about nudism in the wood and the end which is a piece of propaganda in favour of something which, outside of D. H. L.'s country at any rates, makes all the propaganda for itself.
 1931 On D H Lawrence's *Lady Chatterley's Lover*. Letter to Harriet Weaver, 17 Dec.

35 That ideal reader suffering from an ideal insomnia.
 1939 *Finnegans Wake*.

36 Gentes and laitymen, fullstoppers and semicolonials, hybreds and lubberds!
 1939 *Finnegans Wake*.

37 All moanday, tearsday, wailsday, thumpsday, frightday, shatterday till the fear of the Law.
 1939 *Finnegans Wake*.

Joyce, Nora 1884–1951
Wife of James Joyce.

38 Well, Jim, I haven't read any of your books but I'll have to someday because they must be good considering how well they sell.
 To her husband James Joyce. Recalled on her death, 12 Apr 1951.

Joyce, William known as Lord Haw Haw 1906–46
British traitor. He fled to Germany before World War II, from where he broadcast anti-British propaganda in his upper-class drawl until captured at Flensburg and executed.

39 The Twenty Thousand Thieves.
 c.1941 Of the Australian 9th Division troops who were besieged at Tobruk, North Africa. Radio broadcast from Nazi Germany.

Julian of Norwich known as Lady Julian c.1342–1416
English anchoress, who spent much of her life enclosed in a cell attached to the Church of St Julian, Norwich. In 1373 she experienced a series of religious visions which she set down in her *Revelations of Divine Love*.

40 He showed me something small, no bigger than a hazelnut, lying in the palm of my hand, as it seemed to

me, and it was as round as a ball. I looked at it with the eye of my understanding, and thought: What can this be? I was amazed that it could last, for I thought that because of its littleness it would suddenly have fallen into nothing. And I was answered in my understanding: It lasts and always will, because God loves it; and thus every thing has being through the love of God.
1373–c.1393 *Revelations of Divine Love*, ch.5.

41 It is true that sin is the cause of all this pain; but all shall be well, and all shall be well, and all manner of things shall be well.
1373–c.1393 *Revelations of Divine Love*, ch.27.

42 Pray inwardly, even though you do not enjoy it. It does good though you feel nothing, even though you think you are doing nothing.
1373–c.1393 *Revelations of Divine Love*, ch.41.

Jumblatt, Walid 1949–
Lebanese politician and hereditary Druze chieftain, who succeeded his father Jumblatt on the latter's assassination in 1977.

43 Here, even the law of the jungle has broken down.
1985 Of the situation in Beirut, in the *Sunday Times*, 29 Dec.

Juncker, Jean-Claude 1954–
Luxembourgish politician. Leader of the Christian Social People's Party, he was Prime Minister of Luxembourg (1995–2013) before being elected President of European Commission in 2014.

44 We all know what to do, we just don't know how to get re-elected after we've done it.
2007 Referring to economic reform, quoted in John Micklethwait, *The Fourth Revolution: The Global Race to Reinvent the State*.

45 When it becomes serious, you have to lie.
2011 Referring to the economic crisis in Greece.

Jung, Carl Gustav 1875–1961
Swiss psychiatrist. After collaborating with Sigmund Freud he published *The Psychology of the Unconscious* (1911–12), departing from Freud's psychosexual emphasis. Subsequently he developed analytical psychology and the concept of the 'collective unconscious'.

46 The pendulum of the mind oscillates between sense and nonsense, not between right and wrong.
1962 *Memories, Dreams and Reflections*.

47 Show me a sane man and I will cure him for you.
Quoted in the *Observer*, 19 Jul 1975.

'Junius' possibly the pseudonym of Sir Philip Francis (1740–1818)
The identity of Junius, whose scathing political letters were printed in the *Public Advertiser* between 1769 and 1771 and collected in 1772, has never been established. Sir Philip Francis is a favourite candidate.

48 There is a holy mistaken zeal in politics as well as in religion. By persuading others, we convince ourselves.
1769 *Public Advertiser*, 19 Dec, Letter 35.

49 Let it be impressed upon your minds, let it be instilled into your children, that the liberty of the press is the *Palladium* of all the civil, political, and religious rights of an Englishman.
1772 *Letters*, Dedication to the Authorized Edition.

Just, Ward Swift 1935–
US journalist and writer. He was a correspondent with *Newsweek* (1963–5) and the *Washington Post* (1965–70), before turning full time to fiction with works such as *Echo House* (1997), *An Unfinished Season* (2004) and *American Romantic* (2014).

50 The place where bulls and foxes dine very well, but lambs end up head down on the hook.
1988 Of Chicago. *Jack Gance*.

Justinian I AD 482–565
Emperor of the East Roman Empire (from 527). His reign saw the restoration of the Roman Empire to its ancient limits and many legal reforms, collected in the *Corpus Juris Civilis*, which had a considerable influence on European law.

51 Justice is the constant and perpetual wish to render to every one his due.
AD 533 *Institutiones*, pt.1.

Juvenal full name Decimus Iunius Iuvenalis c.55–c.140 AD
Roman lawyer and satirist. He was banished to Egypt for some years by Domitian for his 16 verse satires (c.100–128 AD), which deal with the corruption and immorality of the times.

52 *Difficile est saturam non scribere.*
It is difficult not to write satire.
Satirae, no.1, 1.30.

53 *Quis tulerit Gracchos de seditione querentes?*
Who can bear the Gracchi deploring revolution?
Satirae, no.2, 1.24. The brothers Gaius and Tiberius Sempronius Gracchus (2c BC) attempted radical agrarian reforms, and were both killed by political opponents.

54 *Nil habet infelix paupertas durius in se*
Quam quod ridiculos homines facit.
The hardest thing to bear in poverty is the fact that it makes men ridiculous.
Satirae, no.3, 1.152–3 (translated by Peter Green).

55 *Sed quis custodiet ipsos custodes?*
But who is to guard the guards themselves?
Satirae, no.6, 1.347.

56 *Cantabit vacuus coram latrone viator.*
Travel light and you can sing in the robber's face.
Satirae, no.10, 1.22.

57 *Nam qui dabat olim*
imperium, fasces, legiones, omnia, nunc se
continet atque duas tantum res anxius optat,
panem et circenses.
Time was when their plebiscite elected generals, Heads of State, commanders of legions: but now they've pulled in their horns, there's only two things that concern them: bread and games.
Of the people of Rome. *Satirae*, no.10, 1.78–81 (translated by Peter Green). 'Panem et circenses' is sometimes translated as 'bread and circuses'.

58 *Orandum est ut sit mens sana in corpore sano.*
One should pray to have a sound mind in a sound body.
Satirae, no.10, 1.356.

59 *Maxima debetur puero reverentia, si quid*
turpe paras.
If you are planning any misdeed, never forget that a child has a first claim on your respect.
Satirae, no.14, 1.47 (translated by Peter Green).

Kael

Kael, Pauline 1919–2001
US film critic. She was film critic of the *New Yorker* from 1968 to 1991.

1 The words 'Kiss Kiss Bang Bang' which I saw on an Italian movie poster, are perhaps the briefest statement imaginable of the basic appeal of movies.
   1968 *Kiss Kiss Bang Bang*.

2 Good movies make you care, make you believe in possibilities again.
   1970 *Going Steady*.

Kafka, Franz 1883–1924
Czech novelist and short-story writer who wrote in German. After studying law he worked in Prague at a workers' accident insurance company. He is best known for his bleak studies of the absurdity of the human condition.

3 *Ich glaube, mann sollte überhaupt nur solche Bücher lesen, die einen beißen und stechen.*
   I think we ought to read only the kind of books that wound and stab us.
   1904 Letter to Oskar Pollack. Collected in Richard and Clara Winston (eds and trans) *Letters to Friends, Family, and Editors* (1977).

4 *Ist es schwer und kann es ein Außenseiter begreifen, dass man eine Geschichte von ihrem Anfang in sich erlebt, vom fernen Punkt bis zu der heranfahrenden Lokomotive aus Stahl, Kohl und Dampf, sie aber auch jetzt noch nicht verlässt, sondern von ihr gejagt wird und aus eigenem Schwung vor ihr läuft, wohin sie nur stößt und wohin man sie lockt.*
   It is so difficult and can an outsider understand that you experience a story within yourself from its beginning, from the distant point up to the approaching locomotive of steel, coal and steam, and you don't abandon it even now, but want to be pursued by it and have time for it, therefore are pursued by it and of your own volition run before it wherever it may thrust and wherever you may lure it.
   1911 Diary entry, Aug. Collected in Max Brod (ed) *The Diaries of Franz Kafka, 1910–1913* (1948).

5 *Als Gregor Samsa eines Morgens aus unruhigen Träumen erwachte, fand er sich in seinem Bett zu einem ungeheueren Ungeziefer verwandelt.*
   When Gregor Samsa awoke one morning from uneasy dreams he found himself transformed in his bed into a gigantic insect.
   1915 *Metamorphosis*, ch.1.

6 *Es ist oft besser, in Ketten als frei zu sein.*
   It is often safer to be in chains than to be free.
   1925 *Der Prozess* (translated as *The Trial*, 1937).

7 *Ich bin so weit, dass ich Gewissheit gar nicht haben will.*
   I have reached the stage where I no longer wish to have certainty.

'Der Bau', collected in Nahum N Glatzer (ed) *The Complete Stories* (1971).

8 *Er lächelte und sagte: 'Von mir willst du den Weg erfahren?' 'Ja,' sagte ich, 'da ich ihn selbst nich finden kann.' 'Gibs auf, gibs auf,' sagte er und wandte sich mit einem großen Schwunge ab, so wie Leute, die mit ihrem Lachen allein sein wollen.*
   He smiled and said: 'You asking me the way?' 'Yes,' I said, 'since I cannot find it myself.' 'Give it up! Give it up!' said he, and turned with a sudden jerk, like someone who wants to be alone with his laughter.
   'Gibs Auf!', collected in Nahum N Glatzer (ed) *The Complete Stories* (1971).

Kahn, Gus 1886–1941
US lyricist and author. He supplied the lyrics for many classic hit songs of the 1920s and 1930s, among them 'Toot, Toot, Tootsie', 'Carolina in the Morning', 'Yes Sir, That's My Baby', and 'Makin' Whoopee'.

9 There's nothing surer,
  The rich get rich and the poor get children.
  In the meantime, in between time,
  Ain't we got fun.
  1921 'Ain't We Got Fun' (with Raymond B Egan).

10 All God's Chillum Got Rhythm.
   1937 Title of song.

Kaiko, Takeshi 1930–89
Japanese novelist. His first novel to be translated into English was *Darkness in Summer* (1972).

11 I don't trust anybody who's never eaten bread with the salt of tears.
   1963 'The Laughing Stock', in *Five Thousand Runaways* (translated by Cecilia Segawa Seigle).

12 Late one morning, I awoke in the capital of a certain country and found myself—not changed overnight into a large brown beetle, nor feeling exactly on top of the world—merely ready to go home.
   1978 'The Crushed Pellet', in *Five Thousand Runaways* (translated by Cecilia Segawa Seigle).

Kames, Henry Home, Lord 1696–1782
Scottish judge, philosopher and agricultural improver, a central figure of the Scottish Enlightenment.

13 Fare ye a' weel, ye bitches!
   1782 His alleged words on taking leave of his fellow judges in the Court of Session. He died eight days later. Quoted in Robert Chambers *Traditions of Edinburgh* (1824), 'The Parliament House'.

Kandinsky, Wassily 1866–1944
Russian-born painter and writer on art. He was an important pioneer of abstract art. With Franz Marc he edited the *Blaue Reiter Almanac*.

14 The force that propels the human spirit on the clear way forward and upward is the abstract spirit.
   1912 'On the Question of Form', in *Blaue Reiter Almanac*.

15 We should never make a god out of form. We should struggle for form only as long as it serves as a means of expression for the inner sound.
   1912 'On the Question of Form', in *Blaue Reiter Almanac*.

16 Every work of art is the child of its time, often it is the mother of our emotions.
1912 *Concerning the Spiritual in Art.*

17 In general, therefore, color is a means of exerting a direct influence upon the soul. Color is the keyboard. The eye is the hammer. The soul is the piano, with its many strings.
Quoted in K C Lindsay and P Vergo (eds and trans) *Kandinsky: Complete Writings on Art* (1982).

Kant, Immanuel   1724–1804

German philosopher, Professor of Logic and Metaphysics at Konigsberg (1770), who developed a theory of knowledge depending on perception and propounded the 'moral argument' for the existence of God. His great work is the *Kritik der reinen Vernunft* (*Critique of Pure Reason*, 1781).

18 *Der Verstand vermag nichts anzuschauen, und die Sinne nichts zu denken. Nur daraus, dass sie sich vereinigen, kann Erkenntnis entspringen.*
The understanding can intuit nothing, the senses can think nothing. Only through their union can knowledge arise.
1781 *Kritik der reinen Vernunft* (*Critique of Pure Reason*), B75 (translated by N Kemp Smith).

19 *Ich habe also demnach keine Erkenntnis von mir, wie ich bin, sondern bloß, wie ich mir selbst erscheine. Das Bewusstsein seiner selbst ist also noch lange nicht eine Erkenntnis seiner selbst.*
I have no *knowledge* of myself as I am but merely as I appear to myself. The consciousness of myself is thus very far from being a knowledge of the self.
1781 *Kritik der reinen Vernunft* (*Critique of Pure Reason*), B158 (translated by N Kemp Smith).

20 *Eben darin Philosophie besteht, seine Grenzen zu kennen.*
It is precisely in knowing its limits that philosophy consists.
1781 *Kritik der reinen Vernunft* (*Critique of Pure Reason*), B755 (translated by N Kemp Smith).

21 *Sapere aude*, have the courage to know: that is the motto of enlightenment.
1783 His reply to a newspaper's challenge to define enlightenment. Quoted in *The Economist*, 16 Mar 1996.

22 *Aus so krummen Holze, als woraus der Mensch gemacht ist, kann nichts ganz Gerades gezimmert werden.*
Out of the crooked timber of humanity, no straight thing can ever be made.
1784 *Idee zu einer allgemeinen Geschichte in weltbürgerlicher Absicht* (*Idea for a General History with a Cosmopolitan Purpose*), prop.6.

23 *Ich solle niemals anders verfahren, als so, dass ich auch wollen könne, meine Maxime solle ein allgemeines Gesetz werden.*
I ought never to act except in such a way *that I can also will that my maxim should become a universal law.*
1785 *Grundlagen zur Metaphysik der Sitten* (*Groundwork to a Metaphysic of Morals*), ch.1 (translated by H J Paton).

24 *Handle so, dass du die Menschheit, sowohl in deiner Person, als in der Person eines jeden andern, jederzeit zugleich als Zweck, niemals bloß als Mittel brauchst.*
Act in such a way that you always treat humanity, whether in your own person or in the person of any other, never simply as a means, but always at the same time as an end.
1785 *Grundlagen zur Metaphysik der Sitten* (*Groundwork to a Metaphysic of Morals*), ch.2 (translated by H J Paton).

25 *Ich musste also das Wissen aufheben, um zum Glauben Platz zu bekommen.*
I have therefore found it necessary to deny *knowledge*, in order to make room for *faith*.
1787 *Kritik der reinen Vernunft* (*Critique of Pure Reason*), preface to 2nd edn (translated by N Kemp Smith).

26 *Zwei Dinge erfüllen das Gemüt mit immer neuer und zunehmender Bewunderung und Ehrfurcht, je öfter und anhaltender sich das Nachdenken damit beschäftigt: der bestirnte Himmel über mir, und das moralische Gesetz in mir.*
Two things fill the mind with ever new and increasing admiration and awe, the oftener and more steadily we reflect on them: *the starry heavens above me and the moral law within.*
1788 *Kritik der praktischen Vernunft* (*Critique of Practical Reason*) (translated by T K Abbott).

Kapitsa, Peter Leonidovich   1894–1984

Soviet physicist who studied in Britain under Ernest Rutherford. Director of the Institute of Physical Problems, he was dismissed by Stalin for refusing to work on an atomic bomb, but was later reinstated.

27 Theory is a good thing but a good experiment lasts forever.
1980 *Experiment, Theory, Practice.*

Kapoor, Sir Anish   1954–

Indian sculptor, resident in London since the early 1970s.

28 Artists don't make objects. Artists make mythologies.
Attributed.

Karloff, Boris *originally* William Henry Pratt   1887–1969

English-born US film star. He went to Canada and the US aiming at a diplomatic career, but turned to acting, finding fame as the monster in *Frankenstein* (1931) and other horror roles.

29 The monster was indeed the best friend I could ever have.
On his success as Frankenstein's monster. Quoted in *Connoisseur*, Jan 1991.

Karpov, Anatoly   1951–

Russian chess player.

30 Chess is everything—art, science and sport.
Attributed.

Karr, Alphonse   1808–90

French writer and journalist.

31 *Plus ça change, plus c'est la même chose.*
The more things change, the more they stay the same.
1849 *Les Guêpes*, Jan.

Karsh, Yousuf   1908–2002

Turkish-born Canadian portrait photographer.

32 I said, 'Forgive me, sir,' and plucked the cigar out of his mouth. By the time I got back to my camera, he looked

so belligerent he could have devoured me. It was at that instant that I took the photograph. The silence was deafening.
>   **1983** Recalling how he snapped the celebrated 'bulldog' photograph of Sir Winston Churchill in the Speaker's Chambers, House of Commons, Ottawa, on 30 Dec 1941. *Karsh: A Fifty-Year Retrospective.*

Karzai, Hamid 1957–

Afghan politician. After two years as Interim President following the fall of the Taliban, he was elected President of Afghanistan (2004–14).

33 Don't vote for bad people.
>   **2005** His advice to voters in the Afghan elections.

Kaufman, George S(imon) 1889–1961

US playwright, director and journalist, a member of the Algonquin Round Table circle of literary wits. He collaborated on several successful comedies with Moss Hart, notably *The Man Who Came to Dinner* (1939), and also worked with Edna Ferber and George Gershwin.

34 Am sitting in the last row. Wish you were here.
>   **1932** Telegram sent during a performance of *Of Thee I Sing* to the actor William Gaxton, who was taking various liberties with Kaufman's lines while playing the leading role.

35 Massey won't be satisfied until he's assassinated.
>   **1938** Of Raymond Massey in the title role of *Abe Lincoln in Illinois*. Recalled on Kaufman's death, 2 Jun 1961.

36 Satire is what closes Saturday night.
>   Quoted in Howard Teichmann *George S Kaufman* (1972).

37 I saw his play under bad conditions. The curtain was up.
>   Of Alexander Woollcott. Quoted in Scott Meredith *George S Kaufman and His Friends* (1974).

38 Like the Arabs, I fold my tens and silently steal away.
>   On winning at poker. Quoted in Scott Meredith *George S Kaufman and His Friends* (1974).
>   ▶ See Longfellow 535:23.

39 It's what God would have done if he'd had the money.
>   On visiting Pocantico Hills, the Rockefeller family's 3,000-acre Hudson River estate. Quoted in Michael Kramer and Sam Roberts *I Never Wanted to Be Vice-President of Anything!* (1976).

40 God finally caught his eye.
>   Epitaph for a deceased waiter. Quoted in Jon Winokur *The Portable Curmudgeon* (1987).

41 There was scattered laughter in the rear of the theatre, leading to the belief that somebody was telling jokes back there.
>   Play review.

42 Close the play and keep the store open nights.
>   Reply when asked by one of his backers, the owner of Bloomingdale's department store, how the première of Kaufman's latest play had gone. Attributed.

43 Over my dead body.
>   Suggestion for his own epitaph. Attributed.

Kaufman, Sir Gerald 1930–

English Labour politician.

44 We would prefer to see the House run by a philistine with the requisite financial acumen than by the succession of opera and ballet lovers who have brought a great and valuable institution to its knees.
>   **1997** Report of the Commons' Culture, Media and Sport Select Committee on Covent Garden, 3 Dec.

Kaufmann, Christoph 1753–95

Swiss-born German author and critic.

45 *Sturm und Drang.*
>   Storm and stress.
>   **c.1775** Suggested title for a romantic historical play of F M Klinger, adopted as the defining term for late-18c German drama.

Kaunitz-Rietberg, Wenzel Anton, Prince von 1711–94

Austrian statesman, Ambassador to the French court (1750–2). Appointed Chancellor in 1753, he directed Austrian politics for almost 40 years. Active in the ecclesiastical reforms of Joseph II, he was a liberal patron of arts and sciences.

46 That was very good of him.
>   **1790** Attributed, on hearing that Joseph II had died. Quoted in T C W Blanning *Joseph II* (1994), p.198.

Kavanagh, P(atrick) J(oseph Gregory) 1931–

English poet and novelist. His works include the autobiographical *The Perfect Stranger* (1966) and *A Kind of Journal* (2003), a collection of his *Spectator* columns.

47 Charlie Parker...always filled me with a kind of despair, because he played the way I would have liked to write, and this wasn't possible for me or anyone else. He made poetry seem word-bound.
>   **1966** *The Perfect Stranger*, ch.5.

48 Try not to despise yourself too much—it's only a conceit.
>   **1968** *A Song and Dance*, ch.6.

49 But years ago he had decided never to be afraid of the deafeningly obvious, it is always news to somebody.
>   **1968** *A Song and Dance*, ch.6.

50 Mary lived by wondering what lay round the corner. I lived by knowing there was no corner.
>   **1973** *A Happy Man*, ch.12.

Kazantzakis, Nikos 1883–1957

Greek writer, best known for his novel *Zorba the Greek* (1946, filmed 1964) and the long autobiographical narrative poem, *The Odyssey, a Modern Sequel* (1938).

51 My entire soul is a cry, and all my work is a commentary on that cry.
>   **1965** *Report to Greco*.

Kazin, Alfred 1915–98

US writer, best known for influential books of literary criticism such as *On Native Grounds* (1942) and the autobiographical *A Walker in the City* (1951).

52 In a very real sense, the writer writes in order to teach himself, to understand himself, to satisfy himself; the publishing of his ideas, though it brings gratifications, is a curious anti-climax.
>   **1963** In *Think*, Feb.

53 Only power can get people into a position where they may be noble.
>   Quoted in M Korda *Power in the Office* (1976).

Keane, Roy 1971–

Irish footballer.

54 They have a few drinks, and maybe the prawn sandwiches, and they don't realise what's going on out on the pitch.
2000 On spectators in the corporate boxes at Manchester United games. In the *Sunday Times*, 31 Dec.

55 I don't give people hell. I tell them the truth and they think it's hell.
2002 On RTE, 28 May.

Keating, Paul John 1944–

Australian Republican politician. He became President of the New South Wales Labor Party (1979–83) and in 1991 was elected Leader of the Australian Labor Party. He was Prime Minister from 1991 to 1996.

56 A banana republic.
1986 On Australia's balance-of-payments crisis and cycle of recession. Radio broadcast, Radio 2GB, Sydney, 14 May.

57 All tip and no iceberg.
2007 Referring to Treasurer Peter Costello, ABC Radio interview, 5 Mar.

58 He's a pre-Copernican obscurantist.
2007 Referring to Prime Minister John Howard, ABC Radio interview, 1 May.

59 This is a low flying person.
2008 Referring to Treasurer Peter Costello, *7.30 Report*, 6 Aug.

Keats, John 1795–1821

English Romantic poet. His long mythological poem *Endymion* (1818) was fiercely criticized but *Lamia, Isabella, The Eve of St. Agnes and Other Poems* (1820), containing the romances 'The Eve of St Agnes' and 'Lamia', the epic 'Hyperion' and his major odes, was better received. He died of tuberculosis in Rome.

60 Much have I travell'd in the realms of gold.
1815 'On First Looking into Chapman's Homer', l.1. (Published in *The Examiner* 1816.)

61 Then felt I like some watcher of the skies
When a new planet swims into his ken;
Or like stout Cortez when with eagle eyes
He star'd at the Pacific—and all his men
Look'd at each other with a wild surmise—
Silent, upon a peak in Darien.
1815 'On First Looking into Chapman's Homer', l.9–14. (Published in *The Examiner* 1816.)

62 Sweetly they slept
On the blue fields of heaven, and then there crept
A little noiseless noise among the leaves,
Born of the very sign that silence heaves.
1816 'I Stood Tip-Toe upon a Little Hill', l.9–12.

63 Here are sweet peas, on tiptoe for a flight,
With wings of gentle flush o'er delicate white.
1816 'I Stood Tip-Toe upon a Little Hill', l.57–8.

64 Morality
Weighs heavily on me like unwilling sleep.
1817 'On Seeing the Elgin Marbles'.

65 Yet the sweet converse of an innocent mind,
Whose words are images of thoughts refined,
Is my soul's pleasure; and it sure must be
Almost the highest bliss of human-kind,
When to thy haunts two kindred spirits flee.
1817 'O Solitude! If I Must with Thee Dwell'.

66 Stop and consider! life is but a day;
A fragile dew-drop on its perilous way
From a tree's summit; a poor Indian's sleep
While his boat hastens to the monstrous steep
Of Montmorenci.
1817 'Sleep and Poetry', l.85–9.

67 O for ten years, that I may overwhelm
Myself in poesy; so I may do the deed
That my own soul has to itself decreed.
1817 'Sleep and Poetry', l.96–8.

68 They swayed about upon a rocking horse,
And thought it Pegasus.
1817 'Sleep and Poetry', l.186–7.

69 And they shall be accounted poet kings
Who simply tell the most heart-easing things.
1817 'Sleep and Poetry', l.267–8.

70 It keeps eternal whisperings around
Desolate shores—and with its mighty swell
Gluts twice ten thousand Caverns.
1817 'On the Sea'.

71 I had a dove and the sweet dove died;
And I have thought it died of grieving:
O, what could it grieve for? Its feet were tied,
With a silken thread of my own hands' weaving.
1817 'I had a Dove and the Sweet Dove Died'.

72 A long poem is a test of invention which I take to be the Polar star of poetry, as fancy is the sails, and imagination the rudder.
1817 Letter to Benjamin Bailey, 8 Oct.

73 I am certain of nothing but the holiness of the heart's affections and the truth of the imagination—what the imagination seizes as beauty must be truth—whether it existed before or not.
1817 Letter to Benjamin Bailey, 22 Nov.

74 O for a life of sensations rather than of thoughts!
1817 Letter to Benjamin Bailey, 22 Nov.

75 Negative Capability; that is, when a man is capable of being in uncertainties, mysteries, doubts, without any irritable reaching after fact and reason.
1817 Letter to G and T Keats, 21 Dec.

76 Souls of Poets dead and gone
What Elysium have ye known,
Happy field or mossy cavern,
Choicer than the Mermaid Tavern?
1818 'Lines on the Mermaid Tavern'.

77 When I have fears that I may cease to be
Before my pen has gleaned my teeming brain,
Before high-piled books, in charactery,
Hold like rich garners the full ripened grain.
1818 'When I Have Fears That I May Cease to Be'.

78 When I behold, upon the night's starred face
Huge cloudy symbols of a high romance,
And think that I may never live to trace
Their shadows, with the magic hand
  of chance;
And when I feel, fair creature of an hour,
That I shall never look upon thee more,
Never have relish in the faery power
Of unreflecting love;—then on the shore
Of the wide world I stand alone, and think
Till love and fame to nothingness so sink.
1818 'When I Have Fears That I May Cease to Be'.

Keats

79 If poetry comes not as naturally as leaves to a tree it had better not come at all.
   1818 Letter to John Taylor, 27 Feb.

80 Scenery is fine—but human nature is finer.
   1818 Letter to Benjamin Bailey, 13 Mar.

81 It is impossible to live in a country which is continually under hatches... Rain! Rain! Rain!
   1818 Letter to J H Reynolds, 10 Apr.

82 I think I shall be among the English Poets after my death.
   1818 Letter to George and Georgiana Keats, 14 Oct.

83 The imagination of a boy is healthy, and the mature imagination of a man is healthy; but there is a space of life between, in which the soul is in a ferment, the character undecided, the way of life uncertain, the ambition thick-sighted: thence proceeds mawkishness.
   1818 *Endymion*, preface.

84 A thing of beauty is a joy for ever:
   Its loveliness increases; it will never
   Pass into nothingness; but still will keep
   A bower quiet for us, and a sleep
   Full of sweet dreams, and health, and quiet breathing.
   1818 *Endymion*, bk.1, l.1–5.

85 The grandeur of the dooms
   We have imagined for the mighty dead.
   1818 *Endymion*, bk.1, l.20–1.

86 They always must be with us, or we die.
   1818 *Endymion*, bk.1, l.33.

87 Who, of men, can tell
   That flowers would bloom, or that green fruit would swell
   To melting pulp, that fish would have bright mail,
   The earth its dower of river, wood, and vale,
   The meadows runnels, runnels pebble-stones,
   The seed its harvest, or the lute its tones,
   Tones ravishment, or ravishment its sweet,
   If human souls did never kiss and greet?
   1818 *Endymion*, bk.1, l.835–42.

88 Here is wine,
   Alive with sparkles—never, I aver,
   Since Ariadne was a vintager,
   So cool a purple.
   1818 *Endymion*, bk.2, l.441–4.

89 To Sorrow,
   I bade good-morrow,
   And thought to leave her far away behind;
   But cheerly, cheerly,
   She loves me dearly;
   She is so constant to me, and so kind.
   1818 *Endymion*, bk.4, l.173–8.

90 Their smiles,
   Wan as primroses gathered at midnight
   By chilly fingered spring.
   1818 *Endymion*, bk.4, l.969–71.

91 Turn the key deftly in the oiled wards,
   And seal the hushed Casket of my Soul.
   1819 'To Sleep'.

92 Call the world if you please 'The vale of soul-making'.
   1819 Letter to George and Georgiana Keats, 14 Feb.

93 I have met with women whom I really think would like to be married to a poem, and to be given away by a novel.
   1819 Letter to Fanny Brawne, 8 Jul.

94 I have two luxuries to brood over in my walks, your loveliness and the hour of my death. O that I could have possession of them both in the same minute.
   1819 Letter to Fanny Brawne, 25 Jul.

95 My friends should drink a dozen of Claret on my Tomb.
   1819 Letter to Benjamin Bailey, 14 Aug.

96 Give me books, fruit, french wine and fine weather and a little music out of doors, played by somebody I do not know.
   1819 Letter to Fanny Keats, 29 Aug.

97 Fanatics have their dreams, wherewith they weave
   A paradise for a sect.
   1819 'The Fall of Hyperion', l.1–2.
   (Published 1856.)

98 'None can usurp this height,' returned that shade,
   'But those to whom the miseries of the world
   Are misery, and will not let them rest.'
   1819 'The Fall of Hyperion', l.147–9.
   (Published 1856.)

99 The poet and the dreamer are distinct,
   Diverse, sheer opposite, antipodes.
   The one pours out a balm upon the world,
   The other vexes it.
   1819 'The Fall of Hyperion', l.199–202.
   (Published 1856.)

1 Oh what can ail thee, knight at arms,
   Alone and palely loitering;
   The sedge has wither'd from the lake,
   And no birds sing.
   1820 'La Belle Dame Sans Merci', stanza 1.

2 She found me roots of relish sweet,
   And honey wild, and manna dew;
   And sure in language strange she said,
   'I love thee true.'
   1820 'La Belle Dame Sans Merci', stanza 7.

3 I saw pale kings, and princes too,
   Pale warriors, death-pale were they all;
   Who cry'd—'La belle Dame sans Merci
   Hath thee in thrall!'
   1820 'La Belle Dame Sans Merci', stanza 10.

4 She was a gordian shape of dazzling hue,
   Vermilion-spotted, golden, green, and blue;
   Striped like a zebra, freckled like a pard,
   Eyed like a peacock, and all crimson barr'd.
   1820 *Lamia, Isabella, The Eve of St. Agnes and Other Poems*, 'Lamia', pt.1, l.47–50.

5 Real are the dreams of Gods, and smoothly pass
   Their pleasures in a long immortal dream.
   1820 *Lamia, Isabella, The Eve of St. Agnes and Other Poems*, 'Lamia', pt.1, l.127–8.

6 Love in a hut, with water and a crust,
   Is—Love, forgive us!—cinders, ashes, dust;
   Love in a palace is perhaps at last
   More grievous torment than a hermit's fast.
   1820 *Lamia, Isabella, The Eve of St. Agnes and Other Poems*, 'Lamia', pt.2, l.1–4.

7 That purple-lined palace of sweet sin.
   1820 *Lamia, Isabella, The Eve of St. Agnes and Other Poems*, 'Lamia', pt.2, l.31.

8 In pale contented sort of discontent.
   1820 *Lamia, Isabella, The Eve of St. Agnes and Other Poems*, 'Lamia', pt.2, l.135.

9   Do not all charms fly
    At the mere touch of cold philosophy?
    There was an awful rainbow once in heaven:
    We know her woof, her texture; she is given
    In the dull catalogue of common things.
    Philosophy will clip an Angel's wings.
    1820 *Lamia, Isabella, The Eve of St. Agnes and Other Poems*, 'Lamia', pt.2, l.229–34.

10 Why were they proud? again we ask aloud,
    Why in the name of Glory were they proud?
    1820 *Lamia, Isabella, The Eve of St. Agnes and Other Poems*, 'Isabella; or, The Pot of Basil', stanza 16.

11 So the two brothers and their murdered man
    Rode past fair Florence.
    1820 *Lamia, Isabella, The Eve of St. Agnes and Other Poems*, 'Isabella; or, The Pot of Basil', stanza 27.

12 And she forgot the stars, the moon, and sun,
    And she forgot the blue above the trees,
    And she forgot the dells where waters run,
    And she forgot the chilly autumn breeze;
    She had no knowledge when the day was done,
    And the new morn she saw not: but in peace
    Hung over her sweet Basil evermore,
    And moistened it with tears unto the core.
    1820 *Lamia, Isabella, The Eve of St. Agnes and Other Poems*, 'Isabella; or, The Pot of Basil', stanza 53.

13 'To steal my Basil-pot away from me.'
    1820 *Lamia, Isabella, The Eve of St. Agnes and Other Poems*, 'Isabella; or, The Pot of Basil', stanza 62.

14 St. Agnes' Eve—Ah, bitter chill it was!
    The owl, for all his feathers, was a-cold;
    The hare limped trembling through the
       frozen grass,
    And silent was the flock in woolly fold.
    1820 *Lamia, Isabella, The Eve of St. Agnes and Other Poems*, 'The Eve of St. Agnes', stanza 1.

15 The silver, snarling trumpets 'gan to chide.
    1820 *Lamia, Isabella, The Eve of St. Agnes and Other Poems*, 'The Eve of St. Agnes', stanza 4.

16 And soft adorings from their loves receive
    Upon the honeyed middle of the night.
    1820 *Lamia, Isabella, The Eve of St. Agnes and Other Poems*, 'The Eve of St. Agnes', stanza 6.

17 The music, yearning like a God in pain.
    1820 *Lamia, Isabella, The Eve of St. Agnes and Other Poems*, 'The Eve of St. Agnes', stanza 7.

18 Sudden a thought came like a full-blown rose,
    Flushing his brow, and in his painted heart
    Made purple riot.
    1820 *Lamia, Isabella, The Eve of St. Agnes and Other Poems*, 'The Eve of St. Agnes', stanza 16.

19 A poor, weak, palsy-stricken, churchyard thing.
    1820 *Lamia, Isabella, The Eve of St. Agnes and Other Poems*, 'The Eve of St. Agnes', stanza 18.

20 A casement high and triple-arched there was,
    All garlanded with carven imag'ries
    Of fruits, and flowers, and bunches of knot-grass,
    And diamonded with panes of quaint device,
    Innumerable of stains and splendid dyes,
    As are the tiger-moth's deep-damasked wings.
    1820 *Lamia, Isabella, The Eve of St. Agnes and Other Poems*, 'The Eve of St. Agnes', stanza 24.

21 Full on this casement shone the wintry moon,
    And threw warm gules on Madeleine's fair breast,
    As down she knelt for heaven's grace and boon;
    Rose-bloom fell on her hands, together prest,
    And on her silver cross soft amethyst,
    And on her hair a glory like a saint:
    She seemed a splendid angel, newly drest,
    Save wings, for heaven.
    1820 *Lamia, Isabella, The Eve of St. Agnes and Other Poems*, 'The Eve of St. Agnes', stanza 25.

22 By degrees
    Her rich attire creeps rustling to her knees.
    1820 *Lamia, Isabella, The Eve of St. Agnes and Other Poems*, 'The Eve of St. Agnes', stanza 26.

23 As though a rose should shut, and be a bud
       again.
    1820 *Lamia, Isabella, The Eve of St. Agnes and Other Poems*, 'The Eve of St. Agnes', stanza 27.

24 And still she slept an azure-lidded sleep,
    In blanched linen, smooth, and lavendered,
    While he from forth the closet brought a heap
    Of candied apple, quince, and plum, and gourd;
    With jellies soother than the creamy curd,
    And lucent syrops, tinct with cinnamon;
    Manna and dates, in argosy transferred
    From Fez; and spiced dainties, every one,
    From silken Samarcand to cedared Lebanon.
    1820 *Lamia, Isabella, The Eve of St. Agnes and Other Poems*, 'The Eve of St. Agnes', stanza 30.

25 He played an ancient ditty, long since mute,
    In Provence called, 'La belle dame sans mercy'.
    1820 *Lamia, Isabella, The Eve of St. Agnes and Other Poems*, 'The Eve of St. Agnes', stanza 33.

26 And the long carpets rose along the gusty floor.
    1820 *Lamia, Isabella, The Eve of St. Agnes and Other Poems*, 'The Eve of St. Agnes', stanza 40.

27 And they are gone: aye, ages long ago
    These lovers fled away into the storm.
    1820 *Lamia, Isabella, The Eve of St. Agnes and Other Poems*, 'The Eve of St. Agnes', stanza 42.

28 Deep in the shady sadness of a vale
    Far sunken from the healthy breath of morn,
    Far from the fiery noon and eve's one star,
    Sat gray-haired Saturn, quiet as a stone,
    Still as the silence round about his lair.
    1820 *Lamia, Isabella, The Eve of St. Agnes and Other Poems*, 'Hyperion', bk.1, l.1–5.

29 Where the dead leaf fell, there did it rest.
    1820 *Lamia, Isabella, The Eve of St. Agnes and Other Poems*, 'Hyperion', bk.1, l.10.

30 But oh! How unlike marble was that face.
    1820 *Lamia, Isabella, The Eve of St. Agnes and Other Poems*, 'Hyperion', bk.1, l.34.

31 That large utterance of the early Gods.
    1820 *Lamia, Isabella, The Eve of St. Agnes and Other Poems*, 'Hyperion', bk.1, l.51.

32 Season of mists and mellow fruitfulness,
    Close bosom-friend of the maturing sun;
    Conspiring with him how to load and bless
    With fruit the vines that round the thatch-eaves run.
    1820 *Lamia, Isabella, The Eve of St. Agnes and Other Poems*, 'To Autumn', stanza 1.

33 Where are the songs of Spring? Ay, where are they?
   Think not of them, thou hast thy music too.
   1820 *Lamia, Isabella, The Eve of St. Agnes and Other Poems*, 'To Autumn', stanza 3.

34 Thou still unravished bride of quietness,
   Thou foster-child of silence and slow time.
   1820 *Lamia, Isabella, The Eve of St. Agnes and Other Poems*, 'Ode on a Grecian Urn', stanza 1.

35 What men or Gods are these? What maidens loth?
   What mad pursuit? What struggle to escape?
   What pipes and timbrels? What wild ecstasy?
   1820 *Lamia, Isabella, The Eve of St. Agnes and Other Poems*, 'Ode on a Grecian Urn', stanza 1.

36 Heard melodies are sweet, but those unheard
   Are sweeter; therefore, ye soft pipes, play on;
   Not to the sensual ear, but, more endeared,
   Pipe to the spirit ditties of no tone.
   1820 *Lamia, Isabella, The Eve of St. Agnes and Other Poems*, 'Ode on a Grecian Urn', stanza 2.

37 She cannot fade, though thou hast not thy bliss,
   For ever wilt thou love, and she be fair!
   1820 *Lamia, Isabella, The Eve of St. Agnes and Other Poems*, 'Ode on a Grecian Urn', stanza 2.

38 O Attic shape! Fair attitude!
   1820 *Lamia, Isabella, The Eve of St. Agnes and Other Poems*, 'Ode on a Grecian Urn', stanza 5.

39 Thou, silent form, dost tease us out of thought
   As doth eternity: Cold Pastoral!
   1820 *Lamia, Isabella, The Eve of St. Agnes and Other Poems*, 'Ode on a Grecian Urn', stanza 5.

40 'Beauty is truth, truth beauty,'—that is all
   Ye know on earth, and all ye need to know.
   1820 *Lamia, Isabella, The Eve of St. Agnes and Other Poems*, 'Ode on a Grecian Urn', stanza 5.

41 My heart aches, and a drowsy numbness pains
   My sense, as though of hemlock I had drunk,
   Or emptied some dull opiate to the drains
   One minute past, and Lethe-wards had sunk:
   'Tis not through envy of thy happy lot,
   But being too happy in thine happiness
   That thou, light-winged Dryad of the trees,
   In some melodious plot
   Of beechen green, and shadows numberless,
   Singest of summer in full-throated ease.
   1820 *Lamia, Isabella, The Eve of St. Agnes and Other Poems*, 'Ode to a Nightingale', stanza 1.

42 O, for a draught of vintage! that hath been
   Cooled a long age in the deep-delved earth,
   Tasting of Flora and the country green,
   Dance, and Provençal song, and sunburnt mirth!
   O for a beaker full of the warm South,
   Full of the true, the blushful Hippocrene,
   With beaded bubbles winking at the brim,
   And purple-stained mouth;
   That I might drink, and leave the world unseen,
   And with thee fade away into the forest dim.
   1820 *Lamia, Isabella, The Eve of St. Agnes and Other Poems*, 'Ode to a Nightingale', stanza 2.

43 Fade far away, dissolve, and quite forget
   What thou among the leaves hast never known,
   The weariness, the fever, and the fret
   Here, where men sit and hear each other groan;
   Where palsy shakes a few, sad, last grey hairs,
   Where youth grows pale, and spectre-thin, and dies;
   Where but to think is to be full of sorrow
   And leaden-eyed despairs.
   1820 *Lamia, Isabella, The Eve of St. Agnes and Other Poems*, 'Ode to a Nightingale', stanza 3.

44 Already with thee! tender is the night.
   1820 *Lamia, Isabella, The Eve of St. Agnes and Other Poems*, 'Ode to a Nightingale', stanza 4.

45 Fast fading violets covered up in leaves;
   And mid-May's eldest child,
   The coming musk-rose, full of dewy wine,
   The murmurous haunt of flies on summer eves.
   1820 *Lamia, Isabella, The Eve of St. Agnes and Other Poems*, 'Ode to a Nightingale', stanza 5.

46 Darkling I listen; and, for many a time
   I have been half in love with easeful Death,
   Called him soft names in many a musèd rhyme,
   To take into the air my quiet breath;
   Now more than ever seems it rich to die,
   To cease upon the midnight with no pain,
   While thou art pouring forth thy soul abroad
   In such an ecstasy!
   1820 *Lamia, Isabella, The Eve of St. Agnes and Other Poems*, 'Ode to a Nightingale', stanza 6.

47 Thou wast not born for death, immortal Bird!
   1820 *Lamia, Isabella, The Eve of St. Agnes and Other Poems*, 'Ode to a Nightingale', stanza 7.

48 Forlorn! the very word is like a bell
   To toll me back from thee to my sole self!
   Adieu! the fancy cannot cheat so well
   As she is famed to do, deceiving elf.
   1820 *Lamia, Isabella, The Eve of St. Agnes and Other Poems*, 'Ode to a Nightingale', stanza 8.

49 I know the colour of that blood; it is arterial blood;
   I cannot be deceived in that colour; that drop of blood
   is my death-warrant—I must die.
   1821 On examining a drop of blood that fell from his mouth as he lay dying from tuberculosis. Quoted in John Sutherland *The Oxford Book of Literary Anecdotes* (1975).

50 Here lies one whose name was writ in water.
   Epitaph for himself. Quoted in Richard Monckton Milnes *Life, Letters and Literary Remains of John Keats* (1848), vol.2.

Keble, John 1792–1866

English churchman, the father of the Tractarian movement. He was also influential in the Oxford Movement after J H Newman's secession to Rome.

51 New every morning is the love
   Our wakening and uprising prove.
   1827 *The Christian Year*, 'Morning'.

Keenan, Brian 1950–

Northern Irish teacher and writer. He was kidnapped on 11 April 1986 while working at the American University of Beirut by Iranian terrorists and held hostage for four years.

52 I'm going to visit every country in the world, eat all the food of the world, drink all the drink of the world—and, I hope, make love to every woman in the world. Then I might get a good night's sleep.
   1990 Said on his release, BBC T V, 25 Aug.

Keillor, (Gary Edward) Garrison 1942–

US humorous writer and broadcaster. In 1974 he began his live radio show, *A Prairie Home Companion*, telling tales of small-town Minnesota set in fictional Lake Wobegon. His works include *Lake Wobegon Days* (1985) and *Love Me* (2004).

53 Where all the women are strong, all the men are good-looking, and all the children are above average.
   from 1974 His description of the fictional mid-Western town Lake Wobegon, used regularly in *A Prairie Home Companion*.

54 Peanut butter has survived everything that has been done to improve it.
   1990 In NPR broadcast, 29 Dec.

55 Public radio is a ghetto of good taste.
   1991 In National Public Radio broadcast, 9 Feb.

56 March is the month that God designed to show those who don't drink what a hangover is like.
   1991 In NPR broadcast, 1 Dec.

57 It's a play that after you've been there for a short while, you wonder how long this is going to take.
   1995 Of Edward Albee's *Three Tall Women*. In *New York*, 2 Jan.

58 I look like a tree toad who was changed into a boy but not completely.
   2001 *Lake Wobegon Summer 1956*.

59 One reads books in order to gain the privilege of living more than one life. People who don't read are trapped in a mine shaft, even if they think the sun is shining.
   2005 'The More Noble Prize', *Salon.com*, 30 Nov.

60 There is almost no marital problem that can't be helped enormously by taking off your clothes.
   2005 'The Old Scout', *The Writer's Almanac*, 4 Oct.

61 Jesus said the meek would inherit the earth, but so far all we've gotten is Minnesota and North Dakota.
   2006 'When I'm 64', *Salon.com*, 8 Aug.

62 Why do we work so hard to get what we don't even want?
   2006 *A Prairie Home Companion*.

63 Life is a struggle, and if you should feel really happy, be patient: this will pass.
   2006 *A Prairie Home Companion*.

64 You get old and you realize there are no answers, just stories.
   2007 *Pontoon: A Novel of Lake Wobegon*.

Keller, Helen Adams 1880–1968

US writer. She became deaf and blind at 19 months, but educated by Anne Sullivan she learned to speak, graduated in 1904 and became a distinguished lecturer and writer.

65 Everything has its wonders, even darkness and silence, and I learn, whatever state I may be in, therein to be content.
   1902 *The Story of My Life*.

66 As the eagle was killed by the arrow winged with its own feather, so the hand of the world is wounded by its own skill.
   1912 In the *American Magazine*, Dec.

Kelman, James 1946–

Scottish novelist, whose novels and short stories set in working-class Glasgow are characterized by an uncompromising vernacular style and vocabulary. In 1994 his novel *How late it was, how late* won the Booker Prize.

67 Theoretical webs, dirty webs, fusty webs, old and shrivelling away into nothingness, a fine dust. Who needs that kind of stuff. Far far better getting out into the open air and doing it, actually doing it, something solid and concrete and unconceptualisable.
   1989 *A Disaffection*.

68 Yes, they say, go and write whatever story you want, but don't use whatever language is necessary... By implication those in authority ask the writer to censor and suppress her or his own work. They demand it. If you don't comply then your work isn't produced.
   1992 *Some Recent Attacks*, 'The Importance of Glasgow in My Work'.

69 My culture and my language have the right to exist, and no one has the authority to dismiss that.
   1994 Speech at the Booker Prize award ceremony, 11 Oct.

70 Ye wake in a corner and stay there hoping yer body will disappear, the thoughts smothering ye; these thoughts; but ye want to remember and face up to things, just something keeps ye from doing it, why can ye no do it; the words filling yer head: then the other words; there's something far far wrong; ye're no a good man, ye're just no a good man.
   1994 *How late it was, how late*, opening words.

Kelvin, William Thomson, 1st Baron 1824–1907

Irish-born Scottish physician and mathematician, who developed the temperature scale named after him.

71 At what time does the dissipation of energy begin?
   When his wife proposed an afternoon walk. Quoted in A Fleming *Memories of a Scientific Life* (1934).

Kemble, Charles 1775–1854

English actor-manager. A celebrated comic actor, he became manager of Covent Garden in 1822 but subsequently ran into financial difficulties, mitigated in the early 1830s when he presented his daughter Fanny Kemble's stage debut.

72 Sir, I now pay you this exorbitant charge, but I must ask you to explain to Her Majesty that she must not in future look upon me as a source of income.
   When reluctantly obliged to pay overdue income tax. Attributed.

Kemble, John Philip 1757–1823

English actor-manager, brother of Sarah Siddons and Charles Kemble. A successful tragic actor, he was manager of the Theatre Royal, Drury Lane and subsequently of Covent Garden, where riots greeted his decision to raise ticket prices.

73 Ladies and gentlemen, unless the play is stopped, the child cannot possibly go on.
   Addressing the audience during a performance that was being much disrupted by a child crying. Attributed.

Kempis, St Thomas à c.1380–1471

German monk and author. In 1400 he entered the Augustinian convent of Agnetenberg, near Zwolle, where he was Sub-Prior at the time of his death.

74 *Vere magnus est, qui magnam habet caritatem.*
   He is truly great who has great charity.
   c.1413 *De Imitatione Christi*, bk.1, ch.4, section 6.

75 *Quam cito transit gloria mundi.*
   How quickly the glory of the world passes.
   c.1413 *De Imitatione Christi*, bk.1, ch.4, section 6.

76 *Homo proponit, sed Deus disponit.*
Man proposes, but God disposes.
c.1413 *De Imitatione Christi*, bk.1, ch.19, section 2.

77 *Nemo secure præcipit, nisi qui bene obedire didicit.*
Nobody rules safely, but he who has learned well how to obey.
c.1413 *De Imitatione Christi*, bk.1, ch.20, section 2.

78 *Transeunt omnia, et tu cum eis pariter.*
All things perish, and you along with them.
c.1413 *De Imitatione Christi*, bk.2, ch.1, section 4.

79 *Gloria boni hominis, testimonium bonæ conscientiæ.*
The testimony of a good conscience is the good man's glory.
c.1413 *De Imitatione Christi*, bk.2, ch.6, section 1.

80 *In cruce salus, in cruce vita.*
In the cross is salvation, in the cross is life.
c.1413 *De Imitatione Christi*, bk.2, ch.12, section 2.

81 *Si libenter crucem portas, portabit te.*
If you bear your cross willingly, it will bear you.
c.1413 *De Imitatione Christi*, bk.2, ch.12, section 5.

82 *De duobus malis minus est semper eligendum.*
Of two evils the lesser should always be chosen.
c.1413 *De Imitatione Christi*, bk.3, ch.12, section 2.

Ken, Thomas 1637–1711

English churchman and royal chaplain. He became Bishop of Bath and Wells (1685), and was deposed in 1691 when he refused to take the oath of allegiance to William III.

83 Awake my soul, and with the sun
Thy daily stage of duty run.
1709 *Manual of Prayers for the use of the Scholars of Winchester College.*

84 Praise God, from whom all blessings flow,
Praise Him, all creatures here below,
Praise Him above, ye heavenly host,
Praise Father, Son, and Holy Ghost.
1709 *Manual of Prayers for the use of the Scholars of Winchester College.*

Kendall, Henry Clarence 1839–82

Australian poet who worked variously as a civil servant, freelance writer, timber merchant and inspector of forests. His great love of the Australian countryside is evident in his collections *Poems and Songs* (1862), *Leaves from Australian Forests* (1869), and *Songs from the Mountains* (1880).

85 Through breaks of the cedar and sycamore bowers
Struggles the light that is love to the flowers;
And, softer than slumber and sweeter than singing,
The notes of the bell-birds are running and ringing.
The silver-voiced bell-birds, the darlings of daytime!
They sing in September their songs of the May-time.
1869 *Leaves from Australian Forests*, 'Bell-Birds'.

Kennan, George Frost 1904–2005

US diplomat and historian, adviser to Secretary of State Dean Acheson (1949–52) and US Ambassador in Moscow (1952–53) and Yugoslavia (1961–63). Initially in favour of 'containment' of the USSR, he later called for US disengagement from Europe.

86 The best that an American can look forward to is the lonely pleasure of one who stands at long last on a chilly and inhospitable mountain top where few have been, where few can follow, and where few will consent to believe that he has been.
On negotiating with the Soviets. Quoted in Walter Isaacson and Evan Thomas *The Wise Men* (1986).

87 A guest of one's time and not a member of the household.
Of the feeling of being viewed as a pragmatist. Quoted in Walter Isaacson and Evan Thomas *The Wise Men* (1986).

88 Fig leaves of democratic procedure to hide the nakedness of Stalinist dictatorship.
Of postwar agreements to govern Eastern Europe. Quoted in Walter Isaacson and Evan Thomas *The Wise Men* (1986).

Kennedy, A(lison) L(ouise) 1965–

Scottish novelist. Her short stories and novels have established her as a leading writer of her generation.

89 Night Geometry and the Garscadden Trains.
1990 Title of short story collection.

90 Words just say what you want them to; they don't know any better.
1990 'The Role of Notable Silences in Scottish History'.

91 4. The chosen and male shall go forth unto professions while the chosen and female shall be homely, fecund, docile and slightly artistic.
1993 *Looking for the Possible Dance*, 'The Scottish Method for the Perfection of Children'.

92 7. Joy is fleeting, sinful and the forerunner of despair.
1993 *Looking for the Possible Dance*, 'The Scottish Method for the Perfection of Children'.

93 We all have it in us to be an opium for every conceivable mass.
1995 *So I Am Glad*, ch.1.

94 I am not calm, I am unspontaneous. When something happens to me, I don't know how to feel.
1995 *So I Am Glad*, ch.1.

95 They have all kinds of things in them—liver, spleen, perhaps recklessly inserted lightbulbs. Whether you want any of those things to be removed and then sold to strangers is the question.
2008 Her reply when asked if everyone has a novel in them, in *The Observer*, 2 Mar.

Kennedy, Edward M(oore) 1932–2009

US Democratic politician, son of Joseph and brother of John and Robert. His political career was dogged by his involvement in a car accident at Chappaquiddick in 1969, in which a female companion was drowned, and he withdrew as presidential candidate in 1980.

96 I don't mind not being President. I just mind that someone else is.
1986 Speech, Washington, 22 Mar.

97 Sunlight is the best disinfectant.
1990 On sponsoring legislation for the disclosure of graduation rates and crime figures on campuses. In the *New York Times*, 8 Oct.

98 We are the most hated nation in the world as a result of this disastrous policy in the prisons.
2004 Following news coverage of the abuse of Iraqi prisoners by US soldiers, 13 May.

Kennedy, John F(itzgerald) 1917–63

US Democratic politician, 35th President. His *Profiles in Courage* (1956) won the Pulitzer Prize. The first Catholic, and the youngest person, to be elected President (1961–3), he initiated education and civil rights reform and induced the USSR to withdraw its missiles from Cuba (1962). He was assassinated, allegedly by Lee Harvey Oswald, while being driven in an open car through Dallas, Texas.

99 We stand today on the edge of a new frontier. But the new frontier of which I speak is not a set of promises. It is a set of challenges. It sums up not what I intend to offer the American people, but what I intend to ask of them. It appeals to their pride, not their pocketbook—it holds out the promise of more sacrifice instead of more security.
1960 On accepting the Democratic Convention's presidential nomination, 15 Jul.

1 Let us never negotiate out of fear, but let us never fear to negotiate. Together let us explore the stars.
1961 Inaugural address, Washington, 20 Jan.

2 All this will not be finished in the first 100 days, nor will it be finished in the first 1,000 days, nor in the life of this Administration—nor even, perhaps, in our lifetime on this planet. But let us begin.
1961 Inaugural address, Washington, 20 Jan.

3 Let the word go forth from this time and place, to friend and foe alike, that the torch has been passed to a new generation of Americans, born in this century, tempered by war, disciplined by a hard and bitter peace, proud of our ancient heritage, and unwilling to witness or permit the slow undoing of those human rights to which this nation has always been committed, and to which we are committed today at home and around the world. Let every nation know, whether it wishes us well or ill, that we shall pay any price, bear any burden, meet any hardship, support any friend, oppose any foe, to assure the survival and success of liberty.
1961 Inaugural address, Washington, 20 Jan.

4 And so, my fellow Americans, ask not what your country can do for you. Ask what you can do for your country.
1961 Inaugural address, Washington, 20 Jan.

5 I believe that this nation should commit itself to achieving the goal, before this decade is out, of landing a man on the moon and returning him safely to earth.
1961 State of the Union message to Congress, May.

6 Now we have a problem in making our power credible, and Vietnam is the place.
1961 Attributed remark to journalist James Reston, following Kennedy's meeting with Khrushchev, Jun.

7 A form of atomic blackmail.
1961 On the Soviet decision to resume nuclear testing, 31 Aug.

8 The cold reaches of the universe must not become the new area of an even colder war.
1961 Address to the United Nations, 25 Sep.

9 Mankind must put an end to war or war will put an end to mankind.
1961 Address to the United Nations, 25 Sep.

10 Those who make peaceful revolution impossible will make violent revolution inevitable.
1962 Speech to Latin American diplomats, 12 Mar.

11 This is the most extraordinary collection of talent, of human knowledge, that has ever been gathered in the White House—with the possible exception of when Thomas Jefferson dined alone.
1962 Address at a dinner for 49 Nobel laureates, 29 Apr.

12 The cost of freedom is always high, but Americans have always paid it. And one path we shall never choose, and that is the path of surrender, or submission.
1962 Address to the nation, 22 Oct.

13 If you take the wrong course…the President bears the burden of the responsibility quite rightly. The advisers may move on—to new advice.
1962 Comment to White House Special Counsel Theodore C Sorensen, Dec, after the ill-fated Bay of Pigs invasion of Cuba.

14 His stately ship of life, having weathered the severest storms of a troubled century, is anchored in tranquil waters, proof that courage and faith and zest for freedom are truly indestructible. The record of his triumphant passage will inspire free hearts all over the globe.
1963 On conferring honorary US citizenship on Winston Churchill, 9 Apr.

15 [Winston Churchill] mobilized the English language and sent it into battle.
1963 On conferring honorary US citizenship on Winston Churchill, 9 Apr.

16 Equality of opportunity does not mean equality of responsibility.
1963 Address at Vanderbilt University, 19 May.

17 Man is still the most extraordinary computer of all.
1963 Speech, 21 May.

18 History teaches us that enmities between nations…do not last forever. We must conduct our affairs in such a way that it becomes in the communists' interests to agree on a genuine peace…to let each nation choose its own future, so long as that choice does not interfere with the choices of others. If we cannot now end our differences, at least we can help make the world safe for diversity.
1963 Speech, American University, Washington DC, 10 Jun.

19 The rights of every man are diminished when the rights of one man are threatened.
1963 On sending national guardsmen to ensure peaceful integration at the University of Alabama. Address to the nation, 11 Jun.

20 He [John Hoban] believed by incorporating several features of the Dublin style he would make it more home-like for any President of Irish descent. It was a long wait, but I appreciate his efforts.
1963 On the Irish-American architect's design of the White House. Speech to the Irish Parliament reported in the *New York Times*, 19 Jun.

21 Let it not be said of this Atlantic generation that we left ideals and visions to the past, nor purpose and determination to our adversaries. We have come too far, we have sacrificed too much to disdain the future now.
1963 Speech to the West German Parliament, Frankfurt, 25 Jun.

22 There are many people in the world who really don't understand, or say they don't, what is the great issue between the free world and the Communist world. Let them come to Berlin!
1963 Address in Berlin's Rudolf Wilde Platz, 26 Jun, 22 months after the erection of the wall dividing the city.

23 We have never had to put a wall up to keep our people in, to prevent them from leaving us.
1963 Address in Berlin's Rudolf Wilde Platz, 26 Jun, 22 months after the erection of the wall dividing the city.

24 All free men, wherever they may live, are citizens of Berlin, and therefore, as a free man, I take pride in the words, 'Ich bin ein Berliner.' I am a Berliner!

Kennedy

1963 Speech at West Berlin City Hall, Rudolf Wilde Platz, 26 Jun. Unfortunately for Kennedy, his phrase translated into colloquial German as 'I am a doughnut.'

25 For the first time, we have been able to reach an agreement which can limit the dangers of this age.
1963 On the ratification of a treaty to limit nuclear testing, 7 Oct.

26 The highest duty of the writer, the composer, the artist is to remain true to himself... In serving his vision of the truth, the artist best serves his nation.
1963 At the dedication of Amherst College Robert Frost Library, 25 Oct.

27 When power leads man towards arrogance, poetry reminds him of his limitations. When power narrows the area of man's concern, poetry reminds him of the richness and diversity of existence. When power corrupts, poetry cleanses.
1963 At the dedication of Amherst College Robert Frost Library, 25 Oct.

28 I look forward to...a future in which our country will match its military strength with our moral restraint; its wealth with our wisdom; its power with our purpose.
1963 Last major public speech, Amherst College, 26 Oct.

29 The definition of happiness of the Greeks...is full use of your powers along lines of excellence. I find, therefore, the Presidency provides some happiness.
1963 News conference, 31 Oct.

30 We're heading into nut country today.
1963 Spoken to his wife in Fort Worth a few hours before the assassination in Dallas. Quoted in William Manchester *The Death of a President* (1967).

31 We in this country, in this generation, are—by destiny, rather than choice—the watchmen on the walls of the world.
1963 Address prepared for Dallas luncheon on the day he was assassinated, 22 Nov.

32 What your government believes is its own business; what it does in the world is the world's business.
Letter to Nikita Khrushchev. Quoted in Theodore C Sorensen *Kennedy* (1965).

33 The three most overrated things in the world are the state of Texas, the FBI, and hunting trophies.
Quoted in William Manchester *The Death of a President* (1967).

34 You don't fire God.
Expressing reluctance to replace FBI Director J Edgar Hoover. Reported after Kennedy's death in Senate committee findings on US intelligence activities, 1976.

35 You never know what's hit you. A gunshot is the perfect way.
Comment on methods of assassination. Quoted in Peter Collier and David Horowitz *The Kennedys* (1984).

Kennedy, Joseph Patrick 1888–1969

US businessman and diplomat, a supporter of Roosevelt and the 'New Deal'. The grandson of an Irish immigrant, he placed his fortune at the political disposal of his nine children, all of whom except the eldest son, killed in a flying accident, achieved international fame.

36 With the money I spent I could have elected my chauffeur.
Of his contributions to John F Kennedy's presidential campaign. Quoted in Nigel Hamilton *JFK: Reckless Youth* (1992).

37 Don't get mad, get even.
Attributed.

Kennedy, Joseph P(atrick) II 1952–

Former US Democratic congressman (1987–99) and founder of the Citizens Energy Corporation. He is the son of Joseph Patrick Kennedy.

38 I've had a tough time learning how to act like a Congressman. Today I accidentally spent some of my own money.
1987 In *Newsweek*, 9 Feb.

Kennedy, Nigel 1956–

English violinist.

39 I'd never accept a knighthood because the Queen knows nothing about music, man. How can she say I'm good or bad?
2004 In *The Independent*, 17 Jun.

Kennedy, Robert F(rancis) 1925–68

US politician, son of Joseph. Manager of his brother John's presidential campaign, he became Attorney-General (1961–4) and Senator for New York from 1965. In 1968 he was assassinated after winning the California primary election.

40 Courage is the most important attribute of a lawyer.
1962 Speech at the University of San Francisco Law School, 29 Sep.

41 One fifth of the people are against everything all the time.
1964 In the *Observer*, May.

42 My thanks to you all—and now it's on to Chicago, and let's win there.
1968 Last public remark after winning the Californian primary for the Democratic presidential nomination in Los Angeles, before being assassinated as he left the rally, 4 Jun.

43 It isn't the first step that concerns me, but both sides escalating to the fourth or fifth step—and we don't go to the sixth because there is no one around to do so.
On the possibility of initiating nuclear warfare. *Thirteen Days* (published 1969).

44 Many times...I had heard the military take positions which, if wrong, had the advantage that no one would be around at the end to know.
Recalling discussions on Soviet placement of nuclear missiles in Cuba. *Thirteen Days* (published 1969).

45 Well, we Kennedys, we eat Rockefellers for breakfast.
Quoted in Peter Collier and David Horowitz *The Rockefellers* (1976).

Kennedy, Roger George 1926–2011

Former director, US National Park Service (1993–97). He was also a correspondent for NBC and Director, National Museum of American History, Smithsonian Institution. He wrote books on architecture, houses and historic America.

46 How do you put a price on the Washington Monument?
1995 On presenting his annual budget to Congress and being asked to produce a price list setting a market value on each of the nation's 368 park units. Reported in the *US News and World Report*, 3 Apr.

Kennedy, William (Joseph) 1928–

US novelist and screenwriter. He won a Pulitzer Prize for *Ironweed* (1983).

47 I don't hold no grudges more'n five years.
   1983 Francis Phelan. *Ironweed*.

48 That year an ill wind blew over the city and threatened to destroy flowerpots, family fortunes, reputations, true love, and several types of virtue.
   2002 *Roscoe*, opening lines.

Kent, Bruce 1929–

British peace campaigner and former cleric, Chairman (1987–90) and Vice-President (1990–) of the Campaign for Nuclear Disarmament.

49 Preparing for suicide is not a very intelligent means of defence.
   1989 Speech.

Kent, Corita known as 'Sister Corita' 1918–86

US artist, best remembered for her prints and her 'Love' postage stamp (1985).

50 Women's liberation is the liberation of the feminine in the man and the masculine in the woman.
   1974 In the *Los Angeles Times*, 11 Jul.

Kent, Rockwell 1882–1971

US artist and writer, best known for his stark woodcuts, often accompanying his travel writing. His major works include the paintings *Toilers of the Sea* and *Winter* and writings such as *Wilderness* (1921).

51 Sledgehammer sentimentality.
   Of his wholesome depiction of contemporary America. Quoted in the *Washington Post*, 6 Jun 1993

Kerouac, Jack (John) 1922–69

US novelist. His fast-moving, stream of consciousness novel *On The Road* (1957) became the quintessential text of the Beat Generation.

52 All of life is a foreign country.
   1949 Letter, 24 Jun.

53 But then they danced down the street like dingle-dodies, and I shambled after as I've been doing all my life after people who interest me, because the only people for me are the mad ones, the ones who are mad to live, mad to talk, mad to be saved, desirous of everything at the same time, the ones who never yawn or say a commonplace thing, but burn, burn, burn, like fabulous yellow roman candles exploding like spiders across the stars and in the middle you see the blue centerlight pop and everybody goes 'Awww!'
   1957 *On The Road*, pt.1, ch.1.

54 I have nothing to offer anybody except my own confusion.
   1957 *On The Road*, pt.2, ch.3.

55 The road is life.
   1957 *On The Road*, pt.3, ch.5.

56 John Clellon Holmes…and I were sitting around trying to think up the meaning of the Lost Generation and the subsequent Existentialism and I said, 'You know, this is really a beat generation' and he leapt up and said, 'That's it, that's right!'
   1959 Interview in *Playboy*, Jun.

57 Desolation Angels.
   1965 Title of novel.

Kerr, Jean *née Collins* 1923–2003

US playwright. Her works include successful Broadway plays and humorous autobiographies. She collaborated with her husband Walter Kerr on several projects, including an adaptation of Werfel's *Song of Bernadette* (1946).

58 Even though a number of people have tried, no one has yet found a way to drink for a living.
   1964 *Poor Richard*, act 1.

Kerry, John F 1943–

US politician. Senator for Massachusetts, he ran against President George W Bush in the 2004 presidential election. In 2013 he became Secretary of State under President Barack Obama.

59 No young American in uniform should ever be held hostage to America's dependence on oil from the Middle East.
   2004 Speech in New Hampshire, 27 Jan.

60 Like father, like son, one term and you're done.
   2004 Referring to his contender's chances in the presidential election.

61 I have big heels to fill.
   2013 Referring to Hillary Clinton, his predecessor as Secretary of State.

Kesey, Ken Elton 1935–2001

US novelist. He achieved a major success with his novel *One Flew Over the Cuckoo's Nest* (1962), set in a mental hospital, and became a hero of the US counter-culture in the 1960s.

62 One Flew Over the Cuckoo's Nest.
   1962 Title of novel, derived from a traditional rhyme.

63 But it's the truth even if it didn't happen.
   1962 *One Flew Over The Cuckoo's Nest*, pt.1.

64 I'd rather be a lightning rod than a seismograph.
   Quoted in Tom Wolfe *The Electric Kool-Aid Acid Test* (1968), ch.1.

65 We are always acting on what just finished happening. It happened at least 1/30th of a second ago. We think we're in the present, but we aren't. The present we know is only a movie of the past.
   Quoted in Tom Wolfe *The Electric Kool-Aid Acid Test* (1968), ch.11.

66 You don't lead by pointing and telling people some place to go. You lead by going to that place and making a case.
   1970 Interview in *Esquire*, Jun.

Kethe, William d. c.1608

English divine, army chaplain and hymnwriter. His hymns are characteristically written in metre, like psalms.

67 All people that on earth do dwell,
   Sing to the Lord with cheerful voice;
   Him serve with fear, His praise forth tell,
   Come ye before Him, and rejoice.
   1560 *Daye's Psalter*, 'All People That on Earth Do Dwell'.

Key, Francis Scott 1779–1843

US lawyer and poet, best known for his devotional verse and prose. His poem 'The Star-Spangled Banner' was officially adopted as the national anthem of the US in 1931.

68 O say, can you see, by the dawn's early light,
   What so proudly we hailed at the twilight's last gleaming—

Whose broad stripes and bright stars, through the
  clouds of the fight,
O'er the ramparts we watched were so gallantly
  streaming!
And the rocket's red glare, the bombs bursting in air,
Gave proof through the night that our flag was still there;
O! say, does that star-spangled banner yet wave
O'er the land of the free, and the home of the brave?

1814 'The Star-Spangled Banner', originally published as 'The Defence of Fort M'Henry' in the *Baltimore Patriot*, 20 Sep; it commemorates the bombardment of Fort McHenry, Baltimore, by the British, 13–14 Sep.

Keynes (of Tilton), John Maynard, 1st Baron
1883–1946

English economist. His major works, *A Treatise on Money* (1930) and the revolutionary *General Theory of Employment, Interest and Money* (1936), were inspired by the unemployment crisis. His views influenced Roosevelt's 'New Deal' administration and underpin modern macroeconomics.

69 I work for a government I despise for ends I think criminal.
1917 Letter to Duncan Grant, 15 Dec.

70 Like Odysseus, the President looked wiser when he was seated.
1919 Of Woodrow Wilson. *The Economic Consequences of the Peace.*

71 Lenin was right. There is no subtler, no surer means of overturning the existing basis of society than to debauch the currency. The process engages all the hidden forces of economic law on the side of destruction, and does it in a manner which not one man in a million is able to diagnose.
1919 *The Economic Consequences of the Peace.*

72 England still stands outside Europe. Europe's voiceless tremors do not reach her. Europe is apart, and England is not of her flesh and body.
1919 *The Economic Consequences of the Peace.*

73 The *long run* is a misleading guide to current affairs. *In the long run*, we are all dead. Economists set themselves too easy, too useless a task if in tempestuous seasons they can only tell us that when the storm is long past the ocean is flat again.
1923 *A Tract on Monetary Reform.*

74 If Enterprise is afoot, Wealth accumulates whatever may be happening to Thrift; and if Enterprise is asleep, Wealth decays, whatever Thrift may be doing.
1930 *A Treatise on Money.*

75 A 'sound' banker, alas! is not one who foresees danger and avoids it, but one who, when he is ruined, is ruined in a conventional and orthodox way along with his fellows, so that no one can really blame him.
1931 *Essays in Persuasion.*

76 It is *not* a correct deduction from the Principles of Economics that enlightened self-interest always operates in the public interest… Experience does *not* show that individuals when they make up a social unit are always less clear-sighted than when they act separately.
1931 *Essays in Persuasion.*

77 I agree that our methods of control are unlikely to be sufficiently delicate or sufficiently powerful to maintain continuous full employment. I should be quite content with a reasonable approximation to it, and in practice I should probably relax my expansionist measures a little before technical full employment had actually been reached.
1936 Letter to E F M Durbin, 30 Apr.

78 It might have been supposed that competition between expert professionals, possessing judgement and knowledge beyond that of the average private investor, would correct the vagaries of the ignorant individual left to himself. It happens, however, that the energies and skills of the professional investor and speculator are mainly occupied elsewhere. For most of these persons are, in fact, largely concerned, not with making superior long-term forecasts of the probable yield on an investment over its whole life, but with foreseeing changes in the conventional bias of valuation a short time ahead of the general public… This battle of wits to anticipate the basis of conventional valuation a few months hence, rather than the prospective yield of an investment over a long term of years, does not even require gulls amongst the public to feed the maws of the professional; it can be played by professionals amongst themselves.
1936 *The General Theory of Employment, Interest, and Money.*

79 Speculators may do no harm as bubbles on a steady stream of enterprise. But the position is serious when enterprise becomes the bubble on a whirlpool of speculation. When the capital development of a country becomes a by-product of the activities of a casino, the job is likely to be ill-done.
1936 *The General Theory of Employment, Interest, and Money.*

80 If the Treasury were to fill old bottles with banknotes, bury them at suitable depths in disused coalmines which are then filled up to the surface with town rubbish, and leave it to private enterprise on well-tried principles of *laissez-faire* to dig the notes up again…there need be no more unemployment and, with the help of the repercussions, the real income of the community, and its capital wealth also, would probably become a good deal greater than it actually is. It would, indeed, be more sensible to build houses and the like; but as there are political and practical difficulties in the way of this, the above would be better than nothing.
1936 *The General Theory of Employment, Interest and Money.*

81 The ideas of economists and political philosophers, both when they are right and when they are wrong, are more powerful than is commonly understood. Indeed the world is ruled by little else. Practical men, who believe themselves to be quite exempt from any intellectual influences, are usually the slaves of some defunct economist. Madmen in authority, who hear voices in the air, are distilling their frenzy from some academic scribbler of a few years back. I am sure the power of vested interests is vastly exaggerated compared with the gradual encroachment of ideas.
1936 *The General Theory of Employment, Interest and Money.*

82 The outstanding faults of the economic society in which we live are its failure to provide for full employment and its arbitrary and inequitable distribution of wealth and incomes.
1936 *The General Theory of Employment, Interest and Money.*

83 We take it as a fundamental psychological rule of any modern community that, when its real income is increased, it will not increase its consumption by an equal absolute amount.
1936 *The General Theory of Employment, Interest, and Money.*

84 Worldly wisdom teaches us that it is better for the reputation to fail conventionally than to succeed unconventionally.
1936 *The General Theory of Employment, Interest and Money.*

85 I believe that there is social and psychological justification for significant inequalities of incomes and wealth, but not for such large disparities as exist today.
1936 *The General Theory of Employment, Interest and Money.*

Khayyám, Omar c.1050–c.1123

Persian poet and scholar. Born in Nishapur, he was summoned to Merv by the sultan, where he reformed the Muslim calendar. A renowned astronomer, he also composed mathematical treatises, and is best remembered for his *Rubáiyát* (c.1100).

86 Know yourself as a snowdrift on the sand
Heaped for two days, or three, then thawed and gone.
c.1100 *Rubáiyát*, stanza 16 (translated by Robert Graves and Omar Ali-Shah, 1972).

87 Never anticipate tomorrow's sorrow;
Live always in this paradisal now.
c.1100 *Rubáiyát*, stanza 21 (translated by Robert Graves and Omar Ali-Shah, 1972).

88 The cheerful bird of youth flutters away—
I hardly noticed how it came or went.
c.1100 *Rubáiyát*, stanza 103 (translated by Robert Graves and Omar Ali-Shah, 1972).

Khomeini, Ayatollah Ruhollah 1900–89

Iranian religious and political leader. Exiled in 1964, he returned to Iran in 1979 after the collapse of the Shah's government and became virtual head of state. He instigated a fundamentalist 'Islamic Revolution'.

89 Music is no different from opium. Music affects the human mind in a way that makes people think of nothing but music and sensual matters… Music is a treason to the country, a treason to our youth, and we should cut out all this music and replace it with something instructive.
1979 Ramadan speech, 23 Jul. Quoted in Lebrecht *Discord* (1982).

Khrushchev, Nikita Sergeyevich 1894–1971

Soviet politician. On the death of Stalin he became First Secretary of the Communist Party (1953–64), and subsequently denounced Stalinism. His period of office was marked by the 1956 Poznan riots, the Hungarian uprising, and the Cuban missile crisis (1962).

90 Those who wait for the USSR to reject Communism must wait until a shrimp learns to whistle.
1955 Speech in Moscow, 17 Sep.

91 Whether you like it not, history is on our side. We will bury you.
1956 Remark to Western diplomats at the Kremlin, 18 Nov. Khrushchev later claimed that he had meant 'We will overtake you [economically]', rather than this more sinister version.

92 Politicians are the same all over. They promise to build a bridge even where there is no river.
1960 Press conference, New York, Oct.

93 When you are skinning your customers, you should leave some skin on to grow so that you can skin them again.
1961 Speech to British industrialists, May.

94 They talk about who won and who lost. Human reason won. Mankind won.
1962 Of the ending of the Cuban missile crisis. In the *Observer*, 11 Nov.

95 We had no use for the teachings of the Gospels: if someone slaps you, just turn the other cheek. We had shown that anyone who slapped us on our cheek would get his head kicked off.
1970 *Khrushchev Remembers*. This biography, published in the West, is of dubious authenticity.

96 What the scientists have in their briefcases is terrifying.
Attributed.

Kidder, Tracy 1945–

US author. He won a Pulitzer Prize for *The Soul of a New Machine* (1981), which was also awarded a National Book Award.

97 The Soul of A New Machine
1981 Book title.

Kierkegaard, Sören Aabye 1813–55

Danish philosopher and religious thinker, who attacked dogmatism and the established Lutheran church and foreshadowed Existentialism.

98 The thing is to find a truth *for me*, to find *the idea for which I can live and die.*
1835 Journal entry (translated by Alexander Dru, 1938).

99 There are many people who reach their conclusions about life like schoolboys; they cheat their master by copying the answer out of a book without having worked out the sum for themselves.
1837 Journal entry (translated by Alexander Dru, 1938).

1 Without risk there is no faith.
1846 *Concluding Unscientific Postscript*, bk.2, pt.2, ch.2 (translated by Swenson and Lowrie).

2 The ethical reality of the individual is the only reality.
1846 *Concluding Unscientific Postscript*, bk.2, pt.2, ch.3 (translated by Swenson and Lowrie).

3 If a man in truth *will* the Good then he must be willing to suffer *for* the Good.
1846 *Purity Of Heart Is To Will One Thing* (translated by D Steere, 1938).

4 It is perfectly true, as philosophers say, that life must be understood backwards. But they forget the other proposition, that it must be lived forwards. And if one thinks over that proposition it becomes more and more evident that life can never really be understood in time simply because at no particular moment can I find the necessary resting-place from which to understand it—backwards.
Journal entry (translated by Alexander Dru, 1938).

5 Father in Heaven, when the thought of Thee wakes in our hearts, let it not awaken like a frightened bird that flies about in dismay, but like a child waking from its sleep with a heavenly smile.
Journal entry (translated by Alexander Dru, 1938).

6 Most people really believe that the Christian commandments (e.g. to love one's neighbour as oneself) are intentionally a little too severe—like putting the

clock on half an hour to make sure of not being late in the morning.
Journal entry (translated by Alexander Dru, 1938).

7 The bird on the branch, the lily in the meadow, the stag in the forest, the fish in the sea, the countless joyful creatures sing, God is Love. But beneath all these sopranos, as it were a sustained bass part, is the *De profundis* of the Sacrificed, God is Love.
Journal entry (translated by Alexander Dru, 1938).

Killy, Jean-Claude 1943–

French ski racer. He won the downhill and combined gold medals at the World Championship in Chile in 1966 and a further three gold medals at the Winter Olympics in 1968, after which he turned professional.

8 Skiing is a battle against yourself, always to the frontiers of the impossible. But most of all, it must give you pleasure. It is not an obligation but a joy.
1968 In *Sports Illustrated*, 18 Nov.

Kilmer, Joyce 1886–1918

US poet.

9 I think that I shall never see
A poem lovely as a tree.
1914 'Trees'.

Kilmer, Val 1959–

US actor.

10 On set, you've got 50 people asking if you want a cup of coffee. You throw your shoes in a corner, someone puts them neatly together. It's corrupting.
2004 In the *Observer*, 9 May.

Kilpatrick, James J 1920–2010

US writer and broadcaster.

11 A whore may be *naked*, but a mistress is *nude*. We are talking class.
1993 *Fine Print: Reflections on the Writing Art*.

Kim Il Sung 1912–94

North Korean soldier and political leader. After proclaiming his country a Republic in 1948 he remained in political control until his death. Within his country he was regarded with awe by the majority of citizens.

12 Everything is decided by a person's thoughts and if he is ideologically motivated, there is nothing he cannot do.
1969 Speech, 20 Apr. Collected in *Selected Works* (1992), vol.1, 'Work with Artists Should be Carried Out in Line with Political Principles'.

Kimball, Donald M

US business executive.

13 There's no place where success comes before work, except in the dictionary.
1986 In *USA Today*, 21 Apr.

Kincaid, Jamaica originally Elaine Potter Richardson 1949–

Antiguan writer; living in the US. Her works include *At the Bottom of the River* (1983), *Annie John* (1985), *Mr Potter* (2002) and a critique of colonialism and tourism, *A Small Place* (1988).

14 There was nothing noble-minded men could not do when they discovered they could slap time on their wrists just like that.
1988 *A Small Place*.

15 A tourist is an ugly human being.
1988 *A Small Place*.

King, Anthony 1934–

Canadian academic and political commentator. Professor of Government at the University of Essex since 1969.

16 It is an asteroid hitting the planet and destroying practically all life on earth.
1997 Attempting to define the scale of Labour's victory in the general election, on BBC1's 'Election Night', 2 May.

King, Billie Jean *née Moffitt* 1943–

US tennis player, who won 20 titles at Wimbledon (1965–80).

17 Ask Nureyev to stop dancing, ask Sinatra to stop singing, then you can ask me to stop playing.
1982 Quoted in Colin Jarman *The Guinness Dictionary of Sports Quotations* (1990).

18 If you're up against a girl with big boobs, bring her to the net and make her hit backhand volleys.
1982 *Billie Jean King*.

King, Carlyle 1907–88

Canadian political scientist and socialist.

19 The main business of socialist parties is not to form governments but to change minds.
Attributed, 1940s.

King, Don 1932–

US boxing promoter.

20 Only in America could a Don King happen.
Quoted in Colin Jarman *The Guinness Dictionary of Sports Quotations* (1990). King adopted 'Only in America' as a catchphrase, billing himself as Don 'Only in America' King.

21 This fight is bigger than life itself.
2001 On the heavyweight title bout between Lennox Lewis and Hasim Rahman. In the *Observer*, 30 Dec.

King, Martin Luther Jr 1929–68

US civil rights leader. He advocated passive resistance to segregation and led a boycott (1955–6) against segregated bus lines in Montgomery, Alabama. In 1964 he received both the Kennedy and Nobel peace prizes. He was assassinated by James Earl Ray.

22 He who passively accepts evil is as much involved in it as he who helps to perpetuate it.
1958 *Strides Towards Freedom*.

23 It may be true that the law cannot make a man love me, but it can keep him from lynching me, and I think that's pretty important.
1962 Speech at Cornell College, Mt Vernon, Iowa. Reported in the *Wall Street Journal*, 13 Nov.

24 Injustice anywhere is a threat to justice everywhere.
1963 Letter from Birmingham jail, Alabama, 16 Apr.

25 I have a dream. I have a dream that my four little children will one day live in a nation where they will not

be judged by the colour of their skin but by the content of their character.
1963 Washington civil rights rally, 15 Jun.

26 If a man hasn't discovered something he will die for, he isn't fit to live.
1963 Speech in Detroit, 23 Jun.

27 When the architects of our republic wrote the magnificent words of the Constitution and the Declaration of Independence, they were signing a promissory note to which every American was to fall heir... America has defaulted on this promissory note insofar as her citizens of color are concerned.
1963 Speech at the Lincoln Memorial, 28 Aug, during the March on Washington.

28 We have...come to this hallowed spot to remind America of the fierce urgency of now.
1963 Speech at the Lincoln Memorial, 28 Aug, during the March on Washington.

29 Let us not seek to satisfy our thirst for freedom by drinking from the cup of bitterness and hatred...[nor] allow our creative protests to degenerate into physical violence.
1963 Speech at the Lincoln Memorial, 28 Aug, during the March on Washington.

30 You have been the victim of creative suffering.
1963 Speech at the Lincoln Memorial, 28 Aug, during the March on Washington.

31 I have a dream that one day...the sons of former slaves and the sons of former slave owners will be able to sit together at the table of brotherhood.
1963 Speech at the Lincoln Memorial, 28 Aug, during the March on Washington.

32 We have genuflected before the god of science only to find that it has given us the atomic bomb, producing fears and anxieties that science can never mitigate.
1963 *Strength to Love*, ch.13.

33 The church must be reminded that it is not the master or servant of the state, but rather the conscience of the state.
1963 *Strength to Love*.

34 Discrimination is a hellhound that gnaws at negroes in every waking moment of their lives, to remind them that the lie of their inferiority is accepted as truth in the society dominating them.
1967 Speech at the Christian leadership conference, Atlanta, 16 Aug.

35 I've been to the mountain top. I've looked over, and I've seen the promised land. I may not get there with you, but I want you to know tonight that we as a people will get to the promised land. So, I'm happy tonight. Mine eyes have seen the glory of the coming of the Lord.
1968 Speech at Memphis, 3 Apr, the day before he was assassinated.

36 Love is the only force capable of transforming an enemy into a friend.
Attributed, collected in *The Words of Martin Luther King*.

King, Stephen 1947–

US author, known for his highly suspenseful horror novels. His works include *Carrie* (1974), *The Shining* (1976), *Misery* (1988), *Bag of Bones* (1998) and *Under the Dome* (2009).

37 Terror...often arises from a pervasive sense of disestablishment; that things are in the unmaking.
1981 *Danse Macabre*.

38 I believe there is an unseen world all around us.
1993 *Nightmares and Dreamscapes*, introduction.

39 If I know anything, I know scary. And giving this president and this out-of-control Congress two more years to screw up our future is downright terrifying. Thankfully, this national nightmare is one we can end.
2006 Referring to George W. Bush, *Newsweek*, 24 Oct.

40 You should never trust a person who prays in public.
2008 *Duma Key*.

41 When it comes to the past, everyone writes fiction.
2013 *Joyland*.

King, William Lyon Mackenzie 1874–1950

Canadian Liberal politician, Prime Minister 1921–6, 1926–30 and 1935–48. His view that the dominions should be autonomous within the British Empire resulted in the Statute of Westminster (1931).

42 If some countries have too much history, we have too much geography.
1936 Address to the House of Commons, Ottawa, 18 Jun.

Kingsley, Charles 1819–75

English writer. Among his best-known works are the historical novels *Westward Ho!* (1855), and the children's book *The Water Babies* (1863). A Christian Socialist, he also published an immense number of articles on current topics.

43 'Oh Mary, go and call the cattle home,
And call the cattle home,
And call the cattle home,
Across the sands of Dee.'
The western wind was wild and dank with foam,
And all alone went she.
1850 *Alton Locke*, ch.26, 'The Sands of Dee'.

44 Come; and strong within us
Stir the Vikings' blood;
Bracing brain and sinew;
Blow, thou wind of God!
1857 'Ode to the North-East Wind'.

45 Be good, sweet maid, and let who will be clever;
Do noble things, do not dream them, all day long:
And so make life, death, and that vast for-ever
One grand, sweet song.
1858 'A Farewell'.

46 Once upon a time there was a little chimney-sweep, and his name was Tom.
1863 *The Water Babies*, ch.1.

47 The great elm-trees in the gold-green meadows were fast asleep above, and the cows fast asleep beneath them; nay, the few clouds which were about were fast asleep likewise, and so tired that they had lain down on the earth to rest, in long white flakes and bars, among the stems of the elm-trees, and along the tops of the alders by the stream.
1863 *The Water Babies*, ch.1.

48 When all the world is young, lad,
And all the trees are green;
And every goose a swan, lad,

And every lass a queen;
Then hey for boot and horse, lad,
And round the world away:
Young blood must have its course, lad,
And every dog his day.
1863 Song. *The Water Babies*, ch.2.

49 He was as thorough an Englishman as ever coveted his neighbour's goods... [He was] chief professor of Necrobioneopalaeonthydrochthonanthropopithekology.
1863 Professor Ptthmllnsprts. *The Water Babies*, ch.4.

50 The healthiest situation in England, on Easthampstead Plain. Free run of Windsor Forest. *The Times* every morning. A double-barrelled gun and pointers, and leave to shoot three Wellington College boys a week (not more) in case black game was scarce.
1863 The reward for criminal lunacy. *The Water Babies*, ch.4.

51 I am the ugliest fairy in the world, and I shall be till people behave themselves as they ought to do. And then I shall grow as handsome as my sister...Mrs Doasyouwouldbedoneby.
1863 Mrs Bedonebyasyoudid. *The Water Babies*, ch.5.

52 How long would it take a school-inspector of average activity to tumble head over heels from London to York?
1863 *The Water Babies*, ch.8.

53 So Tom went home with Ellie...and he is now a great man of science...and knows everything about everything, except why a hen's egg don't turn into a crocodile, and two or three other little things which no one will know till the coming of the Cocqcigrues. And all this from what he learnt when he was a water-baby, underneath the sea.
'And of course, Tom married Ellie?' My dear child, what a silly notion! Don't you know that no one ever marries in a fairy tale, under the rank of a prince or a princess?
1863 *The Water Babies*, ch.8.

54 We have used the Bible as if it was a constable's handbook—an opium-dose for keeping beasts of burden patient while they are being overloaded.
Letters to the Chartists, no.2.

55 To be discontented with the divine discontent, and to be ashamed with the noble shame, is the very germ and first upgrowth of all virtue.
1874 *Health and Education*.

Kingsley, Mary Henrietta 1862–1900

English writer and traveller. After the death of her invalid parents she travelled to West Africa (1893 and 1895), living among the natives, and wrote accounts of both journeys. She died of enteric fever while serving as a nurse in the second Boer War.

56 A certain sort of friendship soon arose between the Fans and me. We each recognized that we belonged to that same section of the human race with whom it is better to drink than to fight. We knew we would each have killed the other, if sufficient inducement were offered, and so we took a certain amount of care that the inducement should not arise.
1893 *Travels in West Africa* (published 1899).

57 It is at these times that you realise the blessings of a good thick skirt... Save for a good many bruises, here I was with the fulness of my skirt tucked under me, sitting on nine ebony spikes some twelve inches long, in comparative comfort.
1893 *Travels in West Africa* (published 1899).

58 The sooner the Crown Colony system is removed from the sphere of practical politics and put under a glass case in the South Kensington Museum, labelled 'Extinct', the better for everyone.
1899 *West African Studies*.

59 West Africa today is just a quarry of paving stones for Hell, and those stones were cemented in place with men's blood mixed with wasted gold.
1899 *West African Studies*.

Kington, Miles 1941–2008

British writer and columnist. He was best known as a humorist, and also wrote on jazz.

60 Nobody has ever been able to define jazz satisfactorily. This is probably because anyone who was capable of doing so never really wanted to, knowing how much you would have to leave out of the definition.
1992 *The Jazz Anthology*, ch.1

Kinnock (of Bedwellty), Neil Gordon, Baron 1942–

Welsh Labour politician. In 1983 he succeeded Michael Foot as Party leader, but resigned after the 1992 election defeat. He was Vice-President of the European Commission until 2004, subsequently becoming Chair of the British Council (2004–9).

61 We cannot remove the evils of capitalism without taking its source of power: ownership.
1975 In *Tribune*.

62 I want to retire at 50. I want to play cricket in the summer and geriatric football in the winter, and sing in the choir.
1980 In *The Times*, 28 Jul.

63 Like Brighton Pier—all right as far as it goes, but inadequate for getting to France.
1981 On Conservative European policy, House of Commons, 2 Feb.

64 It's a pity others had to leave theirs on the ground at Goose Green to prove it.
1983 Reply to a heckler who had said Mrs Thatcher had shown 'guts' in the Falklands Crisis. Quoted in *The Times*, 6 Jun.

65 If Margaret Thatcher wins on Thursday, I warn you not to be ordinary, I warn you not to be young, I warn you not to fall ill, I warn you not to get old.
1983 Speech one day before polling, Jun.

66 I have a lot of sympathy with him. I too was once a young, bald Leader of the Opposition.
1999 On William Hague. In *The Independent*, 3 Oct.

Kinsella, W(illiam) P(atrick) 1935–

Canadian novelist.

67 There was silence in the room. Then a voice, stunning as thunder, clear and common as a train whistle—the voice of a ball-park announcer: 'If you build it, he will come.'
1980 'Shoeless Joe Jackson Comes to Iowa', a short story later expanded into the novel *Shoeless Joe* (1982) and filmed as *Field of Dreams* (1989).

Kipling, (Joseph) Rudyard 1865–1935

English writer, born in Bombay, who lived for several years in India. His verse both celebrated and satirized the British Imperial presence, and won him widespread popularity, while the stories in *The Jungle Book* (1894) are considered classics of their kind. He also wrote novels and a biography, and was awarded the Nobel prize in 1907.

68 The toad beneath the harrow knows
Exactly where each tooth-point goes;
The butterfly upon the road
Preaches contentment to that toad.
1886 'Pagett, MP'.

69 Never praise a sister to a sister, in the hope of your compliments reaching the proper ears.
1888 *Plain Tales from the Hills*, 'False Dawn'.

70 Take my word for it, the silliest woman can manage a clever man; but it takes a very clever woman to manage a fool.
1888 *Plain Tales from the Hills*, 'Three and—an Extra'.

71 Every one is more or less mad on one point.
1888 *Plain Tales from the Hills*, 'On the Strength of a Likeness'.

72 The Man who Would be King.
1888 *Wee Willie Winkie*, title of short story.

73 Being kissed by a man who didn't wax his moustache was—like eating an egg without salt.
1888 *The Story of the Gadsbys*, 'Poor Dear Mamma'.

74 Down to Gehenna or up to the Throne,
He travels fastest who travels alone.
1888 *The Story of the Gadsbys*, 'L'Envoi'. The poem was later renamed 'The Winners' (1912).

75 We're poor little lambs who've lost our way,
Baa! Baa! Baa!
We're little black sheep who've gone astray,
Baa-aa-aa!
Gentlemen-rankers out on the spree,
Damned from here to eternity,
God ha' mercy on such as we,
Baa! Yah! Bah!
1889 'The Gentlemen-Rankers'.

76 Oh, East is East, and West is West, and never the twain shall meet,
Till earth and sky stand presently at God's great Judgement seat;
But there is neither East nor West, Border, nor Breed, nor Birth,
When two strong men stand face to face, tho' they come from the ends of the earth.
1889 'The Ballad of East and West'.

77 A man lives well and happily until he begins to feel unwell. Then he feels worse because the climate allows him no chance of pulling himself together—and then he dies.
1889 Of life in Singapore. *From Sea to Sea*.

78 The Japanese should have no concern with business.
1889 *From Sea to Sea*.

79 Moulmein is situated up the mouth of a river which ought to flow through South America.
1889 *From Sea to Sea*.

80 By the old Moulmein Pagoda, lookin' eastward to the sea,
There's a Burma girl a-settin', and I know she thinks o' me;
For the wind is in the palm trees, an' the temple bells they say:
'Come you back, you British soldier'; come you back to Mandalay!'
1890 'Mandalay'.

81 Come you back to Mandalay,
Where the old Flotilla lay:
Can't you 'ear their paddles chunkin' from Rangoon to Mandalay?
On the road to Mandalay,
Where the flyin'-fishes play,
An' the dawn comes up like thunder outer China 'crost the Bay!
1890 'Mandalay'.

82 An' I seed her first a-smokin' of a whackin' white cheroot,
An' a-wastin' Christian kisses on an 'eathen idol's foot.
1890 'Mandalay'.

83 Ship me somewhere east of Suez, where the best is like the worst,
Where there aren't no Ten Commandments an' a man can raise a thirst.
1890 'Mandalay'.

84 For they're hangin' Danny Deever, you can hear the Dead March play,
The regiment's in 'ollow square—they're hangin' him to-day;
They've taken of his buttons off an' cut his stripes away,
An' they're hangin' Danny Deever in the mornin'.
1890 'Danny Deever'.

85 O it's Tommy this, an' Tommy that, an' 'Tommy, go away';
But it's 'Thank you, Mister Atkins,' when the band begins to play.
1890 'Tommy'.

86 Then it's Tommy this, an' Tommy that, and 'Tommy 'ow's yer soul?'
But it's 'Thin red line of 'eroes' when the drums begin to roll.
1890 'Tommy'.
▶ See Russell 735:50.

87 For it's Tommy this, an' Tommy that, and 'Chuck him out, the brute!'
But it's 'Saviour of 'is country' when the guns begin to shoot.
1890 'Tommy'.

88 When you're wounded and left on Afghanistan's plains
And the women come out to cut up what remains
Just roll to your rifle and blow out your brains
An' go to your Gawd like a soldier.
1890 'The Young British Soldier'.

89 So 'ere's *to* you, Fuzzy-Wuzzy, at your 'ome in the Soudan;
You're a pore benighted 'eathen but a first-class fightin' man;
An' 'ere's *to* you, Fuzzy-Wuzzy, with your 'ayrick 'ead of 'air—
You big black boundin' beggar—for you broke a British square!
1890 'Fuzzy-Wuzzy'.

90 The uniform 'e wore
Was nothin' much before,
An' rather less than 'arf o' that be'ind.
1890 'Gunga Din'.

91 Though I've belted you and flayed you,
By the livin' Gawd that made you,
You're a better man than I am, Gunga Din!
1890 'Gunga Din'.

92 'Ave you 'eard o' the Widow at Windsor
With a hairy gold crown on 'er 'ead?
She 'as ships on the foam—she 'as millions at 'ome,
An' she pays us poor beggars in red.
1890 'The Widow at Windsor'.

93 And the talk slid north, and the talk slid south,
With the sliding puffs from the hookah-mouth.
Four things greater than all things are,—
Women and Horses and Power and War.
1890 'The Ballad of the King's Jest'.

94 Winds of the World, give answer! They are whimpering to and fro—
And what should they know of England who only England know?—
The poor little street-bred people that vapour and fume and brag.
1891 'The English Flag'.

95 If I were damned of body and soul,
I know whose prayers would make me whole,
Mother o' mine, O mother o' mine.
1891 *The Light That Failed*, dedication.

96 There ain't twelve hundred people in the world who understand pictures. The others pretend and don't care.
1891 *The Light That Failed*.

97 When the flush of a new-born sun fell first on Eden's green and gold,
Our father Adam sat under the Tree and scratched with a stick in the mould;
And the first rude sketch that the world had seen was joy to his mighty heart,
Till the Devil whispered behind the leaves, 'It's pretty, but is it Art?'
1892 'The Conundrum of the Workshops'.

98 We know that the tail must wag the dog, for the horse is drawn by the cart;
But the Devil whoops, as he whooped of old: 'It's clever, but is it Art?'
1892 'The Conundrum of the Workshops'.

99 And the end of the fight is a tombstone white, with the name of the late deceased,
And the epitaph drear: 'A fool lies here who tried to hustle the East.'
1892 *The Naulahka*, ch.5.

1 For the sin ye do by two and two ye must pay for one by one!
1892 'Tomlinson'.

2 There be triple ways to take, of the eagle or the snake,
Or the way of a man with a maid;
But the sweetest way to me is a ship's upon the sea
In the heel of the North-East Trade.
1892 'The Long Trail'.

3 There are nine and sixty ways of constructing tribal lays,
And—every—single—one—of—them—is—right!
1892 'In the Neolithic Age'.

4 A man-cub is a man-cub, and he must learn *all* the Law of the Jungle.
1894 *The Jungle Book*, 'Kaa's Hunting'.

5 'We be one blood, thou and I', Mowgli answered. 'I take my life from thee to-night. My kill shall be thy kill if ever thou art hungry, O Kaa.'
1894 *The Jungle Book*, 'Kaa's Hunting'.

6 Brother, thy tail hangs down behind!
1894 *The Jungle Book*, 'The Road Song of the Bandar-Log'.

7 Now this is the Law of the Jungle—as old and as true as the sky;
And the Wolf that shall keep it may prosper, but the Wolf that shall break it must die.
1895 *The Second Jungle Book*, 'The Law of the Jungle'.

8 Keep ye the law—be swift in all obedience—
Clear the land of evil, drive the road and bridge the ford.
Make ye sure to each his own
That he reap where he hath sown;
By the peace among our peoples let men know we serve the Lord!
1896 'A Song of the English'.

9 We have fed our sea for a thousand years
And she calls us, still unfed,
Though there's never a wave of all her waves
But marks our English dead.
1896 'A Song of the Dead'.

10 If blood be the price of admiralty
Lord God, we ha' paid in full!
1896 'A Song of the Dead'.

11 I've taken my fun where I've found it,
An' now I must pay for my fun,
For the more you 'ave known o' the others
The less will you settle for one;
1896 'The Ladies'.

12 For the Colonel's Lady an' Judy O'Grady
Are sisters under their skins!
1896 'The Ladies'.

13 The 'eathen in 'is blindness bows down to wood an' stone;
'E don't obey no orders unless they is 'is own.
1896 'The 'Eathen'.

14 The 'eathen in 'is blindness must end where 'e began.
But the backbone of the Army is the non-commissioned man!
1896 'The 'Eathen'.

15 And only the Master shall praise us, and only the Master shall blame;
And no one shall work for money, and no one shall work for fame,
But each for the joy of working, and each, in his separate star,
Shall draw the Thing as he sees It for the God of Things as They are!
1896 'When Earth's Last Picture is Painted'.

16 The tumult and the shouting dies—
The captains and the kings depart—
Still stands Thine ancient Sacrifice,
An humble and a contrite heart.
Lord God of Hosts, be with us yet,
Lest we forget—lest we forget!
1897 'Recessional'.
▶ See Bible 101:74.

17 If, drunk with sight of power, we loose
Wild tongues that have not Thee in awe—

Such boasting as the Gentiles use,
Or lesser breeds without the Law.
1897 'Recessional'.

18 What the horses o' Kansas think to-day, the horses of America will think tomorrow; an' I tell *you* that when the horses of America rise in their might, the day o' the Oppressor is ended.
1898 *The Day's Work*, 'A Walking Delegate'.

19 Take up the White Man's burden—
Send forth the best ye breed—
Go, bind your sons to exile
To serve your captives' need.
1899 'The White Man's Burden'.

20 Your new-caught, sullen peoples,
Half devil and half child.
1899 'The White Man's Burden'.

21 By all ye will or whisper,
By all ye leave or do,
The silent sullen peoples
Shall weigh your God and you.
1899 'The White Man's Burden'.

22 When you've shouted 'Rule Britannia', when you've sung 'God save the Queen'—
When you've finished killing Kruger with your mouth—
Will you kindly drop a shilling in my little tambourine
For a gentleman in *Kharki* ordered South?
1899 *The Absent-Minded Beggar*.

23 Mr Raymond Martin, beyond question, was born in the gutter, and bred in a Board-School, where they played marbles. He was further (I give the barest handful from great store) a Flopshus Cad, an Outrageous Stinker, a Jelly-bellied Flag-flapper (this was Stalky's contribution), and several other things which it is not seemly to put down.
1899 *Stalky & Co*.

24 Being human, she must have been afraid of something, but one never found out what it was.
c.1900 Of Mary Kingsley (1862–1900), the enterprising English traveller in West Africa. Attributed.

25 Little Friend of all the World.
1901 Kim's nickname. *Kim*, ch.1.

26 Men are as chancy as children in their choice of playthings.
1901 *Kim*, ch.10.

27 One does not own to the possession of money in India.
1901 *Kim*, ch.11.

28 'Noble and generous Cetacean, have you ever tasted Man?' 'No,' said the Whale. 'What is it like?' 'Nice,' said the small 'Stute Fish. 'Nice but nubbly.'
1902 *Just So Stories*, 'How the Whale Got His Throat'.

29 You must not forget the suspenders, Best Beloved.
1902 *Just So Stories*, 'How the Whale Got His Throat'.

30 He had his Mummy's leave to paddle, or else he would never have done it, because he was a man of infinite-resource-and-sagacity.
1902 *Just So Stories*, 'How the Whale Got His Throat'.

31 The camel's hump is an ugly lump
Which well you may see at the Zoo;
But uglier yet is the hump we get
From having too little to do.
1902 *Just So Stories*, 'How the Camel Got His Hump'.

32 The cure for this ill is not to sit still,
Or frowst with a book by the fire;
But to take a large hoe and a shovel also,
And dig till you gently perspire.
1902 *Just So Stories*, 'How the Camel Got His Hump'.

33 Most 'scruciating idle.
1902 *Just So Stories*, 'How the Camel Got His Hump'.

34 'Humph yourself!'
And the Camel humphed himself.
1902 *Just So Stories*, 'How the Camel Got His Hump'.

35 There lived a Parsee from whose hat the rays of the sun were reflected in more-than-oriental splendour.
1902 *Just So Stories*, 'How the Rhinoceros Got His Skin'.

36 But there was one Elephant—a new Elephant—an Elephant's Child—who was full of 'satiable curtiosity, and that means he asked ever so many questions.
1902 *Just So Stories*, 'The Elephant's Child'.

37 The great grey-green, greasy Limpopo River, all set about with fever-trees.
1902 *Just So Stories*, 'The Elephant's Child'.

38 Led go! You are hurtig be!
1902 *Just So Stories*, 'The Elephant's Child'.

39 And I'd like to roll to Rio
Some day before I'm old!
1902 *Just So Stories*, 'The Beginning of the Armadilloes'.

40 'You are making my spots ache,' said Painted Jaguar.
1902 *Just So Stories*, 'The Beginning of the Armadillos'.

41 But the wildest of all the wild animals was the Cat. He walked by himself, and all places were alike to him.
1902 *Just So Stories*, 'The Cat That Walked By Himself'.

42 And he went back through the Wet Wild Woods, waving his wild tail and walking by his wild lone. But he never told anybody.
1902 *Just So Stories*, 'The Cat That Walked By Himself'.

43 He would surprise them out of their jumpsome lives.
1902 *Just So Stories*, 'How the Leopard Got His Spots'.

44 Something lost behind the Ranges.
1903 *The Five Nations*, 'The Explorer'.

45 Who hath desired the Sea?—the sight of salt water unbounded—
The heave and the halt and the hurl and the crash of the comber wind-hounded?
The sleek-barrelled swell before storm, grey, foamless, enormous, and growing—
Stark calm on the lap of the Line or the crazy-eyed Hurricane blowing.
1903 'The Sea and the Hills'.

46 And here the sea-fogs lap and cling,
And here, each warning each,
The sheep-bells and the ship-bells ring
Along the hidden beach.
1903 'Sussex'.

47 God gives all men all earth to love,
But since man's heart is small,
Ordains for each one spot shall prove
Belovèd over all.
1903 'Sussex'.

48 Each to his choice, and I rejoice
The lot has fallen to me

    In a fair ground—in a fair ground—
    Yea, Sussex by the sea!
    1903 'Sussex'.
    ▶ See Book of Common Prayer 148:8.

49 Then ye returned to your trinkets; then ye contented your souls
    With the flannelled fools at the wicket or the muddied oafs at the goals.
    1903 'The Islanders'.

50 An' it all goes into the laundry
    But it never comes out in the wash.
    1903 'Stellenbosh'.

51 'Tisn't beauty, so to speak, nor good talk necessarily. It's just It. Some women'll stay in a man's memory if they once walked down a street.
    1904 *Traffics and Discoveries*, 'Mrs Bathhurst'.

52 The God who Looks after Small Things had caused the visitor that day to receive two weeks' delayed mails in one.
    1904 *Traffics and Discoveries*, 'The Captive'.

53 Of all the trees that grow so fair,
    Old England to adorn,
    Greater are none beneath the Sun,
    Than Oak, and Ash, and Thorn.
    1906 *Puck of Pook's Hill*, 'Tree Song'.

54 England shall bide till Judgement Tide
    By Oak, and Ash, and Thorn.
    1906 *Puck of Pook's Hill*, 'Tree Song'.

55 What is a woman that you forsake her,
    And the hearth-fire and the home-acre,
    To go with the old grey Widow-maker?
    1906 *Puck of Pook's Hill*, 'Harp Song of the Dane Women'.

56 If you wake at midnight, and hear a horse's feet,
    Don't go drawing back the blind, or looking in the street,
    Them that asks no questions isn't told a lie.
    Watch the wall, my darling, while the Gentlemen go by!
    1906 *Puck of Pook's Hill*, 'Smuggler's Song'.

57 Land of our birth, we pledge to thee
    Our love and toil in the years to be;
    When we are grown and take our place,
    As men and women with our race.
    1906 *Puck of Pook's Hill*, 'Children's Song'.

58 Teach us delight in simple things
    And mirth that has no bitter springs;
    Forgiveness free of evil done,
    And love to all men 'neath the sun!
    1906 *Puck of Pook's Hill*, 'Children's Song'.

59 But I consort with long-haired things
    In velvet collar-rolls,
    Who talk about the Aims of Art,
    And 'theories' and 'goals',
    And moo and coo with women-folk
    About their blessed souls.
    1909 'In Partibus'.

60 There is sorrow enough in the natural way
    From men and women to fill our day;
    But when we are certain of sorrow in store,
    Why do we always arrange for more?
    Brothers and Sisters, I bid you beware
    Of giving your heart to a dog to tear.
    1909 'The Power of the Dog'.

61 They shut the road through the woods
    Seventy years ago.
    Weather and rain have undone it again,
    And now you would never know
    There was once a road through the woods.
    1910 *Rewards and Fairies*, 'The Way Through the Woods'.

62 If you can keep your head when all about you
    Are losing theirs and blaming it on you;
    If you can trust yourself when all men doubt you,
    But make allowance for their doubting too;
    If you can wait and not be tired by waiting,
    Or being lied about, don't deal in lies,
    Or being hated, don't give way to hating,
    And yet don't look too good, nor talk too wise;
    If you can dream—and not make dreams your master;
    If you can think—and not make thoughts your aim,
    If you can meet with Triumph and Disaster
    And treat those two imposters just the same.
    1910 *Rewards and Fairies*, 'If—'.

63 If you can talk with crowds and keep your virtue,
    Or walk with Kings—nor lose the common touch,
    If neither foes nor loving friends can hurt you,
    If all men count with you, but none too much;
    If you can fill the unforgiving minute
    With sixty seconds' worth of distance run,
    Yours is the Earth and everything that's in it.
    And—which is more—you'll be a Man, my son!
    1910 *Rewards and Fairies*, 'If—'.

64 One man in a thousand, Solomon says,
    Will stick more close than a brother.
    1910 *Rewards and Fairies*, 'The Thousandth Man'.

65 It is always a temptation to a rich and lazy nation,
    To puff and look important and to say:
    'Though we know we should defeat you, we have not the time to meet you,
    We will therefore pay you cash to go away.'

    And that is called paying the Dane-geld;
    But we've proved it again and again,
    That if once you have paid him the Dane-geld
    You never get rid of the Dane.
    1911 'Dane-Geld'.

66 'Oh, where are you going to, all you Big Steamers,
    With England's own coal, up and down the salt seas?'
    'We are going to fetch you your bread and your butter,
    Your beef, pork, and mutton, eggs, apples and cheese.'
    1911 'Big Steamers'.

67 Our England is a garden that is full of stately views,
    Of borders, beds and shrubberies and lawns and avenues,
    With statues on the terraces and peacocks strutting by;
    But the Glory of the Garden lies in more than meets the eye.
    1911 'The Glory of the Garden'.

68 Our England is a garden, and such gardens are not made
    By singing:—'Oh, how beautiful!' and sitting in the shade,
    While better men than we go out and start their working lives
    At grubbing weeds from gravel paths with broken dinner-knives.
    1911 'The Glory of the Garden'.

69 Oh, Adam was a gardener, and God who made him sees
   That half a proper gardener's work is done upon his
     knees,
   So when your work is finished, you can wash your hands
     and pray
   For the Glory of the Garden that it may not pass away!
   1911 'The Glory of the Garden'.

70 We know the war prepared
   On every peaceful home,
   We know the hells declared
   For such as serve not Rome,
   The terror, threats and dread
   In market, hearth and field:
   We know when all is said
   We perish if we yield.
   1912 'Ulster'.

71 For all we have and are,
   For all our children's fate,
   Stand up and take the war.
   The Hun is at the gate!
   1914 'For All We Have and Are'.

72 There is but one task for all—
   For each one life to give.
   What stands if freedom fall?
   Who dies if England live?
   1914 'For All We Have and Are'.

73 It's north you may run to the rime-ringed sun,
   Or south to the blind Horn's hate;
   Or east all the way into Mississippi Bay,
   Or west to the Golden Gate.
   1918 *Twenty Poems*, 'The Long Trail'.

74 Pull out, pull out on the Long Trail—the trail that is
     always new!
   1918 *Twenty Poems*, 'The Long Trail'.

75 Their Name Liveth for Evermore.
   1919 His suggestion for the text to be carved over the lists of
   the dead in the Commonwealth war cemeteries after World
   War I.
   ▶ See Bible 113:11.

76 If any question why we died,
   Tell them, because our fathers lied.
   1919 *Rudyard Kipling's Verse*, 'Common Form'.

77 The female of the species is more deadly than the
     male.
   1919 *Rudyard Kipling's Verse*, 'The Female of the Species'.

78 Words are, of course, the most powerful drug used by
     mankind.
   1923 Speech, 14 Feb, collected in *A Book of Words*.

79 As it will be in the future, it was at the birth of Man—
   There are only four things certain since Social Progress
     began:—
   That the Dog returns to his Vomit and the Sow returns to
     her Mire,
   And the burnt Fool's bandaged finger goes wabbling
     back to the Fire.
   1927 *Rudyard Kipling's Verse*, 'The Gods of the Copybook
   Headings'.

80 England's on the anvil—hear the hammers ring—
   Clanging from the Severn to the Tyne!
   1927 *Rudyard Kipling's Verse*, 'The Anvil'.

Kirkland, (Joseph) Lane 1922–99

US labour leader.

81 My pappy told me never to bet my bladder against a
   brewery or get into an argument with people who buy
   ink by the barrel.
   Quoted in David Olive *Business Babble* (1993).

Kirkup, James 1923–2009

English poet. He held academic posts in Japan from the early
1960s, and his work was greatly influenced by Japanese culture
and literature.

82 But the river remains unchanged, sad, refusing
   rehabilitation.
   1962 'No More Hiroshimas'.

Kishen fl.c.1840

Chinese diplomatist.

83 It appears to Your Majesty's slave that we are very
   deficient in means, and have not the shells and rockets
   used by the barbarians. We must, therefore, adopt other
   methods to stop them, which will be easy, as they have
   opened negotiations.
   1841 Report, Mar, to the Chinese Emperor during the 1st Opium
   War, 1839–42.

Kissinger, Henry Alfred 1923–

US academic and statesman. He was the main US figure in the
negotiations to end the Vietnam War (for which he shared the
1973 Nobel peace prize), and Secretary of State (1973–7). His
'shuttle diplomacy', aimed at improving Israeli–Egyptian relations,
had much success.

84 It is not often that nations learn from the past—even rarer
   that they draw the correct conclusions from it. For the
   lessons of historical experience, as of personal
   experience, are contingent. They teach the
   consequences of certain actions, but they cannot force a
   recognition of comparable situations.
   1957 *A World Restored: Castlereagh, Metternich and the
   Restoration of Peace, 1812–22*.

85 We lost sight of one of the cardinal maxims of guerrilla
   war: the guerrilla wins if he does not lose. The
   conventional army loses if it does not win.
   1969 On the Vietnam War. In *Foreign Affairs*, Jan.

86 Power is the ultimate aphrodisiac.
   1969 Comment at the end of his first year as head of the National
   Security Council. Quoted in Walter Isaacson *Kissinger* (1992).

87 We are all the President's men, and we must behave
   accordingly.
   1970 On the US invasion of Cambodia, alluding to the
   nursery rhyme *Humpty Dumpty* ('All the king's men…'). The
   phrase was used in the title of the book by *Washington Post*
   reporters Bob Woodward and Carl Bernstein on the Watergate
   scandal.

88 No foreign policy, no matter how ingenious, has any
   chance of success if it is born in the minds of a few and
   carried in the heart of none.
   1973 Speech to International Platform Association, 2 Aug.

89 Every civilization that has ever existed has ultimately
   collapsed.
   1974 In the *New York Times*, 13 Oct.

90 History is a tale of efforts that failed…aspirations that weren't realized, or wishes that were fulfilled and then turned out to be different from what one expected.
1974 In the *New York Times*, 13 Oct.

91 There can't be any crisis next week. My schedule is already full.
1977 In *Time*, Jan.

92 High office teaches decision-making, not substance. It consumes intellectual capital; it does not create it. Most high officials leave office with the perceptions and insights with which they entered: they learn how to make decisions, but not what decisions to make.
1979 *The White House Years*.

93 The statesman's duty is to bridge the gap between his nation's experience and his vision.
1982 *Years of Upheaval*.

94 The nice thing about being a celebrity is that when you bore people, they think that it's their fault.
Quoted in *Reader's Digest*, Apr 1985.

95 Whatever must happen ultimately should happen immediately.
1986 Of the Iran–Contra scandal. In *Time*, 8 Oct.

96 Any people who have been persecuted for 2,000 years must be doing something wrong.
Of Israel, after its attack on Egypt. Quoted in Walter Isaacson *Kissinger* (1992).

97 I'd do anything for caviar and probably did.
On his visit to Moscow. Quoted in Walter Isaacson *Kissinger* (1992).

Kitchener of Khartoum and Broome, (Horatio) Herbert, 1st Earl 1850–1916

British field marshal. He served in Palestine, Cyprus and the Sudan, which he regained for the British Empire at Omdurman (1898), and was chief-of-staff and commander-in-chief in the Boer War. In World War I he was Secretary of State for War, but was drowned when HMS *Hampshire* struck a mine.

98 You are ordered abroad as a soldier of the King to help our French comrades against the invasion of a common enemy… In this new experience you may find temptations both in wine and women. You must entirely resist both temptations, and while treating all women with perfect courtesy, you should avoid any intimacy. Do your duty bravely. Fear God. Honour the King.
1914 Message to the soldiers of the British Expeditionary Force, reported in *The Times*, 19 Aug.

99 I don't mind your being killed, but I object to your being taken prisoner.
1914 To the Prince of Wales, later Edward VIII, who had asked to be allowed to the Front, 18 Dec.

Klee, Paul 1874–1940

Swiss painter and graphic artist, one of the most influential teachers of the German Bauhaus.

1 I have now reached the point where I can look over the great art of antiquity and its Renaissance. But, for myself, I cannot find any artistic connection with our own times. And to want to create something outside of one's own age strikes me as suspect.
1901–2 *The Diaries of Paul Klee 1898–1918*, entry 294.

2 The worst state of affairs is when science begins to concern itself with art.
1906 Collected in *The Notebooks of Paul Klee* (published 1957).

3 Color possesses me. I don't have to pursue it. It will possess me always, I know it. That is the meaning of this happy hour: Color and I are one. I am a painter.
1914 *The Diaries of Paul Klee 1898–1918*, entry 926.

4 Art is like Creation: it holds good on the last day as on the first.
1916 *The Diaries of Paul Klee 1898–1918*, entry 1008.

5 *Kunst gibt nicht das Sichtbare wieder, sondern macht sichtbar.*
Art does not reproduce the visible; rather it makes visible.
1920 'Creative Credo', in *Inward Vision* (1958).

Klein, Calvin Richard 1942–

US fashion designer.

6 You have to take things to an extreme and then bring them back to reality.
1988 On the fluctuating length of hemlines. In the *New York Times*, 9 Mar.

Kline, Nancy 1955–

US writer

7 Withholding information from someone is an act of intellectual imperialism. Not bothering to seek accurate information is an act of intellectual recklessness.
1999 *Time to Think*.

Kneller, Godfrey 1646–1723

German-born painter who spent most of his working life in England, particularly renowned as a portrait painter.

8 Painters of history make the dead live, and do not begin to live themselves till they are dead. I paint the living, and they make me live!
When asked why he preferred portraits to more prestigious history scenes. Quoted in A Cunningham *The Lives of the Most Eminent Painters, Sculptors and Architects* (1829).

Knight, Frank Hyneman 1885–1972

US economist, Professor at the University of Chicago (1927–58) and an opponent of social planning. His most famous works were *Risk, Uncertainty and Profit* and *The Ethics of Competition*.

9 Costs merely register competing attractions.
1921 *Risk, Uncertainty and Profit*.

10 I have been increasingly moved to wonder whether my job is a job or a racket, whether economists, and particularly economic theorists, may not be in the position that Cicero, citing Cato, ascribed to the augurs of Rome—that they should cover their faces or burst into laughter when they met on the street.
1950 Collected in *Essays on the History and Method of Economics* (1956).

11 Sociology is the science of talk, and there is only one law in sociology. Bad talk drives out good.
Quoted in Paul A Samuelson *The Samuelson Sampler* (1973).

Knobel, Steven Maxwell 1965–

US businessman.

12 It was the Wild West. If you were alive, they would give you a loan. Actually, I think if you were dead, they would still give you a loan.
  2008 Referring to the behaviour of US banks before the economic crash, 29 Dec.

Knox, John c.1513–1572

Scottish Protestant reformer and architect of the Church of Scotland, whose single-minded determination to establish Presbyterianism brought him into conflict with the Catholic Queen Mary.

13 The Monstrous Regiment of Women.
  1558 From the title of his pamphlet, *The First Blast of the Trumpet Against the Monstrous Regiment of Women*.

14 To promote a woman to bear rule, superiority, dominion, or empire above any realm, nation, or city, is repugnant to nature, contumely to God, a thing most contrarious to his revealed will and approved ordinance; and, finally, it is the subversion of good order, of all equity and justice.
  1558 *First Blast of the Trumpet against the Monstrous Regiment of Women*.

15 If there be not in her, a proud mind, a crafty wit, and an indurate heart against God and his truth, my judgment faileth me.
  1561 After his first meeting with Mary, Queen of Scots. *History of the Reformation in Scotland*, vol.2.

16 *Un homme avec Dieu est toujours dans la majorité.*
  One man with God is always a majority.
  Inscription on the Reformation Monument, Geneva, attributed to Knox.

Knox, Philander Chase 1853–1921

US lawyer and politician. He served as US Attorney General (1901–4) and Secretary of State (1909–13).

17 Oh, Mr President, do not let so great an achievement suffer from any taint of legality.
  1903 Quoted in Tom Buckley *Violent Neighbours* (1983), alluding to Theodore Roosevelt's desire to find legal grounds for the seizure of the Panama Canal by the US.

Knox, Ronald Arbuthnot 1888–1957

English writer and Roman Catholic theologian. He wrote many theological works and Bible translations, and also detective novels.

18 There was once a man who said 'God
  Must think it exceedingly odd
  If he finds that this tree
  Continues to be
  When there's no-one about in the Quad.'
  Attributed. Quoted in Langford Reed *Complete Limerick Book* (1924).
  The limericks summarise Bishop George Berkeley's philosophy that everything is dependent at all times on the will of God.
  ▶ See Anonymous 24:11.

19 It is stupid of modern civilization to have given up believing in the devil, when he is the only explanation of it.
  1939 *Let Dons Delight*, ch.8.

20 A loud noise at one end and no sense of responsibility at the other.
  His definition of a baby. Attributed.

Knudsen, Semon Emil 1912–98

US automotive executive.

21 Before you tell someone how good you are, you must tell him how bad you used to be.
  1959 In *Time* magazine, 25 May.

Koch, Edward I(rving) 1924–2013

US lawyer and Mayor of New York City (1978–89).

22 You're not a nice guy if you have a gun, even if you are a nice guy.
  1980 In *Time*, 3 Mar.

23 Each diploma is a lighted match… Each one of you is a fuse.
  1983 Addressing students at NY State University. In the *New York Times*, 10 Jun.

24 I don't want to leave Manhattan, even when I'm gone. This is my home. The thought of having to go to New Jersey was so distressing to me.
  2008 Explaining why he had bought himself a burial plot in the Trinity Cemetery, Manhattan.

25 It's not soaring, beautiful, handsome, like the George Washington or the Verrazano. It's rugged, it's hard working—and that's me.
  2011 His reaction to the 59th Street Bridge being named after him.

Koestler, Arthur 1905–83

Hungarian-born British writer and journalist. He wrote on science and parapsychology, and is best known for his anti-communist novel *Darkness at Noon* (1940). He and his wife committed suicide after he became terminally ill.

26 The definition of an individual was: a multitude of one million divided by one million.
  1940 *Darkness at Noon*, 'The Grammatical Fiction', pt.2.

27 A writer's ambition should be…to trade a hundred contemporary readers for ten readers in ten years' time and for one reader in a hundred years.
  1951 In the *New York Times Book Review*, 1 Apr.

28 Space-ships and time machines are no escape from the human condition. Let Othello subject Desdemona to a lie-detector test; his jealousy will still blind him to the evidence. Let Oedipus triumph over gravity; he won't triumph over his fate.
  1953 'The Boredom of Fantasy', collected in *The Trail of the Dinosaur* (1955), pt.2.

29 Among all forms of mentation, verbal thinking is the most articulate, the most complex, and the most vulnerable to infectious diseases. It is liable to absorb whispered suggestions, and to incorporate them as hidden persuaders into the code.
  1964 *The Act of Creation*.

30 Creativity in science could be described as the act of putting two and two together to make five.
  1964 *The Act of Creation*.

31 The most persistent sound that reverberates through men's history is the beating of war drums.
  1978 *Janus; A Summing Up*, 'Prologue: The New Calendar', sect.1.

Koffler, Murray 1924–

Canadian pharmacist and philanthropist.

32 Dress British, look Irish, think Yiddish.
His formula for success, quoted in Frank Rasky *Just a Simple Pharmacist: The Story of Murray Koffler, Builder of the Shoppers Drug Mart Empire* (1988).

Koh, Harold Hongju 1954–
US lawyer, Professor of International Law at Yale University.

33 Silence has a sound, and the sound is 'no.'
1991 Testimony to the US Senate Judiciary Committee on the presidential right to enter the Gulf War without congressional approval. Quoted by Senator Joseph R Biden, Jr in NPR broadcast, 10 Jan.

Kohl, Helmut 1930–
German statesman. He was Chancellor from 1982 to 1998.

34 The policy of European integration is in reality a question of war and peace in the 21st century.
1996 Speech, 2 Feb.

Kohlberg, Jerome, Jr 1925–
US investment banker.

35 An ethic is not an ethic, and a value not a value without some sacrifice for it. Something given up, something not gained.
Quoted in Sarah Bartlett *The Money Machine* (1991).

Kollwitz, Käthe 1867–1945
German sculptor and graphic artist. She had two sons, Peter and Hans. Peter was killed at the beginning of World War I, in 1914.

36 As you, the children of my body, have been my tasks, so too are my other works.
1915 Letter to her son Hans, 21 Feb.

37 I have never done any work cold... I have always worked with my blood, so to speak.
1917 Letter to her son Hans, 16 Apr.

The Koran
All quotations are taken from the Arthur J Arberry (1955) translation of The Koran. Line numbers refer to the standard numeration.

38 In the name of God, the Merciful, the Compassionate.
Praise belongs to God, the Lord of all Being,
the All-merciful, the All-compassionate
the Master of the Day of Doom.
Thee only we serve; to Thee alone we pray for succour.
Guide us in the straight path,
the path of those whom Thou hast blessed,
not of those against whom Thou art wrathful,
nor of those who are astray.
Sura 1, l.1–7.

39 We have sent among you, of yourselves, a Messenger, to recite Our signs to you and to purify you, and to teach you the Book and the Wisdom, and to teach you that you knew not. So remember Me, and I will remember you; and be thankful to Me; and be you not ungrateful towards Me.
Sura 2, l.151–2.

40 O all you who believe, seek you help in patience and prayer; surely God is with the patient.
Sura 2, l.153.

41 Surely in the creation of the heavens and the earth and the alternation of night and day and the ship that runs in the sea with profit to men, and the water God sends down from heaven therewith reviving the earth after it is dead and His scattering abroad in it all manner of crawling thing, and the turning about of the winds and the clouds compelled between heaven and earth— surely there are signs for a people having understanding.
Sura 2, l.164.

42 It is not piety that you turn your faces to the East and to the West. True piety is this: to believe in God, and the Last Day, the angels, the Book, and the Prophets, to give of one's substance, however cherished, to kinsmen, and orphans, the needy, the traveller, beggars, and to ransom the slave, to perform the prayer, to pay the alms.
Sura 2, l.177.

43 And fight in the way of God with those who fight with you, but aggress not: God loves not the aggressors.
Sura 2, l.190.

44 God charges no soul save to its capacity; standing to account is what it has earned, and against its account what it has merited.
Sura 2, l.286.

45 And when the angels said: 'Mary, God has chosen thee, and purified thee; He has chosen thee above all women. Mary be obedient to thy Lord, prostrating and bowing before Him.'
Sura 3, l.42–3.

46 You will not attain piety until you expend of what you love.
Sura 3, l.92.

47 It was by some mercy of God that thou wast gentle to them; hadst thou been harsh and hard of heart, they would have scattered from about thee. So pardon them, and pray forgiveness for them, and take counsel with them in the affair; and when thou art resolved, put thy trust in God.
Sura 3, l.159.

48 Every soul shall taste of death; you shall surely be paid in full your wages on the Day of Resurrection. Whosoever is removed from the Fire and admitted to Paradise, shall win the triumph. The present life is but the joy of delusion.
Sura 3, l.185.

49 Surely in the creation of the heavens and earth and in the alternation of night and day there are signs for men possessed of minds who remember God, standing and sitting and on their sides, and reflect upon the creation of the heavens and the earth. 'Our Lord, thou has not created this for vanity!'
Sura 3, l.191.

50 Mankind, fear your Lord, who created you of a single soul, and from it created its mate, and from the pair of them scattered abroad many men and women; and fear God by whom you demand one of another, and the wombs; surely God ever watches over you.
Sura 4, l.1.

51 God commands you to deliver trusts back to their owners.
Sura 4, l.58.

52 How is it with you, that you do not fight in the way of God, and for the men, women, and children who, being

abased, say, 'Our Lord, bring us forth from this city whose people are evildoers, and appoint to us a protector from Thee?'
Sura 4, l.75.

53 O believers, be you securers of justice, witnesses for God, even though it be against yourselves, or your parents and kinsmen, whether the man be rich or poor.
Sura 4, l.135.

54 We have revealed to thee as We revealed to Noah, and the Prophets after him, and We revealed to Abraham, Ishmael, Isaac, Jacob, and the Tribes, Jesus and Job, Jonah and Aaron and Solomon, and We gave to David Psalms, and Messengers We have already told thee of before, and Messengers We have not told thee of; and unto Moses God spoke directly—Messengers bearing good tidings, and warning, so that mankind might have no argument against God, after the Messengers; God is All-mighty, All-wise.
Sura 4, l.163–4.

55 People of the Book, go not beyond the bounds in your religion, and say not as to God but the truth. The Messiah, Jesus son of Mary, was only the Messenger of God, and His Word that He committed to Mary, and a spirit from Him. So believe in God and His Messengers, and say not, 'Three'. Refrain; better is it for you. God is only One God. Glory be to Him—that He should have a son! To Him belongs all that is in the heavens and the earth; God suffices for a guardian. The Messiah will not disdain to be a servant of God, neither the angels who are near stationed to Him.
Sura 4, l.171–2.

56 O believers, be you securers of justice, witnesses for God. Let not detestation for a people move you not to be equitable.
Sura 5, l.8.

57 No creature is there crawling on the earth, no bird flying with its wings, but they are nations like unto yourselves.
Sura 6, l.38.

58 With Him are the keys of the Unseen; none knows them but He. He knows what is in land and sea; not a leaf falls, but He knows it.
Sura 6, l.59.

59 It is God who splits the grain and the date-stone, brings forth the living from the dead; He brings for the dead too from the living. So that then is God; then how are you perverted? He splits the sky into dawn, and has made the night for a repose, and the sun and moon for a reckoning.
Sura 6, l.96–7.

60 Say: 'As for me, my Lord has guided me to a straight path, a right religion, the creed of Abraham, a man of pure faith; he was no idolater.' Say: 'My prayer, my ritual sacrifice, my living, my dying—all belongs to God, the Lord of all Being.'
Sura 6, l.162.

61 To every nation a term; when their term comes they shall not put it back by a single hour nor put it forward.
Sura 7, l.34.

62 Of the people of Moses there is a nation who guide by the truth, and by it act with justice.
Sura 7, l.159.

63 And when thy Lord took from the Children of Adam, from their loins, their seed, and made them testify touching themselves, 'Am I not your Lord?' They said, 'Yes, we testify'—lest you should say on the Day of Resurrection, 'As for us, we were heedless of this.'
Sura 7, l.172.

64 To God belong the Names Most Beautiful; so call Him by them.
Sura 7, l.180.

65 O believers, fear God, and be with the truthful ones.
Sura 9, l.119.

66 And God summons to the Abode of Peace.
Sura 10, l.26.

67 Surely God wrongs not men anything, but themselves men wrong.
Sura 10, l.45.

68 And the king said: 'I saw in a dream seven fat kine, and seven lean ones devouring them; likewise seven green ears of corn, and seven withered. My counsellors, pronounce to me upon my dream, if you are expounders of dreams.' 'A hotchpotch of nightmares!' they said.
Sura 12, l.43–4.

69 It is He who shows you the lightning, for fear and hope, and produces the heavy clouds; the thunder proclaims His praise, and the angels, in awe of Him.
Sura 13, l.13.

70 Hast thou not seen how God has struck a similitude? A good word is as a good tree—its roots are firm, and its branches are in heaven; it gives its produce every season by the leave of its Lord. So God strikes similitudes for men; haply they will remember. And the likeness of a corrupt word is as a corrupt tree—uprooted from the earth, having no stablishment. God confirms those who believe with the firm word, in the present life and in the world to come.
Sura 14, l.24–7.

71 And when thy Lord said to the angels, 'See, I am creating a mortal of a clay of mud moulded. When I have shaped him, and breathed My spirit in him, fall you down, bowing before him!'
Sura 15, l.28–9.

72 He created man of a sperm-drop; and behold, he is a manifest adversary.
Sura 16, l.4.

73 Man prays for evil, as he prays for good; man is ever hasty.
Sura 17, l.11.

74 Thy Lord has decreed you shall not serve any but Him, and to be good to parents, whether one or both of them attains old age with thee; say not to them 'Fie' neither chide them, but speak unto them words respectful, and lower to them the wing of humbleness out of mercy and say: 'My Lord, have mercy on them, as they raised me up when I was little.'
Sura 17, l.23–4.

75 They will question thee concerning the Spirit. Say: 'The Spirit is of the bidding of my Lord. You have been given of knowledge nothing except a little.'
Sura 17, l.85.

76 Say: 'If the sea were ink for the Words of my Lord, the sea would be spent before the Words of my Lord are spent.'
Sura 18, l.110.

77 Whosoever turns away from My remembrance, his shall be a life of narrowness.
Sura 20, l.124.

78 God is the Light of the heavens and the earth; the likeness of His Light is as a niche wherein is a lamp (the lamp in a glass, the glass as it were a glittering star) kindled from a Blessed Tree, an olive that is neither of the East nor of the West whose oil wellnigh would shine, even if no fire touched it; Light upon Light; (God guides to His Light whom He will). (And God strikes similitudes for men, and God has knowledge of everything.)
Sura 24, l.35.

79 Hast thou not seen how that whatsoever is in the heavens and in the earth extols God, and the birds spreading their wings? Each—He knows its prayer and its extolling.
Sura 24, l.41.

80 And of His signs is that He created for you, of yourselves, spouses, that you might repose in them, and He has set between you love and mercy.
Sura 30, l.21.

81 And of His signs is the creation of the heavens and the earth and the variety of your tongues and hues.
Sura 30, l.22.

82 Not a nation there is, but there has passed away in it a warner.
Sura 35, l.24.

83 And when We bless man, he turns away and withdraws aside; but when evil visits him, he is full of endless prayers.
Sura 41, l.51.

84 Hast thou seen him who has taken his caprice to be his God?
Sura 45, l.23.

85 They say: 'There is nothing but our present life; we die, and we live, and nothing but Time destroys us.' Of that they have no knowledge; they merely conjecture.
Sura 45, l.24.

86 Find not fault with one another, neither revile one another by nicknames.
Sura 49, l.11.

87 O mankind, We have created you male and female, and appointed you races and tribes, that you may know one another. Surely the noblest among you in the sight of God is the most godfearing of you. God is All-knowing, All-aware.
Sura 49, l.13.

88 Be not as those who forgot God, and so He caused them to forget their souls.
Sura 59, l.18.

89 They fulfil their vows, and fear a day whose evil is upon the wing; they give food, for the love of Him, to the needy, the orphan, the captive: 'We feed you only for the Face of God; we desire no recompense from you, no thankfulness.'
Sura 76, l.7–9.

90 But as for him who feared the Station of his Lord and forbade the soul its caprice, surely Paradise shall be the refuge.
Sura 79, l.40.

91 When the sun shall be darkened, when the stars shall be thrown down, when the mountains shall be set moving, when the pregnant camels shall be neglected, when the savage beasts shall be mustered, when the seas shall be set boiling, when the souls shall be coupled, when the buried infant shall be asked for what sin she was slain, when the scrolls shall be unrolled, when heaven shall be stripped off, when Hell shall be set blazing, when Paradise shall be brought nigh, then shall a soul know what it has produced.
Sura 81, 1–14.

92 No! I swear by the slinkers, the runners, the sinkers, by the night swarming, by the dawn sighing, truly this is the word of a noble Messenger.
Sura 81, 15–19.

93 By heaven of the returning rain, by earth splitting with verdure, surely it is a decisive word; it is no merriment.
Sura 86, l.11–14.

94 By the snorting chargers, by the strikers of fire, by the dawn raiders blazing a trail of dust, cleaving there with a host! Surely Man is ungrateful to his Lord.
Sura 100, 1–6.

95 Woe to those that pray and are heedless of their prayers, to those who make display and refuse charity.
Sura 107, l.4–7.

Korda, Sir Alexander 1893–1956

Hungarian-born British film producer. He worked in Vienna, Berlin and Hollywood before coming to Britain in the early 1930s where he founded London Film Productions and the Denham Studios.

96 One can be unhappy before eating caviar, even after, but at least not *during*.
1979 In *Newsweek*, 26 Nov.

97 Inside every banker, even the governor of the Bank of England, there lies a gambling streak. In me, they recognise one of their own kind.
Quoted in Michael Wilding and Pamela Wilcox *Apple Sauce* (1982).

98 It's not enough to be Hungarian, you must have talent too.
Attributed. The predominance of Eastern European employees at Denham Studios in the 1930s was a topical joke.

Korn, Arthur 1891–1978

German-born architect, planner and teacher.

99 A new glass age has begun, which is equal in beauty to the old one of Gothic windows.
1926 *Glas im Bau und als Gebrauchsgegenstand* (translated as *Glass in Modern Architecture*, 1967).

Korthals, Robert 1933–

Canadian bank president (1981–95).

1 The easiest way to steal from a bank is to own one.
Quoted by Diane Francis in *Controlling Interest: Who Owns Canada?* (1986).

Kosinski, Jerzy Nikodem 1933–91

Polish-born US novelist. His best-known books are *The Painted Bird* (1965) and *Being There* (1971).

2 I rent everything, other than the gift of life itself, which was given to me without any predictable lease, a gift that can be withdrawn at any time.
1991 Interview given three days before his suicide, in the Weekend Guardian, *25–6 May.*

Kramer, Larry (Lawrence) 1935–

US novelist, playwright and screenwriter. He is best known for his controversial gay novel *Faggots* (1978), and his plays dealing with AIDS, notably *The Normal Heart* (1985).

3 We're all going to go crazy, living this epidemic every minute, while the rest of the world goes on out there, all around us, as if nothing is happening, going on with their own lives and not knowing what it's like, what we're going through. We're living through war, but where they're living it's peacetime, and we're all in the same country.
1985 Ned speaking of gay men with AIDS. The Normal Heart, *act 2, sc.11.*

Krasna, Norman 1909–84

US playwright and screenwriter. He won an Academy Award for *Princess O'Rourke* (1943). Other films include *Bachelor Mother* (1939) and *Indiscreet* (1958).

4 How dare he make love to me and not be a married man?
1958 Line delivered by Ingrid Bergman in Indiscreet.

Kraus, Karl 1874–1936

Austrian critic and dramatist, publisher and sole writer of the radical satirical magazine *Die Fackel* ('The Torch', 1899–1936). He wrote the apocalyptic satirical play *The Last Days of Mankind* (1919), and collections of aphorisms.

5 Today's literature: prescriptions written by patients.
Aphorism collected in Heinrich Fischer (ed) Beim Wort genommen *(1955). Translated by Harry Zohn in* Half-truths and one-and-a-half truths *(1986).*

6 Why didn't Eternity have this deformed age aborted ? Its birthmark is the stamp of a newspaper, its medium is printer's ink, and in its veins flows ink.
Aphorism collected in Heinrich Fischer (ed) Beim Wort genommen *(1955). Translated by Harry Zohn in* Half-truths and one-and-a-half truths *(1986).*

7 The making of a journalist: no ideas and the ability to express them.
Aphorism collected in Heinrich Fischer (ed) Beim Wort genommen *(1955). Translated by Harry Zohn in* Half-truths and one-and-a-half truths *(1986).*

8 A historian is often only a journalist facing backwards.
Aphorism collected in Heinrich Fischer (ed) Beim Wort genommen *(1955). Translated by Harry Zohn in* Half-truths and one-and-a-half truths *(1986).*

9 How is the world ruled and led to war? Diplomats lie to journalists and believe these lies when they see them in print.
Aphorism collected in Heinrich Fischer (ed) Beim Wort genommen *(1955). Translated by Harry Zohn in* Half-truths and one-and-a-half truths *(1986).*

10 One ought to acknowledge the significance for mankind of the simultaneous invention of gunpowder and printer's ink.
Aphorism collected in Heinrich Fischer (ed) Beim Wort genommen *(1955). Translated by Harry Zohn in* Half-truths and one-and-a-half truths *(1986).*

Krishnamurti, Jiddu 1895–1986

Indian-born mystic and spiritual teacher. The theosophist Annie Besant in 1925 proclaimed him Messiah and from then on he travelled the world, teaching a way of life free from the conditioning of culture, race or religion.

11 I maintain that truth is a pathless land, and you cannot approach it by any path whatsoever, by any religion, by any sect.
1929 Speech in Holland. Quoted in Terry Lynn Taylor Messengers of Light, *ch.32.*

12 The authority of a belief imposed by religion surely destroys the discovery of reality. One relies on authority because one is afraid to stand alone.
1970 BBC interview, 7 Dec.

Kristol, Irving 1920–2009

US economist and academic, often considered as the founder of neoconservatism.

13 History does not provide us with any instance of a society that repressed the economic liberties of the individual while being solicitous of his other liberties.
1978 Two Cheers for Capitalism, *introduction.*

14 The fact of affluence is indisputable... Nevertheless, not many of us *feel* that well off. The instinct for contentment seems to have withered even as our economic condition has radically improved.
1978 Two Cheers for Capitalism, *ch.1.*

15 The elitist attitude is basically suspicious of, and hostile to, the market precisely because the market is so vulgarly democratic—one dollar, one vote.
1978 Two Cheers for Capitalism, *ch.2.*

Kroc, Ray(mond) A 1902–84

US entrepreneur, developer of the McDonald's fast-food chain.

16 Luck is a dividend of sweat. The more you sweat, the luckier you get.
1988 Quoted by Penny Moser 'The McDonald's Mystique', in Fortune, *4 Jul.*

17 If they were drowning to death, I would put a hose in their mouth.
1988 On competitors. In Fortune, *4 Jul.*

Kronecker, Leopold 1823–91

German mathematician, who worked in algebraic number theory and the foundations of analysis, and lectured widely. He held that mathematics should be based on whole numbers, rejecting the infinite, irrational and imaginary.

18 God made the integers, man made the rest.
Quoted in F Cajori A History of Mathematics *(1919).*

Kronenberger, Louis 1904–80

US writer, lecturer and critic. His books include novels and autobiographical reminiscences as well as critical works on literature and culture, and biographies.

19 Kings and Desperate Men.
   1942 Title of book on 18c England.

20 The trouble with our age is that it is all signpost and no destination.
   1954 Company Manners, 'The Spirit of The Age'.

Kruger, Paulus   1825–1904

South African soldier and statesman, President of the Transvaal (1883–1902) and head of the provisional government in the first Boer War. During the second Boer War he was forced to flee to Europe, and he died in Switzerland.

21 They have asked me for my trousers, and I have given them; for my coat, and I have given that also; now they want my life, and that I cannot give.
   1899 Speech in the Raad, 7 Sep, at the beginning of the second Boer War, 1899–1902.

Krugman, Paul R   1953–

US economist and columnist, Professor of Economics and International Affairs at Princeton University. In 2008 he won the Nobel memorial prize in economic sciences.

22 The trouble with poverty, as an issue, is that it has basically exhausted the patience of the general public.
   1992 The Age of Diminished Expectations.

23 Given that the deepest problem with the US economy is slow productivity growth, it is difficult to argue for tax increases that might reduce incentives... There seems to be a public consensus that Donald Trump is the price of progress.
   1992 The Age of Diminished Expectations.

24 The exchange rate is only a statistic, not a symbol of national honor and virility.
   1994 Quoted in the New York Times, 26 Jun.

25 There are no atheists in foxholes and there are no libertarians in financial crises.
   2008 On HBO's Real Time.

26 When it comes to the all-too-human problem of recessions and depressions, economists need to abandon the neat but wrong solution of assuming that everyone is rational and markets work perfectly. The vision that emerges as the profession rethinks its foundations may not be all that clear; it certainly won't be neat; but we can hope that it will have the virtue of being at least partly right.
   2009 'How did economists get it so wrong?', New York Times, 2 Sep.

27 Politics determine who has the power, not who has the truth.
   2010 The Australian Financial Review, 6 Sep.

28 Sometimes economists in official positions give bad advice; sometimes they give very, very bad advice; and sometimes they work at the OECD.
   2013 'The Conscience of a Liberal', blog at the New York Times, 30 Apr.

Krutch, Joseph Wood   1893–1970

US author, teacher and critic. He is the author of The Modern Temper (1929) and The Measure of Man (1954).

29 A tragic writer does not have to believe in God, but he must believe in man.
   1929 The Modern Temper, 'The Tragic Fallacy'.

30 Electronic calculators can solve problems which the man who made them cannot solve; but no government subsidized commission of engineers and physicists could create a worm.
   1949 The Twelve Seasons, 'February'.

31 The most serious charge which can be brought against New England is not Puritanism but February.
   1949 The Twelve Seasons, 'February'.

32 Cats seem to go on the principle that it never does any harm to ask for what you want.
   1949 The Twelve Seasons, 'February'.

Kubrick, Stanley   1928–99

US screenwriter, film producer and director. His films include Spartacus (1960), 2001: A Space Odyssey (1969), the controversial A Clockwork Orange (1971) and Full Metal Jacket (1987).

33 Gentlemen, you can't fight in here. This is the war room.
   1963 Dr Strangelove: or How I stopped worrying and learned to love the bomb (with Terry Southern and Peter George).

34 The great nations have always acted like gangsters, and the small nations like prostitutes.
   1963 In The Guardian.

35 The very meaninglessness of life forces man to create his own meaning. If it can be written or thought, it can be filmed.
   Quoted in Halliwell's Filmgoer's and Video Viewer's Companion (1999).

Kuhn, Maggie   1905–95

US writer and social reformer, founder of the Gray Panthers.

36 The ultimate indignity is to be given a bedpan by a stranger who calls you by your first name.
   1978 In the Observer, 20 Aug.

Kuhn, Thomas S(amuel)   1922–96

US historian and philosopher of science. His major work is The Structure of Scientific Revolutions (1962), a cornerstone of modern approaches to the philosophy and history of science.

37 Effective research scarcely begins before a scientific community thinks it has acquired firm answers to questions like the following: What are the fundamental entities of which the universe is composed? How do these interact with each other and with the senses? What questions may legitimately be asked about such entities and what techniques employed in seeking solutions?
   1962 The Structure of Scientific Revolutions.

Kundera, Milan   1929–

Czech-born French novelist.

38 The Unbearable Lightness of Being.
   1984 Title of novel.

Küng, Hans   1928–

Swiss Roman Catholic theologian. His questioning of received doctrine aroused controversy, and the Vatican withdrew his authority to teach as a Catholic theologian in 1979. He defended himself in Why I Am Still A Christian (1987).

39 A Church which abandons the truth abandons itself.
   Die Kirche (translated by Ray and Rosalee Ockenden as The Church, 1967).

Kunitz, Stanley Jasspon 1905–2006
US poet and editor, whose style was at once intellectual and passionate. His poetry collections include *Selected Poems, 1928–1958* (1958, Pulitzer Prize winner) and *Next-to-Last Things: New Poems and Essays* (1985). In 2000 he became the US Poet Laureate.

40 A poem is at once the most primitive and most sophisticated use of language, but my emphasis is on the former.
1985 *Next-to-Last Things*, 'The Wisdom of the Body'.

41 The deepest thing I know is that I am living and dying at once, and my conviction is to report that dialogue.
1987 In the *New York Times*, 11 Mar.

Kuralt, Charles 1934–97
US writer and broadcaster.

42 It takes an earthquake to remind us that we walk on the crust of an unfinished earth.
1994 In *Sunday Morning*, CBS T V, 23 Jan.

Kurosawa, Akira 1910–98
Japanese film director and winner of numerous international awards for his films. Best known in the West for his full-blooded adaptations of Shakespeare.

43 Like a steak spread with butter and topped with good, rich, broiled eels.
1965 His concept of a great film. In *Japan Quarterly*, vol.12.

44 The Japanese see self-assertion as immoral and self-sacrifice as the sensible course to take in life.
1982 *Something like an Autobiography*.

Kushner, Tony 1956–
US playwright, whose highly political plays include the two-part *Angels in America* (1991–2, Pulitzer Prize 1993), on the effects of AIDS in NewYork.

45 I wanted to attempt something of ambition and size even if that meant I might be accused of straying too close to ambition's ugly twin, pretentiousness.
1993 Of his *Angels in America*, written in two parts. In the *New York Times*, 21 Nov.

Kurz, Mordecai 1934–
US economist, Professor at Stanford University.

46 There is only one truth, and many opinions. Therefore, most people are wrong most of the time.
1985 In *Fortune*, 3 Apr.

Kyd, Thomas 1558–94
English dramatist.

47 In time the savage bull sustains the yoke;
In time all haggard hawks will stoop to lure;
In time small wedges cleave the hardest oak,
In time the flint is pierced with softest shower,
And she in time will fall from her disdain,
And rue the sufferance of your friendly pain.
c.1589 *The Spanish Tragedy*, act 2, sc.1.

48 Where words prevail not, violence prevails;
But gold doth more than either of them both.
c.1589 *The Spanish Tragedy*, act 2, sc.1.

49 Oh eyes, no eyes, but fountains fraught with tears;
Oh life, no life, but lively form of death;
Oh world, no world, but mass of public wrongs.
c.1589 *The Spanish Tragedy*, act 3, sc.2.

50 I'll trust myself, myself shall be my friend.
c.1589 *The Spanish Tragedy*, act 3, sc.2.

51 Thus must we toil in other men's extremes,
That know not how to remedy our own.
c.1589 *The Spanish Tragedy*, act 3, sc.6.

52 For what's a play without a woman in it?
c.1589 *The Spanish Tragedy*, act 4, sc.1.

Labé, Louise 1526–66
A poet of the École Lyonnaise who wrote sonnets, elegies and a prose work, *Débat de Folie et d'Amour* (1555, 'Debate Between Folly and Love').

1 *Quelque rigueur qui loge en votre coeur,*
Amour s'en peut un jour rendre vainqueur.
That little harshness which resides in your heart,
Love will vanquish someday.
1555 *Elégies*, no.1.

2 *Où donc es-tu, ô âme bien-aimée?*
Where are you now, oh soul desired?
1555 *Sonnets*, no.6.

3 *Je vis, je meurs; je me brûle et me noie.*
I live, I die; I am on fire and I drown.
1555 *Sonnets*, no.8.

4 *Ne reprenez, dame, si j'ai aimé,*
Si j'ai senti mille torches ardentes,
Mille travaux, mille douleurs mordantes,
Si, en pleurant, j'ai mon temps consumé.
Do not blame me, madam, if I loved,
If I felt one thousand burning torches,
One thousand labours, or one thousand scathing pains,
If, in crying, I spent all my time.
1555 *Sonnets*, no.24.

Labouchère, Henry Du Pré 1831–1912
English radical journalist and politician. A Liberal MP (1865–8, 1880–1906), in 1876 he founded the investigative journal *Truth*.

5 Nothing has conduced more to shake that decent respect for the living symbol of the state that goes by the name of royalty than the ever-recurring rattle of the money box.
1884 In the *Fortnightly Review*, Feb.

La Bruyère, Jean de 1645–96
French moralist author who tutored Louis de Bourbon, grandson of the Great Condé. His *Caractères de Théophraste* (1688) made his reputation but won him many enemies.

6 *Tout est dit, et l'on vient trop tard depuis plus de sept mille ans qu'il y a des hommes et qui pensent.*

La Bruyère

Everything has been said. After seven thousand years of human thought, we have come too late.
1688 *Les Caractères ou les mïurs de ce siècle*, 'Des ouvrages de l'esprit', no.1.

7 *C'est un métier que de faire un livre, comme de faire une pendule; il faut plus que de l'esprit pour être auteur.*
It is as much a trade to write a book as it is to make a watch; it takes more than wit to make an author.
1688 *Les Caractères ou les mïurs de ce siècle*, 'Des ouvrages de l'esprit', no.3.

8 *Une belle femme qui a les qualités d'un honnête homme est ce qu'il y a au monde d'un commerce plus délicieux: l'on trouve en elle tout le mérite des deux sexes.*
A beautiful woman who has the qualities of a gentleman is the most pleasing person in all the world: one finds in her all the merit of both sexes.
1688 *Les Caractères ou les mïurs de ce siècle*, 'Des femmes', no.13.

9 *Les femmes sont extrêmes: elles sont meilleures ou pires que les hommes.*
Women are all in extremes: they are either better or worse than men.
1688 *Les Caractères ou les mïurs de ce siècle*, 'Des femmes', no.53.

10 *Un homme est plus fidèle au secret d'autrui qu'au sien propre; une femme au contraire garde mieux son secret que celui d'autrui.*
A man keeps another person's secret better than his own; a woman, on the contrary, keeps her own secrets better than those of others.
1688 *Les Caractères ou les mïurs de ce siècle*, 'Des femmes', no.58.

11 *Une femme insensible est celle qui n'a pas encore vu celui qu'elle doit aimer.*
A dispassionate woman is one who has yet to see the one she should love.
1688 *Les Caractères ou les mïurs de ce siècle*, 'Des femmes', no.81.

12 *Le temps, qui fortifie les amitiés, affaiblit l'amour.*
Time, which strengthens friendships, weakens love.
1688 *Les Caractères ou les mïurs de ce siècle*, 'Du cœur', no.4.

13 *L'amour et l'amitié s'excluent l'un l'autre.*
Love and friendship exclude one another.
1688 *Les Caractères ou les mïurs de ce siècle*, 'Du cœur', no.7.

14 *L'amour qui naît subitement est le plus long à guérir.*
Love which strikes suddenly takes the longest to cure.
1688 *Les Caractères ou les mïurs de ce siècle*, 'Du cœur', no.12.

15 *Les amours meurent par le dégoût, et l'oubli les enterre.*
Loves die from disgust, and forgetting buries them.
1688 *Les Caractères ou les mïurs de ce siècle*, 'Du cœur', no.32.

16 *Qu'il est difficile d'être content de quelqu'un!*
How difficult it is to be happy with someone!
1688 *Les Caractères ou les mïurs de ce siècle*, 'Du cœur', no.65.

17 *L'esclave n'a qu'un maître; l'ambitieux en a autant qu'il y a des gens utiles à sa fortune.*
A slave has but one master; an ambitious person has as many as he needs to make his fortune.
1688 *Les Caractères ou les mïurs de ce siècle*, 'Du cœur', no.70.

18 *Il fera demain ce qu'il fait aujourd'hui et ce qu'il fit hier; et il meurt ainsi après avoir vécu.*
What he does tomorrow will be what he did today and yesterday; and he shall die after having lived this way.
1688 *Les Caractères ou les mïurs de ce siècle*, 'De la ville', no.12.

19 *La vie est courte et ennuyeuse: elle se passe toute à désirer.*
Life is short and bothersome: all we do is desire what we do not have.
1688 *Les Caractères ou les mïurs de ce siècle*, 'De l'homme', no.19.

20 *Si la vie est misérable, elle est pénible à supporter; si elle est heureuse, il est horrible de la perdre. L'un revient à l'autre.*
If life is miserable, it is difficult to endure; if it is happy, it is horrible to lose. They come to the same thing.
1688 *Les Caractères ou les mïurs de ce siècle*, 'De l'homme', no.33.

21 *A parler humainement, la mort a un bel endroit, qui est de mettre fin à la vieillesse.*
To speak humanely, death has a useful function: it puts an end to old age.
1688 *Les Caractères ou les mïurs de ce siècle*, 'De l'homme', no.45.

22 *Il n'y a pour l'homme que trois événements: naître, vivre et mourir. Il ne se sent pas naître, il souffre à mourir, et il oublie de vivre.*
There are only three great events for a person: to be born, to live and to die. He does not feel his own birth, he suffers upon death and he forgets to live.
1688 *Les Caractères ou les mïurs de ce siècle*, 'De l'homme', no.48.

23 *Les enfants sont hautains, dédaigneux, colères, envieux, curieux, intéressés, paresseux, volages, timides, intempérants, menteurs, dissimulés…ils ne veulent point souffrir de mal, et aiment à en faire: ils sont déjà des hommes.*
Children are haughty, disdainful, angry, envious, curious, interested, lazy, fickle, shy, self-indulgent, liars, deceivers…they do not wish to suffer evil, but like to do evil: they are already adults.
1688 *Les Caractères ou les mïurs de ce siècle*, 'De l'homme', no.50.

24 *Les enfants n'ont ni passé ni avenir, et, ce qui ne nous arrive guère, ils jouissent du présent.*
Children have neither past nor future. They live in the present, something which rarely happens to us.
1688 *Les Caractères ou les mïurs de ce siècle*, 'De l'homme', no.51.

25 *Il y a une espèce de honte d'être heureux à la vue de certaines misères.*
There is a type of shame which comes from being happy at another's distress.
1688 *Les Caractères ou les mïurs de ce siècle*, 'De l'homme', no.82.

26 *La plupart des hommes emploient la meilleure partie de leur vie à rendre l'autre misérable.*
Most people spend the greater part of their lives making others miserable.
1688 *Les Caractères ou les mïurs de ce siècle*, 'De l'homme', no.102.

27 *Le flatteur n'a pas assez bonne opinion de soi ni des autres.*
The flatterer does not have a good opinion of himself or of others.
1688 *Les Caractères ou les mïurs de ce siècle*, 'Des jugements', no.90.

28 *Ceux qui emploient mal leur temps sont les premiers à se plaindre de sa brièveté.*
Those who make poor use of their time are the first to complain of its brevity.
1688 *Les Caractères ou les mïurs de ce siècle*, 'Des jugements', no.101.

29 *L'impossibilité où je suis de prouver que Dieu n'est pas me découvre son existence.*

The impossibility I find myself in to prove that God does not exist proves to me his existence.
1688 *Les Caractères ou les mœurs de ce siècle*, 'Des esprits forts', no.13.

Laclos, Pierre-Ambroise Choderlos de 1741–1803

French artillery officer, best known for his study of human vices and virtues in *Les Liaisons dangereuses* (1782), as well as his advocacy of women's education in *De l'Education des femmes* (1785).

30 *J'ai bien besoin d'avoir cette femme, pour me sauver du ridicule d'en être amoureux.*
I need to possess this woman in order to save myself from the absurdity of being in love with her.
1782 *Les Liaisons dangereuses*, letter 4.

31 *Nos deux passions favorites, la gloire de la défense et le plaisir de la défaite.*
The glory of the resistance and the pleasure of the defeat are our two favourite passions.
1782 *Les Liaisons dangereuses*, letter 10.

32 *Il ne faut se permettre d'excès qu'avec les gens qu'on veut quitter bientôt.*
We should never permit ourselves to behave in excess except with those whom we will leave soon.
1782 *Les Liaisons dangereuses*, letter 10.

33 *En vérité, plus je vis, et plus je suis tenté de croire qu'il n'y a que vous et moi dans le monde, qui valions quelque chose.*
In truth, the more I live, the more I am tempted to believe that only you and I are of any value at all in the world.
1782 *Les Liaisons dangereuses*, letter 100.

34 *J'avoue bien que l'argent ne fait pas le bonheur; mais il faut avouer aussi qu'il le facilite beaucoup.*
I will admit that money does not bring happiness, but it must also be admitted that it facilitates much.
1782 *Les Liaisons dangereuses*, letter 104.

35 *Ce n'est pas assez pour moi de la posséder, je veux qu'elle se livre.*
It's not enough to possess her. I want her to abandon herself.
1782 *Les Liaisons dangereuses*, letter 110.

36 *La haine est toujours plus clairvoyante et plus ingénieuse que l'amitié.*
Hate is always more clairvoyant and ingenious than friendship.
1782 *Les Liaisons dangereuses*, letter 113.

37 *Pour les hommes, l'infidélité n'est pas l'inconstance.*
For men, infidelity is not inconstancy.
1782 *Les Liaisons dangereuses*, letter 134.

38 *On s'ennuie de tout, mon Ange, c'est une loi de la Nature; ce n'est pas ma faute.*
One gets bored of everything, my Angel, it's a law of nature; it's not my fault.
1782 *Les Liaisons dangereuses*, letter 141.

39 *Quand une femme frappe dans le coeur d'une autre, elle manque rarement de trouver l'endroit sensible, et la blessure est incurable.*
When one woman touches another's heart, she rarely has trouble finding the sensitive spot and the wound is incurable.
1782 *Les Liaisons dangereuses*, letter 145.

40 *Apprenez qu'on ne sort de l'esclavage que par une grande révolution.*
Learn that one never escapes slavery except by a great revolution.
1785 *De l'Éducation des femmes*.

Ladd, Alan 1913–64

US film star, best known for *The Blue Dahlia* (1946), *The Great Gatsby* (1949) and *Shane* (1953).

41 A man's gotta do what a man's gotta do.
1953 Line delivered in *Shane* (screenplay by A B Guthrie).

La Fayette, Marie-Madeleine Pioche de La Vergne 1634–93

French novelist. Although married to François Motier, she lived with La Rochefoucauld.

42 *L'amour était toujours mêlé aux affaires et les affaires à l'amour.*
Love has always mixed with politics and politics with love.
1678 *La Princesse de Clèves*.

43 *On persuade aisément une vérité agréable.*
It is easy to persuade one with an agreeable truth.
1678 *La Princesse de Clèves*.

44 *Les passions peuvent me conduire; mais elles ne sauraient m'aveugler.*
Passions can lead me on, but never blind me.
1678 *La Princesse de Clèves*.

45 *La honte est la plus violente de toutes les passions.*
Shame is the most violent of all the passions.
1678 *La Princesse de Clèves*.

La Fontaine, Jean de 1621–95

French poet and moralist. His *Contes et nouvelles en vers* ('Tales and Novels in Verse', 1665) was followed by *Fables choisies mises en vers* ('Selected Fables in Verse', 1668–94).

46 *Je me sers d'animaux pour instruire les hommes.*
I use animals to educate people.
1668 *Fables, à Monseigneur le Dauphin*.

47 *Nous n'écoutons d'instincts que ceux qui sont les nôtres,*
Et ne croyons le mal que quand il est venu.
We only trust our own instincts
And only believe the worst when it comes true.
1668 *Fables*, pt.1, no.8, 'L'hirondelle et les petits oiseaux'.

48 *La raison du plus fort est toujours la meilleure.*
The reason of the strongest is always the best.
1668 *Fables*, pt.1, no.10, 'Le loup et l'agneau'.

49 *Il accusait toujours les miroirs d'être faux.*
He was always blaming mirrors for being untrue.
1668 *Fables*, pt.1, no.11, 'L'homme et son image'.

50 *Plutôt souffrir que mourir,*
C'est la devise des hommes.
It is better to suffer than to die.
That is the motto of mankind.
1668 *Fables*, pt.1, no.16, 'La mort et le bûcheron'.

51 *Je plie, et ne romps pas.*
I bend but do not break.
1668 *Fables*, pt.1, no.22, 'Le chêne et le roseau'. The reed speaks to the oak tree.

52 *Le mensonge et les vers de tout temps sont amis.*
   Lies and literature have always been friends.
   1668 *Fables*, pt.2, no.1, 'Contre ceux qui ont le goût difficile'.

53 *Patience et longueur de temps*
   Font plus que force ni que rage.
   Patience and longevity
   Are worth more than force and rage.
   1668 *Fables*, pt.2, no.11, 'Le lion et le rat'.

54 *C'est double plaisir de tromper le trompeur.*
   It's doubly sweet to deceive the deceiver.
   1668 *Fables*, pt.2, no.15, 'Le coq et le renard'.

55 *Tout au monde est mêlé d'amertume et de charmes:*
   La guerre a ses douceurs, l'hymen a ses alarmes.
   Everything in the world is a mixture of the sweet and the sour:
   War has its own sweetness and marriage its alarms.
   1668 *Fables*, pt.3, no.1, 'Le meunier, son fils et l'âne'.

56 *En toute chose il faut considérer la fin.*
   One must consider the end in everything.
   1668 *Fables*, pt.3, no.5, 'Le renard et le bouc'.

57 *Amour est un étrange maître.*
   Heureux qui peut ne le connaître
   Que par récit, lui ni ses coups!
   Love is a cruel conqueror.
   Happy is he who knows him through stories
   And not by his blows!
   1668 *Fables*, pt.4, no.1, 'Le lion amoureux'.

58 *Le geai paré des plumes du paon.*
   A bluejay in peacock feathers.
   1668 *Fables*, pt.4, no.9, 'Le geai paré des plumes du paon'.

59 *Chacun se dit ami; mais fol qui s'y repose:*
   Rien n'est plus commun que ce nom,
   Rien n'est plus rare que la chose.
   Everyone calls himself a friend; foolish is he who believes it:
   Nothing is more common than the name friend,
   And nothing is more rare than the real thing.
   1668 *Fables*, pt.4, no.17, 'Parole de Socrate'.

60 *Ne possédait pas l'or; mais l'or le possédait.*
   He never owned his gold; his gold owned him.
   1668 *Fables*, pt.4, no.20, 'L'avare qui a perdu son trésor'.

61 *Une ample Comédie à cent actes divers,*
   Et dont la scène est l'Univers.
   A grand comedy in one hundred different acts,
   On the stage of the universe.
   1668 *Fables*, pt.5, no.1, 'Le bûcheron et Mercure'.

62 *Un auteur gâte tout quand il veut trop bien faire.*
   An author spoils everything when he wants too much to do good.
   1668 *Fables*, pt.5, no.1, 'Le bûcheron et Mercure'.

63 *Garde-toi, tant que tu vivras,*
   De juger des gens sur la mine.
   Beware as long as you live,
   Of judging others according to appearance alone.
   1668 *Fables*, pt.6, no.5, 'Le cochet, le chat et le souriceau'.

64 *Sur les ailes du Temps la tristesse s'envole.*
   Grief is carried off by the wings of time.
   1668 *Fables*, pt.6, no.21, 'La jeune veuve'.

65 *Quand l'eau courbe un bâton, ma raison la redresse.*
   When water curves a stick, my reason straightens it out.
   1668 *Fables*, pt.7, no.18, 'Un animal dans la lune'.

66 *Fortune aveugle suit aveugle hardiesse.*
   Blind fortune pursues inconsiderate rashness.
   1668 *Fables*, pt.10, no.13, 'Les deux aventuriers et le talisman'.

67 *Tout est mystère dans l'Amour.*
   Everything about love is a mystery.
   1668 *Fables*, pt.12, no.14, 'L'Amour et la folie'.

68 *Tous chemins vont à Rome.*
   All roads lead to Rome.
   1668 *Fables*, pt.12, no.29, 'Le juge arbitre, l'hospitalier, et le solitaire'.

Lagerfeld, Karl 1933–
German-born French fashion designer.

69 She never wanted to be sexy, but in those days ambitions were different, and she was the most ambitious of them all.
   1993 Of Wallis Simpson, Duchess of Windsor. In the *New York Times*, 19 Sep.

70 Fashion is the image of an age and can tells its story better than a speech.
   1994 In the *Daily Telegraph*, 20 Oct.

71 Fantasy is often better than reality. It's much more inspiring not to go to places than to go.
   2011 *The Guardian*, 12 Dec.

Lamartine, Alphonse Marie Louis de 1790–1869
French poet and revolutionary politician, a minister in the provisional government after 1848. His best-known work is his first volume of lyrical poems, *Méditations poétiques* (1820). His historical works include the *Histoire de la Révolution de 1848* (1849).

72 *Un seul être vous manque, et tout est dépeuplé.*
   One being only is wanting, and your whole world is bereft of people.
   1820 *Méditations poétiques*, 'L'Isolement'.

73 France is revolutionary or she is nothing at all. The revolution of 1789 is her political religion.
   1847 *Histoire des Girondins*.

74 At its birth, the republic gave voice to three words—Liberty, Equality, Fraternity! If Europe is wise and just, each of those words signifies Peace.
   1848 *A Manifesto to the Powers*, 4 Mar.

Lamb, Lady Caroline 1785–1828
English novelist and aristocrat, daughter of the Earl of Bessborough and wife of Prime Minister William Lamb, 2nd Viscount Melbourne, notorious for her nine-month devotion (1812–3) to Lord Byron.

75 Mad, bad, and dangerous to know.
   1812 Of Byron. Journal entry, Mar, after meeting the poet at a ball. Quoted in Elizabeth Jenkins *Lady Caroline Lamb* (1932), ch.6.

Lamb, Charles 1775–1834
English essayist and critic. Together with his sister Mary, he wrote *Tales from Shakespeare* (1807), and his *Specimens of English Dramatic Poets* (1808) contributed to a revival of interest in Elizabethan plays. As 'Elia', he contributed essays to the *London Magazine* from 1820.

76 I have something more to do than feel.
   1796 Letter to Samuel Taylor Coleridge, 27 Sep, on the death of his mother at his sister Mary's hands. Collected in E. W. Marrs *Letters of Charles and Mary Lamb*, vol.1 (1975).

77 Cultivate simplicity, Coleridge.
1796 Letter to Samuel Taylor Coleridge, 8 Nov. Collected in E W Marrs *Letters of Charles and Mary Lamb*, vol.1 (1975).

78 The man must have a rare recipe for melancholy, who can be dull in Fleet Street.
1802 Letter to Thomas Manning, 15 Feb. Collected in E W Marrs *Letters of Charles and Mary Lamb*, vol.2 (1975).

79 Nursed amid her noise, her crowds, her beloved smoke—what have I been doing all my life, if I have not lent out my heart with usury to such scenes?
1802 Of London. Letter to Thomas Manning, 15 Feb. Collected in E W Marrs *Letters of Charles and Mary Lamb*, vol.2 (1975).

80 Gone before
To that unknown and silent shore.
1803 'Hester', stanza 7.

81 Nothing puzzles me more than time and space; and yet nothing troubles me less, as I never think about them.
1806 Letter to Thomas Manning, 2 Jan. Collected in E W Marrs (ed) *Letters of Charles and Mary Lamb*, vol.3 (1978).

82 A child's a plaything for an hour.
1809 'Parental Recollections'. This is often attributed to his sister Mary.

83 Anything awful makes me laugh.
1815 Letter to Robert Southey, 9 Aug. Collected in E W Marrs (ed) *Letters of Charles and Mary Lamb*, vol.3 (1978).

84 This very night I am going to leave off tobacco! Surely there must be some other world in which this unconquerable purpose shall be realized.
1815 Letter to Thomas Manning, 26 Dec. Collected in E W Marrs (ed) *Letters of Charles and Mary Lamb*, vol.3 (1978).

85 An Archangel a little damaged.
1816 Of Coleridge. Letter to Wordsworth, 26 Apr. Collected in E W Marrs (ed) *Letters of Charles and Mary Lamb*, vol.3 (1978).

86 The rogue gives you Love Powders, and then a strong horse drench to bring 'em off your stomach that they mayn't hurt you.
1816 Of Coleridge. Letter to Wordsworth, 23 Sep. Collected in E W Marrs (ed) *Letters of Charles and Mary Lamb*, vol.3 (1978).

87 Fanny Kelly's divine plain face.
1818 Letter to Mary Wordsworth, 18 Feb. Collected in H H Harpter (ed) *Letters of Charles Lamb*, vol.4 (1905).

88 Newspapers always excite curiosity. No one ever lays one down without a feeling of disappointment.
1822 In the *London Magazine*, May–Jul. Collected in *Essays of Elia*, 'Detached Thoughts of Books and Reading'.

89 Who first invented work—and tied the free
And holy-day rejoicing spirit down
To the ever-haunting importunity
Of business?
1822 Letter to Bernard Barton, 11 Sep. Collected in H H Harpter (ed) *Letters of Charles Lamb*, vol.4 (1905).

90 I hate a man who swallows it, affecting not to know what he is eating. I suspect his taste in higher matters.
1823 *Essays of Elia*, 'Grace Before Meat'.

91 In everything that relates to science, I am a whole Encyclopedia behind the rest of the world.
1823 *Essays of Elia*, 'The Old and the New Schoolmaster'.

92 I know that a sweet child is the sweetest thing in nature…but the prettier the kind of a thing is, the more desirable it is that it should be pretty of its kind.
1823 *Essays of Elia*, 'A Bachelor's Complaint of the Behaviour of Married People'.

93 If the husband be a man with whom you have lived on a friendly footing before marriage,—if you did not come in on the wife's side,—if you did not sneak into the house in her train, but were an old friend in first habits of intimacy before their courtship was so much as thought on,—look about you… Every long friendship, every old authentic intimacy, must be brought into their office to be new stamped with their currency, as a sovereign Prince calls in the good old money that was coined in some reign before he was born or thought of, to be new marked and minted with the stamp of his authority, before he will let it pass current in the world.
1823 *Essays of Elia*, 'A Bachelor's Complaint of the Behaviour of Married People'.

94 Ceremony is an invention to take off the uneasy feeling which we derive from knowing ourselves to be less the object of love and esteem with a fellow-creature than some other person is. It endeavours to make up, by superior attentions in little points, for that invidious preference which it is forced to deny in the greater.
1823 *Essays of Elia*, 'A Bachelor's Complaint of the Behaviour of Married People'.

95 Sentimentally I am disposed to harmony. But organically I am incapable of a tune.
1823 *Essays of Elia*, 'A Chapter on Ears'.

96 I have no ear.
1823 *Essays of Elia*, 'A Chapter on Ears'.

97 Presents, I often say, endear Absents.
1823 *Essays of Elia*, 'A Dissertation upon Roast Pig'.

98 She unbent her mind afterwards—over a book.
1823 *Essays of Elia*, 'Mrs Battle's Opinions on Whist'.

99 A votary of the desk—a notched and cropt scrivener—one that sucks his substance, as certain sick people are said to do, through a quill.
1823 *Essays of Elia*, 'Oxford in the Vacation'.

1 The uncommunicating muteness of fishes.
1823 *Essays of Elia*, 'A Quakers' Meeting'.

2 The human species, according to the best theory I can form of it, is composed of two distinct races, the men who borrow, and the men who lend.
1823 *Essays of Elia*, 'The Two Races of Men'.

3 Your *borrowers of books*—those mutilators of collections, spoilers of the symmetry of shelves, and creators of odd volumes.
1823 *Essays of Elia*, 'The Two Races of Men'.

4 Not many sounds in life, and I include all urban and rural sounds, exceed in interest a knock at the door.
1823 *Essays of Elia*, 'Valentine's Day'.

5 Credulity is the man's weakness, but the child's strength.
1823 *Essays of Elia*, 'Witches and Other Night-Fears'.

6 How sickness enlarges the dimensions of a man's self to himself.
1823 *Essays of Elia*, 'The Convalescent'.

7 If dirt were trumps, what hands you would hold!
1828 Quoted in Leigh Hunt *Lord Byron and his Contemporaries*, p.299.

8 How sickness enlarges the dimensions of a man's self to himself.
1833 *Last Essays of Elia*, 'The Convalescent'.

9 The drinking man is never less himself than during his sober intervals.
   1833 *Last Essays of Elia*, 'Confessions of a Drunkard'.

10 Books think for me.
   1833 *Last Essays of Elia*, 'Detached Thoughts on Books and Reading'.

11 Things in book's clothing.
   1833 *Last Essays of Elia*, 'Detached Thoughts on Books and Reading'.

12 A poor relation is the most irrelevant thing in nature.
   1833 *Last Essays of Elia*, 'Poor Relations'.

13 A pistol let off at the ear; not a feather to tickle the intellect.
   1833 Of puns. *Last Essays of Elia*, 'Popular Fallacies', no.9.

14 The greatest pleasure I know, is to do good action by stealth, and to have it found out by accident.
   1834 'Table Talk by the late Elia', in *The Athenaeum*, 1834.

15 The last breath I drew in he wished might be through a pipe and exhaled in a pun.
   Quoted in W Toynbee *Diaries of William Charles Macready 1833–1851* (1912).

Lamb, Marjorie 1949–
Canadian ecologist.

16 Suppose our ancestors had discovered nuclear power in the middle ages, and had decided to bury their radioactive fuel.
   1990 *Two Minutes a Day for a Greener Planet*.

Lambert, Constant 1905–51
English composer, conductor and critic. His first success came with the ballet *Romeo and Juliet*, commissioned by Diaghilev in 1926. Subsequently he worked as conductor for the Camargo Society and for Sadler's Wells Ballet.

17 The Appalling Popularity of Music.
   1934 *Music Ho!*, chapter title.

18 There is a definite limit to the length of time a composer can go on writing in one dance rhythm. This limit is obviously reached by Ravel toward the end of *La Valse* and toward the beginning of *Boléro*.
   1934 *Music Ho!*

19 To put it vulgarly, the whole trouble with a folk song is that once you have played it through there is nothing much you can do except play it over again and play it rather louder.
   1934 *Music Ho!*

Lamming, George Eric 1927–
Barbadian novelist. Winner of the Somerset Maugham Prize for literature for his novel *In the Castle of My Skin* (1953), he has also published *The Emigrants* (1954), *Seasons of Adventure* (1960), and *Natives of My Person* (1972).

20 Histr'y ain't got eyes to see everything.
   1953 *In the Castle of My Skin*, ch.6.

21 If you aren't native to a place you have an excellent chance of becoming a gentleman in it.
   1953 *In the Castle of My Skin*, ch.14.

Lamport, Allan 1903–99
Canadian politician, Mayor of Toronto (1952–42) and a renowned malapropist.

22 If somebody's gonna stab me in the back, I wanna be there.
   1990 *Quotations from Chairman Lamport*.

Lancaster, Sir James c.1554–1618
English navigator, soldier and merchant. He visited the East Indies in 1591–4 and in 1595 captured Pernambuco. In 1600–3 he commanded the first fleet of the East India Company to visit the East Indies. He promoted the voyages of Hudson, Baffin and others in search of the Northwest Passage.

23 I cannot tell where you should look for me, if you send out any pinnace to seek me; because I live at the devotion of the wind and seas. And thus fare you well; desiring God to send us a merry meeting in this world, if it be his good will and pleasure.
   c.1594 Letter to the East India Company written on the homeward voyage when the two English ships ran into storms off the Cape of Good Hope. Lancaster's ship lost her rudder. Unwilling to risk the other ship, Lancaster ordered her captain to sail straight home, taking the letter with him. *A voyage with three tall ships, the Penelope, admirall, the Marchant Royall, vice-admiral, and the Edward Bonaventure, rear-admiral, to the East Indies... Begun By M. George Raymond, in the yeere 1591, and performed by M. James Lancaster; and written from the mouth of Edmund Barker of Ipswich (his lieutenant in the sayd voyage) by M. Richard Hakluyt.*

Lance, Bert 1931–2013
Former US White House Budget Director.

24 Go out on the front porch of the house, turn the *Washington Post* over with your big toe, and if your name's above the fold, you know you're not going to have a good day.
   1993 Of the Bert Lance Toe Test which he devised for his nine months in the Carter administration. In the *Washington Post*, 6 Oct.

Landers, Ann 1918–2002
US newspaper columnist and 'agony aunt', who offered advice and information on topics such as family life, marriage, social issues and health.

25 Women complain about sex more often than men. Their gripes fall into two major categories: (1) Not enough. (2) Too much.
   1968 *Truth Is Stranger...*, ch.2.

Landor, Walter Savage 1775–1864
English writer and poet. His *Imaginary Conversations of Literary Men and Statesmen* (1824–9) was celebrated in its day but has lost popularity. Other works include *Hellenics* (1847) and *Dry Sticks Fagoted* (1858).

26 Ah, what avails the sceptred race!
   Ah, what the form divine!
   1806 'Rose Aylmer'.

27 Clear writers, like clear fountains, do not seem so deep as they are; the turbid look the most profound.
   1824 *Imaginary Conversations of Literary Men and Statesmen*, 'Southey and Porson'.

28 Fleas know not whether they are upon the body of a giant or upon one of ordinary size.
   1824 *Imaginary Conversations of Literary Men and Statesmen*, 'Southey and Porson'.

29 Past ruined Ilion Helen lives,
Alcestis rises from the shades;
Verse calls them forth; 'tis verse that gives
Immortal youth to mortal maids.
1831 'To Ianthe'.

30 There is delight in singing, tho' none hear
Beside the singer.
1846 'To Robert Browning'.

31 Thee gentle Spenser fondly led;
But me he mostly sent to bed.
1846 'To Wordsworth: Those Who Have Laid the Harp Aside'.

32 There are no fields of amaranth on this side of the grave.
1846 *Imaginary Conversations of Literary Men and Statesmen*, 'Aesop and Rhodope'.

33 Death stands above me, whispering low
I know not what into my ear;
Of his strange language all I know
Is, there is not a word of fear.
1853 'Death stands above me'.

34 I strove with none; for none was worth my strife;
Nature I loved, and, next to Nature, Art.
1853 'Dying Speech of an Old Philosopher'.

35 Ireland never was contented...
Say you so? You are demented.
Ireland was contented when
All could use the sword and pen,
And when Tara rose so high
That her turrets split the sky,
And about her courts were seen
Liveried Angels robed in green,
Wearing, by St. Patrick's bounty,
Emeralds big as half a county.
1853 'Ireland never was contented'.

36 Prose on certain occasions can bear a great deal of poetry: on the other hand, poetry sinks and swoons under a moderate weight of prose.
1853 *Imaginary Conversations of Greeks and Romans*, 'Archdeacon Hare and Walter Landor'.

Landowska, Wanda 1879–1959

Polish pianist, harpsichordist and musical scholar, who founded the École de Musique Ancienne near Paris in 1927, and stimulated a new interest in the harpsichord. She also composed songs and piano and orchestral pieces and wrote on music.

37 You play Bach your way and I'll play him *his* way.
Refusing to adapt her technique to suit another Bach specialist. Quoted in Clifton Fadiman *The Faber Book of Anecdotes* (1985).

Lane, Anthony 1962–

English journalist, film critic at the *New Yorker* since 1993.

38 There is more suspense, more dramatic torque, in one page of [Nathaniel] Hawthorne's heart-racked ruminations on the Christian conscience than in all Demi Moore's woodland gallops and horizontal barn dancing.
On the film adaptation of *The Scarlet Letter*, directed by Roland Joffé. In *Nobody's Perfect: Writings from The New Yorker* (2002).

39 If you are going to spend two hundred million dollars on a movie, this is the way to do it.
Admiring the film *Titanic*. In *Nobody's Perfect: Writings from The New Yorker* (2002).

Lang, Andrew 1844–1912

Scottish man of letters. He specialized in mythology, famously arguing against Max Müller that folktale was the foundation of literary mythology. He also wrote history texts, popular fairy books, studies of literary figures and poetry.

40 Politicians use statistics in the same way that a drunk uses lamp-posts—for support rather than illumination.
1910 Speech. Quoted in Alan L Mackay *The Harvest of a Quiet Eye* (1977).

41 If the wild bowler thinks he bowls
Or if the batsman thinks he's bowled,
They know not, poor misguided souls,
They too shall perish unconsoled.
I am the batsman and the bat,
I am the bowler and the ball,
The umpire, the pavilion cat,
The roller, pitch, and stumps and all.
'Brahma'. Quoted by Alan Richardson in a letter to *The Times*, 18 May, 1963.
▶ See Emerson 325:85.

Lang, Fritz 1890–1976

Austrian-born US film director. His many films include *Metropolis* (1926), *You Only Live Once* (1937) and *Beyond a Reasonable Doubt* (1956).

42 Don't forget the western is not only the history of this country, it is what the Saga of the Nibelungen is for the European.
Quoted in Peter Bogdanovich *Fritz Lang in America* (1967).

Langbridge, Frederick 1849–1923

English religious writer.

43 Two men look out through the same bars:
One sees the mud, and one the stars.
1896 *A Cluster of Quiet Thoughts*.

Langland, William c.1332–c.1400

English poet. Little is known of his life but he seems to have been in London in 1362 when he began his only known work, the long poem *Vision of William concerning Piers the Plowman*, the greatest poem of the Middle English Alliterative Revival. It deals with the themes of truth, integrity and social justice. Three versions survive in over 60 manuscipts. It was first printed in 1550.

44 In a somer seson, whan softe was the sonne,
I shoop me into shroudes as I a sheep were,
In habite an heremite unholy of werkes,
Went wide in this world wondres to here.
c.1377 *Piers Plowman* (B text), prologue, l.1–4.
(shoop = got, shroudes = garments)

45 A gloten of wordes.
c.1377 *Piers Plowman* (B text), prologue, l.139.
(gloten = glutton)

46 'Though we hadde ykilled the cat, yat sholde there come another
To cracchen us ans al oure kynde, though we cropen under benches.'
c.1377 The wise mouse advises against belling the cat. *Piers Plowman* (B text), prologue, l.185–6.
(cracchen = scratch, cropen = crept)

47 He was bitelbrowed and baberlipped, with two blered eighen,

And as a letheren purs lolled his chekes.
　　　　c.1377 A description of the sin of Envy. *Piers Plowman* (B text), 'Passus 5,' l.188–9. (eighen = eyes, letheren = leather)

48　Al the povere peple tho pescoddes fetten;
　　　Benes and baken apples thei broghte in hir lappe,
　　　Chibolles and chervelles and ripe chiries manye,
　　　And profrede Piers this present to plese with Hunger.
　　　　c.1378 A description of the sin of Envy. *Piers Plowman* (B text), 'Passus 6,' l.291–4.
　　　　(pescoddes = pea-pod, fetten = fetched, chibolles = spring-onions, chervelles = chervil, plese with Hunger = please hunger with)

49　Ac thorugh his science soothy was nevere no soule ysaved,
　　　Ne broght by hir bokes to blisse ne to joye.
　　　　c.1378 *Piers Plowman* (B text), 'Passus 12', l.134–5.
　　　　The 'science' and 'books' are those of pagan scholars who developed natural science from empirical observation only.

50　'Counseilleth me, Kynde,' quod I, 'what craft be best to lerne?'
　　　'Lerne to love,' quod kynde, 'and leef alle othere.'
　　　　c.1378 *Piers Plowman* (B text), 'Passus 20', l.207–8.

Langner, Lawrence 1890–1962
Co-founder, US Theater Guild.

51　I have no interest in anything but *genius*, so please sit down.
　　　To Tennessee Williams. Recalled in Williams *Memoirs* (1975).

Lanier, Sidney 1842–81
US poet. He fought in the Civil War for the Confederacy. His critical study *The Science of English Verse* (1880) establishes a musical basis for poetry which he tries to exemplify in his verse.

52　Music is Love in search of a word.
　　　1875 *The Symphony*.

Lanyer, Aemilia 1569–1645
English poet. One of the very few professional early female poets, she was unable to secure patronage and published only one work, *Salve Deus Ex Judaeorum* (1611). It has been argued (unconvincingly) that she is the 'dark lady' of Shakespeare's *Sonnets*.

53　Our mother Eve, who tasted of the tree,
　　　Giving to Adam what she held most dear,
　　　Was simply good, and had no power to see.
　　　　1611 *Salve Deus Ex Judaeorum*, 'Eve's Apology in Defense of Women'.

54　But surely Adam cannot be excused;
　　　Her fault though great, yet he was most to blame;
　　　What weakness offered, strength might have refused,
　　　Being lord of all, the greater was the shame.
　　　　1611 *Salve Deus Ex Judaeorum*, 'Eve's Apology in Defense of Women'.

55　Not Eve, whose fault was only too much love,
　　　Which made her give this present to her dear,
　　　That what she tasted he likewise might prove,
　　　Whereby his knowledge might become more clear;
　　　He never sought her weakness to reprove
　　　With those sharp words which he of God did hear;
　　　Yet men will boast of knowledge, which he took
　　　From Eve's fair hand, as from a learned book.
　　　　1611 *Salve Deus Ex Judaeorum*, 'Eve's Apology in Defense of Women'.

56　Then let us have our liberty again,
　　　And challenge to yourselves no sovereignty.
　　　You came not in the world without our pain,
　　　Make that a bar against your cruelty;
　　　Your fault being greater, why should you disdain
　　　Our being your equals, free from tyranny?
　　　　1611 *Salve Deus Ex Judaeorum*, 'Eve's Apology in Defense of Women'.

57　Farewell (sweet *Cooke-ham*) where I first obtained
　　　Grace from that grace where perfect grace remained;
　　　And where the muses gave their full consent,
　　　I should have power the virtuous to content;
　　　Where princely palace willed me to indite,
　　　The sacred story of the soul's delight.
　　　　1611 *Salve Deus Ex Judaeorum*, 'The Description of Cooke-ham'. Probably the first 'country-house' poem in English, this work is dedicated to Margaret Russell Clifford, Countess of Cumberland, and her daughter, Anne Clifford, whose family home was Cookham.

58　Never shall my sad eyes again behold
　　　Those pleasures which my thoughts did then unfold.
　　　　1611 *Salve Deus Ex Judaeorum*, 'The Description of Cooke-ham'.

LaPierre, Wayne Robert 1948–
US lobbyist, CEO and executive vice-president of the National Rifle Association (1991–).

59　The only thing that stops a bad guy with a gun is a good guy with a gun.
　　　2012 News briefing, 21 Dec.

Lao-Tzu 6c BC
Chinese philosopher regarded as the inspiration for Taoism. Its major work, the *Tao-te Ching* was compiled some 300 years after his death but is traditionally ascribed to him.

60　Free from desire, you realise the mystery.
　　　Caught in desire, you see only the manifestations.
　　　　c.250 BC *Tao-te Ching*, no.1 (translated by Stephen Mitchell, 1988).

61　He who defines himself can't know who he really is.
　　　　c.250 BC *Tao-te Ching*, no.24 (translated by Stephen Mitchell, 1988).

62　Even in victory, there is no beauty, and he who calls it beautiful is one who delights in slaughter.
　　　　c.250 BC *Tao-te Ching*, no.31. Collected in Lin Yutang (trans and ed) *The Wisdom of China and India* (1942).

63　A victory should be celebrated with the funeral rite.
　　　　c.250 BC *Tao-te Ching*, no.31. Collected in Lin Yutang (trans and ed) *The Wisdom of China and India* (1942).

64　When two equally matched armies meet, it is the man of sorrow who wins.
　　　　c.250 BC *Tao-te Ching*, no.69. Collected in Lin Yutang (trans and ed) *The Wisdom of China and India* (1942).

Lardner, Dionysus 1793–1859
Irish scientific writer, Professor of Natural Philosophy and Astronomy at University College London (1827). He is best known as the originator and editor of *Lardner's Cabinet Cyclopaedia* (133 vols, 1829–49).

65　Men might as well project a voyage to the Moon as attempt to employ steam navigation against the stormy North Atlantic Ocean.
　　　　1838 Speech to the British Association for the Advancement of Science, London.

Lardner, James

US journalist, former staff writer for the *New Yorker*. He is the director and founder of Inequality.org, a non-profit organization.

66 If...Americans do not succeed in engineering an economic revival, we can look forward to being remembered as, of all the nations that have prospered and declined, the one that has done so in the highest state of self-awareness.
1993 'The Declining Middle', in the *New Yorker*, 3 May.

Lardner, Ring(old Wilmer)   1885–1933

US short story writer, novelist and columnist. He is best known for his vernacular, comic, satirical and usually pessimistic short stories.

67 Are you lost daddy I arsked tenderly.
Shut up he explained.
1920 *The Young Immigrunts*, ch.10.

68 I have known what it was like to be hungry, but I always went right to a restaurant.
1927 *The Lardners: My Family Remembered*, ch.1.

69 'Babe' Ruth and Old Jack Dempsey,
Both Sultans of Swat,
One hits where the other people are,
The other where they're not.
Attributed.

Larionov, Mikhail   1881–1964

Russian painter and designer.

70 We declare: the genius of our days to be: trousers, jackets, shoes, tramways, buses, aeroplanes, railways, magnificent ships—what an enchantment—what a great epoch unrivalled in world history.
1913 'Rayonnist Manifesto', quoted in C Gray *The Russian Experiment in Art* (revised edn 1986).

Larkin, Philip Arthur   1922–85

English poet, novelist and essayist. He was librarian at Hull University, and a jazz critic. His meticulously phrased, frequently pessimistic but often tongue-in-cheek poems include 'The Whitsun Weddings' (1964) and 'High Windows' (1974).

71 Always too eager for the future, we
Pick up bad habits of expectancy.
1951 'Next, Please'.

72 What are days for?
Days are where we live.
They come, they wake us
Time and time over.
They are to be happy in:
Where can we live but days?
1953 'Days'.

73 What calls me is that lifted, rough-tongued bell
(Art, if you like) whose individual sound
Insists I too am an individual.
1953 'Reasons for Attendance'.

74 And the case of butterflies so rich it looks
As if all summer settled there and died.
1953 'Autumn'.

75 Nothing, like something, happens anywhere.
1954 'I Remember, I Remember'.

76 On me your voice falls as they say love should,
Like an enormous yes.
1954 'For Sidney Bechet'.

77 Hatless, I take off
My cycle-clips in awkward reverence.
1954 'Church Going'.

78 A serious house on serious earth it is,
In whose blent air all our compulsions meet,
Are recognised, and robed as destinies.
1954 'Church Going'.

79 Why should I let the toad *work*
Squat on my life?
Can't I use my wit as a pitchfork
And drive the brute off?
Six days of the week it soils
With its sickening poison—
Just for paying a few bills!
That's out of proportion.
1954 'Toads'.

80 Marrying left your maiden name disused.
1955 'Maiden Name'.

81 Time has transfigured them into
Untruth. The stone fidelity
They hardly meant has come to be
Their final blazon, and to prove
Our almost-instinct almost true:
What will survive of us is love.
1956 'An Arundel Tomb'.

82 Never such innocence,
Never before or since,
As changed itself to past
Without a word—the men
Leaving the gardens tidy,
The thousands of marriages
Lasting a little while longer:
Never such innocence again.
1960 'MCMXIV'.

83 Get stewed:
Books are a load of crap.
1960 'A Study of Reading Habits'.

84 The widening river's slow presence,
The piled gold clouds, the shining gull-marked mud,
Gathers to the surprise of a large town:
Here domes and statues, spires and cranes cluster
Beside grain-scattered streets, barge-crowded water,
And residents from raw estates.
1961 Of Hull. 'Here'.

85 Give me your arm, old toad;
Help me down Cemetery Road.
1962 'Toads Revisited'.

86 Life is first boredom, then fear.
1963 'Dockery and Son'.

87 I thought of London spread out in the sun,
Its postal districts packed like squares of wheat.
1964 'The Whitsun Weddings'.

88 Sexual intercourse began
In nineteen sixty-three
(Which was rather late for me)—
Between the end of the *Chatterly* ban
And the Beatles' first LP.
1967 'Annus Mirabilis'.

89 They fuck you up, your mum and dad.
They may not mean to, but they do.
They fill you with the faults they had
And add some extra, just for you.
1971 'This Be the Verse'.

90 Man hands on misery to man.
It deepens like a coastal shelf.
Get out as early as you can,
And don't have any kids yourself.
1971 'This Be the Verse'.

91 I should never call myself a book lover, any more than a people lover: it all depends what's inside them.
1972 In the London Antiquarian Book Fair programme.

92 Perhaps being old is having lighted rooms
Inside your head, and people in them, acting.
People you know, yet can't quite name.
1973 'The Old Fools'.

93 You can't put off being young until you retire,
And however you bank your screw, the money you save
Won't in the end buy you more than a shave.
1973 'Money'.

94 And beyond it, the deep blue air, that shows
Nothing, and is nowhere, and is endless.
1974 'High Windows'.

95 That sure extinction that we travel to
And shall be lost in always. Not to be here,
Not to be anywhere,
And soon; nothing more terrible, nothing more true.
1977 'Aubade'.

96 That vast moth-eaten musical brocade
Created to pretend we never die.
1977 Of religion. 'Aubade'.

97 Far too many relied on the classic formula of a beginning, a muddle, and an end.
1978 On judging the Booker Prize entries for 1977, in *New Fiction*, no.15, Jan.

98 Deprivation is for me what daffodils were for Wordsworth.
1983 *Required Writing*.

La Rochefoucauld, François, 6th Duc de 1613–80

French writer. A supporter of the queen, Marie de Médicis, and an opponent of Richelieu, he was entangled in a series of amorous adventures and political intrigues. His *Mémoires*, published secretly in 1662, caused wide offence and were followed by his *Réflexions, ou sentences et maximes morales* (1664).

99 The love of justice in most men is simply the fear of suffering injustice.
1664 *Réflexions, ou sentences et maximes morales*, no.78.

1 Dans l'adversité de nos meilleurs amis, nous trouvons toujours quelque chose qui ne nous déplaît pas.
In the misfortune of our best friends, we always find something which is not displeasing to us.
1664 *Réflexions, ou sentences et maximes morales*, no.99.

2 On n'est jamais si malheureux qu'on croit, ni si heureux qu'on espère.
One is never as unhappy as one thinks, nor as happy as one hopes.
1664 *Réflexions, ou sentences et maximes morales*, no.128.

3 Nous avons tous assez de force pour supporter les maux d'autrui.
We are all strong enough to bear the misfortunes of others.
1678 *Maximes*, no.19.

4 L'hypocrisie est un hommage que le vice rend à la vertu.
Hypocrisy is a tribute which vice pays to virtue.
1678 *Maximes*, no.218.

5 L'absence diminue les médiocres passions, et augmente les grandes, comme le vent éteint les bougies, et allume le feu.
Absence diminishes commonplace passions, and increases great ones, as wind extinguishes candles and kindles fire.
1678 *Maximes*, no.276.

6 L'accent du pays où l'on est né demeure dans l'esprit et dans le cïur comme dans le langage.
The accent of the place in which one was born lingers in the mind and in the heart as it does in one's speech.
1678 *Maximes*, no.342.

Larwood, Harold 1904–95

English cricketer. He became notorious in the 1932–3 tour of Australia, employed by D R Jardine to bowl 'Bodyline', which led to several batsmen being seriously hurt. He retired from Test cricket as a result of the ensuing furore and eventually settled in Australia.

7 A cricket tour in Australia would be a most delightful period in one's life if one was deaf.
1933 *Body-line*.

8 Bodyline was devised to stifle Bradman's batting genius. They said I was a 'killer with the ball', without taking into account that Bradman, with the bat, was the greatest killer of all.
1965 Of the 'Bodyline' controversy. Quoted in Colin Jarman *The Guinness Dictionary of Sports Quotations* (1990).

9 I darned near bowled him that time.
Attributed. Said to an umpire who had disallowed two previous appeals, on clean bowling a batsman, knocking down the entire wicket.

Lasky, Jesse 1880–1958

US film pioneer. He formed his own production company in 1914 and had his first hit with *The Squaw Man*, going on to produce for Paramount, Fox and Warner.

10 I yearned to trespass on Quality Street.
On his desire to produce better films. Quoted in the *New Yorker*, 21 Mar 1994.

Lassels, Richard c.1603–1668

English classical scholar and priest. As tutor to the young English nobility, he travelled widely in Europe. His *Voyage of Italy* was published posthumously in Paris in 1670, and in London in 1698.

11 Pick out of every country what's best in it.
c.1650 *The Voyage of Italy, or a Compleat Journey through Italy* (published 1670).

12 [Travel] preserves my young nobleman from surfeiting of his parents, and weans him from a dangerous fondness of his mother. It teacheth him wholesome hardship... Whereas the country gentleman that never travelled, can

scarce go to London without making his will, at least without wetting his handkerchief.
c.1650 *The Voyage of Italy, or a Compleat Journey through Italy* (published 1670).

Latimer, Hugh c.1485–1555
English theologian, Bishop of Worcester and Protestant martyr. After Mary I's accession he was tried for heresy and burned at the stake in Oxford.

13 Be of good comfort Master Ridley, and play the man. We shall this day light such a candle by God's grace in England, as (I trust) shall never be put out.
1555 Spoken to Nicholas Ridley, as they waited together to be burned at the stake, 16 Oct. Quoted in Foxe *Acts and Monuments* (1563).

Lauder, Sir Harry (Hugh MacLennan) 1870–1950
Scottish comedian and music-hall entertainer.

14 Will yer stop yer tickling, Jock!
Oh, stop yer tickling, Jock!
Dinna mak' me laugh so hearty, or you'll mak' me choke.
Oh! I wish you'd stop yer nonsense—just look at all the folk.
Will yer stop yer tickling—tickle-ickle-ickle-ing—
Stop yer tickling, Jock!
1904 'Stop Yer Tickling, Jock!', chorus.

15 I love a lassie, a bonnie, bonnie lassie,
She's as pure as the lily in the dell.
She's as sweet as the heather
The bonnie bloomin' heather—
Mary, ma Scotch Bluebell.
1905 'I Love a Lassie', or 'Ma Scotch Bluebell', chorus.

16 Roamin' in the gloamin' on the bonnie banks o' Clyde.
Roamin' in the gloamin' wae my lassie by my side.
When the sun has gone to rest,
That's the time that we love best—
O, it's lovely roamin' in the gloamin'!
1911 'Roamin' in the Gloamin', chorus.

17 Keep right on to the end of the road,
Keep right on to the end.
Tho' the way be long let your heart be strong,
Keep right on round the bend.
Tho' you're tired and weary
Still journey on, till you come to your happy abode,
Where all you love you've been dreaming of
Will be there, at the end of the road.
1924 'The End of the Road', chorus.

Laughlin, J Laurence 1850–1933
US economist, Professor at the University of Chicago.

18 Anything from plumbing to philosophy.
His definition of the scope of sociology. Quoted in Joseph Dorfman *Thorstein Veblen and his America* (1934), p.93.

Laughton, Charles 1899–1962
British actor. His many roles include Henry VIII in *The Private Life of Henry VIII* (1933), Captain Bligh in *Mutiny on the Bounty* (1935) and Quasimodo in *The Hunchback of Notre Dame* (1939).

19 But they can't censor the gleam in my eye.
1934 Of his role of Mr Barrett in *The Barretts of Wimpole Street*.

Lauren, Ralph 1939–
US fashion designer.

20 I don't design clothes, I design dreams.
1986 In the *New York Times*, 19 Apr.

Laurence, Margaret 1926–87
Canadian novelist. Her first works were set in Africa, where she lived for seven years. In London she wrote the five Manawaka novels (1964–74). She has received numerous honours, including the Order of Canada.

21 Privacy is a privilege not granted to the aged or the young.
1964 *The Stone Angel*, ch.1.

22 Even if heaven were real, and measured as Revelation says, so many cubits this way and that, how gimcrack a place it would be, crammed with its pavements of gold, its gates of pearl and topaz, like a gigantic chunk of costume jewelry.
1964 *The Stone Angel*, ch.4.

23 In bygone days, Morag had once believed that nothing could be worse than killing a person. Now she perceived river-slaying as something worse.
1974 *The Diviners*, ch.1.

Laurencin, Marie 1885–1956
French artist, best known for her portraits of women in misty pastel colours. She also illustrated many books with watercolours and lithographs. She exhibited at the Salon des Indépendants in 1907.

24 My ambition is that men should have a voluptuous feeling when they look at the portraits I paint of women. Love interests me more than painting. My pictures are the love stories I tell to myself and which I want to tell others.
Quoted in Gabrielle Buffet 'Marie Laurencin', in *The Arts 3* (1903).

Lautréamont, Comte de *properly* Isidore Ducasse 1846–70
French writer, hailed by the Surrealists as one of their forerunners for his psychological poetry. His death at the age of twenty-four remains a mystery.

25 *Il n'était pas menteur, il avouait la vérité et disait qu'il était cruel.*
He was not a liar. He admitted the truth and said that he was cruel.
1868 *Les Chants de Maldoror*, pt.1.

26 *Oui, quel est le plus profond, le plus impénétrable des deux: l'océan ou le cïur humain?*
What is deeper, more impenetrable: the ocean or the human heart?
1868 *Les Chants de Maldoror*, pt.1.

27 *Moi, je n'aime pas les femmes! Ni même les hermaphrodites! Il me faut des êtres qui me ressemblent, sur le front desquels la noblesse humaine soit marquée en caractères plus tranchés et ineffaçables!*
Me, I do not like women! Nor even hermaphrodites! I need beings who resemble me, on whose foreheads nobility is engraved in sharp and unerasable characters.
1868 *Les Chants de Maldoror*, pt.5.

28 *Si vous êtes malheureux, il ne faut pas le dire au lecteur. Gardez cela pour vous.*
If you are miserable, you should not say so to the reader. Keep it for yourself.
1870 *Poésies*, pt.1.

29 *Il faut que la critique attaque la forme, jamais le fond de vos idées, de vos phrases. Arrangez-vous.*
A critic must attack the form, never the foundation of your ideas and phrases. See to it.
1870 *Poésies*, pt.1.

30 *Si la morale de Cléopâtre eût été moins courte, la face du monde aurait changé. Son nez n'en serait pas devenu plus long.*
If Cleopatra's morality had been less short, the face of the world would have been altered. Her nose would not thereby have grown longer.
1870 *Poésies*, pt.2.

31 *La poésie doit être faite par tous. Non par un. Pauvre Hugo!*
Poetry should be composed by everyone. Not by one. Poor Hugo!
1870 *Poésies*, pt.2.

32 *On ne peut juger de la beauté de la vie que par celle de la mort.*
One can only judge the beauty of life through death.
1870 *Poésies*, pt.2.

Laver, James 1899–1975
English poet, writer and art critic, and Keeper at the Victoria and Albert Museum (1922–59). He made a substantial contribution to the history of English costume.

33 The same costume will be
Indecent...10 years before its time
Shameless...5 years before its time
Outré (daring)...1 year before its time
Smart
Dowdy...1 year after its time
Hideous...10 years after its time
Ridiculous...20 years after its time
Amusing...30 years after its time
Quaint...50 years after its time
Charming...70 years after its time
Romantic...100 years after its time
Beautiful...150 years after its time.
1937 *Taste and Fashion*, ch.18.

34 A visitor from Mars contemplating a man in a frock coat and top hat and a woman in a crinoline might well have supposed that they belonged to different species.
1969 *The Concise History of Costume and Fashion*, ch.8.

Lavoisier, Antoine Laurent 1743–94
French chemist and physicist, one of the fathers of modern chemistry. He was one of the first to use effective quantitative methods to study chemical reactions.

35 We must trust to nothing but facts. These are presented to us by Nature, and cannot deceive. We ought, in every instance, to submit our reasoning to the test of experiment, and never to search for truth but by the natural road of experiment and observation.
1789 *Traité élémentaire de la chimie* ('Elements of Chemistry', translated by Robert Kerr).

Law, (Andrew) Bonar 1858–1923
Canadian-born British Unionist politician. He was Chancellor of the Exchequer (1916–18) and from 1916 Leader of the House of Commons. He retired in 1921, but returned to serve as Prime Minister (1922–3).

36 I can imagine no length of resistance to which Ulster can go in which I should not be prepared to support them, and in which, in my belief, they would not be supported by the overwhelming majority of the British people.
1912 During the Irish Home Rule crisis, 27 Jul.

Law, William 1686–1761
English divine, whose writings expounded the mysticism of Jakob Boehme.

37 I take it for granted that every Christian that is in health is up early in the morning; for it is much more reasonable to suppose a person up early because he is a Christian than because he is a labourer or a tradesman or a servant or has business that wants him.
1728 *A Serious Call to a Devout and Holy Life.*

38 If, therefore, a man will so live as to show that he feels and believes the most fundamental doctrines of Christianity, he must live above the world.
1728 *A Serious Call to a Devout and Holy Life.*

Lawrence, D(avid) H(erbert) 1885–1930
English novelist, poet and essayist. He was the son of a miner, and much of his fiction reflected his upbringing. His candid treatment of emotion and physical love led to prosecution for obscenity with *The Rainbow* in 1915, and *Lady Chatterley's Lover* in 1928 (and 1961). He lived in Italy and Mexico from 1919.

39 'Be a good animal, true to your instincts,' was his motto.
1911 *The White Peacock*, pt.2, ch.2.

40 Curse the blasted, jelly-boned swines, the slimy, the belly-wriggling invertebrates, the miserable sodding rotters, the flaming sods, the snivelling, dribbling, dithering, palsied, pulse-less lot that make up England today.
1913 Letter to Edward Garnett, 3 Jul, after the rejection of *Sons and Lovers* by Heinemann.

41 I like to write when I feel spiteful; it's like having a good sneeze.
1913 Letter to Lady Cynthia Asquith, Nov.

42 You mustn't look in my novel for the old stable *ego* of the character.
1914 Letter to Edward Garnett, 5 Jun.

43 People are not fallen angels, they are merely people.
1916 Letter to J Middleton Murry and Katherine Mansfield, 17 Feb.

44 I am only half there when I am ill, and so there is only half a man to suffer. To suffer in one's whole self is so great a violation, that it is not to be endured.
1916 Letter to Catherine Carswell, 16 Apr.

45 Not I, not I, but the wind that blows through me!
A fine wind is blowing the new direction of Time.
1917 'Song of a Man Who Has Come Through'.

46 The glamour
Of childish days is upon me, my manhood is cast
Down in the flood of remembrance, I weep like a child for the past.
1918 'Piano'.

47 Don't you find it a beautiful clean thought, a world empty of people, just uninterrupted grass, and a hare sitting up?
1920 *Women in Love*, ch.11.

48 In China the bat is a symbol of happiness
Not for me!
1921 'Bat'.

49 I like Australia less and less. The hateful newness, the democratic conceit, every man a little pope of perfection.
1922 Letter, 28 May.

50 Morality which is based on ideas, or on an ideal, is an unmitigated evil.
1922 *Fantasia of the Unconscious*, ch.7.

51 Every race which has become self-conscious and idea-bound in the past has perished.
1922 *Fantasia of the Unconscious*, ch.7.

52 Death is the only pure, beautiful conclusion of a great passion.
1922 *Fantasia of the Unconscious*, ch.15.

53 Better passion and death than any more of these 'isms'. No more of the old purpose done up in aspic. Better passion and death.
1922 *Fantasia of the Unconscious*, ch.15.

54 In the *established* sense it is socially nil. Happy-go-lucky, don't-you-bother, we're-in-Australia. But there also seems to be no inside life of any sort: just a long lapse and drift. A rather fascinating indifference, a *physical* indifference to what we call soul or spirit. It's really a weird show.
1922 Of Australia. Letter, collected in A Huxley (ed) *The Letters of D H Lawrence* (1932).

55 I do not want peace nor beauty nor even freedom from pain. I want to fight and to feel new gods in the flesh.
1922 Letter to E H Brewster, 2 Jan.

56 The wonderful Southern night-sky that makes a man feel so lonely, alien: with Orion standing on his head in the west, and his sword-belt upside down, and his Dog-star prancing in mid-heaven, high above him; and with the Southern Cross insignificantly mixed in with the other stars, democratically inconspicuous.
1923 Of night over Sydney. *Kangaroo*, ch.1.

57 What do the facts we know *about* a man amount to? Only two things we can know of him, and this by pure soul-intuition: we can know if he is true to the flame of life and love which is inside his heart, or if he is false to it.
1923 *Kangaroo*, ch.7.

58 The indifference—the fern-dark indifference of this remote golden Australia. Not to care—from the bottom of one's soul not to care.
1923 *Kangaroo*, ch.10.

59 Life makes no absolute statement. It is all Call and Answer.
1923 *Kangaroo*, ch.10.

60 And so, I missed my chance with one of the lords
Of life.
And I have something to expiate;
A pettiness.
1923 'Snake'.

61 Men! The only animal in the world to fear.
1923 'Mountain Lion'.

62 Hanging upside down like rows of disgusting old rags
And grinning in their sleep.
1923 'Bats'.

63 Evil, what is evil?
There is only one evil, to deny life.
1923 'Cypresses'.

64 The dead don't die. They look on and help.
1923 Letter to J Middleton Murry, 2 Feb, on the death of Katherine Mansfield.

65 Never trust the artist. Trust the tale.
1924 *Studies in Classic American Literature*, ch.1.

66 I want to go south, where there is no autumn, where the cold doesn't crouch over one like a snow-leopard waiting to pounce. The heart of the North is dead, and the fingers of cold are corpse fingers.
1924 Letter to J Middleton Murry, 3 Oct.

67 The identifying ourselves with the visual image of ourselves has become an instinct; the habit is already old. The picture of me, the me that is *seen*, is me.
1925 'Art and Morality'.

68 Damn all absolutes. Oh damn, damn, damn all absolutes!
1925 'The Novel'.

69 After the funeral, my father struggled through half a page, and it might as well have been Hottentott. 'And what dun they gi'e thee for that, lad?' 'Fifty pounds, father.' 'Fifty pounds!' He was dumbfounded, and looked at me with shrewd eyes, as if I were a swindler. 'Fifty pounds! An' tha's niver done a day's hard work in thy life.'
1925 Preface to Edward D McDonald (ed) *A Bibliography of D. H. Lawrence*.

70 I'm not sure if a mental relation with a woman doesn't make it impossible to love her. To know the *mind* of a woman is to end in hating her.
1927 Letter to Dr Trigant Burrow, 3 Aug.

71 You have to have something vicious in you to be a creative writer… God save me from being 'nice'.
1927 Book review, reprinted in *Phoenix*.

72 Ours is essentially a tragic age, so we refuse to take it tragically.
1928 *Lady Chatterley's Lover*, ch.1.

73 John Thomas says goodnight to Lady Jane, a little droopingly, but with a hopeful heart.
1928 *Lady Chatterley's Lover*, ch.19.

74 My God, what a clumsy *olla putrida* James Joyce is! Nothing but old fags and cabbage-stumps of quotations from the Bible and the rest, stewed in the juice of deliberate, journalistic dirty-mindedness.
1928 Letter to Aldous and Maria Huxley, 15 Aug.

75 Sentimentalism is the working off on yourself of feelings you haven't really got.
1928 'John Galsworthy'.

76 I am tired of being told there is no such animal by animals who are merely different.
1929 Letter to J Middleton Murry, 20 May.

77 How beastly the bourgeois is
Especially the male of the species.
1929 'How Beastly the Bourgeois Is'.

78 I never saw a wild thing
Sorry for itself.
1929 'Self-Pity'.

79 When I read Shakespeare I am struck with wonder
That such trivial people should muse and thunder
In such lovely language.
1929 'When I Read Shakespeare'.

80 Pornography is the attempt to insult sex, to do dirt on it.
1929 'Pornography and Obscenity'.

81 Now man cannot live without some vision of himself. But still less can he live with a vision that is not true to his inner experience and inner feeling.
1929 'The Risen Lord'.

82 Now it is autumn and the falling fruit
And the long journey towards oblivion...
Have you built your ship of death, O have you?
1932 'The Ship of Death'.

83 To the Puritan all things are impure, as somebody says.
1932 *Etruscan Places*, 'Cerveteri'.

84 And being a novelist, I consider myself superior to the saint, the scientist, the philosopher, and the poet, who are all great masters of different bits of man alive, but never get the whole hog.
1936 'Why The Novel Matters'.

85 Nothing is more difficult than to determine what a child takes in, and does not take in, of its environment and its teaching. This fact is brought home to me by the hymns which I learned as a child, and never forgot. They mean more to me almost than the finest poetry, and they have for me a more permanent value, somehow or other.
Collected in *Phoenix II: Uncollected, Unpublished and Other Prose Works* (1968).

86 The sense of wonder
that is the sixth sense.
And it is the natural religious sense.
'Hymns in a Man's Life'. Collected in *Phoenix II: Uncollected, Unpublished and Other Prose Works* (1968).

Lawrence, Gertrude 1898–1952

English actress. A star of revue on both sides of the Atlantic, she was highly popular as the lead in Noël Coward's comedies. She died while appearing in the hit Broadway musical *The King and I*.

87 Pardon my long preamble. It's like a chorus girl's tights—it touches everything and covers nothing.
During an after-dinner speech. Attributed.

Lawrence, T(homas) E(dward) known as Lawrence of Arabia 1888–1935

Anglo-Irish soldier and writer. In World War I he worked for army intelligence in North Africa (1914–16). Espousing the Arab cause, he led the Arabs in their revolt against the Turks.

88 I loved you, so I drew these tides of men into my hands
—and wrote my will across the sky in stars
To earn you Freedom, the seven pillared worthy house,
—that your eyes might be shining for me
When we came.
1926 *Seven Pillars of Wisdom*, dedication.

89 All men dream, but not equally. Those who dream by night in the dusty recesses of their minds wake in the day to find that it was vanity; but the dreamers of the day are dangerous men, for they may act their dream with open eyes, to make it possible.
1926 *Seven Pillars of Wisdom*, introductory chapter.

90 We were a self-centred army without parade or gesture, devoted to freedom, the second of man's creeds, a purpose so ravenous that it devoured all our strength, a hope so transcendent that our earlier ambitions faded in its glare.
1926 *Seven Pillars of Wisdom*, ch.1.

91 Many men would take the death sentence without a whimper to escape the life-sentence which fate carries in her other hand.
1936 *The Mint*, pt.1, ch.4.

92 A man hates to be moved to folly by a noise.
1936 Of the emotion aroused by the military trumpets. *The Mint*, pt.3, ch.9.

93 The test of nomadism, that most deeply biting of social disciplines.
Introduction to an edition of Charles Montagu Doughty *Travels in Arabia Deserta*.

Lawson, Henry Hertzberg 1867–1922

Australian writer, son of the writer and feminist Louisa Lawson. His writings for the *Bulletin*, 'The Bushman's Bible', have been collected in *Short Stories in Prose and Verse* (1894) and *While the Billy Boils* (1896).

94 And the sun sank again on the grand Australian bush—
the nurse and tutor of eccentric minds, the home of the weird, and of much that is different from things in other lands.
1892 'The Bush Undertaker', first published in *The Antipodean*.

95 The departed was a 'Roman', and the majority of the town were otherwise—but unionism is stronger than creed. Drink, however, is stronger than unionism; and, when the hearse presently arrived, more than two-thirds of the funeral were unable to follow.
1893 'The Union Buries its Dead', first published in *Truth*, Apr.

96 Type of a coming nation,
In the land of cattle and sheep,
Worked on Middleton's station,
'Pound a week and his keep.'
'Middleton's Rouseabout', collected in Colin Roderick (ed) *Henry Lawson: Collected Verse* (3 vols, 1967–9).

97 Have you seen the bush by moonlight, from the train, go running by?
Blackened log and stump and sapling, ghostly trees all dead and dry;
Here a patch of glassy water; there a glimpse of mystic sky?
Have you heard the still voice calling—yet so warm, and yet so cold:
'I'm the Mother-Bush that bore you! Come to me when you are old'?
'On the Night Train', collected in Colin Roderick (ed) *Henry Lawson: Collected Verse* (3 vols, 1967–9).

Layamon fl.c.1190

English author and priest who lived at Arley Regis in Worcestershire. He wrote the *Brut*, the first English version of the story of Arthur, largely based on Wace's French *Roman de Brut*.

98 And I will fare to Avalun, to the fairest of all maidens, to Argante the queen, an elf most fair, and she shall make my wounds all sound.
   c.1190 *Brut* (translated by Eugene Mason, 1912).

Layton, Irving 1912–2006
Romanian-born Canadian poet, who came to Montreal as an infant. His 35 books of poetry include *The Black Huntsman* (1951), *The Cold Green Element* (1955) and *A Red Carpet for the Sun* (1959).

99 Death is a name for beauty not in use.
   1953 'Composition in Late Spring', collected in *The Collected Poems of Irving Layton* (1971).

1 It amazes me that organs that piss
   Can give human beings such perfect bliss.
   1969 *The Whole Bloody Bird*, 'Aphs'.

2 Only the tiniest fracton of mankind want freedom. All the rest want someone to tell them they are free.
   1969 *The Whole Bloody Bird*.

Lazarus, Emma 1849–87
US poet, a champion of oppressed Jewry. Her poems include *Songs of a Semite* (1882) and *By the Waters of Babylon* (1887). She is best known for her sonnet, 'The New Colossus' which is inscribed on the Statue of Liberty.

3 Give me your tired, your poor,
   Your huddled masses yearning to breathe free,
   The wretched refuse of your teeming shore,
   Send these, the homeless, tempest-tossed, to me:
   I lift my lamp beside the golden door.
   1883 'The New Colossus', inscribed at the foot of the Statue of Liberty, New York harbour, 1886.

4 Still on Israel's head forlorn
   Every nation heaps its scorn.
   1886 'The World's Justice'.

Leach, Jim (James Albert Smith) 1942–
US Republican politician.

5 The only thing the Balkans export is history.
   1995 WAMU broadcast, Washington, 25 Nov.

Leacock, Stephen Butler 1869–1944
English-born Canadian humorist and economist. Head of Economics at McGill University from 1908, he wrote several books on economics and literary biographies, and is usually remembered for his short stories, essays and parodies, which include *Literary Lapses* (1910), *Nonsense Novels* (1911) and *Winsome Winnie* (1920).

6 There are no handles to a horse, but the 1910 model has a string to each side of its face for turning its head when there is anything you want it to see.
   1910 *Literary Lapses*, 'Reflections on Riding'.

7 It takes a good deal of physical courage to ride a horse. This, however, I have. I get it at about forty cents a flask, and take it as required.
   1910 *Literary Lapses*, 'Reflections on Riding'.

8 The great man...walks across his century and leaves the marks of his feet all over it, ripping out the dates on his galoshes as he passes.
   1910 *Literary Lapses*, 'The Life of John Smith'.

9 I detest life-insurance agents; they always argue that I shall some day die, which is not so.
   1910 *Literary Lapses*, 'Insurance Up to Date'.

10 The landlady of a boarding-house is a parallelogram—that is, an oblong angular figure, which cannot be described, but which is equal to anything.
   1910 *Literary Lapses*, 'Boarding-House Geometry'.

11 Astronomy teaches the correct use of the sun and the planets.
   1910 *Literary Lapses*, 'A Manual of Education'.

12 Electricity is of two kinds, positive and negative. The difference is, I presume, that one comes a little more expensive, but is more durable; the other is a cheaper thing, but the moths get into it.
   1910 *Literary Lapses*, 'A Manual of Education'.

13 Get your room full of good air, then shut up the windows and keep it. It will keep for years. Anyway, don't keep using your lungs all the time. Let them rest.
   1910 *Literary Lapses*, 'How to Live to Be 200'.

14 Lord Ronald said nothing; he flung himself from the room, flung himself upon his horse and rode madly off in all directions.
   1911 *Nonsense Novels*, 'Gertrude the Governess: or, Simple Seventeen'.

15 When you meet Mr. Smith first you think he looks like an over-dressed pirate. Then you begin to think him a character. You wonder at his enormous bulk. Then the utter hopelessness of knowing what Smith is thinking by merely looking at his features gets on your mind and makes the Mona Lisa seem an open book and the ordinary human countenance as superficial as a puddle in the sunlight.
   1912 *Sunshine Sketches of a Little Town*, 'The Hostelry of Mr. Smith'.

16 His life was one round of activity which he himself might deplore but was powerless to prevent.
   1912 *Sunshine Sketches of a Little Town*, 'The Ministrations of the Rev. Mr. Drone'.

17 The classics are only primitive literature. They belong to the same class as primitive machinery and primitive music and primitive medicine.
   1913 *Behind the Beyond*, 'Homer and Humbug'.

18 The parent who could see his boy as he really is, would shake his head and say: 'Willie is no good; I'll sell him.'
   1916 *Further Foolishness*, 'The Lot of the Schoolmaster'.

19 A decision of the courts decided that the game of golf may be played on a Sunday, not being a game within the view of the law, but being a form of moral effort.
   1923 *Over the Footlights*, 'Why I Refuse to Play Golf'.

20 Advertising may be described as the science of arresting human intelligence long enough to get money from it.
   1924 *The Garden of Folly*, 'The Perfect Salesman'.

21 The general idea, of course, in any first-class laundry, is to see that no shirt or collar ever comes back twice.
   1926 *Winnowed Wisdom*, ch.6.

22 I am what is called a *professor emeritus*—from the Latin *e*, 'out', and *meritus*, 'so he ought to be'.
   1938 *Here are my Lectures*, ch.14.

23 A sportsman is a man who, every now and then, simply has to go out and kill something. Not that he's cruel. He wouldn't hurt a fly. It's not big enough.
   1942 *My Remarkable Uncle*.

24 Presently I shall be introduced as 'this venerable old gentleman' and the axe will fall when they raise me to the degree of 'grand old man'. That means on our continent any one with snow-white hair who has kept out of jail till eighty.
   1942 *My Remarkable Uncle*, 'Three Score and Ten'.

25 I have a suspicion it's inevitable, but give me my stick. I'll face it.
   1942 On being asked what he thought about death, following a serious throat operation, quoted in John Stevens's introduction to *My Remarkable Uncle* (1965 edn).

Leadbelly pseudonym of Huddie William Ledbetter 1889–1949
US blues and folk singer, songwriter and guitarist. He was 'discovered' while serving one of several prison sentences. His recordings include 'Midnight Special' and 'Rock Island Line'.

26 No white man ever had the blues.
   Quoted in Joachim Berendt *The Jazz Book* (1984).

Lear, Edward 1812–88
English artist, humorist and traveller, famous for his nonsense verse such as that collected in *A Book of Nonsense* (1846, enlarged 1861, 1863 and 1870), as well as his illustrations and landscapes.

27 There was an Old Man with a beard,
   Who said, 'It is just as I feared!—
   Two Owls and a Hen,
   Four Larks and a Wren,
   Have all built their nest in my beard!'
   1846 *A Book of Nonsense*.

28 When awful darkness and silence reign
   Over the great Gromboolian plain,
   Through the long, long wintry nights,
   When the angry breakers roar
   As they beat on the rocky shore—
   When storm-clouds brood on the towering heights
   Of the Hills of the Chankly Bore.
   1871 *Nonsense Songs, Stories, Botany and Alphabets*, 'The Dong with a Luminous Nose'.

29 And those who watch at that midnight hour
   From Hall or Terrace or lofty Tower,
   Cry as the wild light passes along,
   'The Dong!—the Dong!
   The wandering Dong through the forest goes!
   The Dong!—the Dong!
   The Dong with a Luminous Nose!'
   1871 *Nonsense Songs, Stories, Botany and Alphabets*, 'The Dong with a Luminous Nose'.

30 They went to sea in a sieve, they did
   In a sieve they went to sea.
   1871 *Nonsense Songs, Stories, Botany and Alphabets*, 'The Jumblies'.

31 Far and few, far and few,
   Are the lands where the Jumblies live;
   Their heads are green, and their hands are blue,
   And they went to sea in a Sieve.
   1871 *Nonsense Songs, Stories, Botany and Alphabets*, 'The Jumblies'.

32 They called aloud 'Our Sieve ain't big,
   But we don't care a button! We don't care a fig!'
   1871 *Nonsense Songs, Stories, Botany and Alphabets*, 'The Jumblies'.

33 And they brought an Owl, and a useful Cart,
   And a pound of Rice, and a Cranberry Tart,
   And a hive of silvery Bees.
   And they brought a Pig, and some green Jack-daws,
   And a lovely Monkey with lollipop paws, and forty Bottles of Ring-Bo-Ree,
   And no end of Stilton Cheese.
   1871 *Nonsense Songs, Stories, Botany and Alphabets*, 'The Jumblies'.

34 Till Mrs Discobbolos said
   'Oh! W! X! Y! Z!
   It has just come into my head—
   Suppose we should happen to fall!!!!
   Darling Mr Discobbolos?'
   1871 *Nonsense Songs, Stories, Botany and Alphabets*, 'Mr and Mrs Discobbolos'.

35 The Owl and the Pussy-Cat went to sea
   In a beautiful pea-green boat.
   They took some honey, and plenty of money,
   Wrapped up in a five-pound note.
   The Owl looked up to the Stars above
   And sang to a small guitar,
   'Oh lovely Pussy! O Pussy, my love,
   What a beautiful Pussy you are'.
   1871 *Nonsense Songs, Stories, Botany and Alphabets*, 'The Owl and the Pussy-Cat'.

36 Pussy said to the Owl, 'You elegant Fowl!
   How charmingly sweet you sing!
   O let us be married! too long we have tarried:
   But what shall we do for a ring?'
   They sailed away for a year and a day,
   To the land where the Bong-tree grows,
   And there in a wood a Piggy-wig stood
   With a ring at the end of his nose.
   1871 *Nonsense Songs, Stories, Botany and Alphabets*, 'The Owl and the Pussy-Cat'.

37 'Dear Pig, are you willing to sell for one shilling
   Your ring?' Said the Piggy, 'I will.'
   1871 *Nonsense Songs, Stories, Botany and Alphabets*, 'The Owl and the Pussy-Cat'.

38 They dined on mince, and slices of quince,
   Which they ate with a runcible spoon;
   And hand in hand, on the edge of the sand,
   They danced by the light of the moon.
   1871 *Nonsense Songs, Stories, Botany and Alphabets*, 'The Owl and the Pussy-Cat'.

39 The Pobble who has no toes
   Had once as many as we;
   When they said, 'Some day you may lose them all';
   He replied—'Fish fiddle de-dee!'
   His Aunt Jobiska made him drink
   Lavender water tinged with pink,
   For she said, 'The world in general knows
   There's nothing so good for a Pobble's toes!'
   1871 *Nonsense Songs, Stories, Botany and Alphabets*, 'The Pobble Who Has No Toes'.

40 When boats or ships came near him
   He tinkledy-binkledy-winkled a bell.
   1871 *Nonsense Songs, Stories, Botany and Alphabets*, 'The Pobble Who Has No Toes'.

41 He has gone to fish, for his Aunt Jobiska's
   Runcible Cat with crimson whiskers!

1871 *Nonsense Songs, Stories, Botany and Alphabets,* 'The Pobble Who Has No Toes'.

42 'But the longer I live on this Crumpetty Tree
  The plainer than ever it seems to me
  That very few people come this way
  And that life on the whole is far from gay!'
  Said the Quangle-Wangle Quee.
  1871 *Nonsense Songs, Stories, Botany and Alphabets,* 'The Quangle Wangle's Hat'.

43 And what can we expect if we haven't any dinner,
  But to lose our teeth and eyelashes and keep on growing thinner?
  1871 *Nonsense Songs, Stories, Botany and Alphabets,* 'The Two Old Bachelors'.

44 Nasticreechia Krorluppia.
  1872 *More Nonsense, Pictures, Rhymes, Botany Etc,* 'Nonsense Botany'.

45 There was an old person of Ware,
  Who rode on the back of a bear:
  When they asked, 'Does it trot?'
  He said, 'Certainly not!
  He's a Moppsikon Floppsikon bear.'
  1872 *More Nonsense, Pictures, Rhymes, Botany Etc,* 'One Hundred Nonsense Pictures and Rhymes'.

46 There was an old man of Thermopylae,
  Who never did anything properly;
  But they said, 'If you choose
  To boil eggs in your shoes,
  You shall never remain in Thermopylae.'
  1872 *More Nonsense, Pictures, Rhymes, Botany Etc,* 'One Hundred Nonsense Pictures and Rhymes'.

Leary, Timothy Francis 1920–96

US psychologist, Professor at the Universities of California and Harvard, best known for his advocacy of the drug LSD and his association with the counter-cultural movement of the 1960s and 1970s.

47 My advice to people today is as follows: If you take the game of life seriously, if you take your nervous system seriously, if you take your sense organs seriously, if you take the energy process seriously, you must turn on, tune in, and drop out.
  1966 Lecture, Jun, collected in *The Politics of Ecstasy* (1968), ch.21.

48 Science is all metaphor.
  1980 Interview, 24 Sep, collected in *Contemporary Authors* vol.107.

Lease, Mary Elizabeth Cylens 1853–1933

US reformer, who spoke out for women's suffrage, Irish Home Rule, prohibition and other causes.

49 The farmers of Kansas must raise less corn and more hell.
  1890 Speech, Kansas. This phrase became the slogan of the Populist Party.

Leavis, F(rank) R(aymond) 1895–1978

English critic. He taught at Cambridge University, and was a hugely influential figure, although his ideas have now been superseded by new approaches to textual and cultural criticism.

50 Poetry can communicate the actual quality of experience with a subtlety and precision unapproachable by any other means.
  1932 *New Bearings in English Poetry,* ch.2.

51 The Sitwells belong to the history of publicity rather than of poetry.
  1932 *New Bearings in English Poetry,* ch.2.

52 It is well to start by distinguishing the few really great—the major novelists who count in the same way as the major poets, in the sense that they not only change the possibilities of the art for practitioners and readers, but that they are significant in terms of the human awareness they promote; awareness of the possibilities of life.
  1948 *The Great Tradition,* ch.1.

53 The only way to escape misrepresentation is never to commit oneself to any critical judgement that makes an impact—that is, never *say anything.*
  1948 *The Great Tradition,* ch.1.

Leavis, Q(ueenie) D(orothy) 1906–81

British literary critic.

54 Really I suppose what I hate myself most on is showing other people where to dig, not having time to do intensive and exclusive digging myself. I am a dowser and not a navvy.
  Quoted in the *Times Literary Supplement,* 8 Sep 1989.

Le Bon, Gustave 1841–1931

French psychologist and sociologist, whose works aim to identify national characteristics and thereby racial superiority.

55 Science has promised us truth—an understanding of such relationships as our minds can grasp; it has never promised us either peace or happiness.
  1895 *Psychologie des foules,* introduction.

Lebowitz, Fran(ces Ann) 1951–

US writer. Her work is marked by an aphoristic sensibility and a caustic, world-weary and rather cynical wit.

56 There is no such thing as inner peace. There is only nervousness or death. Any attempt to prove otherwise constitutes unacceptable behaviour.
  1978 *Metropolitan Life,* 'Manners'.

57 Nothing succeeds like address.
  1978 *Metropolitan Life,* 'The Nail Bank'.

58 Sleep is death without the responsibility.
  1978 *Metropolitan Life,* 'Why I Love Sleep'.

59 It is by this painstaking method of careful examination and eventual rejection that we reach a conclusion: life is something to do when you can't get to sleep.
  1978 *Metropolitan Life,* 'Mars'.

60 Salad is not a meal. It is a style.
  1978 *Metropolitan Life,* 'Food For Thought and Vice Versa'.

61 Perhaps the least cheering statement ever made on the subject of art is that life imitates it.
  1978 *Metropolitan Life,* 'Arts'.

62 Original thought is like original sin: both happened before you were born to people you could not possibly have met.
  1981 *Social Studies,* 'People'.

63 Great people talk about ideas, average people talk about things, and small people talk about wine.
  1981 *Social Studies,* 'People'.

64 The opposite of talking isn't listening. The opposite of talking is waiting.
   1981 *Social Studies*, 'People'.

65 There are two modes of transport in Los Angeles: car and ambulance. Visitors who wish to remain inconspicuous are advised to choose the latter.
   1981 *Social Studies*, 'Lesson One'.

66 If you're going to America, bring your own food.
   1981 *Social Studies*, 'Fran Lebowitz's Travel Hints'.

67 Being offended is the natural consequence of leaving one's home.
   1981 *Social Studies*, 'When Smoke Gets In Your Eyes…Shut Them'.

68 War is, undoubtedly, hell, but there is no earthly reason why it has to start so early in the morning.
   1981 *Social Studies*, 'War Stories'.

69 There's no such thing as advice to the lovelorn. If they took advice, they wouldn't be lovelorn.
   1997 In *Index Magazine*.

Leboyer, Frédérick 1918–

French gynaecologist and obstetrician, who first drew attention to birth trauma, and has always emphasized the intimate associations between sex, depression and anxiety.

70 Making love is the sovereign remedy for anguish.
   1991 *Birth without Violence*.

Le Carré, John *pseudonym of* David John Moore Cornwell 1931–

English novelist. He taught at Eton and entered the Foreign Service, resigning in 1964 to become a full-time writer. His works, many of which have been filmed, are set in the dark underworld of international diplomacy and espionage.

71 The Spy who Came in from the Cold.
   1963 Title of novel.

72 A committee is an animal with four back legs.
   1974 *Tinker, Tailor, Soldier, Spy*, pt.3, ch.34.

73 Sometimes…we have to do a thing in order to find out the reason for it. Sometimes our actions are questions, not answers.
   1986 *A Perfect Spy*, ch.1.

74 The only decent diplomat is a deaf Trappist.
   1986 *A Perfect Spy*, ch.3.

75 A society that admires its shock troops had better be bloody careful about where it's going.
   1986 *A Perfect Spy*, ch.18.

76 Publishers can get their minds halfway round anything.
   1989 *The Russia House*, ch.5.

77 One long act of sadism.
   1991 On his boyhood at Sherborne School. In *The Times*, 21 Feb.

78 As a maker of fictions, I invent versions of myself, never the real thing, if it exists.
   2002 In the *New Yorker*, 18 Feb.

79 How Bush and his junta succeeded in deflecting America's anger from Bin Laden to Saddam Hussein is one of the great public relations conjuring tricks in history.
   2003 In *Time*, 27 Jan.

Le Corbusier *pseudonym of* Charles Édouard Jeanneret 1887–1965

Swiss architect, co-author of the Purist manifesto. His buildings, which demonstrate the interrelation of machine forms and architectural techniques, include the Cité Universitaire, Paris, and his city planning designs include Buenos Aires (1938). His books have had a worldwide influence.

80 It is a question of building which is at the root of the social unrest of today: architecture or revolution.
   1923 *Vers une architecture* (translated as *Towards a New Architecture*, 1927).

81 The day consists of twenty-four hours only. This regulates the size of the house and the rôle it has to fulfil. For the twenty-four hour day is short, and our acts and thoughts are spurred on *by time*. If we were taught to regard the hand of the clock as a beneficent but implacable god, we should order our lives more rationally.
   1930 'Twentieth-century living and twentieth-century building'. Collected in Dennis Sharp (ed) *The Rationalists: Theory and Design in the Modern Movement* (1978).

82 Architecture provides the framework for a civilization (housing, work, leisure, circulation); so architecture is also town planning. It is no longer possible to separate architecture and town planning—they are one and the same thing.
   1943 'If I had to teach you architecture'. Collected in Dennis Sharp (ed) *The Rationalists: Theory and Design in the Modern Movement* (1978).

Ledger, Heath Andrew 1979–2008

Australian film actor.

83 If you're good at something, never do it for free.
   2008 As The Joker in *The Dark Knight* (screenplay by Jonathan Nolan and Christopher Nolan).

Lee, Gypsy Rose *stage-name of* Rose Louise Hovick 1914–70

US actress. Her career as a striptease artist in burlesque on Broadway in the 1930s provided the basis for the film *Gypsy* (1959).

84 I know men aren't attracted to me by my mind. They're attracted by what I don't mind.
   Attributed.

85 God is love, but get it in writing.
   Attributed.

Lee, (Nelle) Harper 1926–

US writer. Her novel, *To Kill a Mockingbird* (1960, Pulitzer Prize 1961), became a classic of its time.

86 Until I feared I would lose it, I never loved to read. One does not love breathing.
   1960 Scout. *To Kill A Mockingbird*, pt.1, ch.2.

87 Shoot all the bluejays you want, if you can hit 'em, but remember it's a sin to kill a mockingbird.
   1960 Atticus Finch. *To Kill A Mockingbird*, pt.1, ch.10.

88 The one thing that doesn't abide by majority rule is a person's conscience.
   1960 Atticus Finch. *To Kill A Mockingbird*, pt.1, ch.11.

89 Folks don't like to have somebody around knowin' more than they do. It aggravates 'em.
   1960 Calpurnia. *To Kill A Mockingbird*, pt.2, ch.12.

90 A court is only as sound as its jury, and a jury is only as sound as the men who make it up.
1960 Atticus Finch. *To Kill A Mockingbird*, pt.2, ch.20.

91 As you grow older, you'll see white men cheat black men every day of your life, but let me tell you something and don't you forget it—whenever a white man does that to a black man, no matter who he is, how rich he is, or how fine a family he comes from, that white man is trash.
1960 Atticus Finch. *To Kill A Mockingbird*, pt.2, ch.23.

Lee, Hsien Loong 1952–

Singaporean politician, son of the former Prime Minister Lee Kuan Yew. He became Prime Minister himself in 2004.

92 In Singapore you don't volunteer to go into politics—you are invited to enter.
1984 Remark. Quoted in Alan Chong *Goh Tok Chong* (1991), ch.4.

Lee, Kuan Yew 1923–2015

Singaporean politician, the country's first Prime Minister (1959–90), renowned for his authoritarianism and intolerance of political opponents.

93 I have decided that we shall make and build and never give way.
1966 Remark, 27 Dec. Quoted in James Minchin *No Man is an Island* (1986), ch.8.

94 Even from my sick bed, even if you are going to lower me into the grave, and I feel something is wrong, I will get up.
1988 Remark, Aug. Quoted in C M Turnbull *A History of Singapore* (1989).

Lee, Laurie 1914–97

English writer. He fought in the Spanish Civil War, but is best known for *Cider With Rosie* (1959), his evocative account of growing up in an English village between the wars.

95 Such a morning it is when love
leans through geranium windows
and calls with a cockerel's tongue.
1947 'Day of these Days'.

96 I was set down from the carrier's cart at the age of three; and there with a sense of bewilderment and terror my life in the village began.
1959 *Cider With Rosie*, 'First Light'.

97 Effie M. was a monster. Six foot high and as strong as a farm horse. No sooner had she decided that she wanted Uncle Tom than she knocked him off his bicycle and told him.
1959 *Cider With Rosie*, 'The Uncles'.

98 As for me—for me, the grass grew longer, and more sorrowful, and the trees were surfaced like flesh, and girls were no longer to be treated lightly but were creatures of commanding sadness, and all journeys through the valley were now made alone, with passion in every bush, and the motions of wind and cloud and stars were suddenly for myself alone, and voices elected me of all men living and called me to deliver the world, and I groaned from solitude, blushed when I stumbled, loved strangers and bread and butter, and made long trips through the rain on my bicycle, stared wretchedly through lighted windows, grinned wryly to think how little I was known, and lived in a state of raging excitement.
1959 *Cider With Rosie*, 'Last Days'.

Lee, Robert E 1807–70

US Confederate General. He fought in the Mexican War and in Texas. During the Civil War, although he defeated McClellan at Richmond, he surrendered to General Grant at Appomatox, Virginia in 1865.

99 It is well that war is so terrible. We should grow too fond of it.
1862 Attributed, after the Battle of Fredericksburg, Dec.

Lee-Potter, Lynda 1935–2005

British journalist.

1 Powerful men often succeed through the help of their wives. Powerful women only succeed in spite of their husbands.
1984 In the *Daily Mail*, 16 May.

Lees-Milne, James 1908–97

English diarist and founding Secretary of the National Trust's Country House Scheme.

2 All creatures give out a smell when aroused, it seems; certainly humans do.
Ancient as the Hills: Diaries, 1973–1974 (1997).

3 Watched [Vladimir] Horowitz playing his first concert in England for over thirty years. His fingers turn up at the ends, like a pig's nose.
Holy Dread: Diaries, 1982–1984 (2001).

Lees-Smith, Hastings Bernard 1878–1941

British politician. He was associated with Ruskin College, Oxford from its foundation in 1899. He was Liberal MP for Northampton (1910–18), and joined the Labour Party in 1919. He was Labour MP for Keighley (1922–23, 1924–31 and 1935–41).

4 Security can only be obtained by a scheme by which the nations of Europe and outside agree together that all will guarantee each, and each will guarantee all. The purposes of the war will be attained if there is a League of Nations with an absolute and decisive veto upon any mere aggression, and consideration of any legitimate claims that any of the countries engaged in the war may be able to make good.
1916 House of Commons, 21 Oct.

Leeson, Nick 1967–

British derivatives trader, who lost over £600 million trading on the Tokyo stockmarket and caused the collapse of Barings Bank.

5 My sincere apologies for the predicament I have left you in.
1995 Part of a faxed letter of resignation.

Léger, Fernand 1881–1946

French painter, a major force in the Cubist movement, although his paintings are more 'tubist' than 'cubist'. He executed murals for the UN building in New York (1952).

6 Modern man lives more and more in a preponderantly geometric order. All human creation mechanical or industrial is dependent upon geometric intentions.
1924 'The Aesthetic of the Machine', in *Bulletin de l'Effort Moderne*.

7 The thing depicted is less stationary, even the object in itself is less discernible than it used to be. A landscape

broken into and traversed in a car or an express train loses in descriptive value but gains in synthetic value; the window of the railroad carriage or the windshield of the car, combined with the speed at which you are traveling, have changed the familiar look of things. Modern man registers one hundred times more impressions than did an eighteenth century artist.
Quoted in D Cooper *The Cubist Epoch* (1970).

Le Guin, Ursula née Kroeber 1929–

US writer. She is best known for her literate, politically aware works of science fiction, and her children's fantasy novels, notably the *Earthsea* series (1968–2001) including its overtly feminist instalment, *Tehanu* (1990).

8 It is a terrible thing, this kindness that human beings do not lose. Terrible because when we are finally naked in the dark and cold, it is all we have.
1969 *The Left Hand of Darkness*, ch.13.

9 To be, the will to power must increase with each fulfilment, making the fulfilment only a step to a further one. The vaster the power gained the vaster the appetite for more.
1971 *The Lathe of Heaven*, ch.9.

10 In so far as one denies what is, one is possessed by what is not, the compulsions, the fantasies, the terrors that flock to fill the void.
1971 *The Lathe of Heaven*, ch.10.

11 The years before and after the menstrual years are vestigial: the only meaningful condition left to women is that of fruitfulness.
1976 'The Space Crone', in *The Co-Evolution Quarterly*, Summer.

12 To me the 'female principle' is, or at least historically has been, basically anarchic. It values order without constraint, rule by custom not by force. It has been the male who enforces order, who constructs power structures, who makes, enforces, and breaks laws.
'Is Gender Necessary?', in Anderson and McIntyre (eds) *Aurora* (1976).

13 The preservation of life seems to be rather a slogan than a genuine goal of the anti-abortion forces; what they want is control. Control over behavior: power over women.
1982 Address to the National Abortion Rights Action League, Jan. Collected as 'The Princess' in *Dancing at the Edge of the World* (1989).

14 Success is the American Dream we can keep dreaming because most people in most places, including thirty million of ourselves, live wide awake in the terrible reality of poverty.
1983 Address at Mills College. Collected as 'A Left-Handed Commencement Address' in *Dancing at the Edge of the World* (1989).

15 We are volcanoes. When we women offer our experience as our truth, as human truth, all the maps change. There are new mountains.
1983 Address at Mills College. Collected as 'A Left-Handed Commencement Address' in *Dancing at the Edge of the World* (1989).

16 The children of the revolution are always ungrateful, and the revolution must be grateful that it is so.
1983 Address to Folger Library Poetry Series, Washington. Collected as 'Reciprocity of Prose and Poetry' in *Dancing at the Edge of the World* (1989).

17 When either the political or the scientific discourse announces itself as the voice of reason, it is playing God, and should be spanked and stood in the corner.
1986 Commencement address at Bryn Mawr College. Collected in *Dancing at the Edge of the World* (1989).

18 My imagination makes me human and makes me a fool; it gives me all the world and exiles me from it.
1990 'Winged Creatures On My Mind', in *Harper's*, Aug.

19 The reason literacy is important is that literature is the operating instructions. The best manual we have. The most useful guide to the country we're visiting, life.
2004 *The Wave in the Mind*.

Lehmann-Haupt, Christopher Charles Herbert 1934–

US literary critic, born in Scotland. He was senior book reviewer on the *New York Times*.

20 One misses the hiss of acid.
1984 On Gore Vidal's biography *Lincoln* (1984). In the *New York Times*, 30 May.

21 We breathe, we think, we conceive of our lives as narratives.
1984 On Peter Brooks *Reading for the Plot* (1984). In the *New York Times*, 11 Jul.

22 The beginning of a plot…is the prompting of desire.
1984 On Peter Brooks *Reading for the Plot* (1984). In the *New York Times*, 11 Jul.

23 Happiest when he is trying to sculpture fog.
1989 On Robert C Christopher. In the *New York Times*, 29 May.

24 Stevenson's convictions were sometimes too complex for the binary political arena to which he devoted his life.
1989 In the *New York Times*, 31 Jul.

25 The only trouble with this book is that its covers are too close together.
1992 On Florence King *With Charity Toward None* (1992). In the *New York Times*, 9 Apr.

Lehrer, Tom (Thomas Andrew) 1928–

US teacher, songwriter and social satirist.

26 In one word he told me the secret of success in mathematics: Plagiarize…only be sure always to call it please 'research'.
1953 'Lobachevski', satirical song.

27 We'll all go together when we go,
Every Hottentot and every Eskimo,
When the air becomes uranious,
We'll all go simultaneous,
Yes, we'll all go together when we go.
1953 'We'll All Go Together When We Go', satirical song.

Leisen, Mitchell 1898–1972

US film director. His films include *Hold Back the Dawn* (1941), *Frenchman's Creek* (1944) and *Kitty* (1945).

28 He was God out there. He wanted it a certain way, that was the MGM style, and that's what you got.
On working for Cedric Gibbons on *Young Man with Ideas* (1952), quoted in David Chierichetti *Hollywood Director* (1972).

Lekota, Mosiuoa 1948–

South African Defence Minister (1999–2008) and President and Leader of the Congress of the People (2008–).

29 When will we cease to be Africans, Coloureds, Indians and Whites and merely South Africans? This is the question we must ask ourselves.
2004 Briefing the South African parliament's portfolio committee on defence, 1 Jun.

LeMay, Curtis Emerson 1906–90
US general and air force chief. After commanding in World War II he became air force Chief of Staff (1961–5) and ran unsuccessfully for Vice-President as George Wallace's running mate, 1968.

30 My solution to the problem would be to tell them that they've got to draw in their horns, or we're going to bomb them into the Stone Age.
Of the North Vietnamese. *Mission with LeMay* (1965).

31 A man should have dinner with his friends, and the commanding general has no friends.
On declining to dine with a group of colonels. Recalled on his death, 1 Oct 1990.

Lemmon, Jack (John Uhler) 1925–2001
US actor. He made his film debut in *It Should Happen to You* (1954), beginning a career as a comic, bittersweet underdog which won him eight Academy Award nominations and two Oscars.

32 I won't quit until I get run over by a truck, a producer or a critic.
1986 In *Newsweek*, 5 May.

33 I would rather play Hamlet with no rehearsal than TV golf.
Quoted in Michael Hobbs *The Golf Quotation Book* (1992).

34 If you think it's hard to meet new people, try picking up the wrong golf ball.
Attributed.

Lemmy (Ian Fraser Kilmister) 1945–
English heavy metal singer and bass player, member of the band Motörhead.

35 People don't know how to be outrageous any more.
2004 In *The Guardian*, 31 May.

L'Engle, Madeleine *married name* Mrs Hugh Franklin 1918–2007
US writer, best known for her children's trilogy *A Wrinkle in Time* (1962), *A Wind in the Door* (1973) and *A Swiftly Tilting Planet* (1978). Her many other works include *Troubling the Star* (1994) and the autobiographical *Summer of Great-Grandmother* (1974).

36 Artistic temperament...sometimes seems a battleground for a dark angel of destruction and a bright angel of creativity wrestling.
1982 *A Severed Wasp*.

Lenin, Vladimir Ilyich *originally* Vladimir Ilyich Ulyanov 1870–1924
Russian Marxist revolutionary and politician. After the Feb 1917 revolution he urged the proletariat to seize power, and in Oct 1917 led the Bolshevik Revolution and headed the first Soviet government. After the Civil War (1918–21) he introduced the New Economic Policy, which his critics saw as a retreat from strict socialism.

37 A small, compact core, consisting of reliable, experienced and hardened workers, with responsible agents...connected by all the rules of strict secrecy with the organisations of revolutionists, can, with the wide support of the masses and without an elaborate set of rules, perform all the functions of a trade union.
1902 *What Is to be Done?*

38 One Step Forward, Two Steps Back
1904 Title of book.

39 I greet you as the advance guard of the world proletarian army. The hour is not far off when...the German people will turn their weapons against their capitalist exploiters. The sun of the socialist revolution has already risen.
1917 Speech, Petrograd, 16 Apr.

40 We will now proceed to the building of socialism.
1917 Speech, Oct. Quoted in A J P Taylor *From the Boer War to the Cold War: Essays on Twentieth-Century Europe* (1995), p.192.

41 A good man fallen among Fabians.
Of George Bernard Shaw. Quoted in Arthur Ransome *Six Weeks in Russia in 1919* (1919).

42 Chess is the gymnasium of the mind.
Quoted in Colin Jarman *The Guinness Dictionary of Sports Quotations* (1990).

Lennon, John Winston 1940–80
English rock singer, guitarist and songwriter. A member of The Beatles, he wrote with Paul McCartney many of the hits of the 1960s. He later established himself as a solo artist. He was shot dead by a deranged fan outside his Manhattan apartment.

43 On this next number I want you all to join in. Would those in the cheap seats clap their hands? The rest of you can rattle your jewellery.
1963 Addressing the audience during a Royal Command performance. Quoted in Bill Harry *The Ultimate Beatles Encyclopedia* (1992).

44 We're more popular than Jesus Christ now. I don't know which will go first, rock and roll or Christianity.
1966 In the *Evening Standard*.

45 All we are saying is give peace a chance.
1969 Song (with his wife, Yoko Ono), used widely in protests against the Vietnam War.

46 Imagine there's no heaven,
It's easy if you try,
No hell below us,
Above us only sky,
Imagine all the people
Living for today.
1971 'Imagine'.

47 Women should be obscene and not heard.
Attributed.

Lennon, John Winston and McCartney, Sir (James) Paul 1940–80, 1942–
English songwriters and composers who formed The Beatles in 1960. They gained international fame with their songs and performances. They disbanded in 1970.

48 For I don't care too much for money,
For money can't buy me love.
1964 'Can't Buy Me Love'.

49 It's been a hard day's night,
And I've been working like a dog.
1964 'A Hard Day's Night'.

50 She's got a ticket to ride, but she don't care.
   1965 'Ticket to Ride'.

51 Eleanor Rigby picks up the rice in a church where a
      wedding has been,
   Lives in a dream.
   Waits at the window, wearing the face that she keeps in
      a jar by the door,
   Who is it for?
   All the lonely people, where do they all come from?
   1966 'Eleanor Rigby'.

52 Oh I get by with a little help from my friends,
   Mm, I get high with a little help from my friends.
   1967 'With a Little Help From My Friends'.

53 Will you still need me, will you still feed me,
   When I'm sixty four?
   1967 'When I'm Sixty Four'.

54 Strawberry fields forever.
   1967 Title of song.

55 Back in the USSR.
   1968 Title of song.

Leno, Jay (James Douglas Muir) 1950–

US comedian, host of *The Tonight Show* (1992–2009 and 2010–14).

56 Now, today is the day we honour, of course, the presidents, ranging from George Washington, who couldn't tell a lie, to George Bush, who couldn't tell the truth, to Bill Clinton, who couldn't tell the difference.
   2007 Marking Presidents' Day, 19 Feb.

57 The auto industry is not doing well. In fact, the Big Three right now are Matchbox, Tonka and Hot Wheels.
   2008 On *The Tonight Show*, 12 Nov.

58 The good news is, the stock market is closed and it can't hurt us again until tomorrow.
   2011 On *The Tonight Show*, 8 Aug.

59 A new poll shows only three per cent strongly approve of the job Congress is doing, with a margin of error of four per cent, so it's possible that less than no one thinks they're doing a good job.
   2011 On *The Tonight Show*, 6 Oct.

Lenthall, William 1591–1662

English lawyer and parliamentarian, Speaker of the Long Parliament (1640–53) and Master of the Rolls from 1643. He was again made Speaker in 1654 and 1659, and in 1657 became one of Cromwell's peers.

60 May it please your Majesty, I have neither eye to see nor tongue to speak in this place, but as this House is pleased to direct me, whose servant I am.
   1642 To Charles I, on his arrival in the Chamber to arrest five Members, House of Commons, 4 Jan.

Leonard, Elmore John 1925–2013

US novelist and screenwriter. He wrote mainly in the field of crime fiction, where he was widely regarded as the foremost practitioner of his era.

61 The Chekhov of the suburbs.
   Of John Cheever. Quoted in *The Annual Obituary 1982* (1983).

62 I try to leave out the parts that people skip.
   1985 In *Publisher's Weekly*, 8 Mar.

63 If it sounds like writing, I rewrite it.
   1985 In *Newsweek*, 22 Apr.

64 Easy on the Adverbs, Exclamation Points and Especially Hooptedoodle.
   2003 Essay title.

Leonard, Sugar Ray 1956–

US boxer.

65 We're all endowed with certain God-given talents. Mine happens to be punching people in the head.
   Quoted in Colin Jarman *The Guinness Dictionary of Sports Quotations* (1990).

Leonardo da Vinci 1452–1519

Italian painter, sculptor, architect and engineer, the epitome of the 'Renaissance' man. He entered the service of Cesare Borgia in 1500 as architect and engineer, working alongside Michelangelo, and worked for Louis XII of France in 1506.

66 To devise is the work of the master, to execute the act of the servant.
   Treatise on Painting (published 1651, translated by A P McMahon, 1956).

67 I do not find any difference between painting and sculpture except that the sculptor pursues his work with greater physical fatigue than the painter and the painter pursues his with greater mental fatigue.
   Treatise on Painting (published 1651, translated by A P McMahon, 1956).

68 Shun those studies in which the work that results dies with the worker.
   The Notebooks of Leonardo da Vinci (translated by Edward MacCurdy, 1938), vol.1, pt.1.

69 Painting is poetry which is seen and not heard, and poetry is a painting which is heard but not seen.
   Quoted in J P and Irma A Richter *The Literary Works of Leonardo da Vinci* (2 vols, 1939).

70 Force is the same throughout and the whole is in every part of it. Force is a spiritual power, an invisible energy which is imparted by violence from without to all bodies out of their natural balance.
   Quoted in Jean-Paul Richter (ed) *The Literary Works of Leonardo da Vinci* (1939).

71 If a man have a tent made in linen of which the apertures have all been stopped up, and it be twelve *braccia* across and twelve in depth, he will be able to throw himself down from any great height without sustaining injury.
   Description of a parachute. *Notebooks*. Quoted in Vincent Cronin *The Flowering of the Renaissance* (1969).

72 The air moves like a river and carries the clouds with it; just as running water carries all the things that float upon it.
   Notebooks. Quoted in Vincent Cronin *The Flowering of the Renaissance* (1969).

73 He is a poor disciple who does not excel his master.
   Quoted in Irma A Richter (ed) *Selections from the Notebooks of Leonardo da Vinci* (1977).

74 A good painter has two chief objects to paint, man and the intention of his soul; the former is easy, the latter harder, because he has to represent it by the attitudes and movements of the limbs.

Quoted in Irma A Richter (ed) *Selections from the Notebooks of Leonardo da Vinci* (1977).

75 Perspective is the bridle and rudder of painting.
Quoted in Irma A Richter (ed) *Selections from the Notebooks of Leonardo da Vinci* (1977).

76 The span of a man's outspread arms is equal to his height.
Quoted in Irma A Richter (ed) *Selections from the Notebooks of Leonardo da Vinci* (1977).

77 Do not despise my opinion, when I remind you that it should not be hard for you to stop sometimes and look into the stains of walls, or ashes of a fire, or clouds, or mud or like places, in which, if you consider them well, you may find really marvellous ideas.
Quoted in Irma A Richter (ed) *Selections from the Notebooks of Leonardo da Vinci* (1977).

78 Just as a stone flung into the water becomes the centre and cause of many circles, and as sound diffuses itself in circles in the air; so any object, placed in the luminous atmosphere, diffuses itself in circles, and fills the surrounding air with infinite images of itself.
Quoted in Irma A Richter (ed) *Selections from the Notebooks of Leonardo da Vinci* (1977).

79 The painter who draws by practice and judgement of the eye without the use of reason is like a mirror which copies everything placed in front of it without knowledge of the same.
Quoted in Irma A Richter (ed) *Selections from the Notebooks of Leonardo da Vinci* (1977).

Leonidas d.480 BC

King of Sparta, commander of the Greeks when the Persian army of Xerxes invaded mainland Greece. At the narrow pass of Thermopylae he made a heroic stand with 300 Spartans.

80 Come and take them.
Attributed reply when Xerxes summoned him to surrender his weapons at Thermopylae. Quoted in Plutarch, *Apophthegmata Laconica*.

Lerner, Alan Jay 1918–86

US lyricist, screenwriter and producer. He frequently worked in collaboration with Frederick Loewe, and is best known for *Brigadoon* (1955), *Gigi* (1958), *My Fair Lady* (1964) and *Camelot* (1967).

81 Those little eyes so helpless and appealing
One day will flash and send you crashing through the ceiling.
1958 'Thank Heaven for Little Girls', in the musical *Gigi* (music by Frederick Loewe).

82 We met at nine
—We met at eight
I was on time
—No, you were late
Ah yes! I remember it well.
1958 'I Remember it Well', in the musical *Gigi* (music by Frederick Loewe).

83 I've Grown Accustomed To Her Face.
1964 Title of song, in *My Fair Lady* (music by Marcus Loewe).

84 Oozing charm from every pore
He oiled his way around the floor.
1964 'You Did It', from *My Fair Lady* (music by Marcus Loewe).

85 Why can't a woman be more like a man?
Men are so honest, so thoroughly square;
Eternally noble, historically fair;
Who, when you win, will always give your back a pat.
Why can't a woman be like that?
1964 'A Hymn to Him', from *My Fair Lady* (music by Frederick Loewe).

86 Because it saves time.
When Andrew Lloyd Webber asked him 'Why do people take an instant dislike to me?' Quoted by Leah Garchik in the *San Francisco Chronicle*, 27 Nov 1990.

Le Sage, Alain René 1668–1747

French novelist and playwright. He is best remembered for his play *Turcaret* (1709), which satirized the financial world, and the picaresque novel *Gil Blas de Santillane* (1715–35).

87 Justice is such a fine thing that we cannot pay too dearly for it.
1707 *Crispin rival de son maître*, pt.9.

Leslie, David 1601–82

Scottish soldier. He fought at Marston Moor (1644), and defeated Montrose at Philiphaugh (1645). Routed by Cromwell at Dunbar in 1650, he was subsequently imprisoned and held in the Tower until the Restoration. He was made Lord Newark in 1651.

88 How glorious it would be in the eyes of God and men, if we managed to hunt the Catholics from England, follow them to France, and, like the bold King of Sweden, rouse the Protestants in France, plant our religion in Paris by agreement or force, and go from there to Rome to chase the Antichrist and burn the town whence superstition comes.
1643 Said to Lord Hume, Council of Scottish Nobles, Aug.

Lessing, Doris May née Tayler 1919–2013

Rhodesian writer, born in Iran. She lived much of her adult life in England after being exiled for her opposition to the white Southern Rhodesian government. She was a communist for a time, and later an icon of the women's movement. Her best-known works are the novel sequence *Children of Violence* (1952–69), *The Golden Notebook* (1962) and *The Good Terrorist* (1985).

89 When old settlers say 'One has to understand the country,' what they mean is, 'You have to get used to our ideas about the native.' They are saying, in effect, 'Learn our ideas, or otherwise get out; we don't want you.'
1950 *The Grass Is Singing*, ch.1.

90 When a white man in Africa by accident looks into the eyes of a native and sees the human being (which it is his chief preoccupation to avoid), his sense of guilt, which he denies, fumes up in resentment and he brings down the whip.
1950 *The Grass Is Singing*, ch.8.

91 I had learned that if one cannot call a country to heel like a dog, neither can one dismiss the past with a smile in an easy gush of feeling, saying: I could not help it, I am also a victim.
1951 *This was the Old Chief's Country*, 'The Old Chief Mshlanga'.

92 For she was suffering that misery peculiar to the young, that they are going to be cheated by circumstances out of the full life every nerve and instinct is clamouring for.
1952 *Martha Quest*, pt.1, ch.1.

93 She was thinking—for, since she had been formed by literature, she could think in no other way—that all this

had been described in Dickens, Tolstoy, Hugo, Dostoevsky, and a dozen others. All that noble and terrific indignation had done nothing, achieved nothing, the shout of anger from the nineteenth century might as well have been silent—for here came the file of prisoners, handcuffed two by two, and on their faces was that same immemorial look of patient, sardonic understanding.
1952 *Martha Quest*, ch.2.

94 In every city there is a group of middle-aged and elderly women who in fact run it. The extent to which they are formally organised is no gauge of their real power. The way in which they respond to danger is that gauge; and from the frankness with which they express their intentions can be measured the extent of the danger.
1954 *A Proper Marriage*, pt.3, ch.1.

95 Martha and Jasmine smiled at each other…the future they dreamed of seemed just around the corner; they could almost touch it. Each saw an ideal town, clean, noble and beautiful, soaring up over the actual town they saw, which consisted in this area of sordid little shops and third-rate cafés.
1958 *A Ripple from the Storm*, pt.1, ch.1.

96 There is only one real sin, and that is to persuade oneself that the second-best is anything but the second-best.
1962 *The Golden Notebook*, 'The Blue Notebook'.

97 It occurred to her that she was going mad… Yet it did not seem to her that she was even slightly mad; but rather that people who were not as obsessed as she was with the inchoate world mirrored in the newspapers were all out of touch with an awful necessity.
1962 *The Golden Notebook*, 'Free Women 5'.

98 But this novel was not a trumpet for Women's Liberation. It described many female emotions of aggression, hostility, resentment. It put them into print. Apparently what many women were thinking, feeling, experiencing came as a great surprise.
1971 *The Golden Notebook*, preface to new edition.

99 Briefing for a Descent into Hell.
1971 Title of novel.

1 It does no harm to repeat, as often as you can, 'Without me the literary industry would not exist'.
1980 In *The Author*, spring.

2 To be in love with a country or a political regime is a tricky business. You get your heart broken even more surely than by being in love with a person.
1992 *African Laughter*, 'Next Time 1988'.

3 Writers do not come out of houses without books.
2013 In the *Los Angeles Times*.

Lessing, Gotthold Ephraim 1729–81

German philosopher and playwright, an important Enlightenment figure, best known for his essay on aesthetics, *Laokoon* (1766).

4 *Wie manches würde in der Theorie unwidersprechlich scheinen, wenn es dem Genie nicht gelungen wäre, das Widerspiel durch die Tat zu erweisen.*
How many things would have appeared incontestable in theory if genius had not proved them wrong in practice.
1766 *Laokoon: an essay upon the limits of painting and poetry*, pt.4.

5 *Ein einziger dankbarer Gedanke gen Himmel ist das vollkommenste Gebet.*
One single grateful thought raised to heaven is the most perfect prayer.
1767 *Minna von Barnhelm*, act 2, sc.7.

6 *Wer richtig räsonniert, erfindet auch; und wer erfinden will, muss räsonnieren können. Nur die glauben, dass sich das eine von dem anderen trennen lasse, die zu keinem von beiden aufgelegt sind.*
The man who can reason properly can invent; and anyone who wants to invent must be able to reason. The only people who think that the one can be separated from the other are those who have no inclination for either.
1769 *Hamburgische Dramaturgie*.

7 *Es ist nicht wahr, dass die kürzeste Linie immer die Gerade ist.*
It is not true that the shortest line is always the straight one.
1780 *Die Erziehung des Menschengeschlechts*.
▶ See also Brecht 157:92.

L'Estrange, Sir Roger 1616–1704

English journalist and pamphleteer. During the Restoration he was Licenser of the Press.

8 Supposing the Press in order, the people in their right wits, and news or no news to be the question, a Public Mercury should not have my Vote, because I think it makes the Multitude too familiar with the actions and counsels of their superiors, too pragmatical and censorious, and gives them not only an itch but a kind of colourable right to be meddling with the government.
1663 *The Intelligencer*, 31 Aug.

Lette, Kathy 1958–

Australian-born British novelist.

9 I am allergic to domestic goddesses. Men would prefer a woman with a dirty mind to a clean house.
2008 Quoted in *The Funniest Things You Never Said 2*, 2011.

10 I am not allowed to sing, dance, laugh or wear short skirts. Having a teenage daughter is like living with the Taliban.
2013 In *The Telegraph*, 22 Apr.

Letterman, David Michael 1947–

US talk show host and comedian.

11 How long have you been a black man?
2009 Interviewing President Barack Obama, quoted in *The Washington Post*, 22 Sep.

12 This is only phase one of the scandal. Phase two: I go on Oprah and so do.
2009 Admitting on *The Late Show* that he had been blackmailed for having sex with his staff, 5 Oct.

13 I got into the car this morning and the navigation lady wasn't speaking to me.
2009 On *The Late Show*, 5 Oct.

Leupold, Jakob 1674–1727

German mechanic, machinery constructor and government mining commissioner, who wrote a large and comprehensive work on the tasks the engineer faced.

14 As in earlier days were our mechanics, such today are our engineers, who may be required not only to tear down a fortress, and then to build it up again, but also to produce all sorts of engines based on mechanical principles, and with equal ease to defend or to annihilate a fortress.
1724 *Theatrum machinarum.*

15 The best machines and to be chosen above all others are those which consist of the fewest parts or which are the simplest, which produce the least friction; which are not too heavily loaded, and where the power can be conveniently applied without any waste.
1724 *Theatrum machinarum.*

Levant, Oscar 1906–72

US composer, pianist, writer, actor and conductor. He played Gershwin's 'Rhapsody in Blue' on its first performance in 1932.

16 It's a right step in the wrong direction.
1935 Attributed remark at the first performance of George Gershwin's *Porgy and Bess*. He in fact had the deepest respect for Gershwin's music.

17 Chutzpah—that quality which enables a man who has murdered his mother and father to throw himself on the mercy of the court as an orphan.
1968 *The Unimportance of Being Oscar.*

Levenson, Michael

US literary critic, a professor of English at the University of Virginia.

18 Although Brooke never succeeded in becoming the first modern poet, he may deserve to be called the first modern undergraduate, a title of comparable significance.
1987 Of Rupert Brooke. 'Budding Brooke', in the *New Republic*, 31 Aug.

Levenstein, Ros

US copywriter.

19 I'm only here for the beer.
1971 British advertising slogan for Double Diamond beer.

Leverson, Ada 1895–1936

English novelist and journalist, she was friendly with Beerbohm and Wilde, who called her 'the Sphinx'. She wrote six novels.

20 You don't know a woman until you have had a letter from her.
1912 *Tenterhooks*, ch.7.

21 He seemed at ease and to have the look of the last gentleman in Europe.
1930 Of Oscar Wilde. *Letters to the Sphinx.*

Levertov, Denise 1923–97

English-born US poet. She is associated with the Black Mountain group of poets led by Charles Olsen, but has a distinctive voice of her own, reflected in numerous collections.

22 Let's go—much as that dog goes,
intently haphazard.
1958 *Overland to the Islands*, 'Overland to the Islands'.

23 Pergo Park knew me, and Clavering, and Havering-atte-Bower,
Stanford Rivers lost me in osier-beds, Stapleford Abbots sent me safe home on the dark road after Simeon-quiet evensong,
Wanstead drew me over and over into its basic poetry,
in its serpentine lake I saw bass-viols among the golden dead
leaves,
through its trees the ghost of a great house.
1961 *The Jacob's Ladder*, 'A Map of the Western Part of the County of Essex in England'.

24 The world is
not with us enough.
1964 *O Taste and See*, 'O Taste and See'.
▶ See Wordsworth 958:87.

25 Death and pain dominate this world, for though many are cured, they leave still weak,

still tremulous, still knowing mortality
has whispered to them; have seen in the folding
of white bedspreads according to rule

the starched pleats of a shroud.
1972 *Footprints*, 'The Malice of Innocence'.

Levi, Primo 1919–87

Italian writer and the author of a series of major works of remembrance and analysis of his experiences in Nazi concentration camps in World War II.

26 The future of humanity is uncertain, even in the most prosperous countries, and the quality of life deteriorates; and yet I believe that what is being discovered about the infinitely large and infinitely small is sufficient to absolve this end of the century and millennium. What a very few are acquiring in knowledge of the physical world will perhaps cause this period not to be judged as a pure return of barbarism.
1985 *Other People's Trades*, 'News from the Sky' (translated by Raymond Rosenthal, 1989).

Levin, (Henry) Bernard 1928–2004

English writer, journalist and critic. In 1985 he crossed the Alps on foot, following the path of the Carthaginian general, Hannibal.

27 The musical equivalent of blancmange.
1983 Of the music of Frederick Delius. *Enthusiasms.*

28 I dislike almost all dogs, but Alsatians, I do truly believe, should be prohibited by law in any civilised country… The more I see of dogs, the more I admire men.
1985 *Hannibal's Footsteps.*

29 Baedeker is astonishingly enduring; travellers can use nineteenth-century editions with confidence, providing they take some elementary precautions. Many hotels will long since have disappeared, and the prices will be somewhat different, but if Baedeker says 'On leaving the tunnel, the best view is on the right', it probably still is, unless somebody has shifted the mountain, and his descriptions of scenery and where to go to see it at its best are still valid, as is practically all of his potted history.
1985 *Hannibal's Footsteps.*

Levitt, Steven David 1967–

US economist and criminologist.

30 Morality, it could be argued, represents the way that people would like the world to work, whereas economics represents how it actually does work.
   2005 *Freakonomics: A Rogue Economist Explores the Hidden Side of Everything.*

31 Information is a beacon, a cudgel, an olive branch, a deterrent—all depending on who wields it and how.
   2005 *Freakonomics: A Rogue Economist Explores the Hidden Side of Everything.*

32 The swimming pool is almost one hundred times more likely to kill a child than the gun is.
   2005 *Freakonomics: A Rogue Economist Explores the Hidden Side of Everything.*

33 Don't listen to what people say; watch what they do.
   2014 (with Stephen J. Dubner) *Think Like a Freak.*

34 Solving a problem is hard enough; it gets that much harder if you've decided beforehand it can't be done.
   2014 (with Stephen J. Dubner) *Think Like a Freak.*

Lévis, Duc de   1764–1830
French soldier and writer.

35 *Noblesse oblige.*
   Nobility brings obligations.
   1812 *Maximes et réflexions,* 'Morale: Maximes et Préceptes', no.73.

Lévi-Strauss, Claude   1908–2009
French social anthropologist.

36 *La langue est une raison humaine qui a ses raisons, et que l'homme ne connaît pas.*
   Language is a form of human reason, and has its reasons which are unknown to man.
   1962 *La Pensée sauvage,* ch.9.
   ▶ See Pascal 667:80.

37 The scientific mind does not so much provide the right answers as ask the right questions.
   1964 *The Raw and the Cooked* (translated by John and Doreen Weightman 1983).

38 I can't help thinking that science would be more appealing if it had no practical use.
   1964 *The Raw and the Cooked* (translated by John and Doreen Weightman 1983).

Lewin, Albert   1895–1968
US screenwriter and director. His films include *The Moon and Sixpence* (1943), *The Picture of Dorian Gray* (1945) and *Pandora and the Flying Dutchman* (1950).

39 The measure of love is what one is willing to give up for it.
   1950 *Pandora and the Flying Dutchman.*

Lewis, C(live) S(taples)   1898–1963
English novelist, literary scholar and theological writer. His most widely read works include the children's series *The Chronicles of Narnia* (1950–6), several allegorical science-fiction novels, and the Christian apologetics, *The Screwtape Letters* (1942).

40 Humanity does not pass through phases as a train passes through stations: being alive, it has the privilege of always moving yet never leaving anything behind.
   1936 *The Allegory of Love,* ch.1.

41 Out of the Silent Planet.
   1938 Title of novel.

42 There is wishful thinking in Hell as well as on earth.
   1942 *The Screwtape Letters,* preface.

43 Gratitude looks to the past and love to the present: fear, avarice, lust and ambition look ahead.
   1942 *The Screwtape Letters,* no.15.

44 He has a vulgar mind.
   1942 Of God. *The Screwtape Letters,* no.22.

45 She's the sort of woman who lives for others—you can always tell the others by their hunted expression.
   1942 *The Screwtape Letters,* no.26.

46 Fatigue makes women talk more and men less.
   1942 *The Screwtape Letters,* no.30.

47 Courage is not simply one of the virtues but the form of every virtue at the testing point.
   Quoted in Cyril Connolly *The Unquiet Grave* (1944), ch.3.

48 I remember summing up what I took to be our destiny, in conversation with my best friend at Chartres, by the formula, 'Term, holidays, term, holidays, till we leave school, and then work, work, work till we die.'
   1955 *Surprised by Joy,* ch.4.

49 A sick society must think much about politics, as a sick man must think much about his digestion.
   1980 *The Weight of Glory.*

50 All except the best men would rather be called wicked than vulgar.
   Quoted in *The Guardian,* 21 Aug 1980.

Lewis, Esther   *married name* Clark   fl.1747–89
English poet.

51 Are simple women only fit
   To dress, to darn, to flower or knit,
   To mind the distaff, or the spit?
   Why are the needle and the pen
   Thought incompatible by men?
   1754 'A Mirror for Detractors', l.146–50.

Lewis, Joe E   1902–71
US comedian.

52 I distrust camels and anyone else who can go a week without a drink.
   Recalled on his death, 4 Jun 1971.

Lewis, John L(lewellyn)   1880–1969
US labour leader.

53 No tin hat brigade of goose-stepping vigilantes or bibblebabbling mob of blackguarding and corporation-paid scoundrels will prevent the onward march of labor, or divert its purpose to play its natural and rational part in the development of the economic, political, and social life of our nation.
   1937 Address, 3 Sep. Recalled on his death 11 Jun 1969.

54 All forms of government fall when it comes up to the question of bread—bread for the family, something to eat. Bread to a man with a family comes first—before his union, before his citizenship, before his church affiliation. Bread!
   1963 In the *Saturday Evening Post,* 12 Oct.

Lewis, (Harry) Sinclair 1885–1951

US novelist. His novels satirized the materialism and intolerance of US small-town life. He is best known for his novel *Babbitt* (1922), a study of middle-class philistinism. In 1930 he became the first American to receive the Nobel prize for literature.

55 He never put on BVDs without thanking the God of Progress that he didn't wear tight, long, old-fashioned undergarments.
    1922 *Babbitt*, ch.1, section 4. BVD is a trademark for a brand of US underwear.

56 His name was George F. Babbitt. He was forty-six years old now, in April, 1920, and he made nothing in particular, neither butter nor shoes nor poetry, but he was nimble in the calling of selling houses for more than people could afford to pay.
    1922 *Babbitt*, ch.1.

57 To George F. Babbitt, as to most prosperous citizens of Zenith, his motor car was poetry and tragedy, love and heroism. The office was his pirate ship but the car his perilous excursion ashore.
    1922 *Babbitt*, ch.3.

58 In other countries, art and literature are left to a lot of shabby bums living in attics and feeding on booze and spaghetti, but in America the successful writer or picture-painter is indistinguishable from any other decent business man.
    1922 *Babbitt*, ch.14.

59 Damn the great executives, the men of measured merriment, damn the men with careful smiles, damn the men that run the shops, oh, damn their measured merriment.
    1925 *Arrowsmith*, ch.25.

60 Our American professors like their literature clear and cold and pure and very dead.
    1930 Nobel prize address, 12 Dec.

61 Intellectually I know that America is no better than any other country; emotionally I know she is better than every other country.
    1930 Interview in Berlin, 29 Dec.

62 It Can't Happen Here.
    1935 Title of novel.

63 A man takes a drink, a drink takes another, and the drink takes the man.
    Words to his future wife, Dorothy Thompson. Quoted in Vincent Sheean *Dorothy and Red* (1963).

Lewis, (Percy) Wyndham 1882–1957

English novelist, painter and critic. He co-founded the Vorticist movement with Ezra Pound, and remained an important experimental writer and painter between the wars. He became blind in 1951, but continued to write. His works include *The Apes of God* (1930) and the autobiographical *The Self Condemned* (1954).

64 'Dying for an idea,' again, sounds well enough, but why not let the idea die instead of you?
    1926 *The Art of Being Ruled*, pt.1, ch.1.

65 When we say 'science' we can either mean any manipulation of the inventive and organizing power of the human intellect: or we can mean such an extremely different thing as the religion of science, the vulgarized derivative from this pure activity manipulated by a sort of priestcraft into a great religious and political weapon.
    1926 *The Art of Being Ruled*.

66 The puritanical potentialities of science have never been forecast. If it evolves a body of organized rites, and is established as a religion, hierarchically organized, things more than anything else will be done in the name of 'decency'. The coarse fumes of tobacco and liquors, the consequent tainting of the breath and staining of white fingers and teeth, which is so offensive to many women, will be the first things attended to.
    1926 *The Art of Being Ruled*.

67 The revolutionary simpleton is everywhere.
    1927 *Time and Western Man*, pt.1, ch.6.

68 Gertrude Stein's prose song is a cold, black suet-pudding...of fabulously reptilian length.
    1927 *Time and Western Man*, pt.1, ch.13.

69 If you must go nowhere, step out.
    1928 *The Childermass*, final words.

70 It is to what I have called the Apes of God that I am drawing your attention—those prosperous mountebanks who alternately imitate and mock at and traduce those figures they at once admire and hate.
    1930 *The Apes of God*, pt.3.

71 The soul started at the knee-cap and ended at the navel.
    1930 *The Apes of God*, pt.12.

72 Give me the *outside* of all things, I am a fanatic for the externality of things.
    1937 *Blasting and Bombardiering*, ch.1.

73 Then down came the lid—the day was lost, for art, at Sarajevo. World-politics stepped in, and a war was started which has not ended yet: 'a war to end war'. But it merely ended art. It did not end war.
    1937 *Blasting and Bombardiering*, pt.5, 'Toward an Art-Less Society'.

74 'The Art of Being Ruled' might be described from some points of view as an infernal Utopia.
    1950 *Rude Assignment*, ch.31.

75 An account...of the decadence occupying the trough between the two world wars introduces us to a moronic inferno of insipidity and decay.
    1950 *Rude Assignment*, ch.31.

LeWitt, Sol 1928–2007

US artist, one of the developers of the branch of Conceptual art referred to as 'Minimalism'.

76 In Conceptual art the idea or concept is the most important aspect of the work...all planning and decisions are made beforehand and the execution is a perfunctory affair. The idea becomes the machine that makes the art.
    1967 'Paragraphs on Conceptual Art', in *Artforum*, summer.

77 One usually understands the art of the past by applying the conventions of the present thus misunderstanding the art of the past.
    1969 'Sentences on Conceptual Art', in *Art-Language*, vol.1, no.1, May.

Lewontin, Richard Charles 1929–

US evolutionary biologist, geneticist and writer, Professor of Zoology at Harvard.

Leybourne

78 It is characteristic of the design of scientific research that exquisite attention is devoted to methodological problems that can be solved, while the pretense is made that the ones that cannot be solved are really nothing to worry about.
1995 'Sex, Lies, and Social Science', in the *New York Review of Books*, 20 Apr.

79 The social scientist is in a difficult, if not impossible position. On the one hand there is the temptation to see all of society as one's autobiography writ large, surely not the path to general truth. On the other hand, there is the attempt to be general and objective by pretending that one knows nothing about the experience of being human, forcing the investigator to pretend that people usually know and tell the truth about important issues, when we all know from our own lives how impossible that is.
1995 'Sex, Lies, and Social Science', in the *New York Review of Books*, 20 Apr.

Leybourne, George *pseudonym of* Joseph Saunders 1842-84

English singer, entertainer and songwriter, a star of the Victorian music-hall.

80 O, he flies through the air with the greatest of ease,
This daring young man on the flying trapeze.
1868 'The Daring Young Man on the Flying Trapeze'.

Lezama Lima, José 1910-76

Cuban poet, novelist and essayist. His autobiographical novel *Paradiso* (1966) is considered his masterpiece, and he is the key figure of Cuban neo-Baroque literature.

81 *Más que una costumbre, parece como un conjuro para una divinidad que todos desconocemos, que al reunirse varios cubanos...se permanece en un silencio de suspensión, hasta que se oye una voz cualquiera que dice o canta algo, que no tiene relación con la convocatoria para la reunión.*
Rather than custom, it feels more like an invocation to an unknown deity when Cubans get together...they hold a suspenseful silence until any voice is heard saying or singing something that has nothing to do with the purpose of the meeting.
1966 *Paradiso*, ch.3.

Li Po 701-62

Chinese poet, patronized by Emperor Ming Huang until banished from the court. He is said to have drowned after falling intoxicated from a barge, in an attempt to embrace the moon's reflection in the water.

82 Since Life is but a Dream,
Why toil to no avail?
c.750 'A Homily on Ideals in Life, Uttered in Springtime on Rising from a Drunken Slumber', collected in *A Golden Treasury of Chinese Poetry* (translated by John Turner, 1967).

Liberace *pseudonym of* Wladziu Valentino Liberace 1919-87

US pianist and entertainer, renowned for his flamboyant lifestyle.

83 What you said hurt me very much. I cried all the way to the bank.
1973 Responding to a hostile critic. *Autobiography*.

Liberman, Alexander 1912-99

Russian-born US artist and editor, artistic director of Vogue (1943-62). His works include *Olympic Iliad* (1984) and *Faith* (1987). He published *The Artist in his Studio* (1960).

84 All art is solitary and the studio is a torture area.
1979 In the *New York Times*, 13 May.

Lichtenberg, Georg Christoph 1742-99

German scientist and philosopher, a lecturer at the University of Göttingen. His philosophical reputation rests on his aphorisms, collected in notebooks throughout his adult life.

85 Every man also has his moral backside which he refrains from showing unless he has to and keeps covered as long as possible with the trousers of decorum.
c.1770 *Aphorisms*, Notebook B (translated by R J Hollingdale, 1990).

86 If an angel were ever to tell us anything of his philosophy I believe many propositions would sound like 2 times 2 equals 13.
c.1770 *Aphorisms*, Notebook B (translated by R J Hollingdale, 1990).

87 When a book and a head collide and a hollow sound is heard, must it always have come from the book?
c.1773-1775 *Aphorisms*, Notebook D (translated by R J Hollingdale, 1990).

88 What they call 'heart' lies much lower than the fourth waistcoat button.
c.1776-1779 *Aphorisms*, Notebook F (translated by R J Hollingdale, 1990).

89 It is almost impossible to bear the torch of truth through a crowd without singeing someone's beard.
c.1779-1783 *Aphorisms*, Notebook G (translated by R J Hollingdale, 1990).

90 To err is human also in so far as the animals seldom or never err, or at least only the cleverest of them do so.
c.1779-1783 *Aphorisms*, Notebook G (translated by R J Hollingdale, 1990).

91 Once he has stolen his 100,100 thalers a rogue can walk through the world an honest man.
c.1784-1788 *Aphorisms*, Notebook H (translated by R J Hollingdale, 1990).

92 A golden rule: we must judge men, not by their opinions, but by what their opinions make of them.
c.1791 *Aphorisms*, Notebook J (translated by R J Hollingdale, 1990).

93 Doubt everything at least once, even the proposition that two times two equals four.
c.1796 *Aphorisms*, Notebook K (translated by R J Hollingdale, 1990).

Lichtenstein, Roy 1923-97

US painter, a key figure of Pop Art. He moved from Abstract Expressionism in the 1950s to illustrations from popular magazines and cartoon strips, duplicating the dots of newspaper reproduction in colourful, large-scale works.

94 Paintings are Rorschach ink blots. They are what you want them to be.
1993 In *The Times*, 27 Mar.

Liebermann, Max 1847-1935

German painter and graphic artist. His early works are open-air studies and sentimental scenes of humble life, and he later found a more colourful, romantic style, influenced by Impressionism.

95 The art of drawing is the art of omission.
   Quoted in Paul Klee *On Modern Art* (1979).

Liebman, David 1946–
US jazz saxophonist, highly regarded as a performer and teacher.

96 A jazz performance centers upon the process of creation. The final objective is not only the finished product, but the path and process taken towards it.
   1988 *Self-Portrait of a Jazz-Artist*, ch.3.

Ligne, Charles Joseph, Prince de 1735–1814
Belgian soldier and man of letters, who served in the Seven Year's War (1756–63) and the Russo-Turkish war (1787–93). A skilful diplomat and royal favourite, he also wrote extensively.

97 *Le congrès ne marche pas, il danse.*
   The Congress makes no progress; it dances.
   1814 On the Congress of Vienna (1814–15). Quoted in Auguste de la Garde-Chambonas *Souvenirs du Congrès de Vienne, 1814–1815* (1820), ch.1.

98 One could forgive the fiend for becoming a torrent, but to become an earthquake was really too much.
   1814 Of Napoleon I. Attributed.

Lillie, Beatrice Gladys *stage-name of* Constance Sylvia Munston, Lady Peel 1898–1989
Canadian-born actress. A star of light comedy and revue, she married Sir Robert Peel in 1920 and published an autobiography, *Every Other Inch a Lady* (1973).

99 Heard there was a party. Came.
   Explaining her presence after staggering to the nearest house, that of film actor John Gilbert, when she was involved in a car accident in Hollywood. Attributed.

Lillo, George 1693–1739
English dramatist and jeweller, of Dutch extraction. His seven plays were among the first to put middle-class rather than royal characters on the English stage.

1 There's sure no passion in the human soul,
   But finds its food in music.
   1736 *Fatal Curiosity*, act 1, sc.2.

Lin Yutang 1895–1976
Chinese author and philologist. He lived mainly in the US and was Chancellor of Singapore University (1954–5). He is best known for his novels and essays on Chinese culture and wisdom.

2 All women's dresses, in every age and country, are merely variations on the eternal struggle between the admitted desire to dress and the unadmitted desire to undress.
   1945 In the *Ladies Home Journal*.

Lincoln, Abraham 1809–65
US Republican statesman, 16th President (1861–5) and opponent of slavery. In the Civil War he defined the issue in terms of national integrity, not anti-slavery, but proclaimed freedom for all slaves in areas of rebellion. He was shot at Ford's Theatre, Washington, by John Wilkes Booth, an actor, and he died next morning.

3 No man is good enough to govern another man without that other's consent.
   1854 Speech, Peoria, 16 Oct.

4 'A house divided against itself cannot stand': I believe that this Government cannot endure permanently half-slave and half-free. I do not expect the Union to be dissolved. I do not expect the house to fall—but I do expect it will cease to be divided. It will become all one thing, or all the other.
   1858 Speech, Springfield, 16 Jun.

5 You can fool some of the people some of the time, and some of the people all the time, but you cannot fool all the people all of the time.
   1858 Speech, Clinton, 8 Sep.

6 The patent system…added the fuel of *interest* to the *fire* of genius.
   1859 Collected in Roy B Basler (ed) *Collected Works* (1953).

7 What is conservatism? Is it not adherence to the old and tried, against the new and untried?
   1860 Speech, New York, 27 Feb.

8 Let us have faith that right makes might; and in that faith let us to the end dare to do our duty as we understand it.
   1860 Speech, New York, 27 Feb.

9 Four score and seven years ago our fathers brought forth upon this continent a new nation, conceived in liberty and dedicated to the proposition that all men are created equal…we here highly resolve that the dead shall not have died in vain; that this nation, under God, shall have a new birth of freedom; and that government of the people, by the people, and for the people, shall not perish from the earth.
   1863 Dedication address, Gettysburg National Cemetery, 19 Nov.

10 The brave men, living and dead, who struggled here, have consecrated [this ground], far above our poor power to add or detract. The world will little note, nor long remember what we say here, but it can never forget what they did here.
   1863 Dedication address, Gettysburg National Cemetery, 19 Nov.

11 With malice toward none, with charity for all, with firmness in the right, as God gives us to see the right, let us strive on to finish the work we are in, to bind up the nation's wounds, to care for him who shall have borne the battle, and for his widow and his orphan, to do all which may achieve and cherish a just and and lasting peace among ourselves, and with all nations.
   1865 Second inaugural address, 4 Mar, a month before the end of the Civil War.

Lindbergh, Anne Spencer Morrow 1906–2001
US writer, widow of the aviator Charles Augustus Lindbergh. Her works include *North to the Orient*, an account of flights with her husband (1935), and an essay collection, *Earth Shine* (1970).

12 Thoughts die and are buried in the silences between sentences.
   1980 Of the conversational style of US Secretary of State John Foster Dulles. *War Within and Without*.

Lindbergh, Charles A(ugustus) 1902–74
US aviator who made the first solo, non-stop transatlantic flight in *The Spirit of St Louis*, landing in Paris on 21 May 1927. He spoke in favour of isolationism at the beginning of World War II, but subsequently flew in combat missions.

13 I have seen the science I worshipped and the aircraft I loved, destroying the civilization I expected them to serve.
   1967 In *Time*, 26 May.

Lindsay, John Vliet 1921–2000
US politician, Mayor of New York City (1966–74).

14 You'll make the mummies dance.
   To Thomas Hoving, new director of the Metropolitan Museum of Art, who later adopted the phrase as a book title. Quoted in Thomas Hoving *Making the Mummies Dance* (1993).

Lindsay, (Nicholas) Vachel 1879–1931
US poet. He functioned for a time almost as a travelling troubadour across the US, trading his incantatory verses for hospitality. He suffered serious depression in later years, and committed suicide.

15 Booth led boldly with his big brass drum—
   (Are you washed in the blood of the Lamb?)
   The saints smiled gravely and they said 'He's come.'
   1913 *General Booth Enters Into Heaven*, 'General Booth Enters Into Heaven'.

16 Drabs from the alleyways and drug fiends pale—
   Minds still passion-ridden, soul-power frail:—
   Vermin-eaten saints with moldy breath,
   Unwashed legions with the ways of Death—
   (Are you washed in the blood of the Lamb?)
   1913 *General Booth Enters Into Heaven*, 'General Booth Enters Into Heaven'.

17 Booth died blind and still by faith he trod,
   Eyes still dazzled by the ways of God.
   1913 *General Booth Enters Into Heaven*, 'General Booth Enters Into Heaven'.

18 Then I saw the Congo, creeping through the black,
   Cutting through the forest with a golden track.
   1914 *The Congo and Other Poems*, 'The Congo', pt.1.

19 Mumbo-Jumbo is dead in the jungle.
   1914 *The Congo and Other Poems*, 'The Congo', pt.3.

20 It is portentous, and a thing of state
   That here at midnight, in our little town
   A mourning figure walks, and will not rest,
   Near the old courthouse pacing up and down.
   1914 *The Congo and Other Poems*, 'Abraham Lincoln Walks At Midnight'.

21 And who will bring white peace
   That he may sleep upon his hill again?
   1914 *The Congo and Other Poems*, 'Abraham Lincoln Walks At Midnight'.

22 The flower-fed buffalos of the spring
   In the days of long ago,
   Ranged where the locomotives sing
   And the prairie flowers lie low.
   1926 *Going to the Stars*, 'The Flower-Fed Buffaloes'.

23 They gore no more, they bellow no more,
   They trundle around the hills no more:—
   With the Blackfeet, lying low,
   With the Pawnees, lying low,
   Lying low.
   1926 *Going to the Stars*, 'The Flower-Fed Buffaloes'.

Linklater, Eric Robert 1889–1974
Scottish journalist and writer, born in Wales. While in the US (1928–30) he wrote *Poet's Pub* (1929), the first of a series of satirical novels which include *Juan in America* (1931) and *Private Angelo* (1946). Other works include books for children, such as *The Wind on the Moon* (1944), plays and memoirs.

24 All I've got against it is that it takes you so far from the club house.
   1929 Of golf. *Poet's Pub*, ch.3.

25 Authors and uncaptured criminals…are the only people free from routine.
   1929 *Poet's Pub*, ch.23.

26 With a heavy step Sir Matthew left the room and spent the morning designing mausoleums for his enemies.
   1931 *Juan in America*, prologue.

27 It is notorious that we speak no more than half-truths in our ordinary conversation, and even a soliloquy is likely to be affected by the apprehension that walls have ears.
   1931 *Juan in America*, bk.2, pt.4.

28 She looks like a million dollars, but she only knows a hundred and twenty words and she's only got two ideas in her head. The other one's hats.
   1931 *Juan in America*, bk.2, pt.5.

29 There won't be any revolution in America… The people are all too clean. They spend all their time changing their shorts and washing themselves. You can't feel fierce and revolutionary in a bathroom.
   1931 Isadore. *Juan in America*, bk.5, pt.3.

30 I dislike burdens…and at my back I often hear Time's winged chariot changing gear.
   1937 Juan. *Juan in China*, 'End-Piece'.
   ▶ See Marvell 577:91.

31 Wanting to know an author because you like his books is like wanting to know a goose because you like pâté.
   Quoted by Kenneth Murphy in the *Washington Post*, 27 Nov 1994.

Linnaeus, Carolus 1707–78
Swedish botanist and taxonomist, the founder of modern scientific classification of plants and animals.

32 Nature does not make jumps.
   1750 *Philosophia Botanica*, no.77.

33 Minerals grow, plants grow and live, animals grow and live and feel.
   'Systema Naturae', collected in E A Hackel *Generelle Morphologie* (1866).

Lippard, Lucy 1937–
US art critic and feminist.

34 The New York Pop artists are often asked whether or not they like their subjects. This, as Dorothy Seckler has noted, is as irrelevant as asking whether Cézanne liked apples, Géricault corpses, or Picasso guitars.
   1966 *Pop Art*.

Lippmann, Walter 1899–1974
US journalist, a columnist with the New York *Herald Tribune*, awarded a Pulitzer Prize for international reporting (1962). He also wrote *Public Opinion* (1922) and *The Cold War* (1947).

35 The present crisis of Western democracy is a crisis in journalism.
   1920 *Liberty and the News*, 'Journalism and the Higher Law'.

36 There can be no higher law in journalism than to tell the truth and shame the devil.
1920 *Liberty and the News*, 'Journalism and the Higher Law'.
▶ See Shakespeare 771:49.

37 The news of the day as it reaches the newspaper office is an incredible medley of fact, propaganda, rumor, suspicion, clues, hopes, and fears, and the task of selecting and ordering that news is one of the truly sacred and priestly offices in a democracy. For the newspaper is in all literalness the bible of democracy, the book out of which a people determines its conduct.
1920 *Liberty and the News*, 'What Modern Liberty Means'.

38 Newspapers necessarily and inevitably reflect, and therefore, in greater or lesser measure, intensify, the defective organization of public opinion.
1922 *Public Opinion*, ch.1.

39 Usually it is the stereotyped shape assumed by an event at an obvious place that uncovers the run of the news.
1922 *Public Opinion*, ch.23.

40 The news is not a mirror of social conditions, but the report of an aspect that has obtruded itself.
1922 *Public Opinion*, ch.23.

41 The function of news is to signalize an event, the function of truth is to bring to light the hidden facts, to set them into relation with each other, and make a picture of reality on which men can act. Only at those points, where social conditions take recognizable and measurable shape, do the body of truth and the body of news coincide.
1922 *Public Opinion*, ch.23.

42 Successful politicians…are insecure and intimidated men. They advance politically only as they placate, appease, bribe, seduce, bamboozle, or otherwise manage to manipulate the demanding and threatening elements in their constituencies.
1955 *The Public Philosophy*, ch.2, sect.4.

43 The public interest may be presumed to be what men would choose if they saw clearly, thought rationally, acted disinterestedly and benevolently.
1955 *The Public Philosophy*, ch.4.

Lispector, Clarice 1925–77

Brazilian novelist, born in the Ukraine. Her artistic vision transcends time and place, and her characters (often female) are only incidentally modern or Brazilian.

44 *Dessa civilização só pode sair quem tem como função especial a de sair: a um cientista é dada a licença, a um padre é dada a permissão. Mas não a uma mulher que nem sequer tem as garantias de um título.*
Only he whose special function is departure can depart from that civilization: a scientist is given license, a priest is given permission. But these are not given to a woman who does not even have the guarantee of a title.
1964 *A Paixão Segundo G.H.* (*The Passion According to G.H.*).

45 *O bom era ter uma inteligência e não entender. Era uma bênção estranha como a de ter loucura sem ser doida. Era um desinteresse manso em relação às coisas ditas do intelecto, uma doçura de estupidez.*
What was good was to have intelligence and yet not understand. It was a strange blessing like experiencing madness without being mad. It was a gentle lack of interest with respect to the so-called things of the intellect, a sweet stupidity.
1969 *Uma Aprendizagem ou O Livro dos Prazeres*, 'Luminescência' (translated as *An Apprenticeship or The Book of Delights*, 1986).

Liszt, Franz 1811–86

Hungarian composer and pianist. An acclaimed technical and lyrical player, his works include symphonic poems, sacred works, masses and vocal and piano works in which he often experimented with new musical forms.

46 *Ich kann warten.*
I can wait.
When it was suggested to him that his music was being neglected. Quoted in F Lamond *Memoirs* (1949).

Littlewood, John Edensor 1885–1977

English mathematician, whose research included the distribution of prime numbers and ballistics (in World War I). Depite a severe nervous affliction, he continued working into old age. He published the popular *Mathematician's Miscellany* (1953).

47 They are not clever school boys or scholarship candidates, but 'Fellows of another college'.
1953 Of the ancient Greeks. *A Mathematician's Miscellany*.

Lively, Penelope (Margaret) 1933–

English writer. She is best known as a novelist, and has also written a memoir of her early childhood in Egypt, children's books, and an introduction to landscape history.

48 One never, of course, knows what people in portraits are thinking.
1982 *Next to Nature, Art*, ch.10.

49 Wars are fought by children—conceived by their mad demonic elders, and fought by boys.
1987 *Moon Tiger*, ch.8.

50 I believe that the experience of childhood is irretrievable. All that remains, for any of us, is a handful of brilliant frozen moments, already dangerously distorted by the wisdoms of maturity.
1994 *Oleander, Jacaranda*, preface.

51 All habits are geared towards the linear, the sequential, but memory refuses such orderliness.
1994 *Oleander, Jacaranda*, ch.3.

52 Literature has a lot to answer for, where concepts of the countryside are concerned.
2001 *A House Unlocked*.

53 There's a fearful term that's in fashion at the moment—closure. People apparently believe it is desirable and attainable.
2011 *How It All Began*.

54 It seems to me that anyone whose library consists of a Kindle lying on a table is some sort of bloodless nerd.
Attributed.

Livingstone, Dr David 1813–73

Scottish missionary, doctor and explorer. He devoted his life to fighting the Portuguese slave trade, and to establishing settlements for missions in central Africa. He also explored widely, discovering Lakes Ngami, Shirwa and Nyasa and exploring the course of the Zaire River.

55 The mere animal pleasure of travelling in a wild unexplored country is also great... The effect of travel on a man whose heart is in the right place is that the mind is made more self-reliant: it becomes more confident of its own resources—there is greater presence of mind... The sweat of one's brow is no longer a curse when one works for God: it proves a tonic to the system, and actually a blessing. No one can truly appreciate the charm of repose unless he has undergone severe exertion.
Collected in H Waller (ed) *The Last Journals of David Livingstone in Central Africa; continued by a narrative of his last moments and sufferings, obtained from his faithful servants, Chuma and Susi* (1874).

Livingstone, Ken 1945–

English Labour politician. He was leader of the Greater London Council from 1981 to 1986, and in 2000 was elected to the newly created post of Mayor of London.

56 The problem is that many MPs never see the London that exists beyond the wine bars and brothels of Westminster.
1987 In *The Times*, 19 Feb.

57 I feel like Galileo going before the Inquisition to explain that the Sun doesn't revolve around the Earth. I hope I have more success.
1999 Before his interview for selection as Labour's nominee for Mayor of London.

58 I've met serial killers and professional assassins and nobody scared me as much as Mrs T.
2000 On Margaret Thatcher. In *The Times*, 7 Mar.

59 Every year the international finance system kills more people than the Second World War. But at least Hitler was mad, you know.
2000 In the *Sunday Times*, 'Talking Heads', 16 Apr.

60 In this city three hundred languages are spoken and the people that speak them live side by side in harmony. This city typifies what I believe is the future of the human race and a future where we grow together and we share and we learn from each other.
2005 Press conference, 8 Jul.

Livy full name Titus Livius 59 BC–AD 17

Roman historian, admitted to the court of Augustus c.29 BC. His *Ab urbe condita libri* (History of Rome from its Foundations) consisted of 142 books, of which only parts have survived.

61 *Vae victis!*
Down with the defeated!
Attributed to the Gallic King Brennus, who had captured Rome in 390 BC, bk.5, ch.48.

62 *Dum Romae consulitur, Saguntum expugnatur.*
While they were deliberating in Rome, Saguntum was captured.
Oral tradition deriving from Livy's description of the siege and capture of the Spanish city of Saguntum by the Carthaginians in 219 BC. The Roman senate deliberated endlessly before deciding to take action when it was already too late. Cf. Livy 21.7.1 'Dum ea Romani parant consultantque, iam Saguntum summa vi oppugnabatur'.

Llewellyn, Richard originally Richard Doyle Vivian Llewellyn Lloyd 1907–83

Welsh author, who made his name with *How Green was my Valley* (1939), set in a Welsh mining village and later filmed.

63 How Green was my Valley.
1939 Title of book.

Lloyd, Henry Demarest 1847–1903

US journalist, financial writer and editor with the *Chicago Tribune* (1872–85). He crusaded against monopoly, and was a pioneer 'muckraker' journalist.

64 Monopoly is Business at the end of its journey.
1894 *Wealth against Commonwealth*, ch.1.

Lloyd, John 1946–

British journalist and author.

65 There are few hauteurs higher than foreign reporters' disdain for those who have not shared their craft.
2004 *What the Media Are Doing to Our Politics*.

Lloyd, Marie stage-name of Matilda Alice Victoria Wood 1870–1922

English singer. Known simply as 'Our Marie', she became a major star of music hall and pantomime, notorious for her suggestive delivery of such songs as 'A Little of What You Fancy Does You Good'.

66 If we didn't laugh at him, we'd cry our eyes out.
c.1891 Of the singer and comedian Dan Leno, who died insane in 1904. Attributed.

Lloyd George (of Dwyfor), David, 1st Earl 1863–1945

British Liberal Prime Minister. Elected MP for Caernarvon in 1890. President of the Board of Trade 1905–8 and Chancellor of the Exchequer 1905–15. Secretary of War in 1916 and coalition Prime Minister in the same year. After the war, his downfall came when he conceded the Irish Free State in 1921.

67 You cannot feed the hungry on statistics.
1904 Speech advocating tariff reform.

68 This is the trusty mastiff that is to watch over our interests, but which runs away at the first snarl of the trade unions. A mastiff? It is the right honourable gentleman's poodle. It fetches and carries for him. It barks for him. It bites anybody that he sets it on.
1908 Speech to the House of Commons, 21 Dec, referring to the obstructive Conservative majority in the House of Lords exploited by the then Tory leader, A J Balfour.

69 There are no credentials. They do not even need a medical certificate. They need not be sound either in body or mind. They only require a certificate of birth—just to prove that they were the first of the litter. You would not choose a spaniel on those principles.
1909 Referring to the House of Lords, Budget speech, Mar.

70 We are placing the burdens on the broadest shoulders. I made up my mind that, in forming the Budget, no cupboard should be barer, no lot should be harder to bear.
1909 Speech on the People's Budget, London, 30 Jul.

71 Four spectres haunt the poor—old age, accident, sickness, and unemployment. We are going to exorcise them. We are going to drive hunger from the hearth. We mean to banish the workhouse from the horizon of every workman in the land.
1910 Speech, Reading, 1 Jan.

72 We have been too comfortable and too indulgent—many, perhaps, too selfish—and the stern hand of fate has scoured us to an elevation where we can see the great everlasting things that matter for a nation; the great peaks we had forgotten, of honour, duty, patriotism, and, clad in glittering white, the great pinnacle of sacrifice pointing like a rugged finger to Heaven. We shall descend into the valleys again, but as long as men and women of this generation last, they will carry in their hearts the image of those great mountain peaks, whose foundations are not shaken, though Europe rock and sway in the convulsions of a great war.
1914 Speech, London, 19 Sep.

73 By the test of our faith the highest standard of civilization is the readiness to sacrifice for others.
1914 Speech in Queen's Hall, London, 21 Sep.

74 It is a great war for the emancipation of Europe from the thralldom of a military caste which has thrown its shadows upon two generations of men, and is now plunging the world into a welter of bloodshed and death.
1914 Speech in Queen's Hall, London, 21 Sep.

75 At eleven o'clock this morning came to an end the cruellest and most terrible war that has ever scourged mankind. I hope we may say that thus, this fateful morning, came to an end all wars.
1918 Speech in the House of Commons, 11 Nov, announcing the armistice.

76 What is our task? To make Britain a fit country for heroes to live in.
1918 Speech at Wolverhampton, Nov, at the end of World War I.

77 Give it because it is right. Give it because it is just. Give it because it is good for Ireland and good for the United Kingdom. Give it because it brings peace and good will, but do not give it because you are bullied by assassins.
1920 Speech on an Irish settlement, Caernarvon, 9 Oct.

78 Every man has a House of Lords in his own head. Fears, prejudices, misconceptions—those are the peers, and they are hereditary.
1927 Speech, Cambridge.

79 It is the old trouble—too late in dealing with Czechoslovakia, too late with Poland, and certainly too late with Finland. It is always too late, or too little, or both. That is the road to disaster.
1940 House of Commons, 13 Mar.

80 A good lord mayor of Birmingham in a lean year.
Of Neville Chamberlain. Quoted in A J P Taylor *From the Boer War to the Cold War: Essays on Twentieth-Century Europe* (1995), p.363

81 A politician is a person with whose politics you don't agree; if you agree with him, he is a statesman.
Attributed.

Lloyd Webber, Julian 1951–
English cellist.

82 Cello players, like other great athletes, must keep their fingers exercised.
2001 In the *Observer*, 30 Dec.

Loach, Ken 1936–
English film-maker. As well as television work, he has directed such films as *Kes* (1969), *Raining Stones* (1993), *The Wind That Shakes the Barley* (2006) and *Jimmy's Hall* (2014).

83 If the cinema is any kind of force for social change, then it's a force for the bad, because most films are about one guy with a gun solving a problem.
1998 In *Cineaste*, Winter issue.

Lochhead, Liz 1947–
Scottish poet and dramatist.

84 Sexual Etiquette
Sexual Etiquette
How to get more of it
and get more out of what you get.
2003 *The Colours of Black & White: Poems 1984–2000*, 'Sexual Etiquette'.

Locke, John 1632–1704
English philosopher, a formative influence on British Empiricism and on theories of liberal democracy. His most important work is the *Essay Concerning Human Understanding*, published in 1690. His treatises *On Government* (1690) were also influential, inspiring both American and French revolutionaries.

85 Government has no other end but the preservation of property.
1681 *Second Treatise on Civil Government* (published anonymously 1690).

86 Every man has a property in his person. This no body has any right to but himself. The labour of his body, and the work of his hands, we may say, are properly his.
1681 *Second Treatise on Civil Government* (published anonymously 1690).

87 Freedom of men under government is to have a standing rule to live by, common to every one of that society, and made by the legislative power vested in it; a liberty to follow my own will in all things where the rule prescribes not, and not to be subject to the inconstant, uncertain, unknown, arbitrary rule of another man.
1681 *Second Treatise on Civil Government* (published anonymously 1690).

88 It is ambition enough to be employed as an under-labourer in clearing ground a little, and removing some of the rubbish that lies in the way to knowledge.
1690 *Essay Concerning Human Understanding*, 'Epistle to the Reader'.

89 Let us then suppose the mind to be, as we say, white paper, void of all characters, without any ideas; how comes it to be furnished? Whence comes it by that vast store which the busy and boundless fancy of man has painted on it with an almost endless variety? Whence has it all the materials of reason and knowledge? To this I answer, in one word, from *experience*.
1690 *Essay Concerning Human Understanding*, bk.2, pt.1, section 2.

90 These two, I say, viz. external material things, as the objects of SENSATION, and the operations of our own minds within, as the objects of REFLECTION, are to me the only originals from whence all our ideas take their beginnings.
1690 *Essay Concerning Human Understanding*, bk.2, pt.1, section 4.

91 For should the soul of a prince enter and inform the body of a cobbler, as soon as deserted by his own soul, everyone sees he would be the same *person* with the

prince, accountable only for the prince's actions; but who would say it was the same *man*?
1690 *Essay Concerning Human Understanding*, bk.2, pt.27, section 15.

92 A sound mind in a sound body is a short but full description of a happy state in this world. He that has those two, has little more to wish for; and he that wants either of them will be little the better for anything else.
1693 *Some Thoughts Concerning Education*, opening words.
▶ See Juvenal 471:58.

Lodge, David John 1935–
English novelist, playwright and critic. His best-known novels are set in academic circles, such as *Changing Places* (1975). Other works include *Thinks* (2001) and *Author, Author: A Novel* (2004).

93 Literature is mostly about having sex and not much about having children. Life is the other way round.
1965 *The British Museum is Falling Down*, ch.4.

94 The British, he thought, must be gluttons for satire: even the weather forecast seemed to be some kind of spoof, predicting every possible combination of weather for the next twenty-four hours without actually committing itself to anything specific.
1975 *Changing Places*, ch.2.

95 He understood...Walt Whitman, who laid end to end words never seen in each other's company before outside of a dictionary, and Herman Melville who split the atom of the traditional novel in the effort to make whaling a universal metaphor.
1975 *Changing Places*, ch.5.

96 Conversation is like playing tennis with a ball made of Krazy Putty that keeps coming back over the net in a different shape.
1984 *Small World*, pt.1, ch.1.

97 The world is a global campus, Hilary, you'd better believe it. The American Express card has replaced the library pass.
1984 *Small World*, pt.1, ch.2.

98 I gave up screwing around a long time ago. I came to the conclusion that sex is a sublimation of the work instinct.
1984 *Small World*, pt.1, ch.2.

99 Another law of academic life: *it is impossible to be excessive in flattery of one's peers.*
1984 *Small World*, pt.3, ch.1.

1 As to our universities, I've come to the conclusion that they are élitist where they should be egalitarian, and egalitarian where they should be élitist.
1988 *Nice Work*, pt.5, ch.4.

Lodge, Henry Cabot 1850–1924
US Republican politician and Senator.

2 The businessman dealing with a large political question is really a painful sight. It does seem to me that businessmen, with a few exceptions, are worse when they come to deal with politics than men of any other class.
1902 Letter to Theodore Roosevelt, 20 Oct.

Loengard, John Borg 1934–
US photographer, picture editor of *Life* (1973–87). His works include *Pictures Under Discussion* (1987) and many essays in *Life*.

3 A bit like God confessing he'd never gotten the hang of the thunderstorms.
1987 On Henri Cartier-Bresson's remark that he was only good at casual photography. In *Life*, Dec.

Lofthouse, Nat 1925–2011
English footballer. A star centre-forward with Bolton Wanderers in the 1950s, he led the team to victory in the 1958 FA Cup final and also scored 30 goals in 33 internationals for England.

4 There was plenty of fellers who would kick your bollocks off. The difference was that at the end they'd shake your hand and help you look for them.
Comparing football in the 1950s with that of later eras. Quoted in Peter Ball and Phil Shaw *The Book of Football Quotations* (1989).

Logau, Friedrich von 1605–55
German writer, author of epigrams.

5 *Gottes Mühlen mahlen langsam, mahlen aber trefflich klein;*
Ob aus Langmut Er sich säumet, bringt mit Schärf' Er alles ein.
Though the mills of God grind slowly, yet they grind exceeding small;
Though with patience He stands waiting, with exactness grinds He all.
1654 *Sinngedichte*, bk.3, pt.2, no.24 (translated as *Retribution* by Henry Wadsworth Longfellow). Logau used an anonymous classical source for the first line.

Lombardi, Vince(nt Thomas) 1913–70
US American football coach.

6 Winning isn't everything; it's the only thing.
Attributed. His exact words were 'Winning isn't everything, but making the effort is'. Some sources attribute the saying to Red Sanders, coach of the University of California team.

7 If you aren't fired with enthusiasm, you'll be fired with enthusiasm.
Attributed.

8 Once you learn to quit, it becomes a habit.
Attributed.

London, Jack (John Griffith) 1876–1916
US writer. His books, such as *The Call of the Wild* (1903) and *White Fang* (1907), reflect his experiences as a sailor, tramp, gold miner in the Klondike and alcoholic. He also wrote a futuristic political novel *The Iron Heel* (1907).

9 The Call of the Wild.
1903 Title of book.

10 In an English ship, they say, it is poor grub, poor pay, and easy work; in an American ship, good grub, good pay, and hard work. And this is applicable to the working populations of both countries.
1903 *The People of the Abyss*, ch.20.

Longden, Robert Paton 1903–40
English classical scholar and historian, writer of limericks on famous figures of Roman history.

11 The Emperor Caligula
's Habits were somewhat irrigula.

When he sat down to lunch
He got drunk at onch.
Quoted and first published in Arnold Silcock *Verse and Worse* (1952), 'Potted Biography'.

12 The Emperor Claudius
Used to keep a baudius.
When he got more criminal
He ran a den on the Viminal.
1952 Quoted and first published in Arnold Silcock, *Verse and Worse* (1952), 'Potted Biography'.

Longfellow, Henry Wadsworth 1807–82

US poet, Professor of Modern Languages and Literature at Harvard for nearly 18 years. His narrative skill made him one of the most popular poets of his day. His best-known poems include *Evangeline* (1847), *Hiawatha* (1855) and *Tales of a Wayside Inn* (1863).

13 Music is the universal language of mankind.
1835 *Outre Mer*. Also attributed to Christopher North (1865–1954).

14 Life is real, life is earnest!
And the grave is not its goal;
Dust thou art, to dust returnest,
Was not spoken of the soul.
1838 'A Psalm of Life'. In *Knickerbocker or New York Monthly Magazine*, Sep. Collected in *Voices of the Night* (1839).

15 Art is long, and time is fleeting,
And our hearts, though stout and brave,
Still, like muffled drums, are beating
Funeral marches to the grave.
1838 'A Psalm of Life', stanza 4. In *Knickerbocker or New York Monthly Magazine*, Sep. Collected in *Voices of the Night* (1839).

16 Lives of great men all remind us
We can make our lives sublime,
And departing, leave behind us
Footprints on the sands of time.
1838 'A Psalm of Life', stanza 7. In *Knickerbocker or New York Monthly Magazine*, Sep. Collected in *Voices of the Night* (1839).

17 Under a spreading chestnut-tree
The village smithy stands;
The smith a mighty man is he,
With large and sinewy hands;
And the muscles of his brawny arms
Are strong as iron bands.
1840 'The Village Blacksmith', stanza 1. Collected in *Ballads and other Poems* (1841).

18 His brow is wet with honest sweat,
He earns whate'er he can,
And looks the whole world in the face,
For he owes not any man.
1840 'The Village Blacksmith', stanza 2. Collected in *Ballads and other Poems* (1841).

19 Each morning sees some task begin,
Each evening sees it close;
Something attempted, something done,
Has earned a night's repose.
1840 'The Village Blacksmith', stanza 7. Collected in *Ballads and other Poems* (1841).

20 It was the schooner Hesperus,
That sailed the wintry sea.
1841 *Ballads and other Poems*, 'The wreck of the Hesperus'.

21 The shades of night were falling fast,
As through an Alpine village passed
A youth, who bore, 'mid snow and ice,
A banner with a strange device,
Excelsior!
1841 'Excelsior'.

22 I like that ancient Saxon phrase, which calls,
The burial-ground God's-Acre.
1841 'God's-Acre'.

23 And the night shall be filled with music,
And the cares, that infest the day,
Shall fold up their tents like Arabs,
And as silently steal away.
1844 *The Waif*, 'The Day Is Done', stanza 11.
▶ See Kaufman 474:38.

24 I shot an arrow into the air,
It fell to earth, I knew not where.
1845 'The Arrow and the Song'.

25 This is the forest primeval.
1847 *Evangeline*, prologue.

26 Sorrow and silence are strong, and patient endurance is godlike.
1847 *Evangeline*, pt.2, section 1.

27 Thou, too, sail on, O Ship of State!
Sail on, O UNION, strong and great!
Humanity with all its fears,
With all the hopes of future years,
Is hanging breathless on thy fate!
1849 *The Seaside and Fireside*, 'The Building of the Ship', l.377–81.

28 In the moonlight and the starlight,
Fair Nokomis bore a daughter.
And she called her name Wenonah,
As the first-born of her daughters.
1855 The naming of Hiawatha's mother. *The Song of Hiawatha*, pt.3, 'Hiawatha's Childhood'. The name is now usually spelt Winona.

29 By the shore of Gitche Gumee
By the shining Big-Sea-Water,
Stood the wigwam of Nokomis,
Daughter of the Moon, Nokomis.
Dark behind it rose the forest,
Rose the black and gloomy pine-trees,
Rose the firs with cones upon them;
Bright before it beat the water,
Beat the clear and sunny water,
Beat the shining Big-Sea-Water.
1855 *The Song of Hiawatha*, pt.3, 'Hiawatha's Childhood'.

30 From the waterfall he named her,
Minnehaha, Laughing Water.
1855 *The Song of Hiawatha*, pt.4, 'Hiawatha and Mudjekeewis'.

31 A boy's will is the wind's will,
And the thoughts of youth are long, long thoughts.
1855 'My Lost Youth', in *Putnam's Monthly Magazine*, vol.6, Aug. Collected in *The Courtship of Miles Standish and Other Poems*, 1858. In his diary Longfellow notes that these lines are from an 'old Lapland song'.

32 But ah! what once has been shall be no more!
The groaning earth in travail and in pain
Brings forth its races, but does not restore,
And the dead nations never rise again.
1855 'The Jewish Cemetery at Newport'.

33 A Lady with a Lamp shall stand
In the great history of the land,

A noble type of good,
Heroic womanhood.
1857 Of Florence Nightingale. 'Santa Filomena'.

34 Between the dark and the daylight,
When the night is beginning to lower,
Comes a pause in the day's occupations,
That is known as the Children's Hour.
1863 'The Children's Hour', stanza 1.

35 Listen, my children, and you shall hear
Of the midnight ride of Paul Revere,
On the eighteenth of April in Seventy-five.
1863 *Tales of a Wayside Inn*, pt.1, 'The Landlord's Tale: Paul Revere's Ride'.

36 Our ingress into the world
Was naked and bare;
Our progress through the world
Is trouble and care.
1872 *Tales of a Wayside Inn*, pt.2, 'The Student's Tale: The Cobbler of Hagenau'.

37 Ships that pass in the night, and speak each other in passing,
Only a signal shown and a distant voice in the darkness;
So on the ocean of life, we pass and speak one another,
Only a look and a voice, then darkness again and a silence.
1873 *Tales of a Wayside Inn*, pt.3. 'The Theologian's Tale: Elizabeth'.

38 If you would hit the mark, you must aim a little above it;
Every arrow that flies feels the attraction of earth.
1881 *Elegiac Verse*, stanza 9.

39 The men that women marry,
And why they marry them, will always be
A marvel and a mystery to the world.
1883 *Michael Angelo*, pt.1, sc.5.

40 There was a little girl
Who had a little curl
Right in the middle of her forehead;
And when she was good
She was very, very good,
But when she was bad, she was horrid.
Attributed to Longfellow by Blanch Roosevelt Tucker Macchetta in *The Home Life of Henry W. Longfellow* (1882).

Longworth, Alice Roosevelt 1884–1980

US political hostess, daughter of Theodore Roosevelt, renowned for her wit.

41 If you can't say something good about someone, sit right here by me.
Motto embroidered on a sofa pillow. Quoted in *Time*, 9 Dec 1966.

Lonsdale, Hugh Cecil Lowther, 5th Earl of 1857–1944

English sportsman. As president of the National Sporting Club, he founded and presented the 'Lonsdale belts' for boxing.

42 I have always considered that boxing really combines all the finest and highest inclinations of a man—activity, endurance, science, temper, and, last, but not least, presence of mind.
1915 Foreword in Eugene Corri *Thirty Years a Boxing Referee*.

Loos, Adolf 1870–1933

Austrian architect and design theorist, a major figure of the 'Modern Movement', whose designs reflect his rejection of ornament and an emphasis on elegant functionalism.

43 I have emerged victorious from my thirty years of struggle. I have freed mankind from superfluous ornament.
1930 *Trotzdem 1900–1930*.

44 The evolution of culture is synonymous with the removal of ornament from utilitarian objects.
1931 *Trotzdem 1900–1930*.

Loos, Anita c.1893–1981

US writer, best known for her satirical novel *Gentleman Prefer Blondes* (1925). She also wrote plays, screenplays and memoirs.

45 Gentlemen Prefer Blondes.
1925 Title of novel, and subsequently a film starring Marilyn Monroe and Jane Russell (1953).

46 So this gentleman said a girl with brains ought to do something more with them besides think.
1925 *Gentlemen Prefer Blondes*, ch.1.

47 Gentlemen always seem to remember blondes.
1925 *Gentlemen Prefer Blondes*, ch.1.

48 She said she always believed in the old adage, 'Leave them while you're looking good.'
1925 *Gentlemen Prefer Blondes*, ch.1.

49 You have got to be a Queen to get away with a hat like that.
1925 *Gentlemen Prefer Blondes*, ch.4.

50 Any girl who was a lady would not even think of having such a good time that she did not remember to hang on to her jewelry.
1925 *Gentlemen Prefer Blondes*, ch.4.

51 The Eyefull Tower is devine.
1925 *Gentlemen Prefer Blondes*, ch.4.

52 So I really think that American gentlemen are the best after all, because kissing your hand may make you feel very very good but a diamond and safire bracelet lasts forever.
1925 *Gentlemen Prefer Blondes*, ch.4.

53 Fun is fun but no girl wants to laugh all of the time.
1925 *Gentlemen Prefer Blondes*, ch.4

54 So then Dr Froyd said that all I needed was to cultivate a few inhibitions and get some sleep.
1925 *Gentlemen Prefer Blondes*, ch.5.

55 So then he said that he used to be a member of the choir himself, so who was he to cast the first rock at a girl like I.
1925 *Gentlemen Prefer Blondes*, ch.5.

56 Tallulah never bored anyone, and I consider that humanitarianism of a very high order indeed.
1968 Eulogy at Tallulah Bankhead's funeral. Reported in the *New York Times*, 17 Dec.

57 I'm furious about the Woman's Liberationists. They keep getting up on soap-boxes and proclaiming that women are brighter than men. That's true, but it should be kept very quiet or it ruins the whole racket.
Quoted in the *Observer*, 30 Dec 1973.

Lorca, Federico García 1898–1936

Spanish poet and playwright, assassinated on the order of the Nationalist Civil Governor early in the Civil War. He is best known for his gypsy songs and powerful, elemental tragedies such as *Bodas de Sangre* (1933, translated as *Blood Wedding*, 1947).

58 Verde que te quiero verde.
Verde viento. Verdes ramas.
El barco sobre la mar
y el caballo en la montaña.
Green how I love you green.
Green wind. Green boughs.
The ship on the sea
and the horse on the mountain.
1924–7 *Romance sonámbulo.*

59 Spain is the only country where death is the national spectacle.
Quoted in Colin Jarman *The Guinness Dictionary of Sports Quotations* (1990).

Loren, Sophia *pseudonym of* Sofia Scicolone 1934–

Italian actress. Her films include *El Cid* (1961) and *Two Women* (1961), for which she won an Academy Award.

60 Everything you see I owe to spaghetti.
Attributed.

Lorenz, Konrad 1903–89

Austrian zoologist and ethnologist. Lorenz studied the organization of individual animal and group behaviour patterns. He shared the 1973 Nobel prize in physiology or medicine with Karl von Frisch.

61 Überhaupt ist es für den Forscher ein guter Morgensport, täglich vor dem Frühstück eine Lieblingshypothese einzustampfen—das erhält jung.
It is a good morning exercise for a research scientist to discard a pet hypothesis every day before breakfast. It keeps him young.
1963 *Das sogenannte Böse* ('The So-Called Evil', translated by Marjorie Latzke as *On Aggression*, 1966), ch.2.

62 Man appears to be the missing link between anthropoid apes and human beings.
1965 In the *New York Times*, 11 Apr.

Louis IX *also called* St Louis 1214–70

King of France (1226–70). He led the Seventh Crusade (1248), but was defeated, imprisoned and ransomed. On his return to France (1254) he carried out reforms and encouraged the arts and literature. He began a new Crusade in 1270, but died of plague in Tunis.

63 I would rather have a Scot come from Scotland to govern the people of this kingdom well and justly, than that you should govern them ill in the sight of all the world.
1244 To his son, Louis, at Fontainebleau.

Louis XI 1423–83

King of France (1461–83). By a mixture of force and cunning, he broke the power of the nobility and by 1483 had united most of France under the Crown.

64 I have chased the English out of France more easily than my father ever did, for my father drove them out by force of arms, whereas I have driven them out with venison pies and good wine.
1475 Said after the signing of the Treaty of Picquigny, Sep.

Louis XIV *known as* the Great *or* le Roi Soleil [the Sun King] 1638–1715

King of France (1643–1715). His aggressive foreign and commercial policies and his attempt to create a Franco–Spanish Bourbon bloc led to the War of the Spanish Succession (1701–13). Although his old age saw military disaster and its financial toll, he was a model of royal absolutism and courtly brilliance.

65 Everyone knows how much trouble your meetings have caused in my State, and how many dangerous results they have had. I have learnt that you intend to continue them. I have come here expressly to forbid you to do this, which I do absolutely.
1655 Address to the Parlement of Paris, 13 Apr.

66 L'État, c'est moi.
I am the State.
1655 Address to the Parlement of Paris, 13 Apr. This is probably apocryphal.

67 Every time that I fill a high office, I make one hundred men discontented and one ungrateful.
c.1669 After the disgrace of the Duke of Lauzun. Quoted in Voltaire *Le Siècle de Louis XIV* (1751), ch.26.

68 How could God do this to me after all I have done for him?
1704 On hearing the news of the French defeat at Blenheim, Aug. Quoted in L Norton *Saint-Simon at Versailles* (1958).

69 The function of kings consists primarily of using good sense, which always comes naturally and easily. Our work is sometimes less difficult than our amusements.
Mémoires for the Instruction of the Dauphin.

Louis XVI 1754–93

King of France (1774–93), deposed during the Revolution. He was tried before the National Convention for conspiracy with foreign powers, and executed in Paris.

70 Louis XVI: Is this a revolt?
Duke of Rochefoucauld-Liancourt: No, sir, it's a revolution.
1789 Exchange after the fall of the Bastille, 14 Jul. Quoted in F Dreyfus *La Rochefoucauld-Liancourt* (1903), ch.2, section 3.

Louis XVIII *originally* Stanislas Xavier 1755–1824

King of France (from 1795). He fled to Belgium in 1791, proclaiming himself Regent for Louis XVII in 1793 and King in 1795. On the fall of Napoleon, he landed at Calais (1814) and began a severe rule, until Napoleon's return for the Hundred Days (1815). His rule was subsequently more moderate.

71 L'exactitude est la politesse des rois.
Punctuality is the politeness of kings.
Quoted in *Souvenirs de J Lafitte* (1844), bk.1, ch.3.

Louis Philippe *known as* the Citizen King 1773–1850

King of France (1830–48). Eldest son of the Duc d'Orléans, he renounced his titles and fought in the wars of the Republic, becoming 'Citizen King' after the Revolution of 1830. Demands for electoral reform led to the uprising of 1848 and his forced abdication.

72 Died, has he? Now I wonder what he meant by that.
1838 Said on the death of Talleyrand, his calculating and self-serving adviser, 18 Mar.

73 The entente cordiale.
1843 Speech, 27 Dec. Quoted in Collingham *The July Monarchy* (1988), p.320.

74 What perished in France in 1830 was not respect for a dynasty, but respect for anything.
Of the Revolution which brought him to power. Quoted in A J P Taylor *From Napoleon to the Second International* (1993).

Louis, Joe *pseudonym of* Joseph Louis Barrow 1914–81

US boxer. Known as the 'Brown Bomber', he won the world heavyweight title in 1937 and held it for a record 12 years, defending it 25 times. He retired in 1949, attempting two unsuccessful comebacks (1950–1). In all he won 68 of his 71 professional fights.

75 He can run, but he can't hide.
1941 Said during a bout against Billy Conn.

76 Everybody wants to go to heaven, but nobody wants to die.
1965 In *Sports Illustrated*, 'Scorecard', 19 Jul.

77 Every man's got to figure to get beat some time.
Quoted in Colin Jarman *The Guinness Dictionary of Sports Quotations* (1990).

78 I don't like money, actually, but it quiets my nerves.
Quoted in Colin Jarman *The Guinness Dictionary of Sports Quotations* (1990).

79 Why should I? When somebody insulted Caruso, did he sing an aria for him?
When a friend asked why he did not punch a motorist who swore at him following a minor traffic accident. Quoted in Colin Jarman *The Guinness Dictionary of Sports Quotations* (1990).

Love, James *pseudonym of* James Dance 1722–74

English actor and writer.

80 Hail Cricket! glorious, manly, British game!
First of all Sports! be first alike in fame!
1744 'Cricket: An Heroic Poem'.

Lovelace, Richard 1618–58

English Cavalier poet. Twice imprisoned (1642 and 1648–49) by the Puritans for his Royalist sympathies, he spent much of his time behind bars writing poetry, which he published in 1649 as the collection *Lucasta*.

81 When I lie tangled in her hair,
And fettered to her eye;
The Gods, that wanton in the air
Know no such liberty.
1649 *Lucasta*, 'To Althea, from Prison'.

82 Stone walls do not a prison make,
Nor iron bars a cage;
Minds innocent and quiet take
That for a hermitage;
If I have freedom in my love,
And in my soul am free;
Angels along that soar above,
Enjoy such liberty.
1649 *Lucasta*, 'To Althea, from Prison'.

83 If to be absent were to be
Away from thee;
Or that when I am gone,
You or I were alone;
Then my *Lucasta* might I crave
Pity from blust'ring wind, or swallowing wave.
1649 *Lucasta*, 'To Lucasta, Going beyond the Seas'.

84 *Amarantha* sweet and fair,
Ah braid no more that shining hair!
As my curious hand or eye,
Hovering round thee let it fly.
1649 *Lucasta*, 'To Amarantha, That She Would Dishevel Her Hair'.

85 Tell me not, Sweet, I am unkind,
That from the nunnery
Of thy chaste breast, and quiet mind,
To war and arms I fly.
1649 *Lucasta*, 'To Lucasta, Going to the Wars'.

86 I could not love thee, Dear, so much,
Loved I not honour more.
1649 *Lucasta*, 'To Lucasta, Going to the Wars'.

87 Thus did they live: Thus did they love,
Repeating only joys above;
And Angels were, but with clothes on,
Which they would put off cheerfully,
To bathe them in the galaxy,
Then gird them with the Heavenly zone.
1649 *Lucasta*, 'Love Made in the First Age'.

88 The asp doth on his feeder feed.
1649 *Lucasta*, 'A Fly Caught in a Cobweb'.

Loveless, George 1805–40

English Methodist preacher, who in 1833 organized the agricultural labourers of Tolpuddle, Dorset, into a trade union. When the men were convicted of taking illegal oaths and transported, a public outcry ensued and they were eventually pardoned.

89 If we have violated any law, it was not done intentionally. We have injured no man's reputation, character, person, or property. We were meeting together to preserve ourselves, our wives, and our children from utter degradation and starvation.
1833 Statement to the Dorchester Assizes, Mar, on behalf of the Tolpuddle martyrs.

Lovell, Sir (Alfred Charles) Bernard 1913–2012

English astronomer. He was the instigator of the funding, construction and use of the radio telescope at Jodrell Bank.

90 The fate of human civilization will depend on whether the rockets of the future carry the astronomer's telescope or a hydrogen bomb.
1959 *The Individual and the Universe*.

91 A study of history shows that civilizations that abandon the quest for knowledge are doomed to disintegration.
1972 In the *Observer*, 'Sayings of the Week', 14 May.

Lovelock, James Ephraim 1919–

English scientist, environmentalist, and futurologist. He is best known for the Gaia hypothesis, which describes the earth in terms of a living organism.

92 Unfortunately, we are a species with schizoid tendencies, and like an old lady who has to share her house with a growing and destructive group of teenagers, Gaia grows angry, and if they do not mend their ways she will evict them.
2006 *The Revenge of Gaia: Earth's Climate Crisis and the Fate of Humanity*.

93 We are no more qualified to be the stewards or developers of the Earth than are goats to be gardeners.
2006 *The Revenge of Gaia: Earth's Climate Crisis and the Fate of Humanity*.

94 Even the best democracies agree that when a major war approaches, democracy must be put on hold for the time being. I have a feeling that climate change may be an issue as severe as a war. It may be necessary to put democracy on hold for a while.
2010 In *The Guardian*, 29 Mar.

Lowe, Emily fl.1850s
Englishwoman, who travelled in Norway with her mother.

95 The only use of a gentleman in travelling is to look after the luggage.
1857 *Unprotected Females in Norway*.

Lowell, Amy 1874–1925
US poet. A descendant of James Russell Lowell, she was associated with the Imagist movement, and wrote free verse in a style she named 'unrhymed cadence'. She also wrote prose and criticism.

96 For books are more than books, they are the life
The very heart and core of ages past,
The reason why men lived and worked and died,
The essence and quintessence of their lives.
1912 'The Boston Atheneum'.

97 All books are either dreams or swords,
You can cut, or you can drug, with words.
1914 'Sword Blades and Poppy Seeds'.

98 And the softness of my body will be guarded by embrace
By each button, hook, and lace.
For the man who should loose me is dead,
Fighting with the Duke in Flanders,
In a pattern called a war.
Christ! What are patterns for?
1916 'Patterns'.

99 A man must be sacrificed now and again
To provide for the next generation of men.
1922 'A Critical Fable'.

1 I must be mad, or very tired,
When the curve of a blue bay beyond a railroad track
Is shrill and sweet to me like the sudden springing of a tune,
And the sight of a white church above thin trees in a city square
Amazes my eyes as though it were the Parthenon.
1925 'Meeting-House Hill'.

Lowell, James Russell 1819–91
US poet, essayist and diplomat. His popular satiric poems in Yankee dialect were published as *The Biglow Papers* (1848 and 1867). A lecturer at Harvard, he was also editor of the *Atlantic Monthly* and US Minister to Spain (1877–80) and Britain (1880–85).

2 It is mediocrity which makes laws and sets mantraps and spring-guns in the realm of free song, saying thus far shall you go and no further.
1843 'Elizabethan Dramatists, Omitting Shakespeare: John Webster'.

3 Once to every man and nation comes the moment to decide,
In the strife of Truth with Falsehood, for the good or evil side.
1844 'The Present Crisis', in the *Boston Courier*, 11 Dec. Collected in *Poems: Second Series*, 1848. The poem was written in the midst of the controversy over whether Texas should be annexed and slavery extended.

4 They talk about their Pilgrim blood,
Their birthright high and holy!
A mountain-stream that ends in mud
Methinks is melancholy.
1846 'An Interview with Miles Standish', stanza 11.

5 Ez fer war, I call it murder,—
There you hev it plain an' flat;
I don't want to go no furder
Than my Testyment fer that;
God hez sed so plump an' fairly,
It's ez long ez it is broad,
An' you've gut to git up airly
Ef you want to take in God.
1846 'A Letter'. In the *Boston Courier*, 17 Jun. Collected in *The Biglow Papers, First Series* (1848), no.1.

6 'Slavery's a thing thet depends on complexion,
It's God's law thet fetters on black skins don't chafe;
Ef brains wuz to settle it (horrid reflection!)
Wich of our onnable body'd be safe?'
1848 'The Debate in the Sennit', in the *Boston Courier*, 3 May, collected in *The Biglow Papers: First Series* (1848), no. 5.

7 And what is so rare as a day in June?
Then, if ever come perfect days.
1848 'The Vision of Sir Launfal', prelude.

8 There comes Poe, with his raven, like Barnaby Rudge,
Three-fifths of him genius and two-fifths sheer fudge.
1848 'A Fable for Critics'.

9 A reading machine, always wound up and going,
He mastered whatever was not worth knowing.
1848 Of a scholar. 'A Fable for Critics'.

10 Books are the bees which carry the quickening pollen from one to another mind.
1849 'Nationality in Literature', in the *North American Review*, Jul.

11 Every man feels instinctively that all the beautiful sentiments in the world weigh less than a single lovely action.
1867 'Rousseau and the Sentimentalists', in the *North American Review*, Jul.

12 The mind can weave itself warmly in the cocoon of its own thoughts, and dwell a hermit anywhere.
1869 'On a Certain Condescension in Foreigners', in the *Atlantic Monthly*, Jan.

13 Sorrow, the great idealizer.
1876 *Among My Books*, 'Spenser'.

14 There is no good in arguing with the inevitable. The only argument available with an east wind is to put on your overcoat.
1884 'On Democracy', Lowell's inaugural address when he became president of the Birmingham and Midland Institute, 6 Oct.

15 Compromise makes a good umbrella but a poor roof.
1884 'On Democracy', speech in Birmingham, 6 Oct.

16 As life runs on, the road grows strange
With faces new,—and near the end
The milestones into headstones change,
'Neath every one a friend.
1887 'Sixty-Eighth Birthday'.

Lowell, Robert Traill Spence, Jr 1917–77
US poet. His poems are intensely personal and confessional. His public involvement and outspoken comments, especially during

the Vietnam War, have made him one of the best known of all contemporary poets.

17 Let there pass
    A minute, ten, ten trillion; but the blaze
    Is infinite, eternal: this is death.
    To die and know it. This is the Black Widow, death.
    1950 'Mr Edwards and the Spider'.

18 They died
    When time was open-eyed,
    Wooden and childish; only bones abide
    There, in the nowhere, where their boats were tossed
    Sky-high, where mariners had fabled news
    of IS, the whited monster.
    1950 'The Quaker Graveyard in Nantucket', pt.3.

19 This is the end of the whaleroad and the whale
    Who spewed Nantucket bones on the thrashed swell
    And stirred the troubled waters to whirlpools
    To send the Pequod packing off to hell
    1950 'The Quaker Graveyard in Nantucket', pt.4. The Pequod was the ship that sailed after Moby Dick in Melville's novel.

20 The Lord survives the rainbow of his will.
    1950 'The Quaker Graveyard in Nantucket', last line.

21 I keep no rank nor station.
    Cured, I am frizzled, stale and small.
    1956 'Home After Three Months Away'.

22 I myself am hell.
    1956 'Skunk Hour'.

23 I often sigh still
    for the dark downward and vegetating kingdom
    of the fish and reptile.
    1964 'For the Union Dead'.

24 William James could almost hear the bronze Negroes breathe.

    Their monument sticks like a fishbone
    in the city's throat.
    1964 'For The Union Dead'.

25 Everywhere,
    giant finned cars nose forward like fish;
    a savage servility
    slides by on grease.
    1964 'For the Union Dead'.

26 He is out of bounds now. He rejoices in man's lovely peculiar power to choose life and die—
    when he leads his black soldiers to death,
    he cannot bend his back.
    1964 'For The Union Dead'. 'He' refers to Colonel Shaw, the white commander of the black regiment commemorated in the monument.

27 The man is killing time—there's nothing else.
    1964 'The Drinker'.

28 But I suppose even God was born
    too late to trust the old religion—
    all those settings out
    that never left the ground,
    beginning in wisdom, dying in doubt.
    1964 'Tenth Muse'.

29 The elect, the elected...they come here bright as dimes,
    and die dishevelled and soft.
    1964 'July in Washington'.

30 Yours the lawlessness
    of something simple that has lost its law.
    1964 'Caligula'.

31 O that the spirit could remain
    tinged but untarnished by its strain!
    1967 'Waking Early Sunday Morning'.

32 Pity the planet, all joy gone
    from this sweet volcanic cone
    1967 'Waking Early Sunday Morning'.

33 Life is too short to silver over this tarnish.
    The gods, employed to haunt and punish husbands,
    have no hand for trigger-fine distinctions,
    their myopia makes all error mortal.
    1968 'New Year's Eve'.

34 My Darling, prickly hedgehog of the heart,
    chocolates, cherries, hairshirts, pinks and glass—
    when we joined in the sublime blindness of courtship
    loving lost all its vice with half its virtue.
    1968 'New Year's Eve'.

35 Age is our reconciliation with dullness.
    1973 'Last Summer at Milgate'.

36 We feel the machine slipping from our hands
    As if someone else were steering;
    If we see the light at the end of the tunnel,
    It's the light of the oncoming train.
    1977 *Day by Day*, 'Since 1939'.

37 Those blessed structures, plot and rhyme —
    why are they no help to me now
    I want to make
    something imagined, not recalled?
    1977 *Day by Day*, 'Epilogue'.

38 Pray for the grace of accuracy
    Vermeer gave to the sun's illumination
    stealing like the tide across a map
    to his girl solid with yearning.
    1977 *Day by Day*, 'Epilogue'.

Lowenthal, Leo   1900–93
German-born US sociologist.

39 We call the heroes of the past heroes of production. We feel entitled to call the present day magazine heroes 'idols of consumption'. Indeed, almost every one of them is directly, or indirectly, related to the sphere of leisure time.
    1944 'The Triumph of Mass Idols', collected in *Literature and Mass Culture* (1984).

Lowndes, William   1652–1724
English politician.

40 Take care of the pence, and the pounds will take care of themselves.
    Quoted by Lord Chesterfield in a letter to his son, 5 Feb 1750. In an earlier letter, 6 Nov 1747, he refers to the same adage in the form '*for* the pounds'.

Lowry, (Clarence) Malcolm   1909–57
English novelist. He went to sea as a young man and lived in Mexico and Vancouver. He is best known for his novel, *Under the Volcano* (1947), one of the great 20c explorations of alcoholism. He died after choking in his sleep.

41 Nothing in the world was more terrible than an empty bottle! Unless it was an empty glass.
   1947 Under the Volcano, ch.3.

42 Where are the children I might have had?... Drowned to the accompaniment of the rattling of a thousand douche bags.
   1947 Under the Volcano, ch.10.

43 How alike are the groans of love to those of the dying.
   1947 Under the Volcano, ch.12.

44 Dark as the Grave Wherein my Friend is Laid.
   Title of novel, published posthumously (1968).

Lucan full name Marcus Annaeus Lucanus AD 39–65

Latin poet, born in Spain, nephew of the philosopher Seneca. A favourite at the court of Nero, he lost imperial favour and in AD 65 joined Piso's conspiracy against Nero, but was betrayed and compelled to commit suicide. His epic poem *Bellum Civile* (or *Pharsalia*) deals with the civil war between Caesar and Pompey.

45 *Victrix causa deis placuit, sed victa Catoni.*
   A victorious case pleased the gods, but a lost one Cato.
   Pharsalia, bk.1, 1.126.

46 *Stat magni nominis umbra.*
   There stands the shade of a great name.
   Of Pompey. *Pharsalia*, bk.1, 1.135.

47 *Coniunx est mihi, sunt nati: dedimus tot pignora fatis.*
   I have a wife, I have sons: we have given so many hostages to the fates.
   Pharsalia, bk.6, 1.661–2.
   ▸ See Bacon 51:70.

Lucas, E(dward) V(errell) 1868–1938

English essayist and biographer. He was assistant editor of *Punch*, and wrote novels and travel books.

48 I have noticed that people who are late are often so much jollier than the people who have to wait for them.
   1926 365 Days and One More.

49 Readers of novels are strange folk, upon whose probable or even possible tastes no wise book-maker would ever venture.
   1932 Reading, Writing and Remembering, ch.1.

50 There can be no defence like elaborate courtesy.
   1932 Reading, Writing and Remembering, ch.8.

Lucas, F(rank) L(awrence) 1894–1967

English teacher, critic and poet.

51 Unintelligible, the borrowings cheap and the notes useless.
   1923 On T S Eliot's *The Waste Land*, in the *New Statesman and Nation*, Nov.

52 The virtues common to good living and good poetry seem to me not so much matters of what used to be called 'virtue' as, above all, of sane vitality.
   1936 The Decline and Fall of the Romantic Ideal, ch.1.

53 Human temperaments are too diverse; we can never agree how drunk we like our art to be.
   1951 Literature and Psychology, ch.10.

54 Every author's fairy godmother should provide him not only with a pen but also with a blue pencil.
   1955 Style, introduction.

Lucas, George 1944–

US film-maker, best known for the series of *Star Wars* and *Indiana Jones* films.

55 May the Force be with you.
   1977 Line delivered by Alec Guinness as Obi-Wan Kenobi in *Star Wars*.

56 Art is the retelling of certain themes in a new light, making them accessible to the public of the moment.
   1988 In the *New York Times*, 9 Jun.

Luce, Clare Booth 1903–87

US writer, socialite and wit, associate editor of *Vogue* (1930), US Ambassador to Italy (1953–7) and author of several Broadway successes including *Kiss the Boys Goodbye* (1938).

57 Communism is the opiate of the intellectuals, with no cure except as a guillotine might be called a cure for dandruff.
   1955 In *Newsweek*, 24 Jan.

Lucretius full name Titus Lucretius Carus 98–c.55 BC

Roman poet and philosopher, author of *De Rerum Natura*, a hexameter poem in six books expounding the physical system of Epicurus, in which release from fear, and the mortality of the soul, are central concerns.

58 *Nil posse creari*
   De nilo.
   Nothing can be created from nothing.
   De Rerum Natura, bk.1, line 155–6.

59 *Suave, mari magno turbantibus aequora ventis,*
   E terra magnum alterius spectare laborem;
   Non quia vexari quemquamst iucunda voluptas,
   Sed quibus ipse malis careas quia cernere suave est.
   Suave etiam belli certamina magna tueri
   Per campos instructa tua sine parte pericli.
   Sed nil dulcius est, bene quam munita tenere
   Edita doctrina sapientum templa serena,
   Despicere unde queas alios passimque videre
   Errare atque viam palantis quaerere vitae,
   Certare ingenio, contendere nobilitate,
   Noctes atque dies niti praestante labore
   Ad summas emergere opes rerumque potiri.
   What joy it is, when out at sea the stormwinds are lashing the waters, to gaze from the shore at the heavy stress some other man is enduring. Not that anyone's afflictions are in themselves a source of delight; but to realize from what troubles you yourself are free is joy indeed. What joy, again, to watch opposing hosts marshalled on the field of battle when you have yourself no part in their peril! But this is the greatest joy of all: to possess a quiet sanctuary, stoutly fortified by the teaching of the wise, and to gaze down from that elevation on others wandering aimlessly in search of a way of life, pitting their wits one against another, disputing for precedence, struggling night and day with unstinted effort to scale the pinnacles of wealth and power.
   De Rerum Natura, bk.2, lines 1–13 (translated by R. E. Latham).

60 *Vitaque mancipio, nulli datur, omnibus usu.*
   To none is life given in freehold; to all on lease.
   De Rerum Natura, bk.3, line 971 (translated by R. E. Latham).

61 *Ut quod ali cibus est aliis fuat acre venenum.*
   What is food to one may be literally poison to others.
   De Rerum Natura, bk.4, line 637 (translated by R. E. Latham).

Lugones, Leopoldo 1874–1938

Argentinian poet and critic. As a socialist journalist, he joined the *Modernista* group, later becoming a conservative nationalist and, in 1929, a Fascist.

62 *Si tengo la fortuna*
   de que con tu alma mi dolor se integre,
   te diré entre melancólico y alegre
   las singulares cosas de la luna.
   If I am fortunate enough
   for your soul to mix with my sorrow,
   I will tell you, half with melancholy, half with gladness,
   Unique things about the moon.
   1909 *Lunario sentimental,* 'Divagación lunar' ('Lunar digression').

Lukács, Georg 1885–1971

Hungarian-born Marxist scholar, philosopher and aesthetician.

63 Nature is a social category.
   1923 *History and Class Consciousness.*

Lumière, Auguste Marie Louis Nicolas 1862–1954

French film pioneer, brother of Louis Lumière. The brothers owned a factory in Lyons where photographic products were made. They invented the first successful cine camera and projector and presented their film of workers leaving the Lumière factory in 1895.

64 *Mon frère, en une nuit, avait inventé le cinématographe.*
   My brother, in one night, had invented the cinema.
   Of the night his brother Louis had a flash of inspiration which resulted in the 'Kinetoscope de projection' patented in 1895. Quoted in C W Ceram *Archaeology of the Cinema* (1965).

Lurie, Alison 1926–

US novelist and academic. She has written a number of acutely observed novels, often with academic settings, as well as non-fiction and children's literature.

65 That is the worst thing about being a middle-class woman…you have more knowledge of yourself and the world: you are equipped to make choices, but there are none left to make.
   1974 *The War Between The Tates,* ch.3.

66 Fashion is free speech, and one of the privileges, if not always one of the pleasures, of a free world.
   1981 *The Language of Clothes.*

67 The most desirable mental state for a potential consumer…is a kind of free-floating anxiety and depression, combined with a nice collection of unrealistic goals and desires.
   1983 Of advertising. In the *New York Review of Books*, 2 Jun.

Luther, Martin 1483–1546

German theologian. Originally an Augustinian monk, he became the leader of Protestant Reformation in Europe. When he publicly burned the Papal Bull against him he was summoned before the Diet at Worms and banned. His followers later founded the Lutheran Church.

68 *Hier stehe ich. Ich kann nicht anders. Gott helfe mir. Amen.*
   Here I stand; I can do no other; God help me; Amen.
   1521 Speech in defence of his doctrines at the Diet of Worms, 18 Apr. The Diet subsequently denounced his ideas as heretical.

69 I cannot and will not recant anything, for to go against conscience is neither right nor safe.
   1521 Speech in defence of his doctrines at the Diet of Worms, 18 Apr.

70 *Esto peccator et pecca fortiter, sed fortius fide et gaude in Christo.*
   Be a sinner and sin boldly, but more boldly believe and rejoice in Christ.
   1521 Letter to Melanchthon.

71 *Wenn ich gewusst hätte, dass so viel Teufel auf mich gezielet hätten, als Ziegel auf den Dächern waren zu Worms, wäre ich dennoch eingeritten.*
   I would have gone into Worms though there were as many devils as tiles on the roof.
   1524 Letter to Frederick, Elector of Saxony, 21 Aug.

72 It is better that all of these peasants should be killed rather than that the sovereigns and magistrates should be destroyed, because the peasants take up the sword without God's authority.
   1525 Letter to Nicholas von Ansdorf, 30 May.

73 *Ein' feste Burg ist unser Gott,*
   Ein' gute Wehr und Waffen.
   A safe stronghold our God is still,
   A trusty shield and weapon.
   1529 *Ein' feste Burg ist unser Gott* (translated by Thomas Carlyle).

74 *Wo rauff du nu…dein Hertz engest und verlessest, das ist eygentlich dein Gott.*
   Whatever your heart clings to and confides in, that is really your God.
   1529 *Large Catechism,* 'The First Commandment'.

75 Rough, boisterous, stormy and altogether warlike, I am born to fight against innumerable monsters and devils.
   Quoted in Vincent Cronin *The Flowering of the Renaissance* (1969).

76 *Wer nicht liebt Wein, Weib und Gesang,*
   Der bleibt ein Narr sein Leben lang.
   Who loves not woman, wine and song
   Remains a fool his whole life long.
   Attributed. This was inscribed in the Luther room at Wartburg, but is probably apocryphal.

Lutyens, Sir Edwin Landseer 1869–1944

English architect. His designs include the Cenotaph, Whitehall and Liverpool Roman Catholic Cathedral.

77 There will never be great architects or great architecture without great patrons.
   1915 In *Country Life*, 8 May.

Lydgate, John c.1370–c.1451

English poet and Benedictine monk, who travelled widely in Europe. In 1423 he became Prior of the monastery of Hatfield Broadoak. His many works include *The Siege of Thebes* (1420–2) and *The Fall of Princes* (1431–8).

78 Off our language he was the lodesterre.
   1431–8 Of Chaucer. *The Fall of Princes*, prologue, l.252.

79 Lat no man booste of conning nor vertu,
   Of tresour, richesse, nor of sapience,

Of worldly support, for all cometh of Jesu.
c.1450 'Lat no man booste', l.1-3.

80 Woord is but wynd; leff woord and tak the dede.
Secrets of Old Philosophers, l.224.

Lyly, John   c.1554–1606

English writer and dramatist. He published his prose romance *Euphues, or the Anatomy of Wit* in 1578, and wrote eight plays between 1584 and 1590, including *Endymion, or The Man in the Moon* (1588).

81 Be valiant, but not too venturous. Let thy attire be comely, but not costly.
1578 *Euphues, or the Anatomy of Wit*.

82 What bird so sings, yet so does wail?
O 'tis the ravished nightingale.
Jug, jug, jug, jug, tereu, she cries,
And still her woes at midnight rise.
1584 *Campaspe*, act 5, sc.1.

83 How at heaven's gates she claps her wings,
The morn not waking till she sings.
1584 Of the lark. *Campaspe*, act 5, sc.1.

84 A heat full of coldness, a sweet full of bitterness, a pain full of pleasantness, which maketh thoughts have eyes and hearts ears, bred by desire, nursed by delight, weaned by jealousy, killed by dissembling, buried by ingratitude, and this is love. Fair lady, will you any?
1588 *Gallathea*, act 1, sc.2. The passage gently satirizes the conventions of love sonnets, and is characterized by the yoked opposites called Euphuisms, after Lyly's earlier work, a style later used by the metaphysical poets.

85 If love be a god, why should not lovers be virtuous?
1588 *Gallathea*, act 3, sc.1.

86 Yield, ladies, yield to love, ladies, which lurketh under your eyelids whilst you sleep and playeth with your heartstrings whilst you wake, whose sweetness never breedeth satiety, labour weariness, nor grief bitterness.
1588 *Gallathea*, epilogue.

87 Night hath a thousand eyes.
1600 *The Maydes Metamorphosis*, act 3, sc.1.
▶ See Bourdillon 153:94.

Lynch, David Keith   1946–

US film director, writer and actor.

88 I don't think that people accept the fact that life doesn't make sense. I think it makes people terribly uncomfortable. It seems like religion and myth were invented against that, trying to make sense out of it.
Quoted in Jason Rogers, *My Love Affair with David Lynch and Peachy Like Nietzsche: Dark Clown Porn Snuff for Terrorists and Gorefiends* (2005).

89 Ideas are like fish. If you want to catch little fish, you can stay in the shallow water. But if you want to catch the big fish, you've got to go deeper. Down deep, the fish are more powerful and more pure. They're huge and abstract. And they're very beautiful.
2007 *Catching the Big Fish: Meditation, Consciousness, and Creativity*.

Lynd, Robert   1879–1949

Irish essayist and critic, literary editor of the *Daily News* and a contributor to the *New Statesman* (1913–45). His essay collections include *The Art of Letters* (1920), *The Blue Lion* (1923) and *In Defence of Pink* (1939).

90 It may be that all games are silly. But then, so are humans.
Quoted in Colin Jarman *The Guinness Dictionary of Sports Quotations* (1990).

91 It is almost impossible to remember how tragic a place this world is when one is playing golf.
Attributed.

Lyndon, Neil   1946–

British journalist and writer. His critique of feminism, *No More Sex War: The Failures of Feminism*, was published in 1992.

92 The cardinal tenets of feminism divided my generation, effectively disempowering and disenfranchising its members. It does make me bitterly angry that my generation, which prided itself so complacently on its soul, on its powers of intelligence and analysis, should have fallen so cloddishly for totalitarian simplicities which declared a war of eternal opposition between men and women.
1992 *No More Sex War: The Failures of Feminism*.

Lyte, Henry Francis   1793–1847

Scottish hymn writer, curate of Lower Brixham, Devon, from 1823.

93 Praise, my soul, the King of Heaven;
To his feet thy tribute bring.
Ransomed, healed, restored, forgiven,
Who like me his praise should sing?
1834 'Praise, my Soul, the King of Heaven'.

94 Abide with me; fast falls the eventide;
The darkness deepens; Lord, with me abide;
When other helpers fail and comforts flee,
Help of the helpless, O, abide with me.
1847 *Remains*, 'Abide with Me' (published 1850).

Lyttelton, Humphrey Richard Adeane   1921–2008

English jazz trumpeter, bandleader and broadcaster. An Old Etonian and former guardsman, he was the *doyen* of the English jazz scene, both as a musician and as a writer and broadcaster.

95 It is this tendency to play with manic enthusiasm on every possible occasion that distinguishes the amateur jazz musician from the professional, often to the public detriment of the latter, who are regarded as snooty and unfriendly.
1984 *Why No Beethoven?*, ch.1.

McAleese, Mary   1951–

Irish politician, President of Ireland (1997–2011).

1 Apart from shamrock, the President should not wear emblems or symbols of any kind.
1997 On why she would not be wearing a poppy at her inauguration on 11 Nov. In *The Guardian*, 13 Apr.

2 The day of the dinosaurs is over. The future belongs to the bridge-builders, not the wreckers.
  1998 On the Northern Ireland Assembly. In *The Irish Times*, 27 Jun.

MacArthur, Douglas 1880–1964

US soldier. He commanded troops in the Far East (1941) in World War II, directed the recapture of the SW Pacific (1942–5), formally accepted Japan's surrender, and commanded its occupation (1945–51). He led the UN forces in the Korean War, but was relieved of command when he tried to continue the war against China.

3 I came through and I shall return.
  1942 On reaching Australia, having broken through Japanese lines en route from Corregidor, 20 Mar. Reported in the *New York Times*, 21 Mar.

4 There lies the Holy Grail.
  1943 Remark, 6 May, one year after the fall of Corregidor to the Japanese, recalled in *A Soldier Speaks*.

5 A great tragedy has ended. A great victory has been won. A new era is upon us... We have had our last chance. If we do not devise some greater and more equitable system, Armageddon will be at our door.
  1945 National radio broadcast on the surrender of Japan, 2 Sep.

6 An unsinkable air-craft carrier.
  1950 Of Taiwan's military significance for the US. Remark, 27 Aug, recalled in *A Soldier Speaks*.

7 In war, indeed, there can be no substitute for victory.
  1951 Address to Congress, 19 Apr. In the *Congressional Record*, vol.97, pt.3, p.4125.

8 The world has turned over many times since I took the oath on the plain at West Point...but I still remember the refrain of one of the most popular ballads of that day which proclaimed most proudly that old soldiers never die; they just fade away.
  1951 Address to Congress after being relieved of his duty by President Truman, 19 Apr.

9 I now close my military career and just fade away, an old soldier who tried to do his duty as God gave him the light to see that duty.
  1951 Address to Congress after being relieved of his duty by President Truman, 19 Apr.

10 It isn't just dust that is settling in Korea, Senator, it is American blood.
  1951 During the Senate inquiry on MacArthur's dismissal. Reported in the *New York Times*, 2 May.

11 He'll make a fine president. He was the best clerk who ever served under me.
  1952 On Dwight D Eisenhower's election as President. In news summaries, 31 Dec.

12 The chickens are coming home to roost, and you happen to have just moved into the chicken house.
  Comment to John F Kennedy on the presidential crisis. Kennedy enjoyed the remark and often quoted it. Quoted in Theodore C Sorensen *Kennedy* (1965).

Macarthur, James 1937–2010

Actor, only son of Helen Hayes.

13 What a wonderful sight, a full house—my mother would have loved it!
  1993 Speaking at the memorial service at New York's Shubert's Theater for his mother, Helen Hayes. Reported in the *New York Times*, 19 Jun.

Macaulay, Dame (Emilie) Rose 1881–1958

English novelist and travel writer whose book, *Pleasure of Ruins* (1953), includes an account of her visit to Cambodia and the ruins of Angkor.

14 You should always believe all you read in newspapers, as this makes them more interesting.
  1925 *A Casual Commentary*, 'Problems of a Reader's Life'.

15 My point of view has sadly changed. For now, should all the books in the world be laid before me, my problem would be how many of them I could avoid. Most books are like that.
  1925 *A Casual Commentary*, 'Problems of a Reader's Life'.

16 Here is one of the points about this planet which should be remembered; into every penetrable corner of it, and into most of the impenetrable corners, the English will penetrate.
  1926 *Crewe Train*, pt.1, ch.1.

17 Gentlemen know that fresh air should be kept in its proper place—out of doors—and that, God having given us indoors and out-of-doors, we should not attempt to do away with that distinction.
  1926 *Crewe Train*, pt.1, ch.5.

18 All is now desolate, fantastic, and ambushed with ghosts; the archaeologists twitter among them like bats.
  1953 Of Angkor Thom. *Pleasure of Ruins*.

19 'Take my camel, dear,' said my aunt Dot, as she climbed down from this animal on her return from High Mass.
  1956 *The Towers of Trebizond*, ch.1.

Macaulay (of Rothley), Thomas Babington Macaulay, 1st Baron 1800–59

English essayist and historian, an MP from 1830 and a skilful orator in the Reform Bill debates. He wrote the highly popular *Lays of Ancient Rome* (1842) and contributed to the *Edinburgh Review*, but his major work was the *History of England from the Accession of James II* (1848–61, fifth volume unfinished).

20 Then, beneath the nine-tailed cat
  Shall they who use it writhe, sir;
  And curates lean, and rectors fat,
  Shall dig the ground they tithe, sir.
  Down with your Bayleys, and your Bests,
  Your Giffords, and your Gurneys;
  We'll clear the island of the pests,
  Which mortals name attorneys.
  1820 'A Radical War Song', stanza 8. The names are those of lawyers and judges who figured in the trial of the Cato Street conspirators.

21 Free trade, one of the greatest blessings which a government can confer on a people, is in almost every country unpopular.
  1824 'Essay on Mitford's *History of Greece*', collected in *Works* (published 1906), vol.7, p.688–9.

22 The men of our time are not to be converted or perverted by quartos.
  1825 'Milton', in the *Edinburgh Review*, Aug.

23 Perhaps no person can be a poet, or can even enjoy poetry, without a certain unsoundness of mind.
  1825 'Milton', in the *Edinburgh Review*, Aug.

24 There is only one cure for the evils which newly acquired freedom produces; and that is freedom... The blaze of truth and liberty may at first dazzle and bewilder

nations which have become half blind in the house of bondage. But let them gaze on, and they will soon be able to bear it.
1825 'Milton', in the *Edinburgh Review*, Aug.

25 Many politicians of our time are in the habit of laying it down as a self-evident proposition, that no people ought to be free till they are fit to use their freedom. The maxim is worthy of the fool in the old story, who resolved not to go into the water till he had learnt to swim. If men are to wait for liberty till they become wise and good in slavery, they may indeed wait for ever.
1825 'Milton', in the *Edinburgh Review*, Aug.

26 Every man who has seen the world knows that nothing is so useless as a general maxim.
1827 'Machiavelli', in the *Edinburgh Review*, Mar.

27 It has lately been brought to my knowledge
That the Ministers fully design
To suppress each cathedral and college,
And eject every learned divine.
To assist this detestable scheme
Three nuncios from Rome are come over;
They left Calais on Monday by steam,
And landed to dinner at Dover.
1827 'The Country Clergyman's Trip to Cambridge', stanza 2. A satirical poem against the opposition to Catholic emancipation.

28 Knowledge advances by steps, and not by leaps.
1828 'History' in the *Edinburgh Review*, May.

29 History, at least in its ideal state of perfection, is a compound of poetry and philosophy.
1828 'Hallam's *Constitutional History*' in the *Edinburgh Review*, Sep.

30 We know of no spectacle so ridiculous as the British public in one of its periodical fits of morality.
1828 In the *Edinburgh Review*.

31 The gallery in which the reporters sit has become a fourth estate of the realm.
1828 'Hallam's *Constitutional History*' in the *Edinburgh Review*, Sep.
▶ See Hazlitt 403:45.

32 His writing bears the same relation to poetry which a Turkey carpet bears to a picture.
1830 'Robert Montgomery', in the *Edinburgh Review*, Apr.

33 Mr Robert Montgomery's genius [is] far too free and aspiring to be shackled by the rules of syntax... [His] readers must take such grammar as they can get and be thankful.
1830 'Robert Montgomery', in the *Edinburgh Review*, Apr.

34 From the poetry of Lord Byron they drew a system of ethics, compounded of misanthropy and voluptuousness, a system in which the two great commandments were, to hate your neighbour, and to love your neighbour's wife.
1831 Of the young Byron enthusiasts who emulated and hero-worshipped him. 'Moore's *Life of Lord Byron*', in the *Edinburgh Review*, Jun.

35 Many of the greatest men that ever lived have written biography. Boswell was one of the smallest men that ever lived and he has beaten them all.
1831 'Croker's new edition of *The Life of Samuel Johnson*', in the *Edinburgh Review*, Sep.

36 In the foreground is that strange figure which is as familiar to us as the figures of those among whom we have been brought up, the gigantic body, the huge massy face, seamed with the scars of disease, the brown coat, the black worsted stockings, the grey wig with the scorched foretop, the dirty hands, the nails bitten and pared to the quick.
1831 Of Dr Samuel Johnson. 'Croker's new edition of *The Life of Samuel Johnson*', in the *Edinburgh Review*, Sep.

37 Dark and terrible beyond any season within my remembrance of political affairs was the day of their flight. Far darker and more terrible will be the day of their return.
1831 On the defeat of the Tory Government, House of Commons, 20 Sep.

38 He [John Hampden] knew that the essence of war is violence, and that moderation in war is imbecility.
1831 'Lord Nugent's *Memorials of Hampden*', in the *Edinburgh Review*, Dec.

39 It is not easy to make a simile go on all fours.
1831 Of the task of the allegorist. 'Robert Southey's edition of Bunyan's *Pilgrims Progress*', in the *Edinburgh Review*, Dec.

40 A broken head in Cold Bath Fields produces a greater sensation among us than three pitched battles in India.
1833 House of Commons, 20 Sep.

41 There was a time when the most powerful of human intellects were deluded by the gibberish of the astrologer and the alchemist... But time advances; facts accumulate; doubts arise... The highest intellects, like the tops of mountains, are the first to catch and to reflect the dawn.
1835 'Sir James Mackintosh's *History of the Revolution in England, in 1688*' in the *Edinburgh Review*, Jul.

42 The history of England is emphatically the history of progress.
1835 'Sir James Mackintosh's *History of the Revolution in England, in 1688*' in the *Edinburgh Review*, Jul.

43 But even Archimedes was not free from the prevailing notion that geometry was degraded by being employed to produce anything useful. It was with difficulty that he was induced to stoop from speculation to practice. He was half ashamed of those inventions which were the wonder of hostile nations, and always spoke of them slightingly as mere amusements, as trifles in which a mathematician might be suffered to relax his mind after intense application to the higher parts of his science.
1837 'Basil Montagu's edition of *The Works of Francis Bacon, Lord Chancellor of England*', in the *Edinburgh Review*, Jul.

44 Lars Porsena of Clusium
By the nine gods he swore
That the great house of Tarquin
Should suffer wrong no more.
1842 *Lays of Ancient Rome*, 'Horatius', stanza 1.

45 Then out spake brave Horatius,
The Captain of the Gate:
'To every man upon this earth
Death cometh soon or late.
And how can man die better
Than facing fearful odds,
For the ashes of his fathers
And the temples of his God?'
1842 *Lays of Ancient Rome*, 'Horatius', stanza 27.

46 'Now who will stand on either hand,
And keep the bridge with me?'
1842 *Lays of Ancient Rome*, 'Horatius', stanza 29.

McAuliffe

47 Was none who would be foremost
To lead such dire attack;
But those behind cried 'Forward!'
And those before cried 'Back!'
1842 *Lays of Ancient Rome*, 'Horatius', stanza 50.

48 Alone stood brave Horatius,
But constant still in mind;
Thrice thirty thousand foes before,
And the broad flood behind.
1842 *Lays of Ancient Rome*, 'Horatius', stanza 57.

49 And even the ranks of Tuscany
Could scarce forbear to cheer.
1842 *Lays of Ancient Rome*, 'Horatius', stanza 60.

50 With weeping and with laughter
Still is the story told,
How well Horatius kept the bridge
In the brave days of old.
1842 *Lays of Ancient Rome*, 'Horatius', stanza 70.

51 The rugged miners poured to war from Medip's sunless caves.
1842 'The Armada', in the *Quarterly Magazine*.

52 And broader still became the blaze, and louder still the din,
And fast from every village round the horse came spurring in.
1842 'The Armada', in the *Quarterly Magazine*.

53 We hardly know any instance of the strength and weakness of human nature so striking, and so grotesque, as the character of this haughty, vigilant, resolute, sagacious blue-stocking—half Mithridates and half Trissotin, bearing up against a world in arms, with an ounce of poison in one pocket, and a quire of bad verses in the other.
1843 Of Frederick the Great. *Historical Essays*. 'Frederic the Great', in the *Edinburgh Magazine*, Apr.

54 Forget all feuds, and shed one English tear
O'er English dust. A broken heart lies here.
1845 'A Jacobite's Epitaph', closing lines.

55 I hardly know which is the greater pest to society: a paternal Government; that is to say, a prying meddlesome Government, which intrudes itself into every part of human life and which thinks that it can do everything for everybody better than anyone can do for himself, or a careless, lounging Government, which suffers grievances, such as it could at once remove, to grow and multiply, and which to all complaint and remonstrance has only one answer, 'We must let things take their course, we must let things find their own level.'
1846 House of Commons, 22 May.

56 Persecution produced its natural effect on them. It found them a sect; it made them a faction.
1846 On the Puritans, House of Commons, 22 May.

57 The history of England is emphatically the history of progress.
1846 House of Commons, 22 May.

58 Thus our democracy was, from an early period, the most aristocratic, and our aristocracy the most democratic in the world.
1848 *History of England*, vol.1, ch.1.

59 The Puritan hated bear-baiting, not because it gave pain to the bear, but because it gave pleasure to the spectators.
1849 *History of England*, vol.1, ch.2.

60 The Mountjoy began to move, and soon passed safe through the broken stakes and floating spars. But her brave master was no more. A shot from one of the batteries had struck him; and he died by the most enviable of all deaths, in sight of the city which was his birthplace, which was his home, and which had just been saved by his courage and self-devotion from the most frightful form of destruction.
1849 *History of England*, on the relief of Londonderry, vol.2, ch.12.

McAuliffe, Anthony 1898–1975
US soldier, a general in World War II.

61 Nuts!
1944 Replying to the German demand for surrender at Bastogne, Belgium, 23 Dec. His response was reported in this form in the *New York Times*, 28 Dec; the original may have been more explicit.

MacBeth, George Mann 1932–92
Scottish writer. He is best known as a poet, but also wrote novels and children's books.

62 To leave great themes unfinished is
Perhaps the most satisfying exercise
Of power.
1963 'The Spider's Nest'.

63 No one can read a poem unless he realises that it is a physical object as well as an abstract vehicle for conveying ideas. A poem has a material existence like a piece of music or sculpture or a plate of meat.
1967 Introduction to *Poetry 1900 to 1965*.

64 Heap high the
groaning platter with pink fillets, sucking pig and thick gammon, celestial chef. Be generous with the crackling. Let your hand slip with the gravy trough, dispensing plenty.
1977 'An Ode to English Food'.

MacCaig, Norman Alexander 1910–96
Scottish poet. He was a school-teacher for much of his working life. He was one of Scotland's most distinguished poets.

65 A man's boots with a woman in them
Clatter across the floor.
1960 'Crofter's Kitchen, Evening'.

66 The stone remains, and the cross, to let us know
Their unjust, hard demands, as symbols do.
1960 'Celtic Cross'.

67 A cubic inch of some stars
weighs a hundred tons—Blue tit,
who could measure the power
of your tiny spark of energy?
1980 'Blue Tit on a String of Peanuts'.

McCain, John 1936–
US Republican politician, Senator from Arizona.

68 I will not take the low road to the highest office in the land.
2000 Conceding victory in the South Carolina primary to George W Bush. In *The Guardian*, 24 Feb.

69 We have enemies for whom no attack is too cruel.
2008 Speaking while campaigning for the Republican nomination for President.

70 I looked into his eyes and saw three letters: a K, a G and a B.
2008 Referring to Vladimir Putin.

71 I can only express satisfaction that the Dear Leader is joining the likes of Gaddafi, Bin Laden, Hitler, and Stalin in a warm corner of hell.
2011 Responding to news of the death of North Korean leader Kim Jong-il, 19 Dec.

72 We can't get any lower in the polls. We're down to blood relatives and paid staffers now.
2013 Commenting upon the popularity of Congress during the government shutdown, 13 Oct.

73 Russia is a gas station masquerading as a country. It's kleptocracy, it's corruption, it's a nation that's really only dependent upon oil and gas for their economy.
2014 On CNN, 16 Mar.

McCann, M(ichael) J(oseph) 1824–1883
Irish teacher, journalist and ballad-writer.

74 Proudly the note of the trumpet is sounding,
Loudly the war-cries arise on the gale,
Fleetly the steed by Loc Suilig is bounding
To join the thick squadrons in Saimear's green vale.
On, every mountaineer,
Strangers to flight and fear:
Rush to the standard of dauntless Red Hugh!
Bonnought and gallowglass,
Throng from each mountain-pass!
On for old Erin—O'Donnell abu!
1845 *The Spirit of the Nation*, 'O'Donnell Abu'.

75 Wildly o'er Desmond the war-wolf is howling,
Fearless the eagle sweeps over the plain,
The fox in the streets of the city is prowling—
All, all who would scare them are banished or slain!
1845 *The Spirit of the Nation*, 'O'Donnell Abu'.

McCarthy, Cormac *originally Charles McCarthy* 1933–
US novelist, playwright, and screenwriter. He won the Pulitzer Prize and the James Tait Black Memorial Prize for Fiction for *The Road* (2006); subsequent novels have included *Blood Meridian* (1985), *No Country for Old Men* (2005) and *All the Pretty Horses* (1992).

76 There is no such joy in the tavern as upon the road thereto.
1985 *Blood Meridian*.

Hell ain't half full.
1985 *Blood Meridian*.

77 Each man is the bard of his own existence.
1998 *Cities of the Plain*.

78 When the lies are all told and forgot the truth will be there yet.
2005 *No Country for Old Men*.

79 I don't think goodness is something that you learn. If you're left adrift in the world to learn goodness from it, you would be in trouble.
2009 In *The Washington Post*, 13 Nov.

McCarthy, Eugene J(oseph) 1916–2005
US Democratic politician, Senator from Minnesota (1958–70). An opponent of the Vietnam War, in 1968 he challenged President Johnson for nomination but the bid failed and he left politics to devote himself to teaching and writing.

80 The war in Vietnam…[is] of questionable loyalty and constitutionality…diplomatically indefensible…morally wrong.
1967 Speech to the Conference of Concerned Democrats, 2 Dec, an address noted for crystallizing dissent against the Vietnam War.

81 The message from the administration today is a message of fear—even a message of fear of fear.
1967 Speech to the Conference of Concerned Democrats, 2 Dec.

82 Let us pick up again these lost strands and weave them again into the fabric of America…sort out the music from the sounds and again respond to the trumpet and the steady drum.
1967 Speech to Conference of Concerned Democrats, 2 Dec.

83 Being in politics is like being a football coach. You have to be smart enough to know the game and stupid enough to think it is important.
1991 In the *Los Angeles Times*, 7 Dec.

McCarthy, Joseph R(aymond) 1909–57
US Republican politician and inquisitor. As Chairman of the Permanent Subcommittee on Investigations from 1953, he used hectoring cross-examination and innuendo to arraign many often innocent citizens for communist sympathies.

84 While I cannot take time off to name all the men in the State Department who have been named as members of the Communist Party and members of a spy ring, I have here in my hand a list of 205 that were known to the Secretary of State as being members of the Communist Party, and who nevertheless are still working and shaping the policy of the State Department.
1950 Speech at Wheeling, West Virginia, 9 Feb, which marked the beginning of the McCarthy 'witch hunts' for communists.

85 McCarthyism is Americanism with its sleeves rolled.
1952 Re-election campaign slogan.

McCarthy, Mary Thérèse 1912–89
US writer, critic and social commentator. She is best known for her novel *The Group* (1963).

86 When an American heiress wants to buy a man, she at once crosses the Atlantic. The only really materialistic people I have ever met have been Europeans.
1947 'America the Beautiful', in *Commentary*, Sep.

87 The American character looks always as if it just had a rather bad haircut, which gives it, in our eyes at any rate, a greater humanity than the European, which even among its beggars has an all too professional air.
1947 'America the Beautiful', in *Commentary*, Sep.

88 American life, in large cities, is a perpetual assault on the senses and the nerves; it is out of asceticism, out of unworldliness, precisely, that we bear it.
1947 'America the Beautiful', in *Commentary*, Sep.

89 The happy ending is our national belief.
1947 'America the Beautiful', in *Commentary*, Sep.

90 Liberty, as it is conceived by current opinion, has nothing inherent about it; it is a sort of gift or trust bestowed on the individual by the state pending *good behavior*.
1952 Speech. Collected as 'The Contagion of Ideas', in *On the Contrary* (1961).

91 Every age has a keyhole to which its eye is pasted.
1953 'My Confession'. Collected in *On the Contrary* (1961).

92 In the unreal realms of the canals, as in a Swiftian Lilliput, the real world, with its contrivances, appears as a vast folly.
1956 Of Venice. *Venice Observed*, ch.1.

93 To care for the quarrels of the past, to identify oneself passionately with a cause that became, politically speaking, a losing cause with the birth of the modern world, is to experience a kind of straining against reality, a rebellious nonconformity that, again, is rare in America, where children are instructed in the virtues of the system they live under, as though history had achieved a happy ending in American civics.
1957 Of Catholicism. *Memories of a Catholic Girlhood*, 'To the Reader'.

94 Bureaucracy, the rule of no one, has become the modern form of despotism.
1958 'Vita Activa', in the *New Yorker*, 18 Oct.

95 There are no new truths, but only truths that have not been recognized by those who have perceived them without noticing.
1958 'Vita Activa', in the *New Yorker*, 18 Oct.

96 The labor of keeping house is labor in its most naked state, for labor is toil that never finishes, toil that has to be begun again the moment it is completed, toil that is destroyed and consumed by the life process.
1958 'Vita Activa', in the *New Yorker*, 18 Oct.

97 In violence, we forget who we are.
1961 *On the Contrary*, 'Characters in Fiction'.

98 An interviewer asked me what book I thought best represented the modern American woman. All I could think of to answer was: *Madame Bovary*.
1961 *On the Contrary*, 'Characters in Fiction'.

99 Being abroad makes you conscious of the whole imitative side of human behavior. The ape in man.
1965 *Birds of America*, 'Epistle from Mother Carey's Chicken'.

1 In politics, it seems, retreat is honorable if dictated by military considerations and shameful if even *suggested* for ethical reasons.
1967 *Vietnam*, 'Solutions'.

2 I once said in an interview that every word she writes is a lie, including 'and' and 'the'.
1980 In response to Lillian Hellman's memoir, *Scoundrel Time*, in the *New York Times*, 16 Feb.

McCartney, Sir (James) Paul 1942–

British rock singer, musician and songwriter. With fellow-Beatle John Lennon, he formed the most successful songwriting team of the 1960s.

3 Pop music is the classical music of now.
Quoted in Tony Palmer *All You Need Is Love* (1976).
▶ See also Lennon 521:44.

4 You can't reheat a souffle.
Explaining why The Beatles would not be reforming. Quoted in *Chronicle of the 20th Century* (1977).

5 Life is an energy field, a bunch of molecules. And these particular molecules formed to make these four guys, who then formed into this band called the Beatles and did all that work. I have to think that was something metaphysical. Something alchemic. Something that must be thought of as magic.
2007 In *Rolling Stone*, 3 May.

McCarty, Maclyn 1911–2005

US biologist.

6 An alternative device for the recovery of bacteria from large volumes of culture had become available by modification of a machine originally designed as a cream separator.
1985 *The Transforming Principle: Discovering that Genes Are Made of DNA*.

McClellan, George Brinton 1826–85

Union general in the American Civil War, given command of troops in and around Washington after the Battle of Bull Run in 1861. He ran unsuccessfully for election against Abraham Lincoln and resigned from the army in 1864.

7 All quiet along the Potomac.
1862 Attributed.

MacColl, Ewan James Miller 1915–89

English folksinger, composer, collector, author, playwright and socialist, whose work was an important influence on the Scottish and worldwide folk music revivals of the 1950s and 1960s.

8 The first time ever I saw your face
I thought the sun rose in your eyes,
And the moon and the stars were the gifts you gave
To the dark and the empty skies.
1962 'The First Time Ever I Saw Your Face', stanza 1.

McCourt, Frank 1931–2009

US author known for the bestselling memoir *Angela's Ashes* (1996).

9 Worse than the ordinary miserable childhood is the miserable Irish childhood, and worse yet is the miserable Irish Catholic childhood.
1996 *Angela's Ashes*, ch.1.

McCoy, John B(onnet) 1943–

US banker.

10 I was trying to make it as friendly as you can make an unfriendly offer.
1995 On his unsolicited $5 billion bid in an unsuccessful attempt to acquire the Bank of Boston. In *Fortune*, 21 Aug.

McCrae, John 1872–1915

Canadian soldier, physician, and poet, First Brigade surgeon in the Canadian Field Artillery. His most famous poem, 'In Flanders Fields', was written during the Second Battle of Ypres, Belgium, 3 May 1915.

11 In Flanders fields the poppies blow
Between the crosses, row on row,
That mark our place; and in the sky
The larks, still bravely singing, fly
Scarce heard amid the guns below.
1915 'In Flanders Fields', stanza 1.

McCullers, (Lula) Carson née Smith 1917–67

US writer. Her novels, tragic and often symbolic, have been labelled Southern Gothic. She also wrote a novella, *The Ballad of the Sad Café* (1951) as well as short stories and plays.

12 The Heart Is A Lonely Hunter.
   1940 Title of novel.

13 All men are lonely. But sometimes it seems to me that we Americans are the loneliest of all. Our hunger for foreign places and new ways has been with us almost like a national disease.
   1940 'Look Homeward, Americans', in *Vogue*, 1 Dec.

14 There's nothing that makes you so aware of the improvisation of human existence as a song unfinished. Or an old address book.
   1951 *The Ballad of the Sad Café*, 'The Sojourner'.

15 Nothing is so musical as the sound of pouring bourbon for the first drink on a Sunday morning. Not Bach or Schubert or any of those masters.
   1953 *Clock Without Hands*.

McCurry, Michael D 1954–
Clinton White House Press Secretary (1995–98).

16 There are people around here who think Hillary Clinton is responsible for the weather.
   1995 In the *New York Times*, 7 Jan. New revelations about the First Lady's role in Whitewater land sales and the firing of the presidential travel office had coincided with a heavy Washington snowfall.

MacDiarmid, Hugh *pseudonym of* Christopher Murray Grieve 1892–1978
Scottish poet, nationalist and communist, the driving-force behind the modern Scottish literary Renaissance. He used complex forms of both Scots and English in his lyrical, philosophical and polemical verse.

17 I myself believe that we have lost this war—in everything but actuality. When I see scores of sheep go to a slaughter-house I do not feel constrained to admire their resignation.
   1918 Letter to George Ogilvie, 12 Nov.

18 Earth, thou bonnie broukit bairn!
   1925 *Sangschaw*, 'The Bonnie Broukit Bairn'. Broukit = neglected.

19 But greet, an' in your tears ye'll droun
   The haill clanjamfrie.
   1925 *Sangschaw*, 'The Bonnie Broukit Bairn'.

20 An' see the deid come loupin' owre
   The auld grey wa's.
   1925 *Sangschaw*, 'Crowdieknowe', stanza 1.

21 I met ayont the cairney
   A lass wi' tousled hair
   Singin' till a bairnie
   That was nae langer there.
   1926 *Penny Wheep*, 'Empty Vessel', stanza 1.

22 No' wan in fifty kens a wurd Burns wrote
   But misapplied is a'body's property
   1926 *A Drunk Man Looks at the Thistle*, l.41–2.

23 I'll hae nae hauf-way hoose, buy aye be whaur
   Extremes meet—it's the only way I ken
   To dodge the curst conceit o' bein' richt
   That damns the vast majority o' men.
   1926 *A Drunk Man Looks at the Thistle*, l.141–4.

24 The thistle yet'll unite
   Man and the Infinite!
   1926 *A Drunk Man Looks at the Thistle*, l.481–2.

25 To be yersel's—and to mak' that worth bein'.
   Nae harder job to mortals has been gi'en.
   1926 *A Drunk Man Looks at the Thistle*, l.745–6.

26 A'thing that ony man can be's
   A mockery o' his soul at last.
   1926 *A Drunk Man Looks at the Thistle*, l.1415–7.

27 Be like the thistle, O my soul,
   Heedless o' praise and quick to take affront
   1926 *A Drunk Man Looks at the Thistle*, l.1709–10.

28 'Let there be Licht,' said God, and there was
   A little: but He lacked poo'er
   To licht up mair than pairt o' space at aince,
   And there is lots o' darkness that's the same
   As gin He'd never spoken
   1926 *A Drunk Man Looks at the Thistle*, l.2101–5.

29 And Jesus and a nameless ape
   Collide and share the selfsame shape
   That nocht terrestial can escape?
   1926 *A Drunk Man Looks at the Thistle*, l.2476–8.

30 He canna Scotland see wha yet
   Canna see the Infinite,
   And Scotland in true scale to it.
   1926 *A Drunk Man Looks at the Thistle*, l.2527–9.

31 O wha's the bride that cairries the bunch
   O' thistles blinterin' white?
   Her cuckold bridegroom little dreids
   What he sall ken this nicht.
   1926 *A Drunk Man Looks at the Thistle*.

32 The number of people who can copulate properly may be few; the number who can write well are infinitely fewer.
   1928 Review of D H Lawrence's *Lady Chatterley's Lover* in *The New Age*, 27 Sep. This may very well have been the first published review of Lawrence's novel.

33 Lourd on my hert as winter lies
   The state that Scotland's in the day.
   Spring to the North has aye come slow
   But noo dour winter's like to stay
   For guid,
   And no' for guid!
   1930 *To Circumjack Cencrastus, or The Curly Snake*.

34 Better a'e gowden lyric
   Than a social problem solved.
   1930 *To Circumjack Cencrastus, or The Curly Snake*.

35 Are my poems spoken in the factories and fields,
   In the streets o' the toon?
   Gin they're no', then I'm failin' to dae
   What I ocht to ha' dune.
   1932 *Second Hymn to Lenin*.

36 Scotland is not wholly surrounded by the sea—unfortunately.
   1934 *Scottish Scene*, 'The Sea'.

37 We must reconcile ourselves to the stones,
   Not the stones to us.
   1934 'On a Raised Beach'.

38 The rose of all the world is not for me.
   I want for my part
   Only the little white rose of Scotland
   That smells sharp and sweet—and breaks the heart.
   1934 *Stony Limits and other poems*, 'The Little White Rose'.

39 My aim all along has been (in Ezra Pound's term) the most drastic *desuetization* of Scottish life and letters, and, in particular, the de-Tibetanization of the Highlands and Islands, and getting rid of the whole gang of high mucky-mucks, famous fatheads, old wives of both sexes, stuffed shirts, hollow men with headpieces stuffed with straw, bird-wits, lookers-under-beds, trained seals, creeping Jesuses, Scots Wha Ha'evers, village idiots, policemen, leaders of white-mouse factions and noted connoisseurs of bread and butter, glorified gangsters, and what 'Billy' Phelps calls Medlar Novelists (the medlar being a fruit that becomes rotten before it is ripe), Commercial Calvinists, makers of 'noises like a turnip', and all the touts and toadies and lickspittles o the English Ascendancy, and their infernal women-folk, and all their skunkoil skulduggery.
1943 *Lucky Poet*, ch.3, 'The Kind of Poetry I Want'.

40 We do not like the confiding, the intimate, the ingratiating, the hail-fellow-well-met, but prefer the unapproachable, the hard-bitten, the recalcitrant, the sinister, the malignant, the saturnine, the cross-grained and the cankered, and the howling wilderness to the amenities of civilization, the irascible to the affable, the prickly to the smooth. We have no damned fellow-feeling at all.
1952 'The Dour Drinkers of Glasgow', in *The American Mercury*, Mar.

41 So this is what our lives have been given to find,
A language that can serve our purposes,
A marvellous lucidity, a quality of fiery aery light,
Flowing like clear water, flying like a bird
Burning like a sunlit landscape.
1955 'The Task'.

42 My job, as I see it, has never been to lay a tit's egg, but to erupt like a volcano emitting not only flame but a lot of rubbish.
1964 Letter to George Bruce, 1 Jul.

43 Scotland small? Our multiform, infinite Scotland small?
1974 'Direadh'.

McDonald, Alonzo L 1928–
US government official and businessman, former chief executive officer of McKinsey & Company and of the Bendix Corporation and staff director at the White House (1979–81).

44 Very few factors help produce economies of scale. Technology may be one, but not people. When it comes to motivating people and using their brainpower, you hit diseconomies of scale early. At that point, bigger isn't better.
1986 'Of Floating Factories and Mating Dinosaurs', in the *Harvard Business Review*, Nov/Dec.

MacDonald, George 1824–1905
Scottish pastor, poet and novelist who wrote fantastical and allegorical works for both adults and children.

45 Here lie I, Martin Elginbrodde:
Hae mercy o' my soul, Lord God;
As I wad do, were I Lord God,
And ye were Martin Elginbrodde.
1863 *David Elginbrod*, bk.1, ch.13.

46 The love of our neighbour is the only door out of the dungeon of self, where we mope and mow, striking sparks, and rubbing phosphorescence out of the walls, and blowing our own breath in our own nostrils, instead of issuing to the fair sunlight of God, the sweet winds of the universe.
1867 *Unspoken Sermons*.

47 Where did you come from, baby dear?
Out of the everywhere into here.
1871 *At the Back of the North Wind*, ch.33, 'Song'.

48 They all were looking for a king
To slay their foes and lift them high:
Thou cam'st, a little baby thing
That made a woman cry.
1883 'That Holy Thing', stanza 1.

49 There is no strength in unbelief. Even the unbelief of what is false is no source of might. It is the truth shining from behind that gives the strength to disbelieve.
The Marquis of Lossie (published 1906).

50 To be trusted is a greater compliment than to be loved.
The Marquis of Lossie (published 1906).

Macdonald, (James) Ramsay 1866–1937
Scottish politician, Prime Minister and Foreign Secretary of the first British Labour government (1924, 1929–31). He met the financial crisis of 1931 by forming a 'National' coalition government, which he led after a general election (1931–5).

51 The League of Nations grows in moral courage. Its frown will soon be more dreaded than a nation's arms, and when that happens, you and I shall have security and peace.
1929 Speech, London, 9 Nov.

52 We hear war called murder. It is not: it is suicide.
1930 Quoted in the *Observer*, 3 May.

MacDonnell, A(rchibald) G(ordon) 1895–1941
Scottish writer who lived most of his life in England, the subject of his best-known satirical novel.

53 England, their England.
1933 Title of novel.
▶ See Henley 411:7.

MacDougall, Ranald 1915–73
US screenwriter whose credits include *The Hasty Heart* (1949), *The Naked Jungle* (1954), *Queen Bee* (1955) and *The Mountain* (1956).

54 Alligators have the right idea, they eat their young.
1945 *Mildred Pierce* (with Catherine Turney).

McElligott, Tom (Thomas James) 1943–2003
US advertising executive.

55 You're never too bad to win.
1987 In the *Wall Street Journal*, 26 Mar.

McEnroe, John Patrick 1959–
US tennis player. He won four US Open singles titles and three Wimbledon titles. He was known for temperamental behaviour on court.

56 You cannot be serious!
1981 In protest at an umpire's decision at Wimbledon.

57 Being a celebrity is like being raped, and there's absolutely nothing a player can do about it.

Quoted in Colin Jarman *The Guinness Dictionary of Sports Quotations* (1990).

McEwan, Ian Russell 1948–

English writer. He established his reputation with two volumes of short stories before turning to novels. He has also written screenplays.

58 Her eyes, nose, mouth, skin, all might have been designed in committee to meet the barest requirements of feasibility.
   1981 *The Comfort of Strangers*, ch.6.

59 Shall there be womanly times? Or shall we die?
   1983 Refrain from *Or Shall We Die*, an oratorio.

60 Looking after children is one of the ways of looking after yourself.
   1992 *Black Dogs*, preface.

61 You can tell a lot from a person's nails. When a life starts to unravel, they're among the first to go.
   2005 *Saturday*.

62 When anything can happen, everything matters.
   2005 *Saturday*.

63 This is how the entire course of a life can be changed: by doing nothing.
   2007 *On Chesil Beach*.

McFadden, Robert D(ennis) 1937–

US journalist and writer. He has worked for the *New York Times* as a senior journalist since 1961, and is the author of two journalism-related books. His numerous press awards have included a Pulitzer Prize (1996).

64 That rarest of political creatures—a Labor leader who could actually win elections.
   1995 Of Harold Wilson. In the *New York Times*, 25 May.

65 He was rotund, provincial, resolutely middle-class, studiously ambiguous and sometimes wavering in his opinions.
   1995 Of Harold Wilson. In the *New York Times*, 25 May.

66 In an era of precipitous decline for Britain and its once-global empire, Harold Wilson was a fixture for 30 years, a solid workingman's socialist in a rumpled ready-to-wear suit and his trademark Gannex mackintosh.
   1995 Of Harold Wilson. In the *New York Times*, 25 May.

67 The silver-haired, pipe-smoking northerner was a consummate British politician: tenacious, shrewd, manipulative, a blend of homespun tastes, acid wit and pragmatic, often shifting policies…the symbol of an emerging middle-class Briton.
   1995 Of Harold Wilson. In the *New York Times*, 25 May.

McFarlane, J A, and Clements, Warren 1944–, 1952–

Canadian journalists.

68 Say *quotes* from the shortstop or the Prime Minister, but *quotations* from the Bible, Browning or Churchill.
   1990 *The Globe and Mail Style Book*.

69 The patron saint of journalists, officially named by the church, is St. Francis de Sales. The traditional patron saint of editors is St. John Bosco. (The protector of computer-age journalists may well be St. Anthony of Padua, patron saint of searchers for lost articles.)
   1990 *The Globe and Mail Style Book*.

McFarlane, Robert 'Bud' Carl 1937–

US government official. After serving with the Marines, he became National Security adviser to President Reagan (1983–5) and later founder of Global Energy Investors (GEI).

70 He knows so little and accomplishes so much.
   Of President Reagan. Quoted in George P Shultz *Turmoil and Triumph* (1993).

MacGill, Patrick 1890–1963

Irish navvy, novelist and poet. Sold into servitude by his farming parents, he escaped to Scotland where he laboured and hawked his verses before coming to literary attention. He emigrated to the US in 1930, where he fell into poverty and developed muscular sclerosis.

71 All the night the frogs go chuckle, all the day the birds are singing
   In the pond beside the meadow, by the roadway poplar-lined,
   In the field between the trenches are a million blossoms springing
   'Twixt the grass of silver bayonets where the lines of battle wind
   Where man has manned the trenches for the maiming of his kind.
   1917 *Soldier Songs*, 'The Trench'.

McGonagall, William c.1825–1902

Scottish self-styled 'poet and tragedian' from Dundee, most of his work was doggerel. The majority of his poems were originally produced as broadsheets and not collected until after his death.

72 Alas! Lord and Lady Dalhousie are dead, and buried at last,
   Which causes many people to feel a little downcast.
   1890 *Poetic Gems*, 'The Death of Lord and Lady Dalhousie', stanza 1.

73 Beautiful Railway Bridge of the Silv'ry Tay!
   Alas! I am very sorry to say
   That ninety lives have been taken away
   On the last Sabbath day of 1879,
   Which will be remember'd for a very long time.
   1890 *Poetic Gems*, 'The Tay Bridge Disaster', stanza 1.

74 Ye lovers of the picturesque, if ye wish to drown your grief,
   Take my advice, and visit the ancient town of Crieff;
   The climate is bracing, and the walks lovely to see
   Besides, ye can ramble over the district, and view the beautiful scenery.
   More Poetic Gems (published 1962), 'Beautiful Crieff', stanza 1.

75 The man that gets drunk is little else than a fool,
   And is in the habit, no doubt, of advocating for Home Rule;
   But the best Home Rule for him, as far as I can understand,
   Is the abolition of strong drink from the land.
   Last Poetic Gems (published 1968), 'The Demon Drink', stanza 9.

McGough, Roger 1937–

English poet, playwright and performer, associated with the 1960s Liverpool pop scene. His poetry is characterized by a dry, ironic wit and a feeling for the diction and rhythms of the street. He has also written children's books.

76 Let me die a youngman's death
not a clean and in-between-
the-sheets, holy-water death.
1967 'Let Me Die A Youngman's Death'.

77 Discretion is the better part of Valerie
(though all of her is nice).
1969 'Discretion'.

78 by thus keeping one pace ahead of myself
I need never catch up with the truth.
1973 'unlikely now'.

79 I could never begin a poem: 'When I am dead'
In case it tempted Fate, and Fate gave way.
1982 'When I Am Dead'.

80 Do people who wave at trains
Wave at the driver, or at the train itself?
Or, do people who wave at trains
Wave at the passengers? Those hurtling strangers,
The unidentifiable flying faces?
1982 'Waving At Trains'.

81 This is the mother
who one day chose
to smother the child
with kisses, and blows and blows and blows.
1982 'Kisses and Blows'.

MacGowan, Shane 1957–
English singer, member of The Pogues.

82 They died in their hundreds with no sign to mark where
Save the brass in the pocket of the entrepreneur
By landslide and rockblast they got buried so deep
That in death if not life they'll have peace while they sleep.
1985 'Navigator' (co-written with Jim Finer).

83 You're a bum
You're a punk
You're an old slut on junk
Lying there almost dead on a drip in that bed
You scumbag, you maggot
You cheap lousy faggot
Happy Christmas your arse I pray God it's our last.
1988 'Fairytale of New York' (co-written with Jim Finer).

84 Never mind Dylan and the Dead, this'll be Dylan and the Nearly Dead.
1997 On a gig in which he was to be support act for Bob Dylan. Quoted in *Q Magazine*, Apr.

85 Cram as much pleasure as you can into life, and rail against the pain that you have to suffer as a result.
1997 In *Loaded*, Nov.

86 I don't believe in the Hebrew God, some big hairy bastard with thunderbolts.
1999 In the *Irish Voice*, 9 Jun.

McGovern, George S(tanley) 1922–2012
US Democratic politician, Senator for South Dakota (1963–81). He made a bid for the presidential nomination in 1968, and unsuccessfully opposed Nixon in the 1972 presidential election. He tried again for the presidential nomination in 1984, but withdrew.

87 To those who charge that liberalism has been tried and found wanting, I answer that the failure is not in the idea but in the course of recent history. The New Deal was ended by World War II. The New Frontier was closed by Berlin and Cuba even before it was opened. And the Great Society lost its greatness in the jungles of Indochina.
1973 Lecture at Oxford University, 21 Jan.

McGregor, Ewan 1971–
Scottish actor.

88 I'm sometimes asked 'Can you lose the accent?' and I say 'No, but I can put on another one'.
2001 In *In Style*, Sep.

McGuigan, Barry 1961–
Irish boxer.

89 There is nothing like wealth for dulling desire.
2003 In *The Independent*, 29 Dec.

Machado de Assis, Joaquim Maria 1839–1908
Brazilian poet and novelist, writer of romantic stories and poems. *Memórias Póstumas de Brás Cubas* (1881) marks the beginning of his mature style, informed by both pessimism and wit.

90 *Cada estação da vida é uma edição, que corrige a anterior, e que será corrigida também, até a edição definitiva, que o editor dá de graça aos vermes.*
Each stage in life is an edition that supersedes the previous one and will also be superseded until the definitive edition: the one that the editor gives to the worms.
1881 *Memórias Póstumas de Brás Cubas*, ch.27 (translated as *Epitaph of a Small Winner*, 1952).

91 *A vida é tão bela que a mesma idéia da morte precisa de vir primeiro a ela, antes de se ver cumprida. Já me vás entendendo; lê agora outro capítulo.*
Life is so beautiful that even the idea of death must be born before it can be realized. You must already understand. Now read another chapter.
1899 *Dom Casmurro*, ch.133.

Machiavelli, Niccolò di Bernardo dei 1469–1527
Italian politician and political theorist. Obliged to withdraw from public life after an accusation of conspiracy (1513), he devoted himself to literature. His masterpiece is the pragmatic manual for statesmen, *Il Principe* ('The Prince', written in 1513, published in 1532).

92 *Gli uomini si debbano o vezzeggiare o spegnere; perché si vendicano delle leggeri offese, delle gravi non possono.*
Men should be either treated generously or destroyed, because they take revenge for slight injuries—for heavy ones they cannot.
1513 *Il Principe*, ch.3 (translated by Alan Gilbert).

93 *Nasce da questo una disputa: s'egli è meglio essere amato che temuto, o è converso. Rispondesi che si vorrebbe essere l'uno e l'altro; ma perché egli è difficile accozzarli insieme, è molto più sicuro essere temuto che amato, quando si abbia a mancare dell'uno de'due.*
This leads to a debate: is it better to be loved than feared, or the reverse? The answer is that it is desirable to be both, but because it is difficult to join them together, it is

much safer for a prince to be feared than loved, if he is to fail in one of the two.
1513 *Il Principe*, ch.8 (translated by Alan Gilbert).

94 It never or rarely happens that a republic or monarchy is well constituted, or its old institutions entirely reformed, unless it is only done by one individual.
1513–17 *Discourses on First Ten Books of Livy*.

McIlvanney, William Angus 1936–

Scottish writer. He is best known for his Ayrshire novels *Docherty* (1975) and *The Big Man* (1985), and his series of crime novels featuring the Glaswegian detective, Laidlaw. He has also written poetry, essays and short stories.

95 There is a kind of laughter people laugh at public events, as if a joke were a charity auction and they want to be seen to be bidding.
1985 *The Big Man*, ch.1.

96 That would have been a nice place, inside an idea, but it wasn't a place to live. It was necessary to live where the idea and the fact collided.
1985 *The Big Man*, ch.8.

McInerney, Jay 1955–

US author.

97 I'm glad I don't have a book coming out this month.
2001 Comment made by Jay McInerney to Brett Easton Ellis on 11 Sep, when the World Trade Center was destroyed. Ellis replied, 'I was just thinking the same thing'. Quoted in *The Guardian*, 15 Sep.

MacInnes, Colin 1914–79

English writer. He gave a voice to sections of society often ignored. He is best known for his novel *Absolute Beginners* (1959).

98 And I thought, 'My lord, one thing is certain, and that's that they'll make musicals one day about the glamour-studded 1950s.' And I thought, my heaven, one thing is certain too, I'm miserable.
1959 *Absolute Beginners*.

99 Tradition, if not constantly recreated, can be as much a millstone as a mill-wheel.
1961 *England, Half English*, 'England, Half English'.

1 In England, pop art and fine art stand resolutely back to back.
1961 *England, Half English*, 'Pop Songs and Teenagers'.

2 A coloured man can tell, in five seconds dead, whether a white man likes him or not. If the white man *says* he does, he is instantly—and usually quite rightly—mistrusted.
1961 *England, Half English*, 'A Short Guide for Jumbles'.

3 The decorations are like those of the embassy of a nation about to go into voluntary liquidation.
1961 *England, Half English*, 'See You At Mabel's'.

MacInnis, Joseph 1937–

Canadian doctor, environmentalist and undersea explorer.

4 The larger the island of knowledge, the longer the shoreline of wonder.
Quoted by Donald Grant in *The Globe and Mail*, 8 Nov 1986.

Mackay, Alan Lindsay 1926–

British scientist and Fellow of the Royal Society.

5 How can we have any new ideas or fresh outlooks when 90 per cent of all the scientists who have ever lived have still not died?
1969 In *Scientific World*, vol.13.

McKay, Claude originally Festus Claudius 1890–1948

Jamaican born US writer. He wrote poetry, novels, autobiography and a study of life in Harlem, and was a key figure in the Harlem Renaissance of the 1920s.

6 If we must die, let it not be like hogs
  Hunted and penned in an inglorious spot
  While round us bark the mad and hungry dogs,
  Making their mock at our accursed lot.
1922 *Harlem Shadows*, 'If We Must Die'.

7 Like men we'll face the murderous cowardly pack,
  Pressed to the wall, dying, but fighting back!
1922 *Harlem Shadows*, 'If We Must Die'.

Mackaye, Dorothy Disney 1904–92

US journalist and agony aunt, best known for editing the 'Can This Marriage be Saved?' column for the *Ladies Home Journal* for more than 30 years.

8 'He never listens' is universal in the institution of marriage.
Recalled on her death, 5 Sep 1992.

Macke, August 1887–1914

German painter, one of the founder members of the *Blaue Reiter* group of Expressionist artists.

9 To create forms means: to live. Are not children more creative in drawing directly from the secret of their sensations than the imitator of Greek forms? Are not savages artists who have forms of their own powerful as the form of thunder?
1912 *The Blaue Reiter Almanac*.

Mackellar, (Isobel Marion) Dorothea 1885–1968

Australian popular poet and novelist. Her works include *The Witch Maid* (1914), *Dreamharbour* (1923) and the novel *The Little Blue Devil* (1912). She wrote little after the mid-1920s, but translated widely from various European poets.

10 The love of field and coppice,
  Of green and shaded lanes,
  Of ordered woods and gardens
  Is running in your veins.
  Strong love of grey-blue distance
  Brown streams and soft, dim skies—I know
  but cannot share it,
  My love is otherwise.

  I love a sunburnt country,
  A land of sweeping plains,
  Of ragged mountain ranges,
  Of droughts and flooding rains.
  I love her far horizons,
  I love her jewel-sea,
  Her beauty and her terror—
  The wide brown land for me!
1905 'Core of My Heart', first published in the London *Spectator*. Collected as 'My Country' in *The Closed Door, and Other Verses* (1911).

McKellen, Sir Ian Murray 1939–
English stage and film actor and director.

11 I can't be absolutely certain, 30 years ago when I made the decision to become an actor, but certainly one of the reasons was it was the way to meet other queer men.
Quoted in Blake Green 'A Kingly McKellen as a Fascist in *Richard II*', in the Pink Pages, *San Francisco Chronicle*, 16 Aug 1992.

12 You can always pick out stage actors at the Oscars: they know how to walk.
2002 In the *Observer*, 17 Feb.

MacKenzie, Sir (Edward Montague) Compton 1883–1972
English writer and editor. His best-known books are *Sinister Street* (1913–14) and *Whisky Galore* (1947), which became a famous film.

13 Prostitution. Selling one's body to keep one's soul...one might say of most modern marriages that they were selling one's soul to keep one's body.
1918 *The Adventures of Sylvia Scarlett*, bk.2, ch.5.

14 You are offered a piece of bread and butter that feels like a damp handkerchief and sometimes, when cucumber is added to it, like a wet one.
1927 *Vestal Fire*, bk.1, ch.3.

15 Women do not find it difficult nowadays to behave like men, but they often find it extremely difficult to behave like gentlemen.
1933 *Literature in My Time*, ch.22.

MacKenzie, Lewis W 1940–
Canadian Major-General, retired, United Nations Chief of Staff for peacekeeping in Sarajevo, Bosnia-Herzegovina.

16 Countries that have soldiers in charge seem, more often than not, to be the ones where democracy is but a flickering candle sitting in an open window with a forecast of rain.
1993 Letter about his retirement, in *The Globe and Mail*, 21 Jan.

Mackintosh, Sir James 1765–1832
Scottish writer, philosopher and historian. He studied medicine, but settled in London as a journalist. His *Vindiciae Gallicae* (1791) was a defence of the French Revolution (he later recanted his views, 1815). He spent seven years in Bombay, becoming an MP on his return.

17 Men are never so good or so bad as their opinions.
1830 *Dissertation on the Progress of Ethical Philosophy*, section 6, 'Jeremy Bentham'.

18 Henry VIII perhaps approached as nearly to the ideal standard of perfect wickedness as the infirmities of human nature will allow.
1831 Of Henry's actions in executing Thomas More and Anne Boleyn. *History of England*, vol.2.

MacLaine, Shirley *pseudonym of* Shirley MacLean Beatty 1934–
US actress, sister of Warren Beatty. Her films include *The Apartment* (1959), *Irma La Douce* (1963), *Sweet Charity* (1968), *Terms of Endearment* (1983) and *Steel Magnolias* (1989).

19 I've played so many hookers they don't pay me in the regular way any more. They leave it on the dresser.
1989 In *New Woman*, Jul.

20 A person who knows how to laugh at himself will never cease to be amused.
2005 In *Family Circle* magazine, 9 Aug.

McLean, Don 1945–
US singer and songwriter. He enjoyed a series of hits in the early 1970s, among them the classic singles 'American Pie' (1972) and 'Vincent' (1972). He later concentrated on country music.

21 I can't remember if I cried
When I read about his widowed bride.
Something touched me deep inside
The day the music died.
1972 Of the death of Buddy Holly. 'American Pie'.

22 So bye, bye, Miss American Pie,
Drove my Chevy to the levee
But the levee was dry.
Them good old boys was drinkin' whiskey and rye
Singin' 'This'll be the day that I die.'
1972 'American Pie'.

23 And the three men I admired most,
The Father, Son and Holy Ghost,
They caught the last train for the coast
The day the music died.
1972 'American Pie'.

Maclean, Sir Fitzroy Hew 1911–96
English diplomat, soldier and traveller. Sent at his own request to Moscow, he travelled in Central Asia. During World War II he joined the Special Air Service in North Africa and later he was parachuted into Yugoslavia as Churchill's personal representative to contact Tito, then a guerrilla leader.

24 At first sight, landing by plane had seemed an infinitely more normal and agreeable method of entering the country than what Mr Churchill called 'jumping out of a parachute'.
1949 *Eastern Approaches*.

25 A spirit of contradiction has always, to some extent, guided my behaviour.
1949 *Eastern Approaches*.

26 It was unhealthy and unsafe, and of no interest whatever. 'But what,' I said, 'about the tigers?' 'Tigers, perhaps,' he replied pityingly, 'but no culture.'
1949 Of Lenkoran, Azerbaijan, in discussion with an Armenian official. *Eastern Approaches*.

Maclean, John 1879–1923
Scottish Marxist and revolutionary of almost legendary status in Glasgow, appointed Soviet Consul on the Clyde after the Russian Revolution. Ill health accentuated by frequent prison sentences led to his early death.

27 No government is going to take from me my right to speak, my right to protest against wrong, my right to do everything that is for the benefit of mankind. I am not here, then, as the accused; I am here as the accuser of capitalism dripping with blood from head to foot.
1918 Speech at his trial at the High Court, Edinburgh, 9 May, quoted in Nan Milton *John Maclean* (1973), ch.3.

MacLean, Sorley *Gaelic name* **Somhairle MacGill-Eain** 1911–96

Scottish poet. He wrote in Gaelic, in which language he was the most important late 20th century poet, and prepared his own English translations.

28 Ma thubhairt ar cainnt gu bheil a' chiall
co-ionann ris a' ghaol
chan fhior dhi.
If our language has said that reason
is identical with love,
it is not speaking the truth.
1943 'A Chiall's a Ghràidh' ('Reason and Love').

29 Mairg an t-sòil a chì air fairge
ian mór marbh na h-albann.
Pity the eye that sees on the ocean
the great dead bird of Scotland.
1943 'An t-Eilean', 'The Island'.

30 Tha tìm, am fiadh, an coille Hallaig.
Time, the deer, is in the wood of Hallaig.
1970 'Hallaig', epitaph.

31 Mura tig's ann theànas ni a Hallaig
a dh' ionnsaigh sàbaid nam marbh,
far a bheil an sluagh a' tathaich,
gach aon ghinealach a dh' fhalbh.
If it does not, I will go down to Hallaig,
to the Sabbath of the dead,
where the people are frequenting,
every single generation gone.
1970 'Hallaig'.

MacLeish, Archibald 1892–1982

US poet, Librarian of Congress (1939–44), Assistant Secretary of State (1944–5) and Professor of Rhetoric at Harvard (1949–62). He won Pulitzer Prizes for *Conquistador* (1932), *Collected Poems 1917–52* (1952) and his verse drama *J.B.* (1958).

32 A Poem should be palpable and mute
As a globed fruit.
1926 'Ars Poetica'.

33 A poem should be wordless
As the flight of birds.
1926 'Ars Poetica'.

34 A poem should not mean
But be.
1926 'Ars Poetica'.

35 We have learned the answers, all the answers:
It is the question that we do not know.
1928 'The Hamlet of A. MacLeish'.

36 If the poem can be improved by its author's explanations, it should never have been published.
1933 Author's note in *Poems*.

37 Keepers of books, keepers of print and paper on the shelves, librarians are keepers also of the records of the human spirit—the records of men's watch upon the world and on themselves.
1941 A Time to Speak, 'Of the Librarian's Profession'.

38 The dissenter is every human being at those moments in his life when he resigns momentarily from the herd and thinks for himself.
1956 'In Praise of Dissent', in the *New York Times*, 16 Dec.

39 Anything can make us look, only art can make us see.
1961 *Poetry and Experience*. 'Riverside'.

40 History, like a badly constructed concert hall, has occasional dead spots where the music can't be heard.
1967 In the *Observer*, 12 Feb.

41 Wildness and silence disappeared from the countryside, sweetness fell from the air, not because anyone wished them to vanish or fall but because throughways had to floor the meadows with cement to carry the automobiles which advancing technology produced.
1968 'The Great American Frustration', in the *Saturday Review*, 9 Jul.

42 To see the earth as we now see it, small and beautiful in that eternal silence where it floats, is to see ourselves as riders on the earth together, brothers on that bright loveliness in the unending night—brothers who *see* now they are truly brothers.
1968 On the first pictures from the moon. In the *New York Times*, 25 Dec.

43 The business of the law is to make sense of the confusion of what we call human life—to reduce it to order but at the same time to give it possibility, scope, even dignity.
1972 'Apologia', in the *Harvard Law Review*, Jun.

44 Poets…are literal-minded men who will squeeze a word till it hurts.
1972 'Apologia', in the *Harvard Law Review*, Jun.

45 We are great as our belief in human liberty—no greater. And our belief in human liberty is only ours when it is larger than ourselves.
1976 'Now Let Us Address The Main Question: Bicentennial of What?', in the *New York Times*, 3 Jul.

46 Poetry is the art of understanding what it is to be alive.
Recalled on his death, 20 Apr 1982.

47 If the art of poetry is…the art of making sense of the chaos of human experience, it's not a bad thing to see a lot of chaos.
On his work in government. Quoted in Scott Donaldson *Archibald MacLeish* (1992).

48 Mr Morgan struck me as a healthy and childish Britisher probably inhabiting the early 19th century.
Of financier J P Morgan. Quoted in Scott Donaldson *Archibald MacLeish* (1992).

MacLennan, Hugh 1927–90

Canadian novelist and essayist.

49 Boy Meets Girl in Winnipeg and Who Cares?
1960 Title of a magazine article in *Scotchman's Return and Other Essays*. It refers to the preference of Canadian editors, publishers, and readers for romance and drama set in foreign locales.

Macleod, Fiona

▶ *See* Sharp, William

Macleod, Iain Norman 1913–70

English Conservative politician, Chairman of the Conservative Party (1961–3). He refused to serve under Lord Home (having supported R A Butler's leadership claim), and spent two years editing the *Spectator*. He was shadow Chancellor under Heath (1965–70), and briefly Chancellor (1970).

50 The Socialists can scheme their schemes and the Liberals can dream their dreams, but we, at least, have work to do.
   1960 Speech at the Conservative Party Conference.

51 We now have the worst of both worlds—not just inflation on the one side or stagnation on the other, but both of them together. We have a sort of stagflation situation.
   1965 Speech in the House of Commons, Nov.

McLuhan, (Herbert) Marshall 1911–80

Canadian critic and cultural theorist. He claimed that it is the communication media *per se*, not the information and ideas which they broadcast, that influence society. His books include *The Gutenberg Galaxy* (1962) and *The Medium is the Message* (1969).

52 For tribal man space was the uncontrollable mystery. For technological man it is time that occupies the same role.
   1951 *The Mechanical Bride*, 'Magic that Changes Mood'.

53 The medium is the message.
   1959 Speech at the University of British Columbia, 30 Jun, following a symposium in Vancouver on the subject of music and the mass media. The phrase was later used as the title of ch.1 in *Understanding Media* (1964), and as a book title (1969).

54 The new electronic independence recreates the world in the image of a global village.
   1962 *The Gutenberg Galaxy*.

55 The car has become an article of dress without which we feel uncertain, unclad, and incomplete in the urban compound.
   1964 *Understanding Media*, ch.22.

56 Persons grouped around a fire or candle for warmth or light are less able to pursue independent thoughts, or even tasks, than people supplied with electric light. In the same way, the social and educational patterns latent in automation are those of self-employment and artistic autonomy.
   1964 *Understanding Media*, ch.33.

57 If the nineteenth century was the age of the editorial chair, ours is the century of the psychiatrist's couch.
   1964 *Understanding Media*.

58 Canada is the only country in the world that knows how to live without an identity.
   1967 'Canada: A Borderline Case', CBC radio broadcast, 29 May.

59 Life. Consider the alternative.
   1968 *War and Peace in the Global Village*.

60 Television brought the brutality of war into the comfort of the living room. Vietnam was lost in the living rooms of America, not on the battlefields of Vietnam.
   1975 Quoted in the *Montreal Gazette*, May.

61 Gutenburg made everybody a reader. Xerox makes everybody a publisher.
   1977 In the *Guardian Weekly*, 12 Jun.

Macmillan, Sir (Maurice) Harold, 1st Earl of Stockton 1894–1986

English Conservative politician. He succeeded Eden as Prime Minister (1957), and was re-elected in 1959. He resigned through ill health in 1963.

62 We have not overthrown the divine right of kings to fall down for the divine right of experts.
   1950 Speech, Strasbourg, 16 Aug.

63 I thought that the best thing to do was to settle up these little local difficulties, and then turn to the wider vision of the Commonwealth.
   1956 On departing for a Commonwealth conference, after sacking several members of his Cabinet in his Night of the Long Knives, Jan.

64 Forever poised between a cliché and an indiscretion.
   1956 On the role of a Foreign Secretary, in *Newsweek*, Apr.

65 Let us be frank about it. Most of our people have never had it so good. Go around the country, go to the industrial towns, go to the farms, and you will see a state of prosperity such as we have never had in my lifetime—nor indeed ever in the history of this country.
   1957 Speech, Bedford, 20 Jul. This is the original form of the oft-misquoted 'You never had it so good'.

66 At home, you always have to be a politician. When you are abroad, you almost feel yourself to be a statesman.
   1958 Speech during the first visit of a British Prime Minister to Australia, 17 Feb.

67 The most striking of all the impressions that I have formed since I left London a month ago is of the strength of African national consciousness. In different places it may take different forms, but it is happening everywhere. The wind of change is blowing through this continent. Whether we like it or not, the growth of national consciousness is a political fact.
   1960 Speech to the South African Parliament, 3 Feb.

68 Are we so sure that with 15 representatives...in NATO, acting under the unanimity rule, the deterrent would continue to deter? There may be one finger on the trigger, but there will be 15 fingers on the safety catch.
   1960 House of Commons, 30 May.

69 I was determined that no British government should be brought down by the action of two tarts.
   1963 On the Profumo scandal, referring specifically to Christine Keeler and Mandy Rice-Davies, Jul.

70 I have never found, in a long experience of politics, that criticism is ever inhibited by ignorance.
   1963 In the *Wall Street Journal*, 13 Aug.

71 A man who trusts nobody is apt to be the kind of man whom nobody trusts.
   1963 In the *New York Herald Tribune*, 17 Dec.

72 Tradition does not mean that the living are dead; it means that the dead are living.
   1963 In the *Manchester Guardian*, 18 Dec.

73 There are three bodies no sensible man directly challenges: the Roman Catholic Church, the Brigade of Guards, and the National Union of Mineworkers.
   1981 In the *Observer*, 22 Feb.

74 There is a growing division in our comparatively prosperous society between the South and the North and Midlands, which are ailing, that cannot be allowed to continue. There is a general sense of tension. The old English way might be to quarrel and have battles, but they were friendly. I can only describe as wicked the hatred that has been introduced, and which is to be found among different types of people today. Not merely an intellectual but a moral effort is required to get rid of it.
   1984 Maiden speech as the Earl of Stockton (60 years after first entering the House of Commons), House of Lords, 13 Nov.

75 First of all the Georgian Silver goes, and then all that nice furniture that used to be in the salon. Then the Canalettos go.
1985 Speech at a private dinner of the Tory Reform Group, 8 Nov, in a reference to privatization and the selling of profitable state-owned enterprises.

76 Margaret Thatcher is a brilliant tyrant surrounded by mediocrities.
1986 In *Newsweek*, 12 Oct.

77 A man who was alleged to have the rigidity of a poker without its occasional warmth.
Of Charles de Gaulle, whose nickname was 'Ramrod'. Quoted by Henry Fairlie in the *New Republic*, 20 Mar 1989.

78 If people want a sense of purpose, they should get it from their archbishop, they should certainly not get it from their politicians.
Quoted in *The Life of Politics*.

79 You've reached the stage where you must decide whether you're going to be a good writer or a good public servant. You can't be both.
Attributed comment to Michael O'Donovan (real name of the writer Frank O'Connor).

McMurtry, Larry Jeff   1936–

US novelist. Several of his novels have been filmed successfully, but his most significant work is the epic fusion of generic western and historical novel in *Lonesome Dove* (1985).

80 The Last Picture Show.
1966 Title of novel, subsequently filmed.

81 Terms of Endearment.
1975 Title of novel, subsequently filmed.

82 'We'll be the Indians, if we last another twenty years,' Augustus said. 'The way this place is settling up it'll be nothing but churches and dry-goods stores before you know it. Next thing you know they'll have to round us old rowdies and stick us on a reservation to keep us from scaring the ladies.'
1985 *Lonesome Dove*, ch.42

83 The cowboys had lived for months under the great bowl of the sky, and yet the Montana skies seemed deeper than the skies of Texas or Nebraska. Their depth and blueness robbed even the sun of its harsh force—it seemed smaller, in the vastness, and the whole sky no longer turned white at noon as it had in the lower plains. Always, somewhere to the north, there was a swath of blueness, with white cloads floating in it like petals in a pond.
1985 *Lonesome Dove*, ch.93.

84 Self-parody is the first portent of age.
1989 *Some Can Whistle*, pt.1, ch.14.

85 But the sorrowing are nomads, on a plain with few landmarks and no boundaries; sorrow's horizons are vague and its demands are few.
1989 *Some Can Whistle*, pt.4, ch.9.

McNamara, Robert Strange   1916–2009

US Democratic politician and businessman, Secretary of Defense in the Kennedy administration (1961) during the Vietnam War. He resigned to become President of the World Bank (1968–81), and later emerged as a critic of the nuclear arms race and of the Vietnam conflict, expressing regret for his role in the latter.

86 I don't object to it being called 'McNamara's war'… It is a very important war and I am pleased to be identified with it and do whatever I can to win it.
1964 On the Vietnam War. In the *New York Times*, 25 Apr.

87 A test case of US capacity to help a nation meet a Communist 'war of liberation'.
1964 Of the Vietnam War. Quoted in N Sheehan *The Pentagon Papers*.

88 Neither conscience nor sanity itself suggests that the United States is, or should or could be the global gendarme.
1966 Speech to US newspaper editors. Reported in the *New York Times*, 19 May.

89 I wondered if I'd ever see another Saturday night.
On the threat of nuclear war from Russian warheads in Cuba, Oct 1962. Quoted in Elie Abel *Missile Crisis* (1966).

90 One cannot fashion a credible deterrent out of an incredible action.
1968 On nuclear weapons. *The Essence of Security*.

91 We had a two-track approach, one political and the other military, and the military was designed to move us along the political track.
On the Vietnam War in late 1967. Quoted in Deborah Shapley *Promise and Power* (1993).

92 We tend to justify our actions and in a sense we color history to achieve that objective.
Quoted in Robert Siegel (ed) *The NPR Interviews* (1994).

93 Although we sought to do the right thing—and believed we were doing the right thing—in my judgement, hindsight proves us wrong.
1995 *In Retrospect: The tragedy and lessons of Vietnam* (with Brian Van de Mark).

MacNeice, (Frederick) Louis   1907–63

Irish poet born in Belfast. He was closely associated with the British left-wing poets of the 1930s, especially W H Auden with whom he wrote *Letters from Iceland* (1937). He also wrote radio drama, including *The Dark Tower* (broadcast 1946, published 1947). His *Collected Poems* was published in 1966.

94 Something of glass about her, of dead water,
Chills and holds us,
Far more fatal than painted flesh or the lodestone of live hair
This despair of crystal brilliance.
1935 *Poems*, 'Circe'.

95 World is crazier and more of it than we think,
Incorrigibly plural.
1935 *Poems*, 'Snow'.

96 The little sardine men crammed in a monster toy
Who tilt their aggregate beast against our crumbling Troy.
1935 *Poems*, 'Turf-stacks'.

97 It's no go the merrygoround, it's no go the rickshaw,
All we want is a limousine and a ticket for the peepshow.
Their knickers are made of crêpe-de-chine, their shoes are made of python,
Their halls are lined with tiger rugs and their walls with the heads of bison.
1937 'Bagpipe Music', stanza 1.

98 It's no go my honey love, it's no go my poppet;
Work your hands from day to day, the winds will blow the profit.

McNeil

The glass is falling hour by hour, the glass will fall for ever,
But if you break the bloody glass, you won't hold up the weather.
1937 'Bagpipe Music', stanza 10.

99 And the gods are absent and the men are still—
Noli me tangere, my soul is forfeit.
Some are now happy in the hive of home,
Thigh over thigh and a light in the night nursery,
And some are hungry under the starry dome
And some sit turning handles.
1938 *Autumn Journal*, part 2.

1 Spider, spider, spin
Your register and let me sleep a little,
Not now in order to end but to begin
The task begun so often.
1938 *Autumn Journal*, part 2.

2 All of London littered with remembered kisses.
1938 *Autumn Journal*, part 4.

3 Tonight we sleep
On the banks of Rubicon—the die is cast;
There will be time to audit
The accounts later, there will be sunlight later
And the equation will come out at last.
1938 *Autumn Journal*, part 24.

4 Time was away and somewhere else.
1939 'Meeting Point'. Collected in *Collected Poems 1925–1948* (1949).

5 In my childhood trees were green
And there was plenty to be seen.
Come back early or never come.
1941 *Plant and Phantom*, 'Autobiography', l.1–3.

6 The dark was talking to the dead;
The lamp was dark beside my bed.
1941 *Plant and Phantom*, 'Autobiography', l.13–14.

7 The best people never land, sir.
1946 Steward to Roland. *The Dark Tower* (published 1947).

8 For the last blossom is the first blossom
And the first blossom is the best blossom
And when from Eden we take our way
The morning after is the first day.
'Apple Blossom', in *Collected Poems*, 1966.

9 His father gave him a box of truisms
Shaped like a coffin, then his father died;
The truisms remained on the mantelpiece.
'The Truisms', in *Collected Poems*, 1966.

McNeil, Robert

Scottish journalist.

10 Mein Banff.
Suggested title for a biography of Alex Salmond, leader of the Scottish Nationalist Party and MP for Banff and Buchan.

MacQueen, Robert, Lord Braxfield 1722–99

Scottish judge who presided over many famous trials in Edinburgh. Notorious for his harsh sentencing and cruel humour, he was known as the 'hanging judge', and was the original for R L Stevenson's Lord Hermiston in *Weir of Hermiston*.

11 Muckle he made o' that; he was hanget.
1794 Riposte at the trial of a political reformer, when the defendant remarked that all great men had been reformers, 'even our Saviour himself'. Quoted in Lord Cockburn *Memorials of his Time* (1856), ch.2.

12 Ye're a verra clever chiel', man, but ye wad be nane the waur o' a hanging.
Quoted in John G Lockhart *Memoirs of the Life of Sir Walter Scott, Bart.* (1837–8), ch.48.

13 Let them bring me prisoners, and I'll find them law.
Quoted in Lord Cockburn *Memorials of his Time* (1856), ch.2.

MacRéamoinn, Sean Seamas Criostoir 1921–2007

Irish broadcaster and journalist.

14 I am becoming like the Irish Census, broken down by Age, Sex, and Religion.
1991 Chairing a lecture on Parnell, Merriman Summer School.

Madan, Geoffrey 1895–1947

English aphorist.

15 Conservative ideal of freedom and progress: everyone to have an unfettered opportunity of remaining exactly where they are.
Collected in *Geoffrey Madan's Notebooks* (published 1981).

Madison, James 1751–1836

US politician and 4th President (1809–17), co-author of the *Federalist Papers* (1787–8). Originator of the Virginia Plan, his compromise measure on the status of slaves ensured adoption of the Constitution in slave states. He presided over the 1812 war with Britain.

16 The diversity in the faculties of men, from which the rights of property originate, is not less an insuperable obstacle to a uniformity of interests. The protection of those faculties is the first object of government.
1787 *The Federalist*, Nov.

17 What is government itself but the greatest of all reflections on human nature? If men were angels, no government would be necessary. If angels were to govern men, neither external nor internal controls on government would be necessary.
1788 *The Federalist*, Jan.

Madoff, Bernie (Bernard Lawrence) 1938–

US financier, imprisoned for fraud in 2009 for 150 years after being found guilty of the largest financial fraud in US history.

18 I left a legacy of shame. It is something I will live with for the rest of my life.
2009 Speaking in court after being sentenced.

Madonna *full name* Madonna Louise Veronica Ciccone 1958–

US pop singer and actress.

19 We are living in a material world
And I am a material girl.
1985 'Material Girl'.

20 Many people see Eva Perón as either a saint or as the incarnation of Satan. That means I can definitely identify with her.
1996 On playing Eva Perón in the film *Evita*. Quoted in *Newsweek*, 5 Feb.

21 If I had known I would be so universally misunderstood, maybe I wouldn't have been so rebellious and outspoken.
Quoted in the *Guinness Rockopedia* (1998).

22 Sure, I like to provoke to get a reaction, but there's always a reason behind it. There's always some minds that need to get opened, some ears that need to listen, some ideals that need to change.
2014 Quoted on thestar.com, 26 Dec.

23 Sometimes you have to be a bitch to get things done.
Attributed.

Maeterlinck, Maurice 1862–1949

Belgian playwright and poet. The success enjoyed by his play *Pelléas et Mélisande* (1892) established him as the leading playwright of the Symbolist movement. He was awarded a Nobel prize in 1911.

24 *L'Oiseau bleu.*
The Blue Bird.
1908 Title of play.

Magidson, Herb 1906–86

US songwriter.

25 Music, Maestro, Please.
1938 Title of song.

Magna Carta

The Great Charter obtained from King John in 1215, the basis of English political and personal liberty.

26 *Nullius liber homo capiatur, vel imprisonetur, aut dissaisiatur, aut utlagetur, aut exuletur, aut aliquo modo destruator, nec super eum ibimus, nec super eum mittemus, nisi per legale judicium parium suorum vel per legem terrae.*
No free man shall be taken or imprisoned or dispossessed, or outlawed or exiled, or in any way destroyed, nor will we go upon him, nor will we send against him except by the lawful judgement of his peers or by the law of the land.
1215 Clause 39.

27 *Nulli vendemus, nulli negabimus aut differemus, rectum aut justitiam.*
To no man will we sell, or deny, or delay, right or justice.
1215 Clause 40.

Mahathir, Mohamad 1925–

Malaysian politician and the country's longest serving Prime Minister, holding office from 1981 to 2003.

28 I'm brash and abrasive but that's because I've noticed when people are nice and polite they never get anywhere.
c.1990 Quoted in the *Eastern Express*, 24 Apr 1995.

29 If you can't be famous, at least you can be notorious.
c.1994 Quoted in the *Eastern Express*, 24 Apr 1995.

30 We need an opposition to remind us if we are making mistakes. When you are not opposed you think everything you do is right.
2005 Quoted in *The Star*, 11 Dec.

Mahler, Gustav 1860–1911

Austrian composer, conductor and artistic director at the Vienna State Opera (1897). He resigned after 10 years to conduct the New York Philharmonic (1908–11). He is best known for the song-symphony *Das Lied von der Erde* ('The Song of the Earth').

31 A symphony must be like the world, it must embrace everything.
1907 In conversation with Sibelius. Quoted in Ian Crofton and Donald Fraser *A Dictionary of Musical Quotations* (1985).

32 *Endlich fortissimo!*
Fortissimo at last!
1907 On seeing the Niagara Falls. Quoted in Charles Osborne *The Dictionary of Composers* (1977).

33 He is young and perhaps he is right. Maybe my ear is not sensitive enough.
Of Schoenberg's music. Quoted in Lebrecht *Discord* (1982).

Mahony, Francis Sylvester *pseudonym* Father Prout 1804–66

Irish priest and humorous writer. He became a Jesuit priest but was expelled after a late-night frolic. After a spell as a priest in Italy, he turned to journalism in London.

34 And cymbals glorious
Swinging uproarious
In the gorgeous turrets
Of Notre Dame.
'The Bells of Shandon'.

35 O the bells of Shandon
Sound far more grand on
The pleasant waters
Of the River Lee.
'The Bells of Shandon'.

Mailer, Norman Kingsley 1923–2007

US novelist and journalist. An inveterate polemicist and high-profile public figure, he was arguably the most controversial figure in post-war US letters.

36 The Naked and the Dead.
1948 Title of novel.

37 Hip is the sophistication of the wise primitive in a giant jungle.
1957 In *Dissent*, Summer.

38 Each day a few more lies eat into the seed with which we are born, little institutional lies from the print of newspapers, the shock waves of television, and the sentimental cheats of the movie screen.
1959 *Advertisements for Myself*, 'First Advertisement for Myself'.

39 America is a hurricane, and the only people who do not hear the sound are those fortunate if incredibly stupid and smug White Protestants who live in the center, in the serene eye of the big wind.
1959 *Advertisements for Myself*, 'Advertisement for "Games and Ends"'.

40 There is probably no sensitive heterosexual alive who is not preoccupied with his latent homosexuality.
1959 *Advertisements for Myself*, 'The Homosexual Villain'.

41 The final purpose of art is to intensify, even, if necessary, to exacerbate, the moral consciousness of people.
1959 'Hip, Hell, and The Navigator', in *Western Review*, no.23, Winter.

42 Every moment of one's existence one is growing into more or retreating into less. One is always living a little more or dying a little bit.
1959 'Hip, Hell, and The Navigator', in *Western Review*, no. 23, Winter.

43 Once a newspaper touches a story, the facts are lost forever, even to the protagonists.
1960 In *Esquire*, Jun.

44 A modern democracy is a tyranny whose borders are undefined; one discovers how far one can go only by traveling in a straight line until one is stopped.
1963 *The Presidential Papers*, preface.

45 In America few people will trust you unless you are irreverent.
1963 *The Presidential Papers*, preface.

46 Ultimately a hero is a man who would argue with the gods, and so awakens devils to contest his vision.
1963 *The Presidential Papers*, preface.

47 In America all too few blows are struck into flesh. We kill the spirit here, we are experts at that. We use psychic bullets and kill each other cell by cell.
1963 *The Presidential Papers*, 'Fourth Presidential Paper'.

48 A high church for the true mediocre.
1963 Of the FBI. *The Presidential Papers*, 'Sixth Presidential Paper'.

49 Writing books is the closest men ever come to childbearing.
1965 'Mr Mailer Interviews Himself', in the *New York Times Book Review*, 17 Sep.

50 The sense of a long last night over civilization is back again.
1966 *Cannibals and Christians*, 'Introducing Our Argument'.

51 Sentimentality is the emotional promiscuity of those who have no sentiment.
1966 *Cannibals and Christians*, 'My Hope For America'.

52 There is one expanding horror in American life. It is that our long odyssey toward liberty, democracy and freedom-for-all may be achieved in such a way that utopia remains forever closed, and we live in freedom and hell, debased of style, not individual from one another, void of courage, our fear rationalized away.
1966 *Cannibals and Christians*, 'My Hope For America'.

53 What characterizes a member of a minority group is that he is forced to see himself as both exceptional and insignificant, marvelous and awful, good and evil.
1966 *Cannibals and Christians*, 'A Speech At Berkeley on Vietnam Day'.

54 The surest way not to be remembered is to talk about the way you want to be.
1968 Interview in *Playboy*, Aug.

55 New York is one of the capitals of the world and Los Angeles is a constellation of plastic. San Francisco is a lady, Boston has become Urban Renewal, Philadelphia and Baltimore and Washington blink like dull diamonds in the smog of Eastern Megapolis, and New Orleans is unremarkable past the French Quarter. Detroit is a one-trade town, Pittsburgh has lost its golden triangle. St Louis has become the golden arch of the corporation, and nights in Kansas City close early. The oil depletion allowance makes Houston and Dallas naught but checkerboards for this sort of game. But Chicago is a great American city. Perhaps it is the last of the great American cities.
1969 *Miami and the Siege of Chicago*, 'The Siege of Chicago'.

56 The horror of the Twentieth Century was the size of each event, and the paucity of its reverberation.
1970 *Of A Fire On The Moon*, pt.1, ch.2.

57 The difference between writing a book and being on television is the difference between conceiving a child and having a baby made in a test tube.
1971 'The Siege of Mailer: Hero to Historian', in *Village Voice*, 21 Jan.

58 So we think of Marilyn who was every man's love affair with America, Marilyn Monroe who was blonde and beautiful and had a sweet little rinky-dink of a voice and all the cleanliness of all the clean American backyards.
1973 *Marilyn*.

59 No physical activity is so vain as boxing. A man gets into the ring to attract admiration. In no sport, therefore, can you be more humiliated.
1976 *The Fight*.

60 The true religion of America has always been America.
1984 Interview in *Time Out*, 27 Sep–3 Oct.

61 All the security around the American President is just to make sure the man who shoots him gets caught.
1990 In the *Sunday Telegraph*, 4 Mar.

62 When a novel comes, it's a grace. Something in the cosmos has forgiven you long enough so that you can start.
1991 In *The Guardian*, 5 Oct.

63 Writing a best-seller with conscious intent to do so is, after all, a state of mind that is not without comparison to the act of marrying for money only to discover that the absence of love is more onerous than anticipated.
2003 *The Spooky Art: Some Thoughts on Writing*.

64 Movies are more likely than literature to reach deep feelings in people.
2003 *The Spooky Art: Some Thoughts on Writing*.

65 Heaven and Hell make no sense if the majority of humans are a complex mixture of good and evil. There's no reason to receive a reward if you're 57/43—why sit around forever in an elevated version of Club Med? That's almost impossible to contemplate.
2007 *On God*.

66 One of my basic notions for a long, long time is that there is this mysterious mountain out there called reality. We novelists are always trying to climb it. We are mountaineers, and the question is, Which face do you attack? Different faces call for different approaches, and some demand a knotty and convoluted interior style. Others demand great simplicity. The point is that style is an attack on the nature of reality.
2007 In *The Paris Review*, Summer issue.

Maillart, Ella Kini 1903–97

Swiss explorer, writer, actress and athlete. She captained the Swiss women's hockey team and represented Switzerland in skiing and sailing. In 1932 she travelled alone to Russian Turkestan and in 1934 to northeastern China.

67 No. Cost what it may I am determined to go East. The nomad's life enthralls me. Its restlessness pursues me: it is as much part of me as of the sailor. All parts and none are home to me, and all arriving only a new setting forth.
1934 *Des Monts Célestes aux Sables Rouges* (translated by John Rodder as *Turkestan Solo: One Woman's Expedition from the Tien Shan to the Kizil Kum*).

68 Wherever I go, it is always the secret life of such simple, straightforward races that I seek, people whom a fair face

is sufficient to content. Only by returning to their way of life, can we ever hope to find a way out of the bogs in which we vainly stumble.
>**1934** *Des Monts Célestes aux Sables Rouges* (translated by John Rodder as *Turkestan Solo: One Woman's Expedition from the Tien Shan to the Kizil Kum*).

69 So far I like India.
>**1935** On crossing the Mintaka Pass at the extreme border of China. Quoted in Peter Fleming *News from Tartary* (1936).

Maimonides *properly* Moses ben Maimon 1135–1204
Spanish-born Jewish philosopher, rabbi and physician, one of the greatest Hebrew scholars. His philosophical work *Guide to the Perplexed* (1190) attempts to reconcile Greek philosophy and Judaism.

70 There is one [disease] which is widespread, and from which men rarely escape. This disease varies in degree in different men… I refer to this: that every person thinks his mind…more clever and more learned than it is… I have found that this disease has attacked many an intelligent person… They…express themselves [not only] upon the science with which they are familiar, but upon other sciences about which they know nothing… If met with applause…so does the disease itself become aggravated.
>*Aphorisms*. Quoted in *Bulletin of the History of Medicine*, vol.3, p.555 (1935).

Maintenon, Françoise d'Aubigné, Marquise de
known as **Madame de Maintenon** 1635–1719

Second wife of Louis XIV of France. Impoverished widow of the crippled poet Paul Scarron, in 1669 she became governess to Louis' sons. After the queen's death (1683) he married her secretly. She retired to her educational foundation at St-Cyr after his death.

71 You must make use of people according to their abilities, and realize that absolutely no one is perfect.
>**1679** Letter to Count d'Aubigné, 25 Sep.

Major, Sir John 1943–
English Conservative politician and Prime Minister (1990–7). He rose quickly under Margaret Thatcher to become Chancellor of the Exchequer on Lawson's resignation (1989). After Thatcher's downfall he became Prime Minister, and his government was re-elected in 1992.

72 I hope…to build a society of opportunity. By opportunity, I mean an open society—a society in which what people fulfil will depend upon their talent, their application, and their good fortune. What people achieve should depend particularly on those things, and I hope increasingly in the future that that will be the case.
>**1990** Address on entering No.10 Downing Street for the first time as Prime Minister, 27 Nov.

73 I think that we had better start again, somewhere else.
>**1991** Attributed remark during a Cabinet meeting when the Cabinet Room was rocked by an IRA mortar attack on No.10 Downing Street, 7 Feb.

74 Only in Britain could it be thought a defect to be 'too clever by half'. The probability is that too many people are too stupid by three-quarters.
>**1991** Quoted in the *Observer*, 7 Jul.

75 When the final curtain comes down, it's time to get off the stage.

>**1997** Outside 10 Downing Street on 2 May, leaving office as Prime Minister and announcing that he would resign as Party Leader. In *The Guardian*, 3 May.

76 So right. OK. We lost.
>**1997** On election night. In *The Guardian*, 3 May.

77 Margaret has been at her happiest confronting political dragons: I chose consensus.
>**1999** On the difference between his approach to politics and that of Margaret Thatcher. In *The Autobiography*.

78 Oh, Lord, if I must die today,
Please make it after Close of Play.
For this, I know, if nothing more,
I will not go, without the score.
>**2005** 'A Cricket Prayer', in *The Times*, 5 Sep.

79 If the answer is more politicians, you are asking the wrong question.
>**2007** Attributed by Vernon Bogdanor in *The Sunday Telegraph*, 11 Feb.

Makin, Bathsua b. c.1600
English poet and educator. She was appointed tutor to Princess Elizabeth in the 1640s, a post usually held by a man.

80 A Learned Woman is thought to be a Comet, that bodes Mischief, when ever it appears.
>**1673** *An Essay to Revive the Antient Education of Gentlewomen In Religion, Manners, Art and Tongues, With An Answer to the Objections against this Way of Education*.

Makwetu, Clarence 1931–
South African politician, president of the radical Pan-Africanist Congress (1990–7). Initially opposed to negotiation, he agreed to talks with other parties in the early 1990s.

81 We are determined to confront the oppressor with one voice.
>**1991** Addressing the first formal joint meeting for 30 years of the PAC and the rival African National Congress, 15 Apr.

Malamud, Bernard 1914–86
US Jewish writer. Novels including *The Assistant* (1957), *The Fixer* (1966), *Dublin's Lives* (1979) and *God's Grace* (1982) established his reputation as one of the finest novelists of the post-war period.

82 Levin wanted friendship and got friendliness; he wanted steak and they offered spam.
>**1961** *A New Life*, pt.6.

83 'Mourning is a hard business,' Cesare said. 'If people knew there'd be less death.'
>**1963** *Idiot's First*, 'Life Is Better Than Death'.

84 There comes a time in a man's life when to get where he has to go—if there are no doors or windows he walks through a wall.
>**1973** *Rembrandt's Hat*, 'The Man in the Drawer'.

85 I think I said 'All men are Jews except they don't know it.' I doubt I expected anyone to take the statement literally. But I think it's an understandable statement and a metaphoric way of indicating how history, sooner or later, treats all men.
>'An Interview', in L and J Fields (eds) *Bernard Malamud* (1975).

86 Comedy, I imagine, is harder to do consistently than tragedy, but I like it spiced in the wine of sadness.
>**1975** Interview in *Paris Review*, Spring.

Malcolm X

87 I love metaphor. It provides two loaves where there seems to be one. Sometimes it throws in a load of fish.
1975 Interview in *Paris Review*, Spring.

88 The past exudes legend: one can't make pure clay of time's mud. There is no life that can be recaptured wholly; as it was. Which is to say that all biography is ultimately fiction.
1979 *Dubin's Lives*.

Malcolm X originally Malcolm Little 1925–65

US black nationalist leader. Converted to the Black Muslims while in prison, on his release he assumed a new name and promoted the sect. He later founded his own organization, for Afro-American Unity, and in the resulting factional feuding was assassinated.

89 If you're born in America with a black skin, you're born in prison.
1963 Interview, Jun.

90 It has always been my belief that I, too, will die by violence. I have done all that I can to be prepared.
1965 *The Autobiography of Malcolm X*.

91 We didn't land on Plymouth Rock. It landed on us.
Quoted in *Life*, Fall issue 1990.

Malevich, Kasimir 1878–1935

Russian painter and designer. A pioneer of abstract art.

92 Only when the habit of one's consciousness to see in paintings bits of nature, madonnas and shameless nudes has disappeared, shall we see a pure-painting composition.
1915 Manifesto, quoted in C Gray *The Russian Experiment in Art* (rev edn 1986).

Mallarmé, Stéphane 1842–98

French poet, a leading writer in the Symbolist movement.

93 *Il n'y a que la Beauté—et elle n'a qu'une expression parfaite, la Poésie.*
There is only beauty—and it has only one perfect expression, poetry.
1867 Letter to Cazalis.

94 *Le vierge, le vivace et le bel aujourd'hui.*
The virgin, the vibrant and the beautiful today.
1881 *Plusieurs Sonnets*, no.1.

95 *La Poésie est l'expression, par le langage humain ramenée à son rythme essentiel, du sens mystérieux des aspects de l'existence; elle doue ainsi d'authenticité notre séjour et constitue la seule tâche spirituelle.*
Poetry is an expression, through human language restored to its essential rhythm, of the mysteriousness of existence; it endows our life with authenticity and constitutes our only spiritual task.
1884 Letter to M. Léo d'Orfer, 27 Jun.

96 *La chair est triste, hélas! et j'ai lu tous les livres.*
The flesh is sad, alas! and I've read all the books.
1887 'Brise marine', in *Poésies, Du Parnasse Contemporain* (1893).

97 *Dire au peintre qu'il faut prendre la nature comme elle est, vaut de dire au virtuose qu'il peut s'asseoir sur le piano.*
Telling a painter that he must take nature as it is is like telling a virtuoso that he can sit on the piano.
1888 *Le 'ten o'clock' de M. Whistler*.

98 *Nuit blanche de glaçons et de neige cruelle!*
White night of icicles and bitter snow!
1893 *Poésies, Hérodiade*, 'La Nourrice'.

99 *Donner un sens plus pur aux mots de la tribu.*
Bestow a purer sense on the language of the horde.
1893 *Poésies, Hommages et Tombeaux*, 'Le Tombeau d'Edgar Poe' (translated by Henry Weinfield, 1994).

1 *Tel qu'en Lui-même enfin l'éternité le change.*
As for Himself at last eternity changes him.
1893 *Poésies, Hommages et Tombeaux*, 'Le Tombeau d'Edgar Poe' (translated by Henry Weinfield, 1994).

2 *Un coup de dés n'abolira jamais le hasard.*
A throw of the dice will never abolish chance.
1914 Title of poem, in *Cosmopolis*, May.

Mallet-Stevens, Robert 1886–1945

French architect.

3 Architecture is an art which is basically geometrical. The cube is the basis of architecture because the right angle is necessary—the steps of a staircase consist of vertical and horizontal planes and the corners of rooms are nearly always right angles. We need right angles.
1924 'Architecture and Geometry', in *Bulletin de la Vie Moderne*, Paris.

Mallory, George Leigh 1886–1924

English mountaineer. He disappeared while attempting to climb Everest.

4 Because it's there.
1923 When asked 'Why do you want to climb Mount Everest?'. Quoted in the *New York Times*, 18 Mar.

Malory, Sir Thomas d.1471

English writer. His masterpiece, the *Morte d'Arthur*, a cycle of Arthurian legends, influenced Tennyson and other. It was completed c.1470 and a version was printed by Caxton in 1485.

5 The third sister, Morgan le Fey, was put to scole in a nonnery, and ther she lerned so moche that she was a grete clerke of nygromancye.
c.1470 *Morte d'Arthur*, bk.1, ch.2.

6 So the child was delyverd unto Merlyn, and so he bare it forth unto syre Ector and made an holy man to crysten hym and named hym Arthur.
c.1470 *Morte d'Arthur*, bk.1, ch.2.

7 'WHOSO PULLETH OUTE THIS SWERD OF THIS STONE AND ANVYLD IS RIGHTWYS KYNGE BORNE OF ALL ENGLOND'
c.1470 *Morte d'Arthur*, bk.1, ch.4. Inscription on the sword. Arthur was able to remove the sword with ease, and thus became king.

8 And there had Arthure the firste syght of queene Gwenyvere, the kyngis doghter of the londe of Camylarde, and ever afftir he loved hir.
c.1470 *Morte d'Arthur*, bk.1, ch.18.

9 'That is the Ladye of the Lake,' seyde Merlion. 'There ys a grete roche, and therein ys as fayre a paleyce as ony on erthe, and rychely besayne. And thys damesel woll come to you anone, and than speke ye fayre to hir, that she may gyff you that swerde.'
c.1470 To Arthur. *Morte d'Arthur*, bk.1, ch.25.

10 And so kyng Lodgreaunce delyverd hys doughtir Gwenyver unto Merlion, and the Table Rounde.
c.1470 *Morte d'Arthur*, bk.3, ch.1.

11 'What tydynges at Camelot?' seyde that on knyght. 'By my hede, there have I been and aspied the courte of kynge Arthure, and there ys such a felyshyp that they may never be brokyn, and well-nyghe all the world holdith with Arthure, for there ys the floure of chevalry.'
c.1470 *Morte d'Arthur*, bk.3, ch.14.

12 And so at that tyme sir Launcelot had the grettyste name of ony knyght of the worlde, and moste he was honoured of hyghe and lowe.
c.1470 *Morte d'Arthur*, bk.6, ch.18.

13 'But one thyng begyled us, that we myght nat se the Holy Grayle hit was so preciously coverde. Wherefore I woll make here a vow that to-morne, withoute longer abydynge, I shall laboure in the queste of the Sankgreall.'
c.1470 Sir Gawain. *Morte d'Arthur*, bk.13, ch.7.

14 And thus hit passes on frome Candylmas untyll Ester, that the moneth of May was com, whan every lusty harte begynnith to blossom and to burgyne. For, lyke as trees and erbys burgenyth and florysshyth in May, lyke wyse every lusty harte that is ony maner of lover spryngith, burgenyth, buddyth, and florysshyth in lusty dedis.
c.1470 *Morte d'Arthur*, bk.18, ch.25.

15 And there he bounde the gyrdyll aboute the hyltis, and threw the swerde as farre into the watir as he myght. And there cam an arme and an honde above the watir, and toke hit and cleyght hit, and shoke hit thryse and braundysshed, and than vanysshed with the swerde into the watir.
c.1470 *Morte d'Arthur*, bk.21, ch.5.

16 Yet som men say in many partys of Inglonde that kynge Arthur ys nat dede...and men say that he shall com agayne, and he shall win the Holy Crosse. Yet I woll nat say that hit shall be so, but rather I wolde sey: here in thys there ys wrytten upon the tumbe thys: HIC IACET ARTHURUS, REX QUONDAM REXQUE FUTURUS. [Here lies Arthur, the once and future king].
c.1470 *Morte d'Arthur*, bk.21, ch.7.

17 Herein may be seen noble chyvalrye, curtosye, humanyté, frendlynesse, hardynesse, love, frendshyp, cowardyse, murdre, hate, vertue, and synne.
c.1485 *Morte d'Arthur*, Caxton's preface.

Malouf, David 1934–

Australian novelist and librettist, of Lebanese and English extraction. His works include *An Imaginary Life* (1978), *Remembering Babylon* (1993) and *Dream Stuff* (2000).

18 'Do not shoot,' it shouted. 'I am a B-b-british object!'
1993 *Remembering Babylon*, ch.1.

Malthus, Thomas Robert 1766–1834

English economist. His anonymous *Essay on the Principle of Population* (1798) argued that population tends to increase faster than the means of subsistence, and that efforts should be made to cut the birth rate. He also wrote *Principles of Political Economy* (1820).

19 Population, when unchecked, increases in geometrical ratio. Subsistence only increases in arithmetical ratio.
1798 *An Essay on the Principle of Population*.

20 All the immediate checks to population—seem to be resolvable into moral restraint, vice and misery.
1798 *An Essay on the Principle of Population*.

21 The perpetual struggle for room and food.
1798 *An Essay on the Principle of Population*.

22 A man who is born into a world already possessed, if he cannot get subsistence from his parents on whom he has a just demand, and if the society do not want his labour, has no claim of *right* to the smallest portion of food, and, in fact, has no business to be where he is.
1803 *An Essay on the Principle of Population* (revised edn).

23 The employment of the poor in roads and public works, and a tendency among landlords and persons of property to build, to improve and beautify their grounds, and to employ workmen and menial servants, are the means most within our power and most directly calculated to remedy the evils arising from disturbance in the balance of produce and consumption.
1820 *Principles of Political Economy*.

Mamet, David Alan 1947–

US dramatist, screenwriter and director. His demotic language and hard-hitting social observation have made him a significant voice in modern US theatre. He has translated works by Chekhov and written various screenplays. He has also directed films and published essay collections.

24 Sexual Perversity in Chicago.
1976 Title of play.

25 We respond to a drama to that extent to which it corresponds to our dream life.
1986 *Writing in Restaurants*, 'A National Dream-Life'.

26 We live in oppressive times. We have, as a nation, become our own thought police; but instead of calling the process by which we limit our expression of dissent and wonder 'censorship', we call it 'concern for commercial viability'.
1986 *Writing in Restaurants*, 'Radio Drama'.

27 Policemen so cherish their status as keepers of the peace and protectors of the public that they have occasionally been known to beat to death those citizens or groups who question that status.
1986 *Writing in Restaurants*, 'Some Thoughts On Writing In Restaurants'.

28 In a world we find terrifying, we ratify that which doesn't threaten us.
1986 *Writing in Restaurants*, 'Notes For a Catalogue for Raymond Saunders'.

29 We recipients of the boon of liberty have always been ready, when faced with discomfort, to discard any and all first principles of liberty, and, further, to indict those who do not freely join with us in happily arrogating those principles.
1986 *Writing in Restaurants*, 'First Principles'.

30 The product of the artist has become less important than the *fact* of the artist. We wish to absorb this person. We wish to devour someone who has experienced the tragic. In our society this person is much more important than anything he might create.
1986 *Writing in Restaurants*, 'Exuvial Magic: An Essay Concerning Magic'.

31 The absence of the urge to create is decadence.
1986 *Writing in Restaurants*, 'Decadence'.

32 Our semantic chickens have come home to roost... We have come to accept all sorts of semantic inversions, just as George Orwell told us we would.
1986 *Writing in Restaurants*, 'Semantic Chickens'.

33 We live in a world ruined by Reason.
1986 *Writing in Restaurants*, 'Oscars'.

34 We Americans have always considered Hollywood, at best, a sinkhole of depraved venality. And, of course, it is. It is not a Protective Monastery of Aesthetic Truth.
1986 *Writing in Restaurants*, 'A Playwright in Hollywood'.

35 There is such a thing as luck. There is such a thing as a *run of luck*. This is an instructive insight I have gained from poker—that all things have a rhythm, even the most seemingly inanimate of statistics.
1986 *Writing in Restaurants*, 'Things I Have Learned Playing Poker On The Hill'.

36 The poker player learns that sometimes both science and common sense are wrong; that the bumblebee *can* fly; that, perhaps, one should never trust an expert; that there are more things in heaven and earth than are dreamt of by those with an academic bent.
1986 *Writing in Restaurants*, 'Things I Have Learned Playing Poker On The Hill'.

37 All plays are about decay... That is why the theater has always been essential to human psychic equilibrium.
1986 *Writing in Restaurants*, 'Decay: Some Thoughts for Actors'.

38 The problems of the world, AIDS, cancer, nuclear war, pollution, are, finally, no more solvable than the problems of a tree which has borne fruit: the apples are overripe and they are falling—what can be done?... What can be done about the problems which beset our life? *Nothing* can be done, and nothing needs to be done. Something *is* being done—the organism is preparing to rest.
1986 *Writing in Restaurants*, 'Decay: Some Thoughts for Actors'.

39 The Film Industry is the American Monarchy: it is strict entailed succession and Horatio Alger in one. Except for the money manipulators and speculators on the top, it is a society built on work, achievement, and fealty to those in power.
1986 *Writing in Restaurants*, 'Observations of a Backstage Wife'.

40 Life in the movie business is like the beginning of a new love affair: it's full of surprises and you are constantly getting fucked.
1988 Charlie. *Speed The Plough*, sc.1.

41 A good film script should be able to do completely without dialogue.
1988 In *The Independent*, 11 Nov.

42 Film is the least realistic of art forms.
1989 In *The Guardian*, 16 Feb.

43 All of us write plays in our heads all the time...before we're going to visit our girl friend, before we're going to talk to a boss—we rehearse.
Quoted in Susan Stamberg *Talk* (1993).

44 The mind is a mill which can incessant turn, 'til its mere operation focus the stress inward and the stones grind themselves to dust.
2004 *Faustus*.

45 When we fear things I think that we wish for them ... every fear hides a wish.
2005 *Edmond*.

46 The first rule of tinkering is, of course, 'save all the parts'.
2011 *The Secret Knowledge: On the Dismantling of American Culture*.

Manchester, William Raymond 1922–2004

US novelist, foreign correspondent and contemporary historian, born in Attleboro, Massachusetts. His chief work was *The Death of a President* (1967), a landmark account written at the behest of the Kennedys.

47 A leader cut from whipcord.
1967 Of Governor John B Connally Jr. *The Death of a President*.

48 Johnson approached a strongly fortified position by outflanking it, or burrowing under it, or surprising the defenders from the rear, or raining down obstacles upon them from the sky, or starving them into submission... Rarely, and then only reluctantly, would he proceed directly from A to B, to him the shortest distance between two points was a tunnel.
1967 Of Lyndon B Johnson. *The Death of a President*.

49 His critics called him a wheeler-dealer. They overlooked the subtlety of Johnsonian strategy, his use of wheels within wheels.
1967 Of Lyndon B Johnson. *The Death of a President*.

50 Actors who have tried to play Churchill and MacArthur have failed abysmally because each of those men was a great actor playing himself.
1983 In *Book of the Month Club News*, Jun.

51 He resolved to lead Britain and her fading empire in one last great struggle...to arm the nation, not only with weapons but also with the mace of honor, creating in every English breast a soul beneath the ribs of death.
1988 Of Winston Churchill. *The Last Lion*.

52 It would be inaccurate to say that Churchill and I conversed. Like Gladstone speaking to Victoria, he addressed me as though I were a one-man House of Commons.
1988 *The Last Lion*.

Mandela, Nelson Rolihlahla 1918–2013

African Nationalist leader, sentenced to life imprisonment in 1964. A potent symbol of black resistance, he was released in Feb 1990, and elected President (1991) of the ANC. In 1993 he was jointly awarded the Nobel peace prize with F W de Klerk, and in 1994 became South Africa's first black President. His term ended in 1999.

53 During my lifetime I have dedicated my life to this struggle of the African people. I have fought against white domination, and I have fought against black domination. I have cherished the ideals of a democratic and free society in which all persons live together in harmony with equal opportunities. It is an ideal which I hope to live for, and to see realized. But My Lord, if needs be, it is an ideal for which I am prepared to die.
1964 Speech in court, 20 Apr, when charged under the Suppression of Communism Act and facing the death penalty.

54 We are not a political party. We have not changed at all. On the contrary, the ANC is a Government in waiting.
1991 Interviewed for BBC T V, Feb.

55 My fellow South Africans, today we are entering a new era for our country and its people. Today we celebrate not the victory of a party, but a victory for all the people of South Africa.

1994 Speech after his election to the presidency, Cape Town, 9 May.

56 No one is born hating another person because of the colour of his skin, or his background, or his religion. People must learn to hate, and if they can learn to hate, they can be taught to love, for love comes more naturally to the human heart than its opposite.
1994 *Long Walk to Freedom*.

57 One of the things I learnt when I was negotiating was that until I changed myself I could not change others.
2000 In the *Sunday Times*, 16 Apr.

58 I do not want to be presented as some deity. I would like to be remembered as an ordinary human being with virtues and vices.
2005 Interview, *Readers Digest*.

59 Your victory has demonstrated that no person anywhere in the world should not dare to dream of wanting to change the world for a better place.
2008 Letter to Barack Obama on the latter's election as US President.

60 Lead from the back—and let others believe they are in front.
Attributed.

Mandela, (Nomzano) Winnie 1934–

South African civil rights activist, who joined her husband Nelson Mandela in his work with the ANC and on release from prison became controversially involved in the militant politics of the townships. She was divorced by her husband in 1996.

61 With that stick of matches, with our necklaces, we shall liberate this country.
1986 Speech in the black townships, reported in *The Guardian*, 15 Apr. The 'necklaces' were home-made bombs, car tyres filled with petrol.

Mandelson (of Foy), Peter, Baron 1953–

English Labour politician, who helped create 'New Labour' in the 1990s. He has since been a European Commissioner (2004–8) and First Secretary of State (2009–10).

62 Few politicians are good at taking the high ground and throwing themselves off it.
1996 Of Tony Blair and the revision of Clause Four. In the *New Yorker*, 5 Feb.

63 You'll say that I'm in charge of a Mickey Mouse project.
1998 Declining to be photographed holding a balloon at Disney World, while in charge of the ill-fated Millennium Dome project. In the *Daily Telegraph*, 5 Jan.

64 Perhaps we need not more people looking round more corners but the same people looking round more corners more thoroughly to avoid the small things detracting from the big things the Prime Minister is getting right.
2009 Speaking about the MPs' expenses scandal at the Houses of Parliament.

Mandeville, Bernard 1670–1733

Dutch-born English satirist. After obtaining an MD degree from Leiden in 1691 he practised as a physician in London. He was widely denounced for encouraging immorality through his principle 'private vices are public benefits'.

65 The root of Evil, Avarice
That damn'd ill-natur'd, baneful Vice,
Was Slave to Prodigality,
That noble Sin; whilst Luxury
Employed a Million of the Poor,
And odious Pride a Million more;
Envy itself, and Vanity,
Were Ministers of Industry;
Their darling Folly, Fickleness,
In Diet, Furniture and Dress
That strange ridic'lous Vice, was made
That very Wheel that turned the Trade.
1723 *The Fable of the Bees, or, Private Vices, Publick Benefits* (2nd edn.).

Manguel, Alberto 1948–
Argentinian-born Canadian writer.

66 The world that is a book is devoured by a reader who is a letter in the world's text; thus a circular metaphor is created for the endlessness of reading; We are what we read.
1996 *A History of Reading*.

67 Maybe this is why we read, and why in moments of darkness we return to books: to find words for what we already know.
2004 *A Reading Diary: A Passionate Reader's Reflections on a Year of Books*.

68 In the light, we read the inventions of others; in the darkness we invent our own stories.
2006 *The Library at Night*.

Manilow, Barry 1946–
US singer and songwriter.

69 I think my music is like anchovies—some people love it, some people get nauseous.
2003 In *Readers Digest*, Mar.

Mankiewicz, Herman 1897–1953

US journalist, screenwriter and film producer. He initially worked in newspapers as a foreign correspondent in Berlin and as a drama editor in New York, moving to Hollywood in 1926 where he worked on his screenplays. He is best remembered for his Academy Award-winning film *Citizen Kane* (1941), although Orson Welles originally claimed this script as his own work. He is the elder brother of the film director Joseph Mankiewicz.

70 Old age…it's the only disease you don't look forward to being cured of.
1941 *Citizen Kane* (with Orson Welles).

71 Rosebud.
1941 Kane's last word, the opening word of the film, and referred to throughout. *Citizen Kane* (with Orson Welles).

72 Don't believe everything you hear on the radio.
1941 *Citizen Kane* (with Orson Welles).

73 There are millions to be grabbed out here and your only competition is idiots. Don't let this get around.
Cable to Ben Hecht in the early days of Hollywood. Quoted in the *New York Times*, 8 Jan 1993.

Mankiewicz, Joseph 1909–93

US director, producer and writer, brother of Herman. He won an Oscar for the script of *A Letter for Three Wives* (1949) and an Oscar for the direction and script of *All About Eve* (1950).

74 Fasten your seat belts, it's going to be a bumpy night!
1950 Bette Davis as Margo Channing in *All About Eve*.

75 We are a breed apart from the rest of humanity, we theatre folk. We are the original displaced personalities, concentrated gatherings of neurotics, egomaniacs, emotional misfits and precocious children.
1950 George Sanders as Addison De Witt in All About Eve.

Mann, Thomas 1875–1955

German novelist and short story writer who left Germany during World War II and settled in California. He received the Nobel prize for literature in 1929.

76 *Wahrscheinlich sind sie der interessanteste Reiz und Stoff unseres Nachdenkens und unserer Tätigkeit.*
Probably they are the most interesting stimulus and object of our meditation and our activity.
1924 Of illnesses. Der Zauberberg (The Magic Mountain), vol.1.

77 *Bier, Tabak und Musik. Da haben wir Ihr Vaterland!*
Beer, tobacco, and music. There we have the Fatherland!
1924 Der Zauberberg (The Magic Mountain), vol.1.

78 *Leben ist, dass im Wechsel der Materie die Form erhalten bleibt.*
Life is that the form is maintained through the change of substance.
1924 Der Zauberberg (The Magic Mountain), vol.1.

79 *Dass nicht alles auf einmal da ist, bleibt als Bedingung des Lebens und der Erzählung zu achten, und man wird sich doch wohl gegen die gottgegebenen Formen menschlicher Erkenntnis nich auflehnen wollen.*
Let us not forget the condition of life as narration: that we can never see the whole picture at once—unless we propose to throw overboard all the God-conditioned forms of human knowledge.
1924 Der Zauberberg (The Magic Mountain), vol.2.

80 *Zum Leben gibt es zwei Wege: Der eine ist der gewöhnliche, direkte und brave. Der andere ist schlimm, er führt über den Tod, und das ist der geniale Weg!*
There are two paths in life: one is the regular one, direct, honest. The other is bad, it leads through death—that is the way of genius!
1924 Der Zauberberg (The Magic Mountain), vol.2.

81 *Und wenn man sich für das Leben interessiert, so interessiert man sich namentlich für den Tod.*
If a person concerns himself with life, he also concerns himself with death.
1924 Der Zauberberg (The Magic Mountain), vol.2.

82 *Die Zeit hat in Wirklichkeit keine Einschnitte, es gibt kein Gewitter oder Drommetengetön beim Beginn eines neuen Monats oder Jahres, und selbst bei dem eines neuen Säkulums ist es nur wir Menschen, die schießen und läuten.*
Time has no divisions to mark its passage, there is never a thunderstorm or blare of trumpets to announce the beginning of a new month or year. Even when a new century begins it is only we mortals who ring bells and fire off pistols.
1924 Der Zauberberg (The Magic Mountain), ch.4, section 4 (translated by H T Lowe-Porter).

83 *Unser Sterben ist mehr eine Angelegenheit der Weiterlebenden als unserer selbst.*
A man's dying is more the survivors' affair than his own.
1924 Der Zauberberg (The Magic Mountain), ch.6, section 8 (translated by H T Lowe-Porter).

84 *Die Zeit ist das Element der Erzählung, wie sie das Element des Lebens ist,—unlösbar damit verbunden, wie mit den Körpern im Raum. Sie ist auch das Element der Musik, als welche die Zeit misst und gliedert, sie kurzweilig und kostbar auf einmal macht.*
For time is the medium of narration, as it is the medium of life. Both are inextricably bound up with it, as are bodies in space. Similarly, time is the medium of music; music divides, measures, articulates time, and can shorten it, yet enhance its value, both at once.
1924 Der Zauberberg (The Magic Mountain), ch.7, section 1 (translated by H T Lowe-Porter).

85 *Liebe zu sich selbst ist immer der Anfang eines romanhaften Lebens.*
Self-love is always the beginning of a novelistic affair.
1933 Joseph und seine Brüder ('Joseph and his Brothers').

86 *Man kann sehr wohl in einer Geschichte sein, ohne sie zu verstehen.*
A person can be fully involved in a story without understanding it.
1933 Joseph und seine Brüder ('Joseph and his Brothers').

87 *Denn dem Menschen ist am Wiedererkennen gelegen; er möchte das Alte im Neuen wiederfinden und das Typische im Individuellen.*
For man always searches for recognition: he would like to find the old in the new and the ordinary in the individual.
1936 Freud und die Zukunft.

88 *Ist die Liebe das Beste im Leben, so ist in der Liebe das Beste der Kuss.*
If love is the best thing in life, then the best part of love is the kiss.
1939 Lotte im Weimar.

89 *Das Seelische [ist] immer das Primäre und eigentlich Motivierende; die politische Aktion ist zweiter Ordnung, Reflex, Ausdruck, Instrument.*
The mental state is always the primary and ultimately the motivating state. Political action is of second rank, reflex, expression, instrument.
1947 Doktor Faustus.

Mann, Thomas Edward 1944–

US political scientist. He is Senior Fellow in Governance Studies at the Brookings Institution and is the author and co-editor of many books on American political science and congressional election studies, such as *Renewing Congress* (1992) and *Vital Statistics on Congress* (2002).

90 He's a great ex-president. It's a shame he couldn't have gone directly to the ex-presidency.
1994 Of Jimmy Carter and his successful visit to Korea. In Newsweek, *27 Jun.*

Mannheim, Karl 1893–1947

Hungarian-born German sociologist, who taught at the University of Heidelberg until expelled by Hitler and later at the LSE, known for his contributions to the sociology of knowledge.

91 Even the categories in which experiences are subsumed, collected, and ordered vary according to the social position of the observer.
1936 Ideology and Utopia.

Manning, Henry Edward 1808–92

English Roman Catholic prelate. He succeeded as Archbishop of Westminster in 1865 and became a cardinal in 1875. Noted for his support for the temperance and benevolent movements, he was also a keen cricketer and captained the Harrow Eleven team.

92 That bat that you were kind enough to send,
Seems (for as yet I have not tried it) good:
And if there's anything on earth can mend
My wretched play, it is that piece of wood.
1826 Verse sent to Charles Wordsworth, nephew of the poet William Wordsworth, after the latter sent him the present of a cricket bat.

93 To put labour and wages first and human or domestic life second is to invert the order of God and of nature.
1889 On the London dock strike.

Mansfield, Katherine *pseudonym of* Kathleen Mansfield Beauchamp 1881–1923

New Zealand writer. She moved to London to pursue a literary career and married John Middleton Murry. She died prematurely of tuberculosis. She is best known for her finely crafted short stories, in collections such as *Bliss and Other Stories* (1920). Her *Journal* was published in 1927.

94 Talk of our enlightened days and our emancipated country—pure nonsense! We are firmly held with the self-fashioned chains of slavery. Yes, now I see that they *are* self-fashioned, and must be self-removed.
1908 Journal entry, May.

95 The trouble with women like me is—they can't keep their nerves out of the job in hand… I walk about with a mind full of ghosts of saucepans and primus stoves and 'Will there be enough to go round?' I loathe myself, today. I detest this woman who 'superintends' you and rushes about, slamming doors and slopping water—all untidy with her blouse out and her nails grimed.
1913 Letter to John Middleton Murry, summer.

96 Why haven't I got a real 'home'—a real life—why haven't I got a Chinese nurse with green trousers and two babies who rush at me and clasp my knees? I'm not a girl—I'm a woman. I *want* things… all this love and joy that fights for outlet—and all this life drying up, like milk in an old breast.
1915 Letter to John Middleton Murry, 23 Mar.

97 I want for one moment to make our undiscovered country leap into the eyes of the Old World. It must be mysterious, as though floating. It must take the breath. It must be 'one of those islands…'.
1916 Journal entry, 22 Jan.

98 E M Forster never gets any further than warming the teapot. He's a rare fine hand at that. Feel this teapot. Is it not beautifully warm? Yes, but there ain't going to be no tea. And I can never be perfectly certain whether Helen was got with child by Leonard Bast or by his fatal forgotten umbrella. All things considered, I think it must have been the umbrella.
1917 Journal entry, May.

99 Her underlip protruded a little; she had a way of sucking it in that somebody else had told her was awfully fascinating.
1920 Bliss and Other Stories, 'Prelude'.

1 True to oneself! Which self? Which of my many… hundreds of selves?… There are moments when I feel I am nothing but the small clerk of some hotel without a proprietor, who has all his work cut out to enter the names and hand the keys to the wilful guests.
1920 Journal entry, Apr.

2 I believe that people are like portmanteaux—packed with certain things, started going, thrown about, tossed away, dumped down, lost and found, half emptied suddenly, or squeezed fatter than ever, until finally the Ultimate Porter swings them on to the Ultimate Train and away they rattle.
1920 Bliss and Other Stories, 'Je Ne Parle Pas Français'.

3 Is it not possible that the rage for confession, autobiography, especially for memories of earliest childhood, is explained by our persistent yet mysterious belief in a self which is continuous and permanent; which, untouched by all we acquire and all we shed, pushes a green spear through the dead leaves and through the mould, thrusts a scaled bud through years of darkness until, one day, the light discovers it and shakes the flower free and—we are alive—we are flowering for our moment upon the earth? This is the moment which after all, we live for—the moment of direct feeling when we are most ourselves and least personal.
1920 Journal entry, Apr.

4 If there was one thing he hated more than another it was the way she had of waking him in the morning… It was her way of establishing her grievance for the day.
1920 Bliss and Other Stories, 'Mr Reginald Peacock's Day'.

5 The aloe seemed to ride… like a ship with the oars lifted. Bright moonlight hung upon the lifted oars like water, and on the green wave glittered the dew.
1920 Bliss and Other Stories, 'Prelude'.

6 He stands, smiling encouragement, like a clumsy dentist.
1922 The Garden Party and Other Stories, 'Bank Holiday'.

7 She couldn't possibly go back to the gentleman's flat; she had no right to cry in strangers' houses.
1922 The Garden Party and Other Stories, 'The Life of Ma Parker'.

8 What would father say when he found out? For he was bound to find out sooner or later. He always did. 'Buried. You two girls had me *buried*!' She heard his stick thumping. Oh, what would they say? What possible excuse could they make? It sounded such an appallingly heartless thing to do. Such a wicked advantage to take of a person because he happened to be helpless at the moment.
1922 The Garden Party and Other Stories, 'The Daughters of the Late Colonel'.

9 Whenever I prepare for a journey I prepare as though for death. Should I never return, all is in order. This is what life has taught me.
1922 Journal entry, 29 Jan.

10 The longer I live the more I turn to New Zealand. I thank God I was born in New Zealand. A young country is a real heritage, though it takes one time to recognize it.

But New Zealand is in my very bones. What I wouldn't give to have a look at it!
1922 Letter to her father, Sir Harold Beauchamp, 18 Mar.

11 Looking back, I imagine I was always writing. Twaddle it was, too. But better far write twaddle or anything, anything, than nothing at all.
1922 Journal entry.

Mansfield, Michael Joseph 1903–2001

US Democratic senator and ambassador. A professor of history and political science (1933–42), he became a congressional member (1943–53) and Senator for Montana (1953–77). As US Ambassador to Japan (1977–89) in Tokyo, he represented the US on several trips to China.

12 A half-creature of the Senate and a half-creature of the executive.
1969 On the role of the Vice-President as the Senate's presiding officer. In *Time*, 14 Nov.

Mansfield, William Murray, 1st Earl 1705–93

English judge and MP. He was chief-justice of the king's Bench (1756) and a member of the Cabinet. His rulings developed the law of maritime contracts, insurance and bills, and influenced international law.

13 We must not regard political consequences, however formidable they may be. If rebellion was the certain consequence, we are bound to say, 'Justitia fiat, ruat coelum' (Let Justice be done, though the skies may fall).'
1768 Judgement against the sentence imposed on John Wilkes for publishing the anti-ministerial political newspaper *North Briton*, 28 Apr.
▶ See Ferdinand I 332:73.

14 Every man who comes to England is entitled to the protection of the English law, whatever oppression he may heretofore have suffered, and whatever may be the colour of his skin, whether it is black or whether it is white.
1772 Judgement on the Somersett slavery case, May.

Mantel, Dame Hilary Mary 1952–

English novelist. She became the first woman to win the Booker Prize twice, for *Wolf Hall* (2009) and *Bring Up the Bodies* (2012), both about the life of Thomas Cromwell.

15 The reader may ask how to tell fact from fiction. A rough guide: anything that seems particularly unlikely is probably true.
1992 *A Place of Greater Safety*.

16 At some point on your road you have to turn and start walking back towards yourself. Or the past will pursue you, and bite the nape of your neck, leave you bleeding in the ditch. Better to turn and face it with such weapons as you possess.
2005 *Beyond Black*.

17 Some of these things are true and some of them lies. But they are all good stories.
2009 *Wolf Hall*.

18 It is the absence of facts that frightens people: the gap you open, into which they pour their fears, fantasies, desires.
2009 *Wolf Hall*.

19 Beneath every history, another history.
2009 *Wolf Hall*.

20 The word 'however' is like an imp coiled beneath your chair. It induces ink to form words you have not yet seen, and lines to march across the page and overshoot the margin. There are no endings. If you think so you are deceived as to their nature. They are all beginnings. Here is one.
2012 *Bring Up the Bodies*.

21 The things you think are the disasters in your life are not the disasters really. Almost anything can be turned around: out of every ditch, a path, if you can only see it.
2012 *Bring Up the Bodies*.

22 A statute is written to entrap meaning, a poem to escape it.
2012 *Bring Up the Bodies*.

23 I'm not very conscious of having to mine my own past or anything like that. But that doesn't mean I don't do it unconsciously. I think of it as putting the bucket down into the well and wondering how deep and dark I'm going to go this time, what horrible things will come up.
2014 Quoted on thestar.com, 26 Dec.

Mao Zedong or Mao Tse-tung 1893–1976

Chinese military and political leader who became the first Chairman (1949) of the People's Republic. After the failure of the 1958–60 'Great Leap Forward' economic programme, his hold on power was weakened but he regained control by launching the 1966–9 'Cultural Revolution'.

24 But just think how good communism is! The state won't bother us anymore.
1919 Attributed remark. Quoted in Ross Terrill *Mao: A Biography* (1980), ch.4.

25 A revolution is not a dinner party.
1927 *The Little Red Book*, section 2.

26 A single spark can start a forest fire. Our forces, although small at present, will grow rapidly.
1930 Letter, 5 Jan.

27 If you want to know the taste of a pear, you must taste the pear by eating it for yourself. If you want to know the theory and methods of revolution, you must take part in revolution. All genuine knowledge originates in direct experience.
1937 Address to the Anti-Japanese Military and Political College, Jul.

28 Politics is war without bloodshed; war is politics with bloodshed.
1938 'On Protracted War', speech, May.

29 Every Communist must grasp the truth that political power grows out of the barrel of a gun.
1938 'Problems of War and Strategy', speech, 6 Nov.

30 China has stood up.
1949 Proclaiming the establishment of the People's Republic of China, 1 Oct.

31 When a man reaches old age, he will die and the same is true of a party.
1950 Collected in *Selected Works* (1975), vol.4.

32 If the worst came to the worst and half of mankind died, the other half would remain while imperialism would be razed to the ground and the whole world could become socialist.
1954 Quoted in the *Peking Review*, 9 Jun 1963.

33 All the so-called powerful reactionaries are paper tigers, for they are cut off from their people. Was not Hitler a paper tiger, and was he not overthrown? US imperialism has not yet been overthrown, and it has atomic bombs—but I believe that it too will be overthrown. It, too, is a paper tiger.
  1957 Speech to Communist International Congress, Moscow, Nov.

34 Letting a hundred flowers blossom and a hundred schools of thought contend is the policy for promoting the progress of the arts and the sciences and a flourishing culture in our land.
  1957 Speech, Peking, 27 Feb.

35 The east wind prevails over the west wind.
  1957 Spoken at an international conference of Communist leaders in Moscow. Quoted in Ross Terrill *Mao: A Biography* (1980), ch.14.

36 People of the world, unite and defeat the US aggressors and all their running dogs.
  1958 Speech, Jul.

37 I have seen Lenin's manuscripts, which are filled with changes. He too made mistakes.
  1959 Quoted in Ross Terrill *Mao: A Biography* (1980), ch.15.

38 Water too pure breeds no fish.
  Quoted in Han Suyin *Wind in the Tower* (1974).

39 The more books one reads, the more stupid one becomes.
  1976 Quoted in Ross Terrill *Mao: A Biography* (1980), ch.22.

Map, Walter   c.1140–c.1209
Welsh poet and ecclesiast, author of *De Nugis Curialium* (c.1181) and possibly new versions of the Arthurian Romances.

40 *Dura est manus cirurgi, sed sanans.*
  The hand of the surgeon is hard, but healing.
  c.1181 *De Nugis Curialium*, Distinction 4, ch.4.

41 *Numquam enim audiendi quod aliquis monachus super puerum incubuisset, quin statim post ipsum surrexisset puer.*
  I have heard before of a monk throwing himself on a boy, but the boy always rose again afterwards.
  c.1181 On hearing of an unsuccessful attempt by Saint Bernard of Clairvaux to revive a dead boy by throwing himself on the body and praying. *De Nugis Curialium*, Distinction 4, ch.5.

42 *Hoc solum deliqui, quod uiuo.*
  My only fault is that I am alive.
  c.1181 On the refusal of many of his contemporaries to believe that his *Dissuasio Valerii ad Rufinum* could have been composed by a modern writer. *De Nugis Curialium*, Distinction 4, ch.5.

Maradona, Diego   1960–
Argentinian footballer.

43 It was the hand of God.
  1986 To reporters after Argentina's World Cup defeat of England in which he scored a goal with his hand, 22 Jun.

Maraniss, David   1949–
US journalist and author. As a journalist for the *Washington Post* (of which he later became an associate editor) he received the Pulitzer Prize for national reporting in 1993, and has written a biography of President Bill Clinton.

44 It is…classic Bill Clinton, sincere and deceptive at the same time, requiring a careful reading between the lines.

1995 On President Clinton's letter as a graduate student, 3 Dec 1969, to arrange ROTC enlistment to avoid being drafted for the Vietnam War, a position that was to haunt his future campaigning. *First in His Class.*

45 Natural politicians are skilled actors, recreating reality, adjusting and ad-libbing, synthesizing the scenes, saying the same thing over and over again and making it seem that they are saying it for the first time.
  1995 Of Bill Clinton. *First in His Class.*

46 At 34, he fit the ironic description of the quintessential Rhodes Scholar: someone with a great future behind him.
  1995 Of Bill Clinton, the youngest defeated state governor in US history. *First in His Class.*

47 He is a congenital campaigner.
  1995 Predicting that Bill Clinton would always be a candidate for office or an advocate. CNBC broadcast, 7 Mar.

Marc, Franz   1880–1916
German painter, founder member of the Munich-based Blaue Reiter (Blue Rider) group. Most of his paintings were of animals (eg *Blue Horses*, 1911) portrayed in forceful colours. He was killed at Verdun during World War I.

48 Today art is moving in a direction of which our fathers would never even have dreamed. We stand before the new pictures as in a dream and we hear the apocalyptic horsemen in the air.
  1912 Subscription prospectus of the *Blaue Reiter Almanac*, Jan.

49 Art will liberate itself from the needs and desires of men. No longer will we paint a forest or a horse as we like or as they appear to us, but as they really are.
  1914–15 *Aphorisms.*

50 Traditions are lovely things—to create traditions, that is, not to live off them.
  1914–15 *Aphorisms.*

51 Who is able to paint the existence of a dog as Picasso paints the existence of a cubic shape?
  Quoted in *Briefe, Aufzeichnungen und Aphorismen* (2 vols, 1920), translated by Chipp in his *Theories of Modern Art* (1968).

Marceau, Marcel   1923–2007
French mime artist. Celebrated for his performances in the role of the white-faced Bip, he was the foremost exponent of the mime theatre of Charles Dullin and Jean-Louis Barrault.

52 Life is a cycle, and mime is particularly suitable for showing fluidity, transformation, metamorphosis. Words can keep people apart; mime can be a bridge between them.
  Attributed.

Marcos, Ferdinand Edralin   1917–89
Filipino politician, elected President in 1965 and again in 1969. His years of office became increasingly notorious for widespread corruption but US backing helped keep him in power. He declared martial law in 1972 but was overthrown in 1986 by a popular 'People's Power' campaign.

53 It is easier to run a revolution than a government.
  1977 In *Time*, 6 Jun.

54 Some people say the president is incapable of enforcing the law. Let them say that once more and I will set the tanks on them.

1986 Quoted in 'The Snap Revolution', in James Fenton *All the Wrong Places*.

55 History isn't through with me yet.
1986 Remark, quoted in Sterling Seagrave *The Marcos Dynasty*.

Marcos, Imelda Romualdez 1927–

Wife of President Ferdinand Marcos of the Philippines, with whom she fled in 1986. She later faced charges of theft and corruption.

56 Some are smarter than others.
c.1985 Her reply to a question about the great wealth she had accumulated. Quoted in Sterling Seagrave *The Marcos Dynasty*.

57 The real index of this country is the smiles of the people, not the economic index.
c.1985 Quoted in Sterling Seagrave *The Marcos Dynasty*.

58 If you know how much you've got, you probably haven't got much.
Attributed.

Marcus Aurelius *full name* Marcus Aelius Aurelius Antoninus AD 121–180

Roman emperor and philosopher. His spiritual reflections, the *Meditations*, are considered a classic work of Stoicism.

59 Nothing is so conducive to greatness of mind as the ability to examine systematically and honestly everything that meets us in life.
Meditations, vol.3, pt.2 (translated by Charles Reginald Haines, 1901).

Margrethe II 1940–

Queen of Denmark (1972–).

60 There is nothing so clever as people you agree with.
2012 Quoted by Helle Thorning-Schmidt in speech on Margrethe II's Ruby Jubilee, 15 Jan.

Marguerite d'Angoulême 1492–1549

Queen of Navarre and sister of François I. She was a patron of the arts, and wrote poetry.

61 *Je n'ai plus ni père, ni mère,*
Ni sïur, ni frère
Sinon Dieu seul auquel j'espère.
I no longer have a father, nor a mother,
Nor a sister, nor a brother.
I only have God to trust in.
1547 *Cantique spirituel*.

62 *Plus j'ai d'amour plus j'ai de fâcherie.*
The more I love, the more I quarrel.
1547 *Dizains*.

63 *Depuis qu'Ève fit pécher Adam, toutes les femmes ont pris possession de tourmenter, tuer et damner les hommes.*
Ever since Eve made Adam sin, women have taken it upon themselves to torment, kill and damn men.
1558 *Heptaméron*, pt.1.

64 *Seulement les sots sont punis, et non les vicieux.*
Only the foolish are punished, never the truly vicious.
1558 *Heptaméron*, pt.13.

65 *Un malheureux cherche l'autre.*
One unhappy person seeks out another.
1558 *Heptaméron*, pt.21.

66 *Le scandale est souvent pire que le péché.*
The scandal is often worse than the sin itself.
1558 *Heptaméron*, pt.25.

67 *Votre plaisir gît déshonorer les femmes, et votre honneur tuer les hommes en guerre; qui sont deux points formellement contraires à la loi de Dieu.*
Your pleasure lies in dishonouring women and your honour lies in killing men at war; two acts which stand in contradiction to the law of God.
1558 *Heptaméron*, pt.26.

68 *Mariage est un état de si longue durée qu'il ne doit être commencé légèrement, ni sans l'opinion de nos meilleurs amis et parents.*
Marriage is a state of such long duration that it should not begin lightly, nor without the opinion of our best friends and parents.
1558 *Heptaméron*, pt.40.

69 *L'amour n'est pas un feu que l'on tient dans la main.*
Love is not a flame that one holds in the hand.
1558 *Heptaméron*, pt.47.

70 *À force de jurer, on engendre quelque doute à la vérité.*
When forced to swear an oath, one can encounter doubt about the truth.
1558 *Heptaméron*, pt.61.

Marhabal fl.216 BC

Carthaginian soldier, a cavalry commander under Hannibal at the Battle of Cannae (216 BC).

71 You know how to gain a victory, Hannibal: you know not how to use one.
216 BC Comment to Hannibal after victory at Cannae. Quoted in Livy *Ab urbe condita*, bk.22.

Mariátegui, José Carlos 1895–1930

Peruvian political leader and essayist, who applied Marxist principles to Peruvian problems, while acknowledging the value of religion and myth to the indigenous peoples.

72 *Mientras en Norteamérica la colonización depositó los gérmenes de un espíritu y una economía que se plasmaban entonces en Europa y a los cuales pertenecía el porvenir, a la América española trajo los efectos y los métodos de un espíritu y una economía que declinaban ya y a los cuales no pertenecía sino el pasado.*
Whereas in North America colonization planted the seeds of the spirit and economy then growing in Europe and representing the future, the Spaniard brought to America the effects and methods of an already declining spirit and economy that belonged to the past.
1928 *Siete ensayos de interpretación de la realidad peruana*, 'El problema de la tierra' (translated as *Seven Interpretive Essays on Peruvian Reality*, 1971).

Marie de France fl.1160–70

French poet, author of *Lais* and *Fables*. Born in Normandy, she spent most of her life in England. Her *Lais* in particular were of great influence on French literature.

73 *Qui Deus a duné esciënce*
e de parler bone eloquence,
ne s'en deit taisir ne celer,
ainz se deit volunters mustrer.

Whoever God has given knowledge and eloquence in speaking, should not be silent or secretive, but should willingly show it.
c.1170 *Lais*, prologue, l.1–4.

74 *Ki qu'en plurt ne ki qu'en chant, le dreit estuet aler avant.*
Whether it makes one cry or sing, justice must be carried out.
c.1170 *Lanval*, l.437–8.

75 *Mult est fole, ki hume creit.*
She is a fool, who trusts a man.
c.1170 *Eliduc*, l.1084.

Marinetti, Emilio Filippo Tomasso 1876–1944

Italian dramatist, novelist and poet. He published his influential manifesto for Futurism in *Figaro* in 1909, and became a Fascist in 1919. His writings glorify war, the machine age and dynamism, disparaging all traditional forms of art.

76 We sing the love of danger. Courage, rashness, and rebellion are the elements of our poetry. Hitherto literature has tended to exalt thoughtful immobility, ecstasy, and sleep, whereas we are for aggressive movement, febrile insomnia, mortal leaps, and blows with the fist. We proclaim that the world is richer for a new beauty of speed, and our praise is for the man at the wheel. There is no beauty now save in struggle, no masterpiece can be anything but aggressive, and hence we glorify war, militarism and patriotism.
1909 *Manifesto of Futurism*. Quoted in Denis Mack Smith *Italy: A Modern History* (1959), p.270.

77 We affirm that the world's magnificence has been enriched by a new beauty: the beauty of speed. A racing car whose hood is adorned with great pipes, like serpents of explosive breath—a roaring car that seems to ride on grapeshot is more beautiful than the *Victory of Samothrace*.
1909 *Manifesto of Futurism*.

78 It is from Italy that we launch through the world this violently upsetting incendiary manifesto of ours. With it, today, we establish *Futurism*, because we want to free this land from its smelly gangrene of professors, archaeologists, *ciceroni* and antiquarians. For too long has Italy been a dealer in second-hand clothes. We mean to free her from the numberless museums that cover her like so many graveyards.
1909 *Manifesto of Futurism*.

Marion, Frances *originally* Frances Marion Owens
1888–1973

US screenwriter and novelist. She wrote prolifically for the silent screen before working as a war correspondent, and subsequently translated her skills to talking pictures. She later turned to novel writing.

79 Gimme visky...ginger ale on the side. And don't be stingy baby.
1931 Opening lines delivered by Greta Garbo in *Anna Christie*.

80 I read somewhere that machinery is going to take the place of every profession.
Oh my dear that's something you'll never have to worry about.

1933 Dialogue between Jean Harlow and Marie Dressler in *Dinner At Eight* (with Herman Mankiewicz).

Maritain, Jacques 1882–1973

French philosopher and critic. He converted from Protestantism to Catholicism (1906) and gained renown for his interpretations of St Thomas Aquinas. He based his own philosophy on Aristotle and Aquinas.

81 Poetry proceeds from the totality of man, sense, imagination, intellect, love, desire, instinct, blood and spirit together.
Quoted in Robert Fitzgerald (ed) *Enlarging the Change* (1985).

82 The poet knows himself only on the condition that things resound in him, and that in him, at a single awakening, they and he come forth together out of sleep.
Quoted in Robert Fitzgerald (ed) *Enlarging the Change* (1985).

Marivaux, Pierre Carlet de Chamblain de
1688–1763

French author best known for his comedies in which language, more than characters, dictates the action.

83 *Un mari porte un masque avec le monde, et une grimace avec sa femme.*
A husband wears a mask in the world and a smirk with his wife.
1730 *Le jeu de l'amour et du hasard*, act 1, sc.2.

84 *Dans ce monde, il faut être un peu trop bon pour l'être assez.*
In this world, one must be a little too good in order to be good enough.
1730 *Le jeu de l'amour et du hasard*, act 1, sc.2.

85 *Les bienfaits des hommes sont accompagnés d'une maladresse si humiliante pour les personnes qui les reçoivent!*
The generosity of men is accompanied by such a humiliating embarrassment for those who benefit from it.
1731 *La vie de Marianne*, ch.1.

86 *C'est presque toujours le péché qui prêche la vertu dans nos chaires.*
It's almost always sin which preaches virtue in our pulpits.
1731 *La vie de Marianne*, ch.4.

87 *Qu'est-ce qu'une charité qui n'a point de pudeur avec le misérable, et qui, avant de le soulager, commence par écraser son amour-propre.*
What is that charity worth which does not spare the wretched person's feelings, which instead, before providing comfort, begins by wiping out his self-esteem.
1731 *La vie de Marianne*, ch.14.

88 *L'âme se raffine à mesure qu'elle se gâte.*
The soul refines itself in proportion to how it spoils itself.
1735 *Le paysan parvenu*, ch.4.

Markham, Dewey 'Pigmeat' 1906–81

US songwriter and comedy writer.

89 Here comes the judge.
1968 Song title, co-written with Dick Alen, Bob Astor and Sarah Harvey. Often quoted as a vaudeville catchphrase, 'Here come de judge'.

Marks, Leo 1920–2001

British writer. He acted as adviser on the film *Carve Her Name With Pride* (1958), partly based on his own wartime work in cryptography. He also wrote the script of *Peeping Tom* (1960).

90 The life that I have is all that I have
and the life that I have is yours
The love that I have of the life that I have
Is yours and yours and yours.
1958 Poem recited by Virginia McKenna as Violette Szabo in *Carve Her Name With Pride*.

Marlborough, John Churchill, 1st Duke of 1650–1722

English general. He helped quell Monmouth's rebellion at Sedgemoor, but deserted to William of Orange in 1688. Under Queen Anne he was appointed supreme commander of British forces in the War of the Spanish Succession, rewarded for his success with a dukedom.

91 I have not time to say any more, but to beg you will give my duty to the Queen, and let her know her army has had a glorious victory. Monsieur Tallard and two other generals are in my coach, and I am following the rest.
1704 Note written on a tavern bill to his wife, Sarah, 13 Aug, after the Battle of Blenheim.

Marley, Bob (Robert Nesta) 1945–81

Jamaican singer, guitarist, and composer of reggae music. His hits include 'No woman, no cry', 'I Shot the Sheriff', and 'Exodus'. Among his albums were *Catch a Fire* (1972), *Rastaman Vibration* (1976) and *Uprising* (1980).

92 Get up, stand up
Stand up for your rights
Get up, stand up
Don't give up the fight.
1973 'Get Up, Stand Up'.

93 Don't just move to the music, listen to what I'm saying.
Quoted in Johnson and Pines *Reggae* (1982).

Marlowe, Christopher 1564–93

English poet and playwright. It is thought that he was a spy for the English in the Netherlands, and that he was killed in a tavern brawl. His many dramatic works include *Doctor Faustus* (1592), and his poems include the unfinished *Hero and Leander* and lyrics such as 'The Passionate Shepherd to his Love'.

94 From jigging veins of rhyming mother-wits,
And such conceits as clownage keeps in pay,
We'll lead you to the stately tents of war.
1587 *Tamburlaine the Great* (published 1590), pt.1, prologue.

95 Come, lady, let not this appall your thoughts.
1587 *Tamburlaine the Great* (published 1590), pt.1, act 1, sc.2.

96 Tamburlaine!—
A Scythian shepherd so embellishèd
With nature's pride and richest furniture!
His looks do menace heaven and dare the gods.
His fiery eyes are fixed upon the earth.
1587 *Tamburlaine the Great* (published 1590), pt.1, act 1, sc.2.

97 Accurst be he that first invented war.
1587 *Tamburlaine the Great* (published 1590), pt.1, act 2, sc.4.

98 A god is not so glorious as a king.
I think the pleasure they enjoy in Heaven,
Cannot compare with kingly joys in earth.
To wear a crown enchased with pearl and gold,
Whose virtues carry with it life and death;
To ask and have, command and be obeyed;
When looks breed love, with looks to gain the prize,
Such power attractive shines in princes' eyes!
1587 *Tamburlaine the Great* (published 1590), pt.1, act 2, sc.5.

99 Nature that framed us of four elements,
Warring within our breasts for regiment,
Doth teach us all to have aspiring minds:
Our souls, whose faculties can comprehend
The wondrous architecture of the world,
And measure every wandering planet's course,
Still climbing after knowledge infinite,
And always moving as the restless spheres,
Wills us to wear ourselves, and never rest,
Until we reach the ripest fruit of all,
That perfect bliss and sole felicity,
The sweet fruition of an earthly crown.
1587 *Tamburlaine the Great* (published 1590), pt.1, act 2, sc.7.

1 Virtue is the fount whence honour springs.
1587 *Tamburlaine the Great* (published 1590), pt.1, act 4, sc.4.

2 What is beauty, saith my sufferings, then?
If all the pens that ever poets held
Had fed the feeling of their masters' thoughts,
And every sweetness that inspired their hearts,
Their minds, and muses on admirèd themes;
If all the heavenly quintessence they still
From their immortal flowers of poesy,
Wherein, as in a mirror, we perceive
The highest reaches of a human wit;
If these had made one poem's period,
And all combined in beauty's worthiness,
Yet should there hover in their restless heads
One thought, one grace, one wonder, at the least,
Which into words no virtue can digest.
1587 *Tamburlaine the Great* (published 1590), pt.1, act 5, sc.1.

3 And every warrior that is rapt with love
Of fame, of valour, and of victory,
Must needs have beauty beat on his conceits:
I thus conceiving and subduing both,
That which hath stopped the tempest of the gods,
Even from the fiery-spangled veil of heaven,
To feel the lovely warmth of shepherds' flames,
And march in cottages of strowèd weeds,
Shall give the world to note, for all my birth,
That virtue solely is the sum of glory,
And fashions men with true nobility.
1587 *Tamburlaine the Great* (published 1590), pt.1, act 5, sc.1.

4 Helen, whose beauty summoned Greece to arms,
And drew a thousand ships to Tenedos.
1587 *Tamburlaine the Great* (published 1590), pt.2, l.3055–6.

5 More childish valorous than manly wise.
1587 *Tamburlaine the Great* (published 1590), pt.2, l.3690.

6 Holla, ye pampered Jades of Asia;
What, can ye draw but twenty miles a day?
1587 *Tamburlaine the Great* (published 1590), pt.2, l.3980–1.

7 I count religion but a childish toy,
And hold there is no sin but ignorance.
c.1589 *The Jew of Malta* (published 1633), 'Prologue to the Stage, At the Cock-pit'.

8   Might first made kings, and laws were then most sure
    When...they were writ in blood.
    c.1589 *The Jew of Malta* (published 1633), 'Prologue'.

9   Thus methinks should men of judgement frame
    Their means of traffic from the vulgar trade,
    And as their wealth increaseth, so enclose
    Infinite riches in a little room.
    c.1589 *The Jew of Malta* (published 1633), act 1, sc.1.

10 The sad presaging raven, that tolls
    The sick man's passport in her hollow beak,
    And in the shadow of the silent night
    Doth shake contagion from her sable wings.
    c.1589 *The Jew of Malta* (published 1633), act 2, sc.1.

11 As for myself, I walk abroad o'nights
    And kill sick people groaning under walls:
    Sometimes I go about and poison wells.
    c.1589 *The Jew of Malta* (published 1633), act 2, sc.3.

12 Barnardine: Thou hast committed—
    Barabas: Fornication—but that was in another country;
    and besides, the wench is dead.
    c.1589 *The Jew of Malta* (published 1633), act 4, sc.1.

13 'My father is deceased. Come, Gaveston,
    And share the kingdom with thy dearest friend.'
    Ah, words that make me surfeit with delight!
    What greater bliss can hap to Gaveston
    Than live and be the favourite of a king?
    Sweet prince, I come; these, these thy amorous lines
    Might have enforced me to have swum from France,
    And, like Leander, gasped upon the sand,
    So thou would'st smile, and take me in thy arms.
    c.1591 Gaveston is reading a letter from King Edward. *Edward II*
    (published 1594), act 1, sc.1.

14 My men, like satyrs grazing on the lawns,
    Shall with their goat feet dance an antic hay.
    c.1591 *Edward II* (published 1594), act 1, sc.1.

15 The griefs of private men are soon allayed,
    But not of kings.
    c.1591 *Edward II* (published 1594), act 5, sc.1.

16 But what are kings, when regiment is gone,
    But perfect shadows in a sunshine day?
    c.1591 *Edward II* (published 1594), act 5, sc.1.

17 He hath a body able to endure
    More than we can inflict: and therefore now
    Let us assail his mind another while.
    c.1591 *Edward II* (published 1594), act 5, sc.4.

18 Sweet Analytics, 'tis thou has ravished me!
    c.1592 *Doctor Faustus* (published 1604), act 1, sc.1.

19 I'll have them fly to India for gold,
    Ransack the ocean for orient pearl.
    c.1592 *Doctor Faustus* (published 1604), act 1, sc.1.

20 Is, to dispute well, logic's chiefest end?
    Affords this art no greater miracle?
    c.1592 *Doctor Faustus* (published 1604), act 1, sc.1.

21 Oh, what a world of profit and delight,
    Of power, of honour, and omnipotence,
    Is promised to the studious artisan!
    c.1592 *Doctor Faustus* (published 1604), act 1, sc.1.

22 All things that move between the quiet poles
    Shall be at my command: emperors and kings
    Are but obeyed in their several provinces,
    Nor can they raise the wind, or rend the clouds;
    But his dominion that exceeds in this
    Stretcheth as far as doth the mind of man;
    A sound magician is a demi-god.
    c.1592 *Doctor Faustus* (published 1604), act 1, sc.1.

23 How am I glutted with conceit of this!
    Shall I make spirits fetch me what I please,
    Resolve me of all ambiguities,
    Perform what desperate enterprise I will?
    I'll have them fly to India for gold,
    Ransack the ocean for orient pearl,
    And search all corners of the new found world
    For pleasant fruits and princely delicates.
    c.1592 *Doctor Faustus* (published 1604), act 1, sc.1.

24 Why, this is hell, nor am I out of it:
    Thinkst thou that I who saw the face of God,
    And tasted the eternal joys of heaven,
    Am not tormented with ten thousand hells
    In being deprived of everlasting bliss!
    c.1592 *Doctor Faustus* (published 1604), act 1, sc.3.

25 Hell hath no limits, nor is circumscribed
    In one self place; but where we are is hell,
    And where hell is, there must we ever be:
    And, to be short, when all the world dissolves,
    And every creature shall be purified,
    All places shall be hell that is not heaven.
    c.1592 *Doctor Faustus* (published 1604), act 2, sc.1.

26 But think'st thou heaven is such a glorious thing?
    I tell thee, Faustus, it is not half so fair
    As thou, or any man that breathes on earth.
    c.1592 *Doctor Faustus* (published 1604), act 2, sc.2.

27 Have I not made blind Homer sing to me?
    c.1592 *Doctor Faustus* (published 1604), act 2, sc.2.

28 O gentle Faustus, leave this damnèd art,
    This magic, that will charm thy soul to hell.
    c.1592 *Doctor Faustus* (published 1604), act 5, sc.1.

29 Was this the face that launched a thousand ships,
    And burnt the topless towers of Ilium?
    Sweet Helen, make me immortal with a kiss!
    Her lips suck forth my soul: see, where it flies!
    Come Helen, come give me my soul again.
    Here will I dwell, for heaven be in these lips,
    And all is dross that is not Helena.
    c.1592 *Doctor Faustus* (published 1604), act 5, sc.1.

30 Now hast thou but one bare hour to live,
    And then thou must be damned perpetually!
    Stand still, you ever-moving spheres of heaven,
    That time may cease, and midnight never come.
    Fair nature's eye, rise, rise, again, and make
    Perpetual day; or let this hour be but
    A year, a month, a week, a natural day,
    That Faustus may repent and save his soul!
    O lente, lente currite, noctis equi:
    The stars move still, time runs, the clock will strike,
    The devil will come, and Faustus must be damned.
    Oh, I'll leap up to my God!—Who pulls me down?—
    See, see, where Christ's blood streams in the
        firmament!
    One drop would save my soul, half a drop, ah, my
    Christ.
    c.1592 *Doctor Faustus* (published 1604), act 5, sc.2.

31 You stars that reigned at my nativity,
    Whose influence hath allotted death and hell,
    Now draw up Faustus like a foggy mist,
    Into the entrails of yon labouring cloud,
    That when you vomit forth into the air,
    My limbs may issue from your smoky mouths,
    So that my soul may but ascend to heaven.
    c.1592 *Doctor Faustus* (published 1604), act 5, sc.2.

32 Ah, Pythagoras' metempsychosis, were that time,
    This soul should fly from me, and I be changed
    Unto some brutish beast.
    c.1592 *Doctor Faustus* (published 1604), act 5, sc.2.

33 Cut is the branch that might have grown full
          straight,
    And burnèd is Apollo's laurel bough,
    That sometime grew within this learned man.
    c.1592 *Doctor Faustus* (published 1604), epilogue.

34 Where Venus in her naked glory strove
    To please the careless and disdainful eyes
    Of proud Adonis.
    1593 *Hero and Leander* (published 1598), pt.1, l.12–14.

35 So lovely fair was Hero, Venus' nun,
    As Nature wept, thinking she was undone.
    1593 *Hero and Leander* (published 1598), pt.1, l.45–6.

36 His body was as straight as Circe's wand;
    Jove might have sipped out nectar from his hand.
    1593 *Hero and Leander* (published 1598), pt.1, l.61–2.

37 It lies not in our power to love, or hate,
    For will in us is overruled by fate.
    When two are stripped, lo ere the course begin
    We wish that one should lose, the other win;
    And one especially do we affect
    Of two gold ingots, like in each respect.
    The reason no man knows, let it suffice,
    What we behold is censured by our eyes.
    Where both deliberate, the love is slight;
    Who ever loved, that loved not at first sight?
    1593 *Hero and Leander* (published 1598), pt.1, l.167–76.

38 Virginity, albeit some highly prize it,
    Compared with marriage, had you tried them both,
    Differs as much as wine and water doth.
    1593 *Hero and Leander* (published 1598), pt.1, l.268–9.

39 And as she wept, her tears to pearl he turned,
    And wound them on his arm, and for her mourned.
    1593 The mourner is Cupid. *Hero and Leander* (published 1598), pt.1, l.375–6.

40 And to this day is every scholar poor;
    Gross gold from them runs headlong to the boor.
    1593 *Hero and Leander* (published 1598), pt.1, l.477–8.

41 Come live with me and be my love,
    And we will all the pleasures prove
    That valleys, groves, hills, and fields,
    Woods, or steepy mountain yields.

    And we will sit upon the rocks,
    Seeing shepherds feed their flocks,
    By shallow rivers to whose falls
    Melodious birds sing madrigals.

    And I will make thee beds of roses
    And a thousand fragrant posies,
    A cap of flowers, and a kirtle
    Embroidered all with leaves of myrtle.
    'The Passionate Shepherd to His Love' (published 1599).
    ▶ See Raleigh 705:43.

Marples, Morris 1901–
English writer and traveller.

42 The soul of a journey is liberty, perfect liberty to think, feel, do just as one pleases. We go on a journey chiefly to be free of all impediments and of all inconveniences; to leave ourselves behind, much more to get rid of others. It is because I want a little breathing space to muse on different matters…that I absent myself from the town for a while.
    Quoted in John Hillaby *Journey through Britain* (1968).

Marquand, John P(hillips) 1893–1960
US novelist. He began as a writer of popular stories for magazines, and later turned to realist novels in the manner of Sinclair Lewis.

43 His father watched him across the gulf of years and pathos which always must divide a father from his son.
    1937 *The Late George Apley*, ch.10.

Marqués, René 1919–79
Puerto Rican playwright, short-story writer and nationalist. Most of his plays and essays are concerned with the problem of national identity in relation to language, literature and the prevailing social conditions of Puerto Rico.

44 *Hombre, tienes un hijo, un hijo que te hicieron creer podría inmortalizarte llevando el germen de ti mismo por siglos de generaciones… Tu carne, Hombre, carne deleznable, carne podrida que no puede soportar el peso de tu inmortalidad. No, no hay nada de ti mismo en esa carne. ¡Tu hijo no te hará inmortal!'*
    Man, you have a son, a son who they made you believe would make you immortal by carrying your seed through centuries of generations… Your flesh, O man, your despicable and rotten flesh that cannot bear the sight of your immortality. No: there's nothing of yourself in that flesh. Your son won't make you immortal!'
    1948 *El hombre y sus sueños* ('Man and His Dreams'), act 2.

Marquis, Don(ald Robert Perry) 1878–1937
US novelist, playwright and poet. He worked as a journalist and wrote serious work, but is remembered for his comic poems, notably in the *archy and mehitabel* series, the tales of a cockroach who can't reach the upper-case keys of the typewriter, and an alley cat.

45 but wotthehell wotthehell
    oh i should worry and fret
    death and I will coquette
    there s a dance in the old dame yet
    toujours gai toujours gai.
    1927 *archy and mehitabel*, 'the song of mehitabel'.

46 live so that you
    can stick out your tongue
    at the insurance.
    1927 *archy and mehitabel*, 'certain maxims of archy'.

47 procrastination is the
    art of keeping
    up with yesterday.
    1927 *archy and mehitabel*, 'certain maxims of archy'.

48 millionaires and
bums taste
about alike to me.
1927 archy and mehitabel, 'certain maxims of archy'.

49 an optimist is a guy
that has never had
much experience.
1927 archy and mehitabel, 'certain maxims of archy'.

50 coarse
jocosity
catches the crowd
shakespeare
and i
are often
low browed
1927 archy and mehitabel, 'archy confesses'.

51 persian pussy from over the sea
demure and lazy and smug and fat
none of your ribbons and bells for me
ours is the zest of the alley cat
1927 archy and mehitabel, 'mehitabels extensive past'.

52 but wotthehell archy wotthehell
jamais triste archy jamais triste
that is my motto.
1927 archy and mehitabel, 'mehitabel sees paris'.

53 honesty is a good
thing but
it is not profitable to
its possessor
unless it is
kept under control.
1933 archys life of mehitabel, 'archygrams'.

54 did you ever
notice that when
a politician
does get an idea
he usually
gets it all wrong.
1933 archys life of mehitabel, 'archygrams'.

55 now and then
there is a person born
who is so unlucky
that he runs into accidents
which started to happen
to somebody else.
1933 archys life of mehitabel, 'archy says'.

56 boss there is always
a comforting thought
in time of trouble when
it is not our trouble
1935 archy does his part, 'comforting thoughts'.

57 Writing a book of poetry is like dropping a rose petal down the Grand Canyon and waiting for the echo.
Quoted in E. Anthony *O Rare Don Marquis* (1962), ch.6.

58 The art of newspaper paragraphing is to stroke a platitude until it purrs like an epigram.
Quoted in E. Anthony *O Rare Don Marquis* (1962), ch.11.

59 By the time a bartender knows what drink a man will have before he orders, there is little else about him worth knowing.
Quoted in E. Anthony *O Rare Don Marquis* (1962), ch.11.

60 Bores bore each other, too; but it never seems to teach them anything.
Quoted in E. Anthony *O Rare Don Marquis* (1962), ch.11.

61 A demagogue is a person with whom we disagree as to which gang should mismanage the country.
Quoted in E. Anthony *O Rare Don Marquis* (1962), ch.11.

62 Fishing is a delusion entirely surrounded by liars in old clothes.
Attributed.

Marshall, George C(atlett) 1880–1959

US soldier and statesman. He directed the US army throughout the war as chief of staff (1939–45), and as Secretary of State (1947–9) he originated the Marshall Aid plan for the post-war reconstruction of Europe. He was awarded the Nobel peace prize in 1953.

63 Our policy is directed not against any country or doctrine, but against hunger, poverty, desperation and chaos. The purpose shall be the revival of a working economy in the world so as to permit the emergence of political and social conditions in which free institutions can exist.
1947 Speech at Harvard, 5 Jun, announcing the European Recovery Plan (ERA) that became known as the Marshall Plan.

64 We want you to feel unhampered tactically and strategically to proceed north of the 38th parallel.
1950 Telegram to General Douglas MacArthur during the Korean War, Sep, later used by MacArthur as justification for continuing operations after the Chinese had made their presence known. Quoted in David S McLellan *Dean Acheson: The State Department Years* (1976).

Marshall, Thurgood 1908–93

US jurist and civil rights advocate. He worked with the National Association for the Advancement of Colored People and the Court of Appeals (1961–5). Solicitor General (1965–7), he became the first black Justice of the US Supreme Court (1967–91).

65 If the United States is indeed the great melting pot, the negro either didn't get in the pot or he didn't get melted down.
1987 In the *New York Times*, 9 Sep.

Martel, Yann 1963–

Canadian author. His novel *Life of Pi* (2002) was awarded the Booker Prize.

66 If we, citizens, do not support our artists, then we sacrifice our imagination on the altar of crude reality and we end up believing in nothing and having worthless dreams.
2002 Life of Pi.

67 In the literature can be found legions of examples of animals that could escape but did not, or did and returned.
2002 Life of Pi.

68 A work of art works because it is true, not because it is real.
2010 Beatrice and Virgil.

69 Artists risk it all and sometimes they get nothing in return, and wind up being bitter and aging, and teaching creative writing.
2014 Quoted on thestar.com, 26 Dec.

Martí, José 1853–95

Cuban national hero. A journalist, editor and poet, he was a key figure in Cuba's struggle for independence. Exiled for his revolutionary activities, he travelled in Europe and the Americas. He died fighting at Boca de Dos Ríos.

70 ¡Robaron los conquistadores una página al Universo! Aquellos eran los pueblos que llamaban a la Vía Láctea 'el camino de las almas'; para quienes el Universo estaba lleno del Grande Espíritu, en cuyo seno se encerraba toda luz.
The conquistadores stole a page from the Universe! Those were the good people who called the Milky Way 'the souls' path'; for them the Universe was full of the Great Spirit, within which all light was contained.
1884 *Obra literaria*, 'El hombre antiguo de América y sus artes primitivas' ('Ancient Man in America and his Primitive Arts').

71 Yo soy un hombre sincero
De donde crece la palma,
Y antes de morirme quiero
Echar mis versos del alma.
I am a sincere man
from where the palm tree grows;
and before I die I want
to loose my verses from my heart.
1891 *Versos sencillos* ('Simple Verses'), no.1.

Martial *full name* Marcus Valerius Martialis c. 40–104 AD

Latin poet, born in Spain. He went to Rome and became an associate of Lucan and the younger Seneca, who were also Spanish. Martial's most important work is the twelve books of *Epigrams*, each a concise expression of one idea or theme.

72 *Non est, crede mihi, sapientis dicere 'Vivam':
Sera nimis vita est crastina: vive hodie.*
Believe me, wise men do not say 'I shall live on.'
Tomorrow's life's too late; live today.
Epigrams, bk.1, no.15.

73 *Non amo te, Sabidi, nec possum dicere quare:
Hoc tantum possum dicere, non amo te.*
I do not love you, Sabidius, and I can't tell you why; all I can say is this, I don't love you.
Epigrams, bk.1, no.32.

74 *Laudant illa sed ista legunt.*
They praise those works, but read these.
Epigrams, bk.4, no.49, l.9–10.

75 *Bonosque
Soles effugere atque abire sentit,
Qui nobis pereunt et imputantur.*
Each of us feels the good days speed and depart, and they're lost to us and counted against us.
Epigrams, bk.5, no.20, l.11–13.

76 *Non est vivere, sed valere vita est.*
Life is not just to be alive, but to be well.
Epigrams, bk.6, no.70.

77 *Difficilis facilis, iucundus acerbus es idem:
Nec tecum possum vivere nec sine te.*
Difficult or easy, pleasant or bitter, you are the same: I cannot live with you—or without you.
Epigrams, bk.12, no.46.

78 *Rus in urbe.*
Country in the town.
Epigrams, bk.12, no.57, l.21.

Martin, Sir George 1926–

English record producer, particularly known for his association with The Beatles.

79 If you were poor fifty years ago, it meant you didn't have enough to eat. If you're poor now, it means you only have one car.
2003 In *Esquire*, Jan.

Martin, George R(aymond) R(ichard) 1948–

US novelist. He is best known for the *Game of Thrones* series of fantasy adventure novels that began with *A Song of Ice and Fire* (1996).

80 When you tear out a man's tongue, you are not proving him a liar, you're only telling the world that you fear what he might say.
1998 *A Clash of Kings*.

81 'A reader lives a thousand lives before he dies,' said Jojen. 'The man who never reads lives only one.'
2011 *A Dance with Dragons*.

82 Ruling is hard. This was maybe my answer to Tolkien, whom, as much as I admire him, I do quibble with. *Lord of the Rings* had a very medieval philosophy: that if the king was a good man, the land would prosper. We look at real history and it's not that simple… Real-life kings had real-life problems to deal with… My people who are trying to rule don't have an easy time of it. Just having good intentions doesn't make you a wise king.
2014 Interview in *Rolling Stone*, 13 Jun.

Marvell, Andrew 1621–78

English poet. Educated at Cambridge, he held various government posts. His poems cover a variety of genres and classical forms, but he also published anonymously political and satirical prose works.

83 The inglorious arts of peace.
1650 'An Horatian Ode upon Cromwell's Return from Ireland'.

84 He nothing common did or mean
Upon that memorable scene:
But with his leener eye
The axe's edge did try.
1650 Of Charles I. 'An Horatian Ode upon Cromwell's Return from Ireland'.

85 How fit he is to sway
That can so well obey.
1650 'An Horatian Ode upon Cromwell's Return from Ireland'.

86 See how the Orient dew,
Shed from the bosom of the morn
Into the blowing roses,
Yet careless of its mansion new;
For the clear region where 'twas born
Round in its self encloses:
And in its little globes extent,
Frames as it can its native element.
c.1650–1652 'On a Drop of Dew' (published 1681).

87 There is not such another in
The world, to offer for their sin.
c.1650–1652 'The Nymph Complaining for the Death of her Fawn' (published 1681).

88 Had it lived long, it would have been
Lilies without, roses within.

    c.1650–1652 'The Nymph Complaining for the Death of her Fawn' (published 1681)

89 I have a garden of my own,
    But so with roses overgrown,
    And lilies, that you would it guess
    To be a little wilderness.
    c.1650–1652 'The Nymph Complaining for the Death of her Fawn' (published 1681).

90 Had we but world enough, and time,
    This coyness Lady were no crime.
    We would sit down, and think which way
    To walk, and pass our long love's day.
    Thou by the Indian Ganges' side
    Shouldst rubies find: I by the tide
    Of Humber would complain. I would
    Love you ten years before the flood.
    c.1650–1652 'To His Coy Mistress' (published 1681).

91 My vegetable love should grow
    Vaster than empires, and more slow,
    An hundred years should go to praise
    Thine eyes, and on thy forehead gaze.
    Two hundred to adore each breast:
    But thirty thousand to the rest.
    An age at least to every part,
    And the last age should show your heart.
    For Lady you deserve this state;
    Nor would I love at lower rate.
    But at my back I always hear
    Time's winged chariot hurrying near:
    And yonder all before us lie
    Deserts of vast eternity.
    c.1650–1652 'To His Coy Mistress' (published 1681).

92 Then worms shall try
    That long preserved virginity:
    And your quaint honour turn to dust;
    And into ashes all my lust.
    The grave's a fine and private place,
    But none I think do there embrace.
    c.1650–1652 'To His Coy Mistress' (published 1681).

93 Now let us sport us while we may;
    And now, like amorous birds of prey,
    Rather at once our time devour,
    Than languish in his slow-chapped power.
    c.1650–1652 'To His Coy Mistress' (published 1681).

94 Let us roll all our strength, and all
    Our sweetness, up into one ball:
    And tear our pleasures with rough strife,
    Through the iron gates of life.
    Thus, though we cannot make our sun
    Stand still, yet we will make him run.
    c.1650–1652 'To His Coy Mistress' (published 1681), closing lines.

95 My love is of a birth as rare
    As 'tis for object strange and high:
    It was begotten by Despair
    Upon Impossibility.

    Magnanimous Despair alone
    Could show me so divine a thing,
    Where feeble Hope could ne'er have flown
    But vainly flapped its tinsel wing.
    c.1650–1652 'The Definition of Love' (published 1681).

96 As lines so loves oblique may well
    Themselves in every angle greet
    But ours so truly parallel,
    Though infinite can never meet.

    Therefore the love which doth us bind,
    But fate so enviously debars,
    Is the conjunction of the mind,
    And opposition of the stars.
    c.1650–1652 'The Definition of Love' (published 1681).

97 Ye living lamps, by whose dear light
    The nightingale does sit so late,
    And studying all the summer night,
    Her matchless songs does meditate.
    c.1650–1652 'The Mower to the Glo-Worms' (published 1681).

98 And now, when I have summed up all my store,
    Thinking (so I myself deceive)
    So rich a chaplet thence to weave
    As never yet the King of Glory wore,
    Alas! I find the serpent old,
    That, twining in his speckled breast,
    About the flowers disguised does fold
    With wreaths of fame and interest.
    c.1650–1652 'The Coronet' (published 1681).

99 My mind was once the true survey
    Of all these meadows fresh and gay;
    And in the greenness of the grass
    Did see its hopes as in a glass.
    c.1650–1652 'The Mower's Song' (published 1681).

1 How vainly men themselves amaze
    To win the palm, the oak, or bays;
    And their uncessant labours see
    Crown'd from some single herb or tree.
    Whose short and narrow verged shade
    Does prudently their toils upbraid;
    While all flow'rs and all trees do close
    To weave the garlands of repose.
    c.1650–1652 'The Garden' (published 1681).

2 Fair quiet, have I found thee here,
    And Innocence thy Sister dear!
    Mistaken long, I sought you then
    In busy companies of men.
    c.1650–1652 'The Garden' (published 1681).

3 Society is all but rude,
    To this delicious solitude.
    c.1650–1652 'The Garden' (published 1681).

4 What wondrous life is this I lead!
    Ripe apples drop about my head;
    The luscious clusters of the vine
    Upon my mouth do crush their wine;
    The nectarine, and curious peach,
    Into my hands themselves do reach;
    Stumbling on melons, as I pass,
    Ensnared with flowers, I fall on grass.
    c.1650–1652 'The Garden' (published 1681), stanza 5.

5 Annihilating all that's made
    To a green thought in a green shade.
    c.1650–1652 'The Garden' (published 1681), stanza 6.

6 Such was that happy garden-state,
    While man there walked without a mate.
    c.1650–1652 'The Garden' (published 1681), stanza 8.

7   'Twas beyond a mortal's share
    To wander solitary there:
    Two paradises 'twere in one
    To live in paradise alone.
    c.1650–1652 'The Garden' (published 1681), stanza 8.

8   No creature loves an empty space;
    Their bodies measure out their place.
    c.1650–1652 'Upon Appleton House, to My Lord Fairfax'
    (published 1681), stanza 2.

9   'Tis not, what once it was, the world;
    But a rude heap together hurl'd.
    c.1650–1652 'Upon Appleton House, to My Lord Fairfax'
    (published 1681), stanza 96.

10 Oh thou, that dear and happy isle
    The garden of the world ere while,
    Thou paradise of four seas,
    Which heaven planted us to please,
    But, to exclude the world, did guard
    With watery if not flaming sword;
    What luckless apple did we taste,
    To make us mortal, and thee waste?
    c.1650–1652 'Upon Appleton House, to My Lord Fairfax'
    (published 1681), stanza 41.

11 What should we do but sing the praise
    That led us through the watery maze,
    Unto an isle so long unknown,
    And yet far kinder than our own?
    c.1653 'Bermudas' (published 1681).

Marvell, Holt originally Eric Maschwitz 1901–69
English songwriter.

12 These Foolish Things Remind Me of You.
    1935 Title of song.

Marx, Chico originally Leonard Marx 1891–1961
US film comedian, one of the Marx Brothers, best known as the piano player.

13 I wasn't kissing her, I was just whispering in her mouth.
    Explanation to his wife, on being discovered in a compromising position with a chorus girl. Quoted in Groucho Marx and Richard J Anobile Marx Brothers Scrapbook (1973), ch.24.

Marx, Groucho originally Julius Henry Marx 1895–1977
US film comedian, one of the Marx Brothers. He appeared in many films including Animal Crackers (1930), Monkey Business (1931), Horse Feathers (1932) and Duck Soup (1933).

14 What's a thousand dollars? Mere chicken feed. A poultry matter.
    1929 Line delivered in The Cocoanuts (screenplay by George Kaufman and Morrie Ryskind).

15 One morning I shot an elephant in my pyjamas. How he got into my pyjamas I don't know.
    1930 Line delivered in Animal Crackers (screenplay by George Kaufman and Morrie Ryskind).

16 You go Uruguay and I'll go mine.
    1930 Line delivered in Animal Crackers (screenplay by George Kaufman and Morrie Ryskind).

17 I could dance with you till the cows come home. On second thoughts I'll dance with the cows and you come home.
    1933 Line delivered in Duck Soup (screenplay by Bert Kalmar, Harry Ruby and Arthur Sheekman).

18 There ain't no Sanity Claus.
    1935 Line delivered in A Night at the Opera (screenplay by George Kaufman and Morrie Ryskind).

19 Either he's dead or my watch has stopped.
    1937 Line delivered in A Day at the Races (screenplay by George Seaton, Robert Pirosh and George Oppenheimer).

20 Marry me and I'll never look at another horse.
    1937 Line delivered in A Day at the Races (screenplay by George Seaton, Robert Pirosh and George Oppenheimer).

21 Please accept my resignation. I don't want to belong to any club that will accept me as a member.
    1959 Recalled in his autobiography, Groucho and Me (1959), ch.26.

22 When's the game itself going to begin?
    While watching a game of cricket at Lord's. Quoted in Colin Jarman The Guinness Dictionary of Sports Quotations (1990).

Marx, Harpo originally Adolf Marx 1893–1961
US film comedian, one of the Marx Brothers. His role within the team was that of dumb clown and harp maestro. He published an autobiography in 1961.

23 No worse than a bad cold.
    His winning suggestion when a critic set up a competition for readers' reviews of the long-running play Abie's Irish Rose by Anne Nichols. Attributed.

Marx, Karl Heinrich 1818–83
German-born political and economic theorist who began his career as a journalist in 1843. With his lifelong literary collaborator Friedrich Engels he wrote The Communist Manifesto (1848), and settled in London the next year, where he began his unfinished Das Kapital (vol.1, 1867, the rest posthumously).

24 Religion is the sigh of the oppressed creature, the feelings of a heartless world, and the spirit of conditions that are unspiritual. It is the opium of the people.
    1843–4 A Contribution to the Critique of Hegel's Philosophy of Right.

25 The worker becomes poorer the more wealth he produces and the more his production increases in power and extent. The worker becomes an ever cheaper commodity the more good he creates. The *devaluation* of the human world increases in direct relation with the *increase in value* of the world of things. Labour does not only create goods; it also produces itself and the worker *as a commodity*, and indeed in the same proportion as it produces goods.
    1844 Collected in T B Bottomore (trans and ed) Early Writings (1964), p.121.

26 Political economy thus does not recognize the unoccupied worker, the working man so far as he is outside this work relationship. Swindlers, thieves, beggars, the unemployed, the starving, poverty-stricken and criminal working man, are figures which do not exist for political economy, but only for other eyes; for doctors, judges, grave-diggers, beadles, etc. They are ghostly figures outside the domain of political economy.
    1844 Collected in T B Bottomore (trans and ed) Early Writings (1964), p.137–9.

27 The *division of labour* is nothing but the *alienated* establishment of human activity.
    1844 Collected in T B Bottomore (trans and ed) Early Writings (1964), p.181.

28 The philosophers have only interpreted the world in various ways; the point is to change it.
   1845 *Theses on Feuerbach*, no.11.

29 In communist society, where nobody has one exclusive sphere of activity but each can become accomplished in any branch he wishes, society regulates the general production and thus makes it possible for me to do one thing today and another tomorrow, to hunt in the morning, fish in the afternoon, rear cattle in the evening or criticize after dinner, just as I desire, without ever becoming hunter, fisherman, shepherd or critic.
   1845 *The German Ideology* (with Friedrich Engels).

30 Assume a particular state of development in the productive facilities of man and you will get a particular form of commerce and consumption. Assume particular stages of development in production, commerce and consumption and you will have a corresponding social constitution, a corresponding organisation of the family, of orders or of classes, in a word, a corresponding civil society. Assume a particular civil society and you will get particular political conditions which are only the official expression of civil society.
   1846 Letter to P V Annenkov, 26 Dec.

31 The history of all hitherto existing society is the history of class struggles.
   1848 *The Communist Manifesto* (with Friedrich Engels, translated by Samuel Moore, 1888), opening sentence.

32 The theory of the Communists may be summed up in the single sentence: Abolition of private property.
   1848 *The Communist Manifesto* (with Friedrich Engels, translated by Samuel Moore, 1888).

33 A spectre is haunting Europe—the spectre of communism. All the powers of old Europe have entered into a holy alliance to exorcise this spectre; Pope and Tsar, Metternich and Guizot, French Radicals and German police spies.
   1848 *The Communist Manifesto* (with Friedrich Engels, translated by Samuel Moore, 1888).

34 Let the ruling classes tremble at a communist revolution. The proletarians have nothing to lose but their chains. they have a world to win. Working men of all countries, unite!
   1848 *The Communist Manifesto* (with Friedrich Engels, translated by Samuel Moore, 1888), closing words. This translation was approved by Engels, but the phrase is also known as 'Workers of the world, unite'. The literal translation of the German is 'Proletarians of all lands, unite.'

35 If capital is growing rapidly, wages may rise; the profit of capital rises incomparably more rapidly. The material position of the worker has improved, but at the cost of his social position. The social gulf that divides him from the capitalist has widened.
   1849 'Wage Labour and Capital', collected in Robert C Tucker (ed) *The Marx–Engels Reader* (2nd edn, 1972), p.211.

36 Hegel says somewhere that all great events and personalities in the world reappear in one fashion or another. He forgot to add: the first time as tragedy, the second as farce.
   1852 *The Eighteenth Brumaire of Louis Bonaparte*, section 1.

37 All our inventions have endowed material forces with intellectual life and degraded human life into material force.
   1856 Speech, 14 Apr.

38 Society does not consist of individuals; it expresses the sum of connections and relationships in which individuals find themselves.
   1857–8 *The Grundrisse* (translated by David McLellan, 1971), p.77.

39 The product of mental labour—science—always stands far below its value, because the labour-time necessary to reproduce it has no relation at all to the labour-time required for its original production.
   1862 *Theory of Surplus Value*.

40 The production of surplus-value, or the extraction of surplus labour, is the specific end and aim, the sum and substance, of capitalist production.
   1867 *Das Kapital*.

41 The instruments of labour, when they assume the form of machinery, acquire a kind of material existence which involves the replacement of human forces by the forces of Nature, and of rule-of-thumb methods by the purposeful application of natural science.
   1867 *Das Kapital*.

42 In manufacture and in handicrafts, the worker uses a tool; in the factory, he serves a machine.
   1867 *Das Kapital*.

43 Only in a higher phase of communist society...can the narrow horizon of bourgeois right be crossed in its entirety, and society inscribe on its banners, 'From each according to his ability, to each according to his needs!'
   1875 Critique of the Gotha Programme, May.
   ▶ See Bakunin 56:9.

44 All I know is that I am not a Marxist.
   Recalled by Friedrich Engels in letter to Conrad Schmidt, 3 Aug 1890.

45 What I did that was new was to prove that the existence of classes is only bound up with particular, historical phases in the development of production; that the class struggle necessarily leads to the dictatorship of the proletariat; and that dictatorship itself only constitutes the transition to the abolition of all classes and to a classless society.
   In Karl Marx and Friedrich Engels *Correspondence* (1934).

Mary of Teck *formerly* Princess Victoria Mary Augusta Louise Olga Pauline Claudine Agnes *known as* Princess May
1867–1953

Queen-Consort of George V of Britain (married 1893). She helped mould her husband into a 'people's king' and throughout her son's reign was involved in women's war work and philanthropy.

46 God grant that we may not have a European war thrust upon us, and for such a stupid reason too, no I don't mean stupid, but to have to go to war on account of tiresome Serbia beggars belief.
   1914 Letter to her aunt Princess Augusta, Grand-Duchess of Mecklenburg-Strelitz, 28 Jul.

Mary, Queen of Scots 1542–87

Queen of Scotland, the daughter of James V. A Catholic, she succeeded to the throne at the age of one week but was forced to sign an act of abdication in favour of her son James VI in 1567. She fled to England and was imprisoned by Elizabeth I for 20 years before being executed.

47 *En ma fin git mon commencement.*
   In my end is my beginning.

Mary Tudor also known as Mary I 1516–58

Queen of England and Ireland (from 1553). On Edward VI's death she ousted Lady Jane Grey with popular support and repealed anti-Catholic legislation. Public anger at her persecutions of Protestants and her unpopular marriage, and the loss of Calais to the French, broke her down.

48 When I am dead and opened, you shall find 'Calais' lying in my heart.
Quoted in Holinshed *Chronicles* (1808), vol.4.

Embroidered motto, quoted in Antonia Fraser *Mary Queen of Scots* (1969), ch.21, 'My Norfolk'.

Masaryk, Tomás Garrigue 1850–1937

Czechoslovak statesman. An ardent Slovak, while in exile during World War I he organized the Czech independence movement. As the first President of Czechoslovakia (1918–35), he was re-elected on three occasions.

49 Our whole history inclines us towards the democratic powers. Our renaissance is a logical link between us and the democracies of the west.
1918 Inaugural address, 23 Dec.

Masefield, John Edward 1878–1967

English poet and novelist. He served his apprenticeship in the merchant navy, before ill-health forced him to concentrate on writing about the sea rather than sailing it. He became Poet Laureate in 1930.

50 I must down to the seas again, to the lonely sea and the sky,
And all I ask is a tall ship and a star to steer her by,
And the wheel's kick and the wind's song and the white sail's shaking,
And a grey mist on the sea's face and a grey dawn breaking.
1902 'Sea Fever'.

51 I must down to the seas again, for the call of the running tide
Is a wild call and a clear call that may not be denied.
1902 'Sea Fever'.

52 I must down to the seas again, to the vagrant gypsy life,
To the gull's way and the whale's way where the wind's like a whetted knife;
And all I ask is a merry yarn from a laughing fellow-rover,
And quiet sleep and a sweet dream when the long trick's over.
1902 'Sea Fever'.

53 It's a warm wind, the west wind, full of bird's cries;
I never hear the west wind but tears are in my eyes.
1902 'West Wind'.

54 It is good to be out on the road, and going one knows not where.
1902 'Tewkesbury Road'.

55 Quinquireme of Nineveh from distant Ophir
Rowing home to haven in sunny Palestine,
With a cargo of ivory,
And apes and peacocks,
Sandalwood, cedarwood, and sweet white wine.
1903 'Cargoes'.

56 Dirty British coaster with a salt-caked smoke-stack,
Butting through the Channel in the mad March days.
1903 'Cargoes'.

57 I have seen dawn and sunset on moors and windy hills
Coming in solemn beauty like slow old tunes of Spain.
1903 'Beauty'.

58 Oh some are fond of Spanish wine, and some are fond of French,
And some'll swallow tay and stuff fit only for a wench.
1903 'Captain Stratton's Fancy'.

59 Most roads lead men homewards,
My road leads me forth.
1903 'Roadways'.

60 My road leads me seawards
To the white dipping sails.
1903 'Roadways'.

61 Death opens unknown doors. It is most grand to die.
1910 *Pompey the Great*, act 2.

62 In the dark room where I began
My mother's life made me a man.
Through all the months of human birth
Her beauty fed my common earth.
I cannot see, nor breathe, nor stir,
But through the death of some of her.
1910 'C.L.M.'.

63 Out into the street I ran uproarious
The devil dancing in me glorious.
1911 'The Everlasting Mercy'.

64 And he who gives a child a treat
Makes joy-bells ring in Heaven's street,
And he who gives a child a home
Builds palaces in Kingdom come,
And she who gives a baby birth
Brings Saviour Christ again to Earth.
1911 'The Everlasting Mercy'.

65 In this life he laughs longest who laughs last.
1912 *The Widow in Bye Street*, ch.4.

66 The days that make us happy make us wise.
1914 'Biography'.

67 Life's battle is a conquest for the strong;
The meaning shows in the defeated thing.
1914 'The Wanderer'.

68 I have seen flowers come in stony places
And kind things done by men with ugly faces,
And the gold cup won by the worst horse at the races,
So I trust, too.
1914 'An Epilogue'.

69 And all the way that wild high crying,
To cold his blood with the thought of dying.
1919 *Reynard the Fox*, pt.2, stanza 49.

70 People who leave their own time out of their work cannot be surprised if their time fails to find them interesting.
1925 'With the Living Voice'.

Massinger, Philip 1583–1640

English dramatist. He attended Oxford, but left to join Henslowe's company. He collaborated with Thomas Dekker, Ben Jonson and George Chapman, and particularly John Fletcher, with whom he is buried. His works include *A New Way to Pay Old Debts* (1633).

71 He that would govern others, first should be
The master of himself.
1623 *The Bondman*, act 1, sc.3.

72 Soar not too high to fall; but stoop to rise.
  1623 *The Duke of Milan*, act 1, sc.2.

73 Oh that thou hadst like others been all words,
  And no performance.
  1624 *The Parliament of Love*, act 4, sc.2.

74 Pleasures of worse natures
  Are gladly entertained, and they that shun us
  Practice in private sports the stews would blush at.
  1626 Of the theatre. *The Roman Actor*, act 1, sc.1.

75 Nay, droop not, fellows; innocence should be bold.
  1626 *The Roman Actor*, act 1, sc.1.

76 They are only safe
  That know to soothe the prince's appetite
  And serve his lusts.
  1626 *The Roman Actor*, act 1, sc.1.

77 O master doctor, he is past recovery;
  A lethargy hath seized him.
  1626 *The Roman Actor*, act 2, sc.1.

78 How strangely hopes delude men.
  1626 *The Roman Actor*, act 5, sc.2.

79 Greatness, with private men
  Esteem'd a blessing, is to me a curse;
  And we, whom, for our high births, they conclude
  The happy freemen, are the only slaves.
  Happy the golden mean!
  1627 *The Great Duke of Florence*, act 1, sc.1.

80 Virgin me no virgins!
  I must have you lose that name, or you lose me.
  1633 *A New Way to Pay Old Debts*, act 3, sc.2.

Masters, Edgar Lee 1869–1950

US poet. Although he wrote a number of books of both poetry and prose, he is chiefly remembered for the satirical free verse epitaphs on real and imaginary occupants of a midwestern cemetery in *Spoon River Anthology* (1915).

81 Where are Elmer, Herman, Bert, Tom and Charley,
  The weak of will, the strong of arm, the clown, the boozer, the fighter?
  All, all, are sleeping on the hill.
  1915 *Spoon River Anthology*, 'The Hill'.

82 Why, a moral truth is a hollow tooth
  Which must be propped with gold.
  1915 *Spoon River Anthology*, 'Sersmith the Dentist'.

83 Your eight-page paper—behind which you huddle,
  Bawling through the megaphone of big type:
  'This is I, the giant.'
  1915 *Spoon River Anthology*, 'Editor Whedon'.

Matak, Sirik c.1930–1975

Cambodian politician and business leader who joined with Lol Nol to overthrow Sihanouk in 1970. Prime Minister of the US-backed Khmer Republic (1970–5), he was executed by the Khmer Rouge after refusing to leave with the US Ambassador.

84 But mark it well, if I shall die here on the spot and in my country that I love, it is too bad because we are all born and must die one day. I have only committed this mistake of believing in you, the Americans.
  1975 Letter to John Dean, US Ambassador to Cambodia (1974–5), Apr.

Mathew, Sir James Charles 1830–1908

Irish judge. He was appointed judge (1881–1901) and Lord Justice of Appeal (1901–6).

85 In England, justice is open to all—like the Ritz Hotel.
  Quoted in R E Megarry *Miscellany-at-Law* (1955). Sometimes attributed to Lord Darling.

Mathews, Harry Burchell 1930–

US writer and translator. His fiction is marked by a rich vein of lexical experiment and unconventional fantasy. He also translates and has written original literary works in French.

86 Translation is the paradigm, the exemplar of all writing... It is translation that demonstrates most vividly the yearning for transformation that underlies every act involving speech, that supremely human gift.
  1980 *Country Cooking and Other Stories*, 'The Dialect of the Tribe'.

87 Syntax and vocabulary are overwhelming constraints—the rules that run us. Language is using *us* to talk—we think we're using the language, but language is doing the thinking, we're its slavish agents.
  1988 Interview in *City Limits*, 26 May.

Mathias, Charles McCurdy, Jr 1922–2010

US lawyer and Republican politician. He was a Congressman (1961–69), then Senator from Maryland (1969–87).

88 Most of us are honest all the time, and all of us are honest most of the time.
  1967 Of congressional ethics. In *Time*, 31 Mar.

Mathison, Melissa 1949–

US screenwriter, best known for *E.T.—the Extraterrestrial* (1982).

89 E.T. phone home.
  1982 *E.T.—the Extraterrestrial*.

90 How do you explain school to a higher intelligence?
  1982 *E.T.—the Extraterrestrial*.

Matisse, Henri Émile Benoît 1869–1954

French painter, sculptor, designer and graphic artist, from 1904 leader of the Fauves. His paintings typically display bold use of colour organized within a rhythmic two-dimensional design.

91 Expression, for me, does not reside in passions glowing in a human face or manifested by violent movement. The entire arrangement of my picture is expressive: the place occupied by the figures, the empty spaces around them, the proportions, everything has its share.
  1908 'Notes d'un peintre', in *La Grande Revue*.

92 What I dream of is an art of balance, of purity and serenity...a soothing, calming influence on the mind, rather like a good armchair which provides relaxation from physical fatigue.
  1908 'Notes d'un peintre', in *La Grande Revue*.

93 If drawing belongs to the realm of the Spirit and colour to that of the Senses, you must draw first, to cultivate the Spirit and to be able to lead colour through the paths of the Spirit.
  1948 Letter to Henry Clifford, quoted in Jack D Flam *Matisse on Art* (1973).

Matlovich, Leonard 1943–88
US soldier, the first active-duty soldier openly to acknowledge his homosexuality.

94 A Gay Vietnam Veteran—They gave me a medal for killing two men, and a discharge for loving one.
Tombstone inscription. Quoted in the *Washington Post*, 22 Apr 1988.

Matos, Gregório de c.1623–1696
Brazilian poet and epigrammatist, born into the slave-owning gentry. His scandalous private life brought him into conflict with the clergy, government and respectable society, but his frankness and rebellious spirit made him a cultural hero.

95 De dois ff se compõe
Esta cidade a meu ver:
Um furtar, outro foder.
Of two f's,
as I see it,
is this city composed:
one fraud, the other fornication.
'Define a sua cidade' ('He defines his city'), collected in *Crônica do viver bahiano* (published 1882).

Matthews, Christopher J 1945–
US journalist. Former political aide and speechwriter for President Carter. He has written several books, including *Kennedy Nixon: The Rivalry that Shaped Postwar America* (1996).

96 Hang a lantern on your problem.
1987 Advice to political candidates to expose their personal frailties before they can be discovered by the media. In the *New York Times*, 10 Jul.

97 The key is to be a porcupine—have a reputation for being difficult.
Advice for success in the political world. Quoted in Hedrick Smith *The Power Game* (1988).

Matthews, Sir Stanley 1915–2000
English footballer. He was acclaimed the finest winger of his generation and won a total of 54 caps before his eventual retirement in 1955.

98 I played 33 years and never got cautioned. I like that.
1995 Television interview, on his 80th birthday.

Matthiessen, Peter 1927–2014
US writer, naturalist and explorer. His novels included *Far Tortuga* (1975) and *Killing Mister Watson* (1990). He also wrote non-fiction and he won a National Book Award in 1978 for his account of a mystical journey through Tibet, *The Snow Leopard*.

99 At Play In The Fields Of The Lord.
1965 Title of novel.

1 For some time I watch the coming of the night... Above is the glistening galaxy of childhood, now hidden in the Western world by air pollution and the glare of artificial light; for my children's children, the power, peace and healing of the night will be obliterated.
1978 Of the night sky in Nepal. *The Snow Leopard*, 'Northward, October 18'.

Mature, Victor 1915–99
US actor whose credits include *Samson and Delilah* (1949), *Androcles and the Lion* (1952) and *The Robe* (1953).

2 Actually, I am a golfer. That is my real occupation. I never was an actor; ask anybody, particularly the critics.
Attributed.

Maugham, W(illiam) Somerset 1874–1965
British writer, born in Paris of Irish descent. He served as a secret agent in World War II, and travelled widely in south-east Asia. His works include the autobiographical novel *Of Human Bondage* (1915) and his satirical masterpiece, *Cakes and Ale* (1930).

3 At a dinner party one should eat wisely but not too well, and talk well but not too wisely.
1896 *A Writer's Notebook* (published 1949).

4 Impropriety is the soul of wit.
1919 *The Moon and Sixpence*.

5 I hate people who play bridge as though they were at a funeral and knew their feet were getting wet.
1921 Quoted in Colin Jarman *The Guinness Dictionary of Sports Quotations* (1990).

6 Hypocrisy is the most difficult and nerve-racking vice that any man can pursue; it needs an unceasing vigilance and a rare detachment of spirit. It cannot, like adultery or gluttony, be practised at spare moments; it is a whole-time job.
1930 *Cakes and Ale*, ch.1.

7 There is no silence in the East.
1930 *The Gentleman in the Parlour*.

8 Mandalay has its name; the falling cadence of the lovely word has gathered about itself the chiaroscuro of romance.
1930 *The Gentleman in the Parlour*.

9 The Chinese are the aristocracy of the East.
1930 *The Gentleman in the Parlour*.

10 They are like a face full of character that intrigues and excites you, but that on closer acquaintance you discover is merely the mask of a vulgar soul. Such is Tourane.
1930 Of Tourane, now Da Nang, Vietnam. *The Gentleman in the Parlour*.

11 Observing these people I am no longer surprised that there is such a scarcity of domestic servants at home.
1960 Said in an uncharacteristically loud voice after being refused entry to the premier British expatriate club in Singapore. Quoted in Robert Calder *Willie* (1989).

Maupassant, Guy de 1850–93
French writer, best known for his captivating short stories which explored a wide range of characters and, often, the supernatural world.

12 L'histoire, cette vieille dame exaltée et menteuse.
History, this old, honoured and lying woman.
1876 *Sur l'eau*.

13 Le talent provient de l'originalité, qui est une manière spéciale de penser, de voir, de comprendre et de juger.
Talent comes from originality which is a special manner of thinking, of seeing, of understanding and of judging.
1888 *Pierre et Jean*, préface.

14 Raconter tout serait impossible.
To tell all would be impossible.
1888 *Pierre et Jean*, préface.

15 *Les grands artistes sont ceux qui imposent à l'humanité leur illusion particulière.*
Great artists impose their particular illusion on humanity.
1888 *Pierre et Jean*, préface.

16 *La moindre chose contient un peu d'inconnu. Trouvons-le.*
The least thing contains something mysterious. Find it.
1888 *Pierre et Jean*, préface.

17 *On finirait par devenir fou, ou par mourir, si on ne pouvait pas pleurer.*
We would end by becoming crazy or by dying, if we could not cry.
1889 *Fort comme la mort*, bk.2, ch.1.

Maxton, James 1885–1946

Socialist politician, born in Glasgow, elected as a Labour MP in 1922. One of the group of 'Red Clydesiders', he was a brilliant and colourful orator rather than a skilful political tactician.

18 In the interests of economy they condemned hundreds of children to death and I call it murder.
1923 Speech against the withdrawal of child benefits, including the supply of milk, in Scotland. In *Hansard*, 27 Jun.

19 All I say is, if you cannot ride two horses you have no right in the circus.
1931 On the Scottish Independent Labour Party's proposed disaffiliation from the Labour Party. In the *Daily Herald*, 12 Jan.

May, Elaine *originally Elaine Berlin* 1932–

US actress, director and screenwriter. She wrote screenplays for *A New Leaf* (1971) and *Primary Colours* (1998).

20 All I am or was is rich, and that's all I ever wanted to be.
1971 Line delivered by Walter Matthau in *A New Leaf*.

Mayakovsky, Vladimir 1894–1930

Russian Futurist poet, a supporter of the Bolsheviks in the 1917 Revolution. His works include plays, poems and satirical plays. He committed suicide in Moscow.

21 I'll be irreproachably tender;
not a man, but—a cloud in trousers!
1915 'The Cloud in Trousers' (translated by Samuel Charteris).

22 We do not need art museums to worship dead works, we need living factories of the soul—in the streets, in the trams, in the factories, in studios, and in the workers' houses.
1918 Quoted in *Futurismo e Futurismi* (1986).

23 To us love says humming that the heart's stalled motor has begun working again.
1928 'Letter from Paris to Comrade Kostorov on the Nature of Love' (translated by Samuel Charteris).

Maybeck, Bernard Ralph 1862–1957

US architect, renowned for his eclectic combinations of styles and materials. His works include the Palace of Fine Arts, San Francisco (1915) and Clyde, a town in California (1917).

24 Let the thing fall down in peace.
On the crumbling remains of his Corinthian classic Palace of Fine Arts, designed for San Francisco's 1915 Panama–Pacific Exposition. Recalled in the *New York Times*, 9 May 1965.

Mayer, Louis B(urt) *originally Eliezer Mayer* 1885–1957

Russian-born US film mogul. A co-founder of Metro Films in 1915, he joined with Sam Goldwyn to form Metro-Goldwyn-Mayer (MGM) in 1924. He received an honorary Academy Award in 1950.

25 We are the only company whose assets all walk out the gates at night.
Quoted in Leslie Halliwell *The Filmgoer's Book of Quotes* (1973).

Mayhew, Alex

Professor of Political Science, Georgetown University.

26 The future of America is based on one generation sacrificing for the next.
Quoted by David Maraniss in CNBC broadcast, 7 Mar 1995. The phrase was popularized by Mayhew's former student, Bill Clinton.

Mayo, Charles Horace 1865–1939

US surgeon. An authority on the treatment of goitre, he co-founded the Mayo Clinic with his brother in 1905 within what is now St Mary's Hospital, Rochester.

27 The definition of a specialist as one who 'knows more and more about less and less' is good and true.
1939 In *Modern Hospital*, Sep.

Mazarin, Jules, Cardinal 1602–61

Neapolitan statesman. He entered Louis XIII's service in 1639, and succeeded Richelieu as Chief Minister (1642), becoming the lover of Anne of Austria. His domestic policy was problematic, but he negotiated the Peace of Westphalia (1648) and the Treaty of the Pyrenees (1659).

28 The French are nice people. I allow them to sing and to write, and they allow me to do whatever I like.
Attributed by the Duchess of Orléans in a letter dated 25 Oct 1715.

Mazzini, Giuseppe 1805–72

Italian patriot, a leader of the Risorgimento and founder of the revolutionary Young Italy Association. His underground journal, *La Giovine Italia*, fomented revolt throughout Europe.

29 Insurrection—by means of guerrilla bands—is the true method of warfare for all nations desirous of emancipating themselves from a foreign yoke.
1833 *General Instructions for the Members of Young Italy*, section 4.

30 I had thought to evoke the soul of Italy but all I find before me is its corpse.
Attributed. Quoted in Denis Mack Smith *Italy: A Modern History* (1959).

31 A nation is the universality of citizens speaking the same tongue.
In *La Giovine Italia* ('Young Italy').

Mead, Margaret 1901–78

US anthropologist. After expeditions to Samoa and New Guinea she wrote books on her experiences, arguing that personality characteristics are shaped by conditioning rather than heredity.

32 The greatest invention since the novel.
1974 Of television. Comment, 31 Dec.

Meat Loaf (Michael Lee Aday) 1947–

US rock singer.

33 I don't have a rock voice. I have to force it. I am like an opera singer.
2003 In the *Observer*, 7 Dec.

Medawar, Sir Peter Brian 1915–87
British zoologist and immunologist, born in Rio de Janeiro. Professor of Anatomy at University College London, he pioneered experiments in immunological toleration and skin and organ grafting, winning a Nobel prize with Sir Macfarlane Burnet in 1960.

34 I cannot give any scientist of any age better advice than this: the intensity of a conviction that a hypothesis is true has no bearing over whether it is true or not.
1979 *Advice to a Young Scientist*.

35 A scientist soon discovers that he has become a member of the cast of 'them' in the context 'what mischief are they up to now?'
1979 *Advice to a Young Scientist*.

36 Good scientists often possess old-fashioned virtues of the kind school teachers have always professed to despair of ever inculcating in us. These are: a sanguine temperament that expects to solve a problem; power of application and the kind of fortitude that keeps scientists erect in the face of much that might otherwise cast them down; and above all, persistence, a refusal bordering upon obstinacy to give in and admit defeat.
1984 *The Limits of Science*.

Meijer, Frederik 1919–2011
US retail executive and Chairman Emeritus of Meijer Inc.

37 I am more poor than you think.
On trying to secure a low profile. Quoted in *Forbes*, 19 Oct 1992.

Meilhac, Henri 1831–97
French playwright. From 1855 he produced a long series of light comedies, often in conjunction with Ludovic Halévy, with whom he also wrote the librettos for Offenbach's operettas and Bizet's *Carmen*.

38 L'amour est un oiseau rebelle
Que nul ne peut apprivoiser.
Love's a bird that will live in freedom
That no man ever learned to tame.
1875 The *Habañera. Carmen*, act 1.

39 La fleur que tu m'avais jetée
Here is the flower that you threw me
1875 *Carmen*, act 2, 'Flower Song' (Don José).

40 Toreador, en garde!
1875 *Carmen*, act 2, 'Couplets' (Escamillo).

Meir, Golda 1898–1978
Israeli politician. She was elected Prime Minister in 1969, but her efforts for peace in the Middle East were halted by the fourth Arab–Israeli War (1973) and she resigned in 1974.

41 Those that perished in Hitler's gas chambers were the last Jews to die without standing up to defend themselves.
1967 Speech in New York, 11 Jun.

42 Women's Liberation is just a lot of foolishness. It's the men who are discriminated against. They can't bear children. And no-one's likely to do anything about that.
1972 In *Newsweek*, 23 Oct.

Melba, Dame Nellie *real name* Helen Mitchell 1861–1931
Australian soprano, who took her stage name from her native Melbourne. Notorious for her many 'farewell' performances, her earthy Australian character contrasted oddly with the graces she adopted in her stage persona.

43 What are you going to sing? All I can say is—sing 'em muck! It's all they can understand!
c.1907 Advice to Dame Clara Butt on her first tour of Australia. Quoted in Winifred Ponder *Clara Butt: Her Life-Story* (1928).

44 If you wish to understand me at all (and to write an autobiography is only to open a window into one's heart) you must understand first and foremost, that I am an Australian… I shall always come back to rest in the shadow of the blue mountains, in the heart of this vast, deserted continent which gave me birth.
1925 *Melodies and Memories*, ch.1.

45 The first rule in opera is the first rule in life: see to everything yourself.
1925 *Melodies and Memories*.

46 If I'd been a housemaid I'd have been the best in Australia—I couldn't help it. It's got to be perfection for me.
Said to the conductor Fritz Hart. Quoted in John Thompson *On Lips of Living Men* (1962).

Melbourne, William Lamb, 2nd Viscount 1779–1848
English statesman, Chief Secretary for Ireland (1827–8), Home Secretary (1830–4), and Whig Prime Minister (1834, 1835–41), a confidante of the young Queen Victoria. Defeated in the election of 1841, he resigned and thereafter took little part in public affairs.

47 I wish that I was as cocksure of anything as Tom Macaulay is of everything.
1889 Attributed by Earl Cowper.

Melchett, Peter Robert Henry Mond, Baron 1948–
English Labour peer, executive director of Greenpeace UK (1989–2000).

48 The menu could not guarantee GM-free food but I ate vegetarian shepherd's pie.
1999 After spending two days in prison for leading a raid to destroy GM crops. In the *Sunday Times*, 'Talking Heads', 1 Aug.

Mellor, D(avid) H(ugh) 1938–
British Emeritus Professor of Philosophy at Cambridge University. He has written several books on philosophy.

49 Appeals to rationality are mostly bluff. There is no good theory of what it is nor of how to recognize it.
1983 'Objective Decision Making', in *Social Theory and Practice*, Summer–Fall.

Melly, George 1926–2007
English jazz singer.

50 Jazz is an impure art. There's a great deal of romantic nostalgia involved.
1965 *Owning Up*, ch.2.

Melville, Andrew 1545–c.1622
Scottish religious and educational reformer, consolidating the Presbyterianism of the reformed Church of Scotland, and a fierce

critic of royal authority where it impinged on that of the Kirk. In 1596 he headed a deputation to 'remonstrate' with James VI.

51 God's silly vassal.
1596 Said of (and to) King James VI, as reported in his nephew James Melville's *Diary*: 'Mr Andrew bore him down and uttered the commission as from the mighty God, calling him but "God's silly vassal".'

Melville, Herman 1819–91

US novelist. Between 1839 and 1844 he spent time at sea, working as a cabin-boy and on whaling ships. His experiences gave him material for many of his best-known books, including *Typee* (1846) and his masterpiece, *Moby Dick* (1851).

52 We may have civilized bodies and yet barbarous souls.
1849 Redburn, ch.58.

53 Toil is man's allotment; toil of brain, or toil of hands, or a grief that's more than either, the grief and sin of idleness.
1849 Mardi, ch.63.

54 Call me Ishmael.
1851 Moby Dick, ch.1, opening words.

55 Better sleep with a sober cannibal than a drunken Christian.
1851 Moby Dick, ch.3.

56 Faith, like a jackal, feeds among the tombs, and even from these dead doubts she gathers her most vital hope.
1851 Moby Dick, ch.7.

57 A whale ship was my Yale College and my Harvard.
1851 Moby Dick, ch.24.

58 Old age is always wakeful; as if, the longer linked with life, the less man has to do with aught that looks like death.
1851 Moby Dick, ch.29.

59 All visible objects, man, are but as pasteboard masks. But in each event—in the living act, the undoubted deed—there, some unknown but still reasoning thing puts forth the mouldings of its features from behind the unreasoning mask. If man will strike, strike through the mask!
1851 Captain Ahab. *Moby Dick*, ch.36.

60 Though in many of its aspects this visible world seems formed in love, the invisible spheres were formed in fright.
1851 Moby Dick, ch.42.

61 It was the whiteness of the whale that above all things appalled me…for all these accumulated associations, with whatever is sweet, and honourable, and sublime, there yet lurks an elusive something in the innermost idea of this hue, which strikes more of a panic to the soul than that redness which affrights in blood.
1851 Ishmael. *Moby Dick*, ch.42.

62 It may seem strange that of all men sailors should be tinkering at their last wills and testaments, but there are no people in the world more fond of that diversion.
1851 Moby Dick, ch.49.

63 There is a wisdom that is woe; but there is a woe that is madness.
1851 Moby Dick, ch.96.

64 To produce a mighty book, you must choose a mighty theme. No great and enduring volume can ever be written on the flea, though many there be who have tried it.
1851 Moby Dick, ch.104.

65 For whatever is truly wonderous and fearful in man, never yet was put into words or books.
1851 Moby Dick, ch.110.

66 Come; let us squeeze hands all round; nay, let us all squeeze ourselves into each other; let us squeeze ourselves universally into the very milk and sperm of kindness.
1851 Ishmael. *Moby Dick*, ch.114.

67 Warmest climes but nurse the cruellest fangs: the tiger of Bengal crouches in spiced groves of ceaseless verdure.
1851 Moby Dick, ch.119.

68 Oh God! that man should be a thing for immortal souls to sieve through!
1851 Captain Ahab. *Moby Dick*, ch.125.

69 Let me look into a human eye; it is better than to gaze into sea or sky; better than to gaze upon God.
1851 Captain Ahab. *Moby Dick*, ch.132.

70 Guinea-coast slavery of solitary command!
1851 Captain Ahab. *Moby Dick*, ch.132.

71 He says NO! in thunder; but the Devil himself cannot make him say yes. For all men who say *yes*, lie; and all men who say *no*,—why, they are in the happy condition of judicious, unencumbered travellers in Europe; they cross the frontiers into Eternity with nothing but a carpet bag.
1851 Of Nathaniel Hawthorne.

72 The calm, the coolness, the silent grass-growing mood in which a man *ought* always to compose,—that, I fear, can seldom be mine. Dollars damn me; and the malicious Devil is forever grinning in upon me, holding the door ajar… What I feel most moved to write, that is banned,—it will not pay. So the product is a final hash, and all my books are botches.
1851 Letter to Nathaniel Hawthorne, Jun.

73 Why, ever since Adam, who has got to the meaning of this great allegory—the world? Then we pygmies must be content to have our paper allegories but ill comprehended.
1851 Letter to Nathaniel Hawthorne, Nov.

74 Nothing so aggravates an earnest person as a passive resistance.
1853 'Bartleby the Scrivener', in *Putnam's Monthly Magazine*, Nov–Dec.

75 If some books are deemed most baneful and their sale forbid, how, then, with deadlier facts, not dreams of doting men? Those whom books will hurt will not be proof against events. Events, not books, should be forbid.
1854 'The Encantadas, Sketch Eighth', in *Putnam's Monthly Magazine*, May.

76 Who in the rainbow can draw the line where the violet tint ends and the orange tint begins? Distinctly we see the difference of the colors, but where exactly does the one first blendingly enter into the other? So with sanity and insanity.
1891 Billy Budd, Foretopman (first published 1924), ch.21.

77 There is nothing nameable but that some men will, or undertake to, do it for pay.
1891 Billy Budd, Foretopman (first published 1924), ch.21.

Menander c.343–291 BC

Greek comic poet, born in Athens. He wrote more than 100 comedies, most of which are lost. Various fragments and one complete play (*Dyscolus*) have been rediscovered in recent times.

78 He whom the gods love dies young.
Dis Exapaton, fragment 4.

79 The man who runs away will fight again.
Fragment quoted in Aulus Gellius *Noctes Atticae*, 17.21.31 (translated by J C Rolfe, 1967).

Mencius *properly Meng-tzu* c.371–c.289 BC

Chinese philosopher and sage. He helped to develop and popularize Confucian ideas and founded a school to promote their study. His sayings were recorded by his pupils after his death, and included proposals for social and political reform.

80 If the king loves music, there is little wrong in the land.
3c BC *Discourses*.

Mencken, H(enry) L(ouis) 1880–1956

US journalist and critic. He wrote much literary and political criticism as editor of *The Smart Set* (1914–23) and co-founder and editor of the *American Mercury* (1924–33), and various essays were collected in *Prejudices* (6 vols, 1919–27). Other publications included autobiographical writings and *The American Language* (1919).

81 Democracy is the theory that the common people know what they want, and deserve to get it good and hard.
1916 *Little Book in C Major*.

82 Conscience: the inner voice which warns us that someone may be looking.
1916 *Little Book in C Major*.

83 I can't remember a single masculine figure created by a woman who is not, at bottom, a booby.
1918 *In Defence of Women*, ch.1, pt.1.

84 All successful newspapers are ceaselessly querulous and bellicose.
1919 *Prejudices*, 1st series, ch.13.

85 If, after I depart this vale, you ever remember me and have thought to please my ghost, forgive some sinner and wink your eye at some homely girl.
1921 In *The Smart Set*, Dec.

86 Poetry is a comforting piece of fiction set to more or less lascivious music.
1922 *Prejudices*, 3rd series, ch.7.

87 Faith may be defined briefly as an illogical belief in the occurrence of the improbable.
1922 *Prejudices*, 3rd series, ch.14.

88 The man who boasts that he habitually tells the truth is simply a man with no respect for it. It is not a thing to be thrown about loosely, like small change; it is something to be cherished and hoarded, and disbursed only when absolutely necessary.
1922 *Prejudices*, 3rd series, ch.14.

89 [Jeremy] Bentham held no post at the mercy of bankers and tripe sellers; he was a man of independent means, a lawyer and politician and a heretic in general practice. It is impossible to imagine such a man occupying a chair at Harvard or Princeton. He had a hand in too many pies; he was too rebellious and contumacious; he had too little respect for authority, either academic or worldly. Moreover, his mind was too wide for a professor; he could never remain safely in a groove; the whole field of social organization invited his inquiries and experiments.
1922 'The Dismal Science', in *The Smart Set*, Jun.

90 Hygiene is the corruption of medicine by morality.
1922 *Prejudices*.

91 The opera...is to music what a bawdy house is to a cathedral.
1925 Letter to Isaac Goldberg.

92 No one in this world, so far as I know—and I have searched the record for years, and employed agents to help me—has ever lost money by underestimating the intelligence of the great masses of the plain people.
1926 'Notes on Journalism' in the *Chicago Sunday Tribune*, 19 Sep. The phrase is commonly quoted as 'No one ever went broke underestimating the intelligence of the American people.'

93 The saddest life is that of a political aspirant under democracy. His failure is ignominious and his success is disgraceful.
1929 In the *Baltimore Evening Sun*, 9 Dec.

94 Here, indeed, was his one peculiar Fach, his one really notable talent. He slept more than any other President, whether by day or night. Nero fiddled, but Coolidge only snored.
1933 Of Calvin Coolidge. In the *American Mercury*, Apr.

95 Roosevelt will probably go down into American history as a great hero. It is one of our Heavenly Father's characteristic jokes upon the American people, and in the usual bad taste.
1944 Journal entry. Collected in *The Diary of H. L. Mencken* (published 1990).

96 I've made it a rule never to drink by daylight and never to refuse a drink after dark.
1945 In the *New York Post*, 18 Sep.

97 When women kiss it always reminds one of prize-fighters shaking hands.
1949 *Chrestomathy*, ch.30.

98 Love is the delusion that one woman differs from another.
1949 *Chrestomathy*, ch.30.

99 Men have a much better time of it than women. For one thing, they marry later. For another thing, they die earlier.
1949 *Chrestomathy*, ch.30

1 Puritanism. The haunting fear that someone, somewhere, may be happy.
1949 *Chrestomathy*, ch.30.

2 He is a man who sits in the outer office of the White House hoping to hear the President sneeze.
Of the Vice-President. Recalled on his death, 29 Jan 1956.

3 Science, at bottom, is really anti-intellectual. It always distrusts pure reason, and demands the production of objective fact.
'Minority Report'. Collected in *Notebooks* (1956).

4 Some people read too much: the bibliobuli...who are constantly drunk on books, as other men are drunk on whiskey or religion. They wander through the most diverting and stimulating of worlds in a haze, seeing nothing and hearing nothing.
'Minority Report'. Collected in *Notebooks* (1956).

5 We must respect the other fellow's religion, but only in the sense and to the extent that we respect his theory that his wife is beautiful and his children smart.
'Minority Report'. Collected in *Notebooks* (1956).

6 Men always try to make virtues of their weaknesses. Fear of death and fear of life become piety.
'Minority Report'. Collected in *Notebooks* (1956).

7 It is now quite lawful for a Catholic woman to avoid pregnancy by a resort to mathematics, though she is still forbidden to resort to physics and chemistry.
'Minority Report'. Collected in *Notebooks* (1956).

8 The capacity of human beings to bore one another seems to be vastly greater than that of any other animals. Some of their most esteemed inventions have no other apparent purpose, for example, the dinner party of more than two, the epic poem, and the science of metaphysics.
'Minority Report'. Collected in *Notebooks* (1956).

9 Men are the only animals who devote themselves assiduously to making one another unhappy. It is, I suppose, one of their godlike qualities.
'Minority Report'. Collected in *Notebooks* (1956).

10 War will never cease until babies begin to come into the world with larger cerebrums and smaller adrenal glands.
'Minority Report'. Collected in *Notebooks* (1956).

11 Whenever one comes to close grips with so-called idealism, as in war time, one is shocked by its rascality.
'Minority Report'. Collected in *Notebooks* (1956).

12 I hate all sports as rabidly as a person who likes sports hates common sense.
Quoted in Fred Metcalfe *The Penguin Dictionary of Modern Humorous Quotations* (1986).

13 The greatest of all the contributions of the American way of life to the salvation of humanity.
Of the cocktail. Quoted by William Grimes in 'The American Cocktail', *Americana*, Dec 1992.

14 The varnishers and veneerers have been busily converting Abe into a plaster saint...to pump all his human weaknesses out of him, and so leave him a mere moral apparition, a sort of amalgam of John Wesley and the Holy Ghost.
Of popular perceptions of Abraham Lincoln. Quoted in Fred Hobson *Mencken: A Life* (1994).

15 His whole carcass seemed to be made of iron. There was no give in him—no bounce, no softness. He sailed through American history like a steel ship loaded with monoliths made of granite.
Of President Grover Cleveland. Quoted in Fred Hobson *Mencken: A Life* (1994).

16 A third-rate political wheel-horse, with the face of a moving-picture actor, the intelligence of a respectable agricultural implement dealer, and the imagination of a lodge joiner...a benign blank—a decent, harmless, laborious, hollow-headed mediocrity.
Of President Warren G Harding. Quoted in Fred Hobson *Mencken: A Life* (1994).

17 His English reminds me of tattered washing on the line...of stale bean-soup, of college yells, of dogs barking idiotically through endless nights. It is so bad that a sort of grandeur creeps into it.
Of President Warren G Harding. Quoted in Fred Hobson *Mencken: A Life* (1994).

18 He was, on his plane, as insufferable as a Methodist on his.
Of Oscar Wilde. Introduction to a new edition of Wilde *A House of Pomegranates*.

Menzies, Sir Robert Gordon   1894–1978

Australian statesman, Prime Minister (1939–41), Leader of the Opposition (1943–9) and thereafter Premier of the coalition government. He headed the Five Nations Committee which sought a settlement with Nasser on the question of Suez (1956).

19 What Great Britain calls the Far East is to us the near north.
1939 Quoted in the *Sydney Morning Herald*, 27 Apr. Menzies was one of the first Australian statesmen to recognize the importance to his country of Asia.

20 If I were the Archangel Gabriel, madam, I'm afraid you would not be in my constituency.
Attributed reply to a woman who had heckled him with the words 'I wouldn't vote for you if you were the Archangel Gabriel'. Quoted in Ray Robinson *The Wit of Robert Menzies* (1966).

Mercer, David   1928–80

English playwright. Such plays as *A Climate of Fear* (1962) and *In Two Minds* (1967) explored his fascination with mental health, psychiatry and his struggle to reconcile a belief in socialism with the repression revealed during his stays in Eastern Europe. Other writings included the films *Morgan* (1965) and *Providence* (1977) and several plays for television.

21 A Suitable Case for Treatment.
1962 Play title.

Mercer, Johnny   1909–76

US songwriter. His songs include 'Accentuate the Positive', 'Black Magic', 'In the Cool Cool of the Evening' and 'Something's Gotta Give'.

22 Hooray for Hollywood.
1937 Title of song which first appeared in the film *Hollywood Hotel*, performed by Johnny Davis and Frances Langford.

Meredith, George   1828–1909

English novelist and poet. He married the daughter of Thomas Love Peacock but she left him for the painter Henry Wallis, for whose *Death of Chatterton* Meredith was the model. His volumes of poetry include *Modern Love* (1862) and *Poems and Lyrics of the Joy of the Earth* (1883). His novels include *The Ordeal of Richard Feverel* (1859), *Evan Harrington* (1860) and *The Egoist* (1879).

23 Lovely are the curves of the white owl sweeping
Wavy in the dusk lit by one large star.
Lone on the fir-branch, his rattle-note unvaried,
Brooding o'er the gloom, spins the brown eve-jar.
1851 *Poems*, 'Love in the Valley', stanza 5. The poem was revised and republished in 1878.

24 Happy happy time, when the white star hovers
Low over dim fields fresh with blooming dew,
Near the face of dawn, that draws athwart the darkness,
Threading it with colour, like yewberries the yew.
1851 *Poems*, 'Love in the Valley', stanza 7. The poem was revised and republished in 1878.

25 I expect that Woman will be the last thing civilized by Man.
1859 *The Ordeal of Richard Feverel*, ch.1.

26 Away with systems! Away with a corrupt world! Let us breathe the air of the Enchanted island. Golden lie the meadows; golden run the streams; red gold is on the pine-stems. The sun's coming down to earth, and walks the fields and the waters. The sun is coming down to earth, and the fields and the waters shout to him golden shouts.
1859 *The Ordeal of Richard Feverel*, ch.19.

Mérimée

27 Kissing don't last: cookery do!
   1859 *The Ordeal of Richard Feverel*, ch.28.

28 Speech is the small change of silence.
   1859 *The Ordeal of Richard Feverel*, ch.34.

29 It became known that death had taken Mr Melchisedec Harrington, and struck one off the list of living tailors.
   1860 *Evan Harrington*, ch.1.

30 He fainted on his vengefulness, and strove
   To ape the magnanimity of love.
   1862 *Modern Love*, 2.

31 O have a care of natures that are mute!
   1862 *Modern Love*, 35.

32 Much benevolence of the passive order may be traced to a disinclination to inflict pain upon oneself.
   1866 *Vittoria*, ch.24.

33 A dainty rogue in porcelain.
   1879 *The Egoist*, ch.5

34 Cynicism is intellectual dandyism.
   1879 *The Egoist*, ch.7.

35 'But do care a bit for flattery, my lady,' said De Craye. ''Tis the finest of the Arts; we might call it moral sculpture. Adepts in it can cut their friends to any shape they like.'
   1879 De Craye to Lady Busshe. *The Egoist*, ch.36.

36 Enter these enchanted woods,
   You who dare.
   1883 *Poems and Lyrics of the Joy of Earth*, 'The Woods of Westermain'.

37 Soaring through wider zones that pricked his scars
   With memory of the old revolt from Awe,
   He reached the middle height, and at the stars,
   Which are the brain of heaven, he looked, and sank.
   Around the ancient track marched, rank on rank,
   The army of unalterable law.
   1883 *Poems and Lyrics of the Joy of Earth*, 'Lucifer in Starlight'.

38 For singing till his heaven fills
   'Tis love of earth that he instils,
   And ever winging up and up,
   Our valley is his golden cup,
   And he the wine which overflows.
   1883 *Poems and Lyrics of the Joy of Earth*, 'The Lark Ascending'.

39 'Tis Ireland gives England her soldiers, her generals too.
   1885 *Diana of the Crossways*, ch.2.

40 Affairs of the world he could treat competently; he had a head for high politics and the management of men; the feminine half of the world was a confusion and a vexation to his intelligence, characterless; and one woman at last appearing decipherable, he fancied it must be owing to her possession of character, a thing prized the more in women because of his latent doubt of its existence.
   1885 Percy Dacier's opinion of Diana. *Diana of the Crossways*, ch.28.

41 A wind sways in the pines,
   And below
   Not a breath of wild air;
   Still as the mosses that glow
   On the flooring and over the lines
   Of the roots here and there.
   The pine tree drops its dead;
   They are quiet, as under the sea.
   Overhead, overhead
   Rushes life in a race,
   As the clouds the clouds chase;
   And we go,
   And we drop like the fruits of the tree,
   Even we,
   Even so.
   1888 *A Reading of Earth*, 'Dirge in the Woods'.

Mérimée, Prosper 1803–70

French novelist, Inspector-General of Historical Remains in France (1833) and a Senator (1853). He wrote many short stories and novels, including *Colomba* (1841) and *Carmen* (1847), as well as archaeological and historical dissertations and travel stories.

42 A colossal bore... I feel I could write something like it tomorrow, if my cat inspired me by walking over the piano.
   1861 Of Wagner's opera *Tannhäuser*, after the disastrous première of its revised version at the Paris Opéra, 13 Mar. Quoted in Joanna Richardson *La Vie Parisienne* (1971), p.262.
   ▶ See Gounod 380:78.

Merkel, Angela Dorothea 1954–

German politician. She became leader of the Christian Democratic Union in 2000 and Chancellor of Germany in 2005, the first woman to hold either post.

43 The euro is much, much more than a currency. The euro is the guarantee of a united Europe. If the euro fails, then Europe fails.
   2011 Speech in the German Parliament, reported in *Der Spiegel*, 7 Sep.

44 The lesson of this crisis is more Europe, not less Europe.
   2012 Speaking after a meeting with other leaders in Rome to discuss Europe's debt crisis, 22 Jun.

45 Islam is part of Germany.
   2015 Press conference with Turkish Prime Minister Ahmet Davutoglu in Berlin, 12 Jan.

Merman, Ethel *stage-name of* Ethel Agnes Zimmermann 1909–84

US singer and actress. Nicknamed 'The Golden Foghorn' because of her powerful singing voice, she established her reputation in cabaret and subsequently starred in such musicals as *Annie Get Your Gun* (1946) and *Hello, Dolly!* (1970).

46 She's OK, if you like talent.
   1958 Of Mary Martin. In *Theater Arts*, Sep.

47 Can you imagine the name Zimmermann in bright lights? It would burn you to death!
   Explaining why she took a stage-name. Attributed.

Merrifield, D(udley) Bruce 1921–

US former government official and Professor Emeritus of the Wharton Business School. He was Assistant Secretary of Commerce in the Reagan administration.

48 Innovate, automate—or evaporate!
   1987 Address at London's Guildhall to Britain's senior industrialists and bankers. Reported in *The Times*, 19 Feb.

Merrill, James Ingram 1926–95

US poet, the 'ouija poet', whose interest in the occult led him to use a ouija board to communicate with the spirit world. The experience is recorded in an epic poem, *The Changing Light at Sandover* (1982, rev 1992). His collections include *Nights and Days* (1966) and *Divine Comedies* (1976, Pulitzer Prize), and he also wrote plays and novels.

49 Here one is in Later Life, and it's perfectly pleasant really, not for a moment that garden of cactus and sour grapes I'd always assumed it *must* be.
1972 Letter to a friend at age 46.

50 What one wants in this world isn't so much to 'live' as to...*be* lived, to be used by life for its own purposes.
Quoted in the *New Yorker*, 27 Mar 1995.

Merrin, Edward H
Antiquities dealer.

51 The price was quite reasonable. It just happened to be a lot of money.
1989 In the *New York Times*, 16 Jul. On paying $2.09 million for a nine-inch, 5,000-year-old Greek head.

Merton, Paul 1957–
English comedian.

52 They say the closer you sit to the stage, the better chance you have of winning. Angus Deayton is sitting in Row G—at the Theatre Royal, Drury Lane.
2003 At the BAFTA television awards night at the London Palladium—assessing his fellow TV presenter's chances, 13 Apr.

53 I don't consider myself a fashion victim. I consider fashion a victim of me.
2003 In the *Daily Telegraph*, 21 Apr.

Merton, Robert King 1910–2003
US sociologist, Columbia University (1941–2003). He was awarded the National Medal of Science in 1994.

54 The self-fulfilling prophecy is, in the beginning, a *false* definition of the situation evoking a new behavior which makes the originally false conception come *true*. The specious validity of the self-fulfilling prophecy perpetuates a reign of error.
1948 'The Self-Fulfilling Prophecy', in *Social Theory and Social Structure* (rev. edn, 1968), p.477. This is the first use of the phrase 'self-fulfilling prophecy'.

55 It would be a curious reading of the history of thought to suggest that the absence of disagreement testifies to a developing discipline.
1961 Defending internal disputes among sociologists. 'Now the Case *for* Sociology', in the *New York Times Magazine*, 16 Jul.

56 The sociologists of knowledge have been among those raising high the banner which reads: 'We don't know if what we say is true, but it is at least significant.' The sociologists and psychologists engaged in the study of public opinion and mass communications are most often found in the opposed camp of the empiricists... 'We don't know that what we say is particularly significant, but it is at least true.'
1968 *Social Theory and Social Structure* (rev. edn), pt.3, introduction.

Merwin, W(illiam) S(tanley) 1927–
US poet. His poetry includes *A Mask for Janus* (1952), *The Carrier of Ladders* (1970, Pulitzer Prize), *Opening the Hand* (1983) and *The River Sound* (1999). He is also a translator, notably of *The Cid* (1959).

57 The thing that makes poetry different from all of the other arts... [is] you're using language, which is what you use for everything else—telling lies and selling socks, advertising, and conducting law. Whereas we don't write little concerts or paint little pictures.
1994 On receiving the $100,000 Tanning Prize for Poetry. In the *Washington Post*, 30 Sep.

Metternich, Prince Clemens Lothar Wenzel
1773–1859
Austrian statesman, Foreign Minister from 1809. He was a powerful influence for conservatism in Europe, contributing to the tension that produced the upheavals of 1848 and popular rebellions in many countries.

58 When Paris sneezes, Europe catches cold.
1830 Letter, 26 Jan.

59 Italy is a geographical expression.
1847 Letter, 6 Aug.

60 I have been a rock of order.
1859 Attributed, shortly before his death. Quoted in Andrew Milne *Metternich* (1975).

61 Error has never approached my spirit.
Said to Guizot on the steps of the British Museum. Quoted in A J P Taylor *From the Boer War to the Cold War: Essays on Twentieth-Century Europe* (1995).

Meyer, Andrew William 1986–
US student. While at the University of Florida he was tasered by campus police after protesting that he was not being allowed to speak at a public meeting at which Senator John Kerry was the chief guest. The incident made the international headlines.

62 Don't tase me, bro.
2007 His response when threatened with a taser; the phrase subsequently swept the nation, 17 Sep.

Meyer, Karl Ernest 1937–
US journalist and author, formerly of the *Washington Post* and the *New York Times*.

63 Whatever his private behavior, the man and his work existed in different realms. Mencken's defects were commonplace; his virtues were not. So wonderfully uninhibited was his style that even a single sentence in a routine article proclaimed its begetter.
1994 Of H L Mencken. In the *New York Times Book Review*, 8 May.

Michael, George originally Georgios Kyriacos Panayiotou
1963–
English pop singer and songwriter.

64 I have never felt any ethnic connection between the Greeks and me other than how hairy I am.
2004 In *Scotland on Sunday*, 14 Mar.

Michelangelo full name Michelangelo Buonarroti
1475–1564
Italian painter, sculptor, architect, draughtsman and poet. Born near Florence, he is one of the most important figures of the Italian Renaissance.

65 I've finished that chapel I was painting. The Pope is quite satisfied.
   1512 Letter written to his father after 18 months of painting the vault of the Sistine Chapel, quoted in Robert J Clements (ed) *Michelangelo: A Self-Portrait* (1968).

66 Nothing the greatest artist can conceive
   That every marble block doth not confine
   Within itself; and only its design
   The hand that follows intellect can achieve.
   c.1538 Quoted in Robert J Clements (ed) *Michelangelo: A Self-Portrait* (1968).

67 Your Lordship sends to tell me that I should paint and have no doubts. I answer that painting is done with the brain, not the hands.
   1542 Letter written to a Cardinal, Oct, collected in Creighton Gilbert (ed and trans) *Complete Poems and Selected Letters of Michelangelo* (1963).

68 I have only too much of a wife in this art of mine, who has always kept me in tribulation, and my children shall be the works I leave, which, even if they are naught, will live a while.
   In response to a priest and friend who had said it was a pity he had not married and had children to whom he could leave his works. Attributed in Giorgio Vasari *Lives of the Artists* (1568).

69 They are so beautiful that they would grace the entrance to Paradise.
   Of Ghiberti's doors for the Florence Baptistery. Quoted in Giorgio Vasari *Lives of the Artists* (1568).

70 In my opinion painting should be considered excellent in proportion as it approaches the effect of relief, while relief should be considered bad in proportion as it approaches the effect of painting.
   Quoted in Robert J Clements (ed) *Michelangelo: A Self-Portrait* (1968).

Middleton, Thomas c. 1570–1627

English dramatist, who collaborated with Dekker, Webster, Rowley, Massinger, Beaumont and Fletcher and probably Shakespeare. His works include *A Mad World, My Masters* (1608), *Women Beware Women* (1620–7) and *A Chaste Maid in Cheapside* (published 1630). He also wrote pageants and masques for the city of London.

71 But you are dull, nothing comes nimbly from you; you dance like a plumber's daughter and deserve two thousand pound in lead to your marriage, and not in goldsmith's ware.
   1613 *A Chaste Maid in Cheapside* (published 1630), act 1, sc.1.

72 Lie soft, sleep hard, drink wine, and eat good cheer.
   1613 *A Chaste Maid in Cheapside* (published 1630), act 1, sc.1.

73 Nay, good sir, be not so violent; with speed
   I cannot render satisfaction
   Unto the dear companion of my soul,
   Virginity, whom I thus long have lived with,
   And part with it so rude and suddenly.
   Can such friends divide, never to meet again,
   Without a solemn farewell?
   1622 *The Changeling* (with William Rowley), act 1, sc.1.

74 Our eyes are sentinels unto our judgements
   And should give certain judgement what they see;
   But they are rash sometimes and tell us wonders
   Of common things, which when our judgements find,
   They can then check the eyes and call them blind.
   1622 *The Changeling* (with William Rowley), act 1, sc.1.

75 Now I know
   She had rather wear my pelt tanned in a pair
   Of dancing pumps.
   1622 *The Changeling* (with William Rowley), act 1, sc.1.

76 There's scarce a thing but is both loved and loathed.
   1622 *The Changeling* (with William Rowley), act 1, sc.1.

77 I shall run mad with joy.
   1622 *The Changeling* (with William Rowley), act 2, sc.2.

78 I'm up to the chin in heaven.
   1622 *The Changeling* (with William Rowley), act 2, sc.2.

79 Paper blushes not.
   1622 *The Changeling* (with William Rowley), act 3, sc.4.

80 Y'are the deed's creature.
   1622 *The Changeling* (with William Rowley), act 3, sc.4.

81 Beneath the stars, upon yon meteor
   Ever hung my fate, 'mongst things corruptible;
   I ne'er could pluck it from him. My loathing
   Was prophet to the rest, but ne'er believed.
   1622 *The Changeling* (with William Rowley), act 5, sc.3.

Midler, Bette 1945–

US comedienne, singer and actress, whose bawdy nightclub act led to a successful career on Broadway and then in films.

82 There comes a time when you have to let your clothes go out in the world and try to make it on their own.
   1987 On relinquishing the mermaid costume she wore in the 1970s film *Clams on the Half Shell*. In *People*, 31 Aug.

83 When it's three o'clock in New York, it's still 1938 in London.
   Attributed.

84 Give a girl the right shoes, and she can conquer the world.
   Attributed.

Mies van der Rohe, Ludwig 1886–1969

German-born US architect and furniture designer, a pioneer of glass skyscrapers. He was director of the Bauhaus in Dessau (1930–3) and emigrated to the US in 1937.

85 Architecture is the will of the age conceived in spatial terms.
   1922 *De Stijl*, vol.6.

Mikes, George 1912–87

Hungarian-born writer who wrote humorous books about his experience of being a foreigner in England.

86 On the Continent people have good food; in England people have good table manners.
   1946 *How to Be an Alien*.

87 Many continentals think life is a game, the English think cricket is a game.
   1946 *How to be an Alien*.

Milestone, Lewis *pseudonym of* Levis Milstein 1895–1980

US film director, best known for *All Quiet on the Western Front* (1930), which won an Academy Award.

88 I've got your happy ending. We'll let the Germans win the war.
   c.1929 Response when asked to provide an upbeat ending for *All Quiet on the Western Front*.

Miliband, Ed(ward Samuel) 1969–

English politician. Elected MP for Doncaster North in 2005, he served in Gordon Brown's Cabinet (2007–10) before succeeding Brown as leader of the Labour Party (2010–).

89 I suppose not everyone has a dad who wrote a book saying he didn't believe in the Parliamentary road to socialism.
2011 Speech to the Labour Party conference.

90 While there's capitalism, there'll be socialism, because there is always a response to injustice.
2012 In The Telegraph, 15 Sep.

Milius, John 1944–

US screenwriter and director. His writing credits include *The Life and Times of Judge Roy Bean* (1973), *Magnum Force* (1973), *Apolcalyse Now* (co-writer, 1979) and *The Wind and the Lion* (1975) which he also directed.

91 I know the law since I have spent my entire life in its flagrant disregard.
1972 The Life and Times of Judge Roy Bean.

Mill, James 1773–1836

Scottish philosopher, historian and economist. He was a friend of Jeremy Bentham and an enthusiastic proponent of Utilitarianism.

92 The government and the people are under a moral necessity of acting together; a free press compels them to bend to one another.
1811 In the Edinburgh Review, May–Aug.

Mill, John Stuart 1806–73

English empiricist philosopher, MP (1863–8) and reformer, a supporter of women's suffrage (*Subjection of Women*, 1869) and liberalism. His works include *System of Logic* (1843), *Principles of Political Economy* (1848), *On Liberty* (1859) and *Utilitarianism* (1863).

93 Unlike the Laws of Production, those of Distribution are partly of human institution, since the manner in which wealth is distributed in any given society, depends on the statutes or usages therein obtaining.
1848 Principles of Political Economy, with Some Applications to Social Philosophy.

94 A stationary condition of capital and population implies no stationary state of human improvement. There could be as much scope as ever for all kinds of mental culture, and moral and social progress.
1848 Principles of Political Economy, with Some Applications to Social Philosophy.

95 Happily, there is nothing in the laws of value which remains for the present or any future writer to clear up; the theory of the subject is complete.
1848 Principles of Political Economy, with Some Applications to Social Philosophy.

96 I am not charmed with the ideal of life held out by those who think that the normal state of human beings is that of struggling to get on. I know not why it should be a matter of congratulation that persons who are already richer than any one needs to be, should have doubled their means of consuming things which give little or no pleasure except as representative of wealth.
1848 Principles of Political Economy, with Some Applications to Social Philosophy.

97 The average condition of the people improving or deteriorating, depends upon whether population is advancing faster than improvement, or improvement than population.
1848 Principles of Political Economy, with Some Applications to Social Philosophy.

98 That the whole or any part of the education of the people should be in State hands, I go so far as anyone in deprecating… A general State education is a mere contrivance for molding people to be exactly like one another.
1856 Utilitarianism, Liberty and Representative Government.

99 The only purpose for which power can be rightfully exercised over any member of a civilized community, against his will, is to prevent harm to others.
1859 On Liberty.

1 A party of order or stability, and a party of progress or reform, are both necessary elements of a healthy state of political life.
1859 On Liberty.

2 Everyone who receives the protection of society owes a return for the benefit, and the fact of living in a society renders it indispensable that each should be bound to observe a certain line of conduct towards the rest. That conduct consists…in each person bearing his share of the labours and sacrifices incurred for defending the society or its members from injury and molestation.
1859 On Liberty.

3 If all mankind minus one were of one opinion, and only one person were of the contrary opinion, mankind would no more be justified in silencing that one person than he, if he had the power, would be justified in silencing mankind.
1859 On Liberty.

4 If the roads, the railways, the banks, the insurance offices, the great joint-stock companies, the universities, and the public charities, were all of them branches of government; if, in addition, the municipal corporations and local boards, with all that now devolves on them, became departments of the central administration; if the employees of all these different enterprises were appointed and paid by the government, and looked to the government for every rise in life; not all the freedom of the press and popular constitution of the legislature would make this or any other country free otherwise than in name.
1859 On Liberty.

5 The Conservatives, as being by the law of their existence the stupidest party.
1861 Considerations on Representative Government, ch.7, note.

6 The worth of the State, in the long run, is the worth of the individuals composing it.
1861 Considerations on Representative Government.

7 It is better to be a human being dissatisfied than a pig satisfied; better to be Socrates dissatisfied than a fool satisfied.
1863 Utilitarianism, ch.2.

8 The creed which accepts as the foundation of morals, Utility, or the Greatest Happiness Principle, holds that actions are right in proportion as they tend to promote

happiness, wrong as they tend to produce the reverse of happiness.
1863 *Utilitarianism*, ch.2.

9 The sole evidence it is possible to produce that anything is desirable, is that people do actually desire it.
1863 *Utilitarianism*, ch.4.

10 If the universe had a beginning, its beginning, by the very condition of the cases, was supernatural; the laws of Nature cannot account for their own origin.
1865 *Auguste Comte and Positivism*.

11 It is always easy to find fault with a classification. There are a hundred ways of arranging any set of objects, and something may almost always be said against the best, and in favour of the worst of them. But the merits of a classification depend on the purposes to which it is instrumental.
1865 *Auguste Comte and Positivism*.

12 I never was a boy, never played at cricket; it is better to let Nature take her course.
1867 *Autobiography*.

13 It may be asserted without scruple, that no other class of dependants have had their character so entirely distorted from its natural proportions by their relations with their masters.
1869 *The Subjection of Women*, ch.1.

14 With equality of experience and of general faculties, a woman usually sees much more than a man of what is immediately before her.
1869 *The Subjection of Women*, ch.3.

15 Women cannot be expected to devote themselves to the emancipation of women, until men in considerable number are prepared to join with them in the undertaking.
1869 *The Subjection of Women*, ch.3.

16 Marriage is the only actual bondage known to our law. There remain no legal slaves, except the mistress of every house.
1869 *The Subjection of Women*, ch.4.

17 The self-worship of the monarch, or of the feudal superior, is matched by the self-worship of the male.
1869 *The Subjection of Women*, ch.4.

Millay, Edna St Vincent 1892–1950

US poet. Despite her contemporary subject matter, she was a formalist and her poems show a strong technical skill. Her collections include *The Harp-Weaver* (1923), which won a Pulitzer Prize.

18 World, world, I cannot get thee close enough!
Long have I known a glory in it all,
But never knew like this;
Here such a pattern is
As stretcheth me apart. Lord, I do fear
Thou'st made the world too beautiful this year:
My soul is all but out of me—let fall
No burning leaf; prithee, let no bird call.
1917 *God's World*.

19 My candle burns at both ends;
It will not last the night;
But ah, my foes, and oh, my friends—
It gives a lovely light.
1920 *A Few Figs From Thistles*, 'First Fig'.

20 Safe upon solid rock the ugly houses stand:
Come and see my shining palace built upon the sand.
1920 *A Few Figs From Thistles*, 'Second Fig'.

21 Death devours all lovely things;
Lesbia with her sparrow
Shares the darkness—presently
Every bed is narrow.
1921 *Second April*, 'Passer Mortuus Est'.

22 After all, my erstwhile dear,
My no longer cherished,
Need we say it was not love,
Now that love is perished?
1921 *Second April*, 'Passer Mortuus Est'.

23 What lips my lips have kissed, and where, and why,
I have forgotten, and what arms have lain
Under my head till morning; but the rain
Is full of ghosts tonight, that tap and sigh
Upon the glass and listen for reply
1923 *Harp-Weaver and Other Poems*, 'Sonnet 19: What lips my lips have kissed'.

24 Thus in the winter stands the lonely tree,
Nor knows what birds have vanished one by one,
Yet knows its boughs more silent than before
1923 *Harp-Weaver and Other Poems*, 'Sonnet 19: What lips my lips have kissed'.

25 I only know that summer sang in me
A little while, that in me sings no more.
1923 *Harp-Weaver and Other Poems*, 'Sonnet 19: What lips my lips have kissed'.

26 Euclid alone
Has looked on Beauty bare. Fortunate they
Who, though once only and then but far away,
Have heard her massive sandal set on stone.
1923 *Harp-Weaver and Other Poems*, 'Sonnet 22: Euclid alone has looked on Beauty bare'.

27 Down, down, down into the darkness of the grave
Gently they go, the beautiful, the tender, the kind;
Quietly they go, the intelligent, the witty, the brave.
I know. But I do not approve. And I am not resigned.
1928 *The Buck in the Snow*, 'Dirge Without Music'.

28 It's not true that life is one damn thing after another—it's one damn thing over and over.
1930 Letter to Arthur Davison Ficke, 24 Oct.

29 Love is not all; it is not meat nor drink.
1931 *Fatal Interview*, title of poem.

30 Childhood is not from birth to a certain age and at a certain age
The child is grown, and puts away childish things.
Childhood is the kingdom where nobody dies.
Nobody that matters, that is.
1934 *Wine From These Grapes*, 'Childhood is the Kingdom where Nobody dies'.

Miller, Arthur 1915–2005

US playwright. *Death of a Salesman* (1949) won a Pulitzer Prize and established him as a leading contemporary playwright, dealing with the realities of family life. Subsequent plays included *After the Fall* (1964), thought to have been inspired by his unhappy marriage to Marilyn Monroe.

31 A small man can be just as exhausted as a great man.
1949 Linda. *Death of a Salesman*, act 1.

32 Willie was a salesman. And for a salesman, there is no rock bottom to life… He's a man way out there in the blue, riding on a smile and a shoeshine. And when they start not smiling back—that's an earthquake.
1949 Charley. *Death of a Salesman*, 'Requiem'.

33 A salesman is got to dream, boy. It comes with the territory.
1949 Charley. *Death of a Salesman*, 'Requiem'.

34 They believed, in short, that they held in their steady hands the candle that would light the world. We have inherited this belief, and it has helped and hurt us.
1953 Of the settlers in Salem in 1692. *The Crucible*, act 1.

35 Spare me! You forget nothin' and forgive nothin'. Learn charity, woman. I have gone tiptoe in this house all seven month since she is gone. I have not moved from there to there without I think to please you, and still an everlasting funeral marches around your heart.
1953 Proctor to Elizabeth. *The Crucible*, act 2.

36 Theology, sir, is a fortress; no crack in a fortress may be accounted small.
1953 Hale. *The Crucible*, act 2.

37 Oh, no, the machine, the machine is necessary. A man comes into a great hotel and says, I am a messenger. Who is this man? He disappears walking, there is no noise, nothing. Maybe he will never come back, maybe he will never deliver the message. But a man who rides up on a great machine, this man is responsible, this man exists. He will be given messages.
1955 Rodolpho. *A View From the Bridge*, act 1.

38 A genuine invention in the realm of ideas must first emerge as an abstruse and even partial concept… At first blush a new idea appears to be very close to insanity because to be new it must reverse important basic beliefs and assumptions which, in turn, have been institutionalized and are administered by one or another kind of priesthood with a vested interest in an old idea.
1958 *The Collected Plays*, 'Introduction, II'.

39 A good newspaper, I suppose, is a nation talking to itself.
1961 In the *Observer*, 26 Nov.

40 How few the days are that hold the mind in place; like a tapestry hanging on four or five hooks. Especially the day you stop becoming; the day you merely are. I suppose it's when the principles dissolve, and instead of the general gray of what ought to be you begin to see what is… The word 'Now' is like a bomb through the window, and it ticks.
1964 Quentin. *After the Fall*, act 1.

41 A suicide kills two people, Maggie. That's what it's for.
1964 Quentin. *After the Fall*, act 2.

42 Part of knowing who we are is knowing we are not someone else. And Jew is only the name we give to that stranger, the agony we cannot feel, the death we look at like a cold abstraction. Each man has his Jew; it is the other.
1964 Leduc. *Incident at Vichy*, act 1.

43 The concentration camp is the final expression of human separateness and its ultimate consequence. It is organized abandonment.
1966 Interview in the *Paris Review*, Summer.

44 Success, instead of giving freedom of choice, becomes a way of life.
1966 Interview in the *Paris Review*, Summer.

45 [Plays that would] cut through time like a knife through a layer cake or a road through a mountain revealing its geologic layers.
1987 Describing the plays he always wished to write. *Timebends: A Life*.

46 Without alienation, there can be no politics.
1988 In *Marxism Today*, Jan.

47 I'm the end of the line; absurd and appalling as it may seem, serious New York theater has died in my lifetime.
1989 In *The Times*, 11 Jan.

48 Maybe all one can do is hope to end up with the right regrets.
1991 Tom. *The Ride Down Mount Morgan*, act 1.

49 Witch-hunts are always spooked by women's horrifying sexuality awakened by the superstud Devil.
1998 On President Clinton's relationship with Monica Lewinsky. In the *New York Times*, 15 Oct.

50 Mr Clinton, according to Toni Morrison, the Nobel prize-winning novelist, is our first black President, the first to come from the broken home, the alcoholic mother, the under-the-bridge shadows of our ranking system.
1998 In the *New York Times*, 15 Oct.

Miller, Henry Valentine 1891–1980

US novelist. An exile in Paris in the 1930s, he later returned to live in California. His novels, notorious for sexual explicitness, include *Tropic of Cancer* (1934) and *Tropic of Capricorn* (1939), both at one time banned in the US.

51 The wallpaper with which the men of science have covered the world of reality is falling to tatters.
1934 *The Tropic of Cancer*.

52 This is not a book in the ordinary sense of the word. No, this is a prolonged insult, a gob of spit in the face of Art, a kick in the pants to God, Man, Destiny, Time, Love, Beauty…what you will. I am going to sing for you, a little off-key perhaps, but I will sing.
1934 *Tropic of Cancer*.

53 Chaos is the score upon which reality is written.
1934 *Tropic of Cancer*.

54 Every man with a bellyful of the classics is an enemy of the human race.
1934 *Tropic of Cancer*.

55 We live in the mind, in ideas, in fragments.
1936 *Black Spring*, 'The Fourteenth Ward'.

56 There are passages of Ulysses which can be read only in the toilet—if one wants to extract the full flavour of their content.
1936 *Black Spring*, 'A Saturday Afternoon'.

57 The world is the mirror of myself dying.
1936 *Black Spring*, 'Third or Fourth Day of Spring'.

58 I see America as a black curse upon the world. I see a long night settling in and that mushroom which has poisoned the world withering at the roots.
1936 *Black Spring*, 'Third or Fourth Day of Spring'.

59 What does it matter how one comes by the truth so long as one pounces upon it and lives by it.
1939 *Tropic of Capricorn*.

60 The artist does not tinker with the universe; he recreates it out of his own experience and understanding of life.
1939 *The Cosmological Eye*, 'An Open Letter to Surrealists Everywhere'.

61 Example moves the world more than doctrine.
1939 The Cosmological Eye, 'An Open Letter to Surrealists Everywhere'.

62 Life has no other discipline to impose, if we would but realize it, than to accept life unquestioningly... Every moment is a golden one for him who has the vision to recognize it as such.
1940 The World of Sex.

63 Morally, spiritually, we are fettered. What have we achieved in mowing down mountain ranges, harnessing the energy of mighty rivers, or moving whole populations about like chess pieces, if we ourselves remain the same restless, miserable, frustrated creatures we were before. To call such activity progress is utter delusion.
1940 The World of Sex.

64 Until we do lose ourselves there is no hope of finding ourselves.
1940 The World of Sex.

65 All that matters is that the miraculous becomes the norm.
1940 The World of Sex.

66 Though I've never read a line of Homer I believe the Greek of today is essentially unchanged. If anything he is more Greek than he ever was.
1941 The Colossus of Maroussi, pt.1.

67 If men cease to believe that they will one day become gods then they will surely become worms.
1941 The Colossus of Maroussi, pt.3.

68 To live without killing is a thought which could electrify the world, if men were only capable of staying awake long enough to let the idea soak in.
1944 Sunday After The War, 'Reunion in Brooklyn'.

69 No man would set a word down on paper if he had the courage to live out what he believed in.
1945 Sexus, ch.1.

70 The world has *not* to be put in order: the world *is* order incarnate. It is for us to put ourselves in unison with this order.
1945 Sexus, ch.9.

71 The great joy of the artist is to become aware of a higher order of things, to recognize by the compulsive and spontaneous manipulation of his own impulses the resemblance between human creation and what is called 'divine' creation.
1945 Sexus, ch.9.

72 Imagination is the voice of daring. If there is anything Godlike about God it is that. He dared to imagine everything.
1945 Sexus, ch.14.

73 Nowhere have I encountered such a dull, monotonous fabric of life as here in America. Here boredom reaches its peak.
1945 The Air-Conditioned Nightmare, preface.

74 Man has demonstrated that he is master of everything—except his own nature.
1945 The Air-Conditioned Nightmare, 'With Edgar Varèse in the Gobi Desert'.

75 The world goes on because a few men in every generation believe in it utterly, accept it unquestioningly, underwrite it with their lives.
1945 The Air-Conditioned Nightmare, 'With Edgar Varèse in the Gobi Desert'.

76 Back of every creation, supporting it like an arch, is faith. Enthusiasm is nothing: it comes and goes. But if one *believes*, then miracles occur.
1945 The Air-Conditioned Nightmare, 'With Edgar Varèse in the Gobi Desert'.

77 The study of crime begins with the knowledge of oneself. All that you despise, all that you loathe, all that you reject, all that you condemn and seek to convert by punishment springs from you.
1945 The Air-Conditioned Nightmare, 'The Soul of Anaesthesia'.

78 Art is only a means to life, to the life more abundant. It is not in itself the life more abundant... In becoming an end it defeats itself.
1947 The Wisdom of the Heart, 'Reflections on Writing'.

79 I have always looked upon decay as being just as wonderful an expression of life as growth.
1947 The Wisdom of the Heart, 'Reflections on Writing'.

80 It is the creative nature of man which has refused to let him lapse back into that unconscious unity with life which characterizes the animal world from which he made his escape.
1947 The Wisdom of the Heart, 'Creative Death'.

81 The poem is the dream made flesh, in a two-fold sense: as work of art, and as life, which is a work of art.
1947 The Wisdom of the Heart, 'Creative Death'.

82 All growth is a leap in the dark, a spontaneous unpremeditated act without benefit of experience.
1947 The Wisdom of the Heart, 'The Absolute Collective'.

83 Life, as it is called, is for most of us one long postponement.
1947 The Wisdom of the Heart, 'The Enormous Womb'.

84 It is the American vice, the democratic disease which expresses its tyranny by reducing everything unique to the level of the herd.
1947 On democracy. *The Wisdom of the Heart*, 'Raimu'.

85 History is the myth, the true myth, of man's fall made manifest in time.
1949 Plexus, ch.12.

86 In this age, which believes that there is a short cut to everything, the greatest lesson to be learned is that the most difficult way is, in the long run, the easiest.
1951 The Books in My Life, preface.

87 Every genuine boy is a rebel and an anarch.
1951 The Books in My Life, ch.4.

88 Words divested of their magic are but dead hieroglyphs.
1951 The Books in My Life, ch.7.

89 If we are always arriving and departing, it is also true that we are eternally anchored. One's destination is never a place but rather a new way of looking at things.
1957 Big Sur and the Oranges of Hieronymous Bosch, 'The Oranges of the Millennium'.

90 We resist only what is inevitable.
1957 Big Sur and the Oranges of Hieronymous Bosch, 'Paradise Lost'.

91 Obscenity is a cleansing process, whereas pornography only adds to the murk.
1962 Interview in the *Paris Review*, Summer.

92 The word 'civilization' to my mind is coupled with death. When I use the word, I see civilization as a

crippling, thwarting thing, a stultifying thing…
Civilization is the arteriosclerosis of culture.
1962 Interview in the *Paris Review*, Summer.

93 The moment you praise a book too highly you waken a resistance in your listener.
1957 *The Books in My Life*.

94 One has to be a lowbrow, a bit of a murderer, to be a politician; ready and willing to see people sacrificed, slaughtered, for the sake of an idea—whether a good one or a bad one.
In Malcolm Crowley (ed) *Writers at Work* (1958).

Miller, Jonathan Wolfe 1934–
British stage and opera director and writer, trained as a doctor.

95 In fact, I'm not really a *Jew*. Just Jew-*ish*. Not the whole hog you know.
1960 *Beyond the Fringe*, 'Real Class'.

96 The human species is, to some extent, the result of mistakes which arrested our development and prevented us from assuming the somewhat unglamorous form of our primitive ancestors.
1977 *The Body in Question*.

97 I wasn't driven into medicine by a social conscience but by rampant curiosity.
1983 In the *Observer*, 5 Feb.

Miller, William 1810–72
Scottish poet, born in Glasgow, known as the 'Laureate of the Nursery' for his children's rhymes, of which only 'Willie Winkie' is now remembered.

98 Wee Willie Winkie rins through the toun,
Up stairs and doun stairs in his nicht-gown,
Tirling at the window, crying at the lock,
'Are the weans in their bed, for it's now ten
  o' clock?'
1841 'Willie Winkie', stanza 1.

Millett, Kate (Katherine) *née* Murray 1934–
US feminist critic, activist and sculptor. Her PhD thesis was published as *Sexual Politics* (1970). Other works include the autobiographical *Flying* (1974), *The Loony Bin Trip* (1991) and *Mother Millett* (2001).

99 Patriarchy's chief institution is the family. It is both a mirror of and a connection with the larger society; a patriarchal unit within a patriarchal whole.
1970 *Sexual Politics*, ch.2, 'Theory of Sexual Politics'.

1 Aren't women prudes if they don't and prostitutes if they do?
1975 Speech at the Women Writers' Conference, Los Angeles, 22 Mar.

Milligan, Spike 1918–2002
Irish humorist.

2 Money couldn't buy friends but you got a better class of enemy.
1963 *Puckoon*, ch.6.

3 I am not going to thank anybody—because I did it all myself.
1994 Acceptance speech after being awarded the British Comedy Award for Lifetime Achievement.

4 Dúirt mé leat go raibh mé breoite.
2002 Gaelic inscription on his gravestone at Winchelsea, East Sussex. English translation: I told you I was ill.

Millman, Dan 1946–
US writer, who was world trampoline champion before meeting a remarkable gas station attendant called Socrates. He now writes self-help books and runs courses helping athletes and others make the most of their potential.

5 There are no ordinary moments.
1980 *The Way of the Peaceful Warrior*.

Mills, C(harles) Wright 1916–62
US sociologist, a professor at Columbia University.

6 No social study that does not come back to the problems of biography, of history and of their intersections within a society has completed its intellectual journey.
1959 *The Sociological Imagination*, ch.1.

7 In so far as the family as an institution turns women into darling little slaves and men into their chief providers and unweaned dependents, the problem of a satisfactory marriage remains incapable of purely private solution.
1959 *The Sociological Imagination*, ch.1.

8 If everything is caused by innumerable 'factors,' then we had best be very careful in any practical actions we undertake. We must deal with many details, and so it is advisable to proceed to reform this little piece and see what happens, before we reform that little piece too.
1959 *The Sociological Imagination*, ch.4.

Mills, Irving 1884–1985
US jazz manager, music publisher and lyricist.

9 It don't mean a thing
If it ain't got that swing.
1932 Song (music by Duke Ellington).

Mills, Sir John Lewis Ernest Watts 1908–2005
English actor, known for his stiff-upper-lip heroes in such films as *In Which We Serve* (1942), *Scott of the Antarctic* (1948) and *The Colditz Story* (1954). He won an Academy Award for his role in *Ryan's Daughter* (1970).

10 I played the young Earl of Dudley and was beheaded in the third reel—not, in my opinion, a moment too soon.
1980 Of his role in the 1936 film *Tudor Rose*. *Up in the Clouds, Gentlemen Please*.

Milne, A(lan) A(lexander) 1882–1956
English writer. He was an editor at *Punch* and wrote comedies and light essays. His works for children, which he began writing for his son Christopher Robin, are *When We Were Very Young* (1924), *Winnie-the-Pooh* (1926), *Now We Are Six* (1927) and *The House at Pooh Corner* (1928).

11 It is impossible to win gracefully at chess. No man has yet said 'Mate!' in a voice which failed to sound to his opponent bitter, boastful and malicious.
1919 *Not That It Matters*.

12 They're changing guard at Buckingham Palace—
Christopher Robin went down with Alice.
Alice is marrying one of the guard.

'A soldier's life is terribly hard,'
Says Alice.
1924 *When We Were Very Young*, 'Buckingham Palace'.

13 Little Boy kneels at the foot of the bed,
Droops on the little hands, little gold head;
Hush! Hush! Whisper who dares!
Christopher Robin is saying his prayers.
1924 *When We Were Very Young*, 'Vespers'.

14 The King said
'Butter, eh?'
And bounced out of bed.
1924 *When We Were Very Young*, 'The King's Breakfast'.

15 I have just been thinking, and I have come to a very important decision. *These are the wrong sort of bees.*
1926 *Winnie-the-Pooh*, ch.1.

16 Would you read a Sustaining Book, such as would help and comfort a Wedged Bear in Great Tightness?
1926 Pooh, stuck in the entrance to Rabbit's house after eating too much honey. *Winnie-the-Pooh*, ch.2.

17 I am a Bear of Very Little Brain, and long words Bother me.
1926 *Winnie-the-Pooh*, ch.4.

18 'Help, help!' cried Piglet, 'a Heffalump, a Horrible Heffalump!' and he scampered off as hard as he could, still crying out, 'Help, help, a Herrible Hoffalump! Hoff, Hoff, a Hellible Horralump! Holl, Holl, a Hoffable Hellerump!'
1926 *Winnie-the-Pooh*, ch.5.

19 'I ought to say,' explained Pooh as they walked down to the shore of the island, 'that it isn't just an ordinary sort of boat. Sometimes it's a Boat, and sometimes it's more of an Accident. It all depends.'
'Depends on what?'
'On whether I'm on the top of it or underneath it.'
1926 *Winnie-the-Pooh*, ch.9.

20 The more it
SNOWS-tiddely-pom,
The more it
GOES-tiddely-pom
The more it
GOES-tiddely-pom
On
Snowing.
1928 *The House at Pooh Corner*, ch.1.

21 'It's snowing still,' said Eeyore gloomily.
'So it is.'
'*And* freezing.'
'Is it?'
'Yes,' said Eeyore. 'However,' he said, brightening up a little, 'we haven't had an earthquake lately.'
1928 *The House at Pooh Corner*, ch.1.

22 But whatever his weight in pounds, shillings, and ounces,
He always seems bigger because of the bounces.
1928 Pooh's song about Tigger. *The House at Pooh Corner*, ch.2.

23 I could spend a happy morning
Seeing Roo,
I could spend a happy morning
Being Pooh,
For it doesn't seem to matter,
If I don't get any fatter
(And I don't get any fatter),
What I do.
1928 *The House at Pooh Corner*, ch.4.

24 Then he dropped two in at once, and leant over the bridge to see which of them would come out first; and one of them did; but as they were both the same size, he didn't know if it was the one which he wanted to win, or the other one. So the next time he dropped one big one and one little one, and the big one came out first, which was what he had said it would do, and the little one came out last, which was what he had said it would do, so he had won twice... And that was the beginning of the game called Poohsticks.
1928 *The House at Pooh Corner*, ch.6.

25 But what care I? It's the game that calls me—
Simply to be on the field of play;
How can it matter what fate befalls me,
With ten good fellows and one good day!
Quoted in Helen Exley *Cricket Quotations* (1992).

26 Golf is so popular simply because it is the best game in the world at which to be bad.
Attributed.

Milner, Alfred, 1st Viscount Milner 1854–1925

English statesman. He held a succession of top administrative posts, including High Commissioner for South Africa during the Boer Wars, Secretary for War (1918–19) and Colonial Secretary (1921). He recommended virtual independence for Egypt.

27 If we believe a thing to be bad, and if we have a right to prevent it, it is our duty to try to prevent it and damn the consequences.
1909 On the blocking by the Conservative majority in the House of Lords of the Liberal Government's budget. Speech at Glasgow, Nov.

Milosevic, Slobodan 1941–2006

Serbian politician. He became President of Serbia in 1988. In 1996 he was re-elected amidst furious accusations of electoral rigging and from 1998 onwards oversaw Serb military incursions into the province of Kosovo. This led to NATO air strikes and the establishment of a NATO-led peacekeeping force in the province, forcing a Serb withdrawal. He was defeated at the polls in 2000 by opposition candidate Vojislav Kostunica. He was subsequently arrested in 2001 for crimes against humanity by the International Criminal Tribunal in the Hague and died while facing trial.

28 Kosovo is not a part of Serbia. It is the very heart of Serbia.
Quoted in Dusko Doder and Louise Branson *Milosevic: Portrait of a Tyrant* (1999).

29 I'm the Ayatollah Khomeini of Serbia. The Serbs will follow me no matter what!
Quoted in Dusko Doder and Louise Branson *Milosevic: Portrait of a Tyrant* (1999).

Milton, John 1608–74

English poet and controversial pamphleteerist, official apologist for the Commonwealth. Blind from 1652, he devoted himself to poetry after the Restoration. His best-known work is the religious epic *Paradise Lost* (1667), followed by *Paradise Regained* and *Samson Agonistes* (both 1671).

30 This is the month, and this the happy morn
Wherein the son of Heaven's eternal King,

Of wedded maid and virgin mother born,
Our great redemption from above did bring.
1629 'On the Morning of Christ's Nativity', 'The Hymn', stanza 1.

31 It was the winter wild
While the Heaven born child
All meanly wrapped in the rude manger lies;
Nature in awe to him
Had doffed her gaudy trim
With her great Master so to sympathize;
It was no season then for her
To wanton with the sun, her lusty paramour.
1629 'On the Morning of Christ's Nativity', 'The Hymn', stanza 3.

32 But peaceful was the night
Wherein the Prince of Light
His reign of peace upon the earth began:
The winds, with wonder whist,
Smoothly the waters kissed,
Whispering new joys to the mild oceàn,
Who now hath quite forgot to rave,
While birds of calm sit brooding on the charmèd wave.
1629 'On the Morning of Christ's Nativity', 'The Hymn', stanza 3.

33 The stars with deep amaze
Stand fixed in steadfast gaze.
1629 'On the Morning of Christ's Nativity', 'The Hymn', stanza 6.

34 Nature that heard such sound
Beneath the hollow round
Of Cynthia's seat, the airy region thrilling,
Now was almost won
To think her part was done,
And that her reign had here its last fulfilling;
She knew such harmony alone
Could hold all heaven and earth in happier uniòn.
1629 'On the Morning of Christ's Nativity', 'The Hymn', stanza 10.

35 Ring out, ye crystal spheres,
Once bless our human ears
(If ye have power to touch our senses so),
And let your silver chime
Move in melodious time,
And let the bass of Heaven's deep organ blow;
And with your ninefold harmony
Make up full consort to th'angelic symphony.
1629 'On the Morning of Christ's Nativity', 'The Hymn', stanza 13.

36 For if such holy song
Enwrap our fancy long,
Time will run back, and fetch the age of gold,
And speckled vanity
Will sicken soon and die.
1629 'On the Morning of Christ's Nativity', 'The Hymn', stanza 14.

37 The oracles are dumb;
No voice or hideous hum
Runs through the archèd roof in words deceiving.
1629 'On the Morning of Christ's Nativity', 'The Hymn', stanza 19.

38 But see! the Virgin blessed
Hath laid her Babe to rest.
Time is our tedious song should here have ending.
1629 'On the Morning of Christ's Nativity', 'The Hymn', stanza 27.

39 What needs my Shakespeare for his honoured bones
The labour of an age in pilèd stones,
Or that his hallowed relics should be hid
Under a star-y-pointing pyramid?
Dear son of memory, great heir of fame,
What need'st thou such weak witness of thy name?
Thou in our wonder and astonishment
Hast built thyself a livelong monument.
1630 'On Shakespeare'.

40 And so sepùlchered in such pomp dost lie,
That kings for such a tomb would wish to die.
1630 'On Shakespeare'.

41 Hence loathèd Melancholy,
Of Cerberus and blackest midnight born,
In Stygian cave forlorn
'Mongst horrid shapes, and shrieks, and sights unholy,
Find out some uncouth cell,
Where brooding Darkness spreads his jealous wings,
And the night-raven sings.
c.1631 *L'Allegro*, opening lines.

42 The frolic wind that breathes the spring,
Zephyr with Aurora playing,
As he met her once a-Maying,
There on beds of violets blue,
And fresh-blown roses washed in dew,
Filled her with a daughter fair,
So buxom, blithe, and debonair.
c.1631 *L'Allegro*, l.18–24. The 'daughter fair' is Euphrosyne, or Mirth, one of the Three Graces.

43 Come, and trip it as ye go
On the light fantastic toe.
c.1631 *L'Allegro*, l.33–4.

44 While the cock with lively din
Scatters the rear of darkness thin,
And to the stack or the barn door,
Stoutly struts his dames before.
c.1631 *L'Allegro*, l.49–52.

45 Straight mine eye hath caught new pleasures
Whilst the landscape round it measures,
Russet lawns and fallows grey,
Where the nibbling flocks do stray,
Mountains on whose barren breast
The labouring clouds do often rest;
Meadows trim with daisies pied,
Shallow brooks, and rivers wide.
c.1631 *L'Allegro*, l.69–76.

46 Then to the spicy nut-brown ale.
c.1631 *L'Allegro*, l.100.

47 Towered cities pleased us then,
And the busy hum of men,
Where throngs of knights and barons bold
In weeds of peace high triumphs hold,
With store of ladies, whose bright eyes
Rain influence, and judge the prize
Of wit or arms, while both contend
To win her grace, whom all commend.
c.1631 *L'Allegro*, l.117–24.

48 Such sights as youthful poets dream
On summer eves by haunted stream.
c.1631 *L'Allegro*, l.129–30.

49 Hence vain deluding Joys,
The brood of Folly without father bred,
How little you bestead,
Or fill the fixèd mind with all your toys;
Dwell in some idle brain,
And fancies fond with gaudy shapes possess,

As thick and numberless
As the gay motes that people the sunbeams.
c.1631 *Il Penseroso*, opening lines.

50 But hail thou Goddess sage and holy,
Hail, divinest Melancholy,
Whose saintly visage is too bright
To hit the sense of human sight,
And therefore to our weaker view
O'erlaid with black, staid Wisdom's hue.
c.1631 *Il Penseroso*, l.11–16.

51 There held in holy passion still,
Forget thyself to marble.
c.1631 *Il Penseroso*, l.37–8.

52 Sweet bird that shunn'st the noise of folly,
Most musical, most melancholy!
c.1631 Of the nightingale. *Il Penseroso*, l.61–2.

53 And missing thee, I walk unseen
On the dry smooth-shaven green,
To behold the wandering moon,
Riding near her highest noon,
Like one that had been led astray
Through the heaven's wide pathless way;
And oft as if her head she bowed,
Stooping through a fleecy cloud.
c.1631 *Il Penseroso*, l.65–72.

54 Where glowing embers through the room
Teach light to counterfeit a gloom,
Far from all resort of mirth.
Save the cricket on the hearth.
c.1631 *Il Penseroso*, l.79–82.

55 Or bid the soul of Orpheus sing
Such notes as, warbled to the string,
Drew iron tears down Pluto's cheek,
And made Hell grant what Love did seek.
c.1631 *Il Penseroso*, l.105–8.

56 Where more is meant than meets the ear.
c.1631 *Il Penseroso*, l.120.

57 Till civil-suited Morn appear,
Not tricked and frounced as she was wont
With the Attic boy to hunt,
But kerchiefed in a comely cloud.
c.1631 *Il Penseroso*, l.122–5.

58 There in close covert by some brook,
Where no profaner eye may look,
Hide me from day's garish eye,
While the bee with honied thigh,
That at her flowery work doth sing,
And the waters murmuring
And such consort as they keep,
Entice the dewy-feathered Sleep.
c.1631 *Il Penseroso*, l.139–46.

59 But let my due feet never fail
To walk the studious cloister's pale,
And love the high embowèd roof,
With antic pillars massy proof,
And storied windows richly dight
Casting a dim religious light.
c.1631 *Il Penseroso*, l.155–60.

60 And may at last my weary age
Find out the peaceful hermitage,
The hairy gown and mossy cell,

Where I may sit and rightly spell
Of every star that heaven doth shew,
And every herb that sips the dew,
Till old experience do attain
To something like prophetic strain.
c.1631 *Il Penseroso*, l.167–74.

61 Such sweet compulsion doth in music lie.
1633 *Arcades*.

62 Before the starry threshold of Jove's court
My mansion is, where those immortal shapes
Of bright aerial spirits live insphir'd
In regions mild of calm and serene air,
Above the smoke and stir of this dim spot,
Which men call earth.
1634 *Comus, A Mask*, opening lines.

63 All other parts remaining as they were,
And they, so perfect in their misery,
Not once perceive their foul disfigurement,
But boast themselves more comely than before
And all their friends, and native home forget
To roll with pleasure in a sensual sty.
1634 Of Odysseus's men changed to beasts by Circe. *Comus, A Mask*, l.72–7.

64 The star that bids the shepherd fold,
Now the top of heav'n doth hold,
And the gilded car of day,
His glowing axle doth allay
In the steep Atlantic stream.
1634 *Comus, A Mask*, l.93–7.

65 What hath night to do with sleep?
1634 *Comus, A Mask*, l.122.

66 Come, knit hands, and beat the ground,
In a light fantastic round.
1634 *Comus, A Mask*, l.143–4.

67 Thus I hurl
My dazzling spells into the spongy air.
1634 *Comus, A Mask*, l.153–4.

68 A thousand fantasies
Begin to throng into my memory
Of calling shapes, and beckoning shadows dire,
And airy tongues, that syllable men's names
On sands, and shores, and desert wildernesses.
1634 *Comus, A Mask*, l.204–8.

69 These thoughts may startle well, but not astound
The virtuous mind, that ever walks attended
By a strong siding champion conscience.
1634 *Comus, A Mask*, l.209–11.

70 Sweet Echo, sweetest nymph, that liv'st unseen
Within thy airy shell
By slow meander's margent green,
And in the violet-embroidered vale.
1634 *Comus, A Mask*, l.230–3.

71 How sweetly did they float upon the wings
Of silence, through the empty-vaulted night
At every fall smoothing the raven down
Of darkness till it smil'd.
1634 *Comus, A Mask*, l.248–51.

72 Virtue could see to do what Virtue would
By her own radiant light, though sun and moon
Were in the flat sea sunk. And Wisdom's self
Oft seeks to sweet retired solitude,

Where with her best nurse contemplation
She plumes her feathers, and lets grow her wings
That in the various bustle of resort
Were all too ruffl'd, and sometimes impair'd.
He that has light within his own clear breast
May sit i' the centre, and enjoy bright day,
But he that hides a dark soul, and foul thoughts
Benighted walks under the midday sun;
Himself is his own dungeon.
1634 *Comus, A Mask*, l.372–83.

73 Yet where an equal poise of hope and fear
Does arbitrate the event, my nature is
That I incline to hope, rather than fear,
And gladly banish squint suspicion.
1634 *Comus, A Mask*, l.410–13.

74 Of dire chimeras and enchanted isle
And rifted rocks whose entrance leads to Hell,—
For such there be, but unbelief is blind.
1634 *Comus, A Mask*, l.515–17.

75 A pleasing fit of melancholy.
1634 *Comus, A Mask*, l.545.

76 And filled the air with barbarous dissonance.
1634 *Comus, A Mask*, l.550.

77 I was all ear,
And took in strains that might create a soul.
Under the ribs of Death.
1634 *Comus, A Mask*, l.560–2.

78 Thou canst not touch the freedom of my mind
With all thy charms, although this corporal rind
Thou hast immanacl'd, while heav'n sees good.
1634 *Comus, A Mask*, l.663–5.

79 The unexempt condition
By which all mortal frailty must subsist,
Refreshment after toil, ease after pain.
1634 *Comus, A Mask*, l.684–6.

80 But now my task is smoothly done,
I can fly, or I can run
Quickly to the green earth's end,
Where the bow'd welkin slow doth bend,
And from thence can soar as soon
To the corners of the Moon.
1634 *Comus, A Mask*, l.1011–16.

81 Mortals that would follow me,
Love virtue, she alone is free,
She can teach ye how to climb
Higher than the sphery chime;
Or if virtue feeble were,
Heav'n itself would stoop to her.
1634 *Comus, A Mask*, l.1017–22.

82 Yet once more, O ye laurels, and once more
Ye myrtles brown, with ivy never-sere
I come to pluck your berries harsh and crude,
And with forc'd fingers rude,
Shatter your leaves before the mellowing year.
Bitter constraint, and sad occasion dear,
Compels me to disturb your season due
For Lycidas is dead, dead ere his prime
Young Lycidas, and hath not left his peer.
1637 *Lycidas*, opening lines.

83 For we were nursed upon the self-same hill,
Fed the same flock; by fountain, shade, and rill.
1637 *Lycidas*, l.23–4.

84 But O the heavy change, now thou art gone,
Now thou art gone, and never must return!
Thee shepherd, thee the woods, and desert caves,
With wild thyme and the gadding vine o'ergrown,
And all their echoes mourn.
1637 *Lycidas*, l.37–41.

85 Where were ye Nymphs when the remorseless deep
Clos'd o'er the head of your lov'd Lycidas?
1637 *Lycidas*, l.50–1.

86 Alas! What boots it with uncessant care
To tend the homely slighted Shepherd's trade,
And strictly meditate the thankless muse;
Were it not better done as others use,
To sport with Amaryllis in the shade,
Or with the tangles of Neaera's hair?
Fame is the spur that the clear spirit doth raise
(That last infirmity of noble mind)
To scorn delights, and live laborious days;
But the fair guerdon when we hope to find,
And think to burst out into sudden blaze,
Comes the blind Fury with th' abhorred shears,
And slits the thin-spun life.
1637 *Lycidas*, l.64–76.

87 Fame is no plant that grows on mortal soil.
1637 *Lycidas*, l.78.

88 Blind mouths! that scarce themselves know how to hold
A sheep-hook.
1637 *Lycidas*, l.119–20.

89 They are sped;
And when they list, their lean and flashy songs
Grate on their scrannel Pipes of wretched straw,
The hungry sheep look up, and are not fed,
But swollen with wind, and the rank mist they draw,
Rot inwardly, and foul contagion spread,
Besides what the grim wolf with privy paw
Daily devours apace, and nothing said,
But that two-handed engine at the door,
Stands ready to smite once, and smite no more.
1637 *Lycidas*, l.122–31.

90 Ye valleys low where the mild whispers use,
Of shades and wanton winds, and gushing brooks,
On whose fresh lap the swart star sparely looks,
Throw hither all your quaint enameled eyes,
That on the green turf such the honeyed showers,
And purple all the ground with vernal flowers.
1637 *Lycidas*, l.136–41.

91 Bring the rathe primrose that forsaken dies,
The tufted crow-toe, and pale gessamine,
The white pink, and the pansy freaked with jet,
The glowing violet,
The musk-rose, and the well attir'd woodbine,
With cowslips wan that hang the pensive head,
And every flower that sad embroidery wears:
Bid amaranthus all his beauty shed,
And daffadillies fill their cups with tears,
To strew the laureate hearse where Lycid lies.
1637 *Lycidas*, l.142–51. rathe = early.

92 For to interpose a little ease,
Let our frail thoughts dally with false surmise.
1637 *Lycidas*, l.152–3.

Milton Lycidas

93 Look homeward Angel, now, and melt with ruth.
   1637 *Lycidas*, l.163. The phrase was used by Thomas Clayton Wolfe for his 1929 novel, *Look Homeward Angel*.

94 Weep no more, woeful shepherds, weep no more,
   For Lycidas your sorrow is not dead,
   Sunk though he be beneath the watery floor,
   So sinks the day-star in the ocean bed,
   And yet anon repairs his drooping head,
   And tricks his beams, and with new spangled ore,
   Flames in the forehead of the morning sky:
   So Lycidas sunk low, but mounted high,
   Through the dear might of Him that walked the waves.
   1637 *Lycidas*, l.165–73.

95 There entertain him all the saints above,
   In solemn troops, and sweet societies
   That sing, and singing in their glory move,
   And wipe the tears for ever from his eyes.
   1637 *Lycidas*, l.178–81.

96 At last he rose, and twitched his mantle blue:
   Tomorrow to fresh woods, and pastures new.
   1637 *Lycidas*, l.192–3.

97 This manner of writing wherein knowing myself inferior to myself… I have the use, as I may account it, but of my left hand.
   1642 Of his use of prose. *The Reason of Church Government*, bk.2, introduction, 'Plans and Projects'.

98 Beholding the bright countenance of truth in the quiet and still air of delightful studies.
   1642 *The Reason of Church Government*, bk.2, introduction, 'Plans and Projects'.

99 As good almost kill a man as kill a good book: who kills a man kills a reasonable creature, God's image; but he who destroys a good book, kills reason itself, kills the image of God, as it were in the eye.
   1644 *Areopagitica: a speech for the liberty of unlicensed printing*.

1 Promiscuous reading is necessary to the constituting of human nature. The attempt to keep out evil doctrine by licensing is like the exploit of that gallant man who thought to keep out the crows by shutting the park gate.
   1644 *Areopagitica: a speech for the liberty of unlicensed printing*.

2 A good book is the precious life-blood of a master spirit, embalmed and treasured up on purpose to a life beyond life.
   1644 *Areopagitica: a speech for the liberty of unlicensed printing*.

3 It was from out the rind of one apple tasted, that the knowledge of good and evil, as two twins cleaving together, leaped forth into the world.
   1644 *Areopagitica: a speech for the liberty of unlicensed printing*.

4 Where there is much to learn, there of necessity will be much arguing, much writing, many opinions; for opinion in good men is but knowledge in the making.
   1644 *Areopagitica: a speech for the liberty of unlicensed printing*.

5 As therefore the state of man now is, what wisdom can there be to choose, what continence to forbear, without the knowledge of good and evil?
   1644 *Areopagitica: a speech for the liberty of unlicensed printing*.

6 Give me the liberty to know, to utter, and to argue freely according to conscience, above all liberties.
   1644 *Areopagitica: a speech for the liberty of unlicensed printing*.

7 And though all the winds of doctrine were let loose to play upon the earth, so Truth be in the field, we do injuriously by licensing and prohibiting to misdoubt her strength. Let her and Falsehood grapple; who ever knew Truth put to the worse in a free and open encounter?
   1644 *Areopagitica: a speech for the liberty of unlicensed printing*.

8 I cannot praise a fugitive and cloistered virtue, unexercised and unbreathed, that never sallies out and sees her adversary, but slinks out of the race where that immortal garland is to be run for, not without dust and heat. Assuredly we bring not innocence into the world, we bring impurity much rather; that which purifies us is trial, and trial is by what is contrary.
   1644 *Areopagitica: a speech for the liberty of unlicensed printing*.

9 For who knows not that Truth is strong next to the Almighty? She needs no policies, nor stratagems, nor licensings to make her victorious.
   1644 *Areopagitica: a speech for the liberty of unlicensed printing*.

10 That virtue therefore which is but a youngling in the contemplation of evil, and knows not the utmost that vice promises to her followers, and rejects it, is but a blank virtue, not a pure; her whiteness is but an excremental whiteness.
   1644 *Areopagitica: a speech for the liberty of unlicensed printing*.

11 Since therefore the knowledge and survey of vice is in this world so necessary to the constituting of human virtue, and the scanning of error to the confirmation of truth, how can we more safely, and with less danger, scout into the regions of sin and falsity than by reading all manner of tractates and hearing all manner of reason? And this is the benefit which may be had of books promiscuously read.
   1644 *Areopagitica: a speech for the liberty of unlicensed printing*.

12 When God gave [Adam] reason, he gave him freedom to choose, for reason is but choosing; he had been else a mere artificial Adam.
   1644 *Areopagitica: a speech for the liberty of unlicensed printing*.

13 Wherefore did he [God] create passions within us, pleasures round about us, but that these rightly tempered are the very ingredients of virtue?
   1644 *Areopagitica: a speech for the liberty of unlicensed printing*.

14 They are not skilful considerers of human things, who imagine to remove sin by removing the matter of sin.
   1644 *Areopagitica: a speech for the liberty of unlicensed printing*.

15 We ourselves esteem not of that obedience, or love, or gift, which is of force: God therefore let him free, set before him a provoking object, ever almost in his eyes; herein consisted his merit, herein the right of his reward, the praise of his abstinence.
   1644 *Areopagitica: a speech for the liberty of unlicensed printing*.

16 Though ye take from a covetous man all his treasure, he has yet one jewel left: ye cannot bereave him of his covetousness.
   1644 *Areopagitica: a speech for the liberty of unlicensed printing*.

17 Truth indeed came once into the world with her divine Master, and was a perfect shape most glorious to look on: but…a wicked race of deceivers…took the virgin Truth, hewed her lovely form into a thousand pieces, and scattered them to the four winds. From that time ever since, the sad friends of Truth, such as durst appear, imitating the careful search that Isis made for the mangled body of Osiris, went up and down gathering up limb by limb, still as they could find them. We have not

yet found them all...nor ever shall do, till her Master's second coming; he shall bring together every joint and member, and shall mould them into an immortal feature of loveliness and perfection.
1644 *Areopagitica: a speech for the liberty of unlicensed printing.*

18 Lords and Commons of England, consider what nation it is whereof ye are, and whereof ye are the governors: a nation not slow and dull, but of a quick, ingenious, and piercing spirit, acute to invent, subtle and sinewy to discourse, not beneath the reach of any point the highest that human capacity can soar to.
1644 *Areopagitica: a speech for the liberty of unlicensed printing.*

19 God is decreeing to begin some new and great period in his Church, even to the reforming of Reformation itself. What does he then but reveal Himself to his servants, and as his manner is, first to his Englishmen?
1644 *Areopagitica: a speech for the liberty of unlicensed printing.*

20 Methinks I see in my mind a noble and puissant nation rousing herself like a strong man after sleep, and shaking her invincible locks: methinks I see her as an eagle mewing her mighty youth, and kindling her undazzled eyes at the full midday beam; purging and unscaling her long-abused sight at the fountain itself of heavenly radiance; while the whole noise of timorous birds, with those also that love the twilight, flutter about, amazed at what she means.
1644 *Areopagitica: a speech for the liberty of unlicensed printing.*

21 I did but prompt the age to quit their clogs
By the known rules of ancient liberty,
When strait a barbarous noise environs me
Of owls and cuckoos, asses, apes and dogs.
c.1646 'On the Detraction Which Follow'd Upon My Writing Certain Treatises'.

22 None can love freedom heartily, but good men; the rest love not freedom, but licence.
1648–9 *The Tenure of Kings and Magistrates.*

23 No man who knows aught, can be so stupid to deny that all men naturally were born free.
1648–9 *The Tenure of Kings and Magistrates.*

24 The power of kings and magistrates is nothing else but what is only derivative; transformed and committed to them in trust from the people to the common good of them all, in whom the power yet remains fundamentally, and cannot be taken from them without a violation of their natural birthright.
1648–9 *The Tenure of Kings and Magistrates.*

25 Yet much remains
To conquer still; peace hath her victories
No less renowned then war, new foes arise
Threatening to bind our souls with secular chains:
Help us to save free conscience from the paw
Of hireling wolves whose gospel is their maw.
1652 'To the Lord General Cromwell'.

26 When I consider how my light is spent,
E're half my days, in this dark world and wide,
And that one talent which is death to hide,
Lodg'd with me useless, though my soul more bent
To serve therewith my Maker, and present
My true account, least he returning chide,
Doth God exact day-labour, light denied,
I fondly ask; But patience to prevent

That murmur, soon replies, God doth not need
Either man's work or his own gifts, who best
Bear his mild yoke, they serve him best, his state
Is kingly. Thousands at his bidding speed
And post o'er land and ocean without rest:
They also serve who only stand and wait.
c.1652 *Sonnets*, no.16, 'When I Consider'.

27 Methought I saw my late espoused Saint
Brought to me like Alcestis from the grave,
c.1658 *Sonnets*, no.19, 'Methought I Saw'.

28 But O as to embrace me she enclin'd
I wak'd, she fled, and day brought back my night.
c.1658 *Sonnets*, no.19, 'Methought I Saw'.

29 Of man's first disobedience, and the fruit
Of that forbidden tree, whose mortal taste
Brought death into the world, and all our woe,
With loss of Eden, till one greater Man
Restore us, and regain the blissful seat.
1665 *Paradise Lost* (published 1667), bk.1, opening lines.

30 Things unattempted yet in prose or rhyme.
1665 *Paradise Lost* (published 1667), bk.1, l.15.

31 And chiefly thou O spirit, that does prefer
Before all temples th'upright heart and pure,
Instruct me, for thou know'st; thou from the first
Wast present, and with mighty wings outspread
Dove-like sat'st brooding on the vast abyss
And mad'st it pregnant: what in me is dark
Illumine, what is low raise and support;
That to the highth of this great argument
I may assert Eternal Providence,
And justify the ways of God to men.
1665 *Paradise Lost* (published 1667), bk.1, l.16–25.

32 Who first seduced them to that foul revolt?
1665 *Paradise Lost* (published 1667), bk.1, l.33.

33 Him the Almighty Power
Hurled headlong flaming from th' ethereal sky
With hideous ruin and combustion down
To bottomless perdition, there to dwell
In adamantine chains and penal fire.
1665 *Paradise Lost* (published 1667), bk.1, l.44–8.

34 Now the thought
Both of lost happiness and lasting pain
Torments him.
1665 Of Satan. *Paradise Lost* (published 1667), bk.1, l.54–6.

35 A dungeon horrible, on all sides round
As one great furnace flamed; yet from those flames
No light, but rather darkness visible
Served only to discover sights of woe,
Regions of sorrow, doleful shades, where peace
And rest can never dwell, hope never comes
That comes to all.
1665 Of Hell. *Paradise Lost* (published 1667), bk.1, l.61–7.

36 O how fall'n! how changed
From him, who in the happy realms of light
Clothed with transcendent brightness didst outshine
Myriads though bright.
1665 Of Satan. *Paradise Lost* (published 1667), bk.1, l.84–7.

37 United thoughts and counsels, equal hope
And hazard in the glorious enterprise.
1665 *Paradise Lost* (published 1667), bk.1, l.88–9.

38 What though the field be lost?
All is not lost; the unconquerable will,
And study of revenge, immortal hate,
And courage never to submit or yield.
1665 Satan addressing the fallen angels. *Paradise Lost* (published 1667), bk.1, l.105–8.

39 Vaunting aloud, but racked with deep despair.
1665 *Paradise Lost* (published 1667), bk.1, l.126.

40 To be weak is miserable
Doing or suffering, but of this be sure,
To do aught good never will be our task,
But ever to do ill our sole delight.
1665 *Paradise Lost* (published 1667), bk.1, l.157–60.

41 If then his providence
Out of our evil seek to bring forth good,
Our labour must be to pervert that end,
And out of good still to find means of evil.
1665 *Paradise Lost* (published 1667), bk.1, l.162–5.

42 What reinforcement we may gain from hope;
If not, what resolution from despair.
1665 *Paradise Lost* (published 1667), bk.1, l.190–1.

43 Forthwith upright he rears from off the pool
His mighty stature; on each hand the flames
Driv'n backward slope their pointing spires, and rolled
In billows, leave i' th' midst a horrid vale.
1665 Of Satan. *Paradise Lost* (published 1667), bk.1, l.221.

44 The mind is its own place, and in itself
Can make a heav'n of hell, a hell of heav'n.
1665 *Paradise Lost* (published 1667), bk.1, l.254–5.

45 Better to reign in hell, than serve in heav'n.
1665 Satan. *Paradise Lost* (published 1667), bk.1, l.263.

46 For Spirits when they please
Can either sex assume, or both; so soft
And uncompounded is their essence pure,
Not tied or manacled with joint or limb,
Nor founded on the brittle strength of bones,
Like cumbrous flesh; but in what shape they choose
Dilated or condensed, bright or obscure,
Can execute their airy purposes,
And works of love or enmity fulfil.
1665 *Paradise Lost* (published 1667), bk.1, l.423–31.

47 And when night
Darkens the streets, then wander forth the sons
Of Belial, flown with insolence and wine.
1665 *Paradise Lost* (published 1667), bk.1, l.500–2.

48 With high words, that bore
Semblance of worth, not substance, gently raised
Their fainting courage, and dispelled their fears.
1665 *Paradise Lost* (published 1667), bk.1, l.528–30.

49 A shout that tore hell's concave, and beyond
Frighted the reign of Chaos and old Night.
1665 *Paradise Lost* (published 1667), bk.1, l.542–3.

50 For who can yet believe, though after loss,
That all these puissant legions, whose exile
Hath emptied heav'n, shall fail to reascend
Self-raised, and repossess their native seat?
1665 *Paradise Lost* (published 1667), bk.1, l.631–4.

51 Who overcomes
By force, hath overcome but half his foe.
1665 *Paradise Lost* (published 1667), bk.1, l.648–9.

52 War then, war
Open or understood must be resolved.
1665 Satan. *Paradise Lost* (published 1667), bk.1, l.661–2.

53 Let none admire
That riches grow in hell; that soil may best
Deserve the precious bane.
1665 *Paradise Lost* (published 1667), bk.1, l.690–2.

54 Pandemonium, the high capital
Of Satan and his peers.
1665 *Paradise Lost* (published 1667), bk.1, l.756–7.

55 Satan exalted sat, by merit raised
To that bad eminence; and from despair
Thus high uplifted beyond hope.
1665 *Paradise Lost* (published 1667), bk.2, l.5–7.

56 Where there is then no good
For which to strive, no strife can grow up there
From faction; for none sure will claim in hell
Precedence, none, whose portion is so small
Of present pain, that with ambitious mind
Will covet more.
1665 Satan. *Paradise Lost* (published 1667), bk.2, l.30–5.

57 His trust was with the eternal to be deemed
Equal in strength, and rather than be less
Cared not to be at all; with that care lost
Went all his fear.
1665 Of Moloch. *Paradise Lost* (published 1667), bk.2, l.46–9.

58 He seemed
For dignity composed and high exploit:
But all was false and hollow; though his tongue
Dropped manna, and could make the worse appear
The better reason.
1665 Of Belial. *Paradise Lost* (published 1667), bk.2, l.110–14.

59 To be no more; sad cure; for who would lose,
Though full of pain, this intellectual being,
Those thoughts that wander through eternity,
To perish rather, swallowed up and lost
In the wide womb of uncreated night,
Devoid of sense and motion?
1665 Belial. *Paradise Lost* (published 1667), bk.2, l.146–51.

60 Thus Belial with words clothed in reason's garb
Counselled ignoble ease, and peaceful sloth,
Not peace.
1665 *Paradise Lost* (published 1667), bk.2, l.226–8.

61 Our torments also may in length of time
Become our elements, these piercing fires
As soft as now severe, our temper changed
Into their temper.
1665 Mammon. *Paradise Lost* (published 1667), bk.2, l.274–7.

62 There is a place
(If ancient and prophetic fame in heav'n
Err not) another world, the happy seat
Of some new race called Man.
1665 Beelzebub. *Paradise Lost* (published 1667), bk.2, l.345–8.

63 This would surpass
Common revenge.
1665 Beelzebub speaking of the plan to tempt Man away from God. *Paradise Lost* (published 1667), bk.2, l.370–1.

64 When his darling sons
Hurled headlong to partake with us, shall curse

Their frail original, and faded bliss,
Faded so soon.
1665 Beelzebub. *Paradise Lost* (published 1667), bk.2, l.373–6.

65 Who shall tempt with wand'ring feet
The dark unbottomed infinite abyss
And through the palpable obscure find out
His uncouth way, or spread his aery flight
Upborne with indefatigable wings
Over the vast abrupt, ere he arrive
The happy isle.
1665 Beelzebub. *Paradise Lost* (published 1667), bk.2, l.404–10.

66 Long is the way
And hard, that out of hell leads up to light.
1665 *Paradise Lost* (published 1667), bk.2, l.432–3.

67 O shame to men! Devil with devil damned
Firm concord holds, men only disagree
Of creatures rational.
1665 *Paradise Lost* (published 1667), bk.2, l.496–8.

68 Meanwhile the Adversary of God and man,
Satan with thoughts inflamed of highest design,
Puts on swift wings, and towards the gates of hell
Explores his solitary flight.
1665 *Paradise Lost* (published 1667), bk.2, l.629–32.

69 Chaos umpire sits,
And by decision more embroils the fray
By which he reigns; next him high arbiter
Chance governs all.
1665 *Paradise Lost* (published 1667), bk.2, l.681–4.

70 Whence and what art thou, execrable shape?
1665 *Paradise Lost* (published 1667), bk.2, l.681.

71 A race of upstart creatures.
1665 Satan speaks to his daughter, Sin, of Man. *Paradise Lost* (published 1667), bk.2, l.834.

72 And fast by hanging in a golden chain
This pendent world.
1665 *Paradise Lost* (published 1667), bk.2, l.1051–2.

73 Hail holy Light, offspring of Heav'n first-born.
Bright effluence of bright essence increate.
1665 *Paradise Lost* (published 1667), bk.3, l.5–6.

74 Thee I revisit safe,
And feel thy sovran vital lamp; but thou
Revisit'st not these eyes, that roll in vain
To find thy piercing ray, and find no dawn;
So thick a drop serene hath quenched their orbs,
Or dim suffusion veiled.
1665 Of his blindness. *Paradise Lost* (published 1667), bk.3, l.22–7.

75 Thus with the year
Seasons return, but not to me returns
Day, or the sweet approach of ev'n or morn,
Or sight of vernal bloom, or summer's rose,
Or flocks, or herds, of human face divine;
But cloud instead, and ever-during dark
Surrounds me, from the cheerful ways of men
Cut off, and for the book of knowledge fair
Presented with a universal blank
Of nature's works to me expunged and razed,
And wisdom at one entrance quite shut out.
1665 *Paradise Lost* (published 1667), bk.3, l.40–50.

76 Our two first parents, yet the only two
Of mankind, in the happy garden placed,
Reaping immortal fruits of joy and love,
Uninterrupted joy, unrivalled love
In blissful solitude.
1665 *Paradise Lost* (published 1667), bk.3, l.65–9.

77 So bent he seems
On desperate revenge, that shall redound
Upon his own rebellious head.
1665 Of Satan. *Paradise Lost* (published 1667), bk.3, l.84–6.

78 Whose fault?
Whose but his own? Ingrate, he had of me
All he could have; I made him just and right,
Sufficient to have stood, though free to fall.
1665 God speaking of Satan. *Paradise Lost* (published 1667), bk.3, l.96–9.

79 Freely they stood who stood, and fell who fell.
1665 *Paradise Lost* (published 1667), bk.3, l.102.

80 I formed them free, and free they must remain,
Till they enthrall themselves
1665 *Paradise Lost* (published 1667), bk.3, l.124–5.

81 And I will place within them as a guide
My umpire conscience, whom if they will hear
Light after light well used they shall attain,
And to the end persisting, safe arrive.
1665 *Paradise Lost* (published 1667), bk.3, l.194–7.

82 Die he or justice must.
1665 *Paradise Lost* (published 1667), bk.3, l.210.

83 Behold me then, me for him, life for life
I offer, on me let thine anger fall;
Account me man; I for his sake will leave
Thy bosom, and this glory next to thee
Freely put off, and for him lastly die
Well pleased, on me let Death wreck all his rage.
1665 Christ speaking to God. *Paradise Lost* (published 1667), bk.3, l.236–241.

84 O thou
My sole complacence!
1665 God speaking to Christ. *Paradise Lost* (published 1667), bk.3, l.275–6.

85 So on this windy sea of land, the Fiend
Walked up and down alone bent on his prey.
1665 *Paradise Lost* (published 1667), bk.3, l.440–1.

86 Into a limbo large and broad, since called
The Paradise of Fools, to few unknown.
1665 *Paradise Lost* (published 1667), bk.3, l.495–6.

87 The pure marble air.
1665 *Paradise Lost* (published 1667), bk.3, l.564.

88 For neither man nor angel can discern
Hypocrisy, the only evil that walks
Invisible, except to God alone,
By his permissive will, through heav'n and earth.
1665 *Paradise Lost* (published 1667), bk.3, l.681–4.

89 Horror and doubt distract
His troubled thoughts, and from the bottom stir
The hell within him, for within him hell
He brings, and round about him, nor from hell
One step no more than from himself can fly.
1665 Of Satan. *Paradise Lost* (published 1667), bk.4, l.18–22.

90 Now conscience wakes despair
That slumbered, wakes the bitter memory
Of what he was, what is, and what must be
Worse; of worse deeds worse sufferings must ensue.
1665 Of Satan. *Paradise Lost* (published 1667), bk.4, l.23–6.

Milton Paradise Lost

91 A grateful mind
  By owing owes not, but still pays, at once
  Indebted and discharged; what burden then?
  1665 *Paradise Lost* (published 1667), bk.4, l.55–7.

92 Which way I fly is hell; myself am hell;
  And in the lowest deep a lower deep
  Still threat'ning to devour me opens wide,
  To which the hell I suffer seems a heav'n.
  1665 Satan. *Paradise Lost* (published 1667), bk.4, l.75–8.

93 The lower still I fall, only supreme
  In misery; such joy ambition finds.
  1665 Satan. *Paradise Lost* (published 1667), bk.4, l.91–2.

94 For never can true reconcilement grow
  Where wounds of deadly hate have pierced so deep.
  1665 Satan. *Paradise Lost* (published 1667), bk.4, l.98–9.

95 So clomb this first grand thief into God's fold:
  So since into his church lewd hirelings climb.
  Thence up he flew, and on the Tree of Life,
  The middle tree and highest there that grew,
  Sat like a cormorant.
  1665 Of Satan. *Paradise Lost* (published 1667), bk.4, l.192–6.

96 Out of the fertile ground he caused to grow
  All trees of noblest kind for sight, smell, taste;
  And all amid them stood the Tree of Life,
  High eminent, blooming ambrosial fruit
  Of vegetable gold; and next to life
  Our death the Tree of Knowledge grew fast by,
  Knowledge of good bought dear by knowing ill.
  1665 *Paradise Lost* (published 1667), bk.4, l.218–24.

97 Flowers of all hue, and without thorn the rose.
  1665 *Paradise Lost* (published 1667), bk.4, l.256.

98 Two of far nobler shape erect and tall,
  God-like erect, with native honor clad
  In naked majesty seemed lords of all.
  1665 Of Adam and Eve. *Paradise Lost* (published 1667), bk.4, l.288–90.

99 Though both
  Not equal, as their sex not equal seemed;
  For contemplation he and valour formed,
  For softness she and sweet attractive grace,
  He for God only, she for God in him.
  1665 Of Adam and Eve. *Paradise Lost* (published 1667), bk.4, l.295–9.

1 Yielded with coy submission, modest pride,
  And sweet reluctant amorous delay.
  1665 Of Eve. *Paradise Lost* (published 1667), bk.4, l.310–11.

2 Ah gentle pair, ye little think how nigh
  Your change approaches, when all these delights
  Will vanish and deliver ye to woe,
  More woe, the more your taste is now of joy.
  1665 *Paradise Lost* (published 1667), bk.4, l.366–9.

3 Sole partner and sole part of all these joys.
  1665 Adam to Eve. *Paradise Lost* (published 1667), bk.4, l.411.

4 These two
  Emparadised in one another's arms
  The happier Eden, shall enjoy their fill
  Of bliss on bliss.
  1665 Of Adam and Eve. *Paradise Lost* (published 1667), bk.4, l.505–8.

5 Man hath his daily work of body or mind
  Appointed, which declares his dignity,
  And the regard of Heav'n on all his ways.
  1665 Adam to Eve. *Paradise Lost* (published 1667), bk.4, l.618–20.

6 God is thy law, thou mine: to know no more
  Is woman's happiest knowledge and her praise.
  With thee conversing I forget all time.
  1665 Eve to Adam. *Paradise Lost* (published 1667), bk.4, l.637–9.

7 Millions of spiritual creatures walk the earth
  Unseen, both when we wake, and when we sleep.
  1665 *Paradise Lost* (published 1667), bk.4, l.677–8.

8 Iris all hues, roses, and jessamine
  Reared high their flourished heads between, and wrought
  Mosaic; underfoot the violet,
  Crocus, and hyacinth with rich inlay
  Broidered the ground, more coloured than with stone
  Of costliest emblem: other creature here
  Beast, bird, insect, or worm durst enter none;
  Such was their awe of man.
  1665 *Paradise Lost* (published 1667), bk.4, l.698–705.

9 Nor turned I ween
  Adam from his fair spouse, nor Eve the rites
  Mysterious of connubial love refused:
  Whatever hypocrites austerely talk
  Of purity and place and innocence,
  Defaming as impure what God declares
  Pure, and commands to some, leaves free to all.
  1665 *Paradise Lost* (published 1667), bk.4, l.741–7.

10 Hail, wedded love, mysterious law, true source
  Of human offspring, sole propriety
  In Paradise of all things common else.
  1665 *Paradise Lost* (published 1667), bk.4, l.750–2.

11 Him there they found
  Squat like a toad, close at the ear of Eve.
  1665 *Paradise Lost* (published 1667), bk.4, l.799–800.

12 When I am thy captive talk of chains,
  Proud limitary cherub.
  1665 *Paradise Lost* (published 1667), bk.4, l.970–1.

13 But wherefore thou alone? Wherefore with thee
  Came not all hell broke loose?
  1665 *Paradise Lost* (published 1667), bk.4, l.917–18.

14 My fairest, my espoused, my latest found,
  Heav'n's last best gift, my ever new delight.
  1665 Adam to Eve. *Paradise Lost* (published 1667), bk.5, l.18–19.

15 Best image of myself and dearer half.
  1665 Adam to Eve. *Paradise Lost* (published 1667), bk.5, l.95.

16 Nor jealousy
  Was understood, the injured lover's hell.
  1665 *Paradise Lost* (published 1667), bk.5, l.449–50.

17 In contemplation of created things
  By steps we may ascend to God.
  1665 Adam to Raphael. *Paradise Lost* (published 1667), bk.5, l.511–12.

18 God made thee perfect, not immutable.
  1665 Raphael to Adam. *Paradise Lost* (published 1667), bk.5, l.524.

19 Hear all ye angels, progeny of light,
  Thrones, dominations, princedoms, virtues, powers.
  1665 *Paradise Lost* (published 1667), bk.5, l.600–1.

20 All seemed well pleased, all seemed, but were not all.
  1665 *Paradise Lost* (published 1667), bk.5, l.616.

21 Servant of God, well done, well hast thou fought
The better fight.
1665 God to his faithful angels. *Paradise Lost* (published 1667), bk.6, l.29–30.

22 Proud, art thou met?
1665 Abdiel to Satan. *Paradise Lost* (published 1667), bk.6, l.131.

23 This is servitude,
To serve th' unwise, or him who hath rebelled
Against his worthier, as thine now serve thee,
Thyself not free, but to thyself enthralled.
1665 Abdiel to Satan. *Paradise Lost* (published 1667), bk.6, l.178–81.

24 But pain is perfect misery, the worst
Of evils, and excessive, overturns
All patience.
1665 *Paradise Lost* (published 1667), bk.6, l.461–3.

25 On war and mutual slaughter bent.
1665 Of Mankind. *Paradise Lost* (published 1667), bk.6, l.506.

26 Headlong themselves they threw
Down from the verge of heaven, eternal wrath
Burnt after them to the bottomless pit.
1665 Pursued to the wall of Heaven by the Messiah, Satan and his rebelling angels fall to their punishment as the wall opens. *Paradise Lost* (published 1667), bk.6, l.864–6.

27 Standing on earth, not rapt above the pole,
More safe I sing with mortal voice, unchanged
To hoarse or mute, though fall'n on evil days,
On evil days though fallen, and evil tongues.
1665 *Paradise Lost* (published 1667), bk.7, l.23–6.

28 But knowledge is as food, and needs no less
Her temperance over appetite, to know
In measure what the mind may well contain,
Oppresses else with surfeit, and soon turns
Wisdom to folly, as nourishment to wind.
1665 *Paradise Lost* (published 1667), bk.7, l.126–30.

29 Necessity and chance
Approach not me, and what I will is fate.
1665 God. *Paradise Lost* (published 1667), bk.7, l.172–3.

30 He took the golden compasses, prepared
In God's eternal store, to circumscribe
This universe, and all created things:
One foot he centred, and the other turned
Round through the vast profundity obscure,
And said, 'Thus far extend, thus far thy bounds
This be thy just circumference, O world.'
1665 *Paradise Lost* (published 1667), bk.7, l.225–31.

31 And the earth self-balanced on her centre hung.
1665 *Paradise Lost* (published 1667), bk.7, l.242.

32 The great creator from his work returned
Magnificent, his six days' work, a world.
1665 *Paradise Lost* (published 1667), bk.7, l.567–8.

33 Witness this new-made world, another heav'n
From heaven gate not far, founded in view
On the clear hyaline, the glassy sea;
Of amplitude almost immense, with stars
Numerous, and every star perhaps a world
Of destined habitation.
1665 *Paradise Lost* (published 1667), bk.7, l.617–22.

34 O when meet now
Such pairs, in love and mutual honour joined?
1665 *Paradise Lost* (published 1667), bk.8, l.57–8.

35 He his fabric of the heavens
Hath left to their disputes, perhaps to move
His laughter at their quaint opinions wide
Hereafter, when they come to model heaven
And calculate the stars, how they will wield
The mighty frame, how build, unbuild, contrive
To save appearances, how gird the sphere
With centric and eccentric scribbled o'er,
Cycle and epicycle, orb in orb.
1665 *Paradise Lost* (published 1667), bk.8, l.76–84.

36 Heaven is for thee too high
To know what passes there; be lowly wise:
Think only what concerns thee and thy being.
Dream not of other worlds, what creatures there
Live, in what state, condition, or degree,
Contented that thus far hath been revealed
Not of earth only but of highest heav'n.
1665 Raphael to Adam. *Paradise Lost* (published 1667), bk.8, l.172–8.

37 For man to tell how human life began
Is hard; for who himself beginning knew?
1665 Adam to Raphael. *Paradise Lost* (published 1667), bk.8, l.250–1.

38 In solitude
What happiness, who can enjoy alone,
Or all enjoying, what contentment find?
1665 Adam. *Paradise Lost* (published 1667), bk.8, l.364–6.

39 Among unequals what society
Can sort, what harmony or true delight?
1665 Adam. *Paradise Lost* (published 1667), bk.8, l.383–4.

40 Yet when I approach
Her loveliness, so absolute she seems
And in herself complete, so well to know
Her own, that what she wills to do or say,
Seems wisest, virtuousest, discreetest, best.
1665 Adam speaking of Eve. *Paradise Lost* (published 1667), bk.8, l.546–50.

41 All higher knowledge in her presence falls
Degraded, wisdom in discourse with her
Loses discount'nanced, and like folly shows.
1665 Adam speaking of Eve. *Paradise Lost* (published 1667), bk.8, l.551–3.

42 Love refines
The thoughts, and heart enlarges, hath his seat
In reason, and is judicious, is the scale
By which to heav'nly love thou may'st ascend,
Not sunk in carnal pleasure, for which cause
Among the beasts no mate for thee was found.
1665 Raphael to Adam. *Paradise Lost* (published 1667), bk.8, l.589–94.

43 My celestial patroness, who deigns
Her nightly visitation unimplored,
And dictates to me slumbering, or inspires
Easy my unpremeditated verse:
Since first this subject for heroic song
Pleased me long choosing, and beginning late.
1665 *Paradise Lost* (published 1667), bk.9, l.21–6.

44 And the more I see
Pleasures about me, so much more I feel
Torment within me.
1665 Satan. *Paradise Lost* (published 1667), bk.9, l.119–21.

Milton Paradise Lost

45 This man of clay, son of despite.
1665 Satan speaking of Adam. *Paradise Lost* (published 1667), bk.9, l.176.

46 For nothing lovelier can be found
In woman, than to study household good,
And good works in her husband to promote.
1665 Adam to Eve. *Paradise Lost* (published 1667), bk.9, l.232–4.

47 For solitude sometimes is best society,
And short retirement urges sweet return.
1665 Paradise Lost (published 1667), bk.9, l.249–50.

48 That space the Evil One abstracted stood
From his own evil, and for the time remained
Stupidly good, of enmity disarmed,
Of guile, of hate, of envy, of revenge.
1665 Satan gazes upon Eve. *Paradise Lost* (published 1667), bk.9, l.463–6.

49 She fair, divinely fair, fit love for gods.
1665 Satan speaking of Eve. *Paradise Lost* (published 1667), bk.9, l.489.

50 Her rash hand in evil hour
Forth reaching to the fruit, she plucked, she ate:
Earth felt the wound, and nature from her seat
Sighing through all her works gave signs of woe,
That all was lost.
1665 Paradise Lost (published 1667), bk.9, l.781–5.

51 O fairest of creation, last and best
Of all God's works, creature in whom excelled
Whatever can to sight or thought be formed,
Holy, divine, good, amiable, or sweet!
How art thou lost, how on a sudden lost,
Defaced, deflow'red, and now to death devote?
1665 Adam to Eve. *Paradise Lost* (published 1667), bk.9, l.896–91.

52 Flesh of flesh,
Bone of my bone thou art, and from thy state
Mine never shall be parted, bliss or woe.
1665 Adam to Eve. *Paradise Lost* (published 1667), bk.9, l.914–16.

53 What thou art is mine;
Our state cannot be severed, we are one,
One flesh; to lose thee were to lose my self.
1665 Adam to Eve. *Paradise Lost* (published 1667), bk.9, l.957–9.

54 Linked in love so dear,
To undergo with me one guilt, one crime,
If any be, of tasting this fair fruit.
1665 Eve to Adam. *Paradise Lost* (published 1667), bk.9, l.970–2.

55 As with new wine intoxicated both
They swim in mirth, and fancy that they feel
Divinity within them breeding wings
Wherewith to scorn the earth.
1665 Paradise Lost (published 1667), bk.9, l.1007–10.

56 Thus they in mutual accusation spent
The fruitless hours, but neither self-condemning,
And of their vain contést appeared no end.
1665 Paradise Lost (published 1667), bk.9, l.1187–9.

57 Yet I shall temper so
Justice with mercy.
1665 Paradise Lost (published 1667), bk.10, l.77–8.

58 Love was not in their looks, either to God
Or to each other.
1665 Paradise Lost (published 1667), bk.10, l.111–12.

59 Adorned
She was indeed, and lovely to attract
Thy love, not thy subjection.
1665 Christ speaking to Adam of Eve. *Paradise Lost* (published 1667), bk.10, l.151–3.

60 Now possess,
As lords, a spacious world, to our native heaven
Little inferior, by my adventure hard
With peril great achieved.
1665 Satan, returning triumphantly from Earth to Hell after tempting Eve. *Paradise Lost* (published 1667), bk.10, l.466–9.

61 He hears
On all sides, from innumerable tongues
A dismal universal hiss, the sound
Of public scorn.
1665 Satan and the rebel angels are turned to snakes. *Paradise Lost* (published 1667), bk.10, l.506–9.

62 O fleeting joys
Of Paradise, dear bought with lasting woes!
1665 Adam's lament. *Paradise Lost* (published 1667), bk.10, l.741–2.

63 But say
That death be not one stroke, as I supposed,
Bereaving sense, but endless misery
From this day onward, which I feel begun
Both in me, and without me, and so last
To perpetuity; ay me, that fear
Comes thund'ring back with dreadful revolution
On my defenceless head; both Death and I
Am found eternal, and incorporate both,
Nor I on my part single, in me all
Posterity stands cursed: fair patrimony
That I must leave ye, sons; O were I able
To waste it all myself, and leave ye none!
1665 Adam muses on death. *Paradise Lost* (published 1667), bk.10, l.808–20.

64 O why did God,
Creator wise, that peopled highest heav'n
With Spirits masculine, create at last
This novelty on earth, this fair defect
Of nature, and not fill the world at once
With men as angels without feminine,
Or find some other way to generate
Mankind?
1665 Adam speaking of Eve. *Paradise Lost* (published 1667), bk.10, l.888–95.

65 Let us seek Death, or he not found, supply
With our own hands his office on ourselves;
Why stand we longer shivering under fears,
That show no end but death, and have the power,
Of many ways to die the shortest choosing,
Destruction with destruction to destroy.
1665 Eve. *Paradise Lost* (published 1667), bk.10, l.1001–6.

66 So send them forth, though sorrowing, yet in peace.
1665 God speaking to Michael of Adam and Eve. *Paradise Lost* (published 1667), bk.11, l.117.

67 Moping melancholy
And moon-struck madness.
Michael shows Adam a vision of what will happen before the Flood. *Paradise Lost* (published 1667), bk.11, l.485–6.

68 So may'st thou live, till like ripe fruit thou drop
Into thy mother's lap, or be with ease

Gathered, not harshly plucked, for death mature:
This is old age; but then thou must outlive
Thy youth, thy strength, thy beauty, which will change
To withered weak and grey.
1665 Michael to Adam. *Paradise Lost* (published 1667), bk.11, l.535–40.

69 Nor love thy life, nor hate; but what thou liv'st
Live well, how long or short permit to heaven.
1665 *Paradise Lost* (published 1667), bk.11, l.553–4.

70 Now I see
Peace to corrupt no less than war to waste.
1665 *Paradise Lost* (published 1667), bk.11, l.783–4.

71 O goodness infinite, goodness immense!
That all this good of evil shall produce,
And evil turn to good; more wonderful
Than that which by creation first brought forth
Light out of darkness!
1665 Adam to Michael. *Paradise Lost* (published 1667), bk.12, l.470–4.

72 This having learnt, thou hast attained the sum
Of wisdom; hope no higher, though all the stars
Thou knew'st by name, and all th' ethereal powers,
All secrets of the deep, all nature's works,
Or works of God in heav'n, air, earth, or sea,
And all the riches of this world enjoy'dst,
And all the rule, one empire; only add
Deeds to thy knowledge answerable, add faith,
Add virtue, patience, temperance, add love,
By name to come called charity, the soul
Of all the rest: then wilt thou not be loath
To leave this Paradise, but shalt possess
A paradise within thee, happier far.
1665 Michael to Adam. *Paradise Lost* (published 1667), bk.12, l.575–87.

73 Let us descend now therefore from this top
Of speculation.
1665 *Paradise Lost* (published 1667), bk.12, l.588–9.

74 Some natural tears they dropped, but wiped them soon;
The world was all before them, where to choose
Their place of rest, and Providence their guide:
They hand in hand with wand'ring steps and slow,
Through Eden took their solitary way.
1665 *Paradise Lost* (published 1667), bk.12, l.645–9.

75 For what can I increase
Or multiply, but curses on my head?
1665 Adam's lament. *Paradise Lost* (published 1667), bk.10, l.731–2.

76 Skill'd to retire, and in retiring draw
Hearts after them tangled in amorous nets.
1671 *Paradise Regained*, bk.2, l.161–2.

77 The childhood shows the man,
As morning shows the day. Be famous then
By wisdom; as thy empire must extend,
So let extend thy mind o'er all the world.
1671 *Paradise Regained*, bk.4, l.220–3.

78 The first and wisest of them all professed
To know this only, that he nothing knew.
1671 Of Socrates. *Paradise Regained*, bk.4, l.293–4.

79 Athens, the eye of Greece, mother of arts
And eloquence, native to famous wits
1671 *Paradise Regained*, bk.4, l.240–1.

80 Who reads
Incessantly, and to his reading brings not
A spirit and judgement equal or superior
(And what he brings, what needs he elsewhere seek?)
Uncertain and unsettled still remains,
Deep-versed in books and shallow in himself.
1671 *Paradise Regained*, bk.4, l.322–7.

81 But here I feel amends,
The breath of Heav'n fresh-blowing, pure and sweet,
With day-spring born; here leave me to respire.
1671 *Samson Agonistes*, l.9–11.

82 Ask for this great deliverer now, and find him
Eyeless in Gaza at the mill with slaves.
1671 *Samson Agonistes*, l.40–1.

83 O impotence of mind, in body strong!
But what is strength without a double share
Of wisdom, vast, unwieldy, burdensome,
Proudly secure, yet liable to fall
By weakest subtleties, not made to rule,
But to subserve where wisdom bears command.
1671 *Samson Agonistes*, l.52–7.

84 O loss of sight, of thee I most complain!
Blind among enemies, O worse than chains,
Dungeon, or beggary, or decrepit age!
Light the prime work of God to me is extinct,
And all her various objects of delight
Annull'd, which might in part my grief have eas'd,
Inferior to the vilest now become
Of man or worm; the vilest here excel me,
They creep, yet see, I dark in light expos'd
To daily fraud, contempt, abuse and wrong,
Within doors, or without, still as a fool,
In power of others, never in my own;
Scarce half I seem to live, dead more than half.
1671 *Samson Agonistes*, l.67–79.

85 If it be true
That light is in the soul,
She all in every part; why was the sight
To such a tender ball as th' eye confin'd?
1671 *Samson Agonistes*, l.91–4.

86 To live a life half dead, a living death.
1671 *Samson Agonistes*, l.100.

87 Thou art become (O worst imprisonment!)
The Dungeon of thy self.
1671 *Samson Agonistes*, l.155–6.

88 Salve to thy sores, apt words have power to suage
The tumours of a troubl'd mind,
And are as Balm to fester'd wounds.
1671 *Samson Agonistes*, l.184–6.

89 Just are the ways of God,
And justifiable to men;
Unless there be who think not God at all.
1671 *Samson Agonistes*, l.293–5.

90 So much I feel my genial spirits droop,
My hopes all flat, nature within me seems
In her functions weary of herself.
1671 *Samson Agonistes*, l.594–6.

91 My race of glory run, and race of shame,
And I shall shortly be with them that rest.
1671 *Samson Agonistes*, l.597–8.

92 God of our Fathers, what is man!
    That thou towards him with hand so various,
    Or might I say contrarious,
    Temperst thy providence through his short course,
    Not evenly, as thou rul'st
    The angelic orders and inferior creatures mute,
    Irrational and brute.
    1671 *Samson Agonistes*, l.667–73.

93 That grounded maxim
    So rife and celebrated in the mouths
    Of wisest men; that to the public good
    Private respects must yield.
    1671 *Samson Agonistes*, l.865–8.

94 In argument with men a woman ever
    Goes by the worse, whatever be her cause.
    1671 *Samson Agonistes*, l.903–4.

95 At distance I forgive thee, go with that.
    1671 *Samson Agonistes*, l.954.

96 Yet beauty, though injurious, hath strange power,
    After offence returning, to regain
    Love once possessed.
    1671 *Samson Agonistes*, l.1003–5.

97 Love-quarrels oft in pleasing concord end.
    1671 *Samson Agonistes*, l.1008.

98 Lords are lordliest in their wine.
    1671 *Samson Agonistes*, l.1418.

99 Evil news rides post, while good news baits.
    1671 *Samson Agonistes*, l.1538.

1   Death to life is crown or shame.
    1671 *Samson Agonistes*, l.1579.

2   Not willingly, but tangl'd in the fold
    Of dire necessity.
    1671 *Samson Agonistes*, l.1665–6.

3   Nothing is here for tears, nothing to wail
    Or knock the breast, no weakness, no contempt,
    Dispraise, or blame, nothing but well and fair,
    And what may quiet us in a death so noble.
    1671 Of Samson's heroic death. *Samson Agonistes*, l.1721–4.

4   All is best, though we oft doubt,
    What the unsearchable dispose
    Of highest wisdom brings about,
    And ever best found in the close.
    1671 *Samson Agonistes*, l.1745–8.

5   Calm of mind, all passion spent.
    1671 *Samson Agonistes*, l.1758.

Min, Anchee 1957–

Chinese writer who left China for America in 1984. Her autobiography *Red Azalea* (1993) is named after Madame Mao's propaganda film in which Min was an actress.

6   My parents lived like—as the neighbours described them—a pair of chopsticks, always in harmony.
    1993 *Red Azalea*.

7   The Chairman looked dissatisfied lying on his death bed.
    1993 Of Mao Zedong. *Red Azalea*.

Mingus, Charles 1922–79

US composer and bass player. He was one of the great idiosyncratic geniuses of modern jazz, and his musical legacy is only now being fully absorbed.

8   Today musicians listen to see who makes the most money on a style, and then they set to copying him. And they don't copy the ones that are beautiful, creative and good.
    1977 Interview in Enstice and Rubin *Jazz Spoken Here* (1992).

Minot, Laurence d. c.1352

English poet.

9   War yit with the Skottes, for thai er ful of gile.
    early to mid 14c 'Skottes out of Berwik', l.6.

Minow, Newton Norman 1926–

US lawyer, author and communications executive. Named Chair of the Federal Communications Commission (1961–3) by President Kennedy, he was noted for his controversial criticism of television broadcasting standards in the US. Since 1987 he has been director of the Annenberg Washington Program in Communications Policy Studies of Northwestern University in Washington.

10 When television is good, nothing is better. When it's bad, nothing is worse.
    1961 Speech to the National Association of Broadcasters. Reported in the *New York Times*, 10 May.

11 You will observe a vast wasteland.
    1961 Speech to the National Association of Broadcasters, inviting them to watch a full day of television. Reported in the *New York Times*, 10 May.

Minsky, Marvin Lee 1927–

US computer scientist and artificial intelligence researcher.

12 Logic doesn't apply to the real world.
    1981 In Douglas R Hofstadter and Daniel C Dennett (eds) *The Mind's I: fantasies and reflections on self and soul*.

13 Every system that we build will surprise us with new kinds of flaws until those machines become clever enough to conceal their faults from us.
    2006 *The Emotion Machine*.

Mirabeau, Honoré Gabriel Riqueti, Comte de 1749–91

French revolutionary politician. After the publication of his *Essai sur le despotisme*, he was sentenced to death, but only served three years in prison. He espoused the Revolution, and died soon after he was elected President of the Assembly in 1791.

14 War is the national industry of Prussia.
    1788 Attributed to Mirabeau by Albert Sorel (1842–1906), suggested by Mirabeau's introduction to *De la monarchie prussienne sous Frédéric le Grand*.

15 We will only leave our places by the force of the bayonet!
    1789 Speech at the *Séance Royale*. Quoted in Webster *The French Revolution* (1919), p.50.

16 To administer is to govern; to govern is to reign. That is the problem.
    1790 Memorandum, 3 Jul.

Miró, Joán 1893–1983

Spanish painter, graphic artist and designer.

17 I will break their guitar.
    Of the Cubists and their reliance upon the still-life. Attributed in Saranne Alexandrian *Surrealist Art* (1970).

Mirren, Dame Helen Lydia 1945–
English actress.

18 She's very known, but she's also very unknown, seen a lot but never really looked at.
   2007 Referring to Elizabeth II, whom she played when she won an Oscar in *The Queen* (2006).

Mishan, E J 1917–2014
British economist.

19 If frequent teabreaks and other manifestations of disguised leisure are regarded as goods—and economics suggests that they be so regarded—their inclusion in any index of output per capita might go some way to enhance Britain's comparative performance.
   Quoted in Alex Rubner *Three Sacred Cows of Economics* (1970), p.47.

Mishima, Yukio *pseudonym of* Hiraoka Kimitake 1925–70
Japanese writer of novels, plays and short stories. A keen advocate of the chivalrous ideals of Imperial Japan, he committed suicide by performing *seppuku* after a token effort at rallying his country to the right-wing nationalist traditions of pre-war Japan.

20 Teachers—a bunch of men all armed with the same information.
   Acts of Worship, 'Cigarette' (translated by John Bester, 1989).

21 Held in the custody of childhood is a locked chest; the adolescent, by one means or another, tries to open it. the chest is opened: inside, there is nothing.
   Acts of Worship, 'Cigarette' (translated by John Bester, 1989).

22 He'd been mistaken in thinking that if he killed himself the sordid bourgeois world would perish with him.
   Acts of Worship, 'Raisin Bread' (translated by John Bester, 1989).

23 As he saw it, there was only one choice—to be strong and upright, or to commit suicide.
   Acts of Worship, 'Sword' (translated by John Bester, 1989).

24 Human beings...they go on being born and dying, dying and being born. It's kind of boring, isn't it?
   Acts of Worship, 'Sword' (translated by John Bester, 1989).

Mitchel, John 1815–75
Irish patriot. After starting the *United Irishman* (1848) he was tried for 'treason-felony' and transported, but in 1853 he escaped from Van Diemen's Land (Tasmania) to the USA. He returned to Ireland in 1874, and was elected to parliament but declared ineligible.

25 Surely, it is in youth man is most thoroughly depraved. Hell lies about us in our infancy. The youthful innocence sung by aged poets (who forget their first childhood) is nothing but ignorance of evil. As the child comes to know evil, he loves it.
   1849 In the *Jail Journal*, 13 Apr.

Mitchell, Adrian 1932–2008
English writer. His poetry was populist and political in nature. He also wrote novels, plays, and works for children.

26 Most people ignore most poetry because most poetry ignores most people.
   1964 *Poems*, introduction.

27 The man who believes in giraffes would swallow anything.
   1971 'Loose Leaf Poem'.

28 Poetry is an extra hand. It can caress or tickle. It can clench and fight.
   1972 'Poetry Lives', in the *Sunday Times*, 13 Feb.

Mitchell, Austin 1934–
English Labour politician.

29 Welcome to Britain's New Political Order. No passion... No Right. No Left. Just multi-hued blancmange.
   1999 In the *Observer*, 'Sayings of the Week', 11 Apr.

Mitchell, David Stephen 1969–
English novelist. His novels *number9dream* (2001) and *Cloud Atlas* (2004) were both shortlisted for the Booker Prize.

30 A book you finish reading is not the same book it was before you read it.
   2001 *number9dream*.

31 My life amounts to no more than one drop in a limitless ocean. Yet what is any ocean, but a multitude of drops?
   2004 *Cloud Atlas*.

32 Travel far enough, you meet yourself.
   2004 *Cloud Atlas*.

33 History admits no rules; only outcomes.
   2004 *Cloud Atlas*.

34 It's not just the person who fills a house, it's their I'll be back later!s, their toothbrushes and unused hats and coats, their belongingnesses.
   2006 *Black Swan Green*.

35 Trees're always a relief, after people.
   2006 *Black Swan Green*.

Mitchell, Joni (Roberta Joan) née Anderson 1943–
Canadian singer and songwriter. Her highly original and personal compositions made her a central figure in the folk movement of the 1960s. Her albums include *Ladies of the Canyon* (1970) and *Blue* (1971).

36 Woke up, it was a Chelsea morning, and the first thing that I knew
   There was milk and toast and honey and a bowl of oranges, too.
   And the sun poured in like butterscotch and stuck to all my senses.
   1967 'Chelsea Morning'.

37 Don't it always seem to go
   That you don't know what you've got
   Till it's gone.
   They paved paradise
   And put up a parking lot.
   1970 'Big Yellow Taxi'.

Mitchell, Margaret 1900–49
US writer. She worked as a journalist with the Atlanta *Constitution*. Her only novel, *Gone with the Wind* (written 1926–36, published 1936, Pulitzer Prize), rapidly became a bestseller and was made into a celebrated film in 1939.

38 I'm tired of everlastingly being unnatural and never doing anything I want to do...and I'm tired of pretending I don't know anything, so men can tell me things and feel important while they're doing it.
   1936 Scarlett O'Hara. *Gone with the Wind*, ch.5.

39 Land is the only thing in the world worth working for, worth fighting for, worth dying for, because it's the only thing that lasts. It will come to you, this love of the land.
1939 *Gone with the Wind.*

40 Young misses whut eats heavy mos' gener'ly doan never ketch husbands.
1936 Mammy. *Gone with the Wind*, ch.5.

41 Until you've lost your reputation, you never realize what a burden it was or what freedom really is.
1936 Rhett Butler. *Gone with the Wind*, ch.9.

42 I'm going to live through this, and when it's over, I'm never going to be hungry again. No, nor any of my folks. If I have to steal or kill—as God is my witness, I'm never going to be hungry again.
1936 Scarlett O'Hara. *Gone with the Wind*, ch.25.

43 Fighting is like champagne. It goes to the heads of cowards as quickly as of heroes. Any fool can be brave on a battlefield when it's be brave or else be killed.
1936 Ashley Wilkes. *Gone with the Wind*, ch.31.

44 Southerners can never resist a losing cause.
1936 Rhett Butler. *Gone with the Wind*, ch.34.

45 Death and taxes and childbirth! There's never any convenient time for any of them!
1936 Scarlett O'Hara. *Gone with the Wind*, ch.38.

46 What is broken is broken, and I'd rather remember it as it was at its best than mend it and see broken places as long as I lived... I wish I could care what you do or where you go, but I can't. My dear, I don't give a damn.
1936 Rhett Butler's parting speech to Scarlett O'Hara. *Gone with the Wind*, ch.63; the more famous version of the final line from the film script by Sidney Howard (1939, spoken by Clark Gable) ran 'Frankly, my dear, I don't give a damn'.

47 Tomorrow, I'll think of some other way to get him back. After all, tomorrow is another day.
1936 Scarlett O'Hara's final words. *Gone with the Wind*, ch.63.

Mitchell, Warren 1926–
English actor.

48 You don't retire in this business. You just notice that the phone has not rung for ten years.
2000 In *The Guardian*, 31 Dec.

Mitford, Mary Russell 1787–1855
English novelist and dramatist, best known for her sketches of country manners, scenery and character that were collected as *Our Village* (1824–32). Other publications include *Recollections of a Literary Life* (1852).

49 To think of playing cricket for hard cash! Money and gentility would ruin any pastime under the sun.
1823 Letter to R B Haydon, 24 Aug.

50 Who would think that a little bit of leather, and two pieces of wood, had such a delightful and delighting power!
1824–32 *Our Village.*

Mitford, Nancy Freeman 1904–73
English writer. A daughter of the aristocracy, she achieved a considerable reputation for her witty novels.

51 Like all the very young we took it for granted that making love is child's play.
1945 *The Pursuit of Love*, ch.3.

52 Aunt Sadie...so much disliked hearing about health that people often took her for a Christian Scientist, which, indeed, she might have become had she not disliked hearing about religion even more.
1945 *The Pursuit of Love*, ch.4.

53 I have only ever read one book in my life, and that is *White Fang*. It's so frightfully good I've never bothered to read another.
1945 *The Pursuit of Love*, ch.9.

54 Abroad is unutterably bloody and foreigners are fiends.
1945 Uncle Matthew. *The Pursuit of Love*, ch.15.

55 'Always be civil to the girls, you never know who they may marry' is an aphorism which has saved many an English spinster from being treated like an Indian widow.
1949 *Love in a Cold Climate*, pt.1, ch.2.

56 'Twenty three and a quarter minutes past,' Uncle Matthew was saying furiously, 'in precisely six and three-quarter minutes the damned fella will be late.'
1949 *Love in a Cold Climate*, pt.1, ch.13.

57 When the loo paper gets thicker and the writing paper thinner, it's always a bad sign, at home.
1949 *Love in a Cold Climate*, pt.2, ch.2.

58 An aristocracy in a republic is like a chicken whose head has been cut off: it may run about in a lively way, but in fact it is dead.
1956 *Noblesse Oblige.*

Mitsuharu, Kaneko 1895–1975
Japanese poet, noted for his unconventionality. He spent a number of years in Belgium and France and wrote a poem, 'Awa' ('Foam'), about Japanese atrocities in China.

59 The sky snivels green snot.
There is war.
c.1938 *Shijin* (Poet), 'Awa' (translated by A R Davies, 1988).

Mizner, Wilson 1876–1933
US dramatist and wit.

60 Be nice to people on your way up because you'll meet them on your way down.
Quoted in A Johnston *The Legendary Mizners* (1953).

61 Working for Warner Brothers was like fucking a porcupine—it's a hundred pricks against one.
Quoted in David Niven *Bring on the Empty Horses* (1975).

62 A trip through a sewer in a glass-bottomed boat.
1979 Of life in Hollywood. Quoted in Gary Herman *The Book of Hollywood Quotes* (1979).

Mo Yan *pseudonym of* Guan Moye 1955–
Chinese writer and the winner of nearly all the prestigious literary awards in China. He has written a number of novels. *Red Sorghum* (1993), his fourth novel, is set principally during the 1930s when Japanese forces occupied the country. In 2012 he was awarded the Nobel prize in Literature.

63 Words spoken on the road are heard by snakes in the grass.
1993 *Red Sorghum* (translated by Howard Goldblatt).

64 Where there's life, death is inevitable. Dying's easy; it's living that's hard. The harder it gets, the stronger the will to live. And the greater the fear of death, the greater the struggle to keep on living.
1996 *Big Breasts and Wide Hips*, first English publication, 2005.

Mo, Timothy 1950–

British novelist. He was born in Hong Kong, and achieved prominence with *Sour Sweet*, set in the Chinese community in London.

65 The Chens had been living in the UK for four years, which was long enough to have lost their place in the society from which they had emigrated but not long enough to feel comfortable in the new.
   1982 *Sour Sweet*, opening words.

66 It's all honourable enough in its way, but it creates societies which simply cannot sustain any kind of democratic structure. It always leads to totalitarian and corrupt tyrannies... There's no tradition of moral individual courage in Chinese culture.
   1982 Of Chinese tradition. In *The Fiction Magazine*, vol.1, no.4.

67 The assaying of tea is an art and not a science. It is the man, and not his instruments, which is the most important. There can be no substitute for my experience and intuited knowledge.
   1986 *An Insular Possession*, ch.4.

68 I see you belong to the category, old friend, which will have things in the round, which does love an end, causes, the balance sheet drawn and equalled. But, my dear Gid, the world is not like that—it *is* untidy, there are no reasons, the final sum never balances.
   1986 *An Insular Possession*, ch.44.

69 There's no such thing as a hero—only ordinary people asked extraordinary things in terrible circumstances —and delivering.
   1991 *The Redundancy of Courage*, ch.30.

Modersohn-Becker, Paula née Becker 1876–1907

German painter, a member of the Worpswede artists' colony near Bremen and an early Expressionist. In her later works naturalism gives way to simple forms and strong lyrical colour. She died soon after the birth of her first child.

70 In art one is usually totally alone with oneself.
   1906 Diary entry, Paris, 18 Nov, quoted in Gillian Perry *Paula Modersohn-Becker* (1979).

Mola, Emilio 1887–1937

Spanish general, a nationalist leader during the Spanish Civil War.

71 *La quinta columna.*
   The fifth column.
   1936 Speech, Oct. Of the rebel sympathizers within Madrid who would help the four columns of nationalist rebels besieging it. Quoted in Hugh Thomas *The Spanish Civil War* (1961), ch.4, p.317.

Molière, Jean Baptiste Poquelin 1622–73

French actor and playwright who formed a theatrical company in 1643 and toured the provinces until 1658. He gained the patronage of the Duc d'Orléans and later of Louis XIV.

72 *On ne meurt qu'une fois, et c'est pour si longtemps!*
   We only die once; and it's for such a long time!
   1656 *Le dépit amoureux*, act 5, sc.3.

73 *Hors de Paris, il n'y a point de salut pour les honnêtes gens.*
   Outside of Paris, there is no salvation for gentlemen.
   1659 *Les précieuses ridicules*, sc.9.

74 *Les verrous et les grilles
   Ne font pas la vertu des femmes ni des filles.*
   Bolts and bars will not keep wives and daughters chaste.
   1661 *L'École des maris*, act 1, sc.2.

75 *Le siècle s'encanaille furieusement.*
   Our times have become vulgar.
   1663 *La critique de l'École des femmes*, sc.6.

76 *Je voudrais bien savoir si la grande règle de toutes les règles n'est pas de plaire.*
   I shouldn't be surprised if the greatest rule of all weren't to give pleasure.
   1663 *La critique de l'École des femmes*, sc.6.

77 *Le Ciel défend, de vrai, certains contentements;
   Mais on trouve avec lui des accommodements.*
   True, heaven forbids us certain pleasures;
   But we always find a way to arrange things.
   1664 *Le Tartuffe*, act 4, sc.5.

78 *Le scandale du monde est ce qui fait l'offense,
   Et ce n'est pas pécher que pécher en silence.*
   A scandal is that which gives offence to the world.
   To sin in private is not to sin at all.
   1664 *Le Tartuffe*, act 4, sc.5.

79 *Qui vit sans tabac n'est pas digne de vivre.*
   Anyone who lives without tobacco is not worthy of living.
   1665 *Dom Juan*, act 1, sc.1.

80 *La naissance n'est rien où la vertu n'est pas.*
   Birth counts for little when virtue is lacking.
   1665 *Dom Juan*, act 4, sc.4.

81 *L'ami du genre humain n'est point du tout mon fait.*
   I have no use at all for the friend of mankind.
   1666 *Le misanthrope*, act 1, sc.1.

82 *J'aime mieux un vice commode
   Qu'une fatigante vertu.*
   I prefer easygoing vice to tiresome virtue.
   1668 *Amphitryon*, act 1, sc.4.

83 *Quand il y a à manger pour huit, il y en a bien pour dix.*
   When there is enough food for eight, there is enough for ten.
   1668 *L'Avare*, act 3, sc.1.

84 *Il faut manger pour vivre, et non pas vivre pour manger.*
   One should eat to live, not live to eat.
   1668 *L'Avare*, act 3, sc.1.

85 *Ils commencent ici par faire pendre un homme, et puis ils lui font son procès.*
   Here they hang a men first, and try him afterwards.
   1669 In Paris. *Monsieur de Pourceaugnac*, act 3, sc.2.

86 *Par ma foi! il y a plus de quarante ans que je dis de la prose sans que j'en susse rien!*
   Good heavens! I've been speaking prose for forty years without knowing it!
   1670 *Le bourgeois gentilhomme*, act 2, sc.4.

87 *La grammaire qui sait régenter jusqu'aux rois.*
   Even kings must bow to grammar.
   1672 *Les femmes savantes*, act 2, sc.6.

88 *Je vis de bonne soupe, et non de beau langage.*
   It's good food and not fine words that keeps me alive.
   1672 *Les femmes savantes*, act 2, sc.7.

89 *Un sot savant est sot plus qu'un sot ignorant.*
A learned fool is more foolish than an ignorant fool.
1672 *Les femmes savantes*, act 4, sc.3.

90 *Presque tous les hommes meurent de leurs remèdes, et non de leurs maladies.*
Almost all men die from their medicines and not from their illnesses.
1673 *Le malade imaginaire*, act 3, sc.3.

91 We reason with one another; he prescribes the remedies; I omit to take them and I recover.
On his relationship with his doctor, Mauvillan, in the presence of Louis XIV. Quoted in Vincent Cronin *Louis XIV* (1964), p.291.

Moltke, Helmuth von, Count 1800–91
Prussian general. Chief of the General Staff of the Prussian army 1858—88. He presided over successful wars with Denmark (1863–4), Austria (1866) and France (1870–1).

92 Everlasting peace is a dream, and not even a pleasant one; and war is a necessary part of God's arrangement with the world... Without war the world would deteriorate into materialism.
1880 Letter to Dr J K Bluntschi, 11 Dec, collected in *Helmuth von Moltke as a Correspondent* (1893).

93 What our sword has won in half a year, our sword must guard for half a century.
1891 *The Franco-Prussian War of 1870–71*.

Mondale, Walter F(rederick) 1928–
US Democratic politician and lawyer. He served under President Carter as Vice-President (1977–81), and was the Democratic nominee for President in 1984, when he lost to Ronald Reagan. He was US Ambassador to Japan (1993–6).

94 I don't want to spend the next two years in Holiday Inns.
1976 On withdrawing from the presidential campaign.

95 In our system, at about 11.30pm on election night, they just push you off the edge of the cliff—and that's it. You might scream on the way down, but you're going to hit the bottom, and you're not going to be in office.
1984 On losing to Ronald Reagan in the presidential elections, in the *New York Times*, 4 Mar.

Mondrian, Piet 1872–1944
Dutch painter, one of the most important artists in the development of abstract painting.

96 I hate everything approaching temperamental inspiration, 'sacred fire' and all those attributes of genius which serve only as cloaks for untidy minds.
Quoted in F Elgar *Mondrian* (1968).

97 Why should art continue to follow nature when every other field has left nature behind?
Quoted in F Elgar *Mondrian* (1968).

98 The unconscious in us warns us that in art we have to follow one particular path. And if we follow it, it is not the sign of an unconscious act. On the contrary, it shows that there is in our ordinary consciousness a greater awareness of our unconsciousness.
Quoted in F Elgar *Mondrian* (1968).

Monet, Claude 1840–1926
French Impressionist painter. One of the creators of Impressionism, it was his *Impression: soleil levant* (1872) that gave the movement its name. He spent the last years of his life as a recluse in Giverny.

99 When you go out to paint, try to forget what objects you have before you—a tree, a house, a field, or whatever. Merely think, here is a little square of blue, here an oblong of pink, here a streak of yellow, and paint it just as it looks to you, the exact colour and shape, until it gives your own naive impression of the scene before you.
Attributed, in reminiscences written in 1927 by the young American artist Lilla Cabot Perry.

1 It was as if a veil had been torn suddenly away; I had understood, I had grasped what painting could be.
After painting with the artist Boudin in the open air. Quoted in J Isaacson *Claude Monet* (1978).

Monod, Jacques 1910–76
French biologist and author. He proposed (1961) the concepts of messenger RNA. He shared the 1965 Nobel prize in physiology or medicine.

2 There are living systems; there is no 'living matter'.
1967 Lecture, College of France.

3 The scientific attitude implies...the postulate of objectivity—that is to say, the fundamental postulate that there is no plan; that there is no intention in the universe.
1970 *Le Hasard et la Necéssité*.

Monro, Harold Edward 1879–1932
English poet. He founded the influential *Poetry Review* in 1912. A *Collected Poems* appeared in 1933.

4 When the tea is brought at five o'clock,
And all the neat curtains are drawn with care,
The little black cat with bright green eyes
Is suddenly purring there.
1914 'Milk for the Cat'.

5 The white saucer like some full moon descends
At last from the clouds of the table above.
1914 'Milk for the Cat'.

Monroe, Marilyn pseudonym of Norma Jean Baker 1926–62
US film actress. Her sex appeal was exploited in films such as *How to Marry a Millionaire* and *Gentlemen Prefer Blondes* (both 1953), but she went on to light comedy (eg *Some Like It Hot*, 1959) and more serious roles such as *The Misfits* (1961), written by her third husband, Arthur Miller. Her suicide made her an icon, and a symbol of Hollywood's ruthlessness.

6 He's not a director, he's a dictator.
c.1959 On Billy Wilder, the director of *Some Like It Hot*, attributed.

7 He's the only person I know who's in worse shape than I am.
1961 On Montgomery Clift, her co-star in *The Misfits*.

Montagu, (Alexander) Victor Edward Paulet 1906–95
Conservative politician, private secretary to Stanley Baldwin (1932–4) and chairman of the Tory Reform Committee (1943–4). He succeeded as 10th Earl of Sandwich in 1962 but disclaimed his peerage for life the next year. His publications include *The Conservative Dilemma* (1970).

8 Lord Hailsham said the other day that the machinery of Government was creaking. My Lords, it is not even moving sufficiently to emit a noise of any kind.
1963 House of Lords, 20 Apr, shortly before disclaiming his peerage.

Montagu, Ashley *originally Israel Ehrenberg* 1905–99

English-born US anthropologist, author of a number of scholarly and popular works. He has been closely associated with the view that cultural phenomena are not the result of genetics.

9 As the god of contemporary man's idolatry, science is a two-handed engine, and as such science is too important a human activity to leave to the scientists.
1964 Book review in the *New York Times*, 26 Apr.

Montagu, Lady Mary Wortley *née Pierrepoint* 1689–1762

English writer and socialite. She accompanied her ambassador husband to Constantinople (1716–18), writing there many entertaining letters. She introduced smallpox inoculation into England, and settled in Italy with her husband in 1739.

10 'Tis certain we have but very imperfect accounts of the manners and religion of these people; this part of the world being seldom visited, but by merchants, who mind little but their own affairs; or travellers, who make too short a stay to be able to report anything exactly of their own knowledge.
c.1716 Of Turkey. Collected in Lord Wharncliffe (ed) *The Letters and Works of Lady Mary Wortley Montagu* (1837).

11 Thus you see, Sir, that these people are not so unpolished as we represent them. 'Tis true, their magnificence is of a different taste from ours, and perhaps of a better. I am almost of opinion, they have a right notion of life. They consume it in music, gardens, wine, and delicate eating, while we are tormenting our brains with some scheme of politics, or studying some science to which we can never attain, or, if we do, cannot persuade other people to set that value upon it we do ourselves... We die or grow old before we can reap the fruit of our labours. Considering what short-lived weak animals men are, is there any study so beneficial as the study of present pleasure?
c.1716 Collected in Lord Wharncliffe (ed) *The Letters and Works of Lady Mary Wortley Montagu* (1837).

12 I was here convinced of the truth of a reflection I had often made, that if it was the fashion to go naked, the face would be hardly observed.
c.1716 In a Turkish bath in Sofia. Collected in Lord Wharncliffe (ed) *The Letters and Works of Lady Mary Wortley Montagu* (1837).

13 If your daughters are inclined to love reading, do not check their inclination by hindering them of the diverting part of it. It is as necessary for the amusement of women as the reputation of men; but teach them not to expect any applause from it... Ignorance is as much the fountain of vice as idleness, and indeed generally produces it. People that do not read or work for a livelihood have many hours they know not how to employ, especially women, who commonly fall into vapours or something worse.
1750 Letter, Jan. Collected in R Halsband (ed) *Selected Letters of Lady Mary Wortley Montagu* (1970).

14 Their whole business abroad (as far as I can perceive) being to buy new clothes, in which they shine in some obscure coffee-house, where they are sure of meeting only one-another... I look upon them as the greatest blockheads.
1763 On those making the Grand Tour. Quoted in Eric Newby (ed) *A Book of Travellers' Tales* (1985).

Montague, C(harles) E(dward) 1867–1928

English novelist and essayist of Irish parentage. He wrote various novels, a collection of essays and many articles for the *Manchester Guardian* (1890–1925).

15 War hath no fury like a non-combatant.
1922 *Disenchantment*, ch.16.
▶ See Congreve 251.52.

16 I was born below par to the extent of two whiskies.
1923 'Fiery Particles'.

17 The Swiss are inspired hotel-keepers. Some centuries since, when the stranger strayed into one of their valleys, their simple forefathers would kill him and share out the little money he might have about him. Now they know better. They keep him alive and writing cheques.
1926 *The Right Place*.

Montaigne, Michel Eyquem de 1533–92

French essayist. He was a city counsellor of Bordeaux and later its Mayor. From 1571 he lived the life of a country gentleman and started composing his *Essais* (1580), a classic of French literature.

18 *Certes, c'est un sujet merveilleusement vain, divers et ondoyant, que l'homme.*
Man (in good earnest) is a marvellous vain, fickle, and unstable subject.
1580 *Essais*, bk.1, ch.1 (translated by Charles Cotton).

19 *Il faut estre tousjours boté et prest à partir.*
We should always be booted and spurred, and ready to go.
1580 *Essais*, bk.1, ch.20 (translated by Charles Cotton).

20 *Que la mort me trouve plantant mes choux, mais nonchalant d'elle, et encore plus de mon jardin imparfait.*
I would like death to come to me while I am planting cabbages, caring little for death and even less for the imperfection of my garden.
1580 *Essais*, bk.1, ch.20 (translated by Charles Cotton).

21 *Si on me presse de dire pourquoy je l'aymois, je sens que cela ne se peut exprimer, qu'en respondant: 'Parce que c'estoit luy; par ce que c'estoit moy.'*
If a man should importune me to give a reason why I loved him, I find it could no otherwise be expressed, than by making answer: because it was he, because it was I.
1580 *Essais*, bk.1, ch.28 (translated by Charles Cotton).

22 *Or la fin, ce crois-je, en est tout'une, d'en vivre plus à loisir et à son aise.*
Now the end, I take it, is all one, to live at more leisure and at one's ease.
1580 *Essais*, bk.1, ch.39 (translated by Charles Cotton).

23 *Il se faut reserver une arriere boutique toute nostre, toute franche, en laquelle nous establissons nostre vraye liberté et principale retraite et solitude.*
We must reserve a backshop, wholly our own and

entirely free, wherein to settle our true liberty, our principle solitude and retreat.
1580 *Essais*, bk.1, ch.39 (translated by Charles Cotton).

24 *La plus grande chose du monde, c'est de sçavoir estre à soy.*
The greatest thing in the world is for a man to know that he is his own.
1580 *Essais*, bk.1, ch.39 (translated by Charles Cotton).

25 *La gloire et le repos sont choses qui ne peuvent loger en mesme giste.*
Fame and tranquillity are two things that can't live under the same roof.
1580 *Essais*, bk.1, ch.39 (translated by Charles Cotton).

26 *Mon mestier et mon art, c'est vivre.*
My trade and art is to live.
1580 *Essais*, bk.2, ch.6 (translated by Charles Cotton).

27 *Quand je me jouë à ma chatte, qui sçait si elle passe son temps de moy plus que je ne fay d'elle?*
When I play with my cat, who knows whether I do not make her more sport than she makes me?
1580 *Essais*, bk.2, ch.12 (translated by Charles Cotton).

28 *L'homme est bien insensé. Il ne sçauroit forger un ciron, et forge des Dieux à douzaines.*
Man is quite insane. He wouldn't know how to make a maggot, and he makes Gods by the dozen.
1580 *Essais*, bk.2, ch.12 (translated by Charles Cotton).

29 *Nous veillons dormants, et veillants dormons.*
We wake sleeping, and sleep waking.
1580 *Essais*, bk.2, ch.12 (translated by Charles Cotton).

30 *Il n'y a point de fin en nos inquisitions. Nostre fin est en l'autre monde.*
There is no end to our researches; our end is in the other world.
1588 *Essays*, bk.3, ch.13 (translated by Donald M Frame).

31 *Nous sommes par tout vent.*
We are all wind throughout.
1588 *Essais*, bk.3, ch.13 (translated by Charles Cotton).

32 *Nostre grand et glorieux chef-d'iuvre, c'est vivre à propos.*
The great and glorious masterpiece of man is to know how to live to purpose.
1588 *Essais*, bk.3, ch.13 (translated by Charles Cotton).

Montcalm, Marquis de 1712–59

French Governor of Quebec, who unsuccessfully defended the city against General Wolfe's English troops in the Battle of the Plains of Abraham, 13 Sep 1759.

33 I am happy that I shall not live to see the surrender of Quebec.
1759 Spoken to his aides, 13 Sep. He died the following day. Quoted in Francis Parkman *Montcalm and Wolfe* (1884).

Monterroso, Augusto 1921–2003

Guatemalan writer who lived in exile in Mexico from 1944. His works are mainly collections of short stories in which paradox and a whimsical sense of humour are prominent.

34 *La Historia no se detiene nunca. Día y noche su marcha es incesante. Querer detenerla sería como querer detener la Geografía.*
History never stops. It progresses ceaselessly day and night. Trying to stop it is like trying to stop Geography.

1978 *Lo demás es silencio* ('The Rest is Silence'),'Aforismos, dichos, etc'.

Montesquieu, Charles Louis de Secondat, Baron de la Brède et de 1689–1755

French philosopher and jurist, who turned from law to scientific research and literary work. His study of legal and social issues *De l'Esprit des lois* (1748, 'The Spirit of Laws') was very influential in 18c Europe.

35 *Si l'on vient à savoir mon nom, dès ce moment je me tais. Je connais une femme qui marche assez bien, mais qui boite dès qu'on la regarde.*
Once someone wants to know my name, I become quiet. I know a woman who walks rather well, but who limps once she sees someone watching her.
1721 *Lettres persanes*, introduction.

36 *Il n'y a jamais eu de royaume où il y ait eu tant de guerres civiles que dans celui du Christ.*
No kingdom has ever been so divided by civil wars as that of Christ.
1721 *Lettres persanes*, no.29.

37 *Il faut pleurer les hommes à leur naissance, et non pas à leur mort.*
A person should be mourned at his birth, not at his death.
1721 *Lettres persanes*, no.40.

38 *Si les triangles faisaient un dieu, ils lui donneraient trois côtés.*
If triangles had made a god, it would have three sides.
1721 *Lettres persanes*, no.59.

39 *Le droit des gens est naturellement fondé sur ce principe: que les diverses nations doivent se faire, dans la paix, le plus de bien, et, dans la guerre, le moins de mal qu'il est possible, sans nuire à leurs véritables intérêts.*
Law is naturally founded on this principle: that different nations should do, in peace and as far as best as they can in war, the least harm as possible, without harming their true interests.
1748 *De l'esprit des lois*, vol.1, ch.3.

40 *Le gouvernement est comme toutes les choses du monde; pour le conserver, il faut l'aimer.*
Government is like everything else in the world; to conserve it, we must love it.
1748 *De l'esprit des lois*, vol.4, ch.5.

41 *L'amour de la démocratie est celui de l'égalité.*
Love of democracy is love of equality.
1748 *De l'esprit des lois*, vol.5, ch.3.

42 *Les républiques finissent par le luxe; les monarchies, par la pauvreté.*
Republics end by wealth; monarchies end by poverty.
1748 *De l'esprit des lois*, vol.7, ch.4.

43 *La liberté est le droit de faire tout ce que les lois permettent.*
Freedom is the right to do anything the laws permit.
1748 *De l'esprit des lois*, vol.11, ch.3.

44 *Il en est de la luxure comme de l'avarice: elle augmente sa soif par l'acquisition des trésors.*
The same rule applies for lust, as for avarice: it increases its thirst by the acquisition of wealth.
1748 *De l'esprit des lois*, vol.16, ch.6.

45 *Le divorce a ordinairement une grande utilité politique; et quant à l'utilité civile, il est établi pour le mari et pour la femme, et n'est pas toujours favorable aux enfants.*

Divorce generally has a great political use; as for its civil use, it is established for the husband and wife and is not always favourable to the children.
1748 *De l'esprit des lois*, vol.16, ch.15.

46 *Les lois inutiles affaiblissent les lois nécessaires.*
Useless laws weaken the necessary ones.
1748 *De l'esprit des lois*, vol.29, ch.16.

Montgomery of Alamein, Bernard Law, 1st Viscount 1887–1976

British field marshal. He led the 8th Army in World War II, defeating Rommel at El Alamein (1942), and was Commander-in-Chief of Allied ground forces for the invasion of Normandy (1944), Chief of the Imperial General Staff (1946–8) and Supreme Commander of Nato forces in Europe (1951–8).

47 Rule 1, on page 1 of the book of war is: 'Do not march on Moscow'... [Rule 2] is: 'Do not go fighting with your land armies in China.'
1962 Speech in the House of Lords, 30 May.

Montgomery, L(ucy) M(aud) 1874–1942

Canadian novelist. Her first book was the phenomenally successful *Anne of Green Gables* (1908), the story of an orphan girl adopted in error for a boy by an elderly brother and sister. She followed it with several sequels.

48 The point of good writing is knowing when to stop.
1917 *Anne's House of Dreams*, ch.24.

Montrose, James Graham, 1st Marquis of 1612–50

Scottish soldier and poet, who, after first supporting the National Covenant in 1638, fought a brilliant campaign for Charles I during the Civil War from 1644 to 1645. Captured in 1650 after an abortive attempt to win Scotland for Charles II, he was hanged in Edinburgh.

49 My dear and only love, I pray
That little world of thee
Be governed by no other sway
Than purest monarchy.
c.1642 'My Dear and Only Love', stanza 1.

50 He either fears his fate too much,
Or his deserts are small,
That dares not put it to the touch,
To gain or lose it all.
c.1642 'My Dear and Only Love', stanza 2.

51 Let them bestow on every airth a limb,
Then open all my veins that I may swim
To thee, my Maker, in that crimson lake;
Then place my parboiled head upon a stake,
Scatter my ashes, strew them in the air—
Lord! since thou knowest where all these atoms are,
I'm hopeful thou'lt recover once my dust,
And confident thou'lt raise me with the just.
1650 'Lines Composed on the Eve of his Execution'.

Moodie, Susanna née Strickland 1803–85

English-born Canadian writer of fiction, non-fiction, poetry and letters. She reluctantly emigrated to Canada with her husband in 1832 and wrote for many magazines but is best remembered for *Roughing it in the Bush* (1852) and *Life in the Clearing, versus the Bush* (1853).

52 Dear husband! I take shame to myself that my purpose was less firm, that my heart lingered so far behind yours in preparing for this great epoch in our lives; that like Lot's wife, I still turned and looked back, and clung with all my strength to the land I was leaving. It was not the hardships of an emigrant's life I dreaded. I could bear mere physical privations philosophically enough; it was the loss of society in which I had moved, the want of congenial minds, of persons engaged in congenial pursuits, that made me so reluctant to respond to my husband's call.
1852 *Roughing It in the Bush; or, A Life in Canada*, vol.1, ch.11, 'The Charivari'.

53 Speaking of the coldness of one particular day, a genuine brother Jonathan remarked, with charming simplicity, that it was thirty degrees below zero that morning, and it would have been much colder if the thermometer had been longer.
1852 'Brother Jonathan' refers to a typical Yankee. *Roughing It in the Bush; or, A Life in Canada*, vol.2, ch.9, 'The Fire'.

54 If these sketches should prove the means of deterring one family from sinking their property, and shipwrecking all their hopes, by going to reside in the backwoods of Canada, I shall consider myself amply repaid for revealing the secrets of the prison-house, and feel that I have not toiled and suffered in the wilderness in vain.
1852 *Roughing It in the Bush; or, A Life in Canada*, vol.2, ch.14, 'Adieu to the Woods'.

55 In most instances, emigration is a matter of necessity, not of choice.
1854 *Roughing It in the Bush; or, A Life in Canada*, introduction to the 3rd edition.

56 Will they ever forgive me for writing *Roughing It*? They know that it was the truth, but have I not been a mark for every vulgar editor of a village journal, throughout the length and breadth of the land to hurl a stone at, and point out as the enemy to Canada.
1856 Letter to her publisher, Richard Bentley, 19 Aug.

Moody, William Vaughn 1869–1910

US poet and playwright. He taught at the University of Chicago. His best-known prose play, *The Sabine Woman* (1906), was highly successful and focuses on the contrast between a puritanical woman and a free-thinking man. It was retitled *The Great Divide* (1909).

57 A man's a fool to look at things too near:
They look back, and begin to cut up queer.
1901 'The Menagerie'.

Moore, Brian 1921–99

Northern Irish-born writer, who emigrated to Canada in 1948, and also lived in California and New York. His first novel, *The Lonely Passion of Judith Hearne* (1955), was filmed in 1989. Later works include *Black Robe* (1985, filmed 1991), *Lies of Silence* (1990) and *The Statement* (1995).

58 He bathes daily in a running tap of words.
1987 Of a military colonel's desk work. *The Color of Blood*.

Moore, Charles W(illard) 1925–93

US architect, Professor of Architecture at UCLA, California (1975–85). His writings include *The Place of Houses* (1974) and *The Poetics of Gardens* (1988).

59 You bind the goods and trappings of your life together with your dreams to make a place that is uniquely your own.
   1974 *The Place of Houses,* introduction.

Moore, Clement 1779–1863

US writer and poet.

60 'Twas the night before Christmas, when all through the house
   Not a creature was stirring, not even a mouse.
   1822 *The Night Before Christmas.*

61 The stockings were hung by the chimney with care,
   In hopes that St. Nicholas soon would be there;
   The children were nestled all snug in their beds,
   While visions of sugarplums danced in their heads.
   1822 *The Night Before Christmas.*

62 The moon on the breast of the new-fallen snow,
   Gave the lustre of midday to objects below,
   When, what to my wondering eyes should appear,
   But a miniature sleigh, and eight tiny reindeer.
   1822 *The Night Before Christmas.*

63 More rapid than eagles his coursers they came,
   And he whistled, and shouted, and called them by name;
   'Now, *Dasher!* Now, *Dancer!* Now, *Prancer* and *Vixen!*
   On, *Comet!* On, *Cupid!* On, *Donder* and *Blitzen!*
   To the top of the porch! To the top of the wall!
   Now dash away! Dash away! Dash away all!'
   1822 *The Night Before Christmas.*

64 He was dressed all in fur, from his head to his foot,
   And his clothes were all tarnished with ashes and soot;
   A bundle of toys he had flung on his back,
   And he looked like a pedlar just opening his pack.
   1822 *The Night Before Christmas.*

65 He sprang to his sleigh, to his team gave a whistle,
   And away they all flew like the down of a thistle.
   But I heard him exclaim, ere he drove out of sight,
   'Happy Christmas to all. And to all a good night.'
   1822 *The Night Before Christmas.*

Moore, G(eorge) E(dward) 1873–1958

English Empiricist philosopher. He studied and taught at Cambridge, where he was Professor of Mental Philosophy and Logic (1925–39). His most famous and influential work was *Principia Ethica* (1903).

66 'Good', then, if we mean by it that quality which we assert to belong to a thing, when we say that the thing is good, is incapable of any definition, in the most important sense of the word.
   1903 *Principia Ethica,* ch.1.

67 By far the most valuable things, which we know or can imagine, are certain states of consciousness, which may be roughly described as the pleasures of human intercourse and the enjoyment of beautiful objects.
   1903 *Principia Ethica,* ch.6.

Moore, George 1852–1933

Irish novelist, poet and playwright. A co-founder of the Irish Literary Theatre with W B Yeats, he collaborated with Yeats on such poetic dramas as *The Bending of the Bough* (1900) and *Diarmuid and Grania* (1901).

68 A year passed; a year of art and dissipation—one part art, two parts dissipation. We mounted and descended at pleasure the rounds of society's ladder.
   1870 *Confessions of a Young Man* (published 1888).

69 Acting is therefore the lowest of the arts, if it be an art at all.
   1891 *Impressions and Opinions,* 'Mummer-Worship'.

Moore, Henry Spencer 1898–1986

English sculptor and graphic artist. He travelled widely in Europe and was an official war artist (1940–2). His sculptures, mainly semi-abstract figures and groups, are influenced by landscape forms and primitive art.

70 Sculpture in stone should look honestly like stone…to make it look like flesh and blood, hair and dimples is coming down to the level of the stage conjuror.
   1930 In the *Architectural Association Journal.*

Moore, Jo 1963–

British political adviser.

71 It's now a very good day to get out anything we want to bury.
   2001 E-mail sent on 11 Sep, after hijacked planes destroyed the World Trade Center in New York.

Moore, John 1729–1802

Scottish physician and writer. He travelled with Douglas, Duke of Hamilton (1772–8), writing accounts of these journeys, then settled in London. His novel *Zeluco* (1789) was the inspiration for Byron's *Childe Harold.*

72 There is no manner of doubt that a town surrounded by water is a very fine sight; but a town surrounded by land is much finer. Can there be any comparison in point of beauty, between the dull monotony of a watery surface, and the delightful variety of gardens, meadows, hills and woods ?
   c.1780 *A View of Society and Manners in Italy.*

Moore, Lorrie 1957–

US writer. Her writings, such as *Who Will Run the Frog Hospital?* (1994), *Birds of America* (1998) and *Bark: Stories* (2014), include novels and short stories.

73 Literature…is lonely and waited for, brilliant and pure and frightened, a marriage of birds, a conversation of the blind.
   1988 In the *New York Times,* 10 Jul.

74 Love is the answer, said the songs, and that's OK. It was OK, I supposed, as an answer. But no more than that. It was not a solution; it wasn't really even an answer, just a reply.
   2009 *A Gate at the Stairs.*

75 You emptied the top rack of the dishwasher but not the bottom, so the clean dishes have gotten all mixed up with the dirty ones—and now you want to have sex?
   2009 *A Gate at the Stairs.*

Moore, Marianne Craig 1887–1972

US poet, whose crisp language, wit and idiosyncratic style established her as a leading literary figure. Her works include *Observations* (1924, rev 1925), *Collected Poems* (1951, Pulitzer Prize) and *Complete Poems* (1967, rev 1981).

76 It comes to this: of whatever sort it is,
   it must be 'lit with piercing glances into the life of things';
   it must acknowledge the spiritual forces which have made it.
   1921 *Poems*, 'When I Buy Pictures'.

77 I, too, dislike it: there are things that are important beyond all this fiddle.
   Reading it, however, with a perfect contempt for it, one discovers in
   it, after all, a place for the genuine.
   1921 *Poems*, 'Poetry'.

78 If 'compression is the first grace of style,'
   you have it.
   1924 *Observations*, 'To A Snail'.

79 My father used to say,
   'Superior people never make long visits,
   have to be shown Longfellow's grave
   or the glass flowers at Harvard.'
   1924 *Observations*, 'Silence'.

80 Nor was he insincere in saying, 'Make my house your inn.'
   Inns are not residences.
   1924 *Observations*, 'Silence'.

81 You are menaced by the goodness of your mechanics.
   1937 To fellow-poet Elizabeth Bishop. Quoted in David Kalstone *Becoming a Poet* (1989), p.57.

82 A place as kind as it is green,
   the greenest place I've never seen.
   Every name is a tune.
   1941 *What Are Years*, 'Spencer's Ireland'.

83 I do not write for money or fame... One writes because one has a burning desire to objectify what it is indispensible to one's happiness to express.
   1956 Ewing Lecture, University of California, 3 Oct.

84 Omissions are not accidents.
   1956 Ewing Lecture, University of California, 3 Oct.

85 O to be a dragon,
   a symbol of the power of Heaven—of silkworm size or immense; at times invisible.
   Felicitous phenomenon!
   1959 *O To Be A Dragon*, 'O To Be A Dragon'.

86 A connoisseur of tame excitement.
   1960 Self-description, in *Vogue*, 1 Aug.

87 Any writer overwhelmingly honest about pleasing himself is almost sure to please others.
   1963 In *Vogue*, 15 Aug.

88 I am governed by the pull of the sentence as the pull of a fabric is governed by gravity.
   Quoted in Louis Untermeyer 'Five Famous Poetesses', in *Ladies' Home Journal*, May 1964.

89 Subjects choose me... I lie in wait like a leopard on a branch-strained metaphor.
   Quoted in Louis Untermeyer 'Five Famous Poetesses', in *Ladies' Home Journal*, May 1964.

90 Omissions are not accidents.
   1967 Epigraph to *Complete Poems*.

91 To cite passages is to pull one quill from a porcupine.
   Quoted in Patricia C Willis (ed) *The Complete Prose of Marianne Moore* (1986).

Moore, Michael 1954–
US film-maker and writer.

92 The things I believe in, I believe strongly enough in them and I think I'm right. When I'm wrong, then I change my mind and I'm right again.
   2002 In a question and answer session at the National Film Theatre, London, 11 Nov.

93 We live in a time when we have fictitious election results that elect a fictitious president, a time where we have a man sending us to war for fictitious reasons. We are against this war, Mr Bush. Shame on you, Mr Bush. Shame on you.
   2003 At the 76th Academy Awards, where he was awarded an Oscar for Best Documentary Director.

94 I had an unusually large-sized head, though this was not uncommon for a baby in the Midwest. The craniums in our part of the country were designed to leave a little extra room for the brain to grow in case one day we found ourselves exposed to something we didn't understand, like a foreign language, or a salad.
   2011 *Here Comes Trouble*.

95 It is the responsibility of every human to know their actions and the consequences of their actions and to ask questions and to question things when they are wrong.
   2011 *Here Comes Trouble*.

96 Guns don't kill people—Americans kill people.
   2012 On *The Ed Show*, MSNBC, 22 Mar.

Moore, Sir Patrick 1923–2012
English astronomer, author and broadcaster. He began his popular television series, *The Sky at Night*, in 1957, and it continued after his death.

97 The Moon is a splendid object in our skies, and we naturally tend to think of it as important.
   1976 *Guide to the Moon*.

98 I get up, drink my usual four coffees, have a look at the obituaries in *The Times* and, if I'm not in them, I'll get on with the day's work.
   2012 Describing his morning routine.

Moore, Thomas 1780–1852
Irish poet, songwriter and biographer. He wrote a number of patriotic songs and poems as well as lives of Sheridan, Byron (a close friend) and others. He also wrote satirical pieces and novels, including *The Fudge Family in Paris* (1818). He is remembered for *Lallah Rookh* (1817), a series of oriental tales in verse, and for the popular songs 'The Harp that once through Tara's Halls', 'The Minstrel-boy', and 'Tis the Last Rose of Summer'.

99 There is not in the wide world a valley so sweet
   As that vale in whose bosom the bright waters meet;
   Oh! the last rays of feeling and life must depart
   Ere the bloom of that valley shall fade from my heart.
   1807 *Irish Melodies*, 'The Meeting of the Waters'.

1 Let Erin remember the days of Old,
   Ere her faithless sons betrayed her;
   When Malachi wore the collar of gold
   Which he won from her proud invader;
   When her kings, with standards of green unfurled,
   Led the Red-Branch Knights to danger;

Ere the emerald gem of the western world
Was set in the crown of a stranger.
1807 *Irish Melodies*, 'Let Erin Remember'.

2 The Minstrel-boy to the war is gone,
In the ranks of death you'll find him;
His father's sword he has girded on,
And his wild harp slung behind him.
1807 *Irish Melodies*, 'The Minstrel-boy'.

3 'Tis the last rose of summer
Left blooming alone;
All her lovely companions
Are faded and gone.
1807 *Irish Melodies*, ''Tis the Last Rose of Summer'.

4 The harp that once through Tara's halls
The soul of music shed,
Now hangs as mute on Tara's walls
As if that soul were fled.
1807 *Irish Melodies*, 'The Harp that once through Tara's Halls'.

5 No, there's nothing half so sweet in life
As love's young dream.
1807 *Irish Melodies*, 'Love's Young Dream'.

6 Oh! ever thus, from childhood's hour,
I've seen my fondest hopes decay;
I never loved a tree or flower,
But 'twas the first to fade away.
I never nursed a dear gazelle,
To glad me with its soft black eye,
But when it came to know me well,
And love me, it was sure to die!
1817 *Lallah Rookh*, 'The Fire Worshippers'.

7 Yet, who can help loving the land that has taught us
Six hundred and eighty-five ways to dress eggs?
1818 *The Fudge Family in Paris*, letter 8.

Moorhouse, Geoffrey 1931–2009

English writer and traveller. He attempted to cross the Sahara from Mauretania to the Nile, but in March 1973, having travelled 2,000 miles (3,200km), 300 miles (480km) on foot after the last of his camels died, he reached Tamanrasset and gave up.

8 There was nothing but pain in the desert, for human beings and animals alike. Life was pain. Only in death was there relief.
1974 *The Fearful Void*.

Moran, Richard John McMoran Wilson, 2nd Baron 1924–2014

British diplomat and soldier. He filled a succession of diplomatic posts, including High Commissioner in Canada (1981–4). As John Wilson he wrote a Whitbread Award-winning biography of Sir Henry Campbell-Bannerman (1973).

9 Courage is a moral quality; it is not a chance gift of nature, like an aptitude for games. It is a cold choice between two alternatives; the fixed resolve not to quit, an act of renunciation that must be made not once but many times by the power of the will.
1945 *The Anatomy of Courage*.

More, Sir Thomas 1478–1534

English statesman, scholar and writer. Educated at Oxford in the new humanism, he was appointed Lord Chancellor by Henry VIII. He refused to take the oath of supremacy and was executed. His most famous work is *Utopia* (1516; translated into English 1556); other works include *History of King Richard III* (1513) and meditations in prison.

10 In the first place, most princes apply themselves to the arts of war, in which I have neither ability nor interest, instead of to the good arts of peace. They are generally more set on acquiring new kingdoms by hook or by crook than on governing well those that they already have.
1516 *Utopia* (English translation 1556), bk.1.

11 It is only natural, of course, that each man should think his own opinions best: the old crow loves his fledglings, and the ape his cubs.
1516 *Utopia* (English translation 1556), bk.1.

12 Such proud, obstinate, ridiculous judgements I have encountered many times, and once even in England.
1516 *Utopia* (English translation 1556), bk.1.

13 Severe and terrible punishments are enacted against theft, when it would be much better to enable every man to earn his own living, instead of being driven to the awful necessity of stealing and then dying for it.
1516 *Utopia* (English translation 1556), bk.1.

14 The law of Moses is harsh and severe, as for an enslaved and stubborn people, but it punishes theft with a fine, not death. Let us not think that in his new law of mercy, where he treats us with the tenderness of a father, God has given us greater license to be cruel to one another.
1516 *Utopia* (English translation 1556), bk.1.

15 A king who wants to maintain an army can never have too much gold.
1516 *Utopia* (English translation 1556), bk.1.

16 A king has no dignity when he exercises authority over beggars, only when he rules over prosperous and happy subjects.
1516 *Utopia* (English translation 1556), bk.1.

17 The only real thing they accomplish that I can see is to make men feel a little more secure in their consciences about doing evil.
1516 Of preachers. *Utopia* (English translation 1556), bk.1.

18 Hardly any of the women, who are a full half of the population, work; or if they do, then as a rule their husbands lie snoring in bed.
1516 *Utopia* (English translation 1556), bk.2.

19 For where money is the standard of everything, many vain, superfluous trades are bound to be carried on simply to satisfy luxury and licentiousness.
1516 *Utopia* (English translation 1556), bk.2.

20 The chief aim of their constitution is that, whenever public needs permit, all citizens should be free, so far as possible, to withdraw their time and energy from the service of the body, and devote themselves to the freedom and culture of the mind. For that, they think, is the real happiness of life.
1516 *Utopia* (English translation 1556), bk.2.

21 They find pearls by the seashore, diamonds and rubies in certain cliffs, but never go out of set purpose to look for them. If they happen to find some, they polish them, and give them to the children who, when they are small, feel proud and pleased with such gaudy decorations. But after, when they grow a bit older, and notice that only

babies like such toys, they lay them aside. Their parents don't have to say anything, they simply put these trifles away out of a shamefaced sense that they're no longer suitable, just as our children when they grow up put away their rattles, marbles and dolls.
1516 *Utopia* (English translation 1556), bk.2.

22 Thus they say that nature herself prescribes for us a joyous life, in other words, pleasure, as the goal of our actions; and living according to her prescriptions is to be defined as virtue.
1516 *Utopia* (English translation 1556), bk.2.

23 Two evils—greed and faction—are the destruction of all justice.
1516 *Utopia* (English translation 1556), bk.2.

24 Is not this house as nigh heaven as my own?
c.1534 Of the Tower of London. Attributed in William Roper *Life of Sir Thomas More* (ed E V Hitchcock, 1935).

25 I pray you, master Lieutenant, see me safe up, and my coming down let me shift for myself.
1535 On mounting the scaffold. Attributed in William Roper *Life of Sir Thomas More* (ed E V Hitchcock, 1935).

26 This hath not offended the king.
1535 Said on the scaffold as he drew his beard to one side. Attributed in William Roper *Life of Sir Thomas More* (ed E V Hitchcock, 1935).

Morell, Thomas 1703–84
English poet and librettist.

27 See, the conquering hero comes!
Sound the trumpets, beat the drums!
1747 *Judas Maccabeus*, 'A Chorus of Youths'.

Morey, Larry 1905–71
US lyricist who frequently worked with Frank Churchill. Best known for contributing to *Snow White and the Seven Dwarfs* (1937) and *Bambi* (1941).

28 Heigh ho, heigh ho
It's off to work we go.
1937 First lines of the song 'Heigh-Ho' from the film *Snow White and the Seven Dwarfs*. Music by Frank Churchill.

29 Whistle While You Work.
1937 Title of song from the film *Snow White and the Seven Dwarfs*. Music by Frank Churchill.

Morgan, Edwin George 1920–2010
Scottish poet and critic, Professor Emeritus of English at Glasgow University. One of the most important Scottish writers, he was a skilled translator as well as an original poet.

30 Many things are unspoken
in the life of a man, and with a place
there is an unspoken love also
in undercurrents, drifting, waiting its time.
1968 'The Second Life'.

31 And later, wondering farmers as they passed would hear
beyond the lighted window in the autumn evening
two handsome yellow-bosomed basset-hounds
howling to a melodious basset-horn.
1968 'An Addition to the Family'.

32 Deplore what is to be deplored,
and then find out the rest.
1968 'King Billy'.

33 The man lies late since he has lost his job,
smokes on one elbow, letting his coughs fall
thinly into an air too poor to rob.
1973 'Glasgow Sonnets, I'.

34 No deliverer ever rose
from these stone tombs to get the hell they made unmade.
1973 'Glasgow Sonnets, II'.

Morgan, Elaine 1920–2003
British science writer, journalist and playwright. She worked on the award-winning television screening of Vera Brittain's *Testament of Youth* (1980). Her controversial book *The Descent of Woman* (1972), which explores the origins of mankind, with special reference to women's evolution, was followed by *The Aquatic Ape* (1982).

35 It takes two to make a woman into a sex object.
1972 *The Descent of Woman*, ch.11.

Moritz, Karl Philipp 1756–93
German writer, an early Romantic. After travelling in England and Italy he wrote *Reisen eines Deutschen in England* (1783) and *Reisen eines Deutschen in Italien* (1792–3). His autobiographical novel *Anton Reise* (1785–90) influenced Goethe.

36 When you see how in this happy country the lowest and poorest member of society takes an interest in all public affairs; when you see how high and low, rich and poor, are all willing to declare their feelings and convictions; when you see how a carter, a common sailor, a beggar is still a man, nay, even more, an Englishman—then, believe me, you find yourself very differently affected from the experience you feel when staring at our soldiers drilling in Berlin.
1782 Letter to a friend after observing a London by-election.

Morley, Christopher Darlington 1890–1957
US writer and poet, founder and editor (1924–41) of the *Saturday Review*. His many novels include *Parnassus on Wheels* (1917).

37 Life is a foreign language: all men mispronounce it.
1925 *Thunder on the Left*, ch.14.

38 Dancing is a wonderful training for girls, it's the first way you learn to guess what a man is going to do before he does it.
1939 *Kitty Foyle*, ch.11.

39 When you sell a man a book, you don't sell him 12 ounces of paper and ink and glue—you sell him a whole new life.
Recalled on his death, 28 Mar 1957.

Morley, Robert 1908–92
English actor. A popular comic actor, he also made many film and television appearances, including *Beat the Devil* (1953), *Oscar Wilde* (1960) and *Who is Killing the Great Chefs of Europe?* (1978).

40 The French are a logical people, which is one reason the English dislike them so intensely. The other is that they own France, a country which we have always judged to be much too good for them.
1974 *A Musing Morley*, 'France and the French'.

41 It is a great help for a man to be in love with himself. For an actor, it is absolutely essential.
1979 In *Playboy*.

42 I started off in films as a king—a French king, admittedly, but nevertheless a king in *Marie Antoinette*—and stayed in that sort of income bracket.
Quoted in *The Best of Robert Morley* (1981).

43 Anyone who works is a fool. I don't work: I merely inflict myself on the public.
Attributed.

Morris, Desmond John 1928–

British ethologist and writer. His interest in primate behaviour led to his best-known work, the popular *The Naked Ape* (1967).

44 The Human Zoo.
1969 Title of book.

45 Clearly, then, the city is not a concrete jungle, it is a human zoo.
1969 *The Human Zoo*, introduction.

Morris, Jan formerly *James Morris* 1926–

English reporter and writer. As James Morris he wrote books and essays on travel. He accompanied the 1953 first ascent of Everest, covering it for *The Times*. As Jan Morris she has written a moving account of her sex change *Conundrum* (1974), the *Pax Britannica* trilogy (1968–78) and other novels. She was made a CBE in 1999.

46 Venice will linger in your mind…and wherever you go in life you will feel somewhere over your shoulder, a pink, castellated, shimmering presence, the domes and riggings and crooked pinnacles of the Serenissima. There's romance for you! There's the lust and dark wine of Venice! No wonder George Eliot's husband fell into the Grand Canal.
1960 *Venice*.

47 The genius of Canada remains essentially a deflationary genius.
1976 'On the Confederation Special,' in *Travels*.

48 If I was an aspirant litterateur, I was also an aspirant anarchist. I have disliked Authority always, though sometimes seduced by its resplendence.
2003 *A Writer's World: Travels 1950–2000*, prologue.

Morris, John 1895–1980

English writer, traveller and academic. He travelled in Asia and Africa, and took part in two Everest expeditions. He taught at Keio University in Japan (1938–42) and later became Head of the Far Eastern Service then Controller of the Third Programme at the BBC (1952–8).

49 The Japanese…have a saying that there are two kinds of fool: those who have never climbed Mount Fuji, and those who have climbed it more than once.
1943 *Traveller from Tokyo*.

Morris, Sir Lewis 1833–1907

Engish versifier.

50 We hold a vaster Empire than has been.
'Song of Empire', written to celebrate Queen Victoria's Jubilee, 20 Jun. The words were printed on Canada's first commemorative postage stamp, 1898.

Morris, William 1834–96

English craftsman and poet, associated with the Pre-Raphaelite Brotherhood, a major figure in the Arts and Crafts Movement. He joined the Social Democratic Federation in 1883, and organized the Socialist League. In 1890 he set up the private Kelmscott Press.

51 The Socialist papers…came out full to the throat of well-printed matter…admirable and straightforward expositions of the doctrines and practice of Socialism, free from haste and spite and hard words…with a kind of May-day freshness amidst the worry and terror of the moment.
1890 *News from Nowhere*.

52 Between complete socialism and communism there is no difference whatever in my mind. Communism is in fact the completion of socialism; when that ceases to be militant and becomes triumphant, it will be communism.
1893 Addressing Hammersmith Socialist Society.

Morris, Wright Marion 1910–98

US writer. He wrote novels, short stories, memoirs and critical essays. He was an accomplished photographer, and published several books marrying text with photographs.

53 A Bill of Rites, A Bill of Wrongs, A Bill of Goods.
1968 Title of essay collection.

Morrison, R F

54 Just a wee deoch-an-doris,
Just a wee yin, that's a'.
Just a wee deoch-an-doris,
Afore we gang awa'.
There's a wee wifie waitin'
In a wee but-an-ben;
If ye can say 'It's a braw bricht moonlicht nicht',
Ye're a' richt, ye ken.
1911 'Just a Wee Deoch-an-Doris', chorus. The song was popularized by Sir Harry Lauder.

Morrison, Toni Chloe Anthony *née* Wofford 1931–

US novelist. Her novels have reflected black American experience and consciousness through a sophisticated literary sensibility. She was awarded the Nobel prize for literature in 1993.

55 We have to acknowledge that the thing we call 'literature' is more pluralistic now, just as society ought to be. The melting pot never worked.
1981 In *Newsweek*, 30 Mar.

56 How soon country people forget. When they fall in love with a city it is forever, and it is like forever… There, in a city, they are not so much new as themselves: their stronger, riskier selves.
1991 *Jazz*, ch.2.

57 In this country American means white. Everybody else has to hyphenate.
1992 In *The Guardian*, 29 Jan.

58 Slavery broke the world in half, it broke it in every way. It broke Europe. It made them into something else, it made them slave masters, it made them crazy. You can't do that for hundreds of years and it not take a toll. They had to dehumanize, not just the slaves but themselves.
Quoted in Paul Gilroy *Small Acts* (1993), 'Living memory: a meeting with Toni Morrison'.

59 I have always wanted to develop a way of writing that was irrevocably black. I don't have the resources of a musician but I thought that if it was truly black literature,

it would not be black because I was, it would not even be black because of its subject matter. It would be something intrinsic, indigenous, something in the way it was put together—the sentences, the structure, texture and tone—so that anyone who read it would realize.
Quoted in Paul Gilroy *Small Acts* (1993), 'Living memory: a meeting with Toni Morrison'.

60 To be given dominion over another is a hard thing; to wrest dominion over another is a wrong thing; to give dominion of yourself to another is a wicked thing.
2008 *A Mercy*.

Morrissey full name Steven Patrick Morrissey 1959–

English singer and songwriter, former member of The Smiths.

61 Heaven Knows I'm Miserable Now.
1984 Song title.

62 No—he lives next door to me.
2002 When asked whether it was true that he lived next door to Johnny Depp. In the *Observer*, 15 Sep.

63 My best friend is myself... It's a lifelong relationship and divorce will never come into it.
2002 In the *Observer*, 15 Sep.

Morse, Samuel F(inley) B(reese) 1791–1872

US inventor and painter, who demonstrated (1844) the practicability of an electrical telegraph device to Congress. He had earlier trained as an artist.

64 Alas! My dear sir, the very name of *pictures* produces a sadness of heart I cannot describe. Painting has been a smiling mistress to many, but she has been a cruel jilt to me.
1849 Letter to his friend the writer James Fenimore Cooper, 20 Nov.

Mortimer, Sir John Clifford 1923–2009

English playwright, novelist and barrister. Called to the bar in 1948, he took part in several celebrated civil cases before achieving wider fame as a writer, notably as creator of the fictitious barrister Horace Rumpole. His other publications include volumes of autobiography, novels such as *Paradise Postponed* (1985) and *Summer's Lease* (1988) and several plays.

65 No brilliance is needed in the law. Nothing but common sense, and relatively clean finger nails.
1971 *A Voyage Round My Father*, act 1.

66 The law seems like a sort of maze through which a client must be led to safety, a collection of reefs, rocks, and underwater hazards through which he or she must be piloted.
1982 *Clinging to the Wreckage*, ch. 7.

67 They do you a decent death in the hunting field.
1985 *Paradise Postponed*, ch. 18.

68 The shelf life of the modern hardback writer is somewhere between the milk and the yoghurt.
1987 In the *Observer*, 28 Jun.

69 Life itself is a mystery which defies solution.
1990 In the *Sunday Times*, 1 Apr.

70 But plots come from—God knows where. They can't be summoned at will. They come reluctantly, unexpectedly, stealthily, when you have given up hope of them ever paying you a visit.

1993 'A Plot at Last', in Brown and Munro (eds) *Writers Writing* (1993).

Mortimer, (Charles) Raymond Bell 1895–1980

English literary and art critic.

71 People don't learn to enjoy pictures because they seldom look at them; and they seldom look at pictures because they have never learnt to enjoy them.
1976 *Try Anything Once*.

Morton, Jelly Roll (Ferdinand) 1890–1941

US jazz pianist. He was an important pioneer of the New Orleans jazz style, but was much given to making extravagant claims about his role in it.

72 It is evidently known, beyond contradiction, that New Orleans is the cradle of *jazz*, and I, myself, happened to be the creator in the year 1902... *Jazz* music is a style, not compositions; any kind of music may be played in *jazz*, if one has the knowledge.
1938 In *Downbeat*, Aug.

Morton, J(ohn Cameron Andrieu) B(ingham Michael) pseudonym Beachcomber 1893–1979

English writer. He wrote many books of humour, fantasy, satire and history, but is chiefly remembered for his humorous columns in the *Daily Express*, under the nom de plume 'Beachcomber'.

73 One disadvantage of being a hog is that at any moment some blundering fool may try to make a silk purse out of your wife's ear.
1931 *By the Way*.

74 Hush, hush!
Nobody cares!
Christopher Robin
Has
Fallen
Down
Stairs.
1931 *By the Way*.

75 The Doctor is said also to have invented an extraordinary weapon which will make war less brutal. It is described as a very powerful liquid which rots braces at a distance of a mile.
1936 'Bracerot'.

Morton, Rogers Clark Ballard 1914–1979

US former Republican politician. He was president of a flour manufacturing company and representative for Maryland in the 88th–92nd Congresses. He was Secretary of the Interior (1971–5) and a counsellor to the President on economic and domestic matters (1976–7).

76 I have no intention of rearranging the furniture on the deck of the Titanic.
1976 On declining to rescue President Ford's disastrous election campaign.

Morton, Thomas c.1764–1838

English playwright. He is usually remembered for his comedy *Speed the Plough* (1798).

77 What will Mrs Grundy say? What will Mrs Grundy think?
1798 *Speed the Plough*.

Moses, Anna Mary Robertson known as 'Grandma Moses' 1860–1961

US painter. The wife of a farmer in New York state, with no art training, she did not begin painting until in her 70s. Her primitive paintings are colourful, simple scenes of everyday rural life.

78 Paintin's not important. What's important is keepin' busy.
1954 In news summaries, 2 Jan.

Moses, Ed(win) 1955–

US track athlete. He was unbeaten in any 400-metre hurdle race from August 1977 to June 1987, and was Olympic champion in 1976 and 1984 and four times world record holder.

79 There are three universal languages: love, music and sports.
2004 In the Boston Herald, 12 May.

Mosk, Stanley 1912–2001

US lawyer and Justice of State Supreme Court. He practised law in Los Angeles until 1939 and was Attorney General of California 1959–64. He was a Justice of the Supreme Court of California from 1964 until his death.

80 Little old ladies in tennis shoes.
Characterizing older, activist women. Quoted in William Safire Safire's Political Dictionary (1975).

Moss, Gary

US marketing coach, a former vice-president of marketing communications, Campbell Soup Co.

81 You can teach an elephant to dance, but the likelihood of its stepping on your toes is very high.
1993 On the decline of the advertising agencies' monopoly in marketing. In Forbes, 15 Mar.

Moss, Kate 1974–

English model.

82 Nothing tastes as good as skinny feels.
2009 Her personal motto, which drew criticism from eating-disorder experts.

Moss, Sir Stirling 1929–

English racing driver. Although he never won the World Championship, he became one of the most celebrated of all drivers, winning numerous Grand Prix races driving for a variety of teams. He retired in 1962 after a serious crash.

83 It is necessary to relax your muscles when you can. Relaxing your brain is fatal.
1955 In Newsweek, 16 May.

84 There are two things no man will admit he can't do well—drive and make love.
Quoted in Colin Jarman The Guinness Dictionary of Sports Quotations (1990).

Motherwell, Robert 1915–91

US painter and writer, an exponent of Abstract Realism. His works typically consist of large, amorphous blocks of strong colour, such as his most famous series, *Elegies to the Spanish Republic* (1975).

85 One of the most striking of abstract art's appearance is her nakedness, an art stripped bare.

1951 Paper given at a symposium, 5 Feb, at the Museum of Modern Art, New York, published in What Abstract Art Means to Me: Bulletin of the Museum of Modern Art (Spring 1951).

86 Every intelligent painter carries the whole culture of modern painting in his head...everything he paints is both an homage and a critique.
1977 In the Los Angeles Times, 31 Jul.

87 All my life I've been working on the work—every canvas a sentence or paragraph of it. Each picture is only an approximation of what I want.
Recalled on his death, 16 Jul 1991.

Motion, Andrew 1952–

English poet and biographer, Poet Laureate (1999–2009).

88 Earth's axle creeks; the year jolts on; the trees
begin to slip their brittle leaves, their flakes of rust;
and darkness takes the edge off daylight, not
because it wants to—never that. Because it must.
1997 'Mythology', written for the funeral of Diana, Princess of Wales. Published in Public Property (2002).

89 O Jonny the power of your boot
And the accurate heart-stopping route
Of your goal as it ghosts
Through Australian posts
Is a triumph we gladly salute.
2004 'A Song for Jonny', written to commemorate England winning the rugby World Cup and the player Jonny Wilkinson.

Motson, John 1946–

English football commentator.

90 It's Arsenal 0 Everton 1 and the longer it stays like that the more you've got to fancy Everton.
Quoted in Motson's National Obsession (2004).

91 Nearly all the Brazilian supporters are wearing yellow shirts— it's a fabulous kaleidoscope of colour.
Quoted in Motson's National Obsession (2004).

92 For those of you watching in black and white, Spurs are in the all-yellow strip.
Quoted in Motson's National Obsession (2004).

Mountbatten of Burma, Louis Francis Albert Victor Nicholas, 1st Earl 1900–79

English admiral and statesman, chief of Combined Operations Command (1942) in World War II. As Supreme Commander, SE Asia, he received the Japanese surrender at Singapore, and in 1947 became last Viceroy of India. He returned to the Admiralty as First Sea Lord (1954) and Chief of the Defence Staff (1959). He retired in 1965 and in 1979 was assassinated by Irish Republican terrorists.

93 As a military man who has given half a century of active service, I say in all sincerity that the nuclear arms race has no military purpose. Wars cannot be fought with nuclear weapons; their existence only adds to our perils because of the illusions that they have generated. The world now stands on the brink of the final abyss. Let us all resolve to take all possible practicable steps to ensure that we do not, through our own folly, go over the edge.
1979 Speech at the Council of Europe in Strasbourg, 11 May.

Mourinho (Félix), José Mário dos Santos 1963–

Portuguese football manager. His hugely successful international career has included spells at Porto (2002–4), Real Madrid (2010–13), and Chelsea (2004–7 and 2013–).

94 I have top players and I'm sorry, we have a top manager. Please do not call me arrogant because what I say is true. I'm European champion, I'm not one out of the bottle, I think I'm a special one.
2004 Speaking to the press as the new manager of Chelsea.

95 Look, we're not entertaining? I don't care; we win.
2007 Dismissing criticism of Chelsea's performance.

96 It is like having a blanket that is too small for the bed. You pull the blanket up to keep your chest warm and your feet stick out. I cannot buy a bigger blanket because the supermarket is closed. But I am content because the blanket is cashmere. It is no ordinary blanket.
2007 Discussing his difficulties as Chelsea when his squad was reduced by injury, 31 Jan.

97 It's not important how we play. If you have a Ferrari and I have a small car, to beat you in a race I have to break your wheel or put sugar in your tank.
2010 Explaining his management strategy.

98 I believe in freedom of speech: you make a speech and I'll give you your freedom.
Pep talk to his players. Attributed.

Mowlam, Mo (Marjorie) 1949–2005

English Labour politician. She was Secretary of State for Northern Ireland from 1997 to 1999.

99 Ian Paisley said he pitied my husband having to put up with 'the sinner', which is what he often called me.
2000 In the *Sunday Times*, 16 Apr.

Moynihan, Daniel Patrick 1927–2003

US sociologist and diplomat, adviser to Presidents Kennedy, Johnson, Nixon and Ford. He was Ambassador to India (1973–5), US representative to the UN (1975–6), and subsequently a Senator (1976–2001). His writings include *Beyond the Melting Pot* (with Nathan Glazer, 1963).

1 We've come full circle but the best remains the heart of the city, the greatest center of the greatest city, our Acropolis, where our Christmas tree is lighted.
1991 On New York's Rockefeller Centre. In the *New York Times*, 15 Mar.

2 Things become complicated if there are enough people to complexify them.
1991 Of the 19,000-member congressional back-up staff. In the *New York Times*, 12 Nov.

3 They live off secrecy... [it] keep the mistakes secret.
1993 Of government intelligence agencies. *President Kennedy*.

4 The Lord looks after drunks and Americans.
1995 Of the avoidance of casualties in the Haitian intervention. In the *US News and World Report*, 9 Jan.

Mozart, (Johann Chrysostom) Wolfgang Amadeus 1756–91

Austrian composer. An infant prodigy, who suffered throughout his life from poverty and overwork, his many compositions include symphonies, concertos, string quintets, string quartets, numerous piano and violin sonatas, choral works and operas such as *The Marriage of Figaro* (1786), *Don Giovanni* (1787), *Cosìì fan tutte* (1790) and *The Magic Flute* (1791).

5 It is much easier to play a thing quickly than to play it slowly.
1778 Letter.

6 Melody is the very essence of music. When I think of a good melodist I think of a fine race horse. A contrapuntist is only a post-horse.
1786 Letter to Michael Kelly.

Mugabe, Robert Gabriel 1924–

Zimbabwean politician. He co-founded ZANU (Zimbabwe African National Union, 1963), and on Zimbabwe's independence in 1980 became first Prime Minister (1980–7) and subsequently President (1987–).

7 Cricket? It civilises people and creates good gentlemen. I want everyone to play cricket in Zimbabwe. I want ours to be a nation of gentlemen.
Quoted in Helen Exley *Cricket Quotations* (1992).

8 We are not going to give up our country because of a mere X. How can a ballpoint fight with a gun?
2008 Shrugging off the possibility of electoral defeat.

Muggeridge, Malcolm 1903–90

English journalist. He was Editor of *Punch* from 1953 to 1957, and appeared frequently on television as reporter and interviewer. In his later years he became a Roman Catholic.

9 The orgasm has replaced the cross as the focus of longing and the image of fulfilment.
1966 *Tread Softly for You Tread on My Jokes*.

10 The media have, indeed, provided the Devil with perhaps the greatest opportunity accorded him since Adam and Eve were turned out of the Garden of Eden.
1976 *Christ and the Media*, introduction.

11 Future historians will surely see us as having created in the media a Frankenstein monster whom no one knows how to control or direct, and marvel that we should have so meekly subjected ourselves to its destructive and often malign influence.
1976 *Christ and the Media*, 'Lecture 1'.

12 It's very nearly impossible to tell the truth in television.
1976 *Christ and the Media*, 'Questions following the 3rd lecture'.

Muir, Edwin 1887–1959

Scottish writer and translator. He is best known as a poet, but also wrote literary and cultural criticism, and an autobiography.

13 The curse of Scottish literature is the lack of a whole language, which finally means the lack of a whole mind.
1936 *Scott and Scotland*, introduction.

14 The hills and towers
Stood otherwise than they should stand,
And without fear the lawless roads
Ran wrong throughout the land.
1937 *Journeys and Places*, 'Hölderlin's Journey', stanza 11.

15 There is a road that turning always
Cuts off the country of Again.
Archers stand there on every side
And as it runs time's deer is slain,
And lies where it has lain.
1937 'The Road'.

16 All through that summer at ease we lay,
And daily from the turret wall
We watched the mowers in the hay
And the enemy half a mile away.
They seemed no threat to us at all.
1946 The Voyage, 'The Castle', stanza 1.

17 It was not meant for human eyes,
That combat on the shabby patch
Of clods and trampled earth that lies
Somewhere beneath the sodden skies
For eye of toad or adder to catch.
1949 The Labyrinth, 'The Combat'.

18 Oh these deceits are strong almost as life.
Last night I dreamt I was in the labyrinth,
And woke far on. I did not know the place.
1949 The Labyrinth, 'The Labyrinth'.

19 We have seen
Good men made evil wrangling with the evil,
Straight minds grown crooked fighting crooked minds.
Our peace betrayed us; we betrayed our peace.
Look at it well. This was the good town once.
1949 The Labyrinth, 'The Good Town'.

20 Kindness and courage can repair time's faults,
And serving him breeds patience and courtesy
In us, light sojourners and passing subjects.
1949 The Labyrinth, 'The Good Town'.

21 The life of every man is an endlessly repeated
performance of the life of man.
1954 An Autobiography, ch.1.

22 Since then they have pulled our ploughs and borne our loads.
But that free servitude still can pierce our hearts.
Our life is changed; their coming our beginning.
1956 One Foot in Eden, 'The Horses'.

23 Barely a twelvemonth after
The seven days war that put the world to sleep,
Late in the evening the strange horses came.
1956 One Foot in Eden, 'The Horses'.

24 One foot in Eden still, I stand
And look across the other land.
The world's great day is growing late,
Yet strange these fields that we have planted
So long with crops of love and hate.
1956 One Foot in Eden, 'One Foot in Eden'.

Muir, John 1838-1914

Scottish naturalist. He emigrated with his family to America as a boy, and became a champion of wilderness areas and the establishment of National Parks in the US. He is regarded as the father of the environmental movement.

25 The tendency nowadays to wander in wildernesses is delightful to see. Thousands of tired, nerve-shaken, over-civilized people are beginning to find out that going to the mountains is going home; that wildness is a necessity; and that mountain parks and reservations are useful not only as fountains of timber and irrigating rivers, but as fountains of life.
1901 Our National Parks, ch.1, 'The Wild Parks and Forest Reservations of the West'.

26 When we contemplate the whole globe as one great dewdrop, striped and dotted with continents and islands, flying through space with other stars all singing and shining together as one, the whole universe appears as an infinite storm of beauty.
Travels in Alaska, ch.1, 'The Puget Sound and British Columbia' (published 1915).

27 I have precious little sympathy for the selfish propriety of civilized man, and if a war of races should occur between the wild beasts and Lord Man, I would be tempted to sympathise with the bears.
A Thousand-Mile Walk to the Gulf, ch.5, 'Through Florida Swamps and Forests' (published 1916).

Muir, Willa (Wilhelmina) Johnstone née Anderson also known as Agnes Neill Scott 1890-1970

Scottish poet, novelist and translator, wife of the poet Edwin Muir whose unconventional religious beliefs forced her resignation from a teaching position in 1915. Her published works include many translations, several novels and a book of poetry.

28 Apparently the average man sees woman alternately as an inferior being and as an angel.
1925 Women: An Inquiry, pt.1, published as Hogarth Essay no.10 in *The Hogarth Essays* (Second Series, 1926).

29 A man can be a parent without knowing it: a woman cannot.
1925 Women: An Inquiry, pt.1, published as Hogarth Essay no.10 in *The Hogarth Essays* (Second Series, 1926).

Mullan, Peter 1960-

Scottish actor and director.

30 Worst script I've ever read.
2003 On Braveheart. In *The Herald,* 1 Feb.

31 There's no such thing as an actor giving positive criticism to a director. The minute you say 'Don't you think it would look nicer...', that director's going to hate your guts. Particularly if it's a good idea.
2003 In a question and answer session at the National Film Theatre, London, 4 Nov.

32 Nine out of ten delinquents are frustrated actors.
2003 In a question and answer session at the National Film Theatre, London, 4 Nov.

Muller, Herbert Joseph 1905-80

US writer.

33 Few have probably ever heard of Fra Luca Pacioli, the inventor of double-entry bookkeeping; but he has probably had much more influence on human life than has Dante or Michelangelo.
1957 Uses of the Past, ch.8.

Mulroney, (Martin) Brian 1939-

Canadian Conservative politician, Prime Minister (1984-93). His radical reforms included the Meech Lake Accords (which aimed at settling disputes between the provinces and the centre, but which later collapsed) and a free-trade agreement with the US.

34 In politics, madame, you need two things: friends, but above all an enemy.
1990 Remark made to a journalist following the by-election victory of Liberal leader Jean Chrétien, 10 Dec, quoted two days later by Graham Fraser in The Globe and Mail.

Mumford, Lewis 1895–1990

US sociologist and author. A literary critic and journal editor, he began to write on architecture and urbanization in such works as *The Story of Utopias* (1922) and *The City in History* (1961), stressing the dehumanizing effects of technology.

35 Every generation revolts against its fathers and makes friends with its grandfathers.
1931 *The Brown Decades*, p.3.

36 However far modern science and technics have fallen short of their inherent possibilities, they have taught mankind at least one lesson: Nothing is impossible.
1934 *Technics and Civilization*.

37 The Fujiyama of Architecture…at once a lofty mountain and a national shrine.
1953 Of Frank Lloyd Wright. 'A Phoenix Too Infrequent', in the *New Yorker*, 28 Nov.

38 Our national flower is the concrete cloverleaf.
Collected in *Quote Magazine*, 8 Oct 1961.

39 The life-efficiency and adaptability of the computer must be questioned. Its judicious use depends upon the availability of its human employers quite literally to keep their own heads, not merely to scrutinize the programming but to reserve for themselves the right of ultimate decision. No automatic system can be intelligently run by automatons—or by people who dare not assert human intuition, human autonomy, human purpose.
1970 *The Myth of the Machine*.

40 As full of flavor as hickory smoke.
1994 Of geotechnic expert Benton MacKaye. In *Harvard University Magazine*, Jul.

Munch, Edvard 1863–1944

Norwegian painter and graphic artist.

41 One evening, I was walking along a path, the city was on one side and the fjord below. I felt tired and ill. I stopped and looked out over the fjord—the sun was setting, and the clouds turning blood red. I sensed a scream passing through nature; it seemed to me that I heard the scream. I painted this picture, painted the clouds as actual blood. The colour shrieked. This became The Scream.
1889 *Diary*.

Münch, Richard Friedrich 1945–

German sociologist, professor emeritus at the University of Bamberg.

42 Social life is mutual negotiation and society, social order, relies on this mutual negotiation between individuals; this represents both creed and particular reality in American society. In no other society is this creed and the corresponding reality as prominent as the United States.
1986 'The American Creed in Sociological Theory', in *Sociological Theory*, vol.4, issue 43.

Mundy, Peter c.1596–1667

English trader and seafarer. He was sent to France at the age of 12 to learn French. At 15 he went to sea and travelled continually thereafter. His journal was edited by the Hakluyt Society.

43 We all three got up on our elephant which brought us hither. For my own part I found [it] very uneasy riding, being badly seated and not accustomed (he had such a shuffling, jogging justling pace), sitting hindermost on the ridge of his monstrous massy chine bones, and nothing at all under me (nor they neither) that I wished myself on foot and would have let myself fall off but that it was somewhat too high. In fine, we alighted off from his back into the upper galleries of the house and saved the labour going upstairs.
c.1620 On riding on an elephant. *Travels* (pubished c.1650).

44 So that finding myself at present in or about one hundred and twenty degrees off east longitude from England, it bred in me a desire to proceed on the same easterly course till I had ended where I began, and so to have once made one circle round the globe of the earth, which would have been a voyage of voyages.
c.1640 Objections were raised and Mundy was unable to fulfil this aim. *Travels* (published c.1650).

Munger, Charlie (Charles Thomas) 1924–

US businessman. As Vice-Chairman of Berkshire Hathaway Corporation he is a close associate of financier Warren Buffett.

45 The best armour of old age is a well spent life perfecting it.
2005 *Poor Charlie's Almanack: The Wit and Wisdom of Charles T. Munger*.

46 When the tiger gets out and starts creating damage, it's insane to blame the tiger—it's the idiot tiger keeper.
2010 Discussing responsibility for the financial crash of 2008.

Munro, Alice *née Laidlaw* 1931–

Canadian short-story writer whose awards for such short story collections as *Who Do You Think You Are?* (1978) and *The Progress of Love* (1986) have included the 2009 Man Booker international prize and the 2013 Nobel prize for literature.

47 Boys' hate was dangerous, it was keen and bright, a miraculous birthright, like Arthur's sword snatched out of the stone.
1971 *Lives of Girls and Women*, 'Changes and Ceremonies'.

48 I thought of my mother, who would publicly campaign for birth control but would never even think she needed to talk to me, so firmly was she convinced that sex was something no woman—no *intelligent* woman—would ever submit to unless she had to.
1971 *Lives of Girls and Women*, 'Baptizing'.

49 She had reached an age where she thought she could not stand to know any more…she pushed any discovery aside with embarassment.
1978 *Lives of Girls and Women*, 'Royal Beatings'.

50 Country manners. Even if somebody phones up to tell you your house is burning down, they ask first how you are.
1987 *The Progress of Love*, 'The Progress of Love'.

51 Hatred is always a sin, my mother told me. Remember that. One drop of hatred in your soul will spread and discolor everything like a drop of black ink in white milk. I was struck by that and meant to try it, but knew I shouldn't waste the milk.
1987 *The Progress of Love*, 'The Progress of Love'.

52 People live within winter in a way outsiders do not understand. They are watchful, provident, fatigued, exhilarated.
1987 *The Progress of Love*, 'Fits'.

53 Do such moments really mean, as they seem to, that we have a life of happiness with which we only occasionally, knowingly, intersect? Do they shed such light before and after that all that has happened in our lives—or that we've made to happen—can be dismissed?
1987 The Progress of Love, 'The Moon in the Orange Street Skating Rink'.

54 She was learning, quite late, what many people around her appeared to have known since childhood, that life can be perfectly satisfying without major achievements.
2009 Too Much Happiness.

55 She read modern fiction too. Always fiction. She hated to hear the word 'escape' used about fiction. She might have argued, not just playfully, that it was real life that was the escape. But this was too important to argue about.
2009 Too Much Happiness.

56 Who can ever say the perfect thing to the poet about his poetry?
2012 Dear Life: Stories.

Münster, Count Georg 1794–1868
Hanoverian diplomat.

57 An intelligent Russian once remarked to me, 'Every country has its own Constitution. Ours is absolutism moderated by assassination.'
Political Sketches of the State of Europe 1814–1867

Murakami, Haruki 1949–
Japanese novelist and translator. His best-selling books of Kafkaesque fiction and non-fiction include *A Wild Sheep Chase* (1982), *Norwegian Wood* (1987), *Kafka on the Shore* (2002), and *1Q84* (2009–10).

58 Whether you take the doughnut hole as a blank space or as an entity unto itself is a purely metaphysical question and does not affect the taste of the doughnut one bit.
1982 A Wild Sheep Chase.

59 If you only read the books that everyone else is reading, you can only think what everyone else is thinking.
1987 Norwegian Wood.

60 Waste is the highest virtue one can achieve in advanced capitalist society.
1988 Dance, Dance, Dance.

61 Anyone who falls in love is searching for the missing pieces of themselves.
2002 Kafka on the Shore.

62 Memories are what warm you up from the inside. But they're also what tear you apart.
2002 Kafka on the Shore.

63 Pain is inevitable. Suffering is optional.
2008 What I Talk About When I Talk About Running.

Murdoch, Dame (Jean) Iris 1919–99
Irish novelist and philosopher, of Anglo-Irish descent. Her novels, exploring human relationships with subtlety and humour, include *The Sea, The Sea* (1978) and *The Philosopher's Pupil* (1983).

64 All our failures are ultimately failures in love.
1958 The Bell.

65 Love is the extremely difficult realisation that something other than oneself is real. Love, and so art and morals, is the discovery of reality.
1959 'The Sublime and the Good'.

66 What can one do with the past? Forgive it. Let it enter into you in peace.
1968 The Nice and the Good.

67 He was a sociologist; he had gotten into an intellectual muddle early on in life and never managed to get out.
1983 The Philosopher's Pupil, 'The Events in Our Town'.

Murdoch, (Keith) Rupert 1931–
Australian-born US newspaper publisher. He expanded his publishing empire first in Australia, then in Britain, buying the *News of the World* in 1969, *The Times* and the *Sunday Times* in 1981. He moved into the US market in 1976 and created the Fox Network, later adding to his empire with HarperCollins and *The Wall Street Journal*. He resigned as director of News International in 2012 amid allegations of bribery and corruption. He became a US citizen in 1985.

68 I did not come all this way not to interfere.
c.1969 Quoted in S Somerfield *Banner Headlines* (1979). Somerfield was editor of the *News of the World* and complained that Murdoch, who had recently bought the paper, was interfering with his editorial role.

69 I have heard cynics who say he's a very political old monk shuffling around in Gucci shoes.
1999 On the Dalai Lama. In the Daily Telegraph, 7 Sep.

70 We are perhaps the only independent newspaper in this business.
2012 Referring to the *Sun* newspaper while giving evidence to the Leveson Inquiry into press standards, 23 Apr.

71 I'm a curious person who's interested in the great issues of the day, and I'm not good at holding my tongue.
2012 Giving evidence to the Leveson Inquiry, 23 Apr.

Murkowski, Frank H 1933–
US Governor of Alaska (2002–6). Former Vice-Chair, US Senate Select Committee on Intelligence.

72 Low morale and high indigestion.
1991 Of the mood of the Senate confirming CIA Director Robert M Gates. In the *New York Times*, 12 Nov.

Murphy, Dervla 1931–
Irish writer and traveller. In 1963 she cycled to India, where she worked with Tibetan children.

73 On my tenth birthday a bicycle and an atlas coincided as presents and a few days later I decided to cycle to India.
1965 Full Tilt: Ireland to India with a Bicycle.

74 It is on occasions such as these that I thank God for my sanguine temperament, which refuses to allow me to believe in disaster until it is finally manifest.
1965 Full Tilt: Ireland to India with a Bicycle.

75 Each human spirit is immortal—for time cannot destroy whatever element within us reverences the glory of a dawn in the mountains.
1968 In Ethiopia with a Mule.

76 Never before had I embarked on a journey that required courage.
1978 On embarking on travels and research into the problems of Northern Ireland. *A Place Apart.*

Murphy, Ian
Architect, lecturer at the University of Westminster.

77 The technology of decentralization can be the saviour or assassin of contemporary and future society. The role of architects may be uncertain, but the role of architecture is not. In order to look forward society may sometimes have to look back. This it should do in order to learn from previous mistakes and oversights and to preclude similar eventualities in the future. This does not imply historical dependency, as some would assert. The symbiosis of architecture and technology should prevail, engendered by honesty and integrity. The task will not be easy.
1993 'The impact of the environment: the shock of the new', in Ben Farmer and Hentie Louw (eds) *Companion to Contemporary Architectural Thought* (1993).

Murphy, Tom (Thomas) S 1925–
US media company executive, president (1964–72) and chair (1966–96) of ABC Inc.

78 If you hire mediocre people, they will hire mediocre people.
1991 In *Fortune*, 6 May.

Murray, Les(lie Allan) 1938–
Australian poet and writer whose exuberant verse reflects both his farming background and his preoccupation with language. His collections include *The Ilex Tree* (1965), *The Weatherboard Cathedral* (1969), *Subhuman Redneck Poems* (1996) and *Conscious and Verbal* (1999).

79 The houses there wear verandahs out of shyness.
1986 *Selected Poems*, 'Driving Through Sawmill Towns'.

80 If the cardinal points of costume
are Robes, Tato, Rig and Scunge,
where are shorts in this compass?

They are the never Robes
as other bareleg outfits have been:
the toga, the kilt, the lava-lava,
the Mahatma's cotton dhoti;

archbishops and field marshals
at their ceremonies never wear shorts.
The very word
means underpants in North America.
1986 *Selected Poems*, 'The Dream of Wearing Shorts Forever'.

81 A for adrenalin, the original A-bomb, fuel
and punishment of aspiration, the Enlightenment's
air-burst
Back when God made me, I had no script. It was better.
For all the death, we also die unrehearsed.
In *Collected Poems* (1998).

Murray, Mike (Michael) c.1956–
US computer executive and philanthropist. Vice-President of Human Resources and Administration at Microsoft until 1999.

82 If Microsoft were a car it would have a large gas pedal and a small but workable brake. It would not have a rear-view mirror.
1994 In *Newsweek*, 11 Jul.

Murrow, Edward (Edgar) R(oscoe) 1908–65
US journalist and broadcaster. As CBS correspondent from Britain from 1937, he conveyed wartime spirit to the US. He became a producer of current affairs television programmes after the war, and his questioning of Joseph McCarthy contributed to the Senator's fall from grace.

83 He mobilized the English language and sent it into battle to steady his fellow countrymen and hearten those Europeans upon whom the long dark night of tyranny had descended.
1954 Of Churchill. Broadcast, 30 Nov, quoted in *In Search of Light* (1967).

84 The people you have seen have the strength to harvest your fruit and vegetables. They do not have the strength to influence legislation. Maybe you do.
1960 *Harvest of Shame*, CBS TV documentary on migrant labour, 25 Nov, concluding words.

85 The politician is trained in the art of inexactitude. His words tend to be blunt or rounded, because if they have a cutting edge they may later return to wound him.
Attributed.

Muschamp, Herbert 1957–2007
Architecture critic for the *New York Times*.

86 Red-and-gold disease…an itch, the theater a place to scratch it…a yearning for the wider world.
1995 In the *New York Times*, 30 Jul. The phrase 'red-and-gold disease' was coined by Lincoln Kirstein's mother when her son began haunting theatres.

Musgrove, F(rank) 1923–2011
English educationalist.

87 It is the business of education to eliminate the influence of parents on the life-chances of the young.
1966 *The Family, Education and Society*.

Mussolini, Benito also called Il Duce [the Leader] 1883–1945
Italian politician and Prime Minister (1922). By 1925 he had established himself as dictator. His declaration of war on Britain and France exposed Italy's military unpreparedness, and was followed by a series of defeats; his popularity waned, and he was overthrown and arrested (Jul 1943). Rescued by German paratroopers to head the puppet Italian Social Republic, in 1945 he was captured by the Italian Resistance and shot.

88 I could have transformed this grey assembly hall into an armed camp of Blackshirts, a bivouac for corpses. I could have nailed up the doors of Parliament.
1922 Inaugural speech to the Lower House as Prime Minister, 16 Nov.

89 If I advance, follow me. If I retreat, kill me. If I die, avenge me.
1926 Said to senior officials after an attempt on his life, 6 Apr.

90 Better one day as a lion than a hundred years as a sheep.
c.1930 Quoted in Denis Mack-Smith *Mussolini's Roman Empire* (1976), p.47.

91 War alone can carry to the maximum tension all human energies and imprint with the seal of nobility those people who have the courage to confront it; every other test is a mere substitute.

c.1930 Quoted in Denis Mack-Smith *Mussolini's Roman Empire* (1976), p.47.

92 Words are beautiful things, but muskets and machine guns are even more beautiful.
c.1932 Quoted in Denis Mack-Smith *Mussolini's Roman Empire* (1976).

93 A nation, to remain healthy, should make war every twenty-five years.
1934 Quoted in Denis Mack-Smith *Mussolini's Roman Empire* (1976), p.63.

94 War is to man as maternity to women.
1934 Speech, May. Quoted in Denis Mack-Smith *Mussolini's Roman Empire* (1976), p.54.

95 When the war in Spain is over I shall have to find something else: the Italian character has to be formed through fighting.
1936 Quoted in Thomas *The Spanish Civil War*, p.226.

96 Fascism accepts the individual only insofar as his interests coincide with the state's.
Quoted in the *Enciclopedia Italiana*.

Myers, Mike 1963–
US actor.

97 Party on, dude!
1992 As Wayne Campbell in *Wayne's World*.

98 Yeah, baby!
1997 As Austin Powers in *Austin Powers International Man of Mystery*.

Myrdal, (Karl) Gunnar 1898–1987
Swedish economist. Professor of Economics, Stockholm University (1933–9, 1961–5). A prominent member of the 'Stockholm School' of macroeconomics of the 1930s. Swedish Minister for Trade and Commerce (1945–7) and Executive Secretary of the UN Economic Commerce (1947–57). In 1974 he was jointly awarded the Nobel prize for economics with Friedrich Hayek. His wife Alva was awarded the Nobel prize for peace in 1982 with Alfonso Garcia Robles.

99 Quantities defined in terms of measurements made at the end of the period in question are referred to as *ex post*; quantities defined in terms of action planned at the beginning of the period in question are referred to as *ex ante*.
1939 *Monetary Equilibrium*.

Nabokov, Vladimir 1899–1977
Russian-born US writer. He left Russia in 1917 and began writing in English in the 1940s. His most widely known novel is *Lolita* (1955). His work is multi-layered and highly literary.

1 There are aphorisms that, like airplanes, stay up only while they are in motion.
1937 *The Gift*, ch.1.

2 Poor Knight! he really had two periods, the first—a dull man writing broken English, the second—a broken man writing dull English.
1941 *The Real Life of Sebastian Knight*, ch.1.

3 The cradle rocks above an abyss, and common sense tells us that our existence is but a brief crack of light between two eternities of darkness.
1951 *Conclusive Evidence* (revised as *Speak, Memory*, 1966), ch.1.

4 Lolita, light of my life, fire of my loins. My sin, my soul. Lo-lee-ta: the tip of the tongue taking a trip of three steps down the palate to tap, at three, on the teeth. Lo. Lee. Ta.
1955 Humbert Humbert. *Lolita*, pt.1, ch.1.

5 You can always count on a murderer for a fancy prose style.
1955 Humbert Humbert. *Lolita*, ch.1.

6 The tiny madman in his padded cell.
1955 Humbert Humbert's description of an embryo. *Lolita*, ch.11.

7 Like so many ageing college people, Pnin had long ceased to notice the existence of students on campus.
1957 *Pnin*, ch.3, section 6.

8 As to the rest, I am no more guilty of imitating 'real life' than 'real life' is responsible for plagiarizing me.
1958 *Nabokov's Dozen*, bibliographical note.

9 Life is a great surprise. I do not see why death should not be an even greater one.
1962 *Pale Fire*.

10 Human life is but a series of footnotes to a vast, obscure unfinished masterpiece.
1962 *Pale Fire*, 'Commentary'.

11 Solitude is the playfield of Satan.
1962 *Pale Fire*, 'Commentary'.

12 I know more than I can express in words, and the little I can express would not have been expressed, had I not known more.
1964 Interview in *Playboy*, Jan.

13 A novelist is, like all mortals, more fully at home on the surface of the present than in the ooze of the past.
1964 Interview in *Playboy*, Jan.

14 A work of art has no importance whatever to society. It is only important to the individual, and only the individual reader is important to me.
1964 Interview in *Playboy*, Jan.

15 Style and structure are the essence of a book; great ideas are hogwash.
1967 Interview in the *Paris Review*, Summer.

16 Derivative writers seem versatile because they imitate many others, past and present. Artistic originality has only itself to copy.
1967 Interview in the *Paris Review*, Summer.

17 Satire is a lesson, parody is a game.
1967 Interview in *Wisconsin Studies in Contemporary Literature*, Spring.

18 Those Eggheads are terrible Philistines. A real good head is not oval but round.
1967 Interview in *Wisconsin Studies in Contemporary Literature*, Spring.

19 A good laugh is the best pesticide.
1968 Interview on BBC television. Reported in *The Listener*, 10 Oct.

20 I think like a genius, I write like a distinguished author, and I speak like a child.
1973 *Strong Opinions*, foreword.

21 Her exotic daydreams do not prevent her from being small-town bourgeois at heart, clinging to conventional ideas or committing this or that conventional violation of the conventional, adultery being a most conventional way to rise above the conventional.
'Madame Bovary'. Collected in *Lectures on Literature* (published 1980).

22 My answer to your question 'Does the writer have a social responsibility?' is NO. You owe me ten cents, sir.
Letter to an editor who had offered him $200 for 2,000 words. Quoted by Eleanor Blau in the *New York Times*, 24 Aug 1989.

Nader, Ralph   1934–

US lawyer and Green Party political activist. As part of his campaigning on a range of humanitarian, political and environmental issues he has run for US President on five occasions.

23 We must strive to become good ancestors.
2004 *The Good Fight*.

24 Half of democracy is about just showing up.
2004 *The Good Fight*.

25 Advertisements that say they are lying are telling the truth.
2011 *The Greatest Movie Ever Sold*.

26 Your best teacher is your last mistake.
Attributed.

Naipaul, Sir V(idiadhar) S(urajprasad)   1932–

Trinidadian writer. His works include *The Mystic Masseur* (1957, John Llewelyn Rhys Memorial Prize), *Miguel Street* (1959, Somerset Maugham Award), *A House for Mr. Biswas* (1961), *A Bend in the River* (1979, Booker Prize) and the autobiographical *Finding the Centre* (1984). He was awarded the Nobel prize for literature in 2001.

27 Worse, to have lived without even attempting to lay claim to one's portion of the earth; to have lived and died as one had been born, unnecessary and unaccommodated.
1961 *A House for Mr. Biswas*, prologue.

28 All that I know of our history and the history of the Indian Ocean I have got from books written by Europeans… Without Europeans, I feel, all our past would have been washed away, like the scuff marks of fishermen on the beach.
1979 *A Bend in the River*, ch.1, 'The Second Rebellion'.

29 I do not regard the knighthood as a social accomplishment.
1993 Quoted in 'Kingdom of Naipaul' by Zoë Heller in the *Independent on Sunday Review*, 28 Mar.

30 Take it on the chin and move on.
Attributed comment to Paul Theroux after their friendship ended. In *Sir Vidia's Shadow: A Friendship Across Five Continents* by Paul Theroux (1998).

31 It is wrong to have an ideal view of the world. That's where the mischief starts. That's where everything starts unravelling.
2004 *Magic Seeds*.

Nairne, Caroline, Lady   1766–1845

Scottish songwriter, who collected traditional airs and wrote lyrics to them, often on Jacobite themes.

32 The laird o' Cockpen, he's proud an' he's great,
His mind is ta'en up wi' things o' the State.
'The Laird o' Cockpen', stanza 1.

33 I'm wearin' awa', John
Like snaw-wreaths in thaw, John,
I'm wearin' awa'
To the land o' the leal.
'The Land o' the Leal', stanza 1.

34 Bonnie Charlie's now awa,
Safely owre the friendly main;
Mony a heart will break in twa,
Should he ne'er come back again.

Will ye no come back again?
Will ye no come back again?
Better lo'ed ye canna be,
Will ye no come back again?
'Will Ye No Come Back Again?', stanza 1 and chorus.

Namath, Joe Willie (Joseph William)   1943–

US football player. Known as 'Broadway Joe', he was an outstanding quarterback with Alabama University and, from 1965, the New York Jets. In 1969 he led the Jets to unexpected victory in the Superbowl.

35 When you win, nothing hurts.
Quoted in Colin Jarman *The Guinness Dictionary of Sports Quotations* (1990).

Napier, Sir Charles James   1782–1853

Scottish soldier, born in London. He served in Ireland, Portugal, against the US and in 1841 was sent to India, where he broke the power of the amirs at the Battle of Meeanee and became Governor of Sind.

36 *Peccavi.*
I have sinned [Sind].
1843 Attributed encoded message, 24 Mar, sent after the Battle of Hyderabad and the capture of Sind.

Napoleon I   1769–1821

French general and Emperor. Born in Corsica, he rose to prominence during the French Revolution, and was appointed to command the army of Italy in 1796. Campaigns in Egypt and Austria followed, and his successes allowed him to lead a coup against the government and become dictator. Although he was exiled to Elba by the Allies in 1814, he returned in 1815, when he was finally defeated at Waterloo and exiled to St Helena.

37 *Soldats, songez que, du haut de ces pyramides, quarante siècles vous contemplent.*
Soldiers, think that, from the summit of these pyramids, forty centuries look down upon you.
1798 Speech to the Army of Egypt, before the Battle of the Pyramids, 21 Jul. Quoted in Gaspard Gourgaud *Mémoires* (1823), vol.2, 'Egypte, Bataille des Pyramides'.

38 China? There lies a sleeping giant. Let him sleep! For when he wakes he will move the world.
c.1800 Attributed.

39 Wisdom and policy dictate that we must do as destiny demands and keep peace with the irresistible march of events.
1808 Said to Alexander I of Russia, 2 Feb.

40 In war, three-quarters turns on moral considerations; the balance of actual forces counts only for the remaining quarter.

1808 Comment, 27 Apr. Quoted in *Observations sur les affaires de l'Espagne, Saint Cloud*, in *Correspondance de Napoleon 1er* (1858–69), vol.17.

41 France has more need of me than I have of France.
   1813 Speech to Corps Législatif, Paris, 31 Dec.

42 How beautifully the English fight! But they must give way.
   1815 Attributed, at the Battle of Waterloo, 18 Jun.

43 The English conquered us; but they are far from being our equals.
   1815 Letter to Gaspar Gourgaud from St Helena, after the Battle of Waterloo.

44 An army marches on its stomach.
   1816 Attributed. Probably condensed from a long passage dated 14 Nov in E A de Las Cases *Le Mémoriale de Sainte-Hélène* (1823), vol.4.

45 In war, as in love, we must come into contact before we can triumph.
   Quoted in A G De Liancourt (ed) *Maximes de Napoleon* (1842).

46 William behaved like a bashful girl, who is afraid of her lover's bad reputation and therefore avoids being alone with him.
   Of William I of Prussia, who invited other German Princes to attend a meeting with Napoleon at Baden-Baden in June originally intended to be a private discussion on the possibility of a joint alliance with Russia. Quoted in A J P Taylor *Struggle for Mastery in Europe 1848–1918* (1954), p.121.

47 England is a nation of shopkeepers.
   Attributed while in exile on St Helena.

48 Power is my mistress. I have worked too hard in conquering her to allow anyone to take her from me, or even to covet her.
   The Journal of Roederer.

49 Prussia was hatched from a cannon-ball.
   Attributed.

Napoleon III until *1852* Louis-Napoleon in full Charles Louis Napoleon Bonaparte 1808–73

President of the Second French Republic (1848–52) and Emperor of the French (1852–70). He encouraged economic expansion and modernization, and presided over the Crimean conflict (1854–6) and the ill-starred intervention in Mexico (1861–7). After defeat by Prussia in 1870, the remainder of his life was spent in exile in England.

50 For too long, society has resembled a pyramid that has been turned upside down and made to rest on its summit. I have replaced it on its base.
   1852 Speech to the Legislative Assembly, 29 Mar.

51 We must not seek to fashion events, but let them happen of their own accord.
   1865 In conversation with Bismarck, Biarritz, 4 Oct.

52 When a man of my name is in power, he must do great things.
   Quoted in A J P Taylor *From Napoleon to the Second International* (1993).

Narogin, Mudrooroo formerly Colin Jackson 1938–

Australian writer and poet, who has piloted Aboriginal literature courses at several Australian universities. His works include *Dr. Wooreddy's Prescription for Enduring the Ending of the World* (1983), the song cycle *Dalwurra: The Black Bittern* (1988), the anthology *Writing from the Fringe* (1990) and *The Promised Land* (2000).

53 The Aboriginal writer is a Janus-type figure with one face turned to the past and the other to the future while existing in a postmodern, multicultural Australia in which he or she must fight for cultural space.
   1990 *Writing from the Fringe*, ch.1, 'Writing from the Fringe'.

Nash, (Frederic) Ogden 1902–71

US light versifier. His popular verse was published frequently in the *New Yorker* and helped establish its sophisticated tone. His collections include *Hard Lines* (1931) and *Boy is a Boy* (1960).

54 The cow is of the bovine ilk;
   One end is moo, the other, milk.
   1931 *Free Wheeling*, 'The Cow'.

55 The song of canaries
   Never varies,
   And when they're moulting
   They're pretty revolting.
   1931 *Free Wheeling*, 'The Canary'.

56 A bit of talcum
   Is always walcum.
   1931 *Free Wheeling*, 'The Baby'.

57 One would be in less danger
   From the wiles of a stranger
   If one's own kin and kith
   Were more fun to be with.
   1931 *Hard Lines*, 'Family Court'.

58 A girl whose cheeks are covered with paint
   Has an advantage with me over one whose ain't.
   1931 *Hard Lines*, 'Biological Reflection'.

59 Candy
   Is dandy
   But liquor
   Is quicker.
   1931 *Hard Lines*, 'Reflections on Ice-Breaking'.

60 The turtle lives 'twixt plated decks
   Which practically conceal its sex.
   I think it clever of the turtle
   In such a fix to be so fertile.
   1931 *Hard Lines*, 'Autres Bêtes, Autres Moeurs'.

61 It's better to be dead, or even perfectly well, than to suffer from the wrong affliction. The man who owns up to arthritis in a beri-beri year is as lonely as a woman in a last month's dress.
   1933 'How's Your Sacro-iliac?', in the *Saturday Evening Post*, 14 Oct.

62 Any kiddie in school can love like a fool,
   But hating, my boy, is an art.
   1933 *Happy Days*, 'Plea for Less Malice Toward None'.

63 I think that I shall never see
   A billboard lovely as a tree.
   Perhaps, unless the billboards fall,
   I'll never see a tree at all.
   1933 *Happy Days*, 'Song of the Open Road'.
   ▶ See Kilmer 486:9.

64 Children aren't happy with nothing to ignore
   And that's what parents were created for.
   1933 *Happy Days*, 'The Parent'.

65 Home is heaven and orgies are vile,
   But you *need* an orgy, once in a while.
   1935 *The Primrose Path*, 'Home, 9944/100% Sweet Home'.

66 The camel has a single hump;
   The dromedary, two;
   Or else the other way around,
   I'm never sure. Are you?
   1936 *The Bad Parents' Garden of Verse*, 'The Camel'.

67 Let us pause to consider the English,
   Who when they pause to consider themselves they get all reticently thrilled and tinglish,
   Because every Englishman is convinced of one thing, viz.:
   That to be an Englishman is to belong to the most exclusive club there is.
   1938 *I'm a Stranger Here Myself*, 'England Expects'.

68 There was a young belle of old Natchez
   Whose garments were always in patchez.
   When comment arose
   On the state of her clothes,
   She drawled, When Ah itchez, Ah scratchez.
   1938 *I'm a Stranger Here Myself*, 'Requiem'.

69 The trouble with a kitten is
   THAT
   Eventually it becomes a
   CAT.
   1940 *The Face Is Familiar*, 'The Kitten'.

70 One day he missed his loving bride.
   She had, the guide informed him later,
   Been eaten by an alligator.
   Professor Twist could not but smile.
   'You mean,' he said, 'a crocodile.'
   1940 *The Face Is Familiar*, 'The Purist'.

71 Oh, what a tangled web do parents weave
   When they think that their children are naïve.
   1940 *The Face Is Familiar*, 'Baby, What Makes the Sky Blue'.

72 This infant whose middle
   Is diapered still
   Will want to marry
   My daughter Jill.

   Oh sweet be his slumber and moist his middle!
   My dreams, I fear, are infanticiddle.
   1940 *The Face Is Familiar*, 'Song to be Sung by the Father of Infant Female Children'.

73 Sure, deck your lower limbs in pants;
   Yours are the limbs, my sweeting.
   You look divine as you advance—
   Have you seen yourself retreating?
   1940 *The Face Is Familiar*, 'What's The Use'.

74 Life is not having been told that the man has just waxed the floor.
   1942 *Good Intentions*, 'You and Me and P. B. Shelley'.

75 Beneath this slab
   John Brown is stowed.
   He watched the ads,
   And not the road.
   1942 *Good Intentions*, 'Lather As You Go'.

76 I have a bone to pick with Fate.
   Come here and tell me, girlie,
   Do you think my mind is maturing late,
   Or simply rotted early?
   1942 *Good Intentions*, 'Lines On Facing Forty'.

77 I test my bath before I sit,
   And I'm always moved to wonderment
   That what chills the finger not a bit
   Is so frigid upon the fundament.
   1942 *Good Intentions*, 'Samson Agonistes'.

78 Women would rather be right than be reasonable.
   1942 *Good Intentions*, 'Frailty, Thy Name is a Misnomer'.

79 Parsley
   Is gharsely.
   1942 *Good Intentions*, 'Further Reflections on Parsley'.

80 God in His wisdom made the fly
   And then forgot to tell us why.
   1942 *Good Intentions*, 'The Fly'.

81 One thing that literature would be greatly the better for
   Would be a more restricted employment by authors of simile and metaphor.
   1945 *Many Long Years Ago*, 'Very Like A Whale'.

82 He tells you when you've got on too much lipstick,
   And helps you with your girdle when your hips stick.
   1949 *Versus*, 'The Perfect Husband'.

83 All winter long,
   I am one for whom the bell is tolling;
   I can arouse no interest in basketball,
   Indoor fly casting or bowling;
   The sports pages are strictly no soap!
   And until the cry Play Ball! I simply mope.
   1957 Quoted in Colin Jarman *The Guinness Dictionary of Sports Quotations* (1990).

84 It is a fact that a lady wants to be dressed exactly like everybody else but she gets pretty upset if she sees anybody else dressed exactly like her.
   1964 *Marriage Lines*, 'Thoughts Thought on an Avenue'.

85 My verse represents a handle I can grasp in order not to yield to the centrifugal forces which are trying to throw me off the world.
   Recalled on his death, 9 May 1971.

86 Basketball, a game which won't be fit for people until they set the basket umbilicus-high and return the giraffes to the zoo.
   Quoted in Colin Jarman *The Guinness Dictionary of Sports Quotations* (1990).

87 I eat my peas with honey;
   I've done it all my life.
   They do taste kinda funny,
   but it keeps 'em on the knife.
   Attributed.

Nashe, Thomas 1567–1601

English dramatist and satirist. His play *The Isle of Dogs* (1597, now lost) was so scathing on the subject of state abuses that it was suppressed, the theatre closed down and he himself thrown into Fleet prison. *The Unfortunate Traveller* (1594) is a picaresque tale, one of the earliest of its kind.

88 'New herrings, new!' we must cry, every time we make ourselves public, or else we shall be christened with a hundred new titles of idiotism.
   1592 *Pierce Penniless, His Supplication to the Devil*, 'An Invective Against Enemies of Poetry'.

89 Poetry is the honey of all flowers, the quintessence of all sciences, the marrow of wit, and the very phrase of angels.
   1592 *Pierce Penniless, His Supplication to the Devil*, 'An Invective Against Enemies of Poetry'.

90 If I be evil intreated, or sent away with a flea in mine ear, let him look that I will rail on him soundly; nor for an hour or a day, whiles the injury is fresh in my memory; but in some elaborate polished poem, which I will leave to the world when I am dead, to be a living image to all ages of his beggarly parsimony and ignoble illiberality.
1592 *Pierce Penniless, His Supplication to the Devil*, 'An Invective Against Enemies of Poetry'.

91 I will confer with thee somewhat gravely, although thou beest a goosecap and hast no judgement.
1592 *Strange News of the Intercepting Certain Letters*.

92 Immortal Spenser, no frailty hath thy fame but the imputation of this idiot's friendship!
1592 *Strange News of the Intercepting Certain Letters*.

93 Spring, the sweet spring, is the year's pleasant king,
Then blooms each thing, then maids dance in a ring,
Cold doth not sting, the pretty birds do sing:
Cuckoo, jug-jug, pu-we, to-witta-woo!
1592 *Summer's Last Will and Testament*, 'Song'.

94 Fair summer droops, droop men and beasts therefore:
So fair a summer look for never more.
All good things vanish, less than in a day,
Peace, plenty, pleasure, suddenly decay.
Go not yet away, bright soul of the sad year;
The earth is hell when thou leav'st to appear.
1592 *Summer's Last Will and Testament*, 'Song'.

95 From winter, plague and pestilence, good lord, deliver us!
1592 *Summer's Last Will and Testament*.

96 Beauty is but a flower
Which wrinkles will devour;
Brightness falls from the air;
Queens have died young and fair;
Dust hath closèd Helen's eye.
I am sick, I must die.
Lord, have mercy on us!
1592 'A Litany in Time of Plague'.

97 He that is a traveller must have the back of an ass to bear all, a tongue like the tail of a dog to flatter all, the mouth of a hog to eat all what is set before him, the ear of a merchant to hear all and say nothing; and if this be not the highest step of thraldom, there is no liberty or freedom.
1594 *The Unfortunate Traveller, or the Life of Jack Wilton*.

Nathan, George Jean 1882–1958
US theatre critic. He was co-editor of *The Smart Set* (1914–24) and founded the *American Mercury* with H L Mencken in 1924. Among the emerging playwrights to whom he gave support was Eugene O'Neill.

98 The most loyal and faithful woman indulges her imagination in a hypothetical liaison whenever she dons a new street frock for the first time.
1921 *The Theatre, the Drama, the Girls*, 'Woman'.

99 The test of a real comedian is whether you laugh at him before he opens his mouth.
Quoted in *American Mercury*, Sep 1929.

1 I always said that I'd like Barrymore's acting till the cows came home. Well, ladies and gentlemen, last night the cows came home.
1939 Review of John Barrymore's performance in *My Dear Children*.

2 Impersonal criticism...is like an impersonal fist fight or an impersonal marriage, and as successful.
Quoted in Charles Angoff (ed) *The World of George Jean Nathan* (1952).

3 The dramatic critic who is without prejudice is on the plane with the general who does not believe in taking human life.
Attributed.

Nation, Carry Amelia née Moore 1846–1911
US temperance agitator. She went on saloon-smashing expeditions with a hatchet and was frequently imprisoned for breach of the peace.

4 A woman is stripped of everything by them [saloons]. Her husband is torn from her; she is robbed of her sons, her home, her food, and her virtue; and then they strip her clothes off and hang her up bare in these dens of robbery and murder. Truly does the saloon make a woman bare of all things!
c.1893 Quoted in Carleton Beals *Cyclone Carry* (1962), ch.14.

Naughton, Bill 1910–92
Irish novelist and screenwriter. His screen credits include *Alfie* (1966), *The Family Way* (1966) and *Spring and Port Wine* (1970).

5 It seems to me if they ain't got you one way they got you another. So what's the answer? That's what I keep asking myself. What's it all about? Know what I mean?
1966 Line delivered by Michael Caine in *Alfie*.

Neale, J(ames) M(ason) 1818–66
English clergyman and hymn writer.

6 All glory, laud and honour
To Thee, Redeemer, King,
To whom the lips of children
Made sweet hosannas ring.
1851 'All Glory, Laud and Honour'.

7 Jerusalem the golden,
With milk and honey blessed,
Beneath thy contemplation
Sink heart and voice oppressed.
I know not, O I know not
What joys await us there,
What radiancy of glory,
What light beyond compare.
1858 'Jerusalem the Golden', translated from the original Latin of St Bernard of Cluny.

Neeson, Liam John 1952–
Northern Irish film actor. His many performances have ranged from the title roles in *Schindler's List* (1993) and *Michael Collins* (1996) to starring parts in the adventure movies *Taken* (2008), *Clash of the Titans* (2010) and *The Grey* (2011).

8 I will look for you, I will find you, and I will kill you.
2008 As Bryan Mills in *Taken* (screenplay by Luc Besson and Robert Mark Kamen).

Nehru, Jawaharlal 1889–1964
Indian statesman, President of the Indian National Congress (1929) and India's first Prime Minister (1947–64). Neutral in the Cold War, he embarked on industrialization, reorganized the states

linguistically and ended the dispute with Pakistan over Kashmir peacefully.

9 Stalin…that great lover of peace, a man of giant stature who moulded, as few other men have done, the destinies of his age… The occasion is not merely the passing away of a great figure but perhaps the ending of an historic era.
1953 Tribute, Indian Parliament, 9 Mar.

Neilson, John Shaw 1872–1942

Australian poet. His first work was published in the *Bulletin* and first collected in *Heart of Spring* (1919), followed by *Ballad and Lyrical Poems* (1923) and *New Poems* (1927). *Collected Poems* (1934) was followed by posthumous collections.

10 The young girl stood beside me. I
Saw not what her young eyes could see:
—A light, she said, not of the sky
Lives somewhere in the Orange Tree.
1923 *Ballad and Lyrical Poems*, 'The Orange Tree', stanza 1.

11 Here is the ecstasy
Of sun-fed wine and song:
Drink! it is melody
Under a kurrajong.
'Under a Kurrajong', stanza 1, in R H Croll (ed) *Collected Poems of John Shaw Neilson* (1934).

Nelson, Horatio, Viscount Nelson 1758–1805

English admiral. In 1794 he commanded at Bastia and Calvi, where he lost the sight of his right eye, and at Santa Cruz in 1796, where he lost his right arm. In 1798 he destroyed Napoleon's fleet in Aboukir Bay, and subsequently began an affair with Emma, Lady Hamilton. In 1805 he defeated the combined French and Spanish fleet at Trafalgar, but was mortally wounded.

12 A fleet of British ships of war are the best negotiators in Europe.
1801 Letter to Lady Hamilton, Mar, before the Battle of Copenhagen.

13 You know, Foley, I have only one eye—I have a right to be blind sometimes… I really do not see the signal.
1801 Said to Captain Foley during the Battle of Copenhagen, 2 Apr. Nelson disregarded the order of his superior, Admiral Hyde-Parker, to break off action and went on to win the engagement.

14 I wish to say Nelson confides that every man will do his duty.
1805 Instructions to the flag officer on HMS *Victory*, 21 Oct. The signal was amended to begin, 'England expects….

15 Kiss me, Hardy.
1805 Attributed, as he lay dying in the cockpit of the *Victory* during the Battle of Trafalgar, 21 Oct.

16 Thank God, I have done my duty.
1805 Last words at the Battle of Trafalgar, quoted in Robert Southey *Life of Nelson* (1813), ch.9.

Nemerov, Howard 1920–91

US poet, novelist and playwright. He was US Poet Laureate from 1988 to 1990, and won a National Book Award for his *Collected Poems* in 1977.

17 Children, to be illustrious is sad.
1958 *Mirrors and Windows*, 'The Statues in the Public Gardens'.

18 Till I, high in the tower of my time
Among familiar ruins, began to cry
For accident, sickness, justice, war and crime,
Because all died, because I had to die.
The snow fell, the trees stood, the promise kept,
And a child I slept.
1960 *New Poems*, 'The View from an Attic Window'.

19 For a Jewish Puritan of the middle class, the novel is serious, the novel is work, the novel is conscientious application—
why, the novel is practically the retail business all over again.
1965 *Journal of the Fictive Life*, 'Reflexions of the Novelist Felix Ledger'.

20 I've never read a political poem that's accomplished anything. Poetry makes things happen, but rarely what the poet wants.
1988 In the *International Herald Tribune*, 14 Oct.
▶ See Auden 43:91.

Nero AD 37–68

Roman Emperor (AD 54–68). He was adopted by his stepfather Claudius and declared Emperor on Claudius's death. Ancient authors depict him as a debauched tyrant, and accuse him of starting the great fire of Rome in AD 64 (he blamed the Christians). A coup in AD 68 brought Galba to the throne, and Nero committed suicide.

21 *Qualis artifex pereo!*
Dead! And so great an artist!
Attributed words on the point of taking his life. Quoted in Suetonius *Nero*, 49.1 (translated by Robert Graves, 1957).

Neruda, Pablo *pseudonym of* Neftalí Ricardo Reyes Basoalto 1904–73

Chilean poet, essayist and diplomat, who travelled widely as a diplomat. His poetic themes range from subjective love to socially committed epic poems influenced by a communist ideology. He was awarded a Nobel prize in 1971.

22 *Sucede que me canso de mis pies y mis uñas
y mi pelo y mi sombra.
Sucede que me canso de ser hombre.*
I happen to be tired of my feet and my nails
and my hair and my shadow.
I happen to be tired of being a man.
1935 *Residencia en la tierra*, 'Walking Around' (translated as *Residence on Earth*, 1946).

23 *A nosotros nos enseñaron a respetar la iglesia,
a no toser, a no escupir en el atrio,
a no lavar la ropa en el altar
y no es así: la vida rompe las religiones.*
We were taught respect for the church,
no hawking and spitting on porticos,
don't soak your socks on the altar—
but things are different: life smashes religions.
1973 *La rosa separada*, 'Los hombres' (translated as *The Separate Rose*, 'The Men', 1985).

Nerval, Gérard de *pseudonym of* Gérard Labrunie 1808–55

French poet, novelist and author of critical essays, he was admired later by the Surrealists for his fantastic short tales.

24 *Philosophie! dont la lumière, comme celle des enfers de Milton, ne sert qu'à rendre les ténèbres visibles.*
Philosophy! In whose light, like that in Milton's hell, only serves to make the shadows visible.
1852 *Fragments*, 'Paradoxe et vérité'.

Nervo

25 *Il n'y a qu'un seul vice dont on ne voie personne se vanter, c'est l'ingratitude.*
There is only one vice of which no one boasts—ingratitude.
1852 *Fragments*, 'Paradoxe et vérité'.

26 *La vie d'un poète est celle de tous.*
The life of the poet is the life of everyone.
1855 *Petits Châteaux de Bohême*, 'À un ami'.

Nervo, Amado *pseudonym of* Juan Crisóstomo Ruiz de Nervo 1870–1919

Mexican poet and diplomat. He abandoned the priesthood in 1888 to work as a journalist. He studied Buddhist philosophy in depth, and his introspective poetry is characterized by deep religious feeling and simple form.

27 *No te juzgues incompleto porque no responden a tus ternuras; el amor lleva en sí su propia plenitud. Siempre que haya un hueco en tu vida, llénalo de amor.*
Don't judge yourself incomplete when your tenderness gets no response; love carries within itself its own plenitude.
Whenever there is a void in your life, fill it with love.
1918 *Plenitud*, 'Llénalo de amor' (translated as 'Fill It with love', 1928).

Netanyahu, Benjamin 1949–

Israeli politician. After service with the Israel Defence Forces, he joined the Likud Party and became Israeli Ambassador to the United Nations (1984–8). He has since served as Foreign Affairs Minister (2002–3) and Finance Minister (2003–5) and been twice elected as Prime Minister of Israel (1996–9 and 2009–).

28 The truth is that if Israel were to put down its arms there would be no more Israel. If the Arabs were to put down their arms there would be no more war.
2006 Speech in the Knesset at the end of the 2006 Israel–Lebanon conflict, quoted in *The Globes*, 14 Aug.

29 We could find that an Arab Spring turns into an Iranian winter.
2011 Warning about the possible consequences of pro-democracy Arab uprisings.

30 The difference between us is that we're using missile defence to protect our civilians and they're using their civilians to protect their missiles.
2014 Discussing the threat from Hamas on *Face the Nation*, CBS, 12 Jul.

Nevelson, Louise 1900–88

Russian-born US sculptor. Her work incorporates pieces of wood, found objects, cast metal, and other materials, creating great mysterious walls or boxes of complex, abstract forms. Her autobiography, *Dawns and Dusks*, was published in 1976.

31 There's no denying that Caruso came with a voice…that Beethoven came with music in his soul, Picasso was drawing like an angel in the crib. You're born with it.
1976 *Dawns and Dusks*.

Neville, Katherine 1945–

US novelist.

32 'In Scotland,' Tavish muttered, picking up my bags, 'the *women* do the hod carrying while we blokes retire to the nearest pub—to deliberate upon the role of labour in society.'
1992 *A Calculated Risk*.

New York Times

First published 1851 as the *New-York Daily Times*.

33 Who owns history? The public servants who make it, or the people who hire them and to whom they are accountable?
1983 'Who Owns History?', editorial, 19 Nov.

34 Armed with a notebook, ingratiating grin and fine intelligence, he grew to be a most discerning witness of America's most distinctive rite, not just the election but the making of our presidents.
1986 Of journalist Theodore H White. 'Teddy White, the Maker of Epics', editorial, 17 May.

35 The best way to read [a poem] is off the top of your head, and out of the corner of your eye.
1987 *Noted With Pleasure*, in the *New York Times*, 16 Mar.

36 For Palestinians, PLO is a homeland of the mind.
1988 Editorial, 20 Mar.

37 Empty luggage may be easier to carry, but it's still empty.
1988 Of Michael S Dukakis's presidential campaign. 'The Painless Platform', editorial, 20 Jul.

38 Millions drew up before the international hearth of television.
1991 On international media coverage of the Allied deadline for Iraq's withdrawal from Kuwait. 'With Our Own Eyes', editorial, 24 Feb.

39 Lightning rods have had it better than Nancy Reagan.
1991 On the publication of Kitty Kelley's unauthorized biography *Nancy Reagan*. 'Scratching at the Teflon', editorial, 10 Apr.

40 Who is quickest on the drawl?
1992 On claims to Texas by both George Bush and rival presidential aspirant Ross Perot. Editorial, 9 Jun.

41 When it comes to the final judgements on political conduct, history is not merciful. It is just.
1994 'Justice and Mercy in Arkansas', editorial, 17 Dec.

Newman, Arnold 1918–2006

US photographer.

42 We don't take our pictures with cameras. We take them with our hearts, and we take them with our minds.
1992 In *Sunday Morning*, CBS T V, 2 Aug.

Newman, James R 1907–66

US mathematician and mathematical historian. He was the compiler of the magnum opus *The World of Mathematics* (1956).

43 There are two ways to teach mathematics. One is to take real pains toward creating understanding—visual aids, that sort of thing. The other is the old British style of teaching until you're blue in the face.
1956 Quoted in the *New York Times*, 30 Sep.

Newman, John Henry 1801–90

English theologian, active in Oxford in the Tractarian movement of the Church of England. He converted to the Roman Catholic faith in 1845 and was appointed Cardinal by Pope Leo XIII in 1879.

44 It is as absurd to argue men, as to torture them, into believing.

1831 'The Usurpations of Reason', collected in *Oxford University Sermons* (1843).

45 Lead, kindly Light, amid the encircling gloom,
Lead thou me on;
The night is dark, and I am far from home,
Lead thou me on.
Keep Thou my feet; I do not ask to see
The distant scene; one step enough for me.
1833 'Lead, kindly Light'.

46 May He support us all the day long, till the shades lengthen, and the evening comes, and the busy world is hushed, and the fever of life is over, and our work is done! Then in His mercy may He give us a safe lodging, and a holy rest, and peace at the last.
1834 'Wisdom and Innocence', collected in *Sermons Bearing on Subjects of the Day*.

47 *We can believe what we choose*. We are answerable for what we choose to believe.
1848 Letter to Mrs William Froude, 27 Jun.

48 It is very difficult to get up resentment towards persons whom one has never seen.
1864 *Apologia pro Vita Sua*, 'Mr Kingsley's Method of Disputation'.

49 Praise to the Holiest in the height,
And in the depth be praise;
In all His words most wonderful,
Most sure in all His ways.
1865 *The Dream of Gerontius*. In *The Month* (published in book form in 1866).

Newman, Paul Leonard 1925–2008

US film actor. His many awards included an Oscar for *The Color of Money* (1986); other films included *Cat on a Hot Tin Roof* (1958), *The Hustler* (1961), *Hud* (1963), *Butch Cassidy and the Sundance Kid* (1969) and *The Sting* (1973).

50 I'm like a good cheese. I'm just getting mouldy enough to be interesting.
2005 In *The Guardian*, 10 Apr.

51 The embarrassing thing is that my salad dressing is out-grossing my films.
2008 Referring to the successful food company he founded to raise money for charity, *The Times Online*, 26 Jan.

Newman, Peter C 1929–

Austrian-born Canadian author and political columnist.

52 And what I've learned is not to believe in magical leaders any more; that character and compassion are more important than ideology; and that even if it's absurd to think you can change things, it's even more absurd to think that it's foolish and unimportant to try.
1973 *Home Country: People, Places, and Power Politics*.

53 The rich don't have children; they have heirs.
1982 *The Establishment Man: A Portrait of Power*.

News of the World

First published 1843. It ceased publication in 2011 after admitting to illegal phone hacking.

54 All human life is there.
Motto.

55 Quite simply, we lost our way.
2011 Editorial in final edition, 10 Jul.

Newton, Sir Isaac 1642–1727

English mathematician and physicist, considered the greatest scientist of modern time. Newton was Professor of Mathematics (1669–1701) at Cambridge. Between 1664 and 1666 he discovered the law of gravitation, and began to develop differential calculus.

56 *Corpus omne perseverare in statu suo quiescendi vel movendi uniformiter in directum, nisi quatenus illud a viribus impressis cogitur statum suum mutare.*
Every body continues in its state of rest, or of uniform motion in a right line, unless it is compelled to change that state by forces impressed thereon.
1687 First Law of Motion. *Philosophiae Naturalis Principia Mathematica* (translated by Andrew Motte, 1729).

57 *Mutationem motus proportionalem esse vi motrici impressae et fieri secundum lineam rectam qua vis illa imprimitur.*
The alteration of motion is ever proportional to the motive force impressed; and is made in the direction of the right line in which that force is impressed.
1687 Second Law of Motion. *Philosophiae Naturalis Principia Mathematica* (translated by Andrew Motte, 1729).

58 We are to admit no more causes of natural things than such as are both true and sufficient to explain their appearances... Nature is pleased with simplicity, and affects not the pomp of the superfluous causes.
1687 Newton's First Rule of Reasoning in Philosophy. *Philosophiae Naturalis Principia Mathematica* (translated by Andrew Motte, 1729).

59 *Actioni contrarium semper et aequalem esse reactionem: sive corporum duorum actiones in se mutuo semper esse aequales et in partes contrarias dirigi.*
To every action there is always opposed an equal reaction: or, the mutual actions of two bodies upon each other are always equal, and directed to contrary parts.
1687 Third Law of Motion. *Philosophiae Naturalis Principia Mathematica* (translated by Andrew Motte, 1729).

60 Geometry is that part of universal mechanics which accurately proposes and demonstrates the art of measuring.
1687 *Philosophiae Naturalis Principia Mathematica* (translated by Andrew Motte, 1729).

61 I know not what I may appear to the world, but to myself I seem to have been only like a boy playing on the sea shore, and diverting myself in now and then finding a smoother pebble or a prettier shell than ordinary, whilst the great ocean of truth lay all undiscovered before me.
Quoted in D Brewster (ed) *Memoirs of Newton* (1855), vol.2, ch.27.

62 In the absence of any other proof, the thumb alone would convince me of God's existence.
Attributed.

Newton, John 1725–1807

English divine and writer, who converted to Christianity in 1748 and became Curate of Olney, Buckinghamshire, in 1764.

63 Amazing grace! How sweet the sound
That saved a wretch like me!
I once was lost, but now am found,
Was blind, but now I see.
1779 *Olney Hymns*, 'Amazing Grace'.

Ngũgĩ wa Thiong'o

64 Glorious things of thee are spoken,
Zion, city of our God!
1779 Olney Hymns, 'Glorious things of thee are spoken'.

65 How sweet the name of Jesus sounds
In a believer's ear!
1779 Olney Hymns, 'How sweet the name of Jesus sounds'.

Ngũgĩ wa Thiong'o *originally* James Ngũgĩ 1938–

Kenyan writer. His early works were written in English, but he now chooses to write solely in his native Gikuyu. Works include *Weep Not Child* (1964), *The River Between* (1965), *A Grain of Wheat* (1967), *Matigari* (1987) and *Wizard of the Crow* (2006).

66 Today, children, I am going to tell you about the history of Mr. Blackman in three sentences. In the beginning he had the land and the mind and the soul together. On the second day, they took the body away to barter it for silver coins. On the third day, seeing that he was still fighting back, they brought priests and educators to bind his mind and soul so that these foreigners could more easily take his land and produce.
1977 Petals of Blood, ch.8.

67 He who produces should be able to control that which he produces.
1990 Quoted in Carol Sicherman *Nguũgõũ wa Thiong'o: The Making of a Rebel,* pt.1, ch.2, 'Nguũgõũ on Nguũgõũ' (by Nguũgõũ himself).

Nguyen, Xuan Oanh 1921–2003

Vietnamese economist who rose to become South Vietnam's acting Prime Minister briefly in 1964. After the country was reunited in 1975 he remained in limbo for ten years before his ideas for economic change were accepted. He is now regarded as the unofficial architect of Vietnam's economic reforms.

68 There is no such thing as communism versus capitalism. There are only degrees of communism and degrees of capitalism.
1995 In the *Eastern Express,* 17 May.

69 Patriotism in Vietnam took the communist road because it was the only one available. It had the appeal of a dream, a dream of social justice.
1995 In the *Eastern Express,* 17 May.

Nicholas I 1796–1855

Tsar of Russia (from 1825). During his reign, wars with Persia and Turkey increased Russia's territory. He died during the Crimean War, when Russia's attempts to absorb Turkey were resisted by Britain and France.

70 Russia has two generals in whom she can confide—Janvier and Février.
1855 Referring to the severe Russian winter climate. Quoted in *Punch,* 10 Mar.

Nicholas II 1868–1919

Last Emperor of Russia (1894–1917), whose reign was marked by alliance with France (1894), *entente* with Britain, disastrous war with Japan (1904–5) and the establishment of the Duma (1906). He fought against the Central Powers in 1915. Forced to abdicate at the Revolution, he was shot with his family by the Red Guards.

71 There are senseless dreams of the participation of local government representatives in the affairs of internal administration. I shall maintain the principle of autocracy just as firmly and unflinchingly as it was upheld by my own, ever to be remembered dead father.
1896 Declaration, 17 Jan.

Nichols, Grace 1950–

Guyanese poet, novelist and journalist, married to the poet John Agard; her publications include *Trust You, Wriggly!* (1981) and *The Poet Cat* (2000) for children, and the poetry sequences *i is a long memoried woman* (1983) (Commonwealth Poetry Prize) and *The Fat Black Woman's Poems* (1984).

72 I have crossed an ocean
I have lost my tongue
from the root of the old one
a new one has sprung
1983 i is a long memoried woman, epilogue.

73 IT'S BETTER TO DIE IN THE FLESH OF HOPE
THAN TO LIVE IN THE SLIMNESS OF DESPAIR.
1984 The Fat Black Woman's Poems, 'The Fat Black Woman's Motto on Her Bedroom Door'.

Nichols, Mike *originally* Michael Peschowsky 1931–2004

American stage and film director. He won the first of many Tony Awards with the play *Barefoot in the Park* (1963). In 1968 he won an Academy Award for *The Graduate*; subsequent films included *Catch-22* (1969), *Silkwood* (1983), *Working Girl* (1988), *Postcards from the Edge* (1990), *Birdcage* (1995), *Primary Colors* (1998) and *Charlie Wilson's War* (2007). He also won Emmy awards for the television adaptations of *Wit* (2001) and *Angels in America* (2003), making him one of the few directors to win Tony, Oscar and Emmy awards.

74 Style is beginning something in the manner which will make it necessary for things that happen later to happen.
1991 In *Film Comment,* May.

Nicholson, Bill 1919–2004

English footballer and manager. He played with Tottenham Hotspur, and as manager of the club achieved the double of the FA Cup and the League Championship (1961). He won two more FA Cup titles (1962 and 1967), the European Cup Winners' Cup (1963), two more League Championships (1971 and 1973) and the UEFA Cup (1972).

75 I prefer players not to be too good or clever at other things. It means they concentrate on football.
1973 Quoted in Peter Ball and Phil Shaw *The Book of Football Quotations* (1989).

Nicholson, Jack 1937–

US film actor. An office boy at MGM, he made his film debut in *Cry Baby Killer* (1958) and survived a decade of low-budget exploitation films before *Easy Rider* (1969) established his reputation. He has received twelve Academy Award nominations, winning three Oscars.

76 Here's Johnny!
1980 As Jack Torrance in *The Shining* (screenplay by Stanley Kubrick and Diane Johnson).

77 She's like a delicate fawn, crossed with a Buick.
1984 Of actress Jessica Lange. In *Vanity Fair,* Oct.

78 I don't want to be a product of my environment, I want my environment to be a product of me.
2006 As Frank Costello in *The Departed* (screenplay by William Monahan).

Nicholson, Vivian 1936–
English housewife. In 1961 her husband Keith won £152,000 on the football pools, but the couple subsequently had difficulty coping with their fortune. Keith died in a car crash and Viv spent the money in just four years and turned to religion after several failed marriages and alcohol and drug abuse.

79 I want to spend, and spend, and spend!
   1961 Quoted in the *Daily Herald*, 28 Sep, when asked what her plans were on winning the pools. The words 'Spend, spend, spend!' were later used as the title of her autobiography and for a biographical television play by Jack Rosenthal in 1977.

Nicias c.470–413 BC
Athenian statesman and soldier, who negotiated a short-lived peace with Sparta (421 BC). He was a commander in the disastrous naval expedition against Sicily in 418 BC, and following a siege of Syracuse was captured and put to death.

80 For it is men that make a city, and not its walls, nor its ships empty of men.
   413 BC Speech to the defeated Athenian army. Quoted in Thucydides 7.77.

Nicklaus, Jack William known as 'the Golden Bear' 1940–
US golfer. He won the US Open Championship in 1962, the first of 20 major tournaments. He went into semi-retirement in 1986 and is now in demand as a golf course designer.

81 Golf is not and never has been a fair game.
   Quoted in Colin Jarman *The Guinness Dictionary of Sports Quotations* (1990).

82 I think I fail a bit less than everyone else.
   Quoted in Michael Hobbs *The Golf Quotation Book* (1992).

Nicolle, Charles Jules Henri 1866–1936
French physician and microbiologist, Director of the Pasteur Institute in Tunis, Tunisia and Professor of Bacteriology at the Collège de France. He was awarded a Nobel prize in 1928 for demonstrating the transmission of typhus by lice.

83 All method is imperfect. Error is all around it, and at the least opportunity invades it… But what can we do? There is no other way.
   1932 *Biologie de l'Invention*.

Nicolson, Sir Harold 1886–1968
English diplomat, author and critic, born in Tehran. A distinguished diplomat (1909–29), he turned to journalism and was a National Liberal MP (1935–45). He wrote works of literary criticism and literary and historical biography.

84 My first impression is of a slightly bearded spinster: my second is of Willie King made up like Philip II: my third of some thin little bird, peeking, crooked, reserved, violent and timid.
   1931 On meeting James Joyce. Diary entry, 30 Jul.

85 I feel pretty glum and devote myself to reviewing. There is Joyce's *Finnegans Wake*. I try very hard indeed to understand that book but fail completely. It is almost impossible to decipher, and when one or two lines of understanding emerge like telegraph poles above a flood, they are at once countered by other poles going in the opposite direction.
   1939 Diary entry, 29 Apr.

Niebuhr, Reinhold 1892–1971
US theologian, Professor at the Union Theological Seminary, New York.

86 All men who live with any degree of serenity live by some assurance of grace.
   1934 *Reflections on the End of Our Era*.

87 Perhaps the most sublime insights of the Jewish prophets and the Christian gospel is the knowledge that since perfection is love, the apprehension of perfection is at once the means of seeing one's imperfections and the consoling assurance of grace which makes this realization bearable. This ultimate paradox of high religion is not an invention of theologians or priests. It is constantly validated by the most searching experiences of life.
   1934 *Reflections on the End of an Era*.

88 The pretensions of final truth are always partly an effort to obscure a darkly felt consciousness of the limits of human knowledge.
   1941 *The Nature and Destiny of Man*, vol.1.

89 God, give us grace to accept with serenity the things that cannot be changed, courage to change the things that should be changed, and the wisdom to distinguish the one from the other.
   In Richard Wightman Fox *Reinhold Neibuhr* (1985), ch.12. Attributed to Neibuhr, but more probably 18c German.

Nielsen, Carl August 1865–1931
Danish composer, who experimented with polytonality and developed a characteristic contrapuntal style.

90 Music is life, and, like it, inextinguishable.
   1916 Symphony No. 4, motto.

Niemöller, Martin 1892–1984
German submarine commander, pastor and theologian, leader of Christian opposition to Nazism.

91 When Hitler attacked the Jews I was not a Jew, therefore, I was not concerned. And when Hitler attacked the Catholics, I was not a Catholic, and therefore, I was not concerned. And when Hitler attacked the unions and the industrialists, I was not a member of the unions and I was not concerned. Then, Hitler attacked me and the Protestant church—and there was nobody left to be concerned.
   1944 *Children of Light and Darkness*, foreword.

Nietzsche, Friedrich Wilhelm 1844–1900
German philosopher, scholar and writer. Professor of Classical Philology at the University of Basel (1868–78), he resigned in ill health. From 1872 he produced a stream of brilliant, unclassifiable works, rejecting Christianity for a new, heroic morality. In 1889 he had a complete mental and physical breakdown, from which he never recovered. His reputation suffered when his ideas were adopted in a distorted form by the Nazis, but he is now regarded as a major influence on 20c thought.

92 *Überzeugungen sind gefährlichere Feinde der Wahrheit als Lügen.*
   Convictions are more dangerous enemies of truth than lies.
   1878 *Menschliches, Allzumenschliches* (*Human, All Too Human*), section 483 (translated by R J Hollingdale).

93 The press, the machine, the railway, the telegraph are premises whose thousand-year conclusion no one has yet dared to draw.
1880 *The Wanderer and His Shadow*, aphorism 278.

94 *Gott ist tot: aber so wie die Art der Menschen ist, wird es vielleicht noch Jahrtausende lang Höhlen geben, in denen man seinen Schatten zeigt.—Und wir—wir müssen auch noch seinen Schatten besiegen!*
God is dead; but given the way of men, there may still be caves for thousands of years in which his shadow will be shown.—And we—we still have to vanquish his shadow, too.
1882 *Die fröhliche Wissenschaft* (*The Gay Science*), section 108 (translated by W Kaufmann). This is the first occurrence of the famous phrase, which appears elsewhere in Nietzsche's work.

95 *Moralität ist Herden-Instinkt im Einzelnen.*
Morality is herd instinct in the individual.
1882 *Die fröhliche Wissenschaft* (*The Gay Science*), section 116 (translated by W Kaufmann).

96 *Und, alles in allem und großem: ich will irgendwann einmal nur noch ein Jasagender sein!*
And all in all and on the whole: some day I wish to be only a Yes-sayer.
1882 *Die fröhliche Wissenschaft* (*The Gay Science*), section 276 (translated by W Kaufmann).

97 *Glaubt es mir!—das Geheimnis, um die größte Fruchtbarkeit und den größten Genuss vom Dasein einzuernten, heißt: gefährlich leben!*
For believe me: the secret for harvesting from existence the greatest fruitfulness and the greatest enjoyment is—to live dangerously.
1882 *Die fröhliche Wissenschaft* (*The Gay Science*), section 283 (translated by W Kaufmann).

98 *Eins ist not.—Seinem Charakter 'Stil geben'.*
One thing is needful.—To 'give style' to one's character.
1882 *Die fröhliche Wissenschaft* (*The Gay Science*), section 290 (translated by W Kaufmann).

99 *Ich lehre euch den Übermenschen. Der Mensch ist Etwas, das überwunden werden soll.*
I teach you the Superman. Man is something that should be surpassed.
1883–92 *Also sprach Zarathustra* (*Thus Spake Zarathustra*), prologue, section 3 (translated by R J Hollingdale).

1 *Der Mensch ist ein Seil, geknüpft zwischen Tier und Übermensch,—ein Seil über einem Abgrunde.*
Man is a rope, fastened between animal and Superman—a rope over an abyss.
1883–92 *Also sprach Zarathustra* (*Thus Spake Zarathustra*), prologue, section 4 (translated by R J Hollingdale).

2 *Was groß ist am Menschen, das ist, dass er eine Brücke und kein Zweck ist.*
What is great in man is that he is a bridge and not a goal.
1883–92 *Also sprach Zarathustra* (*Thus Spake Zarathustra*), prologue, section 4 (translated by R J Hollingdale).

3 *Ich sage euch: man muss noch Chaos in sich haben, um einem tanzenden Stern gebären zu können.*
I tell you: one must have chaos in one, to give birth to a dancing star.
1883–92 *Also sprach Zarathustra* (*Thus Spake Zarathustra*), prologue, section 5 (translated by R J Hollingdale).

4 *Du gehst zu Frauen? Vergiss die Peitsche nicht!*
You are going to women? Do not forget the whip!
1883–92 *Also sprach Zarathustra* (*Thus Spake Zarathustra*), bk.1 (translated by R J Hollingdale).

5 Distrust all in whom the impulse to punish is powerful.
1883–92 *Also sprach Zarathustra* (*Thus Spake Zarathustra*) (translated by R J Hollingdale).

6 *Gesetzt, wir wollen Wahrheit: warum nicht lieber Unwahrheit? Und Ungewissheit? Selbst Unwissenheit?*
Granted we want truth: why not rather untruth? And uncertainty? Even ignorance?
1886 *Jenseits von Gut und Böse* (*Beyond Good and Evil*), section 1 (translated by R J Hollingdale).

7 *Allmählich hat sich mir herausgestellt, was jede große Philosophie bisher war: nämlich das Selbstbekenntnis ihres Urhebers und eine Art ungewollter und unvermerkter mémoires.*
It has gradually become clear to me what every great philosophy has hitherto been: a confession on the part of its author and a kind of involuntary and unconscious memoir.
1886 *Jenseits von Gut und Böse* (*Beyond Good and Evil*), section 6 (translated by R J Hollingdale).

8 *Sie schafft immer die Welt nach ihrem Bilde, sie kann nicht anders; Philosophie ist dieser tyrannische Treib selbst, der geistigste Wille zur Macht, zur 'Schaffung der Welt'.*
It [philosophy] always creates the world in its own image, it cannot do otherwise; philosophy is this tyrannical drive itself, the most spiritual will to power, to 'creation of the world'.
1886 *Jenseits von Gut und Böse* (*Beyond Good and Evil*), section 9 (translated by R J Hollingdale).

9 *Alles, was tief ist, liebt die Maske.*
Everything profound loves the mask.
1886 *Jenseits von Gut und Böse* (*Beyond Good and Evil*), section 40 (translated by R J Hollingdale).

10 The thought of suicide is a great source of comfort across many a bad night.
1886 *Jenseits von Gut und Böse* (*Beyond Good and Evil*), section 157 (translated by R J Hollingdale).

11 *Das moralische Urteilen und Verurteilen ist die Lieblings-Rache der Geistig-Beschränkten an denen, die es weniger sind.*
Moral judgement and condemnation is the favourite form of revenge of the spiritually limited on those who are less so.
1886 *Jenseits von Gut und Böse* (*Beyond Good and Evil*), section 219 (translated by R J Hollingdale).

12 *Durch schlechte Köchinnen—durch den vollkommenen Mangel an Vernunft in der Küche ist die Entwicklung des Menschen am längsten aufgehalten, am schlimmsten beeinträchtigt worden.*
Through bad female cooks—through the entire lack of reason in the kitchen—the development of mankind has been longest retarded and most interfered with.
1886 *Jenseits von Gut und Böse* (*Beyond Good and Evil*), section 234 (translated by Helen Zimmern, 1907).

13 *Herren-Moral und Sklaven-Moral.*
Master morality and slave morality.
1886 *Jenseits von Gut und Böse* (*Beyond Good and Evil*), section 260 (translated by R J Hollingdale).

14 Oh, how much is today hidden by science! Oh, how much it is expected to hide!
1887 *The Genealogy of Morals*, essay 3, 'What Do Ascetic Ideals Mean?'

15 *Hat je sich ein Weib, das sich gut bekleidet wusste, erkältet?*
Has a woman who knew she was well dressed ever caught a cold?
1889 *Die Götzen-Dämmerung* (*Twilight of the Idols*), 'Maxims and Arrows', no.25 (translated by R J Hollingdale).

16 Without music, life would be a mistake.
1889 *Die Götzen-Dämmerung* (*Twilight of the Idols*, translated by R J Hollingdale)

17 *Das, worin man die nationalen Unterschiede findet, ist viel mehr, als man bis jetzt eingesehen hat, nur der Unterschied verschiedener Kulturstufen und zum geringsten Teile etwas Bleibendes (und auch dies nicht in einem strengen Sinne).*
National differences consist, far more than has hitherto been observed, only in the differences of various grades of culture, and are only to a very small extent permanent (and not even that in a strict sense).
Nachgelassene Fragmente.

Nightingale, Benedict 1939–

British author and theatre critic. He was chief theatre critic for *The Times* (1990–2010).

18 He handles symbolism rather like an Olympic weight lifter, raising it with agonizing care, brandishing it with a tiny grunt of triumph, then dropping it with a terrible clang.
1984 Of playwright William Inge. In the *New York Times*, 28 Jul.

Nightingale, Florence 1820–1910

English nurse and hospital reformer during the Crimean War. She subsequently formed an institution for the training of nurses in London.

19 Why have women Passion, intellect, moral activity—these three—and a place in society where no one of the three can be exercised?
1852 'Cassandra' pt.1, part of an unpublished work *Suggestions for Thought to Searchers after Religious Truth* (revised and privately printed 1859). Published as an appendix in Ray Strachey *The Cause: A Short History of the Women's Movement in Great Britain* (1928).

20 Give us back our suffering, we cry to Heaven in our hearts—suffering rather than indifferentism; for out of nothing comes nothing... Better have pain than paralysis!
1852 'Cassandra' pt.1, part of an unpublished work *Suggestions for Thought to Searchers after Religious Truth* (revised and privately printed 1859). Published as an appendix in Ray Strachey *The Cause: A Short History of the Women's Movement in Great Britain* (1928).

21 Look at the poor lives we lead. It is a wonder that we are so good as we are, not that we are so bad.
1852 'Cassandra' pt.2, part of an unpublished work *Suggestions for Thought to Searchers after Religious Truth* (revised and privately printed 1859). Published as an appendix in Ray Strachey *The Cause: A Short History of the Women's Movement in Great Britain* (1928).

22 Marriage is the only chance (and it is but a chance) offered to women for escape from this death...and how eagerly and how ignorantly it is embraced.
1852 'Cassandra' pt.3, part of an unpublished work *Suggestions for Thought to Searchers after Religious Truth* (revised and privately printed 1859). Published as an appendix in Ray Strachey *The Cause: A Short History of the Women's Movement in Great Britain* (1928).

23 The next Christ will perhaps be a female Christ.
1852 'Cassandra' pt.4, part of an unpublished work *Suggestions for Thought to Searchers after Religious Truth* (revised and privately printed 1859). Published as an appendix in Ray Strachey *The Cause: A Short History of the Women's Movement in Great Britain* (1928).

24 No *man*, not even a doctor, ever gives any other definition of what a nurse should be than this—'devoted and obedient'. This definition would do just as well for a porter. It might even do for a horse. It would not do for a policeman.
1859 *Notes on Nursing.*

Nimitz, Admiral Chester (William) 1885–1966

US naval officer. He was Commander-in-Chief of the Pacific Fleet (1941–5), contributing significantly to the defeat of Japan. As fleet admiral he signed the Japanese surrender documents in Tokyo Bay (1945). He was chief of naval operations (1945–7).

25 A ship is always referred to as 'she' because it costs so much to keep her in paint and powder.
1959 In the *New York Times*, 24 May.

Nin, Anaïs 1903–77

US writer, born in Paris to parents of Spanish–Cuban descent. Her works explored sexuality and feminism with a frankness unusual in her era.

26 I stopped loving my father a long time ago. What remained was the slavery to a pattern.
1944 *Under a Glass Bell*, 'Birth'.

Nisbet, Robert 1913–96

US sociologist.

27 Countless works in the social sciences reveal the inability of their authors to bear in mind the crucial difference between what may properly be called the *logic of discovery* and the *logic of demonstration*. The second is properly subject to rules and prescriptions; the first isn't.
1976 *Sociology as an Art Form*, introduction.

28 With all allowance made for Marx's erudition and his historic impact upon the social sciences, especially sociology, it is as an art united with prophecy, virtually religious prophecy, that Marxism survives.
1976 *Sociology as an Art Form*, ch.5.

Niven, David originally *James David Graham Nevins* 1910–83

English actor. Signed by Samuel Goldwyn, he developed into a polished light comedian in films such as *The Charge of the Light Brigade* (1936), *The Dawn Patrol* (1938) and *Bachelor Mother* (1939). He won an Academy Award for *Separate Tables* (1958).

29 He passed rapidly through his marriages to Virginia Cherrill, Barbara Hutton and Betsy Drake and filled in the lonely gaps between them by falling in and out of love with most of his leading ladies, which, as his output of films was prodigious, underlined the excellence of his physical condition.
1975 Of Cary Grant. *Bring on the Empty Horses.*

Nixon, Pat 1912–93

Wife of President Richard M Nixon. She financed herself through college and taught typing until she married Nixon in 1940. She bore two daughters and was known for her gracious hospitality during her years in the White House. She was unswervingly loyal to her husband during and after his resignation in 1974.

30 The hearings are just like a snake about to devour people.
1973 On Watergate. Letter to a friend, quoted in Julie Nixon Eisenhower *Pat Nixon* (1986).

31 Dick, I don't know how you get up in the morning!
To her husband, who later wrote that he replied 'I do it to confound my enemies'. Quoted in Julie Nixon Eisenhower *Pat Nixon* (1986).

Nixon, Richard M(ilhous) 1913–94

US Republican politician and 37th President (1969–74). He resigned under threat of impeachment after the implication of leading members of his government in the Watergate affair. As President, he sought to end the Vietnam War and had diplomatic success with China and the USSR.

32 I don't believe that I ought to quit because I am not a quitter.
1952 National TV broadcast after allegations that he was financing his vice-presidential candidacy from a secret fund, Sep.

33 Tonight—to you, the great silent majority of my fellow Americans—I ask for your support.
1969 Appeal to the nation, 3 Nov, for support in the Vietnam War.

34 This is not an invasion of Vietnam.
1970 Television address to the nation announcing the invasion of Cambodia, 30 Apr.

35 I don't give a shit what happens. I want you all to stonewall…plead the Fifth Amendment, cover-up, or anything else. If that will save it, save the plan.
1973 From the White House tapes relating to the Watergate scandal, recorded Mar.

36 There will be no whitewash in the White House.
1973 Statement on the Watergate affair, 17 Apr.

37 In giving you these tapes, blemishes and all, I am placing my trust in the basic fairness of the American people.
1974 National address, 30 May, on relinquishing the Watergate tapes after the House Judiciary Committee warned him that refusal 'might constitute a ground for impeachment'.

38 Well, I screwed it up real good, didn't I?
1974 Comment to Chief of Staff Alexander M Haig and Press Secretary Ronald L Zeigler, 3 Aug, on beginning work on his resignation address. Recalled in *RN: The Memoirs of Richard Nixon* (1978).

39 When the president does it, that means that it is not illegal… But I brought myself down. I gave them a sword and they stuck it in and twisted it with relish. And I guess that if I had been in their position, I'd have done the same thing.
1977 Interviewed by David Frost, May.

40 American people don't believe anything until they see it on television.
1994 In *Newsweek*, 2 May. He estimated that 80% of US citizens get their news from television.

Noble, Richard 1946–

English car racer. He established a new land-speed record of 1,019.467kmph (633.468mph) in 1983 in the specially built *Thrust 2*.

41 We did it for Britain and for the hell of it.
1983 After setting a new world land-speed record. Quoted in the *Sunday Times*, 'The Week in Words', 9 Oct.

Nofziger, Lyn (Franklin) 1924–2006

Press secretary and later Chief of the White House Office of Political Affairs in the Reagan administration.

42 Cashing in. That's what we all do. It's called experience.
1988 In *This Week*, 31 Jul.

Nolan, Sir Sidney Robert 1917–92

Australian painter. He made his name with a series of *Ned Kelly* paintings (begun 1946), followed by an 'explorer' series.

43 I wanted to know the true nature of the 'otherness' I had been born into. It was not a European thing. I wanted to paint the great purity and implacability of the landscape. I wanted a visual form of the 'otherness' of the thing not seen.
1971 Quoted in E Lynn *Sidney Nolan—Australia* (1979).

Noonan, Peggy 1950–

US writer. She was speechwriter for President Reagan (1984–9) and has since been a columnist for *Newsweek*, the *New York Times* and *Time* and contributing editor to the *Wall Street Journal*. She has written several books.

44 The battle for the mind of Ronald Reagan was like the trench warfare of World War I. Never have so many fought so hard for such barren terrain.
1990 What I Saw at the Revolution.

45 A speech is poetry: cadence, rhythm, imagery, sweep…and reminds us that words, like children, have the power to make dance the dullest beanbag of a heart.
1990 What I Saw at the Revolution.

46 Lent began yesterday, and I mean to give up a great deal, as you would too if you were me. One of the things I mean to give up is the habit of thinking it and not saying it. A lady has some rights, and this happens to be one I can assert. 'You are embarrassing the angels.' This is what I intend to say for the next forty days whenever I see someone who is hurting the culture, hurting human dignity, denying the stature of a human being.
2006 In *The Wall Street Journal*, 2 Mar.

47 Many of the indices for the GOP are dreadful, especially that they lost the vote of two-thirds of those aged 18 to 29. They lost a generation! If that continues in coming years, it will be a rolling wave of doom.
2008 In *The Wall Street Journal*, 7 Nov.

48 The thing political figures fear most is a terror event that will ruin their careers. The biggest thing they fear is that a bomb goes off and it can be traced to something they did or didn't do, an action they did or didn't support. They all fear being accused of not doing enough to keep the citizenry safe.
2013 In *The Wall Street Journal*, 8 Jun.

Noonuccal, Oodgeroo formerly Kath Walker née Kathleen Jean Mary Ruska 1920–93

Australian poet and Aboriginal rights activist. Her works include *We Are Going* (1964), the first book by an Aboriginal writer to be published in English. She returned an MBE awarded to her in 1970, in protest at planned Australian bicentennial celebrations.

49 Do you know, Mr Menzies, that where I come from you could be gaoled for supplying alcohol to an Aborigine?
   1962 Remark to the then Prime Minister of Australia, Robert Menzies, when he offered her and other Aboriginal delegates a drink after a meeting. Quoted in Kathie Cochrane *Oodgeroo* (1994), pt.1, 'Protest'.

50 What can I tell you, son of mine?
   I could tell you of heartbreak, hatred blind,
   I could tell of crimes that shame mankind,
   Of brutal wrong and deeds malign,
   Of rape and murder, son of mine;
   But I'll tell instead of brave and fine
   When lives of black and white entwine,
   And men in brotherhood combine—
   This would I tell you, son of mine.
   1964 *We Are Going*, 'Son of Mine'.

51 No more boomerang
   No more spear;
   Now all civilized—
   Colour-bar and beer.
   1970 *My People*, 'No More Boomerang'.

Norden, Denis 1922–
English broadcaster and humorist.

52 It's a funny kind of month, October. For the really keen cricket fan it's when you realise that your wife left you in May.
   Quoted in *She* magazine, 1977.

Norman, Barry 1933–
English journalist and broadcaster. He made his name as an influential film critic through the television series that began with *Film '73* (1973–81, 1983–98).

53 The worst films were always bad but now they are bad in a more cynical way. They pander to an audience of 12–24 year olds, mostly male and mostly governed by raging testosterone. Dialogue is kept to a minimum because it holds up the action. Ditto characterisation and the building of it. As for wit, let's not bother with wit.
   2002 *And Why Not?*.

Norman, Greg 1955–
Australian golfer. He won the Open championships in 1986 and 1993. The only player of modern times to have competed in a grand slam of playoffs, unfortunately he lost them all.

54 In the tournament of life, which is the biggest major, I have one of the best records ever.
   2003 In *Golf Magazine*, Jul.

Norman, Major Mike 1943–
British marine. He was commanding officer of the 68 Royal marines who comprised the Falklands garrison at the time of the Argentinian invasion.

55 We've never surrendered before. It's not part of our training.
   1982 Comment, Apr. Quoted in The Sunday Times Insight Team *The Falklands War* (1982), p.7.

Norris, Frank Benjamin Franklin 1870–1902
US novelist. He worked for the San Francisco *Chronicle* and while reporting became involved in the Jameson raid in South Africa. He was influenced by Zola and was one of the first US naturalist writers. His novels include *McTeague* (1899) and *The Pit* (1903).

56 The kind of a man that *men* like—not women—is the kind of man that makes the best husband.
   1903 *The Pit*, ch.2.

57 Here, of all her cities, throbbed the true life—the true power and spirit of America; gigantic, crude with the crudity of youth, disdaining rivalry; sane and healthy and vigorous; brutal in its ambition, arrogant in the new-found knowledge of its giant strength, prodigal of its wealth, infinite in its desires.
   1903 Of Chicago. *The Pit*, ch.2.

North, Christopher pseudonym of John Wilson 1785–1854
Scottish critic and essayist, Professor of Moral Philosophy at Edinburgh University (1820–51), and regular contributor to *Blackwood's Magazine* under the pseudonym 'Christopher North'.

58 His Majesty's dominions, on which the sun never sets.
   1829 'Noctes Ambrosianae', no.42, in *Blackwood's Magazine*, Apr.

59 Laws were made to be broken.
   1830 'Noctes Ambrosianae', no.49, in *Blackwood's Magazine*, May.

60 It may be divided into three parts; in one you cannot hear, in another you cannot see, and in the third you can neither see nor hear. I remember once sitting alone in the third division—and never before or since have I had such a profound feeling of the power of solitude.
   1832 Of the Theatre Royal, Glasgow. 'Noctes Ambrosianae', no.64, in *Blackwood's Magazine*, Nov.

61 Such accidents will happen in the best-regulated families.
   1834 'Noctes Ambrosianae', no.67, in *Blackwood's Magazine*, Aug.

North, Oliver 1943–
US soldier, later columnist and broadcaster. He was a National Security official involved in the 1986 Iran-Contra scandal (the supporting of anti-government Contra rebels in Nicaragua with the proceeds of secret arms sales to Iran). Despite appeals to patriotism, he was convicted on three of twelve charges, which were later dropped on appeal.

62 I don't think there's another person in America that wants to tell this story as much as I do.
   1986 Invoking the Fifth Amendment at the House Committee investigating arms sales to Iran, 10 Dec.

63 I thought using the Ayatollah's money to support the Nicaraguan resistance...was a neat idea.
   1987 Testimony at the House Committee investigating arms sales to Iran, 8 Jul.

Novak, Michael 1933–
US critic, writer and philosopher.

64 Baseball is a Lockean game, a kind of contract theory in ritual form, a set of atomic individuals who assent to patterns of limited co-operation in their mutual interest.
   1976 *The Joys of Sport*, pt.1.

Novalis pseudonym of Friedrich von Hardenberg 1772–1801
German poet, a leading early Romantic. The early death of the woman he loved left a lasting impression on him, and he wrote

the prose lyrics of *Hymnen an die Nicht* (1800) in her memory. He died of tuberculosis.

65 *Der Tod ist das romantisierende Prinzip unsers Lebens. Der Tod ist—das Leben. Durch den Tod wird das Leben verstärkt.*
Death is the romantic principle of Life. Death is—life. Through death life is intensified.
1802 *Schriften, II, Fragmente.*

66 *Ein Charakter ist ein vollkommen gebildeter Willen.*
A character is a perfectly cultivated will.
1802 *Schriften, II, Fragmente.*

67 *Jeder Engländer ist eine Insel.*
Every Englishman is an island.
1802 *Schriften, II, Fragmente.*

68 *Mensch werden ist eine Kunst.*
To become human is art.
1802 *Schriften, II, Fragmente.*

Noyes, Alfred 1880–1958

English writer. He was best known for his florid poems, and especially his sea poems, but also wrote literary essays, plays and memoirs.

69 Go down to Kew in lilac-time (it isn't far from London!)
And you shall wander hand in hand with love in summer's wonderland.
1904 'The Barrel-Organ'.

70 The wind was a torrent of darkness among the gusty trees,
The moon was a ghostly galleon tossed upon cloudy seas,
The road was a ribbon of moonlight over the purple moor,
And the highwayman came riding—
Riding—riding—
The highwayman came riding, up to the old inn-door.
1907 'The Highwayman'.

71 Watch for me by moonlight;
I'll come to thee by moonlight, though hell should bar the way.
1907 'The Highwayman'.

Nozick, Robert 1938–2002

US philosopher, Professor at Harvard University.

72 The socialist society would have to forbid capitalist acts between consenting adults.
1974 *Anarchy, State, and Utopia*, p.163.

Nugent, Ted 1949–

US rock guitarist. His albums include *Free For All* (1976), *Cat Scratch Fever* (1977) and *Take No Prisoners* (2003).

73 If it's too loud, you're too old.
Quoted in David Pickering *Brewer's Twentieth-Century Music* (1994).

Nunn, Sir Trevor 1940–

English stage director. He was artistic director of the Royal Shakespeare Company (1968–86) and of the National Theatre (1997–2003).

74 The National [Theatre] is an organisation that benefits directly from taxpayers' money. I know of no edict that says that only those taxpayers with degrees in English literature pay for this place.
2001 In the *New Statesman*, 22 Oct.

Nuttgens, Patrick 1930–2004

British architect and educationalist. Director of Leeds Polytechnic (1969–86), his works include *The Landscape of Ideas* (1972) and *Understanding Modern Architecture* (1988).

75 In the final analysis, all architecture reveals the application of human ingenuity to the satisfaction of human needs. And among these needs are not only shelter, warmth and accommodation, but also the needs, felt at every moment in every part of the world in endlessly different ways, for something more profound, evocative and universal, for beauty, for permanence, for immortality.
1993 'The Nature of Architecture', in Ben Farmer and Hentie Louw (eds) *Companion to Contemporary Architectural Thought* (1993).

Nye, Joseph S, Jr 1937–

Professor of International Relations and Dean of the Kennedy School, Harvard. Formerly Assistant Secretary of Defense for International Security Affairs and Chair of the National Intelligence Council.

76 Not their style to say no. But when you listen…you don't hear yes.
1994 On asking for Saudi Arabia's help with the $500-million cost of US troop buildup in the Gulf. In the *New York Times*, 4 Nov.

Oakeshott, Michael Joseph 1901–90

English philosopher and political theorist, Professor of Political Science at the London School of Economics (1951–69). His key philosophical work was *Experience and its Modes* (1933), a broadly idealistic view which he developed in economic theory.

1 The politics of our society are a conversation in which past, present and future each has a voice; and though one or other of them may on occasion properly prevail none permanently dominates, and on this account we are free.
1962 *Rationalism in Politics*.

2 We consider ourselves to be free because no one in our society is allowed unlimited power—no leader, faction, party or 'class', no majority, no government, church, corporation, trade, or professional association or trade union. The secret of its freedom is that it is composed of a multitude of organisations in the constitution of the best of which is reproduced that diffusion of power which is characteristic of the whole.
1962 *Rationalism in Politics*.

3 It is difficult to think of any circumstances where learning may be said to be impossible.
Quoted in R S Peters (ed) *The Concept of Education* (1966), ch.10, 'Learning and Teaching'.

4 Every human being is born an heir to an inheritance to which he can succeed only in a process of learning.
Quoted in R S Peters (ed) *The Concept of Education* (1966), ch.10, 'Learning and Teaching'.

50 Let us pause and give thanks for the fact that Nelson Mandela lived—a man who took history in his hands, and bent the arc of the moral universe toward justice.
2013 Speaking after the death of Nelson Mandela, paraphrasing Martin Luther King's 'The arc of the moral universe is long, but it bends towards justice', 5 Dec.

51 It took a man like Madiba to free not just the prisoner, but the jailer as well to show that you must trust others so that they may trust you; to teach that reconciliation is not a matter of ignoring a cruel past, but a means of confronting it with inclusion and generosity and truth.
2013 Speaking at the memorial service for Nelson Mandela, First National Bank Stadium, Johannesburg, South Africa, 10 Dec.

52 This year let's all come together, Congress, the White House, businesses from Wall Street to Main Street, to give every woman the opportunity she deserves, because I believe when women succeed, America succeeds.
2014 State of the Union Address, 28 Jan.

53 Treat people with respect, whoever they are, and expect your governments to treat everybody with respect. And if you do that, then you're going to be okay.
2014 Speech to Young Southeast Asian Leaders Initiative, University of Malaya, Kuala Lumpur, Malaysia, 27 Apr.

54 We tortured some folks. We did some things that are contrary to our values.
2014 Referring to interrogations carried out by the CIA, press conference, 1 Aug.

Obama, Michelle LeVaughn Robinson 1964–

US First Lady. A lawyer, she married Barack Obama (1992), who became President in 2009.

55 I am desperate for change—now—not in eight years or twelve years, but right now. We don't have time to wait. We need big change—not just the shifting of power among insiders. We need to change the game, because the game is broken. When I think about the country I want to give my children, it's not the world we have now. All I have to do is look into the faces of my children, and I realize how much work we need to do.
2007 Campaign speech, quoted in *Vanity Fair*, 27 Dec.

56 Let me tell you something. For the first time in my adult life, I am proud of my country, because it feels like hope is finally making a comeback.
2008 Speech at campaign rally, Milwaukee, 18 Feb.

57 Being president doesn't change who you are—it reveals who you are.
2012 Speech at the Democratic National Convention, 4 Sep.

58 How hard you work matters more than how much you make.
2012 Speech at the Democratic National Convention, 4 Sep.

59 He's not Spider-Man. He's not a superhero; he's a human. So he needs your help.
2012 Speech at fundraiser event in support of her husband, Beverly Hills, California, 12 Aug.

60 A lot of young people think they're invincible, but the truth is young people are knuckleheads.
2014 On *The Tonight Show*, 21 Feb.

O'Brien, (Donal) Conor (Dermod David Donat) Cruise 1917–2008

Irish historian, diplomat, critic and politician. He wrote *To Katanga and Back* (1962), an autobiographical narrative of the Congo crisis. He was a newspaper editor and wrote numerous books of biography, politics and history.

61 Irishness is not primarily a question of birth or blood or language: it is the condition of being involved in the Irish situation, and usually of being mauled by it. On that definition Swift is more Irish than Goldsmith or Sheridan, although by the usual tests they are Irish and he is pure English.
1959 Reviewing *The Oxford Book of Irish Verse* in the *New Statesman*, 17 Jan (written under the pseudonym Donat O'Donnell).

62 Of history and its consequences it may be said: 'Those who can, gloat; those who can't, brood.' Englishmen are born gloaters; Irishmen born brooders. There are, it is true, brooders who take to gloating, and they did much to build the Empire. Yet the brooder-gloater, such as the Irishman turned Englishman, is not, as a human type, altogether a success. He is a little too much on his guard, like an excessively assimilated Jew, or a son of Harlem who has decided to 'pass'. The past of the Irishman, the Jew, the Negro, is, psychologically, too explosive to be buried.
1962 *To Katanga and Back: a UN case history*.

63 In any case you Papists have no right to complain! If you won't have contraception how can you control the population without the assistance of Herod? You ought to be grateful.
1970 *King Herod Explains*.

64 We dislike the IRA, most of us, and fear it. We are a peaceful and democratic people. But our history, our idealistic pretensions and our fatal ambivalence have stuck us with an ideology that is warlike and anti-democratic, and calls increasingly for further human sacrifice.
1985 In the *New York Review of Books*, 29 Apr.

65 The United Nations cannot do anything, and never could. It is not an animate entity or agent. It is a place, a stage, a forum and a shrine…a place to which powerful people can repair when they are fearful about the course on which their own rhetoric seems to be propelling them.
1985 In *New Republic*, 4 Nov.

O'Brien, Edna 1932–

Irish novelist, short-story writer and playwright. Her works include *The Country Girls* (1960), *The Lonely Girl* (1962), *Girls in Their Married Bliss* (1964), *House of Splendid Isolation* (1994), *Wild Decembers* (1999) and *Saints and Sinners* (2011).

66 Ordinary life bypassed me, but I also bypassed it. It couldn't have been any other way. Conventional life and conventional people are not for me.
In Annalena Mc Afee (ed) *Lives and Works: Profiles of Leading Novelists, Poets and Playwrights* (2002).

67 It's not the vote women need, we should be armed.
2012 *Country Girl: A Memoir*.

O'Brien, Flann pseudonym of Brian O'Nolan also known as Myles na Gopaleen 1911–66

Irish writer who worked in the Irish Civil Service until 1953. In 1940 he began writing for *The Irish Times* under the pseudonym of Myles na Gopaleen and developed a reputation for being an eccentric and idiosyncratic columnist. He is best known for his novel, *At Swim-Two-Birds* (1939).

68 When things go wrong and will not come right,
Though you do the best you can,
When life looks black as the hour of night—
A PINT OF PLAIN IS YOUR ONLY MAN.
1939 *At Swim-Two-Birds*, ch.1, 'The Workman's Friend' (as Flann O'Brien).

69 There was a frightful, appalling row.
As a matter of fact the Pope told us all to go to hell. He threatened to silence Father Fahrt.
1961 *The Hard Life*.

70 And now the curse has come upon us, because I have personally met in the streets of Ireland persons who are clearly out of Synge's plays. They talk and dress like that, and damn the drink they'll swally but the mug of porter in the long nights after Samhain.
1968 *The Best of Myles*.

O'Brien, John J

Washington correspondent, Philadelphia *Inquirer*.

71 The only candidate who can whistle Dixie while humming the *Battle Hymn of the Republic*.
1976 Of President Johnson. Quoted in Harold Brayman (ed) *The President Speaks Off the Record* (1976).

O'Brien, (Angela Maxine) Margaret 1937–

US child actress, best known for her performance in *Meet Me in St Louis* (1944).

72 When I cry, shall I let the tears run all the way down my face or shall I stop them halfway down?
1944 Attributed remark to director Henry Koster when making *Music for Millions* (1944). Quoted by Larry Adler in *It Ain't Necessarily So* (1984).

O'Brien, Virginia

Manhattan office worker.

73 Crouch, swivel, tug, pull and plop.
1987 Advice on how to seat oneself at a picnic while wearing a mini-skirt. In the *New York Times*, 17 Jul.

O'Brien, William 1852–1928

Irish journalist and politician, born a Catholic but educated at a Protestant college. He founded the Land League journal *United Ireland* (1881) and became a Nationalist MP (1883–95, 1900–18).

74 What are we learning French or the piano for, I would like to know, if it is not to be sold to a man some day... We have to cringe, and manoeuvre, and grimace for a husband—a husband who may be deaf or have a hump if he is rich—a husband that may attack you in *delirium tremens* to-day if he makes a devout act of contrition for it to-morrow.
1890 *When We Were Boys*.

Ó Bruadair, Dáibhídh c.1625–1698

Irish-Gaelic poet, who recorded the destruction of his culture. His patrons were exiled by wars and proscription, and he became a farm labourer.

75 I will sing no more songs: the pride of my country I sang
Through forty long years of good rhyme, without any avail;
And no one cared even as much as the half of a hang
For the song or the singer, so here is an end of the tale.
Adapted from the Irish by James Stephens.

O'Casey, Sean 1884–1964

Irish playwright. His early plays, including *Juno and the Paycock* (1924), deal with Dublin working-class life and were written for the Abbey Theatre. His later, more experimental, plays include *Cockadoodle Dandy* (1949).

76 Th' whole worl's in a state o' chassis!
1924 Boyle speaking. *Juno and the Paycock*, act 1.

77 JUNO: Sacred Heart o' Jesus, take away our hearts o' stone, and give us hearts o' flesh! Take away this murdherin' hate, an' give us Thine own eternal love!
1924 *Juno and the Paycock*, act 3.

78 She dhresses herself to keep him with her, but it's no use—afther a month or two, th' wondher of a woman wears off.
1926 *The Plough and the Stars*, act 1.

79 There's no reason to bring religion into it. I think we ought to have as great a regard for religion as we can, so as to keep it out of as many things as possible.
1926 *The Plough and the Stars*, act 1.

80 English literature's performing flea.
Of P G Wodehouse. In P G Wodehouse *Performing Flea* (1953).

Occam, William of c.1285–c.1349

English philosopher, theologian and political writer. He was perhaps the most influential of later medieval philosophers.

81 *Entia non sunt multiplicanda praeter necessitatem.*
No more things should be presumed than is necessary.
This principle of intellectual economy, known as Occam's Razor, is not found in this form in his writings. Similar expressions can be found, eg *Pluralitas non est ponenda sine necessitate* ('Plurality should not be posited unnecessarily'), in *Scriptum in Librum Primum Sententiarum*.

O'Connell, Daniel known as the Liberator 1775–1847

Irish Catholic political leader, able to take his Commons seat only after Catholic Emancipation (1829). He fought against tithes and in 1840 founded the Repeal Association, agitating to end the union with Britain. In 1844 he was imprisoned on a charge of sedition, and his influence subsequently waned.

82 Let us never tolerate the slightest inroad on the discipline of our holy Church. Let us never consent that she should be made the hireling of the Ministry. Our forefathers would have died—nay, perished in hopeless slavery—rather than consent to such degradation.
1814 Speech, Dublin, 23 Feb.

83 Not for all the universe contains would I, in the struggle for what I conceive to be my country's cause, consent to the effusion of a single drop of human blood, except my own.
1843 Speech, 18 Feb.

84 While I have a tongue I'll abuse you, you most inimitable periphery. Look at her, boys! there she stands—a convicted perpendicular in petticoats! There's contamination in her circumference, and she trembles with guilt down to the extremities of her corollaries. Ah! you're found out, you rectilineal antecedent, and equiangular old hag! 'Tis with you the devil will fly

away, you porter-swiping similitude of the bisection of a vortex!
Winning thrust in a vituperation contest with Dublin's champion virago, Biddy Moriarty, reported by Daniel Owen-Madden in *Revelations of Ireland* (1877).

O'Connor, Edwin 1918–68

US novelist, originally a radio announcer and producer, best known for his novel *The Last Hurrah* (1956). *The Edge of Sadness* (1961) won a Pulitzer Prize.

85 The Last Hurrah.
1956 Title of novel, based on the career of politician James M Curley.

O'Connor, (Mary) Flannery 1925–64

US novelist and short-story writer. Her fiction, set in the Deep South, reflects a mordant sense of humour. Her works include two novels and two volumes of short stories.

86 I preach there are all kinds of truth, your truth and somebody else's. But behind all of them there is only one truth and that is that there's no truth.
1952 Hazel Motes. *Wise Blood*, ch.10.

87 While the South is hardly Christ-centred, it is most certainly Christ-haunted.
1960 'Some Aspects of the Grotesque in Southern Fiction'. Paper read at Wesleyan College, Fall.

88 There was a time when the average reader read a novel simply for the moral he could get out of it, and however naïve that may have been, it was a good deal less naïve than some of the limited objectives he has now.
1960 'Some Aspects of the Grotesque in Southern Fiction'. Paper read at Wesleyan College, Fall.

89 It's like building a nest. First she thinks about it, then she begins to gather the materials, then she begins to put it together.
On her mother's two-month process of making a fruit cake. Quoted in Sally Fitzgerald (ed) *The Habit of Being* (1979).

O'Connor, Frank *pseudonym of* Michael O'Donovan 1903–66

Irish writer, a member of the IRA in his teens and imprisoned after the War of Independence. His ideal medium was the short story, but he also wrote plays and literary criticism.

90 Every time I leave the old man I feel like a thousand dollars.
1948 Of Yeats. Quoted in Richard Ellmann *Yeats: the Man and the Masks* (1948).

O'Connor, Cardinal John Joseph 1920–2000

Catholic Archbishop of New York.

91 It is increasingly rare for many of us…to believe that people can be poor, but honest, poor but deserving of respect. Poverty is no longer blamed on anyone but the poor themselves. Contempt for the poor has become a virtue.
1994 In *Catholic New York*, quoted in the *New York Times*, 24 Nov.

Odets, Clifford 1906–63

US playwright and actor, an important figure in the US theatre of the 1930s.

92 Go out and fight so life shouldn't be printed on dollar bills.
1935 Jacob. *Awake and Sing*, act 1.

93 Music is the great cheer-up in the language of all countries.
1937 Mr Bonaparte. *Golden Boy*, act 1, sc.2.

O'Donnell, Kenneth P(hillip) 1924–77

Special Assistant to President Kennedy.

94 Mr President, the president is dead.
1963 To Lyndon B Johnson after the assassination of John F Kennedy, 22 Nov.

Oerter, Al(fred) 1936–2007

US athlete and discus-thrower. He won an unsurpassed four gold medals for the discus, at Melbourne (1956), Rome (1960), Tokyo (1964) and Mexico (1968).

95 I never had technique.
1978 In the *New York Times*, 16 May.

O'Faolain, Sean 1900–91

Irish writer and educator. He began writing in and translating from Gaelic. A successful novel, *A Nest of Simple Folk* (1933), was followed by biographies of Irish figures.

96 If we turn to early Irish literature, as we naturally may, to see what sort of people the Irish were in the infancy of the race, we find ourselves wandering in delighted bewilderment through a darkness shot with lightning and purple flame.
1947 *The Irish*.

97 He was like a man who takes a machine-gun to a shooting gallery. Everybody falls flat on his face, the proprietor at once takes to the hills, and when you cautiously peep up, you find that he has wrecked the place but got three perfect bull's-eyes.
On Frank O'Connor (pseudonym of Michael O'Donovan), attributed.

O'Flaherty, Liam 1897–1984

Irish Republican writer. He went to London in 1922 to become a writer, finding fame with his novel *The Informer* (1926). In addition to other novels, he wrote three volumes of autobiography (1930–4).

98 When the parish priest rebuked him for his celibacy, saying it would lead him into debauchery and sin, he said that a man who had to be muzzled by a wife as a protection against debauchery was not worthy of the joy of innocence. After that people began to treat him with priestly respect.
'The Mermaid'.

Ogden, Frank *also known as* 'Dr Tomorrow' 1920–2012

Canadian futurist.

99 Although I am a futurist today, if I don't change tomorrow, I will be a historian.
1994 *Ogdenisms: The Frank Ogden Quote Book*.

1 As the planet globalizes, groups tribalize.
1994 *Ogdenisms: The Frank Ogden Quote Book*.

2 Holidays are the greatest learning experience unknown to man.
1994 *Ogdenisms: The Frank Ogden Quote Book*.

3 Technology breaks the laws and makes the laws.
   1994 *Ogdenisms: The Frank Ogden Quote Book.*

4 My idea of long-range planning is lunch.
   1994 *Ogdenisms: The Frank Ogden Quote Book.*

Ogilvy, David 1911–99
British-born US advertising executive, founder of Ogilvy and Mather.

5 It is the professional duty of the advertising agent to conceal his artifice. When Aeschines spoke, they said, 'How well he speaks', but when Demosthenes spoke, they said 'Let us march against Philip.'
   1963 *Confessions of an Advertising Man,* ch.5.

6 The consumer isn't a moron. She's your wife.
   1963 *Confessions of an Advertising Man,* ch.5.

Ogilvy, James, 1st Earl of Seafield 1644–1730
Scottish advocate, MP and political manager. He was one of the Scottish commissioners appointed to negotiate the Union of Parliaments.

7 There's ane end of ane auld sang.
   1707 On signing the Treaty of Union between Scotland and England. Quoted in George Lockhart of Carnwath *Memoir of the Affairs of Scotland* (1714), vol.1.

O'Hagan, John *pseudonym* Sliabh Cuilinn 1822–90
Irish lawyer and poet.

8 My native heath is brown beneath,
   My native waters blue;
   But crimson red o'er both shall spread,
   Ere I am false to you,
   Dear land!
   Ere I am false to you.
   1845 'Dear Land' in *The Spirit of the Nation.*

O'Hanlon, Redmond 1947–
English naturalist, critic and traveller. With James Fenton, he made an expedition into the heart of Borneo in 1983 and wrote entertainingly about the land and its people.

9 The Iban, when they decide that something is really funny, and know that they are going to laugh for a long time, lie down first.
   Dana, Leon and Inghai lay down.
   1984 *Into the Heart of Borneo.*

O'Hara, Frank 1926–66
US poet and art critic. He published several volumes of poetry, which were closely linked to the New York environment in which he moved.

10 and I am sweating a lot by now and thinking of
   leaning on the john door in the 5 SPOT
   while she whispered a song along the keyboard
   to Mal Waldron and everyone and I stopped breathing
   1964 Of Billie Holiday. *Lunch Poems,* 'The Day Lady Died'.

O'Hara, John Henry 1905–70
US novelist and short-story writer. His best-known works, several of which were successfully filmed, included *Appointment in Samarra* (1934), *Butterfield 8* (1935) and *Pal Joey* (1940).

11 George Gershwin died last week. I don't have to believe it if I don't want to.
   1937 Quoted in Ian Crofton and Donald Fraser *A Dictionary of Musical Quotations* (1985).

12 But whats the use of being old if you cant be dumb?
   1940 *Pal Joey,* ch.1.

13 I am making a little trip to N.Y. in the near future and we will have a little talk and you can explain your positon, altho the way I feel now if I saw you now your positon would be horizonte.
   1940 *Pal Joey,* ch.2.

14 Illinois is a state of suspended animation and the people live in hibernation from Oct. to whenever it ever gets warmer.
   1940 *Pal Joey,* ch.9.

O Henry *pseudonym of* William Sydney Porter 1862–1910
US writer. He is best known for his comic short stories.

15 Life is made up of sobs, sniffles, and smiles, with sniffles predominating.
   1906 *The Four Million,* 'The Gift of the Magi'.

16 If men knew how women pass the time when they are alone, they'd never marry.
   1906 *The Four Million,* 'Memoirs of a Yellow Dog'.

17 It was beautiful and simple as all truly great swindles are.
   1908 *The Gentle Grafter,* 'The Octopus Marooned'.

18 Whenever he saw a dollar in another man's hands he took it as a personal grudge if he couldn't take it any other way.
   1908 *The Gentle Grafter,* 'The Octopus Marooned'.

19 If ever there was an aviary overstocked with jays it is that Yaptown-on-the-Hudson, called New York.
   1908 *The Gentle Grafter,* 'A Tempered Wind'.

20 A story with a moral appended is like the bite of a mosquito. It bores you, and then injects a stinging drop to irritate your conscience.
   1910 *Strictly Business,* 'The Gold That Glittered'.

21 Turn up the lights; I don't want to go home in the dark.
   Last words. Quoted in Charles Alphonso Smith *O. Henry* (1916), ch.9. The words are taken from the popular song by Harry Williams 'I'm afraid to come home in the dark' (1907).

22 A burglar who respects his art always takes his time before taking anything else.
   Sixes and Sevens, 'Makes The Whole World Kin' (1911).

O'Keeffe, Georgia 1887–1986
US painter, a pioneer of abstract art (eg *Blue and Green Music,* 1919). She later moved towards a more figurative style, painting close-ups of parts of flowers and plants. Her works include *Black Iris* (New York, 1949).

23 Nobody sees a flower—really—it is so small—we haven't time—and to see takes time like to have a friend takes time… So I said to myself —I'll paint what I see—what the flower is to me, but I'll paint it big and they will be surprised into taking time to look at it—I will make even busy New Yorkers take time to see what I see of flowers.
   Quoted in Goodrich and Bry *Georgia O'Keeffe* (1970).

24 The men liked to put me down as the best woman painter. I think I'm one of the best painters.
Quoted in W Chadwick *Women, Art and Society* (1990).

Okri, Ben 1959–
Nigerian writer, winner of the 1987 Commonwealth Prize for Africa for *Incidents at the Shrine* (1986) and the 1991 Booker Prize for *The Famished Road*. Other works include *Songs of Enchantment* (1993), *Dangerous Love* (1996) and *In Arcadia* (2002).

25 We feared the heartlessness of human beings, all of whom are born blind, few of whom ever learn to see.
1991 *The Famished Road*, ch.1.

26 We have not yet arrived, but every point at which we stop requires a re-definition of our destination.
2009 *Tales Of Freedom*.

27 A tolerable hell is better than an impossible heaven.
2009 *Tales Of Freedom*.

28 What you see is what you make. What you see in a people is what you eventually create in them.
2011 *A Time For New Dreams*.

Oldenburg, Claes Thure 1929–
Swedish-born US sculptor. From 1958 he was one of the pioneers of Pop Art. His works include giant hamburgers and other foodstuffs, the *Giant Clothespin* in Philadelphia (1975) and projects in Cologne, Eindhoven, Milan and London.

29 I am for an art that helps old ladies across the street… I am for Kool-art, 7-UP art, Pepsi-art, Sunshine art, 39 cents art, 15 cents art, Vatronol art, Dro-bomb art, Vam art, Menthol art, L & M art, Ex-lax art, Venida art, Heaven Hill art, Pamryl art, San-o-med art, Rx art, 9.99 art, Now art, New art, How art, Fire sale art, Last Chance art, Only art, Diamond art, Tomorrow art, Franks art, Ducks art, Meat-o-rama art.
1961 Written for an exhibition in New York, 1961, quoted in Arts Council of Great Britain *Oldenburg* (1970).

Oldman, Gary 1958–
English actor.

30 The industry has changed. Two years ago I could tell a company I've got Russell Crowe and that would get the film made. Now they'd ask 'And who's the girl?' Just one famous face isn't enough any more.
2004 In *Scotland on Sunday*, 30 May.

O'Leary, Michael 1961–
Irish businessman. In 1994 he was appointed chief executive of the Irish airline Ryanair.

31 One of the weaknesses of the company now is it is a bit cheap and cheerful and overly nasty, and that reflects my personality.
Quoted in Alan Ruddock, *Michael O'Leary: A Life in Full Flight* (2007).

32 The best thing you can do with environmentalists is shoot them. These headbangers want to make air travel the preserve of the rich. They are luddites marching us back into the eighteenth century.
Quoted in Brian Clegg, *Ecologic: The Truth and Lies of Green Economics* (2010).

33 We will double our emissions in the next five years because we are doubling our traffic. If preserving the environment means stopping poor people flying so the rich can fly, then screw it.
Quoted in Suzanne Becken, *Climate Change and Tourism: From Policy to Practice* (2012).

34 Ryanair will never fly the Atlantic route because one cannot get there in a Boeing 737, unless one has a very strong tail wind or passengers who can swim the last hour of the flight.
Attributed.

Oliphant, Margaret née Wilson 1828–97
Scottish novelist, essayist and critic. Widowed and debt-ridden at an early age with a large extended family dependent upon her, she was a prolific writer and maintained a long association with *Blackwood's Magazine* and *The Cornhill* as well as completing over 100 novels.

35 A woman who cannot be a governess or a novel-writer must fall back on that poor little needle, the primitive and original handicraft of femininity.
1858 'The Condition of Women', in *Blackwood's Magazine*, vol.83, Feb.

Oliver, Mary 1935–
US poet. Her work includes *American Primitive* (1983, Pulitzer Prize), *New and Selected Poems* (1992, National Book Award) and *The Leaf and the Cloud* (2000).

36 Poetry happens because of life. Poetry happens because of language. And poetry happens because of other poets.
1992 In the *New York Times*, 20 Nov.

Olivier, Laurence Kerr, Baron 1907–89
English actor, producer and director. A great Shakespearean actor, he also produced, directed and played in films of *Henry V* (1944), *Hamlet* (1948) and *Richard III* (1955). He campaigned for the foundation of the National Theatre.

37 Make up your mind dearheart. Do you want to be a great actor or a household word?
c.1962 Comment to Richard Burton while filming *Cleopatra*. Burton replied 'Both'.

38 Acting is a masochistic form of exhibitionism. It is not quite the occupation of an adult.
1978 Quoted in *Time*, 3 Jul.

39 I'm not so artistic that I despise profit.
Attributed.

40 It looks like rows and rows of empty seats.
On being shown the view of the jungle enjoyed from Noël Coward's house on a Jamaican hillside. Attributed.

41 Shakespeare—the nearest thing in incarnation to the eye of God.
Quoted in *Kenneth Harris Talking To…*, 'Sir Laurence Olivier'.

42 What is the main problem of the actor? It is to keep the audience awake, and not let them go to sleep, then wake up and go home feeling they've wasted their money.
Attributed.

Ollivier, Émile 1825–1913
French politician, charged by Napoleon III to form a constitutional ministry. He rushed into war with Germany, was overthrown on 9 Aug 1870, and withdrew to Italy. He wrote numerous works, including *L'Empire libéral* (16 vols, 1894–1912), a defence of his policy.

43 One is never weaker than when one appears to have everybody's support.
1870 Letters.

Olsen, Tillie 1913–2007
US writer and feminist. She wrote proletarian fiction in the 1930s. In the 1960s she emerged as an advocate of feminism, and her work attracted wide attention for the first time. Her later work includes *Tell Me a Riddle* (1960).

44 Vinegar he poured on me all his life; I am well marinated; how can I be honey now?
1960 *Tell Me a Riddle*, section 1.

Olson, Charles 1910–70
US poet and literary theorist. He taught at Black Mountain College, North Carolina, where his ideas were influential on such poets as Robert Creeley and Robert Duncan. As a poet, he is best known for the sequence *The Maximus Poems* (1953).

45 I take SPACE to be the central fact to man born in America... I spell it large because it comes large here. Large and without mercy.
1947 *Call Me Ishmael*, section 1.

46 But that which matters, that which insists, that which will last,
that! o my people, where shall you find it, how, where, where shall you
listen
when all is become billboards, when, all, even silence, is spray-gunned?
1953 *The Maximus Poems*, 'I, Maximus of Gloucester, To You, 3'.

47 one loves only form,
and form only comes
into existence when
the thing is born.
1953 *The Maximus Poems*, 'I, Maximus of Gloucester, To You, 4'.

Olson, Elder James 1909–92
US poet and critic. In both his formal, cerebral poetry and criticism he adhered to the neo-Aristotelian principles espoused at the University of Chicago, where he taught.

48 We shall never know all about art or the values of art until all art is at an end; meanwhile artists will continue to instruct us.
Quoted in Elmer Borklund (ed) *Contemporary Literary Critics* (1977).

Onassis, Jacqueline Lee Kennedy *née Bouvier* 1929–94
Wife of President John F Kennedy. She supervised the restoration of the White House and wielded a powerful and widespread influence on fashion. After her husband's assassination she returned to private life, and in 1968 she married Aristotle Onassis, the Greek shipping magnate.

49 Put your brilliant mind to work for...dresses for public appearances...that I would wear if Jack were President of France.
1960 Letter to Oleg Cassini, 13 Dec. Quoted in Oleg Cassini *In My Fashion* (1987).

50 I felt like a moth hanging on the window pane.
1961 On her first night in the White House, in *Newsweek*, 1 Jan.

51 Lincoln's bedroom! And you see that great bed, it looks like a cathedral.
1961 On her first night in the White House, in *Newsweek*, 1 Jan.

52 You worked together for the finest things in the finest years... Later on when a series of disastrous Presidents and Prime Ministers...will have botched up everything—people will say 'Do you remember those days—how perfect they were?' The days of you and Jack.
1964 To Harold Macmillan, 31 Jan.

53 I cast only one vote—for Jack. It is a rare thing to be able to vote for one's husband for President and I didn't want to dilute it by voting for anyone else.
On the 1960 elections. Quoted in Arthur M Schlesinger Jr *A Thousand Days* (1965).

54 There'll never be another Camelot again.
On Frederick Lowe's lyrics from Alan Jay Lerner's *Camelot*, a title that became synonymous with the Kennedy administration—'Don't let it be forgot, that once there was a spot, for one brief shining moment that was known as Camelot.' Quoted in Theodore H White *In Search of History* (1978).

55 Uncle Cornpone and his Little Porkchop.
On the Johnsons. Quoted in *Newsweek*, 30 May 1994.

Ondaatje, (Philip) Michael 1943–
Sri Lankan-born Canadian poet and novelist. His poetry includes *Rat Jelly* (1973) and *Secular Love* (1987); other works include novels such as *Running in the Family* (1982), *The English Patient* (1992, Booker Prize), *Anil's Ghost* (2000) and *Divisadero* (2007).

56 There was always, he thought, this pleasure ahead of him, an ace of joy up his sleeve so he could say you can do anything to me, take everything away, put me in prison, but I will know [her] when we are old.
1987 *In the Skin of a Lion*, 'Remorse'.

O'Neal, Shaquille 1972–
US basketball player. As centre for Orlando in 1995, he was the NBA leading scorer with 2,315 points from 79 games. He played for Orlando Magic from 1992 to 1996, when he joined the Los Angeles Lakers.

57 Nietzsche was so intelligent and advanced. And that's how I am. I'm the black, basketball-playing Nietzsche.
2003 On himself, having previously likened himself to Aristotle. In *Book*, Mar/Apr.

O'Neill, Eugene Gladstone 1888–1953
US playwright. His play *Beyond the Horizon* (1920) won a Pulitzer Prize, and he established his reputation with such serious-minded plays as *Mourning Becomes Electra* (1931), *The Iceman Cometh* (1946) and *Long Day's Journey into Night* (1956). He was awarded a Nobel prize in 1936.

58 The action of the play takes place on an island in the West Indies as not yet self-determined by White Mariners. The form of native government is, for the time being, an Empire.
1920 *The Emperor Jones*, scene direction.

59 For de little stealin' dey gits you in jail soon or late. For de big stealin' dey makes you Emperor and puts you in de Hall o' Fame when you croaks.
1921 Jones. *The Emperor Jones*, sc.1.

60 Life is for each man a solitary cell whose walls are mirrors.
1927 Lazarus. *Lazarus Laughed*, act 2, sc.1.

61 When men make gods, there is no God!
1927 Lazarus. *Lazarus Laughed*, act 2, sc.2.

62 Man's loneliness is but his fear of life!
1927 Lazarus. *Lazarus Laughed*, act 3, sc.2.

63 The old—like children—talk to themselves, for they have reached that hopeless wisdom of experience which knows that though one were to cry it in the streets to multitudes, or whisper it in the kiss to one's beloved, the only ears that can ever hear one's secrets are one's own!
1927 Tiberius. *Lazarus Laughed*, act 4, sc.1.

64 Life is perhaps most wisely regarded as a bad dream between two awakenings, and every day is a life in miniature.
1928 Chu-Yin. *Marco Millions*, act 2, sc.2.

65 The devil!...what beastly things our memories insist on cherishing!
1928 Marsden. *Strange Interlude*, pt.1, act 2.

66 Strange interlude! Yes, our lives are merely strange dark interludes in the electrical display of God the Father!
1928 Nina. *Strange Interlude*, pt.2, act 9.

67 Mourning Becomes Electra.
1931 Title of play.

68 The sea hates a coward!
1931 Bryant. *Mourning Becomes Electra*, pt.2, act 4.

69 EDMUND: (*sits down opposite his father—contemptuously*). Yes, facts don't mean a thing, do they? What you want to believe, that's the only truth! (*Derisively*.) Shakespeare was an Irish Catholic, for example.
TYRONE: (*stubbornly*). So he was. The proof is in his plays.
1939–41 *Long Day's Journey Into Night*, act 4 (published 1956).

70 Where do you get your taste in authors—That damned library of yours! (*He indicates the small bookcase at rear*.) Voltaire, Rousseau, Schopenhauer, Nietzsche, Ibsen! Atheists, fools, and madmen! And your poets! This Dowson, and this Baudelaire, and Swinburne and Oscar Wilde, and Whitman and Poe! Whoremongers and degenerates! Pah! When I've three good sets of Shakespeare there (*he nods at the large bookcase*) you could read.
1939–41 Tyrone. *Long Day's Journey Into Night*, act 4 (published 1956).

71 A Long Day's Journey Into Night.
1939–41 Title of play (published 1956).

72 The Iceman Cometh.
1946 Title of play.

73 Little subconscious mind, say I each night, bring home the bacon.
Quoted in Kenneth Tynan *Tynan Right and Left* (1988). Tynan added the question,'But how much of the bacon can we nowadays stomach?'

O'Neill, Martin 1952–
Northern Irish footballer and football manager.

74 I never try to make a right decision. I make a decision and then try to make it right.
2002 In *The Independent*, 20 Dec.

O'Neill, Molly 1952–
US writer, food columnist and restaurant critic.

75 Out of the kitchen, to stew is to fret, to worry, to agitate. In the kitchen, however, to stew is to have great expectations.
1994 In the *New York Times*, 30 Jan.

O'Neill, Thomas P known as 'Tip' 1912–94
US Congressman and Speaker of the House of Representatives.

76 Take advantage of the good cigars. You don't get much else in that job.
1977 Advice to Vice-President Walter P Mondale. Quoted in *Time*, 4 Jun 1984.

77 Ronald Reagan...wasn't without leadership ability, but he lacked most of the management skills that a President needs. But let me give him his due: he would have made a hell of a king.
1987 *Man of the House*.

78 You can teach an old dog new tricks—if the old dog wants to learn.
1989 On working with President Reagan. In NPR broadcast, 2 Jan.

79 Herbert Hoover with a smile, a cheerleader for selfishness.
On President Reagan. Recalled on O'Neill's death in the *New York Times*, 7 Jan 1994.

80 Keep your left hand high.
Recommending the boxer's defensive posture to President Carter. Recalled on O'Neill's death in the *New York Times*, 7 Jan 1994.

81 The Democratic Party has succeeded so well that many of its members are now Republicans.
Quoted in WAMU radio broadcast, Washington, 29 Mar 1995.

Onetti, Juan Carlos 1909–94
Uruguayan novelist. He moved to Buenos Aires in 1943 and later to Madrid, where he spent his final years. In many of his novels he sets the action in the mythical city of Santa María.

82 *Es asombroso ver en qué se puede convertir la revolución rusa a través del cerebro de un comerciante yanqui; basta ver las fotos de las revistas norteamericanas, nada más que las fotos porque no sé leerlas, para comprender que no hay pueblo más imbécil que ése sobre la tierra; no puede haberlo porque también la capacidad de estupidez es limitada en la raza humana.*
It's astonishing to see what the Russian Revolution can become thanks to the brain of a Yankee entrepreneur; you only have to see the photos in North American magazines, only the photos because I can't read them, to realize they're the most stupid people on earth; that's quite possible because even the human race has a limited potential for idiocy.
1939 *El pozo* (translated as *The Pit*, 1991).

Oppenheimer, J(ulius) Robert 1904–67
US physicist, lecturer at the University of California and the California Institute of Technology and from 1947 director of the Institute for Advanced Study at Princeton. He was director (1942–5) of the laboratory at Los Alamos, New Mexico, that designed and built the first atomic bomb.

83 When you see something that is technically sweet, you go ahead and do it and you argue about what to do about it only after you have had your technical success. That is the way it was with the atomic bomb.

1954 'In the Matter of J. Robert Oppenheimer', USAEC transcript of hearing before Personnel Security Board.

84 I remembered the line from the Hindu scripture, the *Bhagavad Gita*... 'I am become death, the destroyer of worlds.'
On the detonation of the first atomic bomb, 16 Jul 1945. Quoted in Len Giovanitti and Fred Freed *The Decision to Drop the Bomb* (1965).

85 Science has, as its whole purpose, the rendering of the physical world understandable and beautiful. Without this you have only tables and statistics.
1966 In *Look* magazine.

86 Science is not everything, but science is very beautiful.
1966 In *Look* magazine.

87 No man should escape our universities without knowing how little he knows.
1967 In *Partisan Review*, Summer issue.

88 The theory of our modern technic shows that nothing is as practical as the theory.
1977 In *Reflex*, Jul.

89 Those two scorpions in a bottle.
On the US and USSR in the early 1950s. Quoted in Anthony Cave Brown *Treason in the Blood* (1994).

O'Rahilly, Egan Gaelic name Aodhagán Ó Rathaille 1670–1726

Gaelic poet. Little is known of his life except that he lived and died in great poverty and was buried at Muckross Abbey. His *Vision* is regarded as one of the finest poems in Irish Gaelic.

90 For the future I cease, Death approaches with little delay,
Since the dragons of Laune and Lane and Lee are destroyed;
I'll follow the heroes far from the light of day,
The princes my ancestors followed before Christ died.
c.1729 Closing lines of his last known poem, translated from the Irish by Owen Dudley Edwards.

91 That my old bitter heart was pierced in this black doom,
That foreign devils have made our land a tomb,
That the sun that was Munster's glory has gone down
Has made me a beggar before you, Valentine Brown.
'Valentine Brown', translated from the Irish by Michael O'Donovan (pseudonym Frank O'Connor).

O'Rourke, P(atrick) J(ake) 1947–

US writer and editor. He has written books and articles on government, politics, social mores and travel.

92 The best thing about the violence in Northern Ireland is that it's all so ancient and honorable... The Irish are in the same terrific position as the Shiites in Lebanon, the peasants in El Salvador, the blacks in America, the Jews in Palestine, the Palestinians in Israel (and everybody everywhere, if you read your history)—enough barbarism has been visited on the Irish to excuse all barbarities by the Irish barbarians.
1988 *Holidays in Hell*.

93 Communism doesn't really starve or execute that many people. Mostly it just bores them to death.
1988 *Holidays in Hell*.

94 Republicans are the party that says government doesn't work, and then they get elected and prove it.
1991 *Parliament of Whores*.

95 Sometimes it's hard to remember that bourgeois property is the real revolutionary force these days. All over the world we're bringing down dictatorships—or at least forcing them to go condo.
1992 *Give War a Chance*.

96 For reasons of high aesthetic principle, I do not write on a computer.
2003 In *Writers on Writing, Volume II: More Collected Essays from the New York Times*.

97 The complexity of economics can be calculated mathematically. Write out the algebraic equation that is the human heart and multiply each unknown by the population of the world.
2007 *On The Wealth of Nations*.

98 What's important about morality in politics is us. We own the chicken farm. We must give our bird-brained, feather-headed politicians morals. Politicians love to think of themselves as 'free-range' but they do not have the capacity to hunt or gather morals in the wild. If we fail to supply them with morality, politicians begin to act very scary in the barnyard. These are enormous headless chickens and they have nukes.
2010 *Don't Vote, It Just Encourages the Bastards*.

99 Sucking the fun out of life has always been an important component of politics.
2010 *Don't Vote, It Just Encourages the Bastards*.

Orozco, José Clemente 1883–1949

Mexican painter, one of the three foremost artists in the revival of monumental fresco painting.

1 The highest, the most logical, the purest and strongest form of painting is the mural... It is, too, the most disinterested form, for it cannot be made a matter of private gain; it cannot be hidden away for the benefit of a certain privileged few. It is for the people. It is for ALL.
1929 *Creative Art*.

Ortega y Gasset, José 1883–1955

Spanish essayist and philosopher, Professor of Metaphysics at Madrid. He gained international fame with *The Revolt of the Masses* (1929), which argued in favour of an intellectual governing elite.

2 The man who discovers a new scientific truth has previously had to smash to atoms almost everything he had learnt, and arrives at the new truth with hands blood stained from the slaughter of a thousand platitudes.
1930 *The Revolt of the Masses*.

Orton, Joe originally John Kingsley 1933–67

English dramatist, known for his blackly comic, outrageous farces such as *Entertaining Mr Sloane* (1964). He was murdered by his lover, Kenneth Halliwell, who then committed suicide.

3 I'd the upbringing a nun would envy... Until I was fifteen I was more familiar with Africa than my own body.
1964 *Entertaining Mr Sloane*, act 1.

4 Every luxury was lavished on you — atheism, breast-feeding, circumcision.
1966 *Loot*, act 1.

5 Reading isn't an occupation we encourage among police officers. We try to keep the paperwork down to a minimum.
1966 *Loot*, act 2.

Orwell, George *pseudonym of* Eric Arthur Blair 1903–50
English novelist, essayist and journalist. He fought in the Spanish Civil War and during World War II worked for the BBC. He developed his own brand of socialism in *The Road to Wigan Pier* (1937) and other essays, but is best known for his satire of totalitarian ideology in *Animal Farm* (1945), and the prophetic novel, *Nineteen Eighty-Four* (1949).

6 While the journalist exists merely as the publicity agent of big business, a large circulation, got by fair means or foul, is a newspaper's one and only aim.
1928 In *G.K.'s Weekly*, 29 Dec.

7 He was an embittered atheist (the sort of atheist who does not so much disbelieve in God as personally dislike Him), and took a sort of pleasure in thinking that human affairs would never improve.
1933 *Down and Out in Paris and London*, ch.30.

8 Keep the Aspidistra Flying.
1936 Title of novel.

9 In the early morning the mill girls clumping down the cobbled street, all in clogs, making a curiously formidable sound, like an army hurrying into battle. I suppose this is the typical sound of Lancashire.
1936 Diary entry, 18 Feb. He used this as material for his book *The Road to Wigan Pier* (1937).

10 It is only because miners sweat their guts out that superior persons can remain superior.
1937 *The Road to Wigan Pier*, ch.2.

11 A thousand influences constantly press a working man into a *passive* role. He does not act, he is acted upon.
1937 *The Road to Wigan Pier*, ch.3.

12 A person of bourgeois origin goes through life with some expectation of getting what he wants, within reasonable limits. Hence the fact that in times of stress 'educated' people tend to come to the front.
1937 *The Road to Wigan Pier*, ch.3.

13 I sometimes think the price of liberty is not so much eternal vigilance as eternal dirt.
1937 *The Road to Wigan Pier*, ch.4.

14 In a Lancashire cotton-town you could probably go for months on end without once hearing an 'educated' accent, whereas there can hardly be a town in the South of England where you could throw a brick without hitting the niece of a bishop.
1937 *The Road to Wigan Pier*, ch.7.

15 As with the Christian religion, the worst advertisement for Socialism is its adherents.
1937 *The Road to Wigan Pier*, ch.11.

16 To the ordinary working man, the sort you would meet in any pub on Saturday night, Socialism does not mean much more than better wages and shorter hours and nobody bossing you about.
1937 *The Road to Wigan Pier*, ch.11.

17 The underlying motive of many Socialists is, I believe, a hypertrophied sense of order…what they desire, basically, is to reduce the world to something resembling a chessboard.
1937 *The Road to Wigan Pier*, ch.11.

18 The high-water mark, so to speak, of Socialist literature is W.H. Auden, a sort of gutless Kipling.
1937 *The Road to Wigan Pier*, ch.11.

19 Cease to use your hands, and you have lopped off a huge chunk of your consciousness.
1937 *The Road to Wigan Pier*, ch.12.

20 It is usual to speak of the Fascist objective as the 'beehive state', which does a grave injustice to bees. A world of rabbits ruled by stoats would be nearer the mark.
1937 *The Road to Wigan Pier*, ch.12.

21 We of the sinking middle class…have nothing to lose but our aitches.
1937 *The Road to Wigan Pier*, ch.13.

22 The era of free speech is closing down. The freedom of the press in Britain was always something of a fake, because in the last resort, money controls opinion; still, so long as the legal right to say what you like exists, there are always loopholes for an unorthodox writer.
1938 In the *New Leader*, 24 Jun.

23 Roughly speaking it was the sensation of being *at the centre* of an explosion… I fancy you would feel much the same if you were struck by lightning. I knew immediately that I was hit, but because of that seeming bang and flash, I thought it was a rifle nearby that had gone off accidentally and shot me.
1938 Of his wounding during the Spanish Civil War. *Homage to Catalonia*, ch.12.

24 When you have had a glimpse of such a disaster as this…the result is not necessarily disillusionment and cynicism. Curiously enough, the whole experience has left me with not less but more belief in the decency of human beings.
1938 *Homage to Catalonia*, ch.14.

25 Down here it was still the England I had known in my childhood:…all sleeping the deep, deep sleep of England, from which I sometimes fear that we shall never wake till we are jerked out of it by the roar of bombs.
1938 *Homage to Catalonia*, ch.14.

26 I'm fat, but I'm thin inside. Has it ever struck you that there's a thin man inside every fat man, just as they say there's a statue inside every block of stone?
1939 *Coming Up For Air*, pt.1, ch.3.
▶ See Connolly 243:13.

27 Before the war, and especially before the Boer War, it was summer all the year round.
1939 *Coming Up For Air*, pt.2, ch.1.

28 If the war didn't happen to kill you it was bound to start you thinking. After that unspeakable idiotic mess you couldn't go on regarding society as something eternal and unquestionable, like a pyramid. You knew it was just a balls-up.
1939 *Coming Up For Air*, pt.2, ch.8.

29 Most revolutionaries are potential Tories, because they imagine that everything can be put right by altering the *shape* of society; once that change is effected, as it sometimes is, they see no need for any other.
1939 'Charles Dickens', collected in *Inside the Whale* (1940).

30 The novel is practically a Protestant form of art; it is the product of the free mind, of the autonomous individual.
1940 *Inside the Whale*, 'Inside The Whale'.

31 Contrary to popular belief, the past was not more eventful than the present. If it seems so it is because when you look backward things that happened years apart are telescoped together, and because very few of your memories come to you genuinely virgin.
1940 *Inside the Whale*, 'My Country Right or Left'.

32 As I write, highly civilized human beings are flying overhead, trying to kill me.
1941 *The Lion and the Unicorn: Socialism and the English Genius*, pt.1, 'England Your England'.

33 England is not the jewelled isle of Shakespeare's much-quoted passage, nor is it the inferno depicted by Dr Goebbels. More than either it resembles a family, a rather stuffy Victorian family, with not many black sheep in it but with all its cupboards bursting with skeletons.
1941 *The Lion and the Unicorn: Socialism and the English Genius*, pt.3, 'Shopkeeper at War'.

34 A family with the wrong members in control—that, perhaps, is as near as one can come to describing England in a phrase.
1941 *The Lion and the Unicorn: Socialism and the English Genius*, pt.3, 'The English Revolution'.

35 Probably the battle of Waterloo *was* won on the playing-fields of Eton, but the opening battles of all subsequent wars have been lost there. One of the dominant facts in English life during the past three-quarters of a century has been the decay of ability in the ruling class.
1941 *The Lion and the Unicorn: Socialism and the English Genius*, pt.4.

36 The great enemy of clear language is insincerity. When there is a gap between one's real and one's declared aims, one turns instinctively to long words and exhausted idioms—like cuttlefish squirting out ink.
1941 *The Lion and the Unicorn: Socialism and the English Genius*.

37 I believe that the BBC, in spite of the stupidity of its foreign propaganda and the unbearable voices of its announcers, is very truthful. It is generally regarded here as more reliable than the press.
1941 In the *Partisan Review*, 15 Apr. Reprinted in *Collected Essays, Journalism and Letters*, vol.2.

38 All propaganda is lies, even when one is telling the truth.
1942 Diary entry, 14 Mar.

39 Whatever is funny is subversive, every joke is ultimately a custard pie... A dirty joke is not, of course, a serious attack upon morality, but it is a sort of mental rebellion, a momentary wish that things were otherwise.
1942 'The Art of Donald McGill'.

40 On the whole, human beings want to be good, but not too good, and not all the time.
1942 'The Art of Donald McGill'.

41 Reminds me of nothing so much as a recently-dead fish before it has had time to stiffen.
1942 Of Clement Attlee. Diary entry, 19 May.

42 Any daily journalist will tell you that one of the most important secrets of his trade is the trick of making it appear that there is news when there is no news.
1944 In the *Tribune*, 21 Apr.

43 To blame someone like Northcliffe for making money in the quickest way is like blaming a skunk for stinking.
1944 In the *Tribune*, 21 Apr.

44 Cricket is a game full of forlorn hopes and sudden dramatic changes of fortune and its rules are so ill-defined that their interpretation is partly an ethical business.
1944 *Raffles and Miss Blandish*.

45 If liberty means anything at all, it means the right to tell people what they do not want to hear.
1945 Written for a rejected preface to *Animal Farm*.

46 Man is the only creature that consumes without producing.
1945 *Animal Farm*, ch.1.

47 Four legs good, two legs bad.
1945 *Animal Farm*, ch.3.

48 Napoleon had commanded that once a week there should be held something called a Spontaneous Demonstration.
1945 *Animal Farm*, ch.9.

49 All animals are equal but some animals are more equal than others.
1945 *Animal Farm*, ch.10.

50 The creatures outside looked from pig to man, and from man to pig, and from pig to man again; but already it was impossible to say which was which.
1945 *Animal Farm*, ch.10.

51 No modern Irish writer, even of the stature of Yeats or Joyce, is completely free from traces of nationalism.
1945 'Notes on Nationalism'.

52 In broadcasting your audience is conjectural, but it is an audience of *one*.
1945 'Poetry and the Microphone'.

53 Poetry on the air sounds like the Muses in striped trousers.
1945 'Poetry and the Microphone'.

54 To walk through the ruined cities of Germany is to feel actual doubt about the continuity of civilization.
1945 In the *Observer*, 8 Apr.

55 The books one reads in childhood, and perhaps most of all the bad and good bad books, create in one's mind a sort of false map of the world, a series of fabulous countries into which one can retreat at odd moments throughout the rest of life, and which in some cases can even survive a visit to the real countries which they are supposed to represent.
1946 'Riding Down from Bangor'.

56 Prolonged, indiscriminate reviewing of books involves constantly inventing reactions towards books about which one has no spontaneous feelings whatever.
1946 'Confessions of A Book Reviewer'.

57 The atom bombs are piling up in the factories, the police are prowling through the cities, the lies are streaming from the loudspeakers, but the earth is still going round the sun, and neither the dictators nor the bureaucrats, deeply as they disapprove of the process, are able to prevent it.
1946 'Some Thoughts on the Common Toad'.

58 To see what is in front of one's nose needs a constant struggle.
1946 'In Front of Your Nose'.

59 Good prose is like a window pane.
1946 'Why I Write'.

60 All writers are vain, selfish and lazy, and at the very bottom of their motives lies a mystery.
1946 'Why I Write'.

61 In our time, political speech and writing are largely the defence of the indefensible.
   1946 'Politics and the English Language', collected in *Shooting an Elephant* (1950).

62 The inflated style is itself a kind of euphemism.
   1946 'Politics and the English Language', collected in *Shooting an Elephant* (1950).

63 The great enemy of clear language is insincerity.
   1946 'Politics and the English Language', collected in *Shooting an Elephant* (1950).

64 In prose, the worst thing one can do with words is surrender to them.
   1946 'Politics and the English Language', collected in *Shooting an Elephant* (1950).

65 Political language...is designed to make lies sound truthful and murder respectable, and to give an appearance of solidity to pure wind.
   1946 'Politics and the English Language', collected in *Shooting an Elephant* (1950).

66 The Catholic and the Communist are alike in assuming that an opponent cannot be both honest and intelligent.
   1946 'The Prevention of Literature', in *Polemic*, Jan.

67 The controversy over freedom of speech and of the press is at the bottom a controversy over the desirability, or otherwise, of telling lies. What is really at issue is the right to report events truthfully, or as truthfully as is consistent with the ignorance, bias and self-deception from which every observer necessarily suffers.
   1946 'The Prevention of Literature', in *Polemic*, Jan.

68 The friends of totalitarianism in this country tend to argue that since absolute truth is not attainable, a big lie is no worse than a little lie.
   1946 'The Prevention of Literature', in *Polemic*, Jan.

69 Literature is doomed if liberty of thought perishes.
   1946 'The Prevention of Literature', in *Polemic*, Jan.

70 The quickest way of ending a war is to lose it.
   1946 'Second Thoughts on James Burnham', in *Polemic*, May.

71 It was a bright cold day in April, and the clocks were striking thirteen.
   1949 *Nineteen Eighty-Four*, pt.1, ch.1.

72 On each landing, opposite the lift shaft, the poster with the enormous face gazed from the wall. It was one of those pictures which are so contrived that the eyes follow you about when you move. BIG BROTHER IS WATCHING YOU, the caption beneath it ran.
   1949 *Nineteen Eighty-Four*, pt.1, ch.1.

73 War is peace. Freedom is slavery. Ignorance is strength.
   1949 *Nineteen Eighty-Four*, pt.1, ch.1.

74 'Who controls the past,' ran the Party slogan, 'controls the future: who controls the present controls the past.'
   1949 *Nineteen Eighty-Four*, pt.1, ch.3.

75 Freedom is the freedom to say that two plus two make four. If that is granted, all else follows.
   1949 *Nineteen Eighty-Four*, pt.1, ch.7.

76 *Doublethink* means the power of holding two contradictory beliefs in one's mind simultaneously, and accepting both of them.
   1949 *Nineteen Eighty-Four*, pt.2, ch.9.

77 If you want a picture of the future, imagine a boot stamping on a human face—for ever.
   1949 *Nineteen Eighty-Four*, pt.3, ch.3.

78 Power is not a means, it is an end. One does not establish a dictatorship in order to safeguard a revolution; one makes the revolution in order to establish the dictatorship.
   1949 *Nineteen Eighty-Four*, pt.3, ch.3.

79 Saints should always be judged guilty until they are proved innocent.
   1949 'Reflections on Gandhi', collected in *Shooting an Elephant* (1950).

80 At 50, everyone has the face he deserves.
   1949 Notebook entry, 17 Apr.

81 Serious sport has nothing to do with fair play. It is bound up with hatred, jealousy, boastfulness, disregard of all rules and sadistic pleasure in witnessing violence: in other words it is war minus the shooting...there are quite enough real causes of trouble already, and we need not add to them by encouraging young men to kick each other on the shins amid the roars of infuriated spectators.
   1950 'The Sporting Spirit'.

82 One ought to be able to hold in one's head simultaneously the two facts that Dali is a good draughtsman and a disgusting human being. The one does not invalidate or, in a sense, affect the other.
   Quoted in Michael Shelden *Orwell* (1991).

Osborne, Dorothy 1627–95
Wife of Sir William Temple, English diplomat and essay writer.

83 All letters, methinks, should be free and easy as one's discourse, not studied as an oration, nor made up of hard words like a charm.
   1653 Letter to William Temple.

Osborne, John 1929–94
English playwright and actor. The success of *Look Back in Anger* (1956), with its anti-hero Jimmy Porter, marked a new departure in postwar English drama and identified the author as the most famous of the 'angry young men' of the 1950s. Later works included *The Entertainer* (1957), *Luther* (1961), *Inadmissible Evidence* (1964) and *A Patriot for Me* (1969).

84 She's so clumsy. I watch for her to do the same things every night. The way she jumps on the bed, as if she were stamping on someone's face, and draws the curtains back with a great clatter, in that casually destructive way of hers. It's like someone launching a battleship. Have you ever noticed how noisy women are? Have you? The way they kick the floor about, simply walking over it? Or have you watched them sitting at their dressing tables, dropping their weapons and banging down their bits of boxes and brushes and lipsticks?
   1956 *Look Back in Anger*.

85 Don't clap too hard—it's a very old building.
   1957 *The Entertainer*, 7.

86 There will be a quick rash of hairy American filth, but it shouldn't threaten the existence of decent, serious British filth.
   1967 On the opening of the US musical *Hair*, in *Time* magazine.

Osler, Sir William 1849–1919
Canadian physician.

87 The greater the ignorance the greater the dogmatism.
   1902 Quoted in *Montreal Medical Journal*, Sep.

88 The desire to take medicine is perhaps the greatest feature which distinguishes man from animals.
   Quoted in H Cushing *Life of Sir William Osler* (1925), vol.1, ch.14.

89 One of the first duties of the physician is to educate the masses not to take medicine.
   Collected in W B Bean (ed) *Sir William Osler: Aphorisms from His Bedside Teachings and Writings* (1950).

90 Failure to examine the throat is a glaring sin of omission, especially in children. One finger in the throat and one in the rectum makes a good diagnostician.
   Collected in W B Bean (ed) *Sir William Osler: Aphorisms from His Bedside Teachings and Writings* (1950).

91 To talk of diseases is a sort of *Arabian Nights* entertainment.
   Quoted in Oliver Sacks *The Man Who Mistook his Wife for a Hat*, epigraph (1985).

Otis, James 1725–83
American politician and patriot. As Advocate General he refused to assist royal revenue officers to search individual's homes and resigned to fight for popular rights. In 1769 he was beaten by revenue officers and received a head wound from which he never really recovered.

92 Taxation without representation is tyranny.
   c.1761 His defence, which became a rallying call of the American Revolution.

O'Toole, Peter 1932–2013
Irish actor. His performance in *Lawrence of Arabia* (1962) made him an international star. Later films included *The Lion in Winter* (1968) and *My Favorite Year* (1982).

93 I'm one of the younger oldies. I'm in the prime of senility.
   2000 In *The Guardian*, 31 Dec.

Otway, Thomas 1652–85
English dramatist. Educated at Oxford. His first play was the tragedy *Alcibiades* (1675); in it his alleged lover, Elizabeth Barry, made her debut. His most famous play is *Venice Preserved, or a Plot Discovered* (1682).

94 Ere man's corruptions made him wretched, he
   Was born most noble that was born most free;
   Each of himself was lord; and unconfin'd
   Obey'd the dictates of his godlike mind.
   1676 *Don Carlos*, act 2.

95 You wags that judge by rote, and damn by rule.
   1677 *Titus and Berenice*, prologue.

96 And for an apple damn'd mankind.
   1680 *The Orphan*, act 3.

97 I may boldly speak
   In right, though proud oppression will not hear me!
   1682 *Venice Preserved, or a Plot Discovered*, act 1, sc.1.

98 May the hard hand of a vexatious need
   Oppress and grind you; till at last you find
   The curse of disobedience all your portion.
   1682 *Venice Preserved, or a Plot Discovered*, act 1, sc.1.

99 Home I would go
   But that my doors are hateful to my eyes,
   Fill'd and damm'd up with gaping creditors,
   Watchful as fowlers when their game will spring.
   1682 *Venice Preserved, or a Plot Discovered*, act 1, sc.1.

1 I'm thinking…how that damn'd starving quality
   Call'd honesty, got footing in the world.
   1682 *Venice Preserved, or a Plot Discovered*, act 1, sc.1.

2 Honesty was a cheat invented first
   To bind the hands of bold deserving rogues,
   That fools and cowards might sit safe in power,
   And lord it uncontroll'd above their betters.
   1682 *Venice Preserved, or a Plot Discovered*, act 1, sc.1.

3 'Tis a ragged virtue.
   1682 *Venice Preserved, or a Plot Discovered*, act 1, sc.1.

4 If love be treasure, we'll be wondrous rich.
   1682 *Venice Preserved, or a Plot Discovered*, act 1, sc.1.

5 Is the world
   Reform'd since our last meeting?
   1682 *Venice Preserved, or a Plot Discovered*, act 1, sc.1.

6 No praying, it spoils Business.
   1682 *Venice Preserved, or a Plot Discovered*, act 2, sc.1.

7 Give but an Englishman his whore and ease,
   Beef and a sea-coal fire, he's yours forever.
   1682 *Venice Preserved, or a Plot Discovered*, act 2, sc.3.

8 The poor sleep little.
   1682 *Venice Preserved, or a Plot Discovered*, act 2, sc.3.

9 No, this vile world and I have long been jangling,
   And cannot part on better terms than now,
   When only men like thee are fit to live in't.
   1682 *Venice Preserved, or a Plot Discovered*, act 4, sc.2.

Oud, J(acobus) J(ohannes) P(ieter) 1890–1963
Dutch architect, a pioneer of the modern architectural style based on simplified forms and pure planes.

10 If I was not optimistic, I would not be an architect.
   Quoted in the *New York Times*, 4 Dec 1994.

Overbury, Sir Thomas 1581–1613
English poet and courtier.

11 He disdains all things above his reach, and preferreth all countries before his own.
   1632 'An Affected Traveller', collected in *Miscellaneous Works*.

Overton, Robert fl.1642–68
English soldier. He fought for Parliament in the English Civil War and was made governor of Hull. He was imprisoned in 1656 for two years after he fought under Cromwell in Scotland and was suspected of planning an insurrection against the government. When Cromwell fell, Overton was released, but the doubts about him remained and his further support for a republic led to imprisonment for almost the rest of his life. The date and place of his death are unknown.

12 Whatever our forefathers were, or whatever they did or suffered, or were enforced to yield unto, we are the men of the present age, and ought to be absolutely free from all kinds of exorbitancies, molestations, or arbitrary power.
   1646 Remonstrance to the House of Commons.

Ovid full name Publius Ovidius Naso 43 BC–AD 17
Roman poet, who trained for law but turned to poetry. His many works include the *Ars Amatoria*, the *Metamorphoses* and the

Fasti. He was banished by Augustus in AD 8 to Tomi on the Black Sea, where he wrote the *Tristia*.

13 *Procul omen abesto!*
Far away be that fate!
Amores, bk.1, no.14, l.41.

14 *Iuppiter ex alto periuria ridet amantum.*
Jupiter from above laughs at lovers' perjuries.
Ars Amatoria, bk.1, l.633.

15 *Iam seges est ubi Troia fuit.*
Now there are cornfields where Troy once was.
Heroides, no.1, l.53.

16 *Chaos, rudis indigestaque moles.*
Chaos, a rough unordered mass.
Metamorphoses, bk.1, l.7.

17 *Medio tutissimus ibis.*
You will go most safely by the middle way.
Daedalus speaking to his son, Icarus. *Metamorphoses*, bk.2, l.137 (translated by Peter Green).

18 *Inopem me copia fecit.*
Plenty has made me poor.
Metamorphoses, bk.3, l.466.

19 *Video meliora, proboque;*
Deteriora sequor.
I see the better things, and approve; I follow the worse.
Metamorphoses, bk.7, l.20–1 (translated by Peter Green).

20 *Tempus edax rerum.*
Time the devourer of everything.
Metamorphoses, bk.15, l.234 (translated by Peter Green).

21 *Nec species sua cuique manet, rerumque novatrix*
ex aliis alias reddit natura figuras.
nec perit in toto quidquam, mihi credite, mundo,
sed variat faciemque novat, nascique vocatur
incipere esse aliud, quam quod fuit ante, morique,
desinere illud idem. cum sint huc forsitan illa,
haec translata illuc, summa tamen omnia constant.
No species remains constant: that great renovator of matter Nature, endlessly fashions new forms from old: there's nothing
in the whole universe that perishes, believe me; rather it renews and varies its substance. What we describe as birth
is no more than incipient change from a prior state, while dying
is merely to quit it. Though the parts may be transported hither and thither, the sum of all matter is constant.
Metamorphoses, bk.15, l.252–8 (translated by Peter Green).

22 *Donec eris felix, multos numerabis amicos*
Tempora si fuerint nubila, solus eris.
So long as you are fortunate, you will count many friends; if your life should become clouded, you will be alone.
Tristia, bk.1, no.9, l.5–6.

Owen, David Anthony Llewellyn Owen, Baron 1938–

English politician, one of the 'Gang of Four' who formed the Social Democratic Party (SDP) in 1981, becoming its leader in 1983. He resigned in 1987 rather than merge with the Liberal party, and led a minority, reconstituted SDP, dissolved in 1990. From 1992 to 1995 he was co-chairman (initially with Cyrus R Vance) of the international peace conference on the former Yugoslavia.

23 We are fed up with fudging and nudging, with mush and slush.
1980 Speech to Labour's national conference shortly before leaving the party to found the Social Democratic Party, Oct.

Owen, Robert 1771–1858

Welsh social reformer and philanthropist.

24 All the world is queer save thee and me, and even thou art a little queer.
Attributed. Said to his partner W Allen when they ended their business relationship.

Owen, Wilfred 1893–1918

English poet. Injured in the trenches in 1917, he met Siegfried Sassoon while recuperating in Edinburgh. He died in the last week of the war, and most of his poems were published posthumously. Their vivid and unsentimental realism is a powerful indictment of war, and they were memorably used by Benjamin Britten in his *War Requiem*, first performed in Coventry Cathedral (1962).

25 What passing-bells for these who die as cattle?
Only the monstrous anger of the guns.
Only the stuttering rifles' rapid rattle
Can patter out their hasty orisons.
1917 'Anthem for Doomed Youth'.

26 The pallor of girls' brows shall be their pall;
Their flowers the tenderness of patient minds,
And each slow dusk a drawing-down of blinds.
1917 'Anthem for Doomed Youth'.

27 Red lips are not so red
As the stained stones kissed by the English dead.
1917 'Greater Love'.

28 This book is not about heroes. English poetry is not yet fit to speak of them.
1918 *Poems* (published 1920), preface.

29 Above all, this book is not concerned with Poetry. The subject of it is War, and the pity of War. The Poetry is in the pity.
1918 *Poems* (published 1920), preface.

30 All the poet can do today is to warn.
That is why the true Poet must be truthful.
1918 *Poems* (published 1920), preface.

31 If you could hear, at every jolt, the blood
Come gargling from the froth-corrupted lungs,
Bitter as the cud
Of vile, incurable sores on innocent tongues,—
My friend, you would not tell with such high zest
To children ardent for some desperate glory
The old Lie: Dulce et decorum est
Pro patria mori.
1918 'Dulce et Decorum Est', collected in *Poems* (published 1920).
▶ See Horace 430:10.

32 It seemed that out of battle I escaped
Down some profound dull tunnel, long since scooped
Through granites which titanic wars had groined.
1918 'Strange Meeting', collected in *Poems* (published 1920).

33 And by his smile, I knew that sullen hall,
By his dead smile I knew we stood in Hell.
1918 'Strange Meeting', collected in *Poems* (published 1920).

34 'Strange friend,' I said, 'here is no cause to mourn.'
'None,' said the other, 'save the undone years,

The hopelessness. Whatever hope is yours
Was my life also; I went hunting wild
After the wildest beauty in the world.'
1918 'Strange Meeting', collected in *Poems* (published 1920).

35 I am the enemy you killed, my friend.
1918 'Strange Meeting', collected in *Poems* (published 1920).

36 Move him into the sun—
Gently its touch awoke him once,
At home, whispering of fields unsown.
1918 'Futility', collected in *Poems* (published 1920).

37 If anything might rouse him now
The kind old sun will know.
1918 'Futility', collected in *Poems* (published 1920).

38 Was it for this the clay grew tall?
—O what made fatuous sunbeams toil
To break earth's sleep at all?
1918 'Futility', collected in *Poems* (published 1920).

39 So secretly, like wrongs hushed-up, they went.
1918 'The Send-Off', collected in *Poems* (published 1920).

40 Whatever mourns when many leave these shores:
Whatever shares
The eternal reciprocity of tears.
1918 'Insensibility', collected in *Poems* (published 1920).

Owens, Jesse James Cleveland 1913–80

US athlete. The greatest sprinter of his generation, he won four gold medals at the Berlin Olympics in 1936, embarrassing the Nazi hosts, who had hoped to demonstrate the supremacy of Aryan athletes.

41 I let my feet spend as little time on the ground as possible. From the air, fast down, and from the ground, fast up.
Quoted in Colin Jarman *The Guinness Dictionary of Sports Quotations* (1990).

Ozick, Cynthia 1928–

US writer. She claimed to have begun her first novel, *Trust* (1966), an American writer and finished it six and a half years later a Jewish one. Other works include the short stories *The Shawl* (1989) and the novel *The Puttermesser Papers* (1997).

42 Yiddish is a household tongue, and God, like other members of the family, is sweetly informal in it.
1989 *Metaphor and Memory*.

43 Admittedly, there is always a golden age, the one not ours, the one that once was or will someday be. One's own time is never satisfactory, except to the very rich or the smugly oblivious.
2006 *The Din in the Head: Essays*.

Pacheco, José Emilio 1939–2014

Mexican poet, novelist, critic and translator. His poetry expresses his metaphysical concerns in brilliant images. The novel *Morirás lejos* (1967) documents the purges of Jews throughout history.

1 *Porque todo es irreal en este cuento. Nada sucedió como se indica. Hechos y sitios se deformaron por el empeño de tocar la verdad mediante una ficción, una mentira. Todo irreal, nada sucedió como aquí se refiere. Pero fue un pobre intento de contribuir a que el gran crimen nunca se repita.*
For everything in this story is unreal. Nothing happened the way it was suggested. Facts and places were distorted by that persistent desire to touch the truth by means of fiction, a lie. All of it is unreal; nothing happened the way it is told here. It was a poor attempt to help ensure that the great crime is never repeated.
1967 *Morirás lejos* (translated as *You Will Die in a Distant Land*, 1991).

Pacino, Al(fredo James) 1940–

US actor. Considered one of the leading film actors of his generation, he has won particular acclaim playing mobsters, most notably Michael Corleone in *The Godfather* trilogy (1972–90), as well as detectives and other unpredictable, hard-nosed characters. More varied roles have included Shakespeare's Shylock.

2 It's not personal, Sonny. It's strictly business.
1972 As Michael Corleone in *The Godfather* (screenplay by Mario Puzo and Francis Ford Coppola).

3 Keep your friends close, but your enemies closer.
1974 As Michael Corleone in *The Godfather Part II* (screenplay by Mario Puzo and Francis Ford Coppola).

4 If anything in this life is certain; if history has taught us anything, it's that you can kill anyone.
1974 As Michael Corleone in *The Godfather Part II* (screenplay by Mario Puzo and Francis Ford Coppola).

5 You wanna play rough? Okay. Come say hello to my little friend.
1983 As Tony Montana in *Scarface* (screenplay by Oliver Stone).

6 Just when I thought I was out… they pull me back in.
1990 As Michael Corleone in *The Godfather Part III* (screenplay by Mario Puzo and Francis Ford Coppola).

Packard, David 1912–96

US businessman.

7 Flexitime is the essence of respect for and trust in people.
1995 *The HP Way*.

Packard, Vance 1914–96

US writer and journalist.

8 The Hidden Persuaders.
1957 Title of a book on advertising.

Packer, Herbert Leslie 1925–72

US Professor of Law, Stanford University (1959–72). He was admitted to the New York Bar in 1950, and later the Supreme Court. He practised law in Washington before teaching at Stanford.

9 Crime is a socio-political artifact, not a natural phenomenon. We can have as much or as little crime as we please, depending on what we choose to count as criminal.
1968 *The Limits of Criminal Sanction*, p.364.

Packer, Kerry 1937–2005

Australian media executive.

10 If a British guy saw someone at the wheel of a Rolls-Royce, he'd say 'come the revolution and we'll take that away from you, mate', where the American would say 'one day I'll have one of those, when I have worked hard enough'. It's unfortunate we Australians inherited the British mentality.
1977 In *The Guardian*, 1 Sep.

Packwood, Bob 1932–
US Republican Senator and lawyer. He was Senator for Oregon from 1969 until his resignation in 1995.

11 I am accused of kissing women...perhaps overeagerly kissing women. And that is the charge, not drugging, not robbing, kissing!
1995 Replying to charges of sexual misconduct, lobbying, and editing diaries subpoenaed by the Senate Ethics Committee. In the *New York Times*, 7 Sep.

12 More than Francis of Assisi...less than Wilt Chamberlain.
1995 Estimating the amount of controversial activity documented in his diaries. In the *New York Times*, 9 Sep.

Paderewski, Ignace Jan 1860–1941
Polish pianist, composer and statesman, director of the Warsaw Conservatory (from 1909). In 1919 he became premier of Poland. He retired from politics to return to his music, but in 1940 was elected President by Poland's provisional parliament in Paris.

13 If I don't practise for one day, I know it; if I don't practise for two days, the critics know it; if I don't practise for three days, the audience knows it.
Quoted in Nat Shapiro *An Encyclopedia of Quotations about Music* (1978).

Page, Geraldine 1924–87
US actress. She made her name with the lead role in Tennessee Williams's *Summer and Smoke* (1954).

14 Name me one character in literature or drama who can't be described as neurotic... We wouldn't want to know the people we get to see on the stage. How would you like to have Medea for dinner? Or Macbeth slurping your soup? Or Oedipus with his bloody, blinded eyes dripping all over your tablecloth?
Attributed.

Pagels, Heinz R(udolf) 1939–88
US theoretical physicist and social activist, the author of several works describing the complexities of modern physics for the public.

15 A good simulation, be it a religious myth or scientific theory, gives us a sense of mastery over experience. To represent something symbolically, as we do when we speak or write, is somehow to capture it, thus making it one's own. But with this appropriation comes the realization that we have denied the immediacy of reality and that in creating a substitute we have but spun another thread in the web of our grand illusion.
1988 *The Dreams of Reason*.

16 Science provides a vision of reality seen from the perspective of reason, a perspective that sees the vast order of the universe, living and non-living matter, as a material system governed by rules that can be known by the human mind. It is a powerful vision, formal and austere but strangely silent about many of the questions that deeply concern us. Science shows us what exists but not what to do about it.
1988 *The Dreams of Reason*.

Paglia, Camille 1947–
US writer, Professor of Humanities at the University of the Arts, Philadelphia. Her works include *Sexual Personae* (1990), *Vamps and Tramps* (1994) and *Glittering Images* (2012).

17 The historical repugnance to woman has a rational basis: disgust is reason's proper response to the grossness of procreative nature.
1990 *Sexual Personae: Art and Decadence from Nefertiti to Emily Dickinson*, ch.1, 'Sex and Violence, or Nature and Art'.

18 No woman has to prove herself a woman in the grim way a man has to prove himself a man. He must perform, or the show does not go on. Social convention is irrelevant. A flop is a flop.
1990 *Sexual Personae: Art and Decadence from Nefertiti to Emily Dickinson*, ch.1, 'Sex and Violence, or Nature and Art'.

19 Feminism has become a catch-all vegetable drawer where bunches of clingy sob sisters can store their moldy neuroses.
1992 'The Return of Carry Nation: Catharine Mackinnon and Andrea Dworkin', in *Playboy*, Oct. Collected in *Vamps and Tramps* (1994).

20 I like Hillary because she's kind of a bitch.
1993 In the *Sunday Times* magazine, 18 Apr. Collected as 'Kind of a Bitch: Why I Like Hillary Clinton' in *Vamps and Tramps* (1994).

21 The only antidote to the magic of images is the magic of words.
2005 *Break, Blow, Burn*.

22 My advice to the reader approaching a poem is to make the mind still and blank. Let the poem speak. This charged quiet mimics the blank space ringing the printed poem, the nothing out of which something takes shape.
2005 *Break, Blow, Burn*.

23 Leaving sex to the feminists is like letting your dog vacation at the taxidermist.
Quoted in Alan, Soble, *Sex from Plato to Paglia: A Philosophical Encyclopedia*, vol.2 (2005).

24 Feminism today just exists as a bunch of mean girls on Twitter.
2014 Quoted on thestar.com, 26 Dec.

Pagnol, Marcel 1895–1974
French dramatist and film director, best known for his popular trilogy about Marseilles, *Marius* (1929), *Fanny* (1931) and *César* (1936).

25 *Les coupables, il vaut mieux les choisir que les chercher.*
It's better to choose the culprits than to seek them out.
1928 *Topaze*, act 1.

26 *L'honneur, c'est comme les allumettes: ça ne sert qu'une fois.*
Honour is like a match, you can use it only once.
1929 *Marius*, act 4, sc.5.

Paige, Satchel (Leroy Robert) 1906–82

US baseball player. One of the first blacks to play in the major leagues, he was a celebrated pitcher with the Cleveland Indians and the St Louis Browns.

27 One has to look out for engineers—they begin with sewing machines and end up with the atomic bomb.
1949 Critique des critiques, ch.3.

28 1. Avoid fried meats which angry up the blood.
2. If your stomach disputes you, lie down and pacify it with cool thoughts.
3. Keep the juices flowing by jangling around gently as you move.
4. Go very light on vices such as carrying on in society. The social ramble ain't restful.
5. Avoid running at all times.
6. Don't look back. Something may be gaining on you.
1976 'Six Rules for a Happy Life', which he had inscribed on business cards, offered to fans seeking his autograph.

Paine, Thomas 1737–1809

English radical political writer. His *Common Sense* (1776) argued for complete American independence, and *The Rights of Man* (1791–2) supported the French Revolution. Arraigned for treason, he fled to Paris, and wrote *The Age of Reason* (1794) in favour of deism.

29 These are the times that try men's souls. The summer soldier and the sunshine patriot will, in this crisis, shrink from the service of his country; but he that stands it *now*, deserves the love and thanks of man and woman.
1776 The Crisis, introduction, Dec.

30 Not all the treasures of the world, so far as I believe, could have induced me to support an offensive war, for I think it murder; but if a thief breaks into my house, burns and destroys my property, and kills or threatens to kill me or those that are in it, and to *'bind me in all cases whatsoever'* to his absolute will, am I to suffer it?
1776 The Crisis, introduction, Dec.

31 Government, even in its best state, is but a necessary evil; in its worst state, an intolerable one. Government, like dress, is the badge of lost innocence; the palaces of kings are built upon the bowers of paradise.
1776 Common Sense, ch.1.

32 As to religion, I hold it to be the indispensable duty of government to protect all conscientious professors thereof, and I know of no other business which government hath to do therewith.
1776 Common Sense, ch.4.

33 Man is not the enemy of Man, but through the medium of a false system of government.
1791-2 The Rights of Man.

34 To establish any mode to abolish war, however advantageous it might be to nations, would be to take from such Government the most lucrative of its branches.
1791-2 The Rights of Man.

35 Persecution is not an original feature of *any* religion; but it is always the strongly marked feature of all law-religions, or religions established by law.
1791-2 The Rights of Man.

36 My country is the world, and my religion is to do good.
1791-2 The Rights of Man.

37 The final event to himself has been, that as he rose like a rocket, he fell like the stick.
1792 Of Edmund Burke. *Letters to the Addressers on the late Proclamation.*

38 It is a fraud of the Christian system to call the sciences human invention; it is only the application of them that is human. Every science has for its basis a system of principles as fixed and unalterable as those by which the universe is regulated and governed. Man cannot make principles, he can only discover them.
1794 The Age of Reason, pt.1.

39 It is necessary to the happiness of man that he be mentally faithful to himself. Infidelity does not consist in believing, or in disbelieving, it consists in professing to believe what one does not believe.
1794 The Age of Reason, pt.1.

40 One step above the sublime, makes the ridiculous; and one step above the ridiculous, makes the sublime again.
1795 The Age of Reason, pt.2.

Paisley, Bob 1919–96

English football manager. He succeeded Bill Shankly as manager of Liverpool in 1974 and led the team through a golden era of League success.

41 Yes, we've had bad times at Anfield; one year we came second.
Quoted in Peter Ball and Phil Shaw *The Book of Football Quotations* (1989).

Paisley, Ian 1926–2014

Northern Irish clergyman and politician, founder of the Free Presbyterian Church of Ulster. A vociferous opponent of Irish unification, he was the object of fanatical devotion from Ulster loyalists.

42 I would rather be British than just.
1971 In the *Sunday Times*, 12 Dec.

43 I will walk on no grave of Ulster's honoured dead to do a deal with the IRA or the British government.
1997 Speech at the annual conference of the Democratic Unionist Party. In *The Irish Times*, 'This Week They Said', 6 Dec.

44 The mother of all treachery.
1998 On the Good Friday agreement. In *The Times*, 16 Apr.

45 She has become a parrot.
1998 On the perceived readiness of the Queen to repeat the views of her Prime Minister. In the *Daily Telegraph*, 27 May.

46 We must not allow our loathing of the tragedies of the past to become a barrier to a better future.
2007 Statement on agreeing a power-sharing deal with Sinn Fein, 26 Mar.

Palacký, František 1798–1876

Czech historian and politician in Prague, and the founder of historiography in Bohemia. He served in the first Austrian Reichstag and campaigned for the formation of a separate Czech nation.

47 If the Austrian Empire did not exist, it would have to be created in the interest of Europe and of humanity.
Quoted in A J P Taylor *From Napoleon to the Second International* (1993), p.169.

Palafox, José de c.1776–1847

Spanish general in the Peninsular War, who defended Saragossa with an improvised garrison of civilians. Despite breaching the city wall, the French were unable to capture the city.

48 *Guerra a cuchillo.*
War to the knife.
1808 His reply to the French suggestion that he surrender during the siege of Saragossa, 4 Aug. The phrase was inscribed on survivors' medals.

Paley, Grace née Goodside 1922–2007

US writer and political activist. She was best known as a writer of short stories, often set in a Jewish milieu in New York, but she also published poetry and collections of essays.

49 The Little Disturbances of Man.
1959 Title of story collection.

50 Enormous Changes at the Last Minute.
1974 Title of story collection.

51 Literature, fiction, poetry, whatever, makes justice in the world. That's why it almost always has to be on the side of the underdog.
1974 In *Ms* magazine.

52 All that is really necessary for survival of the fittest, it seems, is an interest in life, good, bad, or peculiar.
1976 In D L Fitzpatrick (ed) *Contemporary Novelists*.

53 No metaphor reinvents the job of the nurture of children except to muddy or mock.
1992 *Begin Again: New and Collected Poems*, 'Stanzas: Old Age and the Conventions of Retirement Have Driven My Friends from the Work They Love'.

54 Poets!
Madness is a gift
god-given
(though not to me).
1992 *Begin Again: New and Collected Poems*, 'On the Bank Street Pier'.

55 It is the responsibility of society to let the poet be a poet
It is the responsibility of the poet to be a woman.
1992 *Begin Again: New and Collected Poems*, 'Responsibility'.

56 It is the responsibility of the poet to be lazy to hang out and prophesy.
1992 *Begin Again: New and Collected Poems*, 'Responsibility'.

Paley, William 1743–1805

English theologian, Archdeacon of Carlisle (1782) and Sub-Dean of Lincoln (1795). His most popular work was *Natural Theology, or Evidences of the Existence and Attributes of the Deity* (1802).

57 Suppose I had found a *watch* upon the ground, and it should be enquired how the watch happened to be in that place… The inference, we think, is inevitable; that the watch must have had a maker, that there must have existed, at some time and at some place or other, an artificer or artificers, who formed it for the purpose which we find it actually to answer; who comprehended its construction, and designed its use.
1802 *Natural Theology*, ch.1.

Palin, Sarah Louise Heath 1964–

US politician. A staunch Republican, she served as Governor of Alaska (2006–9) and ran unsuccessfully as vice-presidential nominee in the 2008 presidential election.

58 What's the difference between a hockey mom and a pit bull? Lipstick.
2008 Speaking at the Republican National Convention, reported in the *New York Times*, 3 Sep.

59 I'm like, OK, God, if there is an open door for me somewhere, this is what I always pray, I'm like, don't let me miss the open door. Show me where the open door is.
2008 Contemplating running for President in 2012, reported on BBC, 11 Nov.

60 Peaceful Muslims, pls refudiate.
2010 Message on Twitter, which introduced the word 'refudiate' to the world; Palin later explained that she had intended to write 'repudiate', Jul.

61 Polls. They're for strippers and cross-country skiers.
2011 On *The Daily Show*, 28 Sep.

62 I love the smell of emissions.
2011 Referring to the exhaust fumes produced by motorbikes.

63 Well, if I were in charge, they would know that waterboarding is how we baptize terrorists.
2014 Speaking at the Stand and Fight Rally, Indianapolis, 26 Apr.

64 Mr. President, the only thing that stops a bad guy with a nuke is a good guy with a nuke.
2014 Conservative Political Action Conference speech, 8 Mar.

Palmer, Arnold 1929–

US golfer. Between 1958 and 1964 he won the US Masters four times, the British Open twice and the US Open once. He was twice captain of the US Ryder Cup team.

65 Winning isn't everything, but wanting to is.
Quoted in Colin Jarman *The Guinness Dictionary of Sports Quotations* (1990).

66 If Tiger Woods slamming his club into the ground is the biggest worry we have, our sport is in pretty good shape.
2000 Quoted in *Golf Digest*, Jan.

Palmerston, Henry John Temple, 3rd Viscount 1784–1865

English politician, Foreign Secretary (1830–41, 1846–51) and Prime Minister (1855–8, 1859–65). His abrasive, bullying approach to foreign affairs and propensity for brinkmanship made him unpopular with his colleagues and the public.

67 Half the wrong conclusions at which mankind arrive are reached by the abuse of metaphors, and by mistaking general resemblance or imaginary similarity for real identity.
1839 Letter to Henry Bulwer, 1 Sep.

68 Diplomats and protocols are very good things, but there are no better peace-keepers than well-appointed three-deckers.
c.1840 Quoted in Denis Judd *Palmerston* (1975). A three-decker is a warship.

69 We said to the Chinese, 'You have behaved very ill; we have had to teach you better manners; it has cost us something to do it, but we will send our bill in, and you must pay our charges.' That was done, and they have certainly profited by the lesson. They have become free traders too.
1847 On the Opium Wars of 1839–42. Election speech at Tiverton, Devon.

70 We have no eternal allies, and we have no perpetual enemies. Our interests are eternal, and it is our duty to follow them.
1848 Speech, House of Commons, 1 Mar.

71 Large republics seem to be essentially and inherently aggressive.
1848 Letter to the British Ambassador to Paris, 5 Mar.

72 I therefore fearlessly challenge the verdict which this house…is to give on the question now brought before it…whether, as the Roman, in days of old, held himself free from indignity, when he could say *Civis Romanus sum*; so also a British subject, in whatever land he may be, shall feel confident that the watchful eye and the strong arm of England will protect him against injustice and wrong.
1850 From his four-and-a-half hour Don Pacifico speech, Jun. Don Pacifico was a Portuguese Jew resident in Athens, born in Gibraltar and therefore a British subject. In support of his claims for compensation from the Greek government for damage done to his property by a mob, Palmerston sent the British fleet to blockade Piraeus and brought the two countries to the brink of war.

73 You may call it coalition, you may call it the accidental and fortuitous concurrence of atoms…but when gentlemen are in the habit of finding themselves in the same Lobby, it is not unnatural to suppose that they may, under certain circumstances, be ready to unite themselves together for the purpose of forming an Administration and becoming responsible for the opinions that they severally entertain.
1858 Speech on the rumoured Palmerston–Disraeli coalition, 5 Mar.

74 England is one of the greatest powers of the world. No event or series of events bearing on the balance of power, or on probabilities of peace or war, can be matters of indifference to her, and her right to have and to express opinions on matters thus bearing on her interests is unquestionable.
1859 Letter to Queen Victoria, 23 Aug.

Paltrow, Gwyneth Kate 1972–

US film actress, singer and food writer. She won an Oscar for her performance in *Shakespeare in Love* (1998); other notable films have included *Sliding Doors* (1998), *The Talented Mr. Ripley* (1999), *Proof* (2005) and *Iron Man* (2008).

75 I'd rather die than let my kid eat Cup-a-Soup.
2005 In the *New York Daily News*, Aug.

76 I am who I am. I can't pretend to be somebody who makes $25,000 a year.
2009 In *Elle UK* magazine, Jul.

77 I'd rather smoke crack than eat cheese from a tin.
2011 Interviewed at the iTunes Music Festival, 7 Jul.

78 I asked my Dad once, 'How did you and Mum stay married for thirty-three years?' He said, 'Well, we never wanted to get divorced at the same time.'
2013 Quoted in the *Evening Standard*, 2 May.

79 We have always conducted our relationship privately and we hope that as we consciously uncouple and co-parent, we will be able to continue in the same manner.
2014 Announcing on her Goop website her separation from her husband, the singer Chris Martin; the phrase 'conscious uncoupling' subsequently attracted much derision, 25 Mar.

Panama, Norman and Frank, Melvin 1914–2003, 1917–88

US screenwriters, who worked together on films such as *The Road to Utopia* (1945), *The Court Jester* (1955) and *Li'l Abner* (1959).

80 The pellet with the poison's in the chalice from the palace
The flagon with the dragon has the brew that is true.
1955 Lines delivered by Danny Kaye in *The Court Jester*.

Pangkor, Treaty of

The British signed a treaty (1874) with a claimant to the Perak Sultanate on the island of Pangkor, off the west coast of what is now peninsular Malaysia, and thereby formalized their economic and political interest in the region. It led to British control over the whole of the peninsula for the following 83 years.

81 A British officer to be called Resident who shall be accredited to his Court and whose advice must be asked and acted upon on all questions other than those touching Malay religion and custom.
1874 Treaty, Nov.

Pankhurst, Christabel 1880–1958

English suffragette and religious writer. Co-founder with her mother Emmeline Pankhurst of the Women's Social and Political Union (1903), she studied law (LLB 1906) and applied to join Lincoln's Inn, but was rejected, as a woman.

82 How long you women have been trying for the vote. For my part, I mean to get it.
c.1890 Childhood remark, quoted by her mother, Emmeline Pankhurst, in *My Own Story* (1914), ch.2.

Pankhurst, Emmeline *née Goulden* 1858–1928

English suffragette, organizer of the Women's Social and Political Union. A militant campaigner, she was frequently imprisoned and undertook hunger strikes. During World War I she turned her attention to the industrial mobilization of women.

83 Women never took a single step forward without being pushed back first of all by their opponents.
1912 Speech, 14 Jan, during a tour of Canada.

84 There is something that Governments care for far more than human life, and that is the security of property. So it is through property that we shall strike the enemy… Be militant each in your own way… I incite this meeting to rebellion.
1912 Speech, Royal Albert Hall, 17 Oct.

85 Women had always fought for men, and for their children. Now they were ready to fight for their own human rights.
1914 *My Own Story*, ch.3.

86 What is the use of fighting for the vote if we do not have a country to vote in? With that patriotism that has nerved women to endure torture in prison for the national good, we ardently desire that our country shall be victorious.
1914 Declaring a truce on suffragette activities for the duration of World War I, 10 Aug.

87 There are women today who never thought to envy men their manhood, but who would, at least for this purpose, be glad to be men.
1914 Speech appealing for the right to fight, 30 Nov, at a meeting organized by the Women's Social and Political Union, in the Kingsway Hall, London.

Parens, Erik
US academic. He is Associate for Philosophical Studies at the Hastings Center, a bioethics research institute.

88 On Why Talking about Behavioral Genetics Is Important and Difficult.
2004 Subtitle of the Hastings Center Report 'Genetic Differences and Human Identities'.

Pareto, Vilfredo 1848–1923
French-born Swiss economist and sociologist.

89 All governments use force and all assert that they are founded on reason. In fact, whether universal suffrage prevails or not, it is always an oligarchy that governs, finding ways to give to 'the will of the people' the expression which the few desire.
Quoted in Arthur Livingstone (ed) *The Mind and Society* (1935).

Parfitt, Harold Robert 1921–2006
US soldier. He served in Vietnam and advanced through the army grades to reach Major-General in 1971. He was decorated many times. He became governor of the Panama Canal Zone in 1975.

90 There will be no more tomorrows, only yesterdays, for the Canal Zone.
1979 On relinquishing authority as last governor of the Panama Canal Zone. Quoted in *Time*, 15 Oct.

Park, Mungo 1771–1806
Scottish explorer. He explored the Niger in 1796, then returned to Scotland and worked as a doctor, publishing *Travels in the Interior Districts of Africa* (1799), before leaving in 1805 for Africa again, sending back journals and letters.

91 I think it not unlikely but I shall be in England before you receive this—You may be sure that I feel happy at turning my face towards home. We this morning have done with all intercourse with the natives; and the sails are now hoisting for our departure for the coast.
1805 Last letter to his wife before leaving Sansanding on the River Niger. Collected in *Journal of a Mission to the Interior of Africa in the Year 1805* (published 1815). Park and his party reportedly drowned in the river when they were ambushed and their boat sank.

Parker, Charlie known as 'Bird' 1920–55
US saxophonist, bandleader and composer, architect of the bebop style. Despite addiction to heroin and alcohol and recurring mental illness, he led jazz groups until his death. His works include 'Now's the Time' and 'Ornithology'.

92 It's just music. It's trying to play clean and looking for the pretty notes.
1949 On bebop. Quoted in Gary Giddins *Celebrating Bird* (1987), ch.1.

93 There is no boundary line to art. Music is your own experience, your thoughts, your wisdom. If you don't live it, it won't come out of your horn.
1950 Quoted in Ross Russell *Bird Lives!* (1972), pt.4, ch.22.

Parker, Dorothy née Rothschild 1893–1967
US writer and humorist, a central figure of the legendary Algonquin Hotel Round Table. She was an influential book and drama critic, contributing incisive and caustic reviews to the *New Yorker*. Her works include *Enough Rope* (1926) and *Here Lies* (1939).

94 Brevity is the soul of lingerie, as the Petticoat said to the Chemise.
1916 Caption for *Vogue*. Quoted in J Keats *You Might as Well Live* (1970).

95 Excuse My Dust.
1925 Suggested epitaph for herself. Quoted in Alexander Woollcott *While Rome Burns* (1934), 'Our Mrs Parker'. She also suggested 'This is on me' for her tombstone.

96 Lady, lady, should you meet
One whose ways are all discreet,
One who murmurs that his wife
Is the lodestar of his life,
One who keeps assuring you
That he never was untrue,
Never loved another one…
Lady, lady, better run!
1926 Enough Rope, 'Social Note'.

97 Where's the man could ease a heart
Like a satin gown?
1926 Enough Rope, 'The Satin Dress', stanza 1.

98 The affair between Margot Asquith and Margot Asquith will live as one of the prettiest love stories in all literature.
1927 Book review in the *New Yorker*, 22 Oct.

99 If, with the literate, I am
Impelled to try an epigram,
I never seek to take the credit;
We all assume that Oscar said it.
1928 Sunset Gun, 'Oscar Wilde'.

1 And it is that word 'hummy', my darlings, that marks the first place in 'The House at Pooh Corner' at which Tonstant Weader fwowed up.
1928 Book review in the *New Yorker*, 20 Oct.

2 More glutton than artist…he commences to chew up the scenery.
1930 Play review, alluding to an unidentified actor. This is said to have been the origin of the phrase 'chew up the scenery', used to describe an actor who is 'hamming it up'.

3 Now that you've got me right down to it, the only thing I didn't like about *The Barretts of Wimpole Street* was the play.
1931 Play review in the *New Yorker*.

4 *House Beautiful* is play lousy.
1933 Review in the *New Yorker*. Quoted in P Hartnoll *Plays and Players* (1984).

5 How did they know?
1933 Attributed response on hearing of the death of President Calvin Coolidge.

6 Katharine Hepburn runs the gamut of the emotions from A to B.
1933 Remark during the interval of *The Lake* on its Broadway première. Quoted in G Carey *Katharine Hepburn* (1983), ch.6.

7 That woman speaks eighteen languages, and can't say No in any of them.
Quoted in Alexander Woollcott *While Rome Burns* (1934), 'Our Mrs Parker'.

8 And there was that wholesale libel on a Yale prom. If all the girls attending it were laid end to end, Mrs Parker said, she wouldn't be at all surprised.
Quoted in Alexander Woollcott *While Rome Burns* (1934), 'Our Mrs Parker'.

9 Good work, Mary. We all knew you had it in you.
   On the arrival of a baby. Quoted in Alexander Woollcott *While Rome Burns* (1934), 'Our Mrs Parker'.

10 Whose love is given over-well
   Shall look on Helen's face in hell
   Whilst they whose love is thin and wise
   Shall see John Knox in Paradise.
   1937 *Not So Deep as A Well*, 'Partial Comfort'.

11 Why is it no one ever sent me yet
   One perfect limousine, do you suppose?
   Ah no, it's always just my luck to get
   One perfect rose.
   1937 *Not So Deep as A Well*, 'One Perfect Rose'.

12 Four be the things I'd been better without:
   Love, curiosity, freckles, and doubt.
   1937 *Not So Deep as A Well*, 'Inventory'.

13 By the time you say you're his,
   Shivering and sighing
   And he vows his passion is
   Infinite, undying—
   Lady, make a note of this:
   One of you is lying.
   1937 *Not So Deep as A Well*, 'Unfortunate Coincidence'.

14 Oh, life is a glorious cycle of song,
   A medley of extemporanea;
   And love is a thing that can never go wrong;
   And I am Marie of Roumania.
   1937 *Not So Deep as A Well*, 'Comment'.

15 Drink and dance and laugh and lie,
   Love, the reeling midnight through,
   For tomorrow we shall die!
   (But, alas, we never do).
   1937 *Not So Deep as A Well*, 'The Flaw in Paganism'.
   ▶ See Bible 127:59.

16 He lies below, correct in cypress wood,
   And entertains the most exclusive worms.
   1937 *Not So Deep as A Well*, 'Tombstones in the Starlight'.

17 Men seldom make passes
   At girls who wear glasses.
   1937 *Not So Deep as A Well*, 'News Item'.

18 Scratch a lover, and find a foe.
   1937 *Not So Deep as A Well*, 'Ballade of a Great Weariness'.

19 Razors pain you
   Rivers are damp;
   Acids stain you;
   And drugs cause cramp.
   Guns aren't lawful;
   Nooses give;
   Gas smells awful;
   You might as well live.
   1937 *Not So Deep as A Well*, 'Résumé'.

20 Sorrow is tranquillity remembered in emotion.
   1939 *Here Lies*, 'Sentiment'.
   ▶ See Wordsworth 958:93.

21 And I'll stay off Verlaine, too; he was always chasing Rimbauds.
   1939 *Here Lies*, 'The Little Hours'.

22 You can always tell that the crash is coming when I start getting tender about Our Dumb Friends. Three highballs and I think I'm St Francis of Assisi.
   1939 *Here Lies*, 'Just a Little One'.

23 There's a hell of a distance between wise-cracking and wit. Wit has truth in it; wise-cracking is simply callisthenics with words.
   1956 In the *Paris Review*, Summer.

24 All those writers who write about their childhood! Gentle God, if I wrote about mine you wouldn't sit in the same room with me.
   1956 In the *Paris Review*, Summer.

25 It serves me right for putting all my eggs in one bastard.
   On her abortion. Quoted in J Keats *You Might as Well Live* (1970).

26 You can lead a horticulture, but you can't make her think.
   Response to a challenge to use 'horticulture' in a sentence. Quoted in J Keats *You Might as Well Live* (1970).

27 One more drink and I'd have been under the host.
   Quoted in H Teichmann *George S Kaufman* (1972).

28 That should assure us of at least forty-five minutes of undisturbed privacy.
   Attributed, after pressing the button marked 'nurse' when her secretary came to visit her in hospital. Quoted in Clifton Fadiman *The Faber Book of Anecdotes* (1985).

29 Three be the things I shall never attain:
   Envy, content, and sufficient champagne.
   Quoted in Marion Meade *Dorothy Parker* (1988).

30 All writers are either 29 or Thomas Hardy.
   On being asked Hemingway's age. Quoted in Marion Meade *Dorothy Parker* (1988).

31 As American as a sawed-off shotgun.
   Of Dashiell Hammett. Quoted in Marion Meade *Dorothy Parker* (1988).

32 Upon my honour, I saw a Madonna
   Standing in a niche
   Above the door of the private whore
   Of the world's worst son of a bitch.
   Jotted into the visitor's book of William Randolph Hearst's house at San Simeon after she had seen a Della Robbia Madonna over the entrance to Marion Davies's bedroom. Quoted in R Hughes *Culture of Complaint* (1994).

Parker, Hubert Lister 1900–72
English judge. He served as Lord Chief Justice of England.

33 A judge is not supposed to know anything about the facts of life until they have been presented in evidence and explained to him at least three times.
   1961 Quoted in the *Observer*, 12 Mar.

Parker, John 1729–75
Commander of the Lexington militia company in the opening engagement of the American Revolution.

34 Stand your ground. Don't fire unless fired upon, but if they mean to have a war, let it begin here!
   1775 Attributed command before the Battle of Lexington, 19 Apr.

Parker, Ross and Charles, Hugh 1914–74, 1907–95
British songwriters.

35 There'll always be an England
   While there's a country lane,
   Wherever there's a cottage small
   Beside a field of grain.
   1939 Song.

Parker, Stewart 1941–88

Northern Irish playwright. A lecturer at Cornell University, he turned to full-time writing for the stage, TV and radio. His best-known plays are *Spokesong* (1976) and *Pentecost* (1987).

36 The Kamikaze Ground Staff Re-union Dinner.
   1979 Title of play.

Parkes, Sir Henry 1815–96

English-born Australian statesman, who emigrated to New South Wales in 1839. A member of the colonial parliament in 1854, he held various offices, from 1872 was repeatedly Prime Minister, and was identified with free trade.

37 Why should not the name of an Australian be equal to that of a Briton...to that of a citizen of the proudest country under the sun? Make yourselves a united people, appear before the world as one, and the dream of going 'home' will die away.
   1880 Speech to the Australian Federation Conference, Feb.

Parkinson, C(yril) Northcote 1909–93

English political scientist and Professor of History, best remembered for his seriocomic tilt at bureaucratic malpractices, *Parkinson's Law: the Pursuit of Progress* (1958).

38 Work expands so as to fill the time available for its completion.
   1958 *Parkinson's Law: the Pursuit of Progress*, ch.1.

39 Time spent on any item of the agenda will be in inverse proportion to the sum involved.
   1958 *Parkinson's Law: the Pursuit of Progress*, ch.3.

40 Men enter local politics solely as a result of being unhappily married.
   1958 *Parkinson's Law: the Pursuit of Progress*, ch.10.

41 Expenditure rises to meet income.
   1960 *The Law and the Profits*, ch.1.

Parkinson, Norman originally Ronald William Parkinson Smith 1913–90

English magazine photographer.

42 A photographer without a magazine behind him is like a farmer without fields.
   1984 In the *New Yorker*, 10 Dec.

43 The camera can be the most deadly weapon since the assassin's bullet. Or it can be the lotion of the heart.
   1984 In the *New Yorker*, 10 Dec.

Parks, Rosa Lee née McCauley 1913–2005

US civil rights protester.

44 All I was doing was trying to get home from work.
   On refusing to give up her seat to a white man in Montgomery, Alabama, which led to the 1955 Montgomery bus boycott and in turn to a Supreme Court ruling that bus segregation was unconstitutional, and fuelled the civil rights movement. Quoted in *Time*, 15 Dec 1975.

45 People always say that I didn't give up my seat because I was tired, but that isn't true. I was not tired physically, or no more tired than I usually was at the end of a working day... No, the only tired I was, was tired of giving in.
   Quoted in Jeanne Theoharis, *The Rebellious Life of Mrs. Rosa Parks* (2013).

Parnell, Charles Stewart 1846–91

Irish politician, elected President of the Irish National Land League (1878). In 1886 he allied with the Liberals in support of Gladstone's Home Rule bill, but was forced to retire as leader of the Irish Nationalists in 1890 in disgrace when cited as co-respondent in a divorce case.

46 When a man takes a farm from which another has been evicted, you must show him on the roadside when you meet him; you must show him in the streets of the town; you must show him in the fair and the market place; and even in the house of worship, by leaving him severely alone—by putting him into a moral Coventry, by isolating him from his kind as if he were a leper of old. You must show him your detestation of the crimes that he has committed.
   1880 Speech that established the practice of boycotting, Ennis, 19 Sep.

47 And it is a good sign that this masquerading knight-errant, this pretended champion of the rights of every other nation except those of the Irish nation, should be obliged to throw off the mask today, and to stand revealed as the man who by his own utterances is prepared to carry fire and sword into your homesteads unless you humbly abase yourselves before him, and before the landlords of the country.
   1881 Speech successfully inciting Gladstone to arrest him, 9 Oct.

48 No man has a right to fix the boundary of the march of a nation. No man has a right to say to his country, 'Thus far thou shalt go and no further.'
   1885 Speech, Cork, 21 Jan.

Parra, Nicanor 1914–

Chilean physicist, poet and lecturer. He addresses common problems in a clear and direct language, with black humour and a highly ironic vision.

49 *Padre nuestro que estás en el cielo*
   Lleno de toda clase de problemas
   Con el ceño fruncido
   Como si fueras un hombre vulgar y corriente
   No pienses más en nosotros.
   Our Father who art in Heaven
   Full of all kinds of problems
   Ceaselessly frowning
   As if you were a simple man:
   Stop thinking about us.
   1969 *Obra gruesa*, 'Padre nuestro' ('Our Father').

Parr-Davies, Harry 1914–55

Welsh songwriter, best known for the songs he wrote for Gracie Fields. His credits include 'Sing As We Go' (1934), 'Queen of Hearts' (1936) and 'Shipyard Sally' (1939).

50 Wish me luck, as you wave me goodbye—
   Cheerio, here I go, on my way.
   1939 Sung by Gracie Fields in *Shipyard Sally*.

Parris, Matthew 1949–

British author, journalist and broadcaster, former Conservative MP (1979–86).

51 Wilde's captors were the police. But his persecutors were to be found on the letters page of the *Daily Telegraph*.
   1993 In *The Times*, 7 Apr.

52 Being an MP feeds your vanity and starves your self-respect.
   1994 In *The Times*, 9 Feb.

53 Bring on the fruitcakes, we want a fruitcake for an unlovable seat.
   1997 On the day before the Kensington and Chelsea Conservatives chose Alan Clark as their parliamentary candidate. In the *Daily Mail*, 26 Jan.

54 I want to see hedge-fund managers tipped into cage fights with naked Gypsies; bank managers wrestle with lions in the O2 arena; failed regulators thrown to alligators in the Royal Docks; short sellers in pits of snakes; and distinguished City economists try their luck with sharks. They've had their heyday, their bonuses, their Porsches, their fine wines and oafish ostentation—they've had their fun. Now for ours. To the guillotine!
   2008 In *The Times*, 18 Dec.

Parry, Sir Charles Hubert Hastings 1848–1918

English composer. Director of the Royal College of Music from 1895, he composed the oratorios *Judith* (1888), *Job* (1892) and *King Saul* (1894); an opera, symphonies, quartets and cantatas. He also wrote various books on music.

55 Look out for this man's music; he has something to say and knows how to say it.
   1899 After the première of Elgar's *Enigma Variations*. Quoted in Ian Crofton and Donald Fraser *A Dictionary of Musical Quotations* (1985).

Parsons, Talcott 1902–79

US sociologist and social theorist. A member of the faculty of Harvard University (1927–74), his chief works include *The Social System* (1951) and *Sociological Theory and Modern Society* (1967).

56 Science is intimately integrated with the whole social structure and cultural tradition. They mutually support one another—only in certain types of society can science flourish, and conversely without a continuous and healthy development and application of science such a society cannot function properly.
   1951 *The Social System*, ch.8.

Parton, Dolly 1946–

US country singer, songwriter and actress.

57 Some people say that less is more. But I think more is more.
   Attributed.

58 You'd be surprised how much it costs to look this cheap.
   Attributed.

59 If I see something sagging, bagging and dragging, I'm going to nip it, tuck it and suck it.
   Attributed.

60 I describe my look as a blend of Mother Goose, Cinderella, and the local hooker.
   2012 *Dream More: Celebrate the Dreamer in You*.

Parvin, Landon 1948–

US speechwriter. He was formerly speechwriter to President Reagan. He runs his own speechwriting and communications consultancy.

61 What you do is take the truth and just skew it a bit.
   1991 On creating political wit for the Washington press's annual Gridiron dinners. In the *New York Times*, 29 Mar.

Pascal, Blaise 1623–62

French philosopher, mathematician and physicist, whose inventions included a calculating machine, barometer, hydraulic press and syringe, and who pioneered probability theory. An ascetic Christian and member of the Jansenist movement, he wrote much spiritual literature. Notes found after his death were published as *Pensées* in 1670.

62 *Il y a deux sortes d'esprits, l'un géométrique, et l'autre que l'on peut appeler de finesse. Le premier a des vues lentes, dures et inflexibles; mais le dernier a une souplesse de pensée.*
   There are two kinds of mind, one mathematical, the other what one might call the intuitive. The first takes a slow, firm, inflexible view, but the latter has flexibility of thought.
   c.1653 *Discours sur les passions de l'amour* (*Discourse on the Passions of Love*). This is usually attributed to Pascal.

63 *Dans une grande âme tout est grand.*
   In a great soul everything is great.
   c.1653 *Discours sur les passions de l'amour* (*Discourse on the Passions of Love*). This is usually attributed to Pascal.

64 *Quelque étendue d'esprit que l'on ait, l'on n'est capable que d'une grande passion.*
   However vast a man's spirit, he is only capable of one great passion.
   c.1653 *Discours sur les passions de l'amour* (*Discourse on the Passions of Love*). This is usually attributed to Pascal.

65 *La netteté de l'esprit cause aussi la netteté de la passion; c'est pourquoi un esprit grand et net aime avec ardeur, et il voit distinctement ce qu'il aime.*
   Clarity of mind results in clarity of passion; that is why a great mind loves ardently and sees distinctly what it loves.
   c.1653 *Discours sur les passions de l'amour* (*Discourse on the Passions of Love*). This is usually attributed to Pascal.

66 *L'on a beau se cacher à soi-même, l'on aime toujours.*
   We vainly conceal from ourselves the fact that we are always in love.
   c.1653 *Discours sur les passions de l'amour* (*Discourse on the Passions of Love*). This is usually attributed to Pascal.

67 *La vraie éloquence se moque de l'éloquence, la vraie morale se moque de la morale.*
   True eloquence has no time for eloquence, true morality has no time for morality.
   c.1654–1662 *Pensées*, no.4 (translated by A Krailsheimer).

68 *La dernière chose qu'on trouve en faisant un ouvrage, est de savoir celle qu'il faut mettre la première.*
   The last thing one discovers in composing a work is what to put first.
   c.1654–1662 *Pensées*, no.19 (translated by A Krailsheimer).

69 *Quand on voit le style naturel, on est tout étonné et ravi, car on s'attendait de voir un auteur, et on trouve un homme.*
   When we see a natural style we are quite amazed and delighted, because we expected to see an author and find a man.
   c.1654–1662 *Pensées*, no.29 (translated by A Krailsheimer).

70 *L'homme n'est qu'un sujet plein d'erreur, naturelle et ineffaçable sans la grâce.*

Man is nothing but a subject full of natural error that cannot be eradicated except through grace.
c.1654–1662 *Pensées*, no.83 (translated by A Krailsheimer).

71 *Condition de l'homme: inconstance, ennui, inquiétude.*
Man's condition. Inconstancy, boredom, anxiety.
c.1654–1662 *Pensées*, no.127 (translated by A Krailsheimer).

72 *Notre nature est dans le mouvement; le repos entier est la mort.*
Our nature consists in movement; absolute rest is death.
c.1654–1662 *Pensées*, no.129 (translated by A Krailsheimer).

73 *Tout le malheur des hommes vient d'une seule chose, qui est de ne savoir pas demeurer en repos, dans une chambre.*
The sole cause of man's unhappiness is that he does not know how to stay quietly in his room.
c.1654–1662 *Pensées*, no.139 (translated by A Krailsheimer).

74 *Le nez de Cléopâtre: s'il eût été plus court, toute la face de la terre aurait changé.*
Cleopatra's nose: if it had been shorter the whole face of the earth would have been different.
c.1654–1662 *Pensées*, no.162 (translated by A Krailsheimer).

75 *Le silence éternel de ces espaces infinis m'effraie.*
The eternal silence of these infinite spaces fills me with dread.
c.1654–1662 *Pensées*, no.206 (translated by A Krailsheimer).

76 *Combien de royaumes nous ignorent!*
How many kingdoms know nothing of us!
c.1654–1662 *Pensées*, no.207 (translated by A Krailsheimer).

77 *Le dernier acte est sanglant, quelque belle que soit la comédie en tout le reste; on jette enfin de la terre sur la tête, et en voilà pour jamais.*
The last act is bloody, however fine the rest of the play. They throw earth over your head and it is finished forever.
c.1654–1662 *Pensées*, no.210 (translated by A Krailsheimer).

78 *Pesons le gain et la perte, en prenant croix que Dieu est. Estimons ces deux cas: si vous gagnez, vous gagnez tout; si vous perdez, vous ne perdez rien. Gagez donc qu'il est, sans hésiter.*
Let us weigh up the gain and loss involved in calling heads that God exists. Let us assess the two cases: if you win you win everything, if you lose you lose nothing. Do not hesitate then; wager that he does exist.
c.1654–1662 *Pensées*, no.233 (translated by A Krailsheimer).

79 *Tout notre raisonnement se réduit à céder au sentiment.*
All our reasoning comes down to surrendering to feeling.
c.1654–1662 *Pensées*, no.274 (translated by A Krailsheimer).

80 *Le cœur a ses raisons, que la raison ne connaît point.*
The heart has its reasons of which reason knows nothing.
c.1654–1662 *Pensées*, no.277 (translated by A Krailsheimer).

81 *L'homme n'est qu'un roseau, le plus faible de la nature; mais c'est un roseau pensant.*
Man is only a reed, the weakest in nature, but he is a thinking reed.
c.1654–1662 *Pensées*, no.347 (translated by A Krailsheimer).

82 *Le moi est haïssable.*
The self is hateful.
c.1654–1662 *Pensées*, no.455 (translated by A Krailsheimer).

83 *À mesure qu'on a plus d'esprit, on trouve qu'il y a plus d'hommes originaux. Les gens du commun ne trouvent pas de différence entre les hommes.*
The more intelligent one is, the greater the differences one finds among men. Ordinary persons do not perceive differences among men.
c.1654–1662 *Pensées*, pt.1, no.7.

84 *Éloquence qui persuade par douceur, non par empire, en tyran, non en roi.*
Eloquence should persuade gently, not by force or like a tyrant or king.
c.1654–1662 *Pensées*, pt.1, no.15.

85 *Qu'est-ce que l'homme dans la nature? Un néant à l'égard de l'infini, un tout à l'égard du néant, un milieu entre rien et tout.*
What is man in nature? Nothing in comparison to the infinite, all in comparison to nothing, a mean between nothing and everything.
c.1654–1662 *Pensées*, pt.2, no.72.

86 *La chose la plus importante à toute la vie est le choix du métier: le hasard en dispose.*
The most important thing in life is to choose a profession: chance arranges for that.
c.1654–1662 *Pensées*, pt.2, no.97.

87 Knowledge of physical science will not console me for ignorance of morality in time of affliction, but knowledge of morality will always console me for ignorance of physical science.
c.1654–1662 *Pensées*, no.23.

88 *L'homme n'est ni ange ni bête, et le malheur veut que qui veut faire l'ange fait la bête.*
Man is neither angel nor beast. Unfortunately, he who wants to act the angel often acts the beast.
c.1654–1662 *Pensées*, pt.6, no.358.

89 *En un mot, l'homme connaît qu'il est misérable: il est donc misérable, puisqu'il l'est; mais il est bien grand, puisqu'il le connaît.*
In one word, man knows that he is miserable and therefore he is miserable because he knows it; but he is also worthy, because he knows his condition.
c.1654–1662 *Pensées*, pt.6, no.416.

90 *Il n'y a que deux sortes d'hommes: les uns justes, qui se croient pécheurs; les autres pécheurs, qui se croient justes.*
There are only two types of people: the virtuous who believe themselves to be sinners and the sinners who believe themselves to be virtuous.
c.1654–1662 *Pensées*, pt.7, no.534.

91 *Il est non seulement impossible, mais inutile de connaître Dieu sans Jésus-Christ.*
It is not only impossible, but also useless to recognize God without Jesus.
c.1654–1662 *Pensées*, pt.7, no.549.

92 *Je ne crois que les histoires dont les témoins se feraient égorger.*
I only believe in histories told by witnesses who would have had their throats slit.
c.1654–1662 *Pensées*, pt.9, no.593.

93 *Le silence est la plus grande persécution: jamais les saints ne se sont tus.*

Silence is the greatest of all persecutions: no saint was ever silent.
c.1654–1662 *Pensées*, pt.14, no.920.

94 *Console-toi, tu ne me chercherais pas si tu ne m'avais trouvé.*
Comfort yourself. You would not seek me if you had not found me.
c.1654–1662 *Pensées*, pt.7, no.553 (translated by L Braunschvicg, 1909).

95 *Je n'ai fait plus longue que parce que je n'ai pas eu le loisir de la faire plus courte.*
I have made this letter longer than usual, only because I have not had the time to make it shorter.
1657 *Lettres provinciales*, letter 16.

96 FEU. *Dieu d'Abraham, Dieu d'Isaac, Dieu de Jacob, non des philosophes et savants. Certitude. Certitude. Sentiment. Joie. Paix.*
FIRE. God of Abraham, God of Isaac, God of Jacob, not of the philosophers and scholars. Certainty. Certainty. Feeling. Joy. Peace.
c.1662 Note found after his death on a parchment stitched to his coat.

Passell, Peter
US financial journalist, editor of the Milken Institute Review.

97 Six percent unemployment only looks good from the vantage point of the other 94 percent.
1994 In the *New York Times*, 31 Mar.

Pasternak, Boris 1890–1960
Russian poet and novelist. He was awarded a Nobel prize for literature in 1958, but refused it.

98 Yet the order of the acts is planned
And the end of the way inescapable.
I am alone; all drowns in the Pharisees' hypocrisy.
1958 *Doctor Zhivago*.

99 The whole wide world is a cathedral;
I stand inside, the air is calm,
And from afar at times there reaches
My ear the echo of a psalm.
1958 *When It Clears Up* (translated by Lydia Pasternak Slater).

Pasteur, Louis 1822–95
French chemist, the father of modern bacteriology. He promoted inoculation as a means of preventing diseases, and in 1888 he founded the Institut Pasteur and served as its first director.

1 *Dans les champs de l'observation le hasard ne favorise que les esprits préparés.*
Where observation is concerned, chance favours only the prepared mind.
1854 Speech at the inauguration of the Faculty of Science, University of Lille, 7 Dec.

2 Science proceeds by successive answers to questions more and more subtle, coming nearer and nearer to the very essence of phenomena.
c.1856 *Études sur la bière*, ch.6 (translated by René Dubois).

3 *Il n'existe pas de sciences appliquées, mais seulement des applications de la science.*
There are no such things as applied sciences, only applications of science.
1872 Speech, Lyons, 11 Sep.

4 I am imbued with two deep impressions; the first, that science knows no country; the second, which seems to contradict the first, although it is really a direct consequence of it…that science is the highest personification of the nation. Science knows no country because knowledge belongs to humanity, and is the torch which illuminates the world. Science is the highest personification of the nation because that nation will remain the first which carries the furthest the works of thought and intelligence.
1876 Toast at the banquet of the International Congress of Sericulture (translated by René Dubois).

5 Outside their laboratories, the physician and chemist are soldiers without arms on the field of battle.
Some Reflections on Science in France, pt.1.

Patchen, Kenneth 1911–72
US author, playwright and poet. His many verse collections, illustrated by him, include *Before the Brave* (1936) and *Hallelujah Anyway* (1967), and his novels include *Memoirs of a Shy Pornographer* (1945).

6 For greatness is only the drayhorse that coaxes
The built cart out; and where we go is reason.
But genius is an enormous littleness, a trickling
Of heart that covers alike the hare and the hunter.
1939 *First Will and Testament*, 'The Character of Love Seen as a Search for the Lost'.

7 Dogs with broken legs are shot; men with broken souls write through the night.
1941 *The Journal of Albion Moonlight*.

8 God must have loved the People in Power, for he made them so very like their own image of him.
Quoted by Adrian Mitchell in *The Guardian*, 1 Feb 1972.

Pater, Walter 1839–94
English critic and essayist, whose highly polished prose style was very influential. He wrote many essays on Renaissance art, and won a wider audience with a romance, *Marius the Epicurean* (1885).

9 She is older than the rocks among which she sits; like the vampire, she has been dead many times, and learned the secrets of the grave.
1873 Of the *Mona Lisa*. 'Leonardo da Vinci' in *Studies in the History of the Renaissance*.

10 All art constantly aspires towards the condition of music.
1873 'The School of Giorgione' in *Studies in the History of the Renaissance*.

11 Of such wisdom, the poetic passion, the desire of beauty, the love of art for its own sake, has most. For art comes to you proposing frankly to give nothing but the highest quality to your moments as they pass, and simply for those moments' sake.
1873 'Conclusion' in *Studies in the History of the Renaissance*.

Paterson, Banjo (Andrew Barton) 1864–1941
Australian poet and journalist. He worked on a station near Yass and later practised as a solicitor, contributing to the satirical weekly *Bulletin* as 'The Banjo'. His first collection of bush ballads, *The Man from Snowy River* (1895), gained him massive popularity.

12 Oh there once was a swagman camped in the billabongs,

Under the shade of a Coolibah tree;
And he sang as he looked at the old billy boiling,
'Who'll come a-waltzing Matilda with me.'

Who'll come a-waltzing Matilda, my darling,
Who'll come a-waltzing Matilda with me.
Waltzing Matilda and leading a water-bag,
Who'll come a-waltzing Matilda with me.
1885 'Waltzing Matilda', in the *Bulletin*, Apr.

13 I had written him a letter which I had, for want of better
Knowledge, sent to where I met him, down the Lachlan,
years ago.
He was shearing when I knew him, so I sent the letter
to him,
Just 'on spec', addressed as follows: 'Clancy, of the
Overflow'.
And an answer came directed in a writing unexpected,
(And I think the same was written with a thumbnail
dipped in tar)
'Twas his shearing mate who wrote it, and verbatim I will
quote it:
'Clancy's gone to Queensland droving, and we don't
know where he are.'
1895 'Clancy of the Overflow', first published in the *Bulletin*,
collected in *The Man from Snowy River and Other Verses* (1895).

14 In all museums throughout the world one may see
plaster casts of footprints of weird animals, footprints
preserved for posterity, not because the animals were
particularly good of their sort, but because they had the
luck to walk on the lava while it was cooling. There is
just a faint hope that something of the same sort may
happen to us.
Of Henry Lawson and himself writing in a new land. Quoted in
Rosamund Campbell and Philippa Harvie *A Literary Heritage:
'Banjo' Paterson* (1988), introduction.

Patmore, Coventry Kersey Dighton 1823–96

English poet. He was associated with the Pre-Raphaelite
brotherhood. His best work, *The Angel in the House* (4 vols.
1854–63), was a poetic treatment of married love which delighted
a generation devoid of cynicism to whom he and his first wife,
Emily, epitomized Victorian values.

15 Oh, wasteful woman, she who may
On her sweet self set her own price,
Knowing man cannot choose but pay,
How has she cheapened paradise:
How given for naught her priceless gift,
How spoiled the bread and spilled the wine,
Which, spent with due, respective thrift,
Had made brutes men, and men divine.
1854 *The Angel in the House*, bk.1, *The Betrothal*, canto 3, prelude
3, 'Unthrift'.

16 Love wakes men, once a lifetime each:
They lift their heavy lids, and look;
And, lo, what one sweet page can teach,
They read with joy, then shut the book.
1854 *The Angel in the House*, bk.1, *The Betrothal*, canto 8, prelude
2, 'The Revelation'.

17 'I saw you take his kiss!' 'Tis true.'
'O modesty!' ''Twas strictly kept:
He thought me asleep—at least, I knew
He thought I thought he thought I slept.'
1854 *The Angel in the House*, bk.2, *The Espousal*, canto 8, prelude
3, 'The Kiss'.

18 A woman is a foreign land.
1854 *The Angel in the House*, bk.2, *The Espousal*, canto 9, prelude
2, 'The Foreign Land'.

19 It was not like your great and gracious ways!
Do you, that have naught other to lament,
Never, my love, repent.
1877 *To the Unknown Eros*, bk.1, no.8, 'Departure'.

20 With all my will, but much against my heart,
We two now part.
1877 *To the Unknown Eros*, bk.1, no.16, 'A Farewell'.

21 'O say,
Shall we no voluntary bars
Set to our drift? I, Sister of the Stars,
And Thou, my glorious, course-compelling Day!'
1877 *To the Unknown Eros*, bk.2, no.2, 'The Contract'.

22 No writer, sacred or profane, ever uses the words 'he' or
'him' of the soul. It is always 'she' or 'her'; so universal is
the intuitive knowledge that the soul, with regard to God
who is her life, is feminine.
1896 *The Rod, the Root, and the Flower*, 'Aurea Dicta', no.21.

23 Those who know God know that it is a quite a mistake to
suppose that there are only five senses.
1896 *The Rod, the Root, and the Flower*, 'Aurea Dicta', no.142.

24 May I know by love and speak by silence.
1896 *The Rod, the Root, and the Flower*, 'Aphorisms and Extracts'.

25 He that but once too nearly hears
The music of forfended spheres
Is thenceforth lonely, and for all
His days as one who treads the Wall
Of China, and, on this hand, sees
Cities and their civilities
And, on the other, lions.
1863 *The Victories of Love*, bk.1.

26 Some dish more sharply spiced than this
Milk-soup men call domestic bliss.
Olympus (published 1906).

Paton, Alan 1903–88

South African writer and educator. President of the South African
Liberal Party (1953–60), he is best remembered for his novel *Cry,
the Beloved Country* (1948), on racial divisions in South Africa.

27 Cry, the Beloved Country.
1948 Title of book.

28 No second Johannesburg is needed upon the earth. One
is enough.
1948 *Cry, the Beloved Country*, bk.2, section 6.

St Patrick 5c AD

Bishop and Apostle of Ireland.

29 Christ for my guardianship today: against poison, against
burning, against drowning, against wounding, that there
may come to me a multitude of rewards;
Christ with me,
Christ before me,
Christ behind me,
Christ in me,
Christ over me,
Christ to right of me,

Christ to left of me,
Christ in lying down,
Christ in sitting,
Christ in rising up,
Christ in the heart of every person who may think
  of me,
Christ in the mouth of every person who may speak
  of me,
Christ in every eye, which may look on me!
Christ in every ear, which may hear me!
St Patrick's Breastplate, traditionally attributed to the saint.

Patrick, John *pseudonym of* John Patrick Goggan 1905–95

US playwright and screenwriter. He received the Pulitzer Prize for the play *The Teahouse of the August Moon* (1953) and his screenplays include *Three Coins in the Fountain* (1954) and *Love is a Many Splendoured Thing* (1955).

30 Punctuality is the vice of virtuous women.
  1954 Line delivered by Clifton Webb in *Three Coins in the Fountain*.

Patton, George Smith *known as* Old Blood and Guts 1885–1945

US soldier, a daring and flamboyant commander in World War II. He led numerous expeditions, including the 3rd Army invasion of France, and was killed in a road accident in Germany soon after being appointed general.

31 The object of war is not to die for your country. The object of war is to make damn sure the other sonofabitch dies for *his*.
  Attributed.

Paul, Leslie 1905–85

Irish writer and poet.

32 Angry Young Man.
  1951 Title of book. Later associated with John Osborne.

Pauli, Wolfgang 1900–58

Austrian–Swiss theoretical physicist and Nobel prize winner (1945).

33 I don't mind your thinking slowly: I mind your publishing faster than you think.
  Attributed.

Pauling, Linus Carl 1901–94

US chemist. He was Professor at the California Institute of Technology and won the Nobel prize for chemistry in 1954. He was awarded the Nobel peace prize in 1962.

34 Science is a search for truth—it is not a game in which one tries to best his opponent, to do harm to others.
  1958 *No More War*.

Pavarotti, Luciano 1935–2007

Italian tenor.

35 If I could live my life over again there is one thing I would change. I would want to be able to eat less.
  1997 In *The Times*, 8 Dec.

36 Horse riding is a perfect comparison with singing. You must know where the double fences are.
  2002 In *The Guardian*, 7 Jan.

37 I believe that a life lived for music is an existence spent wonderfully, and this is what I have dedicated my life to.
  2007 His last words, spoken to his manager Terri Robson, reported in the *New York Times*, 6 Sep.

Pavlov, I(van) P(etrovich) 1849–1936

Russian physiologist and experimental psychologist, famed for his work on the physiology of the digestive system. He received the 1904 Nobel prize for physiology or medicine.

38 Learn the ABC of science before you try to ascend to its summit.
  1936 *Bequest to the Academic Youth of Soviet Russia*.

Pavlov, Valentin Sergeyevich 1937–2003

Russian politician. He was Prime Minister from January 1991 until August of that year, when he was arrested as an accomplice in the failed coup d'état against Mikhail Gorbachev. He was granted amnesty by parliament in 1994.

39 Privatization must come after the liberalization of prices… How on earth can you privatize or denationalize anything if you have no means of assessing the value of assets before offering them on the market?
  1991 Interview, *The Independent*, 18 Apr.

40 Civil war is impossible in the Soviet Union.
  1991 Interview, *The Independent*, 18 Apr.

41 It is no use making revolutionary cavalry charges against the problems that we are facing.
  1991 On Boris Yeltsin's proposals for economic republican autonomy. Interview, *The Independent*, 18 Apr.

Pavlova, Anna 1882–1931

Russian ballerina.

42 Although one may fail to find happiness in theatrical life, one never wishes to give it up after having once tasted its fruits. To enter the School of the Imperial Ballet is to enter a convent whence frivolity is banned, and where merciless discipline reigns.
  Quoted in A H Franks (ed) *Pavlova: A Biography*, 'Pages of My Life' (1956).

Paxman, Jeremy 1950–

English journalist and broadcaster. He is perhaps best known as the presenter of such current affairs programmes as *Panorama* (1979–85), and *Newsnight* (1989–2014).

43 Did you threaten to overrule him?
  1997 Question asked 14 times of Conservative politician Michael Howard, relating to the sacking of a prison governor by the director of the Prison Service, Derek Lewis. On BBC's *Newsnight*.

44 Once upon a time the English knew who they were.
  1998 *The English: A Portrait of a People*.

45 Scots are Jocks, Welshmen Taffies, and Irishmen Paddies or Micks but…it is noticeable there is no similar designation for the English.
  1998 *The English: A Portrait of a People*.

46 The more you look back into English history, the more you are forced to the conclusion that alongside civility and the deeply held convictions about individual rights, the English have a natural taste for disorder.
  1998 *The English: A Portrait of a People*.

Paz, Octavio 1914–98

Mexican poet, writer and diplomat. He sided with the Republican cause during the Spanish Civil War. In Paris, he was strongly influenced by the Surrealist movement. He was awarded a Nobel prize in 1990.

47 *Amar es combatir, es abrir puertas,*
dejar de ser fantasma con un número
a perpetua cadena condenado
por un amo sin rostro.
To love is to battle, to open doors,
to cease to be a ghost with a number
forever in chains, forever condemned
by a faceless master.
1949 *Libertad bajo palabra*, 'Piedra de sol' (translated as 'The Sun Stone', 1963).

48 *Sin duda la cercanía de la muerte y la fraternidad de las armas producen, en todos los tiempos y en todos los países, una atmósfera propicia a lo extraordinario, a todo aquello que sobrepasa la condición humana y rompe el círculo de soledad que rodea a cada hombre.*
No doubt the nearness of death and the brotherhood of men-at-wars, at whatever time and in whatever country, always produce an atmosphere favorable to the extraordinary, to all that rises above the human condition and breaks the circle of solitude that surrounds each one of us.
1950 *El laberinto de la soledad*, pt.1 (translated as *The Labyrinth of Solitude*, 1961).

49 Technology is not an image of the world but a way of operating on reality. The nihilism of technology lies not only in the fact that it is the most perfect expression of the will to power…but also in the fact that it lacks meaning.
1967 *Alternating Current*.

Peace Pilgrim *real name* Mildred Norman c.1908–1981

US writer and mystic. From 1952 to 1981 she walked through North America, carrying only the bare minimum of necessities and teaching wherever she went; her intention was to stop walking only when there was total peace in the world.

50 I never give out my zodiac sign. Do you honestly think I can be pushed around by a planet? Good heavens, your divine nature is always free.
Quoted in Susan Hayward and Malcolm Cohen *The Bag of Jewels* (1988).

Peacock, Thomas Love 1785–1866

English novelist. He entered the service of the East India Company (1819–56) after producing three satirical romances, attacking common prejudices and affectations, and produced further works along similar lines.

51 Marriage may often be a stormy lake, but celibacy is almost always a muddy horsepond.
1817 *Melincourt*, ch.7.

52 Laughter is pleasant, but the exertion is too much for me.
1818 *Nightmare Abbey*, ch.5.

53 Sir, I have quarrelled with my wife; and a man who has quarrelled with his wife is absolved from all duty to his country.
1818 *Nightmare Abbey*, ch.11.

54 The mountain sheep are sweeter,
But the valley sheep are fatter;
We therefore deemed it meeter
To carry off the latter.
We made an expedition;
We met a host, and quelled it;
We forced a strong position,
And killed the men who held it.
1829 *The Misfortunes of Elphin*, 'The War-Song of Dinas Vawr'.

55 But though first love's impassioned blindness
Has passed away in colder light,
I still have thought of you with kindness,
And shall do, till our last goodnight.
The ever-rolling silent hours
Will bring a time we shall not know,
When our young days of gathering flowers
Will be an hundred years ago.
1860 'Love and Age'.

Pearson, Karl 1857–1936

English mathematician and Professor of Mathematics and Eugenics at University College London. Pearson is generally considered one of the founders of modern statistical theory.

56 When every fact, every present or past phenomenon of [the] universe, every phase of present or past life therein, has been examined, classified, and coordinated with the rest, then the mission of science will be completed. What is this but saying that the task of science can never end till man ceases to be, till history is no longer made, and development itself ceases?
1892 *The Grammar of Science*, pt.1, ch.5.

Pearson, Lester Bowles 1897–1972

Canadian politician, president of the UN General Assembly (1952–3). He won the Nobel peace prize (1957). Opposition leader from 1958, he was Prime Minister 1963–8.

57 The grim fact, however, is that we prepare for war like precocious giants and for peace like retarded pygmies.
1957 Acceptance speech on receiving the Nobel peace prize, 11 Dec.

58 Politics is the skilled use of blunt objects.
Quoted in Canadian Broadcasting Corporation tribute on his death, 1972.

Peary, Robert Edwin 1856–1920

US admiral and explorer. He made eight Arctic voyages by the Greenland coast. In 1906 he reached latitude 87° 6 mins N and on 6 Apr 1909 was the first to reach the North Pole.

59 I have got the North Pole out of my system after twenty-three years of effort, hard work, disappointments, hardships, privations, more or less suffering, and some risks… The work is the finish, the cap and climax of nearly four hundred years of effort, loss of life, and expenditure of fortunes by the civilized nations of the world, and it has been accomplished in a way that is thoroughly American. I am content.
1909 Diary entry, Apr. Quoted in *The North Pole* (published 1910).

60 In a march of only a few hours, I had passed from the western to the eastern hemisphere and had verified my position at the summit of the world. It was hard to realise that on the first miles of the brief march we had been travelling due north, while on the last few miles of the same march we had been travelling due south, although

we had all the time been travelling precisely in the same direction.
1909 Description of crossing and then passing the Pole. *The North Pole* (published 1910).

Peck, M(organ) Scott 1936–2005
US writer and psychiatrist, author of the seminal self-help work *The Road Less Traveled* (1978). Later works, combining Christian teaching with psychiatric principles, include *The Different Drum* (1987).

61 Once we truly know that life is difficult—once we understand and accept it—then life is no longer difficult. Because once it is accepted, it no longer matters.
1978 *The Road Less Traveled*, ch.1.

62 The evil in this world is committed by the spiritual fat cats who think that they are without sin because they are unwilling to suffer the discomfort of significant self-examination.
1985 *What Return Can I Make?*

63 What being a Christian means, at the very least, is that whenever there is a decision to be made, which may be several times a day, an alternative should not be discarded simply because it is sacrificial.
1985 *What Return Can I Make?*

64 Simply seek happiness, and you are not likely to find it. Seek to create and love without regard to your happiness, and you will likely be happy much of the time.
1987 *The Different Drum*.

65 The healthy life is hardly one marked by an absence of crises. In fact, an individual's psychological health is distinguished by how early he or she can meet crisis.
1987 *The Different Drum*.

Peel, Sir Robert 1788–1850
English Tory statesman, Secretary for Ireland (1812–18), known as 'Orange Peel' for his strong anti-Catholic spirit. As Home Secretary (1822–7, 1828–30), he carried through the Catholic Emancipation Act (1829) and reorganized the London police force (the 'Peelers' or 'Bobbies'). As Prime Minister (1834–5, 1841–6), his decision to repeal the Corn Laws (1846) split his party, and precipitated his resignation, though he remained in Parliament as leader of the 'Peelites'.

66 If the spirit of the Reform Bill implies merely a careful review of institutions, civil and ecclesiastical, undertaken in a friendly temper, combining with the firm maintenance of established rights the correction of private abuses and the redress of real grievances, I can for myself and my colleagues undertake to act in such a spirit and with such intentions.
1834 *The Tamworth Manifesto*.

67 During my tenure of power, my earnest wish has been to impress the people of this country with a belief that the legislature was animated by a sincere desire to frame its legislation upon the principles of equity and justice... Deprive me of power tomorrow, but you can never deprive me of the consciousness that I have exercised the powers committed to me from no corrupt or interested motives, from no desire to gratify ambition, or to attain any personal object.
1846 On the repeal of the Corn Laws, House of Commons, 15 May.

68 It asks more steadiness, self-control, ay, and manly courage, than any other exercise. You must take as well as give—eye to eye, toe to toe, and arm to arm.
Of boxing. Quoted in John Boyle O'Reilly *Ethics of Boxing and Manly Sport* (1888).

Peele, George c.1556–1596
English dramatist and poet.

69 Fair and fair, and twice so fair,
As fair as any may be;
The fairest shepherd on our green,
A love for any lady.
1584 *The Arraignment of Paris*, act 1, sc.5.

70 What thing is love for (well I wot) love is a thing.
It is a prick, it is a sting,
It is a pretty, pretty thing;
It is a fire, it is a coal
Whose flame creeps in at every hole.
c.1591 *The Hunting of Cupid*.

Pei, I(eoh) M(ing) 1917–
Chinese-born US architect. He emigrated to the US in 1935 and was naturalized in 1954. A controversial and adventurous designer, his works include Mile High Center, Denver and the glass pyramid at the Louvre, Paris.

71 Let's do it right. This is for the ages.
1978 Quoted by J Carter Brown, Director, National Gallery of Art, Washington, in the *Washington Post*, 27 Aug 1995. On his design for the gallery's East Building which was soaring to an unbudgeted cost of $94.4m.

72 *Comment respecter la tradition, et innover en même temps? Quel pari difficile!*
How to respect tradition and to innovate at the same time? What a difficult challenge!
1989 *Les Grands desseins du Louvre* (with E J Biasini).

73 *L'architecture est le miroir même de la vie. Il n'est que de jeter les yeux sur des édifices pour sentir la présence du passé, l'esprit d'un lieu; ils sont le reflet de la société.*
Architecture is the very mirror of life. You only have to cast your eyes on buildings to feel the presence of the past, the spirit of a place; they are the reflection of society.
1989 *Les Grands desseins du Louvre* (with E J Biasini).

Pelé pseudonym of Edson Arantes do Nascimento 1940–
Brazilian footballer. He won World Cup medals with Brazil (1958 and 1970) and scored over 1,000 goals in first-class football.

74 A penalty is a cowardly way to score.
Quoted in Peter Ball and Phil Shaw *The Book of Football Quotations* (1989).

75 I was born for soccer, just as Beethoven was born for music.
Quoted in Colin Jarman *The Guinness Dictionary of Sports Quotations* (1990).

76 Football is like a religion to me. I worship the ball, and I treat it like a god. Too many players think of a football as something to kick. They should be taught to caress it and to treat it like a precious gem.
Quoted in David Pickering *The Cassell Soccer Companion* (1994).

Pelosi, Nancy Patricia D'Alesandro 1940–
US politician. A Democrat, she became the first woman to serve as Speaker of the House of Representatives (2007–11). She has also served as Minority Leader of the House of Representatives (2003–7, 2011–).

77 But we have to pass the bill so you can find out what's in it, away from the fog of controversy.
>2010 Referring to an imminent health care reform bill in a speech to the Legislative Conference for the National Association of Counties, 9 Mar.

Penecuik, Dr Alex 1652–1722
Scottish poet.

78 To curle on the ice, does greatly please,
Being a manly Scottish exercise;
It clears the Brains, stirs up the Native Heat,
And gives a gallant appetite for Meat.
>1715 Quoted in Colin Jarman *The Guinness Dictionary of Sports Quotations* (1990).

Penfield, Wilder Graves 1891–1976
US-born Canadian neurosurgeon, who worked mainly at Montreal's Allan Memorial Institute, where he was first director (1934–60). He famously worked on the exposed brains of living human subjects, and on retirement turned to writing fiction and biography.

79 In all our studies of the brain, no mechanism has been discovered that can force the mind to think, or the individual to believe, anything. The mind continues free. That is a statement I have long considered. I have made every effort to disprove it, without success.
>1970 *Second Thoughts: Science, the Arts, and the Spirit.*

Peniakoff, Vladimir 1897–1951
Belgian-born soldier and writer.

80 A message came on the wireless for me. It said: 'SPREAD ALARM AND DESPONDENCY'. So the time had come, I thought, Eighth Army was taking the offensive. The date was, I think, May 18th, 1942.
>1950 *Popski's Private Army.*

Penn, William 1644–1718
English Quaker, imprisoned for his beliefs. In 1681, in settlement of Charles II's debt to his father, he was granted land in America, and founded the colony of Pennsylvania as a refuge for persecuted Quakers.

81 This day my country was confirmed to me under the great seal of England, with large powers and privileges, by the name of *Pennsylvania*; a name the king would give it in honor of my father.
>1681 Letter to Robert Turner, 14 Mar.

82 Inquire often, but judge rarely, and thou wilt not often be mistaken.
>1693 *Some Fruits of Solitude.*

People's Daily
The official daily newspaper of the Communist Party of China. Speaking for the Chinese government, in 1979 a series of articles denounced the Democracy Wall Movement. Changan Road in Beijing had been a centre for posters and news-sheets demanding democratic rights.

83 The imperialists brought the Chinese people cannons rather than flowers, death instead of 'human rights'... How can they be in a position to instruct us on 'civil rights'?
>1979 *People's Daily*, 22 Mar.

Pepys, Samuel 1633–1703
English civil servant and diarist. He rose in the naval service to become Secretary to the Admiralty, 1672. His diary, covering the years 1660 to 1669, is an important historical and social document.

84 Boys do now cry 'Kiss my Parliament!' instead of 'Kiss my arse!' so great and general a contempt is the Rump come to among all men, good and bad.
>1660 Diary entry, 7 Feb. The Rump Parliament was that which persisted after the fall of Richard Cromwell, and before the restoration of Charles II.

85 And so to bed.
>1660 Diary entry, 20 Apr and passim.

86 A silk suit, which cost me much money, and I pray God to make me able to pay for it.
>1660 Diary entry, 1 Jul.

87 I went out to Charing Cross to see Major-General Harrison hanged, drawn and quartered—which was done there—he looking as cheerfully as any man could do in that condition... Thus it was my chance to see the King beheaded at Whitehall and to see the first blood shed in revenge for the blood of the King at Charing Cross.
>1660 Diary entry, 13 Oct.

88 A good honest and painful sermon.
>1661 Diary entry, 17 Mar.

89 But methought it lessened my esteem of a king, that he should not be able to command the rain.
>1662 Diary entry, 19 Jul.

90 I see it is impossible for the King to have things done as cheap as other men.
>1662 Diary entry, 21 Jul.

91 To the King's Theatre, where we saw *Midsummer Night's Dream*, which I had never seen before, nor shall ever again, for it is the most insipid, ridiculous play that ever I ever saw in my life.
>1662 Diary entry, 29 Sep.

92 But Lord! to see the absurd nature of Englishmen, that cannot forbear laughing and jeering at everything that looks strange.
>1662 Diary entry, 27 Nov.

93 Then over the park (where I first in my life, it being a great frost, did see people sliding with their skates, which is a very pretty art).
>1662 Diary entry, 1 Dec.

94 My wife, who, poor wretch, is troubled with her lonely life.
>1662 Diary entry, 19 Dec.

95 After dinner to the Duke's house, and there saw *Twelfth Night* acted well, though it be but a silly play.
>1663 Diary entry, 6 Jan.

96 Most of their discourse was about hunting, in a dialect I understand very little.
>1663 Diary entry, 22 Nov.

97 To the Tennis Court, and there saw the King play at tennis and others; but to see how the King's play was extolled, without any cause at all, was a loathsome sight.
1664 Diary entry, 4 Jan.

98 Up, and by coach to Sir Ph. Warwickes, the street being full of footballs, it being a great frost.
1665 Diary entry, 3 Jan. Frost restricted the amount of horse traffic in the streets of London, making football a possibility.

99 This day, much against my will, I did in Drury Lane see two or three houses marked with a red cross upon the doors, and 'Lord have mercy upon us' writ there—which was a sad sight to me, being the first of that kind that to my remembrance I ever saw.
1665 Diary entry, 7 Jun. The houses were afflicted with bubonic plague, which lasted in London until the summer of 1666.

1 Up, all of us, and to Billiards.
1665 Diary entry, 17 Jul.

2 The people die so, that now it seems they are fain to carry the dead to be buried by daylight, the nights not sufficing to do it in. And my Lord Mayor commands people to be within at 9 at night, all (as they say) that the sick may have liberty to go abroad for ayre.
1665 Diary entry, 12 Aug.

3 And it is a wonder what will be the fashion after the plague is done as to periwigs, for nobody will dare to buy any haire for fear of the infection—that it had been cut off the heads of people dead of the plague.
1665 Diary entry, 3 Sep.

4 Strange to say what delight we married people have to see these poor fools decoyed into our condition.
1665 Diary entry, 25 Dec.

5 Music and women I cannot but give way to, whatever my business is.
1666 Diary entry, 9 Mar.

6 Poor people staying in their houses as long as till the very fire touched them, and then running into boats or clambering from one pair of stair by the waterside to another. And among other things, the poor pigeons I perceive were loath to leave their houses, but hovered about the windows and balconies till they were some of them burned, their wings, and fell down.
1666 Diary entry, 2 Sep. The Great Fire of London continued for four days, destroying four-fifths of the total area of the city.

7 A most horrid malicious bloody flame... It made me weep to see it.
1666 Observing the Great Fire of London. Diary entry, 2 Sep.

8 Hardly one lighter or boat in three that had the goods of a house in, but there was a pair of virginalls in it.
1666 Describing the chaos on the Thames as people attempted to rescue their possessions from the flames. Diary entry, 2 Sep.

9 But it is pretty to see what money will do.
1668 Diary entry, 21 Mar.

Percy, Walker 1916–90

US novelist. His best-known work of fiction is *The Moviegoer* (1961), but he wrote several novels, and volumes of collected essays and non-fiction.

10 As Einstein once said, ordinary life in an ordinary day in the modern world is a dreary business. I mean *dreary*. People will do anything just to escape this dreariness.
1977 Interview in *Esquire*, Dec.

11 Unlike God the artist does not start with nothing and make something of it. He starts with himself as nothing and makes something of the nothing with the things at hand.
1977 Interview in *Esquire*, Dec.

Perdue, Franklin P 1920–2005

US businessman, former chief executive of Perdue Farms Inc.

12 I hate pudgy poultry.
1987 In the *New Yorker*, 6 Jul.

Perelman, S(ydney) J(oseph) 1904–79

US humorist. He was a scriptwriter, and later one of the circle of wits who wrote for the *New Yorker*. He published a number of books.

13 I have Bright's disease and he has mine, sobbed the panting palooka.
1929 In *Judge*, 16 Nov. A palooka is US slang for a clumsy person, especially in sports.

14 Crazy Like a Fox.
1944 Title of book.

15 A feeling of emulsion swept over me.
1944 Crazy Like a Fox, 'The Love Decoy'.

16 He bit his lip in a manner which immediately awakened my maternal sympathy, and I helped him bite it.
1944 Crazy Like a Fox, 'The Love Decoy'.

17 I guess I'm just an old mad scientist at bottom. Give me an underground laboratory, half a dozen atomsmashers, and a beautiful girl in a diaphanous veil waiting to be turned into a chimpanzee, and I care not who writes the nation's laws.
1944 Crazy Like a Fox, 'Captain Future, Block That Kick'.

18 She had the rippling muscles of a panther, the solidity of a water buffalo, and the lazy insolence of a shoe salesman.
1944 Crazy Like a Fox, 'Kitchen Bouquet'.

19 For years I have let dentists ride roughshod over my teeth; I have been sawed, hacked, chopped, whittled, bewitched, bewildered, tattooed, and signed on again; but this is cuspid's last stand.
1944 Crazy Like a Fox, 'Nothing But the Tooth'.

20 You've got a sharp tongue in your head, Mr Essick. Look out it doesn't cut your throat.
1961 The Rising Gorge, 'All Out...'.

21 English life, while very pleasant, is rather bland. I expected kindness and gentility and I found it, but there is such a thing as too much couth.
1971 In the *Observer*, 24 Sep.

22 The dogs had eaten the upholstery of a Packard convertible that afternoon, and were consequently somewhat subdued.
1981 The Last Laugh, 'The Last Laugh'.

Peres, Shimon 1923–

Israeli statesman and politician. In 1994 he shared the Nobel peace prize with Yasser Arafat and Yitzhak Rabin.

23 Television has made dictatorship impossible, but democracy unbearable.
1995 In the *Financial Times*, 31 Jan.

Pericles c.490–429 BC

Athenian statesman, who initiated democratic reforms and a great building programme (including the Parthenon). His famous *epitaphios* (Funerary Oration on the death of the first year of the Peloponnesian War) was reported by Thucydides. He died of the plague which struck Athens in 430 BC.

24 Famous men have the whole earth as their memorial.
   Quoted in Thucydides *History of the Peloponnesian War*, 2.43 (translated by R Warner, 1961).

25 Your great glory is not to be inferior to what you have been given by nature, and the greatest glory of a woman is to be least talked about by men, whether they are praising or criticizing you.
   Address to women in the Funerary Oration. Quoted in Thucydides *History of the Peloponnesian War*, 2.45.2 (translated by R Warner, 1961).

Perkins, Carl 1932–98

US songwriter and composer. A key figure of early rock 'n' roll, his guitar playing combined blues and country music.

26 Don't you step on my blue suede shoes.
   1956 'Blue Suede Shoes'.

Perkins, Frances 1882–1965

US social reformer and politician. Educated at Mount Holyoke College, Massachusetts, she was the first woman to hold Cabinet rank in the US. She was appointed US Secretary of Labor (1933–45) in President Franklin D Roosevelt's Cabinet.

27 No one had any measure of its progress; no one had any plan for stopping it. Everyone tried to get out of its way.
   On the depression of the 1930s which inspired her to set up the Social Security system. Recalled on her death, 14 May 1965.

Perry, Grayson 1960–

English potter who won the Turner Prize in 2003.

28 It's about time a transvestite potter won the Turner Prize.
   2003 In his acceptance speech, referring to his habit of dressing as his alter ego, Claire.

29 Contemporary art often plays to the part of us that is very uncomfortable with not being sure, that cannot maintain a state of 'don't know'. The over-prioritising of meaning gets in the way of just experiencing the art in a more sensual way. Judging quality purely from an intuitive emotional response needs more confidence and experience than just working it out like a crossword clue.
   2008 In *The Observer*, 2 Mar.

Persius *properly* Aulus Persius Flaccus AD 34–62

Roman satirist and Stoic. Only one book of satires has survived.

30 *Quis leget haec?*
   Who'll read that sort of thing?
   Satirae, no.1, 1.2 (translated by W S Merwin, 1961).

Perth, James, 4th Earl of 1648–1716

Scottish Justice-General (1682) and Chancellor (1684). He was imprisoned in Stirling Castle (1688–96), after the fall of James II and VII, but then joined the exiled court of the King at St Germain, where he remained for the rest of his life. He was created Duke of Perth and Knight of the Garter.

31 I have been here a fortnight and I think I shall be here fifteen or twenty days longer, although I do not very much like the place, for this puddling in a tub continually is no charm to me.
   On Venice. Collected in *Letters to his sister the Countess of Erroll, and other members of his family*.

Pessoa, Fernando António Nogueira 1888–1935

Portuguese poet, an important figure in the Modernist movement.

32 *Sê plural como o universo!*
   Be plural, like the universe!
   Páginas Íntimas e de Auto-interpretação.

33 *Estrangeiro aqui como em toda a parte.*
   I'm a stranger here, as I am everywhere.
   1926 *Lisbon Revisited*.

34 *Não sou nada.*
   Nunca serei nada.
   Não posso querer ser nada.
   À parte isso, tenho em mim todos os sonhos do mundo.
   I am not nothing.
   I will never be nothing.
   I cannot ever want to be nothing.
   Apart from that, I have in me all the dreams of the world.
   1928 *Tabacaria* ('The Tobacconist's').

Pétain, (Henri) Philippe 1856–1951

French soldier and politician. In World War I his defence of Verdun (1916) made him a national hero, and he became Commander-in-Chief (1917) and Marshal of France (1918). When France collapsed in 1940, he negotiated the armistice with Germany and Italy, became chief of state, and collaborated with Germany in an attempt to keep France out of the war. He is regarded by some as a patriot, by others as a traitor.

35 They shall not pass.
   This phrase came to symbolize the stubborn defence of Verdun against Ludendorf's siege, which cost 300,000 German and 400,000 French troops.
   ▶ See Ibarruri Gomez 444:5.

36 I was with you in the days of glory. At the head of the Government, I shall remain with you during the days of darkness. Stay by my side.
   1940 Radio broadcast announcing his intention to seek an armistice, 20 Jun.

Peter, Laurence J 1919–90

Canadian academic and writer, professor at the University of South California.

37 In a hierarchy every employee tends to rise to his level of incompetence; the cream rises until it sours.
   1969 *The Peter Principle*, ch.1 (with Raymond Hull).

38 Bureaucracy defends the status quo long past the time when the quo has lost its status.
   1978 In the *San Francisco Chronicle*, 29 Jan.

Peters, Richard Stanley 1919–2011

English educationalist, Professor of the Philosophy of Education at the University of London Institute of Education (1962–82). He wrote widely on education.

39 What matters is not what any individual thinks, but what is true. A teacher who does not equip his pupils with the

Petersen, Henry Edward 1921–91

US Assistant Attorney General for Prosecutions. He went from clerk to chief of the organized crime and racketeering section of the FBI, Washington (1948–69).

40 What you have just said, Mr President, speaks very well of you as a man. It does not speak well of you as a president.
1973 On President Nixon's remark that he would need proof of the guilt of aides John Ehrlichman and H R Hadelman on the Watergate break-in and cover-up before he could fire them. Quoted in Richard M Nixon *RN: The Memoirs of Richard Nixon* (1978).

Petersen, Wolfgang 1941–

German film director.

41 It has been condensed and moved around a bit. And we left out the gods.
2004 On how he adapted Homer to make the film *Troy*. Quoted in *The Scotsman*, 14 May.

Petrarch (Francesco Petrarca) 1304–74

Italian poet and classical scholar, responsible for the discovery of several works, including Cicero's letters and two of his orations, and a portion of Quintilian's *De Oratio*. In 1341 he was crowned Poet Laureate in Rome. Most famous for the lyrics of his *Canzionere*, he also composed prose treatises, historical works, and letters.

42 *Continue morimur, ego dum hec scribo, tu dum leges, alii dum audient dumque non audient, ego quoque dum hec leges moriar, tu moreris dum hec scribo, ambo morimur, omnes morimur, semper morimur.*
We are dying continuously: I while I write this, you while you read it, others while they hear or do not hear it. I will be dying as you read this, you will be dying as I write it. We are both dying, we are all dying, we are always dying.
c.1360 Letter to Philippe de Cabassoles.

Petronius Arbiter d. AD 66

Roman satirical writer, usually thought to be the Gaius Petronius whom Tacitus calls the 'arbiter elegantiae' at the court of Nero. His *Satyricon* wittily depicts the licentious life of the moneyed class of freedmen in southern Italy.

43 *Abiit ad plures.*
He has gone to the majority.
(ie He has died.) *Satyricon*, 42.

44 *Qualis dominus talis est servus.*
Like master like man.
Satyricon, 58.

Petty, Sir William 1623–87

English physician and pioneer economist. From humble beginnings he rose to become Professor of Anatomy at Oxford and of Music at Gresham's College, London. As Physician-General to Cromwell's army he acquired an immense fortune, and he was a founder of the Royal Society of London.

45 If a man bring to London an ounce of Silver out of the Earth in Peru in the same time that he can produce a bushel of Corn, then one is the natural price of the other.
1662 Treatise of Taxes.

46 Labour is the Father and active principle of Wealth, as lands are the Mother.
1662 Treatise of Taxes.

47 Instead of using only comparative Words and intellectual Arguments, I have taken the course… to express myself in Terms of Number, Weight, or Measure; to use only Arguments of Sense, and to consider only such Causes, as have visible Foundations in Nature.
1690 Political Arithmetick.

Phelps, Edward John 1822–1900

US lawyer and diplomat.

48 The man who makes no mistakes does not usually make anything.
1889 In a speech given in London.

Phelps, Michael Fred 1985–

US swimmer. With a total of 22 medals, he is the most decorated competitor in Olympic history.

49 You can't put a limit on anything. The more you dream, the farther you get.
2009 In *Woman's Day*, 1 Apr.

Philby, Kim 1912–88

British double-agent.

50 To betray, you must first belong.
1967 In the *Sunday Times*, 17 Dec.

Philip II 1527–98

King of Spain (1556–98), Naples and Sicily (1554–98) and Portugal (1580–98). He married Mary I in 1554, becoming joint sovereign of England until her death in 1558. A secular champion of the Counter-Reformation, he had more success against Turks than Protestant Dutch and English.

51 England's chief defence depends upon the navy being always ready to defend the realm against invasion.
c.1555 Submission to the Privy Council while King-Consort of England.

Philips, Ambrose c.1675–1749

English poet.

52 The flowers anew, returning seasons bring;
But beauty faded has no second spring.
1708 The First Pastoral, 'Lobbin'.

Philips, Katherine née Fowler 1632–64

English poet. Her reputation was greater during her brief life, when she was known as 'the Matchless Orinda', than after her death, but she proved a significant model to later female poets. Her poems were surreptitiously printed in 1664 and issued in 1667.

53 Thus our twin souls in one shall grow,
And teach the world new love,
Redeem the age and sex, and show
A flame fate dares not move:

And courting death to be our friend,
Our lives, together too, shall end.
1664 'To Mrs. M. A. at Parting'.

54 I did but see him, and he disappeared,
I did but touch the rosebud, and it fell;
A sorrow unforeseen and scarcely feared,
So ill can mortals their afflictions spell.
'On the Death of My First and Dearest Child, Hector Philips'. (Issued 1667).

Phillips, Arthur Angell 1900–85

Australian academic and literary critic. He wrote for the Melbourne literary journal *Meanjin* and much of his critical writing was collected as *Responses* (1971).

55 Cultural Cringe.
1950 On Australia's reliance on British cultural values. In *Meanjin*.

Phillips, Edward O 1931–

Canadian novelist.

56 To grow older is to realize the universe is Copernican, not Ptolemaic, and that self and the loved one do not form the epicentre of the solar system.
1990 *Sunday Best*.

Phillips, Wendell 1811–84

US abolitionist, born in Boston, Massachusetts. Called to the Bar in 1834, by 1837 he was chief orator of the anti-slavery party, associated with William Lloyd Garrison.

57 Some doubt the courage of the Negro. Go to Haiti and stand on those fifty thousand graves of the best soldiers France ever had, and ask them what they think of the Negro's sword.
1861 Address on Toussaint l'Ouverture, referring to the War of Haitian Independence, 1804.

Picasso, Pablo Ruiz y 1881–1973

Spanish painter, graphic artist, sculptor and ceramicist. The melancholy studies of his early 'blue period' (1902–4) gave way to a life-affirming 'pink period' (1904–6). In later works he moved towards Cubism, along with Georges Braque.

58 There is no abstract art. You must always start with something. Afterward you can remove all traces of reality.
1935 In an interview with Christian Zervos, editor of *Cahiers d'Art*, translated by Alfred H Barr Jr in his *Picasso: Fifty Years of His Art* (1946).

59 Art is not the application of a canon of beauty but what the instinct and the brain can conceive beyond any canon. When we love a woman we don't start measuring her limbs.
1935 In an interview with Christian Zervos, editor of *Cahiers d'Art*, translated by Alfred H Barr Jr in his *Picasso: Fifty Years of His Art* (1946).

60 No, painting is not done to decorate apartments. It is an instrument of war for attack and defense against the enemy.
1945 Responding to claims that his Communism was a mere caprice. Quoted in Alfred H Barr Jr *Picasso: Fifty Years of His Art* (1946).

61 I paint objects as I think them, not as I see them.
Quoted in John Golding *Cubism* (1959).

62 God is really only another artist. He invented the giraffe, the elephant, and the cat. He has no real style. He just goes on trying other things.
Quoted in F Gilot and C Lake *Life with Picasso* (1964), pt.1.

63 We all know that art is not truth. Art is a lie that makes us realize truth.
Quoted in Dore Ashton *Picasso on Art* (1972).

Pickens, T(homas) Boone, Jr 1928–

US oilman and hydrocarbon investor, a geologist with Phillips Petroleum Co (1951–5) then founder and chair of Mesa Petroleum Co until 1996.

64 Work eight hours and sleep eight hours and make sure they are not the same.
1992 In NPR broadcast, 28 May.

Pickford, Mary *originally* Gladys Mary Smith 1893–1979

US actress, born in Canada. Known as 'America's sweetheart', she played innocent heroines in a series of silent films (1909–29), and made her sound debut in 1929.

65 Adding sound to movies would be like putting lipstick on the Venus de Milo.
Recalled on her death, 29 May 1979.

Pierce, C(harles) S(aunders) 1839–1914

US philosopher.

66 It is the man of science, eager to have his every opinion regenerated, his every idea rationalized, by drinking at the fountain of fact, and devoting all the energies of his life to the cult of truth, not as he understands it, but as he does not yet understand it, that ought properly to be called a philosopher.
Selected Writings, 'Lessons on the History of Science'.

Piercy, Marge 1936–

US novelist and poet. Novels including *Woman on the Edge of Time* (1975) trace the emerging feminist consciousness of the post-1960s generation. Later works include the novels *Gone to Soldiers* (1988) and *Three Women* (1999) and the volume of poetry *Colors Passing Through Us* (2003).

67 Burning dinner is not incompetence but war.
1983 *Stone, Paper, Knife*, 'What's that smell in the kitchen?'

68 Your anger was a climate I inhabited
like a desert in a dry frigid weather
of high thin air and ivory sun,
sand dunes the wind lifted into stinging
clouds that blinded and choked me
where the only ice was in the blood.
1983 *Stone, Paper, Knife*, 'The Weight'.

69 On this twelfth day of my diet
I would rather die satiated
than slim.
1983 *Stone, Paper, Knife*, 'On Mental Corsets'.

70 Art is a game only if you play at it,
a mirror that reflects from the inside out.
1983 *Stone, Paper, Knife*, 'Stone, Paper, Knife'.

71 Hope sleeps in our bones like a bear
waiting for spring to rise and walk.
1983 *Stone, Paper, Knife*, 'Stone, Paper, Knife'.

Piero della Francesca c.1420–1492
Italian Renaissance painter.

72 Painting is nothing but a representation of surfaces and solids foreshortened or enlarged, and put on the plane of the picture in accordance with the fashion in which the real objects seen by the eye appear on this plane.
c.1480–1490 *De Prospectiva Pingendi.*

Piggott, Lester Keith 1935–
English jockey. He became champion jockey 11 times, from 1948, and totalled 30 Classic winners, including nine Derbies.

73 People ask me why I ride with my bottom in the air. Well, I've got to put it somewhere.
Quoted in Colin Jarman *The Guinness Dictionary of Sports Quotations* (1990).

74 When I won the Derby on Never Say Die I went home and cut the lawn. I haven't cut the lawn since.
2004 In the *Observer*, 30 May.

Piglia, Ricardo 1941–
Argentinian novelist and critic.

75 *Sencillamente se me ocurre que la parodia se ha desplazado y hoy invade los gestos, las acciones. Donde antes había acontecimientos, experiencias, pasiones, hoy quedan sólo parodias. Eso trataba a veces de decirle a Marcelo en mis cartas: que la parodia ha sustitutido por completo a la historia.*
It's simply that I believe that parody has been displaced and that it now invades all gestures and actions. Where there used to be events, experiences, passions, now there are nothing but parodies. This is what I tried to tell Marcelo so many times in my letters: that parody had completely replaced history.
1980 *Respiración artificial*, pt.2, ch.4 (translated as *Artificial Respiration*, 1994).

Pigou, Arthur Cecil 1877–1959
English economist, a professor at Cambridge (1908–43).

76 If a man marries his housekeeper or his cook, the national dividend is diminished.
1920 *Economics of Welfare.*

Pilger, John 1939–
Australian journalist, writer and film-maker highly regarded for his investigative work in Vietnam and Cambodia. His documentary films include *Year Zero The Silent Death of Cambodia* (1979), *Death of a Nation* (1994), about the slaughter in East Timor, and *Breaking the Silence: Truth and Lies in the War on Terror* (2003).

77 I used to see Vietnam as a war rather than a country.
1978 *Do you remember Vietnam?*

78 What Nixon and Kissinger began, Pol Pot completed.
Collected in *Distant Voices* (1992).

79 The major western democracies are moving towards corporatism. Democracy has become a business plan, with a bottom line for every human activity, every dream, every decency, every hope. The main parliamentary parties are now devoted to the same economic policies—socialism for the rich, capitalism for the poor—and the same foreign policy of servility to endless war. This is not democracy. It is to politics what McDonalds is to food.
2009 Sydney Peace Prize address, Sydney Opera House, 5 Nov.

Pindar c.522–440 BC
Greek lyric poet, born near Thebes in Boeotia.

80 Seek not, my soul, immortal life, but make the most of the resources that are within your reach.
Pythia, 3.109.

Pinochet Ugarte, Augusto 1915–2006
Chilean soldier and dictator. He led the coup that overthrew the government of Salvador Allende (1973) and in 1980 enacted a constitution giving himself an eight-year presidential term (1981–9); he retained his military command until 1998, the year he was arrested in the UK at the request of Spain. General Pinochet was ruled unfit to face extradition, and in 2000 returned to Chile. Plans to put him on trial there for human rights violations and other crimes ended with his death.

81 I am not a dictator. It's just that I have a grumpy face.
Attributed.

Pinter, Harold 1930–2008
English playwright, director and actor. Such early plays as *The Birthday Party* (1958) were dismissed as obscure, but after *The Caretaker* (1960) his work underwent a reappraisal and he was acknowledged as one of the most interesting playwrights of his generation. Subsequent works for the stage included *The Homecoming* (1965) and *Celebration* (1999). He also wrote numerous filmscripts, including *The Servant* (1963) and *The French Lieutenant's Woman* (1981). In 2005 he won the Nobel prize for literature.

82 If only I could get down to Sidcup! I've been waiting for the weather to break. He's got my papers, this man I left them with, it's got it all down there, I could prove everything.
1960 *The Caretaker*, act 1.

83 The weasel under the cocktail cabinet.
1962 His reply when asked what his plays were about. Quoted in J Russell Taylor *Anger and After.*

84 I no longer feel banished from myself.
1995 On completing his first full-length play in 17 years. In *Newsweek*, 18 Sep.

85 We have brought torture, cluster bombs, depleted uranium, innumerable acts of random murder, misery, degradation, and death to the Iraqi people and call it 'bringing freedom and democracy to the Middle East'.
2005 Pre-recorded acceptance speech for the Nobel Prize for Literature, Stockholm, 7 Dec.

86 Language in art remains a highly ambiguous transaction, a quicksand, a trampoline, a frozen pool which might give way under you... at any time.
2005 Pre-recorded acceptance speech for the Nobel Prize for Literature, Stockholm, 7 Dec.

Pirandello, Luigi 1867–1936
Italian playwright, novelist and short-story writer. His play *Right You Are (If You Think You Are)* (1917) was followed by such innovative works as *Six Characters in Search of an Author* (1921), *Enrico IV* (1922) and *Tonight We Improvise* (1929). He was awarded a Nobel prize in 1934.

87 Six Characters in Search of an Author.
1921 Title of play (translated 1922).

88 Drama is action, sir, action and not confounded philosophy.
1921 *Six Characters in Search of an Author* (translated 1922).

Pirsig, Robert M(aynard) 1928–

US writer. His most noted book is *Zen and the Art of Motorcycle Maintenance* (1974), a rumination on life and technology after a cross-country motorcycle trip.

89 The Buddha, the Godhead, resides quite as comfortably in the circuits of a digital computer or the gears of a cycle transmission as he does at the top of a mountain or in the petals of a flower.
1974 *Zen and the Art of Motorcycle Maintenance*, pt.1, ch.1.

90 When people are fanatically dedicated to political or religious faiths or any other kind of dogmas or goals, it's always because these dogmas or goals are in doubt.
1974 *Zen and the Art of Motorcycle Maintenance*, pt.2, ch.3.

91 Mental reflection is so much more interesting than TV it's a shame more people don't switch over to it. They probably think what they hear is unimportant but it never is.
1974 *Zen and the Art of Motorcycle Maintenance*, pt.3, ch.17.

92 One thing about pioneers that you don't hear mentioned is that they are invariably, by their nature, mess-makers.
1974 *Zen and the Art of Motorcycle Maintenance*, pt.3, ch.21.

93 One geometry can not be more true than another; it can only be more *convenient*. Geometry is not true, it is advantageous.
1974 *Zen and the Art of Motorcycle Maintenance*, pt.3, ch.22.

94 Traditional scientific method has always been at the very *best*, 20-20 hindsight. It's good for seeing where you've been. It's good for testing the truth of what you think you know, but it can't tell you where you *ought* to go.
1974 *Zen and the Art of Motorcycle Maintenance*, pt.3, ch.24.

95 That's the classical mind at work, runs fine inside but looks dingy on the surface.
1974 *Zen and the Art of Motorcycle Maintenance*, pt.3, ch.26.

Pissarro, Camille 1830–1903

French Impressionist artist. Most of his works were painted in or around Paris.

96 But as I see it, the most corrupt art is the sentimental—the art of orange blossoms which make pale women swoon.
1883 Letter to his son Lucien.

97 Watercolour is not especially difficult, but I must warn you to steer clear of those pretty English watercolourists, so skilful and alas so weak, and so often too truthful.
1883 Letter to his son Lucien, Jul.

98 Draw more and more often—remember Degas.
1883 Letter to his son Lucien, Oct.

99 Observe that it is a grave error to believe that all mediums of art are not closely tied to their time.
1898 Letter to his son Lucien.

Pitt, William, 1st Earl of Chatham *known as* the Elder 1708–78

English statesman and orator. In 1756 he became Secretary of State, virtual Prime Minister. Forced to resign in 1757 by George II, he was recalled by public demand but resigned again in 1761 when his Cabinet refused to declare war on Spain. He formed a new ministry in 1766, but resigned in ill health (1768).

1 The atrocious crime of being a young man, which [Walpole] has, with such spirit and decency, charged upon me, I shall neither attempt to palliate nor deny; but content myself with wishing that I may be one of those whose follies cease with their youth, and not of those who continue ignorant in spite of their age and experience.
1741 Speech to the House of Commons, 6 Mar.

2 It is now apparent that this great, this powerful, this formidable kingdom is considered only as a province of a despicable electorate.
1742 Speech to the House of Commons, 10 Dec.

3 I know that I can save this country and that no one else can.
1756 In conversation with one of his private secretaries, Nov.

4 I was called by my sovereign and by the voice of the people to assist the State when others had abdicated the service of it. That being so, no one can be surprised that I will go on no longer, since my advice is not taken. Being responsible, I will direct—and will be responsible for nothing that I do not direct.
1761 On informing Cabinet of his resignation, 3 Oct.

5 I rejoice that America has resisted. Three millions of people, so dead to all the feelings of liberty, as voluntarily to submit to be slaves, would have been fit instruments to make slaves of the rest.
1766 Speech to the House of Commons, 14 Jan.

6 Where laws end, tyranny begins.
1770 Speech to the House of Lords, 2 Mar.

7 The spirit that now resists your taxation in America is…the same spirit that established the great fundamental, essential maxim of your liberties—that no subject of England shall be taxed but by his own consent. The glorious spirit of Whiggism animates three million in America, who prefer poverty with liberty to gilded chains and sordid affluence; and who will die in defence of their rights as men, as free men.
1775 Speech to the House of Lords, 20 Jan.

8 You cannot conquer America.
1777 Speech to the House of Lords, 18 Nov.

9 If I were an American, as I am an Englishman, while a foreign troop was landed in my country, I never would lay down my arms—never—never—never!
1777 Speech to the House of Lords, 18 Nov.

Pitt, William *known as* the Younger 1759–1806

English statesman and Prime Minister (1783–1801, 1804–6), son of William Pitt, the Elder. Elected MP in 1781, he became Chancellor in 1782 and Britain's youngest-ever Prime Minister in 1783. He resigned over the King's opposition to the union with Ireland in 1801 but returned in 1804 to lead a coalition of European powers against Napoleon.

10 I am sure that the immediate abolition of the slave trade is the first, the principal, the most indispensable act of policy, of duty and of justice the legislature of this country has to take, if it is indeed their wish to secure those important objects… For we continue to this hour a barbarous traffic in slaves, we continue it even yet, in spite of all our great and undeniable pretensions as civilisation.

1792 Speech to the House of Commons, 2 Apr. The House did not abolish slavery until 1806.

11 We must recollect...what it is we have at stake, what it is we have to contend for. It is for our property, it is for our liberty, it is for our independence, nay for our existence as a nation; it is for our character, it is for our very name as Englishmen, it is for everything dear and valuable to man on this side of the grave.
1803 Speech, 22 Jul, on the breaking of the Peace of Amiens and the resumption of the war with Napoleon. Quoted in *Speeches of the Rt. Hon. William Pitt* (1806), vol.4.

12 Amid the wreck and the misery of nations it is our just exaltation that we have continued superior to all that ambition or despotism could effect; and our still higher exaltation ought to be that we provide not only for our own safety but hold out a prospect for nations now bending under the yoke of tyranny of what the exertions of a free people can effect.
1804 Speech to the House of Commons, 25 Apr.

13 Roll up that map; it will not be wanted these ten years.
1805 Of a map of Europe. Remark on hearing of Napoleon's victory at Austerlitz, Dec. Quoted in Earl Stanhope *Life of the Rt. Hon. William Pitt*, vol.4 (1862), ch.43.

14 England has saved herself by her exertions, and will, as I trust, save Europe by her example.
1805 Replying to a toast in which he had been described as the saviour of his country in the wars with France. Quoted in R Coupland *War Speeches of William Pitt* (1915).

15 I think that I could eat one of Bellamy's veal pies.
1806 Attributed last words, 23 Jan.

Pittacus of Mytilene 650–570 BC
Greek ruler, one of the Seven Wise Men of Greece.

16 Know thine opportunity.
Attributed. Quoted in *Chambers Biographical Dictionary* (5th edn, 1990).

Pius II *real name* Enea Silvio de Piccolomini 1405–64
Italian-born churchman, Pope from 1458. After entering the service of Emperor Frederick II he took orders, becoming Bishop of Trieste and, on returning to Italy (1456), Cardinal then Pope. He tried unsuccessfully to organize a crusade against the Turks.

17 Of the two lights of Christendom, one has been extinguished.
1453 Attributed, on hearing of the fall of Constantinople to the Turks, 29 May.

18 Glorious deeds are not embraced by democracies, least of all by merchants, who, being by their nature intent on profit, loathe those splendid things that cannot be achieved without expense.
1584 *Commentaries*. Quoted in J H Plumb (ed) *The Horizon Book of the Renaissance* (1961, new edn by Penguin, 1982).

19 Nothing gives the Scots more pleasure than to hear the English abused.
1584 *Commentaries*. Quoted in J H Plumb (ed) *The Horizon Book of the Renaissance* (1961, new edn by Penguin, 1982).

Pius XII *real name* Eugenio Pacelli 1876–1958
Italian-born churchman, Pope from 1939.

20 Sport, rightly conceived, is an occupation carried out by the whole man. It renders the body a more perfect instrument of the soul and at the same time makes the soul itself a finer instrument of the whole man in seeking for Truth and in transmitting it to others. In this way it helps a man to reach that End to which all other ends are subordinate, the service and the greater glory of his Creator.
1945 Speech to the Central School of Sports of the USA, 29 Jul.

Pizzaro, Eddie 1961–
US stonecarver.

21 We're not all perfect, but we can do something perfect.
1990 On his work at New York's Cathedral of St John the Divine. Quoted in the *New York Times*, 14 Jul.

Planck, Max Karl Ernst 1858–1947
German physicist. He hypothesized that atoms emit and absorb energy only in discrete bundles called quanta and laid the foundations for quantum theory, the basis of contemporary theorizing in physics. He received the 1918 Nobel prize in physics for his work on radiation.

22 Science cannot exist without some small portion of metaphysics.
1931 *The Universe in the Light of Modern Physics*, ch.7.

23 Scientific discovery and scientific knowledge have been achieved only by those who have gone in pursuit of them without any practical purpose whatsoever in view.
1932 *Where is Science Going?* pt.4 (translated by James Murphy).

24 Science cannot solve the ultimate mystery of nature. And that is because, in the last analysis, we ourselves are part of nature and therefore part of the mystery that we are trying to solve.
1932 *Where is Science Going?* pt.4 (translated by James Murphy).

25 A new scientific truth does not triumph by convincing its opponents and making them see the light, but rather because its opponents eventually die, and a new generation grows up that is familiar with it.
A Scientific Autobiography and Other Papers (translated by Frank Gaynor, published 1949).

Plante, Jacques 1929–86
Canadian hockey player, a leading goalkeeper.

26 How would you like a job where, every time you make a mistake, a big red light goes on and 18,000 people boo?
Attributed. Quoted in John Robert Colombo (ed) *Colombo's All-Time Great Canadian Quotations* (1994).

Plath, Sylvia 1932–63
US poet who settled in England after her marriage to Ted Hughes. Her poetry and her only novel, *The Bell Jar* (1963), are deeply introspective. She committed suicide, and much of her work was published posthumously.

27 I am afraid of getting married. Spare me from cooking three meals a day—spare me from the relentless cage of routine and rote.
1949 Diary entry, 13 Nov. Collected in Aurelia Schober Plath (ed) *Letters Home by Sylvia Plath*, 'Diary Supplement' (1949).

28 I could never be a complete scholar or a complete housewife or a complete writer: I must combine a little of all, and thereby be imperfect in all.
1956 Letter to her mother, Aurelia Schober Plath, 25 Feb. Collected in Aurelia Schober Plath (ed) *Letters Home by Sylvia Plath* (1949).

29 Apparently, the most difficult feat for a Cambridge male is to accept a woman not merely as feeling, not merely as thinking, but as managing a complex, vital interweaving of both.
1956 Written while a student at Cambridge University, in *Isis*, 6 May.

30 Love set you going like a fat gold watch.
The midwife slapped your footsoles, and your bald cry
Took its place among the elements.
1961 'Morning Song', published posthumously by Ted Hughes (*Ariel*, 1965).

31 A sort of walking miracle, my skin
Bright as a Nazi lampshade.
1962 'Lady Lazarus', published posthumously by Ted Hughes (*Ariel*, 1965).

32 Dying,
Is an art, like everything else.
I do it exceptionally well.
1962 'Lady Lazarus', published posthumously by Ted Hughes (*Ariel*, 1965).

33 Out of the ash
I rise with my red hair
And I eat men like air.
1962 'Lady Lazarus', published posthumously by Ted Hughes (*Ariel*, 1965).

34 Not God but a swastika
So black no sky could squeak through.
Every woman adores a Fascist,
The boot in the face, the brute
Brute heart of a brute like you.
1962 'Daddy', published posthumously by Ted Hughes (*Ariel*, 1965).

35 Daddy, daddy, you bastard, I'm through.
1962 'Daddy', published posthumously by Ted Hughes (*Ariel*, 1965).

36 Winter is for women—
The woman still at her knitting,
At the cradle of Spanish walnut,
Her body a bulb in the cold and too dumb to think.
1962 'Wintering', published posthumously by Ted Hughes (*Ariel*, 1965).

37 I saw my life branching out before me like the green fig-tree in the story.
From the tip of every branch, like a fat purple fig, a wonderful future beckoned and winked. One fig was a husband and a happy home and children, and another fig was a famous poet...I saw myself sitting in the crotch of this fig-tree, starving to death, just because I couldn't make up my mind which of the figs I would choose. I wanted each and every one of them, but choosing one meant losing all the rest, and, as I sat there, unable to decide, the figs began to wrinkle and go black, and, one by one, they plopped to the ground at my feet.
1963 *The Bell Jar*, ch.7.

38 If neurotic is wanting two mutually exclusive things at one and the same time, then I'm neurotic as hell. I'll be flying back and forth between one mutually exclusive thing and another for the rest of my days.
1963 *The Bell Jar*, ch.8.

Platini, Michel 1955–

French footballer. He scored a record 41 goals in 72 games for France (winning the European championship in 1984). He retired as a player in 1987 and was France's manager from then until 1992.

39 What Zidane does with a ball Maradona could do with an orange.
2000 In *The Independent*, 23 Dec.

Plato c.428–c.348 BC

Greek philosopher, a pupil of Socrates and the teacher of Aristotle. He wrote in the form of dialogues, often with Socrates as a leading character. Some 30 philosophical dialogues and some letters (not all considered genuine) have survived.

40 Let no one ignorant of mathematics enter here.
c.380 BC Inscription over the door of the Academy at Athens.

41 The wisest of you men is he who has realized, like Socrates, that in respect of wisdom he is really worthless.
Apology, 23b (translated by H Tredennick).

42 Socrates is guilty of corrupting the minds of the young, and of believing in deities of his own invention instead of the gods recognized by the state.
The formal indictment in Socrates' trial, quoted in the *Apology*, 24b (translated by H Tredennick).

43 For I spend all my time going about trying to persuade you, young and old, to make your first and chief concern not for your bodies nor for your possessions, but for the highest welfare of your souls, proclaiming as I go, Wealth does not bring goodness, but goodness brings wealth and every other blessing, both to the individual and to the state.
Apology, 30b (translated by H Tredennick).

44 The unexamined life is not worth living.
Apology, 38a (translated by H Tredennick).

45 Now it is time that we were going, I to die and you to live, but which of us has the happier prospect is unknown to anyone but God.
Apology, 42a (translated by H Tredennick).

46 It is not living, but living well, which we ought to consider most important.
Crito, 48b (translated by H North Fowler, 1923).

47 Your country is more precious and more to be revered and is holier and in higher esteem among the gods and among men of understanding than your mother and your father and all your ancestors.
Crito, 51a–b (translated by H North Fowler, 1923).

48 Men of sound sense have Law for their god, but men without sense Pleasure.
Epistulae, 8. 354e (translated by R G Bury, 1925).

49 To do wrong is the greatest of evils.
Gorgias, 469b (translated by W D Woodhead). There is a similar remark in the *Crito*, 49b.

50 Much more wretched than lack of health in the body, it is to dwell with a soul that is not healthy, but corrupt.
Gorgias, 479b (translated by W R M Lamb, 1967).

51 No one can escape his destiny.
Gorgias, 512e (translated by W R M Lamb, 1967).

52 All the gold upon the earth and all the gold beneath it, does not compensate for lack of virtue.
Leges, 728a (translated by Trevor J Saunders, 1970).

53 Every unjust man is unjust against his will.
Leges, 731c (translated by Trevor J Saunders, 1970).

54 Is virtue something that can be taught?
Meno, 70a (translated by W K C Guthrie).

55 If we are ever to have pure knowledge of anything, we must get rid of the body and contemplate things by themselves with the soul by itself.
Phaedo, 66d (translated by H Tredennick).

56 One should die in silence.
Phaedo, 117e (translated by D Gallop, 1993).

57 Crito, we ought to offer a cock to Asclepius. See to it, and don't forget.
Phaedo, 118a (translated by H Tredennick).

58 For myself I am fairly certain that no wise man believes anyone sins willingly or willingly perpetrates any evil or base act.
Protagoras, 345e (translated by W K C Guthrie).

59 We must now examine whether just people also live better and are happier than unjust ones. I think it's clear already that this is so, but we must look into it further, since the argument concerns no ordinary topic, but the way we ought to live.
Republic, bk.1, 352d (translated by G M A Grube, revised by C D C Reeve).

60 Justice is superior to injustice.
Republic, bk.1, 367b (translated by P Shorey, 1953).

61 The most important stage of any enterprise is the beginning.
Republic, bk.2, 377b (translated by R Waterfield, 1993).

62 Justice is doing one's work and not meddling with what isn't one's own.
Republic, bk.4, 433a (translated by G M A Grube, revised by C D C Reeve).

63 Until philosophers rule as kings or those who are now called kings and leading men genuinely and adequately philosophize, that is, until political power and philosophy entirely coincide...cities will have no rest from evils, nor, I think, will the human race.
Republic, bk.5, 473c (translated by G M A Grube, revised by C D C Reeve).

64 Every soul pursues the good and does whatever it does for its sake.
Republic, bk.6, 505e (translated by G M A Grube, revised by C D C Reeve).

65 The power to learn is present in everyone's soul, and the instrument with which each learns is like an eye that cannot be turned around from darkness to light without turning the whole body.
Republic, bk.7, 518c (translated by G M A Grube, revised by C D C Reeve).

66 If the study of all these sciences which we have enumerated, should ever bring us to their mutual association and relationship, and teach us the nature of the ties which bind them together, I believe that the diligent treatment of them will forward the objects which we have in view, and that the labor, which otherwise would be fruitless, will be well bestowed.
Republic, bk.7, 531d (translated by G M A Grube, revised by C D C Reeve).

67 Extreme freedom can't be expected to lead to anything but a change to extreme slavery, whether for a private individual or for a city.
Republic, bk.8, 564a (translated by G M A Grube, revised by C D C Reeve).

68 God is a geometrician.
Quoted in Plutarch *Symposium*.

Plautus, Titus Maccius c.250–184 BC
Roman comic poet, who worked as a trader and craftsman before writing plays in middle life. He became the most important Latin adapter of the Greek New Comedy, which dealt with social life to the exclusion of politics. Only 21 of his comedies have survived.

69 *Lupus est homo homini, non homo, quom qualis sit non novit.*
A man is a wolf, and not a man, to another man, for as long as he doesn't know what he is like.
Asinaria, 495. The phrase is often rendered 'Homo homini lupus' ('Man is a wolf to another man').

Pliny full name Gaius Plinius Secundus known as the Elder AD 23–79
Roman statesman, scholar and writer. His only surviving work is his universal encyclopedia, *Historia Naturalis* (37 vols, AD 77). He was killed while observing the eruption of Vesuvius.

70 *Vulgoque veritas iam attributa vino est.*
And truth has come to be proverbially credited to wine.
AD 77 *Historia Naturalis*, bk.14, section 28 (translated by H Rackham). The phrase is often rendered as 'in vino veritas'.

71 *Addito salis grano.*
With the addition of a pinch of salt.
AD 77 *Historia Naturalis*, bk.23, section 8. This is probably a version of a more ancient proverb, commonly rendered 'cum grano salis'.

Plomer, William 1903–73
South African-born British writer.

72 Out of that bungled, unwise war
An alp of unforgiveness grew.
1960 'The Boer War'.

73 On a sofa upholstered in panther skin
Mona did researches in original sin.
1960 'Mews Flat Mona'.

Plout, David

74 Deathbed utterances, like suicide notes, are a powerful coinage, stamped by an awareness that words can outlive us.
1990 In the *Wall Street Journal*, 26 Sep, reviewing J M Coetzee *Age of Iron* (1990).

Plutarch c.46–c.120 AD
Greek historian, biographer and philosopher. His extant writings include the essays in *Opera Moralia*, and the biographical *Bioi paralleloi* (*Parallel Lives*, translated into English by Thomas North in 1759), a major source for Shakespeare.

75 He who cheats with an oath acknowledges that he is afraid of his enemy, but that he thinks little of God.
Parallel Lives, 'Lysander', ch.8.

76 Though others before him had triumphed three times, Pompeius, by having gained his first triumph over Libya, his second over Europe, and this the last over Asia, seemed in a manner to have brought the whole world into his three triumphs.
Referring to Pompey's victories against the Marian party in Africa, in Spain, and against Mithridates in Asia Minor (c.62 BC). *Parallel Lives*, 'Pompeius', ch.45.

Pobedonostsev, Constantin Petrovich 1827–1907
Russian jurist, tutor to Alexander III and Nicholas II. Initially a liberal, he became an uncompromising champion of autocracy

and the supremacy of the Russian Orthodox Church, strongly opposed to westernization.

77 Parliaments are the great lie of our time.
Moskovskii Shornik.

Po Chü-I 772–846

Chinese poet and civil servant who rose to become the Governor of a number of different cities in China.

78 But now that age comes
A moment of joy is harder and harder to get.
812 'The Chrysanthemums in the Eastern Garden' (in *Chinese Poems*, translated by Arthur Waley, 1946).

79 Deeper and deeper, one's love of old friends;
Fewer and fewer, one's dealings with young men.
835 *Old Age*.

Poe, Edgar Allan 1809–49

US poet and short-story writer, a pioneer of the modern detective story, whose poetry emphasizes the beauty of melancholy. He is best known for stories such as 'The Tell-Tale Heart' (1843) and his poem 'The Raven' (1845).

80 I know not how it was—but, with the first glimpse of the building, a sense of insufferable gloom pervaded my spirit... There was an iciness, a sinking, a sickening of the heart—an unredeemed dreariness of thought which no goading of the imagination could torture into aught of the sublime.
1839 'The Fall of the House of Usher', in the *Gentleman's Magazine*, Sep.

81 As the strong man exults in his physical ability, delighting in such exercises as call his muscles into action, so glories the analyst in that moral activity which *disentangles*.
1841 Of detective work. 'The Murders in the Rue Morgue', in the *Gentleman's Magazine*, Apr.

82 It will be found, in fact, that the ingenious are always fanciful, and the *truly* imaginative never otherwise than analytic.
1841 'The Murders in the Rue Morgue', in the *Gentleman's Magazine*, Apr.

83 And now was acknowledged the presence of the Red Death. He had come like a thief in the night. And one by one dropped the revellers in the blood-bedecked halls of their revel, and died each in the despairing posture of his fall.
1842 'The Masque of the Red Death', in the *Gentleman's Magazine*, May.

84 There is something in the unselfish and self-sacrificing love of a brute, which goes directly to the heart of him who has had frequent occasion to test the paltry friendship and gossamer fidelity of mere *Man*.
1843 'The Black Cat', in the *United States Saturday Post*, 19 Aug.

85 I have no faith in human perfectibility... Man is now only more active—not more happy—nor more wise, than he was 6,000 years ago.
1844 Letter to James Russell Lowell, 2 Jul.

86 On desperate seas long wont to roam,
Thy hyacinth hair, thy classic face,
Thy Naiad airs have brought me home
To the glory that was Greece,
And the grandeur that was Rome.
1845 'To Helen', stanza 2.

87 Yes, Heaven is thine; but this
Is a world of sweets and sours;
Our flowers are merely—flowers.
1845 'Israfel', stanza 7.

88 'Take thy beak from out my heart, and take thy form from off my door!'
Quoth the raven, 'Nevermore.'
1845 'The Raven', stanza 17. In *American Review*, Feb 1845.

89 The death...of a beautiful woman is, unquestionably, the most poetical topic in the world.
1846 'The Philosophy of Composition', in *Graham's Magazine*, Apr.

90 Mournful and Never-ending Remembrance.
1846 Of the significance of the bird in his poem 'The Raven'. 'The Philosophy of Composition', in *Graham's Magazine*, Apr.

91 To be *thoroughly* conversant with a Man's heart is to take our final lesson in the iron-clasped volume of despair.
1849 'Marginalia', in the *Southern Literary Messenger*, Jun.

92 The nose of a mob is its imagination. By this, at any time, it can be quietly led.
1849 'Marginalia', in the *Southern Literary Messenger*, Jul.

93 To vilify a great man is the readiest way in which a little man can himself attain greatness.
1849 *Marginalia 1844–49*.

94 Thank Heaven! the crisis—
The danger is past,
And the lingering illness
Is over at last—
And the fever called 'Living'
Is conquered at last.
1850 'For Annie'.

Poelzig, Hans 1869–1936

German Expressionist architect, Professor of Architecture at Breslau Academy of Arts (1900) and later director.

95 We cannot do without the past in solving the architectural problems of our own day.
1906 *Das Deutsche Kunstgewerbe 1906*.

Poincaré, (Jules) Henri 1854–1912

French mathematician and physicist. In his research in the theory of functions he contributed greatly to the field of mathematical physics.

96 If we ought not to fear mortal truth, still less should we dread scientific truth. In the first place it can not conflict with ethics... But if science is feared, it is above all because it can give no happiness... Man, then, can not be happy through science but today he can much less be happy without it.
1904 *The Value of Science*.

97 Science is facts. Just as houses are made of stones, so science is made of facts. But a pile of stones is not a house and a collection of facts is not necessarily a science.
1905 *Science and Hypothesis*, ch.9.

98 The scientist does not study nature because it is useful to do so. He studies it because he takes pleasure in it, and he takes pleasure in it because it is beautiful.
1909 *Science and Method*, vol.1, ch.1 (translated by Francis Maitland).

Poindexter, John Marlan 1936–

US naval officer and statesman, chief of naval operations in the 1970s. He became Reagan's National Security Adviser in 1985. He resigned (Nov 1986) after implication in the Irangate scandal, and was later convicted. His sentence was overturned by the Federal appeals court in 1991. He was head of the Pentagon's controversial Information Awareness Office until 2003.

1 I made a very deliberate decision not to ask the President, so that I could insulate him from the decision and provide some future deniability for him if it ever leaked out.
1987 On his action in diverting funds from arms sales at Iran–Contra hearings, 15 Jul.

Polanski, Roman 1933–

French–Polish film director, scriptwriter and actor, known for such films as *Rosemary's Baby* (1968), *Chinatown* (1974), *The Tenant* (1976), *Frantic* (1988) and *The Pianist* (2002).

1 The best films are the best because of no one but the director.
Quoted in *Halliwell's Filmgoer's Book of Quotes* (1973).

Pollock, (Paul) Jackson 1912–56

US artist, best known for his technique of pouring or dripping paint on the canvas. A leader of 'action painting' and the Abstract Expressionist movement, his works include the enormous *One* and the monochrome *Echo* and *Blue Poles*.

2 On the floor I am more at ease, I feel nearer, more a part of the painting, since this way I can walk around it, work from the four sides and literally be 'in' the painting.
1947 Quoted in Italo Tomassoni *Pollock* (1968).

3 Abstract painting is abstract. It confronts you.
Quoted in Francis V O'Connor *Jackson Pollock* (1967).

Polo, Marco c.1254–1324

Venetian trader and traveller. In 1271–5 he accompanied his father and uncle to China and stayed on for 16 years, becoming the envoy of Kublai Khan. He returned to Venice in 1295 and, imprisoned by the Genoese, used his time to dictate his memoirs.

4 Now it came to pass...that the Tartars made them a King whose name was Chinghis Kaan [Genghis Khan]. He was a man of great worth, and of great ability, and valour. And as soon as the news that he had been chosen King was spread abroad through those countries, all the Tartars in the world came to him and owned him for their Lord.
c.1310 Quoted in Col. Henry Yule (ed and trans) *The Book of Ser Marco Polo, the Venetian, Concerning the Kingdoms and Marvels of the East* (1871), 2 vols.

5 I have not told even the half of the things that I have seen.
c.1320 On being accused of exaggeration in his accounts of China. Quoted in R H Poole and P Finch (eds) *Newnes Pictorial Knowledge* (1950), vol.2.

Pol Pot *real name* Saloth Sar 1925–98

Cambodian political and military leader whose Khmer Rouge army took over Cambodia in 1975. Prime Minister of Kampuchea (1976–8), he presided over the deaths of over a million people, by starvation or murder, before Vietnam liberated the country in Dec 1978.

6 We will burn the old grass and the new will grow.
c.1975 Quoted in John Pilger *Distant Voices* (1992), section 5.

7 If our people can build Angkor Wat they can do anything.
1979 Quoted by Dennis Bloodworth in the *Observer*, 20 Jan 1980.

Pol-Roger, Christian 1940–

French vintner.

8 Champagne! In victory, one deserves it; in defeat, one needs it.
1988 'Champagne, a Magnum Opus', in the *New York Times*, 31 Dec.

Pomfret, John 1667–1702

English clergyman and poet.

9 We live and learn, but not the wiser grow.
1700 'Reason'.

Pompadour, Madame de *full name* Jeanne Antoinette Poisson, Marquise de Pompadour 1721–64

French mistress of Louis XV. Installed at Versailles (1745), she assumed control of public affairs and swayed state policy, appointing her favourites. She was a lavish patron of the arts and literature.

10 The Duke takes a town in the same light-hearted way as he seduces a woman.
1756 Of Cardinal Duc de Richelieu, following his capture of the reputedly impregnable Fort St Phillip, Minorca, by taking his men up a cliff face to surprise the defenders. Quoted in Nancy Mitford *Madame de Pompadour* (1954), p.201.

11 *Après nous le déluge.*
After us the deluge.
1757 Quoted in Madame de Hausset *Mémoires* (1824).

Pompéia, Raul d'Avila 1863–95

Brazilian novelist, best known for *O Ateneú* (1888), the story of life in an oppressive boarding school. Unable to cope any longer with his emotional problems, he committed suicide at the age of 32.

12 *O tédio é a grande enfermidade da escola, o tédio corruptor que tanto se pode gerar da monotonia do trabalho como da ociosidade.*
Tedium is the worst disease in schools, the corrupting tedium that comes equally from monotony, work or leisure.
1888 *O Ateneú* ('The Atheneum'), ch.7.

Pompidou, Georges 1911–74

Second President (1969–74) of the Fifth French Republic. He served in the Resistance during World War II, and was a member of Charles de Gaulle's staff (1944–6) before taking control of the provisional government.

13 There are three roads to ruin—women, gambling and technicians. The most pleasant is women, the quickest is with gambling, but the surest is with technicians.
1968 In the *Sunday Telegraph*.

Pop, Iggy 1947–

US rock singer and songwriter.

14 What seems to pass for guitar more and more now is some wimp with a fuzz box. Somewhere around

Hendrix, the line was crossed. Hendrix had both: he had the hands and he had the fuzz box. Now all they have is the fuzz box.
2004 In *Rolling Stone*, 15 Apr.

Pope, Alexander 1688–1744
English poet and essayist, crippled at 12 by a tubercular infection of the spine. His work, distinguished by its technical brilliance and skilful satire, includes *The Rape of the Lock* (1712, enlarged 1714), *The Dunciad* (1728, revised 1742) and *An Essay on Man* (1732–4).

15 Where'er you walk, cool gales shall fan the glade,
Trees where you sit, shall crowd into a shade:
Where'er you tread, the blushing flowers shall rise,
And all things flourish where you turn your eyes.
1709 *Pastorals*, 'Summer', l.73–6.

16 Some are bewildered in the maze of schools,
And some made coxcombs Nature meant but fools.
1711 *An Essay on Criticism*, l.26–7.

17 Some have at first for wits, then poets passed,
Turned critics next, and proved plain fools at last.
1711 *An Essay on Criticism*, l.36–7.

18 First follow Nature, and your judgement frame
By her just standard, which is still the same:
Unerring Nature, still divinely bright,
One clear, unchanged, and universal light,
Life, force and beauty must to all impart,
At once the source and end and test of art.
1711 *An Essay on Criticism*, l.68–73.

19 A little learning is a dangerous thing;
Drink deep, or taste not the Pierian spring:
There shallow draughts intoxicate the brain,
And drinking largely sobers us again.
1711 *An Essay on Criticism*, l.215–8.

20 Poets like painters, thus unskilled to trace
The naked nature and the living grace,
With gold and jewels cover ev'ry part,
And hide with ornaments their want of art.
True wit is Nature to advantage dressed,
What oft was thought, but ne'er so well expressed.
1711 *An Essay on Criticism*, l.293–8.

21 Expression is the dress of thought.
1711 *An Essay on Criticism*, l.318.

22 In Words, as Fashions, the same rule will hold;
Alike Fantastic, if too New, or Old;
Be not the *first* by whom the New are try'd,
Nor the *last* to lay the Old aside.
1711 *An Essay on Criticism*, l.333–6.

23 As some to church repair,
Not for the doctrine, but the music there.
1711 *An Essay on Criticism*, l.342–3.

24 True ease in writing comes from art, not chance,
As those move easiest who have learned to dance.
'Tis not enough no harshness gives offence,
The sound must seem an echo to the sense.
1711 *An Essay on Criticism*, l.362–5.

25 To err is human; to forgive, divine.
1711 *An Essay on Criticism*, l.525.

26 All seems infected that th'infected spy,
As all looks yellow to the jaundiced eye.
1711 *An Essay on Criticism*, l.558–9.

27 The bookful blockhead, ignorantly read,
With loads of learned lumbers in his head.
1711 *An Essay on Criticism*, l.612–3.

28 For fools rush in where angels fear to tread.
1711 *An Essay on Criticism*, l.625.

29 What dire offence from am'rous causes springs,
What mighty contests rise from trivial things.
1714 *The Rape of the Lock*, canto 1, l.1–2.

30 Now lap-dogs give themselves the rousing shake,
And sleepless lovers, just at twelve, awake.
1714 *The Rape of the Lock*, canto 1, l.15–16.

31 They shift the moving Toyshop of their heart.
1714 *The Rape of the Lock*, canto 1, l.100.

32 Bright as the sun, her eyes the gazers strike,
And, like the sun, they shine on all alike.
1714 *The Rape of the Lock*, canto 2, l.13–14.

33 If to her share some female errors fall,
Look on her face, and you'll forget 'em all.
1714 *The Rape of the Lock*, canto 2, l.17–18.

34 Belinda smiled, and all the world was gay.
1714 *The Rape of the Lock*, canto 2, l.52.

35 Whether the nymph shall break Diana's law,
Or some frail china jar receive a flaw,
Or stain her honour, or her new brocade,
Forget her pray'rs, or miss a masquerade.
1714 *The Rape of the Lock*, canto 2, l.105–8.

36 Here thou, great Anna! whom three realms obey,
Dost sometimes counsel take—and sometimes tea.
1714 *The Rape of the Lock*, canto 3, l.7–8.

37 At ev'ry word a reputation dies.
1714 *The Rape of the Lock*, canto 3, l.16.

38 The hungry judges soon the sentence sign,
And wretches hang that jury-men may dine.
1714 *The Rape of the Lock*, canto 3, l.21–2.

39 Let spades be trumps! she said, and trumps they were.
1714 *The Rape of the Lock*, canto 3, l.46.

40 Not louder shrieks to pitying heav'n are cast,
When husbands or when lapdogs breathe their last.
1714 *The Rape of the Lock*, canto 3, l.157–8.

41 Sir Plume, of amber snuff-box justly vain,
And the nice conduct of a clouded cane.
1714 *The Rape of the Lock*, canto 4, l.123–4.

42 Beauties in vain their pretty eyes may roll;
Charms strike the sight, but merit wins the soul.
1714 *The Rape of the Lock*, canto 5, l.33–4.

43 Happy the man, whose wish and care
A few paternal acres bound,
Content to breathe his native air,
In his own ground.
1717 'Ode on Solitude'.

44 Is there no bright reversion in the sky,
For those who greatly think or bravely die?
1717 *Elegy to the Memory of an Unfortunate Lady*, l.9–10.

45 On all the line a sudden vengeance waits,
And frequent hearses shall besiege your gates.
1717 *Elegy to the Memory of an Unfortunate Lady*, l.37–8.

46 By foreign hands thy dying eyes were closed,
By foreign hands thy decent limbs composed,

By foreign hands thy humble grave adorned,
By strangers honoured, and by strangers mourned.
1717 *Elegy to the Memory of an Unfortunate Lady*, l.51–4.

47 Oh happy state! when souls each other draw,
When love is liberty, and nature, law:
All then is full, possessing, and possessed,
No craving void left aching in the breast.
1717 'Eloisa to Abelard'.

48 No, make me mistress to the man I love;
If there be yet another name more free,
More fond than mistress, make me that to thee!
1717 'Eloisa to Abelard'.

49 Of all affliction taught a lover yet,
'Tis sure the hardest science to forget!
How shall I lose the sin, yet keep the sense,
And love th'offender, yet detest th'offence?
How the dear object from the crime remove,
Or how distinguish penitence from love?
1717 'Eloisa to Abelard'.

50 How happy is the blameless Vestal's lot!
The world forgetting, by the world forgot.
1717 'Eloisa to Abelard'.

51 And wine can of their wits the wise beguile,
Make the sage frolic, and the serious smile.
1726 *Odyssey*, bk.14, l.520–1.

52 Welcome the coming, speed the parting guest.
1726 *Odyssey*, bk. 15, l.83.

53 To endeavour to work upon the vulgar with fine sense, is like attempting to hew blocks with a razor.
1727 *Miscellanies*, 'Thoughts on Various Subjects', vol.2.

54 A man should never be ashamed to own he has been in the wrong, which is but saying, in other words, that he is wiser to-day than he was yesterday.
1727 *Miscellanies*, 'Thoughts on Various Subjects', vol.2.

55 It is with narrow-souled people as with narrow-necked bottles: the less they have in them, the more noise they make in pouring it out.
1727 *Miscellanies*, 'Thoughts on Various Subjects', vol.2.

56 When men grow virtuous in their old age, they only make a sacrifice to God of the devil's leavings.
1727 *Miscellanies*, 'Thoughts on Various Subjects', vol.2.

57 The most primitive men are the most credulous.
1727 *Miscellanies*, 'Thoughts on Various Subjects', vol.2.

58 Consult the genius of the place in all.
1731 *Epistles to Several Persons*, 'To Lord Burlington', l.57.

59 Still follow sense, of ev'ry art the soul,
Parts answering parts shall slide into a whole.
1731 *Epistles to Several Persons*, 'To Lord Burlington', l.65–6.

60 No pleasing Intricacies intervene,
No artful wildness to perplex the scene;
Grove nods at grove, each a mirror of the other.
The suff'ring eye inverted Nature sees,
Trees cut to Statues, Statues thick as trees,
With here a Fountain, never to be play'd,
And there a Summer-house, that knows no shade;
Here Amphitrite sails thro' myrtle bow'rs
There Gladiators fight, or die, in flow'rs
Un-water'd see the drooping sea-horse mourn,
And swallows roost in Nilus' dusty Urn.
1731 *Epistles to Several Persons*, 'To Lord Burlington', l.115–25.

61 To rest, the cushion and soft Dean invite,
Who never mentions Hell to ears polite.
1731 *Epistles to Several Persons*, 'To Lord Burlington', l.149–50.

62 Another age shall see the golden ear
Imbrown the slope, and nod on the parterre,
Deep harvests bury all his pride has planned,
And laughing Ceres re-assume the land.
1731 *Epistles to Several Persons*, 'To Lord Burlington', l.173–6.

63 'Tis use alone that sanctifies expense,
And splendour borrows all her rays from sense.
1731 *Epistles to Several Persons*, 'To Lord Burlington', l.179–80.

64 How often are we to die before we go quite off this stage? In every friend we lose a part of ourselves, and the best part.
1732 Letter to Swift, 5 Dec.

65 Who shall decide, when doctors disagree,
And soundest casuists doubt, like you and me?
1733 *Epistles to Several Persons*, 'To Lord Bathurst', l.1–2.

66 But thousands die, without or this or that,
Die, and endow a college, or a cat.
1733 *Epistles to Several Persons*, 'To Lord Bathurst', l.95–6.

67 The ruling passion be it what it will,
The ruling passion conquers reason still.
1733 *Epistles to Several Persons*, 'To Lord Bathurst', l.155–6.

68 Who sees pale Mammon pine amidst his store,
Sees but a backward steward for the poor;
This year a reservoir, to keep and spare,
The next a fountain, spouting through his heir,
In lavish streams to quench a country's thirst,
And men and dogs shall drink him 'till they burst.
1733 *Epistles to Several Persons*, 'To Lord Bathurst', l.173–8.

69 In the worst inn's worst room, with mat half-hung,
The floors of plaister, and the walls of dung,
On once a flock-bed, but repaired with straw,
With tape-tied curtains, never meant to draw,
The George and Garter dangling from that bed
Where tawdry yellow strove with dirty red,
Great Villiers lies.
1733 *Epistles to Several Persons*, 'To Lord Bathurst', l.229–35.

70 Awake, my St. John! leave all meaner things
To low ambition, and the pride of kings.
Let us (since Life can little more supply
Than just to look about us and to die)
Expatiate free o'er all this scene of man;
A mighty maze! but not without a plan.
1733 *An Essay on Man*, epistle 1, l.1–6.

71 Eye Nature's walks, shoot Folly as it flies,
And catch the Manners living as they rise.
Laugh where we must, be candid where we can;
But vindicate the ways of God to man.
1733 *An Essay on Man*, epistle 1, l.13–16.
▶ See Milton 601:31.

72 Observe how system into system runs,
What other planets circle other suns.
1733 *An Essay on Man*, epistle 1, l.25–6.

73 Who sees with equal eye, as God of all,
A hero perish, or a sparrow fall,
Atoms or systems into ruin hurled,
And now a bubble burst, and now a world.
1733 *An Essay on Man*, epistle 1, l.87–90.

74 Hope springs eternal in the human breast:
Man never Is, but always To be blest.
1733 *An Essay on Man*, epistle 1, l.95–6.

75 Lo! the poor Indian, whose untutored mind
Sees God in clouds, or hears him in the wind;
His soul proud Science never taught to stray
Far as the solar walk, or milky way;
Yet simple Nature to his hope has giv'n,
Behind the cloud-topped hill, an humbler heav'n.
1733 *An Essay on Man*, epistle 1, l.99–104.

76 Pride still is aiming at the blest abodes,
Men would be angels, angels would be gods.
1733 *An Essay on Man*, epistle 1, l.125–6.

77 The spider's touch, how exquisitely fine!
Feels at each thread, and lives along the line.
1733 *An Essay on Man*, epistle 1, l.217–8.

78 All are but parts of one stupendous whole,
Whose body, Nature is, and God the soul.
1733 *An Essay on Man*, epistle 1, l.267–8.

79 All nature is but art, unknown to thee;
All chance, direction, which thou canst not see;
All discord, harmony, not understood;
All partial evil, universal good:
And, spite of Pride, in erring Reason's spite,
One truth is clear, 'Whatever Is, is RIGHT.'
1733 *An Essay on Man*, epistle 1, l.289–94.

80 Know then thyself, presume not God to scan;
The proper study of mankind is man.
Placed on this isthmus of a middle state,
A being darkly wise, and rudely great:
With too much knowledge for the sceptic side,
With too much weakness for the stoic's pride,
He hangs between; in doubt to act or rest,
In doubt to deem himself a god, or beast;
In doubt his mind or body to prefer,
Born but to die, and reas'ning but to err;
Alike in ignorance, his reason such,
Whether he thinks too little, or too much.
1733 *An Essay on Man*, epistle 2, l.1–12.

81 Created half to rise, and half to fall;
Great lord of all things, yet a prey to all;
Sole judge of truth, in endless error hurled;
The glory, jest, and riddle of the world!
1733 *An Essay on Man*, epistle 2, l.15–18.

82 Vice is a monster of so frightful mien,
As, to be hated, needs but to be seen;
Yet seen too oft, familiar with her face,
We first endure, then pity, then embrace.
1733 *An Essay on Man*, epistle 2, l.217–19.

83 The learn'd is happy nature to explore,
The fool is happy that he knows no more.
1733 *An Essay on Man*, epistle 2, l.263–4.

84 For forms of government let fools contest;
Whate'er is best administered is best.
1733 *An Essay on Man*, epistle 3, l.303–4.

85 In faith and hope the world will disagree,
But all mankind's concern is charity.
1733 *An Essay on Man*, epistle 3, l.307–8.

86 Thus God and nature linked the gen'ral frame,
And bade self-love and social be the same.
1733 *An Essay on Man*, epistle 3, l.317–18.

87 Oh Happiness! our being's end and aim!
Good, pleasure, ease, content! whate'er thy name:
That something still which prompts th' eternal sigh,
For which we bear to live, or dare to die.
1734 *An Essay on Man*, epistle 4, l.1–4.

88 Order is Heaven's first law.
1733 *An Essay on Man*, epistle to 4, l.49.

89 A wit's a feather, and a chief a rod;
An honest man's the noblest work of God.
1734 *An Essay on Man*, epistle 4, l.247–8.

90 If parts allure thee, think how Bacon shined,
The wisest, brightest, meanest of mankind:
Or ravished with the whistling of a name,
See Cromwell, damned to everlasting fame!
1734 *An Essay on Man*, epistle 4, l.281–4.

91 Slave to no sect, who takes no private road,
But looks thro' Nature, up to Nature's God.
1734 *An Essay on Man*, epistle 4, l.331–2.

92 All our knowledge is, ourselves to know.
1734 *An Essay on Man*, epistle 4, l.398.

93 Alas! in truth the man but changed his mind,
Perhaps was sick, in love, or had not dined.
1734 *Epistles to Several Persons*, 'To Lord Cobham', l.127–8.

94 'Tis from high life high characters are drawn;
A saint in crape is twice a saint in lawn.
1734 *Epistles to Several Persons*, 'To Lord Cobham', l.134–6.

95 Search then the Ruling Passion: There, alone,
The wild are constant and the cunning known;
The fool consistent, and the false sincere;
Priests, princes, women, no dissemblers here.
This clue once found, unravels all the rest.
1734 *Epistles to Several Persons*, 'To Lord Cobham', l.174–8.

96 Odious! in woollen! 'twould a saint provoke!
1734 *Epistles to Several Persons*, 'To Lord Cobham', l.246.

97 Shut, shut the door, good John! fatigued I said,
Tie up the knocker; say I'm sick, I'm dead.
The Dog-star rages!
1735 'An Epistle to Dr Arbuthnot', l.1–3.

98 You think this cruel? take it for a rule,
No creature smarts so little as a fool.
Let peals of laughter, Codrus! round thee break,
Thou unconcerned canst hear the mighty crack.
Pit, box, and gallery in convulsions hurled,
Thou stand'st unshook amidst a bursting world.
1735 'An Epistle to Dr Arbuthnot', l.83–8.

99 Destroy his fib, or sophistry; in vain,
The creature's at his dirty work again.
1735 'An Epistle to Dr Arbuthnot', l.91–2.

1 Pretty! in amber to observe the forms
Of hairs, or straws, or dirt, or grubs, or worms!
The things, we know are neither rich nor rare,
But wonder how the Devil they got there.
1735 'An Epistle to Dr Arbuthnot', l.169–72.

2 And he, whose fustian's so sublimely bad,
It is not poetry, but prose run mad.
1735 'An Epistle to Dr Arbuthnot', l.187–8.

3 Damn with faint praise, assent with civil leer,
And without sneering, teach the rest to sneer;

Willing to wound, and yet afraid to strike,
Just hint a fault, and hesitate dislike.
1735 Of Addison. 'An Epistle to Dr Arbuthnot', l.201–4.

4 But still the great have kindness in reserve,
He helped to bury whom he helped to starve.
1735 Of a patron. 'An Epistle to Dr Arbuthnot', l.247–8.

5 Let Sporus tremble—'What? that thing of silk,
Sporus, that mere white curd of ass's milk?
Satire or sense, alas! can Sporus feel?
Who breaks a butterfly upon a wheel?
1735 Of Lord Hervey. 'An Epistle to Dr Arbuthnot', l.305–8.

6 And he himself one vile antithesis.
1735 Of Lord Hervey. 'An Epistle to Dr Arbuthnot', l.325.

7 Unlearn'd, he knew no schoolman's subtle art,
No language, but the language of the heart.
1735 Of Pope's father. 'An Epistle to Dr Arbuthnot', l.398–9.

8 Most women have no characters at all.
1735 *Epistles to Several Persons*, 'To a Lady', l.2.

9 A very heathen in the carnal part,
Yet still a sad, good Christian at her heart.
1735 *Epistles to Several Persons*, 'To a Lady', l.67–8.

10 Chaste to her husband, frank to all beside,
A teeming mistress, but a barren bride.
1735 *Epistles to Several Persons*, 'To a Lady', l.71–2.

11 'With every pleasing, every prudent part,
Say, what can Cloe want?'—She wants a heart.
1735 *Epistles to Several Persons*, 'To a Lady', l.159–60.

12 Virtue she finds too painful an endeavour,
Content to dwell in decencies for ever.
1735 *Epistles to Several Persons*, 'To a Lady', l.163–4.

13 In men, we various ruling passions find,
In women, two almost divide the kind;
Those, only fixed, they first or last obey
The love of pleasure, and the love of sway.
1735 *Epistles to Several Persons*, 'To a Lady', l.207–10.

14 Men, some to business, some to pleasure take;
But every woman is at heart a rake:
Men, some to quiet, some to public strife;
But every lady would be Queen for life.
1735 *Epistles to Several Persons*, 'To a Lady', l.215–8.

15 Still round and round the ghosts of Beauty glide,
And haunt the places where their honour died.
See how the world its veterans rewards!
A youth of frolics, an old age of cards.
1735 *Epistles to Several Persons*, 'To a Lady', l.241–4.

16 Woman's at best a contradiction still.
1735 *Epistles to Several Persons*, 'To a Lady', l.270.

17 Who now reads Cowley? if he pleases yet,
His moral pleases, not his pointed wit.
1737 *Imitations of Horace*, bk.2, epistle 1, l.75–6.

18 The people's voice is odd,
It is, and it is not, the voice of God.
1737 *Imitations of Horace*, bk.2, epistle 1, l.89–90.

19 But those who cannot write, and those who can,
All rhyme, and scrawl, and scribble, to a man.
1737 *Imitations of Horace*, bk.2, epistle 1, l.187–8.

20 Ev'n copious Dryden, wanted, or forgot,
The last and greatest art, the art to blot.
1737 *Imitations of Horace*, bk.2, epistle 1, l.280–1.

21 There still remains, to mortify a wit,
The many-headed monster of the pit.
1737 *Imitations of Horace*, bk.2, epistle 1, l.304–5.

22 The more you drink, the more you crave.
1737 *Imitations of Horace*, bk.2, espistle 2, l.212.

23 Not to go back, is somewhat to advance,
And men must walk at least before they dance.
1738 *Imitations of Horace*, bk.1, epistle 1, l.53–4.

24 Not to admire, is all the art I know,
To make men happy, and to keep them so.
1738 *Imitations of Horace*, bk.1, epistle 6, l.1–2.

25 The worst of madmen is a saint run mad.
1738 *Imitations of Horace*, bk.1, epistle 6, l.27.

26 Ask you what provocation I have had?
The strong antipathy of good to bad.
1738 *Imitations of Horace*, epilogue to the satires, dialogue 2, l.197–8.

27 Yes, I am proud; I must be proud to see
Men not afraid of God, afraid of me.
1738 *Imitations of Horace*, epilogue to the satires, dialogue 2, l.208–9.

28 Teach me to feel another's woe;
To hide the fault I see;
That mercy I to others show,
That mercy show to me.
1738 *The Universal Prayer*.

29 Books and the Man I sing, the first who brings
The Smithfield Muses to the Ear of Kings.
Say great Patricians! (since your selves inspire
These wond'rous works; so Jove and Fate require)
Say from what cause, in vain decry'd and curst,
Still Dunce the second reigns like Dunce the first?
1742 *The Dunciad*, bk.1, l.1–6.

30 Poetic Justice, with her lifted scale,
Where, in nice balance, truth with gold she weighs,
And solid pudding against empty praise.
1742 *The Dunciad*, bk.1, l.52–4.

31 Here gay Description Aegypt glads with showers;
Or gives to Zembla fruits, to Barca flowers;
Glitt'ring with ice here hoary hills are seen,
There painted vallies of eternal green.
1742 *The Dunciad*, bk.1, l.71–4.

32 While pensive poets painful vigils keep,
Sleepless themselves, to give their readers sleep.
1742 *The Dunciad*, bk.1, l.93–4.

33 In each she marks her image full exprest,
But chief, in Tibbald's monster-breeding breast;
Sees Gods with Daemons in strange league ingage,
And earth, and heav'n, and hell her battles wage.
1742 *The Dunciad*, bk.1, l.105–8.

34 Or where the pictures for the page atone,
And Quarles is saved by beauties not his own.
1742 *The Dunciad*, bk.1, l.139–40.

35 A brain of feathers, and a heart of lead.
1742 *The Dunciad*, bk.2, l.44.

36 How little, mark! that portion of the ball,
Where, faint at best, the beams of science fall.
1742 *The Dunciad*, bk.3, l.83–4.

37 None need a guide, by sure attraction led,
And strong impulsive gravity of head.
1742 *The Dunciad*, bk.4, l.75–6.

38 A wit with dunces, and a dunce with wits.
  1742 The Dunciad, bk.4, l.90.

39 Leave not a foot of verse, a foot of stone,
  A Page, a Grave, that they can call their own;
  But spread, my sons, your glory thin or thick,
  On passive paper, or on solid brick.
  1742 The Dunciad, bk.4, l.127–30.

40 Whate'er the talents, or howe'er designed,
  We hang one jingling padlock on the mind.
  1742 The Dunciad, bk.4, l.161–2.

41 The Right Divine of Kings to govern wrong.
  1742 The Dunciad, bk.4, l.187.

42 How parts relate to parts, or they to whole,
  The body's harmony, the beaming soul.
  1742 The Dunciad, bk.4, l.235–6.

43 Isles of fragrance, lily-silver'd values.
  1742 The Dunciad, bk.4, l.303.

44 Love-whispering woods, and lute-resounding waves.
  1742 The Dunciad, bk.4, l.306.

45 —She marked thee there,
  Stretched on the rack of a too easy chair,
  And heard thy everlasting yawn confess
  The pains and penalties of idleness.
  1742 The Dunciad, bk.4, l.341–4.

46 O! would the Sons of Men once think their Eyes
  And Reason giv'n them but to study Flies?
  See Nature in some partial narrow shape,
  And let the Author of the Whole escape.
  1742 The Dunciad, bk.4, l.453–6.

47 Religion blushing veils her sacred fires,
  And unawares Morality expires.
  1742 The Dunciad, bk.4, l.649–50.

48 Lo! thy dread empire, Chaos! is restored;
  Light dies before thy uncreating word:
  Thy hand, great Anarch! lets the curtain fall;
  And universal darkness buries all.
  1742 The Dunciad, bk.4, l.653–6.

49 I am his Highness' dog at Kew;
  Pray, tell me sir, whose dog are you?
  'Epigram Engraved on the Collar of a Dog which I gave to His Royal Highness'.

50 Here am I, dying of a hundred good symptoms.
  1744 His response to reassurance from his doctors that his health was showing signs of improvement. Quoted in Joseph Spence *Anecdotes by and about Alexander Pope* (1820).

Popova, Lyubov Sergeyevna 1889–1924
Russian painter and theatre and textile designer.

51 Texture is the content of painterly surfaces.
  Quoted in W Chadwick *Women, Art and Society* (1990).

Popper, Sir Karl Raimund 1902–94
Anglo-Austrian philosopher, professor (1949–69) at the London School of Economics. He expounded his political theory in *The Open Society and Its Enemies* (1945), and his philosophy of science in *The Logic of Scientific Discovery* (1934).

52 It must be possible for an empirical system to be refuted by experience.
  1934 The Logic of Scientific Discovery.

53 Every scientific statement must remain *tentative for ever*.
  1934 The Logic of Scientific Discovery.

54 In order that a new theory should constitute a discovery or step forward it should conflict with its predecessor ...it should contradict its predecessor; it should overthrow it. In this sense, progress in science—or at least striking progress—is always revolutionary.
  1934 The Logic of Scientific Discovery.

55 It is not his possession of knowledge, of irrefutable truth, that makes the man of science, but his persistent and recklessly critical quest for truth.
  1934 The Logic of Scientific Discovery.

56 We may become the makers of our fate when we have ceased to pose as its prophets.
  1945 The Open Society and Its Enemies, introduction.

57 There is no history of mankind, there are only many histories of all kinds of aspects of human life. And one of these is the history of political power. This is elevated into the history of the world.
  1945 The Open Society and Its Enemies, vol.2, ch.25.

58 The belief that we can start with pure observations alone, without anything in the nature of a theory, is absurd.
  1953 Conjectures and Refutations (published 1963), ch.1.

59 Observation is always selective. It needs a chosen object, a definite task, an interest, a point of view, a problem.
  1953 Conjectures and Refutations (published 1963), ch.1.

60 There is at least one philosophical problem in which all thinking men are interested. It is the problem of cosmology: *the problem of understanding the world—including ourselves, and our knowledge, as part of the world*. All science is cosmology, I believe, and for me the interest of philosophy, no less than that of science, lies solely in the contributions which it has made to it.
  1959 The Logic of Scientific Discovery (1934), preface to 1959 edition.

61 In so far as a scientific statement speaks about reality, it must be falsifiable: and in so far as it is not falsifiable, it does not speak about reality.
  1959 The Logic of Scientific Discovery (1934), appendix to 1959 edition.

62 What we should do, I suggest, is to give up the idea of ultimate sources of knowledge, and admit that all knowledge is human; that it is mixed with our errors, our prejudices, our dreams, and our hopes; that all we can do is to grope for truth even though it be beyond our reach.
  1960 Conjectures and Refutations (published 1963), introduction.

63 The history of science, like the history of all human ideas, is a history of irresponsible dreams, of obstinacy, and of error. But science is one of the very few human activities—perhaps the only one—in which errors are systematically criticized and fairly often, in time, corrected. This is why we can say that, in science, we often learn from our mistakes, and why we can speak clearly and sensibly about making progress there.
  1960 Conjectures and Refutations (published 1963), ch.10.

64 Science starts only with problems.
  1960 Conjectures and Refutations (published 1963), ch.10.

65 For this, indeed, is the true source of our ignorance—the fact that our knowledge can only be finite, while our ignorance must necessarily be infinite.
1960 Lecture to the British Academy, 20 Jan.

66 Science may be described as the art of systematic oversimplification.
1982 Quoted in the *Observer*, 1 Aug.

Porter, Cole 1891–1964

US composer. He studied law at Harvard before turning to music, composing and writing lyrics for a string of successful stage and screen musicals including *Kiss Me Kate* (1948, filmed 1953), *High Society* (1956) and *Can-Can* (1953, filmed 1960).

67 I get no kick from champagne;
Mere alcohol doesn't thrill me at all.
So tell me why should it be true
That I get a kick out of you?
1934 'I Get a Kick Out of You', from the show *Anything Goes*.

68 In olden days a glimpse of stocking
Was looked on as something shocking.
But now, God knows,
Anything goes.
1934 'Anything Goes', from the show *Anything Goes*.

69 I'm a worthless check, a total wreck, a flop
But if baby I'm the bottom, you're the top.
1936 'You're the Top', from the show *Anything Goes*.

70 You're the top
You're the Louvr' Museum
You're a melody from a symphony by Strauss.
1936 'You're the Top', from the show *Anything Goes*.

71 My sole inspiration is a telephone call from a director.
1955 Interview, 8 Feb.

72 Who wants to be a millionaire?
And go to ev'ry swell affair?
1956 'Who Wants to Be a Millionaire', from the show *High Society*.

Porter, Katherine Anne 1890–1980

US novelist and short-story writer. Her works include the novella *Pale Horse, Pale Rider* (1939) and the long allegorical novel *The Ship of Fools* (1962).

73 Most people won't realize that writing is a craft. You have to take your apprenticeship in it like anything else.
1962 In the *Saturday Review*, 31 Mar.

74 The real sin against life is to abuse and destroy beauty, even one's own—even more, one's own, for that has been put in our care and we are responsible for its well-being.
1962 *Ship of Fools*, pt.3.

75 The pimple on the face of American literature.
On Truman Capote. Quoted in Gerald Clarke *Capote* (1988).

76 Oh, poor Pearl Buck! She has no more bounce than a boiled potato.
Quoted from the journals of Glenway Westcott, in Robert Phelps and Jerry Rosco (eds) *Continuous Lessons* (1990).

Porteus, Beilby 1731–1808

English prelate and poet.

77 One murder made a villain
Millions a hero.
1759 'Death'.

78 War its thousands slays, Peace its ten thousands.
1759 'Death'.

79 Teach him how to live,
And, oh! still harder lesson! how to die.
1759 'Death'.

Portillo, Michael 1953–

English Conservative politician. He lost his seat in the 1997 general election. Victory in a 1999 by-election led to his return to the Commons, until his resignation in 2005.

80 A truly terrible night for the Conservatives.
1997 After losing Enfield South to Labour in the general election, 2 May. Quoted in Brian Cathcart *Were You Still Up for Portillo?*.

Pott, Frances 1832–1909

English cleric and translator.

81 The strife is o'er, the battle done;
Now is the Victor's triumph won;
O let the song of praise be sung;
Alleluia!
1861 Hymn, translated from the original Latin 'Finita iam sunt praelia'.

Potter, Beatrix 1866–1943

English author and illustrator of books for children, whose characters have become classics of children's literature.

82 Don't go into Mr McGregor's garden: your father had an accident there, he was put into a pie by Mr McGregor.
1902 *The Tale of Peter Rabbit*.

83 In the time of swords and periwigs and full-skirted coats with flowered lappets—when gentlemen wore ruffles, and gold-laced waistcoats of paduasoy and taffeta—there lived a tailor in Gloucester.
1903 *The Tailor of Gloucester*.

Potter, Henry Codman 1835–1908

US religious leader. For 15 years he was rector of Grace Church, New York City. He was elected Bishop Co-Adjutor of New York in 1883 and Bishop in 1887. He was known for his diplomacy and was outspoken on corruption.

84 If there be no nobility of descent in a nation, it is all the more indispensable that there should be nobility of ascent; a character in them that bear rule, so fine and high and pure, that as men come within the circle of its influence, they involuntarily pay homage to that which is the one pre-eminent distinction—the royalty of virtue.
1889 Washington centennial address, 30 Apr.

Potter, Stephen 1900–69

English humorous writer.

85 How to be one up—how to make the other man feel that something has gone wrong, however slightly.
1950 *Lifemanship*.

86 Each of us can, by ploy or gambit, most naturally gain the advantage.
1950 *Lifemanship*.

Pound, Ezra Loomis 1885–1972

US poet, a key figure in the Modernist movement, whose chief work was the massive poetic cycle *The Cantos* (collected 1970).

He spent much of his life in Italy, and was committed to an asylum for a time after World War II, during which he espoused Fascist sympathies.

87 Bah! I have sung women in three cities,
But it is all the same;
And I will sing of the sun.
1908 *Personae,* 'Cino'.

88 No good poetry is written in a manner twenty years old, for to write in such a manner shows conclusively that the writer thinks from books, convention and cliché; and not from life.
1912 'Prolegomena', in *The Poetry Review,* Feb.

89 All great art is born of the metropolis.
1913 Letter to Harriet Monroe, 7 Nov.

90 Poetry must be *as well written as prose.*
1915 Letter to Harriet Monroe, Jan.

91 Winter is icummen in,
Lhude sing Goddamm,
Raineth drop and staineth slop,
And how the wind doth ramm!
Sing: Goddamm.
1916 *Lustra,* 'Ancient Music'.
▶ See Anonymous 21:43.

92 The apparition of these faces in the crowd;
Petals on a wet, black bough.
1916 *Lustra,* 'In a Station of the Metro'.

93 She is dying piece-meal
of a sort of emotional anaemia.
And round about there is a rabble
of the filthy, sturdy, unkillable infants
of the very poor.
1916 *Lustra,* 'The Garden'.

94 I make a pact with you, Walt Whitman—
I have detested you long enough.
I come to you as a grown child
Who has had a pig-headed father
I am old enough not to make friends.
1916 *Lustra,* 'A Pact'.

95 Poetry must be read as music and not as oratory.
1917 'Vers Libre and Arnold Dolmetsch', in *The Egoist,* Jul.

96 A chryselephantine poem of immeasurable length which will occupy me for the next four decades unless it becomes a bore.
1917 On beginning the poetic series *The Cantos,* which remained unfinished on his death.

97 A man of genius has a right to any mode of expression.
1918 Letter to J B Yeats, 4 Feb.

98 Of all those young women
Not one has enquired the cause of the world
Nor the modus of lunar eclipses
Nor whether there be any patch left of us
After we cross the infernal ripples.
1919 *Quia Pauper Amavi,* 'Homage to Sextus Propertius'.

99 For three years, out of key with his time,
He strove to resuscitate the dead art
Of poetry; to maintain 'the sublime'
In the old sense. Wrong from the start—

No, hardly, but seeing he had been born
In a half savage country, out of date.
1920 *Hugh Selwyn Mauberley,* pt.1.

1 His true Penelope was Flaubert,
He fished by obstinate isles;
Observed the elegance of Circe's hair
Rather than the mottoes on sundials.
1920 *Hugh Selwyn Mauberley,* pt.1.

2 Better mendacities
Than the classics in paraphrase!
1920 *Hugh Selwyn Mauberley,* pt.2.

3 Christ follows Dionysus
Phallic and ambrosial
Made way for macerations;
Caliban casts out Ariel.
1920 *Hugh Selwyn Mauberley,* pt.3.

4 Died some, *pro patria,*
non 'dulce' non 'et decor'...
walked eye-deep in hell
believing in old men's lies, then unbelieving
came home, home to a lie,
home to many deceits
home to old lies and new infamy;
usury age-old and age-thick
and liars in public places.
1920 *Hugh Selwyn Mauberley,* pt.4.

5 There died a myriad,
And of the best, among them,
For an old bitch gone in the teeth,
For a botched civilization.
1920 *Hugh Selwyn Mauberley,* pt.5.

6 And no one knows, at first sight, a masterpiece.
And give up verse, my boy.
There's nothing in it.
1920 *Hugh Selwyn Mauberley,* 'MR NIXON'.

7 I never mentioned a man but with the view
Of selling my own works.
The tip's a good one, as for literature
It gives no man a sinecure.
1920 *Hugh Selwyn Mauberley,* 'MR NIXON'.

8 The haven from sophistications and contentions
Leaks through its thatch;
He offers succulent cooking;
The door has a creaking latch.
1920 *Hugh Selwyn Mauberley,* pt.10.

9 The curse of me and my nation is that we always think things can be bettered by immediate action of some sort, *any* sort rather than no sort.
1920 Letter to James Joyce, 7–8 Jun.

10 And then went down to the ship,
Set keel to breakers, forth on the godly sea.
1925 *Draft of XVI Cantos,* no.1.

11 And even I can remember
A day when the historians left blanks in their writings,
I mean for things they didn't know.
1930 *Draft of XXX Cantos,* no.13.

12 Great literature is simply language charged with meaning to the utmost possible degree.
1931 *How To Read,* pt.2.

13 Any general statement is like a cheque drawn on a bank. Its value depends on what is there to meet it.
1934 *The ABC of Reading,* ch.1.

14 One of the pleasures of middle age is to *find out* that one WAS right, and that one was much righter than one knew at say 17 or 23.
1934 *The ABC of Reading*, ch.1.

15 Literature is news that STAYS news.
1934 *The ABC of Reading*, ch.2.

16 Real education must ultimately be limited to one who INSISTS on knowing, the rest is mere sheep-herding.
1934 *The ABC of Reading*, ch.8.

17 The author's conviction on this day of New Year is that music begins to atrophy when it departs too far from the dance; that poetry begins to atrophy when it gets too far from music . . .
1934 *The ABC of Reading*, 'Warning'.

18 To the beat of the measure
From star-up to the half-dark
From half-dark to half-dark
Unceasing the measure.
1934 *Eleven New Cantos*, no.34.

19 People find ideas a bore because they do not distinguish between live ones and stuffed ones on a shelf.
1938 *Guide to Kulcher*, pt.1, section 1, ch.5.

20 Man is an over-complicated organism. If he is doomed to extinction he will die out for want of simplicity.
1938 *Guide to Kulcher*, pt.3, section 5, ch.19.

21 Civilization itself is a certain sane balance of values.
1938 *Guide to Kulcher*, pt.3, section 5, ch.20.

22 Adolf Hitler was a Jeanne d'Arc, a saint. He was a martyr. Like many martyrs, he held extreme views.
1945 In the *Philadelphia Record* and *Chicago Sun*, 9 May.

23 What thou lovest well remains,
The rest is dross
What thou lov'st well shall not be reft from thee
What thou lov'st well is thy true heritage.
1948 *The Pisan Cantos*, no.81.

24 The ant's a centaur in his dragon world.
Pull down thy vanity, it is not man
Made courage, or made order, or made grace.
1948 *The Pisan Cantos*, no.81.

25 Learn of the green world what can be thy place
In scaled invention or true artistry,
Pull down thy vanity,
Paquin pull down!
The green casque has outdone your elegance.
1948 *The Pisan Cantos*, no.81.

26 Thou art a beaten dog beneath the hail,
A swollen magpie in a fitful sun,
Half black half white
Nor knowst'ou wing from tail
Pull down thy vanity.
1948 *The Pisan Cantos*, no.81.

27 Tching prayed on the mountain and wrote
  MAKE IT NEW
on his bath tub.
Day by day make it new
cut underbrush,
pile the logs
keep it growing.
1954 *The Cantos*, no.53.

28 Artists are the antennae of the race, but the bullet-headed many will never learn to trust their great artists.
1954 *Literary Essays*, 'Henry James'.

29 How did it go in the madhouse? Rather badly. But what other place could one live in America?
1958 On his release after 13 years in St Elizabeth's Hospital, Washington DC. Recalled on his death, 1 Nov 1972.

30 The worst mistake I made was that stupid, suburban prejudice of anti-Semitism.
1968 Remark to Allen Ginsberg, 7 Jun. Quoted in H Carpenter *A Serious Character* (1988), pt.5.

31 Art very possibly *ought* to be the supreme achievement, the 'accomplished', but there is the other satisfactory effect—that of a man hurling himself at an indomitable chaos and yanking and hauling as much of it as possible into some sort of order (or beauty) aware of it both as chaos and as potential.
Quoted in H Kenner (ed) *The Pound Era* (1973).

32 A dirty book worth reading.
Of Henry Miller *Tropic of Cancer* (1934). Recalled on Miller's death, 7 Jun 1980.

33 All America is an insane asylum.
Quoted in Patricia C Willis (ed) *The Complete Poems of Marianne Moore* (1986).

34 Some poems have form as a tree has form and some as water poured into a vase.
Quoted in Patricia C Willis (ed) *The Complete Poems of Marianne Moore* (1986).

35 The great writer is always the plodder.
Quoted in Patricia C Willis (ed) *The Complete Poems of Marianne Moore* (1986).

36 The true poet is most easily distinguished from the false when he trusts himself to the simplest expression and writes without adjectives.
Quoted in Patricia C Willis (ed) *The Complete Poems of Marianne Moore* (1986).

37 Use no word that under stress of emotion you could not actually say.
Quoted in Patricia C Willis (ed) *The Complete Poems of Marianne Moore* (1986).

38 Great poets seldom make bricks without straw. They pile up all the excellences they can beg, borrow, or steal from their predecessors and contemporaries and then set their own inimitable light atop the mountain.
Quoted in Patricia C Willis (ed) *The Complete Poems of Marianne Moore* (1986).

Pound, (Nathan) Roscoe 1870–1964

US jurist, Professor of Law at Harvard University.

39 Wealth, in a commercial age, is made up largely of promises.
1922 *An Introduction to the Philosophy of Law*, ch.6.

Poussin, Nicolas 1594–1665

French painter who spent most of his working life in Rome. The Classical tradition in French painting developed from his work.

40 The grand manner consists of four elements: subject or theme, concept, structure, and style. The first requirement, fundamental to all the others, is that the subject and the narrative be grandiose, such as battles, heroic actions, and religious themes.

Quoted in Giovanni Pietro Bellori *Lives of the Modern Painters* (1672).

Powell, Anthony Dymoke 1905–2000

English novelist. His major work is the sequence of twelve novels chronicling 20c English upper-middle-class life, collectively known as *A Dance to the Music of Time* (1951–75).

41 All the same, you know parents—especially stepparents—are sometimes a disappointment to their children. They don't fulfil the promise of their early years.
1952 A Buyer's Market, ch.2.

42 There is a strong disposition in youth, from which some individuals never escape, to suppose that everyone else is having a more enjoyable time than we are ourselves.
1952 A Buyer's Market, ch.4.

43 He fell in love with himself at first sight and it is a passion to which he has always remained faithful. Self-love seems so often unrequited.
1955 The Acceptance World, ch.1.

44 Dinner at the Huntercombes possessed 'only two dramatic features—the wine was a farce and the food a tragedy.'
1955 The Acceptance World, ch.4.

45 All men are brothers, but, thank God, they aren't all brothers-in-law.
1957 At Lady Molly's, ch.4.

46 Books Do Furnish a Room.
1971 Title of novel.

47 Growing old is like being increasingly penalised for a crime you haven't committed.
1973 Temporary Kings, ch.1.

48 People think that because a novel's invented, it isn't true. Exactly the reverse is the case.
1975 Hearing Secret Harmonies, ch.3.

49 One of the worst things about life is not how nasty the nasty people are. You know that already. It is how nasty the nice people can be.
1975 Hearing Secret Harmonies, ch.7.

50 In this country it is rare for anyone, let alone a publisher, to take writers seriously.
1979 In the Daily Telegraph, 8 Feb.

51 If you don't spend every morning of your life writing, it's awfully difficult to know what to do otherwise.
1984 In the Observer, 3 Apr.

Powell, Colin Luther 1937–

US army general. He fought in Vietnam, and became National Security Adviser to President Reagan (1987–9). He was appointed chairman of the Joint Chiefs of Staff (1989–93), and controlled US strategy during the Gulf War. He went on to serve as Secretary of State under President George W Bush (2001–5).

52 We have decapitated him from the dictatorship.
1988 On evicting from office Panama's General Manuel Noriega. Quoted in the Washington Post, 21 Dec.

53 The American people do not want their young dying for $1.50 a gallon oil.
1990 Urging caution against interfering with Iraq's invasion of oil-rich Kuwait in a White House meeting 2 Aug. Quoted in the New York Times, 23 Oct 1994.

54 First we're going to cut it off, and then we're going to kill it.
1991 On the opposition to Operation Desert Storm. In the US News and World Report, 4 Feb.

55 I remember the front door. I remember the auditorium. I remember the feeling that you can't make it. But you can.
1991 On revisiting the South Bronx high school from which he graduated in 1954. In the New York Times, 16 Apr.

56 I sleep like a baby too—every two hours I wake up screaming.
2003 On being reminded that George W Bush claims to sleep like a baby. In the New Yorker, 10 Feb.

Powell, (John) Enoch 1912–98

English Conservative and Ulster Unionist politician. Professor of Greek at Sydney University (1937–9), he was elected MP in 1950. Minister of Health (1960–3), he was dismissed from the shadow Cabinet in 1968 for his attitude to immigration. He was returned as an Ulster Unionist in 1974, but lost his seat in 1987. His books include *A Nation Not Afraid* (1965).

57 History is littered with the wars which everybody knew would never happen.
1967 Speech to Conservative Party conference, 19 Oct.

58 As I look ahead, I am filled with much foreboding. Like the Roman, I seem to see 'the River Tiber foaming with much blood'.
1968 Speech at Birmingham on racial tension in Britain, Apr.

59 I was born a Tory, am a Tory, and shall die a Tory. I never yet heard that it was any part of the faith of a Tory to take the institutions and liberties, the laws and customs that his country has evolved over the centuries, and merge them with those of eight other nations into a new-made artificial state—and what is more, to do so without the willing approbation and consent of the nation.
1974 Speech against Britain's entry into the Common Market, Shipley, 25 Feb.

60 All political lives, unless they are cut off in mid-stream at a happy juncture, end in failure, because that is the nature of politics and of human affairs.
1977 Joseph Chamberlain.

Powell, Michael 1905–90

English film-maker. He made various 'quota quickies' in the 1930s and then began a partnership with Emeric Pressburger. Known as 'the Archers', they collaborated on such films as *The Life and Death of Colonel Blimp* (1943), *Black Narcissus* (1947) and *The Red Shoes* (1948).

61 What do they know of England, who only the West End know?
1950 Attributed comment in defence of Gone to Earth.
▸ See Kipling 490:94.

Powys, John Cowper 1872–1963

English novelist and essayist.

62 It is that cricket field that, in all the sharp and bitter moments of life as they come to me now, gives me a sense of wholesome proportion: 'At least I am not playing cricket!'
Quoted in Helen Exley *Cricket Quotations* (1992).

Pratchett, Sir Terry (Terence David John) 1948–2015

English novelist. His best-known novels include the *Discworld* fantasy series, although he also wrote science fiction and children's books.

63 The trouble with having an open mind, of course, is that people will insist on coming along and trying to put things in it.
1990 Diggers.

64 Light thinks it travels faster than anything but it is wrong. No matter how fast light travels, it finds the darkness has always got there first, and is waiting for it.
1991 Reaper Man.

65 Some humans would do anything to see if it was possible to do it. If you put a large switch in some cave somewhere, with a sign on it saying 'End-of-the-World Switch. PLEASE DO NOT TOUCH', the paint wouldn't even have time to dry.
2001 Thief of Time.

Prather, Hugh 1938–2010

US minister, counsellor and writer.

66 If the ocean was pure mind and I was a wave, I would be in terror if I tried to distinguish myself from the water that produced me. What is a wave without water, and what is a mind without God?
1982 The Quiet Answer.

67 Forgive and be happy. That is the ancient secret…the only wisdom ever to be attained.
1982 The Quiet Answer.

Pratt, Edwin John 1882–1964

Canadian poet. Born in Newfoundland, he obtained a PhD in divinity from the University of Toronto and became Professor of English there in 1919. He is best known for his documentary poetry, including *The Titanic* (1935), *Brébeuf and His Brethren* (1940) and *Towards the Last Spike* (1952).

68 It was the same world then as now—the same,
Except for little differences of speed
And power, and means to treat myopia
To show an axe-blade infinitely sharp
Splitting things infinitely small.
1952 Towards the Last Spike. The poet is speaking of the building of the Canadian National Railway, from coast to coast.

Prescott (of Kingston upon Hull), John Leslie, Baron 1938–

English Labour politician, Deputy Prime Minister (1997–2007).

69 People like me were branded, pigeon-holed, a ceiling put on our ambitions.
1996 Speech at Oxford, 13 Jun. Quoted in The Guardian, 14 Jun.

70 Tony will go on and on and on.
2004 On Prime Minister Tony Blair. On BBC Radio 4's Today programme.

Presley, Elvis Aaron 1935–77

US singer and actor.

71 You ain't nothin' but a hound dog
cryin' all the time.
You ain't nothin' but a hound dog
cryin' all the time.
Well, you ain't never caught a rabbit
and you ain't no friend of mine.
1956 'Hound Dog' (written by Jerry Leiber and Mike Stoller).

72 Well since my baby left me
I found a new place to dwell
It's down at the end of lonely street
At Heartbreak Hotel.
1956 'Heartbreak Hotel' (with Mae Boren Axton and Tommy Durden).

73 I learned very early in life that: 'Without a song, the day would never end; without a song, a man ain't got no friend; without a song the road would never bend—without a song'. So I keep on singing. Goodnight. Thank you.
1971 Acceptance speech, Ten Outstanding Men of the Year Awards, 16 Jan.

74 I don't know anything about music—in my line you don't have to.
Quoted in David Pickering Brewer's Twentieth Century Music (1994).

Preston, James E 1933–

US businessman. He joined Avon Products in 1964 as a management trainee, becoming Chief Executive Officer (1988–98) and Chairman (1989–98).

75 A bad reputation is like a hangover. It takes a while to get rid of, and it makes everything else hurt.
1992 In Fortune, 10 Feb.

Previn, André (George) 1929–

German-born US conductor and composer. A US citizen from 1943, he conducted major orchestras around the world from 1967. His own compositions include musicals, film scores and orchestral works.

76 The basic difference between classical music and jazz is that in the former music is always greater than its performance—whereas the way jazz is performed is always more important than what is being played.
1967 Quoted in The Times.

Prévost, Abbé Antoine-François 1697–1763

French novelist, educated in the Jesuit tradition. He enlisted in the army before eventually deciding on a religious life after an unhappy love affair.

77 *Il ne reste donc que l'exemple qui puisse servir de règle à quantité de personnes dans l'exercice de la vertu.*
Most people can learn only by example to be virtuous.
1731 Histoire du chevalier Des Grieux et de Manon Lescaut, Avis de l'auteur.

78 *Crois-tu qu'on puisse être bien tendre lorsqu'on manque de pain?*
Do you believe that a person can be truly affectionate when he is starving?
1731 Histoire du chevalier Des Grieux et de Manon Lescaut, ch.1.

79 *Il faut compter ses richesses par les moyens qu'on a de satisfaire ses désirs.*
We must count our riches by the means we have to satisfy our desires.
1731 Histoire du chevalier Des Grieux et de Manon Lescaut, ch.2.

Prial, Frank J 1930–2012

US writer and wine columnist for the *New York Times*.

80 Macaulay, Gibbon, Tolstoy, Francis Parkman and other immortals...never said anything in two pages that might possibly sound better in 10.
Quoted in the *New York Times*, 31 Mar 1990.

Price, Raymond 1930–

Nixon White House speechwriter.

81 The response is to the image, not to the man, since 99 percent of the voters have no contact with the man.
1967 Memo, 28 Nov. Quoted in the *New York Times*, 31 Oct 1993.

82 It's not what's *there* that counts, it's what's projected —and...it's not what *he* projects but rather what the voter receives... It's not the man we have to change, but rather the *received* impression.
1967 Memo, 28 Nov. Quoted in the *New York Times*, 31 Oct 1993.

Prichard, Katharine Susannah married name Throssell 1883–1969

Australian journalist, novelist and political activist. Western Australia is the background for her later novels including *Coonardoo* (1929).

83 Coonardoo they called it, the dark well, or the well in the shadows.
1929 *Coonardoo*, ch.1.

Priestley, J(ohn) B(oynton) 1894–1984

English writer, whose works include the novel *The Good Companions* (1929) and plays such as *Dangerous Corner* (1932). He achieved national renown as deliverer of radio 'postscripts' during World War II.

84 To say that these men paid their shillings to watch twenty-two hirelings kick a ball is merely to say that a violin is wood and catgut, that *Hamlet* is so much paper and ink. For a shilling the Bruddersford United AFC offered you Conflict and Art.
1929 *The Good Companions*, bk.1, ch.1.

85 The earth is nobler than the world we have put upon it.
1939 *Johnson Over Jordan*, act 3.

86 This little steamer, like all her brave and battered sisters, is immortal. She'll go sailing proudly down the years in the epic of Dunkirk. And our great-great-grand-children, when they learn how we began this war by snatching glory out of defeat, and then swept on to victory, may also learn how the little holiday steamers made an excursion to hell and came back glorious.
1940 Radio broadcast, 5 Jun, quoted in *The Listener*, 13 Jun.

87 An Inspector Calls.
1947 Title of play.

88 The trouble is that we drink too much tea. I see in this the slow revenge of the Orient, which has diverted the Yellow River down our throats.
1949 In the *Observer*, 15 May.

89 Sometimes you might think that the machines we worship make all the chief appointments, promoting the human beings who seem closest to them.
1957 *Thoughts in the Wilderness*.

90 *Finnegans Wake* took him seventeen years to write, a length of time that suggests an elaborate hobby rather than a passionate desire to create something.
1960 Of James Joyce. *Literature and Western Man*.

91 He was a black Irish type, with centuries of rebelliousness behind him, and I decided to chance it.
1961 *Saturn Over the Water*.

92 I can't help feeling wary when I hear anything said about the masses. First you take their faces from 'em by calling 'em the masses and then you accuse 'em of not having any faces.
1961 *Saturn Over the Water*, ch.2.

93 It is hard to tell where the MCC ends and the Church of England begins.
1962 In the *New Statesman*, 20 Jul.

94 Some time ago, in an interview that turned towards the Theatre, I suggested that 'Pubic hair is not an adequate substitute for wit'. My point now is that depending upon shock tactics is easy, whereas writing a good play is difficult.
1974 *Outcries and Asides*, 'Danger of Shock Tactics'.

95 England is not ruined because sinewy brown men from a distant colony sometimes hit a ball further and oftener than our men do.
Quoted in Colin Jarman *The Guinness Dictionary of Sports Quotations* (1990).

Prince in full Prince Roger Nelson 1958–

US pop singer and composer. His works include the album *1999* (1982), and the film and album *Purple Rain* (1984).

96 Maybe at one time they could get Little Richard for a new car and a bucket of chicken. We don't roll like that no more.
2004 In *Rolling Stone*, 27 May.

97 The Internet's completely over. I don't see why I should give my new music to iTunes or anyone else... All these computers and digital gadgets are no good. They just fill your head with numbers and that can't be good for you.
2010 Explaining why he planned to distribute his new album free in British newspapers, in *The Daily Mirror*, 5 Jul.

Prior, Matthew 1664–1721

English poet and diplomat. His verse includes *The Hind and the Panther Transvers'd to the Story of the Country Mouse and the City Mouse* (with Charles Montagu, 1687, a satire on Dryden). He is remembered for his many witty, epigrammatic occasional verses.

98 They never taste who always drink;
They always talk who never think.
1697 'Upon this Passage in Scaligerana'.

99 Nobles and heralds, by your leave,
Here lies what once was Matthew Prior,
The son of Adam and of Eve,
Can Stuart or Nassaw go higher?
1702 'Epitaph'. In a later version 'Stuart' was changed to 'Bourbon'.

1 Be to her virtues very kind;
Be to her faults a little blind;
Let all her ways be unconfined;
And clap your padlock—on her mind.
1705 'An English Padlock'.

2 And of the pangs of absence to remove
By letters, soft interpreters of love.
1708 'Henry and Emma'.

3 But of good household features her person was made,
Nor by faction cry'd up nor of censure afraid,
And her beauty was rather for use than parade.
1708 'Jinny the Just' (first printed 1907). The title was given by A R Waller.

4 Cured yesterday of my disease,
I died last night of my physician.
1714 'The Remedy Worse than the Disease'.

5 Venus, take my votive glass;
Since I am not what I was,
What from this day I shall be
Venus never let me see.
1718 'The Lady Who Offered Her Looking-Glass to Venus'.

6 No, no; for my virginity,
When I lose that, says Rose, I'll die:
Behind the elms last night, cried Dick,
Rose, were you not extremely sick?
1718 'A True Maid'.

7 They walked and eat, good folks: What then?
Why then they walked and eat again:
They soundly slept the night away:
They did just nothing all the day.
1718 'An Epitaph', l.9–12.

8 Their beer was strong; their wine was port;
Their meal was large; their grace was short.
They gave the poor the remnant meat,
Just when it grew not fit to eat.
1718 'An Epitaph', l.29–32.

9 On his death bed poor Lubin lies:
His spouse is in despair.
With frequent sobs and mutual cries
They both express their care.

A different cause, says parson Sly,
The same effect may give:
Poor Lubin fears, that he shall die:
His wife, that he may live.
1718 'A Reasonable Affliction'.

10 What I speak, my fair Chloe, and what I write shows
The difference there is betwixt Nature and Art:
I court others in verse: but I love thee in prose:
And they have my whimsies, but thou hast my heart.
1718 'A Better Answer', stanza 4.

11 So when I am wearied with wandering all day;
To thee my delight in the evening I come:
No matter what beauties I saw in my way:
They were but my visits; but thou art my home.
1718 'A Better Answer', stanza 6.

12 And 'twould be a cruel thing,
When her black eyes have raised desire,
Should she not her bucket bring
And kindly help to quench the fire.
'Chloe Beauty Has and Wit'. (Date unknown. In *Matthew Prior: Literary Works*, edited by H B Wright and M K Spears, 2 vols, 1959.)

13 Rise not till noon, if life be but a dream,
As Greek and Roman poets have exprest:
Add good example to so grave a theme,
For he who sleeps the longest lives the best.
'Epigram'. (Date unknown. In *Matthew Prior: Literary Works*, edited by H B Wright and M K Spears, 2 vols, 1959.)

Pritchett, Sir V(ictor) S(awdon) 1900–97

English writer. He wrote novels and works of literary criticism and biography, but is best known for his short stories.

14 The principle of procrastinated rape is said to be the ruling one in all of the great best-sellers.
1946 *The Living Novel*, 'Clarissa'.

15 A touch of science, even bogus science, gives an edge to the superstitious tale.
1946 *The Living Novel*, 'An Irish Ghost'.

16 The detective novel is...the classic example of a specialized form of art removed from contact with the life it pretends to build on.
1951 In the *New Statesman*, 16 Jun.

17 He watched his restless hands, surprised they had remembered to come with him.
1951 *Mr Beluncle*, ch.15.

18 If evil does not exist, what is going to happen to literature?
1951 *Mr Beluncle*, ch.23.

19 Dickens was not the first or the last novelist to find virtue more difficult to portray than the wish for it.
1953 'Oliver Twist', collected in *Books in General* (1981).

20 It is well known that, when two or three authors meet, they at once start talking about money—like everyone else.
1978 In *The Author*, Spring.

21 What Chekhov saw in our failure to communicate was something positive and precious: the private silence in which we live, and which enables us to endure our own solitude.
1979 *The Myth Makers*, 'Chekhov'.

22 It is the role of the poet to look at what is happening in the world and to know that quite other things are happening.
1979 *The Myth Makers*, 'Pasternak'.

23 The poet is a master of the quotidian, of conveying a whole history in two or three lines that point to an exact past drama and intensify a future one.
1979 *The Myth Makers*, 'Borges'.

24 A short story is always a disclosure.
1981 *The Oxford Book of Short Stories* (edited by Pritchett), introduction.

25 'The firm'—a proud Victorian word. It evokes the lost sense of Victorian regard for the pride of people in their daily trade.
'Betjeman', in the *New Yorker*, 24 Jun.

Private Eye

British satirical magazine, founded 1962.

26 Kill An Argie—Win A Metro!
1982 Front page headline during the Falklands War, parodying the jingoism of tabloid coverage of the conflict.

Proctor, Adelaide Ann *pseudonym of* Mary Berwick 1825–64

English poet. She won renown with her *Legends and Lyrics* (1858–60), and her poem 'The Lost Chord' was set to music by Sir Arthur Sullivan.

27 Seated one day at the organ,
   I was weary and ill at ease,
   And my fingers wandered idly
   Over the noisy keys;
   I know not what I was playing,
   Or what I was dreaming then,
   But I struck one chord of music,
   Like the sound of a great Amen.
   1858 'The Lost Chord'.

Profumo, John Dennis 1915–2006

English Conservative politician, Secretary of State for War in 1960. He resigned in 1963 during the 'Profumo Affair', admitting that he had deceived the House over the nature of his relationship with Christine Keeler, who was at the time also involved with a Russian diplomat. He turned to charitable service, and was awarded the CBE in 1975.

28 There was no impropriety whatsoever in my acquaintanceship with Miss Keeler… I shall not hesitate to issue writs for libel and slander if scandalous allegations are made or repeated outside the House.
   1963 House of Commons, Mar.

Prokofiev, Sergei Sergeyevich 1891–1953

Russian composer, who lived in exile in the West (1918–36). His works include the *Classical Symphony* (1917), the opera *The Love for Three Oranges* (1919), the ballets *The Prodigal Son* (1928) and *Romeo and Juliet* (1936), *Peter and the Wolf* (1936) and the opera *War and Peace* (1943).

29 Bach on the wrong notes.
   Of the music of Stravinsky. Quoted in V Seroff *Sergei Prokofiev* (1968).

Propertius, Sextus 1c BC

Roman poet.

30 *Navita de ventis, de tauris narrat arator,*
   Enumerat miles vulnera, pastor oves.
   The sailor tells stories of the winds, the ploughman of bulls; the soldier lists his wounds, the shepherd his sheep.
   Elegies, bk.2, no.1, l.43–4.

31 *Cedite Romani scriptores, cedite Grai!*
   Nescioquid maius nascitur Iliade.
   Make way, Roman writers, make way, Greeks!
   Something greater than the *Iliad* is born.
   Of Virgil's *Aeneid. Elegies*, bk.2, no.34, l.65–6.

Protagoras c.490–c.420 BC

Greek Sophist and teacher, the first and most famous of the Sophists who, for a fee, offered professional training in public life and other skills. His works survive only as fragments in other writers (notably Plato).

32 Man is the measure of all things, of the existence of the things that are, and the non-existence of the things that are not.
   Fragment quoted in Plato *Theaetetus*, 152a (translated by H North Fowler, 1977).

33 He said that there is no art without practice, and no practice without art.
   Fragment quoted in H Diels and W Kranz (eds) *Die Fragmente der Vorsokratiker*, vol.2 (1952), 268, no.10.

34 Concerning the gods I am not in a position to know either that they are or that they are not, or what they are like in appearance; for there are many things that are preventing knowledge, the obscurity of the matter and the brevity of human life.
   Quoted in G B Kerferd *The Sophistic Movement* (1981), ch.13.

Proudhon, Pierre Joseph 1809–65

French socialist and political theorist, the founder of French radicalism. His works include the great *Système des contradictions économiques* (1846, *System of Economic Contradictions*). Imprisoned for three years in 1849 and again in 1858, he spent the time writing further works arguing for liberty, equality and justice.

35 *La propriété, c'est le vol.*
   Property is theft.
   1840 *Qu'est-ce que la propriété?*.

36 Universal suffrage is counter-revolution.
   On Europe after the 1848 revolution. Quoted in A J P Taylor *From Napoleon to the Second International* (1993).

Proulx, E. Annie 1935–

US author whose works include *The Shipping News* (1993), which won a number of awards including the Pulitzer Prize (1994), and the short story 'Brokeback Mountain' (1997) which was later made into a film.

37 If you get the landscape right, the characters will step out of it, and they'll be in the right place.
   1993 *Time*, 29 Nov.

38 At thirty-six, bereft, brimming with grief and thwarted love, Quoyle steered away to Newfoundland, the rock that had generated his ancestors, a place he had never been nor thought to go.
   1993 *The Shipping News*, ch.1.

Proust, Marcel 1871–1922

French novelist who withdrew from society because of asthma, the death of his parents and disillusionment with the world. He introduced psychological analysis into fiction, notably in his 13-volume novel sequence *À la recherche du temps perdu* (1913–27).

39 *Il vaut mieux rêver sa vie que la vivre, encore que la vivre ce soit encore la rêver.*
   It's better to dream your life than to live it, and even though you live it, you will still dream it.
   1896 *Les Plaisirs et les jours*.

40 *Le bonheur est dans l'amour un état anormal.*
   In love, happiness is abnormal.
   1919 *À la recherche du temps perdu*, 'À l'ombre des jeunes filles en fleurs'.

41 *Nous sommes tous obligés, pour rendre la réalité supportable, d'entretenir en nous quelques petites folies.*
   We must all indulge in a few follies if we are to make reality bearable.
   1919 *À la recherche du temps perdu*, 'À l'ombre des jeunes filles en fleurs'.

42 *L'adolescence est le seul temps où l'on ait appris quelque chose.*
   Adolescence is the only time when we can learn something.
   1919 *À la recherche du temps perdu*, 'À l'ombre des jeunes filles en fleurs'.

43 *On devient moral dès qu'on est malheureux.*
We become moral once we are miserable.
1919 À la recherche du temps perdu, 'À l'ombre des jeunes filles en fleurs'.

44 *On ne reçoit pas la sagesse, il faut la découvrir soi-même, après un trajet que personne ne peut faire pour nous, ne peut nous épargner.*
We do not receive wisdom. We must discover it ourselves after experiences which no one else can have for us and from which no one else can spare us.
1919 À la recherche du temps perdu, 'À l'ombre des jeunes filles en fleurs'.

45 *Il n'y avait pas d'anormaux quand l'homosexualité était la norme.*
There was nothing abnormal about it when homosexuality was the norm.
1921 À la recherche du temps perdu, 'Sodome et Gomorrhe'.

46 *La médecine a fait quelques petits progrès dans ses connaissances depuis Molière, mais aucun dans son vocabulaire.*
Medicine has made a few, small advances in knowledge since Molière, but none in its vocabulary.
1921 À la recherche du temps perdu, 'Sodome et Gomorrhe'.

47 Neurosis has an absolute genius for malingering. There is no illness which it cannot counterfeit perfectly.
1922 *Sodom and Gomorrah*.

48 *L'amour, c'est l'espace et le temps rendus sensibles au cŭur.*
Love is space and time made tender to the heart.
1923 À la recherche du temps perdu, 'La Prisonnière'.

49 *La possession de ce qu'on aime est une joie plus grande encore que l'amour.*
Possessing what one loves is an even greater joy than love itself.
1923 À la recherche du temps perdu, 'La Prisonnière'.

50 *On a dit que la beauté est une promesse de bonheur. Inversement, la possibilité du plaisir peut être un commencement de beauté.*
It has been said that beauty is a guarantee of happiness. Conversely, the possibility of pleasure can be the beginning of beauty.
1923 À la recherche du temps perdu, 'La Prisonnière'.

51 *L'adultère introduit l'esprit dans la lettre que bien souvent le mariage eût laissée morte.*
Adultery breathes new life into marriages which have been left for dead.
1923 À la recherche du temps perdu, 'La Prisonnière'.

52 *L'idée qu'on mourra est plus cruelle que mourir, mais moins que l'idée qu'un autre est mort.*
The idea of dying is worse than dying itself, but less cruel than the idea that another has died.
1923 À la recherche du temps perdu, 'La Prisonnière'.

53 [Music] a pederast might hum when raping a choirboy.
Of Fauré's *Romances sans paroles*. Quoted in *Musical Quarterly*, 1924.

54 *Laissons les jolies femmes aux hommes sans imagination.*
Leave the pretty women for the men without imagination.
1925 À la recherche du temps perdu, 'Albertine disparue'.

55 *Le mensonge est essentiel à l'humanité. Il y joue peut-être un aussi grand rôle que la recherche du plaisir, et d'ailleurs est commandé par cette recherche.*
Lies are essential to humanity. They play perhaps as great a role as the pursuit of pleasure, and are indeed controlled by this pursuit.
1925 À la recherche du temps perdu, 'Albertine disparue'.

56 *Si notre vie est vagabonde, notre mémoire est sédentaire.*
Even though our lives wander, our memories remain in one place.
1927 À la recherche du temps perdu, 'Le Temps retrouvé'.

57 *Le temps qui change les êtres ne modifie pas l'image que nous avons gardée d'eux.*
Although time changes people, it cannot change the image we have already made of them.
1927 À la recherche du temps perdu, 'Le Temps retrouvé'.

58 *Le bonheur est salutaire pour les corps, mais c'est le chagrin qui développe les forces de l'esprit.*
Happiness is healthy for the body, but it is sorrow which enhances the forces of the mind.
1927 À la recherche du temps perdu, 'Le Temps retrouvé'.

59 *Le style, pour l'écrivain aussi bien que pour le peintre, est une question non de technique mais de vision.*
For the writer as well as for the painter, style is not a question of technique, but of vision.
1927 À la recherche du temps perdu, 'Le Temps retrouvé'.

60 *Pour écrire ce livre essentiel, le seul livre vrai, un grand écrivain n'a pas, dans le sens courant, à l'inventer puisqu'il existe déjà en chacun de nous, mais à le traduire.*
To write the essential book, the only true book, a great writer does not need to invent because the book already exists inside each one of us and merely needs translation.
1927 À la recherche du temps perdu, 'Le Temps retrouvé'.

61 *En réalité, chaque lecteur est, quand il lit, le propre lecteur de soi-même. L'ouvrage de l'écrivain n'est qu'une espèce d'instrument optique qu'il offre au lecteur afin de lui permettre de discerner ce que, sans ce livre, il n'eût peut-être pas vu en soi-même.*
In reality, each reader reads only what is already within himself. The book is only a kind of optical instrument which the writer offers to the reader to enable him to discover in himself what he could not have found but for the aid of the book.
1927 À la recherche du temps perdu, 'Le Temps retrouvé'.

Prout, Father

▶ See Mahony, Francis Sylvester

Prynne, William 1600–69

English Puritan. An opponent of the theatre, he was imprisoned for publishing *Histrio Mastix: The Players' Scourge, or Actors' Tragedie* (1633), with its criticism of Charles I's queen Henrietta Maria. His ears were cut off as a punishment in 1634 and he was imprisoned again in 1650 for refusing to pay taxes.

62 Stage-plays…are sinfull, heathenish, lewd, ungodly Spectacles and most pernicious Corruptions, condemned in all ages as intolerable Mischiefes to Churches, to Republickes, to the manners, mindes and soules of men. And that the Profession of Play-poets, of

Stage-players; together with the penning, acting and frequenting of Stage-plays are unlawfull, infamous and misbeseeming Christians.
1633 *Histrio Mastix: The Players' Scourge, or Actors' Tragedie.*

Pryor, Richard 1940–2005
US comedian.

63 Two things people throughout history have had in common are hatred and humour. I am proud that I have been able to use humour to lessen people's hatred.
2004 In *The Scotsman*, 5 Jun.

Publilius Syrus 1c BC
Writer of Latin mimes.

64 *Formosa facies muta commendatio est.*
A beautiful face is a dumb commendation.
Sententiae.

65 *Inopi beneficium bis dat qui dat celeriter.*
He who gives quickly gives the poor man twice as much.
Sententiae.

Puccini, Giacomo Antonio Domenico Michele Secondo Maria 1858–1924
Italian composer, best known for his operas *La Bohème* (1896), *Tosca* (1900) and *Madama Butterfly* (1900). His last opera, *Turandot*, was unfinished.

66 Who sent you to me—God?
To Caruso, who was auditioning for him. Quoted in Derek Watson *Music Quotations* (1991).

Puckett, B Earl 1897–1974
US businessman, President of Allied Stores Corp.

67 It is our job to make women unhappy with what they have.
Recalled on his death, in *Newsweek*, 23 Feb 1974.

Pudney, John Sleigh 1909–77
British poet, journalist and novelist. He is best known for his poem 'For Johnny' (1941) and his novel *The Net* (1952).

68 Do not despair
For Johnny Head-in-Air
He sleeps as sound
As Johnny Underground.
1941 'For Johnny', spoken by Sir Michael Redgrave at the end of the film *The Way to the Stars* (1945).

Puig, Manuel 1932–90
Argentinian novelist. He studied cinema in Rome and spent several years in New York. His novels, which often exploit society's popular icons, include *El beso de la mujer araña* (1976), adapted for stage, screen and Broadway musical.

69 *Porque, sí, fuera de la celda están nuestros opresores, pero adentro no. Aquí nadie oprime a nadie. Lo único que hay, de perturbador, para mi mente...cansada, o condicionada o deformada...es que alguien me quiere tratar bien, sin pedir nada a cambio.*
Because, well, outside of this cell we may have our oppressors, yes, but not inside. Here no one oppresses the other. The only thing that seems to disturb me... because I'm exhausted, or conditioned, or perverted...is that someone wants to be nice to me, without asking anything back for it.
1976 *El beso de la mujer araña*, ch.11 (translated as *Kiss of the Spider Woman*, 1978).

Pulitzer, Joseph 1847–1911
Hungarian-born US newspaper proprietor. He emigrated to the US in 1864, became a reporter and began to acquire and revitalize old newspapers, notably the New York *World*. He established the annual Pulitzer prizes.

70 I want to talk to a nation, not to a select committee.
1909 In *Pearson's Magazine*, Mar.

71 We are a democracy, and there is only one way to get a democracy on its feet in the matter of its individual, its social, its municipal, its State, its National conduct, and that is by keeping the public informed about what is going on. There is not a crime, there is not a dodge, there is not a trick, there is not a swindle, there is not a vice which does not live by secrecy. Get these things out in the open, describe them, attack them, ridicule them in the press, and sooner or later public opinion will sweep them away.
c.1910 Quoted in Alleyne Ireland *An Adventure with a Genius*, ch.4.

72 What a newspaper needs in its news, in its headlines, and on its editorial page is terseness, humor, descriptive power, satire, originality, good literary style, clever condensation and accuracy, accuracy, accuracy.
c.1910 Quoted in Alleyne Ireland *An Adventure with a Genius*, ch.4.

Punch
British humorous weekly periodical, founded 1841, closed 2002.

73 Advice to persons about to marry—don't.
1845

74 You pays your money and you takes your choice.
1846

75 Let us be a nation of shopkeepers as much as we please, but there is no necessity that we should become a nation of advertisers.
1848 Quoted in David Ogilvy *Confessions of an Advertising Man* (1963), ch.2.
▶ See Smith 828:87.

76 Never do today what you can put off till tomorrow.
1849

77 Nothink for nothink 'ere, and precious little for sixpence.
1869

78 Sure, the next train has gone ten minutes ago.
1871

79 Go directly—see what she's doing, and tell her she mustn't.
1872

80 There was one poor tiger that hadn't *got* a Christian.
1875

81 I am not hungry; but thank goodness, I am greedy.
1878

82 Nearly all our best men are dead! Carlyle, Tennyson, Browning, George Eliot!—I'm not feeling very well myself.
1891

83 Botticelli isn't a wine, you Juggins! Botticelli's a *cheese!*
1891

84 Sometimes I sits and thinks, and then again I just sits.
1906

Purdy, Al 1918–2000

Canadian poet. Born in rural Ontario, he settled there again after some years away. He published nearly 30 volumes of poetry, including *The Cariboo Horses* (1965), *The Stone Bird* (1981) and *To Paris Never Again: New Poems* (1997).

85 Uneasily the leaves fall at this season,
   forgetting what to do or where to go;
   the red amnesiacs of autumn
   drifting thru the graveyard forest.

   What they have forgotten they have forgotten:
   what they meant to do instead of fall
   is not in earth or time recoverable—
   the fossils of intention, the shapes of rot.
   1962 *Poems for All the Annettes*, 'Pause' (revised 1968).

86 This is the country of defeat.
   1965 *The Cariboo Horses*, 'The Country North of Belleville' (revised 1972).

87 They had their being once
   and left a place to stand on.
   1968 *Poems for All the Annettes*, 'Roblin Mills' (revised 1972).

Pushkin, Aleksandr Sergeyevich 1799–1837

Russian poet and writer. He is best known for the novel in verse *Eugene Onegin* (1833) and the tragic drama *Boris Godunov* (1825). He also wrote ballads and prose pieces. He was killed in a duel with his brother-in-law.

88 Moscow…what surge that sound can start
   In every Russian's inmost heart!
   1833 *Eugene Onegin*, ch.7, stanza 36 (translated by Adrian Room, 1995).

Pussy Riot

Russian feminist punk rock group. In 2012, after voicing opposition to the government of Vladimir Putin in a concert in Moscow, three members of the band were arrested and imprisoned on charges of hooliganism, leading to international protests.

89 Virgin Mary, Mother of God, become a feminist…Virgin Mary, Mother of God, drive Putin away.
   2012 Lyrics of the 'punk prayer' for which members of the band were imprisoned, delivered in the Cathedral of Christ the Saviour, Moscow, 21 Feb.

90 Like Solzhenitsyn, I believe that in the end, words will break cement. Solzhenitsyn wrote, 'So the word is more sincere than concrete? So the word is not a trifle? Then may noble people begin to grow, and their word will break cement.'
   Nadezhda Tolokonnikova, imprisoned member of Pussy Riot, quoted in Masha Gessen, *Words Will Break Cement: The Passion of Pussy Riot* (2014).

Putin, Vladimir Vladimirovich 1952–

Russian politician. A former officer in the KGB, he moved rapidly up the political ranks to become Prime Minister (1999–2000) and then President of Russia (2000–8). Subsequently he gave up the Presidency to become Prime Minister for a second term (2008–12) and ultimately President once more (2012–). His authoritarian stance on both domestic and foreign matters has attracted international criticism.

91 There is no such thing as a former KGB man.
   2000 Commenting after Prime Minister Sergei Stepashin called himself a former KGB officer, May.

92 Above all, we should acknowledge that the collapse of the Soviet Union was a major geopolitical disaster of the century.
   2005 Televised speech in parliament, reported in the *San Diego Union Tribune*, 25 Apr.

93 People in Russia say that those who do not regret the collapse of the Soviet Union have no heart, and those that do regret it have no brain.
   2005 Interview, German television channel ARD and ZDF, May.

94 Comrade wolf knows who to eat, as the saying goes. He knows who to eat and is not about to listen to anyone.
   2006 Referring to the US, annual presidential address to the Federal Senate, 10 May.

95 There is no one to talk to since Mahatma Gandhi died.
   2007 Press interview, G8 summit meeting, 4 Jun.

96 You don't understand, George, that Ukraine is not even a state. What is Ukraine? Part of its territories is Eastern Europe, but the greater part is a gift from us.
   2008 Discussing Ukrainian sovereignty with George H. Bush at the NATO Bucharest Summit, 4 Apr.

97 In any case, I'd rather not deal with such questions, because anyway it's like shearing a pig—lots of screams but little wool.
   2013 Explaining why he refused to deal with the US, specifically over whistleblower Edward Snowden, quoted in *The Guardian*, 25 Jun.

98 President Obama hasn't been elected by the American people in order to be pleasant to Russia. And your humble servant hasn't been elected by the people of Russia to be pleasant to someone either.
   2013 Interview with Associated Press and Channel 1 television, 3 Sep.

99 It is extremely dangerous to encourage people to see themselves as exceptional.
   2013 Referring to Syria. Quoted in the *New York Times*, 12 Sep.

1 Russia's partners… should understand it's best not to mess with us. Thank God, I think no one is thinking of unleashing a large-scale conflict with Russia. I want to remind you that Russia is one of the leading nuclear powers.
   2014 Speech at youth camp near Moscow, 29 Aug.

Putnam, Israel 1718–90

American general in the American Revolution.

2 Men, you are all marksmen—don't one of you fire until you see the white of their eyes.
   1775 Order before the Battle of Bunker Hill. Quoted in R Frothingham *History of the Siege of Boston* (1873), ch.5.

Pu Yi 1906–67

Chinese puppet emperor. He was proclaimed Emperor at the age of two, but after the Chinese Revolution (1911) he was given a pension and a summer palace. He eventually became a private citizen. The story of his life was made into a film, *The Last Emperor*, in 1988.

3 For the past 40 years I had never folded my own quilt, made my own bed, or poured out my own

washing. I had never even washed my own feet or tied my shoes.
1964 *From Emperor to Citizen: The Autobiography of Aisin-Gioro Pu Yi* (translated by W J F Jenner).

Puzo, Mario 1920–99

US novelist. His breakthrough as a writer came with his novel about the Mafia, *The Godfather* (1969). It became a bestseller and the basis of a trilogy of films directed by Francis Ford Coppola.

4 I'll make him an offer he can't refuse.
1969 *The Godfather*, bk.1, ch.1.

5 A lawyer with a briefcase can steal more than a hundred men with guns.
1969 *The Godfather*, bk.1, ch.1.

6 Like many businessmen of genius he learned that free competition was wasteful, monopoly efficient. And so he simply set about achieving that efficient monopoly.
1969 *The Godfather*, bk.3, ch.14.

7 Show me a gambler and I'll show you a loser, show me a hero, and I'll show you a corpse.
1978 *Fools Die*, ch.2.

8 Our own death wish is our only real tragedy.
1978 *Fools Die*, ch.55.

9 No, I never heard nothing about it, but when they name any disease after two guys, it's got to be terrible!
On Guillain-Barré syndrome. Quoted in Heller and Vogel *No Laughing Matter* (1986).

Pyke, Magnus 1908–92

British scientist and broadcaster.

10 Once a man or woman begins to take a serious interest in the way the universe works—that is to say in science—there is no telling what may turn up.
1976 *Butter Side Up*.

Pynchon, Thomas Ruggles 1937–

US novelist. His acclaimed, highly complex, novels include *V* (1963), *Gravity's Rainbow* (1974), *Mason & Dixon* (1997) and *Bleeding Edge* (2013).

11 Life's single lesson: that there is more accident to it than a man can ever admit to in a lifetime and stay sane.
1963 *V*.

12 Keep cool but care.
1963 *V*.

13 Everybody gets told to write about what they know. The trouble with many of us is that at the earlier stages of life we think we know everything—or to put it more usefully, we are often unaware of the scope and structure of our ignorance.
1984 *Slow Learner: Early Stories*.

14 Paranoia's the garlic in life's kitchen, right, you can never have too much.
2013 *Bleeding Edge*.

Pyrrhus of Epirus 319–272 BC

Greek king, renowned for his wars against the Romans. From 281 BC he fought Rome on behalf of the Tarentines and won battles in 280 BC and 279 BC, but with very high casualties (hence the expression a 'Pyrrhic victory'). He was killed in a street fight in Argos during a war with the Macedonians.

15 One more such victory, and we are lost!
279 BC After defeating the Romans at Asculum. Quoted in Plutarch *Regum et imperatorum apophthegmata*, 184c.

Pythagoras 6c BC

Greek philosopher and mathematician. He founded a school in Crotona but was persecuted there and settled in Lucania. He taught an abstemious way of life and a doctrine of transmigration, but is best remembered for his mathematical work.

16 There is geometry in the humming of the strings. There is music in the spacings of the spheres.
Quoted in Aristotle *Metaphysics*.

Qaboos, Bin Said 1940–

Sultan of Oman. On the deposition of his father in 1970 he became Oman's ruler. He is also Prime Minister and Minister of Foreign Affairs, Defence and Finance.

1 Don't wait for schools to be built. Teach the children under the nearest tree.
1995 Quoted by Rosalind Miles in 'An Oxonian in Oman', in *Oxford Today*, vol.7, no.2, Hilary Issue, 1995.

Qian, Zhang

2 They gave us our rice bowl and we don't want it broken.
1993 On the need to avoid offending the government that permitted broadcasts by Shanghai's Radio Orient. In the *New York Times*, 26 Apr.

Quant, Dame Mary 1934–

English fashion designer. She opened a small boutique, Bazaar, in Chelsea in 1955. In the 1960s she became one of the best-known designers of the 'swinging Britain' era when the simplicity of her designs, especially the mini-skirt, and the originality of her colours attracted international attention.

3 A fashionable woman wears clothes; the clothes don't wear her.
1966 *Quant by Quant*.

4 Fashion should be a game.
1966 *Quant by Quant*.

5 A woman is as young as her knee.
Attributed.

Quarles, Francis 1592–1644

English religious poet. His best-known works are *Emblems* (1635), a series of symbolic pictures with verse commentary, and a book of aphorisms, *Enchyridion* (1640).

6 My soul; sit thou a patient looker-on;
Judge not the play before the play is done:
Her plot hath many changes, every day
Speaks a new scene; the last act crowns the play.
1630 *Epigram, Respice Finem*.

Quayle, Dan (James Danforth) 1947-

US politician. He became a member of Congress (1977-81) and the Senate (1981-8) and served as Vice-President under George Bush (1988-92).

7 It doesn't help...when primetime TV has a character...bearing a child alone...just another lifestyle choice.
1992 Criticism of Murphy Brown, played by Candice Bergen. In the *Washington Post*, 21 May. The comment set off a great controversy about single mothers and freedom of choice.
▸ See Bentsen 82:8.

Quennell, Sir Peter Courtney 1905-93

English biographer, Professor of English at Tokyo (1930). He wrote travel books, verse and novels, but is best known for his biographies of literary figures.

8 Every occupation, unless it employs the whole mind and satisfies the human creative instinct, is to some extent absurd; and about the advertising business what I chiefly disliked was not so much the work I did as its general atmosphere of unreality. We dealt in fairy-gold—in fugitive dreams and illusions.
1977 *The Marble Foot: an Autobiography, 1905-1938*, p.227.

Quiller-Couch, Sir Arthur Thomas known as 'Q' 1863-1944

English writer and critic. His prominence as a critic dates from 1900, when he edited the *Oxford Book of English Verse*. He also wrote novels, short stories, children's books and poetry.

9 He that loves but half of Earth
Loves but half enough for me.
1896 'The Comrade'.

10 Not as we wanted it,
But as God granted it.
1896 'To Bearers'.

11 O the Harbour of Fowey
Is a beautiful spot,
And it's there I enjowey
To sail in a yot;
Or to race in a yacht
Round a mark or a buoy—
Such a beautiful spacht
Is the Harbour of Fuoy!
1899 *A Fowey Garland*, 'The Harbour of Fowey'.

12 The best is the best, though a hundred judges have declared it so.
1900 *The Oxford Book of English Verse*, preface.

13 Our fathers have, in process of centuries, provided this realm, its colonies and wide dependencies, with a speech as malleable and pliant as Attic, dignified as Latin, masculine, yet free of Teutonic guttural, capable of being precise as French, dulcet as Italian, sonorous as Spanish, and captaining all these excellences to its service.
1900 *The Oxford Book of English Verse*, preface.

14 Literature is not an abstract science, to which exact definitions can be applied. It is an Art rather, the success of which depends on personal persuasiveness, on the author's skill to give as on ours to receive.
1913 Inaugural lecture as Professor of English at Cambridge University.

15 Gilbert had a baddish streak or two in him; and one in particular which was not only baddish but so thoroughly caddish that no critic can ignore or, in my view, extenuate it. The man, to summarize, was essentially cruel, and delighted in cruelty.
1929 Of W S Gilbert. *Studies in Literature*, 3rd series, 'Lecture on W.S. Gilbert', no.4.

16 There was an old man of St Omer
Who objected, 'This town's a misnomer;
You've no right to translate
And beatificate
A simple digamma in Homer.'
1941 'A Limerick', in *Chanticlere*, Michaelmas Term.

17 Swinburne is just emptiness to me as he gets older, and the more maddening as he goes on exploiting a heavenly gift. I wish he had just shut up, like Coleridge, and left us surmising wonders.
Quoted in A L Rowse *Quiller-Couch: a Portrait of 'Q'* (1988).

Quin, James 1693-1766

English actor. A performer in the tradition of heroic tragedy, whose most acclaimed roles included Falstaff, he outlived the popularity of the bombastic declamatory style of which he was the master but steadfastly refused to change with the times. He was also noted for his fiery temper.

18 If the young fellow is right, I and the rest of the players have been all wrong.
c.1741 Of David Garrick and his revolutionary, more naturalistic acting style. Attributed.

Quindlen, Anna 1953-

US journalist and author. She worked as a reporter for the *New York Times* (1977-81) and is now a syndicated columnist. She won the Pulitzer Prize for Commentary in 1992 and was named Woman of the Year for 1991 by *Glamour* magazine.

19 The purse is the mirror of the soul.
1987 In the *New York Times*, 16 Dec.

20 What is really hard, and really amazing, is giving up being perfect and beginning the work of becoming yourself.
2005 *Being Perfect*.

Quine, Willard Van Orman 1908-2000

US philosopher and logician, Professor of Philosophy at Harvard (1948-78). He wrote many works on logic and language, including *Two Dogmas of Empiricism* (1951), *Word and Object* (1960) and *From Stimulus to Science* (1995).

21 To define an expression is, paradoxically speaking, to explain how to get along without it. To define is to eliminate.
1987 *Quiddities*, 'Definition'.

22 We can applaud the state lottery as a public subsidy of intelligence, for it yields public income that is calculated to lighten the tax burden of us prudent abstainers at the expense of the benighted masses of wishful thinkers.
1987 *Quiddities*, 'Gambling'.

Quinet, Edgar 1803-75

French writer and politician.

23 La famille des Bourbons est un poignard que l'étranger en 1814 a laissé dans le cïur de la France:

changez le manche comme il vous plaira, dorez la lame si vous voulez, le poignard reste poignard.
The Bourbon family is a dagger which the foreigner left in the heart of France in 1814: change the haft if you please, gild the blade if you will, the dagger remains a dagger.
1877 *Éuvres*, vol.3, p.267.

Quinn, Jane Bryant 1939–

US journalist, broadcaster and financial pundit. Her works include *Everyone's Money Book* (1979) and *Making the Most of Your Money* (1991).

24 Half of them don't know what's going to happen tomorrow and the other half don't know they don't know.
1994 Of stock market players. On CNN TV, 4 Apr.

Quintilian *properly* Marcus Fabius Quintilianus
c.35–c.100 AD

Roman rhetorician born in Spain. He studied oratory at Rome and settled there as an advocate and teacher of rhetoric. His pupils included Pliny the Younger. His reputation rests on his *Institutio Oratoria* ('Education of an Orator').

25 *Mendaces memorem esse oportere.*
Liars need to have good memories.
Institutio Oratoria, 4.2.9.1 (translated by H E Butler, 1968).

26 *Scribitur ad narrandum, non ad probandum.*
It is written for the purpose of narrative, not of proof.
Of history. *Institutio Oratoria*, 10.1.31 (translated by H E Butler, 1968).

Quiroga, Horacio 1878–1937

Uruguayan short-story writer, who spent most of his life in the Argentinian province of Misiones, where most of his stories, generally dealing with morbid themes, are set. He committed suicide in a charity hospital.

27 *Se comprende muy bien que el advenimiento del cinematógrafo haya sido para mí el comienzo de un nueva era, por la cual cuento las noches sucesivas en que he salido mareado y pálido del cine, porque he dejado mi corazón…en la pantalla que impregnó por tres cuartos de hora el encanto de Brownie Vernon.*
It is easy to understand that, for me, cinema was the beginning of a new era which marked my nights, one after the other, as I left the theatre, dizzy and pale after leaving my heart on the screen…on that screen that for forty-five minutes was impregnated by Brownie Vernon's charm.
1921 *Anaconda*, 'Miss Dorothy Phillips, mi esposa' ('Miss Dorothy Phillips, My Wife').

Raban, Jonathan 1942–

English writer. He has written novels and literary criticism, but is best known for his travel books. He now lives in the US.

1 The Falklands held a mirror up to our own islands, and it reflected, in brilliantly sharp focus, all our injured belittlement, our sense of being beleaguered, neglected and misunderstood.
1986 *Coasting*, ch.3.

2 If we live inside a bad joke, it is up to us to learn, at best and worst, to tell it well.
1986 *Coasting*, ch.6.

3 Good travel books are novels at heart.
Recalled by Christopher Lehmann-Haupt in the *New York Times*, 26 Jan 1987, reviewing Raban's novel *Coasting* (1986).

4 The mythical America…—that marvellous, heroic, sentimental land—was an object of faith. It challenged you to make the believer's leap over the rude facts at your feet.
1990 *Hunting Mister Heartbreak*, ch.2.

5 It always seems to me odd to call a place a wilderness when every wilderness area in the US bristles with rules and regulations as to how you can behave, what you're allowed to do, and is patrolled by armed rangers enforcing the small print. They're parks, of course, not wildernesses at all.
2008 Interview, *Granta Magazine*, 15 Jul.

Rabelais, François c.1494–c.1553

French humanist and satirist, who began his career as a Franciscan monk. He studied Greek and Latin as well as medicine, law and philology, and wrote two novels under the pseudonym Alcofribas Nasier.

6 *Science sans conscience n'est que ruine de l'âme.*
Science without conscience is the soul's perdition.
1532 *Pantagruel*, bk.2, ch.8.

7 *Il avait soixante et trois manières d'en trouver toujours à son besoin, dont la plus honorable et la plus commune était par façon de larcin furtivement fait.*
He had sixty-three ways to find the money when he needed it, the most honourable and most ordinary of which was to steal secretively.
1532 *Pantagruel*, bk.2, ch.16.

8 *Mieux est de ris que de larmes écrire*
Pour ce que rire est le propre de l'homme.
It is better to write of laughter than of tears
For laughter is the basis of humankind.
1534 *Gargantua*, Aux lecteurs.

9 *L'odeur du vin, ô combien plus est friand, riant, priant, plus céleste et délicieux que d'huile!*
The odour of wine, oh how much sweeter, more cheerful, pleasing, heavenly and delicious it is than oil!
1534 *Gargantua*, Prologue de l'auteur.

10 *Rompre l'os et sucer la substantifique moelle.*
Break the bone and suck out the very substance.
1534 *Gargantua*, Prologue de l'auteur.

11 *L'appétit vient en mangeant.*
Appetite comes with eating.
1534 *Gargantua*, bk.1, ch.5.

12 *Du cheval donné toujours regardait en la gueule.*
Always look a gift horse in the mouth.
1534 *Gargantua*, bk.1, ch.11.

13 *Lever matin n'est point bonheur;*
Boire matin est le meilleur.

Getting up in the morning does not make you happy;
Drinking in the morning is the best.
1534 *Gargantua*, bk.1, ch.22.

14 *Nature n'endure mutations soudaines sans grande violence.*
Nature does not endure sudden changes without great violence.
1534 *Gargantua*, bk.1, ch.23.

15 *Thésauriser est fait de vilain.*
To hoard is a villainous act.
1534 *Gargantua*, bk.1, ch.33.

16 *Jamais je ne m'assujettis aux heures: les heures sont faites pour l'homme, et non l'homme pour les heures.*
I never subject myself to hours: hours are made for men; men are not made for hours.
1534 *Gargantua*, bk.1, ch.41.

17 *En leur règle n'était que cette clause: FAIS CE QUE VOUDRAS.*
In their laws there was but this one clause: DO WHAT YOU WISH.
1534 *Gargantua*, bk.1, ch.57.

18 *Un fol enseigne bien un sage.*
A fool has a lot to teach a wise man.
1546 *Tiers Livre*, pt.37.

19 *O que trois et quatre fois heureux sont ceux qui plantent choux!*
Oh, those who plant cabbages are three and four times happier than the rest of us!
1548 *Quart Livre*, pt.18.

20 *Pantagruélisme…est certaine gaieté d'esprit confite en mépris des choses fortuites.*
Pantagruelism is a certain liveliness of mind made in contempt of chance happenings.
1552 *Quart Livre*, Prologue de l'auteur.

21 *Ignorance est mère de tous les maux.*
Ignorance is the mother of all evils.
1564 *Cinquième Livre*, pt.7.

22 Abandon yourself to Nature's truths, and let nothing in this world be unknown to you.
Quoted in J H Plumb (ed) *The Horizon Book of the Renaissance* (1961).

Rabi, Isidor Isaac 1898–1988

US physicist, born in Austria. He taught physics at Columbia from 1929 and served as an adviser to the US Atomic Energy Commission. Rabi won the 1944 Nobel prize in physics for his discovery and measurement of the radio-frequency spectra of atomic nuclei.

23 It is only in science, I find, that we can get outside ourselves. It's realistic, and to a great degree verifiable, and it has this tremendous stage on which it plays. I have the same feeling—to a certain degree—about some religious expressions…but only to a certain degree. For me, the proper study of mankind is science, which also means that the proper study of mankind is man.
Quoted in Jeremy Bernstein *Experiencing Science* (1978).

Rabin, Yitzhak 1922–95

Israeli soldier and statesman. He was awarded the Nobel peace prize jointly with Shimon Peres and Yasser Arafat in 1994.

24 We say to you today in a loud and a clear voice: enough of blood and tears. Enough.
1993 To the Palestinians. Speech in Washington, 13 Sep.

Rachmaninov, Sergei Vasilevich 1873–1943

Russian composer and pianist, who settled in the US in 1918, best known for his piano music. His style epitomizes the lush romanticism of the later 19c, still apparent in his last major composition, *Rhapsody on a Theme of Paganini* (1934).

25 My dear hands. Farewell, my poor hands.
On being told that he was dying of cancer. Quoted in H Schonberg *The Great Pianists* (1964).

Racine, Jean 1639–99

French court dramatist who studied at Port Royal and went on to write many of his dramatic works for performance there.

26 *Ah! je l'ai trop aimé pour ne le point haïr!*
Oh! I loved him too much not to hate him now!
1667 *Andromaque*, act 2, sc.1.

27 *Les témoins sont fort chers, et n'en a pas qui veut.*
Witnesses are expensive and not everyone can afford them.
1668 *Les Plaideurs*, act 3, sc.3.

28 *J'aimais jusqu'à ses pleurs que je faisais couler.*
I loved even the tears which I made her cry.
1669 *Britannicus*, act 2, sc.2.

29 *J'embrasse mon rival, mais c'est pour l'étouffer.*
If I embrace my rival, it is to strangle him.
1669 *Britannicus*, act 4, sc.3.

30 *Ainsi que la vertu, le crime a ses degrés.*
Crime, like virtue, has its degrees.
1677 *Phèdre*, act 4, sc.2.

31 *Pensez-vous être saint et juste impunément?*
You think you can be holy and righteous with impunity?
1691 *Athalie*, act 1, sc.1.

Radcliffe, Daniel Jacob 1989–

English actor. He became famous playing the title role in the *Harry Potter* films based upon the books by J.K. Rowling, but has since played other roles on both stage and screen, subsequent films including *The Woman in Black* (2012) and *What If* (2013).

32 I'm the only kid in the world who doesn't want an eighth Harry Potter book.
2007 Quoted in *Details* magazine, Aug.

Radisson, Pierre-Esprit 1636–1710

French traveller, explorer of New France (Canada).

33 We were Caesars, there being nobody to contradict us.
Attributed boast of the *coureur de bois* in the Canadian North West. Quoted in Arthur T Adams (ed) *The Explorations of Pierre-Esprit Radisson* (1961).

Rado, James 1939–

US composer and librettist.

34 This is the dawning of the age of Aquarius.
1968 *Hair*, 'Aquarius' (music by Galt MacDermot).

Rae, John 1931–2006

English writer.

35 War is, after all, the universal perversion.
1960 *The Custard Boys*, ch.13.

Rahner, Karl 1904–84
German Jesuit priest, who taught at Innsbruck and Munich and who was widely recognized as a leading Roman Catholic theologian.

36 But there is yet another form of this hidden heresy, and, paradoxically, it can affect those who are proudest of their long-standing and unimpeachable orthodoxy; heresy in the form of indifference.
1963 'Natur und Gnade' in *Fragen der Theologie Heute* (translated by Dinah Wharton as *Nature and Grace*, 1963).

Rainborowe, Thomas 1598–1648
English soldier.

37 The poorest He that is in England hath a life to live as well as the greatest He, and therefore, truly Sirs, I think that every man that is to live under a Government ought first, by his own consent, to put himself under that Government.
1647 Said to Cromwell during the Army Debates, Putney, 29 Oct.

Raine, Craig Anthony 1944–
English poet and critic. His collections include *A Martian Sends a Postcard Home* (1979) and *Collected Poems 1978-1999* (1999).

38 We live in the great indoors:
the vacuum cleaner grazes
over the carpet, lowing,
its udder a swollen wobble.
1978 'An Inquiry into Two Inches of Ivory'.
▶ See Austen 46:80.

39 Caxtons are mechanical birds with many wings and some are treasured for their markings.
1979 'A Martian Sends a Postcard Home'.

40 But time is tied to the wrist
or kept in a box, ticking with impatience.
1979 'A Martian Sends a Postcard Home'.

41 The mind is a museum
to be looted at night.
1984 'The Grey Boy'.

Raine, Kathleen Jessie 1908–2003
English poet and critic. Her poetry reflects a mystical, visionary appreciation of nature, and she was a sympathetic critic of symbolists such as Blake, Hopkins and Yeats.

42 Nowadays harmony comes almost as a shock.
Letter to Arthur Bliss.

Raleigh, Sir Walter 1552–1618
English courtier, navigator and poet. His writings include lyric poems, *The Discovery of Guyana* (1596) and an unfinished *History of the World* (1614). Implicated in a plot to overthrow Queen Elizabeth, his death sentence was suspended until 1618, when he was beheaded.

43 If all the world and love were young,
And truth in every shepherd's tongue
These pretty pleasures might me move
To live with thee and be thy love.
c.1592 'The Nymph's Reply to the Shepherd', a response to Marlowe's 'The Passionate Shepherd to His Love', attributed to Raleigh.
▶ See Marlowe 574:41.

44 Give me my scallop-shell of quiet,
My staff of faith to walk upon,
My scrip of joy, immortal diet,
My bottle of salvation,
My gown of glory, hope's true gage,
And thus I'll take my pilgrimage.
1604 *The Passionate Man's Pilgrimage*.

45 What is our life? a play of passion;
Our mirth the music of division;
Our mothers' wombs the tiring-houses be
Where we are dressed for this short comedy.
Heaven the judicious sharp spectator is,
That sits and marks still who doth act amiss;
Our graves that hide us from the searching sun
Are like drawn curtains when the play is done.
Thus march we, playing, to our latest rest,
Only we die in earnest—that's no jest.
1612 'On the Life of Man'.

46 I shall never be persuaded that God hath shut up all light of learning within the lantern of Aristotle's brain.
1614 *The History of the World*.

47 Even such is Time, which takes in trust
Our youth, our joys, and all we have,
And pays us but with age and dust,
Who in the dark and silent grave
When we have wandered all our ways
Shuts up the story of our days,
And from which earth, and grave, and dust
The Lord shall raise me up, I trust.
1618 'The Author's Epitaph, Made by Himself'. Poem written the night before his death.

Rambert, Dame Marie 1888–1982
Polish-born British ballet dancer and teacher.

48 One is often asked whether his jump was really as high as it is always described. To that I answer: 'I don't know how far from the ground it was, but I know it was near the stars.' Who would watch the floor when he danced?
1960 On Vaslav Nijinsky. *Quicksilver*.

Ramón y Cajal, Santiago 1852–1934
Spanish physician and histologist. He made use of the specialized histological staining techniques of Camillo Golgi, and the two men shared the 1906 Nobel prize for physiology or medicine.

49 In my systematic explorations through the realms of microscopic anatomy, there came the turn of the nervous system, that masterpiece of life.
1937 *Recollections of My Life*.

Ramos, Graciliano 1892–1953
Brazilian novelist. In 1936 he was arrested and imprisoned, and on his release settled in Rio de Janeiro. His work explores the lives of characters shaped by the rural misery of north-east Brazil.

50 *Sempre que os homens sabidos lhe diziam palavras difíceis, ele saía logrado. Sobressaltava-se escutando-as. Evidentemente só serviam para encobrir ladroeiras. Mas eram bonitas.*
Whenever men with book learning used big words in dealing with him, he came out the loser. It startled him

1938 *Vidas secas* (translated as *Barren Lives*, 1965), 'Contas'.

Ramsey, Sir Alf(red) 1922–99

English footballer and manager. A player with Southampton and Tottenham Hotspur, he managed Ipswich Town in the early 1960s and went on to manage the England side that won the World Cup in 1966.

51 I feel like jumping over the moon.
1962 Quoted in Nigel Rees *Dictionary of Popular Phrases* (1990). This is one of the earliest records of the phrase 'over the moon' being used in the context of football.

52 Listen to them moan, but those people will be going mad if we beat West Germany by a goal in the World Cup Final.
1966 Of press criticism after England lost against West Germany in February, several months before England won the World Cup. Quoted in Bryon Butler *The Official History of the Football Association* (1986).

53 You've beaten them once. Now go out and bloody beat them again.
1966 Addressing his players when the World Cup final went into extra time.

Rand, Ayn 1905–82

Russian-born US novelist, screenwriter and ardent propagandist for her philosophy of self-interest against the altruistic tendencies of the welfare state. Her novels include *The Fountainhead* (1943) and *Atlas Shrugged* (1957).

54 The entire history of science is a progression of exploded fallacies, not of achievements.
1957 *Atlas Shrugged*.

Randall, Clarence Beldan 1891–1967

US businessman, Chief Executive Officer of Inland Steel. He wrote several books on business.

55 Every man who has lived his life to the full, should, by the time his senior years are reached, have established a reserve inventory of unfinished thinking.
1963 *Sixty-Five Plus*.

56 The leader must know, must know that he knows and must be able to make it abundantly clear to those about him that he knows.
1964 *Making Good in Management*.

Randall, Dudley 1914–2000

US poet and librarian. He established the Broadside Press, which prints the work of black US poets, including his own books.

57 Musing on roses and revolutions,
I saw night close down on the earth like a great dark wing.
1968 *Cities Burning*, 'Roses and Revolutions'.

58 I saw dawn upon them like the sun a vision
of a time when all men walk proudly through the earth
and the bombs and missiles lie at the bottom of the
  ocean
like the bones of dinosaurs buried under the shale of eras.
1968 *Cities Burning*, 'Roses and Revolutions'.

59 Then washed in the brightness of this vision,
I saw how in its radiance would grow and be nourished
  and suddenly
just to hear those words. Obviously they were just a cover for robbery. But they sounded nice.

burst into terrible and splendid bloom
the blood-red flower of revolution.
1968 *Cities Burning*, 'Roses and Revolutions'.

Ranjitsinhji, Prince 1872–1933

Indian nobleman and England cricketer. A star batsman with Sussex and England, he succeeded as Jam Sahib of Nawanagar in 1906 (Maharaja in 1918), and did much to modernize and improve conditions in his home state.

60 He turned the old one-stringed instrument into a many-chorded lyre… W.G. discovered batting; he turned its many narrow straight channels into one great winding river.
1897 Of W G Grace. *The Jubilee Book of Cricket*.

61 Find out where the ball is, get there; hit it.
Explaining his tactics as a batsman. Quoted in Colin Jarman *The Guinness Dictionary of Sports Quotations* (1990).

Rankin, Ian 1960–

Scottish author, known for his detective novels featuring Inspector Rebus.

62 It was one of those cool, crepuscular days that could have belonged to any of at least three Scottish seasons, a sky like slate roofing and a wind that Rebus's father would have called 'snell'.
2001 *The Falls*.

63 It seemed to him a very Edinburgh thing. Welcoming, but not very.
2007 *Exit Music*.

Rankin, Jeanette 1880–1973

US pacifist and politician, the first woman in Congress. She voted against US entry into both World Wars and demonstrated against the war in Vietnam.

64 As a woman I can't go to war, and I refuse to send anyone else.
Quoted in Hannah Josephson *Lady in Congress* (1974).

65 You can no more win a war than you can win an earthquake.
Quoted in Hannah Josephson *Lady in Congress* (1974).

Ransom, John Crowe 1888–1974

US poet and critic. He was an influential figure in the rise of the New Criticism movement in the US, and an important Southern poet.

66 Here lies a lady of beauty and high degree.
Of chills and fever she died, of fever and chills,
The delight of her husband, her aunts, an infant of three,
And of medicos marvelling sweetly on her ills.
1924 *Chills and Fever*, 'Here Lies a Lady'.

67 The little cousin is dead, by foul subtraction,
A green bough from Virginia's aged tree.
1924 *Chills and Fever*, 'Dead Boy'.

68 Tawny are the leaves turned but they still hold,
And it is harvest; what shall this land produce?
A meagre hill of kernels, a runnel of juice;
Declension looks from our land, it is old.
Therefore let us assemble, dry, gray, spare,
And mild as yellow air.
1924 *Chills and Fever*, 'Antique Harvesters'.

69 The curse of hell upon the sleek upstart
That got the Captain finally on his back
And took the red red vitals of his heart
And made the kites to whet their beaks clack clack.
1924 *Chills and Fever,* 'Captain Carpenter'.

70 Two evils, monstrous either one apart,
Possessed me, and were long and loath at going:
A cry of Absence, Absence, in the heart,
And in the wood the furious winter blowing.
1924 *Chills and Fever,* 'Winter Remembered'.

71 And if no Lethe flows beneath your casement,
And when ten years have not brought full effacement,
Philosophy was wrong, and you may meet.
1924 *Grace after Meat,* 'Parting at Dawn'.

72 Old Hodge stays not his hand, but whips to kennel
The renegade. God's peace betide the souls
Of the pure in heart. But in the box that fennel
Grows around, are two red eyes that stare like coals.
1927 *Two Gentlemen in Bonds,* 'Dog'.

73 God have mercy on the sinner
Who must write with no dinner,
No gravy and no grub,
No pewter and no pub,
No belly and no bowels,
Only consonants and vowels.
1955 *Poems and Essays,* 'Survey of Literature'.

Raphael, Frederic 1931–

British novelist and screenwriter.

74 City of perspiring dreams.
1976 Of Cambridge. *The Glittering Prizes,* ch.3.

Rapoport, Anatol 1911–2007

Russian-born Canadian mathematician, social philosopher and peace advocate.

75 Cooperate on move one; thereafter, do whatever the other player did the previous move.
The two commands for his computer program, Tit for Tat, designed at the University of Toronto. It outperformed all other programs at an international computer tournament in 1979, and it continues to excel in tournaments. The program initiates reciprocal cooperation yet responds in kind to provocation.

Rather, Dan(iel Irvin) 1931–

US newscaster, host of *CBS Evening News* (1981–2005).

76 Not long after I first came to the anchor chair, I briefly signed off using the word, Courage. I want to return to it now, in a different way: to a nation still nursing a broken heart for what happened here in 2001, and especially to those who found themselves closest to the events of September 11; to our soldiers, sailors, airmen and Marines, in dangerous places; to those who have endured the tsunami, and to all who have suffered natural disasters, and must now find the will to rebuild; to the oppressed and to those whose lot it is to struggle in financial hardship or in failing health; to my fellow journalists in places where reporting the truth means risking all; and to each of you, Courage. For *The CBS Evening News,* Dan Rather reporting. Good night.
2005 Final broadcast for *CBS Evening News,* 9 Mar.

77 He couldn't sell watermelons if you gave him the state troopers to flag down traffic.
2010 Referring to President Barack Obama on the Chris Matthews Show, 8 Mar.

Rattigan, Sir Terence 1911–77

English playwright.

78 When you're between any sort of devil and the deep blue sea, the deep blue sea sometimes looks very inviting.
1952 *The Deep Blue Sea.*

79 You can be in the Horseguards and still be common, dear.
1954 *Separate Tables.*

Rauschenberg, Robert 1925–2008

US artist, whose paintings and collages incorporate images and objects from everyday life. *Gloria* (1956) is a typical example of his 'combines', or collages.

80 I don't like masterpieces having one-night stands in collectors' homes between auctions.
1989 On quick-turnover profits on his work. In the *New York Times,* 10 May.

81 Most artists try to break your heart, or they accidentally break their own hearts. But I find the quietness in the ordinary much more satisfying.
2004 In the *New York Times,* 15 Feb.

82 They block the view.
2004 When asked what he had against mountains. In the *New York Times,* 15 Feb.

Ravel, (Joseph) Maurice 1875–1937

French composer. A pupil of Fauré, his innovative early compositions include *Schéhérazade* and the *Pavane pour une infante défunte* (both 1899). Other notable works include the ballet *Daphnis et Chloé* (1912), and *Boléro* (1928).

83 I've still so much music in my head. I have said nothing. I have so much more to say.
1937 Spoken on his deathbed. Quoted in Jourdan-Morhange *Ravel et nous* (1945).

84 A piece for orchestra without music.
Of his *Boléro.* Quoted in R Nichols *Ravel* (1977).

Ravitch, Diane Silvers 1938–

US historian, writer and Research Professor of Education at New York University. She was a member of the US Department of Education from 1991 to 1993.

85 The person who knows 'how' will always have a job. The person who knows 'why' will always be his boss.
1985 Speech at Reed College commencement. Reported in *Time,* 17 Jun.

Rawnsley, Andrew 1962–

English author, broadcaster and journalist.

86 The Millennium Dome was intended to be New Labour's Xanadu and Tony Blair its Kubla Khan.
2000 *Servants of the People: The Inside Story of New Labour.*

Ray, Dixy Lee 1914–94

US politician and administrator.

87 The general public has long been divided into two parts: those who think that science can do anything, and those who are afraid that it will.
1973 In *New Scientist*, 5 Jul.

Ray, James Earl 1928–98

US assassin of Martin Luther King. He was imprisoned in 1960 for armed robbery but escaped in 1967 and shot King. He was apprehended in London and sentenced in Memphis to 99 years.

88 I was in Tennessee 24 hours and got 99 years.
1988 On beginning the 20th year of his prison sentence for the assassination of Martin Luther King. In *Life*, March.

Rayburn, Sam(uel Taliaferro) 1882–1961

US politician. A Democrat, he represented Texas (1913–61) and was Speaker of the House for a record 17 terms between 1940 and 1961. He was a supporter of Roosevelt's New Deal.

89 I like to make running water walk.
Quoted in Valton J Young *The Speaker's Agent* (1956).

90 These…society women never serve chilli.
His reason for not attending parties. Quoted in David Brinkley *Washington Goes to War* (1988).

91 Go along and get along.
On politics as a process of accommodation, recalled by former Speaker Gerald R Ford in the *Washington Times*, 24 May 1995.

Read, Sir Herbert Edward 1893–1968

English poet and art critic. Editor of the *Burlington Magazine* (1933–9) and Professor of Fine Art at Edinburgh (1931–3), he wrote works on art criticism and *Naked Warriors* (1919), a poetry collection inspired by his war experiences.

92 I saw him stab
And stab again
A well-killed Boche.
1919 *Naked Warriors*, 'The Scene of War, 4. The Happy Warrior'.

93 This is the happy warrior,
This is he.
1919 *Naked Warriors*, 'The Scene of War, 4. The Happy Warrior'.

94 It is defiant—the desperate act of men too profoundly convinced of the rottenness of our civilization to want to save a shred of its respectability.
1936 Catalogue of the International Surrealist Exhibition, New Burlington Galleries, London, Jun/Jul, introduction.

95 But one thing we learned: there is no glory in the deed Until the soldier wears a badge of tarnished braid.
1948 'To a Conscript of 1940'.

96 It will be a gay world. There will be lights everywhere except in the minds of men, and the fall of the last civilization will not be heard above the din.
1964 Quoted in Hoggart and Johnston, *An Idea of Europe* (1987), 'Pyramids and Planes'.

Reade, Charles 1814–84

English novelist and playwright.

97 Take courage, my friend, the devil is dead!
1861 *The Cloister and the Hearth*.

Reagan, Nancy 1923–

US actress and First Lady, second wife of US President Ronald Reagan.

98 If the President has a bully pulpit, then the First Lady has a white glove pulpit…more refined, restricted, ceremonial, but it's a pulpit all the same.
1988 In the *New York Times*, 10 Mar.

99 I'm more aware if somebody is trying to end-run him…it just never occurs to him.
1988 On protecting her husband. In *Time*, 28 Nov.

1 For eight years I was sleeping with the President, and if that doesn't give you special access, I don't know what does!
1989 *My Turn* (with William Novack).

Reagan, Ronald Wilson 1911–2004

US Republican politician, 40th President (1981–9), a radio sports announcer and film star. A Democrat turned Republican, he won nomination in 1980, defeating Carter to become President. He introduced economic reform, took a strong anti-communist stand and introduced the Strategic Defence Initiative ('Star Wars'). In 1981 he was wounded in an assassination attempt. Re-elected in 1984, he achieved a major arms-reduction accord with Gorbachev. His reputation was tarnished by the Iran–Contra affair.

2 To sit back hoping that some day, some way, someone will make things right is to go on feeding the crocodile, hoping that he will eat you last—but eat you he will.
1974 CBS News, 7 Nov.

3 Recession is when your neighbour loses his job. Depression is when you lose yours.
1980 Election campaign speech, Jersey City, 1 Sep.
▶ See Truman 899:86.

4 I can tell a lot about a fellow's character by the way that he eats jelly beans.
1981 In the *Daily Mail*, Jan.

5 Honey, I forgot to duck.
1981 Said to his wife, Nancy, after being shot by John R Hinckley, Jr, 30 Mar.
▶ See Dempsey 272:50.

6 Who's minding the store?
1981 After he was shot by John R Hinckley, Jr, 30 Mar.

7 This is not the end of anything. This is the beginning of everything.
1984 On his re-election. In *Time*, Nov.

8 We are not going to tolerate these attacks from outlaw states, run by the strangest collection of misfits, looney tunes and squalid criminals since the advent of the Third Reich.
1985 Speech after terrorist attacks by Shi'ite Muslims, Jul.

9 We must say something but not much because I'm being held out to dry.
1986 Comment at a meeting with National Security Council advisers, 10 Nov. Quoted by Theodore Draper *A Very Thin Line* (1991).

10 We make history and changing it is within our power.
1987 On welcoming Soviet premier Mikhail S Gorbachev to the White House, 8 Dec.

11 We don't know where that money came from and we don't know who had it and we don't know where it went.
1988 Of the Iran–Contra funding. In the *New York Times*, 17 Mar.

12 I paid for this microphone.
1988 To a New Hampshire moderator who tried to keep President Reagan from speaking on behalf of other candidates. Reported in *Congressional Quarterly*, 23 May.

13 There is our little bungalow down there.
  1989 On viewing the White House from a helicopter the day he left office. Quoted in the *Washington Post*, 22 Apr 1991.

14 Washington is a sieve…it was virtually impossible to find out who was doing the leaking and shut them up.
  1990 Deposition on the Iran–Contra arms sales. In the *New York Times*, 23 Feb.

15 Politics is just like show business…a hell of an opening, you coast for a while, you have a hell of a closing.
  1995 In the *New York Times*, 23 Apr.

16 When men fail to drive toward a goal or purpose, but only drift, the drift is always towards barbarism.
  Quoted in Edmund Morris *Dutch: A Memoir of Ronald Reagan* (1999).

Reardon, Ray 1932–

Welsh snooker player. He was world champion in 1970, 1973, 1976 and 1978.

17 I cannot remember anyone ever asking 'Who came second?' Can you?
  Quoted in Colin Jarman *The Guinness Dictionary of Sports Quotations* (1990).

18 If I had to make the choice between staying married and playing snooker, snooker would win.
  Quoted in Colin Jarman *The Guinness Dictionary of Sports Quotations* (1990).

Red Cloud *original name* Mahpiua Luta 1822–1909

Oglala Sioux chief who led the Indian war against the Americans.

19 You have heard the sound of the white soldier's axe on the Little Piney. His presence here is…an insult to the spirits of our ancestors. Are we to give up their sacred graves to be ploughed for corn? Dakotas, I am for war.
  1866 Speech before war council at Fort Laramie, Wyoming.

Redgrave, Vanessa 1937–

English actress. Having established her reputation playing some of the great Shakespeare roles, she became one of the most admired stars of the London and Broadway stages, as well as appearing to acclaim in such films as *Isadora* (1968), *Julia* (1977), *Howards End* (1992) and *The Butler* (2013).

20 The arts stop society going rotten and mad.
  2013 Interview, *FT Magazine*, 26 Apr.

Redmond, John Edward 1856–1918

Irish politician. A champion of Home Rule, he was Chairman of the Nationalist Party in 1900. He declined a seat in Asquith's coalition ministry (1915), but supported World War I, deplored the Irish rebellion, and opposed Sinn Féin.

21 The government may tomorrow withdraw every one of their troops from Ireland. Ireland will be defended by her armed sons from foreign invasion, and for that purpose the armed Catholics in the south will be only too glad to join arms with the armed Protestant Ulsterman. Is it too much to hope that out of this situation a result may spring that will be good not merely for the Empire but for the future welfare and integrity of the Irish nation?
  1914 Speech, House of Commons, 3 Aug.

Redon, Odilon 1840–1916

French Symbolist painter and graphic artist, also well known for his work in pastel.

22 What distinguishes the artist from the dilettante? Only the pain that the artist feels. The dilettante looks only for pleasure in art.
  c.1871 Journal entry, quoted in *Portfolio*, no.8, Spring 1964 (translated by Richard Howard).

23 All my originality consists…in giving life in human fashion to beings which are impossible according to the laws of possibility.
  Quoted in Edward Lucie-Smith *Symbolist Art* (1972).

24 I am repelled by those who voice the word 'nature', without having any trace of it in their hearts.
  Quoted in Edward Lucie-Smith *Symbolist Art* (1972).

Redtenbacher, Ferdinand 1818–83

German engineer, Professor of Mechanical Engineering and author on the construction of machinery.

25 Thanks to his bodily form and thanks to his mind, [man] is a universal machine, capable of an infinite diversity of movement.
  1840 *Resultate fur den Maschinenbau* (published 1848).

Reed, Henry 1914–86

English poet and dramatist. He is best known for his war poems and for his radio plays, notably *The Private Life of Hilda Tablet* (1954). 'Chard Whitlow' (1946) is a parody of T S Eliot's 'Burnt Norton'.

26 Today we have naming of parts. Yesterday,
  We had daily cleaning. And tomorrow morning,
  We shall have what to do after firing. But today,
  Today we have naming of parts. Japonica
  Glistens like coral in all of the neighbouring gardens
  And today we have naming of parts.
  1946 *Lessons of the War*, pt.1, 'Naming of Parts'.

27 We can slide it
  Rapidly backwards and forwards: we call this
  Easing the spring. And rapidly backwards and forwards
  The early bees are assaulting and fumbling the flowers:
  They call it easing the Spring.
  1946 *Lessons of the War*, pt.1, 'Naming of Parts'.

28 There may be dead ground in between; and I may not have got
  The knack of judging a distance; I will only venture
  A guess that perhaps between me and the apparent lovers,
  (Who, incidentally, appear by now to have finished,)
  At seven o'clock from the houses, is roughly a distance
  Of about one year and a half.
  1946 *Lessons of the War*, pt.2, 'Judging Distances'.

29 As we get older we do not get any younger.
  Seasons return, and today I am fifty-five,
  And this time last year I was fifty-four,
  And this time next year I shall be sixty-two.
  1946 'Chard Whitlow (Mr Eliot's Sunday Evening Postscript)', a parody of T S Eliot's style.

30 It is, we believe,
  Idle to hope that the simple stirrup-pump
  Can extinguish hell.
  1946 'Chard Whitlow (Mr Eliot's Sunday Evening Postscript)'.

31 Modest? My word, no… He was an all-the-lights-on man.
  1953 *A Very Great Man Indeed*, radio play.

32 And the sooner the tea's out of the way, the sooner we can get out the gin, eh?
   1954 *The Private Life of Hilda Tablet*, radio play.

33 In a civil war, a general must know—and I'm afraid it's a thing rather of instinct than of practice—he must know exactly when to move over to the other side.
   1959 *Not a Drum Was Heard: The War Memoirs of General Gland*, unpublished radio play.

Reed, Ishmael Scott 1938–

US novelist, poet and publisher. He founded the experimental literary magazine *East Village Other* in New York. His works include the novels *The Free-Lance Pallbearers* (1967) and *Mumbo Jumbo* (1972).

34 When State Magic fails unofficial magic becomes stronger.
   1968 *Yellow Back Radio Broke Down*, 'II. The Loop Garou Kid Comes Back Mad'.

35 Hoo-doo, which in America flowered in New Orleans, was an unorganized religion without ego-games or death worship.
   1968 *Yellow Back Radio Broke Down*, 'V. A Jigsaw of a Last Minute Rescue'.

Reed, John 1887–1920

US writer and journalist. He is best known as a war correspondent in Mexico and Europe, and for his reports from Russia in the wake of the revolution.

36 Ten Days That Shook the World.
   1919 Title of book.

37 In the relations of a weak Government and a rebellious people there comes a time when every act of the authorities exasperates the masses, and every refusal to act excites their contempt.
   1919 *Ten Days That Shook the World*, ch.3.

Rees-Mogg, William Rees-Mogg, Baron 1928–2012

English journalist. He joined the *Financial Times* (1952) and the *Sunday Times* (1960), becoming deputy editor (1964). He was editor of *The Times* (1967–81) and headed the Broadcasting Standards Council (1988–93).

38 Information, free from interest or prejudice, free from the vanity of the writer or the influence of a Government, is as necessary to the human mind as pure air and water to the human body.
   1970 *Christian Science Monitor*, 22 Sep.

Reeve, Christopher 1952–2004

US actor, best known for his role as the superhero in *Superman* (1978) and subsequent films. Paralysed in a horse-riding accident, he became a spokesperson for medical research into treatments and cures for spinal injuries.

39 Every scientist should remove the word 'impossible' from their lexicon.
   2004 In the *Observer*, 15 Feb.

Regan, Donald Thomas 1918–2003

US financier, writer and lecturer. He was chair of Merrill Lynch & Co Inc (1973–81), secretary to the US Treasury Department (1981–85) and White House Chief of Staff (1985–87) for President Reagan. Following the Tower Commission Report on the Iran–Contra affair, he was forced to resign.

40 The buck doesn't even *pause* here.
   1987 Of his job. In the *New York Times*, 31 Jul.
   ▶ See Truman 900:93.

41 I thought I was Chief of Staff to the President, not to his wife.
   1988 On submitting his resignation. *For the Record*.

42 Mistaken in its assumptions, defective in its evidence and wrong in its conclusions.
   1988 Of the congressional report faulting him on lack of direction and public disclosure of Iran–Contra arms sales. *For the Record*.

Reger, Max 1873–1916

German composer. He was Director of Music (1907) and professor (1908) at Leipzig University. His work includes organ music, piano concertos, choral works and songs.

43 Ich sitze in dem kleinsten Zimmer in meinem Hause. Ich habe Ihre Kritik vor mir. Im nächsten Augenblick wird sie hinter mir sein.
   I am sitting in the smallest room of my house. I have your review before me. In a moment it will be behind me.
   1906 Written in response to an unfavourable review by Rudolf Louis. Quoted in Nicolas Slonimsky *Lexicon of Musical Invective* (2nd edn, 1969), p.139.

Reid, Alastair 1926–2014

Scottish-born poet, essayist and translator of Spanish and Latin American literature. After serving in the Navy in World War II, he became a professional itinerant, his only permanent address the *New Yorker*. His witty poetry collections include *Weathering* (1978).

44 The point is the seeing—the grace
   beyond recognition, the ways
   of the bird rising, unnamed, unknown,
   beyond the range of language, beyond its noun.
   Eyes open on growing, flying, happening,
   and go on opening. Manifold, the world
   dawns on unrecognizing, realizing eyes.
   Amazement is the thing.
   Not love, but the astonishment of loving.
   1978 *Weathering*, 'Growing, Flying, Happening'.

Reid, Thomas Mayne 1818–83

Irish writer of boys' stories. After work as a journalist and soldier in the Mexican War of 1847, he won a wide readership with a string of adventure tales, which included such titles as *The Rifle Rangers* (1850), *War Trail* (1857) and *Boy Tar* (1859).

45 Praise the sports of the land
   And water, each one—
   The bath by the beach, or the yacht on the sea—
   But of all the sweet pleasures
   Known under the sun;
   A good game of Croquet's the sweetest to me.
   1863 Quoted in Colin Jarman *The Guinness Dictionary of Sports Quotations* (1990).

Remarque, Erich Maria 1898–1970

German-born US novelist, who served in World War I. His novels were banned by the Nazis in 1933, and he emigrated to the US in 1939.

46 *Im Westen nichts Neues.*
   All Quiet on the Western Front.
   1929 Title of novel.

Renan, (Joseph) Ernest 1823–92
French philologist and historian, whose studies led him to abandon traditional faith. His works include *Histoire général des langues sémitiques* (1854), *Études d'histoire religieuse* (1856) and the controversial *Vie de Jésus* (1863), the first of a series on the history of Christianity.

47 War is a condition of progress; the whip-cut that prevents a country from going to sleep and forces satisfied mediocrity to shake off its apathy.
1871 *La Réforme intellectuelle et morale*.

Reno, Janet 1938–
US politician and lawyer. She was State Attorney in Florida (1978–93) and subsequently US Attorney-General in the Clinton administration (1993–2001).

48 I'm just an awkward old maid with a very great affection for men.
1993 Denying rumours that she was a lesbian. In the *Washington Times*, 22 Feb.

49 Nothing can make me madder than lawyers who don't care about others.
1993 Address to the American Bar Association. In the *New York Times*, 9 Aug.

50 Vengeance is a personal reaction. But not one that government can indulge in.
1994 Opposing the death penalty. In the *New York Times*, 15 May.

51 I made the decision long ago that to be afraid would be to diminish my life.
1995 Interview in NPR broadcast, 18 Jul.

Renoir, Jean 1894–1979
French film director, son of Pierre Auguste Renoir. His *La Grande Illusion* (1937) and *La Bête humaine* (1939) are among the masterpieces of the cinema.

52 A director makes only one film in his life. Then he breaks it into pieces and makes it again.
Quoted in Leslie Halliwell *Halliwell's Filmgoer's Companion* (1993).

53 Goodbye Mr Zanuck. It certainly has been a pleasure working for 16th Century Fox.
On leaving Hollywood. Attributed.

Renoir, Pierre Auguste 1841–1919
French Impressionist painter, born in Limoges. He exhibited with the Impressionists, and his *Moulin de la Galette* (1876) with sunlight filtering through leaves epitomizes his colourful, happy art. His visit to Italy in 1880 was followed by a series of *Bathers* (1884–7) in a more cold and classical style. He then returned to reds, orange and gold to portray nudes in sunlight, a style which he continued to develop until his death. His works include *The Umbrellas* (c.1883) and *The Judgement of Paris* (c.1914).

54 There is something in painting which cannot be explained, and that something is essential. You come to nature with your theories, and nature knocks them all flat.
c.1915 Quoted in Ambroise Vollard *Renoir, an Intimate Record* (1930).

55 I have a horror of the word 'flesh', which has become so shopworn. Why not 'meat' while they're about it? What I like is skin, a young girl's skin that is pink and shows that she has a good circulation.
Quoted in Jean Renoir *Renoir, My Father* (translated by R and D Weaver, 1962).

56 The only reward one should offer an artist is to buy his work.
From Renoir's notebook, quoted in L Nochlin *Impressionism and Post-Impressionism 1874–1904* (1966).

57 It is impossible to repeat in one period what was done in another. The point of view is not the same, any more than are the tools, the ideals, the needs, or the painters' techniques.
From Renoir's notebook, quoted in L Nochlin *Impressionism and Post-Impressionism 1874–1904* (1966).

58 They were madmen, but they had in them that little flame which never dies.
On the Communards. Quoted in A J P Taylor *From Napoleon to the Second International* (1993).

59 Why shouldn't art be pretty? There are enough unpleasant things in the world.
Quoted in Ian Chilvers and Harold Osborne (eds) *The Oxford Dictionary of Art* (1994).

Repplier, Agnes 1858–1950
US writer and social critic.

60 Science may carry us to Mars, but it will leave the Earth peopled as ever by the inept.
1936 *In Pursuit of Laughter*.

Reston, James B(arrett) 1909–95
Scottish-born US journalist and author. He enjoyed a distinguished career with the *New York Times* and his national news reporting in World War II was recognized in a Pulitzer Prize (1945) and in his promotion to Chief of the Washington Bureau (1953–1964). He won a second Pulitzer Prize in 1957. He was vice-president of the *New York Times* (1969–74) and internationally respected for his political analysis.

61 Smarter than most of his colleagues in the Truman cabinet, but not smart enough to hide it.
1991 Of Secretary of State Dean Acheson. *Deadline*.

62 A little shorter than the Washington monument, erect, elegant, dogmatic, and ironically witty.
1991 Of Secretary of State Dean Acheson. *Deadline*.

63 He could strut sitting down.
1991 Of Senator Arthur Vandenberg. *Deadline*.

64 They were always…getting more credit than they deserved, more sorrow than they could bear, climbing into jobs before they were ready and failing just when they were succeeding.
1991 Of John F, Robert F and Edward M Kennedy. *Deadline*.

65 He not only knew a lot about foreign affairs, he *was* a foreign affair.
1991 Of former Secretary of State Henry A Kissinger. *Deadline*.

66 The American people…were like him: cheerful, optimistic, patriotic, inconsistent, and casually inattentive.
1991 Of President Ronald Reagan. *Deadline*.

Revlon, Charles Haskell 1906–75
US cosmetics salesman, founder with his brother Joseph and chemist Charles Lachman of Revlon Inc (1932). His success was due to initiatives such as giving exotic names to colours and also to intimidation and attacks on competitors.

67 I don't meet competition. I crush it.
1958 In *Time*, 16 Jun.

68 In the factory, we make cosmetics; in the store we sell hope.
Quoted in Andrew P Tobias *Fire and Ice* (1976), ch.8.

Reyes, Alfonso 1889–1959

Mexican poet, novelist, essayist, critic, educator and diplomat. His classical background and humanistic approach lend his writings a distinctive elegance.

69 *El orbe hispano nunca se vino abajo, ni siquiera a la caída del imperio español, sino que se ha multiplicado en numerosas facetas de ensanches todavía insospechados… No somos pueblos en estado de candor, que se deslumbren fácilmente con los instrumentos externos de que se acompaña la cultura, sino pueblos que heredan una vieja civilización y exigen la excelencia misma de la cultura.*
The Hispanic world never crumbled, not even after the Spanish Empire fell, but instead has multiplied itself in broad ways that are still largely unknown… Our people are not naive and are not blinded by the external tools that go together with culture; we are rather the inheritors of an old civilization, and we demand the excellence proper to culture itself.
1941 *Páginas escogidas*, 'Valor de la literatura hispanoamericana' (translated as 'The Value of Hispanic American Literature').

Reynolds, Sir Joshua 1723–92

English painter, writer on art and the first President of the Royal Academy. He is one of the most important figures in the history of English painting.

70 A mere copier of nature never produces anything great.
1770 *Discourses on Art*, no.3, 14 Dec.

Rhodes, Cecil John 1853–1902

South African statesman. He entered the Cape House of Assembly, where he secured the charter for the British South Africa Company (1889), whose territory was later named Rhodesia. Prime Minister of Cape Colony (1890–6), he resigned after the Jameson raid (when the Boers defeated Dr Jameson's attempt to reach Johannesburg). During the Boer War of 1899–1902 he organized the defences of Kimberley.

71 Remember that you are an Englishman, and have consequently won first prize in the lottery of life.
Quoted in Peter Ustinov *Dear Me* (1977). This has also been attributed to Lord Milner.

Rhys, Jean *pseudonym of* Ellen Gwendolen Rees Williams 1894–1979

British novelist, born in the West Indies, of Welsh and Creole descent. Of her novels and short stories *Wide Sargasso Sea* (1966), redefining Charlotte Brontë's first Mrs Rochester, is the best known.

72 The perpetual hunger to be beautiful and that thirst to be loved which is the real curse of Eve.
1927 *The Left Bank*, 'Illusion'.

73 I wanted to be black. I always wanted to be black… Being black is warm and gay, being white is cold and sad.
1934 *Voyage in the Dark*, ch.1.

74 It's funny when you feel as if you don't want anything more in your life except to sleep, or else to lie without moving. That's when you can hear time sliding past you, like water running.
1934 *Voyage in the Dark*, ch.2.

75 Cold—cold as truth, cold as life. No, nothing can be as cold as life.
1934 *Voyage in the Dark*, ch.3.

76 The feeling of Sunday is the same everywhere, heavy, melancholy, standing still. Like when they say 'As it was in the beginning, is now, and ever shall be, world without end'.
1934 *Voyage in the Dark*, ch.4, pt.1.

77 We will watch the sun set again—many times, and perhaps we'll see the Emerald Drop, the green flash that brings good fortune.
1966 *Wide Sargasso Sea*, pt.2.

78 There is no looking-glass here and I don't know what I am like now. I remember watching myself brush my hair and how my eyes looked back at me. The girl I saw was myself and yet not quite myself. Long ago when I was a child and very lonely I tried to kiss her. But the glass was between us—hard, cold and misted over with my breath. Now they have taken everything away. What am I doing in this place and who am I?
1966 The consciousness of Antoinette Mason/Bertha Rochester at a point of intersection with the text of *Jane Eyre*. *Wide Sargasso Sea*, pt.3.

Ricardo, David 1772–1823

English political economist. He set up in business as a young man, and in 1817 produced his chief work, *Principles of Political Economy and Taxation*. In 1819 he became an MP, and was influential in the free-trade movement.

79 It is not to be understood that the natural price of labour, estimated even in food and necessaries, is absolutely fixed and constant. It varies at different times in the same country and very materially differs in different countries. It essentially depends on the habits and customs of the people.
1817 *Principles of Political Economy and Taxation*.

80 In every case, agricultural as well as manufacturing profits are lowered by a rise in the price of raw produce, if it be accompanied by a rise of wages_ The natural tendency of profits is to fall; for in the progress of society and wealth, the additional quantity of food required is obtained by the sacrifice of more and more labour.
1817 *Principles of Political Economy and Taxation*.

81 Like all other contracts, wages should be left to the fair and free competition of the market, and should never be controlled by the interference of the legislature.
1817 *Principles of Political Economy and Taxation*.

82 Possessing utility, commodities derive their exchangeable value from two sources: from their scarcity and from the labour required to obtain them. By far the greatest part of those goods which are the objects of desire, are procured by labour.
1817 *Principles of Political Economy and Taxation*.

83 The interest of the landlord is always opposed to the interests of every other class in the community.
1817 *Principles of Political Economy and Taxation*.

84 The natural price of labour is that price which is necessary to enable the labourers, one with another, to

subsist and to perpetuate their race, without either increase or diminution.
1817 *Principles of Political Economy and Taxation.*

Rice, Condoleezza 1954–

US political scientist and diplomat. Having served as National Security Advisor (2001–5) during President George W. Bush's first term, she became Secretary of State (2005–9) in his second administration.

85 For sixty years, my country, the United States, pursued stability at the expense of democracy in this region, here in the Middle East, and we achieved neither.
2005 Speech at the American University, Cairo, 21 Jun.

86 The United States government does not authorise or condone torture of detainees. Torture, and conspiracy to commit torture, are crimes under US law, wherever they may occur in the world.
2005 Responding to allegations that the US was torturing detainees, 5 Dec.

87 It's bad policy to speculate on what you'll do if a plan fails when you're trying to make a plan work.
2007 Speaking before the Senate Foreign Relations Committee, 11 Jan.

88 If you are over-dressed, it is a comment on them. If you are under-dressed, it is a comment on you.
2010 *Extraordinary, Ordinary People: A Memoir of Family.*

Rice, Grantland 1880–1954

US sportswriter and poet. He is remembered for his colourful reporting style and popular verse.

89 For when the One Great Scorer comes
To write against your name,
He marks—not that you won or lost—
But how you played the game.
1941 *Only the Brave,* 'Alumnus Football'.

90 All wars are planned by old men
In council rooms apart.
1955 *The Final Answer,* 'The Two Sides of War'.

91 Play ball! Means something more than runs
Or pitches thudding into gloves!
Remember through the summer suns
This is the game your country loves.
Quoted in Colin Jarman *The Guinness Dictionary of Sports Quotations* (1990).

Rice-Davies, Mandy 1944–2014

Welsh model and show girl.

92 He would, wouldn't he?
1963 On hearing that during the trial of Stephen Ward, Lord Astor had denied her allegations of orgies at his house parties at Cliveden, 29 Jun.

Rich, Adrienne Cecile 1929–2012

US poet. She was one of the most prominent feminist poets of her generation. Her best-known work includes *Diving into the Wreck* (1973).

93 Weather abroad
And weather in the heart alike come on
Regardless of prediction.
1951 *A Change of World,* 'Storm Warnings'.

94 Love only what you do,
And not what you have done.
1955 *The Diamond Cutters and Other Poems,* 'The Diamond Cutters'.

95 Your mind now, moldering like wedding-cake,
heavy with useless experience, rich
with suspicion, rumour, fantasy,
crumbling to pieces under the knife-edge
of mere fact. In the prime of your life.
1963 *Snapshots of a Daughter-in-Law,* 'Snapshots of a Daughter-in-Law, 1'.

96 Only
a fact could be so dreamlike.
1966 *Necessities of Life,* 'Like This Together'.

97 Only where there is language is there world.
1969 *Leaflets,* 'The Demon Lover'.

98 All wars are useless to the dead.
1969 *Leaflets,* 'Implosions'.

99 I am an instrument in the shape
of a woman trying to translate pulsations
into images for the relief of the body
and the reconstruction of the mind.
1971 *The Will to Change,* 'Planetarium'.

1 It's exhilarating to be alive in a time of awakening consciousness; it can also be confusing, disorienting, and painful.
1971 Talk delivered to Forum on 'The Woman Writer in the Twentieth Century'. Collected as 'When We Dead Awaken: Writing as Re-Vision', in *College English,* Oct 1972.

2 the thing I came for:
the wreck and not the story of the wreck
the thing itself and not the myth.
1973 *Diving into the Wreck,* 'Diving into the Wreck'.

3 When did we begin to dress ourselves?
1973 *Diving into the Wreck,* 'Blood-Sister'.

4 Any woman's death diminishes me.
1974 *Poems: Selected and New,* 'From an Old House in America, 16'.
▶ See Donne 293:69.

5 Without contemplating last and late
the true nature of poetry. The drive
to connect. The dream of a common language.
1978 *The Dream of a Common Language,* 'Origins and History of Consciousness'.

6 Since we're not young, weeks have to do time for years of missing each other. Yet only this odd warp in time tells me we're not young.
1978 *The Dream of a Common Language,* 'Twenty-One Love Poems, III'.

7 Anger and tenderness: my selves.
And now I can believe they breathe in me
as angels, not polarities.
1981 *A Wild Patience Has Taken Me This Far,* 'Integrity'.

8 I refuse to become a seeker for cures.
Everything that has ever
helped me has come through what already
lay stored in me.
1986 *Your Native Land, Your Life,* 'Sources, II'.

9 This is the day of atonement; but do my people forgive me?
If a cloud knew loneliness and fear, I would be that cloud.
1986 *Your Native Land, Your Life,* 'Yom Kippur, 1984'.

10 Experience is always larger than language.
   1991 Interview in the *American Poetry Review*, Jan–Feb.

Richard I known as 'the Lionheart' 1157–99
King of England (from 1189). He led the Crusaders in 1190 and after concluding a peace sailed for home (1191), but was captured by Leopold, Duke of Austria and handed over to Emperor Henry VI. Ransomed in 1194, he went to France where he warred against Philip II until he was killed in the siege of Chalus.

11 *Si inuenissem emptorum, Londoniam uendidissem.*
   If I could have found a buyer I would have sold London itself.
   1190 Of his fundraising for the Crusade to Palestine. Quoted in Richard of Devizes *Chronicle of Richard of Devizes of the Time of King Richard I* (c.1192).

Richard of Devizes fl.c.1190
English Benedictine monk and chronicler.

12 *Si nolueris habitare cum turpidis, non habitatis Londonie.*
   If you do not want to live among wicked people, do not live in London.
   c.1192 *Chronicle of Richard of Devizes of the Time of King Richard I.*

Richards, Ann 1933–2006
US Democratic politician. State Treasurer of Texas from 1982 to 1990, she then became Governor of Texas (1991–5).

13 You can put lipstick on a hog, and it's still a pig.
   1992 On Republicans' attempts to enhance their candidates. In *Sunday Morning*, CBS TV broadcast, 25 Oct.

Richards, Sir Gordon 1904–86
English jockey. In 34 seasons (1921–54) he was champion jockey 26 times, and rode 4,870 winners. In 1953 he won his first Derby, on Pinza, and also received a knighthood.

14 Mother always told me my day was coming, but I never realized I'd end up being the shortest knight of the year.
   1953 Quoted in Colin Jarman *The Guinness Dictionary of Sports Quotations* (1990).

Richards, I(vor) A(rmstrong) 1893–1979
English scholar and literary critic. He was the initiator of the influential 'New Criticism' school of textual criticism at Cambridge University in the 1920s.

15 To be forced by desire into any unwarrantable belief is a calamity.
   1924 *Principles of Literary Criticism.*

16 Poetry…is capable of saving us; it is a perfectly possible means of overcoming chaos.
   1926 *Science and Poetry*, ch. 7.

Richardson, Henry Handel pen-name of Ethel Florence Lindesay Robertson née Richardson 1870–1946
Australian novelist, who settled in England in 1904. Her first novel was *Maurice Guest* (1908) but she made her name with a trilogy set in Australia, *The Fortunes of Richard Mahoney* (1917–29). She was nominated for the Nobel prize in 1932.

17 You're blessed with a woman's brain: vague, slippery, inexact, interested only in the personal aspect of a thing.
   1910 *The Getting of Wisdom*, ch.9.

Richardson, Tony (Cecil Antonio) 1928–91
British film and stage director. He made a number of highly acclaimed films at the beginning of the 1960s including *The Entertainer* (1960), *A Taste of Honey* (1961) and *Tom Jones* (1963), which won an Academy Award.

18 People in this country haven't got the cinema in their blood—the real creative talent has been drained off into theatre.
   1961 On Britain. Quoted in the *Monthly Film Bulletin*, Apr 1993.

Richelieu, Armand Jean du Plessis, Duc de known as Cardinal Richelieu 1585–1642
French statesman. A protégé of the regent Marie de Médicis, he became Minister of State (1624), and as Chief Minister to Louis XIV (1624–42) was effective ruler of France. He succeeded in destroying Huguenot power, securing universal obedience to the Bourbon monarchy, checking Habsburg power and enhancing France's international prestige, but his ruthless severity, his intrigues and his high taxes earned him the hatred of many.

19 Not least among the qualities in a great King is a capacity to permit his Ministers to serve him.
   1688 *Testament Politique.*

20 Secrecy is the first essential in the affairs of State.
   1688 *Testament Politique.*

21 When people are too comfortable, it is not possible to restrain them within the bounds of their duty… They may be compared to mules who, being accustomed to burdens, are spoilt by rest rather than labour.
   1688 *Testament Politique.*

22 Wounds inflicted by the sword heal more easily than those inflicted by the tongue.
   1688 *Testament Politique.*

Richler, Mordecai 1931–2001
Canadian novelist, journalist and essayist. His greatest works, including *The Apprenticeship of Duddy Kravitz* (1959), *St Urbain's Horseman* (1971) and *Joshua Then and Now* (1980), are darkly comic novels about the working-class Jewish community in Montreal in which he grew up.

23 Thousands of miles of wheat, indifference, and self-apology.
   1971 Of Canada. *St Urbain's Horseman*, ch.1.

24 Tomorrow country then, tomorrow country now.
   1971 Of Canada. *St Urbain's Horseman*, ch.1.

25 Even in Paris, I remained a Canadian. I puffed hashish, but I didn't inhale.
   1971 *St Urbain's Horseman*, ch.2. The last phrase was later popularized by Bill Clinton, responding to claims that he had taken drugs as a student.

26 The Canadian kid who wants to grow up to be Prime Minister isn't thinking big, he is setting a limit to his ambitions rather early.
   Quoted in *Time* (Canadian edition), 31 May 1971.

Rickword, Edgell 1898–1982
English poet and critic. His early work was influenced by Sassoon. He edited *Left Review* in the 1930s.

27 The oldest griefs of summer seem less sad
   than drone of mowers on suburban lawns

and girls' thin laughter, to the ears that hear
the soft rain falling of the failing stars.
1921 'Regret for the Passing of the Entire Scheme of Things'.

28 My soul's a trampled duelling ground where Sade,
the gallant marquis, fences for his life
against the invulnerable retrograde
Masoch, his shade, more constant than a wife.
1928 'Chronique Scandaleuse'.

29 Why stir the wasps that rim Fame's luscious pot?
Love costs us nothing, satire costs a lot!
1931 'The Contemporary Muse'.

Ridge, W(illiam) Pett 1857–1930

English novelist. He was a prolific writer, publishing over 60 books in total.

30 He took her up in his arms in the way of a bachelor who has had amateur experience of the carrying of nieces.
1902 *Lost Property*, pt.1, ch.8.

31 Ballard admitted he was no hand at giving descriptions; the man was apparently a gentleman and the woman— well, not exactly a lady, although she had a very fine flow of language.
1905 *Mrs Galer's Business*, ch.6.

32 Gertie recommended her to adopt the habit of not magnifying grievances; if you wanted to view trouble, you could take opera-glasses, but you should be careful to hold them the wrong way round.
1912 *Love at Paddington Green*, ch.4.

33 'How did you think I managed at dinner, Clarence?'
'Capitally!'
'I had a knife and two forks left at the end,' she said regretfully.
1912 *Love at Paddington Green*, ch.6.

Riding, Laura née Reichenthal 1901–91

US poet and fiction writer. She was first published by Leonard and Virginia Woolf's Hogarth Press, and is more admired as a poet than for her polemical prose writings.

34 Art, whose honesty must work through artifice, cannot avoid cheating truth.
1975 *Selected Poems: In Five Sets*, preface.

Rifkind, Simon Hirsch 1901–95

US judge. He was a partner in his legal firm and an adviser to General Eisenhower on Jewish matters in the American occupied zone (1945).

35 Impartiality is an acquired taste, like olives. You have to be habituated to it.
1979 In *Time*, 20 Aug.

Rilke, Rainer Maria 1875–1926

German poet who travelled widely and lived throughout Europe.

36 Ach, aber mit Versen ist so wenig getan, wenn man sie früh schreibt. Man sollte warten damit und Sinn und Süßigkeit sammeln ein ganzes Leben lang und ein langes womöglich, und dann, ganz zum Schluss, vielleicht könnte man dann zehn Zeilen schreiben, die gut sind.
Ah, poems amount to so little when you write them too early in your life. You ought to wait and gather sense and sweetness for a whole lifetime, and a long one if possible, and then, at the very end, you might perhaps be able to write ten good lines.
1910 *Die Aufzeichnungen des Malte Laurids Brigge* (translated by Stephen Mitchell in *The Selected Poetry of Rainer Maria Rilke*, 1989).

37 Ich habe um meine Kindheit gebeten, und sie ist wiedergekommen, und ich fühle, dass sie immer noch so schwer ist wie damals, und dass es nichts genützt hat, älter zu werden.
I prayed to rediscover my childhood, and it has come back, and I feel that it is just as difficult as it used to be, and that growing older has served no purpose at all.
1910 *Die Aufzeichnungen des Malte Laurids Brigge* (translated by Stephen Mitchell in *The Selected Poetry of Rainer Maria Rilke*, 1989).

38 Und das Totsein ist mühsam
und voller Nachholn, dass man allmählich ein wenig Ewigkeit spürt.
And being dead is hard work
and full of retrieval before one can gradually feel
a trace of eternity.
1923 *Duinieser Elegien*, no.1 (translated by Stephen Mitchell in *The Selected Poetry of Rainer Maria Rilke*, 1989).

39 Siehe, wir lieben nicht, wie die Blumen, aus einem einzigen Jahr; uns steigt, wo wir lieben, unvordenklicher Saft in die Arme.
No, we don't accomplish our love in a single year
as the flowers do; an immemorial sap
flows up through our arms when we love.
1923 *Duinieser Elegien*, no.3 (translated by Stephen Mitchell in *The Selected Poetry of Rainer Maria Rilke*, 1989).

40 Wer zeigt ein Kind, so wie es steht? Wer stellt es ins Gestirn und gibt das Maß des Abstands ihm in die Hand?
Who shows a child as he really is? Who sets him
in his constellation and puts the measuring-rod
of distance in his hand?
1923 *Duinieser Elegien*, no.4 (translated by Stephen Mitchell in *The Selected Poetry of Rainer Maria Rilke*, 1989).

Rimbaud, (Jean Nicolas) Arthur 1854–91

French poet who wrote his entire work before the age of 20. His relationship with poet Paul Verlaine was notorious. He eventually became an arms trader in Abyssinia.

41 Et j'ai vu quelquefois ce que l'homme a cru voir.
I've sometimes seen what other men have only dreamed of seeing.
1871 *Poésies*, 'Le Bateau ivre'.

42 Je regrette l'Europe aux anciens parapets!
I long for Europe of the ancient parapets!
1871 *Poésies*, 'Le Bateau ivre'.

43 Ô mes petites amoureuses,
Que je vous hais!
Oh my little mistresses,
How I hate you!
1871 *Poésies*, 'Mes petites amoureuses'.

44 On n'est pas sérieux, quand on a dix-sept ans.
When you are seventeen, you are not serious.
1871 *Poésies*, 'Roman', no.1.

45 Le poète est vraiment voleur de feu.
The poet is the true fire-stealer.
1871 Letter to Paul Demeny, 15 May.

46 *La Poésie ne rythmera plus l'action; elle sera en avant.*
Poetry will no longer keep step with the action; it will be ahead of it.
1871 Letter to Paul Demeny, 15 May.

47 *Elle est retrouvée.*
Quoi?—L'Éternité.
C'est la mer allée
Avec le soleil.
It has been recovered.
What?—Eternity.
It is the sea escaping
With the sun.
1872 *Derniers vers, Fêtes de la patience,* 'L'Éternité'.

48 *J'ai fait la magique étude*
Du Bonheur, que nul n'élude.
I studied the magic lore of Happiness
Which no one can escape.
1872 *Derniers vers, Fêtes de la faim,* 'Ô saisons, ô châteaux!'.

49 *Un soir, j'ai assis la Beauté sur mes genoux.—Et je l'ai trouvée amère.—Et je l'ai injuriée.*
One evening, I sat Beauty on my knees.—And I found her bitter.—And I hurt her.
1873 *Une saison en enfer,* 'Jadis, si je me souviens bien'.

50 *Je me crois en enfer, donc j'y suis.*
I believe myself to be in hell; therefore I am.
1873 *Une saison en enfer,* 'Mauvais sang'.

51 *Le Bonheur était ma fatalité, mon remords, mon ver: ma vie serait toujours trop immense pour être dévouée à la force et à la beauté.*
Happiness was my fate, my remorse, my worm: my life would always be too large to be dedicated to force and to beauty.
1873 *Une saison en enfer, Délires,* no.2, 'Alchimie du verbe'.

Rimsky-Korsakov, Nikolai Andreievich 1844–1908

Russian composer. He established his reputation with three great orchestral masterpieces (1887–8), *Capriccio Espagnol, Easter Festival* and *Scheherazade*. He then turned to opera, producing *The Snow Maiden* (1882), *Legend of Tsar Saltan* (1900), *The Invisible City of Kitesh* (1906) and *The Golden Cockerel* (1906).

52 I have already heard it. I had better not go: I will start to get accustomed to it and finally like it.
Of the music of Debussy, when invited to a concert where it was to be performed. Quoted in Igor Stravinsky *Chronicles of My Life* (1936).

Riva, Maria 1924–

Daughter and biographer of Marlene Dietrich.

53 They filled our hall like a monogrammed Stonehenge.
1992 Of the six closet-size wardrobe trunks used by her mother. *Marlene Dietrich*.

Rivera, Diego 1886–1957

Mexican painter, one of the three foremost artists in the revival of monumental fresco painting.

54 The subject is to the painter what the rails are to a locomotive. He cannot do without it.
1929 *Creative Art*.

Rivera, José Eustasio 1889–1928

Colombian lawyer, poet and novelist. A journey through the Amazon jungle with a commission to settle the boundary dispute between Colombia and Venezuela inspired him to write the magnificently descriptive novel *La vorágine* (1924).

55 *Antes que me hubiera apasionado por mujer alguna, jugué mi corazón al azar y me lo ganó la violencia.*
Before I felt passion for any woman, I gambled my heart and lost it to violence.
1924 *La vorágine,* pt.1 (translated as *The Vortex,* 1935).

Rivers, Joan *pseudonym of* Joan Alexandra Molinsky 1933–2014

US comedienne and writer. An acid-tongued stand-up comedienne in the 1960s, she went on to host television shows, as well as directing and appearing in films, recording an album and publishing books.

56 I'm Jewish. I don't work out. If God had wanted us to bend over he'd've put diamonds on the floor.
Quoted in Colin Jarman *The Guinness Dictionary of Sports Quotations* (1990).

57 My body is a temple, and my temple needs redecorating.
2012 Explaining why she was having cosmetic surgery at the age of 78, *Mail Online,* 25 Jan.

58 Every joke I make, no matter how tasteless, is there to draw attention to something I really care about. And if the jokes I make call attention to things that aren't right in the world, that's why I do it.
2014 Quoted on thestar.com, 26 Dec.

Robb, Charles S(pittal) 1939–

US lawyer, Senator for Virginia (1989–2001).

59 The threat to morale comes not from the orientation of a few, but from the closed minds of the many.
1993 On gays in the military. In the *New York Times,* 5 Feb.

Robbe-Grillet, Alain 1922–2008

French novelist, scriptwriter and film director, whose repetitive style blurs the standard narrative distinctions in writing.

60 *On n'échappe pas à son sort.*
One cannot escape destiny.
1953 *Les Gommes*.

61 *Deux mètres—ou un peu plus—séparent donc l'homme de la femme.*
Two metres, or a little more, separates a man from a woman.
1955 *Le Voyeur*.

62 *Le lecteur, lui non plus, ne voit pas les choses du dehors. Il est dans le labyrinthe aussi.*
The reader [as well as the main character] does not view the work from outside. He too is in the labyrinth.
1959 *Dans le labyrinthe*.

63 *Et une fois de plus je m'avançais le long de ces mêmes couloirs, marchant depuis des jours, depuis des mois, depuis des années, à votre rencontre.*
And one more time, I advanced along these same hallways, walking for *days,* for *months,* for *years,* to meet you.
1961 *L'Année dernière à Marienbad*.

64 *Car loin de le [le lecteur] négliger, l'auteur aujourd'hui proclame l'absolu besoin qu'il a de son concours actif, conscient, créateur. Ce qu'il lui demande, ce n'est plus de recevoir tout fait un monde achevé, plein, clos sur lui-même, c'est au*

contraire de participer à une création, d'inventer à son tour l'œuvre—et le monde—et d'apprendre ainsi à inventer sa propre vie.

Far from neglecting him [the reader], the author today proclaims the absolute necessity of the reader's active, conscious and creative assistance. What he demands of the reader is no longer to receive a ready-made world, complete, full, closed in upon itself. On the contrary, the reader is asked to participate in the creation, to invent for himself a work—and the world—and to understand thus how to invent his own life.

1963 *Pour un nouveau roman.*

65 *L'amour est un jeu, la poésie est un jeu, la vie doit devenir un jeu (c'est le seul espoir de nos luttes politiques) et 'la révolution elle-même est un jeu', comme disaient les plus conscients des révolutionnaires de mai.*

Love is a game, poetry is a game, life should become a game (it's the only hope for our political struggles) and 'the revolution itself is a game', as the most aware of the May revolutionaries said.

1970 *Projet pour une révolution à New York.*

66 *Première approximation: j'écris pour détruire, en les décrivant avec précision, des monstres nocturnes qui menacent d'envahir ma vie éveillée.*

First general point: I write to destroy, by describing exactly the nocturnal monsters that threaten to invade my waking life.

1984 *Le Miroir qui revient.*

Robbins, Colonel

US Red Cross representative at Petrograd.

67 A four-kind son-of-a-bitch, but the greatest Jew since Jesus Christ.

Of Leon Trotsky. Quoted by A J P Taylor in the *New Statesman and Nation*, 20 Feb 1954.

Robbins, Lionel Charles, Baron Robbins of Clare Market 1898–1984

English economist, Professor at the London School of Economics and later chairman of the *Financial Times*.

68 Economics is the science which studies human behaviour as a relationship between scarce resources and ends which have alternative uses… It does not attempt to pick out certain *kinds* of behaviour, but focuses attention on a particular *aspect* of behaviour, the form imposed by the influence of scarcity.

1932 *An Essay on the Nature and Significance of Economic Science*, p.16–17.

Robbins, Tim 1958–

US actor and director, whose acting credits include *Jacob's Ladder* (1990), *The Player* (1992) and *The Shawshank Redemption* (1994), *Mystic River* (2003) and *Cinema Verite* (2011).

69 As we applaud the hard-edged realism of the opening battle scene of *Saving Private Ryan*, we cringe at the thought of seeing the same on the nightly news. We are told it would be pornographic.

2003 Speech to the National Press Club, Washington DC, 15 Apr.

70 I had been unaware that baseball was a Republican sport.

2003 In a letter to Dale Petroskey, president of the National Baseball Hall of Fame, after his appearance there was cancelled when he criticized President George W Bush, Apr.

Robert of Clari fl.c.1216

Pickard knight.

71 When they were on that sea and had spread their sails and had their banners set high on the poops of the ships and their ensigns, it seemed indeed as if the sea were all a-tremble and all on fire with the ships they were sailing and the great joy they were making.

1203 Describing the Venetian fleet setting out. *The Conquest of Constantinople* (translated by E H McNeal, 1936), p.42–3.

Roberts, Sir Charles George Douglas 1860–1943

Canadian poet, naturalist, novelist and short-story writer. His first book of poems, *Orion, and Other Poems* (1880), inspired the group later known as 'The Confederation Poets'. In 1892 he published his first animal story, of which there would eventually be about 20 collected volumes. Roberts also translated French–Canadian literature into English.

72 This is the voice of high midsummer's heat.
 The rasping vibrant clamour soars and shrills
 O'er all the meadowy range of shadeless hills,
 As if a host of giant cicadae beat
 The cymbals of their wings with tireless feet,
 Or brazen grasshoppers with triumphing note
 From the long swath proclaimed the fate that
  smote
 The clover and timothy-tops and meadowsweet.

1893 'The Mowing'.

73 When Winter scourged the meadow and the hill
 And in the withered leafage worked his will,
 Then water shrank, and shuddered, and stood still,—
 Then built himself a magic house of glass,
 Irised with memories of flowers and grass,
 Wherein to sit and watch the fury pass.

1898 'Ice'.

74 And I turned and fled, like a soul pursued,
 From the white, inviolate solitude.

1901 'The Skater'.

Robertson (of Port Ellen), George Islay Macneill Robertson, Baron 1946–

Scottish Labour politician, Secretary-General of NATO (1999–2004).

75 Serbs out, Nato in, refugees back.

1999 Summing up the Nato objective in Kosovo, 7 Jun.

Robeson, Paul 1898–1976

US singer, actor and civil rights activist.

76 My father was a slave, and my people died to build this country, and I am going to stay here and have a piece of it, just like you.

1956 Statement to the House of Representatives Committee on Un-American Activities.

Robin, Leo 1899–1985

US lyricist best known for his collaboration with composer Ralph Rainger between 1932 and 1942. After Rainger's death he wrote with various other composers.

77 Thanks for the Memory.
   1937 Title of song, which became Bob Hope's signature tune. Music by Ralph Rainger.

Robinson, (Edward) Austin George 1897–1993
English economist, professor at Cambridge University.

78 All industrial efficiency consists in trying to do with eight men what we have hitherto been doing with ten men. It consists in creating unemployment.
   1931 *The Structure of Competitive Industry*.

Robinson, Casey 1903–79
US screenwriter. His credits include *Captain Blood* (1935), *Now, Voyager* (1942) and *The Snows of Kilimanjaro* (1952).

79 Don't let's ask for the moon. We have the stars.
   1942 Line delivered by Bette Davis to Paul Henreid in *Now, Voyager*.

80 Where's the rest of me?
   1942 Line delivered by Ronald Reagan on discovering his legs have been amputated in *King's Row*.

Robinson, Edward G *pseudonym of* Emanuel Goldenberg 1893–1973
Hungarian-born US actor, whose portrayal of a vicious gangster in *Little Caesar* (1930) brought him stardom. Other films include *The Whole Town's Talking* (1935), *Double Indemnity* (1944) and *Key Largo* (1948).

81 Mother of Mercy, is this the end of Rico?
   1930 Line delivered by him in *Little Caesar* (screenplay by Francis Faragoh and Robert E Lee).

Robinson, Edwin Arlington 1869–1935
US poet. He created a fictional New England village, Tilbury Town, in which his best poetry is set. He won three Pulitzer Prizes (1922, 1925 and 1928).

82 In fine, we thought that he was everything
   To make us wish that we were in his place.

   So on we worked, and waited for the light,
   And went without meat, and cursed the bread;
   And Richard Cory, one calm summer night,
   Went home and put a bullet through his head.
   1897 *The Children of the Night*, 'Richard Cory'.

83 Friends
   To borrow my books and set wet glasses on them.
   1902 *Captain Craig*, 'Captain Craig', pt.2.

84 Miniver Cheevy, child of scorn,
   Grew lean while he assailed the seasons;
   He wept that he was ever born,
   And he had reasons.
   1910 *The Town down the River*, 'Miniver Cheevy'.

85 Miniver loved the Medici,
   Albeit he had never seen one;
   He would have sinned incessantly
   Could he have been one.
   1910 *The Town down the River*, 'Miniver Cheevy'.

86 Miniver Cheevy, born too late,
   Scratched his head and kept on thinking;
   Miniver coughed, and called it fate,
   And kept on drinking.
   1910 *The Town down the River*, 'Miniver Cheevy'.

87 The world is…a kind of kindergarten, where millions of bewildered infants are trying to spell God with the wrong blocks.
   1917 *Literature in the Making*.

88 I shall have more to say when I am dead.
   1920 *The Three Taverns*, 'John Brown'.

89 Below him, in the town among the trees,
   Where friends of other days had honored him,
   A phantom salutation of the dead
   Rang thinly till old Eben's eyes were dim.
   1921 *Avon's Harvest*, 'Mr Flood's Party'.

90 The Man Who Died Twice.
   1924 Title of book.

91 Joy shivers in the corner where she knits
   And Conscience always has the rocking-chair,
   Cheerful as when she tortured into fits
   The first cat that was ever killed by Care.
   1925 *Dionysus in Doubt*, 'New England'.

Robinson, Joan Violet *née* Maurice 1903–83
English economist, a leader of the Cambridge school which developed macroeconomic theories of growth and distribution based on the work of Keynes. Her works include *The Economics of Imperfect Competition* (1933) and *Economic Heresies* (1971).

92 The typical entrepreneur is no longer the bold and tireless man of Marshall, or the sly and rapacious Moneybags of Marx, but a mass of inert shareholders, indistinguishable from *rentiers*, who employ salaried managers to run their concerns.
   1947 *An Essay on Marxian Economics*.

93 The purpose of studying economics is not to acquire a set of ready-made answers to economic questions, but to learn how to avoid being deceived by economists.
   1955 Quoted in *Contributions to Modern Economics* (1978), p.75.

94 It is impossible to understand the economic system in which we are living if we try to interpret it as a rational scheme. It has to be understood as an awkward phase in a continuing process of historical development.
   1966 *Economics: an Awkward Corner*.

95 Hitler had already found out how to cure unemployment before Keynes had finished explaining why it occurred.
   1971 Collected in *Contributions to Modern Economics* (1978), p.10.

Robinson, John Arthur Thomas 1919–83
English churchman and radical theologian, Bishop of Woolwich, latterly Dean of Clare College, Cambridge.

96 Jesus never claims to be God, personally, yet he always claims to bring God, completely.
   1963 *Honest to God*.

Robinson, Mary 1944–
Irish Labour politician, President (1990–7) and UN High Commissioner for Human Rights (1997–2002).

97 Instead of rocking the cradle, they rocked the system.
   1990 Paying tribute to Irish women, in her victory speech. Quoted in *The Times*, 10 Nov.

Robson, Sir Bobby 1933–2009

English footballer and football manager. He was manager of Ipswich Town (1969–82), England (1982–90) and Newcastle United (1999–2004).

98 I'd have given my right arm to be a pianist.
   2000 On what he would have done if he were not a football manager. In *The Times*, 26 Dec.

Roche, Sir Boyle 1743–1807

Irish politician. He joined the British army and fought in the war in America. On returning to Ireland he entered parliament in 1776 and remained an MP until the Act of Union (1800). He opposed Catholic emancipation and supported the Union. He was granted a pension for his constant support of the government.

99 Mr Speaker, I think the noble young man has no business to make any apology. He is a gentleman, and none such should be asked to make an *apology*, because no *gentleman* could *mean* to *give offence*.
   c.1796 Debate on motion to expel Lord Edward Fitzgerald from Irish House of Commons, quoted in Sir Jonah Barrington *Personal Sketches and Recollections of his own Times* (1827).

1 Sir, there is no Levitical degrees between nations, and on this occasion I can see neither sin nor shame in *marrying our own sister*.
   c.1800 Debate on the Act of Union between Great Britain and Ireland, Irish House of Commons, quoted in Sir Jonah Barrington *Personal Sketches and Recollections of his own Times* (1827).

2 What, Mr Speaker! and so we are to beggar ourselves for fear of vexing posterity! Now, I would ask the honourable gentleman, and *still more* honourable House, why should we put ourselves out of our way to do anything for *posterity*; for what has *posterity* done for *us*?
   Debate in Irish House of Commons, quoted in Sir Jonah Barrington *Personal Sketches and Recollections of his own Times* (1827).
   ▸ See Addison 7:54.

3 The best way to *avoid* danger is to *meet it plump*.
   Quoted in Sir Jonah Barrington *Personal Sketches and Recollections of his own Times* (1827).

Rochester, John Wilmot, 2nd Earl of 1647–80

English courtier and lyric poet. He is noted for his entertaining letters, for satires, including 'A Satyr Against Mankind' (1674), and for his verses and songs, many of which are sexually frank or defamatory.

4 I hold you six to four I love you with all my heart, if I would bet with other people I'm sure I could get ten to one.
   c.1667 Letter from Newmarket to his wife. In *The Letters of John Wilmot, Earl of Rochester*, edited by Jeremy Treglown (1980).

5 Naked she lay, clasped in my longing arms,
   I filled with love, and she all over charms,
   Both equally inspired with eager fire,
   Melting through kindness, flaming in desire;
   With arms, legs, lips, close clinging to embrace.
   c.1672 'The Imperfect Enjoyment', l.1–6 (published 1680).

6 'Is there no more?'
   She cries. 'All this to love, and rapture's due,
   Must we not pay a debt to pleasure too?'
   c.1672 'The Imperfect Enjoyment', l.22–4 (published 1680).

7 Restless, he rolls about from whore to whore,
   A merry Monarch, scandalous and poor.
   1673 Of Charles II. 'I' th' Isle of Britain', l.14–15. The poem resulted in a brief period of exile for Rochester.

8 Great Negative, how vainly would the wise
   Enquire, define, distinguish, teach, devise,
   Didst thou not stand to point their blind
   Philosophies.
   c.1673 'Upon Nothing', stanza 10 (published 1679).

9 French truth, Dutch prowess, British policy,
   Hibernian learning, Scotch civility,
   Spaniards' dispatch, Danes' wit, are mainly seen in thee.
   c.1673 'Upon Nothing', stanza 16 (published 1679).

10 Were I (who to my loss already am
   One of those strange prodigious creatures, Man)
   A spirit, free to choose for my own share
   What case of flesh and blood I'd choose to wear,
   I'd be a dog, a monkey, or a bear.
   1674 'A Satyr Against Mankind', l.1–5 (published 1679).

11 Reason, an ignis fatuus in the mind,
   Which leaving light of nature, sense behind,
   Pathless and dangerous wandering ways it takes,
   Through error's fenny bogs and thorny brakes;
   Whilst the misguided follower climbs, with pain,
   Mountains of whimsy heaped in his own brain.
   1674 'A Satyr Against Mankind', l.12–17 (published 1679).

12 Then old age and experience, hand in hand,
   Lead him to death, and make him understand,
   After a search so painful and so long,
   That all his life he has been in the wrong.
   Huddled in dirt, the reasoning engine lies,
   Who was so proud, so witty, and so wise.
   1674 'A Satyr Against Mankind', l.25–30 (published 1679).

13 Birds feed on birds, beasts on each other prey,
   But savage man alone does man betray.
   1674 'A Satyr Against Mankind', l.129–30 (published 1679).

14 That cordial drop heaven in our cup has thrown
   To make the nauseous draught of life go down.
   c.1674 Of love. 'A Letter from Artemisia in the Town to Chloe in the Country', l.44–5 (published 1679).

15 What vain, unnecessary things are men,
   How well we do without 'em!
   c.1674–1675 'Fragment of a Satire on Men', l.1–2 (published in full 1953).

16 Dear Madam, You are stark mad, and therefore the fitter for me to love; and that is the reason I think I can never leave to be Your humble servant.
   c.1675 Letter to his mistress, the actress Elizabeth Barry. In *The Letters of John Wilmot, Earl of Rochester*, edited by Jeremy Treglown (1980).

17 To pick out the wildest and most fantastical odd man alive, and to place your kindness there, is an act so brave and daring as will show the greatness of your spirit and distinguish you in love, as you are in all things else, from womankind.
   c.1675 Letter to his mistress, the actress Elizabeth Barry. In *The Letters of John Wilmot, Earl of Rochester*, edited by Jeremy Treglown (1980).

18 They who would be great in our little government seem as ridiculous to me as schoolboys who…climb a crab-tree, venturing their necks for fruit which solid pigs would disdain if they were not starving.
   c.1676 Letter to Henry Savile. In *The Letters of John Wilmot, Earl of Rochester*, edited by Jeremy Treglown (1980).

19 He is a rarity which I cannot but be fond of, as one would be of a hog that could fiddle, or a singing owl.
c.1676 Of Dryden. Letter to Henry Savile. In *The Letters of John Wilmot, Earl of Rochester*, edited by Jeremy Treglown (1980).

20 Son of a whore, God damn you! can you tell
A Peerless Peer the readiest way to Hell?
c.1676 'To the Post-Boy', l.1–2 (published 1926). The postboy's answer is 'The readiest way, my lord, is by Rochester'.

21 My most neglected wife, till you are a much respected widow, I find you will scarce be a contented woman, and to say no more than the plain truth, I do endeavour so fairly to do you that last good service.
c.1677 Letter to his wife, 20 Nov. In *The Letters of John Wilmot, Earl of Rochester*, edited by Jeremy Treglown (1980).

22 There can be no danger in sweetness and youth
Where love is secured by good nature and truth,
On her beauty I'll gaze, and of pleasure complain,
While every kind look adds a link to my chain.
'The Submission', l.13–16 (published 1680).

23 Farewell Woman, I intend,
Henceforth, every night to sit,
With my lewd well natured friend,
Drinking, to engender wit.
'Love a Woman!', l.9–12 (published 1680).

24 Since 'tis nature's law to change,
Constancy alone is strange.
'A Dialogue between Strephon and Daphne', l.31–2 (published 1691).

25 An age in her embraces passed,
Would seem a winter's day;
Where life and light, with envious haste,
Are torn and snatched away.

But, oh how slowly minutes roll,
When absent from her eyes
That feed my love, which is my soul,
It languishes and dies.
'The Mistress', l.1–8 (published 1691).

26 Ancient Person, for whom I
All the flattering youth defy;
Long be it ere thou grow old,
Aching, shaking, crazy, cold;
But still continue as thou art,
Ancient person of my heart.
'A Song of a Young Lady to Her Ancient Lover', stanza 1 (published 1691).

27 God bless our good and gracious King
Whose promise none relies on,
Who never said a foolish thing
Nor ever did a wise one.
Of Charles II (published 1707). The verse was later changed to an epitaph ('Here lies a great and mighty king...').

Rockefeller, David 1915–

US banker and philanthropist, born into the wealthy Rockefeller dynasty, Chairman and Chief Executive Officer of the Chase Manhattan Bank (1969–81).

28 One thing this family does not need to do is make itself resented by thousands more people.
Explaining his reluctance to join the management of the Chase Manhattan Bank. Quoted in Peter Collier and David Horowitz *The Rockefellers* (1976).

29 I was born into wealth and there was nothing I could do about it. It was there like food or air.
1990 In *Merchants and Masterpieces*, WETA TV broadcast, 31 Dec.

30 The supranational sovereignty of an intellectual elite and world bankers is surely preferable to the national auto-determination practised in past centuries.
2002 *Memoirs*.

Rockefeller, John D(avison) 1839–1937

US industrialist and philanthropist. In 1875 he founded with his brother William the Standard Oil Company, securing control of US oil trade. After 1897 he devoted himself to philanthropy, and in 1913 established the Rockefeller Foundation 'to promote the wellbeing of mankind'.

31 The growth of a large business is merely a survival of the fittest... The American Beauty rose can be produced in the splendor and fragrance which bring cheer to its beholder only by sacrificing the early buds which grow up around it.
Quoted in W J Ghent *Our Benevolent Feudalism* (1902).

Rockefeller, John D(avison), Jr 1874–1960

US business and oil magnate. He took over his father's business empire in 1911 and continued the Rockefeller philanthropic tradition. He founded the Rockefeller Center, New York (1931, completed 1939).

32 The secretaries here have an advantage I never had. They can prove to themselves their commercial worth.
1950 Speech to the New York Chamber of Commerce, 6 Apr. Quoted in Peter Collier and David Horowitz *The Rockefellers* (1976).

33 The rendering of useful service is the common duty of mankind, and...only in the purifying fire of sacrifice is the dross of selfishness consumed and the greatness of the human soul set free.
Credo engraved in Rockefeller Center Plaza, New York.

Rockefeller, John D(avison), III 1906–78

US businessman and art collector, Governor of West Virginia.

34 If my name were John D Smith IV I wouldn't have been elected to anything.
1970 On becoming West Virginia's Secretary of State (before moving on to be Governor). In the *New York Times*, 4 Oct.

35 It's like orchestrating a symphony of unhappiness.
1971 On the necessity of compromise in health-care financing. In the *Washington Post*, 1 Jul.

Rockefeller, Laurance S 1910–2004

US businessman, son of John D Rockefeller, Jr. He has been involved with a variety of conservation and environmental organizations.

36 Lyndon gave me that instead of the Hawaii air route.
Of the Medal of Freedom which he received from President Johnson after Eastern Airlines failed to receive permission to fly a coveted route. Quoted in Peter Collier and David Horowitz *The Rockefellers* (1978).

Rockefeller, Nelson A(ldrich) 1908–79

US Republican politician. Director of the Rockefeller Center (1931–58), he became Governor of New York State (1958–73) and Vice-President (1974–7) under Ford, after failing to win the presidential nomination.

37 If there is anything more satisfying than dedicating a new building, it is dedicating eight new buildings.
  1970 On Albany's Government Mall. In the *New York Times*, 13 Mar.

38 When you think of what I had, what else was there to aspire to?
  Of his lifelong ambition to be US President. Quoted in Michael Kramer and Sam Roberts *I Never Wanted to be Vice President of Anything* (1976).

Rockefeller, Winthrop 1912–73

US businessman and politician, son of John D Rockefeller Jr, who ran a farm in Arkansas on experimental principles. He served as Republican Governor of Arkansas (1967–70).

39 In them one can see the spontaneous—and often aesthetic—expression of a people reflected, not in a gilt-framed drawing room mirror, but in an honest glass held up to the face of a nation.
  1962 On an exhibition of American folk art at the US Embassy, London. In news summaries, 31 Jan.

40 In the springtime of America's cultural life, its itinerant folk artists took to the road to record the life and times of a people. Perhaps never again will we have an artistic record created in such direct and unassuming terms.
  1962 On an exhibition of American folk art at the US Embassy, London. In news summaries, 31 Jan.

Rockne, Knute Kenneth 1888–1931

Norwegian-born US football coach. Coach for the University of Notre Dame team after World War I, he dominated US college football until his death in an air crash.

41 When the going gets tough, the tough get going.
  His catchphrase, later adopted by John F Kennedy.

Rockwell, Norman 1894–1978

US popular illustrator, best known for his *Saturday Evening Post* covers. His style is typically anecdotal, idealized scenes of everyday American small-town life.

42 If the public dislikes one of my *Post* covers, I can't help disliking it myself.
  Quoted in the *New York Times*, 28 Sep 1986.

Rodchenko, Alexander 1891–1956

Russian artist who was a leader of the Russian Constructivist painters before he took up photography in 1922 and became active in the field of typography and photographic journalism.

43 Tell me, frankly, what ought to remain of Lenin:
  an art bronze,
  oil portraits,
  etchings,
  watercolours,
  his secretary's diary, his friends' memoirs—
  or
  a file of photographs taken of him at work and rest, archives of his books, writing pads, notebooks, shorthand reports, films, phonograph records?
  I don't think there's any choice.
  Art has no place in modern life... Every cultured modern man must wage war against art, as against opium.

Photograph and be photographed!
  Quoted in Robert Hughes *The Shock of the New* (1980).

Roddenberry, Gene 1921–91

US scriptwriter, producer and director. A former air force pilot, he made his name as the creator of the popular *Star Trek* television series.

44 Space—the final frontier.
  1966 Introductory voiceover to *Star Trek*.

45 To boldly go where no man has gone before.
  1966 The mission of the starship *Enterprise*. Introductory voiceover to *Star Trek*.

46 Beam us up, Mr Scott.
  1966 *Star Trek*, 'Gamesters of Triskelion'. The phrase is often misquoted as 'Beam me up, Scotty'.

Roddick, Andy 1982–

US tennis player.

47 It's only stalking if the other person doesn't like it.
  2009 Admitting to stalking his future wife, *GQ* magazine, Aug.

Roddick, Anita 1942–2007

English retail entrepreneur, founder (in 1976) of the Body Shop.

48 I think that business practices would improve immeasurably if they were guided by 'feminine' principles—qualities like love and care and intuition.
  1991 *Body and Soul*.

Rodgers, Richard and Hart, Lorenz 1902–79; 1896–1943

US composer and songwriter partnership. They wrote a series of popular musicals including *Pal Joey* (1940).

49 Sigmund Freud has often stated
  Dreams and drives are all related.
  Zip, I am such a scholar!
  1940 'Zip', in *Pal Joey*.

Rodgers, T(hurman) J(ohn) 1948–

US businessman. He is founder, president and chief executive officer of Cypress Semiconductor Corporation.

50 Most entrepreneurs who have the guts to take on a big challenge are a lot like Babe Ruth—they set records for both home runs and strike outs.
  1993 Letter about Steven Jobs of Next in the *San Francisco Chronicle*, 6 Dec.

Rodó, José Enrique 1872–1917

Uruguayan essayist and philosopher, a leading stylist and thinker of the Modernist group. His most famous work, *Ariel*, admonishes the youth of South America to cultivate spiritual (Ariel) rather than material (Caliban) values.

51 *La visión de una América deslatinizada por propia voluntad, sin la extorsión de la conquista, y regenerada luego a imagen y semejanza del arquetipo del Norte, flota ya sobre los sueños de muchos sinceros interesados por nuestro porvenir... Tenemos nuestra nordomanía. Es necesario oponerle los límites que la razón y el sentimiento señalan.*
  The vision of an America de-Latinized of its own will, without threat of conquest, and reconstituted in the image and likeness of the North, now looms in the nightmares of many who are genuinely concerned about

our future... We have our *USA-mania*. It must be limited by the boundaries our reason and sentiment jointly dictate.
1900 *Ariel* (translated 1922), pt.5.

Rodriguez, Richard 1944–
US writer and journalist.

52 The genius of American culture and its integrity comes from fidelity to the light. Plain as day, we say. Happy as the day is long. Early to bed, early to rise. American virtues are daylight virtues: honesty, integrity, plain speech. We say yes when we mean yes and no when we mean no, and all else comes from the evil one. America presumes innocence and even the right to happiness.
1990 *Frontiers*, 'Night and Day'.

53 In the modern city, it takes on the status of a cathedral, our Chartres, our Notre Dame, our marble museum of the soul.
1995 On San Francisco's new Museum of Modern Art. In the *MacNeil-Lehrer Report*, 27 Feb.

Rodriguez, Sue 1950–94
Canadian campaigner for euthanasia, who suffered from ALS (amyotrophic lateral sclerosis, or Lou Gehrig's disease, a progressive and terminal illness).

54 I want to ask you gentlemen, if I cannot give consent to my own death, then whose body is this? Who owns my life?
1992 Videotaped presentation to the Justice Committee of the House of Commons, Ottawa, Nov. Reported by Deborah Wilson in *The Globe and Mail*, 5 Dec. The Supreme Court of Canada denied Rodriguez's request for a physician-assisted death.

Roethke, Theodore 1908–63
US poet. Professor of English at the University of Washington from 1948, he won a Pulitzer Prize for his collection *The Waking* (1953).

55 I have known the inexorable sadness of pencils,
Neat in their boxes, dolor of pad and paper-weight,
All the misery of manila folders and mucilage,
Desolation in immaculate public places.
1948 *The Lost Son*, 'Dolor'.

56 And I have seen dust from the walls of institutions,
Finer than flour, alive, more dangerous than silica,
Sift, almost invisible, through long afternoons of tedium.
1948 *The Lost Son*, 'Dolor'.

57 To know that light falls and fills, often without our knowing,
As an opaque vase fills to the brim from quick pouring,
Fills and trembles at the edge yet does not flow over,
Still holding and feeding the stem of the contained flower.
1948 *The Lost Son*, 'The Shape of Fire'.

58 And what a congress of stinks!—
Roots ripe as old bait,
Pulpy stems, rank, silo-rich,
Leaf-mold, manure, lime, piled against slippery planks.
Nothing would give up life:
Even the dirt kept breathing a small breath.
1948 *The Lost Son*, 'Root Cellar'.

59 I wake to sleep, and take my waking slow.
I feel my fate in what I cannot fear.
I learn by going where I have to go.
1953 *The Waking*, 'The Waking'.

60 Over this damp grave I speak the words of my love;
I, with no rights in this matter,
Neither father nor lover.
1953 Poem addressed to a dead student. *The Waking*, 'Elegy for Jane'.

61 Of her choice virtues only gods should speak,
Or English poets who grew up on Greek
(I'd have them sing in chorus, cheek to cheek).
1958 *Words for the Wind*, 'I Knew a Woman'.

62 What's freedom for? To know eternity.
I swear she cast a shadow white as stone.
But who would count eternity in days?
These old bones live to learn her wanton ways:
(I measure time by how a body sways).
1958 *Words for the Wind*, 'I Knew a Woman'.

63 In a dark time the eye begins to see.
1963 *Sequence, Sometimes Metaphysical*, 'In a Dark Time'.

64 The self persists like a dying star,
In sleep, afraid.
1964 *The Far Field*, 'Meditation at Oyster River'.

Rogers, Carl Ransom 1902–87
US psychologist and pioneer of client-centred counselling. His *Client-Centred Therapy* (1951) and *On Becoming a Person* (1961) emphasized the value of genuine empathy with the patient.

65 Unconditional positive regard.
c.1950 The slogan of the Rogerian counselling movement.

Rogers, Richard George Rogers, Baron 1933–
English architect, concerned with advancing technology in architecture and pushing the limits of design. His works include the Beaubourg or Pompidou Centre, Paris (1971–9, with Renzo Piano), Lloyds Building, London (1979–85), the Millennium Dome (1999) and the National Assembly for Wales (1999).

66 'Form follows profit' is the aesthetic principle of our times. Thus, design skill is measured today by the architect's ability to build the largest possible enclosure for the smallest investment in the quickest time.
1990 22nd annual Walter Neurath lecture. Collected in *Architecture: a Modern View*.

67 Architects cannot work in a vacuum; unlike other artists they are totally dependent on a site, a brief and finance.
1990 22nd annual Walter Neurath lecture. Collected in *Architecture: a Modern View*.

68 The problem is not style but quality, not aesthetics but ethics.
1990 22nd annual Walter Neurath lecture. Collected in *Architecture: a Modern View*.

69 The high street is where society comes into itself.
2013 In *The Guardian*, 11 Jul.

Rogers, Will 1879–1935
US actor, rancher and humorist. Best known for his ready wisecracks, he had a syndicated column, and wrote a number of books, including a posthumously compiled *Autobiography*.

70 Will you please tell me what you do with all the vice presidents a bank has?... The United States is the biggest business institution in the world and they only have one vice president and nobody has ever found anything for him to do.
1922 Speech, International Bankers' Association.

71 Well, all I know is what I read in the papers.
1923 In the *New York Times*, 30 Sep.

72 You know everybody is ignorant, only on different subjects.
1924 In the *New York Times*, 31 Aug.

73 The more you read and observe about this Politics thing, you got to admit that each party is worse than the other. The one that's out always looks the best.
1924 *The Illiterate Digest*, 'Breaking into the Writing Game'.

74 Everything is funny as long as it is happening to Somebody Else.
1924 *The Illiterate Digest*, 'Warning to Jokers: Lay Off the Prince'.

75 The Income Tax return has made more Liars out of the American people than Golf has. Even when you make one out on the level, you don't know when it's through if you are a Crook or a Martyr.
1924 *The Illiterate Digest*, 'Helping the Girls with Their Income Taxes'.

76 I bet you if I had met him and had a chat with him, I would have found him a very interesting and human fellow, for I never yet met a man that I didn't like.
1926 On Trotsky. In the *Saturday Evening Post*, 6 Nov.

77 Communism is like prohibition, it's a good idea but it won't work.
1927 Syndicated column, Nov. Collected in *The Weekly Articles*, vol. 3 (1981).

78 You can't say civilization don't advance, however, for in every war they kill you in a new way.
1929 In the *New York Times*, 23 Dec.

79 Half our life is spent trying to find something to do with the time we have rushed through life trying to save.
1930 In the *New York Times*, 29 Apr.

80 The United States is the only country ever to go to the poorhouse in an automobile.
c.1930 Attributed.

81 I was born because it was a habit in those days, people didn't know anything else.
The Autobiography of Will Rogers (published 1949), ch.1.

82 There is only one thing that can kill the Movies, and that is education.
The Autobiography of Will Rogers (published 1949), ch.6.

83 When a man goes in for politics over here, he has no time to labour, and any man that labours has no time to fool with politics. Over there, politics is an obligation; over here it's a business.
On Britain electing a Labour government. *The Autobiography of Will Rogers* (published 1949), ch.14.

84 It's great to be great but it's greater to be human.
The Autobiography of Will Rogers (published 1949), ch.15.

85 Being a hero is about the shortest-lived profession on earth.
Quoted in 'A Rogers Thesaurus' in *The Saturday Review*, 25 Aug 1962. Another form of the quote appeared in a syndicated newspaper article, 15 Feb 1925: 'Heroing is one of the shortest-lived professions there is'.

86 I don't make jokes—I just watch the government and report the facts.
Quoted in 'A Rogers Thesaurus' in *The Saturday Review*, 25 Aug 1962.

87 I guess there is nothing that will get your mind off everything like golf. I have never been depressed enough to take up the game but they say you get so sore at yourself you forget to hate your enemies.
Quoted in Michael Hobbs *The Golf Quotation Book* (1992).

Rogers, William Pierce 1913–2001

US lawyer and government official. As Deputy Attorney General (1953–7) he supported the 1957 Civil Rights Act, becoming Attorney General (1957–61). As Secretary of State (1969–73) he brought about a Middle East ceasefire.

88 Making foreign policy is like pornographic movies...more fun doing it than watching it.
1982 On becoming Under-Secretary of State for Economic Affairs, 7 Jun.

Rolleston, Humphrey 1862–1944

English physician.

89 Medicine is a noble profession but a damn bad business.
1944 Quoted in *Who Said What When* (1988).

Rollins, Sonny (Theodore Walter) 1930–

US jazz saxophonist. He is a leading figure in the development of jazz in the post-bebop era.

90 America is deeply rooted in Negro culture: its colloquialisms, its humour, its music. How ironic that the Negro, who more than any other people can claim America's culture as his own, is being persecuted and repressed, that the Negro, who has exemplified the humanities in his very existence, is being rewarded with inhumanity.
1958 Statement on sleeve of *Freedom Suite*.

Romani, Felice 1788–1865

Italian librettist, poet, essayist and critic. He provided libretti for more than 100 composers, striking a balance between Classicism and Romanticism. He is best known for his collaborations with Donizetti and Bellini.

91 *Casta Diva.*
Chaste goddess.
1831 Norma's aria. *Norma*, act 1 (music by Bellini, published 1832).

92 *Una furtiva lagrima.*
A furtive tear.
1832 Nemorino's aria. *L'Elisir d'Amore*, act 2 (music by Donizetti).

Romney, George W 1907–95

US politician. He was Governor of Michigan (1963–9) and member of the Nixon administration (1969–73).

93 I didn't say I didn't say it. I said I didn't say I said it. I want to make that very clear.
1967 Clarifying his policy. In the *National Review*, 12 Dec.

Romney, (Willard) Mitt 1947–

US businessman and politician. A Republican, he served as Governor of Massachusetts (2003–7) and ran unsuccessfully as the Republican candidate against Barack Obama in the 2012 presidential election.

94 Religious tolerance would be a shallow principle indeed if it were reserved only for faiths with which we agree.
2006 'Faith in America' speech, George Herbert Walker Bush Presidential Library, Texas, reported in the *New York Times*, 6 Dec.

95 I am convinced that unless America changes course, we will become the France of the 21st Century—still a great nation, but no longer the leader of the world.
2008 BBC News, 8 Feb.

96 I believe in an America where millions of Americans believe in an America that's the America millions of Americans believe in. That's the America I love.
2012 CBS News, 23 Jan.

97 I love this state. The trees are the right height.
2012 Campaign speech in Michigan, Feb.

98 I'm not familiar precisely with what I said, but I'll stand by what I said, whatever it was.
2012 Quoted in *The Washington Post*, 17 May.

Roosevelt, (Anna) Eleanor 1884–1962

US humanitarian and diplomat, wife and adviser of Franklin D Roosevelt. After his death she was US delegate to the UN (1945–53, 1961), chair of the Human Rights Commission (1946–51) and US representative to the General Assembly (1946–52).

99 You always admire what you don't really understand.
1956 In *Meet the Press*, NBC TV broadcast, 16 Sep.

1 She can talk beautifully about democracy but doesn't know how to live democracy.
Of Madame Chiang Kai-shek. Recalled on Mrs Roosevelt's death, 7 Nov 1962.

2 Where, after all, do human rights begin? They begin in small places, close to home—so close and so small that they cannot be seen on any map of the world.
1965 Quoted in the *New York Times*, 26 Dec.

3 A woman is like a tea bag; when she is in hot water she just gets stronger.
Quoted by Hillary Rodham Clinton in the *Wall Street Journal*, 30 Sep 1994.

Roosevelt, Franklin D(elano) 1882–1945

US Democratic statesman, 32nd President (1933–45) despite being stricken with polio in 1921. He introduced a 'New Deal' for national recovery (1933), and was re-elected three times. He entered World War II after Pearl Harbor (1941), meeting Churchill and Stalin at Teheran (1943) and Yalta (1945), but died just before the German surrender.

4 I pledge you, I pledge myself, to a New Deal for the American people.
1932 Speech accepting the Democratic Convention's presidential nomination, Chicago, 2 Jul.

5 In the field of world policy, I would dedicate this nation to the policy of the good neighbour.
1933 Inaugural address, 4 Mar.

6 Let me assert my belief that the only thing that we have to fear is fear itself—nameless, unreasoning, unjustified terror that paralyses needed efforts to convert retreat into advance.
1933 Inaugural address, 4 Mar.

7 Better the occasional faults of a Government that lives in a spirit of charity than the consistent omissions of a Government frozen in the ice of its own indifference.
1936 Renomination acceptance speech, Philadelphia, 27 Jun.

8 I have seen war... I hate war.
1936 Speech at Chantauqua, New York, 14 Aug.

9 When peace has been broken anywhere, the peace of all countries is in danger.
1939 Radio broadcast, 3 Sep.

10 A conservative is a man with two perfectly good legs who has never learned to walk forwards. A reactionary is a somnambulist walking backwards. A radical is a man with both feet planted firmly in the air.
1939 Radio broadcast, Oct.

11 I have said this before, but I shall say it again and again and again: Your boys are not going to be sent into any foreign wars.
1940 Speech in Boston, 30 Oct.

12 We have the men—the skill—the wealth—and above all, the will... We must be the great arsenal of democracy.
1940 'Fireside chat' radio broadcast, 29 Dec.

13 In the future days, which we seek to make secure, we look forward to a world founded upon four essential freedoms. The first is freedom of speech and expression, everywhere in the world. The second is the freedom of every person to worship God in his own way, everywhere in the world. The third is freedom from want... The fourth is freedom from fear.
1941 Third inaugural address, 6 Jan.

14 Yesterday, December 7, 1941—a date which will live in infamy—the United States of America was suddenly and deliberately attacked by naval and air forces of the Empire of Japan.
1941 Address to Congress, 8 Dec, following the Japanese attack on Pearl Harbor.

Roosevelt, Theodore 1858–1919

US Republican statesman and 26th President (1901–9). Elected Vice-President in 1900, he became President on McKinley's assassination and was re-elected in 1904. His expansionist policies included a strong navy, the regulation of trusts and monopolies, and his 'Square Deal' policy for social reform.

15 There is a homely adage that runs, 'Speak softly and carry a big stick, and you will go far.' If the American nation will speak softly and yet build, and keep at a pitch of the highest training, the Monroe Doctrine will go far.
1901 Vice-presidential speech, Sep.

16 In the western hemisphere, the adherence of the United States to the Monroe Doctrine may force the United States, however reluctantly, in flagrant cases of wrongdoing or impotence, to the exercise of an international police power.
1904 Message to Congress, 6 Dec.

17 The men with the muck-rakes are often indispensable to the well-being of society, but only if they know when to stop raking the muck.
1906 House of Representatives, 14 Apr.

18 I stand for the square deal...not merely for fair play under the present rules of the game, but for having those rules changed, so as to work for a more substantial equality of opportunity and of reward for equally good service.
1910 Speech, Osawatomie, 31 Aug.

19 Do not hit at all if it can be avoided, but never hit softly.
1913 *Theodore Roosevelt: an Autobiography*.

20 Practical efficiency is common, and lofty idealism is not uncommon; it is the combination that is necessary, and that combination is rare.
1913 *Theodore Roosevelt: an Autobiography.*

21 There is no reason why people should not call themselves Cubists, or Octagonists, or Parallelopipedonists, or Knights of the Isosceles Triangle, or Brothers of the Cosine, if they so desire; as expressing anything serious and permanent, one term is as fatuous as another.
1913 His opinion on the *International Exhibition of Modern Art* in New York, popularly known as *The Armoury Show.* 'A Layman's Views of an Art Exhibition', in *The Outlook* (9 Mar).

22 We are fighting in the quarrel of civilization against barbarism, of liberty against tyranny. Germany has become a menace to the whole world. She is the most dangerous enemy of liberty now existing.
1917 Speech at Oyster Bay, Long Island, Apr.

23 We have room in this country but for one flag, the Stars and Stripes. We have room for but one loyalty, loyalty to the United States. We have room for but one language, the English language.
1919 Message to the American Defense Society two days before his death, 3 Jan.

Rosebery, Archibald Philip Primrose, 5th Earl of 1847–1929

English statesman, Foreign Secretary (1886, 1892–4) under Gladstone, whom he succeeded as Prime Minister for a brief period in 1894 before the Liberals lost the election of 1895. He was noted for his racehorse stables, and as a biographer of British statesmen.

24 It is beginning to be hinted that we are a nation of amateurs.
1900 Rectorial address, Glasgow University, 16 Nov.

25 For the present at any rate, I must proceed alone. I must plough my own furrow alone—but before I get to the end of that furrow, it is possible that I may not find myself alone.
1901 On breaking from the Liberal Party, Jul.

Rosenberg, Harold 1906–78

US critic of the modern movement in painting and literature.

26 At a certain moment the canvas began to appear to one American painter after another as an arena in which to act—rather than as a space in which to reproduce, re-design, analyze or 'express' an object, actual or imagined. What was to go on the canvas was not a picture but an event.
1952 'The American Action Painters', in *Art News*, no.51, Dec.

27 A painting that is an act is inseparable from the biography of the artist.
1952 'The American Action Painters', in *Art News*, no.51, Dec.

28 Everyone knows that the label Modern Art no longer has any relation to the words that compose it. To be Modern Art a work need not be either modern nor art; it need not even be a work. A three-thousand-year-old mask from the South Pacific qualifies as Modern and a piece of wood found on a beach becomes Art.
1952 'The American Action Painters', in *Art News*, no.51, Dec.

29 As we have seen Modern Art does not have to be actually new; it only has to be new to somebody—to the last lady who found out about the driftwood.
1952 'The American Action Painters', in *Art News*, no.51, Dec.

Rosenberg, Isaac 1890–1918

English poet and artist. He published two volumes of poems before being killed in action in France. A third appeared posthumously, and his *Collected Works* (1937, rev edn 1973) revived his reputation.

30 The darkness crumbles away—
It is the same old druid Time as ever.
1916 'Break of Day in the Trenches'.

31 Droll rat, they would shoot you if they knew
Your cosmopolitan sympathies.
1916 'And God Knows What Antipathies'.

32 Earth has waited for them,
All the time of their growth
Fretting for their decay:
Now she has them at last.
1917 'Dead Man's Dump'.

33 Death could drop from the dark
As easily as song.
1917 'Returning, We Hear the Larks'.

Rosenblum, Robert 1927–2006

US art historian. His works include *Cubism and Twentieth Century Art* (1960) and *Andy Warhol: Portrait of the 70s* (1981).

34 She transformed junkyards of secular carpentry into almost sacred altarpieces.
1988 On sculptor Louise Nevelson. In *Time*, 26 Dec.

Ross, Edward Alsworth 1866–1951

US sociologist, Professor at the University of Wisconsin.

35 A society...which is riven by a dozen oppositions along lines running in every direction, may actually be in less danger of being torn with violence or falling to pieces than one split along just one line. For each new cleavage contributes to narrow the cross clefts, so that one might say that society is *sewn together* by its internal conflicts.
1920 *The Principles of Sociology*.

Rossetti, Christina Georgina 1830–94

English poet and sister of Dante Gabriel Rossetti. She helped found with her brother the Pre-Raphaelite Brotherhood. A devout Christian, her poetry has a melancholic and religiously intense quality.

36 Because the birthday of my life
Is come, my love is come to me.
1862 *Goblin Market and Other Poems*, 'A Birthday'.

37 Come to me in the silence of the night;
Come in the speaking silence of a dream;
Come with soft rounded cheeks and eyes as bright
As sunlight on a stream;
Come back in tears,
O memory, hope, love of finished years.
1862 *Goblin Market and Other Poems*, 'Echo'.

38 For there is no friend like a sister
In calm or stormy weather;
To cheer one on the tedious way,
To fetch one if one goes astray,

    To lift one if one totters down,
    To strengthen whilst one stands.
    1862 *Goblin Market and Other Poems*, 'Goblin Market'.

39 The hope I dreamed of was a dream,
    Was but a dream; and now I wake,
    Exceeding comfortless, and worn, and old,
    For a dream's sake.
    1862 *Goblin Market and Other Poems*, 'Mirage'.

40 Oh roses for the flush of youth,
    And laurel for the perfect prime;
    But pluck an ivy branch for me
    Grown old before my time.
    1862 *Goblin Market and Other Poems*, 'Oh Roses for the Flush of Youth'.

41 Remember me when I am gone away,
    Gone far away into the silent land.
    1862 *Goblin Market and Other Poems*, 'Remember'.

42 Better by far you should forget and smile
    Than that you should remember and be sad.
    1862 *Goblin Market and Other Poems*, 'Remember'.

43 O Earth, lie heavily upon her eyes;
    Seal her sweet eyes weary of watching, Earth.
    1862 *Goblin Market and Other Poems*, 'Rest'.

44 Silence more musical than any song.
    1862 *Goblin Market and Other Poems*, 'Rest'.

45 Does the road wind up-hill all the way?
    Yes, to the very end.
    Will the day's journey take the whole long day?
    From morn to night, my friend.
    1862 *Goblin Market and Other Poems*, 'Up-Hill'.

46 When I am dead, my dearest,
    Sing no sad songs for me;
    Plant thou no roses at my head,
    Nor shady cypress tree:
    Be the green grass above me
    With showers and dewdrops wet;
    And if thou wilt, remember,
    And if thou wilt, forget.
    1862 *Goblin Market and Other Poems*, 'When I Am dead'.

47 In the bleak mid-winter
    Frosty wind made moan,
    Earth stood hard as iron,
    Water like a stone;
    Snow had fallen, snow on snow,
    Snow on snow,
    In the bleak mid-winter,
    Long ago.
    1875 'Mid-Winter'.

48 Love came down at Christmas,
    Love all lovely, Love Divine;
    Love was born at Christmas,
    Star and angels gave the sign.
    1893 *Verses*, 'Love Came Down at Christmas'.

Rossetti, Dante Gabriel 1828–82

English painter and poet, who with his sister Christina Rossetti, Millais and Holman Hunt, founded the Pre-Raphaelite Brotherhood. His poetic works include *Poems* (1870) and *Ballads and Sonnets* (1881).

49 The blessed damozel leaned out
    From the gold bar of Heaven;
    Her eyes were deeper than the depth
    Of waters stilled at even;
    She had three lilies in her hand,
    And the stars in her hair were seven.
    1870 *Poems*, 'The Blessed Damozel', stanza 1.

50 Her hair that lay along her back
    Was yellow like ripe corn.
    1870 *Poems*, 'The Blessed Damozel', stanza 2.

51 As low as where this earth
    Spins like a fretful midge.
    1870 *Poems*, 'The Blessed Damozel', stanza 6.

52 And the souls mounting up to God
    Went by her like thin flames.
    1870 *Poems*, 'The Blessed Damozel', stanza 7.

53 'We two,' she said, 'will seek the groves
    Where the lady Mary is,
    With her five handmaidens, whose names
    Are five sweet symphonies,
    Cecily, Gertrude, Magdalen,
    Margaret and Rosalys.'
    1870 *Poems*, 'The Blessed Damozel', stanza 18.

54 I have been here before,
    But when or how I cannot tell:
    I know the grass beyond the door,
    The sweet keen smell,
    The sighing sound, the lights around the shore.
    1870 *Poems*, 'Sudden Light'.

55 A sonnet is a moment's monument,—
    Memorial from the Soul's eternity
    To one dead deathless hour.
    1881 *The House of Life*, introduction.

56 'Tis visible silence, still as the hour-glass.
    1881 *The House of Life*, 'Silent Noon', pt.1.

57 Deep in the sun-searched growths the dragon-fly
    Hangs like a blue thread loosened from the sky:—
    So this winged hour is dropt to us from above.
    Oh! clasp we to our hearts, for deathless dower,
    This close-companioned inarticulate hour
    When twofold silence was the song of love.
    1881 *The House of Life*, 'Silent Noon', pt.1.

58 Lo! as that youth's eyes burned at thine, so went
    Thy spell through him, and left his straight neck bent
    And round his heart one strangling golden hair.
    1881 *The House of Life*, 'Body's Beauty', pt.2.

59 They die not,—for their life was death,—but cease;
    And round their narrow lips the mould falls close.
    1881 *The House of Life*, 'The Choice', pt.1.

60 I do not see them here; but after death
    God knows I know the faces I shall see,
    Each one a murdered self, with low last breath.
    'I am thyself,—what hast thou done to me?'
    'And I—and I—thyself,' (lo! each one saith,)
    'And thou thyself to all eternity!'
    1881 *The House of Life*, 'Lost Days', pt.2.

61 Give honour unto Luke Evangelist;
    For he it was (the aged legends say)
    Who first taught Art to fold her hands and pray.
    1881 *The House of Life*, 'Old and New Art', pt.2.

62 When vain desire at last and vain regret
    Go hand in hand to death, and all is vain,

What shall assuage the unforgotten pain
And teach the unforgetful to forget?
1881 *The House of Life*, 'The One Hope', pt.2.

63 Look in my face; my name is Might-have-been;
I am also called No-more, Too-late, Farewell.
1881 *The House of Life*, 'A Superscription', pt.2.

64 Sleepless with cold commemorative eyes.
1881 *The House of Life*, 'A Superscription', pt.2.

65 Unto the man of yearning thought
And aspiration, to do nought
Is in itself almost an act.
1881 *Ballads and Sonnets*, 'Soothsay', stanza 10.

Rossini, Gioacchino Antonio 1792–1868

Italian composer. His early operas including *La Scala de seta* (1812) and *L'Italiana in Algeri* (1813) were followed by his masterpiece, *Il Barbiere de Seviglia* (1816). His later works, mostly written in Paris, include *La Gazza Ladra* (1817), *Semiramide* (1823) and *Guillaume Tell* (1829).

66 I was born for *opera buffa*, as well Thou knowest. Little skill, a little heart, and that is all. So be Thou blessed and admit me to Paradise.
1863 Manuscript inscription on the score of his 'Petite Messe Solennelle'.

67 Monsieur Wagner has good moments, but awful quarters of an hour!
1867 Quoted in Emile Naumann *Italienische Tondichter* (1883).

Rosso, Medardo 1858–1928

Italian sculptor. Sometimes known as the 'Impressionist' sculptor, he was a major influence on the Italian Futurists.

68 When I make a portrait, I cannot limit it to the lines of the head, for that head belongs to a body, it exists in a setting which influences it, it is part of a totality that I cannot suppress. The impression you produce upon me is not the same if I catch sight of you alone in a garden or if I see you in the midst of a group of other people, in a living room or on the street.
Quoted in Edmond Claris *De l'impressionisme en sculpture*, 'Medardo Rosso' (1902).

69 One does not walk around a statue any more than one walks around a painting, because one does not walk around a figure to receive an impression from it. Nothing is material in space.
Quoted in Edmond Claris *De l'impressionisme en sculpture*, 'Medardo Rosso' (1902).

Rostand, Jean 1894–1977

French biologist and writer.

70 A body of work such as Pasteur's is inconceivable in our time: no man would be given a chance to create a whole science. Nowadays a path is scarcely opened up when the crowd begins to pour in.
1939 'Pensées d'un Biologiste', collected in *The Substance of Man* (translated by Irma Brandeis, 1962).

71 Nothing leads the scientist so astray as a premature truth.
1939 'Pensées d'un Biologiste', collected in *The Substance of Man* (translated by Irma Brandeis, 1962).

Rosten, Leo Calvin 1908–97

US writer, humorist and anthologist. He is best known for his humorous compendium *The Joys of Yiddish* (1968), but has also written novels and stage plays (some as Leonard Ross).

72 The only thing I can say about W C Fields, whom I have admired since the day he advanced upon Baby LeRoy with an ice pick, is this: any man who hates dogs and babies can't be all bad.
1939 Speech at a Hollywood dinner in honour of W C Fields, 16 Feb.

73 The only reason for being a professional writer is that you just can't help it.
In D L Kirkpatrick (ed) *Contemporary Novelists* (1976).

Roth, Guenther 1931–

German-born US sociologist, professor emeritus at Columbia University.

74 My draft-dodging father proved that in the struggle for survival the fittest are most likely to get killed off.
'Partisanship and Scholarship', collected in Bennett Berger (ed) *Authors of Their Own Lives* (1990).

Roth, Henry 1906–95

US novelist. His novel of Jewish life in New York, *Call It Sleep* (1934), was rediscovered on its paperback publication in 1962. Apart from the shorter writings collected in *Shifting Landscape* (1987), he did not publish another until the first part of a massive six-book project, *Mercy of a Rude Stream* (1994).

75 The mind shuttles and reminds: we go this way only once; and shuttles again and rejoins: once is enough.
1960 'The Dun Dakotas', in *Commentary*, 30 Aug.

76 Detach the writer from the milieu where he has experienced his greatest sense of belonging, and you have created a discontinuity within his personality, a short circuit in his identity. The result is his originality, his creativity comes to an end. He becomes the one-book novelist or the one-trilogy writer.
1987 'The Eternal Plebeian and Other Matters', in *Shifting Landscape*.

Roth, Philip Milton 1933–

US novelist. His *succès de scandale*, *Portnoy's Complaint* (1969), was followed by a series of highly literary novels featuring his fictional alter ego, Nathan Zuckerman, all dealing with questions of Jewish identity. In 2011 he was awarded the Man Booker international prize.

77 Since I was a little girl I always wanted to be Very Decent to People. Other little girls wanted to be nurses and pianists. They were less dissembling.
1962 *Letting Go*, pt.1, ch.1.

78 It's the little questions from women about tappets that finally push men over the edge.
1962 *Letting Go*, pt.1, ch.1.

79 It's a family joke that when I was a tiny child I turned from the window out of which I was watching a snowstorm, and hopefully asked, 'Momma, do we believe in winter?'
1969 *Portnoy's Complaint*, 'The Most Unforgettable Character I've Ever Met'.

80 A Jewish man with parents alive is a fifteen-year-old boy, and will remain a fifteen-year-old boy until *they die*!
1969 *Portnoy's Complaint*, 'Cunt Crazy'.

81 Doctor, doctor, what do you say, LET'S PUT THE ID BACK IN YID!
   1969 *Portnoy's Complaint*, 'Cunt Crazy'.

82 Know that famous proverb? When the prick stands up, the brains get buried in the ground!
   1969 *Portnoy's Complaint*, 'Cunt Crazy'.

83 My Life as a Man.
   1974 Title of novel.

84 Satire is moral outrage transformed into comic art.
   1975 *Reading Myself and Others*, 'On Our Gang'.

85 The road to hell is paved with works-in-progress.
   1979 In the *New York Times Book Review*, 15 Jul.

86 In America everything goes and nothing matters, while in Europe nothing goes and everything matters.
   1983 Interview in *Time*, Nov.

87 In Israel it's enough to live—you don't have to do anything else and you go to bed exhausted. Have you ever noticed that Jews shout? Even one ear is more than you need.
   1987 *The Counterlife*, ch.2.

88 What makes you a normal Jew, Nathan, is how you are riveted by Jewish abnormality.
   1987 *The Counterlife*, ch.2.

89 Is an intelligent human being likely to be much more than a large-scale manufacturer of misunderstanding?
   1987 *The Counterlife*, ch.5.

90 For me, as for most novelists, every genuine imaginative event begins down there, with the facts, with the specific, and not with the philosophical, the ideological, or the abstract.
   1988 *The Facts: A Novelist's Autobiography*, 'Dear Zuckerman'.

91 In our lore, the Jewish family was an inviolate haven against every form of menace, from personal isolation to gentile hostility. Regardless of internal friction and strife, it was assumed to be an indissoluble consolidation... Family indivisibility, the first commandment.
   1988 *The Facts: A Novelist's Autobiography*, 'Dear Zuckerman'.

92 I write fiction and I'm told it's autobiography, I write autobiography and I'm told it's fiction, so since I'm so dim and they're so smart, let *them* decide what it is or it isn't.
   1990 Of critics. *Deception*, 'Philip'.

93 It was the summer when a president's penis was on everyone's mind, and life, in all its shameless impurity, once again confounded America.
   2001 *The Human Stain*.

94 I want to make it clear that it wasn't impotence that led me in to a reclusive existence.
   2001 *The Human Stain*.

95 I would be wonderful with a 100-year moratorium on literature talk, if you shut down all literature departments, close the book reviews, ban the critics. The readers should be alone with the books, and if anyone dared to say anything about them, they would be shot or imprisoned right on the spot. Yes, shot. A 100-year moratorium on insufferable literary talk. You should let people fight with the books on their own and rediscover what they are and what they are not. Anything other than this talk.
   2005 In *The Guardian*, 13 Dec.

96 Old age isn't a battle; old age is a massacre.
   2006 *Everyman*.

97 It's best to give while your hand is still warm.
   2006 *Everyman*.

98 At a certain stage of misery, you'll try anything to explain what's going on with you, even if you know it doesn't explain a thing and it's one failed explanation after another.
   2009 *The Humbling*.

99 Suicide is the role you write for yourself. You inhabit it and you enact it. All carefully staged—where they will find you and how they will find you. But one performance only.
   2009 *The Humbling*.

1 You have a conscience, and a conscience is a valuable attribute, but not if it begins to make you think you were to blame for what is far beyond the scope of your responsibility.
   2010 *Nemesis*.

Roth, William V, Jr 1921–2003

US senator. A member of Congress for Delaware (1967–71), he became a Senator (1971–2001) and a member of the finance government affairs committee.

2 If only trimmed, it inevitably creeps back...thicker and more deeply rooted than before.
   1995 Of bureaucracy, compared to crab grass. In the *Washington Times*, 19 May.

Rothko, Mark originally Marcus Rothkovitch 1903–70

Latvian-born painter, who emigrated to the US as a child. A largely self-taught artist, he moved from Surrealism to a distinctively meditative form of Abstract Expressionism, filling large canvases with blocks of pure colour.

3 I am not interested in relationships of color or form or anything else... I am interested only in expressing the basic human emotions—tragedy, ecstasy, doom, and so on—and the fact that lots of people break down and cry when confronted with my pictures shows that I *communicate* with those basic human emotions. The people who weep before my pictures are having the same religious experience I had when I painted them. And if you, as you say, are moved only by their color relationships, then you miss the point!
   Quoted in R Rosenblum *Modern Painting and the Northern Romantic Tradition* (1975).

Rothwell, Talbot 1916–74

British screenwriter who wrote for film and television, best known for his contribution to many of the *Carry On...* films.

4 Infamy! Infamy! They've all got it in for me!
   1964 Line delivered by Kenneth Williams as Julius Caesar in *Carry On Cleo*.

5 The eunuchs are on strike. They are complaining about loss of assets.
   1964 *Carry On Cleo*.

Rotten, Johnny stage name of John Lydon 1956–

English punk singer, member of The Sex Pistols.

6 Ever get the feeling you've been cheated?
   1978 Having walked offstage at the Winterland Ballroom during The Sex Pistols tour of the US, 14 Jan.

Rouault, Georges Henri 1871–1958

French painter and engraver. Apprenticed to a stained-glass designer in his youth, he retained the characteristic glowing colour outlined in black in his later work. He joined the Fauves c.1904. His works include the large religious engravings *Miserere* and *Guerre*.

7 Decorative art does not exist—only art, intimate, heroic, or epic.
1937 *La Renaissance*.

Rous, Sir Stanley 1895–1986

English football administrator. A former player and referee, he became Secretary of the Football Association in 1934 and President of FIFA in 1961. His codification of the rules of football into 17 laws is still followed today.

8 If this can be termed the century of the common man, then soccer, of all sports, is surely his game… In a world haunted by the hydrogen and napalm bomb, the football field is a place where sanity and hope are still left unmolested.
1952 Quoted in Bryon Butler *The Official History of the Football Association* (1986).

Rousseau, Jean Jacques 1712–78

French political philosopher, educationalist and writer. The father of French Romanticism, he wrote in many different genres. He is best known for his novel *Julie, ou la Nouvelle Héloïse* (1761), his autobiography, his posthumously published *Confessions*, and for *Du contrat social* (*The Social Contract*, 1762).

9 *Le premier qui, ayant enclos un terrain, s'avisa de dire: 'Ceci est à moi' et trouva des gens assez simples pour le croire, fut le vrai fondateur de la société civile.*
The first person who fenced in a piece of land, ventured to say: 'This is mine,' and found others simple enough to believe him, was the true founder of civil society.
1755 *Discours sur l'origine et les fondements de l'inégalité parmi les hommes*, ch.1.

10 *L'homme est né libre, et partout il est dans les fers.*
Man is born free, yet everywhere he is in chains.
1762 *Du contrat social* (*The Social Contract*), bk.1, ch.1 (translated by M Cranston).

11 *La force a fait les premiers esclaves, leur lâcheté les a perpétués.*
Force made the first slaves; their cowardice perpetuated slavery.
1762 *Du contrat social* (*The Social Contract*), bk.1, ch.2 (translated by M Cranston).

12 *Si l'on recherche en quoi consiste précisément le plus grand bien de tous, qui doit être le fin de tout système de législation, on trouvera qu'il se réduit à ces deux objets principaux, la liberté et l'égalité.*
If we enquire wherein lies precisely the greatest good of all, which ought to be the goal of every system of law, we shall find that it comes down to two main objects, *freedom* and *equality*.
1762 *Du contrat social* (*The Social Contract*), bk.2, ch.11 (translated by M Cranston).

13 *L'éducation de l'homme commence à sa naissance; avant de parler, avant que d'entendre, il s'instruit déjà.*
A man's education begins when he is born; before speaking, before understanding, he is already teaching himself.
1762 *Émile ou de l'éducation*, pt.1.

14 *J'aime mieux être homme à paradoxes qu'homme à préjugés.*
I would rather be a man of paradoxes than of prejudices.
1762 *Émile ou de l'éducation*, pt.2.

15 *C'est dans le cïur de l'homme qu'est la vie du spectacle de la nature; pour le voir, il faut le sentir.*
The spectacle of nature is in the heart of a man; to see it, he must feel it.
1762 *Émile ou de l'éducation*, pt.3.

16 *L'homme dit ce qu'il sait, la femme dit ce qui plaît.*
A man says what he knows, a woman says what pleases.
1762 *Émile ou de l'éducation*, pt.5.

17 War, then, is not a relationship between man and man, but between State and State, in which private persons are only enemies accidentally.
Quoted in A J P Taylor *From the Boer War to the Cold War: Essays on Twentieth-Century Europe* (1995), 'War and Peace', p.15.

Rowbotham, Sheila 1943–

English social historian and feminist. Together with Segel and Wainwright, she wrote the controversial *Beyond the Fragments: Feminism and the Making of Socialism* (1979). She has also written *Women, Resistance and Revolution* (1972) and *Women Resist Globalization: Mobilizing for Livelihood and Rights* (2001).

18 There is no 'beginning' of feminism in the sense that there is no beginning to defiance in women.
1972 *Women, Resistance and Revolution*, ch.1.

Rowland, Helen 1876–1950

US journalist, writer and humorist.

19 When you see what some girls marry, you realize how they must hate to work for a living.
1909 *Reflections of a Bachelor Girl*.

20 Never trust a husband too far, or a bachelor too near.
1915 *The Rubaiyat of a Bachelor*.

21 A husband is what is left of the lover after the nerve has been extracted.
1922 *A Guide to Men*.

22 The follies which a man regrets most in his life are those which he didn't commit when he had the opportunity.
1922 *A Guide to Men*.

Rowling, J K 1965–

English author whose first children's book, *Harry Potter and the Philosopher's Stone* (1997, published in the US as *Harry Potter and the Sorcerer's Stone*, 1998), set in the Hogwarts School of Witchcraft and Wizardry, was an immediate success, and was followed by equally successful sequels and film versions.

23 Before we begin our banquet, I would like to say a few words. And here they are: Nitwit! Blubber! Oddment! Tweak!
1997 *Harry Potter and the Philosopher's Stone* (published in the US as *Harry Potter and the Sorcerer's Stone*, 1998), ch.7.

24 Harry Potter was a highly unusual boy in many ways. For one thing, he hated the summer holidays more than any other time of year. For another, he really

wanted to do his homework, but was forced to do it in secret, in the dead of night. And he also happened to be a wizard.
1999 *Harry Potter and the Prisoner of Azkaban*, opening lines.

25 Those who choose not to empathize enable real monsters, for without ever committing an act of outright evil ourselves we collude with it through our apathy.
2008 Speech to the Harvard Alumni Association, 5 Jun.

26 We do not need magic to change the world. We carry all the power we need inside ourselves already: we have the power to imagine better.
2008 Speech to the Harvard Alumni Association, 5 Jun.

Roy, Arundhati 1960–
Indian author and environmental activist. Her first novel, *The God of Small Things* (1997), won the Booker Prize.

27 The whole of contemporary history, the World Wars, the War of Dreams, the Man on the Moon, science, literature, philosophy, the pursuit of knowledge—was no more than a blink of the Earth Woman's eye.
1997 *The God of Small Things*.

28 Flags are bits of coloured cloth that governments use first to shrink-wrap people's minds and then as ceremonial shrouds to bury the dead.
2003 *War Talk*.

29 Capitalism is destroying the planet. The two old tricks that dug it out of past crises—War and Shopping—simply will not work.
2014 *Capitalism: A Ghost Story*.

Roy, Gabrielle 1909–83
Canadian novelist and memoirist.

30 Every writer must eventually write his Ninth Symphony or give in to despair.
1973 Letter, 1 Aug, quoted in Joan Hind-Smith *Three Voices* (1975).

Royden, (Agnes) Maude 1876–1956
English social worker and preacher who took a religious and moral approach to women's suffrage.

31 The Church of England should no longer be satisfied to represent only the Conservative Party at prayer.
1917 Address to the Life and Liberty Movement, London, 16 Jul.

Rubenstein, Helena 1870–1965
Polish cosmetics businesswoman. She developed and sold the first tinted foundation and face powder when she moved to New York in World War I and pioneered the use of silk in cosmetics. She used methods of mass production and marketing to attract customers who were intimidated by the cosmetics of her biggest rival—Elizabeth Arden.

32 Some women won't buy anything unless they can pay a lot.
1965 In *Time*, 9 Apr.

Ruckelshaus, William D(oyle) 1932–
US government administrator, lawyer and businessman. He served Indiana in the House of Representatives (1967–9) and was majority leader and was administrator of the new Environmental Protection Agency, Washington (1970–3, 1983–5).

33 Everybody wants you to pick it up, and nobody wants you to put it down.
1988 Articulating 'the First Law of Garbage'. In *Fortune*, 21 Nov.

Rudd, Kevin Michael 1957–
Australian politician. A member of the Labor Party, he has served two terms as Prime Minister of Australia (2007–10 and 2013).

34 For the pain, suffering and hurt of these stolen generations, their descendants and for their families left behind, we say sorry. To the mothers and the fathers, the brothers and the sisters, for the breaking up of families and communities, we say sorry. And for the indignity and degradation thus inflicted on a proud people and a proud culture, we say sorry.
2008 Issuing an official government apology for the mistreatment of Australia's aboriginal peoples, 13 Feb.

Rudofsky, Bernard 1905–88
Austrian-born architect, engineer and critic. He studied in Vienna, but worked in New York.

35 For it seems that long before the first enterprising man bent some twigs into a leaky roof, many animals were already accomplished builders.
1964 *Architecture without Architects*.

36 There is much to learn from architecture before it became an expert's art.
1964 *Architecture without Architects*.

Ruether, Rosemary Radford 1936–
US theologian, leading Roman Catholic exponent of feminist and liberation theology.

37 Indeed, if one can say that Christ comes to the oppressed and the oppressed especially hear him, then it is women within these marginal groups who are often seen both as the oppressed of the oppressed and also as those particularly receptive to the gospel.
1981 *To Change the World: Christology and Cultural Criticism*.

Ruiz, Juan c.1290–c.1350
Spanish poet, arch-priest of Hita. He was a vagabond for several years before entering the Church. In 1337 he was imprisoned for 13 years by the Archbishop of Toledo, Don Gil de Ardonoz.

38 *El amor siempre fabla mentiroso.*
Love is always a liar.
c.1330 *Libro de Buen Amor*, stanza 161.

39 *Por las verdades se pierden los amigos, e per las non dezir se fazen desamigos.*
Telling the truth loses you friends; not telling it gains you enemies.
c.1330 *Libro de Buen Amor*, stanza 165.

Rulfo, Juan 1918–86
Mexican writer. He grew up in the rural countryside that provides the setting for his two masterpieces, the short story collection *El llano en llamas* (1953) and the novel *Pedro Páramo* (1955). Although his writing output is slim, it has been enormously influential.

40 *Sólo yo entiendo lo lejos que está el cielo de nosotros; pero conozco cómo acortar las veredas. Todo consiste en morir, Dios mediante, cuando uno* quiera y no cuando Él lo disponga. O, si tú quieres, forzarlo a disponer antes de tiempo.

I know how far away Heaven is, all right, but I know the shortcuts. You just die, God willing, when you want to, not when He arranges it. Or if you want you can make Him arrange it earlier.
1955 *Pedro Páramo* (translated 1959).

Rumsfeld, Donald 1932–

US politician. He was US ambassador to NATO (1973–4), White House Chief of Staff (1974–5) and Secretary of Defense (1975–7), and in 2001 was appointed Secretary of Defense for a second time by George W Bush (2001–6).

41 Reports that say that something hasn't happened are always interesting to me, because as we know, there are known knowns; there are things we know we know. We also know there are known unknowns; that is to say we know there are some things we do not know. But there are also unknown unknowns — the ones we don't know we don't know.
2002 Responding to a reporter's question at a US Department of Defense news briefing, 12 Feb.

42 You're thinking of Europe as Germany and France. I don't. I think that's old Europe.
2003 Responding to questions about European hostility to military intervention in Iraq, 22 Jan.

43 They seem to be a country that disagrees with a lot of other countries.
2003 Discussing the French standpoint on Iraq. In *Time*, 17 Feb.

44 Answering the question as to whether we are winning— that is a very difficult one.
2004 Television interview, 27 Jun.

45 We don't seek empires. We're not imperialistic.
Quoted in Niall Ferguson *Colossus: The Rise and Fall of the American Empire* (2004).

46 I am not going to give you a number for it because it's not my business to do intelligent work.
2005 His reply to Congress when asked how many Iraqi insurgents there were.

47 I have benefitted greatly from criticism, and at no time have I suffered a lack thereof.
2006 Speaking on his resignation.

Runcie, Robert Alexander Kennedy Runcie, Baron 1921–2000

English Anglican prelate and Archbishop of Canterbury (1980–91). His career was marked by a papal visit to Canterbury, controversies over homosexuality and women in the Church, the Falklands War, and his envoy Terry Waite's captivity in Beirut (1987–91).

48 Royalty puts a human face on the operations of government.
1980 Sermon at a service to mark the Queen Mother's 80th birthday, St Paul's Cathedral, 15 Jul.

49 Those who dare to interpret God's will must never claim Him as an asset for one nation or group rather than another. War springs from the love and loyalty that should be offered to God being applied to some God substitute—one of the most dangerous being nationalism.
1982 Sermon at Thanksgiving Service after the Falklands War, St Paul's Cathedral, 26 Jul.

Runciman, Sir Steven 1903–2000

English historian of the Crusades. His works include *The Fall of Constantinople, 1453* (1965) and *Byzantine Style and Civilization* (1975).

50 The triumphs of the Crusades were the triumphs of faith. But faith without wisdom is a dangerous thing.
1954 *A History of the Crusades*, vol.3.

Runge, Philipp Otto 1777–1810

German painter and draughtsman, a member of the German Romantic movement.

51 Art of all periods teaches us that humanity changes, and that a period, once past, never returns.
1802 Letter, Feb. Quoted in L Eitner *Neoclassicism and Romanticism 1750–1850* (1964).

52 But could we not reach the point of highest perfection in a new kind of art, in this art of landscape, and perhaps reach a higher beauty than existed before?
1802 Letter, quoted in L Eitner *Neoclassicism and Romanticism 1750–1850* (1964).

53 Colour is the ultimate in art. It is still and will always remain a mystery to us, we can only apprehend it intuitively in flowers.
1802 Letter, quoted in L Eitner *Neoclassicism and Romanticism 1750–1850* (1964).

54 We must become children again if we wish to achieve the best.
1802 Letter, quoted in R Rosenblum *Modern Painting and the Northern Romantic Tradition* (1975).

Runyon, (Alfred) Damon 1884–1946

US journalist, sportswriter and humorist. He is remembered for the colourful argot of his New York stories, which have been gathered in several collections, and provided the basis of the musical *Guys and Dolls* (1931).

55 'My boy,' he says, 'always try to rub up against money, for if you rub up against money long enough, some of it may rub off on you.'
1931 *Guys and Dolls*, 'A Very Honourable Guy'.

56 'You are snatching a hard guy when you snatch Bookie Bob. A very hard guy, indeed. In fact,' I say, 'I hear the softest thing about him is his front teeth.'
1933 *Blue Plate Special*, 'Snatching of Bookie Bob'.

57 Any time you see him he is generally by himself because being by himself is not apt to cost him anything.
1933 *Blue Plate Special*, 'Little Miss Marker'.

58 The best thing to do right now is to throw a feed into her as the chances are that her stomach thinks her throat is cut.
1933 *Blue Plate Special*, 'Little Miss Marker'.

59 'In fact,' Sam the Gonoph says, 'I long ago come to the conclusion that all life is 6 to 5 against.'
1935 *Money from Home*, 'A Nice Price'.

60 I do not approve of guys using false pretences on dolls, except, of course, when nothing else will do.
1935 *Money from Home*, 'It Comes Up Mud'.

61 He is without strict doubt a Hoorah Henry, and he is generally figured as nothing but a lob as far as doing anything useful in this world is concerned.
1935 *Money from Home*, 'Tight Shoes'.

62 I always claim the mission workers came out too early to catch any sinners on this part of Broadway. At such an hour the sinners are still in bed resting up from their sinning of the night before, so they will be in good shape for more sinning a little later on.
1944 *Runyon à la Carte*, 'The Idyll of Miss Sarah Brown'.

63 You can keep the things of bronze and stone and give me one man to remember me just once a year.
1946 Last words.

Rushdie, Sir (Ahmed) Salman 1947–

British novelist, born in Bombay. His works include *Midnight's Children* (1981, Booker Prize), *The Moor's Last Sigh* (1995) and *Fury* (2001) and *Shalimar the Clown*. His novel *The Satanic Verses* (1988) provoked Iran's Ayatollah Khomeini to issue a fatwa against him (1989) forcing Rushdie to live in hiding for several years.

64 Most of what matters in your life takes place in your absence.
1981 *Midnight's Children*, 'Alpha and Omega', bk.2.

65 A poet's work… To name the unnamable, to point at frauds, to take sides, start arguments, shape the world and stop it from going to sleep.
1988 *The Satanic Verses*, pt.2.

66 To burn a book is not to destroy it. One minute of darkness will not make us blind.
1989 Book review in the *Weekend Guardian*, 14–15 Oct.

67 No story comes from nowhere; new stories are born from old—it is the new combinations that make them new.
1990 *Haroun and the Sea of Stories*.

68 Books have to teach their readers how to read them.
1995 Quoted in the *Observer Review*, 16 Apr.

69 We are the lethal voyeurs.
1997 Reflecting on the death of Diana, Princess of Wales.

70 I know of very few great film-makers who might have been good novelists—Satyajit Ray, Ingmar Bergman, Woody Allen, Jean Renoir, and that's about it.
2002 *Step Across This Line: Collected Non-Fiction 1992–2002*.

71 [Charlton] Heston thinks America should arm its teachers; he seems to believe that schools would be safer if staff had the power to gun down children in their charge.
2002 *Step Across This Line: Collected Non-Fiction 1992–2002*.

72 I knew a man whose thing it was to wreck the toilets in office buildings and write a slogan on the ruined walls: 'If the cistern cannot be changed it must be destroyed.' I'm beginning to understand how he felt.
2002 *Step Across This Line: Collected Non-Fiction 1992–2002*.

73 What is freedom of expression? Without the freedom to offend, it ceases to exist.
2004 Quoted in the *BBC News Magazine*, 21 Dec.

74 There is no right in the world not to be offended. That right simply doesn't exist. In a free society, an open society, people have strong opinions, and these opinions very often clash. In a democracy, we have to learn to deal with this. And this is true about novels, it's true about cartoons, it's true about all these products.
2012 Interview in *The Hindu*, 8 Oct.

75 The art of telling a story is keeping an audience sitting there and from throwing things at you.
2014 Speaking at Symphony Space's Selected Shorts literary event, New York, Dec.

76 Literature happens at the level of the sentence.
2014 Speaking at Symphony Space's Selected Shorts literary event, New York, Dec.

Rushworth, John c.1612–1690

English historian, whose *Historical Collections of Private Passages of State* (8 vols, 1659–1701) cover the period 1618–48. Clerk-assistant to the House of Commons in the Long Parliament (1640), and a parliamentary secretary, in 1684 he was imprisoned for debt.

77 His Majesty entered the House, and as he passed up towards the Chair, he cast his eye on the right hand near the Bar of the House where Mr Pym used to sit; but His Majesty, not seeing him there (knowing him well) went up to the Chair and said, 'By your leave, Mr Speaker, I must borrow your chair a little.'
1642 His account of the attempt made by Charles I to arrest five Members of Parliament on 4 Jan.

Rusk, (David) Dean 1909–94

US politician. As Secretary of State under Kennedy and Johnson (1961–9), he played a major role in the Cuban Missile Crisis of 1962.

78 We were eyeball to eyeball and the other fellow just blinked.
1962 Recalling his words on the retreat of Soviet ships during the Cuban Missile Crisis. In the *Saturday Evening Post*, 8 Dec.

79 Communications today puts a special emphasis on what happens next, for an able, sophisticated and competitive press knows that what happens today is no longer news—it is what is going to happen tomorrow that is the object of interest and concern.
1963 At *Time*'s 40th anniversary dinner, 17 May.

80 We looked into the mouth of the cannon, the Russians flinched.
Of the Cuban Missile Crisis. Quoted in Robert F Kennedy *Thirteen Days* (1969).

Ruskin, John 1819–1900

English author, the major art critic and social philosopher of his day, champion of Turner and the pre-Raphaelites and an opponent of Utilitarianism. His most famous works are *Modern Painters* (1843–60) and *Seven Lamps of Architecture* (1849).

81 I believe the right question to ask, respecting all ornament, is simply this: Was it done with enjoyment—was the carver happy while he was about it?
1849 *Seven Lamps of Architecture*, 'The Lamp of Life', sect.24.

82 Better the rudest work that tells a story or records a fact, than the richest without meaning.
1849 *Seven Lamps of Architecture*, 'The Lamp of Memory', sect.7.

83 When we build, let us think that we build for ever.
1849 *Seven Lamps of Architecture*, 'The Lamp of Memory', sect.10.

84 Remember that the most beautiful things in the world are the most useless; peacocks and lilies for instance.
1851–3 *The Stones of Venice*, vol.i, ch.2.

85 But for me, the Alps and their people were alike beautiful in their snow, and their humanity; and I wanted, neither for them nor myself, sight of any thrones in heaven but the rocks, or of any spirits in heaven but the clouds.
1851–3 *The Stones of Venice*, vol.i, ch.2.

86 The purest and most thoughtful minds are those which love colour the most.
1851–3 *The Stones of Venice*, vol.ii, ch.5.

87 All things are literally better, lovelier, more beloved for the imperfections which have been divinely appointed.
1851–3 *The Stones of Venice*, vol.ii, ch.6.

88 No person who is not a great sculptor or painter can be an architect. If he is not a sculptor or painter, he can only be a *builder*.
1854 *Lectures on Architecture and Painting*.

89 What is poetry?... The suggestion, by the imagination, of noble grounds for the noble emotions.
1856 *Modern Painters*, vol.3, pt.4, ch.1.

90 All violent feelings...produce in us a falseness in all our impressions of external things, which I would generally characterize as the 'Pathetic Fallacy'.
1856 *Modern Painters*, vol.3, pt.4, ch.12.

91 Mountains are the beginning and the end of all natural scenery.
1856 *Modern Painters*, vol.4, pt.5, ch.20.

92 Fine art is that in which the hand, the head, and the heart of man go together.
1859 *The Two Paths*, lecture 2.

93 Not only is there but one way of *doing* things rightly, but there is only one way of *seeing* them, and that is, seeing the whole of them.
1859 *The Two Paths*, lecture 2.

94 Nobody cares much at heart about Titian; only there is a strange undercurrent of everlasting murmur about his name, which means the deep consent of all great men that he is greater than they.
1859 *The Two Paths*, lecture 2.

95 It ought to be quite as natural and straightforward a matter for a labourer to take his pension from his parish, because he has deserved well of his parish, as for a man in higher rank to take his pension from his country, because he has deserved well of his country.
1862 *Unto this Last*, preface.

96 The force of the guinea you have in your pocket depends wholly on the default of a guinea in your neighbour's pocket. If he did not want it, it would be of no use to you.
1862 *Unto this Last*, essay 2.

97 Political economy (the economy of a State, or of citizens) consists simply in the production, preservation, and distribution, at fittest time and place, of useful or pleasurable things.
1862 *Unto this Last*, essay 2.

98 Soldiers of the ploughshare as well as soldiers of the sword.
1862 *Unto this Last*, essay 3.

99 Government and co-operation are in all things the laws of life; anarchy and competition the laws of death.
1862 *Unto this Last*, essay 3.

1 Whereas it has long been known and declared that the poor have no right to the property of the rich, I wish it also to be known and declared that the rich have no right to the property of the poor.
1862 *Unto this Last*, essay 3.

2 There is no wealth but life.
1862 *Unto this Last*, essay 4.

3 All books are divided into two classes, the books of the hour, and the books of all time.
1865 *Sesame and Lilies*, 'Of Kings' Treasures'.

4 Be sure that you go to the author to get at his meaning, not to find yours.
1865 *Sesame and Lilies*, 'Of Kings' Treasures'.

5 Which of us...is to do the hard and dirty work for the rest—and for what pay? Who is to do the pleasant and clean work, and for what pay?
1865 *Sesame and Lilies*, 'Of Kings' Treasures'.

6 You hear of me, among others, as a respectable architectural man-milliner; and you send for me, that I may tell you the leading fashion.
1866 *The Crown of Wild Olive*, 'Traffic', lecture 2.

7 Labour without joy is base. Labour without sorrow is base. Sorrow without labour is base. Joy without labour is base.
1867 *Time and Tide*, letter 5.

8 Your honesty is *not* to be based either on religion or policy. Both your religion and policy must be based on *it*.
1867 *Time and Tide*, letter 8.

9 The first duty of a state is to see that every child born therein shall be well housed, clothed, fed and educated, till it attain years of discretion.
1867 *Time and Tide*, letter 13.

10 Life without industry is guilt, and industry without art is brutality.
1870 *Lectures on Art*, 'The Relation of Art to Morals', lecture 3, section 95.

11 Engraving then, is, in brief terms, the Art of Scratch.
1870–85 *Ariadne Florentina*, lecture 1.

12 Thackeray settled like a meat-fly on whatever one had got for dinner, and made one sick of it.
1873 *Fors Clavigera* (published 1871–84), letter no.31, 1 Jul.

13 English artists are usually entirely ruined by residence in Italy.
1873 *Modern Painters*, vol.1, pt.1, 'Of General Principles'.

14 The greatest thing a human soul ever does in this world is to *see* something, and tell what it *saw* in a plain way. Hundreds of people can talk for one who can think, but thousands can think for one who can see. To see clearly is poetry, prophecy, and religion, all in one.
1873 *Modern Painters*, vol.3, pt.4, ch.16.

15 I have seen, and heard, much of Cockney impudence before now; but never expected to hear a coxcomb ask two hundred guineas for flinging a pot of paint in the public's face.
1877 On Whistler's *Nocturne in Black and Gold*. *Fors Clavigera* (published 1871–84), letter no.79, 18 Jun.

16 Men don't and can't live by exchanging articles, but by producing them. They don't live by trade, but by work. Give up that foolish and vain title of Trades Unions; and take that of Labourers' Unions.
1880 Open letter to English Trades Unions, 29 Sep.

17 Beethoven always sounds to me like the upsetting of a bag of nails, with here and there an also dropped hammer.
1881 Letter.

18 Of all the affected, sapless, soulless, beginningless, endless, topless, bottomless, topsiturviest, scrannel-pipiest, tongs and boniest doggerel of sounds I ever endured the deadliest of, that eternity of nothing was the deadliest.

1882 Of Wagner's *Die Meistersinger*. Letter to Mrs Burne-Jones, 30 Jun.

19 There was a rocky valley between Buxton and Bakewell...divine as the vale of Tempe; you might have seen the gods there morning and evening—Apollo and the sweet Muses of the Light... You enterprised a railroad...you blasted its rocks away... And, now, every fool in Buxton can be at Bakewell in half-an-hour, and every fool in Bakewell at Buxton.
1886-8 *Praeterita*, vol.3, pt.4, 'Joanna's Cave', note.

Russell, Bertrand Arthur William Russell, 3rd Earl
1872-1970

English philosopher and mathematician, a controversial public figure ('an enemy of religion and morality') who produced a stream of popular and provocative works on social, moral and religious issues. After 1949 he championed nuclear disarmament, and engaged in correspondence with several world leaders. He won the Nobel prize for literature in 1950.

20 Mathematics possesses not only truth, but supreme beauty—a beauty cold and austere, like that of sculpture.
1903 *The Principles of Mathematics*.

21 Philosophy, if it cannot *answer* so many questions as we could wish, has at least the power of *asking* questions which increase the interest of the world, and show the strangeness and wonder lying just below the surface even in the commonest things of daily life.
1912 *The Problems of Philosophy*, ch.1.

22 The essential characteristic of philosophy, which makes it a study distinct from science, is *criticism*. It examines critically the principles employed in science and in daily life; it searches out any inconsistencies there may be in these principles, and it only accepts them when, as the result of a critical inquiry, there is no reason for rejecting them.
1912 *The Problems of Philosophy*, ch.14.

23 Philosophy is to be studied, not for the sake of any definite answers to its questions, since no definite answers can, as a rule, be known to be true, but rather for the sake of the questions themselves; because these questions enlarge our conception of what is possible, enrich our intellectual imagination, and diminish the dogmatic assurance which closes the mind against speculation; but above all because, through the greatness of the universe which philosophy contemplates, the mind also is rendered great, and becomes capable of that union with the universe which constitutes its highest good.
1912 *The Problems of Philosophy*, ch.14.

24 Every proposition which we can understand must be composed wholly of constituents with which we are acquainted.
1917 *A Free Man's Worship*, 'Knowledge by Acquaintance and Knowledge by Description'.

25 The true spirit of delight, the exaltation, the sense of being more than man, which is the touchstone of the highest excellence, is to be found in mathematics as surely as in poetry.
1917 *Mysticism and Logic*.

26 The typical Westerner wishes to be the cause of as many changes as possible in his environment; the typical Chinese wishes to enjoy as much and as delicately as possible.
1922 *The Problems of China*.

27 In science men have discovered an activity of the very highest value in which they are no longer, as in art, dependent for progress upon the appearance of continually greater genius, for in science the successors stand upon the shoulders of their predecessors; where one man of supreme genius has invented a method, a thousand lesser men can apply it.
1923 *A Free Man's Worship and Other Essays*.

28 Machines are worshipped because they are beautiful, and valued because they confer power; they are hated because they are hideous, and loathed because they impose slavery.
1928 *Sceptical Essays*.

29 The scientific attitude of mind involves a sweeping away of all other desires in the interest of the desire to know.
1930 Interview in the *New Statesman*, 24 May.

30 It is, of course, clear that a country with a large foreign population must endeavour, through its schools, to assimilate the children of immigrants... It is, however, unfortunate that a large part of this process should be effected by means of a somewhat blatant nationalism.
1935 *In Praise of Idleness*, 'Modern Homogeneity'.

31 No rules, however wise, are a substitute for affection and tact.
1935 *In Praise of Idleness*, 'Education and Discipline'.

32 I think modern educational theorists are inclined to attach too much importance to the negative virtue of not interfering with children, and too little to the positive merit of enjoying their company.
1935 *In Praise of Idleness*, 'Education and Discipline'.

33 Two men who differ as to the ends of life cannot hope to agree about education.
1935 *In Praise of Idleness*, 'Education and Discipline'.

34 Can a society in which thought and technique are scientific persist for a long period, as, for example, ancient Egypt persisted, or does it necessarily contain within itself forces which must bring either decay or explosion?
1949 'Can a Scientific Community Be Stable?', Lloyd Roberts lecture to the Royal Society of Medicine, 29 Nov.

35 There is only one constant preoccupation: I have throughout been anxious to discover how much we can be said to know and with what degree of certainty or doubtfulness.
1959 *My Philosophical Development*, ch.1.

36 I do not think it possible to get anywhere if we start from scepticism. We must start from a broad acceptance of whatever seems to be knowledge and is not rejected for some specific reason.
1959 *My Philosophical Development*, ch.16.

37 Ever since I was engaged on *Principia Mathematica*, I have had a certain method of which at first I was scarcely conscious, but which has gradually become more explicit in my thinking. The method consists in an attempt to build a bridge between the world of sense and the world of science.
1959 *My Philosophical Development*, ch.16.

38 This idea of weapons of mass extermination is utterly horrible, and is something that no one with a spark of

humanity can tolerate. I will not pretend to obey a Government that is organizing a mass massacre of mankind.
1961 Speech urging civil disobedience in support of nuclear disarmament, Birmingham, 15 Apr.

39 Obscenity is what happens to shock some elderly and ignorant magistrate.
1961 Quoted in *Look* magazine.

40 I've got a one-dimensional mind.
Quoted in R Crawshay-Williams *Russell Remembered* (1970), ch.2.

Russell, Dora 1894–1986

English feminist and pacifist, second wife of Bertrand Russell. In her many works she advocated sexual freedom and birth control.

41 We want better reasons for having children than not knowing how to prevent them.
1925 *Hypatia: or Women and Knowledge*, ch.4.

Russell, George William pseudonym Æ 1867–1935

Irish poet, painter, writer and economist. He met Yeats in Dublin and turned from his art studies to theosophy. His first book *Homeward: Songs by the Way* (1894) established his role in the Irish literary renaissance. He edited the *Irish Homestead* (1906–23) and subsequently the *Irish Statesman* (1923–30).

42 As Michael read the Gaelic scroll
It seemed the story of the soul;
And those who wrought, lest there should fail
From earth the legend of the Gael,
Seemed warriors of Eternal Mind
Still holding in a world gone blind,
From which belief and hope had gone,
The lovely magic of its dawn.
1922 *The Interpreters*, 'Michael'.

43 In ancient shadows and twilights
Where childhood had strayed,
The world's great sorrows were born
And its heroes were made.
In the lost boyhood of Judas,
Christ was betrayed.
1930 *Enchantment and Other Poems*, 'Germinal'.

44 No blazoned banner we unfold—
One charge alone we give to youth,
Against the sceptred myth to hold,
The golden heresy of truth.
'On Behalf of Some Irishmen not Followers of Tradition'.

Russell, John Russell, 1st Earl 1792–1878

English Whig politician, proposer of the first Reform Bill (1832) and Prime Minister (1846–52, 1865–6).

45 If peace cannot be maintained with honour, it is no longer peace.
1853 Speech, Greenock, 19 Sep.
▶ See Cecil 210:27, Chamberlain 212:64, Disraeli 288:66.

Russell, John 1919–2008

English-born US art critic. He was art critic for the *Sunday Times* (1949–74) and the *New York Times* (1974–2001). His many books include *The Meanings of Modern Art* (1981) and *Matisse: Father and Son* (1999).

46 It was not in Dalí's nature to play Gilbert to someone else's Sullivan.
1989 On Salvador Dalí's death. In the *New York Times*, 24 Jan.

47 When Dalí hallucinated...the whole world hallucinated with him.
1989 On Salvador Dalí's death. In the *New York Times*, 24 Jan.

Russell, Mary Annette Russell, Countess née Beauchamp pseudonym Elizabeth 1866–1941

New Zealand-born writer, cousin of Katherine Mansfield. She came to Britain in 1871 and in 1891 married Count Von Arnim and moved to Germany, where she wrote her best-known novel, *Elizabeth and her German Garden* (1898). After his death in 1910 she married Francis, 2nd Earl Russell, brother of Bertrand (1916, separated 1919). In later life she spent much time in the US, where she enjoyed considerable popularity.

48 Far from being half a woman, a widow is the only complete example of her sex. In fact, the finished article.
1936 *All the Dogs of My Life*, pt.2, dog 9, 'Coco'.

Russell, Rosalind 1911–76

US actress. A graduate, she started her acting career in summer stock. After a contract with MGM, she formed the production company Independent Artists with her husband in 1947 and appeared in 51 films. She starred in the Broadway shows *Wonderful Town* (1953) and *Auntie Mame* (1956).

49 Flops are a part of life's menu, and I've never been a girl to miss out on any of the courses.
1957 In the *New York Herald Tribune*, 11 Apr.

Russell, Sir William Howard 1820–1907

Irish-born British war correspondent. He joined *The Times* in 1843, and wrote despatches from the Crimean War (1854–5) which swayed British public opinion against the conflict. He subsequently wrote from the Indian Mutiny (1858), the American Civil War (1861) and the Austro-Prussian War (1866).

50 They dashed on towards that thin red line tipped with steel.
1877 Of the Russians charging the British at the Battle of Balaclava, 14 Nov 1854. *The British Expedition to the Crimea*.

Russell, Willy (William) 1947–

English playwright, best known for *Educating Rita* (1979) and *Shirley Valentine* (1986).

51 Of course I'm drunk—you don't really expect me to teach this stuff when I'm sober.
1979 *Educating Rita*.

Rutherford, Ernest, Baron Rutherford of Nelson 1871–1937

New Zealand-born English physicist, who taught at McGill, Montreal and the University of Manchester (1907–19). In 1919 he became director of the Cavendish Laboratory, Cambridge. Rutherford researched radiation and received the 1908 Nobel prize in chemistry.

52 All science is either physics or stamp collecting.
Quoted in J B Birks *Rutherford at Manchester* (1962).

53 We haven't got the money, so we've got to think.
Quoted in *Bulletin of the Institute of Physics*, vol.13, 1962.

Ryan, Desmond 1893–1964

Irish journalist. He fought at the GPO in the 1916 Rising and became a journalist on his release from internment. His books include *The Man Called Pearse* (1919), *The Phoenix Flame* (1937) and *The Rising* (1949).

54 The triumph of failure.
   1949 Of the Irish uprising of 1916. *The Rising*, closing words.

Rybczynski, Witold Marian 1943–

Scottish-born Canadian architect and writer, professor at the University of Pennsylvania. His works include *Home: A Short History of an Idea* (1986) and *The Look of Architecture* (2001).

55 The most beautiful house in the world is the one that you build for yourself.
   Quoted by Pamela Young in *Maclean's*, 19 Jun 1989.

56 It is truly a place for self-presentation—of oneself, to oneself. A fitting sign of the self-absorbed 1980s.
   1992 On the increasing luxuriousness of bathrooms. *Looking Around*.

Ryder, Albert Pinkham 1847–1917

US painter, whose works are characterized by dreamlike figures and landscapes, evoking a romantic, lonely mood, such as *Toilers of the Sea*. His experimental technique of loading paint on the canvas caused many works to deteriorate. He became misanthropic in later life.

57 The artist needs but a roof, a crust of bread, and his easel, and all the rest God gives him in abundance. He must live to paint and not paint to live.
   Quoted in Sherman *Albert Pinkham Ryder* (1920).

58 The artist should fear to become the slave of detail. He should strive to express his thought and not the surface of it. What avails a storm cloud accurate in form and colour if the storm is not therein?
   Quoted in Goodrich *Albert Pinkham Ryder* (1959).

Ryle, Gilbert 1900–76

English philosopher and Professor of Philosophy at Oxford. His most famous work was *The Concept of Mind* (1949) in which he denounced Cartesian ideas of mind.

59 The dogma of the Ghost in the Machine.
   1949 *The Concept of Mind*.

60 The sorts of things that I can find out about myself are the same as the sorts of things that I can find out about other people and the methods of finding them out are much the same.
   1949 *The Concept of Mind*.

61 As every teacher, like every drill-sergeant or animal trainer, knows in his practice, teaching and training have virtually not yet begun, so long as the pupil is too young, too stupid, too scared or too sulky to respond—and to respond is not just to yield. Where there is a modicum of alacrity, interest or anyhow docility in the pupil, where he tries, however faintheartedly, to get things right rather than awkward, where, even, he registers even a slight contempt for the poor performances of others, of chagrin at his own, pleasure at his own successes and envy of those of others, then he is, in however slight a degree, co-operating and so self-moving.
   Quoted in R S Peters (ed) *The Concept of Education* (1966), ch.7.

S

Saarinen, Aline Bernstein née Loucheim 1914–72

US art critic. In 1955 she married the architect Eero Saarinen, who was one of the leaders of a trend in experimentation in American architecture in the 1950s.

1 He meant to gather for America an undreamed-of collection of art so great and complete that a trip to Europe would be superfluous.
   1991 On the philanthropist and collector John Pierpont Morgan. In *Antiques*, Oct.

Sábato, Ernesto 1911–2011

Argentinian novelist, journalist and essayist. Trained in physics, he increasingly devoted himself to literature. *El túnel* (1948) is a typical existential novel that confronts the problem of the condition of human life.

2 *Había un solo túnel, oscuro y solitario: el mío, el túnel en que había transcurrido mi infancia, mi juventud, toda mi vida… Y entonces, mientras yo avanzaba siempre por mi pasadizo, ella vivía afuera su vida normal, la vida agitada que llevan esas gentes que viven afuera.*
   There was only one tunnel, dark and solitary: mine, the tunnel in which I had spent my childhood, my youth, my entire life… And then, while I kept moving through my passageway, she lived her normal life outside, the exciting life of people who live outside.
   1948 *El túnel*, ch.36 (translated as *The Outsider*, 1950).

Sachar, Abram Leon 1899–1993

US educator, president of Brandeis University, Massachusetts (1948–68), chancellor there (1968–82, emeritus from 1982). His works include *A History of the Jews* (1929) and *The Redemption of the Unwanted* (1983).

3 A university where, at last, the Jews are hosts, and not guests as we have always been before.
   1956 Of Brandeis University, on its 10th anniversary. Speech, 19 Nov.

Sacks (of Aldgate), Sir Jonathan, Baron 1948–

English rabbi, Chief Rabbi of Great Britain (1991–2013).

4 Religious law is like the grammar of language. Any language is governed by such rules; otherwise it ceases to be a language. But within them, you can say many different sentences and write many different books.
   1994 In *The Independent*, 30 Jun.

5 After the destruction of the Second Temple Jews lived by an ancient and fundamental insight, that God does not live in buildings but in the human heart.
   1995 *Community of Faith*.

Sacks, Oliver Wolf 1933–

English-born US neurologist and writer.

6 The Man Who Mistook His Wife for a Hat.
1985 Title of book.

7 We have no idea where the world is going, except that it's going there very fast.
2009 Speech to Kenan Ethics department.

Sackville-West, Vita (Victoria Mary) 1892–1962

English novelist. The daughter of the 3rd Baron Sackville, she married the diplomat Harold Nicolson. She wrote novels, poetry and memoirs, and a regular gardening column for the *Observer*.

8 Forget not bees in winter, though they sleep,
For winter's big with summer in her womb.
1926 *The Land*, 'Spring'.

9 All craftsmen share a knowledge.
They have held
Reality down fluttering to a bench.
1926 *The Land*, 'Summer'.

10 The country habit has me by the heart,
For he's bewitched for ever who has seen,
Not with his eyes but with his vision, Spring
Flow down the woods and stipple leaves with sun.
1926 *The Land*, 'Winter'.

11 The greater cats with golden eyes
Stare out between the bars.
Deserts are there, and different skies,
And night with different stars.
1929 'The Greater Cats with Golden Eyes'.

12 I have come to the conclusion, after many years of sometimes sad experience, that you cannot come to any conclusion at all.
1953 'In Your Garden Again'.

Sadat, Anwar el- 1918–81

Egyptian soldier and politician, jointly awarded the Nobel peace prize with Menachem Begin in 1978.

13 Peace is much more precious than a piece of land.
1978 *In Search of Identity*.

Sade, Donatien Alphonse François, Marquis de 1740–1814

French libertine who expressed his critique of society and the Enlightenment through his controversial behaviour. He spent most of his adult life in the prisons of Vincennes, was released during the Revolution, and eventually died in confinement.

14 La cruauté, bien loin d'être un vice, est le premier sentiment qu'imprime en nous la nature; l'enfant brise son hochet, mord le téton de sa nourrice, étrangle son oiseau, bien avant que d'avoir l'âge de raison.
Far from being a vice, cruelty is the primary feeling that nature imprints in us. The infant breaks its rattle, bites its nurse's nipple, and strangles a bird, well before reaching the age of reason.
1795 *La Philosophie dans le boudoir*.

15 Quand l'athéisme voudra des martyrs, qu'il le dise et mon sang est tout prêt.
When atheism wants martyrs, let it say so and my blood will be ready.
1797 *La Nouvelle Justine*.

Safer, Morley 1931–

Canadian-born journalist and broadcaster, who moved to the US in 1964. His distinguished career includes work for Reuters, London (1955), the BBC (1961) and CBS, as Vietnam correspondent (1964–71) and as co-host of *60 Minutes* news (1970–). He has 12 Emmy and several Peabody awards.

16 BBC Radio is a never-never land of broadcasting, a safe haven from commercial considerations, a honey pot for every scholar and every hare-brained nut to stick a finger into.
1985 In *60 Minutes*, CBS TV broadcast, 15 Sep.

Safire, William 1929–2009

US journalist and author. A correspondent for radio and TV, he ran his own public relations company before President Nixon made him a special assistant (1969–73). A Pulitzer Prize winner for distinguished commentary (1978), he was a columnist for the *New York Times* (1973–2005).

17 The new, old, and constantly changing language of politics is a lexicon of conflict and drama…ridicule and reproach…pleading and persuasion.
1968 *Safire's Political Dictionary*, introduction.

18 Color and bite permeate a language designed to rally many men, to destroy some, and to change the minds of others.
1968 *Safire's Political Dictionary*, introduction.

19 Cover your ass—the bureaucrat's method of protecting his posterior from posterity.
1968 *Safire's Political Dictionary*, introduction.

20 A man who lies, thinking it is the truth, is an honest man, and a man who tells the truth, believing it to be a lie, is a liar.
1975 *After the Fall*, referring to Watergate and the resignation of Richard M Nixon.

21 President Reagan is a rhetorical roundheels, as befits a politician seeking empathy with his audience.
1990 *Language Maven Strikes Again*.

22 The remarkable legion of the unremarked, whose individual opinions are not colorful or different enough to make news, but whose collective opinion, when crystallized, can make history.
1993 Of the so-called 'silent majority'. *Safire's New Political Dictionary*.

23 I was egregiously wrong.
1995 Of serving as a speech-writer for President Nixon. In *USA Today*, 30 Aug.

Sagan, Carl Edward 1934–96

US astronomer and popularizer of science. He has advised NASA on interplanetary probes, was president of the Planetary Society (1979–96) and was a strong proponent of SETI, the search for extraterrestrial intelligence.

24 There is a lurking fear that some things are not meant 'to be known', that some inquiries are too dangerous for human beings to make.
1979 *Broca's Brain*.

25 Science is a way of thinking much more than it is a body of knowledge.
1979 'Can We Know the Universe? Reflections on a Grain of Salt'.

26 Sceptical scrutiny is the means, in both science and religion, by which deep thoughts can be winnowed from deep nonsense.
1980 Interview in *The Times*, 20 Oct.

Sagan, Françoise 1935–2004
French novelist.

27 Art must take reality by surprise.
1958 *Writers at Work*.

28 To jealousy, nothing is more frightful than laughter.
1965 *La Chamade*, ch.9.

Sage, Lorna 1943–2001
British literary critic and author.

29 The night I finished *Dracula* was a lot more exciting than Saturday night at the Regal.
2000 *Bad Blood*.

Saifoutdinov, Anvar 1963–
Russian artist.

30 Life is not easy. I paint the memory of happiness.
Quoted by M S Mason in *Christian Science Monitor*, 19 Nov 1992.

Saint-Exupéry, Antoine de 1900–44
French author and aviator. A commercial and wartime pilot, his works include *Vol de nuit* (1931) and the children's fable *Le Petit Prince* (1943). He was declared missing after a flight to North Africa in 1944.

31 *Il n'y a pas de fatalité extérieure. Mais il y a une fatalité intérieure.*
There is no exterior fatality, only an interior one.
1931 *Vol de nuit*.

32 *L'expérience nous montre qu'aimer ce n'est point nous regarder l'un l'autre mais regàrder ensemble dans la même direction.*
Life has taught us that love does not consist in gazing at each other but in looking together in the same direction.
1939 *Terre des hommes*.

33 *Quand une femme me paraît belle, je n'ai rien à en dire. Je la vois sourire, tout simplement. Les intellectuels démontent le visage, pour l'expliquer par les morceaux, mais ils ne voient plus le sourire.*
When I find a woman attractive, I have nothing at all to say. I simply watch her smile. Intellectuals take apart her face in order to explain it bit by bit, but they no longer see the smile.
1942 *Pilote de guerre*.

34 *Je combattrai pour l'Homme. Contre ses ennemis. Mais aussi contre moi-même.*
I shall fight for mankind. Against his enemies. But also against myself.
1942 *Pilote de guerre*.

35 *Les grandes personnes ne comprennent jamais rien toutes seules, et c'est fatigant, pour les enfants, de toujours et toujours leur donner des explications.*
Adults never understand anything for themselves, and it is tiresome for children to be always and forever explaining things to them.
1943 *Le Petit Prince*.

36 *On est un peu seul dans le désert.*
—On est seul aussi chez les hommes.
One is a little bit alone in the desert.
One is also alone among others.
1943 *Le Petit Prince*.

37 *On ne voit bien qu'avec le cïur. L'essentiel est invisible pour les yeux.*
Only with the heart can a person see rightly; what is essential is invisible to the eye.
1943 *Le Petit Prince*.

38 *Un sourire est souvent l'essentiel. On est payé par un sourire. On est récompensé par un sourire. On est animé par un sourire. Et la qualité d'un sourire peut faire que l'on meure.*
A smile is often the key thing. One is paid with a smile. One is rewarded with a smile. One is brightened by a smile. And the quality of a smile can make one die.
1943 *Lettre à un otage*.

39 *La vie crée l'ordre, mais l'ordre ne crée pas la vie.*
Life creates order, but order does not create life.
1943 *Lettre à un otage*.

40 *Je suis triste pour ma génération qui est vide de toute substance humaine.*
I am sad for my generation which is empty of all human substance.
1944 *Lettre au général*, no.10. Published 10 Apr 1948 in *Le Figaro littéraire*.

41 *J'aime l'homme délivré par sa religion et vivifié par les dieux que je fonde en lui.*
I admire the person freed from his religion and inspired by the gods inside of himself.
Citadelle (published 1948).

42 *L'homme, c'est ce qui est, non point ce qui s'exprime.*
Man is who he is, not how he expresses himself.
Citadelle (published 1948).

43 *Car l'homme, je te le dis, cherche sa propre destinée et non pas son bonheur.*
Because man, I tell you, is looking for his own destiny, not his own happiness.
Citadelle (published 1948).

44 *Prendre conscience, disait ailleurs mon père, c'est d'abord acquérir un style.*
To become conscious, as my father said, one must first acquire a style.
Citadelle (published 1948).

45 *Quiconque craint la contradiction et demeure logique tue en lui la vie.*
Whoever fears contradiction and remains logical kills life within himself.
Carnets (published 1953).

46 *La vérité, pour l'homme, c'est ce qui fait de lui un homme.*
Truth, for a human, is what makes him or her a human being.
Un Sens à la vie (unedited texts collected by Claude Reynal, published 1956).

Saint Laurent, Louis 1882–1973
Canadian politician, Prime Minister (1948–57). He was fluently bilingual, having a French father and an English mother.

47 I didn't know at first that there were two languages in Canada. I just thought that there was one way to speak to my father and another to talk to my mother.
Attributed. Quoted in Dale C Thomson *Louis St. Laurent* (1967).

48 Socialists are Liberals in a hurry.
Attributed. Quoted in Dale C Thomson *Louis St. Laurent* (1967).

Saint-Saëns, (Charles) Camille 1835–1921

French composer, music critic, pianist and organist. Founder of the Société Nationale de Musique in 1871, he composed widely and prolifically.

49 There are two kinds: one takes the music too fast, and the other too slow. There is no third!
   Of conductors. Quoted in Sir Thomas Beecham *A Mingled Chime* (1944).

Saki *pseudonym of* Hector Hugh Munro 1870–1916

British novelist and short-story writer. His short stories are humorous, macabre, and filled with eccentric wit. He was a gifted satirist of the Edwardian world. His collections include *Reginald* (1904) and *The Chronicles of Clovis* (1911). He was killed in World War I.

50 I always say beauty is only sin deep.
   1904 *Reginald*, 'Reginald's Choir Treat'.

51 People can say what they like about the decay of Christianity; the religious system that produced green Chartreuse can never really die.
   1904 *Reginald*, 'Reginald on Christmas Presents'.

52 Her frocks are built in Paris, but she wears them with a strong English accent.
   1904 *Reginald*, 'Reginald on Worries'.

53 The young have aspirations that never come to pass, the old have reminiscences of what never happened.
   1904 *Reginald*, 'Reginald at the Carlton'.

54 There may have been disillusionments in the lives of the medieval saints, but they would scarcely have been better pleased if they could have foreseen that their names would be associated nowadays chiefly with racehorses and the cheaper clarets.
   1904 *Reginald*, 'Reginald at the Carlton'.

55 The cook was a good cook, as cooks go; and as good cooks go, she went.
   1904 *Reginald*, 'Reginald on Besetting Sins'.

56 But, good gracious, you've got to educate him first. You can't expect a boy to be vicious till he's been to a good school.
   1910 *Reginald in Russia*, 'The Baker's Dozen'.

57 'Is your maid called Florence?' 'Her name is Florinda.' 'What an extraordinary name to give a maid!' 'I did not give it to her; she arrived in my service already christened'. 'What I mean is,' said Mrs Riversedge, 'that when I get maids with unsuitable names I call them Jane; they soon get used to it.' 'An excellent plan,' said the aunt of Clovis coldly; 'unfortunately I have got used to being called Jane myself. It happens to be my name.'
   1911 *The Chronicles of Clovis*, 'The Secret Sin of Septimus Brope'.

58 The censorious said that she slept in a hammock and understood Yeats's poems, but her family denied both stories.
   1911 *The Chronicles of Clovis*, 'The Jesting of Arlington Stringham'.

59 The people of Crete unfortunately make more history than they can consume locally.
   1911 *The Chronicles of Clovis*, 'The Jesting of Arlington Stringham'.

60 You needn't tell me that a man who doesn't love oysters and asparagus and good wines has got a soul, or a stomach either. He's simply got the instinct for being unhappy highly developed.
   1911 *The Chronicles of Clovis*, 'The Match-Maker'.

61 His socks compelled one's attention without losing one's respect.
   1911 *The Chronicles of Clovis*, 'Ministers of Grace'.

62 There's nothing in Christianity or Buddhism that quite matches the sympathetic unselfishness of an oyster.
   1911 *The Chronicles of Clovis*, 'The Match-Maker'.

63 All decent people live beyond their incomes nowadays, and those who aren't respectable live beyond other peoples'. A few gifted individuals manage to do both.
   1911 *The Chronicles of Clovis*, 'The Match-Maker'.

64 One of the great advantages of Ireland as a place of residence is that a large number of excellent people never go there.
   1914 Ludovic. *The Watched Pot, or The Mistress of Briony*.

65 'But why should you want to shield him?' cried Egbert; 'the man is a common murderer.'
   'A common murderer, possibly, but a very uncommon cook.'
   1914 *Beasts and Super-Beasts*, 'The Blind Spot'.

66 'Waldo is one of those people who would be enormously improved by death,' said Clovis.
   1914 *Beasts and Super-Beasts*, 'The Feast of Nemesis'.

67 'I believe I take precedence,' he said coldly; 'you are merely the Club Bore: I am the Club Liar.'
   1914 *Beasts and Super-Beasts*, 'A Defensive Diamond'.

68 I should be the last person to say anything against temptation, naturally, but we have a proverb down here 'in baiting a mouse-trap with cheese, always leave room for the mouse'.
   The Square Egg, 'The Infernal Parliament' (published 1924).

69 A little inaccuracy sometimes saves tons of explanation.
   The Square Egg, 'Clovis on the Alleged Romance of Business' (published 1924).

Sala, George Augustus Henry 1828–95

English journalist, book illustrator and novelist, born in London of Italian ancestry. He was in the US during the Civil War, in Italy with Garibaldi, in France in 1870–71, in Russia in 1876 and in Australia in 1885.

70 The foaminess of the Falls, together with the tinge of tawny yellow in the troubled waters, only reminded me of so much unattainable soda and sherry, and made me feel thirstier than ever.
   1865 On seeing Niagara Falls for the first time. *My Diary in America in the Midst of War*.

Salinger, J(erome) D(avid) 1919–2010

US novelist. His novel *The Catcher in the Rye* (1951) is one of the most widely read novels of the era. He published little else, and lived as a recluse in New Hampshire.

71 If you really want to hear about it, the first thing you'll probably want to know is where I was born, and what my lousy childhood was like, and how my parents were occupied and all before they had me, and all that David Copperfield kind of crap, but I don't feel like going into it.
   1951 *The Catcher in the Rye*, ch.1.

72 What really knocks me out is a book that, when you're all done reading it, you wish the author that wrote it was

a terrific friend of yours and you could call him up on the phone whenever you felt like it.
1951 *The Catcher in the Rye*, ch.3.

73 Sex is something I really don't understand too hot. You never know *where* the hell you are. I keep making up these sex rules for myself, and then I break them right away.
1951 *The Catcher in the Rye*, ch.9.

74 That's the thing about girls. Every time they do something pretty, even if they're not much to look at, or even if they're sort of stupid, you fall half in love with them, and then you never know *where* you are.
1951 *The Catcher in the Rye*, ch.10.

75 He looked like the kind of guy that wouldn't talk to you much unless he wanted something off you. He had a lousy personality.
1951 *The Catcher in the Rye*, ch.11.

76 The thing is it's really hard to be room-mates with people if your suitcases are much better than theirs—if yours are really good and theirs aren't. You think if they're intelligent and all, the other person, and have a good sense of humour, that they don't give a damn whose suitcases are better, but they do.
1951 *The Catcher in the Rye*, ch.15.

77 The trouble with me is, I always have to read that stuff by myself. If an actor reads it out, I hardly listen. I keep worrying about whether he's going to do something phoney every minute.
1951 Of Hamlet. *The Catcher in the Rye*, ch.16.

78 Take most people, they're crazy about cars... I'd rather have a goddam horse. A horse is at least *human*, for God's sake.
1951 *The Catcher in the Rye*, ch.17.

79 The trouble with girls is, if they like a boy, no matter how big a bastard he is, they'll say he has an inferiority complex, and if they don't like him, no matter how nice a guy he is, or how big an inferiority complex he has, they'll say he's conceited. Even smart girls do it.
1951 *The Catcher in the Rye*, ch.18.

80 Sally said I was a sacrilegious atheist. I probably am. The thing that Jesus *really* would've liked would be the guy that plays the kettle drums in the orchestra.
1951 *The Catcher in the Rye*, ch.18.

81 Anyway, I keep picturing all these little kids playing some game in this big field of rye and all. Thousands of little kids, and nobody's around—nobody big, I mean—except me. And I'm standing on the edge of some crazy cliff. What I have to do, I have to catch everybody if they start to go over the cliff—I mean if they're running and they don't look where they're going I have to come out from somewhere and catch them. That's all I'd do all day. I'd just be the catcher in the rye and all. I know it's crazy, but that's the only thing I'd really like to be.
1951 *The Catcher in the Rye*, ch.22.

82 Never tell anyone anything. If you do you start missing everyone.
1951 *The Catcher in the Rye*, last words.

83 For Esmé—with Love and Squalor.
1953 Title of story.

84 Poetry, surely, is a crisis, perhaps the only actionable one we can call our own.
1959 'Seymour: An Introduction'.

85 A confessional passage has probably never been written that didn't stink a little bit of the writer's pride in having given up his pride.
1959 'Seymour: An Introduction'.

86 One of the reasons that I quit going to the theatre when I was about twenty was that I resented like hell filing out of the theatre because some playwright was forever slamming down his silly curtain.
1959 'Seymour: An Introduction'.

87 There's no more to Holden Caulfield. Read the book again. It's all there. Holden Caulfield is only a frozen moment in time.
2009 In the *New York Times*, 14 Aug.

Salisbury, Robert Arthur Talbot Gascoyne Cecil, 3rd Marquis of 1830–1903

English Conservative statesman. He succeeded Disraeli as Leader of the Opposition, and was subsequently Prime Minister (1885–6, 1886–92, 1895–1902), as well as holding other posts. He was head of government during the Boer War (1889–1902).

88 Horny-handed sons of toil.
1873 In the *Quarterly Review*, Oct.

89 No lesson seems to be so deeply inculcated by the experience of life as that you should never trust experts. If you believe the doctors, nothing is wholesome: if you believe the theologians, nothing is innocent: if you believe the soldiers, nothing is safe. They all require to have their strong wine diluted by a very large admixture of insipid common sense.
1877 Letter to Lord Lytton, 15 Jun. Quoted in Lady Gwendolen Cecil *Life of Robert, Marquis of Salisbury* (1921–32), vol.2, ch.4.

90 We are part of the community of Europe and we must do our duty as such.
1888 Speech at Caernarvon, 10 Apr. In *The Times*, 11 Apr.

91 By office boys for office boys.
Of the *Daily Mail*. The phrase recalls Thackeray's Pendennis who started a newspaper 'by gentlemen for gentlemen'. Quoted in S J Taylor *The Great Outsiders: Northcliffe, Rothermere and the Daily Mail* (1966), ch.2.

Sallust *in full* Gaius Sallustius Crispus 86–34 BC

Roman historian and politician. As Governor of Numidia he enriched himself enormously. He wrote *Bellum Catilinae, Bellum Iugurthinum* and *Historiarum libri quinque*, of which only fragments survive.

92 *Alieni appetens, sui profusus.*
Greedy for the belongings of others, extravagant with his own.
Bellum Catilinae, 5.

93 *Esse quam videri bonus malebat.*
He preferred to be good, rather than seem good.
Of Cato. *Bellum Catilinae*, 54.

94 *Punica fide.*
With Punic faith.
Used ironically (meaning treacherously) of the Numidian Bocchus, a double agent between Iugurtha and Sulla. *Bellum Iugurthinum*, 108.3.

Salter, Sir (James) Arthur, 1st Baron Salter 1881–1975

English economist and international civil servant.

95 The normal economic system works itself.
   Quoted in Ronald H Coase *Essays on Economics and Economists* (1994), p.6.

Salvianus c.400–c.470 AD

Christian writer from Gaul. His surviving works include nine epistles, *Ad Ecclesiam* and the unfinished *De Gubernatione Dei*. He urged that all estates be bequeathed to the poor, and denounced inherited wealth.

96 *Quot curiales, tot tyranni.*
   As many councillors, so many tyrants.
   De Gubernatione Dei, 5.18.27.

Sampson, Anthony (Terrell Seward) 1926–2004

English journalist and writer. His most influential book was *The Anatomy of Britain* (1962), which was followed by other titles on the same theme. He was a staff member of the *Observer* (1955–66).

97 In America journalism is apt to be regarded as an extension of history: in Britain, as an extension of conversation.
   1965 *The Anatomy of Britain Today*, ch.9.

Samuel, Herbert Louis, 1st Viscount Samuel 1870–1963

English Liberal statesman and philosophical writer, Home Secretary (1916, 1931–2) and High Commissioner for Palestine (1920–5). His philosophical works include *Practical Ethics* (1935), *Belief and Action* (1937) and *In Search of Reality* (1957).

98 The House of Lords must be the only institution in the world that is kept efficient by the persistent absenteeism of its members.
   1948 In *American News Review*, 5 Feb.

99 Hansard is history's ear, already listening.
   1949 House of Lords, Dec.

Samuelson, Paul Anthony 1915–2009

US economist and journalist, professor at Massachusetts Institute of Technology (1940–85). His works include *Foundations of Economic Analysis* (1947) and the classic *Economics* (1948). He won the Nobel prize for economics in 1970.

1 The consumer, so it is said, is the king...each is a voter who uses his money as votes to get the things done that he wants done.
   1948 *Economics*.

2 Commentators quote economic studies alleging that market downturns predicted four out of the last five recessions. That is an understatement. Wall Street indexes predicted nine out of the last five recessions!
   1966 Quoted in *The Samuelson Sampler* (1973).

Samuelson, Sir Sydney 1925–

British film commissioner. He started in the film industry in 1939 and worked as a cinema projectionist, editor and cameraman. He founded Samuelson Film Service and in 1991 was appointed the first British Film Commissioner.

3 We welcome all enquiries about the UK climate—after all, we have more weather available in this country than anywhere else.
   1994 *Check Book*.

Sand, George *pseudonym of* Amandine Aurore Lucille Dupin, Baronne Dudevant 1804–76

French novelist, the illegitimate daughter of Marshal de Saxe, known for her scandalous bohemian lifestyle and her liaisons with Musset and Chopin, and later with prominent politicians.

4 *L'amour, heurtant son front aveugle à tous les obstacles de la civilisation.*
   Love, knocking its blind forehead against all of civilization's obstacles.
   1832 *Indiana*, preface.

5 *En France particulièrement, les mots ont plus d'empire que les idées.*
   In France particularly, words reign over ideas.
   1832 *Indiana*, pt.1, ch.2.

6 *L'homme qui a un peu usé ses émotions est plus pressé de plaire que d'aimer.*
   The person who has used his emotions even a little is more anxious to please than to love.
   1832 *Indiana*, pt.1, ch.5.

7 *La société ne doit rien exiger de celui qui n'attend rien d'elle.*
   Society should not ask anything of the person who expects nothing from society.
   1832 *Indiana*, conclusion.

8 *Nous ne pouvons arracher une seule page de notre vie, mais nous pouvons jeter le livre au feu.*
   We cannot tear out a single page from our life, but we can throw the entire book in the fire.
   1832 *Mauprat*.

9 *Nulle créature humaine ne peut commander à l'amour.*
   No human being can give orders to love.
   1833 *Jacques*.

10 *Le vrai est trop simple, il faut y arriver toujours par le compliqué.*
   Truth is too simple; it must always be arrived at in a complicated manner.
   1867 Letter to Armand Barbès, May.

11 *L'art pour l'art est un vain mot. L'art pour le vrai, l'art pour le beau et le bon, voilà la religion que je cherche.*
   Art for art's sake is an empty phrase. Art for the sake of the true, art for the sake of the good and the beautiful, that is the faith I search for.
   1872 Letter to Alexandre Saint-Jean.

Sandburg, Carl 1878–1967

US poet, originally a journalist in Chicago. His volumes of poetry, celebrating US life in free verse, include *Chicago Poems* (1916) and *Good Morning, America* (1928). He also published a collection of folk-songs, *The American Songbag* (1927), and a *Life of Abraham Lincoln* (6 vols, 1926–39, Pulitzer Prize). He was awarded another Pulitzer Prize for his *Complete Poems* (1950).

12 The ache to utter and see in word
   The silhouette of a brooding soul.
   1904 Describing the poet's motivation. *In Reckless Ecstasy*.

13 Hog Butcher for the World,
   Tool Maker, Stacker of Wheat,
   Player with Railroads and the Nation's Freight Handler;
   Stormy, husky, brawling,
   City of the Big Shoulders.
   1916 *Chicago Poems*, 'Chicago'.

14 The fog comes
on little cat feet.

It sits looking
over harbor and city
on silent haunches
and then moves on.
1916 *Chicago Poems*, 'Fog'.

15 (All the coaches shall be scrap and rust and all the men
and women
laughing in the diners and sleepers shall pass to ashes.)
I ask a man in the smoker where he is going and he
answers: 'Omaha'.
1916 *Chicago Poems*, 'Limited'.

16 I tell you the past is a bucket of ashes.
1918 *Cornhuskers*, 'Prairie'.

17 When Abraham Lincoln was shovelled into the tombs,
he forgot the copperheads and the assassin…
in the dust, in the cool tombs.
1918 *Cornhuskers*, 'Cool Tombs'.

18 Pile the bodies high at Austerlitz and Waterloo.
Shovel them under and let me work—
I am the grass; I cover all.
1918 *Cornhuskers*, 'Grass'.

19 Why is there always a secret singing
When a lawyer cashes in?
Why does a hearse horse snicker
Hauling a lawyer away?
1920 *Smoke and Steel*, 'The Lawyers Know Too Much'.

20 Look how you use proud words,
When you let proud words go, it is not easy to call them
back,
They wear long boots, hard boots; they walk off proud;
they can't hear you calling—
look out how you use proud words.
1922 *Slabs of the Sunburnt West*, 'Primer Lesson'.

21 Poetry is the opening and closing of a door, leaving
those who look through to guess about what is seen
during a moment.
1923 'Poetry Considered', in the *Atlantic Monthly*, Mar.

22 Poetry is the achievement of the synthesis of hyacinths
and biscuits.
1923 'Poetry Considered', in the *Atlantic Monthly*, Mar.

23 The people will live on.
The learning and blundering will live on.
They will be tricked and sold and again sold
And go back to the nourishing earth for rootholds.
1936 *The People, Yes*.

24 I never made a mistake in grammar but once
in my life and as soon as I done it I seen it.
1936 *The People, Yes*.

25 'Would you just as soon get off the earth?'
holding ourselves aloof in pride of distinction
saying to ourselves this costs us nothing
as though hate has no cost
as though hate ever grew anything worth growing.
1936 On 'the red men'. *The People, Yes*.

26 or we may hold them in respect and affection
as fellow creepers on a commodious planet
saying, 'Yes you too you too are people'.
1936 On 'the red men'. *The People, Yes*.

27 Sometime they'll give a war and nobody will come.
1936 *The People, Yes*.

28 The people know what the land knows.
1936 *The People, Yes*.

29 I am still studying verbs and the mystery of how they
connect nouns. I am more suspicious of adjectives than
at any other time in all my born days.
c.1940 On receiving nearly a dozen honorary doctorates for his
biography of Lincoln. Quoted in *The Complete Poems of Carl
Sandburg* (1986), 'Notes for a Preface'.

30 A baby is God's opinion that life should go on.
1948 *Remembrance Rock*, ch.2.

31 Slang is a language that rolls up its sleeves, spits on its
hands and goes to work.
1959 In the *New York Times*, 13 Feb.

32 In these times you have to be an optimist to open your
eyes when you wake in the morning.
1960 In the *New York Post*, 9 Sep.

33 The simple dignity of a child drinking a bowl of milk
embodies the fascination of an ancient rite.
Quoted in *Personalia, the Complete Poems of Carl Sandburg*
(1970).

34 In the spacious highways of books major or minor, each
poet is allowed the stride that will get him where he
wants to go if, God help him, he can hit that stride and
keep it.
Quoted in *The Complete Poems of Carl Sandburg* (1986), 'Notes for
a Preface'.

35 The more rhyme there is in poetry the more danger of
its tricking the writer into something other than the urge
in the beginning.
Quoted in *The Complete Poems of Carl Sandburg* (1986), 'Notes for
a Preface'.

36 There is a formal poetry perfect only in form…the
number of syllables, the designated and required stresses
of accent, the rhymes if wanted—they come off with the
skill of a solved crossword puzzle.
Quoted in *The Complete Poems of Carl Sandburg* (1986), 'Notes for
a Preface'.

Sandburg, Sheryl Kara 1969–

US businesswoman, Chief Operating Officer of Facebook since 2014.

37 Lean In.
2013 Title of book, which encourages women to play a bigger role
in the professional world.

Sanders, George 1906–72

British actor who became renowned for playing cads and sophisticated villains. Among his many roles, his parts in *Rebecca* (1940), *The Moon and Sixpence* (1942), *The Picture of Dorian Gray* (1944), *All About Eve* (1950) and *A Shot in the Dark* (1964) were particularly notable.

38 Dear World, I am leaving because I am bored. I feel I
have lived long enough. I am leaving you with your
worries in this sweet cesspool. Good luck.
1972 His suicide note.

Sandys, George 1578–1644

English translator and traveller, youngest son of the Archbishop of York. He published a verse translation of Ovid's *Metamorphoses*, written while treasurer to the colony in Virginia. He also wrote poetic versions of the *Psalms* (1636) and the *Song of Solomon* (1641).

39 Men ignorant of letters, studious for their bellies, and ignominiously lazy.
   1610 On the monks of Patmos. *Relation of a Journey Begun An. Dom. 1610.*

Santayana, George *originally* Jorge Augustín Nicolás Ruiz de Santayana 1863–1952

Spanish–US philosopher, poet and novelist, Professor of Philosophy at Harvard (1907–12). His writing career began as a poet with *Sonnets and Other Verses* (1894), but he later became known as a philosopher and stylist, in such works as *The Life of Reason* (5 vols, 1905–6), *Realms of Being* (4 vols, 1927–40), and his novel *The Last Puritan* (1935). He moved to Europe in 1912, stayed at Oxford during World War I, then settled in Rome.

40 Fashion is something barbarous, for it produces innovation without reason and imitation without benefit.
   1905–6 *The Life of Reason*, 'Reason in Religion'.

41 Those who cannot remember the past are condemned to repeat it.
   1905–6 *The Life of Reason*.

42 For an idea ever to be fashionable is ominous, since it must afterwards be always old-fashioned.
   1913 *Winds of Doctrine*, 'Modernism and Christianity'.

43 Philosophy to him was rather like a maze in which he happened to find himself wandering, and what he was looking for was the way out.
   1920 Of William James. *Character and Opinion in the United States.*

44 The empiricist…thinks he believes only what he sees, but he is much better at believing than at seeing.
   1955 *Scepticism and Animal Faith.*

45 Art is dedicated echo.
   Quoted in John Gassner and Sidney Thomas (eds) *The Nature of Art* (1964).

46 Nothing is so poor and melancholy as an art that is interested in itself and not in its subject.
   Quoted in John Gassner and Sidney Thomas (eds) *The Nature of Art* (1964).

47 A building without ornamentation is like a heaven without stars.
   Quoted in the *Christian Science Monitor*, 14 Dec 1990.

48 Pure poetry is pure experiment…memorable nonsense.
   Quoted in Helen Gardner (ed) *The New Oxford Book of English Verse* (1991).

Sappho 7c BC

Greek lyric poetess, born on Lesbos. Most of her surviving poems are from papyrus fragments discovered in recent times.

49 He looks to me to be in heaven, that man who sits across from you and listens near you to your soft speaking, your laughing lovely: that, I vow, makes the heart leap in my breast; for watching you a moment, speech fails me, my tongue is paralysed, at once a light fire runs beneath my skin, my eyes are blinded, and my ears drumming, the sweat pours down me, and I shake all over, sallower than grass: I feel as if I'm not far off dying.
   D L Page (ed) *Lyrica Graeca Selecta* (1968), no.199 (translated by M L West).

50 Just as the sweet-apple reddens on the high branch, high on the highest, and the apple-pickers missed it, or rather did not miss it out, but could not reach it.
   Of a girl before her marriage. D L Page (ed) *Lyrica Graeca Selecta* (1968), no.224.

Sarduy, Severo 1937–93

Cuban novelist and essayist. He left his country for Paris in 1960. A practitioner and a theoretician of so-called neo-Baroque, he used in his novels a variety of experimental techniques, satire, parody and a carnivalistic approach.

51 ¡Ah sí, ponerse a escribir otra vez, qué vomitivo! ¸Como si todo esto sirviera para algo, como si todo esto fuera a entrar en alguna cabezota, a entretener a alguno de los lectores babosos, ovillados en sus poltronas, frente al sopón soporífero de cada día!
   Ah yes, going back to writing, how disgusting! As if all this had some purpose, as if all this would penetrate some thick skull, amuse some drivelling reader curled up in his armchair before the soporific stew of every day!
   1967 *De donde son los cantantes* (translated as *From Cuba with a Song*, 1972), 'La Dolores Rondón'.

Sargent, John Singer 1856–1925

US painter.

52 Every time I paint a portrait I lose a friend.
   Attributed.

Sargent, Sir (Harold) Malcolm Watts 1895–1967

English conductor. Originally trained as an organist, he was conductor of the Royal Choral Society from 1928, was in charge of the Liverpool Philharmonic Orchestra (1942–48) and led the BBC Symphony Orchestra (1950–57).

53 Just a little more reverence, please, and not so much astonishment.
   Attributed, admonishing a choir singing Handel's 'For Unto Us a Child is Born'.

Sarkozy, Nicolas 1955–

French politician. Having previously been appointed to several ministerial positions, he served as President of France (2007–12) before being charged with corruption by the French courts.

54 Europe is not a choice, it is a necessity, but it needs to be rethought, refounded.
   2011 Speaking at EU debt talks in Paris, 2 Dec.

Sarnoff, David 1891–1971

Russian-born US radio and television pioneer. He began with the Marconi Wireless Co, covering the Titanic disaster (1912), and became president (1930) and chairman of the board (1947) of the Radio Corporation of America, a key figure in the development of television.

55 Seldom is it given to one generation to have such an opportunity to rise again, but now before you is that opportunity in television—a larger, richer, broader opportunity than ever existed in radio.
   c.1948 Speech to NBC station affiliates. Recalled on his death, 12 Dec 1971.

56 Competition brings out the best in products and the worst in people.
   Attributed.

Saroyan, William 1908–81
US playwright and novelist. He was awarded the Pulitzer Prize in 1939 for his best-known play, *The Time of Your Life*.

57 The Daring Young Man on the Flying Trapeze.
1934 Title of story collection.

58 The events of life have never fallen into the form of the short story or the form of the poem, or into any other form. Your own consciousness is the only form you need.
1934 *The Daring Young Man on the Flying Trapeze*, 'A Cold Day'.

59 Now what?
1981 Last words.

Sarraute, Nathalie 1902–99
French novelist and literary critic.

60 *Le mot 'psychologie' est un de ceux qu'aucun auteur d'aujourd'hui ne peut entendre prononcer à son sujet sans baisser les yeux et rougir.*
The word 'psychology' is one that no author today can hear said about her work without lowering her eyes and blushing.
1956 *L'Ère du soupçon*.

61 *Vous savez qu'on doit se sentir heureux. Tous les vrais écrivains ont éprouvé ce sentiment. Quand on ne l'éprouve pas, je suis obligé de vous en avertir, c'est mauvais signe.*
You know that one should feel happy. All the true writers have experienced this feeling. When one does not experience it, I am obliged to tell you that it is a bad sign.
1968 *Entre la vie et la mort*.

62 *Chacun peut éprouver en soi ce double mouvement: désir de s'intégrer à la société, besoin de se réaliser par soi-même en dehors d'elle.*
We all have this double impulse within ourselves: the desire to integrate into society, and the need to fulfil ourselves outside of it, through our own efforts.
La Quinzaine littéraire, 50.

Sarton, George A 1884–1956
US academic and historian of science.

63 Definition—Science is systematized positive knowledge, what has been taken as such in different ages and in different places. Theorem—The acquisition and systematization of positive knowledge are the only human activities which are truly cumulative and progressive. Corollary—The history of science is the only history which can illustrate the progress of mankind. In fact, progress has no definite and unquestionable meaning in other fields than the field of science.
1957 *The Study of the History of Science*.

Sarton, May 1912–95
US poet and novelist. Her poetry collections include *Inner Landscape* (1939), *The Land of Silence* (1953) and *The Silence Now* (1988), and she wrote other works such as *Mrs Stevens Hears the Mermaids Singing* (1965).

64 The poet must be free to love or hate as the spirit moves him, free to change, free to be a chameleon, free to be an *enfant terrible*. He must above all never worry about his effect on other people. Power requires that one do just that all the time. Power requires that the inner person never be unmasked. No, we poets have to go naked. And since this is so, it is better that we stay private people; a naked public person would be rather ridiculous, what?
1965 Hilary Stevens. *Mrs Stevens Hears the Mermaids Singing*, pt.2.

65 I write poems, have always written them, to transcend the painfully personal and reach the universal.
Quoted in *Encore: A Journal of the 80th Year* (1993).

66 When you're a poet, you're a poet first. When it comes, it's like an angel.
Quoted by Mel Gussow in her obituary, in the *New York Times*, 18 Jul 1995.

Sartre, Jean-Paul 1905–80
French existentialist philosopher and writer, a prominent intellectual and friend of Simone de Beauvoir. His works include the trilogy *Les Chemins de la liberté* (1945–9, *The Roads to Freedom*) and many plays. His philosophy is presented in *L'Être et le néant* (1943, *Being and Nothingness*). In 1964 he published his autobiography *Les Mots* (*Words*), and was awarded (but declined) the Nobel prize for literature.

67 *Trois heures, c'est toujours trop tard ou trop tôt pour tout ce qu'on veut faire.*
Three o'clock is always either too late or too early for anything one might want to do.
1938 *La Nausée*, 'Vendredi'.

68 *L'homme est une passion inutile.*
Man is a useless passion.
1943 *L'Être et le néant* (*Being and Nothingness*, 1957) pt.4, ch.2, section 3 (translated by Hazel Barnes).

69 *L'Enfer, c'est les Autres.*
Hell is other people.
1945 *Huis clos*.

70 *Est-ce qu'au fond, ce qui fait peur, dans la doctrine que je vais essayer de vous exposer, ce n'est pas le fait qu'elle laisse une possibilité de choix à l'homme?*
For at bottom, what is alarming in the doctrine that I am about to try to explain to you is—is it not?—that it confronts man with a possibility of choice.
1946 *L'Existentialisme est un humanisme* (*Existentialism and Humanism*, 1948) (translated by Philip Mairet).

71 *Ce qu'ils ont en commun, c'est simplement le fait qu'ils estiment que l'existence précède l'essence, ou, si vous voulez, qu'il faut partir de la subjectivité.*
What [existentialists] have in common is simply the fact that they believe that *existence* comes before *essence*—or, if you will, that we must begin from the subjective.
1946 *L'Existentialisme est un humanisme* (*Existentialism and Humanism*, 1948) (translated by Philip Mairet).

72 *Qu'est-ce que signifie que l'existence précède l'essence? Cela signifie que l'homme existe d'abord, se rencontre, surgit dans le monde, et qu'il se définit après.*
What do we mean by saying that existence precedes essence? We mean that man first of all exists, encounters himself, surges up in the world—and defines himself afterwards.
1946 *L'Existentialisme est un humanisme* (*Existentialism and Humanism*, 1948) (translated by Philip Mairet).

73 *L'homme n'est rien d'autre que ce qu'il se fait. Tel est le premier principe de l'existentialisme.*
   Man is nothing else but that which he makes of himself. That is the first principle of existentialism.
   1946 *L'Existentialisme est un humanisme* (*Existentialism and Humanism*, 1948) (translated by Philip Mairet).

74 *L'homme est condamné à être libre.*
   Man is condemned to be free.
   1946 *L'Existentialisme est un humanisme* (*Existentialism and Humanism*, 1948) (translated by Philip Mairet).

75 *Un homme n'est rien d'autre qu'une série d'entreprises.*
   A man is no other than a series of undertakings.
   1946 *L'Existentialisme est un humanisme* (*Existentialism and Humanism*, 1948) (translated by Philip Mairet).

76 *Il n'y a pas d'autre univers qu'un univers humain, l'univers de la subjectivité humaine.*
   There is no other universe except the human universe, the universe of human subjectivity.
   1946 *L'Existentialisme est un humanisme* (*Existentialism and Humanism*, 1948) (translated by Philip Mairet).

77 *Vous êtes libre, choisissez, c'est-à-dire, inventez. Aucune morale générale ne peut vous indiquer ce qu'il y a à faire.*
   You are free, therefore choose—that is to say, invent. No rule of general morality can show you what you ought to do.
   1946 *L'Existentialisme est un humanisme* (*Existentialism and Humanism*, 1948) (translated by Philip Mairet).

78 The status of 'native' is a nervous condition introduced and maintained by the settler among colonized people with their consent.
   1961 Preface to Franz Fanon *Les Damnés de la terre* (*The Wretched of the Earth*, 1967, translated by Constance Farrington). Tsitsi Dangarembga uses this sentence to supply both epigraph and title of her 1988 novel *Nervous Conditions*.

Sassoon, Siegfried Louvain 1886–1967

English poet and novelist. He established his reputation as a war poet while serving in World War I. He wrote a semi-autobiographical trilogy, *The Memoirs of George Sherston* (1928–36), and several volumes of actual memoirs.

79 I am making this statement as an act of wilful defiance of military authority, because I believe that the War is being deliberately prolonged by those who have the power to end it.
   1917 'A Soldier's Declaration'. Statement sent to his commanding officer which was read out in the House of Commons and printed in *The Times*.

80 I'd like to see a Tank come down the stalls,
   Lurching to rag-time tunes, or 'Home sweet Home',—
   And there'd be no more jokes in Music-halls
   To mock the riddled corpses round Bapaume.
   1917 'Blighters'.

81 How right it seemed that he should reach the span
   Of comfortable years allowed to man!
   Splendid to eat and sleep and choose a wife,
   Safe with his wound, a citizen of life.
   He hobbled blithely through the garden gate,
   And thought: 'Thank God they had to amputate!'
   1917 'The One-Legged Man'.

82 We'd gained our first objective hours before
   While dawn broke like a face with blinking eyes,
   Pallid, unshaved and thirsty, blind with smoke.
   1918 'Counter-Attack'.

83 Soldiers are citizens of death's grey land,
   —Drawing no dividend from time's to-morrows.
   In the great hour of destiny they stand,
   —Each with his feuds, and jealousies, and sorrows.
   Soldiers are sworn to action; they must win
   —Some flaming, fatal climax with their lives.
   Soldiers are dreamers; when the guns begin
   —They think of firelit homes, clean beds and wives.
   1918 'Dreamers'.

84 If I were fierce and bald and short of breath
   I'd live with scarlet Majors at the Base,
   And speed glum heroes up the line to death.
   1918 'Base Details'.

85 And when war is done and youth stone dead
   I'd toddle safely home and die—in bed.
   1918 'Base Details'.

86 'Good-morning; good-morning!' the General said
   When we met him last week on our way to the line.
   Now the soldiers he smiled at are most of 'em dead,
   And we're cursing his staff for incompetent swine.
   'He's a cheery old card,' grunted Harry to Jack
   As they slogged up to Arras with rifle and pack.

   But he did for them both by his plan of attack.
   1918 'The General'.

87 Does it matter?—losing your sight?...
   There's such splendid work for the blind;
   And people will always be kind
   As you sit on the terrace remembering
   And turning your face to the light.
   1918 'Does It Matter'.

88 From you, Beethoven, Bach, Mozart,
   The substance of my dreams took fire.
   You built cathedrals in my heart,
   And lit my pinnacled desire.
   1918 'Dead Musicians'.

89 You have no part with lads who fought
   And laughed and suffered at my side.
   Your fugues and symphonies have brought
   No memory of my friends who died.
   1918 'Dead Musicians'.

90 Why do you lie with your legs ungainly huddled,
   And one arm bent across your sullen cold
   Exhausted face?
   1918 'The Dug-Out'.

91 You are too young to fall asleep for ever;
   And when you sleep you remind me of the dead.
   1918 'The Dug-Out'.

92 Everyone suddenly burst out singing;
   And I was filled with such delight
   As prisoned birds must find in freedom,
   1919 'Everyone Sang'.

93 But the past is just the same,—and
   War's a bloody game.
   1919 'Aftermath'.

94 When all is said and done, leading a good life is more important than keeping a good diary.
   1923 Diary entry, 8 Jul.

95 In me the tiger sniffs the rose.
   1928 *The Heart's Journey*, pt.7, 'In me, past, present, future meet'.

96 And what is time but shadows that were cast
   By these storm-sculptured stones while centuries fled?
   The stones remain; their stillness can outlast
   The skies of history hurrying overhead.
   1928 *The Heart's Journey*, pt.9, 'What is Stonehenge? It is the roofless past'.

97 *Alone...* The word is life endured and known.
   It is the stillness where our spirits walk
   And all but inmost faith is overthrown.
   1928 *The Heart's Journey*, pt.11, '"When I'm alone"—the words tripped off his tongue'.

98 They have spoken lightly of my deathless friends,
   (Lamps for my gloom, hands guiding where I stumble,)
   Quoting, for shallow conversational ends,
   What Shelley shrilled, what Blake once wildly muttered...
   How can they use such names and be not humble?
   1928 *The Heart's Journey*, pt.15, 'Grandeur of Ghosts'.

99 Who will remember, passing through this Gate,
   The unheroic Dead who fed the guns?
   Who shall absolve the foulness of their fate,—
   Those doomed, conscripted, unvictorious ones?
   1928 *The Heart's Journey*, pt.21, 'On Passing the New Menin Gate'.

1 Here Vaughan lies dead, whose name flows on for ever
   Through pastures of the spirit washed with dew
   And starlit with eternities unknown.
   1928 *The Heart's Journey*, pt.23, 'At the Grave of Henry Vaughan'.

2 The skull that housed white angels and had vision
   Of daybreak through the gateways of the mind.
   1928 *The Heart's Journey*, pt.23, 'At the Grave of Henry Vaughan'.

3 A man may be born a poet, but he has to make himself an artist as well.
   1939 *On Poetry*.

Satie, Erik Alfred Leslie 1866–1925

French composer. A pupil of Vincent d'Indy and Albert Roussel, he wrote ballets, lyric dramas and numerous whimsical pieces in which he rebelled against Wagnerism and orthodoxy in general. His music had some influence on Debussy, Ravel and others.

4 Before I compose a piece, I walk round it several times, accompanied by myself.
   Quoted in *Bulletin des éditions musicales* (1913).

5 To be played with both hands in the pocket.
   Instruction on one of his piano compositions. Quoted in Oscar Levant *The Unimportance of Being Oscar* (1968).

6 It is not enough to refuse the Legion d'Honneur. One should never have deserved it.
   Of Maurice Ravel, who had declined the honour. Quoted by Alister Kershaw in *The Australian*, 1991.

Sayers, Dorothy L(eigh) 1893–1957

English detective-story writer. Her hero, Lord Peter Wimsey, is one of the most popular of the great detectives, and her books are distinguished by realistically created settings as well as stylish wit. She also wrote plays and poems.

7 I admit it is more fun to punt than to be punted, and that a desire to have all the fun is nine-tenths of the law of chivalry.
   1935 *Gaudy Night*, ch.14.

8 I can't see that she could have found anything nastier to say if she'd thought it out with both hands for a fortnight.
   1937 'Prothalamion'.

9 Plain lies are dangerous.
   1937 'The Psychology of Advertising', in *The Spectator*, 19 Nov.

10 Those who prefer their English sloppy have only themselves to thank if the advertisement writer uses his mastery of vocabulary and syntax to mislead their weak minds.
   1937 'The Psychology of Advertising', in *The Spectator*, 19 Nov.

11 The moral of all this...is that we have the kind of advertising we deserve.
   1937 'The Psychology of Advertising', in *The Spectator*, 19 Nov.

12 As I grow older and older,
   And totter towards the tomb,
   I find that I care less and less
   Who goes to bed with whom.
   'That's Why I Never Read Modern Novels', collected in Janet Hitchman *Such a Strange Lady* (1975), ch.12.

Scargill, Arthur 1938–

English trade union leader, president of the National Union of Mineworkers (1981–2002). A powerful orator, his strong defence of miners and his socialist politics led to conflict with government, particularly in the miners' strike of 1984–5. He started a new socialist party in 1996.

13 My father still reads the dictionary every day. He says that your life depends on your power to master words.
   1982 In the *Sunday Times*, 10 Jan.

14 I speak of that most dangerous duo—President Ray-Gun and the plutonium blonde, Margaret Thatcher.
   1984 Quoted in *Time*, 3 Dec.

15 I wouldn't vote for Ken Livingstone if he were running for mayor of Toytown.
   2000 In *The Guardian*, 3 May.

Scève, Maurice c.1510–c.1564

French poet of the École Lyonnaise. His most famous collection of poems, *Délie, objet de plus haute vertu* (1544), is a meditation on love.

16 *Car loi d'Amour est de l'un captiver,*
   L'autre donner d'heureuse liberté.
   The law of love is to captivate one,
   And to give another joyous freedom.
   1544 *Délie*, no.40.

17 *En toi je vis, où que tu sois absente;*
   En moi je meurs, où que je sois présent.
   Tant loin sois-tu, toujours tu es présente;
   Pour près que sois, encore suis-je absent.
   I live in you, wherever you are, when you are absent;
   I die in myself wherever I am.
   No matter how far away you are, you are always present;
   And no matter how near you are, I am always absent.
   1544 *Délie*, no.144.

18 *Tu es le Corps, Dame, et je suis ton ombre.*
   You are the body, lady, and I am your shadow.
   1544 *Délie*, no.376.

Schacht, Hjalmar Horace Greely 1877–1970

German financier. As president of the Reichsbank (1923) he ended inflation, and recalled by the Nazis from resignation in 1933, he restored the German trade balance by unorthodox methods. Dismissed after disagreement with Hitler, he was later acquitted at Nuremberg of crimes against humanity.

19 I wouldn't believe that Hitler was dead, even if he told me himself.
   1945 Attributed remark, 8 May.

Schaw, Janet b.c.1730

Scottish traveller. She was distantly related to Sir Walter Scott and was well educated, but little is known of her other than what is told in her *Journal of a Lady of Quality*, an account of her travels in the West Indies in 1774–6.

20 At last America is in my view; a dreary waste of white barren sand, and melancholy, nodding pines. In the course of many miles, no cheerful cottage has blest my eyes. All seems dreary, savage and desert; and was it for this such sums of money, such streams of British blood have been lavished away? Oh, thou dear land, how dearly hast thou purchased this habitation for bears and wolves. Dearly has it been purchased, and at a price far dearer still it will be kept. My heart dies within me, while I view it.
   c.1776 On her first sight of the country around Cape Fear. *Journal of a Lady of Quality; Being the Narrative of a Journey from Scotland to the West Indies, North Carolina, and Portugal, in the years 1774 to 1776.*

Scheckter, Jody 1950–

South African Formula One driver.

21 Fewer girls, more technology.
   1997 On how Formula One had changed since he won the world championship in 1979. In *The Times*, 29 Dec.

Schiaparelli, Elsa 1890–1973

Italian fashion designer who opened one of the first couture boutiques in Paris in 1935. She was known for introducing the colour 'shocking pink' into the fashion world.

22 So fashion is born by small facts, trends, or even politics, never by trying to make little pleats and furbelows, by trinkets, by clothes easy to copy, or by the shortening or lengthening of a skirt.
   1954 *A Shocking Life*, ch.9.

23 A good cook is like a sorceress who dispenses happiness.
   1954 *A Shocking Life*, ch.21.

Schiller, Friedrich 1759–1805

German poet and playwright who was briefly a surgeon before turning his attention to writing and travelling.

24 *In seinen Göttern malt sich der Mensch.*
   Humankind is reflected in its gods.
   1789 *Was heit und zu welchem Ende studiert man Universalgeschichte?*

25 *Alle anderen Dinge müssen; der Mensch ist das Wesen, welches will.*
   All other things must; man is the being who wills.
   1794 *Über das Erhabene.*

26 *Man kann den Menschen nicht verwehren,
   Zu denken, was sie wollen.*
   One cannot prevent people from thinking what they please.
   1800 *Maria Stuart*, act 1, sc.8.

27 *Was man scheint,
   Hat jedermann zum Richter; was man ist, hat keine.*
   What we appear to be is subject to the judgement Of all mankind, and what we truly are, of no one.
   1800 *Maria Stuart*, act 2, sc.5.

28 *Was man nicht aufgibt, hat man nie verloren.*
   What is not abandoned is never completely lost.
   1800 *Maria Stuart*, act 2, sc.5.

29 *Das Leben ist
   Nur ein Moment, der Tod ist auch nur einer.*
   Life is but a moment. Death is but a moment, too.
   1800 *Maria Stuart*, act 3, sc.6.

30 *Den stolzen Sieger stürzt sein eignes Glück.*
   The victor is often vanquished by his own success.
   1801 *Die Jungfrau von Orléans*, act 1, sc.5.

31 *Mehr als das Leben lieb' ich meine Freiheit.*
   More than life, I cherish freedom.
   1801 *Die Jungfrau von Orléans*, act 2, sc.2.

32 *Mitt der Dummheit kämpfen Götter selbst vergebens.*
   Even the gods themselves struggle in vain against stupidity.
   1801 *Die Jungfrau von Orléans*, act 3, sc.6.

Schlesinger, Arthur Meier 1888–1965

US historian. His works include *New Viewpoints in American History* (1922) and a *History of American Life* (13 vols, 1928–43).

33 The military struggle may frankly be regarded for what it actually was, namely a war for independence, an armed attempt to impose the views of the revolutionists on the British government and large sections of the colonial population at whatever cost to freedom of opinion or the sanctity of life and property.
   1919 'The American Revolution Reconsidered', in *Political Science Quarterly*, Mar.

Schlesinger, Arthur M(eier), Jr 1917–2007

US historian and special assistant to President Kennedy (1961–3). His works include the Pulitzer prize-winning *The Age of Jackson* (1945) and *A Thousand Days: John F Kennedy in the White House* (1965). He became president of the American Institute of Arts and Letters (1981).

34 He read partly for information, partly for comparison, partly for insight, partly for the sheer joy of felicitous statement. He delighted particularly in quotations which distilled the essence of an argument.
   1965 Of John F Kennedy. *A Thousand Days.*

35 Ceremony, circus, farce, melodrama, tragedy...nothing else offers all at once the whirl, the excitement, the gaiety, the intrigue and the anguish.
   1965 On national political conventions. *A Thousand Days.*

36 At the time it is all a confusion; in retrospect...all a blur.
   1965 On national political conventions. *A Thousand Days.*

37 The things people had once held against her... unconventional beauty...un-American elegance, the taste for French clothes and French food—were suddenly no longer liabilities but assets.

1965 On Jacqueline Kennedy's post-election image. *A Thousand Days*.

38 Television has spread the habit of instant reaction and has stimulated the hope of instant results.
1970 In *Newsweek*, 6 Jul.

Schlesinger, James R(odney) 1929–2014

US economist and public servant who was Secretary of Defense (1973–5) under Presidents Nixon and Ford.

39 The notion of a defence that will protect American cities is one that will not be achieved, but it is that goal that supplies the political magic in the President's vision.
1987 Senate Foreign Relations Committee, 6 Feb.

Schmitt, Wolfgang Rudolph 1944–

German-born US businessman. He joined houseware manufacturers Rubbermaid Inc in 1966, becoming president in 1991.

40 Innovation most of the time is simply taking A, B, C and D, which already exist, and putting them together in a form called E.
1994 In *Fortune*, 14 Nov.

Schnabel, Artur 1882–1951

Austrian pianist and composer. He studied under Leschetizsky and made his debut at the age of eight. Subsequently he toured throughout Europe and the US, where he settled in 1939. He was an authoritative player of a small range of German classics—notably Beethoven, Mozart and Schubert.

41 The notes I handle no better than many pianists. But the pauses between the notes—ah, that is where the art resides.
1958 In the *Chicago Daily News*, 11 Jun.

42 Applause is a receipt, not a bill.
Explaining why he did not play encores. Quoted in I Kolodin *The Musical Life* (1958).

43 I know two kinds of audience only—one coughing and one not coughing.
1961 *My Life and Music*.

44 I don't think there was ever a piece of music that changed a man's decision on how to vote.
1961 *My Life and Music*.

45 When a piece gets difficult make faces.
Quoted in Oscar Levant *The Unimportance of Being Oscar* (1968).

46 The sonatas of Mozart are unique; they are too easy for children, and too difficult for artists.
Quoted in Nat Shapiro *An Encyclopedia of Quotations about Music* (1978).

Schoenbaum, Thomas J 1939–

Research Professor of Law at George Washington University and professor emeritus, University of Georgia.

47 [He] made himself the rock against which crashed the successive waves of dissent.
1988 Of Secretary of State Dean Rusk during the Vietnam War. *Waging Peace and War*.

Schoenberg, Arnold Franz Walter 1874–1951

Austrian composer, conductor and teacher. A self-taught pioneer of atonality, his works include the tone poem *Pelleas und Melisande* (1903), the song cycle *Pierrot Lunaire* (1912), operas, chamber music and other choral and orchestral pieces. He lived in the US from 1933.

48 Harmony! Harmony!
1951 Attributed last words.

49 My music is not modern, it is merely badly played.
Quoted in C Rosen *Schoenberg* (1976).

50 If it is art it is not for all, and if it is for all it is not art.
Quoted in Ian Crofton and Donald Fraser *A Dictionary of Musical Quotations* (1985).

Schopenhauer, Arthur 1788–1860

German philosopher, whose work is often characterized as a systematic philosophical pessimism. His major work was *Die Welt als Wille und Vorstellung* (*The World as Will and Representation*), published in 1819. A second enlarged edition followed in 1844.

51 *Alle Befriedigung, oder was man gemeinhin Glück nennt, ist eigentlich und wesentlich immer nur negativ und durchaus nie positiv.*
All satisfaction, or what is commonly called happiness, is really and essentially always *negative* only, and never positive.
1819 *Die Welt als Wille und Vorstellung* (*The World as Will and Representation*), vol.1, bk.4, ch.58 (translated by E F J Payne).

52 *Wir tappen im Labyrinth unsers Lebenswandels und im Dunkel unserer Forschungen umher: helle Augenblicke erleuchten dabei wie Blitze unsern Weg.*
We grope about in the labyrinth of our life and in the obscurity of our investigations; bright moments illuminate our path like flashes of lightning.
1844 *Die Welt als Wille und Vorstellung* (*The World as Will and Representation*), vol.2, ch.15 (translated by E F J Payne).

53 *Das Ganze der Erfahrung gleicht einer Geheimschrift und die Philosophie der Entzifferung derselben.*
The whole of experience is like a cryptograph, and philosophy is like the deciphering of it.
1844 *Die Welt als Wille und Vorstellung* (*The World as Will and Representation*), vol.2, ch.17 (translated by E F J Payne).

54 *Ist es an und für sich absurd, das Nichtsein für ein Übel zu halten; da jedes Übel wie jedes Gut das Dasein zur Voraussetzung hat, ja sogar das Bewusstsein.*
It is in and by itself absurd to regard non-existence as an evil; for every evil, like every good, presupposes existence, indeed even consciousness.
1844 *Die Welt als Wille und Vorstellung* (*The World as Will and Representation*), vol.2, ch.41 (translated by E F J Payne).

55 *Unsterblichkeit der Individualität verlangen heißt eigentlich einen Irrtum ins Unendliche perpetuieren wollen. Denn im Grunde ist doch jede Individualität nur ein spezieller Irrtum, Fehltritt, etwas, das besser nicht wäre, ja wovon uns zurückzubringen der eigentliche Zweck des Lebens ist.*
To desire immortality for the individual is really the same as wanting to perpetuate an error for ever; for at bottom every individuality is really only a special error, a false step, something that it would be better should not be, in fact something from which it is the real purpose of life to bring us back.
1844 *Die Welt als Wille und Vorstellung* (*The World as Will and Representation*), vol.2, ch.41 (translated by E F J Payne).

56 *Alle Verliebtheit [...] wurzelt allein im Geschlechtstriebe.*
All amorousness [...] is rooted in the sexual impulse alone.

1844 *Die Welt als Wille und Vorstellung* (*The World as Will and Representation*), vol.2, ch.44 (translated by E F J Payne).

57 Was man auch sagen mag, der glücklichste Augenblick des Glücklichen ist doch der seines Einschlafens wie der unglücklichste des Unglücklichen der seines Erwachens.
Whatever we may say, the happiest moment of the happy man is that of his falling asleep, just as the unhappiest moment of the unhappy man is that of his awakening.
1844 *Die Welt als Wille und Vorstellung* (*The World as Will and Representation*), vol.2, ch.46 (translated by E F J Payne).

58 Es gibt nur einen Irrtum, und es ist der, dass wir dasind, um glücklich zu sein.
There is only one inborn error, and that is the notion that we exist in order to be happy.
1844 *Die Welt als Wille und Vorstellung* (*The World as Will and Representation*), vol.2, ch.49 (translated by E F J Payne).

59 Die Szenen unsers Lebens gleichen den Bildern in großer Mosaik, welche in der Nähe keine Wirkung tun, sondern von denen man fern stehn muss, um sie schön zu finden.
The scenes of our life resemble pictures in rough mosaic; they are ineffective from close up, and have to be viewed from a distance if they are to seem beautiful.
1851 *Parerga und Paralipomena*, ch.11 (translated by R J Hollingdale).

60 Jede Trennung gibt einen Vorgeschmack des Todes—und jedes Wiedersehen einen Vorgeschmack der Auferstehung.
Every parting is a foretaste of death, and every reunion a foretaste of resurrection.
1851 *Parerga und Paralipomena*, ch.26 (translated by R J Hollingdale).

Schreiner, Olive Emily Albertina *pseudonym* Ralph Iron 1855–1920

South African feminist, novelist and polemicist. Educated at home against a strict religious background, she is best known for her semi-autobiographical novel, *The Story of an African Farm* (1883), which rejects the spiritual aridity of colonial life and loveless marriage.

61 This pretty ring… I will give it to the first man who tells me he would like to be a woman. It is delightful to be a woman; but every man thanks the Lord devoutly that he isn't one.
1883 *The Story of an African Farm*, ch.17, 'Lyndall'.

62 We are cursed, Waldo, born cursed from the time our mothers bring us into the world till the shrouds are put on us.
1883 Lyndall. *The Story of an African Farm*, ch.17, 'Lyndall'.

63 We sit…and look out at the boys in their happy play…we kneel still with one little cheek wistfully pressed against the pane…and we go and stand before the glass. We see the complexion we were not to spoil, and the white frock… Then the curse begins to act upon us. It finishes its work when we are grown women, who no more look out wistfully at a more healthy life; we are contented. We fit our sphere as a Chinese woman's foot fits her shoe, exactly, as though God made both—and yet he knows nothing of either.
1883 Lyndall. *The Story of an African Farm*, ch.17, 'Lyndall'.

64 Men are like the earth and we are the moon; we turn always one side to them, and they think there is no other, because they don't see it—but there is.
1883 Lyndall. *The Story of an African Farm*, ch.17, 'Lyndall'.

65 Give us labour and the training which fits for labour! We demand this, not for ourselves alone, but for the race.
1911 *Women and Labour*, ch.1.

66 With each generation the entire race passes through the body of its womanhood as through a mould, reappearing with the indelible marks of that mould upon it, that as the *os cervix* of woman, through which the head of the human infant passes at birth, forms a ring, determining for ever the size at birth of the human head…so exactly the intellectual capacity, the physical vigour, the emotional depth of woman, forms also an untranscendable circle, circumscribing with each successive generation the limits of expansion of the human race.
1911 *Women and Labour*, ch.3.

Schroeder, Patricia Scott 1940–

US Congresswoman and lawyer. She practised law in Denver and then became a faculty member of the University of Colorado (1969–72), before being elected to Congress (1972–96).

67 I was cooking breakfast this morning for my kids and I thought, 'He's just like Teflon. Nothing sticks to him.'
1984 Of President Ronald Reagan. In the *Boston Globe*, 24 Oct.

68 Washington is awash in post-war testosterone.
1991 On her decision not to seek presidential nomination in the wake of victory in the Gulf War. In the *New York Times*, 30 Jun.

Schulberg, Budd Wilson 1914–2009

US novelist and scritpwriter. He is best known for his screenplay for the film *On the Waterfront* (1954).

69 What Makes Sammy Run?
1941 Title of novel.

70 You don't understand. I could have had class. I could have been a contender. I could have been somebody—instead of a bum, which is what I am, let's face it.
1954 Lines spoken by Marlon Brando. *On the Waterfront*.

Schultz, Howard 1952–

US businessman.

71 Retail is detail.
1994 On building Starbucks, the largest US coffee-bar chain and mail-order business. In the *New York Times*, 14 Dec.

Schulz, Charles Monroe 1922–2000

US cartoonist. He created the syndicated comic strip *Peanuts* (1950), internationally loved for its characters of Charlie Brown, Snoopy, Lucy, Linus, Schroeder, Peppermint Patty, Pigpen, Marcie and the bird Woodstock.

72 Jogging is very beneficial. It's very good for your legs and your feet. It's also very good for the ground. It makes it feel needed.
Quoted in Colin Jarman *The Guinness Dictionary of Sports Quotations* (1990).

Schumacher, E(rnst) F(riedrich) 1911–77
British economist and public servant, member of the Control Commission in Germany (1946–50) and economist of the National Coal Board (1950–70).

73 Small Is Beautiful: a Study of Economics as if People Mattered.
1973 Title of book.

74 I have no doubt that it is possible to give a new direction to technological development, a direction that shall lead it back to the real needs of man, and that also means: to the actual size of man. Man is small, and, therefore, small is beautiful. To go for giantism is to go for self-destruction.
1973 *Small Is Beautiful*.

Schumacher, Michael 1969–
German Formula One driver, winner of the world championship in 1994 and 1995, and 2000–4.

75 To control 800 horse power relying just on arm muscles and foot sensitivity can turn out to be a dangerous exercise.
2003 In the *Observer*, 2 Mar.

Schumpeter, Joseph Alois 1883–1950
Austrian-born US economist, who emigrated to the US in 1932 and later became professor at Harvard. He emphasized the importance of the entrepreneur in the business cycle and traced the economic history of capitalism.

76 When I was a young man, I wanted to be three things: I wanted to be the world's greatest horseman, the world's greatest economist, and the world's greatest lover. Unfortunately I never became the world's greatest horseman.
1940s Attributed, Harvard oral tradition.

77 The cold metal of economic theory is in Marx's pages immersed in such a wealth of steaming phrases as to acquire a temperature not naturally its own.
1942 *Capitalism, Socialism, and Democracy*, p.21.

78 Can capitalism survive? No, I do not think it can.
1942 *Capitalism, Socialism, and Democracy*, p.61.

79 Queen Elizabeth owned silk stockings. The capitalist achievement does not typically consist in providing more silk stockings for queens but in bringing them within the reach of factory girls in return for steadily decreasing amount of effort.
1942 *Capitalism, Socialism, and Democracy*, p.67.

80 The question that is so clearly in many potential parents' minds: 'Why should we stunt our ambitions and impoverish our lives in order to be insulted and looked down upon in our old age?'
1942 *Capitalism, Socialism, and Democracy*, ch. 14.

81 Bureaucracy is not an obstacle to democracy but an inevitable complement to it.
1942 *Capitalism, Socialism, and Democracy*, ch. 18.

Schwartz, Eugene M 1927–95
US art collector, known for amassing one of the nation's leading collections of contemporary art and giving it away with almost as much zeal.

82 Collecting is the only socially commendable form of greed.
1995 In the *New York Times*, 7 Sep.

Schwartz, Sanford 1946–
US writer.

83 Dalí's importance for the Surrealists at that time, and for art historians now, is that he found a way to put Freud on canvas.
1994 In the *New Republic*, 17 Oct.

Schwarzenegger, Arnold 1947–
Austrian-born US actor and politician. He began as a body builder, winning the Mr Universe title, and became a Hollywood star in adventure films such as *The Terminator* (1984) and *True Lies* (1994). He served as Republican Governor of California (2003–11).

84 Posing is a performing art.
Quoted in *The Guardian*, 1975.

85 I'll be back.
1984 *The Terminator*.

86 Hasta la vista, baby.
1991 *Terminator 2: Judgment Day*.

87 I am humbled, I am honoured and I am moved beyond words to be your governor.
2003 On being sworn in as Governor of California, 17 Nov.

88 Just remember, you can't climb the ladder of success with your hands in your pockets.
2009 Speech at the University of Southern California, 15 May.

Schwarzkopf, H Norman, Jr 1934–2012
US army general. He served in the Vietnam War and as deputy commander in Grenada (1983), and in 1991 commanded allied troops in the Gulf War. He retired the following year.

89 We are not going after Saddam Hussein. If I can eliminate his ability to communicate with his forces, I would be entirely satisfied with that result.
1991 Press briefing on the start of the Gulf War, 15 Jan.

90 I don't consider myself dovish and I certainly don't consider myself hawkish. Maybe I would describe myself as owlish—that is wise enough to understand that you want to do everything possible to avoid war.
1991 In the *New York Times*, 28 Jan.

91 I asked you to be the thunder and lightning of Desert Storm. You were all of that and more.
1991 Message to US units on the cease-fire that ended the Gulf War.

92 Seven months ago I could give a single command and 541,000 people would immediately obey it. Today I can't get a plumber to come to my house.
1991 In *Newsweek*, 11 Nov.

Schweikart, Russell 1935–
US astronaut.

93 The most beautiful sight in orbit…is a urine dump at sunset, because as the stuff comes out and as it hits the exit nozzle it instantly flashes into ten million little ice crystals which go out almost in a hemisphere… It's really a spectacular sight.
1981 *The Next Whole Earth Catalog*.

Schweitzer, Albert 1875–1965
German medical missionary, theologian, musician and philosopher. In 1896 he vowed to live for science and art until he was 30, and then devote his life to serving humanity. He became

principal of a theological college (1903) and wrote *Von Reimarus zu Wrede* (1906, *The Quest for the Historical Jesus*) and major works on St Paul. Despite his international reputation in music and theology, he turned to medicine in 1905, and with his wife set up a hospital in French Equatorial Africa. He was awarded the Nobel peace prize in 1952.

94 He comes to us as One unknown, without a name, as of old, by the lakeside, He came to those who knew Him not. He speaks to us the same word: 'Follow thou me!' and sets us to the tasks which He has to fulfil for our time. He commands. And to those who obey Him, whether they be wise or simple, He will reveal Himself in the toils, the conflicts, the sufferings which they shall pass through in His fellowship, and, as an ineffable mystery, they shall learn in their own experience who He is.
1906 *Von Reimarus zu Wrede* (translated by W Montgomery as *The Quest for the Historical Jesus*, 1910).

95 An optimist is a person who sees a green light everywhere, while the pessimist sees only the red stop-light. The truly wise person is colour-blind.
1965 Quoted in CBS News tribute, 14 Jan.

Scorsese, Martin 1942–

US film director. With films such as *Taxi Driver* (1976) and *Raging Bull* (1980), he established himself as one of the foremost directors of his generation.

96 I always tell the younger film-makers and students: Do it like the painters used to… Study the old masters. Enrich your palette. Expand the canvas. There's always so much more to learn.
1997 *Scorsese: A Personal Journey Through American Movies*.

97 Cinema is a matter of what's in the frame and what's out.
1997 *Scorsese: A Personal Journey Through American Movies*.

Scott, C(harles) P(restwich) 1846–1932

English newspaper editor and Liberal MP (1895–1906). At the age of 26 he became editor of the *Manchester Guardian*, and made it a serious liberal rival of *The Times* by a highly independent and often controversial editorial policy and high literary standards.

98 The newspaper is of necessity something of a monopoly, and its first duty is to shun the temptations of a monopoly. Its primary office is the gathering of News. At the peril of its soul it must see that the supply is not tainted. Neither in what it gives, nor in what it does not give, nor in the mode of presentation, must the unclouded face of Truth suffer wrong. Comment is free, but facts are sacred.
1921 Of the newspaper industry. In the *Manchester Guardian*, special centenary issue, 6 May.

99 One of the virtues, perhaps almost the chief virtue, of a newspaper is its independence. Whatever its position or character, at least it should have a soul of its own.
1921 In the *Manchester Guardian*, special centenary issue, 6 May.

Scott, Duncan Campell 1862–1947

Canadian poet. One of the 'Confederation Poets', he also wrote short stories, biographies and a play.

1 How strange the stars have grown;
The presage of extinction glows on their crests
And they are beautied with impermanence.
1916 'The Height of Land'.

Scott, F(rancis) R(eginald) 1899–1985

Canadian poet. A lawyer, professor and politician (a founder of the Canadian social democratic party, the Co-operative Commonwealth Federation), he established several important literary reviews. His collected poems were published in 1981.

2 I have sat by night beside a cold lake
And touched things smoother than moonlight on still water,
But the moon on this cloud sea is not human,
And here is no shore, no intimacy,
Only the start of space, the road to suns.
1945 'Trans Canada'.

3 Hidden in wonder and snow, or sudden with summer,
This land stares at the sun in a huge silence
Endlessly repeating something we cannot hear.
Inarticulate, arctic,
Not written on by history, empty as paper,
It leans away from the world with songs in its lakes
Older than love, and lost in the miles.
1954 Of Canada. 'Laurentian Shield'.

4 Newspapers are born free and everywhere are in chains.
1973 Aphorism, collected in John Robert Colombo (ed) *Colombo's Canadian Quotations* (1974).
▶ See Rousseau 729:10.

Scott, Robert Falcon 1868–1912

English Antarctic explorer. In 1900–4 he commanded the National Antarctic Expedition to the Ross Sea. On his second expedition he reached the South Pole (Jan 1912), only to discover that Amundsen had beaten him by a month. He and his party died on the way back; their bodies and diaries were found by a search party eight months later.

5 Great God! This is an awful place and terrible enough for us to have laboured to it without the reward of priority.
1912 Journal entry, 18 Jan. *Scott's Last Expedition: The Personal Journals of Captain R F Scott, CVO, RN, on His Journey to the South Pole* (published 1923).

6 Had we lived, I should have had a tale to tell of the hardihood, endurance, and courage of my companions which would have stirred the heart of every Englishman. These rough notes and our dead bodies must tell the tale.
1912 Message to the public. Quoted in *The Times*, 11 Feb 1913.

7 It seems a pity but I do not think I can write more. For God's sake look after our people.
1912 Last entry in journal, 29 Mar. In *Scott's Last Expedition: The Personal Journals of Captain R F Scott, CVO, RN, on His Journey to the South Pole* (published 1923).

Scott, Rose 1847–1925

Australian feminist.

8 Life is too short to waste on the admiration of one man.
Her habitual response to offers of marriage. Quoted in Jennifer Uglow (ed) *The Macmillan Dictionary of Women's Biography* (2nd edn, 1989).

Scott, Sir Walter 1771–1832

Scottish novelist and poet. He studied law and became an advocate and later a sheriff, but achieved worldwide fame as a writer of epic poetry and as the author of the *Waverley Novels*, promoting a fundamentally romantic image of history and in particular of Scotland's past.

9 The way was long, the wind was cold,
   The Minstrel was infirm and old;
   His withered cheek, and tresses grey,
   Seemed to have known a better day;
   The harp, his sole remaining joy,
   Was carried by an orphan boy,
   The last of all the Bards was he,
   Who sung of Border chivalry.
   1805 *The Lay of the Last Minstrel*, introduction.

10 He poured, to lord and lady gay,
   The unpremeditated lay.
   1805 *The Lay of the Last Minstrel*, introduction.

11 And said I that my limbs were old,
   And said I that my blood was cold,
   And that my kindly fire was fled,
   And my poor withered heart was dead,
   And that I might not sing of Love?
   1805 *The Lay of the Last Minstrel*, canto 1, stanza 1.

12 If thou would'st view fair Melrose aright,
   Go visit it by the pale moonlight.
   1805 *The Lay of the Last Minstrel*, canto 2, stanza 1.

13 The woodland brook he bounding crossed,
   And laughed, and shouted, 'Lost! lost! lost!'
   1805 *The Lay of the Last Minstrel*, canto 3, stanza 13.

14 The Harper smiled, well pleased; for ne'er
   Was flattery lost on poet's ear:
   A simple race! they waste their toil
   For the vain tribute of a smile.
   1805 *The Lay of the Last Minstrel*, canto 4, conclusion.

15 Call it not vain:—they do not err
   Who say, that when the Poet dies,
   Mute Nature mourns her worshipper,
   And celebrates his obsequies.
   1805 *The Lay of the Last Minstrel*, canto 5, stanza 1.

16 Breathes there the man, with soul so dead,
   Who never to himself hath said,
   This is my own, my native land!
   Whose heart hath ne'er within him burned,
   As home his footsteps he hath turned
   From wandering on a foreign strand!
   1805 *The Lay of the Last Minstrel*, canto 6, stanza 1.

17 O Caledonia! stern and wild,
   Meet nurse for a poetic child!
   Land of brown heath and shaggy wood,
   Land of the mountain and the flood.
   Land of my sires! what mortal hand
   Can e'er untie the filial band
   That knits me to thy rugged strand!
   1805 *The Lay of the Last Minstrel*, canto 6, stanza 2.

18 November's sky is chill and drear,
   November's leaf is red and sear.
   1808 *Marmion*, canto 1, introduction.

19 And come he slow, or come he fast,
   It is but Death who comes at last.
   1808 *Marmion*, canto 2, stanza 30.

20 Still is thy name in high account,
   And still thy verse has charms,
   Sir David Lindesay of the Mount,
   Lord Lion King-at-arms!
   1808 *Marmion*, canto 4, stanza 7.

21 O, young Lochinvar is come out of the west,
   Through all the wide Border his steed was the best;
   And save his good broadsword he weapon had
     none,
   He rode all unarmed, and he rode all alone.
   So faithful in love, and so dauntless in war,
   There never was knight like the young Lochinvar.
   1808 *Marmion*, canto 5, stanza 12, 'Lochinvar'.

22 Heap on more wood!—the wind is chill;
   But let it whistle as it will,
   We'll keep our Christmas merry still.
   1808 *Marmion*, canto 6, introduction.

23 And dar'st thou then
   To beard the lion in his den,
   The Douglas in his hall?
   1808 *Marmion*, canto 6, stanza 14.

24 Oh what a tangled web we weave,
   When first we practise to deceive!
   1808 *Marmion*, canto 6, stanza 17.

25 O Woman! in our hours of ease,
   Uncertain, coy, and hard to please,
   And variable as the shade
   By the light quivering aspen made;
   When pain and anguish wring the brow,
   A ministering angel thou!
   1808 *Marmion*, canto 6, stanza 30.

26 The stubborn spearmen still made good
   Their dark impenetrable wood,
   Each stepping where his comrade stood
   The instant that he fell.
   1808 *Marmion*, canto 6, stanza 34.

27 Still from the sire the son shall hear
   Of the stern strife, and carnage drear,
   Of Flodden's fatal field,
   Where shivered was fair Scotland's spear,
   And broken was her shield!
   1808 *Marmion*, canto 6, stanza 34.

28 The stag at eve had drunk his fill,
   Where danced the moon on Monan's rill.
   1810 *The Lady of the Lake*, canto 1, stanza 1.

29 Hail to the Chief who in honour advances!
   Honoured and bless'd be the evergreen Pine!
   1810 *The Lady of the Lake*, canto 2, stanza 19, 'Boat Song'.

30 Time rolls his ceaseless course.
   1810 *The Lady of the Lake*, canto 3, stanza 1.

31 He is gone on the mountain,
   He is lost to the forest,
   Like a summer-dried fountain,
   When our need was the sorest.
   1810 *The Lady of the Lake*, canto 3, stanza 16, 'Coronach'.

32 Like the dew on the mountain,
   Like the foam on the river,
   Like the bubble on the fountain,
   Thou art gone, and for ever!
   1810 *The Lady of the Lake*, canto 3, stanza 16, 'Coronach'.

33 Merry it is in the good greenwood,
   When the mavis and merle are singing,
   When the deer sweeps by, and the hounds are in cry,
   And the hunter's horn is ringing.
   1810 *The Lady of the Lake*, canto 4, stanza 12, 'Alice Brand'.

34 O, Brignal banks are wild and fair,
And Greta woods are green
And you may gather garlands there
Would grace a summer queen.
  1813 *Rokeby*, canto 3, stanza 16.

35 A weary lot is thine, fair maid,
A weary lot is thine!
To pull the thorn thy brow to braid,
And press the rue for wine!
  1813 *Rokeby*, canto 3, stanza 28, 'Song'.

36 Look back, and smile at perils past!
  1813 *The Bridal of Triermain*, introduction.

37 He that steals a cow from a poor widow, or a stirk from a cottar, is a thief; he that lifts a drove from a Sassenach laird, is a gentleman-drover. And, besides, to take a tree from the forest, a salmon from the river, a deer from the hill, or a cow from a Lowland strath, is what no Highlander need ever think shame upon.
  1814 Evan Dhu Maccombich to Edward Waverley. *Waverley*, ch.18.

38 I am heartily glad you continued to like Waverley to the end—the hero is a sneaking piece of imbecility and if he had married Flora she would have set him up upon the chimney-piece as Count Boralaski's wife used to do with him.
  1814 Letter to John Morritt, 28 Jul. Joseph Borowlaski was a Polish dwarf known as 'The Little Count' who left France at the Revolution and exhibited himself at fairs throughout Britain.

39 Then strip lads, and to it, though sharp be the weather,
And if, by mischance, you should happen to fall,
There are worse things in life than a tumble on the heather
And life is itself a game of football.
  1815 On a match between the Scottish teams Ettrick and Selkirk, published in the *Edinburgh Journal*.

40 But ruffian stern, and soldier good,
The noble and the slave,
From various cause the same wild road,
On the same bloody morning, trode,
To that dark inn—the Grave!
  1815 *The Lord of the Isles*, canto 6, stanza 26.

41 Pro-di-gi-ous!
  1815 Dominie Sampson. *Guy Mannering*, ch.8.

42 'That sounds like nonsense, my dear.'
'Maybe so, my dear; but it may be very good law for all that.'
  1815 Mrs and Mr Bertram in conversation. *Guy Mannering*, ch.9.

43 Gin by pailfuls, wine in rivers,
Dash the window-glass to shivers!
For three wild lads were we, brave boys,
And three wild lads were we;
Thou on the land, and I on the sand,
And Jack on the gallows-tree!
  1815 *Guy Mannering*, ch.34.

44 The frolicsome company had begun to practise the ancient and now forgotten pastime of *High Jinks*.
  1815 *Guy Mannering*, ch.36.

45 'Why weep ye by the tide, ladie?
Why weep ye by the tide?
I'll wed ye to my youngest son,
And ye sall be his bride:
And ye sall be his bride, ladie,
Sae comely to be seen'—

But aye she loot the tears down fa'
For Jock of Hazeldean.
  1816 'Jock of Hazeldean', stanza 1.

46 'A chain of gold ye sall not lack,
Nor braid to bind your hair;
Nor mettled hound, nor managed hawk,
Nor palfrey fresh and fair.'
  1816 'Jock of Hazeldean', stanza 3.

47 They sought her baith by bower and ha';
The ladie was not seen!
She's o'er the Border and awa'
Wi' Jock of Hazeldean.
  1816 'Jock of Hazeldean', stanza 4.

48 Prætorian here, prætorian there, I mind the bigging o't.
  1816 Edie Ochiltree to Jonathan Oldbuck. *The Antiquary*, ch.4.

49 It's no fish ye're buying—it's men's lives.
  1816 Maggie Mucklebackit to Oldbuck. *The Antiquary*, ch.11.

50 It's weel wi' you gentles, that can sit in the house wi' handkerchers at your een when ye lose a friend; but the like o' us maun to our wark again, if our hearts were beating as hard as my hammer.
  1816 Saunders Mucklebackit to Oldbuck. *The Antiquary*, ch.34.

51 He that is without name, without friends, without coin, without country, is still at least a man; and he that has all these is no more.
  1817 Rob Roy to Francis Osbaldistone. *Rob Roy*, ch.21.

52 Come fill up my cup, come fill up my cann,
Come saddle my horses, and call up my man;
Come open your gates, and let me gae free,
I daurna stay langer in Bonny Dundee!
  1817 *Rob Roy*, ch.23.

53 If your honour disna ken when ye hae a gude servant, I ken when I hae a gude master, and the deil be in my feet gin I leave ye.
  1817 Andrew Fairservice to Francis Osbaldistone. *Rob Roy*, ch. 24.

54 It's ill taking the breeks aff a Hielandman.
  1817 Andrew Fairservice to Bailie Nicol Jarvie. *Rob Roy*, ch.27.

55 There's a gude time coming.
  1817 Rob Roy to the Duke. *Rob Roy*, ch.32.

56 Speak out, sir, and do not Maister or Campbell me—my foot is on my native heath, and my name is MacGregor!
  1817 Rob Roy to Francis Osbaldistone. *Rob Roy*, ch.34.

57 Ye ken weel eneugh that women and gear are at the bottom of a' the mischief in this warld.
  1817 Rob Roy to Francis Osbaldistone. *Rob Roy*, ch.35.

58 The hour's come, but not the man.
  1818 *The Heart of Midlothian*, ch.4, motto.

59 'I dinna ken muckle about the law,' answered Mrs Howden; 'but I ken, when we had a king, and a chancellor, and parliament-men o' our ain, we could aye peeble them wi' stanes when they werena gude bairns—But naebody's nails can reach the length o' Lunnon.'
  1818 *The Heart of Midlothian*, ch.4.

60 Jock, when ye hae naething else to do, ye may be aye sticking in a tree; it will be growing, Jock, when ye're sleeping.
  1818 The Laird of Dumbiedikes to his son. *The Heart of Midlothian*, ch.8.

61 Never mind my grace, lassie; just speak out a plain tale, and show you have a Scotch tongue in your head.
   1818 The Duke of Argyle to Jeanie Deans. *The Heart of Midlothian*, ch.35.

62 Dinna be chappit back or cast down wi' the first rough answer.
   1818 Jeanie Deans to the Duke of Argyle. *The Heart of Midlothian*, ch.35.

63 Proud Maisie is in the wood,
   Walking so early;
   Sweet Robin sits on the bush,
   Singing so rarely.
   1818 *The Heart of Midlothian*, ch.40 (Madge Wildfire's song).

64 Look not thou on beauty's charming,—
   Sit thou still when kings are arming.—
   Taste not when the wine-cup glistens,—
   Speak not when the people listens,—
   Stop thine ear against the singer,—
   From the red gold keep thy finger,—
   Vacant heart, and hand, and eye,—
   Easy live and quiet die.
   1819 *The Bride of Lammermoor*, ch.3 (Lucy Ashton's song).

65 But no one shall find me rowing against the stream. I care not who knows it—I write for the general amusement.
   1822 *The Fortunes of Nigel*, introductory epistle.

66 For a con-si-de-ra-tion.
   1822 Trapbois. *The Fortunes of Nigel*, ch.22.

67 O Geordie, Jingling Geordie, it was grand to hear Baby Charles laying down the guilt of dissimulation and Steemie lecturing on the turpitude of incontinence.
   1822 *The Fortunes of Nigel*, ch.31.

68 Carle, now the King's come!
   Carle, now the King's come!
   Thou shalt dance, and I will sing,
   Carle, now the King's come!
   1822 'Carle, Now the King's Come', written in celebration of George IV's visit to Edinburgh.

69 Ah! County Guy, the hour is nigh,
   The sun has left the lea,
   The orange flower perfumes the bower,
   The breeze is on the sea.
   1823 *Quentin Durward*, ch.4.

70 Fair, fat, and forty.
   1823 *St Ronan's Well*, ch.7.

71 It's ill speaking between a fou man and a fasting.
   1824 *Redgauntlet*, letter 11, 'Wandering Willie's Tale'.

72 The ae half of the warld thinks the tither daft.
   1824 Peter Peebles to Justice Foxley. *Redgauntlet*, ch.7.

73 'Then, gentlemen,' said Redgauntlet, clasping his hands together as the words burst from him, 'the cause is lost for ever!'
   1824 *Redgauntlet*, ch.23.

74 Widowed wife, and married maid,
   Betrothed, betrayer, and betrayed!
   1825 *The Betrothal*, ch.15.

75 Came through cold roads to as cold news.
   1826 *Journal*, 16 Jan, referring to the financial collapse of his publisher, Constable, which led directly to Scott's own bankruptcy.

76 We had better remain in union with England, even at the risk of becoming a subordinate species of Northumberland, as far as national consequence is concerned, than remedy ourselves by even hinting the possibility of a rupture. But there is no harm in wishing Scotland to have just so much ill-nature, according to her own proverb, as may keep her good-nature from being abused.
   1826 *Letters of Malachi Malagrowther on the Proposed Change of Currency*, letter 1.

77 If I can but get the sulky Scottish spirit set up, the devil won't turn them.
   1826 *Journal*, 25 Feb.

78 The Big Bow-wow strain I can do myself like any now going; but the exquisite touch, which renders ordinary commonplace things and characters interesting, from the truth of description and the sentiment, is denied to me.
   1826 On Jane Austen. *Journal*, 14 Mar.

79 But if you *unscotch* us you will find us damned mischievous Englishmen.
   1826 Letter to J W Croker, 19 Mar.

80 I would like to be there, were it but to see how the cat jumps. One knows nothing of the world, if you are absent from it so long as I have been.
   1826 *Journal*, 7 Oct, expressing frustration and wonder at the machinations of London bureaucracy which prevented him accessing government papers for his *Life of Napoleon*.

81 Long life to thy fame and peace to thy soul, Rob Burns! When I want to express a sentiment which I feel strongly, I find the phrase in Shakespeare—or thee. The blockheads talk of my being like Shakespeare—not fit to tie his brogues.
   1826 *Journal*, 11 Dec.

82 To the Lords of convention 'twas Claver'se who spoke,
   'Ere the King's crown shall fall there are crowns to be broke;
   So let each Cavalier who loves honour and me,
   Come follow the bonnet of Bonny Dundee.'
   1830 *The Doom of Devorgoil*, act 2, sc.2, 'Bonny Dundee', stanza 1.

83 No repose for Sir Walter but in the grave. Friends, don't let me expose myself—get me to bed—that's the only place.
   1832 Quoted in John G Lockhart *Memoirs of the Life of Sir Walter Scott, Bart.* (1837–8). Scott had fallen asleep in his bath-chair while trying to write a few words.

84 Be a good man—be virtuous—be religious—be a good man. Nothing else will give you any comfort when you come to lie here.
   1832 Last words, addressed to Lockhart, quoted in John G Lockhart *Memoirs of the Life of Sir Walter Scott, Bart.* (1837–8). Scott concluded by saying 'God bless you all.'

Scottish Metrical Psalms

85 The Lord's my shepherd, I'll not want.
   He makes me down to lie
   In pastures green: he leadeth me
   the quiet waters by.
   My soul he doth restore again:
   and me to walk doth make

Within the paths of righteousness,
ev'n for his own name's sake.

Yea, though I walk in death's dark vale,
yet will I fear no ill:
For thou art with me; and thy rod
and staff me comfort still.
1650 Translation of Psalm 23:1–4.

86 God is our refuge and our strength,
in straits a present aid;
Therefore, although the earth remove,
we will not be afraid.
1650 Psalm 46:1–2.

87 How lovely is thy dwelling-place
O Lord of hosts, to me!
The tabernacles of thy grace
how pleasant, Lord, they be!
1650 Psalm 84:1.

88 All people that on earth do dwell,
Sing to the Lord with cheerful voice.
Him serve with mirth, his praise forth tell,
Come ye before him and rejoice.
Know that the Lord is God indeed;
Without our aid he did us make:
We are his folk, he doth us feed,
And for his sheep he doth us take.
1650 Psalm 100:1–3.

89 I to the hills will lift mine eyes,
from whence doth come mine aid.
My safety cometh from the Lord,
Who heav'n and earth hath made.
1650 Psalm 121:1–2.

Scribner, Charles, Jr 1921–95

US publisher, chairman of Charles Scribner's Sons (1977–8) and Scribner Book Companies from 1978. His autobiography is *In the Company of Writers: Life in Publishing* (1991).

90 Nowadays a sales conference resembles a Passion play: everybody is invited to participate and marvel at the drama.
1991 *In the Company of Writers: A Life in Publishing.*

Seaborg, Glenn 1912–99

US atomic scientist. His principal work was with Enrico Fermi's team, which achieved the first chain reaction in uranium-235 in 1942. He shared the 1951 Nobel prize for chemistry.

91 People must understand that science is inherently neither a potential for good nor for evil. It is a potential to be harnessed by man to do his bidding.
1964 Interview, 29 Sep.

Seacole, Mary c.1805–1884

Jamaican nurse and adventurer.

92 I wonder if the people of other countries are as fond of carrying with them everywhere their home habits as the English. I think not.
1857 *Wonderful Adventures of Mrs Seacole in Many Lands.*

Seaton, George pseudonym of George Stenius 1911–79

US screenwriter and director. He won Academy Awards for both *Miracle on 34th Street* (1947) and *The Country Girl* (1954).

93 For those who believe in God no explanation is necessary. For those who do not believe in God no explanation is possible.
1943 Prologue to *The Song of Bernadette.*

Sedaris, David Raymond 1956–

US humorist and writer. His best-selling publications include *Me Talk Pretty One Day* (2000), *Dress Your Family in Corduroy and Denim* (2004) and *When You Are Engulfed in Flames* (2008).

94 A broken heart is a rite of passage and, looking back, I must have wanted one pretty badly. 'Kick me,' I demanded, and when somebody finally did, I burst like a cheap piñata.
2007 In *O Magazine*, Feb.

95 Art isn't about following the rules. It's about breaking them.
2008 *When You Are Engulfed in Flames.*

96 Sometimes the sins you haven't committed are all you have to hold on to. If you're really desperate, you might need to grope, saying, for example, 'I've never killed anyone *with a hammer*' or 'I've never stolen from anyone *who didn't deserve it.*'
2008 *When You Are Engulfed in Flames.*

97 I'm not afraid to write about madness. I always figure that whatever most embarrasses you is something that everyone can relate to, really… because we're just not that different. So if you think, 'Oh my god, this is so embarrassing. I can't possibly talk about that,' and you write about it, the audience is gonna be like, 'that happened to me!'
2013 Interview with Dutch television channel VPRO, 22 Sep.

Sedighi, Hojatoleslam Kazem 1951–

Iranian cleric.

98 Many women who do not dress modestly lead young men astray, corrupt their chastity and spread adultery in society, which increases earthquakes.
2010 Quoted in the *Daily Mail*, 19 Apr.

Seeger, Alan 1888–1916

US poet. He settled in Paris, and enlisted in the French Foreign Legion when World War I broke out. He was killed at the Battle of the Somme.

99 I have a rendezvous with Death
At some disputed barricade,
When Spring comes round with rustling shade
And apple blossoms fill the air.
I have a rendezvous with Death
When Spring brings back blue days and fair.
1916 'I Have a Rendezvous with Death', in the *North American Review*, Oct.

Seeger, Pete 1919–2014

US folk singer and songwriter.

1 Where have all the flowers gone?
1961 Title of song.

Seeley, Sir John Robert 1834–95

English historian, Professor of Modern History at Cambridge (1869). His *Ecce Homo* (1865), a popular life of Christ, caused much controversy. Other works include the authoritative *Life and Times of Stein* (1874), *Natural Religion* (1882) and *The Expansion of England* (1883).

2 We [the English] seem to have conquered and peopled half the world in a fit of absence of mind.
   1883 *The Expansion of England*.

Segal, Erich 1937–2010

US novelist. He is known for the popular success of *Love Story*, which was both a bestselling novel and a major film.

3 Love means not ever having to say you're sorry.
   1970 *Love Story*, ch.13.

Segovia, Andrés 1893–1987

Spanish guitarist. Influenced by the Spanish nationalist composers, he evolved a revolutionary guitar technique permitting the performance of a wide range of music, and many composers wrote works for him.

4 Electric guitars are an abomination, whoever heard of an electric violin? An electric cello? Or for that matter an electric singer?
   Quoted in Rick Friedman *The Beatles: Words without Music* (1968).

Seibel, Cathy 1960–

US federal judge.

5 Just because you're rich doesn't mean you're not cheap.
   1989 On the prosecution of hotel owner Leona Helmsley. In the *New York Times*, 24 Aug.

Seinfeld, Jerry 1954–

US comedian.

6 Everybody lies about sex. People lie during sex. If it weren't for lies, there'd be no sex.
   1998 In the *New York Times*, 18 Dec.

Selden, John 1584–1654

English jurist, historian and antiquary. A member of the Long Parliament in 1640, he withdrew from politics after the execution of Charles I, of which he disapproved. His many writings on constitutional matters included *Titles of Honour* (1614), *Analecton Britannicon* (1615) and *History of Tithes* (1618). The most notable of his many tracts and treatises was the posthumous *Table Talk* (published 1689).

7 Every law is a contract between the king and the people and therefore to be kept.
   Table Talk (published 1689).

8 Ignorance of the law excuses no man; not that all men know the law, but because 'tis an excuse every man will plead, and no man can tell how to confute him.
   Table Talk (published 1689).

9 Those that govern most make least noise.
   Table Talk (published 1689).

Self, Will 1961–

English novelist, columnist and critic. He was a cartoonist with the *New Statesman*, but turned to writing fiction. His novel *Umbrella* (2012) was shortlisted for the Man Booker prize.

10 No one ever complains if a great artist says that he was driven to create a masterpiece by a hunger for recognition and money. But a scientist? Well, he is meant to be disinterested, pure, his ambition merely to descry the cement of the universe. He isn't meant to use it to start laying his own patio.
    1991 *The Quantity Theory of Insanity and Five Supporting Propositions*, 'The Quantity Theory of Insanity'.

11 I think in retrospect that all those 'alternative' modes of living were little more than exercises in arrested development.
    1991 *The Quantity Theory of Insanity and Five Supporting Propositions*, 'The Quantity Theory of Insanity'.

12 I make no apology for preoccupying myself with architecture, television, conceptual art, restaurants and Jane Asher's cakes.
    2001 *Feeding Frenzy*.

13 I have a healthy appetite for solitude. If you don't, you have no business being a writer.
    2007 In *The Guardian*, 9 May.

Sellar, W(alter) C(arruthers) and Yeatman, R(obert) J(ulian) 1898–1951, 1897–1968

British humorous writers.

14 [Gladstone] spent his declining years trying to guess the answer to the Irish Question. Unfortunately, whenever he was getting warm, the Irish secretly changed the question.
    1930 *1066 and All That*.

15 The National Debt is a very Good Thing, and it would be dangerous to pay it off for fear of Political Economy.
    1930 *1066 and All That*.

Sellars, Peter 1957–

US theatre director.

16 Post Traumatic Stress Disorder. I disagree with that last word. If you've killed a lot of people and you don't feel good about it, that's a sign of order to me. That's the correct human response. The sign of your humanity is that you can't get over what you just did.
    2014 Quoted on thestar.com, 26 Dec.

Sellers, Peter 1925–80

English actor and comedian. He came to prominence in the *Goon Show* on radio, but is perhaps best remembered as the incompetent French detective Inspector Clouseau in a series of films that began with *The Pink Panther* (1963).

17 If you ask me to play myself, I will not know what to do. I do not know who or what I am.
    Attributed.

Selye, Hans 1907–83

Austrian-born Canadian endocrinologist, founder of Montreal's Institute of Experimental Medicine.

18 Stress is the state manifested by a specific syndrome which consists of all the nonspecifically inducted changes within a biologic system.
    1956 *The Stress of Life*.

Selznick, David O(liver) 1902–65

US cinema mogul. He founded his own company in 1936, producing the screen adaptation of *Gone with the Wind* in 1939. Other successes include *Rebecca* (1940), *Duel in the Sun* (1946) and *A Farewell to Arms* (1957).

19 This is the story of the unconquerable fortress—the American home.
1944 Since You Went Away, opening line.

20 If they will only do their job...that is all that they are being overpaid for.
Of his stars, while filming *The Garden of Allah*. Quoted in Maria Riva *Marlene Dietrich* (1992).

Seneca *full name* Lucius Annaeus Seneca *called* the Younger c.4 BC–65 AD

Roman Stoic philosopher, statesman and tragedian, son of the orator Seneca the Elder. He tutored Nero and for a time enjoyed considerable political influence, but he lost favour and was forced to commit suicide. His works include the *Epistulae morales ad Lucilium*, the *Apocolocyntosis divi Claudii* (literally 'The Pumpkinification of the Divine Claudius'), and several tragedies.

21 *Utrumque enim vitium est, et omnibus credere et nulli.*
It is equally unsound to trust everyone and to trust no one.
Epistulae, 3.4.

22 *Longum iter est per praecepta, breve et efficax per exempla.*
The way is long if one follows precepts, but short and helpful, if one follows patterns.
Epistulae, 6.5 (translated by R M Gummere).

23 *Homines dum docent discunt.*
Men learn while they teach.
Epistulae 7.8 (translated by R M Gummere).

24 *Vitae, non scholae discimus.*
It is for life, not for school that we learn.
Oral tradition based on Seneca's conclusion of a letter to Lucilius which says the opposite: 'Non vitae, sed scholae discimus', *Epistulae*, 106.12.

25 *Qui timide rogat, docet negare.*
Who makes timid requests, invites denial.
Phaedra, 593–4 (translated by F J Miller).

Senghor, Léopold Sédar 1906–2001

Senegalese poet who explored the theme of black African culture.

26 *J'ai choisi mon peuple noir peinant, mon peuple paysan, toute la race paysanne, par le monde.*
I chose my black people struggling, my country people, all country people, in the world.
1945 Chants d'ombre, 'Que m'accompagnent kára et balafong, 3'.

27 *Seul le rythme provoque le court-circuit poétique et transmue le cuivre en or, la parole en verbe.*
Only rhythm brings about a poetic short-circuit and transforms the copper into gold, the words into life.
1956 Éthiopiques, postface.

28 *Au contraire de l'Européen classique, le Négro-Africain ne se distingue pas de l'objet, il ne le tient pas à distance, il ne le regarde pas, il ne l'analyse pas... Il le touche, il le palpe, il le sent.*
Unlike the classical European, the Black-African does not distinguish himself from an object. He does not hold it at a distance, he does not look at it, he does not examine it... He touches it, he fingers it, he *feels* it.
1960 Au Congrès de l'Union nationale de la Jeunesse du Mali, Dakar.

29 *Danser, c'est découvrir et recréer, surtout lorsque la danse est danse d'amour. C'est, en tout cas, le meilleur mode de connaissance.*
To dance is to discover and to recreate, above all when the dance is the dance of love. It is the best mode of knowledge.
1960 Au Congrès de l'Union nationale de la Jeunesse du Mali, Dakar.

Senior, Nassau William 1790–1864

English economist. He stressed the importance of the last hour's work in the cotton factories and opposed the trade unions. His works include *On the Cost of Obtaining Money* (1830), *An Outline of the Science of Political Economy* (1836) and *Value of Money* (1840).

30 This barbarous feeling of nationality...has become the curse of Europe.
1850 Diary, 20 May.

Senna, Ayrton 1960–94

Brazilian Formula One driver. World champion in 1988, 1990, and 1991, he died after crashing during the San Marino Grand Prix.

31 To survive in grand prix racing, you need to be afraid. Fear is an important feeling. It helps you to race longer and live longer.
1994 In *The Times*, 3 May.
▶ *See Berger 83:19.*

Serling, Rod

32 Every writer is a frustrated actor who recites his lines in the hidden auditorium of his skull.
1957 In *Vogue*, 1 Apr.

Service, Robert William 1874–1958

English-born poet. He emigrated to Canada, and became famous for his popular ballads of life in the Canadian wilderness, which earned him the nickname 'The Canadian Kipling'. He also wrote several novels.

33 This is the law of the Yukon, that only the Strong shall thrive;
That surely the Weak shall perish, and only the Fit survive.
1907 Songs of a Sourdough, 'The Law of the Yukon'.

34 A promise made is a debt unpaid, and the trail has its own stern code.
1907 Songs of a Sourdough, 'The Cremation of Sam McGhee'.

35 Back of the bar, in a solo game, sat dangerous Dan McGrew,
And watching his luck was his light-o'-love, the lady that's known as Lou.
1907 Songs of a Sourdough, 'The Shooting of Dan McGrew'.

36 Ah! The clock is always slow;
It is later than you think.
1921 Ballads of a Bohemian, 'It Is Later Than You Think'.

37 When we, the Workers, all demand: What are WE fighting for?
Then we'll end that stupid crime, that devil's madness—War.
1921 Ballads of a Bohemian, 'Michael'.

Seuss, Dr *pseudonym of* Theodor Seuss Geisel 1904–91

US children's author and illustrator, remembered for his 'Beginner Books', intended to help teach reading, starting with *The Cat in the Hat* (1957).

38 We looked!
Then we saw him step in on the mat!

We looked!
And we saw him!
The Cat in the Hat!
1957 *The Cat in the Hat.*

39 You will see something new.
Two things. And I call them
Thing One and Thing Two.
1957 *The Cat in the Hat.*

40 Do you like green eggs and ham?
1960 *Green Eggs and Ham.*

Sévigné, Marie de Rabutin-Chantal, Marquise de
1626–96

French writer famed for her letters which recounted daily life at court and in her family. They were collected by her daughter and published in 1725.

41 La grande amitié n'est jamais tranquille.
Great friendship is never peaceful.
1671 Letter to Mme de Grignan, 16 Sep.

42 Le temps vole et m'emporte malgré moi; j'ai beau vouloir le retenir, c'est lui qui m'entraîne; et cette pensée me fait grande peur: vous devinez à peu près pourquoi.
Time flies and takes me with it despite my efforts; I'd like to hold it back, but it keeps dragging me along and this thought frightens me greatly: you can perhaps guess why.
1691 Letter to the Comte de Bussy-Rabutin, 12 Jul.

Sexton, Anne née Harvey 1928–74

US poet, lecturer, and writer of children's books. Her works include *To Bedlam and Part Way Back* (1962), *All My Pretty Ones* (1962), *Live or Die* (1966), for which she won a Pulitzer Prize (1967), and *The Death Notebooks* (1974). She committed suicide.

43 Go child, who is my sin and nothing more.
1962 *To Bedlam and Part Way Back*, 'Unknown Child in the Maternity Ward'.

44 Now I fold you down, my drunkard, my navigator, my first lost keeper, to love or look at later.
1962 On photographs of her dead father. *All My Pretty Ones*, 'All My Pretty Ones'.

45 Whether you are pretty or not, I outlive you, bend down my strange face to yours and forgive you.
1962 *All My Pretty Ones*, 'All My Pretty Ones'.

46 In a dream you are never eighty.
1962 *All My Pretty Ones*, 'Old'.

47 But suicides have a special language.
Like carpenters they want to know *which* tools.
They never ask *why* build.
1964 'Wanting To Die', dated 3 Feb. Collected in *Live or Die* (1966).

48 I was tired of being a woman,
tired of the spoons and the pots,
tired of my mouth and my breasts
tired of the cosmetics and the silks...
I was tired of the gender of things.
1966 *Live or Die*, 'Consorting with Angels'.

49 The sea is mother-death and she is a mighty female, the one who wins, the one who sucks us all up.
1971 Journal entry, 19 Nov, in *The Poet's Story*, 'A Small Journal'.

50 It doesn't matter who my father was; it matters who I remember he was.
1972 Journal entry, 1 Jan, in *The Poet's Story*, 'A Small Journal'.

51 The Awful Rowing Toward God.
1975 Title of book.

52 God owns heaven
but He craves the earth.
1975 *The Awful Rowing Toward God*, 'The Earth'.

Shaffer, Sir Peter 1926–

English dramatist. His best-known plays include *Equus* (1973) and *Amadeus* (1979).

53 All my wife has ever taken from the Mediterranean—from that whole vast intuitive culture—are four bottles of Chianti to make into lamps.
1973 *Equus*, act 1, sc.18.

54 We keep saying old people are square. Then when they aren't—we don't like it!
1973 *Equus*, act 2, sc.31.

Shakespeare, William 1564–1616

English poet, playwright and actor. He lived in Stratford-upon-Avon, the home of his wife and children, and in London, where he worked in the theatre, becoming England's greatest playwright. His influence on literature and language throughout the world has been immense. The dates of composition of many of the plays are uncertain. Line numbers conform to *The Oxford Shakespeare* (Oxford University Press, 1988).

55 Home-keeping youth have ever homely wits.
1590–1 Valentine. *The Two Gentlemen of Verona*, act 1, sc.1, l.2.

56 He was more than over-shoes in love.
1590–1 Proteus, of Lysander. *The Two Gentlemen of Verona*, act 1, sc.1, l.24.

57 I have no other but a woman's reason:
I think him so because I think him so.
1590–1 Lucetta, explaining her preference for Proteus. *The Two Gentlemen of Verona*, act 1, sc.2, l.23–4.

58 O, how this spring of love resembleth
The uncertain glory of an April day,
Which now shows all the beauty of the sun,
And by and by a cloud takes all away.
1590–1 Proteus. *The Two Gentlemen of Verona*, act 1, sc.3, l.84–7.

59 I was in love with my bed.
1590–1 Speed. *The Two Gentlemen of Verona*, act 2, sc.1, l.76.

60 What, gone without a word?
Ay, so true love should do. It cannot speak,
For truth hath better deeds than words to grace it.
1590–1 Proteus. *The Two Gentlemen of Verona*, act 2, sc.2, l.16–18.

61 A fine volley of words, gentlemen, and quickly shot off.
1590–1 Silvia to Thurio and Valentine. *The Two Gentlemen of Verona*, act 2, sc.4, l.32.

62 When I was sick, you gave me bitter pills,
And I must minister the like to you.
1590–1 Proteus to Valentine. *The Two Gentlemen of Verona*, act 2, sc.4, l.147–8.

63 For love, thou know'st, is full of jealousy.
1590–1 Valentine. *The Two Gentlemen of Verona*, act 2, sc.4, l.175.

64 As one nail by strength drives out another,
So the remembrance of my former love
Is by a newer object quite forgotten.
1590–1 Proteus. *The Two Gentlemen of Verona*, act 2, sc.4, l.191–3.

65 Didst thou but know the inly touch of love
Thou wouldst as soon go kindle fire with snow
As seek to quench the fire of love with words.
1590–1 Julia to Lucetta. *The Two Gentlemen of Verona*, act 2, sc.7, l.18–20.

66 Win her with gifts if she respects not words.
Dumb jewels often in their silent kind
More than quick words do move a woman's mind.
1590–1 Valentine to Duke. *The Two Gentlemen of Verona*, act 3, sc.1, l.89–91.

67 Love is like a child
That longs for everything that he can come by.
1590–1 Duke to Valentine. *The Two Gentlemen of Verona*, act 3, sc.1, l.124–5.

68 Except I be by Silvia in the night
There is no music in the nightingale.
Unless I look on Silvia in the day
There is no day for me to look upon.
1590–1 Valentine. *The Two Gentlemen of Verona*, act 3, sc.1, l.178–81.

69 Slander Valentine
With falsehood, cowardice, and poor descent,
Three things that women highly hold in hate.
1590–1 Proteus to Duke. *The Two Gentlemen of Verona*, act 3, sc.2, l.31–3.

70 You must lay lime to tangle her desires
By wailful sonnets.
1590–1 Proteus to Thurio. *The Two Gentlemen of Verona*, act 3, sc.2, l.68–9.

71 Who is Silvia? What is she,
That all our swains commend her?
1590–1 Song. *The Two Gentlemen of Verona*, act 4, sc.2, l.38–9.

72 How use doth breed a habit in a man!
1590–1 Valentine. *The Two Gentlemen of Verona*, act 5, sc.4, l.1.

73 O heaven, were man
But constant, he were perfect!
1590–1 Proteus. *The Two Gentlemen of Verona*, act 5, sc.4, l.109–10.

74 My thoughts are whirlèd like a potter's wheel;
I know not where I am, nor what I do.
1592 Talbot. *Henry VI Part One*, act 1, sc.7, l.19–20.

75 I have heard it said, 'Unbidden guests
Are often welcomest when they are gone'.
1592 Bedford. *Henry VI Part One*, act 2, sc.2, l.55–6.

76 Faith, I have been a truant in the law,
And never yet could frame my will to it,
And therefore frame the law unto my will.
1592 Suffolk. *Henry VI Part One*, act 2, sc.4, l.7–9.

77 We will bestow you in some better place,
Fitter for sickness and for crazy age.
1592 Talbot to Bedford. *Henry VI Part One*, act 3, sc.5, l.47–8.

78 I owe him little duty and less love.
1592 Somerset, of York. *Henry VI Part One*, act 4, sc.4, l.34.

79 Beauty's princely majesty is such,
Confounds the tongue, and makes the senses rough.
1592 Suffolk. *Henry VI Part One*, act 5, sc.5, l.26–7.

80 She's beautiful, and therefore to be wooed;
She is a woman, therefore to be won.
1592 Suffolk, of Margaret. *Henry VI Part One*, act 5, sc.5, l.34–5.

81 To be a queen in bondage is more vile
Than is a slave in base servility,
For princes should be free.
1592 Margaret. *Henry VI Part One*, act 5, sc.5, l.68–70.

82 Marriage is a matter of more worth
Than to be dealt in by attorneyship.
1592 Suffolk. *Henry VI Part One*, act 5, sc.7, l.55–6.

83 O Lord that lends me life,
Lend me a heart replete with thankfulness.
1592 Henry of Queen Margaret. *Henry VI Part Two*, act 1, sc.1, l.19–20.

84 All his mind is bent to holiness,
To number Ave-Maries on his beads.
1592 Queen Margaret of Henry. *Henry VI Part Two*, act 1, sc.3, l.58–9.

85 Could I come near your beauty with my nails,
I'd set my ten commandments in your face.
1592 Duchess to Queen Margaret. *Henry VI Part Two*, act 1, sc.3, l.144–5.

86 How irksome is this music to my heart!
When such strings jar, what hope of harmony?
1592 Henry. *Henry VI Part Two*, act 2, sc.1, l.59–60.

87 God shall be my hope,
My stay, my guide, and lantern to my feet.
1592 Henry. *Henry VI Part Two*, act 2, sc.3, l.24–5.

88 Smooth runs the water where the brook is deep,
And in his simple show he harbours treason.
1592 Suffolk to Henry. *Henry VI Part Two*, act 3, sc.1, l.53–4.

89 The fox barks not when he would steal the lamb.
1592 Suffolk. *Henry VI Part Two*, act 3, sc.1, l.55.

90 The commons, like an angry hive of bees
That want their leader, scatter up and down
And care not who they sting.
1592 Warwick to Henry. *Henry VI Part Two*, act 3, sc.2, l.125–7.

91 What stronger breastplate than a heart untainted?
Thrice is he armed that hath his quarrel just;
And he but naked, though locked up in steel,
Whose conscience with injustice is corrupted.
1592 Henry. *Henry VI Part Two*, act 3, sc.2, l.232–5.

92 Forbear to judge, for we are sinners all.
1592 Henry. *Henry VI Part Two*, act 3, sc.3, l.31.

93 The gaudy, babbling, and remorseful day
Is crept into the bosom of the sea.
1592 Captain. *Henry VI Part Two*, act 4, sc.1, l.1–2.

94 I say it was never merry world in England since gentlemen came up.
1592 Second rebel. *Henry VI Part Two*, act 4, sc.2, l.9–10.

95 There shall be in England seven halfpenny loaves sold for a penny, the three-hooped pot shall have ten hoops, and I will make it felony to drink small beer.
1592 Cade. *Henry VI Part Two*, act 4, sc.2, l.67–9.

96 The first thing we do let's kill all the lawyers.
1592 The Butcher. *Henry VI Part Two*, act 4, sc.2, l.78.

97 And Adam was a gardener.
1592 Cade. *Henry VI Part Two*, act 4, sc.2, l.133.

98 Thou hast most traitorously corrupted the youth of the realm in erecting a grammar school; and, whereas before, our forefathers had no other books but the score and the tally, thou hast caused printing to be used and, contrary to the King his crown and dignity, thou hast

built a paper-mill. It will be proved to thy face that thou
hast men about thee that usually talk of a noun and a
verb and such abominable words as no Christian ear can
endure to hear.
1592 Cade. *Henry VI Part Two*, act 4, sc.7, l.30–8.

99 Ignorance is the curse of God,
Knowledge the wing wherewith we fly to heaven.
1592 Saye. *Henry VI Part Two*, act 4, sc.7, l.72–3.

1 It is great sin to swear unto a sin,
But greater sin to keep a sinful oath.
1592 Salisbury to Henry. *Henry VI Part Two*, act 5, sc.1, l.180–1.

2 Farewell, faint-hearted and degenerate king,
In whose cold blood no spark of honour bides.
1592 Westmorland to Henry. *Henry VI Part Three*, act 1, sc.1, l.184–5.

3 O tiger's heart wrapped in a woman's hide!
1592 York to Margaret. *Henry VI Part Three*, act 1, sc.4, l.138.

4 Women are soft, mild, pitiful and flexible—
Thou stern, obdurate, flinty, rough, remorseless.
1592 York to Margaret. *Henry VI Part Three*, act 1, sc.4, l.142–3.

5 Many strokes, though with a little axe,
Hews down and fells the hardest-timbered oak.
1592 Messenger to Richard telling of his father York's death. *Henry VI Part Three*, act 2, sc.1, l.54–5.

6 To weep is to make less the depth of grief;
Tears, then, for babes—blows and revenge for me!
1592 Richard. *Henry VI Part Three*, act 2, sc.1, l.85–6.

7 This battle fares like to the morning's war,
When dying clouds contend with growing light,
What time the shepherd, blowing of his nails,
Can neither call it perfect day nor night.
1592 Henry. *Henry VI Part Three*, act 2, sc.5, l.1–4.

8 O God! Methinks it were a happy life
To be no better than a homely swain.
To sit upon a hill, as I do now;
To carve out dials quaintly, point by point.
1592 Henry. *Henry VI Part Three*, act 2, sc.5, l.21–4.

9 Thereby to see the minutes how they run:
How many makes the hour full complete,
How many hours brings about the day,
How many days will finish up the year,
How many years a mortal man may live.
1592 Henry. *Henry VI Part Three*, act 2, sc.5, l.25–9.

10 Gives not the hawthorn bush a sweeter shade
To shepherds looking on their seely sheep
Than doth a rich embroidered canopy
To kings that fear their subjects' treachery?
1592 Henry. *Henry VI Part Three*, act 2, sc.5, l.42–5.

11 The common people swarm like summer flies.
1592 Clifford. *Henry VI Part Three*, act 2, sc.6, l.8.

12 I know I am too mean to be your queen,
And yet too good to be your concubine.
1592 Lady Gray to Edward. *Henry VI Part Three*, act 3, sc.2, l.97–8.

13 Hasty marriage seldom proveth well.
1592 Richard of Gloucester. *Henry VI Part Three*, act 4, sc.1, l.18.

14 What fates impose, that men must needs abide.
It boots not to resist both wind and tide.
1592 Edward. *Henry VI Part Three*, act 4, sc.4, l.31–2.

15 Fearless minds climb soonest unto crowns.
1592 Richard of Gloucester. *Henry VI Part Three*, act 4, sc.8, l.62.

16 My pity hath been balm to heal their wounds.
1592 Henry. *Henry VI Part Three*, act 4, sc.10, l.9.

17 Lo now my glory smeared in dust and blood.
My parks, my walks, my manors that I had,
Even now forsake me, and of all my lands
Is nothing left me but my body's length.
1592 Warwick wounded and dying. *Henry VI Part Three*, act 5, sc.2, l.23–6.

18 Why, courage, then—what cannot be avoided
'Twere childish weakness to lament or fear.
1592 Margaret. *Henry VI Part Three*, act 5, sc.4, l.37–8.

19 Down, down to hell; and say I sent thee thither!
1592 Richard of Gloucester to Henry. *Henry VI Part Three*, act 5, sc.6, l.67.

20 Since the heavens have shaped my body so,
Let hell make crooked my mind to answer it.
I had no father, I am like no father;
I have no brother, I am like no brother;
And this word, 'love', which greybeards call divine,
Be resident in men like one another
And not in me—I am myself alone.
1592 Richard of Gloucester. *Henry VI Part Three*, act 5, sc.6, l.78–84.

21 Wilt thou draw near the nature of the gods?
Draw near them then in being merciful.
1592 Tamora to Titus. *Titus Andronicus*, act 1, sc.1, l.117–18.

22 Give me a staff of honour for mine age,
But not a sceptre to control the world.
1592 Titus. *Titus Andronicus*, act 1, sc.1, l.198–9.

23 Vengeance is in my heart, death in my hand,
Blood and revenge are hammering in my head.
1592 Aaron to Tamora. *Titus Andronicus*, act 2, sc.3, l.38–9.

24 Dost thou not perceive
That Rome is but a wilderness of tigers?
1592 Titus to Lucius. *Titus Andronicus*, act 3, sc.1, l.52–3.

25 To weep with them that weep doth ease some deal,
But sorrow flouted at is double death.
1592 Marcus. *Titus Andronicus*, act 3, sc.1, l.243–4.

26 My heart, all mad with misery,
Beats in the hollow prison of my flesh.
1592 Titus. *Titus Andronicus*, act 3, sc.2, l.9–10.

27 I'll to thy closet and go read with thee
Sad stories chancèd in the times of old.
1592 Titus to Lavinia. *Titus Andronicus*, act 3, sc.2, l.81–2.

28 I have heard my grandsire say full oft
Extremity of griefs would make men mad.
1592 Young Lucius. *Titus Andronicus*, act 4, sc.1, l.18–19.

29 The eagle suffers little birds to sing,
And is not careful what they mean thereby,
Knowing that with the shadow of his wings
He can at pleasure stint their melody.
1592 Tamora to Saturninus. *Titus Andronicus*, act 4, sc.4, l.83–6.

30 If one good deed in all my life I did
I do repent it from my very soul.
1592 Aaron. *Titus Andronicus*, act 5, sc.3, l.188–9.

31 Now is the winter of our discontent
Made glorious summer by this son of York.
1592–3 Richard. *Richard III*, act 1, sc.1, l.1–2.

32 Grim-visaged war hath smoothed his wrinkled front,
And now—instead of mounting barbèd steeds
To fright the souls of fearful adversaries—

He capers nimbly in a lady's chamber
To the lascivious pleasing of a lute.
But I, that am not shaped for sportive tricks
Nor made to court an amorous looking-glass.
1592–3 Richard. Richard III, act 1, sc.1, l.9–15.

33 Cheated of feature by dissembling nature,
Deformed, unfinished, sent before my time
Into this breathing world scarce half made up.
1592–3 Richard. Richard III, act 1, sc.1, l.19–21.

34 I in this weak piping time of peace
Have no delight to pass away the time,
Unless to spy my shadow in the sun
And descant on mine own deformity.
1592–3 Richard. Richard III, act 1, sc.1, l.24–7.

35 Teach not thy lip such scorn, for it was made
For kissing, lady, not for such contempt.
1592–3 Richard to Lady Anne. Richard III, act 1, sc.2, l.159–60.

36 Was ever woman in this humour wooed?
Was ever woman in this humour won?
1592–3 Richard. Richard III, act 1, sc.2, l.215–16.

37 Were you snarling all before I came,
Ready to catch each other by the throat,
And turn you all your hatred now on me?
1592–3 Margaret. Richard III, act 1, sc.3, l.185–7.

38 They that stand high have many blasts to shake them,
And if they fall they dash themselves to pieces.
1592–3 Margaret. Richard III, act 1, sc.3, l.257–8.

39 And thus I clothe my naked villainy
With odd old ends, stol'n forth of Holy Writ,
And seem a saint when most I play the devil.
1592–3 Richard. Richard III, act 1, sc.3, l.334–6.

40 O Lord! Methought what pain it was to drown,
What dreadful noise of waters in my ears,
What sights of ugly death within my eyes.
Methoughts I saw a thousand fearful wrecks,
Ten thousand men that fishes gnawed upon,
Wedges of gold, great ouches, heaps of pearl,
Inestimable stones, unvalued jewels,
All scattered in the bottom of the sea.
1592–3 Clarence, shortly before he is murdered. Richard III, act 1, sc.4, l.21–8.

41 Woe to that land that's governed by a child.
1592–3 Third Citizen. Richard III, act 2, sc.3, l.11.

42 So wise so young, they say, do never live long.
1592–3 Richard, aside. Richard III, act 3, sc.1, l.79.

43 Talk'st thou to me of 'ifs'? Thou art a traitor.—
Off with his head.
1592–3 Richard. Richard III, act 3, sc.4, l.75–6.

44 I am not in the giving vein today.
1592–3 Richard. Richard III, act 4, sc.2, l.119.

45 Thou cam'st on earth to make the earth my hell.
1592–3 Duchess of York to Richard. Richard III, act 4, sc.4, l.167.

46 True hope is swift, and flies with swallows' wings.
1592–3 Henry, Earl of Richmond. Richard III, act 5, sc.2, l.23.

47 The King's name is a tower of strength.
1592–3 Richard. Richard III, act 5, sc.3, l.12.

48 Give me another horse! Bind up my wounds!
Have mercy, Jesu!—Soft, I did but dream.
O coward conscience, how dost thou afflict me?
1592–3 Richard. Richard III, act 5, sc.5, l.131–3.

49 Richard loves Richard; that is, I am I.
1592–3 Richard. Richard III, act 5, sc.5, l.137.

50 My conscience hath a thousand several tongues,
And every tongue brings in a several tale,
And every tale condemns me for a villain.
1592–3 Richard. Richard III, act 5, sc.5, l.147–9.

51 There is no creature loves me,
And if I die no soul will pity me.
Nay, wherefore should they?—Since that I myself
Find in myself no pity to myself.
1592–3 Richard. Richard III, act 5, sc.5, l.154–7.

52 Methought the souls of all that I had murdered
Came to my tent, and every one did threat
Tomorrow's vengeance on the head of Richard.
1592–3 Richard on the eve of the Battle of Bosworth. Richard III, act 5, sc.5, l.158–60.

53 Conscience is but a word that cowards use,
Devised at first to keep the strong in awe.
Our strong arms be our conscience; swords,
  our law.
March on, join bravely! Let us to't, pell mell—
If not to heaven, then hand in hand to hell.
1592–3 Richard. Richard III, act 5, sc.6, l.39–43.

54 A thousand hearts are great within my bosom.
Advance our standards! Set upon the foes!
Our ancient word of courage, fair Saint George,
Inspire us with the spleen of fiery dragons.
Upon them! Victory sits on our helms!
1592–3 Richard. Richard III, act 5, sc.6, l.77–81.

55 A horse! A horse! My kingdom for a horse!
1592–3 Richard. Richard III, act 5, sc.7, l.7.

56 Slave, I have set my life upon a cast,
And I will stand the hazard of the die.
1592–3 Richard. Richard III, act 5, sc.7, l.9–10.

57 Frame your mind to mirth and merriment,
Which bars a thousand harms, and lengthens life.
1593 Messenger to Sly. The Taming of the Shrew, Induction 2, l.131–2.

58 Think'st thou, Hortensio, though her father be very rich,
any man is so very a fool to be married to hell?
1593 Gremio. The Taming of the Shrew, act 1, sc.1, l.122–4.

59 There's small choice in rotten apples.
1593 Hortensio to Gremio. The Taming of the Shrew, act 1, sc.1, l.133–4.

60 I come to wive it wealthily in Padua;
If wealthily, then happily in Padua.
1593 Petruccio to Hortensio. The Taming of the Shrew, act 1, sc.2, l.74–5.

61 O this learning, what a thing it is!
1593 Gremio. The Taming of the Shrew, act 1, sc.2, l.157.

62 She is your treasure, she must have a husband.
I must dance barefoot on her wedding day,
And for your love to her lead apes in hell.
1593 Katherine. The Taming of the Shrew, act 2, sc.1, l.32–4.

63 I am rough, and woo not like a babe.
1593 Petruccio. The Taming of the Shrew, act 2, sc.1, l.137.

64 Good morrow, Kate, for that's your name, I hear.
1593 Petruccio. The Taming of the Shrew, act 2, sc.1, l.182.

65 You are called plain Kate,
And bonny Kate, and sometimes Kate the curst,

Shakespeare The Taming of the Shrew

But Kate, the prettiest Kate in Christendom,
Kate of Kate Hall, my super-dainty Kate.
1593 Petruccio. *The Taming of the Shrew*, act 2, sc.1, l.185–8.

66 Your father hath consented
That you shall be my wife, your dowry 'greed on,
And will you, nill you, I will marry you.
1593 Petruccio to Kate. *The Taming of the Shrew*, act 2, sc.1, l.263–5.

67 We will have rings, and things, and fine array;
And kiss me, Kate. We will be married o' Sunday.
1593 Petruccio. *The Taming of the Shrew*, act 2, sc.1, l.319–20.

68 Preposterous ass, that never read so far
To know the cause why music was ordained!
Was it not to refresh the mind of man
After his studies or his usual pain?
1593 Lucentio to Hortensio. *The Taming of the Shrew*, act 3, sc.1, l.9–12.

69 Old fashions please me best. I am not so nice
To change true rules for odd inventions.
1593 Bianca to Hortensio. *The Taming of the Shrew*, act 3, sc.1, l.78–9.

70 Go, girl. I cannot blame thee now to weep.
For such an injury would vex a very saint.
1593 Baptista. *The Taming of the Shrew*, act 3, sc.2, l.27–8.

71 To me she's married, not unto my clothes.
1593 Petruccio. *The Taming of the Shrew*, act 3, sc.2, l.117.

72 He took the bride about the neck
And kissed her lips with such a clamorous smack
That at the parting all the church did echo.
1593 Gremio, of Petruccio. *The Taming of the Shrew*, act 3, sc.3, l.50–2.

73 This is a way to kill a wife with kindness.
1593 Petruccio. *The Taming of the Shrew*, act 4, sc.1, l.194.

74 How say you to a fat tripe finely broiled?
1593 Grumio to Katherine. *The Taming of the Shrew*, act 4, sc.3, l.20.

75 What, is the jay more precious than the lark
Because his feathers are more beautiful?
Or is the adder better than the eel
Because his painted skin contents the eye?
1593 Petruccio to Kate. *The Taming of the Shrew*, act 4, sc.3, l.173–6.

76 Your plainness and your shortness please me well.
1593 Baptista to Pedant. *The Taming of the Shrew*, act 4, sc.4, l.38.

77 Then God be blessed, it is the blessèd sun,
But sun it is not when you say it is not,
And the moon changes even as your mind.
What you will have it named, even that it is,
And so it shall be still for Katherine.
1593 Katherine. *The Taming of the Shrew*, act 4, sc.6, l.19–23.

78 Thy husband is thy lord, thy life, thy keeper,
Thy head, thy sovereign.
1593 Katherine. *The Taming of the Shrew*, act 5, sc.2, l.151–2.

79 I am ashamed that women are so simple
To offer war where they should kneel for peace.
1593 Katherine. *The Taming of the Shrew*, act 5, sc.2, l.166–7.

80 Come on, and kiss me, Kate.
1593 Katherine. *The Taming of the Shrew*, act 5, sc.2, l.185.

81 Hunting he loved, but love he laughed to scorn.
1593 *Venus and Adonis*, stanza 1, l.4.

82 Make use of time; let not advantage slip.
Beauty within itself should not be wasted.
Fair flowers that are not gathered in their prime
Rot, and consume themselves in little time.
1593 *Venus and Adonis*, stanza 22, l.129–32.

83 Bid me discourse, I will enchant thine ear.
1593 *Venus and Adonis*, stanza 25, l.145.

84 Love is a spirit all compact of fire,
Not gross to sink, but light, and will aspire.
1593 *Venus and Adonis*, stanza 25, l.149–50.

85 Affection is a coal that must be cooled;
Else, suffered, it will set the heart on fire.
1593 *Venus and Adonis*, stanza 65, l.387–8.

86 Dismiss your vows, your feignèd tears, your flatt'ry;
For where a heart is hard they make no batt'ry.
1593 *Venus and Adonis*, stanza 71, l.425–6.

87 Melodious discord, heavenly tune harsh sounding,
Ear's deep-sweet music, and heart's deep-sore wounding.
1593 *Venus and Adonis*, stanza 72, l.431–2.

88 Love comforteth, like sunshine after rain.
1593 *Venus and Adonis*, stanza 134, l.799.

89 Their copious stories, oftentimes begun,
End without audience, and are never done.
1593 *Venus and Adonis*, stanza 141, l.845–6.

90 I to the world am like a drop of water
That in the ocean seeks another drop.
1594 Antipholus of Syracuse. *The Comedy of Errors*, act 1, sc.2, l.35–6.

91 They say this town is full of cozenage,
As nimble jugglers that deceive the eye,
Dark-working sorcerers that change the mind,
Soul-killing witches that deform the body.
1594 Antipholus of Syracuse. *The Comedy of Errors*, act 1, sc.2, l.97–100.

92 Am I so round with you as you with me,
That like a football you do spurn me thus?
You spurn me hence, and he will spurn me hither.
If I last in this service, you must case me in leather.
1594 Dromio of Ephesus. *The Comedy of Errors*, act 2, sc.1, l.81–4.

93 They brought one Pinch, a hungry lean-faced villain,
A mere anatomy, a mountebank,
A threadbare juggler, and a fortune-teller,
A needy, hollow-eyed, sharp-looking wretch,
A living dead man.
1594 Antipholus of Ephesus. *The Comedy of Errors*, act 5, sc.1, l.238–42.

94 Respect and reason wait on wrinkled age!
1594 *The Rape of Lucrece*, stanza 39, l.275.

95 Thy beauty hath ensnared thee to this night.
1594 *The Rape of Lucrece*, stanza 70, l.485.

96 To show the beldame daughters of her daughter,
To make the child a man, the man a child,
To slay the tiger that doth live by slaughter,
To tame the unicorn and lion wild,
To mock the subtle in themselves beguiled,
To cheer the ploughman with increasing crops,
And waste huge stones with little water drops.
1594 *The Rape of Lucrece*, stanza 137, l.953–9.

97 Like an unpractised swimmer plunging still,
With too much labour drowns for want of skill.
1594 *The Rape of Lucrece*, stanza 157, l.1098–9.

98 It cannot be, I find,
But such a face should bear a wicked mind.
1594 *The Rape of Lucrece*, stanza 220, l.1539–40.

99 Let fame, that all hunt after in their lives,
Live registered upon our brazen tombs,
And then grace us in the disgrace of death
When, spite of cormorant devouring time,
Th' endeavour of this present breath may buy
That honour which shall bate his scythe's keen edge
And make us heirs of all eternity.
1594–5 King. *Love's Labour's Lost*, act 1, sc.1, l.1–7.

1 Study is like the heavens' glorious sun,
That will not be deep searched with saucy looks.
1594–5 Biron. *Love's Labour's Lost*, act 1, sc.1, l.84–5.

2 Small have continual plodders ever won,
Save base authority from others' books.
1594–5 Biron to King. *Love's Labour's Lost*, act 1, sc.1, l.86–7.

3 How well he's read, to reason against reading!
1594–5 King. *Love's Labour's Lost*, act 1, sc.1, l.94.

4 At Christmas I no more desire a rose
Than wish a snow in May's new-fangled shows.
1594–5 Biron. *Love's Labour's Lost*, act 1, sc.1, l.105–6.

5 Necessity will make us all forsworn.
1594–5 Biron. *Love's Labour's Lost*, act 1, sc.1, l.147.

6 A man in all the world's new fashion planted,
That hath a mint of phrases in his brain.
One who the music of his own vain tongue
Doth ravish like enchanting harmony.
1594–5 King, of Armado. *Love's Labour's Lost*, act 1, sc.1, l.162–5.

7 A child of our grandmother Eve, a female, or, for thy
more sweet understanding, a woman.
1594–5 Armado's letter. *Love's Labour's Lost*, act 1, sc.1, l.255.

8 Assist me, some extemporal god of rhyme, for I am sure I
shall turn sonnet. Devise wit, write pen, for I am for
whole volumes, in folio.
1594–5 Armado. *Love's Labour's Lost*, act 1, sc.2, l.174–6.

9 This wimpled, whining, purblind, wayward boy,
This Signor Junior, giant dwarf, Dan Cupid,
Regent of love-rhymes, lord of folded arms,
Th' anointed sovereign of sighs and groans,
Liege of all loiterers and malcontents,
Dread prince of plackets, king of codpieces,
Sole imperator and great general
Of trotting paritors—O my little heart!
1594–5 Biron. *Love's Labour's Lost*, act 3, sc.1, l.174–81.

10 A giving hand, though foul, shall have fair praise.
1594–5 Princess. *Love's Labour's Lost*, act 4, sc.1, l.23.

11 O thou monster ignorance, how deformed dost thou look!
1594–5 Holofernes, to Dull. *Love's Labour's Lost*, act 4, sc.2, l.23.

12 He hath never fed of the dainties that are bred in a book.
He hath not eat paper, as it were, he hath not drunk ink.
1594–5 Nathaniel, of Dull. *Love's Labour's Lost*, act 4, sc.2, l.24–5.

13 The elegancy, facility, and golden cadence of poesy.
1594–5 Holofernes. *Love's Labour's Lost*, act 4, sc.2, l.123.

14 By heaven, I do love; and it hath taught me to rhyme,
and to be melancholy.
1594–5 Biron. *Love's Labour's Lost*, act 4, sc.3, l.11.

15 What fool is not so wise
To lose an oath to win a paradise?
1594–5 Longueville. *Love's Labour's Lost*, act 4, sc.3, l.69–70.

16 Love's feeling is more soft and sensible
Than are the tender horns of cockled snails.
1594–5 Biron. *Love's Labour's Lost*, act 4, sc.3, l.313–14.

17 And when love speaks, the voice of all the gods
Make heaven drowsy with the harmony.
1594–5 Biron. *Love's Labour's Lost*, act 4, sc.3, l.320–1.

18 Never durst poet touch a pen to write
Until his ink were tempered with love's sighs.
1594–5 Biron. *Love's Labour's Lost*, act 4, sc.3, l.322–3.

19 From women's eyes this doctrine I derive.
They sparkle still the right Promethean fire.
They are the books, the arts, the academes
That show, contain, and nourish all the world,
Else none at all in aught proves excellent.
1594–5 Biron. *Love's Labour's Lost*, act 4, sc.3, l.326–30.

20 He draweth out the thread of his verbosity finer than the
staple of his argument.
1594–5 Holofernes, of Armado. *Love's Labour's Lost*, act 5, sc.1, l.16.

21 O, they have lived long in the alms-basket of words.
I marvel thy master hath not eaten thee for a word,
for thou art not so long by the head as
honorificabilitudinitatibus. Thou art easier swallowed
than a flapdragon.
1594–5 Costard. *Love's Labour's Lost*, act 5, sc.1, l.38–42.

22 A light heart lives long.
1594–5 Catherine. *Love's Labour's Lost*, act 5, sc.2, l.18.

23 There's no such sport as sport by sport o'erthrown.
1594–5 Princess. *Love's Labour's Lost*, act 5, sc.2, l.152.

24 Taffeta phrases, silken terms precise,
Three-piled hyperboles, spruce affectation,
Figures pedantical—these summer flies
Have blown me full of maggot ostentation.
1594–5 Biron. *Love's Labour's Lost*, act 5, sc.2, l.406–10.

25 Mirth cannot move a soul in agony.
1594–5 Biron. *Love's Labour's Lost*, act 5, sc.2, l.843.

26 A jest's prosperity lies in the ear
Of him that hears it, never in the tongue
Of him that makes it.
1594–5 Rosaline. *Love's Labour's Lost*, act 5, sc.2, l.847–9.

27 When icicles hang by the wall,
And Dick the shepherd blows his nail,
And Tom bears logs into the hall,
And milk comes frozen home in pail;
When blood is nipped, and ways be foul,
Then nightly sings the staring owl:
Tu-whit, tu-whoo!—a merry note,
While greasy Joan doth keel the pot.
1594–5 Winter's song. *Love's Labour's Lost*, act 5, sc.2, l.897–904.

28 When all aloud the wind doth blow,
And coughing drowns the parson's saw,
And birds sit brooding in the snow,
And Marian's nose looks red and raw;
When roasted crabs hiss in the bowl.
1594–5 Winter's song. *Love's Labour's Lost*, act 5, sc.2, l.905–9.

29 Our doctors say this is no time to bleed.
1595 Richard. *Richard II*, act 1, sc.1, l.157.

30 I am disgraced, impeached, and baffled here,
Pierced to the soul with slander's venomed spear.
1595 Mowbray to Richard. *Richard II*, act 1, sc.1, l.170–1.

31 Lions make leopards tame.
1595 Richard. *Richard II*, act 1, sc.1, l.174.

32 The purest treasure mortal times afford
Is spotless reputation; that away,
Men are but gilded loam, or painted clay.
A jewel in a ten-times barred-up chest
Is a bold spirit in a loyal breast.
Mine honour is my life. Both grow in one.
Take honour from me, and my life is done.
1595 Mowbray to Richard. *Richard II*, act 1, sc.1, l.177–83.

33 As gentle and as jocund as to jest
Go I to fight. Truth hath a quiet breast.
1595 Mowbray. *Richard II*, act 1, sc.3, l.95–6.

34 This must my comfort be:
That sun that warms you here shall shine on me.
1595 Bolingbroke to Richard. *Richard II*, act 1, sc.3, l.138–9.

35 How long a time lies in one little word!
Four lagging winters and four wanton springs
End in a word: such is the breath of kings.
1595 Bolingbroke. *Richard II*, act 1, sc.3, l.206–8.

36 O, who can hold a fire in his hand
By thinking on the frosty Caucasus,
Or cloy the hungry edge of appetite
By bare imagination of a feast,
Or wallow naked in December snow
By thinking on fantastic summer's heat?
1595 Bolingbroke. *Richard II*, act 1, sc.3, l.257–62.

37 Methinks I am a prophet new-inspired,
And thus, expiring, do foretell of him.
His rash, fierce blaze of riot cannot last,
For violent fires soon burn out themselves.
1595 John of Gaunt, to Richard. *Richard II*, act 2, sc.1, l.31–4.

38 Small showers last long, but sudden storms are short.
1595 John of Gaunt. *Richard II*, act 2, sc.1, l.35.

39 With eager feeding food doth choke the feeder.
1595 John of Gaunt. *Richard II*, act 2, sc.1, l.37.

40 This royal throne of kings, this sceptred isle,
This earth of majesty, this seat of Mars,
This other Eden, demi-paradise,
This fortress built by nature for herself
Against infection and the hand of war,
This happy breed of men, this little world,
This precious stone set in the silver sea,
Which serves it in the office of a wall,
Or as a moat defensive to a house
Against the envy of less happier lands;
This blessèd plot, this earth, this realm, this England.
1595 John of Gaunt. *Richard II*, act 2, sc.1, l.40–50.

41 England that was wont to conquer others
Hath made a shameful conquest of itself.
1595 John of Gaunt. *Richard II*, act 2, sc.1, l.65–6.

42 Each substance of a grief hath twenty shadows,
Which shows like grief itself.
1595 Bushy. *Richard II*, act 2, sc.2, l.14–15.

43 Comfort's in heaven, and we are on the earth,
Where nothing lives but crosses, cares, and griefs.
1595 York. *Richard II*, act 2, sc.2, l.78–9.

44 Hope to joy is little less in joy
Than hope enjoyed.
1595 Northumberland. *Richard II*, act 2, sc.3, l.15–16.

45 I count myself in nothing else so happy
As in a soul rememb'ring my good friends.
1595 Bolingboke. *Richard II*, act 2, sc.3, l.46–7.

46 Things past redress are now with me past care.
1595 York. *Richard II*, act 2, sc.3, l.170.

47 Not all the water in the rough rude sea
Can wash the balm from an anointed king.
1595 Richard. *Richard II*, act 3, sc.2, l.50–1.

48 O, call back yesterday, bid time return,
And thou shalt have twelve thousand fighting men.
Today, today, unhappy day too late.
1595 Salisbury. *Richard II*, act 3, sc.2, l.65–7.

49 Time hath set a blot upon my pride.
1595 Richard. *Richard II*, act 3, sc.2, l.77.

50 Cry woe, destruction, ruin, loss, decay;
The worst is death, and death will have his day.
1595 Richard. *Richard II*, act 3, sc.2, l.98–9.

51 And nothing can we call our own but death,
And that small model of the barren earth
Which serves as paste and cover to our bones.
1595 Richard. *Richard II*, act 3, sc.2, l.148–50.

52 For God's sake, let us sit upon the ground,
And tell sad stories of the death of kings—
How some have been deposed, some slain in war,
Some haunted by the ghosts they have deposed,
Some poisoned by their wives, some sleeping killed,
All murdered. For within the hollow crown
That rounds the mortal temples of a king
Keeps Death his court; and there the antic sits,
Scoffing his state and grinning at his pomp,
Allowing him a breath, a little scene,
To monarchize, be feared, and kill with looks,
Infusing him with self and vain conceit,
As if this flesh which walls about our life
Were brass impregnable; and humoured thus,
Comes at the last, and with a little pin
Bores through his castle wall; and farewell, king.
1595 Richard. *Richard II*, act 3, sc.2, l.151–166.

53 O, that I were as great
As is my grief, or lesser than my name,
Or that I could forget what I have been,
Or not remember what I must be now!
1595 Richard. *Richard II*, act 3, sc.3, l.135–8.

54 What must the King do now? Must he submit?
The King shall do it. Must he be deposed?
The King shall be contented. Must he lose
The name of King? A God's name, let it go.
I'll give my jewels for a set of beads,
My gorgeous palace for a hermitage,
My gay apparel for an almsman's gown,
My figured goblets for a dish of wood,
My sceptre for a palmer's walking staff,
My subjects for a pair of carvèd saints,
And my large kingdom for a little grave.
1595 Richard. *Richard II*, act 3, sc.3, l.142–52.

55 Alack, why am I sent for to a king
Before I have shook off the regal thoughts
Wherewith I reigned? I hardly yet have learned

To insinuate, flatter, bow, and bend my knee.
Give sorrow leave awhile to tutor me
To this submission. Yet I well remember
The favours of these men. Were they not mine?
Did they not sometime cry. 'All hail!' to me?
So Judas did to Christ. But He in twelve
Found the truth in all but one; I, in twelve thousand,
none.
God save the King! Will no man say 'Amen'?
Am I both the priest and clerk? Well then, Amen.
1595 Richard. *Richard II*, act 4, sc.1, l.153–164.

56 You may my glories and my state depose,
But not my griefs; still am I king of those.
1595 Richard. *Richard II*, act 4, sc.1, l.182–3.

57 Mine eyes are full of tears; I cannot see.
And yet salt water blinds them not so much
But they can see a sort of traitors here.
Nay, if I turn mine eyes upon myself
I find myself a traitor with the rest.
1595 Richard. *Richard II*, act 4, sc.1, l.234–8.

58 I am sworn brother, sweet,
To grim necessity, and he and I
Will keep a league till death.
1595 Richard. *Richard II*, act 5, sc.1, l.20–1.

59 The love of wicked friends converts to fear;
That fear to hate.
1595 Richard. *Richard II*, act 5, sc.1, l.66–7.

60 Had not God, for some strong purpose steeled
The hearts of men, they must perforce have melted.
1595 York. *Richard II*, act 5, sc.2, l.34–5.

61 Say 'Pardon', king. Let pity teach thee how.
The word is short, but not so short as sweet;
No word like 'Pardon' for kings' mouths so meet.
1595 Duchess of York. *Richard II*, act 5, sc.3, l.115–16.

62 Thoughts tending to ambition, they do plot
Unlikely wonders: how these vain weak nails
May tear a passage through the flinty ribs
Of this hard world.
1595 Richard. *Richard II*, act 5, sc.5, l.18–21.

63 How sour sweet music is
When time is broke and no proportion kept.
So is it in the music of men's lives.
1595 Richard. *Richard II*, act 5, sc.5, l.42–4.

64 Mount, mount, my soul; thy seat is up on high,
Whilst my gross flesh sinks downward, here to die.
1595 Richard. *Richard II*, act 5, sc.5, l.111–12.

65 From forth the fatal loins of these two foes
A pair of star-crossed lovers take their life.
1595 Chorus. *Romeo and Juliet*, Prologue, l.5–6.

66 Alas that love, so gentle in his view,
Should be so tyrannous and rough in proof.
1595 Benvolio to Romeo. *Romeo and Juliet*, act 1, sc.1, l.166–7.

67 'Tis not hard, I think,
For men so old as we to keep the peace.
1595 Capulet. *Romeo and Juliet*, act 1, sc.2, l.2–3.

68 Such comfort as do lusty young men feel
When well-apparell'd April on the heel
Of limping winter treads.
1595 Capulet. *Romeo and Juliet*, act 1, sc.2, l.24–6.

69 Is love a tender thing? It is too rough,
Too rude, too boist'rous, and it pricks like thorn.
1595 Romeo. *Romeo and Juliet*, act 1, sc.4, l.25–6.

70 She is the fairies' midwife, and she comes
In shape no bigger than an agate stone
On the forefinger of an alderman,
Drawn with a team of little atomi
Athwart man's noses as they lie asleep.
1595 Mercutio. *Romeo and Juliet*, act 1, sc.4, l.55–9.

71 Her chariot is an empty hazelnut
Made by the joiner squirrel or old grub,
Time out o' mind the fairies' coachmakers.
And in this state she gallops night by night
Through lovers' brains, and then they dream of love.
1595 Mercutio. *Romeo and Juliet*, act 1, sc.4, l.68–72.

72 I talk of dreams,
Which are the children of an idle brain,
Begot of nothing but vain fantasy.
1595 Mercutio. *Romeo and Juliet*, act 1, sc.4, l.96–8.

73 You and I are past our dancing days.
1595 Capulet to his cousin. *Romeo and Juliet*, act 1, sc.5, l.31.

74 O, she doth teach the torches to burn bright!
It seems she hangs upon the cheek of night
As a rich jewel in an Ethiope's ear—
Beauty too rich for use, for earth too dear.
1595 Romeo of Juliet. *Romeo and Juliet*, act 1, sc.5, l.43–6.

75 Did my heart love till now? Forswear it, sight,
For I ne'er saw true beauty till this night.
1595 Mercutio. *Romeo and Juliet*, act 1, sc.5, l.51–2.

76 My only love sprung from my only hate!
Too early seen unknown, and known too late!
1595 Juliet. *Romeo and Juliet*, act 1, sc.5, l.137–8.

77 He jests at scars that never felt a wound.
But soft, what light through yonder window breaks?
It is the east, and Juliet is the sun.
1595 Romeo. *Romeo and Juliet*, act 2, sc.1, l.43–5.

78 O, speak again, bright angel; for thou art
As glorious to this night, being o'er my head,
As is a wingèd messenger of heaven.
1595 Romeo of Juliet. *Romeo and Juliet*, act 2, sc.1, l.68–70.

79 O Romeo, Romeo, wherefore art thou Romeo?
Deny thy father and refuse thy name,
Or if thou will not, be but sworn my love,
And I'll no longer be a Capulet.
1595 Juliet. *Romeo and Juliet*, act 2, sc.1, l.75–8.

80 What's in a name? That which we call a rose
By any other word would smell as sweet.
1595 Juliet. *Romeo and Juliet*, act 2, sc.1, l.85–6.

81 Call me but love and I'll be new baptized.
Henceforth I never will be Romeo.
1595 Romeo. *Romeo and Juliet*, act 2, sc.1, l.93–4.

82 If thou think'st I am too quickly won,
I'll frown and be perverse and say thee nay,
So thou wilt woo.
1595 Juliet. *Romeo and Juliet*, act 2, sc.1, l.137–9.

83 O swear not by the moon, th'inconstant moon
That monthly changes in her circled orb,
Lest that thy love prove likewise variable.
1595 Juliet. *Romeo and Juliet*, act 2, sc.1, l.151–3.

Shakespeare Romeo and Juliet

84 My bounty is as boundless as the sea,
My love as deep. The more I give to thee
The more I have, for both are infinite.
1595 Juliet. *Romeo and Juliet*, act 2, sc.1, l.175–7.

85 Parting is such sweet sorrow
That I shall say good-night till it be morrow.
1595 Juliet. *Romeo and Juliet*, act 2, sc.1, l.229–30.

86 Sleep dwell upon thine eyes, peace in thy breast.
1595 Romeo. *Romeo and Juliet*, act 2, sc.1, l.231.

87 O mickle is the powerful grace that lies
In plants, herbs, stones, and their true qualities,
For nought so vile that on the earth doth live
But to the earth some special good doth give.
1595 Friar Laurence. *Romeo and Juliet*, act 2, sc.2, l.15–18.

88 Virtue itself turns vice, being misapplied,
And vice sometime's by action dignified.
1595 Friar Laurence. *Romeo and Juliet*, act 2, sc.2, l.21–2.

89 Care keeps his watch in every old man's eye.
1595 Friar Laurence to Romeo. *Romeo and Juliet*, act 2, sc.2, l.35.

90 Wisely and slow. They stumble that run fast.
1595 Friar Laurence to Romeo. *Romeo and Juliet*, act 2, sc.2, l.94.

91 A gentleman, Nurse, that loves to hear himself talk, and will speak more in a minute than he will stand to in a month.
1595 Romeo. *Romeo and Juliet*, act 2, sc.3, l.138–9.

92 These violent delights have violent ends.
1595 Friar Laurence. *Romeo and Juliet*, act 2, sc.5, l.9.

93 Thy head is as full of quarrels as an egg is full of meat.
1595 Mercutio to Benvolio. *Romeo and Juliet*, act 3, sc.1, l.20.

94 A plague o' both your houses.
They have made worms' meat of me.
1595 Mercutio, dying stabbed by Tybalt. *Romeo and Juliet*, act 3, sc.1, l.106–7.

95 Come, civil night,
Thou sober-suited matron all in black.
1595 Juliet. *Romeo and Juliet*, act 3, sc.2, l.10–11.

96 So tedious is this day
As is the night before some festival
To an impatient child that hath new robes
And may not wear them.
1595 Juliet. *Romeo and Juliet*, act 3, sc.2, l.28–31.

97 Steal immortal blessing from her lips.
1595 Romeo. *Romeo and Juliet*, act 3, sc.3, l.37.

98 Hang up philosophy!
Unless philosophy can make a Juliet.
1595 Romeo. *Romeo and Juliet*, act 3, sc.3, l.57–8.

99 A joy past joy calls out on me.
1595 Romeo. *Romeo and Juliet*, act 3, sc.3, l.172.

1 It was the nightingale, and not the lark,
That pierced the fear-full hollow of thine ear.
Nightly she sings on yon pom'granate tree.
1595 Juliet to Romeo. *Romeo and Juliet*, act 3, sc.5, l.2–4.

2 Night's candles are burnt out, and jocund day
Stands tiptoe on the misty mountaintops.
I must be gone and live, or stay and die.
1595 Romeo to Juliet. *Romeo and Juliet*, act 3, sc.5, l.9–11.

3 O, fortune, fortune, all men call thee fickle.
1595 Juliet. *Romeo and Juliet*, act 3, sc.5, l.60.

4 Mistress minion, you,
Thank me no thankings, nor proud me no prouds,
But fettle your fine joints 'gainst Thursday next
To go with Paris to Saint Peter's Church,
Or I will drag thee on a hurdle thither.
Out, you green-sickness carrion! Out, you baggage,
You tallow-face!
1595 Capulet, to Juliet, ordering her marriage to Paris. *Romeo and Juliet*, act 3, sc.5, l.151–7.

5 Is there no pity sitting in the clouds,
That sees into the bottom of my grief?
1595 Juliet. *Romeo and Juliet*, act 3, sc.5, l.196–7.

6 I think it best you married with the County.
O, he's a lovely gentleman!
Romeo's a dishclout to him.
1595 Nurse to Juliet. *Romeo and Juliet*, act 3, sc.5, l.217–19.

7 'Tis an ill cook that cannot lick his own fingers.
1595 Servingman to Capulet. *Romeo and Juliet*, act 4, sc.2, l.6.

8 I have a faint cold fear thrills through my veins
That almost freezes up the heat of life.
1595 Juliet. *Romeo and Juliet*, act 4, sc.3, l.15–16.

9 Out, alas, she's cold.
Her blood is settled, and her joints are stiff.
Life and these lips have long been separated.
Death lies on her like an untimely frost
Upon the sweetest flower of all the field.
1595 Capulet, of Juliet, as she feigns death. *Romeo and Juliet*, act 4, sc.4, l.52–6.

10 She's not well married that lives married long,
But she's best married that dies married young.
1595 Friar Laurence. *Romeo and Juliet*, act 4, sc.4, l.104–5.

11 I dreamt my lady came and found me dead—
Strange dream, that gives a dead man leave to think!—
And breathed such life with kisses in my lips
That I revived and was an emperor.
1595 Romeo. *Romeo and Juliet*, act 5, sc.1, l.6–9.

12 Art thou so bare and full of wretchedness,
And fear'st to die? Famine is in thy cheeks,
Need and oppression starveth in thy eyes,
Contempt and beggary hangs upon thy back.
The world is not thy friend, nor the world's law.
1595 Romeo to Apothecary. *Romeo and Juliet*, act 5, sc.1, l.68–72.

13 Give me thy hand,
One writ with me in sour misfortune's book.
1595 Romeo to Paris, whom he has just killed. *Romeo and Juliet*, act 5, sc.3, l.81–2.

14 Here, here will I remain
With worms that are thy chambermaids. O, here
Will I set up my everlasting rest,
And shake the yoke of inauspicious stars
From this world-wearied flesh.
1595 Romeo. *Romeo and Juliet*, act 5, sc.3, l.108–12.

15 Never was a story of more woe
Than this of Juliet and her Romeo.
1595 Prince. *Romeo and Juliet*, act 5, sc.3, l.308–9.

16 To you your father should be as a god.
1595 Theseus to Hermia. *A Midsummer Night's Dream*, act 1, sc.1, l.47.

17 The course of true love never did run smooth.
1595 Lysander to Hermia. *A Midsummer Night's Dream*, act 1, sc.1, l.134.

18 Your eyes are lodestars, and your tongue's sweet air
More tuneable than lark to shepherd's ear
When wheat is green, when hawthorn buds appear.
1595 Helena. *A Midsummer Night's Dream*, act 1, sc.1, l.183–5.

19 Love looks not with the eyes, but with the mind,
And therefore is winged Cupid painted blind.
1595 Helena. *A Midsummer Night's Dream*, act 1, sc.1, l.234–5.

20 Marry, our play is The Most Lamentable Comedy and Most Cruel Death of Pyramus and Thisbe.
1595 Quince. *A Midsummer Night's Dream*, act 1, sc.2, l.11–12.

21 That will ask some tears in the true performing of it. If I do it, let the audience look to their eyes. I will move stones.
1595 Bottom. *A Midsummer Night's Dream*, act 1, sc.2, l.21–3.

22 Nay, faith, let not me play a woman. I have a beard coming.
1595 Flute, on his reluctance to act the role of Thisbe. *A Midsummer Night's Dream*, act 1, sc.2, l.43–4.

23 SNUG: Have you the lion's part written? Pray you, if it be, give it me; for I am slow of study.
QUINCE: You may do it extempore, for it is nothing but roaring.
BOTTOM: Let me play the lion too. I will roar that I will do any man's heart good to hear me. I will roar that I will make the Duke say 'Let him roar again; let him roar again'.
1595 *A Midsummer Night's Dream*, act 1, sc.2, l.62–69.

24 I will roar you as gently as any sucking dove. I will roar you an 'twere any nightingale.
1595 Bottom. *A Midsummer Night's Dream*, act 1, sc.2, l.77–8.

25 Over hill, over dale,
Thorough bush, thorough brier,
Over park, over pale,
Thorough flood, thorough fire:
I do wander everywhere
Swifter than the moon's sphere,
And I serve the Fairy Queen
To dew her orbs upon the green.
The cowslips tall her pensioners be.
In their gold coats spots you see;
Those be rubies, fairy favours;
In those freckles live their savours.
I must go seek some dewdrops here,
And hang a pearl in every cowslip's ear.
1595 Fairy. *A Midsummer Night's Dream*, act 2, sc.1, l.2–15.

26 Ill met by moonlight, proud Titania.
1595 Oberon. *A Midsummer Night's Dream*, act 2, sc.1, l.60.

27 Yet marked I where the bolt of Cupid fell.
It fell upon a little western flower—
Before, milk-white; now, purple with love's wound—
And maidens call it love-in-idleness.
1595 Oberon. *A Midsummer Night's Dream*, act 2, sc.1, l.165–8.

28 I'll put a girdle round about the earth
In forty minutes.
1595 Robin Goodfellow. *A Midsummer Night's Dream*, act 2, sc.1, l.175–6.

29 We cannot fight for love as men may do;
We should be woo'd, and were not made to woo.
1595 Helena. *A Midsummer Night's Dream*, act 2, sc.1, l.241–2.

30 I know a bank where the wild thyme blows,
Where oxlips and the nodding violet grows,
Quite overcanopied with luscious woodbine,
With sweet musk-roses, and with eglantine.
1595 Oberon. *A Midsummer Night's Dream*, act 2, sc.1, l.249–52.

31 You spotted snakes with double tongue,
Thorny hedgehogs, be not seen;
Newts and blindworms, do no wrong;
Come not near our Fairy Queen.
1595 First Fairy. *A Midsummer Night's Dream*, act 2, sc.2, l.9–12.

32 A surfeit of the sweetest things
The deepest loathing to the stomach brings.
1595 Lysander. *A Midsummer Night's Dream*, act 2, sc.2, l.143–4.

33 A lion among ladies is a most dreadful thing.
1595 Bottom. *A Midsummer Night's Dream*, act 3, sc.1, l.28.

34 FLUTE: (as Thisbe)
Most radiant Pyramus, most lily-white of hue,
Of colour like the red rose on triumphant brier;
Most bristly juvenile, and eke most lovely Jew,
As true as truest horse that yet would never tire:
I'll meet thee, Pyramus, at Ninny's tomb.
QUINCE: Ninus' tomb, man!
1595 *A Midsummer Night's Dream*, act 3, sc.1, l.87–92.

35 What angel wakes me from my flow'ry bed?
1595 Titania, of Bottom. *A Midsummer Night's Dream*, act 3, sc.1, l.122.

36 I pray thee, gentle mortal, sing again.
Mine ear is much enamoured of thy note;
So is mine eye enthrallèd to thy shape;
And thy fair virtue's force perforce doth move me
On the first view to say, to swear, I love thee.
1595 Titania. *A Midsummer Night's Dream*, act 3, sc.1, l.130–4.

37 I go, I go—look how I go,
Swifter than arrow from the Tartar's bow.
1595 Robin Goodfellow to Oberon. *A Midsummer Night's Dream*, act 3, sc.2, l.100–1.

38 Lord, what fools these mortals be!
1595 Robin Goodfellow. *A Midsummer Night's Dream*, act 3, sc.2, l.115.

39 Sleep, that sometimes shuts up sorrow's eye,
Steal me a while from mine own company.
1595 Helena. *A Midsummer Night's Dream*, act 3, sc.3, l.23–4.

40 I must to the barber's, monsieur, for methinks I am marvellous hairy about the face; and I am such a tender ass, if my hair do but tickle me I must scratch.
1595 Bottom. *A Midsummer Night's Dream*, act 4, sc.1, l.23–6.

41 Methinks I have a great desire to a bottle of hay. Good hay, sweet hay, hath no fellow.
1595 Bottom. *A Midsummer Night's Dream*, act 4, sc.1, l.32–3.

42 My Oberon, what visions have I seen!
Methought I was enamoured of an ass.
1595 Titania. *A Midsummer Night's Dream*, act 4, sc.1, l.75–6.

43 I have had a dream past the wit of man to say what dream it was.
1595 Bottom. *A Midsummer Night's Dream*, act 4, sc.1, l.202–3.

44 Lovers and madmen have such seething brains,
Such shaping fantasies, that apprehend
More than cool reason ever comprehends.
1595 Theseus. *A Midsummer Night's Dream*, act 5, sc.1, l.4–6.

45 The lunatic, the lover, and the poet
Are of imagination all compact.
One sees more devils than vast hell can hold:
That is the madman. The lover, all as frantic,
Sees Helen's beauty in a brow of Egypt.
The poet's eye, in a fine frenzy rolling,
Doth glance from heaven to earth, from earth to heaven,
And as imagination bodies forth
The forms of things unknown, the poet's pen

Turns them to shapes, and gives to airy nothing
A local habitation and a name.
Such tricks hath strong imagination
That if it would but apprehend some joy
It comprehends some bringer of that joy;
Or in the night, imagining some fear,
How easy is a bush supposed a bear!
1595 Theseus. *A Midsummer Night's Dream*, act 5, sc.1, l.7–22.

46 [LYSANDER] (reads)
'A tedious 'brief' scene of young Pyramus
And his love Thisbe: very tragical mirth.'
THESEUS:
'Merry' *and* 'tragical'? 'Tedious' *and* 'brief'?—
That is, hot ice and wondrous strange black snow.
1595 *A Midsummer Night's Dream*, act 5, sc.1, l.56–9.

47 A play there is, my lord, some ten words long,
Which is as brief as I have known a play;
But by ten words, my lord, it is too long.
1595 [Egeus]. *A Midsummer Night's Dream*, act 5, sc.1, l.61–3.

48 Anon comes Pyramus, sweet youth and tall,
And finds his trusty Thisbe's mantle slain;
Whereat with blade—with bloody, blameful blade—
He bravely broached his boiling bloody breast;
And Thisbe, tarrying in mulberry shade,
His dagger drew and died.
1595 Quince's prologue to Pyramus and Thisbe. *A Midsummer Night's Dream*, act 5, sc.1, l.143–8.

49 O dainty duck, O dear!
Thy mantle good,
What, stained with blood?
Approach, ye furies fell.
O fates, come, come,
Cut the thread and thrum,
Quail, crush, conclude, and quell.
1595 Bottom (as Pyramus). *A Midsummer Night's Dream*, act 5, sc.1, l.276–82.

50 His eyes were green as leeks.
1595 Flute (as Thisbe). *A Midsummer Night's Dream*, act 5, sc.1, l.330.

51 If we shadows have offended,
Think but this, and all is mended:
That you have but slumbered here,
While these visions did appear.
1595 Robin Goodfellow. *A Midsummer Night's Dream*, act 5, sc.2, l.1–4.

52 By how much unexpected, by so much
We must awake endeavour for defence,
For courage mounteth with occasion.
1596 Duke of Austria. *King John*, act 2, sc.1, l.80–2.

53 Well, whiles I am a beggar I will rail,
And say there is no sin but to be rich,
And being rich, my virtue then shall be
To say there is no vice but beggary.
Since kings break faith upon commodity,
Gain, be my lord, for I will worship thee.
1596 Bastard. *King John*, act 2, sc.1, l.594–9.

54 I will instruct my sorrows to be proud,
For grief is proud and makes his owner stoop.
1596 Constance. *King John*, act 2, sc.2, l.68–9.

55 My grief's so great
That no supporter but the huge firm earth
Can hold it up. Here I and sorrows sit.
1596 Constance. *King John*, act 2, sc.2, l.71–3.

56 Bell, book, and candle shall not drive me back
When gold and silver becks me to come on.
1596 Bastard. *King John*, act 3, sc.3, l.12–13.

57 Grief fills the room up of my absent child,
Lies in his bed, walks up and down with me.
1596 Constance. *King John*, act 3, sc.4, l.93–4.

58 Life is as tedious as a twice-told tale
Vexing the dull ear of a drowsy man.
1596 Louis the Dauphin. *King John*, act 3, sc.4, l.108–9.

59 When Fortune means to men most good,
She looks upon them with a threat'ning eye.
1596 Pandolf. *King John*, act 3, sc.4, l.119–20.

60 He that stands upon a slipp'ry place
Makes nice of no vile hold to stay him up.
1596 Pandolf. *King John*, act 3, sc.4, l.137–8.

61 Strong reasons make strange actions.
1596 Louis the Dauphin. *King John*, act 3, sc.4, l.182.

62 To gild refinèd gold, to paint the lily,
To throw a perfume on the violet,
To smooth the ice, or add another hue
Unto the rainbow, or with taper-light
To seek the beauteous eye of heaven to garnish,
Is wasteful and ridiculous excess.
1596 Salisbury. *King John*, act 4, sc.2, l.11–16.

63 The rich advantage of good exercise?
1596 Pembroke. *King John*, act 4, sc.2, l.60.

64 Think you I bear the shears of destiny?
Have I commandment on the pulse of life?
1596 John. *King John*, act 4, sc.2, l.91–2.

65 Entreat the north
To make his bleak winds kiss my parchèd lips,
And comfort me with cold. I do not ask you much;
I beg cold comfort.
1596 John to Prince Henry. *King John*, act 5, sc.7, l.39–42.

66 This England never did, nor never shall,
Lie at the proud foot of a conqueror.
1596 Bastard. *King John*, act 5, sc.7, l.112–3.

67 Now, by two-headed Janus,
Nature hath framed strange fellows in her time:
Some that will evermore peep through their eyes
And laugh like parrots at a bagpiper.
1596–7 Solanio. *The Merchant of Venice*, act 1, sc.1, l.50–3.

68 I hold the world but as the world, Graziano;
A stage where every man must play a part,
And mine a sad one.
1596–7 Antonio. *The Merchant of Venice*, act 1, sc.1, l.77–9.

69 Let me play the fool.
With mirth and laughter let old wrinkles come.
1596–7 Graziano to Antonio. *The Merchant of Venice*, act 1, sc.1, l.79–80.

70 O my Antonio, I do know of these
That therefore only are reputed wise
For saying nothing.
1596–7 Graziano. *The Merchant of Venice*, act 1, sc.1, l.95–7.

71 Fish not with this melancholy bait
For this fool gudgeon, this opinion.
1596–7 Graziano. *The Merchant of Venice*, act 1, sc.1, l.101–2.

72 For silence is only commendable
    In a neat's tongue dried and a maid not vendible.
    1596–7 Graziano. *The Merchant of Venice*, act 1, sc.1, l.111–2.

73 Graziano speaks an infinite deal of nothing, more than any man in all Venice. His reasons are as two grains of wheat hid in two bushels of chaff: you shall seek all day ere you find them, and when you have them they are not worth the search.
    1596–7 Bassanio to Antonio. *The Merchant of Venice*, act 1, sc.1, l.114–18.

74 They are as sick that surfeit with too much as they that starve with nothing.
    1596–7 Nerissa. *The Merchant of Venice*, act 1, sc.2, l.5–6.

75 I can easier teach twenty what were good to be done than to be one of the twenty to follow mine own teaching.
    1596–7 Portia. *The Merchant of Venice*, act 1, sc.2, l.15–17.

76 The brain may devise laws for the blood, but a hot temper leaps o'er a cold decree.
    1596–7 Portia. *The Merchant of Venice*, act 1, sc.2, l.17–18.

77 He doth nothing but talk of his horse.
    1596–7 Portia. *The Merchant of Venice*, act 1, sc.2, l.39–40.

78 I fear he will prove the weeping philosopher when he grows old, being so full of unmannerly sadness in his youth.
    1596–7 Portia, of her suitor the County Palatine. *The Merchant of Venice*, act 1, sc.2, l.47–9.

79 God made him, and therefore let him pass for a man.
    1596–7 Portia, of her suitor M. le Bon. *The Merchant of Venice*, act 1, sc.2, l.54–5.

80 I will do anything, Nerissa, ere I will be married to a sponge.
    1596–7 Portia. *The Merchant of Venice*, act 1, sc.2, l.95–6.

81 There is not one among them but I dote on his very absence, and I pray God grant them a fair departure.
    1596–7 Portia, of the suitors. *The Merchant of Venice*, act 1, sc.2, l.106–8.

82 Yes, to smell pork, to eat of the habitation which your prophet the Nazarite conjured the devil into! I will buy with you, sell with you, talk with you, walk with you, and so following, but I will not eat with you, drink with you, nor pray with you.
    1596–7 Shylock, invited to dine with Bassanio. *The Merchant of Venice*, act 1, sc.3, l.31–5.

83 How like a fawning publican he looks.
    I hate him for he is a Christian.
    1596–7 Shylock, of Antonio. *The Merchant of Venice*, act 1, sc.3, l.39–40.

84 The devil can cite Scripture for his purpose.
    An evil soul producing holy witness
    Is like a villain with a smiling cheek,
    A goodly apple rotten at the heart.
    O, what a goodly outside falsehood hath!
    1596–7 Antonio. *The Merchant of Venice*, act 1, sc.3, l.97–101.

85 Signor Antonio, many a time and oft
    In the Rialto you have rated me
    About my moneys and my usances.
    Still have I borne it with a patient shrug,
    For suff'rance is the badge of all our tribe.
    1596–7 Shylock. *The Merchant of Venice*, act 1, sc.3, l.105–109.

86 If thou wilt lend this money, lend it not
    As to thy friends; for when did friendship take
    A breed for barren metal of his friend?
    1596–7 Antonio to Shylock. *The Merchant of Venice*, act 1, sc.3, l.130–3.

87 I like not fair terms and a villain's mind.
    1596–7 Bassanio. *The Merchant of Venice*, act 1, sc.3, l.178.

88 It is a wise father that knows his own child.
    1596–7 Lancelot. *The Merchant of Venice*, act 2, sc.2, l.72–3.

89 I'll take my leave of the Jew in the twinkling.
    1596–7 Lancelot to Gobbo. *The Merchant of Venice*, act 2, sc.2, l.161–2.

90 Alack, what heinous sin is it in me
    To be ashamed to be my father's child!
    But though I am a daughter to his blood,
    I am not to his manners.
    1596–7 Jessica. *The Merchant of Venice*, act 2, sc.3, l.16–19.

91 Then it was not for nothing that my nose fell a-bleeding on Black Monday.
    1596–7 Lancelot. *The Merchant of Venice*, act 2, sc.5, l.23–5.

92 There is some ill a-brewing towards my rest,
    For I did dream of money-bags tonight.
    1596–7 Shylock. *The Merchant of Venice*, act 2, sc.5, l.17–18.

93 But love is blind, and lovers cannot see
    The pretty follies that themselves commit.
    1596–7 Jessica. *The Merchant of Venice*, act 2, sc.6, l.36.

94 I will not choose what many men desire,
    Because I will not jump with common spirits
    And rank me with the barbarous multitudes.
    1596–7 Aragon. *The Merchant of Venice*, act 2, sc.9, l.30–2.

95 O, that estates, degrees, and offices
    Were not derived corruptly, and that clear honour
    Were purchased by the merit of the wearer!
    1596–7 Aragon. *The Merchant of Venice*, act 2, sc.9, l.40–2.

96 The ancient saying is no heresy;
    Hanging and wiving goes by destiny.
    1596–7 Nerissa. *The Merchant of Venice*, act 2, sc.9, l.81–2.

97 A day in April never came so sweet,
    To show how costly summer was at hand.
    1596–7 Messenger, of Bassanio's arrival. *The Merchant of Venice*, act 2, sc.9, l.92.

98 The bird was fledged; and then it is the complexion of them all to leave the dam.
    1596–7 Solanio, of Jessica. *The Merchant of Venice*, act 3, sc.1, l.27.

99 Let him look to his bond.
    1596–7 Shylock, of Antonio. *The Merchant of Venice*, act 3, sc.1, l.45–6.

1   Hath not a Jew eyes? Hath not a Jew hands, organs, dimensions, senses, affections, passions; fed with the same food, hurt with the same weapons, subject to the same diseases, healed by the same means, warmed and cooled by the same winter and summer as a Christian is? If you prick us do we not bleed? If you tickle us do we not laugh? If you poison us do we not die? And if you wrong us shall we not revenge? If we are like you in the rest, we will resemble you in that.
    1596–7 Shylock. *The Merchant of Venice*, act 3, sc.1, l.54–63.

2   Let music sound while he doth make his choice.
    Then if he lose he makes a swanlike end,
    Fading in music.
    1596–7 Portia to Bassanio. *The Merchant of Venice*, act 3, sc.2, l.43–5.

3 There is no vice so simple but assumes
Some mark of virtue on his outward parts.
1596-7 Bassiano, aside. *The Merchant of Venice*, act 3, sc.2, l.81–2.

4 Look on beauty
And you shall see 'tis purchased by the weight,
Which therein works a miracle in nature,
Making them lightest that wear most of it.
1596-7 Bassanio, aside. *The Merchant of Venice*, act 3, sc.2, l.88–91.

5 Thou gaudy gold,
Hard food for Midas, I will none of thee.
1596-7 Bassiano, aloud. *The Merchant of Venice*, act 3, sc.2, l.101–2.

6 An unlessoned girl, unschooled, unpractisèd,
Happy in this, she is not yet so old
But she may learn.
1596-7 Portia, of herself. *The Merchant of Venice*, act 3, sc.2, l.159–61.

7 Madam, you have bereft me of all words.
Only my blood speaks to you in my veins.
1596-7 Bassanio to Portia. *The Merchant of Venice*, act 3, sc.2, l.175–6.

8 Here are a few of the unpleasant'st words
That ever blotted paper.
1596-7 Bassanio, reading of Antonio's misfortunes. *The Merchant of Venice*, act 3, sc.2, l.249–50.

9 Let it serve for table-talk.
Then, howsome'er thou speak'st, 'mong other things
I shall digest it.
1596-7 Lorenzo. *The Merchant of Venice*, act 3, sc.5, l.83–5.

10 Some men there are love not a gaping pig,
Some that are mad if they behold a cat,
And others when the bagpipe sings i'th' nose
Cannot contain their urine.
1596-7 Shylock. *The Merchant of Venice*, act 4, sc.1, l.46–49.

11 We turned o'er many books together.
1596-7 Bellario's letter of recommendation for Portia (as Balthasar). *The Merchant of Venice*, act 4, sc.1, l.154–5.

12 The quality of mercy is not strained.
It droppeth as the gentle rain from heaven
Upon the place beneath. It is twice blest:
It blesseth him that gives, and him that takes.
1596-7 Portia. *The Merchant of Venice*, act 4, sc.1, l.181–4.

13 It is enthronèd in the hearts of kings;
It is an attribute to God himself,
And earthly power doth then show likest God's
When mercy seasons justice.
1596-7 Portia. *The Merchant of Venice*, act 4, sc.1, l.190–4.

14 A Daniel come to judgement, yea, a Daniel!
O wise young judge, how I do honour thee!
1596-7 Shylock, of the disguised Portia. *The Merchant of Venice*, act 4, sc.1, l.220–1.

15 Antonio, I am married to a wife
Which is as dear to me as life itself,
But life itself, my wife, and all the world
Are not with me esteemed above thy life.
I would lose all, ay, sacrifice them all
Here to this devil, to deliver you.
1596-7 Bassanio. *The Merchant of Venice*, act 4, sc.1, l.279–84.

16 Take thou thy pound of flesh.
1596-7 Portia to Shylock. *The Merchant of Venice*, act 4, sc.1, l.305.

17 Nay, take my life and all, pardon not that.
You take my house when you do take the prop
That doth sustain my house; you take my life
When do you take the means whereby I live.
1596-7 Shylock to the Duke. *The Merchant of Venice*, act 4, sc.1, l.371–4.

18 How sweet the moonlight sleeps upon this bank!
Here will we sit, and let the sounds of music
Creep in our ears.
1596-7 Lorenzo to Jessica. *The Merchant of Venice*, act 5, sc.1, l.54–6.

19 Look how the floor of heaven
Is thick inlaid with patens of bright gold.
There's not the smallest orb which thou behold'st
But in his motion like an angel sings.
1596-7 Lorenzo to Jessica. *The Merchant of Venice*, act 5, sc.1, l.58–61.

20 I am never merry when I hear sweet music.
1596-7 Jessica. *The Merchant of Venice*, act 5, sc.1, l.69.

21 The man that hath no music in himself,
Nor is not moved with concord of sweet sounds,
Is fit for treasons, stratagems, and spoils.
1596-7 Lorenzo. *The Merchant of Venice*, act 5, sc.1, l.83–5.

22 How far that little candle throws his beams—
So shines a good deed in a naughty world.
1596-7 Portia. *The Merchant of Venice*, act 5, sc.1, l.90–1.

23 A substitute shines brightly as a king
Until a king be by.
1596-7 Portia. *The Merchant of Venice*, act 5, sc.1, l.94–5.

24 The crow doth sing as sweetly as the lark
When neither is attended.
1596-7 Portia. *The Merchant of Venice*, act 5, sc.1, l.102–3.

25 A light wife doth make a heavy husband.
1596-7 Portia. *The Merchant of Venice*, act 5, sc.1, l.130.

26 O, that it could be proved
That some night-tripping fairy had exchanged
In cradle clothes our children where they lay.
1596-7 King Henry of his son, Harry, and Northumberland's son, Hotspur. *Henry IV Part One*, act 1, sc.1, l.85–7.

27 What a devil hast thou to do with the time of the day? Unless hours were cups of sack, and minutes capons, and clocks the tongues of bawds, and dials the signs of leaping-houses, and the blessed sun himself a fair hot wench in flame-coloured taffeta, I see no reason why thou shouldst be so superfluous to demand the time of the day.
1596-7 Prince Harry to Falstaff. *Henry IV Part One*, act 1, sc.2, l.6–12.

28 How now, how now, mad wag? What, in thy quips and thy quiddities? What a plague have I to do with a buff jerkin?
1596-7 Falstaff to Prince Harry. *Henry IV Part One*, act 1, sc.2, l.44–6.

29 I would to God thou and I knew where a commodity of good names were to be bought.
1596-7 Falstaff. *Henry IV Part One*, act 1, sc.2, l.82–3.

30 'Tis my vocation, Hal. 'Tis no sin for a man to labour in his vocation.
1596-7 Falstaff, of stealing. *Henry IV Part One*, act 1, sc.2, l.104–5.

31 What says Monsieur Remorse? What says Sir John, sack-and-sugar Jack? How agrees the devil and thee about thy

soul, that thou soldest him on Good Friday last, for a cup of Madeira and a cold capon's leg?
1596–7 Poins to Falstaff. *Henry IV Part One*, act 1, sc.2, l.111–15.

32 He was never yet a breaker of proverbs: he will give the devil his due.
1596–7 Prince Harry. *Henry IV Part One*, act 1, sc.2, l.117–8.

33 He made me mad
To see him shine so brisk, and smell so sweet,
And talk so like a waiting gentlewoman
Of guns, and drums, and wounds, God save the mark!
And telling me the soverign'st thing on earth
Was parmacity for an inward bruise,
And that it was great pity, so it was,
This villainous saltpetre should be digged
Out of the bowels of the harmless earth,
Which many a good tall fellow had destroyed
So cowardly, and but for these vile guns
He would himself have been a soldier.
1596–7 Hotspur. *Henry IV Part One*, act 1, sc.3, l.52–63.

34 To put down Richard, that sweet lovely rose,
And plant this thorn, this canker, Bolingbroke?
1596–7 Hotspur. *Henry IV Part One*, act 1, sc.3, l.173–4.

35 If he fall in, good night, or sink or swim.
1596–7 Hotspur. *Henry IV Part One*, act 1, sc.3, l.192.

36 —O, the blood more stirs
To rouse a lion than to start a hare!
1596–7 Hotspur. *Henry IV Part One*, act 1, sc.3, l.195–6.

37 By heaven, methinks it were an easy leap
To pluck bright honour from the pale-faced moon,
Or dive into the bottom of the deep,
Where fathom-line could never touch the ground,
And pluck up drownèd honour by the locks.
1596–7 Hotspur. *Henry IV Part One*, act 1, sc.3, l.199–203.

38 I am joined with no foot-landrakers, no longstaff sixpenny strikers, none of these mad mustachio purple-hued maltworms, but with nobility and tranquillity, burgomasters and great 'oyez'-ers; such as can hold in, such as will strike sooner than speak, and speak sooner than drink, and drink sooner than pray.
1596–7 Gadshill. *Henry IV Part One*, act 2, sc.1, l.73–8.

39 I am bewitched with the rogue's company. If the rascal have not given me medicines to make me love him, I'll be hanged.
1596–7 Falstaff, of Prince Harry. *Henry IV Part One*, act 2, sc.2, l.17–20.

40 A plague upon't when thieves cannot be true one to another.
1596–7 Falstaff. *Henry IV Part One*, act 2, sc.2, l.27–8.

41 Hang thyself in thine own heir-apparent garters!
1596–7 Falstaff to Prince Harry. *Henry IV Part One*, act 2, sc.2, l.43.

42 Out of this nettle danger we pluck this flower safety.
1596–7 Hotspur. *Henry IV Part One*, act 2, sc.4, l.9–10.

43 Constant you are,
But yet a woman; and for secrecy
No lady closer, for I well believe
Thou wilt not utter what thou dost not know.
1596–7 Hotspur to Kate. *Henry IV Part One*, act 2, sc.4, l.105–8.

44 I am not yet of Percy's mind, the Hotspur of the North —he that kills me some six or seven dozen of Scots at a breakfast, washes his hands, and says to his wife, 'Fie upon this quiet life! I want work.'
1596–7 Prince Harry. *Henry IV Part One*, act 2, sc.5, l.102–6.

45 There lives not three good men unhanged in England, and one of them is fat and grows old.
1596–7 Falstaff, of himself. *Henry IV Part One*, act 2, sc.5, l.130–1.

46 Give you a reason on compulsion? If reasons were as plentiful as blackberries, I would give no man a reason upon compulsion.
1596–7 Falstaff. *Henry IV Part One*, act 2, sc.5, l.242–4.

47 PRINCE HARRY: This sanguine coward, this bed-presser, this horse-backbreaker, this huge hill of flesh—
SIR JOHN: 'Sblood, you starveling, you elf-skin, you dried neat's tongue, you bull's pizzle, you stock-fish—O, for breath to utter what is like thee!—you tailor's yard, you sheath, you bow-case, you vile standing tuck.
1596–7 *Henry IV Part One*, act 2, sc.5, l.245–52.

48 SIR JOHN: Sweet Jack Oldcastle, kind Jack Oldcastle, true Jack Oldcastle, valiant Jack Oldcastle, and therefore more valiant being, as he is, old Jack Oldcastle
Banish not him thy Harry's company,
Banish not him thy Harry's company.
Banish plump Jack, and banish all the world.
PRINCE HARRY: I do; I will.
1596–7 Falstaff. *Henry IV Part One*, act 2, sc.5, l.480–6.

49 I can teach thee, coz, to shame the devil,
By telling truth: 'Tell truth, and shame the devil'.
1596–7 Hotspur to Glyndwr. *Henry IV Part One*, act 3, sc.1, l.55–6.

50 Mincing poetry.
'Tis like the forced gait of a shuffling nag.
1596–7 Hotspur. *Henry IV Part One*, act 3, sc.1, l.130–1.

51 I understand thy kisses, and thou mine,
And that's a feeling disputation.
1596–7 Mortimer to his wife. *Henry IV Part One*, act 3, sc.1, l.200–1.

52 Now I perceive the devil understands Welsh;
And 'tis no marvel, he is so humorous.
1596–7 Hotspur. *Henry IV Part One*, act 3, sc.1, l.226–7.

53 Swear me, Kate, like a lady as thou art,
A good mouth-filling oath.
1596–7 Hotspur. *Henry IV Part One*, act 3, sc.1, l.249–50.

54 Do thou amend thy face, and I'll amend my life.
1596–7 Falstaff to Bardolph. *Henry IV Part One*, act 3, sc.3, l.23.

55 Thou knowest in the state of innocency Adam fell, and what should poor Jack Oldcastle do in the days of villainy? Thou seest I have more flesh than another man, and therefore more frailty.
1596–7 Falstaff. *Henry IV Part One*, act 3, sc.3, l.165–7.

56 I am as vigilant as a cat to steal cream.
1596–7 Falstaff. *Henry IV Part One*, act 4, sc.2, l.58–9.

57 Rebellion lay in his way, and he found it.
1596–7 Falstaff, of Worcester. *Henry IV Part One*, act 5, sc.1, l.28.

58 I would 'twere bed-time, Hal, and all well.
1596–7 Falstaff. *Henry IV Part One*, act 5, sc.1, l.125.

59 Honour pricks me on. Yea, but how if honour prick me off when I come on? How then?
1596–7 Falstaff. *Henry IV Part One*, act 5, sc.1, l.129–131.

60 What is honour? A word.
1596–7 Flastaff. *Henry IV Part One*, act 5, sc.1, l.133–4.

61 Who hath it [honour]? He that died o' Wednesday.
1596–7 Falstaff. *Henry IV Part One*, act 5, sc.1, l.135–6.

Shakespeare 1 Henry IV

62 Treason is but trusted like the fox,
    Who, ne'er so tame, so cherished and locked up,
    Will have a wild trick of his ancestors.
    1596-7 Worcester. *Henry IV Part One*, act 5, sc.2, l.9-11.

63 O gentlemen, the time of life is short.
    To spend that shortness basely were too long
    If life did ride upon a dial's point,
    Still ending at the arrival of an hour.
    1596-7 Hotspur. *Henry IV Part One*, act 5, sc.2, l.81-4.

64 Sound all the lofty instruments of war,
    And by that music let us all embrace,
    For, heaven to earth, some of us never shall
    A second time do such a courtesy.
    1596-7 Hotspur. *Henry IV Part One*, act 5, sc.2, l.97-100.

65 I am as hot as molten lead, and as heavy too.
    1596-7 Falstaff. *Henry IV Part One*, act 5, sc.3, l.33-4.

66 Time, that takes survey of all the world,
    Must have a stop.
    1596-7 Hotspur. *Henry IV Part One*, act 5, sc.4, l.81-2.

67 Fare thee well, great heart.
    Ill-weaved ambition, how much art thou shrunk!
    When that this body did contain a spirit,
    A kingdom for it was too small a bound,
    But now two paces of the vilest earth
    Is room enough.
    1596-7 Prince Harry, of Hotspur. *Henry IV Part One*, act 5, sc.4, l.86-91.

68 The better part of valour is discretion, in the which better part I have saved my life.
    1596-7 Falstaff. *Henry IV Part One*, act 5, sc.4, l.118-20.

69 In poison there is physic; and these news,
    Having been well, that would have made me sick,
    Being sick, have in some measure made me well.
    1597-8 Northumberland. *Henry IV Part Two*, act 1, sc.1, l.137-9.

70 I am not only witty in myself, but the cause that wit is in other men.
    1597-8 Falstaff. *Henry IV Part Two*, act 1, sc.2, l.9-10.

71 Your lordship, though not clean past your youth, hath yet some smack of age in you, some relish of the saltness of time.
    1597-8 Falstaff, of the Lord Justice. *Henry IV Part Two*, act 1, sc.2, l.98-9.

72 I am as poor as Job, my lord, but not so patient.
    1597-8 Falstaff. *Henry IV Part Two*, act 1, sc.2, l.128.

73 If it be a hot day and I brandish anything but my bottle, would I might never spit white again.
    1597-8 Falstaff. *Henry IV Part Two*, act 1, sc.2, l.211-13.

74 It was alway yet the trick of our English nation, if they have a good thing, to make it too common.
    1597-8 Falstaff. *Henry IV Part Two*, act 1, sc.2, l.215-17.

75 I can get no remedy against this consumption of the purse. Borrowing only lingers and lingers it out, but the disease is incurable.
    1597-8 Falstaff. *Henry IV Part Two*, act 1, sc.2, l.237-9.

76 [He] lined himself with hope,
    Eating the air on promise of supply.
    1597-8 Lord Bardolph, of Hotspur. *Henry IV Part Two*, act 1, sc.3, l.27-8.

77 Away, you scullion, you rampallion, you fustilarian! I'll tickle your catastrophe!
    1597-8 Page to Mistress Quickly. *Henry IV Part Two*, act 2, sc.1, l.61-2.

78 He hath eaten me out of house and home.
    1597-8 Mistress Quickly, of Falstaff. *Henry IV Part Two*, act 2, sc.1, l.75-6.

79 Thus we play the fools with the time, and the spirits of the wise sit in the clouds and mock us.
    1597-8 Prince Harry. *Henry IV Part Two*, act 2, sc.2, l.133-5.

80 He was indeed the glass
    Wherein the noble youth did dress themselves.
    1597-8 Lady Percy, of Hotspur. *Henry IV Part Two*, act 2, sc.3, l.21-2.

81 Shall pack-horses
    And hollow pampered jades of Asia,
    Which cannot go but thirty mile a day,
    Compare with Caesars and with cannibals,
    And Trojan Greeks?
    Nay, rather damn them with King Cerberus,
    And let the welkin roar.
    1597-8 Pistol. *Henry IV Part Two*, act 2, sc.4, l.160-6.

82 Thou whoreson little tidy Bartholomew boar-pig, when wilt thou leave fighting o'days, and foining o'nights, and begin to patch up thine old body for heaven?
    1597-8 Doll Tearsheet, of Falstaff. *Henry IV Part Two*, act 2, sc.4, l.232-5.

83 Is it not strange that desire should so many years outlive performance?
    1597-8 Poins. *Henry IV Part Two*, act 2, sc.4, l.262-3.

84 O sleep, O gentle sleep,
    Nature's soft nurse, how have I frighted thee,
    That thou no more wilt weigh my eyelids down.
    1597-8 King Henry. *Henry IV Part Two*, act 3, sc.1, l.5-7.

85 Canst thou, O partial sleep, give thy repose
    To the wet sea-boy in an hour so rude,
    And in the calmest and most stillest night,
    With all appliances and means to boot,
    Deny it to a king? Then happy low, lie down.
    Uneasy lies the head that wears a crown.
    1597-8 King Henry. *Henry IV Part Two*, act 3, sc.1, l.25-31.

86 Death, as the Psalmist saith, is certain to all: all shall die.
    How a good yoke of bullocks at Stamford fair?
    1597-8 Shallow. *Henry IV Part Two*, act 3, sc.2, l.35-6.

87 We have heard the chimes at midnight, Master Shallow.
    1597-8 Falstaff. *Henry IV Part Two*, act 3, sc.2, l.211.

88 A man can die but once. We owe God a death.
    1597-8 Feeble. *Henry IV Part Two*, act 3, sc.2, l.233-4.

89 Lord, Lord, how subject we old men are to this vice of lying!
    1597-8 Falstaff. *Henry IV Part Two*, act 3, sc.2, l.298-9.

90 When a was naked, he was for all the world like a forked radish, with a head fantastically carved upon it with a knife.
    1597-8 Falstaff, of Shallow. *Henry IV Part Two*, act 3, sc.2, l.305-7.

91 An iron man,
    Cheering a rout of rebels with your drum,
    Turning the word to sword, and life to death.
    1597-8 Prince John. *Henry IV Part Two*, act 4, sc.1, l.234-6.

92 Sudden sorrow
    Serves to say thus: some good thing comes tomorrow.
    1597-8 Westmorland. *Henry IV Part Two*, act 4, sc.1, l.309-10.

93 A peace is of the nature of a conquest,
For then both parties nobly are subdued,
And neither party loser.
1597–8 Archbishop of York. *Henry IV Part Two*, act 4, sc.1, l.315–17.

94 He saw me, and yielded, that I may justly say, with the hook-nosed fellow of Rome, 'I came, saw, and overcame'.
1597–8 Falstaff. *Henry IV Part Two*, act 4, sc.2, l.39–41.

95 A man cannot make him laugh. But that's no marvel; he drinks no wine.
1597–8 Falstaff. *Henry IV Part Two*, act 4, sc.2, l.85–6.

96 Will fortune never come with both hands full,
But write her fair words still in foulest letters?
1597–8 Henry, receiving good news when ill. *Henry IV Part Two*, act 4, sc.3, l.103–4.

97 How quickly nature falls into revolt
When gold becomes her object!
1597–8 King Henry, of his son Harry. *Henry IV Part Two*, act 4, sc.3, l.195–6.

98 Revel the night, rob, murder, and commit
The oldest sins the newest kind of ways?
1597–8 King Henry to Harry. *Henry IV Part Two*, act 4, sc.3, l.254–5.

99 I know thee not, old man. Fall to thy prayers.
How ill white hairs becomes a fool and jester!
1597–8 The newly-crowned King Harry, rejecting Falstaff. *Henry IV Part Two*, act 5, sc.5, l.47–8.

1 Here will be an old abusing of God's patience and the King's English.
1597–8 Mistress Quickly. *The Merry Wives of Windsor*, act 1, sc.4, l.4–5.

2 His worst fault is that he is given to prayer; he is something peevish that way.
1597–8 Mistress Quickly. *The Merry Wives of Windsor*, act 1, sc.4, l.11–12.

3 Why, then the world's mine oyster, which I with sword will open.
1597–8 Pistol. *The Merry Wives of Windsor*, act 2, sc.2, l.4–5.

4 Thinkst thou I'll endanger my soul gratis?
1597–8 Falstaff. *The Merry Wives of Windsor*, act 2, sc.2, l.16–17.

5 If money go before, all ways do lie open.
1597–8 Ford (as Brooke). *The Merry Wives of Windsor*, act 2, sc.2, l.164–5.

6 Money is a good soldier, sir, and will go on.
1597–8 Falstaff. *The Merry Wives of Windsor*, act 2, sc.2, l.166.

7 There is money. Spend it, spend it; spend more.
1597–8 Ford (as Brooke). *The Merry Wives of Windsor*, act 2, sc.2, l.223–4.

8 I cannot tell what the dickens his name is.
1597–8 Mistress Page. *The Merry Wives of Windsor*, act 3, sc.2, l.16.

9 He capers, he dances, he has eyes of youth; he writes verses, he speaks holiday, he smells April and May. He will carry't, he will carry't; 'tis in his buttons he will carry't.
1597–8 Host, of Master Fenton. *The Merry Wives of Windsor*, act 3, sc.2, l.61–4.

10 O, what a world of vile ill-favoured faults
Looks handsome in three hundred pounds a year!
1597–8 Anne. *The Merry Wives of Windsor*, act 3, sc.4, l.31–2.

11 A woman would run through fire and water for such a kind heart.
1597–8 Mistress Quickly. *The Merry Wives of Windsor*, act 3, sc.4, l.101–2.

12 Have I lived to be carried in a basket like a barrow of butcher's offal, and to be thrown in the Thames? Well, if I be served such another trick, I'll have my brains ta'en out and buttered, and give them to a dog for a New Year's gift. 'Sblood, the rogues slighted me into the river with as little remorse as they would have drowned a blind bitch's puppies, fifteen i'th' litter! And you may know by my size that I have a kind of alacrity in sinking.
1597–8 Falstaff. *The Merry Wives of Windsor*, act 3, sc.5, l.4–12.

13 They say there is divinity in odd numbers, either in nativity, chance, or death.
1597–8 Falstaff. *The Merry Wives of Windsor*, act 5, sc.1, l.3–4.

14 Let the sky rain potatoes, let it thunder to the tune of 'Greensleeves'.
1597–8 Falstaff. *The Merry Wives of Windsor*, act 5, sc.5, l.17–18.

15 A victory is twice itself when the achiever brings home full numbers.
1598 Leonato. *Much Ado About Nothing*, act 1, sc.1, l.8–9.

16 How much better is it to weep at joy than to joy at weeping!
1598 Leonato. *Much Ado About Nothing*, act 1, sc.1, l.27–8.

17 He wears his faith but as the fashion of his hat, it ever changes with the next block.
1598 Beatrice, of Benedick. *Much Ado About Nothing*, act 1, sc.1, l.71–3.

18 He is sooner caught than the pestilence.
1598 Beatrice, of Claudio. *Much Ado About Nothing*, act 1, sc.1, l.82.

19 I wonder that you will still be talking, Signor Benedick. Nobody marks you.
1598 Beatrice. *Much Ado About Nothing*, act 1, sc.1, l.110–11.

20 What, my dear Lady Disdain! Are you yet living?
1598 Benedick to Beatrice. *Much Ado About Nothing*, act 1, sc.1, l.112–13.

21 I had rather hear my dog bark at a crow than a man swear he loves me.
1598 Beatrice. *Much Ado About Nothing*, act 1, sc.1, l.125–6.

22 Were she other than she is she were unhandsome, and being no other but as she is, I do not like her.
1598 Benedick, of Hero. *Much Ado About Nothing*, act 1, sc.1, l.166–7.

23 If he send me no husband, for the which blessing I am at him upon my knees every morning and evening. Lord, I could not endure a husband with a beard on his face. I had rather lie in the woollen.
1598 Beatrice. *Much Ado About Nothing*, act 2, sc.1, l.24–7.

24 He shows me where the bachelors sit, and there live we as merry as the day is long.
1598 Beatrice, of St Peter. *Much Ado About Nothing*, act 2, sc.1, l.42–4.

25 I have a good eye, uncle. I can see a church by daylight.
1598 Beatrice to Leonato. *Much Ado About Nothing*, act 2, sc.1, l.74–5.

26 Beauty is a witch
Against whose charms faith melteth into blood.
1598 Claudio. *Much Ado About Nothing*, act 2, sc.1, l.169–70.

27 She speaks poniards, and every word stabs. If her breath were as terrible as her terminations, there were no living near her, she would infect to the North Star.
1598 Benedick, of Beatrice. *Much Ado About Nothing*, act 2, sc.1, l.231–4.

28 Will your grace command me any service to the world's end? I will go on the slightest errand now to the Antipodes that you can devise to send me on. I will fetch you a tooth-picker now from the furthest inch of Asia, bring you the length of Prester John's foot, fetch you a hair off the Great Cham's beard, do you any embassage to the pigmies, rather than hold three words' conference with this harpy.
1598 Benedick, of Beatrice. *Much Ado About Nothing*, act 2, sc.1, l.246–53.

29 O God, sir, here's a dish I love not. I cannot endure my Lady Tongue.
1598 Benedick, of Beatrice. *Much Ado About Nothing*, act 2, sc.1, l.256–7.

30 Silence is the perfectest herald of joy. I were but little happy if I could say how much.
1598 Claudio. *Much Ado About Nothing*, act 2, sc.1, l.287–8.

31 Your silence most offends me, and to be merry best becomes you; for out o' question, you were born in a merry hour.
1598 Don Pedro to Beatrice. *Much Ado About Nothing*, act 2, sc.1, l.310–12.

32 But then there was a star danced, and under that was I born.
1598 Beatrice. *Much Ado About Nothing*, act 2, sc.1, l.313–14.

33 There's little of the melancholy element in her, my lord. She is never sad but when she sleeps, and not ever sad then; for I have heard my daughter say she hath often dreamt of unhappiness and waked herself with laughing.
1598 Leonato, of Beatrice. *Much Ado About Nothing*, act 2, sc.1, l.321–5.

34 If they were but a week married they would talk themselves mad.
1598 Leonato, of Beatrice and Benedick. *Much Ado About Nothing*, act 2, sc.1, l.330–1.

35 Time goes on crutches till love have all his rites.
1598 Claudio. *Much Ado About Nothing*, act 2, sc.1, l.334–5.

36 He was wont to speak plain and to the purpose, like an honest man and a soldier, and now is he turned orthography. His words are a very fantastical banquet, just so many strange dishes.
1598 Benedick, of Claudio. *Much Ado About Nothing*, act 2, sc.3, l.18–21.

37 Is it not strange that sheep's guts should hale souls out of men's bodies?
1598 Benedick. *Much Ado About Nothing*, act 2, sc.3, l.57–9.

38 Sigh no more, ladies, sigh no more.
Men were deceivers ever,
One foot in sea, and one on shore,
To one thing constant never.
1598 Balthasar's song. *Much Ado About Nothing*, act 2, sc.3, l.61–4.

39 He doth indeed show some sparks that are like wit.
1598 Don Pedro, of Benedick. *Much Ado About Nothing*, act 2, sc.3, l.178–9.

40 I will be horribly in love with her.
1598 Benedick, of Beatrice, having been tricked into thinking she secretly loves him. *Much Ado About Nothing*, act 2, sc.3, l.222–3.

41 Look where Beatrice like a lapwing runs
Close by the ground to hear our conference.
1598 Hero to Ursula. *Much Ado About Nothing*, act 3, sc.1, l.24–5.

42 From the crown of his head to the sole of his foot he is all mirth.
1598 Don Pedro, of Benedick. *Much Ado About Nothing*, act 3, sc.2, l.7–9.

43 He hath twice or thrice cut Cupid's bow-string, and the little hangman dare not shoot at him. He hath a heart as sound as a bell, and his tongue is the clapper, for what his heart thinks his tongue speaks.
1598 Don Pedro, of Benedick. *Much Ado About Nothing*, act 3, sc.2, l.9–13.

44 Everyone can master a grief but he that has it.
1598 Benedick. *Much Ado About Nothing*, act 3, sc.2, l.26–7.

45 The barber's man hath been seen with him, and the old ornament of his cheek hath already stuffed tennis balls.
1598 Claudio, of Benedick. *Much Ado About Nothing*, act 3, sc.2, l.41–3.

46 Seest thou not, I say, what a deformed thief this fashion is, how giddily a turns about all the hot-bloods between fourteen and five-and-thirty…?
1598 Borachio to Conrad. *Much Ado About Nothing*, act 3, sc.3, l.126–9.

47 The fashion wears out more apparel than the man.
1598 Conrad to Borachio. *Much Ado About Nothing*, act 3, sc.3, l.134–5.

48 Comparisons are odorous.
1598 Dogberry to Verges. *Much Ado About Nothing*, act 3, sc.5, l.15.

49 As they say, when the age is in, the wit is out.
1598 Dogberry. *Much Ado About Nothing*, act 3, sc.5, l.32–3.

50 Well, God's a good man. An two men ride of a horse, one must ride behind.
1598 Dogberry to Verges. *Much Ado About Nothing*, act 3, sc.5, l.35–6.

51 O, what authority and show of truth
Can cunning sin cover itself withal!
1598 Claudio, of Hero. *Much Ado About Nothing*, act 4, sc.1, l.35–6.

52 'Tis all men's office to speak patience
To those that wring under the load of sorrow.
1598 Leonato. *Much Ado About Nothing*, act 5, sc.1, l.27–8.

53 There was never yet philosopher
That could endure the toothache patiently.
1598 Leonato. *Much Ado About Nothing*, act 5, sc.1, l.35–6.

54 Though care killed a cat, thou hast mettle enough in thee to kill care.
1598 Claudio, of Benedick. *Much Ado About Nothing*, act 5, sc.1, l.133–4.

55 Marry, sir, they have committed false report, moreover they have spoken untruths, secondarily they are slanders, sixth and lastly they have belied a lady, thirdly they have verified unjust things, and to conclude, they are lying knaves!
1598 Dogberry to Don Pedro. *Much Ado About Nothing*, act 5, sc.1, l.208–12.

56 I can find out no rhyme to 'lady' but 'baby', an innocent rhyme; for 'scorn' 'horn', a hard rhyme; for 'school' 'fool', a babbling rhyme. Very ominous endings. No, I was not born under a rhyming planet, nor I cannot woo in festival terms.
1598 Benedick. *Much Ado About Nothing*, act 5, sc.2, l.35–9.

57 If a man do not erect in this age his own tomb ere he dies, he shall live no longer in monument than the bell rings and the widow weeps.
1598 Benedick. *Much Ado About Nothing*, act 5, sc.2, l.69–72.

58 Good morrow, Benedick. Why, what's the matter
That you have such a February face,
So full of frost, of storm and cloudiness?
1598 Don Pedro. *Much Ado About Nothing*, act 5, sc.4, l.40–2.

59 Let's have a dance ere we are married, that we may
lighten our own hearts and our wives' heels.
1598 Benedick. *Much Ado About Nothing*, act 5, sc.4, l.116–18.

60 Prince, thou art sad, get thee a wife, get thee
a wife.
1598 Benedick to Don Pedro. *Much Ado About Nothing*, act 5, sc.4, l.121–2.

61 O for a muse of fire, that would ascend
The brightest heaven of invention.
1598–9 Chorus. *Henry V*, prologue to act 1, l.1–2.

62 When we have matched our rackets to these balls,
We will in France, by God's grace, play a set
Shall strike his father's crown into the hazard.
1598–9 King Harry, on the gift of tennis balls from the Dauphin. *Henry V*, act 1, sc.2, l.261–3.

63 'Tis ever common
That men are merriest when they are from home.
1598–9 King Harry. *Henry V*, act 1, sc.2, l.271–2.

64 Now all the youth of England are on fire,
And silken dalliance in the wardrobe lies.
1598–9 Chorus. *Henry V*, prologue to act 2, l.1–2.

65 O England! model to thy inward greatness,
Like little body with a mighty heart,
What might'st thou do, that honour would thee do,
Were all thy children kind and natural.
1598–9 Chorus. *Henry V*, prologue to act 2, l.16–19.

66 Though Patience be a tired mare, yet she will plod.
1598–9 Nim. *Henry V*, act 2, sc.1, l.22–3.

67 Treason and murder ever kept together,
As two yoke-devils sworn to either's purpose.
1598–9 King Harry. *Henry V*, act 2, sc.2, l.102–3.

68 I saw him fumble with the sheets, and play with flowers,
and smile upon his finger's end.
1598–9 Hostess, describing Falstaff's death. *Henry V*, act 2, sc.3, l.13–15.

69 NIM: They say he cried out of sack.
HOSTESS: Ay, that a did.
BARDOLPH: And of women.
HOSTESS: Nay, that a did not.
BOY: Yes, that a did, and said they were devils incarnate.
HOSTESS: A could never abide carnation, 'twas a colour he never liked.
1598–9 Of Falstaff's death. *Henry V*, act 2, sc.3, l.26–32.

70 Look to my chattels and my movables.
Let senses rule. The word is 'Pitch and pay'.
Trust none, for oaths are straws, men's faiths are wafer-cakes,
And Holdfast is the only dog, my duck.
1598–9 Pistol to Nim. *Henry V*, act 2, sc.3, l.45–8.

71 Let us do it with no show of fear,
No, with no more than if we heard that England
Were busied with a Whitsun morris dance.
For, my good liege, she is so idly kinged,
Her sceptre so fantastically borne
By a vain, giddy, shallow, humorous youth,
That fear attends her not
1598–9 Dauphin, to King Charles. *Henry V*, act 2, sc.4, l.23–9.

72 In cases of defence 'tis best to weigh
The enemy more mighty than he seems.
1598–9 Dauphin. *Henry V*, act 2, sc.4, l.43–4.

73 Self-love, my liege, is not so vile a sin
As self-neglecting.
1598–9 Dauphin, to King Charles. *Henry V*, act 2, sc.4, l.73–4.

74 Once more unto the breach, dear friends, once more,
Or close the wall up with our English dead.
In peace there's nothing so becomes a man
As modest stillness and humility.
But when the blast of war blows in our ears,
Then imitate the action of the tiger.
Stiffen the sinews, conjure up the blood,
Disguise fair nature with hard-favoured rage.
1598–9 King Harry rallying his men at the siege of Harfleur. *Henry V*, act 3, sc.1, l.1–8.

75 I see you stand like greyhounds in the slips,
Straining upon the start. The game's afoot.
1598–9 King Harry rallying his men at the siege of Harfleur. *Henry V*, act 3, sc.1, l.31–2.

76 Cry, 'God for Harry! England and Saint George!'
1598–9 King Harry rallying his men at the siege of Harfleur. *Henry V*, act 3, sc.1, l.34.

77 FLUELLEN: Captain Macmorris, I think, look you, under your correction, there is not many of your nation—
MACMORRIS: Of my nation? What ish my nation? Ish a villain and a bastard and a knave and a rascal? What ish my nation? Who talks of my nation?
1598–9 *Henry V*, act 3, sc.3, l.64–8.

78 From camp to camp through the foul womb of night
The hum of either army stilly sounds.
1598–9 Chorus. *Henry V*, prologue to act 4, l.4–5.

79 A little touch of Harry in the night.
1598–9 Chorus. *Henry V*, prologue to act 4, l.47.

80 There is some soul of goodness in things evil,
Would men observingly distil it out.
1598–9 King Harry. *Henry V*, act 4, sc.1, l.4–5.

81 The King's a bawcock and a heart-of-gold,
A lad of life, an imp of fame,
Of parents good, of fist most valiant.
I kiss his dirty shoe, and from my heartstring
I love the lovely bully.
1598–9 Pistol to King Harry, disguised. *Henry V*, act 4, sc.1, l.45–9.

82 Every subject's duty is the King's, but every subject's soul is his own.
1598–9 King Harry. *Henry V*, act 4, sc.1, l.175–6.

83 Be friends, you English fools, be friends. We have French quarrels enough, if you could tell how to reckon.
1598–9 Bates. *Henry V*, act 4, sc.1, l.220–1.

84 Upon the King.
'Let us, our lives, our souls, our debts, our care-full wives,
Our children, and our sins, lay on the King.'
1598–9 King Harry. *Henry V*, act 4, sc.1, l.227–9.

85 O God of battles, steel my soldiers' hearts.
1598–9 King Harry, before Agincourt. *Henry V*, act 4, sc.1, l.286.

86 O that we now had here
But one ten thousand of those men in England
That do no work today.
1598–9 Warwick, before Agincourt. *Henry V*, act 4, sc.3, l.16–18.

87 If it be a sin to covet honour
    I am the most offending soul alive.
    1598-9 King Harry. *Henry V*, act 4, sc.3, l.28-9.

88 He which hath no stomach to this fight,
    Let him depart.
    1598-9 King Harry, before Agincourt. *Henry V*, act 4, sc.3, l.35.

89 He that shall see this day and live t'old age,
    Will yearly on the vigil feast his neighbours
    And say, 'Tomorrow is Saint Crispian.'
    1598-9 King Harry, before Agincourt. *Henry V*, act 4, sc.3, l.44-6.

90 Then will he strip his sleeve and show his scars
    And say, 'These wounds I had on Crispin's day.'
    Old men forget; yet all shall be forgot,
    But he'll remember.
    1598-9 King Harry, before Agincourt. *Henry V*, act 4, sc.3, l.47-50.

91 Then shall our names,
    Familiar in his mouth as household words...
    Be in their flowing cups freshly remembered.
    1598-9 King Harry, before Agincourt. *Henry V*, act 4, sc.3, l.51-5.

92 This story shall the good man teach his son,
    And Crispin Crispian shall ne'er go by
    From this day to the ending of the world
    But we in it shall be rememberèd,
    We few, we happy few, we band of brothers.
    1598-9 King Harry, before Agincourt. *Henry V*, act 4, sc.3, l.56-60.

93 He today that sheds his blood with me
    Shall be my brother; be he ne'er so vile.
    1598-9 King Harry, before Agincourt. *Henry V*, act 4, sc.3, l.61-2.

94 And gentlemen in England now abed
    Shall think themselves accursed they were not here,
    And hold their manhoods cheap whiles any speaks
    That fought with us upon Saint Crispin's day.
    1598-9 King Harry, before Agincourt. *Henry V*, act 4, sc.3, l.64-7.

95 Let life be short, else shame will be too long.
    1598-9 Bourbon, returning to the battle. *Henry V*, act 4, sc.5, l.19.

96 There is occasions and causes why and wherefore in all things.
    1598-9 Fluellen. *Henry V*, act 5, sc.1, l.3-4.

97 Not for Cadwallader and all his goats.
    1598-9 Pistol, refusing to eat leeks. *Henry V*, act 5, sc.1, l.27.

98 An angel is like you, Kate, and you are like an angel.
    1598-9 King Harry, wooing Catherine. *Henry V*, act 5, sc.2, l.109-10.

99 Thou wouldst find me such a plain king that thou wouldst think I had sold my farm to buy my crown.
    1598-9 King Harry, wooing Catherine. *Henry V*, act 5, sc.2, l.125-7.

1 You have witchcraft in your lips, Kate. There is more eloquence in a sugar touch of them than in the tongues of the French Council.
   1598-9 King Harry, wooing Catherine. *Henry V*, act 5, sc.2, l.274-6.

2 God, the best maker of all marriages,
   Combine your hearts in one, your realms in one.
   1598-9 Queen Isabel, on the marriage of King Harry and Catherine. *Henry V*, act 5, sc.2, l.354-5.

3 Hence, home, you idle creatures, get you home!
   1599 Flavius. *Julius Caesar*, act 1, sc.1, l.1.

4 You blocks, you stones, you worse than senseless things!
   O, you hard hearts, you cruel men of Rome,
   Knew you not Pompey?
   1599 Murellus, to the citizens of Rome. *Julius Caesar*, act 1, sc.1, l.34-7.

5 Beware the ides of March.
   1599 Soothsayer to Caesar. *Julius Caesar*, act 1, sc.2, l.19.

6 Poor Brutus, with himself at war,
   Forgets the shows of love to other men.
   1599 Brutus. *Julius Caesar*, act 1, sc.2, l.48-9.

7 Set honour in one eye and death i' the other,
   And I will look on both indifferently.
   1599 Brutus. *Julius Caesar*, act 1, sc.2, l.88-9.

8 I cannot tell what you and other men
   Think of this life; but for my single self,
   I had as lief not be, as live to be
   In awe of such a thing as I myself.
   I was born free as Caesar, so were you.
   1599 Cassius to Brutus. *Julius Caesar*, act 1, sc.2, l.95-9.

9 He doth bestride the narrow world
   Like a Colossus, and we petty men
   Walk under his huge legs, and peep about
   To find ourselves dishonourable graves.
   Men at sometime were masters of their fates.
   The fault, dear Brutus, is not in our stars,
   But in ourselves, that we are underlings.
   1599 Cassius, of Caesar. *Julius Caesar*, act 1, sc.2, l.136-42.

10 Brutus and Caesar: what should be in that 'Caesar'?
   Why should that name be sounded more than yours?
   Write them together: yours is as fair a name.
   Sound them: it doth become the mouth as well.
   Weigh them: it is as heavy. Conjure with 'em:
   'Brutus' will start a spirit as soon as 'Caesar'.
   1599 Cassius to Brutus. *Julius Caesar*, act 1, sc.2, l.143-8.

11 Upon what meat doth this our Caesar feed
   That he is grown so great?
   1599 Cassius to Brutus. *Julius Caesar*, act 1, sc.2, l.150-1.

12 Let me have men about me that are fat;
   Sleek-headed men, and such as sleep o'nights;
   Yond Cassius has a lean and hungry look;
   He thinks too much: such men are dangerous.
   1599 Caesar. *Julius Caesar*, act 1, sc.2, l.193-6.

13 Seldom he smiles, and smiles in such a sort
   As if he mocked himself.
   1599 Caesar, of Cassius. *Julius Caesar*, act 1, sc.2, l.206-7.

14 Cassius from bondage will deliver Cassius.
   Therein, ye gods, you make the weak most strong;
   Therein, ye gods, you tyrants do defeat.
   Nor stony tower, nor walls of beaten brass,
   Nor airless dungeon, nor strong links of iron,
   Can be retentive to the strength of spirit;
   But life, being weary of these worldly bars,
   Never lacks power to dismiss itself.
   1599 Cassius. *Julius Caesar*, act 1, sc.3, l.89-96.

15 It is the bright day that brings forth the adder,
   And that craves wary walking.
   1599 Brutus. *Julius Caesar*, act 2, sc.1, l.14-15.

16 Between the acting of a dreadful thing
   And the first motion, all the interim is
   Like a phantasma or a hideous dream.
   1599 Brutus. *Julius Caesar*, act 2, sc.1, l.63-5.

17 Let's carve him as a dish fit for the gods,
   Not hew him as a carcass fit for hounds.
   1599 Brutus, of Caesar. *Julius Caesar*, act 2, sc.1, l.173-4.

18 Am I your self
But as it were in sort or limitation?
To keep with you at meals, comfort your bed,
And talk to you sometimes? Dwell I but in the suburbs
Of your good pleasure? If it be no more,
Portia is Brutus' harlot, not his wife.
1599 Portia. *Julius Caesar*, act 2, sc.1, l.281–6.

19 You are my true and honourable wife,
As dear to me as are the ruddy drops
That visit my sad heart.
1599 Brutus to Portia. *Julius Caesar*, act 2, sc.1, l.287–9.

20 When beggars die there are no comets seen;
The heavens themselves blaze forth the death of princes.
1599 Calpurnia. *Julius Caesar*, act 2, sc.2, l.30–1.

21 Cowards die many times before their deaths;
The valiant never taste of death but once.
1599 Caesar. *Julius Caesar*, act 2, sc.2, l.32–3.

22 Of all the wonders that I yet have heard,
It seems to me most strange that men should fear,
Seeing that death, a necessary end,
Will come when it will come.
1599 Caesar. *Julius Caesar*, act 2, sc.2, l.34–7.

23 Danger knows full well
That Caesar is more dangerous than he.
1599 Caesar. *Julius Caesar*, act 2, sc.2, l.44–5.

24 The cause is in my will; I will not come.
1599 Caesar. *Julius Caesar*, act 2, sc.2, l.71.

25 Ay me! How weak a thing
The heart of woman is!
1599 Portia. *Julius Caesar*, act 2, sc.4, l.41–2.

26 I could be well moved if I were as you.
If I could pray to move, prayers would move me.
But I am constant as the Northern star,
Of whose true fixed and resting quality
There is no fellow in the firmament.
The skies are painted with unnumbered sparks;
They are all fire, and every one doth shine;
But there's but one in all doth hold his place.
So in the world: 'tis furnished well with men,
And men are flesh and blood, and apprehensive;
Yet in the number I do know but one
That unassailable holds on his rank,
Unshaked of motion; and that I am he
Let me a little show it even in this—
That I was constant Cimber should be banished,
And constant do remain to keep him so.
1599 Caesar. *Julius Caesar*, act 3, sc.1, l.58–73.

27 Et tu, Bruté?—Then fall Caesar.
1599 *Julius Caesar*, act 3, sc.1, l.76.

28 Ambition's debt is paid.
1599 Brutus, after he has killed Caesar. *Julius Caesar*, act 3, sc.1, l.82.

29 Fates, we will know your pleasures.
That we shall die, we know; 'tis but the time
And drawing days out that men stand upon.
1599 Brutus. *Julius Caesar*, act 3, sc.1, l.99–101.

30 He that cuts off twenty years of life
Cuts off so many years of fearing death.
1599 Casca. *Julius Caesar*, act 3, sc.1, l.102–3.

31 How many ages hence
Shall this our lofty scene be acted over,
In states unborn and accents yet unknown!
1599 Cassius, of the murder of Caesar. *Julius Caesar*, act 3, sc.1, l.112–14.

32 O mighty Caesar! Dost thou lie so low?
Are all thy conquests, glories, triumphs, spoils,
Shrunk to this little measure?
1599 Antony. *Julius Caesar*, act 3, sc.1, l.149–51.

33 O pardon me, thou bleeding piece of earth,
That I am meek and gentle with these butchers.
1599 Antony. *Julius Caesar*, act 3, sc.1, l.257–8.

34 Caesar's spirit, ranging for revenge,
With Ate by his side come hot from hell,
Shall in these confines with a monarch's voice
Cry 'havoc!', and let slip the dogs of war,
That this foul deed shall smell above the earth
With carrion men, groaning for burial.
1599 Antony. *Julius Caesar*, act 3, sc.1, l.273–8.

35 This is my answer: not that I loved Caesar less, but that I loved Rome more.
1599 Brutus, explaining his reasons for killing Caesar. *Julius Caesar*, act 3, sc.2, l.20–1.

36 As Caesar loved me, I weep for him. As he was fortunate, I rejoice at it. As he was valiant, I honour him. But as he was ambitious, I slew him.
1599 Brutus. *Julius Caesar*, act 3, sc.2, l.24–7.

37 Friends, Romans, countrymen, lend me your ears.
I come to bury Caesar, not to praise him.
The evil that men do lives after them;
The good is oft interrèd with their bones.
So let it be with Caesar. The noble Brutus
Hath told you Caesar was ambitious.
If it were so, it was a grievous fault,
And grievously hath Caesar answered it.
Here, under leave of Brutus and the rest—
For Brutus is an honourable man,
So are they all, all honourable men—
Come I to speak in Caesar's funeral.
He was my friend, faithful and just to me.
1599 Antony. *Julius Caesar*, act 3, sc.2, l.74–86.

38 When that the poor have cried, Caesar hath wept.
Ambition should be made of sterner stuff.
1599 Antony. *Julius Caesar*, act 3, sc.2, l.92–3.

39 O judgement! thou art fled to brutish beasts,
And men have lost their reason!
1599 Antony. *Julius Caesar*, act 3, sc.2, l.105–6.

40 Bear with me.
My heart is in the coffin there with Caesar,
And I must pause till it come back to me.
1599 Antony. *Julius Caesar*, act 3, sc.2, l.106–8.

41 But yesterday the word of Caesar might
Have stood against the world. Now lies he there,
And none so poor to do him reverence.
1599 Antony. *Julius Caesar*, act 3, sc.2, l.119–21.

42 If you have tears, prepare to shed them now.
1599 Antony. *Julius Caesar*, act 3, sc.2, l.167.

43 This was the most unkindest cut of all.
For when the noble Caesar saw him stab,
Ingratitude, more strong than traitors' arms,
Quite vanquished him.
1599 Antony of Brutus. *Julius Caesar*, act 3, sc.2, l.181–4.

Shakespeare   Julius Caesar

44 O now you weep, and I perceive you feel
The dint of pity. These are gracious drops.
1599 Antony to the crowd. *Julius Caesar*, act 3, sc.2, l.191–2.

45 I am no orator as Brutus is,
But, as you know me all, a plain blunt man.
1599 Antony. *Julius Caesar*, act 3, sc.2, l.212–13.

46 Fortune is merry,
And in this mood will give us anything.
1599 Antony. *Julius Caesar*, act 3, sc.2, l.259–60.

47 Good reasons must of force give place to better.
1599 Brutus. *Julius Caesar*, act 4, sc.2, l.255.

48 There is a tide in the affairs of men
Which, taken at the flood, leads on to fortune;
Omitted, all the voyage of their life
Is bound in shallows and in miseries.
1599 Brutus. *Julius Caesar*, act 4, sc.2, l.270–3.

49 We'll along ourselves, and meet them at Philippi.
1599 Cassius. *Julius Caesar*, act 4, sc.2, l.277.

50 I should not urge thy duty past thy might.
1599 Brutus to Lucius. *Julius Caesar*, act 4, sc.2, l.312.

51 Good words are better than bad strokes.
1599 Brutus to Octavius. *Julius Caesar*, act 5, sc.1, l.29.

52 Blow wind, swell billow, and swim bark.
The storm is up, and all is on the hazard.
1599 Cassius, at Philippi. *Julius Caesar*, act 5, sc.1, l.67–8.

53 Since the affairs of men rest still incertain,
Let's reason with the worst that may befall.
1599 Cassius to Brutus. *Julius Caesar*, act 5, sc.1, l.95–6.

54 O that a man might know
The end of this day's business ere it come!
But it sufficeth that the day will end,
And then the end is known.
1599 Brutus. *Julius Caesar*, act 5, sc.1, l.123–6.

55 I prithee, Strato, stay thou by thy lord.
Thou art a fellow of a good respect.
Thy life hath had some smatch of honour in it.
Hold then my sword, and turn away thy face
While I do run upon it.
1599 Brutus, killing himself. *Julius Caesar*, act 5, sc.5, l.44–8.

56 Caesar, now be still,
I killed not thee with half so good a will.
1599 Brutus, killing himself. *Julius Caesar*, act 5, sc. 5, l.50–1.

57 This was the noblest Roman of them all.
All the conspirators save only he
Did that they did in envy of great Caesar.
He only in a general honest thought
And common good to all made one of them.
His life was gentle, and the elements
So mixed in him that nature might stand up
And say to all the world 'This was a man'.
1599 Antony, of Brutus. *Julius Caesar*, act 5, sc.5, l.67–74.

58 Let us sit and mock the good housewife Fortune from her wheel, that her gifts may henceforth be bestowed equally.
1599–1600 Celia to Rosalind. *As You Like It*, act 1, sc.2, l.30–2.

59 Where is this young gallant that is so desirous to lie with his mother earth?
1599–1600 Charles to Orlando. *As You Like It*, act 1, sc.2, l.188–9.

60 My pride fell with my fortunes.
1599–1600 Rosalind. *As You Like It*, act 1, sc.2, l.241.

61 Fare you well.
Hereafter, in a better world than this,
I shall desire more love and knowledge of you.
1599–1600 Le Beau to Orlando. *As You Like It*, act 1, sc.2, l.273–4.

62 Thy words are too precious to be cast away upon curs.
Throw some of them at me.
1599–1600 Celia to Rosalind. *As You Like It*, act 1, sc.3, l.4–6.

63 Thou art thy father's daughter—there's enough.
1599–1600 Duke Frederick to Rosalind, explaining why he does not trust her. *As You Like It*, act 1, sc.3, l.57.

64 What danger will it be to us,
Maids as we are, to travel forth so far!
Beauty provoketh thieves sooner than gold.
1599–1600 Rosalind to Celia. *As You Like It*, act 1, sc.3, l.107–9.

65 Sweet are the uses of adversity
Which, like the toad, ugly and venomous,
Wears yet a precious jewel in his head.
1599–1600 Duke Senior. *As You Like It*, act 2, sc.1, l.12–14.

66 And this our life, exempt from public haunt,
Finds tongues in trees, books in the running brooks,
Sermons in stones, and good in everything.
1599–1600 Duke Senior. *As You Like It*, act 2, sc.1, l.15–17.

67 Sweep on, you fat and greasy citizens.
1599–1600 First Lord, quoting Jaques. *As You Like It*, act 2, sc.1, l.55.

68 I love to cope him in these sullen fits,
For then he's full of matter.
1599–1600 Duke Senior, of Jaques. *As You Like It*, act 2, sc.1, l.67–8.

69 Unregarded age in corners thrown.
1599–1600 Adam. *As You Like It*, act 2, sc.3, l.43.

70 He that doth the ravens feed,
Yea providently caters for the sparrow,
Be comfort to my age.
1599–1600 Adam to Orlando. *As You Like It*, act 2, sc.3, l.44–6.

71 Though I look old, yet I am strong and lusty,
For in my youth I never did apply
Hot and rebellious liquors in my blood,
Nor did not with unbashful forehead woo
The means of weakness and debility.
Therefore my age is as a lusty winter.
1599–1600 Adam to Orlando. *As You Like It*, act 2, sc.3, l.48–53.

72 Thou art not for the fashion of these times,
Where none will sweat but for promotion.
1599–1600 Orlando, of Adam. *As You Like It*, act 2, sc.3, l.60–1.

73 I think you have no money in your purse.
1599–1600 Touchstone to Celia. *As You Like It*, act 2, sc.4, l.12.

74 Now I am in Ardenne; the more fool I. When I was at home I was in a better place; but travellers must be content.
1599–1600 Touchstone. *As You Like It*, act 2, sc.4, l.14–15.

75 Under the greenwood tree
Who loves to lie with me,
And turn his merry note
Unto the sweet bird's throat.
1599–1600 Amiens's song. *As You Like It*, act 2, sc.5, l.1–4.

76 I can suck melancholy out of a song as a weasel sucks eggs.
1599–1600 Jaques. *As You Like It*, act 2, sc.5, l.11–12.

77 I'll go sleep if I can. If I cannot, I'll rail against all the firstborn of Egypt.
1599–1600 Jaques. *As You Like It*, act 2, sc.5, l.57–8.

78 A fool, a fool, I met a fool i'th' forest,
A motley fool—a miserable world!—
As I do live by food, I met a fool,
Who laid him down and basked him in the sun,
And railed on Lady Fortune in good terms,
In good set terms, and yet a motley fool.
1599–1600 Jaques. *As You Like It*, act 2, sc.7, l.12–17.

79 'Thus we may see', quoth he, 'how the world wags.
'Tis but an hour ago since it was nine,
And after one hour more 'twill be eleven.
And so from hour to hour we ripe and ripe,
And then from hour to hour we rot and rot;
And thereby hangs a tale.'
1599–1600 Jaques, quoting Touchstone. *As You Like It*, act 2, sc.7, l.23–8.

80 All the world's a stage,
And all the men and women merely players.
They have their exits and their entrances,
And one man in his time plays many parts.
1599–1600 Jaques. *As You Like It*, act 2, sc.7, l.139–42.

81 The whining schoolboy with his satchel
And shining morning face.
1599–1600 Jaques. *As You Like It*, act 2, sc.7, l.145–6.

82 Jealous in honour, sudden, and quick in quarrel,
Seeking the bubble reputation
Even in the cannon's mouth.
1599–1600 Jaques, of the soldier. *As You Like It*, act 2, sc.7, l.151–3.

83 Second childishness and mere oblivion,
Sans teeth, sans eyes, sans taste, sans everything.
1599–1600 Jaques, of old age. *As You Like It*, act 2, sc.7, l.165–6.

84 Blow, blow, thou winter wind,
Thou art not so unkind
As man's ingratitude.
1599–1600 Amiens singing. *As You Like It*, act 2, sc.7, l.175–7.

85 Most friendship is feigning, most loving, mere folly.
1599–1600 Amiens. *As You Like It*, act 2, sc.7, l.182.

86 These trees shall be my books
And in their barks my thoughts I'll character.
1599–1600 Orlando. *As You Like It*, act 3, sc.2, l.5–6.

87 Run, run, Orlando; carve on every tree
The fair, the chaste, and unexpressive she.
1599–1600 Orlando. *As You Like It*, act 3, sc.2, l.9–10.

88 Hast any philosophy in thee, shepherd?
1599–1600 Touchstone to Corin. *As You Like It*, act 3, sc.2, l.21–2.

89 I earn that I eat, get that I wear; owe no man hate, envy no man's happiness.
1599–1600 Corin. *As You Like It*, act 3, sc.2, l.71–2.

90 This is the very false gallop of verses.
1599–1600 Touchstone, of Orlando's poem. *As You Like It*, act 3, sc.2, l.111.

91 I was never so berhymed since Pythagoras' time that I was an Irish rat, which I can hardly remember.
1599–1600 Rosalind. *As You Like It*, act 3, sc.2, l.172–4.

92 O wonderful, wonderful, and most wonderful-wonderful, and yet again wonderful, and after that out of all whooping!
1599–1600 Celia, on the arrival of Orlando. *As You Like It*, act 3, sc.2, l.187–9.

93 Do you not know that I am a woman? When I think, I must speak.
1599–1600 Rosalind to Celia. *As You Like It*, act 3, sc.2, l.244–5.

94 I do desire we may be better strangers.
1599–1600 Orlando to Jaques. *As You Like It*, act 3, sc.2, l.253.

95 Time travels in divers paces with divers persons.
1599–1600 Rosalind. *As You Like It*, act 3, sc.2, l.301–2.

96 Love is merely a madness, and, I tell you, deserves as well a dark house and a whip as madmen do.
1599–1600 Rosalind to Orlando. *As You Like It*, act 3, sc.2, l.386–8.

97 I would the gods had made thee poetical.
1599–1600 Touchstone to Audrey. *As You Like It*, act 3, sc.3, l.12–13.

98 The truest poetry is the most feigning.
1599–1600 Touchstone to Audrey. *As You Like It*, act 3, sc.3, l.16–17.

99 Honesty coupled to beauty is to have honey a sauce to sugar.
1599–1600 Touchstone to Audrey. *As You Like It*, act 3, sc.3, l.26–7.

1 His kissing is as full of sanctity as the touch of holy bread.
1599–1600 Rosalind. *As You Like It*, act 3, sc.4, l.12–13.

2 Mistress, know yourself; down on your knees
And thank heaven, fasting, for a good man's love.
1599–1600 Rosalind, in disguise, to Phoebe. *As You Like It*, act 3, sc.5, l.58–9.

3 I pray you do not fall in love with me,
For I am falser than vows made in wine.
Besides, I like you not.
1599–1600 Rosalind, in disguise, to Phoebe. *As You Like It*, act 3, sc.5, l.73–5.

4 Dead shepherd, now I find thy saw of might:
'Who ever loved that loved not at first sight?'
1599–1600 Phoebe, in love with Rosalind (disguised as a young man). *As You Like It*, act 3, sc.5, l.82–3.

5 It is a melancholy of mine own, compounded of many simples, extracted from many objects, and indeed the sundry contemplation of my travels.
1599–1600 Jaques. *As You Like It*, act 4, sc.1, l.15–17.

6 A traveller! By my faith, you have great reason to be sad. I fear you have sold your own lands to see other men's.
1599–1600 Rosalind to Jaques. *As You Like It*, act 4, sc.1, l.20–2.

7 I had rather have a fool to make me merry than experience to make me sad—and to travel for it too!
1599–1600 Rosalind to Jaques. *As You Like It*, act 4, sc.1, l.25–7.

8 JAQUES: Nay then, God b'wi'you an you talk in blank verse.
ROSALIND: Farewell, Monsieur Traveller. Look you lisp, and wear strange suits; disable all the benefits of your own country; be out of love with your nativity, and almost chide God for making you that countenance you are, or I will scarce think you have swam in a gondola.
1599–1600 *As You Like It*, act 4, sc.1, l.29–36.

9 Come, woo me, woo me, for now I am in a holiday humour, and like enough to consent.
1599–1600 Rosalind, in disguise, to Orlando. *As You Like It*, act 4, sc.1, l.64–5.

10 Men have died from time to time, and worms have eaten them, but not for love.
1599–1600 Rosalind, in disguise, to Orlando. *As You Like It*, act 4, sc.1, l.99–101.

11 Can one desire too much of a good thing?
1599–1600 Rosalind, in disguise, to Orlando. *As You Like It*, act 4, sc.1, l.115–16.

12 Men are April when they woo, December when they wed. Maids are May when they are maids, but the sky changes when they are wives.
  1599–1600 Rosalind, in disguise, to Orlando. *As You Like It*, act 4, sc.1, l.139–41.

13 Make the doors upon a woman's wit, and it will out at the casement. Shut that, and 'twill out at the key-hole. Stop that, 'twill fly with the smoke out at the chimney.
  1599–1600 Rosalind, in disguise, to Orlando. *As You Like It*, act 4, sc.1, l.153–4.

14 'Tis no matter how it be in tune, so it make noise enough.
  1599–1600 Jaques. *As You Like It*, act 4, sc.2, l.8–9.

15 The horn, the horn, the lusty horn
Is not a thing to laugh to scorn.
  1599–1600 Lords, singing. *As You Like It*, act 4, sc.2, l.18–19.

16 I do now remember a saying: 'The fool doth think he is wise, but the wise man knows himself to be a fool.'
  1599–1600 Touchstone to William. *As You Like It*, act 5, sc.1, l.29–31.

17 To wit, I kill thee, make thee away, translate thy life into death, thy liberty into bondage. I will deal in poison with thee, or in bastinado, or in steel. I will bandy with thee in faction, I will o'errun thee with policy. I will kill thee a hundred and fifty ways. Therefore tremble, and depart.
  1599–1600 Touchstone. *As You Like It*, act 5, sc.1, l.51–6.

18 [They] no sooner looked but they loved; no sooner loved but they sighed; no sooner sighed but they asked one another the reason; no sooner knew the reason but they sought the remedy.
  1599–1600 Rosalind, of Celia and Oliver. *As You Like It*, act 5, sc.2, l.32–5.

19 How bitter a thing it is to look into happiness through another man's eyes.
  1599–1600 Orlando. *As You Like It*, act 5, sc.2, l.41–2.

20 I can live no longer by thinking.
  1599–1600 Orlando. *As You Like It*, act 5, sc.2, l.48.

21 It was a lover and his lass,
With a hey, and a ho, and a hey-nonny-no,
That o'er the green cornfield did pass
In spring-time, the only pretty ring-time,
When birds do sing, hey ding-a-ding ding,
Sweet lovers love the spring.
  1599–1600 Pages' song. *As You Like It*, act 5, sc.3, l.15–20.

22 A poor virgin, sir, an ill-favoured thing, sir, but mine own.
  1599–1600 Touchstone, of Audrey. *As You Like It*, act 5, sc.4, l.57–8.

23 I durst go no further than the Lie Circumstantial, nor he durst not give me the Lie Direct; and so we measured swords, and parted.
  1599–1600 Touchstone. *As You Like It*, act 5, sc.4, l.83–5.

24 O sir, we quarrel in print, by the book, as you have books for good manners. I will name you the degrees. The first, the Retort Courteous; the second, the Quip Modest; the third, the Reply Churlish; the fourth, the Reproof Valiant; the fifth, the Countercheck Quarrelsome; the sixth, the Lie with Circumstance; the seventh, the Lie Direct.
  1599–1600 Touchstone. *As You Like It*, act 5, sc.4, l.88–94.

25 Your 'if' is the only peacemaker; much virtue in 'if'.
  1599–1600 Touchstone. *As You Like It*, act 5, sc.4, l.100–1.

26 He uses his folly like a stalking-horse, and under the presentation of that he shoots his wit.
  1599–1600 Duke Senior, of Touchstone. *As You Like It*, act 5, sc.4, l.104–5.

27 If it be true that good wine needs no bush, 'tis true that a good play needs no epilogue.
  1599–1600 Rosalind. *As You Like It*, epilogue.

28 For this relief much thanks. 'Tis bitter cold,
And I am sick at heart.
  1600–1 Francisco. *Hamlet*, act 1, sc.1, l.6–7.

29 Thus twice before, and just at this dead hour,
With martial stalk hath he gone by our watch.
  1600–1 Marcellus, of the ghost of Hamlet's father. *Hamlet*, act 1, sc.1, l.64–5.

30 And then it started like a guilty thing
Upon a fearful summons.
  1600–1 Horatio, of the ghost. *Hamlet*, act 1, sc.1, l.129–30.

31 The head is not more native to the heart,
The hand more instrumental to the mouth,
Than is the throne of Denmark to thy father.
  1600–1 Claudius to Laertes. *Hamlet*, act 1, sc.2, l.47–9.

32 A little more than kin and less than kind.
  1600–1 Hamlet, of Claudius. *Hamlet*, act 1, sc.2, l.65.

33 I am too much i' th' sun.
  1600–1 Hamlet. *Hamlet*, act 1, sc.2, l.67.

34 Good Hamlet, cast thy nightly colour off,
And let thine eye look like a friend on Denmark.
Do not for ever with thy vailèd lids
Seek for thy noble father in the dust.
  1600–1 Gertrude. *Hamlet*, act 1, sc.2, l.68–71.

35 Seems, madam? Nay, it *is*. I know not 'seems'.
  1600–1 Hamlet to Gertrude. *Hamlet*, act 1, sc.2, l.76.

36 But I have that within which passeth show—
These but the trappings and the suits of woe.
  1600–1 Hamlet to Gertrude. *Hamlet*, act 1, sc.2, l.85–6.

37 O that this too too solid flesh would melt,
Thaw, and resolve itself into a dew,
Or that the Everlasting had not fixed
His canon 'gainst self-slaughter!
  1600–1 Hamlet. *Hamlet*, act 1, sc.2, l.129–32.

38 How weary, stale, flat, and unprofitable
Seem to me all the uses of this world!
  1600–1 Hamlet. *Hamlet*, act 1, sc.2, l.133–4.

39 So loving to my mother
That he might not beteem the winds of heaven
Visit her face too roughly!
  1600–1 Hamlet, of his father. *Hamlet*, act 1, sc.2, l.140–3.

40 Frailty, thy name is woman.
  1600–1 Hamlet, of Gertrude. *Hamlet*, act 1, sc.2, l.146.

41 We'll teach you to drink deep ere you depart.
  1600–1 Hamlet to Horatio. *Hamlet*, act 1, sc.2, l.174.

42 Thrift, thrift, Horatio. The funeral baked meats
Did coldly furnish forth the marriage tables.
  1600–1 Hamlet to Horatio, on the reason for his mother's swift marriage to Claudius. *Hamlet*, act 1, sc.2, l.179–80.

43 A was a man. Take him for all in all,
I shall not look upon his like again.
  1600–1 Hamlet, of his father. *Hamlet*, act 1, sc.2, l.186–7.

44 A countenance more
In sorrow than in anger.

1600–1 Horatio, of Hamlet's father's ghost. *Hamlet*, act 1, sc.2, l.228–9.

45 I doubt some foul play. Would the night were come.
Till then, sit still, my soul. Foul deeds will rise,
Though all the earth o'erwhelm them, to men's eyes.
1600–1 Hamlet. *Hamlet*, act 1, sc.2, l.255–7.

46 And keep within the rear of your affection,
Out of the shot and danger of desire.
1600–1 Laertes to Ophelia. *Hamlet*, act 1, sc.3, l.34–5.

47 The chariest maid is prodigal enough
If she unmask her beauty to the moon.
1600–1 Laertes to Ophelia. *Hamlet*, act 1, sc.3, l.36–7.

48 Do not, as some ungracious pastors do,
Show me the steep and thorny way to heaven,
Whilst, like a puffed and reckless libertine
Himself the primrose path of dalliance treads.
1600–1 Ophelia to Laertes. *Hamlet*, act 1, sc.3, l.47–50.

49 The friends thou hast, and their adoption tried,
Grapple them to thy soul with hoops of steel.
1600–1 Polonius to Laertes. *Hamlet*, act 1, sc.3, l.62–3.

50 Beware
Of entrance to a quarrel, but being in,
Bear't that th' opposèd may beware of thee.
1600–1 Polonius to Laertes. *Hamlet*, act 1, sc.3, l.65–7.

51 Give every man thine ear but few thy voice.
Take each man's censure, but reserve thy
judgement.
1600–1 Polonius to Laertes. *Hamlet*, act 1, sc.3, l.68–9.

52 Costly thy habit as thy purse can buy,
But not expressed in fancy; rich not gaudy;
For the apparel oft proclaims the man.
1600–1 Polonius to Laertes. *Hamlet*, act 1, sc.3, l.70–2.

53 Neither a borrower nor a lender be.
1600–1 Polonius to Laertes. *Hamlet*, act 1, sc.3, l.75.

54 This above all—to thine own self be true,
And it must follow, as the night the day,
Thou canst not then be false to any man.
1600–1 Polonius to Laertes. *Hamlet*, act 1, sc.3, l.78–80.

55 Ay, springes to catch woodcocks. I do know
When the blood burns how prodigal the soul
Lends the tongue vows.
1600–1 Polonius. *Hamlet*, act 1, sc.3, l.115–7.

56 And to my mind, though I am native here
And to the manner born, it is a custom
More honoured in the breach than the observance.
1600–1 Hamlet. *Hamlet*, act 1, sc.4, l.16–18.

57 Be thou a spirit of health or goblin damned,
Bring with thee airs from heaven or blasts from hell,
Be thy intents wicked or charitable,
Thou com'st in such a questionable shape
That I will speak to thee.
1600–1 Hamlet to the ghost. *Hamlet*, act 1, sc.4, l.21–5.

58 I do not set my life at a pin's fee,
And for my soul, what can it do to that,
Being a thing immortal as itself?
1600–1 Hamlet. *Hamlet*, act 1, sc.4, l.46–8.

59 Something is rotten in the state of Denmark.
1600–1 Marcellus. *Hamlet*, act 1, sc.4, l.67.

60 I could a tale unfold whose lightest word
Would harrow up thy soul, freeze thy young blood,
Make thy two eyes like stars start from their spheres,
Thy knotty and combinèd locks to part,
And each particular hair to stand on end
Like quills upon the fretful porcupine.
1600–1 Ghost to Hamlet. *Hamlet*, act 1, sc.5, l.15–20.

61 Murder most foul, as in the best it is,
But this most foul, strange, and unnatural.
1600–1 Ghost to Hamlet. *Hamlet*, act 1, sc.5, l.27–8.

62 O my prophetic soul! Mine uncle?
1600–1 Hamlet to the ghost. *Hamlet*, act 1, sc.5, l.41.

63 [My] love was of that dignity
That it went hand-in-hand even with the vow
I made to her in marriage.
1600–1 Ghost, of Gertrude. *Hamlet*, act 1, sc.5, l.48–50.

64 In the porches of mine ears.
1600–1 Ghost. *Hamlet*, act 1, sc.5, l.63.

65 Let not the royal bed of Denmark be
A couch for luxury and damnèd incest.
1600–1 Ghost to Hamlet. *Hamlet*, act 1, sc.5, l.82–4.

66 O all you host of heaven! O earth! What else?
And shall I couple hell? O fie! Hold, hold, my heart,
And you, my sinews, grow not instant old,
But bear me stiffly up. Remember thee?
Ay, thou poor ghost, while memory holds a seat
In this distracted globe.
1600–1 Hamlet. *Hamlet*, act 1, sc.5, l.92–7.

67 My tables—meet it is I set it down
That one may smile and smile and be a villain.
1600–1 Hamlet. *Hamlet*, act 1, sc.5, l.108–9.

68 There's ne'er a villain dwelling in all Denmark
But he's an arrant knave.
1600–1 Hamlet. *Hamlet*, act 1, sc.5, l.127–8.

69 Well said, old mole. Canst work i'th' earth so fast?
1600–1 Hamlet. *Hamlet*, act 1, sc.5, l.164.

70 There are more things in heaven and earth, Horatio,
Than are dreamt of in our philosophy.
1600–1 Hamlet. *Hamlet*, act 1, sc.5, l.168–9.

71 The time is out of joint. O cursèd spite
That ever I was born to set it right!
1600–1 Hamlet. *Hamlet*, act 1, sc.5, l.189–90.

72 Lord Hamlet, with his doublet all unbraced,
No hat upon his head, his stockings fouled,
Ungartered, and down-gyvèd to his ankle.
1600–1 Ophelia. *Hamlet*, act 2, sc.1, l.79–81.

73 This is the very ecstasy of love,
Whose violent property fordoes itself
And leads the will to desperate undertakings.
1600–1 Polonius, of Hamlet. *Hamlet*, act 2, sc.1, l.103–5.

74 Brevity is the soul of wit.
1600–1 Polonius. *Hamlet*, act 2, sc.2, l.91.

75 More matter with less art.
1600–1 Gertrude to Polonius, urging him to speak more plainly.
Hamlet, act 2, sc.2, l.96.

76 'To the celestial and my soul's idol, the most beautified
Ophelia'—that's an ill phrase, a vile phrase, 'beautified'
is a vile phrase.
1600–1 Polonius to Gertrude, quoting Hamlet's letter to Ophelia.
Hamlet, act 2, sc.2, l.110–12.

77 Doubt thou the stars are fire,
Doubt that the sun doth move,

Doubt truth to be a liar,
But never doubt I love.
1600–1 Polonius to Gertrude, quoting Hamlet's letter to Ophelia. *Hamlet*, act 2, sc.2, l.116–19.

78 If circumstances lead me I will find
Where truth is hid, though it were hid indeed
Within the centre.
1600–1 Polonius, of Hamlet's madness. *Hamlet*, act 2, sc.2, l.159–61.

79 To be honest, as this world goes, is to be one man picked out of ten thousand.
1600–1 Hamlet to Polonius. *Hamlet*, act 2, sc.2, l.180–1.

80 POLONIUS: What do you read, my lord?
HAMLET: Words, words, words.
1600–1 *Hamlet*, act 2, sc.2, l.193–5.

81 Though this be madness, yet there is method in't.
1600–1 Polonius (aside), of Hamlet. *Hamlet*, act 2, sc.2, l.207–8.

82 POLONIUS: My lord, I will take my leave of you.
HAMLET: You cannot, sir, take from me anything that I will more willingly part withal—except my life, my life, my life.
1600–1 *Hamlet*, act 2, sc.2, l.215–19.

83 [We are] happy in that we are not over-happy,
On Fortune's cap we are not the very button.
1600–1 Guildenstern to Hamlet. *Hamlet*, act 2, sc.2, l.230–1.

84 HAMLET: What's the news?
ROSENCRANTZ: None, my lord, but that the world's grown honest.
HAMLET: Then is doomsday near.
1600–1 *Hamlet*, act 2, sc.2, l.238–41.

85 There is nothing either good or bad, but thinking makes it so.
1600–1 Hamlet. *Hamlet*, act 2, sc.2, l.251–2.

86 I could be bounded in a nutshell and count myself a king of infinite space, were it not that I have bad dreams.
1600–1 Hamlet. *Hamlet*, act 2, sc.2, l.256–8.

87 I hold ambition of so airy and light a quality that it is but a shadow's shadow.
1600–1 Rosencrantz. *Hamlet*, act 2, sc.2, l.263–4.

88 I have of late—but wherefore I know not—lost all my mirth, forgone all custom of exercise; and indeed it goes so heavily with my disposition that this goodly frame, the earth, seems to me a sterile promontory. This most excellent canopy the air, look you, this brave o'erhanging, this majestical roof fretted with golden fire—why, it appears no other thing to me than a foul and pestilent congregation of vapours.
1600–1 Hamlet. *Hamlet*, act 2, sc.2, l.296–304.

89 What a piece of work is a man! How noble in reason, how infinite in faculty, in form and moving how express and admirable, in action how like an angel, in apprehension how like a god—the beauty of the world, the paragon of animals! And yet to me what is this quintessence of dust?
1600–1 Hamlet. *Hamlet*, act 2, sc.2, l.305–10.

90 Man delights not me—no, nor woman neither.
1600–1 Hamlet. *Hamlet*, act 2, sc.2, l.310–11.

91 If you delight not in man what lenten entertainment the players shall receive from you.
1600–1 Rosencrantz. *Hamlet*, act 2, sc.2, l.317–19.

92 There is something in this more than natural, if philosophy could find it out.
1600–1 Hamlet. *Hamlet*, act 2, sc.2, l.367–9.

93 I am but mad north-north-west; when the wind is southerly, I know a hawk from a handsaw.
1600–1 Hamlet to Guildenstern. *Hamlet*, act 2, sc.2, l.380–1.

94 The best actors in the world, either for tragedy, comedy, history, pastoral, pastoral-comical, historical-pastoral, tragical-historical, tragical-comical-historical-pastoral, scene individable, or poem unlimited.
1600–1 Polonius. *Hamlet*, act 2, sc.2, l.398–401.

95 Thy face is valanced since I saw thee last. Com'st thou to beard me in Denmark?
1600–1 Hamlet to one of the players. *Hamlet*, act 2, sc.2, l.426–7.

96 The play, I remember, pleased not the million. 'Twas caviare to the general.
1600–1 Hamlet to one of the players. *Hamlet*, act 2, sc.2, l.438–40.

97 Will you see the players well bestowed? Do ye hear? —let them be well used, for they are the abstracts and brief chronicles of the time.
1600–1 Hamlet to Polonius. *Hamlet*, act 2, sc.2, l.524–7.

98 Use every man after his desert, and who should scape whipping?
1600–1 Hamlet to Polonius. *Hamlet*, act 2, sc.2, l.532–3.

99 O, what a rogue and peasant slave am I!
Is it not monstrous that this player here,
But in a fiction, in a dream of passion,
Could force his soul so to his whole conceit
That from her working all his visage wanned,
Tears in his eyes, distraction in 's aspect,
A broken voice, and his whole function suiting
With forms to his conceit? And all for nothing.
For Hecuba!
What's Hecuba to him, or he to Hecuba,
That he should weep for her?
1600–1 Hamlet. *Hamlet*, act 2, sc.2, l.552–62.

1 But I am pigeon-livered and lack gall
To make oppression bitter
1600–1 Hamlet. *Hamlet*, act 2, sc.2, l.579–80.

2 Why, what an ass am I? Ay, sure, this is most brave,
That I, the son of the dear murderèd,
Prompted to my revenge by heaven and hell,
Must, like a whore, unpack my heart with words.
1600–1 Hamlet. *Hamlet*, act 2, sc.2, l.585–8.

3 Murder, though it have no tongue, will speak
With most miraculous organ.
1600–1 Hamlet. *Hamlet*, act 2, sc.2, l.595–6.

4 The spirit I have seen
May be the devil, and the devil hath power
T'assume a pleasing shape.
1600–1 Hamlet. *Hamlet*, act 2, sc.2, l.600–2.

5 The play's the thing
Wherein I'll catch the conscience of the King.
1600–1 Hamlet. *Hamlet*, act 2, sc.2, l.606–7.

6 The harlot's cheek, beautied with plast'ring art,
Is not more ugly to the thing that helps it
Than is my deed to my most painted word.
1600–1 Claudius. *Hamlet*, act 3, sc.1, l.53–5.

7 To be, or not to be; that is the question:
Whether 'tis nobler in the mind to suffer

The slings and arrows of outrageous fortune,
Or to take arms against a sea of troubles,
And, by opposing, end them. To die, to sleep—
No more, and by a sleep to say we end
The heartache and the thousand natural shocks
That flesh is heir to—'tis a consummation
Devoutly to be wished. To die, to sleep.
To sleep, perchance to dream. Ay, there's the rub,
For in that sleep of death what dreams may come
When we have shuffled off this mortal coil
Must give us pause. There's the respect
That makes calamity of so long life,
For who would bear the whips and scorns of time,
Th'oppressor's wrong, the proud man's contumely,
The pangs of disprized love, the law's delay,
The insolence of office, and the spurns
That patient merit of th'unworthy takes,
When he himself might his quietus make
With a bare bodkin? Who would these fardels bear,
To grunt and sweat under a weary life,
But that the dread of something after death,
The undiscovered country from whose bourn
No traveller returns, puzzles the will,
And makes us rather bear those ills we have
Than fly to others that we know not of?
Thus conscience does make cowards of us all,
And thus the native hue of resolution
Is sicklied o'er with the pale cast of thought,
And enterprises of great pith and moment
With this regard their currents turn awry,
And lose the name of action.
1600–1 Hamlet. *Hamlet*, act 3, sc.1, l.58–90.

8 To the noble mind
Rich gifts wax poor when givers prove unkind.
1600–1 Ophelia to Hamlet. *Hamlet*, act 3, sc.1, l.102–4.

9 The power of beauty will sooner transform honesty from
what it is to a bawd than the force of honesty can
translate beauty into his likeness.
1600–1 Hamlet to Ophelia. *Hamlet*, act 3, sc.1, l.113–15.

10 Get thee to a nunnery. Why wouldst thou be a breeder of
sinners?
1600–1 Hamlet to Ophelia. *Hamlet*, act 3, sc.1, l.123–4.

11 I am very proud, revengeful, ambitious, with more
offences at my beck than I have thoughts to put them in,
imagination to give them shape, or time to act them in.
1600–1 Hamlet. *Hamlet*, act 3, sc.1, l.126–9.

12 What should such fellows as I do crawling between
heaven and earth?
1600–1 Hamlet. *Hamlet*, act 3, sc.1, l.129–31.

13 Let the doors be shut upon him, that he may play the fool
nowhere but in's own house.
1600–1 Hamlet, of Polonius. *Hamlet*, act 3, sc.1, l.134–5.

14 God has given you one face, and you make yourselves
another.
1600–1 Hamlet, of women. *Hamlet*, act 3, sc.1, l.145–7.

15 I say we will have no more marriages; those that are
married already—all but one—shall live. The rest shall
keep as they are.
1600–1 Hamlet to Ophelia. *Hamlet*, act 3, sc.1, l.150–2.

16 O what a noble mind is here o'erthrown!
1600–1 Ophelia, of Hamlet. *Hamlet*, act 3, sc.1, l.153.

17 Madness in great ones must not unwatched go.
1600–1 Claudius, of Hamlet. *Hamlet*, act 3, sc.1, l.191.

18 Speak the speech, I pray you, as I pronounced it to you
—trippingly on the tongue; but if you mouth it, as many
of your players do, I had as lief the town-crier had spoke
my lines.
1600–1 Hamlet to the players. *Hamlet*, act 3, sc.2, l.1–4.

19 Hold as 'twere the mirror up to nature, to show virtue her
own feature, scorn her own image.
1600–1 Hamlet to the players. *Hamlet*, act 3, sc.2, l.22–3.

20 Let those that play your clowns speak no more than is set
down for them.
1600–1 Hamlet to the players. *Hamlet*, act 3, sc.2, l.38–9.

21 A man that Fortune's buffets and rewards
Hath ta'en with equal thanks.
1600–1 Hamlet, of Horatio. *Hamlet*, act 3, sc.2, l.65–6.

22 Give me that man
That is not passion's slave, and I will wear him
In my heart's core.
1600–1 Hamlet. *Hamlet*, act 3, sc.2, l.69–71.

23 OPHELIA: 'Tis brief, my lord.
HAMLET: As woman's love.
1600–1 *Hamlet*, act 3, sc.2, l.146–7.

24 Our wills and fates do so contrary run
That our devices still are overthrown.
1600–1 Player King. *Hamlet*, act 3, sc.2, l.202–3.

25 The lady protests too much, methinks.
1600–1 Gertrude to Hamlet, of the Player Queen. *Hamlet*, act 3, sc.2, l.219.

26 No, no, they do but jest, poison in jest.
1600–1 Hamlet, of the play. *Hamlet*, act 3, sc.2, l.224.

27 KING CLAUDIUS: What do you call the play?
HAMLET: *The Mousetrap*.
1600–1 *Hamlet*, act 3, sc.2, l.225–6.

28 Let the galled jade wince, our withers are
unwrung
1600–1 Hamlet, of the play. *Hamlet*, act 3, sc.2, l.231.

29 'Sblood, do you think I am easier to be played on than a
pipe?
1600–1 Hamlet to Guildenstern. *Hamlet*, act 3, sc.2, l.357–8.

30 'Tis now the very witching time of night,
When churchyards yawn and hell itself breathes out
Contagion to this world.
1600–1 Hamlet. *Hamlet*, act 3, sc.2, l.377–9.

31 I will speak daggers to her, but use none;
My tongue and soul in this be hypocrites.
1600–1 Hamlet, of Gertrude. *Hamlet*, act 3, sc.2, l.385–6.

32 O, my offence is rank! It smells to heaven.
1600–1 Claudius. *Hamlet*, act 3, sc.3, l.36.

33 Try what repentance can. What can it not?
Yet what can it when one cannot repent?
1600–1 Claudius. *Hamlet*, act 3, sc.3, l.65–6.

34 O limèd soul that, struggling to be free,
Art more engaged! Help, angels! make assay.
1600–1 Claudius. *Hamlet*, act 3, sc.3, l.68–9.

35 My words fly up, my thoughts remain below.
Words without thoughts never to heaven go.
1600–1 Claudius. *Hamlet*, act 3, sc.3, l.97–8.

36 You shall not budge.
You go not till I set you up a glass
Where you may see the inmost part of you.
1600–1 Hamlet to Gertrude. *Hamlet*, act 3, sc.4, l.18–20.

37 How now, a rat? Dead for a ducat, dead.
1600–1 Hamlet, hearing Polonius behind the arras. *Hamlet*, act 3, sc.4, l.23.

38 A bloody deed—almost as bad, good-mother,
As kill a king and marry with his brother.
1600–1 Hamlet. *Hamlet*, act 3, sc.4, l.27–8.

39 Thou wretched, rash, intruding fool, farewell.
I took thee for thy better.
1600–1 Hamlet to Polonius, whom Hamlet has just stabbed. *Hamlet*, act 3, sc.4, l.29–31.

40 You cannot call it love, for at your age
The heyday in the blood is tame.
1600–1 Hamlet to Gertrude. *Hamlet*, act 3, sc.4, l.67–8.

41 To flaming youth let virtue be as wax
And melt in her own fire.
1600–1 Hamlet to Gertrude. *Hamlet*, act 3, sc.4, l.74–5.

42 Nay, but to live
In the rank sweat of an enseamèd bed,
Stewed in corruption, honeying and making love
Over the nasty sty.
1600–1 Hamlet to Gertrude. *Hamlet*, act 3, sc.4, l.81–4.

43 Confess yourself to heaven;
Repent what's past, avoid what is to come.
1600–1 Hamlet to Gertrude. *Hamlet*, act 3, sc.4, l.140–1.

44 In the fatness of these pursy times
Virtue itself of vice must pardon beg.
1600–1 Hamlet to Gertrude. *Hamlet*, act 3, sc.4, l.144–5.

45 Assume a virtue if you have it not.
1600–1 Hamlet to Gertrude. *Hamlet*, act 3, sc.4, l.151.

46 I'll lug the guts into the neighbour room.
1600–1 Hamlet, of Polonius, whom he has killed. *Hamlet*, act 3, sc.4, l.186.

47 A man may fish with the worm that hath eat of a king, and eat of the fish that hath fed of that worm.
1600–1 Hamlet to Claudius. *Hamlet*, act 4, sc.3, l.27–8.

48 He is dead and gone, lady,
He is dead and gone.
At his head a grass-green turf,
At his heels a stone.
1600–1 Ophelia, singing. *Hamlet*, act 4, sc.5, l.29–32.

49 We know what we are, but know not what we may be.
1600–1 Ophelia. *Hamlet*, act 4, sc.5, l.42–3.

50 Good night, ladies, good night, sweet ladies, good night, good night.
1600–1 Ophelia. *Hamlet*, act 4, sc.5, l.71–2.

51 When sorrows come they come not single spies,
But in battalions.
1600–1 Claudius to Gertrude. *Hamlet*, act 4, sc.5, l.76–7.

52 The people muddied,
Thick and unwholesome in their thoughts and whispers.
1600–1 Claudius to Gertrude. *Hamlet*, act 4, sc.5, l.78–9.

53 There's such divinity doth hedge a king
That treason can but peep to what it would.
1600–1 Claudius to Gertrude. *Hamlet*, act 4, sc.5, l.122–3.

54 O, how the wheel becomes it!
1600–1 Ophelia. *Hamlet*, act 4, sc.5, l.172.

55 There's rosemary, that's for remembrance. Pray, love, remember. And there is pansies; that's for thoughts.
1600–1 Ophelia. *Hamlet*, act 4, sc.5, l.175–7.

56 Where th'offence is, let the great axe fall.
1600–1 Claudius. *Hamlet*, act 4, sc.5, l.216.

57 There is a willow grows aslant a brook
That shows his hoar leaves in the glassy stream.
Therewith fantastic garlands did she make
Of crow-flowers, nettles, daisies, and long purples,
That liberal shepherds give a grosser name,
But our cold maids do dead men's fingers call them.
1600–1 Gertrude, describing the scene of Ophelia's death. *Hamlet*, act 4, sc.7, l.138–42.

58 Her garments, heavy with their drink,
Pulled the poor wretch from her melodious lay
To muddy death.
1600–1 Gertrude, describing how Ophelia drowned. *Hamlet*, act 4, sc.7, l.153–5.

59 Too much of water hast thou, poor Ophelia,
And therefore I forbid my tears.
1600–1 Laertes. *Hamlet*, act 4, sc.7, l.158–9.

60 There is no ancient gentlemen but gardeners, ditchers, and gravemakers; they hold up Adam's profession.
1600–1 First Clown. *Hamlet*, act 5, sc.1, l.29–31.

61 This might be the pate of a politician which this ass o'er-offices, one that would circumvent God, might it not?
1600–1 Hamlet to Horatio. *Hamlet*, act 5, sc.1, l.77–9.

62 HAMLET: Ay, marry, why was he [Hamlet] sent into England?
FIRST CLOWN: Why, because a was mad. A shall recover his wits there; or if a do not, 'tis no great matter there.
HAMLET: Why?
FIRST CLOWN: 'Twill not be seen in him there. There the men are as mad as he.
1600–1 *Hamlet*, act 5, sc.1, l.146–152.

63 Alas, poor Yorick. I knew him, Horatio—a fellow of infinite jest, of most excellent fancy. He hath borne me on his back a thousand times; and now, how abhorred my imagination is! My gorge rises at it.
1600–1 Hamlet, of Yorick's skull. *Hamlet*, act 5, sc.1, l.180–4.

64 HAMLET: Dost thou think Alexander looked o' this fashion i'th' earth?
HORATIO: E'en so.
HAMLET: And smelt so? Pah!
1600–1 *Hamlet*, act 5, sc.1, l.193–6.

65 Imperial Caesar, dead and turned to clay,
Might stop a hole to keep the wind away.
1600–1 Hamlet. *Hamlet*, act 5, sc.1, l.208–9.

66 Hold off the earth a while,
Till I have caught her once more in mine arms.
1600–1 Laertes, of Ophelia, at her burial. *Hamlet*, act 5, sc.1, l.245–6.

67 For though I am not splenative and rash,
Yet have I something in me dangerous,
Which let thy wiseness fear.
1600–1 Hamlet to Laertes. *Hamlet*, act 5, sc.1, l.258–9.

68 Let Hercules himself do what he may,
The cat will mew, and dog will have his day.
1600–1 Hamlet to Laertes. *Hamlet*, act 5, sc.1, l.288–9.

69 There's a divinity that shapes our ends,
Rough-hew them how we will.
1600-1 Hamlet to Horatio. *Hamlet*, act 5, sc.2, l.10-11.

70 The bravery of his grief did put me
Into a tow'ring passion.
1600-1 Hamlet, of Laertes. *Hamlet*, act 5, sc.2, l.80-1.

71 A hit, a very palpable hit.
1600-1 Osric. *Hamlet*, act 5, sc.2, l.232.

72 I am more an antique Roman than a Dane.
Here's yet some liquor left.
1600-1 Horatio, intending to drink from the poisoned chalice. *Hamlet*, act 5, sc.2, l.294-5.

73 Absent thee from felicity a while,
And in this harsh world draw thy breath in pain
To tell my story.
1600-1 Hamlet to Horatio. *Hamlet*, act 5, sc.2, l.299-301.

74 O, I die, Horatio!
The potent poison quite o'ercrows my spirit.
1600-1 Hamlet. *Hamlet*, act 5, sc.2, l.304-5.

75 The rest is silence.
1600-1 Hamlet's last words. *Hamlet*, act 5, sc.2, l.310.

76 Good night, sweet prince,
And flights of angels sing thee to thy rest.
1600-1 Horatio. *Hamlet*, act 5, sc.2, l.312-13.

77 If music be the food of love, play on,
Give me excess of it that, surfeiting,
The appetite may sicken and so die.
That strain again, it had a dying fall.
O, it came o'er my ear like the sweet sound
That breathes upon a bank of violets,
Stealing and giving odour. Enough, no more,
'Tis not so sweet now as it was before.
1601 Orsino. *Twelfth Night*, act 1, sc.1, l.1-8.

78 O spirit of love, how quick and fresh art thou
That, notwithstanding thy capacity
Receiveth as the sea, naught enters there,
Of what validity and pitch so e'er,
But falls into abatement and low price
Even in a minute! So full of shapes is fancy
That it alone is high fantastical.
1601 Orsino. *Twelfth Night*, act 1, sc.1, l.9-15.

79 O, when mine eyes did see Olivia first
Methought she purged the air of pestilence;
That instant was I turned into a hart,
And my desires, like fell and cruel hounds,
E'er since pursue me.
1601 Orsino. *Twelfth Night*, act 1, sc.1, l.18-22.

80 He plays o'th' viol-de-gamboys, and speaks three or four languages word for word without book, and hath all the good gifts of nature.
1601 Sir Toby, of Sir Andrew. *Twelfth Night*, act 1, sc.3, l.23-6.

81 He's a great quarreller, and but that he hath the gift of a coward to allay the gust he hath in quarrelling, 'tis thought among the prudent he would quickly have the gift of a grave.
1601 Maria, of Sir Andrew. *Twelfth Night*, act 1, sc.3, l.28-31.

82 I'll drink to her as long as there is a passage in my throat and drink in Illyria.
1601 Sir Toby. *Twelfth Night*, act 1, sc.3, l.36-8.

83 I am a great eater of beef, and I believe that does harm to my wit.
1601 Sir Andrew. *Twelfth Night*, act 1, sc.3, l.83-4.

84 I have unclasped
To thee the book even of my secret soul.
1601 Orsino to Viola, disguised as Cesario. *Twelfth Night*, act 1, sc.4, l.13-14.

85 Many a good hanging prevents a bad marriage.
1601 Orsino. *Twelfth Night*, act 1, sc.5, l.18.

86 'Better a witty fool than a foolish wit.'
1601 Feste. *Twelfth Night*, act 1, sc.5, l.32-3.

87 Virtue that transgresses is but patched with sin.
1601 Feste. *Twelfth Night*, act 1, sc.5, l.44-5.

88 (*He belches*) A plague o' these pickle herring!
1601 Sir Toby. *Twelfth Night*, act 1, sc.5, l.116-17.

89 I would be loath to cast away my speech, for besides that it is excellently well penned, I have taken great pains to con it.
1601 Viola, in disguise, to Olivia. *Twelfth Night*, act 1, sc.5, l.165-7.

90 O sir, I will not be so hard-hearted. I will give out divers schedules of my beauty. It shall be inventoried and every particle and utensil labelled to my will, as *item*, two lips, indifferent red; *item*, two grey eyes, with lids to them; *item*, one neck, one chin, and so forth. Were you sent hither to praise me?
1601 Olivia to Viola (disguised as a young man). *Twelfth Night*, act 1, sc.5, l.233-8.

91 Make me a willow cabin at your gate
And call upon my soul within the house,
Write loyal cantons of contemnèd love,
And sing them loud even in the dead of night;
Halloo your name to the reverberate hills,
And make the babbling gossip of the air
Cry out 'Olivia!' O, you should not rest
Between the elements of air and earth
But you should pity me.
1601 Viola, describing how she would woo Olivia, were she in love with her. *Twelfth Night*, act 1, sc.5, l.258-65.

92 O mistress mine, where are you roaming?
O stay and hear, your true love's coming,
That can sing both high and low.
Trip no further, pretty sweeting,
Journeys end in lovers meeting,
Every wise man's son doth know.
1601 Feste's song. *Twelfth Night*, act 2, sc.3, l.38-43.

93 What is love? 'Tis not hereafter,
Present mirth hath present laughter.
What's to come is still unsure.
In delay there lies no plenty,
Then come kiss me, sweet and twenty.
Youth's a stuff will not endure.
1601 Feste's song. *Twelfth Night*, act 2, sc.3, l.46-51.

94 Is there no respect of place, persons, nor time in you?
1601 Malvolio to Feste, Sir Andrew and Sir Toby. *Twelfth Night*, act 2, sc.3, l.88-9.

95 Dost thou think because thou art virtuous there shall be no more cakes and ale?
1601 Sir Toby to Feste. *Twelfth Night*, act 2, sc.3, l.110-11.

96 Let still the woman take
An elder than herself. So wears she to him;
So sways she level in her husband's heart.
1601 Orsino. *Twelfth Night*, act 2, sc.4, l.28-30.

97 Then let thy love be younger than thyself,
Or thy affection cannot hold the bent;
For women are as roses, whose fair flower
Being once displayed, doth fall that very hour.
1601 Orsino. *Twelfth Night*, act 2, sc.4, l.35–8.

98 Now the melancholy god protect thee, and the tailor make thy doublet of changeable taffeta, for thy mind is a very opal.
1601 Feste to Orsino. *Twelfth Night*, act 2, sc.4, l.72–4.

99 My father had a daughter loved a man
As it might be, perhaps, were I a woman
I should your lordship.
1601 Viola, in disguise, to Orsino. *Twelfth Night*, act 2, sc.4, l.107–9.

1 She never told her love,
But let concealment, like a worm i' th' bud,
Feed on her damask cheek.
1601 Viola, in disguise, to Orsino. *Twelfth Night*, act 2, sc.4, l.110–12.

2 With a green and yellow melancholy
She sat like patience on a monument,
Smiling at grief.
1601 Viola, in disguise, to Orsino. *Twelfth Night*, act 2, sc.4, l.113–15.

3 By my life, this is my lady's hand. These be her very c's, her u's, and her t's, and thus makes she her great P's. It is in contempt of question her hand.
1601 Malvolio. *Twelfth Night*, act 2, sc.5, l.84–7.

4 Be not afraid of greatness. Some are born great, some achieve greatness, and some have greatness thrust upon 'em.
1601 Malvolio. *Twelfth Night*, act 2, sc.5, l.139–41.

5 He will come to her in yellow stockings, and 'tis a colour she abhors, and cross-gartered, a fashion she detests.
1601 Maria, of Malvolio. *Twelfth Night*, act 2, sc.5, l.192–4.

6 Fools are as like husbands as pilchards are to herrings—the husband's the bigger.
1601 Feste to Viola. *Twelfth Night*, act 3, sc.1, l.32–4.

7 Now Jove in his next commodity of hair send thee a beard.
1601 Feste to Viola. *Twelfth Night*, act 3, sc.1, l.43–4.

8 Most excellent accomplished lady, the heavens rain odours on you.
1601 Viola to Olivia. *Twelfth Night*, act 3, sc.1, l.83–4.

9 O world, how apt the poor are to be proud!
1601 Olivia. *Twelfth Night*, act 3, sc.1, l.126.

10 Then westward ho!
1601 Viola. *Twelfth Night*, act 3, sc.1, l.133.

11 O, what a deal of scorn looks beautiful
In the contempt and anger of his lip!
1601 Olivia, of Viola (as Cesario). *Twelfth Night*, act 3, sc.1, l.143–4.

12 Love sought is good, but given unsought, is better.
1601 Olivia. *Twelfth Night*, act 3, sc.1, l.154.

13 You are now sailed into the north of my lady's opinion, where you will hang like an icicle on a Dutchman's beard unless you do redeem it by some laudable attempt either of valour or policy.
1601 Fabian, of Sir Toby. *Twelfth Night*, act 3, sc.2, l.24–8.

14 There is no love-broker in the world can more prevail in man's commendation with woman than report of valour.
1601 Sir Toby to Sir Andrew. *Twelfth Night*, act 3, sc.2, l.34–6.

15 For Andrew, if he were opened and you find so much blood in his liver as will clog the foot of a flea, I'll eat the rest of th'anatomy.
1601 Sir Toby. *Twelfth Night*, act 3, sc.2, l.58–60.

16 Why, this is very midsummer madness.
1601 Olivia, of Malvolio. *Twelfth Night*, act 3, sc.4, l.54.

17 If this were played upon a stage now, I could condemn it as an improbable fiction.
1601 Fabian. *Twelfth Night*, act 3, sc.4, l.125–6.

18 Still you keep o' th' windy side of the law.
1601 Fabian. *Twelfth Night*, act 3, sc.4, l.162.

19 A terrible oath, with a swaggering accent sharply twanged off, gives manhood more approbation than ever proof itself would have earned him.
1601 Sir Toby to Sir Andrew. *Twelfth Night*, act 3, sc.4, l.176–8.

20 I am sure no man hath any quarrel to me. My remembrance is very free and clear from any image of offence done to any man.
1601 Viola (as Cesario) to Sir Toby. *Twelfth Night*, act 3, sc.4, l.221–3.

21 In nature there's no blemish but the mind.
None can be called deformed but the unkind.
1601 Antonio. *Twelfth Night*, act 3, sc.4, l.359–60.

22 There is no darkness but ignorance.
1601 Feste to Malvolio. *Twelfth Night*, act 4, sc.2, l.43–4.

23 Thus the whirligig of time brings in his revenges.
1601 Feste. *Twelfth Night*, act 5, sc.1, l.373.

24 I'll be revenged on the whole pack of you.
1601 Malvolio. *Twelfth Night*, act 5, sc.1, l.374.

25 When that I was and a little tiny boy,
With hey, ho, the wind and the rain,
A foolish thing was but a toy,
For the rain it raineth every day.
1601 Feste. *Twelfth Night*, act 5, sc.1, l.385–8.

26 Then everything includes itself in power,
Power into will, will into appetite;
And appetite, an universal wolf.
1602 Ulysses. *Troilus and Cressida*, act 1, sc.3, l.119–21.

27 The general's disdained
By him one step below; he, by the next;
That next, by him beneath. So every step,
Exampled by the first pace that is sick
Of his superior, grows to an envious fever
Of pale and bloodless emulation.
1602 Ulysses. *Troilus and Cressida*, act 1, sc.3, l.129–134.

28 The nature of the sickness found, Ulysses,
What is the remedy?
1602 Agamemnon. *Troilus and Cressida*, act 1, sc.3, l.140–1.

29 In such indices, although small pricks
To their subsequent volumes, there is seen
The baby figure of the giant mass
Of things to come at large.
1602 Nestor. *Troilus and Cressida*, act 1, sc.3, l.337–40.

30 The common curse of mankind, folly and ignorance, be thine.
1602 Thersites. *Troilus and Cressida*, act 2, sc.3, l.26–7.

31 He that is proud eats up himself. Pride is his own glass, his own trumpet, his own chronicle.
1602 Agamemnon. *Troilus and Cressida*, act 2, sc.3, l.153–5.

32 To make a sweet lady sad is a sour offence.
1602 Helen to Pandarus. *Troilus and Cressida*, act 3, sc.1, l.71.

33 I am giddy. Expectation whirls me round.
Th'imaginary relish is so sweet
That it enchants my sense.
1602 Troilus, on the prospect of an assignation with Cressida. *Troilus and Cressida*, act 3, sc.2, l.16–18.

34 Words pay no debts.
1602 Pandarus to Troilus. *Troilus and Cressida*, act 3, sc.2, l.54.

35 This is the monstruosity in love, lady—that the will is infinite and the execution confined; that the desire is boundless and the act a slave to limit.
1602 Troilus to Cressida. *Troilus and Cressida*, act 3, sc.2, l.77–80.

36 Some men creep in skittish Fortune's hall
Whiles others play the idiots in her eyes.
1602 Ulysses. *Troilus and Cressida*, act 3, sc.3, l.129–30.

37 Time hath, my lord,
A wallet at his back, wherein he puts
Alms for oblivion.
1602 Ulysses to Achilles. *Troilus and Cressida*, act 3, sc.3, l.139–41.

38 Perseverance, dear my lord,
Keeps honour bright. To have done is to hang
Quite out of fashion, like a rusty mail
In monumental mock'ry.
1602 Ulysses. *Troilus and Cressida*, act 3, sc.3, l.144–7.

39 One touch of nature makes the whole world kin.
1602 Ulysses to Achilles. *Troilus and Cressida*, act 3, sc.3, l.169.

40 I see my reputation is at stake.
My fame is shrewdly gored.
1602 Achilles. *Troilus and Cressida*, act 3, sc.3, l.220–1.

41 The busy day,
Waked by the lark, hath roused the ribald crows,
And dreaming night will hide our joys no longer.
1602 Troilus to Cressida. *Troilus and Cressida*, act 4, sc.2, l.10–11.

42 The kiss you take is better than you give.
1602 Cressida to Menelaus. *Troilus and Cressida*, act 4, sc.6, l. 39.

43 With too much blood and too little brain these two may run mad.
1602 Thersites, of Achilles and Patroclus. *Troilus and Cressida*, act 5, sc.1, l.45–7.

44 Lechery, lechery, still wars and lechery! Nothing else holds fashion.
1602 Thersites. *Troilus and Cressida*, act 5, sc.2, l.197–8.

45 Words, words, mere words, no matter from the heart.
1602 Troilus, on his letter from Cressida. *Troilus and Cressida*, act 5, sc.3, l.111.

46 Scare Troy out of itself. But march away.
1602 Troilus. *Troilus and Cressida*, act 5, sc.11, l.21.

47 Heaven doth with us as we with torches do,
Not light them for themselves.
1603 Duke. *Measure for Measure*, act 1, sc.1, l.32–3.

48 I had as lief have the foppery of freedom as the morality of imprisonment.
1603 Lucio to Claudio. *Measure for Measure*, act 1, sc.2, l.125–6.

49 Our doubts are traitors,
And makes us lose the good we oft might win,
By fearing to attempt.
1603 Lucio to Isabella. *Measure for Measure*, act 1, sc.4, l.77–9.

50 We must not make a scarecrow of the law,
Setting it up to fear the birds of prey,
And let it keep one shape till custom make it
Their perch, and not their terror.
1603 Angelo. *Measure for Measure*, act 2, sc.1, l.1–4.

51 'Tis one thing to be tempted, Escalus,
Another thing to fall.
1603 Angelo. *Measure for Measure*, act 2, sc.1, l.17–18.

52 I not deny
The jury passing on the prisoner's life
May in the sworn twelve have a thief or two
Guiltier than him they try.
1603 Angelo. *Measure for Measure*, act 2, sc.1, l.18–21.

53 The jewel that we find, we stoop and take't
Because we see it, but what we do not see
We tread upon.
1603 Angelo. *Measure for Measure*, act 2, sc.1, l.24–26.

54 Some rise by sin, and some by virtue fall.
1603 Escalus. *Measure for Measure*, act 2, sc.1, l.38.

55 The law hath not been dead, though it hath slept.
1603 Angelo to Isabella. *Measure for Measure*, act 2, sc.2, l.92.

56 ISABELLA: Yet show some pity,
ANGELO: I show it most of all when I show justice,
For then I pity those I do not know.
1603 *Measure for Measure*, act 2, sc.2, l.101–3.

57 O, it is excellent
To have a giant's strength, but it is tyrannous
To use it like a giant.
1603 Isabella to Angelo. *Measure for Measure*, act 2, sc.2, l.109–11.

58 But man, proud man,
Dressed in a little brief authority,
Most ignorant of what he's most assured,
His glassy essence, like an angry ape
Plays such fantastic tricks before high heaven
As makes the angels weep.
1603 Isabella to Angelo. *Measure for Measure*, act 2, sc.2, l.120–5.

59 Great men may jest with saints; 'tis wit in them,
But in the less, foul profanation.
1603 Isabella to Angelo. *Measure for Measure*, act 2, sc.2, l.130–1.

60 Thieves for their robbery have authority,
When judges steal themselves.
1603 Angelo. *Measure for Measure*, act 2, sc.2, l.181–2.

61 When men were fond, I smiled, and wondered how.
1603 Angelo. *Measure for Measure*, act 2, sc.2, l.191–2.

62 When I would pray and think, I think and pray
To several subjects; heaven hath my empty words,
Whilst my invention, hearing not my tongue,
Anchors on Isabel.
1603 Angelo. *Measure for Measure*, act 2, sc.4, l.1–4.

63 The miserable have no other medicine
But only hope.
1603 Claudio to the Duke. *Measure for Measure*, act 3, sc.1, l.2–3.

64 Reason thus with life
If I do lose thee, I do lose a thing
That none but fools would keep.
1603 Duke to Claudio. *Measure for Measure*, act 3, sc.1, l.6–8.

65 If thou art rich, thou'rt poor,
For like an ass whose back with ingots bows,
Thou bear'st thy heavy riches but a journey,
And death unloads thee.
1603 Duke to Claudio. *Measure for Measure*, act 3, sc.1, l.25–8.

66 The sense of death is most in apprehension,
And the poor beetle that we tread upon
In corporal sufferance finds a pang as great
As when a giant dies.
1603 Isabella to Claudio. *Measure for Measure*, act 3, sc.1, l.76–9.

67 If I must die,
I will encounter darkness as a bride,
And hug it in mine arms.
1603 Claudio to Isabella. *Measure for Measure*, act 3, sc.1, l.81–3.

68 Sure it is no sin,
Or of the deadly seven it is the least.
1603 Claudio to Isabella, of fornication. *Measure for Measure*, act 3, sc.1, l.109–10.

69 Ay, but to die, and go we know not where;
To lie in cold obstruction, and to rot.
1603 Claudio. *Measure for Measure*, act 3, sc.1, l.118–19.

70 The weariest and most loathèd worldly life
That age, ache, penury, and imprisonment
Can lay on nature is a paradise
To what we fear of death.
1603 Claudio to Isabella. *Measure for Measure*, act 3, sc.1, l.129–32.

71 Virtue is bold, and goodness never fearful.
1603 Duke to Isabella. *Measure for Measure*, act 3, sc.1, l.210.

72 Take, O take thy lips away
That so sweetly were forsworn.
1603 Boy, singing. *Measure for Measure*, act 4, sc.1, l.1–2.

73 Music oft hath such a charm
To make bad good, and good provoke to harm.
1603 Duke. *Measure for Measure*, act 4, sc.1, l.14–15.

74 You weigh equally; a feather will turn the scale.
1603 Provost to Abhorson. *Measure for Measure*, act 4, sc.2, l.28–29.

75 Every true man's apparel fits your thief.
1603 Abhorson. *Measure for Measure*, act 4, sc.2, l.41.

76 Drunk many times a day, if not many days entirely drunk.
1603 Provost, of Barnardine. *Measure for Measure*, act 4, sc.2, l.151–2.

77 Death's a great disguiser.
1603 Duke to Provost. *Measure for Measure*, act 4, sc.2, l.175.

78 If she be mad, as I believe no other,
Her madness hath the oddest frame of sense.
1603 Duke to Isabella. *Measure for Measure*, act 5, sc.1, l.60–1.

79 Haste still pays haste, and leisure answers leisure;
Like doth quit like, and measure still for measure.
1603 Duke. *Measure for Measure*, act 5, sc.1, 407–8.

80 They say best men are moulded out of faults,
And, for the most, become much more the better
For being a little bad. So may my husband.
1603 Mariana, of Angelo. *Measure for Measure*, act 5, sc.1, l.436–8.

81 In following him I follow myself.
1603–4 Iago, of Othello. *Othello*, act 1, sc.1, l.58.

82 For when my outward action doth demonstrate
The native act and figure of my heart
In compliment extern, 'tis not long after
But I will wear my heart upon my sleeve
For daws to peck at. I am not what I am.
1603–4 Iago. *Othello*, act 1, sc.1, l.60–5.

83 Though he in a fertile climate dwell,
Plague him with flies.
1603–4 Iago, of Brabanzio. *Othello*, act 1, sc.1, l.70–1.

84 Even now, now, very now, an old black ram
Is tupping your white ewe.
1603–4 Iago to Brabanzio. *Othello*, act 1, sc.1, l.88–89.

85 I am one, sir, that comes to tell you your daughter and the Moor are now making the beast with the two backs.
1603–4 Iago to Brabanzio. *Othello*, act 1, sc.1, l.117–9.

86 Though in the trade of war I have slain men,
Yet do I hold it very stuff o'th' conscience
To do no contrived murder. I lack iniquity,
Sometime, to do me service. Nine or ten times
I had thought to've yerked him here, under the ribs.
1603–4 Iago. *Othello*, act 1, sc.2, l.1–5.

87 But that I love the gentle Desdemona
I would not my unhousèd free condition
Put into circumscription and confine
For the seas' worth.
1603–4 Othello. *Othello*, act 1, sc.2, l.25–8.

88 Whether a maid so tender, fair, and happy,
So opposite to marriage that she shunned
The wealthy curlèd darlings of our nation,
Would ever have, t'incur a general mock,
Run from her guardage to the sooty bosom
Of such a thing as thou.
1603–4 Brabanzio to Othello. *Othello*, act 1, sc.2, l.67–72.

89 My particular grief
Is of so floodgate and o'erbearing nature
That it engluts and swallows other sorrows,
And it is still itself.
1603–4 Brabanzio, learning of Desdemona's marriage. *Othello*, act 1, sc.3, l.55–8.

90 For nature so preposterously to err,
Being not deficient, blind, or lame of sense,
Sans witchcraft could not.
1603–4 Brabanzio, of Desdemona's marriage. *Othello*, act 1, sc.3, l.62–4.

91 Rude am I in my speech,
And little blessed with the soft phrase of peace.
1603–4 Othello. *Othello*, act 1, sc.3, l.81–2.

92 A maiden never bold,
Of spirit so still and quiet that her motion
Blushed at herself—and she in spite of nature,
Of years, of country, credit, everything,
To fall in love with what she feared to look on!
It is a judgement maimed and most imperfect
That will confess perfection so could err
Against all rules of nature.
1603–4 Brabanzio of Desdemona. *Othello*, act 1, sc.3, l.94–100.

93 The Anthropophagi, and men whose heads
Do grow beneath their shoulders.
1603–4 Othello. *Othello*, act 1, sc.3, l.143–4.

94 She gave me for my pains a world of kisses.
She swore in faith 'twas strange, 'twas passing strange,
'Twas pitiful, 'twas wonderous pitiful.
She wished she had not heard it, yet she wished
That heaven had made her such a man.
1603–4 Othello, of his courtship of Desdemona. *Othello*, act 1, sc.3, l.158–162.

95 She loved me for the dangers I had passed,
And I loved her that she did pity them.
1603–4 Othello, of Desdemona. *Othello*, act 1, sc.3, l.166–7.

96 My noble father,
I do perceive here a divided duty.
1603–4 Desdemona. *Othello*, act 1, sc.3, l.179–80.

97 For your sake, jewel,
I am glad at soul I have no other child,
For thy escape would teach me tyranny,
To hang clogs on 'em.
1603–4 Brabanzio to Desdemona. *Othello*, act 1, sc.3, l.194–7.

98 When remedies are past, the griefs are ended
By seeing the worst which late on hopes depended.
To mourn a mischief that is past and gone
Is the next way to draw new mischief on.
1603–4 Duke to Brabanzio. *Othello*, act 1, sc.3, l.201–4.

99 The robbed that smiles steals something from the thief;
He robs himself that spends a bootless grief.
1603–4 Duke. *Othello*, act 1, sc.3, l.207–8.

1 But words are words. I never yet did hear
That the bruised heart was piercèd through the ear.
1603–4 Brabanzio. *Othello*, act 1, sc.3, l.217–8.

2 I never found man that knew how to love himself. Ere I would say I would drown myself for the love of a guinea-hen, I would change my humanity with a baboon.
1603–4 Iago to Roderigo. *Othello*, act 1, sc.3, l.313–6.

3 Virtue? A fig! 'Tis in ourselves that we are thus or thus. Our bodies are our gardens, to the which our wills are gardeners.
1603–4 Iago to Roderigo. *Othello*, act 1, sc.3, l.319–21.

4 Make all the money thou canst. If sanctimony and a frail vow betwixt an erring barbarian and a super-subtle Venetian be not too hard for my wits and all the tribes of hell, thou shalt enjoy her.
1603–4 Iago to Roderigo. *Othello*, act 1, sc.3, l.352–6.

5 The Moor is of a free and open nature,
That thinks men honest that but seem to be so,
And will as tenderly be led by th' nose
As asses are.
I ha't. It is ingendered. Hell and night
Must bring this monstrous birth to the world's light.
1603–4 Iago. *Othello*, act 1, sc.3, l.391–6.

6 You are pictures out of doors,
Bells in your parlours; wildcats in your kitchens,
Saints in your injuries; devils being offended,
Players in your housewifery, and hussies in your beds.
1603–4 Iago of women. *Othello*, act 2, sc.1, l.112–15.

7 With as little web as this will I ensnare as great a fly as Cassio.
1603–4 Iago (aside). *Othello*, act 2, sc.1, l.171–2.

8 If it were now to die
'Twere now to be most happy, for I fear
My soul hath her content so absolute
That not another comfort like to this
Succeeds in unknown fate.
1603–4 Othello to Desdemona. *Othello*, act 2, sc.1, l.190–4.

9 The heavens forbid
But that our loves and comforts should increase
Even as our days do grow.
1603–4 Desdemona to Othello. *Othello*, act 2, sc.1, l.194–6.

10 [I'll] make the Moor thank me, love me, and reward me
For making him egregiously an ass.
1603–4 Iago. *Othello*, act 2, sc.1, l.307–8.

11 Reputation, reputation, reputation! O—I ha' lost my reputation, I ha' lost the immortal part of myself, and what remains is bestial.
1603–4 Cassio to Iago. *Othello*, act 2, sc.3, l.256–8.

12 Reputation is an idle and most false imposition, oft got without merit and lost without deserving.
1603–4 Iago to Cassio. *Othello*, act 2, sc.3, l.262–4.

13 O God, that men should put an enemy in their mouths to steal away their brains!
1603–4 Cassio, of wine. *Othello*, act 2, sc.3, l.283–5.

14 So will I turn her virtue into pitch,
And out of her own goodness make the net
That shall enmesh them all.
1603–4 Iago. *Othello*, act 2, sc.3, l.351–3.

15 How poor are they that ha' not patience!
What wound did ever heal but by degrees?
1603–4 Iago to Roderigo. *Othello*, act 2, sc.3, l.360–1.

16 Excellent wretch! Perdition catch my soul
But I do love thee, and when I love thee not,
Chaos is come again.
1603–4 Othello, of Desdemona. *Othello*, act 3, sc.3, l.91–3.

17 I know thou'rt full of love and honesty,
And weigh'st thy words before thou giv'st them breath.
1603–4 Othello to Iago. *Othello*, act 3, sc.3, l.123–4.

18 Good name in man and woman, dear my lord,
Is the immediate jewel of their souls.
Who steals my purse steals trash; 'tis something, nothing;
'Twas mine, 'tis his, and has been slave to thousands.
But he that filches from me my good name
Robs me of that which not enriches him
And makes me poor indeed.
1603–4 Iago to Othello. *Othello*, act 3, sc.3, l.160–6.

19 O, beware, my lord, of jealousy,
It is the green-eyed monster which doth mock
The meat it feeds on.
1603–4 Iago to Othello. *Othello*, act 3, sc.3, l.169–71.

20 Poor and content is rich, and rich enough,
But riches fineless is as poor as winter
To him that ever fears he shall be poor.
1603–4 Iago to Othello. *Othello*, act 3, sc.3, l.176–8.

21 I humbly do beseech you of your pardon
For too much loving you.
1603–4 Iago to Othello. *Othello*, act 3, sc.3, l.216–7.

22 If I do prove her haggard,
Though that her jesses were my dear heart-strings
I'd whistle her off and let her down the wind
To prey at fortune.
1603–4 Othello. *Othello*, act 3, sc.3, l.264–7.

23 If she be false, O then heaven mocks itself!
I'll not believe't.
1603–4 Othello, of Desdemona. *Othello*, act 3, sc.3, l.282–3.

24 Trifles light as air
Are to the jealous confirmations strong
As proofs of holy writ.
1603–4 Iago. *Othello*, act 3, sc.3, l.326–8.

25 Not poppy nor mandragora
Nor all the drowsy syrups of the world
Shall ever medicine thee to that sweet sleep
Which thou owedst yesterday.
1603–4 Iago, of Othello. *Othello*, act 3, sc.3, l.334–7.

Shakespeare Othello

26 He that is robbed, not wanting what is stol'n,
Let him not know't and he's not robbed at all.
1603–4 Othello to Iago. *Othello*, act 3, sc.3, l.347–8.

27 I had been happy if the general camp,
Pioneers and all, had tasted her sweet body,
So I had nothing known. O, now for ever
Farewell the tranquil mind, farewell content,
Farewell the plumèd troops and the big wars
That makes ambition virtue! O, farwell,
Farewell the neighing steed and the shrill trump,
The spirit-stirring drum, th'ear-piercing fife,
The royal banner, and all quality,
Pride, pomp, and circumstance of glorious war!
And O, you mortal engines whose rude throats
Th'immortal Jove's dread clamours counterfeit,
Farewell! Othello's occupation's gone.
1603–4 Othello. *Othello*, act 3, sc.3, l.350–62.

28 But this denoted a foregone conclusion.
1603–4 Othello. *Othello*, act 3, sc.3, l.433.

29 My bloody thoughts with violent pace
Shall ne'er look back, ne'er ebb to humble love,
Till that a capable and wide revenge
Swallow them up.
1603–4 Othello to Iago. *Othello*, act 3, sc.3, l.460–3.

30 Jealous souls will not be answered so.
They are not ever jealous for the cause,
But jealous for they're jealous. It is a monster
Begot upon itself, born on itself.
1603–4 Emilia to Desdemona. *Othello*, act 3, sc.4, l.156–9.

31 But yet the pity of it, Iago. O, Iago, the pity of it, Iago!
1603–4 Othello. *Othello*, act 4, sc.1, l.191–2.

32 Do it not with poison. Strangle her in her bed.
1603–4 Iago to Othello. *Othello*, act 4, sc.1, l.202–3.

33 Is this the noble Moor whom our full senate
Call all-in-all sufficient? Is this the nature
Whom passion could not shake, whose solid virtue
The shot of accident nor dart of chance
Could neither graze nor pierce?
1603–4 Lodovico. *Othello*, act 4, sc.1, l.266–70.

34 O thou weed,
Who art so lovely fair, and smell'st so sweet,
That the sense aches at thee—would thou hadst ne'er
been born!
1603–4 Othello, of Desdemona. *Othello*, act 4, sc.2, l.69–72.

35 I cry you mercy then.
I took you for that cunning whore of Venice
That married with Othello.
1603–4 Othello to Desdemona. *Othello*, act 4, sc.2, l.93–4.

36 I will be hanged, if some eternal villain,
Some busy and insinuating rogue,
Some cogging, cozening slave, to get some office,
Have not devised this slander.
1603–4 Emilia. *Othello*, act 4, sc.2, l.134–7.

37 Mine eyes do itch. Doth that bode weeping?
1603–4 Desdemona to Emilia. *Othello*, act 4, sc.3, l.56–7.

38 Let husbands know
Their wives have sense like them. They see, and smell,
And have their palates both for sweet and sour,
As husbands have.
1603–4 Emilia to Desdemona. *Othello*, act 4, sc.3, l.92–5.

39 It is the cause, it is the cause, my soul.
Let me not name it to you, you chaste stars.
It is the cause. Yet I'll not shed her blood,
Nor scar that whiter skin of hers than snow,
And smooth as monumental alabaster.
Yet she must die, else she'll betray more men.
Put out the light, and then put out the light.
1603–4 Othello. *Othello*, act 5, sc.2, l.1–7.

40 When I have plucked thy rose
I cannot give it vital growth again.
It needs must wither. I'll smell thee on the tree.
1603–4 Othello. *Othello*, act 5, sc.2, l.13–15.

41 Had all his hairs been lives, my great revenge
Had stomach for 'em all.
1603–4 Othello, of Cassio. *Othello*, act 5, sc.2, l.81–2.

42 Kill me tomorrow; let me live tonight.
1603–4 Desdemona to Othello. *Othello*, act 5, sc.2, l.87.

43 It is the very error of the moon,
She comes more nearer earth than she was wont,
And makes men mad.
1603–4 Othello. *Othello*, act 5, sc.2, l.118–20.

44 Not Cassio killed? Then murder's out of tune,
And sweet revenge grows harsh.
1603–4 Othello. *Othello*, act 5, sc.2, l.124–5.

45 She's like a liar gone to burning hell.
'Twas I that killed her.
1603–4 Othello. *Othello*, act 5, sc.2, l.138–9.

46 May his pernicious soul
Rot half a grain a day.
1603–4 Emilia, of Iago. *Othello*, act 5, sc.2, l.162–3.

47 Thou hast not half that power to do me harm
As I have to be hurt. O gull, O dolt,
As ignorant as dirt!
1603–4 Emilia to Othello. *Othello*, act 5, sc.2, l.169–71.

48 Here is my journey's end, here is my butt
And very sea-mark of my utmost sail.
1603–4 Othello. *Othello*, act 5, sc.2, l.274–5.

49 O ill-starred wench,
Pale as thy smock! When we shall meet at count
This look of thine will hurl my soul from heaven,
And fiends will snatch at it.
1603–4 Othello, of Desdemona. *Othello*, act 5, sc.2, l.279–2.

50 Demand me nothing. What you know, you know.
From this time forth I never will speak word.
1603–4 Iago to Othello. *Othello*, act 5, sc.2, l.309–10.

51 I pray you, in your letters,
When you shall these unlucky deeds relate,
Speak of me as I am. Nothing extenuate,
Nor set down aught in malice. Then must you speak
Of one that loved not wisely but too well,
Of one not easily jealous but, being wrought,
Perplexed in the extreme; of one whose hand,
Like the base Indian, threw a pearl away
Richer than all his tribe; of one whose subdued eyes,
Albeit unusèd to the melting mood,
Drops tears as fast as the Arabian trees
Their medicinable gum. Set you down this,
And say besides that in Aleppo once,
Where a malignant and a turbaned Turk
Beat a Venetian and traduced the state,

I took by th' throat the circumcisèd dog
And smote him thus.
1603–4 Othello's speech as he stabs himself. *Othello*, act 5, sc.2, l.349–65.

52 I kiss thee ere I killed thee. No way but this:
Killing myself, to die upon a kiss.
1603–4 Othello. *Othello*, act 5, sc.2, l.368–9.

53 Be checked for silence,
But never taxed for speech.
1604–5 Countess to Bertram. *All's Well That Ends Well*, act 1, sc.1, l.64–5.

54 'Twere all one
That I should love a bright particular star
And think to wed it, he is so above me.
1604–5 Helen, of Bertram. *All's Well That Ends Well*, act 1, sc.1, l.84–6.

55 The hind that would be mated by the lion
Must die for love.
1604–5 Helen, of Bertram. *All's Well That Ends Well*, act 1, sc.1, l.90–1.

56 Virginity is peevish, proud, idle, made of self-love
—which is the most inhibited sin in the canon. Keep it not.
1604–5 Paroles to Helen. *All's Well That Ends Well*, act 1, sc.1, l.141–3.

57 Get thee a good husband, and use him as he uses thee.
1604–5 Paroles to Helen. *All's Well That Ends Well*, act 1, sc.1, l.209–10.

58 Our remedies oft in ourselves do lie
Which we ascribe to heaven.
1604–5 Helen. *All's Well That Ends Well*, act 1, sc.1, l.212.

59 Though honesty be no puritan, yet it will do no hurt.
1604–5 Lavatch. *All's Well That Ends Well*, act 1, sc.3, l.91–2.

60 He and his physicians
Are of a mind: he, that they cannot help him;
They, that they cannot help.
1604–5 Countess, of the King. *All's Well That Ends Well*, act 1, sc.3, l.235–7.

61 They say miracles are past, and we have our philosophical persons to make modern and familiar things supernatural and causeless. Hence it is that we make trifles of terrors, ensconcing ourselves into seeming knowledge when we should submit ourselves to an unknown fear.
1604–5 Lafeu. *All's Well That Ends Well*, act 2, sc.3, l.1–6.

62 Why, these balls bound, there's noise in it. 'Tis hard:
A young man married is a man that's marred.
1604–5 Paroles. *All's Well That Ends Well*, act 2, sc.3, l.294–5.

63 The soul of this man is his clothes.
1604–5 Lafeu. *All's Well That Ends Well*, act 2, sc.5, l.43.

64 No legacy is so rich as honesty.
1604–5 Mariana to Diana. *All's Well That Ends Well*, act 3, sc.5, l.12–13.

65 'Tis not the many oaths that make the truth,
But the plain single vow that is vowèd true.
1604–5 Diana. *All's Well That Ends Well*, act 4, sc.2, l.22–3.

66 My chastity's the jewel of our house,
Bequeathèd down from many ancestors,
Which were the greatest obloquy i' th' world
In me to lose.
1604–5 Diana. *All's Well That Ends Well*, act 4, sc.2, l.47–50.

67 A heaven on earth I have won by wooing thee.
1604–5 Bertram to Diana. *All's Well That Ends Well*, act 4, sc.2, l.67.

68 The web of our life is of mingled yarn, good and ill together.
1604–5 First Lord Dumaine. *All's Well That Ends Well*, act 4, sc.3, l.74–5.

69 Drunkenness is his best virtue, for he will be swine-drunk, and in his sleep he does little harm, save to his bedclothes.
1604–5 Paroles, of the Duke. *All's Well That Ends Well*, act 4, sc.3, l.257–9.

70 'Twas a good lady, 'twas a good lady. We may pick a thousand salads ere we light on such another herb.
1604–5 Lafeu, of Helen. *All's Well That Ends Well*, act 4, sc.5, l.13–15.

71 I am for the house with the narrow gate, which I take to be too little for pomp to enter. Some that humble themselves may, but the many will be too chill and tender, and they'll be for the flow'ry way that leads to the broad gate and the great fire.
1604–5 Lavatch to Lafeu. *All's Well That Ends Well*, act 4, sc.5, l.50–5.

72 Praising what is lost
Makes the remembrance dear.
1604–5 King. *All's Well That Ends Well*, act 5, sc.3, l.19–20.

73 Th'inaudible and noiseless foot of time.
1604–5 King. *All's Well That Ends Well*, act 5, sc.3, l.42.

74 I wonder men dare trust themselves with men.
1605 Apemantus. *Timon of Athens*, act 1, sc.2, l.42.

75 Grant I may never prove so fond
To trust man on his oath or bond.
1605 Apemantus' grace. *Timon of Athens*, act 1, sc.2, l.63–4.

76 Men shut their doors against a setting sun.
1605 Apemantus. *Timon of Athens*, act 1, sc.2, l.141.

77 Every man has his fault, and honesty is his.
1605 Lucullus, of Timon. *Timon of Athens*, act 3, sc.1, l.27–8.

78 Men must learn now with pity to dispense,
For policy sits above conscience.
1605 First Stranger. *Timon of Athens*, act 3, sc.2, l.87–8.

79 Nothing emboldens sin so much as mercy.
1605 First Senator. *Timon of Athens*, act 3, sc.6, l.3.

80 This yellow slave
Will knit and break religions, bless th' accursed.
1605 Timon, of gold. *Timon of Athens*, act 4, sc.3, l.34–5.

81 Thanks I must you con
That you are thieves professed, that you work not
In holier shapes; for there is boundless theft
In limited professions.
1605 Timon to thieves. *Timon of Athens*, act 4, sc.3, l.426–30.

82 Trust not the physician;
His antidotes are poison, and he slays
More than you rob.
1605 Timon to thieves. *Timon of Athens*, act 4, sc.3, l.433–5.

83 Rich men deal gifts,
Expecting in return twenty for one?
1605 Timon to Flavius. *Timon of Athens*, act 4, sc.3, l.510–11.

84 I cannot heave
My heart into my mouth. I love your majesty
According to my bond, nor more nor less.
1605–6 Cordelia to Lear. *King Lear*, act 1, sc.1, l.91–3.

Shakespeare King Lear

85 Thy youngest daughter does not love thee least,
Nor are those empty-hearted whose low sounds
Reverb no hollowness.
1605–6 Kent to Lear. *King Lear*, act 1, sc.1, l.152–4.

86 If for I want that glib and oily art
To speak and purpose not—since what I well intend,
I'll do't before I speak—that you make known
It is no vicious blot, murder, or foulness,
No unchaste action or dishonoured step
That hath deprived me of your grace and favour,
But even the want of that for which I am richer—
A still-soliciting eye, and such a tongue
That I am glad I have not, though not to have it
Hath lost me in your liking.
1605–6 Cordelia to Lear. *King Lear*, act 1, sc.1, l.224–33.

87 Time shall unfold what pleated cunning hides.
1605–6 Cordelia. *King Lear*, act 1, sc.1, l.280.

88 Fine word, 'legitimate'.
Well, my legitimate, if this letter speed
And my invention thrive, Edmond the base
Shall to th' legitimate. I grow, I prosper.
Now gods, stand up for bastards!
1605–6 Edmond. *King Lear*, act 1, sc.2, l.18–22.

89 We make guilty of our disasters the sun, the moon, and stars, as if we were villains on necessity, fools by heavenly compulsion, knaves, thieves, and treachers by spherical predominance, drunkards, liars, and adulterers by an enforced obedience of planetary influence, and all that we are evil in by a divine thrusting on. An admirable evasion of whore-master man, to lay his goatish disposition on the charge of a star!
1605–6 Edmond. *King Lear*, act 1, sc.2, l.118–26.

90 You base football player.
1605–6 Kent to Oswald. *King Lear*, act 1, sc.4, l.84–5.

91 Have more than thou showest,
Speak less than thou knowest,
Lend less than thou owest.
1605–6 Fool to Kent. *King Lear*, act 1, sc.4, l.117–19.

92 The hedge-sparrow fed the cuckoo so long
That it's had it head bit off by it young.
1605–6 Fool, singing to Lear. *King Lear*, act 1, sc.4, l.198–9.

93 As you are old and reverend, should be wise.
1605–6 Goneril to Lear. *King Lear*, act 1, sc.4, l.218.

94 Ingratitude, thou marble-hearted fiend,
More hideous when thou show'st thee in a child
Than the sea-monster.
1605–6 Lear. *King Lear*, act 1, sc.4, l.237–9.

95 How sharper than a serpent's tooth it is
To have a thankless child.
1605–6 Lear. *King Lear*, act 1, sc.4, l.268–9.

96 O, let me not be mad, not mad, sweet heaven!
Keep me in temper. I would not be mad!
1605–6 Lear. *King Lear*, act 1, sc.5, l.45–6.

97 Thou whoreson Z, thou unnecessary letter.
1605–6 Kent. *King Lear*, act 2, sc.2, l.63.

98 I have seen better faces in my time
Than stands on any shoulder that I see
Before me at this instant.
1605–6 Kent. *King Lear*, act 2, sc.2, l.91–3.

99 A good man's fortune may grow out at heels.
1605–6 Kent. *King Lear*, act 2, sc.2, l.148.

1 All the stored vengeances of heaven fall
On her ingrateful top!
1605–6 Lear to Regan. *King Lear*, act 2, sc.2, l.334–5.

2 Return to her, and fifty men dismissed?
No, rather I abjure all roofs, and choose
To be a comrade with the wolf and owl,
To wage against the enmity o'th' air,
Necessity's sharp pinch!
1605–6 Lear, of Goneril. *King Lear*, act 2, sc.2, l.380–4.

3 Touch me with noble anger,
And let not women's weapons, water-drops,
Stain my man's cheeks. No, you unnatural hags,
I will have such revenges on you both
That all the world shall—I will do such things—
What they are, yet I know not; but they shall be
The terrors of the earth. You think I'll weep.
No, I'll not weep. I have full cause of weeping,
But this heart shall break into a hundred thousand flaws
Or ere I'll weep.—O Fool, I shall go mad!
1605–6 Lear. *King Lear*, act 2, sc.2, l.450–9.

4 Blow, winds, and crack your cheeks! Rage, blow,
You cataracts and hurricanoes, spout
Till you have drenched our steeples, drowned the cocks!
1605–6 Lear. *King Lear*, act 3, sc.2, l.1–3.

5 Thou all-shaking thunder,
Strike flat the thick rotundity o' th' world.
1605–6 Lear. *King Lear*, act 3, sc.2, l.6–7.

6 There was never yet fair woman, but she made mouths in a glass.
1605–6 Fool. *King Lear*, act 3, sc.2, l.35–6.

7 I am a man
More sinned against than sinning.
1605–6 Lear to Kent. *King Lear*, act 3, sc.2, l.59–60.

8 How dost, my boy? Art cold?
I am cold myself.—Where is this straw, my fellow?
The art of our necessities is strange,
And can make vile things precious.
1605–6 Lear to Fool. *King Lear*, act 3, sc.2, l.68–71.

9 He that has and a little tiny wit,
With heigh-ho, the wind and the rain,
Must make content with his fortunes fit,
Though the rain it raineth every day.
1605–6 Fool. *King Lear*, act 3, sc.2, l.74–7.

10 O, that way madness lies.
1605–6 Lear. *King Lear*, act 3, sc.4, l.21.

11 Poor naked wretches, wheresoe'er you are,
That bide the pelting of this pitiless storm,
How shall your houseless heads and unfed sides,
Your looped and windowed raggedness, defend you
From seasons such as these?
1605–6 Lear. *King Lear*, act 3, sc.4, l.28–32.

12 Child Roland to the dark tower came,
His word was still 'Fie, fo, and fum;
I smell the blood of a British man.'
1605–6 Edgar. *King Lear*, act 3, sc.4, l.170–2.

13 Let them anatomize Regan; see what breeds about her heart. Is there any cause in nature that makes these hard-hearts?
1605–6 Lear. *King Lear*, act 3, sc.6, l.34–6.

14 Out, vile jelly!
Where is thy lustre now?
1605–6 Cornwall, pulling out Gloucester's other eye. *King Lear*, act 3, sc.7, l.81–2.

15 Turn out that eyeless villain. Throw this slave
Upon the dunghill.
1605–6 Cornwall to his servants. *King Lear*, act 3, sc.7, l.94–5.

16 The worst is not
So long as we can say 'This is the worst'.
1605–6 Edgar. *King Lear*, act 4, sc.1, 27–8.

17 As flies to wanton boys are we to th' gods;
They kill us for their sport.
1605–6 Gloucester. *King Lear*, act 4, sc.1, l.37–8.

18 GONERIL: I have been worth the whistling.
ALBANY: O Goneril,
You are not worth the dust which the rude wind
Blows in your face.
1605–6 *King Lear*, act 4, sc.2, l.29–32.

19 Alack, 'tis he! Why, he was met even now,
As mad as the vexed sea, singing aloud,
Crowned with rank fumitor and furrow-weeds,
With burdocks, hemlock, nettles, cuckoo-flowers,
Darnel, and all the idle weeds that grow
In our sustaining corn.
1605–6 Cordelia, of Lear. *King Lear*, act 4, sc.3, l.1–6.

20 GLOUCESTER: The trick of that voice I do well remember.
Is't not the King?
LEAR: Ay, every inch a king.
1605–6 *King Lear*, act 4, sc.5, l.106–7.

21 When I do stare, see how the subject quakes!
I pardon that man's life. What was thy cause?
Adultery? Thou shalt not die. Die for adultery!
No, the wren goes to't, and the small gilded fly
Does lecher in my sight. Let copulation thrive.
1605–6 Lear. *King Lear*, act 4, sc.5, l.108–12.

22 Down from the waist
They're centaurs, though women all above.
But to the girdle do the gods inherit;
Beneath is all the fiend's. There's hell, there's darkness,
there is the sulphurous pit, burning, scalding stench,
consumption. Fie, fie, fie; pah, pah! Give me an
ounce of civet, good apothecary, sweeten my
imagination.
1605–6 Lear. *King Lear*, act 4, sc.5, l.121–7.

23 O ruined piece of nature! This great world
Shall so wear out to naught. Dost thou know me?
1605–6 Gloucester to Lear. *King Lear*, act 4, sc.5, l.130–1.

24 Hark in thine ear. Change places, and handy-dandy,
which is the justice, which is the thief?
1605–6 Lear. *King Lear*, act 4, sc.5, l.148–50.

25 A dog's obeyed in office.
Thou rascal beadle, hold thy bloody hand.
Why dost thou lash that whore? Strip thy own back.
Thou hotly lusts to use her in that kind
For which thou whip'st her.
1605–6 Lear. *King Lear*, act 4, sc.5, l.154–9.

26 Get thee glass eyes,
And, like a scurvy politician, seem
To see the things thou dost not.
1605–6 Lear. *King Lear*, act 4, sc.5, l.166–8.

27 When we are born, we cry that we are come
To this great stage of fools.
1605–6 Lear to Gloucester. *King Lear*, act 4, sc.5, l.178–9.

28 I know thee well—a serviceable villain.
1605–6 Edgar, of Oswald. *King Lear*, act 4, sc.5, l.250.

29 Mine enemy's dog though he had bit me, should have
stood
That night against my fire.
1605–6 Cordelia. *King Lear*, act 4, sc.6, l.30–1.

30 You do me wrong to take me out o'th' grave.
Thou art a soul in bliss, but I am bound
Upon a wheel of fire, that mine own tears
Do scald like molten lead.
1605–6 Lear to Cordelia. *King Lear*, act 4, sc.6, l.38–41.

31 Pray do not mock.
I am a very foolish, fond old man,
Fourscore and upward,
Not an hour more nor less; and to deal plainly,
I fear I am not in my perfect mind.
1605–6 Lear to Cordelia. *King Lear*, act 4, sc.6, l.52–6.

32 Men must endure
Their going hence even as their coming hither.
Ripeness is all.
1605–6 Edgar. *King Lear*, act 5, sc.2, l.9–11.

33 [We'll] take upon 's the mystery of things
As if we were God's spies.
1605–6 Lear to Cordelia. *King Lear*, act 5, sc.3, l.16–17.

34 The gods are just, and of our pleasant vices
Make instruments to plague us.
1605–6 Edgar to Edmond. *King Lear*, act 5, sc.3, l.161–2.

35 The wheel is come full circle. I am here.
1605–6 Edmond to Edgar. *King Lear*, act 5, sc.3, l.165.

36 His flawed heart—
Alack, too weak the conflict to support—
'Twixt two extremes of passion, joy and grief,
Burst smilingly.
1605–6 Edgar, of Gloucester. *King Lear*, act 5, sc.3, l.188–91.

37 Howl, howl, howl, howl! O, you are men of stones.
Had I your tongues and eyes, I'd use them so
That heaven's vault should crack.
1605–6 Lear, grief-stricken at the death of Cordelia. *King Lear*, act 5, sc.3, l.232–4.

38 Her voice was ever soft,
Gentle, and low, an excellent thing in woman.
1605–6 Lear, of Cordelia. *King Lear*, act 5, sc.3, l.247–8.

39 Why should you a dog, a horse, a rat have life,
And thou no breath at all? Thou'lt come no more.
Never, never, never, never, never.
Pray you, undo this button.
1605–6 Edgar. *King Lear*, act 5, sc.3, l.282–5.

40 The weight of this sad time we must obey,
Speak what we feel, not what we ought to say.
The oldest hath borne most. We that are young
Shall never see so much, nor live so long.
1605–6 Edgar. *King Lear*, act 5, sc.3, l.299–302.

41 His captain's heart,
Which in the scuffles of great fights hath burst
The buckles on his breast.
1606 Philo, of Antony. *Antony and Cleopatra*, act 1, sc.1, l.6–8.

42 The triple pillar of the world transformed
Into a strumpet's fool. Behold and see.
1606 Philo, of Antony. *Antony and Cleopatra*, act 1, sc.1, l.12–13.

43 There's beggary in the love that can be reckoned.
1606 Antony to Cleopatra. *Antony and Cleopatra*, act 1, sc.1, l.15.

44 Let Rome in Tiber melt, and the wide arch
Of the ranged empire fall.
1606 Antony to Cleopatra. *Antony and Cleopatra*, act 1, sc.1, l.35–6.

45 In nature's infinite book of secrecy
A little I can read.
1606 Soothsayer. *Antony and Cleopatra*, act 1, sc.2, l.9–10.

46 I love long life better than figs.
1606 Charmian. *Antony and Cleopatra*, act 1, sc.2, l.28.

47 The tears live in an onion that should water this sorrow.
1606 Enobarbus, of the death of Fulvia. *Antony and Cleopatra*, act 1, sc.2, l.161–2.

48 In time we hate that which we often fear.
1606 Charmian. *Antony and Cleopatra*, act 1, sc.3, l.12.

49 Eternity was in our lips and eyes,
Bliss in our brow's bent; none our parts so poor
But was a race of heaven.
1606 Cleopatra to Antony. *Antony and Cleopatra*, act 1, sc.3, l.35–7.

50 The strong necessity of time commands
Our services a while, but my full heart
Remains in use with you.
1606 Antony to Cleopatra. *Antony and Cleopatra*, act 1, sc.3, l.42–4.

51 Age from folly could not give me freedom.
1606 Cleopatra. *Antony and Cleopatra*, act 1, sc.3, l.57.

52 Sir, you and I must part; but that's not it.
Sir, you and I have loved; but there's not it;
That you know well. Something it is I would—
O, my oblivion is a very Antony,
And I am all forgotten.
1606 Cleopatra to Antony. *Antony and Cleopatra*, act 1, sc.3, l.88–92.

53 Now I feed myself
With most delicious poison.
1606 Cleopatra, thinking of Antony. *Antony and Cleopatra*, act 1, sc.5, l.26–7.

54 My salad days,
When I was green in judgement.
1606 Cleopatra. *Antony and Cleopatra*, act 1, sc.5, l.72–3.

55 The barge she sat in, like a burnished throne
Burned on the water. The poop was beaten gold;
Purple the sails, and so perfumèd that
The winds were love-sick with them. The oars were
 silver,
Which to the tune of flutes kept stroke, and made
The water which they beat to follow faster,
As amorous of their strokes. For her own person,
It beggared all description.
1606 Enobarbus, of Cleopatra. *Antony and Cleopatra*, act 2, sc.2, l.198–205.

56 Antony,
Enthroned i'th' market-place, did sit alone,
Whistling to th'air, which but for vacancy
Had gone to gaze on Cleopatra too,
And made a gap in nature.
1606 Enobarbus. *Antony and Cleopatra*, act 2, sc.2, l.221–5.

57 I saw her once
Hop forty paces through the public street,
And having lost her breath, she spoke and panted,
That she did make defect perfection.
1606 Enobarbus, of Cleopatra. *Antony and Cleopatra*, act 2, sc.2, l.235–8.

58 Age cannot wither her, nor custom stale
Her infinite variety.
1606 Enobarbus, of Cleopatra. *Antony and Cleopatra*, act 2, sc.2, l.241–2.

59 If thou dost play with him at any game
Thou art sure to lose; and of that natural luck
He beats thee 'gainst the odds.
1606 Soothsayer. *Antony and Cleopatra*, act 2, sc.3, l.23–5.

60 Give me some music—music, moody food
Of us that trade in love.
1606 Cleopatra. *Antony and Cleopatra*, act 2, sc.5, l.1–2.

61 Let it alone. Let's to billiards.
1606 Cleopatra. *Antony and Cleopatra*, act 2, sc.5, l.3.

62 I laughed him out of patience, and that night
I laughed him into patience, and next morn,
Ere the ninth hour, I drunk him to his bed.
1606 Cleopatra, of Antony. *Antony and Cleopatra*, act 2, sc.5, l.19–21.

63 There is gold, and here
My bluest veins to kiss—a hand that kings
Have lipped, and trembled kissing.
1606 Cleopatra to a messenger bringing news of Antony. *Antony and Cleopatra*, act 2, sc.5, l.28–30.

64 I will praise any man that will praise me.
1606 Enobarbus. *Antony and Cleopatra*, act 2, sc.6, l.90.

65 If I lose mine honour,
I lose myself.
1606 Antony to Octavia. *Antony and Cleopatra*, act 3, sc.4, l.22–3.

66 We have kissed away
Kingdoms and provinces.
1606 Scarus. *Antony and Cleopatra*, act 3, sc.10, l.7–8.

67 I have offended reputation;
A most unnoble swerving.
1606 Antony. *Antony and Cleopatra*, act 3, sc.11, l.48–9.

68 Thou knew'st too well
My heart was to thy rudder tied by th' strings,
And thou should'st tow me after.
1606 Antony. *Antony and Cleopatra*, act 3, sc.11, l.56–8.

69 Fortune knows
We scorn her most when most she offers blows.
1606 Antony. *Antony and Cleopatra*, act 3, sc.11, l.74–5.

70 He wears the rose
Of youth upon him.
1606 Antony, of Caesar. *Antony and Cleopatra*, act 3, sc.13, l.19–20.

71 I dare him therefore
To lay his gay caparisons apart
And answer me declined, sword against sword,
Ourselves alone.
1606 Antony's message to Caesar. *Antony and Cleopatra*, act 3, sc.13, l.24–7.

72 Let's have one other gaudy night. Call to me
All my sad captains. Fill our bowls once more.
Let's mock the midnight bell.
1606 Antony. *Antony and Cleopatra*, act 3, sc.13, l.185–7.

73 Never anger
Made good guard for itself.
1606 Maecenas. *Antony and Cleopatra*, act 4, sc.1, l.9–10.

74 To business that we love we rise betime,
And go to't with delight.
1606 Antony. *Antony and Cleopatra*, act 4, sc.4, l.20–1.

75 O sovereign mistress of true melancholy,
The poisonous damp of night disponge upon me,
That life, a very rebel to my will,
May hang no longer on me.
1606 Enobarbus. *Antony and Cleopatra*, act 4, sc.10, l.11–14.

76 There is left us
Ourselves to end ourselves.
1606 Antony to Eros. *Antony and Cleopatra*, act 4, sc.15, l.21–2.

77 All strange and terrible events are welcome,
But comforts we despise.
1606 Cleopatra. *Antony and Cleopatra*, act 4, sc.16, l.3–4.

78 Is it sin
To rush into the secret house of death
Ere death dare come to us?
1606 Cleopatra. *Antony and Cleopatra*, act 4, sc.16, l.82–4.

79 But I will be
A bridegroom in my death, and run into't
As to a lover's bed.
1606 Antony. *Antony and Cleopatra*, act 4, sc.15, l.99–101.

80 Let him that loves me strike me dead.
1606 Antony. *Antony and Cleopatra*, act 4, sc.15, l.108.

81 So it should be,
That none but Antony should conquer Antony.
1606 Cleopatra. *Antony and Cleopatra*, act 4, sc.16, l.16–17.

82 Of many thousand kisses the poor last
I lay upon thy lips.
1606 Antony to Cleopatra. *Antony and Cleopatra*, act 4, sc.16, l.21–2.

83 Shall I abide
In this dull world, which in thy absence is
No better than a sty?
1606 Cleopatra to Antony. *Antony and Cleopatra*, act 4, sc.16, l.62–4.

84 There is nothing left remarkable
Beneath the visiting moon.
1606 Cleopatra, of the death of Antony. *Antony and Cleopatra*, act 4, sc.16, l.69–70.

85 What's brave, what's noble,
Let's do it after the high Roman fashion,
And make death proud to take us.
1606 Cleopatra. *Antony and Cleopatra*, act 4, sc.16, l.88–90.

86 It is great
To do that thing that ends all other deeds.
1606 Cleopatra. *Antony and Cleopatra*, act 5, sc.2, l.4–5.

87 I dreamt there was an Emperor Antony,
O, such another sleep, that I might see
But such another man!
1606 Cleopatra. *Antony and Cleopatra*, act 5, sc.2, l.75–7.

88 His legs bestrid the ocean; his reared arm
Crested the world.
1606 Cleopatra, of Antony. *Antony and Cleopatra*, act 5, sc.2, l.81–2.

89 The bright day is done,
And we are for the dark.
1606 Iras. *Antony and Cleopatra*, act 5, sc.2, l.189–90.

90 Hast thou the pretty worm
Of Nilus there, that kills and pains not?
1606 Cleopatra. *Antony and Cleopatra*, act 5, sc.2, l.238–9.

91 His biting is immortal; those that do die of it do seldom or ever recover.
1606 Clown. *Antony and Cleopatra*, act 5, sc.2, l.241–3.

92 Give me my robe. Put on my crown. I have
Immortal longings in me.
1606 Cleopatra. *Antony and Cleopatra*, act 5, sc.2, l.275–6.

93 Husband, I come.
Now to that name my courage prove my title.
1606 Cleopatra. *Antony and Cleopatra*, act 5, sc.2, l.282–3.

94 If thou and nature can so gently part,
The stroke of death is as a lover's pinch,
Which hurts and is desired. Dost thou lie still?
If thus thou vanishest, thou tell'st the world
It is not worth leave-taking.
1606 Cleopatra. *Antony and Cleopatra*, act 5, sc.2, l.289–93.

95 A lass unparalleled. Downy windows, close,
And golden Phoebus never be beheld
Of eyes again so royal.
1606 Charmian. *Antony and Cleopatra*, act 5, sc.2, l.310–12.

96 When shall we three meet again?
In thunder, lightning, or in rain?
1606 First Witch. *Macbeth*, act 1, sc.1, l.1–2.

97 Fair is foul, and foul is fair,
Hover through the fog and filthy air.
1606 Witches. *Macbeth*, act 1, sc.1, l.10–11.

98 Fortune on his damnèd quarry smiling
Showed like a rebel's whore.
1606 Captain. *Macbeth*, act 1, sc.2, l.14–15.

99 A sailor's wife had chestnuts in her lap,
And munched, and munched, and munched. 'Give me,'
quoth I.
'Aroint thee, witch,' the rump-fed runnion cries.
Her husband's to Aleppo gone, master o'th' Tiger.
But in a sieve I'll thither sail,
And like a rat without a tail
I'll do, I'll do, and I'll do.
1606 First Witch. *Macbeth*, act 1, sc.3, l.3–9.

1 I'll drain him dry as hay.
Sleep shall neither night nor day
Hang upon his penthouse lid.
He shall live a man forbid.
Weary sennights nine times nine
Shall he dwindle, peak, and pine.
Though his barque cannot be lost,
Yet it shall be tempest-tossed.
1606 First Witch. *Macbeth*, act 1, sc.3, l.17–23.

2 The weird sisters hand in hand,
Posters of the sea and land,
Thus do go about, about.
1606 Witches. *Macbeth*, act 1, sc.3, l.30–2.

3 So foul and fair a day I have not seen.
1606 Macbeth. *Macbeth*, act 1, sc.3, l.36.

4 Live you, or are you aught
That man may question? You seem to understand me
By each at once her choppy finger laying
Upon her skinny lips. You should be women,
And yet your beards forbid me to interpret
That you are so.
1606 Banquo. *Macbeth*, act 1, sc.3, l.40–4.

5 If you can look into the seeds of time
And say which grain will grow and which will not,
Speak then to me.
1606 Banquo to the witches. *Macbeth*, act 1, sc.3, l.56–9.

6 To be king
Stands not within the prospect of belief.
1606 Macbeth to the witches. *Macbeth*, act 1, sc.3, l.71–2.

7 The earth hath bubbles, as the water has,
And these are of them.
1606 Banquo, of the witches. *Macbeth*, act 1, sc.3, l.77–8.

8 What, can the devil speak true?
1606 Banquo, hearing that the first of the witches' predictions has come true. *Macbeth*, act 1, sc.3, l.105.

9 The Thane of Cawdor lives. Why do you dress me
In borrowed robes?
1606 Macbeth. *Macbeth*, act 1, sc.3, l.106–7.

10 Come what come may,
Time and the hour runs through the roughest day.
1606 Macbeth. *Macbeth*, act 1, sc.3, l.145–6.

11 Nothing in his life
Became him like the leaving of it. He died
As one that had been studied in his death
To throw away the dearest thing he owed
As 'twere a careless trifle.
1606 Malcolm, of Cawdor. *Macbeth*, act 1, sc.4, l.7–11.

12 There's no art
To find the mind's construction in the face.
He was a gentleman on whom I built
An absolute trust.
1606 King Duncan, of Cawdor. *Macbeth*, act 1, sc.4, l.11–14.

13 Yet do I fear thy nature;
It is too full o'th' milk of human kindness
To catch the nearest way.
1606 Lady Macbeth, of Macbeth. *Macbeth*, act 1, sc.5, l.15–17.

14 Thou wouldst be great,
Art not without ambition, but without
The illness should attend it.
1606 Lady Macbeth, of Macbeth. *Macbeth*, act 1, sc.5, l.17–19.

15 Come, you spirits
That tend on mortal thoughts, unsex me here,
And fill me from the crown to the toe top-full
Of direst cruelty.
1606 Lady Macbeth. *Macbeth*, act 1, sc.5, l.39–42.

16 Your face, my thane, is as a book where men
May read strange matters.
1606 Lady Macbeth to Macbeth. *Macbeth*, act 1, sc.5, l.61–2.

17 Bear welcome in your eye,
Your hand, your tongue; look like the innocent
 flower,
But be the serpent under't.
1606 Lady Macbeth to Macbeth. *Macbeth*, act 1, sc.5, l.63–5.

18 KING DUNCAN: This castle hath a pleasant seat. The air
Nimbly and sweetly recommends itself
Unto our gentle senses.
BANQUO: This guest of summer,
The temple-haunting marlet, does approve
By his loved mansionry that the heavens' breath
Smells wooingly here. No jutty, frieze,
Buttress, nor coign of vantage but this bird
Hath made his pedant bed and procreant cradle;
Where they most breed and haunt I have observed
The air is delicate.
1606 *Macbeth*, act 1, sc.6, l.1–10.

19 If it were done when 'tis done, then 'twere well
It were done quickly. If th'assassination
Could trammel up the consequence, and catch
With his surcease success: that but this blow
Might be the be-all and the end-all, here,
But here upon this bank and shoal of time,
We'd jump the life to come. But in these cases
We still have judgement here, that we but teach
Bloody instructions which, being taught, return
To plague th'inventor.
1606 Macbeth, on the prospect of murdering Duncan. *Macbeth*, act 1, sc.7, l.1–10.

20 Besides, this Duncan
Hath borne his faculties so meek, hath been
So clear in his great office, that his virtues
Will plead like angels, trumpet-tongued against
The deep damnation of his taking-off,
And pity, like a naked new-born babe,
Striding the blast, or heaven's cherubin, horsed
Upon the sightless couriers of the air,
Shall blow the horrid deed in every eye
That tears shall drown the wind. I have no spur
To prick the sides of my intent, but only
Vaulting ambition which o'erleaps itself
And falls on th'other.
1606 Macbeth. *Macbeth*, act 1, sc.7, l.16–29.

21 Wouldst thou have that
Which thou esteem'st the ornament of life,
And live a coward in thine own esteem,
Letting 'I dare not' wait upon 'I would',
Like the poor cat i'th' adage?
1606 Lady Macbeth to Macbeth. *Macbeth*, act 1, sc.7, l.41–45.

22 I dare do all that may become a man;
Who dares do more is none.
1606 Macbeth to Lady Macbeth. *Macbeth*, act 1, sc.7, l.46–7.

23 Screw your courage to the sticking-place
And we'll not fail.
1606 Lady Macbeth to Macbeth. *Macbeth*, act 1, sc.7, l.60–1.

24 Bring forth men-children only,
For thy undaunted mettle should compose
Nothing but males.
1606 Macbeth to Lady Macbeth. *Macbeth*, act 1, sc.7, l.72–4.

25 Away, and mock the time with fairest show.
False face must hide what the false heart doth know.
1606 Macbeth. *Macbeth*, act 1, sc.7, l.81–2.

26 There's husbandry in heaven,
Their candles are all out.
1606 Banquo. *Macbeth*, act 2, sc.1, l.4–5.

27 Is this a dagger which I see before me,
The handle toward my hand? Come, let me clutch thee.
I have thee not, and yet I see thee still.
1606 Macbeth. *Macbeth*, act 2, sc.1, l.33–5.

28 Mine eyes are made the fool o'th' other senses,
Or else worth all the rest.
1606 Macbeth. *Macbeth*, act 2, sc.1, l.44–5.

29 Whiles I threat, he lives.
Words to the heat of deeds too cold breath gives.
I go, and it is done. The bell invites me.

Hear it not, Duncan; for it is a knell
That summons thee to heaven or to hell.
1606 Macbeth, steeling himself to murder Duncan. *Macbeth*, act 2, sc.1, l.60–4.

30 That which hath made them drunk hath made me bold.
What hath quenched them hath given me fire.
1606 Lady Macbeth. *Macbeth*, act 2, sc.2, l.1–2.

31 Th'attempt and not the deed
Confounds us.
1606 Lady Macbeth. *Macbeth*, act 2, sc.2, l.10–11.

32 I laid their daggers ready;
He could not miss 'em. Had he not resembled
My father as he slept, I had done't.
1606 Lady Macbeth, of Duncan. *Macbeth*, act 2, sc.2, l.11–13.

33 I had most need of blessing, and 'Amen'
Stuck in my throat.
1606 Macbeth. *Macbeth*, act 2, sc.2, l.30–1.

34 Methought I heard a voice cry 'Sleep no more,
Macbeth does murder sleep'—the innocent sleep,
Sleep that knits up the ravelled sleave of care.
1606 Macbeth. *Macbeth*, act 2, sc.2, l.33–5.

35 Still it cried 'Sleep no more' to all the house,
'Glamis hath murdered sleep, and therefore Cawdor
Shall sleep no more, Macbeth shall sleep no more.'
1606 Macbeth. *Macbeth*, act 2, sc.2, l.39–41.

36 Infirm of purpose!
Give me the daggers. The sleeping and the dead
Are but as pictures. 'Tis the eye of childhood
That fears a painted devil.
1606 Lady Macbeth. *Macbeth*, act 2, sc.2, l.50–4.

37 Will all great Neptune's ocean wash this blood
Clean from my hand? No, this my hand will rather
The multitudinous seas incarnadine,
Making the green one red.
1606 Macbeth. *Macbeth*, act 2, sc.2, l.58–61.

38 A little water clears us of this deed.
1606 Lady Macbeth. *Macbeth*, act 2, sc.2, l.65.

39 But this place is too cold for hell. I'll devil-porter it no further. I had thought to have let in some of all professions that go the primrose way to th'everlasting bonfire.
1606 Porter. *Macbeth*, act 2, sc.3, l.15–18.

40 The labour we delight in physics pain.
1606 Macbeth. *Macbeth*, act 2, sc.3, l.49.

41 Confusion now hath made his masterpiece.
Most sacreligious murder hath broke ope
The Lord's anointed temple and stole thence
The life o'th' building.
1606 Macduff, announcing Duncan's murder. *Macbeth*, act 2, sc.3, l.65–8.

42 There's daggers in men's smiles.
1606 Donalbain. *Macbeth*, act 2, sc.3, l.139.

43 Go not my horse the better,
I must become a borrower of the night
For dark hour or twain.
1606 Banquo. *Macbeth*, act 3, sc.1, l.26–8.

44 I could
With barefaced power sweep him from my sight.
1606 Macbeth, of Banquo. *Macbeth*, act 3, sc.1, l.119–20.

45 Things without all remedy
Should be without regard. What's done is done.
1606 Lady Macbeth. *Macbeth*, act 3, sc.2, l.13–14.

46 Duncan is in his grave.
After life's fitful fever he sleeps well.
Treason has done his worst.
1606 Macbeth. *Macbeth*, act 3, sc.2, l.24–5.

47 Come, seeling night,
Scarf up the tender eye of pitiful day.
1606 Macbeth. *Macbeth*, act 3, sc.2, l.47–8.

48 Light thickens, and the crow
Makes wing to th' rooky wood.
Good things of day begin to droop and drowse,
Whiles night's black agents to their preys do rouse.
1606 Macbeth. *Macbeth*, act 3, sc.2, l.51–4.

49 Thou canst not say I did it. Never shake
Thy gory locks at me.
1606 Macbeth to Banquo's ghost. *Macbeth*, act 3, sc.4, l.49–50.

50 You make me strange
Even to the disposition that I owe,
When now I think you can behold such sights
And keep the natural ruby of your cheeks,
When mine is blanched with fear.
1606 Macbeth to Lady Macbeth. *Macbeth*, act 3, sc.4, l.111–15.

51 I am in blood
Stepped in so far that, should I wade no more,
Returning were as tedious as go o'er.
1606 Macbeth. *Macbeth*, act 3, sc.4, l.135–7.

52 Double, double, toil and trouble,
Fire burn, and cauldron bubble.
1606 Witches. *Macbeth*, act 4, sc.1, l.10–11.

53 By the pricking of my thumbs,
Something wicked this way comes.
1606 Second witch. *Macbeth*, act 4, sc.1, l.61–2.

54 MACBETH: How now, you secret, black, and midnight hags,
What is't you do?
WITCHES: A deed without a name.
1606 *Macbeth*, act 4, sc.1, l.63–5.

55 Be bloody, bold, and resolute. Laugh to scorn
The power of man, for none of woman born
Shall harm Macbeth.
1606 Second apparition to Macbeth. *Macbeth*, act 4, sc.1, l.95–7.

56 Macbeth shall never vanquished be until
Great Birnam Wood to high Dunsinane Hill
Shall come against him.
1606 Third Apparition. *Macbeth*, act 4, sc.1, l.108–10.

57 No boasting like a fool;
This deed I'll do before this purpose cool.
1606 Macbeth, intending to murder Macduff's family. *Macbeth*, act 4, sc.1, l.169–70.

58 Our fears do make us traitors.
1606 Lady Macduff. *Macbeth*, act 4, sc.2, l.4.

59 He loves us not,
He wants the natural touch.
1606 Lady Macduff, of Macduff. *Macbeth*, act 4, sc.2, l.8–9.

60 Each new morn
New widows howl, new orphans cry, new sorrows
Strike heaven on the face.
1606 Macduff. *Macbeth*, act 4, sc.3, l.4–6.

61 MACDUFF: Stands Scotland where it did?
ROSS: Alas, poor country,
Almost afraid to know itself.
1606 *Macbeth*, act 4, sc.3, l.165–6.

62 MACDUFF: He has no children. All my pretty ones?
Did you say all? O hell-kite! All?
What, all my pretty chickens and their dam
At one fell swoop?
MALCOLM: Dispute it like a man.
MACDUFF: I shall do so,
But I must also feel it as a man.
I cannot but remember such things were
That were most precious to me. Did heaven look on
And would not take their part?
1606 Macduff, of his murdered wife and children. *Macbeth*, act 4, sc.3, l.217–26.

63 The night is long that never finds the day.
1606 Malcolm. *Macbeth*, act 4, sc.3, l.242.

64 It is an accustomed action with her, to seem thus washing her hands. I have known her continue in this a quarter of an hour.
1606 Gentlewoman, of Lady Macbeth. *Macbeth*, act 5, sc.1, l.27–9.

65 Out, damned spot; out, I say. One, two,—why, then 'tis time to do't. Hell is murky. Fie, my lord, fie, a soldier and afeard? What need we fear who knows it when none can call our power to account? Yet who would have thought the old man to have had so much blood in him?
1606 Lady Macbeth, sleepwalking, of the murdered Duncan. *Macbeth*, act 5, sc.1, l.33–8.

66 The Thane of Fife had a wife. Where is she now? What, will these hands ne'er be clean?
1606 Lady Macbeth. *Macbeth*, act 5, sc.1, l.40–1.

67 Now does he feel
His secret murders sticking on his hands.
Now minutely revolts upbraid his faith-breach.
Those he commands move only in command,
Nothing in love. Now does he feel his title
Hang loose about him, like a giant's robe
Upon a dwarfish thief.
1606 Angus, of Macbeth. *Macbeth*, act 5, sc.2, l.16–22.

68 The devil damn thee black, thou cream-faced loon!
1606 Macbeth to his servant. *Macbeth*, act 5, sc.3, l.11.

69 I have lived long enough. My way of life
Is fall'n into the sere, the yellow leaf,
And that which should accompany old age,
As honour, love, obedience, troops of friends,
I must not look to have.
1606 Macbeth. *Macbeth*, act 5, sc.3, l.24–8.

70 Canst thou not minister to a mind diseased,
Pluck from the memory a rooted sorrow,
Raze out the written troubles of the brain,
And with some sweet oblivious antidote
Cleanse the fraught bosom?
1606 Macbeth to the doctor, of Lady Macbeth. *Macbeth*, act 5, sc.3, l.42–5.

71 Throw physic to the dogs; I'll none of it.
1606 Macbeth. *Macbeth*, act 5, sc.3, l.49.

72 What rhubarb, cyme, or what purgative drug
Would scour these English hence?
1606 Macbeth to the doctor. *Macbeth*, act 5, sc.3, l.57–8.

73 I have supped full with horrors.
Direness, familiar to my slaughterhouse thoughts,
Cannot once start me.
1606 Macbeth. *Macbeth*, act 5, sc.5, l.13–14.

74 She should have died hereafter.
There would have been a time for such a word.
Tomorrow, and tomorrow, and tomorrow
Creeps in this petty pace from day to day
To the last syllable of recorded time,
And all our yesterdays have lighted fools
The way to dusty death. Out, out, brief candle.
Life's but a walking shadow, a poor player
That struts and frets his hour upon the stage,
And then is heard no more. It is a tale
Told by an idiot, full of sound and fury,
Signifying nothing.
1606 Macbeth, hearing of Lady Macbeth's death. *Macbeth*, act 5, sc.5, l.16–27.

75 They have tied me to a stake. I cannot fly,
But bear-like I must fight the course.
1606 Macbeth. *Macbeth*, act 5, sc.7, l.1–2.

76 YOUNG SIWARD: What is thy name?
MACBETH: Thou'lt be afraid to hear it.
YOUNG SIWARD: No, though thou call'st thyself a hotter name
Than any in hell.
MACBETH: My name's Macbeth.
1606 *Macbeth*, act 5, sc.7, l.5–8.

77 Macduff was from his mother's womb
Untimely ripped.
1606 Macduff. *Macbeth*, act 5, sc.10, l.15–16.

78 Lay on, Macduff,
And damned be him that first cries 'Hold, enough!'
1606 Macbeth. *Macbeth*, act 5, sc.10, l.33–4.

79 Your cause of sorrow
Must not be measured by his worth, for then
It hath no end.
1606 Ross to Siward. *Macbeth*, act 5, sc.11, l.10–12.

80 Kings are earth's gods; in vice their law's their will,
And if Jove stray, who dares say Jove doth ill?
1607 Pericles. *Pericles*, sc.1, l.146–7.

81 They do abuse the King that flatter him,
For flatt'ry is the bellows blows up sin.
1607 Helicanus. *Pericles*, sc.2, l.43–4.

82 'Tis time to fear when tyrants seems to kiss.
1607 Pericles. *Pericles*, sc.2, l.84.

83 We'll mingle our bloods together in the earth
From whence we had our being and our birth.
1607 Helicanus to Pericles. *Pericles*, sc.2, l.118–9.

84 I'll take thy word for faith, not ask thine oath;
Who shuns not to break one will sure crack both.
1607 Pericles to Helicanus. *Pericles*, sc.2, l.125–6.

85 Shall we rest us here
And, by relating tales of others' griefs,
See if 'twill teach us to forget our own?
1607 Cleon to Dioniza. *Pericles*, sc.4, l.1–3.

86 One sorrow never comes but brings an heir
That may succeed as his inheritor.
1607 Cleon. *Pericles*, sc.4, l.62–3.

87 He's a very dog to the commonalty.
1608 Fourth citizen. *Coriolanus*, act 1, sc.1, l.27.

88 What's the matter, you dissentious rogues,
That, rubbing the poor itch of your opinion,
Make yourselves scabs?
1608 Martius. *Coriolanus*, act 1, sc.1, l.162–4.

89 They threw their caps
As they would hang them on the horns o'th' moon.
1608 Martius. *Coriolanus*, act 1, sc.1, l.210–11.

90 Nature teaches beasts to know their friends.
1608 Sicinius. *Coriolanus*, act 2, sc.1, l.6.

91 [I am] one that loves a cup of hot wine with not a drop of allaying Tiber in't.
1608 Menenius. *Coriolanus*, act 2, sc.1, l.47–8.

92 What I think, I utter, and spend my malice in my breath.
1608 Menenius. *Coriolanus*, act 2, sc.1, l.52–3.

93 That's a brave fellow, but he's vengeance proud and loves not the common people.
1608 First Officer, of Coriolanus. *Coriolanus*, act 2, sc.2, l.5–6.

94 He seeks their hate with greater devotion than they can render it him.
1608 First Officer, of Coriolanus. *Coriolanus*, act 2, sc.2, l.18–19.

95 Ingratitude is monstrous, and for the multitude to be ingrateful were to make a monster of the multitude.
1608 Third Citizen. *Coriolanus*, act 2, sc.3, l.9–10.

96 'Shall remain'?
Hear you this Triton of the minnows? Mark you His absolute 'shall'?
1608 Coriolanus. *Coriolanus*, act 3, sc.1, l.91–3.

97 On both sides more respect.
1608 Menenius. *Coriolanus*, act 3, sc.1, l.183.

98 You common cry of curs, whose breath I hate
As reek o'th' rotten fens, whose loves I prize
As the dead carcasses of unburied men
That do corrupt my air: I banish you.
1608 Coriolanus to the citizens. *Coriolanus*, act 3, sc.3, l.124–7.

99 Now we have shown our power,
Let us seem humbler after it is done.
1608 Brutus. *Coriolanus*, act 4, sc.2, l.3–4.

1 Anger's my meat, I sup upon myself,
And so shall starve with feeding.
1608 Volumnia. *Coriolanus*, act 4, sc.2, l.53–4.

2 He'll shake your Rome about your ears.
1608 Cominius. *Coriolanus*, act 4, sc.6, l.103.

3 Like a dull actor now
I have forgot my part, and I am out
Even to a full disgrace.
1608 Coriolanus. *Coriolanus*, act 5, sc.3, l.40–2.

4 O, a kiss
Long as my exile, sweet as my revenge!
1608 Coriolanus to Virgilia. *Coriolanus*, act 5, sc.3, l.44–5.

5 O mother, mother!
What have you done? Behold, the heavens do ope,
The gods look down, and this unnatural scene
Thay laugh at.
1608 Coriolanus. *Coriolanus*, act 5, sc.3, l.183–6.

6 Cut me to pieces, Volsces. Men and lads,
Stain all your edges on me. 'Boy'! False hound,
If you have writ your annals true, 'tis there
That, like an eagle in a dove-cot, I
Fluttered your Volscians in Corioles.
Alone I did it. 'Boy'!
1608 Coriolanus. *Coriolanus*, act 5, sc.6, l.112–7.

7 We were, fair Queen,
Two lads that thought there was no more behind
But such a day tomorrow as today,
And to be boy eternal.
1609 Polixenes to Hermione. *The Winter's Tale*, act 1, sc.2, l.63–6.

8 One good deed dying tongueless
Slaughters a thousand waiting upon that.
1609 Hermione. *The Winter's Tale*, act 1, sc.2, l.94–5.

9 He makes a July's day as short as December.
1609 Polixenes, of Mamillius. *The Winter's Tale*, act 1, sc.2, l.170.

10 Should all despair
That have revolted wives, the tenth of mankind
Would hang themselves.
1609 Leontes. *The Winter's Tale*, act 1, sc.2, l.199–201.

11 I saw his heart in's face.
1609 Polixenes, of Leontes. *The Winter's Tale*, act 1, sc.2, l.447.

12 A sad tale's best for winter.
1609 Mamillius. *The Winter's Tale*, act 2, sc.1, l.27.

13 It is an heretic that makes the fire,
Not she which burns in't.
1609 Paulina. *The Winter's Tale*, act 2, sc.3, l.115–6.

14 *Exit, pursued by a bear.*
1609 Stage Direction. *The Winter's Tale*, act 3, sc.3, l.57.

15 A snapper-up of unconsidered trifles.
1609 Autolycus, of himself. *The Winter's Tale*, act 4, sc.3, l.25–6.

16 Jog on, jog on, the footpath way,
And merrily hent the stile-a.
A merry heart goes all the day,
Your sad tires in a mile-a.
1609 Autolycus, singing. *The Winter's Tale*, act 4, sc.3, l.123–6.

17 Let's be red with mirth.
1609 Florizel. *The Winter's Tale*, act 4, sc.4, l.54.

18 Blasts of January
Would blow you through and through.
1609 Perdita, of Camillo. *The Winter's Tale*, act 4, sc.4, l.111–12.

19 Daffodils,
That come before the swallow dares, and take
The winds of March with beauty.
1609 Perdita. *The Winter's Tale*, act 4, sc.4, l.118–20.

20 When you speak, sweet,
I'd have you do it ever; when you sing,
I'd have you buy and sell so, so give alms,
Pray so; and for the ord'ring your affairs,
To sing them too. When you do dance, I wish you
A wave o'th' sea, that you might ever do
Nothing but that, move still, still so,
And own no other function. Each your doing,
So singular in each particular,
Crowns what you are doing in the present deeds,
That all your acts are queens.
1609 Florizel to Perdita. *The Winter's Tale*, act 4, sc.4, l.136–46.

21 Good sooth, she is
The queen of curds and cream.
1609 Camillo, of Perdita. *The Winter's Tale*, act 4, sc.4, l.160–1.

22 Garlic to mend her kissing with!
1609 Dorcas, of Mopsa. *The Winter's Tale*, act 4, sc.4, l.162–3.

23 He says he loves my daughter:
I think, so too, for never gazed the moon
Upon the water as he'll stand and read,
As 'twere, my daughter's eyes.
1609 Old Shepherd. *The Winter's Tale*, act 4, sc.4, l.172–5.

Shakespeare The Winter's Tale

24 He has the prettiest love songs for maids, so without
bawdry, which is strange, with such delicate burdens of
dildos and fadings, 'Jump her, and thump her'; and
where some stretch-mouthed rascal would, as it were,
mean mischief and break a foul gap into the matter, he
makes the maid to answer, 'Whoop, do me no harm,
good man!'
1609 Servant. *The Winter's Tale*, act 4, sc.4, l.193–200.

25 Lawn as white as driven snow.
1609 Autolycus. *The Winter's Tale*, act 4, sc.4, l.219.

26 If I were not in love with Mopsa thou shouldst take no
money of me, but being enthralled as I am, it will also be
the bondage of certain ribbons and gloves.
1609 Clown to Autolycus (in disguise). *The Winter's Tale*, act 4,
sc.4, l.231–3.

27 I love a ballad in print, alife, for then we are sure they are
true.
1609 Mopsa to Autolycus (in disguise). *The Winter's Tale*, act 4,
sc.4, l.258–9.

28 Though I am not naturally honest, I am so sometimes by
chance.
1609 Autolycus. *The Winter's Tale*, act 4, sc.4, l.712–13.

29 Stars, stars,
And all eyes else, dead coals!
1609 Leontes. *The Winter's Tale*, act 5, sc.1, l.67–8.

30 Women will love her that she is a woman
More worth than any man; men, that she is
The rarest of all women.
1609 Servant, of Perdita. *The Winter's Tale*, act 5, sc.1, l.110–12.

31 My lord, your sorrow was too sore laid on,
Which sixteen winters cannot blow away,
So many summers dry. Scarce any joy
Did ever so long live.
1609 Camillo to Leontes. *The Winter's Tale*, act 5, sc.3, l.49–52.

32 O, she's warm!
If this be magic, let it be an art
Lawful as eating.
1609 Leontes, of the now animated statue of Hermione. *The Winter's Tale*, act 5, sc.3, l.109–11.

33 Thou art thy mother's glass, and she in thee
Calls back the lovely April of her prime.
1609 *Sonnets*, sonnet 3.

34 Music to hear, why hear'st thou music sadly?
Sweets with sweets war not, joy delights in joy.
Why lov'st thou that which thou receiv'st not gladly?
1609 *Sonnets*, sonnet 8.

35 For thou art so possessed with murd'rous hate
That 'gainst thyself thou stick'st not to conspire.
1609 *Sonnets*, sonnet 10.

36 If I could write the beauty of your eyes
And in fresh numbers number all your graces,
The age to come would say 'This poet lies;
Such heavenly touches ne'er touched earthly faces.'
1609 *Sonnets*, sonnet 17.

37 Shall I compare thee to a summer's day?
Thou art more lovely and more temperate.
Rough winds do shake the darling buds of May,
And summer's lease hath all too short a date.
Sometime too hot the eye of heaven shines,
And often is his gold complexion dimmed,
And every fair from fair sometime declines,
By chance or nature's changing course untrimmed;
But thy eternal summer shall not fade
Nor lose possession of that fair thou ow'st,
Nor shall death brag thou wander'st in his shade
When in eternal lines to time thou grow'st.
So long as men can breathe or eyes can see,
So long lives this, and this gives life to thee.
1609 *Sonnets*, sonnet 18.

38 Yet do thy worst, old time; despite thy wrong
My love shall in my verse ever live young.
1609 *Sonnets*, sonnet 19.

39 A woman's face with nature's own hand painted
Hast thou, the master-mistress of my passion.
1609 *Sonnets*, sonnet 20.

40 My glass shall not persuade me I am old
So long as youth and thou are of one date;
But when in thee time's furrows I behold,
Then look I death my days should expiate.
1609 *Sonnets*, sonnet 22.

41 Presume not on thy heart when mine is slain:
Thou gav'st me thine not to give back again.
1609 *Sonnets*, sonnet 22.

42 O let my books be then the eloquence
And dumb presagers of my speaking breast,
Who plead for love, and look for recompense
More than that tongue that more hath more expressed.
O learn to read what silent love hath writ;
To hear with eyes belongs to love's fine wit.
1609 *Sonnets*, sonnet 23.

43 Now see what good turns eyes for eyes have done:
Mine eyes have drawn thy shape, and thine for me
Are windows to my breast, wherethrough the sun
Delights to peep, to gaze therein on thee.
Yet eyes this cunning want to grace their art:
They draw but what they see, know not the heart.
1609 *Sonnets*, sonnet 24.

44 The painful warrior famousèd for might,
After a thousand victories once foiled
Is from the book of honour razèd quite,
And all the rest forgot for which he toiled.
1609 *Sonnets*, sonnet 25.

45 Weary with toil I haste me to my bed,
The dear repose for limbs with travel tired;
But then begins a journey in my head
To work my mind when body's work's expired.
1609 *Sonnets*, sonnet 27.

46 When, in disgrace with fortune and men's eyes,
I all alone beweep my outcast state,
And trouble deaf heaven with my bootless cries,
And look upon myself and curse my fate,
Wishing me like to one more rich hope,
Featured like him, like him with friends possessed,
Desiring this man's art and that man's scope,
With what I most enjoy contented least:
Yet in these thoughts myself almost despising,
Haply I think on thee, and then my state,
Like to the lark at break of day arising
From sullen earth, sings hymns at heaven's gate;
For thy sweet love remembered such wealth brings
That then I scorn to change my state with kings'.
1609 *Sonnets*, sonnet 29.

47 When to the sessions of sweet silent thought
   I summon up remembrance of things past,
   I sigh the lack of many a thing I sought,
   And with old woes new wail my dear time's waste.
   Then can I drown an eye unused to flow
   For precious friends hid in death's dateless night,
   And weep afresh love's long-since-cancelled woe,
   And moan th'expense of many a vanished sight.
   Then can I grieve at grievances foregone,
   And heavily from woe to woe tell o'er
   The sad account of fore-bemoanèd moan,
   Which I new pay as if not paid before.
   But if the while I think on thee, dear friend,
   All losses are restored, and sorrows end.
   1609 *Sonnets*, sonnet 30.

48 Full many a glorious morning have I seen
   Flatter the mountain tops with sovereign eye,
   Kissing with golden face the meadows green.
   1609 *Sonnets*, sonnet 33.

49 As a decrepit father takes delight
   To see his active child do deeds of youth,
   So I, made lame by fortune's dearest spite,
   Take all my comfort of thy worth and truth.
   1609 *Sonnets*, sonnet 37.

50 All days are nights to see till I see thee,
   And nights bright days when dreams do show
      thee me.
   1609 *Sonnets*, sonnet 43.

51 O how much more doth beauty beauteous seem
   By that sweet ornament which truth doth give!
   1609 *Sonnets*, sonnet 54.

52 The rose looks fair, but fairer we it deem
   For that sweet odour which doth in it live.
   1609 *Sonnets*, sonnet 54.

53 Not marble nor the gilded monuments
   Of princes shall outlive this powerful rhyme,
   But you shall shine more bright in these contents
   Than unswept stone besmeared with sluttish time.
   1609 *Sonnets*, sonnet 55.

54 So, till the judgement that yourself arise,
   You live in this, and dwell in lovers' eyes.
   1609 *Sonnets*, sonnet 55.

55 Being your slave, what should I do but tend
   Upon the hours and times of your desire?
   I have no precious time at all to spend,
   Nor services to do, till you require;
   Nor dare I chide the world-without-end hour
   Whilst I, my sovereign, watch the clock for you,
   Nor think the bitterness of absence sour
   When you have bid your servant once adieu.
   Nor dare I question with my jealous thought
   Where you may be, or your affairs suppose,
   But like a sad slave stay and think of naught
   Save, where you are, how happy you make those.
   So true a fool is love that in your will,
   Though you do anything, he thinks no ill.
   1609 *Sonnets*, sonnet 57.

56 Like as the waves make towards the pebbled
      shore,
   So do our minutes hasten to their end.
   1609 *Sonnets*, sonnet 60.

57 Since brass, nor stone, nor earth, nor boundless sea,
   But sad mortality o'ersways their power,
   How with this rage shall beauty hold a plea,
   Whose action is no stronger than a flower?
   O how shall summer's honey breath hold out
   Against the wrackful siege of battering days
   When rocks impregnable are not so stout,
   Nor gates of steel so strong, but time decays?
   O fearful meditation! where, alack,
   Shall time's best jewel from time's chest lie hid,
   Or what strong hand can hold his swift foot back,
   Or who his spoil of beauty can forbid?
   O none, unless this miracle have might:
   That is black ink my love may still shine bright.
   1609 *Sonnets*, sonnet 65.

58 Right perfection wrongfully disgraced.
   1609 *Sonnets*, sonnet 66.

59 Simple truth miscalled simplicity.
   1609 *Sonnets*, sonnet 66.

60 They look into the beauty of thy mind,
   And that in guess they measure by thy deeds.
   1609 *Sonnets*, sonnet 69.

61 No longer mourn for me when I am dead
   Than you shall hear the surly sullen bell
   Give warning to the world that I am fled
   From this vile world with vilest worms to dwell.
   Nay, if you read this line, remember not
   The hand that writ it; for I love you so
   That I in your sweet thoughts would be forgot
   If thinking on me then should make you woe.
   O, if, I say, you look upon this verse
   When I perhaps compounded am with clay,
   Do not so much as my poor name rehearse,
   But let your love even with my life decay,
   Lest the wise world should look into your moan
   And mock you with me after I am gone.
   1609 *Sonnets*, sonnet 71.

62 That time of year thou mayst in me behold
   When yellow leaves, or none, or few, do hang
   Upon those boughs which shake against the cold,
   Bare ruined choirs where late the sweet birds sang.
   In me thou seest the twilight of such day
   As after sunset fadeth in the west,
   Which by and by black night doth take away,
   Death's second self, that seals up all in rest.
   1609 *Sonnets*, sonnet 73.

63 O know, sweet love, I always write of you,
   And you and love are still my argument.
   1609 *Sonnets*, sonnet 76.

64 For as the sun is daily new and old,
   So is my love, still telling what is told.
   1609 *Sonnets*, sonnet 76.

65 Thy glass will show thee how thy beauties wear,
   Thy dial how thy precious minutes waste,
   The vacant leaves thy mind's imprint will bear,
   And of this book this learning mayst thou taste:
   The wrinkles which thy glass will truly show
   Of mouthèd graves will give thee memory;
   Thou by thy dial's shady stealth mayst know
   Time's thievish progress to eternity.
   1609 *Sonnets*, sonnet 77.

66 Who is it that says most which can say more
Than this rich praise: that you alone are you.
1609 *Sonnets*, sonnet 84.

67 Farewell—thou art too dear for my possessing,
And like enough thou know'st thy estimate.
The charter of thy worth gives thee releasing;
My bonds in thee are all determinate.
For how do I hold thee but by thy granting,
And for that riches where is my deserving?
The cause of this fair gift in me is wanting,
And so my patent back again is swerving.
Thyself thou gav'st, thy own worth then not
  knowing,
Or me to whom thou gav'st it else mistaking;
So thy great gift, upon misprision growing,
Comes home again, on better judgement making.
Thus have I had thee as a dream doth flatter:
In sleep a king, but waking no such matter.
1609 *Sonnets*, sonnet 87.

68 So shall I live supposing thou art true
Like a deceived husband; so love's face
May still seem love to me, though altered new.
1609 *Sonnets*, sonnet 93.

69 They that have power to hurt and will do none,
That do not do the thing they most do show,
Who moving others are themselves as stone,
Unmovèd, cold, and to temptation slow—
They rightly do inherit heaven's graces,
And husband nature's riches from expense;
They are the lords and owners of their faces,
Others but stewards of their excellence.
1609 *Sonnets*, sonnet 94.

70 For sweetest things turn sourest by their deeds:
Lilies that fester smell far worse than weeds.
1609 *Sonnets*, sonnet 94.

71 How like a winter hath my absence been
From thee, the pleasure of the fleeting year!
What freezings have I felt, what dark days seen.
What old December's bareness everywhere.
1609 *Sonnets*, sonnet 97.

72 From you have I been absent in the spring
When proud-pied April, dressed in all his trim,
Hath put a spirit of youth in everything.
1609 *Sonnets*, sonnet 98.

73 Nor did I wonder at the lily's white,
Nor praise the deep vermilion in the rose.
1609 *Sonnets*, sonnet 98.

74 To me, fair friend, you never can be old;
For as you were when first your eye I eyed,
Such seems your beauty still.
1609 *Sonnets*, sonnet 104.

75 Kind is my love today, tomorrow kind,
Still constant in a wondrous excellence.
1609 *Sonnets*, sonnet 105.

76 Not mine own fears nor the prophetic soul
Of the wide world dreaming on things to come
Can yet the lease of my true love control,
Supposed as forfeit to a confined doom.
1609 *Sonnets*, sonnet 107.

77 What's in the brain that ink may character
Which hath not figured to thee my true spirit?
What's new to speak, what now to register,
That may express my love or thy dear merit?
Nothing, sweet boy; but yet like prayers divine
I must each day say o'er the very same,
Counting no old thing old, thou mine, I thine,
Even as when first I hallowed thy fair name.
1609 *Sonnets*, sonnet 108.

78 O never say that I was false of heart,
Though absence seemed my flame to qualify.
1609 *Sonnets*, sonnet 109.

79 Then give me welcome, next my heaven the best,
Even to thy pure and most loving breast.
1609 *Sonnets*, sonnet 110.

80 Let me not to the marriage of true minds
Admit impediments. Love is not love
Which alters when it alteration finds,
Or bends with the remover to remove.
O no, it is an ever fixèd mark
That looks on tempests and is never shaken;
It is the star to every wand'ring barque,
Whose worth's unknown although his height be
  taken.
Love's not time's fool, though rosy lips and
  cheeks
Within his bending sickle's compass come;
Love alters not with his brief hours and weeks,
But bears it out even to the edge of doom.
If this be error and upon me proved,
I never writ, nor no man ever loved.
1609 *Sonnets*, sonnet 116.

81 What potions have I drunk of siren tears
Distilled from limbecks foul as hell within,
Applying fears to hopes and hopes to fears,
Still losing when I saw myself to win!
1609 *Sonnets*, sonnet 119.

82 For if you were by my unkindness shaken,
As I by yours, you've passed a hell of time.
1609 *Sonnets*, sonnet 120.

83 My mistress' eyes are nothing like the sun;
Coral is far more red than her lips' red.
If snow be white, why then her breasts are dun;
If hairs be wires, black wires grow on her head.
I have seen roses damasked, red and white,
But no such roses see I in her cheeks;
And in some perfumes is there more delight
Than the breath that from my mistress reeks.
I love to hear her speak, yet well I know
That music hath a far more pleasing sound.
I grant I never saw a goddess go:
My mistress when she walks treads on the ground.
And yet, by heaven, I think my love as rare
As any she belied with false compare.
1609 *Sonnets*, sonnet 130.

84 Whoever hath her wish, thou hast thy Will,
And Will to boot, and Will in overplus.
1609 *Sonnets*, sonnet 135.

85 So thou, being rich in Will, add to thy Will
One will of mine to make thy large Will more.
Let no unkind no fair beseechers kill;
Think all but one, and me in that one Will.
1609 *Sonnets*, sonnet 135.

86 When my love swears that she is made of truth
I do believe her though I know she lies.
1609 *Sonnets*, sonnet 138.

87 Two loves I have, of comfort and despair,
Which like two spirits do suggest me still.
The better angel is a man right fair,
The worser spirit a woman coloured ill.
1609 *Sonnets*, sonnet 144.

88 My love is as a fever, longing still
For that which longer nurseth the disease,
Feeding on that which doth preserve the ill,
Th'uncertain sickly appetite to please.
My reason, the physician to my love,
Angry that his prescriptions are not kept,
Hath left me, and I desperate now approve
Desire is death, which physic did except.
Past cure I am, now reason is past care,
And frantic mad with evermore unrest.
My thoughts and my discourse as madmen's are,
At random from the truth vainly expressed;
For I have sworn thee fair, and thought thee bright,
Who art as black as hell, as dark as night.
1609 *Sonnets*, sonnet 147.

89 Was there ever man had such luck? When I kissed the jack upon an upcast to be hit away! I had a hundred pound on't, and then a whoreson jackanapes must take me up for swearing.
1610 Cloten. *Cymbeline*, act 2, sc.1, l.1–4.

90 When a gentleman is disposed to swear it is not for any standers-by to curtail his oaths.
1610 Cloten. *Cymbeline*, act 2, sc.1, l.10–11.

91 On her left breast
A mole, cinque-spotted, like the crimson drops
I'th' bottom of a cowslip.
1610 Giacomo, of Innogen. *Cymbeline*, act 2, sc.2, l.37–9.

92 I am advised to give her music o' mornings; they say it will penetrate.
1610 Cloten, of Innogen. *Cymbeline*, act 2, sc.3, l.11–12.

93 Hark, hark, the lark at heaven gate sings,
And Phoebus gins arise.
1610 Musician, singing. *Cymbeline*, act 2, sc.3, l.19–20.

94 Is there no way for men to be, but women
Must be half-workers? We are bastards all.
1610 Posthumus. *Cymbeline*, act 2, sc.5, l.1–2.

95 I thought her
As chaste as unsunned snow.
1610 Posthumus, of Innogen. *Cymbeline*, act 2, sc.5, l.12–13.

96 I am stale, a garment out of fashion.
1610 Innogen. *Cymbeline*, act 3, sc.4, l.51.

97 Against self-slaughter
There is a prohibition so divine
That cravens my weak hand.
1610 Innogen. *Cymbeline*, act 3, sc.4, l.76–8.

98 Thus may poor fools
Believe false teachers.
1610 Innogen. *Cymbeline*, act 3, sc.4, l.84–5.

99 Though those that are betrayed
Do feel the treason sharply, yet the traitor
Stands in worse case of woe.
1610 Innogen. *Cymbeline*, act 3, sc.4, l.85–7.

1 Hath Britain all the sun that shines? Day, night,
Are they not but in Britain? I'th' world's volume
Our Britain seems as of it but not in't,
In a great pool a swan's nest.
1610 Innogen to Pisanio. *Cymbeline*, act 3, sc.4, l.137–40.

2 Thou art all the comfort
The gods will diet me with.
1610 Innogen to Pisanio. *Cymbeline*, act 3, sc.4, l.180–1.

3 Weariness
Can snore upon the flint when resty sloth
Finds the down pillow hard.
1610 Belarius. *Cymbeline*, act 3, sc.6, l.33–5.

4 By Jupiter, an angel—or, if not,
An earthly paragon.
1610 Belarius, of Innogen in disguise. *Cymbeline*, act 3, sc.6, l.42–3.

5 All gold and silver rather turn to dirt.
1610 Arviragus. *Cymbeline*, act 3, sc.6, l.52.

6 Society is no comfort
To one not sociable.
1610 Innogen. *Cymbeline*, act 4, sc.2, l.12–13.

7 Fear no more the heat o'th' sun,
Nor the furious winter's rages.
Thou thy worldly task hast done,
Home art gone and ta'en thy wages.
Golden lads and girls all must,
As chimney-sweepers, come to dust.
1610 Guiderius. *Cymbeline*, act 4, sc.2, l.259–64.

8 By medicine life may be prolonged, yet death
Will seize the doctor too.
1610 Cymbeline. *Cymbeline*, act 5, sc.6, l.29–30.

9 The power that I have on you is to spare you.
1610 Posthumus to Giacomo. *Cymbeline*, act 5, sc.6, l.419.

10 What seest thou else
In the dark backward and abyss of time?
1611 Prospero to Miranda. *The Tempest*, act 1, sc.2, l.49–50.

11 I find my zenith doth depend upon
A most auspicious star, whose influence
If now I court not, but omit, my fortunes
Will ever after droop.
1611 Prospero to Miranda. *The Tempest*, act 1, sc.2, l.182–5.

12 Thou art inclined to sleep; 'tis a good dullness,
And give it way. I know thou canst not choose.
1611 Prospero to Miranda. *The Tempest*, act 1, sc.2, l.186–7.

13 You taught me language, and my profit on't
Is I know how to curse.
1611 Caliban to Miranda. *The Tempest*, act 1, sc.2, l.365–6.

14 Come unto these yellow sands,
And then take hands.
1611 Ariel, singing. *The Tempest*, act 1, sc.2, l.377–8.

15 This music crept by me upon the waters,
Allaying both their fury and my passion
With its sweet air.
1611 Ferdinand. *The Tempest*, act 1, sc.2, l.394–6.

16 Full fathom five thy father lies.
Of his bones are coral made.
1611 Ariel. *The Tempest*, act 1, sc.2, l.399–400.

17 Nothing of him that doth fade
But doth suffer a sea-change
Into something rich and strange.
1611 Ariel. *The Tempest*, act 1, sc.2, l.402–4.

18 He receives comfort like cold porridge.
  1611 Sebastian, of Alonso. *The Tempest*, act 2, sc.1, l.11.

19 Look, he's winding up the watch of his wit.
  By and by it will strike.
  1611 Sebastian, of Gonzalo. *The Tempest*, act 2, sc.1, l.13–14.

20 Misery acquaints a man with strange bedfellows.
  1611 Trinculo, of Caliban. *The Tempest*, act 2, sc.2, l.39.

21 'Ban, 'ban, Cacaliban
  Has a new master.—Get a new man!
  1611 Caliban. *The Tempest*, act 2, sc.2, l.183–4.

22 FERDINAND: I do beseech you,
  Chiefly that I might set it in my prayers,
  What is your name?
  MIRANDA: Miranda. O my father,
  I have broke your hest to say so!
  FERDINAND: Admired Miranda!
  Indeed the top of admiration, worth
  What's dearest to the world.
  1611 *The Tempest*, act 3, sc.1, l.36–9.
  Shakespeare invented the name Miranda, taking it from the Latin word meaning 'worthy to be admired'.

23 Remember
  First to possess his books, for without them
  He's but a sot as I am, nor hath not
  One spirit to command–they all do hate him
  As rootedly as I. Burn but his books.
  1611 Caliban, of Prospero. *The Tempest*, act 3, sc.2, l.92–6.

24 He that dies pays all debts.
  1611 Stefano. *The Tempest*, act 3, sc.2, l.134.

25 The isle is full of noises,
  Sound, and sweet airs, that give delight and hurt not.
  1611 Caliban. *The Tempest*, act 3, sc.2, l.138–9.

26 Thou shalt find that she will outstrip all praise,
  And make it halt behind her.
  1611 Prospero, of Miranda. *The Tempest*, act 4, sc.1, l.10–11.

27 The cloud-capped towers, the gorgeous palaces,
  The solemn temples, the great globe itself,
  Yea, all which it inherit, shall dissolve;
  And, like this insubstantial pageant faded,
  Leave not a rack behind.
  1611 Prospero. *The Tempest*, act 4, sc.1, l.152–6.

28 We are such stuff
  As dreams are made on, and our little life
  Is rounded with a sleep.
  1611 Prospero. *The Tempest*, act 4, sc.1, l.156–8.

29 They were red-hot with drinking;
  So full of valour that they smote the air
  For breathing in their faces.
  1611 Ariel. *The Tempest*, act 4, sc.1, l.171–3.

30 This rough magic
  I here abjure.
  1611 Prospero. *The Tempest*, act 5, sc.1, l.50–1.

31 I'll break my staff,
  Bury it certain fathoms in the earth,
  And deeper than did ever plummet sound
  I'll drown my book.
  1611 Prospero. *The Tempest*, act 5, sc.1, l.54–7.

32 Where the bee sucks, there suck I:
  In a cowslip's bell I lie;
  There I couch when owls do cry.
  On the bat's back I do fly
  After summer merrily.
  Merrily, merrily shall I live now
  Under the blossom that hangs on the bough.
  1611 Ariel's song. *The Tempest*, act 5, sc.1, l.88–94.

33 How beauteous mankind is! O brave new world
  That hath such people in't!
  1611 Miranda. *The Tempest*, act 5, sc.1, l.186–7.

34 What a thrice-double ass
  Was I to take this drunkard for a god,
  And worship this dull fool!
  1611 Caliban. *The Tempest*, act 5, sc.1, l.299–301.

35 Now my charms are all o'erthrown,
  And what strength I have's mine own.
  1611 Prospero. *The Tempest*, epilogue, l.1–2.

36 Heat not a furnace for your foe so hot
  That it do singe yourself.
  1613 Norfolk. *Henry VIII*, act 1, sc.1, l.140–1.

37 Travelled gallants
  That fill the court with quarrels, talk, and tailors.
  1613 Lovell. *Henry VIII*, act 1, sc.3, l.19–20.

38 Good company, good wine, good welcome
  Can make good people.
  1613 Guildford. *Henry VIII*, act 1, sc.4, l.6–7.

39 Two women placed together makes cold weather.
  1613 Lord Chamberlain. *Henry VIII*, act 1, sc.4, l.22.

40 If I chance to talk a little wild, forgive me.
  I had it from my father.
  1613 Sands. *Henry VIII*, act 1, sc.4, l.26–7.

41 Those you make friends
  And give your hearts to, when they once perceive
  The least rub in your fortunes, fall away
  Like water from ye.
  1613 Buckingham. *Henry VIII*, act 2, sc.1, l.128–31.

42 I would not be a queen
  For all the world.
  1613 Anne Boleyn. *Henry VIII*, act 2, sc.3, l.45–6.

43 You have many enemies that know not
  Why they are so, but, like to village curs,
  Bark when their fellows do.
  1613 Henry to Wolsey. *Henry VIII*, act 2, sc.4, l.155–7.

44 Orpheus with his lute made trees,
  And the mountain tops that freeze,
  Bow themselves when he did sing.
  1613 Gentlewoman, singing. *Henry VIII*, act 3, sc.1, l.3–5.

45 Everything that heard him play,
  Even the billows of the sea,
  Hung their heads, and then lay by.
  In sweet music is such art,
  Killing care and grief of heart
  Fall asleep, or hearing, die.
  1613 Gentlewoman, singing. *Henry VIII*, act 3, sc.1, l.9–14.

46 Methought
  I stood not in the smile of heaven.
  1613 Henry. *Henry VIII*, act 2, sc.4, l.183–4.

47 In sweet music is such art,
  Killing care and grief of heart
  Fall asleep, or hearing die.
  1613 Gentlewoman. *Henry VIII*, act 3, sc.1, l.13–15.

48 Yet I know her for
A spleeny Lutheran, and not wholesome to
Our cause.
1613 Cardinal Wolsey, of Anne Boleyn. *Henry VIII*, act 3, sc.2, l.99–101.

49 Nature does require
Her times of preservation.
1613 Wolsey to Henry. *Henry VIII*, act 3, sc.2, l.147–8.

50 I have touched the highest point of all my greatness,
And from that full meridian of my glory
I haste now to my setting.
1613 Wolsey. *Henry VIII*, act 3, sc.2, l.224–6.

51 I feel within me
A peace above all earthly dignities,
A still and quiet conscience.
1613 Wolsey. *Henry VIII*, act 3, sc.2, l.379–81.

52 This is the state of man. He puts forth
The tender leaves of hopes; tomorrow blossoms,
And bears his blushing honours thick upon him;
The third day comes a frost, a killing frost,
And when he thinks, good easy man, full surely
His greatness is a-ripening, nips his root,
And then he falls, as I do.
1613 Wolsey. *Henry VIII*, act 3, sc.2, l.353–9.

53 Had I but served my God with half the zeal
I served my King, He would not in mine age
Have left me naked to mine enemies.
1613 Wolsey. *Henry VIII*, act 3, sc.2, l.456–8.

54 Still in thy right hand carry gentle peace
To silence envious tongues.
1613 Wolsey. *Henry VIII*, act 3, sc.2, l.446–7.

55 An old man broken with the storms of state
Is come to lay his weary bones among ye.
Give him a little earth, for charity.
1613 Griffith, recalling Wolsey. *Henry VIII*, act 4, sc.2, l.21–3.

56 Men's evil manners live in brass, their virtues
We write in water.
1613 Griffith. *Henry VIII*, act 4, sc.2, l.45–6.

57 That comfort comes too late,
'Tis like a pardon after execution.
1613 Katherine. *Henry VIII*, act 4, sc.2, l.121–2.

58 Good grows with her.
In her days every man shall eat in safety
Under his own vine what he plants, and sing
The merry songs of peace to all his neighbours.
1613 Cranmer, of Elizabeth. *Henry VIII*, act 5, sc.4, l.32–5.

Shange, Ntozake *originally* Paulette Williams 1948–

Black US writer, who adopted a Zulu name for political reasons. She has written mainly for the stage, often adopting a multimedia approach combining poetry, dance and music.

59 For coloured girls who have considered suicide / when the rainbow is enuf.
1975 Title of 'choreo-poem'.

Shankly, Bill (William) 1913–81

Scottish footballer and manager. A player with Preston North End and Scotland, he established a reputation as one of the finest managers of his generation through his management of Liverpool in the 1960s and was widely known for his grim determination and biting wit.

60 Some people think football is a matter of life and death. I don't like that attitude. I can assure them it is much more serious than that.
Quoted in the *Sunday Times*, 4 Oct 1981.

61 I don't drop players, I make changes.
Quoted in Peter Ball and Phil Shaw *The Book of Football Quotations* (1990).

62 If Everton were playing down at the bottom of my garden, I'd draw the curtains.
Quoted in Colin Jarman *The Guinness Dictionary of Sports Quotations* (1990).

63 If you're in the penalty area and aren't sure what to do with the ball, just stick it in the net, and we'll discuss your options afterwards.
Quoted in Colin Jarman *The Guinness Dictionary of Sports Quotations* (1990).

64 Of course I didn't take my wife to see Rochdale as an anniversary present. It was her birthday. Would I have got married during the football season? And anyway it wasn't Rochdale, it was Rochdale reserves.
Quoted in Peter Ball and Phil Shaw *The Book of Football Quotations* (1990).

65 This town has two great teams—Liverpool and Liverpool reserves.
Deliberately ignoring rival team Everton. Quoted in Colin Jarman *The Guiness Dictionary of Sports Quotations* (1990).

66 We murdered them 0–0.
Quoted in Colin Jarman *The Guiness Dictionary of Sports Quotations* (1990).

67 Me having no education, I had to use my brains.
Quoted in David Pickering *The Cassell Soccer Companion* (1994)

Shapin, Steven 1955–

US sociologist

68 The very power of science to hold knowledge as collective knowledge is founded upon a degree and a quality of trust which are arguably unparalleled elsewhere in our culture... Scientists know so much about the natural world by knowing so much about whom they can trust.
1994 *A Social History of Truth*.

Sharansky, Natan Anatoly Borisovich 1948–

Ukrainian-born Soviet dissident, human rights activist and politician. He was imprisoned (1977–86) by the Soviet government. As a Jew, he applied for emigration rights to Israel in 1975, but was harassed by the KGB and discharged from his job. He was arrested in 1977 and accused of treason and espionage. On his release from prison he was allowed to go to Israel, where he became a politician.

69 All the resources of a superpower cannot isolate a man who hears the voice of freedom; a voice that I heard from the very chamber of my soul.
1986 Speech, New York, 11 May, shortly after his release following nine years in a Soviet labour colony.

Sharp, William *pseudonym* Fiona Macleod 1855–1905

Scottish writer and traveller. He published poetry and literary criticism, but he is best known as the author of a series of neo-Celtic romantic tales written under the pseudonym he systematically refused to acknowledge.

70 My heart is a lonely hunter that hunts on a lonely hill.
   1896 'The Lonely Hunter', stanza 6. Carson McCullers adapted the phrase as the title of a 1940 novel, *The Heart Is a Lonely Hunter*.

Sharpe, Tom (Thomas Ridley) 1928–2013

English novelist. His early works were plays written in South Africa. He returned to England in 1961, and became known for the vigorous satire of his comic novels.

71 The South African police would leave no stone unturned to see that nothing disturbed the even terror of their lives.
   1973 *Indecent Exposure*, ch.1.

72 Skullion had little use for contraceptives at the best of times. Unnatural, he called them, and placed them in the lower social category of things along with elastic-sided boots and made-up bow ties. Not the sort of attire for a gentleman.
   1974 *Porterhouse Blue*, ch.9.

73 And besides, Mrs Forthby in the flesh was a different kettle of fish to Mrs Forthby in his fantasies. In the latter she had a multitude of perverse inclinations, which corresponded exactly with his own unfortunate requirements, while possessing a discretion that would have done credit to a Trappist nun. In the flesh she was disappointingly different.
   1975 *Blott on the Landscape*, ch.3.

74 In the lotus position at her yoga class she managed to exude energy, and her attempts at Transcendental Meditation had been likened to a pressure-cooker on simmer.
   1976 *Wilt*, ch.1.

75 God, in his view, had created a perfect world if the book of Genesis was to be believed and it had been going downhill ever since.
   1976 *Wilt*, ch.17.

76 All you had to do was tell people what they wanted to hear and they would believe you no matter how implausible your story might be.
   1976 *Wilt*, ch.18.

77 The Rev St John Froude put the phone down thoughtfully. The notion that he was sharing the house with a disembodied and recently murdered woman was not one that he had wanted to put to his caller. His reputation for eccentricity was already sufficiently widespread without adding to it.
   1976 *Wilt*, ch.19.

78 If any writer thinks the world is full of middle-class people of nice sensibilities, then he is out of his mind.
   1985 In the *Observer*, 3 Feb.

Shaw, George Bernard 1856–1950

Anglo-Irish dramatist and socialist. He moved to London in 1876 and in 1882 joined the Fabian Society. He wrote over 40 plays including *Arms and the Man* (1894, published 1898), *Candida* (1895), *Man and Superman* (1903), *Pygmalion* (1913), *Saint Joan* (1923, published 1924) and *The Apple Cart* (1929). He was also a lifelong advocate of vegetarianism, and a passionate supporter of spelling reform. In 1935 he was awarded the Nobel prize for literature.

79 Money is indeed the most important thing in the world: and all sound and successful personal and national morality should have this fact for its basis.
   1880 *The Irrational Knot*, preface.

80 Reminiscences make one feel so deliciously aged and sad.
   1880 *The Irrational Knot*, ch.14.

81 A man who has no office to go to—I don't care who he is—is a trial of which you can have no conception.
   1880 *The Irrational Knot*, ch.18.

82 'Do you know what a pessimist is?'
   'A man who thinks everybody is as nasty as himself, and hates them for it.'
   1887 *An Unsocial Socialist*, ch.5.

83 Don't ask me for promises until I know what I am promising.
   1894 Catherine to Raina. *Arms and the Man*, act 1.

84 You can always tell an old soldier by the inside of his holsters and cartridge boxes. The young ones carry pistols and cartridges; the old ones, grub.
   1894 The Man to Raina. *Arms and the Man*, act 1.

85 Oh, you are a very poor soldier—a chocolate cream soldier!
   1894 Raina to The Man. *Arms and the Man*, act 1.

86 You're not a man, you're a machine.
   1894 Sergius to Bluntschli. *Arms and the Man*, act 3.

87 We have no more right to consume happiness without producing it than to consume wealth without producing it.
   1895 Morell to Lexy. *Candida*, act 1.

88 Do you think that the things people make fools of themselves about are any less real and true than the things they behave sensibly about? They are more true: they are the only things that are true.
   1895 Marchbanks to Morell. *Candida*, act 1.

89 It is easy—terribly easy—to shake a man's faith in himself. To take advantage of that to break a man's spirit is devil's work.
   1895 Morell to Marchbanks. *Candida*, act 1.

90 Wicked people means people who have no love: therefore they have no shame. They have the power to ask for love because they don't need it: they have the power to offer it because they have none to give. But we, who have love, and long to mingle it with the love of others: we cannot utter a word. You find that, don't you?
   1895 Marchbanks to Proserpine. *Candida*, act 2.

91 I'm only a beer teetotaller, not a champagne teetotaller.
   1895 Proserpine. *Candida*, act 3.

92 I no longer desire happiness: life is nobler than that.
   1895 Marchbanks. *Candida*, act 3.

93 We're from Madeira, but perfectly respectable, so far.
   1896 Philip Clandon to Valentine. *You Never Can Tell*, act 1.

94 We don't bother much about dress and manners in England, because, as a nation, we don't dress well and we've no manners.
   1896 Valentine to Dolly and Philip Clandon. *You Never Can Tell*, act 1.

95 The great advantage of a hotel is that it's a refuge from home life.
   1896 Waiter. *You Never Can Tell*, act 2.

96 Well, sir, you never can tell. That's a principle in life with me, sir, if you'll excuse my having such a thing, sir.
   1896 Waiter to Fergus Crampton. *You Never Can Tell*, act 2.

97 There is nothing so bad or so good that you will not find Englishmen doing it; but you will never find an Englishman in the wrong. He does everything on principle. He fights you on patriotic principles; he robs you on business principles; he enslaves you on imperial principles; he bullies you on manly principles; he supports his king on loyal principles and cuts off his head on republican principles.
1897 *The Man of Destiny.*

98 The worst sin towards our fellow creatures is not to hate them, but to be indifferent to them: that's the essence of inhumanity.
1897 Pastor Anderson to Judith Anderson. *The Devil's Disciple*, act 2.

99 Martyrdom...the only way in which a man can become famous without ability.
1897 *The Devil's Disciple*, act 3.

1 I never expect a soldier to think, sir.
1897 Richard Dudgeon to Major Swindon. *The Devil's Disciple*, act 3.

2 'I can't believe it! What will History say?'
'History, sir, will tell lies as usual.'
1897 Major Swindon and Gen Burgoyne. *The Devil's Disciple*, act 3.

3 Your friend the British soldier can stand up to anything except the British War Office.
1897 Gen Burgoyne to Major Swindon. *The Devil's Disciple*, act 3.

4 Brains are not everything.
1898 Rev Samuel Gardner. *Mrs Warren's Profession*, act 1.

5 If there is anything I hate in a woman, it's want of character.
1898 Mrs Warren. *Mrs Warren's Profession*, act 2.

6 The only way for a woman to provide for herself decently is for her to be good to some man that can afford to be good to her.
1898 Mrs Warren to Vivie Warren. *Mrs Warren's Profession*, act 2.

7 There are no secrets better kept than the secrets everybody guesses.
1898 Sir George Crofts. *Mrs Warren's Profession*, act 3.

8 'Damn you!'
'You need not. I feel among the damned already.'
1898 Sir George Crofts and Vivie Warren. *Mrs Warren's Profession*, act 3.

9 Miss Warren is a great devotee of the Gospel of Getting On.
1898 Praed. *Mrs Warren's Profession*, act 4.

10 He is a barbarian, and thinks that the customs of his tribe and island are the laws of nature.
1899 Of the Briton. Caesar to Theodotus. *Caesar and Cleopatra*, act 2.

11 When a stupid man is doing something he is ashamed of, he always declares that it is his duty.
1899 Apollodorus. *Caesar and Cleopatra*, act 3.

12 A man of great common sense and good taste, meaning thereby a man without originality or moral courage.
1899 Of Caesar. *Caesar and Cleopatra*, notes.

13 But a lifetime of happiness! No man alive could bear it: it would be hell on earth.
1903 John Tanner. *Man and Superman*, act 1.

14 I am proud of your contempt for my character and opinions, sir.
1903 Roebuck Ramsden to John Tanner. *Man and Superman*, act 1.

15 The more things a man is ashamed of, the more respectable he is.
1903 John Tanner. *Man and Superman*, act 1.

16 Vitality in a woman is a blind fury of creation.
1903 John Tanner to Octavius Robinson. *Man and Superman*, act 1.

17 Of all human struggles there is none so treacherous and remorseless as the struggle between the artist man and the mother woman.
1903 John Tanner. *Man and Superman*, act 1.

18 A sensitive boy's humiliations may be very good fun for ordinary thick-skinned grown-ups; but to the boy himself they are so acute, so ignominious, that he cannot confess them—cannot but deny them passionately.
1903 John Tanner. *Man and Superman*, act 1.

19 There is no love sincerer than the love of food.
1903 John Tanner to Octavius Robinson. *Man and Superman*, act 1.

20 That damnable woman's trick of heaping obligations on a man, of placing yourself so entirely and helplessly at his mercy that at last he dare not take a step without running to you for leave. I know a poor wretch whose one desire in life is to run away from his wife. She prevents him by threatening to throw herself in front of the engine of the train he leaves her in. That is what all women do. If we try to go where you do not want us to go there is no law to prevent us; but when we take the first step your breasts are under our foot as it descends: your bodies are under our wheels as we start. No woman shall ever enslave me in that way.
1903 John Tanner to Ann Whitefield. *Man and Superman*, act 1.

21 You think that you are Ann's suitor; that you are the pursuer and she the pursued... Fool: it is you who are pursued, the marked down quarry, the destined prey.
1903 John Tanner to Octavius Robinson. *Man and Superman*, act 2.

22 'I am a brigand: I live by robbing the rich.'
'I am a gentleman: I live by robbing the poor.'
1903 Mendoza and John Tanner. *Man and Superman*, act 3.

23 Hell is full of musical amateurs: music is the brandy of the damned.
1903 Don Juan to the Devil. *Man and Superman*, act 3.

24 Englishmen never will be slaves: they are free to do whatever the Government and public allow them to do.
1903 The Devil to Ann Whitefield. *Man and Superman*, act 3.

25 An Englishman thinks he is moral when he is only uncomfortable.
1903 The Devil. *Man and Superman*, act 3.

26 In the arts of life man invents nothing; but in the arts of death he outdoes Nature herself, and produces by chemistry and machinery all the slaughter of plague, pestilence and famine.
1903 The Devil to Don Juan. *Man and Superman*, act 3.

27 In the arts of peace Man is a bungler.
1903 The Devil to Don Juan. *Man and Superman*, act 3.

28 As an old soldier I admit the cowardice: it's as universal as sea sickness, and matters just as little.
1903 The Statue. *Man and Superman*, act 3.

29 Sexually, Woman is Nature's contrivance for perpetuating its highest achievement.
1903 Don Juan to Ana. *Man and Superman*, act 3.

30 When the military man approaches, the world locks up its spoons and packs off its womankind.
1903 Don Juan. *Man and Superman*, act 3.

31 What is virtue but the Trade Unionism of the married?
1903 Don Juan to Ann Whitefield. *Man and Superman*, act 3.

32 Marriage is the most licentious of human institutions.
1903 Don Juan. *Man and Superman*, act 3.

33 Those who talk most about the blessings of marriage and the constancy of its vows are the very people who declare that if the claim were broken and the prisoners were left free to choose, the whole social fabric would fly asunder. You can't have the argument both ways. If the prisoner is happy, why lock him in? If he is not, why pretend that he is?
1903 Don Juan to Ann Whitefield. *Man and Superman*, act 3.

34 Beauty is all very well at first sight; but who ever looks at it when it has been in the house three days?
1903 Ann Whitefield. *Man and Superman*, act 4.

35 Revolutions have never lightened the burden of tyranny: they have only shifted it to another shoulder.
1903 *Man and Superman*, 'The Revolutionist's Handbook and Pocket Companion, by John Tanner', foreword.

36 The art of government is the organization of idolatry.
1903 *Man and Superman*, 'Maxims for Revolutionists: Idolatry'.

37 Democracy substitutes election by the incompetent many for appointment by the corrupt few.
1903 *Man and Superman*, 'Maxims for Revolutionists: Democracy'.

38 Liberty means responsibility. That is why most men dread it.
1903 *Man and Superman*, 'Maxims for Revolutionists: Liberty and Equality'.

39 He who can, does. He who cannot, teaches.
1903 *Man and Superman*, 'Maxims for Revolutionists: Education'.

40 Marriage is popular because it combines the maximum of temptation with the maximum of opportunity.
1903 *Man and Superman*, 'Maxims for Revolutionists: Marriage'.

41 Titles distinguish the mediocre, embarrass the superior, and are disgraced by the inferior.
1903 *Man and Superman*, 'Maxims for Revolutionists: Titles'.

42 When domestic servants are treated as human beings it is not worth while to keep them.
1903 *Man and Superman*, 'Maxims for Revolutionists: Servants'.

43 If you strike a child take care that you strike it in anger, even at the risk of maiming it for life. A blow in cold blood neither can nor should be forgiven.
1903 *Man and Superman*, 'Maxims for Revolutionists: How to Beat Children'.

44 Beware of the man whose God is in the skies.
1903 *Man and Superman*, 'Maxims for Revolutionists: Religion'.

45 The most intolerable pain is produced by prolonging the keenest pleasure.
1903 *Man and Superman*, 'Maxims for Revolutionists: Beauty and Happiness'.

46 Economy is the art of making the most of life.
1903 *Man and Superman*, 'Maxims for Revolutionists: Virtues and Vices'.

47 Self-denial is not a virtue: it is only the effect of prudence on rascality.
1903 *Man and Superman*, 'Maxims for Revolutionists: Virtues and Vices'.

48 A moderately honest man with a moderately faithful wife, moderate drinkers both, in a moderately healthy house: that is the true middle-class unit.
1903 *Man and Superman*, 'Maxims for Revolutionists: Moderation'.

49 The reasonable man adapts himself to the world: the unreasonable one persists in trying to adapt the world to himself. Therefore all progress depends on the unreasonable man.
1903 *Man and Superman*, 'Maxims for Revolutionists: Reason'.

50 The man who listens to Reason is lost: Reason enslaves all whose minds are not strong enough to master her.
1903 *Man and Superman*, 'Maxims for Revolutionists: Reason'.

51 Decency is Indecency's conspiracy of silence.
1903 *Man and Superman*, 'Maxims for Revolutionists: Decency'.

52 Life levels all men: death reveals the eminent.
1903 *Man and Superman*, 'Maxims for Revolutionists: Fame'.

53 Home is the girl's prison and the woman's workhouse.
1903 *Man and Superman*, 'Maxims for Revolutionists: Women in the Home'.

54 Every man over forty is a scoundrel.
1903 *Man and Superman*, 'Maxims for Revolutionists: Stray Sayings'.

55 Youth, which is forgiven everything, forgives itself nothing: age, which forgives itself everything, is forgiven nothing.
1903 *Man and Superman*, 'Maxims for Revolutionists: Stray Sayings'.

56 Take care to get what you like or you will be forced to like what you get.
1903 *Man and Superman*, 'Maxims for Revolutionists: Stray Sayings'.

57 Beware of the man who does not return your blow: he neither forgives you nor allows you to forgive yourself.
1903 *Man and Superman*, 'Maxims for Revolutionists: Stray Sayings'.

58 Self-sacrifice enables us to sacrifice other people without blushing.
1903 *Man and Superman*, 'Maxims for Revolutionists: Self-Sacrifice'.

59 Do not do unto others as you would they should do to you. Their tastes may not be the same.
1903 *Man and Superman*, 'Maxims for Revolutionists: The Golden Rule'.

60 The golden rule is that there are no golden rules.
1903 *Man and Superman*, 'Maxims for Revolutionists: The Golden Rule'.

61 When a man wants to murder a tiger he calls it sport; when a tiger wants to murder him he calls it ferocity.
1903 *Man and Superman*, 'Maxims for Revolutionists: Crime and Punishment'.

62 An Irishman's imagination never lets him alone, never convinces him, never satisfies him; but it makes him that he can't face reality nor deal with it nor handle it nor conquer it: he can only sneer at them that do, and be 'agreeable to strangers', like a good-for-nothing woman on the streets.
1904 Larry Doyle to Tom Broadbent. *John Bull's Other Island*, act 1.

63 An Irishman's heart is nothing but his imagination.
   1904 Larry Doyle to Tom Broadbent. *John Bull's Other Island*, act 1.

64 The poor silly-clever Irishman takes off his hat to God's Englishman.
   1904 Larry Doyle. *John Bull's Other Island*, act 1.

65 My way of joking is to tell the truth. It's the funniest joke in the world.
   1904 Peter Keegan to Nora Reilly. *John Bull's Other Island*, act 2.

66 I am sincere; and my intentions are perfectly honourable. I think you will accept the fact that I'm an Englishman as a guarantee that I am not a man to act hastily or romantically.
   1904 Tom Broadbent to Nora Reilly. *John Bull's Other Island*, act 2.

67 You just keep your air on and listen to me. You Awrish people are too well off: thet's wots the matter with you.
   1904 Hodson to Matthew Haffigan. *John Bull's Other Island*, act 3.

68 There are only two qualities in the world: efficiency and inefficiency, and only two sorts of people: the efficient and the inefficient.
   1904 Tom Broadbent. *John Bull's Other Island*, act 4.

69 In my dreams is a country where the State is the Church and the Church the people: three in one and one in three. It is a commonwealth in which work is play and play is life: three in one and one in three. It is a temple in which the priest is the worshipper and the worshipper the worshipped: three in one and one in three. It is a godhead in which all life is human and all humanity divine: three in one and one in three. It is, in short, the dream of a madman.
   1904 Of Heaven, Keegan speaking. *John Bull's Other Island*, act 4.

70 The greatest of evils and the worst of crimes is poverty...our first duty—a duty to which every other consideration should be sacrificed—is not to be poor.
   1905 *Major Barbara*, preface.

71 Nobody can say a word against Greek: it stamps a man at once as an educated gentleman.
   1905 Lady Britomart Undershaft to Stephen. *Major Barbara*, act 1.

72 I am a Millionaire. That is my religion.
   1905 Undershaft to Barbara Undershaft. *Major Barbara*, act 2.

73 I can't talk religion to a man with bodily hunger in his eyes.
   1905 Barbara Undershaft. *Major Barbara*, act 2.

74 Alcohol is a very necessary article... It makes life bearable to millions of people who could not endure their existence if they were quite sober. It enables Parliament to do things at eleven at night that no sane person would do at eleven in the morning.
   1905 Undershaft to Barbara Undershaft. *Major Barbara*, act 2.

75 It's nao good: you cawnt get rahnd me nah. Aw downt blieve in it; and Awve seen tody that Aw was rawt. Sao long, aol soupkitchener! Ta, ta, Mijor Earl's Grendorter! Wot prawce selvytion nah? Snobby Prawce! Ha! ha!
   1905 Bill Walker to Barbara Undershaft. *Major Barbara*, act 2.

76 He knows nothing; and he thinks he knows everything. That points clearly to a political career.
   1905 Undershaft speaking of Stephen. *Major Barbara*, act 3.

77 Like all young men, you greatly exaggerate the difference between one young woman and another.
   1905 Undershaft about Adolphus Cusins. *Major Barbara*, act 3.

78 Fashions, after all, are only induced epidemics.
   1906 *The Doctor's Dilemma*, 'Preface on Doctors: Fashions and Epidemics'.

79 Science becomes dangerous only when it imagines that it has reached its goal.
   1906 *The Doctor's Dilemma*, preface, 'The Latest Theories'.

80 There is at bottom only one genuinely scientific treatment for all diseases, and that is to stimulate the phagocytes.
   1906 BB (Sir Ralph Bloomfield Bonington). *The Doctor's Dilemma*, act 1.

81 All professions are conspiracies against the laity.
   1906 Sir Patrick Cullen. *The Doctor's Dilemma*, act 1.

82 A man's behaviour may be quite harmless and even beneficial, when he is morally behaving like a scoundrel. And he may do great harm when he is morally acting on the highest principles.
   1906 BB. *The Doctor's Dilemma*, act 3.

83 The criminal law is no use to decent people.
   1906 Sir Patrick. *The Doctor's Dilemma*, act 3.

84 There's almost as many different sorts of marriage as there's different sorts of people. There's the young things that marry for love, not knowing what they're doing, and the old things that marry for money and comfort and companionship. There's the people that marry for children. There's the people that don't intend to have children and that aren't fit to have them. There's the people that marry because they're so much run after by the other sex that they have to put a stop to it somehow. There's the people that want to try a new experience, and the people that want to have done with experiences.
   1908 Bill Collins. *Getting Married*.

85 Home life as we understand it is no more natural to us than a cage is natural to a cockatoo.
   1908 *Getting Married*, preface, 'Hearth and Home'.

86 The one point on which all women are in furious secret rebellion against the existing law is the saddling of the right to a child with the obligation to become the servant of a man.
   1908 *Getting Married*, preface, 'The Right to Motherhood'.

87 Physically there is nothing to distinguish human society from the farmyard except that children are more troublesome and costly than chickens and calves, and that men and women are not so completely enslaved as farm stock.
   1908 *Getting Married*, preface, 'The Personal Sentimental Basis of Monogamy'.

88 You see, family life is all the life she knows: she's like a bird born in a cage, that would die if you let it loose in the woods.
   1908 Bill Collins about his wife. *Getting Married*.

89 A man is like a phonograph with half-a-dozen records. You soon get tired of them all; and yet you have to sit at table whilst he reels them off to every new visitor. In the end you have to be content with his common humanity.
   1908 The Bishop of Chelsea. *Getting Married*.

90 I am a snob, not only in fact, but on principle.
   1908 St John Hotchkiss. *Getting Married*.

91 Optimistic lies have such immense therapeutic value that a doctor who cannot tell them convincingly has mistaken his profession.
1910 *Misalliance*, preface.

92 Anybody on for a game of tennis?
1910 *Misalliance*. This may be the origin of 'Anyone for tennis?', as used in archetypal theatrical drawing-room comedies.

93 The English have no respect for their language, and will not teach their children to speak it. They spell it so abominably that no man can teach himself what it sounds like. It is impossible for an Englishman to open his mouth without making some other Englishman hate or despise him.
1913 *Pygmalion*, Preface.

94 He's a gentleman: look at his boots.
1913 Bystander. *Pygmalion*, act 1.

95 I don't want to talk grammar, I want to talk like a lady.
1913 Eliza Doolittle. *Pygmalion*, act 2.

96 Have you ever met a man of good character where women are concerned?
1913 Higgins to Pickering. *Pygmalion*, act 2.

97 'Have you no morals, man?'
'Can't afford them, Governor.'
1913 Col Pickering and Alfred Doolittle. *Pygmalion*, act 2.

98 I'm one of the undeserving poor...up agen middle-class morality all the time... What is middle-class morality? Just an excuse for never giving me anything.
1913 Alfred Doolittle. *Pygmalion*, act 2.

99 Gin was mother's milk to her.
1913 Eliza, speaking of her Aunt. *Pygmalion*, act 3.

1 Walk! Not bloody likely. I am going in a taxi.
1913 Eliza to Freddy. *Pygmalion*, act 3.

2 The secret of being miserable is to have leisure to bother about whether you are happy or not. The cure for it is occupation.
1914 *Parents and Children*.

3 A perpetual holiday is a good working definition of hell.
1914 *Parents and Children*.

4 I am a woman of the world, Hector; and I can assure you that if you will only take the trouble always to do the perfectly correct thing, and to say the perfectly correct thing, you can do just what you like.
1919 Lady Utterword to Hector Hushabye. *Heartbreak House*, act 1.

5 It's prudent to gain the whole world and lose your own soul. But don't forget that your soul sticks to you if you stick to it; but the world has a way of slipping through your fingers.
1919 Captain Shotover. *Heartbreak House*, act 2.

6 There are only two classes in good society in England: the equestrian classes and the neurotic classes.
1919 Lady Utterword. *Heartbreak House*, act 3.

7 Go anywhere in England where there are natural, wholesome, contented, and really nice English people; and what do you always find? That the stables are the real centre of the household.
1919 Lady Utterword. *Heartbreak House*, act 3.

8 This souls' prison we call England.
1919 Hector Hushabye. *Heartbreak House*, act 3.

9 The captain is in his bunk, drinking bottled ditch-water; and the crew is gambling in the forecastle. She will strike and sink and split. Do you think the laws of God will be suspended in favour of England because you were born in it?
1919 Captain Shotover. *Heartbreak House*, act 3.

10 Everyone can see that the people who hunt are the right people and the people who don't are the wrong ones.
1919 Lady Usherword to Mrs Hushabye. *Heartbreak House*, act 3.

11 All great truths begin as blasphemies.
1919 *Annajanska*.

12 I enjoy convalescence. It is the part that makes illness worth while.
1921 *Back to Methuselah*.

13 Silence is the most perfect expression of scorn.
1921 *Back to Methuselah*.

14 If ever I utter an oath again may my soul be blasted to eternal damnation!
1923 Captain La Hire. *Saint Joan*, sc.2.

15 No Englishman is ever fairly beaten.
1923 The Chaplain. *Saint Joan*, sc.4.

16 How can what an Englishman believes be heresy? It is a contradiction in terms.
1923 The Chaplain to Peter Cauchon. *Saint Joan*, sc.4.

17 Some men are born kings; and some are born statesmen. The two are seldom the same.
1923 Peter Cauchon. *Saint Joan*, sc.4.

18 Must then a Christ perish in torment in every age to save those that have no imagination?
1923 *Saint Joan*, epilogue.

19 Idiots are always in favour of inequality of income (their only chance of eminence), and the really great in favour of equality.
1928 *The Intelligent Woman's Guide to Socialism and Capitalism*.

20 Many men would hardly miss their heads, there is so little in them.
1929 King Magnus. *The Apple Cart*, act 1.

21 One man that has a mind and knows it can always beat ten men who haven't and don't.
1929 Joe Proteus. *The Apple Cart*, act 1.

22 As interesting as a wall can be.
c.1930 Asked what he thought of the Great Wall after his flight over China. Quoted in Hesketh Pearson *Bernard Shaw: His Life and Personality* (1961).

23 The fact is, there are no rules and there never were any rules, and there never will be any rules of musical composition except rules of thumb; and thumbs vary in length, like ears.
1931 *Music in London, 1890–1894*.

24 [The Red Flag] is the funeral march of a fried eel.
Quoted by Winston Churchill in *Great Contemporaries* (1937).

25 A perpendicular expression of a horizontal desire.
Of dancing. Quoted in the *New Statesman*, 23 Mar 1962.

26 That's the difference between us. You talk of art Mr Goldwyn, I think of money.
To Samuel Goldwyn. Quoted in David Niven *Bring on the Empty Horses* (1975).

27 Baseball has the great advantage over cricket of being sooner ended. It combines the best features of that primitive form of cricket known as Tip-and-Run with those of lawn tennis, Puss-in-the-corner and Handel's Messiah.

Quoted in Colin Jarman *The Guinness Dictionary of Sports Quotations* (1990).

28 No sportsman wants to kill a fox or the pheasant as I want to kill him when I see him doing it.
Quoted in Colin Jarman *The Guinness Dictionary of Sports Quotations* (1990).

29 There is no reason why the infield should not try to put the batter off his stride at the critical moment, by neatly-timed disparagements of his wife's fidelity and his mother's respectability.
Alluding to baseball. Quoted in Colin Jarman *The Guinness Dictionary of Sports Quotations* (1990).

30 Who is this 'Babe' Ruth? And what does she do?
Of the legendary baseball star 'Babe' Ruth. Quoted in Colin Jarman *The Guinness Dictionary of Sports Quotations* (1990).

31 England and America are two countries divided by a common language.
Attributed.

32 If all the economists in the world were laid end to end, they would not reach a conclusion.
Attributed.

33 To begin with, I was born with an unreasonably large stock of relations, who have increased and multiplied ever since. My aunts and uncles were legion, and my cousins as the sands of the sea without number. Consequently, even a low death-rate meant, in the course of mere natural decay, a tolerably steady supply of funerals for a by no means affectionate but exceedingly clannish family to go to. Add to this that the town we lived in, being divided in religious opinion, buried its dead in two great cemeteries, each of which was held by the opposite faction to be the ante-chamber of perdition, and by its own patrons to be the gate of paradise.
'Music in London'.

34 You see things, and you say, 'Why?' But I dream things that never were; and I say 'Why not?'
The Serpent

35 [Lord Rosebery] was a man who never missed an occasion to let slip an opportunity.
Quoted by Winston Churchill in *Great Contemporaries* (1937).

Shawcross, Sir Hartley William, Baron Shawcross 1902–2003

English jurist, Attorney General (1945–51) and President of the Board of Trade (1951). He established his reputation as chief British prosecutor at the Nuremberg Trials (1945–6), and as prosecutor in the Fuchs atom spy case (1950). He was made a life peer in 1959.

36 We are the masters at the moment, and not only at the moment, but for a very long time to come.
1946 Alluding to Labour's victory in the general election, House of Commons, 2 Apr.

37 The so-called new morality is too often the old immorality condoned.
1963 In the *Observer*, 17 Jul.

Shawcross, Paul

US public official, Chief of the Science and Space Branch, White House Office of Management and Budget.

38 The administration does not support blowing up planets.
2013 Rejecting a mass petition calling for the US to build a Death Star weapon, as featured in the *Star Wars* films, 11 Jan.

Shawcross, William 1946–

English journalist whose book *Sideshow* (1979) detailed US involvement in Cambodia up to 1975.

39 Cambodia was not a mistake; it was a crime. The world is diminished by the experience.
1979 *Sideshow*, afterword.

Sheehy-Skeffington, Francis 1878–1916

Irish pacifist and feminist.

40 A crank is a small engine that causes revolutions.
On being described as a crank, quoted by his son Owen.

Sheen, Charlie *pseudonym of* Carlos Irwin Estevez 1965–

US film and television actor. The youngest son of actor Martin Sheen, he established himself as a popular leading man in such films as *Platoon* (1986), *Wall Street* (1987) and *Being John Malkovich* (1999) and consolidated his success in such television series as *Two and a Half Men* and *Anger Management*, but has subsequently become equally well known for his eccentric behaviour off stage.

41 I am on a drug. It's called Charlie Sheen. It's not available because if you try it once, you will die. Your face will melt off and your children will weep over your exploded body.
2011 His reaction when dropped from *Two and a Half Men*, interview on ABC News, Feb.

42 Can't is the cancer of happen.
2011 On *Good Morning America*, 28 Feb.

43 It ain't a party till something gets broken.
Attributed.

Sheen, Fulton John 1895–1979

US Roman Catholic prelate, who argued strenuously against Communism and birth control.

44 Our Lord…said that if men withheld their praise of him, 'the very stones would cry out', which they did as, later, they burst into Gothic cathedrals.
1962 *These Are the Sacraments*.

Shelley, Mary Godwin 1797–1851

English novelist, who married Percy Bysshe Shelley (1816). Her most famous work is *Frankenstein* (1818), written when she was only 19. After her husband's death she wrote *Valperga* (1823), *The Last Man* (1826), *Perkin Warbeck* (1830), *Lodore* (1835) and *Falkner* (1837) and edited her husband's works.

45 You seek for knowledge and wisdom as I once did; and I ardently hope that the gratification of your wishes may not be a serpent to sting you, as mine has been.
1818 *Frankenstein*, letter 4.

46 I was their plaything and their idol, and something better—their child.
1818 *Frankenstein*, speaking of his parents. *Frankenstein*, ch.1.

47 So much has been done, exclaimed the soul of Frankenstein—more, far more, will I achieve; treading the steps already marked, I will pioneer a new way,

explore unknown powers, and unfold to the world the deepest mysteries of creation.
1818 *Frankenstein*, ch.3.

48 All men hate the wretched; how, then, must I be hated, who am miserable beyond all living things! Yet you, my creator, detest and spurn me, thy creature, to whom thou art bound by ties only dissoluble by the annihilation of one of us.
1818 Frankenstein's monster. *Frankenstein*, ch.10.

49 Everywhere I see bliss, from which I alone am irrevocably excluded.
1818 Frankenstein's monster. *Frankenstein*, ch.10.

Shelley, Percy Bysshe 1792–1822

English lyric poet, who eloped with and later married Mary Godwin. He was a leading light of the Romantic movement and a lifelong atheist. His early poems include *Queen Mab* (1813). He later wrote tragedies such as *The Cenci* (1818), lyrical poems such as 'Ode to the West Wind' (1819) and lyric dramas such as *Prometheus Unbound* (1820).

50 The discussion of any subject is a right that you have brought into the world with your heart and tongue. Resign your heart's blood before you part with this inestimable privilege of man.
1812 *An Address to the Irish People*.

51 Titles are tinsel, power a corrupter, glory a bubble, and excessive wealth a libel on its possessor.
1812 *Declaration of Rights*, article 27.

52 That sweet bondage which is freedom's self.
1813 *Queen Mab*, canto 9.

53 There is no disease, bodily or mental, which adoption of vegetable diet and pure water has not infallibly mitigated, wherever the experiment has been fairly tried.
1813 'A Vindication of Natural Diet'.

54 Mont Blanc yet gleams on high: the power is there,
The still and solemn power of many sights
And many sounds, and much of life and death.
In the long glare of day, the snows descend
Upon that Mountain; none beholds them there,
Nor when the flakes burn in the sinking sun,
Or the sunbeams dart through them.
1816 'Mont Blanc'.

55 The awful shadow of some unseen Power
Floats though unseen among us,—visiting
This various world with as inconstant wing
As summer winds that creep from flower to flower.
1816 'Hymn to Intellectual Beauty'.

56 While yet a boy I sought for ghosts, and sped
Through many a listening chamber, cave and ruin,
And starlight wood, with fearful steps pursuing
Hopes of high talks with the departed dead.
1816 'Hymn to Intellectual Beauty'.

57 The day becomes more solemn and serene
When noon is past—there is a harmony
In autumn, and a lustre in its sky,
Which through the summer is not heard or seen,
As if it could not be, as if it had not been!
1816 'Hymn to Intellectual Beauty'.

58 Nought may endure but Mutability.
1816 'Mutability'.

59 In honoured poverty thy voice did weave
Songs concentrate to truth and liberty,—
Deserting these, thou leavest me to grieve,
Thus having been, that thou shouldst cease to be.
1816 'To Wordsworth'.

60 I love all waste
And solitary places; where we taste
The pleasure of believing what we see
Is boundless, as we wish our souls to be.
1818 'Julian and Maddalo', l.14–16.

61 Thou Paradise of exiles, Italy!
1818 'Julian and Maddalo', l.57.

62 Me—who am as a nerve o'er which do creep
The else unfelt oppressions of this earth.
1818 'Julian and Maddalo', l.449–50.

63 Most wretched men
Are cradled into poetry by wrong:
They learn in suffering what they teach in song.
1818 'Julian and Maddalo', l.544–7.

64 Beneath is spread like a green sea
The waveless plain of Lombardy,
Bounded by the vaporous air,
Islanded by cities fair;
Underneath Day's azure eyes,
Ocean's nursling, Venice lies,—
A peopled labyrinth of walls,
Amphitrite's destined halls.
1818 'Lines written amongst the Euganean Hills', l.90–7.

65 Sun-girt city, thou hast been
Ocean's child, and then his queen;
Now is come a darker day,
And thou soon must be his prey.
1818 'Lines written amongst the Euganean Hills', l.115–18.

66 The City's voice itself is soft like Solitude's.
1818 'Stanzas Written in Dejection, near Naples'.

67 I see the waves upon the shore,
Like light dissolved in star-showers, thrown.
1818 'Stanzas Written in Dejection, near Naples'.

68 Alas! I have nor hope nor health,
Nor peace within nor calm around,
Nor that content surpassing wealth
The sage in meditation found.
1818 'Stanzas Written in Dejection, near Naples'.

69 With hue like that when some great painter dips
His pencil in the gloom of earthquake and eclipse.
1818 'The Revolt of Islam'.

70 An old, mad, blind, despised, and dying king.
1819 'England in 1819' (published in 1839).

71 His big tears, for he wept well,
Turned to mill-stones as they fell.
And the little children, who
Round his feet played to and fro,
Thinking every tear a gem,
Had their brains knocked out by them.
1819 Of Fraud (ie, Lord Eldon). 'The Mask of Anarchy'.

72 I met Murder on the way—
He had a mask like Castlereagh.
1819 'The Mask of Anarchy', alluding to English foreign secretary Viscount Castlereagh, who was held responsible for the Peterloo Massacre in 1819.

73 On his brow this mark I saw—
'I AM GOD, AND KING, AND LAW!'
1819 'The Mask of Anarchy'.

74 Rise like Lions after slumber
In unvanquishable number—
Shake your chains to earth like dew
Which in sleep has fallen on you—
Ye are many—they are few.
1819 'The Mask of Anarchy'.

75 I wield the flail of the lashing hail,
And whiten the green plains under,
And then again I dissolve it in rain,
And laugh as I pass in thunder.
1819 'The Cloud'.

76 That orbèd maiden, with white fire laden,
Whom mortals call the Moon.
1819 'The Cloud'.

77 I am the daughter of Earth and Water,
And the nursling of the Sky;
I pass through the pores of the ocean and shores;
I change, but I cannot die,
For after the rain when with never a stain
The pavilion of Heaven is bare,
And the winds and sunbeams with their convex gleams
Build up the blue dome of air,
I silently laugh at my own cenotaph,
And out of the caverns of rain,
Like a child from the womb, like a ghost from the tomb,
I arise and unbuild it again.
1819 'The Cloud'.

78 The fountains mingle with the river,
And the rivers with the ocean;
The winds of heaven mix for ever
With a sweet emotion;
Nothing in the world is single;
All things, by a law divine,
In one spirit meet and mingle.
Why not I with thine?
1819 'Love and Philosophy'.

79 O wild West Wind, thou breath of Autumn's being,
Thou, from whose unseen presence the leaves dead
Are driven, like ghosts from an enchanter fleeing.
1819 'Ode to the West Wind', l.1–3.

80 Wild Spirit, which art moving everywhere;
Destroyer and preserver; hear, oh, hear!
1819 'Ode to the West Wind', l.13–4.

81 Thou who didst waken from his summer dreams
The blue Mediterranean, where he lay,
Lulled by the coil of his crystalline streams

Beside a pumice isle in Baiae's bay,
And saw in sleep old palaces and towers
Quivering within the wave's intenser day,

All overgrown with azure moss and flowers
So sweet, the sense faints picturing them.
1819 'Ode to the West Wind', l.29–36.

82 Oh, lift me as a wave, a leaf, a cloud!
I fall upon the thorns of life! I bleed!
1819 'Ode to the West Wind', l.53–4.

83 Make me thy lyre, even as the forest is:
What if my leaves are falling like its own!
The tumult of thy mighty harmonies
Will take from both a deep, autumnal tone,
Sweet though in sadness.
1819 'Ode to the West Wind', l.57–61.

84 And, by the incarnation of this verse,
Scatter, as from an unextinguished hearth
Ashes and sparks, my words among mankind!
Be through my lips to unawakened earth

The trumpet of a prophecy! O, Wind,
If Winter comes, can Spring be far behind?
1819 'Ode to the West Wind', l.65–70.

85 I met a traveller from an antique land
Who said: Two vast and trunkless legs of stone
Stand in the desert.
1819 'Ozymandias'.

86 'My name is Ozymandias, king of kings:
Look on my works, ye Mighty, and despair!'
Nothing beside remains. Round the decay
Of that colossal wreck, boundless and bare
The lone and level sands stretch far away.
1819 'Ozymandias'.

87 Hell is a city much like London—
A populous and smoky city.
1819 'Peter Bell the Third' pt.3, stanza 1.

88 But from the first 'twas Peter's drift
To be a kind of moral eunuch,
He touched the hem of Nature's shift,
Felt faint—and never dared uplift
The closest, all-concealing tunic.
1819 'Peter Bell the Third', pt.4, stanza 11.

89 Men of England, wherefore plough
For the lords who lay you low?
1819 'Song to the Men of England'.

90 Hail to thee, blithe Spirit!
Bird thou never wert,
That from Heaven, or near it,
Pourest thy full heart
In profuse strains of unpremeditated art.
1820 'To a Skylark', stanza 1.

91 Higher still and higher
From the earth thou springest
Like a cloud of fire;
The blue deep thou wingest
And singing still dost soar, and soaring ever singest.
1820 'To a Skylark', stanza 2.

92 In the golden lightning
Of the sunken sun
O'er which clouds are brightening,
Thou dost float and run
Like an unbodied joy whose race is just begun.
1820 'To a Skylark', stanza 3.

93 Keen as are the arrows
Of that silver sphere,
Whose intense lamp narrows
In the white dawn clear
Until we hardly see, we feel that it is there.
1820 'To a Skylark', stanza 5.

Shelley

94 Like a Poet hidden
In the light of thought,
Singing hymns unbidden,
Till the world is wrought
To sympathy with hopes and fears it heeded not.
1820 'To a Skylark', stanza 8.

95 What objects are the fountains
Of thy happy strain?
What fields, or waves, or mountains?
What shapes of sky or plain?
What love of thine own kind? What ignorance of pain?
1820 'To a Skylark', stanza 15.

96 With thy clear keen joyance
Languor cannot be:
Shadow of annoyance
Never came near thee:
Thou lovest—but ne'er knew love's sad satiety.
1820 'To a Skylark', stanza 16.

97 We look before and after,
And pine for what is not:
Our sincerest laughter
With some pain is fraught:
Our sweetest songs are those that tell of saddest thought.
1820 'To a Skylark', stanza 18.

98 Better than all measures
Of delightful sound,
Better than all treasures
That in books are found,
Thy skill to poet were, thou scorner of the ground!
1820 'To a Skylark', stanza 21.

99 Teach me half the gladness
That thy brain must know,
Such harmonious madness
From my lips would flow
The world should listen then—as I am listening now.
1820 'To a Skylark', stanza 21.

1 Chameleons feed on light and air:
Poet's food is love and game.
1820 'An Exhortation'.

2 London, that great sea, whose ebb and flow
At once is deaf and loud, and on the shore
Vomits its wrecks, and still howls on for more.
1820 'Letter to Maria Gisborne', l.193–5.

3 You will see Coleridge—he who sits obscure
In the exceeding lustre and the pure
Intense irradiation of a mind,
Which, through its own internal lighting blind,
Flags wearily through darkness and despair—
A cloud-encircled meteor of the air,
A hooded eagle among blinking owls—
You will see Hunt—one of those happy souls
Which are the salt of the earth, and without whom
This world would smell like what it is—a tomb.
1820 'Letter to Maria Gisborne' l.202–11.

4 Have you not heard
When a man marries, dies, or turns Hindoo,
His best friends hear no more of him?
1820 'Letter to Maria Gisborne' l.235–7.

5 His fine wit
Makes such a wound, the knife is lost in it.
1820 Of Thomas Love Peacock. 'Letter to Maria Gisborne', l.240–1.

6 Ere Babylon was dust,
The Magus Zoroaster, my dead child,
Met his own image walking in the garden,
That apparition, sole of men, he saw.
1820 Prometheus Unbound, act 1, l.191–4.

7 Cruel he looks, but calm and strong,
Like one who does, not suffers wrong.
1820 Prometheus Unbound, act 1, l.238–9.

8 It doth repent me: words are quick and vain:
Grief for a while is blind, and so was mine.
I wish no living thing to suffer pain.
1820 Prometheus Unbound, act 1, l.303–5.

9 Kingly conclaves stern and cold,
Where blood with guilt is bought and sold.
1820 Prometheus Unbound act 1, l.530–1.

10 The good want power, but to weep barren tears.
The powerful goodness want: worse need for them.
The wise want love; and those who love want
 wisdom.
1820 Prometheus Unbound act 1, l.625–7.

11 Peace is in the grave.
The grave hides all things beautiful and good:
I am a God and cannot find it there.
1820 Prometheus Unbound act 1, l.638–40.

12 The dust of creeds outworn.
1820 Prometheus Unbound act 1, l.697.

13 On a poet's lips I slept
Dreaming like a love-adept
In the sound his breathing kept.
1820 Prometheus Unbound, act 1, l.737–9.

14 To be
Omnipotent but friendless is to reign.
1820 Prometheus Unbound, act 2, sc.4, l.47–8.

15 He gave man speech, and speech created thought,
Which is the measure of the universe.
1820 Prometheus Unbound, act 2, sc.4, l.72–3.

16 Fate, Time, Occasion, Chance, and Change?
 To these
All things are subject but eternal love.
1820 Prometheus Unbound, act 2, sc.4, l.119–20.

17 My soul is an enchanted boat,
Which, like a sleeping swan, doth float
Upon the silver waves of thy sweet singing.
1820 Prometheus Unbound, act 2, sc.5, l.72–4.

18 The loathsome mask has fallen, the man remains
Sceptreless, free, uncircumscribed, but man
Equal, unclassed, tribeless, and nationless,
Exempt from awe, worship, degree, the king
Over himself; just, gentle, wise: but man
Passionless?—no, yet free from guilt or pain,
Which were, for his will made or suffered them,
Nor yet exempt, though ruling them like slaves,
From chance, and death, and mutability,
The clogs of that which else might oversoar
The loftiest star of unascended heaven,
Pinnacled dim in the intense inane.
1820 Prometheus Unbound, act 3, sc.4, l.193–204.

19 A traveller from the cradle to the grave
Through the dim night of this immortal day.
1820 Prometheus Unbound, act 4, l.551–2.

20 To suffer woes which Hope thinks infinite;
To forgive wrongs darker than death or night;
To defy Power, which seems omnipotent:
To love, and bear; to hope till Hope creates
From its own wreck the thing it contemplates;
Neither to change, nor falter, nor repent;
This, like thy glory, Titan, is to be
Good, great and joyous, beautiful and free;
This is alone Life, Joy, Empire and Victory.
1820 *Prometheus Unbound*, act 4, l.570–8.

21 A Sensitive Plant in a garden grew.
1820 'The Sensitive Plant', pt.1, l.1.

22 And the rose like a nymph to the bath addressed,
Which unveiled the depth of her glowing breast,
Till, fold after fold, to the fainting air
The soul of her beauty and love lay bare.
1820 'The Sensitive Plant', pt.1, l.29–32.

23 And the jessamine faint, and the sweet tuberose,
The sweetest flower for scent that blows.
1820 'The Sensitive Plant', pt.1, l.37–8.

24 A lovely lady, garmented in light
From her own beauty.
1820 'The Witch of Atlas', stanza 5.

25 For she was beautiful—her beauty made
The bright world dim, and everything beside
Seemed like the fleeting image of a shade.
1820 'The Witch of Atlas', stanza 12.

26 The cemetery is an open space among the ruins, covered in winter with violets and daisies. It might make one in love with death, to think that one should be buried in so sweet a place.
1821 *Adonais*, preface.

27 I weep for Adonais—he is dead!
O, weep for Adonais! though our tears
Thaw not the frost which binds so dear a head!
1821 *Adonais*, stanza 1.

28 He died,
Who was the Sire of an immortal strain,
Blind, old and lonely.
1821 *Adonais*, stanza 4.

29 To that high Capital, where kingly Death
Keeps his pale court in beauty and decay,
He came.
1821 *Adonais*, stanza 7.

30 The quick Dreams,
The passion-winged Ministers of thought.
1821 *Adonais*, stanza 9.

31 Lost Angel of a ruined Paradise!
She knew not 'twas her own; as with no stain
She faded, like a cloud which had outwept its rain.
1821 *Adonais*, stanza 10.

32 Ah, woe is me! Winter is come and gone,
But grief returns with the revolving year.
1821 *Adonais*, stanza 18.

33 From the great morning of the world when first
God dawned on Chaos.
1821 *Adonais*, stanza 19.

34 Alas! that all we loved of him should be,
But for our grief, as if it had not been,
And grief itself be mortal!
1821 *Adonais*, stanza 21.

35 Whence are we, and why are we? Of what scene
The actors or spectators?
1821 *Adonais*, stanza 21.

36 A pard-like Spirit, beautiful and swift—
A love in desolation masked;—a Power
Girt round with weakness;—it can scarce uplift
The weight of the superincumbent hour;
It is a dying lamp, a falling shower,
A breaking billow;—even whilst we speak
Is it not broken?
1821 *Adonais*, stanza 32.

37 Our Adonais has drunk poison—oh!
What deaf and viperous murderer could crown
Life's early cup with such a draught of woe?
1821 *Adonais*, stanza 36.

38 He wakes or sleeps with the enduring dead;
Thou canst not soar where he is sitting now—
Dust to the dust! but the pure spirit shall flow
Back to the burning fountain whence it came,
A portion of the Eternal.
1821 *Adonais*, stanza 38.

39 He hath awakened from the dream of life—
'Tis we, who lost in stormy visions, keep
With phantoms an unprofitable strife,
And in mad trance, strike with our spirit's knife
Invulnerable nothings.
1821 *Adonais*, stanza 39.

40 He has out-soared the shadow of our night;
Envy and calumny and hate and pain,
And that unrest which men miscall delight,
Can touch him not and torture not again;
From the contagion of the world's slow stain
He is secure, and now can never mourn
A heart grown cold, a head grown grey in vain.
1821 *Adonais*, stanza 40.

41 He lives, he wakes,—'tis Death is dead, not he.
1821 *Adonais*, stanza 41.

42 He is a portion of the loveliness
Which once he made more lovely.
1821 *Adonais*, stanza 43.

43 The One remains, the many change and pass;
Heaven's light forever shines, Earth's shadows fly:
Life, like a dome of many-coloured glass,
Stains the white radiance of Eternity,
Until Death tramples it to fragments.
1821 *Adonais*, stanza 52.

44 I never was attached to that great sect,
Whose doctrine is that each one should select
Out of the crowd a mistress or a friend,
And all the rest, though fair and wise, commend
To cold oblivion.
1821 'Epipsychidion', l.149–53.

45 The beaten road
Which those poor slaves with weary footsteps tread,
Who travel to their home among the dead
By the broad highway of the world, and so
With one chained friend, perhaps a jealous foe,
The dreariest and the longest journey go.
1821 'Epipsychidion', l.154–9.

46 True Love in this differs from gold and clay,
   That to divide is not to take away.
   1821 'Epipsychidion', l.160–1.

47 An isle under Ionian skies
   Beautiful as a wreck of Paradise.
   1821 'Epipsychidion', l.422–3.

48 I pant, I sink, I tremble, I expire!
   1821 'Epipsychidion', l.591.

49 The vanity of translation; it were as wise to cast a violet into a crucible that you might discover the formal principle of its colour and odour, as seek to transfuse from one language to another the creations of a poet. The plant must spring again from its seed, or it will bear no flower.
   1821 *A Defence of Poetry*.

50 The great instrument of moral good is the imagination; and poetry administers to the effect by acting on the cause.
   1821 *A Defence of Poetry*.

51 A single word even may be a spark of inextinguishable thought.
   1821 *A Defence of Poetry*.

52 Poetry is a record of the best and happiest moments of the happiest and best minds.
   1821 *A Defence of Poetry*.

53 Poets are the hierophants of an unapprehended inspiration; the mirrors of the gigantic shadows which futurity casts upon the present; the words which express what they understand not; the trumpets which sing to battle, and feel not what they inspire; the influence which is moved not, but moves. Poets are the unacknowledged legislators of the world.
   1821 *A Defence of Poetry*.

54 Death will come when thou art dead,
   Soon, too soon—
   Sleep will come when thou art fled;
   Of neither would I ask the boon
   I ask of thee, belovèd Night—
   Swift be thine approaching flight,
   Come soon, soon!
   1821 'To Night'.

55 Life may change, but it may fly not,
   Hope may vanish, but can die not;
   Truth be veiled, but still it burneth;
   Love repulsed,—but it returneth!
   1822 'Hellas', l.34–7.

56 Let there be light! Said Liberty,
   And like sunrise from the sea,
   Athens arose!
   1822 'Hellas', l.682–4.

57 The world's great age begins anew,
   The golden years return,
   The earth doth like a snake renew
   Her winter weeds outworn;
   Heaven smiles, and faiths and empires gleam,
   Like wrecks of a dissolving dream.
   1822 'Hellas', l.1060–5.

58 O cease! must hate and death return,
   Cease! must men kill and die?
   Cease! drain not to its dregs the urn
   Of bitter prophecy.
   The world is weary of the past,
   Oh, might it die or rest at last!
   1822 'Hellas', l.1096–101.

59 I dreamed that, as I wandered by the way,
   Bare Winter suddenly was changed to Spring,
   And gentle odours led my steps astray,
   Mixed with a sound of water's murmuring
   Along a shelving bank of turf, which lay
   Under a copse, and hardly dared to fling
   Its green arms round the bosom of the stream,
   But kissed it and then fled, as thou mightst in dream.
   1822 'The Question', stanza 1.

60 Daisies, those pearled Arcturi of the earth,
   The constellated flower that never sets.
   1822 'The Question', stanza 2.

61 And in the warm hedge grew lush eglantine,
   Green cowbind and the moonlight-coloured may.
   1822 'The Question', stanza 3.

62 Less oft peace in Shelley's mind,
   Than calm in waters seen.
   1822 'To Jane: The Recollection'.

63 Music when soft voices die,
   Vibrates in the memory—
   Odours, when sweet violets sicken,
   Live within the sense they quicken.
   'To—: Music when soft voices die' (published 1824).

64 I pursued a maiden and clasped a reed:
   Gods and men, we are all deluded thus!
   It breaks in our bosom and then we bleed.
   'Hymn of Pan' (published 1824).

65 Swiftly walk o'er the western wave,
   Spirit of Night!
   Out of the misty eastern cave,
   Where, all the long and lone daylight,
   Thou wovest dreams of joy and fear,
   Which make thee terrible and dear,
   Swift be thy flight!
   'To Night' (published 1824).

66 Art thou pale for weariness
   Of climbing heaven, and gazing on the earth,
   Wandering companionless
   Among the stars that have a different birth,—
   And ever-changing, like a joyless eye
   That finds no object worth its constancy?
   'To the Moon' (published 1824).

67 And like a dying lady, lean and pale,
   Who totters forth, wrapped in a gauzy veil.
   'The Waning Moon' (published 1824).

Sheridan, Philip Henry 1831–88

American Union cavalry commander in the Civil War and the American-Indian wars.

68 The only good Indian is a dead Indian.
   1869 Attributed comment at Fort Cobb, Jan.

69 We took away their country and their means of support, broke up their mode of living, their habits of life, introduced disease and decay among them and it was for this and against this they made war. Could anyone expect less?
   c.1870 Quoted in Thomas C Leonard *Above the Battle* (1978).

Sheridan, Richard Brinsley 1751–1816

Irish dramatist. His major plays, *The Rivals*, *The Duenna*, and *The Critic*, were produced between 1775 and 1779. He became an MP and in 1782 under-secretary for foreign affairs, a renowned orator. He lost his seat in 1812.

70 Promise to forget this fellow—to illiterate him, I say, quite from your memory.
   1775 Mrs Malaprop to Lydia. *The Rivals*, act 1, sc.2.

71 What business have you, miss, with preference and aversion?...You ought to know, that as both always wear off, 'tis safest in matrimony to begin with a little aversion.
   1775 Mrs Malaprop to Lydia. *The Rivals*, act 1, sc.2.

72 Madam, a circulating library in a town is as an evergreen tree of diabolical knowledge!... Depend upon it, Mrs Malaprop, that they who are so fond of handling the leaves, will long for the fruit at last.
   1775 Sir Anthony Absolute. *The Rivals*, act 1, sc.2.

73 I'll make my old clothes know who's master. I shall straightaway cashier the hunting-frock, and render my leather breeches incapable. My hair has been in training some time.
   1775 Bob Acres. *The Rivals*, act 2, sc.1.

74 Though one eye may be very agreeable, yet as the prejudice has always run in favour of two, I would not wish to affect a singularity in that article.
   1775 Jack Absolute. *The Rivals*, act 3, sc.1.

75 He is the very pine-apple of politeness.
   1775 Mrs Malaprop of Jack Absolute. *The Rivals*, act 3, sc.3.

76 Sure, if I reprehend anything in this world it is the use of my oracular tongue, and a nice derangement of epitaphs.
   1775 Mrs Malaprop. *The Rivals*, act 3, sc.3.

77 She's as headstrong as an allegory on the banks of the Nile.
   1775 Mrs Malaprop of Lydia Languish. *The Rivals*, act 3, sc.3.

78 That's too civil by half.
   1775 Bob Acres to Sir Lucius O' Trigger. *The Rivals*, act 3, sc.4.

79 Pray, sir, be easy; the quarrel is a very pretty quarrel as it stands; we should only spoil it by trying to explain it.
   1775 Sir Lucius O'Trigger to Jack Absolute. *The Rivals*, act 4, sc.3.

80 [To] have an unmannerly fat clerk ask the consent of every butcher in the parish to join John Absolute and Lydia Languish, spinster. Oh that I should live to hear myself called spinster!
   1775 Lydia Languish, who had hoped for a romantic elopement. *The Rivals*, act 5, sc.1.

81 Oh, poor Dolly! I never shall see her like again; such an arm for a bandage—veins that seemed to invite the lancet.
   1775 Dr Rosy. *St Patrick's Day*, act 1, sc.1.

82 A bumper of good liquor,
   Will end a contest quicker
   Than justice, judge or vicar.
   1775 *The Duenna*, act 2, sc.3.

83 Conscience has no more to do with gallantry than it has with politics.
   1775 Isaac to Don Antonio. *The Duenna*, act 2, sc.4.

84 BERINTHIA: Your lordship, I suppose, is fond of music?
   LORD FOP: Oh, passionately, on Tuesdays and Saturdays.
   1777 *A Trip to Scarborough*, act 2, sc.1.

85 Ah, Amanda, it's a delicious thing to be a young widow!
   1777 *A Trip to Scarborough*, act 2, sc.1.

86 Alas! the devil's sooner raised than laid.
   So strong, so swift, the monster there's no gagging:
   Cut Scandal's head off, still the tongue is wagging.
   1777 *The School for Scandal*, prologue.

87 I think you will like them, when you shall see them on a beautiful quarto page, where a neat rivulet of text shall meander through a meadow of margin.
   1777 Sir Benjamin Backbite, of his love elegies to Maria. *The School for Scandal*, act 1, sc.1.

88 I'm called away by particular business. But I leave my character behind me.
   1777 Sir Peter Teazle, leaving a gathering of gossips. *The School for Scandal*, act 2, sc.2.

89 I hate to see prudence clinging to the green suckers of youth; 'tis like ivy round a sapling, and spoils the growth of the tree.
   1777 Sir Oliver Surface. *The School for Scandal*, act 2, sc.3.

90 Here's to the maiden of bashful fifteen;
   Here's to the widow of fifty;
   Here's to the flaunting extravagant quean;
   And here's to the housewife that's thrifty.
   Chorus. Let the toast pass,
          Drink to the lass—
   I'll warrant she'll prove an excuse for a glass!
   1777 Song. *The School for Scandal*, act 3, sc.3.

91 Wine does but draw forth a man's natural qualities.
   1777 Charles Surface. *The School for Scandal*, act 3, sc.3.

92 When a scandalous story is believed against one, there is certainly no comfort like the conscience of having deserved it.
   1777 Joseph Surface. *The School for Scandal*, act 4, sc.3.

93 There needs no small degree of address to gain the reputation of benevolence without incurring the expense.
   1777 Joseph Surface. *The School for Scandal*, act 5, sc. 1.

94 The *newspapers! Sir, they are the most villainous—licentious—abominable—infernal—Not that I ever read them—No—I make it a rule never to look into a newspaper.*
   1779 *The Critic*, act 1, sc.1.

95 If there is anything to one's praise, it is a foolish vanity to be gratified at it; and, if it is abuse—why one is always sure to hear of it from one damned good-natured friend or other!
   1779 Sir Fretful Plagiary, of newspaper criticism. *The Critic*, act 1, sc.1.

96 Mr Dangle, here are two very civil gentlemen trying to make themselves understood, and I don't know which is the interpreter.
   1779 Mrs Dangle. *The Critic*, act 1, sc.2.

97 Puffing is of various sorts; the principal are, the puff direct, the puff preliminary, the puff collateral, the puff collusive, and the puff oblique, or puff by implication.
   1779 Mr Puff. *The Critic*, act 1, sc.2.

98 The number of those who undergo the fatigue of judging for themselves is very small indeed.
   1779 Mr Puff. *The Critic*, act 1, sc.2.

99 The puff collusive is the newest of any; for it acts in the disguise of determined hostility. It is much used by bold

booksellers and enterprising poets.
1779 Mr Puff. *The Critic*, act 1, sc.2.

1 No scandal about Queen Elizabeth, I hope?
1779 Mr Sneer, of Mr Puff's tragedy 'The Spanish Armada'. *The Critic*, act 2, sc.1.

2 I open with a clock striking, to beget an awful attention in the audience: it also marks the time, which is four o'clock in the morning, and saves a description of the rising sun, and a great deal about gilding the eastern hemisphere.
1779 Mr Puff, of his tragedy 'The Spanish Armada'. *The Critic*, act 2, sc.2.

3 BEEFEATER: [a character in Mr Puff's play within a play, 'The Spanish Armada'] Perdition catch my soul but I do love thee.
SNEER: Haven't I heard that line before?
PUFF: No, I fancy not.—Where pray?
DANGLE: Yes, I think there is something like it in *Othello*.
PUFF: Gad! now you put me in mind on't, I believe there is—but that's of no consequence; all that can be said is, that two people happened to hit upon the same thought—and Shakespeare made use of it first, that's all.
1779 *The Critic*, act 3, sc.1.

4 When a heroine goes mad, she always goes into white satin.
1779 Mr Puff. *The Critic*, act 3, sc.1.

5 An oyster may be crossed in love!
1779 Tilburnia's 'mad' speech from 'The Spanish Armada'. *The Critic*, act 3, sc.1.

6 Give me the liberty of the Press, and I will give the Minister a venal House of Peers, I will give him a corrupt and servile House of Commons...armed with the liberty of the Press, I will go forth to meet him undismayed.
1810 Speech, House of Commons.

Sherman, Richard M and Robert B 1928–, 1925–2012

US song-writing brothers, who wrote songs for Disney films from 1959 and also complete scores for musicals. Among their best-known films are *Mary Poppins* (1964) and *Chitty Chitty Bang Bang* (1968).

7 Supercalifragilisticexpialidocious.
1964 Title of song from *Mary Poppins*.

8 Protocoligorically Correct.
1976 Title of song from *The Slipper and the Rose*.

Sherman, William Tecumseh 1820–91

US general. He was Union commander during the American Civil War, when he captured Atlanta in 1864 and divided Confederate forces by his 'march to the sea', hastening the surrender of the South.

9 There is many a boy here today who looks on war as all glory, but, boys, it is all hell.
1880 Speech at Columbus, Ohio, 11 Aug. Quoted in Lloyd Lewis *Sherman Fighting Prophet* (1932).

Sherriff, R(obert) C(edric) 1896–1975

British playwright, novelist and screenwriter. He achieved an international reputation with his first play *Journey's End* (1929). He also wrote screenplays for films such as *The Invisible Man* (1933), *Goodbye Mr Chips* (1939) and *The Odd Man Out* (1947).

10 Even the moon is frightened of me, frightened to death! The whole world is frightened to death!
1933 Line delivered by Claude Rains in *The Invisible Man* (with Philip Wylie).

Shevardnadze, Eduard Ambrosievich 1928–2014

Georgian-born Soviet politician. In 1978 he was inducted into the Politburo and was appointed Foreign Minister in 1985. He rapidly overhauled the Soviet foreign policy machine for a new era of détente. In 1992 he returned to Georgia, where he became Chairman of the Supreme Council and Head of State (1992–95) then President (1995–2003).

11 Democrats are fleeing in all directions. Reformers are going into hiding. A dictatorship is beginning, and no one knows what shape it will take or who will come to power.
1990 On the increasing disarray in the USSR caused by failing Soviet reforms, rivalry between the Gorbachev and Yeltsin factions and unrest in the Baltic states, in the *Sunday Times*, 23 Dec.

Shinwell, Emanuel Shinwell, Baron 1884–1986

English Labour politician. A 'street-corner' socialist in Glasgow, he became Secretary of State for War (1947) and Minister of Defence (1950–1). Known for his belligerence, he mellowed into a backbench 'elder statesman'. He wrote several autobiographical works.

12 We know that you, the organized workers of the country, are our friends... As for the rest, they do not matter a tinker's curse.
1947 Trade union conference, 7 May.

Shipton, Eric Earle 1908–77

British mountaineer, explorer and writer. The foremost mountain explorer of his generation, he facilitated the successful ascent of Everest in 1953. He wrote seven books, including an autobiography, *That Untravelled World* (1969).

13 I have never been able to decide whether, in mountain exploration, it is the prospect of tackling an unsolved problem, or the performance of the task itself, or the retrospective enjoyment of successful effort, which affords the greatest amount of pleasure.
1936 *Nanda Devi*.

14 Whatever may have been my enthusiasm or impatience to be up and doing on the night before, the hour for getting up always finds me with no other ambition in the world than to be permitted to lie where I am and sleep, sleep, sleep. Not so Tilman. I have never met anyone with such a complete disregard for the sublime comforts of the early morning bed. However monstrously early we might decide, the night before, to get up, he was about at least half an hour before the time. He was generally very good about it, and used to sit placidly smoking his pipe over the fire.
1936 On climbing with H W (Bill) Tilman. *Nanda Devi*.

15 We were now actually in the inner sanctuary of the Nanda Devi Basin, and at each step I experienced that subtle thrill which anyone of imagination must feel when treading hitherto unexplored country... My most blissful dream as a child was to be in some such valley, free to wander where I liked, and discover for myself some hitherto unrevealed glory of Nature. Now the reality was no less wonderful than that half-forgotten dream; and of how many childish fancies can that be said, in this age of disillusionment?
1936 *Nanda Devi*.

Shirley, James 1596-1666

English dramatist. Educated at Oxford and Cambridge, he took holy orders but renounced them upon conversion to Catholicism. He died in the Great Fire of London. He wrote plays and masques, including the comedies *Hyde Park* (1634) and *The Lady of Pleasure* (1635), the tragedy *The Cardinal* (1641), and the masque *The Contention of Ajax and Ulysses* (1659).

16 How little room
  Do we take up in death, that, living know
  No bounds?
  1626 *The Wedding*, act 4, sc.4.

17 'Tis no shame for men
  Of his high birth to love a wench; his honour
  May privilege more sins. Next to a woman,
  He loves a running-horse.
  1634 *Hyde Park*, act 1, sc.1.

18 RIDER: …we can be but
  What we are.
  VENTURE: A pair of credulous fools.
  1634 *Hyde Park*, act 1, sc.1.

19 I presume you're mortal, and may err.
  1635 *The Lady of Pleasure*, act 2, sc.2.

20 The glories of our blood and state
  Are shadows, not substantial things;
  There is no armour against fate;
  Death lays his icy hand on kings:
  Scepter and crown
  Must tumble down,
  And in the dust be equal made
  With the poor crooked scythe and spade.
  1659 *The Contention of Ajax and Ulysses*, act 1, sc.3.

Shultz, George P(ratt) 1920-

US Former Secretary of State. A Professor of Chicago University's graduate business school (1957-68), he was US Secretary of Labor (1969-70), then assistant to President Nixon (1972-4). He was Secretary of State to President Reagan (1982-89). A fellow of the Hoover Institution, Stanford University (1989-) he is a distinguished author and was awarded the Seoul Peace Prize (1992).

21 He made a combative apology.
  1987 On the ability of Elliott Abrams, Assistant Secretary for Inter-American Affairs, to acknowledge a sensitive question without giving a definite reply. In the *New York Times*, 25 Jul.

22 Gardening…is one of the most underrated aspects of diplomacy.
  1993 On the need to meet people 'on their own turf'. *Turmoil and Triumph*.

23 Washington is a resigning town. Nothing else holds the special excitement of a rumored resignation.
  1993 *Turmoil and Triumph*.

24 The way to keep weeds from overwhelming you is to deal with them constantly and in their early stages.
  1993 *Turmoil and Triumph*.

25 The Soviet game is chess…ours is poker. We will have to play a creative mixture of both games.
  1993 Comment to President Reagan. Recalled in *Turmoil and Triumph*.

26 Better to use force when you *should* rather than when you *must*.
  1993 On Soviet alarm at the prospect of US science 'turned on' and venturing into the realm of space defence. *Turmoil and Triumph*.

27 Agreement reached by the negotiators…usually starts to collapse in the hands of those who implement it, no matter how carefully cleared at the top.
  1993 On negotiating the release of Russian political prisoners. *Turmoil and Triumph*.

28 The decision makers face each other. No safety screen stands between the issues and the highest authorities.
  1993 Of summit meetings, particularly that between the US and the Soviets at Reykjavik, Iceland, 9-12 Oct 1986. *Turmoil and Triumph*.

29 A 'staffocracy' has been created.
  1993 On the National Security Council. *Turmoil and Triumph*.

30 You can't figure him out like a fact, because to Reagan the main fact was a vision… He came from the heartland of the country, where people could be down-to-earth yet feel that the sky is the limit—not ashamed of, or cynical about, the American dream.
  1993 Of Ronald Reagan. *Turmoil and Triumph*.

Shute, Nevil *originally* Nevil Shute Norway 1899-1960

English writer. An aeronautical engineer, he began to write novels in 1926 and after World War II emigrated to Australia, the setting for most of his later books, notably *A Town Like Alice* (1949) and *On the Beach* (1957).

31 A Town Like Alice
  1949 Title of book.

Sidgwick, Henry 1838-1900

British economist, Professor at Cambridge.

32 We cannot not say how much wealth there is in a country till we know how it is shared among its inhabitants.
  1883 *Principles of Political Economy*.

Sidmouth, Henry Addington, 1st Viscount 1757-1844

English statesman and Tory Prime Minister (1801-4) after the resignation of William Pitt the Younger. As Home Secretary (1812-21) he had to deal with the Luddite riots and the 'Peterloo Massacre' in Manchester (1819).

33 I hate liberality. Nine times out of ten it is cowardice—and the tenth time, lack of principle.
  Attributed.

Sidney, Algernon 1622-83

English Whig politician. He fought for the Parliamentary army in the English Civil War and in 1645 entered Parliament, but he resented Cromwell's assumption of power, and retired to Penshurst (1653-9). In exile after the Restoration, in 1677 he was pardoned and returned, but was implicated in the Rye House Plot (1683) and beheaded.

34 Liars ought to have good memories.
  Discourses Concerning Government (published 1689).

Sidney, Sir Philip 1554-86

English poet and patron. Educated at Oxford, he travelled widely; in 1585 he was made Governor of Flushing. He died after being wounded in the battle of Zutphen. His sonnet sequence *Astrophel and Stella* (published 1591) was an early example of the genre in English, as was his prose romance *The Arcadia* (*The Old Arcadia*, as it is called, was not published during Sidney's lifetime; a revised version, *The New Arcadia*, was first published in 1590); his *Defence of Poetry* (published 1595) was the first English essay on literary criticism.

35 I readily admit that I am often more serious than I should be at my age or in my present circumstances, yet I know from experience that I am never less given to melancholy than when I am keenly applying the feeble powers of my mind to some arduous and difficult matter.
1574 Letter to Hubert Languet, 4 Feb.

36 O wretched state of man in self-division!
1581 *The Old Arcadia*, 'First Eclogues'.

37 She was stricken with most obstinate love to a young man.
1581 *The Old Arcadia*, 'First Eclogues'.

38 What allurements she used indifferently were long to tell.
1581 *The Old Arcadia*, 'Second Eclogues'.

39 What be the fruits of speaking art? What grows by the words?
1581 *The Old Arcadia*, 'Second Eclogues'.

40 My true love hath my heart and I have his,
By just exchange one for the other giv'n;
I hold his dear, and mine he cannot miss,
There never was a better bargain driv'n.
1581 *The Old Arcadia*, 'Third Eclogues'.

41 O sweet, on a wretch wilt thou be revenged?
Shall such high planets tend to the loss of a worm?
1581 *The Old Arcadia*, 'Fourth Eclogues'.

42 A lamentable tune is the sweetest music to a woeful mind.
1590 *Arcadia*, pt.2.

43 Loving in truth, and vain in verse my love to show,
That she (dear she) might take some pleasure of my pain,
Pleasure might cause her read, reading might make her know;
Knowledge might pity win, and pity grace obtain.
1591 *Astrophel and Stella*, sonnet 1.

44 But words came halting forth, wanting Invention's stay;
Invention, Nature's child, fled step-dame Study's blows…
Biting my truant pen, beating myself for spite,
'Fool,' said my muse to me; 'look in thy heart, and write.'
1591 *Astrophel and Stella*, sonnet 1.

45 Your rhubarb words.
1591 *Astrophel and Stella*, sonnet 14.

46 Come sleep, O sleep, the certain knot of peace,
The baiting place of wit, the balm of woe,
The poor man's wealth, the prisoner's release,
The indifferent judge between the high and low.
1591 *Astrophel and Stella*, sonnet 39.

47 That sweet enemy, France.
1591 *Astrophel and Stella*, sonnet 41.

48 Hope, art thou true, or dost thou flatter me?
1591 *Astrophel and Stella*, sonnet 67.

49 Oh heav'nly fool, thy most kiss-worthy face
Anger invests with such a lovely grace
That Anger's self I needs must kiss again.
1591 *Astrophel and Stella*, sonnet 73.

50 I am no pick-purse of another's wit.
1591 *Astrophel and Stella*, sonnet 74.

51 Stella, think not that I by verse seek fame;
Who seek, who hope, who love, who live, but thee:
Thine eyes my pride, thy lips my history;
If thou praise not, all other praise is shame.
1591 *Astrophel and Stella*, sonnet 90.

52 I have just cause to make a pitiful defence of poor poetry, which from almost the highest estimation of learning is fallen to be the laughing stock of children.
1595 *The Defence of Poetry*.

53 And truly, even Plato, whosoever well considereth shall find that in the body of his work, though the inside and strength were philosophy, the skin as it were and beauty depended most on poetry.
1595 *The Defence of Poetry*.

54 [Nature's] world is brazen, the poets only deliver a golden.
1595 *The Defence of Poetry*.

55 Poetry therefore, is an art of imitation… A speaking picture, with this end: to teach and delight.
1595 *The Defence of Poetry*.

56 With a tale forsooth he cometh unto you, with a tale which holdeth children from play, and old men from the chimney corner.
1595 Of the poet. *The Defence of Poetry*.

57 Comedy is an imitation of the common errors of our life, which he representeth in the most ridiculous and scornful sort that may be, so as it is impossible that any beholder can be content to be such a one.
1595 *The Defence of Poetry*.

58 I…am admitted into the company of paper-blurrers.
1595 *The Defence of Poetry*.

59 [This] much curse I must send you, in the behalf of all poets, that while you live, you live in love, and never get favour for lacking skill of a sonnet, and, when you die, your memory die from the earth for want of an epigraph.
1595 *The Defence of Poetry*.

Siegel, Jerome 1914–92
US writer, co-creator of Superman.

60 I'm lying in bed counting sheep when all of a sudden it hits me…a character like Samson, Hercules and all the strong men I heard tell of rolled into one. Only more so.
Recalling the inspiration behind Superman, created 1938. Quoted in *Time*, 14 Mar 1988.

61 Faster than a speeding bullet! More powerful than a locomotive! Able to leap tall buildings in a single bound!
Introduction for the Superman radio serial. Quoted in *Time*, 14 Mar 1988.

Sièyes, Emmanuel Joseph, Comte also called Abbé Sièyes 1748–1836
French cleric and political theorist. His pamphlet, *Qu'est-ce que le tiers-état?* ('What is the Third Estate?', 1789) was very popular with the bourgeoisie. He helped organize the revolution of 18th Brumaire (in which Napoleon overthrew the Directory, 1799). Exiled at the Restoration (1815), he returned after the July Revolution (1830).

62 Who will dare deny that the Third Estate contains within itself all that is needed to constitute a nation?… What would the Third Estate be without the privileged classes? It would be a whole in itself, and a prosperous one.

Nothing can be done without it, and everything would be done far better without the others.
1789 *Qu'est-ce que le tiers-état?*

Sigismund 1368–1437
Holy Roman Emperor from 1433. He became King of Hungary in 1387 and as Emperor presided over the Council of Constance, which ended the Great Schism (1414–18).

63 Only do always in health what you have often promised to do when you are sick.
His advice for a happy life, quoted in Clifton Fadiman *Faber Book of Anecdotes* (1985).

Sigourney, Lydia Howard née Huntley 1791–1865
American poet. Her pious, sentimental poetry made her the most popular woman poet of her generation. She was an important campaigner in the cause of higher education for women. Her collections include *Moral Pieces in Prose and Verse* (1815).

64 Ye say, they all have passed away,
That noble race and brave,
That their light canoes have vanished
From off the crested wave;
That 'mid the forests where they roamed
There rings no hunter's shout;
But their name is on your waters,
Ye may not wash it out.
1848 *Select Poems*, 'Indian Names'.

Sihanouk, Prince Norodom 1922–2012
Cambodian politician who as Prime Minister tried but failed to keep his country out of the Vietnam War. He was deposed in 1970 by a military coup but returned in 1993 and was elected king. He attacked the intensive US bombing of his country.

65 What is the difference between burning and gassing people in ovens and doing it to a whole nation out in the open?
1973 Of the US bombing of Cambodia. *My War with the CIA* (with W Burchett).

66 The humble people of Cambodia are the most wonderful in the world. Their great misfortune is that they always have terrible leaders who make them suffer. I am not sure I was much better myself, but perhaps I was the least bad.
1978 In an interview with William Shawcross, author of *Sideshow* (1979).

Sikorski, Gerry 1948–
US politician.

67 Like a toothless terrier on Valium.
1987 On the workings of the Office of Government Ethics. In the *New York Times*, 8 Jul.

Sikorsky, Igor Ivan 1889–1972
Russian-born US aeronautical engineer. He built and flew the first four-engined aeroplane (1913), then founded the Sikorsky Aero Engineering Corporation in the USA (1923). He built several flying boats, and in 1939 produced the first successful helicopter.

68 The work of the individual still remains the spark that moves mankind ahead, even more than teamwork.
Quoted in his *New York Times* obituary, 27 Oct 1972.

Sillitoe, Alan 1928–2010
English novelist. Several of his novels set in the north of England have been adapted as successful films, notably *Saturday Night and Sunday Morning* (1960).

69 The Loneliness of the Long Distance Runner.
1962 Title of book.

Silva, José Asunción 1865–96
Colombian poet whose life was marked by financial reverses, the death of loved ones, and the loss of his manuscripts in a shipwreck. His poetry is characteristically melancholy, and after only ten years of writing he committed suicide.

70 *Y si evitas la sífilis, siguiendo
la sabia profilaxia,
al llegar los cuarenta irás sintiendo
un principio de ataxia.*
And if you manage to avoid syphilis
by following a wise course of prophylaxis,
when you turn forty you will feel
the beginnings of ataxia.
1908 *Gotas amargas*, 'Filosofías' ('Philosophies').

Silvers, Phil originally Philip Silver 1912–85
US comic actor. His success in films and on Broadway led to the *Phil Silvers Show* (1955–9) on television, where he introduced the character of Sergeant Bilko. He won three Emmy awards during his career, and a Tony Award for his performance in *A Funny Thing Happened on the Way to the Forum* (1972).

71 Be funny on a golf course? Do I kid my best friend's mother about her heart condition?
Quoted in Michael Hobbs *The Golf Quotation Book* (1992).

Silvester, David
English politician. A town councillor in Henley-on-Thames, he left the Conservatives in order to join the United Kingdom Independence Party in 2013 but was suspended from UKIP in January 2014.

72 Since the passage of the Marriage (Same Sex Couples) Act, the nation has been beset by serious storms and floods. One recent one caused the worst flooding for 60 years. The Christmas floods were the worst for 127 years. Is this just global warming or is there something more serious at work?
2014 Letter to the *Henley Standard* that led to his suspension from UKIP, Jan.

Simon, Caroline K(lein) 1900–93
Judge, NY State Court of Claims.

73 Look like a girl, act like a lady, think like a man and work like a dog.
Comment the year after her candidacy for Postmaster General was barred by federal officials who claimed the job was unsuited to a woman. Recalled on her death, in the *New York Times*, 30 Jul 1993.

Simon, Herbert A 1916–2001
US psychologist and economist; awarded a Nobel prize in economics (1978).

74 It is a fatal defect of current principles of administration that, like proverbs, they occur in pairs. For almost every

principle one can find an equally plausible and acceptable contradictory principle. Although the two principles of the pair will lead to exactly opposite recommendations, there is nothing in the theory to indicate which is the appropriate one to apply.
1945 *Administrative Behavior.*

Simon (of Stackpole Elidor), John Allsebrook Simon, 1st Viscount 1873–1954
English Liberal politician and lawyer. Attorney-General (1913–15) and Home Secretary (1915–16), he resigned from the Cabinet over conscription. Deserting the Liberals to form the Liberal National Party, he supported Ramsay MacDonald's coalition governments and became Foreign Secretary (1931–5), Home Secretary (1935–7), Chancellor of the Exchequer (1937–40) and Lord Chancellor (1940–5).

75 If Joan of Arc had been born in Austria and worn a moustache, she might have conveyed much the same impression.
1935 Letter to George V, referring to his first meeting with Adolf Hitler, 27 Mar.

Simon, (Marvin) Neil 1927–
US playwright. His plays and musicals include *Barefoot in the Park* (1963), *The Odd Couple* (1965) and the semi-autobiographical trilogy *Brighton Beach Memoirs* (1983), *Biloxi Blues* (1984) and *Broadway Bound* (1986). More recent works include *Lost in Yonkers* (1991), which won him a Pulitzer Prize and a Tony Award, and *London Suite* (1995).

76 I've already had medical attention—a dog licked me when I was on the ground.
1982 *Only When I Laugh.*

77 I would have been disappointed if I hung up my pen without ever getting one... [and] now I hope to get one every 30 years like clockwork.
1991 On receiving the Pulitzer Prize for *Lost in Yonkers.* In the *Washington Post,* 10 Apr.

Simone, Nina *pseudonym of* Eunice Waymon 1933–2003
US singer and pianist. She was a gifted classical pianist as a teenager, but her career was blocked by the racial prejudice of the time, and she went on to become a cult figure in jazz, gospel and soul music.

78 It wasn't a matter of becoming interested in music; music is a gift and a burden I've had since I can remember who I was. I was born into music. The decision was how to make the best use of it.
Quoted in Art Taylor *Notes and Tones* (1977), 'Nina Simone'.

Simonides of Ceos c.556–468 BC
Greek lyric poet. His poetry survives only in fragments, but he is known to have written epitaphs for Greeks who fell in the Persian Wars, and in 489 BC he beat Aeschylus in a competition for the best elegy on those who fell at Marathon.

79 Go, stranger, and tell the Spartans that here we lie, obedient to their commands.
c.480 BC Epitaph for the Spartan army dead after the Battle of Thermopylae. Quoted in Herodotus *Histories,* bk.7, ch.228.

80 Man's strength is but little, and futile his concerns.
Lyrica Graeca Selecta, (ed. D L Page), no.354.

Simons, Henry C 1899–1946
US economist, Professor at the University of Chicago.

81 Monopoly power must be abused. It has no use save abuse.
1944 *Economic Policy for a Free Society,* p.129.

Simple, Peter *pseudonym of* Michael Wharton 1913–2006
English newspaper columnist.

82 Rentacrowd Ltd—the enterprising firm that supplies crowds for all occasions, and has done so much to keep progressive causes in the public eye.
1962 In the *Daily Telegraph.*

Simpson, Alan (Kooi) 1931–
US senator and lawyer. He was a member of the US Senate for Wyoming (1978–97). In 2010 he was appointed co-chair of the National Commission on Fiscal Responsibility and Reform.

83 Like giving dry birth to a porcupine.
1989 On the passage of immigration reform bill. In the *Washingtonian,* Mar.

84 I come from a state where gun control is just how steady you hold your weapon.
1991 In *Fortune,* 30 Dec.

Simpson, Kirke L 1881–1972
US journalist. He was awarded a Pulitzer Prize in 1921 for his article on the Unknown Soldier.

85 Chosen by a group of men in a smoke-filled room.
Of Warren G Harding, presidential candidate. Recalled on Simpson's death in the *New York Times,* 17 Jun 1972. The 'smoke-filled room' became a common phrase in presidential nomination.

Simpson, O J (Orenthal James) 1947–
US former professional football player, actor and sports commentator. He joined the Buffalo Bills professionally in 1969, and retired in 1979 to become an actor and broadcaster. In 1995 he was tried and controversially acquitted for the murders of his estranged wife Nicole and Ronald Goodman. In 2007 he stood trial once more on charges including armed robbery and kidnapping. He was found guilty and sentenced to 33 years' imprisonment.

86 Absolutely 100 per cent not guilty.
1994 Plea on arraignment for the murder of his estranged wife. Reported in the *New York Times,* 23 Jul. Simpson was later found not guilty.

Simpson, Tom 1938–67
English cyclist. In 1962 he became the first Briton ever to wear the leader's yellow jersey in the Tour de France. He died from heart failure during the Tour de France.

87 Put me back on my bike.
1967 Last words.

Sinatra, Frank (Francis Albert) 1915–98
US singer and actor. He began with the Tommy Dorsey orchestra (1940–2), and starred on radio and in films (eg *Anchors Aweigh,* 1945). His recordings (1956–65) include *Songs For Swinging Lovers, Come Fly With Me,* and *That's Life.* His highly publicized and controversial personal life included four marriages (amongst them, to Ava Gardner and Mia Farrow).

88 My greatest teacher was not a vocal coach, not the work of other singers, but the way Tommy Dorsey breathed and phrased on the trombone.
Foreword to George T Simon *The Big Bands* (1967).

Singer, Isaac Bashevis 1904–91
US Yiddish writer of novels and short stories. Awarded the Nobel prize for literature (1978).

89 Children...have no use for psychology.
1978 Speech on receiving his Nobel prize.

Singh, Vijay 1963–
Fijian golfer whose wins include the US Masters in 2000 and the PGA Championship in 1998 and 2004.

90 Golf is to Fiji what cricket is to America.
2000 In The Independent, 23 Dec.

Sisco, Joseph John 1919–2004
US diplomat and businessman. He set up his own management consultancy, and also acted as a consultant and adviser to the UN.

91 Welcome to shuttle diplomacy!
1995 Comment to reporters Marvin Kalb and Ted Koppel on Henry A Kissinger's first trip to the Middle East after the Yom Kippur War. Reported in the New York Times, 29 Oct.

Sisson, C(harles) H(erbert) 1914–2003
English poet and critic. One of the leading poets of the period, he also wrote novels and an autobiography.

92 Here lies a civil servant. He was civil
To everyone, and servant to the devil.
1961 'Civil Servant'.

Sitting Bull *real name* Tatanka Iyotake 1834–90
Chief of the Dakota Sioux, who led the defeat of Custer at Little Big Horn, 1876. He later featured in Buffalo Bill Cody's Wild West Show, 1885, but was killed evading arrest during the 'ghost dance' uprising of 1890.

93 When I was a boy the Sioux owned the world; the sun rose and set on their land; they sent ten thousand men to battle. Where are the warriors today? Who slew them? Where are our lands? Who owns them?... What law have I broken? Is it wrong for me to love my own? Is it wicked for me because my skin is red? Because I am a Sioux; because I was born where my father lived; because I would die for my country?
c.1866 Quoted in T C McLuhan Touch the Earth (1973).

Sitwell, Dame Edith Louisa 1887–1964
English poet and essayist, sister of Osbert and Sacheverell Sitwell. Her poems were designed to shock her audiences and revitalize English poetry. Her numerous prose works reflect her interest in English history. Her books include *Façade* (1923, set to music by Walton), *English Eccentrics* (1933), and *Fanfare of Elizabeth* (1946).

94 Lady Venus on the settee of the horsehair sea!
1923 Façade, 'Hornpipe'.

95 This minx, of course,
  Is as sharp as any lynx and blacker—deeper than the drinks and quite as
  Hot as any hottentot, without remorse!
1923 Façade, 'Hornpipe'.

96 An admiral red, whose only notion,
(A butterfly poised on a pigtailed ocean)
Is of the peruked sea whose swell
Breaks on the flowerless rocks of Hell.
1923 Façade, 'En Famille'.

97 The Admiral said, 'You could never call—
I assure you it would not do at all!
She gets down from the table without saying 'please',
Forgets her prayers and to cross her T's,
In short, her scandalous reputation
Has shocked the whole of the Hellish nation'.
1923 Façade, 'En Famille'.

98 Those trains will run over their tails, if they can,
Snorting and sporting like porpoises. Flee
The burly, the whirligig wheels of the train,
As round as the world and as large again.
1923 Façade, 'Mariner Man'.

99 The light is braying like an ass.
1923 Façade, 'Long Steel Grass'.

1 Through gilded trellises
Of the heat, spangles
Pelt down through the tangles
Of bell-flowers.
1923 Façade, 'Through Gilded Trellises'.

2 But a word stung him like a mosquito...
For what they hear, they repeat!
1923 Façade, 'Tango-Pasodoble'.

3 In a room of the palace
Black Mrs Behemoth
Gave way to wrath
And the wildest malice.
1923 Façade, 'Black Mrs Behemoth'.

4 Where the satyrs are chattering, nymphs with their flattering
Glimpse of the forest enhance
All the beauty of marrow and cucumber narrow
And Ceres will join in the dance.
1923 Façade, 'Tarantella'.

5 That hobnailed goblin, the bob-tailed Hob,
said, 'It is time I began to rob'.
1923 Façade, 'Country Dance'.

6 And shade is on the brightest wing,
And dust forbids the birds to sing.
1923 Façade, 'Popular Song'.

7 Came the great Popinjay
Smelling his nosegay:
In cage like grots
The birds sing gavottes.
1923 Façade, 'Came the Great Popinjay'.

8 Jane, Jane,
Tall as a crane,
The morning light creaks down again.
1923 Façade, 'Aubade'.

9 The fire was furry as a bear.
1923 Façade, 'Dark Song'.

10 Daisy and Lily,
Lazy and silly,
Walk by the shore of the wan grass sea,—
Talking once more 'neath a swan-bosomed tree.
1923 Façade 'Valse'.

11 Still falls the Rain—
Dark as the world of man, black as our loss—
Blind as the nineteen hundred and forty nails
Upon the cross.
1942 'The Raids, 1940. Night and Dawn'.

12 The Englishwoman's clothes, too, have improved out of all knowledge...no longer are our hats, as in Victorian days, a kind of Pageant of Empire, whereon the products of all the colonies battle for precedence.
1942 *English Women*.

13 I have often wished I had time to cultivate modesty... But I am too busy thinking about myself.
1950 In the *Observer*, 30 Apr.

14 I enjoyed talking to her, but thought *nothing* of her writing. I considered her 'a beautiful little knitter'.
1955 Of Virginia Woolf. Letter to Geoffrey Singleton, 11 Jul.

15 Mr Lewis's pictures appeared, as a very great painter said to me, to have been painted by a mailed fist in a cotton glove.
1965 On Wyndham Lewis. *Taken Care Of*, ch.11.

16 I wish the Government would put a tax on pianos for the incompetent.
Collected in *Letters, 1916-1964* (1970).

Sitwell, Sir (Francis) Osbert 1892–1969

English writer. He was the brother of Edith and Sacheverell Sitwell, and a friend of Eliot, Pound and Wyndham Lewis, whose radical aesthetic he shared.

17 The British Bourgeosie
Is not born
And does not die,
But, if it is ill,
It has a frightened look in its eyes.
1921 *At the House of Mrs Kinfoot*.

18 But what is Dust,
Save Time's most lethal weapon,
Her faithful ally and our sneaking foe?
1927 'Mrs Southern's Enemy'.

19 *Educated: during the holidays from Eton*.
1929 From his entry in *Who's Who*.

20 Now the nimble fingers are no more nimble,
And the silver thimble lies cold and tarnished black.
1931 'Mrs Mew's Windowbox'.

21 But he was never, well,
What I call
A Sportsman:
For forty days
He went out into the desert
—And never shot anything.
1931 Of Jesus Christ. 'Old Fashioned Sportsmen'.

22 The artist, like the idiot or clown, sits on the edge of the world, and a push may send him over it.
1946 *The Scarlet Tree*, bk.4, ch.2.

23 A word is the carving and colouring of a thought, and gives it permanence.
1949 *Laughter in the Next Room*, ch.7.

24 In reality, killing time
Is only the name for another of the multifarious ways
By which Time kills us.
1958 'Milordo Inglese'.

25 Hunting the author, painter and musician is a traditional and popular sport. In this country poet-baiting at an early stage assumed the place of bull-baiting.
1963 'What It Feels Like to be an Author'.

Sixtus V originally Felice Peretti 1521–90

Franciscan preacher and a professor of theology, created cardinal in 1570. Elected Pope in 1585, because of his presumed feebleness, he implemented vigorous moral, legal and financial reforms.

26 Just see how well she governs! She is only a woman, only the mistress of half an island, and yet she makes herself feared by Spain, by France, by the Empire, by all!
1588 Of Elizabeth I. Quoted in L von Pastor *The History of the Popes* (edited by Kerr R F, 1932), vol.22, p.34.

Skelton, John c.1460–1529

English poet. Educated at Oxford and Cambridge, he was tutor to Prince Henry (later Henry VIII). He began his poetic career with translations and elegies, but turned to writing satirical vernacular poetry, including *Colin Clout* (1521) and *Why Come Ye Not to Court?* (1521), both of which were attacks on Cardinal Wolsey.

27 The sovereign'st thing that any man may have
Is little to say, and much to hear and see.
1499 *The Bouge of Court*, l. 211.

28 With Mannerly Margery milk and ale.
1523 'Mannerly Margery Milk and Ale'.

29 Far may be sought
Erst that ye can find
So courteous, so kind,
As Merry Margaret,
This midsummer flower,
Gentle as falcon
Or hawk of the tower.
1523 *The Garland of Laurel*, 'To Mistress Margaret Hussey'.

30 With lullay, lullay, like a child,
Thou sleepest too long, thou art beguiled.
1527 'Lullay, Lullay, Like a Child'.

31 What dreamest thou, drunkard, drowsy pate?
Thy lust and liking is from thee gone.
Thou blinkard blowboll, thou wakest too late.
1527 'Lullay, Lullay, Like a Child'.

Skelton, (Archibald) Noel 1880–1935

Scottish-born politician and lawyer. He was MP for Perth (1922–3 and 1924–31) and Parliamentary Under-Secretary in the Scottish Office (1931–5).

32 To state as clearly as may be what means lie ready to develop a property-owning democracy, to bring the industrial and economic status of the wage-earner abreast of his political and educational status, to make democracy stable and four-square.
1923 In *The Spectator*, 19 May.

Skelton, Red (Richard) 1913–97

US comedian. A star of radio and television, he also made a few films in the 1940s, among them *Whistling in the Dark* (1941) and *DuBarry Was a Lady* (1943).

33 Exercise? I get it on the golf course. When I see my friends collapse, I run for the paramedics.
Attributed.

Skelton, Robin 1925–97

English-born Canadian poet and aphorist.

34 When someone says, 'It is good business', you may be sure it is bad morality.
1991 *A Devious Dictionary*.

35 Some part of us still believes that men should kill.
1991 *A Devious Dictionary*.

36 Death is the only mystery we all solve.
1991 *A Devious Dictionary*.

37 Never believe what you cannot doubt.
1991 *A Devious Dictionary*.

38 Headlines pass; breadlines continue.
1991 *A Devious Dictionary*.

39 Anything said off the cuff has usually been written on it first.
1991 *A Devious Dictionary*.

40 It requires less skill to love than to be loved.
1991 *A Devious Dictionary*.

41 When one hears of progress one should ask for whom.
1991 *A Devious Dictionary*.

42 Procrustes was an editor.
1991 *A Devious Dictionary*.

43 Kneel to nobody; bow to everyone.
1991 *A Devious Dictionary*.

44 Those who have the habit of revelation lose the habit of thought.
1991 *A Devious Dictionary*.

45 More dreams are destroyed in bed than are ever found there.
1991 *A Devious Dictionary*.

Skinner, B(urrhus) F(rederic) 1904–90

US psychologist and social philosopher, developer and exponent of behaviourism, which views human behaviour and learning as physiological responses. His works include *Walden Two* (1961) and *The Technology of Teaching* (1968).

46 Education is what survives when what has been learnt has been forgotten.
1964 In *New Scientist*, 21 May.

47 The real problem is not whether machines think but whether men do.
1969 *Contingencies of Reinforcement*, ch.9.

Skinner, Cornelia Otis 1902–79

US actress, singer and writer.

48 It's as though some poor devil were to set out for a large dinner party with the knowledge that the following morning he would be hearing exactly what each of the other guests thought of him.
1959 Of opening night reviews. *The Ape In Me*.

49 There are compensations for growing older. One is the realization that to be sporting isn't at all necessary. It is a great relief to reach this stage of wisdom.
Attributed.

Skinner, John 1721–1807

Jacobite songwriter and Episcopalian minister in Aberdeenshire, whose 'Tullochgorum' was described by Robert Burns as 'the best Scotch song ever Scotland saw'.

50 Come, gie's a sang, Montgomery cry'd,
And lay your disputes a' aside;
What signifies't for folks to chide
For what's been done before them?
Let Whig and Tory a' agree,
Whig and Tory, Whig and Tory,
Whig and Tory a' agree
To drop their whigmigmorum;
Let Whig and Tory a' agree
To spend this night wi' mirth and glee,
And cheerfu' sing, alang wi' me,
The Reel o' Tullochgorum.
'Tullochgorum', stanza 1.

Skirving, Adam 1719–1803

Scottish composer of Jacobite songs.

51 Hey, Johnnie Cope, are ye wauking yet?
Or are your drums a-beating yet?
If ye were wauking I wad wait
To gang to the coals i' the morning.
1745 'Johnnie Cope', chorus (commemorating the Battle of Prestonpans and General Cope's flight to Newcastle).

Slessor, Kenneth Adolf 1901–71

Australian poet and journalist. In 1924 he published *Thief of the Moon* and in 1926 *Earth-Visitors*. *Darlinghurst Nights and Morning Glories* (1933) celebrates 'The Cross', the bohemian district of Sydney where he lived for most of his life. His verse was collected in *One Hundred Poems: 1919–1939* (1944, reissued as *Poems*, 1957), and his prose in *Bread and Wine* (1970).

52 Time that is moved by little fidget wheels
Is not my Time, the flood that does not flow.
Between the double and the single bell
Of a ship's hour, between a round of bells
From the dark warship riding there below,
I have lived many lives, and this one life
Of Joe, long dead, who lives between five bells.
1939 *Five Bells*, title poem. The poem was written as an elegy for Joe Lynch, a friend who fell overboard from a Sydney ferry.

Slezak, Leo 1873–1946

Czech tenor. Tall and commanding, he was internationally famous as an interpreter of the heroes of Wagnerian opera.

53 *Wann geht der nächste Schwan?*
What time's the next swan?
1900 When the swan-boat failed to arrive to take him off in Wagner's *Lohengrin*. Quoted in Hugh Vickers *Great Operatic Disasters* (1979).

Sloan, John French 1871–1951

US painter of the Ashcan school, painting everyday subjects, particularly street life in New York City. His works include *Sunday, Women Drying Their Hair* (1912) and *Backyards, Greenwich Village* (1914).

54 Facility is a dangerous thing. Where there is too much technical ease the brain stops criticising. Don't let the hand fall into a smart way of putting the mind to sleep.
1939 *Gist of Art*.

55 Artists are the only people in the world who really live. The others have to hope for heaven.
Recalled on his death, 7 Sep 1951, and quoted in the *Smithsonian*, Apr 1988.

Slovo, Gillian 1952–
South African writer.

56 In most families it is the children who leave home. In mine it was the parents.
1997 Both her parents, Joe Slovo and Ruth First, were anti-apartheid activists. In *Every Secret Thing*.

Small, Albion W 1854–1926
US sociologist; first head of the first department of sociology in the US, at the University of Chicago.

57 Sociology was born of the modern ardor to improve society.
1894 *An Introduction to the Study of Society* (with George E Vincent, 1894).

58 The social problem of the twentieth century is whether civilized nations can restore themselves to sanity after their nineteenth-century aberrations of individualism and capitalism.
1914 'A Vision of Social Efficiency', in the *American Journal of Sociology*, Jan.

Smart, Christopher 1722–71
English poet. He made a precarious living as a writer, helped by Dr Johnson and others, but suffered from bouts of insanity. His poetry includes *The Hilliad* (1753, a satire on doctors modelled on *The Dunciad*) and the structurally complex *A Song To David* (1763). During one of his confinements in a private madhouse he wrote the extraordinary and highly allusive *Jubliate Agno* (1758–63, first published as *Rejoice in the Lamb* 1939, edited by W F Stead).

59 Night, with all her negro train,
  Took possession of the plain;
  In an hearse she rode reclined,
  Drawn by screech-owls slow and blind:
  Close to her, with printless feet,
  Crept Stillness, in a winding sheet.
1748 'A Night-Piece; or, Modern Philosophy', stanza 2. In the *London Magazine*, no.14, Dec. Collected in *Poems on Several Occasions* (1752).

60 Let Eli rejoice with Leucon—he is an honest fellow, which is a rarity.
  For I have seen the White Raven and Thomas Hall of Willingham and am myself a greater curiosity than both.
  Let Jemuel rejoice with Charadrius, who is from the HEIGHT and the sight of him is good for the jaundice.
  For I look up to heaven which is my prospect to escape envy by surmounting it.
1758–63 *Jubilate Agno*, fragment B, stanzas 25–6 (first published 1939). Both the white raven and Thomas Hall, a giant of four feet at the age of three, were curiosities exhibited in the 1740s.

61 For every word has its marrow in the English tongue for order and for delight.
  For the dissyllables such as able table &c are the fiddle rhymes.
  For all dissyllables and some trissyllables are fiddle rhymes.
  For the relations of words are in pairs first.
  For the relations of words are sometimes in oppositions.
  For the relations of words are according to their distances from the pair.
1758–63 *Jubilate Agno*, fragment B, l.595–600. (First published 1939.)

62 For I will consider my cat Jeoffry.
  For he is the servant of the Living God duly and daily serving him.
  For at the first glance of the glory of God in the East he worships in his way.
1758–63 Of his cat Jeoffry. *Jubilate Agno*, fragment B, l.695–7. (First published 1939.)

63 For he counteracts the powers of darkness by his electrical skin and glaring eyes.
  For he counteracts the Devil, who is death, by brisking about the life.
  For in his morning orisons he loves the sun and the sun loves him.
  For he is of the tribe of Tiger.
1758–63 Of his cat Jeoffry. *Jubilate Agno*, fragment B, l.719–22. (First published 1939.)

64 For ADORATION seasons change,
  And order, truth, and beauty range,
  Adjust, attract, and fill:
  The grass the polyanthus cheques;
  And polished porphyry reflects,
  By the descending rill.
1763 *A Song to David*, stanza 52.

65 Strong is the lion—like a coal
  His eye-ball—like a bastion's mole
  His chest against the foes:
  Strong, the gier-eagle on his sail,
  Strong against tide, th'enormous whale
  Emerges as he goes.
1763 *A Song to David*, stanza 76.

66 Beauteous the fleet before the gale;
  Beauteous the multitudes in mail,
  Rank'd arms and crested heads:
  Beauteous the garden's umbrage mild,
  Walk, water, meditated wild,
  And all the bloomy beds.
1763 *A Song to David*, stanza 78.

67 Glorious the northern lights astream;
  Glorious the song, when God's the theme;
  Glorious the thunder's roar:
  Glorious hosanna from the den;
  Glorious the catholic amen;
  Glorious the martyr's gore.
1763 *A Song to David*, stanza 85.

68 Lo, thro' her works gay nature grieves
  How brief she is and frail,
  As ever o'er the falling leaves
  Autumnal winds prevail.
  Yet still the philosophic mind
  Consolatory food can find,
  And hope her anchorage maintain:
  We never are deserted quite;
  'Tis by succession of delight
  That love supports his reign.
1764 *Ode to the Earl of Northumberland, with Some Other Pieces*, 'On a Bed of Guernsey Lilies: written in September 1763', stanza 2.

Smiles, Samuel 1812–1904
Scottish writer and social reformer who settled as a surgeon in Leeds, and published works encouraging self-improvement such as *Self-Help* (1859), *Character* (1871), *Thrift* (1875) and *Duty* (1880).

69 The spirit of self-help is the root of all genuine growth in the individual.
1859 Self-Help, ch.1.

70 The shortest way to do many things is to do only one thing at once.
1859 Self-Help, ch.9.

71 The healthy spirit of self-help created among working people would, more than any other measure, serve to raise them as a class; and this, not by pulling down others, but by levelling them up to a higher and still advancing standard of religion, intelligence, and virtue.
1859 Self-Help, ch.10.

72 We often discover what *will* do, by finding out what will not do; and probably he who never made a mistake never made a discovery.
1859 Self-Help, ch.11.

Smith, A J M   1902–80
Canadian-born US poet and anthologist.

73 McLuhan put a telescope to his ear;
What a lovely smell, he said, we have here.
1967 Poems, 'The Taste of Space'. When McLuhan first heard this couplet, his response was 'Synaesthesia!'

Smith, Adam   1723–90
Scottish economist and philosopher. His *Inquiry into the Nature and Causes of the Wealth of Nations* (1776), the first major work of political economy, examined in detail the consequences of economic freedom—division of labour, the function of markets and the international implications of a *laissez-faire* economy. He was Professor of Moral Philosophy at the University of Glasgow.

74 In ease of body, peace of mind, all the different ranks of life are nearly upon a level and the beggar who suns himself by the side of the highway, possesses that security which kings are fighting for.
1759 The Theory of Moral Sentiments.

75 The greatest improvement in the productive powers of labour, and the greater part of the skill, dexterity and judgement with which it is any where directed, as applied, seem to have been the effects of the division of labour.
1776 An Inquiry into the Nature and Causes of the Wealth of Nations, bk.1, ch.1.

76 It is not from the benevolence of the butcher, the brewer, or the baker, that we expect our dinner, but from their regard to their own interest.
1776 An Inquiry into the Nature and Causes of the Wealth of Nations, bk.1, ch.2.

77 The difference between the most dissimilar characters, between a philosopher and a common street porter, seems to arise not so much from nature, as from habit, custom and education
1776 An Inquiry into the Nature and Causes of the Wealth of Nations, bk.1, ch.2.

78 The word VALUE, it is to be observed, has two different meanings, and sometimes the utility of some particular object, and sometimes the power of purchasing other goods which the possession of that object conveys. This one may be called 'value in use'; the other, 'value in exchange'. The things which have the greatest value in use have frequently little or no value in exchange; and on the contrary, those which have the greatest value in exchange have frequently little or no value in use. Nothing is more useful than water: but it will purchase scarce any thing; scarce any thing can be had in exchange for it. A diamond, on the contrary, has scarce any value in use; but a very great quantity of other goods may frequently be had in exchange for it.
1776 An Inquiry into the Nature and Causes of the Wealth of Nations, bk.1, ch.4.

79 The real price of everything, what everything really costs to the man who wants to acquire it, is the toil and trouble of acquiring it. Labour was the first price, the original purchase money that was paid for all things.
1776 An Inquiry into the Nature and Causes of the Wealth of Nations, bk.1, ch.5.

80 The common wages of labour depends every where upon the contract usually made between those two parties whose interests are by no means the same…Masters are always and every where in a sort of tacit, but constant and uniform combination, not to raise the wages of labour above their actual rate.
1776 An Inquiry into the Nature and Causes of the Wealth of Nations, bk.1, ch.8.

81 People of the same trade seldom meet together, even for merriment and diversion, but the conversation ends in a conspiracy against the public, or in some contrivance to raise prices.
1776 An Inquiry into the Nature and Causes of the Wealth of Nations, bk.1, ch.10, pt.2.

82 The rate of profit does not, like rent and wages, rise with the prosperity, and fall with the declension, of the society. On the contrary, it is naturally low in rich, and high in poor countries, and it is always highest in the countries which are going fastest to ruin.
1776 An Inquiry into the Nature and Causes of the Wealth of Nations, bk.1, ch.11, conclusion.

83 Capitals are increased by parsimony, and diminished by prodigality and misconduct. By what a frugal man annually saves he not only affords maintenance to an additional number of productive hands…but…he establishes as it were a perpetual fund for the maintenance of an equal number in all times to come.
1776 An Inquiry into the Nature and Causes of the Wealth of Nations, bk.2, ch.3.

84 The principle which prompts to save is the desire of bettering our condition—a desire which…comes with us from the womb and never leaves us till we go into the grave.
1776 An Inquiry into the Nature and Causes of the Wealth of Nations, bk.2, ch.3.

85 It is the maxim of every prudent master of a family never to attempt to make at home what it will cost him more to make than to buy. The taylor does not attempt to make his own shoe… All of them find it for their interest to employ their whole industry in a way in which they have some advantage over their neighbours and to purchase with a part of its produce…whatever else they have occasion for… What is prudence in the conduct of every private family, can scarce be folly in that of a great kingdom… Would it be a reasonable law to prohibit the importation of all foreign wines, merely to encourage the making of claret and burgundy in Scotland?

1776 *An Inquiry into the Nature and Causes of the Wealth of Nations*, bk.4, ch.2.

86 Every individual...intends only his own gain, and he is in this as in many other cases led by an invisible hand to promote an end which was no part of his intention... By pursuing his own interest he frequently promotes that of the society more effectually than when he really intends to promote it. I have never known much good done by those who affected to trade for the publick good.
1776 *An Inquiry into the Nature and Causes of the Wealth of Nations*, bk.4, ch.3.

87 To found a great Empire for the sole purpose of raising up a people of customers, may at first sight appear a project fit only for a nation of shopkeepers. It is, however, a project altogether unfit for a nation of shopkeepers; but extremely fit for a nation that is governed by shopkeepers.
1776 *An Inquiry into the Nature and Causes of the Wealth of Nations*, bk.4, ch.7, pt.3.
▶ See Napoleon 630:47, Punch 699:75, Stoppard 856:20.

88 Consumption is the sole end and purpose of all production.
1776 *An Inquiry into the Nature and Causes of the Wealth of Nations*, bk.4, ch.8.

89 The man whose life is spent in performing a few simple operations of which the effects too are, perhaps, always the same or very nearly the same, has no occasion to exert his understanding, or to exercise his invention. He generally becomes as stupid and ignorant as it is possible for a human creature to become.
1776 *An Inquiry into the Nature and Causes of the Wealth of Nations*, bk.5, ch.1, pt.3, article 2.

90 Science is the great antidote to the poison of enthusiasm and superstition.
1776 *An Inquiry into the Nature and Causes of the Wealth of Nations*, bk.5, ch.1, pt.3, article 3.

91 There is no art which one government sooner learns of another than that of draining money from the pockets of the people.
1776 *An Inquiry into the Nature and Causes of the Wealth of Nations*, bk.5, ch.2.

Smith, Al(fred) Emmanuel 1873–1944
US Democrat politician, who rose from newsboy to be Governor of New York State (1919–20, 1923–8). He was defeated as Democratic candidate for the Presidency in 1928.

92 Nobody shoots Santa Claus.
1936 Denouncing criticisms of the US aid programme.

93 No matter how thin you slice it, it's still baloney.
1936 Election campaign speech, October.

Smith, Alexander McCall 1949–
Scottish Professor of Medical Law and author of numerous works of fiction and non-fiction.

94 The No.1 Ladies' Detective Agency.
1998 Novel title.

95 There are many women whose lives would be immeasurably improved by widowhood, but one should not always point that out.
2005 *Espresso Tales*.

96 If your ceiling should fall down, then you have lost a room, but gained a courtyard. Think of it that way.
2006 *The Right Attitude to Rain*.

Smith, Arthur 1954–
English comedian and broadcaster.

97 On paper, England are a good cricket team. The trouble is they play on grass.
Attributed.

Smith, Dodie 1896–1990
English playwright, novelist and theatre producer, whose works include the highly popular children's book *The Hundred and One Dalmatians* (1956).

98 The family—that dear octopus from whose tentacles we never quite escape.
1938 *Dear Octopus*.

Smith, Godfrey 1926–
English writer and columnist. He was Associate Editor of the *Sunday Times* from 1972 to 1991 and has written novels and books about English social life and customs. He has also compiled anthologies.

99 A scoop of pure honey set in a green bowl.
1984 Of Bath. *The English Companion*.

1 Try as one may to stress the cultural and historical role of the place...it still conveys one overwhelmingly powerful image to your average Englishman: the dirty weekend.
1984 Of Brighton. *The English Companion*.

Smith, Iain Crichton Gaelic name *Blain Mac A'Ghobhainn* 1928–98
Scottish poet and novelist, who wrote in both English and Gaelic. His novels include *Consider the Lilies* (1968). His *Collected Poems* were published in 1992.

2 Here they have no time for the fine graces
of poetry, unless it freely grows
in deep compulsion, like water in the well,
woven into the texture of the soil
in a strong pattern.
1955 'Poem of Lewis'.

3 And she, being old, fed from a mashed plate
as an old mare might droop across a fence
to the dull pastures of her ignorance.
Her husband held her upright while he prayed

to God who is all-forgiving to send down
some angel somewhere who might land perhaps
in his foreign wings among the gradual crops.
She munched, half dead, blindly searching the spoon.
1961 *Thistles and Roses*, 'Old Woman', stanzas 1–2.

4 This is the land God gave to Andy Stewart—we have our inheritance.
There shall be no ardour, there shall be indifference.
There shall not be excellence, there shall be the average.
We shall be the intrepid hunters of golf balls.
1969 'The White Air of March'.

5 I tremble in this factory of books.
What love he must have lost to write so much.

Smith, Iain Duncan 1954–

English Conservative politician, leader of the Conservative Party from 2001 to 2003. In 2010 he was appointed Secretary of State for Work and Pensions.

6 The quiet man is here to stay, and he's turning up the volume!
2003 At the Conservative Party Conference, Oct.

Smith, Ian Douglas 1919–2007

Zimbabwean (Rhodesian) politician, a founder of the pro-independence Rhodesian Front. Prime Minister from 1964, he unilaterally declared independence in 1965. Britain applied sanctions, and in 1979 majority rule was granted. He was suspended from government (1987) for South African links.

7 We have the happiest Africans in the world.
1971 In the *Observer*, 28 Nov.

8 Let me say it again, I don't believe in black majority rule ever in Rhodesia. Not in a thousand years.
1976 Radio broadcast, 20 Mar.

Smith, John 1938–94

Scottish politician. He was called to the Bar in 1967, and made a QC in 1983. He became MP for Lanarkshire North in 1970, and for Monklands East in 1983. He served as a cabinet minister under Harold Wilson and James Callaghan, and in the shadow cabinet (1972–92). He succeeded Neil Kinnock as leader of the Labour Party in 1992.

9 The settled will of the Scottish people.
1994 Of the creation of a Scottish parliament, in a speech at the Scottish Labour Conference, 11 Mar.

10 We will do our best to reward your faith in us, but please give us the opportunity to serve our country, that is all we ask.
1994 Address to a European Gala Dinner, 11 May. They were his final public words; he died the next morning of a heart attack.

Smith, Logan Pearsall 1865–1946

US-born British writer, who took British nationality in 1913. He is best known for his polished essays and aphorisms, gathered in books such as *Afterthoughts* (1931); he also wrote criticism and short stories.

11 The denunciation of the young is a necessary part of the hygiene of older people, and greatly assists the circulation of their blood.
1931 *Afterthoughts*, 'Age and Death'.

12 There are two things to aim at in life: first, to get what you want; and, after that, to enjoy it. Only the wisest of mankind achieve the second.
1931 *Afterthoughts*, 'Life and Human Nature'.

13 How awful to reflect that what people say of us is true!
1931 *Afterthoughts*, 'Life and Human Nature'.

14 There are few sorrows, however poignant, in which a good income is of no avail.
1931 *Afterthoughts*, 'Life and Human Nature'.

15 An improper mind is a perpetual feast.
1931 *Afterthoughts*, 'Life and Human Nature'.

16 There is more felicity on the far side of baldness than young men can possibly imagine.
1931 *Afterthoughts*, 'Age and Death'.

17 What music is more enchanting than the voices of young people, when you can't hear what they say?
1931 *Afterthoughts*, 'Age and Death'.

18 Most people sell their souls, and live with a good conscience on the proceeds.
1931 *Afterthoughts*, 'Other People'.

19 A friend who loved perfection would be the perfect friend, did not that love shut his door on me.
1931 *Afterthoughts*, 'Other People'.

20 All Reformers, however strict their social conscience, live in houses just as big as they can pay for.
1931 *Afterthoughts*, 'Other People'.

21 When they come downstairs from their Ivory Towers, Idealists are very apt to walk straight into the gutter.
1931 *Afterthoughts*, 'Other People'.

22 Married women are kept women, and they are beginning to find it out.
1931 *Afterthoughts*, 'Other People'.

23 A best-seller is the gilded tomb of a mediocre talent.
1931 *Afterthoughts*, 'Art and Letters'.

24 People say that life is the thing, but I prefer reading.
1931 *Afterthoughts*, 'Myself'.

25 Thank heavens, the sun has gone in, and I don't have to go out and enjoy it.
1931 *Afterthoughts*, 'Myself'.

26 What I like in a good author is not what he says, but what he whispers.
1933 *All Trivia*, 'Afterthoughts'.

Smith, Margaret Chase 1897–1995

US Senator. Elected to the US Senate in 1948, she served four terms and continued to be politically active afterwards. She supported the draft for women, was a teacher and a syndicated columnist. She held 95 honorary degrees from various universities and colleges.

27 The greatest deliberative body in the world...has too often been debased to the level of a forum of hate and character assassination sheltered by the shield of congressional immunity.
1950 'Declaration of Conscience' address to the Senate, 1 Jun, denouncing accusations by Senator Joseph R McCarthy.

Smith, Dame Maggie (Margaret Natalie) 1934–

English actress. She has won equal acclaim as a stage actress and in the cinema, appearing in such films as *The Prime of Miss Jean Brodie* (1969), *California Suite* (1978), *A Room with a View* (1986), *Gosford Park* (2001) and *The Best Exotic Marigold Hotel* (2012).

28 They always seem to think that I'm scary, and I understand that totally. Old people are scary. And I have to face it, I am old and I am scary. And I'm very, very sorry about it, but I don't know what you do.
2013 On *60 Minutes*, CBS, 2 Jun.

Smith, Patti 1946–

US singer, songwriter, poet and political activist.

29 Everybody's got to reclaim these things—poetry, rock'n'roll, political activism—and it's got to be done over and over again. It's like eating: you can't say, 'Oh, I ate yesterday'. You have to eat again.
2004 In *Rolling Stone*, 27 May.

Smith, Red 1905–82

US sportswriter.

30 It was an ideal day for football—too cold for the spectators and too cold for the players.
   1963 Reporting on a match between the Chicago Bears and the New York Giants.

Smith, Samuel Francis 1808–95

US clergyman and poet.

31 My country, 'tis of thee,
   Sweet land of liberty,
   Of thee I sing:
   Land where my fathers died,
   Land of the pilgrims' pride,
   From every mountain-side
   Let the freedom ring.
   1831 'America'.

Smith, Stevie (Florence Margaret) 1902–71

English poet and novelist. She lived most of her life with her aunt in a London suburb, and much of her work reflected that setting. Loneliness is a persistent theme, but she was also adept at dealing wittily with serious matters.

32 If you cannot have your dear husband for a comfort and a delight, for a breadwinner and a crosspatch, for a sofa, chair or a hot-water bottle, one can use him as a Cross to be Borne.
   1936 Novel On Yellow Paper.

33 A Good Time was Had By All.
   1937 Title of poetry collection.

34 This Englishwoman is so refined
   She has no bosom and no behind.
   1937 A Good Time was Had By All, 'This Englishwoman'.

35 Here is all straight and narrow as a tomb
   Oh shut me not within a little room.
   1950 Harold's Leap, 'The Commuted Sentence'.

36 Let all the little poets be gathered together in classes
   And let prizes be given to them by the Prize Asses.
   1950 Harold's Leap, 'To School!'

37 Oh, no, no, no, it was too cold always
   (Still the dead one lay moaning)
   I was much too far out all my life
   And not waving but drowning.
   1957 Not Waving but Drowning, 'Not Waving but Drowning'.

38 People who are always praising the past
   And especially the times of faith as best
   Ought to go and live in the Middle Ages
   And be burnt at the stake as witches and sages.
   1957 Not Waving but Drowning, 'The Past'.

39 Shall I tell you the signs of a New Age coming?
   It is a sound of drubbing and sobbing
   Of people crying, We are old, we are old
   And the sun is going down and becoming cold.
   1957 Not Waving but Drowning, 'The New Age'.

40 Why does my Muse only speak when she is unhappy?
   She does not, I only listen when I am unhappy
   When I am happy I live and despise writing
   For my Muse this cannot but be dispiriting.
   1962 Selected Poems, 'My Muse'.

41 I long for the Person from Porlock
   To bring my thoughts to an end.
   I am growing impatient to see him
   I think of him as a friend.
   1962 Selected Poems, 'Thoughts About the Person from Porlock' (a reference to the 'person from Porlock' mentioned in Coleridge's preliminary note to 'Kubla Khan').

42 Private Means is dead
   God rest his soul, officers and fellow-rankers said.
   1962 Selected Poems, 'Private Means is Dead'.

43 'This night shall thy soul be required of thee.'
   My soul is never required of me
   It always has to be somebody else of course.
   Will my soul be required of me tonight perhaps?
   1972 Scorpion, 'Scorpion'.
   ▶ See Bible 121:85.

44 Scorpion so wishes to be gone.
   1972 Scorpion, 'Scorpion'.

45 Oh I am a cat that likes to
   Gallop about doing good.
   1972 Scorpion, 'The Galloping Cat'.

Smith, Rev Sydney 1771–1845

English journalist, clergymen and preacher and lecturer on moral philosophy, also one of the founders of the Edinburgh Review. He wrote letters and pamphlets in favour of Catholic emancipation, the ballot, the abolition of prison abuses and other causes, and is best known as a conversationalist and wit.

46 The moment that the very name of Ireland is mentioned, the English seem to bid adieu to common feeling, common prudence, and common sense, and to act with the barbarity of tyrants and the fatuity of idiots.
   1807-8 Peter Plymley's Letters.

47 I look upon Switzerland as an inferior sort of Scotland.
   1815 Letter to Lord Holland, [August]. In The Letters of Sydney Smith edited by Nowell C Smith (1953), vol. 1.

48 What two ideas are more inseparable than Beer and Britannia.
   1823 In the Edinburgh Review, quoted in H Pearson The Smith of Smiths (1934), ch.11.

49 Alas, alas, how easily a priest begets children and with what difficulty he provides for them; a priest I mean who is extravagant enough to keep a conscience; a point wherein our profession commits (I must say) little excess.
   1825 Letter to Lord Holland, 14 Jul. In The Letters of Sydney Smith edited by Nowell C Smith (1953), vol. 1.

50 He who drinks a tumbler of London Water has literally in his stomach more animated beings than there are men, Women and Children on the face of the globe.
   1834 Letter to Lady Grey, 19 Nov.

51 No furniture so charming as books.
   Quoted in Lady Holland Memoir (1855), vol I, ch. 9.

52 Take short views, hope for the best, and trust in God.
   Quoted in Lady Holland Memoir (1855), vol I, ch. 6.

53 That knuckle-end of England—that land of Calvin, oat-cakes and sulphur.
   Quoted in Lady Holland Memoir (1855), vol I, ch. 2.

54 I heard him [Jeffrey] speak disrespectfully of the Equator!
   Quoted in Lady Holland Memoir (1855), vol.I, ch.2.

55 As the French say, there are three sexes—men, women, and clergymen.
   Quoted in Lady Holland Memoir (1855), vol.I, ch.9.

56 He is like a book in breeches.
Of Lord Macaulay. Quoted in Lady Holland *Memoir* (1855), vol.1, ch.11.

57 He has occasional flashes of silence that make his conversation perfectly delightful.
Of Lord Macaulay. Quoted in Lady Holland *Memoir* (1855), vol.1, ch.11.

58 My definition of marriage... It resembles a pair of shears, so joined that they cannot be separated; often moving in opposite directions, yet always punishing anyone who comes between them.
Quoted in Lady Holland *Memoir* (1855), vol.1, ch.11.

59 Let onion atoms lurk within the bowl,
And, half-suspected, animate the whole.
'Receipt for a Salad', quoted in Lady Holland *Memoir* (1855), vol.1, ch.11.

60 Serenely full, the epicure would say,
'Fate cannot harm me, I have dined today.'
'Receipt for a Salad', concluding lines, quoted in Lady Holland *Memoir*, (1855), vol.1, ch.11.

61 My idea of heaven is, eating *paté de foie gras* to the sound of trumpets.
Quoted in H Pearson *The Smith of Smiths*, (1934), ch.10.

62 What a pity it is we have no amusements in England but vice and religion!
Quoted in H Pearson *The Smith of Smiths*, (1934), ch.10.

63 I am just going to pray for you at St Paul's, but with no very lively hope of success.
Quoted in H Pearson *The Smith of Smiths*, (1934), ch.10.

Smith, Sydney Goodsir 1915–75

New Zealand-born Scottish poet and critic, who played an important part in the 20c revival of poetry in the Scots language. His first volume, *Skail Wind* (1941), was followed by several others. He also edited works on Scottish literature.

64 This rortie wretched city
Sair come down frae its auld hiechts
—The hauf o't smug, complacent,
Lost til all pride of race or spirit,
The tither wild and rouch as ever
In its secret hairt
But lost alsweill, the smeddum tane,
The man o'independent mind has cap in hand the day
—Sits on its craggy spine
And drees the wind and rain
That nourished all its genius
—Weary wi centuries
This empty capital snorts like a great beast
Caged in its sleep, dreaming of freedom.
1954 Of Edinburgh. 'Kynd Kittock's Land' (Kynd Kittock is a character in the poetry of the 16c Scottish poet William Dunbar.) rortie=splendid, smeddum=spirit, drees=endures.

Smith, Walter Chalmers 1824–1908

Scottish clergyman and poet.

65 Immortal, invisible, God only wise,
In light inaccessible hid from our eyes,
Most blessèd, most glorious, the Ancient of Days,
Almighty, victorious, Thy great name we praise.
1867 'Immortal, Invisible', hymn.

Smollett, Tobias George 1721–71

Scottish novelist. He wrote a history of England and from 1753 edited the *Critical Review*, which led to his being imprisoned for libel in 1760. His unfavourable account of his travels in France and Italy, which he was ordered to visit for the sake of his health, earned him Sterne's designation as 'Smelfungus'. His novel *Humphrey Clinker* (1771) remains popular.

66 I think for my part one half of the nation is mad—and the other not very sound.
1762 *The Adventures of Sir Launcelot Greaves*, ch.6.

67 They have no education, no taste for reading, no housewifery, nor, indeed, any earthly occupation but that of dressing their hair, and adorning their bodies. They hate walking, and would never go abroad, if they were not stimulated by the vanity of being seen... Nothing can be more parsimonious than the economy of these people. They live upon soup and bouille, fish and salad.
1766 Of the nobility of Boulogne. *Travels through France and Italy*.

68 The capital is become an overgrown monster; which, like a dropsical head, will in time leave the body and extremities without nourishment and support.
1771 Of London. Letter from Matthew Bramble, 29 May, *Humphrey Clinker*, vol.1.

69 I am pent up in frowzy lodgings, where there is not room enough to swing a cat.
1771 Letter from Matthew Bramble, 8 Jun, *Humphrey Clinker*, vol.1.

Smuts, Jan Christian 1870–1950

South African general and statesman, Prime Minister (1919–24). A significant figure at Versailles, he was instrumental in the founding of the League of Nations. As Minister of Justice under Hertzog, his coalition with the Nationalists in 1934 produced the United Party, and he became Premier again (1939–48).

70 Perhaps it is God's will to lead the people of South Africa through defeat and humiliation to a better future and a brighter day.
1902 Speech at the Vereeniging peace talks, 31 May.

71 What was everybody's business in the end proved to be nobody's business. Each one looked to the other to take the lead, and the aggressors got away with it.
1943 Explaining the failure of the League of Nations to the Empire Parliamentary Association, London, 25 Nov.

Snagge, John 1904–96

English radio commentator.

72 I can't tell who's leading—it's either Oxford or Cambridge.
1949 Radio commentary on the Boat Race, when the engine of Snagge's launch broke down. Quoted in C Dodd *Oxford and Cambridge Boat Race* (1983), ch.14.

Snow, Carmel 1887–1961

Irish-born US journalist. She was fashion editor (1932–35) and then editor-in-chief (1935–57) of *Harper's Bazaar*.

73 Elegance is good taste *plus* a dash of daring.
1962 *The World of Carmel Snow*.

Snow, C(harles) P(ercy), 1st Baron 1905–80

English novelist and physicist. His works include a cycle of novels portraying English life from 1920, including *Strangers and Brothers* (1940), *The Masters* (1951), *The New Men* (1954) and *Corridors of*

Power (1964). In his controversial *Two Cultures* (Rede lecture, 1959) he discussed the need for closer contact of science and literature.

74 Drinking the best tea in the world in an empty cricket ground—that, I think, is the final pleasure left to man.
   1932 Quoted in Colin Jarman *The Guinness Dictionary of Sports Quotations* (1990).

75 The official world, the corridors of power, the dilemmas of conscience and egotism—she disliked them all.
   1956 *Homecomings*, ch.22. This phrase was later used as the title of his 1964 novel, *Corridors of Power*.

76 A good many times I have been present at gatherings of people who...are thought highly educated and who have...been expressing their incredulity at the illiteracy of scientists. Once or twice I have been provoked and have asked the company how many of them could describe the Second Law of Thermodynamics. The response was cold: it was also negative.
   1959 *The Two Cultures*, Rede Lecture, ch.1.

77 I believe the intellectual life of the whole of western society is increasingly being split into two polar groups... Literary intellectuals at one pole—at the other scientists, and as the most representative, the physical scientists. Between the two a gulf of mutual incomprehension.
   1959 *The Two Cultures*, Rede Lecture.

78 'I grant you that he's not two-faced,' I said. 'But what's the use of that when the one face he has got is so peculiarly unpleasant?'
   1960 *The Affair*, ch.4.

79 Technology...is a queer thing. It brings you great gifts with one hand, and it stabs you in the back with the other.
   1971 In the *New York Times*, 15 Mar.

80 There have been many crimes committed in the name of duty and obedience—many more than in the name of dissent.
   1971 'Testimony of Four Peers', in *Esquire*, Dec.

81 Writers are much more esteemed in Russia, they play a much larger part in society than they do in the West. The advantage of not being free is that people listen to you.
   1971 Interview on Radio Moscow.

82 In not much over a generation, physicists have changed our world.
   1981 *The Physicists* (published posthumously).

83 There are no secrets in science.
   1981 *The Physicists* (published posthumously).

Snow, Clyde Collins 1928–2014

Forensic anthropologist.

84 The ground is like a beautiful woman. If you treat her gently, she'll tell you all her secrets.
   1991 On exploring the massacre of thousands of Mayan Indians in Guatemala in the early 1980s. In the *Washington Post*, 18 Dec.

Snowden, Ed(ward Joseph) 1983–

US computer analyst, who in 2013 caused a sensation by releasing thousands of classified documents he had obtained access to while working at the Defense Intelligence Agency. Threatened with imprisonment in the US, he fled to Hong Kong and then Moscow, where he remains.

85 Much of what I saw in Geneva really disillusioned me about how my government functions and what its impact is in the world. I realized that I was part of something that was doing far more harm than good.
   2013 In *The Guardian*, 9 Jun.

86 I don't see myself as a hero, because what I'm doing is self-interested; I don't want to live in a world where there's no privacy and, therefore, no room for intellectual exploration and creativity.
   2013 In *The Guardian*, 9 Jun.

87 My sole motive is to inform the public as to that which is done in their name and that which is done against them.
   2013 In *The Guardian*, 9 Jun.

Snowden, Philip Snowden, 1st Viscount 1864–1937

English Labour statesman, crippled in a cycling accident. A socialist MP from 1906, he opposed conscription and as Chancellor of the Exchequer from 1924 aggravated the financial crises. A free trader, he resigned in 1932, and wrote an *Autobiography* (1934).

88 The Labour Party's election programme...is the most fantastic and impracticable programme ever put before the electors. This is not socialism. It is bolshevism run mad.
   1931 Radio broadcast, 17 Oct.

Snyder, Gary Sherman 1930–

US poet. The 'Japhy Ryder' of Kerouac's *The Dharma Bums*, his writings reflect an almost sacramental vision of man's relationship to his natural environment.

89 I cannot remember things I once read
   A few friends, but they are in cities.
   Drinking cold snow-water from a tin cup
   Looking down for miles
   Through high still air.
   1959 *Riprap*, 'Mid-August at Sourdough Mountain Lookout'.

90 A clear, attentive mind
   Has no meaning but that
   Which sees is truly seen.
   1959 *Riprap*, 'Piute Creek'.

91 In ten thousand years the Sierras
   Will be dry and dead, home of the scorpion.
   Ice-scratched slabs and bent trees.
   No paradise, no fall,
   Only the weathering land
   The wheeling sky,
   Man, with his Satan
   Scouring the chaos of the mind.
   Oh Hell!
   1959 *Riprap*, 'Milton By Firelight (Piute Creek, August 1955)'.

92 After weeks of watching the roof leak
   I fixed it tonight
   by moving a single board.
   1968 *The Back Country*, 'Hitch Haiku'.

93 Down for a new radio, to Ross Lake, and back up. Three days walking. Strange how unmoved this place leaves one;
   neither articulate or worshipful; rather the pressing need to look
   within and adjust the mechanism of perception.
   1969 *Earth House Hold*, 'Lookout's Journal, Crater Shan 28 July'.

94 Beware of anything that promises freedom or enlightenment—traps for eager and clever fools—a dog has a keener nose—every creature in a cave can justify himself. Three-fourths of philosophy and literature is the talk of people trying to convince themselves that they really like the cage they were tricked into entering.
1969 *Earth House Hold*, 'Japan First Time Around, 24: X'.

95 I recalled when I worked in the woods
and the bars of Madras, Oregon.
That short-haired joy and roughness—
America—your stupidity.
I could almost love you again.
1974 *Turtle Island*, 'I Went Into The Maverick Bar'.

Socrates 469–399 BC

Greek philosopher. Our knowledge of his life and teaching derives mainly from the work of his pupil Plato, in dialogues including the *Republic*, and the *Apology*, *Crito* and *Phaedo*, which describe Socrates' trial for 'corrupting the young' and his death by drinking hemlock.

96 I am so far like the midwife that I cannot myself give birth to wisdom, and the common reproach is true, that, though I question others, I can myself bring nothing to light because there is no wisdom in me.
Quoted in Plato *Theaetetus*, 150c (translated by F M Cornford).

97 This sense of wonder is the mark of the philosopher. Philosophy indeed has no other origin.
Quoted in Plato *Theaetetus*, 150c (translated by F M Cornford).

98 How many things I can do without!
On viewing goods for sale. Quoted in Diogenes Laertius *Vitae Philosophorum*, 2.25 (translated by R D Hicks, 1950).

99 The unexamined life is not worth living.
Quoted in Plato *Apology*, 38a.

1 There is only one good, knowledge, and only one evil, ignorance.
Quoted in Diogenes Laertius *Vitae Philosophorum*, 2.31 (translated by R D Hicks, 1950).

Solon c.640–c.559 BC

Athenian lawgiver and poet. Archon in 594 BC (or 591 BC), he reformed the constitution, abolishing debt-slavery and admitting a fourth class to the Assembly. After 10 years of voluntary exile he returned to Athens in 580 BC

2 As I grow older, I constantly learn more.
Quoted in Bergk (ed) *Poetae Lyrici Graeci*, 'Solon', no.18.

Solow, Robert M 1924–

US economist, winner of the Nobel prize (1987).

3 Thinking precisely and systematically about something as complex and irregular as a modern economy is very difficult, maybe impossible.
1984 In the *New York Times Book Review*, 30 Dec.

4 Merely to adopt the more powerful assumption is no more than to assume the more powerful conclusion.
1994 In the *Journal of Economic Perspectives*, 8:53.

Solzhenitsyn, Aleksandr Isayevich 1918–2008

Russian writer, a labour camp prisoner (1945–53). His *One Day in the Life of Ivan Denisovich* (1962) was widely acclaimed, but his subsequent denunciation of Soviet censorship led to the banning of his novels *Cancer Ward* (1968) and *The First Circle* (1968). He was awarded the Nobel prize for literature in 1970 (received 1974). After *The Gulag Archipelago* (3 vols, 1973–6), an account of the Stalinist terror, he was exiled (1974). His citizenship was restored in 1990, and the treason charges against him dropped in 1991. In 1994 he returned to Russia.

5 You only have power over people so long as you do not take everything away from them. But when you have robbed man of everything, he is no longer in your pocket—he is free.
1968 *The First Circle*.

6 In our country the lie has become not just a moral category but a pillar of the State.
1974 Quoted in the *Observer*, 29 Dec.

7 For us in Russia, communism is a dead dog, while, for many people in the West, it is still a living lion.
1979 In the *Listener*, 15 Feb.

Somerville, Edith (Anna Oenone) and Martin, Violet Florence née Ross who wrote under the pseudonym Martin Ross 1858–1949; 1862–1915

Irish cousins who first met in 1886. They formed a lasting successful literary partnership and are both known for a series of novels that makes fun of the Irish.

8 'May the divil choke ye!' says he, pleasant enough, but I knew by the blush he had he was vexed.
1898 *Some Experiences of an Irish R.M.*, 'Lisheen Races, Second-Hand'.

9 'I call it a criminal thing in any one's great-great-grandfather to rear up a preposterous troop of sons and plant them all out in his own country', Lady Knox said to me with apparent irrelevance. 'I detest collaterals. Blood may be thicker than water, but it is also a great deal nastier.'
1898 *Some Experiences of an Irish R.M.*, 'Philippa's Fox-Hunt'.

10 Every known class of refusal was successfully exhibited. One horse endeavoured to climb the rails into the Grand Stand; another, having stopped dead at the critical point, swung round, and returned in consternation to the starting-point, with his rider hanging like a locket around his neck. Another, dowered with a sense of humour unusual among horses, stepped delicately over the furze-bushes, and, amidst rounds of applause, walked through the lime with a stoic calm.
1908 *Further Experiences of an Irish R.M.*, 'A Royal Command'.

Somoza, (García) Anastasio 1925–80

Nicaraguan dictator, educated in the US. As Chief of the National Guard he established himself in supreme power in the early 1930s, and retained it until assassinated, when the rule passed to his sons.

11 You won the elections. But I won the count.
1977 In *The Guardian*, 17 Jun.

Sontag, Susan 1933–2004

US writer and critic. Although she emerged first as an experimental fiction writer her main impact was as a critic. Her essays in leading journals were expanded into books including *On Photography* (1976) and *Illness As Metaphor* (1978). Later publications include the novels *The Volcano Lover* (1992) and *In America* (2000), and a play, *Alice in Bed* (1993).

12 Ambition if it feeds at all, does so on the ambition of others.
1963 *The Benefactor*, ch.1.

13 Interpretation is the revenge of the intellect upon art.
1964 In *The Evergreen Review*, Dec.

14 Perversity is the muse of modern literature.
1966 *Against Interpretation*, 'Camus' Notebooks'.

15 What pornography is really about, ultimately, isn't sex but death.
1967 In *Partisan Review*, Spring.

16 The white race *is* the cancer of human history, it is the white race, and it alone—its ideologies and inventions—which eradicates autonomous civilizations wherever it spreads, which has upset the ecological balance of the planet, which now threatens the very existence of life itself.
1967 In *Partisan Review*, Winter.

17 The camera makes everyone a tourist in other people's reality, and eventually in one's own.
1974 In the *New York Review of Books*, 18 Apr. Later published in book form as *On Photography* (1976).

18 When we're afraid we shoot. But when we're nostalgic we take pictures.
1974 In the *New York Review of Books*, 18 Apr.

19 The most interesting ideas are heresies.
1975 Interview in *Salmagundi*, Fall–Winter.

20 Illness is the night-side of life, a more onerous citizenship. Everyone who is born holds dual citizenship, in the kingdom of the well and in the kingdom of the sick. Although we all prefer to use only the good passport, sooner or later each of us is obliged, at least for a spell, to identify ourselves as citizens of that other place.
1978 In the *New York Review of Books*, 26 Jan.

21 It seems the very model of all the catastrophes privileged populations feel await them.
1989 Of AIDS. *AIDS and Its Metaphors*, ch.8.

22 I envy paranoids; they actually feel people are paying attention to them.
1992 In *Time Out*, 19 Aug.

23 In the matter of courage (a morally neutral virtue): whatever may be said of the perpetrators of Tuesday's slaughter, they were not cowards.
2001 Reflecting on the 11 Sep terrorist attacks in New York. In the *New Yorker*, 24 Sep.

Sophocles c.496–405 BC

Athenian playwright. He wrote well over 100 plays, of which seven tragedies have survived, including *Oedipus Tyrannus*.

24 Woman, silence makes a woman beautiful.
Ajax, 293 (translated by H Lloyd-Jones, 1994).

25 Hope has often caused the love of gain to ruin men.
Antigone, 222 (translated by H Lloyd-Jones, 1994).

26 Many things are formidable, and none more formidable than man.
Antigone, 332–3 (translated by H Lloyd-Jones, 1994).

27 One must obey the man whom the city sets up in power in small things and in justice and in its opposite.
Creon speaking. *Antigone*, 666–7 (translated by H Lloyd-Jones, 1994).

28 You see how when rivers are swollen in winter those trees that yield to the flood retain their branches, but those that offer resistance perish, trunk and all.
Haemon speaking. *Antigone*, 712–14 (translated by H Lloyd-Jones, 1994).

29 Love invincible in battle.
Antigone, 781–90 (translated by H Lloyd-Jones, 1994).

30 Remember there is no success without hard work.
Electra, 945 (translated by H Lloyd-Jones, 1994).

31 When I do not understand, I like to say nothing.
Oedipus Tyrannus, 569 (translated by H Lloyd-Jones, 1994).

32 It is best to live anyhow, as one may; do not be afraid of marriage with your mother! Many have lain with their mothers in dreams too. It is he to whom such things are nothing who puts up with life best.
Jocasta to Oedipus, her son and husband, before they both discover the truth of the prophecy. *Oedipus Tyrannus*, 979–83 (translated by H Lloyd-Jones, 1994).

Sorley, Charles Hamilton 1895–1915

Scottish poet, killed in action during World War I.

33 When you see millions of the mouthless dead
Across your dreams in pale battalions go,
Say not soft things as other men have said,
That you'll remember. For you need not so.
Give them not praise. For, deaf, how should they know
It is not curses heaped on each gashed head?
Marlborough and Other Poems, 'A Sonnet' (published 1916).

Soros, George originally György Schwartz 1930–

Hungarian-born US businessman, philanthropist, and political activist. Chairman of the Soros Fund Management and Open Society Foundations, he is revered for his financial acumen.

34 Markets are constantly in a state of uncertainty and flux and money is made by discounting the obvious and betting on the unexpected.
2005 Quoted on TeenAnalyst.com, 5 May.

35 We witnessed the collapse of the financial system… it was placed on life support, and it's still on life support. There's no sign that we are anywhere near a bottom.
2009 Quoted by Reuters, 21 Feb.

36 Revolutions usually start with enthusiasm and end in tears.
2011 In *The Washington Post*, 3 Feb.

37 I'm only rich because I know when I'm wrong.
Attributed.

Soule, John Babsone Lane 1815–91

US teacher, cleric and journalist.

38 Go West, young man, go West!
Terre Haute Express.

Sousa, John Philip 1854–1932

US composer and bandmaster. He became conductor of the United States Marine Band in 1880 and formed his own band, which built up an international reputation, 12 years later. As well as more than a hundred popular marches, he composed 10 comic operas.

39 Jazz will endure just as long as people hear it through their feet instead of their brains.
c.1920 Attributed.

Soutar, William 1898–1943

Scottish poet and diarist, who was confined to bed for the last 13 years of his life with a form of spondylitis. His poems in Scots for adults and children were praised by Hugh MacDiarmid and others.

40 O luely, luely cam she in
And luely she lat doun:
I kent her be her caller lips
And her breists sae sma' an' roun'.

A' thru the nicht we spak nae word
Nor sinder'd bane frae bane:
A' thru the nicht I heard her hert
Gang soundin' wi' my ain.
1932 'The Tryst', stanzas 1-2.

41 Sae luely, luely, cam she in
Sae luely was she gaen
And wi' her a' my simmer days
Like they had never been.
1932 'The Tryst', stanza 4.

Southey, Robert   1774–1843

English poet and writer and friend of Wordsworth. His epics include *Thalaba* (1801) and *Madoc* (1805). His shorter poems are 'The Battle of Blenheim' and 'The Inchcape Rock'. He also wrote a *Life of Nelson* (1813), and became Poet Laureate in 1813.

42 She has made me in love with a cold climate, and frost and snow, with a northern moonlight.
1797 On Mary Wollstonecraft. Letter to his brother Thomas Southey, 28 Apr.

43 You are old, Father William, the young man cried,
The few locks which are left you are grey;
You are hale, Father William, a hearty old man,
Now tell me the reason, I pray.
1799 'The Old Man's Comforts'.
▶ See Carroll 203:66.

44 In the days of my youth I remembered my God!
And He hath not forgotten my age.
1799 'The Old Man's Comforts'.

45 It was a summer evening,
Old Kasper's work was done,
And he before his cottage door
Was sitting in the sun,
And by him sported on the green
His little grandchild Wilhelmine.
1800 'The Battle of Blenheim'.

46 Now tell us all about the war,
And what they fought each other for.
1800 'The Battle of Blenheim'.

47 'And everybody praised the Duke,
Who this great fight did win.'
'But what good came of it at last?'
Quoth little Peterkin.
'Why that I cannot tell,' said he,
'But 'twas a famous victory.'
1800 'The Battle of Blenheim'.

48 Blue, darkly, deeply, beautifully blue.
1805 *Madoc*, 'Lincoya', pt.1, canto 5, 1.102.

49 We wage no war with women nor with priests.
1805 *Madoc*, 'The Excommunication', pt.1, canto 15, 1.65.

50 Curses are like young chickens, they always come home to roost.
1810 *The Curse of Kehama*, motto.

51 Thou has been called, O Sleep! the friend of Woe,
But 'tis the happy who have called thee so.
1810 *The Curse of Kehama*, canto 15, stanza 12.

52 Your true lover of literature is never fastidious.
1812 *The Doctor*, ch.12.

53 Show me a man who cares no more for one place than another, and I will show you in that same person one who loves nothing but himself. Beware of those who are homeless by choice.
1812 *The Doctor*, ch.34.

54 Live as long as you may, the first twenty years are the longest half of your life.
1812 *The Doctor*, ch.130.

55 The death of Nelson was felt in England as something more than a public calamity; men started at the intelligence, and turned pale, as if they had heard of the loss of a dear friend.
1813 *The Life of Nelson*, ch.9.

56 My name is Death: the last best friend am I.
1816 'The Lay of the Laureate', stanza 87.

57 The arts babblative and scribblative.
1829 *Colloquies on the Progress and Prospects of Society*, no.10, pt.2.

58 The march of intellect.
1829 *Colloquies on the Progress and Prospects of Society*, no.14.

Soyinka, Wole   *pseudonym of* **Akinwande Oluwole Soyinka**
1934–

Nigerian dramatist, poet and novelist. He was held as a political prisoner for two years (1967–9). His writing is concerned with the tension between old and new in modern Africa, and includes his first novel, *The Interpreters* (1964), the poetic collection *A Shuttle in the Crypt* (1972), the mostly prose 'prison notes', *The Man Died* (1973) and the play *The Beatification of Area Boy* (1995). He was awarded the Nobel prize for literature in 1986.

59 But the skin of progress
Masks, unknown, the spotted wolf of sameness.
1959 *The Lion and the Jewel* (published 1962), 'Night'.

60 Americans expect to be loved.
1964 *The Interpreters*.

Spacey, Kevin   1959–

US actor. His film appearances include *Glengarry Glen Ross* (1992), *The Usual Suspects* (1995), *LA Confidential* (1997), *American Beauty* (1999) and *The Shipping News* (2001).

61 The less you know about me the easier it is to convince you that I'm the character on screen.
2004 In *The Scotsman*, 20 Apr.

Spark, Dame Muriel Sarah   *née* **Camberg**   1918–2006

Scottish novelist, poet, playwright and writer of short stories. Her many works include biographical studies on Mary Wollstonecraft Shelley (1951) and Emily Brontë (1953) and her best-known novel, *The Prime of Miss Jean Brodie* (1961). She converted to Catholicism in 1954 and lived for many years in Italy.

62 The one certain way for a woman to hold a man is to leave him for religion.
1957 *The Comforters*, ch.1.

63 Parents learn a lot from their children about coping with life.
1957 *The Comforters*, ch.6.

64 Selwyn MacGregor, the nicest boy who ever committed the sin of whisky.
1958 *The Go-Away Bird*, 'A Sad Tale's Best for Winter'.

65 She doesn't have anything to do with youth clubs. There are classes within classes in Peckham.
1960 The Ballad of Peckham Rye, ch.3.

66 A short neck denotes a good mind... You see, the messages go quicker to the brain because they've shorter to go.
1960 The Ballad of Peckham Rye, ch.7.

67 I am putting old heads on your young shoulders...all my pupils are the crème de la crème.
1961 The Prime of Miss Jean Brodie, ch.1.

68 One's prime is elusive. You little girls, when you grow up, must be on the alert to recognise your prime at whatever time of your life it may occur. You must live it to the full.
1961 The Prime of Miss Jean Brodie, ch.1.

69 Give me a girl at an impressionable age, and she is mine for life.
1961 The Prime of Miss Jean Brodie, ch.1.

70 'Whoever has opened the window has opened it too wide,' said Miss Brodie. 'Six inches is perfectly adequate. More is vulgar.'
1961 The Prime of Miss Jean Brodie, ch.3.

71 All the nice people were poor; at least, that was a general axiom, the best of the rich being poor in spirit.
1963 The Girls of Slender Means, ch.1.

72 A nice girl should only fall in love once in her life.
1963 The Girls of Slender Means, ch.2.

73 Every communist has a fascist frown, every fascist a communist smile.
1963 The Girls of Slender Means.

74 Well, it's about everything in particular, isn't it?
1988 Of Proust. A Far Cry from Kensington, ch.6.

75 Beware of men bearing flowers.
Her personal motto, quoted by John Cornwell in the *Sunday Times*, 15 May 1994.

76 Writing a novel you have to be quite aware that what you are writing is not all true. Such a character did not cross the road at such a time; this is not true.
In John Tusa *On Creativity: Interviews Explaining the Process* (2003).

77 I believe I have liberated the novel in many ways, showing how anything whatsoever can be narrated, including sheer damn cheek. I think I have opened doors and windows in the mind, and challenged fears—especially the most inhibiting fears about what a novel should be.
2004 In the *Sunday Herald*, 22 Feb.

78 The dedication of an artist involves willing oblivion to everybody else while the art is being practised, and for the hours ambiguous to it.
2004 The Finishing School.

79 Most marriages, where both or one is an artist, are rickety.—Most marriages of this kind comprise one failed artist.
2004 The Finishing School.

Sparshott, Francis 1926–
Canadian philosopher and professor.

80 For every philosopher, in every age, the first question must be: Just what is philosophy?
1972 Looking for Philosophy, 'Speculation and Reflection'.

Speke, John Hanning 1827–64
English explorer. In 1854, with Richard Burton, he searched for the equatorial lakes of Africa. While travelling alone he discovered Victoria Nyanza, source of the Nile, and in 1860 tracked the Nile flowing out of it. His findings were controversial, and on the day he was to meet with Burton to discuss them he was killed by a shot from his own rifle.

81 The expedition had now performed its functions. I saw that old father Nile without any doubt rises in the Victoria Nyanza, and as I had foretold, that lake is the great source of the holy river which cradled the first expounder of our religious belief.
1863 Journal of the Discovery of the Source of the Nile.

82 As fattening is the first duty of fashionable female life, it must be duly enforced by the rod if necessary. I got up a bit of flirtation with missy, and induced her to rise and shake hands with me. Her face was lovely, but her body was as round as a ball.
1863 In Karagwe, west of Lake Victoria, among the Galla people. *Journal of the Discovery of the Source of the Nile.*

Spencer, Charles, Earl 1964–
English writer and broadcaster.

83 I pledge that we, your blood family, will do all we can to continue the imaginative way in which you were steering these two exceptional young men [the princes, William and Harry] so that their souls are not simply immersed by duty and tradition, but can sing openly as you planned.
1997 Oration at the funeral of his sister, Diana, Princess of Wales, 6 Sep.

Spencer, Herbert 1820–1903
English philosopher. He expounded his evolutionary theories in *Principles of Psychology* (1855), and was a leading advocate of 'Social Darwinism'. Other works included *Social Statics* (1851), *System of Synthetic Philosophy* (1862–93) and an *Autobiography* (1904).

84 No one can be perfectly free until all are free; no one can be perfectly moral till all are moral; no one can be perfectly happy till all are happy.
1851 Social Statics, pt.4, ch.30, section 16.

85 Science is organized knowledge.
1861 Education, ch. 2.

86 The preservation of health is a *duty*. Few seem conscious that there is such a thing as physical morality.
1861 Education, ch.4.

87 It cannot but happen...that those will survive whose functions happen to be most nearly in equilibrium with the modified aggregate of external forces... This survival of the fittest implies multiplication of the fittest.
1865 Principles of Biology, pt.3, ch.12, sect.164.

88 How often misused words generate misleading thoughts.
1879 Principles of Ethics, bk.1, pt.2, ch.8, sect.152.

89 The liberty that the citizen enjoys is to be measured not by the governmental machinery that he lives under, whether representative or otherwise, but by the paucity of restraints that it imposes upon him.
1884 The Man Versus the State.

90 The Republican form of government is the highest form of government; but because of this, it requires the highest

type of human nature—a type nowhere at present existing.
'The Americans', collected in *Essays* (1891).

91 It was remarked to me by the late Mr Charles Roupell... that to play billiards well was a sign of an ill-spent youth.
Quoted in Duncan *Life and Letters of Spencer*, ch.20. Robert Louis Stevenson has also been credited with this observation.

Spender, Sir Stephen Harold 1909–95
English poet and critic. A liberal idealist, he served in the Spanish Civil War, and was a fireman in London during the Blitz. He co-edited *Horizon* (with Cyril Connolly) and later *Encounter*, and published several volumes of poetry and criticism, as well as journals and memoirs.

92 I think continually of those who were truly great.
1933 'I Think Continually of Those'.

93 The names of those who in their lives fought for life,
Who wore at their hearts the fire's centre.
Born of the sun they travelled a short while towards the sun,
And left the vivid air signed with their honour.
1933 'I Think Continually of Those'.

94 What I had not foreseen
Was the gradual day
Weakening the will
Leaking the brightness away
1933 'What I Expected, Was'.

95 For I had expected always
Some brightness to hold in trust,
Some final innocence
To save from dust
1933 'What I Expected, Was'.

96 They lounge at corners of the street
And greet friends with a shrug of shoulder
And turn their pockets out,
The cynical gestures of the poor.
1933 'Moving Through the Silent Crowd'.

97 Never being, but always at the edge of Being.
1933 'Never Being'.

98 My parents kept me from children who were rough
Who threw words like stones and who wore torn clothes
1933 'My Parents Kept Me from Children Who Were Rough'.

99 Who live under the shadow of war,
What can I do that matters?
1933 'Who Live Under the Shadow'.

1 After the first powerful plain manifesto
The black statement of pistons, without more fuss,
But gliding like a queen, she leaves the station.
1933 'The Express'.

2 Pylons, those pillars
Bare like nude, giant girls that have no secret.
1933 'Pylons'.

3 Different living is not living in different places
But creating in the mind a map.
1933 'Different Living'.

4 Consider: only one bullet in ten thousand kills a man.
Ask: was so much expenditure justified
On the death of one so young and so silly
Stretched under the olive trees, Oh, world, Oh, death?
1939 'Regum Ultimo Ratio'.

5 Their collected
Hearts wound up with love, like little watch springs.
1939 'The Past Values'.

6 The light in the window seemed perpetual
Where you stayed in the high room for me
1942 'The Room Above The Square'.

7 The poet shares with other artists the faculty of seeing things as though for the first time.
1942 *Life and the Poet*.

8 Poetry cannot take sides except with life.
1942 *Life and the Poet*.

9 My uncle was famous for his balanced point of view. At the time of which I am writing (when he was nearly seventy) it had become so balanced, that the act of balancing seemed rather automatic. One had only to offer him an opinion for him to balance it with a counter-opinion of exactly the same weight, as a grocer puts a pound weight against a pound of sugar.
1951 *World within World*, p.77.

10 My brothers and sister and I were brought up in an atmosphere which I would describe as 'Puritan decadence'. Puritanism names the behaviour which is condemned; Puritan decadence regards the name itself as indecent, and pretends that the object behind that name does not exist until it is named.
1951 *World within World*, p.314–15.

11 People sometimes divide others into those you laugh at and those you laugh with. The young Auden was someone you could laugh-at-with.
1973 Address at Auden's Memorial Service, Oxford, 27 Oct.

12 But reading is not idleness...it is the passive, receptive side of civilization without which the active and creative world would be meaningless. It is the immortal spirit of the dead realised within the bodies of the living. It is sacramental.
1980 Journal entry, 4 Jan.

13 We were obsessed by the feeling that this was the supreme cause of our time. The cause of poets and of writers. The cause of freedom. And that unless the cause of anti-Fascism was won, unless Fascism was defeated, we would be unable to exist as writers.
1982 Speaking on the ITV series *The Spanish Civil War*, no.3, 'Battleground for idealists'.

Spenser, Edmund c.1552–1599
English poet. Educated at Cambridge, he held positions in government, including secretary to the lord deputy in Ireland during a period of rebellion, for most of his life, although he died in poverty. His epic Protestant romance, *The Faerie Queen*, was published in two instalments, Books I–III (1590) and Books IV–VI (1596). Other works include *The Shepherd's Calendar* (1579), *Colin Clout's Come Home Again* (1595), *Amoretti* and *Epithalamion* (1595), and *Four Hymns* (1596).

14 Go little book, thy self present,
As child whose parent is unkent:
To him that is the president
Of noblesse and of chivalry,
And if that Envy bark at thee,
As sure it will, for succour flee.
1579 *The Shepherd's Calendar*, 'To His Book'.

15 Bring hither the pink and purple columbine,
With gillyflowers:
Bring coronation, and sops in wine,
Worn of paramours.
Strew me the ground with daffadowndillies,
And cowslips, and kingcups, and loved lilies.
1579 The Shepherd's Calendar, 'April', l.136–41.

16 And he that strives to touch the stars,
Oft stumbles at a straw.
1579 The Shepherd's Calendar, 'July', l.99–100.

17 Uncouth unkist, said the old famous poet Chaucer.
1579 The Shepherd's Calendar, 'Letter to Gabriel Harvey'.

18 So now they have made our English tongue a gallimaufry or hodgepodge of all other speeches.
1579 The Shepherd's Calendar, 'Letter to Gabriel Harvey'.

19 A gentle knight was pricking on the plain.
1590 The Faerie Queen, bk.1, canto 1, stanza 1.

20 The sailing pine, the cedar proud and tall,
The vine-prop elm, the poplar never dry,
The builder oak, sole king of forests all,
The aspen good for staves, the cypress funeral.

The laurel, meed of mighty conquerors
And poets sage, the fir that weepeth still,
The willow worn of forlorn paramours,
The ewe obedient to the benders will,
The birch for shafts, the sallow for the mill,
The myrrh sweet bleeding in the bitter wound,
The warlike beech, the ash for nothing ill,
The fruitful olive, and the platan round,
The carver holme, the maple seldom inward sound.
1590 The Faerie Queen, bk.1, canto 1, stanzas 8–9. plantan=plane tree; holme=holly.

21 Oft fire is without smoke.
1590 The Faerie Queen, bk.1, canto 1, stanza 12.

22 A stately palace built of squarèd brick,
Which cunningly was without mortar laid,
Whose walls were high, but nothing strong, nor thick,
And golden foil all over them displayed,
That purest sky with brightness they dismayed.
1590 Of the palace of pride. The Faerie Queen, bk.1, canto 4, stanza 4.

23 And by his side rode loathsome Gluttony,
Deformèd creature, on a filthy swine.
1590 The Faerie Queen, bk.1, canto 4, stanza 21.

24 Fretting grief the enemy of life.
1590 The Faerie Queen, bk.1, canto 4, stanza 35.

25 But who can turn the stream of destiny,
Or break the chain of strong necessity?
1590 Night argues against the necessity of faith. The Faerie Queen, bk.1, canto 5, stanza 25.

26 What worlds delight, or joy of living speech
Can heart, so plunged in sea of sorrows deep,
And heapèd with so huge misfortunes, reach?
The careful cold beginneth for to creep,
And in my heart his iron arrow steep,
Soon as I think upon my bitter bale.
1590 The Faerie Queen, bk.1, canto 7, stanza 39.

27 Still as he fled, his eye was backward cast,
As if his fear still followed him behind.
1590 The Faerie Queen, bk.1, canto 9, stanza 21.

28 Sleep after toil, port after stormy seas,
Ease after war, death after life does greatly please.
1590 The Faerie Queen, bk.1, canto 9, stanza 40.

29 Where justice grows, there grows eke greater grace.
1590 The Faerie Queen, bk.1, canto 9, stanza 53

30 His iron coat all overgrown with rust,
Was underneath envelopèd with gold,
Whose glistering gloss darkened with filthy dust,
Well yet appearèd, to have been of old
A work of rich entail, and curious mold,
Woven with antics and wild imagery.
1590 Of Mammon. The Faerie Queen, bk.2, canto 7, stanza 4.

31 And all for love, and nothing for reward.
1590 The Faerie Queen, bk.2, canto 8 stanza 2.

32 Of all God's works, which do this world adorn,
There is no one more fair and excellent,
Then is mans body both for power and form,
Whiles it is kept in sober government.
1590 The Faerie Queen, bk.2, canto 9, stanza 1.

33 So passeth, in the passing of a day,
Of mortal life the leaf, the bud, the flower,
No more doth flourish after first decay,
That erst was sought to deck both bed and bower,
Of many a lady, and many a paramour:
Gather therefore the rose, whilst yet is prime,
For soon comes age, that will her pride deflower:
Gather the rose of love, whilst yet is time,
Whilst loving thou mayst lovèd be with equal crime.
1590 The Faerie Queen, bk.2, canto 12, stanza 75.

34 Nought so of love this looser dame did skill,
But as a coal to kindle fleshly flame,
Giving the bridle to her wanton will,
And treading underfoot her honest name.
1590 Of Malecasta. The Faerie Queen, bk.3, canto 1, stanza 50.

35 But as it falleth, in the gentlest hearts
Imperious love hath highest set his throne,
And tyrannizeth in the bitter smarts
Of them, that to him buxom are and prone.
1590 The Faerie Queen, bk.3, canto 2, stanza 23.
buxom = 'yielding'.

36 Most sacred fire, that burnest mightily
In living breasts, ykindled first above,
Amongst th'eternal spheres and lamping sky,
And thence poured into men, which men call Love.
1590 The Faerie Queen, bk.3, canto 3, stanza 1.

37 Where is the antique glory now become,
What whilom wont in women to appear?
Where be the brave achievements doen by some?
Where be the battles, where the shield and spear,
And all the conquests, which them high did rear,
That matter made for famous poet's verse,
And boastful men so oft abashed to hear?
Bene they all dead, and laid in doleful hearse?
Or doen they only sleep, and shall again reverse?
1590 The Faerie Queen, bk.3, canto 4, stanza 1.

38 But ah, who can deceive his destiny,
Or ween by warning to avoid his fate?
1590 The Faerie Queen, bk.3, canto 4, stanza 27.

39 There is continual spring, and harvest there
Continual, both meeting at one time:
For both the boughs do laughing blossoms bear,

And with fresh colours deck the wanton prime,
And eke attonce the heavy trees they climb,
Which seem to labour under their fruits load:
The whiles the joyous birds make their pastime
Amongst the shady leaves, their sweet above,
And their true loves without suspicion tell abroad.
1590 Of the Garden of Adonis. *The Faerie Queen*, bk.3, canto 6, stanza 42.

40 Yet never can he die, but dying lives,
And doth himself with sorrow new sustain,
That death and life attonce unto him gives,
And painful pleasure turns to pleasing pain.
1590 *The Faerie Queen*, bk.3, canto 10, stanza 60.

41 And as she looked about, she did behold,
How over that same door was likewise writ,
Be bold, be bold, and everywhere Be bold…
At last she spied at that room's upper end
Another iron door, on which was writ
Be not too bold.
1590 *The Faerie Queen*, bk.3, canto 11, stanza 54.

42 Of such deep learning little had he need,
Ne yet of Latin, ne of Greek that breed
Doubts 'mongst divines, and difference of texts,
From when arise diversity of sects,
And hateful heresies.
1591 *Prosopopoia*, l.385–9.

43 Most glorious Lord of Life! that, on this day,
Didst make Thy triumph over death and sin;
And having harrowed hell, didst bring away
Captivity thence captive, us to win:
1595 *Amoretti*, sonnet 68.

44 But when I plead, she bids me play my part,
And when I weep, she says tears are but water:
And when I sigh, she says I know the art,
And when I wail, she turns herself to laughter.
1595 *Amoretti*, sonnet 18.

45 The merry cuckoo, messenger of Spring,
His trumpet shrill hath thrice already sounded.
1595 *Amoretti*, sonnet 19.

46 Most glorious Lord of Life! that, on this day,
Didst make Thy triumph over death and sin;
And having harrowed hell, didst bring away
Captivity thence captive, us to win:
1595 *Amoretti*, sonnet 68.

47 One day I wrote her name upon the strand,
But came the waves and washèd it away;
Again I wrote it with a second hand,
But came the tide, and made my pains his prey.
'Vain man,' said she, 'that doest in vain assay
A mortal thing so to immortalise,
For I my self shall like to this decay,
And eke my name be wipèd out likewise.'
'Not so,' quod I, 'let baser things devise
To die in dust, but you shall live by fame:
My verse your virtues rare shall eternise,
And in the heavens write your glorious name.
Where when as death shall all the world subdue,
Our love shall live, and later life renew.'
1595 *Amoretti*, sonnet 75.

48 In youth, before I waxèd old,
The blind boy, Venus' baby,

For want of cunning made me bold,
In bitter hive to grope for honey.
1595 *Amoretti*, 'Anacreontics', no.1.

49 Open the temple gates unto my love,
Open them wide that she may enter in.
1595 *Epithalamion*, section 12.

50 Pour out the wine without restraint or stay,
Pour not by cups, but by the belly full,
Pour out to all that will,
And sprinkle all the posts and walls with wine,
That they may sweat, and drunken be withal.
1595 *Epithalamion*, section 14.

51 Ah when will this long weary day have end,
And lend me leave to come unto my love?
How slowly do the hours their numbers spend!
How slowly does sad Time his feathers move!
1595 *Epithalamion*, section 16.

52 Dan Chaucer, well of English undefiled,
On Fame's eternal beadroll worthy to be filed.
1596 *The Faerie Queen*, bk.4, canto 2, stanza 32.

53 O sacred hunger of ambitious minds.
1596 *The Faerie Queen*, bk.5, canto 12, stanza 1.

54 A monster, which the Blatant beast men call,
A dreadful fiend of gods and men ydrad.
1596 *The Faerie Queen*, bk.5, canto 12, stanza 37.

55 Me seems the world is run quite out of square,
And being once amiss grows daily worse and worse.
1596 *The Faerie Queen*, bk.5, proem, stanza 1.

56 For that which all men then did virtue call,
Is now called vice; and that which vice was hight,
Is now hight virtue, and so used of all:
Right now is wrong, and wrong that was is right,
1596 *The Faerie Queen*, bk.5, proem, stanza 4.

57 Yet is that glass so gay, that it can blind
The wisest sight, to think gold that is brass.
1596 Of the mirror of fashion. *The Faerie Queen*, bk.6, proem, stanza 5.

58 The gentle mind by gentle deeds is known.
For a man by nothing is so well bewrayed,
As by his manners.
1596 *The Faerie Queen*, bk.6, canto 3, stanza 1.

59 Sweet Thames, run softly, till I end my song.
1596 *Prothalamion*, l.1.

60 What man that sees the ever-whirling wheel
Of Change, the which all mortal things doth sway,
But that thereby doth find, and plainly feel,
How mutability in them doth play
Her cruel sports, to many men's decay?
1609 *The Faerie Queen*, 'Mutability', canto 6, stanza 1.

61 First, sturdy March with brows full sternly bent,
And armèd strongly, rode upon a ram,
The same which over Hellespontus swam:
Yet in his hand a spade he also hent,
And in a bag all sorts of seeds ysame,
Which on the earth he strowèd as he went,
And filled her womb with fruitful hope of nourishment.
1609 *The Faerie Queen*, 'Mutability', canto 7, stanza 32.
hent = grasped; ysame = together.

62 Jolly June, arrayed
All in green leaves, as he a Player were.
1609 *The Faerie Queen*, 'Mutability', canto 7, stanza 35.

63 Next was November, he full gross and fat,
As fed with lard, and that right well might seem;
For, he had been a fatting hogs of late.
1609 *The Faerie Queen*, 'Mutability', canto 7, stanza 40.

64 I was promised on a time,
To have reason for my rhyme;
From that time unto this season,
I received nor rhyme nor reason.
'Lines on his Pension.' Attributed.

Spielberg, Steven 1947–

US film-maker. His many films include *Jaws* (1975), *Close Encounters of the Third Kind* (1977), *The Color Purple* (1985), *Schindler's List* (1993), *Men in Black* (1997), *Saving Private Ryan* (1998) and *Lincoln* (2012).

65 I hope we're such a communal society that we'll always insist on sharing an adventure in the dark with strangers, no matter what the platform hardware. That's my wish and dream—that we never give up the communal experience. It started a long time ago with cave paintings and I hope it doesn't go away.
2002 On whether cinema has a future. Quoted on www.filmmonthly.com, 12 Dec.

66 Technology can be our best friend, and technology can also be the biggest party pooper of our lives. It interrupts our own story, interrupts our ability to have a thought or a daydream, to imagine something wonderful because we're too busy bridging the walk from the cafeteria back to the office on the cell phone.
2002 In *Wired*, Jun.

67 Movies are always in a state of locomotion. You start with a general idea of how it should feel and then you find you've got a runaway train. You have to race to catch up: the movie is telling you what it wants to become, and when that happens there's no greater feeling.
2011 In *Newsweek*, 19 Dec.

Spillane, Mickey *properly* Frank Morrison Spillane
1918–2006

US popular novelist. He wrote for pulp magazines to pay for his education, and produced his first novel *I, the Jury* in 1947. His private detective character Mike Hammer inspired many films and a television series.

68 There are more salted peanuts consumed than caviar.
Defending his low-brow fiction. Quoted in Neil J Jones (ed) *A Book of Days for the Literary Year* (1984).

Spinoza, Baruch *also known as* Benedict de Spinoza
1632–77

Dutch philosopher, of Jewish descent. The *Tractatus Theologico-Politicus* was published in 1670, and the more famous *Ethics* in 1677. His pantheistic monism led to accusations of atheism but was influential in the development of metaphysics.

69 *Sedulo curavi, humanas actiones non ridere, non lugare, neque detestari, sed intelligere.*
I have striven not to laugh at human actions, not to weep at them, nor to hate them, but to understand them.
1670 *Tractatus Theologico-Politicus*, bk.1, pt.4.

70 *Quicquid est, in Deo est, et nihil sine Deo esse necque concipi potest.*
Whatever is, is in God, and nothing can exist or be conceived without God.
1677 *Ethics*, bk.1, prop.15.

71 *In rerum natura nullum datur contingens; sed omnia ex necessitate divinae naturae determinata sunt ad certo modo existandum et operandum.*
In the nature of things nothing contingent is granted, but all things are determined by the necessity of divine nature for existing and working in a certain way.
1677 *Ethics*, bk.1, prop.29.

72 *Nempe falluntur homines, quod se liberos esse putant; quae opinio in hoc solo consistit, quod suarum actionum sint conscii, et ignari causarum, a quibus determinantur. Haec ergo est eorum libertatis idea, quod suarum actionum nullam cognoscant causam.*
Men are mistaken in thinking themselves free; and this opinion consists of this alone, that they are conscious of their actions and ignorant of the causes by which they are determined. This, therefore, is their idea of liberty, that they should know no cause of their actions.
1677 *Ethics*, bk.2, prop.35, note.

73 *Veritas norma sua est.*
Truth is its own standard.
1677 *Ethics*, bk.2, prop.43, note.

74 *De natura Rationis est, res sub quadam aeternitatis specie percipere.*
It is the nature of reason to perceive things under a certain species of eternity.
1677 *Ethics*, bk.2, prop.44, corollary 2.

75 *Unaquaeque res, quantum in se est, in suo esse perseverare conatur.*
Everything in so far as it is in itself endeavours to persist in its own being.
1677 *Ethics*, bk.3, prop.6.

76 *Nihil nos conari, velle, appetere, neque cupere, quia id bonum esse judicamus; sed contra, nos propterea aliquid bonum esse judicare, quia id conamur, volumus, appetimus, atque cupimus.*
We endeavour, wish, desire, or long for nothing because we deem it good; but on the other hand, we deem a thing good because we endeavour, wish for, desire, or long for it.
1677 *Ethics*, bk.3, prop.9, note.

77 *Nempe Amor nihil aliud est, quam Laetitia concomitante idea causae externae; et Odium nihil aliud est, quam Tristitia concomitante idea causae externae.*
Love is nothing else than pleasure accompanied by the idea of an external cause; and hate pain accompanied by the idea of an external cause.
1677 *Ethics*, bk.3, prop.13, note.

78 *Ex virtute absoluto agere nihil aliud in nobis est, quam ex ductu Rationis agere, vivere, suum esse conservare (haec tria idem significant) ex fundamento proprium utile quaerendi.*
To act absolutely according to virtue is nothing else in us than to act under the guidance of reason, to live so, and to preserve one's being (these three have the same meaning) on the basis of seeking what is useful to oneself.
1677 *Ethics*, bk.4, prop.24.

79 *Summum Mentis bonum est Dei cognitio, et summa Mentis virtus Deum cognoscere.*
The greatest good of the mind is the knowledge of God, and the greatest virtue of the mind is to know God.
1677 *Ethics*, bk.4, prop.28.

80 *Homo liber de nulla re minus quam de morte cogitat; et ejus sapienta non mortis, sed vitae meditatio est.*
A free man thinks of nothing less than of death, and his wisdom is a meditation not of death but of life.
1677 *Ethics*, bk.4, prop.67.

81 *In vita itaque apprime utile est, intellectum seu Rationem, quantum possumus, perficere, et in hoc uno summa hominis felicitas seu beatitudo consistit; quippe beatitudo nihil aliud est, quam ipsa animi acquiescentia quae ex Dei intuitiva cognitione oritur.*
It is therefore extrememly useful in life to perfect as much as we can the intellect or reason, and of this alone does the greatest happiness or blessedness of man exist: for blessedness is nothing else than satisfaction of mind which arises from the intuitive knowledge of God.
1677 *Ethics*, bk.4, appendix.

82 *Ex tertio cognitionis genere oritur necessario Amor Dei intellectualis.*
From the third kind of knowledge [intuition] arises necessarily the intellectual love of God.
1677 *Ethics*, bk.5, prop.32, corollary.

83 *Per Deum intelligo ens absolute infinitum, hoc est, substantiam constantem infinitis attributis, quorum unumquodque aeternam et infinitam essentiam exprimit.*
By God I mean a being absolutely infinite—that is, a substance consisting in infinite attributes, of which each expresses eternal and infinite essentiality.
1677 *Ethics*.

Spock, Dr Benjamin McLane 1903–98

US paediatrician. His *Common Sense Book of Baby and Child Care* (1946) sold over 30 million copies, transforming childcare. He gave up psychiatry to devote himself to pacifism, and ran for the presidency in 1972.

84 You know more than you think you do.
1946 *The Common Sense Book of Baby and Child Care*, opening words.

85 To win in Vietnam, we will have to exterminate a nation.
1968 *Dr Spock on Vietnam*, ch.7.

Springer, Jerry (Gerald Norman) 1944–

English-born US television presenter. Formerly Democratic mayor of Cincinnati, Ohio, he has hosted *The Jerry Springer Show* since 1991.

86 Until next time, take care of yourself and each other.
His catchphrase.

Spring-Rice, Sir Cecil Arthur 1858–1918

English diplomat.

87 I vow to thee, my country—all earthly things above— Entire and whole and perfect, the service of my love.
1918 *I Vow To Thee, My Country*.

Springsteen, Bruce 1949–

US rock singer and guitarist. His albums include *Born To Run* (1975) and *Born In The USA* (1984).

88 We gotta get out while we're young 'Cause tramps like us, baby, we were born to run.
1975 'Born to Run'.

Spurgeon, Charles Haddon 1834–92

English Baptist preacher, famous for his eloquent sermons. A strong Calvinist, he left the Evangelical Alliance (1864) and Baptist Union (1887) over doctrinal differences and a concern for orthodoxy.

89 If you want truth to go round the world you must hire an express train to pull it; but if you want a lie to go round the world, it will fly: it is as light as a feather, and a breath will carry it. It is well said in the old proverb, 'a lie will go round the world while truth is pulling its boots on'.
Collected in *Gems from Spurgeon* (1859).

Squire, Sir J(ohn) C(ollings) 1884–1958

English poet and editor. He was an influential anti-modernist figure in the 1920s, with a gift for amusing parody.

90 It did not last: the Devil howling 'Ho! Let Einstein be!' restored the status quo.
1926 'In Continuation of Pope on Newton'.

91 But I'm not so think as you drunk I am.
1931 'Ballade of Soporific Absorption'.

Staël, Germaine Necker, Baronne de 1766–1817

French author of important critical, political and philosophical essays as well as novels and plays seen as precursors of Romanticism. She was an opponent of Napoleon.

92 *L'amour est l'histoire de la vie des femmes, c'est un épisode dans celle des hommes.*
Love is the story of a woman's life, but only an episode in the life of a man.
1796 *De l'influence des passions sur le bonheur des individus et des nations*.

93 *La force de l'esprit ne se développe toute entière qu'en attaquant la puissance.*
The mind fully develops its faculties when it attacks power.
1800 *De la littérature considererée dans ses rapports avec les institutions sociales*.

94 *En cherchant la gloire, j'ai toujours espéré qu'elle me ferait aimer.*
I have pursued fame always in the hope of winning her love.
1807 *Corinne ou de l'Italie*.

95 *Quand une fois on a tourné l'enthousiasme en ridicule, on a tout défait, excepté l'argent et le pouvoir.*
Once we have made enthusiasm ridiculous, there is nothing left but money and power.
1807 *Corinne ou de l'Italie*.

96 *Les païens ont divinisé la vie, et les chrétiens ont divinisé la mort.*
Pagans deified life and Christians deified death.
1807 *Corinne ou de l'Italie*.

97 *On dirait que l'âme des justes donne, comme les fleurs, plus de parfums vers le soir.*
It seems that the soul of the just gives off, like flowers, a stronger scent towards evening.
1807 *Corinne ou de l'Italie.*

98 *On cesse de s'aimer si quelqu'un ne nous aime.*
We stop loving ourselves when no one loves us.
1810 *De l'Allemagne.*

99 *La première condition pour écrire, c'est une manière de sentir vive et forte.*
The primary requirement for a writer is to feel keenly and strongly.
1810 *De l'Allemagne.*

1 *En France, on étudie les hommes; en Allemagne, les livres.*
In France, they study men; in Germany, books.
1810 *De l'Allemagne.*

2 *La poésie est le langage naturel de tous les cultes.*
Poetry is the natural language of all religions.
1810 *De l'Allemagne.*

3 *Le sentiment de l'infini est le véritable attribut de l'âme.*
To feel the infinite is the true attribute of the soul.
1810 *De l'Allemagne.*

Stalin, Joseph *originally Iosif Vissarionovich Dzhugashvili* 1879–1953

Soviet leader. Appointed General Secretary to the Communist Party Central Committee (1922), enabling him to take power after Lenin's death in 1924. His collectivization was responsible for millions of deaths, as were his political purges (1934–38). Although he signed a non-aggression pact with Hitler (1939), he declared war, joining the Allies, when Hitler threatened the Soviet Union in 1941.

4 In the name of the Constitution, Cromwell took up arms, executed the king, dissolved Parliament, imprisoned some, and beheaded others.
1934 In conversation with H G Wells, Moscow.

5 To attempt to export revolution is nonsense.
1936 Said to Roy Howard, US newspaper proprietor, 1 Mar.

6 History shows that there are no invincible armies.
1941 Radio broadcast, 3 Jul, announcing the declaration of war against Germany, three weeks before Hitler invaded.

7 Communism fits Germany as a saddle fits a cow.
1944 In conversation with the Polish politician, Stanislaw Mikolajcik, Aug.

Stallone, Sylvester 1946–

US actor and film director, best known for his roles in action films such as *Rocky* (1976) and *Rambo* (1985) and their sequels.

8 Playing polo is like trying to play golf during an earthquake.
1990 Quoted in Colin Jarman *The Guinness Dictionary of Sports Quotations* (1990).

9 Peace is an accident, war is natural. Old men start it, young men fight it, everybody in the middle dies, and nobody tells the truth.
2007 As John Rambo in *Rambo IV* (screenplay by Art Monterastelli and Sylvester Stallone).

Stamp, Sir Josiah Charles, Baron Stamp of Shortlands 1880–1941

British economist and statistician, who published early estimates of the British national income.

10 The first argument that is brought against every new proposal departing from conventional lines is nearly always that it is impracticable.
1921 *Fundamental Principles of Taxation*, p.95.

Stanley, Sir Henry Morton *originally John Rowlands* 1841–1904

Welsh-born US explorer and journalist. He fought on both sides in the American Civil War and then, as a journalist, was commissioned by the *New York Herald* to lead an expedition in search of Dr David Livingstone, who was rumoured to have died while exploring rivers in Central Africa. On one of the three subsequent expeditions he travelled the length of the Congo.

11 I would have run to him, only I was a coward in the presence of such a mob—would have embraced him, only, he being an Englishman, I did not know how he would receive me; so I did what cowardice and false pride suggested was the best thing—walked deliberately to him, took off my hat, and said:
'Dr Livingstone, I presume?'
'Yes,' said he, with a kind smile, lifting his cap slightly.
I replace my hat on my head, and he puts on his cap, and we both grasp hands, and I then say aloud:
'I thank God, Doctor, I have been permitted to see you.'
He answered, 'I feel thankful that I am here to welcome you.'
1872 *How I Found Livingstone in Central Africa.*

Stanton, Elizabeth *née Cady* 1815–1902

US reformer and suffragette; organizer of the first Women's Rights Convention, Seneca Falls, US (1848). She is remembered chiefly as co-author of *The History of Woman Suffrage* (1881–6) and she also wrote *The Women's Bible* (1895).

12 We hold these truths to be self-evident: that all men and women are created equal; that they are endowed by their Creator with certain inalienable rights; that among these are life, liberty, and the pursuit of happiness.
1848 'Declaration of Sentiments', Seneca Falls Women's Rights Convention, 19–20 Jul. This is modelled on the American Declaration of Independence of 4 Jul 1776.

13 Quite as many false ideas prevail as to woman's true position in the home as to her status elsewhere. Womanhood is the great fact in her life; wifehood and motherhood are but incidental relations.
1881 *The History of Woman Suffrage 1848–61*, vol.1, introduction.

14 Men are the Brahmin, women the Pariahs, under our existing civilization.
1881 *The History of Woman Suffrage 1848–61*, vol.1, ch.1, 'Preceding Causes'.

15 Although woman has performed much of the labor of the world, her industry and economy have been the very means of increasing her degradation.
1881 *The History of Woman Suffrage 1848–61*, vol.1, ch.1, 'Preceding Causes'.

16 As to woman's subjection…it is important to note that equal dominion is given to woman over every living

thing, but not one word is said giving man dominion over woman.
1895 *The Woman's Bible*, pt.1, ch.1, 'Comments on Genesis'.

17 The Old Testament makes woman a mere after-thought in creation; the author of evil; cursed in her maternity; a subject in marriage; and all female life, animal and human, unclean.
1898 *The Woman's Bible*, pt.2, preface.

18 'Self-development is a higher duty than self-sacrifice', should be a woman's motto henceforward.
1898 *The Woman's Bible*, pt.2, 'Comments on Mark'.

Stanwyck, Barbara *originally* Ruby Stevens 1907–90

American film, television and radio actress. She was a dancer in the Ziegfeld Follies at the age of 13 and went on to play gutsy, pioneering women in westerns such as *Annie Oakley* (1935), as well as sultry femmes fatales in films noirs, including *Double Indemnity* (1944). She became a successful radio star in the 1960s.

19 To eat, to survive and to have a good coat.
1987 Her three goals in life, recalled on receiving the American Film Institute Life Achievement Award. Reported in the *New York Times*, 11 Apr.

Stapledon, Olaf 1886–1950

English writer and social philosopher. He used science fiction as a means of embodying his social theories.

20 That strange blend of the commercial traveller, the missionary, and the barbarian conqueror, which was the American abroad.
1930 *Last and First Men*, ch.3.

Stark, Dame Freya Madeleine 1893–1993

English writer and traveller, born in Paris. She studied Arabic and made her first journey to the Middle East in 1928, after which she travelled extensively in Europe, the Middle East and Asia, writing over 30 books.

21 The great and almost only comfort about being a woman is that one can always pretend to be more stupid than one is and no one is surprised.
1934 *The Valley of the Assassins*.

22 I came to the conclusion that some more ascetic reason than mere enjoyment should be found if one wishes to travel in peace: to do things for fun smacks of levity, immorality almost, in our utilitarian world. And though personally I think the world is wrong, and I know in my heart of hearts that it is a most excellent reason to do things merely because one likes the doing of them, I would advise all those who wish to see unwrinkled brows in passport offices to start out ready labelled as entomologists, anthropologists, or whatever other -ology they think suitable and propitious.
1936 *The Valleys of the Assassins and other Persian Travels*.

23 The true call of the desert, of the mountains, or the sea, is their silence—free from the networks of dead speech.
1948 *Perseus in the Wind*.

24 This is the prospect from the watershed, and when the traveller reaches it, it is a good thing to take an hour's leisure and look out on the visible portions of the journey, since never in one's life can one see the same view twice.
1948 *Perseus in the Wind*.

25 The *inscrutability* of the East is, indeed, I believe a myth… The ordinary inhabitant is incomprehensible merely to people who never trouble to have anything much to do with them.
1963 *The Journey's Echo*.

Stark, John 1728–1822

American revolutionary commander. He saw service in the French and Indian war (1754–9), and at Bunker Hill (1775) and Bennington (1777) during the American Revolution.

26 We beat them today or Molly Stark's a widow.
1777 Speech before the Battle of Bennington, 16 Aug. Quoted in *Cyclopaedia of American Biography*, vol.5.

Starr, Roger 1918–2001

US businessman, housing administrator and journalist.

27 A busy man who can keep up a daily journal resembles a person preparing for bed with the shades up… When such a man publishes parts of his journal, the reader must conclude he always knew the lights were on.
1989 On George F Kennan *Sketches From a Life* (1989). In the *Washington Post*, 8 May.

Steacie, E W 1900–62

Canadian government official, President of the National Research Council of Canada (1952).

28 The academic atmosphere, produced mainly by the humanities, is the only atmosphere in which pure science can flourish.
1956 Collected in J D Babbitt (ed) *Science in Canada: Selections from the Speeches of E. W. Steacie* (1965).

29 An efficient organization is one in which the accounting department knows the exact cost of every useless administrative procedure which they themselves have initiated.
Quoted by J D Babbitt in his introduction to Steacie's *Science in Canada* (published posthumously, 1965).

Stead, William Thomas 1849–1912

English journalist and reformer. Editor of the *Pall Mall Gazette* (1883–90). He drowned in the *Titanic* disaster.

30 The Press is at once the eye and the ear and the tongue of the people. It is the visible speech, if not the voice, of the democracy. It is the phonograph of the world.
1886 'Government by Journalism', in the *Contemporary Review*, May. Collected in *A Journalist on Journalism* (1892).

31 He may be more potent than any other man. The damnable iteration day after day of earnest conviction wears like the dropping of the water upon the stone.
1886 Of the journalist. 'Government by journalism', in the *Contemporary Review*, May. Collected in *A Journalist on Journalism* (1892).

32 An editor is the uncrowned king of an educated democracy.
1886 'Government by Journalism', in the *Contemporary Review*, May. Collected in *A Journalist on Journalism* (1892).

33 The duty of a journalist is the duty of a watchman.
1886 'Government by Journalism', in the *Contemporary Review*, May. Collected in *A Journalist on Journalism* (1892).

34 It is the great inspector, with a myriad eyes, who never sleeps, and whose daily reports are submitted, not to a functionary or department, but to the whole people.

1886 Of a newspaper. 'Government by Journalism', in the *Contemporary Review*, May. Collected in *A Journalist on Journalism* (1892).

35 What a marvellous opportunity for attacking the devil!
Letter of appointment to the *Northern Echo*, quoted by Harold Evans in his preface to Ray Boston *The Essential Fleet Street* (1990).

Steel, David Martin Scott Steel, Baron 1938–

Scottish Liberal politician. He sponsored a controversial bill to reform abortion laws (1966–7), and was active in the anti-apartheid movement. The last Liberal leader (1976–88), he led the Liberals into an Alliance with the Social Democrats (1981) and later negotiated their merger. From 1999 to 2003 he was the Presiding Officer of the Scottish Parliament.

36 I have the good fortune to be the first Liberal for over half a century who is able to say to you at the end of our annual Assembly, go back to your constituencies and prepare for government.
1981 Speech at party conference, 18 Sep.

37 [Margaret Thatcher] has turned the British bulldog into a Reagan poodle.
1986 In *Time*, 28 Apr.

38 I trust that the Duke of Edinburgh will not disagree that this ancient capital whose name he bears, with its legal and ecclesiastical headquarters and its worldwide reputation for quality education and financial management has nonetheless until now seemed like a body with its heart missing.
1999 At the opening of the Scottish Parliament, 12 May.

Steele, Sir Richard 1672–1729

Irish essayist, dramatist and politician. His plays include *The Funeral* (1701). He founded the *Tatler* (1709–11), a periodical published three times a week, on which he was joined by Joseph Addison. Together they founded the *Spectator*, a daily which ran from 1711 to 1712 under their joint editorship.

39 Dear Prue,
If a servant I sent last night got to Hampton-court, you received 29 walnuts and a letter from me. I inclose the Gazette; and am, with all my soul,
Your passionate lover, and faithful husband,
RICH. STEELE
1708 Letter, 20 Sep (published 1787).

40 I am, dear Prue, a little in drink, but at all times your faithful husband,
RICH. STEELE
1708 Letter, 27 Sep (published 1787).

41 It is to be noted that when any part of this paper appears dull there is a design in it.
1709 In the *Tatler*, no.38, 7 Jul.

42 To love her is a liberal education.
1709 Of Lady Elizabeth Hastings *Tatler*, no.49, 2 Aug.

43 Every man is the maker of his own fortune
1709 In the *Tatler*, no.52, 9 Aug.

44 It gave me a great notion of the credit of our present government and administration, to find people press as eagerly to pay money as they would to receive it; and, at the same time, a due respect for that body of men who have found out so pleasing an expedient for carrying on the common cause, that they have turned a tax into a diversion.
1710 On the first state lottery of 1710. In the *Tatler*, no.124, 24 Jan.

45 Reading is to the mind what exercise is to the body.
1710 In the *Tatler*, no.147, 18 Mar. Also attributed to Addison.

46 Let your precept be, Be Easy.
1710 In the *Tatler*, no.196, 11 Jul.

47 I was undone by my Auxiliary; when I had once called him in, I could not subsist without Dependance on him.
1711 Of Addison's contribution to the *Tatler*. Preface to vol.4 of the collected edition.

48 I have heard Will Honeycomb say, A Woman seldom Writes her Mind but in her Postscript.
1711 In the *Spectator*, no.79, 30 May.

49 We were in some little time fixed in our seats, and sat with that dislike which people not too good-natured usually conceive of each other at first sight.
1711 Embarking on a coach journey. In the *Spectator*, no.132, 1 Aug.

50 I am confident that no boy, who will not be allured to letters without blows, will ever be brought to anything with them.
1711 On flogging in schools. In the *Spectator*, no.157, 30 Aug.

51 Those grave fellows are my aversion who sift everything with the utmost nicety, and find the malignity of a lie in a piece of humour, pushed a little beyond exact truth.
1713 In the *Guardian*, no.42, 29 Apr.

Stefansson, Vilhjalmur 1879–1962

Canadian Arctic explorer and author.

52 There are two kinds of Arctic problems, the imaginary and the real. Of the two, the imaginary are the most real.
1945 *The Arctic in Fact and Fable*.

53 What is the difference between unethical and ethical advertising? Unethical advertising uses falsehoods to deceive the public; ethical advertising uses truth to deceive the public.
Discovery (published 1964).

54 A land may be said to be discovered the first time a European, presumably an Englishman, sets foot on it.
Discovery (published 1964).

Steffens, (Joseph) Lincoln 1866–1936

US journalist. While editor of *McClure's Magazine* (1902–6), his revision of an article on city corruption led to a series published as *The Shame of the Cities* (1904), a key work in urban reform. His *Struggle for Self-Government* (1906) analysed corruption and reform at state level.

55 I have seen the future and it works.
1919 On his visit to post-Revolutionary Russia, in *Autobiography* (2 vols, 1931).
▶ See Toynbee 895:76.

Stegner, Wallace Earle 1909–93

US novelist. Professor of English at Stanford University.

56 A political animal can be defined as a body that will go on circulating a petition even with its heart cut out.
1954 *Beyond the Hundredth Meridian*.

57 If you're going to get old, you might as well get as old as you can get.

1989 On his 80th birthday. Reported in the *San Francisco Chronicle*, 6 Mar.

Steichen, Edward Jean 1879–1973

Belgian-born US photographer, credited with developing photography as an art form. He also pioneered aerial and naval photography during World Wars I and II.

58 Photography was conceived as a mirror of the universal elements and emotions of the everydayness of life—as a mirror of the essential oneness of mankind throughout the world.
Quoted in *Dialogue*, May 1989.

Stein, Gertrude 1874–1946

US writer, influential in the development of Modernism. She settled in Paris in 1903, where with her friend Alice B Toklas she dominated expatriate life. Her less experimental works include *The Autobiography of Alice B. Toklas* (1933) and *Everybody's Autobiography* (1937).

59 You are so afraid of losing your moral sense that you are not willing to take it through anything more dangerous than a mud-puddle.
1903 'Q.E.D.', bk.1. Collected in *Fernhurst, Q.E.D., and Other Early Writings* (1971).

60 Rose is a rose is a rose is a rose, is a rose.
1914 *Tender Buttons*, 'Sacred Emily'.

61 You are all a lost generation.
Quoted as epigraph in Ernest Hemingway *The Sun Also Rises* (1926).

62 He had added to his stories a little story of meditations and in these he said that The Enormous Room was the greatest book he had ever read. It was then that Gertrude Stein said, Hemingway, remarks are not literature.
1933 *The Autobiography of Alice B. Toklas*, ch.7.

63 Pigeons on the grass alas.
1934 *Four Saints in Three Acts*, act 3, sc.2.

64 Disillusionment in living is the finding out nobody agrees with you . . . Complete disillusionment is when you realise that no one can for they can't change.
1934 *The Making of Americans*, ch.5.

65 In the United States there is more space where nobody is than where anybody is. That is what makes America what it is.
1936 *The Geographical History of America*.

66 Native always means people who belong somewhere else, because they had once belonged somewhere. That shows that the white race does not really think they belong anywhere because they think of everybody else as native.
1937 *Everybody's Autobiography*, ch.1.

67 Anything scares me, anything scares anyone but really after all considering how dangerous everything is nothing is really very frightening.
1937 *Everybody's Autobiography*, ch.2.

68 It takes a lot of time to be a genius, you have to sit around so much doing nothing, really doing nothing.
1937 *Everybody's Autobiography*, ch.2.

69 What was the use of my having come from Oakland it was not natural to have come from there yes write about it if I like or anything if I like but not there, there is no there there.
1937 *Everybody's Autobiography*, ch.4.

70 Two things are always the same the dance and war.
1937 *Everybody's Autobiography*, ch.5.

71 Everybody gets so much information all day long that they lose their common sense.
1959 'Reflection on the Atomic Bomb', collected in Robert A Goodwin (ed) *Readings in World Politics* (1959).

72 Nature is commonplace. Imitation is more interesting.
Quoted in Sir Charles Spencer Chaplin *My Autobiography* (1964).

73 You should only read what is truly good or what is frankly bad.
Quoted in Ernest Hemingway *A Moveable Feast* (1964), ch.3.

74 Anyone who marries three girls from St Louis hasn't learned much.
Of Ernest Hemingway. Quoted in R Mellow *Charmed Circle* (1974), ch.16.

75 Just before she died she asked, 'What is the answer?' No answer came. She laughed and said, 'In that case what is the question?' Then she died.
Last words, as quoted in D Sutherland *Gertrude Stein* (1951), ch.6.

76 She said he was a village explainer, excellent if you were a village, but if you were not, not.
Of Ezra Pound. Quoted in J Hobhouse *Everyone Who Was Anybody* (1975), ch.6.

Stein, Herbert 1916–99

US economist, member of the Council of Economic Advisers under Nixon, Ford and Reagan.

77 *Consumer*: A person who is capable of choosing a president but incapable of choosing a bicycle without help from a government agency.
1979 *Washington Bedtime Stories*.

78 Whatever may be the distribution of uncertainty among economists, the public only gets to hear from those who have certain opinions.
1979 *Washington Bedtime Stories*.

79 A few weeks ago I had a revelation and told my secretary that I could give him a synthesis of forty-six years of living with economic policy. It is: 'Economic policy is random with respect to the performance of the American economy, but, thank God, there isn't much of it.'
1979 *Washington Bedtime Stories*.

Steinbeck, John Ernest 1902–68

US novelist. His works include *Of Mice and Men* (1937), *The Grapes of Wrath* (1939) and *East of Eden* (1952). He received the Nobel prize for literature in 1962.

80 Man, unlike any other thing organic or inorganic in the universe, grows beyond his work, walks up the stairs of his concepts, emerges ahead of his accomplishments.
1939 *The Grapes of Wrath*, ch.14.

81 I know this—a man got to do what he got to do.
1939 *The Grapes of Wrath*, ch.18.

82 Okie use' ta mean you was from Oklahoma. Now it means you're a dirty son-of-a-bitch. Okie means you're scum. Don' mean nothing itself, it's the way they say it.
1939 *The Grapes of Wrath*, ch.18.

83 Well, maybe like Casy says, a fellow ain't got a soul of his own, but on'y a piece of a big one—an then—... Then it don' matter. Then I'll be all aroun' in the dark. I'll

be everywhere—wherever you look. Wherever they's a fight so hungry people can eat, I'll be there. Wherever they's a cop beatin' up a guy, I'll be there. If Casy knowed, why, I'll be in the way guys yell when they're mad an'—I'll be in the way kids laugh when they're hungry an' they know supper's ready. An' when our folks eat the stuff they raise an' live in the houses they build—why, I'll be there. See?
1939 *The Grapes of Wrath*, ch.28.

84 All Americans believe that they are born fishermen. For a man to admit a distaste for fishing would be like denouncing mother-love or hating moonlight.
1954 Quoted in Colin Jarman *The Guinness Dictionary of Sports Quotations* (1990).

85 Unless the bastards have the courage to give you unqualified praise, I say ignore them.
1958 Of critics. Quoted in J K Galbraith *The Affluent Society* (1977), introduction.

86 I pulled to the side of the street and got out my book of road maps. But to find where you are going, you must know where you are, and I didn't.
1962 *Travels With Charley In Search of America*.

87 A journey is like a marriage. The certain way to be wrong is to think you control it.
1962 *Travels With Charley In Search of America*, pt.1.

88 It is the nature of a man as he grows older, a small bridge in time, to protest against change, particularly change for the better.
1962 *Travels With Charley In Search of America*, pt.2.

89 The profession of book writing makes horse racing seem like a solid, stable business.
1962 In *Newsweek*, 24 Dec.

90 A good writer always works at the impossible.
Recalled on his death, 20 Dec 1968.

Steinem, Gloria 1934–

US feminist and writer. She emerged as a leading figure in the women's movement in the 1960s, and as a campaigner against the Vietnam War and racism. She co-founded the Women's Action Alliance (1970) and *Ms* magazine (1971).

91 A woman needs a man like a fish needs a bicycle.
c.1970 Attributed, in various forms.

92 This is what forty looks like. We've been lying so long who would know?
c.1974 Response when complimented by a reporter on not looking forty years old, quoted by Lisa Jardine in 'Still Angry After All These Years', in the *Sunday Times*, 15 May 1994.

93 What would happen if…men could menstruate and women could not? Clearly, menstruation would become an enviable, boast-worthy, masculine event: Men would brag about how long and how much. Young boys would talk about it as the envied beginning of manhood… Generals, right-wing politicians, and religious fundamentalists would cite …'*mens*-truation' as proof that only men could serve God and country in combat… If men could menstruate, the power justifications would go on and on. If we let them.
1978 'If Men could Menstruate', collected in *Outrageous Acts and Everyday Rebellions* (1983).

94 I've finally figured out why soap operas are, and logically should be, so popular with generations of housebound women. *They are the only place in our culture where grown-up men take seriously all the things that grown-up women have to deal with all day long.*
1980 'Night Thoughts of a Media Watcher', collected in *Outrageous Acts and Everyday Rebellions* (1983).

95 There's no such thing as post-feminism. It's like saying post-democracy, excuse me, what does that mean? We're nowhere near equality, so the very idea of post-feminism is ridiculous. The same people who thirty to forty years ago said the women's movement is not necessary, 'it's going against nature, my wife is not interested', are the same people now saying 'well, it used to be necessary but not anymore'. The very invention of the word post-feminism is the current form of resistance.
2009 Radio interview.

96 Labelling makes the invisible visible, but it's limiting. Categories are the enemy of connecting. Link, don't rank.
Quoted in Katie Couric, *The Best Advice I Ever Got* (2011).

97 You can't do it all. No one can have two full-time jobs, have perfect children and cook three meals and be multi-orgasmic 'till dawn … Superwoman is the adversary of the women's movement.
Quoted in Oprah Winfrey, 'Gloria Steinem on Progress and Women's Rights', Oprah Winfrey Network (2012).

Steiner, George 1929–

French-born US literary critic and scholar.

98 Where God's presence is no longer a tenable proposition and where his absence is no longer a felt, indeed overwhelming weight, certain dimensions of thought and creativity are no longer attainable.
1989 *Real Presences*.

Steinmetz, Charles Proteus 1865–1923

German-born US electrical engineer and inventor, whose most notable work was the development of alternating current.

99 In the realm of science, all attempts to find any evidence of supernatural beings, of metaphysical concepts, as God, immortality, infinity, etc have thus far failed, and if we are honest, we must confess that in science there exists no God, no immortality, no soul or mind, as distinct from the body.
1941 In the *American Freeman*, Jul.

Steloff, Frances 1887–1989

US bookseller. She worked at Loeser's Department Store, New York City, then at Bretanos where she ran the drama department (1917–19). She founded Gotham Book Mart, New York City, in 1920.

1 Wise men fish here.
Sign for Gotham Book Mart. Quoted in the *New York Times*, 30 Dec 1987.

Stendhal *pseudonym of* Henri Beyle 1783–1842

French writer who lived many years in Italy, he wrote novels and treatises on literature. He held a modernist concept of Romanticism and was opposed to those who sought literary models from the past.

2 *L'esprit et le génie perdent vingt-cinq pour cent de leur valeur, en débarquant en Angleterre.*

The mind and genius lose twenty-five percent of their value on entry into England.
1830 *Le Rouge et le noir*, bk.2, ch.7.

3 *La politique au milieu des intérêts d'imagination, c'est un coup de pistolet au milieu d'un concert.*
Politics mixed with the imagination is like a shot fired in the middle of a concert.
1830 *Le Rouge et le noir*, bk.2, ch.22.

4 *Grand Dieu! Pourquoi suis-je moi?*
Great God! Why am I me?
1830 *Le Rouge et le noir*, bk.2, ch.28.

5 *Le pire des malheurs en prison, pensa-t-il, c'est de ne pouvoir fermer sa porte.*
The worst of prison life, he thought, was not being able to close his door.
1830 *Le Rouge et le noir*, bk.2, ch.44.

6 *Les gens qu'on honore ne sont que des fripons qui ont eu le bonheur de n'être pas pris en flagrant délit.*
Respected people are only rascals who have had the good fortune not to be caught in the act.
1830 *Le Rouge et le noir*, bk.2, ch.44.

Stengel, Casey (Charles Dillon) 1890–1975

US baseball player and manager. An outfielder with the Brooklyn Dodgers and other teams, he became manager of the New York Yankees (1949–62), leading them to seven World Series victories, and of the New York Mets (1962–5).

7 The secret of managing a ball club is to keep the five guys who hate you away from the five who are undecided.
Quoted in Colin Jarman *The Guinness Dictionary of Sports Quotations* (1990).

8 There's three things you can do in a baseball game—you can win, you can lose, or it can rain.
Quoted in Colin Jarman *The Guinness Dictionary of Sports Quotations* (1990).

9 Without losers, where would the winners be?
Quoted in Colin Jarman *The Guinness Dictionary of Sports Quotations* (1990).

10 Not bad. Most people my age are dead. You could look it up.
Attributed, when asked how he was. 'You could look it up' was one of his catchphrases.

Stephen, J(ames) K(enneth) 1859–92

English lawyer and journalist, a cousin of Virginia Woolf. He began a weekly paper, *The Reflector* in 1888 and was a successful parodist and light versifier.

11 Two voices are there: one is of the deep;
It learns the storm-clouds thundrous melody,
Now roars, now murmurs with the changing sea,
Now bird-like pipes, now closes soft in sleep:
And one is of an old half-witted sheep
Which bleats articulate monotony,
And indicates that two and one are three,
That grass is green, lakes damp, and mountains steep
And, Wordsworth, both are thine.
1896 *Lapsus Calami*, 'A Sonnet'.

12 Will there never come a season
Which shall rid us of the curse
Of a prose which knows no reason
And an unmelodious verse...
When there stands a muzzled stripling,
Mute, beside a muzzled bore:
When the Rudyards cease from kipling
And the Haggards Ride no more.
'To R K'.

Stephenson, Bette 1924–

Former President of the Canadian Medical Association and Ontario Minister of Health.

13 Men are very fragile creatures. Their psyches are so closely tied to their epididymis.
1975 Interviewed by Christina McCall Newman in *The Globe and Mail*, 12 Jul. The epididymis is the tube carrying sperm out from the testicle.

Sterling, Bruce 1954–

US science fiction writer.

14 Unfortunately, computers are...stupid. Unlike human beings, computers possess the truly profound stupidity of the inanimate.
1992 *The Hacker Crackdown: law and disorder on the electronic frontier*.

15 It's a truism in technological development that no silver lining comes without its cloud.
1993 Opening statement to the House Subcommittee on Telecommunications and Finance, Washington DC, 29 Apr.

16 Cyberspace is the funhouse mirror of our own society.
1993 National Academy of Sciences Convocation on Technology and Education, Washington DC, 10 May.

17 Tomorrow composts today.
2005 *Shaping Things*.

Stern, Robert A(rthur) M(orton) 1939–

US architect and writer, author of *New Directions in American Architecture* (1969, revised 1977) and *The House that Bob Built* (1991).

18 The dialogue between client and architect is about as intimate as any conversation you can have because, when you're talking about building a house, you're talking about dreams.
1985 'The Trend-Setting Traditionalism of Architecture', in the *New York Times*, 13 Jan.

19 Our greatest responsibility is not to be pencils of the past.
1985 'The Trend-Setting Traditionalism of Architecture', in the *New York Times*, 13 Jan.

Sterne, Laurence 1713–68

Irish novelist. He extended the scope of the novel with his major work *Tristram Shandy* (1759–67). As his health failed, he spent much of his time in France and Italy and published *A Sentimental Journey through France and Italy* in 1768.

20 I wish either my father or my mother, or indeed both of them, as they were in duty both equally bound to it, had minded what they were about when they begot me.
1759–67 *Tristram Shandy*, bk.1, ch.1.

21 'Pray, my dear,' quoth my mother, 'have you not forgot to wind up the clock?'—'Good G—?' cried my father, making an exclamation, but taking care to moderate his voice at the same time,—'Did ever woman, since the

creation of the world, interrupt a man with such a silly question?'
1759–67 *Tristram Shandy*, bk.1, ch.6.

22 As we jog on, either laugh with me, or at me, or in short do anything,—only keep your temper.
1759–67 Tristram to reader. *Tristram Shandy*, bk.1, ch.6.

23 Have not the wisest of men in all ages, not excepting Solomon himself,—have they not had their Hobby-Horses…and so long as a man rides his Hobby-Horse peaceably and quietly along the King's highway, and neither compels you or me to get up behind him,—pray, Sir, what have either you or I to do with it?
1759–67 *Tristram Shandy*, bk.1, ch.7.

24 He was in a few hours of giving his enemies the slip for ever.
1759–67 Of Eugenis. *Tristram Shandy*, bk.1, ch.12.

25 'Tis known by the name of perseverance in a good cause,—and of obstinacy in a bad one.
1759–67 Toby. *Tristram Shandy*, bk.1, ch.17.

26 What is the character of a family to an hypothesis? my father would reply.
1759–67 *Tristram Shandy*, bk.1, ch.21.

27 My uncle Toby would never offer to answer this by any other kind of argument, than that of whistling half a dozen bars of Lillabullero.
1759–67 *Tristram Shandy*, bk.1, ch.21.

28 Digressions, incontestably, are the sunshine;—they are the life, the soul of reading;—take them out of this book for instance,—you might as well take the book along with them.
1759–67 *Tristram Shandy*, bk.1, ch.22.

29 I should have no objection to this method, but that I think it must smell too strong of the lamp.
1759–67 Toby. *Tristram Shandy*, bk.1, ch.23.

30 Writing, when properly managed (as you may be sure I think mine is) is but a different name for conversation.
1759–67 *Tristram Shandy*, bk.2, ch.11.

31 'I'll not hurt thee,' says my uncle Toby, rising from his chair, and going across the room, with the fly in his hand, 'I'll not hurt a hair of thy head:—Go,' says he, lifting up the sash, and opening his hand as he spoke, to let it escape;—'go, poor devil, get thee gone, why should I hurt thee?—This world surely is wide enough to hold both thee and me.'
1759–67 *Tristram Shandy*, bk.2, ch.12.

32 Whenever a man talks loudly against religion,—always suspect that it is not his reason, but his passions which have got the better of his creed.
1759–67 Trim. *Tristram Shandy*, bk.2, ch.17.

33 It is the nature of an hypothesis, when once a man has conceived it, that it assimilates everything to itself, as proper nourishment; and, from the first moment of your begetting it, it generally grows the stronger by every thing you see, hear, read, or understand.
1759–67 *Tristram Shandy*, bk.2, ch.19.

34 'Our armies swore terribly in Flanders,' cried my uncle Toby,—'but nothing to this.'
1759–67 *Tristram Shandy*, bk.3, ch.11.

35 The corregiescity of Corregio.
1759–67 *Tristram Shandy*, bk.3, ch.12.

36 Of all the cants which are canted in this canting world,—though the cant of hypocrites may be the worst,—the cant of criticism is the most tormenting.
1759–67 *Tristram Shandy*, bk.3, ch.12.

37 Is this a fit time, said my father to himself, to talk of Pensions and Grenadiers?
1759–67 *Tristram Shandy*, bk.4, ch.5.

38 True *Shandeism*, think what you will against it, opens the heart and lungs, and like all those affections which partake of its nature, it forces the blood and other vital fluids of the body to run freely through its channels, and makes the wheel of life run long and cheerfully round.
1759–67 *Tristram Shandy*, bk.4, ch.32.

39 'There is no terror, brother Toby, in its looks, but what it borrows from groans and convulsions—and the blowing of noses, and the wiping away of tears with the bottoms of curtains, in a dying man's room—Strip it of these, what is it?'—'Tis better in battle than in bed,' said my uncle Toby.
1759–67 Of death. *Tristram Shandy*, bk.5, ch.3.

40 There is a North-west passage to the intellectual World.
1759–67 *Tristram Shandy*, bk.5, ch.42.

41 To say a man is fallen in love,—or that he is deeply in love,—or up to the ears in love,—and sometimes even over head and ears in it,—carries an idiomatical kind of implication, that love is a thing below a man:—this is recurring again to Plato's opinion, which, with all his divinityship,—I hold to be damnable and heretical:—and so much for that. Let love therefore be what it will,—my uncle Toby fell into it.
1759–67 *Tristram Shandy*, bk.6, ch.37.

42 My brother Toby, quoth she, is going to be married to Mrs Wadman. Then he will never, quoth my father, lie *diagonally* in his bed again as long as he lives.
1759–67 *Tristram Shandy*, bk.6, ch.39.

43 Now hang it! quoth I, as I look'd towards the French coast—a man should know something of his own country too, before he goes abroad.
1759–67 Tristram. *Tristram Shandy*, bk.7, ch.2.

44 And who are you? Said he.—Don't puzzle me, said I.
1759–67 Tristram to the commissary. *Tristram Shandy*, bk.7, ch.33.

45 'A soldier,' cried my uncle Toby, interrupting the corporal, 'is no more exempt from saying a foolish thing, Trim, than a man of letters.'—'But not so often, an' please your honour,' replied the corporal.
1759–67 *Tristram Shandy*, bk.8, ch.19.

46 Everything presses on—whilst thou art twisting that lock,—see! it grows grey; and every time I kiss thy hand to bid adieu, and every absence which follows it, are preludes to that eternal separation which we are shortly to make.
1759–67 Tristram to Jenny. *Tristram Shandy*, bk.9, ch.8.

47 '—d!' said my mother, 'what is all this story about?'—'A Cock and a Bull,' said Yorick.
1759–67 *Tristram Shandy*, bk.9, ch.33.

48 A man cannot dress, but his ideas get cloath'd at the same time.
1759–67 *Tristram Shandy*, bk.9, ch.13.

49 This sad vicissitude of things.
1767 *Sermons*, 'The Character of Shimei', no.16.

50 They order, said I, this matter better in France.
1768 A Sentimental Journey, opening words.

51 As an Englishman does not travel to see Englishmen, I retired to my room.
1768 A Sentimental Journey, 'Preface. In the Desobligeant'.

52 I pity the man who can travel from Dan to Beersheba, and cry, 'tis all barren.
1768 A Sentimental Journey, 'In the Street. Calais'.

53 I had had an affair with the moon, in which there was neither sin nor shame.
1768 A Sentimental Journey, 'The Monk, Calais'.

54 If ever I do a mean action, it must be in some interval betwixt one passion and another.
1768 A Sentimental Journey, 'Montriul'.

55 Vive l'amour! Et vive la bagatelle!
1768 A Sentimental Journey, 'The Latter'.

56 Hail, ye small sweet courtesies of life.
1768 A Sentimental Journey, 'The Pulse, Paris'.

57 There are worse occupations in this world than feeling a woman's pulse.
1768 A Sentimental Journey, 'The Pulse, Paris'.

58 God tempers the wind, said Maria, to the shorn lamb.
1768 A Sentimental Journey, 'Maria'. This is an allusion to an old French proverb.

59 Dear sensibility! Source inexhausted of all that's precious in our joys, or costly in our sorrows!
1768 A Sentimental Journey, 'The Bourbonnois'.

Steuart (later Denham), Sir James 1712–80

Scottish advocate and economist. A fervent Jacobite who was a member of the Council of Prince Charles Edward Stuart in 1745 and subsequently in exile until 1763, travelling extensively on the Continent and studying political economy. His *Principles of Political Oeconomy* (1767) was soon eclipsed by the *Wealth of Nations* of Adam Smith.

60 To preserve a trading state from decline, the greatest care must be taken, to support a perfect balance between the hands employed in work and the demand for their labour.
1767 Inquiry into the Principles of Political Oeconomy.

61 It is the business of a statesman to judge of the expediency of different schemes of economy, and by degrees to model the minds of his subjects so as to induce them from the allurement of private interest to concur in the execution of his plan.
1767 Inquiry into the Principles of Political Oeconomy.

Stevens, Brooks 1911–95

US industrial designer.

62 Our whole economy is based on planned obsolescence... We make good products, we induce people to buy them, and then the next year we deliberately introduce something that will make these products old-fashioned, out of date, obsolete.
Quoted in Vance Packard *The Waste Makers* (1960), ch.6. This is thought to be the first use of the phrase 'planned obsolescence'.

Stevens, Roger Lacey 1910–98

US theatrical producer. He worked as a real estate broker (1934–60) but was increasingly involved as a producer in over 200 theatrical productions. He was Chair of the National Council on the Arts (1965–9), and a member of the President's Committee on Arts and Humanities.

63 Whenever I think, I make a mistake.
1955 In 'How Businessmen Make Decisions', *Fortune*, Aug.

Stevens, Wallace 1879–1955

US poet. He began as a journalist and lawyer, then joined an insurance company. *Harmonium*, his first collection of philosophical verse, appeared in 1923. Further works include *The Man with the Blue Guitar* (1937) and *Collected Poems* (1954, winner of a Pulitzer Prize).

64 I placed a jar in Tennessee,
And round it was, upon a hill.
It made the slovenly wilderness
Surround that hill.
1923 Harmonium, 'Anecdote of the Jar'.

65 Poetry is the supreme fiction, madame.
Take the moral law and make a nave of it
And from the nave build haunted heaven.
1923 Harmonium, 'A High-Toned Old Christian Woman'.

66 Call the roller of big cigars,
The muscular one, and bid him whip
In kitchen cups of concupiscent curds.
1923 Harmonium, 'The Emperor of Ice-Cream'.

67 The only emperor is the emperor of ice-cream.
1923 Harmonium, 'The Emperor of Ice-Cream'.

68 I shall whisper
Heavenly labials in a world of gutterals.
It will undo him.
1923 Harmonium, 'The Plot Against the Giant'.

69 Complacencies of the peignoir, and late
Coffee and oranges in a sunny chair,
And the green freedom of a cockatoo
Upon a rug mingle to dissipate
The holy hush of ancient sacrifice.
1923 Harmonium, 'Sunday Morning', pt.1.

70 What is divinity if it can come
Only in silent shadows and in dreams?
1923 Harmonium, 'Sunday Morning', pt.2.

71 And, in the isolation of the sky,
At evening, casual flocks of pigeons make
Ambiguous undulations as they sink,
Downward to darkness, on extended wings.
1923 Harmonium, 'Sunday Morning', pt.8.

72 Chieftain Iffucan of Azcan in caftan
Of tan with henna hackles, halt!
1923 Harmonium, 'Bantams in Pine-Woods'.

73 Just as my fingers on these keys
Make music, so the self-same sounds
On my spirit make a music, too.

Music is feeling, then, not a sound;
And thus it is that what I feel,
Here in this room, desiring you,

Thinking of your blue-shadowed silk,
Is music.
1923 Harmonium, 'Peter Quince at the Clavier', pt.1.

74 I do not know which to prefer,
The beauty of inflections
Or the beauty of innuendoes,
The blackbird whistling
or just after.
1923 *Harmonium*, 'Thirteen Ways of Looking At A Blackbird', pt.5.

75 I know noble accents
And lucid, inescapable rhythms;
But I know, too,
That the blackbird is involved
In what I know.
1923 *Harmonium*, 'Thirteen Ways of Looking At A Blackbird', pt.8.

76 What counted was the mythology of self,
Blotched out beyond unblotching.
1923 *Harmonium*, 'The Comedian as the Letter C', pt.1.

77 Like a dull scholar, I behold, in love,
An ancient aspect touching a new mind.
It comes, it blooms, it bears its fruit and dies.
This trivial trope reveals a way of truth.
Our bloom is gone. We are the fruit thereof.
1923 *Harmonium*, 'Le Monocle de Mon Oncle', pt.8.

78 Only, here and there, an old sailor,
Drunk and asleep in his boots,
Catches tigers
In red weather.
1923 *Harmonium*, 'Disillusionment of Ten O'Clock'.

79 It was her voice that made
The sky acutest at its vanishing.
She measured to the hour its solitude.
She was the single artificer of the world
In which she sang.
1935 *Ideas of Order*, 'The Idea of Order at Key West'.

80 They said, 'You have a blue guitar,
You do not play things as they are.'
The man replied, 'Things as they are
Are changed upon a blue guitar.'
1937 *The Man with the Blue Guitar and Other Poems*, title poem.

81 It has to be living, to learn the speech of the place,
It has to face the man of the time.
1942 *Parts of a World*, 'Of Modern Poetry'.

82 The first idea was not our own.
1942 *Notes Toward A Supreme Fiction*, 'It Must Be Abstract'.

83 There was a muddy centre before we breathed
There was a myth before the myth began,
Venerable and articulate and complete.
1942 *Notes Toward A Supreme Fiction*, 'It Must Be Abstract'.

84 They will get it straight one day at the Sorbonne.
We shall return at twilight from the lecture
Pleased that the irrational is rational.
1942 *Notes Toward A Supreme Fiction*, 'It Must Give Pleasure'.

85 Not evocations but last choirs, last sounds,
With nothing else compounded, carried full,
Pure rhetoric of a language without words.
1947 *Transport to Summer*, 'Credences of Summer'.

86 Sentimentality is a failure of feeling.
1957 *Opus Posthumous*, Aphorisms, 'Adagia'.

87 Poetry is a means of redemption.
1957 *Opus Posthumous*, Aphorisms, 'Adagia'.

88 Literature is based not on life but on propositions about life, of which this is one.
1957 *Opus Posthumous*, Aphorisms, 'Adagia'.

89 Poetry must resist the intelligence almost successfully.
1957 *Opus Posthumous*, Aphorisms, 'Adagia'.

90 All poetry is experimental poetry.
1957 *Opus Posthumous*, Aphorisms, 'Adagia'.

91 Ethics are no more a part of poetry than they are of painting.
1957 *Opus Posthumous*, Aphorisms, 'Adagia'.

92 The poet makes silk dresses out of worms.
1957 *Opus Posthumous*, Aphorisms, 'Adagia'.

93 After one has abandoned a belief in God, poetry is the essence which takes its place as life's redemption.
1957 *Opus Posthumous*, Aphorisms, 'Adagia'.

94 Authors are actors, books are theatres.
1957 *Opus Posthumous*, Aphorisms, 'Adagia'.

95 The poet represents the mind in the act of defending us against itself.
1957 *Opus Posthumous*, Aphorisms, 'Adagia'.

96 Poetry is a rich, full-blooded whistle, cracked ice crunching in pails, the night that numbers the leaf, the duet of two nightingales, the sweet pea, that has run wild, Creation's tears in shoulder blades.
Quoted in *Life*, 13 Jun 1960.

97 Money is a kind of poetry.
Quoted in *Harper's*, Oct 1985.

98 Words of the world are the life of the world.
Quoted in Brendan Gill *A New York Life* (1990).

99 Poetry is the supreme fiction, madame.
Quoted in Helen Gardner (ed) *The New Oxford Book of English Verse* (1991).

Stevenson, Adlai E(wing) 1900–65

US Democratic politician, Governor of Illinois (1948). He helped to found the United Nations (1946), stood twice against Eisenhower as presidential candidate (1952, 1956), and was the US Delegate to the UN (1961–5).

1 A lie is an abomination unto the Lord, and a very present help when in trouble.
1951 Speech, Washington, Jan.

2 It is often easier to fight for principles than to live up to them.
1952 Speech, New York, 27 Aug.

3 If Republicans will stop telling lies about the United States, we will stop telling the truth about them.
1952 Speech at Bakersfield, California. Quoted in *Time*, 10 Sep.

4 Looking back, I am content. Win or lose I have told you the truth as I see it. I have said what I meant and meant what I said.
1952 Concluding his campaign. Reported in *Time*, 10 Sep.

5 Man has wrested from nature the power to make the world a desert or to make the deserts bloom. There is no evil in the atom—only in men's souls.
1952 Speech, Connecticut, 18 Sep.

6 When political ammunition runs low, inevitably the rusty artillery of abuse is wheeled into action.
1952 Speech, New York, 22 Sep.

7 My definition of a free society is a society in which it is safe to be unpopular.
   1952 Speech, Detroit, Oct.

8 Eggheads of the world unite; you have nothing to lose but your yolks.
   1952 Presidential election campaign speech.

9 Via ovum cranium difficilis est. The way of the egghead is hard.
   1954 Reply to charges that he was too intellectual. Lecture at Harvard, 17 Mar.

10 Shouting is not a substitute for thinking and reason is not the subversion but the salvation of freedom.
   1954 Lecture at Harvard, 17 Mar.

11 Technology, while adding daily to our physical ease, throws daily another loop of fine wire around our souls. It contributes hugely to our mobility, which we must not confuse with freedom. The extensions of our senses, which we find so fascinating, are not adding to the discrimination of our minds, since we need increasingly to take the reading of a needle on a dial to discover whether we think something is good or bad, or right or wrong.
   1955 'My Faith in Democratic Capitalism', in *Fortune*, Oct.

12 You will find that the truth is often unpopular and the contest between agreeable fancy and disagreeable fact is unequal. For, in the vernacular, we Americans are suckers for good news.
   1958 Speech, Michigan, 8 Jun.

13 Freedom is not an ideal; it is not even a protection, if it means nothing more than the freedom to stagnate.
   1960 *Putting First Things First*.

14 We have confused the free with the free and easy.
   1960 *Putting First Things First*.

15 The Republican Party needs to be dragged kicking and screaming into the 20th century.
   Quoted in Kenneth Tynan *Curtains* (1961).

16 It will be helpful in our mutual objective to allow every man in America to look his neighbour in the face and see a man—not a colour.
   1964 In the *New York Times*, 22 Jun.

17 He who slings mud generally loses ground.
   Recalled on his death, 14 Jul 1965.

18 You can't teach an underdog new tricks.
   On presidential hopeful Estes Kefauver's replay of his anti-bossism theme. Quoted in *Newsweek*, 1 Nov 1971.

19 The best politics is good government.
   Quoted by New York Governor Mario Cuomo in the *New York Times*, 26 Aug 1990.

20 A politician is a statesman who approaches every question with an open mouth.
   Attributed.

21 He is the kind of politician who would cut down a redwood tree and then mount the stump to make a speech for conservation.
   On Richard M Nixon. Attributed.

22 In America, any boy may become president. I suppose that's just one of the risks that he takes.
   Attributed.

Stevenson, Robert Louis 1850–94

Scottish author. He wrote travel sketches, essays, short stories, serials and romantic thrillers, including *Treasure Island* (1883), *The Strange Case of Dr Jekyll and Mr Hyde* (1886) and *Kidnapped* (1886). In his early years he toured Belgium and northern France by canoe and the Cévennes by donkey, described in *Travels with a Donkey in the Cévennes* (1879). He struggled for many years against tuberculosis and spent the last five years of his life living on his estate in Samoa.

23 For will anyone dare to tell me that business is more entertaining than fooling among boats? He must have never seen a boat, or never seen an office, who says so. And for certain the one is a great deal better for the health.
   1878 *An Inland Voyage*, 'The Royal Sport Nautique'.

24 Respectability is a very good thing in its way, but it does not rise superior to all considerations. I would not for a moment venture to hint that it was a matter of taste; but I think I will go as far as this: that if a position is admittedly unkind, uncomfortable, unnecessary, and superfluously useless, although it were as respectable as the Church of England, the sooner a man is out of it, the better for himself, and all concerned.
   1878 *An Inland Voyage*, 'At Maubeuge'.

25 The gauger walked with willing foot,
   And aye the gauger played the flute;
   And what should Master Gauger play
   But *Over the hills and far away*?
   1878 'A Song of the Road', stanza 1 (dated 'Forest of Montargis, 1878'), collected in *Underwoods* (1887), bk.1, no.2.

26 If a man knows he will sooner or later be robbed upon a journey, he will have a bottle of the best in every inn, and look upon all his extravagances as so much gained upon the thieves.
   1878 *An Inland Voyage*, 'The Oise in Flood'.

27 The most patient people grow weary at last with being continually wetted with rain; except, of course, in the Scottish Highlands, where there are not enough fine intervals to point the difference.
   1878 *An Inland Voyage*, 'Down the Oise: to Compiègne'.

28 For my part, I travel not to go anywhere, but to go. I travel for travel's sake. The great affair is to move.
   1879 *Travels with a Donkey*, 'Cheylard and Luc'.

29 I opened a tin of Bologna sausage and broke a cake of chocolate, and that was all I had to eat. It may sound offensive, but I ate them together, bite by bite, by way of bread and meat. All I had to wash down this revolting mixture was neat brandy; a revolting beverage in itself. But I was rare and hungry; ate well, and smoked one of the best cigarettes in my experience. Then I put a stone in my straw hat, pulled the flap of my fur cap over my neck and eyes, put my revolver ready to hand, and snuggled well down among the sheepskins.
   1879 *Travels with a Donkey*.

30 I own I like definite form in what my eyes are to rest upon; and if landscapes were sold, like the sheets of characters of my boyhood, one penny plain and twopence coloured, I should go the length of twopence every day of my life.
   1879 *Travels with a Donkey*, 'Father Apollinaris'.

31 To live out of doors with the woman a man loves is of all lives the most complete and free.
   1879 *Travels with a Donkey*, 'A Night Among the Pines'.

32 The fact is, we are much more afraid of life than our ancestors, and cannot find it in our hearts either to marry

or not to marry. Marriage is terrifying, but so is a cold and forlorn old age.
1881 *Virginibus Puerisque*, 'Virginibus Puerisque', pt.1.

33 In marriage, a man becomes slack and selfish, and undergoes a fatty degeneration of his moral being.
1881 *Virginibus Puerisque*, 'Virginibus Puerisque', pt.1.

34 I see women marry indiscriminately with staring burgesses and ferret-faced, white-eyed boys, and men dwell in contentment with noisy scullions, or taking into their lives acidulous vestals.
1881 *Virginibus Puerisque*, 'Virginibus Puerisque', pt.1.

35 And you have only to look these happy couples in the face, to see they have never been in love, or in hate, or in any other high passion all their days.
1881 *Virginibus Puerisque*, 'Virginibus Puerisque', pt.1.

36 Even if we take marriage at its lowest, even if we regard it as no more than a sort of friendship recognised by the police.
1881 *Virginibus Puerisque*, 'Virginibus Puerisque', pt.1.

37 Lastly (and this is, perhaps, the golden rule) no woman should marry a teetotaller, or a man who does not smoke.
1881 *Virginibus Puerisque*, 'Virginibus Puerisque', pt.1.

38 Marriage is a step so grave and decisive that it attracts light-headed, variable men by its very awfulness.
1881 *Virginibus Puerisque*, 'Virginibus Puerisque', pt.1.

39 Marriage is like life in this—that it is a field of battle, and not a bed of roses.
1881 *Virginibus Puerisque*, 'Virginibus Puerisque', pt.1.

40 Times are changed with him who marries; there are no more by-path meadows, where you may innocently linger, but the road lies long and straight and dusty to the grave. Idleness, which is often becoming and even wise in the bachelor, begins to wear a different aspect when you have a wife to support.
1881 *Virginibus Puerisque*, 'Virginibus Puerisque', pt.2.

41 To marry is to domesticate the Recording Angel. Once you are married, there is nothing left for you, not even suicide, but to be good.
1881 *Virginibus Puerisque*, 'Virginibus Puerisque', pt.2.

42 Man is a creature who lives not upon bread alone, but principally by catchwords.
1881 *Virginibus Puerisque*, 'Virginibus Puerisque', pt.2.

43 The cruellest lies are often told in silence.
1881 *Virginibus Puerisque*, 'Truth of Intercourse'.

44 Most of our pocket wisdom is conceived for the use of mediocre people, to discourage them from ambitious attempts, and generally console them in their mediocrity.
1881 *Virginibus Puerisque*, 'Crabbed Age and Youth'.

45 Old and young, we are all on our last cruise.
1881 *Virginibus Puerisque*, 'Crabbed Age and Youth'.

46 It is better to be a fool than to be dead.
1881 *Virginibus Puerisque*, 'Crabbed Age and Youth'.

47 For God's sake give me the young man who has brains enough to make a fool of himself!
1881 *Virginibus Puerisque*, 'Crabbed Age and Youth'.

48 To travel hopefully is a better thing than to arrive, and the true success is to labour.
1881 *Virginibus Puerisque*, 'El Dorado'.

49 Books are good enough in their own way, but they are a mighty bloodless substitute for life.
1881 *Virginibus Puerisque*, 'An Apology for Idlers'.

50 Extreme *busyness*, whether at school or college, kirk or market, is a symptom of a deficient vitality; and a faculty for idleness implies a catholic appetite and a strong sense of personal identity.
1881 *Virginibus Puerisque*, 'An Apology for Idlers'.

51 There is no duty we so much underrate as the duty of being happy.
1881 *Virginibus Puerisque*, 'An Apology for Idlers'.

52 We live the time that a match flickers; we pop the cork of a ginger-beer bottle, and the earthquake swallows us on the instant. Is it not odd, is it not incongruous, is it not, in the highest sense of human speech, incredible, that we should think so highly of the ginger-beer, and regard so little the devouring earthquake?
1881 *Virginibus Puerisque*, 'Aes Triplex'.

53 Think of the heroism of Johnson, think of that superb indifference to mortal limitation that set him upon his dictionary, and carried him through triumphantly until the end! Who, if he were wisely considerate of things at large, would ever embark upon any work much more considerable than a halfpenny post-card? Who would project a serial novel, after Thackeray and Dickens had each fallen in mid-course? Who would find heart enough to begin to live, if he dallied with the consideration of death?
1881 *Virginibus Puerisque*, 'Aes Triplex'.

54 Even if the doctor does not give you a year, even if he hesitates about a month, make one brave push and see what can be accomplished in a week.
1881 *Virginibus Puerisque*, 'Aes Triplex'.

55 Though we are mighty fine fellows nowadays, we cannot write like Hazlitt.
1881 *Virginibus Puerisque*, 'Walking Tours'.

56 We are in such haste to be doing, to be writing, to be gathering gear, to make our voice audible a moment in the derisive silence of eternity, that we forget that one thing, of which these are but the parts—namely, to live.
1881 *Virginibus Puerisque*, 'Walking Tours'.

57 It seems he had no design except to appear respectable, and here he keeps a private book to prove that he was not.
1882 Of Samuel Pepys and his *Diary. Familiar Studies of Men and Books.*

58 Politics is perhaps the only profession for which no preparation is thought necessary.
1882 *Familiar Studies of Men and Books*, 'Yoshida-Torajiro'.

59 Fifteen men on a dead man's chest—
Yo-ho-ho, and a bottle of rum!
Drink and the devil had done for the rest—
Yo-ho-ho, and a bottle of rum!
1883 *Treasure Island*, ch.1, 'The Old Sea-Dog at the 'Admiral Benbow''.

60 Pieces of eight!
1883 *Treasure Island*, ch.10, 'The Voyage'.

61 You mightn't happen to have a piece of cheese about you, now? No? Well, many's the long night I've dreamed of cheese—toasted, mostly—and woke up again, and here I were.
1883 Ben Gunn to Jim Hawkins. *Treasure Island*, ch.15, 'The Man of the Island'.

62 Under the wide and starry sky,
  Dig the grave and let me lie.
  Glad did I live and gladly die,
  And I laid me down with a will.

  This be the verse you grave for me:
  Here he lies where he longed to be,
  Home is the sailor, home from sea,
  And the hunter home from the hill.
  1884 'Requiem' (dated 'Hyères, May 1884'), collected in *Underwoods* (1887), bk.1, no.21.

63 In winter I get up at night
  And dress by yellow candle-light.
  In summer, quite the other way,
  I have to go to bed by day.

  I have to go to bed and see
  The birds still hopping on the tree,
  Or hear the grown-up people's feet
  Still going past me in the street.
  1885 *A Child's Garden of Verses*, no.1, 'Bed in Summer', stanzas 1–2.

64 A child should always say what's true,
  And speak when he is spoken to,
  And behave mannerly at table:
  At least as far as he is able.
  1885 *A Child's Garden of Verses*, no.5, 'Whole Duty of Children'.

65 Whenever the moon and stars are set,
  Whenever the wind is high,
  All night long in the dark and wet,
  A man goes riding by.
  Late in the night when the fires are out,
  Why does he gallop and gallop about?
  1885 *A Child's Garden of Verses*, no.9, 'Windy Nights', stanza 1.

66 When I am grown to man's estate
  I shall be very proud and great,
  And tell the other girls and boys
  Not to meddle with my toys.
  1885 *A Child's Garden of Verses*, no.12, 'Looking Forward'.

67 Whenever Auntie moves around,
  Her dresses make a curious sound;
  They trail behind her up the floor,
  And trundle after through the door.
  1885 *A Child's Garden of Verses*, no.15, 'Auntie's Skirts'.

68 When I was sick and lay a-bed,
  I had two pillows at my head,
  And all my toys beside me lay
  To keep me happy all the day.
  1885 *A Child's Garden of Verses*, no.16, 'The Land of Counterpane', stanza 1.

69 I have a little shadow that goes in and out with me,
  And what can be the use of him is more than I can see.
  1885 *A Child's Garden of Verses*, no.18, 'My Shadow', stanza 1.

70 The world is so full of a number of things,
  I'm sure we should all be as happy as kings.
  1885 *A Child's Garden of Verses*, no.24, 'Happy Thought'.

71 Children, you are very little,
  And your bones are very brittle;
  If you would grow great and stately,
  You must try to walk sedately.
  1885 *A Child's Garden of Verses*, no.27, 'Good and Bad Children', stanza 1.

72 My tea is nearly ready and the sun has left the sky;
  It's time to take the window to see Leerie going by;
  For every night at tea-time and before you take your seat,
  With lantern and with ladder he comes posting up the street.
  1885 *A Child's Garden of Verses*, no.30, 'The Lamplighter', stanza 1.

73 Must we to bed indeed? Well then,
  Let us arise and go like men,
  And face with an undaunted tread
  The long black passage up to bed.
  1885 *A Child's Garden of Verses*, XLI, 'North-West Passage', pt.1, 'Good Night', stanza 3.

74 In the Land of Nod at last.
  1885 *A Child's Garden of Verses*, XLI, 'North-West Passage', pt.3, 'In Port', stanza 3.

75 Am I no a bonny fighter?
  1886 Alan Breck to David Balfour. *Kidnapped*, ch.10.

76 Even though his tongue acquire the Southern knack, he will still have a strong Scots accent of the mind.
  1887 *Memories and Portraits*, ch.1, 'The Foreigner at Home'.

77 I have thus played the sedulous ape to Hazlitt, to Lamb, to Wordsworth, to Sir Thomas Browne, to Defoe, to Hawthorne, to Montaigne, to Baudelaire and to Obermann.
  1887 *Memories and Portraits*, ch.4, 'A College Magazine'.

78 Every one lives by selling something, whatever be his right to it.
  1888 'Beggars', originally published in *Scribner's Magazine*.

79 Here lies one who meant well, tried a little, failed much:—surely that may be his epitaph, of which he need not be ashamed.
  1892 *Across the Plains*, 'A Christmas Sermon', pt.4.

80 The bright face of danger.
  1892 *Across the Plains*, 'The Lantern-Bearers', pt.4.

81 Life is not all Beer and Skittles. The inherent tragedy of things works itself out from white to black and blacker, and the poor things of a day look ruefully on. Does it shake my cast-iron faith? I cannot say it does. I believe in an ultimate decency of things: ay, and if I woke in hell, should still believe it!
  1893 Letter to Sidney Colvin, 23 Aug.

82 Give to me the life I love,
  Let the lave go by me,
  Give the jolly heaven above
  And the byway nigh me.
  Bed in the bush with the stars to see,
  Bread I dip in the river—
  There's the life for a man like me,
  There's the life for ever.
  1894 *Songs of Travel* (published 1896), no.1, 'The Vagabond', stanza 1.

83 Wealth I ask not, hope nor love,
  Nor a friend to know me.
  All I ask, the heaven above,
  And the road below me.
  1894 *Songs of Travel* (published 1896), no.1, 'The Vagabond', stanza 4.

84 I will make you brooches and toys for your delight
  Of bird-song at morning and star-shine at night.
  I will make a palace fit for you and me

Of green days in forests and blue days at sea.
I will make my kitchen, and you shall keep your room,
Where white flows the river and bright blows the broom,
And you shall wash your linen and keep your body white
In rainfall at morning and dewfall at night.
1894 *Songs of Travel* (published 1896), no.11, stanza 1.

85 In the highlands, in the country places,
Where the old plain men have rosy faces,
And the young fair maidens
Quiet eyes.
1894 *Songs of Travel* (published 1896), no.16.

86 Trusty, dusky, vivid, true,
With eyes of gold and bramble-dew,
Steel-true and blade-straight,
The great artificer
Made my mate.
1894 *Songs of Travel* (published 1896), 'My Wife'.

87 Blows the wind to-day, and the sun and the rain are flying,
Blows the wind on the moors to-day and now,
Where about the graves of the martyrs the whaups are crying,
My heart remembers how!
1894 *Songs of Travel* (published 1896), no.45, 'To S.R. Crockett (in reply to a dedication)', stanza 1.

88 Be it granted to me to behold you again in dying,
Hills of home! and to hear again the call;
Hear about the graves of the martyrs the peeweets crying,
And hear no more at all.
1894 *Songs of Travel* (published 1896), no.45, 'To S.R. Crockett (in reply to a dedication)', stanza 3.

89 And all that I could think of, in the darkness and the cold,
Was just that I was leaving home and my folks were growing old.
1894 'Christmas at Sea', stanza 11.

90 I saw rain falling and the rainbow drawn
On Lammermuir. Hearkening I heard again
In my precipitous city beaten bells
Winnow the keen sea wind. And here afar,
Intent on my own race and place, I wrote.
1894 *Weir of Hermiston* (published 1896), Dedication 'To My Wife'.

91 It seemed unprovoked, a wilful convulsion of brute nature...
1894 *Weir of Hermiston* (published 1896), ch.9, 'At the Weaver's Stone'. These are the last words of the unfinished novel, dictated by Stevenson on the morning of his death from a blood-clot on the brain.

92 The *bourgeoisie's* weapon is starvation. If as a writer or artist you run counter to their narrow notions they simply and silently withdraw your means of subsistence. I sometimes wonder how many people of talent are executed in this way every year.
Quoted by Lloyd Osbourne in 'The Death of Stevenson', preface to Tusitala edition of *Weir of Hermiston* (published 1924).

93 The saddest object in civilization, and to my mind the greatest confession of its failure, is the man who can work, who wants work, and who is not allowed to work.
Quoted by Lloyd Osbourne in 'The Death of Stevenson', preface to Tusitala edition of *Weir of Hermiston* (published 1924).

Stewart, John Innes Mackintosh 1906–94
Scots-born academic, author and critic, Chair of Literature at Adelaide University (1935–45). His sequence of novels on life at Oxford, *A Staircase in Surrey*, began in 1974 with *The Gaudy*. As 'Michael Innes' he wrote erudite detective novels.

94 I am most grateful to the CLF [Commonwealth Literary Fund] for providing the funds to give these lectures in Australian literature, but unfortunately they have neglected to provide any literature. I will lecture therefore on D H Lawrence's 'Kangaroo'.
1940 Quoted in the *London Magazine*, Nov 1985.

95 On the platform stood a policeman of normal proportions, and instead of a revolver and a truncheon he carried a copy of *Ben Hur* translated into Irish, which he was evidently studying for an examination important to his professional advancement. Mr Thewless realised that the imperial might of Great Britain lay behind him and that in front was the philosophic republic of Mr de Valera.
1949 *The Journeying Boy*.

96 'In about half a mile you cross the river by an Irish bridge—'
'Whatever is that?'
'It's just a bridge, but built under the water instead of over it.'
'Extremely sensible.'
1969 *A Family Affair*.

Stigler, George Joseph 1911–91
US economist, University of Chicago; awarded a Nobel prize (1982).

97 The branch of economics dealing with how to enrich a new nation ('economic development' was the title) was actually forbidden by the courts, on the grounds that no university could pay for the damage its teachers did.
1973 'The History of Truth in Teaching', in *The Intellectual and the Marketplace* (1984).

Still, Bayrd 1906–92
US historian and archivist.

98 The tombstone of capitalism...with windows.
1956 Of the Rockefeller Center. *Mirror for Gotham*.

Stilwell, General Joseph 1883–1946
US general, commander in the Far East during World War II, who led the successful attack against the Japanese in Myanmar (1943–4). His acerbic manner earned him the nickname of 'Vinegar Joe'.

99 This little book contains none of your damn business.
Note on flyleaf of 1906 diary. Quoted in Barbara Tuchman *General Stilwell and the American Experience in China* (1970).

Stinchcombe, Arthur Leonard 1933–
US sociologist, University of Chicago.

1 The question of how to apply social theory to historical materials, as it is usually posed, is ridiculous. One does not apply theory to history; rather one uses history to develop theory.
1978 *Theoretical Methods in Social History*, p.1.

Sting originally Gordon Matthew Sumner 1951–
English singer-songwriter and actor, also known as a campaigner to save Brazilian rainforests.

2   If I were a Brazilian without land or money or the means to feed my children, I would be burning the rainforest too.
    1989 In the *International Herald Tribune*, 14 Apr.

Stipe, Michael 1960–
US singer and songwriter, member of the band REM.

3   Everybody hurts sometimes
    Everybody cries
    1992 'Everybody Hurts' (co-written by members of REM).

4   We don't get groupies. We get teenagers who want to read us their poetry.
    1994 In *Q*, 1 Sep.

5   There is always something of the writer in the work but I don't think Melville had to be swallowed by a whale to write a great novel. If I had lived the lives of all the characters of the songs I've written, that would truly be an extraordinary story.
    2001 In the *Daily Telegraph*, 20 Oct.

Stockton, Philip
US sound editor.

6   I want to thank everybody who is here tonight, and everybody who isn't, and everybody who has ever been born or may be born or be born again or reborn. If I've forgotten anybody then you probably know who you are.
    2012 Accepting the Academy Award for Best Sound Editing for *Hugo*, 26 Feb.

Stockwood, (Arthur) Mervyn 1913–95
English cleric. As Bishop of Southwark (1959–80) he was renowned for his liberal writings on the uniformity of faith and the communality of belief.

7   A psychiatrist is a man who goes to the Folies-Bergère and looks at the audience.
    1961 In the *Observer*, 15 Oct.

Stoker, Bram 1847–1912
Irish writer best remembered for the classic vampire story *Dracula* (1897).

8   The mouth, so far as I could see it under the heavy moustache, was fixed and rather cruel-looking, with peculiarly sharp white teeth; these protuded over the lips, whose remarkable ruddiness showed astonishing vitality in a man of his years.
    1897 Describing Count Dracula. *Dracula*, ch.2.

Stokowski, Leopold *pseudonym of* Antoni Stanislaw Boleslawowich 1882–1977
US conductor of Polish origin. He built up an international reputation as conductor of the Philadelphia Symphony Orchestra (1912–36), the New York Philharmonic (1946–50) and the Houston Symphony Orchestra (1955–60). He also worked in films and founded the American Symphony Orchestra in New York in 1962.

9   Musicians paint their pictures on silence—we provide the music, and you provide the silence.
    Addressing an audience at Carnegie Hall. Quoted in Derek Watson *Music Quotations* (1991).

Stone, Robert Anthony 1937–2015
US novelist and screenwriter. His best-known book is the novel *Dog Soldiers* (1974).

10 People are getting to be a disgrace to the planet.
    1982 *A Flag for Sunrise*, ch.6.

Stone, Samuel John 1839–1900
English cleric and hymnwriter

11 The Church's one foundation
    Is Jesus Christ, her Lord;
    She is his new creation
    By water and the word;
    From heaven he came and sought her
    To be his holy bride,
    With his own blood he bought her.
    And for her life he died.
    1866 *Lyra fidelium*.

Stopes, Marie 1880–1958
British birth-control pioneer and palaeobotanist.

12 An impersonal and scientific knowledge of the structure of our bodies is the surest safeguard against prurient curiosity and lascivious gloating.
    1918 *Married Love*, ch.5.

13 Each coming together of a man and wife, even if they have been mated for many years, should be a fresh adventure; each winning should necessitate a fresh wooing.
    1918 *Married Love*, ch.10.

Stoppard, Sir Tom *originally* Tom Straussler 1937–
Czech-born British dramatist. After writing for radio, he made his name with *Rosencrantz and Guildenstern are Dead* (1967) at the Edinburgh Festival. Other plays include the philosophical satire *Jumpers* (1972), *Travesties* (1974) and *Arcadia* (1993). He shared an Academy Award with Marc Norman for the screenplay of *Shakespeare in Love* (1998).

14 The House of Lords, an illusion to which I have never been able to subscribe—responsibility without power, the prerogative of the eunuch throughout the ages.
    1966 *Lord Malquist and Mr Moon*, pt.6.
    ▶ See Baldwin 57:30.

15 To sum up: your father, whom you love, dies, you are his heir, you come back to find that hardly was the corpse cold before his younger brother popped on to his throne and into his sheets, thereby offending both legal and natural practice. Now why exactly are you behaving in this extraordinary manner.
    1967 To Hamlet. *Rosecrantz and Guildenstern are Dead*, act 1.

16 Sometimes I dream of revolution, a bloody *coup d'état* by the second rank—troupes of actors slaughtered by their understudies, magicians sawn in half by indefatigably smiling glamour girls, cricket teams wiped out by marauding bands of twelfth men.
    1968 *The Real Inspector Hound*.

17 It's not the voting that's democracy; it's the counting.
    1972 *Jumpers*.

18 War is capitalism with the gloves off.
    1974 *Travesties*.

19 I learned three things in Zurich during the war... Firstly you're either a revolutionary or you're not, and if you're not you might as well be an artist as anything else. Secondly, if you can't be an artist, you might as well be a revolutionary... I forget the third thing.
   1974 *Travesties*, final lines.

20 Maybe Napoleon was wrong when he said we were a nation of shopkeepers... Today England looked like a nation of goalkeepers.
   1977 *Professional Foul*.
   ▶ See Napoleon 630:47.

21 Ambushing the audience is what theatre is all about.
   1984 In *Newsweek*, 16 Jan.

22 I don't think I can be expected to take seriously a game which takes less than three days to reach its conclusion.
   1984 Of baseball. In *The Guardian*, 24 Dec.

23 We're better at predicting events at the edge of the galaxy or inside the nucleus of an atom than whether it'll rain on auntie's garden party three Sundays from now.
   1993 *Arcadia*.

24 A lot of people would say, 'I would rather have a heart attack at the height of sexual passion.' On the whole, I would prefer to be killed by a bookcase.
   2010 In *The Daily Telegraph*, 4 Sep.

25 Something you might chance to read in the paper that morning can change the direction in which the play you're writing is going. It's like eating sushi in one of those little restaurants with a train going by. You just take what goes by at the moment and looks appealing.
   2014 Quoted in thestar.com, 26 Dec.

Storr, Robert 1949–
US art administrator, curator and writer on art. He was curator of painting and sculpture at the Museum of Modern Art from 1990 to 2002.

26 It's a letting go of distances.
   1995 On the necessity of establishing an intimacy and trust between artist and sitter. In the *New York Times*, 1 Jan.

Stowe, Harriet (Elizabeth) née Beecher 1811–96
US novelist. Her novel *Uncle Tom's Cabin* (1852) was written in anger after the passage of the Fugitive Slave Law. She caused a furore with *Lady Byron Vindicated* (1870) in which she accused Byron of having an incestuous relationship with his sister.

27 What makes saintliness in my view, as distinguished from ordinary goodness, is a certain quality of magnanimity and greatness of soul that brings life within the circle of the heroic.
   1846 'The Cathedral', in the *Atlantic Monthly*, Dec.

28 So long as the law considers all these human beings, with beating hearts and living affections, only as so many *things* belonging to the master—so long as the failure, or misfortune, or imprudence, or death of the kindest owner, may cause them any day to exchange a life of kind protection and indulgence for one of hopeless misery and toil—so long is it impossible to make anything beautiful or desirable in the best-regulated administration of slavery.
   1852 *Uncle Tom's Cabin*, ch.1.

29 I've got just as much conscience as any man in business can afford to keep,—just a little, you know, to swear by, as 't were.
   1852 *Uncle Tom's Cabin*, ch.1.

30 'Do you know who made you?'
   'Nobody, as I knows on,' said the child...I 'spect I grow'd. Don't think nobody never made me.'
   1852 *Uncle Tom's Cabin*, ch.20. The child is Topsy.

31 Whipping and abuse are like laudanum; you have to double the dose as the sensibilities decline.
   1852 *Uncle Tom's Cabin*, ch.20.

32 The longest day must have its close,—the gloomiest night will wear on to a morning. An eternal, inexorable lapse of moments is ever hurrying the day of the evil to an eternal night, and the night of the just to an eternal day.
   1852 *Uncle Tom's Cabin*, ch.40.

33 The bitterest tears shed over graves are for words left unsaid and deeds left undone.
   1865 *Little Foxes*, ch.3.

34 The obstinacy of cleverness and reason is nothing to the obstinacy of folly and inanity.
   1865 *Little Foxes*, ch.4.

Strachey, (Evelyn) John 1901–63
British writer and political leader.

35 If socialists lose sight of the central importance of social ownership of the means of production, they will cease, in a very real sense, to be socialists at all: they will subside into the role of well-intentioned, amiable, rootless, drifting social reformers.
   1956 *Contemporary Capitalism*.

Strachey, (Giles) Lytton 1880–1932
English writer. He is best known for his biographies, especially *Eminent Victorians* (1918), which challenged established concepts of the Victorian age.

36 The history of the Victorian age will never be written: we know too much about it. For ignorance is the first requisite of the historian—ignorance, which simplifies and clarifies, which selects and omits, with a placid perfection unattainable by the highest art.
   1918 *Eminent Victorians*, preface.

37 The time was out of joint, and he was only too delighted to have been born to set it right.
   1918 Of Hurrell Froude. *Eminent Victorians*, 'Cardinal Manning'.

38 'Before she came,' said a soldier, 'there was cussin' and swearin', but after that it was 'oly as a church.' The most cherished privilege of the fighting man was abandoned for the sake of Miss Nightingale.
   1918 *Eminent Victorians*, 'Florence Nightingale'.

39 Yet her conception of God was certainly not orthodox. She felt towards Him as she might have felt towards a glorified sanitary engineer; and in some of her speculations she seems hardly to distinguish between the Deity and the Drains.
   1918 *Eminent Victorians*, 'Florence Nightingale'.

40 His legs, perhaps, were shorter than they should have been.
   1918 *Eminent Victorians*, 'Dr Arnold'.

41 Johnson's aesthetic judgements are almost invariably subtle, or solid, or bold; they have always some good quality to recommend them—except one: they are never right.
1922 On Samuel Johnson. *Books and Characters*, 'Lives of the Poets'.

42 Asked by the chairman the usual question: 'I understand, Mr Strachey, that you have a conscientious objection to war?' he replied (in his curious falsetto voice), 'Oh no, not at all, only to *this* war.' Better than this was his reply to the chairman's other stock question, which had previously never failed to embarrass the claimant. 'Tell me, Mr Strachey, what would you do if you saw a German soldier trying to violate your sister?' With an air of noble virtue: 'I would try to get between them.'
On his appearance before a military tribunal, in Robert Graves *Goodbye To All That* (1929), ch.23.

43 If this is dying, then I don't think much of it.
1932 Last words, attributed.

Strafford, Thomas Wentworth, 1st Earl of
1593–1641

English statesman. As Lord Deputy of Ireland from 1632 he imposed firm rule, and in 1639 became the King's principal adviser. After failing to suppress the rebellion in Scotland (1639–40), he was impeached by the Long Parliament and executed despite a famous defence.

44 Divide not between Protestant and Papist. Divide not nationally, betwixt English and Irish. The King makes no distinction betwixt you.
1634 To the Irish Parliament, 15 Jul.

45 I would desire that every man would lay his hand on his heart, and consider seriously whether the beginnings of the people's happiness should be written in letters of blood.
1641 At his execution on Tower Hill, 12 May.

Stravinsky, Igor Fedorovich 1882–1971

Russian composer, who achieved fame with his ballet *The Firebird* (1910). Other ballets include *Petrushka* (1911) and the innovative *Rite of Spring* (1913). Among his significant later works are *The Soldier's Tale* (1918), *Orpheus* (1948, using the 12-tone system), *Oedipus Rex* (1927) and the opera *The Rake's Progress* (1951). He lived in France from 1934 and finally settled in the US (1945).

46 My music is best understood by children and animals.
1961 In the *Observer*, 8 Oct.

47 The most perfect of Swiss clockmakers.
Of Ravel. Quoted in R Nichols *Ravel* (1977).

Streep, Meryl Louise 1949–

US film actress. Having won three Academy Awards, she is considered among the finest film actors in the history of cinema. Her many notable films include *Kramer vs. Kramer* (1979), *Sophie's Choice* (1982), *Silkwood* (1983), *Out of Africa* (1985), *A Cry in the Dark* (1988), *The Bridges of Madison County* (1995), *Julie & Julia* (2009) and *Into the Woods* (2014).

48 Women are the last group anyone cares about in Hollywood.
2009 In *The Telegraph*, 19 Jan.

49 I gotta thank everybody in England that let me come and trample over their history.

2012 Accepting her eighth Golden Globe Award, for her performance of Margaret Thatcher in *The Iron Lady*.

50 You can't get spoiled if you do your own ironing.
Attributed.

Streeton, Sir Arthur Ernest 1867–1943

Australian landscape painter, one of the founders of the influential Heidelberg School and a contributor to the *9x5 Impression Exhibition* (1889), Australia's first Impressionist exhibition. He was official war artist in France in World War I.

51 Nature's scheme of colour in Australia is gold and blue.
Quoted in William Moore *The Story of Australian Art* (1934), vol. 1.

Streisand, Barbra 1942–

US actress, director and bestselling singer.

52 We elected a President, not a Pope.
1998 Referring to Bill Clinton. To journalists at the White House, 5 Feb.

Strindberg, August 1849–1912

Swedish dramatist and novelist, regarded as Sweden's greatest modern writer.

53 Family!… the home of all social evil, a charitable institution for comfortable women, an anchorage for house-fathers, and a hell for children.
1886 *The Son of a Servant*.

Strong, L(eonard) A(lfred) G(eorge) 1896–1958

English novelist and poet.

54 Have I a wife? Bedam I have! But we was badly mated. I hit her a great clout one night And now we're separated.
And mornin's going to me work I meets her on the quay: 'Good mornin' to you, ma'am!' says I, 'To hell with ye!' says she.
1921 *Dublin Days*, 'The Brewer's Man'.

Strong, Sir Roy Colin 1935–

English art historian, museum curator, writer, broadcaster and landscape designer. He became director of the National Portrait Gallery (1967–73) and of the Victoria and Albert Museum (1973–87).

55 Style has gone out of fashion.
2011 In the *Evening Standard*, 15 Sep.

Stuart, Francis 1902–2000

Australian-born Irish novelist and poet. He was interned by the Free State government as an Irish republican (1922–3), and by the Germans during World War II after he taught at Berlin University. He later lived and wrote in Paris, London and Ireland.

56 Those are old patterns, faded and bleached in the glare of the pressing present moments in the story.
'Jacob: An Episode from a Theme Based upon the Biblical Story of Jacob, Laban and Two Daughters'.

Stuart, John McDouall 1815–66

Scottish-born explorer, who emigrated to Australia aged 25. He led six expeditions from Adelaide (1858–62), becoming in 1860 the first European to reach the centre of the continent and in 1862 the first to cross Australia from south to north. His health was wrecked by his adventures.

57 To-day I find from my observations of the sun...that I am now camped in the centre of Australia. I have marked a tree and planted the British flag there. There is a high mount about two miles and a half to the north-north-east. I wish it had been in the centre; but on it to-morrow I will raise a cone of stones, and plant the flag there, and name it 'Central Mount Stuart'.
1860 Journal entry, 22 Apr. On reaching the centre of Australia, at Small Gum Creek. Collected in W. Hardman (ed) *Journals of John McDou'all Stuart during the Years 1858, 1859, 1860, 1861 and 1862*.

58 If this country is settled, it will be one of the finest Colonies under the Crown, suitable for the growth of any and everything.
1862 On reaching the sea at the Gulf of Carpentaria. Journal entry, Jul.

Stuart, Mary known as Mary, Queen of Scots 1542–87

Daughter of James V of Scotland, she married the Dauphin of France in 1558. During her stormy rule, she attempted to support Roman Catholicism in Reformation Scotland, was deposed and fled to England, eventually being imprisoned and executed for treason against her cousin, Queen Elizabeth I of England.

59 O Domine Deus! speravi in Te;
   O care mi Jesu! nunc libera me;
   In dura catena, in misera poena,
   Desidero Te,
   Languendo, gemendo, et genu flectendo
   Adoro, imploro, ut liberes me!
   O Lord my God, I hope in thee;
   My dear Lord Jesus, set me free;
   In chains, in pains
   On bended knee
   I adore thee, implore thee
   To set me free.
1587 Poem composed just before her execution (translated by E Milner-White and G W Briggs, 1941).

Stubbes, Philip 1543–93

English Puritan pamphleteer. His *Anatomie of Abuses in the Realme of England* (1583) was a vehement denunciation of the luxury of the times.

60 Lord, remove these exercises from the Sabbath. Any exercise which withdraweth from godliness either upon the Sabbath or on any other day, is wicked and to be forbidden.
1583 *Anatomie of Abuses in the Realme of England*.

61 For as concerning football playing, I protest unto you it may be rather called a friendly kind of fight than a play or recreation, a bloody or murmuring practice than a fellowy sport or pastime.
1583 *Anatomie of Abuses in the Realme of England*.

62 Football causeth fighting, brawling, contention, quarrel-picking, murder, homicide, and a great effusion of blood, as daily experiences teaches.
1583 *Anatomie of Abuses in the Realme of England*.

Studdert Kennedy, G(eoffrey) A(nketell) known as 'Woodbine Willie' 1883–1929

Army chaplain, theologian and poet of World War I.

63 Waste of Blood, and waste of Tears,
   Waste of youth's most precious years,
   Waste of ways the saints have trod,
   Waste of Glory, waste of God,
   War!
1919 *More Rough Rhymes of a Padre*, 'Waste'.

64 When Jesus came to Birmingham they simply passed Him by,
   They never hurt a hair of him, they only let Him die.
   For men had grown more tender and they would not give Him pain,
   They only just passed down the street, and left Him in the rain.
1921 *Peace Rhymes of a Padre*, 'Indifference'.

Su Wu fl.c.100 BC

Chinese general whose poem *To his Wife* expresses his dismay at their forced parting when he was called to battle.

65 With all your might enjoy the spring flowers,
   But do not forget the time of our love and pride
c.100 BC *To his Wife* (translated by Arthur Waley).

Suckling, Sir John 1609–41

English poet and playwright. His father was Secretary of State, and he served as ambassador, but upon his inheritance devoted himself to extravagance and court life. Works include the plays *Aglaura* (1638) and *The Goblins* (by 1641), the mock-ballad *The Wits* (1637) and shorter lyrics. By 1641 he had fled to France, where Aubrey says he committed suicide.

66 Why so pale and wan, fond lover?
   Prithee, why so pale?
   Will, when looking well can't move her,
   Looking ill prevail?
1637 *Aglaura*, act 4, sc.1, 'Song'.

67 'Tis love in love that makes the sport.
c.1638 Sonnet no.2.

68 'Tis not the meat; but 'tis the appetite
   Makes eating a delight.
c.1638 Sonnet no.2.

69 Women enjoyed (whatsoe'er before they've been)
   Are like romances read, or sights once seen:
   Fruition's dull, and spoils the play much more
   Than if one read or knew the plot before;
   'Tis expectation makes a blessing dear;
   It were not heaven, if we knew what it were.
1646 'Against Fruition'.

70 The maid (and thereby hangs a tale)
   For such a maid no Whitson-ale
   Could ever yet produce:
   No grape that's kindly ripe, could be
   So round, so plump, so soft as she,
   Nor half so full of juice.
1646 'Ballad: Upon a Wedding'.

71 Love is the fart
   Of every heart:
   It pains a man when 'tis kept close,
   And others doth offend, when 'tis let loose.
1646 'Love's Offence'.

72 Out upon it! I have loved
   Three whole days together;
   And am like to love three more,
   If it prove fair weather.
1656 'Out Upon It!'

Sugar, Lord Alan Michael 1947–
English businessman. Having made a fortune in consumer electronics and other businesses, he became the presiding host of the BBC TV series *The Apprentice* (2005–).

73 If you take care of your character, your reputation will take care of itself.
2009 On *The Apprentice*, BBC television, 3 Jun.

Sullivan, Andrew 1963–
English journalist and writer, based in the US.

74 From the moment she danced with John Travolta, she became an honorary American.
1997 On Diana, Princess of Wales. In the *Sunday Times*, 7 Sep.

75 If religion is about truth, why is it so afraid of error?
2008 On his blog *The Daily Dish*, 30 Sep.

76 I occasionally used to day-dream about a 'one-nation' Tory US president, a second Eisenhower of a sort. Little did I know he would be a black man with a funny name.
2010 In *The Atlantic*, 19 Dec.

77 Obama is looking good because he kept his nerve and retained his restraint. That's a tough combo: nerve and restraint. It takes a cold-bloodedness to pull this off, and there are times when ice seems to run through the man's veins.
2010 In *The Atlantic*, 19 Dec.

Sullivan, Anne 1866–1936
US educator, best known as the teacher of Helen Keller, whom she taught using the manual alphabet and touch-teaching.

78 Language grows out of life, out of its needs and experiences.
1894 Speech to the American Association to Promote the Teaching of Speech to the Deaf, Jul.

79 *Language* and *knowledge* are indissolubly connected; they are interdependent. Good work in language presupposes and depends on a real knowledge of things.
1894 Speech to the American Association to Promote the Teaching of Speech to the Deaf, Jul.

Sullivan, Timothy Daniel 1827–1914
Irish nationalist, politician, journalist and poet.

80 High upon the gallows tree
Swung the noble-hearted three
By the vengeful tyrant stricken in their bloom;
But they met him face to face
With the courage of their race,
And they went with souls undaunted to their doom.
'God save Ireland!' said the heroes;
'God save Ireland', say they all:
Whether on the scaffold high
Or the battlefield we die,
Oh, what matter when for Erin dear we fall.
1867 'God Save Ireland'.

Sumner, William Graham 1840–1910
US sociologist, formerly an Episcopal rector, Professor of Political and Social Science at Yale University. He was a disciple of Herbert Spencer, and a strong believer in laissez-faire and free economy.

81 It would be hard to find a single instance of a direct assault by positive effort upon poverty, vice, and misery which has not either failed or, if it has not failed directly and entirely, has not entailed other evils greater than the one which it removed.
1881 'Sociology', collected in *War and Other Essays* (1911).

82 The law of the survival of the fittest was not made by man and cannot be abrogated by man. We can only by interfering with it, produce the survival of the unfittest.
1881 'Sociology', collected in *War and Other Essays* (1911).

83 Society needs first of all to be free from meddlers—that is, to be let alone.
Attributed.

The Sun
British tabloid newspaper.

84 GOTCHA!
1982 Headline, 4 May, reporting the sinking of the Argentinian battleship *General Belgrano* by the British nuclear submarine *HMS Conqueror*. It was withdrawn after the first edition.

85 UP YOURS DELORS
1990 Headline, 1 Nov, supporting Margaret Thatcher's speech in defiance of European Commission president Jacques Delors' wish for Britain to adopt the Ecu.

86 IT'S THE SUN WOT WON IT
1992 Headline, 11 Apr, after the general election victory by the Conservatives.

Sun Tzu c.500–c.320 BC
Name used by the Chinese authors of the *Art of War*. The core text was probably written by one person, perhaps a feudal warrior, but the exact date is unknown. It includes many commentaries by later Chinese philosophers.

87 The art of war is of vital importance to the state.
c.500–320 BC *The Art of War*, ch.1, 'Laying Plans', section 1 (translated by James Clavell, 1981).

88 All warfare is based on deception.
c.500–320 BC *The Art of War*, ch.1, 'Laying Plans', section 18 (translated by James Clavell, 1981).

89 There is no instance of a country having benefitted from prolonged warfare.
c.500–320 BC *The Art of War*, ch.2, 'Waging War', section 6 (translated by James Clavell, 1981).

90 Know the enemy and know yourself; in a hundred battles, you will never be defeated.
c.500 BC *Art of War*, ch.3 (translated by Yuan Shibang, 1987).

91 A victorious general is able to make his soldiers fight with the effect of pent-up waters which, suddenly released, plunge into a bottomless abyss.
c.500 BC *Art of War*, ch.4 (translated by Yuan Shibang, 1987).

92 The business of a general is to kick away the ladder behind soldiers when they have climbed up a height.
c.500 BC *Art of War*, ch.10 (translated by Yuan Shibang, 1987).

93 The general who advances without coveting fame and retreats without fearing disgrace, whose only thought is to protect the country and do good service to his sovereign, is the jewel of the kingdom.
c.500–320 BC *The Art of War*, ch.10, 'Terrain', section 24 (translated by James Clavell, 1981).

94 There is no place where espionage is not possible.
c.500 BC *Art of War*, ch.13 (translated by Yuan Shibang, 1987).

Sun Yat-Sen or Sun Yixian 1867–1925

Chinese non-Communist revolutionary, regarded as the father of the Chinese Republic. Founder and early leader of China's Nationalist Party, he founded the Society for the Revival of China, but was kidnapped by the Chinese legation in London. After his release he organized risings in South China. The assassination of his follower, Sung Chiao-Jen, led to civil war (1913), and he set up a separate government at Guangzhou (Canton).

95 Modern European culture is nothing but a culture of natural sciences.
1924 Speech, Nov, calling for a union of Japan and China to liberate Asia from European influence. Quoted in John Wu Sun Yat-Sen: The Man and His Ideas (1971).

96 The foundation of the government of a nation must be built upon the rights of the people, but the administration must be entrusted to experts. We must not look upon those experts as stately and grand presidents and ministers, but simply as our chauffeurs, guards at the gate, cooks, physicians, carpenters, or tailors.
1927 The Three Principles of the People.

Surrey, Henry Howard, Earl of c.1517–1547

English poet; of royal blood, he served Henry VIII at court and in France. In the turmoil over the succession, he became the target of the rival Seymour family, and was arrested and executed on trumped-up charges. He, with Wyatt, introduced the sonnet to England. *Tottel's Miscellany* (1557) contained forty of his poems.

97 Love, that doth reign and live within my thought,
And built his seat within my captive breast,
Clad in the arms wherein with me he fought,
Oft in my face he doth his banner rest.
1557 'Love, that doth reign'.

98 Alas! so all things now do hold their peace,
Heaven and earth disturbed in no thing…
Calm is the sea, the waves work less and less;
So am not I whom love, alas, doth wring,
Bringing before my face the great increase
Of my desires, whereat I weep and sing,
In joy and woe, as in a doubtful ease.
For my sweet thoughts sometime do pleasure bring,
But by and by the cause of my disease
Gives me a pang that inwardly doth sting,
When that I think what grief it is again
To live and lack the thing should rid my pain.
1557 'Alas! so all things now do hold their peace'.

99 Wyatt resteth here, that quick could never rest;
Whose heavenly gifts increased by disdain,
And virtue sank the deeper in his breast;
Such profit he of envy could obtain.
1557 'Wyatt resteth here'.

1 So cruel prison how could betide, alas,
As proud Windsor? Where I in lust and joy
With a king's son my childish years did pass
In greater feast than Priam's sons of Troy.
1557 'So cruel prison'.

2 London, hast thou accused me
Of breach of laws, the root of strife?
Within whose breast did boil to see,
So fervent hot, thy dissolute life,
That even the hate of sins that grow
Within thy wicked walls so rife,
For to break forth did convert so
That terror could it not repress.
1557 'London, hast thou accused me'.

3 O happy dames, that may embrace
The fruit of your delight,
Help to bewail the woeful case
And eke the heavy plight
Of me, that wonted to rejoice
The fortune of my pleasant choice.
Good ladies, help to fill my mourning voice.
1557 'O happy dames'.

4 Set me whereas the sun doth parch the green,
Or where his beams may not dissolve the ice,
In temperate heat, where he is felt and seen,
With proud people, in presence sad and wise;
Set me in base, or yet in high degree,
In the long night, or in the shortest day,
In clear weather, or where mists thickest be,
In lusty youth, or when my hairs be grey…
Yours will I be, and with that only thought
Comfort myself when that my hap is nought.
'Set me whereas the sun doth parch the green'.

Surtees, Robert Smith 1803–64

English journalist and novelist. Founder of the *New Sporting Magazine* in 1831, he introduced the popular Cockney character John Jorrocks. Later works include *Jorrocks' Jaunts and Jollities* (1838) and *Hillingdon Hall* (1845).

5 The horse loves the hound, and I loves both.
Quoted in Colin Jarman The Guinness Dictionary of Sports Quotations (1990).

6 There is no secret so close as that between a rider and his horse.
Attributed.

Sutherland, Arthur Jr 1902–73

US lawyer, Professor of Law at Harvard University.

7 One can scarcely imagine a speaker at a meeting of a county medical society discussing the possible elimination of some disease by public health measures, and then qualifying his observations by the statement that many practitioners make a living out of treating the disease in question; and that unless the physicians are vigilant to prevent the adoption of such measures, this source of business will be taken from them. Yet speakers at bar association meetings are frequently heard to make similar observations about the effect of proposed reforms.
1938 'A New Society and an Old Calling,' in the Cornell Law Quarterly.

Swanson, Gloria originally Gloria May Josephine Svensson 1897–1983

US film actress. She rose from an extra in silent films in 1915 to leading roles as a chic sophisticate in the front line of the battle of the sexes, under the direction of Cecil B de Mille in the 1920s.

8 Arriving Monday… Arrange ovation.
Transatlantic cable to Adolf Zukor. Quoted in the New Yorker, 21 Mar 1994.

Sweetenham, Bill 1950–

Australian swimming coach.

9 The Romans conquered the world not because they held committees but because they killed the opposition. That's where I'm coming from.
2003 In *The Independent*, 29 Dec.

Sweezy, Paul Malor 1910–2004
Independent US Marxist economist, founder of the *Monthly Review* (1949).

10 Capitalism only works well when it has a strong opposition, because that forces it to be more egalitarian than it wants to be.
1992 Interview in *The Progressive*, May.

Swettenham, Sir Frank Athelstane 1850–1946
English colonial administrator, serving as the British Resident in Selangor and Perak before being appointed the Resident General in the Federated Malay States (1896–1901).

11 The Malay Peninsula, with the climate of a perpetual Turkish bath.
1906 *British Malaya*.

Swift, Graham 1949–
English writer. He has written several novels including *Waterland* (1983), which was shortlisted for the Booker Prize, and *Last Orders*, which won the Booker Prize in 1996.

12 Life is one-tenth Here and Now, nine-tenths a history lesson. For most of the time the Here and Now is neither now nor here.
1983 *Waterland*, ch.8.

13 People die when curiosity goes. People have to find out, people have to know. How can there be any true revolution till we know what we're made of?
1983 *Waterland*, ch.27.

14 How quick and rushing life can sometimes seem, when at the same time it's so slow and sweet and everlasting.
2007 *Tomorrow*.

Swift, Jonathan 1667–1745
Anglo-Irish poet, novelist, essayist, pamphleteer and letter writer. Born in Ireland, he became a satirist in London but returned to Dublin to become Dean of St Patrick's. His works, characterized by biting wit, include *Gulliver's Travels* (1726), a satire on religious dissension, *A Tale of a Tub* (1704), *A Modest Proposal* (1729) and *Drapier's Letters* (1724), in which he campaigned for Irish liberty.

15 Th' artillery of words.
1692 'My Lady's Lamentation'.

16 Philosophy! the lumber of the schools.
1692 'Ode to Dr William Sancroft'.

17 Satire is a sort of glass, wherein beholders do generally discover everybody's face but their own.
1704 *The Battle of the Books*, preface.

18 Instead of dirt and poison we have rather chosen to fill our hives with honey and wax; thus furnishing mankind with the two noblest of things, which are sweetness and light.
1704 *The Battle of the Books*.

19 Books, like men their authors, have no more than one way of coming into the world, but there are ten thousand to go out of it, and return no more.
1704 *A Tale of a Tub*, 'Epistle Dedicatory'.

20 Satire, being levelled at all, is never resented for an offence by any.
1704 *A Tale of a Tub*, 'Author's Preface'.

21 What though his head be empty, provided his commonplace book be full.
1704 *A Tale of a Tub*, 'Digression in praise of digression', ch.7.

22 Last week I saw a woman flayed, and you will hardly believe, how much it altered her person for the worse.
1704 *A Tale of a Tub*, ch.9.

23 Laws are like cobwebs, which may catch small flies, but let wasps and hornets break through.
1709 *A Critical Essay upon the Faculties of the Mind*.

24 There is nothing in this world constant, but inconstancy.
1709 *A Critical Essay upon the Faculties of the Mind*.

25 Surely mortal man is a broomstick!
1710 *A Meditation upon a Broomstick*.

26 We are so fond of one another, because our ailments are the same.
1711 *Journal to Stella*, 1 Feb.

27 Will she pass in a crowd? Will she make a figure in a country church?
1711 *Journal to Stella*, 9 Feb.

28 I love good creditable acquaintance; I love to be the worst of the company.
1711 *Journal to Stella*, 17 May.

29 He was a fiddler, and consequently a rogue.
1711 *Journal to Stella*, 25 July.

30 He showed me his bill of fare to tempt me to dine with him; poh, said I, I value not your bill of fare, give me your bill of company.
1711 *Journal to Stella*, 2 Sep.

31 We have just enough religion to make us hate, but not enough to make us love one another.
1711 *Thoughts on Various Subjects*.

32 When a true genius appears in the world, you may know him by this sign, that the dunces are all in confederacy against him.
1711 *Thoughts on Various Subjects*.

33 What they do in heaven we are ignorant of: what they do *not* we are told expressly, that they neither marry, nor are given in marriage.
1711 *Thoughts on Various Subjects*.

34 The stoical scheme of supplying our wants, by lopping off our desires, is like cutting off our feet when we want shoes.
1711 *Thoughts on Various Subjects*.

35 The reason why so few marriages are happy, is, because young ladies spend their time in making nets, not in making cages.
1711 *Thoughts on Various Subjects*.

36 We were to do more business after dinner, but after dinner is after dinner—an old saying and a true, 'much drinking, little thinking'.
1712 *Journal to Stella*, 26 Feb.

37 Proper words in proper places, make the true definition of style.
1720 *Letter to a Young Gentleman lately entered into Holy Orders*.

38 Indeed the arguments on both sides were invincible; for in reason, all government without the consent of the

governed is the very definition of slavery; but in fact eleven men well armed will certainly subdue one single man in his shirt.
1724 Fourth letter to…Ireland, written under the pseudonym of 'M B Drapier'.

39 I have heard of a man who had a mind to sell his house, and therefore carried a piece of brick in his pocket, which he shewed as a pattern to encourage purchasers.
1724 Drapier's Letters, no.2.

40 In Church your grandsire cut his throat;
To do the job too long he tarried,
He should have had my hearty vote,
To cut his throat before he married.
1724 'Verses on the Upright Judge'.

41 'Libertas et natale solum':
Fine words! I wonder where you stole 'em.
1724 'Whitshed's motto on his Coach'.

42 He is taller by almost the breadth of my nail than any of his court, which alone is enough to strike an awe into the beholders.
1726 Of the Emperor. Gulliver's Travels, 'A Voyage to Lilliput', ch.2.

43 It is alleged indeed, that the high heels are most agreeable to our ancient constitution: but however this be, his Majesty hath determined to make use of only low heels in the administration of the government.
1726 Gulliver's Travels, 'A Voyage to Lilliput', ch.4.

44 I cannot but conclude the bulk of your natives to be the most pernicious race of little odious vermin that nature ever suffered to crawl upon the surface of the earth.
1726 Gulliver's Travels, 'A Voyage to Brobdingnag', ch.6.

45 And he gave it for his opinion, that whoever could make two ears of corn or two blades of grass to grow upon a spot of ground where only one grew before, would deserve better of mankind, and do more essential service to his country than the whole race of politicians put together.
1726 Gulliver's Travels, 'A Voyage to Brobdingnag', ch.7.

46 He had been eight years upon a project for extracting sun-beams out of cucumbers, which were to be put into vials hermetically sealed, and let out to warm the air in raw inclement summers.
1726 Gulliver's Travels, 'A Voyage to Laputa, etc.' ch.5.

47 These unhappy people were proposing schemes for persuading monarchs to choose favourites upon the score of their wisdom, capacity and virtue; of teaching ministers to consult the public good; of rewarding merit, great abilities and eminent services; of instructing princes to know their true interest by placing it on the same foundation with that of their people: of choosing for employment persons qualified to exercise them; with many other wild impossible chimeras, that never entered before into the heart of man to conceive, and confirmed in me the old observation, that there is nothing so extravagant and irrational which some philosophers have not maintained for truth.
1726 Gulliver's Travels, 'A Voyage to Laputa, etc.' ch.6.

48 He replied that I must needs be mistaken, or that I *said the thing which was not*. (For they have no word in their language to express lying or falsehood.)
1726 Gulliver's Travels, 'A Voyage to the Houyhnhnms', ch.3.

49 I told him…that we ate when we were not hungry, and drank without the provocation of thirst.
1726 Gulliver's Travels, 'A Voyage to the Houyhnhnms', ch.6.

50 Few are qualified to shine in company; but it is in most men's power to be agreeable.
1727 Thoughts on Various Subjects (enlarged edn).

51 Every man desires to live long; but no man would be old.
1727 Thoughts on Various Subjects (enlarged edn).

52 A nice man is a man of nasty ideas.
1727 Thoughts on Various Subjects (enlarged edn).

53 Old men and comets have been reverenced for the same reason; their long beards, and pretences to foretell events.
1727 Thoughts on Various Subjects (enlarged edn).

54 How haughtily he lifts his nose,
To tell what every schoolboy knows.
1727 'The Journal', l.81–2.

55 Walls have tongues, and hedges ears.
1727 'A Pastoral Dialogue between Richmond Lodge and Marble Hill', l.8.

56 Hail fellow, well met,
All dirty and wet:
Find out, if you can,
Who's master, who's man.
1728 'My Lady's Lamentation', l.171.

57 These *Mothers*, instead of being able to work for their honest livelihood, are forced to beg Sustenance for their *helpless Infants*; who, as they grow up either turn *Thieves* for want of Work; or leave their dear native country, to fight for the *Pretender* in Spain; or sell themselves to the *Barbadoes*.
1729 A Modest Proposal for Preventing the Children of Ireland from being a Burden to their Parents or Country.

58 I have been assured by a very knowing American of my Acquaintance in London; that a young healthy Child, well nursed, is, at a Year old, a most delicious, nourishing, and wholesome Food; whether Stewed, Roasted, Baked, or Boiled; and, I make no doubt, that it will equally serve in a Fricassee, or a Ragout.
1729 A Modest Proposal for Preventing the Children of Ireland from being a Burden to their Parents or Country.

59 A Child will make two Dishes at an Entertainment for Friends; and when the Family dines alone, the fore or hind Quarter will make a reasonable Dish; and seasoned with a little Pepper or Salt, will be very good Boiled on the fourth Day, especially in Winter.
1729 A Modest Proposal for Preventing the Children of Ireland from being a Burden to their Parents or Country.

60 Say, Britain, could you ever boast,—
Three poets in an age at most?
Our chilling climate hardly bears
A sprig of bays in fifty years.
1733 'On Poetry', l.5–8.

61 Then, rising with Aurora's light,
The Muse invoked, sit down to write;
Blot out, correct, insert, refine,
Enlarge, diminish, interline.
1733 'On Poetry', l.85–8.

62 As learned commentators view
In Homer than Homer knew.
1733 'On Poetry', l.103–4.

63 So geographers, in Afric-maps,
   With savage-pictures fill their gaps;
   And o'er unhabitable downs
   Place elephants for want of towns.
   1733 'On Poetry', l.177–80.

64 He gives direction to the town,
   To cry it up, or run it down.
   1733 'On Poetry', l.269–70.

65 Hobbes clearly proves, that every creature
   Lives in a state of war by nature.
   1733 'On Poetry', l.319–20.

66 So, naturalists observe, a flea
   Hath smaller fleas on him prey;
   And these have smaller fleas to bite 'em,
   And so proceed *ad infinitum*.
   Thus every poet, in his kind,
   Is bit by him that comes behind.
   1733 'On Poetry', l.337–42.

67 I mean, you lie—under a mistake.
   1738 *Polite Conversation*, dialogue 1.

68 I think she was cut out for a Gentlewoman, but she was spoiled in the making. She wears her clothes as if they were thrown on with a pitchfork; and, for the fashion, I believe they were made in the days of Queen Bess.
   1738 *Polite Conversation*, dialogue 1.

69 The more careless, the more modish.
   1738 *Polite Conversation*, dialogue 1.

70 I won't quarrel with my Bread and Butter.
   1738 *Polite Conversation*, dialogue 1.

71 He was a bold Man that first ate an Oyster.
   1738 *Polite Conversation*, dialogue 2.

72 Faith, that's as well said, as if I had said it myself.
   1738 *Polite Conversation*, dialogue 2.

73 I always love to begin a journey on Sundays, because I shall have the prayers of the church, to preserve all that travel by land, or by water.
   1738 *Polite Conversation*, dialogue 2.

74 Lord, I wonder what fool it was that first invented kissing!
   1738 *Polite Conversation*, dialogue 2.

75 Promises and pie-crust are made to be broken.
   1738 *Polite Conversation*.

76 Be she barren, be she old,
   Be she slut, or be she scold,
   Eat my oysters, and lie near her,
   She'll be fruitful, never fear her.
   1746 'Verses Made for the Women Who Cry Oysters'.

77 I never saw, heard, nor read, that the clergy were beloved in any nation where Christianity was the religion of the country. Nothing can render them popular, but some degree of persecution.
   1765 *Thoughts on Religion*.

78 I must complain the cards are ill shuffled till I have a good hand.
   Quoted in Colin Jarman *The Guinness Dictionary of Sports Quotations* (1990).

Swinburne, Algernon Charles 1837–1909

English playwright and poet. He made his name with *Poems and Ballads* (1866). Later works include *A Song of Italy* (1867), *Erechtus* (1876) and *Tristam of Lyonesse* (1882).

79 Swallow, my sister, O sister swallow,
   How can thine heart be full of the spring?
   A thousand summers are over and dead.
   What hast thou found in the spring to follow?
   What hast thou found in thine heart to sing?
   What wilt thou do when the summer is shed?
   1864 'Itylus'.

80 Till life and death remember,
   Till thou remember and I forget.
   1864 'Itylus'.

81 Maiden, and mistress of the months and stars
   Now folded in the flowerless fields of heaven.
   1865 *Atlanta in Calydon*, l.1

82 When the hounds of spring are on winter's traces,
   The mother of months in meadow or plain
   Fills the shadows and windy places
   With lisp of leaves and ripple of rain;
   And the brown bright nightingale amorous
   Is half assured for Itylus,
   For the Thracian ships and the foreign faces,
   The tongueless vigil and all the pain.
   1865 *Atlanta in Calydon*, chorus, 'When the hounds of spring'.

83 For winter's rains and ruins are over,
   And all the season of snows and sins;
   The days dividing lover and lover,
   The light that loses, the night that wins;
   And time remembered is grief forgotten,
   And frosts are slain and flowers begotten,
   And in green underwood and cover
   Blossom by blossom the spring begins.
   1865 *Atlanta in Calydon*, chorus, 'When the hounds of spring'.

84 And soft as lips that laugh and hide
   The laughing leaves of the tree divide,
   And screen from seeing and leave in sight
   The god pursuing, the maiden hid.
   1865 *Atlanta in Calydon*, chorus 'When the hounds of spring'.

85 Before the beginning of years
   There came to the making of man
   Time with a gift of tears,
   Grief with a glass that ran.
   1865 *Atlanta in Calydon*, chorus, 'Before the beginning of years'.

86 Strength without hands to smite,
   Love that endures for a breath;
   Night, the shadow of light,
   And Life, the shadow of death.
   1865 *Atlanta in Calydon*, chorus, 'Before the beginning of years'.

87 For words divide and rend;
   But silence is most noble till the end.
   1865 *Atlanta in Calydon*, chorus, 'Who hath given man speech'.

88 Ah, yet would God this flesh of mine might be
   Where air might wash and long leaves cover me;
   Where tides of grass break into foam of flowers,
   Or where the wind's feet shine along the sea.
   1866 'Laus Veneris'.

89 Superflux of pain.
   1866 *Poems and Ballads*, 'Anactoria'

90 We shift and bedeck and bedrape us,
   Thou art noble and nude and antique.
   1866 *Poems and Ballads*, 'Dolores', stanza 7.

91 Change in a trice
   The lilies and languors of virtue
   For the raptures and roses of vice.
   1866 *Poems and Ballads*, 'Dolores', stanza 9.

92 O splendid and sterile Dolores,
   Our Lady of Pain.
   1866 *Poems and Ballads*, 'Dolores', stanza 9.

93 Ah beautiful passionate body
   That never has ached with a heart!
   1866 *Poems and Ballads*, 'Dolores', stanza 11.

94 For the crown of our life as it closes
   Is darkness, the fruit thereof dust;
   No thorns go as deep as a rose's,
   And love is more cruel than lust.
   Time turns the old days to derision,
   Our loves into corpses or wives;
   And marriage and death and division
   Make barren our lives.
   1866 *Poems and Ballads*, 'Dolores', stanza 20.

95 I shall remember while the light lives yet
   And in the night time I shall not forget.
   1866 *Poems and Ballads*, 'Erotion'.

96 Pale, beyond porch and portal,
   Crowned with calm leaves, she stands
   Who gathers all things mortal
   With cold immortal hands.
   1866 *Poems and Ballads*, 'The Garden of Proserpine'.

97 Here, where the world is quiet,
   Here, where all trouble seems
   Dead winds' and spent waves' riot
   In doubtful dreams of dreams.
   1866 *Poems and Ballads*, 'The Garden of Proserpine'.

98 Yea, is not even Apollo, with hair and harpstring of gold,
   A bitter God to follow, a beautiful God to behold?
   1866 *Poems and Ballads*, 'Hymn to Proserpine'.

99 Thou hast conquered, O pale Galilean; the world has
     grown grey from Thy breath;
   We have drunken of things Lethean, and fed on the
     fullness of death.
   1866 *Poems and Ballads*, 'Hymn to Proserpine'.

1 Though these that were Gods are dead, and thou being
    dead art God,
  Though before thee the throned Cytherean be fallen,
    and hidden her head,
  Yet thy kingdom shall pass, Galilean, thy dead shall go
    down to thee dead.
  1866 *Poems and Ballads*, 'Hymn to Proserpine'.

2 I remember the way we parted,
  The day and the way we met;
  You hoped we were both broken-hearted,
  And knew we should both forget.
  1866 *Poems and Ballads*, 'An Interlude'.

3 And the best and the worst of this is
  That neither is most to blame
  If you have forgotten my kisses
  And I have forgotten your name.
  1866 *Poems and Ballads*, 'An Interlude'.

4 If love were what the rose is,
  And I were like the leaf,
  Our lives would grow together
  In sad or singing weather,
  Blown fields or flowered closes,
  Green pleasure or grey grief.
  1866 *Poems and Ballads*, 'A Match'.

5 I will go back to the great sweet mother,
  Mother and lover of men, the sea.
  I will go down to her, I and no other,
  Close with her, kiss her and mix her with me.
  1866 *Poems and Ballads*, 'The Triumph of Time'.

6 I shall sleep, and move with the moving ships,
  Change as the winds change, veer in the tide.
  1866 *Poems and Ballads*, 'The Triumph of Time'.

7 There lived a singer in France of old
  By the tideless dolorous midland sea.
  In a land of sand and ruin and gold
  There shone one woman, and none but she.
  1866 *Poems and Ballads*, 'The Triumph of Time'.

8 O slain and spent and sacrificed
  People, the grey-grown speechless Christ.
  1871 *Songs before Sunrise*, 'Before a Crucifix'.

9 But God, if a God there be, is the substance of men
  which is man.
  1871 *Songs before Sunrise*, 'Hymn of Man'.

10 Glory to Man in the highest! for Man is the master of
   things.
   1871 *Songs before Sunrise*, 'Hymn of Man'.

11 There was a poor poet named Clough,
   Whom his friends all united to puff,
   But the public, though dull,
   Had not such a skull
   As belonged to believers in Clough.
   1875 *Essays and Studies*, 'Matthew Arnold'.

12 For a day and a night Love sang to us, played with us,
   Folded us round from the dark and the light;
   And our hearts were fulfilled with the music he made
     with us,
   Made with our hands and our lips while he stayed
     with us,
   Stayed in mid passage his pinions from flight
   For a day and a night.
   1878 *Poems and Ballads* (2nd edn), 'At Parting'.

13 The deep division of prodigious breasts,
   The solemn slope of mighty limbs asleep.
   1878 *Poems and Ballads* (2nd edn), 'Ave Atque Vale', stanza 6.

14 Sleep; and if life was bitter to thee, pardon,
   If sweet, give thanks; thou hast no more to live;
   And to give thanks is good, and to forgive.
   1878 *Poems and Ballads* (2nd edn), 'Ave Atque Vale', stanza 17.

15 Villon, our sad bad glad mad brother's name.
   1878 *Poems and Ballads* (2nd edn), 'Ballad of François Villon'.

16 In a coign of the cliff between lowland and highland,
   At the sea-down's edge between windward and lee,
   Walled round with rocks as an inland island,
   The ghost of a garden fronts the sea.
   1878 *Poems and Ballads* (2nd edn), 'A Forsaken Garden'.

17 As a god self-slain on his own strange altar,
   Death lies dead.
   1878 *Poems and Ballads* (2nd edn), 'A Forsaken Garden'.

18 Fiddle, we know, is diddle: and diddle, we take it, is dee.
   1880 *The Heptalogia*, 'The Higher Pantheism in a Nutshell'.

Symington, Stuart 1901–88

US Senator. In 1939 he became President and Chairman of the Emerson Electric Manufacturing Company. He was the first Secretary of the Air Force (1945–48) and was elected Senator for Missouri in 1952.

19 I found out that he was a bachelor, as was his father before him.
1960 On hiring a speechwriter. Address to Washington's Gridiron Club, 12 Mar, quoted in Harold Brayman *The President Speaks-off-the-Record* (1976).

Synge, John Millington 1871–1909

Irish dramatist. On the advice of W B Yeats he travelled to the Aran Islands and there found materials for his plays which include *Riders to the Sea* (1904) and his masterpiece, *The Playboy of the Western World* (1907), which caused riots when it was first staged in Dublin.

20 No man at all can be living for ever, and we must be satisfied.
1904 *Riders to the Sea.*

21 They're all gone now, and there isn't anything more the sea can do to me.
1904 Maurya speaking. *Riders to the Sea.*

22 Well, if the worst comes in the end of all, it'll be great game to see if there's none to pity him but a widow woman, the like of me, has buried her children and destroyed her man.
1907 Widow Quin. *The Playboy of the Western World*, act 2.

23 Drink a health to the wonders of the western world, the pirates, preachers, poteen-makers, with the jobbing jockies; parching peelers, and the juries fill their stomachs selling judgments of the English law.
1907 *The Playboy of the Western World*, act 2.

24 I'll say, a strange man is a marvel, with his mighty talk; but what's a squabble in your back-yard, and the blow of a loy, have taught me that there's a great gap between a gallous story and a dirty deed.
1907 Pegeen Mike. *The Playboy of the Western World*, act 3.

25 Oh my grief, I've lost him surely. I've lost the only Playboy of the Western World.
1907 Pegeen Mike. *The Playboy of the Western World*, act 3, closing words.

Szasz, Thomas Stephen 1920–2012

Hungarian-born US psychiatrist. His books argue that disease is physical, hence mental illness is a myth, that the individual should be allowed complete freedom within the law, and all psychiatric therapy should be contractual.

26 Formerly, when religion was strong and science weak, men mistook magic for medicine, now, when science is strong and religion weak, men mistake medicine for magic.
1974 *The Second Sin.*

27 Men are rewarded and punished not for what they do, but rather for how their acts are defined. This is why men are more interested in better justifying themselves than in better behaving themselves.
1974 *The Second Sin.*

28 Psychiatrists classify a person as neurotic if he suffers from his problems in living, and a psychotic if he makes others suffer.
1974 *The Second Sin.*

Szent-Györgyi, Albert von Nagyrapolt 1893–1986

Hungarian-born US biochemist, authority on the processes of biological combustion. He was educated at the universities of Budapest and Cambridge. In 1947, he migrated to the US to join the Marine Biological Laboratories, Massachusetts. He was awarded the 1937 Nobel prize in physiology or medicine.

29 Discovery consists of seeing what everybody has seen and thinking what nobody has thought.
Quoted in Irving Good (ed) *The Scientist Speculates* (1962).

30 Knowledge is a sacred cow, and my problem will be how we can milk her while keeping clear of her horns.
1964 In *Science*, vol.146.

Szilard, Leo 1898–1964

Hungarian-born US nuclear physicist, who contributed to the development of controlled nuclear fission. He left the University of Berlin with the advent of Hitler, jointing Columbia University in 1938. He urged Albert Einstein to write to President Roosevelt warning of the possible military use of atomic energy by the Nazis.

31 We turned the switch, saw the flashes, watched for ten minutes, then switched everything off and went home. That night I knew the world was headed for sorrow.
1939 After an early experiment at Columbia University which proved the possibility of splitting the atom. Quoted in James B Simpson *Simpson's Contemporary Quotations* (1988).

32 Don't lie if you don't have to.
1972 In *Science*, vol.176, p.966.

Taaffe, Eduard Franz Josef, Graf von 1833–95

Austrian statesman, Minister of the Interior (1867) and Chief Minister (1869–70, 1879–93).

1 As a Minister, it is my policy to keep all the nationalities within the Habsburg monarchy in a balanced state of well-modulated dissatisfaction.
1881 Letters.

Tacitus, Cornelius *full name* Publius *or* Gaius Cornelius Tacitus AD 55–c.120

Roman historian and orator, who lived under Domitian, Nerva, Trajan and Hadrian. He wrote a biography of his father-in-law Agricola. His major historical works are the *Historiae* (Histories), of which only the first four books survive whole, and the *Annales* (Annals), of which only eight books survive.

2 *Solitudinem faciunt pacem appellant.*
They make a wilderness and they call it peace.
Speech of the British chieftain Calgacus, before the battle of Mons Graupius, referring to the Romans. *Agricola*, ch.30.

3 *Proprium humani ingenii est odisse quem laeseris.*
It is part of human nature to hate a man you have hurt.
Agricola, ch.42.

4 *Perdomita Britannia et statim omissa.*
Britain was conquered and immediately lost.
Referring to Agricola's conquest of Britain, and the loss of much of it under Domitian. *Histories*, bk.1, ch.2.

5 *Deos fortioribus adesse.*
The gods support those who are stronger.
Histories, bk.4, ch.17.

6 *Miseram pacem vel bello bene mutari.*
Even war is preferable to a shameful peace.
Annals, bk.3, ch.44.

7 *Auctor nominis eius Christus, Tiberio imperitante, per procuratorem Pontium Pilatum, supplicio affectus erat.*
Christ, the leader of the sect, had been put to death by the procurator Pontius Pilate in the reign of Tiberius.
Annals, bk.15, ch.44.

8 *Elegantiae arbiter.*
The arbiter of taste.
Of Petronius. *Annals*, bk.16, ch.18.

Taft, Robert A(lphonso) 1889–1953

US politician. Son of US President William Howard Taft, he entered the Senate in 1932 and was a prominent isolationist. He co-sponsored the Taft-Hartley Act (1947), which acted against the 'closed shop' power of trade unions. He failed three times (1940, 1948, 1952) to gain the Republican nomination for the US presidency.

9 Lending arms is like lending chewing gum. You don't get it back.
On the lend-lease agreement. Quoted in David Brinkley *Washington Goes to War* (1988).

Taft, William Howard 1857–1930

US Republican politician and 27th US President. Secretary of War (1904–8) and provisional governor of Cuba (1906), he became President in 1909 and remained in the post until 1913, when he was defeated by Woodrow Wilson. Subsequently he became US Chief Justice (1921).

10 There are a great many people who are in favor of conservation no matter what it means.
Quoted in J W Milliman *Land Economics* (1962).

11 Golf is in the interest of good health and good manners. It promotes self-restraint and affords a chance to play the man and act the gentleman.
Quoted in Michael Hobbs *The Golf Quotation Book* (1992).

Takuboku, Ishikawa 1886–1902

Japanese poet whose first book of poems, *Akogare* (Longing), was published in 1905. Five years later, a second collection, *Ichiaku no Suna* (A Handful of Dust), broke new ground by writing about aspects of everyday life.

12 There are some lives duller
Than dusty glass
1910 *Ichiaku no Suna* (translated by Sakanishi Shio).

13 Like a stone
That rolls down a hill,
I have come to this day.
1910 *Ichiaku no Suna* (translated by Sakanishi Shio).

Talbot, Godfrey Walker 1908–2000

English broadcaster and writer. He was the BBC's war correspondent in World War II and their court correspondent from 1948 to 1969. He wrote articles on the Royal Family and an autobiography, *Ten Seconds from Now* (1973).

14 A man who, until he made the journey from London, thought that woad began at Watford.
1973 *Ten Seconds from Now*, ch.3. An early reference to the 'north of Watford' concept, in which Watford is regarded as the limit of 'civilization' northwards from London.

Talese, Gay 1932–

US writer and journalist. His works include *New York: A Serendipiter's Journey* (1961), *Fame and Obscurity* (1970) and *Unto the Sons* (1992).

15 New glass skyscrapers stand shoulder to shoulder, reflecting one another narcissistically.
1965 In the *New York Times*, 23 Jun.

Talleyrand-Périgord, Charles-Maurice de, Prince of Benevento 1754–1838

French statesman, President of the Assembly (1790). He lived in exile until the fall of Robespierre. As Foreign Minister under the Directory (1797–1807) he helped consolidate Napoleon's position, but alarmed by his ambitions resigned in 1807 to become leader of the anti-Napoleonic faction. Foreign Minister under Louis XVIII, he represented France at the Congress of Vienna (1814–15). He was Louis Philippe's chief adviser at the July Revolution, and Ambassador to England (1830–4).

16 *Ils n'ont rien appris, ni rien oublié.*
They have learned nothing, and forgotten nothing.
Attributed.

17 *Voilà le commencement de la fin.*
This is the beginning of the end.
Attributed.

18 The allies are too frightened to fight each other, too stupid too agree.
1814 Congress of Vienna, Nov.

Tally, Ted 1952–

US screenwriter, best known for *The Silence of the Lambs* (1991) for which he won an Academy Award for Best Adapted Screenplay.

19 A census taker once tried to test me, I ate his liver with some fava beans and a nice Chianti.
1991 Anthony Hopkins as Dr Hannibal Lecter ('Hannibal the Cannibal') in *The Silence of the Lambs*.

20 I do wish we could chat longer but I'm having an old friend for dinner.
1991 Anthony Hopkins as Dr Hannibal Lecter ('Hannibal the Cannibal') in *The Silence of the Lambs*.

Talma, François-Joseph 1763–1826

French actor-manager. He established his reputation as a powerful tragedian in the central role of Chénier's *Charles IX* in 1789, which caused a sensation; subsequently he formed his own company and staged admired productions of Corneille, Shakespeare and others. As head of the French national theatre under Napoleon he introduced various important reforms.

21 *Voltaire! Comme Voltaire, toujours comme Voltaire.*
Voltaire! Like Voltaire, always like Voltaire.
1826 Last words.

Tanaka, Kakuei 1918–93

Japanese politician who rose through the ranks of the Liberal Democratic party to become Prime Minister. Arrested in 1976 for bribery, he resigned the premiership, although he remained influential.

22 The politics of numbers.
   1983 Describing democracy, in an interview with the *Nihon Keizai Shimbun*, 25 Jan.

23 Why should not a large shareholder sometimes name the president?
   1983 Responding to criticism that candidates for the premiership must win his approval. Quoted in the *Financial Times*, 11 Oct.

Tannahill, Robert 1774–1810

Scottish poet and songwriter, born in Paisley, the son of a weaver.

24 The sun has gane down o'er the lofty Benlomond,
   And left the red clouds to preside o'er the scene,
   While lanely I stray, in the calm simmer gloamin',
   To muse on sweet Jessie, the flower o' Dunblane.
   How sweet is the brier wi' its saft faulding blossom,
   And sweet is the birk, wi' its mantle o' green;
   Yet sweeter, and fairer, and dear to this bosom,
   Is lovely young Jessie, the flower o' Dunblane.
   1807 'Jessie, the Flower o' Dunblane', stanza 1.

T'ao Ch'ien AD 372–427

Chinese poet about whom little is known.

25 I beg you listen to this advice—
   When you get wine, be sure to drink it.
   c.400 AD Collected in *Substance, Shadow and Spirit*, translated by Arthur Waley.

Tarantino, Quentin 1963–

US director and screenwriter, known for the brutality and violent escapism of his films. One of his many scripts was made into his debut film as director, *Reservoir Dogs* (1993). In 1994 his second film, *Pulp Fiction*, won the Palme d'Or at the Cannes Film Festival. Later films include *Jackie Brown* (1997), *Inglourious Basterds* (2009) and *Django Unchained* (2012).

26 Violence in real life is terrible; violence in movies can be cool. It's just another colour to work with.
   1994 In the *Observer*, 'Sayings of the Week', 16 Oct.

27 Violence is fun, man.
   2004 In *The Times*, 17 May.

28 It's not for the chicken to speak of his own soup.
   2009 When asked his opinion of his movie *Inglourious Basterds*.

Tarkington, (Newton) Booth 1869–1946

US novelist, best known for his Penrod books, *Penrod* (1914) and *Seventeen* (1916). His novel *The Magnificent Ambersons* (1918) won the Pulitzer Prize and was made into a successful film by Orson Welles.

29 There are two things that will be believed of any man whatsoever, and one of them is that he has taken to drink.
   1914 *Penrod*, ch.10.

30 The Magnificent Ambersons.
   1918 Title of novel.

31 An ideal wife is any woman who has an ideal husband.
   1924 *Looking Forward And Others*, 'The Hopeful Pessimist'.

Tarrant, Chris 1946–

English radio and television presenter.

32 Is that your final answer?
   Catchphrase on the television show *Who Wants To Be A Millionaire?*.

Tartt, Donna 1963–

US author. She achieved widespread succes with her first novel, *The Secret History* (1992). Her second novel, *The Little Friend* (2002), appeared a decade later. *The Goldfinch* (2013) won a Pulitzer prize.

33 The snow in the mountains was melting and Bunny had been dead for several weeks before we came to understand the gravity of our situation.
   1992 *The Secret History*.

34 I'd love to write a book a year, but I don't think I'd have any fans.
   2002 In the *Sunday Times*, 2 Jun.

35 Birds—birds, everywhere, great black cawing explosions of them, like radioactive fall-out, like shrapnel.
   2002 *The Little Friend*.

36 Caring too much for objects can destroy you. Only—if you care for a thing enough, it takes on a life of its own, doesn't it? And isn't the whole point of things—beautiful things—that they connect you to some larger beauty?
   2013 *The Goldfinch*.

37 Stay away from the ones you love too much. Those are the ones who will kill you.
   2013 *The Goldfinch*.

Tate, (John Orley) Allen 1899–1979

US poet, critic and biographer. He was the editor of the influential *Sewanee Review* (1944–7). His own poetry was strongly influenced by T S Eliot.

38 Row upon row with strict impunity
   The headstones yield their names to the element.
   1948 *Poems 1922–1947*, 'Ode to the Confederate Dead'.

39 Autumn is desolation in the plot
   Of a thousand acres, where these memories grow
   From the inexhaustible bodies that are not
   Dead, but feed the grass, row after rich row.
   1948 *Poems 1922–1947*, 'Ode to the Confederate Dead'.

40 The brute curiosity of an angel's stare
   Turn you like them to stone.
   1948 *Poems 1922–1947*, 'Ode to the Confederate Dead'.

41 I've heard the wolves scuffle, and said: So this
   Is man; so—what better conclusion is there—
   The day will not follow night, and the heart
   Of man has a little dignity, but less patience
   Than a wolf's, and a duller sense that cannot
   Smell its own mortality.
   1948 *Poems 1922–1947*, 'The Wolves'.

Tate, Greg

US writer and music critic.

42 Commodity fetishism is the true God of this nation.
   1992 In *Vibe*, reported in *USA Today*, 14 Sep.

Tawney, R(ichard) H(enry) 1880–1962

British economic historian, active in the Workers' Educational Association at Rochdale, Lancashire, and its President (1928–44).

He was Professor of Economic History at London (1931–49) and wrote a number of studies in English economic history.

43 The instinct of mankind warns it against accepting at their face value spiritual demands that cannot satisfy themselves by practical achievements. The road along which the organized workers, like any other class, must climb to power starts from the provision of a more effective economic service than their masters, as their grip upon industry becomes increasingly vacillating and uncertain, are able to supply.
1926 *The Acquisitive Society.*

44 As long as men are men, a poor society cannot be too poor to find a right order of life; nor a rich society too rich to have need to seek it.
1926 *The Acquisitive Society.*

Taylor, A(lan) J(ohn) P(ercivale) 1906–90

English historian, whose major work was *The Struggle for Mastery in Europe 1848–1918* (1954). His controversial revisionist *Origins of the Second World War* (1961) argued against a grand design. Other works include *English History 1914–1945* (1965), *The Trouble Makers* (1957), on critics of British foreign policy, and *A Personal History* (1983).

45 Crimea: The War That Would Not Boil.
1952 *Rumours of Wars,* ch.6, chapter title.

46 Human blunders usually do more to shape history than human wickedness.
1961 *The Origins of the Second World War.*

47 The First World War had begun—imposed on the statesmen of Europe by railway timetables. It was an unexpected climax to the railway age.
1963 *The First World War,* ch.1.

48 Like most of those who study history, Napoleon learned from the mistakes of the past how to make new ones.
1963 BBC radio broadcast, 6 Jun.

49 History gets thicker and thicker as it approaches recent times.
1965 *English History 1914–1945.*

Taylor, Dwight 1902–86

US screenwriter. Best known for his screenplays for two of the Fred Astaire/Ginger Rogers musicals *Top Hat* (1935) and *Follow the Fleet* (1936).

50 Are you sure you didn't forget yourself in the park? Positive. If I ever forget myself with that girl I'd remember it.
1935 Dialogue between Edward Everett Horton and Fred Astaire in *Top Hat* (with Allan Scott).

Taylor, Elizabeth Rosemond 1932–2011

English-born US film actress. She graduated from child star to screen goddess in films such as *A Place in the Sun* (1951), *Raintree County* (1957), *Butterfield 8* (1960), *Cleopatra* (1962) and *Who's Afraid of Virginia Woolf?* (1966). She has had seven husbands, most famously Richard Burton, whom she married twice.

51 It will be fun to be the first Jewish Queen of Egypt.
c.1962 On taking the title role in *Cleopatra.* Attributed.

52 If someone was stupid enough to offer me a million dollars to make a picture—I was certainly not dumb enough to turn it down.
Quoted in David Niven *The Moon's a Balloon* (1975).

53 Success is a great deodorant.
1977 ABC TV broadcast, 6 Apr.

54 You help them get elected, and then the Senate becomes the wife, the mistress. That was one lady I couldn't begin to fight. She was too tough.
1987 After her marriage to Senator John Warner. In *Cosmopolitan,* Sep.

55 Some of my best leading men have been horses and dogs.
Attributed.

Taylor, Graham 1944–

English football manager. Manager of Aston Villa and other sides, he succeeded Bobby Robson as manager of England in 1990 but resigned three years later after England failed to qualify for the 1994 World Cup.

56 Agents do nothing for the good of football. I'd like to see them lined up against a wall and machine-gunned …some accountants and solicitors with them.
1983 Quoted in Peter Ball and Phil Shaw *The Book of Football Quotations* (1989).

57 Do I not like that!
1993 During England defeat to Norway, recorded in television documentary.

Taylor, Jeremy 1613–67

English divine, whose sermons and devotional writings are masterpieces and considered to be of sacred eloquence.

58 Faith gives new light to the soul, but it does not put our eyes out; and what God hath given us in our nature could never be intended as a snare to Religion, or engage us to believe a lie.
1660 *The Worthy Communicant.*

Taylor, John Vernon 1914–2001

English cleric and writer, Bishop of Winchester (1974–84).

59 The Holy Spirit is the invisible third party who stands between me and the other, making us mutually aware.
1972 *The Go-Between God.*

60 [God's] changelessness means that he cannot cease to be what he is, but it does not preclude his doing some new thing to express what he is.
1992 *The Christlike God.*

Taylor, Maxwell Davenport 1901–87

US soldier, air commander in World War II and superintendent of West Point (1945–9). After commanding in Korea and the Far East, he was appointed army chief of staff (1955–9) but resigned when his proposals for army reorganization were disregarded. He was instrumental in securing US support for the war in Vietnam.

61 They didn't know how it ran, where you put in the gas, where you put in the oil, where you turn the throttle.
On the Kennedy White House and the botched invasion of Cuba's Bay of Pigs. Quoted in Ralph G Martin *A Hero for Our Time* (1983).

Teal, Clare 1973–

English jazz singer.

62 Jazz is a small word for a vast sound.
2002 In *The Guardian,* 29 Dec.

Tebbit, Norman (Beresford) Tebbit, Baron 1931–

English Conservative politician, Employment Secretary (1981–3) and Secretary for Trade and Industry (1983–5). In 1984 he and his wife were injured by an IRA bomb in Brighton. In 1985 he became Chairman of the Party, but after 1987 he returned to the backbenches until his retirement in 1992.

63 He didn't riot. He got on his bike and looked for work, and he kept looking till he found it.
1981 Speaking of his father after criticism of high unemployment under the Conservative Government, party conference, 15 Oct.

64 The cricket test—which side do they cheer for?
1990 On the loyalties of immigrants in Britain. In the *Los Angeles Times*, Apr.

Te Kanawa, Dame Kiri 1944–

New Zealand soprano.

65 When men reach about the age of 50 they tend to digress and don't want to do anything. You can't inspire them to do anything—they almost go to sleep in their bodies.
2001 In *The Mail on Sunday*, 25 Nov.

Teller, Edward 1908–2003

Hungarian-born US physicist, called the father of the hydrogen bomb. He was born in Budapest, and educated in Germany. In 1941 he became a US citizen and joined the US atomic bomb development project known as the Manhattan Project.

66 If there ever was a misnomer, it is 'exact science'. Science has always been full of mistakes; they require a genius to correct them. Of course, we do not see our own mistakes.
1991 Conversations on the Dark Secrets of Physics.

Temple, William 1881–1944

English prelate. Headmaster of Repton School (1910–14), he became a bishop in 1921, Archbishop of York in 1919, and succeeded as Archbishop of Canterbury in 1942. He was an outspoken advocate of social reform.

67 Personally, I have always looked upon cricket as organized loafing.
c.1914 Address to parents of pupils at Repton School, Derbyshire.

68 Christianity is the most materialist of all great religions.
1939 Readings in St John's Gospel, vol.1.

69 I believe in the Church, one Holy Catholic and Apostolic Church; and nowhere does it exist.
Attributed.

Templeton, Charles 1915–2001

Canadian media personality and author.

70 You are born with two things: existence and opportunity, and these are the raw materials out of which you can make a successful life.
1989 Succeeding.

Tennyson, Alfred, 1st Baron *also called* Alfred, Lord Tennyson 1809–92

English lyric poet, a master of rhythm, mood and imagery. He became Poet Laureate in 1850. Among the finest poems are *Morte d'Arthur* (1842), the elegiac *In Memoriam* (1850) and *The Idylls of the King* (1859).

71 Below the thunders of the upper deep;
Far, far beneath in the abysmal sea,
His ancient, dreamless, uninvaded sleep
The Kraken sleepeth.
1830 Poems, Chiefly Lyrical, 'The Kraken', l.1–4.

72 There hath he lain for ages and will lie
Battening upon huge seaworms in his sleep
Until the latter fire shall heat the deep.
1830 Poems, Chiefly Lyrical, 'The Kraken', l.11–13.

73 Vex not thou the poet's mind
With thy shallow wit:
Vex not thou the poet's mind;
For thou canst not fathom it.
1830 Poems, Chiefly Lyrical, 'The Poet's Mind', l.1–4.

74 Airy, fairy Lilian.
1830 Poems, 'Lilian', l.1.

75 A daughter of the gods, divinely tall,
And most divinely fair.
1832 Poems, 'A Dream of Fair Women', l.87–8.

76 O Love, O fire! once he drew
With one long kiss my whole soul through
My lips, as sunlight drinketh dew.
1832 Poems, 'Fatima', stanza 3.

77 On either side the river lie
Long fields of barley and of rye,
That clothe the wold and meet the sky;
And through the field the road runs by
To many-towered Camelot.
1832 Poems, 'The Lady of Shalott' (revised 1842), pt.1, l.1–5.

78 Willows whiten, aspens quiver,
Little breezes dusk and shiver.
1832 Poems, 'The Lady of Shalott' (revised 1842), pt.1, l.10–11.

79 Four grey walls, and four grey towers,
Overlook a space of flowers,
And the silent isle imbowers
The Lady of Shalott.
1832 Poems, 'The Lady of Shalott' (revised 1842), pt.1, l.15–18.

80 Only reapers, reaping early
In among the bearded barley,
Hear a song that echoes cheerly
From the river winding clearly,
Down to towered Camelot.
1832 Poems, 'The Lady of Shalott' (revised 1842), pt.1, l.28–32.

81 And moving through a mirror clear
That hangs before her all the year,
Shadows of the world appear.
1832 Poems, 'The Lady of Shalott' (revised 1842), pt.2, l.46–8.

82 Or when the moon was overhead,
Came two young lovers lately wed;
'I am half sick of shadows,' said
The Lady of Shalott.
1832 Poems, 'The Lady of Shalott' (revised 1842), pt.2, l.69–72.

83 A bow-shot from her bower-eaves,
He rode between the barley-sheaves,
The sun came dazzling through the leaves,
And flamed upon the brazen greaves
Of bold Sir Lancelot.
A red-cross knight forever kneeled
To a lady in his shield,
That sparkled on the yellow field,
Beside remote Shalott.
1832 Poems, 'The Lady of Shalott' (revised 1842), pt.3, l.73–81.

84 All in the blue unclouded weather
   Thick-jewelled shone the saddle leather,
   The helmet and the helmet-feather
   Burned like one burning flame together,
   As he rode down to Camelot.
   1832 *Poems*, 'The Lady of Shalott' (revised 1842), pt.3, l.91–5.

85 She left the web, she left the loom,
   She made three paces through the room,
   She saw the water-lily bloom,
   She saw the helmet and the plume,
   She looked down to Camelot.
   Out flew the web and floated wide;
   The mirror cracked from side to side;
   'The curse is come upon me', cried
   The Lady of Shalott.
   1832 *Poems*, 'The Lady of Shalott' (revised 1842), pt.3, l.109–17.

86 Down she came and found a boat
   Beneath a willow left afloat,
   And round about the prow she wrote
   The Lady of Shalott.
   1832 *Poems*, 'The Lady of Shalott' (revised 1842), pt.4, l.123–6.

87 But Lancelot mused a little space;
   He said, 'She has a lovely face;
   God in his mercy lend her grace,
   The Lady of Shalott.'
   1832 *Poems*, 'The Lady of Shalott' (revised 1842), pt.4, l.168–71.

88 'Courage!' he said, and pointed toward the land,
   'This mounting wave will roll us shoreward soon.'
   In the afternoon they came unto a land
   In which it seemèd always afternoon.
   All round the coast the languid air did swoon,
   Breathing like one that hath a weary dream.
   1832 *Poems*, 'The Lotos-Eaters', l.1–6.

89 There is sweet music here that softer falls
   Than petals from blown roses on the grass,
   Or night dews on still waters between walls
   Of shadowy granite, in a gleaming pass;
   Music that gentlier on the spirit lies,
   Than tired eyelids upon tired eyes.
   1832 *Poems*, 'The Lotos-Eaters', Choric Song, stanza 1, l.46–51.

90 There is no joy but calm!
   1832 *Poems*, 'The Lotos-Eaters', Choric Song, stanza 2, l.68.

91 Death is the end of life; ah, why
   Should life all labour be?
   1832 *Poems* 'The Lotos-Eaters', Choric Song, stanza 4, l.86–87.

92 Live and lie reclined
   On the hills like Gods together, careless of mankind.
   For they lie beside their nectar, and the bolts are hurled
   Far below them in the valleys, and the clouds are lightly curled
   Round their golden houses, girdled with the gleaming world.
   1832 *Poems*, 'The Lotos-Eaters', Choric Song, stanza 8, l.154–8.

93 Surely, surely, slumber is more sweet than toil, the shore
   Than labour in the deep mid-ocean, wind and wave and oar;
   Oh rest ye, brother mariners, we will not wander more.
   1832 *Poems*, 'The Lotos-Easters', Choric Song, stanza 8, l.171–3.

94 I built my soul a lordly pleasure-house,
   Wherein at ease for aye to dwell.
   1832 *Poems*, 'The Palace of Art', stanza 1, l.1–2.

95 And 'while the world runs round and round,' I said,
   'Reign thou apart, a quiet king,
   Still as, while Saturn whirls, his steadfast shade
   Sleeps on his luminous ring.'
   1832 *Poems*, 'The Palace of Art', stanza 4, l.13–16.

96 An English home—grey twilight poured
   On dewy pasture, dewy trees,
   Softer than sleep—all things in order stored,
   A haunt of ancient Peace.
   1832 *Poems*, 'The Palace of Art', stanza 22, l.85–8.

97 It little profits that an idle king
   By this still hearth, among these barren crags,
   Matched with an agèd wife, I mete and dole
   Unequal laws unto a savage race,
   That hoard, and sleep, and feed, and know not me.
   1833 *Poems*, 'Ulysses' (published 1842), l.1–5.

98 I cannot rest from travel: I will drink
   Life to the lees: all times I have enjoyed
   Greatly, have suffered greatly, both with those
   That loved me, and alone; on shore, and when
   Through scudding drifts the rainy Hyades
   Vext the dim sea: I am become a name;
   For always roaming with a hungry heart
   Much have I seen and known; cities of men
   And manners, climates, council, governments,
   Myself not least, but honoured of them all;
   And drunk delight of battle with my peers,
   Far on the ringing plains of windy Troy.
   I am part of all that I have met;
   Yet all experience is an arch wherethrough
   Gleams that untravelled world, whose margin fades
   For ever and for ever when I move.
   How dull it is to pause, to make an end,
   To rust unburnished, not to shine in use!
   As though to breathe were life.
   1833 *Poems*, 'Ulysses' (published 1842), l.6–24.

99 This grey spirit yearning in desire
   To follow knowledge like a sinking star,
   Beyond the utmost bound of human thought.
   1833 *Poems*, 'Ulysses' (published 1842), l.30–2.

1 This is my son, mine own Telemachus.
   1833 *Poems*, 'Ulysses' (published 1842), l.33.

2 There lies the port; the vessel, puffs her sail:
   There gloom the dark broad seas. My mariners,
   Souls that have toiled, and wrought, and thought with me—
   That ever with a frolic welcome took
   The thunder and the sunshine, and opposed
   Free hearts, free foreheads—you and I are old:
   Old age hath yet his honour and his toil;
   Death closes all: but something ere the end,
   Some work of noble note, may yet be done,
   Not unbecoming men that strove with gods.
   The lights begin to twinkle from the rocks:
   The long day wanes: the slow moon climbs: the deep
   Moans round with many voices. Come, my friends,
   'Tis not too late to seek a newer world.
   Push off, and sitting well in order smite
   The sounding furrows: for my purpose holds
   To sail beyond the sunset, and the baths
   Of all the western stars, until I die.
   It may be that the gulfs will wash us down:

It may be we shall touch the Happy Isles,
And see the great Achilles, whom we knew.
Though much is taken, much abides: and though
We are not now that strength which in old days
Moved earth and hearth: that which we are, we are:
One equal temper of heroic hearts,
Made weak by time and fate, but strong in will
To strive, to seek, to find, and not to yield.
1833 *Poems*, 'Ulysses' (published 1842), l.44–70.

3 Break, break, break,
On thy cold grey stones, O Sea!
And I would that my tongue could utter
The thoughts that arise in me.
1842 *Poems*, 'Break, Break, Break', stanza 1.

4 And the stately ships go on
To their haven under the hill;
But O for the touch of a vanished hand,
And the sound of a voice that is still!
1842 *Poems*, 'Break, Break, Break', stanza 3.

5 'Tis not your work, but Love's. Love, unperceived,
A more ideal Artist he than all,
Came, drew your pencil from you, made those eyes
Darker than the darkest pansies, and that hair
More black than ashbuds in the front of March.
1842 *Poems*, 'The Gardener's Daughter', l.24–8.

6 A sight to make an old man young.
1842 *Poems*, 'The Gardener's Daughter', l.140.

7 Then she rode forth, clothed on with chastity.
1842 *Poems*, 'Godiva', l.53.

8 With twelve great shocks of sound, the shameless noon
Was clashed and hammered from a hundred towers.
1842 *Poems*, 'Godiva', l.74–5.

9 At me you smiled, but unbeguiled
I saw the snare, and I retired:
The daughter of a hundred Earls,
You are not one to be desired.
1842 *Poems*, 'Lady Clara Vere de Vere', stanza 1, l.5–8.

10 From yon blue heavens above us bent
The gardener Adam and his wife
Smile at the claims of long descent.
Howe'er it be, it seems to me,
'Tis only noble to be good.
Kind hearts are more than coronets,
And simple faith than Norman blood.
1842 *Poems*, 'Lady Clara Vere de Vere', stanza 7, l.50–6.

11 In the Spring a fuller crimson comes upon the robin's breast;
In the Spring the wanton lapwing gets himself another crest
In the Spring a livelier iris changes on the burnished dove;
In the Spring a young man's fancy lightly turns to thoughts of love.
1842 *Poems*, 'Locksley Hall', l.17–20.

12 And our spirits rushed together at the touching of the lips.
1842 *Poems*, 'Locksley Hall', l.38.

13 He will hold thee, when his passion shall have spent its novel force,
Something better than his dog, a little dearer than his horse.
1842 *Poems*, 'Locksley Hall', l.49–50.

14 This is truth the poet sings,
That a sorrow's crown of sorrow is remembering happier things.
1842 *Poems*, 'Locksley Hall', l.75–6.

15 Like a dog, he hunts in dreams.
1842 *Poems*, 'Locksley Hall', l.79.

16 But the jingling of the guinea helps the hurt that Honour feels.
1842 *Poems*, 'Locksley Hall', l.105.

17 Men, my brothers, men the workers, ever reaping something new:
That which they have done but earnest of the things that they shall do:

For I dipped into the future, far as human eye could see,
Saw the vision of the world, and all the wonder that would be;

Saw the heaven fill with commerce, argosies of magic sails,
Pilots of the purple twilight, dropping down with costly bales;

Heard the heavens fill with shouting, and there rained a ghastly dew
From the nations' airy navies grappling in the central blue;

Far along the world-wide whisper of the south-wind rushing warm,
With the standards of the peoples plunging through the thunder-storm;

Till the war-drum throbbed no longer, and the battle-flags were furled
In the Parliament of man, the Federation of the world.
1842 *Poems*, 'Locksley Hall', l.117–28.

18 Science moves, but slowly slowly, creeping on from point to point.
1842 *Poems*, 'Locksley Hall', l.134.

19 Yet I doubt not through the ages one increasing purpose runs,
And the thoughts of men are widened with the process of the suns.
1842 *Poems*, 'Locksley Hall', l.137–8.

20 Knowledge comes, but wisdom lingers, and I linger on the shore,
And the individual withers, and the world is more and more.
1842 *Poems*, 'Locksley Hall', l.141–2.

21 I will take some savage woman, she shall rear my dusky race.
1842 *Poems*, 'Locksley Hall', l.168.

22 I the heir of all the ages, in the foremost files of time.
1842 *Poems*, 'Locksley Hall', l.178.

23 Forward, forward let us range,
Let the great world spin for ever down the ringing grooves of change.
1842 *Poems*, 'Locksley Hall', l.181–2.

24 Better fifty years of Europe than a cycle of Cathay.
1842 *Poems*, 'Locksley Hall', l.184.

25 This truth within thy mind rehearse,
That in a boundless universe
Is boundless better, boundless worse.
1842 Poems, 'The Two Voices', stanza 9, l.25–7.

26 No life that breathes with human breath
Has ever truly longed for death.
1842 Poems, 'The Two Voices', stanza 132, l.395–6.

27 Fill the cup, and fill the can:
Have a rouse before the morn:
Every moment dies a man,
Every moment one is born.
1842 Poems, 'The Vision of Sin', pt.4, stanza 9, l.95–8.

28 I grow in worth, and wit, and sense,
Unboding critic-pen,
Or that eternal want of pence,
Which vexes public men.
1842 Poems, 'Will Waterproof's Lyrical Monologue', stanza 6, l.41–4.

29 A land of settled government,
A land of just and old renown,
Where Freedom slowly broadens down
From precedent to precedent.
1842 Poems, 'You ask me, why, though ill at ease', stanza 3, l.9–12.

30 But we grow old, Ah! when shall all men's good
Be each man's rule, and universal peace
Lie like a shaft of light across the land,
And like a lane of beams athwart the sea,
Through all the circle of the golden year.
1846 'The Golden Year', l.47–51.

31 With prudes for proctors, dowagers for deans,
And sweet girl-graduates in their golden hair.
1847 The Princess, 'Prologue', l.141–2.

32 A classic lecture, rich in sentiment,
With scraps of thundrous Epic lilted out
By violet-hooded Doctors, elegies
And quoted odes, and jewels five-words-long,
That on the stretched forefinger of all Time
Sparkle for ever.
1847 The Princess, pt.2, l.352–7.

33 Man is the hunter; woman is his game:
The sleek and shining creatures of the chase,
We hunt them for the beauty of their skins;
They love us for it, and we ride them down.
1847 The Princess, pt.5, l.147–50.

34 The woman is so hard
Upon the woman.
1847 The Princess, pt.6, l.205–6.

35 No little lily-handed baronet he,
A great broad-shouldered genial Englishman,
A lord of fat prize-oxen and of sheep,
A raiser of huge melons and of pine,
A patron of some thirty charities,
A pamphleteer on guano and on grain.
1847 The Princess, 'Conclusion', l.84–9.

36 And blessings on the falling out
That all the more endears,
When we fall out with those we love
And kiss again with tears!
1850 The Princess, pt.2, added song, l.6–9.

37 Sweet and low, sweet and low,
Wind of the western sea,
Low, low, breathe and blow,
Wind of the western sea!
Over the rolling waters go,
Come from the dying moon, and blow,
Blow him again to me;
While my little one, while my pretty one, sleeps.

Sleep and rest, sleep and rest,
Father will come to thee soon;
Rest, rest, on mother's breast,
Father will come to thee soon;
Father will come to his babe in the nest,
Silver sails all out of the west
Under the silver moon:
Sleep, my little one, sleep, my pretty one, sleep.
1850 The Princess, pt.3, added song, stanzas 1–2.

38 The splendour falls on castle walls
And snowy summits old in story:
The long light shakes across the lakes,
And the wild cataract leaps in glory.
Blow, bugle, blow, set the wild echoes flying,
Blow, bugle; answer, echoes, dying, dying, dying.
1850 The Princess, pt.4, added song, stanza 1.

39 O hark, O hear! how thin and clear
And thinner, clearer, farther going!
O sweet and far from cliff and scar
The horns of Elfland faintly blowing!
Blow, let us hear the purple glens replying:
Blow, bugle; answer, echoes, dying, dying, dying.
1850 The Princess, pt.4, added song, stanza 2.

40 O love, they die in yon rich sky,
They faint on hill or field or river:
Our echoes roll from soul to soul,
And grow for ever and for ever.
1850 The Princess, pt.4, added song, stanza 3.

41 Tears, idle tears, I know not what they mean,
Tears from the depth of some divine despair
Rise in the heart, and gather to the eyes,
In looking on the happy autumn-fields,
And thinking of the days that are no more.
1850 The Princess, pt.4, added song, stanza 1.

42 So sad, so fresh, the days that are no more.
1850 The Princess, pt.4, added song, stanza 2.

43 Ah, sad and strange as in dark summer dawns
The earliest pipe of half-awakened birds
To dying ears, when unto dying eyes
The casement slowly grows a glimmering square;
So sad, so strange, the days that are no more.

Dear as remembered kisses after death,
And sweet as those by hopeless fancy feigned
On lips that are for others; deep as love,
Deep as first love, and wild with all regret;
O Death in Life, the days that are no more.
1850 The Princess, pt.4, added song, stanzas 3–4.

44 O Swallow, Swallow, flying, flying South,
Fly to her, and fall upon her gilded eaves,
And tell her, tell her, what I tell to thee.
O tell her, Swallow, thou that knowest each,
That bright and fierce and fickle is the South,
And dark and true and tender is the North.
1850 The Princess, pt.4, added song, stanzas 1–2.

45 O tell her, Swallow that thy brood is flown:
   Say to her, I do but wanton in the South,
   But in the North long since my nest is made.
   1850 The Princess, pt.4, added song, stanza 6.

46 Home they brought her warrior dead.
   She nor swooned, nor uttered cry:
   All her maidens, watching said,
   'She must weep or she will die.'
   1850 The Princess, pt.6, added song, stanza 1.

47 Rose a nurse of ninety years,
   Set his child upon her knee–
   Like summer tempest came her tears–
   'Sweet my child, I live for thee.'
   1850 The Princess, pt.6, added song, stanza 4.

48 Ask me no more: what answer should I give?
   I love not hollow cheek or faded eye:
   Yet, O my friend, I will not have thee die!
   Ask me no more, lest I should bid thee live.
   1850 The Princess, pt.7, added song, stanza 2.

49 Now sleeps the crimson petal, now the white;
   Nor waves the cypress in the palace walk;
   Nor winks the gold fin in the porphyry font:
   The fire-fly wakens: waken thou, with me.

   Now droops the milk-white peacock like
     a ghost,
   And like a ghost she glimmers on to me.
   Now lies the Earth all Danaë to the stars,
   And all thy heart lies open unto me.

   Now slides the silent meteor on, and leaves
   A shining furrow, as thy thoughts in me.

   Now folds the lily all her sweetness up,
   And slips into the bosom of the lake:
   So fold thyself, my dearest, thou, and slip
   Into my bosom and be lost in me.
   1850 The Princess, pt.7, added song, complete.

50 Come down, O maid, from yonder mountain
     height:
   What pleasure lives in height?
   1850 The Princess, pt.7, added song, l.1–2.

51 For love is of the valley, come thou down
   And find him; by the happy threshold, he,
   Or hand in hand with Plenty in the maize,
   Or red with spirited purple of the vats,
   Or foxlike in the vine; nor cares to walk
   With Death and Morning on the silver horns.
   1850 The Princess, pt.7, added song, l.184–9.

52 Sweet is every sound,
   Sweeter thy voice, but every sound is sweet;
   Myriads of rivulets hurrying through the lawn,
   The moan of doves in immemorial elms,
   With murmuring of innumerable bees.
   1850 The Princess, pt.7, added song, l.203–7.

53 Come not, when I am dead,
   To drop thy foolish tears upon my grave,
   To trample round my fallen head,
   And vex the unhappy dust thou wouldst not save.
   There let the wind sweep and the plover cry;
   But thou, go by.

   Child, if it were thine error or thy crime
   I care no longer, being all unblest;
   Wed whom thou wilt, but I am sick of Time,
   And I desire to rest.
   Pass on, weak heart, and leave me where I lie:
   Go by, go by.
   1850 'Come not, when I am dead', complete poem.

54 Strong Son of God, immortal Love,
   Whom we, that have not seen thy face,
   By faith, and faith alone, embrace,
   Believing where we cannot prove.
   1850 In Memoriam A.H.H., prologue, l.1–4.

55 Thou madest man, he knows not why,
   He thinks he was not made to die;
   And thou hast made him: thou art just.
   1850 In Memoriam A.H.H., prologue, l.10–12.

56 Our little systems have their day;
   They have their day and cease to be;
   They are but broken lights of thee,
   And thou, O Lord, art more than they.
   1850 In Memoriam A.H.H., prologue, l.17–20.

57 Let knowledge grow from more to more,
   But more of reverence in us dwell;
   That mind and soul, according well,
   May make one music as before.
   1850 In Memoriam A.H.H., prologue, l.25–8.

58 I sometimes hold it half a sin
   To put in words the grief I feel;
   For words, like Nature, half reveal
   And half conceal the Soul within.

   But, for the unquiet heart and brain,
   A use in measured language lies;
   The sad mechanic exercise,
   Like dull narcotics, numbing pain.
   1850 In Memoriam A.H.H., canto 5, l.1–8.

59 And common is the commonplace,
   And vacant chaff well meant for grain.
   1850 In Memoriam A.H.H., canto 6, l.3–4.

60 Never morning wore
   To evening, but some heart did break.
   1850 In Memoriam A.H.H., canto 6, l.7–8.

61 His heavy-shotted hammock-shroud
   Drops in his vast and wandering grave.
   1850 In Memoriam A.H.H., canto 6, l.15–16.

62 Dark house, by which once more I stand
   Here in the long unlovely street,
   Doors, where my heart was used to beat
   So quickly, waiting for a hand.
   1850 In Memoriam A.H.H., canto 7, l.1–4.

63 And ghastly through the drizzling rain
   On the bald street breaks the blank day.
   1850 In Memoriam A.H.H., canto 7, l.11–12.

64 The last red leaf is whirled away,
   The rooks are blown about the skies.
   1850 In Memoriam A.H.H., canto 15, l.3–4.

65 There twice a day the Severn fills;
   The salt sea-water passes by,
   And hushes half the babbling Wye,
   And makes a silence in the hills.
   1850 In Memoriam A.H.H., canto 19, l.5–8.

Tennyson In Memoriam A.H.H.

66 The Shadow cloaked from head to foot,
   Who keeps the keys of all the creeds.
   1850 *In Memoriam A.H.H.*, canto 23, l.4–5.

67 And Thought leapt out to wed with Thought
   Ere Thought could wed itself with Speech.
   1850 *In Memoriam A.H.H.*, canto 23, l.15–16.

68 I envy not in any moods
   The captive void of noble rage,
   The linnet born within the cage,
   That never knew the summer woods.
   1850 *In Memoriam A.H.H.*, canto 27, l.1–4.

69 I hold it true, whate'er befall;
   I feel it, when I sorrow most;
   'Tis better to have loved and lost
   Than never to have loved at all.
   1850 *In Memoriam A.H.H.*, canto 27, l.13–16.

70 A solemn gladness even crowned
   The purple brows of Olivet.
   1850 *In Memoriam A.H.H.*, canto 31, l.11–12.

71 Who trusted God was love indeed
   And love Creation's final law—
   Though Nature, red in tooth and claw
   With ravine, shrieked against his creed.
   1850 *In Memoriam A.H.H.*, canto 31.

72 Her eyes are homes of silent prayer.
   1850 *In Memoriam A.H.H.*, canto 32, l.1.

73 Short swallow-flights of song, that dip
   Their wings in tears, and skim away.
   1850 *In Memoriam A.H.H.*, canto 48, l.15–16.

74 Be near me when my light is low,
   When the blood creeps, and the nerves prick
   And tingle; and the heart is sick,
   And all the wheels of Being slow.

   Be near me when the sensuous frame
   Is racked with pains that conquer trust;
   And Time, a maniac scattering dust,
   And Life, a Fury slinging flame.
   1850 *In Memoriam A.H.H.*, canto 50, l.1–8.

75 Oh yet we trust that somehow good
   Will be the final goal of ill.
   1850 *In Memoriam A.H.H.*, canto 54, l.1–2.

76 That nothing walks with aimless feet;
   That not one life shall be destroyed,
   Or cast as rubbish to the void,
   When God hath made the pile complete.
   1850 *In Memoriam A.H.H.*, canto 54, l.5–8.

77 Behold, we know not anything;
   I can but trust that good shall fall
   At last—far off—at last, to all,
   And every winter change to spring.

   So runs my dream: but what am I?
   An infant crying in the night:
   An infant crying for the light:
   And with no language but a cry.
   1850 *In Memoriam A.H.H.*, canto 54, l.13–20.

78 So careful of the type she seems,
   So careless of the single life.
   1850 Of Nature. *In Memoriam A.H.H.*, canto 55, l.7–8.

79 The great world's altar-stairs
   That slope through darkness up to God.
   1850 *In Memoriam A.H.H.*, canto 55, l.15–16.

80 Man, her last work, who seemed so fair,
   Such splendid purpose in his eyes,
   Who rolled the psalm to wintry skies,
   Who built him fanes of fruitless prayer,
   Who trusted God was love indeed
   And love Creation's final law—
   Though Nature, red in tooth and claw
   With ravine, shrieked against his creed.
   1850 *In Memoriam A.H.H.*, canto 56, l.9–16.

81 Peace; come away: the song of woe
   Is after all an earthly song:
   Peace; come away: we do him wrong
   To sing so wildly: let us go.
   1850 *In Memoriam A.H.H.*, canto 57, l.1–4.

82 O Sorrow, wilt thou live with me
   No casual mistress, but a wife.
   1850 *In Memoriam A.H.H.*, canto 59, l.1–2.

83 Dost thou look back on what hath been,
   As some divinely gifted man,
   Whose life in low estate began
   And on a simple village green;

   Who breaks his birth's invidious bar,
   And grasps the skirts of happy chance,
   And breasts the blows of circumstance,
   And grapples with his evil star.
   1850 *In Memoriam A.H.H.*, canto 64, l.1–8.

84 So many worlds, so much to do,
   So little done, such things to be.
   1850 *In Memoriam A.H.H.*, canto 73, l.1–2.

85 Death has made
   His darkness beautiful with thee.
   1850 *In Memoriam A.H.H.*, canto 74, l.11–12.

86 And round thee with the breeze of song
   To stir a little dust of praise.
   1850 *In Memoriam A.H.H.*, canto 75, l.11–12.

87 O last regret, regret can die!
   1850 *In Memoriam A.H.H.*, canto 78, l.17.

88 Laburnums, dropping-wells of fire.
   1850 *In Memoriam A.H.H.*, canto 83, l.12.

89 God's finger touched him, and he slept.
   1850 *In Memoriam A.H.H.*, canto 85, l.20.

90 He brought an eye for all he saw;
   He mixed in all our simple sports;
   They pleased him, fresh from brawling courts
   And dusty purlieus of the law.
   1850 *In Memoriam A.H.H.*, canto 89, l.9–12.

91 You tell me, doubt is Devil-born.
   1850 *In Memoriam A.H.H.*, canto 96, l.4.

92 There lives more faith in honest doubt,
   Believe me, than in half the creeds.
   1850 *In Memoriam A.H.H.*, canto 96, l.11–12.

93 Their meetings made December June,
   Their every parting was to die.
   1850 *In Memoriam A.H.H.*, canto 97, l.11–12.

94 He seems so near and yet so far.
   1850 *In Memoriam A.H.H.*, canto 97, l.23.

95 Ring out, wild bells, to the wild sky,
    The flying cloud, the frosty light:
    The year is dying in the night;
    Ring out, wild bells, and let him die.

    Ring out the old, ring in the new,
    Ring, happy bells, across the snow:
    The year is going, let him go;
    Ring out the false, ring in the true.
    1850 *In Memoriam A.H.H.*, canto 106, l.1–8.

96 Ring out the want, the care, the sin,
    The faithless coldness of the times;
    Ring out, ring out my mournful rhymes,
    But ring the fuller minstrel in.

    Ring out false pride in place and blood,
    The civic slander and the spite;
    Ring in the love of truth and right,
    Ring in the common love of good.

    Ring out old shapes of foul disease;
    Ring out the narrowing lust of gold;
    Ring out the thousand wars of old,
    Ring in the thousand years of peace.

    Ring in the valiant man and free,
    The larger heart, the kindlier hand;
    Ring out the darkness of the land;
    Ring in the Christ that is to be.
    1850 *In Memoriam A.H.H.*, canto 106, l.17–32.

97 Not the schoolboy heat,
    The blind hysterics of the Celt.
    1850 *In Memoriam A.H.H.*, canto 109, l.15–16.

98 Now fades the last streak of snow,
    Now burgeons every maze of quick
    About the flowering squares, and thick
    By ashen roots the violets blow.
    1850 *In Memoriam A.H.H.*, canto 115, l.1–4.

99 And drowned in yonder living blue
    The lark become a sightless song.
    1850 *In Memoriam A.H.H.*, canto 115, l.7–8.

1   There, where the long street roars, hath been
    The stillness of the central sea.
    1850 *In Memoriam A.H.H.*, canto 123, l.3–4.

2   And thou art worthy; full of power;
    As gentle; liberal-minded, great,
    Consistent; wearing all that weight
    Of learning lightly like a flower.
    1850 *In Memoriam A.H.H.*, epilogue, l.37–40.

3   One God, one law, one element,
    And one far-off divine event,
    To which the whole creation moves.
    1850 *In Memoriam A.H.H.*, epilogue, l.142–4.

4   He clasps the crag with crooked hands;
    Close to the sun in lonely lands,
    Ringed with the azure world, he stands.

    The wrinkled sea beneath him crawls;
    He watches from his mountain walls,
    And like a thunderbolt he falls.
    1851 'The Eagle', complete poem.

5   Gigantic daughter of the West,
    We drink to thee across the flood,
    We know thee most, we love thee best,
    For art thou not of British blood?
    1852 'Hands all Round', stanza 4, l.37–40.

6   The last great Englishman is low.
    1852 'Ode on the Death of the Duke of Wellington', stanza 3, l.18.

7   O good grey head which all men knew!
    1852 'Ode on the Death of the Duke of Wellington', stanza 4, l.35.

8   O fall'n at length that tower of strength
    Which stood four-square to all the winds that blew!
    1852 'Ode on the Death of the Duke of Wellington', stanza 4, l.38–9.

9   That world-earthquake, Waterloo!
    1852 'Ode on the Death of the Duke of Wellington', stanza 6, l.133.

10 Who never sold the truth to serve the hour,
    Nor paltered with Eternal God of power.
    1852 'Ode on the Death of the Duke of Wellington', stanza 7, l.179–80.

11 Half a league, half a league,
    Half a league onward,
    All in the valley of Death
    Rode the six hundred.
    1854 'The Charge of the Light Brigade', l.1–4.

12 'Forward, the Light Brigade!'
    Was there a man dismayed?
    Not though the soldier knew
    Some one had blundered:
    Their's not to make reply,
    Their's not to reason why,
    Their's but to do and die:
    Into the valley of Death
    Rode the six hundred.

    Cannon to right of them,
    Cannon to left of them,
    Cannon in front of them
    Volleyed and thundered.
    1854 'The Charge of the Light Brigade', l.9–21.

13 Into the jaws of Death,
    Into the mouth of Hell
    Rode the six hundred.
    1854 'The Charge of the Light Brigade', l.24–6.

14 Faultily faultless, icily regular, splendidly null,
    Dead perfection, no more.
    1855 *Maud*, pt.1, sect.2, l.82–3.

15 The passionate heart of the poet is whirled into folly and vice.
    1855 *Maud*, pt.1, sect.4, stanza 7, l.139.

16 And most of all would I flee from the cruel madness of love,
    The honey of poison-flowers and all the measureless ill.
    1855 *Maud*, pt.1, sect.4, stanza 10, l.156–7.

17 That jewelled mass of millinery,
    That oiled and curled Assyrian Bull.
    1855 *Maud*, pt.1, sect.6, stanza 6, l.232–3.

18 She came to the village church,
    And sat by a pillar alone;
    An angel watching an urn
    Wept over her, carved in stone.
    1855 *Maud*, pt.1, sect.8, l.301–4.

Tennyson Maud

19 I heard no longer
    The snowy-banded, dilettante,
    Delicate-handed priest intone.
    1855 *Maud*, pt.1, sect.8, l.309–11.

20 Ah God, for a man with heart, head, hand,
    Like some of the simple great ones gone
    For ever and ever by,
    One still strong man in a blatant land,
    Whatever they call him, what care I,
    Aristocrat, democrat, autocrat—one
    Who can rule and dare not lie.
    1855 *Maud*, pt.1, sect.10, stanza 5, l.389–95.

21 And ah for a man to arise in me
    That the man I am may cease to be!.
    1855 *Maud*, pt.1, sect.10, stanza 6, l.396–7.

22 I kissed her slender hand,
    She took the kiss sedately;
    Maud is not seventeen,
    But she is tall and stately.
    1855 *Maud*, pt.1, sect.12, stanza 4, l.424–7.

23 Gorgonised me from head to foot
    With a stony British stare.
    1855 *Maud*, pt.1, sect.13, stanza 2, l.464–5.

24 A livelier emerald twinkles in the grass,
    A purer sapphire melts into the sea.
    1855 *Maud*, pt.1, sect.18, stanza 6, l.649–50.

25 Come into the garden, Maud,
    For the black bat, night, has flown,
    Come into the garden, Maud,
    I am here at the gate alone;
    And the woodbine spices are wafted
      abroad,
    And the musk of the rose is blown.

    For a breeze of morning moves,
    And the planet of Love is on high,
    Beginning to faint in the light that she loves
    On a bed of daffodil sky.
    1855 *Maud*, pt.1, sect.22, stanza 1, l.850–9.

26 All night has the casement jessamine stirred
    To the dancers dancing in tune;
    Till a silence fell with the waking bird,
    And a hush with the setting moon.
    1855 *Maud*, pt.1, sect.22, stanza 3, l.864–7.

27 Queen rose of the rosebud garden of girls.
    1855 *Maud*, pt.1, sect.22, stanza 9, l.902.

28 There has fallen a splendid tear
    From the passion-flower at the gate.
    She is coming, my dove, my dear;
    She is coming, my life, my fate;
    The red rose cries, 'She is near, she is near;'
    And the white rose weeps, 'She is late;'
    The larkspur listens, 'I hear, I hear;'
    And the lily whispers, 'I wait.'

    She is coming, my own, my sweet;
    Were it ever so airy a tread,
    My heart would hear her and beat,
    Were it earth in an earthy bed;
    My dust would hear her and beat,
    Had I lain for a century dead;

Would start and tremble under her feet,
And blossom in purple and red.
1855 *Maud*, pt.1, sect.22, stanzas 10–11, l. 908–23.

29 O that 'twere possible
    After long grief and pain
    To find the arms of my true love
    Round me once again!
    1855 *Maud*, pt.2, sect.4, stanza 1, l.141–4.

30 Dead, long dead,
    Long dead!
    And my heart is a handful of dust,
    And the wheels go over my head.
    1855 *Maud*, pt.2, sect.5, stanza 1, l.239–42.

31 But the churchmen fain would kill their church,
    As the churches have killed their Christ.
    1855 *Maud*, pt.2, sect.5, stanza 2, l.266–7.

32 O me, why have they not buried me deep enough?
    Is it kind to have made me a grave so rough,
    Me, that was never a quiet sleeper?
    1855 *Maud*, pt.2, sect. 5, stanza 11, l.334–6.

33 My life has crept so long on a broken wing
    Through cells of madness, haunts of horror and fear,
    That I come to be grateful at last for a little thing.
    1855 *Maud*, pt.3, sect.6, stanza 1, l.1–3.

34 When the face of night is fair on the dewy downs,
    And the shining daffodil dies.
    1855 *Maud*, pt.3, sect.6, stanza 1, l.5–6.

35 And now by the side of the Black and the Baltic deep,
    And deathful-grinning mouths of the fortress, flames
    The blood-red blossom of war with a heart of fire.
    1855 *Maud*, pt.3, sect.6, stanza 4, l.51–3.

36 It is better to fight for the good, than to rail at the ill;
    I have felt with my native land, I am one with my kind,
    I embrace the purpose of God, and the doom assigned.
    1855 *Maud*, pt.3, sect.6, stanza 5, l.57–9.

37 I come from haunts of coot and hern,
    I make a sudden sally
    And sparkle out among the fern,
    To bicker down a valley.
    1855 'The Brook', l.23–6.

38 For men may come and men may go,
    But I go on for ever.
    1855 'The Brook', l.33–4.

39 That a lie which is all a lie may be met and fought with
      outright,
    But a lie which is part a truth is a harder matter to
      fight.
    1859 'The Grandmother', stanza 8, l.31–2.

40 Wearing the white flower of a blameless life,
    Before a thousand peering littlenesses,
    In that fierce light which beats upon a throne,
    And blackens every blot.
    1859 *Idylls of the King*, dedication, l.24–7.

41 For man is man and master of his fate.
    1859 *Idylls of the King*, 'The Marriage of Geraint', l.355.

42 Our hoard is little, but our hearts are great.
    1859 *Idylls of the King*, 'The Marriage of Geraint', l.374.

43 They take the rustic murmur of their bourg
    For the great wave that echoes round the world.
    1859 *Idylls of the King*, 'The Marriage of Geraint', l.419–20.

44 It is little rift within the lute,
   That by and by will make the music mute,
   And ever widening slowly silence all.
   1859 *Idylls of the King*, 'Merlin and Vivien', l.388–90.

45 And trust me not at all or all in all.
   1859 *Idylls of the King*, 'Merlin and Vivien', l.396.

46 Man dreams of fame while woman wakes to love.
   1859 *Idylls of the King*, 'Merlin and Vivien', l.458.

47 With this for motto, 'Rather use than fame'.
   1859 *Idylls of the King*, 'Merlin and Vivien', l.478.

48 Where blind and naked Ignorance
   Delivers brawling judgements, unashamed,
   On all things all day long.
   1859 *Idylls of the King*, 'Merlin and Vivien', l.662–4.

49 But every page having an ample marge,
   And every marge enclosing in the midst
   A square of text that looks a little blot.
   1859 *Idylls of the King*, 'Merlin and Vivien', l.667–9.

50 Elaine the fair, Elaine the loveable,
   Elaine the lily maid of Astolat.
   1859 *Idylls of the King*, 'Lancelot and Elaine'.

51 He is all fault who hath no fault at all:
   For who loves me must have a touch of earth.
   1859 *Idylls of the King*, 'Lancelot and Elaine', l.132–3.

52 In me there dwells
   No greatness, save it be some far-off touch
   Of greatness to know well I am not great.
   1859 *Idylls of the King*, 'Lancelot and Elaine', l.447–9.

53 I know not if I know what true love is,
   But if I know, then, if I love not him,
   I know there is none other I can love.
   1859 *Idylls of the King*, 'Lancelot and Elaine', l.672–4.

54 The shackles of an old love straitened him,
   His honour rooted in dishonour stood,
   And faith unfaithful kept him falsely true.
   1859 *Idylls of the King*, 'Lancelot and Elaine', l.870–2.

55 —Never yet
   Was noble man but made ignoble talk.
   He makes no friend who never made a foe.
   1859 *Idylls of the King*, 'Lancelot and Elaine', l.1081–2.

56 To reverence the King, as if he were
   Their conscience, and their conscience as their
     King,
   To break the heathen and uphold the Christ,
   To ride abroad redressing human wrongs,
   To speak no slander, no, nor listen to it,
   To honour his own words as if his God's.
   1859 *Idylls of the King*, 'Guinevere', l.465–70.

57 To love one maiden only, cleave to her,
   And worship her by years of noble deeds,
   Until they won her; for indeed I knew
   Of no more subtle master under heaven
   Than is the maiden passion for a maid,
   Not only to keep down the base in man,
   But teach high thought, and aimable words
   And courtliness, and the desire of fame,
   And love of truth, and all that makes man.
   1859 *Idylls of the King*, 'Guinevere', l.472–80.

58 I thought I could not breathe in that fine air
   That pure severity of perfect light—
   I yearned for warmth and colour which I found
   In Lancelot.
   1859 *Idylls of the King*, 'Guinevere', l.640–3.

59 It was my duty to have loved the highest;
   It surely was my profit had I known:
   It would have been my pleasure had I seen.
   We needs must love the highest when we see it,
   Not Lancelot, nor another.
   1859 *Idylls of the King*, 'Guinevere', l.652–6.

60 The woods decay, the woods decay and fall,
   The vapours weep their burthen to the ground,
   Man comes and tills the field and lies beneath,
   And after many a summer dies the swan.
   Me only cruel immortality
   Consumes: I wither slowly in thine arms,
   Here at the quiet limit of the world.
   1860 'Tithonus' (revised 1864), l.1–7.

61 Why wilt thou ever scare me with thy tears,
   And make me tremble lest a saying learnt,
   In days far-off, on that dark earth, be true?
   'The gods themselves cannot recall their gifts.'
   1860 'Tithonus' (revised 1864), l.46–9.

62 Of happy men that have the power to die,
   And grassy barrows of the happier dead.
   1860 'Tithonus' (revised 1864), l.70–1.

63 O mighty-mouthed inventor of harmonies,
   O skilled to sing of Time or Eternity,
   God-gifted organ-voice of England,
   Milton, a name to resound for ages.
   1863 'Milton: Alcaics', l.1–4.

64 All that bowery loneliness,
   The brooks of Eden mazily murmuring.
   1863 'Milton: Alcaics', l.9–10.

65 O you chorus of indolent reviewers.
   1863 'Milton: Hendecasyllabics', l.1.

66 And when they buried him the little port
   Had seldom seen a costlier funeral.
   1864 'Enoch Arden', closing words.

67 The voice of the dead was a living voice to me.
   1864 'In the Valley of Cauteretz', l.10.

68 I saw the flaring atom-streams
   And torrents of her myriad universe,
   Ruining along the illimitable inane
   Fly on to clash together again, and make
   Another and another frame of things
   For ever.
   1868 'Lucretius', l.38–40.

69 Nor at all can tell
   Whether I mean this day to end myself,
   Or lend an ear to Plato where he says,
   That men like soldiers may not quit the post
   Allotted by the Gods.
   1868 'Lucretius', l.145–9.

70 Passionless bride, divine Tranquillity,
   Yearned after by the wisest of the wise,
   Who fail to find thee, being as thou art
   Without one pleasure and without one pain.
   1868 'Lucretius', l.265–8.

71 Speak to Him thou for He hears, and Spirit with Spirit
   can meet—

Closer is He than breathing, and nearer than hands and feet.
1869 'The Higher Pantheism', l.11–12.

72 Man's word is God in man.
1869 *Idylls of the King*, 'The Coming of Arthur', l.132.

73 Clothed in white samite, mystic, wonderful.
1869 *Idylls of the King*, 'The Coming of Arthur', l.284.

74 Rain, rain, and sun! a rainbow in the sky!
A young man will be wiser by and by;
An old man's wit may wander ere he die.
1869 *Idylls of the King*, 'The Coming of Arthur', l.402–4.

75 From the great deep to the great deep he goes.
1869 *Idylls of the King*, 'The Coming of Arthur', l.410.

76 Blow trumpet, for the world is white with May.
1869 *Idylls of the King*, 'The Coming of Arthur', l.481.

77 For good ye are and bad, and like to coins,
Some true, some light, but every one of you
Stamped with the image of the King.
1869 *Idylls of the King*, 'The Holy Grail', l.25–7.

78 I will be deafer than the blue-eyed cat,
And thrice as blind as any noonday owl,
To holy virgins in their ecstasies.
1869 *Idylls of the King*, 'The Holy Grail', l.862–4.

79 I found Him in the shining of the stars,
I marked Him in the flowering of His fields,
But in His ways with men I find Him not.
1869 *Idylls of the King*, 'The Passing of Arthur', l.9–11.

80 So all day long the noise of battle rolled
Among the mountains by the winter sea.
1869 *Idylls of the King*, 'The Passing of Arthur', l.170–1.

81 On one side lay the Ocean, and on one
Lay a great water, and the moon was full.
1869 *Idylls of the King*, 'The Passing of Arthur', l.179–80.

82 Authority forgets a dying king.
1869 *Idylls of the King*, 'The Passing of Arthur', l.289.

83 Clothed with his breath, and looking, as he walked,
Larger than human on the frozen hills.
He heard the deep behind him, and a cry
Before.
1869 *Idylls of the King*, 'The Passing of Arthur', l.350–3.

84 And the days darken round me, and the years,
Among new men, strange faces, other minds.
1869 *Idylls of the King*, 'The Passing of Arthur', l.405–6.

85 The old order changeth, yielding place to new,
And God fulfils himself in many ways,
Lest one good custom should corrupt the world.
1869 *Idylls of the King*, 'The Passing of Arthur', l.408–10.

86 If thou shouldst never see my face again,
Pray for my soul. More things are wrought by prayer
Than this world dreams of. Wherefore, let thy voice
Rise like a fountain for me night and day.
For what are men better than sheep or goats
That nourish a blind life within the brain,
If, knowing God, they lift not hands of prayer
Both for themselves and those who call them friend?
For so the whole round earth is every way
Bound by gold chains about the feet of God.
1869 *Idylls of the King*, 'The Passing of Arthur', l.414–23.

87 I am going a long way
With these thou se'st—if indeed I go
(For all my mind is clouded with a doubt)—
To the island-valley of Avilion;
Where falls not hail, or rain, or any snow,
Nor ever wind blows loudly; but it lies
Deep-meadowed, happy, fair with orchard lawns
And bowery hollows crowed with summer sea,
Where I will heal me of my grievous wound.
1869 *Idylls of the King*, 'The Passing of Arthur', l.424–32.

88 Like some full-breasted swan
That, fluting a wild carol ere her death,
Ruffles her pure cold plume, and takes the flood
With swarthy webs.
1869 *Idylls of the King*, 'The Passing of Arthur', l.434–7.

89 But I knaw'd a Quaäker feller as often 'as towd ma this:
'Doänt thou marry for munny, but goä wheer munny is!'
1869 'Northern Farmer. New Style', stanza 5.

90 Taäke my word for it, Sammy, the poor in a loomp is bad.
1869 'Northern Farmer. New Style', stanza 12.

91 The dirty nurse, Experience, in her kind
Hath fouled me.
1871 *Idylls of the King*, 'The Last Tournment', l.317–18.

92 The greater man, the greater courtesy.
1871 *Idylls of the King*, 'The Last Tournment', l.628.

93 Live pure, speak true, right wrong, follow the King—
Else, wherefore born?
1872 *Idylls of the King*, 'Gareth and Lynette', l.117–18.

94 The city is built
To music, therefore never built at all,
And therefore built for ever.
1872 *Idylls of the King*, 'Gareth and Lynette', l.272–4.

95 At Flores in the Azores Sir Richard Grenville lay,
And a pinnace, like a fluttered bird, came flying from far away:
'Spanish ships of war at sea! We have sighted fifty-three!'
Then sware Lord Thomas Howard: "Fore God I am no coward;
But I cannot meet them here, for my ships are out of gear,
And the half my men are sick. I must fly, but follow quick.
We are six ships of the line; can we fight with fifty-three?'

Then spake Sir Richard Grenville: 'I know you are no coward;
You fly them for a moment to fight with them again.
But I've ninety men and more that are lying sick ashore.
I should count myself the coward if I left them, my Lord Howard,
To these Inquisition dogs and the devildoms of Spain.'

So Lord Howard passed away with five ships of war that day,
Till he melted like a cloud in the silent summer heaven.
1878 'The Revenge', stanzas 1–3, l.1–14.

96 And Sir Richard said again: 'We be all good English men.
Let us bang these dogs of Seville, the children of the devil,
For I never turned my back upon Don or devil yet.'
1878 'The Revenge', stanza 4, l.29–31.

97 And the sun went down, and the stars came out far over the summer sea,
But never a moment ceased the fight of the one and the fifty-three.
1878 'The Revenge', stanza 9, l.56–7.

98 'Sink me the ship, Master Gunner—sink her, split her in
twain!
Fall into the hands of God, not into the hands of Spain!'

And the gunner said 'Ay, ay,' but the seamen made reply:
'We have children we have wives,
And the Lord hath spared our lives.'
1878 'The Revenge', stanzas 11–12, l.89–93.

99 And they praised him to his face with their courtly
foreign grace;
But he rose upon their decks, and he cried:
'I have fought for Queen and Faith like a valiant man and
true;
I have only done my duty as a man is bound to do:
With a joyful spirit I Sir Richard Grenville die!'
And he fell upon their decks, and he died.
1878 'The Revenge', stanza 13, l.99–104.

1 And little Revenge herself went down by the island crags
To be lost evermore in the main.
1878 'The Revenge', stanza 14, l.118–19.

2 That man's the true Conservative
Who lops the mouldered branch away.
1882 'Hands All Round', l.7–8.

3 Pray God our greatness may not fail
Through craven fears of being great.
1882 'Hands All Round', l.31–2.

4 For nothing worthy proving can be proven,
Nor yet disproven: wherefore thou be wise,
Cleave ever to the sunnier side of doubt.
1885 'The Ancient Sage', l.66–8.

5 France had shown a light to all men, preached a Gospel,
all men's good;
Celtic Demos rose a Demon, shriek'd and slaked the
light with blood.
1886 'Locksley Hall Sixty Years After', l.89–90.

6 Twilight and evening bell,
And after that the dark!
And may there be no sadness of farewell,
When I embark;

For though from out our bourne of Time and Place
The flood may bear me far,
I hope to see my Pilot face to face
When I have crossed the bar.
1889 'Crossing the Bar', l.9–16. This was Tennyson's last
poem.

7 The mellow lin-lan-lone of evening bells.
1889 'Far-Far-Away', l.5.

8 Launch your vessel,
And crowd your canvas,
And, ere it vanishes
Over the margin,
After it, follow it,
Follow The Gleam.
1889 'Merlin and The Gleam', stanza 9, l.126–31.

9 What is it all but a trouble of ants in the gleam of a
million million of suns?
1889 'Vastness', stanza 2, l.4.

10 A louse in the locks of literature.
Of Churton Collins. Quoted in Evan Charteris *Life and Letters of Sir
Edmund Gosse* (1931), ch.14.

Tenzing Norgay *known as* Sherpa Tenzing 1914–86

Nepalese mountaineer. He took part in several Himalayan expeditions before accompanying Edmund Hillary to the summit of Everest in 1953. Subsequently he became head of the Institute of Mountaineering in Darjeeling and President of the Sherpa Association.

11 We done the bugger!
1953 On reaching the summit of Everest, 29 May.

Terence *full name* Publius Terentius Afer 185–159 BC

Roman comic dramatist. A freed slave, he enjoyed his first success with *Andria* ('The Andrian Girl', 166 BC). His six surviving comedies are Greek in origin and scene, and four are directly based on Menander. Many of his conventions were later used by European dramatists.

12 *Homo sum: nihil humani a me alienum puto.*
I am a man, I regard nothing that is human alien to me.
163 BC *Heauton timorumenos*, 77.

13 *Fortis fortuna adiuvat.*
Fortune favours the brave.
161 BC *Phormio*, 203.

14 *Nil est dictu facilius.*
Nothing is easier to say.
161 BC *Phormio*, 300.

15 *Quot homines tot sententiae: suo quoique mos.*
There are as many opinions as there are people: each
has his own view.
161 BC *Phormio*, 454.

Terentianus Maurus 2/3c BC

Latin grammarian from north Africa. He is remembered for his didactic poem *De litteris syllabis et metris*.

16 *Pro captu lectoris habent sua fata libelli.*
Depending on the reception of the reader, books have
their own fate.
De litteris syllabis et metris, 1286. The phrase is often incorrectly
attributed to Horace.

Terry, Quinlan 1937–

English architect.

17 An architect is only really a glorified tailor and if people
want a suit—as long as they don't ask for three sleeves or
something—it's do-able.
2004 In the *Observer*, 7 Mar.

Tertullian *full name* Quintus Septimius Florens Tertullianus c.160–c.220 AD

Christian theologian, a lawyer in Rome until he converted in c.196 AD, an opponent of worldliness in the Church and leader of the Montanist sect (c.207 AD). His most famous work is *Apologeticus* (c. 197 AD), an impassioned defence of Christianity against pagan charges of immorality, economic worthlessness and political subversion.

18 *Plures efficimus quoties metimur a vobis, semen est
sanguis Christianorum.*
As often as we are mown down by you, the more
we grow in numbers; the blood of the Christians is
the seed.
Apologeticus, ch.50, section 13. The phrase is often quoted as 'The
blood of the martyrs is the seed of the church.'

19 *Certum est quia impossibile est.*
It is certain because it is impossible.
De Carne Christi, ch.5. The phrase is commonly rendered 'It is so extraordinary that it must be true.'

Tessimond, A(rthur) S(eymour) J(ohn) 1902–62

20 Cats, no less liquid than their shadows,
Offer no angles to the wind.
They slip, diminished, neat, through loopholes
Less than themselves.
'Cats', pt.2.

Thackeray, William Makepeace 1811–63

English novelist. He earned his living from journalism, working for *Punch* from 1842–54. He provided a complex view of the changing nature of English society with its mingling of rich parvenus and decadent upper class. His best-known novels include *Vanity Fair* (1847–8) and *Henry Esmond* (1852).

21 'A chilli,' said Rebecca, gasping, 'Oh, yes!' She thought a chilli was something cool, as its name imported, and was served with some. 'How fresh and green they look,' she said, and put one into her mouth. It was hotter than the curry; flesh and blood could bear it no longer. She laid down her fork. 'Water, for Heaven's sake, water!' she cried.
1847–8 *Vanity Fair*, ch.3

22 A woman with fair opportunities and without a positive hump, may marry whom she likes.
1847–8 Rebecca Sharp. *Vanity Fair*, ch.4.

23 Whenever he met a great man he grovelled before him, and my-lorded him as only a free-born Briton can do.
1847–8 Of Old Osbourne. *Vanity Fair*, ch.13.

24 If a man's character is to be abused, say what you will, there's nobody like a relation to do the business.
1847–8 Miss Crawley. *Vanity Fair*, ch.19.

25 Them's my sentiments!
1847–8 Fred Bullock. *Vanity Fair*, ch.21.

26 Darkness came down on the field and city: and Amelia was praying for George, who was lying on his face, dead, with a bullet through his heart.
1847–8 *Vanity Fair*, ch.32.

27 Nothing like blood, sir, in hosses, dawgs, and men.
1847–8 James Crawley. *Vanity Fair*, ch.35.

28 How to Live Well on Nothing a Year.
1847–8 *Vanity Fair*, ch.36, title of chapter.

29 I think I could be a good woman if I had five thousand a year.
1847–8 *Vanity Fair*, ch.36.

30 Ah! Vanitas Vanitatum! Which of us is happy in this world? Which of us has his desire? or, having it, is satisfied?—Come, children, let us shut up the box and the puppets, for our play is played out.
1847–8 Concluding words. *Vanity Fair*, ch.67.

31 He who meanly admires mean things is a Snob.
1848 *The Book of Snobs*, ch.2.

32 Yes, I am a fatal man, Madame Fribsbi. To inspire hopeless passion is my destiny.
1848–50 Mirobolant. *Pendennis*, ch.23.

33 Remember, it is as easy to marry a rich woman as a poor woman.
1848–50 *Pendennis*, ch.28.

34 The Pall Mall Gazette is written by gentlemen for gentlemen.
1848–50 *Pendennis*, ch.32.

35 For a slashing article, sir, there's nobody like the Capting.
1848–50 Mr Bungay. *Pendennis*, ch.32.

36 'Tis not the dying for a faith that's so hard, Master Harry—every man of every nation has done that—'tis the living up to it that is difficult.
1852 *The History of Henry Esmond*, bk.1, ch.6.

37 'Tis strange what a man may do, and a woman yet think him an angel.
1852 *The History of Henry Esmond*, bk.1, ch.7.

38 What money is better bestowed than that of a school-boy's tip?
1853–5 *The Newcomes*, vol.1, ch.16.

39 He lifted up his head a little, and quickly said, 'Adsum!' and fell back... He, whose heart was as that of a little child, had answered to his name, and stood in the presence of The Master.
1853–5 *The Newcomes*, vol.1, ch.80.

40 Werther had a love for Charlotte
Such as words could never utter;
Would you know how first he met her?
She was cutting bread and butter.
1855 'Sorrows of Werther'.

41 Business first; pleasure afterwards
1855 *The Rose and the Ring*, ch.1.

Tharp, Twyla 1941–

US dancer and choreographer.

42 The notion of doing something impossibly new usually turns out to be an illusion.
1995 In *The Independent*, 8 Dec.

43 Before you can think out of the box, you have to start with a box.
2003 *The Creative Habit*.

44 In the end all collaborations are love stories.
2009 *The Collaborative Habit: Life Lessons for Working Together*.

45 When it all comes together, a creative life has the nourishing power we normally associate with food, love, and faith.
2013 Quoted in Mason Currey, *Daily Rituals: How Artists Work*.

Thatcher, Margaret Hilda Thatcher, Baroness 1925–2013

English Conservative politician and Prime Minister (1979–90). A research chemist, she entered Parliament (1959) and was Minister of Education (1970–4), becoming party leader in 1975. As premier she instituted privatization of nationalized industries and utilities. She resigned (Nov 1990) after a leadership challenge following controversy over economic union with Europe.

46 No woman in my time will be Prime Minister or Chancellor of the Exchequer or Foreign Secretary—not the top jobs. Anyway, I would not want to be Prime Minister; you have to give yourself 100 per cent.
1969 On her appointment as a junior Education Minister, in the *Sunday Telegraph*, 26 Oct.

47 I owe nothing to Women's Lib.
1974 Quoted in the *Observer*, 1 Dec.

48 In politics, if you want anything said, ask a man. If you want anything done, ask a woman.
1975 *People*, 15 Sep.

49 Let our children grow tall, and some taller than others if they have it in them to do so.
1975 Speech, Oct.

50 I stand before you tonight in my green chiffon evening gown, my face softly made up, my fair hair gently waved…the Iron Lady of the Western World? Me? A Cold War warrior? Well, yes—if that is how they wish to interpret my defence of values and freedoms fundamental to our way of life.
1976 Speech, Dorking. Alluding to the title bestowed upon her by the Soviet defence journal, in *Red Star*, 31 Jan.

51 We want a society in which we are free to make choices, to make mistakes, to be generous and compassionate. That is what we mean by a moral society—not a society in which the State is responsible for everything, and no one is responsible for the State.
1977 Speech, Zurich University, 14 Mar.

52 Let us make this country safe to work in. Let us make this a country safe to walk in. Let us make it a country safe to grow up in. Let us make it a country safe to grow old in.
1979 General election party broadcast, 30 Apr.

53 Unless we change our ways and our direction, our greatness as a nation will soon be a footnote in the history books, a distant memory of an offshore island, lost in the mist of time like Camelot, remembered kindly for its noble past.
1979 General election campaign speech, Bolton, 2 May.

54 Where there is discord, may we bring harmony. Where there is error, may we bring truth. Where there is doubt, may we bring faith. Where there is despair, may we bring hope.
1979 Said on entering No.10 Downing Street for the first time as Prime Minister; 4 May. A misquotation of St Francis of Assisi.
▶ See St Francis 347:99.

55 Any woman who understands the problems of running a home will be nearer to understanding the problems of running a country.
1979 Interviewed by the *Observer* four days after becoming Britain's first woman Prime Minister, 8 May.

56 Pennies don't fall from heaven. They have to be earned here on earth.
1979 Quoted in the *Observer*, 'Sayings of the Week', 18 Nov.
▶ See Burke 176:59.

57 There is no easy popularity, in that I believe that people accept that there is no alternative.
1980 On her Government's stringent economic policies. Speech at the Conservative Women's Conference, 21 May.

58 To those who wait with bated breath for that favourite media catchphrase, the U-turn, I have only this to say. You turn if you want to. The lady's not for turning.
1980 Address to the Conservative Party Conference.
▶ See Fry 353:31.

59 It is exciting to have a real crisis on your hands, when you have spent half your political life dealing with humdrum issues like the environment.
1982 Of the Falklands conflict. Speech to the Scottish Conservative Party Conference, 14 May.

60 This is the day that I was meant not to see.
1984 On attending church the Sunday after she had narrowly escaped being killed in the IRA bomb explosion at the Grand Hotel, Brighton, Oct.

61 I like Mr Gorbachev. We can do business together.
1984 Said on her first meeting with him, before he became premier, 17 Dec.

62 Democracies must try to find ways to starve the terrorist and the hijackers of the oxygen of publicity on which they depend.
1985 Speech to the American Bar Association meeting in London, referring in particular to increasing British press coverage of IRA terrorist activities, 15 Jul.

63 I always cheer up immensely if an attack is particularly wounding because…it means that they have not a single political argument left.
1986 In the *Daily Telegraph*, 21 Mar.

64 If you want to cut your own throat, don't come to me for a bandage.
1986 Comment to Robert Mugabe, Prime Minister of Zimbabwe, when he pressed for sanctions against South Africa. Quoted in *Time*, 7 Jul.

65 To wear your heart on your sleeve isn't a very good plan. You should wear it inside, where it functions best.
1987 Interview, ABC TV, 18 Mar.

66 There is no such thing as society. There are individual men and women, and there are families.
1987 In *Woman's Own*, 31 Oct.

67 I don't mind how much my Ministers talk—as long as they do what I say.
1987 In *The Times*.

68 If one leads a country such as Britain—a strong country that has taken a lead in world affairs in good times and bad, that is always reliable, then you must have a touch of iron about you.
1987 In *The Times*.

69 We have become a grandmother.
1989 *The Times*, 4 Mar.

70 I seem to smell the stench of appeasement in the air.
1990 Describing the western attitude to the Gulf crisis. In *The Independent*, 31 Oct.

71 After three general election victories, leading the only party with clear policies, resolutely carried out, I intend to continue.
1990 On Michael Heseltine's challenge for the leadership of the Conservative Party, in the *Sunday Times*, 18 Nov.

72 I shall fight. I will fight on.
1990 To reporters, on learning that she had not won the necessary majority to secure her re-election as party leader, two days before announcing her decision to step down, 21 Nov.

73 There is no way in which one can buck the market.
1990 Speech to the Commons on 10 Mar, before the Budget, complaining about what she called 'excessive' intervention in the exchange markets which would lead to inflation.

74 If you are guided by opinion polls, you are not practising leadership—you are practising followship.
1991 US TV interview, 5 Mar.

75 Marxism is at the root of debunking journalism.
Quoted in John Birt *The Harder Path* (2002).

76 Is he one of us?
Attributed comment on considering a candidate for office in her new Government.

77 I am not a consensus politician. I am a conviction politician.
Quoted in Iain Dale, *Margaret Thatcher* (2005).

78 Being powerful is like being a lady. If you have to tell people you are, you aren't.
Quoted in Iain Dale and Grant Tucker, *The Margaret Thatcher Book of Quotations* (2012).

Theophilus c.10c

Greek writer and courtier. His *Diversarum Artium Schedula* was the most important art book of the Middle Ages, describing the methods of ecclesiastical art of his time.

79 All arts are taught by degrees. The first process in art of the painter is the composition of colours. Let your mind be afterwards applied to the study of the mixtures.
An Essay Upon Various Arts (translated by Robert Hendrie, 1847), bk.1, preface.

Theophrastus c.372–286 BC

Greek philosopher. A student of Aristotle, he succeeded him as head of the Lyceum from 322. Most of his prolific output is lost; among the writings that survive is a volume of *Characters*, containing 30 sketches of different moral types, which has been widely translated and imitated.

80 The sound of the flute will cure epilepsy and sciatic gout.
Quoted in David Pickering *Brewer's Twentieth-Century Music* (1994).

Theresa (of Calcutta), Mother *originally* Agnes Gonxha Bojaxhiu 1910–97

Roman Catholic nun, born in Yugoslavia. She went to India in 1928 and in 1948 left a convent school to work in the slums. She founded the Missionaries of Charity sisterhood (1950) and a House for the Dying (1952), and in 1957 began work with lepers and in disaster areas of the world. She was awarded the Pope John XXIII Peace Prize in 1971, and the Nobel peace prize in 1979.

81 The biggest disease today is not leprosy or tuberculosis, but rather the feeling of being unwanted.
Quoted in the *Observer*, 3 Oct 1971.

82 To keep a lamp burning, we have to keep putting oil in it.
1975 In *Time*, 29 Dec.

83 There should be less talk; a preaching point is not a meeting point. What do you do then? Take a broom and clean someone's house. That says enough.
1975 *A Gift for God*, 'Carriers of Christ's Love'.

84 We need to find God, and he cannot be found in noise and restlessness. God is the friend of silence. See how nature—trees, flowers, grass—grows in silence; see the stars, the moon and the sun, how they move in silence… We need silence to be able to touch souls.
1975 *A Gift for God*, 'Willing Slaves to the Will of God'.

Theron, Charlize 1975–

South African–US film actress.

85 Women are not allowed to be complicated in our society. We still very much have a Madonna–whore complex. We're comfortable seeing women as great mothers, and then we're comfortable seeing them as hookers, but there's no in-between.
2008 In *Glamour Magazine*, Jul.

Theroux, Paul Edward 1941–

US novelist and travel writer. His best-known novel is *The Mosquito Coast* (1982), but he is particularly regarded for his travel writings, notably those concerned with epic rail journeys.

86 Extensive travelling induces a feeling of encapsulation, and travel, so broadening at first, contracts the mind.
1975 *The Great Railway Bazaar*, ch.21.

87 Nothing happens in Burma, but then nothing is expected to happen.
1975 *The Great Railway Bazaar*, ch.23.

88 I went to Vietnam to take the train: people have done stranger things in that country.
1975 *The Great Railway Bazaar*, ch.24.

89 The Japanese have perfected good manners and made them indistinguishable from rudeness.
1975 *The Great Railway Bazaar*, ch.28.

90 Like a lower form of life, like the cross-eyed planarian or squashed amoeba, the sort of creature that can't die even when it is cut to pieces.
1975 Of Laos. *The Great Railway Bazaar*.

91 In Turkey it was always 1952, in Malaysia 1937; Afghanistan was 1910 and Bolivia 1949. It is twenty years ago in the Soviet Union, ten in Norway, five in France. It is always last year in Australia and next week in Japan.
1983 *The Kingdom By The Sea*, ch.1.

92 Fogeydom is the last bastion of the bore and reminiscence is its anthem. It is futile to want the old days back, but that doesn't mean one should ignore the lessons of the visitable past.
2007 In the *International Herald Tribune*, 2 Jan.

93 Most travel, and certainly the rewarding kind, involves depending on the kindness of strangers, putting yourself into the hands of people you don't know and trusting them with your life.
2008 *Ghost Train to the Eastern Star*.

94 Delay and dirt are the realities of the most rewarding travel.
2008 *Ghost Train to the Eastern Star*.

95 The wish to travel seems to me characteristically human: the desire to move, to satisfy your curiosity or ease your fears, to change the circumstances of your life, to be a stranger, to make a friend, to experience an exotic landscape, to risk the unknown.
2011 *The Tao of Travel: Enlightenments from Lives on the Road*.

Thesiger, Sir Wilfred Patrick 1910–2003

English explorer. He twice crossed the Empty Quarter (Rub'al Khali) between 1946 and 1949 and wrote sensitively about the Bedu and their changing way of life.

96 For me, exploration was a personal venture. I did not go to the Arabian desert to collect plants nor to make a map; such things were incidental. At heart I knew that to write or even to talk of my travels was to tarnish the achievement. I went there to find peace in the hardship of desert travel and the company of desert people. I set myself a goal on these journeys, and, although the goal itself was unimportant, its attainment had to be worth every effort and sacrifice.
1959 *Arabian Sands*.

Thiers, (Louis) Adolphe 1797–1877

French statesman, twice Prime Minister (1836, 1839). He supported Napoleon in 1848, but was banished in the *coup d'état* of 1851 and re-entered the Chamber in 1863 as a critic. After the collapse of the Second Empire he suppressed the Paris Commune and became first President of the Third Republic (1871–3). Defeated by monarchists, he resigned in 1873. He wrote *L'histoire du consulat et de l'empire* ('History of the Consulate and the Empire', 20 vols, 1845–62).

97 The Republic will be conservative, or it will be nothing.
1872 Presidential address to the French National Assembly, Nov.

Thomas, (Walter) Brandon 1857–1914

English playwright, actor and songwriter. He is usually remembered for his classic farce, *Charley's Aunt* (1892).

98 Where the nuts come from.
1892 Of Brazil. *Charley's Aunt.*

Thomas, D(onald) M(itchell) 1935–

English writer. He made his initial reputation as a poet, but became better known as the author of the novel *The White Hotel* (1981).

99 Freud becomes one of the dramatis personae, in fact, as discoverer of the great and beautiful modern myth of psychoanalysis. By myth, I mean a poetic, dramatic expression of a hidden truth; and in placing this emphasis, I do not intend to put into question the scientific validity of psychoanalysis.
1981 *The White Hotel*, author's note.

1 She was cut off from the past and therefore did not live in the present. But suddenly, as she stood close against a pine tree and breathed in its sharp, bitter scent, a clear space opened to her childhood, as though a wind had sprung from the sea, clearing a mist. It was not a memory from the past, it was the past itself, as alive, as real; and she knew that she and the child of forty years ago were the same person.
1981 *The White Hotel*, ch.4.

2 The soul of man is a far country, which cannot be approached or explored. Most of the dead were poor and illiterate. But every single one of them had dreamed dreams, seen visions and had amazing experiences, even the babes in arms (perhaps especially the babes in arms).
1981 *The White Hotel*, ch.5.

Thomas, Dylan Marlais 1914–53

Welsh poet. The son of a schoolmaster, he worked as a journalist for a time. He also wrote short stories and novels, and later turned to drama, notably the celebrated radio play *Under Milk Wood* (published 1954). His tempestuous lifestyle culminated in his death from alcohol abuse on a lecture tour of the US.

3 The force that through the green fuse drives the flower
Drives my green age; that blasts the roots of trees
Is my destroyer.
And I am dumb to tell the crooked rose
My youth is bent by the same wintry fever.
1934 'The Force That Through the Green Fuse Drives the Flower'.

4 Light breaks where no sun shines;
Where no sea runs, the waters of the heart
Push in their tides.
1934 'Light Breaks Where No Sun Shines'.

5 Man be my metaphor.
1934 'If I Were Tickled by The Rub of Love'.

6 I am getting more obscure day by day.
1934 Letter to Pamela Hansford Johnson, 9 May.

7 Though they go mad they shall be sane
Though they sink through the sea they shall rise again;
Though lovers be lost love shall not;
And death shall have no dominion.
1936 'And Death Shall Have No Dominion'.

8 The hand that signed the paper felled a city;
Five sovereign fingers taxed the breath,
Doubled the globe of dead and halved a country;
These five kings did a king to death.
1936 'The Hand That Signed the Paper Felled a City'.

9 The hand that signed the treaty bred a fever,
And famine grew, and locusts came;
Great is the hand that holds dominion over
Man by a scribbled name.
1936 'The Hand That Signed the Paper Felled a City'.

10 What is the metre of the dictionary?
1936 'Altarwise by Owl-light'.

11 Shall gods be said to thump the clouds
When clouds are cursed by thunder?
1936 'Shall Gods be Said to Thump the Clouds'.

12 I hold a beast, an angel and a madman within me, and my enquiry is as to their working, and my problem is their subjugation and victory, downthrow and upheaval, and my effort is their self expression.
1938 Letter to Henry Treece.

13 Her fist of a face died clenched on a round pain;
And sculptured Ann is seventy years of stone.
1939 'After the Funeral'.

14 I don't think it does any harm to the artist to be lonely as an artist.
1939 Letter to Pennar Davies.

15 Portrait of the Artist as a Young Dog.
1940 Title of book.

16 And the wild boys innocent as strawberries.
1946 'The Hunchback in the Park'.

17 Now as I was young and easy under the apple boughs
About the lilting house and happy as the grass was green.
1946 'Fern Hill'.

18 Oh as I was young and easy in the mercy of his means,
Time held me green and dying
Though I sang in my chains like the sea.
1946 'Fern Hill'.

19 After the first death, there is no other.
1946 'A Refusal to Mourn the Death, By Fire, of a Child in London'.

20 It was my thirtieth year to heaven
Woke to my hearing from harbour and neighbour wood
And the mussel pooled and the heron
Priested shore.
1946 'Poem in October'.

21 Pale rain over the dwindling harbour
And over the sea wet church the size of a snail
With its horns through mist and the castle
Brown as owls.
1946 'Poem in October'.

22 And I rose
In rainy autumn
And walked abroad in the shower of all my days.
1946 'Poem in October'.

23 I hear John Arlott's voice every weekend, describing cricket matches. He sounds like Uncle Tom Cobleigh reading Neville Cardus to the Indians.
1947 Letter to Margaret Taylor, 11 Jul.

24 The joy and function of poetry is, and was, the celebration of man, which is also the celebration of God.
1951 Letter to a student.

25 If you want a definition of poetry, say: 'Poetry is what makes me laugh or cry or yawn, what makes my toenails twinkle, what makes me want to do this or that or nothing' and let it go at that.
1951 Letter to a student.

26 I fell in love—that is the only expression I can think of—at once, and am still at the mercy of words, though sometimes now, knowing a little of their behaviour very well, I think I can influence them slightly and have even learned to beat them now and gain, which they appear to enjoy.
1951 Letter to a student.

27 Do not go gentle into that good night,
Old age should burn and rave at close of day;
Rage, rage against the dying of the light.
1952 'Do Not Go Gentle Into That Good Night'.

28 These poems, with all their crudities, doubts, and confusions, are written for the love of Man, and in praise of God, and I'd be a damn' fool if they weren't.
1952 *Collected Poems*, author's note.

29 The land of my fathers. My fathers can have it.
1953 Of Wales. In *Adam*, Dec.

30 I've had eighteen straight whiskies. I think that's the record.
1953 Attributed, supposedly said before lapsing into his final coma.

31 To begin at the beginning: It is spring, moonless night in the small town, starless and bible-black, the cobblestreets silent and the hunched, courters'-and-rabbits' wood limping invisible down to the sloeblack, slow, black, crowblack, fishingboat-bobbing sea.
1954 *Under Milk Wood*, opening words.

32 Oh I'm a martyr to music.
1954 *Under Milk Wood*.

33 The boys are dreaming wicked or of the bucking ranches of the night and the jolly-rogered sea.
1954 *Under Milk Wood*.

34 And before you let the sun in, mind it wipes its shoes.
1954 *Under Milk Wood*.

35 Alone until she dies, Bessie Bighead, hired help, born in the workhouse, smelling of the cowshed, snores bass and gruff on a couch of straw in a loft in Salt Lake Farm and picks a posy of daisies in Sunday Meadow to put on the grave of Gomer Owen who kissed her once by the pig-sty when she wasn't looking and never kissed her again although she was looking all the time.
1954 *Under Milk Wood*.

36 Straightfaced in his cunning sleep he pulls the legs of his dreams.
1954 *Under Milk Wood*.

37 Nothing grows in our garden, only washing. And babies. And where's their fathers live, my love? Over the hills and far away.
1954 *Under Milk Wood*.

38 You're thinking, you're no better than you should be, Polly, and that's good enough for me. Oh, isn't life a terrible thing, thank God?
1954 *Under Milk Wood*.

39 Hullo, Polly, my love, can you hear the dumb goose-hiss of the wives as they huddle and peck or flounce at a waddle away? Who cuddled you when? Which of their gandering hubbies moaned in Milk Wood for your naughty mothering arms and body like a wardrobe, love?
1954 *Under Milk Wood*.

40 The sun hums down through the cotton flowers of her dress into the bell of her heart and buzzes in the honey there and couches and kisses, lazy-loving and boozed, in her red-berried breast.
1954 *Under Milk Wood*.

41 Alone in the hissing laboratory of his wishes, Mr Pugh minces among bad vats and jeroboams, tiptoes through spinneys of murdering herbs, agony dancing in his crucibles, and mixes especially for Mrs Pugh a venomous porridge unknown to toxicologists which will scald and viper through her until her ears fall off like figs, her toes grow big and black as balloons, and steam comes screaming out of her navel.
1954 *Under Milk Wood*.

42 You just wait. I'll sin until I blow up!
1954 *Under Milk Wood*.

43 Too many of the artists of Wales spend too much time talking about the position of the artists of Wales. There is only one position for an artist anywhere: and that is, upright.
1954 *Quite Early One Morning*, 'Wales and the Artist'.

44 The best poem is that whose worked-upon unmagical passages come closest, in texture and intensity, to those moments of magical accident.
1954 *Quite Early One Morning*, 'On Poetry'.

45 A good poem is a contribution to reality. The world is never the same once a good poem has been added to it.
1954 *Quite Early One Morning*, 'On Poetry'.

46 One Christmas was much like another... I can never remember whether it snowed for six days and six nights when I was twelve or whether it snowed for twelve days and twelve nights when I was six.
1954 *A Child's Christmas in Wales*.

47 Years and years ago, when I was a boy, when there were wolves in Wales, and birds the colour of red-flannel petticoats whisked past the harp-shaped hills, when we sang and wallowed all night and day in caves that smelt like Sunday afternoons in damp front farmhouse parlours, and we chased, with the jawbones of deacons, the English and the bears, before the motor car, before the wheel, before the duchess-faced horse, when we rode the daft and happy hills bareback, it snowed and it snowed.
1954 *A Child's Christmas in Wales*.

Thomas, (Philip) Edward 1878–1917

English nature writer and poet. His poetry was all written during World War I, in which he was killed in action at Arras. Very few poems were published in his lifetime, but posthumous collections established his reputation as a great nature poet.

48 A merely great intellect can produce great prose, but not poetry, not one line.
1908 Letter to Gordon Bottomley, 26 Feb.

49 When Gods were young
This wind was old.
1914 'The Mountain Chapel'.

50 The Past is a strange land, most strange.
1915 'Parting'.

51 Yes; I remember Adlestrop—
The name, because one afternoon
Of heat the express-train drew up there
Unwontedly. It was late June.
1915 'Adlestrop'.

52 And for that minute a blackbird sang
Close by, and round him, mistier,
Farther and farther, all the birds
Of Oxfordshire and Gloucestershire.
1915 'Adlestrop'.

53 The men, the music piercing that solitude
And silence, told me truths I had not dreamed,
And have forgotten since their beauty passed.
1915 'Tears'.

54 The last light has gone out of the world, except
This moonlight lying on the grass like frost
Beyond the brink of the tall elm's shadow.
1915 'Liberty'.

55 This is no case of petty right or wrong
That politicians or philosophers
Can judge. I hate not Germans, nor grow hot
With love of Englishmen, to please newspapers.
1915 'This Is No Case of Petty Right Or Wrong'.

56 The dark-lit stream has drowned the Future and the Past.
1915 'The Bridge'.

57 The new moon hangs like an ivory bugle
In the naked frosty blue.
1915 'The Penny Whistle'.

58 It is a fine world and I wish I knew how to make £200 a year in it.
1915 Letter to Gordon Bottomley, 16 Jun.

59 The past is the only dead thing that smells sweet,
The only sweet thing that is not also fleet.
1916 'Early One Morning'.

60 For the life in them he loved most living things,
But a tree chiefly.
1916 'Bob's Lane'.

61 That girl's clear eyes utterly concealed all
Except that there was something to reveal.
1916 'That Girl's Clear Eyes'.

62 I have come to the borders of sleep,
The unfathomable deep
Forest, where all must lose
Their way, however straight
Or winding, soon or late;
They cannot choose.
1916 'Lights Out'.

63 As well as any bloom upon a flower
I like the dust on the nettles, never lost
Except to prove the sweetness of a shower.
1916 'Tall Nettles'.

64 Now all the roads lead to France
And heavy is the tread
Of the living: but the dead
Returning lightly dance.
1916 'Roads'.

65 Out in the dark over the snow
The fallow fawns invisible go
With the fallow doe;
And the winds blow
Fast as the stars are slow.
1916 'Out in the Dark'.

66 The sorrow of true love is a great sorrow
And true love parting blackens a bright morrow.
1917 'Last Poem'.

Thomas, Sir George 1881–1972
English badminton administrator, founder and first president of the International Badminton Federation.

67 The art of badminton is to deceive.
Quoted in *The Guinness Book of Badminton* (1983).

Thomas, John Parnell 1895–1970
US congressman. He was an insurance broker before entering Congress (1937–49). He served as Chairman of the Committee on Un-American Activities.

68 Are you now, or have you ever been, a member of the Communist Party?
1947–57 Stock question to those called before the House of Representatives Committee on Un-American Activities.

Thomas, Michael M 1936–
US novelist.

69 Bankers' genes were Wall St. genes, especially in the big cities. If the banks were conservative just now [1955], it was because bankers still awoke in the middle of the night, trembling and sweaty with thoughts of the Crash. But in time a new generation would take over: ambitious, overcompetitive young men to whom 1929 would be merely a date on a page; such men would sever the roots of memory as if with an ax, not realizing that those tendrils were also the rudder cables.
1987 *The Ropespinner Conspiracy*.

Thomas, R(onald) S(tuart) 1913–2000
Welsh poet and priest. His poetry characteristically deals with the themes of nature, religion and his love of Wales.

70 We were a people taut for war; the hills
Were no harder, the thin grass
Clothed them more warmly than the coarse
Shirts our small bones.
1952 'Welsh History'.

71 An impotent people,
Sick with inbreeding.
Worrying the carcase of an old song.
1952 'Welsh Landscape'.

72 We will listen to the wind's text
Blown through the roof, or the thrush's song
In the thick bush that proved him wrong,

Wrong from the start, for nature's truth
Is primary and her changing seasons
Correct out of a vaster reason
The vague errors of the flesh.
1953 'The Minister'.

73 For the first twenty years you are still growing,
Bodily that is; as a poet, of course,
You are not born yet. It's the next ten
You cut your teeth on to emerge smirking
For your brash courtship of the muse.
1963 'To A Young Poet'.

74 Prompt me, God,
But not yet. When I speak
Though it be you who speak
Through me, something is lost.
The meaning is the waiting.
1968 'Kneeling'.

75 The poem in the rock and
The poem in the mind
Are not one.
It was in dying
I tried to make them so.
1972 'The Epitaph'.

76 Among the forests
Of metal the one human
Sound was the lament of
The poets for deciduous language.
1972 'Postscript'.

77 Life is not hurrying
on to a receding future, nor hankering after
an imagined past. It is the turning
aside like Moses to the miracle
of the lit bush, to a brightness
that seemed as transitory as your youth
once, but is the eternity that awaits you.
1976 *Laboratories of the Spirit*, 'The Bright Field'.

78 We are beginning to see
now it is matter is the scaffolding
of spirit; that the poet emerges
from morphemes and phonemes; that
as form in sculpture is the prisoner
of the hard rock, so in everyday life
it is the plain facts and natural happenings
that conceal God and reveal him to us
little by little under the mind's tooling.
1978 *Frequencies*, 'Emerging'.

Thompson, E P 1924–93
British historian.

79 This going into Europe will not turn out to be the thrilling mutual exchange supposed. It is more like nine middle-aged couples with failing marriages meeting in a darkened bedroom in a Brussels hotel for a group grope.
1975 On Britain's entry into the EEC, in the *Sunday Times*, 27 Apr.

Thompson, Francis 1859–1907
English poet. His poems, mainly religious in theme and collected in such publications as *Poems* (1893) and *Sister Songs* (1895), include the well-known 'The Hound of Heaven'.

80 The fairest things have fleetest end,
  Their scent survives their close:
But the rose's scent is bitterness
To him that loved the rose.
'Daisy' (published 1890).

81 I fled Him, down the nights and down the days;
I fled Him, down the arches of the years;
I fled Him, down the labyrinthine ways
Of my own mind; and in the midst of tears
I hid from Him, and under running laughter.
1893 *Poems*, 'The Hound of Heaven'.

82 I said to Dawn: Be sudden—to Eve: Be soon.
1893 *Poems*, 'The Hound of Heaven'.

83 O world invisible, we view thee,
O world intangible, we touch thee,
O world unknowable, we know thee,
Inapprehensible, we clutch thee!
1897 'In No Strange Land'.

84 It is little I repair to the matches of the Southron folk,
Though my own red roses there may blow;
It is little I repair to the matches of the Southron folk,
Though the red roses crest the caps, I know.
For the field is full of shades as I near the shadowy coast,
And a ghostly batsman plays to the bowling of a ghost,
And I look through my tears on a soundless-clapping host
As the run-stealers flicker to and fro,
To and fro:—
O my Hornby and my Barlow long ago!
1907 'At Lord's', poem dedicated to friends to explain why he could not attend a match at Lord's at their invitation for fear of the sadness it would cause him, remembering the long-dead friends who had played there (for Lancashire) back in 1878.

85 There is no expeditious road
To pack and label men for God,
And save them by the barrel-load,
Some may perchance, with strange surprise,
Have blundered into Paradise.
1913 'A Judgment in Heaven', epilogue.

86 Wake! for the Ruddy Ball has taken flight
That scatters the slow Wicket of the Night;
And the swift Batsman of the Dawn has driven
Against the Star-spiked Rails a fiery smite.
'Wake! for the Ruddy Ball has Taken Flight', parody of Edward Fitzgerald, quoted in J C Squire *Apes and Parrots* (1929).
▶ See Fitzgerald 337:68.

Thompson, Hunter S(tockton) 1939–2005
US writer, inventor of a semi-fictionalized participatory journalism he dubbed 'gonzo'. His work for *Rolling Stone* magazine made him a cult figure. He sometimes wrote as 'Raoul Duke'.

87 Weird heroes and mould-breaking champions exist as living proof to those who need it that the tyranny of 'the rat race' is not yet final.
1969 'Those Daring Young Men In Their Flying Machines...Ain't What They Used To Be!', in *Pageant*, Sep.

88 History is hard to know...but...it seems entirely reasonable to think that every now and then the energy of a whole generation comes to a head in a long fine flash, for reasons that nobody really understands at the time—and which never explain, in retrospect, what actually happened.
1971 *Fear and Loathing in Las Vegas*, ch.8.

89 Absolute truth is a very rare and dangerous commodity in the context of professional journalism.
   1973 'Fear and Loathing at the Superbowl', in *Rolling Stone*, 15 Feb.

90 In a nation ruled by swine, all pigs are upwardly-mobile—and the rest of us are fucked until we can put our acts together: not necessarily to win, but mainly to keep from losing completely. We owe that to ourselves and our crippled self-image as something better than a nation of panicked sheep.
   1979 *The Great Shark Hunt*, 'Jacket Copy for *Fear and Loathing in Las Vegas*'.

91 Going to trial with a lawyer who considers your whole life-style a Crime in Progress is not a happy prospect.
   1990 Letter to *The Champion*, a legal journal, Jul.

Thompson, James R 1936–

US lawyer and politician, Republican governor of Illinois (1977–91).

92 It is not so much who you elect, it's who you throw out.
   1981 On the campaign to clean up government. In the *Chicago Tribune*, 26 Jul.

Thompson, Robert 1914–97

Canadian politician, leader of the Social Credit Party of Canada (1961–7) and renowned malapropist.

93 The Americans are our best friends, whether we like it or not.
   Oft-quoted remark recalled by Peter C Newman in *Home Country* (1973).

Thompson, Tommy 1913–85

Canadian public official, Parks Commissioner, Metropolitan Toronto.

94 Please Walk on the Grass
   1960 Message on a sign erected in Toronto's Edwards Gardens, which attracted national and then international attention for its 'hands-on' approach to public parks.

Thomson, David 1914–88

Scottish writer. His often autobiographical books include *Woodbrook* and *Nairn in Darkness and Light*.

95 The vice of meanness, condemned in every other country, is in Scotland translated into a virtue called 'thrift'.
   1987 *Nairn in Darkness and Light*.

96 Even stroking a cat may be regarded by strict Presbyterians as a carnal sin.
   1987 *Nairn in Darkness and Light*.

Thomson, James 1700–48

Scottish poet. He studied for the ministry but moved to London to become a writer. His chief works were *The Castle of Indolence* (1748) and *The Seasons*, an early nature poem extensively revised between 1730 and 1746.

97 When Britain first, at heaven's command,
   Arose from out the azure main,
   This was the charter of the land,
   And guardian angels sung this strain:
   'Rule, Britannia, rule the waves;
   Britons never will be slaves.'
   1740 *Alfred: a Masque*, act 2, sc.5.

98 Delightful task! to rear the tender thought,
   To teach the young idea how to shoot.
   1746 *The Seasons*, 'Spring', l.1152–3.

99 An elegant sufficiency, content,
   Retirement, rural quiet, friendship, books,
   Ease and alternate labour, useful life,
   Progressive virtue, and approving Heaven!
   1746 *The Seasons*, 'Spring', l.1161–4.

1 Or sighed and looked unutterable things.
   1746 *The Seasons*, 'Summer', l.188.

2 Poor is the triumph o'er the timid hare!
   1746 *The Seasons*, 'Autumn', l.401.

3 Welcome, kindred glooms!
   Congenial horrors, hail!
   1746 *The Seasons*, 'Winter', l.5–6.

4 There studious let me sit,
   And hold high converse with the mighty dead.
   1746 *The Seasons*, 'Winter', l.431–2.

5 A little round, fat, oily man of God,
   Was one I chiefly marked among the fry:
   He had a roguish twinkle in his eye.
   1748 *The Castle of Indolence*, canto 1, stanza 69.

Thomson, James *pseudonym* 'BV', Byssbe Vanolis 1834–82

Scottish poet born in Port Glasgow. He trained as an army schoolmaster but was dismissed from army service in 1862 for alcoholism. He worked in London as a poet, journalist and critic, and published his greatest work *The City of Dreadful Night* in 1874.

6 As we rush, as we rush in the train,
   The trees and the houses go wheeling back,
   But the starry heavens above that plain
   Come flying on our track.
   1863–5 'Sunday at Hampstead', stanza 10.

7 The City is of Night, but not of Sleep;
   There sweet Sleep is not for the weary brain;
   The pitiless hours like years and ages creep,
   A night seems termless hell.
   1874 *The City of Dreadful Night*, pt.1.

8 The City is of Night; perchance of Death,
   But certainly of Night.
   1874 *The City of Dreadful Night*, pt.1.

9 As I came through the desert thus it was,
   As I came through the desert: All was black,
   In heaven no single star, on earth no track;
   A brooding hush without a stir or note;
   The air so thick it clotted in my throat.
   1874 *The City of Dreadful Night*, pt.4.

10 Yet I strode on austere;
   No hope could have no fear.
   1874 *The City of Dreadful Night*, pt.4.

Thomson, Roy Herbert, 1st Baron Thomson of Fleet 1894–1976

Canadian-born British newspaper and television magnate. After setting up his first radio station in 1931 and buying many Canadian and US newspapers, he settled in Edinburgh on acquiring *The Scotsman* (1952), and bought the Kemsley newspapers (1959) and *The Times* (1966).

11 A TV licence is a licence to print money.
   1957 On being awarded the licence to operate Scottish Television Ltd, 19 Jun. Recalled in his memoirs *After I Was Sixty* (1975).

Thomson, Virgil 1896–1989

US composer and critic. His work, notable for its simplicity of style, includes the operas *Four Saints in Three Acts* (1934) and *The Mother of Us All* (1947) in addition to symphonies, ballets, choral, chamber and film music. He was music critic of the *New York Herald* (1940–54).

12 A libretto that should never have been accepted on a subject that should never have been chosen by a man who should never have attempted it.
   1935 Of Gershwin's *Porgy and Bess. Modern Music.*

13 The way to write American music is simple. All you have to do is be an American and then write any kind of music you wish.
   Quoted in Machlis *Introduction to Contemporary Music* (1963).

Thoreau, Henry David 1817–62

US essayist and poet, known as 'the hermit of Walden'. In 1839 he began his nature studies, and lived as a hermit (1845–7). His works include *Walden, or Life in the Woods* (1854) and his nature observations, beginning with *Early Spring in Massachusetts* (1881). His essay *Civil Disobedience* (1849) was provoked by his opposition to the Mexican war.

14 We seem but to linger in manhood to tell the dreams of our childhood, and they vanish out of memory ere we learn the language.
   1841 Journal entry, 19 Feb.

15 Being is the great explainer.
   1841 Journal entry, 26 Feb.

16 Men reverence one another, not yet God.
   1849 *A Week on the Concord and Merrimack Rivers,* 'Sunday'.

17 Under a government which imprisons any unjustly, the true place for a just man is also a prison.
   1849 *Civil Disobedience.*

18 Read the best books first, or you may not have a chance to read them at all.
   1849 *A Week on the Concord and Merrimack Rivers,* 'Sunday'.

19 The lawyer's truth is not Truth, but consistency or a consistent expediency.
   1849 *Civil Disobedience.*

20 It takes two to speak the truth,—one to speak, and another to hear.
   1849 *A Week on the Concord and Merrimack Rivers,* 'Wednesday'.

21 A truly good book is something as wildly natural and primitive, mysterious and marvelous, ambrosial and fertile, as a fungus or a lichen.
   1850 Journal entry, 16 Nov. In Bradford Torrey and F H Allen (eds) *The Journals of Henry David Thoreau* (1906).

22 Some circumstantial evidence is very strong, as when you find a trout in the milk.
   1850 Journal entry, 11 Nov.

23 How many a man has dated a new era in his life from the reading of a book!... The at present unutterable things we may find somewhere uttered.
   1854 *Walden, or Life in the Woods,* 'Reading'.

24 If we knew all the laws of Nature, we should need only one fact, or the description of one actual phenomenon, to infer all the particular results at that point. Now we know only a few laws, and our result is vitiated, not, of course, by any confusion or irregularity in Nature, but by our ignorance of essential elements in the calculation. Our notions of law and harmony are commonly confined to those instances which we detect; but the harmony which results from a far greater number of seemingly conflicting, but really concurring, laws, which we have not detected, is still more wonderful. The particular laws are as our points of view, as, to the traveler, a mountain outline varies with every step, and it has an infinite number of profiles, though absolutely but one form. Even when cleft or bored through it is not comprehended in its entireness.
   1854 *Walden, or Life in the Woods,* 'The Pond in Winter'.

25 Every man is the builder of a temple, called his body, to the god he worships, after a style purely his own, nor can he get off by hammering marble instead. We are all sculptors and painters, and our material is our own flesh and blood and bones.
   1854 *Walden, or Life in the Woods,* 'Higher Laws'.

26 It is a part of the destiny of the human race, in its gradual improvement, to leave off eating animals, as surely as the savage tribes have left off eating each other when they come in contact with the more civilized.
   1854 *Walden, or Life in the Woods,* 'Higher Laws'.

27 We can never have enough of nature. . . . We need to witness our own limits transgressed, and some life pasturing freely where we never wander.
   1854 *Walden, or Life in the Woods,* 'Spring'.

28 There is no odor so bad as that which arises from goodness tainted.
   1854 *Walden, or Life in the Woods,* 'Economy'.

29 The mass of men lead lives of quiet desperation.
   1854 *Walden, or Life in the Woods,* 'Economy'.

30 Our inventions are wont to be pretty toys, which distract our attention from serious things. They are but improved means to an unimproved end.
   1854 *Walden, or Life in the Woods,* 'Economy'.

31 Men have become the tools of their tools.
   1854 *Walden, or Life in the Woods,* 'Economy'.

32 I have yet to hear the first syllable of valuable or even earnest advice from my seniors.
   1854 *Walden, or, Life in the Woods,* 'Economy'.

33 As for Doing-good, that is one of the professions which are full.
   1854 *Walden, or Life in the Woods,* 'Economy'.

34 I say, beware of all enterprises that require new clothes, and not rather a new wearer of clothes.
   1854 *Walden, or Life in the Woods,* 'Economy'.

35 Every generation laughs at the old fashions, but follows religiously the new.
   1854 *Walden, or Life in the Woods,* 'Economy'.

36 As long as possible live free and uncommitted. It makes but little difference whether you are committed to a farm or the county jail.
   1854 *Walden, or Life in the Woods,* 'Where I Lived, and What I Lived For'.

37 I went to the woods because I wished to live deliberately, to front only the essential facts of life, and

see if I could not learn what it had to teach, and not, when I came to die, discover that I had not lived.
1854 Walden, or Life in the Woods, 'Where I Lived, and What I Lived For'.

38 Our life is frittered away by detail.
1854 Walden, or Life in the Woods, 'Where I Lived, and What I Lived For'.

39 We do not ride on the railroad; it rides upon us.
1854 Walden, or Life in the Woods, 'Where I Lived and What I Lived For'.

40 Will you be a reader, a student merely, or a seer? Read your fate, see what is before you, and walk on into futurity.
1854 Walden, or Life in the Woods, 'Sounds'.

41 I never found the companion that was so companionable as solitude.
1854 Walden, or Life in the Woods, 'Solitude'.

42 I was determined to know beans.
1854 Walden, or Life in the Woods, 'The Bean-Field'.

43 If a man does not keep pace with his companions, perhaps it is because he hears a different drummer.
1854 Walden, or Life in the Woods, 'Conclusion'.

44 Why level downward to our dullest perception always, and praise that as common sense?
1854 Walden, or Life in the Woods, 'Conclusion'.

45 As for style of writing—if one has anything to say, it drops from him simply and directly, as a stone falls to the ground.
1857 Letter to Daniel Ricketson, 18 Aug.

46 I fear that I have not got much to say about Canada, not having seen much; what I got by going to Canada was a cold.
1866 A Yankee in Canada.

47 A gun gives you the body, not the bird.
Quoted in Colin Jarman *The Guinness Dictionary of Sports Quotations* (1990).

Thorndike, Dame (Agnes) Sybil 1882–1976

English actress. She made her stage debut in 1904 and went on to distinguish herself in both modern and classical tragedies. Her most famous roles included Medea, George Bernard Shaw's St Joan and Shakespeare's Volumnia. She was married to the actor and director Sir Lewis Casson.

48 You're never too old to play Saint Joan; you're only too young.
Quoted in *Julie Harris Talks to Young Actors* (1971).

Thorne, James 1815–81

English antiquary. He contributed topographical articles to many publications and spent many years researching material for his *Handbook to the Environs of London* (1876), in which he combines factual knowledge with entertaining passages on places and personalities of local interest.

49 An unenviable reputation for dirt and ill odours.
1876 Of Brentford, Middlesex, now in Greater London. *Handbook to the Environs of London.*

50 A town of narrow streets, old houses, shops curiously low, with little in it to interest any one.
1876 Of Hatfield, Hertfordshire. *Handbook to the Environs of London.*

51 A waste of modern tenements, mean, monotonous, and wearisome.
1876 On Penge, Surrey, now in Greater London. *Handbook to the Environs of London.*

52 A populous railway town of hideous brick shops and habitations.
1876 Of Redhill, Surrey. *Handbook to the Environs of London.*

53 Twickenham is one of those happy places which is not burdened with a history.
1876 Handbook to the Environs of London.

Thorneycroft, Lord (George Edward) Peter 1909–94

English politician. He entered the House of Commons in 1938, and was President of the Board of Trade (1951–7). Appointed Chancellor of the Exchequer in 1957, he resigned a year later, in disagreement with the government's financial policy, and lost his seat in 1966. He was created a life peer in 1967, and was Chairman of the Conservative Party (1975–81).

54 The choice in politics isn't usually between black and white. It is between two horrible shades of grey.
1979 In the *Sunday Telegraph*, 11 Feb.

55 Some men go through life absolutely miserable because, despite the most enormous achievements, they just didn't do one thing—like the architect who didn't build St Paul's. I didn't quite build St Paul's, but I stood on more mountain tops than possibly I deserved.
1979 In the *Sunday Telegraph*, 11 Feb.

Thornton, Sir Henry 1871–1933

Canadian pioneer of public broadcasting.

56 It is essential that broadcasting be surrounded with such safeguards as will prevent the air becoming what might be described as an atmospheric billboard.
1926 Address to the Advertising Clubs of the World, Philadelphia, 21 Jun. Quoted in E Austin Weir *The Struggle for National Broadcasting in Canada* (1965).

Thorpe, (John) Jeremy 1929–2014

English politician. Leader of the Liberal Party from 1967, he resigned in 1976 following allegations concerning a previous homosexual relationship with a Mr Norman Scott and was later acquitted of charges of conspiracy and incitement to murder Mr Scott.

57 Greater love hath no man than this, that he lay down his friends for his life.
1962 On Harold Macmillan's sacking of several Cabinet members, House of Commons.

58 Looking around the House, one realizes that we are all minorities now.
1974 On the absence of a clear party majority, House of Commons, 6 Mar.
▶ See Shawcross 811:36.

Thrasymachus 5c BC

Greek sophist and rhetorician from Chalcedon in Bithynia, he figures in Plato's *Republic* defending the proposition that might is right.

59 Morality is nothing other than the advantage of the stronger party.
Quoted in Plato *Republic*, 338b (translated by Robin Waterfield, 1993).

Thubron, Colin Gerald Dryden 1939–
English travel writer, novelist and film-maker.

60 Around me, around them [the dissidents], the total, all-eclipsing Soviet world, which renders any other world powerless and far away, had become profoundly, morally hostile.
1983 *Among the Russians* (published in the US as *Where the Nights are Longest*).

Thucydides c.460–c.400 BC
Athenian politician and historian. As a naval commander in the Peloponnesian war he failed to relieve the Amphipolis in 424, and was exiled from Athens. He began a *History of the Peloponnesian War*, but died before its completion.

61 Ktema es aei.
A possession intended to last for ever.
Of his *History of the Peloponnesian War*, 1.22.4.

Thurber, James Grover 1894–1961
US humorist and cartoonist. In 1927 he was appointed managing editor of the *New Yorker* where he published many sketches and cartoons. Collections of his work include *Men Women and Dogs* (1943). His best-known short story is *The Secret Life of Walter Mitty* (1939) which was later filmed (1946).

62 It takes that *je ne sais quoi* which we call sophistication for a woman to be magnificent in a drawing-room when her faculties have departed but she herself has not yet gone home.
1930 In the *New Yorker*, 2 Aug.

63 All right, have it your own way—you heard a seal bark!
1932 Cartoon caption, in the *New Yorker*, 30 Jan.

64 That's my first wife up there and this is the *present* Mrs Harris.
1933 Cartoon caption, in the *New Yorker*, 16 Mar.

65 I myself have accomplished nothing of excellence except a remarkable and, to some of my friends, unaccountable expertness in hitting empty ginger ale bottles with small rocks at a distance of thirty paces.
1933 *My Life and Hard Times*, preface.

66 They lead, as a matter of fact, an existence of jumpiness and apprehension. They sit on the edge of the chair of Literature. In the house of Life they have the feeling that they have never taken off their overcoats.
1933 On humorists. *My Life and Hard Times*, preface.

67 I suppose that the high-water mark of my youth in Colombus, Ohio, was the night the bed fell on my father.
1933 *My Life and Hard Times*, ch.1.

68 Her own mother lived the latter years of her life in the horrible suspicion that electricity was dripping invisibly all over the house.
1933 *My Life and Hard Times*, ch.2.

69 The war between men and women.
1934 Title of series of cartoons in the *New Yorker*, 20 Jan–28 Apr.

70 The Middle-Aged Man on the Flying Trapeze.
1935 Title of book.

71 It's a naïve domestic Burgundy without any breeding, but I think you'll be amused by its presumption.
1937 Cartoon caption, in the *New Yorker*, 27 Mar.

72 Well, if I called the wrong number, why did you answer the phone?
1937 Cartoon caption, in the *New Yorker*, 5 Jun.

73 There is no safety in numbers, or in anything else.
1939 'The Fairly Intelligent Fly', in the *New Yorker*, 4 Feb.

74 Early to rise and early to bed makes a male healthy and wealthy and dead.
1939 'The Shrike and the Chipmunks', in the *New Yorker*, 18 Feb.

75 It's our *own* story *exactly*! He bold as a hawk, she soft as the dawn.
1939 Cartoon caption, in the *New Yorker*, 28 Feb.

76 Then, with that faint fleeting smile playing about his lips, he faced the firing squad; erect and motionless, proud and disdainful, Walter Mitty, the undefeated, inscrutable to the last.
1939 'The Secret Life of Walter Mitty', in the *New Yorker*, 18 Mar.

77 You might as well fall flat on your face as lean over too far backward.
1939 'The Bear Who Let It Alone', in the *New Yorker*, 29 Apr.

78 You can fool too many of the people too much of the time.
1939 'The Owl Who Was God', in the *New Yorker*, 29 Apr.
▶ See Lincoln 529:5.

79 Art—the one achievement of Man which has made the long trip from all fours seem well advised.
1939 In *Forum and Century* magazine, Jun.

80 It is better to have loafed and lost than never to have loafed at all.
1940 *Fables for Our Time*, 'The Courtship of Arthur and Al'.

81 No oyster ever profited from its pearl.
1940 *Fables for Our Time*, 'The Philosopher and the Oyster'.

82 My World—And Welcome To It.
1942 Title of book.

83 If he knew where he was going, it is not apparent from this distance. He fell down a great deal during this period, because of a trick he had of walking into himself.
1945 Of his young self. *The Thurber Carnival*, preface.

84 I suppose that even the most pleasurable of imaginable occupations, that of batting baseballs through the windows of the RCA Building, would pall a little as the days ran on.
1945 *The Thurber Carnival*, 'Memoirs of a Drudge'.

85 He who hesitates is sometimes saved.
1945 *The Thurber Carnival*, 'The Glass in the Field'.

86 She developed a persistent troubled frown which gave her the expression of someone who is trying to repair a watch with his gloves on.
1948 *The Beast In Me and Other Animals*, 'Look Homeward, Jeannie'.

87 'We all have flaws,' he said, 'and mine is being wicked.'
1950 *The 13 Clocks*, ch.8.

88 'For God, for Country and for Yale', the outstanding single anti-climax in the English language.
1951 In *Time*, 11 Jun.

89 The theater is the primary evidence of a nation's culture.
1952 In the *New York Times*, 27 Jul.

90 Try to imagine a famous witty saying that is not immediately clear.
1954 Letter to Malcolm Cowley, 11 Mar.

91 With sixty staring me in the face, I have developed inflammation of the sentence structure and definite hardening of the paragraphs.
1955 In the *New York Post*, 30 Jun.

92 Seeing is deceiving. It's eating that's believing.
1956 *Further Fables for Our Time.*

93 'I think this calls for a drink' has long been one of our national slogans.
1957 *Alarms and Diversions,* 'Merry Christmas'.

94 'Poe,' I said, 'was perhaps the first great nonstop literary drinker of the American nineteenth century. He made the indulgences of Coleridge and De Quincey seem like a bit of mischief in the kitchen with the cooking sherry.
1957 *Alarms and Diversions,* 'The Moribundant Life, or, Grow Old Along with Whom?'.

95 I was seized by the stern hand of Compulsion, that dark, unseasonable Urge that impels women to clean house in the middle of the night.
1957 *Alarms and Diversions,* 'There's A Time For Flags'.

96 The laughter of man is more terrible than his tears, and takes more forms—hollow, heartless, mirthless, maniacal.
1958 In the *New York Times Magazine,* 7 Dec.

97 The power that created the poodle, the platypus and people has an integrated sense of both comedy and tragedy.
1959 Letter to Frances Glennon, Jun.

98 'Humour,' he said, 'is emotional chaos remembered in tranquillity.'
1960 In the *New York Post,* 29 Feb.
▶ See Wordsworth 958:93.

99 Ours is a precarious language, as every writer knows, in which the merest shadow line often separates affirmation from negation, sense from nonsense, and one sex from another.
1961 Of English. *Lanterns and Lances,* 'Such a Phrase as Drifts Through Dreams'.

1 Writers of comedy have outlook, whereas writers of tragedy have, according to them, insight.
1961 *Lanterns and Lances,* 'The Case for Comedy'.

2 The only rules comedy can tolerate are those of taste, and the only limitations those of libel.
1961 *Lanterns and Lances,* 'The Duchess and the Bugs'.

3 God bless... God damn!
1961 Last words.

4 I have the reputation of having read all of Henry James, which would argue a misspent youth *and* middle age.
Recalled on his death, 2 Nov 1961.

5 Word has somehow got around that the split infinitive is always wrong. That is of a piece with the outworn notion that it is always wrong to strike a lady.
Recalled on his death, 2 Nov 1961.

6 Unless [artists] can remember what it was to be a little boy, they are only half complete as artist and as man.
Quoted in Helen Thurber and Edward Weeks (eds) *Selected Letters of James Thurber* (1981).

7 Laughter need not be cut out of anything, since it improves everything.
Quoted in Helen Thurber and Edward Weeks (eds) *Selected Letters of James Thurber* (1981).

8 There is something about a poet which leads us to believe that he died, in many cases, as long as 20 years before his birth.
Quoted in Helen Thurber and Edward Weeks (eds) *Selected Letters of James Thurber* (1981).

9 Some American writers who have known each other for years have never met in the daytime or when both were sober.
Quoted in Neil T Jones (ed) *A Book of Days for the Literary Year* (1984).

10 It had only one fault. It was kind of lousy.
Of a play he had recently seen. Attributed.

Thurow, Lester C(arl)   1938–

US economist, former dean of the Sloan School of Management, Massachusetts Institute of Technology.

11 America no longer lives behind its great wall. Economically, Genghis Khan has arrived.
1992 *Head to Head.*

Tilden, Bill (William Tatem II)   1893–1953

US tennis player. One of the greatest players of his time, he was Wimbledon singles champion three times (1920, 1921, 1930) and doubles champion (1927). He was also six times US singles champion and four times doubles champion in the 1920s.

12 Never change a winning game: always change a losing one.
Quoted in Colin Jarman *The Guinness Dictionary of Sports Quotations* (1990).

Tillich, Paul Johannes   1886–1965

German pastor, theologian and philosopher. Dismissed from his professorship by Nazis in 1933, he left to teach in the US. His theories blend philosophical and psychoanalytical elements with the theological.

13 Neurosis is the way of avoiding non-being by avoiding being.
1952 *The Courage to Be.*

14 Faith comprises both itself and doubt of itself.
1955 *Biblical Religion and the Search for Ultimate Reality.*

15 Faith is the state of being ultimately concerned.
1957 *Dynamics of Faith.*

16 I had the honor to be the first non-Jewish professor dismissed from a German university.
Recalled on his death, 22 Oct 1965.

Tilman, Bill (Harold William)   1898–1977

English mountaineer, explorer and sailor. He went to Kenya as a planter and there met Eric Shipton, with whom he made many notable explorations and climbs. After serving in World War II he took up sailing in remote areas such as Patagonia, the Arctic and the Antarctic. He disappeared on a voyage to the South Shetland Islands in 1977.

17 We live and learn, and big mountains are stern teachers.
1949 *Two Mountains and a River.*

Time

US news periodical.

18 The old man puffed into sight like a venerable battlewagon pressing up over the horizon. First a smudge of smoke, then the long cigar, then the familiar, stoop-shouldered hulk that a generation has come to know as the silhouette of greatness.
1952 Of Winston Churchill disembarking from the *Queen Mary.* 14 Jan.

19 The mighty US suddenly seemed as impotent as a beached whale.

1968 On the fall of 28 of South Vietnam's 44 provincial capitals. 15 Feb.

20 His career was a text book example of the rise of a patrician in the snug embrace of the American establishment.
1971 Of Dean Acheson. 25 Oct.

21 The rescuers had to rescue themselves.
1980 On the ill-fated helicopter attempt to free the hostages held in Iran. 5 May.

The Times

British newspaper, founded as the *Daily Universal Register* on 1 Jan 1785. It changed its name to *The Times* on 1 Jan 1788.

22 Of all journals, and of all writers, those will obtain the largest measure of public support who have told the truth most constantly and most fearlessly.
1852 Leading article, 6 Feb.

23 The first duty of the press is to obtain the earliest and most correct intelligence of the events of the time, and by disclosing them, to make them the common property of the nation.
1852 Leading article, 6 Feb.

Tintoretto *real name* Jacopo Robusti 1518–94

Venetian painter.

24 In judging paintings, you should consider whether the first impression pleases the eye and whether the artist has followed the rules; as for the rest, everyone makes some mistakes.
Quoted in Carlo Ridolfi *Life of Tintoretto* (1642).

Tobin, James 1918–2002

US economist, winner of the Nobel prize in economics (1981) and a professor at Yale University.

25 Why do so many talented economic theorists believe and teach elegant fantasies so obviously refutable by plainly evident facts?
1992 'An Old Keynesian Counterattacks', in the *Eastern Economic Journal*, Fall issue.

Tocqueville, Alexis Charles Henri Clérel de 1805–59

French historian and politician, Minister of Foreign Affairs for a few months in 1849. His major works are *De la Démocratie en Amérique* (1835–40, *Democracy in America*) and *L'Ancien Régime et la Révolution* (1856, *The Old Regime and the Revolution*).

26 Why, as civilization spreads, do outstanding men become fewer? Why, when attainments are the lot of all, do great intellectual talents become rarer? Why, when there are no longer lower classes, are there no longer upper classes? Why, when knowledge of how to rule reaches the masses, is there a lack of great abilities in the direction of society? America clearly poses these questions. But who can answer them?
1831 Translated by George Lawrence. Quoted in J P Mayer (ed) *Journey to America* (1960).

27 From this foul drain the greatest stream of human industry flows out to fertilize the whole world. From this filthy sewer pure gold flows. Here humanity attains its most complete development and its most brutish, here civilization works its miracles and civilized man is turned almost into a savage.
1835 Of Manchester. Journal entry, 2 Jul. *Journeys to England and Ireland* (translated by George Lawrence and J P Mayer, 1958).

28 *En matière de presse, il n'y a donc réellement pas de milieu entre la servitude et la licence. Pour recueillir les biens inestimables qu'assure la liberté de la presse, il faut savoir se soumettre aux maux inévitables qu'elle fait naître.*
As for the press, there is no middle way between servitude and extreme licence. In order to enjoy the invaluable benefits ensured by freedom of the press, it is necessary to submit to the inevitable evils that it engenders.
1835–40 *De la Démocratie en Amérique* (*Democracy in America*), vol.1, pt.2, ch.3.

29 *C'est un axiome de la science politique aux États-Unis, que le seul moyen de neutraliser les effets des journaux est d'en multiplier le nombre.*
It is an axiom of politics in the United States, that the only means of neutralising the effects of newspapers is to increase their number.
1835–40 *De la Démocratie en Amérique* (*Democracy in America*), vol.1, pt.2, ch.3.

30 *La presse exerce encore un immense pouvoir en Amérique. Elle fait circuler la vie politique dans toutes les portions de ce vaste territoire. C'est elle dont l'ïil toujours ouvert met sans cesse à nu les secrets ressorts de la politique, et force les hommes publics à venir tour à tour comparaître devant le tribunal de l'opinion. C'est elle qui rallie les intérêts autour de certaines doctrines et formule le symbole des partis; c'est par elle que ceux-ci se parlent sans se voir, s'entendent sans être mis en contact.*
The press has enormous power in America. It is the press that circulates political life through all parts of this vast territory. Its eye is always open, and making known the secret springs of politics, thus forcing public men to appear before the tribunal of public opinion. It is the press which rallies the interests of the community round certain principles and forms the creed of different parties. Through the press these parties can speak to each other without seeing each other, can listen without meeting.
1835–40 *De la Démocratie en Amérique* (*Democracy in America*), vol.1, pt.2, ch.3.

31 *Le journal représente l'association; l'on peut dire qu'il parle à chacun de ses lecteurs au nom de tous les autres, et il les entraîne d'autant plus aisément qu'ils sont individuellement plus faibles. L'empire des journaux doit donc croître à mesure que les hommes s'égalisent.*
A newspaper represents an association; one might say that it addresses each of its readers in the name of all the others, and influences them in proportion to their individual weakness. The power of newspapers should therefore increase as men become more equal.
1835–40 *De la Démocratie en Amérique* (*Democracy in America*), vol.2, pt.2, ch.6.

32 *Il n'y a qu'un journal qui puisse venir déposer au même moment dans mille esprits la même pensée.*
Only a newspaper can place at the same time in a thousand minds the same thought.
1835–40 *De la Démocratie en Amérique* (*Democracy in America*), vol.2, pt.2, ch.6.

33 *Un journal est un conseiller qu'on n'a pas besoin d'aller chercher, mais qui se présente de lui-même et qui vous parle tous les jours et brièvement de l'affaire commune, sans vous déranger de vos affaires particulières.*
A newspaper is an adviser whom one does not need to seek out, but one who comes of his own accord and speaks to you every day, briefly, of public affairs, without disturbing you from your own.
1835–40 *De la Démocratie en Amérique* (*Democracy in America*), vol.2, pt.2, ch.6.

34 *Ce serait diminuer leur importance que de croire qu'ils ne servent qu'à garantir la liberté; ils maintiennent la civilisation.*
It would diminish the importance [of newspapers] to believe that they only serve to guarantee freedom; they maintain civilization.
1835–40 *De la Démocratie en Amérique* (*Democracy in America*), vol.2, pt.2, ch.6.

Todd, Mike 1907–58
US theatre and film producer.

35 No gals, no gags, no chance.
1943 On attending rehearsals for *Oklahoma!* Quoted in the *US News and World Report*, 12 Apr 1993, on the 50th anniversary of the musical that ran six years, won a Pulitzer Prize, and was to have 750 revivals in 1993.

Todd, Ron(ald) 1927–2005
English trade union leader, a member of the Transport and General Workers' Union. He became General-Secretary in 1985, with strong left-wing support.

36 You don't have power if you surrender all your principles—you have office.
1988 Speech, London, Jun.

Toffler, Alvin 1928–
US writer and journalist, one of the most successful trend-spotters of the age. Toffler coined the phrase 'future shock' and convinced a sizable number of the reading public and policy administrators that what ailed them was the fact that everything was changing so fast.

37 'Future shock'…the shattering stress and disorientation that we induce in individuals by subjecting them to too much change in too short a time.
1970 *Future Shock*.

38 That great, growing engine of change—technology.
1970 *Future Shock*.

39 Technology feeds on itself. Technology makes more technology possible.
1970 *Future Shock*.

Tóibín, Colm 1955–
Irish novelist, playwright, journalist, and poet.

40 A novelist could probably run a military campaign with some success. They could certainly run a country.
2013 In *The Guardian*, 19 Feb.

Tojo, Hideki 1885–1948
Japanese soldier who rose to become Minister of War (1940–1) and from 1941 premier and dictator of Japan. He was sentenced to death in 1948.

41 This is farewell.
I shall wait beneath the moss
Until the flowers are fragrant
In this island country of Japan.
1948 His final statement before execution, 23 Dec. Quoted in R J C Butow *Tojo and the Coming War* (1961).

Tolkien, J(ohn) R(onald) R(euel) 1892–1973
English writer and philologist. He was born in South Africa, educated in England, and he taught at Oxford. He wrote scholarly books, but is famous for his hugely popular fantasy novels *The Hobbit* (1937) and *The Lord of the Rings* trilogy (1954–6).

42 In a hole in the ground there lived a hobbit. Not a nasty, dirty, wet hole, filled with the ends of worms and an oozy smell, nor yet a dry, bare, sandy hole with nothing in it to sit down on or to eat: it was a hobbit-hole, and that means comfort.
1937 *The Hobbit*, ch.1.

43 My political opinions lean more and more to anarchy (philosophically understood, meaning abolition of control not whiskered men with bombs)… The most improper job of any man is bossing other men.
1943 Letter to Christopher Tolkien, 29 Apr.

44 There is only one bright spot and that is the growing habit of disgruntled men of dynamiting factories and power stations. I hope that, encouraged now as patriotism, it may remain a habit! But it won't do any good, if it is not universal.
1943 Letter to Christopher Tolkien, 29 Apr.

45 One Ring to rule them all, One Ring to find them,
One Ring to bring them all and in the darkness bind them.
In the Land of Mordor where the Shadows lie.
1954 *The Fellowship of the Ring*, epigraph and passim.

46 But I cordially dislike allegory in all its manifestations, and always have done so since I grew old and wary enough to detect its presence. I much prefer history, true or feigned, with its varied applicability to the thought and experience of readers.
1954 *The Fellowship of the Ring*, foreword.

47 Hobbits are an unobtrusive but very ancient people, more numerous formerly than they are today; for they love peace and quiet and good tilled earth: a well-ordered and well-farmed countryside was their favourite haunt… Even in ancient days they were, as a rule, shy of 'the Big Folk', as they call us, and now they avoid us with dismay and are becoming hard to find.
1954 *The Fellowship of the Ring*, prologue.

48 Do not meddle in the affairs of Wizards, for they are subtle and quick to anger.
1954 Gandalf. *The Fellowship of the Ring*, bk.1, ch.3.

49 Where iss it, where iss it: my Precious, my Precious? It's ours, it is, and we wants it.
1955 Gollum. *The Two Towers*, ch.1.

Tolstoy, Leo Nikolayevich 1828–1910
Russian novelist, social philosopher, social critic and sometime mystic. His best-known works are *War and Peace* (1868–9) and *Anna Karenina* (1875–7).

50 Our body is a machine for living. It is organized for that, it is its nature. Let life go on in it unhindered and let it

defend itself, it will do more than if you paralyse it by encumbering it with remedies.
1869 *War and Peace*, bk.10, ch.29.

51 All happy families resemble each other; each unhappy family is unhappy in its own way.
1874 *Anna Karenina*, opening words.

52 I sit on a man's back, choking him and making him carry me, and yet assure myself and others that I am very sorry for him and wish to ease his lot by all possible means—except by getting off his back.
1886 *What Then Must We Do?*, ch.16 (translated by Maude).

53 What is called science today consists of a haphazard heap of information, united by nothing, often utterly unnecessary, and not only failing to present one unquestionable truth, but as often as not containing the grossest errors today put forward as truths, and tomorrow overthrown.
1898 *What is Art?* (translated by V Tchertkoff).

54 I am convinced that the history of so-called scientific work in our famous centers of European civilization will, in a couple of hundred years, represent an inexhaustible source of laughter and sorrow for future generations. The learned men of the small western part of our European continent lived for several centuries under the illusion that the eternal blessed life was the West's future. They were interested in the problem of when and where this blessed life would come. But they never thought of how they were going to make their life better.
1898 *What is Art?* (translated by V Tchertkoff).

Tomé Pires c.1480–1525

Portuguese scholar and diplomat who came to Malacca in 1512, shortly after his country's conquest of the region. Portuguese control of new sea routes meant that valuable spices no longer needed to travel via Venice to reach Europe.

55 Whoever is Lord of Malacca has his hand on the throat of Venice.
1512–15 *The Suma Oriental of Tomé Pires* (translated by Armando Cortasao, 1944).

Tomlinson, (Alfred) Charles 1927–

English poet and critic. Emeritus Professor of English, University of Bristol. His publications include *Poems* (1964) and *The Flood* (1981).

56 Everything we see
Teaches the time that we are living in.
1984 'Poem for My Father'.

Tomlinson, H(enry) M(ajor) 1873–1958

English writer. He wrote novels, travel books, memoirs and a biography of Norman Douglas.

57 I will never believe again that the sea was ever loved by anyone whose life was married to it.
1912 *The Sea and the Jungle*, ch.1.

Toole, John Kennedy 1937–69

US novelist. He published nothing in his lifetime, and committed suicide. His novel *A Confederacy of Dunces* was published to great acclaim in 1980, and *The Neon Bible* in 1989.

58 Her logic was a combination of half-truths and clichés, her worldview a compound of misconceptions deriving from a history of our nation as written from the perspective of a subway tunnel.
A Confederacy of Dunces (published 1980), ch.5, pt.3.

59 The human desire for food and sex is relatively equal. If there are armed rapes why should there not be armed hot dog thefts?
A Confederacy of Dunces (published 1980), ch.7, pt.1.

60 You can always tell employees of the government by the total vacancy which occupies the space where most other people have faces.
A Confederacy of Dunces (published 1980), ch.9, pt.1.

Toplady, Augustus Montague 1740–78

English clergyman and hymn writer.

61 Rock of Ages, cleft for me,
Let me hide myself in Thee,
Let the water and the blood,
From thy riven side which flowed,
Be of sin the double cure,
Cleanse me from its guilt and power.
1776 Hymn.

Torrance, Sam 1953–

Scottish golfer, captain of the successful European Ryder Cup team in 2002.

62 I just led them to the water—and they drank copiously.
2002 On his victorious European Ryder Cup team. In *The Times*, 28 Dec.

Toscanini, Arturo 1867–1957

Italian conductor. He made his debut at La Scala in 1898 and remained there until 1908, returning between 1920 and 1929. He conducted many major orchestras, and created the National Broadcasting Orchestra of America (1937–53). He had a reputation as a tyrannical perfectionist.

63 God tells me how he wants this music played—and you get in his way.
1930 Berating players in his orchestra. Quoted in Howard Tubman *Etude*.

64 After I die I am coming back to earth as the doorkeeper of a bordello. And I won't let a one of you in.
To an uncooperative orchestra. Quoted in Norman Lebrecht *Discord* (1982).

Towne, Robert 1936–

US screenwriter. His credits include *The Tomb of Ligeia* (1964), *Chinatown* (1974), *Greystoke: the Legend of Tarzan* (1984), *Mission: Impossible* (1996) and *Mission: Impossible II* (2000).

65 Why are you doing it? What can you buy that you can't already afford?
The future, Mr Gittes, the future.
1974 *Chinatown*.

66 Forget it, Jake, it's Chinatown.
1974 *Chinatown*, closing line.

Townsend, Sue 1945–2014

English writer. She wrote novels and plays, but is best known for her 'Adrian Mole' books.

67 The Secret Diary of Adrian Mole Aged 13¾.
1982 Title of book.

68 I have decided to be a poet. My father said there isn't a suitable career structure for poets and no pensions and other boring things, but I am quite decided.
   1982 *The Secret Diary of Adrian Mole Aged 13¾*, 'Monday, May 25th'.

69 I think it's essential for comic writers to have a hate figure, a despot, a regime to react against, and I think Thatcher was perfect for me, I loathed everything she stood for.
   2002 In the *Observer*, 24 Mar.

Townshend, Pete 1945–
British rock musician.

70 Hope I die before I get old.
   1966 'My Generation'.

Toynbee, Arnold 1852–83
English economic historian and social reformer, best known as the author of *The Industrial Revolution in England* (1884). Toynbee Hall, Whitechapel was founded in his memory in 1885.

71 The Industrial Revolution.
   1880–1 Title of Oxford lectures, published posthumously in 1884. The phrase passed into common usage.

Toynbee, Arnold Joseph 1889–1975
English historian, nephew of Arnold Toynbee. His greatest work is *A Study of History*, published in 10 volumes (1934–54).

72 No annihilation without representation.
   1947 Advocating greater British representation at the United Nations.
   ▶ See Otis 656:92.

73 America is a large, friendly dog in a very small room. Every time it wags its tail, it knocks over a chair.
   1949 Letter, 26 Oct.

74 Civilisation is a movement and not a condition; a voyage and not a harbour.
   Quoted in *Reader's Digest*, Oct 1958.

75 Angkor is perhaps the greatest of Man's essays in rectangular architecture that has yet been brought to life.
   1958 *East to West*.

Toynbee, (Theodore) Philip 1916–81
English novelist and journalist, son of the historian Arnold Joseph Toynbee. An experimental writer, his semi-autobiographical Pantaloon sequence is particularly innovative.

76 I have seen the future and it does not work.
   1974 Of the USA. In the *Observer*, 27 Jan.
   ▶ See Steffens 844:55.

77 He was the type of man who was always trying to live beyond his moral means.
   1975 Of J Middleton Murry. In the *Observer*, 12 Jan.

78 The basic command of religion is not 'do this!' or 'do not do that!' but simply 'look!'.
   1978 Journal entry, 15 Feb. Collected in *Part of a Journey* (1981).

79 The primary duty of a serious biographer is to illuminate his subject's life work, not to play the spy in his bedroom.
   1979 Book review in the *Observer*, 18 Mar.

Toynbee, Polly 1946–
English journalist, columnist at *The Guardian* (1977–88, 1998–).

80 I hate to join the chortling ranks of [Millennium] Dome rubbishers in the right-wing press…but, alas, I have to admit the Dome is a lemon.
   2000 In *The Guardian*, 5 Jan.

Traherne, Thomas c.1636–1674
English poet and mystic. Educated at Oxford, he took holy orders and in 1667 became Chaplain to the Lord Keeper of the Great Seal. He wrote religious prose, including *Roman Forgeries* (1673), *Christian Ethics* (1675) and *Centuries of Religious Meditations* (published 1908); his poetry was not published until 1903.

81 In unexperienc'd Infancy
   Many a sweet mistake doth lie.
   'Shadows in the Water' (published 1903).

82 Some unknown joys there be
   Laid up in store for me.
   'Shadows in the Water' (published 1903).

83 Sleep is cousin-german unto death:
   Sleep and death differ, no more, than a carcass
   And a skeleton.
   'A Serious and a Curious Night-Meditation' (published 1903).

84 A Stranger here
   Strange things doth meet, strange glories see;
   Strange Treasures lodg'd in this fair world appear,
   Strange all, and New to me,
   But that they mine should be, who nothing was,
   That Strangest is of all, yet brought to pass.
   The Salutation (published 1903).

85 You never enjoy the world aright, till the sea itself floweth in your veins, till you are clothed with the heavens, and crowned with the stars: and perceive yourself to be the sole heir of the whole world.
   Centuries of Meditations, 'First Century', section 29 (published 1908).

Travers, Ben 1886–1980
English dramatist and screenwriter.

86 The really great batsmen fall into two categories. One comes to the wicket saying to the bowlers 'I am going to slaughter you'. The other comes to the wicket saying 'You can't get me out'.
   1981 *94 Declared Cricket Reminiscences*.

Travers, P(amela) L(yndon) 1906–96
British writer. She worked as a journalist, actress and dancer, and for the British Ministry of Information in the US during World War II. *Mary Poppins* was published in 1934; subsequent titles include *Mary Poppins Comes Back* (1935), *Mary Poppins Opens the Door* (1943) and *Mary Poppins in the Park* (1952).

87 'Now,' she said, 'spit-spot into bed.'
   1934 *Mary Poppins*, ch.1.

88 From the [empty] carpet-bag she took out seven flannel night-gowns, four cotton ones, a pair of boots, a set of dominoes, two bathing-caps and a postcard album. Last of all came a folding camp-bedstead with blankets and eiderdown complete.
   1934 *Mary Poppins*, ch.1.

89 Mary Poppins looked down at her feet and rubbed the toe of one shoe along the pavement two or three times. Then she smiled at the shoe in such a way that the shoe knew quite well that the smile wasn't meant for it.
   1934 *Mary Poppins*, ch.2.

90 'Don't you know,' she said pityingly, 'that everybody's got a Fairyland of their own?'
1934 *Mary Poppins*, ch.2.

91 If I laugh on that particular day I become so filled with Laughing Gas that I simply can't keep on the ground. Even if I smile it happens. The first funny thought, and I'm up like a balloon. And until I can think of something serious I can't get down again.
1934 Mr Wigg, Mary Poppins's uncle. The 'particular day' is when his birthday falls on a Friday. *Mary Poppins*, ch.3.

92 Oh, my Gracious, Glorious, Galumphing Goodness!
1934 Mr Wigg. *Mary Poppins*, ch.3.

93 The Red Cow was very respectable, she always behaved like a perfect lady and she knew What was What. To her a thing was either black or white—there was no question of it being grey or perhaps pink. People were good or they were bad—there was nothing in between. Dandelions were either sweet or sour—there were never any moderately nice ones.
1934 *Mary Poppins*, ch.5.

94 He could smell her crackling white apron and the faint flavour of toast that always hung about her so deliciously.
1934 Michael's impressions of Mary Poppins. *Mary Poppins*, ch.6.

95 Feed the Birds, Tuppence a Bag! Feed the Birds, Tuppence a Bag!
1934 *Mary Poppins*, ch.7.

96 Trouble trouble and it will trouble you!
1934 Mary Poppins. *Mary Poppins*, ch.12.

Tree, Sir Herbert (Draper) Beerbohm 1852–1917

English actor-manager. He played a wide range of roles, of which the most successful included Svengali in George du Maurier's *Trilby*, Higgins in George Bernard Shaw's *Pygmalion* and Charles Dickens's Fagin. He assumed the management of the Comedy Theatre in London in 1887 and then spent a prosperous 10 years as manager of the Haymarket before opening Her Majesty's in 1897. He was also the founder of the Royal Academy of Dramatic Art (1904).

97 Ladies, just a little more virginity, if you don't mind.
To actresses playing the roles of ladies-in-waiting. Quoted in Alexander Woollcott *Shouts and Murmurs* (1923), 'Capsule Criticism'.

98 He is an old bore. Even the grave yawns for him.
Of Israel Zangill. Quoted in Hesketh Pearson *Beerbohm* (1956).

99 It is difficult to live up to one's poster… When I pass my name in large letters I blush, but at the same time instinctively raise my hat.
Quoted in Hesketh Pearson *Beerbohm* (1956).

1 The national sport of England is obstacle-racing. People fill their rooms with useless and cumbersome furniture, and spend the rest of their lives trying to dodge it.
Quoted in Hesketh Pearson *Beerbohm* (1956).

Treitschke, Georg Friedrich 1776–1842

German librettist and translator best known for revising the libretto for the final version (1814) of Beethoven's opera *Fidelio* from earlier versions by Stefan von Breuning (1806) and Joseph Sonnleithner (1805).

2 Abscheulicher!
Perfidious wretch!
1814 Leonora's recitative and aria. *Fidelio*, act 1.

3 O welche Lust!
Oh what delight!
1814 The prisoners' chorus. *Fidelio*, act 1.

Trevelyan, George Macaulay 1876–1962

English historian. After serving in World War I, he became Professor of Modern History at Cambridge (1927–40). A pioneer social historian, he wrote *English Social History* (1944)—a companion volume to his *History of England* (1926).

4 Disinterested intellectual curiosity is the life-blood of real civilisation.
1944 *English Social History*.

5 Village cricket spread fast through the land. In those days, before it became scientific, cricket was the best game in the world to watch—each ball a potential crisis.
Quoted in Helen Exley *Cricket Quotations* (1992).

Trevelyan, John 1904–85

British executive. He was secretary of the British Board of Film Censors between 1958 and 1970.

6 Censors are paid to have dirty minds.
1970 Attributed.

Trevino, Lee Buck 1939–

US golfer. He won his first US Open in 1968 and in 1971 established a record by winning three Open titles (the US, Canadian and British) in the same year, retaining his British title the following year.

7 I'm not saying my golf game went bad, but if I grew tomatoes they'd come up sliced.
Quoted in *Scholastic Coach*, 'Coaches' Corner', Dec 1982.

8 If my IQ had been two points lower, I'd have been a plant somewhere.
Quoted in Colin Jarman *The Guinness Dictionary of Sports Quotations* (1990).

9 I'm hitting the driver so good, I gotta dial the operator for long distance after I hit it.
Attributed.

Trevor-Roper, Hugh Redwald, Baron Dacre of Glanton 1914–2003

English historian, known for his vivid reconstruction of *The Last Days of Hitler* (1947). He was Professor at Oxford (1957–80) and Master of Peterhouse, Cambridge (1980–7).

10 Any society, so long as it is, or feels itself to be, a working society, tends to invest in itself: a military society tends to become more military, a bureaucratic society more bureaucratic, a commercial society more commercial, as the status and profits of war or office or commerce are enhanced by success, and institutions are framed to forward it. Therefore, when such a society is hit by a general crisis, it finds itself partly paralyzed by the structural weight of increased social investment. The dominant military or official or commercial classes cannot easily change their orientation: and their social dominance, and the institutions through which it is exercised, prevent other classes from securing power or changing policy.
1965 *The Rise of Christian Europe*.

Trillin, Calvin Marshall 1935–
US journalist and author.

11 A shelf life somewhere between butter and yoghurt.
   1987 On the plethora of new book titles. In the *New York Times*, 14 Jun.

12 Math was my worst subject because I could never persuade the teacher that my answers were meant ironically.
   1990 In the *New York Times*, 7 Oct.

Trilling, Lionel 1905–75
US literary critic whose works, such as *The Liberal Imagination* (1950) and *Beyond Culture* (1965), gained him a reputation for scholarly and astute social comment. He also wrote a novel, *The Middle of the Journey* (1947).

13 Literature is the human activity that takes the fullest and most precise account of variousness, possibility, complexity, and difficulty.
   1950 *The Liberal Imagination*, preface.

14 We are all ill: but even a universal sickness implies an idea of health.
   1950 *The Liberal Imagination*, 'Art and Neurosis'.

15 We who are liberal and progressive know that the poor are our equals in every sense except that of being equal to us.
   1950 *The Liberal Imagination*, 'Princess Casamassima'.

16 It would seem that Americans have a kind of resistance to looking closely at society.
   1950 *The Liberal Imagination*, 'Manners, Morals and the Novel'.

17 The poet…may be used as a barometer, but let us not forget that he is also part of the weather.
   1950 *The Liberal Imagination*.

18 The function of literature through all its mutations, has been to make us aware of the particularity of selves, and the high authority of the self in its quarrel with its society and its culture. Literature is in that sense subversive.
   1965 *Beyond Culture*, introduction.

Trinder, Tommy 1909–89
English comedian and actor, whose famous catchphrase was 'You lucky people'.

19 Overpaid, overfed, oversexed, and over here.
   Of US troops stationed in Britain during World War II. This phrase is associated with Trinder, but was probably not his invention.

Trollope, Anthony 1815–82
English novelist. He is best known for his two novel sequences, the Barchester novels and the 'Palliser' novels, both of which chronicle the life of a region and are distinguished by their slow pace and quiet comedy. His novels include *Barchester Towers* (1857) and *Can You Forgive Her?* (1864).

20 The tenth Muse, who now governs the periodical press.
   1855 *The Warden*, ch.14.

21 She was rich in apparel, but not bedizened with finery… She well knew the great architectural secret of decorating her constructions, and never descended to construct a decoration.
   1857 Of Mrs Stanhope. *Barchester Towers*, ch.9.

22 There is no road to wealth so easy and respectable as that of matrimony.
   1858 *Doctor Thorne*, ch.16.

23 Let no man boast himself that he has got through the perils of winter till at least the seventh of May.
   1858 *Doctor Thorne*, ch.47.

24 Those who have courage to love should have courage to suffer.
   1859 *The Bertrams*, ch.27.

25 For the most of us, if we do not talk of ourselves, or at any rate of the individual circles of which we are the centres, we can talk of nothing. I cannot hold with those who wish to put down the insignificant chatter of the world.
   1861 *Framley Parsonage*, ch.10.

26 We cannot bring ourselves to believe it possible that a foreigner should in any respect be wiser than ourselves. If any such point out to us our follies, we at once claim those follies as the special evidence of our wisdom.
   1862 Stavely. *Orley Farm*, ch.18.

27 It is because we put up with bad things that hotel-keepers continue to give them to us.
   1862 Stavely. *Orley Farm*, ch.18.

28 As for conceit, what man will do any good who is not conceited? Nobody holds a good opinion of a man who has a low opinion of himself.
   1862 *Orley Farm*, ch.22.

29 Mr Palliser was one of those politicians in possessing whom England has perhaps more reason to be proud than of any other of her resources, and who, as a body, give to her that exquisite combination of conservatism and progress which is her present strength and best security for the future.
   1864 *Can You Forgive Her?*, ch.24.

30 To think of one's absent love is very sweet; but it becomes monotonous… I doubt whether any girl would be satisfied with her lover's mind if she knew the whole of it.
   1864 *The Small House at Allington*, ch.4.

31 Why is it that girls so constantly do this, so frequently ask men who have loved them to be present at their marriages with other men? There is no triumph in it. It is done in sheer kindness and affection. They intend to offer something which shall soften and not aggravate the sorrow that they have caused… I fully appreciate the intention, but in honest truth, I doubt the eligibility of the proffered entertainment.
   1864 John Eames. *The Small House at Allington*, ch.9.

32 It may almost be a question whether such wisdom as many of us have in our mature years has not come from the dying out of the power of temptation, rather than as the results of thought and resolution.
   1864 *The Small House at Allington*, ch.14.

33 Never think that you're not good enough yourself. A man should never think that. My belief is that in life people will take you much at your own reckoning.
   1864 Lord De Guest to Johnny. *The Small House at Allington*, ch.32.

34 With many women I doubt whether there be any more effectual way of touching their hearts than ill-using them and then confessing it. If you wish to get the sweetest fragrance from the herb at your feet, tread on it and bruise it.
   1865 *Miss Mackenzie*, ch.10.

35 It was manifest to me that there was something in the Roman Catholic religion which made the priests very

dear to the people; for I doubt whether in any village in England, had such an accident happened to the rector, all the people would have roused themselves at midnight to wreak their vengeance on the assailant.
1866 *Argosy*, 'Father Giles of Ballymoy', May.

36 How I did respect you when you dared to speak the truth to me! Men don't know women, or they would be harder to them.
1867 *The Claverings*, ch.15.

37 She understood how much louder a cock can crow in its own farmyard then elsewhere.
1867 *The Last Chronicle of Barset*, ch.17.

38 It's dogged as does it. It ain't thinking about it.
1867 *The Last Chronicle of Barset*, ch.61, 'Giles Hoggett'.

39 They who do not understand that a man may be brought to hope that which of all things is the most grievous to him, have not observed with sufficient closeness the perversity of the human mind.
1869 Of Trevelyan's paranoia about his wife's fidelity. *He Knew He Was Right*, ch.38.

40 A faineant government is not the worst government that England can have. It has been the great fault of our politicians that they have all wanted to do something.
1869 *Phineas Finn*, ch.13.

41 Mr Turnball had predicted evil consequences...and was now doing the best in his power to bring about the verification of his own prophecies.
1869 *Phineas Finn*, ch.25.

42 Perhaps there is no position more perilous to a man's honesty than that...of knowing himself to be quite loved by a girl whom he almost loves himself.
1869 *Phineas Finn*, ch.50.

43 She knew how to allure by denying, and to make the gift rich by delaying it.
1869 *Phineas Finn*, ch.57.

44 We cannot have heroes to dine with us. There are none. And were those heroes to be had, we should not like them...the persons whom you cannot care for in a novel, because they are so bad, are the very same that you so dearly love in your life, because they are so good.
1873 Of Frank Greystock. *The Eustace Diamonds*, ch.35.

45 What man thinks of changing himself so as to suit his wife? And yet men expect that women shall put on altogether new characters when they are married, and girls think that they can do so.
1874 Lady Chiltern to Mr Maule. *Phineas Redux*, ch.3.

46 It is the necessary nature of a political in this country to avoid, as long as it can be avoided, the consideration of any question which involves a great change... The best carriage horses are those which can most steadily hold back against the coach as it trundles down the hill.
1874 *Phineas Redux*, ch.4.

47 Is it not singular how some men continue to obtain the reputation of popular authorship without adding a word to the literature of their country worthy of note?... To puff and to get one's self puffed have become different branches of a new profession.
1875 *The Way We Live Now*, ch.1.

48 Love is like any other luxury. You have no right to it unless you can afford it.
1875 *The Way We Live Now*, ch.84.

49 Equality would be a heaven, if we could attain it.
1876 Prime Minister to Phineas. *The Prime Minister*, ch.68.

50 I hold that gentleman to be the best dressed whose dress no one observes.
1879 *Thackeray*, ch.9.

51 A man's mind will very generally refuse to make itself up until it be driven and compelled by emergency.
1881 Houston. *Ayala's Angel*, ch.41.

52 He must have known me had he seen me as he was wont to see me, for he was in the habit of flogging me constantly. Perhaps he did not recognize me by my face.
1883 *Autobiography*, ch.1.

53 She was neither clear-sighted nor accurate; and in her attempts to describe morals, manners, and even facts, was unable to avoid the pitfalls of exaggeration.
1883 Of his mother, Frances Trollope, author of *The Domestic Manners of the Americans*. *Autobiography*, ch.2.

54 Take away from English authors their copyrights, and you would very soon take away from England her authors.
1883 *Autobiography*, ch.6.

55 It is admitted that a novel can hardly be made interesting or successful without love... It is necessary because the passion is one which interests or has interested all. Everyone feels it, has felt it, or expects to feel it.
1883 *Autobiography*, ch.12.

56 Three hours a day will produce as much as a man ought to write.
1883 *Autobiography*, ch.15.

57 I think that Plantagenet Palliser, Duke of Omnium, is a perfect gentleman. If he be not, then I am unable to describe a gentleman.
1883 *Autobiography*, ch.20.

Trollope, Joanna 1943–

English writer. She is best known for her novels set in rural English communities, but also writes historical fiction and, under the name Caroline Harvey, romances.

58 Contentment and fulfilment don't make for very good fiction.
1994 In *The Times*, 25 Jun.

59 People have to throw away this absurd Vera Wang shopping list which says of a man that he has to earn £100,000 a year, that he has to be able to cut down a tree, play the Spanish guitar, make love all night and cook me a cheese soufflé. This is a ridiculously impossible wish list.
2010 In *The Daily Mail*, 15 Apr.

60 You're stuck with yourself, so you might as well try and be someone you can stand to live with.
2013 *Sense and Sensibility*.

Trotsky, Leon originally Lev Davidovich Bronstein
1879–1940

Russian Jewish revolutionary, born in Ukraine. Already a noted revolutionary, he played a major role in the October Revolution (1917), and created the Red Army. After Lenin's death (1924) his influence began to decline and under Stalin he was expelled from the Soviet Union (1929) and sentenced to death (1937). He was assassinated in Mexico by one of Stalin's agents.

61 You have played out your role. Go where you belong: to the dustheap of history.
   1917 To the Mensheviks, at the first Congress of Soviets following the October Revolution. Quoted in A J P Taylor *From the Boer War to the Cold War: Essays on Twentieth-Century Europe* (1995), p.271.

62 A cossack's whip wrapped in the parchment of a constitution.
   1905 On the October Manifesto, a package of limited constitutional reforms conceded by the Tzarist government following the strikes and civil unrest of early October 1905. Quoted in Lionel Kochan *Russia in Revolution* (1967).

63 The Soviet Republic needs an army that will be able to fight and conquer.
   1918 Speech to the Moscow Soviet of Workers', Soldiers' and Peasants' Deputies, 19 Mar.

64 It was the supreme expression of the mediocrity of the apparatus that Stalin himself rose to his position.
   1930 *My Life*, p.501.

65 Civilization has made the peasantry its pack animal. The bourgeoisie in the long run only changed the form of the pack.
   1934 *History of the Russian Revolution* (translated by Max Eastman, 1934), vol.3, pt.3.

66 Old age is the most unexpected of all things that happens to a man.
   1935 *Diary in Exile*.

67 In a country that is economically backward, the proletariat can take power earlier than in countries where capitalism is advanced.
   1931 *The Permanent Revolution*.

68 Marxism is, above all, a method of analysis.
   1931 *The Permanent Revolution*.

69 The end may justify the means, as long as there is something that justifies the end.
   Attributed.

Trudeau, Pierre Elliott 1919–2000

Canadian politician. As Minister of Justice and Attorney-General (1967) he opposed the separation of Quebec from Canada. He became Liberal Prime Minister (1968–79, 1980–4), urging independence from US influence and home economic control. He proposed a new constitution for complete Canadian independence, secured Apr 1982.

70 The state has no place in the bedrooms of the nation.
   1967 Of the liberalization of the Criminal Code. Interview in Ottawa, 22 Dec. The remark is based on similar words written by the journalist Martin O'Malley in an unsigned editorial in the *Globe and Mail*, 12 Dec 1967.

71 Living next to you is like sleeping with an elephant. No matter how friendly and even-tempered the beast, one is affected by every twitch and grunt.
   1969 Of the US. Speech, National Press Club, Washington DC, 25 Mar. Quoted in Lawrence Martin *The Presidents and the Prime Ministers* (1982).

72 Fuddle-duddle.
   1971 Neologism coined by Trudeau when accused of uttering a 'four-letter word' in the House of Commons, Ottawa, 16 Feb. 'No, it was fuddle-duddle,' replied Trudeau. The reply led an opposition Member of Parliament to observe, 'Mr. Trudeau wants to be obscene but not heard.'

Trueman, Fred (Frederick Sewards) 1931–2006

English cricketer, a notoriously fast bowler. He played for Yorkshire (1949–68) and made 67 Test appearances for England (1952–65). He took a record 307 Test wickets.

73 If there is any game in the world that attracts the half-baked theorist more than cricket I have yet to hear of it.
   1964 *Freddie Trueman's Book of Cricket*.

74 The difference between a fast bowler and a good fast bowler is not extra muscle but extra brains.
   1964 *Freddie Trueman's Book of Cricket*.

75 We didn't have metaphors in my day. We didn't beat about the bush.
   1996 Quoted in the *Sunday Times*, 22 Dec.

Truman, Harry S 1884–1972

US Democratic statesman, 33rd President (1945–53), responsible for the first atom bombing on Japan, the postwar loan to Britain, the establishment of NATO (1949) and the sending of US troops to South Korea (1950). He gave military and economic aid to countries threatened by communist interference, and introduced a 'Fair Deal' of economic reform at home.

76 When I first came to Washington, for the first six months I wondered how the hell I ever got here. For the next six months, I wondered how the hell the rest of them ever got here.
   1940 Speech, Apr.

77 Every segment of our population, and every individual, has a right to expect from his Government a Fair Deal.
   1945 Speech to Congress, 6 Sep.

78 If you think somebody is telling a big lie about you, the only way to answer is with the whole truth.
   1950 On Senator Joseph R McCarthy. Quoted in John Hersey *Aspects of the Presidency* (1980).

79 The only thing you have to worry about is bad luck. I never had bad luck.
   1950 After an assassination attempt, 1 Nov.

80 If you can't stand the heat you better get out of the kitchen.
   1952 Address to the Aero Club of Washington, 27 Dec, quoting a colleague from his days as a county judge.

81 Why, this fellow doesn't know any more about politics than a pig on Sunday.
   1952 Of presidential hopeful Eisenhower. Quoted in Richard M Nixon *RN: Memoirs of Richard Nixon* (1978).

82 In 1945 we did much more than draft an international agreement among 50 nations. We set down on paper the only principles that will enable civilized human life to continue to survive on this globe.
   1955 On the 10th anniversary of the United Nations, 24 Jun.

83 Party platforms are contracts with the people.
   1956 *Memoirs: Years of Trial and Hope*.

84 I never give them hell. I just tell the truth and they think it is hell.
   1956 Interview, in *Look*, 3 Apr.

85 A politician is a man who understands government, and it takes a politician to run a Government. A statesman is a politician who has been dead 10 or 15 years.
   1958 New York World Telegram, 12 Apr.

86 It's a recession when your neighbour loses his job; it's a depression when you lose yours.

87 Too many…pass judgement on wartime decisions in the luxury of a peacetime environment.
1963 Reply to a Boston University official who had criticized Truman's use of the atomic bomb. Truman Library archives, 23 Sep.

88 The President hears a hundred voices telling him that he is the greatest man in the world. He must listen carefully indeed to hear the one voice that tells him he is not.
1964 In *This Week*, 5 Apr.

89 Being criticized…he never did get it through his head that that's what politics is all about.
Of President Eisenhower. Quoted in Merle Miller (ed) *Plain Speaking* (1974).

90 Can't somebody bring me a one-handed economist?
Recalled on the death of his economic adviser Edwin Nourse, 9 Apr 1974. Nourse had been fond of saying 'on one hand…but on the other'.

91 I told him to fire away. He did and it is dynamite.
On asking Joseph Stalin for the Soviet agenda at the Potsdam Conference. Quoted in the *New York Times*, 2 Jun 1980.

92 Being president is like riding a tiger…keep on riding or be swallowed.
Quoted in the *New York Times*, 28 Dec 1984.

93 The buck stops here.
Motto displayed on a sign on his desk. Quoted in William Safire *Safire's New Political Dictionary* (1993).

94 I don't much care for your law, but, by golly, this bourbon is good.
To US Supreme Court Justice William O Douglas. Attributed.

1958 In the *Observer*, 13 Apr.
▸ See Reagan 708:3.

Trump, Donald 1946–
US businessman, renowned for his flamboyant and sometimes controversial dealings in real estate. His best-known developments include Trump Tower, New York City, and Trump Castle, Trump Plaza and the Taj Mahal casino in Atlantic City.

95 I like thinking big. If you're going to be thinking anyway, you might as well think big.
1989 In *Time*, 16 Jan.

96 A gambler is someone who plays slot machines. I prefer to own slot machines.
1990 On the opening of his Atlanta City Taj Mahal casino. In *Time*, 9 Apr.

97 See that gold Cadillac down the street? That's the color I want those handrails. Gold. Cadillac Gold. Not yellow like a daisy.
Of the handrails in Manhattan's Trump Tower. Quoted by Paul Trachtman in the *Smithsonian*, Mar 1995, reviewing Alexander Theroux *The Primary Colors*.

98 You're fired!
2004 His catchphrase on *The Apprentice*.

99 Without passion, you don't have energy; without energy, you have nothing. Nothing great in the world has been accomplished without passion.
Quoted in Michael Volkin, *Social Networking for Authors: Untapped Possibilities for Wealth* (2009).

1 It's important to focus on the solution, not the problem.
2012 In the *Washington Times*, 28 Jan.

Truss, Lynne 1955–
English writer and broadcaster.

2 The Zero Tolerance Approach to Punctuation.
2003 Subtitle of *Eats, Shoots & Leaves*.

3 It used to be just CIA agents with ear-pieces who walked round with preoccupied, faraway expressions, and consequently regarded all the little people as irrelevant scum. Now, understandably, it's nearly everybody.
2005 *Talk to the Hand: The Utter Bloody Rudeness of the World Today (or Six Good Reasons to Stay Home and Bolt the Door)*.

Truth, Sojourner *née* Isabella c.1797–1883
American abolitionist. Born a slave, she gained her freedom and later became an ardent evangelist. In 1843 she changed her name to Sojourner Truth and campaigned against slavery and for woman suffrage.

4 Well, chilern, whar dar is so much racket dar must be something out o' kilter. I tink dat 'twixt de niggers of de Souf and de women at de Norf all a talkin' 'bout rights, de white men will be in a fix pretty soon.
1851 Women's Rights Convention, Akron, Ohio. Quoted in *Narrative of Sojourner Truth* (1875), pt.2, 'Book of Life'.

5 Look at me! Look at my arm!… I have plowed, and planted, and gathered into barns, and no man could head me—and ar'n't I a woman? I could work as much and eat as much as a man (when I could get it), and bear de lash as well—and ar'n't I a woman? I have borne thirteen chilern and seen 'em mos' all sold off into slavery, and when I cried out with a mother's grief, none but Jesus heard—and ar'n't I a woman?
1851 Women's Rights Convention, Akron, Ohio. Quoted in *Narrative of Sojourner Truth* (1875), pt.2, 'Book of Life'.

Ts'ao Sung c.830–910
Chinese poet from Anhui about whom very little is known. He was in his seventies before finally passing a set of literary examinations.

6 I charge thee, sir, not to talk of high honours,
A single general achieves fame on the rotting bones of ten thousand.
c.879 'Written in the year Chi hai (879)', collected in *A Book of Chinese Verse* (translated by N L Smith and R H Kotewall).

Tsongas, Paul Efthemios 1941–97
US politician, Senator from Massachusetts and a candidate for Democratic presidential nomination.

7 We are becoming an economic colony. America is up for sale. One percent of Japan's manufacturing base is foreign-owned; 2 per cent of Germany's is; 3 per cent of France's. Ours is 18 per cent and growing rapidly.
1992 Quoted in the *Los Angeles Times*, 17 Mar.

8 You cannot be pro-jobs and anti-government at the same time. You cannot love employees and despise employers. You cannot redistribute wealth that you never created. No goose, no golden egg.
1992 Quoted in the *Los Angeles Times*, 19 Feb.

Tu Fu 712–70
Chinese poet who never achieved a settled existence and is known to have spent a large part of his life travelling in a state of hardship.

9 Sundered by peaks unscalable,
Tomorrow shall we strangers be.
c.750 'Visiting an Old Friend', collected in *A Golden Treasury of Chinese Poetry* (translated by John Turner, 1967).

Tuchman, Barbara W(ertheim) 1912–89
US historian, best known for *The Guns of August* (1962, Pulitzer Prize), tracing the origins of World War I, and *Stilwell and the American Experience in China* (1970, Pulitzer Prize). Other works include *A Distant Mirror* (1978).

10 Dead battles, like dead generals, hold the military mind in their dead grip.
   1962 *The Guns of August*, ch.2.

11 No more distressing moment can ever face a British Government than that which requires it to come to a hard and fast and specific decision.
   1962 *The Guns of August*, ch.9.

12 Reasonable orders are easy enough to obey; it is capricious, bureaucratic or plain idiotic demands that form the habit of discipline.
   1970 *Stilwell and the American Experience in China*, pt.1, ch.1.

13 Most people are relieved to find a superior on whose judgment they can rest. That, indeed, is the difference between most people and Generals.
   1972 Address at US Army War College, Apr. Collected in *Practising History* (1981).

14 To a historian libraries are food, shelter, and even muse.
   1981 *Practising History*, 'The Houses of Research'.

Tucker, Sophie pseudonym of **Sophia Abuza** 1884–1966
US jazz singer, born in Russia. A legendary star of cabaret and vaudeville in the 1920s, she included among her biggest hits such songs as 'Some of These Days' (1926) and 'My Yiddische Momma' (1928). She led her own band in the 1930s and made several appearances on Broadway and in musical films.

15 I've been rich and I've been poor. Believe me, honey, rich is better.
   1945 *Some of These Days*.

16 The Last of the Red-Hot Mamas.
   Title of song, adopted by Tucker as her nickname.

Turgenev, Ivan 1818–83
Russian novelist. His best-known work is the novel *Fathers and Sons* (1862).

17 Nature is not a temple, but a workshop, and man's the workman in it.
   1862 *Fathers and Sons* (translated by Rosemary Edmonds), ch.9.

18 I share no one's ideas. I have my own.
   1862 *Fathers and Sons* (translated by Rosemary Edmonds), ch.13.

19 Whatever a man prays for, he prays for a miracle. Every prayer reduces itself to this: Great God, grant that twice two be not four.
   1881 *Poems in Prose*, 'Prayer'.

Turner, Bruce 1922–93
British jazz saxophonist. He played in the Humphrey Lyttelton Band for many years, as well as leading his own groups.

20 Jazz musicians are not demigods. They are warm, vulnerable human beings with a desperate need to go on paying the rent.
   1984 *Hot Air, Cool Music*, ch.10.

Turner, Joseph Mallard William 1775–1851
English painter, one of Britain's most important 19c artists.

21 This is the end of Art. I am glad I have had my day.
   Attributed, on first seeing a daguerrotype. Quoted in J G Links *Canaletto and his Patrons* (1977).

Tutu, Desmond Mpilo 1931–
Black South African prelate, the first black Bishop of Johannesburg (1984) and Archbishop of Cape Town (1986). A fierce critic of apartheid, advocating international sanctions, he also condemned the use of violence, seeking instead a negotiated solution. He was awarded the Nobel peace prize in 1984.

22 Be nice to whites. They need you to rediscover their humanity.
   1984 In the *New York Times*, 19 Oct.

23 I am not interested in picking up crumbs of compassion thrown from the table of someone who considers himself to be my master. I want the full menu of rights.
   1985 NBC News, 9 Jan.

24 We don't want apartheid liberalized. We want it dismantled. You can't improve something that is intrinsically evil.
   1985 Speech, Mar.

25 I have struggled against tyranny. I didn't do that in order to substitute one tyranny with another.
   1998 In *The Irish Times*, 'This Week They Said', 31 Oct.

26 If you are neutral in situations of injustice, you have chosen the side of the oppressor. If an elephant has its foot on the tail of a mouse and you say that you are neutral, the mouse will not appreciate your neutrality.
   Quoted in William P. Quigley, *Ending Poverty As We Know It: Guaranteeing a Right to a Job at a Living Wage* (2003).

27 I give great thanks to God that he has created a Dalai Lama. Do you really think, as some have argued, that God will be saying: 'You know, that guy, the Dalai Lama, is not bad. What a pity he's not a Christian'? I don't think that is the case—because, you see, God is not a Christian.
   2006 BBC News, 2 Jun.

28 Sometimes you want to whisper in God's ear, 'God, we know you are in charge, but why don't you make it slightly more obvious?'
   2008 Wallenberg Lecture, University of Michigan, 29 Oct.

29 I'm absolutely, utterly, and completely certain that God wouldn't be homophobic. I'd much rather go to hell—I really would much rather go to hell—than go to a homophobic heaven.
   2014 On NBC News, 27 Jun.

Twain, Mark pseudonym of **Samuel Langhorne Clemens** 1835–1910
US writer. He worked as a steamboat pilot and took his pen-name from a term used for measuring the depth of the Mississippi. His novel *Huckleberry Finn* (1884) is a classic. His work ranges from the lightly comic *The Innocents Abroad* (1869) to the darkly pessimistic *What is Man?* (1906).

30 No woman can look as well out of the fashion as in it.
   1867 Letter, 16 Apr, quoted in Franklin Walker and G Ezra Dane (eds) *Mark Twain's Travels with Mr. Brown* (1940), letter 14.

31 I must have a prodigious quantity of mind; it takes me as much as a week to make it up.
   1869 *The Innocents Abroad*, ch.7.

32 They spell it Vinci and pronounce it Vinchy; foreigners always spell better than they pronounce.
1869 *The Innocents Abroad*, ch.19.

33 The French are polite, but it is often mere ceremonious politeness. A Russian imbues his polite things with a heartiness that compels belief in their sincerity.
1869 *The Innocents Abroad*.

34 Lump the whole thing! Say that the Creator made Italy from designs by Michael Angelo!
1869 *The Innocents Abroad*.

35 Travel is fatal to prejudice.
1869 *The Innocents Abroad*, conclusion.

36 Soap and education are not as sudden as a massacre, but they are more deadly in the long run.
1872 *A Curious Dream*, 'Facts Concerning the Recent Resignation'.

37 Nothing helps scenery like ham and eggs.
1872 *Roughing It*, ch.17.

38 Well-a-well, man that is born of woman is of few days and full of trouble, as the Scripture says.
1876 Aunt Polly. *The Adventures of Tom Sawyer*, ch.1.

39 I reckon you're a kind of singed cat, as the saying is—better'n you look.
1876 Aunt Polly to Tom. *The Adventures of Tom Sawyer*, ch.1.

40 He was not the Model Boy of the village. He knew the model boy very well though—and loathed him.
1876 *The Adventures of Tom Sawyer*, ch.1.

41 Tom turned in without the added vexation of prayers.
1876 *The Adventures of Tom Sawyer*, ch.3.

42 He held curls to be effeminate, and his own filled his life with bitterness.
1876 *The Adventures of Tom Sawyer*, ch.4.

43 Often, the less there is to justify a traditional custom, the harder it is to get rid of it.
1876 *The Adventures of Tom Sawyer*, ch.5.

44 Church ain't shucks to a circus.
1876 *The Adventures of Tom Sawyer*, ch.7.

45 So they inwardly resolved that so long as they remained in the business, their piracies should not again be sullied with the crime of stealing.
1876 *The Adventures of Tom Sawyer*, ch.13.

46 There comes a time in every rightly constructed boy's life when he has a raging desire to go somewhere and dig for hidden treasure.
1876 *The Adventures of Tom Sawyer*, ch.25.

47 The cross of the Legion of Honour has been conferred upon me. However, few escape that distinction.
1880 *A Tramp Abroad*, ch.8.

48 An Irishman is lined with copper, and the beer corrodes it. But whiskey polishes the copper and is the saving of him.
1883 *Life on the Mississippi*, ch.23.

49 In the South, the war is what AD is elsewhere: they date from it.
1883 Of the American Civil War. *Life on the Mississippi*, ch.45.

50 Persons attempting to find a motive in this narrative will be prosecuted; persons attempting to find a moral in it will be banished; persons attempting to find a plot in it will be shot.
1884 *The Adventures of Huckleberry Finn*, 'Notice'.

51 She allowed she would sivilize me.
1884 *The Adventures of Huckleberry Finn*, ch.1.

52 If you are with the quality, or at a funeral, or trying to go to sleep when you ain't sleepy…why you itch all over in upward of a thousand places.
1884 *The Adventures of Huckleberry Finn*, ch.2.

53 You think you're a good deal of a big-bug, *don't* you.
1884 Huck's Pap to Huck. *The Adventures of Huckleberry Finn*, ch.5.

54 [He] reckoned a body could reform the old man with a shotgun, maybe, but he didn't know no other way.
1884 Judge Thatcher's opinion of Pap. *The Adventures of Huckleberry Finn*, ch.5.

55 Pap warn't in a good humor—so he was his natural self.
1884 *The Adventures of Huckleberry Finn*, ch.6.

56 A body would 'a thought he was Adam—he was just all mud.
1884 *The Adventures of Huckleberry Finn*, ch.6.

57 After supper Pap took the jug, and said he had enough whisky there for two drunks and one delirium tremens.
1884 *The Adventures of Huckleberry Finn*, ch.6.

58 How slow and still the time did drag along.
1884 *The Adventures of Huckleberry Finn*, ch.6.

59 I's rich now, come to look at it. I owns myself, en I's wuth eight hund'd dollars.
1884 Jim. *The Adventures of Huckleberry Finn*, ch.8.

60 But it warn't no time to be sentimentering.
1884 *The Adventures of Huckleberry Finn*, ch.13.

61 It was fifteen minutes before I could work myself up to go and humble myself to a nigger—but I done it, and I warn't ever sorry for it afterwards, neither. I didn't do him no more mean tricks, and I wouldn' done that one if I'd a knowed it would make him feel that way.
1884 Huck, of Jim. *The Adventures of Huckleberry Finn*, ch.15.

62 Jim said it made him all over trembly and feverish to be so close to freedom.
1884 *The Adventures of Huckleberry Finn*, ch.16.

63 To be, or not to be; that is the bare bodkin
That makes calamity of so long life;
For who would fardels bear, till Birnam Wood do come to Dunsinane,
But that the fear of something after death
Murders the innocent sleep,
Great nature's second course,
And makes us rather sling the arrows of outrageous fortune
Than fly to others that we know not of.
There's the respect must give us pause:
Wake Duncan with thy knocking! I would thou couldst;
For who would bear the whips and scorns of time,
The oppressor's wrong, the proud man's contumely,
The law's delay, and the quietus which his pangs might take,
In the dead waste and middle of the night, when Churchyards yawn
In customary suits of solemn black,
But that the undiscovered country from whose bourne no traveler returns,
Breathes forth contagion on the world,
And thus the native hue of resolution, like the poor cat i' the adage,

Is sicklied o'er with care,
And all the clouds that lowered o'er our housetops,
With this regard their currents turn awry,
And lose the name of action.
'Tis a consummation devoutly to be wished.
But soft you, the fair Ophelia:
Ope not thy ponderous and marble jaws,
But get thee to a nunnery—go!
1884 The Duke's version of Hamlet's soliloquy, combining elements of other speeches by Hamlet and pieces of *Macbeth. The Adventures of Huckleberry Finn*, ch.21.
▶ See Shakespeare 782:7.

64 All kings is mostly rapscallions.
1884 *The Adventures of Huckleberry Finn*, ch.22.

65 Hain't we got all the fools in town on our side? And ain't that a big enough majority in any town?
1884 *The Adventures of Huckleberry Finn*, ch.26.

66 It don't make no difference whether you do right or wrong, a person's conscience ain't got no sense, and just goes for him *anyway*. If I had a yaller dog that didn't know no more than a person's conscience does I would poison him. It takes up more room than all the rest of a person's insides, and yet ain't no good, nohow. Tom Sawyer he says the same.
1884 *The Adventures of Huckleberry Finn*, ch.33.

67 But that's always the way; it don't make no difference whether you do right or wrong, a person's conscience ain't got no sense, and just goes for him *anyway*.
1884 Huck. *The Adventures of Huckleberry Finn*, ch.33.

68 But I reckon I got to light out for the territory ahead of the rest, because Aunt Sally she's going to adopt me and sivilize me, and I can't stand it. I been there before.
1884 Huck. *The Adventures of Huckleberry Finn*, closing words.

69 The boy's mouth is a trifle more Irishy than is necessary.
1884 Letter to his publishers.

70 An experienced, industrious, ambitious, and often quite picturesque liar.
1885 'The Private History of a Campaign That Failed'.

71 Many a small thing has been made large by the right kind of advertising.
1889 *A Connecticut Yankee in King Arthur's Court*, ch.22.

72 The master minds of all nations, in all ages, have sprung in affluent multitude from the mass of the nation, and from the mass of the nation only—not from its privileged classes.
1889 *A Connecticut Yankee in King Arthur's Court*, ch.25.

73 If you pick up a starving dog and make him prosperous, he will not bite you. This is the principal difference between a dog and a man.
1894 *Pudd'nhead Wilson*, ch.16.

74 Few things are harder to put up with than the annoyance of a good example.
1894 *Pudd'nhead Wilson*, ch.19.

75 Familiarity breeds contempt—and children.
c.1894 Quoted in Albert Bigelow Paine (ed) *Mark Twain's Notebook* (1935).

76 What marriage is to morality, a properly conducted licensed liquor traffic is to sobriety.
1895 Quoted in Albert Bigelow Paine (ed) *Mark Twain's Notebook* (1935), ch.23.

77 When in doubt, tell the truth.
1897 *Following the Equator*, ch.2.

78 I admire him, I frankly confess it; and when his time is come I shall buy a piece of the rope for a keepsake.
1897 Of Cecil Rhodes. *Following the Equator*, ch.2.

79 Man is the Only Animal that Blushes. Or needs to.
1897 *Following the Equator*, ch.27.

80 When people do not respect us we are sharply offended; yet deep down in his private heart no man much respects himself.
1897 *Following the Equator*, ch.29.

81 The man with a new idea is a crank until the idea succeeds.
1897 *Following the Equator*, ch.32.

82 There are several good protections against temptation but the surest is cowardice.
1897 *Following the Equator*, ch.36.

83 It takes your enemy and your friend, working together, to hurt you to the heart; the one to slander you and the other to get the news to you.
1897 *Following the Equator*, ch.45.

84 Human nature is the same everywhere; it deifies success, it has nothing but scorn for defeat.
1897 *Joan of Arc*, bk.1, ch.8.

85 Education consists mainly in what we have unlearned.
c.1897 Quoted in Albert Bigelow Paine (ed) *Mark Twain's Notebook* (1935).

86 There are many scapegoats for our blunders, but the most popular one is Providence.
c.1897 Quoted in Albert Bigelow Paine (ed) *Mark Twain's Notebook* (1935).

87 The report of my death was an exaggeration.
1897 In the *New York Journal*, 2 Jun. This was the substance of Twain's cable to the Associated Press in response to the news item that he had died.

88 I am a democrat only on principle, not by instinct—nobody is *that*. Doubtless some people *say* they are, but this world is grievously given to lying.
1898 *Notebook*, ch.31, Feb–Mar.

89 A classic...something that everybody wants to have read and nobody wants to read.
1900 Speech on 'The Disappearance of Literature' at the Nineteenth Century Club, 20 Nov. Quoted in Albert Bigelow Paine (ed) *Mark Twain's Speeches* (1910).

90 Always do right. This will gratify some people, and astonish the rest.
1901 Speech, Brooklyn, 16 Feb.

91 The man who is a pessimist before 48 knows too much; if he is an optimist after it, he knows too little.
1902 Notebook, ch.33, Dec.
▶ See also Willkie 947:33.

92 Of the delights of this world man cares most for sexual intercourse. He will go any length for it—risk fortune, character, reputation, life itself.
c.1906 Quoted in Albert Bigelow Paine (ed) *Mark Twain's Notebook* (1935).

93 Scientists have odious manners, except when you prop up their theory; then you can borrow money off them.
The Bee (published 1917).

94 I have been told that Wagner's music is better than it sounds.
Autobiography (published in 1924).

95 I have never taken any exercise, except sleeping and resting, and I never intend to take any. Exercise is loathsome.
Quoted in Colin Jarman *The Guinness Dictionary of Sports Quotations* (1990).

96 Golf is a good walk spoiled.
Attributed.

97 I don't know anything that mars good literature so completely as too much truth.
'The Savage Club Dinner'. Quoted in Albert Bigelow Paine (ed) *Mark Twain's Speeches* (1923).

98 A habit cannot be tossed out of the window, it must be coaxed down the stairs one step at a time.
Attributed.

Tynan, Kenneth 1927–80

English theatre critic. Writing for the *Observer* and for the *New Yorker*, he argued strongly for the foundation of the National Theatre and lent his support to many talented radical playwrights. He was also the moving force behind the stylish erotic revue *Oh, Calcutta!* (1969).

99 There was a heated division of opinion in the lobbies during the interval but a small conservative majority took the view that it might be as well to remain in the theatre.
1953 Reviewing the play *The Glorious Days*.

1 A good many inconveniences attend play-going in any large city, but the greatest of them is usually the play itself.
1957 In the *New York Herald Tribune*.

2 A novel is a static thing that one moves through; a play is a dynamic thing that moves past one.
1961 *Curtains*.

3 Forty years ago he was Slightly in *Peter Pan*, and you might say that he has been wholly in *Peter Pan* ever since.
1961 Of Noël Coward. *Curtains*.

4 A critic is a man who knows the way but can't drive the car.
1966 In the *New York Times Magazine*, 9 Jan.

5 A good drama critic is one who perceives what is happening in the theatre of his time. A great drama critic also perceives what is *not* happening.
1967 *Tynan Right and Left*, foreword.

6 I doubt if I could love anyone who did not wish to see *Look Back in Anger*.
1956 In the *Observer*, 13 May.

7 A useful word previously unknown to me: 'ergophobia', meaning 'fear or hatred of work'. At last I can define myself in one word.
The Diaries of Kenneth Tynan (2001), entry for 26 Oct 1975.

8 Dichotomy = operation performed on lesbians to make them normal.
The Diaries of Kenneth Tynan (2001), entry for 11 Oct 1977.

Tyson, Don(ald) John 1930–2011

US businessman, chairman and chief executive officer of Tyson Foods Inc, Arkansas.

9 If you can take $20,000 in one-hundred-dollar bills and walk up on a windy hill and tear them up and watch them blow away, and it doesn't bother you, then you should go into the commodities market.
1994 In the *New Yorker*, 30 May.

Tyson, Mike 1966–

US boxer.

10 Everybody in America is so money-hungry. It's like a rat race and even when you win you're still a freaking rat.
2000 In *The Times*, Dec 26.

11 I'm not Mother Teresa. I'm not Charles Manson either.
2002 In *The Independent*, 20 Dec.

12 My main objective is to be professional, but to kill him.
2002 On Lennox Lewis. In *The Independent*, 20 Dec.

13 Man is not meant to be humble, he's meant to be humbled.
2013 *Undisputed Truth*.

14 Religion is for people who are scared of hell. I'm spiritual because I've already been to hell.
2014 Quoted on thestar.com, 26 Dec.

Tzara, Tristan *pseudonym of* Samy Rosenstock 1896–1963

Romanian-born poet, essayist and editor in Paris, a leader of the Dadaist movement.

15 *La mort serait un beau long voyage et les vacances illimitées de la chair des structures et des os.*
Death should be a long, beautiful voyage and limitless vacations of the flesh.
1923 *De nos oiseaux*, 'La mort de Guillaume Apollinaire'.

16 *Dada ne signifie rien.*
Dada means nothing.
1924 *Sept manifestes Dada*, 'Manifeste Dada 1918'.

17 *Liberté:* DADA DADA DADA, *hurlement de couleurs crispées, entrelacements des contraires et de toutes les contradictions, des grotesques, des inconséquences:* LA VIE.
Freedom: DADA DADA DADA, a howl of unnerving colours, intertwinings of contrarities and contradictions, of the grotesque, of inconsistencies: LIFE.
1924 *Sept manifestes Dada*, 'Manifeste Dada 1918'.

18 All pictorial or plastic art is useless; art should be a monster which casts servile minds into terror.
Quoted in Saranne Alexandrian *Surrealist Art* (1970).

19 Dada began not as an art form but as a disgust.
Quoted in Saranne Alexandrian *Surrealist Art* (1970).

U

Uccello, Paolo 1397–1475

Florentine painter. One of the first Italian painters of the Renaissance to explore the use of perspective.

1 O what a lovely thing this perspective is!
Attributed in Giorgio Vasari *Lives of the Artists* (1568, translated by George Bull, 1965).

Umaseo, Tadao 1920–2010
Japanese intellectual who wrote about and commented on his country's social and political traditions.

2 In terms of communication, Japan is like the black hole of the universe. It receives signals but does not emit them.
Quoted in David Halberstam *The Reckoning* (1986).

Unamuno, Miguel de 1864–1936
Spanish fatalist philosopher and writer. Rector at the University of Salamanca, he first supported and then denounced Franco and subsequently died at the hands of the Fascists.

3 *La vida es duda, y la fe sin la duda es solo muerte.*
Life is doubt, and faith without doubt is nothing but death.
1907 *Poesías*, 'Salmo II'.

4 It is not usually our ideas that make us optimistic or pessimistic, but it is our optimism or pessimism of physiological or pathological origin that makes our ideas.
1913 *The Tragic Sense of Life*.

5 Science is a cemetery of dead ideas.
1913 *The Tragic Sense of Life* (translated by P Smith, 1953).

6 True science teaches, above all, to doubt and to be ignorant.
1913 *The Tragic Sense of Life* (translated by P Smith, 1953).

7 Science robs men of wisdom and usually converts them into phantom beings loaded up with facts.
Collected in *Essays and Soliloquies* (translated by J E Crawford Flitch, 1925).

Unesco Constitution
An organization founded (in 1946) to promote collaboration among nations through education, science and culture.

8 Since wars begin in the minds of men, it is in the minds of men that the defences of peace must be constructed.
1945 Signed 16 Nov. The Unesco Constitution came into force 4 Nov 1946.

United Nations Charter
Drafted during World War II by the US, UK and USSR. Key figures included John Foster Dulles, Ralph Bunche and Field Marshal Jan Smuts.

9 We the Peoples of the United Nations, determined to save succeeding generations from the scourge of war, which twice in our lifetime has brought untold sorrow to mankind, and to reaffirm faith in fundamental human rights, in the dignity and worth of the human person, in the equal rights of men and women and of nations large and small, and to establish conditions under which justice and respect for the obligations arising from treaties and other sources of international law can be maintained, and to promote social progress and better standards of life in larger freedom, and for these ends, to practice tolerance and live together in peace with one another as good neighbours, and to unite our strength to maintain international peace and security, and to ensure by the acceptance of principles and the institution of methods, that armed force shall not be used, save in the common interest, and to employ international machinery for the promotion of the economic and social advancement of all peoples, have resolved to combine our efforts to accomplish these aims.
1945 26 Jun.

Unseld, Siegfried 1924–2002
German publisher, head of Suhrkamp Verlag (Frankfurt).

10 One of the signs of Napoleon's greatness—according to a sociologist who recently wrote to our publishing house—is that he once had a publisher shot.
1978 *The Author and his Publisher* (translated by H and H Hannum, 1980), p.1.

Untermeyer, Louis 1885–1977
US writer and editor, best known as the editor of anthologies such as *Modern American Poetry* (1919), which introduced some important new voices, and *Treasury of Great Poems* (1955).

11 Every poet knows the pun is Pierian, that it springs from the same soil as the Muse…a matching and shifting of vowels and consonants, an adroit assonance sometimes derided as jackassonance.
1965 *Bygones*.

Updike, John Hoyer 1932–2009
US novelist, poet and critic. He is best known for his novels, notably the 'Rabbit' series, but also wrote poetry, short stories, criticism and *Self-Consciousness* (1989), a volume of memoirs.

12 Everybody who tells you how to act has whisky on their breath.
1960 *Rabbit, Run*.

13 The difficulty with humorists is that they will mix what they believe with what they don't; whichever seems likelier to win an effect.
1960 *Rabbit, Run*.

14 Many-maned scud-thumper, tub
of male whales, maker of worn wood, shrub-
ruster, sky-mocker, rave!
portly pusher of waves, wind-slave.
1960 *Telephone Poles and Other Poems*, 'Winter Ocean'.

15 School is where you go between when your parents can't take you and industry can't take you.
1963 *The Centaur*, ch.4.

16 One out of three hundred and twelve Americans is a bore, for instance, and a healthy male adult bore consumes each year one and a half times his own weight in other people's patience.
1965 *Assorted Prose*, 'Confessions of a Wild Bore'.

17 The first breath of adultery is the freest; after it, constraints aping marriage develop.
1968 *Couples*, ch.2.

18 Sex is like money; only too much is enough.
1968 *Couples*, ch.5.

19 Facts are generally overesteemed. For most practical purposes, a thing is what men think it is. When they judged the earth flat, it was flat. As long as men thought slavery tolerable, it was tolerable. We live down here among shadows, shadows among shadows.
1974 *Buchanan. Buchanan Dying*, act 1.

20 To be President of the United States, sir, is to act as advocate for the blind, venomous, and ungrateful client;

still, one must make the best of the case, for the purposes of Providence.
1974 Polk. *Buchanan Dying*, act 2.

21 In general the churches...bore for me the same relation to God that billboards did to Coca-Cola: they promoted thirst without quenching it.
1975 *A Month of Sundays*, ch.2.

22 Americans have been conditioned to respect newness, whatever it costs them.
1975 *A Month of Sundays*, ch.18.

23 One of the last...of the great narrating English virgins.
Of Mildred Lathbury, protagonist of Barbara Pym's *Excellent Women* (1978). Attributed.

24 America is a vast conspiracy to make you happy.
1980 *Problems*, 'How to Love America and Leave It at the Same Time'.

25 Writing criticism is to writing fiction and poetry as hugging the shore is to sailing in the open sea.
1984 *Hugging The Shore*, foreword.

26 Why does one never hear of government funding for the preservation and encouragement of comic strips, girlie magazines and TV soap operas? Because these genres still hold the audience they were created to amuse and instruct.
1985 In the *New York Review of Books*, 18 Jul.

27 There's a crystallization that goes on in a poem which the young man can bring off, but which the middle-aged man can't.
1986 In the *New York Times*, 24 Mar.

28 How circumstantial reality is! Facts are like individual letters, with their spikes and loops and thorns, that make up words: eventually they hurt our eyes, and we long to take a bath, to rake the lawn, to look at the sea.
1989 *Self-Consciousness*, I. 'A Soft Spring Night in Shillington'.

29 A writer's self-consciousness, for which he is much scorned, is really a mode of interestedness, that inevitably turns outward.
1989 *Self-Consciousness*, I. 'A Soft Spring Night in Shillington'.

30 The essential self is innocent, and when it tastes its own innocence knows that it lives forever.
1989 *Self-Consciousness*, I. 'A Soft Spring Night in Shillington'.

31 The throat: how strange, that there is not more erotic emphasis upon it. For here, through this compound pulsing pillar, our life makes its leap into spirit, and in the other direction gulps down what it needs of the material world.
1989 *Self-Consciousness*, III. 'Getting The Words Out'.

32 The great temple of fiction has no well-marked front portal; most devotees arrive through a side door, and not dressed for worship.
1989 *Self-Consciousness*, III. 'Getting The Words Out'.

33 In fact we do not try to picture the afterlife, nor is it our selves in our nervous tics and optical flecks that we wish to perpetuate; it is the self as the window on the world that we can't bear to think of shutting.
1989 *Self-Consciousness*, VI. 'On Being A Self Forever'.

34 Not only are selves conditional but they die. Each day, we wake slightly altered, and the person we were yesterday is dead.
1989 *Self-Consciousness*, VI. 'On Being A Self Forever'.

35 So writing is my sole remaining vice. It is an addiction, an illusory release, a presumptuous taming of reality, a way of expressing lightly the unbearable.
1989 *Self-Consciousness*, VI. 'On Being A Self Forever'.

36 Now that I am sixty, I see why the idea of elder wisdom has passed from currency.
1992 In the *New Yorker*, Nov.

37 [There is] an undercurrent of emotion bred of the deep acquaintance that can take a landscape and its inhabitants to be a vocabulary, a set of wordless symbols effortlessly shared.
1995 On the artist Edward Hopper. In the *Washington Post*, 25 Jun.

38 The United States, democratic and various though it is, is not an easy country for a fiction-writer to enter: the slot between the fantastic and the drab seems too narrow.
1995 *Rabbit Angstrom: The Four Novels*, introduction.

39 Clarence's mind was like a many-legged, wingless insect that had long and tediously been struggling to climb up the walls of a slick-walled porcelain basin; and now a sudden impatient wash of water swept it down the drain.
1996 *In the Beauty of the Lilies*.

40 But when has happiness ever been the subject of fiction? The pursuit of it is just that—a pursuit.
2003 *The Early Stories: 1953–1975*, foreword.

41 God Himself is simple, and employs simple men to shape the world.
2006 *Terrorist*.

Urey, Harold Clayton 1893–1981

US chemist and discoverer of deuterium, or heavy hydrogen. He taught at the Universities of Montana, John Hopkins, Columbia, Chicago and Oxford, and was awarded the 1934 Nobel prize in chemistry.

42 I thought it might have a practical use in something like neon signs.
c.1934 Recalling his 1932 discovery of heavy water which proved critical to the development of the atomic bomb.

Ustinov, Sir Peter Alexander 1921–2004

English actor, playwright and director, of Russian descent. He appeared in a wide range of European works, including both comedies and tragedies, and also enjoyed success in plays of his own, among them *The Love of Four Colonels* (1951), *Romanoff and Juliet* (1956) and *Beethoven's Tenth* (1983). His talent as a witty raconteur and his many film appearances also contributed to his international reputation.

43 Critics search for ages for the wrong word, which, to give them credit, they eventually find.
1952 BBC radio broadcast, Feb.

44 A diplomat these days is nothing but a head waiter who's allowed to sit down occasionally.
1956 *Romanoff and Juliet*.

45 Would it have helped Ben Hur if Christ had not been crucified?
1962 Comment when the financiers of his *Billy Budd* expressed their preference for a happy ending. Recalled in his autobiography *Dear Me* (1977).

46 Thanks to the movies, gunfire has always sounded unreal to me, even when being fired at.
1977 *Dear Me*.

47 There is always something engagingly lunatic about Ralph, a Quixotic quality, although his windmills are ditches and his faithful nag a powerful motor-cycle.
1977 Of Sir Ralph Richardson. *Dear Me.*

48 Toronto is a kind of New York operated by the Swiss.
Quoted by John Bentley Mays in the *Globe and Mail*, 1 Aug 1987.

49 I was relieved to hear that your welcome was not excessive.
To the audience, opening a one-man show at the Curran Theater. Quoted in the *San Francisco Chronicle*, 25 Apr 1991.

Uttley, Alison 1884–1976

English writer. She is remembered for her books for children, notably the 'Little Grey Rabbit' series (1929 onwards).

50 For a long time we dreamed of a real leather ball, and at last my brother had one for his birthday. The feel of the leather, the stitching round it, the faint gold letters stamped upon it, the touch of the seam, the smell of it, all affected me so deeply that I still have that ache of beauty when I hold a cricket ball.
1948 *Carts and Candlesticks.*

Vachell, Horace Annesley 1861–1955
British writer.

1 In nature there are no rewards or punishments; there are only consequences.
1906 *The Face of Clay.*

Valenzuela, Luisa 1940–
Argentinian fiction writer.

2 *Siendo el esperar sentada la forma más muerta de la espera muerta, siendo el esperar la forma menos estimulante de muerte.*
To wait, seated in a chair, is the deadest form of dead anticipation, and waiting the most uninspired form of death.
1982 *Cambio de armas*, 'Ceremonias de rechazo' (translated as *Other Weapons*, 'Rituals of Rejection', 1985).

Valéry, Paul 1871–1945
French poet, writer and critic, considered one of the great modern philosophical writers in French verse. He wrote widely on philosophical issues and on the metaphysics of life.

3 *Un poème n'est jamais achevé—c'est toujours un accident qui le termine, c'est-à-dire qui le donne au public.*
A poem is never finished; it is always an accident that puts a stop to it, that gives it to the public.
1930 *Littérature.*

4 *Il faut n'appeler Science que l'ensemble des recettes qui réussissent toujours.—Tout le reste est littérature.*
Science means simply the aggregate of all the recipes that are always successful. All the rest is literature.
1932 *Moralités.*

5 *Dieu créa l'homme, et ne le trouvant pas assez seul, il lui donne une compagne pour lui faire mieux sentir sa solitude.*
God created man and, finding him not sufficiently alone, gave him a companion to make him feel his solitude more keenly.
1941 *Tel Quel 1*, 'Moralités'.

6 *La politique est l'art d'empêcher les gens de se mêler de ce qui les regarde.*
Politics is the art of preventing people from taking part in affairs which concern them.
1943 *Tel Quel 2*, 'Rhumbs'.

Valle y Caviedes, Juan del c.1652–?1695
Peruvian poet born in a small town in Andalusia, Spain. He lived most of his life in Lima. Little is known of his life. His collection *Diente del Parnaso* (1689) is an earthy satire of the medical profession.

7 *Y así, enfermos, ojo alerta,
y a ningún médico admitan;
mueran de gorra, sin dar
un real a la medicina.*
Be careful then, patients,
and don't accept any doctor;
die for free and do not give
a single coin to medicine.
1689 *Diente del Parnaso* ('Parnassus' Tooth'), 'Prólogo al que leyere este tratado'.

Vallejo, César Abraham 1892–1938
Peruvian poet. A first-hand witness to poverty and the injustices done to the indigenous peoples, after the publication of his collection *Trilce* (1922), he left Peru (1923) and spent the rest of his life in France and Spain living in precarious circumstances and without publishing a single poem. He also wrote novels and non-fiction.

8 *Yo nací un día
que Dios estuvo enfermo.*
I was born on a day
God was sick.
1918 *Los heraldos negros* (translated as *The Black Heralds*, 1990), 'Espergesia'.

9 *Absurdo, sólo tú eres puro.
Absurdo, este exceso sólo ante ti se
suda de dorado placer.*
Absurdity, only you are pure.
Absurdity, only before you
is this excess sweated out of golden pleasure.
1922 *Trilce* (translated 1973), no.73.

10 *Me moriré en París con aguacero,
un día del cual tengo ya el recuerdo.
Me moriré en París y no me corro
tal vez un jueves, como es hoy, de otoño.*
I will die in Paris with a sudden shower,
a day I can already remember.
I will die in Paris—and I don't budge—
maybe a Thursday, like today is, in autumn.
1939 *Poemas humanos*, 'Piedra negra sobre una piedra blanca' (translated as 'Black Stone on a White Stone', 1968).

Vance, Paul and Pockriss, Lee 1929–, 1924–2011
US songwriters who composed many popular songs, including 'Catch a Falling Star' which was made popular by Perry Como.

11 Itsy Bitsy Teenie Weenie Yellow Polkadot Bikini.
   1960 Title of song.

van den Berghe, Pierre L 1933–
US sociologist, Emeritus Professor at the University of Washington.

12 I suffer the anthropological malady diagnosed by Lévi-Strauss in *Tristes tropiques*: I find it much more difficult to suspend value judgments about the society in which I normally reside than I do abroad. It takes physical and cultural distance to gain moral detachment and political noncommitment. Relativism implies a solid measure of indifference.
   'From the Popocatepetl to the Limpopo', collected in Bennett Berger (ed) *Authors of their Own Lives* (1990).

13 Sociology seems to have missed every intellectually promising boat in the last half century.
   'From the Popocatepetl to the Limpopo', collected in Bennett Berger (ed) *Authors of their Own Lives* (1990).

Vanderbilt, Amy 1908–74
US hostess and writer, an authority on social etiquette.

14 Breakfast is the one meal at which it is perfectly good manners to read the paper.
   1954 *Amy Vanderbilt's Complete Book of Etiquette.*

van der Post, Sir Laurens 1906–96
South African soldier, explorer, writer and philosopher.

15 Human beings are perhaps never more frightened than when they are convinced beyond doubt that they are right.
   1958 *Lost World of the Kalahari.*

van de Wetering, Janwillem 1931–2008
Dutch murder-mystery writer.

16 The desire to make money is a symptom of all sorts of emotional disturbances—greed is only one of them.
   1988 *The Maine Massacre.*

Van Druten, John William 1901–57
US playwright of Dutch extraction, who was born in London. His mainly light comic plays include *Old Acquaintance* (1940), *Bell, Book and Candle* (1950) and *I Am a Camera* (1951), a stage adaptation of Isherwood's Berlin stories.

17 If I were a woman I'd wear coffee as a perfume.
   Quoted in *Think*, Feb 1963.

van Gogh, Vincent 1853–90
Dutch Post-Impressionist painter. He was an evangelistic preacher in Le Borinage (1878–80) and after studying in Paris he settled in Arles (1888), where the light and colour transformed his art. He became increasingly mentally disturbed, and finally shot himself.

18 There is no blue without yellow and without orange.
   1888 Letter to Émile Bernard, Jun.

19 I have a terrible lucidity at moments when nature is so beautiful. I am not conscious of myself any more, and the pictures come to me as if in a dream.
   1888 Letter to his brother Theo, c.27 Sep.

20 It is no more easy to make a good picture than it is to find a diamond or a pearl. It means trouble and you risk your life for it.
   1888 From a letter to his brother Theo, early Oct.

21 I cannot help it that my paintings do not sell. The time will come when people will see that they are worth more than the price of the paint.
   1888 Letter to his brother Theo, 24 Oct.

Van Hooijdonk, Pierre 1969–
Dutch footballer.

22 £7,000 a week would be fine for the homeless. But not for me.
   1997 Rejecting a new wage deal at Celtic Football Club. Quoted in the *Observer*, 6 Jun 2004.

Van Horne, Harriet 1920–98
US journalist.

23 Cooking is like love. It should be entered into with abandon or not at all.
   1956 *Vogue*, Oct.

24 After nightfall, I wouldn't leave a burning building without an escort.
   1969 On muggings in Manhattan. In the *Washington Post*, 26 Feb.

Varèse, Edgar 1883–1965
US composer of Italo-French parentage. He settled in New York in 1919 and founded the New Symphony Orchestra to further the cause of modern music. In 1921 he founded the international Composers' Guild, which has become the leading organ of progressive musicians. His work is almost entirely orchestral, examples including the largely abstract *Hyperprism* (1923) and *Ionisation* (1931).

25 There is no avant-garde: only some people a bit behind.
   Attributed.

Vargas Llosa, Mario 1936–
Peruvian writer, who spent his early life in Bolivia and moved to Paris in 1959, living in several European cities. He was a defeated candidate for the Peruvian presidency (1990), having declined an offer of the premiership in 1984, and remains active and often controversial in literary and political matters. In 2010 he was awarded the Nobel prize for literature.

26 *Por qué esos personajes que se servían de la literatura como adorno o pretexto iban a ser más escritores que Pedro Camacho, quien sólo vivía para escribir? Porque ellos habían leído (o, al menos, sabían que deberían haber leído) a Proust, a Faulker, a Joyce, y Pedro Camacho era poco más que un analfabeto?*
   Why should those persons who used literature as an ornament or pretext have any more right to be considered real writers than Pedro Camacho, who lived *only* to write? Because they had read (or at least knew that they should have read) Proust, Faulkner, Joyce, while Pedro Camacho was very nearly illiterate?
   1977 *La tía Julia y el escribidor* (translated as *Aunt Julia and the Scriptwriter*, 1982), ch.11.

Vasari, Giorgio 1511–74
Italian painter, architect and author of the first biography of the Italian Renaissance artists.

27 According to Pliny, painting was brought to Egypt by Gyges of Lydia; for he says that Gyges once saw his own shadow cast by the light of a fire and instantly drew his own outline on the wall with a piece of charcoal.
   1568 *Lives of the Artists* (translated by George Bull, 1965).

28 [Michelangelo] Buonarotti commended it [Titian's painting] highly, saying that his colouring and his style pleased him very much but that it was a shame that in Venice they did not learn to draw well from the beginning.
   1568 *Lives of the Artists* (translated by George Bull, 1965).

Vasconcelos, José 1882–1959

Mexican educator, politician, essayist and philosopher, Minister of Education (1920–4). His political activism led to exile on several occasions. His works call for the incorporation of native culture into Mexican life to transcend the limitations of Western culture.

29 *La América Latina debe lo que es al europeo blanco y no va a renegar de él...Sin embargo, aceptamos los ideales superiores del blanco, pero no su arrogancia.*
   Latin America owes its being to the European, and should not deny it...but, while accepting the white man's superior ideals, we do not accept his arrogance.
   1925 *La raza cósmica* (translated as *The Cosmic Race*, 1979), pt.1, ch.2.

Vaughan Williams, Ralph 1872–1958

British composer. He established his reputation with the choral *Sea Symphony* (1910) and promoted the English folksong movement. His works include *Fantasia on a Theme of Tallis* (1909), for strings, the *Pastoral Symphony* (1922), the opera *The Pilgrim's Progress* (1948–9) and many choral works.

30 Misbegotten abortions.
   1930 Of critics. Letter to Holst.

31 I don't know whether I like it, but it's what I meant.
   Of his Fourth Symphony. Quoted in Ian Crofton and Donald Fraser *A Dictionary of Musical Quotations* (1985).

32 It takes perhaps a thousand poor musicians to produce one virtuoso.
   1954 In *The New York Times*, 5 Dec.

Vaughan, Henry 1622–95

Welsh religious poet. Educated at Oxford, he later practised as a physician. His verse publications include *Silex Scintillans* (1650, enlarged 1655) and *Olor Iscansus* (1651); prose meditations include *The Mount of Olives* (1652) and *Flores Solitudinis* (1652).

33 The skin and shell of things
   Though fair
   are not
   Thy wish nor prayer
   but got
   My meer despair
   of wings.
   1650 *Silex Scintillans*, 'The Search'.

34 Happy those early days when I
   Shined in my Angel-infancy.
   Before I understood this place
   Appointed for my second race,
   Or taught my soul to fancy aught
   But a white, celestial thought;
   When yet I had not walked above
   A mile or two from my first love,
   And looking back (at that short space)
   Could see a glimpse of His bright face.
   When on some gilded cloud or flower
   My gazing soul would dwell an hour
   And in those weaker glories spy
   Some shadows of eternity.
   1650 *Silex Scintillans*, 'The Retreat'.

35 Before I taught my tongue to wound
   My conscience with a sinful sound,
   Or had the black art to dispense
   A several sin to every sense,
   But felt through all this fleshly dress
   Bright shoots of everlastingness.
   1650 *Silex Scintillans*, 'The Retreat'.

36 Some men a forward motion love,
   But I by backward steps would move,
   And when this dust falls to the urn
   In that state I came, return.
   1650 *Silex Scintillans*, 'The Retreat'.

37 My soul, there is a country
   Far beyond the stars,
   Where stands a wingèd sentry
   All skilful in the wars;
   1650 *Silex Scintillans*, 'Peace'.

38 King of comforts, King of life,
   Thou hast cheered me,
   And when fears and doubts were rife,
   Thou hast cleared me.

   Not a hook in all my breast
   But thou fill'st it,
   Not a thought in all my rest
   But thou kill'st it.

   Wherefore with my utmost strength
   I will praise thee,
   And as thou giv'st line, and length,
   I will raise thee.
   1650 *Silex Scintillans*, 'Praise'.

39 I saw Eternity the other night
   Like a great ring of pure and endless light,
   All calm, as it was bright,
   And round beneath it, Time in hours, days, years
   Driven by the spheres
   Like a vast shadow moved.
   1650 *Silex Scintillans*, 'The World'.

40 Man is the shuttle, to whose winding quest
   And passage through these looms
   God ordered motion, but ordained no rest.
   1650 *Silex Scintillans*, 'Man'.

41 They are all gone into the world of light,
   And I alone sit lingering here;
   Their very memory is fair and bright,
   And my sad thoughts doth clear.
   1650 *Silex Scintillans*, 'They Are All Gone'.

42 I played with fire, did counsel spurn,
   Made life my common stake;
   But never thought that fire would burn,
   O that a soul could ache.
   1650 *Silex Scintillans*, 'The Garland'.

Vaz de Caminha, Pero   late 15c–early 16c

Portuguese historian, who came to the New World only eight years after Columbus. His account avoids the prevalent hyperbole, striving instead to give a realistic picture of the native peoples.

43 *Esta gente é boa e de boa simplicidade. E imprimir-se-á ligeiramente neles cualquer cunho, que les quiserem dar. E logo lhes, Nosso Senhor, deu bons corpos e bons rostos, como a bons homens, e Ele que nos por aqui trouxe, creio que não foi sem causa. E portanto, Vossa Alteza, pois tanto deseja acrescentar na santa fé católica, deve entender em sua salvação.*
These people are good and simple. You can stamp on them any design that you wish to give them. And Our Lord gave them good bodies and good faces, and I think that it was his plan that we arrive here. Therefore, Your Majesty, since you wish so much to increase Catholic faith, you must provide for their salvation.
Carta (published 1817).

Veblen, Thorstein   1857–1929

US economist and social critic. He attacked commercial values in his best-known work, *Theory of the Leisure Class* (1899). He was instrumental in breaking the hold of neo-classical economic theory and became a leader in the institutional school of economics.

44 The corset is…a mutilation, undergone for the purpose of lowering the subject's vitality and rendering her permanently and obviously unfit for work.
1899 *Theory of the Leisure Class.*

45 When seen in the perspective of half-a-dozen years or more, the best of our fashions strike us as grotesque, if not unsightly.
1899 *Theory of the Leisure Class.*

46 Conspicuous consumption of valuable goods is a means of reputability to the gentleman of leisure.
1899 *Theory of the Leisure Class.*

Vega Carpio, Lope Félix de   1562–1635

Spanish playwright and poet. His prolific output included some 1,800 plays, of which around 600 survive. He served with the Spanish Armada in 1588 and was ordained as a priest in 1614, though he continued to enjoy numerous love affairs.

47 All right, then, I'll say it: Dante makes me sick.
1635 Last words.

Vegetius   full name *Flavius Vegetius Renatus*
fl.c.385–400 AD

Roman military writer under Theodosius I, the Great. After AD 375 he produced the *Epitoma Rei Militaris*, mainly extracted from other authors, which was a supreme authority on warfare during the Middle Ages.

48 *Qui desiderat pacem, praeparat bellum.*
Let him who desires peace prepare for war.
c.380 AD *Epitoma Rei Miltaris*, no.3, prologue. This became familiar in the Middle Ages as *Si vis pacem para bellum* (If you want peace, prepare for war).

Venables, Terry   1943–

English footballer and manager. He was dismissed as manager of Tottenham Hotspur in 1993, but appointed manager of England a year later. He resigned after the 1996 European championships.

49 I had mixed feelings—like watching your mother-in-law drive over a cliff in your car.
1992 Of Paul Gascoigne's move from Tottenham Hotspur to the Italian club Lazio. Quoted in David Pickering *The Cassell Soccer Companion* (1994).

50 Never's a hard call, isn't it? Never-ish.
2000 On whether he would ever manage England again. In *The Times*, 26 Dec.

51 If you can't stand the heat in the dressing room, get out of the kitchen.
Attributed.
▶ *Truman 868:32.*

Venturi, Robert Charles   1925–

US architect, renowned for his eclectic and sometimes humorous designs, a key figure of the postmodernist school.

52 [It is] drawing a moustache on a madonna.
1977 On designing an addition to Oberlin College's 1917 Allen Memorial Art Museum. In the *New York Times*, 30 Jan.

53 Less is a bore.
Attributed.

Vergniaud, Pierre Victurnien   1753–93

French revolutionary politician, leader of the Girondists. When the Girondists clashed with the Montagnards, who wished to retain dictatorial power, he and his party were arrested and guillotined.

54 *Il a été permis de craindre que la Révolution, comme Saturne, dévorât successivement tous ses enfants.*
There is reason to fear that the Revolution may, like Saturn, devour each of her children one by one.
1793 Spoken at his trial, Oct.

Verlaine, Paul   1844–96

French poet who befriended and promoted the poetry of Arthur Rimbaud with whom he had a volatile relationship.

55 *Les sanglots longs*
Des violons
De l'automne
Blessent mon cïur
D'une langueur
Monotone.
Slow sobs
Of the violins
Of autumn
Wound my heart
With a monotonous languor.
1866 *Poèmes saturniens, Paysages tristes, V*: 'Chansons d'Automne'.

56 *Un vaste et tendre*
Apaisement
Semble descendre
Du firmament . . .
C'est l'heure exquise.
A vast and tender
Calm
Seems to descend
From the heavens . . .
This is the exquisite hour.
1866 *Poèmes saturniens*, 'La Bonne Chanson, no.6'.

57 *Il pleure dans mon cïur*
Comme il pleut sur la ville.

The tears fall in my heart
As the rain over the town.
1874 *Romances sans paroles,* 'Ariettes oubliées, no.3'.

58 *Voici des fruits, des fleurs, des feuilles et des branches
Et puis voici mon cïur qui ne bat que pour vous.*
Here are fruits, flowers, leaves and branches
And here also is my heart which beats only for you.
1874 *Romances sans paroles,* 'Aquarelles, Green'.

59 *Pas la Couleur, rien que la Nuance!*
No colour, only nuance!
1884 *Jadis et naguère,* 'Art poétique'.

60 *Prends l'éloquence et tords-lui son cou!*
Take eloquence and break its neck!
1884 *Jadis et naguère,* 'Art poétique'.

61 *Que ton vers soit la bonne aventure
Éparse au vent crispé du matin
Qui va fleurant la menthe et le thym.
Et tout le reste est littérature.*
May your verse be a glorious adventure
Strewn by the crisp morning air
Which helps the mint and the thyme grow.
Everything else is mere literature.
1884 *Jadis et naguère,* 'Art poétique'.

Verne, Jules 1828–1905
French novelist. His best-known works include *A Journey to the Centre of the Earth* (1864), *Twenty Thousand Leagues Under the Sea* (1869) and *Around the World in Eighty Days* (1873).

62 An Englishman does not joke about such an important matter as a bet.
1873 *Around the World in Eighty Days.*

Versace, Donatella 1955–
Italian fashion designer.

63 I'd like to dress the Queen. She can handle anything. Maybe in black with a little leather, a little rock 'n' roll.
Attributed.

Vespasian *full name* Titus Flavius Vespasianus AD 9–79
Roman Emperor, commander of the legions in the East when Nero was deposed. He was proclaimed emperor by his troops in Alexandria, and after defeating his rival Vitellius (AD 69) reached Rome and restored order. He began an ambitious building programme, including the Colosseum, and extended and consolidated the Empire.

64 *Pecunia non olet.*
Money does not smell.
Attributed. His son Titus had objected to a tax on the contents of the city's urinals (used by fullers). Vespasian held a coin to Titus's nose, asking him whether it smelled. When Titus said no he replied 'Atqui e lotio est' ('And yet, it comes from urine'). Quoted in Suetonius *Vespasian,* 23.

65 *Vae, puto deus fio.*
Dear me, I must be turning into a god.
AD 79 Attributed last words. Quoted in Suetonius *Vespasian,* 23 (translated by Robert Graves, 1967).

Vettel, Sebastian 1987–
German racing driver. He has won the Formula One championship four times (2010, 2011, 2012, 2013).

66 The chequered flag is really just a stupid wooden stick and a piece of cloth. It's a small thing, but it means so much when you cross the line at moments like that. It was unbelievable.
2007 On finishing fourth in China.

Vettriano, Jack 1951–
Scottish artist whose works have proved particularly popular as prints and posters.

67 Rather the poster on the student's wall than the original unseen on a shelf in a big gallery storeroom.
2004 In *The Times,* 13 Mar.

Vian, Boris 1920–59
French novelist associated with the Surrealist movement.

68 *Les gens ne changent pas. Ce sont les choses qui changent.*
People do not change. Things change.
1947 *L'Écume des jours.*

69 *Les masses ont tort et les individus toujours raison.*
The masses are wrong; individuals are always right.
1947 *L'Écume des jours.*

70 *Mais enfin, bande de critiques, les livres que vous ne comprenez pas ne vaudraient-ils pas au moins que vous les signaliez?*
For heaven's sake, gang of critics, don't the books which you do not understand at least deserve recognition?
1948 In *La Seine,* 19 Apr.

71 *Rien n'est plus parfait, plus achevé qu'un cadavre.*
Nothing is more perfect, more complete than a corpse.
1950 *L'Herbe rouge.*

72 *Savoir qu'il existe des passions et ne pas le ressentir, c'est affreux.*
To know that there are passions and to not feel any, that is horrible.
1950 *L'Herbe rouge.*

73 *Les femmes et les hommes ne vivent pas sur le même plan.*
Women and men do not live according to the same design.
1953 *L'Arrache-cïur.*

74 *Un poète
C'est un être unique
À des tas d'exemplaires
Qui ne pense qu'en vers
Et n'écrit qu'en musique
Sur des sujets divers
Des rouges ou des verts
Mais toujours magnifiques.*
A poet
Is a unique being
From an exemplary multitude
Who only thinks in verse
And only writes in music
On diverse subjects
Reds and greens
But always magnificently.
1962 *Je voudrais pas crever.*

Vicious, Sid *pseudonym of* **John Simon Ritchie** 1957–79

British rock bassist. He played with the notorious punk rock group The Sex Pistols in the 1970s, and died of a drug overdose while awaiting trial for the murder of his girlfriend, Nancy Spungen, in the US.

75 You just pick a chord, go twang, and you've got music.
  1976 In *The Sun*.

Victoria *in full* **Alexandrina Victoria** 1819–1901

Queen of Great Britain (1837–1901). She married Prince Albert of Saxe-Coburg and Gotha (1840), and bore him nine children. After his death (1861) she neglected her duties, but her recognition as Empress of India (1876) and the celebratory Golden (1887) and Diamond (1897) Jubilees restored her prestige. She had strong preferences for certain Prime Ministers (eg Melbourne and Disraeli) over others (notably Peel and Gladstone).

76 This mad, wicked folly of 'Women's Rights' with all its attendant horrors, on which her poor sex is bent, forgetting every sense of womanly feeling and propriety. Lady Amberley ought to get a good whipping.
  1870 Letter to Sir Theodore Martin, 29 Mar. The feminist Lady Amberley was Bertrand Russell's mother.

77 Oh, if the Queen were a man, she would like to go and give those Russians, whose word one cannot believe, such a beating! We shall never be friends again till we have it out.
  1878 Letter to Lord Beaconsfield, 10 Jan.

78 Please understand that there is no one depressed in this house. We are not interested in the possibilities of defeat; they do not exist.
  1899 On the 2nd Boer War. Comment to the Prime Minister, Arthur Balfour, Dec. Quoted in Lady Gwendolen Cecil *Life of Robert, Marquis of Salisbury* (1931), vol.3, ch.6.

79 A strange, horrible business, but I suppose good enough for Shakespeare's day.
  Attributed comment after watching a performance of *King Lear*.

80 He speaks to Me as if I were a public meeting.
  Of Gladstone. Attributed in G W E Russell *Collections and Recollections*.

81 We are not amused.
  Attributed.

Vidal, Gore *originally* **Eugene Luther Vidal, Jr** 1925–2012

US writer and polemicist. He ran for congress in 1960 and spent some time as a TV commentator. His novels include the satirical comedies *Myra Breckenridge* (1968) and *Duluth* (1983), and the historical trilogy *Burr* (1974), *1876* (1976) and *Lincoln* (1984). He published his memoirs, *Palimpsest*, in 1995.

82 A talent for drama is not a talent for writing, but is an ability to articulate human relationships.
  1956 In the *New York Times*, 17 Jun.

83 I'm all for bringing back the birch. But only between consenting adults.
  1966 Interview on *The Frost Programme*.

84 It is the spirit of the age to believe that any fact, no matter how suspect, is superior to any imaginative exercise, no matter how true.
  1967 'French Letters: Theories of the New Novel', in *Encounter*, Dec.

85 Astronauts! Rotarians in space!
  1968 *Myra Breckenridge*.

86 There is something about a bureaucrat that does not like a poem.
  1968 *Sex, Death and Money*, preface.
  ▶ See Frost 352:90.

87 People who obtain power do so because it delights them for its own sake and for no other reason.
  1970 In *Esquire*, Sep.

88 From primeval ooze to the stars, we killed anything that stood in our way, including each other.
  1970 On the human race. In *Esquire*, Sep.

89 Whenever a friend succeeds, a little something in me dies.
  1973 In the *Sunday Times Magazine*, 16 Sep.

90 It is not enough to succeed. Others must fail.
  Quoted in G Irvine *Antipanegyric for Tom Driberg* (1976).

91 A triumph of the embalmer's art.
  1981 Of Ronald Reagan. Quoted in the *Observer*, 26 Apr.

92 But to ignore the absence of evidence is the basis of true faith.
  1981 'Pink Triangle and Yellow Star', in the *Nation*, 14 Nov.

93 For certain people, after fifty, litigation takes the place of sex.
  1981 Quoted in the *Evening Standard*.

94 Democracy is supposed to give you the feeling of choice, like Painkiller X and Painkiller Y. But they're both just aspirin.
  1982 Interview in the *Observer*, 7 Feb.

95 It's a country evenly divided between conservatives and reactionaries.
  1984 Of the US. In the *Observer*, 16 Sep.

96 American men do not read novels because they feel guilty when they read books which do not have facts in them.
  1984 In *Saturday Review*, 18 Jun.

97 The century that began with a golden age in all the arts (or at least the golden twilight of one) is ending not so much without art as without the idea of art.
  Introduction to Logan Pearsall Smith *All Trivia* (1984).

98 Fifty per cent of them won't vote and the other half doesn't read newspapers. I hope it's the same.
  1991 In *Emmy*, May.

99 When it comes to getting things wrong, the English are born masters.
  1991 'Reflections on Glory Reflected and Otherwise', in the *Threepenny Review*, Spring.

1 Meanwhile, let us give Clinton his due. Lincoln to one side, he does better funerals than any American president in an increasingly murderous history.
  1997 *Virgin Islands: Essays 1992–1997*.

2 We are, said President Clinton, the one indispensable—or was it indisposable?—nation.
  1997 *Virgin Islands: Essays 1992–1997*.

3 There are as many good writers as ever there were. The problem is that there are so few good readers.
  2003 Quoted in *Writers on Writing, Volume II: More Collected Essays from the New York Times*.

4 As societies grow decadent, the language grows decadent, too. Words are used to disguise, not to illuminate, action: you liberate a city by destroying it. Words are to confuse, so that at election time people will solemnly vote against their own interests.

2004 *Imperial America: Reflections on the United States of Amnesia.*

5 He was interesting because he was interested. He had a way of approaching subjects that was never boring.
2007 Responding to the death of Norman Mailer.

Vidor, King Wallis 1894–1982

US film director, born in Galveston, Texas. In Hollywood from 1915, he worked as a writer and extra before moving into directing. His many films include *The Big Parade* (1925), *The Crowd* (1928), *Our Daily Bread* (1934) and *The Fountainhead* (1949).

6 The crowd laughs with you always but it will cry with you for only a day.
1929 *The Crowd* (with John V A Weaver and Harry Behn).

Vieira, Antônio 1608–97

Jesuit missionary, orator, diplomat and writer, condemned by the Inquisition and briefly imprisoned. His sermons, letters and state papers are a valuable index to the climate of opinion in 17c Brazil and Portugal.

7 *Que coisa é a formosura, senão uma caveira bem vestida, a que a menor enfermidade tira a cor, e antes de a a morte a despir de todo, os anos lhe vão mortificando a graça daquela exterior e aparente superfície, de tal sorte, que, se os olhos pudessem penetrar o interior dela, o não poderiam ver sem horror?*
What is beauty, but a well-dressed skull that loses colour with the slightest illness, and, before death robs it of everything, the grace of its external and apparent surface is mortified by the years in such a way that, if eyes could penetrate within beauty, they could watch it only full of horror?
c.1666 *Sermões*, 'Sermão do dem⁴nio mudo' ('Sermon of the Silent Devil').

Villon, François 1431–63

French poet, member of the criminal organization 'The Brotherhood of the Cocquille'. Several times sentenced to death for various crimes, he was repeatedly pardoned. In 1463 he received his final death sentence, but this was commuted to banishment.

8 *Mais où sont les neiges d'antan?*
But where are last year's snows?
1461 'Ballade des Dames du Temps Jadis', refrain.

St Vincent of Lérins *known as* Vincentius Lerinensis
d.c.450 AD

A native of Gaul, and monk on the island of Lerna (Lérins).

9 *Quod ubique, quod semper, quod ab omnibus creditum est.*
What is everywhere, what is always, what is by all people believed.
Commonitorium Primum, section 2 (translated by Heurtley, 1895).

Viner, Jacob 1892–1970

US economist, a professor at the University of Chicago and Princeton University.

10 The classical economists were not wholly free from error, for they were only mortals, even if of a superior species.
1930 *The Long View and the Short.*

Virgil *full name* Publius Vergilius Maro 70–19 BC

Roman poet, under the patronage of Maecenas and Augustus. He published the *Eclogues*, a collection of pastorals, in 37 BC, and the *Georgics* (a didactic poem on husbandry in four books) in 30 BC. The *Aeneid*, a national epic based on the legendary founder of the Roman nation, was published posthumously.

11 *Arma virumque cano, Troiae qui primus ab oris Italiam fato profugus Laviniaque venit Litora.*
This is a tale of arms and of a man. Fated to be an exile, he was the first to sail from the land of Troy and reach Italy, at its Lavinian shore.
Aeneid, opening lines (translated by W F Jackson Knight).

12 *Non ignara mali, miseris succurrere disco.*
No stranger to trouble myself, I am learning to help those who are in distress.
Dido, queen of Carthage. *Aeneid*, bk.1, l.630.

13 *Conticuere omnes intentique ora tenebant Inde toro pater Aeneas sic orsus ab alto.*
They fell silent, every one, and each face was turned intently towards him. From high on the dais Aeneas, Troy's Chieftain, began to speak.
Aeneid, bk.2, l.1–2 (translated by W F Jackson Knight).

14 *Quidquid id est, timeo Danaos et dona ferentis.*
Whatever it may be, I fear the Greeks, even when bearing gifts.
Spoken by Laocoon, a Trojan prince and priest of Apollo, warning the city against the wooden horse left by the Greeks. *Aeneid*, bk.2, l.49.

15 *Una salus victis nullam sperare salutem.*
Nothing can save the conquered but the knowledge that they cannot now be saved.
Aeneid, bk.2, l.354 (translated by W F Jackson Knight).

16 *Dis aliter visum.*
The gods thought otherwise.
Aeneid, bk.2, l.428.

17 *Fama, malum qua non aliud velocius ullum.*
Rumour is of all pests the swiftest.
Aeneid, bk.4, l.174 (translated by W F Jackson Knight).

18 *Quis fallere possit amantem?*
Who can deceive a lover?
Aeneid, bk.4, l.296.

19 *Varium et mutabile semper femina.*
Women were ever things of many changing moods.
Aeneid, bk.4, l.569–70 (translated by W F Jackson Knight).

20 *Audentis Fortuna iuvat!*
Fortune helps those who dare.
Aeneid, bk.10, l.284. The phrase is often rendered as 'Fortune favours the brave'.

21 *Experto credite.*
Believe one who has experienced it.
Aeneid, bk.11, l.283.

22 *Latet anguis in herba.*
A snake lurks in the grass.
Eclogues, 3.93.

23 *Sicelides Musae, paulo maiora canamus. Non omnis arbusta iuvant humilesque myricae.*
Sicilian Muses, let us sing a somewhat loftier strain. Not all do orchards please and the lowly tamarisks.
Eclogues, 4.1–2 (translated by H Rushton Fairclough).

24 *Non omnia possumus omnes.*
We cannot all do everything.
Eclogues, 8.63 (translated by H Rushton Fairclough).

25 *Omnia vincit amor.*
Love conquers all things.
Eclogues, 10.69.

26 *Labor omnia vicit*
improbus et duris urgens in rebus egestas.
Toil conquered the world, unrelenting toil, and want that pinches when life is hard.
Georgics, 1.145-6 (translated by H Rushton Fairclough).

27 *Felix qui potuit rerum cognoscere causas.*
Blessed is he who has been able to win knowledge of the causes of things.
Georgics, 2.490 (translated by H Rushton Fairclough).

28 *Mantua me genuit, Calabri rapuere, tenet nunc Parthenope; cecini pascua rura duces.*
Mantua brought me life, Calabria death; now Naples holds me: I sang of flocks and farms and heroes.
19 BC Epitaph on his tomb near Naples, supposedly dictated on his deathbed. Quoted in Donatus *Vita Vergilii*, 'Life of Virgil'.

Vitruvius full name Marcus Vitruvius Pollio c.70 BC–25 BC

Roman architect and engineer whose ten books on architecture, *De Architectura*, are the oldest surviving work on the subject.

29 Neither talent without instruction, nor instruction without talent can produce the perfect craftsman.
c.25 BC *On Architecture*.

Vlaminck, Maurice de 1876–1958

French painter, graphic artist and writer.

30 Good painting is like good cooking: it can be tasted, but not explained.
Attributed.

Voltaire pseudonym of François Marie Arouet 1694–1778

French philosopher. He was imprisoned for lampooning the Duc d'Orleans, 1717–18, and later went into exile in England, 1726–9. He returned to France, but moved to Berlin in 1750 to the court of Frederick the Great. His works include *Édipe* (1718), *Candide* (1759) and the *Dictionnaire philosophique* (1764).

31 *Le superflu, chose très nécessaire.*
The superfluous, a very necessary thing.
1736 *Le Mondain*.

32 *Dans ce pays-ci il est bon de tuer de temps en temps un amiral pour encourager les autres.*
In this country it is considered a good thing to kill an admiral from time to time, to encourage the others.
1759 Of England. Reference to the execution of Admiral Byng following his failure to engage the French at Menorca, 1757. *Candide*, ch.23.

33 *Tout est pour le mieux dans le meilleur des mondes possibles.*
All is for the best in the best of all possible worlds.
1759 *Candide*, ch.30.

34 *Cela est bien dit, répondit Candide, mais il faut cultiver notre jardin.*
'Well said', Candide replied, 'but we must cultivate our own garden.'
1759 *Candide*, ch.30.

35 I am the best-tempered man there ever was, yet I have killed three men, and two of them were priests!
1759 *Candide*, ch.15.

36 You know that these two nations have been at war over a few acres of snow near Canada, and that they are spending on this fine struggle more than Canada itself is worth.
1759 Of the French and English struggle in Quebec. *Candide*, ch.23.

37 Men will always be mad, and those who think they can cure them are the maddest of all.
1762 Letter.

38 *La superstition met le monde entier en flammes; la philosophie les éteint.*
Superstition sets the whole world in flames; philosophy puts out the fire.
1764 *Dictionnaire philosophique*, 'Superstition'.

39 *En effet, l'histoire n'est que le tableau des crimes et des malheurs.*
In fact, history is nothing but a tableau of crimes and misfortunes.
1767 *L'Ingénu*, ch.10.

40 *Ce corps qui s'appelait et qui s'appelle encore le saint empire romain n'était en aucune manière ni saint, ni romain, ni empire.*
This state which was called and is still called the Holy Roman Empire, was not in any way holy, or Roman or an Empire.
1769 *Essai sur Les Moeurs et l'Ésprit des Nations*.

41 *La foi consiste à croire ce que la raison ne croit pas… Il ne suffit pas qu'une chose soit possible pour la croire.*
Faith consists in believing what reason cannot…In order to believe something, it is not enough that it should be possible.
1770 *Questions sur l'Encyclopédie*.

42 *Le mieux est l'ennemi du bien.*
The best is the enemy of the good.
1772 *Contes*, 'La Bégueule', I.2. He is quoting an Italian proverb, *Il meglio è l'inimico del bene*.

43 This enormous dunghill.
1776 Of the works of William Shakespeare. Letter to d'Argental, 19 Jul.

44 *On doit des égards aux vivants; on ne doit aux morts que la vérité.*
We should be considerate to the living; to the dead we owe only the truth.
'Première Lettre sur Œdipe'. In *Œuvres*, vol.1 (published 1785).

45 *Dieu n'est pas pour les gros bataillons, mais pour ceux qui tirent le mieux.*
God is on the side not of the big battalions, but of the best shots.
In *Voltaire's Notebooks*, edited by Th. Besterman (1952).

46 *Il faut, dans le gouvernement, des bergers et des bouchers.*
Governments need both shepherds and butchers.
In *Voltaire's Notebooks*, edited by Th. Besterman (1952).

47 One goes to see a tragedy to be moved, to the opera one goes either for want of any other interest or to facilitate digestion.
Quoted in J Wechsberg *The Opera* (1972).

48 *Si Dieu n'existait pas, il faudrait l'inventer.*
If God did not exist, it would be necessary to invent him.
Epîtres,'À l'Auteur du Livre des Trois Imposteurs'.

49 The art of medicine consists of amusing the patient while Nature cures the disease.
Attributed.

50 I disapprove of what you say, but I will defend to the death your right to say it.
Attributed.

Vonnegut, Kurt, Jr 1922–2007

US novelist. *Player Piano* (1952) was his first novel and there were another three before *Slaughterhouse-Five* (1969), the central event of which is the destruction of Dresden during World War II, an event witnessed by the author as a prisoner-of-war.

51 The British had no way of knowing it, but the candles and the soap were made from the fat of rendered Jews and Gypsies and fairies and communists, and other enemies of the state. So it goes.
1969 *Slaughterhouse-Five*, ch.5.

52 Their only English-speaking guard told them to memorize their simple address, in case they got lost in the city. Their address was this: 'Schlachthof-fünf'. *Schlachthof* meant *slaughterhouse*. *Fünf* was good old five.
1969 *Slaughterhouse-Five*, ch.6.

53 Our leaders are sick of all the solid information that has been dumped on humanity by honest research and excellent scholarship and investigative reporting. They want to put us back on the snake-oil standard.
2006 In *Rolling Stone*, 24 Aug.

54 Those who believe in telekinetics, raise my hand.
Attributed.

Vorster, John *originally* Balthazar Johannes Vorster 1915–83

South African Nationalist politician, an extreme Afrikaner. As Prime Minister (1966–78) he maintained a policy of apartheid and protected white interests. In 1978 he became President, but resigned over a financial scandal.

55 As far as criticism is concerned, we don't resent that unless it is absolutely biased—as it is in most cases.
1969 In the *Observer*, 9 Nov.

Vreeland, Diana *originally* Diana Dalziel 1906?–1989

US journalist, editor of *Vogue*. Born in Paris, she married Thomas Vreeland in 1924 in New York and joined Vogue as editor-in-chief in 1962. She transformed the high-fashion magazine into a society journal. She also acted as consultant to the costume institute at the Metropolitan Museum of Art.

56 A little bad taste is like a splash of paprika. We all need a splash of bad taste—it's hearty, it's healthy, it's physical.
1984 *D.V.* (her autobiography, edited by George Plimpton and Christopher Hemphill).

57 The biggest thing since the atom bomb.
1990 On the bikini. In her obituary in the *New York Times*, 1 Apr.

58 People who eat white bread have no dreams.
Quoted in Annette Tapert and Diana Edkins *The Power of Style* (1994).

Vukovich, Bill 1918–55

US motor-racing driver. He won the Indianapolis 500 in 1953 and 1954 but was killed in the race while in the lead the following year.

59 There's no secret. You just press the accelerator to the floor and steer left.
1954 Of his tactics in the Indianapolis 500. Quoted in Colin Jarman *The Guinness Dictionary of Sports Quotations* (1990).

Waddington, Miriam 1917–2004

Canadian poet and critic. Of Russian-Jewish origin, she was a social worker in Montreal and taught at York University, Toronto. Her works include poetry such as *The Glass Trumpet* (1966), *The Price of Gold* (1976) and *The Visitants* (1981), and short stories and essays.

1 Keep bees and
grow asparagus,
watch the tides
and listen to the
wind instead of
the politicians
make up your own
stories and believe
them if you want to
live the good life.
1972 *Driving Home: Poems New and Selected*, 'Advice to the Young'.

Wagner, Otto 1841–1918

Austrian architect and teacher, considered the founder of the modern movement.

2 The whole basis of the views of architecture prevailing today must be displaced by the recognition that the only possible point of departure for our artistic creation is modern life.
1895 *Modern Architecture* (1895), preface.

Wagner, Robert Ferdinand, Jr 1944–93

US former deputy mayor of New York City.

3 When in danger, ponder. When in trouble, delegate. And when in doubt, mumble.
1991 In the *New York Times*, 17 Feb.

Wain, John Barrington 1925–94

English writer. He is known primarily as a critic and novelist, but he also wrote poetry, plays and a biography of Samuel Johnson.

4 Poetry is to prose as dancing is to walking.
1976 BBC radio broadcast, 13 Jan.

Waite, Terry (Terence Hardy) 1939–

English religious adviser, envoy of Archbishop of Canterbury Robert Runcie from 1980. On 20 Jan 1987, while making inquiries in Beirut about European hostages, he was kidnapped. Following worldwide efforts to secure his release and that of his fellow hostages, 1,763 days later he was freed.

5 Politics come from man. Mercy, compassion, and justice come from God.
1985 In the *Observer*, 13 Jan.

6 Freeing hostages is like putting up a stage set—which you do with the captors, agreeing on each piece as you slowly put it together. Then you leave an exit through which both the captor and the captive can walk with sincerity and dignity.
1986 Interviewed on ABC news, 3 Nov.

Waits, Tom 1949–
US singer, songwriter, musician and actor. His albums include *Heartattack and Vine* (1980), *Swordfishtrombones* (1983) and *Mule Variations* (1999).

7 There's a lot of intelligence in the hands. When you pick up a shovel, the hands know what to do. The same thing's true of sitting at the piano.
1999 In the *Dallas Observer*, 6 May.

8 There's truths there that spiral out of what appears to be just a word game. That's what I find mystifying about the meanings of things: they kind of unscrew themselves from the practical words.
2011 In the *New York Times*, 20 Oct.

Walcott, Derek Alton 1930–
West Indian poet and dramatist. He founded the Trinidad Theatre Workshop in 1959 and is Visiting Professor of English at Boston University. His poetry includes *In A Green Night* (1962), *Castaway* (1965), *The Gulf* (1969), *Omeros* (1990) and *White Egrets* (2010). He was awarded the Nobel prize for literature in 1992.

9 I who have cursed
  The drunken officer of British rule, how choose
  Between this Africa and the English tongue I love?
  Betray them both, or give back what they give?
  How can I face such slaughter and be cool?
  How can I turn from Africa and live?
1962 *In a Green Night*, 'A Far Cry from Africa'.

10 I'm just a red nigger who love the sea,
   I had a sound colonial education,
   I have Dutch, nigger, and English in me,
   and either I'm nobody or I'm a nation.
1980 *The Star-Apple Kingdom*, 'The Schooner *Flight*', pt.1.

11 Who knows
   who his grandfather is, much less his name?
1980 *The Star-Apple Kingdom*, 'The Schooner *Flight*', pt.5.

12 But we live like our names and you would have
   to be colonial to know the difference,
   to know the pain of history words contain.
1980 *The Star-Apple Kingdom*, 'The Schooner *Flight*', pt.6.

13 I see these islands and I feel to bawl,
   'area of darkness" with V.S. Nightfall.
1982 *The Fortunate Traveller*, 'The Spoiler's Return'.

14 The English language is nobody's special property. It is the property of the imagination: it is the property of the language itself.
Interviewed in George Plimpton (ed) *Writers at Work* (8th series, 1988).

15 every 'I'
   is a fiction finally.
1990 *Omeros*, bk.1, ch.5, section 2.

16 Time is the metre, memory the only plot.
1990 *Omeros*, bk.2, ch.24, section 2.

17 'We were the colour of shadows when we came down with tinkling leg-irons to join the chains of the sea, for the silver coins multiplying on the sold horizon.'
1990 *Omeros*, bk.3, ch.28, section 1.

18 The worst crime is to leave a man's hands empty. Men are born makers, with that primal simplicity in every maker since Adam.
1990 *Omeros*, bk.3, ch.28, section 2.

19 Art is History's nostalgia, it prefers a thatched roof to a concrete factory, and the huge church above a bleached village.
1990 *Omeros*, bk.6, ch.45, section 2.

20 Poetry…is perfection's sweat but most seen as fresh as the raindrops on a statue's brow.
1992 In the *New York Times*, 8 Dec.

21 The fate of poetry is to fall in love with the world, in spite of History.
1992 In the *New York Times*, 8 Dec.

22 The process of poetry is one of excavation and of self-discovery.
1992 In the *New York Times*, 8 Dec.

23 V S Nightfall.
Nickname for V S Naipaul. Attributed to Derek Walcott by Paul Theroux, in *Sir Vidia's Shadow: A Friendship Across Five Continents* (1998).

Wald, George 1906–97
US biochemist and member of the faculty at Harvard University. He shared the 1967 Nobel prize in physiology or medicine and became known widely for his view opposing the War in Vietnam.

24 We are the products of editing, rather than of authorship.
1975 'The Origin of Optical Activity', in *Annals of the New York Academy of Sciences*, vol.69.

Wald, Jerry 1911–62
US writer and producer. His films include *Mildred Pierce* (1945), *Johnny Belinda* (1948) and *The Glass Menagerie* (1950).

25 He used to be a big shot.
1939 The words of Panama Smith (Gladys George) as Eddie Bartlett (James Cagney) dies on the steps of the church in *The Roaring Twenties*. With Richard Macauley and Robert Rossen.

Waldron, Hicks 1924–
Chair, Boardroom Consultants Inc.

26 People do what you pay them to do, not what you ask them to do.
1991 In the *Wall Street Journal*, 17 Apr.

Walesa, Lech 1943–
Polish trade unionist, politician and President. A former shipyard worker, he became leader of the independent trade union, Solidarity, which openly challenged the government's policies, and was imprisoned under martial law (1981). Released in 1982, he was awarded the Nobel peace prize in 1983. He was President from 1990 to 1995.

27 He who once became aware of the power of Solidarity and who breathed the air of freedom will not be crushed.
1983 Nobel peace prize lecture, read on his behalf, 11 Dec.

28 The English are all right. They're quiet, they're slow, they count things carefully, they hesitate—and I'm switching to their track.
1991 In *The Times*, 17 Apr, on the eve of his state visit to London.

29 The Soviet Union remains a superpower in the military and nuclear sense—only its economy is in difficulty. People want me to lead the troops out or to chuck them over the border, but I have neither the strength nor the will to do it.
1991 In *The Times*, 17 Apr.

30 I'm lazy. But it's the lazy people who invented the wheel and the bicycle because they didn't like walking or carrying things.
Attributed.

Waley, Arthur David 1889–1966

English poet and Sinologist. He was a distinguished translator of Chinese and Japanese literature.

31 It is not difficult to censor foreign news.
What is difficult today is to censor one's own thoughts,—
To sit by and see the blind man
On the sightless horse, riding into the bottomless abyss.
1940 'Censorship'.

Walken, Christopher 1943–

US actor. His numerous films include *The Deer Hunter* (1978), *A View to a Kill* (1985), *True Romance* (1993), *Sleepy Hollow* (1999) and *Catch Me If You Can* (2002).

32 I'm better off not socialising. I make a better impression if I'm not around.
2004 In *The Scotsman*, 12 Jun.

Walker, Alice Malsenior 1944–

US writer. She has written poetry and non-fiction, and established her reputation with her novels, notably *The Color Purple* (1983, filmed 1985).

33 The gift of loneliness is sometimes a radical vision of society or one's people that has not previously been taken into account.
1973 Interview in J O'Brien (ed) *Interviews with Black Writers*.

34 It is healthier, in any case, to write for the adults one's children will become than for the children one's 'mature' critics often are.
1976 'A Writer Because of, Not in Spite of, Her Children', in *Ms.*, Jan.

35 Writing saved me from the sin and inconvenience of violence.
1979 '*One* Child of One's Own', in *Ms.*, Aug.

36 The good news may be that Nature is phasing out the white man, but the bad news is that's who She thinks we all are.
1982 'Nuclear Madness: What You Can Do', in *Black Scholar*, Spring.

37 Anybody can observe the Sabbath, but making it holy surely takes the rest of the week.
1983 *In Search of Our Mothers' Gardens*, 'To the Editors of *Ms.* Magazine'.

38 The trouble with our people is as soon as they got out of slavery they didn't want to give the white man nothing else. But the fact is, you got to give 'em something. Either your money, your land, your woman or your ass.
1985 Pa. *The Color Purple*.

39 She say, Celie, tell the truth, have you ever found God in church? I never did. I just found a bunch of folks hoping for him to show. Any God I ever felt in church I brought in with me. And I think all the other folks did too. They come to church to *share* God, not find God.
1985 Shug. *The Color Purple*.

40 There are those who believe Black people possess the secret of joy and that it is this which will sustain them through any spiritual or moral or physical devastation.
1992 *Possessing the Secret of Joy*, epigraph.

41 How anyone cannot see that Nature is God is amazing to me: that they'd rather worship something that can only exist, really, in their own minds.
2013 *The Cushion in the Road: Meditation and Wandering as the Whole World Awakens to Being in Harm's Way*.

42 The harm that you do to others is the harm that you do to yourself and you cannot think then that you can cause wars in other parts of the world and destroy people and drone them without this having a terrible impact on your own soul and your own consciousness.
2013 *The Cushion in the Road: Meditation and Wandering as the Whole World Awakens to Being in Harm's Way*.

43 Hard times require furious dancing.
2013 *The Cushion in the Road: Meditation and Wandering as the Whole World Awakens to Being in Harm's Way*.

Wall Street Journal

Leading US financial newspaper.

44 God is registered to vote for Hollywood as a Republican. However, Jesus Christ is a Democrat from Santa Monica.
1995 'God Lives in Hollywood', editorial on California's voter registration lists, 12 Jul.

Wall, Mervyn 1908–97

Irish writer.

45 The Bishop gave vent to a long-drawn sigh.
'Did it ever occur to you to wonder why God created women?' he asked. 'It's the one thing that tempts me at times to doubt His infinite goodness and wisdom.'
1946 *The Unfortunate Fursey*.

46 The odour of sanctity was clearly discernible from his breath and person.
1946 *The Unfortunate Fursey*.

47 'Did you ever hear the like?' said the Devil, and a hard note crept into his voice. 'If there's one thing I can't stand', he said, 'it's superstition.'
1946 *The Unfortunate Fursey*.

Wallace, George Corley 1919–98

US Democratic lawyer and politician, opponent of the civil rights movement and Governor of Alabama (1963–7, 1971–4, 1975–8 and 1983–7). A presidential bid ended with an as-sassination attempt, on 15 May 1972, which left him paralyzed.

48 Segregation now, segregation tomorrow, and segregation for ever.
1963 Inaugural speech as Governor of Alabama, 19 Feb.

49 I've climbed my last political mountain.
   1972 On retiring after being crippled in an assassination attempt. Quoted in the *New York Times*, 3 Apr 1986.

50 A great deal has been lost and a great deal gained...may your message be heard...your lessons never be forgotten.
   1995 Reversing the 'segregation for ever' stance of 1963. In news reports, 11 Mar.

Wallace, Henry Agard 1888–1965

US agriculturist and statesman, editor of *Wallace's Farmer* (1933–40) until nominated Vice-President to Roosevelt. Chairman of the Board of Economic Welfare (1941–5) and Secretary of Commerce (1945–6), he stood unsuccessfully as President in 1948.

51 The century on which we are entering, the century that will come out of this war, can be and must be the century of the common man.
   1942 Speech, New York, 8 May.

Wallace, William Ross 1819–81

US poet. Only a few of his poems, mostly militant patriotic songs, have survived as anthology works. He practised as a lawyer in New York from 1841 until his death and was a contributor to Harper's magazine. Stimulated by the American Civil War, he wrote *Sword of Bunker Hill* (1861) and *The Liberty Bell* (1862).

52 The hand that rocks the cradle
   Is the hand that rules the world.
   c.1865 *John o' London's Treasure Trove*.

Wallach, Eli 1915–2014

US actor. A star of both stage and screen, he appeared in such films as *The Moonspinners* (1964), *The Tiger Makes Out* (1967) and *The Sentinel* (1977). On the stage he won particular acclaim in plays by Tennessee Williams and others.

53 There's something about a crowd like that that brings a lump to my wallet.
   1964 Observing the crowds that were gathering at the box office to see the highly successful Broadway show *Luv*. Attributed.

54 Having the critics praise you is like having the hangman say you've got a pretty neck.
   Attributed.

Waller, Edmund 1606–87

English poet and politician. Educated at Cambridge, he went on to be an MP; his involvement in a plot against Parliament during the Civil War led to his banishment in 1643. His collected poems were published in 1645.

55 Go, lovely rose,
   Tell her that wastes her time and me,
   That now she knows,
   When I resemble her to thee,
   How sweet and fair she seems to be.
   1645 'Go, lovely rose'.

56 Small is the worth
   Of beauty from the light retir'd;
   Bid her come forth,
   Suffer her self to be desir'd,
   And not blush to be admir'd.
   1645 'Go, lovely rose'.

57 Phillis, why shou'd we delay
   Pleasures shorter than the day?
   1645 'To Phillis'.

58 Since thou wouldst needs, bewitched with some ill charms,
   Be buried in those monumental arms:
   As we can wish, is, may that earth lie light
   Upon thy tender limbs, and so good night.
   1645 'To One Married to an Old Man'.

59 Poets may boast (as safely-vain)
   Their work shall with the world remain:
   Both bound together, live, or die,
   The verses and the prophecy.

   But who can hope his lines shou'd long
   Last, in a daily changing tongue?
   While they are new, envy prevails,
   And as that dies, our language fails.
   1645 'Of English Verse'.

60 We write in sand, our language grows,
   And like our tide ours overflows.
   1645 'Of English Verse'.

61 Verse thus design'd has no ill fate,
   If it arrive but at the date
   Of fading beauty, if it prove
   But as long-liv'd as present love.
   1645 'Of English Verse'.

Waller, Fats (Thomas Wright) 1904–43

US jazz pianist, composer and entertainer. A professional musician at 15, he began his recording career in 1922. Among the jazz standards he wrote were 'Ain't Misbehavin'' and 'Honeysuckle Rose'.

62 Madam, if you don't know by now, don't mess with it!
   When asked what jazz was. Quoted in Marshall Stearns *The Story of Jazz* (1956).
   ▶ See Armstrong 32:48.

Wallis, Hal 1898–1986

US producer. He worked in Hollywood for many years and then became an independent producer.

63 Louis, I think this is the beginning of a beautiful friendship.
   1942 Closing words of *Casablanca*, one of his contributions to a script largely written by the Epstein twins and Howard Koch.

Walpole, Horace, 4th Earl of Orford 1717–97

English writer and politician. Architectural pursuits, correspondence, writing, visits to Paris, his house, Strawberry Hill, and the establishment of a private press were the main occupations of his life. He exchanged more than 1600 letters with Mme du Deffand between 1769 and 1797 and corresponded also with Sir Horace Mann and the Countess of Upper Ossory.

64 We were eight days in coming hither from Lyons; the four last in crossing the Alps. Such uncouth rocks, and such uncomely inhabitants!
   1739 Letter to Richard West. Collected in P Cunningham (ed) *The Letters of Horace Walpole, Fourth Earl of Orford* (1857–9).

65 I am very glad that I see Rome while it yet exists; before a great number of years are elapsed, I question whether it will be worth seeing. Between the ignorance and poverty of the present Romans, every thing is neglected and falling to decay.
   1740 Letter. Collected in P Cunningham (ed) *The Letters of Horace Walpole, Fourth Earl of Orford* (1857–9).

66 It is a little plaything-house that I got out of Mrs Chevenix's shop, and it is the prettiest bauble you ever saw. It is set in enamelled meadows with filigree hedges…barges as solemn as Barons of the Exchequer move under my window… Thank God! the Thames is between me and the Duchess of Queensberry.
1747 Of Strawberry Hill, the first 'Gothic' cottage, a showplace in its day. Letter to Henry Seymour Conway, 8 Jun. In W S Lewis (ed) *Selected Letters of Horace Walpole* (1973). Mrs Chevenix kept a well-known toy-shop.

67 Every drop of ink in my pen ran cold.
1752 Letter to George Montague, 30 Jul. In *The Correspondence of Horace Walpole* (Yale edition, 1937–8).

68 One of the greatest geniuses that ever existed, Shakespeare, undoubtedly wanted taste.
1764 Letter to Christopher Wren, 9 Aug. In *The Correspondence of Horace Walpole* (Yale edition, 1937–8).

69 It is charming to totter into vogue.
1765 Letter to George Selwyn, 2 Dec. In *The Correspondence of Horace Walpole* (Yale edition, 1937–8).

70 Wondrously clean, but as evidently an actor as Garrick.
1766 Of the Methodist preacher John Wesley. Letter to John Chute, 10 Oct. In William Hadley (ed) *The Letters of Horace Walpole* (1926).

71 It was easier to conquer it than to know what to do with it.
1772 Of the Orient. Letter to Sir Horace Mann, 27 Mar. In *The Correspondence of Horace Walpole* (Yale edition, 1937–8).

72 The way to ensure summer in England is to have it framed and glazed in a comfortable room.
1774 Letter to William Cole, 28 May. In *The Correspondence of Horace Walpole* (Yale edition, 1937–8).

73 By the waters of Babylon we sit down and weep, when we think of thee, O America!
1775 Letter to William Mason, 12 Jun. In *The Correspondence of Horace Walpole* (Yale edition, 1937–8).

74 The world is a comedy to those that think, a tragedy to those that feel.
1776 Letter to Lady Ossory, 11 Dec. In W S Lewis (ed) *Selected Letters of Horace Walpole* (1973).

75 Your daughters, I hope, will be married to Americans, and not in this dirty, despicable little island.
1777 Letter to Lady Ossory, 11 Dec. In W S Lewis (ed) *Selected Letters of Horace Walpole* (1973).

76 When will the world know that peace and propagation are the two most delightful things in it?
1778 Letter to Sir Horace Mann, 7 Jul. In *The Correspondence of Horace Walpole* (Yale edition, 1937–8).

77 It is the story of a mountebank and his zany.
1785 Of Boswell's account of his *Tour of the Hebrides* with Dr Johnson. Letter to Henry Conway, 6 Oct. In *The Correspondence of Horace Walpole* (Yale edition, 1937–8).

78 All the sensible Tories that I ever knew were either Jacobites or became Whigs; those that remained Tories remained fools.
Memoirs of the Reign of King George III (published 1845).

79 Virtue knows to a farthing what it has lost by not being vice.
Quoted in L Kronenberger *The Extraordinary Mr Wilkes* (1973).

80 A fertile pedant.
Of Margaret Cavendish, Duchess of Newcastle. Quoted in Nicholas T Parsons *The Joy of Bad Verse* (1988).

Walpole, Sir Robert, 1st Earl of Orford 1676–1745

English statesman and leading minister of George I and II. Elected as a Whig MP in 1701, he became Secretary for War (1708), Treasurer of the Navy (1710) and Chancellor of the Exchequer (1715). Recognized as England's first Prime Minister from 1721, he resigned in 1742, when a war he had opposed broke out.

81 Madam, there are fifty thousand men slain this year in Europe, and not one an Englishman.
1734 To Queen Caroline, on avoiding British participation in the War of the Polish Succession. Quoted in John Hervey *Memoirs 1734–43* (1848), vol.1.

82 They may ring their bells now; before long they will be wringing their hands.
1739 Remark on hearing church bells celebrating the declaration of war against Spain, 19 Oct.

83 I have lived long enough in the world to know that the safety of a Minister lies in his having the approbation of this House. Former Ministers neglected that and therefore they fell; I have always made it my first study to obtain it, and therefore I hope to stand.
1739 Speech, House of Commons, 21 Nov.

84 Patriots spring up like mushrooms. I could raise 50 of them within the four and twenty hours. I have raised many of them in one night. It is but refusing to gratify an immeasurable or insolent demand, and up starts a patriot.
1741 Speech, House of Commons, 13 Feb.

85 All those men have their price.
Quoted in William Coxe *Memoirs of Sir Robert Walpole* (1798).

Walters, Julie 1950–

English actress. On television she has appeared in both comedy and drama, and her films include *Educating Rita* (1983) and *Billy Elliot* (2000).

86 There's something great about going through the menopause and being in your 50s. You trade in that youthful thing, where everything is brand new. You swap it hopefully for some kind of wisdom; all the stuff you've learned. And I think HRT and plastic surgery kind of stopped that.
2003 In *The Guardian*, 1 Sep.

Walther Von der Vogelweide c.1170–1230

German poet. One of the most celebrated poets of his time, he found particular favour at the Austrian court, and was awarded a small estate by Emperor Frederick II.

87 *Jâ leider desn mac nicht gesîn,*
Das guot und wertlich êre
Und gotes hulde mêre
Zesamene in ein herze komen.
It is sadly impossible
For wealth and a good name,
along with God's favour,
to be united in one heart.
c.1195 'Ich sass ûf eime steine', l.16–19.

Walton, Izaak 1593–1683

English writer. He is remembered for *The Compleat Angler* (1653), which discusses the business of fishing and is interspersed with scraps of dialogue, moral reflections, quaint old verses, songs and sayings, and idyllic glimpses of country life.

88 But God, who is able to prevail, wrestled with him, as the Angel did with Jacob, and marked him; marked him for his own.
1653 *Of Donne. Life of John Donne.*

89 Angling may be said to be so like mathematics, that it can never be fully learnt.
1653 *The Compleat Angler,* 'Epistle to the Reader'.

90 I shall stay [the reader] no longer than to wish him a rainy day to read this...discourse; and that if he be an honest angler, the east wind may never blow when he goes a-fishing.
1653 *The Compleat Angler,* 'Epistle to the Reader'.

91 Angling is somewhat like poetry, men are to be born so: I mean with inclination to it.
1653 *The Compleat Angler,* pt.1, ch.1.

92 Sir Henry Wotton...was also a most dear lover, and a frequent practiser of the art of angling; of which he would say, 'it was an employment for his idle time...a rest to his mind, a cheerer of his spirits, a diverter of sadness, a calmer of unquiet thoughts, a moderator of passions, a procurer of contentedness; and that it begat habits of peace and patience in those that professed and practised it.'
1653 *The Compleat Angler,* pt.1, ch.1.

93 An excellent angler, and now with God.
1653 *Of Sir George Hastings, The Compleat Angler,* pt.1, ch.4.

94 She and I both love all anglers, they be such honest, civil quiet men.
1653 *The milkwoman. The Compleat Angler,* pt.1, ch.4.

95 No life, my honest scholar, no life so happy and so pleasant, as the life of a well-governed angler; for when the lawyer is swallowed up with business, and the statesman is preventing or contriving plots, then we sit on cowslip-banks, hear the birds sing, and possess ourselves in as much quietness as these silver streams, which we now see glide so quietly by us.
1653 *The Compleat Angler,* pt.1, ch.5.

96 He would often say, Religion does not banish mirth, but only moderates and sets rules to it.
1670 *Of George Herbert. Life of George Herbert.*

Walton, Sir William Turner 1902–83

British composer. His works include *Façade* (1923), designed to accompany verses by Edith Sitwell, the *Sinfonia Concertante* (1927), the biblical cantata *Belshazzar's Feast* (1931), the opera *Troilus and Cressida* (1954) and much incidental music for films.

97 I seriously advise all sensitive composers to die at the age of thirty-seven. I know I've gone through the first halcyon period, and am just about ripe for my critical damnation.
1939 Letter.

Wang Xizhe 1956–

Chinese dissident, released from prison in 1993 after 12 years for his role in the Democracy Wall Movement.

98 You may keep me under surveillance until the year 2000, but will you even be able to hold on to power until then?
1995 Quoted in the *Eastern Express,* 10 May.

Ward, Artemus *pseudonym of* Charles Farrar Browne 1834–67

US humorist. In 1857 he began to publish letters from 'Artemus Ward' in the Cleveland *Plain Dealer*. His backwoods humour was an immediate success, and Lincoln interrupted a Cabinet meeting to read from him. In 1866 he moved to England where he worked for *Punch* and became a popular lecturer.

99 Traters...are a unfortunate class of people. If they wasn't they wouldn't be traters. They conspire to bust up a country—they fail, and they're traters. They bust her, and they become statesmen and heroes.
1867 *Artemus Ward in London and Other Papers,* 'The Tower of London'.

1 Let us all be happy, and live within our means, even if we have to borrow the money to do it with.
1867 *Artemus Ward in London, and Other Papers,* 'Science and Natural History'.

2 I am happiest when I am idle.
I could live for months without performing any kind of labour, and at the expiration of that time I should feel fresh and vigorous enough to go right on in the same way for numerous more months.
1867 *Artemus Ward in London, and Other Papers,* 'Pyrotechny', 3.

3 Why care for grammar as long as we are good?
1867 *Artemus Ward in London, and Other Papers,* 'Pyrotechny', 5.

4 He [Brigham Young] is dreadfully married. He's the most married man I ever saw in my life.
1869 *Artemus Ward's Lecture,* 'Brigham Young's Palace'.

5 'Why is this thus? What is the reason of this thusness?'
1869 *Artemus Ward's Lecture,* 'Heber C. Kimball's Harem'.

Warhol, Andy 1928–87

US graphic artist, painter and film-maker. He was one of the most controversial figures in American Pop Art.

6 If you want to know all about Andy Warhol, just look at the surface of my paintings and films and me, there I am. There's nothing behind it!
1967 Quoted in Gretchen Berg 'Andy: My True Story', in the *LA Free Press,* 17 Mar.

7 In the future everybody will be world famous for fifteen minutes.
Quoted in Andy Warhol, Kasper König, Pontus Hultén and Olle Granath (eds) *Andy Warhol* (1968).

8 The Pop artists did images that anybody walking down Broadway could recognize in a split second—comics, picnic tables, men's trousers, celebrities, shower curtains, refrigerators, Coke bottles—all the great modern things that the Abstract Expressionists tried so hard not to notice at all.
Quoted in Andy Warhol and Pat Hackett *POPism: The Warhol '60s* (1980).

9 When you think about it, department stores are kind of like museums.
1985 *America.*

Warner, Marina Sarah 1946–

British writer and literary and social critic. Her works include *Alone of All Her Sex* (1976) and *From the Beast to the Blonde* (1994), and novels such as *Indigo* (1992). In 1994 she delivered the Reith Lectures, later published as *Managing Monsters* (1994).

10 Although Mary cannot be a model for the New Woman, a goddess is better than no goddess at all, for the sombre-suited masculine world of the Protestant religion is altogether too much like a gentlemen's club to which the ladies are only admitted on special days.
   1976 *Alone of All Her Sex: the Myth and Cult of the Virgin Mary*, epilogue.

Warner, Sir Pelham Plum 1873–1963

English cricketer, born in Trinidad. He played for Middlesex and captained England on tours of Australia and South Africa. He was secretary (1939–45) and president (1950) of the MCC and was knighted in 1937.

11 Cricket is the greatest game that the wit of man has yet devised.
   Quoted in Colin Jarman *The Guinness Dictionary of Sports Quotations* (1990).

Warren, Earl 1891–1974

US politician and judge. As chief justice of the US Supreme Court (1943–53) he was a liberalizing influence, ending segregation in schools and protecting accused persons from police abuses. He headed the Commission into the assassination of John F Kennedy (1963–4).

12 We conclude that in the field of public education the doctrine of 'separate but equal' has no place.
   1954 Ruling to declare segregated schools unconstitutional, 17 May.

13 The freedom to marry has long been recognized as one of the vital personal rights essential to the orderly pursuit of happiness by free men.
   1957 2 Jun. Unanimous ruling against a Virginian law forbidding intermarriage of blacks and whites.

14 I always turn to the sports section first. The sports page records people's accomplishments; the front page has nothing but man's failures.
   1968 In *Sports Illustrated*, 'Scorecard', 22 Jul.

Warren, Harry *pseudonym of* Salvatore Guaragno 1893–1981

US songwriter, born in Brooklyn. During the 1930s, he collaborated with Al Dubin on several Busby Berkeley movies. During the war years he worked with Mark Gordon for Fox and then also for MGM.

15 Walk two Oscars behind me.
   1975 Comment to Harold Arlen on winning a second Oscar for *On the Atchison, Topeka and the Santa Fe*. Quoted in Tony Thomas *Harry Warren*.

Warren, Robert Penn 1905–89

US writer, Professor of English at Louisiana, Minnesota and Yale. He established an international reputation with his novel *All the King's Men* (1943, filmed 1949), and wrote several other novels, short stories and volumes of poetry.

16 The poem…is a little myth of man's capacity of making life meaningful. And in the end, the poem is not a thing we see—it is, rather, a light by which we may see—and what we see is life.
   1958 In the *Saturday Review*, 22 Mar.

17 The urge to write poetry is like having an itch. When the itch becomes annoying enough, you scratch it.
   1969 In the *New York Times*, 16 Dec.

18 How do poems grow? They grow out of your life.
   1985 In the *New York Times*, 12 May.

19 What is a poem but a hazardous attempt at self-understanding? It is the deepest part of autobiography.
   1985 In the *New York Times*, 12 May.

20 I don't expect you'll hear me writing any poems to the greater glory of Ronald and Nancy Reagan.
   1986 On being appointed the first US Poet Laureate. In the *Washington Post*, 27 Feb.

21 He woke me from the torpor of the accustomed.
   On familiar scenes more fully realized through Walker Evans's realistic photographs. Quoted in Belinda Rathbone *Walker Evans* (1995).

Washington, Booker Taliaferro 1856–1915

African-American educationalist, born a slave in Virginia. He became principal of the Tuskegee Institute in Alabama in 1881 and was a moderate in the negro movement. His autobiography, *Up from Slavery*, was published in 1901.

22 No race can prosper until it learns that there is as much dignity in tilling a field as in writing a poem. It is at the bottom of life we must begin, and not at the top.
   1895 'The Atlanta Exposition Address', in *Up from Slavery* (1901), ch.14.

23 In all things that are purely social we can be as separate as the fingers, yet one as the hand in all things essential to mutual progress.
   1895 'The Atlanta Exposition Address', in *Up from Slavery* (1901), ch.14.

Washington, George 1732–99

American soldier and statesman, first President. As commander of American forces in the War of Independence he displayed great powers of leadership, suffering defeats at Brandywine and Germantown, but holding his army together through the winter of 1777–8 at Valley Forge. After the alliance with France (1778), he forced the surrender of Cornwallis (1781) then retired to Mount Vernon, and sought strong constitutional government. In 1787 he presided over the Constitutional Convention and became President, eventually joining the Federalist Party, and retired in 1797.

24 Father, I cannot tell a lie. I did it with my little hatchet.
   In childhood, on admitting to vandalizing a cherry tree, attributed by Mason Locke Weems (Parson Weems) in his *Life and Memorable Actions of George Washington* (5th edn, c.1810). Weems claimed to have heard the tale from an elderly lady, a distant relation of Washington's, 20 years earlier.

25 When we assumed the soldier, we did not lay aside the citizen.
   1775 Address to the New York legislature, 26 Jun.

26 I can answer for but three things: a firm belief in the justice of our cause, close attention in the prosecution of it, and the strictest integrity.
   1775 On being elected Commander of the Unionist Army, 19 Jun.

27 The time is now near at hand which must probably determine whether Americans are to be freemen or slaves… The fate of unborn millions will now depend, under God, on the courage and conduct of this army. Our cruel and unrelenting enemy leaves us only the choice of brave resistance or abject submission. We have, therefore, to resolve to conquer or die.

1776 General orders, 2 Jul. Quoted in J C Fitzpatrick (ed) *Writings of George Washington* (1932), vol.5.

28 An old-fashioned Virginia fox hunt, gentlemen.
1777 Comment on the skirmish at Princeton, 3 Jan. Attributed.

29 The preservation of the sacred fire of liberty, and the destiny of the republican model of government, are justly considered as deeply, perhaps as finally staked, on the experiment entrusted to the hands of the American people.
1789 Inaugural address, 30 Apr.

30 To be prepared for war is one of the most effective means of preserving peace.
1790 First Annual Address, 8 Jan.

31 It is our true policy to steer clear of permanent alliance with any portion of the foreign world.
1796 Farewell address to the union, 17 Sep.

Washington Post
US newspaper.

32 The Closest of Strangers.
1994 Headline, 9 Jan, on the sharing of Nobel peace prize by South Africa's F W de Klerk and Nelson Mandela.

Washington Times
US newspaper.

33 Cool is Hot.
1988 Headline, 9 May, on Massachusetts Governor Michael Dukakis's low-key campaign for Democratic presidential nomination.

34 There's no crime like the present.
1995 In the week in which three persons jumped the White House fence, 25 May.

Waterhouse, Keith Spencer 1929–2009
English novelist, dramatist, humorist and journalist. His whimsical novel *Billy Liar* (1959) was adapted for the stage the next year and filmed in 1963, and he continued writing mordantly humorous novels, such as *Jubb* (1963) and *Office Life* (1978). Later works include *Unsweet Charity* (1992), a novel, and two volumes of autobiography, *City Lights* (1994) and *Streets Ahead* (1995).

35 Lying in bed, I abandoned the facts again and was back in Ambrosia.
1959 *Billy Liar*, opening sentence.

36 I cannot bring myself to vote for a woman who has been voice-trained to speak to me as though my dog has just died.
1978 On Margaret Thatcher, attributed.

37 The 50s face was angry, the 60s face was well-fed, the 70s face was foxy. Perhaps it was the right expression: there was a lot to be wary about.
1979 In the *Observer Magazine*, 30 Dec.

38 Why should it take three times longer to elect a Mayor for London as it does to set up an entire Scottish Parliament?
1999 In the *Observer*, 'They Said What...?', 24 Oct.

Waterman, Pete 1947–
English pop record producer, one of the founder members of Stock Aitken and Waterman (1984–93).

39 I wish there was a formula. I'd be billionaire instead of a millionaire.
2003 On making hit records. In *Varsity*, 28 Nov.

Watson, James D(ewey) 1928–
US biochemist who with Francis Crick helped to determine the structure of the nucleic acid known as DNA. Crick, Maurice Wilkins and Watson shared the 1962 Nobel prize in physiology or medicine. Watson wrote *The Double Helix* (1968), the story of the discovery of the structure of DNA.

40 We wish to suggest a structure for the salt of deoxyribose nucleic acid (DNA).
1953 First sentence of the paper describing the structure of DNA, with Francis Crick. *Nature*, 25 Apr.

41 [Science] seldom proceeds in the straightforward logical manner imagined by outsiders. Instead, its steps forward...are often very human events in which personalities and cultural traditions play major roles.
1968 *The Double Helix*.

Watson, Thomas John 1874–1956
US businessman and computing pioneer, president of IBM.

42 I think there is a world market for about five computers.
1943 Quoted in Christopher Cerf and Victor Navasky *The Experts Speak* (1984).

Watson, Thomas John, Jr 1914–93
US businessman, president (1952–61), chairman (1961–71) and chairman of the executive board (1972–9) at IBM. He also served as Ambassador to the USSR (1979–81).

43 Solve it quickly, solve it right or wrong.
1977 His advice on dealing with problems. In *Fortune*.

Watson, William c.1559–1603
English Catholic conspirator and secular priest.

44 Fiat justitia et ruant coeli.
Let justice be done, though the heavens may fall.
1602 *A Decacordon of Ten Quodlibeticall Questions Concerning Religion and State*. This was an influential reworking of Ferdinand I's motto.
▶ See Ferdinand I 332:73.

Watt, James 1736–1819
Scottish inventor and mechanical engineer, best remembered for his refinements to the steam engine.

45 That vessel in which the powers of steam are to be employed to work the engine, which is called the Cylinder in common fire engines, and which I call the Steam Vessel, must, during the whole time the engine is at work, be kept as hot as the steam that enters it; first, by enclosing it in a case of wood, or any other materials that transmit heat slowly; secondly, by surrounding it with steam or other heated bodies; and thirdly, by suffering neither water nor any other substance colder than steam to enter and touch it during that time.
1769 Specification of patent, 5 Jan, for a new method of lessening the consumption of steam and fuel in fire engines.

Watts, Isaac 1674–1748
English independent preacher and hymn writer.

46 When I survey the wondrous cross
On which the prince of glory died,
My richest gain I count but loss,
And pour contempt on all my pride.

1707 *Hymns and Spiritual Songs*, 'Crucifixion to the World, by the Cross of Christ'.

47 Jesus shall reign where'er the sun
Does his successive journeys run;
His kingdom stretch from shore to shore,
Till moons shall wax and wane no more.
1719 *The Psalms of David Imitated*, Psalm 72.

48 Our God, our help in ages past
Our hope for years to come,
Our shelter from the stormy blast
And our eternal home.
1719 *The Psalms of David Imitated*, Psalm 90 (in 1738 John Wesley substituted 'O God' for 'Our God').

Waugh, Auberon Alexander 1939–2001

English writer and editor, the eldest son of Evelyn Waugh. He was a journalist and novelist, and the editor of the *Literary Review*.

49 I will endeavour to put the word sex in capital letters on the cover of every issue of the *Literary Review* under my editorship, regardless of its actual contents... My purpose is simply to embolden booksellers.
1986 In the *Daily Telegraph*, 9 May.

50 It was inevitable that as soon as we had enjoyed a few days of reasonable summer weather, the country would suffer an acute water shortage. It can rain for 100 days, but if the sun shines on the 101st there will be hosepipe restrictions on the 102nd.
1997 *Way of the World: The Forgotten Years: 1995–6*.

51 Those who argue that the free supply of heroin to elderly addicts in Denmark would help to cut the crime rate—nine out of 10 burglaries are thought to be drug-related—ignore an important question. How many Copenhagen burglaries are committed by the elderly?
1997 *Way of the World: The Forgotten Years: 1995–6*.

Waugh, Evelyn Arthur St John 1903–66

English novelist. He enjoyed great success with his first novel, *Decline and Fall* (1928), the first of a series of barbed satirical novels which included *Vile Bodies* (1930) and *Scoop* (1938). Preoccupied with the decline of English civilization, his works include *Brideshead Revisited* (1945) and the *Sword of Honour* trilogy (1952–61). A supreme stylist, and considered one of the great comic novelists, he also wrote travel books and biographies.

52 I expect you'll be becoming a schoolmaster, sir. That's what most of the gentlemen does, sir, that gets sent down for indecent behaviour.
1928 *Decline and Fall*, Prelude.

53 'We class schools, you see, into four grades: Leading School, First-rate School, Good School, and School. Frankly,' said Mr Levy, 'School is pretty bad.'
1928 *Decline and Fall*, pt.1, ch.1.

54 That's the public-school system all over. They may kick you out but they never let you down.
1928 *Decline and Fall*, pt.1, ch.3.

55 You can't get into the soup in Ireland, do what you like.
1928 *Decline and Fall*, pt.1, ch.3.

56 Meanwhile, you will write an essay on 'self-indulgence'. There will be a prize of half a crown for the longest essay, irrespective of any possible merit.
1928 *Decline and Fall*, pt.1, ch.5.

57 For generations the British bourgeoisie have spoken of themselves as gentlemen, and by that they have meant, among other things, a self-respecting scorn of irregular perquisites. It is the quality that distinguishes the gentleman from both the artist and the aristocrat.
1928 *Decline and Fall*, pt.1, ch.6.

58 There aren't many left like him nowadays, what with education and whisky the price it is.
1928 *Decline and Fall*, pt.1, ch.7.

59 'I often think,' he continued, 'that we can trace almost all the disasters of English history to the influence of Wales!'
1928 *Decline and Fall*, pt.1, ch.8.

60 I have noticed again and again since I have been in the Church that lay interest in ecclesiastical matters is often a prelude to insanity.
1928 *Decline and Fall*, pt.1, ch.8.

61 I have often observed in women of her type a tendency to regard all athletics as inferior forms of fox-hunting.
1928 *Decline and Fall*, pt.1, ch.10.

62 I'm one of the blind alleys off the main road of procreation.
1928 *Decline and Fall*, pt.1, ch.12.

63 I haven't been to sleep for over a year. That's why I go to bed early. One needs more rest if one doesn't sleep.
1928 *Decline and Fall*, pt.2, ch.3.

64 There is a species of person called a 'Modern Churchman' who draws the full salary of a beneficed clergyman and need not commit himself to any religious belief.
1928 *Decline and Fall*, pt.2, ch.4.

65 Instead of this absurd division into sexes, they ought to class people as static and dynamic.
1928 *Decline and Fall*, pt.2, ch.7.

66 I came to the conclusion many years ago that almost all crime is due to the repressed desire for aesthetic expression.
1928 *Decline and Fall*, pt.3, ch.1.

67 Anyone who has been to an English public school will always feel comparatively at home in prison. It is the people brought up in the gay intimacy of the slums, Paul learned, who find prison so soul-destroying.
1928 *Decline and Fall*, pt.3, ch.4.

68 Creative Endeavour lost her wings, Mrs Ape.
1930 *Vile Bodies*, ch.1.

69 Particularly against books the Home Secretary is. If we can't stamp out literature in the country, we can at least stop it being brought in from outside.
1930 *Vile Bodies*, ch.2.

70 When the war broke out she took down the signed photograph of the Kaiser and, with some solemnity, hung it in the men-servants' lavatory; it was her one combative action.
1930 *Vile Bodies*, ch.3.

71 All this fuss about sleeping together. For physical pleasure I'd sooner go to my dentist any day.
1930 *Vile Bodies*, ch.6.

72 'The Beast stands for strong mutually antagonistic governments everywhere,' he said. 'Self-sufficiency at home, self-assertion abroad.'
1938 *Scoop*, bk.1, ch.1.

73 Mr Salter's side of the conversation was limited to expressions of assent. When Lord Copper was right, he

said, 'Definitely, Lord Copper'; when he was wrong, 'Up to a point.'
1938 *Scoop*, bk.1, ch.1.

74 'He's supposed to have a particularly high-class style: "Feather footed through the plashy fen passes the questing vole"…would that be it?' 'Yes,' said the Managing Editor. 'That must be good style.'
1938 *Scoop*, bk.1, ch.1.

75 News is what a chap who doesn't care much about anything wants to read. And it's only news until he's read it. After that it's dead.
1938 *Scoop*, bk.1, ch.5.

76 'I will not stand for being called a woman in my own house,' she said.
1938 *Scoop*, bk.2, ch.1.

77 Other nations use 'force'; we Britons alone use 'might'.
1938 *Scoop*, bk.2, ch.5.

78 Lady Peabury was in the morning room reading a novel; early training gave a guilty spice to this recreation, for she had been brought up to believe that to read a novel before luncheon was one of the gravest sins it was possible for a gentlewoman to commit.
1939 'An Englishman's Home'.

79 Like German opera, too long and too loud.
1941 Of warfare. Attributed.

80 I do not think I shall ever forget the sight of Etna at sunset… Nothing I have ever seen in Art or Nature was quite so revolting.
1946 *Labels*.

81 The historic destiny of the Irish is being fulfilled on the other side of the Atlantic, where they have settled in their millions, bringing with them all their ancient grudges and the melancholy of the bogs, but also their hard, ancient wisdom. They alone of the newcomers are never for a moment taken in by the multifarious frauds of modernity. They have been changed from peasants and soldiers into townsmen. They have learned some of the superficial habits of 'good citizenship', but at heart they remain the same adroit and joyless race that broke the hearts of all who ever tried to help them.
1947 'The American Epoch in the Catholic Church'.

82 You never find an Englishman among the underdogs—except in England, of course.
1948 *The Loved One*, ch.1.

83 In the dying world I come from, quotation is a national vice. No one would think of making an after-dinner speech without the help of poetry. It used to be classics, now it's lyric verse.
1948 *The Loved One*, ch.9.

84 Words should be an intense pleasure, just as leather should be to a shoemaker.
1950 In the *New York Times*, 19 Nov.

85 Most writers in the course of their careers become thick-skinned and learn to accept vituperation, which in any other profession would be unimaginably offensive, as a healthy counterpoise to unintelligent praise.
1952 In the *New York Times Magazine*, 30 Nov.

86 He sat at the cocktail bar… It wore the air of a fashion magazine, once stiff and shiny, which too many people had handled.
1955 *Officers and Gentlemen*, bk.1, ch.8.

87 Enclosing every thin man, there's a fat man demanding elbow room.
1955 *Officers and Gentlemen*, interlude.
▶ See Connolly 243:13, Orwell 653:26.

88 He did not, even in his extremity, quite abandon his faith in the magic of official forms. In bumf lay salvation.
1955 *Officers and Gentlemen*, bk.2, ch.5.

89 We are all American at puberty; we die French.
1961 Diary note, 18 Jul.

90 Most of the world's troubles seem to come from people who are too busy. If only politicians and scientists were lazier, how much happier we should all be.
1962 *Seven Deadly Sins*.

91 Punctuality is the virtue of the bored.
1962 Diary note, 26 Mar.

92 Manners are especially the need of the plain. The pretty can get away with anything.
1962 In the *Observer*, 15 Apr.

93 One can write, think and pray exclusively of others; dreams are all egocentric.
1962 Diary entry, 5 Oct.

94 One forgets words as one forgets names. One's vocabulary needs constant fertilizing or it will die.
1962 Diary entry, 25 Dec.

95 All fictional characters are flat.
1963 'The Art of Fiction XXX: Evelyn Waugh', in *The Paris Review*, no.8, Summer/Fall.

96 No writer before the middle of the 19th century wrote about the working classes other than as grotesques or as pastoral decorations. Then when they were given the vote certain writers started to suck up to them.
1963 'The Art of Fiction XXX: Evelyn Waugh', in *The Paris Review*, no.8, Summer/Fall.

97 Only when one has lost all curiosity has one reached the age to write an autobiography.
1964 *A Little Learning*, opening words.

98 With a thorough knowledge of the Bible, Shakespeare and Wisden, you cannot go far wrong.
1964 *A Little Learning*.

99 Randolph Churchill went into hospital…to have a lung removed. It was announced that the trouble was not 'malignant'. Seeing Ed Stanley in White's, on my way to Rome, I remarked that it was a typical triumph of modern science to find the only part of Randolph that was not malignant and remove it.
1964 Diary note, Mar.

1 To watch him fumbling with our rich and delicate English language is like seeing a Sèvres vase in the hands of a chimpanzee.
Of Sir Stephen Spender. Quoted by Eric Pace in Spender's obituary in the *New York Times*, 18 Jul 1995.

Wavell, Archibald Percival, 1st Earl 1883–1950

British field-marshal. He held the Middle East Command from 1939 and was Viceroy of India 1943–7. His *Generals and Generalship* (1941) served as a combat handbook to his most formidable opponent, Erwin Rommel.

2 For sheer courage and endurance, physical and mental, the two men stand together as examples of what toughness the body will find, if the spirit within it is tough; and as very worthy representatives of our national capacity for individual enterprise, which it is hoped even the modern craze for regulating every detail of our lives will never stifle.
1948 Of F Spencer Chapman and T E Lawrence. Quoted in foreword to F Spencer Chapman *The Jungle is Neutral* (1950).

3 The story of Colonel Chapman's adventures is typical of the British way of war, and therefore begins with a complete lack of preparation.
1948 Quoted in foreword to F Spencer Chapman *The Jungle is Neutral* (1950).

Waxman, Howard
Editor of the *Ice Cream Reporter*.

4 The relation between the human tongue, the human psyche and butterfat is not very complex. The first two love the third.
1992 In *Newsweek*, 30 Nov.

Weatherill, (Bruce) Bernard Weatherill, Baron
1920–2007

English politician, chair of the Ways and Means Committee (1979–1983) and Speaker of the House of Commons (1987–1992). He oversaw with enthusiasm the televising of parliamentary proceedings.

5 Mine is one of the jobs that, if you want it, you will never get it—and if you're seen to want it you will certainly never get it.
1991 In *The House Magazine*, Jan.

Webb, (Martha) Beatrice née Potter 1858–1943
English social reformer, social historian, and economist. She wrote many studies with her husband, Sidney Webb.

6 His sensuality has all drifted into sexual vanity, delight for being the candle to the moths, with a dash of intellectual curiosity to give flavour to his tickled vanity… His incompleteness as a thinker, his shallow and vulgar view of many human relationships—the lack of a sterner kind of humour which would show him the dreariness of his farce and the total absence of proportion and inadequateness in some of his ideas—all these defects came largely from the flippant and worthless self-complacency brought about by the worship of rather second-rate women.
1897 Of George Bernard Shaw. Diary entry, 8 May.

7 All along the line, physically, mentally, morally, alcohol is a weakening and deadening force, and it is worth a great deal to save women and girls from its influence.
1917 *Health of Working Girls*, ch.10.

Webb, Phyllis 1927–
Canadian poet, university teacher and broadcaster. Her poetry includes *The Sea is Also a Garden* (1962), *Naked Poems* (1965) and *Wilson's Bowl* (1980); she has also published a collection of her essays.

8 Some people swim lakes, others climb flagpoles, some join monasteries, but we, my friends, who have considered suicide take our daily walk with death and are not lonely.
In the end it brings more honesty and care than all the democratic parliaments of tricks.
1956 *Even Your Right Eye*, 'To Friends Who Have Also Considered Suicide'.

Webb, Sidney James 1859–1947
English social reformer, historian and economist. A lawyer and Fabian, he wrote many powerful tracts and in 1892 married fellow socialist Beatrice Potter. They wrote a classic *History of Trade Unionism* (1894) and *English Local Government* (1906–29, 9 vols), and began the *New Statesman* (1913). He became President of the Board of Trade (1924), Dominions and Colonial Secretary (1929–30) and Colonial Secretary (1930–1).

9 No philosopher now looks for anything but the gradual evolution of the new order from the old… History shows us no example of the sudden substitutions of Utopian and revolutionary romance.
1889 *Fabian Essays*.

10 How anyone can fear that the British electorate, whatever mistakes it can make or may condone, can ever go too far or too fast is incomprehensible… The Labour Party, when in due course it comes to be entrusted with power, will naturally not want to do everything at once. Once we face the necessity of putting our principles into execution from one end of the kingdom to the other, the inevitability of gradualness cannot fail to be appreciated.
1923 Labour Party Conference, 26 Jun.

Weber, Max 1864–1920
German sociologist and economist.

11 In Baxter's view, the care of external goods should only lie on the shoulders of the 'saint like a light cloak, which can be thrown aside at any moment.' But fate decreed that the cloak should become an iron cage.
1904–5 *The Protestant Ethic and the Spirit of Capitalism* (translated by Talcott Parsons, 1930), ch.5. Richard Baxter (1615–91) was an eminent Puritan, chaplain of Cromwell's army.

12 The impulse to acquisition, pursuit of gain, of money, of the greatest possible amount of money, has in itself nothing to do with capitalism. This impulse exists among waiters, physicians, coachmen, artists, prostitutes, dishonest officials, soldiers, nobles, crusaders, gamblers, and beggars. One may say that it has been common to all sorts and conditions of men at all times and in all cultures of the earth, wherever the objective possibility of it is or has been given.
1904–5 *The Protestant Ethic and the Spirit of Capitalism* (translated by Talcott Parsons, 1930).

13 Capital accounting in its formally most rational shape…presupposes *the battle of man with man*.
1922 Collected in Guenther Roth and Claus Wittich (eds) *Economy and Society* (1978), ch.1.

14 However many people may complain about the 'red tape', it would be sheer illusion to think for a moment that continuous administrative work can be carried out in any field except by means of officials working in offices… The choice is only that between bureaucracy and dilettantism in the field of administration.
1922 Collected in Guenther Roth and Claus Wittich (eds) *Economy and Society* (1978), ch.3.

Webster, Daniel 1782–1852

US lawyer and statesman, one of the greatest of US orators. As Secretary of State (1840–3) he negotiated the Webster–Ashburton treaty with Great Britain. A supporter of free trade, nationality and established institutions, he was unwilling to break the Union to abolish slavery.

15 [Alexander Hamilton] smote the rock of the national resources, and abundant streams of revenue gushed forth. He touched the dead corpse of the public credit, and it sprang upon its feet.
1831 Speech, New York, 10

16 There is always room at the top.
On being advised against joining the overcrowded legal profession, attributed.

Webster, John c.1580–c.1625

English dramatist. He collaborated with Dekker, Drayton, Marston and others. He is best known for two great tragedies, *The White Devil* (1612) and *The Duchess of Malfi* (1623).

17 Fortune's a right whore:
If she give aught, she deals it in small parcels,
That she may take away all at one swoop.
1612 The White Devil, act 1, sc.1.

18 All the damnable degrees
Of drinking have you staggered through.
1612 The White Devil, act 1, sc.1.

19 Perfumes, the more they are chafed, the more they render
Their pleasing scents; and so affliction
Expresseth virtue fully.
1612 The White Devil, act 1, sc.1.

20 Oh, they are politic: they know our desire is increased by the difficulty of enjoying, whereas satiety is a blunt, weary, and drowsy passion.
1612 Of women. The White Devil, act 1, sc.1.

21 See, the curse of children!
In life they keep us frequently in tears,
And in the cold grave leave us in pale fears.
1612 The White Devil, act 1, sc.2.

22 'Tis just like a summer birdcage in a garden; the birds that are without despair to get in, and the birds that are within despair, and are in a consumption, for fear they shall never get out.
1612 The White Devil, act 1, sc.2.

23 Lust carries her sharp whip
At her own girdle.
1612 The White Devil, act 2, sc.1.

24 See, a good habit makes a child a man,
Whereas a bad one makes a man a beast.
1612 The White Devil, act 2, sc.1.

25 A mere tale of a tub, my words are idle.
1612 The White Devil, act 2, sc.1.

26 Only the deep sense of some deathless shame.
1612 The White Devil, act 2, sc.1.

27 Find me but guilty, sever head from body,
We'll part good friends.
1612 The White Devil, act 3, sc.2.

28 For your names
Of whores and murderers, they proceed from you,
As if a man should spit against the wind;
The filth returns in's face.
1612 The White Devil, act 3, sc.2.

29 Sum up my faults, I pray, and you shall find,
That beauty, and gay clothes, a merry heart,
And a good stomach to a feast, are all,
All the poor crimes that you can charge me with.
1612 The White Devil, act 3, sc.2.

30 VITTORIA: A rape! a rape!
MONTICELSO: How!
VITTORIA: Yes, you have ravished justice,
Forced her to do your pleasure.
1612 The White Devil, act 3, sc.2.

31 Woman to man
Is either a God or a wolfe.
1612 The White Devil, act 4, sc.2.

32 For your gifts,
I'll return them all; and I do wish
That I could make you full executor
To all my sins.
1612 The White Devil, act 4, sc.2.

33 He could not have invented his own ruin,
Had he despaired, with more propriety.
1612 The White Devil, act 5, sc.1.

34 They that sleep with dogs shall rise with fleas.
1612 The White Devil, act 5, sc.1.

35 O, the rare tricks of a Machiavellian!
He doth not come, like a gross plodding slave,
And buffet you to death; no, my quaint knave,
He tickles you to death, makes you die laughing.
1612 The White Devil, act 5, sc.3.

36 Call for the robin-red-breast and the wren,
Since o'er shady groves they hover,
And with leaves and flowers do cover
The friendless bodies of unburied men.
1612 The White Devil, act 5, sc.4.

37 I have heard grief named the eldest child of sin.
1612 The White Devil, act 5, sc.4.

38 Are you grown an atheist? Will you turn your body,
Which is the goodly palace of the soul,
To the soul's slaughter-house? Oh, the cursèd devil,
Which doth present us with all other sins
Thrice-candied o'er.
1612 The White Devil, act 5, sc.6.

39 Oh, yes, thy sins
Do run before thee to fetch fire from hell,
To light thee thither.
1612 The White Devil, act 5, sc.6.

40 I myself have heard a very good jest, and have scorned to seem to have so silly a wit as to understand it.
1623 The Duchess of Malfi, act 1, sc.1.

41 Then the law to him
Is like a foul black cobweb to a spider;
He makes it his dwelling, and a prison
To entangle those shall feed him.
1623 The Duchess of Malfi, act 1, sc.1.

42 DUCHESS: Diamonds are of most precious value
They say, that have passed through most jewellers' hands.
FERDINAND: Whores, by that rule, are precious.
1623 The Duchess of Malfi, act 1, sc.1.

43 Wisdom begins at the end.
　1623 *The Duchess of Malfi*, act 1, sc.1.

44 DUCHESS: What do you think of marriage?
　ANTONIO: I take't, as those that deny purgatory,
　It locally contains or heaven, or hell;
　There's no third place in't.
　1623 *The Duchess of Malfi*, act 1, sc.2.

45 Ambition, madam, is a great man's madness,
　That is not kept in chains, and close-pent rooms,
　But in fair lightsome lodgings, and is girt
　With the wild noise of prattling visitants,
　Which makes it lunatic beyond all cure.
　1623 *The Duchess of Malfi*, act 1, sc.1.

46 I have long served virtue,
　And never ta'en wages of her.
　1623 *The Duchess of Malfi*, act 1, sc.1.

47 The misery of us, that are born great,
　We are forced to woo because none dare woo us.
　1623 *The Duchess of Malfi*, act 1, sc.1.

48 I hope in time 'twill grow into a custom
　That noblemen shall have with cap and knee
　To purchase a night's lodging of their wives.
　1623 *The Duchess of Malfi*, act 3, sc.2.

49 I would sooner swim to the Bermudas on
　Two politicians' rotten bladders, tied
　Together with an intelligencer's heartstring,
　Than depend on so changeable a prince's favour.
　1623 *The Duchess of Malfi*, act 3, sc.2.

50 A politician is the devil's quilted anvil,
　He fashions all sins on him, and the blows
　Are never heard.
　1623 *The Duchess of Malfi*, act 3, sc.2.

51 Love mixed with fear is sweetness.
　1623 *The Duchess of Malfi*, act 3, sc.2.

52 That curious engine, your white hand.
　1623 *The Duchess of Malfi*, act 3, sc.2.

53 Why should only I…
　Be cased up, like a holy relic? I have youth
　And a little beauty.
　1623 *The Duchess of Malfi*, act 3, sc.2.

54 You have shook hands with Reputation
　And made him invisible.
　1623 *The Duchess of Malfi*, act 3, sc.2.

55 Her melancholy seems to be fortified
　With a strange disdain.
　1623 *The Duchess of Malfi*, act 4, sc.1.

56 Other sins only speak; murder shrieks out.
　1623 *The Duchess of Malfi*, act 4, sc.2.

57 What's this flesh? A little crudded milk, fantastical puff-paste.
　1623 *The Duchess of Malfi*, act 4, sc.2. crudded = curdled.

58 What would it pleasure me, to have my throat cut
　With diamonds? Or to be smothered
　With cassia? Or to be shot to death, with pearls?
　1623 *The Duchess of Malfi*, act 4, sc.2.

59 O, that it were possible,
　We might but hold some two days' conference
　With the dead!
　1623 *The Duchess of Malfi*, act 4, sc.2.

60 I am Duchess of Malfi still.
　1623 *The Duchess of Malfi*, act 4, sc.2.

61 I know death hath ten thousand several doors
　For men to take their exits.
　1623 *The Duchess of Malfi*, act 4, sc.2.

62 FERDINAND: Cover her face; mine eyes dazzle: she died young.
　BOSOLA: I think not so; her infelicity
　Seemed to have years too many.
　1623 *The Duchess of Malfi*, act 4, sc.2.

63 Physicians are like kings,—they brook no contradiction.
　1623 *The Duchess of Malfi*, act 5, sc.2.

64 We are merely the stars' tennis-balls, struck and bandied
　Which way please them.
　1623 *The Duchess of Malfi*, act 5, sc.4.

Webster, Margaret 1905–72
US actress and director.

65 You must not wear your heart on your sleeve for daws to pick at.
　c.1940 To Tennessee Williams on the out-of-town closing of his first professionally produced play *Battle of Angels*. Recalled by Williams in the *New York Times*, 17 Mar 1957.
　▶ See Shakespeare 788:82.

Wei Jingsheng 1950–
Chinese dissident, considered one of the fathers of the Chinese dissident movement, released in 1993 after serving a 14-year jail sentence for his role in the Democracy Wall Movement. He was arrested again in April 1994 and was released in 1997.

66 No leader deserves the unconditional confidence of his people.
　1979 Part of a statement appearing on Democracy Wall under the pseudonym 'Voice of Today'. Quoted in Uli Franz *Deng Xiaoping* (1988).

Weighell, Sidney 1922–2002
British trade union leader. He was General Secretary of the National Union of Railwaymen (1975–83) and a member of the Trades Union General Council (1975–83). He joined the LNER in 1938 and became a full-time union official in 1954.

67 If you…believe in the philosophy of the pig trough—that those with the biggest snouts should get the largest share—I reject it.
　1978 Labour Party Conference, 10 Apr.

68 I don't see how we can talk with Mrs Thatcher… I will say to the lads, 'Come on, get your snouts in the trough.'
　1979 Speech, London, 10 Apr.

Weil, Simone 1909–43
French philosophical writer and mystic, who undertook manual labour to experience working-class life and served as a Republican in the Spanish Civil War (1936). A mystic Catholic who distrusted organized religion, she worked for the Free French in London, and starved herself to death in sympathy with the victims of war. Her works include *La Pesanteur et la Grâce* (*Gravity and Grace*, 1947) and *Attente de Dieu* (*Waiting for God*, 1950).

69 To us, men of the West, a very strange thing happened at the turn of the century; without noticing it, we lost science, or at least the thing that had been called by that name for the last four centuries. What we now have in place of it is something different, radically different, and we don't know what it is. Nobody knows what it is.

1941 *On Science, Necessity and the Love of God,* 'Classical Science and After' (translated by Richard Rees, 1968).

70 Science is voiceless; it is the scientists who talk.
1941 *On Science, Necessity and the Love of God* (translated by Richard Rees, 1968).

71 The future is made of the same stuff as the present.
1941 *On Science, Necessity, and the Love of God* (translated by Richard Rees, 1968).

72 *Tous les péchés sont des tentatives pour combler des vides.*
All sins are attempts to fill voids.
La Pesanteur et la Grâce (published 1947).

73 The beauty of the world is almost the only way by which we can allow God to penetrate us...the beauty of the world is the commonest, easiest and most natural way of approach.
Attente de Dieu (translated as *Waiting for God*, 1951).

74 Bourgeois society is infected by monomania: the monomania of accounting. For it, the only thing that has value is what can be counted in francs and centimes. It never hesitates to sacrifice human life to figures which look well on paper, such as national budgets or industrial balance sheets.
La condition ouvrière, 'La rationalisation' (published 1951).

75 One might lay down as a postulate: All conceptions of God which are incompatible with the movement of pure charity are false.
Letter to a Priest (translated by A F Wills, published 1954).

76 The word 'revolution' is a word for which you kill, for which you die, for which you send the labouring masses to their deaths; but which does not contain any content.
Oppression and Liberty (translated by A F Wills and J Petrie, published 1958).

Weinberger, Caspar Willard 1917–2006

American politician. A former lawyer, he was state finance director of California when Ronald Reagan was Governor (1968–9), served in the administrations of Presidents Nixon and Ford, then became Secretary of Defense under President Reagan (1981–87).

77 Wishful thinking is equally as effective for arms control as it is for birth control.
1986 In *USA Today,* 6 Oct.

Weizsäcker, Richard Freiherr, Baron von 1920–2015

German politician. A member of the conservative Christian Democratic Union, he served as CDU Deputy Chairman (1972–9) and Mayor of West Berlin (1981–4) until being elected President of the Federal Republic of Germany (1984, re-elected 1989). In 1990 he signed the treaty that reunited East and West Germany. He served as President of Germany from 1990 to 1994.

78 There were many ways of not burdening one's conscience, of shunning responsibility, looking away, keeping silent. When the unspeakable truth of the Holocaust became known at the end of the war, all too many of us claimed that they had not known anything about it, or even suspected anything... Whoever refuses to remember the inhumanity is prone to new risks of infection... Seeking to forget makes exile all the longer; the secret of redemption lies in remembrance.
1985 On the 40th anniversary of the end of World War II, in the *New York Times,* 12 May.

Weldon, Fay *originally* Franklin Birkinshaw 1931–

English writer, an advertising copywriter before turning to novels and screenplays. She is best known for her fiction, which deal with recurring themes, including the nature of women's sexuality and experience in a patriarchal world. Her works include *Female Friends* (1974), *The Life and Loves of a She-Devil* (1983), *The Cloning of Joanna May* (1989) and *The Bulgari Connection* (2001).

79 Go to work on an egg.
1957 Advertising slogan for the British Egg Marketing Board.

80 The Life and Loves of a She-Devil.
1983 Title of novel.

81 It will do us no harm to retool our imaginations. AIDS is a major revolution in how writers write... Our heroes and heroines will have to change. The only thing AIDS is good for is fiction. Writers will have to think differently.
1987 In *The Guardian,* 7 Mar.

82 Pride comes before a fall; a sense of sisterhood with sad experience.
1987 *The Heart of the Country,* 'Chomp, Chomp, Grittle-Grax, Gone!'

83 Christianity is really a man's religion: there's not much in it for women except docility, obedience, who-sweeps-the-room-as-for-thy-cause, downcast eyes and death in childbirth. For the men it's better: all power and money and fine robes, the burning of the heretics—fun, fun, fun!—and the Inquisition fulminating from the pulpit.
1987 *The Heart of the Country,* 'Love Your Enemy'.

84 To journey is better than to arrive—or so say those who have already arrived.
1987 *The Heart of the Country,* 'Doing It All Wrong'.

85 It's full time work being on social security. They really make you earn your living.
1987 *The Heart of the Country,* 'Driven Mad'.

86 Men are so romantic, don't you think? They look for a perfect partner when what they should be looking for is perfect love.
1987 In the *Sunday Times,* 6 Sep.

87 I didn't set out to be a feminist writer. I just look at the sheep out of the window and watch their behaviour.
1989 In the *Observer,* 30 Apr.

88 I think if you had ever written a book you were absolutely pleased with, you'd never write another. The same probably goes for having children.
1991 In *The Guardian,* 28 Nov.

89 Nature's only interest is in having you procreate, then it throws you away.
1992 In *The Guardian,* 15 Jan.

90 One sort of believes in recycling. But one believes in it as a kind of palliative to the gods.
2009 In *The Observer Magazine,* 30 Aug.

91 I am not cynical. I am just old. I know what is going to happen next.
2009 *Chalcot Crescent.*

Welland, Colin 1934–

British actor and writer. Best known for his screenplays for *Yanks* (1979, with Walter Bernstein) and *Chariots of Fire* (1981), for the second of which he won an Academy Award.

92 The British are coming.
1982 At the Academy Award ceremony in Los Angeles, 29 Mar.

Welles, (George) Orson 1915-85

US director and actor. He is best known for his radio production of H G Wells's *The War of the Worlds* (1938), and for the films *Citizen Kane* (1941), a masterpiece of cinema technique, and his adaptation of Booth Tarkington's *The Magnificent Ambersons* (1942).

93 In Italy for thirty years under the Borgias they had warfare, terror, murder, bloodshed—they produced Michelangelo, Leonardo da Vinci and the Renaissance. In Switzerland they had brotherly love, five hundred years of democracy and peace, and what did they produce? The cuckoo clock.
   1949 Harry Lime's speech to Holly Martins as he leaves the great wheel, *The Third Man*. This phrase was added to the script by Welles who played Harry Lime.

94 A film is never really good unless the camera is an eye in the head of a poet.
   1958 'Un ruban de rêves' in *L'Express*, 5 Jun. Reprinted in English in *International Film Annual*, no.2.

95 A typewriter needs only paper; a camera uses film, requires subsidiary equipment by the truckload and several hundreds of technicians. That is always the central fact about the filmmaker as opposed to any other artist: he can never afford his own tools.
   1958 Letter in the *New Statesman*.

96 I started at the top and worked down.
   Attributed.

97 Every actor in his heart believes everything bad that's printed about him.
   Attributed.

Wellington, Arthur Wellesley, 1st Duke of 1769-1852

British soldier and statesman. He was made a duke after his defeat of French forces in the Peninsular War, and took command of British forces again after Napoleon's escape from Elba in 1815. After victory at Waterloo, he went into politics, becoming Prime Minister in 1828. His dispatches and other papers were published in three series (1834-80).

98 As Lord Chesterfield said of the generals of his day, 'I only hope that when the enemy reads the list of their names, he trembles as I do'.
   1810 Letter, 29 Aug, during the Peninsular War. Collected in *Supplementary Despatches* (1860).

99 We have in the service the scum of the earth as common soldiers.
   1813 Comment 21 Jun, before the Battle of Vitoria. Quoted in Elizabeth Longford *Wellington: The Years of the Sword*, p.321.

1 Hard pounding this, gentlemen, let's see who will pound longest.
   1815 At the Battle of Waterloo, 18 Jun. Quoted in Sir Walter Scott *Paul's Letters* (1816), letter 8.

2 Up guards and at them!
   1815 Attributed shout at the Battle of Waterloo, 18 Jun.

3 It has been a damned serious business—Blucher and I have lost 30,000 men. It has been a damned nice thing—the nearest run thing you ever saw in your life... By God! I don't think it would have done if I had not been there!
   1815 Comment to Thomas Creevey at Brussels, 19 Jun, the day after the Battle of Waterloo. Quoted in Sir Thomas Creevey *The Creevey Papers* (edited by Sir H Maxwell, 1904), p.142.

4 Napoleon did not manoeuvre at all. He just moved forward in the old style, in columns, and was driven off in the old style.
   1815 Letter to Sir William Beresford, 2 Jul.

5 Next to a battle lost, the greatest misery is a battle gained.
   1815 Of the Battle of Waterloo. Comment to Lady Shelley, Jul. Quoted in Richard Edgecumbe (ed) *The Diary of Frances, Lady Shelley* (1912), vol.1, ch.9, p.102.

6 The history of a battle is not unlike the history of a ball. Some individuals may recollect all the little events of which the great result is the battle won or lost; but no individual can recollect the order in which, or the exact moment at which, they occurred, which makes all the difference.
   1815 Of the Battle of Waterloo. Letter, 8 Aug.

7 Beginning reform is beginning revolution.
   1830 Attributed remark, 7 Nov.

8 I used to say of him that his presence on the field made the difference of 40,000 men.
   1831 Of Napoleon. Comment, 2 Nov. Quoted in Philip Henry Stanhope *Notes of Conversations with the Duke of Wellington* (1888).

9 Our course in the House of Lords ought to be very firm and uncompromising but moderate...an example of what has since been called the politics of the extreme centre.
   1832 Conduct of Opposition speech, Dec.

10 There is no such thing as a little war for a great nation.
   1838 House of Lords, 16 Jan.

11 All the business of war, and indeed all the business of life, is to endeavour to find out what you don't know by what you do; that's what I call 'guessing what was at the other side of the hill'.
   Quoted in John Wilson Croker *The Croker Papers* (edited by Bernard Pool, 1885), vol.3, ch.28.

12 Don't quote Latin; say what you have to say, and then sit down.
   Advice to a new member of Parliament.

13 The Battle of Waterloo was won on the playing fields of Eton.
   Attributed, and probably apocryphal. Quoted in Count Charles de Montalembert *De l'Avenir politique de l'Angleterre* (1856), ch.10: 'C'est ici qu'a été gagné la bataille de Waterloo'.

14 There is no mistake; there has been no mistake, and there shall be no mistake.
   Quoted in William Fraser *Words on Wellington* (1889).

15 Publish and be damned.
   To the publisher of the *Memoirs* of the courtesan Hariette Wilson, attempting blackmail. Attributed.

16 If you believe that, you'll believe anything.
   Attributed.

Wells, H(erbert) G(eorge) 1866-1946

English writer and Fabian, best known for his scientific fantasies *The Time Machine* (1895) and *The War of the Worlds* (1898). He also wrote popular comic novels, notably *Kipps* (1905) and *The History of Mr Polly* (1910), and socio-political works on science and world peace (*The Outline of History*, 1920 and *The Work, Wealth and Happiness of Mankind*, 1931).

17 He was a practical electrician but fond of whisky, a heavy, red-haired brute with irregular teeth. He doubted

the existence of the Deity but accepted Carnot's cycle, and he had read Shakespeare and found him weak in chemistry.
1894 'The Lord of the Dynamos'.

18 Bah! the thing is not a nose at all, but a bit of primordial chaos clapped on to my face.
1895 *Select Conversations with an Uncle*, 'The Man with a Nose'.

19 Yet, across the gulf of space, minds that are to our minds as ours are to the beasts that perish, intellects vast and cool and unsympathetic, regarded this earth with envious eyes, and slowly and surely drew their plans against us.
1898 *The War of the Worlds*, bk.1, ch.1.

20 At times I suffer from the strangest sense of detachment from myself and the world about me; I seem to watch it all from the outside, from somewhere inconceivably remote, out of time, out of space, out of the stress and tragedy of it all.
1898 *The War of the Worlds*, bk.1, ch.7.

21 The Social Contract is nothing more or less than a vast conspiracy of human beings to lie to and humbug themselves and one another for the general Good. Lies are the mortar that bind the savage individual man into the social masonry.
1900 *Love and Mrs Lewisham*, ch.23.

22 Notice the smug suppressions of his face. In his mouth are Lies in the shape of false teeth.
1900 *Love and Mrs Lewisham*, ch.23.

23 In the country of the blind, the one-eyed man is king.
1904 'The Country of the Blind', collected in *The Country of the Blind and Other Stories* (1911).

24 Of course we can Learn even from Novels, Nace Novels that is, but it isn't the same thing as serious reading.
1905 *Kipps*, bk.2, ch.2.

25 He found that a fork in his inexperienced hand was an instrument of chase rather than capture.
1905 *Kipps*, bk.2, ch.7.

26 'I expect,' he said, 'I was thinking jest what a Rum Go everything is.'
1905 *Kipps*, bk.3, ch.3.

27 'You're a Christian?' 'Church of England,' said Mr Polly. 'Mm,' said the employer, a little checked. 'For good all round business work, I should have preferred a Baptist.'
1909 *The History of Mr Polly*, ch.3, pt.2.

28 Arson, after all, is an artificial crime... A large number of houses deserve to be burnt.
1909 *The History of Mr Polly*, ch.10, pt.1.

29 Once they heard someone call for 'Snooks'. 'I always thought that name was invented by novelists,' said Miss Winchelsea. 'Fancy! Snooks. I wonder which is Mr. Snooks?' Finally they picked out a stout and resolute little man in a large check suit. 'If he isn't Snooks, he ought to be,' said Miss Winchelsea.
1913 *Tales of Life and Adventure*, 'Miss Winchelsea's Heart'.

30 The War that will End War.
1914 Title of book.

31 Moral indignation is jealousy with a halo.
1914 *The Wife of Sir Isaac Harman*, ch.9.

32 The uglier a man's legs are, the better he plays golf. It's almost a law.
1915 *Bealby*.

33 He had the face of a saint, but he had rendered this generally acceptable by growing side-whiskers.
1915 'The Story of The Last Trump'.

34 Cynicism is humour in ill-health.
1915 'The Story of The Last Trump'.

35 Human history becomes more and more a race between education and catastrophe.
1920 *The Outline of History*, vol.2, ch.41.

36 Now it is on the whole more convenient to keep history and theology apart.
1922 *A Short History of the World*, ch.37.

37 I am reported to be 'pessimistic' about broadcasting... [The] truth is that I have anticipated its complete disappearance—confident that the unfortunate people, who must now subdue themselves to 'listening-in', will soon find a better pastime for their leisure.
1928 *The Way the World is Going*.

38 In England we have come to rely upon a comfortable time-lag of fifty years or a century intervening between the perception that something ought to be done and a serious attempt to do it.
1931 *The Work, Wealth and Happiness of Mankind*, ch.2.

39 The Shape of Things to Come.
1933 Title of book.

40 If his thinking has been sound, then this world is at the end of its tether. The end of everything we call life is close at hand and cannot be evaded.
1945 *Mind at the End of Its Tether*, ch.1.

Welsh, Irvine 1958–

Scottish writer. He scored a major critical success with his first novel, *Trainspotting* (1993, filmed 1995).

41 I grew up in what was not so much a family as a genetic disaster.
1995 *Marabou Stork Nightmares*, ch.2.

42 A symbol of all that's perfectly hideous about Scotland
1996 On the poet Hugh MacDiarmid. In *Scotland on Sunday*, 28 Jan.

43 There's fuck-all to say about my books other than what's written in them.
Quoted in Annalena McAfee *Lives and Works: Profiles of Leading Novelists, Poets and Playwrights* (2002).

44 Now, for the first time, he's seeing that there really is a way out of this, and it's all so simple. You don't have to run away. You just meet somebody special and step sideways into a parallel universe.
2012 *Skagboys*.

45 Without this kickstart to my day, I'd be lost. A day without a morning run is a day you fumble through, rather than one you attack.
2014 *The Sex Lives of Siamese Twins*.

Welty, Eudora 1909–2001

US novelist and short-story writer. She wrote five novels, set in her native Mississippi, and several collections of short stories, issued as *Collected Stories* (1981).

46 I have been told, both in approval and accusation, that I seem to love all my characters. What I do in writing of any character is to try to enter into the mind, heart and skin of a human being who is not myself. Whether this

happens to be a man or a woman, old or young, with skin black or white, the primary challenge lies in making the jump itself. It is the act of a writer's imagination that I set most high.
1981 *The Collected Stories of Eudora Welty*, preface.

47 It had been startling and disappointing to me to find out that story books had been written by *people*, that books were not natural wonders, coming up themselves like green grass.
1984 *One Writer's Beginnings*, I. 'Listening'.

48 The events in our lives happen in a sequence in time, but in their significance to ourselves they find their own order, a timetable not necessarily—perhaps not possibly—chronological… It is the continuous thread of revelation.
1984 *One Writer's Beginnings*, II. 'Learning to See'.

49 A sheltered life can be a daring life as well. For all serious daring starts from within.
1984 *One Writer's Beginnings*, III. 'Finding a Voice'.

Wenger, Arsène 1949–

French footballer and football manager. He has been manager of Arsenal since 1996.

50 A football team is like a beautiful woman. When you do not tell her so, she forgets she is beautiful.
2002 In *The Times*, 28 Dec.

51 When you're dealing with someone who only has a pair of underpants on, if you take his underpants off, he has nothing left—he's naked. You're better off trying to find him a pair of trousers to complement him rather than change him.
2007 Explaining his methods.

Wentworth, Peter 1530–96

English parliamentarian. He was a prominent Puritan in the reign of Elizabeth I, to whom he presented challenges on the issues of religion and royal succession. He supported the liberties of parliament against encroachments by Elizabeth I. His speech to Parliament in 1576 was examined by the Star Chamber and he was sent to the Tower of London for it. He was imprisoned twice more, and it is thought he never regained his freedom the second time.

52 In this House, which is termed a place of free speech, there is nothing so necessary for the preservation of the Prince and State as free speech; and without it, it is a scorn and a mockery to call it a Parliament House, for in truth it is none but a very school of flattery and dissimulation, and so fit a place to serve the devil and his angels in, and not to glorify God and benefit the Commonwealth.
1576 House of Commons, 8 Feb.

Wentworth, William Charles 1790–1872

Statesman and explorer, born aboard a convict ship on which his mother was being transported for theft. One of the first to explore successfully beyond the Blue Mountains, he established the first Australian newspaper and was one of the founders of Sydney University. His *Australasia* (1823) was the first book of verse by a native-born Australian.

53 Illustrious Cook, Columbus of our shore,
To whom was left this unknown world t'explore,
Its untraced bounds on faithful chart to mark,
And leave a light where all before was dark.
1823 *Australasia*.

Werefkin, Marianne 1860–1938

Russian-born painter who emigrated to Germany just before 1900. She was a founding member of the Blaue Reiter group in Munich.

54 Art is not made only one way, art is a point of view… Rembrandt in our days would be Rembrandt again, because the work of the master is his self. But in order to be Rembrandt in our days he would have used new ways that would give a new culture.
1902 *Lettres à un Inconnu* (1901–05). Translated by Mara R Witzling (ed) in *Voicing Our Visions: Writings by Women Artists* (1992).

55 There is no history of art—there is the history of artists.
1905 *Lettres à un Inconnu* (1901–05). Translated by Mara R Witzling (ed) in *Voicing Our Visions: Writings by Women Artists* (1992).

Wesker, Sir Arnold 1932–

English playwright.

56 And then I saw the menu… It said 'Chips with everything'. Chips with every damn thing. You breed babies and you eat chips with everything.
1962 *Chips with Everything* act 1, sc.2

Wesley, Charles 1707–88

English Methodist hymn writer and preacher, brother of John Wesley.

57 Long my imprisoned spirit lay
Fast bound in sin and nature's night;
Thine eye diffused a quickening ray—
I woke, the dungeon flamed with light,
My chains fell off, my heart was free,
I rose, went forth, and followed thee.
1738 Hymn. 'And Can it Be'.

58 Hark! how all the welkin rings,
Glory to the King of kings.
Peace on earth and mercy mild,
God and sinners reconciled.
1739 'Hymn for Christmas'. In *Hymns and Sacred Poems*. The first two lines were changed to 'Hark! the herald-angels sing/Glory to the new born king' in Whitfield's *Hymns for Social Worship* (1753).

59 Jesu, lover of my soul,
Let me to thy bosom fly,
While the nearer waters roll,
While the tempest still is high;
Hide me, O my Saviour, hide,
Till the storm of life is past;
Safe into the haven guide,
O receive my soul at last.
1740 'In Temptation', collected in *Hymns and Sacred Poems*.

60 Gentle Jesus, meek and mild,
Look upon a little child;
Pity my simplicity,
Suffer me to come to thee.
1742 'Gentle Jesus', collected in *Hymns and Sacred Poems*.

61 Rejoice, the Lord is King!
Your Lord and King adore;

Mortals, give thanks and sing,
And triumph evermore:
Lift up your heart, lift up your voice;
Rejoice, again, I say rejoice.
1746 'Rejoice, the Lord is King'. In *Hymns for our Lord's Resurrection*.

62 Love divine, all loves excelling,
Joy of heav'n, to earth come down,
Fix in us thy humble dwelling,
All thy faithful mercies crown.
Jesu, thou art all compassion,
Pure unbounded love thou art;
Visit us with thy salvation,
Enter every trembling heart.
1747 'Love Divine', collected in *Hymns for those that seek…Redemption*.

63 Forth in thy name, O Lord, I go,
My daily labour to pursue.
Thee, only thee, resolved to know,
In all I think or speak or do.
1749 'Forth in Thy Name', collected in *Hymns and Sacred Poems*.

64 Lo! He comes with clouds descending,
Once for favoured sinners slain;
Thousand thousand Saints attending
Swell the triumph of His train.
1758 'Lo! He Comes'. In *Hymns of Intercession for all Mankind*.

Wesley, John 1703–91

English evangelist, preacher and writer. Although he himself remained loyal to the Church of England, he is recognized as the principal founder of Methodism. He published his *Rules* for the Methodist Societies in 1743.

65 I felt my heart strangely warmed. I felt I did trust in Christ, Christ alone for salvation; and an assurance was given me that he had taken away *my* sins, even *mine*, and saved *me* from the law of sin and death.
1738 Journal entry, 24 May.

66 Thou hidden love of God, whose height,
Whose depth unfathomed no man knows,
I see from far thy beauteous light,
Only I sigh for thy repose.
1738 *A Collection of Psalms and Hymns*, 'Divine Love'.

67 I look upon all the world as my parish.
1739 Journal entry, 11 Jun.

68 Do all the good you can
By all the means you can
In all the ways you can
In all the places you can
To all the people you can
As long as ever you can.
1743 'Rules of Conduct'.

69 Lord, let me not live to be useless!
1763 Journal entry, 22 Dec.

70 Sure a more consummate coxcomb never saw the sun! How amazingly full of himself! Whatever he speaks, he pronounces as an oracle.
1770 Of Rousseau. Journal entry, 3 Feb.

71 I have none of the infirmities of old age, and have lost several I had in my youth. The grand cause is, the good pleasure of God, who does whatever pleases him. The chief means are: 1. My constantly rising at four, for about fifty years. 2. My generally preaching at five in the morning; one of the most healthy exercises in the world. 3. My never travelling less, by sea or land, than four thousand five hundred miles in a year.
1774 Journal entry, 28 Jun.

72 I spent two hours with that great man, Dr Johnson, who is sinking into the grave by a gentle decay.
1783 Journal entry, 18 Dec.

73 The best of all is, God is with us!
1791 Quoted in *John Wesley's Journal*, edited by Robert Backhouse (1993), p.256.

74 Beware you be not swallowed up in books! An ounce of love is worth a pound of knowledge.
Quoted in R Southey *Life of Wesley* (1820), ch.16.

West, Benjamin 1738–1820

US painter who spent most of his working life in England.

75 Always remember, sir, that light and shadow never stand still.
Advice to the young John Constable, attributed in C R Leslie *Memoirs of the Life of John Constable* (1845).

West, Kanye Omari 1977–

US rap artist noted for his eccentric public statements.

76 Aids is a man-made disease. It was placed in Africa just like crack was placed in the black community to break up the Black Panthers.
2005 During a Live 8 concert, Philadelphia.

77 George Bush doesn't care about black people.
2005 During Hurricane Katrina fundraiser on NBC, 2 Sep.

78 There's certain things that black people are the best at and certain things that white people are the best at. Whatever we as black people are the best at, I'ma go get that. Like, on Christmas I don't want any food that tastes white. And when I go to purchase a house, I don't want my credit to look black.
2007 In *Spin*, Dec.

79 I am the number one human being in music. That means any person that's living or breathing is number two.
2007 On *The Wendy Williams Show*.

80 I'm doing pretty good as far as geniuses go… I'm like a machine. I'm a robot. You cannot offend a robot… I'm going down as a legend, whether or not you like me or not. I am the new Jim Morrison. I am the new Kurt Cobain… The Bible had twenty, thirty, forty, fifty characters in it. You don't think that I would be one of the characters of today's modern Bible?
2008 Radio interview.

81 My greatest pain in life is that I will never be able to see myself perform live.
2009 *VH1 Storytellers*.

82 I'm like a tree. I feed the branches of the people.
2010 In *The Daily Mirror*.

83 And the thing is, for me to say I wasn't a genius, I would just be lying to you and to myself.
2013 On *Jimmy Kimmel Live*, 9 Oct.

West, Mae 1893–1980

US vaudeville and film actress born in Brooklyn, New York. She wrote many of the plays she starred in, including *Sex* (1929) and

Diamond Lil (1928) later filmed as *She Done Him Wrong* (1933). Other films included *I'm No Angel* (1933) and *My Little Chickadee* (1940).

84 'Goodness what beautiful diamonds!'
'Goodness had nothing to do with it.'
1932 *Night After Night* (screenplay by Vincent Lawrence).

85 Why don't you come up sometime, see me?
1933 As Lou in *She Done Him Wrong*. The line is popularly rendered 'Come up and see me sometime.'

86 When I'm good I'm very very good, but when I'm bad I'm better.
1933 *I'm No Angel*.

87 Beulah, peel me a grape.
1933 *I'm No Angel*.

88 A man has one hundred dollars and you leave him with two dollars, that's subtraction.
1940 Line spoken in *My Little Chickadee*.

89 Lieutenant, is that your sword, or are you just glad to see me?
1944 Ad-libbed when her stage lover in *Catherine Was Great* became entangled with his sword scabbard as he attempted to embrace her. Attributed.

90 Catherine had three hundred lovers. I did the best I could do in a couple of hours.
1944 Curtain speech at the end of her play *Catherine Was Great*. Attributed.

91 I've been in Who's Who and I know what's what, but it's the first time I ever made the dictionary.
Reputedly said on learning that a life jacket was to be named after her.

92 It isn't what I do, but how I do it.
It isn't what I say, but how I say it—
And how I look when I do and say it.
Attributed.

West, Nathanael *pseudonym of* Nathan Wallenstein Weinstein 1903–40

US novelist, who lived for two years in Paris. After he wrote his most famous novel *Miss Lonelyhearts*, he spent his last five years writing scripts for a Hollywood film studio, which provided the material for a final masterpiece, *The Day of the Locust* (1939, filmed 1975).

93 Prayers for the condemned man will be offered on an adding machine. Numbers constitute the only universal language.
1933 *Miss Lonelyhearts*.

West, Dame Rebecca *formerly* Cecily Isabel Fairfield 1892–1983

Anglo-Irish novelist, journalist, biographer and critic. She trained for the stage but her involvement with the suffragettes led her into journalism, and her studies arising out of the Nuremberg war trials include *The Meaning of Treason* (1947) and *A Train of Powder* (1955). She bore a son to H G Wells during an affair which lasted 10 years.

94 Women know the damnation of charity because the habit of civilisation has always been to throw them cheap alms rather than give them good wages.
1912 'The Personal Service Association: Work for Idle Hands to Do', in *The Clarion*, 13 Dec.

95 Antifeminists, from Chesterton down to Dr Lionel Tayler, want women to specialise in virtue. While men are rolling round the world having murderous and otherwise sinful adventures of an enjoyable nature, in commerce, exploration or art, women are to stay at home earning the promotion of the human race to a better world.
1912 'The Personal Service Association: Work for Idle Hands to Do', in *The Clarion*, 13 Dec.

96 I saw in my own education some of the things which eat the power out of women.
1913 'Training in Truculence: The Working Women's College', in *The Clarion*, 14 Feb.

97 We have asked men for votes, they have given us advice. At present they are also giving us abuse.
1913 'The Sex War: Disjointed Thoughts on Men', in *The Clarion*, 18 Apr.

98 I have horrible nightmares of Sir Almwroth Wright's limp sentences wandering through the arid desert of his mind looking for dropped punctuation marks.
1913 'Lynch Law: The Tragedy of Ignorance', in *The Clarion*, 17 Oct. Almwroth Wright was one of the most vocal opponents of women's suffrage.

99 Who is there in that lot one would want as a father, except perhaps Mrs Thatcher? That choice would be irregular but safe.
1982 Of British Prime Ministers. *1900*, introduction.

1 There is, of course, no reason for the existence of the male sex except that one sometimes needs help with moving the piano.
Attributed.

Wharton, Edith Newbold *née* Jones 1861–1937

US novelist. She wrote more than 50 books in all, but is best known for her sophisticated novels of manners, which include *The House of Mirth* (1905) and *The Age of Innocence* (1920).

2 I despair of the Republic!… What a horror it is for a whole nation to be developing without a sense of beauty, and eating bananas for breakfast.
1904 On the US. Letter to Sara Norton, 19 Aug.

3 If I were shabby no one would have me: a woman is asked out as much for her clothes as for herself.
1905 *The House of Mirth*, bk.1, ch.1.

4 She was like a disembodied spirit who took up a great deal of room.
1905 *The House of Mirth*, bk.1, ch.2.

5 Of course, being fatally poor and dingy, it was wise of Gerty to have taken up philanthropy and symphony concerts.
1905 *The House of Mirth*, bk.1, ch.8.

6 Miss Farish, who was accustomed, in the way of happiness, to such scant light as shone through the cracks of other people's lives.
1905 *The House of Mirth*, bk.1, ch.14.

7 She keeps on being Queenly in her own room, with the door shut.
1905 *The House of Mirth*, bk.2, ch.1.

8 Paying for what she doesn't get rankles so dreadfully with Louisa; I can't make her see that it's one of the preliminary steps to getting what you haven't paid for.
1905 *The House of Mirth*, bk.2, ch.2.

9 Almost everyone in the neighbourhood had 'troubles', frankly localized and specified; but only the chosen had 'complications'. To have them was in itself a distinction,

though it was also, in most cases, a death warrant. People struggled on for years with 'troubles', but they almost always succumbed to 'complications'.
1911 *Ethan Frome*, ch.7.

10 Mrs Ballinger is one of the ladies who pursue Culture in bands, as though it were dangerous to meet it alone.
1916 *Xingu and Other Stories*, 'Xingu'.

11 An unalterable and unquestioned law of the musical world required that the German text of French operas sung by Swedish artists should be translated into Italian for the clearer understanding of English speaking audiences.
1920 *The Age of Innocence*, bk.1, ch.1.

12 What can you expect of a girl who was allowed to wear black satin at her coming-out ball?
1920 *The Age of Innocence*, bk.1, ch.5.

13 Blessed are the pure in heart for they have so much more to talk about.
1932 In *John O'London's Weekly*, 10 Apr.

14 There is no such thing as old age, there is only sorrow.
1934 *A Backward Glance*, 'A First Word'.

Whately, Richard 1787–1863
English scholar and prelate, Archbishop of Dublin (1831), writer of treatises on logic and rhetoric. A founder of the Broad Church party, he supported Catholic emancipation and rejected sectarianism, but his caustic wit and outspokenness made him unpopular.

15 Preach not because you have to say something, but because you have something to say.
1854 *Apophthegms*.

16 Happiness is no laughing matter.
1854 *Apophthegms*.

Whistler, James (Abbott) McNeill 1834–1903
US artist, who moved to Paris and later London, where he was controversially received. He is best known for his 'nocturnes', including *Old Battersea Bridge* (1872–5, Tate, London), and the portrait of his mother (*The Artist's Mother*, 1871–2, Louvre, Paris).

17 I am not arguing with you—I am telling you.
1890 *The Gentle Art of Making Enemies*.

18 A picture is finished when all trace of the means used to bring about the end has disappeared.
1890 *The Gentle Art of Making Enemies*.

19 A life passed among pictures makes not a painter—else the policeman in the National Gallery might assert himself.
1890 *The Gentle Art of Making Enemies*.

20 To say to the painter, that Nature is to be taken as she is, is to say to the player, that he may sit on the piano.
1890 *The Gentle Art of Making Enemies*.

21 The imitator is a poor kind of creature. If the man who paints only the tree, or a flower, or other surface he sees before him were an artist, the king of artists would be the photographer.
1890 *The Gentle Art of Making Enemies*.

22 Art should be independent of all clap-trap—should stand alone, and appeal to the artistic sense of eye or ear, without confounding this with emotions entirely foreign to it, as devotion, pity, love, patriotism and the like. All these have no kind of concern with it; and that is why I insist on calling my works 'arrangements' and 'harmonies'.
1890 *The Gentle Art of Making Enemies*.

23 Poor lawyers, like poor paintings, are dear at any price.
On the cost and quality of some of the lawyers he had hired. Quoted in Arthur Jerome Eddy *Recollections and Impressions of J.A.M. Whistler* (1903).

Whitbread, Samuel 1758–1815
English radical Whig politician, founder of the famous brewing firm. The intimate friend of Fox, under Pitt he was Leader of the Opposition, and in 1805 headed the attack on the treasurer of the navy, Viscount Melville.

24 The nation suspects that the regular ministerial majorities in Parliament are bought, and that the Crown has made a purchase of the House with the money of the people. Hence the ready, tame and servile compliance to every royal verdict issued by Lord North... It is almost universally believed that this debt has been contracted in corrupting the representatives of the people.
1777 House of Commons, 16 Apr.

25 In a political point of view, nothing can possibly afford greater stability to a popular Government than the education of the people.
1807 House of Commons, 19 Feb.

White, Andrew Dickson 1832–1918
US educationalist. President of Cornell University.

26 I will not permit thirty men to travel four hundred miles to agitate a bag of wind.
On refusing permission for a team from Cornell University to visit Michigan to play a game of American football. Quoted in D Wallechinsky *The People's Almanac* (1975).

White, Edmund 1940–
US writer. His sensitive assessments of gay life have appeared in novels including *A Boy's Own Story* (1982) and *The Beautiful Room Is Empty* (1988), as well as in his essays.

27 In fact, they are the classic scapegoats. Our old fears about our sissiness, still with us though masked by the new macho fascism, are now located, isolated, quarantined through our persecution of the transvestite.
1980 *States of Desire: Travels in Gay America*, ch.2.

28 Those who believe machismo reeks of violence alone choose to forget it once stood for honor as well.
1980 *States of Desire: Travels in Gay America*, ch.5.

29 The AIDS epidemic has rolled back a big rotting log and revealed all the squirming life underneath it, since it involves, all at once, the main themes of our existence: sex, death, power, money, love, hate, disease and panic. No American phenomenon has been so compelling since the Vietnam War.
1986 'Afterword—AIDS: An American Epidemic', added to later editions of *States of Desire: Travels in Gay America*.

30 Paris is a city where even the most outrageous story of incest and murder is greeted with a verbal shrug: 'Mais c'est normal!'
2001 In *The Flâneur*.

31 I'd rather come back with a few transcendent memories than an album of snapshots.
2012 *Jack Holmes and His Friend*.

White, E(lwyn) B(rooks) 1899–1985

US essayist, children's novelist, poet and parodist. He was closely associated with the rise and development of the *New Yorker* magazine.

32 MOTHER: It's broccoli, dear.
   CHILD: I say it's spinach, and I say the hell with it.
   1928 Cartoon caption, in the *New Yorker*, 8 Dec.

33 All poets who, when reading from their own works, experience a choked feeling, are major. For that matter, all poets who read from their own works are major, whether they choke or not.
   1939 *Quo Vadimus?*, 'How To Tell A Major Poet From A Minor Poet'.

34 It is easier for a man to be loyal to his club than to his planet; the by-laws are shorter, and he is personally acquainted with the other members.
   1942 *One Man's Meat*, 'One Man's Meat'.

35 The duty of a democracy is to know then what it knows now.
   1942 *One Man's Meat*, 'One Man's Meat'.

36 A poet's pleasure is to withhold a little of his meaning, to intensify by mystification. He unzips the veil from beauty, but does not remove it.
   1942 *One Man's Meat*, 'Poetry'.

37 Democracy is the recurrent suspicion that more than half the people are right more than half the time.
   1944 In the *New Yorker*, 3 Jul.

38 You can see in pantomime the puppets fumbling with their slips of paper...see them pick up their phone...see the noiseless, ceaseless capital of memoranda, in touch with Calcutta, in touch with Reykjavik, and always fooling with something.
   1949 On office windows at twilight. *Here Is New York*.

39 I'm less than two months old and I'm tired of living.
   1952 Wilbur the pig. *Charlotte's Web*, ch.3.

40 I can surely fool a man. People are not as smart as bugs.
   1952 Charlotte. *Charlotte's Web*, ch.10.

41 It was the best place to be, thought Wilbur, this warm delicious cellar, with the garrulous geese, the changing seasons, the heat of the sun, the passage of swallows, the nearness of rats, the sameness of sheep, the love of spiders, the smell of manure, and the glory of everything.
   1952 *Charlotte's Web*, ch.22.

42 It is not often that someone comes along who is a true friend and a good writer. Charlotte was both.
   1952 *Charlotte's Web*, ch.22.

43 The time not to become a father is eighteen years before a war.
   1954 *The Second Tree from the Corner*, 'The Second Tree from the Corner'.

44 Thurber did not write the way a surgeon operates, he wrote the way a child skips rope, the way a mouse waltzes.
   1961 In the *New Yorker*, 11 Nov. Tribute to James Thurber.

45 A man who publishes his letters becomes a nudist—nothing shields him from the world's gaze except his bare skin.
   1975 Letter to Corona Macheiner, 11 Jun.

46 She would write 8 or 10 words, then draw her gun and shoot them down.
   1979 On his wife and fellow editor Katharine S White. *Onward and Upward in the Garden*.

47 Commuter—one who spends his life
   In riding to and from his wife;
   A man who shaves and takes a train,
   And then rides back to shave again.
   1982 *Poems and Sketches*, 'The Commuter'.

White, George Malcolm 1920–2011

US architect, designer of the Capitol, Washington.

48 The fact that you don't buy a teenager new clothes doesn't mean he isn't going to grow.
   1987 On the need for a fourth Senate office building. In *Connoisseur*, Apr.

White, Patrick Victor Martindale 1912–90

Australian novelist, born in London, who went to Australia as an infant and settled there after World War II. He received the Nobel prize for literature in 1973, and numerous other awards, particularly for *Voss* (1957).

49 She would imprison the child in her house by the force of love.
   1955 *The Tree of Man*, ch.7.

50 So that in the end there were the trees. The boy walking through them with his head drooping as he increased in stature. Putting out shoots of green thought. So that, in the end, there was no end.
   1955 *The Tree of Man*, ch.26.

51 The mystery of life is not solved by success, which is an end in itself, but in failure, in perpetual struggle, in becoming.
   1957 *Voss*, ch.10.

52 Perhaps true knowledge only comes of death by torture in the country of the mind.
   1957 *Voss*, ch.16.

53 There is nothing like a rain of bombs to start one trying to assess one's own achievement.
   1958 Essay on his literary career, in *Australian Letters*, 'The Prodigal Son', vol.1, no.3, Apr.

54 In all directions stretched the Great Australian Emptiness, in which the mind is the least of possessions...and the march of material ugliness does not raise a quiver from the average nerves. It was the exaltation of the 'average' that made me panic most.
   1958 Essay on his literary career, in *Australian Letters*, 'The Prodigal Son', vol.1, no.3, Apr.

55 Above all I was determined to prove that the Australian novel is not necessarily the dreary, dun-coloured offspring of journalistic realism.
   1958 Essay on his literary career, in *Australian Letters*, 'The Prodigal Son', vol.1, no.3, Apr.

White, Theodore H(arold) 1915–86

US journalist and political commentator. His *The Making of the President, 1960* (1961), with its characteristic reportage style, won a Pulitzer Prize in 1962.

56 Chafing in action when his nature yearned to act, conscious of indignities real and imagined, Johnson went through three years of slow burn.
   Of Lyndon B Johnson as John F Kennedy's Vice President. Quoted in Arthur M Schlesinger, Jr *A Thousand Days* (1965).

57 The best time to listen to a politician is when he is on a street corner, in the rain, late at night, when he's exhausted. Then he doesn't lie.
  1969 In the *New York Times*, 5 Jan.

58 He was almost a force of nature, like a slumbering volcano, wreathed in clouds, occasionally emitting smoke which soothsayers attempted to interpret.
  1969 Of Nelson Rockefeller. *The Making of the President, 1968*.

59 The epitaph on the Kennedy administration became Camelot—a magic moment in American history, when gallant men danced with beautiful women, when great deeds were done, when artists, writers and poets met at the White House and the barbarians beyond the walls were held back.
  1978 *In Search of History*.

60 Eisenhower has...a magic in American politics that is peculiarly his: he makes people happy.
  Of Dwight D Eisenhower's appearances during Richard M Nixon's 1960 presidential campaign. Quoted in Michael R Beschloss *Eisenhower* (1990).

White, Thomas 1550–1624
English Puritan.

61 The cause of plagues is sin, if you look to it well; and the cause of sin are plays; therefore the cause of plagues are plays.
  Attributed.

Whitehead, Alfred North 1861–1947
English mathematician and philosopher. He taught at Imperial College London and later at Harvard University. With his former pupil Bertrand Russell he wrote *Principia Mathematica* (1910–13).

62 It is a safe rule to apply that, when a mathematical or philosophical author writes with a misty profundity, he is talking nonsense.
  1911 *Introduction to Mathematics*.

63 Knowledge does not keep any better than fish.
  1916 'The Aims of Education; a plea for reform', address as president of the Mathematical Association.

64 Familiar things happen, and mankind does not bother about them. It requires a very unusual mind to undertake the analysis of the obvious.
  1925 *Science and the Modern World*.

65 Religion is something which stands beyond, behind, and within the passing flux of immediate things; something which is real, and yet waiting to be realized; something which is a remote possibility, and yet the greatest of present facts; something that gives meaning to all that passes, and yet eludes apprehension; something whose possession is the final good, and yet is beyond all reach; something which is the ultimate ideal, and the hopeless quest.
  1925 *Science and the Modern World*.

66 The worship of God is not a rule of safety—it is an adventure of the spirit, a flight after the unattainable. The death of religion comes with the repression of the high hope of adventure.
  1925 *Science and the Modern World*.

67 Mathematics is thought moving in the sphere of complete abstraction from any particular instance of what it is talking about.
  1925 *Science And the Modern World*.

68 Religion is what a man does with his solitariness.
  1926 *Religion in the Making*.

69 The safest general characterization of the European philosophical tradition is that it consists of a series of footnotes to Plato.
  1929 *Process and Reality*, pt.2, ch.1, section 1.

70 The power of Christianity lies in its revelation in act, of that which Plato divined in theory.
  1938 *Adventures of Ideas*.

71 The essence of Christianity is the appeal to the life of Christ as a revelation of the nature of God and of his agency in the world. The record is fragmentary, inconsistent and uncertain... But there can be no doubt as to the elements in the record that have evoked the best in human nature. The Mother, the Child and the bare manger: the lowly man, homeless and self-forgetful, with his message of peace, love and sympathy: the suffering, the agony, the tender words as life ebbed, the final despair: and the whole with the authority of supreme victory.
  1938 *Adventures of Ideas*.

72 What is morality in any given time or place? It is what the majority then and there happen to like, and immorality is what they dislike.
  1941 Conversation, 30 Aug. Collected in *Dialogues* (1954).

Whitehead, Hal
Canadian marine biologist.

73 'Scientific whaling' is like the prostitution of the profession: using the name of science for a totally bogus purpose.
  2004 *New Scientist*, May.

Whitehorn, Katharine 1926–
English journalist.

74 Hats divide generally into three classes: offensive hats, defensive hats, and shrapnel.
  1963 *Shouts and Murmurs*.

Whitelaw, William Stephen Ian, 1st Viscount
1918–99

Scottish Conservative politician, Leader of the House of Commons (1970–2), Secretary of State for Northern Ireland (1972–3) and Employment (1973–4) and Home Secretary (1979–83). Loyal to Heath and then Thatcher, he led the House of Lords until 1988.

75 I do not intend to prejudge the past.
  1973 On arriving in Ulster for the first time as Secretary of State for Northern Ireland, 2 Dec.

76 He is going round the country stirring up apathy.
  1974 Of Harold Wilson during the general election campaign. Attributed.

77 A short, sharp shock.
  1979 At the Conservative Party Conference, 10 Oct, on the need for more effective treatment of young offenders.
  ▶ See Gilbert 369:64.

Whiteman, Paul 1891–1967
US bandleader. A pioneer of 'sweet style' jazz in the 1920s, he recruited such talents as trumpeter Bix Beiderbecke. He developed Gershwin's 'symphonic jazz' experiments, commissioning *Rhapsody in Blue* in 1924.

78 Jazz came to America three hundred years ago in chains.
   1926 *Jazz*.

Whiteread, Rachel 1963–
English sculptor. In 1993 she came to prominence when she made a cast of an entire disused house in East London. She won the 1993 Turner Prize.

79 When I visited concentration camps, I was more interested in how people responded to the camps than in the actual places. I watched kids picnicking on the ovens and other people stricken with grief.
   2001 From an interview on www.guggenheim.org, 18 Apr.

80 I don't want to make plop art—sculpture that just gets plopped down in places. I wouldn't want to litter every corner of the world with my sculpture.
   2005 Quoted in *The Guardian*, 16 Oct.

Whiting, George 1884–1943
US songwriter.

81 When You're All Dressed Up and Have No Place To Go.
   1912 Title of song (music by Newton Harding).

Whitlam, (Edward) Gough 1916–2014
Australian politician, leader of the Labor Party from 1967 and Prime Minister (1972–5). He resigned in 1978 to move into academia. His works include *The Italian Inspiration in English Literature* (1980).

82 The importance of an historical event lies not in what happened but in what later generations believe to have happened.
   1973 Speech at Ballarat, Victoria, 3 Dec.

83 I do not mind the Liberals, still less do I mind the Country party, calling me a bastard. In some circumstances, I am only doing my job if they do. But I hope that you will not publicly call me a bastard, as some bastards in the Caucus have.
   1974 Speech to the Australian Labor Party, 9 Jun.

84 We may say 'God Save the Queen', because nothing will save the Governor-General… Maintain your rage and your enthusiasm for the election now to be held and until polling day.
   1975 On the Governor-General Sir John Kerr's action in dissolving the Australian Parliament, 11 Nov. Whitlam lost the subsequent election.

Whitman, Christine Todd 1946–
US Republican politician, Governor of New Jersey (1994–2001) and Administrator of the Environmental Protection Agency (2001–3).

85 The states are the laboratories of democracy.
   1995 In the *New York Times*, 29 Jan.

86 When you're dealing with people who think that Sponge Bob Square Pants is more important than social security, you have a problem.
   2005 On *The Daily Show*, Jan.

87 Anyone who thinks that they are too small to make a difference has never tried to fall asleep with a mosquito in the room.
   Attributed.

Whitman, Walt(er) 1819–91
US poet. He was editor of the *Brooklyn Eagle* and worked as a nurse during the Civil War. His poetry reflected his mystical faith in democracy and was attacked for indecency because it addressed many taboo subjects. It is collected in *Leaves of Grass* (1855–92).

88 The Americans of all nations at any time upon the earth have probably the fullest poetical nature. The United States themselves are essentially the greatest poem.
   1855 *Leaves of Grass*, preface.

89 As soon as histories are properly told there is no more need of romances.
   1855 *Leaves of Grass*, preface.

90 I celebrate myself, and sing myself,
   And what I assume you shall assume,
   For every atom belonging to me as good belongs to you.
   1855 *Leaves of Grass*, 'Song of Myself', section 1.

91 All goes onward and outward, nothing collapses,
   And to die is different from what any one supposed, and luckier.
   1855 *Leaves of Grass*, 'Song of Myself', section 6.

92 I believe a leaf of grass is no less than the journey-work of the stars.
   1855 *Leaves of Grass*, 'Song of Myself', section 31.

93 I think I could turn, and live with animals, they are so placid and self-contain'd.
   1855 *Leaves of Grass*, 'Song of Myself', section 32.

94 I have said that the soul is not more than the body,
   And I have said that the body is not more than the soul,
   And nothing, not God, is greater to one than one's self is.
   1855 *Leaves of Grass*, 'Song of Myself', section 48.

95 Do I contradict myself?
   Very well then I contradict myself,
   (I am large, I contain multitudes.)
   1855 *Leaves of Grass*, 'Song of Myself', section 51.

96 I too am not a bit tamed, I too am untranslatable,
   I sound my barbaric yawp over the roofs of the world.
   1855 *Leaves of Grass*, 'Song of Myself', section 52.

97 How beggarly appear arguments before a defiant deed!
   1855 Leaves of Grass, 'Broad-Axe Song', later 'Song of the Broad-Axe' (from 1867).

98 If anything is sacred the human body is sacred.
   1855 *Leaves of Grass*, 'Children of Adam', 'I Sing the Body Electric', section 8.

99 I do not think seventy years is the time of a man or woman,
   Nor that seventy millions of years is the time of a man or woman,
   Nor that years will ever stop the existence of me, or any one else.
   1855 *Leaves of Grass*, 'Autumn Rivulets', 'Who Learns My Lesson Complete?'.

1 Henceforth I whimper no more, postpone no more, need nothing,
   Done with indoor complaints, libraries, querulous criticisms,
   Strong and content I travel the open road.
   1856 *Leaves of Grass*, 'Song of the Open Road', section 1.

2 What can ever be more stately and admirable to me than mast-hemm'd Manhattan?
   1856 *Leaves of Grass*, 'Crossing Brooklyn Ferry', section 8.

3   He or she is greatest who contributes the greatest
    original practical example.
    1856 *Leaves of Grass*, 'By Blue Ontario's Shores', section 13.

4   And I will show that nothing can happen more
    beautiful than death.
    1860 *Leaves of Grass*, 'Proto-Leaf', later renamed 'Starting From Paumanok' (from 1867).

5   I hear it was charged against me that I sought to destroy
    institutions,
    But really I am neither for nor against institutions.
    1860 *Leaves of Grass*, 'Calamus', 'I Hear It Was Charged Against Me'.

6   Camarado, this is no book,
    Who touches this touches a man.
    1860 *Leaves of Grass*, 'Songs of Parting', 'So Long!'

7   O Captain! my Captain! our fearful trip is done,
    The ship has weather'd every rack, the prize we sought
    is won,
    The port is near, the bells I hear, the people all exulting.
    1865 *Leaves of Grass*, 'Memories of President Lincoln', 'O Captain! My Captain!'

8   When lilacs last in the dooryard bloom'd,
    And the great star early droop'd in the western sky in the
    night,
    I mourn'd, and yet shall mourn with ever-returning
    spring.
    1865–66 *Leaves of Grass*, 'Memories of President Lincoln', 'When Lilacs Last in the Dooryard Bloom'd', section 1.

9   Come lovely and soothing death,
    Undulate round the world, serenely arriving, arriving,
    In the day, in the night, to all, to each,
    Sooner or later delicate death.
    1865–66 *Leaves of Grass*, 'Memories of President Lincoln', 'When Lilacs Last in the Dooryard Bloom'd', section 14.

10 The Past—the dark unfathom'd retrospect!
    The teeming gulf—the sleepers and the shadows!
    The past! the infinite greatness of the past!
    For what is the present after all but a growth out
    of the past?
    1871 *Passage to India*, opening verse.

11 Political democracy, as it exists and practically works in
    America, with all its threatening evils, supplies a
    training-school for making first-class men. It is life's
    gymnasium, not of good only, but of all.
    1871 *Democratic Vistas*.

12 In this broad earth of ours,
    Amid the measureless grossness and the slag,
    Enclosed and safe within its central heart,
    Nestles the seed perfection.
    1874 *Leaves of Grass*, 'Birds of Passage', 'Song of the Universal', section 1.

13 After you have exhausted what there is in business,
    politics, conviviality, love, and so on—and found that
    none of these finally satisfy, or permanently wear—what
    remains? Nature remains.
    1876–77 *Speciman Days*, 'New Themes Entered Upon'.

14 Youth, large, lusty, loving—youth full of grace, force,
    fascination,
    Do you know that Old Age may come after you with
    equal grace, force, fascination?
    1881 *Leaves of Grass*, 'Youth, Day, Old Age and Night', stanza 1.

15 Have you not learn'd great lessons from those who reject
    you,
    and brace themselves against you? or who treat you
    with
    contempt, or dispute the passage with you?
    1888 *Leaves of Grass*, 'Sands at Seventy', 'Stronger Lessons'.

16 No one will get at my verses who insists upon viewing
    them as a literary performance.
    1888 'A Backward Glance O'er Travel'd Roads'.

Whittier, John Greenleaf   1807–92

US poet and abolitionist. A Quaker, he devoted himself to the cause of emancipation. His ballads and sentimental poems, such as 'Barbara Freitchie', which was included in *In War Time* (1864), were extremely popular in their day. His best work is the nostalgic narrative poem, *Snow-Bound* (1866).

17 When the care-wearied man seeks his mother once
    more,
    And the worn matron smiles where the girl smiled
    before,
    What moistens the lip and what brightens the eye?
    What calls back the past, like the rich Pumpkin pie?
    1844 'The Pumpkin', stanza 3.

18 When faith is lost, when honor dies,
    The man is dead!
    1850 'Ichabod', stanza 8.

19 Beneath her torn hat glowed the wealth
    Of simple beauty and rustic health.
    1854 'Maud Muller', l.3–4.

20 For of all sad words of tongue or pen,
    The saddest are these: 'It might have been!'
    1854 'Maud Muller', l.105–6.

21 The age is dull and mean. Men creep,
    Not walk.
    1855 'Lines, Inscribed to Friends Under Arrest for Treason Against the Slave Power', stanza 1.

22 Up from the meadows rich with corn,
    Clear in the cool September morn.
    1863 'Barbara Frietchie', opening lines.

23 'Shoot, if you must this old grey head,
    But spare your country's flag,' she said.
    1863 'Barbara Frietchie', l.35–36.

24 Dear Lord and Father of mankind,
    Forgive our foolish ways!
    Re-clothe us in our rightful mind,
    In purer lives thy service find,
    In deeper reverence praise
    1872 'The Brewing of Soma'.

Whitton, Charlotte   1896–1975

Canadian politician, Mayor of Ottawa (1951–6, 1960–4), the first woman to serve as mayor of a Canadian city.

25 Whatever women do they must do twice as well as men
    to be thought half so good...luckily, it's not difficult.
    1963 In *Canada Month*, Jun.

Whymper, Edward   1840–1911

English wood-engraver and mountaineer. In 1860–9 he conquered several hitherto unscaled peaks of the Alps, including the Matterhorn. He later published several books based on his travels in the Alps and elsewhere.

26 Do nothing in haste, look well to each step, and from the
beginning think what may be the end.
1871 *Scrambles Amongst the Alps.*

Widdecombe, Anne 1947–

English Conservative politician and novelist.

27 He has something of the night in him.
1997 Of fellow Conservative Michael Howard. In the *Sunday Times*, (electronic edition) 11 May.

Wiener, Norbert 1894–1964

US academic, who studied mathematics with Bertrand Russell and taught at MIT. His work contributed to the development of the understanding of information systems. He coined the word *cybernetics* to describe the science of feedback control in systems.

28 The automatic machine, whatever we think of any feelings it may or may not have, is the precise economic equivalent of the slave.
1949 *The Human Use of Human Beings.*

29 The new industrial revolution is a two-edged sword. It may be used for the benefit of humanity, assuming that humanity survives long enough to reach a period in which such a benefit is possible. If, however, we proceed along the clear and obvious lines of our traditional behavior, and follow our traditional worship of progress and the fifth freedom—the freedom to exploit—it is practically certain that we shall have to face a decade or more of ruin and despair.
1949 *The Human Use of Human Beings.*

30 Scientific discovery consists in the interpretation for our own convenience of a system of existence which has been made with no eye to our convenience at all.
1949 *The Human Use of Human Beings.*

Wiesel, Elie 1928–

Romanian-born US writer and political activist. His writing reflects his early experiences as an inmate of Nazi concentration camps.

31 There are victories of the soul and spirit. Sometimes, even if you lose, you win.
Attributed in Diana Doroftei and Matthew Cross (eds.), *The Little Book of Romanian Wisdom* (2011).

Wiggins, Sir Bradley Marc 1980–

English cyclist. The first British winner of the Tour de France, in 2012 he also became the most decorated British Olympian.

32 It's the stuff of dreams. As a child, being a fan of the sport, I never imagined that one day I'd be in this position. Kids from Kilburn don't become favourite for the Tour de France. You're supposed to become a postman or a milkman or work in Ladbrokes.
2012 In *The Guardian*, 2 Nov.

Wilberforce, Samuel 1805–73

English prelate, Canon of Winchester, later Dean of Westminster and Bishop of Oxford.

33 If I were a cassowary
 On the plains of Timbuctoo,
 I would eat a missionary,
 Cassock, band, and hymn-book too.
Attributed.

Wilbur, Richard 1921–

US poet. He taught at Harvard and Wesleyan Universities, and wrote a significant body of poems. He also contributed lyrics to Leonard Bernstein's opera, *Candide* (1957).

34 We milk the cow of the world, and as we do
 We whisper in her ear, 'You are not true.'
1950 *Ceremony and Other Poems*, 'Epistemology'.

35 Forgive the hero, you who would have died
 Gladly with all you knew; he rode that tide
 To Ararat; all men are Noah's sons.
1950 *Ceremony and Other Poems*, 'Still, Citizen Sparrow'.

36 Outside the open window
 The morning air is all awash with angels.
1956 *Things of This World*, 'Love Calls Us to the Things of This World'.

37 The soul shrinks
 From all that it is about to remember,
 From the punctual rape of every blessèd day
1956 *Things of This World*, 'Love Calls Us to the Things of This World'.

38 Columbus and his men, they say,
 Conveyed the virus hither
 Whereby my features rot away
 And vital powers wither;
 Yet had they not traversed the seas
 And come infected back,
 Why, think of all the luxuries
 That modern life would lack.
1957 'Pangloss's Song', from *Candide*.

39 It is not tricks of sense
 But the time's fright within me which distracts
 Least fancies into violence
1969 *Walking to Sleep*, 'On the Marginal Way'.

40 All night, this headland
 Lunges into the rumpling
 Capework of the wind.
1976 *The Mind Reader*, 'Sleepless at Crown Point'.

41 Writing is…waiting for the word that may not be there until next Tuesday.
1987 In the *Los Angeles Times*, 13 Oct.

42 Most women know that sex is good for headaches.
1987 Quoted in the *Observer*, 1 Nov.

Wilcox, Ella Wheeler 1850–1919

US poet who wrote over 30 volumes of sentimental verse. Her temperance poems were collected in *Drops of Water* (1872). *Poems of Passion* (1883) was attacked for its immorality.

43 Laugh, and the world laughs with you:
 Weep, and you weep alone;
 For the sad old earth must borrow its mirth,
 It has trouble enough of its own.
1883 *Poems of Passion*, 'Solitude'.

Wilde, Jane Francesca née Elgee 1826–96

Irish Poet and folklorist, mother of Oscar Wilde. She was an ardent nationalist and contributed verse and prose to the *Nation* under the pen name 'Speranza'.

44 'Tis midnight, falls the lamp-light dull and sickly
 On a pale and anxious crowd,
 Through the court, and round the judges thronging thickly,

With prayers they dare not speak aloud—
Two youths, two noble youths, stand prisoners at the bar—
You can see them through the gloom—
In the pride of life and manhood's beauty, there they are
Awaiting their death-doom.
'The Brothers'.

45 Weary men, what reap ye?—Golden corn for the stranger.
What sow ye?—Human corpses that wait for the avenger.
Fainting forms, hunger stricken, what see ye in the offing?
Stately ships to bear our food away, amid the stranger's scoffing.
There's a proud array of soldiers—what do they round your door?
They guard our master's granaries from the thin hands of the poor.
Pale mothers, wherefore weeping? Would to God that we were dead—
Our children swoon before us, and we cannot give them bread.
'The Famine Year'.

Wilde, Oscar Fingal O'Flahertie Wills 1854–1900

Anglo-Irish poet and dramatist, renowned for his wit and flamboyant lifestyle. His works include *The Picture of Dorian Gray* (1891), *Lady Windermere's Fan* (1892), *An Ideal Husband* (1895), *The Importance of Being Earnest* (1895) and *The Ballad of Reading Gaol* (1898). He was ruined by a trial arising from his homosexual relationships.

46 To make a good salad is to be a brilliant diplomatist—the problem is entirely the same in both cases. To know exactly how much oil one must put with one's vinegar.
1880 *Vera, or The Nihilists*, act 2.

47 I have nothing to declare except my genius.
1882 On passing through US customs on a lecture tour. Quoted in F Harris, *Oscar Wilde* (1918), p.75.

48 Over the piano was printed a notice: 'Please do not shoot the pianist. He is doing his best.'
1883 *Impressions of America: Leadville*.

49 What captivity was to the Jews, exile has been to the Irish: America and American influence have educated them. Their first practical leader is an Irish-American.
1889 Of Charles Stewart Parnell. 'The Two Chiefs of Dunboy: or, an Irish Romance of the Last Century' in *Pall Mall Gazette*, 13 Apr.

50 Books of poetry by young writers are usually promissory notes that are never met. Now and then, however, one comes across a volume that is so far above the average that one can hardly resist the fascinating temptation of recklessly prophesying a fine future for its author. Such a book Mr Yeats's *Wanderings of Oisin* certainly is. Here we find nobility of treatment and nobility of subject-matter, delicacy of poetic instinct and richness of imaginative resource.
1889 In the *Pall Mall Gazette*, 12 Jul.

51 Newspapers have degenerated. They may now be absolutely relied upon.
1889 'The Decay of Lying', first published in the *Nineteenth Century Review*.

52 Art never expresses anything but itself.
1889 'The Decay of Lying', first published in the *Nineteenth Century Review*.

53 After playing Chopin, I feel as if I had been weeping over sins that I had never committed.
1891 *Intentions*, 'The Critic as Artist'.

54 Every great man nowadays has his disciples, and it is always Judas who writes the biography.
1891 *Intentions*, 'The Critic as Artist'.

55 Meredith is a prose Browning, and so is Browning.
1891 *Intentions*, 'The Critic as Artist'.

56 The one duty we owe to history is to rewrite it.
1891 *Intentions*, 'The Critic as Artist'.

57 It is through Art, and through Art only, that we can realise our perfection; through Art, and through Art only, that we can shield ourselves from the sordid perils of actual existence.
1891 *Intentions*, 'The Critic as Artist'.

58 All art is immoral.
1891 *Intentions*, 'The Critic as Artist'.

59 A little sincerity is a dangerous thing, and a great deal of it is absolutely fatal.
1891 *Intentions*, 'The Critic as Artist'.

60 Modern journalism justifies its own existence by the great Darwinian principle of the survival of the vulgarest.
1891 *Intentions*, 'The Critic as Artist'.

61 All that I desire to point out is the general principle that Life imitates Art far more than Art imitates Life.
1891 *Intentions*, 'The Decay of Lying'.

62 There is no such thing as a moral or an immoral book. Books are well written, or badly written.
1891 *The Picture of Dorian Gray*, preface.

63 The nineteenth century dislike of Realism is the rage of Caliban seeing his own face in the glass.
1891 *The Picture of Dorian Gray*, preface.

64 The moral life of man forms part of the subject matter of the artist, but the morality of art consists in the perfect use of an imperfect medium.
1891 *The Picture of Dorian Gray*, preface.

65 There is only one thing in the world worse than being talked about, and that is not being talked about.
1891 *The Picture of Dorian Gray*, ch.1.

66 A man cannot be too careful in the choice of his enemies.
1891 *The Picture of Dorian Gray*, ch.1.

67 I like Wagner's music better than anybody's. It is so loud that one can talk the whole time without other people hearing what one says.
1891 *The Picture of Dorian Gray*, ch.4.

68 If one hears bad music, it is one's duty to drown it by one's conversation.
1891 *The Picture of Dorian Gray*, ch.4.

69 A cigarette is the perfect type of a perfect pleasure. It is exquisite, and it leaves one unsatisfied. What more can one want?
1891 *The Picture of Dorian Gray*, ch.6.

70 It is better to be beautiful than to be good. But...it is better to be good than to be ugly.
1891 *The Picture of Dorian Gray*, ch.17.

71 Anybody can be good in the country.
1891 *The Picture of Dorian Gray*, ch.19.

72 Murder is always a mistake... One should never do anything that one cannot talk about after dinner.
1891 *The Picture of Dorian Gray*, ch.19.

73 As for the virtuous poor, one can pity them, of course, but one cannot possibly admire them.
1891 'The Soul of Man under Socialism'.

74 Democracy means simply the bludgeoning of the people by the people for the people.
1891 'The Soul of Man under Socialism'.

75 I can resist everything except temptation.
1892 Lord Darlington. *Lady Windermere's Fan*, act 1.

76 Many a woman has a past, but I am told that she has at least a dozen, and that they all fit.
1892 Said by Duchess of Berwick. *Lady Windermere's Fan*, act 1.

77 Do you know, Mr Hopper, dear Agatha and I are so much interested in Australia. It must be so pretty with all the dear little kangaroos flying about. Agatha has found it on the map. What a curious shape it is! Just like a large packing case.
1892 Duchess of Berwick to Mr Hopper. *Lady Windermere's Fan*, act 2.

78 We are all in the gutter, but some of us are looking at the stars.
1892 Said by Lord Darlington. *Lady Windermere's Fan*, act 3.

79 There is nothing in the whole world so unbecoming to a woman as a Nonconformist conscience.
1892 Cecil Graham. *Lady Windermere's Fan*, act 3.

80 A man who knows the price of everything and the value of nothing.
1892 Lord Darlington's definition of a cynic. *Lady Winderemere's Fan*, act 3.

81 Experience is the name everyone gives to their mistakes.
1892 Dumby. *Lady Windermere's Fan*, act 3.

82 The play was a great success, but the audience was a disaster.
1892 Attributed comment after the poor reception of *Lady Windermere's Fan*.

83 LORD ILLINGWORTH: The Book of Life begins with a man and a woman in a garden.
MRS ALLONBY: It ends with Revelations.
1893 *A Woman of No Importance*, act 1.

84 The English country gentleman galloping after a fox–the unspeakable in full pursuit of the uneatable.
1893 Lord Illingworth. *A Woman of No Importance*, act 1.

85 MRS ALLONBY: They say, Lady Hunstanton, that when good Americans die they go to Paris.
LADY HUNSTANTON: Indeed? And when bad Americans die, where do they go to?
LORD ILLINGWORTH: Oh, they go to America.
1893 *A Woman of No Importance*, act 1.

86 The youth of America is their oldest tradition. It has been going on now for three hundred years.
1893 Lord Illingworth. *A Woman of No Importance*, act 1.

87 One should never trust a woman who tells one her real age. A woman who would tell one that, would tell one anything.
1893 Lord Illingworth. *A Woman of No Importance*, act 1.

88 Children begin by loving their parents; after a time they judge them; rarely, if ever, do they forgive them.
1893 Lord Illingworth. *A Woman of No Importance*, act 2.

89 After a good dinner one can forgive anybody, even one's own relations.
1893 Lady Caroline. *A Woman of No Importance*, act 2.

90 GERALD: I suppose society is wonderfully delightful!
LORD ILLINGWORTH: To be in it is merely a bore. But to be out of it is simply a tragedy.
1893 *A Woman of No Importance*, act 3.

91 No woman should have a memory. Memory in a woman is the beginning of dowdiness.
1893 Lord Illingworth. *A Woman of No Importance*, act 3.

92 You should study the Peerage, Gerald... It is the best thing in fiction the English have ever done.
1893 Lord Illingworth. *A Woman of No Importance*, act 3.

93 A man who can dominate a London dinner-table can dominate the world.
1893 Lord Illingworth. *A Woman of No Importance*, act 3.

94 I'm afraid I play no outdoor games at all, except dominoes. I have sometimes played dominoes outside a French café.
1895 Quoted by Gelett Burgess in 'A Talk with Mr Oscar Wilde' in *The Sketch*, 9 Jan.

95 JACK: I think Jack, for instance, a charming name.
GWENDOLEN: Jack?... No, there is very little music in the name Jack, if any at all, indeed. It does not thrill. It produces absolutely no vibrations... I have known several Jacks, and they all, without exception, were more than usually plain. Besides, Jack is a notorious domesticity for John! And I pity any woman who is married to a man called John. She would probably never be allowed to know the entrancing pleasure of a single moment's solitude. The only really safe name is Ernest.
1895 *The Importance of Being Earnest*, act 1.

96 Really, if the lower orders don't set us a good example, what on earth is the use of them?
1895 Algernon. *The Importance of Being Earnest*, act 1.

97 It is very vulgar to talk like a dentist when one isn't a dentist. It produces a false impression.
1895 Jack. *The Importance of Being Earnest*, act 1.

98 The truth is rarely pure, and never simple.
1895 Algernon. *The Importance of Being Earnest*, act 1.

99 In married life three is company and two none.
1895 Algernon. *The Importance of Being Earnest*, act 1.

1 Ignorance is like a delicate exotic fruit; touch it and the bloom is gone. The whole theory of modern education is radically unsound. Fortunately, in England, at any rate, education produces no effect whatsoever.
1895 Lady Bracknell. *The Importance of Being Earnest*, act 1.

2 To lose one parent, Mr Worthing, may be regarded as a misfortune; to lose both looks like carelessness.
1895 Lady Bracknell. *The Importance of Being Earnest*, act 1.

3 All women become like their mothers. That is their tragedy. No man does. That's his.
1895 Algernon. *The Importance of Being Earnest*, act 1, also in *A Woman of No Importance* (1893), act 2.

4 The good ended happily, and the bad unhappily. That is what fiction means.
1895 Miss Prism. *The Importance of Being Earnest*, act 2.

5 The chapter on the fall of the Rupee you may omit. It is somewhat too sensational.
1895 Miss Prism. *The Importance of Being Earnest*, act 2.

6 I hope you have not been leading a double life, pretending to be wicked and being really good all the time. That would be hypocrisy.
1895 Said by Cecily. *The Importance of Being Earnest*, act 2.

7 Charity, dear Miss Prism, charity! None of us are perfect. I myself am peculiarly susceptible to draughts.
1895 Dr Chasuble. *The Importance of Being Earnest*, act 2.

8 CECILY: When I see a spade I call it a spade.
GWENDOLEN: I am glad to say that I have never seen a spade.
1895 *The Importance of Being Earnest*, act 3.

9 Thirty-five is a very attractive age. London society is full of women of the very highest birth who have, of their own free choice, remained thirty-five for years.
1895 Lady Bracknell. *The Importance of Being Earnest*, act 3.

10 She wore far too much rouge last night, and not quite enough clothes. That is always a sign of despair in a woman.
1895 Lord Goring. *An Ideal Husband*, act 2.

11 Nothing is so dangerous as being too modern. One is apt to grow old-fashioned quite suddenly.
1895 Lord Markby. *An Ideal Husband*, act 2.

12 Fashion is what one wears oneself. What is unfashionable is what other people wear.
1895 Lord Goring. *An Ideal Husband*, act 3.

13 If one could only teach the English how to talk, and the Irish how to listen, society here would be quite civilised.
1895 Mrs Cheveley speaking. *An Ideal Husband*, act 3.

14 If this is the way Queen Victoria treats her prisoners she doesn't deserve to have any.
1895 On being obliged to stand in the rain as he awaited transport to take him to prison. Attributed.

15 He did not wear his scarlet coat,
For blood and wine are red,
And blood and wine were on his hands
When they found him with the dead.
1898 *The Ballad of Reading Gaol*, pt.1, stanza 1.

16 I never saw a man who looked
With such a wistful eye
Upon that little tent of blue
Which prisoners call the sky.
1898 *The Ballad of Reading Gaol*, pt.1, stanza 3.

17 Yet each man kills the thing he loves,
By each let this be heard,
Some do it with a bitter look,
Some with a flattering word.
The coward does it with a kiss,
The brave man with a sword!
1898 *The Ballad of Reading Gaol*, pt.1, stanza 7.

18 The Governer was strong upon
The Regulation Act:
The Doctor said that Death was but
A scientific fact:
And twice a day the Chaplain called,
And left a little tract.
1898 *The Ballad of Reading Gaol*, pt.3, stanza 3.

19 Something was dead in each of us,
And what was dead was Hope.
1898 *The Ballad of Reading Gaol*, pt.3, stanza 31.

20 And the wild regrets, and the bloody sweats,
None knew so well as I:
For he who lives more lives than one
More deaths than one must die.
1898 *The Ballad of Reading Gaol*, pt.3, stanza 37.

21 I know not whether Laws be right,
Or whether Laws be wrong;
All that we know who lie in gaol
Is that the wall is strong;
And that each day is like a year,
A year whose days are long.
1898 *The Ballad of Reading Gaol*, pt.5, stanza 1.

22 How else but through a broken heart
May Lord Christ enter in?
1898 *The Ballad of Reading Gaol*, pt.5, stanza 14.

23 I am dying, as I have lived, beyond my means.
1900 Accepting a glass of champagne shortly before his death. Attributed.

24 Either that wallpaper goes or I do.
1900 As he lay dying in a Paris hotel bedroom. Attributed.

25 Football is all very well as a game for rough girls, but it is hardly suitable for delicate boys.
Quoted in Alvin Redman *The Epigrams of Oscar Wilde* (1952).

26 The only possible form of exercise is to talk, not to walk.
Quoted in Alvin Redman *The Epigrams of Oscar Wilde* (1952).

27 Mr Bernard Shaw has no enemies, but is intensely disliked by all his friends.
Quoted in W B Yeats *Autobiographies* (1955).

28 It requires one to assume such indecent postures.
His reason for not playing cricket. Quoted in *Bloomsbury Thematic Dictionary of Quotations* (1988)

29 Work is the curse of the drinking classes.
Attributed.

30 Henry James wrote fiction as if it were a painful duty.
Attributed.

31 The three women I have admired most are Queen Victoria, Sarah Bernhardt and Lillie Langtry. I would have married any one of them with pleasure.
Attributed.

Wilder, Billy (Samuel) 1906–2002

Austrian-born writer and director who moved to Hollywood in 1934. He won Academy Awards for *The Lost Weekend* (1945), *Sunset Boulevard* (1950) and *The Apartment* (1960). Other successes include *Double Indemnity* (1944), *The Seven Year Itch* (1955) and *Some Like It Hot* (1959).

32 Johnny, keep it out of focus. I want to win the foreign picture award.
1950 Remark to cameraman John Seitz during the making of *Sunset Boulevard*.

33 Making a picture with Marilyn Monroe was like going to the dentist. It was hell at the time, but after it was all over it was wonderful.
Quoted in Doug McClelland *Star Speak* (1987).

34 No one ever leaves a star.
1950 *Sunset Boulevard*.

35 Fasten your cigarettes.
1972 Avanti (with I A L Diamond).

36 I don't object to foreigners speaking a foreign language; I just wish they'd all speak the same foreign language.
1972 Avanti (with I A L Diamond).

37 Hindsight is always twenty-twenty.
Attributed.

Wilder, Thornton Niven 1897–1975

US playwright and novelist. His most successful plays included *Our Town* (1938) and *The Skin of Our Teeth* (1942), while his other writings included the novel *The Bridge of San Luis Rey* (1927). His play *The Matchmaker* (1954) provided the basis for the hit musical *Hello, Dolly!*

38 From what human ill does not dawn seem to be an alleviation.
1927 The Bridge of San Luis Rey, ch.3.

39 Most everybody in the world climbs into their graves married.
1938 Our Town, act 2.

40 Marriage is a bribe to make a housekeeper think she's a householder.
1939 The Merchant of Yonkers, act 1.

41 The fights are the best part of married life. The rest is merely so-so.
1939 The Merchant of Yonkers, act 2.

42 My advice to you is not to inquire why or whither, but just enjoy your ice-cream while it's on your plate,—that's my philosophy.
1942 The Skin of Our Teeth, act 1.

43 When you're at war you think about a better life; when you're at peace you think about a more comfortable one.
1942 The Skin of Our Teeth, act 1.

44 We'll trot down to the movies and see how girls with wax faces live.
1942 The Skin of Our Teeth, act 3.

45 I've never forgotten for long at a time that living is a struggle. I know that every good and excellent thing in the world stands moment by moment on the razor-edge of danger and must be fought for—whether it's a field, or a home, or a country.
1942 The Skin of Our Teeth, act 3.

46 Literature is the orchestration of platitudes.
1953 In *Time,* 12 Jan.

47 A living is made, Mr Kemper, by selling something that everybody needs at least once a year. Yes, sir! And a million is made by producing something that everybody needs every day. You artists produce something that nobody needs at any time.
1954 The Matchmaker, act 1.

48 Ninety-nine percent of the people in the world are fools, and the rest of us are in great danger of contagion.
1954 The Matchmaker, act 1.

49 Never support two weaknesses at the same time. It's your combination sinners—your lecherous liars and your miserly drunkards—who dishonour the vices and bring them into bad repute.
1954 The Matchmaker, act 3.

50 But there comes a time in everybody's life when he must decide whether he'll live among human beings or not—a fool among fools or a fool alone.
1954 The Matchmaker, act 4.

51 I am not interested in the ephemeral—such subjects as the adulteries of dentists. I am interested in those things that repeat and repeat in the lives of the millions.
1961 In the *New York Times,* 6 Mar.

52 The less seen, the more heard. The eye is the enemy of the ear in real drama.
1961 In the *New York Times,* 6 Nov.

53 The process of learning is accompanied by alternations of pain and brief quickenings that resemble pain.
1967 The Eighth Day.

Wilding, Michael 1912–79

English actor. He is usually remembered for his performances in such films as *Piccadilly Incident* (1946) and *Spring in Park Lane* (1948).

54 You can pick out actors by the glazed look that comes into their eyes when the conversation wanders away from themselves.
Attributed.

Wilhelm II, Kaiser 1859–1941

Kaiser and King of Prussia 1888–1918. Dismissed Bismarck in 1890, beginning a long period of personal rule. Although his bellicosity contributed to the origins of World War I, he became a figurehead during the course of it. He abdicated at the end of the war and settled in the Netherlands.

55 We have…fought for our place in the sun and have won it. It will be my business to see that we retain this place in the sun unchallenged.
1901 Speech in Hamburg, 18 Jun. Quoted in *The Times,* 20 Jun.

56 You will be home before the leaves have fallen from the trees.
1914 Address to German troops leaving for the Front, Aug.

57 We draw the sword with a clean conscience and with clean hands.
1914 Address from the throne, Berlin, 4 Aug.

58 The machine is running away with him as it ran away with me.
1939 Of Adolf Hitler at the start of World War II, said to Sir Robert Bruce-Lockhart, 27 Aug.

Wilkinson, Anne 1910–61

Canadian poet. One of the founders of the important literary magazine, *The Tamarack Review,* she published poetry (*Counterpoint to Sleep,* 1951, and *The Hangman Ties the Holly,* 1955), a family history (*Lions in the Way,* 1956) and a children's book. Her collected poems were published in 1968.

59 Fabulous the insects
Stud the air
Or walk on running water,
Klee-drawn saints
And bright as angels are.
1955 The Hangman Ties the Holly, 'In June and Gentle Oven'.

60 Our hearts, unrisen, yield a heavy bread.
1955 The Hangman Ties the Holly, 'Topsoil to the Wind'.

Wilkinson, Jonny 1979–
English rugby player, member of the successful England Rugby World Cup team (2003).

61 The first game I ever played I scored a goal from the halfway line. Didn't have a clue what I was doing. Ball just came to me, so I whacked it.
2002 On his childhood attempts to play football. Quoted in *The Guardian*, 28 Jan.

62 I play with the fear of letting people down. That's what motivates me.
2004 Quoted on www.bbc.co.uk.

Will, George Frederick 1941–
US journalist and author.

63 What the federal government does basically is borrow money from people and mail it to people.
1993 Of entitlement programs. ABC TV broadcast, 19 Sep.

William of Poitiers 11c.
French chronicler of the life of William the Conqueror.

64 A strange manner of battle, where one side works by constant motion and ceaseless charges, while the other can but endure passively as it stands fixed to the sod. The Norman arrow and sword worked on: in the English ranks the only movement was the dropping of the dead: the living stood motionless.
c.1071 Of the Battle of Hastings, 14 Oct 1066. *Gesta Guillelmi ducis Normannorum et regis Anglorum* (edited by R Foreville, 1952).

William of Wykeham 1324–1404
Bishop of Winchester and Chancellor of England.

65 Manners makyth man.
Proverb common from the 14th century and said to be Wykeham's motto.

William III *also called* William of Orange 1650–1702
Dutch-born King of Great Britain (1689–1702), and Stadholder of the United Provinces (1672–1702). Husband of Mary, daughter of James II, he was invited by Protestant elements to assume the throne in the Glorious Revolution of 1688.

66 People in Parliament occupy themselves with private animosities and petty quarrels, and think little of the national interest. It is impossible to credit the serene indifference with which they consider events outside their own country.
1699 Letter, Jan.

67 The eyes of all England are on this Parliament. If you do in good earnest wish to see England hold the balance of Europe and to be indeed at the head of the Protestant interest, it will appear by your right improving the present opportunity.
1701 At the State Opening of Parliament, Dec.

68 Every bullet has its billet.
Quoted by John Wesley, journal entry, 6 Jun 1765.

William, Duke of Cambridge, Prince 1982–
HRH Prince William, eldest son of Charles, Prince of Wales, and Diana, Princess of Wales.

69 Never being able to say 'Mummy' again in your life seems a small thing. However, for many, including me, it's now really just a word—hollow and evoking only memories.
2009 Speaking about Princess Diana, who died prematurely in a car crash in Paris.

Williams, (Hiram) Hank 1923–53
US country singer, the 'Father of Country Music'. His hits include 'Lovesick Blues', 'Hey, Good Lookin'', 'Jambalaya' and 'Your Cheatin' Heart'. His death was the result of alcoholism and drug abuse.

70 You got to have smelt a lot of mule manure before you can sing like a hillbilly.
Quoted in *Rolling Stone*, 1969.

Williams, Harry Abbott 1919–2006
English cleric and scholar, a member of the Anglican Community of the Resurrection. In his theological writings he combined theology with insights from psychology.

71 The prelude to resurrection as we experience it in this life is always powerlessness. We cannot raise ourselves by our own bootstraps.
1972 *The True Resurrection*.

Williams, Raymond 1921–88
Welsh critic and novelist. He is best known for his works mixing socio-cultural and literary criticism, including *The Long Revolution* (1966) and *The Country and the City* (1973).

72 The human crisis is always a crisis of understanding: what we genuinely understand we can do.
1958 *Culture and Society*, ch.3.

73 When art communicates, a human experience is actively offered and actively received. Below this activity threshold there can be no art.
1966 *The Long Revolution*, pt.1, ch.1.

Williams, Robin 1952–2014
US comedian and film actor. He starred in the TV series *Mork and Mindy* (1970s) and in such films as *The World According to Garp* (1982), *Good Morning, Vietnam* (1987), *Dead Poets Society* (1989), *The Fisher King* (1991), *Mrs Doubtfire* (1993), *The Birdcage* (1995) and *Good Will Hunting* (1997).

74 I thought lacrosse was what you find in la church.
1982 Interview in *Playboy*.

75 Cricket is baseball on valium.
Quoted in Colin Jarman *The Guinness Dictionary of Sports Quotations* (1990).

76 Spring is nature's way of saying, 'Let's party!'
2007 In *Woman's Day Magazine*, 1 Apr.

77 Marriage is a triumph of imagination over intelligence.
2013 As Father Monighan in *The Big Wedding* (screenplay by Justin Zackham).

Williams, Shirley Vivien Teresa Brittain Williams, Baroness 1930–
English politician, a Labour MP from 1964. She lost her seat in 1979, co-founded the Social Democratic Party in 1981 and became its first elected MP. She lost her seat in 1983 but remained as SDP President (1982–8), and supported the merger with the Liberal Party in 1988. A professor at Harvard University, she remains active in British politics.

78 The British Civil Service…is a beautifully designed and effective braking mechanism.

1980 Speech at the Royal Institute of Public Administration, 11 Feb.

Williams, Tennessee Thomas Lanier 1911–83

US playwright. He won recognition as a leading contemporary writer with his play *The Glass Menagerie* (1945), which was followed by such intense, atmospheric and often brutal dramas as *A Streetcar Named Desire* (1947), *The Rose Tattoo* (1951), *Cat On A Hot Tin Roof* (1955), *Suddenly Last Summer* (1958) and *The Night of the Iguana* (1962).

79 In memory everything seems to happen to music.
   1945 Tom. *The Glass Menagerie*, sc.1.

80 I didn't go to the moon, I went much further—for time is the longest distance between two places.
   1945 Tom. *The Glass Menagerie*, sc.7.

81 I can't stand a naked light bulb, any more than I can a rude remark or a vulgar action.
   1947 Blanche. *A Streetcar Named Desire*, sc.3

82 I have always depended on the kindness of strangers.
   1947 Blanche. *A Streetcar Named Desire*, sc.11.

83 The only thing worse than a liar is a liar that's also a hypocrite!
   1951 Rosa. *The Rose Tattoo*, act 3.

84 It is a terrible thing for an old woman to outlive her dogs.
   1953 *Camino Real*, prologue.

85 Caged birds accept each other but flight is what they long for.
   1953 Marguerite. *Camino Real*, block 7.

86 Bohemia has no banner. It survives by discretion.
   1953 Marguerite. *Camino Real*, block 7.

87 We have to distrust each other. It's our only defence against betrayal.
   1953 Marguerite. *Camino Real*, block 10.

88 We're all of us guinea pigs in the laboratory of God. Humanity is just a work in progress.
   1953 The Gipsy. *Camino Real*, block 12.

89 Some mystery should be left in the revelation of character in a play, just as a great deal of mystery is always left in the revelation of character in life, even in one's own character to himself.
   1955 *Cat on a Hot Tin Roof*, stage direction.

90 What is the victory of a cat on a hot tin roof?—I wish I knew… Just staying on it, I guess, for as long as she can.
   1955 Maggie. *Cat on a Hot Tin Roof*, act 1.

91 You can be young without money but you can't be old without it.
   1955 Maggie. *Cat on a Hot Tin Roof*, act 1.

92 A drinking man's someone who wants to forget he isn't still young an' believing.
   1955 *Cat on a Hot Tin Roof*, act 2.

93 BRICK: Well, they say nature hates a vacuum, Big Daddy.
   BIG DADDY: That's what they say, but sometimes I think that a vacuum is a hell of a lot better than some of the stuff that nature replaces it with.
   1955 *Cat on a Hot Tin Roof*, act 2.

94 Mendacity is a system that we live in. Liquor is one way out an' death's the other.
   1955 Brick. *Cat on a Hot Tin Roof*, act 2.

95 At the age of 14 I discovered writing as an escape from…being called a sissy by the neighborhood kids, and Miss Nancy by my father.
   1957 In the *New York Times*, 17 Mar.

96 The world is a funny paper read backwards. And that way it isn't so funny.
   1957 In the *Observer*, 7 Apr.

97 Don't look forward to the day you stop suffering, because when it comes you'll *know* you're dead.
   1958 In the *Observer*, 26 Jan.

98 We're all of us sentenced to solitary confinement inside our own skins, for life!
   1958 Val. *Orpheus Descending*, act 2, sc.1.

99 It haunts me, the passage of time. I think time is a merciless thing. I think life is a process of burning oneself out and time is the fire that burns you. But I think the spirit of man is a good adversary.
   1958 In the *New York Post*, 30 Apr.

1 He was meddling too much in my private life.
   1961 Explaining why he had dispensed with the services of his psychoanalyst. Attributed.

2 All cruel people describe themselves as paragons of frankness!
   1963 Mrs Goforth. *The Milk Train Doesn't Stop Here Anymore*, sc.1.

3 Life is all memory except for the one present moment that goes by you so quick you hardly catch it going.
   1963 Mrs Goforth. *The Milk Train Doesn't Stop Here Anymore*, sc.3

4 We all live in a house on fire, no fire department to call; no way out, just the upstairs window to look out of while the fire burns the house down with us trapped, locked in it.
   1963 Chris. *The Milk Train Doesn't Stop Here Anymore*, sc.6.

Williams, Venus 1980–

US tennis player. Her first Grand Slam singles victory came in 2000 when she won the Wimbledon title. As well as other singles titles, she has won numerous doubles titles with her sister Serena.

5 I guess there's always going to be jobs that pay more than others, and I suppose I have one of those.
   2002 In the *Observer*, 9 Jun.

Williams, William Carlos 1883–1963

US poet, a paediatrician as well as a writer. His poetry and objectivist aesthetic made him a major Modernist figure. He also wrote novels, stories, plays, literary and cultural essays and memoirs.

6 I will teach you my townspeople
   how to perform a funeral
   for you have it over a troop
   of artists—
   unless one should scour the world—
   you have the ground sense necessary.
   1917 *Al Que Quiere!*, 'Tract'.

7 Covertly the hands of a great clock
   go round and round! Were they to
   move quickly and at once the whole
   secret would be out and the shuffling
   of all ants be done forever.
   1921 *Sour Grapes*, 'Overture to a Dance of Locomotives'.

8 Lifeless in appearance, sluggish
dazed spring approaches—

They enter the new world naked,
cold, uncertain of all
save that they enter.
1923 *Spring and All*, 'Spring and All'.

9 One by one the objects are defined—
It quickens: clarity, outline of leaf

But now the stark dignity of
entrance—Still, the profound change
has come upon them: rooted, they
grip down and begin to awaken.
1923 *Spring and All*, 'Spring and All'.

10 so much depends
upon

a red wheel
barrow

glazed with rain
water

beside the white
chickens.
1923 *Spring and All*, 'The Red Wheelbarrow'.

11 —through metaphor to reconcile
the people and the stones.
1944 *The Wedge*, 'A Sort of Song'.

12 Is it any better in Heaven, my friend Ford,
Than you found it in Provence?
1944 *The Wedge*, 'To Ford Madox Ford in Heaven'.

13 To make a start,
out of particulars
and make them general, rolling
up the sum, by defective means—
Sniffing the trees, just another dog
among a lot of dogs. What
else is there? And to do?
1946 *Paterson*, bk.1, preface.

14 For the beginning is assuredly
the end—since we know nothing, pure
and simple, beyond
our own complexities.
1946 *Paterson*, bk.1, preface.

15 Minds like beds always made up
(more stony than a shore)
unwilling or unable.
1946 *Paterson*, bk.1, preface.

16 Say it, no ideas but in things.
1946 *Paterson*, bk.1, 'The Delineaments of the Giants', 1.

17 Divorce is
the sign of knowledge in our time.
1946 *Paterson*, bk.1, 'The Delineaments of the Giants', 2.

18 Without invention nothing is well-spaced.
1948 *Paterson*, bk.2, 'Sunday in the Park', 1.

19 Unless there is
a new mind there cannot be a new
line, the old will go on
repeating itself with recurring
deadliness:
1948 *Paterson*, bk.2, 'Sunday in the Park', 1.

20 Beyond the gap where the river
plunges into the narrow gorge, unseen

—and the imagination soars, as a voice
beckons, a thundrous voice, endless
—as sleep: the voice
that has ineluctably called them—
that unmoving roar!
1948 *Paterson*, bk.2, 'Sunday in the Park', 1.

21 For what we cannot accomplish, what
is denied to love,
what we have lost in the anticipation—
a descent follows,
endless and indestructible.
1948 *Paterson*, bk.2, 'Sunday in the Park', 1.

22 For there is a wind or a ghost of wind
in all books echoing the life
there, a high wind that fills the tubes
of the ear until we think we hear a wind,
actual.
1949 *Paterson*, bk.3, 'The Library'.

23 and there grows in the mind
a scent, it may be, of locust blossoms
whose perfume is itself a wind moving
to lead the mind away.
1949 *Paterson*, bk.3, 'The Library'.

24 It isn't what he says that counts as a work of art, it's what he makes with such intensity of perception that it lives with an intrinsic movement of its very own to verify the authenticity.
Of the poet. Quoted by Richard Eberhart in the *New York Times*, 17 Dec 1950.

25 I have never been one to write by rule, not even by my own rules.
1954 Letter to Richard Eberhart, 23 May.

26 Love is that common tone
shall raise his fiery head
and sound his note.
1954 *The Desert Music*, 'The Orchestra'.

27 All writing is a disease. You can't stop it.
Quoted in *Newsweek*, 7 Jan 1957.

28 Nothing whips my blood like verse.
Quoted in John Thirlwall (ed) *The Selected Letters of William Carlos Williams* (1957).

29 Though he is approaching death he is possessed by many poems.
1958 *Paterson*, bk.5.

30 Anything is good material for poetry. Anything.
1958 *Paterson*, bk.5.

Williamson, Roy 1937–90

Scottish folksinger and musician, a partner in the Corries with Ronnie Browne from 1961, and composer of 'Flower of Scotland', adopted by many as an unofficial Scottish national anthem.

31 O flower of Scotland, when will we see your like again,
That fought and died for your wee bit hill and glen

And stood against him, proud Edward's army,
And sent him homeward tae think again.
1968 'Flower of Scotland', stanza 1.

Willis, Bruce 1955–

US actor. He has appeared in a number of action-man roles in such films as *Die Hard* (1988) and its sequels, as well as taking character parts.

32 Frankly, reviews are mostly for people who still read. Like most of the written word, it is going the way of the dinosaur.
1997 In *Time*, 19 May.

Willkie, Wendell Lewis 1892–1944

US politician, Republican candidate for the presidency (1940).

33 Any man who is not something of a Socialist before he is forty has no heart. Any man who is still a Socialist after he is forty has no head.
Quoted in Richard Norton Smith *Thomas E. Dewey and his Times* (1982), p.294.
▶ See Twain 903:91.

Wilmer, Val(erie) 1941–

English writer and photographer. Her books on jazz include *Jazz People* (1970), *As Serious As Your Life* (1977) and the autobiographical *Mama Said There'd Be Days Like This* (1989).

34 A rather bitter British musician once remarked sourly to a friend of mine: 'Oh, all *she* knows about music she learned in bed with musicians.' To that, I can only add, what better place to learn?
1989 *Mama Said There'd Be Days Like This*, ch.3.

Wilson, A(ndrew) N(orman) 1950–

English writer. He has written novels, criticism, journalism and biography, including the controversial *Jesus* (1992).

35 It had never occurred to Giles that there was something perfectly sensible about wanting to hold onto innocence. He had always gone in for the idea that since we only pass this way once, *experience* counts for everything.
1982 *Wise Virgins*, ch.6.

36 Religion is the tragedy of mankind… But I do know, from the inside as well as from personal observation, that religion appeals to something deep and irrational and strong within us, and that is what makes it so dangerous.
1991 *Against Religion*, no.19.

37 I should prefer to have a politician who regularly went to a massage parlour than one who promised a laptop computer for every teacher.
1999 In the *Observer*, 21 Mar.

Wilson, Sir Angus Frank Johnstone 1931–91

English writer. He wrote literary criticism, short stories and a play, but was best known for his novels including *Anglo-Saxon Attitudes* (1956) and *The Old Men in the Zoo* (1961).

38 'God knows how you Protestants can be expected to have any sense of direction,' she said. 'It's different with us, I haven't been to mass for years, I've got every mortal sin on my conscience, but I know when I'm doing wrong. I'm still a Catholic, it's there, nothing can take it away from me.' 'Of course, duckie,' said Jeremy… 'once a Catholic always a Catholic.'
1949 *The Wrong Set*, 'Significant Experience'.

39 She was more than ever proud of the position of the bungalow, so almost in the country.
1957 'A Flat Country Christmas'.

40 All fiction is for me a kind of magic and trickery—a confidence trick, trying to make people believe something is true that isn't.
1957 In *The Paris Review*, no.17.

41 The impulse to write a novel comes from a momentary unified vision of life.
1963 *The Wild Garden*.

42 I have no concern for the common man except that he should not be so common.
1967 *No Laughing Matter*.

43 My theme is always *humanistic*. Life today is junglelike…it is complex, it is inhuman in its materialism.
1972 Letter to David Farrer, his publisher, Jul. Quoted in Margaret Drabble *Angus Wilson—A Biography* (1995).

44 All are deceptions, substitutes for the hard job of using reason and industry and intuition and compassion to solve even a little bit of the muddle with humaneness and awe for the natural world and the complexity of human beings.
1972 Letter to David Farrer, his publisher, Jul. Quoted in Margaret Drabble *Angus Wilson—A Biography* (1995).

45 People are able to live with only half a heart, to live without real compassion, because they are able to use words that are only forms.
1972 Interview in *Iowa Review*, no.3, Fall.

46 The novelist must be his own most harsh critic and also his own most loving admirer—and about both he must say nothing.
1976 Author's comment in D L Kirkpatrick (ed) *Contemporary Novelists*.

Wilson, Charles called 'Engine Charlie' 1890–1961

President of General Motors and Secretary of Defense. He was nicknamed 'Engine Charlie' to distinguish him from 'Electric Charlie' Wilson, president of General Electric.

47 For years I thought what was good for our country was good for General Motors, and vice versa. The difference did not exist. Our company is too big. It goes with the welfare of the country.
1953 Statement to US Senate, Committee on Armed Services, Jan.

Wilson, David Gordon 1928–

English-born US mechanical engineer and bicycling enthusiast.

48 You must invent because you enjoy it.
2004 On making his first recumbent bicycle in 1955.

Wilson, Edmund 1895–1972

US literary critic, social commentator, and novelist. Although his own fiction, plays and poems are now little read, he was an influential critic with a wide-ranging perspective on art, history and society.

49 In a sense, one can never read the book that the author originally wrote, and one can never read the same book twice.
1938 The Triple Thinkers, introduction.

50 Of all the great Victorian writers, he was probably the most antagonistic to the Victorian age itself.
1941 Of Dickens. *The Wound and the Bow*, 'Dickens: The Two Scrooges'.

Wilson, Edward O(sborne) 1929–

US biologist, Professor of Entomology at Harvard University. His works include *Insect Societies* (1971), *Sociobiology: The New Synthesis* (1975) and *Biophilia* (1984).

51 It came by a lightning flash like knowledge from the gods.
1975 On the 1953 discovery of the DNA molecule. *Sociobiology*.

52 Important science is not just any similarity glimpsed for the first time. It offers analogies that map the gateways to unexplored terrain.
1984 Biophilia.

53 To a considerable degree science consists in originating the maximum amount of information with the minimum expenditure of energy.
1984 Biophilia.

54 Karl Marx was right, socialism works, it is just that he had the wrong species.
1990 Concluding that Marxism is more suited to ants than humans, *The Ants*.

55 We have created a Star Wars civilization, with Stone Age emotions, medieval institutions, and godlike technology.
2013 The Social Conquest of Earth.

56 The most successful scientist thinks like a poet—wide-ranging, sometimes fantastical—and works like a bookkeeper. It is the latter role that the world sees.
2014 The Meaning of Human Existence.

Wilson, Ernest 1876–1930

English plant hunter.

57 Smoke That Thunders.
1927 Book title, referring to Victoria Falls.

Wilson of Rievaulx, (James) Harold Wilson, Baron 1916–95

English Labour politician and Prime Minister (1964–70, 1974–6). A renowned debater, his economic plans were hampered by a balance of payments crisis. He faced too the problems of Rhodesian independence, opposition to Britain's proposed entry into the Common Market, and conflict within the Party. After a third general election victory, he resigned in 1976.

58 The school that I went to in the north was a school where more than half the children in my class never had any boots or shoes to their feet. They wore clogs, because they lasted longer than shoes of comparable price.
1948 Speech, Birmingham, 28 Jul.
▶ See Bulmer-Thomas 173:61.

59 All the little gnomes in Zurich and other finance centres.
1956 Speech, House of Commons, 12 Nov.

60 Every time that Mr Macmillan comes back from abroad, Mr Butler goes to the airport and grips him warmly by the throat.
1957 Attributed.

61 We are redefining and restating our socialism in terms of the scientific revolution… The Britain that will be forged in the white heat of this revolution will be no place for restrictive practices or outdated methods on either side of industry.
1963 Labour Party Conference, 1 Oct. His phrase has since been memorably rendered as 'the white heat of the technological revolution'.

62 The Labour Party is a moral crusade, or it is nothing.
1964 Scottish Labour Party conference, 5 Sep.

63 A week is a long time in politics.
1964 Comment to lobby correspondents, Oct. As such meetings are off the record, there is no exact source for this famous phrase.

64 Given a fair wind, we will negotiate our way into the Common Market, head held high, not crawl in… Negotiations? Yes. Unconditional acceptance of whatever terms we are offered? No.
1966 Speech, Bristol, 20 Mar.

65 In a recent interview, I was asked what, above all, I associated with socialism in this modern age. I answered that if there was one word I would use to identify modern socialism, it was 'Science'.
1967 Speech, 17 Jun.

66 From now on the pound abroad is worth 14 per cent or so less in terms of other currencies. That does not mean, of course, that the pound here in Britain—in your pocket or purse, or in your bank—has been devalued.
1967 National broadcast, 19 Nov. The speech gave rise to the well-known phrase, 'the pound in your pocket'.

67 We are creating a Britain of which we can be proud, and the world knows it. The world's tourists are coming here in their millions…because the new Britain is exciting. Yes, Britain with a Labour Government is an exciting place.
1969 Speech, Labour Party Conference, 30 Sep.

68 One man's wage rise is another man's price increase.
1970 In the *Observer*, 11 Jan.

69 Have you ever noticed how we only win the World Cup under a Labour government?
1971 Quoted in Peter Ball and Phil Shaw *The Book of Football Quotations* (1989).

70 The greatest asset that a head of state can have is the ability to get a good night's sleep.
1975 BBC Radio 4 broadcast, 16 Apr.

71 The party must protect itself against the activities of small groups of inflexible political persuasion…having in common only their arrogant dogmatism… I have no wish to lead a party of political zombies.
1975 Labour Party Conference, 30 Sep.

72 The main essentials of a successful Prime Minister are sleep and a sense of history.
1976 The Governance of Britain.

73 A constant effort to keep a party together, without sacrificing either principle or the essentials of basic strategy, is the very stuff of political leadership. Macmillan was canonized for it.
1979 Final Term: The Labour Government 1974–76.

Wilson, Michael 1937–

Canadian Minister of Finance in the 1980s.

74 No matter how we define the term, Canada has an acute shortage of rich people.

1985 Giving one reason why taxing the wealthy would not ensure the continuation of Canada's social programs, at the Canadian Economics Association, Montreal, 30 May.

Wilson, (Thomas) Woodrow 1856–1924

US statesman and 28th President (1913–21). He was twice elected Democratic President. His administration was chiefly remembered for Prohibition, woman's suffrage, US entry into World War I, and his championing of the League of Nations. He was awarded the Nobel peace prize (1919).

75 The feelings with which we face this new age of right and opportunity sweep across our heartstrings like some air out of God's own presence, where justice and mercy are reconciled, and the judge and the brother are one.
1913 Inaugural address, 4 Mar.

76 Human rights, national integrity, and opportunity as against material interests…are the issues that we now must face. I take this occasion to say that the United States will never again seek one additional foot of territory by conquest.
1913 Speech, Alabama, 27 Oct.

77 The people of the United States are drawn from many nations, and chiefly from the nations now at war. Some will wish one nation, others another, to succeed in this monumental struggle. I venture to speak a solemn word of warning. The United States must be neutral in fact as well as in name during these days that are to try men's souls. We must be impartial in thought as well as in action.
1914 Message to the Senate, 19 Aug.

78 There is such a thing as a man being too proud to fight; there is such a thing as a nation being so right that it does not need to convince others by force that it is right.
1915 Speech in Philadelphia, 10 May.

79 We are constantly thinking of the great war…which saved the Union…but it was a war which did a great deal more than that. It created in this country what had never existed before—a national consciousness.
1915 Memorial Day Address at Arlington National Cemetery, Virginia, 31 May.

80 America cannot be an ostrich, with its head in the sand.
1916 Speech, New Mexico, 1 Feb.

81 Nations should with one accord adopt the doctrine of President Monroe as the doctrine of the world; that every people should be left free to determine its own policy, its own way of development, unhindered, unthreatened, unafraid—the little along with the great and powerful. Those are American principles, American policies. We could stand for no others. They are also the principles of mankind, and must prevail.
1917 Speech to the Senate, 22 Jan.

82 Armed neutrality is ineffectual enough at best.
1917 Speech before a joint session of Congress, 2 Apr, to request a declaration that a state of war exists between Germany and the US.

83 The world must be made safe for democracy. Its peace must be planted on the tested foundations of political liberty.
1917 Speech before a joint session of Congress, 2 Apr, to request a declaration that a state of war exists between Germany and the US.

84 It is not an army that we must train for war; it is a nation.
1917 Speech, Washington, 12 May.

85 In this war, we demand nothing that is peculiar to ourselves; only that the world be made fit and safe to live in. The programme of the world's peace, therefore, is our programme.
1918 The 'Fourteen Points' speech to Congress, 8 Jan.

86 People and provinces must not be bartered about from sovereign to sovereign as if they were chattels, or pawns in a game. Self-determination is not a mere phrase. It is an imperative principle, which statesmen will henceforth ignore at their peril.
1918 Address to Congress, 11 Feb.

87 People call me an idealist. That is how I know that I am an American. America is the only idealistic nation in the world.
1919 Speech, Sioux Falls, 8 Sep.

Wimperis, Arthur 1874–1953

British screenwriter. He provided the screenplays for such movies as *The Private Life of Henry VIII* (1932) and *Mrs Miniver* (1942).

88 My dear fellow, a unique evening! I wouldn't have left a turn unstoned.
After watching a vaudeville show. Quoted in E Short *Fifty Years of Vaudeville* (1946).

Winchell, Walter 1897–1972

US theatre critic and actor. His publications included *Broadway Thro' a Keyhole* (1933).

89 A newspaperman, whose sweetheart ran away with an actor.
Defining a drama critic. Attributed.

Winfrey, Oprah 1954–

US actress, talk-show host and businesswoman. She was the first woman to own and produce her own talk show and the first African-American to own a large television studio.

90 I am a product of every other black woman before me who has done or said anything worthwhile. Recognizing that I am part of history is what allows me to soar.
Quoted in Brian Lanker *I Dream a World: Portraits of Black Women Who Changed America* (1989).

91 It felt like a new day.
2004 Her response to Barack Obama's speech at the Democratic convention, quoted on Oprah.com, 19 Jan. 2005.

92 What I learned at a very early age was that I was responsible for my life. And as I became more spiritually conscious, I learned that we all are responsible for ourselves, that you create your own reality by the way you think and therefore act. You cannot blame apartheid, your parents, your circumstances, because you are not your circumstances. You are your possibilities. If you know that, you can do anything.
2007 In *O Magazine*, Jan.

93 People never fail to amaze me. They face the unimaginable with a shot of grace and a rush of adrenaline; they steel their nerves; they summon their cool or anger or faith or whatever it takes to pull them through, and they go on to live another day.
2007 In *O Magazine*, Apr.

94 What other people label or might try to call failure, I have learned is just God's way of pointing you in a new direction.
2007 Speech at Howard University, 12 May.

95 Mr. Right's coming, but he's in Africa, and he's walking!
Quoted in Tuchy Palmieri, *Oprah, In Her Words: Our American Princess* (2008).

96 Be thankful for what you have—you'll end up having more.
Quoted in Tuchy Palmieri, *Oprah, In Her Words: Our American Princess* (2008).

97 We are better than the cynicism and the pessimism that is regurgitated throughout Washington and the 24-hour cable news cycle.
2013 Speech at Harvard University, 30 May.

Winkworth, Catherine 1827–78

English hymn writer and translator.

98 Now thank we all our God,
With heart and hands and voices,
Who wondrous things hath done,
In whom his world rejoices;
Who from our mother's arms
Hath blessed us on our way
With countless gifts of love,
And still is ours to-day.
1858 *Lyra Germanica* (translated from the original German of Martin Rinkart 'Nun danket alle Gott', c.1636).

Winner, Langdon 1944–

US academic and social critic with an interest in issues relating to technology and society.

99 The map of the world shows no country called Technopolis, yet in many ways we are already its citizens.
1986 *The Whale and the Reactor*.

Winner, Michael 1935–2013

British director. Credits include *Chato's Land* (1972), *Death Wish* (1974) and *The Wicked Lady* (1983).

1 Who says that actors are cattle? Show me a cow who can earn a million dollars a film.
Quoted by David Lewin in *Cinema Today*, 1 Jul 1970.

2 Keeping awake for ten weeks at a stretch.
1970 When asked what is the hardest part of directing. John Player Lecture, London, Sep.

3 A writer of talent needs only a typewriter and paper, a painter only needs brushes, canvas and paint, but I need a million dollars or more to be in business. That's a hell of a business to be in.
1974 In the *Observer Magazine*, 7 Jul.

4 I don't go to restaurants, I go to tables.
2004 In the *Observer*, 25 Jan.

5 A team effort is a lot of people doing what I say.
Attributed.

Winterson, Jeanette 1959–

English novelist. Her autobiographical first novel, *Oranges Are Not the Only Fruit* (1985), described her upbringing as an Evangelical Pentecostalist and her subsequent realization of her homosexuality. Subsequent novels include *Sexing the Cherry* (1989), *Written on the Body* (1992), *Art and Lies* (1994) and *The.PowerBook* (2000).

6 I asked why he was a priest and he said that if you have to work for anybody an absentee boss is best.
1987 *The Passion*, ch.1.

7 Adults talk about being happy because largely they are not.
1987 *The Passion*, ch.1.

8 I call him Jordan and it will do. He has no other name before or after. What was there to call him, fished as he was from the stinking Thames? A child can't be called Thames, no and not Nile either, for all his likeness to Moses. But I wanted to give him a river name, a name not bound to anything, just as the waters aren't bound to anything.
1989 *Sexing the Cherry*.

9 I have met a great many people on their way towards God and I wonder why they have chosen to look for him rather than themselves.
1989 *Sexing the Cherry*.

10 I don't hate men, I just wish they'd try harder. They all want to be heroes and all we want is for them to stay at home and help with the housework and the kids. That's not the kind of heroism they enjoy.
1989 *Sexing the Cherry*.

11 When I was born, my father wanted to drown me, but my mother persuaded him to let me live in disguise, to see if I could bring any wealth to the household.
2000 *The.PowerBook*.

12 In this life you have to be your own hero.
2000 *The.PowerBook*.

13 I don't know which is worse: to be wrongfully accused or mistakenly understood.
2007 *The Stone Gods*.

14 Only the impossible is worth the effort.
2007 *The Stone Gods*.

15 Pain is very often a maimed creature without a mouth.
2008 In *The Guardian*, 14 Nov.

16 The trouble with a book is that you never know what's in it until it's too late.
2011 *Why Be Happy When You Could Be Normal?*

17 Yes, the past is another country, but one that we can visit, and once there we can bring back the things we need.
2011 *Why Be Happy When You Could Be Normal?*

Wisdom, Sir Norman 1915–2010

English comedian, born in London. He made his stage debut in 1946 and his first film appearance in *Trouble in Store* (1953). This was followed by a string of successes including *Man of the Moment* (1955), *Just My Luck* (1958) and *Follow a Star* (1959).

18 They don't seem to realize that I have grown up and can get laughs without falling downstairs.
1991 Quoted in Richard Dacre *Trouble in Store: Norman Wisdom, a Career in Comedy* (1991).

Witte, Sergei Yulevich 1849–1915

Russian politician. As Minister of Finance (1892) he encouraged capitalism and industrialization, making Russia a leading industrial power. He became first Prime Minister (1905–6) in the Revolution of 1905, but was unable to satisfy either conservatives or liberals.

19 The world is in flames today for a cause that interests Russia first and foremost; a cause that is essentially the

cause of the Slavs, and which is of no concern to France or to England.
1914 Said to the French Ambassador, 10 Sep.

Wittgenstein, Ludwig Josef Johann 1889–1951

Austrian-born British philosopher who became one of the most influential and charismatic figures in British philosophy in this century. He was Professor of Philosophy at Cambridge (1939–47), and published only one book in his lifetime, the *Tractatus Logico-Philosophicus* (1921). Of his many posthumous publications, by far the most important is the *Philosophical Investigations* (1953).

20 *Was sich überhaupt sagen lässt, lässt sich klar sagen; und wovon man nicht reden kann, darüber muss man schweigen.*
What can be said at all can be said clearly; and whereof one cannot speak thereof one must be silent.
1921 *Tractatus Logico-Philosophicus*, preface (translated by Frank Ramsey).

21 *Die Welt ist alles, was der Fall ist.*
The world is all that is the case.
1921 *Tractatus Logico-Philosophicus*, prop.1 (translated by Pears and McGuinness).

22 *Die Welt ist die Gesamtheit der Tatsachen, nicht der Dinge.*
The world is the totality of facts, not of things.
1921 *Tractatus Logico-Philosophicus*, prop.1.1 (translated by Pears and McGuinness).

23 *Der Tod ist kein Ereignis des Lebens. Den Tod erlebt man nicht.*
Death is not an event in life: we do not live to experience death.
1921 *Tractatus Logico-Philosophicus*, prop 6.4311 (translated by Pears and McGuinness).

24 *Die Probleme werden gelöst, nicht durch Beibringen neuer Erfahrung, sondern durch Zusammenstellung des längst Bekannten. Die Philosophie ist ein Kampf gegen die Verhexung unseres Verstandes durch die Mittel unserer Sprache.*
The problems are solved, not by giving new information, but by arranging what we have always known. Philosophy is a battle against the bewitchment of our intelligence by means of language.
1945 *Philosophische Untersuchungen* (*Philosophical Investigations*), section 109 (translated by G E M Anscombe).

25 *Ein philosophisches Problem hat die Form: 'Ich kenne mich nicht aus'.*
A philosophical problem has the form: 'I don't know my way about'.
1945 *Philosophische Untersuchungen* (*Philosophical Investigations*), section 123 (translated by G E M Anscombe).

26 *Der Philosoph behandelt eine Frage wie eine Krankheit.*
The philosopher's treatment of a question is like the treatment of an illness.
1945 *Philosophische Untersuchungen* (*Philosophical Investigations*), section 255 (translated by G E M Anscombe).

27 *Was ist dein Ziel in der Philosophie? — 'Der Fliege den Ausweg aus dem Fliegenglas zeigen'.*
What is your aim in philosophy?—To show the fly the way out of the fly-bottle.
1945 *Philosophische Untersuchungen* (*Philosophical Investigations*), section 309 (translated by G E M Anscombe).

28 *Ein 'innerer Vorgang' bedarf äußerer Kriterien.*
An 'inner process' stands in need of outward criteria.
1945 *Philosophische Untersuchungen* (*Philosophical Investigations*), section 580 (translated by G E M Anscombe).

29 *Wenn ein Löwe sprechen könnte, wir könnten ihn nicht verstehen.*
If a lion could talk, we could not understand him.
1945 *Philosophische Untersuchungen* (*Philosophical Investigations*), pt.2, section 11 (translated by G E M Anscombe).

Wittig, Monique 1935–2003

French feminist novelist who questioned traditional gender stereotypes in her writing.

30 *L'expérience…d'une femme écrivain est complètement schizophrénique. Il faut toujours faire coupure entre les deux: d'une part, employer un langage qui n'est pas le nôtre…et la lutte qu'on mène sur un autre plan, qui tend à casser tout ça, à essayer de faire à travers et dans le langage autre chose.*
The experience…of the woman writer is completely schizophrenic. One is always torn between two approaches: on the one hand, to use a language that is not ours…and on the other, the battle one fights to break all this up, in order to do something else through and in language.
Quoted in Jean-François Josselin 'Lettre à Sapho' in *Le Nouvel Observateur* (1973).

Wodehouse, Sir P(elham) G(renville) also known as Plum 1881–1975

Anglo-American writer, renowned for his humorous stories of the English country aristocracy. He lived in the US after World War II, taking citizenship in 1955, but never shed his quintessential Englishness.

31 An English peer of the right sort can be bored nearer to the point where mortification sets in, without showing it, than anyone else in the world.
1915 *Something Fresh*, ch.3.

32 She fitted into my biggest arm-chair as if it had been built round her by someone who knew they were wearing arm-chairs tight about the hips that season.
1919 *My Man Jeeves*, 'Jeeves and the Unbidden Guest'.

33 What with excellent browsing and sluicing and cheery conversation and what-not, the afternoon passed quite happily.
1919 *My Man Jeeves*, 'Jeeves and the Unbidden Guest'.

34 'What ho!' I said.
'What ho!' said Motty.
'What ho! What ho!'
'What ho! What ho! What ho!'
After that it seemed rather difficult to go on with the conversation.
1919 *My Man Jeeves*, 'Jeeves and the Unbidden Guest'.

35 In this matter of shimmering into rooms the chappie is rummy to a degree… He moves from point to point with as little uproar as a jellyfish.
1919 *My Man Jeeves*, 'Jeeves and the Hard-Boiled Egg'.

36 Chumps always make the best husbands. When you marry, Sally, grab a chump. Tap his forehead first, and if it rings solid, don't hesitate. All the unhappy marriages come from the husbands having brains. What good are brains to a man? They only unsettle him.
1920 *The Adventures of Sally*, ch.10.

37 I turned to Aunt Agatha, whose demeanour was now rather like that of one who, picking daisies on the railway, has just caught the down express in the small of the back.
1923 *The Inimitable Jeeves*, ch.4.

38 Jeeves coughed one soft, low, gentle cough like a sheep with a blade of grass stuck in its throat.
1923 *The Inimitable Jeeves*, ch.13.

39 As a rule, you see, I'm not lugged into Family Rows. On the occasions when Aunt is calling to Aunt like mastodons bellowing across the primeval swamps...the clan has a tendency to ignore me. It's one of the advantages I get from being a bachelor—and, according to my nearest and dearest, practically a half-witted bachelor at that.
1923 *The Inimitable Jeeves*, ch.16.

40 It was my Uncle George who discovered that alcohol was a food well in advance of medical thought.
1923 *The Inimitable Jeeves*, ch.16.

41 'Alf Todd,' said Ukridge, soaring to an impressive burst of imagery, 'has about as much chance as a one-armed blind man in a dark room trying to shove a pound of melted butter into a wild cat's left ear with a red-hot needle.'
1924 *Ukridge*, ch.5.

42 Honoria...is one of those robust, dynamic girls with the muscles of a welter-weight and a laugh like a squadron of cavalry charging over a tin bridge.
1925 *Carry On, Jeeves*, 'The Rummy Affair of Old Biffy'.

43 He looked haggard and careworn, like a Borgia who has suddenly remembered that he has forgotten to shove the cyanide in the consommé, and the dinner-gong due any moment.
1925 *Carry On, Jeeves*, 'Clustering Around Young Bingo'.

44 To my daughter Leonora without whose never-failing sympathy and encouragement this book would have been finished in half the time.
1926 *The Heart of a Goof*, dedication.

45 The Right Hon was a tubby little chap who looked as if he had been poured into his clothes and had forgotten to say 'When!'
1930 *Very Good, Jeeves*, 'Jeeves and the Impending Doom'.

46 I have at last come to a momentous decision. I am going to give up my press-clippings agency. I find that even a favourable notice makes me feel sick nowadays, while an unfavourable one, even from a small provincial newspaper, puts me off my work for days.
1934 Letter to Denis Mackail, 15 Oct.

47 Into the face of the young man...had crept a look of furtive shame, the shifty, hangdog look which announces that an Englishman is about to talk French.
1935 *The Luck of the Bodkins*, ch.1.

48 It is never difficult to distinguish between a Scotsman with a grievance and a ray of sunshine.
1935 *Blandings Castle and Elsewhere*, 'The Custody of the Pumpkin'.

49 I can't do with any more education. I was full up years ago.
1938 *The Code of the Woosters*, ch.1.

50 He spoke with a certain what-is-it in his voice, and I could see that, if not actually disgruntled, he was far from being gruntled.
1938 *The Code of the Woosters*, ch.1.

51 Slice him where you like, a hellhound is always a hellhound.
1938 *The Code of the Woosters*, ch.1.

52 Roderick Spode? Big chap with a small moustache and the sort of eye that can open an oyster at sixty paces?
1938 *The Code of the Woosters*, ch.2.

53 He felt like a man who, chasing rainbows, has had one of them suddenly turn and bite him in the leg.
1940 *Eggs, Beans and Crumpets*, 'Anselm Gets His Chance'.

54 My war history has been a simple one. I have just sat in my chair and written all the time.
1946 Letter to Ira Gershwin, 24 Jan.

55 Ice formed on the butler's upper slopes.
1952 *Pigs Have Wings*, ch.5.

56 Has anyone ever seen a dramatic critic in the daytime? Of course not. They come out after dark, up to no good.
1955 In the *New York Mirror*, 27 May.

57 There'll always be an England, but who wants an England full of morons reading the *Express*?
1959 Letter to Denis Mackail, 22 Apr.

Wogan, Sir Terry 1938–
Irish broadcaster and writer.

58 People confuse longevity with merit. Look at Cliff Richard.
2004 In the *Observer*, 28 Mar.

59 Ah, to be able to recognise when the tide is going out, when to get off the beach.
2004 On deciding when to retire. In the *Observer*, 28 Mar.

Wolf, Naomi 1962–
US writer; she was a Rhodes Scholar in 1986. *The Beauty Myth* (1990) and *Fire with Fire* (1993) examine the relationship between patriarchal power and female beauty. Later books include the bestselling *The End of America* (2007).

60 The more legal and material hindrances women have broken through, the more strictly and heavily and cruelly images of female beauty have come to weigh upon them.
1990 *The Beauty Myth*, ch.1, 'The Beauty Myth'.

61 'Beauty' is a currency like the gold standard. Like any economy it is determined by politics, and in the modern age in the West it is the last, best belief system that keeps male domination intact.
1990 *The Beauty Myth*, ch.1, 'The Beauty Myth'.

62 When women breached the power structure in the 1980s...two economies finally merged. Beauty was no longer just a symbolic form of currency: it literally *became* money.
1990 *The Beauty Myth*, ch.2 'Work'.

63 Many of the signals that either stoke or diminish female desire have to do with the female brain's question: Is it safe here?
2012 *Vagina: A New Biography*.

Wolfe, James 1727–59
English general. He fought against the Jacobites at Culloden and was sent to Canada in 1756. Promoted to general after his

prominence in the capture of Louisberg, he commanded the British force which took Quebec.

64 Gentlemen, I would rather have written those lines than take Quebec tomorrow.
1759 To his troops, 12 Sep, after reciting Thomas Gray's 'Elegy, Written in a Country Churchyard' the evening before storming the ramparts of Quebec and dying a hero's death on the Plains of Abraham the following day. Quoted in Francis Parkman *Montcalm and Wolfe* (1884).

65 Now God be praised, I will die in peace.
1759 Last words, on hearing of the defeat of the French at Quebec. Quoted in J Knox *Historical Journal of the Campaigns in North America* (1909), ch.17.

Wolfe, Thomas Clayton 1900–38

US novelist. Unsuccessful in drama, he wrote a series of sprawling, uneven but often powerful novels, two of which were published posthumously.

66 Most of the time we think we're sick, it's all in the mind.
1929 Look Homeward, Angel, pt.1, ch.1.

67 'Where they got you stationed now, Luke?'... 'At the p-p-p-present time in Norfolk at the Navy base,' Luke answered, 'm-m-making the world safe for hypocrisy.'
1929 Look Homeward, Angel, pt.3, ch.36.

68 My efforts to cut out 50,000 words may sometimes result in my adding 75,000.
1929 Letter to his editor, Maxwell Perkins.

69 If a man has a talent and cannot use it, he has failed. If he has a talent and uses only half of it, he has partly failed. If he has a talent and learns somehow to use the whole of it, he has gloriously succeeded, and won a satisfaction and a triumph few men ever know.
The Web and the Rock (published 1939), ch.29.

70 It was a cruel city, but it was a lovely one, a savage city, yet it had such tenderness, a bitter, harsh, and violent catacomb of stone and steel and tunnelled rock, slashed savagely with light, and roaring, fighting a constant ceaseless warfare of men and machinery; and yet it was so sweetly and so delicately pulsed, as full of warmth, of passion, and of love, as it was full of hate.
1939 The Web and the Rock (published 1939), ch.30.

71 You Can't Go Home Again.
Title of novel (published 1940).

Wolfe, Tom (Thomas Kennerley) 1931–

US journalist and novelist. He was a leading proponent of the New Journalism, with a propensity for a racy style and attention-grabbing titles. His book on the astronauts, *The Right Stuff* (1979), was filmed, as was his novel *The Bonfire of the Vanities* (1987).

72 The Electric Kool-Aid Acid Test
1968 Title of book.

73 Radical chic invariably favors radicals who seem primitive, exotic and romantic.
1970 Radical Chic.

74 Not 'Seeing is Believing', you ninny, but 'Believing is Seeing'. For modern art has become completely literary: the paintings and other works exist only to illustrate the text.
1975 The Painted Word, ch.1.

75 The idea was to prove at every foot of the way up...that you were one of the elected and anointed ones who had the right stuff and could move higher and higher and even—ultimately, God willing, one day—that you might be able to join that special few at the very top, that elite who had the capacity to bring tears to men's eyes, the very Brotherhood of the Right Stuff itself.
1979 The Right Stuff.

76 A cult is a religion with no political power.
1980 In Our Time, ch.2.

77 From Bauhaus to Our House.
1981 Title of book.

78 Today educated people look upon traditional religious ties—Catholic, Episcopal, Presbyterian, Methodist, Baptist, Jewish—as matters of social pedigree. It is only art that they look upon religiously.
1984 'The Worship of Art: Notes on the New God', in *Harper's*, Oct.

79 Yes, the labour movement was truly religious, like Judaism itself. It was one of those things you believed in for all mankind and didn't care about for a second in your own life.
1987 The Bonfire of the Vanities, ch.8.

80 A liberal is a conservative who has been arrested.
1987 The Bonfire of the Vanities, ch.24.

81 Pornography was the great vice of the Seventies; plutography—the graphic depiction of the acts of the rich—is the great vice of the Eighties.
1988 In the *Sunday Times Magazine*, 10 Jan.

82 The Versailles of American corporate culture.
1992 Of Manhattan's Four Seasons restaurant, in the *New York Times*, 14 Nov.

83 In the year 2000, a Tolstoy or a Flaubert wouldn't have stood a chance in the United States.
2000 Hooking Up.

84 They were Archer's second set of children and paragons of contemporary teenage cynicism. They enjoyed setting fire to the tails of tender thoughts.
2004 I am Charlotte Simmons.

Wollstonecraft, Mary *also known as* Mrs Godwin 1759–97

Anglo-Irish feminist and writer. Her *Vindication of the Rights of Man* (1790) was followed by *Vindication of the Rights of Woman* (1792), advocating gender equality. After bearing an illegitimate daughter to Captain Gilbert Imlay (1794) she married political writer William Godwin (1797) but died on the birth of their daughter, Mary Wollstonecraft Shelley.

85 I now speak of the sex in general. Many individuals have more sense than their male relatives; and...some women govern their husbands without degrading themselves, because intellect will always govern.
1792 A Vindication of the Rights of Woman, introduction.

86 Men, in general, seem to employ their reason to justify prejudices, which they have imbibed, they can scarcely trace how, rather than root them out.
1792 A Vindication of the Rights of Woman, pt.1, ch.1.

87 Men, indeed, appear to me to act in a very unphilosophical manner when they try to secure the good conduct of women by attempting to keep them always in a state of childhood.
1792 A Vindication of the Rights of Woman, pt.1, ch.2.

88 Strengthen the female mind by enlarging it, and there will be an end to blind obedience; but as blind

obedience is ever sought for by power, tyrants and sensualists are in the right when they endeavour to keep women in the dark, because the former only want slaves, and the latter a play-thing.
1792 *A Vindication of the Rights of Woman*, pt.1, ch.2.

89 Gentleness, docility, and a spaniel-like affection are, on this ground, consistently recommended as the cardinal virtues of the sex; and, disregarding the arbitrary economy of nature, one writer has declared that it is masculine for a woman to be melancholy. She was created to be the toy of man, his rattle, and it must jingle in his ears, whenever, dismissing reason, he chooses to be amused.
1792 *A Vindication of the Rights of Woman*, pt.1, ch.2.

90 Liberty is the mother of virtue, and if women be, by their very constitution, slaves, and not allowed to breathe the sharp invigorating air of freedom, they must ever languish like exotics, and be reckoned beautiful flaws in nature.
1792 *A Vindication of the Rights of Woman*, pt.1, ch.2.

91 The *divine right* of husbands, like the divine right of kings, may it is to be hoped, in this enlightened age, be contested without danger.
1792 *A Vindication of the Rights of Woman*, pt.1, ch.3.

92 A king is always a king—and a woman always a woman; his authority and her sex, ever stand between them and rational converse.
1792 *A Vindication of the Rights of Woman*, pt.1, ch.4.

93 I do not wish them to have power over men; but over themselves.
1792 Of women. *A Vindication of the Rights of Woman*, pt.1, ch.4.

94 Necessity never makes prostitution the business of men's lives; though numberless are the women who are thus rendered systematically vicious.
1792 *A Vindication of the Rights of Woman*, pt.1, ch.4.

95 Let woman share the rights and she will emulate the virtues of man, for she must grow more perfect when emancipated.
1792 *A Vindication of the Rights of Woman*, pt.1, ch.13.

Wolpert, Lewis 1929–
British developmental biologist.

96 The physics of motion provides one of the clearest examples of the counter-intuitive and unexpected nature of science.
1992 *The Unnatural Nature of Science*.

Wolstenholme, Kenneth 1920–2002
English football commentator. He broadcast for the BBC from 1948 to 1971, covering 22 FA Cup finals and five World Cups.

97 There are people on the pitch…they think it's all over…it is now!
1966 Radio commentary on the last goal of the World Cup final, in which England beat West Germany at Wembley.

Wood, Victoria 1953–
English playwright, lyricist and comedienne. Her comic plays include *Talent* (1979) and *Happy Since I Met You* (1981), and her television work is collected in *Mens Sana in Thingummy Doodah* (1991).

98 Jogging is for people who aren't intelligent enough to watch Breakfast TV.
1989 Victoria Wood, television series. Published in *Mens Sana in Thingummy Doodah* (1991).

99 LILL: My massage was marvellous. I feel really relaxed. And my masseur, Harold—
VICTORIA: You can't have a masseur called Harold. It's like having a member of the Royal Family called Ena.
1989 Victoria Wood, television series. Published in *Mens Sana in Thingummy Doodah* (1991).

Woodcock, George 1912–95
Canadian writer, poet, social critic and biographer. He also wrote several travel books. He has been described as a philosophical anarchist.

1 Well-founded fear, which takes one through the valley of the shadow of death without abandoning one there, is what makes the worst of worse journeys; the situation is made all the more intense when the fear is somehow mingled with delight.
'My Worst Journeys', collected in Keath Fraser (ed) *Worst Journeys: The Picador Book of Travel* (1991).

Woodman, Marion 1928–
Canadian therapist and author.

2 To strive for perfection is to kill love because perfection does not recognize humanity.
1982 *Addition to Perfection: The Still Unravished Bride*.

Woodroofe, Thomas 1899–1978
British naval officer.

3 The whole fleet's lit up. When I say 'lit up', I mean by fairy lamps.
1937 BBC radio commentary of the Spithead review, 20 May, Britain's first live outside broadcast. 'Lit up' was a common euphemism for 'drunk'.

Woods, Donald 1933–2001
South African editor and Black civil rights campaigner.

4 When I left South Africa, I arrogantly predicted that within seven years, apartheid would be gone. It has taken a bit longer than that.
1991 BBC TV broadcast, Feb.

Woods, Tiger 1975–
US golfer. He has won numerous events, including the US Masters (1997, 2001, 2002, 2005), the British Open (2000, 2005, 2006) and the US Open (2000, 2002, 2008).

5 Growing up, I came up with this name: I'm a Cablinasian.
1997 Explaining his dissatisfaction with the term 'African-American' to describe his own Caucasian, African-American, Native American, Chinese and Thai ancestry. In an interview with Oprah Winfrey, 21 Apr.

6 My dad once told me: no matter what anyone says or writes, really, none of those people have to hit your four-foot putt. You have to go do it yourself.
2001 *Quotable Tiger*.

7 Hockey is a sport for white men. Basketball is a sport for black men. Golf is a sport for white men dressed like black pimps.
Attributed.

Woodsworth, James Shaver 1874–1942

Canadian politician, socialist and pacifist. An MP from 1921, in 1932 he founded the Co-operative Commonwealth Federation, serving as its chairman and parliamentary leader.

8 I take my place with the children.
1939 Casting the sole dissenting voice to ratify Canada's entry into World War II, in the House of Commons, Ottawa, 9 Sep.

Wooldridge, Adrian 1959–

English journalist with *The Economist* (London).

9 America has mitigated poverty by massively increasing pauperism.
1995 'Damned Statistics', in the *Wall Street Journal*, 27 Jul.

Woolf, (Adeline) Virginia née Stephen 1882–1941

English novelist, critic and essayist. Daughter of Sir Leslie Stephen and sister of Vanessa Bell, she married Leonard Woolf and in 1917 they formed the Hogarth Press. Her experimental novels include *Mrs. Dalloway* (1925) and *To the Lighthouse* (1927). *A Room of One's Own* (1929) is a feminist classic. She committed suicide by drowning.

10 Life…is a luminous halo, a semi-transparent envelope surrounding us from the beginning of consciousness to the end.
1919 'Modern Fiction'.

11 Each had his past shut in him like the leaves of a book known to him by heart; and his friends could only read the title.
1922 Jacob's Room, ch.5.

12 It's not catastrophes, murders, deaths, diseases, that age and kill us; it's the way people look and laugh, and run up the steps of omnibuses.
1922 Jacob's Room, ch.6.

13 Never did I read such tosh.
1922 On James Joyce's *Ulysses*. Letter to Lytton Strachey, 24 Apr.

14 I believe that all novels…deal with character, and that it is to express character—not to preach doctrines, sing songs, or celebrate the glories of the British Empire, that the form of the novel, so clumsy, verbose, and undramatic, so rich, elastic, and alive, has been evolved.
1924 'Mr Bennett and Mrs Brown'.

15 Life itself, every moment of it, every drop of it, here, this instant, now, in the sun, in Regent's Park, was enough. Too much, indeed.
1925 Mrs Dalloway.

16 It is vain and foolish to talk of knowing Greek.
1925 The Common Reader, 'On Not Knowing Greek'.

17 The interest in life does not lie in what people do, nor even in their relations to each other, but largely in the power to communicate with a third party, antagonistic, enigmatic, yet perhaps persuadable, which one may call life in general.
1925 The Common Reader, 'On Not Knowing Greek'.

18 For the self-centred and self-limited writers have a power denied the more catholic and broad-minded… Nothing issues from their minds which has not been marked with their own impress.
1925 The Common Reader, 'Jane Eyre and Wuthering Heights'.

19 A good essay must have this permanent quality about it; it must draw its curtain round us, but it must be a curtain that shuts us in not out.
1925 The Common Reader, 'The Modern Essay'.

20 We are nauseated by the sight of trivial personalities decomposing in the eternity of print.
1925 The Common Reader, 'The Modern Essay'.

21 *Middlemarch*, the magnificent book which with all its imperfections is one of the few English novels for grown up people.
1925 The Common Reader, 'George Eliot'.

22 London is enchanting. I step out upon a tawny coloured magic carpet, it seems, and get carried into beauty without raising a finger… People pop in and out, lightly, divertingly like rabbits; and I look down Southampton Row, wet as a seal's back or red and yellow with sunshine, and watch the omnibuses going and coming and hear the old crazy organs. One of these days I will write about London, and how it takes up the private life and carries it on, without any effort.
1926 Diary entry, 26 May.

23 So that is marriage, Lily thought, a man and a woman looking at a girl throwing a ball.
1927 To the Lighthouse, pt.1, ch.13.

24 She faded…became more inconspicuous than ever, in her little grey dress.
1927 To the Lighthouse, pt.1, ch.17.

25 One cannot think well, love well, sleep well, if one has not dined well.
1929 A Room of One's Own, ch.1.

26 A woman must have money and a room of her own if she is to write fiction.
1929 A Room of One's Own, ch.1.

27 Women have served all these centuries as looking-glasses possessing the magic and delicious power of reflecting the figure of man at twice its natural size.
1929 A Room of One's Own, ch.2.

28 I would venture to guess that Anon, who wrote so many poems without signing them, was often a woman.
1929 A Room of One's Own, ch.3.

29 Literature is strewn with the wreckage of men who have minded beyond reason the opinion of others.
1929 A Room of One's Own, ch.3.

30 It is obvious that the values of women differ very often from the values which have been made by the other sex… Yet it is the masculine values that prevail.
1929 A Room of One's Own, ch.4.

31 We think back through our mothers if we are women.
1929 A Room of One's Own, ch.4.

32 For there is a spot the size of a shilling at the back of the head which one can never see for oneself. It is one of the good offices that sex can discharge for sex—to describe that spot.
1929 A Room of One's Own, ch.5.

33 For all the dinners are cooked; the plates and cups washed; the children sent to school and gone out into the world. Nothing remains of it all. All has vanished. No biography or history has a word to say about it.
1929 A Room of One's Own, ch.5.

34 I am not trying to tell a story. Yet perhaps it might be done in that way. A mind thinking. They might be islands of light—islands in the stream that I am trying to convey; life itself going on.
1929 Diary entry, 28 May.

35 Killing the Angel in the House was part of the occupation of a woman writer.
1931 'Professions for Women', lecture to the National Society for Women's Service, 21 Jan. Woolf's solution was to throw the inkpot at the Angel (the embodiment of stereotyped Victorian femininity) whenever she appeared.

36 Things have dropped from me. I have outlived certain desires; I have lost friends, some by death—Percival—others through sheer inability to cross the street.
1931 *The Waves*.

37 Yes, always keep the Classics at hand to prevent flop.
1937 Diary entry, 23 Jun.

38 Somewhere, everywhere, now hidden, now apparent in whatever is written down, is the form of a human being. If we seek to know him, are we idly occupied?
The Captain's Death Bed, 'Reading' (published 1950).

39 The poet gives us his essence, but prose takes the mould of the body and mind entire.
The Captain's Death Bed, 'Reading' (published 1950).

Woollcott, Alexander Humphreys 1887–1943

US critic, writer, actor and broadcaster. He became theatre critic for the *New York Times* in 1914 and subsequently became one of the celebrated Algonquin Round Table of wits and literary figures. Noted for his biting humour, he was the inspiration for Kaufman and Hart's play *The Man Who Came to Dinner*.

40 She is so odd a blend of Little Nell and Lady Macbeth. It is not so much the familiar phenomenon of a hand of steel in a velvet glove as a lacy sleeve with a bottle of vitriol concealed in its folds.
1934 Of Dorothy Parker. *While Rome Burns*, 'Our Mrs Parker'.

41 I have no need of your God-damned sympathy. I only wish to be entertained by some of your grosser reminiscences.
1942 Letter to Rex O'Malley. Quoted in Samuel Adams *Alexander Woollcott* (1945), ch.34.

42 A broker is a man who takes your fortune and runs it into a shoestring.
Quoted in Samuel Adams *Alexander Woollcott* (1945), ch.15.

43 Harold Ross...had a contempt for anything he didn't understand, which was practically everything.
Quoted in James Thurber *The Years With Ross* (1959), ch.15.

44 All the things I really like to do are either illegal, immoral or fattening.
Quoted in R Drennan *Wit's End* (1968).

45 The play left a taste of lukewarm parsnip juice.
Play review. Quoted in H Techmann *Smart Alex* (1976).

46 My doctor forbids me to play, unless I win.
Of croquet. Quoted in Colin Jarman *The Guinness Dictionary of Sports Quotations* (1990).

47 It is no game for the soft of sinew and the gentle of spirit. The higher and dirtier croquet-player can use the guile of a cobra and the inhumanity of a boa constrictor.
Quoted in Colin Jarman *The Guinness Dictionary of Sports Quotations* (1990).

48 Always a godfather, never a god!
On serving as godfather at a christening celebration for the 19th time. Attributed.

49 Just what God would do if he had the money.
On being shown round Moss Hart's splendid country retreat. Attributed.

50 The scenery was beautiful, but the actors got in front of it.
Play review.

Wordsworth, William 1770–1850

English poet. At first given to agnosticism and a revolutionary passion for social justice, he then turned to exploring the lives of humble people living in contact with nature. He succeeded Robert Southey as Poet Laureate in 1843.

51 Now, in this blank of things, a harmony,
Home-felt, and home-created, comes to heal
That grief for which the senses still supply
Fresh food.
1786 'Calm is all nature as a resting wheel', l.7–10. Published in the *Morning Post*, 13 Feb. 1802.

52 In this universe,
Where the least things control the greatest, where
The faintest breath that breathes can move a world.
1795–6 Oswald. *The Borderers*, act 3, l.1562–4 (published 1842).

53 These beauteous forms,
Through a long absence, have not been to me
As is a landscape to a blind man's eye:
But oft, in lonely rooms, and 'mid the din
Of towns and cities, I have owed to them,
In hours of weariness, sensations sweet,
Felt in the blood, and felt along the heart.
1798 'Lines composed a few miles above Tintern Abbey, on revisiting the banks of the Wye', l.22–8.

54 That best portion of a good man's life,
His little, nameless, unremembered, acts
Of kindness and of love.
1798 'Lines composed a few miles above Tintern Abbey, on revisiting the banks of the Wye', l.33–5.

55 For I have learned
To look on nature, not as in the hour
Of thoughtless youth; but hearing often-times
The still, sad music of humanity,
Nor harsh nor grating, though of ample power
To chasten and subdue. And I have felt
A presence that disturbs me with the joy
Of elevated thoughts; a sense sublime
Of something far more deeply interfused,
Whose dwelling is the light of setting suns,
And the round ocean and the living air,
And the blue sky, and in the mind of man.
1798 'Lines composed a few miles above Tintern Abbey, on revisiting the banks of the Wye', l.88–99.

56 Therefore am I still
A lover of the meadows and the woods,
And mountains; and of all that we behold
From this green earth; of all the mighty world
Of eye, and ear,—both what they half create
And what perceive.
1798 'Lines composed a few miles above Tintern Abbey, on revisiting the banks of the Wye', l.102–6.

57 Away we go—and what care we
For treasons, tumults, and for wars?

We are as calm in our delight
As is the crescent moon so bright
Among the scattered stars.
1798 'Peter Bell', prologue, stanza 5 (published 1819).

58 Books! 'tis a dull and endless strife:
Come, hear the woodland linnet
How sweet his music! on my life
There's more of wisdom in it.
1798 'The Tables Turned', stanza 3.

59 One impulse from a vernal wood
May teach you more of man,
Of moral evil and of good,
Than all the sages can.

Sweet is the lore which Nature brings;
Our meddling intellect
Mis-shapes the beauteous forms of things:—
We murder to dissect.

Enough of science and of art;
Close up those barren leaves;
Come forth and bring with you a heart
That watches and receives.
1798 'The Tables Turned', stanzas 6–8.

60 I heard a thousand blended notes,
While in a grove I sate reclined,
In that sweet mood when pleasant thoughts
Bring sad thoughts to the mind.
1798 'Lines Written in Early Spring', stanza 1.

61 To her fair works did Nature link
The human soul that through me ran;
And much it grieved my heart to think
What man has made of man.
1798 'Lines Written in Early Spring', stanza 2.

62 She dwelt among the untrodden ways
Beside the springs of Dove,
A maid whom there were none to praise
And very few to love:

A violet by a mossy stone
Half hidden from the eye!
—Fair as a star, when only one
Is shining in the sky.

She lived unknown, and few could know
When Lucy ceased to be;
But she is in her grave, and, oh,
The difference to me!
1799 'She dwelt among the untrodden ways', complete poem (published 1800).

63 Three years she grew in sun and shower,
The Nature said, 'A lovelier flower
On earth was never sown;
This Child I to myself will take;
She shall be mine, and I will make
A Lady of my own.'
1799 'Three Years she grew in sun and shower', stanza 1 (published 1800).

64 A slumber did my spirit seal;
I had no human fears:
She seemed a thing that could not feel
The touch of earthly years.

No motion has she now, no force;
She neither hears nor sees;
Rolled round in earth's diurnal course
With rocks, and stones and trees.
1799 'A slumber did my spirit seal', complete poem (published 1800).

65 Physician art thou?—one, all eyes,
Philosopher!—a fingering slave,
One that would peep and botanize
Upon his mother's grave?
1799 'A Poet's Epitaph', stanza 5 (published 1800).

66 One to whose smooth-rubbed soul can cling
Nor form, nor feeling, great or small;
A reasoning, self-sufficing thing,
An intellectual All-in-all!
1799 'A Poet's Epitaph', stanza 8 (published 1800).

67 Shut close the door; press down the latch;
Sleep in thy intellectual crust;
Nor lose ten tickings of thy watch
Near this unprofitable dust.
1799 'A Poet's Epitaph', stanza 9 (published 1800).

68 In common truths that round us lie
Some random truths he can impart,—
The harvest of a quiet eye
That broods and sleeps on his own heart.
1799 'A Poet's Epitaph', stanza 13 (published 1800).

69 Wisdom and Spirit of the universe!
Thou soul, that art the eternity of thought,
And giv'st to forms and images a breath
And everlasting motion.
1799 'Influence of Natural Objects', l.1–4 (published in *The Friend* 28 Dec 1809).

70 Leaving the tumultuous throng,
To cut across the reflex of a star;
Image that, flying still before me, gleamed
Upon the glassy plain.
1799 'Influence of Natural Objects', l.49–52 (published in *The Friend* 28 Dec 1809).

71 When we had given our bodies to the wind,
And all the shadowy banks on either side
Came sweeping through the darkness, spinning still
The rapid line of motion, then at once
Have I, reclining back upon my heels,
Stopped short; yet still the solitary cliffs
Wheeled by me—even as if the earth had rolled
With visible motion her diurnal round!
1799 'Influence of Natural Objects', l.53–60 (published in *The Friend* 28 Dec 1809).

72 Oh there is blessing in this gentle breeze,
A visitant that while it fans my cheek
Doth seem half conscious of the joy it brings
From the green fields, and from yon azure sky.
Whate'er its mission, the soft breeze can come
To none more grateful than to me; escaped
From the vast city, where I long had pined
A discontented sojourner: now free,
Free as a bird to settle where I will.
1799–1805 *The Prelude*, bk.1, l.1–9 (published 1850).

73 I, methought, while the sweet breath of heaven
Was blowing on my body, felt within
A correspondent breeze, that gently moved
With quickening virtue, but is now become

A tempest, a redundant energy,
Vexing its own creation.
1799–1805 *The Prelude*, bk.1, l.33–8 (published 1850).

74 Either still I find
Some imperfection in the chosen theme,
Or see of absolute accomplishment
Much wanting, so much wanting, in myself,
That I recoil and droop, and seek repose
In listlessness from vain perplexity,
Unprofitably travelling towards the grave.
1799–1805 *The Prelude*, bk.1, l.261–7 (published 1850).

75 Fair seed-time had my soul, and I grew up
Fostered alike by beauty and by fear.
1799–1805 *The Prelude*, bk.1, l.301–2 (published 1850).

76 Dust as we are, the immortal spirit grows
Like harmony in music; there is a dark
Inscrutable workmanship that reconciles
Discordant elements, makes them cling together
In one society.
1799–1805 *The Prelude*, bk.1, l.340–4 (published 1850).

77 Then, the calm
And dead still water lay upon my mind
Even with a weight of pleasure, and the sky,
Never before so beautiful, sank down
Into my heart, and held me like a dream.
1799–1805 *The Prelude*, bk.2, l.70–4 (published 1850).

78 I was taught to feel, perhaps too much,
The self-sufficing power of Solitude.
1799–1805 *The Prelude*, bk.2, l.76–7 (published 1850).

79 Science appears but what in truth she is,
Not as our glory and our absolute boast,
But as a succedaneum, and a prop
To our infirmity.
1799–1805 *The Prelude*, bk.2, l.212–15 (published 1850).

80 That false secondary power
By which we multiply distinctions, then
Deem that our puny boundaries are things
That we perceive, and not that we have made.
1799–1805 *The Prelude*, bk.2, l.216–19 (published 1850).

81 A babe, by intercourse of touch
I held mute dialogues with my Mother's heart.
1799–1805 *The Prelude*, bk.2, l.267–8 (published 1850).

82 From my pillow, looking forth by light
Of moon or favouring stars, I could behold
The antechapel where the statue stood
Of Newton with his prism and silent face,
The marble index of a mind for ever
Voyaging through strange seas of Thought alone.
1799–1805 *The Prelude*, bk.3, l.58–63 (published 1850).

83 There's not a man
That lives who hath not known his god-like hours.
1799–1805 *The Prelude*, bk.3, l.190–1 (published 1850).

84 Visionary power
Attends the motions of the viewless winds,
Embodied in the mystery of words.
1799–1805 *The Prelude*, bk.5, l.595–7 (published 1850).

85 Even forms and substances are circumfused
By that transparent veil with light divine,
And, through the turnings intricate of verse,
Present themselves as objects recognised,
In flashes, and with glory not their own.
1799–1805 *The Prelude*, bk.5, l.601–5 (published 1850).

86 An open place it was, and overlooked,
From high, the sullen water far beneath,
On which a dull red image of the moon
Lay bedded, changing oftentimes its form
Like an uneasy snake.
1799–1805 *The Prelude*, bk.6, l.703–7 (published 1850).

87 In the very world, which is the world
Of all of us,—the place where, in the end,
We find our happiness, or not at all!
1799–1805 *The Prelude*, bk.11, l.142–4 (published 1850).

88 I shook the habit off
Entirely and for ever, and again
In Nature's presence stood, as now I stand,
A sensitive being, a *creative* soul.
1799–1805 *The Prelude*, bk.12, l.204–7 (published 1850).

89 A balance, an ennobling interchange
Of action from without and from within;
The excellence, pure function, and best power
Both of the object seen, and eye that sees.
1799–1805 *The Prelude*, bk.13, l.375–8 (published 1850).

90 The thought of death sits easy on the man
Who has been born and dies among the mountains.
c.1800 The Priest. 'The Brothers', l.182–3.

91 The moving accident is not my trade;
To freeze the blood I have no ready arts:
'Tis my delight, alone in summer shade,
To pipe a simple song for thinking hearts.
1800 'Hart-Leap Well', part 2, l.97–100.

92 I travelled among unknown men
In lands beyond the sea;
Nor England! did I know till then
What love I bore to thee.
1801 'I Travelled Among Unknown Men', stanza 1 (published 1807).

93 Poetry is the spontaneous overflow of powerful feelings: it takes its origin from emotion recollected in tranquillity.
1802 Preface to *Lyrical Ballads* (2nd ed. 1802; *Lyrical Ballads* first published 1798, preface added 1800, enlarged 1802).

94 Milton! thou shouldst be living at this hour:
England hath need of thee: she is a fen
Of stagnant waters: altar, sword and pen,
Fireside, the heroic wealth of hall and bower,
Have forfeited their ancient English dower
Of inward happiness. We are selfish men;
Oh! raise us up, return to us again;
And give us manners, virtue, freedom, power.
Thy soul was like a star, and dwelt apart;
Thou hadst a voice whose sound was like the sea:
Pure as the naked heavens, majestic, free,
So didst thou travel on life's common way,
In cheerful godliness; and yet thy heart
The lowliest duties on herself did lay.
1802 'Milton! thou shouldst be living at this hour', complete poem (published 1807).

95 Thrice welcome, darling of the Spring
Even yet thou are to me
No bird, but an invisible thing,
A voice, a mystery.
1802 'To the Cuckoo', stanza 4 (published 1807).

96 It is a beauteous evening, calm and free,
The holy time is quiet as a nun
Breathless with adoration; the broad sun
Is sinking down in its tranquillity;
The gentleness of heaven broods o'er the sea:
Listen! the mighty being is awake,
And doth with his eternal motion make
A sound like thunder—everlastingly.
1802 'It is a beauteous evening calm and free', l.1–8 (published 1807).

97 With little here to do or see
Of things that in the great world be,
Sweet Daisy! oft I talk to thee
For thou art worthy,
Thou unassuming commonplace
Of Nature, with that homely face,
And yet with something of a grace
Which love makes for thee!
1802 'To the Daisy', stanza 1 (published 1807).

98 My heart leaps up when I behold
A rainbow in the sky:
So was it when my life began;
So is it now I am a man;
So be it when I shall grow old,
Or let me die!
The Child is father of the Man;
And I could wish my days to be
Bound each to each by natural piety.
1802 'My heart leaps up when I behold', complete poem (published 1807).

99 My whole life have I lived in pleasant thought,
As if life's business were a summer mood;
As if all needful things would come unsought
To genial faith, still rich in genial good.
1802 'Resolution and Independence', stanza 6 (published 1807).

1 I thought of Chatterton, the marvellous boy,
The sleepless soul that perished in his pride.
Of him who walked in glory and in joy
Following his plough along the mountainside:
By our own spirits are we deified.
We poets in our youth begin in gladness;
But thereof comes in the end despondency and madness.
1802 Of the poet Thomas Chatterton, who committed suicide at the age of 17. 'Resolution and Independence', stanza 7 (published 1807).

2 The fear that kills;
And hope that is unwilling to be fed.
1802 'Resolution and Independence', stanza 17 (published 1807).

3 Earth hath not anything to show more fair:
Dull would he be of soul who could pass by
A sight so touching in its majesty:
This City now doth like a garment wear
The beauty of the morning; silent, bare,
Ships, towers, domes, theatres, and to the sky;
All bright and glittering in the smokeless air.
Never did sun more beautifully steep
In his first splendour, valley, rock, or hill;
Ne'er saw I, never felt, a calm so deep!
The river glideth at his own sweet will;
Dear God! the very houses seem asleep;
And all that mighty heart is lying still!
1802 Of London. 'Composed upon Westminster Bridge', complete poem. (Published 1807).

4 Once did she hold the gorgeous East in fee,
And was the safeguard of the West: the worth
Of Venice did not fall below her birth,
Venice, the eldest child of Liberty.
1802 Of Venice. 'On the Extinction of the Venetian Republic', l.1–4 (published 1807).

5 There was a time when meadow, grove, and stream,
The earth, and every common sight,
To me did seem
Apparelled in celestial light,
The glory and the freshness of a dream.
It is not now as it hath been of yore;—
Turn whereso'er I may,
By night or day,
The things which I have seen I now can see no more.
c.1802–1803 'Ode. Intimations of Immortality from Recollections of Early Childhood', stanza 1 (published 1807).

6 Thou Child of Joy,
Shout round me, let me hear thy shouts.
c.1802–1803 'Ode. Intimations of Immortality from Recollections of Early Childhood', stanza 3 (published 1807).

7 But there's a tree, of many, one,
A single field which I have looked upon,
Both of them speak of something that is gone:
The pansy at my feet
Doth the same tale repeat:
Whither is fled the visionary gleam?
Where is it now, the glory and the dream?
c.1802–1803 'Ode. Intimations of Immortality from Recollections of Early Childhood', stanza 4 (published 1807).

8 Our birth is but a sleep and a forgetting:
The soul that rises with us, our life's star,
Hath had elsewhere its setting,
And cometh from afar:
Not in entire forgetfulness
And not in utter nakedness,
But trailing clouds of glory do we come
From God, who is our home:
Heaven lies about us in our infancy!
Shades of the prison-house begin to close
Upon the growing boy,
But he beholds the light, and whence it flows,
He sees it in his joy;
The youth, who daily farther from the east
Must travel, still is nature's priest,
And by the vision splendid
Is on his way attended;
At length the man perceives it die away,
And fade into the light of common day.
c.1802–1803 'Ode. Intimations of Immortality from Recollections of Early Childhood', stanza 5 (published 1807).

9 O joy! that in our embers
Is something that doth live,
That nature yet remembers
What was so fugitive!
c.1802–1803 'Ode. Intimations of Immortality from Recollections of Early Childhood', stanza 9 (published 1807).

10 Those obstinate questionings
Of sense and outward things,
Fallings from us, vanishings;

Blank misgivings of a creature
Moving about in worlds not realised,
High instincts before which our mortal nature
Did tremble like a guilty thing surprised.
c.1802–1803 'Ode. Intimations of Immortality from Recollections of Early Childhood', stanza 9 (published 1807).

11 Our noisy years seem moments in the being
Of the eternal silence: truths that wake,
To perish never:
Which neither listlessness, nor mad endeavour,
Nor man nor boy,
Nor all that is at enmity with joy,
Can utterly abolish or destroy!
Hence in a season of calm weather,
Though inland far we be,
Our souls have sight of that immortal sea
Which brought us hither,
Can in a moment travel thither,
And see the children sport upon the shore,
And hear the mighty waters rolling evermore.
c.1802–1803 'Ode. Intimations of Immortality from Recollections of Early Childhood', stanza 9 (published 1807).

12 Though nothing can bring back the hour
Of splendour in the grass, of glory in the flower;
We will grieve not.
c.1802–1803 'Ode. Intimations of Immortality from Recollections of Early Childhood', stanza 10 (published 1807).

13 Thanks to the human heart by which we live,
Thanks to its tenderness, its joys, and fears,
To me the meanest flower that blows can give
Thoughts that do often lie too deep for tears.
c.1802–1803 'Ode. Intimations of Immortality from Recollections of Early Childhood', stanza 11 (published 1807).

14 Let beeves and home-bred kine partake
The sweets of Burn-mill meadow;
The swan on still St Mary's Lake
Float double, swan and shadow!
We will not see them; will not go,
To-day, nor yet to-morrow;
Enough if in our hearts we know
There's such a place as Yarrow.

Be Yarrow stream unseen, unknown;
It must, or we shall rue it:
We have a vision of our own,
Ah! why should we undo it?
The treasured dreams of times long past,
We'll keep them, winsome Marrow!
For when we're there, although 'tis fair,
'Twill be another Yarrow!
1803 'Yarrow Unvisited', stanzas 6–7 (published 1807).

15 For thou wert still the poor man's stay,
The poor man's heart, the poor man's hand;
And all the oppressed, who wanted strength,
Had thine at their command.
1803 'Rob Roy's Grave', l. 109–12 (published 1807).

16 Thy friends are exultations, agonies,
And love, and man's unconquerable mind.
1803 'To Toussaint L'Ouverture', l.13–14 (published in the *Morning Post* 2 Feb).

17 What, you are stepping westward?
1803–5 'Stepping Westward', l.1 (published 1807).

18 Behold her, single in the field,
Yon solitary Highland Lass!
Reaping and singing by herself;
Stop here, or gently pass!
1803–5 'The Solitary Reaper', l.1–4 (published 1807).

19 She was a Phantom of delight
When first she gleamed upon my sight;
A lovely apparition sent
To be a moment's ornament.
1804 'She was a Phantom of delight', l.1–4 (published 1807).

20 And now I see with eye serene
The very pulse of the machine;
A being breathing thoughtful breath,
A traveller between life and death;
The reason firm, the temperate will,
Endurance, foresight, strength, and skill;
A perfect woman, nobly planned,
To warn, to comfort, and command.
1804 'She was a Phantom of delight', l.21–8 (published 1807).

21 Chains tie us down by land and sea;
And wishes, vain as mine, may be
All that is left to comfort thee.
1804 'The Affliction of Margaret', stanza 8 (published 1807).

22 My apprehensions come in crowds;
I dread the rustling of the grass;
The very shadows of the clouds
Have power to shake me as they pass.
1804 'The Affliction of Margaret', stanza 10 (published 1807).

23 Oh! pleasant exercise of hope and joy!
For mighty were the auxiliars which then stood
Upon our side, we who were strong in love!
Bliss it was in that dawn to be alive,
But to be young was very heaven!
1804 'The French Revolution as it appeared to enthusiasts at its commencement', l.1–5 (published in *The Friend*, 26 Oct. 1809).

24 I wandered lonely as a cloud
That floats on high o'er vales and hills,
When all at once I saw a crowd,
A host, of golden daffodils;
Beside the lake, beneath the trees,
Fluttering and dancing in the breeze.
1804 'I wandered lonely as a cloud', stanza 1 (published 1807).

25 Continuous as the stars that shine
And twinkle on the milky way
They stretched in never-ending line
Along the margin of a bay:
Ten thousand saw I at a glance,
Tossing their heads in sprightly dance.
1804 'I wandered lonely as a cloud', stanza 2 (published 1807).

26 The waves beside them danced; but they
Out-did the sparkling waves in glee:
A poet could not but be gay,
In such a jocund company:
I gazed—and gazed—but little thought
What wealth the show to me had brought.
1804 'I wandered lonely as a cloud', stanza 3 (published 1807).

27 For oft, when on my couch I lie
In vacant or in pensive mood,
They flash upon that inward eye
Which is the bliss of solitude;

And then my heart wih pleasure fills,
And dances with the daffodils.
1804 'I wandered lonely as a cloud', stanza 4 (published 1807).

28 If mine had been the painter's hand,
To express what then I saw; and add the gleam,
The light that never was, on sea or land,
The consecration, and the poet's dream.
1805 'Elegiac Stanzas: suggested by a picture of Peele Castle in a storm', stanza 4 (published 1807).

29 Not for a moment could I now behold
A smiling sea, and be what I have been.
1805 'Elegiac Stanzas: suggested by a picture of Peele Castle in a storm', stanza 10 (published 1807).

30 The world is too much with us; late and soon,
Getting and spending we lay waste our powers:
Little we see in nature that is ours;
We have given our hearts away, a sordid boon!
The sea that bares her bosom to the moon;
The winds that will be howling at all hours,
And are up-gathered now like sleeping flowers;
For this, for everything, we are out of tune;
It moves us not.—Great God! I'd rather be
A pagan suckled in a creed outworn;
So might I, standing on this pleasant lea,
Have glimpses that would make me less forlorn;
Have sight of Proteus rising from the sea;
Or hear old Triton blow his wreathèd horn.
1806 'The world is too much with us; late and soon', complete poem (published 1807).

31 Two voices are there; one is of the sea,
One of the mountains; each a mighty voice:
In both from age to age thou didst rejoice,
They were thy chosen music, Liberty!
1807 'Thought of a Briton on the Subjugation of Switzerland', l.1–4.

32 These people in the senseless hurry of their idle lives do not *read* books, they merely snatch a glance at them that they may talk about them. And even if this were not so, never forget what I believe was observed by Coleridge, that every great and original writer, in proportion as he is great or original, must himself create the taste by which he is to be relished.
1807 Letter to Lady Beaumont, 21 May, on his *Poems in Two Volumes* (1807). In *The Letters of William Wordsworth* edited by Alan G Hill (1984).

33 Surprised by joy—impatient as the wind
I turned to share the transport—Oh! with whom
But thee, deep buried in the silent tomb,
That spot which no vicissitude can find?
c.1812 'Surprised by joy—impatient as the wind', l.1–4 (published 1815). The poet's second daughter, Catherine, who died in June 1812, is the 'thee' referred to in the poem.

34 On Man, on Nature, and on Human Life,
Musing in solitude, I oft perceive
Fair trains of images before me rise,
Accompanied by feelings of delight
Pure, or with no unpleasing sadness mixed.
1814 'The Excursion', preface, l.1–5.

35 Not Chaos, not
The darkest pit of lowest Erebus
Nor aught of blinder vacancy, scooped out
By help of dreams—can breed such fear and awe
As fall upon us often when we look
Into our Minds, into the Mind of Man—
My haunt, and the main region of my song.
1814 'The Excursion', preface, l.35–41.

36 What soul was his, when, from the naked top
Of some bold headland, he beheld the sun
Rise up, and bathe the world in light!
He looked—
Ocean and earth, the solid frame of earth
And ocean's liquid mass, in gladness lay
Beneath him:—Far and wide the clouds were touched,
And in their silent faces he could read
Unutterable love.
1814 'The Excursion', bk.1, l.198–205.

37 This dull product of a scoffer's pen.
1814 Of Voltaire's novel *Candide*. 'The Excursion', bk.2, l.484.

38 Compassed round by pleasure, sighed
For independent happiness; craving peace,
The central feeling of all happiness,
Not as a refuge from distress or pain,
A breathing-time, vacation, or a truce,
But for its absolute self.
1814 'The Excursion', bk.3, l.380–5.

39 Society became my glittering bride,
And airy hopes my children.
1814 'The Excursion', bk.3, l.735–6.

40 'To every Form of being is assigned,'
Thus calmly spake the venerable Sage,
'An *active* Principle:—howe'er removed
From sense and observation, it subsists
In all things, in all natures.'
1814 'The Excursion', bk.9, l.1–5.

41 For all the startled scaly tribes that slink
Into his coverts, and each fearless link
Of dancing insects forged upon his breast.
1820 *The River Duddon*, no.28, 'Journey Renewed', l.6–8.

42 Still glides the stream, and shall for ever glide;
The Form remains, the function never dies;
While we, the brave, the mighty, and the wise,
We Men, who in our morn of youth defied
The elements, must vanish;—be it so!
1820 *The River Duddon*, no.34, 'After-Thought', l.5–9.

43 Enough, if something from our hands have power
To live, and act, and serve the future hour;
And if, as toward the silent tomb we go,
Through love, through hope, and faith's transcendent dower,
We feel that we are greater than we know.
1820 *The River Duddon*, no.34, 'After-Thought', l.10–14.

44 Ethereal minstrel! pilgrim of the sky!
Dost thou despise the earth where cares abound?
Or, while the wings aspire, are heart and eye
Both with thy nest upon the dewy ground?
1825 'To a Skylark', l.1–4 (published 1827).

45 Type of the wise who soar, but never roam;
True to the kindred points of Heaven and Home!
1825 'To a Skylark', l.11–12 (published 1827).

46 But who is innocent? By grace divine,
Not otherwise, O Nature! we are thine.
1834 'Evening Voluntaries', no.4, l.16–17 (published 1835).

47 Even so for me a vision sanctified
The sway of death; long ere my eyes had seen

Thy countenance—the still rapture of thy mien—
When thou, dear Sister! wert become death's bride:
No trace of pain or languor could abide
That change—age on thy brow was smoothed—thy cold
Wan cheek at once was privileged to unfold
A loveliness to living youth denied.
Oh! if within me hope should e'er decline,
The lamp of faith, lost Friend! too faintly burn;
The may that heaven-revealing smile of thine,
The bright assurance, visibly return:
And let my spirit in that power divine
Rejoice, as, through that power, it ceased to mourn.
1836 'November 1836', complete poem (published 1837).

48 The softest breeze to fairest flowers gives birth:
Think not that Prudence dwells in dark abodes,
She scans the future with the eye of gods.
1837 'At Bologna, In Remembrance of the Late Insurrections: Continued', l.12–14 (published 1842).

49 Before us lay a painful road,
And guidance have I sought in duteous love
From Wisdom's heavenly Father. Hence hath flowed
Patience, with trust that, whatsoe'er the way
Each takes in this high matter, all may move
Cheered with the prospect of a brighter day.
1839–40 *Sonnets upon the Punishment of Death*, no.14, 'Apology', l.9–14 (published in the *Quarterly Review* 1841).

50 With what nice care equivalents are given,
How just, how bountiful, the hand of Heaven.
1840 'Poor Robin', l.35–6 (published 1842).

51 That to this mountain-daisy's self were known
The beauty of its star-shaped shadow, thrown
On the smooth surface of this naked stone!
1844 'So fair so sweet', stanza 2 (published 1845).

52 21st May—a glorious day for beauty. I wish you could see how lovely our country is at this fine season.
1846 Letter to William Boxall, 21 May.

Worley, Helen

53 Dance, little words, on the end of your string. I can make you do most anything I want to. I can hide anywhere and watch you say the things I would never dare.
1982 *The Soul Survivor*, 'Puppetry and Poetry'.

Wotton, Sir Henry 1568–1639

English traveller, diplomat, scholar and poet. A trusted ambassador of James I and VI, he served in Venice and Germany. His tracts and letters were collected as *Reliquiae Wottonianae* (1651).

54 An ambassador is an honest man sent to lie abroad for the good of his country.
Quoted in Izaak Walton's *Life* (1651).

Wozniak, Stephen Gary 1950–

US computer engineer. In 1976 he became a co-founder, with Steve Jobs, of Apple Computer and went on to design the first Apple computers.

55 Wherever smart people work, doors are unlocked.
2004 Speech to the Fifth Hope Conference, 10 Jul.

56 Artists work best alone. Work alone.
2006 *iWoz*.

57 All of a sudden, we've lost a lot of control. We can't turn off our internet; we can't turn off our smartphones; we can't turn off our computers. You used to ask a smart person a question. Now, who do you ask? It starts with g-o, and it's not God.
2010 Interview on *CNN*, 8 Dec.

58 Never trust a computer you can't throw out a window.
Attributed.

Wragg, Ted (Edward) Conrad 1938–2005

English educator, a Professor of Education at the University of Exeter.

59 Nobody loves a bad teacher.
1986 *Education: an Action Guide for Parents*.

Wright, Sir Almroth Edward 1861–1947

English bacteriologist and Professor of Experimental Pathology, known for his work on parasitic diseases. A vocal opponent of the suffragettes, he wrote *The Unexpurgated Case against Woman Suffrage* (1913).

60 The recruiting field for the militant suffragists is the million of our excess female population—that million which had better long ago have gone out to mate with its complement of men beyond the sea.
1912 Letter to *The Times*, 28 Mar.

61 The primordial argument against giving woman the vote is that that vote would not represent physical force.
1913 *The Unexpurgated Case against Woman Suffrage*, pt.2.

62 The woman voter would be pernicious to the State not only because she could not back her vote by physical force, but also by reason of her intellectual defects.
1913 *The Unexpurgated Case against Woman Suffrage*, pt.2.

63 Practically every man feels that there is in woman…an element of unreason which, when you come upon it, summarily puts an end to purely intellectual intercourse.
1913 *The Unexpurgated Case against Woman Suffrage*, pt.5.

Wright, Betsey 1943–

Aide to President Clinton.

64 Bimbo eruptions.
1994 On an explosion of charges of sexual harassment against President Clinton. In the *Washington Post*, 30 May.

Wright, Frank Lloyd 1867–1959

US architect, known for his original and controversial designs exploiting modern technology and cubist spatial concepts. His works include the Imperial Hotel, Tokyo (1916–20) and the Guggenheim Museum of Art, New York (1959).

65 Architecture is man's great sense of himself embodied in a world of his own making. It may rise as high in quality only as its source because great art is great life.
1930 In Frederick Gutheim (ed) *Frank Lloyd Wright on Architecture: selected writings (1894–1940)*.

66 I know we can't have a great architecture while it is only for the landlord.
1932 In Frederick Gutheim (ed) *Frank Lloyd Wright on Architecture: selected writings (1894–1940)*.

67 The physician can bury his mistakes, but the architect can only advise his client to plant vines.
1953 In the *New York Times*, 4 Oct.

Wright, James C, Jr 1922–

US Congressman, former speaker of the US House of Representatives.

68 The boiling, churning caldron of America.
   1987 On the House of Representatives. In *Life*.

69 I know how that pancake feels when you pour the syrup all over it.
   1991 Of his official portrait, unveiled two years after he was forced to resign. In the *International Herald Tribune*, 12 Jul.

Wright, Judith Arundell *also known as* Judith Wright McKinney 1915–2000

Australian poet and conservationist, whose awards include the Robert Frost Memorial Prize (1976). Selected works have been published in *A Human Pattern* (1990).

70 The easy Eden-dreamtime then
   in a country of birds and trees
   made me your shadow-sister, child,
   dark girl I couldn't play with.
   1990 *A Human Pattern*, 'Two Dreamtimes', stanza 14. The poem is dedicated to Kath Walker (now Oodgeroo Noonuccal).

71 I am born of the conquerors,
   you of the persecuted.
   Raped by rum and an alien law,
   progress and economics,

   are you and I and a once-loved land
   peopled by tribes and trees;
   doomed traders and stock-exchanges,
   bought by faceless strangers.
   1990 *A Human Pattern*, 'Two Dreamtimes', stanzas 17–18. The poem is dedicated to Kath Walker (now Oodgeroo Noonuccal).

Wright, Kenyon 1932–99

Scottish Methodist minister, General Secretary of the Scottish Council of Churches since 1981, and Executive of the Scottish Constitutional Convention (1989–99).

72 What if that other single voice we know so well responds by saying, 'We say no, and we are the State'? Well, we say yes—and we are the people.
   1989 Calling for a Scottish Parliament. Speech at the inaugural meeting of the Scottish Constitutional Convention, 30 Mar. The 'single voice' is that of Prime Minister Margaret Thatcher.

Wright, Orville and Wright, Wilbur 1871–1948, 1867–1912

Born in Dayton, Ohio, early mechanics and tinkerers, and eventually self-taught aviation engineers.

73 SUCCESS FOUR FLIGHTS THURSDAY MORNING ALL AGAINST TWENTY-ONE MILE WIND STARTED FROM LEVEL WITH ENGINE POWER ALONE AVERAGE SPEED THROUGH AIR THIRTY-ONE MILES LONGEST 59 SECONDS INFORM PRESS HOME CHRISTMAS.
   1903 Telegram from the brothers at Kitty Hawk, North Carolina to their father, 17 Dec.

Wriston, Walter Bigelow 1919–2005

US banker. He joined Citibank in 1946 and worked his way up to chairman (1970–84).

74 Our banking system grew by accident; and wherever something happens by accident, it becomes a religion.
   1975 In *Business Week*, 20 Jan.

75 When you retire…you go from who's who to who's that.
   1985 In the *New York Times*, 21 Apr.

76 If you put a floor under wages and a ceiling over prices, a free man cannot long stand erect.
   1986 *Risk and Other Four-Letters Words*.

77 The Doomsayers have always had their uses, since they trigger the coping mechanism that often prevents the events they forecast.
   1986 *Risk and Other Four-Letter Words*.

78 Our current tendency to take our economic blood pressure every few minutes…obfuscates thought on many problems.
   1986 *Risk and Other Four-Letter Words*.

79 Banking is a branch of the information business.
   1986 *Risk and Other Four-Letters Words*.

80 It is a maxim of cryptology that what one man can devise, another can unravel. This principle keeps armies of tax lawyers and accountants employed, but adds nothing to our national productivity.
   1986 *Risk and Other Four-Letters Words*.

81 Rising prices or wages do not cause inflation; they only report it. They represent an essential form of economic speech, since money is just another form of information.
   1986 *Risk and Other Four-Letter Words*.

82 Every line in the government's budget has its own constituency.
   1986 *Risk and Other Four-Letter Words*.

83 It's a Texas wrestling match with a new team against you every night.
   1993 On life as a chief executive officer. In the *New York Times*, 25 Apr.

Wu-ti 157–87 BC

Chinese emperor of the Han dynasty who became its sixth ruler at the age of 16. The Han dynasty saw the Chinese expanding their political power westwards into Central Asia.

84 Autumn wind rises; white clouds fly.
   Grass and trees wither; geese go south.
   c.127 BC 'The Autumn Wind' (translated by Arthur Waley). The poem is a lament on leaving his mistress behind while he travelled on official business.

Wyatt, Sir Thomas (the Elder) 1503–42

English courtier and poet under Henry VIII. Twice imprisoned on capital offences—on charges of adultery with Anne Boleyn and for treason—he was twice released. Many of his poems were published in *Tottel's Miscellany* (1557). He is credited with introducing the sonnet form to English; many of his are translations from Petrarch.

85 In lusty leas at liberty I walk.
   1536 'Mine Own John Poins'.

86 But here I am in Kent and Christendom,
   Among the Muses, where I read and rhyme.
   1536 'Mine Own John Poins'.

87 Farewell, Love, and all thy laws forever,
   Thy baited hooks shall tangle me no more.
   1557 'Farewell, Love'.

88 And graven with diamonds in letters plain
   There is written, her fair neck round about:

Noli me tangere, for Caesar's I am,
And wild for to hold, though I seem tame.
1557 'Whoso List to Hunt'. The subject of the poem is thought to be Anne Boleyn.
▶ See Bible 125:66.

89 My lute, awake! Perform the last
Labour that thou and I shall waste,
And end that I have now begun;
For when this song is sung and past,
My lute, be still, for I have done.
1557 'My Lute, Awake!'

90 They flee from me, that sometime did me seek,
With naked foot, stalking in my chamber.
I have seen them gentle, tame, and meek,
That now are wild, and do not remember
That sometime they put themselves in danger
To take bread at my hand; and now they range,
Busily seeking with a continual change.
1557 'They Flee from Me'.

91 But all is turned, through my gentleness,
Into a strange fashion of forsaking.
1557 'They Flee from Me'.

Wycherley, William c.1640-1716

English dramatist. Educated at Oxford and Middle Temple. Although a successful playwright who garnered attention and support from both Charles II and James II, his fortunes were unsteady. Plays include *The Gentleman Dancing-Master* (1672), *Love in a Wood* (1671), *The Country Wife* (1675) and *The Plain Dealer* (1677), the last two of which were based on plays by Molière.

92 Fy! madam, do you think me so ill bred as to love a husband?
1671 *Love in a Wood*, act 3, sc.4.

93 A good name is seldom got by giving it one's self.
1675 *The Country Wife*, act 1, sc.1.

94 A mistress should be like a little country retreat near the town, not to dwell in constantly, but only for a night and away.
1675 *The Country Wife*, act 1, sc.1.

95 Your virtue is your greatest affectation.
1675 *The Country Wife*, act 1, sc.1.

96 Women serve but to keep men from better company.
1675 *The Country Wife*, act 1, sc.1.

97 Mistresses are like books. If you pore upon them too much, they doze you, and make you unfit for company; but if used discreetly, you are the fitter for conversation by 'em.
1675 *The Country Wife*, act 1, sc.1.

98 'Tis as hard to be a good fellow, a good friend, and a lover of women, as 'tis to be a good fellow, a good friend, and a lover of money.
1675 *The Country Wife*, act 1, sc.1.

99 Wine gives you liberty, love takes it away.
1675 *The Country Wife*, act 1, sc.1.

1 For my part, I will have only those glorious manly pleasures of being very drunk and very slovenly.
1675 *The Country Wife*, act 1, sc.1.

2 Wit is more necessary than beauty; and I think no young woman ugly that has it, and no handsome woman agreeable without it.
1675 *The Country Wife*, act 1, sc.1.

3 He's a fool that marries; but he's a greater that does not marry a fool.
1675 *The Country Wife*, act 1, sc.1.

4 Poetry in love is no more to be avoided than jealousy.
1675 *The Country Wife*, act 3, sc.2.

5 I love to be envied, and would not marry a wife that I alone could love; loving alone is as dull as eating alone.
1675 *The Country Wife*, act 3, sc.2.

Wycliffe, John c.1330-1384

English religious reformer. His many popular vernacular tracts attacked Church hierarchy, priestly powers, and the doctrine of transubstantiation, and he issued the first English translation of the Bible. Although condemned, his teaching was influential in its insistence on inward religion instead of formalism. His followers were derisively known as 'Lollards'.

6 Christ during His life upon earth was of all men the poorest, casting from Him all worldly authority. I deduce from these premises...that the Pope should surrender all temporal authority to the civil power and advise his clergy to do the same.
1384 Dismissing an order to appear before the Papal Court.

Wyeth, Andrew Newell 1917-2009

US painter, known for his meticulous depictions of the Pennsylvanian and Maine countryside. His most famous work is *Christina's World* (1948).

7 I get excited by the shape of a person's nose, the tone of their eyes, or the way their back looks when they're turned away from me. That's my reason for painting.
1991 In *National Geographic*, Jul.

Wylie, Betty Jane 1931-

Canadian dramatist and writer.

8 First deal with your own tears; tomorrow do something about acid rain.
1986 *Successfully Single*.

9 There are all kinds of ways of being unfaithful, not the worst of them with your body.
1988 *All in the Family: A Survival Guide for Living and Loving in a Changing World*.

10 Listening is one of the lesser-known skills that mistresses offer.
1988 *All in the Family: A Survival Guide for Living and Loving in a Changing World*.

11 There is a line between sexuality and promiscuity, and the line is closer to celibacy than not.
1988 *All in the Family: A Survival Guide for Living and Loving in a Changing World*.

12 Poverty isn't being broke; poverty is never having enough.
1989 *Everywoman's Money Book* (with Lynne MacFarlane).

Wyman, Jane originally Sarah Jane Fulks 1914-2007

First wife of Ronald Reagan and best known as a film actress, she married Reagan (her second husband) in 1940 and divorced in 1948. She won an Academy Award for *Johnny Belinda* (1948).

13 Ask him what time it is and he'll tell you how the watch was made.
Of Ronald Reagan. Quoted in Jack Finney *From Time to Time* (1995).

X

Xenophon c.435–c.354 BC
Athenian historian and soldier.

1 *Thalatta! Thalatta!*
The sea! The sea!
Anabasis bk. 4, 24. Shouted by the Greek soldiers from the Expedition of Cyrus in 401 BC when they reached the sea after months inland.

Y

Yarborough, Ralph 1903–96
US liberal politician and Governor of Texas (1957–71).

1 It is the only case on record of a man swimming toward a sinking ship.
1973 On former Texas Governor John B Connally's switch from Democratic to the Republican party in his bid for the presidential nomination. Quoted in the *Washington Post*, 18 Jan 1988.

Yeats, Georgie née Hyde-Lees 1892–1968
Wife of Irish poet W B Yeats. Her attempts at automatic writing on their honeymoon in 1917 profoundly influenced Yeats' subsequent writing.

2 After your death people will write of your love affairs, but I shall say nothing, because I will remember how proud you were.
Quoted in Richard Ellman *A Long the Riverrun: Selected Essays* (1988), p.253.

Yeats, W(illiam) B(utler) 1865–1939
Irish poet. He was a prolific writer influenced by Irish mythology and by his close relationships with a number of women, eventually evolving his own system of symbolism which underlies much of his work. He also edited many books, including the controversial *Oxford Book of Modern Verse* (1936), and served as a Senator of the Irish Free State (1922–9).

3 Down by the salley gardens my love and I did meet;
She passed the salley gardens with little snow-white feet.
She bid me take love easy, as the leaves grow on the tree;
But I, being young and foolish, with her would not agree.

In a field by the river my love and I did stand,
And on my leaning shoulder she laid her snow-white hand.
She bid me take life easy, as the grass grows on the weirs;
But I was young and foolish, and now am full of tears.
1888 'Down by the Salley Gardens', complete poem. Collected in *Crossways*.

4 I will arise and go now, and go to Innisfree,
And a small cabin build there, of clay and wattles made:
Nine bean-rows will I have there, a hive for the honey-bee,
And live alone in the bee-loud glade.

And I shall have some peace there, for peace comes dropping slow,
Dropping from the veils of the morning to where the cricket sings;
There midnight's all a-glimmer, and noon a purple glow,
And evening full of the linnet's wings.
1888 'The Lake Isle of Innisfree', stanzas 1–2. Collected in *The Rose* (1893).

5 O Oisin, mount by me and ride
To shores by the wash of the tremulous tide,
Where men have heaped no burial-mounds,
And the days pass by like a wayward tune.
1889 'The Wanderings of Oisin', l.80–3.

6 The brawling of a sparrow in the eaves,
The brilliant moon and all the milky sky,
And all that famous harmony of leaves,
Has blotted out man's image and his cry.
1891 'The Sorrow of Love', stanza 1. Collected in *The Rose* (1893).

7 When you are old and grey and full of sleep,
And nodding by the fire, take down this book,
And slowly read, and dream of the soft look
Your eyes had once, and of their shadows deep;

How many loved your moments of glad grace,
And loved your beauty with love false or true,
But one man loved the pilgrim soul in you,
And loved the sorrows of your changing face;

And bending down beside the glowing bars,
Murmur, a little sadly how Love fled
And paced among the mountains overhead
And hid his face amid a crowd of stars.
1891 'When You Are Old', complete poem. Collected in *The Rose* (1893).

8 Rose of all Roses, Rose of all the World!
The tall thought-woven sails, that flap unfurled
Above the tide of hours, trouble the air,
And God's bell buoyed to be the water's care.
1891 'The Rose of Battle', l.1–4. Collected in *The Rose* (1893).

9 Out-worn heart, in a time out-worn,
Come clear of the nets of wrong and right;
Laugh, heart, again in the grey twilight,
Sigh, heart, again in the dew of the morn.
1893 'Into the Twilight', stanza 1. Collected in *The Wind Among the Reeds* (1899).

10 And walk among long dappled grass,
And pluck till time and times are done
The silver apples of the moon,
The golden apples of the sun.
1897 'The Song of Wandering Aengus', l.21–4. Collected in *The Wind Among the Reeds* (1899).

11 Half close your eyelids, loosen your hair,
And dream about the great and their pride;

They have spoken against you everywhere,
But weigh this song with the great and their pride;
I made it out of a mouthful of air,
Their children's children shall say they have lied.
1898 'He Thinks of Those who have Spoken Evil of His Beloved', complete poem. Collected in *The Wind Among the Reeds* (1899).

12 Had I the heavens' embroidered cloths,
Enwrought with golden and silver light,
The blue and the dim and the dark cloths
Of night and light and the half-light,
I would spread the cloths under your feet:
But I, being poor, have only my dreams;
I have spread my dreams under your feet;
Tread softly because you tread on my dreams.
1899 'He Wishes for the Cloths of Heaven', complete poem. Collected in *The Wind Among the Reeds* (1899).

13 You have disgraced yourselves again. You are rocking the cradle of a new masterpiece.
1907 Addressing the rioting audience at Dublin's Abbey Theatre at the première of J M Synge's *The Playboy of the Western World*.

14 What could have made her peaceful with a mind
That nobleness made simple as a fire,
With beauty like a tightened bow, a kind
That is not natural in an age like this,
Being high and solitary and most stern?
Why, what could she have done, being what she is?
Was there another Troy for her to burn?
1908 'No Second Troy', l.6–12. Collected in *The Green Helmet and Other Poems* (1910).

15 You say, as I have often given tongue
In praise of what another's said or sung,
'Twere politic to do the like by these;
But was there ever dog that praised his fleas?
1909 'To a Poet, who would have me Praise certain Bad Poets, Imitators of His and Mine', complete poem. Collected in *The Green Helmet and Other Poems* (1910).

16 I have made my song a coat
Covered with embroideries
Out of old mythologies
From heel to throat;
But the fools caught it,
Wore it in the world's eyes
As though they'd wrought it.
Song, let them take it,
For there's more enterprise
In walking naked.
1912 'A Coat', complete poem. Collected in *Responsibilities* (1914).

17 Romantic Ireland's dead and gone,
It's with O'Leary in the grave.
1913 'September 1913', refrain. Collected in *Responsibilities* (1914).

18 I have met them at close of day
Coming with vivid faces
From counter or desk among grey
Eighteenth-century houses.
1916 'Easter, 1916', l.1–4. Collected in *Michael Robartes and Dancer* (1921).

19 The horse that comes from the road,
The rider, the birds that range
From cloud to tumbling cloud,
Minute by minute they change;
A shadow of cloud on the stream
Changes minute by minute;
A horse-hoof slides on the brim,
And a horse plashes within it;
The long-legged moor-hens dive,
And hens to moor-cocks call;
Minute by minute they live:
The stone's in the midst of all.
1916 'Easter 1916', l.45–56. Collected in *Michael Robartes and the Dancer* (1921).

20 Too long a sacrifice
Can make a stone of the heart.
1916 'Easter 1916', l.57–8. Collected in *Michael Robartes and the Dancer* (1921).

21 There's nothing but our own red blood
Can make a right Rose Tree.
1917 'The Rose Tree', stanza 3. Collected in *Michael Robartes and the Dancer* (1921).

22 I know that I shall meet my fate
Somewhere among the clouds above;
Those that I fight I do not hate,
Those that I guard I do not love.
1918 'An Irish Airman Foresees his Death', l.1.–4. Collected in *The Wild Swans at Coole* (1919).

23 Very nice, but if I had rehearsed you it would have been much better.
1919 Of Lady Gregory's title-role performance in his *Kathleen Ni Houlihan*. Recorded in Lady Gregory's journal, entry for 19 Mar.

24 Turning and turning in the widening gyre
The falcon cannot hear the falconer;
Things fall apart; the centre cannot hold;
Mere anarchy is loosed upon the world,
The blood-dimmed tide is loosed, and everywhere
The ceremony of innocence is drowned;
The best lack all conviction, while the worst
Are full of passionate intensity.
1919 'The Second Coming', l.1–8. Collected in *Michael Robartes and the Dancer* (1921).
▶ See Achebe 2:20.

25 And what rough beast, its hour come round at last,
Slouches towards Bethlehem to be born?
1919 'The Second Coming', l.21–2. Collected in *Michael Robartes and the Dancer* (1921).

26 An aged man is but a paltry thing,
A tattered coat upon a stick, unless
Soul clap its hands and sing, and louder sing
For every tatter in its mortal dress.
1926 'Sailing to Byzantium', stanza 8. Collected in *The Tower* (1928).

27 O chestnut tree, great-rooted blossomer,
Are you the leaf, the blossom, or the bole?
O body swayed to music, O brightening glance,
How can we know the dancer from the dance?
1927 'Among School Children', stanza 8. collected in *The Tower* (1928).

28 Never to have lived is best, ancient writers say;
Never to have drawn the breath of life, never to have
  looked into the eye of day;
The second best's a gay goodnight and quickly turn
  away.
1927 'From Oedipus at Colonnus', stanza 4. Collected in *The Tower* (1928).

29 The innocent and the beautiful
Have no enemy but time.

1927 'In Memory of Eva Gore-Booth and Con Markiewicz', l.24–5. Collected in *The Winding Stair and Other Poems* (1933).

30 If I make the lashes dark
And the eyes more bright
And the lips more scarlet,
Or ask if all be right
From mirror after mirror,
No Vanity's displayed:
I'm looking for the face I had
Before the world was made.
1928 'A Woman Young and Old', part 2 'Before the World was Made', stanza 1. Collected in *The Winding Stair and Other Poems* (1933).

31 A starlit or a moonlit dome disdains
All that man is,
All mere complexities
The fury and the mire of human veins.
1930 'Byzantium', stanza 1. Collected in *The Winding Stair and Other Poems* (1933).

32 Marbles of the dancing floor
Break bitter furies of complexity,
Those images that yet
Fresh images beget,
That dolphin-torn, that gong-tormented sea.
1930 'Byzantium', stanza 5. Collected in *The Winding Stair and Other Poems* (1933).

33 Only God, my dear,
Could love you for yourself alone
And not your yellow hair.
1930 'For Anne Gregory', l.16–18. Collected in *The Winding Stair and Other Poems* (1933).

34 Grant me an old man's frenzy.
Myself I must remake
Till I am Timon and Lear
Or that William Blake
Who beat upon the wall
Till Truth obeyed his call.
1936 'An Acre of Grass', stanza 3. Collected in *New Poems* (1938).

35 John Bull has gone to India
And all must pay him heed
For histories are there to prove
That none of another breed
Has had a like inheritance,
Or sucked such milk as he,
And there's no luck about a house
If it lacks honesty.
The ghost of Roger Casement
Is beating on the door.
1936 'The Ghost of Roger Casement', stanza 3. Collected in *New Poems* (1938).

36 Now that my ladder's gone,
I must lie down where all the ladders start,
In the foul rag-and-bone shop of the heart.
1937–8 'The Circus Animals' Desertion', part 3, l.6–8. Collected in *Last Poems* (1939).

37 Our master Caesar is in the tent
Where the maps are spread,
His eyes fixed upon nothing,
A hand under his head.

Like a long-legged fly upon the stream
His mind moves upon silence.
1938 'Long-Legged Fly', l.5–10. Collected in *Last Poems* (1939).

38 When Pearse summoned Cuchulain to his side,
What stalked through the Post Office? What intellect,
What calculation, number, measurement, replied?
We Irish, born into that ancient sect
But thrown upon this filthy modern tide
And by its formless spawning fury wrecked,
Climb to our proper dark, that we may trace
The lineaments of a plummet-measured face.
1938 'The Statues', stanza 4. Collected in *Last Poems* (1939).

39 Swear by what the sages spoke
Round the Mareotic Lake
That the Witch of Atlas knew,
Spoke and set the cocks a-crow.
1938 'Under Ben Bulben', stanza 1. Collected in *Last Poems* (1939).

40 Under bare Ben Bulben's head
In Drumcliffe churchyard Yeats is laid,
An ancestor was rector there
Long years ago; a church stands near,
By the road an ancient Cross.
No marble, no conventional phrase,
On limestone quarried near the spot
By his command these words are cut:
Cast a cold eye
On life, on death.
Horseman, pass by!
1938 'Under Ben Bulben', stanza 6. Collected in *Last Poems* (1939). The last three lines were used as his epitaph.

41 Propinquity had brought
Imagination to that pitch where it casts out
All that is not itself. I had grown wild
And wandered murmuring everywhere, 'My child, my child.'
1939 'A Bronze Head', l.18–21. Collected in *Last Poems* (1939).

42 OLD MAN: Do not let him touch you! It is not true
That drunken men cannot beget,
And if he touch he must beget
And you must bear his murderer.
Deaf! Both deaf!
1939 *Purgatory*.

Yellen, Jack 1892–1991
US lyricist.

43 Happy Days are Here Again.
1930 Title of song. It became linked with US Democrat campaigns.

Yeltsin, Boris 1931–2007
President of Russia. He graduated as a construction engineer in 1955 and entered work for the Communist Party. Called to Moscow in 1985 by Gorbachev, he was sacked in 1987 and against Gorbachev's wishes became Chairman of the Russian Parliament. He was elected President in 1991. His programme for a rapid transition to a market economy, support for other republics to be treated equally, and for multiparty democracy, helped him survive the following politically tumultuous years, but his policies caused much domestic criticism. He resigned in 1999 and was replaced by Vladimir Putin.

44 The West has not lived through totalitarianism, with a single ideology for 70 years. We are escaping from the burden of the past, and only after we have done that will we be ready to integrate with Europe—and Europe needs Russia.
1991 Addressing socialist MPs in Strasbourg, 15 Apr.

45 I ask you to forgive me for not fulfilling some hopes of those people who believed that we would be able to jump from the totalitarian past into a bright, rich and civilized future in one go.
   2000 On his retirement. In the *Observer*, 2 Jan.

Yevtushenko, Yevgeny Aleksandrovich 1932–

Russian poet. He emerged as a poet representing the young post-Stalin generation with such works as *The Third Snow* (1955), *Chausée Eutuziastov* (1956) and *The Promise* (1957). Later works have included *Babi Yar* (1962), concerning anti-Semitism in Russia, *Love Poems* (1977), *Ivan the Terrible and Ivan the Fool* (1979) and the novel *Berries* (1981).

46 I love sport because I love life, and sport is one of the basic joys of life.
   1966 In *Sports Illustrated*, 19 Dec.

47 When truth is replaced by silence, the silence is a lie.
   Attributed.

Yokoi, Shoichi 1915–97

Japanese corporal who emerged from the jungles of Guam in 1972 after hiding for 28 years. He was obeying his commanding officer's 1944 order to evade capture by the enemy.

48 I am deeply ashamed at my failure to serve His Majesty.
   1972 Announcement to journalists at Tokyo airport, 2 Feb. Quoted in Edward Behr *Hirohito*, epilogue.

York, Sarah, Duchess of 1959–

English Duchess and children's author, ex-wife of Prince Andrew, Duke of York.

49 Women leave the Royal Family in only one mode—with their heads cleaved from the shoulders.
   1997 *My Story*.

Yost, Elwy 1925–2011

Canadian television personality.

50 If you work very hard, and give life everything you've got, you may not quite make it.
   1990 Comment, 17 Jan.

Young, Arthur 1741–1820

British agriculturalist and writer.

51 Give a man the secure possession of a bleak rock, and he will turn it into a garden; give him a nine years' lease on a garden, and he will convert it into a desert... The magic of PROPERTY turns sand to gold.
   1787 Journal entries, 30 Jul and 7 Nov, published in *Travels in France and Italy* (1794).

Young, Brigham 1801–77

US Mormon leader.

52 This is the place!
   1847 On first seeing Great Salt Lake Valley, Utah, 24 Jul.

Young, Douglas 1913–73

Scottish poet, scholar and nationalist. He was jailed for refusing to serve in the British Army in 1941. After the war he taught classics at universities in Scotland, Canada and the US.

53 The Minister said it wald dee,
   the cypress-buss I plantit.
   But the buss grew til a tree,
   naething dauntit.

   It's growan, stark and heich,
   derk and straucht and sinister,
   kirkyairdielike and dreich.
   But whaur's the Minister?
   1943 *Auntran Blads*, 'Last Lauch'.

Young, Edward 1683–1765

English poet, tragedian and cleric, best known for his satires, *The Love of Fame, the Universal Passion* (1725–8) and the remarkable *Complaint, or Night Thoughts on Life, Death and Immortality* (1742–5), written on the death of his wife.

54 Some, for *renown*, on scraps of learning doat,
   And think they grow immortal as they *quote*.
   1725 *The Love of Fame, the Universal Passion* 'Satire 1'.

Yourcenar, Marguerite *pseudonym of* Marguerite de Crayencour 1903–87

French novelist. Born into aristocracy, she spent her childhood travelling in Europe and in 1937 left for the US, taking dual US–French nationality. She is best known for her historical novel *Mémoires d'Hadrien* (Memoirs of Hadrian, 1951), and for being the first woman elected to the Académie Française.

55 *Un homme qui lit, ou qui pense, ou qui calcule, appartient à l'espèce et non au sexe; dans ses meilleurs moments, il échappe même à l'humain.*
   A person who reads or thinks or calculates, belongs to a kind and not to a gender; in his or her best moments, he or she escapes being human.
   1951 *Mémoires d'Hadrien*.

56 *Les trois quarts de nos exercices intellectuels ne sont plus que broderies sur le vide.*
   Three quarters of our intellectual performances are no more than decorations over a void.
   1951 *Mémoires d'Hadrien*.

57 *Tout bonheur est un chef-d'œuvre: la moindre erreur le fausse, la moindre hésitation l'altère, la moindre lourdeur le dépare, la moindre sottise l'abêtit.*
   Happiness is always a work of art: the least fault distorts it, the least hesitation changes it, a little dullness spoils it, the smallest foolish act makes it idiotic.
   1951 *Mémoires d'Hadrien*.

58 *Entre le rôle de sauveur et celui de complice du bourreau, j'aperçois tout au plus l'incommode emploi de victime.*
   Between the role of saviour and that of butcher's accomplice, all I see left for you is the unsavoury role of victim.
   1963 *Qui n'a pas son Minotaure?*, pt.3.

59 *Que le Dieu qui nous tue nous vienne en aide!*
   God who kills us, come to our rescue!
   1963 *Qui n'a pas son Minotaure?*, pt.3.

60 ARIANE: *Tu n'es que la réponse la plus courte qu'on puisse faire aux questions des hommes.*
   DIEU: *En sais-tu de meilleur?*
   ARIANE: *Oui. Le mot rien est aussi court que le mot Dieu.*

ARIADNE: You are only the shortest possible answer to all the questions of men.
GOD (BACCHUS): Do you know a better one?
ARIADNE: Yes, the word no is just as short as the word God.
1963 *Qui n'a pas son Minotaure?*, pt.9.

61 Out of the debris of a statue thoroughly shattered a new art work is born: a naked foot unforgettably resting on a stone; a candid hand; a bent knee which contains all the speed of the foot race; a torso which has no face to prevent us from loving it.
Quoted in the *New York Times*, 10 May 1992.

Yousafzai, Malala 1997–

Pakistani human rights and education activist. Having narrowly escaped death when shot in the head by Taliban gunmen, she was brought to the UK, where she continued to press for education of all children around the world. In 2014, aged 17, she became the youngest person to receive the Nobel Peace Prize, sharing it with Kailash Satyarthi.

62 One child, one teacher, one book and one pen can change the world. Education is the only solution.
2013 Speech at the UN Youth Assembly, reported in *The Independent*, 12 Jul.

63 They thought bullets would silence us, but they were wrong.
2013 Speech at the UN General Assembly, reported in *The Independent*, 12 Jul.

64 We are human beings, and this is the part of our human nature, that we don't learn the importance of anything until it's snatched from our hands.
2013 Interview on *The Daily Show*, 8 Oct.

65 I believe the gun has no power because a gun can only kill, but a pen can give life.
2013 Speech on accepting a Glamour Award, 12 Nov.

66 Education is neither Eastern nor Western, it is human.
2013 *I Am Malala: The Girl Who Stood Up for Education and Was Shot by the Taliban*.

Yüan Mei 1716–98

Chinese poet who was a magistrate for six years before retiring to live off his writings. Unorthodox and hedonistic, he also championed women poets.

67 If I can rejoice for a moment,
Death at an early age would still be a long life.
c.746 Collected in *A Book of Chinese Verse* (translated by N L Smith and R H Kotewall).

Z

Zangwill, Israel 1864–1926

English writer and leading Zionist, known for his novels on Jewish themes including *Children of the Ghetto* (1892) and *Ghetto Tragedies* (1894). Other works include the early collections of witty tales *The Bachelors' Club* (1891) and *The Old Maids' Club* (1892), and the plays *The Melting Pot* (1908) and *We Moderns* (1925).

1 America is God's Crucible, the great Melting Pot where all the races of Europe are melting and re-forming... God is making the American.
1908 *The Melting Pot*.

Zatopek, Emil 1922–2000

Czech athlete and middle-distance runner. He won the gold medal for the 10,000 metres at the 1948 Olympics in London and subsequently broke 13 world records as well as gold medals in the 10,000 metres and 5,000 metres events at the Helsinki Olympics in 1952.

2 An athlete cannot run with money in his pockets. He must run with hope in his heart and dreams in his head.
Quoted by Christopher Brasher in the *Observer*, 12 Sep 1982.

3 You can't climb up to the second floor without a ladder. When you set your aim too high and don't fulfil it, then your enthusiasm turns to bitterness. Try for a goal that's reasonable, and then gradually raise it. That's the only way to get to the top.
Quoted in Colin Jarman *The Guinness Dictionary of Sports Quotations* (1990).

Zeldin, Theodore 1933–

Historian and writer

4 Brilliant lecturers shouldn't be wasted in lecture rooms: they should appear on TV. We need black market universities, in which people just help each other, and which don't leave out the poor.
1995 Quoted in Christina Hardyment 'Zeldin and the art of human relationships', in *Oxford Today*, vol.7, no.2, Hilary Issue.

Zel'dovich, Yakov 1914–87

Russian astrophysicist.

5 Without publicity there is no prosperity.
Quoted by Tony Rothman in *Bostonia*, summer 1993, p.58.

Zhang Jie 1937–

Chinese writer whose first short story appeared in 1978 and whose writing often sets romantic themes in the contemporary Chinese world of rapid modernization.

6 When we reach communism, will there still be cases of marriage without love?
1979 'Love Must Not Be Forgotten', in *Seven Contemporary Women Writers* (1982).

7 To live single is not such a fearful disaster. I believe it may be a sign of a step forward in culture, education and the quality of life.
1979 'Love Must Not Be Forgotten', in *Seven Contemporary Women Writers* (1982).

Zhao Zhenkai *pen name* Beo Dao 1949–

Chinese writer who has written poetry and fiction and was associated with China's Democracy Movement. He has lived largely in exile since 1989. The use of pen names dates back to the Cultural Revolution when secrecy was often essential.

8 They say the ice age ended years ago.
Why are there icicles everywhere?
c.1989 'Answer', collected in Donald Finkel *A Splintered Mirror* (1991).

9 Freedom is only the distance
between the hunter and his prey.
c.1989 'Answer', collected in Donald Finkel *A Splintered Mirror* (1991).

Zhivkov, Todor 1911–98

Bulgarian statesman, part of the Communist coup d'état of 1944. Prime Minister from 1962 and Chairman of the Council of State from 1971, he was effectively President of the Republic. Conservative and unquestioningly loyal to the USSR, he was ousted in 1989 and expelled from the Party, charged with nepotism, corruption and abuse of power.

10 If I had to do it over again, I would not even be a communist. And if Lenin were alive today, he would say the same thing.
1990 In the *Sunday Times*, 9 Dec.

Zhou Enlai *or* Chou En–Lai 1898–1975

Chinese Communist Party leader, Prime Minister of the People's Republic from its creation in 1949 until his death. Under Mao Zedong he became the Party's chief negotiator and diplomat, and vastly increased China's international influence. In the Cultural Revolution (1966–76), he worked to preserve national unity.

11 For us, it is all right if the talks succeed; and it is all right if they fail.
1971 On President Nixon's visit, 5 Oct.

Zia Ul-Haq, Mohammed 1924–88

Pakistani soldier and politician. He led the military coup against Zulfikar Ali Bhutto (1977), becoming President a year later. He introduced a new policy of Islamization and freer-market economic programme, finally lifting martial law in 1985. He was killed in an aircraft.

12 Cricket can be a bridge and a glue… Cricket for peace is my mission.
Quoted in Helen Exley *Cricket Quotations* (1992).

Zidane, Zinedine 1972–

French footballer and coach, Fifa World Player of the Year in 1998, 2000 and 2003.

13 Every day I think about where I come from and I am still proud to be who I am: first, a Kabyle from La Castellane, then an Algerian from Marseille, and then a Frenchman.
2004 Explaining his identity—his father was a Berber from the Kabylie region of Algeria and Zidane grew up in the Marseille suburb of La Castellane. In the *Observer*, 4 Apr.

Zoeller, Fuzzy 1951–

US golfer, his wins include the US Masters (1979) and the US Open (1984).

14 Even on the mornings when I creak out of bed, I still get pumped up about hitting that silly little white ball.
2001 In *Golf World*, 13 Apr.

Zola, Émile 1840–1902

French novelist, a pioneer of naturalism. His novels include *Thérèse Raquin* (1867) and the great series called *Les Rougon-Macquart*, which depicts all aspects of society under the Second Empire. After impeaching the military authorities over the Dreyfus case, Zola was sentenced to imprisonment (1898), but escaped for a year to England, and was welcomed back as a hero. He died in Paris, accidentally suffocated by charcoal fumes.

15 *J'accuse.*
I accuse.
1898 Title of open letter to the President of France regarding the Dreyfus case.

16 A dead reign…a strange epoch of folly and shame.
On the France of the Second Empire. Quoted in Joanna Richardson *La Vie Parisienne* (1971), p.276.

Zolotow, Maurice 1913–91

US biographer and journalist.

17 There is no more offensive act of theatrical rudeness than coming late to a performance.
1958 In *Theater Arts*, Feb.

Zuckerberg, Mark Elliot 1984–

US software developer. He co-founded the social networking site Facebook in 2004 while still at Harvard and later became chief executive and president of Facebook, Inc.

18 Move fast and break things. Unless you are breaking stuff, you are not moving fast enough.
2009 In *Business Insider*, Oct.

19 The biggest risk is not taking any risk. In a world that's changing really quickly, the only strategy that is guaranteed to fail is not taking risks.
2011 Interview at Stanford University, Oct.

Zuckerman, Solly Zuckerman, Baron 1904–84

South African-born English scientist, zoologist and educator, the author of several studies of primate behavior.

20 Science creates the future without knowing what the future will be. If scientists knew tomorrow's discovery they would make it.
1964 In the *Daily Mirror*.

Zwerin, Mike 1930–2010

US writer and musician. He played trombone, and wrote extensively on jazz.

21 Jazz musicians have some outlaw in them somewhere if they are serious about this music… There is no valid motivation for it other than love—outlaw motivation in a profit-motivated society.
1985 *La Tristesse de Saint Louis: Swing Under the Nazis*, ch.4.

Selected quotations by theme

A modest selection of quotes drawn from the main text, arranged thematically and with a particular emphasis upon quotations added for this new edition of the book, follows. It concludes with additional lists of quotations selected to provide inspiration for readers faced with the daunting prospect of speaking in public.

Art and culture

Abu'l-'Alá Al-Ma'arri
The world's best moment is a calm hour passed
In listening to a friend who can talk well.
c.1000 *Luzūmiyyāt*, stanza 32 (translated by R A Nicholson in *Studies in Islamic Poetry*, 1921).

Addison, Joseph
Nothing is capable of being well set to music that is not nonsense.
1711 In *The Spectator*, no.18.

Antheil, George
Art cannot hold its breath too long without dying.
1945 *Bad Boy of Music*.

Appleton, Sir Edward Victor
I do not mind what language an opera is sung in so long as it is a language I don't understand.
1955 In the *Observer*, 28 Aug.

Banksy
Art should comfort the disturbed and disturb the comfortable.
Attributed.

Carey, Peter
I have travelled widely. I have seen this country in its infancy. I tell you what it will become. The public squares will be occupied by an uneducated class who will not be able to quote a line of Shakespeare.
2010 *Parrot and Olivier in America*.

de Botton, Alain
It is perhaps when our lives are at their most problematic that we are likely to be most receptive to beautiful things.
2006 *The Architecture of Happiness*.

Donahue, Phil
The breasts, the hallmark of our culture. You cannot sell anything in America without the breasts.
1990 On NBC TV, Aug.

Gandhi, Mohandas Karamchand known as Mahatma [great soul]
What do I think of Western civilization? I think that it would be a good idea.
Attributed.

Greer, Germaine
Football is an art more central to our culture than anything the Arts Council deigns to recognize.
1996 In *The Independent*, 28 Jun.

James, Clive
A painter can leave you with nothing left to say. A writer leaves you with everything to say.
2007 *Cultural Amnesia: Necessary Memories from History and the Arts*.

Johst, Hanns
When I hear anyone talk of culture... I take off the safety catch on my Browning!
1933 *Schlageter*, act 1, sc.1. The phrase is often attributed to Hermann Goering, in the form 'Whenever I hear the word culture, I reach for my gun!'.

Kapoor, Sir Anish
Artists don't make objects. Artists make mythologies.
Attributed.

Martel, Yann
A work of art works because it is true, not because it is real.
2010 *Beatrice and Virgil*.

Miller, Henry
The word 'civilization' to my mind is coupled with death. When I use the word, I see civilization as a crippling, thwarting thing, a stultifying thing... Civilization is the arteriosclerosis of culture.
1962 Interview in the *Paris Review*, Summer.

Picasso, Pablo Ruiz y
God is really only another artist. He invented the giraffe, the elephant, and the cat. He has no real style. He just goes on trying other things.
Quoted in F Gilot and C Lake *Life with Picasso* (1964), pt.1.

Punch
Botticelli isn't a wine, you Juggins! Botticelli's a cheese!
1891

Redgrave, Vanessa
The arts stop society going rotten and mad.
2013 Interview, *FT Magazine*, 26 Apr.

Schnabel, Artur
I know two kinds of audience only—one coughing and one not coughing.
1961 *My Life and Music*.

Strong, Sir Roy Colin
Style has gone out of fashion.
2011 In the *Evening Standard*, 15 Sep.

Whiteread, Rachel
I don't want to make plop art—sculpture that just gets plopped down in places. I wouldn't want to litter every corner of the world with my sculpture.
2005 Quoted in *The Guardian*, 16 Oct.

Wilde, Oscar
All art is immoral.
1891 *Intentions*, 'The Critic as Artist'.

Business

Adams, Scott
Give a man a fish, and you'll feed him for a day. Teach a man to fish, and he'll buy a funny hat. Talk to a hungry man about fish, and you're a consultant.
2008 *Stick to Drawing Comics, Monkey Brain!: Cartoonist Ignores Helpful Advice.*

Appel, Jacob M.
The boss is never your friend, even if you're sleeping with him.
2005 *Arborophilia.*

Bezos, Jeff(rey Preston)
Amazon is not happening to book selling, the future is happening to book selling.
2013 On *60 Minutes*, CBS, 1 Dec.

Coolidge, (John) Calvin
The chief business of the American people is business.
1925 Speech to the Society of Newspaper Editors, Washington, 17 Jan.

Forbes, (Malcolm Stevenson) 'Steve', Jr
It is unfortunate we can't buy many business executives for what they are worth and sell them for what they think they are worth.
Quoted in David Mahoney *Confessions of a Street-Smart Manager* (1988).

Franklin, Benjamin
Time is money.
1748 *Advice to a Young Tradesman.*

Gates, Bill (William Henry III)
The Internet is becoming the town square for the global village of tomorrow.
1999 *Business@the Speed of Thought* (co-written with Collins Hemingway).

Hoffman, Dustin
Accountant—according to the word, it must be a cross between a 'counter' and a 'mutant'.
2007 As Mr Edward Magorium in *Mr Magorium's Wonder Emporium* (screenplay by Zack Helm).

Jobs, Steve (Steven Paul)
It's more fun to be a pirate than to join the navy.
1982 Quoted in John A. Byrne, *Odyssey: Pepsi to Apple*, 1987.

Keynes (of Tilton), John Maynard, 1st Baron
A 'sound' banker, alas! is not one who foresees danger and avoids it, but one who, when he is ruined, is ruined in a conventional and orthodox way along with his fellows, so that no one can really blame him.
1931 *Essays in Persuasion.*

Knobel, Steven Maxwell
It was the Wild West. If you were alive, they would give you a loan. Actually, I think if you were dead, they would still give you a loan.
2008 Referring to the behaviour of US banks before the economic crash, 29 Dec.

Marlowe, Christopher
Thus methinks should men of judgement frame
Their means of traffic from the vulgar trade,
And as their wealth increaseth, so enclose
Infinite riches in a little room.
c.1589 *The Jew of Malta* (published 1633), act 1, sc.1.

Merkel, Angela Dorothea
The euro is much, much more than a currency. The euro is the guarantee of a united Europe. If the euro fails, then Europe fails.
2011 Speech in the German Parliament, reported in *Der Spiegel*, 7 Sep.

Puzo, Mario
I'll make him an offer he can't refuse.
1969 *The Godfather*, bk.1, ch.1.

Rather, Dan(iel Irvin)
He couldn't sell watermelons if you gave him the state troopers to flag down traffic.
2010 Referring to President Barack Obama on the *Chris Matthews Show*, 8 Mar.

Roy, Arundhati
Capitalism is destroying the planet. The two old tricks that dug it out of past crises—War and Shopping—simply will not work.
2014 *Capitalism: A Ghost Story.*

Soros, George
I'm only rich because I know when I'm wrong.
Attributed.

Stevenson, Robert Louis
Every one lives by selling something, whatever be his right to it.
1888 'Beggars', originally published in *Scribner's Magazine.*

Stoppard, Sir Tom
War is capitalism with the gloves off.
1974 *Travesties.*

Trump, Donald
You're fired!
2004 His catchphrase on *The Apprentice.*

Celebrities

Prince Albert
I have had wealth, rank and power, but, if these were all I had, how wretched I should be.
1861 Attributed last words.

Current affairs

Brand, Russell Edward

Mostly orphans' tears, old clock parts, lizards' tails, spit, the concept of freedom; all up there, all shooshed up right nice and tight, like a bonfire that's never actually burned... it mutters follicular oddities into my mind.
2007 When asked what he put on his hair, Radio 1 interview, 5 Jul.

Congreve, William

They come together like the Coroner's Inquest, to sit upon the murdered reputations of the week.
1700 Fainall to Mirabell. *The Way of the World*, act 1, sc.1.

Dobson, (Henry) Austin

Fame is a food that dead men eat,
I have no stomach for such meat.
1906 'Fame is a Fool'.

Fitzgerald, F(rancis) Scott Key

When people are taken out of their depths they lose their heads, no matter how charming a bluff they may put up.
1934 *Tender is the Night*, bk.3, ch.12.

Gore, Al

The planet is in distress and all of the attention is on Paris Hilton.
2007 In *The Sun*, 18 Jun.

Greer, Germaine

Diana was never a fashion icon. She dressed to the same demotic standard of elegance as TV anchorwomen do, plus the inevitable hat. This was a desperate woman seeking applause. In death she has it, doled out in huge amounts.
2007 Referring to Princess Diana. Quoted in the *Sydney Morning Herald*, 26 Aug.

Johansson, Scarlett

You work hard making independent films for fourteen years and you get voted best breasts.
2006 In *Esquire* magazine, Nov.

John, Elton Hercules

I think Jesus was a compassionate, super-intelligent gay man who understood human problems.
2010 In *Parade* magazine, 21 Feb.

Jolie, Angelina

Quod me nutrit me destruit.
What nourishes me destroys me.
Tattoo.

Jonson, Ben

Fame and rumour are but toys.
1609 *Volpone*, 'Song', act 3, sc.7.

Kissinger, Henry Alfred

The nice thing about being a celebrity is that when you bore people, they think that it's their fault.
Quoted in *Reader's Digest*, Apr 1985.

Mandela, Nelson

I do not want to be presented as some deity. I would like to be remembered as an ordinary human being with virtues and vices.
2005 Interview, *Reader's Digest*.

Mirren, Dame Helen Lydia

She's very known, but she's also very unknown, seen a lot but never really looked at.
2007 Referring to Elizabeth II, whom she played when she won an Oscar in *The Queen* (2006).

Monroe, Marilyn

He's the only person I know who's in worse shape than I am.
1961 On Montgomery Clift, her co-star in *The Misfits*.

Oates, Joyce Carol

Those whom the gods wish to destroy, they first make famous.
2006 Speech at Mount Holyoke College, 25 Apr.

Rice-Davies, Mandy

He would, wouldn't he?
1963 On hearing that during the trial of Stephen Ward, Lord Astor had denied her allegations of orgies at his house parties at Cliveden, 29 Jun.

Sheen, Charlie

It ain't a party till something gets broken.
Attributed.

West, Kanye Omari

And the thing is, for me to say I wasn't a genius, I would just be lying to you and to myself.
2013 On *Jimmy Kimmel Live*, 9 Oct.

West, Mae

I've been in *Who's Who* and I know what's what, but it's the first time I ever made the dictionary.
Reputedly said on learning that a life jacket was to be named after her.

Current affairs

Adams, Gerry

The hardest negotiation is always with your own side.
2003 In *The Observer*, 9 Nov.

Anonymous

Je suis Charlie.
I am Charlie.
2015 Slogan widely adopted in France and elsewhere in defiance after Islamic terrorists murdered 12 staff of the *Charlie Hebdo* satirical magazine in Paris, 7 Jan.

Anonymous

We are the 99 per cent.

Current affairs

2011 Slogan of the Occupy Movement against corporate greed, inspired by a statistic claiming that most wealth in US society is controlled by one per cent of the population.

Ashcroft, John David

Why are we talking about this in the White House? History will not judge this kindly.
2008 Attributed. Referring to discussion of torture techniques by senior officials, as quoted on *ABC News*, 9 Apr.

Balfour, Arthur James Balfour, 1st Earl

I look forward to a time when Irish patriotism will as easily combine with British patriotism as Scottish patriotism combines now.
1889 Speech, Glasgow, Dec.

Blix, Hans

We have not found any smoking guns.
2003 Of weapons inspections in Iraq. To reporters, 9 Jan.

Bush, George W(alker)

Our war on terror is well begun, but it is only begun. This campaign may not be finished on our watch—yet it must be and it will be waged on our watch.
2002 State of the Union Address, 29 Jan.

Cameron, David William Donald

I am the heir to Blair.
2005 Speaking to newspaper executives, 3 Oct.

Carter, Jimmy

America does not at the moment have a functioning democracy.
2013 Referring to mass surveillance by the US government, quoted in *International Business Times*, 18 Jul.

Clegg, Nick (Nicholas William Peter)

I need to say this—you shouldn't trust any government, actually including this one. You should not trust government—full stop. The natural inclination of government is to hoard power and information; to accrue power to itself in the name of the public good.
Attributed.

de Klerk, F(rederik) W(illem)

Today we have closed the book on apartheid.
1992 On the endorsement of his government's reform programme following a referendum of white South Africans. In *The Independent*, 19 Mar.

Fawkes, Guy

A desperate disease requires a dangerous remedy.
1605 When questioned after his arrest on 5 Nov.

Henry II

Will no one rid me of this turbulent priest?
1170 Of Thomas à Becket. Quoted in WL Warren *Henry II*, p508. Four of Henry's soldiers took his words to heart and proceeded to Canterbury, where they murdered Becket in the cathedral.

Lincoln, Abraham

Four score and seven years ago our fathers brought forth upon this continent a new nation, conceived in liberty and dedicated to the proposition that all men are created equal... we here highly resolve that the dead shall not have died in vain; that this nation, under God, shall have a new birth of freedom; and that government of the people, by the people, and for the people, shall not perish from the earth.
1863 Dedication address, Gettysburg National Cemetery, 19 Nov.

Mao Zedong *or* Mao Tse-tung

Every Communist must grasp the truth that political power grows out of the barrel of a gun.
1938 'Problems of War and Strategy', speech, 6 Nov.

Meyer, Andrew William

Don't tase me, bro.
2007 His response when threatened with a taser; the phrase subsequently swept the nation, 17 Sep.

Mugabe, Robert

We are not going to give up our country because of a mere X. How can a ballpoint fight with a gun?
2008 Shrugging off the possibility of electoral defeat.

Obama, Barack Hussein

It's been a long time coming, but tonight, because of what we did on this date in this election at this defining moment, change has come to America.
2008 Victory speech in US Presidential election, Chicago, 4 Nov.

Palin, Sarah Louise Heath

Well, if I were in charge, they would know that waterboarding is how we baptize terrorists.
2014 Speaking at the Stand and Fight Rally, Indianapolis, 26 Apr.

Putin, Vladimir Vladimirovich

People in Russia say that those who do not regret the collapse of the Soviet Union have no heart, and those that do regret it have no brain.
2005 Interview, German television channel ARD and ZDF, May.

O'Casey, Sean

Th' whole worl's in a state o'chassis!
1924 Boyle speaking. *Juno and the Paycock*, act 1.

Rice, Condoleezza

For sixty years, my country, the United States, pursued stability at the expense of democracy in this region, here in the Middle East, and we achieved neither.
2005 Speech at the American University, Cairo, 21 Jun.

Roosevelt, Franklin D(elano)

Yesterday, December 7, 1941—a date which will live in infamy—the United States of America was suddenly and deliberately attacked by naval and air forces of the Empire of Japan.
1941 Address to Congress, 8 Dec, following the Japanese attack on Pearl Harbor.

Shakespeare, William

There is a tide in the affairs of men
Which, taken at the flood, leads on to fortune;

Omitted, all the voyage of their life
Is bound in shallows and in miseries.
1599 Brutus. *Julius Caesar*, act 4, sc.2.

Walpole, Sir Robert, 1st Earl of Orford

All those men have their price.
Quoted in William Coxe *Memoirs of Sir Robert Walpole* (1798).

Zola, Émile

J'accuse.
I accuse.
1898 Title of open letter to the President of France regarding the Dreyfus case.

Freedom

Achebe, Chinua

We cannot trample upon the humanity of others without devaluing our own. The Igbo, always practical, put it concretely in their proverb *Onye ji onye n'ani ji onwe ya*: 'He who will hold another down in the mud must stay in the mud to keep him down.'
2009 *The Education of a British-Protected Child: Essays.*

Ai Weiwei

I don't see myself as a dissident artist. I see them as a dissident government!
2012 On Twitter, 25 Jan.

Assange, Julian Paul

It is impossible to correct abuses unless we know that they're going on.
2010 Address to the Oslo Freedom Forum, 26–29 Apr.

Burke, Edmund

Liberty too must be limited in order to be possessed.
1777 *Letter to the Sheriffs of Bristol*.

Burns, Robert

A fig for those by law protected!
Liberty's a glorious feast!
Courts for Cowards were erected,
Churches built to please the Priest.
c.1786 'The Jolly Beggars', or 'Love and Liberty, a Cantata', chorus to a song to the tune 'Jolly Mortals, fill your glasses'.

Camus, Albert

What is a rebel? A man who says no.
1951 *L'Homme révolté*.

Clinton, Hillary

Freedom is never granted. It is earned by each generation.
2007 Speaking to Veterans of Foreign Wars, Kansas City, Missouri, 20 Aug.

Crichton, Michael

Do you know what we call opinion in the absence of evidence? We call it prejudice.
2004 *State of Fear*.

Davis, Jefferson

All we ask is to be let alone.
1861 Inaugural address, 18 Feb.

Eisenhower, Dwight D(avid)

History does not long entrust the care of freedom to the weak or the timid.
1953 Inaugural address, 20 Jan.

George, Daniel

O Freedom, what liberties are taken in thy name!
1963 *The Perpetual Pessimist*.

Herbert, Sir A(lan) P(atrick)

Let's find out what everyone is doing
And then stop everyone from doing it.
1930 'Let's Stop Somebody from Doing Something'.

Ibsen, Henrik Johan

You should never have your best trousers on when you turn out to fight for freedom and truth.
1882 *En folkefiende* (*An Enemy of the People*), act 5.

Kennedy, John F(itzgerald)

The rights of every man are diminished when the rights of one man are threatened.
1963 On sending national guardsmen to ensure peaceful integration at the University of Alabama. Address to the nation, 11 Jun.

Orwell, George

If liberty means anything at all, it means the right to tell people what they do not want to hear.
1945 Written for a rejected preface to *Animal Farm*.

Pitt, William, 1st Earl of Chatham known as the Elder

Where laws end, tyranny begins.
1770 Speech to the House of Lords, 2 Mar.

Rushdie, Salman

There is no right in the world not to be offended. That right simply doesn't exist. In a free society, an open society, people have strong opinions, and these opinions very often clash. In a democracy, we have to learn to deal with this. And this is true about novels, it's true about cartoons, it's true about all these products.
2012 Interview in *The Hindu*, 8 Oct.

Sartre, Jean-Paul

Man is condemned to be free.
1946 *L'Existentialisme est un humanisme* (*Existentialism and Humanism*, 1948) (translated by Philip Mairet).

Snowden, Ed(ward Joseph)

My sole motive is to inform the public as to that which is done in their name and that which is done against them.
2013 In *The Guardian*, 9 Jun.

Turgenev, Ivan

I share no one's ideas. I have my own.
1862 *Fathers and Sons* (translated by Rosemary Edmonds), ch.13.

Yevtushenko, Yevgeny

When truth is replaced by silence, the silence is a lie.
Attributed.

History

Barnes, Julian

History is that certainty produced at the point where the imperfections of memory meet the inadequacies of documentation.
2011 *The Sense of an Ending*.

Butler, Samuel

It has been said that although God cannot alter the past, historians can; it is perhaps because they can be useful to Him in this respect that He tolerates their existence.
1901 *Erewhon Revisited*, ch.14.

Drexler, Arthur

History is written for the victors and what they leave out is the losers.
1975 In the *New York Review*, 27 Nov.

Durrell, Lawrence George

History is the endless repetition of the wrong way of living, and it'll start again tomorrow, if it's moved from here today.
1978 In *The Listener*, 20 Apr.

Ferguson, Niall

The law of unintended consequences is the only real law of history.
2012 In *Newsweek*, 18 Jun.

Ford, Henry

History is more or less bunk. It's tradition.
1916 Interview, *Chicago Tribune*, May.

Guedalla, Philip

History repeats itself. Historians repeat each other.
1920 *Supers and Supermen*, 'Some Historians'.

Hartley, L(eslie) P(oles)

The past is a foreign country: they do things differently there.
1953 *The Go-Between*, prologue.

Hawthorne, Nathaniel

The present is burthened too much with the past.
1856 Entry for 27 Mar at the British Museum, collected in *The English Notebooks* (1870).

King, Stephen

When it comes to the past, everyone writes fiction.
2013 *Joyland*.

MacLeish, Archibald

History, like a badly constructed concert hall, has occasional dead spots where the music can't be heard.
1967 In the *Observer*, 12 Feb.

Mantel, Dame Hilary Mary

Beneath every history, another history.
2009 *Wolf Hall*.

Ozick, Cynthia

Admittedly, there is always a golden age, the one not ours, the one that once was or will someday be. One's own time is never satisfactory, except to the very rich or the smugly oblivious.
2006 *The Din in the Head: Essays*.

Pascal, Blaise

I only believe in histories told by witnesses who would have had their throats slit.
c.1654–1662 *Pensées*, pt.9, no.593.

Saki *pseudonym of* Hector Hugh Munro

The people of Crete unfortunately make more history than they can consume locally.
1911 *The Chronicles of Clovis*, 'The Jesting of Arlington Stringham'.

Santayana, George

Those who cannot remember the past are condemned to repeat it.
1905–6 *The Life of Reason*.

Sterling, Bruce

Tomorrow composts today.
2005 *Shaping Things*.

Strachey, (Giles) Lytton

The history of the Victorian age will never be written: we know too much about it. For ignorance is the first requisite of the historian—ignorance, which simplifies and clarifies, which selects and omits, with a placid perfection unattainable by the highest art.
1918 *Eminent Victorians*, preface.

Streep, Meryl Louise

I gotta thank everybody in England that let me come and trample over their history.
2012 Accepting her eighth Golden Globe Award, for her performance of Margaret Thatcher in *The Iron Lady*.

Whitlam, (Edward) Gough

The importance of an historical event lies not in what happened but in what later generations believe to have happened.
1973 Speech at Ballarat, Victoria, 3 Dec.

Human nature

Adams, Scott

Few things are as destructive and limiting as a worldview that assumes people are mostly rational.
2013 *How to Fail at Almost Everything and Still Win Big: Kind of the Story of My Life.*

Attenborough, Sir David

Human beings are good at many things, but thinking about our species as a whole is not one of our strong points.
2009 *How Many People Can Live on Planet Earth?*, BBC *Horizon* programme.

Carey, Peter

Writers are always envious, mean-minded, filled with rage and envy at other's good fortune. There is nothing like the failure of a close friend to cheer us up.
2002 In the *Observer*, 18 Aug.

Dickens, Charles John Huffam

Subdue your appetites, my dears, and you've conquered human nature.
1838–9 *Nicholas Nickleby*, ch.5.

Donleavy, J(ames) P(atrick)

I got disappointed in human nature as well and gave it up because I found it too much like my own.
1973 *A Fairy Tale of New York*, ch.18.

Eco, Umberto

People are never so completely and enthusiastically evil as when they act out of religious conviction.
2010 *The Prague Cemetery.*

Franzen, Jonathan

Integrity's a neutral value. Hyenas have integrity, too. They're pure hyena.
2010 *Freedom.*

Gervais, Ricky Dene

Just because you're offended, doesn't mean you're right.
2011 Quoted on CNN *Tonight* Show, 20 Jan.

Holub, Miroslav

Humankind can generally be divided into hunters and people who cope with consequences.
1990 *The Dimensions of the Present Moment and Other Essays.*

Humphries, (John) Barry

I am a lucky woman because I was born with a priceless gift: the ability to laugh at the misfortunes of others.
2012 As Dame Edna Everage, announcing his retirement.

Keats, John

Scenery is fine—but human nature is finer.
1818 Letter to Benjamin Bailey, 13 Mar.

Lorenz, Konrad

Man appears to be the missing link between anthropoid apes and human beings.
1965 In the *New York Times*, 11 Apr.

Margrethe II

There is nothing so clever as people you agree with.
2012 Quoted by Helle Thorning-Schmidt in speech on Margrethe II's Ruby Jubilee, 15 Jan.

Mitchell, David Stephen

It's not just the person who fills a house, it's their I'll be back later!s, their toothbrushes and unused hats and coats, their belongingnesses.
2006 *Black Swan Green.*

Owen, Robert

All the world is queer save thee and me, and even thou art a little queer.
Attributed. Said to his partner W Allen when they ended their business relationship.

Pynchon, Thomas Ruggles

Paranoia's the garlic in life's kitchen, right, you can never have too much.
2013 *Bleeding Edge.*

Rabelais, François

It is better to write of laughter than of tears
For laughter is the basis of humankind.
1534 *Gargantua*, Aux lecteurs.

Sedaris, David Raymond

Sometimes the sins you haven't committed are all you have to hold on to. If you're really desperate, you might need to grope, saying, for example, 'I've never killed anyone *with a hammer*' or 'I've never stolen from anyone *who didn't deserve it*.'
2008 *When You Are Engulfed in Flames.*

Trollope, Anthony

We cannot have heroes to dine with us. There are none. And were those heroes to be had, we should not like them... the persons whom you cannot care for in a novel, because they are so bad, are the very same that you so dearly love in your life, because they are so good.
1873 Of Frank Greystock. *The Eustace Diamonds*, ch.35.

Wells, H(erbert) G(eorge)

Human history becomes more and more a race between education and catastrophe.
1920 *The Outline of History*, vol.2, ch.41.

Yousafzai, Malala

We are human beings, and this is the part of our human nature, that we don't learn the importance of anything until it's snatched from our hands.
2013 Interview on *The Daily Show*, 8 Oct.

Insults

Asquith, Margot

The t is silent, as in Harlow.
Attributed riposte to Jean Harlow who was having trouble pronouncing her name. The line may actually have been spoken by Margot Grahame, an English actress in Hollywood in the 1930s.

Cable, (John) Vince(nt)

The House has noticed the Prime Minister's remarkable transformation in the past few weeks from Stalin to Mr Bean, creating chaos out of order, rather than order out of chaos.
2007 Referring to Labour Prime Minister Gordon Brown in the House of Commons, 28 Nov.

Charles, Prince of Wales

What is proposed is like a monstrous carbuncle on the face of a much-loved and elegant friend.
1984 On the proposed extension to the National Gallery, London. Speech at the 150th anniversary of the Royal Institute of British Architects, 30 May.

Churchill, Sir Winston Leonard Spencer

An empty taxi arrived at 10 Downing Street, and when the door was opened Attlee got out.
Attributed. Quoted in Kenneth Harris *Attlee* (1982), ch.16.

Clemenceau, Georges

America is the only country in history that miraculously has gone directly from barbarism to decadence without the usual interval of civilization.
Attributed. This has also been attributed to George Bernard Shaw.

Cowell, Simon Phillip

You have the showmanship of a peanut.
2011 *Britain's Got Talent*.

Davis, Bette

She's the original good time who was had by all.
On an anonymous starlet. Attributed.

Dorries, Nadine Vanessa

Two posh boys who don't know the price of milk.
2012 Referring to Prime Minister David Cameron and Chancellor of the Exchequer George Osborne, 23 Apr.

Farage, Nigel Paul

You have the charisma of a damp rag, and the appearance of a low-grade bank clerk.
2010 Addressing Herman Van Rompuy, President of the EU, at the European Parliament, 24 Feb.

Gallagher, Noel

He's like a man with a fork, in a world of soup.
2009 Referring to his brother Liam Gallagher.

Greene, Robert

For there is an upstart crow, beautified with our feathers, that with his tiger's heart wrapped in a player's hide, supposes he is as well able to bombast out a blank verse as the best of you; and being an absolute *Iohannes fac totum*, is in his own conceit the only Shake-scene in a country.
1592 Of Shakespeare. *The Groatsworth of Wit, Bought with a Million of Repentance. Iohannes fac totum* = 'Jack-of-all-trades'.

Hitchens, Peter Jonathan

Frankly, I could carve a better opposition party out of a banana than the Tories.
2009 'Question Time', *The Guardian*, 14 May.

Johnson, Boris

He is like some sherry-crazed old dowager who has lost the family silver at roulette, and who now decides to double up by betting the house as well.
2008 Describing Prime Minister Gordon Brown, quoted on *Mail Online*, 25 Nov.

Johnson, Lyndon B(aines)

So dumb he can't fart and chew gum at the same time.
Of Gerald Ford. Quoted in Richard Reeves *A Ford, Not a Lincoln*. (1975), ch.2.

Johnson, Samuel

The noblest prospect which a Scotchman ever sees, is the high road that leads him to England!
1763 Remark, 6 Jul. Quoted in James Boswell *The Life of Samuel Johnson* (1791), vol.1.

Keating, Paul

All tip and no iceberg.
2007 Referring to Treasurer Peter Costello, ABC Radio interview, 5 Mar.

Napoleon I

England is a nation of shopkeepers.
Attributed while in exile on St Helena.

Parker, Dorothy

Katharine Hepburn runs the gamut of the emotions from A to B.
1933 Remark during the interval of *The Lake* on its Broadway première. Quoted in G Carey *Katharine Hepburn* (1983), ch.6.

Pope, Alexander

A brain of feathers, and a heart of lead.
1742 *The Dunciad*, bk.2, l.44.

Sheridan, Philip Henry

The only good Indian is a dead Indian.
1869 Attributed comment at Fort Cobb, Jan.

Language

Ackerman, Diane

And yet, words are the passkeys to our souls. Without them, we can't really share the enormity of our lives.
2011 *One Hundred Names for Love: A Stroke, a Marriage, and the Language of Healing.*

Banville, (William) John

The sentence is the greatest invention of civilization. To sit all day long assembling these extraordinary strings of words is a marvellous thing. I couldn't ask for anything better. It's as near to godliness as I can get... The great thrill is when a sentence that starts out being completely plain suddenly begins to sing, rising far above itself and above any expectation I might have had for it. That's what keeps me going on those dark December days.
2009 In *The Paris Review*, spring.

Bible (Old Testament)

Be not rash with thy mouth, and let not thine heart be hasty to utter any thing before God: for God is in heaven, and thou upon earth: therefore let thy words be few.
Ecclesiastes 5:2.

Fiennes, Ralph Nathaniel

We're in a world of truncated sentences, soundbites and Twitter... our expressiveness and our ease with some words is being diluted so that the sentence with more than one clause is a problem for us, and the word of more than two syllables is a problem for us.
2011 In *The Daily Mail*, 28 Oct.

Gilbert, Sir W(illiam) S(chwenck)

When you're lying awake with a dismal headache, and repose is taboo'd by anxiety,
I conceive you may use any language you choose to indulge in, without impropriety.
1882 Lord Chancellor's nightmare song, *Iolanthe*, act 2.

James, Henry

Summer afternoon—summer afternoon; to me those have always been the two most beautiful words in the English language.
Quoted in Edith Wharton *A Backward Glance* (1934), ch.10, section 6.

Jong, Erica

Murky language means someone wants to pick your pocket.
2006 *Seducing the Demon: Writing for My Life.*

Jovanovich, William

The most important single thing in publishing is the English sentence, and the editor who cannot contemplate it again and again with a sense of wonder has not yet gained respect for the complexity of learning.
1964 *Now, Barabbas.*

Lively, Penelope

There's a fearful term that's in fashion at the moment—closure. People apparently believe it is desirable and attainable.
2011 *How It All Began.*

Milne, A(lan) A(lexander)

I am a Bear of Very Little Brain, and long words Bother me.
1926 *Winnie-the-Pooh*, ch.4.

Milton, John

Salve to thy sores, apt words have power to suage
The tumours of a troubl'd mind,
And are as Balm to fester'd wounds.
1671 *Samson Agonistes*, l.184–6.

Moore, Marianne Craig

I am governed by the pull of the sentence as the pull of a fabric is governed by gravity.
Quoted in Louis Untermeyer 'Five Famous Poetesses', in *Ladies' Home Journal*, May 1964.

Palin, Sarah Louise Heath

Peaceful Muslims, pls refudiate.
2010 Message on Twitter, which introduced the word 'refudiate' to the world; Palin later explained that she had intended to write 'repudiate', Jul.

Pinter, Harold

Language in art remains a highly ambiguous transaction, a quicksand, a trampoline, a frozen pool which might give way under you... at any time.
2005 Pre-recorded acceptance speech for the Nobel Prize for Literature, Stockholm, 7 Dec.

Sandburg, Carl

Slang is a language that rolls up its sleeves, spits on its hands and goes to work.
1959 In the *New York Times*, 13 Feb.

Shakespeare, William

But words are words. I never yet did hear
That the bruised heart was piercèd through the ear.
1603–4 Brabanzio. *Othello*, act 1, sc.3, l.217–8.

Shaw, George Bernard

England and America are two countries divided by a common language.
Attributed.

Tennyson, Alfred, 1st Baron

I sometimes hold it half a sin
To put in words the grief I feel;
For words, like Nature, half reveal
And half conceal the Soul within.
1850 *In Memoriam A.H.H.*, canto 5, l.1–4.

Walcott, Derek Alton

The English language is nobody's special property. It is the property of the imagination: it is the property of the language itself.

Interviewed in George Plimpton (ed) *Writers at Work* (8th series, 1988).

Waugh, Evelyn Arthur St John

To watch him fumbling with our rich and delicate English language is like seeing a Sèvres vase in the hands of a chimpanzee.

Of Sir Stephen Spender. Quoted by Eric Pace in Spender's obituary in the *New York Times*, 18 Jul 1995.

Last words

Adams, John Quincy

I inhabit a weak, frail, decayed tenement; battered by the winds and broken in on by the storms, and, from all I can learn, the landlord does not intend to repair.

1848 Attributed, as he lay on his deathbed. Quoted in Clifton Fadiman *The Faber Book of Anecdotes* (1985).

Addison, Joseph

See in what peace a Christian can die.

1719 Spoken to his stepson Lord Warwick. Quoted in Edward Young *Conjectures on Original Composition* (1759).

Angelou, Maya

Listen to yourself and in that quietude you might hear the voice of God.

2014 On Facebook, shortly before her death, 23 May.

Best, George

Don't die like I did.

2005 Last words.

Caesar, Gaius Julius

Et tu, Brute?
You too, Brutus?

Attributed last words, when struck by his murderers, Cassius and Brutus. The tradition is based on Suetonius *Lives of the Twelve Caesars*, 'Divus Iulius', section 82: 'Some say that when he saw Marcus Brutus about to deliver the second blow, he reproached him in Greek with: 'You too, my son?' (the Greek is *kai su, teknon*).

Charles II

Let not poor Nelly starve.

c.1685 Worrying on his deathbed about his mistress, Nell Gwynn. Quoted in Bishop Gilbert Burney *History of My Own Time* (1724), vol.1, bk.2.

Ferrier, Kathleen

Now I'll have eine kleine pause.

1953 Quoted in Gerald Moore *Am I Too Loud?* (1962).

Garner, Eric

I can't breathe.

2014 His protest when put in a chokehold by arresting officers, 17 Jul. Garner's last words were subsequently widely adopted by protesters criticizing the court's failure to take action in the case.

George V

Bugger Bognor.

1929 or 1936 Reply to a courtier who had remarked 'Cheer up, your Majesty, you will soon be at Bognor again', either during his convalescence or on his deathbed. Quoted in Kenneth Rose *King George V* (1983), ch.9.

Heaney, Seamus

Noli timere.
Don't be afraid.

2013 Last words, in a text message to his wife, quoted in *The Atlantic*, 4 Sep.

Ibsen, Henrik Johan

On the contrary!

1906 Refuting a nurse's suggestion that he was feeling better.

James, Henry

So here it is at last, the distinguished thing!

Quoted in Edith Wharton *A Backward Glance* (1934), ch.14, section 3.

Jobs, Steve (Steven Paul)

Oh wow, oh wow, oh wow.

2011 Last words, 5 Oct.

Nelson, Horatio, Viscount Nelson

Kiss me, Hardy.

1805 Attributed, as he lay dying in the cockpit of the *Victory* during the Battle of Trafalgar, 21 Oct.

News of the World

Quite simply, we lost our way.

2011 Editorial in final edition, 10 Jul.

Oates, Lawrence Edward Grace

I am just going outside and may be some time.

1912 During Captain Scott's ill-fated Antarctic expedition, Mar.

Pavarotti, Luciano

I believe that a life lived for music is an existence spent wonderfully, and this is what I have dedicated my life to.

2007 His last words, spoken to his manager Terri Robson, reported in the *New York Times*, 6 Sep.

Pitt, William *known as* the Younger

I think that I could eat one of Bellamy's veal pies.

1806 Attributed last words, 23 Jan.

Vega Carpio, Lope Félix de

All right, then, I'll say it: Dante makes me sick.

1635 Attributed.

Wilde, Oscar Fingal O'Flahertie Wills

Either that wallpaper goes or I do.

1900 As he lay dying in a Paris hotel bedroom. Attributed.

Life and death

Ackerman, Diane
No matter how politely one says it, we owe our existence to the farts of blue-green algae.
2004 *An Alchemy of Mind: The Marvel and Mystery of the Brain.*

Allen, Woody
My relationship with death remains the same—I'm strongly against it.
2011 Press conference, Cannes Film Festival.

Arnold, Matthew
Is it so small a thing
To have enjoyed the sun,
To have lived light in the spring,
To have loved, to have thought, to have done.
1852 'Empedocles on Etna', act 1, sc.2, l.397–400.

Banks, Iain M
All you ever were was a little bit of the universe, thinking to itself. Very specific; this bit, here, right now.
2010 *Surface Detail.*

Bennett, Alan
Life is rather like a tin of sardines—we're all of us looking for the key.
1960 *Beyond the Fringe.*

Butler, Samuel
Life is like playing a violin solo in public and learning the instrument as one goes on.
1895 Speech at the Somerville Club, 27 Feb.

Chaucer, Geoffrey
This world nys but a thurghfare ful of wo,
And we been pilgrymes, passynge to and fro.
1387 *Canterbury Tales*, 'The Knight's Tale', l. 2847–8.

Cowley, Abraham
Life is an incurable disease.
1656 'To Dr Scarborough', stanza 6.

Cronenberg, David Paul
Why do I concern myself so much with sex and death? It's simple. Sex is the only way we have of keeping death at bay.
2014 Quoted on thestar.com, 26 Dec.

Didion, Joan
Life changes in the instant. The ordinary instant.
2005 *The Year of Magical Thinking.*

Doctorow, E. L.
Someone dying asks if there is life after death. Yes, comes the answer, only not yours.
2009 *Homer & Langley.*

Eliot, T(homas) S(tearns)
Birth, and copulation, and death.
That's all the facts when you come to brass tacks:
Birth, and copulation, and death.
I've been born, and once is enough.
1932 *Sweeney Agonistes*, 'Fragment of an Agon'.

50 Cent
If you die in an elevator make sure you press the up button.
Attributed.

Fitzgerald, Edward
Drink! for you know not whence you came, nor why:
Drink! for you know not why you go nor where.
1859 *The Rubáiyát of Omar Khayyám of Naishapur*, stanza 74.

Gay, John
Life is a jest; and all things show it.
I thought so once; but now I know it.
1720 'My Own Epitaph'.

Hubbard, Elbert Green
Life is just one damned thing after another.
1909 In *The Philistine*, Dec.

Shakespeare, William
Life is as tedious as a twice-told tale
Vexing the dull ear of a drowsy man.
1596 Louis the Dauphin. *King John*, act 3, sc.4, l.108–9.

Smith, Logan Pearsall
People say that life is the thing, but I prefer reading.
1931 *Afterthoughts*, 'Myself'.

Tennyson, Alfred, 1st Baron
Fill the cup, and fill the can:
Have a rouse before the morn:
Every moment dies a man,
Every moment one is born.
1842 *Poems*, 'The Vision of Sin', pt.4, stanza 9, l.95–8.

Thomas, Dylan Marlais
Do not go gentle into that good night,
Old age should burn and rave at close of day;
Rage, rage against the dying of the light.
1952 'Do Not Go Gentle Into That Good Night'.

Lifestyle

Amis, Martin
Screw-top wine has improved the quality of life by about ten per cent, wouldn't you say?
2010 *The Pregnant Widow.*

Bacall, Lauren

A planned life is a dead life.
2005 Interview, Aug.

Bennett, (Enoch) Arnold

Good taste is better than bad taste, but bad taste is better than no taste, and men without individuality have no taste—at any rate no taste that they can impose on their publics.
1930 In the *Evening Standard*, 21 Aug.

Blanc, Raymond

When you cook it should be an act of love. To put a frozen bag in the microwave for your child is an act of hate.
2001 In *The Daily Telegraph*, 2 Oct.

Cibber, Colley

One had as good be out of the World, as out of the Fashion.
1696 *Love's Last Shift: or, The Fool in Fashion*, act 2, sc.1.

Emerson, Ralph Waldo

Whoso would be a man must be a nonconformist.
1841 *Essays: First Series*, 'Self-Reliance'.

Galbraith, John Kenneth

In the affluent society, no useful distinction can be made between luxuries and necessities.
1958 *The Affluent Society*.

Keillor, Garrison

Why do we work so hard to get what we don't even want?
2006 *A Prairie Home Companion*.

Lovelock, James Ephraim

Unfortunately, we are a species with schizoid tendencies, and like an old lady who has to share her house with a growing and destructive group of teenagers, Gaia grows angry, and if they do not mend their ways she will evict them.
2006 *The Revenge of Gaia: Earth's Climate Crisis and the Fate of Humanity*.

Lucretius *full name* Titus Lucretius Carus

What is food to one may be literally poison to others.
De Rerum Natura, bk.4, line 637 (translated by R. E. Latham).

Moore, Michael

I had an unusually large-sized head, though this was not uncommon for a baby in the Midwest. The craniums in our part of the country were designed to leave a little extra room for the brain to grow in case one day we found ourselves exposed to something we didn't understand, like a foreign language, or a salad.
2011 *Here Comes Trouble*.

Moss, Kate

Nothing tastes as good as skinny feels.
2009 Her personal motto, which drew criticism from eating-disorder experts.

Nader, Ralph

We must strive to become good ancestors.
2004 *The Good Fight*.

O'Leary, Michael

The best thing you can do with environmentalists is shoot them. These headbangers want to make air travel the preserve of the rich. They are luddites marching us back to the eighteenth century.
Quoted in Brian Clegg, *Ecologic: The Truth and Lies of Green Economics* (2010).

Paltrow, Gwyneth Kate

I'd rather die than let my kid eat Cup-a-Soup.
2005 In the *New York Daily News*, Aug.

Potter, Stephen

How to be one up—how to make the other man feel that something has gone wrong, however slightly.
1950 *Lifemanship*.

Shakespeare, William

The play, I remember, pleased not the million. 'Twas caviare to the general.
1600–1 Hamlet to one of the players. *Hamlet*, act 2, sc.2, l.438–40.

Shaw, George Bernard

Fashions, after all, are only induced epidemics.
1906 *The Doctor's Dilemma*, 'Preface on Doctors: Fashions and Epidemics'.

Socrates

How many things I can do without!
On viewing goods for sale. Quoted in Diogenes Laertius *Vitae Philosophorum*, 2.25 (translated by R D Hicks, 1950).

West, Mae

Beulah, peel me a grape.
1933 *I'm No Angel*.

Literature

Abse, Dannie

I want you to go into them sober and come out drunk.
2013 Of his collection of poems *Speak, Old Parrot*.

Bacon, Francis, Viscount St Albans

Some books are to be tasted, others to be swallowed, and some few to be chewed and digested; that is, some books are to be read only in parts; others to be read but not curiously; and some few to be read wholly, and with diligence and attention. Some books also may be read by deputy, and extracts made of them by others.
1625 *Essays*, no. 50, 'Of Studies'.

Banks, Iain M.

The trouble with writing fiction is that it has to make sense, whereas real life doesn't.
2013 In 'Iain Banks: The Final Interview', *The Guardian*, 14 Jun.

Coleridge, Samuel Taylor

Prose = words in their best order;—poetry = the best words in the best order.
1827 *Table Talk* (published 1835), entry for 12 Jul.

Collins, Billy

While the novelist is banging on his typewriter, the poet is watching a fly in the windowpane.
Attributed.

Connolly, Cyril Vernon

Literature is the art of writing something that will be read twice; journalism what will be read once.
1938 *Enemies of Promise*, ch.3.

Cronenberg, David Paul

The only authentic literature of the modern era is the owner's manual.
2014 *Consumed*.

Descartes, René

The reading of good books is like a conversation with the best men of past centuries—in fact like a prepared conversation, in which they reveal their best thoughts.
1637 *Discours de la méthode* (*Discourse on Method*), 1st discourse (translated by G E M Anscombe and Peter Geach).

Duffy, Dame Carol Ann

I like to use simple words, but in a complicated way.
2002 In *The Guardian*.

Ferlinghetti, Lawrence

Poetry is a naked woman, a naked man, and the distance between them.
2007 *Poetry as Insurgent Art*.

Huxley, Aldous Leonard

The proper study of mankind is books.
1921 *Crome Yellow*, ch.28.

Le Guin, Ursula

The reason literacy is important is that literature is the operating instructions. The best manual we have. The most useful guide to the country we're visiting, life.
2004 *The Wave in the Mind*.

Lodge, David John

Literature is mostly about having sex and not much about having children. Life is the other way round.
1965 *The British Museum is Falling Down*, ch.4.

Mantel, Dame Hilary Mary

The reader may ask how to tell fact from fiction. A rough guide: anything that seems particularly unlikely is probably true.
1992 *A Place of Greater Safety*.

Rushdie, Salman

Literature happens at the level of the sentence.
2014 Speaking at Symphony Space's Selected Shorts literary event, New York, Dec.

Stoppard, Tom

A lot of people would say, 'I would rather have a heart attack at the height of sexual passion.' On the whole, I would prefer to be killed by a bookcase.
2010 In *The Daily Telegraph*, 4 Sep.

Twain, Mark

A classic... something that everybody wants to have read and nobody wants to read.
1900 Speech on 'The Disappearance of Literature' at the Nineteenth Century Club, 20 Nov. Quoted in Albert Bigelow Paine (ed) *Mark Twain's Speeches* (1910).

Wain, John Barrington

Poetry is to prose as dancing is to walking.
1976 BBC radio broadcast, 13 Jan.

Wilder, Thornton Niven

Literature is the orchestration of platitudes.
1953 In *Time*, 12 Jan.

Winterson, Jeanette

The trouble with a book is that you never know what's in it until it's too late.
2011 *Why Be Happy When You Could Be Normal?*

Love and sex

Allen, Woody

That was the most fun I ever had without laughing.
1977 Of sex. *Annie Hall* (with Marshall Brickman).

Auden, W(ystan) H(ugh)

O tell me the truth about love.
When it comes, will it come without warning
Just as I'm picking my nose?
Will it knock on my door in the morning,
Or tread in the bus on my toes?
1940 'Twelve Poems', section 12.

Berlusconi, Silvio

When asked if they would like to have sex with me, 30 per cent of women said, 'Yes', while the other 70 per cent replied, 'What, again?'
2011 His reply when quizzed about sex allegations made against him.

Blake, William
Love seeketh not itself to please,
Nor for itself hath any care,
But for another gives its ease,
And builds a heaven in hell's despair.
1794 *Songs of Experience*, 'The Clod and the Pebble'.

Browning, Elizabeth
How do I love thee? Let me count the ways!—
I love thee to the depth and breadth and height
My soul can reach, when feeling out of sight
For the ends of Being and Ideal Grace.
1850 *Poems*, 'Sonnets from the Portuguese', sonnet 43.

Burns, Robert
O my Luve's like a red, red rose
That's newly sprung in June;
O my luve's like the melodie
That's sweetly play'd in tune.
1794 'A red, red rose'.

Campbell, Mrs Patrick
It doesn't matter what you do in the bedroom as long as you don't do it in the street and frighten the horses.
Quoted in Daphne Fielding *The Duchess of Jermyn Street* (1964), ch.2. Sometimes attributed to Edward VII.

Donne, John
Come live with me, and be my love,
And we will some new pleasures prove
Of golden sands, and crystal brooks:
With silken lines, and silver hooks.
c.1595–1605 'The Bait', collected in *Songs and Sonnets* (1633).

Graves, Robert von Ranke
In love as in sport, the amateur status must be strictly maintained.
1950 *Occupation: Writer*, 'Lars Porsena'.

James, P. D.
How odd that sex should be so simple and love such a complication.
2005 *The Lighthouse*.

Jerome, Jerome K(lapka)
Love is like the measles; we all have to go through it.
1886 *Idle Thoughts of an Idle Fellow*, 'On Being in Love'.

Lebowitz, Fran
There's no such thing as advice to the lovelorn. If they took advice, they wouldn't be lovelorn.
1997 In *Index Magazine*.

Moore, Lorrie
You emptied the top rack of the dishwasher but not the bottom, so the clean dishes have gotten all mixed up with the dirty ones—and now you want to have sex?
2009 *A Gate at the Stairs*.

Paltrow, Gwyneth Kate
We have always conducted our relationship privately and we hope that as we consciously uncouple and co-parent, we will be able to continue in the same manner.
2014 Announcing on her Goop website her separation from her husband, the singer Chris Martin; the phrase 'conscious uncoupling' subsequently attracted much derision, 25 Mar.

Parker, Dorothy
By the time you say you're his,
Shivering and sighing
And he vows his passion is
Infinite, undying—
Lady, make a note of this:
One of you is lying.
1937 *Not So Deep as A Well*, 'Unfortunate Coincidence'.

Roddick, Andy
It's only stalking if the other person doesn't like it.
2009 Admitting to stalking his future wife, *GQ* magazine, Aug.

Salinger, J(erome) D(avid)
Sex is something I really don't understand too hot. You never know where the hell you are. I keep making up these sex rules for myself, and then I break them right away.
1951 *The Catcher in the Rye*, ch.9.

Shakespeare, William
Lechery, lechery, still wars and lechery! Nothing else holds fashion.
1602 Thersites. *Troilus and Cressida*, act 5, sc.2, l.197–8.

Twain, Mark
Familiarity breeds contempt—and children.
c.1894 Quoted in Albert Bigelow Paine (ed) *Mark Twain's Notebook* (1935).

Wesley, John
Beware you be not swallowed up in books! An ounce of love is worth a pound of knowledge.
Quoted in R Southey *Life of Wesley* (1820), ch.16.

Winfrey, Oprah
Mr. Right's coming, but he's in Africa, and he's walking!
Quoted in Tuchy Palmieri, *Oprah, In Her Words: Our American Princess* (2008).

Men and Women

Albright, Madeleine Korbel
There is a special place in hell for women who don't help other women.
2006 Speech to Women's National Basketball Association All-Decade Team.

Browning, Guy

Men love women because they are the loveliest things on God's earth. Women love men because chocolate can't mow the lawn.
2004 *Never Hit a Jellyfish with a Spade: How to Survive Life's Smaller Challenges.*

Byron, George Gordon, 6th Baron Byron of Rochdale

Man's love is of man's life a thing apart,
'Tis woman's whole existence.
1819–24 *Don Juan*, canto 1, stanza 194.

Clinton, Hillary

When women participate in politics, it ripples out to the entire society... Women are the world's most underused resource.
2013 Interview, *New York Magazine*, 22 Sep.

Compton-Burnett, Dame Ivy

There is more difference within the sexes than between them.
1955 *Mother and Son*, ch.10.

Connolly, Cyril Vernon

In the sex war thoughtlessness is the weapon of the male, vindictiveness of the female.
1944 *The Unquiet Grave*, pt.1.

de Beauvoir, Simone

One is not born a woman: one becomes a woman.
1949 *Le Deuxième Sexe* (*The Second Sex*), bk.2, pt.1, ch.1.

Enright, Anne Teresa

There is nothing as tentative as an old woman's touch; as loving or as horrible.
2007 *The Gathering*.

Gaga, Lady

Some women choose to follow men, and some women choose to follow their dreams. If you're wondering which way to go, remember that your career will never wake up and tell you that it doesn't love you anymore.
2010 In *Cosmopolitan*, April issue.

Greer, Germaine

If women understand by emancipation the adoption of the masculine role then we are lost indeed.
1970 *The Female Eunuch*, 'Soul: Womanpower'.

Kipling, (Joseph) Rudyard

Take my word for it, the silliest woman can manage a clever man; but it takes a very clever woman to manage a fool.
1888 *Plain Tales from the Hills*, 'Three and—an Extra'.

Lerner, Alan Jay

Why can't a woman be more like a man?
Men are so honest, so thoroughly square;
Eternally noble, historically fair;
Who, when you win, will always give your back a pat.
Why can't a woman be like that?
1964 'A Hymn to Him', from *My Fair Lady* (music by Frederick Loewe).

Meredith, George

I expect that Woman will be the last thing civilized by Man.
1859 *The Ordeal of Richard Feverel*, ch.1.

Paglia, Camille

Feminism today just exists as a bunch of mean girls on Twitter.
2014 Quoted on thestar.com, 26 Dec.

Steinem, Gloria

A woman needs a man like a fish needs a bicycle.
c.1970 Attributed, in various forms.

Tennyson, Alfred, 1st Baron

Man is the hunter; woman is his game:
The sleek and shining creatures of the chase,
We hunt them for the beauty of their skins;
They love us for it, and we ride them down.
1847 *The Princess*, pt.5, l.147–50.

Thackeray, William Makepeace

'Tis strange what a man may do, and a woman yet think him an angel.
1852 *The History of Henry Esmond*, bk.1, ch.7.

Waugh, Evelyn Arthur St John

Instead of this absurd division into sexes, they ought to class people as static and dynamic.
1928 *Decline and Fall*, pt.2, ch.7.

West, Dame Rebecca

There is, of course, no reason for the existence of the male sex except that one sometimes needs help with moving the piano.
Attributed.

Wilde, Oscar Fingal O'Flahertie Wills

All women become like their mothers. That is their tragedy. No man does. That's his.
1895 Algernon. *The Importance of Being Earnest*, act 1, also in *A Woman of No Importance* (1893), act 2.

Money

Adiga, Aravind

It's amazing. The moment you show cash, everyone knows your language.
2008 *The White Tiger*.

Bacon, Francis, Viscount St Albans

Money is like muck, not good except it be spread.
1625 *Essays*, no.15, 'Of Seditions and Troubles'.

Baldwin, James Arthur

Money, it turned out, was exactly like sex, you thought of nothing else if you didn't have it and thought of other things if you did.
1961 'Black Boy Looks at the White Boy', in *Esquire*, May.

Bale, Christian (Charles Philip)

Always take the favour over the money.
2013 As Irving Rosenfeld in *American Hustle* (screenplay by Eric Warren Singer and David O. Russell).

Bible (Old Testament)

A feast is made for laughter, and wine maketh merry: but money answereth all things.
Ecclesiastes 10:19.

Branson, Sir Richard Charles Nicholas

If you want to be a millionaire, start with a billion dollars and launch a new airline.
Attributed.

Buffet, Warren

I made my first investment at age eleven. I was wasting my life up until then.
2009 *The Tao of Warren Buffet*.

Bush, George W(alker)

If money isn't loosened up, this sucker could go down.
2008 Referring to the global economy, 26 Sep.

Cervantes, Miguel de

There are but two families in the world, as my grandmother used to say—the Haves and the Havenots.
1615 *Don Quixote*, pt .2, ch.20.

Chesterton, G(ilbert) K(eith)

The rich are the scum of the earth in every country.
1914 *The Flying Inn*, ch.15.

Clinton, Hillary

Rich people, God bless us. We deserve all the opportunities to make sure our country and our blessings continue to the next generation.
2008 Interview on Fox News, 30 Apr.

Farquhar, George

There is no scandal like rags, nor any crime so shameful as poverty.
1707 *The Beaux' Stratagem*, act 1, sc.1.

Pope Francis

This is what I want, a poor Church for the poor.
2013 First audience at the Vatican, *NBC News*, 16 Mar.

Jones, Rev. Tim

My advice, as a Christian priest, is to shoplift.
2009 Advice to poor and needy parishioners at St Lawrence's Church, York, quoted in *The Telegraph*, 23 Dec.

Lennon, John Winston and McCartney, Sir (James) Paul

For I don't care too much for money,
For money can't buy me love.
1964 'Can't Buy Me Love'.

Milligan, Spike

Money couldn't buy friends but you got a better class of enemy.
1963 *Puckoon*, ch.6.

Smith, Logan Pearsall

Most people sell their souls, and live with a good conscience on the proceeds.
1931 *Afterthoughts*, 'Other People'.

Vespasian

Money does not smell.
Attributed. His son Titus had objected to a tax on the contents of the city's urinals (used by fullers). Vespasian held a coin to Titus's nose, asking him whether it smelled. When Titus said no he replied 'Atqui e lotio est' ('And yet, it comes from urine'). Quoted in Suetonius *Vespasian*, 23.

Ward, Artemus

Let us all be happy, and live within our means, even if we have to borrow the money to do it with.
1867 *Artemus Ward in London, and Other Papers*, 'Science and Natural History'.

Woollcott, Alexander Humphreys

Just what God would do if he had the money.
On being shown round Moss Hart's splendid country retreat. Attributed.

One-liners

Atwood, Margaret

Longed for him. Got him. Shit.
2006 'Very Short Stories', *Wired*, Nov.

Benchley, Robert Charles

STREETS FLOODED. PLEASE ADVISE.
Telegraph message to the US on arriving in Venice. Quoted in R E Drennan (ed) *Wits End* (1973).

Benn, Tony

I got a death threat last year. Hadn't had one for years. I was so chuffed.
2009 In *The Daily Telegraph*, 12 Aug.

Brand, Jo(sephine Grace)

If we aren't supposed to eat animals, then why are they made out of meat?
2009 *Looking Back in Hunger*.

Bryson, Bill

Geologists are never at a loss for paperweights.
2003 *A Short History of Nearly Everything*.

Bush, George Herbert Walker

I have opinions of my own—strong opinions, but I don't always agree with them.
2007 Attributed.

Cameron, David William Donald

Calm down, dear.
2011 Speaking to Angela Eagle MP during Prime Minister's Questions.

Clinton, Hillary

We came, we saw, he died.
2011 On the death of Libyan leader Muammar Gaddafi, CBS News interview, 20 Oct.

Fiennes, Sir Ranulph

There is no bad weather, only inappropriate clothing.
Attributed.

Goldwyn, Sam(uel)

A verbal contract isn't worth the paper it's written on.
Attributed. Quoted in A Scott Berg *Goldwyn* (1989).

Johnson, Boris

Voting Tory will cause your wife to have bigger breasts and increase your chances of owning a BMW M3.
2005 Speaking during the general election, Apr.

Letterman, David Michael

How long have you been a black man?
2009 Interviewing President Barack Obama, quoted in *The Washington Post*, 22 Sep.

Marx, Groucho

Please accept my resignation. I don't want to belong to any club that will accept me as a member.
1959 Recalled in his autobiography, *Groucho and Me* (1959), ch.26.

Milligan, Spike

Dúirt mé leat go raibh mé breoite.
2002 Gaelic inscription on his gravestone at Winchelsea, East Sussex. English translation: I told you I was ill.

Parker, Dorothy

You can lead a horticulture, but you can't make her think.
Response to a challenge to use 'horticulture' in a sentence. Quoted in J Keats *You Might as Well Live* (1970).

Romney, Willard Mitt

I'm not familiar precisely with what I said, but I'll stand by what I said, whatever it was.
2012 Quoted in *The Washington Post*, 17 May.

Rumsfeld, Donald

Reports that say that something hasn't happened are always interesting to me, because as we know, there are known knowns; there are things we know we know. We also know there are known unknowns; that is to say we know there are some things we do not know. But there are also unknown unknowns—the ones we don't know we don't know.
2002 Responding to a reporter's question at a US Department of Defense news briefing, 12 Feb.

Sheridan, Richard Brinsley

She's as headstrong as an allegory on the banks of the Nile.
1775 Mrs Malaprop of Lydia Languish. *The Rivals*, act 3, sc.3.

Twain, Mark

The report of my death was an exaggeration.
1897 In the *New York Journal*, 2 Jun. This was the substance of Twain's cable to the Associated Press in response to the news item that he had died.

Wilde, Oscar Fingal O'Flahertie Wills

The play was a great success, but the audience was a disaster.
1892 Attributed comment after the poor reception of *Lady Windermere's Fan*.

Philosophy and religion

Alan Alda

The good thing about being a hypocrite is that you get to keep your values.
2007 Television interview, 13 Sep.

Adams, Douglas Noël

The Answer to the Great Question Of... Life, the Universe and Everything... Is... Forty-two.
1979 *The Hitch-Hiker's Guide to the Galaxy*, ch.27.

Cicero

There is nothing so absurd that it has not been said by some philosopher.
c.44 BC *De Divinatione*, bk.2, section 58.

Dalai Lama

Fundamentalism is terrifying because it is based purely on emotion, rather than intelligence. It prevents followers from thinking as individuals and about the good of the world.
2006 Quoted in *The Daily Telegraph*, 1 Mar.

Dawkins, Richard

We should be open-minded, but not so open-minded that our brain falls out.
2007 'The Enemies of Reason'.

de Botton, Alain

Travel agents would be wiser to ask us what we hope to change about our lives rather than simply where we wish to go.
2009 *A Week at the Airport: A Heathrow Diary*.

Einstein, Albert

Science without religion is lame, religion without science is blind.
1941 *Science, Philosophy and Religion: A Symposium*, ch.13.

Fry, Stephen John

God once had Bach and Michelangelo on his side, he had Mozart, and now who does he have? People with ginger whiskers and tinted spectacles who reduce the glories of theology to a kind of sharing, you know?
2009 *The Blasphemy Debate*, quoted in *The Guardian*.

Hawking, Stephen

I have noticed even people who claim everything is predestined, and that we can do nothing to change it, look before they cross the road.
2006 Attributed in Rosemarie Jarski, *Words from the Wise*.

Hurt, Sir John Vincent

The clergy is in the same business as actors, just a different department.
2007 In *The Guardian*, 20 Mar.

Johnson, Samuel

'I refute it *thus*.'
1763 Johnson refutes Bishop Berkeley's theory of the nonexistence of matter by kicking a large stone, 6 Aug. Quoted in James Boswell *The Life of Samuel Johnson* (1791), vol.1.

Lynch, David Keith

Ideas are like fish. If you want to catch little fish, you can stay in the shallow water. But if you want to catch the big fish, you've got to go deeper. Down deep, the fish are more powerful and more pure. They're huge and abstract. And they're very beautiful.
2007 *Catching the Big Fish: Meditation, Consciousness, and Creativity.*

Marx, Karl Heinrich

Religion is the sigh of the oppressed creature, the feelings of a heartless world, and the spirit of conditions that are unspiritual. It is the opium of the people.
1843–4 *A Contribution to the Critique of Hegel's Philosophy of Right.*

McEwan, Ian

When anything can happen, everything matters.
2005 *Saturday.*

Merkel, Angela Dorothea

Islam is part of Germany.
2015 Press conference with Turkish Prime Minister Ahmet Davutoglu in Berlin, 12 Jan.

Montaigne, Michel Eyquem de

Man is quite insane. He wouldn't know how to make a maggot, and he makes Gods by the dozen.
1580 *Essais*, bk.2, ch.12 (translated by Charles Cotton).

Murakami, Haruki

Whether you take the doughnut hole as a blank space or as an entity unto itself is a purely metaphysical question and does not affect the taste of the doughnut one bit.
1982 *A Wild Sheep Chase.*

Pratchett, Sir Terry (Terence David John)

The trouble with having an open mind, of course, is that people will insist on coming along and trying to put things in it.
1990 *Diggers.*

Shaw, George Bernard

Well, sir, you never can tell. That's a principle in life with me, sir, if you'll excuse my having such a thing, sir.
1896 Waiter to Fergus Crampton. *You Never Can Tell*, act 2.

Tutu, Desmond

I give great thanks to God that he has created a Dalai Lama. Do you really think, as some have argued, that God will be saying: 'You know, that guy, the Dalai Lama, is not bad. What a pity he's not a Christian'? I don't think that is the case—because, you see, God is not a Christian.
2006 *BBC News*, 2 Jun.

Politics and politicians

Aguirre y Gil de Biedma, Countess of Bornos, Grandee of Spain, Esperanza

When socialism comes through the door, employment jumps out the window.
2011 In *La Razon*, 6 May.

Acheson, Dean Gooderham

Trust him as much as you would a rattlesnake with a silencer on its rattle.
1980 Advice to President Truman on J Edgar Hoover. Quoted in David S McLellan and David C Acheson (eds) *Among Friends: Personal Letters of Dean Gooderham Acheson* (1980).

Acton, John Emerich Edward Dalberg, 1st Baron Acton of Aldenham

Power tends to corrupt, and absolute power corrupts absolutely. Great men are almost always bad men. There is no worse heresy than that the office sanctifies the holder of it.
1887 Letter to Bishop Mandell Creighton, 3 Apr.

Adams, Henry Brooks

Practical politics consists in ignoring the facts.
1907 *The Education of Henry Adams*, ch.22.

Aristotle

Man is by nature a political animal; it is his nature to live in a state.
c.330 BC *Politics*, bk.1, ch.2, 1253a (translated by T A Sinclair).

Blair, Tony

That's the art of leadership. To make sure that what shouldn't happen, doesn't happen.
2007 Interview, *Newsweek*, Feb.

Clinton, Bill

A great democracy does not make it harder to vote than to buy an assault weapon.
2013 Speech at the Lincoln Memorial marking the fiftieth anniversary of the March on Washington, 28 Aug.

Gates, Robert Michael

Most governments lie to each other. That's the way business gets done.
2011 CNN interview, 19 Jun.

Johnson, Boris

All politicians are like crazed wasps in a jam jar, each individually convinced that they are going to make it.
2005 On *Desert Island Discs*, BBC radio, 30 Oct.

Karzai, Hamid

Don't vote for bad people.
2005 His advice to voters in the Afghan elections.

Krugman, Paul

Politics determine who has the power, not who has the truth.
2010 *The Australian Financial Review*, 6 Sep.

Major, John

If the answer is more politicians, you are asking the wrong question.
2007 Attributed by Vernon Bogdanor in *The Sunday Telegraph*, 11 Feb.

Miliband, Ed(ward Samuel)

I suppose not everyone has a dad who wrote a book saying he didn't believe in the parliamentary road to socialism.
2011 Speech to the Labour Party conference.

Nader, Ralph

Half of democracy is about just showing up.
2004 *The Good Fight*.

Obama, Barack Hussein

What is lacking right now is not good ideas. The problem we have is that Washington has become a place where good ideas go to die.
2008 During a public debate with Senator Hillary Clinton at Austin, Texas, 23 Feb.

O'Rourke, P. J.

Sucking the fun out of life has always been an important component of politics.
2010 *Don't Vote, It Just Encourages the Bastards*.

Putin, Vladimir Vladimirovich

It is extremely dangerous to encourage people to see themselves as exceptional.
2013 Referring to Syria. Quoted in the *New York Times*, 12 Sep.

Rogers, Will

The more you read and observe about this Politics thing, you got to admit that each party is worse than the other. The one that's out always looks the best.
1924 *The Illiterate Digest*, 'Breaking into the Writing Game'.

Spencer, Herbert

The Republican form of government is the highest form of government; but because of this, it requires the highest type of human nature—a type nowhere at present existing.
'The Americans', collected in *Essays* (1891).

Stevenson, Adlai E(wing)

A politician is a statesman who approaches every question with an open mouth.
Attributed.

Valéry, Paul

Politics is the art of preventing people from taking part in affairs which concern them.
1943 *Tel Quel 2*, 'Rhumbs'.

Popular culture

Adele (Adele Laurie Blue Adkins)

I don't make music for eyes, I make music for ears.
2011 In *Rolling Stone*, 28 Apr.

Armstrong, Billie Joe

A guy walks up to me and asks 'What's Punk?' So I kick over a garbage can and say 'That's punk!' So he kicks over the garbage can and says 'That's Punk?', and I say 'No, that's trendy!'
2006 Quoted in Matt Doeden, *Green Day: Keeping Their Edge*.

Brown, Gordon

The Arctic Monkeys really wake you up in the morning.
2006 Claiming familiarity with the Sheffield rock band, in *New Woman* magazine, summer issue.

Berlin, Irving

Listen kid, take my advice—never hate a song that has sold half a million copies.
Comment to the young Cole Porter, attributed.

Charles, Prince of Wales

I am not part of the PlayStation generation.
2011 Attributed.

Cher

Singing is like going to a party at someone else's house. Acting is like having the party at your house.
2010 In *Entertainment Weekly*.

Clooney, George Timothy

Theatre actors look down on film actors, who look down on TV actors. Thank God for reality shows or we wouldn't have anybody to look down on.
2008 Attributed.

Collins, Suzanne Marie

May the odds be ever in your favour.
2008 *The Hunger Games.*

Coward, Sir Noël Peirce

Extraordinary how potent cheap music is.
1930 *Private Lives*, act 1.

Godard, Jean-Luc

Photography is truth. And cinema is truth twenty-four times a second.
1960 *Le Petit Soldat.*

Hoffman, Dustin

What would you feel like if you go in for brain surgery and the brain surgeon leans over and says 'I just want you to know that I am not a perfectionist. But don't worry, I'm a nice guy'?
2007 Justifying his reputation for perfectionism.

Jay-Z

Hip-hop is a perfect mix between poetry and boxing.
2010 *Decoded.*

Lennon, John Winston

We're more popular than Jesus Christ now. I don't know which will go first, rock and roll or Christianity.
1966 In the *Evening Standard.*

Neeson, Liam John

I will look for you, I will find you, and I will kill you.
2008 As Bryan Mills in *Taken* (screenplay by Luc Besson and Robert Mark Kamen).

Nixon, Richard M(ilhous)

American people don't believe anything until they see it on television.
1994 In *Newsweek*, 2 May. He estimated that 80% of US citizens get their news from television.

Pickford, Mary

Adding sound to movies would be like putting lipstick on the Venus de Milo.
Recalled on her death, 29 May 1979.

Pussy Riot

Virgin Mary, Mother of God, become a feminist...Virgin Mary, Mother of God, drive Putin away.
2012 Lyrics of the 'punk prayer' for which members of the band were imprisoned, delivered in the Cathedral of Christ the Saviour, Moscow, 21 Feb.

Radcliffe, Daniel Jacob

I'm the only kid in the world who doesn't want an eighth Harry Potter book.
2007 Quoted in *Details* magazine, Aug.

Sousa, John Philip

Jazz will endure just as long as people hear it through their feet instead of their brains.
c.1920 Attributed.

Whitman, Christine Todd

When you're dealing with people who think that Sponge Bob Square Pants is more important than social security, you have a problem.
2005 On *The Daily Show*, Jan.

Science and technology

American Library Association

The computer is a fast idiot, it has no imagination; it cannot originate action. It is, and will remain, only a tool to man.
1964 Statement of the American Library Association regarding the Univac computer exhibited at the New York World's Fair, 1964.

Archimedes

Eureka, Eureka! (I found it, I found it!).
Vitruvius 9.9.10. Attributed, on discovering the principle of upthrust on a floating body while having a bath. Archimedes had been given the task of establishing whether there was the proper weight of gold in the crown of Hieron of Syracuse. One day when entering his bath he noticed the water which flowed over the sides as he entered and he correctly perceived that the weight of the water displaced was that of the weight of his body.

Bryson, Bill

There are three stages in scientific discovery. First, people deny that it is true, then they deny that it is important; finally they credit the wrong person.
2003 *A Short History of Nearly Everything.*

Cameron, David William Donald

Too many twits make a twat.
2009 Referring to Twitter, Absolute Radio interview, 29 Jul.

Clarke, Sir Arthur C(harles)

When a distinguished but elderly scientist states that something is possible he is almost certainly right. When he states that something is impossible, he is very probably wrong.
1962 *Profiles of the Future.*

Coupland, Douglas

TV and the Internet are good because they keep stupid people from spending too much time out in public.
2006 *JPod.*

Darwin, Charles Robert

A mathematician is a blind man in a dark room looking for a black cat which isn't there.
Quoted in John D Barrow *Pie in the Sky, Counting, Thinking and Being* (1992).

Dowd, Maureen

Just because digital technology makes connecting possible doesn't mean you're actually reaching people.
2013 In the *New York Times.*

Gates, Bill

If geek means you're willing to study things, and if you think science and engineering matter, I plead guilty. If your culture doesn't like geeks, you are in real trouble.
2010 In *The Daily Telegraph*, 20 Oct.

Gell-Mann, Murray

If I have seen further than others, it is because I am surrounded by dwarfs.
2009 Parodying Isaac Newton's 'If I have seen further it is only by standing on the shoulders of giants'. Quoted in *New Scientist*, 19 Sep.

Hawking, Stephen

To confine our attention to terrestrial matters would be to limit the human spirit.
2007 Foreword to Lawrence Krauss, *The Physics of Star Trek*.

Hubbard, Elbert Green

One machine can do the work of fifty ordinary men. No machine can do the work of one extraordinary man.
1911 *Thousand and One Epigrams*.

Huxley, T(homas) H(enry)

It is the customary fate of new truths to begin as heresies and to end as superstitions.
1880 *Science and Culture and Other Essays*, 'The Coming of Age of the Origin of the Species'.

Lorenz, Konrad

It is a good morning exercise for a research scientist to discard a pet hypothesis every day before breakfast. It keeps him young.
1963 *Das sogenannte Böse* ('The So-Called Evil', translated by Marjorie Latzke as *On Aggression*, 1966), ch.2.

Mamet, David

The first rule of tinkering is, of course, 'save all the parts'.
2011 *The Secret Knowledge: On the Dismantling of American Culture*.

Minsky, Marvin

Every system that we build will surprise us with new kinds of flaws until those machines become clever enough to conceal their faults from us.
2006 *The Emotion Machine*.

Rogers, Will

You can't say civilization don't advance, however, for in every war they kill you in a new way.
1929 In the *New York Times*, 23 Dec.

Russell, Bertrand Arthur William Russell, 3rd Earl

Machines are worshipped because they are beautiful, and valued because they confer power; they are hated because they are hideous, and loathed because they impose slavery.
1928 *Sceptical Essays*.

Toffler, Alvin

Technology feeds on itself. Technology makes more technology possible.
1970 *Future Shock*.

Wozniak, Stephen Gary

Never trust a computer you can't throw out a window.
Attributed.

Zuckerberg, Mark Elliot

Move fast and break things. Unless you are breaking stuff, you are not moving fast enough.
2009 In *Business Insider*, Oct.

Society

Alcuin

We should not listen to those who like to affirm that the voice of the people is the voice of God, for the tumult of the masses is truly close to madness.
800 Letter to Charlemagne.

Burke, Edmund

The people are the masters.
1780 Speech, House of Commons, 11 Feb.

Carlyle, Thomas

The public is an old woman. Let her maunder and mumble.
1835 Journal entry.

Donne, John

No man is an island, entire of itself; every man is a piece of the continent, a part of the main.
1624 *Devotions upon Emergent Occasions*, Meditation no.17.

Edinburgh, Duke of

Constitutionally I don't exist.
2011 Quoted on *BBC News*, 27 Jan.

Harman, Harriet Ruth

For many young people, social mobility now means a bus down to the job centre.
2011 During House of Commons debate, 5 Apr.

Hitchens, Christopher Eric

A bit of a stomach gives a chap a position in society.
2007 In *Vanity Fair*, Oct. issue.

Juvenal

Time was when their plebiscite elected generals, Heads of State, commanders of legions: but now they've pulled in their horns, there's only two things that concern them: bread and games.
Of the people of Rome. *Satirae*, no.10, l.78–81 (translated by Peter Green). 'Panem et circenses' is sometimes translated as 'bread and circuses'.

Levitt, Steven David

Morality, it could be argued, represents the way that people would like the world to work, whereas economics represents how it actually does work.

2005 *Freakonomics: A Rogue Economist Explores the Hidden Side of Everything.*

Marx, Karl Heinrich

The history of all hitherto existing society is the history of class struggles.
1848 *The Communist Manifesto* (with Friedrich Engels, translated by Samuel Moore, 1888), opening sentence.

Morris, Desmond John

Clearly, then, the city is not a concrete jungle, it is a human zoo.
1969 *The Human Zoo*, introduction.

Rice, Condoleezza

If you are over-dressed, it is a comment on them. If you are under-dressed, it is a comment on you.
2010 *Extraordinary, Ordinary People: A Memoir of Family.*

Rogers, Richard

The high street is where society comes into itself.
2013 In *The Guardian*, 11 Jul.

Sartre, Jean-Paul

Hell is other people.
1945 *Huis clos.*

Sedighi, Hojatoleslam Kazem

Many women who do not dress modestly lead young men astray, corrupt their chastity and spread adultery in society, which increases earthquakes.
2010 Quoted in the *Daily Mail*, 19 Apr.

Shakespeare, William

Society is no comfort
To one not sociable.
1610 Innogen. *Cymbeline*, act 4, sc.2, l.12–13.

Wells, H(erbert) G(eorge)

The Social Contract is nothing more or less than a vast conspiracy of human beings to lie to and humbug themselves and one another for the general Good. Lies are the mortar that bind the savage individual man into the social masonry.
1900 *Love and Mrs Lewisham*, ch.23.

Wilder, Thornton Niven

But there comes a time in everybody's life when he must decide whether he'll live among human beings or not—a fool among fools or a fool alone.
1954 *The Matchmaker*, act 4.

Wilson, Sir Angus Frank Johnstone

I have no concern for the common man except that he should not be so common.
1967 *No Laughing Matter.*

Wilson, Edward O.

We have created a Star Wars civilization, with Stone Age emotions, medieval institutions, and godlike technology.
2013 *The Social Conquest of Earth.*

Sport

Ali, Muhammad

I am the greatest!
1962 In the *Louisville Times*, 16 Nov. This became his catchphrase.

Bacon, Francis, Viscount St Albans

Tennis is a game of no use in itself.
1605 *The Advancement of Learning*, bk.2.

Bernhardt, Sarah

I do so love cricket—it's so very English.
c.1905 On being taken to see a game of football in Manchester. Quoted in R Buckle *Nijinsky* (1971).

Bolt, Usain St Leo

It's what I came here to do, I'm now a legend.
2012 After becoming the first man to retain the 100 and 200m titles, at the London Olympics.

Boycott, Geoffrey

Frankly, he had more chance of picking his nose with his toe.
2007 Describing, as commentator, batsman Andrew Flintoff's chance of doing well against Australian spin bowlers.

Churchill, Sir Winston Leonard Spencer

An ineffectual attempt to direct an uncontrollable sphere into an inaccessible hole with instruments ill adapted for the purpose.
Quoted in Michael Hobbs *The Golf Quotations Book* (1992).

Ferguson, Sir Alex

Sometimes you look in a field and you see a cow and you think it's a better cow than the one you've got in your own field. It's a fact. Right? And it never really works out that way.
2010 Referring to a transfer request from his star player Wayne Rooney. Quoted on *Goal.com*, 20 Oct.

Hillary, Edmund

It's not the mountain we conquer but ourselves.
2007 *O Magazine*, Apr. issue.

Jerrold, Douglas William

The only athletic sport I mastered was backgammon.
Quoted in W Jerrold *Douglas Jerrold* (1914), vol.1, ch.1.

Johnson, Samuel

Fly fishing may be a very pleasant amusement; but angling or float fishing I can only compare to a stick and a string, with a worm at one end and a fool at the other.
Quoted in Hawker *Instructions to Young Sportsmen* (1859). The attribution is doubtful, and Swift has also been credited with the remark.

Jordan, Michael

Limits, like fears, are often just an illusion.
2009 Speaking on the occasion of his induction into the Basketball Hall of Fame.

Success and failure

Kelvin, William Thomson, 1st Baron
At what time does the dissipation of energy begin?
When his wife proposed an afternoon walk. Quoted in A Fleming *Memories of a Scientific Life* (1934).

Levitt, Steven David
The swimming pool is almost one hundred times more likely to kill a child than the gun is.
2005 *Freakonomics: A Rogue Economist Explores the Hidden Side of Everything*.

Mourinho (Félix), José Mário dos Santos
I have top players and I'm sorry, we have a top manager. Please do not call me arrogant because what I say is true. I'm European champion, I'm not one out of the bottle, I think I'm a special one.
2004 Speaking to the press as the new manager of Chelsea.

Norden, Denis
It's a funny kind of month, October. For the really keen cricket fan it's when you realise that your wife left you in May.
Quoted in *She* magazine, 1977.

Orwell, George
Serious sport has nothing to do with fair play. It is bound up with hatred, jealousy, boastfulness, disregard of all rules and sadistic pleasure in witnessing violence: in other words it is war minus the shooting—there are quite enough real causes of trouble already, and we need not add to them by encouraging young men to kick each other on the shins amid the roars of infuriated spectators.
1950 'The Sporting Spirit'.

Palin, Sarah Louise Heath
What's the difference between a hockey mom and a pit bull? Lipstick.
2008 Speaking at the Republican National Convention, reported in the *New York Times*, 3 Sep.

Rice, Grantland
For when the One Great Scorer comes
To write against your name,
He marks—not that you won or lost—
But how you played the game.
1941 *Only the Brave*, 'Alumnus Football'.

Shankly, Bill (William)
Some people think football is a matter of life and death. I don't like that attitude. I can assure them it is much more serious than that.
Quoted in the *Sunday Times*, 4 Oct 1981.

Wilde, Oscar Fingal O'Flahertie Wills
The only possible form of exercise is to talk, not to walk.
Quoted in Alvin Redman *The Epigrams of Oscar Wilde* (1952).

Addison, Joseph
'Tis not in mortals to command success,
But we'll do more, Sempronius; we'll deserve it.
1713 *Cato*, act 1, sc.2, l.43–4.

Banville, (William) John
Doing what you do well is death. Your duty is to keep trying to do things that you don't do well, in the hope of learning.
2009 In *The Paris Review*, spring.

Blair, Tony
Sometimes it is better to lose and do the right thing than to win and do the wrong thing.
2005 Prime Minister's Questions, House of Commons, 9 Nov.

Blinder, Alan
Don't overstate your likely achievements; when in doubt, understate them.
2013 'After the Music Stopped: The Financial Crisis, the Response, and the Work Ahead', 24 Jan.

Brown, Rita Mae
Happiness is pretty simple: someone to love, something to do, something to look forward to.
2011 *Hiss of Death*.

Caesar, Gaius Julius
Veni, vidi, vici.
I came, I saw, I conquered.
46 BC Said to have been written on a *titulus* (placard) carried along in Caesar's triumph after a campaign in Pontus (Asia Minor) during the civil war (46 BC). Quoted in Suetonius *Lives of the Twelve Caesars*, 'Divus Iulius', section 37. Another source reports that Caesar used this expression in a letter to the Senate after the same campaign (cf Plutarch, *Caesar* 50, 3–4).

Chalmers, Patrick Reginald
What's lost upon the roundabouts we pulls up on the swings!
1912 *Green Days and Blue Days*, 'Roundabouts and Swings'.

Clough, Arthur Hugh
'Tis better to have fought and lost,
Than never to have fought at all.
1854 'Peschiera'.

Coubertin, Pierre de, Baron
The most important thing in the Olympic games is not winning but taking part—just as the most important thing in life is not the triumph but the struggle. The essential thing in life is not conquering but fighting well.
1908 Speech to Olympic Games officials, London, 24 Jul.

Dickinson, Emily Elizabeth

Success is counted sweetest
By those who ne'er succeed.
c.1859 *Complete Poems*, no.67 (first published 1890).

Eggers, Dave

Better to be at the bottom of a ladder you want to climb than in the middle of some ladder you don't, right?
2013 *The Circle*.

Hemingway, Ernest Millar

A man can be destroyed but not defeated.
1952 *The Old Man and the Sea*.

Hickson, William Eward

If at first you don't succeed,
Try, try again.
'Try and Try Again'.

Isaacson, Walter

The people who are crazy enough to think they can change the world are the ones who do.
2011 *Steve Jobs*.

Lombardi, Vince(nt Thomas)

Winning isn't everything; it's the only thing.
Attributed. His exact words were 'Winning isn't everything, but making the effort is'. Some sources attribute the saying to Red Sanders, coach of the University of California team.

Marvell, Andrew

How vainly men themselves amaze
To win the palm, the oak, or bays;
And their uncessant labours see
Crown'd from some single herb or tree.
c.1650–1652 'The Garden' (published 1681).

Morell, Thomas

See, the conquering hero comes!
Sound the trumpets, beat the drums!
1747 *Judas Maccabeus*, 'A Chorus of Youths'.

Pyrrhus of Epirus

One more such victory, and we are lost!
279 BC After defeating the Romans at Asculum. Quoted in Plutarch *Regum et imperatorum apophthegmata*, 184c.

Schwarzenegger, Arnold

Just remember, you can't climb the ladder of success with your hands in your pockets.
2009 Speech at the University of Southern California, 15 May.

Winfrey, Oprah

What other people label or might try to call failure, I have learned is just God's way of pointing you in a new direction.
2007 Speech at Howard University, 12 May.

War and peace

Allen, Woody

The lion and the calf shall lie down together but the calf won't get much sleep.
1974 'The Scrolls', in *The New Republic*, 31 Aug.

Astley, Sir Jacob

O Lord! Thou knowest how busy I must be this day: if I forget thee, do not thou forget me.
1642 Prayer before the Battle of Edgehill, 23 Oct. Quoted in Sir Philip Warwick *Memoires* (1702).

Bible (Old Testament)

They shall beat their swords into plowshares, and their spears into pruninghooks: nation shall not lift up sword against nation, neither shall they learn war anymore.
Isaiah 2:4.

Bierce, Ambrose Gwinett

Peace, n. In international affairs, a period of cheating between two periods of fighting.
1906 *The Cynic's Word Book*. Retitled *The Devil's Dictionary* (1911).

Churchill, Sir Winston Leonard Spencer

Those who can win a war well can rarely make a good peace, and those who could make a good peace would never have won the war.
1930 *My Early Life*.

Elizabeth II

It has perhaps always been the case that the waging of peace is the hardest form of leadership of all.
2010 Quoted in *Newsweek*.

Franklin, Benjamin

There never was a good war or a bad peace.
1773 Letter, 11 Sep.

Gorbachev, Mikhail

We had ten years after the Cold War to build a new world order and yet we squandered them. The United States cannot tolerate anyone acting independently. Every US president has to have a war.
2009 In *The Daily Telegraph*, 7 May.

Hardy, Thomas

War makes rattling good history; but Peace is poor reading.
1904 *The Dynasts*, pt.1, act 2, sc.5.

Hosseini, Khaled

There are a lot of children in Afghanistan, but little childhood.
2003 *The Kite Runner*.

Inge, William Ralph

It takes in reality only one to make a quarrel. It is useless for the sheep to pass resolutions in favour of vegetarianism, while the wolf remains of a different opinion.
1919 *Outspoken Essays* (first series), 'Patriotism'.

LaPierre, Wayne Robert

The only thing that stops a bad guy with a gun is a good guy with a gun.
2012 News briefing, 21 Dec.

McCain, John

We have enemies for whom no attack is too cruel.
2008 Speaking while campaigning for the Republican nomination for President.

Netanyahu, Benjamin

The difference between us is that we're using missile defence to protect our civilians and they're using their civilians to protect their missiles.
2014 Discussing the threat from Hamas on *Face the Nation*, CBS, 12 Jul.

Roy, Arundhati

Flags are bits of coloured cloth that governments use first to shrink-wrap people's minds and then as ceremonial shrouds to bury the dead.
2003 *War Talk*.

Shawcross, Paul

The administration does not support blowing up planets.
2013 Rejecting a mass petition calling for the US to build a Death Star weapon, as featured in the *Star Wars* films, 11 Jan.

Unesco Constitution

Since wars begin in the minds of men, it is in the minds of men that the defences of peace must be constructed.
1945 Signed 16 Nov. The Unesco Constitution came into force 4 Nov 1946.

Vegetius

Let him who desires peace prepare for war.
c.380 AD *Epitoma Rei Militaris*, no.3, prologue. This became familiar in the Middle Ages as *Si vis pacem para bellum* (If you want peace, prepare for war).

Wilder, Thornton Niven

When you're at war you think about a better life; when you're at peace you think about a more comfortable one.
1942 *The Skin of Our Teeth*, act 1.

Yousafzai, Malala

I believe the gun has no power because a gun can only kill, but a pen can give life.
2013 Speech on accepting a Glamour Award, 12 Nov.

INSPIRATIONAL QUOTES FOR SPEECHMAKERS:

Apologies, excuses and expressions of thanks

Aung San Suu Kyi

Every thought, every word, and every action that adds to the positive and the wholesome is a contribution to peace. Each and every one of us is capable of making such a contribution. Let us join hands to try to create a peaceful world where we can sleep in security and wake in happiness.
2012 Nobel Peace Prize acceptance speech, Oslo, 16 Jun.

Beerbohm, Sir (Henry) Max(imilian)

When a public man lays his hand on his heart and declares that his conduct needs no apology, the audience hastens to put up its umbrellas against the particularly severe downpour of apologies in store for it. I won't give the customary warning. My conduct shrieks aloud for apology, and you are in for a thorough drenching.
1906 'A Straight Talk' (parody of George Bernard Shaw), in the *Saturday Review*, 22 Dec.

Beresford, Lord Charles

Very sorry can't come. Lie follows by post.
Telegraph to the Prince of Wales, declining a dinner invitation. Quoted in Ralph Nevill *The World of Fashion 1837–1922* (1923), ch.5.

Bible (Old Testament)

Let thy speech be short, comprehending much in few words; be as one that knoweth and yet holdeth his tongue.
Ecclesiasticus 32:8.

Charles I

A rule that may serve for a statesman, a courtier, or a lover—never make a defence or an apology before you be accused.
1636 Letter to Lord Wentworth, 3 Sep.

Holmes, Oliver Wendell

Apology is only egotism wrong side out.
1858–9 *The Professor at the Breakfast Table*, ch.6.

Marlowe, Christopher

Barnardine: Thou hast committed–
Barabas: Fornication—but that was in another country; and besides, the wench is dead.
c.1589 *The Jew of Malta* (published 1633), act 4, sc.1.

Milligan, Spike

I am not going to thank anybody—because I did it all myself.
1994 Acceptance speech after being awarded the British Comedy Award for Lifetime Achievement.

Rudd, Kevin Michael

For the pain, suffering and hurt of these stolen generations, their descendants and for their families left behind, we say sorry. To the mothers and the fathers, the brothers and the sisters, for the breaking up of families and communities, we say sorry. And for the indignity and degradation thus inflicted on a proud people and a proud culture, we say sorry.
2008 Issuing an official government apology for the mistreatment of Australia's aboriginal peoples, 13 Feb.

Segal, Erich

Love means not ever having to say you're sorry.
1970 *Love Story*, ch.13.

Stockton, Philip

I want to thank everybody who is here tonight, and everybody who isn't, and everybody who has ever been born or may be born or be born again or reborn. If I've forgotten anybody then you probably know who you are.
2012 Accepting the Academy Award for Best Sound Editing for *Hugo*, 26 Feb.

Tarantino, Quentin

It's not for the chicken to speak of his own soup.
2009 When asked his opinion of his movie *Inglourious Basterds*.

Washington, George

Father, I cannot tell a lie. I did it with my little hatchet.
In childhood, on admitting to vandalizing a cherry tree, attributed by Mason Locke Weems (Parson Weems) in his *Life and Memorable Actions of George Washington* (5th edn, c.1810). Weems claimed to have heard the tale from an elderly lady, a distant relation of Washington's, 20 years earlier.

Wallach, Eli

Having the critics praise you is like having the hangman say you've got a pretty neck.
Attributed.

Wellington, Arthur Wellesley, 1st Duke of

Don't quote Latin; say what you have to say, and then sit down.
Advice to a new member of Parliament.

Winfrey, Oprah

Be thankful for what you have—you'll end up having more.
Quoted in Tuchy Palmieri, *Oprah, In Her Words: Our American Princess* (2008).

Birthday congratulations

Bennett, Alan

At eighty things do not occur; they recur.
2007 *The Uncommon Reader*.

Cleese, John

You do realise as you grow older that almost nobody knows what they are talking about.
2009 Attributed.

Democritus

Strength and beauty are the blessings of youth; temperance, however, is the flower of old age.
Fragment quoted in H Diels and W Kranz (eds) *Die Fragmente der Vorsokratiker*, vol.2 (1952), no.294.

Dench, Dame Judi(th Olivia)

We get up in the morning. We do our best. Nothing else matters.
2012 As Evelyn Greenslade in *The Best Exotic Marigold Hotel* (screenplay by Ol Parker).

Gilbert, Sir W(illiam) S(chwenck)

She may very well pass for forty-three
In the dusk with a light behind her!
1875 *Trial by Jury*.

Griffiths, Richard

Everyone over fifty, as part of the NHS, should be issued every week with a wet fish in a plastic bag by the Post Office so that whenever you see someone young and happy you can hit them as hard as you can across the face.
2008 In the *Daily Express*, 20 Nov.

Hicks, Sir Edward Seymour

You will recognize, my boy, the first sign of old age: it is when you go out into the streets of London and realize for the first time how young the policemen look.
Quoted in C R D Pulling *They Were Singing* (1952), ch.7.

Holmes, Oliver Wendell

To be seventy years young is sometimes far more cheerful and hopeful than to be forty years old.
1879 Letter to Julia Ward Howe, 27 May.

Irving, Washington

Whenever a man's friends begin to compliment him about looking young, he may be sure that they think he is growing old.
1822 *Bracebridge Hall*, 'Bachelors'.

Johnson, Samuel

At seventy-seven it is time to be in earnest.
1775 *A Journey to the Western Isles of Scotland*, 'Col'.

Lennon, John Winston and McCartney, Sir (James) Paul

Will you still need me, will you still feed me,
When I'm sixty four?
1967 'When I'm Sixty Four'.

Obama, Michelle LeVaughn Robinson

A lot of young people think they're invincible, but the truth is young people are knuckleheads.
2014 On *The Tonight Show*, 21 Feb.

Orwell, George
At 50, everyone has the face he deserves.
1949 Notebook entry, 17 Apr.

Pound, Ezra Loomis
One of the pleasures of middle age is to find out that one WAS right, and that one was much righter than one knew at say 17 or 23.
1934 *The ABC of Reading*, ch.1.

Quant, Mary
A woman is as young as her knee.
Attributed.

Roth, Philip
Old age isn't a battle; old age is a massacre.
2006 *Everyman*.

Shakespeare, William
Age cannot wither her, nor custom stale
Her infinite variety.
1606 Enobarbus, of Cleopatra. *Antony and Cleopatra*, act 2, sc.2, l.241–2.

Walpole, Horace, 4th Earl of Orford
It is charming to totter into vogue.
1765 Letter to George Selwyn, 2 Dec. In *The Correspondence of Horace Walpole* (Yale edition, 1937–8).

Weldon, Fay
I am not cynical. I am just old. I know what is going to happen next.
2009 *Chalcot Crescent*.

Wilde, Oscar Fingal O'Flahertie Wills
One should never trust a woman who tells one her real age. A woman who would tell one that, would tell one anything.
1893 Lord Illingworth. *A Woman of No Importance*, act 1.

Funeral addresses

Ackroyd, Peter
Suffering is intrinsic to human existence. There is no joy without its attendant pain.
2008 *The Casebook of Victor Frankenstein*.

Angelou, Maya
I've learned that people will forget what you said, people will forget what you did, but people will never forget how you made them feel.
2012 In *Beautifully Said Magazine*, Jul.

Ariosto, Ludovico
Nature made him, and then broke the mould.
1516 *Orlando Furioso*, canto 10, stanza 84.

Banksy
I mean, they say you die twice. One time when you stop breathing and a second time, a bit later on, when somebody says your name for the last time.
2010 In *The Sun*.

Beerbohm, Sir (Henry) Max(imilian)
She was one of those born to make chaos cosmic.
1911 *Zuleika Dobson*, ch.2.

Bible (Old Testament)
To every thing there is a season, and a time to every purpose under the heaven:
A time to be born, and a time to die; a time to plant, and a time to pluck up that which is planted…
Ecclesiastes 3:1–8.

Day, Clarence Shepard
'If you don't go to other men's funerals,' he told Father stiffly, 'they won't go to yours.'
1935 *Life With Father*, 'Father interferes'.

Donne, John
Death be not proud, though some have called thee
Mighty and dreadful, for thou art not so,
For those, whom thou think'st thou dost overthrow,
Die not, poor death, nor yet canst thou kill me.
From rest and sleep, which but thy pictures be,
Much pleasure, then from thee much more must flow,
And soonest our best men with thee do go,
Rest of their bones and soul's delivery.
c.1610–1615 *Holy Sonnets*, no.10.

Hardy, Thomas
Woman much missed, how you call to me, call to me,
Saying that now you are not as you were
When you had changed from the one who was all to me,
But as at first, when our day was fair.
1914 'The Voice'.

Holland, Henry Scott
Death is nothing at all; it does not count. I have only slipped away into the next room.
1910 Sermon, Whit Sunday.

Jackson, Jesse
He was born with little, inherited nothing and left a lot.
2007 Eulogy at the burial of soul singer James Brown in Augusta, Georgia.

Obama, Barack Hussein
Let us pause and give thanks for the fact that Nelson Mandela lived—a man who took history in his hands, and bent the arc of the moral universe toward justice.
2013 Speaking after the death of Nelson Mandela, paraphrasing Martin Luther King's 'The arc of the moral universe is long, but it bends towards justice', 5 Dec.

Rossetti, Christina Georgina

Remember me when I am gone away,
Gone far away into the silent land.
1862 *Goblin Market and Other Poems*, 'Remember'.

Shakespeare, William

Good night, sweet prince,
And flights of angels sing thee to thy rest.
1600–1 Horatio. *Hamlet*, act 5, sc.2, l.312–13.

Shelley, Percy Bysshe

He hath awakened from the dream of life—
'Tis we, who lost in stormy visions, keep
With phantoms an unprofitable strife,
And in mad trance, strike with our spirit's knife
Invulnerable nothings.
1821 *Adonais*, stanza 39

Stevenson, Robert Louis

Here he lies where he longed to be,
Home is the sailor, home from sea,
And the hunter home from the hill.
1884 'Requiem' (dated 'Hyères, May 1884'), collected in *Underwoods* (1887), bk.1, no.21.

Tennyson, Alfred, 1st Baron

For though from out our bourne of Time and Place
The flood may bear me far,
I hope to see my Pilot face to face
When I have crossed the bar.
1889 'Crossing the Bar', l.9–16. This was Tennyson's last poem.

Tutu, Desmond

Sometimes you want to whisper in God's ear, 'God, we know you are in charge, but why don't you make it slightly more obvious?'
2008 Wallenberg Lecture, University of Michigan, 29 Oct.

Wedding speeches

Astor (of Hever Castle), Nancy Witcher Astor, Viscountess

I married beneath me. All women do.
1951 Speech, Oldham.

Bacon, Francis, Viscount St Albans

He was reputed one of the wise men that made answer to the question when a man should marry? 'A young man not yet, an elder man not at all.'
1625 *Essays*, no.8, 'Of Marriage and the Single Life'.

Bible (New Testament)

It is better to marry than to burn.
1 Corinthians 7:9.

Biel, Jessica Claire

If you want a man's attention, ignore him.
2008 As Larita Whittaker in *Easy Virtue* (screenplay by Stephan Elliott and Sheridan Jobbins).

Brand, Russell Edward

I like threesomes with two women, not because I'm a cynical sexual predator. Oh no! But because I'm a romantic. I'm looking for 'The One'. And I'll find her more quickly if I audition two at a time.
Attributed.

Campbell, Mrs Patrick

The deep, deep peace of the double-bed after the hurly-burly of the chaise-longue.
Her definition of marriage, quoted in Alexander Woollcott *While Rome Burns* (1934), 'The First Mrs Tanqueray'.

Congreve, William

Thus grief still treads upon the heels of pleasure:
Married in haste, we may repent at leisure.
1693 Sharper to Setter. *The Old Bachelor*, act 5, sc.1.

Disraeli, Benjamin, 1st Earl of Beaconsfield

Every woman should marry—and no man.
1870 *Lothair*, ch.30.

Gabor, Zsa Zsa

A girl must marry for love and keep on marrying until she finds it.
Attributed.

Herbert, Sir A(lan) P(atrick)

The critical period in matrimony is breakfast-time.
1935 *Uncommon Law*, 'Is Marriage Lawful?'.

James, E. L.

At the end of the day, we want someone who is going to do the bloody dishes.
2012 Explaining what women really want in a man.

Johnson, Samuel

The triumph of hope over experience.
1770 On a friend's second marriage shortly after the death of his first, troublesome, wife. Quoted in James Boswell *The Life of Samuel Johnson* (1791), vol.2.

Keillor, Garrison

There is almost no marital problem that can't be helped enormously by taking off your clothes.
2005 'The Old Scout', *The Writer's Almanac*, 4 Oct.

Lette, Kathy

I am allergic to domestic goddesses. Men would prefer a woman with a dirty mind to a clean house.
2008 Quoted in *The Funniest Things You Never Said 2*, 2011.

Paltrow, Gwyneth Kate

I asked my Dad once, 'How did you and Mum stay married for thirty-three years?' He said,

'Well, we never wanted to get divorced at the same time.'
2013 Quoted in the *Evening Standard*, 2 May.

Pepys, Samuel

Strange to say what delight we married people have to see these poor fools decoyed into our condition.
1665 Diary entry, 25 Dec.

Shaw, George Bernard

Marriage is popular because it combines the maximum of temptation with the maximum of opportunity.
1903 *Man and Superman*, 'Maxims for Revolutionists: Marriage'.

Stevenson, Robert Louis

Even if we take marriage at its lowest, even if we regard it as no more than a sort of friendship recognised by the police.
1881 *Virginibus Puerisque*, 'Virginibus Puerisque', pt.I.

Wilder, Thornton Niven

The fights are the best part of married life. The rest is merely so-so.
1939 *The Merchant of Yonkers*, act 2.

Williams, Robin

Marriage is a triumph of imagination over intelligence.
2013 As Father Monighan in *The Big Wedding* (screenplay by Justin Zackham).

Words of advice and encouragement

Altman, Robert

I'll give you the same advice I give my children: Never take advice from anybody.
2004 *Esquire*, Mar.

Angelou, Maya

Nothing will work unless you do.
2014 On Facebook, 2 Jan.

Auster, Paul

Wounds are an essential part of life, and until you are wounded in some way, you cannot become a man.
2010 *Sunset Park*.

Banks, Iain M.

One should never regret one's excesses, only one's failures of nerve.
2012 *The Hydrogen Sonata*.

Bezos, Jeff(rey Preston)

The number one rule has to be: Don't be boring.
2013 Addressing staff at *The Washington Post*, which he had just bought.

Burns, Robert

Liberty's in every blow!
Let us do or die!
1793 'Bruce's Address at Bannockburn', stanza 3.

Chesterfield, Philip Dormer Stanhope, 4th Earl of

Whatever is worth doing at all is worth doing well.
1746 Letter to his son, 10 Mar.

Craig, Daniel Wroughton

Why is it that people who can't take advice always insist in giving it?
2006 As James Bond in *Casino Royale* (screenplay by Neal Purvis, Robert Wade, and Paul Haggis).

Confucius

Man has three ways of acting wisely. First, on meditation; that is the noblest. Secondly, on imitation; that is the easiest. Thirdly, on experience; that is the bitterest.
c.479 BC *The Analects*.

DeGeneres, Ellen Lee

Never follow anyone else's path, unless you're in the woods and you're lost and you can see a path; then, by all means, you should follow that path.
Quoted in Katie Couric, *The Best Advice I Ever Got* (2011).

Emerson, Ralph Waldo

Keep cool: it will be all one a hundred years hence.
1850 *Representative Men*, 'Montaigne; or, The Skeptic'.

Gervais, Ricky Dene

The best advice I've ever received is, 'No one else knows what they're doing either.'
Attributed.

Hopkins, Anthony

If you don't go when you want to go, when you do go, you'll find you've gone.
2005 As Burt Munro in *The World's Fastest Indian* (screenplay by Roger Donaldson).

Rockne, Knute Kenneth

When the going gets tough, the tough get going.
His catchphrase, later adopted by John F Kennedy.

Rowling, J. K.

We do not need magic to change the world. We carry all the power we need inside ourselves already: we have the power to imagine better.
2008 Speech to the Harvard Alumni Association, 5 Jun.

Shakespeare, William

Once more unto the breach, dear friends, once more,
Or close the wall up with our English dead.
In peace there's nothing so becomes a man
As modest stillness and humility.
But when the blast of war blows in our ears,
Then imitate the action of the tiger.
Stiffen the sinews, conjure up the blood,
Disguise fair nature with hard-favoured rage.
1598–9 King Harry rallying his men at the siege of Harfleur. *Henry V*, act 3, sc.1, l.1–8.

Thoreau, Henry David

I have yet to hear the first syllable of valuable or even earnest advice from my seniors.
1854 *Walden, or, Life in the Woods*, 'Economy'.

Trollope, Anthony

It's dogged as does it. It ain't thinking about it.
1867 *The Last Chronicle of Barset*, ch.61, 'Giles Hoggett'.

Trollope, Joanna

You're stuck with yourself, so you might as well try and be someone you can stand to live with.
2013 *Sense and Sensibility*.

Whitman, Christine Todd

Anyone who thinks that they are too small to make a difference has never tried to fall asleep with a mosquito in the room.
Attributed.

accidents

9/11
Rudy Giuliani…9/11 — BIDEN 133:53

99
We are the 99 per cent — ANON 28:45

A

Aaron A. shall bear the judgment — BIBLE 94:68
  rod of A. — BIBLE 94:81
abandon A. all hope — DANTE 262:27
  a. established stereotypes — GORB 378:49
  A. yourself to Nature's truths — RABE 704:22
  don't a. it even now — KAFKA 472:4
  there is pleasure, there is…a. — EGGE 313:67
  want her to a. herself — LACL 503:35
  with a. or not at all — VAN 908:23
abandoned What God a. — HOUS 432:72
  What is not a. — SCHI 747:28
abandonment organized a. — MILL 593:43
abase humbly a. yourselves — PARN 665:47
Abba A., Father — BIBLE 125:18
ABC Learn the A. of science — PAVL 670:33
abdicate Better to a. — FULL 355:77
abducted A. by a French Marquis! — GRAH 380:88
Abe converting A. into a…saint — MENC 587:14
abecedary characters…form the a. — DOMI 290:3
abed in England now a. — SHAK 776:94
Abednego Meshach, and A. — BIBLE 111:39
Abel Where is A. thy brother? — BIBLE 92:3
Aberdour Half-owre, half-owre to A. — BALL 59:72
Aberfeldey birks of A. — BURNS 178:1
aberration not a temporary a. — JAMES 450:32
aberrations nineteenth-century a. — SMALL 826:58
abhorrent The more a. a news item — FOWL 345:64
  war a. to all real women — FOWL 345:61
abhors two things it a. most — HAZL 403:35
abide A. with me — LYTE 543:94
  Shall I a. — SHAK 795:83
abiding there is none a. — BIBLE 98:83
abilities of a brain surgeon — BRES 158:2
  born with instincts and a. — BALZ 61:6
  people according to their a. — MAIN 561:71
  uncommon a. — BAGE 55:80
ability a. nor interest — MORE 618:10
  a. to examine systematically — MARC 570:59
  a. to express them — KRAUS 499:7
  a. to get a good night's sleep — WILS 948:70
  a. to get to the verge — DULL 306:87
  a. to think in quotations — DRAB 298:79
  each according to his a. — MARX 579:43
  eliminate his a. to communicate — SCHW 750:89
  exults in his physical a. — POE 683:81
  famous without a. — SHAW 807:99
  lost your a. — GONC 377:41
abjure a. all roofs — SHAK 792:2
ablaze set the world a. — GILB 369:53
able-bodied every a.-b. man — DORAM 294:84
abnormal if everybody is a. — HUTC 441:50
  Living is a. — IONE 447:53
  nothing a. about…homosexuality — PROU 698:45
abnormality riveted by Jewish a. — ROTH 728:88
abode come to your happy a. — LAUD 511:17
  Divides a. with me — DICK 284:52
  live in a numble a. — DICK 280:44
abodes aiming at the blest a. — POPE 687:76
  Prudence…in dark a. — WORD 962:48
abolished state is not 'a.' — ENGE 326:13
abolition a. of all classes — MARX 579:45
  a. of control — TOLK 893:43
  a. of poverty — HOOV 427:43
  A. of private property — MARX 579:32
  a. of the slave trade — PITT 679:10
abominable A. no-man — ANON 25:74
  are altogether become…a. — BOOK 148:7
abomination Electric guitars…a. — SEGO 756:4
  Great desolation of a. — COBB 233:76
abominations A. Of The Earth — BIBLE 132:17
  commit…all a. — BARN 64:61
Abora Singing of Mount A. — COLE 236:41
aboriginal a. and savage singer — CHOC 222:25
  A. writer is a Janus-type — NARO 630:53
Aborigine alcohol to an A.? — NOON 641:49
abortions Misbegotten a. — VAUG 909:30
about minded what they were a. — STER 847:20
above either a. or below it — GILL 370:83

Unless a. himself he can — DANI 262:33
Abraham carried…into A.'s bosom — BIBLE 121:97
  God of A. — PASC 668:96
Abram when A. was ninety years old — BIBLE 92:20
abrasive brash and a. — MAHA 559:28
abreast gaps even two can pass a. — FROST 352:90
a-brewing some ill a.-b. — SHAK 769:92
abroad A. is bloody — GEOR 364:55
  A. is unutterably bloody — MITF 610:54
  a., you almost feel…a statesman — MACM 556:66
  before he goes a. — STER 848:43
  don't hold with a. — CRISP 254:2
  haven't been a. in so long — BENC 78:5
  honest man sent to lie a. — WOTT 962:54
  lov'd at home, rever'd a. — BURNS 177:76
  No more. I will a. — HERB 414:75
  scattereth a. — BIBLE 117:83
  to go a. for ayre — PEPYS 674:2
  walked a. in the shower — THOM 884:22
  Weather a. — RICH 713:93
  whole business a. — MONT 613:14
  without suspicion tell a. — SPEN 838:39
  would never go a. — SMOL 831:67
Absalom O my son A. — BIBLE 97:49
absence A. diminishes…passions — LARO 510:5
  a. is no longer a felt…weight — STEI 846:98
  A. is to love what wind is to fire — BUSSY 184:55
  a. of the real thing — BERG 83:27
  a. seemed my flame to qualify — SHAK 802:78
  cry of A., A., in the heart — RANS 707:70
  dote on his very a. — SHAK 769:81
  every a. which follows it — STER 848:46
  fit of a. of mind — SEEL 756:2
  like a winter hath my a. been — SHAK 802:71
  marked by an a. of crises — PECK 672:65
  presence of a. — BERG 83:27
  shoot me in my a. — BEHAN 74:9
  takes place in your a. — RUSH 732:64
  the a. of facts — MANT 568:18
  the a. of hope — OBAMA 644:38
  Through a long a. — WORD 956:53
  world, which in thy a. — SHAK 795:83
absent a. are always in the wrong — DEST 275:4
  a. from it so long — SCOTT 754:80
  a. one from another — BIBLE 93:35
  From you have I been a. — SHAK 802:72
  If to be a. — LOVE 538:83
  live in you…when you are a. — SCEVE 746:17
  love the a. — BEHN 75:26
  think of one's a. love — TROL 897:30
absentee a. boss is best — WINT 950:6
absenteeism persistent a. — SAMU 741:98
absentees those cruel a.! — EDGE 311:43
absent-minded motive of the a.-m. — BELL 78:94
absents often say, endear A. — LAMB 505:57
absolute a. rest is death — PASC 667:72
  content so a. — SHAK 789:8
  If a. sovereignty be not necessary — ASTE 39:4
  Reaching no a. — GUNN 390:96
absolutely A. 100 per cent — SIMP 822:86
absolutes damn, damn all a.! — LAWR 513:68
absolutism a. moderated — MUNS 626:57
absolve History will a. me — CAST 208:77
  Who shall a. the foulness — SASS 746:99
abstainers burden of…prudent a. — QUINE 702:22
abstinence almost a sin of a. — DRYD 304:44
  praise of his a. — MILT 600:15
  total a. is easier — AUGU 44:30
abstract A. Expressionists — WARH 920:8
  A. painting…confronts you — POLL 684:3
  contain any a. reasoning — HUME 438:7
  ideological, or the a. — ROTH 728:90
  is the a. spirit — KAND 472:14
  Literature is not an a. science — QUIL 702:14
  pictures known…as Cubist and A. — DAVIS 266:6
  test of an a. picture — BETJ 88:23
  there exists none which is a. — HEIN 407:21
abstraction Art is an a. — GAUG 361:2
  death…like a cold a. — MILL 593:42
  thought moving in…complete a. — WHIT 936:67
abstracts a. and brief chronicles — SHAK 782:97
abstruseness a. in their language — GOWE 380:81
absurd A. in form — GOET 375:58
  a. is born of…confrontation — CAMUS 195:81
  a. is the fundamental idea — CAMUS 195:82
  a. to regard non-existence — SCHO 748:54
  attacked as a. — JAMES 451:75

nothing so a. that it has not been said — CICE 227:33
something rather a. about the past — BEER 73:74
war abhorrent…and a. — FOWL 345:61
absurdist A. plays…in No Man's Land — ADAM 4:70
absurdity a. of being in love — LACL 503:30
  a., only you are pure — VALL 907:9
  fear of being an a. — FIND 336:45
abundance shall have a. — BIBLE 119:34
  sound of a. of rain — BIBLE 97:63
abundant life more a. — MILL 594:78
abuse a.—I thrive on it — DOUG 295:12
  a. of metaphors — PALM 661:67
  a. the King — SHAK 798:81
  also giving us a. — WEST 933:97
  Bad language or a. — GILB 368:32
  contempt, a. and wrong — MILT 607:84
  if it is a. — SHER 817:95
  more dangerous is the a. — BURKE 175:12
  only offer a. — GALL 358:40
  Whipping and a. — STOWE 856:31
abuses correction of private a. — PEEL 672:66
  It is impossible to correct a. — ASSAN 39:95
abusing old a. of God's patience — SHAK 773:1
abyss a. of time? — SHAK 803:10
  brink of the final a. — MOUN 622:93
  brooding on the vast a. — MILT 601:31
  cradle rocks above an a. — NABO 628:3
  facing a deep a. — HUSS 440:37
  mother's heart is an a. — BALZ 61:2
  plunge into a bottomless a. — SUN 859:91
  riding into the bottomless a. — WALEY 917:31
  rope over an a. — NIET 638:1
  secrets of th' a. to spy — GRAY 385:90
  unbottomed infinite a. — MILT 603:65
abysses whatsoever a. Nature leads — HUXL 443:3
Abyssinian In a vision…an A. maid — COLE 236:41
academic a. atmosphere — STEA 843:28
  term of reproach in a. discussions — BERG 83:18
academies A. of Science — FRAN 348:18
academy groves of their a. — BURKE 176:42
accelerator press the a. to the floor — VUKO 915:59
accent a. of the place — LARO 510:6
  Can you lose the a.? — MCGR 552:88
  English without an a. — BENC 78:5
  Scots a. of the mind — STEV 853:76
  stresses of a. — SAND 742:36
  with a strong English a. — SAKI 739:52
  with a swaggering a. — SHAK 786:19
accents a. yet unknown! — SHAK 777:31
  I hear in a. low — GRAY 384:59
  I know noble a. — STEV 850:75
accentuate a. the existing inequities — HARDY 396:98
accept A. who you are. — DEGEN 270:4
  worse…having to a. it — FAUL 331:37
acceptable become a. tomorrow — HELL 408:34
  no longer a. — CLIN 231:24
  see the a. face of capitalism — HEATH 405:87
acceptance a. of a task — GIDE 368:24
  broad a. of whatever — RUSS 734:36
  deserves respect if not enthusiastic a. — ANGE 18:87
access a. to a better life…denied — ANGE 19:94
  doesn't give you special a. — REAG 708:1
accession A. of Commodus — GIBB 366:90
accessories vital a. to my work — BAIN 55:95
accident a. happened to the rector — TROL 897:32
  a. of sex — GILM 371:94
  a., sickness, justice — NEME 633:18
  a. that puts a stop to it — VALE 907:3
  automobile a. — GIBB 376:6
  Body-line…was not an a. — JAMES 450:32
  entire universe…is Pure A. — OATES 643:7
  God enlightens men…purely by a. — CYRA 260:12
  happens by a.…becomes a religion — WRIS 963:74
  have it found out by a. — LAMB 506:14
  moments of magical a. — THOM 884:44
  moving a. is not my trade — WORD 958:91
  old age, a., sickness — LLOY 532:71
  sometimes it's more of an A. — MILNE 596:19
  there is more a. to it — PYNCH 701:11
accidents A.…in the best-regulated
  families — DICK 280:51
  a. will happen — NORTH 641:61
  chapter of a. is a very long one — CHES 219:44
  Omissions are not a. — MOORE 617:84
  Omissions are not a. — MOORE 617:90
  problem of habitual a. — BENC 78:7
  runs into a. — MARQ 575:55

accommodation

accommodation warmth and a. — NUTT 642:75
accomplish a. these aims — UNIT 905:9
  For what we cannot a. — WILL 946:21
  real thing they a. — MORE 618:17
accomplished only become truly a. — ANGE 19:6
accomplishment absolute a. — WORD 958:74
  a. of modern science — GALB 357:20
  a. of what we can do — AGAS 9:86
  knighthood as a social a. — NAIP 629:29
  only a. my education ever bestowed — DRAB 298:79
accomplishments ahead of his a. — STEI 845:80
  reasonable quantity of a. — AUST 46:73
accord comes of his own a. — TOCQ 893:33
accordion A....in harmony — BIER 134:59
account a. for what we do — FENT 332:61
  even when you take into a. — HOFS 422:35
  faithful a. of men and things — ELIOT 315:20
  most precise a. — TRIL 897:13
  thy name in high a. — SCOTT 752:20
accountable a. for its exercise — DISR 287:16
accountant A...a 'counter' and a 'mutant'. — HOFF 422:29
accountants a. and solicitors — TAYL 868:56
accounting a. department — STEA 843:29
  Capital a. in...rational shape — WEBER 925:13
  monomania of a. — WEIL 928:74
accounts everyone's a. but their own — ARON 37:49
accuracy grace of a. — LOWE 540:38
  no fineness or a. of suppression — BELL 77:75
accurate more a. in the beginning — JONS 468:96
  neither clear-sighted nor a. — TROL 898:53
  scrupulously a. instrument — ERNST 327:40
accursed bless th' a. — SHAK 791:80
  think themselves a. — SHAK 776:94
accusation both in approval and a. — WELTY 930:46
  mutual a. spent — MILT 606:56
accuse a. 'em of not having any faces — PRIE 695:92
  I a. — ZOLA 970:15
  justice enough to a. — GOLD 376:91
accused before you be a. — CHAR 215:29
  persons who are a. — DENM 273:72
accustomed It is an a. action — SHAK 798:64
  start to get a. to it — RIMS 716:52
  torpor of being a. — WARR 921:21
ace an a. of joy up his sleeve — ONDA 650:56
  someone else was about to play the a. — FIELD 335:12
ache a. to utter — SAND 741:12
  still have that a. — UTTL 907:50
achieve I can a. it — JACK 448:4
  those who do a. something — HUXL 441:60
  wish to a. the best — RUNGE 731:54
achievement a. its nothingness — HAMM 394:59
  a. suffer from any taint — KNOX 495:17
  Art...the supreme a. — POUND 692:31
  assess one's own a. — WHITE 935:35
  dote on past a. — HAZL 403:47
  lowest...human a. — CART 206:48
  one a. of Man — THUR 890:79
  perpetuating its highest a. — SHAW 808:29
  Poetry is the a. — SAND 742:22
  tarnish the a. — THES 882:96
achievements a....in a...fog — CONR 244:49
  Don't overstate your...a. — BLIN 142:55
  most enormous a. — THOR 889:55
  Where be the brave a. — SPEN 838:37
  without major a. — MUNRO 626:54
achiever a. brings home — SHAK 773:15
Achilles see the great A. — TENN 871:2
acid Electric Kool-Aid A. Test — WOLFE 953:72
  misses the heels of a. — LEHM 520:20
  tomorrow do...a. rain — WYLIE 964:8
acids A. stain you — PARK 664:19
acini a. degenerate leaving Islets — BANT 62:35
acknowledge a. and bewail — BOOK 147:67
  In all thy ways a. him — BIBLE 104:52
acorns hundred a. are planted — CARL 201:16
acquaintance friend...first an a. — CHEK 218:17
  good creditable a. — SWIFT 861:28
  make a new a. — JOHN 464:97
  not make a new a. — JOHN 460:65
  of the deep a. — UPDI 906:37
  repented of having sought his a. — BIRD 136:7
  Should auld a. be forgot — BURNS 178:5
acquainted a. with all my ways — BIBLE 103:43
  a. with the night — FROST 352:6
  constituents with which we are a. — RUSS 734:24
  when we were first a. — BURNS 179:16
acquiesce a. with silence — JOHN 460:72

acquisition a....of positive knowledge — SART 744:63
  by the a. of wealth — MONT 614:44
acquisitiveness jealousy, and a. — JAMES 451:69
acres few paternal a. bound — POPE 685:43
acrimony a. of the last election — DICK 279:2
acrobat poet like an a. — FERL 333:89
Acropolis A., where our Christmas — MOYN 623:1
acrostic province in A. Land — DRYD 301:45
act a. a gridiron — CLIVE 231:38
  A. in such a way — KANT 473:24
  a. like a lady — SIMON 821:73
  a. of a writer's imagination — WELTY 931:46
  a. of balancing — SPEN 837:9
  a. of defending us — STEV 850:95
  A. of Parliament to save...the nation — CONG 241:57
  a. of putting two and two — KOES 495:30
  a. of the servant — LEON 522:56
  A. One, Scene One — HART 400:70
  A small a. is worth — AI WEI 10:4
  a. so brave and daring — ROCH 719:17
  a. without benefit of experience — MILL 594:82
  any evil or base a. — PLATO 682:58
  Between the motion And the a. — ELIOT 318:15
  cut...The second a. — COWA 249:63
  don't have to a. with me — FURT 356:90
  every a. of the authorities — REED 710:37
  first a. on entering this world — BOYD 154:12
  how to a. like a Congressman — KENN 482:38
  I can't a. — HARD 396:95
  indispensable a. of policy — PITT 679:10
  itself almost an a. — ROSS 727:65
  joyous and responsible human a. — FRIE 350:66
  last a. crowns the play — QUAR 701:6
  last a. harsh, and violent — DONNE 290:16
  last a. is bloody — PASC 667:77
  living a. the undoubted deed — MELV 589:55
  nature yearned to a. — WHITE 935:56
  not to be caught in the a. — STEN 847:6
  ought never to a. — KANT 473:23
  painting that is an a. — ROSE 725:27
  second a. and the ending — ANON 26:1
  something for the Third A. — ANON 26:90
  tells you how to a. — UPDI 905:12
  To a....according to virtue — SPIN 840:78
  to a. with your eyes — BONH 145:20
  Troops always ready to a. — FRED 349:37
  Whether you compose or a. — DIDE 285:63
  who doth a. amiss — RALE 705:45
acta A. est fabula — AUGU 45:38
acted a. disinterestedly — LIPP 531:43
  a. so tragic — HARG 398:31
acting a. and frequenting — PRYN 699:62
  a. in its purest form — BONH 145:20
  A. is like having the party — CHER 218:28
  A. is not hard work — CLOO 231:42
  A. is reacting — DEPP 273:80
  A. is therefore the lowest — MOORE 616:69
  a. of a dreadful thing — SHAK 776:16
  a. on what just finished — KESEY 483:65
  convey when you are a. — BARR 65:95
  danger chiefly lies in a. well — CHUR 224:60
  important thing in a. — GOLD 377:37
  Method a.? — BARR 65:3
  robs the mind of all its powers of a. — BURKE 175:6
  when he was off he was a. — GOLD 377:18
action a. and passion — CARL 201:14
  a. from without and from within — WORD 958:89
  A. is consolatory — CONR 244:37
  a. is not sister — BAUD 68:68
  a....most dangerous thing — CLOU 232:58
  a. of some sort, any sort — POUND 691:9
  a. of the tiger — SHAK 775:74
  a. planned at the beginning — MYRD 628:99
  a. takes place in Poland — JARRY 452:92
  an accustomed a. — SHAK 798:64
  by a., not...contemplation — BRON 160:51
  call his muscles into a. — POE 683:81
  Chafing in a. — WHITE 935:56
  deterrent out of an incredible a. — MCNA 557:90
  do good a. by stealth — LAMB 506:14
  doubt...be removed except by A. — CARL 200:97
  Drama is a., sir — PIRA 679:88
  end of man is an a. — CARL 200:95
  every a....is thought to aim — ARIS 31:19
  every a. there is — NEWT 635:59
  glorious in its a. — BYRON 189:84
  If ever I do a mean a. — STER 849:54

acquisition — 1004 —

impartial in thought as well as in a. — WILS 949:77
in a. how like an angel — SHAK 782:89
keep step with the a. — RIMB 716:46
lose the name of a. — SHAK 783:7
made to follow a course of a. — CONF 240:17
Makes it and th' a. fine — HERB 413:60
months of a. worse than inactivity — BYRON 187:31
moves great masses of men to a. — BOUL 152:88
Neither a. nor style — ACHE 3:41
Never confuse movement with a. — HEMI 410:93
No unchaste a. — SHAK 792:86
parents...snap into a. — ALLEN 14:92
precondition to meaningful a. — BART 66:17
representation of an a. — ARIS 31:23
right a. is freedom — ELIOT 320:76
sworn to a. — SASS 745:83
taking...a. to stop small ones — EDEN 311:31
than a single lovely a. — LOWE 539:11
That a. is best — HUTC 441:49
Thought is the child of A. — DISR 287:15
true men of a. — AUDEN 44:10
truth in a. — DISR 288:41
vice sometime's by a. dignified — SHAK 766:88
victim and slave of his a. — EMER 325:81
wheeled into a. — STEV 850:6
Youth, beauty, graceful a. — DRYD 302:85
actionable only a. one we can call — SALI 740:84
actions a. and counsels — LEST 524:8
  a. and the consequences of their a. — MOORE 617:95
  a. are questions — LECA 518:73
  a. are right in proportion — MILL 591:8
  a. of two bodies — NEWT 635:59
  A. receive their tincture — DEFOE 269:73
  advantage...in practical a. — DRAKE 298:97
  conscious of their a. — SPIN 840:72
  consequences of certain a. — KISS 493:86
  goal of our a. — MORE 619:22
  Great a. are not...true sons — BUTL 185:72
  honour and good a. — BACON 52:16
  important legislative a. — JEVO 455:55
  invades all gestures and a. — PIGL 678:75
  man's a. critical a. — ELIOT 315:21
  Men's a. are too strong — EMER 325:81
  my a. are my Ministers' — CHAR 215:34
  poor centre of a man's a. — BACON 52:5
  practical a. we undertake — MILLS 595:8
  Strong reasons make strange a. — SHAK 768:61
  tend to justify our a. — MCNA 557:92
active a. and creative world — SPEN 837:12
  a. child do deeds of youth — SHAK 801:49
  resignation is a. — FITZ 338:3
  take an a. part — JOHN 456:72
activities consequences of their a. — HOBS 421:7
  human a. which are truly cumulative — SART 744:63
activity a. of soul exhibiting excellence — ARIS 31:20
  a. of the very highest — RUSS 734:27
  Imagination...into a separate a. — DUDEK 305:78
  life was one round of a. — LEAC 515:16
  moral a. which disentangles — POE 683:81
  No physical a. is so vain — MAIL 560:59
  one exclusive sphere of a. — MARX 579:29
  untidy a. continues — BISH 136:25
act of God A. o. G. was defined — HERB 412:48
actor a. everywhere but upon the stage — CHES 219:46
  a. giving positive criticism to a director — MULL 624:31
  a. has a natural animosity — BROO 163:12
  a. in his heart believes — WELL 929:97
  a. is a kind of guy — BRAN 156:68
  a great a. or a household word? — OLIV 649:37
  as evidently an a. — WALP 919:70
  better the a. the more stupid — CAPO 197:31
  decent a. waiting for a chance — FLYNN 341:64
  decision to become an a. — MCKE 554:11
  every a. in Hollywood — GIEL 368:26
  Every writer is a frustrated a. — STER 757:32
  face of a moving-picture a. — MENC 587:87
  For an a., it is...essential — MORL 619:41
  great a....walking down the street — COPL 246:99
  greatest vice in an a. — HAZL 403:31
  If an a. reads it out — SALI 740:77
  Like a dull a. — SHAK 799:3
  main problem of the a. — OLIV 649:42
  never was an a. — MATU 582:2
  sweetheart ran away with an a. — WINC 949:89
actors A. are cattle — HITC 419:86
  a. got in front of it — WOOL 956:50
  a. or spectators? — SHEL 815:35

advice

A. who have tried to play Churchill	MANC 564:50	kiss thy hand to bid a.	STER 848:46	a. one's children will become	WALK 917:34
Authors are a.	STEV 850:94	**adjectives** fatigue of a.	BROY 169:88	A. talk about being happy	WINT 950:7
best a. in the world	SHAK 782:94	more suspicious of a.	SAND 742:29	between consenting a.	VIDAL 912:83
clergy is…same business as a.	HURT 440:36	writes without a.	POUND 692:36	Children…are already a.	LABR 502:23
come across a lot with a.	GRANT 381:2	**adjoining** hold down the a.	BELL 77:75	distinction between children and a.	BART 66:13
delinquents are frustrated a.	MULL 624:32	**adjudications** body of a.	FRYE 354:53	**advance** If I a., follow me	MUSS 627:89
Natural politicians are skilled a.	MARA 569:45	**adjusted** happier and more well a.	FALU 329:11	if it does not a.	GIBB 366:97
pick out a. by	WILD 943:54	so well a.	JARR 452:85	If there is technological a.	HARR 398:43
pick out that a. at the Oscars	MCKE 554:12	well a. members of society	CALL 192:28	retreat into a.	ROOS 724:6
says that a. are cattle?	WINN 950:1	**adjustments** clear-eyed a.	DAY 267:28	somewhat to a.	POPE 688:23
troupes of a. slaughtered	STOP 855:16	**Adlai** Madly for A.	ANON 25:33	**advanced** a. in the way	JONS 468:89
actress a. in motion pictures	DAVIS 265:94	**Adlestrop** I remember A.	THOM 885:51	**advances** small a. in knowledge	PROU 698:46
aim of any a.	DAVIS 265:95	**ad-libbing** a.-l., synthesizing	MARA 569:45	**advantage** a. of doing one's praising	BUTL 185:97
For an a. to be a success	BARR 65:98	**administer** a. is to govern	MIRA 608:16	a. of not being free	SNOW 832:81
Next worse to an a.	CARY 207:65	hated by those who a. it	GOLD 376:83	a. of time and place	DRAKE 298:87
schooling any a. needs	GING 371:98	**administered** Whate'er is best a.	POPE 687:84	a. over their neighbours	SMITH 827:85
actresses A. have to…frown	DENEU 272:52	**administration** a. must be entrusted	SUN 860:96	a. that no one would	KENN 482:44
bosoms of your a.	JOHN 459:51	a. of slavery	STOWE 856:28	Baseball has the great a.	SHAW 810:27
acts all your a. are queens	SHAK 799:20	affairs of internal a.	NICH 636:71	essential a. for a poet	ELIOT 319:30
comedy in one hundred different a.	LAFO 504:61	choice…in the field of a.	WEBER 925:14	great a. of a hotel	SHAW 806:95
five a. of Shakespeare's tragedy	FIELD 335:12	criticism of a.	BAGE 54:66	let not a. slip	SHAK 762:82
how their a. are defined	SZASZ 865:27	current principles of a.	SIMON 821:74	Many girls have not the a.	FLEM 340:44
little, nameless, unremembered, a.	WORD 956:54	departments of the central a.	MILL 591:4	Men have every a.	AUST 47:89
put our a. together	THOM 887:90	government and a.	STEE 844:44	most naturally gain the a.	POTT 690:86
the order of the a.	PAST 668:98	life of this A.	KENN 481:2	rich a. of good exercise?	SHAK 768:63
With such a. fill a pen	DRAY 298:95	low heels in the a.	SWIFT 862:43	take a. of that	SHAW 806:89
acute so a., so ignominious	SHAW 807:18	purpose of forming an a.	PALM 662:73	**advantages** a.…from being a bachelor	WODE 952:39
AD what A. is elsewhere	TWAIN 902:49	**administrations** differences of a.	BIBLE 126:51	a. of Ireland	SAKI 739:64
adage believed in the old a.	LOOS 536:48	**admirable** how express and a.	SHAK 782:89	Women are…debarred those a.	ASTE 39:2
homely a. that runs	ROOS 724:15	**admiral** a good thing to kill an a.	VOLT 914:32	**advent** Hark to the A. voice!	OAKL 643:5
poor cat i'th' a.?	SHAK 796:21	An a. red	SITW 823:96	**adventure** a. hard With peril	MILT 606:60
Adam A. and Eve were dispossessed	BOUL 152:91	to kill an a. from time to time	VOLT 914:32	a. is only an inconvenience	CHES 220:73
A. and Eve were turned out	MUGG 623:10	**admiralty** price of a.	KIPL 490:10	a. of the spirit	WHIT 936:66
A. and his wife hid themselves	BIBLE 91:93	**admiration** a. of each other's play	BARR 65:94	But the a.	HEDIN 406:4
A. ate the apple	HUGH 436:37	a. of one man	SCOTT 751:8	death…the most beautiful a.	FROH 351:87
A. cannot be excused	LANY 508:54	ever new and increasing a. and awe	KANT 473:26	pass out into a.	FORS 344:24
A. from his fair spouse	MILT 604:9	near to a.	JOHN 463:73	To die will be an awfully big a.	BARR 65:87
A. knew Eve	BIBLE 92:2	to attract a.	MAIL 560:59	verse be a glorious a.	VERL 911:61
A. like the Lord's First Word	FARJ 330:20	top of a.	SHAK 804:22	**adventurer** by temperament…an a.	FREUD 350:55
A.'s recollection of his fall	BYRON 189:98	**admire** a….don't…understand	ROOS 724:99	**adventurers** two kinds of a.	HEAT 406:93
A. was a gardener	KIPL 493:69	cannot possibly a. them	WILDE 941:73	**adventures** critic…recognizes the a.	FRAN 346:79
A. was a gardener	SHAK 759:97	I a. him	TWAIN 903:78	large spiritual a.	DAVI 265:86
A. was not Adamant!	HOOD 426:29	more things to a. in people	CAMUS 196:89	murderous and otherwise sinful a.	WEST 933:95
as in A. all die	BIBLE 127:57	Not to a., is all the art	POPE 688:24	Unlikely a. require unlikely tools	HOFF 422:30
deep sleep to fall on A.	BIBLE 91:90	Women…a…not understand	CONG 240:45	**adverbs** Easy on the A.	LEON 522:64
Eve made A. sin	MARG 570:63	**admired** a. but never knew	FENT 332:60	glad you like a.	JAMES 451:54
every maker since A.	WALC 916:18	a. by an American	HEPB 412:25	**adversaries** a. claim that	JAMES 451:75
father A. sat	KIPL 490:97	a. through being misunderstood	COCT 233:85	determination to our a.	KENN 481:21
Giving to A. what she held	LANY 508:53	**admirer** own most loving a.	WILS 947:46	souls of fearful a.	SHAK 760:32
hold up A.'s profession	SHAK 784:60	**admires** a. all kinds of things	BEER 74:94	**adversary** mine a. had written	BIBLE 98:10
old A. in this Child	BOOK 147:76	**adolescence** A. is the only time	PROU 697:42	sallies out and sees her a.	MILT 600:8
seeing what A. had seen	HUXL 442:90	petrified as	BEVAN 89:56	your a. the devil	BIBLE 130:73
son of A. and of Eve	PRIOR 695:99	Theory of Permanent A.	CONN 242:5	**adversity** a. doth best discover virtue	BACON 51:66
state of innocency A. fell	SHAK 771:55	to be a poet. A. is enough	CIAR 226:2	a. is not without comforts	BACON 51:65
the gardener A.	TENN 871:10	**adolescent** a….tries to open it	MISH 609:21	A. is sometimes hard	CARL 201:35
thought he was A.	TWAIN 902:56	No a….wants to be understood	FRY 354:42	a. is the blessing	BACON 51:64
When A. delved and Eve span	BALL 58:49	sensibility of a male a.	AUDEN 44:20	A. stretcheth our days	BROW 165:76
Why, ever since A.	MELV 585:73	**Adonais** A.—he is dead!	SHEL 815:37	are the uses of a.	SHAK 778:65
adamant Adam was not A.!	HOOD 426:29	**Adonis** eyes Of proud A.	MARL 574:34	brother is born for a.	BIBLE 105:81
adamantine a. chains and penal fire	MILT 601:33	**adopt** a. me and sivilize me	TWAIN 903:68	faint in the day of a.	BIBLE 105:92
bar thine a. doors	BLAKE 139:83	**adoption** and their a. tried	SHAK 781:49	tested by a.	CART 206:47
adaptability life-efficiency and a.	MUMF 625:39	Spirit of a.	BIBLE 125:18	virtue of a.	BACON 51:63
add whatever we a.	CRUZ 256:39	**adoration** Breathless with a.	WORD 959:96	**advertisement** a. writer	SAYE 746:10
adder a. better than the eel	SHAK 762:75	For A. seasons change	SMART 826:64	patent medicine a.	JERO 454:38
brings forth the a.	SHAK 776:15	**adorings** soft a. from their loves	KEATS 477:16	worst a. for Socialism	ORWE 653:15
deaf a. that stoppeth her ears	BOOK 149:21	**adroit** a. and joyless race	WAUGH 924:81	**advertisements** A. that say they are lying	NADER 629:25
toad or a. to catch	MUIR 624:17	**Adsum** quickly said, 'A.!'	THAC 880:39	– ideals…by its a.	DOUG 295:9
addicted most a. to the belief	JAMES 450:36	**adult** a. American Negro female	ANGE 18:87	**advertisers** become a nation of a.	PUNCH 699:75
wholly a. themselves to her	JONS 468:89	a. slave	GREER 387:43	**advertising** a. business	QUEN 702:8
addiction a. of political groups	GALB 357:15	not quite the occupation of an a.	OLIV 649:38	A….described as the science	LEAC 515:20
It is an a.	UPDI 906:35	**adulteries** all the a. of art	JONS 467:60	a. we deserve	SAYE 746:11
prisoners of a.	ILLI 445:23	**adulterous** is not a.	BENC 78:6	constant flow of fraudulent a.	CHAN 213:87
rape, sodomy and drug a.	COOK 245:68	**adultery** Do not a. commit	CLOU 232:65	duty of the a. agent to conceal	OGIL 648:5
terminal point of a.	AUDEN 44:18	first breath of a.	UPDI 905:17	right kind of a.	TWAIN 903:71
Addington Pitt is to A.	CANN 196:7	have committed a. in my heart	CART 206:46	unethical and ethical a.	STEF 844:53
addition any a. to knowledge	DONNE 293:77	hazards…alcohol and a.	CRIT 255:10	**advice** a. from my seniors	THOR 888:32
address no small degree of a.	SHER 817:93	Liberty, Equality, A.	BELL 77:84	A. is seldom welcome	CHES 219:38
Adenauer dear old Konrad A.	JAY 453:99	like a. or gluttony	MAUG 582:6	A. is what we ask for	JONG 466:36
adequate a. to take care of everybody	FULL 355:74	men call gallantry, and gods a.	BYRON 189:92	a. on the affairs of the world	FLAU 339:23
Six inches is perfectly a.	SPARK 836:70	rather be taken in a.	HUXL 441:54	a. to persons about to marry	PUNCH 699:73
adherents worst advertisement…a.	ORWE 653:15	Sara could commit a.	CARY 207:64	a. to the lovelorn	LEBO 518:69
adhesion Out of association grows a.	BRON 161:70	Thou shalt not commit a.	BIBLE 94:66	a. to you is not to inquire	WILD 943:42
adieu A., a.! my native shore	BYRON 187:35	Thou shalt not commit a.	BIBLE 114:33	aid or a. on any matter	DISR 288:54
A., Farewell	JAME 449:20	What was thy cause? A.	SHAK 793:21	given us a.	WEST 933:97
A. for evermore	BURNS 180:59	**adulthood** If this was a.	ALTH 15:13	give young writers a.	HELL 408:45
A. tristesse	ELUA 324:45	**adulthoods** a. are reaping	ELLI 323:33	I never give any a.	CHES 219:45
English seem to bid a.	SMITH 830:46	**adults** A. never understand anything	SAINT 738:35	Listen kid, take my a.	BERL 84:43

adviser

listen to this a.	TAO 867:25
move on—to new a.	KENN 481:13
my a. is not taken	PITT 679:4
Never take a. from anybody	ALTM 15:18
people who can't take a.	CRAIG 252:49
rendering public a.	GALB 357:23
Some a.	GAUG 361:2
Sometimes economists give...bad a.	KRUG 500:28
strongest possible piece of a.	CURR 259:95
woman seldom asks a.	ADDI 7:42
adviser A newspaper is an a.	TOCQ 893:33
advisers a. may move	KENN 481:13
that the Prime Minister's a. are responsible is absurd	FOLL 341:70
advising a. the former President	BUSH 182:96
advocate a. for the blind, venomous	UPDI 905:20
a. with the Father	BIBLE 130:78
advocates more potent a. of peace	GEOR 364:49
Aeneas A., Troy's Chieftain	VIRG 913:13
aeroplanes century of a.	DEBU 268:63
Aeschines When A. spoke	OGIL 648:5
Aeschylean in A. phrase	HARDY 397:16
Aeson A. had (as Poets fain)	HERR 415:1
Aesop A. was writing for the tortoise	BROO 163:4
prettily devised of A.	BACON 53:42
aesthetic a. judgements	STRA 857:41
desire for a. expression	WAUGH 923:66
enough a. excitement here	BART 66:15
pictures known in a. slang as Cubist	DAVIS 266:5
aestheticism first was a.	HUGH 435:28
aesthetics not a. but ethics	ROGE 722:68
Aetolian Europe to the A. shore	ARNO 35:5
afar and from a.	PAST 668:99
Faintly, faintlier a.	FREE 350:50
affable irascible to the a.	MACD 550:40
more a. than rumour would have it	DAVIS 265:94
affair a. between Margot Asquith	PARK 663:98
an a. with the moon	STER 849:53
And go to ev'ry such a.	PORT 690:72
beginning of a novelistic a.	MANN 566:85
great a. is to move	STEV 851:28
he was a foreign a.	REST 711:65
squalid a.	HAIL 392:18
affairs advice on the a. of the world	FLAU 339:23
a. of men rest still incertain	SHAK 778:53
a. of others	BEAU 70:6
a. of the nation	AMERY 15:27
a. which concern them	VALE 907:6
conduct our a.	KENN 481:18
foreign a.	JOHN 458:19
interest in all public a.	MORI 619:36
knew a lot about foreign a.	REST 711:65
mind little but their own a.	MONT 613:10
mind their own a.	HOUS 432:67
mischief in...ordinary everyday a.	CHUR 224:51
nature of...human a.	POWE 693:60
remembrance of political a.	MACA 545:37
Secrecy...in the a. of State	RICH 714:20
tide in the a. of men	SHAK 778:48
time in which our a. prosper	BIER 134:79
turned to their a.	FROST 352:99
write of your love a.	YEATS 965:2
affect having it a. his mind	HOOV 427:53
affectation so used to a.	ETHE 327:48
too much...for ornament is a.	BACON 53:35
virtue is your greatest a.	WYCH 964:95
affectations a. rise up in his heart	DIDE 285:78
affected a., sapless, soulless	RUSK 733:18
affection A. beaming in one eye	DICK 279:12
A. is a coal	SHAK 762:85
begin our public a. in our families	BURKE 176:49
in respect and a.	SAND 742:26
judgement is...subject to a.	JOHN 463:73
man's a.	GILB 368:38
rear of your a.	SHAK 781:46
Rearrange a 'Wife's a.'!	DICK 284:54
Set your a. on things above	BIBLE 128:10
sheer kindness and a.	TROL 897:31
spaniel-like a.	WOLL 954:89
substitute for a.	RUSS 734:31
what unrequited a. is	DICK 280:36
affectionate a person can be truly a.	PREV 694:78
affections history of the a.	IRVI 447:58
insinuate our selves into men's a.	CAVE 210:21
living a.	STOWE 856:28
not masters of our own a.	ETHE 327:46
strain on the a.	ELIOT 316:47

affirmation a. of...colonial elites	ILLI 445:21
separates a. from negation	THUR 891:99
affirmations a. of the soul	EMER 324:74
afflict mine own a. me	JONS 467:61
afflicted a. by the thought	GALS 358:49
affliction all a. taught a lover	POPE 686:49
in time of a.	PASC 667:87
Remembering mine a.	BIBLE 110:25
some a. or defect	BEER 74:90
suffer from the wrong a.	NASH 630:61
afflictions mortals their a. spell	PHIL 677:54
affluence fact of a. is indisputable	KRIS 499:14
gilded chains and sordid a.	PITT 679:7
affluent a. country	GALB 357:22
In the a. society	GALB 357:16
a. society	GALB 357:22
a. to be good to her	SHAW 807:6
not everyone can a. them	RACI 704:27
that you can't already a.?	TOWNE 894:65
unless you can a. it	TROL 898:48
affront quick to take a.	MACD 549:27
Afghanistan A. was 1910	THER 882:91
hill villages of A.	GLAD 373:38
left on A.'s plains	KIPL 489:88
There are a lot of children in A.	HOSS 430:28
afloat A.. We move: Delicious!	CLOU 232:50
afraid a. of getting married	PLATH 680:27
a. of losing your moral sense	STEIN 845:59
a. of something	KIPL 491:24
a. of the present	GREY 388:63
a., reading this passage now	FENT 332:60
a. to ask...the silent question	FRIE 350:64
a. to strike	POPE 688:3
Almost a. to know itself	SHAK 797:61
be a. and...forget it forever	FAUL 331:35
be not a.	BIBLE 117:99
be not a.	BIBLE 95:6
Be not a. nor dismayed	BIBLE 98:87
do not be a. of marriage	SOPH 834:32
Don't be a.	HEAN 405:82
general public...are a.	RAY 708:87
man...neither tarnished nor a.	CHAN 213:78
never to be a.	KAVA 474:49
not a. of God, a. of me	POPE 688:27
not so much a. of death	BROW 165:62
See all nor be a.!	BROW 168:59
to be a. would be to diminish	RENO 711:51
When we're a.	SONT 834:18
Who's A. of Virginia Woolf?	ALBEE 11:24
will not be a.	SCOT 755:86
you need to be a.	SENNA 757:31
Africa A. and the English tongue	WALC 916:9
all A. and her prodigies	BROW 165:55
Black-A. does not distinguish	SENG 757:28
I am a woman...of A.	EMEC 324:47
map of A. lies in Europe	BISM 137:37
more familiar with A.	ORTON 652:3
Poverty has a home in A.	HEAD 404:63
sands of A.	JOHN 460:86
talking about A.	BUSH 182:14
Till China and A. meet	AUDEN 43:81
West A. today	KING 488:59
What is A. to me	CULL 257:43
What is A. to me?	CULL 257:44
Where A.'s sunny fountains	HEBER 406:1
white man in A.	LESS 523:90
African A. music	GILL 370:87
A. national consciousness	MACM 556:67
As Irish as Black Americans are A.	GELD 362:30
struggle of the A. people	MAND 564:53
Africans happiest A. in the world	SMITH 829:7
Africas I see several A. and one	CESA 211:51
afric-maps So geographers, in A.-m.	SWIFT 863:63
Afro-American replaced the term A.-A.	FEIF 332:56
after not too damn much a.	HEMI 410:74
afterlife picture the a.	UPDI 906:33
afternoon a. or evening cup of tea	HOLM 424:85
a. passed quite happily	WODE 951:33
ceremony known as a. tea	JAMES 450:38
lose the war in an a.	CHUR 225:73
one a. of heat	THOM 885:51
seemed always a.	TENN 870:88
Summer a.—summer a.	JAMES 451:55
afternoons long a. of tedium	ROET 722:36
aftersight urge...to a. and foresight	ELIOT 321:86
afterthought woman a mere a.	STAN 843:17
afterwards man...defines himself a.	SART 744:72

Afton flow gently, sweet A.	BURNS 178:10
again Here we are a.!	GRIM 388:72
against a. everything all the time	KENN 482:41
argument is a. it	JOHN 463:57
death...I'm strongly a. it	ALLEN 14:4
held a. her...unconventional beauty	SCHL 747:37
man...up a. Nature	GABOR 356:1
Agamemnon before A.'s time	HORA 430:12
Agatha A. has found it on the map	WILDE 941:77
turned to Aunt A.	WODE 952:37
age a., ache, penury	SHAK 788:70
a. and at a certain a.	MILL 592:30
a. at least to every part	MARV 577:91
A. cannot wither her	SHAK 794:58
a. conceived in spatial terms	MIES 590:85
A. from folly	SHAK 794:51
a. has a keyhole	MCCA 548:91
a. in her embraces passed	ROCH 720:65
a. is as a lusty winter	SHAK 778:71
A. is deformed	BAST 67:51
a. is dull and mean	WHIT 938:21
a....is forgiven nothing	SHAW 808:55
A. is our reconciliation	LOWE 540:35
A. known by marks	DICK 281:77
a. of chivalry is past	DISR 287:18
a. of prudence	ELIOT 318:11
a. of right and opportunity	WILS 949:75
a....seems to have quickened	CHEE 218:4
a. shall not weary them	BINY 135:1
a. strikes me as suspect	KLEE 494:1
a. to come would say	SHAK 800:36
a. to quit their clogs	MILT 601:21
a. to write an autobiography	WAUGH 924:97
a., which believes	MILL 594:86
a. will flatten a man	JONES 466:27
an a. like this	YEATS 966:14
Another a. shall see the golden ear	POPE 686:62
antagonistic to the Victorian a.	WILS 948:50
Anyone happy in this a.	FULL 355:77
astonishing any of us choose old a.	BAIN 55:92
At the a. of 14	WILL 945:95
at your a., it is right?	CARR 203:66
Be comfort to my a.	SHAK 778:70
before reaching the a. of reason	SADE 737:14
beggary, or decrepit a.	MILT 607:84
Brought up in an a. when	HUXL 441:65
buried in a good old a.	BIBLE 92:18
carefulness bringeth a.	BIBLE 113:3
cart at the a. of three	LEE 519:96
characterise this a. of ours	CARL 200:79
characteristic of the present a.	DISR 288:48
common at your a.	BELL 76:51
complain of the a. we live in	BURKE 175:9
Death at an early a.	YUAN 969:67
differences between youth and a.	BARN 64:77
dress according to your a.	DISR 288:69
dresses, in every a. and country	LIN 529:2
drives my green a.	THOM 883:5
essentially a tragic a.	LAWR 513:72
Every a. has a...universal genius	DRYD 300:18
Every city has a sex and a.	BERG 83:26
every philosopher, in every a.	SPAR 836:80
Fashion is the ima. of an a.	LAGE 504:70
fetch the a. of gold	MILT 597:36
first portent of a.	MCMU 557:84
Fitter...for crazy a.	SHAK 759:77
from a. to a.	WORD 961:37
girl at an impressionable a.	SPARK 836:69
ignorant in spite of their a.	PITT 679:1
in equal proportion to a.	HEMI 410:94
In every a.	GIBB 366:92
in the a. of mass loquacity	AMIS 17:56
Irish Census, broken down by A.	MACR 558:14
language of the a.	GRAY 383:49
last my weary a.	MILT 598:60
leave it to...the next a.	BACON 53:44
Let A. approve of youth	BROW 169:61
love...at your a.	SHAK 784:40
men of the present a.	OVER 656:16
more serious...at my a.	SIDN 820:35
Most people my a.	STEN 847:10
moulded...destinies of his a.	NEHRU 633:9
never mellows with a.	IRVI 447:57
new glass a. has begun	KORN 498:99
nineteenth century was the a.	MCLU 556:57
no such thing as old a.	WHAR 934:14
not catastrophes...that a.	WOOLF 955:12

not forgotten my a. SOUT 835:44
nothing...a little a....will not cure DURA 307:24
not of an a. JONS 468:80
now that a. comes PO 683:78
Of no a. COLE 236:53
Old a. is always wakeful MELV 585:58
Old A. may come after you WHIT 938:14
old plays...disgust this refined a. EVEL 328:71
one fixed point in a changing a. DOYLE 297:72
our present a. JOHN 456:72
Perfection...and confusion...our a. EINS 313:82
perish in torment in every a. SHAW 810:18
poets in an a. SWIFT 862:60
print a woman's a. CHRI 223:35
reached an a. where MUNRO 625:49
Redeem the a. and sex PHIL 676:53
Refuse his a. DRYD 302:73
severest writers of the severest a. DRYD 300:40
some smack of a. in you SHAK 772:71
soon comes a. SPEN 838:33
Soul of the A.! JONS 468:78
Spirit of the A. HAZL 404:49
staff of honour for mine a. SHAK 760:22
tell a woman's a. GILB 369:56
tells one her real a. WILDE 941:87
the a. of Aquarius RADO 704:34
The more of a. HENR 411:16
Thirty-five is a very attractive a. WILDE 942:9
this a. of disillusionment? SHIP 818:15
this deformed a. KRAUS 499:6
This is old a. MILT 607:68
This is the editorial a. BENN 81:80
Time...says us but with a. RALE 705:47
Tis well an old a. is out DRYD 304:58
tragedy of the a. DU 305:67
treasures of a. IRVI 447:56
trouble with our a. KRON 500:20
Unregarded a. in corners thrown SHAK 778:69
violence and ferocity of our a. JAMES 450:32
wait on wrinkled a.! SHAK 762:94
what man's a. is like DENH 272:63
when a., Disease, or sorrow strike CLOU 232:53
When you're my a. GIEL 368:25
When you've reached my a. EPST 327:34
woes that wait on a.? BYRON 187:44
world's great a. begins anew SHEL 816:57
aged An a. man YEATS 966:26
feet of the a. BIBLE 113:1
granted to the a. or the young LAUR 511:21
introduced to the A. DICK 283:9
neither do the a. understand BIBLE 98:11
so deliciously a. and sad SHAW 806:80
ageing A....the only available way AUBER 41:55
agency a. in the world WHIT 936:71
Ladies' Detective A. SMITH 828:94
agenda any item of the a. PARK 665:39
agent a. of the largest HAIG 391:14
agents A. do nothing for TAYL 868:56
CIA a. with ear-pieces TRUSS 900:3
detest life-insurance a. LEAC 515:9
employed a. to help me MENC 586:92
language...we're its slavish a. MATH 581:87
night's black a. SHAK 797:48
people...would not need a. CHAN 213:90
salon for his a. BYRON 191:37
workers, with responsible a. LENIN 521:37
age-old a.-o. and age-thick POUND 691:4
ages a. and a. hence FROST 352:95
doubt not through the a. TENN 871:19
How many a. hence SHAK 777:31
This is for the a. PEI 672:71
Three poets, in three distant a. DRYD 303:19
Throughout the a. ALAN 10:18
wisest of men in all a. STER 848:23
aggrandisement imperial a. CHUR 225:81
aggravates It a. 'em LEE 518:89
aggravating an a. child BELL 77:64
aggregate a. of all the recipes VALE 907:4
modified a. of external forces SPEN 836:87
aggression female emotions of a. LESS 524:98
menace of a. ASQU 38:84
veto upon any mere a. LEES 519:4
aggressive inherently a. PALM 662:71
aggressor ranged against an a. ATTL 40:24
aggressors A. got away with it SMUTS 831:71
God loves not the a. KORAN 496:43
agitators cared for, not by the labor a. BAER 54:62

Agnes St. A.' Eve KEATS 477:14
agnostic appropriate title of 'a.' HUXL 443:4
agnosticism that is all that a. means DARR 263:50
agony a. we cannot feel MILL 593:42
Birth was Hard and bitter a. ELIOT 318:18
only a., and that has ending BROO 162:91
soul in a. SHAK 763:25
agree All colours will a. BACON 50:61
I don't always a. BUSH 182:2
people you a. with MARG 570:60
with her would not a. YEATS 965:3
agreeable a. person...agrees with me DISR 288:58
a. to strangers SHAW 808:62
few hours in life more a. JAMES 450:38
power to be a. SWIFT 862:50
so charming and a. ETHE 327:45
agreed except they be a. BIBLE 111:50
agreeing A. or disagreeing? AUDEN 44:22
agreement able to reach an a. KENN 482:25
A. reached by the negotiators SHUL 819:27
a. signed last night CHAM 212:63
a. that satisfies us both FRED 349:41
draft an international a. TRUM 899:82
full a. with Government policy HOWE 433:89
tacit a. to call all...by one name CARL 199:69
we shall be in full a. DAYAN 267:34
with hell are we at a. BIBLE 108:70
agreements A. in likes and dislikes CATI 208:97
agrees nobody a. with you STEIN 845:64
agriculture bullfighting does to a. HUBB 434:2
Ahab ran before A. BIBLE 97:65
ahem poets get a quizzical a. FULL 355:76
Ahithophel A. saw that his counsel BIBLE 96:48
aid a. or advice on any matter DISR 288:54
Alliteration's artful a. CHUR 224:59
but for the a. of the book PROU 698:61
doth come mine a. SCOT 755:89
in straits a present a. SCOT 755:86
lend us Thine a.! HEBER 406:98
Without our a. he did us make SCOT 755:88
Aïda can't judge Egypt by A. FIRB 336:58
AIDS A....a classic own-goal ANNE 19:14
A., cancer, nuclear war, pollution MAMET 564:38
A. epidemic WHITE 934:29
A. is a major revolution WELD 928:81
I have A. BROD 160:31
One has A. GORB 378:50
stop them catching A. CURR 259:94
ail what can a. thee KEATS 476:1
ailments our a. are the same SWIFT 861:26
aim a. in philosophy WITT 951:27
a. of any actress DAVIS 265:95
a. of every artist FAUL 331:42
a. of science JAMES 451:65
a. of the school of business DEMI 274:27
a....the pursuit of truth DESC 274:94
grand a. of all science EINS 314:89
not make thoughts your a. KIPL 492:62
our being's end and a. POPE 687:87
rivalry of a. ADAMS 5:92
set your a. too high ZATO 969:3
strikes...as an ultimate a. ENGE 326:14
aiming Pride still is a. POPE 687:76
two things worth a. for HIND 419:67
aims accomplish these a. UNIT 905:9
modern life...divided a. ARNO 34:94
real and...declared a. ORWE 654:36
air a. all our compulsions meet LARK 509:78
a. a solemn stillness holds GRAY 384:62
a. becomes uranious LEHR 520:27
a., earth, or sea MILT 607:72
a. is all awash with angels WILB 939:36
a. is not so full of motes DONNE 293:71
a....kept in its proper place MACA 544:17
a. moves like a river LEON 522:72
a. of a man ADDI 6:29
a. of delightful studies MILT 600:98
a. of the Enchanted island MERE 587:26
a. out of God's own presence WILS 949:75
a. pollution and...artificial light MATT 582:1
a. shall note her soft DONNE 291:18
a. that inhabits you ATWO 41:43
a. that kills HOUS 431:51
a. too poor to rob MORG 619:33
a. which is now thoroughly small ELIOT 319:23
a. with barbarous dissonance MILT 599:76
all the untilled a. AUDEN 44:15

among the crowded a. DICK 283:31
apocalyptic horsemen in the a. MARC 569:48
arrow into the a. LONG 535:24
ashes, strew them in the a. MONT 615:51
babbling gossip of the a. SHAK 785:91
beyond it, the deep blue a. LARK 510:94
blue dome of a. SHEL 813:77
Bounded by the vaporous a. SHEL 812:64
breathe his native a. POPE 685:43
breathe in that fine a. TENN 877:58
breathing English a. BROO 162:88
breath of wild a. MERE 588:41
Brightness falls from the a. NASHE 632:96
caste up in the a. ANON 20:40
Castles in the a. IBSEN 444:9
Clear the a.! ELIOT 319:48
cloud-encircled meteor of the a. SHEL 814:3
corrupt my a. SHAK 799:98
Courage is in the a. FROST 353:22
crisp morning a. VERL 911:61
dove descending breaks the a. ELIOT 321:90
Dust in the a. ELIOT 321:84
Eating the a. SHAK 772:76
enmity o'th' a. SHAK 792:2
feet...in the a. ROOS 724:10
fire-folk sitting in the a.! HOPK 428:75
flies through the a. LEYB 528:80
fog and filthy a. SHAK 795:97
foolscaps of a. AVIS 47:1
fresh a., and royalties ASHF 38:73
From the a., fast down OWENS 658:41
glittering in the smokeless a. WORD 959:3
Gods, that wanton in the a. LOVE 538:81
high in a. PIER 677:68
his happy good-night a. HARDY 397:23
I eat men like a. PLATH 681:33
Inebriate of A. DICK 283:33
instead of the Hawaii a. route ROCK 720:36
invigorating a. of freedom WOLL 954:90
left the vivid a. SPEN 837:93
mild as yellow a. RANS 706:68
mouthful of a. YEATS 966:11
music in the a. ELGAR 314:12
natural as the a. we breathe COLE 234:3
Now a. is hushed COLL 238:76
poetry on the a. ORWE 654:53
prevent the a. THOR 889:56
pure a. and water REES 710:38
purged the a. of pestilence SHAK 758:79
raptures were All a. and fire DRAY 299:98
redesigned everything but the a. CALD 192:23
room full of good a. LEAC 515:13
sails...trouble the a. YEATS 965:8
second place of a. and light FRAME 346:76
sightless couriers of the a. SHAK 796:20
smote the a. SHAK 804:29
soft summer a. FOST 345:55
sound...circles in the a. LEON 523:78
spells into the spongy a. MILT 598:67
Stud the a. WILK 943:59
such a conscience-stricken a.? HOUS 433:81
sweetness fell from the a. MACL 555:41
the a. is calm PAST 668:98
The a. Nimbly and sweetly SHAK 796:18
The a. so thick THOM 887:9
The pure marble a. MILT 603:87
Through high still a. SNYD 832:83
to go abroad for a. PEPYS 674:2
too professional a. MCCA 547:87
to the fainting a. SHEL 815:20
to warm the a. SWIFT 862:46
Trifles light as a. SHAK 789:24
unhealthy for want of a. DICK 281:57
vomit forth into the a. MARL 574:31
was there like food or a. ROCK 720:29
web of sunny a. BRON 161:59
what are names but a.? COLE 235:26
where a. might wash SWIN 863:88
Wild a., world-mothering a. HOPK 429:87
With its sweet a. SHAK 803:15
with my bottom in the a. PIGG 678:73
without the help of the a. ETHE 327:48
yelling through the troublous a. COLL 238:77
aircraft a. I loved LIND 530:13
Loud fluttering a. slope above FULL 355:75
unsinkable a.-c. carrier MACA 544:6
air force naval and a. f. ROOS 724:14

airline

Entry	Ref
airline launch a new a.	BRAN 156:74
airplane artist...flown in an a.	DAVIS 266:5
airplanes a....do not make...happier	DE 267:43
aphorisms that, like a.	NABO 628:1
airport pretty as an a.	ADAMS 4:79
airports there aren't enough a.	HARM 398:38
airs a. from heaven	SHAK 781:57
killing a. and gases were bricked in	DICK 282:79
Naiad a. have brought me home	POE 683:86
Sound, and sweet a.	SHAK 804:25
whistle all the a.	GILB 368:40
airt plaidie to the angry a.	BURNS 180:60
air travel A. t. is nature's way	GORE 379:64
airts Of a' the a.	BURNS 178:9
airy A., fairy Lilian	TENN 869:74
so a. and light a quality	SHAK 782:87
aitches nothing to lose but our a.	ORWE 653:21
aits among green a. and meadows	DICK 281:55
alack A., 'tis he!	SHAK 793:19
alacrity kind of a. in sinking	SHAK 773:12
modicum of a.	RYLE 736:61
Alan A. like the flowing on	FARJ 330:20
alarm spread a.	PENI 673:80
alarming what is a. in the doctrine	SART 744:70
alarms confused a. of struggle	ARNO 33:67
dwell in the midst of a.	COWP 250:96
marriage its a.	LAFO 504:55
alas A., a., how easily a priest	SMITH 830:49
May say A. but cannot help	AUDEN 42:76
albatross I shot the A.	COLE 235:10
Albert A. married beneath him	COWA 249:60
Prince A....discovered the impotence	CANN 196:4
albinos a., bonded in their flick	AVIS 47:1
Alcestis A. from the grave	MILT 601:27
A. rises from the shades	LAND 507:29
alchemist astrologer and the a.	MACA 545:41
alchemy all wealth a.	DONNE 291:26
alcohol a. is a...deadening force	WEBB 925:7
A. is a very necessary article	SHAW 809:74
A. is the prince of liquids	BRIL 159:21
a. made the present enough	GEE 362:28
a. produces a delightful social	BENN 81:71
a. to an Aborigine?	NOON 641:49
discovered that a. was a food	WODE 952:40
help of opium or a.	HERZ 416:22
Mere a. doesn't thrill me	PORT 690:67
alcoholic about stray a. drinks	HOOV 427:46
a. has been lightly defined	BARA 63:40
keys...to a confirmed a.	BALL 58:47
Alcoholics Anonymous A. A. might have worked for me	BEST 87:6
Alcoran Talmud, and the A.	BACON 51:78
Aldershot burnish'd by A. sun	BETJ 88:24
ale a.'s the stuff to drink	HOUS 432:57
bliss in a.	CRAB 251:24
drink your a.	HOUS 432:65
fed purely upon a.	FARQ 330:27
Loveth well good a.	ANON 22:62
milk and a.	SKEL 824:28
no more cakes and a.?	SHAK 785:95
send thee good a.	ANON 21:60
spicy nut-brown a.	MILT 597:46
ale-house A.-h. is healthy	BLAKE 140:21
alembic From an antique a.	DOYLE 297:75
Aleppo husband's to A. gone	SHAK 795:99
alert must be on the a.	SPARK 836:68
Alexander A.'s Ragtime Band	BERL 84:36
Dost thou think A.	SHAK 784:64
if I were not A.	ALEX 12:57
Quhen A. oure kyng	ANON 21:44
Alexander Graham Bell 'Did A. G. B. do...market research...?'	ISAAC 447:67
Alexandrian A. lighthouses	GILL 370:77
algae owe our existence to...a.	ACKER 3:58
Alger succession and Horatio A.	MAMET 564:39
alibi always has an a.	ELIOT 320:54
Alice A Town like A.	SHUTE 819:21
alien A. people clutching their gods	ELIOT 318:18
a. planet is Earth	BALL 60:84
democratic principles as a.	AUNG 45:39
nothing that is human a.	TERE 879:12
thou art an a.	AESC 9:82
alienated a. establishment of human	MARX 578:27
alienation Without a....no politics	MILL 593:46
alienists few professional a.	DOCT 289:82
aliens If a. visit us	HAWK 401:95
alive a. for evermore	BIBLE 131:89

Entry	Ref
born into the world a.	GILB 369:52
created for people a.	HERN 414:92
half dead and half a.	BETJ 88:14
he is no longer a.	BENT 82:98
in Christ shall all be made a.	BIBLE 127:57
it's exhilarating to be a.	RICH 713:1
many ways...of being a.	DAWK 266:17
need'st not strive...to keep a.	CLOU 232:64
not just to be a.	MART 576:76
not life-like; it is a.	CECIL 210:23
only fault is that I am a.	MAP 569:42
only mission...to come down a.	HELL 407:26
Sex...keeps us all a.	EWART 328:73
was I dead before I was a.	BROW 165:67
wish they were the only one a.	AUDEN 43:9
Words are taken a.	CIXO 227:46
all A. are needed by each	EMER 324:50
a. for love	SPEN 838:31
A. for one	DUMAS 306:89
a. have to go through it	JERO 454:36
a. is always now	ELIOT 319:44
a. of that and more	SCHW 750:91
a. shall be well	JULI 471:41
a. shall die	SHAK 772:86
A. the Way with LBJ	HOLT 424:90
A. things perish	KEMP 480:78
a. things to a. men	BIBLE 126:43
America I've given you a.	GINS 372:8
Christ is a., and in a.	BIBLE 128:11
feared...by a.!	SIXT 824:26
Goodbye to A. That	GRAV 382:18
If it is for a.	SCHO 748:50
nothing, and yet possessing a.	BIBLE 127:73
silent question—'Is this a.?'	FRIE 350:64
That's a. folks!	FREL 350:51
would that you were a. to me	BROW 168:49
Allah A. is great	CLOU 232:60
allegations scandalous a.	PROF 697:28
allegiance a. to one Crown	GEOR 364:54
flag...has not pledged its a.	BALD 57:23
allegorical all the a. paintings	JOHN 465:3
allegories a. are so much lettuce	GINS 371:4
allegory cordially dislike a.	TOLK 893:46
great a.—the world	MELV 585:73
alley dropped it into the a.	CHAN 213:95
alley cat zest of the a. c.	MARQ 575:51
alleys lowest and vilest a. in London	DOYLE 297:59
not worry about the blind a.	FEYN 334:5
one of the blind a.	WAUGH 923:62
alleyways a. and drug fiends	LIND 530:16
all-forgiving God who is a.-f.	SMITH 828:3
alliance A....union of two thieves	BIER 134:62
steer clear of permanent a.	WASH 922:31
allies a. are too frightened	TALL 866:18
no eternal a.	PALM 662:70
alligator Been eaten by an a.	NASH 631:70
alligators A. have the right idea	MACD 550:54
all-in-all intellectual A.-in-a.!	WORD 957:66
alliteration A.'s artful aid	CHUR 224:59
alliterations drone of a.	BROY 169:87
allotment capable of digging an a.	DORAM 294:84
allowance make a. for their doubting	KIPL 492:62
all right make it a. r.	HAMM 395:70
all-round wonderful a.-r. man	BEER 74:95
All-Souls Christ-Church and A.-S.	JOHN 461:17
allure If parts a. thee	POPE 687:90
to a. by denying	TROL 898:43
allurement a. of private interest	STEU 849:61
allurements What a. she used	SIDN 820:38
alluring little scorn is a.	CONG 241:69
nothing is more a.	CONG 241:73
ally a. of the people	DODD 289:87
help of any a.	GARI 360:72
Her faithful a.	SITW 824:18
infamy of betraying an a.	CECIL 210:28
treacherous desertion of an a.	CHUR 224:70
almighty A. has placed your hand	CURZ 260:5
A. hearkens unto him	FRIE 351:73
A.'s orders to perform	ADDI 6:19
A. would answer me	BIBLE 98:10
find out the A. unto perfection?	BIBLE 98:1
Truth is strong next to the A.	MILT 600:9
work of an A. hand	ADDI 7:40
almond cut an a. rod	BRON 161:59
almonds rod of Aaron...yielded a.	BIBLE 94:81
almost-instinct a.-i. almost true	LARK 509:81
alms A. for oblivion	SHAK 787:37

Entry	Ref
so give a.	SHAK 799:20
throw them cheap a.	WEST 933:94
when thou doest thine a.	BIBLE 115:40
aloe a. seemed to ride	MANS 567:5
alone all a. went she	KING 487:43
All we ask is to be let a.	DAVIS 265:99
A. and palely loitering	KEATS 476:1
A. I did it	SHAK 799:6
a. in a way that no earthling has ever been	COLL 237:66
a. in the desert	SAINT 738:36
a. on earth	BYRON 187:44
A....The word is life	SASS 746:97
a. until she dies	THOM 884:35
a. when he falleth	BIBLE 106:17
a. with his laughter	KAFKA 472:8
and a.; on shore	TENN 870:98
and live a.	YEATS 965:4
Antony...did sit a.	SHAK 794:56
been, shalt be, art, a.	ARNO 35:6
But wherefore thou a.?	MILT 604:13
find himself left a.	JOHN 460:65
Hell is a.	ELIOT 321:97
I am a.	GOET 375:72
imagination never lets him a.	SHAW 808:62
least unpleasant...to live a.	BERN 86:73
lie down a.	HOUS 432:76
live for years a.	AUDEN 43:84
loving a. is as dull as eating a.	WYCH 964:5
may not find myself a.	ROSE 725:25
mortal millions live a.	ARNO 34:81
never to be a.	BALL 58:48
no one exists a.	AUDEN 43:97
not good that the man should be a.	BIBLE 91:89
not sufficiently a.	VALE 907:5
One man a. ain't got	HEMI 410:79
or a fool a.	WILD 943:50
this proves I'm not a.	HIRST 419:81
to be let a.	SUMN 859:83
totally a. with oneself	MODE 611:70
travels fastest who travels a.	KIPL 489:74
want to be a.	GARBO 359:63
when we are a.	GRIS 389:76
Work a.	WOZNI 962:56
you a. are you?	SHAK 802:66
You'll never walk a.	HAMM 395:65
aloof a. in pride of distinction	SAND 742:25
alp an a. of unforgiveness	PLOM 682:72
Alph A., the sacred river	COLE 236:36
alpha A. and Omega	BIBLE 131:87
alpine streams along the A. height	BYRON 188:60
Alps A. and their people	RUSK 732:85
beneath some snow-deep A.	ELIOT 317:87
crossing the A.	WALP 918:64
Alsatians dislike...all dogs, but A.	LEVIN 525:28
altar a., sword and pen	WORD 958:94
broken A.	HERB 411:55
Ever at Thy glowing a.	CULL 257:46
on his own strange a.	SWIN 864:17
socks on the a.	NERU 633:23
altarpieces almost sacred a.	ROSE 725:34
altars even thine a., O Lord	BIBLE 101:88
wings display and a. raise	DRYD 301:45
altar-stairs great world's a.-s.	TENN 874:77
alteration alters when it a. finds	SHAK 802:80
alterations a. on the map of Europe	CHUR 224:68
alternative accept that there is no a.	THAT 881:57
a.' modes of living	SELF 756:11
an a. should not be discarded	PECK 672:63
Life. Consider the a.	MCLU 556:59
alternatives a. that are not their own	BONH 146:26
choice between two a.	MORAN 618:9
ends which have a. uses	ROBB 717:68
exhausted all other a.	EBAN 310:8
ignorance of a.	ANGE 18:87
always a. has to be somebody else	SMITH 830:43
we are a. dying	PETR 676:42
what is a.	VINC 913:9
am I am still proud to be who I am	ZIDA 970:43
I a. that I a.	BIBLE 93:55
I a. what I a.	BIBLE 127:55
know not where I a.	SHAK 759:74
Amalek A. prevailed	BIBLE 94:65
amalgamation out of adhesion is. a.	BRON 161:72
amaranth fields of a.	LAND 507:32
Amaranthus A. sweet and fair	LOVE 538:84
a. all his beauty shed	MILT 599:91

American

Amaryllis A. in the shade — MILT 599:86
kind A., the wanton country maid — CAMP 195:74
amateur a. status — GRAV 382:29
sign of an a. is too much detail — BURG 174:94
amateurs disease that afflicts a. — CHES 220:62
Hell is full of musical a. — SHAW 807:23
that we are a nation of a. — ROSE 725:24
a-Maying met her once a.-M. — MILT 597:42
amaze People never fail to a. me — WINF 949:93
amazement A. is the thing — REID 710:44
often met with a. — ANGE 18:87
Amazon She was an A. — BLAN 141:46
ambassador a. is an honest man — WOTT 962:54
a. that beds a queen — CLEV 230:96
no a. would ever be relieved — HEAN 405:78
ambassadors a. for Christ — BIBLE 127:71
Diplomatic problems…discussed by a. — ACHE 2:26
amber a. to observe the forms — POPE 687:1
of A. Snuff-box — POPE 685:41
turn those a. locks to grey — DRAY 298:93
unzipped fly caught in forever a. — COND 239:13
Amberley Lady A. ought to get — VICT 912:76
Ambersons Magnificent A. — TARK 867:30
ambiguities Resolve me of all a. — MARL 573:23
ambiguity Seven Types of A. — EMPS 326:7
ambiguous a.…in his opinions — MCFA 551:65
ambition all that a.…could effect — PITT 680:12
A.…desire to be vilified — BIER 134:63
A., Distraction, Uglification — CARR 203:78
a. enough to be employed — LOCKE 533:88
A.…great man's madness — WEBS 927:45
a. has been growing steadily — DALI 261:12
A. if it feeds at all — SONT 833:12
a. is that men should have — LAUR 511:24
a. merely to descry — SELF 756:10
a. of an old man — CHUR 224:65
a. of so airy and light — SHAK 782:87
A.'s debt is paid — SHAK 777:28
A. should be made of sterner stuff — SHAK 777:38
attempt something of a. — KUSH 501:45
avarice, lust and a. — LEWIS 526:43
brutal in its a. — NORR 641:57
Ill-weaved a. — SHAK 772:67
in those days a. — LAGE 504:69
Let not A. mock — GRAY 384:66
lilies of a. — DOUG 295:6
meaner things To low a. — POPE 686:70
no desire to gratify a. — PEEL 672:67
no other a. in the world — SHIP 818:11
not without a. — SHAK 796:14
stimulate their a. — CHRI 223:36
such joy a. finds — MILT 604:93
Thoughts tending to a. — SHAK 765:62
Vaulting a. — SHAK 796:20
What argufies pride and a.? — DIBD 276:31
when a. blinds! — DRYD 302:78
writer's a. — KOES 495:37
ambitions a ceiling put on our a. — PRES 694:69
all a. are lawful — CONR 244:46
a. faded in its glare — LAWR 514:90
books…contain our…a. — CONR 244:40
deceives with whispering a. — ELIOT 317:84
limit to his a. — RICH 714:26
not favourable to such a. — DISR 288:63
stunt our a. — SCHU 750:80
ambitious a. attempts — STEV 852:44
a.…needs to make his fortune — LABR 502:17
a. will not be content — CARL 200:77
a.…young men — THOM 885:69
as he was a., I slew him — SHAK 777:36
most a. of them all — LAGE 504:69
too late to be a. — BROW 165:78
Ambrosia back in A. — WATE 922:35
ambrosial Phallic and a. — POUND 691:3
ambulance car and a. — LEBO 518:65
ambushing A. the audience — STOP 856:21
Amelia A. was praying for George — THAC 880:26
amen all the people shall say, A. — BIBLE 95:95
a.'? Stuck in my throat — SHAK 797:33
God help me; a. — LUTH 542:68
sound of a great a. — PROC 697:37
the catholic a. — SMART 826:67
amend a. thy face…a. my life — SHAK 771:54
amended Corrected and a. — FRAN 348:7
amends I must make a. — JOPL 468:98
amenities a. that count — COOKE 245:75
wilderness to the a. — MACD 550:30

amenity Claude's landscape all is…a. — CONS 244:58
America aboriginal…singer of A. — CHOC 222:25
A. as a black curse — MILL 593:58
A. as the paperback version — DELI 271:37
A.…barbarism to decadence — CLEM 230:89
A., bring your own food — LEBO 518:66
A. came up with the idea — HUGH 435:28
A. cannot be an ostrich — WILS 949:80
A. de-Latinized — RODO 721:51
A. gets Hollywood — JONG 466:38
A.! God shed His grace — BATES 68:53
A. had plenty of money — BEHR 75:28
A. has defaulted — KING 487:27
A. has just passed through — BENT 82:7
A. has mitigated poverty — WOOL 955:9
A. has the best-dressed poverty — HARR 398:44
A. I'm putting my queer shoulder — GINS 372:9
A. is a country of young men — EMER 325:98
A. is a friend of each nation — OBAMA 644:33
A. is a hurricane — MAIL 559:39
A. is an insane asylum — POUND 692:33
A. is a vast conspiracy — UPDI 906:24
A. is God's Crucible — ZANG 969:1
A. is in my view — SCHAW 747:20
A. is just ourselves — ARNO 36:26
A. is not…at war with Islam — OBAMA 644:35
A. is not like a blanket — JACK 448:3
A. is now wholly given — HAWT 402:14
A. is…rooted in Negro culture — ROLL 723:90
A. is so money-hungry — TYSON 904:10
A. is up for sale — TSON 900:7
A. I've given you all — GINS 372:8
A.…large, friendly dog — TOYN 895:73
A. makes prodigious mistakes — CUMM 258:60
A.! my new-found-land — DONNE 291:20
A. no longer lives behind — THUR 891:11
A.…only idealistic nation — WILS 949:87
A.—rather, the United States — FERB 332:67
A.'s cultural life — ROCK 721:40
A.'s dependence on oil — KERRY 483:59
A. settles in the mould — JEFF 453:10
A.'s leading socialist — ECON 310:20
A.'s present need — HARD 396:94
A. the beautiful — HUXT 443:14
A., the people are friendly — CRISP 255:8
A. the spirit of Christian France — BOUR 152:93
A., thou half-brother — BAIL 55:88
A.…where all things are possible — OBAMA 644:30
A.—your stupidity — SNYD 833:95
ancient Spanish historians of A. — ECHE 310:14
another person in A. — NORTH 641:62
Black A. reveals — JORD 468:99
born in A. with a black skin — MALC 562:89
cannot conquer A. — PITT 679:8
cannot sell anything in A. — DONA 290:5
change has come to A. — OBAMA 644:31
churning caldron of A. — WRIG 963:68
cuisine here in A. — CHIR 222:22
declared war on A. and Britain — HIRO 419:71
deflecting A.'s anger from Bin Laden
to Saddam Hussein — LECA 518:79
deserts of A. — JOHN 460:86
destroy sex in A. — DOCT 289:82
drill to the tooth of A. — CLIN 230:4
dull…life as here in A. — MILL 594:73
economic insecurity in A. — ELLW 323:39
energy stored up in A. — GERS 365:72
England and A. — GREN 388:59
England and A. — SHAW 811:31
every family in A. — JOHN 458:18
every man in A. — STEV 851:16
every man…in A. — GOLD 377:25
fabric of A. — MCCA 547:82
future of A. is based — MAYH 583:26
gather for A. — SAAR 736:1
God bless A. — ANON 24:9
Golf is to Fiji what cricket is to A. — SINGH 823:90
heart and mind of A. — BARZ 67:40
Heston thinks A. should arm its teachers — RUSH 732:71
history of A. — ADAMS 5:1
Hoo-doo, which in A. flowered — REED 710:35
horses of A. — KIPL 491:18
I feel displaced when I'm back in A. — HYNDE 444:23
If there is poetry in our A. — DARIO 262:44
In A. all too few blows — MAIL 560:80
In A., any boy — STEV 851:22
In A. everything goes — ROTH 728:86

In A. few people will trust — MAIL 560:45
In A. journalism — SAMP 741:97
in A. the…writer — LEWIS 527:58
In A.…two classes of travel — BENC 78:3
I believe in an A. where
if…part of the West can…reboot…it's A. — ROMN 724:96
Intellectually I know that A. — FERG 333:82
I rejoice that A. has resisted — LEWIS 527:61
Jazz came to A.…in chains — PITT 679:5
last true cowboy in A. — WHIT 937:78
Let's get A. moving again — HEAT 406:96
Lost in the living rooms of A. — ANON 25:40
man born in A. — MCLU 556:60
Marilyn…man's love affair with A. — OLSEN 650:45
morning again in A. — MAIL 560:39
New York…cultural centre of A. — ANON 26:86
next to…god a. — BELL 77:86
noises of A. — CUMM 257:58
nonconformity…rare in A. — CUMM 257:51
nothing left to envy about A. — MCCA 548:93
Nothing less…than whole A. — BRAGG 156:55
Only in A. — BURKE 175:16
Patriotism…understand in A. — KING 486:20
power and spirit of A. — COOL 246:82
remind A. — NORR 641:57
resists your taxation in A. — KING 487:28
revolution in A. — PITT 679:7
sailed…Atlantic and found A. — LINK 530:29
symbol for A. — BEHAN 74:10
the blacks in A. — ATWO 41:38
The mythical A. — OROU 652:92
The youth of A. — RABAN 703:4
think of thee, O A.! — WILDE 941:86
true religion of A. — WALP 919:73
typical of life in A. — MAIL 560:60
United States of A. — BALD 56:14
unless A. changes course — ROOS 724:14
What A. does best — ROMN 724:95
what makes A. what it is — FUEN 354:60
willing to grant A. independence — STEIN 845:65
witness of A.'s…rite — GEOR 363:47
American adult A. Negro female — NEW 634:34
All modern A. literature — ANGE 18:87
A. abroad — HEMI 410:76
A. art…sexless — STAP 843:20
A. athlete is superior — ADAMS 5:96
A. at puberty — CALI 192:24
A. Beauty rose — WAUGH 924:89
A. can look forward to — ROCK 720:31
A. Express card — KENN 480:86
A. gentlemen are the best — LODGE 534:97
A. girls turn into A. women — LOOS 536:52
A. heiress — HAMP 395:75
A. history as a great hero — MCCA 547:86
A. history is all about men — MENC 586:95
A. influence…educated them — BRAD 154:26
A. men do not read — WILDE 940:49
A. names — VIDAL 912:96
A. nation will speak — BENET 79:23
A. Negro problem — ROOS 724:15
A. people — BALD 56:13
A. people do not want — GERG 365:65
A. people don't — POWE 693:53
A. people have voted — NIXON 640:40
A. people…were like him — CLIN 230:1
A. phenomenon — REST 711:66
A. politics — WHITE 934:29
A. principles, A. policies — WHITE 936:50
A. professors — WILS 949:81
A. ship, good grub — LEWIS 527:60
A. system — LOND 534:10
A. vice, the democratic — HOOV 427:44
an honorary A. — MILL 594:84
appear to one A. painter — SULL 859:74
As A. as a…shotgun — ROSE 725:26
being an A. — PARK 664:31
building…the A. consciousness — JAMES 450:34
business of the A. people is business — BUSH 182:94
Chicago…last of the great A. cities — COOL 246:79
contributions of the A. way — MAIL 560:55
country A. means white — MENC 587:13
critics are like A. universities — MORR 620:57
expanding horror in A. life — ALBEE 11:28
exploited by A. capital — MAIL 560:52
face of A. literature — INNIS 446:44
faces of most A. women — PORT 690:75
failed promises of A. life — FITZ 338:96
— GILL 370:78

Americanism

fairness of the A. people	NIXON	640:37
fortress—the A. home	SELZ	757:19
free man, an A.	JOHN	458:10
genius of A. culture	RODR	722:52
hairy A. filth	OSBO	655:86
hands of the A. people	WASH	922:29
hardly find a typical A.	BARN	64:59
I am an A.	BELL	77:76
If I were an A.	PITT	679:9
Liars out of the A. people	ROGE	723:75
magic moment in A. history	WHITE	936:59
minds of A. women	FRIE	350:64
Miss A. Pie	MCLE	554:22
most A. artist of all	ADLER	8:68
most beautiful prose paragraph... by any A.	BLOOM	143:67
New Deal for the A. people	ROOS	724:4
not ashamed of...the A. Dream	SHUL	819:30
old-fashioned A. hypocrisy	GALL	358:37
one dirty secret in A. life...racism	CISN	227:40
performance of the A. economy	STEIN	845:79
photos in North A. magazines	ONET	651:82
police dog of A. fiction	FADI	329:7
propaganda arm of the A. Dream	HASK	400:80
protect A. cities	SCHL	748:39
reality in A. society	MUNCH	625:42
sailed through A. history	MENC	587:15
security around the A. President	MAIL	560:61
send A. boys	JOHN	458:13
separating an A.	JOHN	458:32
Some A. writers	THUR	891:9
success happens to an A. writer	AMIS	16:48
Success is the A. Dream	LEGU	520:14
That's A.	HUGH	435:14
the A. establishment	TIME	892:20
To be an A.	FIED	334:10
To be an A.	FRIE	351:72
to write A. music	THOM	888:13
Versailles of A. corporate culture	WOLFE	953:82
very knowing A.	SWIFT	862:58
way that is thoroughly A.	PEARY	671:59
Americanism McCarthyism is A.	MCCA	547:85
Americans All A. believe	STEI	846:84
A. are our best friends	THOM	887:93
A. are polite by telling the truth	BRAD	154:27
A. are...the most self-conscious	JAMES	450:36
A....considered Hollywood	MAMET	564:34
A. do not rear children	JARR	452:89
A. expect to be loved	SOYI	835:60
A. have a kind of resistance	TRIL	897:16
A. have always paid it	KENN	481:12
A. have been conditioned	UPDI	906:22
A. is a bore	UPDI	905:16
A. of all nations	WHIT	937:88
A....tend to protect their children	ACH	2:23
A. want to bomb	ANON	27:34
believing in you, the A.	MATAK	581:84
brave A.	DICK	284:57
drunks and A.	MOYN	623:4
good A. die they go to Paris	WILDE	941:85
Good A., when they die	APPL	30:92
If/...A. do not succeed in engineering	LARD	509:66
Irish A. are about as Irish	GELD	362:30
majority of my fellow A.	NIXON	640:33
married to A.	WALP	919:75
the number of Muslim A	OBAMA	644:34
To A., English manners	JARR	452:86
What makes war interesting for A.	DALL	261:18
when women succeed, A. succeeds	OBAMA	645:52
whether A. are to be freemen	WASH	921:27
which amazes A.	GALL	358:40
amethyst ruby and a. eyes	BRAS	156:77
silver cross soft a.	KEATS	477:21
amiable good, a., or sweet!	MILT	606:51
how a. are thy dwellings	BOOK	149:28
In Claude's landscape all is...a.	CONS	244:58
amiss little disdain is not a.	CONG	241:69
ammunition pass the a.	FORGY	344:19
political a. runs low	STEV	850:6
amnesiacs red a. of autumn	PURDY	700:85
amoeba squashed a.	THER	882:90
amor Salud, Dinero, A....y Tiempo	ANON	27:34
amorous As a. of their strokes	SHAK	794:55
be a., but be chaste	BYRON	187:26
excite my a. propensities	JOHN	459:51
amorousness a....is rooted in	SCHO	748:56
amour beginning of an a.!	BEHN	75:22
amphibious a. ill-born mob	DEFOE	269:70
Amphitrite A. sails thro' myrtle	POPE	686:60
A.'s destined halls	SHEL	812:64
ample a. make this Bed	DICK	284:43
amplitude action...of some a.	ARIS	31:23
amputate Thank God they had to a.!	SASS	745:81
amuse created to a.	UPDI	906:26
amused a. by its presumption	THUR	890:71
instructed and a.	ATLAS	40:20
People mutht be a.	DICK	282:82
We are not a.	VICT	912:81
amusement for the a. of women	MONT	613:13
I write for the general a.	SCOTT	754:65
very pleasant a.	JOHN	465:7
work is less boring than a.	BAUD	69:84
amusements less difficult than our a.	LOUI	537:69
we have no a.	SMITH	831:62
amuses a. the people of England	JOHN	461:90
amusing I am generally rather a.	BEER	73:76
previously a. human beings	COUP	248:35
torture and death...is a.	FROU	353:27
Amynta give A. so much freedom	BEHN	75:19
anabaptist a....I am not a member	FLEM	340:48
anachronistic a., feudal institution	ACHE	2:27
Everything is a. obscene	BART	66:28
anaemia a sort of emotional a.	POUND	691:93
anagram mild a.	DRYD	301:45
analogies a. that map the gateways	WILS	948:52
analogue no a. in space	EDDI	311:24
analysis a., all architecture	NUTT	642:75
a. of the obvious	WHIT	936:64
intelligence and a.	LYND	543:92
in the last a.	PLAN	680:24
method of a.	TROT	899:68
analyst a. in...moral activity	POE	683:81
analytic skilled in a.	BUTL	184:66
analytics Sweet A., 'tis thou	MARL	573:18
analyzer I am an a.	BECK	72:51
anapaestic rolling a. Curled	BROW	166:90
Anarch Thy hand, great A.!	POPE	689:48
anarchic been, basically a.	LEGU	520:12
anarchist an aspirant a.	MORR	620:48
To a real a. a poke in the eye	CARY	207:66
anarchy A. and competition	RUSK	733:99
call it a.	HOBB	420:3
Freedom...cure of a.	BURKE	175:19
Mere a. is loosed	YEATS	966:24
more and more to a.	TOLK	893:43
anatomize Let them a. Regan	SHAK	792:13
anatomy A. is destiny	FREUD	350:59
portions of the human a.	HELP	409:56
ANC A. is a Government in waiting	MAND	564:54
ancestors a. had...nuclear power	LAMB	506:16
Bequeathed down from many a.	SHAK	791:66
form of our primitive a.	MILL	595:96
more...favourable...than your a.	ADAMS	4:71
most obscure of all classes, our a.	CHES	220:69
never look backward to their a.	BURKE	176:36
Not one of your...a. was squashed of life than our a.	BRYS	171:12
	STEV	851:32
princes my a. followed	ORAH	652:90
spirits of our a.	RED	709:19
vices of his a.	FAUL	330:34
We must strive to become good a.	NADER	629:23
wild trick of his a.	SHAK	772:62
ancestral A. voices prophesying war!	COLE	236:40
ancestry delusion about its a.	INGE	445:30
reminds the world of its dark a.	BETH	87:13
whole female line of a.	EDGE	312:47
anchorage hope her a. maintain	SMART	826:68
anchored eternally a.	MILL	594:89
anchorite saintship of an a.	BYRON	187:34
anchors A. on Isabel	SHAK	787:62
ancient an a. aspect	STEV	850:77
a. and prophetic fame	MILT	602:62
A. of Days	GRANT	381:5
A. of Days	SMITH	831:65
a. past?	GARC	360:67
A. Person, for whom I	ROCH	720:26
a. saying is no heresy	SHAK	769:96
a. Spanish historians of America	ECHE	310:14
a. writers	YEATS	966:28
came to the A. of days	BIBLE	111:43
Europe of the a. parapets	RIMB	715:42
Even in a. days	TOLK	893:47
held sway since a. days	AESC	8:76
poetry...in a. items	DARIO	262:44
saying of an a. philosopher	ADDI	6:30
That is the a. secret	PRAT	694:67
What Art was to the A. world	DISR	287:28
With the a. is wisdom	BIBLE	98:3
Anderson John A. my jo	BURNS	179:16
androids Do A. Dream	DICK	277:34
anecdotage man fell into his a.	DISR	288:55
anemones amethyst eyes of a.	BRAS	156:77
Aneurin A. and Taliesin, cruel owls	BUNT	173:68
Anfield bad times at A.	PAIS	660:41
angel an a.'s stare	TATE	867:40
a. and a madman	THOM	883:12
a. came in unto her	BIBLE	120:64
a. departed from her	BIBLE	120:65
a. is like you, Kate	SHAK	776:98
A. of Death has been abroad	BRIG	159:13
a. of the Lord	BIBLE	120:69
a. of the Lord appeared	BIBLE	93:51
a. watching an urn	TENN	875:18
a. will be there	GUST	390:4
battleground for a dark a.	LENG	521:36
being and as an a.	MUIR	624:28
better a. is a man	SHAK	803:87
bored of everything, my A.	LACL	503:38
By Jupiter, an a.	SHAK	803:4
clip an A.'s wings	KEATS	477:9
drawing like an a.	NEVE	634:31
Drew one a.	BROW	168:57
drive a. from your door	BLAKE	139:93
form, so a. fair	BRON	161:54
golden hours, on a. wings	BURNS	178:11
If an a. were ever	LICH	528:86
in action how like an a.	SHAK	782:89
ineffectual a.	ARNO	36:40
in his motion like an a.	SHAK	770:19
is man an ape or an a.?	DISR	288:50
it's like an a.	SART	744:66
Killing the A. in the House	WOOLF	956:55
Look homeward A.	MILT	600:93
Lost A. of a ruined Paradise!	SHEL	815:31
madman bum and a.	GINS	372:5
Man is neither a. nor beast	PASC	667:88
man nor a. can discern	MILT	603:88
may not be an a.	DUBIN	304:63
ministering a. thou!	SCOTT	752:25
my guardian a.	BENE	79:18
O lyric love half a.	BROW	169:72
O, speak again, bright a.	SHAK	765:78
pause...for an a. to pass	FIRB	336:46
send down some a.	SMITH	828:3
She drew an a. down	DRYD	303:35
something of the a....in him	ETHE	327:45
splendid a., newly drest	KEATS	477:21
tarantula on a slice of a. food	CHAN	213:75
the Recording A.	STEV	852:41
to act the A.	PASC	667:88
What a. wakes me	SHAK	767:35
White as an a. is the English child	BLAKE	139:87
woman yet think him an a.	THAC	880:37
wrestled...as the A. did with Jacob	WALT	920:88
angelfish opulent calm of a.	ALLEN	13:74
angel-infancy Shined in my A.-i.	VAUG	909:34
Angelo designs by Michael A.	TWAIN	902:34
angels air is all awash with a.	WILB	939:36
all the holy a. with him	BIBLE	119:35
A. affect us oft	DONNE	291:33
A. along that soar above	LOVE	538:82
a....ascending and descending	BIBLE	93:32
A. can fly	CHES	220:71
a. gave the sign	ROSS	726:48
a. play only Bach	BARTH	66:72
a., progeny of light	MILT	604:19
a....singing out of tune	BYRON	190:31
a. to be lookers on	BACON	49:31
A. were, but with clothes	LOVE	538:87
as the a. of God	BIBLE	118:25
beggar died, and was carried by the a.	BIBLE	121:67
bright as a. are	WILK	943:59
Desolation A.	KERO	483:57
entertained a. unawares	BIBLE	129:46
flights of a. sing	SHAK	785:76
given her to...the a.	FERRE	334:98
Help, a.!	SHAK	783:34
If men were a.	MADI	558:17
invite God, and his A.	DONNE	293:74
joy in the presence of the a.	BIBLE	121:88
kreated a little lower than the a.	BILL	135:95

antiquity

little lower than the a.	BIBLE 99:31	
Liveried A. robed in green	LAND 507:35	
makes the a. weep	SHAK 787:58	
Men would be a., a....gods	POPE 687:76	
murderous a. in his head	DEVL 275:8	
Not Angles, but a.	GREG 387:49	
People are not fallen a.	LAWR 512:43	
plead like a.	SHAK 796:20	
serve the devil and his a.	WENT 931:52	
skull that housed white a.	SASS 746:2	
they breathe in me as a.	RICH 713:7	
tongues of men and of a.	BIBLE 126:52	
very phrase of a.	NASHE 631:89	
where a. fear to tread	POPE 685:28	
Where a. tremble	GRAY 385:90	
with a., and archangels	BOOK 147:70	
Ye holy a. bright	GURN 390:2	
angel-visits Like a.-v., few and far	CAMP 194:64	
anger a. about religion	HALI 393:39	
A. and jealousy can no more	ELIOT 315:30	
A. and tenderness	RICH 713:7	
a. from the nineteenth century	LESS 524:93	
A. invests with such a lovely grace	SIDN 820:49	
A. is never without	HALI 393:35	
a. is outrageous	BIBLE 105:1	
a. of men who have no opinions	CHES 220:63	
A.'s my meat	SHAK 799:1	
contempt and a. of his lip!	SHAK 786:11	
grievous words stir up a.	BIBLE 104:73	
monstrous a. of the guns	OWEN 657:25	
more In sorrow than in a.	SHAK 780:44	
Never a.	SHAK 794:73	
on me let thine a. fall	MILT 603:83	
outer life of telegrams and a.	FORS 344:29	
sense by...degrees of a.	EVANS 328:69	
slow to a.	BIBLE 102:7	
strike it in a.	SHAW 808:43	
Touch me with noble a.	SHAK 792:3	
Your a. was a climate	PIER 677:68	
Angkor A....greatest of Man's	TOYN 895:75	
our people can build A. Wat	POL 684:7	
angle any man may a. to	BERN 86:81	
in every a. greet	MARV 577:96	
angler An excellent a.	WALT 920:93	
honest a.	WALT 920:90	
well-governed a.	WALT 920:95	
anglers a....honest, civil quiet men	WALT 920:94	
angles a. of their bodies	ANGE 19:99	
auspicious a. have been polished	DOUG 295:15	
Not A., but angels	GREG 387:49	
Anglesea A. is the Mother of Wales	FULL 355:79	
angling A. is somewhat like poetry	WALT 920:91	
A....like mathematics	WALT 920:89	
a. or float fishing	JOHN 465:7	
art of a.	WALT 920:92	
Science is a. in the mud	HUXL 442:83	
Anglo-Saxon an A.-S. Messenger	CARR 205:16	
natural idol of the A.-S.	BAGE 54:69	
angry 50s face was a.	WATE 922:37	
a. only when I hit my thumb	AMIS 16:38	
a. with my friend	BLAKE 140:17	
A. Young Man	PAUL 670:32	
Be ye a., and sin not	BIBLE 128:90	
Golf...makes me so damned a.	GEOR 364:53	
reconnected with the a. middle?	ANON 27:28	
whosoever is a. with his brother	BIBLE 114:32	
Angst kein Gemüt, sondern A.	FRIS 351:84	
anguish a....at Rome	AUGU 44:33	
In a. we uplift	DAVI 264:66	
In our a. we struggle	AUDEN 43:2	
love is the...remedy for a.	LEBO 518:70	
pain and a. wring the brow	SCOTT 752:25	
world's a. is eased by people	FAUL 331:38	
animal all female life, a. and human	STAN 843:17	
a. magnetism drew thee and me	BRON 161:71	
a. pleasure of travelling	LIVI 532:55	
a. trainer...knows	RYLE 736:61	
Are you a.—or vegetable	CARR 205:17	
Be a good a.	LAWR 512:39	
between a. and Superman	NIET 638:1	
characterizes the a. world	MILL 594:80	
climbed down from this a.	MACA 544:19	
committee is an a.	LECA 518:72	
essentially the imitative a.	JAMES 451:69	
feminine spouse to the masculine a.	DIAZ 276:26	
making man a political a.	ARIS 31:26	
man...a political a.	ARIS 31:26	

Man is a noble a.	BROW 166:81	
mystical drama of the a. life	AMIS 16:44	
No a. ever invented anything	CHES 220:74	
no such a. by animals	LAWR 513:76	
only a. in the world to fear	LAWR 513:61	
Only A. that Blushes	TWAIN 903:79	
peasantry its pack a.	TROT 899:65	
political a. can be defined	STEG 844:56	
vegetable, a. and mineral	GILB 368:39	
animals All a. are equal	ORWE 654:49	
all a., except man, know	BUTL 185:96	
animal by a. who are merely	LAWR 513:76	
a. could be made human	HEINE 407:15	
a. grow and live	LINN 530:33	
a....on British television screens	ATTE 40:21	
a....perfectly designed pieces of machinery	DAWK 266:14	
a. seldom or never err	LICH 528:90	
a. were already...builders	RUDO 730:35	
a. will not look	AUDEN 42:76	
best subjects...are a. and plants	HEIN 407:20	
could turn, and live with a.	WHIT 937:93	
distinguishes man from a.	OSLER 656:88	
distinguish us from other a.	BEAU 70:9	
eat a.	BRAND 156:59	
fabulous a....who used to sing	DICK 279:9	
footprints of weird a.	PATE 669:14	
greater than...any other a.	MENC 587:8	
human beings and a.	MOOR 618:8	
If...backboned a. were to disappear	ATTE 40:22	
leave off eating a.	THOR 888:26	
Love the a.	DOST 294:94	
Men are the only a.	MENC 587:9	
paragon of a.!	SHAK 782:89	
production of the higher a.	DARW 263:53	
reason men are greater than a.	ELLI 323:32	
short-lived male a. men	MONT 613:11	
understood by children and a.	STRA 857:46	
unique among the a.	BRON 161:53	
use a. to educate people	LAFO 503:46	
Wild a. never kill	FROU 353:27	
wildest of all the wild a.	KIPL 491:41	
animate a. the whole	SMITH 831:59	
animosities private a.	WILL 944:66	
animosity actor has a natural a.	BROO 163:12	
ankle down-gyvèd to his a.	SHAK 781:72	
Anna Here thou. great A.	POPE 685:36	
annals short and simple a.	GRAY 384:66	
writ your a. true	SHAK 799:6	
Annapurna A., to which we had gone	HERZ 416:26	
Anne think that you are A.'s suitor	SHAW 807:21	
Annie held awa to A.	BURNS 178:88	
annihilating A. all that's made	MARV 577:5	
annihilation a. of one of us	SHEL 812:48	
No a. without representation	TOYN 895:72	
anniversary a. of the first request	DARM 263:48	
as an a. present	SHAN 805:64	
anno domini a. d....most fatal	HILT 418:65	
taste my A. D.	FARQ 330:26	
announcer voice of a ball-park a.	KINS 488:67	
announcers voices of its a.	ORWE 654:37	
annoyance a. of a good example	TWAIN 903:74	
Shadow of a.	SHEL 814:96	
annuity Buy an a. cheap	DICK 279:15	
annus horribilis 1992...has turned out to be an a. h.	ELIZ 322:11	
anointed balm from an a. king	SHAK 764:47	
elected and a. ones	WOLFE 953:75	
anomaly singular a.	GILB 369:61	
Anon A....was often a woman	WOOLF 955:28	
another a. one walking beside you	ELIOT 318:9	
do we look for a.?	BIBLE 116:75	
from which a. has been evicted	PARN 665:46	
Never loved a. one	PARK 663:96	
one damned thing after a.	HUBB 434:97	
answer all Call and A.	LAWR 513:59	
already know the a.	JONG 466:36	
an a. came directed	PATE 669:13	
a.: because it was he	MONT 613:21	
a. for but three things	WASH 921:26	
a. me declined	SHAK 794:71	
a. so many questions	RUSS 734:21	
a. that became famous in Deptford	DAVI 265:82	
a. to his simple question	GRAV 383:39	
A. to the Great Question	ADAMS 4:76	
a. to the Irish Question	SELL 756:14	
Beauty was their a.	BRID 158:10	

cast down wi' the first rough a.	SCOTT 754:62	
charm...a way of getting the a. yes	CAMUS 196:94	
copying the a. out	KIER 485:99	
find the a. to that	HAWK 401:88	
give a.!	KIPL 490:94	
how ye ought to a. every man	BIBLE 128:13	
Love is the a.	MOORE 616:74	
men were the a.	BARN 64:69	
more than the wisest man can a.	COLT 238:84	
only way to a.	TRUM 899:78	
on-the-one-hand...a.	BLIN 142:54	
on the way to a pertinent a.	BRON 160:52	
Pilate...would not stay for an a.	BACON 50:55	
Puzzle me the right a.	HEAN 405:73	
right a. to the wrong question	CHRI 224:49	
shortest possible a.	YOUR 969:60	
silver a. rang	BROW 166:92	
soft a. turneth away wrath	BIBLE 104:73	
So what's the a.?	NAUG 632:5	
Speak now, and I will a.	HOUS 431:50	
the a. is more politicians	MAJOR 561:79	
The a. is...to be both	MACH 552:93	
uncle Toby would never offer to a.	STER 848:27	
what a. should I give?	TENN 873:48	
What is the a.?	STEIN 845:75	
your final a.?	TARR 867:32	
answered a. best with silence	JONS 467:52	
Tell them I came, and no one a.	DELA 271:26	
answering don't even remember a.	HAMM 394:57	
answers a. as ask the right questions	LEVI 526:37	
a. to its questions	RUSS 734:23	
a. were meant ironically	TRIL 897:12	
firm a. to questions	KUHN 500:37	
give my friends the incorrect, absurd a.	ELLI 323:36	
learned the a.	MACL 555:35	
looking to other lives for a.	BRAU 157:80	
questions, not a.	LECA 518:73	
resist the easy and preferred a.	BLOOM 142:63	
set of ready-made a.	ROBI 718:93	
successive a. to questions	PAST 668:2	
there are no a.	KEIL 479:64	
ant a.'s a centaur in his...world	POUND 692:24	
Go to the a.	BIBLE 104:58	
men of experiment are like the a.	BACON 50:44	
antagonism a. between Russia	CECIL 210:34	
Antarctica inform you proceeding A.	AMUN 17:64	
antecedents a. are rum, Romanism	BURC 174:86	
antechamber a. of perdition	SHAW 811:33	
antechapel A. where the statue	WORD 958:82	
antennae Artists are the a.	POUND 692:28	
anthologies a. will...continue	JANE 452:79	
anthology well-chosen a.	GRAV 382:35	
Anthony St. A. of Padua	MCFA 551:69	
anthropological a. malady	VAN 908:12	
anthropologists a., or whatever	STARK 843:22	
anthropophagi A., and men	SHAK 788:93	
anti-abortion goal of the a.-a. forces	LEGU 520:13	
Antichrist Rome to chase the A.	LESL 523:88	
anticipation dead a.	VALE 907:2	
intelligent a. of the facts	CURZ 259:4	
lost in the a.	WILL 946:21	
anticipations parts of their a.	BAGE 54:77	
anti-classic A.-c. art	INGR 446:40	
anti-climax a.-c. in the English curious a.-c.	THUR 890:88 KAZIN 474:52	
everything afterward savors of a.-c.	FITZ 337:79	
antics Woven with a.	SPEN 838:30	
antidote a. against the opium of time	BROW 165:79	
Science is the great a.	SMITH 828:90	
sweet oblivious a.	SHAK 798:70	
antidotes a. are poison	SHAK 791:82	
anti-Fascism cause of a.-f.	SPEN 837:13	
antifeminists A., from Chesterton	WEST 933:95	
anti-government a.-g. at the same	TSON 900:8	
anti-intellectual Science...is really a.-i.	MENC 586:3	
antipathy to the noisy Plebeian	CHES 219:49	
strong a. of good to bad	POPE 688:26	
antipodes slightest errand now to the A.	SHAK 774:28	
antiquated as a. as a duel	GOOCH 378:44	
antique more an a. Roman	SHAK 785:72	
nude and a.	SWIN 863:90	
traveller from an a. land	SHEL 813:85	
Where is the a. glory	SPEN 838:37	
antiquities A. are history defaced	BACON 49:26	
museum of a.	ENGE 326:15	
antiquity A....clichéd and boring	FLAU 339:27	
controversy in a.	GERA 364:61	

anti-Semitism

enforced to awake all a.	BACON 49:23	**apostles** a. of equality	ARNO 36:28	rind of one a. tasted	MILT 600:3
great art of a.	KLEE 494:1	A. would have done as they did	BYRON 189:93	**apple-pickers** the a.-p. missed it	SAPP 743:50
man who goes to a.	BAUD 68:72	Cristes lore, and his a. twelve	CHAU 217:79	**apple-pie** make an a.-p.	FOOTE 342:83
rejected all respect for a.	DISR 287:25	least of the a.	BIBLE 127:55	**apples** a. are overripe	MAMET 564:38
anti-Semitism prejudice of a.-S.	POUND 692:30	**apostolic** Holy Catholic and A.	TEMP 869:69	a. began to be golden-skinned	DAVI 264:68
antithesis one vile a.	POPE 688:6	through his a. skin	BYRON 190:32	a. drop about my head	MARV 577:4
true a. to knowledge	DE 273:83	**app** There's an a. for that	ANON 27:43	a. of gold in pictures of silver	BIBLE 105:93
Antonio A., I am married	SHAK 770:15	**appalled** to be a. by our parents	JONG 466:42	as a tree bears a.	EMER 325:88
O my A.	SHAK 768:70	**apparel** a. oft proclaims the man	SHAK 781:52	Benes and baken a.	LANG 508:48
Antony A. should conquer A.	SHAK 795:81	As men their best a. do	BUTL 184:64	Cézanne liked a.	LIPP 530:34
A., who lost the world	DRYD 304:52	fashion wears out more a.	SHAK 774:47	small choice in rotten a.	SHAK 761:59
Emperor A.	SHAK 795:87	rich in a.	TROL 897:21	Stolen, stolen, be your a.	HUNT 439:24
oblivion is a very A.	SHAK 794:52	**apparent** It is now a.	PITT 679:2	The silver a.	YEATS 965:10
ants a. in the gleam	TENN 879:9	me and the a. lovers	REED 709:28	**appliances** all a. and means to boot	SHAK 772:85
Call country a. to harvest offices	DONNE 291:25	**apparition** a. of these faces	POUND 691:92	**application** a. of human ingenuity	NUTT 642:75
shuffling of all a.	WILL 945:7	a., sole of men	SHEL 814:6	a. of science	PARS 666:56
anvil devil's quilted a.	WEBS 927:50	as if I had seen an a.	DEFOE 269:74	a. of them that is human	PAINE 660:38
England's on the a.	KIPL 493:80	lovely a.	WORD 960:19	Art is not the a. of a canon	PICA 677:59
anxiety free-floating a.	LURIE 542:67	mere moral a.	MENC 587:14	novel is conscientious a.	NEME 633:19
Inconstancy, boredom, a.	PASC 667:71	**appeal** books are of…universal a.	FORD 343:91	**applications** only a. of science	PAST 668:3
no comfort, only a.	FRIS 351:84	He has a gay a.	COWA 249:52	**appointed** a. unto men once to die	BIBLE 129:37
taboo'd by a.	GILB 369:54	**appeals** system of a. that pervades	CAPO 197:21	**appointment** a. by the corrupt few	SHAW 808:37
anxious more a. to please	SAND 741:6	**appear** merely as I a. to myself	KANT 473:19	we have kept our a.	BECK 72:44
most a. for its welfare	BURKE 175:8	wish to a. considerable	JOHN 462:23	**appraisal** a. of the drift of public	DAFOE 260:2
pleasing a. being	GRAY 384:74	**appearance** according to a. alone	LAFO 504:63	rough a., but curiously true	ACHE 2:35
woman who is very a.	FREUD 350:58	an a. of solidity	ORWE 655:65	**appreciate** a. his efforts	KENN 481:20
anybody A. on for a game	SHAW 810:92	a. of…greater genius	RUSS 734:27	**appreciated** more loved and a.	ELLI 323:36
anything A. scares me	STEIN 845:67	attractive about her was not her a.	BROO 163:11	**appreciation** object of aesthetic a.	BARR 64:81
ask for a. more	GERS 365:73	gods…what they are like in a.	PROT 697:34	**apprehension** a. of perfection	NIEB 637:87
did not say a.	HEMI 409:64	images in a. remote from each other	JOHN 459:54	articulate a.	GERH 365:70
nobody tells me a.	GALS 358:47	man looketh on the outward a.	BIBLE 96:34	in a. how like a god	SHAK 782:89
now, God knows, A. goes	PORT 690:68	not considered apart from her a.	DE 268:46	Religion…eludes a.	WHIT 936:65
our people…can do a.	POL 684:7	**appearances** contrary to all a.	GOWE 380:80	**apprehensions** a. come in crowds	WORD 960:22
People will do a.	PERCY 674:10	depends…upon their personal a.	HAGG 391:9	**apprentice** time…to become an a.	BEAV 71:31
think that science can do a.	RAY 708:87	explain their a.	NEWT 635:58	**apprenticeship** a. for freedom	BARA 63:43
When a. can happen	MCEW 551:62	Keep up a.	CHUR 224:56	at the very beginning of the a.	CIXO 228:49
anywhere Good done a.	ANGE 19:3	**appears** but by what a.	HARDY 397:12	wonderful a.	JAMES 451:58
apace ready man who write a.	BROW 168:40	since so plainly it a.	CRUZ 256:39	writing…take your a. in it	PORT 690:73
apartheid a. would be gone	WOODS 954:4	**appeasement** stench of a.	THAT 881:70	**approach** a. and depart	HERA 412:33
closed the book on a.	DE 270:17	**appeaser** a.…feeds a crocodile	CHUR 226:13	a. to the meaning	ELIOT 320:73
don't want a. liberalized	TUTU 901:24	**appendix** makes man its a.	FROMM 352:88	two-track a.	MCNA 557:91
apartments painting…to decorate a.	PICA 677:60	**appetite** A. comes with eating	RABE 703:11	**approbation** a. and consent	POWE 693:59
apathetic never flustered, never a.	AURE 45:47	a healthy a. for solitude	SELF 756:13	gives manhood more a.	SHAK 786:19
apathy a. in education	FORS 344:32	a. is keen	EMER 324:70	**appropriate** a. act of creation	FEIN 332:57
shake off its a.	RENAN 711:47	a. may sicken	SHAK 785:77	a. one to apply	SIMON 822:74
stirring up a.	WHIT 936:76	but 'tis the a.	SUCK 858:68	**appropriation** with this a. comes	PAGE 659:15
ape achievement for the neotenic a.	ALDI 12:51	gallant a. for Meat	PENE 673:78	**approval** a. of a course already decided	BIER 134:71
a. his cubs	MORE 618:11	have an a. for submission	ELIOT 316:45	carries no hint of a.	HEND 410:2
a. in man	MCCA 548:99	hungry edge of a.	SHAK 764:36	my a. rating	BUSH 183:40
glassy essence, like an angry a.	SHAK 787:58	men in a.	BACON 53:32	people will not buy…without my a.	BERE 83:15
How like us is…the a.!	ENNI 326:18	Nature or unrestrained a.	CAREW 198:55	**approve** I see…and a.	OVID 657:19
is man an a. or an angel?	DISR 288:50	satisfying a voracious a.	FIEL 335:24	strongly a. of…Congress	LENO 522:59
Jesus and a nameless a.	MACD 549:29	sickly a. to please	SHAK 803:88	**approximation** picture is only an a.	MOTH 622:87
played the sedulous a.	STEV 853:97	vaster the a. for more	LEGU 520:9	reasonable a. to it	KEYN 484:17
story of an a.	HARL 398:36	will into a.	SHAK 786:26	**April** A., 1920	LEWIS 527:56
apertures a. have all been stopped up	LEON 522:71	**appetites** a. as apt to change	DRYD 301:58	A. is the cruellest month	ELIOT 317:95
apes anthropoid a. and human beings	LORE 537:62	more dinners than a.	CHAM 213:70	bright cold day in A.	ORWE 655:71
called the A. of God	LEWIS 527:70	Subdue your a.	DICK 278:77	day in A.	SHAK 769:97
cargo of ivory, And a.	MASE 580:55	**applaud** A.…the comedy is over	BEET 74:5	flag to A.'s breeze unfurled	EMER 324:48
scourge those a.	JONS 466:43	come to a. their money	HIRS 419:76	glory of an A. day	SHAK 758:58
Tarzan of the A.	BURR 180:62	Fish don't a.	HOPE 428:61	lovely A. of her prime	SHAK 800:33
aphorism may marry' is an a.	MITF 610:52	**applause** amidst rounds of a.	SOME 833:10	Men are A.	SHAK 780:12
aphorisms A.…more for your time	DUDEK 305:73	a., delight, the wonder	JONS 468:78	Now that A.'s there	BROW 167:20
a. that, like airplanes	NABO 628:1	a desperate woman seeking a.	GREER 387:47	of A. in Seventy-five	LONG 536:35
one of his questionable a.	ELIOT 315:37	A. is almost a duty	CHAN 214:5	Of A., May, of June	HERR 415:99
translate a. into continuous prose	FRYE 354:56	A. is a receipt	SCHN 748:42	proud-pied A.	SHAK 802:57
aphrodisiac Fame is a powerful a.	GREE 386:16	A.…the echo of a platitude	BIER 134:64	smells A. and May	SHAK 773:9
Power is the ultimate a.	KISS 493:86	a. which he cannot keep	JOHN 459:55	that A. morn	BRID 158:8
truffle is not a true a.	BRIL 159:20	expect any a. from it	MONT 613:13	well-apparell'd A. on the heel	SHAK 765:68
used for…a. purpose	BLISS 142:57	food and shelter and a.	JARR 452:89	Whan that A. with	CHAU 217:69
apocalyptic a. horsemen in the air	MARC 569:48	her own a.	JONS 468:84	**apron** crackling white a.	TRAV 896:94
Apollo A. and the sweet Muses	RUSK 734:19	If met with a.	MAIM 561:70	**aprons** made themselves a.	BIBLE 91:93
A.'s laurel bough	MARL 574:33	purred a.	GRAY 383:51	**apt** how a. the poor are	SHAK 786:9
call the A. a fancy piece?	EMER 324:66	**apple** Adam ate the a.	HUGH 436:37	**Aquarius** the age of A.	RADO 704:34
Yea, is not even A.	SWIN 864:98	And for an a. damn'd	OTWAY 656:96	**Arabia** spell of far A.	DELA 271:28
young A., golden-haired	CORN 247:2	a. a day	ANON 28:49	**Arabian** A. fleet	GIBB 366:95
Apollos A. watered	BIBLE 126:37	a.…better than an insipid peach	HUNT 439:26	A. Nights entertainment	OSLER 656:91
apologies My sincere a.	LEES 519:5	a. blossoms fill the air	SEEG 755:99	to the A. desert to collect	THES 882:96
apology a. for the Devil	BUTL 186:5	a. of his eye	BIBLE 112:59	**Arabs** dirty and ragged little street A.	DOYLE 297:48
A. is only egotism	HOLM 424:79	a. of his eye	BIBLE 95:99	Jews and A. should settle	AUST 47:99
made a combative a.	SHUL 819:21	a. of the eye	BIBLE 99:37	joined with the A., by cracky!	ACHE 3:52
miles of…self-a.	RICH 714:23	a. pressed with specious cant	HOOD 426:29	Like the A.	KAUF 474:38
My conduct shrieks aloud for a.	BEER 73:78	a. that isn't young anymore	GARBO 359:64	up their tents like A.	LONG 535:23
Never make…an a.	CHAR 215:29	easy under the a. boughs	THOM 883:17	**Arab Spring** A. S. turns into…winter	NETAN 634:29
no business to make any a.	ROCHE 719:99	goodly a. rotten at the heart	SHAK 769:84	**Aral** stars…shine upon the A. Sea	ARNO 35:1
apostle a. of the Philistine	ARNO 35:15	luckless a. did we taste	MARV 578:10	**Ararat** rode that tide To A.	WILB 939:35
A.'s advice to use wine	BERN 85:62	millionaires love a baked a.	FIRB 336:48	**arbeit** A. macht frei	ANON 24:20

arbiter a. Chance governs all — MILT 603:69
a. of taste — TACI 866:8
arbitrary accusation of being a. — JAMES 450:42
sociology ruthlessly attaches the adjective 'a.' — ARON 36:48
arc the a. of the moral universe — OBAMA 645:50
arch all experience is an a. — TENN 870:98
a. Of the ranged empire fall — SHAK 794:44
a. to build on — ADAMS 5:87
forgot the a. — DICK 277:42
like an a., is faith — MILL 594:76
night's black a. — BURNS 179:26
St Louis…golden a. — MAIL 560:55
archaeologists a. twitter — MACA 544:18
gangrene of professors, a. — MARI 571:78
archangel A. a little damaged — LAMB 505:85
A. Gabriel, madam — MENZ 587:20
archangels a. with angels, and a. — BOOK 147:70
archbishop a. had come to see me — BURG 174:97
sense of purpose…from their a. — MACM 557:78
archbishops a. and field marshals — MURR 627:80
Archer make…Jeffrey A. rich — BRAD 155:36
archer laughs at the a. — BAUD 68:59
archers A. stand there on — MUIR 623:15
as for you, a., soldiers — JOAN 455:59
arches a. of the years — THOM 886:81
Underneath the A. — FLAN 338:6
Archimedes A. was not free — MACA 545:43
architect A.…advise his client — WRIG 962:67
a. is only really a glorified tailor — TERRY 879:17
a. of his own fate — CLAU 229:73
a.'s ability to build — ROGE 722:66
a. who didn't build St Paul's — THOR 889:55
Art and Assistance of the A. — ALBE 11:33
dialogue between client and a. — STERN 847:18
I would not be an a. — OUD 656:10
painter can be an a. — RUSK 733:88
position of the modern a. — BETJ 88:32
architects A. cannot work — ROGE 722:67
a., engineers and builders — BIRNS 136:21
a. of our republic — KING 487:27
great a. or great architecture — LUTY 542:77
role of a. — MURP 627:77
architectural great a. secret — TROL 897:21
respectable a. man-milliner — RUSK 733:6
architecture analysis, all a. — NUTT 642:75
A. cannot be understood — CASS 207:73
A.…how to waste space — JOHN 459:34
A. is an art — MALL 562:3
A. is man's great sense of himself — WRIG 962:65
A. is the…mirror of life — PEI 672:73
a. is the organization — JOHN 458:29
A. is the will of the age — MIES 590:85
a. of the world — MARL 572:99
a. or revolution — LECO 518:80
A. provides the framework — LECO 518:82
art of a. — JOHN 458:28
can't have a great a. — WRIG 962:66
can't learn a. — JOHN 458:30
co-creator of a social a. — BEUYS 89:49
cuckoo clock style of a. — HEMI 409:59
Fashion is a. — CHAN 214:3
Fujiyama of A. — MUMF 625:37
good a. if it works — JOHN 458:27
Good a. is…efficiency and beauty — HUXT 443:16
great architects or great a. — LUTY 542:77
history of City a. — JOHN 458:31
learn from a. — RUDO 730:36
New styles of a. — AUDEN 42:66
phenomenon of a. — ALLS 14:9
preoccupying myself with a. — SELF 756:12
rectangular a. — TOYN 895:75
rise and fall of English a. — BETJ 88:17
role of a. — MURP 627:77
views of a. — WAGN 915:2
arctic Inarticulate, a. — SCOTT 751:3
seven months of A. weather — ANON 23:93
two kinds of A. problems — STEF 844:52
Arctic Monkeys The A. M.…wake you up — BROWN 164:26
Arcturi daisies, those pearled A. — SHEL 816:60
Ardenne Now I am in A. — SHAK 778:74
ardent children a. for…glory — OWEN 657:31
ardently great mind loves a. — PASC 666:65
ardour a. to improve society — SMALL 826:57
There shall be no a. — SMITH 828:4
are know what we a. — SHAK 784:49

what we truly a. — SCHI 747:27
where you a. — ELIOT 320:63
area consciousness is a staging a. — BELL 78:96
must not become the new a. — KENN 481:8
studio is a torture a. — LIBE 528:84
arena in which to act — ROSE 725:26
binary political a. — LEHM 520:24
Arethusa like the river A. — BROW 165:49
Argante A. the queen, an elf — LAYA 515:98
Argie Kill an A. — PRIV 696:26
argosy a. of crocs and dragons — AMIS 16:46
argue A. for your limitations — BACH 49:13
a. freely according — MILT 600:6
a. from what has been done — ATTL 40:26
can't a. with a river — ACHE 3:46
enemies of freedom do not a. — INGE 445:28
argues a. by increments of noise — BYATT 186:18
arguing In a. too — GOLD 376:2
much a., much writing — MILT 600:4
not a. with you — WHIS 934:17
argument All a. is against it — JOHN 463:57
an impression, not an a. — HARDY 397:17
any other kind of a. — STER 848:27
a. against giving woman the vote — WRIG 962:81
a. concerns no ordinary topic — PLATO 682:59
a. with men a woman — MILT 608:94
a. with people — KIRK 493:81
can't have the a. both ways — SHAW 808:33
detected…use of an a. — BENN 81:69
essence of an a. — SCHL 747:34
first a. that is brought against — STAMP 842:10
found you an a. — JOHN 464:94
good life is a main a. — JONS 468:88
highth of this great a. — MILT 601:31
metre-making a., that makes a poem — EMER 324:69
never without an a. — HALI 393:35
nice knock-down a. for you! — CARR 205:14
not good at precise, coherent a. — BENN 80:55
only a. available — LOWE 539:14
sharpest men in a. — HOLM 424:65
staple of his a. — SHAK 763:20
supporting their guesses by a. — BAGE 54:69
Whigs admit no force but a. — BROW 166:87
you and love are still my a. — SHAK 801:63
arguments in favor of it — JAMES 452:77
a. on both sides — SWIFT 861:38
a. which are brought — JOHN 461:96
beggarly appear a. — WHIT 937:97
couldn't pick holes in our a. — ASSAN 39:97
intellectual A. — PETTY 676:47
start a. — RUSH 732:65
tolerate unlikely a. — FORD 343:3
aria sing an a. for him? — LOUIS 538:79
Ariadne Since A. was a vintager — KEATS 476:88
arias Clear a. of light — DAY 267:36
Ariel Caliban casts out A. — POUND 691:3
arise A., shine — BIBLE 110:5
I will a. and go now — YEATS 965:4
let us a. — STEV 853:73
Napoleons will duly a. — HUXL 442:81
aristocracy a. in a republic — MITF 610:58
a. means government — CHES 221:6
A. of the Moneybag — CARL 201:12
a. preserves us — BAGE 54:69
a. the most democratic — MACA 546:58
Bunyip A. — DENI 273:64
Chinese are the a. — MAUG 582:9
Clover…is A. — DICK 284:51
displeased with a. — HOBB 420:3
Ireland…an absentee a. — DISR 287:31
moneyed a. — BLEST 142:52
possession of a bourgeois a. — ENGE 326:12
relief for the a. of Great Britain — BRIG 159:14
The true a. — BLIX 142:62
aristocrat A., democrat, autocrat — TENN 876:20
a. is the democrat ripe — EMER 325:82
Aristotle Every Poet his own A. — BYRON 189:2
follow this counsel of A. — ASCH 37:52
lantern of A.'s brain — RALE 705:46
arithmetic different branches of A. — CARR 203:78
ark like the A. of the Covenant — JEFF 454:28
Noe entered into the a. — BIBLE 118:31
two and two unto Noah into the a. — BIBLE 92:8
when he made mention of the a. — BIBLE 96:29
won't start with Noah's A. — ECHE 310:14
Arlott hear John A.'s voice — THOM 884:23
arm a. of the Lord revealed? — BIBLE 109:73

a. the weak — FRAN 347:87
a. to a. — PEEL 672:68
auld moon in her a. — BALL 59:70
cam an a. and an honde — MALO 563:15
gather the lambs with his a. — BIBLE 108:80
given my right a. to be a pianist — ROBS 719:98
Heston thinks America should a. its teachers — RUSH 732:71
his reared a. — SHAK 795:88
Human on my faithless a. — AUDEN 43:95
Look at my a.! — TRUTH 900:5
made bare his holy a. — BIBLE 109:91
one a. bent — SASS 745:90
strong a. of England — PALM 662:72
such an a. for a bandage — SHER 817:81
take the skin from the a. — ELIOT 319:48
weak of will, the strong of a. — MAST 581:81
wound them on his a. — MARL 573:49
your a., old toad — LARK 509:85
Armada English against the A. — CUOMO 258:81
Armageddon A. is not a foreign policy — ALBR 11:35
A. will be at our door — MACA 544:5
armaments piling up national a. — ATTL 40:24
armchair A. theorists — ASHD 37:66
a. which provides relaxation — MATI 581:92
drivelling reader curled up in his a. — SARD 743:51
arm-chair fitted into my biggest a.-c. — WODE 951:22
armed a. attempt to impose the views — SCHL 747:33
a. force shall not be used — UNIT 905:9
a. with the liberty of the Press — SHER 818:6
defended by her a. sons — REDM 709:21
armies a. swore terribly in Flanders — STER 848:34
ignorant a. clash by night — ARNO 33:67
land a. in China — MONT 615:47
no invincible a. — STAL 842:6
plenty of money and large a. — ANOU 28:69
two equally matched a. meet — LAO 508:64
whose fingers are ten a. — GINS 372:6
armistice for twenty years — FOCH 341:68
armour a. of light — BOOK 147:51
no a. against fate — SHIR 819:20
Put on the whole a. of God — BIBLE 128:95
armoury castle without an a. — GEOF 363:44
arms a. and the man — ANON 20:25
A., and the man I sing — DRYD 304:37
a. do flourish — BACON 53:43
a. hang down to laugh — ELIOT 317:80
a. of my true love — TENN 876:29
buried in those monumental a. — WALL 918:58
chess with a. and legs — BARZ 67:41
clad in the a. — SURR 860:97
clasped in my longing a. — ROCH 719:5
Come to my a., my beamish boy — CARR 204:90
Cromwell took up a. — STAL 842:4
effective for a. control — WEIN 928:77
Emparadised in one another's a. — MILT 604:4
For the theatre one needs long a. — BERN 86:86
freeing his a. — JOYCE 470:20
from our mother's a. — WINK 950:98
green a. round the bosom — SHEL 816:59
history of a. control — ADEL 8:61
hug it in mine a. — SHAK 788:67
if my love were in my a. — ANON 21:59
I never would lay down my a. — PITT 679:9
in the a. of a chambermaid — JOHN 463:64
laid down his a.! — HOOD 426:19
lay down their a. — GOEB 374:54
Lending a. — TAFT 866:9
lord of folded a. — SHAK 763:9
lore of a. — ANON 21:50
more strong than traitors' a. — SHAK 777:43
muscles of his brawny a. — LONG 535:17
Of seeming a.…a short essay — DRYD 304:47
once more in mine a. — SHAK 784:66
outspread a. is equal — LEON 523:76
prize Of wit or a. — MILT 597:47
Rank'd a. and crested heads — SMART 826:66
sap flows up through our a. — RILKE 715:39
soldiers without a. — PAST 668:5
strong a. be our conscience — SHAK 761:53
take a. against a sea of troubles — SHAK 783:7
take me in thy a. — MARL 573:13
took her up in his a. — RIDGE 715:30
took the ball in his a. — ANON 21:50
To war and a. I fly — LOVE 538:85
underneath are the everlasting a. — BIBLE 95:3
very long a. — HALI 393:36

army

Weep me not dead, in thine a.	DONNE 291:35	A....excludes all competition	FUSE 356:91	A work of a. works	MART 575:68
what a. have lain	MILL 592:23	A. for a.'s sake	CONS 245:62	beauty has in a.	DIDE 285:61
why did we take up a.	CROM 255:19	A. for a.'s sake	FORS 345:44	became an expert's a.	RUDO 730:36
With a., legs, lips	ROCH 719:5	A. for a.'s sake	SAND 741:11	become human is a.	NOVA 642:68
wither slowly in thine a.	TENN 877:60	a. for practitioners and readers	LEAV 517:52	beginning and end of a.	HEIN 407:19
world in a.	MACA 546:53	A., Glory, Freedom fail	BYRON 187:43	better teachers of the A. of Painting	DURER 307:26
army accompanied by all the a.	GRAY 383:44	a. has no place in...life	RODC 721:43	betwixt Nature and A.	PRIOR 696:10
affairs of the a.	JAUR 452:98	A. has to move you	HOCK 421:15	black a. to dispense	VAUG 909:35
a. has had...victory	MARL 572:91	A., if you like	LARK 509:73	boundaries between politics and a.	DANG 262:29
a. hurrying into battle	ORWE 653:9	a., in London	DRYD 300:35	Bullfighting is the only a.	HEMI 409:71
a. marches on its stomach	NAPO 630:44	A. is a game	PIER 677:70	burglar who respects his a.	OHEN 648:22
a. of unalterable law	MERE 588:37	A. is a jealous mistress	EMER 325:87	clever, but is it A.?	KIPL 490:98
a. that we must train for war	WILS 949:84	A. is an abstraction	GAUG 361:2	conceptual a. the idea	LEWI 527:76
a. that will be able	TROT 899:63	A. is a point of view	WERE 931:54	concern itself with a.	KLEE 494:2
a. would be a base rabble	BURKE 175:21	A. is dedicated echo	SANT 743:45	condition of a.	CONR 243:25
backbone of the A.	KIPL 490:14	A. is history's nostalgia	WALC 916:19	Contemporary a.	PERRY 675:29
conduct of this a.	WASH 921:27	A. is like Creation	KLEE 494:4	corner-stones of literary a.	DUDEK 305:73
conventional a. loses	KISS 493:85	a. is long	CARM 202:46	corrupt a. is the sentimental	PISS 679:96
efficiency of an a.	JAY 453:2	A. is long, and time	LONG 535:15	counts as a work of a.	WILL 946:24
honour of the...British A.	CHUR 225:93	A. is not a brassière	BARN 64:67	Dalí's importance...for a. historians	SCHW 750:83
hum of either a.	SHAK 775:78	A. is not...a canon of beauty	PICA 677:59	Decorative a. does not exist	ROUA 729:7
proud Edward's a.	WILL 947:31	A. is nothing without form	FLAU 339:15	delights of a. satisfy me	FUEN 354:59
to maintain an a.	MORE 618:15	A. is not...merely a skill	FRIE 351:76	demonstrates the a. of measuring	NEWT 635:60
were a self-centred a.	LAWR 514:90	A. is not truth	PICA 677:63	destroy genius and a.	HAZL 404:59
world proletarian a.	LENIN 521:39	A. isn't about...rules	SEDA 755:95	deviating from the rules of a.	ADDI 7:55
aroint A. thee, witch	SHAK 795:99	A. is only a means to life	MILL 594:78	difference between...true a.	CAPO 197:26
arrange make Him a. it earlier	RULFO 731:40	a. is only possible	BEUYS 89:49	difficulty of a.	CHAR 215:26
arrangement a. into three reigns	GUED 389:83	a. is pursued with a view to money	BUTL 186:3	Dress is a form of visual a.	HOLL 423:51
arranging a. what we have always		A. is significant deformity	FRY 354:39	drunk we like our a.	LUCAS 541:53
known	WITT 951:24	a. is the child	KAND 473:16	Dying, Is an a.	PLATH 681:32
arrant he's an a. knave	SHAK 781:68	A. is the only work	GRAY 383:42	emotion of a.	ELIOT 317:88
Arras slogged up to A.	SASS 745:86	a. is the perfection of nature	BROW 165:57	end and test of a.	POPE 685:18
arrest neither a. nor movement	ELIOT 319:39	a. is the retelling	LUCAS 541:56	enemy of good a.	CONN 242:99
arrested exercises in a. development	SELF 756:61	a....life imitates it	LEBO 517:61	Europe had plenty of a.	BEHR 75:28
arrive a. where we started	ELIOT 321:91	A. may make a suit	HUME 438:2	ever seen in A. or Nature	WAUGH 924:80
persisting, safe a.	MILT 603:81	A. most cherishes	BROW 168:55	Every a....is thought to aim	ARIS 31:19
rather than striving to a.	HILL 418:58	a. museums to worship dead works	MAYA 583:22	Every true work of a.	FRIE 351:78
arriving always a. and departing	MILL 594:89	A. must take reality by surprise	SAGAN 738:27	expressing emotion in the form of a.	ELIOT 317:90
arrogance do not accept his a.	VASC 909:29	A. never expresses anything	WILDE 940:52	Faustus, leave this damnèd a.	MARL 573:28
power leads man towards a.	KENN 482:27	a., not chance	POPE 685:24	Film a. has a greater influence	BALA 56:10
arrogant most a. and invincible	JONS 467:66	A. of all periods	RUNGE 731:51	final purpose of a.	MAIL 559:41
not often to the a.	JEFF 453:15	a. of angling	WALT 920:92	find in a. and science	HALD 392:25
arrow a. into the air	LONG 535:24	a. of architecture	JOHN 458:28	Fond without a.	DRYD 301:59
a. that flies feels	LONG 536:38	a. of balance, of purity	MATI 581:92	for a shilling...conflict and a.	PRIE 695:84
a. that flieth by day	BIBLE 102:96	a. of drawing	LIEB 529:95	fruits of speaking a.?	SIDN 820:39
draw an a. arbitrarily	EDDI 311:24	a. of getting drunk	JOHN 463:65	future of a.	FLAU 339:17
in my heart his iron a.	SPEN 838:26	a. of government	SHAW 808:36	give their lives to a. and science	EINS 313:76
killed by the a.	KELL 479:66	a. of inexactitude	MURR 627:85	glory and good of A.	BROW 169:79
shot an a.	HAMER 393:44	a. of losing	BISH 137:29	goal of a. is almost divine	HUGO 436:55
Swifter than a.	SHAK 767:37	a. of making the most	SHAW 808:46	good is always a product of a.	BAUD 69:77
arrows a. of desire!	BLAKE 141:42	a. of newspaper paragraphing	MARQ 575:58	great a. is great life	WRIG 962:65
a. of outrageous fortune	TWAIN 902:63	a. of our necessities	SHAK 792:8	Great a. is	HIRST 419:82
As a. are in the hand	BIBLE 103:37	a. of painting cannot be...judged	DURER 307:25	Great a. is the contempt	FITZ 338:1
arse Kiss my a.!	PEPYS 673:84	a. of perceiving	DICK 282:83	great a. of antiquity	KLEE 494:1
politician is an a.	CUMM 258:66	a. of pleasing	HAZL 403:33	Happiness is always a work of a.	YOUR 968:57
arson A....artificial crime	WELLS 930:28	a. of poetry	MACL 555:47	hating, my boy, is an a.	NASH 630:62
art abstract a.'s appearance	MOTH 622:85	A. of Scratch	RUSK 733:11	hide...their want of a.	POPE 685:20
adventures...in great works of a.	FRAN 346:79	a. of systematic over-simplification	POPP 690:66	History...is an a.	FRAN 347:86
adventures of...a.	WEST 933:95	a. of the masses	HALL 393:41	I don't want to make plop a.	WHITE 937:80
Affords this a.	MARL 573:20	a. of the past	LEWI 527:77	If a. does not enlarge...sympathies	ELIOT 315:28
Aims of A.	KIPL 492:59	a. of the writer	APOL 29:80	If a work of a. is to be truly immortal	CHIR 222:23
All a. is immoral	WILDE 940:58	A. pales when compared	AQUI 30:99	If it is a.	SCHO 748:50
All a. is solitary	LIBE 528:84	A. produces ugly things	COCT 233:88	if it may even be called an a.	INGR 446:40
All great a. is born	POUND 691:89	a. reverenced the while	JONS 467:71	In a. economy is always beauty	JAMES 451:52
all mediums of a.	PISS 679:99	a. should be a monster	TZARA 904:18	In a. one is	MODE 611:70
all the adulteries of a.	JONS 467:60	A. should be independent	WHIS 934:22	in a. the best is good enough.	GOET 375:60
American a.	ADAMS 5:96	A. should comfort	BANKS 62:30	in a. we have to follow	MOND 612:98
anything other than ideal a.	BAUD 68:72	A.'s subject is the human clay	AUDEN 42:75	industry without a.	RUSK 733:10
a....achievement of stillness	BELL 77:80	a. that conceals a.	HARDY 397:9	informing them as a.	BLOOM 143:64
A. among a religious race	FUSE 356:93	a. that helps old ladies	OLDE 649:29	In Spenser, and in Jonson, A.	DENH 272:62
A. and Assistance of the Architect	ALBE 11:33	a. that is interested in itself	SANT 743:46	In sweet music is such a.	SHAK 804:45
a. and literature are left	LEWIS 527:58	a., that monopolizes	DUDEK 305:78	In sweet music is such a.	SHAK 804:47
a. and morals	MURD 626:65	A.—the one achievement	THUR 890:79	iron palaces of A.	HUGH 435:22
A. and Religion...two roads	BELL 75:33	A....the supreme achievement	POUND 692:31	Isherwood became...a work of a.	BURU 182:90
A. and Science cannot exist	BLAKE 141:31	A. to fold her hands	ROSS 726:61	Italy...home Of all A.	BYRON 188:59
a. can make us see	MACL 555:39	a. united with prophecy	NISB 639:28	it's only a.	CHAP 214:14
A....cannot avoid cheating	RIDI 715:34	A. was made to disturb	BRAQ 156:75	knows what a work of a. is	FRY 354:38
A. cannot be made...to please	DEGAS 269:87	A....will have a country	APOL 29:84	Language in a.	PINT 678:86
A. cannot hold its breath	ANTH 29:72	A. will liberate itself	MARC 569:49	last and greatest a.	POPE 688:20
A. comes to you proposing	ANON 26:89	a. world is a jungle	HAMM 394:60	least realistic of a. forms	MAMET 564:42
A....communication that insinuates	CALAS 192:22	as in a., dependent	RUSS 734:27	leave a. to us	EPST 326:25
a. constantly aspires	PATER 668:10	assaying of tea is an a.	MO 611:67	let it be an a.	SHAK 800:32
a. continue to follow nature	MOND 612:97	As the a. of reading	JAMES 451:68	Life does not imitate a.	ALLEN 14:2
A. derives a considerable part	JAMES 450:41	attempt to realize A.	HOLM 424:80	Life imitates A. far more	WILDE 940:61
A. does not expand	DEGAS 269:83	Ausonia, skilled in every a.	BYRON 187:28	Like a. and politics	DOCT 289:84
A. does not reproduce	KLEE 494:5	a very pretty a.	PEPYS 673:93	Literature...is an A.	QUIL 702:14
a. doesn't dare	HUST 440:46	a wife in this a. of mine	MICH 590:68	Literature is the a. of writing	CONN 242:95

arts

lost, for a., at Sarajevo	LEWIS 527:73	When a. communicates	WILL 944:73	king of a....photographer	WHIS 934:21
Love...is also an a.	BALZ 61:99	where the a. resides	SCHN 748:41	life of the a. sufficiently miserable	BELL 75:35
love of a. for its own sake	PATER 668:11	Why shouldn't a. be pretty?	RENO 711:59	make himself an a.	SASS 746:3
masterpiece of a. has...a fixed place	EMER 324:66	without the idea of a.	VIDAL 912:97	man who never...is no a..	BLAKE 141:35
men who have failed in...a.	DISR 288:57	work of a.	NABO 628:14	marriages, where both or one is an a.	SPARK 836:79
modern a....completely literary	WOLFE 953:74	work of a., and as life	MILL 594:81	might as well be an a.	STOP 856:19
Modern a. does not	ROSE 725:29	writer's only responsibility is to his a.	FAUL 331:40	More glutton than a.	PARK 663:2
Modern A. no longer	ROSE 725:28	year of a. and dissipation	MOORE 616:68	most American a. of all	ADLER 8:68
Modern a. tends towards	BAUD 69:78	You talk of a.	SHAW 810:26	Never trust the a.	LAWR 513:65
morality of a.	WILDE 940:64	**arterial** it is a. blood	KEATS 478:49	not up to the a....to find	GENET 363:39
More matter with less a.	SHAK 781:75	**arteriosclerosis** a. of culture	MILL 595:92	only become a good a.	INGR 446:41
more than Wisdom, A., or Nature	HERR 415:6	**art-form** a.-f....invented in England	BEER 74:97	pain that the a. feels	REDON 709:22
My religion and my a.	JOHN 456:85	**artful** No a. wildness to perplex	POPE 686:60	Portrait of the A. as	THOM 883:15
nation's a. is greatest	HOPP 429:1	**arthritis** man who owns up to a.	NASH 630:61	product of the a.	MAMET 563:30
Nature in him was almost lost in A.	COLL 237:69	**Arthur** A.'s sword snatched	MUNRO 625:47	qualities essential for the a.	DIDE 285:75
nature is the a. of God	BROW 165:58	A. the firste syght of queene	MALO 562:8	Remember I'm an a.	CARY 207:65
nature's handmaid a.	DRYD 299:15	courte of kynge A.	MALO 563:11	reward none should offer an a.	RENO 711:56
Nature that is above all a.	DANI 262:34	kynge A. ys nat dede	MALO 563:16	special kind of a.	GILL 370:82
never know all about a.	OLSEN 650:48	named hym A.	MALO 562:6	subject matter of the a.	WILDE 940:64
new a. to them is natural	DAVI 264:75	Speak for England, A.!	AMERY 15:26	To be an a.	JOHNS 457:87
new a. work is born	YOUR 969:61	**article** affect a singularity in that a.	SHER 817:74	to be lonely as an a.	THOM 883:14
next to Nature, A.	LAND 507:34	Alcohol is a very necessary a.	SHAW 809:74	what an a. does, is fail	BART 66:19
no a. which one government	SMITH 828:91	a. which nobody wants	HONE 425:12	what style is to an a.	BUEC 172:41
no a. without practice	PROT 697:33	desireus of being the correct a.	ASHF 38:74	writer or a.	STEV 854:92
no boundary line to a.	PARK 663:93	For a slashing a.	THAC 880:35	**artiste** a. with short arms	BERN 86:86
no history of a.	WERE 931:55	In fact, the finished a.	RUSS 735:48	**artistic** A. growth...a refining of the sense	CATH 208:87
no one will take to a.	BELL 75:35	ordinary home-made a.	DICK 281:73	a. sense of eye or ear	WHIS 934:22
no such thing as authentic a.	CUMM 257:50	single sentence in a routine a.	MEYER 589:63	a. temperament is a disease	CHES 220:62
not as an a. form	TZARA 904:19	**articles** a. published in scientific	FEYN 334:5	departure for our a. creation	WAGN 915:2
not the courtier's a.	DRYD 302:88	exchanging a.	RUSK 733:16	slightly a.	KENN 480:91
Not to admire, is all the a.	POPE 688:24	These a. subscribed	CONG 241:75	**artistry** invention or true a.	POUND 692:25
of ev'ry a. the soul	POPE 686:59	**articulate** a. and complete	STEV 850:83	**artists** are not savages a.	MACKE 553:9
oldest a. in the world	CHAP 214:10	neither a. or worshipful	SNYD 832:93	A. and poets	ANON 27:18
only a. that they look upon	WOLFE 953:78	**articulation** A. is the tongue-tied's		A. are the antennae	POUND 692:28
perception of works of a.	DEWEY 276:20	fighting	HARR 399:56	A. are the only people	SLOAN 825:55
perfection in a new kind of a.	RUNGE 731:52	**artifice** Art...through a.	RIDI 715:34	A. don't make... A. make	KAP 473:28
photography...stand in for a.	BAUD 68:71	to conceal his a.	OGIL 648:5	a. go potty as they get older	BLAKE 139:77
Poetry...is an a. of imitation	SIDN 820:55	without a., I...work	ARET 31:11	A....if you copy others	BERN 86:78
Poetry is the a. of understanding	MACL 555:46	**artificer** an a....who formed it	PALEY 661:57	a. must break a hole	HALE 392:28
Politics is the a. of	VALE 907:2	single a. of the world	STEV 850:79	a. produce something that	WILD 943:47
pop a. and fine a.	MACI 553:1	The great a.	STEV 854:86	A. risk it all	MART 575:69
Posing is a performing a.	SCHW 750:84	**artificial** All things are a.	BROW 165:58	a. took to the road	ROCK 721:40
power of all true a.	EINS 313:80	arrest motion...by a. means	FAUL 331:42	a. try to break your heart	RAUS 707:81
preoccupying myself with...a.	SELF 756:12	**artillery** Our light a.	GILB 369:55	a. will...instruct us	OLSEN 650:48
pretty, but is it A.?	KIPL 490:97	rusty a. of abuse	STEV 850:6	a.... want to become inhuman	APOL 29:78
procrastination is the a.	MARQ 574:47	Th' a. of words	SWIFT 861:15	best subjects for a.	HEIN 407:20
profuse strains of unpremeditated a.	SHEL 813:90	**artisan** promised to the studious a.!	MARL 573:21	conceived...by unknown a.	BART 66:22
Protestant form of a.	ORWE 653:30	**artist** aim of every a.	FAUL 331:42	English a....ruined	RUSK 733:13
purpose of a.	GOULD 379:73	A more ideal A.	TENN 871:5	Great a. impose their	MAUP 583:15
reactions to a. or to music	COLE 234:4	And so great an a.	NERO 633:21	history of a..	WERE 931:55
reading...itself an a.	CARY 207:60	an 'a.' must have...suffering	DISKI 287:13	Horrible as successful a.	JONG 466:34
Religion and a....from the same root	CATH 208:95	a. absolute beauty	HALD 392:25	If we...do not support our a.	MART 575:66
revenge of the intellect upon a.	SONT 834:13	a. best serves his nation	KENN 482:26	New York Pop a.	LIPP 530:34
rid of the element of a. in their being	CHES 220:62	a. does not start with nothing	PERCY 674:11	no one wants Fine A.	FULL 355:68
says I know the a.	SPEN 839:44	a. does not tinker	MILL 593:60	over a troop of a.	WILL 945:6
schoolman's subtle a.	POPE 688:7	a....driven by demons	FAUL 331:39	poet shares with other a.	SPEN 837:7
seven...exhibitions of modern a.	DUNL 307:13	a. has followed the rules	TINT 892:24	position of the a. of Wales	THOM 884:43
sharp compassion of the healer's a.	ELIOT 320:64	a. is a spectator	ERNST 327:39	style of most a. and all humbugs	CONN 242:4
shouldn't talk about a.	JOHN 458:30	a. is extremely lucky	BERR 87:4	Summoning a. to participate	FROST 353:21
spare...patience towards...music or a.	GLEN 374:50	a. is in danger of death	HEMI 409:71	ten great a.	GREE 385:1
specialized form of a.	PRIT 696:16	a. is making something exist	BURR 181:68	too difficult for a.	SCHN 748:46
spit in the face of A.	MILL 593:52	a., like the idiot	SITW 824:22	What do these so-called a.	INGR 446:39
start on all this A.	HERB 412:43	a. man and the mother woman	SHAW 807:17	**arts** are the books, the a.	SHAK 763:19
sweet music is such a.	SHAK 804:45	a. must possess the courageous soul	CHOP 223:33	a. are taught by degrees	THEO 882:79
sweet music is such a.	SHAK 804:47	a. needs but a roof	RYDER 736:57	a. babblative and scribblative	SOUT 835:57
symbol of Irish a.	JOYCE 470:22	A. of the Floating World	ISHI 447:71	a. of war	MORE 618:10
Teaching is not a lost a.	BARZ 67:36	a.'s first responsibility is to himself	DAVIS 265:1	brought the a. into rustic Latium	HORA 430:16
than when A.	HERR 416:17	a. should fear	RYDER 736:58	elegant a. are unknown here	BROO 162:83
The a. of war	SUN 859:87	a. should not only paint	FRIE 351:77	finest of the A.	MERE 588:35
the dead a. of poetry	POUND 691:99	a. who has travelled on a steam train	DAVIS 266:5	France, famed in all great a.	ARNO 33:65
the end of A.	TURN 901:21	a. who seeks dignity	ALBE 11:31	France, mother of a.	BELL 76:43
the necessary a.	DULL 306:87	a. will be judged only by...solitude	CONN 243:17	Greece, mother of a.	MILT 607:79
There is no abstract a.	PICA 677:58	a. with true feelings	FRIE 351:73	idea of an a. ghetto	HARR 399:58
third great form of a.	HUGO 437:66	biography of the a.	ROSE 725:27	inglorious a. of peace	MARV 576:83
Though a.'s hid causes	JONS 467:60	critic when he cannot be an a.	FLAU 339:16	In the a. of life	SHAW 807:26
through A....realise our perfection	WILDE 940:57	dedication of an a.	SPARK 836:78	In the a. of peace	SHAW 807:27
Today a. is moving	MARC 569:48	eighteenth century a.	LEGER 520:7	lowest of the a.	MOORE 616:69
trade and a. is to live	MONT 614:26	expect the a. to have more to say	CALAS 192:22	mechanical a. and merchandise	BACON 53:43
transformed into comic a.	ROTH 728:84	filmmaker...other a.	WELL 929:93	mind with a. improve	DONNE 291:27
truth of a. should never be	HUGO 436:54	function of the a.	BETH 87:13	Murder...One of the Fine A.	DE 273:84
ultimate in a.	RUNGE 731:53	God is...another a.	PICA 677:62	no a.; no Letters	HOBB 420:2
unattainable by the highest a.	STRA 856:36	greatest a. can conceive	MICH 590:66	no ready a.	WORD 958:91
undreamed-of collection of a.	SAAR 736:1	half complete as a.	THUR 891:6	progress of the a. and the sciences	MAO 569:34
want that glib and oily a.	SHAK 792:86	I am an a.	FUEN 354:59	servant of...the a.	BAUD 68:71
What a. can wash her guilt	GOLD 376:93	if a great a. says	SELF 756:10	so far advanced in the A.	HAZL 403:47
What A. was to the ancient world	DISR 287:28	innovative and important a.	DAVIS 265:2	The a. stop society	REDG 709:20
What is a. is not likely to be decided	COND 240:14	joy of the a.	MILL 594:71	turn a. education into a system	HUGH 435:27

ascend

ascend
'What do you think about the a.?' ATWO 41:52
ascend a. it then with religion JONS 467:62
Ascendancy o the English A. MACD 550:39
ascent nobility of a. POTT 690:84
The a. of money FERG 333:79
asceticism out of a. MCCA 547:88
Asclepius offer a cock to A. PLATO 682:57
ash alone as a mountain a. DAY 267:38
a. for nothing ill SPEN 838:20
Oak, and A., and Thorn KIPL 492:53
Oak, and A., and Thorn KIPL 492:54
Out of the a. PLATH 681:33
There grows the wild a. CALL 192:32
ashamed a. at my failure to serve YOKOI 968:48
a. of one another CONG 241:74
a. to be my father's child! SHAK 769:90
feel a. of home DICK 282:7
more things a man is a. of SHAW 807:15
not…afraid of death, as a. BROW 165:62
not a. of…the American dream SHUL 819:30
not a. to fail JOHN 459:39
seldom a….that he cannot love ELIOT 316:5
something he is a. of SHAW 807:11
Ashbourn native of A., Derbyshire ANON 23:88
ashbuds More black than a. TENN 871:5
ashes a. all my lust MARV 577:92
A. and sparks, my words SHEL 813:48
a. of an oak DONNE 292:63
a. taken to Australia ANON 23:92
a. to a. BOOK 148:1
a. under Uricon HOUS 431:48
beauty for a. BIBLE 110:6
burnt to a. GRAH 380:87
handful of grey a. CORY 247:9
men and women…shall pass to a. SAND 742:15
past is a bucket of a. SAND 742:16
repent in dust and a. BIBLE 99:23
sat down among the a. BIBLE 98:93
Scatter my a. MONT 615:51
sour grapes and a. ASHF 38:75
splendid in a. BROW 166:81
tarnished with a. and soot MOORE 616:64
ashore perilous excursion a. LEWIS 527:57
water comes a. FROST 352:8
ashtrays a. will become as obsolete BLACK 137:39
Asia dusty catastrophe of A. BROD 160:36
from the furthest inch of A. SHAK 774:28
in A. as elsewhere BALD 57:33
pampered Jades of A. MARL 572:6
seven churches which are in A. BIBLE 131:85
seven churches which are in A. BIBLE 131:87
Sitting as huge as A. BARK 63:52
stabilisation of East A. HIRO 419:71
Asian what A. boys ought JOHN 458:13
aside all gone a. BIBLE 99:33
ask again we a. aloud KEATS 477:10
A., and it shall be given you BIBLE 115:50
a. for my money back HUXL 442:76
a. less than one? JONS 468:83
A. me no more TENN 873:48
a. not what your country KENN 481:4
a. the hard question AUDEN 42:69
If you still have to a. ARMS 32:48
intend to a. of them KENN 481:99
then you can a. me KING 486:17
what you a. them to do WALD 916:26
askew come in a. HEAT 406:92
asking a. too much CANN 197:10
a. 'Who came second?' REAR 709:17
You a. me the way? KAFKA 472:8
asleep Fall a., or hearing die SHAK 804:47
Fall a., or hearing, die SHAK 804:45
fast a. and weary BIBLE 95:11
happiest moment…falling a. SCHO 749:57
never tried to fall a. WHIT 937:87
Not to fall a. is distinguished BELL 78:88
thought me a. PATM 669:17
too young to fall a. SASS 745:91
we are a. in this world BORG 151:58
asp a. doth on his feeder feed LOVE 538:88
child shall play on the hole of the a. BIBLE 108:62
small whisper of the a. BYRON 188:63
asparagus a. of the poor FRAN 347:88
grow a. WADD 915:1
mention A. and it appeared DICK 282:88
oysters and a. and good wines SAKI 739:60
aspect evident a. of things HEID 406:17

aspects a. of human life POPP 689:57
aspen a. good for staves SPEN 838:20
By the light quivering a. made SCOTT 752:25
aspens a. quiver TENN 869:78
Asperges A. me hyssopo BIBLE 132:31
asphalt only monument the a. road ELIOT 319:32
aspic old purpose done up in a. LAWR 513:53
aspidistra Keep the A. Flying ORWE 653:8
aspiration thought and a. ROSS 727:65
aspirations a. that weren't realized KISS 494:90
poetry of our a. CUOMO 258:82
young have a. SAKI 739:53
aspire a. to give…a faithful account ELIOT 315:20
bade me gaze, and there a. ARNO 35:3
light, and will a. SHAK 762:84
what else was there to a. to? ROCK 721:38
aspirin both just a. VIDAL 912:94
Asquith affair between Margot A. PARK 663:98
Herbert A.'s clarity BALF 58:42
ass am such a tender a. SHAK 767:40
back of an a. to bear all NASHE 632:97
braying like an a. SITW 823:99
broaden your a. if not your mind HEMI 410:85
Cover your a. SAFI 737:19
enamoured of an a. SHAK 767:42
Hood an a. with reverend purple JONS 466:48
law is a a. DICK 278:72
law is such an a. CHAP 215:23
like an a. whose back SHAK 787:65
Lord opened the mouth of the a. BIBLE 94:83
making him egregiously an a. SHAK 789:10
part man, part horse's a. ACHE 2:35
Preposterous a. SHAK 762:68
scoreboard is an a. CARD 198:43
this a. o'er-offices SHAK 784:61
thrice-double a. SHAK 804:34
what an a. am I? SHAK 782:2
With the jawbone of an a. BIBLE 96:18
assailant vengeance on the a. TROL 898:35
assailed a. by eyes JAMES 451:67
assassin a.'s bullet PARK 665:43
forgot…the a. SAND 742:17
in harmony…sentiments of an a. BIER 134:59
saviour or a. MURP 627:77
assassinated until he's a. KAUF 474:35
assassination A. has never changed DISR 288:51
moderated by a. MUNS 626:57
assassins because you are bullied by a. LLOY 533:77
assault a.' on the mountain CRAN 253:75
instance of a direct a. SUMN 859:81
assaulting bees are a….the flowers REED 709:27
assay Help, angels! make a. SHAK 783:34
assent ever given his a. HUXL 441:61
expressions of a. WAUGH 923:73
asserted a. itself in her HARDY 397:10
assertions falsehood of his a. JOHN 463:73
asses come out A. BURNS 177:69
given to them by the Prize A. SMITH 830:36
led by th' nose As a. SHAK 789:5
asset greatest a. any country can have CHUR 226:98
greatest a….good night's sleep WILS 948:70
assets assessing the value of a. PAVL 670:39
complaining about loss of a. ROTH 728:5
no longer liabilities but a. SCHL 747:37
assimilation avenue of a. into society DOCT 289:84
assistance Art and A. of the Architect ALBE 11:33
conscious and creative a. ROBBE 717:64
association free and equal a. ENGE 326:15
newspaper represents an a. TOCQ 892:31
Out of a. grows adhesion BRON 161:70
associations all these accumulated a. MELV 585:61
assonance adroit a. UNTE 905:11
assume A. a virtue SHAK 784:45
what I a. you shall a. WHIT 937:90
assumption more powerful a. SOLOW 833:4
assumptions a. of the ordinary man ATTL 40:26
basic beliefs and a. MILL 593:38
Mistaken in its a. REGAN 710:42
assurance a. was given me WESL 932:65
bright a. WORD 962:47
diminish the dogmatic a. RUSS 734:23
old house carried an a. ACHE 2:29
on whom a. sits ELIOT 318:7
some a. of grace NIEB 637:86
the consoling a. of grace NIEB 637:87
assurances greatest a. of safety ACHE 3:55
assure a. the survival KENN 481:3

assured ignorant of what he's most a. SHAK 787:58
Assyrian oiled and curled A. Bull TENN 875:17
asteroid an a. hitting the planet KING 486:16
Astolat lily maid of A. TENN 877:50
astonish A. me! DIAG 276:22
astonished As many were a. at thee BIBLE 109:92
a. at my own moderation! CLIVE 231:40
beyond measure a. BIBLE 119:57
suddenly a. HEYE 417:79
astonishment not so much a. SARG 743:53
the a. of loving REID 710:44
truth which still fills me with a. DAWK 266:15
your a.'s odd ANON 24:11
astound startle well, but not a. MILT 598:69
astounding seek for…the a. BORG 150:55
astray sheep who've gone a. KIPL 489:75
taking quite a liberty in going a. ELIOT 315:16
astrologer gibberish of the a. MACA 545:41
astronauts A.! Rotarians in space! VIDAL 912:85
astronomer no a. can find HUGH 436:42
astronomy A. teaches the correct LEAC 515:11
asunder let no man put a. BOOK 148:94
let not man put a. BIBLE 118:15
asylum America is an insane a. POUND 692:33
as though I were in a lunatic a. CONA 239:10
ataxia beginnings of a. SILVA 821:70
Ate with A. by his side SHAK 777:34
Athalus craftier to pley…Than A. CHAU 216:56
atheism a. is against…our reason BURKE 176:44
Every luxury…a., breast-feeding ORTON 652:4
inclineth Man's mind to a. BACON 51:79
religion, and not a., is the true remedy BURKE 175:19
When a. wants martyrs SADE 737:15
atheist an embittered a. ORWE 653:7
a….no invisible means of support BUCH 171:27
daylight a. BEHAN 74:13
grown an a.? WEBS 926:38
Sally said I was a sacrilegious a. SALI 740:80
Thanks be to God, I am still an a. BUNU 173:70
atheists A., fools, and madmen! ONEI 651:70
a. have nothing to live for GERV 366:85
should make men a. CAREW 198:51
Athens A. arose! SHEL 816:56
A., the eye of Greece MILT 607:79
Burn, with A. CAMP 194:54
Who brings owls to A.? ARIS 31:14
Ye men of A. BIBLE 124:91
athlete American a. is superior CALI 192:25
a. cannot run with money ZATO 969:2
I'm not an a. BRYA 170:99
athletes All pro a. are bilingual HOWE 433:90
athletics regard all a. as inferior WAUGH 923:61
Athlone Great Gun of A. ANON 23:96
Atkins Thank you, Mister A. KIPL 489:85
Atlanta In A., the first question BERE 83:13
Atlantic A. to the Pacific CHUR 225:80
crosses the A. MCCA 547:86
Irish…other side of the A. WAUGH 924:81
Ryanair will never fly the A. OLEA 649:34
sailed across the A. BEHAN 74:10
steep A. stream MILT 598:64
stormy North A. Ocean LARD 508:65
this A. generation KENN 481:21
atlas bicycle and an a. MURP 626:73
discumbered A. of the state COWP 250:92
Witch of A. YEATS 967:39
atmosphere academic a. STEA 843:28
a. favorable to the extraordinary PAZ 671:48
brought up in an a. SPEN 837:10
delightful social a. BENN 81:71
general a. of unreality QUEN 702:8
human creatures breathe an a. DICK 282:92
placed in the luminous a. LEON 523:78
atmospheric a. billboard THOR 889:56
atom a. bombs are piling up ORWE 654:57
a….breathed before BRON 160:49
conceal the power of the a. COLE 234:1
every a. belonging to me WHIT 937:90
Herman Melville who split the a. LODGE 534:95
knowledge of the a. EDDI 311:25
mystery of the a. BRAD 155:43
no evil in the a. STEV 850:5
Protons give an a. its identity BRYS 171:14
since the a. bomb VREE 915:57
atomic end up with the a. bomb PAGN 660:22
forces a. energy on us FROMM 352:88
form of a. blackmail KENN 481:7

authors

given us the a. bomb	KING 487:32	attractive a. about her was not her		**Australians** A. inherited the British	
Hibakusha, a. victims	GEE 362:27	appearance	BROO 163:11	mentality	PACK 659:10
way it was with the a. bomb	OPPE 651:83	a. to the half-baked mind	FORS 344:26	**Austria** A. is a little world	HEBB 406:97
atoms air is not so full…of a.	DONNE 293:71	When I find a woman a.	SAINT 738:33	born in A.	SIMON 822:75
A. or systems into ruin hurled	POPE 686:73	**attractiveness** peculiar a. of each child	ACHE 2:22	**Austrian** A. Empire did not exist	PALA 660:47
fortuitous concourse of a.	FISKE 337:66	**attribute** a. to God himself	SHAK 770:13	**authenticity** verify the a.	WILL 946:24
fortuitous concurrence of a.	PALM 662:73	important a. of a lawyer	KENN 482:40	**author** a. and finisher of our faith	BIBLE 129:43
Let onion a. lurk	SMITH 831:59	true a. of the soul	STAEL 842:3	a. and giver of all good things	BOOK 147:54
Nothing exists except a.	DEMO 272:48	**attributes** consisting in infinite a.	SPIN 847:83	a. because you like his books	LINK 530:31
smash to a….everything he had learnt	ORTE 652:2	**attribution** a. of false motives	BALD 57:35	a. is the first to go	COLL 237:61
atomsmashers half a dozen a.	PERE 674:17	**Auburn** Sweet A., loveliest village	GOLD 376:96	a. of peace	BOOK 146:39
atom-streams saw the flaring a.-s.	TENN 877:68	**auction** a. joke were a charity a.	MCIL 553:95	a. of the play	GILB 370:75
atone pictures for the page a.	POPE 688:34	**auctions** stands…between a.	RAUS 707:80	A. of the Whole escape	POPE 689:46
atonement This is the day of a.	RICH 713:9	**audacity** punished for their a.	CABE 191:4	a.'s fairy godmother	LUCAS 541:54
atrocious a. crime of being…young	PITT 679:1	tactful in a.	COCT 233:84	a.'s mind	GAUG 361:3
A. in content	GOET 375:58	**Auden** A. ran it	BOWL 153:2	a. spoils everything	LAFO 504:62
atrocities a. that horrified us	HELL 408:34	I think I'm A.	EWART 328:75	a. today proclaims	ROBBE 716:64
atrophy a. of the imagination	GELL 363:33	W.H. A., a sort of gutless Kipling	ORWE 653:18	a. who speaks about his own books	DISR 288:61
music begins to a.	POUND 692:17	**audience** Ambushing the a.	STOP 856:21	a. writes with a misty profundity	WHIT 936:62
attach Where people wish to a.	AUST 47:85	and looks at the a.	STOC 855:7	choose an a.	DILL 286:95
attack a….economic legends	GALB 357:17	a. look to their eyes	SHAK 767:21	confession…of its a.	NIET 638:7
a. is particularly wounding	THAT 881:63	a….put up its umbrellas	BEER 73:78	Corrected…By its A.!	FRAN 348:7
French want to a.	ANON 27:34	a.'s power of judgement	HARD 396:95	every other a. may aspire to praise	JOHN 460:67
lead such dire a.	MACA 546:47	a. was a disaster	WILDE 941:80	expected to see an a.	PASC 666:69
no a. is too cruel	MCCA 546:69	a. would immediately be looking	HITC 419:83	fine future for its a.	WILDE 940:50
plan of a.	SASS 745:86	a. yelled, 'You're sublime'	HARG 398:31	first-rate a. wants an exquisite heroine	FITZ 338:2
serious a. upon morality	ORWE 654:39	awful attention in the a.	SHER 818:2	from the a.'s soul	HUXL 441:63
attacks a. from outlaw states	REAG 708:8	best a….a little drunk	BARK 63:55	go to the a.	RUSK 733:4
attain cannot here a. unto them	HOOK 427:40	End without a.	SHAK 762:89	Hunting the a., painter and musician	SITW 824:25
if we could a. it	TROL 898:49	hold the a.	UPDI 906:26	improved by its a.'s explanations	MACL 555:36
attained only wisdom ever to be a.	PRAT 694:67	if I don't practise…the a. knows	PADE 659:13	in Search of an A.	PIRA 678:87
attainments a. are the lot of all	TOCQ 892:26	inviting his a. to discard him	ANNAN 19:11	Literature…depends…on the a.'s skill	QUIL 702:14
attempt a. at deliberate evasion	JONES 465:21	keep the a. awake	OLIV 649:42	more intelligent than its a.	ECO 310:18
die in the a.	HELL 407:26	must have a London a.	AUST 46:70	more than wit to make an a.	LA 502:7
fearing to a.	SHAK 787:49	seeking empathy with his a.	SAFI 737:21	no a. today	SARR 744:60
vain a. to subdue	GILL 370:80	spirits of the a.	BIER 135:88	not only as an a.	GRASS 382:12
attempts a. to display qualities	JOHN 459:55	two kinds of a.	SCHN 748:43	role of the a.	DIDE 285:68
attend Another to a. him	HERB 413:71	your a. is conjectural	ORWE 654:52	sending the a. some small cash token	CONN 242:97
attendant a. and…inmate	CONA 239:10	**audiences** a. come to hear	FREE 349:44	shrimp of an a.	GRAY 385:95
attended When neither is a.	SHAK 770:24	**auditorium** hidden a. of his skull	STER 757:32	This is indeed to be an a.!	HAZL 403:48
attention all of the a. is on		I remember the a.	POWE 693:55	truth about its a.	CHES 220:61
Paris Hilton	GORE 379:62	**August** A. for the people	AUDEN 42:74	What I like in a good a.	SMITH 829:26
an awful a.	SHER 818:2	winter…To recommence in A.	BYRON 190:23	what the a. promised	JOHN 460:64
a. on a particular aspect	ROBB 717:68	**august** a. occasions of the state	FROST 353:21	wish the a….was a terrific friend	SALI 739:72
by paying a.	HUXL 442:86	**Augusta** A….grandmother's maiden name	BERE 83:13	write like a distinguished a.	NABO 628:20
distract our a.	THOR 888:30	**Augustus** A. was a chubby lad	HOFF 422:32	**authoress** dared to be an a.	AUST 46:71
drawing your a.	LEWIS 527:70	**auld** a. lang syne!	BURNS 178:5	**authoritarian** perpetuate a. rule	AUNG 45:39
enough to get any child's a.	BAIL 55:86	**aunt** A. is calling to A.	WODE 952:39	**authoritarianism** 1984 a.	GINS 372:14
fix our a. out of ourselves	HUME 438:94	A. Jane observed	GRAH 380:85	**authorities** a….we do not control	CONN 243:16
husbands…cannot give their entire a.	BENN 81:67	A. Sally she's going to adopt	TWAIN 903:68	between the issues and the highest a.	SHUL 819:28
If you want a man's a.	BIEL 134:57	Her A….from her Earliest Youth	BELL 77:63	every act of the a.	REED 710:37
more a. paid to them	JOHN 462:45	said my a. Dot	MACA 544:19	If civil a. legislate	JOHN 456:73
paying a. to them	SONT 834:22	**Auntie** Whenever A. moves around	STEV 853:67	**authority** a man under a.	BIBLE 116:57
socks compelled one's a.	SAKI 739:61	**aunts** a. and uncles were legion	SHAW 811:33	a., either academic or worldly	MENC 586:89
something worthy of a.	DARW 263:51	cousins, and his a.!	GILB 368:33	A. forgets a dying king	TENN 878:82
undivided a….of the entire nation	BORAH 150:53	her husband, her a.	RANS 706:66	a. in the affairs of the church	BECK 72:54
attentions pleasing a.	AUST 45:56	play bridge with my old maid a.	FIEL 335:29	a. of a belief	KRIS 499:12
superior a. in little points	LAMB 505:94	**aura** a. of one who knows	BANKS 62:21	a. of supreme victory	WHIT 936:71
attic A. boy to hunt	MILT 598:57	**Aurora** rising with A.'s light	SWIFT 862:61	base a. from others' books	SHAK 763:2
little brain a.	DOYLE 297:58	See how A. throws her fair	HERR 415:10	combat general a.	DRYD 300:39
mellow glory of the A. stage	ARNO 33:64	Zephyr with A.	MILT 597:42	Dressed in a little brief a.	SHAK 787:58
O A. shape!	KEATS 478:38	**Ausonia** let A., skilled in every art	BYRON 187:28	enjoying such a. and prestige	BERE 83:15
speech a….pliant as A.	QUIL 702:13	**Austen** Jane A….only novelist	BANKS 62:28	established by the said a.	HOWA 433:86
attics shabby bums living in a.	LEWIS 527:58	**austere** strode on a.	THOM 887:10	exercises a. over beggars	MORE 618:16
attire a. be comely	LYLY 543:81	**austerity** high a. to delight	FREE 350:49	for their robbery have a.	SHAK 787:60
a. for a gentleman	SHAR 806:72	**Austerlitz** Pile the bodies…at A.	SAND 742:18	hardly an a. upon anything	DAFOE 260:7
rich a. creeps rustling	KEATS 477:22	**Australia** always last year in A.	THER 882:91	high a. of the self	TRIL 897:18
attitude don't like that a.	SHAN 805:60	ashes taken to A.	ANON 23:92	his a. and her sex	WOLL 954:92
elitist a. is basically suspicious	KRIS 499:15	Being lost in A.	CHAT 216:53	I have installed A. always	MORR 620:48
enchantingly wavering a.	FITZ 337:75	camped in the centre of A.	STUA 858:57	no one has the a.	KELM 479:69
end up with the a.	JACK 449:8	colour in A. is gold	STRE 857:51	O, what a.	SHAK 774:51
Fair a.!	KEATS 478:38	cricket tour in A.	LARW 510:7	stamp of his a.	LAMB 505:93
not my aptitude but my a.	JACK 448:4	Dead Heart of A.	GREG 387:53	takes on an a.	BAIL 55:83
scientific a. of mind	RUSS 734:29	housemaid…the best in A.	MELBA 584:46	those in a.	KELM 479:68
attitudes a. and movements	LEON 522:74	indifference of…golden A.	LAWR 513:58	vices of a.	BACON 51:89
in-office a. and behavior	COUP 248:28	like A. less and less	LAWR 513:49	you hate a.	BAIL 55:83
number of conflicting a.	ALTH 15:15	postmodern, multicultural A.	NARO 630:53	**authors** ancient a.	BACON 49:23
paid to have a. toward things	HEMI 409:61	so much interested in A.	WILDE 941:77	A. and uncaptured criminals	LINK 530:25
attorney Even an a. of modest talent	CAPO 197:21	Spirit of A.	FIELD 335:11	A. are actors	STEV 850:94
gentleman is an a.	JOHN 462:22	the other in A.	GAY 362:9	a. of simile and metaphor	NASH 631:81
in love with a rich a.'s…daughter	GILB 368:29	**Australian** A. be equal to…a Briton	PARK 665:37	from English a. their copyrights	TROL 898:54
office boy to an a.'s firm	GILB 368:34	A. literature	STEW 854:94	inability of their a.	NISB 639:27
attorneyship dealt in by a.	SHAK 759:82	A. novel is not…dreary	WHITE 935:55	invades a. like a monarch	DRYD 300:21
attracted a. by God, not by Nature	INGE 445:27	first and foremost…an A.	MELBA 584:44	let great a. have their due	BACON 49:20
attraction A. and repulsion	BLAKE 139:94	proud that I am an A.	FRAN 348:23	our a. make a doubt	BUTL 184:63
by sure a. led	POPE 688:37	spirit of an A.	FRAN 348:22	we a. repeat ourselves	FITZ 338:90
attractions register competing a.	KNIG 494:9	stretched the Great A. Emptiness	WHITE 935:54	when two or three a. meet	PRIT 696:20

authorship

your taste in a. ONEI 651:70
authorship popular a. TROL 898:47
products...rather than of a. WALD 916:24
autobiographies A. tell more lies BYATT 186:17
autobiography age to write an a. WAUGH 924:97
a. is an obituary CRISP 255:7
a. is only 'a sort of life' GREE 386:20
a. writ large LEWO 528:79
deepest part of a. WARR 921:19
rage for confession, a. MANS 567:3
told it's a. ROTH 728:92
write an a. is only to open MELBA 584:44
autocracy communism is Tsarist a. HERZ 416:23
principle of a. NICH 636:71
autocrat Aristocrat, democrat, a. TENN 876:20
rebel...turning into an a. DURR 308:36
autographs write for a. GILB 369:60
automate a.—or evaporate! MERR 588:48
automatic a. machine WIEN 939:28
balancing seemed rather a. SPEN 837:9
automation patterns latent in a. MCLU 556:56
automatons intelligently run by a. MUMF 625:39
automobile artist...driven an a. DAVIS 266:5
a. accident GIBB 367:6
a. has practically reached the limit ANON 24:5
a. is the greatest catastrophe JOHN 458:31
a....object of aesthetic appreciation BARR 64:81
poorhouse in an a. ROGE 723:80
autonomous the a. individual ORWE 653:30
autonomy new conception of a. GEOR 364:54
self-employment and artistic a. MCLU 556:56
autumn a. and the falling fruit LAWR 514:82
A. is desolation TATE 867:39
A.'s pleasant weather BURNS 178:91
A. wind rises WU 963:84
breath of A.'s being SHEL 813:79
carry well this A. night BUNT 173:68
descends the a. evening ARNO 36:25
happy a.-f. TENN 872:41
harmony In a. SHEL 812:57
O A., laden with fruit BLAKE 139:82
old A. in the misty morn HOOD 426:18
red amnesiacs of a. PURDY 700:85
rose in rainy a. THOM 884:22
sallow A. fills thy lap COLL 238:77
Slow sobs...of a. VERL 910:55
south, where there is no a. LAWR 513:66
Thursday...in a. VALL 907:10
autumnal pox of her a. face JONS 467:59
auxiliars mighty were the a. WORD 960:23
Auxiliary I was undone by my A. STEE 844:47
avail good income is of no a. SMITH 829:14
Avalun will fare to A. LAYA 515:98
avant-garde chamber of the A.-G. HUGH 435:22
one thing constant...is the a.-g.. JOUV 469:12
There is no a.-g. VARE 908:25
avant-gardism therapeutic a.-g. HUGH 435:28
avarice a.: it increases its thirst MONT 614:44
a., lust and ambition LEWIS 526:43
gratify a., and extend corruption JOHN 460:86
root of Evil, A. MAND 565:65
take up with a. BYRON 189:4
Ave-Maries A.-M. on his beads SHAK 759:84
avenge shalt not a. BIBLE 94:78
avenger still the enemy and the a. BIBLE 99:30
wait for the a. WILDE 940:45
avenue a. I'm taking you to DUBIN 304:59
a. of assimilation into society DOCT 289:84
average children are above a. KEIL 479:53
there shall be the a. SMITH 828:4
aversion gentleman's park is my a. CONS 244:57
Those...fellows are my a. STEE 844:51
with preference and a. SHER 817:71
aviary an a. overstocked with jays OHEN 648:19
avidity Beast ravens in its own a.? EBER 310:12
Avilion island-valley of A. TENN 878:87
avoid a. what is to come SHAK 784:43
manages to a. them HEIS 407:24
avoided what cannot be a. SHAK 760:18
avoiding a. non-being TILL 891:13
Avon Sweet Swan of A.! JONS 468:81
awake a. for sake of Song! FERG 333:83
a. in another one BORG 151:58
A. my soul KEN 480:83
Keeping a. for ten weeks WINN 950:2
let me be a., my God! COLE 235:22
rather sleep...than stay a. ALBEE 11:29

trying to a. JOYCE 470:24
When you're lying a. GILB 369:54
awaken begin to a. WILL 946:9
awakened a. from the dream of life SHEL 815:39
awakening a time of a. consciousness RICH 713:1
single a. MARI 571:82
awakenings dream between two a. ONEI 651:64
aware a. that one's mother JARRY 452:96
I'm more a. REAG 708:99
awareness a. of that revelation FRYE 354:53
a. that words can outlive us PLOUT 682:74
delicate a. of unreasoning things DARK 263:47
terms of the human a. LEAV 517:52
awash Washington is a. SCHR 749:68
away a. we go WORD 956:57
Come, dear children, let us a. ARNO 33:55
People who never get carried a. FORB 342:84
take that a. from me GERS 365:75
take that a. from me GERS 365:76
Take the soup a.! HOFF 422:32
awe a. for the natural world WILS 947:42
ever new and increasing admiration and a. KANT 473:26
Exempt from a., worship, degree SHEL 814:18
fear and a. WORD 961:35
feelings of a. and respect DICK 277:39
In a. of...myself SHAK 776:8
Make this Bed with A. DICK 284:43
no longer...stand rapt in a. EINS 313:80
Stand in a. BIBLE 99:29
The plan is called 'shock and a.' ANON 27:42
With a....I tread CRAB 251:25
awful Anything a. makes me laugh LAMB 505:83
How a. to reflect SMITH 829:1
awfulness by its very a. STEV 852:38
awkward I'm just an a. old maid RENO 711:48
awkwardness regret The a. HEAN 405:75
awoke a. in the capital KAIKO 472:12
a. one morning KAFKA 472:5
So I a. BUNY 174:79
awry Gang aft a.-g. BURNS 177:78
axe a.'s edge did try MARV 576:84
a. will fall when they raise me LEAC 516:24
let the great a. fall SHAK 784:56
Many strokes...with a little a. SHAK 760:5
sound of the white soldier's a. RED 709:19
spinning wheel and the bronze a. ENGE 326:15
stone than with an a. JOHN 463:63
swinging his a. BUNT 173:69
axe-blade a.-b. infinitely sharp PRATT 694:68
axes two a. of the world FRAN 346:81
axiom a enforced by...experience CONN 243:19
A.: Hatred of the bourgeois FLAU 339:24
a. of politics TOCQ 892:29
a. of sports FRAY 349:35
long been an a. of mine DOYLE 297:52
that was a general a. SPARK 836:71
axioms hypotheses or a. EINS 314:89
axis constitute an a. of evil BUSH 183:18
under-belly of the A. CHUR 226:97
axle glowing a. doth allay MILT 598:64
axletree fly sat upon the a. BACON 53:42
Ayatollah A.'s money to support NORTH 641:63
I'm the A. Khomeini of Serbia MILO 596:57
Ayr A....ne'er a town surpasses BURNS 179:20
Azcan A. in caftan STEV 849:72
Azores At Flores in the A. TENN 878:95
azure out the a. main THOM 887:97
overgrown with a. moss SHEL 813:81
rock inlaid with a. glaciers BENU 88:9

B

Baal if B., then follow him BIBLE 97:61
Babbitt name was George F. B. LEWIS 527:56
To George F. B. LEWIS 527:57
babblative arts b. and scribblative SOUT 835:57
babbler What will this b. say? BIBLE 124:90
babbling b. rhyme SHAK 774:76
babe b., by intercourse of touch WORD 958:81
Coleridge lull the b. at nurse BYRON 187:29
find the b. wrapped BIBLE 120:69
his b. in the nest TENN 872:37
laid her b. to rest MILT 597:38
naked new-born b. SHAK 796:20
woo not like a b. SHAK 761:63
Babel name of it called B. BIBLE 92:15
babes As newborn b. BIBLE 130:66

B. reduced to misery BLAKE 140:13
even the b. in arms THOM 883:2
Out of the mouth of b. BIBLE 99:30
Tears, then, for b. SHAK 760:6
babies b....come into the world MENC 587:10
b. like such toys MORE 619:21
b. who rush at me MANS 567:36
bit the b. in the cradles BROW 167:16
hates dogs and b. ROST 727:72
having b. without chloroform BARB 63:48
long hours spent as b. BRAD 154:25
only washing. And b. THOM 884:37
Other people's b. HERB 412:44
putting milk into b. CHUR 226:98
You breed b. and you eat chips WESK 931:56
Bab-lock-hithe Crossing...at B.-l.-h. ARNO 34:90
baboon humanity with a b. SHAK 789:2
morals of a b. CAPO 197:30
baby b., assailed by eyes JAMES 451:67
B. in an ox's stall BETJ 88:36
b. is God's opinion SAND 742:30
b. made in a test tube MAIL 560:57
blind boy, Venus' b. SPEN 839:48
don't be stingy b. MARI 571:79
Every b. born into the world DICK 278:85
Hasta la vista, b. SCHW 750:86
little b. thing MACD 550:48
mother laid her b. ALEX 13:63
no more...than a man can have a b. DRAP 298:89
no rhyme to 'lady' but 'b.' SHAK 774:56
slept like a b. DOLE 290:96
When the first b. laughed BARR 65:85
Where did you come from, b. dear? MACD 550:47
who gives a b. birth MASE 580:64
why...name your b. 'John' GOLD 377:29
Babylon B. be thrown down BIBLE 132:18
B. The Great BIBLE 132:17
By the rivers of B. BIBLE 103:42
By the waters of B. WALP 919:73
Ere B. was dust SHEL 814:6
London is a modern B. DISR 288:40
through the walls of B. COMN 239:96
Baca through the valley of B. BIBLE 101:89
Bacall hint of B.'s slinkiness ALLEN 13:77
Bacchus B. hath drowned more men FULL 355:80
Bach angels play only B. BARTH 66:12
B. on the wrong notes PROK 697:29
not B. or Schubert MCCU 549:15
play B. your way LAND 507:37
bachelor b., a solicitor, a Freemason DOYLE 297:66
b. who has...experience RIDGE 715:30
half-witted b. WODE 952:29
he was a b. SYMI 865:19
makes Legree a b. CHES 219:32
married or a b. ADDI 6:23
Never trust a...b. too near ROWL 729:20
wise in the b. STEV 852:40
bachelors reasons for b. to go out ELIOT 315:26
where the b. sit SHAK 773:24
back and they stared b. GILL 370:78
at my b. in a cold blast ELIOT 318:3
B. and side go bare ANON 21:60
b. the masses GLAD 374:49
b. to nature GOTT 379:71
b. us or sack us CALL 193:30
b. with ingots bows SHAK 787:65
beast on my b. DOUG 295:5
behind his b. JOHN 462:22
coming b. seems possible DICK 284:55
Dost thou look b. TENN 874:82
down express in the small of the b. WODE 952:37
flying b. and forth PLATH 681:38
good coat upon his b. JOHN 461:59
hangs upon thy b. SHAK 766:12
I'll be b. SCHW 750:85
it will come drifting b. HAWES 401:74
Lead from the b. MAND 565:60
lean'd my b. unto an aik BALL 60:79
my b. I always hear MARV 577:91
never turned his b. BROW 169:85
not easy to call them b. SAND 742:27
sit on a man's b. TOLS 894:52
stab me in the b. LAMP 506:22
stabs you in the b. SNOW 832:79
they pull me b. PACI 658:6
thumps upon your b. COWP 251:3
wallet at his b. SHAK 787:37

bank

way their b. looks	WYETH 964:7	b. of lost innocence	PAINE 660:31	history of bat and b.	ARLO 32:31
Will ye no come b. again	NAIR 629:34	Red B. of Courage	CRANE 253:71	impell'd the flying b.	BYRON 186:23
backbone b. of the Army	KIPL 490:14	soldier wears a b.	READ 708:95	I worship the b.	PELE 672:76
backboned If…b. animals…disappear	ATTE 40:22	**badgers** When b. fight	CLARE 228:51	killer with the b.'	LARW 510:8
backgammon sport I mastered…b.	JERR 455:50	**badminton** art of b. is to deceive	THOM 885:67	one b. left!	JOHN 465:10
backhand make her hit b. volleys	KING 486:18	**bads** goods…jointly with b.	BOUL 152:90	Play b.!	RICE 713:91
wonderful b. drive	BETJ 88:21	**Baedeker** B. is astonishingly	LEVIN 525:29	real leather b.	UTTL 907:50
backlash b. against women's rights	FALU 329:12	never Mr B.	HERB 412:46	red b. of fire	AGAWA 9:92
finding of limited use to b. publicists	FALU 329:11	**baffled** b. to fight better	BROW 169:85	roll…up into one b.	MARV 577:94
backs b. to the wall	HAIG 392:15	**bag** agitate a b. of wind	WHITE 934:26	Ruddy B. has taken flight	THOM 886:86
on the b. of his friends	HUGH 435:18	in a b. all sorts of seeds	SPEN 839:61	secret of managing a b. club	STEN 847:7
when our b. are turned	CRISP 254:2	into a b. with holes	BIBLE 111:57	sight To such a tender b.	MILT 607:85
backshop reserve a b.	MONT 613:23	Tuppence a B.!	TRAV 896:95	silly little white b.	ZOEL 970:14
backside moral b.	LICH 528:85	upsetting of a b. of nails	RUSK 733:17	'Sphere of Influence'—the cricket b.	ANON 23:94
skelp across her b.	ANON 25:35	with nothing but a carpet b.	MELV 585:71	swing at the b.	DIMA 286:97
backward b. motion	FROST 352:7	**bagatelle** vive la b.!	STER 849:55	that portion of the b.	POPE 688:36
B. ran sentences	GIBBS 367:12	**bagel** after another like a b.	IGNA 445:17	took the b. in his arms	ANON 23:85
dark b. and abyss of time?	SHAK 803:10	**baggage** believe the b. loves me	CONG 240:24	watch…hirelings kick a b.	PRIE 695:84
fell from off the seat b.	BIBLE 96:29	**bagging** sagging, b. and dragging	PART 666:59	what to do with the b.	SHAN 805:63
too far b.	THUR 890:77	**bagpipe** Twelve Highlanders and a b.	ANON 28:53	wind it into a b.	BLAKE 141:32
when you look b.	ORWE 654:31	when the b. sings i'th' nose	SHAK 770:10	**ballad** love a b. in print	SHAK 800:27
backwards life must be understood b.	KIER 485:4	**bagpiper** laugh like parrots at a b.	SHAK 768:67	**ballads** b., songs and snatches	GILB 369:58
memory that only works b.	CARR 205:4	**bags** picking up my b.	NEVI 634:32	refrain of one of the most popular b.	MACA 544:8
rapidly b. and forwards	REED 709:27	thousand douche b.	LOWRY 541:42	**Ballinger** Mrs B. is one of the ladies	WHAR 934:10
backwoods b. of Canada	MOOD 615:54	**Bah** 'B.!' said Scrooge	DICK 279:3	**balloon** if the moon's a b.	CUMM 257:56
back-yard squabble in your b.-y.	SYNGE 865:24	**Baiae** in B.'s bay	SHEL 813:81	up like a b.	TRAV 896:91
backyards American b.	MAIL 560:58	**bairn** bonnie broukit b.!	MACD 549:18	**balloons** toes grow…as b.	THOM 884:41
Bacon dig up B.	GILB 370:75	**bairnie** Singin' till a b.	MACD 549:21	**ballpoint** How can a b. fight with a gun?	MUGA 623:8
Bacon their lordships asked B.	BENT 82:5	**bairnies** waefu' wife and b. three	BALL 59:64	**balls** elliptical billiard b.	GILB 370:67
think how B. shined	POPE 687:90	**bairns** when they werena gude b.	SCOTT 753:59	golden b. whirring through indigo	AVIS 47:1
bacon bring home the b.	ONEI 651:73	**bait** Roots ripe as old b.	ROET 722:58	hear the bump of the b.	JOYCE 470:19
bacon man who never ate b.	HATT 400:82	**baiting** b. a mouse-trap with cheese	SAKI 739:68	hustling over large b.	EDWA 312:56
bad almost a b., good-mother	SHAK 784:38	b. place of wit	SIDN 820:46	matched our rackets to these b.	SHAK 775:82
as b. as b. can be	JOHN 464:90	**baker** b. rhymes for his pursuit	BROW 169:82	moment the first b. are bowled	HOWE 433:88
b., and like to coins	TENN 878:77	B. Street irregulars	DOYLE 297:48	only three b. and no one watches it	DAVIS 266:4
b. book is as much	HUXL 441:63	**Bakewell** every fool in B. at Buxton	RUSK 734:19	thousand lost golf b.	ELIOT 319:32
b. die late	DEFOE 269:68	**Balaam** ass…said unto B.	BIBLE 94:83	Why, these b. bound	SHAK 791:62
b. guy with a gun	LAPI 508:59	**balance** b., an interchange	WORD 958:89	**balls-up** it was just a b.-u.	ORWE 653:28
b. guy with a nuke	PALIN 661:64	b. between the hands employed	STEU 849:60	**balm** b. from an anointed king	SHAK 764:47
B. laws are the worst sort of tyranny	BURKE 175:31	b. of actual forces	NAPO 629:40	b. in Gilead	BIBLE 110:18
b. poets deface	ELIOT 317:92	bodies out of their natural b.	LEON 522:70	b. of woe	SIDN 820:46
b.'s the best of us	FLET 341:55	causes, the b. sheet	MO 611:68	B. to fester'd wounds	MILT 607:88
b. unhappily	WILDE 941:4	ecological b. of the planet	SONT 834:16	b. upon the world	KEATS 476:99
because they are so b.	TROL 898:44	false b. is abomination	BIBLE 104:64	pity hath been b.	SHAK 760:16
believe a thing to be b.	MILN 596:27	held in b. only by the miracle	HONE 425:14	**balmy** Not with a b. hands his wounds	COLL 237:73
better than b. strokes	SHAK 778:51	hold the b. of Europe	WILL 944:67	**baloney** it's still b.	SMITH 828:93
bring them into b. repute	WILD 943:49	redress the b. of the Old	CANN 197:11	**Baltimore** B.…like dull diamonds	MAIL 560:54
but some b. man	HERB 414:81	sane b. of values	POUND 692:21	**bamboo** Learn about…a b. stalk	BASHO 67:49
can't be all b.	FIEL 335:35	scale…in nice b.	POPE 688:30	**ban** B. the Bomb	ANON 25:34
Don't vote for b. people	KARZ 474:33	the b. of power	PALM 662:74	**banana** b. republic	KEAT 475:56
everything b. that's printed	WELL 929:97	**balances** checks and b.	ANON 26:92	carve a better…party out of a b.	HITCH 420:90
good and b. of every land	BAIL 55:88	weighed in the b.	BIBLE 111:42	**bananas** eating b. for breakfast	WHAR 933:2
good Compensate b. in man	BROW 169:76	**balancing** b. an egg on a spoon	HILL 418:55	Yes, We Have No B.	DORG 294:36
good or they were b.	TRAV 896:93	b. seemed rather automatic	SPEN 837:9	**band** b. begins to play	KIPL 489:85
how b. you used to be	KNUD 495:21	**balconies** prams on concrete b.	BETJ 88:33	cassock, b., and hymn-book	WILB 939:33
How sad and b. and mad	BROW 169:67	**bald** b. as an egg	CHEE 218:10	go tell the b.	GERS 365:74
If we live inside a b. joke	RABAN 703:2	b. as the bare mountain tops	ARNO 36:44	humbler b. of duodecimos	CRAB 251:26
Mad, b., and dangerous to know	LAMB 504:75	brow is b.	BURNS 179:16	mighty folios…a lordly b.	CRAB 251:26
make b. good	SHAK 788:73	fierce and b.	SASS 745:84	**bandage** don't come to me for a b.	THAT 881:64
might also be very b.	HOCK 421:14	fight between two b. men	BORG 151:60	such an arm for a b.	SHER 817:81
never was…a b. peace	FRAN 348:16	Go up, thou b. head	BIBLE 97:73	**Bandersnatch** frumious B.	CARR 204:89
No man…irreclaimably b.	CARL 200:88	Slightly b.	ANON 24:15	**bands** b. of twelfth men	STOP 855:16
nothing either good or b.	SHAK 782:85	young, b. Leader of the Opposition	KINN 488:66	fantastic b.	CRAS 254:84
nothing b. or so good	SHAW 807:97	**baldness** b. full of grandeur	ARNO 36:44	strong as iron b.	LONG 535:17
not really b. at heart	BELL 77:63	far side of b.	SMITH 829:16	**bandy** not for me to b. civilities	JOHN 461:15
not that we are so b.	NIGH 639:21	Rich people spend…money on…b.	GATES 361:96	will b. with thee in faction	SHAK 780:17
obstinacy in b. one	STER 848:25	**bale** think upon my bitter b.	SPEN 838:26	**bane** Deserve the precious b.	MILT 602:53
only good if you can do b.	FORD 343:14	**bales** down with costly b.	TENN 871:17	**Banff** Mein B.	MCNE 558:10
people…not good or b. enough	COMP 239:2	**Balkans** B. export…history	LEACH 515:5	**bang** Not with a b. but a whimper	ELIOT 318:16
perhaps I was the least b.	SIHA 821:66	One of nature's B.	CURR 259:89	**banish** B. not him	SHAK 771:48
put up with b. things	TROL 897:27	some damned silly thing in the B.	BISM 137:36	I b. you	SHAK 799:98
strong antipathy of good to b.	POPE 688:26	**ball** after I have delivered the b.	BARR 65:93	**banished** b. from myself	PINT 678:84
sure it is b. morality	SKEL 825:34	as round as a b.	SPEKE 836:82	moral in it will be b.	TWAIN 902:50
that I have b. dreams	SHAK 782:86	b. made of Krazy Putty	LODGE 534:96	**bank** b. and shoal of time	SHAK 796:19
think something is good or b.	STEV 851:11	bowler and the b.	LANG 507:41	b. president finish the script	EPST 327:35
though it be from b. to worse	IRVI 447:61	chaperoning a b.	GILL 370:79	b. where the wild thyme blows	SHAK 767:30
was b., she was horrid	LONG 536:40	coming-out b.?	WHAR 934:12	beastly to the B. of England	CRIT 255:11
we're not doing too b.	DICK 277:33	cry Play B.!	NASH 631:83	cried all the way to the b.	LIBE 528:83
what is frankly b.	STEIN 845:73	Death's unerring b.	EGAN 313:65	easiest way to steal from a b.	KORT 498:1
what you feel b. after	HEMI 409:70	each b. a potential crisis	TREV 896:5	governor of the B. of England	KORDA 498:97
When b. men combine	BURKE 175:10	Every b. is…the first b.	BRAD 155:48	however you b. your screw	LARK 510:93
when I'm b. I'm better	WEST 933:86	Find out where the b. is	RANJ 706:61	lay on Huntlie b.	BALL 59:74
Where everything is b.	BRAD 155:42	Games played with the b.	JEFF 454:29	like a cheque drawn on a b.	POUND 691:13
world is b. enough	CLOU 232:51	Gave up his bat and b.	EGAN 313:65	moonlight sleeps upon this b.!	SHAK 770:18
baddish Gilbert had a b. streak	QUIL 702:15	girl throwing a b.	WOOLF 955:23	officials with too many b.accounts	DOSP 294:86
badge b. of all our tribe	SHAK 769:85	gown for a dancing-school b.	HUME 438:3	O waly, waly up the b.	BALL 60:79
b. of authority	HERB 414:90	history of a b.	WELL 929:71	pregnant b. swelled up	DONNE 292:41

banker — 1020

shelving b. of turf	SHEL	816:59
upon a b. of violets	SHAK	785:77
vice presidents a b. has?	ROGE	722:70
banker A 'sound' b., alas!	KEYN	484:75
B.' genes	THOM	885:69
become a central b.	GREE	386:34
Inside every b.	KORDA	498:97
bankers Bats have no b.	BERR	87:1
intellectual elite and world b.	ROCK	720:30
mercy of b. and tripe sellers	MENC	586:89
Bankhead Tallulah B. barged	BROWN	164:29
Tallulah B. on the stage	CAMP	194:49
bank-holiday jolly b.-h.	GILB	369:45
banking B. is a branch	WRIS	963:79
b. system grew by accident	WRIS	963:74
banknotes fill old bottles with b.	KEYN	484:80
bankrupt B. of life	DRYD	302:73
bankruptcy Capitalism without b.	BORM	151:62
banks b. and braes o' bonie Doon	BURNS	179:32
b. of every computer	GIBS	367:15
b. were conservative	THOM	885:69
bonnie b. o' Loch Lomond	ANON	22:79
burnis hurlis all their b. doun	DOUG	294:1
lifts me to my b.	DRYD	301:56
On the b. of Rubicon	MACN	558:3
on the bonnie b. o' Clyde	LAUD	511:16
shadowy b. on either side	WORD	954:71
so are b., so is cotton	DICK	279:2
banner b. over me was love	BIBLE	107:41
b. with a strange device	LONG	535:21
blazoned b. we unfold	RUSS	735:44
doth his b. rest	SURR	860:97
fight under his b.	BOOK	147:77
raising high the b. which reads	MERT	589:56
royal b., and all quality	SHAK	790:27
star-spangled b.	KEY	483:68
trails like a b. in defeat	JEFF	453:13
banners b. set high on the poops	ROBE	717:71
society inscribe on its b.	MARX	579:43
banquet b. of happiness	HUGO	437:63
Before we begin our b.	ROWL	729:23
words are a very fantastical b.	SHAK	774:36
banqueting me to the b. house	BIBLE	107:41
bantering this whole matter of b.	ISHI	447:73
Bapaume riddled corpses round B.	SASS	745:80
baptism Sadducees come to his b.	BIBLE	114:20
suffering may well be called a b.	ELIOT	315:25
Baptist who have preferred a B.	WELLS	930:27
baptized Jesus, when he was b.	BIBLE	114:21
bar Back of the b.	SERV	757:35
b. against your cruelty	LANY	508:56
b. association meetings	SUTH	860:7
b. himself in	BIRN	136:19
B. of the House	RUSH	732:17
gold b. of Heaven	ROSS	726:49
I have crossed the b.	TENN	879:6
prisoners at the b.	WILDE	939:44
sat at the cocktail b.	WAUGH	924:86
went to the B.	GILB	369:51
Barabbas B. was a publisher	CAMP	194:69
crowd will always save B.	COCT	233:86
barajar paciencia y b.	CERV	211:49
Barbadoes sell themselves to the B.	SWIFT	862:57
barbarian betwixt an erring b.	SHAK	789:4
He is a b.	SHAW	807:10
barbarians b. beyond the walls	WHITE	936:59
B., Philistines, and Populace	ARNO	36:26
excuse all…Irish b.	OROU	652:92
Fit only for b.	FULL	355:77
rockets used by the b.	KISH	493:83
without any b.	CAVA	210:16
young b. all at play	BYRON	188:66
barbaric b. yawp	WHIT	937:96
people which…becomes b.	ELIOT	319:28
barbarism to decadence	CLEM	230:89
b.…visited on the Irish	OROU	652:92
civilization against b.	ROOS	725:22
drift is always towards b.	REAG	709:16
pure return of b.	LEVI	525:26
wall…separates civilisation from b.	BUCH	171:22
barbarisms colloquial b.	JOHN	459:57
barbarities by the Irish	OROU	652:92
barbarity b. of tyrants	SMITH	830:46
barbarous b. feeling of nationality	SENI	757:30
b. traffic in slaves	PITT	679:10
Fashion is something b.	SANT	743:40
rank me with the b. multitudes	SHAK	769:94

barber b.'s man hath been seen	SHAK	774:45
imprudently married the b.	FOOTE	342:83
must to the b.'s	SHAK	767:40
Barca to B. flowers	POPE	688:31
Barchester table in B. Towers	BROY	169:89
bard the b. of his own existence	MCCA	547:77
voice of the B.!	BLAKE	140:8
Bardie certain B.'s rantin, drinkin	BURNS	177:84
bards last of all the B.	SCOTT	752:9
paint it, and as b. will not	CRAB	252:31
writers and the b.	FERG	333:87
bare art stripped b.	MOTH	622:85
B. like nude	SPEN	837:2
made b. his holy arm	BIBLE	109:91
so b. and full of wretchedness	SHAK	766:12
bareback rode the…hills b.	THOM	884:47
barefaced With b. power	SHAK	797:44
bargain Curse…science into the b.	COOK	245:66
Necessity never made a good b.	FRAN	348:10
never was a better b. driv'n	SIDN	820:40
Will anyone be satisfied with the b.?	COLL	237:65
bargain-basement b.-b. Boadicea	HEAL	404:65
bargains Queens never make b.	CARR	205:25
rule for b.	DICK	279:2
barge The b. she sat in	SHAK	794:55
barges b. as solemn as Barons	WALP	919:66
bark B. when their fellows do	SHAK	804:43
come out as I do, and b.	JOHN	464:84
heard a seal b.!	THUR	890:63
swell billow, and swim b.	SHAK	778:52
Barkis B. is willin'	DICK	280:40
barks in their b. my thoughts	SHAK	779:86
barley among the bearded b.	TENN	869:80
b. and of rye	TENN	869:77
Corn rigs, an' b. rigs	BURNS	178:90
fill his barn with wheat or b.	BUNY	174:84
taste the b. bree	BURNS	178:12
Barleycorn John B. should d.	BURNS	178:99
barley-sheaves between the b.-s.	TENN	869:83
Barlow my Hornby and my B.	THOM	886:84
barn fill his b. with wheat or barley	BUNY	174:84
men from the b. and the forge	HOUS	431:46
stack or the b. door	MILT	597:44
Barnet old B., the minister's man	HOGG	422:42
barns gathered into b.	TRUTH	900:5
barometer poet…used as a b.	TRIL	897:17
baronet lily-handed b. he	TENN	872:35
barons b. and their supporters	INNO	446:48
knights, and b. bold	MILT	597:47
barque Though his b. cannot be lost	SHAK	795:1
barrel buy ink by the b.	KIRK	493:81
dribble…like a leaky b.	ELIOT	315:23
out of the b. of a gun	MAO	568:29
barrel-load save them by the b.-l.	THOM	886:85
barrel-organ kind of human b.-o.	DICK	280:31
barren a b. bride	POPE	688:10
b. thing this Conservatism	DISR	287:27
Be she b.	SWIFT	863:76
breed for b. metal	SHAK	769:86
from Dan to Beersheba…'tis all b.	STER	849:52
make b. our lives	SWIN	864:94
small model of the b. earth	SHAK	764:51
Speech is often b.	ELIOT	315:41
Barrets didn't like about The B. of Wimpole	PARK	663:3
barricade some disputed b.	SEEG	755:99
barriers break down b.	GING	371:99
impenetrable b. of our prison	EDGE	311:41
barrows grassy b.	TENN	877:62
Barrymore B.'s acting till the cows	NATH	632:1
No B. would allow	BARR	65:1
bars b. a thousand harms	SHAK	761:57
b. of Madras, Oregon	SNYD	833:95
Between their silver b.!	FLEC	340:38
Bolts and b. will not	MOLI	611:74
half a dozen b. of Lillabullero	STER	848:27
look out through the same b.	LANG	507:43
Nor iron b. a cage	LOVE	538:82
no voluntary b.	PATM	669:21
Stare out between the b.	SACK	737:11
weary of these worldly b.	SHAK	776:14
bartender By the time a b. knows	MARQ	575:79
good drunk…a good b.	BISH	137:30
bartered People…must not be b.	WILS	949:86
base b. football player	SHAK	792:90
Joy without Labour is b.	RUSK	733:7
Majors at the B.	SASS	745:84
peace, be it never so b.	CROM	255:19

replaced it on its b.	NAPO	630:50
baseball B.…collective chess	BARZ	67:41
b.…free of chivalry	BROUN	163:20
B. has the great advantage	SHAW	810:27
B. is a Lockean game	NOVAK	641:64
better learn b.	BARZ	67:40
Cricket is b. on valium	WILL	944:75
things you can do in a b. game	STEN	847:8
unaware that b. was a Republican sport	ROBB	717:70
baseballs batting b.	THUR	890:84
baseness dignity or b. of a person	CHRI	223:46
basenesses b. are plainer to no eye	CARL	199:73
basest b. of all things	FAUL	331:35
bashfulness in England a particular b.	ADDI	7:17
Basil steal my B.-pot away	KEATS	477:13
sweet B. evermore	KEATS	477:12
basis laughter is the b. of humankind	RABE	703:8
on the b. of our splendid failure	FAUL	331:43
science has for its b.	PAINE	660:38
whole b.…of architecture	WAGN	915:2
basked b. him in the sun	SHAK	779:78
basket egg heads are in one b.	ANON	25:47
like wet crabs in a b.	DURR	308:35
lived to be carried in a b.	SHAK	773:12
set the b. umbilicus-high	NASH	631:85
basketball B., a game	NASH	631:86
I'm the black, b.-playing Nietzsche	ONEAL	650:57
interest in b.	NASH	631:83
bass sustained b. part	KIER	486:5
basset-horn melodious b.-h.	MORG	619:31
basset-hounds yellow-bosomed b	MORG	619:31
Bast got with child by Leonard B.	MANS	567:98
bastard all my eggs in one b.	PARK	664:25
Daddy, daddy, you b.	PLATH	681:35
knocked the b. off!	HILL	418:60
no matter how big a b.	SALI	740:79
publicly call me a b.	WHIT	937:83
bastards gods, stand up for b.!	SHAK	792:88
unless the b. have the courage	STEI	846:85
We are b. all	SHAK	803:94
bastinado or in b., or in steel	SHAK	780:17
bastion like a b.'s mole	SMART	826:65
bat batsman and the b.	LANG	507:41
b. that you were kind	MANN	567:92
b. with tears in your eyes	BRAD	155:45
black b., night	TENN	876:25
Bradman, with the b.	LARW	510:8
click of the b.	COOKE	245:75
come to see me b.	GRACE	380:84
Gave up his b. and ball	EGAN	313:65
history of b. and ball	ARLO	32:51
think he's going to b. on	JOHN	465:10
Twinkle, twinkle, little b.!	CARR	203:71
weak-eyed b.…flits by	COLL	238:76
bath b. by the beach	REID	710:45
B. twice a day	BURG	174:89
I need a b.	COWE	249:70
long to take a b.	UPDI	906:22
nymph to the b. addressed	SHEL	815:22
soaping her breasts in the b.	EWART	328:72
steamed like a b.	JONS	467:55
test my b. before	NASH	631:77
wrote…on his b. tub	POUND	692:27
bathes b. daily in a running	MOORE	615:58
bathing-caps two b.-c.	TRAV	895:88
bathroom as he goes to the b.	BLYT	144:86
revolutionary in a b.	LINK	530:29
baths B. that made him young	HERR	415:1
two walking b.	CRAS	254:81
bats archaeologists…like b.	MACA	544:18
b. have been broken	HOWE	433:88
B. have no bankers	BERR	87:1
covered with the skins of b.	DRAY	299:1
sad b. wheel about the steeple	DEBU	268:59
Suspicions…like b.	BACON	52:18
batsman B. of the Dawn	THOM	886:86
b.'s Willey	JOHN	465:9
b. thinks he's bowled	LANG	507:41
Cricket is a b.'s game	BENA	78:2
ghostly b. plays	THOM	886:84
premium on temperament for a b.	BRAD	155:46
batsmen sending your opening b.	HOWE	433:88
The really great b.	TRAV	895:86
battalions big b.	VOLT	914:45
dreams in pale b.	SORL	834:33
sorrows come…in b.	SHAK	784:51
batter put the b. off his stride	SHAW	811:29

batteries shot from one of the b. MACA 546:60
battery make no b. SHAK 762:86
batting W. G. discovered b. RANJ 706:60
battle army hurrying into b. ORWE 653:9
 b. against yourself KILLY 486:8
 B. decide everything CLAU 229:74
 b. for precedence SITW 824:12
 b. for the mind NOON 640:44
 b. for your all AESC 8:78
 B. Hymn of the Republic OBRI 646:71
 b. is not yours, but God's BIBLE 98:87
 b. of man with man WEBER 925:13
 b. of Waterloo WELL 929:13
 b. of Waterloo was won ORWE 654:35
 b....to break all this up WITT 951:20
 b. to the strong BIBLE 106:29
 b. to the strong DAVI 264:66
 B....untying with the teeth BIER 134:65
 Ben B. was a soldier bold HOOD 426:19
 better in b. than in bed STER 848:39
 borne the b. LINC 529:11
 brave that die in the b. CLOU 232:62
 drunk delight of b. TENN 870:98
 field of b. STEV 852:39
 fights no uphill b. HAZL 403:43
 forefront of the hottest b. BIBLE 96:44
 Goddess of the B. BARK 63:54
 half the b. GOLD 377:14
 history of a b. WELL 929:6
 invincible b. SOPH 834:29
 lines of b. wind MACG 551:71
 lit the b.'s wreck HEMA 409:58
 most serious things…in a b. CARR 205:2
 Next to a b. lost WELL 929:5
 noise of b. rolled TENN 878:80
 Old age isn't a b. ROTH 728:96
 on the field of b. PAST 668:5
 out of b. I escaped OWEN 657:32
 prepared for the b. HUSS 440:39
 See the front o' b. lour BURNS 180:47
 sent it into b. KENN 481:15
 sent it into b. MURR 627:83
 sent ten thousand men to b. SITT 823:93
 smelleth the b. afar off BIBLE 99:19
 strange manner of b. WILL 944:64
 strife is o'er, the b. done POTT 690:81
 This b. fares like SHAK 760:7
 trumpets which sing to b. SHEL 816:53
 Tweedledum…agreed to have a b. CARR 204:96
 we never won a b. DAVIS 266:8
 who shall prepare himself to the b.? BIBLE 126:53
battlefield b. of Vietnam MCLU 556:60
 brave on a b. MITC 610:43
 or the b. we die SULL 859:80
 soldier dying on the b. BISM 137:34
battle-flags b.-f. were furled TENN 871:17
battleground B. for a dark angel LENG 521:36
battlehorse painting…a b. DENIS 273:71
battles b. and death GARI 360:73
 b., heroic actions POUS 692:40
 b...were but desperate and vain appeals CHUR 225:77
 b...with the immortals HOMER 425:1
 Dead b. TUCH 901:10
 exercises are unbloody b. JOSE 469:10
 fought his b. BUNY 174:83
 hell her b. wage POPE 688:33
 in a hundred b. SUN 859:90
 mother of all b. HUSS 440:38
 not called to win b. JENK 454:32
 O God of b. SHAK 775:85
 pitched b. in India MACA 545:40
 quarrel and have b. MACM 556:74
 where be the b. SPEN 838:37
battleship like…launching a b. OSBO 655:84
battlewagon like a venerable b. TIME 891:18
bauble fool's b. CROM 256:23
 prettiest b. you ever saw WALP 919:66
Baudelaire B....Whoremongers ONEI 651:70
 Like Shelley and like B. ISHE 447:69
bauhaus From B. to Our House WOLFE 953:77
bawcock King's a b. SHAK 775:81
bawdry so without b. SHAK 800:24
Baxter In B.'s view WEBER 925:11
bay curve of a blue b. LOWE 539:1
 in Baiae's b. SHEL 813:81
 like a green b.-tree BOOK 149:13
 margin of a b. WORD 960:25

planted a green B.-tree BETH 87:10
Somebody bet on de b. FOST 345:53
Bayleys B., and your Bests MACA 544:20
bayonet b. is a weapon ANON 24:18
 force of the b.! MIRA 608:15
bayonets grass of silver b. MACG 551:71
 throne of b. INGE 445:26
BBC B. Radio is a never-never land SAFER 737:16
 B. 'set its house in order' CRIT 255:11
 the B....is very truthful ORWE 654:37
be can b. but What we are SHIR 819:18
 For what shall b.—yes! HAMM 394:53
 How can I b. who I am? JORD 468:99
 Must it be? It must be! BEET 74:3
 only thing I'd really like to b. SALI 740:81
 only way one can b. BECK 72:50
 or not to b. TWAIN 902:63
 thou shouldst cease to b. SHEL 812:59
 To b., or not to b. SHAK 782:7
 What is there to b. EMPS 326:11
 What we appear to b. SCHI 747:27
 what we may b. SHAK 784:49
 you should not b.? GRAV 382:20
beach Along the hidden b. KIPL 491:46
 dry shell on the b. DU 306:94
 marks of fishermen on the b. NAIP 629:28
 On the B. is a story GARD 360:68
 wood found on a b. ROSE 725:28
beaches fight on the b. CHUR 225:85
beach volleyball women playing b.-v. JOHN 459:99
Beachy Birmingham by way of B. Head CHES 221:94
beadle b. on boxin' day DICK 277:55
 Thou rascal b. SHAK 793:25
beadroll Fame's eternal b. SPEN 839:52
beads jewels for a set of b. SHAK 764:54
 number Ave-Maries on his b. SHAK 759:84
beak b. of preposterous widthlessness CUMM 257:48
 thy b. from out my heart POE 683:88
beaker b. full of the warm South KEATS 478:42
beaks kites to whet their b. RANS 707:69
beam b. that is in thine own eye? BIBLE 115:48
 B. us up, Mr Scott RODD 721:46
 eyes at the full midday b. MILT 601:20
beaming b. soul POPE 689:42
beams b. may not dissolve the ice SURR 860:4
 b. of science fall POPE 688:36
 little candle throws his b. SHAK 770:22
 splendour of his mid-day b. HERR 415:5
 way your smile just b. GERS 365:76
bean Boston...home of the b. BOSS 151:74
 Nine b.-rows YEATS 965:4
 stale b.-soup, of college yells MENC 587:17
beanbag b. of a heart NOON 640:45
beanfields smell of the b. CHAT 216:52
beans b. and peason put within ANON 20:40
 determined to know b. THOR 889:42
 hill of b. GARN 360:78
 hill of b. in this crazy world EPST 327:29
bear b. any burden KENN 481:3
 b. fruit—or wither JAY 453:2
 B. of Very Little Brain MILNE 596:17
 bush supposed a b.! SHAK 767:45
 every b. that ever there was BRAT 157:79
 Exit, pursued by a b. SHAK 799:14
 furry as a b. SITW 823:9
 Grizzly b. is huge HOUS 433:80
 hardest thing to b. JUVE 471:54
 If you b. your cross KEMP 480:81
 last b., shot drinking CRANE 253:60
 many things to say…ye cannot b. BIBLE 123:56
 more sorrow than they could b. REST 711:64
 out of the paw of the b. BIBLE 96:37
 Puritan hated b.-baiting MACA 546:59
 rode on the back of a b. LEAR 517:45
 tree could b. no more FROST 352:98
 Wedged B. in Great Tightness? MILNE 596:16
 Who can b. the Gracchi JUVE 471:53
beard b. the lion in his den SCOTT 752:23
 By thy long grey b. COLE 234:8
 Com'st thou to b. me SHAK 782:95
 endure a husband with a b. SHAK 773:23
 even Aaron's b. BIBLE 103:40
 hairs in the b. GOYA 380:82
 have a b. coming SHAK 767:22
 Loose his b., and hoary hair GRAY 385:81
 off the Great Cham's b. SHAK 774:28
 Old Man with a b. LEAR 516:27

send thee a b. SHAK 786:7
 singeing of the King of Spain's b. DRAKE 298:86
 To shave the b. is a sin IVAN 448:80
 without singeing someone's b. LICH 528:89
bearded b. like a man! DICK 284:54
beards b. forbid me to interpret SHAK 795:4
 their long b. SWIFT 862:53
bearing b. what is laid upon us ELIOT 315:33
bear-like But b.-l. I must fight SHAK 798:75
bears beat out tunes for b. FLAU 339:20
 habitation for b. and wolves SCHAW 747:20
 sympathise with the b. MUIR 624:27
 the English and the b. THOM 884:47
beast And what rough b. YEATS 966:25
 b. imbued with such immortal fire? BYRON 187:39
 b. on my back DOUG 295:5
 B. ravens in its own avidity? EBER 310:12
 Better B. and know your end DEVL 275:8
 Blatant b. SPEN 839:54
 call this b. to mind BELL 76:52
 chase had a b. in view DRYD 304:58
 Cocoa is a vulgar b. CHES 221:88
 deem himself a god, or b. POPE 687:80
 even-tempered the b. TRUD 899:71
 huge inarticulate b. HOFS 422:38
 I hold a b. THOM 883:12
 makes a man a b. WEBS 926:24
 making the b. with the two backs SHAK 788:85
 Man is neither angel nor b. PASC 667:88
 man who lay with a b. HELL 408:33
 marks of the b. HARDY 397:11
 night out for man or b. FIEL 335:30
 number of the b. BIBLE 132:11
 often acts the b. PASC 667:88
 snorts like a great b. SMITH 831:64
 Tam mounts his b. BURNS 179:26
 tilt their aggregate b. MACN 557:96
 Unto some brutish b. MARL 574:32
 who worship the b. BIBLE 132:12
 wild b., or a god BACON 52:12
beastie Wee, sleeket, cowrin…b. BURNS 177:77
beastly b. to the Bank of England CRIT 255:11
 B. to the Germans COWA 249:58
beasts all manner of fourfooted b. BIBLE 124:82
 Among the b. no mate MILT 605:42
 b. are our masters FLET 341:56
 b. of the intellectual domain HOLM 424:62
 b. on each other prey ROCH 719:13
 brute b. that have no understanding BOOK 148:85
 droop men and b. NASHE 632:94
 fled to brutish b. SHAK 777:39
 keeping b. of burden patient KING 488:54
 man's distinctive mark…not the b. BROW 169:64
 minds…to the b. that perish WELLS 930:19
 Music might tame…wild b. GAY 362:23
 Nature teaches b. SHAK 799:90
 round about the throne, were four b. BIBLE 131:96
 small and great b. BIBLE 102:13
 wild b. and Lord man MUIR 624:27
 wild b. ate it BAUD 68:64
beat b. Mr Turgenev HEMI 410:84
 b. my people to pieces BIBLE 107:52
 b. them now and gain THOM 884:26
 b. them today STARK 843:26
 bloody b. them again RAMS 706:53
 Don't b. me, pa! JOYCE 467:9
 figure to get b. some time LOUIS 538:77
 if we b. West Germany RAMS 706:52
 One man…can always b. ten SHAW 810:21
 this is really a b. generation KERO 483:56
 To the b. of the measure POUND 692:18
beaten No Englishman is…fairly b. SHAW 810:15
 The b. road SHEL 815:45
 You've b. them once RAMS 706:53
beatificate translate And b. QUIL 702:16
beating driven by b. ASCH 37:53
 hear the b. of his wings BRIG 159:13
beatings dread of b.! BETJ 89:48
Beatles band called the B. MCCA 548:5
 Chatterly ban And the B. LARK 509:88
Beatrice B. like a lapwing runs SHAK 774:41
beauteous B. the fleet SMART 826:66
 b. things for which CORY 247:11
 How b. mankind is! SHAK 804:33
beautied b. with impermanence SCOTT 751:1
 b. with plast'ring art SHAK 782:6
beauties b. of the fute-ball ANON 22:64

beautified

Entry	Reference
B....their pretty eyes may roll	POPE 685:42
concealed b. of a writer	ADDI 6:32
no matter what b. I saw	PRIOR 696:11
pale, unripened b.	ADDI 7:47
saved by b. not his own	POPE 688:34
Thy b., yet could write	JONS 468:85
beautified b.' is a vile phrase	SHAK 781:76
beautiful appear b. outward	BIBLE 118:28
art for the sake of...the b.	SAND 741:11
b. and death-struck year	HOUS 431:53
b. and frozen, I preserve you	ATWO 41:41
B. and terrible things will happen	BUEC 172:43
B. and the Damned	FITZ 337:77
b., and therefore to be wooed	SHAK 759:80
b. as a wreck	SHEL 816:47
B.! B.!	ALDR 12:55
b. countenance	BIBLE 96:35
B. dreamer	FOST 345:56
B. for situation	BIBLE 100:70
b. is always shocking	BAUD 68:74
b. only when she is loved	EPST 327:32
b. passionate body	SWIN 864:93
b. sentiments	GIDE 368:23
b., the tender, the kind	MILL 592:27
b. things made by renunciation?	DEGAS 269:85
b. woman...qualities of a gentleman	LABR 502:8
beginning of a b. friendship	WALL 918:63
better to be b. than to be good	WILDE 940:70
Black is b.	ANON 25:56
deal of scorn looks b.	SHAK 786:11
desired all b. things	CHES 220:76
feathers are more b.?	SHAK 762:75
football team is like a b. woman	WENG 931:50
For she was b.	SHEL 815:25
Fowey Is a b. spot	QUIL 702:11
grave hides all things b.	SHEL 814:11
ground is like a b. woman	SNOW 832:84
House B. is...lousy	PARK 663:4
How b. the Republic was	DURR 308:34
How b. upon the mountains	BIBLE 109:90
if they are to seem b.	SCHO 749:59
Life...is a b. thing	BURT 181:73
make anything b. or desirable	STOWE 856:28
more b. than death	WHIT 938:4
most b. sight in orbit	SCHW 750:93
most b. things on earth	ISAA 447:63
most b. works	FLAU 339:17
never have a mistress as b.	ARLT 32:35
only b. if it has good grass	BUTL 185:89
only hope of creating something b.	FLAU 339:22
pard-like Spirit, b. and swift	SHEL 815:36
perpetual hunger to be b.	RHYS 712:72
picture that is b.	FRAN 348:5
pleasure...because it is b.	POIN 683:98
saddest and most b. sight	DALG 261:11
science is very b.	OPPE 652:86
silence makes a woman b.	SOPH 834:24
small is b.	SCHU 750:73
The innocent and the b.	YEATS 966:29
things that are b.	DEBU 268:61
too b. to live	DICK 278:79
travel...to find the b.	EMER 324:65
two most b. words	JAMES 451:55
ugly things...frequently become b.	COCT 233:88
When a woman isn't b.	CHEK 218:18
worshipped because they are b.	RUSS 734:28
beauty absolute b.	HALD 392:25
abuse and destroy b.	PORT 690:74
ache of b.	UTTL 907:50
all that b....e'er gave	GRAY 384:66
And order, truth, and b. range	SMART 826:64
Art is not...a canon of b.	PICA 677:59
autumnal face, her pieced b.!	JONS 467:59
b., and gay clothes	WEBS 926:29
B. and the lust for learning	BEER 73:84
b. beat on his conceits	MARL 572:3
B....became money	WOLF 952:62
b. can lie...in days	FOWL 346:65
b. cold and austere	RUSS 734:20
b. depended most on poetry	SIDN 820:53
b. faded	PHIL 676:52
b. for ashes	BIBLE 110:6
b., for permanence	NUTT 642:75
b. from the light retir'd	WALL 918:56
b. has in art	DIDE 285:61
B. has only one form	HUGO 436:51
b. hath ensnared thee	SHAK 762:95
b. in the works of a great genius	ADDI 7:55
b. is a guarantee of happiness	PROU 698:50
b. is a joy for ever	KEATS 476:84
B. is all very well	SHAW 808:34
b. is as summer-fruits	BACON 52:26
B. is a witch	SHAK 773:26
b. is only sin deep	SAKI 739:50
B. is the first test	HARDY 396:97
B. is the lover's gift	CONG 241:63
B. is truth, truth b.	KEATS 478:40
b. is vain	BIBLE 105:8
b. like a tightened bow	YEATS 966:14
B....like the gold standard	WOLF 952:61
B. lives though lilies die	FLEC 340:31
b. made The bright world dim	SHEL 815:25
b. of creatures	AQUI 30:95
b. of holiness	BIBLE 102:3
b. of inflections	STEV 850:74
b. of its...shadow	WORD 962:51
b....of life	ALLEN 13:78
b. of marrow	SITW 823:4
b. of sense objects	AQUI 30:98
b. of speed	MARI 571:76
b. of speed	MARI 571:77
b....of the buildings we burnt	ELGIN 315:13
b. of their s.	TENN 872:33
b. of the morning	WORD 959:3
b. of the world	SHAK 782:89
b. of the world	WEIL 928:73
b. of thy mind	SHAK 801:60
B. pains	HAAS 391:1
B. provoketh thieves	SHAK 778:64
b.'s charming	SCOTT 754:64
B....should not be wasted	SHAK 762:82
b. so old and so new	AUGU 44:27
B.'s princely majesty	SHAK 759:79
b.'s self she is	ANON 22:67
b. than existed before	RUNGE 731:52
b., though injurious	MILT 608:96
B. too rich for use	SHAK 765:74
b. vanishes; b. passes	DELA 271:29
B., virtue, happiness	BERN 86:75
b. was rather for use	PRIOR 696:3
B. was their answer	BRID 158:10
befriended us with b.	CAVE 210:21
behold the b. of the Lord	BIBLE 100:50
best part of b.	BACON 52:28
cannot write of b.	BELL 76:46
carried into b.	WOOLF 955:22
day for b.	WORD 962:52
Death is a name for b.	LAYT 515:99
decay...of b.	CONG 241:58
dedicated to force and to b.	RIMB 716:51
desire of b....has most	PATER 668:11
divers schedules of my b.	SHAK 785:90
doth b. beauteous seem	SHAK 801:51
equal in b. to	KORN 498:99
Euclid alone Has looked on B.	MILL 592:26
fading b.	WALL 918:61
fatal gift of b.	BYRON 188:61
Fostered...by b.	WORD 958:75
ghosts of B. glide	POPE 688:15
Good architecture is...b.	HUXT 443:16
hardships into forms of b.	CAMP 194:56
her...unconventional b.	SCHL 747:37
Honesty coupled to b.	SHAK 779:99
If you get simple b.	BROW 167:28
images of female b.	WOLF 952:60
imagination seizes as b.	KEATS 475:73
In art economy is always b.	JAMES 451:52
in victory, there is no b.	LAO 508:62
I sat b. on my knees	RIMB 716:49
Is there in truth no b.?	HERB 413:72
judge the b. of life	LAUT 512:32
June for b.'s heightening	ARNO 35:17
Kindness is worth more than b.	ARRAS 37:50
Knowledge of ideal b.	BLAKE 141:37
lady of b. and high degree	RANS 706:66
Life, force and b.	POPE 685:18
light...From her own b.	SHEL 815:24
Look on b.	SHAK 770:4
loved your b.	YEATS 965:7
manhood's b.	WILDE 940:44
March with b.	SHAK 799:19
most radiant b.	EINS 313:80
nation...without a sense of b.	WHAR 933:2
no b. that we should desire him	BIBLE 109:93
not b. because it is not nature	CONS 244:57
On her b. I'll gaze	ROCH 720:22
pale court in b. and decay	SHEL 815:29
peace nor b.	LAWR 513:55
power of b.	SHAK 783:9
saw true b. till this night	SHAK 765:75
She walks in b.	BYRON 189:50
simple b. and rustic health	WHIT 938:19
since their b. passed	THOM 885:53
some sort of order (or b.)	POUND 692:31
soul of her b.	SHEL 815:22
Strength and b.	DEMO 272:49
Such seems your b. still	SHAK 802:74
the b. of the thing	GALL 358:44
There is only b.	MALL 562:93
things of b.	CRUZ 256:38
Tisn't b., so to speak	KIPL 492:51
trouble with b.	BASE 67:43
turns all things to b.	JOHN 456:75
unmask her b. to the moon	SHAK 781:47
unzips the veil from b.	WHITE 935:36
What is b.	MARL 572:2
What is b.	VIEI 913:7
where all is order and b.	BAUD 68:65
where B. was	GALS 358:50
whose b. is past change	HOPK 428:73
why talk of b.	CUMM 257:59
wildest b. in the world	OWEN 657:34
Wit is more necessary than b.	WYCH 964:2
world is richer for a new b.	MARI 571:76
write the b. of your eyes	SHAK 800:23
youth and a little b.	WEBS 927:53
Youth, b., graceful action	DRYD 302:85
Beaverbrook B....like the town tart	BAXT 69:92
papers conducted by...Lord B.	BALD 57:30
because B. it's there	MALL 562:4
Becher's deeper foreboding than...B.	FRAN 347:1
beck more offences at my b.	SHAK 783:11
become What's b. of me or you?	EMPS 326:11
bed A b., a b.	BALL 58:56
Ample make this B.	DICK 284:43
And so to b.	PEPYS 673:85
As to a lover's b.	SHAK 795:79
b. fell on my father	THUR 890:67
b. Of crimson joy	BLAKE 140:12
b. of daffodil sky	TENN 876:25
b....the cold, cold grave	BALL 58:58
B....the poor man's opera	HUXL 442:92
Best bloody place is bloody b.	BLAIR 138:48
better in battle than in b.	STER 848:39
bounced out of b.	MILNE 596:14
Chairman...lying on his death b.	MIN 608:7
comforts of the early morning b.	SHIP 818:44
Creep into thy narrow b.	ARNO 35:24
cry in my b.	AGUS 9:98
dark beside my b.	MACN 558:6
deck both b. and bower	SPEN 838:33
destroyed in b.	SKEL 825:45
die—in b.	SASS 745:85
early to b.	THUR 890:74
Early to b., early to rise	RODR 722:52
Every b. is narrow	MILL 592:21
get me to b.	SCOTT 754:83
go to b. by day	STEV 853:63
go to b. early	WAUGH 923:63
go to b. exhausted	ROTH 728:87
go to b. sober	FLET 341:54
haste me to my b.	SHAK 800:23
husbands lie snoring in b.	MORE 618:18
ideal companion in b.	DAVI 265:87
in b. with musicians	WILM 947:34
in love with my b.	SHAK 758:59
in my b. againe	ANON 21:59
lie diagonally in his b.	STER 848:43
lie down on my b.	HILL 418:64
lie o' both sides of the b.	DEKK 270:14
Lies in his b.	SHAK 768:57
Lying in b.	CHES 220:75
Lying in b.	WATE 922:35
lying in b. counting sheep	SIEG 820:60
lying in b., thinking	GINS 372:15
made his pedant b.	SHAK 796:18
make my b. in hell	BIBLE 103:24
manger for his b.	ALEX 13:63
mind is not a b.	AGATE 9:89
mostly sent to b.	LAND 507:31
mother, mother, mak my b.	BALL 58:50

Must we to b. indeed?	STEV 853:73
never...made my own b.	PU 700:3
not a b. of roses	STEV 852:39
not mount the marriage b.	JONS 467:62
now 'tis your b. time	DONNE 291:19
pillow on a b.	DONNE 292:41
preparing for b. with the shades up	STARR 843:27
rouse them from their lowly b.	GRAY 384:64
royal B. of Denmark	SHAK 781:65
sinners are still in b.	RUNY 732:62
sitting at the edge of a hotel b.	CHEE 218:8
spit-spot into b.	TRAV 895:87
stay in b. all day	BENC 78:7
still keeping open b.	HUXL 441:56
Strangle her in her b.	SHAK 790:32
sweat of an enseaméd b.	SHAK 784:42
take up thy b., and walk	BIBLE 122:30
this b.-presser	SHAK 771:47
under the b. for Communists	FOOT 342:80
wakes me from my flow'ry b.?	SHAK 767:35
Welcome to your gory b.	BURNS 180:47
When Harriet goes to b.	BROY 169:90
Who goes to b. with whom	SAYE 746:12
would 'twere b.-time	SHAK 771:58
you see that great b.	ONAS 650:51
bedchamber calls on my b. less	HILL 418:64
bedclothes little harm, save to his b.	SHAK 791:69
bedeck b. and bedrape us	SWIN 863:90
bedevilment Of man's b.	HOUS 432:68
bedfellows strange b.	SHAK 804:20
bedpan b. by a stranger	KUHN 500:36
bedrape bedeck and b. us	SWIN 863:90
bedrock the b. of this nation	OBAMA 643:23
bedroom b. in a Brussels hotel	THOM 886:79
doesn't matter what you do in the b.	CAMP 194:48
Lincoln's b.!	ONAS 650:51
spy in his b.	TOYN 895:79
trying on ties in his b.	CURT 259:98
what belongs in the b.	GOLD 377:30
bedrooms b. of the nation	TRUD 899:70
beds all snug in their b.	MOORE 616:61
hussies in your b.	SHAK 789:6
made the b., shopped for groceries	FRIE 350:64
Minds like b.	WILL 946:15
bedspreads b. according to rule	LEVE 525:25
bee as lightly as the B.	JONS 468:83
b. takes a middle course	BACON 50:44
b. with honied thigh	MILT 598:58
Pedigree...Does not concern the B.	DICK 284:51
sting like a b.	ALI 13:72
Where the b. sucks	SHAK 804:32
beech moss-grown b.	GRAY 383:56
warlike b.	SPEN 838:20
Beecham B.'s Pills are just the thing	BEEC 73:65
beef B. and a sea-coal fire	OTWAY 656:7
b., pork, and mutton	KIPL 492:66
great eater of b.	SHAK 785:83
roast b. of England	FIEL 335:19
beefsteak as English...as a b.	HAWT 402:18
beehive Fascist...b.	ORWE 653:20
been For what has b.—thanks!	HAMM 394:53
It might have b.!	WHIT 938:20
might have b.	HARTE 400:75
what hath b.	TENN 874:83
Where I have b.	GURN 390:99
beer B. and Britannia	SMITH 830:48
b. corrodes it	TWAIN 902:48
B., tobacco, and music	MANN 566:77
b. was strong	PRIOR 696:8
colour-bar and b.	NOON 641:51
embodied spirit of b.	BENN 81:77
ever taste b.?	DICK 279:94
faint stale smells of b.	ELIOT 317:71
felony to drink small b.	SHAK 759:95
Life isn't all b. and skittles	HUGH 436:46
muddy ecstasies of b.	CRAB 251:24
not all B. and Skittles	STEV 853:81
no wine or good b.	GORO 379:67
only b. teetotaller	SHAW 806:91
only here for the b.	LEVE 525:19
Pints and quarts of Ludlow b.	HOUS 432:58
teach the Irish to drink b.	EDGE 311:39
Beersheba from Dan to B.	STER 849:52
bees a grave injustice to b.	ORWE 653:20
angry hive of b.	SHAK 759:90
B. are sometimes drowned	HAWT 401:2
Books are the b.	LOWE 539:10
early b. are assaulting	REED 709:27
Forget not b. in winter	SACK 737:8
hive of silvery B.	LEAR 516:33
innumerable b.	TENN 873:52
Keep b.	WADD 915:1
these are the wrong sort of b.	MILNE 596:15
bees-winged b.-w. eyes?	BETJ 88:18
Beethoven as B. was born for music	PELE 672:75
B. always sounds	RUSK 733:17
B. came with music	NEVE 634:31
B.'s Fifth Symphony	FORS 344:25
difference between B. and Mahler	COPL 246:99
From you, B., Bach, Mozart	SASS 745:88
how much I appreciate B.	HEIF 407:12
Roll over B.	BERRY 87:94
beetle b. wheels his droning flight	GRAY 384:62
b. winds His small but sullen horn	COLL 238:76
into a large brown b.	KAIKO 472:12
poor b. that we tread	SHAK 788:66
beeves Let b. and home-bred kine	WORD 960:14
before B., behind, between, above, below	DONNE 291:20
B. Thee in humility	HAMM 394:55
beset me behind and b.	BIBLE 103:43
those things which are b.	BIBLE 116:76
beg b. in the streets	FRAN 347:89
should not b. in vain	JONS 468:83
beget if he touch he must b.	YEATS 967:42
Is there no way to b.	HERR 415:1
never to b.	HOPK 429:93
begetter proclaimed its b.	MEYER 589:87
beggar a b. before you	ORAH 652:91
b. begrudges b.	HESI 417:31
b. by banqueting upon borrowing	BIBLE 113:96
b. died, and was carried by the angels	BIBLE 121:97
b. is still a man	MORI 619:36
b. who suns himself	SMITH 827:74
black boundin' b.	KIPL 489:89
whiles I am a b.	SHAK 768:53
beggared B. by fools	DRYD 302:84
beggars b....too professional air	MCCA 547:87
exercises authority over b.	MORE 618:16
pays us poor b. in red	KIPL 490:92
tiresome Serbia b. belief	MARY 579:46
When b. die	SHAK 777:20
beggar-woman b.-w. and single	ELIZ 321:98
beggary b. in the love	SHAK 794:43
Contempt and b. hangs	SHAK 766:12
begging nor his seed b. bread	BIBLE 100:60
begin B. at the beginning	CARR 204:85
b. from the subjective	SART 744:71
b. to dress ourselves	RICH 713:3
But let us b.	KENN 481:2
time to b. a new	DRYD 304:58
To b. at the beginning	THOM 884:31
worst of all is to b.	BART 66:16
beginner man ceases to be a b.	COLL 237:60
mere b.	HUGH 434:6
beginning as he was at the b.	HICKS 417:47
As it was in the b.	BOOK 146:35
As it was in the b.	RHYS 712:76
b., a middle, and an end	ARIS 31:24
b., a muddle, and an end	LARK 510:97
b. and end of art	HEIN 407:19
b. is assuredly the end	WILL 946:14
b. is often the end	ELIOT 321:92
b. of everything	REAG 708:7
b.' of feminism	ROWB 729:18
b. of the end	TALL 866:17
b. of wisdom	BIBLE 102:19
coming our b.	MUIR 624:22
each venture...a new b.	ELIOT 320:66
end of the b.	CHUR 226:95
end precedes the b.	ELIOT 319:44
from the b. think	WHYM 939:26
In my b. is my end	ELIOT 320:56
In the b. God created	BIBLE 90:80
In the b. was the Word	BIBLE 122:15
In the b. was the Word	ELIOT 317:79
more accurate in the b.	JONS 468:96
most important...is the b.	PLATO 681:46
my end is my b.	MARY 579:47
Never ending, still b.	DRYD 303:33
pleasure can be the b. of beauty	PROU 698:50
sort of a bad b.	DICK 277:33
urge in the b.	SAND 742:35
voted to make a new b.	CLIN 230:1
beginningless b., endless, topless, bottomless	RUSK 733:18
beginnings b. of ataxia	SILVA 821:70
ends by our b. know	DENH 272:63
mighty things from small b.	DRYD 299:15
begins Fashion constantly b. and ends	HAZL 403:35
where...the Church of England b.	PRIE 695:93
begot b. in fear	GRAV 382:20
when they b. me	STER 847:20
begotten B., not made	BOOK 147:61
beguiled B. again	HART 400:68
thou art b.	SKEL 824:30
Behan My name is B.	BEHAN 74:10
behave b. in excess except	LACL 503:32
b. like a child	BERCO 83:11
How well I did b.	HOUS 431:39
must b. accordingly	KISS 493:87
things they b. sensibly about?	SHAW 806:88
behaving better b. themselves	SZASZ 865:27
expedient in the way of our b.	JAMES 451:76
behaviour abdication...Makes the B.	DICK 284:49
certain kinds of b.	ROBB 717:68
constitutes unacceptable b.	LEBO 517:56
decency and discretion in their b.	BACON 49:22
evoking a new b.	MERT 589:54
Fearful and hostile b.	FULB 355:63
guided my b.	MACL 554:25
in-office attitudes and b.	COUP 248:28
knowing...their b. very well	THOM 884:26
man's b. may be quite harmless	SHAW 809:82
my b. full of rigor	BROW 164:43
Puritanism names the b.	SPEN 837:10
quality of moral b.	HUXL 442:84
social b. displays many features	HOMA 425:92
watch their b.	WELD 928:87
Whatever his private b.	MEYER 589:63
behaviourism Of course, B. 'works'	AUDEN 44:19
beheaded imprisoned...b. others	STAL 842:4
one of our kings who was b.	APPL 30:65
to see the King b.	PEPYS 673:87
behemoth Behold now b.	BIBLE 99:20
Black Mrs B.	SITW 823:3
behind b. your scenes	JOHN 459:51
beset me b. and before	BIBLE 103:43
it will b. me	REGER 710:43
no bosom and no b.	SMITH 830:34
one must ride b.	SHAK 774:50
turn thee b. me	BIBLE 97:76
behold B. and see	SHAK 794:42
beholder cheer to its b.	ROCK 720:31
impossible that any b.	SIDN 820:57
beholders awe into the b.	SWIFT 862:42
beige B.! Just my color	DE 276:21
Beijing every road to B.	CLIN 231:24
being A b. darkly wise	POPE 687:80
at the edge of B.	SPEN 837:97
b. absolutely infinite	SPIN 841:83
b. always with myself	GIRO 373:28
b. and as an angel	MUIR 624:28
B. and Ideal Grace	BROW 166:97
b. and our birth	SHAK 798:83
B. is the great explainer	THOR 888:15
b. is to be perceived	BERK 84:30
b. who...need not even exist	BAUD 69:79
breath of Autumn's b.	SHEL 813:79
by avoiding b.	TILL 891:13
chain of b.	EMER 324:66
concerns thee and thy b.	MILT 605:36
creation, development and b.	HUMB 438:93
how such a b. could exist	ANDR 18:76
intellectual b.	MILT 602:59
live, and move and have our b.	BIBLE 125:93
man is the b. who wills	SCHI 747:25
mighty b. is awake	WORD 959:96
most prostituted b.	BAUD 69:87
part of our very b.	GAND 359:60
persist in its own b.	SPIN 840:95
pleasing anxious b.	GRAY 384:74
poem...once it is in b.	FROST 353:13
preserve one's b.	SPIN 840:78
presuppose a Supreme B.	DOUG 295:22
reason for b.	FRAN 347:84
sensitive b., a creative soul	WORD 958:88
that is the essence of our b.	BUSH 184:51
They had their b. once	PURDY 700:87
Unbearable Lightness of B.	KUND 500:38
very bottom of her b.	ADAMS 4:80

beings

wheels of B. slow	TENN 874:74	
beings b. brighter than have been	BYRON 189:82	
b. which are impossible	REDON 709:23	
evidence of supernatural b.	STEI 846:99	
in his stomach more animated b.	SMITH 830:50	
other b. in the zoological scale	CARB 198:36	
three respectable b.	BAUD 69:86	
Beirut If you liked B.	HEMP 410:98	
beleaguered sense of being b.	RABAN 703:1	
Belgium B. recovers in full measure	ASQU 38:84	
B.'s capital had gathered	BYRON 187:50	
Belial B. with words clothed	MILT 602:60	
forth the sons of B.	MILT 602:47	
belief abandoned a b. in God	STEV 850:93	
abdication of B.	DICK 284:49	
any unwarrantable b.	RICH 714:15	
assert my b. that	ROOS 724:6	
authority of a b.	KRIS 499:12	
b. and hope had gone	RUSS 735:42	
B. consists in affirming	EMER 324:74	
b....founded upon my experience	DOYLE 297:59	
b. in...human beings	ORWE 653:24	
b. in luck	OATES 643:6	
b. in their sincerity	TWAIN 902:33	
b. is for it	JOHN 463:57	
b. is made religious	CUPI 258:85	
b. of truth	BACON 50:56	
b. that we can start	POPP 689:58	
b. which may be right	FORS 344:26	
commit...to any religious b.	WAUGH 923:64	
decline of religious b.	FREUD 350:61	
do not believe in B.	FORS 345:45	
epoch of b.	DICK 282:94	
Faith...an illogical b.	MENC 586:87	
firm b. in the justice of our cause	WASH 921:26	
firm b. that everybody could write	BAIN 55:90	
first expounder of our religious b.	SPEKE 836:81	
impress the people...with a b.	PEEL 672:67	
inherited this b.	MILL 593:34	
last, best b. system	WOLF 952:61	
leading to the b.	KAUF 474:41	
lose b. in this truth	DU 305:69	
My b. is that in life	TROL 897:33	
national b.	MCCA 547:89	
proportions his b. to the evidence	HUME 438:6	
prospect of b.	SHAK 796:6	
Rome...trades on b.	BURG 174:90	
tiresome Serbia beggars b.	MARY 579:46	
beliefs All known religious b.	DURK 308:30	
b., traditions and aspirations	DURK 308:31	
b....we hold sacred	ARON 36:48	
different people, different b.	CART 206:45	
discuss your b.	HELL 408:40	
Home of...forsaken b.	ARNO 35:12	
reverse important basic b.	MILL 593:38	
someone's mistaken b.	ELLI 323:36	
strong b. wounded	BROO 163:9	
two contradictory b.	ORWE 655:76	
believe b. also in me	BIBLE 123:51	
b. and rejoice in Christ	LUTH 542:70	
b., because they so were bred	DRYD 303:16	
B. false teachers	SHAK 803:98	
b. in ideas and die for them	ANOU 28:63	
b. of my own stories	IRVI 447:60	
B. one who has experienced it.	VIRG 913:21	
b. what we choose	NEWM 635:45	
cease to b.	HAMM 394:54	
devils also b.	BIBLE 130:53	
don't b. in preachers	BENE 79:13	
Except I shall see...I will not b.	BIBLE 124:67	
few will consent to b.	KENN 480:86	
For those who b. in God	SEAT 755:93	
fun to b. them	BACH 49:14	
I b. in an A. where	ROMN 724:96	
If you b. that	WELL 927:67	
If you don't b. it	AUGU 44:34	
live by what they b.	HAMP 395:74	
mix what they b.	UPDI 905:13	
Never b. again	SKEL 825:37	
never b. again	TOML 894:57	
those who b.	WALK 917:40	
Those who b. that they are	HUXL 441:60	
what we ourselves b.	GRANT 381:1	
willing to b. what they wish	CAES 192:12	
believer b. will fight another	GREE 386:27	
In a b.'s ear!	NEWT 636:65	
make the b.'s leap	RABAN 703:4	
believers objectionable types of b.	BORN 151:64	
believes one b., then miracles occur	MILL 594:76	
One sort of b. in recycling	WELD 928:90	
thinks he b. only what he sees	SANT 743:44	
what an Englishman b.	SHAW 810:16	
What your government b.	KENN 482:32	
believing B. is Seeing	WOLFE 953:74	
better at b. than at seeing	SANT 743:44	
eating that's b.	THUR 891:92	
pleasure of b. what we see	SHEL 812:60	
torture them, into b.	NEWM 634:44	
We are born b.	EMER 325:88	
Belinda B. smiled, and all the world	POPE 685:34	
belittlement all our injured b.	RABAN 703:1	
belittling not b. the brave pioneer men	FERB 332:46	
bell B., book, and candle	SHAK 768:56	
b. rings and the widow weeps	SHAK 774:57	
b.-rope that gathers God	CRANE 253:70	
binkledy-winkled a b.	LEAR 516:40	
double and the single b.	SLES 825:52	
for whom the b. is tolling	NASH 631:68	
for whom the b. tolls	DONNE 293:69	
God's b. buoyed	YEATS 965:8	
hear the surly sullen b.	SHAK 801:61	
lifted, rough-tongued b.	LARK 509:73	
like b.-bottoms and W. C. Fields	HAWES 401:86	
silver-voiced b.-birds	KEND 480:85	
tangles Of b.-flowers	SITW 823:1	
The b. invites me	SHAK 796:29	
Time and the b.	ELIOT 319:42	
tolling b. Measures time	ELIOT 320:72	
Twilight and evening b.	TENN 879:6	
word is like a b.	KEATS 478:48	
Bellamy one of B.'s veal pies	PITT 680:15	
belle my time, my b. époque	HOLL 423:52	
young b. of old Natchez	NASH 631:68	
bellicose querulous and b.	MENC 586:84	
bellies evil beasts, slow b.	BIBLE 129:31	
studious for their b.	SAND 743:39	
belligerent looked so b.	KARSH 473:32	
belligerents Police...separate the b.	EDEN 311:31	
bellman B. would cry:	CARR 205:29	
bellows flatt'ry is the b.	SHAK 798:81	
bells beaten b.	STEV 854:90	
b. I hear	WHIT 938:7	
B. in your parlours	SHAK 789:6	
b. off San Salvador	CRANE 252:54	
b. of Shandon	MAHO 559:35	
B., the poor man's only music	COLE 235:24	
b. they sound so clear	HOUS 431:43	
church b. hollowing out	BETJ 89:46	
floating many b. down	CUMM 258:69	
lin-lan-lone of evening b.	TENN 879:7	
mortals who ring b.	MANN 566:82	
name is like a ring of b.	BETJ 88:31	
none of your ribbons and b.	MARQ 575:51	
Oh, noisy b., be dumb	HOUS 431:45	
passing-b. for these who die	OWEN 657:25	
Ring out, wild b.	TENN 875:95	
ring the b. of heaven	HODG 421:23	
ring their b.	WALP 919:82	
sleigh b. in the snow	BERL 84:41	
tall building, with a tower and b.	CRAB 252:38	
belly b....send thee good ale	ANON 21:60	
b. was bitter	BIBLE 131:8	
bitter b.-tension	GIBB 361:7	
does not mind his b.	JOHN 461:4	
everything, except this perpetual B.	EMER 325:77	
filled his b. with the husks	BIBLE 121:90	
Gun Fired in the Pope's B.	ANON 23:96	
No b. and no bowels	RANS 707:73	
pour...by the b. full	SPEN 839:50	
upon thy b. thou shalt go	BIBLE 91:96	
whose God is their b.	BIBLE 128:3	
belong b. to Britain	GERA 364:61	
Go where you b.	TROT 899:61	
really b.	GREE 386:8	
To betray, you must first b.	PHIL 676:50	
belonging greatest sense of b.	ROTH 727:76	
belongings b. of others	SALL 740:92	
b. on show	JOYCE 470:32	
beloved b. is mine, and I am his	BIBLE 107:44	
Cry, the B. Country	PATON 669:27	
Dearly b., we are gathered together	BOOK 148:84	
more b. for the imperfections	RUSK 733:87	
the kiss to one's b.	ONEI 651:63	
below either above or b. it	GILL 370:83	
He lies b.	PARK 664:16	
belt could not see a b.	ASQU 38:89	
belted Though I've b. you	KIPL 490:91	
Ben bare B. Bulben's head	YEATS 967:40	
B. Hur translated into Irish	STEW 854:95	
bench designed a b. in a few moments	BELL 76:49	
fluttering to a b.	SACK 737:9	
murd'rous hand a drowsy b. protect	CRAB 252:34	
benches though we cropen under b.?	LANG 507:46	
bend b. but do not break	LAFO 503:51	
b. to the wind	BUCK 172:37	
right on round the b.	LAUD 511:17	
bending nations now b. under...tyranny	PITT 680:12	
beneath B. is spread like a green sea	SHEL 812:64	
B. the visiting moon	SHAK 795:84	
see b. both beauty and ugliness	ELIOT 319:30	
Benedick B. Nobody marks you.	SHAK 773:19	
benedicte B., omnia opera Domini	BIBLE 133:41	
benediction clouds in b.	DAY 267:36	
beneficial harmless and even b.	SHAW 809:82	
Jogging is very b.	SCHU 749:72	
benefit familiar one of social b.	HUGH 435:28	
owes a return for the b.	MILL 591:2	
what b. to the soul	HONO 426:17	
without the b. o' the Clergy	CONG 240:41	
benefits disable all the b.	SHAK 779:8	
so many people...for material b.	COLU 238:91	
Who b.?	CICE 227:31	
benefitted b. from prolonged warfare	SUN 859:89	
I have b. greatly from criticism	RUMS 731:47	
benevolence b. of the butcher	SMITH 827:76	
benevolent what is inexhaustible is b.	FRYE 354:57	
Bengal tiger of b. crouches	MELV 585:67	
benighted b. masses	QUINE 702:22	
must be b. and superstitious	JAMES 452:77	
benign under the b. sky	BRON 162:82	
benison b. of hot water	BROO 162:87	
Benlomond o'er the lofty B.	TANN 867:24	
bent b. the arc of the moral universe	OBAMA 645:50	
Still b. to make some port	ARNO 34:80	
those with an academic b.	MAMET 564:36	
Bentham B. held no post	MENC 586:89	
benumbed faculties of the mind are b.	BROO 162:83	
bequeathèd B. down from many	SHAK 791:66	
bereft b. me of all words	SHAK 770:7	
berhymed never so b.	SHAK 779:91	
Berkeley fell to earth in B. Square	HAMER 393:44	
Berlin Be off with your Irving B.!	GERS 365:74	
B. by Christmas	ANON 24:7	
Isherwood...find himself in B.	BURU 182:90	
Let them come to B.!	KENN 481:24	
New Frontier was closed by B.	MCGO 552:87	
soldiers drilling in B.	MORI 619:36	
Berliner Ich bin ein B.	KENN 481:24	
Berlitz glibness of the B.-school	FIRB 336:56	
Berlusconi B. is unfit to lead Italy	ECON 310:23	
Bermudas swim to the B.	WEBS 927:49	
Bernard B....was rather pious	ASHF 37:71	
Bernhardt admired most...Sarah B.	WILDE 942:31	
berries b. harsh and crude	MILT 599:82	
berry God could have made a better b.	BUTL 186:13	
berserk Sex suppressed will go b.	EWART 328:73	
beryl colour of a b.	BIBLE 110:28	
beseech b. thee, shew me thy glory	BIBLE 94:74	
humbly do b. you	SHAK 789:21	
beside Paul, thou art b. thyself	BIBLE 125:99	
besieging who are b. Orleans	JOAN 455:59	
best All is for the b.	VOLT 914:33	
Always to be b.	HOMER 425:3	
b. actors in the world	SHAK 782:94	
b. and the worst of this	SWIN 864:3	
b. cannot be expected	JOHN 464:96	
b. ends by the b. means	HUTC 441:48	
b. is like the worst	KIPL 489:83	
b. is yet to be	BROW 168:59	
b. lack all conviction	YEATS 966:24	
b. married that dies married young	SHAK 766:10	
b. minds in the world	ACHE 3:52	
b. of all possible worlds	CABE 191:6	
b. of all things	HUXL 443:12	
b. of the rich	SPARK 836:71	
b. that an American	KENN 480:86	
b. that has been known	ARNO 36:32	
b. that is known	ARNO 35:13	
B. thing in eird	HENR 411:20	
b. thing to be up and go	EMPS 326:10	
b....to do what the mob do	DICK 277:49	

bird

B., to forget!		BROW 169:83
Competition brings out the b.		SARN 743:56
doing our b. to re-establish peace		ELIZ 322:10
do our b. to reward your faith		SMITH 829:10
do the b. you can		OBRI 646:68
Drinking the b. tea		SNOW 832:74
English are b.!		FLAN 338:11
He is doing his b.		WILDE 940:48
hope for the b.		SMITH 830:52
It is b. to live		SOPH 834:32
last b. friend		SOUT 835:56
learn, at b. and worst		RABAN 703:2
mediocrity…always at its b.		BEER 74:96
most of everything and the b. of nothing		CHAN 213:85
Mother Knows B.		FERB 332:65
My God must have my b.		HERB 414:84
Never to have lived is b.		YEATS 966:28
one of the very b. means		HUXL 443:11
people are at their b.		GRAY 383:41
record of the b….moments		SHEL 816:52
said against the b.		MILL 592:11
serves his party b.		HAYES 403:28
That action is b.		HUTC 441:49
The b….enemy of the good		VOLT 914:42
The b. is the b.		QUIL 702:12
the b. moment of all		BUSH 183:39
the b. that's possible		BRAND 156:63
the b. words in the b. order		COLE 236:48
very b. and the very worst		FORD 343:91
We do our b.		DENCH 272:53
What America does b.		FUEN 354:60
Why not the b.?		CART 206:43
bestial what remains is b.		SHAK 789:11
bestride b. the narrow world		SHAK 776:9
bestseller b. is the gilded tomb		SMITH 829:23
best-sellers in all of the great b.-s.		PRIT 669:14
bet b. you, Ziggie, a hundred bucks		DILL 286:94
if I would b. with other people		ROCH 719:4
important matter as a b.		VERNE 911:62
beteem b. the winds of heaven		SHAK 780:39
Bethel O God of B.!		DODD 289:91
Bethlehem But thou, B.		BIBLE 111:55
Christ is born in B.		CASW 208:83
Let us now go even unto B.		BIBLE 120:69
Slouches towards B.		YEATS 966:25
when Jesus was born in B.		BIBLE 114:16
betide God's peace b. the souls		RANS 707:72
betray b. them both		WALC 916:9
cruel brother will you b.		BALL 58:59
finds too late that men b.		GOLD 376:93
savage man alone does man b.		ROCH 719:13
To b., you must first belong		PHIL 676:50
betrayal defence against b.		WILL 945:87
betrayed Betrothed, betrayer, and b.!		SCOTT 754:74
but by ourselves, b.		CONG 240:25
by luxury b.		GOLD 376:5
democratic people b.		ATTL 40:25
those that are b.		SHAK 803:99
betrayer Betrothed, b., and betrayed!		SCOTT 754:74
betraying b. my country and b. my friend		FORS 345:46
betrothed B., betrayer, and betrayed!		SCOTT 754:74
better B. a witty fool		SHAK 785:86
b. future and a brighter day		SMUTS 831:70
B. if he had said		HILL 418:61
b. man than I am		KIPL 490:91
b. than bad strokes		SHAK 778:51
b. than light		HASK 400:81
b. that some should		JOHN 463:50
b. to dwell in a corner		BIBLE 105:88
B. to use force		SHUL 819:26
b. world than this		SHAK 778:61
change for the b.		STEI 846:88
don't know any b.		KENN 480:90
Every day…I am getting b.		COUE 248:21
far b. without the others		SIEY 820:62
for b. for worse		BOOK 148:91
from worse to b.		JOHN 460:66
give place to b.		SHAK 778:47
He is no b.		AUST 47:96
I see the b. things		OVID 657:19
kiss you take is b.		SHAK 787:42
Love…unsought, is b.		SHAK 786:12
no b. than you should be		BEAU 71:23
no b. than you should be		THOM 884:34
not sure I was much b.		SIHA 821:66
took thee for thy b.		SHAK 784:39
way to the B. there be		HARDY 397:24

We are b. than…cynicism		WINF 950:97
When you meet someone b.		CONF 240:18
would be b. than nothing		KEYN 484:80
betters lord it…above their b.		OTWAY 656:2
between try to get b. them		STRA 857:42
Bevan nurses and Nye B.		HALD 392:26
beverage revolting b. in itself		STEV 851:29
beware all should cry, B.! B.!		COLE 236:42
B. of anything that promises		SNYD 833:94
B. Of entrance to a quarrel		SHAK 781:50
B. of men		SPARK 836:75
B. of over-great pleasure		FULL 355:65
B. of quotations in Latin		FLAU 339:29
B. of the man		SHAW 808:44
B. of the man		SHAW 808:57
B. of those who are homeless		SOUT 835:53
B. the ides of March		SHAK 776:5
O. b., my lord		SHAK 789:19
bewildered b. like an old lady		ACHE 3:44
by the unprincipled to the utterly b.		CAPP 197:32
without finally getting b.		HAWT 402:6
bewilderment sense of b. and terror		LEE 519:96
wandering in delighted b.		OFAO 647:96
bewitch Do more b. me		HERR 416:17
bewitched b., bothered…am I		HART 400:68
b. for ever		SACK 737:10
b. with some ill charms		WALL 918:58
b. with the rogue's company		SHAK 771:39
bewitching his wine's sae b.!		BURNS 180:61
bewitchment battle against the b.		WITT 951:24
bewrayed man by nothing is so well b.		SPEN 839:58
beyond b. the range of language		REID 710:44
He hath been b.-sea		JONS 466:44
is there anything b.?		BROO 163:99
stands b., behind, and within		WHIT 936:65
bias History must not be written with b.		BETJ 88:34
biases bundle of b.		BALL 60:88
Bible B. as…a constable's handbook		KING 488:54
B. said that nothing was permanent		FRAME 346:78
cursing the bloody b.		HEMI 409:63
do you ever read the B.?		CHAN 213:83
He knows…his B.		ARNO 36:31
Jacobean…who translated the B.		ACHE 2:28
knowledge of the B., Shakespeare		WAUGH 924:98
li'ble To read in the B.		HEYW 417:41
quotations from the B.		LAWR 513:74
quotations from the B., Browning		MCFA 551:68
that book is the B.		ARNO 35:9
Those who talk of the B.		ELIOT 319:35
bible-black starless and b.-b.		THOM 884:31
bibliobuli b….drunk on books		MENC 586:4
bicycle as common use as the b.		ANON 23:1
b. and an atlas		MURP 626:73
fish needs a b.		STEI 846:91
incapable of choosing a b.		STEIN 845:77
journeys were made by b.		JOHN 457:98
knocked him off his b.		LEE 519:97
rain on my b.		LEE 519:98
bid do as you're b.		EDGE 311:40
Bidford Drunken B.		ANON 24:32
bifocals rest of the world wears b.		GOLD 375:82
big b. one holds its tryouts		HEBB 406:97
boxer never sees the b. one		FORE 344:18
Canadian…isn't thinking b.		RICH 714:26
houses just as b.		SMITH 829:20
I like thinking b.		TRUMP 900:95
Motels can be b.		HEAT 406:95
never use a b., b. D—		GILB 368:32
big-bug good deal of a b.-b.		TWAIN 902:53
bigger The b. the organization		JAY 453:3
bigging mind the b. o't		SCOTT 753:48
Bighead Bessie B., hired help		THOM 884:35
bigotry B. may be roughly defined		CHES 220:63
Big Three the B. T. right now		LENO 522:57
bike back on my b.		SIMP 822:87
got on his b.		TEBB 869:63
on my b.		ARMS 32:44
On yer b.!		ANON 26:82
bike lanes compare b. l. to…swimming with the sharks		FORD 344:16
bikini Yellow Polkadot B.		VANCE 908:11
bilbo B.'s the word		CONG 240:26
bile b. was blak		CHAU 217:98
bilingual pro athletes are b.		HOWE 433:90
bilious the ecstatic and the b.		ELIOT 315:17
bilk ought never to b. his part		HAZL 403:31
bill B. for the future government		CHUR 224:65

b. of fare		SWIFT 861:30
b. of rights		JEFF 454:23
B. of Rites, A B. of Death…like a gas b.		MORR 620:53
		BURG 174:95
one more to the plaguey b.?		DONNE 291:28
receipt, not a b.		SCHN 748:42
to pay the b.		HARD 396:91
we will send our b. in		PALM 661:69
billabongs swagman…in the b.		PATE 668:12
billboard atmospheric b.		THOR 889:56
b. lovely as a tree		NASH 630:63
billboards all is become b.		OLSEN 650:46
b. did to Coca-Cola		UPDI 906:21
billet Every bullet has its b.		WILL 944:68
billet-doux b.-d. written in cold blood		ETHE 327:43
billiards and to B.		PEPYS 674:1
B.…three balls and no one watches		DAVIS 266:4
let's to b.		SHAK 794:61
play b. well		SPEN 837:91
billie rhyming, ranting, raving b.		BURNS 177:81
billies chapman b. leave the street		BURNS 179:18
billion b. here, a b. there		DIRK 287:7
billionaire b. instead of a millionaire		WATE 922:39
billow A breaking b.		SHEL 815:36
Blow wind, swell b.		SHAK 778:52
haughty b.'s roar		BYRON 189:6
mirth of the b.		CALL 193:32
billows b. are gone over me		BIBLE 100:65
b. smooth and bright		CARR 204:98
Even the b. of the sea		SHAK 804:45
bills account wife and children…as b.		BACON 51:71
Just for paying a few b.!		LARK 509:79
one-hundred-dollar b.		TYSON 904:9
billy looked at the old b. boiling		PATE 668:12
bimbo B. eruptions		WRIG 962:64
bind b. another to its delight		BLAKE 140:10
b. up the brokenhearted		BIBLE 110:6
in the darkness b. them		TOLK 893:45
only b. the hands		GRIL 388:69
binding b. on the consciences		JOHN 456:73
more blessed or more b.		HELO 408:53
must be b. on the conscience		JOHN 456:73
binge Life itself is the proper b.		CHILD 222:15
Bin Laden deflecting America's anger from B. L. to Saddam Hussein		LECA 518:79
Binnorie bonnie mill-dams o' B.		BALL 58:52
biographer duty of a serious b.		TOYN 895:79
biographies innumerable B.		CARL 201:15
biography all b. is ultimately fiction		MALA 562:88
art of B.		BENT 82:97
Between history and the novel stands b.		HOLR 424:87
B….branch of psychiatry		ASLET 38:82
b. is a kind of frogspawn		HOLR 424:88
b. of the artist		ROSE 725:27
In writing b.		BOWEN 153:95
Judas who writes the b.		WILDE 940:54
less errors…than a b.		GREE 386:20
men…have written b.		MACA 545:35
no history; only b.		EMER 324:58
nothing but b.		DISR 287:19
not the way to write b.		ACHE 3:50
problems of b., of history		MILLS 595:6
why not escapist b.?		GALB 357:26
write his b.		ALLEN 13:76
biologic changes within a b. system		SELYE 756:18
biology b….lagged far behind		CRIC 254:90
birch b. for shafts		SPEN 838:20
bringing back the b.		VIDAL 912:83
climbing a b. tree		FROST 352:98
bird at least some b. would trust		HERB 413:64
awaken like a frightened b.		KIER 485:5
b. born in a cage		SHAW 809:88
b. of the air shall carry the voice		BIBLE 106:33
b. on the branch		KIER 486:7
b. that shunn'st		MILT 598:52
b. that thinks two notes a song		DAVI 265:92
b. thou never wert		SHEL 813:90
b. was fledged		SHAK 769:98
body, not the b.		THOR 889:47
but one small b. to shoot		DEVL 275:8
cheerful b. of youth		KHAY 485:88
death, immortal B.!		KEATS 478:47
flying like a b.		MACD 550:41
Free as a b.		WORD 957:72
gave us the b.		ACHE 3:52
Go, go, go, said the b.		ELIOT 319:38
great dead of b. of Scotland		MACL 555:29

birdcage

know why the caged b. sings!	DUNB 306:96	b. of the modern world	MCCA 548:93	with a b. look	WILDE 942:17
let no b. call	MILL 592:18	b. Of your brave soul	CRAS 254:83	**bitterness** b. in our laughter	EMER 325:83
Like the first b.	FARJ 330:19	b.'s invidious bar	TENN 874:83	b. of his soul	BIBLE 113:85
Love's a b. that will	MEIL 584:38	b. to a dancing star	NIET 638:3	drinking from the cup of b.	KING 487:29
Martin like a flying b.	FARJ 330:20	cannot myself give b. to wisdom	SOCR 833:96	enthusiasm turns to b.	ZATO 969:3
Most musical, most melancholy' b.!	COLE 235:25	died...before his b.	THUR 891:8	filled his life with b.	TWAIN 902:42
No b., but an invisible thing	WORD 958:95	difference of b. or state?	DEKK 270:9	no hatred or b. towards anyone	CAVE 210:19
of b.-song at morning	STEV 853:84	does not feel his own b.	LABR 502:22	nor grief b.	LYLY 543:86
O lyric love...half b.	BROW 169:72	happiness...not with b. born	CHAP 214:17	sweet full of b.	LYLY 543:84
pinnace, like a fluttered b.	TENN 878:95	head...passes at b.	SCHR 749:66	**bivouac** b. for corpses	MUSS 627:88
shot one b. flying	HEMI 409:69	Irishness is not...a question of b.	OBRI 645:61	**black** All was b.	THOM 887:9
strangles a b.	SADE 737:14	Land of our b.	KIPL 492:57	Any color—so long as it's b.	FORD 343:96
The b., the beste	JAME 449:18	led all that way for B. or Death?	ELIOT 318:18	been a b. man	LETT 524:11
The Blue B.	MAET 559:24	Like giving dry b.	SIMP 822:83	between b. and white	THOR 889:54
thin little b., peeking	NICO 637:84	men Of his high b.	SHIR 819:17	B. America	JORD 468:99
Unto the sweet b.'s throat	SHAK 778:75	mourned at his b.	MONT 614:37	b. and blacker	STEV 853:81
ways of the b. rising	REID 710:44	Our b. is but a sleep	WORD 959:8	b. and white entwine	NOON 641:50
west wind, full of b.'s cries	MASE 580:53	points the way to its new b.	BETH 87:13	b. as our loss	SITW 823:11
wet b.-haunted English lawn	ARNO 34:77	riddles of b. and death	FRYE 354:57	B....Baltic deep	TENN 876:35
What b. so sings	LYLY 543:82	stars that have a different b.	SHEL 816:66	b. face	GIOV 372:20
with the waking b.	TENN 876:26	sweet and potent voice, of its own b.	COLE 235:30	B. is beautiful	ANON 25:56
young b.-catcher	GRAV 383:40	**birth certificate** a child without a b. c.	GISC 373:30	B. love	GIOV 372:17
birdcage like a summer b.	WEBS 926:22	**birthday** b. of my life	ROSS 725:36	b. man or a fair man	ADDI 6:23
birds all the b.	THOM 885:52	bitter b. present	DILL 286:91	b. market universities	ZELD 969:4
all the b. are flown	CHAR 215:30	It was her b.	SHAN 805:64	B. Mrs Behemoth	SITW 823:3
all the day the b. are singing	MACG 551:71	my eighty-first b.	BURG 174:97	B. people possess the secret of joy	WALK 917:40
amorous b. of prey	MARV 577:93	one for his b.	UTTL 907:50	b. people with Jesus	GIOV 372:19
And no b. sing	KEATS 476:1	On my tenth b.	MURP 626:73	B. power	ANON 25:57
between fishes and reptiles and b.	BRYAN 170:98	**birthmark** b. is the stamp	KRAUS 499:6	b. promise	HOLM 423:58
B. build	HOPK 429:96	**birthplace** in sight of...his b.	MACA 546:60	B.'s not so b.	CANN 197:8
b., everywhere	TARTT 867:35	**birthright** b. high and holy	LOWE 539:4	b. statement of pistons	SPEN 837:1
B. feed on b.	ROCH 719:13	Esau despised his b.	BIBLE 92:29	born in America with a b. skin	MALC 562:85
b. got to fly	HAMM 394:62	miraculous b.	MUNRO 625:47	called the chess-board...b.	BROW 168:39
b. have vanished	MILL 592:24	sold his b.	BIBLE 92:29	chose my b. people	SENG 757:26
b. of calm sit brooding	MILT 597:32	violation of their natural b.	MILT 601:24	climb b. branches	FROST 352:98
b. of Eden sang?	CULL 257:43	**births** b. column brought bad	HAMER 393:45	cold and tarnished b.	SITW 824:20
b. of the air come and lodge	BIBLE 117:95	b. of time	BACON 52:8	devil damn thee b.	SHAK 798:68
b. of the air have nests	BIBLE 116:59	for our high b., they conclude	MASS 581:79	doesn't care about b. people	WEST 932:77
b. sing gavottes	SITW 823:7	**biscuits** empires break like b.	FULL 355:75	don't believe in b. majority rule	SMITH 829:8
b. sing madrigals	MARL 574:41	synthesis of hyacinths and b.	SAND 742:22	don't want my credit to look b.	WEST 932:78
b. sit brooding in the snow	SHAK 763:28	**bishop** B. gave vent to...sigh	WALL 917:45	either b. or white	TRAV 896:93
b. still hopping on the tree	STEV 853:63	b....must be blameless	BIBLE 129:18	fact parts in b. ink	BOWEN 153:95
b. that are without despair	WEBS 926:22	B. of Rome hath no jurisdiction	BOOK 150:42	fought against b. domination	MAND 564:53
b. that range	YEATS 966:19	Fart for the B. of Cork!	ANON 23:96	he was a b. Irish type	PRIE 695:91
b. the colour of	THOM 884:47	hitting the niece of a b.	ORWE 653:14	I always wanted to be b.	RHYS 712:73
B. warbling all the music	COWP 251:8	Shepherd and B. of your souls	BIBLE 130:69	I am B.	JORD 469:3
Caged b. accept each other	WILL 945:85	**bishops** b. eat from my hand	DUPL 307:23	I am b....my soul is white	BLAKE 139:87
country of b. and trees	WRIG 963:70	May all your sons be b.	BEHAN 74:11	I'm the b., basketball-playing Nietzsche	ONEAL 650:57
fear the b. of prey	SHAK 787:50	lees left by B.	HERZL 416:24	instructed me to hate b. girls	ANON 20:23
Feed the B.	TRAV 896:95	**Bismarck** B. merely shook the tree	GREY 388:60	Irish as B. Americans are African	GELD 362:30
flight of b.	MACL 555:33	**Bison** walls with the heads of B.	MACN 557:97	Japan is like the b. hole	UMAS 905:2
flighty as b.	DAY 267:38	**bit** A b. of a stomach	HITCH 419:87	man has a b. face	EDWA 312:59
forbids the b. to sing	SITW 823:6	a little b. of the universe	BANKS 62:24	More like b. and grey	GREE 386:29
half-awakened b.	TENN 872:43	mouth...held in with b.	BIBLE 100:54	not be b. because I was	MORR 620:59
hear the b. sing	WALT 920:95	though he had b. me	SHAK 793:29	product of every other b. woman	WINF 949:90
joyous b. make their pastime	SPEN 838:39	**bitch** called John a Impudent B.	FLEM 340:45	purchased by the b. man's misery	DOUG 296:24
late the sweet b. sang	SHAK 801:62	four-kind son-of-a-b.	ROBB 717:67	regal b. Women	CULL 257:43
like bats amongst b.	BACON 52:18	Isn't it a b.?	BIDEN 134:56	Southern B. girl	ANGE 18:83
listen to the b.	GIBS 367:14	old b. gone in the teeth	POUND 691:5	strength...in b. women	ANGE 19:90
marriage of b.	MOORE 616:73	she's kind of a b.	PAGL 659:20	suits of solemn b.	TWAIN 902:63
mechanical b. with many wings	RAINE 705:39	Sometimes you have to be a b.	MADO 559:23	the linear b.	HEAN 405:79
nest of singing b.	JOHN 459:36	worst son of a b.	PARK 664:32	those of you watching in b. and white	MOTS 622:70
pretty b. do sing	NASHE 632:93	you've got to have a son of a b.	BRIC 158:7	unnatural red and b.	DICK 282:78
prisoned b. must find in freedom	SASS 745:92	**bitches** Fare ye a' weel, ye b.!	KAME 472:13	When life looks b.	OBRI 646:68
song of the b.	GURN 390:98	**bite** b. some of my other generals	GEOR 363:46	white men cheat b. men	LEE 519:91
What was good for God's b.	HARDY 397:19	b. the hand that fed them	BURKE 176:54	White shall not neutralize the b.	BROW 169:76
When b. do sing	SHAK 780:21	Color and b. permeate a language	SAFI 737:18	Why do you wear b.	CHEK 218:14
whole noise of timorous b.	MILT 601:20	hate to b.	HEAN 405:75	Wishing He I served were b.	CULL 257:46
ye chant, ye little b.	BURNS 179:32	rainbows...turn and b.	WODE 952:53	young, gifted and b.	HANS 396:86
birk sweet is the b.	TANN 867:24	smaller fleas to b. 'em	SWIFT 863:66	**blackberries** reasons...plentiful as b.	SHAK 771:46
birks b. of Aberfeldey	BURNS 178:1	**bitelbrowed** b. and baberlipped	LANG 507:47	**blackbird** B. has spoken	FARJ 330:19
Birmingham B. by...Beachy Head	CHES 221:94	**biting** His b. is immortal	SHAK 795:91	b. is involved	STEV 850:75
lord mayor of B.	LLOY 533:80	**bitter** Because it is B.	OATES 643:10	minute a b. sang	THOM 885:52
no great hopes from B.	AUST 46:78	belly was b.	BIBLE 131:8	the b. whistling	STEV 850:74
When Jesus came to B.	STUD 858:64	be not b. against them	BIBLE 128:12	**Blackfeet** B., lying low	LIND 530:23
BirnamWood B. W....to Dunsinane	TWAIN 902:63	b. cosmic joke	GELL 363:33	**blackguard** b. whose faulty vision	BIER 134:73
Great B. W. to high Dunsinane Hill	SHAK 797:56	b. furies	YEATS 967:32	Sesquipedalian b.	CLOU 232:4
birth as we lay at b.	ARNO 34:75	b. God to follow	SWIN 864:98	**black holes** using b. h. to travel	HAWK 401:90
At its b., the republic	LAMA 504:74	B. is the knowledge	BAUD 68:70	**blackletter** b. man may be	HOLM 424:86
at the b. of Man	KIPL 493:79	b. to thee	SWIN 864:14	**blackmail** form of atomic b.	KENN 481:7
being and our b.	SHAK 798:83	Death's b. cup	ABU 1:14	**Blackman** history of Mr. B.	NGU 636:66
B., and copulation, and death	ELIOT 319:26	How b. a thing it is	SHAK 780:19	**blackness** poverty of b.	DANG 262:28
b. and growth...are ubiquitous	DILL 286:92	I found her b.	RIMB 716:49	**blacks** B....used to play whites	ANGE 19:99
b. and spirit rather took	HERB 413:62	It is b.—b.	CRANE 253:72	don't ask employers...to like b.	BORO 151:68
b. astride of a grave	BECK 72:46	misfortunes more b.	BACON 51:69	It's the same with B.	BIKO 135:94
B. counts for little	MOLI 611:80	pleasant or b.	MART 576:77	the b. in America	OROU 652:92
b. is...incipient change	OVID 657:21	sour with the b.	GOLD 377:36	want to be called b.	FEIF 332:56

blood

whites...ignorant of b.	ANGE 19:98	B. is the almost insensitive tree	DARIO 263:46	wingèd Cupid painted b.	SHAK 767:19
blackshirts armed camp of B.	MUSS 627:88	b. them unaware	COLE 235:16	Ye b. guides	BIBLE 118:27
bladder bet my b. against	KIRK 493:81	b. with a woman's brain	RICH 714:17	**blinded** b. by the external tools	REYES 712:69
get the b. and blow it great	ANON 20:40	b. with such happy manners	AUST 45:57	**blindness** 'eathen in 'is b.	KIPL 490:13
wind out of the b.	ANON 22:83	b. you out of the house	BIBLE 103:23	'eathen in 'is b.	KIPL 490:14
bladders rotten b., tied Together	WEBS 927:25	does not make a man b.	ARIS 31:20	first love's impassioned b.	PEAC 671:55
blade B. on the feather	CORY 247:12	more b. to give than to receive	BIBLE 125:96	**blinds** a drawing-down of b.	OWEN 657:26
b. struck the water	COKE 234:98	wife seems more b.	HELO 408:53	b. let through the day	HOUS 432:69
drive the b. a little forward	CURZ 260:5	**blessèd** Most b., most glorious	SMITH 831:65	**blindworms** Newts and b.	SHAK 767:31
gild the b. if you will	QUIN 702:23	**blessedness** happiness or b. of man	SPIN 841:81	**blink** at one b.	DOUG 294:99
ranting roving b.	ANON 22:72	**blesses** nation b. what undoes it	HUGO 437:73	**blinkard** Thou b. blowboll	SKEL 824:31
taken up the broken b.	DE 270:92	**blessing** b., even life for evermore	BIBLE 103:40	**bliss** Almost the highest b.	KEATS 475:65
Whereat with b.	SHAK 768:48	b. like experiencing madness	LISP 531:45	b. in ale	CRAB 251:24
blades b. pricked the mud	BROW 168:34	b. of God Almighty	BOOK 147:75	B. in our brow's bent	SHAK 794:49
Blair B. is very convincing	CHIR 222:21	continual dew of thy b.	BOOK 146:41	B. it was...to be alive	WORD 960:23
I am the heir to B.	CAM 193:37	for the which b.	SHAK 773:23	b. of solitude	WORD 960:27
I'm just Tony B.	BLAIR 138:55	If this is a b.	CHUR 226:1	deprived of everlasting b.!	MARL 573:24
It will be B., B., B.	BENN 79:34	most need of b.	SHAK 797:33	domestic b.	PATM 669:26
Tony B. its Kubla Khan	RAWN 707:86	Oh there is b.	WORD 957:72	Everywhere I see b.	SHEL 812:49
Blake B. once wildly muttered	SASS 746:98	pour you out a b.	BIBLE 112:63	excels all other b.	DYER 309:47
Till I am...William B.	YEATS 967:34	proceedeth b. and cursing	BIBLE 130:57	faded b., faded so soon	MILT 602:64
blame b. it on the other party	ANON 26:80	Prosperity is the b.	BACON 51:64	fill Of b. on b.	MILT 604:4
b. thee now to weep	SHAK 762:70	steal immortal b. from her lips	SHAK 766:97	gate of b.	CRAS 254:82
Dispraise, or b., nothing	MILT 608:3	Sweet was its b.	COCK 233:81	ignorance is b.	GRAY 383:48
Do not b. me, madam	LABE 501:4	system, and actually a b.	LIVI 532:55	never...parted, b. or woe	MILT 606:52
freeze the heart as much as b.	BUCK 172:36	taken away thy b.	BIBLE 92:13	promise of pneumatic b.	ELIOT 317:78
grief as is the b.	AYTO 48:10	thou shalt be a b.	BIBLE 92:16	thou hast not thy b.	KEATS 478:37
it's insane to b. the tiger	MUNG 625:46	to delight...paid thy utmost b.	DELA 271:34	wingèd hours of b.	CAMP 194:64
moved with the slightest touch of b.	EDGE 311:34	to us a national b.	HAMI 394:47	**blissful** experience is not always b.	HUXL 442:91
neither is most to b.	SWIN 864:3	truly it's a b.	CLOU 232:52	**blisters** shoes...gave her b.	BAIN 55:91
nobody is to b. for anything	AMIS 16:53	**blessings** all the b. of this life	BOOK 147:50	**blithe** b. wi' Comrades dear	BURNS 178:89
no one can really b. him	KEYN 484:75	b. of a good thick skirt	KING 488:57	No b. Irish lad was so happy	CAMP 194:60
only the Master shall b.	KIPL 490:15	b. of marriage	SHAW 808:33	**blitz** of a boy	CAUS 209:14
take all the b.	ASTU 39:12	b. of youth	DEMO 272:49	**block** big black b.	GILB 369:64
yet he was most to b.	LANY 508:54	b. on your frosty pow	BURNS 179:16	changes with the next b.	SHAK 773:17
blanched b. with fear	SHAK 797:50	Free trade, one of the greatest b.	MACA 544:21	chip off the old b.	BURKE 175:32
blancmange equivalent of b.	LEVIN 525:27	from whom all b. flow	KEN 480:84	the biggest coal b.	HEAN 405:79
bland Cruel, but composed and b.	ARNO 35:2	glass of B. standing by	HERB 414:82	**blockade** Navy will run the b.	ANDE 17:67
demeanour nobly b.	GILB 370:72	Life is the greatest of b.	HEINE 407:14	**blockhead** bookful b.	POPE 685:27
blank benign b.—a decent	MENC 587:16	**blest** be for ever b.	HOW 433:84	No man but a b.	JOHN 463:49
b. Of nature's work	MILT 603:75	still be very b.	GOLD 376:8	**blockheads** b. of all ages	CONG 241:57
no blot for us Nor b.;	BROW 167:29	**blew** B. hither	HOUS 431:49	The b. talk	SCOTT 754:81
practically b. as snow	HARDY 397:15	**blight** b. man was born for	HOPK 428:82	the greatest b.	MONT 613:14
this b. of things	WORD 956:51	**Blimber** Doctor B.'s assistant	DICK 280:31	**blocks** hew b. with a razor	POPE 686:53
blanket a b. that is too small	MOUR 623:96	**blind** all...are born b.	OKRI 649:25	spell God with the wrong b.	ROBI 718:87
America is not like a b.	JACK 448:3	birth and growth...ubiquitous and b.	DILL 286:92	You b., you stones	SHAK 776:4
four bare legs under a b.	DAVI 265:81	b. and naked Ignorance	TENN 877:48	**bloke** b. fer showin' off	DENN 273:74
right side of the b.	ASHF 38:74	b. as any noonday owl	TENN 878:78	**blokes** b. retire to the...pub	NEVI 634:32
takes her wet b. with her	BROY 169:90	B. as the...nails	SITW 823:11	**blond** like a b. satan	HAMM 395:69
blankets rough male kiss of b.	BROO 162:86	b. boy, Venus' baby	SPEN 839:48	more b. than you	CUMM 258:62
blanks historians left b.	POUND 691:11	b. dates are a way of life	EPST 327:34	**blonde** b. to make a bishop kick	CHAN 213:76
blare amid the b. of trumpets	EUDA 328:52	b., despised, and dying king	SHEL 812:70	in love with a beautiful b.	FIEL 335:34
blasphemies great truths begin as b.	SHAW 810:11	b. fury of creation	SHAW 807:16	**blondes** Gentlemen Prefer B.	LOOS 536:45
blasphemy All manner of sin and b.	BIBLE 117:84	b. hysterics of the Celt.	TENN 875:97	Gentlemen...seem to remember b.	LOOS 536:47
blast at my back in a cold b.	ELIOT 318:3	b. in the end	BERR 87:96	**blood** always worked with my b.	KOLL 496:37
b. of war blows	SHAK 775:74	b. lead the b.	BIBLE 117:3	angry up the b.	PAIGE 660:28
Striding the b.	SHAK 796:20	b. life within the brain	TENN 878:86	billet-doux written in cold b.	ETHE 327:43
wert thou in the cauld b.	BURNS 180:60	B., old and lonely	SHEL 815:28	B., all price excelling	AQUI 30:96
blasts b. from hell	SHAK 781:57	b. receive their sight	BIBLE 116:76	b. and other vital fluids	STER 848:38
B. of January	SHAK 799:18	b. with smoke	SASS 745:82	B. and revenge...in my head	SHAK 760:23
many b. to shake them	SHAK 761:38	brave sun Die b.	JEFF 453:12	b. and spirit together	MARI 571:81
blatant in a b. land	TENN 876:20	but unbelief is b.	MILT 599:74	b. and water	BIBLE 123:63
blaze b. of branch, or brazier	ELIOT 321:81	chance he might go b.	GREG 387:52	b. and wine are red	WILDE 942:15
broader still became the b.	MACA 546:52	check the eyes and call them b.	MIDD 590:74	b.-bedecked halls of their revel	POE 683:83
out into sudden b.	MILT 599:86	conversation of the b.	MOORE 616:73	b. Come gargling	OWEN 657:31
trillion; but the b.	LOWE 540:17	country of the b.	WELLS 930:23	b. enough upon your penal code	BYRON 187:31
blazon final b., and to prove	LARK 509:81	drawing back the b.	KIPL 492:56	b. from head to foot	MACL 554:27
bleed breaks...and then we b.	SHEL 816:64	eyes of the b. shall be opened	BIBLE 108:76	b. in torrents pour	DAVI 264:67
do we not b.?	SHAK 769:1	Fortune...she be b.	BACON 52:25	b. is settled, and her joints	SHAK 766:9
no time to b.	SHAK 763:29	glass so gay, that it can b.	SPEN 839:57	b. is strong	GALT 359:54
bleeding Beneath the b. hands	ELIOT 320:64	Grief for a while is b.	SHEL 814:8	B. may be thicker than water	SOME 833:9
b. piece of earth	SHAK 777:33	In the country of the b.	ERAS 327:36	b. [may lose] its fire	BYRON 188:64
fell a-b. on Black Monday	SHAK 769:91	it is the b. watchmaker	DAWK 266:16	b. mixed with wasted gold	KING 488:59
blemish lamb shall be without b.	BIBLE 93:58	I was b., now I see	BIBLE 123:43	b. of all the martyrs	IVAN 448:80
no b. but the mind	SHAK 786:21	love is b.	SHAK 769:93	b. of grape	BLAKE 139:82
blemishes tapes, b. and all	NIXON 640:37	Love, knocking its b. forehead	SAND 741:4	B. of our Lord Jesus	BOOK 147:73
blend strange b. of the commercial	STAP 843:20	mathematician is a b. man	DARW 263:60	b. of patriots and tyrants	JEFF 454:22
bless attend and b.	GILB 369:57	not worry about the b. alleys	FEYN 334:5	b. of the Christians	TERT 879:18
except thou b. me	BIBLE 93:36	one-armed b. man	WODE 952:41	b. of the new testament	BIBLE 119:40
Lord b. thee, and keep thee	BIBLE 94:79	one of the b. alleys	WAUGH 923:62	b.-red blossom	TENN 876:35
Rich people, God b. us	CLIN 231:29	Passions can...never b. me	LAFA 503:44	b.-red flower of revolution	RAND 706:59
blessed b. and admit me to Paradise	ROSS 727:66	religion without science is b.	EINS 313:79	b. rolled out	HUGH 435:15
B. are the dead	BIBLE 132:13	right to be b.	NELS 633:13	b.'s a rover	HOUS 431:76
B. are the pure in heart	WHAR 934:13	splendid work for the b.	SASS 745:87	b. speaks to you in my veins	SHAK 770:7
b. be the evergreen Pine!	SCOTT 752:29	through its own internal lighting b.	SHEL 814:3	B. sport...in the gossip columns	INGH 446:34
b. be the name of the Lord	BIBLE 98:31	Was b., but now I see	NEWT 635:63	b., toil, tears and sweat	CHUR 225:84
B. is he who	VIRG 914:37	will not make us b.	RUSH 732:66	b. was cold	SCOTT 752:11

bloodguiltiness 1028

b. was shed for me — ELLI 323:26
b. was sprinkled on the wall — BIBLE 97:80
b. will be ready — SADE 737:15
b. with guilt is bought — SHEL 814:9
b. with the thought of dying — MASE 580:69
blow in cold b. — SHAW 808:43
brand sae drap wi' b. — BALL 59:61
by man shall his b. be shed — BIBLE 92:12
caked in b. — JOHN 457:2
Christ's b. streams in the firmament! — MARL 573:30
cinema in their b. — RICH 714:18
clouds as actual b. — MUNCH 625:41
conjure up the b. — SHAK 775:74
cooling the b. — FLAN 338:8
dark b. dammed within — CULL 257:45
daughter to his b. — SHAK 769:90
dogs licked the b. of Naboth — BIBLE 97:69
drink his b. — BOOK 147:72
dripping b. our only drink — ELIOT 320:65
economic b. pressure — WRIS 963:78
effusion of…human b. — OCON 646:83
enough of b. and tears — RABIN 704:24
Every drop of my b. — GAND 359:57
faints at the sight of b. — BETJ 88:32
faith melteth into b. — SHAK 773:26
find so much b. — SHAK 786:15
Fire, B., and Famine — HENR 411:12
first b. shed in revenge — PEPYS 673:87
flesh and b. — THOR 888:25
flesh and b. — THAC 880:21
freeze thy young b. — SHAK 781:60
glories of our b. and state — SHIR 819:20
glory smeared in dust and b. — SHAK 760:17
great effusion of b. — STUB 858:62
happit flesh and b. — FERG 333:87
heart's b. dyed — CONN 242:84
heyday in the b. — SHAK 784:40
I am in b. — SHAK 797:51
ice was in the b. — PIER 677:68
If b. be the price — KIPL 490:10
in place and b. — TENN 875:96
In whose cold b. — SHAK 760:2
iron and b. — BISM 137:32
joys are more to flesh and b. — DRYD 303:15
know the colour of that b. — KEATS 478:49
laws for the b. — SHAK 769:76
laws…writ in b. — MARL 573:8
liquors in my b. — SHAK 778:71
looked kneaded up with b. — BROW 168:34
look like flesh and b. — MOORE 616:70
love respects no b. — DEKK 270:9
May their b. cease to flow! — DAVIS 266:7
men are flesh and b. — SHAK 772:6
Moloch whose b. is running — GINS 372:6
More b.! More b.! — CRON 256:25
not…a question of birth or b. — OBRI 645:61
Nothing like b., sir — THAC 880:27
not shed her b. — SHAK 790:39
of British b.? — TENN 875:5
one drop of negro b. — HUGH 435:16
one of the b.-suckers — FRAN 348:23
O, the b. more stirs — SHAK 771:36
our own red b. — YEATS 966:21
poet's feverish b. — ARNO 34:79
poison the whole b. stream fills — EMPS 326:8
Politics is a b. sport — BEVAN 90:60
redness which affrights in b. — MELV 585:61
Resign your heart's b. — SHEL 812:50
Senator, it is American b. — MACA 544:10
sensations…Felt in the b. — WORD 956:53
sheds his b. with me — SHAK 776:93
show-business with b. — BELA 75:29
slaked the light with b. — TENN 879:5
smell the b. of a British man — SHAK 792:12
so much b. in him? — SHAK 798:65
so much b. in his liver — SHAK 786:15
stained with b. — SHAK 768:49
Stir the Vikings' b. — KING 487:44
streams of British b. — SCHAW 747:20
sweat and b. and souls — FRAN 348:23
talk about their Pilgrim b. — LOWE 539:4
the circulation of their b. — SMITH 829:11
this is my b. — BIBLE 119:40
Tiber foaming with much b. — POWE 693:58
To freeze the b. — WORD 958:91
tomahawks, wi' b. red-rusted — BURNS 179:28
too much b. — SHAK 787:43

voice of thy brother's b. — BIBLE 92:3
washed in the b. of the Lamb? — LIND 530:15
washed in the b. of the Lamb? — LIND 530:16
wash this b. Clean — SHAK 797:37
Waste of B. — STUD 858:63
water and the b. — TOPL 894:61
We be one b. — KIPL 490:5
welt'ring in his b. — DRYD 303:31
What case of flesh and b. — ROCH 719:10
When b. is nipped — SHAK 763:27
When the b. burns — SHAK 781:55
when the b. creeps — TENN 874:74
whips my b. like verse — WILL 946:28
win…By b. or ink — BYRON 189:97
with hands b. stained — ORTE 652:2
with his own b. he bought — STONE 855:11
Without shedding of b. — BIBLE 129:36
would draw b. — DUNC 307:11
written in letters of b. — STRA 857:45
You cannot wash b. — AHMAD 10:99
Young b. must have its course — KING 487:48
bloodguiltiness Deliver me from b. — BIBLE 101:74
bloodless b. substitute for life — STEV 852:49
bloodmoney Dr B. — DICK 277:32
bloods mingle our b. together — SHAK 798:83
our two b. mingled be — DONNE 291:36
bloodshed Politics is war without b. — MAO 568:28
blood-thirsty b.-t. and deceitful man — BOOK 148:3
bloody battles b. exercises — JOSE 469:10
Be b., bold, and resolute — SHAK 797:55
b. beat them again — RAMS 706:53
B. instructions which, being taught — SHAK 796:19
greet you with b. hands — CORW 247:7
head is b. but unbowed — HENL 411:5
horrid malicious b. flame — PEPYS 674:7
My b. thoughts — SHAK 790:29
On the same b. morning — SCOTT 753:40
Walk! Not b. likely — SHAW 810:1
War's a b. game — SASS 745:93
Bloom Leopold B. ate with relish — JOYCE 470:29
bloom As well as any b. — THOM 885:63
b. is shed — BURNS 179:25
b. of that valley shall — MOORE 617:99
b. sae fresh and fair — BURNS 179:32
Charm…it's a sort of b. — BARR 65:88
Each opening sweet of earliest b. — COLL 237:70
hung with b. along the bough — HOUS 431:33
look at things in b. — HOUS 431:35
Our b. is gone — STEV 850:77
risk of spoiling its b. — CONR 244:51
terrible and splendid b. — RAND 706:59
touch it and the b. is gone — WILDE 941:1
vernal b., or summer's rose — MILT 603:75
with the b. go I — ARNO 35:18
blooms b. each thing, then maids — NASHE 632:93
bloomy all the b. beds — SMART 826:66
blossom Are you…the b. — YEATS 966:27
b. by b. the spring begins — SWIN 863:83
b. in purple and red — TENN 876:28
b. of war — TENN 876:35
full spring-tide of b. — BETJ 88:26
last b. is the first b. — MACN 558:8
saft faulding b. — TANN 867:24
there is a b. about me — BOSW 151:75
Under the b. — SHAK 804:32
blossomer great-rooted b. — YEATS 966:27
blossoms art of orange b. — PISS 679:96
boughs do laughing b. bear — SPEN 838:39
cherry b. in the spring — ANON 24:27
million b. springing — MACG 551:71
of locust b. — WILL 946:23
rod of Aaron…bloomed b. — BIBLE 94:81
strange odours of b. — CONR 244:34
tender leaves…tomorrow b. — SHAK 805:52
blot And blackens every b. — TENN 876:40
b. on the fair face of creation — BRON 161:62
b. upon my pride — SHAK 764:49
It is no vicious b. — SHAK 792:86
text that looks a little b. — TENN 877:49
the art to b. — POPE 688:20
This world's no b. — BROW 167:29
blotched b. out beyond — STEV 850:76
blotted man will be b. out — JEFF 453:12
never b. out a line — JONS 468:90
blouse b. out and her nails grimed — MANS 567:95
blow bless the hand that gave the b. — DRYD 302:98
B. him again to me — TENN 872:37

b. in cold blood — SHAW 808:43
b. of a loy — SYNGE 865:24
b. over the face — AUBR 42:59
b., thou winter wind — SHAK 779:84
B., winds — SHAK 792:4
b. you through and through — SHAK 799:18
Death unfailing will strike the b. — CURR 259:91
first b. is half the battle — GOLD 377:14
Liberty's in every b. — BURNS 180:48
man who does not return your b. — SHAW 808:57
must strike the b.? — BYRON 187:41
put your lips together—and b. — FURT 356:90
receive a knock-down b. — HUNT 439:19
terrible b. — HAMER 393:45
that relaxed alluring b. — HEAN 405:79
until I b. up! — THOM 884:42
blowboll Thou blinkard b. — SKEL 824:31
blowing furious winter b. — RANS 707:70
blown to have b. up the King — HOBY 421:11
blows allured…without b. — STEE 844:50
b. and revenge for me! — SHAK 760:6
fled step-dame Study's b. — SIDN 820:44
It b. so hard — HOUS 431:48
stories And not by his b. — LAFO 504:57
when most she offers b. — SHAK 794:69
Blucher B. and I have lost — WELL 929:3
bludgeoning b. of the people — WILDE 941:74
blue b. and white young man — GILB 369:46
B., darkly, deeply — SOUT 835:48
b-gum nigger — BENET 79:25
b. is all in a rush — HOPK 428:74
b.…Of night — YEATS 966:12
b. ribbon of the turf — DISR 288:44
chic old b.-haired ladies — CAPO 197:29
in yonder living b. — TENN 875:99
naked frosty b. — THOM 885:57
no b. without yellow — VAN 908:18
ocean b. or smoke b. — GALE 357:28
The b. deep — SHEL 813:91
The b. Mediterranean — SHEL 813:81
those b. remembered hills — HOUS 431:51
bluebell Mary, ma Scotch B. — LAUD 511:15
bluebells If you love your b. — GREER 387:48
bluejay b. in peacock feathers — LAFO 504:58
bluejays shoot all the b. — LEE 518:87
blues blue-gum nigger to sing me b. — BENET 79:25
No white man ever had the b. — LEAD 516:26
soul keeps a singin' the b. — BERRY 87:94
Sweet b.! — HUGH 434:10
bluest b. veins to kiss — SHAK 794:63
bluff no matter how charming a b. — FITZ 338:92
blunder frae monie a b. free us — BURNS 177:87
so grotesque a b. — BENT 82:4
Youth is a b. — DISR 287:26
blundered Some one had b. — TENN 875:12
blundering b. will live on — SAND 742:23
blunders b.…shape history — TAYL 868:46
scapegoats for our b. — TWAIN 903:86
woman…Nature's agreeable b. — COWL 250:78
blur in retrospect…all a b. — SCHL 747:36
blush At first b. a new idea — MILL 593:38
b. at your faults — FLET 341:57
bring a b. into the cheek — DICK 283:19
knew by the b. — SOME 833:8
not b. to be admir'd — WALL 918:56
pass my name…I b. — TREE 896:99
with a b. retire — DICK 283:26
blushes B.. Or needs to. — TWAIN 903:79
Who b. at the name? — INGR 446:36
blushing b.…a sign of guilt — CONG 241:60
Religion b. veils — POPE 689:47
sacrifice other people without b. — SHAW 808:58
without lowering her eyes and b. — SARR 744:60
Blyton Enid B. of economics — HOLME 423:56
boa reach for my feather B. — GINS 372:10
Boadicea bargain-basement B. — HEAL 404:65
board bred in a B.-School — KIPL 491:23
ideal b. of directors — DOCH 289:80
moving a single b. — SNYD 832:92
boarding-house landlady of a b.-h. — LEAC 515:10
boarding-school old-fashioned B.-s. — AUST 46:73
boards he who treads the b. — BISH 136:23
boar-pig Bartholomew b.-p. — SHAK 772:82
boast b. not thyself of tomorrow — BIBLE 105:99
b. of heraldry — GRAY 384:66
Boston…hast naught to b. — ANON 22:81
Britain, could you ever b. — SWIFT 862:60

bondage

empty b. of flesh	HABI 391:2
How many people can b. as much	BECK 72:44
Let no man b. himself	TROL 897:23
our absolute b.	WORD 958:79
Such is the patriot's b.	GOLD 376:86
boastful b. men so oft abashed	SPEN 838:37
boasting No b. like a fool	SHAK 797:57
boat beautiful pea-green b.	LEAR 516:35
b....had the goods of a house	PEPYS 674:8
b. wallows in the sea	IGNA 445:18
came and found a b.	TENN 870:86
glass-bottomed b.	MIZN 610:62
intellectually promising b.	VAN 908:13
soul is an enchanted b.	SHEL 814:17
Speed, bonnie b.	BOUL 152:92
While his b. hastens	KEATS 475:66
boathook diplomatic b.	CECIL 210:30
boating Jolly b. weather	CORY 247:12
boatman B., do not tarry	CAMP 194:65
boatmen puny b. do not know how	HERZ 416:21
boats b. against the current	FITZ 338:87
b. began to near the winning post	COKE 234:98
b. or ships came near	LEAR 516:40
b. were tossed	LOWE 540:18
fooling among b.?	STEV 851:23
messing about in b.	GRAH 380:89
running into b.	PEPYS 674:6
bob b.-tail nag	FOST 345:53
meek with thirty b. a week	DAVI 264:64
bobolink B. for a Chorister	DICK 283:35
bobtailed b. Hob	SITW 823:5
Boche stab...A well-killed B.	READ 708:92
bodies actions of two b.	NEWT 635:59
adorning their b.	SMOL 831:67
angles of their b.	ANGE 19:99
b. are buried in peace	BIBLE 113:11
b. are under our wheels	SHAW 807:20
b. in space	MANN 566:84
b. measure out their place	MARV 578:8
b. of the living	SPEN 837:12
b. of those bones	DOMI 290:3
concern not for your b.	PLATO 681:43
embraces of our b. taste	CAREW 198:53
grave keeps b.	DONNE 292:62
house their b.	GIBR 367:13
inexhaustible b.	TATE 867:39
may have civilized b.	MELV 585:52
other heated b.	WATT 922:45
our dead b.	SCOTT 751:6
Pile the b. high	SAND 742:18
present your b. a living sacrifice	BIBLE 125:24
scent of unwashed b.	ACKR 3:60
scorn their b.	BAST 67:51
souls out of men's b.?	SHAK 774:37
souls...to your scattered b. go	DONNE 292:50
the structure of our b.	STOP 855:12
three b. no sensible man	MACM 556:73
well-developed b.	FORS 344:40
women's b. are more delicate	CHRI 223:47
bodily Close your b. eye	FRIE 351:75
Thanks to his b. form	REDT 709:25
bodkin that is the bare b.	TWAIN 902:63
With a bare b.?	SHAK 782:7
body air and water to the human b.	REES 710:38
as it is for the b.	HUXL 441:68
as well as of the b.	HAZL 404:58
beautiful passionate b.	SWIN 864:93
best marriage...of mind and b.	FOWL 346:65
b. able to endure	MARL 573:17
b. and material substance	CARL 201:33
B. and soul	JORD 468:99
b. and substance of his works	COLE 236:53
b. away to barter	NGU 636:66
b. between your knees	CORY 247:12
b. continues in its state	NEWT 635:56
b. could reform	TWAIN 902:54
b. is a machine for living	TOLS 893:50
b. is the temple	BIBLE 126:39
b. like a wardrobe.	THOM 884:39
b. like mine!	ATLAS 40:18
b. meet a b.	BURNS 180:55
b. of a cobbler	LOCKE 533:91
b. of a weak...woman	ELIZ 321:4
b. of Benjamin Franklin	FRAN 348:7
b. of...generalizations	FRIE 351:68
b. of its womanhood	SCHR 749:66
B. of our Lord Jesus	BOOK 147:73
b. of this death?	BIBLE 125:15
b. of truth and the b.	LIPP 531:41
b.'s harmony	POPE 689:42
b....straight as Circe's wand	MARL 574:36
b.'s work's expired	SHAK 800:45
b. that will go on circulating	STEG 844:56
b. was as round	SPEKE 836:82
b. will be guarded	LOWE 539:98
brief loan of his own b.	CABE 191:2
bury my b. in Sussex grass	BENET 79:26
children of my b.	KOLL 496:36
commit his b. to the deep	BOOK 149:39
commit his b. to the ground	BOOK 148:1
damned of b. and soul	KIPL 490:95
dignity or baseness...not in their b.	CHRI 223:46
ease of the b.	SMITH 827:74
Fleas...upon the b.	LAND 506:28
for the relief of the b.	RICH 713:99
get rid of the b.	PLATO 682:55
gun gives you the b.	THOR 889:47
had tasted her sweet b.	SHAK 790:27
Happiness is healthy for the b.	PROU 698:58
harmonies of the b.	BERN 86:74
head belongs to a b.	ROSSO 727:68
Health and an able b.	FLET 341:59
Her b. a bulb	PLATH 681:36
human b. is sacred	WHIT 937:98
I knew her b. there	CRANE 253:62
in time leave the b.	SMOL 831:68
keep your b. white	STEV 853:84
knit together into one b. politic	HENR 411:13
labour of his b.	LOCKE 533:86
lack of health in the b.	PLATO 681:50
language is...the b., of thought	CARL 200:94
liberation of both b. and mind	BANN 62:34
little b. with a mighty heart	SHAK 775:65
live in company with a b.	DELA 271:21
looking for a b. in the coach	HITC 419:83
mans b. both for power	SPEN 838:32
mind, in b. strong!	MILT 607:83
mind or b. grieved	CAMP 195:77
mind or b. to prefer	POPE 687:80
more...Africa than my own b.	ORTON 652:3
most erotic part of the b.	BART 66:25
mystery...Of the glorious B.	AQUI 30:96
Naught broken save this b.	BROO 162:91
not a single molecule of my b.	DIDE 285:69
not be sound...in b. nor mind	LLOY 532:69
nothing...but my b.'s length	SHAK 760:17
not of her flesh and b.	KEYN 484:72
not that thy whole b. should be cast	BIBLE 114:34
O b. swayed to music	YEATS 966:27
one b. and one heart	DOUG 295:4
onnable b.'d be safe?	LOWE 539:6
Over my dead b.	KAUF 474:43
own your own b.	JONG 466:30
patch up thine old b.	SHAK 772:82
prefer shifting my whole b.	HERZ 416:22
prose takes the mould of the b.	WOOLF 956:39
Prostitution. Selling one's b.	MACK 554:13
Punish a b.	DRYD 302:73
renders the b....more perfect	PIUS 680:20
resurrection of the b.	BOOK 146:37
see...my b. without disgust	BAUD 68:69
service of the b.	MORE 618:20
sever head from b.	WEBS 926:27
shaped my b. so	SHAK 760:20
soul is not more than the b.	WHIT 937:94
sound mind in a sound b.	JUVE 471:58
sound mind in a sound b.	LOCKE 534:92
Take, eat: this is my b.	BIBLE 126:49
temple, called his b.	THOR 888:25
that b. of men	STEE 844:44
the gigantic b.	MACA 545:36
this b. did contain a spirit	SHAK 772:67
this is my b.	BIBLE 126:49
this is my b.	BIBLE 119:40
time by how a b. sways	ROET 722:62
too violent for the b.	JEFF 454:29
toughness the b. will find	WAVE 925:2
turning the whole b.	PLATO 682:65
turn your b.	WEBS 926:38
Upon my buried b. lay	BEAU 71:18
use of my b.	BECK 72:47
vital fluids of my b.	STER 848:38
well proportioned b.	AUBR 42:58
what exercise is to the b.	STEE 844:45
Whether I was in my b.	HAND 395:79
whose b. is this?	RODR 722:54
Whose b., Nature is	POPE 687:78
witches that deform the b.	SHAK 762:91
with my b. I thee worship	BOOK 148:93
work of b. or mind	MILT 604:5
written on his b.	ADIGA 8:65
yer b. will disappear	KELM 479:70
You are the b.	SCEVE 746:18
Your b. rocking!	CRANE 253:56
bodyguards Bush has 100 b.	GORB 378:50
bodyline B. was devised to stifle	LARW 510:8
B. was not an incident	JAMES 450:32
Boer before the B. War	ORWE 653:27
Bognor Bugger B.	GEOR 364:51
bogs Brown b. with black water	COLUM 238:89
find a way out of the b.	MAIL 560:68
melancholy of the b.	WAUGH 924:81
bogus science, even b. science	PRIT 696:15
Bohemia B. has no banner	WILL 945:86
boil b. at different degrees	EMER 325:95
War That Would Not B.	TAYL 868:45
boils satan has not geven me b.	FLEM 340:44
bold Be b., be b.	SPEN 839:41
be b., it will not burst thee	BIBLE 113:99
b. as a hawk	THUR 890:75
hath made me b.	SHAK 797:30
He was a b. Man	SWIFT 863:71
lover b. and free	CLEV 230:95
solid, or b.	STRA 857:41
Virtue is b.	SHAK 788:71
want of cunning made me b.	SPEN 839:48
boldness Boldness...always b.!	DANT 262:43
b. is a child of ignorance	BACON 51:90
b. to wealth	HESI 417:33
differ chiefly in the b.	JEVO 455:54
in a young woman, it is b.	HUGO 437:86
bole Are you...the b.?	YEATS 966:27
Boléro toward the beginning of B.	LAMB 506:18
Bolingbroke this canker, B.?	SHAK 771:34
Bolivia and B. 1949	THER 882:91
bollocks who would kick your b.	LOFT 534:4
Boloigne hadde been, and at B.	CHAU 217:77
Bolshevik B. tyranny is the worst	CHUR 224:70
Bolsheviks B. are sincere	DRIB 299:5
bolshevism b. run mad	SNOW 832:88
bolt b. is shot back	ARNO 34:72
b. of Cupid fell	SHAK 767:27
bolts and the b. are hurled	TENN 870:92
B. and bars will not	MOLI 611:74
bomb Americans want to b.	ANON 27:34
Ban the B.	ANON 25:34
B. brought peace	CHUR 226:99
b. the knot off a tree	JENS 454:34
end up with the atomic b.	PAGN 660:27
How We Got Along After The B.	DICK 277:32
hydrogen and napalm b.	ROUS 729:8
Long after the b. falls	JANO 452:80
production of the fission b.	FROMM 352:88
the way it was with the atomic b.	OPPE 651:83
word 'Now' is like a b.	MILL 593:40
bombardment fury of aerial b.	EBER 310:11
bombast swelling into b.	DRYD 300:20
bombed glad we've been b.	ELIZ 322:15
protect him from being b.	BALD 57:31
bombs atom b. are piling up	ORWE 654:57
b. and missiles lie...buried	RAND 706:58
B. away	ANON 25:59
b. bursting in air	KEY 483:68
Come, friendly b.	BETJ 88:20
construction of...powerful b.	EINS 313:78
Ears like b.	CAUS 209:14
rain of b.	WHITE 935:53
the roar of b.	ORWE 653:25
whiskered men with b.	TOLK 893:43
bonbon pink b. stuffed with snow	DEBU 268:62
bond According to my b.	SHAK 791:84
Let him look to his b.	SHAK 769:99
neither b. nor free	BIBLE 127:79
trust man on his oath or b.	SHAK 791:75
bondage Marriage...only actual b.	MILL 592:16
bondage b. of certain ribbons	SHAK 800:26
damn'd to the b. be?	HABI 391:3
from the b. of sins	BHAG 90:78
hold another in b.	FULL 355:66
in the house of b.	MACA 544:24
out of the house of b.	BIBLE 94:66

bonds

queen in b.	SHAK 759:81
spirit of b.	BIBLE 125:18
That sweet b.	SHEL 812:52
bonds draw tight the b.	CHAM 212:57
garters to be b. and shackles	BACON 51:72
bondsmen Hereditary b.!	BYRON 187:41
bone b.-ache disquietude of life	ALLEN 13:78
b. and muscle of my nation	FRAN 348:23
b. of my bones	BIBLE 91:90
B. of my b. thou art	MILT 606:52
Break the b.	RABE 703:10
cricket goes to the b.	ARLO 32:33
dog…with a juicy b.	AUDEN 42:79
every b. a-stare	BROW 168:34
touch his b. and his flesh	BIBLE 98:92
boneless b. wonder	CHUR 225:78
bones all my b. are out of joint	BIBLE 99:43
bodies of those b.	DOMI 290:3
b. are coral made	SHAK 803:16
b. are smitten asunder	BOOK 149:15
b. live to learn	ROET 722:62
brittle strength of b.	MILT 602:46
broken spirit drieth the b.	BIBLE 105:82
can these b. live	BIBLE 111:36
childish; only b. abide	LOWE 540:18
conjuring trick with b.	JENK 454:31
full of dead men's b.	BIBLE 118:28
Hope sleeps in our b.	PIER 677:71
interred with their b.	SHAK 777:37
lay his weary b.	SHAK 805:55
like the b. of dinosaurs	RAND 706:58
maketh the b. fat	BIBLE 104:77
massy china b.	MUNDY 625:43
never mended no broken b.	DICK 277:38
New Zealand is in my very b.	MANS 567:10
O'er his white b.	BALL 60:78
our small b.	THOM 885:70
O ye dry b.	BIBLE 111:37
Parents are the b.	DOUG 295:19
paste and cover to our b.	SHAK 764:51
Picked his b.	ELIOT 318:6
rattle of the b.	ELIOT 318:3
Rest of their b.	DONNE 292:51
rottenness in his b.	BIBLE 104:66
rotting b. of ten thousand	TS 900:6
Smash the scaffold of the b.	HUID 438:91
spewed Nantucket b.	LOWE 540:19
the tongue breaketh the b.	BIBLE 113:2
town of monks and b.	COLE 236:50
until your b. are clean	ADCO 6:14
valley where all of b.	BIBLE 111:35
your b. are very brittle	STEV 853:71
bonfire th'everlasting b.	SHAK 797:39
bonhomie overcame his natural b.	BENT 82:2
bonjour B. tristesse	ELUA 324:45
bonkers stark, staring b.	HAIL 392:19
bonnet b. of Bonny Dundee	SCOTT 754:82
bonnie b. banks o' Loch Lomond	ANON 22:79
b., b. broom	BALL 58:55
b. brow was brent	BURNS 179:16
B. lassie will ye go	BURNS 178:1
b. mill-dams o' Binnorie	BALL 58:52
brisk and a b. lad	ANON 22:72
corn rigs are b.	BURNS 177:88
corn rigs are b.	BURNS 178:90
gin love be b.	BALL 60:79
service to my b. lassie	BURNS 178:8
bonny B. Dundee	SCOTT 753:52
B. Dundee	SCOTT 754:82
honest men and b. lasses	BURNS 179:20
no a b. fighter?	STEV 853:75
bons trucs b. t.…annihilated	CUMM 257:50
boo 18,000 people b.	PLAN 680:26
boobs girl with big b.	KING 486:18
booby who is not, at bottom, a b.	MENC 586:83
booh Sing 'B. to you—	GILB 369:44
book A b. unwritten	HARR 399:53
A b. you finish reading	MITCH 609:30
A good b.	MILT 600:99
a good b. is more intelligent	ECO 310:18
as kill a good b.	MILT 600:99
as much a trade to write a b.	LA 502:7
bad b. is as much	HUXL 441:63
Bell, b., and candle	SHAK 768:56
betray me to a lingering b.	HERB 413:62
b.…a kind of optical instrument	PROU 698:61
b. and a head collide	LICH 528:87
b. and me together	BROW 168:51
b.…finished in half the time	WODE 952:44
b. in the ordinary sense	MILL 593:52
b. is not harmless	ELIOT 319:34
b. of knowledge	MILT 603:75
b. of life	BIBLE 132:22
b.…of my secret soul	SHAK 785:84
b. of road maps	STEI 846:86
b. out of which a people	LIPP 531:37
b. this learning mayst	SHAK 801:65
b.…you're all done reading	SALI 739:72
burn a b.	RUSH 732:66
by the b.	SHAK 780:24
called the b. Men Without Women	HEMI 409:63
commonplace b. be full	SWIFT 861:21
cover of an old b.	FRAN 348:7
dainties…bred in a b.	SHAK 763:12
damned, thick, square b.!	GLOU 374:51
difference between writing a b.	MAIL 560:57
dirty b. worth reading	POUND 692:32
do not throw this b. about	BELL 76:50
drown my b.	SHAK 804:31
Each creature…Is as a b.	ALAN 10:15
essence of a b.	NABO 628:15
Europe…a hardcover b.	DELI 271:37
ever written a b.	WELD 928:88
Every b. is like a purge	DU 306:94
face…is as a b.	SHAK 796:16
find one English b.	ARNO 35:9
Finishing a b.	CAPO 197:28
from the b. of honour razed	SHAK 800:44
frowst with a b.	KIPL 491:32
Go little b.	SPEN 837:14
greatest b. he had ever read	STEIN 845:62
He is like a b. in breeches	SMITH 831:56
ideal companion…a good b.	DAVI 265:87
In the Penguin b.	HEAN 405:75
in thy b. all my members	BIBLE 103:45
little black b. with two players in	CHAR 216:49
little b. out of the angel's hand	BIBLE 131:8
Louvre is the b.	CEZA 212:53
make one b.	JOHN 462:36
man the index of that b.	DONNE 293:79
May my b. teach	GIDE 367:19
men with b. learning	RAMOS 705:50
mind afterwards—over a b.	LAMB 505:98
mine adversary had written a b.	BIBLE 98:10
Mona Lisa seem an open b.	LEAC 515:15
moral or an immoral b.	WILDE 940:62
nature's infinite b. of secrecy	SHAK 794:45
never call myself a b. lover	LARK 510:91
never read the same b. twice	WILS 948:49
nice new little b.	CATU 209:5
no instruction b. came with it	FULL 355:73
of the b. of war	MONT 615:47
old address b.	MCCU 549:14
oldest rule in the b.	CARR 204:86
one b.…can change the world	YOUS 969:62
one-b. novelist	ROTH 727:76
only one b. in them	BARN 64:73
only trouble with this b.	LEHM 520:25
past…like the leaves of a b.	WOOLF 955:11
possession of a b.	BURG 174:93
praise a b. too highly	MILL 595:93
private b. to prove	STEV 852:57
profession of b. writing	STEI 846:89
Publishing a b. is…like	ATWO 41:48
readers who are pleased with a b.	CONN 242:97
reading of a b.!	THOR 888:23
read one b. in my life	MITF 610:53
school history b.	GLAS 374:46
seal the b.	BIBLE 111:44
seldom peruses a b.	ADDI 6:23
sell a man a b.	MORL 619:39
sour misfortune's b.	SHAK 766:13
take down this b.	YEATS 965:7
take them out of this b.	STER 848:28
tastes no wise b.-maker	LUCAS 541:49
The B. of Life	WILDE 941:83
the future is happening to b. selling	BEZOS 90:75
the most important b.	BEZOS 90:70
then shut the b.	PATM 669:16
The physical b.…had a 500-year run	BEZOS 90:72
The trouble with a b. is	WINT 950:16
Things in b.'s clothing	LAMB 506:11
This b. is not about heroes	OWEN 657:28
this b. is not concerned with Poetry	OWEN 657:29
this is no b.	WHIT 938:6
This little b. contains	STIL 854:99
throw the entire b. in the fire	SAND 741:8
To produce a mighty b.	MELV 585:64
to write a really funny b.	HEMI 409:60
To write the essential b.	PROU 698:60
truly good b.	THOR 888:21
understand that b. but fail	NICO 637:25
until he has written a b.	JOWE 469:15
when you read a b.	GAUG 361:3
Who is worthy to open the b.	BIBLE 131:99
word for word without b.	SHAK 785:80
Would you read a Sustaining B.	MILNE 596:16
write a b. a year	TARTT 867:34
writing a b.	GERA 364:60
Writing a b. of poetry	MARQ 575:37
book-case prefer to be killed by a b.	STOP 856:24
red mahogany b.-c.	BETJ 88:19
Bookie snatch B. Bob	RUNY 731:56
bookkeeper works like a b.	WILS 948:56
book-keeping double-entry b.-k.	MULL 624:33
book-learning b.-l. in monasteries	GALL 358:44
books All b. are the Book of Job	ELKIN 322:16
all my b. are botches	MELV 585:72
all the b. you can export	CHIS 222:24
archives of his b.	RODC 721:43
are the b., the arts	SHAK 763:19
author because you like his b.	LINK 530:31
author who speaks about his own b.	DISR 288:61
base authority from others' b.	SHAK 763:2
Before high-piled b.	KEATS 475:77
be not swallowed up in b.!	WESL 932:74
bibliobuli…who are…drunk on b.	MENC 586:4
B. and the man I sing	POPE 688:29
B. are a load of crap	LARK 509:83
B. are cold and certain	HUGO 437:78
b. are divided	RUSK 733:3
b. are either dreams	LOWE 539:97
B. are good enough	STEV 852:49
b. are more than b.	LOWE 539:96
b. are theatres	STEV 850:94
B. are the bees	LOWE 539:10
b.…are the nearest to us	CONR 244:40
B. are the opium	FRAN 346:80
B. are written by martyr-men	CARL 201:29
b., convention and cliché	POUND 691:88
B. do furnish a room	POWE 693:46
b. echoing the life	WILL 946:22
B. from Boots	BETJ 88:22
B. have had their day	BENN 81:81
b. have their own fate	TERE 879:16
b. have to teach	RUSH 732:68
b.…how many of them I could avoid	MACA 544:15
b. in the running brooks	SHAK 778:66
B., like men	SWIFT 861:19
B. make sense of life	BARN 64:68
B. must follow sciences	BACON 53:50
B. of poetry…promissory notes	WILDE 940:50
b. one reads in childhood	ORWE 654:55
b. promiscuously read	MILT 600:11
B.…propose to instruct	DE 273:83
b. teach them	GARC 359:67
b. that everyone else is reading	MURAK 626:59
b. that have a lot of dreck	BART 66:14
b. that influence us	FORS 345:50
b. that wound	KAFKA 472:3
B. think for me	LAMB 506:10
B.! 'tis a dull…strife	WORD 957:58
b. to blisse ne to joye	LANG 508:49
b. were read	BELL 77:71
b. which do not have facts	VIDAL 912:96
b. which you do not understand	VIAN 912:96
b. written by Europeans	NAIP 629:28
borrowers of b.	LAMB 505:3
British…taste for bad b.	BRAD 154:30
cannot learn men from b.	DISR 287:15
Deep-versed in b.	MILT 607:80
everybody could write b.	BAIN 50:97
factory of b.	SMITH 828:5
First to possess his b.	SHAK 804:23
forefathers had no other b.	SHAK 759:98
Forsake thy b., and mateless play	BRON 161:74
Friends To borrow my b.	ROBI 718:83
fuck-all to say about my b.	WELSH 930:43
Give me b., fruit, french wine	KEATS 476:96
God has written all the b.	BUTL 186:5
Good travel b.	RABAN 703:3

bottle

haven't read any of your b.	JOYCE 470:38	
houses without b.	LESS 524:3	
If my b. had been any worse	CHAN 213:80	
In b. lies the soul of the whole Past	CARL 201:33	
indiscriminate reviewing of b.	ORWE 654:56	
in Germany, b.	STAEL 842:1	
I've read all the b.	MALL 562:96	
Keepers of b.	MACL 555:37	
let my b. be...eloquence	SHAK 800:42	
luminous plectrum of b.	BELLI 76:47	
Mistresses are like b.	WYCH 964:97	
more b. one reads	MAO 569:39	
more b. we read	CONN 243:6	
never yet was put into words or b.	MELV 585:65	
of making many b. there is no end	BIBLE 107:37	
old b.	GOLD 376:9	
One reads b.	KEIL 479:59	
people...do not read b.	WORD 961:32	
pictures of obscene b.!	ARLT 32:35	
reading of good b.	DESC 274:92	
Read the best b. first	THOR 888:18	
so charming as b.	SMITH 830:51	
Some b. accrete things	HOLM 423:59	
some b. are deemed most baneful	MELV 585:75	
Some b. are lies	BURNS 177:73	
Some b. are to be tasted	BACON 53:37	
Some b. are undeservedly forgotten	AUDEN 43:8	
spacious highways of b.	SAND 742:34	
spectacles of b.	DRYD 300:20	
story b....written by people	WELTY 931:47	
study of mankind is b.	HUXL 441:53	
trees shall be my b.	SHAK 779:86	
true University...is a collection of b.	CARL 201:34	
turned o'er many b.	SHAK 770:11	
two classes of b.	FORD 343:91	
who has written fine b.	GARR 360:80	
worse crimes than burning b.	BROD 160:41	
Writing b. is the closest men	MAIL 560:49	
booksellers bold b.	SHER 817:99	
embolden b.	WAUGH 923:49	
boomerang b. No more spear	NOON 641:51	
boon for heaven's grace and b.	KEATS 477:21	
Of neither would I ask the b.	SHEL 816:54	
recipients of the b. of liberty	MAMET 563:29	
sordid b.!	WORD 961:30	
boot b. in the face, the brute	PLATH 681:34	
imagine a b. stamping	ORWE 655:77	
power of your b.	MOTI 622:89	
Then hey for b. and horse	KING 487:48	
booted always be b. and spurred	MONT 613:19	
Booth B. died blind	LIND 530:17	
B. led boldly	LIND 530:15	
bootless spends a b. grief	SHAK 789:99	
boots a pair of b.	TRAV 895:68	
asleep in his b.	STEV 850:78	
before the truth has got its b. on	CALL 192:29	
children...never had any b.	WILS 948:58	
elastic-sided b.	SHAR 806:72	
It b. not to resist	SHAK 760:14	
look at his b.	SHAW 810:94	
pantheon of b. and overalls	DUNN 307:14	
truth is pulling its b. on	SPUR 841:89	
wear long b., hard b.	SAND 742:20	
went to school without any b.	BULM 173:61	
when I take my b. off	DICK 280:36	
bootstraps raise ourselves by our own b.	WILL 944:71	
booty none left to play b.	DICK 278:66	
booze B., of course, and then curtains	AMIS 16:41	
feeding on b. and spaghetti	LEWIS 527:58	
man shouldn't fool with b.	FAUL 331:48	
boozer clown, the b., the fighter?	MAST 581:81	
boozes tell a man who b.	BURT 181:71	
bop Playing b. is like playing Scrabble	ELLI 322:20	
Boralaski as Count B.'s wife	SCOTT 753:38	
Borat B....works as a tool	BARON 64:80	
bordello doorkeeper of a b.	TOSC 894:64	
border across the b. to get a drink	ANON 24:9	
chuck them over the b.	WALE 917:29	
Night Mail crossing the b.	AUDEN 42:71	
o'er the B. and awa'	SCOTT 753:47	
sung of B. chivalry	SCOTT 752:9	
Through all the wide B.	SCOTT 752:21	
borders b., beds and shrubberies	KIPL 492:67	
invade the b. of my realm	ELIZ 321:4	
no walls, no b.	ATWO 41:34	
tyranny whose b. are undefined	MAIL 560:44	
bore A colossal b.	MERI 588:42	
beside a muzzled b.	STEP 847:12	
complaints are a b.	ACHE 3:40	
Every hero becomes a b.	EMER 325:79	
healthy male adult b.	UPDI 905:16	
If your husband is a b.	BELL 77:85	
in it is merely a b.	WILDE 941:90	
is an old b.	TREE 896:98	
last bastion of the b.	THER 882:92	
less is a b.	VENT 910:53	
merely the Club B.	SAKI 739:67	
People find ideas a b.	POUND 692:19	
unless it becomes a b.	POUND 691:96	
bored better that aged diplomats be b.	AUST 47:98	
boasting...they are never b.	DRAB 298:84	
b. nearer to...mortification	WODE 951:31	
I am heavy b.	BERR 87:98	
leaving because I am b.	SAND 742:38	
nearly b.	GOSSE 379:69	
Never to be b.	BALL 58:48	
People do not read to be b.	BEAV 71:32	
Punctuality...virtue of the b.	WAUGH 924:91	
so b. with it all	CHUR 226:21	
boredom b. and pain of it	BUEC 172:42	
b., and the horror	ELIOT 319:30	
b. makes you old	CAST 207:75	
effect of b. on a large scale	INGE 445:29	
Here b. reaches its peak	MILL 594:73	
Inconstancy, b., anxiety	PASC 667:71	
increase in world b.	AMIS 17:58	
Life is first b.	LARK 509:86	
not waiting for them to die of b.	BLAN 141:48	
Symmetry is b.	HUGO 437:80	
what makes a journey...horrible is b.	GELL 363:35	
bores B. and Bored	BYRON 190:24	
B. bore each other	MARQ 575:60	
B. have succeeded to dragons	DISR 287:18	
Borgia B. who has suddenly	WODE 952:43	
Borgias dining with the B. tonight	BEER 74:93	
thirty years under the B.	WELL 929:93	
boring Antiquity...clichéd and b.	FLAU 339:27	
Don't be b.	BEZOS 90:74	
Life...is b.	BERR 87:97	
previously amusing...become b.	COUP 248:35	
something curiously b.	HUXL 441:52	
work is less b. than amusement	BAUD 69:84	
born all b. and must die	MATAK 581:84	
as a poet...not b. yet	THOM 886:73	
as if I had insisted on being b.	DICK 282:3	
as natural...to be b.	BACON 50:59	
as soon as we were b.	BIBLE 112:77	
because you were b. in it?	SHAW 810:9	
bird b. in a cage	SHAW 809:88	
blight man was b. for	HOPK 428:82	
b....among the mountains	WORD 958:90	
b. and dying, dying	MISH 609:24	
b., And he had reasons	ROBI 718:84	
b. below par to the extent	MONT 613:16	
B. but to die	POPE 687:80	
b. free as Caesar	SHAK 776:8	
b. in a merry hour	SHAK 774:31	
b. in Canada	JOHN 458:24	
b. in the minds of a few	KISS 493:88	
b. into music	SIMO 822:78	
b. into the world alive	GILB 369:52	
B. of the sun	SPEN 837:93	
b. of woman	TWAIN 902:38	
b. out of due time	BIBLE 127:55	
b. to know you	ELUA 324:44	
b. to run	SPRI 841:88	
b. to set it right	STRA 856:37	
b....when wits were fresh and clear	ARNO 34:94	
b. where my father lived	SITT 823:93	
b. with an unreasonably large stock	SHAW 811:33	
b....with ready-made parents	FRAME 346:77	
b. with two things	TEMP 869:70	
Bred in b. in a brier-patch	HARR 398:46	
British Bourgeosie Is not b.	SITW 824:17	
can't be b., unless it's...in	DICK 280:52	
Else, wherefore b.?	TENN 878:93	
engaged, married, or b.	GALS 358:48	
Every moment one is b.	TENN 872:27	
Except a man be b. again	BIBLE 122:23	
fashion is b. by small facts	SCHI 747:22	
He was b. with little	JACK 448:5	
If...b. were being invented	DOYLE 297:75	
if he had happened to be b....there	FRIE 351:70	
If Joan of Arc had been b.	SIMON 822:75	
in dying that we are b.	FRAN 347:99	
I've been b., and once	ELIOT 319:26	
I was b. on a day	VALL 907:8	
less than to be b.	BEAU 71:14	
misery of us, that are b. great	WEBS 927:47	
none of woman b.	SHAK 797:55	
not a single molecule...when b.	DIDE 285:69	
not b. a parasite	FRAN 348:23	
not b. under a rhyming planet	SHAK 774:56	
Not to be b. is the best	AUDEN 42:77	
One is not b. a woman	DE 268:44	
powerless to be b.	ARNO 35:4	
remember where I was b.	BENET 79:24	
Sociology was b.	SMALL 826:57	
Some men are b. kings	SHAW 810:17	
That ever I was b.	SHAK 781:71	
time to be b.	BIBLE 105:14	
to be b., to live and to die	LABR 502:22	
to the manner b.	SHAK 781:56	
We are all b. crazy	BECK 72:45	
We are b. believing	EMER 325:88	
When I was b.	WINT 950:11	
When we are b.	SHAK 793:27	
where I was b.	SALI 739:71	
why wasn't I b. old	DICK 279:99	
borne hath b. me on his back	SHAK 784:63	
borogove All mimsy were the b.	CARR 204:89	
boroughs bright b.	HOPK 428:75	
borrow know well enough to b. from	BIER 134:60	
poets...beg, b., or steal	POUND 692:38	
borrowed B. garments never fit	FULL 355:81	
b. time, b. money	CALL 192:27	
borrower b. of the night	SHAK 797:43	
Neither a b. nor a lender be	SHAK 781:53	
borrowing banqueting upon b.	BIBLE 113:96	
b. foolishly spent	DUNC 307:7	
borrowings b. cheap and the notes	LUCAS 541:51	
bosom Amputate my freckled B.!	DICK 284:54	
borne, see, on my b.!	BROW 168:57	
b. is actually a millstone	GREER 387:40	
b. of the great English	ARNO 35:11	
b. of the lake	TENN 873:49	
b. of the sea	SHAK 759:93	
b. of the stream	SHEL 816:59	
b. the bright waters meet	MOORE 617:99	
breaks in our b.	SHEL 816:64	
Can a man take fire in his b.	BIBLE 104:60	
charge within the b.	DICK 283:30	
Cleanse the fraught b.?	SHAK 798:70	
Close b.-friend	KEATS 477:32	
dear to this b.	TANN 867:24	
from the b. of the morn	MARV 576:86	
great within my b.	SHAK 761:54	
guardage to the sooty b.	SHAK 788:88	
Here in my b.	JONS 467:74	
in your fragrant b. dies	CAREW 199:58	
Let me to thy b. fly	WESL 931:59	
no b. and no behind	SMITH 830:34	
not a b. to repose upon	DICK 282:86	
sea that bares her b.	WORD 961:30	
shall men give into your b.	BIBLE 120:74	
tribes...slumber in its b.	BRYA 170:2	
will leave Thy b.	MILT 603:83	
bosoms b. of your actresses	JOHN 459:51	
hang and brush their b.?	BROW 168:32	
Quiet to quick b. is a hell	BYRON 187:52	
boss absentee b. is best	WINT 950:6	
b....a comforting thought	MARQ 575:56	
talk to a b.	MAMET 564:43	
The b. is never your friend	APPEL 29:87	
will always be his b.	RAVI 707:85	
Boston B. has become Urban Renewal	MAIL 560:55	
B....hast naught to boast	ANON 22:81	
B....home of the bean and the cod	BOSS 151:74	
B. is a state of mind	APPL 30:93	
B. man is the east wind	APPL 30:94	
B. State-House is the hub	HOLM 424:70	
bottle of B. sea	BENET 79:25	
Boswell B. was one of the smallest	MACA 545:35	
botanize peep and b.	WORD 957:65	
botched Presidents...have b. up	ONAS 650:52	
bother 'b. it' I may Occasionally say	GILB 368:32	
don't b. much about dress	SHAW 806:94	
bothered buzzard...is never b.	FAUL 331:44	
bothersome Life is short and b.	LABR 502:19	
Botticelli B. isn't a wine	PUNCH 700:83	
bottle a little for the b.	DIBD 276:29	

bottles

b. of Boston sea — BENET 79:25
b. of salvation — RALE 705:44
b. of the best — STEV 851:26
brandish anything but my b. — SHAK 772:73
cantaloupe in a coke b. — JONES 466:24
desire to a b. — SHAK 767:41
fly the way out of the fly-b. — WITT 951:27
ginger-beer b. — STEV 852:52
leave the b. on the chimley-piece — DICK 279:16
like magic in a pint b. — DICK 282:88
Poetry in a b. — FADI 329:8
scorpions in a b. — OPPE 652:89
terrible than an empty b. — LOWRY 541:41
vintage wine from a musty old b. — BOYLE 154:18

bottles B. of Ring-Bo-Ree — LEAR 516:33
fill old b. with banknotes — KEYN 484:80
new wine into old b. — BIBLE 116:64

bottom at the b. of a' the mischief — SCOTT 753:57
b. of my grief? — SHAK 766:5
b. stir The hell — MILT 603:89
Better to be at the b. — EGGE 313:68
going to hit the b. — MOND 612:95
I'm the b., you're the top — PORT 690:69
old mad scientist at b. — PERE 674:17
They have…mettle and b. — EMER 325:84
very b. of her being — ADAMS 4:80
will reach the b. first — GRAH 380:86
with my b. in the air — PIGG 678:73

bottomless b., topsiturviest — RUSK 733:18
Law is a b. pit — ARBU 30:1

bottoms b. of my trousers rolled — ELIOT 316:67

bough Apollo's laurel b. — MARL 574:33
blossom that hangs on the b. — SHAK 804:32
b. from Virginia's aged tree — RANS 706:67
bread beneath the b. — FITZ 337:69
Petals on a wet, black b. — POUND 691:92

boughs b. do laughing blossoms bear — SPEN 838:39
b. more silent than before — MILL 592:24
b. off many a tree — HERB 413:59
Green b. — LORCA 537:58
lowest b. and the brushwood sheaf — BROW 167:20
those b. which shake — SHAK 801:62

bouillabaisse B. is only good — DOUG 295:7
bouillion good poem is like a b. cube — DOVE 296:28
boulders spills the upper b. — FROST 352:90
bounce no more b. than…potato — PORT 690:76
bounces bigger because of the b. — MILNE 596:22
bound b. for the same bourn — HOUS 431:53
b. to give it honestly — JOHN 462:29
stream, confined in narrow b. — CRAB 252:43
tall buildings in a single b.! — SIEG 820:61
too small a b. — SHAK 772:67
tranced woman, b. and stark — FREE 350:48

boundaries b. between politics — DANG 262:29
b. of the soul — HERA 412:35
cannot remain within their b. — DANTE 262:40
Deem that our puny b. — WORD 958:80
few landmarks and no b. — MCMU 557:85
step over the b. — HIRST 419:79

boundary b. of the march — PARN 665:48
no b. line to art — PARK 663:93

bounded b. in a nutshell — SHAK 782:86

boundless b., as we wish our souls — SHEL 812:60
b., endless, and sublime — BYRON 188:73
Is b. better, b. worse — TENN 872:25
there is b. theft — SHAK 791:81

bounds Eternity as if it had b. — DUNC 307:10
flaming b. of place and time — GRAY 385:90
is out of b. now — LOWE 540:26
living know No b.? — SHIR 819:16
thus far thy b. — MILT 605:30
untraced b. — WENT 931:53
wider shall thy b. be set — BENS 81:84

bountiful How just, how b. — WORD 962:50
nature…careless as it is b. — DILL 286:92

bounty b. is as boundless — SHAK 766:84
b. of God — BLAKE 140:2
those his former b. fed — DRYD 303:31

bouquets b. keep pouring in — FREUD 350:56

Bourbon B. family is a dagger — QUIN 702:23
bourbon sound of pouring b. — MCCU 549:15
this b. is good — TRUM 900:94

bourgeois astound the b. — BAUD 69:90
beastly the b. is — LAWR 513:77
b. always bounces up — CONN 242:93
B. society is infected — WEIL 928:74
English proletariat…more b. — ENGE 326:11

Hatred of the b. — FLAU 339:24
narrow horizon of b. — MARX 579:43
person of b. origin — ORWE 653:12
small-town b. at heart — NABO 629:21
sordid b. world — MISH 609:22

bourgeoisie b. in the long run — TROT 899:65
b. of all classes, who deny tragedy — BLIX 142:62
Discreet Charm of the B. — BUNU 173:71
fine nervous flower of the b. — BOGAN 144:95
For generations the British b. — WAUGH 923:57
The b.'s weapon — STEV 854:92
The British B. — SITW 824:71
wanted to make the b. a class — HUGO 437:84

bourn bound for the same b. — HOUS 431:53

Bournemouth B. is one of the few — BETJ 88:30

Bovary Madame B. — MCCA 548:98

bovine cow is of the b. — NASH 630:54

bow Ane b. that is ay bent — HENR 411:19
arrow from the Tartar's b. — SHAK 767:37
B., b., ye lower middle classes! — GILB 369:49
b. of burning gold! — BLAKE 141:42
B. themselves when he did sing — SHAK 804:44
b. to everyone — SKEL 825:43
b. was made in England — DOYLE 297:49
breaketh the b. — BIBLE 100:69
breaketh the b. — BOOK 149:17
drew a b. at a venture — BIBLE 97:70
made-up b. ties — SHAR 806:72
set my b. in the cloud — BIBLE 92:13
Thou shalt not b. down thyself — BIBLE 94:66
tightened b. — YEATS 966:14

bowels b. of Christ — CROM 255:20
b. of compassion — BIBLE 130:80
b. were moved for him — BIBLE 107:47
melted in the midst of my b. — BIBLE 99:43
molten b. — BOTT 152:83
No belly and no b. — RANS 707:73

bower b. quiet for us — KEATS 476:84
deck both bed and b. — SPEN 838:33
flower perfumes the b. — SCOTT 754:69
hall and b. — WORD 958:94
sought her baith by b. and ha' — SCOTT 753:47
twa sisters in a b. — BALL 58:52

bowers built upon the b. of paradise — PAINE 660:31
cedar and sycamore b. — KEND 480:85

bowl b. of night — FITZ 337:68
child drinking a b. of milk — SAND 742:33
Come, dear b. — BARL 63:56
great b. of the sky — MCMU 557:83
honey set in a green b. — SMITH 828:99
I b. so slow — BARR 65:93
love in a golden b. — BLAKE 139:84
lurk within the b. — SMITH 831:59
softly in the brimming b. — JOYCE 470:19

bowled darned near b. him — LARW 510:9

bowler b.'s Holding — JOHN 465:9
b. thinks he bowls — LANG 507:41
difference between a fast b. — TRUE 899:74

bowling b. lobs and slow twisters — JOYCE 470:19

bowls bowler thinks he b. — LANG 507:41
B. is a young man's game — BRYA 170:1
b. of fierce desire — CRAS 254:87
Fill our b. once more — SHAK 794:72
playing b. upon a splitting wreck — DAVI 264:65

bow-shot A b.-s. from her — TENN 869:83

bowstring thrice cut Cupid's b. — SHAK 774:43

bow-wow Big B.-w. strain — SCOTT 754:78

box B. about — AUBR 42:59
b. and the puppets — THAC 880:30
b. that fennel Grows around — RANS 707:72
father gave him a b. — MACN 558:9
jack in the b. — ELKIN 322:17
Pit, b., and gallery — POPE 687:98
rattle of the money b. — LABO 501:5
think out of the b. — THARP 880:43
time…kept in a b. — RAINE 705:40

boxer b. never sees the big one — FORE 344:18
With a nation, as with a b. — ACHE 3:55

boxes banging down their bits of b. — OSBO 655:84
Neat in their b. — ROET 722:55

boxing activity is so vain as b. — MAIL 560:59
b. is everything — HEMI 410:97
B. is show-business with blood — BELA 75:29
b. really combines — LONS 536:42
I have covered b. — GALL 358:39
poetry and b. — JAY 453:7
Squash is b. — BARR 65:96

box of chocolates life was like a b. o. c. — HANKS 395:83

boy any b.…become president — STEV 851:22
As a b. — HATT 400:82
Attic b. to hunt — MILT 598:57
blind b., Venus' baby — SPEN 839:48
blitz of a b. — CAUS 209:14
b. always rose again — MAP 569:41
B. Meets Girl in Winnipeg — MACL 555:49
b. playing on the sea — NEWT 635:41
b.'s ideal of a manly career — DISR 287:33
b. stood on the burning deck — HEMA 409:58
b.'s will is the wind's — LONG 535:31
b. walking…head drooping — WHITE 935:50
b. with his father — IHIM 445:19
can't expect a b. to be vicious — SAKI 739:56
changed into a b. — KEIL 479:58
Chatterton, the marvellous b. — WORD 959:1
down to talk poetry, my b. — DICK 277:55
every b. and every gal — GILB 369:52
genuine b. is a rebel — MILL 594:87
Give to your b. — DRYD 301:51
growing b. — WORD 959:8
hating, my b., is an art — NASH 630:62
Her little b. weeping sought — BLAKE 139:92
How dost, my b.? — SHAK 792:8
if they like a b. — SALI 740:79
imagination of a b. — KEATS 476:83
Little B. kneels at the foot — MILNE 596:13
little tiny b. — SHAK 786:25
Mad about the b. — COWA 249:52
many a b. here — SHER 818:9
modest, good-humoured b. — BEER 73:77
My b.,' he says — RUNY 731:55
never was a b. — MILL 592:12
no b.…allured to letters — STEE 844:50
not the Model B. — TWAIN 902:40
office b. — GILB 368:34
parent who could see his b. — LEAC 515:18
plump and hearty, healthy b. — HOFF 422:32
purblind, wayward b. — SHAK 763:9
read to by a b. — ELIOT 317:82
remain a fifteen-year-old b. — ROTH 727:80
Robin was a rovin' B. — BURNS 178:98
salesman is got to dream, b. — MILL 593:33
Selwyn MacGregor, the nicest b. — SPARK 835:64
sensitive b.'s humiliations — SHAW 807:18
Speak roughly to your little b. — CARR 203:68
speak to your little b. — BLAKE 139:91
Than when I was a b. — HOOD 426:23
The b.'s mouth — TWAIN 903:69
this b. will be surrounded — HARD 396:91
to be a little b. — THUR 891:4
to be b. eternal — SHAK 799:7
What a wonderful b. he is! — HOGG 422:42
When I was a b. — SITT 823:93
When I was a b. — THOM 884:47
While yet a b. — SHEL 812:56
with our precious b. — DICK 279:19
You are a human b. — DICK 281:66

boyfriend and have a French b. — HEPB 412:25

boyhood characters of my b. — STEV 851:30
lost b. of Judas — RUSS 735:43

boys As flies to wanton b. — SHAK 793:17
Beautiful b. with bright red guitars — HENRI 411:8
b. are not going to be sent — ROOS 724:11
B. do now cry — PEPYS 673:84
B.' hate was dangerous — MUNRO 625:47
b. in their happy play — SCHR 749:63
b. late at their play! — ARNO 36:25
breaks are beating the b. — GIPP 372:21
By office b. for office b. — SALI 740:91
Christian b. I can scarcely hope — ARNO 36:45
elders, and fought by b. — LIVE 531:49
English…half-little b. — CELI 211:41
give the b. a little tea — ANDE 18:74
Give them the cold steel, b.! — ARMI 32:40
good old b. was drinkin' — MCLE 554:22
hardly suitable for delicate b. — WILDE 942:25
lightfoot b. are laid — HOUS 431:55
loaded guns with b. — CRAB 252:48
only know two sorts of b. — DICK 278:70
other girls and b. — STEV 853:66
school b. or scholarship — LITT 531:47
The b. are dreaming wicked — THOM 884:33
three wild lads…brave b. — SCOTT 753:43
Till the b. come Home — FORD 343:9
what Asian b. ought — JOHN 458:13

Young b. would talk about it	STEI 846:93	steal away their b.!	SHAK 789:13
bra Burn your b.!	ANON 25:70	such seething b.	SHAK 767:44
braccia twelve b. across	LEON 522:71	Through lovers' b.	SHAK 765:71
bracelet diamond and safire b.	LOOS 536:52	tormenting our b.	MONT 613:11
braces liquid which rots b.	MORT 621:75	What good are b. to a man?	WODE 951:36
bracing Skegness is so b.	ANON 24:4	with no b. at all	HERB 412:41
Bradford silk hat on a B. millionaire	ELIOT 318:4	young man who has b.	STEV 852:47
Bradman B.'s batting genius	LARW 510:8	**brain surgeon** the b. s. leans over	HOFF 422:28
Bradyism B....multisibling sensibility	COUP 248:33	**brake** small but workable b.	MURR 627:82
brae waly, waly doun the b.	BALL 60:79	**bramble-dew** eyes of gold and b.-d.	STEV 854:86
braes among thy green b.	BURNS 178:10	**brambles** like the b. in a wild field	DIDE 285:78
banks and b. o' bonie Doon	BURNS 179:32	**branch** accomplished in any b.	MARX 579:29
b. o' Killiecrankie	BURNS 179:17	blaze of b., or brazier	ELIOT 321:81
by yon bonnie b.	ANON 22:79	b. of...antediluvian families	CONG 240:46
brag Men would b.	STEI 846:93	B. shall grow out of his roots	BIBLE 108:61
Brahmin Men are the B.	STAN 842:14	Cut is the b.	MARL 574:33
braid badge of tarnished b.	READ 708:95	Lone on the fir-b.	MERE 587:23
b. to bind your hair	SCOTT 753:46	lops the mouldered b. away	TENN 879:2
O' gude B. Claith	FERG 333:84	neither root nor b.	BIBLE 112:65
thy brow to b.	SCOTT 753:35	pluck an ivy b. for me	ROSS 726:40
brain are the b. of heaven	MERE 588:37	reddens on the high b.	SAPP 743:50
blessed with a woman's b.	RICH 714:17	tip of every b.	PLATH 681:37
blind life within the b.	TENN 878:86	**branches** b. of government	MILL 591:4
Bracing b. and sinew	KING 487:44	climb black b.	FROST 352:98
b. falls out	DAWK 267:24	most lucrative of its b.	PAINE 660:34
b. has Corridors	DICK 284:41	poetry does not swing from the b.	CHOC 222:25
b. may devise laws	SHAK 769:76	retain their b.	SOPH 834:28
b. of feathers	POPE 688:35	**branch-strained** b.-s. metaphor	MOORE 617:89
b. stops criticising	SLOAN 825:54	**brand** b. him either a failure	HOLM 423:57
B....wider than the Sky	DICK 284:39	b. sae drap wi' bluid	BALL 59:61
B....with which we think	BIER 134:67	**brandy** of the damned	SHAW 807:23
children of an idle b.	SHAK 765:72	must drink b.	JOHN 463:66
cobweb of the b.	BUTL 185:76	neat b.	STEV 851:29
Dilutes with drivel every drizzly b.	BYRON 187:33	**brash** when it is b. or noisy	AUDEN 44:16
dislocate my B.!	DICK 284:54	**brashness** a certain b.	GALB 357:17
draughts intoxicate the b.	POPE 685:19	**brass** belly and his thighs of b.	BIBLE 111:38
dry b. in a dry season	ELIOT 317:86	bound him with fetters of b.	BIBLE 96:19
Dwell in some idle b.	MILT 597:49	B. Money	ANON 23:96
eat the b. of clever men	FRAS 349:31	b., nor stone, nor earth	SHAK 801:57
emptying the native's b.	FANON 329:14	evil manners live in b.	SHAK 805:56
gladness...thy b. must know	SHEL 814:99	feet like unto fine b.	BIBLE 131:88
gleaned my teeming b.	KEATS 475:77	nor walls of beaten b.	SHAK 776:14
I feared it might injure the b.	CARR 203:66	serpent of b.	BIBLE 94:82
in my b. I sing it	BROW 168:57	sounding b.	BIBLE 126:52
lantern of Aristotle's b.	RALE 705:46	think gold that is b.	SPEN 839:57
lenses through which the b. explores	DOUG 295:5	**brass-collar** letter'd, braw b.-c.	BURNS 177:80
let the b. lie also	BROW 168:51	**brassière** Art is not a b.	BARN 64:67
little b. attic	DOYLE 297:58	**brat** you horrid b.	BEME 78:1
madness...should possess a poet's b.	DRAY 299:98	**brattle** Wi' bickering b.!	BURNS 177:77
messages go quicker to the b.	SPARK 836:66	**brave** act so b. and daring	ROCH 719:17
no one's b. rejects it	BACON 53:55	b. and battered sisters	PRIE 695:86
not for the weary b.	THOM 887:7	b. and meek with thirty bob a week	DAVI 264:64
painting is done with the b.	MICH 590:67	b., generous...warm-hearted race	BUCH 171:25
passion of the b.	BURT 181:87	b. man with a sword	WILDE 942:17
petrifactions of a plodding b.	BYRON 187:27	b. master was no more	MACA 546:60
phonographs of hades in the b.	CRANE 253:69	B. men are a city's strongest tower	ALCA 11:39
phrases in his b.	SHAK 763:6	b. on a battlefield	MITC 610:43
Purple haze is in my b.	HEND 411:3	b. resistance	WASH 921:27
puzzle their b.	GOLD 376:11	b. that die in the battle	CLOU 232:62
rafters of the b.	HUID 438:91	Fortune favours the b.	TERE 879:13
Relaxing your b. is fatal	MOSS 622:83	home of the b.?	KEY 483:68
shifting my b.	HERZ 416:22	How sleep the b.	COLL 237:71
so small his b.	BUTL 184:63	instead of the b. fine	NOON 641:50
studies of the b.	PENF 673:79	intelligent, the witty, the b.	MILL 592:27
toil of b., or toil of hands	MELV 585:53	make one b. push	STEV 852:54
too little b.	SHAK 787:43	makes e'en the valiant more b.	DIBD 276:30
troubles of the b.	SHAK 798:70	Many b. men lived before	HORA 430:12
unquiet heart and b.	TENN 873:58	more b. than me	CUMM 258:62
What's in the b.	SHAK 802:77	Neither a wise man nor a b. man	EISE 314:93
whimsy heaped in his own b.	ROCH 719:11	noble race and b.	SIGO 821:64
work like madness on the b.	COLE 235:34	None but the b. deserves the fair	DRYD 303:28
brainpower using their b.	MCDO 550:44	O b. new world	SHAK 804:33
brains big feet and no b.	HAGEN 391:5	That's a b. fellow	SHAK 799:93
blow out your b.	KIPL 489:89	The b. may not live forever	BRAN 156:71
Blows out his b. upon the flute	BROW 169:82	the b., the mighty	WORD 961:42
B. are not everything	SHAW 807:4	this is most b.	SHAK 782:2
b. get buried	ROTH 728:82	To fight aloud, is very b.	DICK 283:30
b. go to his head	ASQU 38:91	What's b., what's noble	SHAK 795:85
b. knocked out by them	SHEL 812:71	**braver** b. in another language	BROO 163:7
b. of Minerva	BARR 65:98	**bravery** b. of his grief	SHAK 785:70
b. wuz to settle	LOWE 539:6	**braw** that was b.	BURNS 180:49
but extra b.	TRUE 899:74	**brawling** b. of a sparrow	YEATS 965:6
clears the b.	PENE 673:78	**braying** light is b.	SITW 823:99
feet instead of their b.	SOUSA 834:39	**brazen** [Nature's] world is b.	SIDN 820:54
gentleman said a girl with m.	LOOS 536:46	**brazier** blaze of branch, or b.	ELIOT 321:81
had to use my b.	SHAN 805:67	**Brazil** Science fiction, like B.	DISCH 287:10
have my b. ta'en out and buttered	SHAK 773:12	**Brazilian** a B. without love or more	STING 855:2

Brazilification B....widening gulf	COUP 248:27	**breach** endure not yet A b.	DONNE 292:39
		more unto the b.	SHAK 775:74
		bread After b.	JOHN 458:18
		b. and butter	MACK 554:14
		b. and butter	MACD 550:39
		b. and butter	SWIFT 863:70
		b. and games	JUVE 471:57
		b. and meat	STEV 851:29
		b. and your butter	KIPL 492:66
		b. beneath the bough	FITZ 337:69
		b. eaten in secret	BIBLE 104:62
		b. for the family	LEWIS 526:54
		b. I dip in the river	STEV 853:82
		b.-sauce of the happy ending	JAMES 450:48
		b. to the wise	BIBLE 106:29
		b. which strengtheneth	BIBLE 102:11
		b. with the salt of tears	KAIKO 472:11
		cannot give them b.	WILDE 940:45
		cast my b. on the waters	JACK 448:1
		Cast thy b. upon the waters	BIBLE 106:34
		Cast your b. upon	HAGG 391:6
		Content...To eat dusty b.	BOGAN 144:93
		crust of b.	RYDER 736:57
		cutting b. and butter	THAC 880:40
		did eat of my b.	BIBLE 100:62
		earn my b.	FRAN 348:23
		eat b. to the full	BIBLE 93:64
		eat the b. of sorrows	BIBLE 103:36
		eat thy b. with joy	BIBLE 106:27
		eat thy b. with quaking	BIBLE 110:31
		give him b. to eat	BIBLE 105:95
		Give us this day our daily b.	BIBLE 115:42
		half a loaf was better than no b.	CHES 220:78
		having looked to government for b.	BURKE 176:54
		I am the b. of life	BIBLE 122:34
		if his son ask b.	BIBLE 115:51
		Jesus took b.	BIBLE 119:40
		Jesus...took b.	BIBLE 126:49
		lives not upon b. alone	STEV 852:42
		man doth not live by b. only	BIBLE 95:90
		Man shall not live by b. alone	BIBLE 114:22
		meat, and cursed the b.	ROBI 718:82
		nor his seed begging b.	BIBLE 100:60
		offered a piece of b. and butter	MACK 554:14
		People who eat white b.	VREE 915:58
		ravens brought him b.	BIBLE 97:60
		science as well as b.	JAMES 451:62
		servants...have b. enough	BIBLE 121:90
		shalt thou eat b.	BIBLE 91:99
		Some gave them white b.	CARR 205:15
		spend money for that which is not b.?	BIBLE 109:96
		spoiled the b. and spilled the wine	PATM 669:15
		steal b.	FRAN 347:89
		take b. at my hand	WYATT 964:90
		that b. should be so dear	HOOD 426:32
		touch of holy b.	SHAK 779:1
		Who never ate his b. in sorrow	GOET 375:61
		With the b. eaten	CERV 211:46
		yield a heavy b.	WILK 943:60
		breadlines b. continue	SKEL 825:38
		breadwinner b. and a crosspatch	SMITH 830:32
		break bend but do not b.	LAFO 503:51
		B., b., b.	TENN 871:3
		b. earth's sleep	OWEN 658:38
		b. my staff	SHAK 804:31
		B. the bone	RABE 703:10
		b. them at pleasure	EDGE 311:35
		but they never b.	BUCK 172:37
		Move fast and b. things	ZUCK 970:18
		Never Give...an Even B.	FIEL 335:33
		sex rules...I b.	SALI 740:73
		those that will not b.	HEMI 409:66
		Thou thyself must b.	ARNO 35:24
		time to b. down	BIBLE 105:14
		Words...sometimes b.	ELIOT 319:45
		breaker b. of proverbs	SHAK 771:32
		breaker-beaten b.-b. coast	BYRON 189:6
		breakers angry b. roar	LEAR 516:28
		like b. cliffward leaping!	CRANE 253:66
		Set keel to b.	POUND 691:10
		breakfast bananas for b.	WHAR 933:2
		b., dinner, lunch, and tea	BELL 76:60
		B. is the one meal	VAND 908:14
		cooking b. this morning	SCHR 749:67
		eat Rockefellers for b.	KENN 482:45
		Hope is a good b.	BACON 50:54

breakfasts

hypothesis every day before b.	LORE 537:61
impossible things before b.	CARR 205:6
Where shall we our b. take	BALL 59:76
breakfasts b. on...frosty mornings	GRAH 381:91
breakfast-table well-provisioned b.-t.	HAWT 402:9
breakfast-time critical period...is b.-t.	HERB 413:51
breakneck riding at b. speed	BLAN 141:46
bream Backed lyke a b.	BERN 86:80
breast boiling bloody b.	SHAK 768:48
b. high amid the corn	HOOD 426:24
b. Still tender	HOPE 427:57
broods with warm b.	HOPK 428:71
buckles on his b.	SHAK 793:41
charms to soothe a savage b.	CONG 241:51
craving void...aching in the b.	POPE 686:47
creating in every English b.	MANC 564:51
creep into my b.	BEAU 71:21
crimson...robin's b.	TENN 871:11
deeply implanted in the human b.	DICK 278:68
depth of her glowing b.	SHEL 815:22
forged upon his b.	WORD 961:41
fresh, green b. of the new world	FITZ 338:86
heart leap in my b.	SAPP 743:49
hundred to adore each b.	MARV 577:91
in her red-berried b.	THOM 884:40
Leaning her b.	GIBB 367:7
light within his own clear b.	MILT 598:72
marched b. forward	BROW 169:85
milk in an old b.	MANS 567:96
miss the white b.	JEFF 453:17
moon on the b.	MOORE 616:62
my speaking b.	SHAK 800:42
Not a hook in all my b.	VAUG 909:38
nunnery Of thy chaste b.	LOVE 538:85
On her left b.	SHAK 803:91
on Madeleine's fair b.	KEATS 477:21
on mother's b.	TENN 872:37
peace in thy b.	SHAK 766:86
pepper-pot b. of thrush?	FRAME 346:75
seat within my captive b.	SURR 860:97
shining b.	GORD 378:53
shot...in our b.	ARNO 34:72
soft as the b. of doves	CORN 247:3
spirit in a loyal b.	SHAK 764:32
sweetness fills the b.	CASW 208:81
Tibbald's monster-breeding b.	POPE 688:33
toss him to my b.	HERB 414:83
Truth hath a quiet b.	SHAK 764:33
twining in his speckled b.	MARV 577:98
tyrant of the throbbing b.	GRAY 385:87
wail Or knock the b.	MILT 608:3
what a panic's in thy b.!	BURNS 177:77
whose b. is a cannibal dynamo	GINS 372:6
windows to my b.	SHAK 800:43
Within whose b. did boil	SURR 860:2
wounds are in his b. and face	DAVIS 266:10
breastbone your white b.	CAUS 209:13
breast-feeding atheism, b.-f.	ORTON 652:4
breastplate b. of righteousness	BIBLE 128:95
put in the b. of judgment	BIBLE 94:68
Unpin that spangled b.	DONNE 291:19
What stronger b.	SHAK 759:91
breasts bore within their b. the grief	AYTO 48:13
b. are like two young roes	BIBLE 107:45
b. are under our foot	SHAW 807:20
b., the hallmark of our culture	DONA 290:5
clos'd within each other's b.	DRYD 301:55
could feel my b.	JOYCE 470:33
have bigger b.	JOHN 457:91
In living b.	SPEN 838:36
let her b. satisfy thee	BIBLE 104:57
prodigious b.	SWIN 864:13
soaping her b. in the bath	EWART 328:72
then her b. are dun	SHAK 802:83
voted best b.	JOHAN 456:69
Warring within our b.	MARL 572:99
breath a b. to forms	BYRON 189:82
air my quiet b.	KEATS 478:46
Art cannot hold its b.	ANTH 29:72
before thou giv'st them b.	SHAK 789:17
borne my b. away!	HOOD 426:22
b. And everlasting motion	WORD 957:69
b. can make them	GOLD 376:98
breathed into his nostrils the b. of life	BIBLE 91:86
breathes with human b.	TENN 872:26
b. goes now	DONNE 292:38
breathing a small b.	ROET 722:58

breathing thoughtful b.	WORD 960:20
b. of a buffalo in the winter	HAGG 391:7
b. of Autumn's being	SHEL 813:79
b. of degradation	BYRON 189:84
b. of Heav'n fresh-blowing	MILT 607:81
b. of kings	BURNS 177:76
b. of life	YEATS 966:28
b. Of the night-wind	ARNO 33:66
B.'s a ware	HOUS 431:36
b. that from my mistress reeks	SHAK 802:83
b. were as terrible	SHAK 773:27
b. will carry it	SPUR 841:89
call the fleeting b.?	GRAY 384:67
Clothed with his b.	TENN 878:83
cry that was no more than a b.	CONR 243:30
discernible from his b.	WALL 917:46
draw thy b. in pain	SHAK 785:73
endures for a b.	SWIN 863:86
fluttered and failed for b.	ARNO 34:86
having lost her b.	SHAK 794:57
healthy b. of morn	KEATS 477:28
last b. I drew in	LAMB 506:15
little b.	AURE 45:44
love thee with the b.	BROW 166:98
malice in my b.	SHAK 799:92
Meistersinger...set b. in steel	CRANE 253:67
morn and evening b.	BLAKE 139:80
must take the b.	MANS 567:97
O, for b. to utter	SHAK 771:47
own b. in our own nostrils	MACD 550:46
serpents of explosive b.	MARI 571:177
short of b.	SASS 745:84
sweet b. of heaven	WORD 957:73
tainting of the b.	LEWIS 527:66
taxed the b.	THOM 883:8
The faintest b.	WORD 956:52
Th' endeavour of this present b.	SHAK 763:99
use your b.	FLET 340:53
wait with bated b.	THAT 881:58
while there's b. of life	BISH 136:27
whose b. I hate	SHAK 799:98
with her thick b.	JONS 467:55
with low last b.	ROSS 726:60
breathe as though to b.	TENN 870:98
cannot see, nor b.	MASE 580:62
can't even hear people b.	CRON 256:31
I can't b.	GARN 360:76
they b. in me as angels	RICH 713:7
thought I could not b.	TENN 877:58
When...lapdogs b. their last	POPE 685:40
breathes B. there the man	SCOTT 752:16
hell itself b. out	SHAK 783:30
breathing b. in their faces	SHAK 804:29
B. like one that hath	TENN 870:88
Closer is He than b.	TENN 877:71
does not love b.	LEE 518:86
health, and capture b.	KEATS 476:84
sound his b. kept	SHEL 814:13
Trick is to Keep B.	GALL 358:42
breathing-space want a little b. s.	MARP 574:42
breathing-time b.-t....or a truce	WORD 961:38
breathless B. and bewildered	ACHE 3:44
B., we flung us	BROO 162:84
bred B. en bawn in a brier-patch	HARR 398:46
Bredon summertime in B.	HOUS 431:43
bree A little aboon her b.	BALL 59:73
breeches He is like a book in b.	SMITH 831:56
render my leather b. incapable	SHER 817:73
breed b. apart from...humanity	MANK 566:75
b. for barren metal	SHAK 769:86
B. never dies	BENN 80:46
dogs I b. and sell	GRAV 382:31
none of another b.	YEATS 967:35
not b. one work	HOPK 429:96
Where they most b.	SHAK 796:18
breeder b. of sinners	SHAK 783:10
breeding formed by a different b.	DISR 288:34
guilt, or of ill b.	CONG 241:60
true b. of a gentleman	BYRON 190:14
breeds see what b. about her heart	SHAK 792:13
breeks b. aff a Hielandman	SCOTT 753:54
breeze b. of morning moves	TENN 876:25
b. of song	TENN 874:86
correspondent b.	WORD 957:73
dancing in the b.	WORD 960:24
Each b. from foggy mount	BYRON 187:33
flag to April's b. unfurled	EMER 324:48

fragrance was borne upon the b.	DICK 279:18
gentle b.	WORD 957:72
hay-harvest b.	CORY 247:12
planted...by some unnoticed b.	CARL 201:16
softest b....gives birth	WORD 962:48
The b. is on the sea	SCOTT 754:69
tossing b.	ARNO 35:18
wings of the b.	BRON 161:55
breezes little b. dusk	TENN 869:78
Brendan Saint B....Irish boats	BEHAN 74:10
brent bonie brow was b.	BURNS 179:16
Brer Fox en B. F., he lay low	HARR 398:45
brethren b. to dwell together	BIBLE 103:40
mother and my b.!	BIBLE 117:89
one of the least of these my b.	BIBLE 119:37
presence of all his b.	BIBLE 92:19
sent his b. away	BIBLE 93:47
Breughel B. of the 20th century	ADLER 8:68
brevity B. is the sister of talent	CHEK 218:13
B. is the soul	SHAK 781:74
B. is the soul of lingerie	PARK 663:94
b. of human life	PROT 697:34
first to complain of its b.	LABR 502:28
its body b.	COLE 235:33
brew b. that is true	PANA 662:80
brewery bladder against a b.	KIRK 493:81
brews peer of England b.	HOUS 432:57
briars blinding with b. my joy	BLAKE 140:15
bribe man who offers a b.	GREE 386:18
Marriage is a b.	WILD 943:40
Too poor for a b.	GRAY 385:94
bribes by b. to please	DYER 309:50
How many b. he had taken	BENT 82:5
brick carried a b. in his pocket	JOHN 461:9
men...expect b.	ASTE 39:2
on solid b.	POPE 689:39
palace built of squarèd b.	SPEN 838:22
piece of b. in his pocket	SWIFT 862:29
threw it a b. at a time	HARG 398:31
throw a b....hitting the niece	ORWE 653:14
town of red b.	DICK 282:78
bricks Great poets seldom make b.	POUND 692:38
bridal b. of the earth and sky	HERB 414:80
bride a barren b.	POPE 688:10
as a b. adorned for her husband	BIBLE 132:23
b. and my darling to be?	BALL 59:65
b. of a ducal coronet	DICK 280:25
b. that cairries the bunch	MACD 549:31
death's b.	WORD 961:47
encounter darkness as a b.	SHAK 788:67
jealousy to the b.	BARR 65:84
missed his loving b.	NASH 631:70
my glittering b.	WORD 961:39
Passionless b.	TENN 877:70
read about his widowed b.	MCLE 554:21
So though a virgin, yet a b.	CAREW 199:60
to be his holy b.	STONE 855:11
took the b. about the neck	SHAK 762:72
unravished b. of quietness	KEATS 478:34
virgin-widow...mourning b.	DRYD 304:55
ye sall be his b.	SCOTT 753:45
bridegroom b. in my death	SHAK 795:79
b. little dreids	MACD 549:31
funeral train which the b. sees	CLOU 232:59
Like a b. from his room	AYTO 48:12
bride-grooms Of b.-g., brides	HERR 415:99
bridge Beautiful Railway B.	MCGO 551:73
b. and not a goal	NIET 638:2
b. between the world	RUSS 734:37
brought his b. technique with him	CECIL 210:26
cavalry charging over a tin b.	WODE 952:42
Cricket can be a b.	ZIA 970:12
cross the river by an Irish b.	STEW 854:96
Faith...the Pierless B.	DICK 284:45
Horatius kept the b.	MACA 546:50
keep the b. with me?	MACA 545:46
mime can be a b. between	MARC 569:52
play b. with my old maid aunts	FIEL 335:29
promise to build a b.	KHRU 485:92
rude b. that arched the flood	EMER 324:48
small b. in time	STEI 846:88
that great B.	CRANE 253:67
Venice, on the B. of Sighs	BYRON 188:58
bridges sleep under b.	FRAN 347:89
bridle b. and rudder of painting	LEON 523:75
b. reins a shake	BURNS 180:59
b. to her wanton will	SPEN 838:34

brother

held in with bit and b.	BIBLE 100:54	**Britannia** beer and B.	SMITH 830:48	**broken** A b. heart	SEDA 755:94
Brie-cheese B.-c. poisoning	ADLER 8:69	B., rule the waves	THOM 887:97	b. for you	BIBLE 126:49
brief b. as I have known a play	SHAK 768:47	shouted 'Rule B.'	KIPL 491:22	b. to shivers	BIBLE 131:92
b. quickenings that resemble pain	WILD 943:53	**British** A B. officer	PANG 662:81	b. with the storms of state	SHAK 805:55
hold no b. for private enterprise	BURT 181:72	anything except the B. War Office	SHAW 807:3	Is it not b.?	SHEL 815:36
site, a b. and finance	ROGE 722:67	as…rude as the B.	GALL 358:40	jungle has b. down	JUMB 471:43
Tis b., my lord	SHAK 783:23	Australians inherited the B. mentality	PACK 659:10	made to be b.	SWIFT 863:75
briefcase lawyer with a b. can steal	PUZO 701:5	B-b-b. object	MALO 563:18	Our hearts are b.	GIUL 373:33
briefcases in their b. is terrifying	KHRU 485:96	beneath the B. flag	JOHN 458:24	something gets b.	SHEEN 811:43
briefing B. for a Descent	LESS 524:99	B. are an aggressive nation	ABSE 1:10	staff of this b. reed	BIBLE 108:78
brier How sweet is the b.	TANN 867:24	B. are coming	WELL 928:92	we don't want it b.	QIAN 701:2
instead of the b.…the myrtle	BIBLE 109:2	B. bulldog into a Reagan poodle	STEEL 844:37	What is b. is b.	MITC 610:46
brier-patch Bred en bawn in a b.-p.	HARR 398:46	B. Civil Service	WILL 944:78	**brokenhearted** bind up the b.	BIBLE 110:6
brigade chiefs of the Irish B.	DAVIS 266:9	B. Empire has advanced	GEOR 364:54	**broken-hearted** both b.-h.	SWIN 864:2
No tin hat b.	LEWIS 526:53	B.…gluttons for satire	LODGE 534:94	ne'er been b.-h.	BURNS 179:35
Viva la the New B.!	DAVIS 266:11	B. had no way of knowing it	VONN 915:51	**broker** b.…takes your fortune	WOOL 956:42
brigand I am a b.	SHAW 807:22	B. have more heritage than is good	BRYS 170:6	honest b.	BISM 137:35
Briggs Matilda B.…was a ship	DOYLE 297:74	B. music…perpetual promise	BEEC 73:69	**bronchitis** unless he or she has b.	AGATE 5:69
Bright I have B.'s disease	PERE 674:13	B. public falls for this	HAIL 392:19	**bronze** art b., oil portraits	RODC 721:43
young lady named B.	BULL 173:58	B. soldier can stand up to anything	SHAW 807:3	B. cloud-waves	FREE 350:50
bright b. as angels are	WILK 943:59	B. 'Sphere of Influence'	ANON 23:94	more lasting than b.	HORA 430:11
b. day that brings forth	SHAK 776:15	B. subject, in whatever land	PALM 662:72	things of b. and stone	RUNY 732:63
forgetting the b. speed	ARNO 35:1	B.…taste for bad books	BRAD 154:30	**brooches** I will make you b.	STEV 853:84
leaden interfolds are b.	FREE 350:49	B. want…another meeting	ANON 27:34	**brood** b. over a full nest	ELIOT 315:41
torches to burn b.!	SHAK 765:74	B. won't fight	GALT 359:55	that thy b. is flown	TENN 873:45
westward…the land is b.	CLOU 232:49	broke a B. square!	KIPL 489:89	**brooders** Irishmen born b.	OBRI 645:62
brightened b. by a smile	SAINT 738:38	But B., no, the name's not right	HEAN 405:75	**broods** b. with warm breast	HOPK 428:71
brighter better future and a b. day	SMUTS 831:70	Come you back, you B. soldier	KIPL 489:80	**brook** b. where you had often fished	COWL 250:82
brightest B. and best of the sons	HEBER 406:98	Conversation is never easy for the B.	BRAD 154:33	covert by some b.	MILT 598:58
part with their b. hour	HELL 408:47	deal with the IRA or the B. government	PAIS 660:43	drank of the b.	BIBLE 97:60
wisest, b., meanest of mankind	POPE 687:90	decent, serious B. filth	OSBO 655:86	five smooth stones out of the b.	BIBLE 96:38
bright-eyed b.-e. Mariner	COLE 234:9	Dirty B. coaster	MASE 580:56	never-failing b.	GOLD 376:97
brightness b. of his glory	BIBLE 129:33	Dress B., look Irish	KOFF 496:32	where the b. is deep	SHAK 759:88
b. of this vision	RAND 706:59	face a B. Government	TUCH 901:11	willow grows aslant a b.	SHAK 784:57
b. to hold in trust	SPEN 837:95	fear that the B. electorate	WEBB 925:10	woodland b. he bounding crossed	SCOTT 752:13
Leaking the b. away	SPEN 837:94	fleet of B. ships	NELS 633:12	**Brooke** B. never succeeded	LEVE 525:18
long the b. of the west	BRON 161:60	For generations the B. bourgeoisie	WAUGH 923:57	**Brooklyn** over the B. Bridge	BISH 136:26
no b. in it?	BIBLE 111:53	greatness of the B. Nation	ADDI 7:35	**brooks** books in the running b.	SHAK 778:66
provides the moon with its b.	ANAX 17:65	Hitler never understood…the B.	BULL 173:60	b., and rivers wide	MILT 597:45
purest sky with b.	SPEN 838:22	impose the views…on the B.	SCHL 747:33	b. of Eden	TENN 877:64
transcendent b. didst outshine	MILT 601:36	invade B. territory	HUNT 440:33	b., On whose fresh lap	MILT 599:90
Brighton Like B. Pier	KINN 488:63	irritation with the word B.	BUFO 172:50	b. too broad for leaping	HOUS 432:56
Brignal B. banks are wild and fair	SCOTT 753:34	manly, B. game!	LOVE 538:80	golden sands, and crystal b.	DONNE 292:37
brilliance b. of a lightning storm	FLAU 339:19	Most B. statesmen…drunk too much	GEOR 364:58	sing of b.	HERR 415:99
brilliant b. moon	YEATS 965:6	no B. government	MACM 556:69	**Broom** Beggarly B.	ANON 24:32
everything b. and virgin	DAY 267:38	of B. blood?	TENN 875:5	**broom** b. of Cowdenknowes	BALL 58:55
far less b. pen than mine	BEER 73:75	old B. style of teaching	NEWM 634:43	bright blows the b.	STEV 853:84
brillig Twas b., and the slithy toves	CARR 204:89	planted the B. flag there	STUA 858:57	pods went pop on the b.	DAVI 264:68
brim but sparkles near the b.	BYRON 187:47	rather be B. than just	PAIS 660:42	Take a b. and clean	THER 882:83
full to the b.	DICK 281:76	rather bitter B. musician	WILM 947:34	**broomstick** man is a b.	SWIFT 861:25
brimstone b. and fire	BIBLE 92:23	ridiculous as the B.	MACA 545:30	**broth** cooks spoil the b.	ANON 22:71
brink scared to go to the b.	DULL 306:87	ridiculous as the B. public	MACA 545:30	**brothel** couldn't score in a b.	DOCH 289:81
brisking counteracts…by b. about	SMART 826:63	smell the blood of a B. man	SHAK 792:12	**brothels** b. with bricks of Religion	BLAKE 140:99
Bristol not the Member for B.	BURKE 175:13	stony B. stare	TENN 876:23	Of stews and b. only knew	HERB 414:84
Britain an end to the old B.	BROWN 163:23	streams of B. blood	SCHAW 747:20	**brother** Am I my b.'s keeper?	BIBLE 92:3
a stronger, fairer B.	BROWN 163:22	supported by…the B. people	LAW 512:36	At the hand of every man's b.	BIBLE 92:12
Backing B.	ANON 25:62	The B. Bourgeoisie	SITW 824:17	Be my b., or I kill you	CHAM 213:72
belong to B.	GERA 364:61	the B. public have no regard	EMIN 325:4	BIG B. IS WATCHING YOU	ORWE 655:72
best built city in B.	DEFOE 269:79	typical of the B. way of war	WAVE 925:3	b. came with subtilty	BIBLE 92:31
B. absorbs and adapts	COOK 245:69	United States and the B.	CHUR 226:3	B. can you spare a dime?	HARB 396:87
B. a fit country	LLOY 533:76	Well, B. Public	BROW 169:69	b., in one night	LUMI 542:64
B. and for the hell of it	NOBLE 640:41	**Britisher** healthy and childish B.	MACL 555:48	b. in Shropshire	BARR 65:95
B., could you ever boast	SWIFT 862:60	**Briton** Australian be equal to…a B.	PARK 665:37	b. is born for adversity	BIBLE 105:81
B. had a savage culture	BANDA 61:9	better class of B.	BRAD 154:34	b.'s name	SWIN 864:15
B. has lost an Empire	ACHE 2:33	free-born B.	THAC 880:23	B., thy tail hangs	KIPL 490:6
B. is a Morris Minor country	ANON 26:84	**Britons** B. alone use 'might'	WAUGH 924:77	B. to Death	DANI 262:31
B. must…stand shoulder-to-shoulder	BLAIR 138:59	**Brixton** shoddy streets of B.	ABSE 1:10	B. to Death	FLET 340:52
B.…on borrowed time	CALL 192:27	**broadcasting** essential that b.	THOR 889:56	b. was dead, and is alive again	BIBLE 121:91
B.'s comparative performance	MISH 609:19	In b. your audience is conjectural	ORWE 654:52	darker b.	HUGH 434:8
B. set the world ablaze	GILB 369:53	never-never land of b.	SAFER 737:16	Eat-well is drink-well's b.	FULL 355:82
B.'s New Political Order	MITC 609:29	'pessimistic' about b.	WELLS 930:37	every man against his b.	BIBLE 112:62
B.'s true national dish	COOK 245:69	**broaden** b. your ass if not your mind	HEMI 410:85	friend that sticketh closer than a b.	BIBLE 105:84
B. was conquered	TACI 866:4	**broadsword** save his good b.	SCOTT 752:21	genuine b. Jonathan	MOOD 615:53
B. will not be involved in…war	DAILY 260:4	**Broadway** Has had B.	DAVIS 265:94	how oft shall my b. sin	BIBLE 118:14
end of B.	GAIT 357:13	Lullaby of B.	DUBIN 304:64	I am like no b.	SHAK 760:20
freedom of the press in B.	ORWE 653:22	music of B.	GERS 365:74	I am sworn b.	SHAK 765:58
Graces…not…natives of Great B.	CHES 219:41	sinners on this part of B.	RUNY 732:62	judge and the b. are one	WILS 949:75
Hath B. all the sun	SHAK 803:1	sunny street as this B.!	DICK 279:1	kynges court, my b.	CHAU 217:80
inability in B. to comprehend	HAUG 401:84	walking down B.	WARH 920:8	Life is very sweet, b.	BORR 151:69
journalism…in B.	SAMP 741:97	**brocade** moth-eaten musical b.	LARK 510:96	lo'ed him like a vera b.	BURNS 179:22
lead B. and her fading empire	MANC 564:51	stain…her new b.	POPE 685:35	love God, and hateth his b.	BIBLE 131:84
leads a country such as B.	THAT 881:68	**broccoli** It's b., dear	WHITE 935:32	marry with his b.	SHAK 784:38
most urgent tasks in B.	BEVE 90:63	**brogues** not fit to tie his b.	SCOTT 754:81	more close than a b.	KIPL 492:64
new B. is exciting	WILS 948:67	**broke** it bow'd, and syne it b.	BALL 60:79	mote that is in thy b.'s eye	BIBLE 115:48
Only in B.	MAJOR 561:74	Poverty isn't being b.	WYLIE 964:12	my b. had one	UTTL 907:50
precipitous decline for B.	MCFA 551:66	'Tis true, I'm b.!	JONS 468:87	my fellow man—my b.	BAUD 68:57
When B. first	THOM 887:97	When time is b.	SHAK 765:63	Nor a sister, nor a b.	MARG 570:61

brotherhood

scan your b. Man	BURNS 178:93
seeth his b. have need	BIBLE 130:80
Shall be my b.	SHAK 776:93
Still to my b. turns	GOLD 376:85
went in unto his b.'s wife	BIBLE 93:40
whosoever is angry with his b.	BIBLE 114:32
younger b. popped on to his throne	STOP 865:15
brotherhood Bawling B.	GRAND 381:97
b. of men-at-wars	PAZ 671:48
B. of the Right Stuff	WOLFE 953:75
crown thy good with b.	BATES 67:53
Love the b.	BIBLE 130:68
men in b. combine	NOON 641:50
table of b.	KING 487:31
brotherhoods b. of cedars	BROW 167:10
brothers All men are b.	POWE 693:45
b. be, for a' that	BURNS 180:54
B. of the Cosine	ROOS 725:21
b. on that bright loveliness	MACL 555:42
b. won't mind	COLUM 238:88
happy few, we band of b.	SHAK 776:92
So the two b.	KEATS 477:11
Working for Warner B.	MIZN 610:61
brothers-in-law they aren't all b.-i.-l.	POWE 693:45
brow bonie b. was brent	BURNS 179:16
brotherhoods of cedars on its b.	BROW 167:10
B., bay and tray	DAVI 264:69
b. is wet with	LONG 535:18
b. so grim	ELIOT 319:49
Flushing his b.	KEATS 477:28
Ida's shady b.	BLAKE 139:78
lifted…her white b.	FREE 350:50
meet my Maker b. to b.	CORN 247:5
On his b. this mark	SHEL 813:73
pain and anguish wring the b.	SCOTT 752:25
rugged mountain's b.	GRAH 380:86
speech in that victorious b.	ARNO 33:63
sweat of my b.	FRAN 348:23
sweat of one's b.	LIVI 532:55
thy b. to braid	SCOTT 753:35
thy b. was smoothed	WORD 961:47
wrinkle deeper on the b.?	BYRON 187:44
brown hard, b., nutlike word	BART 66:15
have baked me too b.	CARR 204:83
sinewy b. men	PRIE 695:95
Browning Meredith is a prose B.	WILDE 940:55
quotations from the Bible, B.	MCFA 551:68
safety catch on my B.!	JOHST 465:11
brows b. full sternly bent	SPEN 839:61
Gathering her b.	BURNS 179:19
not seen in either of our b.	DRAY 299:99
pallor of girls' b.	OWEN 657:26
purple b. of Olivet	TENN 874:70
unwrinkled b. in passport offices	STARK 843:22
browsing b. and sluicing	WODE 951:33
Bruce Scots, wham B. has aften led	BURNS 180:47
bruise parmacity for an inward b.	SHAK 771:33
shalt b. his heel	BIBLE 91:96
tread on it and b. it	TROL 897:34
bruised b. for our iniquities	BIBLE 109:94
b. in a new place	IRVI 447:61
b. reed shall he not break	BIBLE 117:82
b. reed shall he not break	BIBLE 109:86
brush b. should not see better	GOYA 380:82
work with so fine a b.	AUST 46:80
brushwood boughs and the b. sheaf	BROW 167:20
brutality without art is b.	RUSK 733:10
Brute Et tu, B.?	CAES 192:16
Et tu, B.?	SHAK 777:27
brute B. heart of a b. like you	PLATH 681:34
Chuck him out, the b.!	KIPL 489:87
creatures…Irrational and b.	MILT 608:92
heavy, red-haired b.	WELLS 929:17
lord of the fowl and the b.	COWP 250:96
never saw a b. I hated so	BROW 168:35
that ugly b., the ape!	ENNI 326:18
treated as a b.	EDWA 312:59
Whatever b. and blackguard	HOUS 432:64
brutes because the b. are dumb?	ELIOT 315:18
Exterminate all the b.!	CONR 243:29
one with the b.	HUXL 443:7
Brutus B. is an honourable man	SHAK 777:37
B.' will start a spirit	SHAK 776:10
no orator as B. is	SHAK 778:45
Poor B., with himself at war	SHAK 776:6
You too, B.?	CAES 192:16
Bubber B. was the first man	ELLI 322:12
bubble break, like a b.	HOLM 424:68
b. burst, and now a world	POPE 686:73
b. on the fountain	SCOTT 752:32
glory a b.	SHEL 812:51
Honour but an empty b.	DRYD 303:33
Seeking the b. reputation	SHAK 779:82
world's a b.	BACON 53:49
bubbles beaded b. winking	KEATS 478:42
dramatic criticism…tattoo soap b.	BROWN 164:30
earth hath b.	SHAK 796:7
no harm as b.	KEYN 484:79
bubbling with b. groan	BYRON 188:72
Buck poor Pearl B.!	PORT 690:76
buck b. doesn't even pause here	REGAN 710:40
b. starts here	GREE 386:35
The b. stops here	TRUM 900:93
bucket not her b. bring	PRIOR 696:12
past is a b. of ashes	SAND 742:16
buckets b. into empty wells	COWP 251:16
Buckingham changing…at B. Palace	MILNE 595:12
buckler b. of the people's cause	DRYD 302:75
shield and b.	BIBLE 101:96
buckles b. on his breast	SHAK 793:41
bucks bet you, Ziggie, a hundred b.	DILL 286:94
bud be a b. again	KEATS 477:23
b. of the spring	DONNE 293:72
b. of thought	DARIO 262:45
like a worm i' th' b.	SHAK 786:1
thrusts a scaled b.	MANS 567:3
Buddha The B., the Godhead, resides	PIRS 679:89
Buddhism Christianity or B.	SAKI 739:62
Buddhist Canadian Hinayana B.	GINS 372:12
budge You shall not b.	SHAK 784:36
budget figures…such as national b.	WEIL 928:74
forming the B.	LLOY 532:70
size of its military b.	BENN 79:31
buds darling b. of May	SHAK 800:37
rod of Aaron…brought forth b.	BIBLE 94:81
sacrificing the early b.	ROCK 720:31
buffalo breath of a b. in the winter	HAGG 391:7
solidity of a water b.	PERE 674:18
where the b. roam	HIGL 419:56
Buffalo Bill B. B.'s defunct	CUMM 257:54
buffalos flower-fed b.	LIND 530:22
buffets Fortune's b. and rewards	SHAK 783:21
buffoon chemist, fiddler…and b.	DRYD 302:83
bugger We done the b.!	TENZ 879:11
bughtin-time b.-t. is near	BURNS 180:45
bugle Blow, b.; answer	TENN 872:38
Blow, b.; answer	TENN 872:39
Blow, b., blow	TENN 872:38
like an ivory b.	THOM 885:57
bugles Blow out, you b.	BROO 162:90
b. of social change	HANDY 395:80
bugs People are not as smart as b.	WHITE 935:40
Buick fawn, crossed with a B.	NICH 636:77
build b. and never give way	LEE 519:93
b. himself a throne	INGE 445:26
but not I b.	HOPK 429:96
If you b. it, he will come	KINS 488:67
life it pretends to b. on	PRIT 696:16
never ask why b.	SEXT 758:47
No more to b.	FROST 352:99
one that you b.	RYBC 736:55
so easy to b., too	IBSEN 444:9
think that we b.	RUSK 732:83
time to b. up	BIBLE 105:14
you didn't b. that	OBAMA 644:44
builder b. of a temple	THOR 888:25
can only be a b.	RUSK 733:88
builders b. have laboured in vain	BIBLE 133:37
Now we are the b.	BEVAN 89:51
building B. is good architecture	JOHN 458:27
b. of God	BIBLE 127:68
b. without ornamentation	SANT 743:47
b.…with tomorrow inside	AKERS 10:11
dedicating a new b.	ROCK 721:37
first glimpse of the b.	POE 683:80
ken by the b. o't	ANON 22:73
My name is on the b.	FORD 343:98
opening the door of the b.	AREN 31:10
question of b.	LECO 518:80
tall b., with a tower and bells	CRAB 252:38
very old b.	OSBO 655:85
Victorians expected every b.	CASS 207:74
wouldn't leave a burning b.	VAN 908:24
buildings Able to leap tall b.	SIEG 820:61
before b. can…touch us	De 268:52
b. of Hong Kong	BOOTH 150:48
cast your eyes on b.	PEI 672:73
magnificence of the b. we burnt	ELGIN 315:13
built And therefore b. for ever	TENN 878:94
b. immovable cathedrals	GIDE 367:18
b. in such a logical way	HOLM 424:74
b. to envious show	JONS 467:71
not what they b.	FENT 332:59
wait for schools to be b.	QABO 701:1
bulb Her body a b.	PLATH 681:36
naked light b.	WILL 945:67
bulk wonder at his enormous b.	LEAC 515:15
Bull John B. has gone to India	YEATS 967:35
bull gone to milk the b.	JOHN 461:97
In time the savage b.	KYD 501:47
take the b.	GOLD 377:28
taking the b. by both horns	ASHF 36:79
you b.'s pizzle	SHAK 771:47
bull-baiting place of b.-b.	SITW 824:25
Buller Captain B. broke a window	JOYCE 470:31
bullet assassin's b.	PARK 665:43
b.…done the job five years ago	COLL 237:65
b. through his head	ROBI 718:82
b. through his heart	THAC 880:26
Each b. has got its commission	DIBD 276:31
Every b. has its billet	WILL 944:68
Faster than a speeding b.!	SIEG 820:61
one b. in ten thousand	SPEN 837:4
bullet-headed B. many b.	POUND 692:28
bullets Better b. than yours	JEFF 453:17
b. made of platinum	BELL 76:53
They thought b. would silence us	YOUS 969:63
use psychic b.	MAIL 560:47
where the b. all go in	CAUS 209:13
bullfighting B. is the only art	HEMI 409:71
that b. does to agriculture	HUBB 434:2
bullfights Spain gets b.	JONG 466:38
bullfrog eyes like a b.	DAVIS 265:97
bullies b. you on manly principles	SHAW 807:97
bull-rushes Divine…in b.-r.	FRIE 351:74
bulls b. and foxes dine very well	JUST 471:50
the ploughman of b.	PROP 697:30
bull's-eyes three perfect b.-e.	OFAO 647:97
bully a…capriciously malevolent b.	DAWK 266:19
If the President has a b. pulpit	REAG 708:98
let a b. come into	JOHN 458:12
love the lovely b.	SHAK 775:81
most heinous b.	HAIG 391:14
bullying 'b.'…not to his taste	ANON 23:89
bum madman b. and angel	GINS 372:5
somebody—instead of a b.	SCHU 749:70
bumblebee b. can fly	MAMET 564:36
bumf In b. lay salvation	WAUGH 924:88
bump don't b. into people	COWA 249:59
bumper b. of good liquor	SHER 817:82
bums millionaires and b. taste	MARQ 575:48
shabby b. living in attics	LEWIS 527:58
bun getting only the b.	COWE 249:68
bunches b. of clingy sob sisters	PAGL 659:19
Buncombe speaking…to B.	CARL 201:41
bundle b. of biases	BALL 60:88
bungalow position of the b.	WILS 947:39
There is our little b.	REAG 709:13
bungler Man is a b.	SHAW 807:27
poor magnificent b.!	BAKER 56:6
bunk captain is in his b.	SHAW 810:9
Exercise is b.	FORD 343:97
History is more or less b.	FORD 343:95
bunyip B. Aristocracy	DENI 273:64
Buonarotti B. commended it	VASA 909:28
burden bear the b.	ARNO 34:76
b. is light	BIBLE 116:81
escaping from the b. of the past	YELT 967:44
heavy b. of responsibility	EDWA 312:61
lay the b. equally	CHUR 225:72
lighten the tax b.	QUINE 702:22
music is a gift and a b.	SIMO 822:78
not so heavy a b.	EISE 314:95
President bears the b.	KENN 481:13
realize what a b.	MITC 610:41
Revolutions…never lightened the b.	SHAW 808:35
what b. then.?	MILT 604:91
White Man's b.	KIPL 491:19
womanhood is a heavy b.	DANG 262:28
Words strain…under the b.	ELIOT 319:45
burdened present is b. too much	HAWT 402:15

burdens b….and at my back	LINK 530:30	
b. on the broadest shoulders	LLOY 532:70	
burdocks With b., hemlock, nettles	SHAK 793:19	
bureaucracy B. defends the status	PETER 675:38	
B. is not an obstacle	SCHU 750:81	
B., the rule of no one	MCCA 548:94	
choice…b. and dilettantism	WEBER 925:14	
bureaucrat b.'s method of protecting something about a b.	SAFI 737:19 VIDAL 912:86	
bureaucratic b. or plain idiotic	TUCH 901:12	
b. society	TREV 896:10	
bureaucrats dictators nor the b.	ORWE 654:57	
burgeoned b. without…directors	GLEI 374:48	
Burger King B. K. and Dairy Queen	HUXT 443:14	
burgers Hold the b.	ANON 28:46	
burgesses with staring b.	STEV 852:34	
burglar b. who respects his art	OHEN 648:22	
burgundy claret and b. in Scotland?	SMITH 827:85	
naïve domestic B.	THUR 890:71	
burial-mounds no b.-m.	YEATS 965:5	
buried in a good old age	BIBLE 92:18	
b. in so sweet a place	SHEL 815:26	
b. under the shale of eras	RAND 706:58	
b. with me	HEWE 417:37	
not b. me deep enough?	TENN 876:32	
not mind its being b.	HOPK 429:93	
Upon my b. body lay	BEAU 71:18	
when they b. him	TENN 877:66	
buries universal darkness b. all	POPE 689:48	
Burma Nothing happens in B.	THER 882:87	
There's a B. girl	KIPL 489:80	
burn better to marry than to b.	BIBLE 126:40	
b. and rave at close of day	THOM 884:27	
B., baby, b.	ANON 25:60	
B., with Athens	CAMP 194:54	
B. your bra!	ANON 25:70	
but b., b., b.	KERO 483:53	
three years of slow b.	WHITE 935:56	
burned bush b. with fire	BIBLE 93:51	
clothes not be b.?	BIBLE 104:60	
got myself b. or hanged	JERO 454:43	
shalt not be b.	BIBLE 109:87	
burnie whare the b. rowes	BURNS 180:51	
burning b. a farthing candle	JOHN 461:2	
b. and gassing people	SIHA 821:65	
B. dinner	PIER 677:67	
B. for b.	BIBLE 94:67	
b. of the leaves	BINY 135:2	
Castletown's b.	HOGG 422:41	
guardianship…against b.	PATR 669:29	
It is like b. an encyclopedia	HAWK 401:90	
Lady's not for B.	FRY 353:31	
burnish thoughts began to b.	HERB 413:73	
Burn-mill B.-m. meadow	WORD 960:14	
Burns kens a wurd B.	MACD 549:22	
burns b. hurlis all their bankis	DOUG 294:1	
Not she which b. in't	SHAK 799:13	
burn-side waly, waly yon b.-s.	BALL 60:79	
burnt had to be b. down	JOHN 459:33	
burst b. into…bloom	RAND 706:59	
B. smilingly	SHAK 793:36	
burthen their b. to the ground	TENN 877:60	
Burton why was B. built on Trent?	HOUS 432:57	
bury b. for nothing	DICK 280:20	
b. them at suitable depths	KEYN 484:80	
b. whom he helped to starve	POPE 688:4	
good day to get out anything we want to b.	MOORE 616:71	
went to b. her	BIBLE 98:81	
We will b. you	KHRU 485:91	
bus drove the b. into the ditch	OBAMA 643:20	
Hitler…missed the b.	CHAM 212:67	
no bloody b.	BLAIR 138:47	
tread in the b. on my toes?	AUDEN 43:83	
tumbled off a b.	GRAH 380:85	
buses men are like bloody b.	COPE 246:94	
Bush B. has 100 bodyguards	GORB 378:50	
How B. and his junta	LECA 518:77	
President B….seems to think	CUOMO 258:80	
the criminal, reckless little B.	HUSS 440:41	
The devil B.	HUSS 440:38	
We are against this war, Mr B.	MOORE 617:93	
bush Bed in the b.	STEV 853:82	
burdened licorice b.	BETJ 89:42	
b. afire with God	BROW 166:3	
b. burned with fire	BIBLE 93:51	
b. supposed a bear!	SHAK 767:45	

child of the mighty b.	FRAN 348:23	
good wine needs no b.	SHAK 780:27	
miracle of the lit b.	THOM 886:77	
Mother-b. that bore you!	LAWS 514:97	
passion in every b.	LEE 519:98	
seen the b. by moonlight	LAWS 514:97	
sun…on the…Australian b.	LAWS 514:94	
Sweet Robin sits on the b.	SCOTT 754:63	
thick b. that proved	THOM 885:72	
Thorough b., thorough brier	SHAK 767:25	
bushel a b. of Corn	PETTY 676:45	
put it under a b.	BIBLE 114:29	
bushels two b. of chaff	SHAK 769:73	
business advertising b.…illusions	QUEN 702:8	
aim of the school of b.	DEMI 272:47	
an ethical b.	ORWE 654:44	
anon we shall dote on b.	ETHE 327:46	
any man in b. can afford	STOWE 856:29	
any other decent b. man	LEWIS 527:58	
broker who really intends to do b.	BISM 137:35	
B. at the end of its journey	LLOYD 532:64	
B. carried on as usual	CHUR 224:68	
B. first; pleasure afterwards	THAC 880:41	
b., industrial and commercial	CARN 202:48	
b. in great waters	BIBLE 102:15	
b. institution in the world	ROGE 722:70	
b. is to appraise	DEWEY 276:20	
b. is very simple	GATES 361:90	
b. meetings…supply people	BOYD 153:9	
b. of a comic poet	CONG 240:34	
b. of a statesman	STEU 849:61	
b. of the American people is b.	COOL 246:79	
b. of the day	DRYD 304:47	
b. of war	GERB 364:64	
b. practices would improve immeasurably	RODD 721:48	
b. that we love	SHAK 795:74	
but a damn bad b.	ROLL 723:89	
buy many b. executives	FORB 342:85	
called away by particular b.	SHER 817:88	
Canada was open for b.	ATWO 41:45	
Corruption…is Chinese b. life	ECON 310:21	
damned serious b.	WELL 929:3	
dare to tell me that b.	STEV 851:23	
do your own b.	BIBLE 128:14	
end of this day's b.	SHAK 778:54	
ever-haunting importunity Of b.	LAMB 505:89	
exhausted what there is in b.	WHIT 938:13	
good all round b. work	WELLS 930:27	
growth of a large b.	ROCK 720:31	
heat of the b. is over!	ETHE 327:43	
hell of a b. to be in	WINN 950:3	
He which hath b.	DONNE 291:34	
horse racing…a solid, stable b.	STEI 846:89	
If everybody minded their own b.	CARR 203:67	
In civil b.; What first?	BACON 51:90	
is the world's b.	KENN 482:32	
It is good b.	SKEL 825:34	
It's strictly b.	PACI 658:2	
jungles of b.	HAMM 394:60	
know…about b. cycles	BECK 71:35	
lawyer…swallowed up with b.	WALT 920:95	
life…is a dreary b.	PERCY 674:10	
life's b.…a summer mood	WORD 959:99	
main b. of socialist parties	KING 486:19	
make b. for itself	DICK 281:72	
Men of b.	BAGE 54:77	
minding my own b.	COOL 246:81	
more b. after dinner	SWIFT 861:36	
my b. to see that we retain	WILH 943:55	
new rule for b.	GATES 361:92	
No B. Like Show B.	BERL 84:42	
no b., no income	GALS 358:47	
no concern with b.	KIPL 489:78	
none of your damn b.	STIL 854:99	
no other b. which government	PAINE 660:32	
No praying, it spoils b.	OTWAY 656:6	
Not slothful in b.	BIBLE 125:25	
over here it's a b.	ROGE 723:83	
paper of b.	HAZL 403:42	
people without b.	DEFOE 269:78	
Pleasure is a thief to b.	DEFOE 269:80	
principal b. of life is to enjoy	BUTL 185:96	
publicity agent of big b.	ORWE 653:6	
remained in the b.	TWAIN 902:62	
retail b. all over again	NEME 633:19	
robs you on b. principles	SHAW 807:97	

servant or has b.	LAW 512:37	
servants of b.	BACON 51:83	
strange, horrible b.	VICT 912:79	
successful in b.	GILL 371:88	
The b. of a general	SUN 859:92	
The rest is not our b.	ELIOT 320:67	
to do the b.	THAC 880:24	
true b. precept	DICK 279:14	
way that b. has structured itself	HARV 400:79	
We can do b. together	THAT 881:61	
What b. have you, miss	SHER 817:71	
whatever my b.	PEPYS 674:5	
What's your b.	BERE 83:13	
What was everybody's b.	SMUTS 831:71	
whin B. gets above sellin' tinpinny	DUNNE 307:19	
businessman I'm not a b.	JAY 453:9	
prominent b.	GALB 357:14	
businessmen b.…take on a science	ASIM 38:81	
like many b. of genius	PUZO 701:6	
message to the b.	CURR 259:94	
more businesslike than b.	FROST 352:1	
busk b. my heid	BALL 60:79	
buskins With b. shortened to descry	HERR 415:8	
busses trolley b. hissing	BETJ 89:28	
bust animated b.	GRAY 384:67	
Uncorseted, her friendly b.	ELIOT 317:78	
busy and insinuating rogue	SHAK 790:36	
b., and the tired	FITZ 337:82	
b. man who can keep up	STARR 843:27	
important is keepin' b.	MOSES 622:78	
Lord! Thou knowest how b.	ASTL 39:8	
Nowhere so b. a man	CHAU 217:76	
busyness Extreme b.	STEV 852:50	
but-an-ben wee b.-a.-b.	MORR 620:54	
butcher benevolence of the b.	SMITH 827:76	
Hog B. for the World	SAND 741:13	
son of a first rate b.	ASHF 38:74	
the consent of every b.	SHER 817:80	
want to know a b. paints	BROW 169:82	
When a b. tells you	JOHN 461:90	
butchered B. to make a…holiday	BYRON 188:66	
butchers gentle with these b.	SHAK 777:33	
sadists…become policemen or b.	CONN 242:96	
shepherds and b.	VOLT 914:46	
Butler Mr B.…grips him warmly	WILS 948:60	
butler A 'great' b. can only be	ISHI 447:72	
Ice formed on the b.'s upper slopes	WODE 952:55	
butlers vagaries of b.	ACHE 2:30	
butter a pound of melted b.	WODE 952:41	
between b. and yoghurt	TRIL 897:11	
bread and b.	MACK 554:14	
bread and b.	MACD 550:39	
bread and b.	SWIFT 863:70	
bread and your b.	KIPL 492:66	
b. in a lordly dish	BIBLE 95:12	
b. nor shoes nor poetry	LEWIS 527:56	
crush these men of b.?	ALBA 11:20	
cutting bread and b.	THAC 880:40	
King said 'B., eh?'	MILNE 596:14	
loved…bread and b.	LEE 519:98	
manage without b.	GOEB 374:53	
offered a piece of bread and b.	MACK 554:14	
rather have b. or guns?	GOER 374:56	
steak spread with b.	KURO 501:43	
buttercup I'm called little B.	GILB 368:31	
buttered b. on both sides	JACK 448:1	
butterflies case of b. so rich it looks	LARK 509:74	
unsympathetic as b.	ELIOT 315:19	
butterfly breaks a b. upon a wheel?	POPE 688:5	
breathing incense into b.'s wings	BASHO 67:47	
b. poised on a pigtailed ocean	SITW 823:96	
b. upon the road	KIPL 489:68	
Float like a b.	ALI 13:72	
guts of a b.	CAPO 197:30	
sharp wings of a b.	HARR 399:55	
butterscotch sun poured in like b.	MITC 609:36	
buttocks Miss Universe's b.	BENE 79:13	
button b., hook, and lace	LOWE 539:98	
But we don't care a b.!	LEAR 516:32	
fourth waistcoat b.	LICH 528:88	
little round b. at top	FOOTE 342:83	
wad na gie a b.	BURNS 179:38	
we are not the very b.	SHAK 782:83	
buttons b. on the screen	JOBS 455:63	
in his b. he will carry't	SHAK 773:9	
taken of his b. off	KIPL 489:84	
buxom b. are and prone	SPEN 838:35	

Buxton

Buxton every fool in Bakewell at B.	RUSK 734:19
buy b. his work	RENO 711:56
b. it of thee	BIBLE 97:50
can't b. many business executives	FORB 342:85
farm to b. my crown	SHAK 776:99
I will b. with you	SHAK 769:82
more to make than to b.	SMITH 827:85
no man might b. or sell	BIBLE 132:11
What can you b.	TOWNE 894:65
buyer If I...found a b.	RICH 714:11
buzzard come back as a b.	FAUL 331:44
buzzing b. about between right	HUXL 443:12
by-and-by lest we should be b.-a.-b.	ALDR 12:53
bygone Her b. simplicity	HARDY 397:9
bygones In commerce b. are for ever b.	JEVO 455:53
by-laws b.-l. are shorter	WHITE 935:34
by-product something....as a b.-p.	HUXL 441:67
Byron B. bore, with haughty scorn	ARNO 35:5
B. is only great as a poet	GOET 375:69
the poetry of Lord b.	MACA 545:34
bystanders b....hope that he will die	EMER 325:86
byway and the b. nigh me	STEV 853:82
byword Israel...a proverb and a b.	BIBLE 97:54

C

cabal killed by the usual c.	DAVI 265:85
cabbage c.-stumps of quotations	LAWR 513:74
cabbage-leaf cut a c.-l.	FOOTE 342:83
cabbages like their c. spherical	BOYD 154:13
Of c.—and kings	CARR 204:1
those who plant c.	RABE 704:19
while I am planting c.	MONT 613:20
cabin a small c. build	YEATS 965:4
sleep...in a log c.	BIRD 136:8
willow c. at your gate	SHAK 785:91
cabinet colleagues in the Truman c.	REST 711:61
Crossed in his C.	DISR 288:46
mislead the C.	ASQU 38:86
cable c. Hitler and ask him	GOLD 377:24
cables also the rudder c.	THOM 885:69
cabooses c. of collier-brigs	DICK 281:55
Cabots Lowells talk to the C.	BOSS 151:74
Cacaliban 'Ban, 'ban, C.	SHAK 804:21
cackle c. w'en he fine a wum	HARR 399:48
cackling when it takes to c.	ELIOT 315:41
cactus garden of c. and sour grapes	MERR 589:49
This is c. land	ELIOT 318:14
cad Flopshus C.	KIPL 491:23
cadence c., a quality of voice	CATH 208:96
golden c. of poesy	SHAK 763:13
cadillac See that gold C.	TRUMP 900:97
Cadogan One-eighty-nine C. Square	BETJ 88:22
cads c. of the most unscrupulous	FRY 353:28
Cadwallader C. and all his goats	SHAK 776:97
Cadwallo Cold is C.'s tongue	GRAY 385:82
Caesar As C. loved me	SHAK 777:36
born free as C.	SHAK 776:8
C. is more dangerous	SHAK 777:23
C., now be still	SHAK 778:56
C.'s I am	WYATT 963:88
C.'s spirit, ranging	SHAK 777:34
C.'s wife must be above suspicion	CAES 192:15
decree from C. Augustus	BIBLE 120:67
doth this our C. feed	SHAK 776:11
Either C. or nothing	BORG 151:61
envy of great C.	SHAK 778:57
from C.'s laurel crown	BLAKE 141:27
Imperial C.	SHAK 784:65
in the coffin there with C.	SHAK 777:40
noble C. saw him stab	SHAK 777:43
O mighty C.!	SHAK 777:32
Our master C.	YEATS 967:37
Religion C. never knew	COWP 250:94
Render therefore unto C.	BIBLE 118:24
speak in C.'s funeral	SHAK 777:37
that C. might be great!	CAMP 194:63
that I loved C.	SHAK 777:35
Then fall C.	SHAK 777:27
what should be in that 'C.'	SHAK 776:10
word of C.	SHAK 777:41
your boy, your C.	DRYD 301:51
Caesars Compare with C.	SHAK 772:81
We were C.	RADI 704:33
worship the C. and Napoleons	HUXL 442:81
café dominoes outside a French c.	WILDE 941:94

In the Garden City C.	BETJ 89:43
cafés shops and third-rate c.	LESS 524:95
caftan Azcan in c.	STEV 849:72
cage bird born in a c.	SHAW 809:88
born within the c.	TENN 874:68
c. like grots	SITW 823:7
c. they were tricked into entering	SNYD 833:94
no more natural...than a c.	SHAW 809:85
Nor iron bars a c.	LOVE 538:82
Over the c. floor	HUGH 435:30
put in a c. if...any sign of fierceness	CARB 198:36
relentless c. of routine	PLATH 680:27
robin red breast in a c.	BLAKE 141:25
cage fights hedge-fund managers...into...c. f.	PARR 666:54
cages not in making c.	SWIFT 861:35
Cain before she conceived of C.	BROW 165:67
C....dwelt in the land of Nod	BIBLE 92:6
conceived and bare C.	BIBLE 93:2
first city C.	COWL 250:76
Had C. been Scot	CLEV 230:92
land God gave to C.	CART 207:55
Lord set a mark upon C.	BIBLE 92:5
tragedy and destiny of C.	JOHN 456:78
cairney ayont the c.	MACD 549:21
cajolery No amount of c.	BEVAN 89:53
cake have your c. and eat it	BARN 64:65
icing that detracts from the c.	AUCH 42:64
layer c. or a road	MILL 593:45
only a certain sized c.	CRIP 254:97
cakes after tea and c. and ices	ELIOT 316:62
c....looked green with worry	FIRB 336:54
no more c. and ale?	SHAK 785:95
preoccupying myself with...Jane Asher's c.	SELF 756:12
Calabria C. death	VIRG 914:28
Calais C.' lying in my heart	MARY 580:48
left C. on Monday	MACA 545:27
shew light at C.	JOHN 461:2
calamities Among the c. of War	JOHN 460:84
C. are of two kinds	BIER 134:68
calamity faint flicker of c.	HOLL 423:52
forced...into...belief is a c.	RICH 714:15
makes c. of so long life	TWAIN 902:63
something more than a public c.	SOUT 835:55
calamus c. saevior ense patet	BURT 181:78
calcine C. its clods	BROW 168:33
calculated c. to lighten the tax burden	QUINE 702:22
calculation c. shining out	DICK 279:12
essential elements in the c.	THOR 888:24
What c., number, measurement	YEATS 967:28
when a c. is made	JOHN 462:35
calculators Electronic c. can solve sophisters, economists, and c.	KRUT 500:30 BURKE 176:40
Calcutta in touch with C.	WHITE 935:38
Caledonia O C.! stern and wild	SCOTT 752:17
calendar kind of Newgate C.	IRVI 447:55
calf bring hither the fatted c.	BIBLE 121:91
c. and the young lion	BIBLE 108:62
lion and the c. shall lie down	ALLEN 14:86
molten c.	BIBLE 94:69
When he killed a c.	AUBR 42:60
Caliban C. casts out Ariel	POUND 691:3
California C.'s power to cloud	BAKER 56:8
C., the department-store state	CHAN 213:85
From C. to the New York Island	GUTH 390:5
Caligula Emperor C.'s Habits	LONG 534:11
call all C. and Answer	LAWR 513:59
c. it the stream of thought	JAMES 451:66
c. me Newt	GING 371:99
c. the shots	IACO 444:3
c. the whole thing off	GERS 365:77
dead men's fingers c. them	SHAK 784:57
true c. of the desert	STARK 843:23
What do you c. the play?	SHAK 783:27
Whatever they c. him	TENN 876:20
wild c. and a clear c.	MASE 580:51
You could never c.	SITW 823:97
called Come when you're c.	EDGE 311:40
how things are c.	HOBB 420:96
I'm c. little Buttercup	GILB 368:31
calling c. him Smith	HOLM 424:76
can't hear you c.	SAND 742:20
high c. of God	BIBLE 128:2
mercenary c.	HOUS 432:71
nimble in the c.	LEWIS 527:56
callisthenics c. with words	PARK 664:23

calm a c. so deep	WORD 959:3
A vast and tender C.	VERL 910:56
C. down, dear	CAM 193:41
c. in our delight	WORD 956:57
c. simmer gloamin'	TANN 867:24
Cruel...but c. and strong	SHEL 814:7
flat c. with drizzling rain	BOWEN 153:96
for a c. unfit	DRYD 301:71
I am not c.	KENN 480:94
in the c. bent up we grow	ANON 22:63
Lush, c. and voluptuous	BAUD 68:65
no joy but c.!	TENN 870:90
Nor peace within nor c. around	SHEL 812:68
opulent c. of angelfish	ALLEN 13:74
something...c. her down	JAGG 449:14
there was a great c.	BIBLE 116:61
tumult dwindled to a c.	BYRON 191:33
with a stoic c.	SOME 833:10
Women are supposed to be very c.	BRON 161:61
world's best moment is a c. hour	ABU 1:13
calmness smallest space of c.	BEDE 72:59
calumnies C. are answered best	JONS 467:52
calumny loud roar of foaming c.	BYRON 188:63
calves c. of the stall	BIBLE 112:65
peculiarly susceptible to c.	HUXL 441:65
Calvin that land of C.	SMITH 830:53
Calvinists Commercial C.	MACD 550:39
Camacho C. was very nearly illiterate?	VARG 908:26
camaraderie c. does not hold	HUGH 435:35
Cambodia C. was not a mistake	SHAW 811:29
humble people of C.	SIHA 821:66
Cambridge C. has always tried	ANON 25:36
C. ladies...furnished souls	CUMM 257:53
C. people rarely smile	BROO 162:95
difficult feat for a C. male	PLATH 681:29
either Oxford or C.	SNAG 831:72
Oxford...more attractive than C.	BAED 54:61
to C. books he sent	BROW 166:87
Ye fields of C.	COWL 250:71
came angel c.	GUST 390:4
c., saw, and overcame	SHAK 773:94
c. to those who knew Him not	SCHW 751:14
I c., I saw	JOHN 456:76
I c., I saw, God conquered	CHAR 215:36
I c., I saw, I conquered	CAES 192:14
know not whence you c.	FITZ 337:71
We c., we saw, he died	CLIN 231:34
where we c. from	HORN 430:23
camel c. has a single hump	NASH 631:66
C. humphed himself	KIPL 491:34
c. is a horse	ISSI 448:78
c.'s hump	KIPL 491:31
easier for a c. to go	BIBLE 118:18
raiment of c.'s hair	BIBLE 114:19
swallow a c.	BIBLE 118:27
Take my c., dear	MACA 544:19
Camelot Kennedy...became C.	WHITE 936:59
looked down to C.	TENN 870:85
lost...like C.	THAT 881:53
many-towered C.	TENN 869:77
never be another C.	ONAS 650:54
rode down to C.	TENN 870:84
to towered C.	TENN 869:80
camels distrust c. and anyone	LEWIS 526:52
camembert c. of time and space	DALI 261:15
camera C. can be the...weapon	PARK 665:43
c. is an eye in the head	WELL 929:94
c. makes everyone a tourist	SONT 834:17
c. relieves...burden of memory	BERG 83:22
c. uses film	WELL 929:95
got back to my c.	KARSH 473:32
I am a c.	ISHE 447:68
cameras pictures with c.	NEWM 634:42
Camilla Prince Charles's right to marry C.	INGH 446:35
camp armed c. of Blackshirts	MUSS 627:88
From c. to c.	SHAK 775:78
happy if the general c.	SHAK 790:2
never fortified a c.	CHRI 223:43
opposed c. of the empiricists	MERT 589:56
campaign after a bloody c.	HAYD 402:23
c. for birth control	MUNRO 625:48
defeat comparable to...military c.	EDIN 312:49
defiant c. of civil disobedience	CHUR 225:79
prospect of another c.	JOHN 457:3
You c. in poetry	CUOMO 258:77
campaigner congenital c.	MARA 569:47

cardinal

camp-bedstead folding c.-b.	TRAV 895:88	**candy** C. Is dandy	NASH 630:59	C. requires people to be pious souls	CHER 219:30
Campbell C.'s Hippocrene	BYRON 189:3	**cane** nice Conduct of a clouded C.	POPE 685:41	C. without bankruptcy	BORM 151:62
do not Maister or C. me	SCOTT 753:56	**canem** Cave c.!	ANON 20:18	c. with the gloves off	STOP 855:18
Campbell-Bannerman Henry C.-B.	BENT 82:6	**cankered** cross-grained and the c.	MACD 550:40	communism versus c.	NGUY 636:68
Campbells C. are comin'	ANON 22:76	**cankerworm** c., and the caterpillar	BIBLE 111:47	definition of c.	HAMP 395:75
camps When I visited concentration c.	WHIT 937:79	**cann** come fill up my c.	SCOTT 753:52	evils of c.	KINN 488:61
campus students on c.	NABO 628:7	**canned** C. music is like...wallpaper	COOKE 245:76	nothing to do with c.	WEBER 925:12
world is a global c.	LODGE 534:97	**Cannes** C....is 10,000 people	ANON 26:88	old-fashioned free-market c.	GLEI 374:48
can fill the c.	TENN 872:27	**cannibal** Better sleep with a sober c.	MELV 585:5	The tombstone of c.	STILL 854:98
He who c., does	SHAW 808:39	**cannibals** c., And Trojan Greeks?	SHAK 772:81	unacceptable face of c.	HEATH 405:86
Pass me the c., lad	HOUS 432:62	c. eat the brains of clever men	FRAS 349:31	where c. is advanced	TROT 899:67
queerer than we c. suppose	HALD 392:23	**cannon** C. to right of them	TENN 875:12	While there's c. there'll be socialism	MILI 591:90
Yes, we c.	OBAMA 643:24	Even in the c.'s mouth	SHAK 779:82	**capitalist** against their c. exploiters	LENIN 521:39
Canaan land of C.	BIBLE 92:21	mouth of the c.	RUSK 732:80	any major crisis of the c. system	EAGL 309:2
Canada as the enemy to C.	MOOD 615:56	**cannonball** c. took off his legs	HOOD 426:19	c. achievement	SCHU 750:79
backwoods of C.	MOOD 615:54	**cannon-ball** hatched from a c.-b.	NAPO 630:49	forbid c. acts	NOZI 642:72
born in C.	JOHN 458:24	**cannot** He who c., teaches	SHAW 808:39	gulf that divides him from the c.	MARX 579:35
C. could have enjoyed	COLO 238:80	**canoe** make love in a c.	BERT 87:5	in advanced c. society	MURAK 626:60
C....hardly exists	BORG 151:59	**canoes** light c. have vanished	SIGO 821:64	patching up the c. system	CONN 243:21
C. has an acute shortage of rich	WILS 948:74	**canon** Art is not...a c. of beauty	PICA 677:59	substance, of c. production	MARX 579:40
C. is not really a place	DAVI 265:86	c. 'gainst self-slaughter!	SHAK 780:37	worker is the slave of c. society	CONN 243:22
C. is paranoid schizophrenia	ATWO 41:36	most inhibited sin in the c.	SHAK 791:56	**capitals** C. are increased	SMITH 827:83
C. moved from colony to nation	INNIS 446:44	**canonization** sort of natural c.	HAZL 403:46	New York is one of the c.	MAIL 560:55
C. only needs to be known	HOPK 429:99	**canonized** c. on earth	BROW 165:61	**Capitol** ruins of the C.	GIBB 366:2
C....the only country	MCLU 556:58	Macmillan was c.	WILS 948:73	**capitulate** will not c.	JOHN 464:98
C. was open for business	ATWO 41:45	**canopy** most excellent c. the air	SHAK 782:88	**capon** cold c.'s leg?	SHAK 770:31
genius of C.	MORR 620:47	rich embroidered c.	SHAK 760:10	**caprice** rule by whim or c.	DOUG 291:21
graduate from C.	FULF 355:64	**cant** C. is the cancer of happen	SHEEN 811:42	**Capricorn** Lady C., he understood	HUXL 441:56
independent Quebec...united C.	DESC 275:3	clear your mind of c.	JOHN 464:89	**caps** always holding their c.	DUNN 307:15
more than C. itself is worth	VOLT 914:36	Cricket...sentimentalism and c.	CARD 198:42	They threw their c.	SHAK 799:89
not got much to say about C.	THOR 889:46	**cantaloupe** put a c. in a coke bottle	JONES 466:24	**captain** broken...by the team c.	HOWE 433:88
One foot in C.	GAY 362:9	**can't-be-bothered** the c.-b.-b.		c. is in his bunk	SHAW 810:9
symbol for C....Survival	ATWO 41:38	working class	GALL 358:36	c. of a mine-sweeper	CATTO 209:4
two languages in C.	SAINT 738:47	**Canterbury** compass of his C. Tales	DRYD 304:40	C. of the Gate	MACA 545:45
Vive le C. franćais!	DE 270:97	**cantos** c. of unvanquished space	CRANE 253:65	c. over his people	BIBLE 96:32
Canadian C. kid who wants	RICH 714:26	**cants** c....canted in this canting world	STER 848:36	c.'s heart	SHAK 793:41
C....make love in a canoe	BERT 87:5	**canty** wad na been sae c.	BURNS 179:17	got the C....on his back	RANS 707:69
I'm a C.	CRON 256:26	**canvas** c. a sentence or paragraph	MOTH 622:87	O C.! my C.!	WHIT 938:7
in Paris, I remained a C.	RICH 714:25	c. is to the painter	BRIL 159:19	plain, russet-coated C.	CROM 255:17
Canadians C....held together	ACHE 3:48	c. was always saying no	BEAR 70:96	well-bred C. of the Pinafore!	GILB 368:32
My generation of C.	FULF 355:64	certain moment the c.	ROSE 725:26	**captains** All my sad c.	SHAK 794:72
special task, as French C.	BOUR 152:93	crowd your c.	TENN 879:8	c. and the kings	KIPL 490:16
canal fell into the Grand C.	MORR 620:46	put Freud on c.	SCHW 750:83	C. of Industry	CARL 201:38
yesterdays, for the C. Zone	PARF 663:90	see and imitate on c.	CUMM 257:50	Star c. glow	FLEC 340:37
Canalettos C. go	MACM 557:75	**cap** but in a fool's c.	HOPK 428:66	**captivate** law of love is to c.	SCEVE 746:16
canals unreal realms of the c.	MCCA 548:92	c. in hand the day	SMITH 831:64	**captive** both the captor and the c.	WAITE 916:6
canaries song of c.	NASH 630:55	flap of my fur c.	STEV 851:29	c. talk of chains	MILT 604:12
cancer AIDS, c., nuclear war	MAMET 564:38	Green jacket, red c.	ALLI 14:6	**captives** proclaim liberty to the c.	BIBLE 110:6
C. is a membership to a club	DRES 299:3	On Fortune's c.	SHAK 782:83	serve your c.' need	KIPL 491:19
C. can be rather fun	HALD 392:26	**capability** Negative C.	KEATS 475:75	**captivity** c. thence captive, us to win	SPEN 839:43
c....close to the presidency	DEAN 267:40	**capable** anyone who was c.	KING 488:60	c. thence captive, us to win	SPEN 839:46
Can't is the c. of happen	SHEEN 811:42	c. of an infinite diversity	REDT 709:25	led c. captive	BIBLE 101:82
dying of throat c.	BECK 72:53	c. of choosing a president	STEIN 845:77	nothing beyond c. and depression	HARD 396:93
political c.	ANON 26:9	c. of higher things	FORS 345:42	What c. was to the Jews	WILDE 940:49
white race is the c.	SONT 834:16	**capacities** vulgar sort of c.	BACON 49:22	**captor** both the c. and the captive	WAITE 916:6
candid be c. where we can	POPE 686:71	**capacity** c. for innocent enjoyment	GILB 368:42	**captors** with the c.	WAITE 916:6
save me, from the c. friend	CANN 197:9	c. for seeing nothing	DUDEK 305:80	**capture** chase rather than c.	WELLS 930:25
candidate c. of probity and integrity	HAGUE 391:11	c. to do	FAUL 331:38	**Capulet** no longer be a C.	SHAK 765:79
c. who can whistle Dixie	OBRI 646:71	How large is the c. of man	AUGU 44:32	**car** bend...with thine iron c.	BLAKE 139:83
potato c.	ANON 27:21	infinite c. for taking pains	ACHE 3:42	buy a used c.	ANON 25:41
candidates boys or scholarship c.	LITT 531:47	infinite c. for taking things	HUXL 442:88	can't drive the c.	TYNAN 904:4
checks go to c.	ANON 26:88	**caparisons** lay his gay c. apart	SHAK 794:71	c. and ambulance	LEBO 518:65
locked c. into ridiculous positions	DANF 261:27	**Capernaum** heard done in C.	BIBLE 120:72	c. has become an article of dress	MCLU 556:55
candied Of c. apple, quince	KEATS 477:24	**capers** He c., he dances	SHAK 773:9	Carol like a rolling c.	FARJ 330:20
candle Bell, book, and c.	SHAK 768:56	**capework** rumpling C. of the wind	WILB 939:40	drive his c. at you at 95 mph	BOYC 153:7
burning a farthing c.	JOHN 461:2	**capital** awoke in the c.	KAIKO 472:12	gilded c. of day	MILT 598:64
day light such a c.	LATI 511:13	c. development	KEYN 484:79	if your c. breaks down	IACO 444:4
delight for being the c.	WEBB 925:6	c. is become an overgrown monster	SMOL 831:68	landscape...traversed in a c.	LEGER 521:7
democracy is but a flickering c.	MACK 554:16	c. of memoranda	WHITE 935:38	Microsoft were a c.	MURR 627:82
fire or c. for warmth	MCLU 556:56	c. punishment tend to the security of		motor c. was poetry	LEWIS 527:57
light a c., and sweep the house	BIBLE 121:88	the people	FRY 353:56	over a cliff in your c.	VENA 910:49
little c. throws his beams	SHAK 770:22	condition of c. and population	MILL 591:94	step out in front of a moving c.	ZERT 277:36
Neither do men light a c.	BIBLE 114:29	consumes intellectual c.	KISS 494:92	work hard and save hard to own a c.	HAGUE 391:12
candle-ends friends called him 'C.-e.'	CARR 205:28	controversy over c. punishment	FISH 336:61	you only have one c.	MART 576:79
candle-flame feel the steady c.-f.	BROW 167:23	empty c. snorts	SMITH 831:64	**caravan** Put up your c.	HODG 421:19
candle-light dress by yellow c.-l.	STEV 853:63	exploited by American c.	INNIS 446:44	**carbuncle** monstrous c. on the face	CHAR 215:40
Fire and fleet and c.-l.	BALL 59:66	fine thing c. punishment is	DICK 278:66	**carbuncular** young man c.	ELIOT 318:4
candles c. are all out	SHAK 796:26	If c. is growing	MARX 579:35	**carcase** c. of an old song	THOM 885:71
c. burns at both ends	MILL 592:19	pandemonium, the high c.	MILT 602:54	**carcass** c. and a skeleton	TRAH 895:83
c. burn their sockets	HOUS 432:69	To that high C.	SHEL 815:29	c. fit for hounds	SHAK 776:17
extinguishes c. and kindles fire	LARO 510:5	**capitalism** aberrations of...c.	SMALL 836:58	c. seemed to be made of iron	MENC 587:15
Night's c. are burnt out	SHAK 766:3	acceptable face of c.	HEATH 405:86	**carcasses** c. of old policies	CECIL 210:31
candlestick-maker C.-m. much		acceptable face of c.	HEATH 405:85	dead c. of unburied men	SHAK 799:98
acquaints	BROW 169:82	accuser of c.	MACL 554:27	**card** American Express c.	LODGE 534:97
candle-making 'C.-m. industry		Can c. survive?	SCHU 750:78	cheery old c.	SASS 745:86
threatened'	GING 371:2	C. is destroying the planet	ROY 730:29	time c. office hours	BAND 61:10
candlesticks midst of the seven c.	BIBLE 131:88	C. only works well	SWEE 861:10	**cardinal** unbecoming for a c.	JOHN 456:77

card-indexes

card-indexes memories are c.-i.	CONN 243:16
cards c. are ill shuffled	SWIFT 863:78
c. as a substitute	ALBEE 11:22
Never play c. with...Doc	ALGR 13:68
old age of c.	POPE 688:15
patience, and shuffle the c.	CERV 211:49
tythe o' what ye waste at c.	BURNS 177:72
Cardus reading Neville C.	THOM 884:23
care agonizing c.	NIGH 639:18
better c. of myself	BLAKE 139:76
boots it with uncessant c.	MILT 599:86
c. and not to c.	ELIOT 319:24
c. beyond to-day	GRAY 383:47
c. for the elderly	FIELD 335:15
c. is like my shadow	ELIZ 321:3
C. keeps his watch	SHAK 766:89
c. killed a cat	SHAK 774:54
c. less and less	SAYE 746:12
c. lost Went all his fear	MILT 602:57
c. of external goods	WEBER 925:11
c. of this world	BIBLE 117:91
Casting all your c. upon him	BIBLE 130:72
cat that was ever killed by C.	ROBI 718:91
dark forgetting of my c.	DANI 262:31
despair and sceptred c.	GRAY 385:88
doesn't c. about black people	WEST 932:77
entrust the c. of freedom	EISE 314:96
greatest c. must be taken	STEU 849:60
Have little c. that Life is brief	CARM 202:46
Keep cool but c.	PYNCH 701:12
Killing c. and grief	SHAK 804:45
Killing c. and grief	SHAK 804:47
lawyers who don't c.	RENO 711:49
life...full of c.	DAVI 265:90
neat, clean...and I didn't c.	CHAN 213:73
neither of them c. for	HALI 393:39
Nor for itself hath any c.	BLAKE 140:9
past redress...past c.	SHAK 764:46
people which ceases to c.	ELIOT 319:28
ravelled sleave of c.	SHAK 797:34
sicklied o'er with c.	TWAIN 902:63
sought it with c.	CARR 206:31
take c. of everybody	FULL 355:74
take c. of yourself	SPRIN 841:86
Take c. to get	SHAW 808:56
the water's c.	YEATS 965:8
took a certain amount of c.	KING 488:56
weary fu' o' c.!	BURNS 179:32
With what nice c.	WORD 962:50
career boy's ideal of a manly c.	DISR 287:33
c....product of that simple observation	BEHR 75:28
c. structure for poets	TOWN 895:68
c. was a text book example	TIME 892:20
close my military c.	MACA 544:9
design c. is a process of learning	BELL 76:48
details...of man and c.	ELTON 323:42
for c. advancement	GRANT 381:2
my c. has just peaked	FIRTH 336:59
my c., my brilliant c.!	FRAN 348:21
Poetry is not a c.	ELIOT 319:29
points clearly to a political c.	SHAW 809:76
satisfying c. choice	COUP 248:24
your c. will never	GAGA 356:5
careerism vulgar c.	GRAV 383:36
careers People don't choose their c.	DOSP 294:87
ruin their c.	NOON 640:48
careful Be c. for nothing	BIBLE 128:4
c. in the choice of his enemies	WILDE 940:66
c. not to drink too much	HAMM 395:71
So c. of the type	TENN 874:78
carefulness c. bringeth age	BIBLE 113:3
careless c. people	FITZ 338:85
So c. of the single life	TENN 874:78
The more c.	SWIFT 863:69
carelessness back into their...vast c.	FITZ 338:85
looks like c.	WILDE 941:2
cares all your c. beguile	DRYD 303:23
c. and pleasures	GIBB 366:92
c. no more for one place	SOUT 835:53
c., that infest the day	LONG 535:23
flesh without c.	CIXO 227:47
soil of his shallow c.!	BRON 162:80
where c. abound	WORD 961:44
caress can c. or tickle	MITC 609:28
curse sound like a c.	FOOT 342:79
careworn haggard and c.	WODE 952:43
cargo c. of ivory, And apes	MASE 580:55
caricatures c....most penetrating	HUXL 441:66
caring C. is the greatest thing	HUGEL 443:5
C. too much for objects	TARTT 867:36
Carle C., now the King's come!	SCOTT 754:68
Carlyle C. has led us all out	CLOU 232:46
let C. and Mrs C. marry	BUTL 185:93
our best men are dead! C.	PUNCH 699:82
carnage c. drear	SCOTT 752:27
carnal heathen in the c. part	POPE 688:9
carnation could never abide c.	SHAK 775:69
carnations musk c. break and swell	ARNO 35:19
Carol C. like a rolling car	FARJ 330:20
carol fluting a wild c.	TENN 878:88
Carolina ham 'n' eggs in C.	GORD 378:56
carollings So little cause for c.	HARDY 397:23
carpe C. diem	HORA 429:6
carpenter Walrus and the C.	CARR 204:99
carpenters Like c. they want to know	SEXT 758:47
Politicians...are professionals, like c.	EICH 313:72
carpentry junkyards of secular c.	ROSE 725:34
carpet c. on the floor	JOHN 458:18
grazes over the c., lowing	RAINE 705:38
Neapolitan c. cleaner	CHEE 218:10
tawny coloured magic c.	WOOLF 955:22
carpets long c. rose along	KEATS 477:26
carriage c. held but just Ourselves	DICK 284:42
sent a c. to bring you back	CH 222:17
window of the railroad c.	LEGER 519:7
carrion c. comfort	HOPK 429:88
green-sickness c.	SHAK 766:4
carrots overdo it with your c..	BECK 72:43
carry c. all he knew	GOLD 376:2
c. knowledge with him	JOHN 463:60
c. us not up hence	BIBLE 94:73
must c. it with us	EMER 324:65
Science may c. us to Mars	REPP 711:60
cars armoured c. of dreams	BISH 136:24
c. and sleeping pills	HALD 392:26
C....supreme creation of an era	BART 66:22
crazy about c.	SALI 740:78
finned c. nose forward	LOWE 540:25
like armoured c.	JANO 452:80
cart carrier's c. at the age of three	LEE 519:96
c. with the home packed	COLL 237:64
coaxes the built C. out	PATC 668:6
Owl, and a useful C.	LEAR 516:33
Carterhaugh come or gae by C.	BALL 59:73
Carthage C. must be destroyed	CATO 209:2
carton the bottom of a c.	DE 268:53
cartons slag-heap covered in...c.	DRAB 298:83
cartridges carry pistols and c.	SHAK 806:84
Caruso C. came with a voice	NEVE 634:31
when somebody insulted C.	LOUIS 538:79
carve c. him as a dish	SHAK 776:17
c. on every tree	SHAK 779:87
carver was the c. happy	RUSK 732:81
carving c. and colouring of a thought	SITW 824:23
C. is interrelated masses	HEPW 412:28
Casbah Come with me to the C.	BOYER 154:15
case c. me in leather	SHAK 762:92
c....not entirely devoid of interest	DOYLE 297:54
c. of butterflies so rich it looks	LARK 509:74
c. of petty right	THOM 885:55
c. sae hard is	FERG 333:87
doctors know a hopeless c.	CUMM 258:68
enclosing it in a c. of wood	WATT 922:45
find in fact to be the c.	HOMA 425:93
heart in a c. o' gowd	BALL 60:80
Just like a large packing c.	WILDE 941:77
make the best of the c.	UPDI 905:20
making a c.	KESEY 483:66
presentation of your fraudulent c.	ADAMS 5:7
put under a glass c.	KING 488:58
slavery...condemned...in one c.	ASTE 39:5
strong c.	BAIL 55:84
Suitable C. for Treatment	MERC 587:21
terrible c. of the Fountainbleus	HUXL 443:13
test c. of US capacity	MCNA 557:87
victorious c. pleased	LUCAN 541:45
When a lady's in the c.	GAY 362:13
world is all that is the c.	WITT 951:21
Casement The ghost of Roger C.	YEATS 967:35
casement All night has the c.	TENN 876:26
c. high and triple-arched	KEATS 477:20
c. slowly grows	TENN 872:43
Lethe flows beneath your c.	RANS 707:71
on this c. shone	KEATS 477:21
out at the c.	SHAK 780:13
cases assess the two c.	PASC 667:78
only two types of c.	BENN 80:48
Casey Mr C., freeing his arms	JOYCE 470:20
cash c. cows to feed your pigs	ANDE 17:68
C. for trash	CLIN 230:98
c. payment...sole nexus	CARL 201:27
pay you c. to go away	KIPL 492:65
playing cricket for hard c.!	MITF 610:49
sold myself for very little c.	CARL 199:70
The moment you show c.	ADIGA 8:64
cashing C. in. That's what	NOFZ 640:42
cash-value practical c.-v.	JAMES 451:74
casino activities of a c.	KEYN 484:79
law courts...as a c.	INGR 446:37
casket C. of My soul	KEATS 476:91
cassia smothered With c.?	WEBS 927:58
Cassius C. has a lean...look	SHAK 776:12
cassock c., band, and hymn-book	WILB 939:33
cassocks We need saints without c.	ANON 27:44
cassowary If I were a c.	WILB 939:33
cast c. fear out	GRAV 382:20
friends of the c.	HIRS 419:76
in no wise c. out	BIBLE 123:35
pale c. of thought	SHAK 782:7
shadows that were c.	SASS 746:96
shrieks to...heav'n are c.	POPE 685:40
caste chair is not a c.	HUGO 437:84
thralldom of a military c.	LLOY 533:74
castle batailled as it were a c. wal	CHAU 217:98
c. brown as owls	THOM 883:21
c. hath a pleasant seat	SHAK 796:18
c. without an armoury	GEOF 363:44
falls on c. walls	TENN 872:38
Look owre the c. Doune	BALL 58:54
man's house is his c.	COKE 234:97
rich man in his c.	ALEX 13:62
swimming through an aquarian c.	ALLEN 13:74
through his c. wall	SHAK 764:52
Castlereagh mask like C.	SHEL 812:72
castles C. in the air	IBSEN 444:9
neurotic builds c.	ANON 24:19
War to the c.	CHAM 212:69
Castletown C.'s burning	HOGG 422:41
castor-oil C. o. of the Palestinian	ANON 27:23
castrate delights of the flesh c. me	FUEN 354:54
casts plaster c. of footprints	PATE 669:14
casualty first c. when war comes	JOHN 457:8
casuists soundest c. doubt	POPE 686:65
Casy maybe like C. says	STEI 845:83
cat Aunt Jobiska's Runcible C.	LEAR 516:41
a wild c.'s left ear	WODE 952:41
black c. which isn't there	DARW 263:60
care killed a c.	SHAK 774:54
c. in profound meditation	ELIOT 320:53
c. is black or white	DENG 272:56
c. must have Three...Names	ELIOT 319:52
C. of such deceitfulness	ELIOT 320:54
c. on a hot tin roof	WILL 945:90
c. that was ever killed by Care	ROBI 718:91
c....walking over the piano	MERI 588:42
c. will mew	SHAK 784:68
c. with bright green eyes	MONRO 612:4
consider my c.	SMART 826:62
deafer than the blue-eyed c.	TENN 878:78
endow a college, or a c.	POPE 686:66
Even stroking a c.	THOM 887:87
Eventually it becomes a C.	NASH 631:69
fog comes on little c. feet	SAND 742:14
Footed lyke a c.	BERN 86:80
God...invented...the c.	PICA 677:62
Had Tiberius been a c.	ARNO 35:2
kind of singed c.	TWAIN 902:39
Like the poor c. i'th' adage?	SHAK 796:21
Massermann, the c. man	ANON 24:30
nine-tailed c.	MACA 544:29
Oh I am a c.	SMITH 830:45
play with my c.	MONT 614:27
poor c. i' the adage	TWAIN 902:63
room to swing a c.	DICK 281:53
support my c.	GRAV 382:31
swing a c.	SMOL 831:69
The C. in the Hat	SEUSS 757:38
to see how the c. jumps	SCOTT 754:80
umpire, the pavilion c.	LANG 507:12
very unique c.	GINS 372:12
vigilant as a c.	SHAK 771:56

What c.'s averse to fish?	GRAY 383:52	Work was like c.	AMIS 16:33	Medip's sunless c.	MACA 546:51
what you did to that poor c.	BEME 78:1	cattle Actors are c.	HITC 419:86	misty eastern c.	SHEL 816:65
wildest…was the C.	KIPL 491:41	All hat and no c.	CONN 242:82	secret c. in which he can kneel	ACKR 3:61
ykilled the c.	LANG 507:46	cursed above all c.	BIBLE 91:96	stand at the jaws of the c.	AMIS 16:45
catacomb c. of stone and steel	WOLFE 953:70	land of c. and sheep	LAWS 514:96	Stygian c. forlorn	MILT 597:41
catalogue dull c. of common things	KEATS 477:9	rear c. in the evening	MARX 579:29	cavern Happy field or mossy c.	KEATS 475:76
catalogues look at flatware c.	COUP 248:35	says that actors are c.?	WINN 950:1	caverns c. measureless to man	COLE 236:40
catalyst occasion, c., or tripwire	ACKE 3:57	these who die as c.	OWEN 657:25	c. measureless to man	COLE 236:36
catamite in bed with my c.	BURG 174:97	cattle-shed Stood a lowly c.-s.	ALEX 13:63	out of the c. of rain	SHEL 813:77
catapult to…c. the propaganda	BUSH 183:33	Caucasus thinking on the frosty C.?	SHAK 764:36	Sand-strewn c., cool and deep	ARNO 33:57
cataract wild c. leaps	TENN 872:38	Caucus some bastards in the C. have	WHIT 937:83	twice ten Thousand C.	KEATS 475:70
cataracts You c. and hurricanoes	SHAK 792:4	caught c. up into the world	HAMI 394:49	caves c. for thousands of years	NIET 638:94
catastrophe dusty c. of Asia	BROD 160:36	hanging around until you've c. on	FROST 353:23	c. that smelt like	THOM 884:47
From such a c.	CHUR 225:74	should have c. it	BEAS 70:97	convictions…are c.	FITZ 337:73
greatest c.	JOHN 458:31	sooner c. than the pestilence	SHAK 773:18	desert c., With wild thyme	MILT 599:84
imminent c.	HUSS 440:37	cauldron c. of our way of life	GOER 374:55	sunny pleasure-dome with c. of ice!	COLE 236:39
race between education and c.	WELLS 930:35	churning c. of America	WRIG 963:68	caviar do anything for c.	KISS 494:97
tickle your c.!	SHAK 772:77	Fire burn, and c. bubble	SHAK 797:52	know about champagne and c.	FERB 332:68
catastrophes c. may be inevitable	ASIM 38:79	cause acting on the c.	SHEL 816:50	more…consumed than c.	SPIL 840:68
model of all the c.	SONT 834:21	A c. is a lie	GASS 361:89	'Twas c. to the general	SHAK 782:96
not c….that age and kill us	WOOLF 955:12	buckler of the people's c.	DRYD 302:75	unhappy before eating c.	KORDA 498:96
catch c. everybody if they start	SALI 740:81	c. is in my will	SHAK 777:24	cavity into the c….cast all weapons	DEKA 270:7
never can c. myself	HUME 438:96	c. is just	DICK 284:58	Cawdor The Thane of C. lives	SHAK 796:9
you hardly c. it going	WILL 945:3	c. is lost for ever!	SCOTT 754:73	Caxtons C. are mechanical birds	RAINE 705:39
Catch-22 only one catch…C.-2.	HELL 407:27	c. is sometimes simpler	HOPE 427:56	cease cannot c. to be	TAYL 868:60
catch-as-catch-can game of c.	FOOTE 342:	c. is the consequence	FANON 329:13	O c.! must hate and death return	SHEL 816:58
catcher c. in the rye	SALI 740:81	c. may be inconvenient	BENN 81:66	whose follies c. with their youth	PITT 679:1
catching c. every air-borne particle	JAMES 450:43	c. of plagues are plays	WHITE 936:61	Cecilia Blessed C., appear in visions	AUDEN 43:99
catchwords principally by c.	STEV 852:42	c. or cure!	GOLD 376:88	Cecily C., Gertrude, Magdalen	ROSS 726:53
catechism c. of comfort	BENE 79:13	c….or the Emerald Isle	DREN 299:2	cedar breaks of the c. and sycamore	KEND 480:85
categorical in order c.	GILB 368:39	c. that interests Russia	WITTE 950:19	moonlit c. what a burst	ARNO 34:84
categories batsmen fall into two c.	TRAV 895:86	c. that perishes with them?	CLOU 232:62	cedars brotherhoods of c.	BROW 167:10
c. in which experiences	MANN 567:91	c. that wit is in other men	SHAK 772:70	cedarwood go of…Sandalwood, c.	MASE 580:55
category c. of human being	ASIM 38:80	c. to write about me	GIOV 372:17	ceiling crashing through the c.	LERN 523:81
c. of truth and falsehood	AYER 48:6	c. why music was ordained!	SHAK 762:68	If your c. should fall down	SMITH 828:96
lower social c.	SHAR 806:72	effect, Whose c. is God	COWP 251:23	long enough to draw on the c.	CHES 220:75
Nature is a social c.	LUKA 542:63	fighting for every c.	COBD 233:80	celebrate c. myself	WHIT 937:90
never fell into the second c.	GEOR 364:58	full c. of weeping	SHAK 792:3	something artists ought to c.	FROST 353:21
not just a moral c.	SOLZ 833:6	grand c.	WESL 932:71	to c. the event	JERR 455:49
to the c., old friend	MO 611:68	idea of an external c.	SPIN 840:77	celebrated solaced and c.	BACON 53:54
caterpillar cankerworm, and the c.	BIBLE 111:47	if any man can shew any just c.	BOOK 148:88	That c….Nobleman	GILB 370:71
world for a moss or a c.	BARB 63:45	I'll try the whole c.	CARR 203:65	celebration c. of man	THOM 884:24
cathedral bawdy house is to a c.	MENC 586:91	important to the c. of science	AGAS 9:86	celebrations make great c.	COLU 238:91
law courts not as a c.	INGR 446:37	jealous for the c.	SHAK 790:30	celebrity a c. is like being raped	MCEN 550:57
pass for a c. doctor	JONS 466:48	just c. to make a pitiful defence	SIDN 820:52	Moriarty of mathematical c.	DOYLE 297:62
status of a c.	RODR 722:53	justice or injustice of the c.	JOHN 462:29	nice thing about being a c.	KISS 494:94
suppress each c. and college	MACA 545:27	never resist a losing c.	MITC 610:44	celery thrives in the dark. Like c.	HUXL 441:57
that great bed…looks like a c.	ONAS 650:51	No man can c. more grief	FAUL 330:34	celestial c. and my soul's idol	SHAK 781:76
the…world is a c.	PAST 668:99	not degrade a First C.	HARDY 397:7	do c. chores	CULL 257:42
cathedrals burst into Gothic c.	SHEEN 811:44	notion of c. and effect	HUME 438:95	high c. flavour	BYRON 190:11
c. in my heart	SASS 745:88	not wholesome to Our c.	SHAK 805:48	white, c. thought	VAUG 909:34
Gothic c….supreme creation	BART 66:22	Obstinacy in a bad c.	BROW 165:59	Celia Come, my C.	JONS 467:56
immovable c.	GIDE 367:18	perseverance in a good c.	STER 848:25	celibacy c. has no pleasures	JOHN 460:87
Catherine C. the Great of Finchley	HEAL 404:66	sole c. of…unhappiness	PASC 667:73	c. is…a muddy horsepond	PEAC 671:51
Catholic C. and the Communist	ORWE 655:66	supreme c. of our time	SPEN 837:13	closer to c. than not	WYLIE 964:11
C. and the Protestant	CONN 243:21	takes up no falling c.	HAZL 403:43	rebuked him for his c.	OFLA 647:98
church he…did not attend was C.	AMIS 16:36	the c. of the world	POUND 691:98	cell Each in his narrow c.	GRAY 384:64
had once been a C.	FITZ 337:75	the common c.	STEE 844:44	Find out some uncouth c.	MILT 597:41
holy C. Church	BOOK 146:37	There is always a c. for fear	CRIC 254:91	for each man a solitary c.	ONEI 650:60
I am a C.	BELL 76:57	various c. the same wild road	SCOTT 753:40	gown and mossy c.	MILT 598:60
it is necessary…he hold the C. Faith	BOOK 146:44	Your c. of sorrow	SHAK 798:79	kill each other c. by c.	MAIL 560:47
lawful for a C. woman	MENC 587:7	causes art's hid c.	JONS 467:60	madman in his padded c.	NABO 628:6
miserable Catholic c. childhood	MCCO 548:9	c., and secret motions	BACON 53:45	Minister's room is like a padded c.	CROS 256:35
Once a C. always a C.	WILS 947:38	c., and secret motions	BACON 50:52	outside of this c.	PUIG 699:69
Shakespeare was an Irish C.	ONEI 651:69	C., as have visible Foundations	PETTY 676:47	tight hot c. of their hearts	BOGAN 144:93
catholic c. appetite	STEV 852:50	c. that they represent	FORS 345:49	cellar born in a c.	CONG 240:42
Holy C. and Apostolic	TEMP 869:69	c. why the execution	JOHN 460:64	warm delicious c.	WHITE 935:41
power denied the more c.	WOOLF 955:18	desire to know c.	HAZL 404:52	cello An electric c.?	SEGO 756:4
the c. amen	SMART 826:67	hate the idea of c.	FORS 345:46	C. players, like other great athletes	LLOY 533:82
to increase C. faith	VAZD 910:43	Home of lost c.	ARNO 35:12	cells These little grey c.	CHRI 223:41
Catholics armed C. in the south	REDM 709:21	ignorant of the c.	SPIN 840:72	Celt hysterics of the C.	TENN 875:97
C., bad harvests, and…fluctuations	ELIOT 315:31	knowledge of the c. of things	VIRG 914:27	celtic C. Demos rose a Demon	TENN 879:5
Hitler attacked the C.	NIEM 637:91	Logic-mill to grind out the true c.	CARL 200:85	C. genius of Wales	ARNO 35:22
hunt the C. from England	LESL 523:88	occasions and c. why	SHAK 776:96	chair of C.	ARNO 35:23
no lapsed C. after…Pavarotti	BURKE 177:64	pomp of the superfluous c.	NEWT 635:58	Rangers and C. had both lost	DODD 289:88
Cato Cicero, citing C.	KNIG 494:10	progressive c. in the public eye	SIMP 822:82	cement c. of the universe	SELF 756:10
gods, but a lost one C.	LUCAN 541:45	tough on the c. of crime	BLAIR 138:49	floor the meadows with c.	MACL 555:41
cats C. and monkeys	JAMES 450:37	caution c. of a sword	CLEV 230:96	words will break c.	PUSSY 700:90
C., no less liquid	TESS 880:20	throw c. to the winds	BENN 80:52	cemented c. with tears	HERB 413:56
C. seem to go on the principle	KRUT 500:32	cautioned 33 years and never got c.	MATT 582:96	cemeteries buried in…two great c.	SHAW 811:33
c. with golden eyes	SACK 737:11	cautious Be c., careful	ITO 448:79	Corde avoided c.	BELL 78:93
evil…committed by the spiritual fat c.	PECK 672:62	cavalier C. who loves honour	SCOTT 754:82	cemetery allot a portion…as a c.	HAWT 402:4
killed the c.	BROW 167:16	cavaliero he was a perfect c.	BYRON 189:85	c. is an open space	SHEL 815:26
lotta to c. copy the Mona Lisa	ARMS 33:50	cavalry c. commander	BRIN 159:24	c. of dead ideas	UNAM 905:5
still…mean to c.	CHEE 218:10	C. of Woe	DICK 283:30	Help me down C. Road	LARK 509:85
wailed like melodious c.	HUXL 442:75	laugh like a squadron c.	WODE 952:42	new plot in the c.	DAY 267:32
windows of the eyes of c.	DRAY 299:1	cave every creature in a c.	SNYD 833:94	only place…is a c.	GENET 363:42

cenotaph 1042

Running a c.	ANON 27:27	c. known as afternoon tea	JAMES 450:38	What a difficult c.!	PEI 672:72
cenotaph laugh at my own c.	SHEL 813:77	c. of innocence is drowned	YEATS 966:24	**challenged** c. you to…leap	RABAN 703:4
censor ask the writer to c.	KELM 479:68	depending on the c.	JOHN 458:29	If one is c.	GALB 357:14
c. foreign news	WALEY 917:31	that reverend c.	JONS 467:62	**challenges** is a set of c.	KENN 481:95
c. the gleam in my eye	LAUG 511:19	**Ceres** C. will join in the dance	SITW 823:4	**chamber** c. of my soul	SHAR 805:69
censorious c. said that she slept	SAKI 739:58	laughing C. re-assume the land	POPE 686:62	in the c. of consciousness	JAMES 450:43
censors C. are paid	TREV 896:6	**certain** c. because it is impossible	TERT 880:19	many a listening c.	SHEL 812:56
censorship conversation, not…c.	JAY 453:8	c. leisure of study	GERB 364:64	nimbly in a lady's c.	SHAK 760:32
instead of…'c.'	MAMET 563:26	c.…something to be sincere about	DRIB 299:5	One need not be a C.	DICK 284:41
censure every trade Save c.	BYRON 186:25	Death…is c. to all	SHAK 772:86	retired into a c.	AUBR 42:61
exposed to c.	JOHN 460:67	laws of mathematics…are not c.	EINS 314:90	stalking in my c.	WYATT 964:90
shame or c. free	JOHN 459:43	nothing can be said to be c.	FRAN 348:19	throw myself down in my C.	DONNE 293:74
Take each man's c.	SHAK 781:51	nothing is c.	BINY 135:4	**Chamberlain** less than Wilt C.	PACK 659:12
census c. taker	TALLY 866:19	**certainties** man will begin with c.	BACON 49:21	Neville C. had greatness	CANN 196:5
Irish C.	MACR 558:14	**certainty** C.. C.. Feeling. Joy	PASC 668:96	**chambermaid** in the arms of a c.	JOHN 463:64
centaur ant's a c. in his…world	POUND 692:24	c. of power	DAY 267:35	**chambermaids** worms that are thy c.	SHAK 766:14
real C.	ACHE 2:35	no longer wish to have c.	KAFKA 472:7	**chambers** c. of the East	BLAKE 139:78
centaurs They're c., though women	SHAK 793:22	**certificate** need a medical c.	LLOY 532:69	whispering c. of Imagination	DICK 280:24
centipede c. was happy quite	CRAS 254:88	**Cervantes** C.…puts me to sleep	GONZ 378:43	**chameleon** c. on plaid	HOOV 427:50
Central Mount Stuart name it 'C.M.S.'	STUA 858:57	**cervix** os c. of woman	SCHR 749:66	free to be a c.	SART 744:64
centre at their hearts the fire's c.	SPEN 837:93	**cesspool** c. deep	CHAP 215:25	**chameleons** C. feed on light	SHEL 814:1
c., and enjoy bright day	MILT 598:72	leaving you…in this sweet c.	SAND 742:38	**champ** C. and chafe	ARNO 33:56
C. and soul of every sphere	HOLM 424:82	London, that great c.	DOYLE 296:38	**champagne** c. and the stars	FITZ 337:80
c. cannot hold	YEATS 966:24	**cetacean** Noble and generous c.	KIPL 491:28	C.!…one deserves it	POL 684:8
c. is giving way	FOCH 341:67	**Cézanne** All C.'s apples I would give	AUDEN 42:75	c. that has stood for five days	ATTL 40:31
c. of true religiousness.	EINS 313:80	C. liked apples	LIPP 530:34	drink c. all night and not get drunk	BOHL 144:99
From the c.…to the sea	COWP 250:96	**chafe** c. and toss in the spray	ARNO 33:56	Fighting is like c.	MITC 610:43
hid…Within the c.	SHAK 782:78	**chaff** see that the c. is printed	HUBB 434:1	I get no kick from c.	PORT 690:67
muddy c. before we breathed	STEV 850:83	two bushels of c.	SHAK 769:73	know about c. and caviar	FERB 332:68
poor c. of a man's actions	BACON 52:5	ungodly…are like the c.	BIBLE 99:25	like c. or high heels	BENN 81:66
proclaiming himself the c.	ATWO 41:34	**chaffinch** c. sings on the orchard	BROW 167:20	not a c. teetotaller	SHAW 806:91
real c. of the household	SHAW 810:7	**chagrin** of c. at his own	RYLE 736:61	sufficient c.	PARK 664:29
self-balanced on her c.	MILT 605:31	**chain** adds a link to my c.	ROCH 720:22	**champion** siding c. conscience	MILT 598:69
slightly left of c.	FRYE 354:58	c. I forged in life	DICK 279:4	this pretended c.	PARN 665:47
system of which they were the c.	DICK 280:27	c. of being	EMER 324:66	**champions** mould-breaking c.	THOM 886:46
centrelight see the blue c. pop	KERO 483:53	c. of gold	SCOTT 753:46	**Champmédy** bury my tongue at C.	BENET 79:26
cents forty c. a flask	LEAC 515:7	c. of strong necessity?	SPEN 838:25	**chance** ain't got…no c.	HEMI 410:79
owe me ten c., sir	NABO 629:22	hanging in a golden c.	MILT 603:72	All c., direction	POPE 687:27
Today I feel like thirty c.	ADE 7:59	lengthening c.	GOLD 376:85	arbiter C. governs all	MILT 603:69
wouldn't give you two c.	BUCH 171:30	Such words as 'c.' or 'train'	JAMES 451:66	art, not c.	POPE 685:24
centuries All c. but this	GILB 369:61	tuppence for your old watch c.	COLL 237:63	c. as a one-armed blind man	WODE 952:41
c. of rebelliousness behind him	PRIE 695:91	**chains** bind our souls with secular c.	MILT 601:25	c. favours only	PAST 668:1
country 'tis of c.	CUMM 257:58	Bound by gold c.	TENN 878:86	c. of being drowned	JOHN 460:88
customs…evolved over the c.	POWE 693:59	captive talk of c.	MILT 604:12	c. to read them at all	THOR 888:17
forty c. look down	NAPO 629:37	C. and Slaverie!	BURNS 180:47	decent actor waiting for a c.	FLYNN 341:64
how I shall lie through c.	BROW 167:23	c. fell off	WESL 931:57	either in nativity, c., or death	SHAK 773:13
in process of c.	QUIL 702:13	c. of one's own transient desires	EINS 313:76	element of c.…is expelled	FISKE 337:66
One three c. removed	CULL 257:44	c. of slavery	GRIL 388:69	entirely a matter of c.	AUST 45:55
Through what wild c.	DELA 271:24	c. of the sea	WALC 916:17	Fate, Time, Occasion, C.	SHEL 814:16
Weary wi c.	SMITH 831:64	C. tie us down	WORD 960:21	From c., and death, and mutability	SHEL 814:18
well-wrought c.	ARLO 32:31	clock with weights and c.	COLUM 238:90	game of c.	CAPO 197:21
while c. fled?	SASS 746:96	everywhere he is in c.	ROUS 729:10	had our last c.	MACA 544:5
centurion c. answered and said	BIBLE 116:57	forever in c.	PAZ 671:47	haven't got a c.	FIEL 335:29
c., which stood over against him	BIBLE 120:62	gilded c. and sordid affluence	PITT 679:7	honest…sometimes by c.	SHAK 800:28
century absolute this end of the c.	LEVI 525:26	in c., in pains	STUA 858:59	I decided to c. it	PRIE 695:91
American nineteenth c.	THUR 891:94	Jazz…in c.	WHIT 937:78	If I c. to talk	SHAK 804:40
anger from the nineteenth c.	LESS 523:93	Man…held only by the slightest c.	EDGE 311:35	in contempt of c. happenings	RABE 704:20
born in this c.	KENN 481:3	Newspapers…everywhere are in c.	SCOTT 751:4	mixture of c. and choice	FRIE 351:70
Britisher…early 19th c.	MACL 555:48	nothing to lose but their c.	MARX 579:34	my c. to see the King beheaded	PEPYS 673:87
c. of active service	MOUN 622:93	not kept in c.	WEBS 927:45	Necessity and c. Approach	MILT 605:29
c. of the common man	ROUS 729:8	not so heavy…as a prisoner's c.	EISE 314:95	No gifts from c.	ARNO 33:60
c. on which we are entering	WALL 918:51	safer to be in c.	KAFKA 472:6	No girls, no legs…no c.	ANON 24:26
c. that began with a golden age	VIDAL 912:97	self-fashioned c. of slavery	MANS 567:11	now to prove our c.	DRAY 298:94
guard for half a c.	MOLT 612:93	Shake your c.	SHEL 813:74	only c. of eminence	SHAW 810:19
horror of the Twentieth C.	MAIL 560:56	woman must wear c.	FARQ 330:29	skirts of happy c.	TENN 874:83
intellectual life of our c.	ARNO 35:12	worse than c., Dungeon	MILT 607:84	through change and c.	BRID 158:9
In the later nineteenth c.	GILL 370:77	**chair** age of the editorial c.	MCLU 556:57	time and c. happeneth	BIBLE 106:29
into the 20th c.	STEV 851:15	a too easy c.	POPE 689:45	Under the bludgeonings of c.	HENL 411:5
man…walks across his c.	LEAC 515:8	c. is not a caste	HUGO 437:84	various turns of c. below	DRYD 303:32
new c. begins	MANN 566:82	c.…judged by one's pants	ANON 25:38	will never abolish c.	MALL 562:2
nineteenth c.	MCLU 556:57	edge of the c. of Literature	THUR 890:66	**chancellor** C. of the Exchequer	HOWE 433:88
nineteenth c. is great	HUGO 437:87	Jumping from the c.	HUNT 439:30	king, and c., and parliament-men	SCOTT 753:59
No writer before the…19th c.	WAUGH 924:96	knocks over a c.	TOYN 895:73	Lord High C. in his High Court	DICK 281:55
problem of the twentieth c.	DU 304:65	passed up towards the C.	RUSH 732:77	**Chancery** C. Lane young man	GILB 369:47
social problem of the twentieth c.	SMALL 826:58	sat in my c. and written	WODE 952:54	**chances** take c. for peace	DULL 306:87
Sociology…in the last half c.	VAN 908:13	seated in a c.	VALE 907:2	**chandeliered** mute c. isolation	CAPO 197:29
strange thing…turn of the c.	WEIL 927:69	sunny c.	STEV 849:69	**change** beyond her c. of life	HOPE 427:57
twentieth c. had a wonderful capacity	DUDEK 305:80	tears, and a sedan c.	DICK 278:58	birth is…incipient c.	OVID 657:21
working for 16th C. Fox	RENO 711:53	The C. she sat in	ELIOT 318:99	bugles of social c.	HANDY 395:80
Cerberus C. and blackest midnight	MILT 597:41	**chairman** Asked by the c.	STRA 857:42	Busily seeking with a continual c.	WYATT 964:90
damn them with King C.	SHAK 772:81	C. looked dissatisfied	MIN 608:7	can't c.	GUIR 389:89
cerebrums c. and smaller adrenal	MENC 587:10	c. of the Senate Ethics Committee	BRYAN 170:96	certain relief in c.	IRVI 447:61
ceremonial refined, restricted, c.	REAG 708:98	**chairmen** hooligans…92 club c.	CLOU 232:68	c., but I cannot die	SHEL 813:77
ceremonies c. never wear shorts	MURR 627:80	**chaise-longue** hurly-burly of the c.-l.	CAMP 193:41	c., continuing c., inevitable c.	ASIM 38:81
ceremonious c. politeness	TWAIN 902:33	**chalice** c. from the palace	PANA 662:80	c. has come to America	OBAMA 644:31
ceremony C., circus, farce	SCHL 747:35	**chalk** c. cliffs of Dover	BALD 57:32	C. in a trice	SWIN 864:91
C. is an invention	LAMB 505:94	**challenge** guts to take on a big c.	RODG 721:50	c. is always nice	EURI 328:63

C. is not a destination	GIUL 373:35	C., a rough unordered mass.	OVID 657:16	stable ego of the c.	LAWR 512:42
C. is not made without	JOHN 460:66	c. is a science	GLEI 374:47	stamp no c. on the mind	JEFF 454:29
c. minds	KING 486:19	C. is come again	SHAK 789:16	style' to one's c.	NIET 638:98
c. my state with kings'	SHAK 800:46	C. is the score	MILL 593:53	take care of your c.	SUGAR 859:73
c. of consciousness	GINS 372:14	c. of human experience	MACL 555:47	tell a lot about a fellow's c.	REAG 708:4
C. proves true	ICHI 444:12	c. often breeds life	ADAMS 5:90	think ourselves wise about his c.	ELIOT 315:21
c. the world	ISAAC 447:66	c. of the mind	SNYD 832:91	to her possession of c.	MERE 588:40
c. the world	MAND 565:59	c. of vacancy	DELA 271:32	true index of a man's c.	CONN 243:14
continual occupation and c.	AUST 47:88	c. remembered in tranquillity	THUR 891:98	Virtue…is a state of c.	ARIS 31:21
didn't come into politics to c. the Labour Party	BLAIR 138:51	C. umpire sits	MILT 603:69	want of c.	SHAW 807:5
doesn't c. who you are	OBAMA 645:57	God dawned on C.	SHEL 815:33	weak spot or two in a c.	HOLM 424:78
don't have to c. the world	JOBS 455:62	means of overcoming c.	RICH 714:16	well as the main c.	ROBBE 716:62
ever-whirling wheel Of C.	SPEN 839:60	must have c. in one	NIET 638:3	Whatever its position or c.	SCOTT 751:99
fundamental c.	GORB 378:47	Not C., not The darkest pit	WORD 961:35	What is c.	JAMES 450:45
great, growing engine of c.	TOFF 893:38	reduce a c. of experience	GREE 386:21	when it most reflects the c.	HOPP 429:1
hope to c. about our lives	DE 268:55	reign of c. and old Night	MILT 602:49	without…stain upon your c.	ADAMS 5:8
how nigh Your c.	MILT 604:2	stillness in the midst of c.	BELL 77:80	women have no c.	POPE 688:8
I am desperate for c.	OBAMA 645:55	thy dread empire, C.!	POPE 689:48	writing of any c.	WELTY 930:46
Ideals survive through c.	BLAIR 138:68	wish for nothing but c.	HITL 420:92	**characteristic** c. of philosophy	RUSS 734:22
leave it to a torrent of c.	CHES 220:70	**chap** Big c. with a small moustache	WODE 952:52	c. of the design	LEWO 528:78
Life may c.	SHEL 816:55	c. seems bent on cheatin'	HALI 393:32	c. of the really great novelist	BENN 80:61
magic to c. the world	ROWL 730:26	c. who doesn't care much	WAUGH 924:75	nothing so c. as its hat	HOLM 424:73
more than eighty years of c.	FRAN 349:29	common old working c.	FYFFE 356:96	one commanding c.	DISR 288:63
more things c.…stay the same	KARR 473:31	decent c. never lets his public down	FLYNN 341:63	one common c.	DURK 308:30
nature's law to c.	ROCH 720:24	My dear c.!	GILB 370:76	**characteristics** c. of the present age	DISR 288:48
necessary not to c.	FALK 329:9	tubby little c.	WODE 952:45	**characterization** safest general c.	WHIT 936:69
Neither to c., nor falter, nor repent	SHEL 815:20	**chapel** c. was built in the midst	BLAKE 140:14	**characters** Absurdist plays…two c.	ADAM 4:70
not the man we have to c.	PRICE 695:82	Devil always builds a c. there	DEFOE 269:69	altogether new c.	TROL 898:45
once that c. is effected	ORWE 653:29	finished that c. I was painting	MICH 590:65	C. in Search of an Author	PIRA 678:87
O the heavy c.	MILT 599:84	**chapels** all the churches or c. in New York	BENN 81:81	c. of hell to trace	GRAY 385:84
people c. and forget	HELL 408:44	**chaperoning** implacably c. a ball	GILL 370:79	c. will step out of it	PROU 697:37
People do not c.	ENRI 326:20	**chaplan** twice a day the C. called	WILDE 942:18	comedy paints c.	HUGO 437:66
protest against c.	STEI 846:88	**chaplet** So rich a c.…to weave	MARV 577:98	consideration of c.	JOHN 462:44
realise…they can't c.	STEIN 845:64	**Chapman** Colonel C.'s adventures	WAVE 925:3	engraved in…unerasable c.	LAUT 511:27
religion, knavery, and c.	BEHN 75:18	**chappie** c. is rummy	WODE 951:35	four c. wide	CHAP 215:25
ringing grooves of c.	TENN 871:23	**chappit** Dinna be c. back	SCOTT 754:62	give wit to your c.	DIDE 284:59
Speech is the small c.	MERE 588:28	**chaps** biography is about C.	BENT 82:97	great c. are formed	ADAMS 4:72
state without the means of some c.	BURKE 176:35	**chapter** approach c. One each year	FRAN 347:1	high c. are drawn	POPE 687:94
the many c. and pass	SHEL 815:43	c. of accidents	CHES 219:44	I describe imperfect c.	BRON 161:67
Things c.	VIAN 911:68	c. on the fall of the Rupee	WILDE 942:5	immense number of their c.	JOHN 463:63
through c. and chance	BRID 158:9	now read another c.	MACH 552:91	learn from those c.	DOMI 290:3
thrown about loosely, like small c.	MENC 586:88	**chapters** Whole c.…one paragraph	CHAN 213:83	most dissimilar c.	SMITH 827:77
Time, Occasion, Chance, and C.?	SHEL 814:16	**character** all novels…deal with c.	WOOLF 955:14	Too many c.	AUST 46:67
too much c. in too short a time	TOFF 893:37	American c.	MCCA 547:87	void of all c.	LOCKE 533:89
until I c.d myself I could not c. others	MAND 565:57	As the c. is	AELI 8:73	**Charadrius** Jemuel rejoice with C.	SMART 826:60
We c. the tools	BEZOS 90:71	begin to think him a c.	LEAC 515:15	**charcoal** drew…with a piece of c.	VASA 909:27
which involves a great c.	TROL 898:46	Being another c.	GIEL 368:27	Philosophy…kind of c. appetite	CLEV 230:94
wonderful c. from wives and work	EWART 328:73	by the content of their c.	KING 486:25	**charge** c. that an idea is radical	GALB 357:14
changed Are we correct to have c.	ASAHI 37:51	c. and compassion	NEWM 635:52	God, we know you are in c.	TUTU 901:28
c. upon a blue guitar	STEV 850:80	c.…bearing a child alone	QUAY 702:7	meant to c. me	GERH 365:68
not c. overnight	KAIKO 472:12	c. in them that bear rule	POTT 690:84	most serious c.	KRUT 500:31
Nothing has c. since	HUGH 435:32	c. is a…cultivated will	NOVA 642:66	One c. alone we give	RUSS 735:44
physicists have c. our world	SNOW 832:82	c. is destiny	ELIOT 315:37	One thing alone I c. you	DU 305:69
shall all be c.	BIBLE 127:62	c. it gives of itself	HAZL 403:41	that is the c.…kissing!	PACK 659:11
changelessness [God's] c. means	TAYL 868:60	c. like Samson, Hercules	SIEG 820:60	this exorbitant c.	KEMB 479:72
changes cause of as many c.	RUSS 734:26	c. of a family	STER 848:26	**charges** ceaseless c.	WILL 944:64
c. in circumstances	FRIE 351:68	c. of those who handle it	AUST 46:76	revolutionary cavalry c.	PAVL 670:41
c. we fear	JOHN 460:72	c.…sagacious blue-stocking	MACA 546:53	**Charing Cross** I went out to C. C.	PEPYS 673:87
c. we think we see	FROST 352:89	c. so entirely distorted	MILL 592:13	**chariot** Bring me my c. of fire!	BLAKE 141:42
c. within a biologic system	SELYE 756:18	c. undecided	KEATS 476:83	burneth the c. in the fire	BIBLE 100:69
c. with the next block	SHAK 773:17	c. who would sell his grandmother	GRANT 381:2	c. is an empty hazelnut	SHAK 765:71
Do not…make any c.	ANON 25:44	contempt for my c. and opinions	SHAW 807:14	c. of fire	BIBLE 97:71
don't drop…make c.	SHAN 805:61	dignity of soul and c.	CARL 200:83	first Sunday in a new c.	CONG 241:74
endure sudden c.	RABE 704:14	do justice to my c.	EMMET 325:6	gal in a bang-up c.	DICK 283:24
Enormous C.	PALEY 661:50	drive…through my c.	ASSAN 39:97	Time's winged c.	LINK 530:30
Her plot hath many c.	QUAR 701:6	effect on the Parisian c.	HAZL 403:44	Time's winged c.	MARV 577:91
monthly c. in her circled orb	SHAK 765:83	emerges a formidable c.	ANGE 18:87	Why is his c. so long in coming?	BIBLE 95:12
Only a fool never c. his mind	BRAN 156:72	even in one's own c. to himself	WILL 945:89	**chariots** burneth the c. in the fire	BOOK 149:17
with foreseeing in c. the	KEYN 484:78	for our c.	PITT 680:11	Some trust in c.	BIBLE 99:40
world's a scene of c.	COWL 250:71	hate and c. assassination	SMITH 829:27	**chariot-wheel** axletree of the c.-w.	BACON 53:42
changing constant in a c. world	JOUV 469:12	hundred pounds…bad for my c.	CONN 242:97	**charisma** C. without substance	CAMP 193:45
loved to be c.	DRAY 298:96	ideas disintegrate, his c. changes	DIDE 285:78	the c. of a damp rag	FARA 330:17
the rules of the game are c.	BLAIR 138:70	identity with the c.	HAZL 403:31	**charitable** single men…more c.	BACON 51:74
Chankly Hills of the C. Bore	LEAR 516:28	leave my c. behind me	SHER 817:88	**charities** cold c. of man to man	CRAB 252:33
channel Butting through the C.	MASE 580:56	man of good c.	SHAW 810:96	some thirty c.	TENN 872:35
going to watch the shopping c.	COUP 248:35	man's c.…abused	THAC 880:24	**charity** called c., the soul	MILT 607:72
hot slimy c. slowly glide	CRAB 252:42	moral c.…was full of promise	DICK 279:11	c. for all	LINC 529:11
channels forced into c. of evil	FAUL 331:38	more c. than the combined heroes	BROY 169:89	C. is the power of defending	CHES 220:59
narrow straight c.	RANJ 706:60	more powerful…than the worth of c.	ALCO 12:43	c. of its silence	EMMET 325:6
run freely through its c.	STER 848:38	my c. I despare for	FLEM 340:47	c. shall cover the multitude of sins	BIBLE 130:71
chant c., ye little birds	BURNS 179:32	my thoughts I'll c.	SHAK 779:86	damnation of c.	WEST 933:94
chaos begged God to have retained C.	EVANS 328:66	one c. in literature	PAGE 659:14	Do not ask me for c.	ADCO 6:14
Be no longer a c.	CARL 200:99	perfection of c.	AURE 45:47	greatest of these is c.	BIBLE 126:52
bit of primordial c.	WELLS 930:18	problems with your main c.	ANON 26:1	little earth, for c.	SHAK 805:55
born to make c. cosmic	BEER 73:79	reputation, c., person	LOVE 538:89	lives in a spirit of c.	ROOS 724:7
		simplification of the human c.	FORS 344:39	mankind's concern is c.	POPE 687:85
		Sports do not build c.	BROUN 163:21	Miss Prism, c.!	WILDE 942:7

Charles

movement of pure c.	WEIL 928:75	cheat c. at cards genteelly	BOSW 152:78	physician and c. are soldiers	PAST 668:5
What is that c. worth	MARI 571:87	c. you yet	BURNS 177:84	sold at ev'ry c.	FORM 344:21
who has great c.	KEMP 479:74	fancy cannot c. so well	KEATS 478:48	chemistry by c. and machinery	SHAW 807:26
Charles grand to hear Baby C.	SCOTT 754:67	Honesty was a c.	OTWAY 656:2	C. followed in the wake of physics	CRIC 254:90
[Prince C.] is entitled to be	JAY 453:5	if both sides agree to c.	FRY 353:29	resort to physics and c.	MENC 587:7
Charlie C. he's my darling	BURNS 180:56	it's so lucrative to c.	CLOU 232:66	Shakespeare...weak in c.	WELLS 929:17
I am C.	ANON 28:48	nothing so monosyllabic as to c.	FRY 353:34	Chens C. had been living in the UK	MO 611:65
Charlie Sheen a drug...called C. S.	SHEEN 811:41	sweet c. gone	DELA 271:32	cheque c. and the postal order	AUDEN 42:71
Charlotte love for C.	THAC 880:40	To c. a man is nothing	GAY 362:21	general statement is like a c.	POUND 691:13
charm c. from every pore	LERN 523:84	cheated feeling you've been c.?	ROTT 728:6	chequered The c. flag	VETT 911:66
c....getting the answer yes	CAMUS 196:94	pleasure...Of being c.	BUTL 185:81	cheques alive and writing c.	MONT 613:17
c. he never so wisely	BOOK 149:21	cheating bent on c. himself	HALI 393:32	cherish love, c., and to obey	BOOK 148:92
C....it's a sort of a bloom	BARR 65:88	cheats all c. and liars	JONES 465:21	to love and to c.	BOOK 148:91
C. never made a rooster	ACHE 3:53	c. of the movie screen	MAIL 559:38	cherished c. and hoarded	MENC 586:88
c. of all power is modesty	ALCO 12:41	checked Be c. for silence	SHAK 791:53	fox...so c. and locked up	SHAK 772:62
c. of novelty	FLAU 339:21	checkerboards Dallas naught but c.	MAIL 560:55	cheroot whackin' white c.	KIPL 489:82
Completing the c.	ELIOT 319:51	checks c. and balances in government	ANON 26:92	cherries c., hairshirts, pinks	LOWE 540:34
Discreet C. of the Bourgeoisie	BUNU 173:71	cheek bring a blush into the c.	DICK 283:19	c....which none may buy	CAMP 195:76
impregnated by Brownie Vernon's c.	QUIR 703:27	c. of night	SHAK 765:74	Cherrill marriages to Virginia C.	NIVEN 639:29
Music oft hath such a c.	SHAK 788:73	c. wistfully pressed against the pane	SCHR 749:63	cherry c. blossoms in the spring	ANON 24:27
no c. to me	PERTH 675:31	chorus, c. to c.	ROET 722:61	c. now Is hung	HOUS 431:35
paused on every c.	GOLD 376:97	Feed on her damask c.	SHAK 786:1	early c.	JONS 467:72
What c. can soothe	GOLD 376:93	gentle breeze...fans my c.	WORD 957:72	see the c. hung with snow	HOUS 431:35
woman loses a c.	JOYCE 470:30	harlot's c.	SHAK 782:6	taste the ripened c.	CAREW 198:54
charmer Were t'other dear c. away!	GAY 362:22	hollow c. or faded eye	TENN 873:48	cherry-stones carve heads upon c.-s.	JOHN 464:92
charming beauty's c.	SCOTT 754:64	slapped us on our c.	KHRU 485:95	cherub Proud limitary c.	MILT 604:12
c. people have something to conceal	CONN 242:1	smite thee on thy right c.	BIBLE 115:35	cherubim heaven's c., horsed	SHAK 796:20
c. thing to meet	JAMES 450:40	tears down Pluto's c.	MILT 598:55	cherubs poor black c.	CULL 257:42
c. to totter into vogue	WALP 919:69	thy cold Wan c.	WORD 961:47	Cheshire cosmic C. cat	HUXL 442:1
no matter how c. a bluff	FITZ 338:92	withered c.	SCOTT 752:9	chess C. is the gymnasium	LENIN 521:42
so c. and agreeable	ETHE 327:45	cheeks c. and eyes as bright	ROSS 725:37	c. tournament disguised	CONN 242:80
so c. as books	SMITH 830:51	c. are covered with paint	NASH 630:58	go mad; but c. players do	CHES 220:66
charms Against whose c.	SHAK 773:26	compare the c....to a rose	DALI 261:14	idea of a contact sport was c.	HUGH 435:29
bewitched with some ill c.	WALL 918:58	crack your c.!	SHAK 792:4	kind of collective c.	BARZ 67:41
c. are all o'erthrown	SHAK 804:35	Famine is in thy c.	SHAK 766:12	Life's too short for c.	BYRON 191:19
C. strike the sight	POPE 685:42	Fat, ruddy c. Augustus had	HOFF 422:32	populations about like c. pieces	MILL 594:63
Do not all c. fly	KEATS 477:9	mask...hides our c.	DUNB 306:95	Soviet game is c.	SHUL 819:25
fields and flocks have c.	CRAB 252:30	natural ruby of your c.	SHAK 797:50	when you make a move in c.	ISHI 448:74
Music alone with sudden c.	CONG 241:77	purs lolled his c.	LANG 507:47	win gracefully at c.	MILNE 595:11
O Solitude! where are the c.	COWP 250:96	roses see I in her c.	SHAK 802:83	chessboard world...a c.	ORWE 653:17
still thy verse has c.	SCOTT 752:20	stain my man's c.	SHAK 792:3	chess-board called the c.-b. white	BROW 168:39
With all thy c.	MILT 599:78	tears run down her c.	ANON 22:62	chessman way you'd look at a c.	JARR 452:87
chart enigma of the fever c.	ELIOT 320:64	cheels Facts are c.	BURNS 177:85	chest best jewel from time's c.	SHAK 801:57
on faithful c. to mark	WENT 931:53	cheer be of good c.	BIBLE 123:57	childhood is a locked c.	MISH 609:21
charter c. of thy worth	SHAK 802:67	c. up immensely	THAT 881:63	dead man's c.	STEV 852:59
condemn the c.	INNO 446:48	C. up—the worst	JOHN 458:25	His c. against	SMART 826:65
chartered through each c. street	BLAKE 140:16	drink wine, and eat good c.	MIDD 590:72	no medals on my c.	EISE 314:4
Chartres best friend at C.	LEWIS 526:48	Greet the unseen with a c.!	BROW 169:86	Chesterton Antifeminists, from C.	WEST 933:95
C., our Notre Dame	RODR 722:53	piped with merry c.	BLAKE 139:85	chestnut O c. tree	YEATS 966:27
Chartreuse produced...green C.	SAKI 739:51	scarce forbear to c.	MACA 546:49	showers betumble the c. spikes	HARDY 397:29
chase c. had a beast in view	DRYD 304:58	cheerful a bit cheap and c.	OLEA 649:31	spreading c.-tree	LONG 535:17
c. rather than capture	WELLS 930:25	C. as when she tortured	ROBI 718:91	chestnuts c. in her lap	SHAK 795:99
creatures of the c.	TENN 872:33	far more c. and hopeful	HOLM 424:84	Chevalier Charlie...the young C.	BURNS 180:56
chaser c. of white and blue	ACHE 3:37	God loveth a c. giver	BIBLE 127:74	Chevy Drove my C.	MCLE 554:22
chasm nuance...is a wide c.	COND 239:12	merry heart maketh a c.	BIBLE 104:74	chewing gum like lending c. g.	TAFT 866:9
save himself from the c.	BANN 62:33	cheerfulness c. fixed and permanent	ADDI 6:34	Chianti a nice C.	TALLY 866:19
chaste be amorous, but be c.	BYRON 187:26	c. was always breaking in	EDWA 312:63	four bottles of C.	SHAF 758:53
c., and unexpressive she	SHAK 779:87	cheeriness chintzy c.	BETJ 88:14	chiaroscuro c. of romance	MAUG 582:8
c. as unsunned snow	SHAK 803:95	cheerio C., here I go	PARR 665:50	chic C. is a convent	BROY 169:69
C. goddess	ROMA 723:91	cheerleader a c. for selfishness	ONEI 651:79	Radical c.	WOLFE 953:73
C. to her husband	POPE 688:10	cheerly But c., c.	KEATS 476:89	Chicago C. is a great American city	MAIL 560:55
English text is c.	GIBB 366:3	cheers give three c.	GILB 368:32	now it's on to C.	KENN 482:42
Never shall be free, Nor ever c.	DONNE 292:55	sounds no more than c.	HOUS 431:41	Sexual Perversity in C.	MAMET 563:24
what is c. in Constantinople	FORD 342:90	two c. for democracy	FORS 345:47	stock-yards at C.	HEMI 409:64
chastity c. of honour	BURKE 176:41	cheer-up Music is the great c.-u.	ODETS 647:93	chicken c. whose head has	MITF 610:58
c.'s the jewel	SHAK 791:66	cheese 246 different types of c.	DE 270:93	Gin and c. helpless	BARK 63:52
clothed on with c.	TENN 871:7	apples and c.	KIPL 492:66	It's not for the c.	TARA 867:28
Grant me c.	AUGU 44:25	baiting a mouse-trap with c.	SAKI 739:68	Mere c. feed	MARX 578:14
chat had a c. with him	ROGE 723:76	Botticelli's a c.!	PUNCH 700:83	Some c., some neck!	CHUR 225:91
wish we could c. longer	TALLY 866:20	C. for dessert	BRAC 154:19	The c. is only	DAWK 267:26
Chatfield bloody ships today, C.	BEAT 70:3	C., milk's leap toward immortality	FADI 329:6	chickens beside the white c.	WILL 946:50
Chattanooga C. Choo-choo	GORD 378:55	eat c. from a tin	PALT 662:77	c. are coming home	MACA 544:12
chattels Look to my c.	SHAK 775:70	I do not like green c.	CHES 221:7	Curses are like young c.	SOUT 835:50
chatter insignificant c. of the world	TROL 897:25	I'm like a good c.	NEWM 635:50	enormous headless c.	OROU 652:98
Women should...avoid idle c.	ANON 20:39	I've dreamed of c.	STEV 852:61	more troublesome and costly than c.	SHAW 809:87
chattering Where the satyrs are c.	SITW 823:4	maggot...born i' the rotten c.	ELIOT 315:22	Our semantic c.	MAMET 564:32
Chatterly C. ban And the Beatles	LARK 509:88	no end of Stilton C.	LEAR 516:33	chid you'll never be c.	EDGE 311:40
Chatterton C., the marvellous boy	WORD 959:1	cheeses ate the c. out of the vats	BROW 167:16	chide almost c. God	SHAK 779:8
Chaucer C., well of English undefiled	SPEN 839:52	Cheevy Miniver C., born too late	ROBI 718:86	channerin' worm doth c.	BALL 60:83
exuberation of C.	HAMER 393:46	Miniver C., child of scorn	ROBI 718:84	snarling trumpets 'gan to c..	KEATS 477:15
old famous poet C.	SPEN 838:17	chef celestial c.	MACB 546:64	will not always c.	BIBLE 102:7
chauffeur could have elected my c.	KENN 482:36	Chekhov C. of the suburbs	LEON 522:61	chief Hail to the C.	SCOTT 752:29
chauffeurs simply as our c.	SUN 860:96	the Russians have C.	DUVA 308:41	sinners; of whom I am c.	BIBLE 129:17
cheap a bit c. and cheerful	OLEA 649:31	What C. saw in our failure	PRIT 696:21	chiefs c. of the Irish Brigade	DAVIS 266:9
doesn't mean you're not c.	SEIB 756:5	Chelsea was a C. morning	MITC 609:36	Confederated C.	DEKA 270:7
flesh and blood so c.!	HOOD 426:32	chemise Petticoat said to the C.	PARK 663:94	chieftain c. to the Highlands bound	CAMP 194:65
life...so astonishingly c.	DILL 286:92	chemist c., fiddler, statesman	DRYD 302:83	Great C. o' the Puddin'-race!	BURNS 178:94

children

chiels couthy c. at e'ening meet	FERG 333:86	naked c. against hungry wolf	DAVI 264:65	write about their c.	PARK 664:24
Chigwell first sense...of God...at C.	AUBR 42:61	nurse for a poetic c.!	SCOTT 752:17	**childhoods** c. are sowing the wind	ELLI 323:33
child A C. will make two Dishes	SWIFT 862:59	Ocean's c., and then his queen	SHEL 812:65	instead of happy c.	HERR 415:96
a c. without a birth certificate	GISC 373:30	old Adam in this C.	BOOK 147:76	**childish** c. weakness to lament	SHAK 760:18
active c. do deeds of youth	SHAK 801:49	On a cloud I saw a c.	BLAKE 139:85	either knavish or c.	JOHN 463:67
am but a little c.	BIBLE 97:53	one for a c.	BEEC 73:65	It was a c. ignorance	HOOD 426:23
an aggravating c.	BELL 77:64	perfect for me this c.	HEAN 404:69	my c. years did pass	SURR 860:1
as a grown c.	POUND 691:94	presence of the cherished c.	ELIOT 315:27	put away c. things	BIBLE 126:52
ashamed to be my father's c.!	SHAK 769:90	promise kept, And a c.	NEME 633:18	**childishness** Second c....oblivion	SHAK 779:83
be a very wicked little c.	DICK 279:93	receive one such little c.	BIBLE 118:11	What c. is it	BISH 136:27
before fact as a little c.	HUXL 443:3	receive this C.	BOOK 147:77	**childlike** keep that c. creativity	HIRS 419:77
Better is a poor and a wise c.	BIBLE 106:19	refuse in respect of our c.	BIBLE 112:71	**children** account...c....as bills	BACON 51:71
Can a woman forget her suckling c.	BIBLE 109:89	room up of my absent c.	SHAK 768:57	airy hopes my c.	WORD 961:39
care for the c.'s rattle	JOHN 461:14	saddling of the right to a c.	SHAW 809:86	All c. have to be deceived	ISHI 448:75
Cheevy, c. of scorn	ROBI 718:84	saw the young c.	BIBLE 114:17	All God's C. got Rhythm	KAHN 472:10
c. a mandrake root	DONNE 291:23	seem to hear a c. weeping	DYSON 309:61	Americans do not rear c.	JARR 452:89
c. cannot possibly go on	KEMB 479:73	send the c. a errand	DICK 279:19	anxious to get c.	FREUD 350:58
c. comes to know evil	MITC 609:25	Set his c.	TENN 873:47	Are not c. more creative	MACKE 553:9
C.! do not throw this book about	BELL 76:50	simpering, whimpering c. again	HART 400:68	asking a man to list his c.	ACHE 2:22
c. from the womb	SHEL 813:77	simple dignity of a c.	SAND 742:33	become as little c.	BIBLE 118:10
c. has a first claim	JUVE 471:59	solitary c. and solitary man	ACKR 3:62	Being constantly with c.	BAIN 55:91
C., if it were thine error	TENN 873:53	something better—their c.	SHEL 811:46	borne thirteen c.	TRUTH 900:5
c. imposes on the man	DRYD 303:16	spare the rod, and spoil the c.	BUTL 185:78	bourgeois...reappears in your c.	CONN 242:93
C. is father of the Man	WORD 959:98	speak like a c.	NABO 628:20	breeds contempt—and c.	TWAIN 903:75
c. is grown, and puts away	MILL 592:30	successful parent...raises a c.	EPHR 326:23	buried her c.	SYNGE 865:22
c. of eight is many-sided	DOUG 295:15	sweet c. is the sweetest thing	LAMB 505:92	c. ardent for...glory	OWEN 657:31
c. of forty years ago	THOM 883:1	that every c. may reach	JONS 467:72	c. are above average	KEIL 479:53
c. of its time	KAND 473:16	There is a man c. conceived	BIBLE 98:94	c. are a kind of discipline	BACON 51:74
c. of our grandmother Eve	SHAK 763:7	This C. I to myself will take	WORD 957:63	c. are an heritage of the Lord	BIBLE 103:3
c. of the mighty bush	FRAN 348:23	Thou C. of Joy	WORD 959:6	c. are dumb to say	GRAV 382:17
C. on earth for me	BETJ 88:36	thought as a c.	BIBLE 126:52	C. are haughty, disdainful, angry	LABR 502:23
c. ought to be of the party	AUST 45:51	took a c. out in the yard	CAPO 197:28	c. are instructed	MCCA 548:93
C. Roland to the dark tower	SHAK 792:12	Train up a c.	BIBLE 105:89	c. are more troublesome	SHAW 809:87
c.'s a plaything for an hour	LAMB 505:82	unsatisfied c.	GRAV 383:39	c. aren't happy	NASH 630:64
c. should always say	STEV 853:64	unto us a c. is born	BIBLE 107:60	C. begin by loving their parents	WILDE 941:88
c. was dear	COLE 234:6	use of a new-born c.?	FRAN 348:20	C. being now come to the years	BOOK 148:82
c. was delyverd unto Merlyn	MALO 562:6	virgin shall be with c.	BIBLE 114:15	c. being taught mathematical	GIBS 367:15
c. whose parent is unkent	SPEN 837:14	weep like a c. for the past	LAWR 512:43	c. fear to go in the dark	BACON 50:57
Come close to me, my darling c.	BRON 161:74	what a c. takes in	LAWR 514:85	c. from utter degradation	LOVE 538:89
communism is the illegitimate c.	ATTL 40:29	what it is like to be a c.	JARR 452:91	c....gone out into the world	WOOLF 955:33
Credulity...the c.'s strength	LAMB 505:5	When Israel was a c.	BIBLE 111:46	c. have lost their innocence	GREER 387:43
devoured the infant c.	HOUS 433:80	when I was a tiny c.	ROTH 727:79	c. have neither past nor future	LABR 502:24
difference between conceiving a c.	MAIL 560:57	When you have a c.	DUFF 305:85	C. have never been very good	BALD 57:17
draw nearer to...the mind of a c.	CHIR 222:23	White as an angel is the English c.	BLAKE 139:87	C....have no use for psychology	SING 823:89
eldest c. of sin	WEBS 926:37	who gives a c. a treat	MASE 580:64	c. I might have had	LOWRY 541:42
Elephant's C.	KIPL 491:36	Who shows a c.	RILKE 715:40	c. inter their parents	HERO 415:95
enough to get any c.'s attention	BAIL 55:86	wondering as a c.	BARB 63:45	c. kind and natural	SHAK 775:65
every c. born therein	RUSK 733:9	wretched c. expires	BELL 76:50	c., let us shut	THAC 880:30
father of the c. cried out	BIBLE 120:59	wrote the way a c. skips	WHITE 935:44	c. like olive plants	BIBLE 103:38
fixity of a thoughtful c.'s	HARDY 397:18	young healthy C.	SWIFT 862:58	c. love you and are learning	ANON 25:44
Go c.	SEXT 758:43	**childbearing** closest...to c.	MAIL 560:49	c....never had any boots	WILS 948:58
God bless the c.	HOLI 423:47	**childbirth** death in c.	WELD 928:83	c....not returnable	CRISP 254:99
good habit makes a c. a man	WEBS 926:24	taxes and c.!	MITC 610:45	c. of an idle brain	SHAK 765:72
Half devil and half c.	KIPL 491:20	**childhood** about my hard c.	GIOV 372:17	c. of God	BIBLE 125:18
have a thankless c.	SHAK 792:95	a lot of children...but little c.	HOSS 430:28	c. of God	BIBLE 114:27
have no other c.	SHAK 789:97	books one reads in c.	ORWE 654:55	c. of immigrants	RUSS 734:30
heart...that of a little c.	THAC 880:39	c....cannot remain a fairy-land	BOGAN 144:94	c. of men put their trust	BIBLE 100:57
Heaven born c.	MILT 597:31	c. does not last as long	AMIS 17:61	c. of my body	KOLL 496:36
Helen was got with c.	MANS 567:98	C. is measured out	BETJ 89:47	c. of the devil	TENN 878:96
hideous when...in a c.	SHAK 792:94	C. is not from birth	MILL 592:30	c. of the kingdom	BIBLE 116:58
I am to have his c.	BURG 174:88	c., my youth, my entire life	SABA 736:2	c. of the poor	DICK 281:61
If you strike a c.	SHAW 808:43	c. shows the man	MILT 607:77	c. of the revolution	LEGU 520:16
imprison her c. in her house	WHITE 935:49	c. trees were green	MACN 558:5	c. of your Father	BIBLE 115:38
Invention, Nature's c.	SIDN 820:44	clear space opened to her c.	THOM 883:1	c. one's 'mature' critics often are	WALK 917:34
is it well with the c.?	BIBLE 97:74	doing things in c.	GONC 377:41	C.'s c. are the crown	BIBLE 105:80
I was a c. and very lonely	RHYS 712:78	dreams of our c.	THOR 888:14	c. shall be the works	MICH 590:68
Jesus Christ her little c.	ALEX 13:63	England...in my c.	ORWE 653:25	C. should acquire their heroes	AUDEN 44:17
keeps a secret like a c.	HUGO 437:81	everything is as it was in my c.	EBER 310:10	c. sport upon the shore	WORD 960:11
knows his own c.	SHAK 769:88	experience of c.	LIVE 531:50	C.'s talent to endure	ANGE 18:84
land that's governed by a c.	SHAK 761:41	From his c. onward	HARD 396:51	C. sweeten labours	BACON 51:69
lay down my life...for a c.	CLOU 232:57	glistening galaxy of c.	MATT 582:1	C., to be illustrious	NEME 633:17
like a c. waking	KIER 485:5	I in c. sweetly slept	CLARE 228:55	c. were nestled all snug	MOORE 616:61
like an old c.	BEET 74:4	in the custody of c.	MISH 609:21	c. who leave home	SLOVO 826:56
Lillian as a c.	FEIB 331:54	keep them always in a state of c.	WOLL 953:87	c. will one day live	KING 486:25
listens like a three years' c.	COLE 234:9	memories of earliest c.	MANS 567:3	C., you are very little	STEV 853:71
little c. shall lead them	BIBLE 108:62	miserable Irish Catholic c.	MCCO 548:9	Come, dear c., let us away	ARNO 33:55
Look upon a little c.	WESL 931:60	Old age is second c.	ARIS 31:15	curse of c.!	WEBS 926:21
Lord B....is a c.	GOET 375:69	one moment in c.	GREE 385:5	devour each of her c.	VERG 910:54
Love is like a c.	SHAK 759:67	prayed to rediscover my c.	RILKE 715:37	disappointment to their c.	POWE 693:41
lullay, lullay, like a c.	SKEL 824:30	prefer to return to c.?	DESAI 274:87	distinction between c. and adults	BART 66:13
Magus Zoroaster, my dead c.	SHEL 814:66	privatize the cost of c.	HEWE 417:38	examine the throat...in c.	OSLER 656:90
make the c. a man	SHAK 762:96	Remember your own c.	CAMP 195:71	exercise the rights of c.	COWP 251:9
making love is c.'s play	MITF 610:51	secret of his c.	ACKR 3:61	father pitieth his c.	BIBLE 102:9
mid-May's eldest c.	KEATS 475:96	'Tis the eye of c.	SHAK 797:36	first class, and with c.	BENC 78:3
most blissful dream as a c.	SHIP 818:15	what my lousy c. was like	SALI 739:71	For all our c.'s fate	KIPL 493:71
mother...chose to smother the c.	MCGO 552:81	where c. had strayed	RUSS 735:43	for my c.'s c., the power	MATT 582:1
murmuring...'My c., my c.'	YEATS 967:41	wove a web in c.	BRON 161:59	for the procreation of c.	BOOK 148:86

Chile

give good gifts unto your c.	BIBLE 115:51	wife is beautiful and his c.	MENC 586:	c. cream soldier!	SHAW 806:85
give them to the c.	MORE 618:21	will not teach their c.	SHAW 810:93	entire box of c. liqueurs	CAPO 197:20
'God's police'—wives and little c.	CHIS 222:24	wiser than the c. of light	BIBLE 121:93	made of c.	BRAND 156:60
happy home and c.	PLATH 681:37	Women...fought...for their c.	PANK 662:85	**chocolates** c., cherries, hairshirts	LOWE 540:34
hates c. and dogs	FIEL 335:35	Women's love...not for their c.	EURI 328:56	**choice** and you takes your c.	PUNCH 699:74
having c.	WELD 928:88	words, like c.	NOON 640:45	any c. in the matter	JOHN 462:44
heart of the c.	BIBLE 112:66	world...begat more c.	BACON 52:21	character concerned with c.	ARIS 31:21
He has no c.	SHAK 798:62	world in which c. have their existence	DICK 282:5	c. between staying married	REAR 709:18
how easily a priest begets c.	SMITH 830:49	Yes, Sir...many c.	JOHN 461:91	c. between two alternatives	MORAN 618:9
hundreds of c. to death	MAXT 583:18	Young c. [are] sooner allured	ASCH 37:53	c. does not interfere	KENN 481:18
impression made upon c.	BRYAN 170:98	Your c. are not your c.	GIBR 367:13	c. virtues only gods	ROET 722:61
In cradle clothes our c.	SHAK 770:26	**Chile** in C. everything yields	BLEST 142:52	c. would be irregular but safe	WEST 933:99
in sorrow thou shalt bring forth c.	BIBLE 91:97	**chill** bitter c. it was!	KEATS 477:14	Each to his c.	KIPL 491:48
interfering with c.	RUSS 734:32	c. down the spine	COOKE 245:75	Europe is not a c.	SARK 743:54
justified of her c.	BIBLE 116:80	November's sky is c.	SCOTT 752:18	feeling of c.	VIDAL 912:94
kill more women and c.	BALD 57:31	wind is c.	SCOTT 752:22	freedom of c.	GITL 373:31
known as the C.'s Hour	LONG 536:34	**chilli** c. was something cool	THAC 880:21	homeless by c.	SOUT 835:53
laughing stock of c.	SIDN 820:52	society women never serve c.	RAYB 708:90	if one had no c.	ANGE 18:86
learn a lot from their c.	SPARK 835:63	**chills** Of c. and fever she died	RANS 706:66	just another lifestyle c.	QUAY 702:7
Let our c. grow tall	THAT 881:49	**Chilterns** C., the North Downs	FORS 344:22	Life's business...the terrible c.	BROW 169:76
like c.—talk to themselves	ONEI 651:63	**chime** began to whirr and c.	AUDEN 43:82	measure and the c.	JOHN 459:49
Literature...about having c.	LODGE 534:93	higher than the sphery c.	MILT 599:81	mixture of chance and c.	FRIE 351:70
little c. died	AUDEN 43:88	let your silver c.	MILT 597:35	only one c.—to be strong	MISH 609:23
little c....Round his feet	SHEL 812:71	that harmonious c.	DONNE 291:19	small c. in rotten apples	SHAK 761:59
Looking after c.	MCEW 551:60	**chimera** Peace without honour...c.	CECIL 210:27	while he doth make his c.	SHAK 769:2
man shall be known in his c.	BIBLE 113:91	**chimeras** wild impossible c.	SWIFT 862:47	**choices** equipped to make c.	LURIE 542:65
man...successful with his c.	EURI 328:64	**chimes** c. ring out with a carol gay	BOND 157:65	free to have c.	THAT 881:51
marry for c.	SHAW 809:84	heard the c. at midnight	SHAK 772:87	sum of all the c. gone before?	DIDI 286:80
Men are as chancy as c.	KIPL 491:26	**chimley** bottle on the c.-piece	DICK 279:16	**choir** c. of saints	DONNE 293:64
Men are but c.	DRYD 301:58	**chimney** by the c. with care	MOORE 616:61	member of the c.	LOOS 536:55
Minister for C.	BERCO 83:11	oak in the c.	DONNE 292:63	sing in the c.	KINN 488:62
misfits and precocious c.	MANK 566:75	old men from the c. corner	SIDN 820:56	**choirboy** when raping a c.	PROU 698:53
mother who talks about her own c.	DISR 288:61	smoke out at the c.	SHAK 780:13	**choirs** Bare ruined c.	SHAK 801:62
multitude of unprofitable c.	BIBLE 113:95	**chimney-piece** upon the c.-p.	SCOTT 753:38	last c., last sounds	STEV 850:85
must become c. again	RUNGE 731:54	**chimneys** Your c. I sweep	BLAKE 139:90	**choke** doth c. the feeder	SHAK 764:39
No c. run to lisp their sire's return	GRAY 384:65	**chimney-sweep** there was a little c.-s.	KING 487:46	poets...whether they c. or not	WHITE 935:33
nor do his c. prattle about	HOMER 425:1	**chimney-sweepers** c.-s., come to dust	SHAK 803:7	**choked** experience a c. feeling	WHITE 935:33
not always favourable to the c.	MONT 615:45	**chimpanzee** girl...turned into a c.	PERE 674:17	**choleric** mild or c. disposition	ADDI 6:23
Novelists...are also c.	DE 275:10	vase in the hands of a c.	WAUGH 924:1	**choose** c. between betraying	FORS 345:46
Our c., and our sins	SHAK 775:84	**chin** obliterated the unimportant c.	CUMM 257:48	c. what many men desire	SHAK 769:94
Our c. swoon before us	WILDE 940:45	one neck, one c.	SHAK 785:90	C. you...whom ye will serve	BIBLE 95:10
parents kept me from c.	SPEN 837:98	Take it on the c.	NAIP 629:30	do not c. our problems	FROMM 352:88
peacemakers...the c. of God	BIBLE 114:27	up to the c. in heaven	MIDD 590:78	free, therefore c.	SART 745:27
poisoning three little c.	DOYLE 296:44	**China** C. asked for a sword	BRID 158:11	not c. not to be	HOPK 429:88
poor get c.	KAHN 472:9	C. has stood up	MAO 568:30	spirit, free to c.	ROCH 719:10
provoke not your c. to wrath	BIBLE 128:93	C.? There lies a sleeping	NAPO 629:38	They cannot c.	THOM 885:62
put to Dickens as c.	BENN 80:50	from C. to Peru	JOHN 459:45	thou canst not c.	SHAK 803:12
Rachel weeping for her c.	BIBLE 110:22	In C., even one million people	DENG 272:58	woman can hardly ever c.	ELIOT 316:42
reasons for having c.	RUSS 735:41	In C. the bat is a symbol	LAWR 513:48	would a man c.	JOHN 464:86
rich don't have c.	NEWM 635:53	land armies in C.	MONT 615:47	**choosing** just c. so	BROW 169:66
secrets...must be kept from c.	DRYD 299:16	outer C. 'crost the Bay!	KIPL 489:81	reason is but c.	MILT 600:12
send his c. away to school	BRAD 154:34	than eat C.'s all our lives	HO 421:13	**Chopin** After playing C.	WILDE 940:43
sins of the fathers upon the c.	BOOK 147:59	the Wall of C.	PATM 669:25	**chopped** c. up in bits	JAMES 451:66
songs as live your c.	BONO 146:30	Till C. and Africa meet	AUDEN 43:81	**chopper** cheap and chippy c.	GILB 369:64
spending my c.'s inheritance	ANON 27:29	yesterday in C.	GORD 378:57	**chopsticks** pair of c....in harmony	MIN 608:6
started life as c.	AMIS 16:37	**Chinatown** Forget it, Jake, it's C.	TOWNE 894:66	**chord** just as they do in a c.	HONO 426:16
STRANGELOVE REPRODUCTION:...c.	COUP 248:34	**Chinese** as much C. as French	FLAU 339:13	pick a c., go twang	VICI 912:75
Suffer little c....to come unto me	BIBLE 118:16	brought the C. people cannons	PEOP 673:83	struck one c. of music	PROC 697:27
Suffer the little c. to come unto me	BIBLE 120:60	C. are the aristocracy	MAUG 582:9	**chords** c. in the human mind	DICK 281:67
take my place with the c.	WOOD 955:8	C. cheap labour	HARTE 400:73	c. of summer	DAY 267:36
tale which holdeth c.	SIDN 820:56	C. nurse with green trousers	MANS 567:96	vasectomy of the vocal c.	ALTH 15:14
Teach the c. under the...tree	QABO 701:1	C. woman's foot fits her shoe	SCHR 749:63	**chores** do celestial c.	CULL 257:42
that their c. are naïve	NASH 631:71	Corruption...is C. business life	ECON 310:21	**chorister** Bobolink for a C.	DICK 283:35
their c.'s c.	YEATS 966:12	courage in C. culture	MO 611:66	**chorus** c. of indolent reviewers	TENN 877:65
the nurture of c.	PALEY 661:53	difficult to trust the C.	DALAI 260:7	like a c. girl's tights	LAWR 514:87
They were privileged c.	BROO 163:8	heathen C. is peculiar	HARTE 400:72	**chorus-ending** c.-e. from Euripides	BROW 168:38
thou shalt have c.	BOOK 149:16	no one can destroy the C. people	BUCK 172:37	**chosen** c. and male	KENN 480:91
tiresome for c.	SAINT 738:35	typical C. wishes	RUSS 734:26	doorman, was the one c.	AREN 31:10
Today, c., I am	NGU 636:66	We said to the C.	PALM 661:69	lesser should always be c.	KEMP 480:82
too easy for c.	SCHN 748:46	**chintzy** c. cheeriness	BETJ 88:14	ye are a c. generation	BIBLE 130:67
To rescue our c.	JORD 469:2	**chip** c. off the old block	BURKE 175:32	**Christ** all at once what C. is	HOPK 429:94
trade union for pensioners and c.	HEATH 405:84	**chips** C. with everything	WESK 931:56	ambassadors for C.	BIBLE 127:71
understood by c. and animals	STRA 857:46	**chivalrous** from all c. actions	ANON 21:50	believe and rejoice in C.	LUTH 542:70
unto us and our c. for ever	BIBLE 95:96	**chivalry** age of c. is gone	BURKE 176:40	bowels of C.	CROM 255:20
victory of the c. of light	BEND 78:12	age of c. is past	DISR 287:18	certainly have despised C.	GREE 386:23
Wars are fought by c.	LIVE 531:49	baseball...free of c.	BROUN 163:20	C. being raised from the dead	BIBLE 125:12
We have c.	TENN 879:98	Belgium's...beauty and her c.	BYRON 187:50	C., borne in to virgynyte	ANON 21:44
Well, c., whar dar is	TRUTH 900:4	may be seen noble c.	MALO 563:17	C. comes to the oppressed	RUET 730:37
what is he doing with the c.	CAUS 209:15	nine-tenths of the law of c.	SAYE 746:7	C. died for us	BIBLE 125:9
what will your c. see?	BETJ 88:33	noble acts of c.	CAXT 210:22	C. follows Dionysus	POUND 691:3
when I look at my c.	CART 207:54	noblesse and of c.	SPEN 837:14	C. had not been crucified?	USTI 906:45
when mum...looks after the c.	FALU 329:11	sung of Border c.	SCOTT 752:9	C. if my love were in my armes	ANON 21:59
When you had c.	ATKIN 40:16	**Chloe** speak, my fair C.	PRIOR 696:10	C. is all, and in all	BIBLE 128:11
whom the lips of c.	NEALE 632:6	what can C. want?	POPE 688:11	C. is born in Bethlehem	CASW 208:83
wife and c.	BACON 51:70	**chloroform** having babies without c.	BARB 63:48	C. laughed or played	FORS 345:51
wife and c.	BACON 51:71	**chocolate** cake of c.	STEV 851:29	C. may dwell in your hearts	BIBLE 127:88
wife and c.	BACON 51:74	chocolate can't mow the lawn	BROW 167:7	C....of all men the poorest	WYCL 964:6

Circe

C. receive thy saule — BALL 59:66
C. risen from the dead — BIBLE 127:57
C.'s blood streams in the firmament! — MARL 573:30
C.'s blood was shed for thee — BOOK 147:74
C.'s lore, and his apostles twelve — CHAU 217:79
C., the leader of the sect — TACI 866:7
C....the self-confession — FEUE 334:1
C. the tiger — ELIOT 317:83
C. was betrayed — RUSS 735:43
C.! What are patterns for? — LOWE 539:98
C. will perhaps be a female — NIGH 639:23
C. with me — PATR 669:29
C. wole we claym of him — CHAU 217:89
churches have killed their C. — TENN 876:31
civil wars as that of C. — MONT 614:36
come, C. — ANON 22:74
do all things through C. — BIBLE 128:7
faith of C. — BOOK 147:77
followed before C. died — ORAH 652:90
Hold to C. — BUTT 186:14
Jesus C., her Lord — STONE 855:11
Jesus C. his only Son our Lord — BOOK 146:37
Jesus C....Word of God — BARTH 65:8
life of C. as a revelation — WHIT 936:71
May Lord C. enter in? — WILDE 942:22
Must then a C. perish — SHAW 810:18
new illnesses brought by C. — GAUT 361:4
O C., O God — HOPK 428:69
Ring in the C. — TENN 875:96
Saviour C. again to Earth — MASE 580:64
Saviour, which is C. the Lord — BIBLE 120:69
So Judas did to C. — SHAK 764:55
speechless C. — SWIN 864:8
the South is hardly C.-centred — OCON 647:87
trust in C. — WESL 932:65
unsearchable riches of C. — BIBLE 127:87
uphold the C. — TENN 877:56
whole state of C.'s Church — BOOK 147:64
words our Saviour C. saith — BOOK 147:68
Christ-Church light in C.-C. hall — ARNO 34:92
study at C.-C. — JOHN 461:17
Christendom C. ought to feel joyful — COLU 238:91
in C. where is the Christian? — EMER 324:52
Kent and C. — WYATT 963:86
live in any place of C. — ELIZ 321:99
prettiest Kate in C. — SHAK 761:65
two lights of C. — PIUS 680:17
christened arrived...already c. — SAKI 739:57
c. with a hundred — NASHE 631:88
christening Like a c., a wedding — COOKE 245:74
Christian As with the C. religion — ORWE 653:15
C. gospel is the knowledge — NIEB 637:87
C. ideal has not been tried — CHES 220:77
C. on a Pound a Week? — HARD 396:92
C. that is in health — LAW 512:37
every C. in Hitler's Europe — FACK 329:1
forgive them as a C. — AUST 46:62
form C. men — ARNO 36:45
fraud of the C. system — PAINE 660:38
fruits of C. civilisation — BIRD 136:10
God is not a C. — TUTU 901:27
honourable style of a C. — BROW 164:42
in Christendom where is the C.? — EMER 324:52
in what peace a C. can die — ADDI 7:57
lawful for C. men — BOOK 150:43
no C. ear can endure — SHAK 759:98
persuadest me to be a C. — BIBLE 125:1
sad, good C. at her heart — POPE 688:9
same...as a C. is? — SHAK 769:1
than a drunken C. — MELV 585:55
tiger that hadn't got a C. — PUNCH 699:80
took her for a C. Scientist — MITF 610:52
What being a C. means — PECK 672:63
You're a C.? — WELLS 930:27
Christianity C. has taught us — HUGEL 434:5
C. is the most materialist — TEMP 869:68
C....man's religion — WELD 928:83
decay of C. — SAKI 739:1
essence of C. — WHIT 936:71
fundamental doctrines of C. — LAW 512:38
gap in C. — FORS 345:51
go first, rock and roll or C. — LENN 521:44
grave of C. — ELIOT 319:35
He who begins by loving C. — COLE 236:46
His C. was muscular — DISR 288:68
If religion is only a garment of C. — BONH 146:24
like C. without hell — BORM 151:62
local thing called C. — HARDY 397:26
nothing in C. or Buddhism — SAKI 739:62
power of C. — WHIT 936:70
Christians blood of the C. — TERT 879:18
C. are frightened — BARTH 66:11
C. are not called — JENK 454:32
C. deified death — STAEL 841:96
C. have burnt each other — BYRON 189:93
C. that travel in Turkey — BUTL 184:62
C. will hence have refreshment — COLU 238:91
dreams of Jews, Muslims and C. — CLIN 230:3
Jews and Arabs...like good C. — AUST 47:99
misbeseeming C. — PRYN 698:62
obstructed by the lives of C. — JOHN 460:86
profess and call themselves C. — BOOK 147:49
Christian Science C. S. explains all cause and effect — EDDY 311:28
Christmas At C. I no more desire Berlin by C. — SHAK 763:4, ANON 24:7
C. should fall out — ADDI 6:31
C.-tree decorated by a Pre-Raphaelite — BEER 74:98
C. tree is lighted — MOYN 623:1
C. without any presents — ALCO 12:40
dreaming of a White C. — BERL 84:41
football is proposed at C. — ANON 23:89
Happy C. to all — MOORE 616:65
inform press home C. — WRIG 963:73
keep our C. merry still — SCOTT 752:22
Love came down at C. — ROSS 726:48
night before C. — MOORE 616:60
One C. was much like another — THOM 884:46
Christopher Robin C. R. Has Fallen — MORT 621:74
C. R. is saying his prayers — MILNE 596:13
C. R. went down with Alice — MILNE 595:12
Christ's College lady of C. C. — AUBR 42:58
chronicle Pride...his own c. — SHAK 786:31
chronicles c. of the time — SHAK 782:97
chryselephantine A c. poem — POUND 691:96
chubby Augustus was a c. lad — HOFF 422:32
chuck C. him out, the brute! — KIPL 489:87
chuckle C....from ear to ear — ELIOT 318:3
irritating c. — GILB 369:56
reading of a white man's c. — ANGE 19:99
chum Nationalism, and its c. — DUNN 307:17
chumps C....the best husbands — WODE 951:36
church a c. stands near — YEATS 967:40
all the c. did echo — SHAK 762:72
a poor c. for the poor — FRAN 347:90
authority in the affairs of the c. — BECK 72:54
before his c. affiliation — LEWIS 526:54
believe in the C. — TEMP 869:69
Broad of C. — BETJ 88:16
Brought you to c. well-dressed — HERB 414:84
build my c. — BIBLE 117:6
came to the village c. — TENN 875:18
C. ain't shucks — TWAIN 902:44
C....asks God only for peace — BONH 145:21
C. clock at ten to three? — BROO 162:97
c. for his mother — CYPR 260:8
c. he...did not attend — AMIS 16:36
C. is cold — BLAKE 140:21
c. is my text — BROW 164:45
c. is of mercies — DONNE 293:71
c. must be reminded — KING 487:33
C. of England — ROYD 730:31
C. of England — WELLS 930:27
c. to God — BYRON 191:37
C. which abandons — KUNG 500:39
churchyard into the c. — DONNE 292:63
Come all to c. — HOUS 431:45
decent c. — GOLD 376:97
discipline of our holy C. — OCON 646:82
excommunicated by the medieval c. — ANON 27:19
fain would kill their c. — TENN 876:31
figure in a country c. — SWIFT 861:27
found God in c.? — WALK 917:39
goes to c. as he goes to the bathroom — BLYT 144:86
great period in his C. — MILT 601:19
Here's a c.! — DICK 283:12
high c. for the true mediocre — MAIL 560:48
holy Catholick C. — BOOK 146:37
huge c. above...village — WALC 916:19
In C. your grandsire — SWIFT 862:40
into his c. hurried — MILT 604:95
Ireland...an alien C. — DISR 287:31
keep the Sabbath going to C. — DICK 283:35
MCC ends and the C. — PRIE 695:93
nearer the C. — ANDR 18:80
neither despair in the c. — FACK 329:1
next to the C. — HOOV 427:52
no government, c., corporation — OAKE 642:2
no salvation outside the c. — CYPR 260:9
noticed...since I have been in the C. — WAUGH 923:60
officially named by the c. — MCFA 551:69
'oly as a c. — STRA 856:38
one Catholick and Apostolick C. — BOOK 147:63
over the sea wet c. — THOM 883:21
Paris to Saint Peter's C. — SHAK 766:4
prayers of the c., to preserve — SWIFT 863:73
respectable as the C. of England — STEV 851:24
rice in a c. — LENN 522:51
see a c. by daylight — SHAK 773:25
sight of a white c. — LOWE 539:1
some to c. repair — POPE 685:23
State is the C. — SHAW 809:69
suffer nobody to sleep in...[the c.] — ADDI 6:28
taught respect for the c. — NERU 633:23
The C.'s one foundation — STONE 855:11
true C. ....lies in the Editors — CARL 199:75
undermining the C's credibility — FRAN 347:92
Unto him be glory in the c. — BIBLE 128:89
What is a c.? — CRAB 252:38
what you find in la c. — WILL 944:74
Where do you go to c.? — BERE 83:13
Where Peter is...is the C. — AMBR 15:22
whole state of Christ's C. — BOOK 147:64
churches all the c. or chapels in New York — BENN 81:81
all the c. you can build — CHIS 222:24
c. and dry-goods stores — MCMU 557:82
C. built to please the Priest — BURNS 177:79
c. have killed their Christ — TENN 876:31
In general the c. — UPDI 906:21
intolerable Mischiefes to C. — PRYN 698:62
seven c. which are in Asia — BIBLE 131:85
seven c. which are in Asia — BIBLE 131:87
Churchill Actors...tried to play C. — MANC 564:50
C. once sponsored the...idea — GALB 357:14
C. on top of the wave — BEAV 71:24
He'll be up there with C. — BLAIR 137:46
inaccurate to say that C. — MANC 564:52
opinion of Winston C. — ELTON 323:42
quotations from...C. — MCFA 551:68
Randolph C. went into hospital — WAUGH 924:99
trousers of Winston C. — BREZ 158:5
churchman As for the British c. — BLYT 144:86
'Modern C.' — WAUGH 923:64
churchmen the c. fain would kill — TENN 876:31
churchyard church into the c. — DONNE 292:63
c. full of sailor's graves — BETJ 89:38
In Drumcliffe c. — YEATS 967:40
nowhere worse taste, than in a c. — JOWE 469:16
palsy-stricken, c. thing — KEATS 477:19
churchyards When c. yawn — SHAK 783:30
When c. yawn — TWAIN 902:63
Chutzpah C.—that quality — LEVA 525:17
Chuzzlewit C. suggested 'Swans' — DICK 279:9
cicadae host of giant c. beat — ROBE 717:72
cicadas c. have been screaming — BOWL 153:1
Cicero C., citing Cato — KNIG 494:10
cigar c. out of his mouth — KARSH 473:32
substitute out of c. stumps — DOUG 295:7
then the long c. — TIME 891:18
cigarette c. is the perfect...pleasure — WILDE 940:69
cigarettes best c. in my experience — STEV 851:29
Fasten your c. — WILD 943:35
cigars I'd like...to smoke c. — DIAZ 276:26
roller of big c. — STEV 849:66
Cimber C. should be banished — SHAK 777:26
cinder how dry a c. this world is — DONNE 292:63
scorched my intellect into a c. — CARL 199:71
Cinderella If I made C. — HITC 419:83
Mother Goose, C. and...phooker — PART 666:60
wand of C.'s Fairy Godmother — DIOR 287:4
cinema c. in their blood — RICH 714:18
C. is a matter of — SCOR 751:97
c. is any kind of force — LOACH 533:83
c. is built along 19th-century models — GREE 385:98
c. is truth — GODA 374:52
c. was...a new era — QUIR 703:27
invented the c. — LUMI 542:64
cinnamon c. and cloves — ANON 22:68
Spicy grove, c. tree — CULL 257:44
Circe body...straight as C.'s wand — MARL 574:36
elegance of C.'s hair — POUND 691:1

circle

circle c. of its influence	POTT 690:84
c. of the golden year	TENN 872:30
c. of the heroic	STOWE 856:27
c. round the globe	MUNDY 625:44
come full c.	MOYN 623:1
firmness makes my c. just	DONNE 292:40
forms…an untranscendable c.	SCHR 749:66
narrow c. of strikes	ENGE 326:14
Round and round the c.	ELIOT 319:51
Sorrow comes as in a c.	CH 222:18
square the c.	HEAN 404:69
Weave a c. round him thrice	COLE 236:42
What other planets c. other suns	POPE 686:72
wheel is come full c.	SHAK 793:35
circles centre and cause of many c.	LEON 523:78
c. of which we are the centres	TROL 897:25
mind skating c.	FROST 353:24
sweep in ever-widening c.	HUXL 442:2
circling c. in his desire	FLAU 339:25
circuit short c. in his identity	ROTH 727:76
Success in C. lies	DICK 284:47
circuits c. of a digital computer	PIRS 679:89
circulation she has a good c.	RENO 711:55
the c. of their blood	SMITH 829:11
work, leisure, c.	LECO 518:82
circumcised c. people	GIBB 366:95
C. the eighth day	BIBLE 128:99
circumcision every luxury…c.	ORTON 652:4
circumference just c., O world	MILT 605:30
circumlocution C.…literary trick	BIER 134:69
C. Office	DICK 282:83
circumstance blows of c.	TENN 874:83
escape from c. to ecstasy	BELL 75:33
foresee no c.	HESE 416:28
In the fell clutch of c.	HENL 411:5
suspect such a c.	AUST 46:72
circumstances cheated by c.	LESS 523:92
difficult to think of any c.	OAKE 642:3
If c. lead me	SHAK 782:78
more serious…in my present c.	SIDN 820:35
pain of particular c.	CART 206:38
things in terrible c.	MO 611:69
circumstantial How c. reality is!	UPDI 906:28
no further than the Lie C.	SHAK 780:23
circus ain't shucks to a c.	TWAIN 902:44
celebrated Barnum's c.	CHUR 225:78
chess tournament disguised as a c.	CONN 242:80
c. remains the same	ASHD 37:65
gets the c. it deserves	JONG 466:38
no right in the c.	MAXT 583:19
cirrhosis end up with c. of the liver	EAGL 309:1
cistern wheel broken at the c.	BIBLE 106:36
cisterns broken c.	BIBLE 110:12
citadel Coketown…ugly c.	DICK 282:79
Troy's sacred c.	HOMER 425:9
cithera universe is arranged like a c.	HONO 426:16
cities American life, in large c.	MCCA 547:88
c. and their civilities	PATM 669:25
c. are divided into two parts	BROW 166:5
c. of men	TENN 870:98
c., throbbed the true life	NORR 641:57
c. will have no rest from evils	PLATO 682:63
do not look in great c.	AUST 46:66
founder of c.!	COLUM 238:87
friends…are in c.	SNYD 832:89
great kings and fine c.	CATU 209:10
hum Of human c. torture	BYRON 187:53
impure love for c.	CASAL 207:69
inquire of all the C.	ALBE 11:33
In today's c.…on the outskirts	GENET 363:42
Islanded by c. fair	SHEL 812:64
Of towns and c.	WORD 956:53
protect American c.	SCHL 748:39
prowling through the c.	ORWE 654:57
ruined c. of Germany	ORWE 654:54
seek a livelihood…in c.	CANT 197:12
Soveraign of c.	DUNB 306:2
streets of a hundred c.	HOOV 427:42
sung women in three c.	POUND 691:87
Towered c. pleased	MILT 597:47
whose c. he saw	HOMER 425:9
citizen am to become a private c.	EISE 314:3
c. of life	SASS 745:81
c. of no mean city	BIBLE 125:97
c. of the proudest country	PARK 665:37
c. of the world	BOSW 152:77
I am a Roman c.	CICE 227:34

liberty that the c. enjoys	SPEN 836:89
No cold relation is a zealous c.	BURKE 176:49
not lay aside the c.	WASH 921:25
Sophia Loren is not a c.	GRAMM 381:95
transformed…into the perfect c.	DOUG 295:15
citizens all c. should be free	MORE 618:20
beat to death those c.	MAMET 563:27
c. dream of the south and west	HARDY 397:29
c. of Berlin	KENN 481:24
c. of death's grey land	SASS 745:83
c. of that other place	SONT 834:20
fat and greasy c.	SHAK 778:67
Healthy c. are the greatest asset	CHUR 226:98
prosperous c. of Zenith	LEWIS 527:57
State, or of c.	RUSK 733:97
universality of c. speaking	MAZZ 583:31
citizenship more onerous c.	SONT 834:20
union, before his c.	LEWIS 526:54
city amid the c.'s jar	ARNO 34:74
balloon, coming out of a keen c.	CUMM 257:56
Beautiful c.!	ARNO 35:12
belonging to a race…a c., a group	DUDEK 305:76
Brave men are a c.'s strongest tower	ALCA 11:39
citizen of no mean c.	BIBLE 125:97
c.…is a human zoo	MORR 620:45
c. is built to music	TENN 878:94
c. now doth look like a garment worn	WORD 959:3
c. of all time	HAWT 402:17
C. of London…clearing-house	CHAM 212:59
C. of perspiring dreams	RAPH 707:74
C. of the Big Shoulders	SAND 741:13
c.…out of step with the century	CHEE 218:4
c. shoulderingly upwards	CUMM 257:51
c. that is set on an hill	BIBLE 114:29
c. there is a group	LESS 524:94
c. was on one side	MUNCH 625:41
c. where most people live	GRAY 383:43
c. will follow you	CAVA 210:18
decline and fall of the C.	GIBB 366:2
depart out of that house or c.	BIBLE 116:68
died…in sight of the c.	MACA 546:60
escaped From the vast c.	WORD 957:72
Every c. has a sex and age	BERG 83:26
except the Lord keep the c.	BIBLE 103:36
fall in love with a c.	MORR 620:56
felled a c.	THOM 883:8
first c. Cain	COWL 250:76
fishbone in the c.'s throat	LOWE 540:24
forbid…in the c. in future	EDWA 312:56
great noise in the c.	EDWA 312:56
hard-boiled c.	CHAN 213:86
heart of the c.	MOYN 623:1
Hell is a c.	SHEL 813:87
history of C. architecture	JOHN 458:31
How doth the c. sit solitary	BIBLE 110:23
if you would know…live in a c.	COLT 238:85
in the c. of our God	BIBLE 100:70
In this c.	LIVI 532:60
Like c. lights, receding	GIBS 367:15
looking over harbor and c.	SAND 742:14
make glad the c. of God	BIBLE 100:68
man whom the c. sets up	SOPH 834:27
men that make a c.	NICI 637:80
modern c., it takes on	RODR 722:53
New York was no mere c.	DIDI 286:81
O c. of God	BIBLE 101:91
Of two f's…is this c.	MATOS 582:95
Once in royal David's c.	ALEX 13:63
on the field and c.	THAC 880:26
Paris is a beast of a c.	HAZL 403:44
play-going in any large c.	TYNAN 904:1
precipitous c.	STEV 854:90
prepared for them a c.	BIBLE 129:41
private individual or for a c.	PLATO 682:67
realm, nation, or c.	KNOX 495:14
roofs of this distracted C.	CARL 200:6
run about through the c.	BOOK 149:22
sacred c. of the mind	CAMP 194:54
streets of the c.	MCCA 547:75
Sun-girt c., thou hast been	SHEL 812:65
that sweet C.	ARNO 35:17
The C. is of Night	THOM 887:7
The C. is of Night	THOM 887:8
The C.'s voice	SHEL 812:66
thin trees in a c. square	LOWE 539:1
This rortie wretched c.	SMITH 831:64
took the c.	BIBLE 95:8

Towery c.	HOPK 428:78
Unless the Lord guards the c.	BIBLE 133:37
Unreal C.	ELIOT 318:97
vastly overrated c.	BURG 174:90
very fine c.	DEFOE 269:79
Without a c. wall	ALEX 13:64
Zion, c. of our God!	NEWT 636:64
civet Give me an ounce of c.	SHAK 793:22
civil as for its c. use	MONT 615:45
assault on our c. liberties	GORE 379:59
British C. Service	WILL 944:78
c. and obliging young woman	AUST 45:49
c., political, and religious	JUNI 471:49
c. servant doesn't make jokes	IONE 447:52
c. servant lyricism	BAND 61:10
C. Service is profoundly deferential	CROS 256:35
c. To everyone	SISS 823:92
C. war is impossible	PAVL 670:40
c. war obstructs the crusade	INNO 446:48
corresponding c. society	MARX 579:30
dire effects from c. discord flow	ADDI 7:53
Here lies a c. servant	SISS 823:92
He was very c., 'Masa	DAVI 265:82
How can I be c.	GERS 365:74
In a c. war, a general must know	REED 710:33
In c. business; What first?	BACON 51:90
Pray, good people, be c.	GWYN 391:8
too c. by half	SHER 817:78
civilians using…c. to protect…missiles	NETAN 634:30
civilities bandy c. with my sovereign	JOHN 461:15
cities and their c.	PATM 669:25
civility Scotch c.	ROCH 719:9
see a wild c.	HERR 416:17
civilization advance the cause of c.	BRIL 159:22
All c. has from time to time	ELLIS 323:29
all of c.'s obstacles	SAND 741:4
amenities of c.	MACD 550:40
as c. spreads	TOCQ 892:26
centers of European c.	TOLS 894:54
c. and profits	COOL 245:77
c. don't advance	ROGE 723:78
C. has made the peasantry	TROT 899:65
C. is a conspiracy	BUCH 171:23
C. is a movement	TOYN 895:74
c. is based on the…materialistic	BONA 145:16
c.…is coupled with death	MILL 594:92
c. is essentially one of property	EMER 325:83
C. itself is a…balance	POUND 692:21
c. of one epoch	CONN 243:11
c. works its miracles	TOCQ 892:27
continuity of c.	ORWE 654:54
curriculum vitae of C.	ANDR 18:77
depart from that c.	LISP 531:44
destroying the c.	LIND 530:13
Every c. that has ever existed	KISS 493:89
fall of the last c.	READ 708:96
farmyard c. of the Fabians	INGE 445:29
fate of human c.	LOVE 538:90
For a botched c.	POUND 691:5
fruits of Christian c.	BIRD 136:10
great movements of…human c.	BENN 81:81
green end of one of c.'s hardest winters	FOWL 345:62
habit of c.	WEST 933:94
highest standard of c.	LLOY 533:73
incompatible with c.	COOP 246:85
inheritors of an old c.	REYES 712:69
life-blood of real c.	TREV 896:4
long last night over c.	MAIL 560:50
mark of high c.	BERL 84:46
passive, receptive side of c.	SPEN 837:12
principal task of c.	FREUD 350:57
quarrel of c. against	ROOS 725:22
rottenness of our c.	READ 708:94
saddest object in c.	STEV 854:93
stupid of modern c.	KNOX 495:19
sweetness of present c.	HUGO 438:89
the greatest invention of c.	BAN 52:9
they maintain c.	TOCQ 893:34
to imbue c.	JOHN 456:72
undeniable pretensions as c.	PITT 679:10
under our existing c.	STAN 842:14
vulgar sort of c.	BURG 174:91
wall…separates c. from barbarism	BUCH 171:22
What do I think of Western c.?	GAND 359:61
whole history of c.	JAMES 451:69
without the usual interval of c.	CLEM 230:89

Clinton

civilizations autonomous c.	SONT 834:16
c. that abandon the quest for knowledge	LOVE 538:91
civilize adopt me and c. me	TWAIN 903:68
allowed she would c. me	TWAIN 902:51
civilized c. human life	TRUM 899:82
contact with the more c.	THOR 888:26
highly c. human beings	ORWE 654:32
I have become c.	BIRD 136:8
society here would be quite c.	WILDE 942:13
the more c....the people	DIDE 285:65
civilizers two c. of man	DISR 288:59
civil-suited c.-s. Morn	MILT 598:57
clack whet their beaks c. c.	RANS 707:69
claim c. on your respect	JUVE 471:59
c. those f.	TROL 897:26
if the c. were broken	SHAW 808:33
no human c....significance	OATES 643:11
on every beauty's c.?	CRUZ 256:38
claimant failed to embarrass the c.	STRA 857:42
clairvoyant Hate is always more c.	LACL 503:36
People also claim to be c.	BOWL 153:5
clamorous with such a c. smack	SHAK 762:72
clamours c. soars and shrills	ROBE 717:72
clan Against the c. M'Tavish	AYTO 46:3
c. has a tendency to ignore me	WODE 952:39
Clancy C., of the Overflow'	PATE 669:13
clanjamfrie haill c.	MACD 549:19
clannish exceedingly c. family	SHAW 811:33
clap Don't c. too hard	OSBO 655:85
trees of the field shall c.	BIBLE 109:1
Clapham safe back to C. Junction?	BUTL 185:1
claret c. and burgundy in Scotland?	SMITH 827:85
C. is the liquor	JOHN 463:66
C. on my Tomb	KEATS 476:95
clarets racehorses and the cheaper c.	SAKI 739:54
clarions Great winds Thy c.	ELLE 322:18
clarity c. is a great liability	BALF 58:42
C. of mind results in	PASC 666:65
universal and unbounded c.	JOHN 459:38
clark c. ther was of Oxenford	CHAU 217:74
clash c. together again	TENN 877:68
class c. lies late and snores	CULL 257:42
c. of declassed women	DUMAS 306:91
c. struggle...leads to the dictatorship	MARX 579:45
could have had c.	SCHU 749:70
decay of ability in the ruling c.	ORWE 654:35
educated c....hate us	CHEL 218:21
Every known c. of refusal	SOME 833:10
every other c. in the community	RICA 712:83
he gave her c.	HEPB 412:27
history of c. struggles	MARX 579:31
like any other c.	TAWN 868:43
lowest c. is literary footmen	HAZL 404:55
make the bourgeoisie a c.	HUGO 437:84
men of any other c.	LODGE 534:2
no other c. of dependants	MILL 592:13
one c. is made to feed	DOUG 296:26
prosperity...through every c.	BRYAN 170:97
raise them as a c.	SMIL 827:71
sector of the liberal middle c.	EAGL 309:2
sinking middle c.	ORWE 653:21
spokesman of a c.	CHAM 212:58
very low c. among the European states	GEOR 363:47
We are talking c.	KILP 486:11
Yuppies as a c.	ADLER 8:69
classes All c. of society	JEVO 455:54
c. of people	GARL 360:74
c. within c. in Peckham	SPARK 836:65
Comfort came in with the middle c.	BELL 75:36
curse of the drinking c.	WILDE 942:29
disappearance of the middle c.	COUP 248:27
divided into c.	RUSK 733:3
equally on all c.	CHUR 225:72
gathered together in c.	SMITH 830:36
General Strike has taught the working c.	BALF 58:40
Let the ruling c.	MARX 579:34
lower c. had such white skins	CURZ 260:6
masses against the c.	GLAD 373:40
patsies for the ruling c.	HELL 408:46
prove that the existence of c.	MARX 579:45
Society is composed of two large c.	CHAM 213:70
sports for the old ruling c.	HOBS 421:10
the privileged c.?	SIEY 820:62
To prove the upper c.	COWA 249:55
two c. in good society	SHAW 810:6
two c. of books	FORD 343:91
two c. of travel	BENC 78:3

wrote about the working c.	WAUGH 924:96
classic A c.	TWAIN 903:89
No c. resembles any previous c.	HEMI 410:89
tread on c. ground	ADDI 6:16
classical c. era was epic	HUGO 436:52
c. music and jazz	PREV 694:76
c. music of now	MCCA 548:3
c. period was healthy	GOET 375:68
C. quotations is the parole	JOHN 464:80
classics bellyful of the c.	MILL 593:54
c. are only primitive literature	LEAC 515:17
keep the c. at hand	WOOLF 956:37
the c. in paraphrase!	POUND 691:2
used to be c.	WAUGH 924:83
classification c. of all things	DURK 308:30
find fault with a c.	MILL 592:11
classless c. society	MARX 579:45
classroom Socrates in every c.	GRIS 389:74
clatter c. of high voices	DOYLE 297:48
draws the curtains...with a great c.	OSBO 655:84
Claudius Emperor C.	LONG 535:12
clause but this one c.	RABE 704:17
Clavell How to frighten Miss C.	BEME 78:99
Clavering c., and Havering	LEVE 525:23
Claver'se 'twas C. who spoke	SCOTT 754:82
claw red in tooth and c.	TENN 874:71
red in tooth and c.	TENN 874:80
claws c. that catch	CARR 204:89
neatly spreads his c.	CARR 203:64
pair of ragged c.	ELIOT 316:64
clay Art's subject is the human c.	AUDEN 42:75
C. blurs the whitewash	AVIS 47:1
c. grew tall	OWEN 658:38
C. lies still	HOUS 431:36
compounded am with c.	SHAK 801:61
dead and turned to c.	SHAK 784:62
feet...of iron and part of c.	BIBLE 111:38
from gold and c.	SHEL 816:46
Honouring itself the c. rears up	BARK 63:53
loam, or painted c.	SHAK 764:32
made of c.	GERS 365:80
of c. and wattles	YEATS 965:4
out of the miry c.	BIBLE 100:61
Potter and c. endure	BROW 168:60
power over the c.	BIBLE 125:23
pure c. of time's mud	MALA 562:88
shall the c. say to him	BIBLE 109:88
clean Bath twice...to be really c.	BURG 174:89
C. from my hand?	SHAK 797:37
c. hands	GALS 358:51
grew more c. and white	BROW 166:96
one more thing to keep c.	FRY 353:32
Then I was c. and brave	HOUS 431:39
though dirty is c.	FLEM 340:48
trying to play c.	PARK 663:92
until your bones are c.	ADCO 6:14
upbringings that were so c.	COUP 248:32
vanished c.	GURN 390:99
will these hands ne'er be c.?	SHAK 798:66
Wondrously c.	WALP 919:70
cleaners father had a chain of dry c.	BENN 80:54
cleanest c. and beautifullest	DEFOE 269:79
cleaning Yesterday, We had daily c.	REED 709:26
cleanliness C. is next to Godliness	DICK 282:2
c. of...backyards	MAIL 560:58
clear c., attentive mind	SNYD 832:90
free and c. from any image	SHAK 786:20
how thin and c.	TENN 872:39
might be too c.	GREE 387:37
not immediately c.	THUR 890:90
so c. and distinct	HUXL 443:5
unduly c.	GREE 386:34
want to make that very c.	ROMN 723:93
cleared no matter how carefully c.	SHUL 819:27
clearer see a little c.	BRAC 154:20
clear-eyed c.-e. adjustments	DAY 267:28
clearing-house c.-h. of the world	CHAM 212:59
clears water c. us of this deed	SHAK 797:38
clear-sighted c.-s. nor accurate	TROL 898:53
not the c.-s. who rule the world	CONR 244:49
cleavage c. contributes to narrow	ROSS 725:35
cleft c. for me	TOPL 894:61
clefts narrow the cross c.	ROSS 725:35
clench can c. and fight	MITC 609:28
clenched held my flower in a c. fist	HOFF 421:25
clenches wit degenerating into c.	DRYD 300:20
Cleopatra C.'s morality	LAUT 512:10

C.'s nose: if it had been shorter	PASC 667:74
down the Nile last night as C.	BROWN 164:29
gone to gaze on C.	SHAK 794:56
in the bed of C.	BROW 166:86
not...less than C.	DRYD 301:51
clergy all the c. you can despatch	CHIS 222:24
c. were beloved	SWIFT 863:77
The c. is in the same business	HURT 440:36
without the benefit o' the C.	CONG 240:41
clergyman salary of a beneficed c.	WAUGH 923:64
clergymen men, women, and c.	SMITH 830:55
clerical features of c. cut	ELIOT 319:49
clerk an unmannerly fat c.	SHER 817:80
both the priest and c.?	SHAK 764:55
grete c. of nygromancye	MALO 562:5
small c. of some hotel	MANS 567:1
small house agent's c.	ELIOT 318:4
was the best c.	MACA 544:11
clerks c. been noght wisest men	CHAU 217:87
clever c., but is it Art?	KIPL 490:98
c. enough to get all that money	CHES 221:96
c. to a fault	BROW 168:40
Everything c. has been thought	GOET 375:64
manage a c. man	KIPL 489:70
too c. by half	MAJOR 561:74
cleverness The obstinancy of c.	STOWE 856:34
cliché books, convention and c.	POUND 691:88
c. and an indiscretion	MACM 556:64
c. of whites being ignorant	ANGE 19:98
It is a c.	FRY 354:43
clichés half-truths and c.	TOOLE 894:58
most c. are true	FRY 354:43
click constant c. and kissing	BETJ 89:38
clicking c. with the subject	EISE 314:9
client c. is fain to hire a lawyer	BUTL 184:62
c. must be led to safety	MORT 621:66
dialogue between c. and architect	STERN 847:18
serving the c.	JOHN 458:28
venomous, and ungrateful c.	UPDI 905:20
cliff drive over a c.	VENA 910:49
edge of some crazy c.	SALI 740:81
far from c. and scar	TENN 872:39
In a coign of the c.	SWIN 864:16
lawyers going over a c.	HUNT 439:18
like jumping off a c.	BRYAN 170:96
off the edge of the c.	MOND 612:95
cliffs chalk c. of D.	BALD 57:32
c. of fall	HOPK 429:91
rubies in certain c.	MORE 618:21
yet still the solitary c.	WORD 957:71
climate c. allows him no chance	KIPL 489:77
c. is bracing	MCGO 551:74
c. of a perpetual Turkish bath	SWET 861:11
c. of Manitoba	ANON 23:93
c. suspends...understanding	BROO 162:83
cloudy c.	BYRON 189:87
common where the c.'s sultry	BYRON 189:92
enquiries about the UK c.	SAMU 741:3
fertile c. dwell	SHAK 788:83
in love with a cold c.	SOUT 835:42
not so much the result of c.	FUSE 356:92
our chilling c.	SWIFT 862:60
spring in their c.	DOUG 295:6
the c. crisis is real	GORE 379:63
whole c. of opinion	AUDEN 43:89
Your anger was a c.	PIER 677:68
climates and manners, c., council	TENN 870:98
climax cap and c. of...years	PEARY 671:59
flaming, fatal c.	SASS 745:83
works its way up to a c.	GOLD 377:31
climb teach ye how to c.	MILT 599:81
climbing c. a birch tree	FROST 352:98
c. into jobs	REST 711:64
C. over rocky mountain	GILB 368:36
clime born in the same c.	BYRON 190:11
Love...no season knows, nor c.	DONNE 291:25
sweet golden c.	BLAKE 140:11
visit our c.	BLAKE 139:80
climes styles for different c.	BROD 160:30
clinging c. blindly to the vices	FAUL 330:34
clingy bunches of c. sob sisters	PAGL 659:19
Clinton classic Bill C., sincere	MARA 569:44
C., the one indispensable...nation	VIDAL 912:2
give C. his due	VIDAL 912:7
Hillary C. is responsible	MCCU 549:16
impeachment against William Jefferson C.	ANON 27:40
Mr C....is our first black President	MILL 593:50

cloak

President C. returned today	DOWD 296:29	good smell of old c.	BROO 162:87	let the c. rain down	BIBLE 133:40
cloak c....an iron cage	WEBER 925:11	Italy been a dealer in second-hand c.	MARI 571:78	Never doubted c. would break	BROW 169:85
knyf under the c.	CHAU 217:84	Kindles in c. a wantonness	HERR 416:17	no pity sitting in the c.	SHAK 766:5
cloaks c. for untidy minds	MOND 612:96	liars in old c.	MARQ 575:62	nor the c. return after the rain	BIBLE 106:36
display of rich c.	DICK 279:1	liquefaction of her c.	HERR 416:16	O c., unfold!	BLAKE 141:42
clock Church c. at ten to three?	BROO 162:97	make a suit of c.	HUME 438:2	O'er which c.	SHEL 812:62
c. is always slow	SERV 757:36	married, not unto my c.	SHAK 762:71	piled gold c.	LARK 509:84
c. with weights and chains	COLUM 238:90	musty odour of old c.	ACKR 3:60	prince of the c.	BAUD 68:89
hands of a great c.	WILL 945:7	not quite enough c.	WILDE 942:10	raise the wind, or rend the c.	MARL 573:22
I open with a c. striking	SHER 818:2	Old C. are not venerable	CARL 200:1	shadows of the c.	WORD 960:22
If you can't turn the c. back	JOHN 457:98	old c. know who's master	SHER 817:73	sit in the c.	SHAK 772:79
produce? The cuckoo c.	WELL 929:93	On the state of her c.	NASH 631:68	slow movement of c.	DAY 267:36
putting the c. on half an hour	KIER 485:6	out of these wet c.	ANON 24:14	Somewhere among the c.	YEATS 966:22
regard the hand of the c.	LECO 518:81	politics with the c. off	BRAD 154:31	the poor Indian...Sees God in c.	POPE 687:75
time runs, the c. will strike	MARL 573:30	poured into his c.	WODE 952:45	Through the dark c.	FORD 343:9
watch the c. for you	SHAK 801:55	require new c.	THOR 888:34	tossing sea of c.	BENU 83:9
wind up the c.?	STER 847:21	soul...is his c.	SHAK 791:63	trailing c. of glory	WORD 959:8
clockmakers Swiss c.	STRA 857:47	take the girl's c. off	CHAN 213:91	When c. are cursed by thunder	THOM 883:11
clocks all the c. in the city	AUDEN 43:82	taking off your c.	KEIL 479:60	white c. floating	MCMU 557:83
c. the tongues of bawds	SHAK 770:27	taste for French c.	SCHL 747:37	white c. fly	WU 963:84
c. were striking thirteen	ORWE 655:71	the c. don't wear her	QUANT 701:3	White c. on the wing	ALLI 14:7
morning c. will ring	HOUS 431:37	time when you have to let your c.	MIDL 590:82	wreathed in c.	WHITE 936:58
Stop all the c.	AUDEN 42:79	walked away with their c.	DISR 288:37	**cloud-topped** Behind the c.-t. hill	POPE 687:77
clockwork c. orange	BURG 174:87	wears her c. as if	SWIFT 863:68	**cloud-waves** Bronze c.-w.	FREE 350:50
every 30 years like c.	SIMON 822:77	Who touched my c.?	BIBLE 119:56	**Clough** poet named C.	SWIN 864:11
clod turned her into the c.	ALTH 15:61	witnesses laid down their c.	BIBLE 124:88	**clout** hit her a great c.	STRO 857:54
clods Calcine its c.	BROW 168:33	wore torn c.	SPEN 837:98	**cloven** espied his c. foot	BALL 58:58
c. and trampled earth	MUIR 624:17	**clothing** Be courtly ay in c.	DUNB 306:1	**clover** c. and timothy-tops	ROBE 717:72
clog c. the foot of a flea	SHAK 786:15	c. affords a glimpse	BART 66:25	C....is Aristocracy	DICK 284:51
clogs age to quit their c.	MILT 601:21	c. for the soul divine	BLAKE 141:26	**cloverleaf** flower is the concrete c.	MUMF 625:38
c....lasted longer than shoes	WILS 948:58	c. of a manservant	HUGO 437:69	**cloves** cinnamon and c.	ANON 22:68
c....which else might oversoar	SHEL 814:18	Gave thee c. of delight	BLAKE 139:86	**Clovis** aunt of C.	SAKI 739:57
clumping...all in c.	ORWE 653:9	inappropriate c.	FIEN 336:39	**clown** c., the boozer, the fighter?	MAST 581:81
To hang c. on 'em	SHAK 789:97	Things in book's c.	LAMB 506:11	like the idiot or c.	SITW 824:22
cloister c. without a library	GEOF 363:44	**cloths** embroidered c.	YEATS 966:12	**clowns** those that play your c.	SHAK 783:20
in the court a c.	AELR 8:74	**cloud** a fair luminous c.	COLE 235:30	**club** any c. that will accept me	MARX 579:24
studious c.'s pale	MILT 598:59	avails a storm c.	RYDER 736:58	belong to the most exclusive c.	NASH 631:67
cloisters quiet collegiate c.	CLOU 232:61	black c. carries the sun away	ELIOT 319:42	best c. in London	DICK 283:22
clones c. have hung	HUGH 435:26	c. instead, and ever-during	MILT 603:75	Cancer is a membership to a c.	DRES 299:3
Clootie Satan, Nick, or C.	BURNS 177:83	c. in trousers!	MAYA 583:21	far from the c. house	LINK 530:24
Cloots auld C., I ken ye're thinkan	BURNS 177:84	From c. to tumbling c.	YEATS 966:19	harte in one hand and a c. in the other	BILL 135:97
close c. of day	YEATS 966:18	great c. came over me	FOX 346:71	I am the C. Liar	SAKI 739:67
C. the play	KAUF 474:42	he melted like a c.	TENN 878:95	man...loyal to his c.	WHITE 935:34
day must have its c.	STOWE 856:32	If a c. knew loneliness	RICH 713:9	No c. has been good enough	BUSBY 182:93
ineffective from c. up	SCHO 749:59	kerchiefed in a comely c.	MILT 598:57	savage wields his c.	HUXL 443:10
Keep your friends c.	PACI 658:3	Like a fiend hid in a c.	BLAKE 140:18	secret of managing a ball c.	STEN 847:7
live too c. to each other	GOLD 375:78	little c. out of the sea	BIBLE 97:64	**clue** Singularity...invariably a c.	DOYLE 297:50
still hasten to a c.	COWP 250:89	moon on this c. sea	SCOTT 751:2	**Clunton** C. and Clunbury	HOUS 431:54
the stock market is c.	LENO 522:58	motions of wind and c.	LEE 519:98	**clusters** c. and constellations of data	GIBS 367:15
closes c. Saturday night	KAUF 474:36	no silver lining...without its c.	STER 847:15	Where we such c. had	HERR 416:18
or flowered c.	SWIN 864:4	On a c. I saw a child	BLAKE 139:85	**clutch** Come, let me c. thee	SHAK 796:27
closest human beings who seem c.	PRIE 695:89	peaks of c.	CIAR 226:22	**clutching** c. the inviolable shade	ARNO 34:95
closet forth the c. brought a heap	KEATS 477:24	pillar of a c.	BIBLE 93:62	**Clyde** on the bonnie banks o' C.	LAUD 511:16
I'll to thy c.	SHAK 760:27	set my bow in the c.	BIBLE 92:13	**coach** generals are in my c.	MARL 572:91
put me in the C.	DICK 284:38	She faded, like a c.	SHEL 815:31	hold back against the c.	TROL 898:46
when thou prayest, enter into thy c.	BIBLE 115:41	so great a c. of witnesses	BIBLE 129:43	looking for a body in the c.	HITC 419:83
closets Out of the C.	ANON 25:68	some gilded c.	VAUG 909:34	politics is like...a football c.	MCCA 547:83
closing opening and c. of a door	SAND 742:21	Stooping through a fleecy c.	MILT 598:53	rattling of a c.	DONNE 293:74
you have a hell of a c.	REAG 709:17	The flying c.	TENN 875:95	Up, and by c.	PEPYS 674:98
closure a fearful term...in fashion...—C.	LIVE 531:53	wandered lonely as a c.	WORD 960:24	**coaches** c. shall be scrap	SAND 742:15
C. is a greasy little word	AMIS 17:57	wild geese lost in c.	BASHO 67:48	**coachmaker** o' mind the fairies' c.	SHAK 765:71
cloth Fine c. is never out of fashion	FULL 355:83	yon labouring c.	MARL 574:31	**coal** Affection is a c.	SHAK 762:85
Flags are...c.	ROY 730:28	**cloud-capped** c.-c. towers	SHAK 804:27	c. to kindle fleshly flame	SPEN 838:34
new c. unto an old garment	BIBLE 116:64	**clouded** if your life should become c.	OVID 657:22	island is made mainly of c.	BEVAN 89:52
On a c. untrue	GILB 370:67	**cloud-encircled** c.-e. meteor	SHEL 814:3	it is a c.	PEELE 672:70
clothe c. my naked villainy	SHAK 761:30	**cloudiness** full of frost...and c.?	SHAK 775:58	like a c.	SMART 826:65
clothed C. with his breath	TENN 878:83	**clouds** After the greatest c.	ALAN 10:16	live c. in his hand	BIBLE 107:55
c. with the heavens	TRAH 895:85	all the c. that lowered	TWAIN 902:63	the biggest c. block	HEAN 405:79
clothes Angels were, but with c.	LOVE 538:87	carries the c. with it	LEON 522:72	With England's own c.	KIPL 492:66
as if she were taking off all her c.	COLE 236:55	c. are deep	FREE 350:49	**coalition** You may call it c.	PALM 662:73
as much for her c. as for herself	WHAR 933:3	c. are lightly curled	TENN 870:92	**coalitions** England does not love c.	DISR 288:43
being to buy new c.	MONT 613:14	c. do often rest	MILT 597:45	**coalminers** keep the c. off the streets	BRES 158:2
brand-new suit of c.	HERB 414:90	c. of his own glory	GREE 385:3	**coalmines** in disused c.	KEYN 484:80
buy a teenager new c.	WHITE 935:48	c. of the table above	MONRO 612:5	**coals** all eyes else, dead c.!	SHAK 800:29
c. and hair were neat	GUNT 390:97	c., or mud or like places	LEON 523:77	Can one go upon hot c.	BIBLE 104:60
C. are our weapons	CART 206:36	c. takes all away	SHAK 758:58	c. thereof are c. of fire	BIBLE 107:49
c. easy to copy	SCHI 747:22	c. that blinded	PIER 677:68	eyes that stare like c.	RANS 707:72
C. make the poor invisible	HARR 398:44	c. the c. chase	BIBLE 131:86	gang to the c. i' the morning	SKIR 825:51
c. off and hang her up	NATI 632:4	c. turning blood red	MUNCH 625:41	heap c. of fire upon his head	BIBLE 105:95
c. possess an influence	ALCO 12:43	c. were touched	WORD 961:36	piles of dry wood with red-hot c.	CISN 227:39
c. were all tarnished	MOORE 616:64	cometh with c.	BIBLE 131:86	**coarse** c. emotion of mankind	ELIOT 316:52
covered him with c.	BIBLE 97:51	dying c. contend	SHAK 760:7	c. warty hands	DONO 293:82
don't design c., I design dreams	LAUR 511:20	gloom of c.	ADDI 6:34	such a c. pattern	HARDY 397:15
earthly interests...held up, by C.	CARL 200:92	heaven but the c.	RUSK 732:85	**coast** c. where souls are lost	ANON 22:81
Englishwoman's c.	SITW 824:12	Heaven is free From c.	BYRON 188:60	last train for the c.	MCLE 554:23
Fine c. are good	JOHN 463:46	He comes with c. descending	WESL 932:64	look'd towards the French c.	STER 848:43
Good c. open all doors	FULL 355:85	left the red c.	TANN 867:24	near the shadowy c.	THOM 886:84

colour

Entry	Reference
People can't die, along the c.	DICK 280:52
round the c. the languid air	TENN 870:88
scarcely visited any c.	JOHN 460:86
wild and breaker-beaten c.	BYRON 189:6
you c. for a while	REAG 709:15
coaster dirty British c.	MASE 580:56
coat brown c., the...stockings	MACA 545:36
c., and I have given that	KRUG 500:21
c. Covered with embroideries	YEATS 966:16
c. of many colours	BIBLE 93:37
did not wear his scarlet c.	WILDE 942:15
eternal Footman hold my c.	ELIOT 316:65
for a riband to stick in his c.	BROW 167:18
good c. upon his back	JOHN 461:95
Grab your c.	FIEL 335:28
have a good c.	STAN 843:19
iron c. all overgrown	SPEN 838:30
love that loves a scarlet c.	HOOD 426:21
tattered c.	YEATS 966:26
coats gold c. spots you see	SHAK 767:25
cobbler body of a c.	LOCKE 533:91
c. stick to his last	APEL 29:76
cobble-stones On c.-s. I lay	FLAN 338:6
cobblestreets the c. silent	THOM 884:31
Cobleigh sounds like Uncle Tom C.	THOM 884:23
Uncle Tom C. and all	BALL 60:81
cobra guile of a c.	WOOL 956:47
cobweb c. of the brain	BUTL 185:76
foul black c.	WEBS 926:41
cobwebs Laws are like c.	SWIFT 861:23
reasoners...make c.	BACON 50:44
weave fine c.	BUTL 184:69
Coca-Cola billboards did to C.-C.	UPDI 906:21
cocaine C. habit-forming?	BANK 61:12
I...was once given c.	JOHN 457:93
cock Before the c. crow	BIBLE 119:41
C. and a Bull	STER 848:47
c. doth craw	BALL 60:83
c. may craw	BURNS 178:12
c.'s shrill clarion	GRAY 384:64
c. who thought the sun had risen	ELIOT 315:24
c. with lively din	MILT 597:44
c. won't fight	BEAV 71:26
louder a c. can crow	TROL 898:37
Nationalism is a silly c.	ALDI 12:48
offer a c. to Asclepius	PLATO 682:57
this night, before the c. crow	BIBLE 119:41
with my old c. linnet	COLL 237:64
cockade lad wi' his white c.	ANON 22:72
cockatoo cage...to a c.	SHAW 809:85
green freedom of a c.	STEV 849:69
cockatrice hand on the c.' den	BIBLE 108:62
cockerel calls with a c.'s tongue	LEE 519:95
cockle like him that soweth c.	BUNY 174:84
Cockney much of C. impudence	RUSK 733:15
cockroaches c. will still be here	JANO 452:80
cocks drowned the c.!	SHAK 792:4
set the c. a-crow	YEATS 967:39
cocksure c....as Tom Macaulay	MELB 584:47
cocktail c. is to...wine	CLAU 229:72
pause...known as the c. hour	DE 275:11
weasel under the c. cabinet	PINT 678:83
cock-up wash-out of a c.-u.	ANON 26:10
cocoa C. is a cad	CHES 221:88
rather have a nice cup of c.	COWA 249:65
cocoon c. of its own thoughts	LOWE 539:12
people live wrapped tight in a c.	CARR 202:55
Cocqcigrues coming of the C.	KING 488:53
Cocteau C. thinks that I am a poor thief	GENET 363:38
cod Boston...home of...the c.	BOSS 151:74
O bely! O stynkyng c.	CHAU 217:94
coddled I have been c. long enough	BUFF 172:48
code c....for those who oppose us	EISE 314:99
rigid c. of immorality	BRAD 154:22
trail has its own stern c.	SERV 757:34
codes rape us with...their c.	FREN 350:53
codfish taste of c. in it	GRIEG 388:65
Codrus peals of laughter, C.!	POPE 687:98
coelacanth like the c.	HOGG 423:44
coffee c. and doughnuts	DAVI 265:84
c. and oranges	STEV 849:69
I like my c. like	DEGEN 270:6
measured out my life with c. spoons	ELIOT 316:63
morning cup of c.	HOLM 424:85
Rock 'n' roll is instant c.	GELD 362:31
wear c. as a perfume	VAN 908:17
went on drinking c.	GREE 385:4
coffee-house some obscure c.-h.	MONT 613:14
coffer litel gold in c.	CHAU 217:75
coffin Bring out the c.	AUDEN 42:79
heart is in the c.	SHAK 777:40
Shaped like a c.	MACN 558:9
silver plate on a c.	CURR 259:93
turns in his c.	GILB 370:75
coffins c. were looking up	DICK 278:65
cogent equally c.	GASK 361:84
cogging Some c., cozening slave	SHAK 790:36
cogitations c. still amaze	ELIOT 317:75
cogito c., ergo sum	DESC 274:96
coherence all c. gone	DONNE 292:60
coign In a c. of the cliff	SWIN 862:15
coil shuffled off this mortal c.	SHAK 782:7
coin single c. to medicine	VALLE 907:7
smallest current c.	BIER 134:61
coinage powerful c.	PLOUT 682:74
coiner c. of sweet words!	ARNO 34:96
coins and like to c.	TENN 878:77
barter it for silver c.	NGU 636:66
glory in large c.	HUGO 437:74
silver c. multiplying	WALC 916:17
coition trivial and vulgar way of c.	BROW 165:70
Coke cantaloupe in a C. bottle	JONES 466:24
C. bottles...great modern things	WARH 920:8
coke Happiness is like c.	HUXL 441:67
Coketown C....ugly citadel	DICK 282:79
cold being white is c. and sad	RHYS 712:73
blood was c.	SCOTT 752:11
blow in c. blood	SHAW 808:43
called a c. a c.	BENN 81:65
Came in from the C.	LECA 518:71
careful c. beginneth	SPEN 838:26
c. and certain friends	HUGO 437:78
c. as truth	RHYS 712:75
c. coming they had of it	ANDR 18:79
c. coming we had of it	ELIOT 318:17
c. doesn't crouch over one	LAWR 513:66
C. doth not sting	NASHE 632:93
C. in the earth	BRON 162:76
c. o' the moon	BROW 169:65
c. reaches of the universe	KENN 481:8
c. roads...c. news	SCOTT 754:75
c., uncertain of all	WILL 946:8
comfort me with c.	SHAK 768:65
dressed ever caught a c.?	NIET 639:15
Europe catches c.	METT 589:58
feel hot and think c.	CARY 207:62
foot and hand go c.	ANON 21:60
Give them the c. steel	ARMI 32:40
glass...hard, c. and misted over	RHYS 712:78
going down and becoming c.	SMITH 806:75
have to do that c.	HEMI 410:77
heart grown c.	SHEL 815:40
hot temper leaps o'er a c. decree	SHAK 769:76
ink in my pen ran c.	WALP 919:67
in love with a c. climate	SOUT 835:42
in the c. grave leave	WEBS 926:21
in the darkness and the c.	STEV 854:87
makes c. weather	SHAK 804:39
my boy? Art c.?	SHAK 792:8
naked in the dark and c.	LEGU 520:8
neither c. nor hot	BIBLE 131:94
No worse than a bad c.	MARX 578:23
silver thimble lies c.	SITW 824:20
'Tis bitter c.	SHAK 780:28
too c. always	SMITH 830:37
too c. for hell	SHAK 797:39
too c. for the spectators	SMITH 830:30
wert thou in the c. blast	BURNS 180:60
what I got...was a c.	THOR 889:44
wind was c.	SCOTT 752:9
yet so warm, and yet so c.	LAWS 514:97
colder even c. war	KENN 481:8
coldness heat full of c.	LYLY 543:84
colds c. a forward spring remove?	DONNE 291:28
Coleridge C....has lately taken wing	BYRON 189:89
C. lull the babe at nurse	BYRON 187:29
Cultivate simplicity, C.	LAMB 505:77
indulgences of C.	THUR 891:94
observed by C.	WORD 961:32
shut up, like C.	QUIL 702:17
You will see C.	SHEL 814:3
Coliseum While stands the C.	BYRON 188:68
collage C. is a supersensitive	ERNST 327:40
C. Agreement...starts to c.	SHUL 819:25
all his plans c.	JOSE 469:8
When I see my friends c.	SKEL 824:33
collapses nothing c.	WHIT 937:91
collar Malachi wore the c.	MOORE 617:1
shirt or c. ever comes back	LEAC 515:21
collarbone silly old c.'s bust	BETJ 89:45
collar-rolls In velvet c.-r.	KIPL 492:59
collaterals I detest c.	SOME 833:9
colleagues former c. are to be believed	HOWE 433:89
for myself and my c.	PEEL 672:66
most eminent of his c.	DISR 288:46
Most of my c. were -ists	HUXL 443:4
Smarter than most of his c.	REST 711:61
collecting what c. is all about	ANNE 20:15
collection c. of unrealistic goals	LURIE 542:67
extraordinary c. of talent	KENN 481:11
collections those mutilators of c.	LAMB 505:3
collective c. opinion...make history	SAFI 737:22
collectors great c. before me	DOUG 295:6
one-night stands in c.' homes	RAUS 707:80
college at school or c.	STEV 852:50
endow a c., or a cat	POPE 686:66
Fellows of another c.	LITT 531:47
Magdalen C.	GIBB 366:98
suppress each cathedral and c.	MACA 545:27
This great C.	HOUS 432:61
collie tither was a ploughman's c.	BURNS 177:81
collier-brigs cabooses of c.-b.	DICK 281:55
Collins if you do not marry Mr C.	AUST 46:58
colloquial clear it from c. barbarisms	JOHN 459:57
colloquialisms c., its humour	ROLL 723:90
collusive the puff c.	SHER 817:97
Cologne wash your city of C.	COLE 236:50
Colombia last optimist left in C.	GARC 359:66
colonel c. comes from Brian's race	DAVIS 266:10
For the C.'s Lady	KIPL 490:12
colonial have to be c. to know	WALC 916:12
large sections of the c. population	SCHL 747:33
colonialism C. forces the people	FANON 330:15
C. is not satisfied	FANON 329:14
colonies finest C. under the Crown	STUA 858:58
In the c. the economic substructure	FANON 329:13
products of all the c.	SITW 824:12
this realm, its c.	QUIL 702:13
colonists Roman c. settled in Britain	HYDE 443:19
colonization c. by any European	ADAMS 5:5
c. planted the seeds	MARI 570:72
colonized among c. people	SART 745:78
Colonus Singer of sweet C.	ARNO 33:64
colony an economic c.	TSON 900:7
brown men from a distant c.	PRIE 695:95
Crown C. system	KING 488:58
founders of a new c.	HAWT 402:4
from c. to nation to c.	INNIS 446:44
Colossus Like a C.	SHAK 776:9
Milton...could cut a C. from a rock	JOHN 464:92
colour abominable c. of his hair	HOUS 433:82
altered the c. of my mind	BRON 162:77
Any c.—so long as it's black	FORD 343:96
Beige! Just my c.	DE 276:21
between the mind and the c.	HEPW 412:28
burned gold was his c.	CHAU 217:98
cast thy nightly c. off	SHAK 780:34
citizens of c. are concerned	KING 487:27
C. and bite permeate a language	SAFI 737:18
c. is a means of exerting	KAND 473:17
c. is the goal	HEIN 407:19
C. is the ultimate	RUNGE 731:53
c. I want those handrails	TRUMP 900:97
c. of a beryl	BIBLE 110:28
c. of my soul is iron-grey	DEBU 268:59
c. of one's skin	BALD 56:15
c. of sand	ASHB 37:56
c. of shadows	WALC 916:17
c. of their skin	KING 486:25
c. of the sky	CRANE 253:75
C. possesses me	KLEE 494:3
c. shrieked	MUNCH 625:81
c. to that of the Senses	MATI 581:93
exact c. and shape	MONET 612:99
formal principle of its c.	SHEL 816:49
for the c. of his hair	HOUS 433:81
heart never knows the c. of the skin	GEOR 364:56
know the c. of that blood	KEATS 478:49
know the c. rose	ABSE 1:7
life is c. and warmth	GREN 388:57
loses c. with the slightest	VIEI 913:2

colour-bar

Nature's scheme of c.	STRE 857:51
No c., only nuance!	VERL 911:59
paint the c. of the wind	BODE 144:91
problem of race and c.	DU 305:70
problem of the c. line	DU 304:65
relationships of c. or form	ROTH 728:3
see a man...not a c.	STEV 851:16
subtle spies Of c.	FREE 350:49
'tis a c. she abhors	SHAK 786:5
'twas a c. he never liked	SHAK 775:69
What c. is your parachute?	BOLL 145:10
yearned for warmth and c.	TENN 877:58
colour-bar c.-b. and beer	NOON 641:51
colour-blind wise person is c.-b.	SCHW 751:95
coloured For c. girls	SHAN 805:59
makes a man c.	HUGH 435:16
Negroes...replaced c. people	FEIF 332:56
shadow over the c.	BUCK 172:33
colouring c. of a thought	SITW 824:23
colourists Painters who are not c.	DELA 271:23
colours All c. will agree	BACON 50:61
coat of many c.	BIBLE 93:37
c. don't quite match your face	ASHF 37:70
c. laid so thick	DRYD 299:10
composition of c.	THEO 882:79
flat surface covered with c.	DENIS 273:71
fresh c. deck the wanton prime	SPEN 838:39
Fresh-quilted c. through the air	HERR 415:10
howl of unnerving c.	TZARA 904:17
I had shown my c.	ACHE 3:37
Lentil-soup c.	HUGH 435:20
more c. in these ten minutes	DICK 279:1
Scents, c., and sounds	BAUD 68:60
see the difference of the c.	MELV 585:76
table of c.	GALE 357:28
troop their c.	BAIN 55:94
colts play left-guard for the C.	BRES 158:2
columbine pink and purple c.	SPEN 838:15
Columbus C. and his men	WILB 939:38
C. of our shore	WENT 931:53
first carnival person was Christopher C.	COLE 234:99
my youth in C., Ohio	THUR 890:67
column The fifth c.	MOLA 611:71
thunderhead-like c.	AGAWA 9:92
urn Throws up a steamy c.	COWP 251:19
columns c. of the old rain forest	AMIS 16:46
Greeks were hiding behind their c.	DE 271:18
moved...in c.	WELL 929:4
coma eight-year c.	BENT 82:7
keep the mothers in a state of c.	DAVI 264:72
comb fight between two bald men over a c.	BORG 151:60
c. my hair	BALL 60:79
combat c. the monster	BALZ 60:90
naval c.	GIBB 366:95
set a c. them between	BALL 58:59
combative made a c. apology	SHUL 819:21
combats causes them to hide their c.	BALZ 61:97
comber c. wind-hounded?	KIPL 491:45
combination c. of half-truths	TOOLE 894:58
c. of outward with inward facts	ELIOT 315:21
c. that is necessary	ROOS 725:20
constant and uniform c.	SMITH 827:80
exquisite c.	TROL 897:29
unbeatable c.	ANGE 18:85
combinations irregular c.	JOHN 459:57
combine C. your hearts in one	SHAK 776:2
sure to c.	JAMES 451:64
combustion ruin and c. down	MILT 601:33
come Art thou he that should c.	BIBLE 116:75
avoid what is to c.	SHAK 784:43
change has c. to America	OBAMA 644:31
c. again with rejoicing	BIBLE 103:35
C. and take them	LEON 523:80
C., seeling night	SHAK 797:47
C. what c. may	SHAK 796:10
hands...remembered to c. with him	PRIT 696:17
know not how to...c. in	BIBLE 97:53
let him c. out	JOHN 464:84
One to c., and one to go	CARR 207:18
shape of things to c.	WELLS 930:39
Surely I c. quickly	BIBLE 132:29
Then c. on, c. on	HERR 415:14
was, and is, and is to c.	BIBLE 131:97
comedian test of a real c.	NATH 632:99
comedians being c.	GREE 386:19
comedies c. are ended	BYRON 190:31

comedy All I need to make a c.	CHAP 214:11
Applaud...the c. is over	BEET 74:5
at a c. we only look	HUXL 442:889
both c. and tragedy	THUR 891:97
c. in one hundred different acts	LAFO 504:61
C. is an imitation	SIDN 820:57
C. is a very serious thing	GARR 360:81
C....is harder to do	MALA 561:86
C. is if I walk into an open sewer	BROO 163:14
C. is more like coke	IZZA 448:84
c. paints characters	HUGO 437:66
c. tells us	GORM 379:65
Farce is nearer tragedy...than c.	COLE 236:52
happier still is that musical c.	AGATE 9:88
make in som c.!	CHAU 216:67
Most Lamentable C.	SHAK 767:20
rules c. can tolerate	THUR 891:2
Talking of the C.	JOHN 464:93
world is a c.	WALP 919:74
Writers of c. have outlook	THUR 891:1
comeliness no form nor c.	BIBLE 109:93
comely boast themselves more c.	MILT 598:63
Sae c. to be seen	SCOTT 753:45
Comet On, C.! On, Cupid!	MOORE 616:63
comet come like a daytime c.	BISH 136:26
Woman is thought to be a C.	MAKIN 561:80
comets Old men and c.	SWIFT 862:53
there are no c. seen	SHAK 777:20
comfort Art should c. the disturbed	BANKS 62:30
Be c. to my age	SHAK 778:70
before providing c.	MARI 571:87
beg cold c.	SHAK 768:65
carrion c.	HOPK 429:88
catechism of c.	BENE 79:13
c. across many a...night	NIET 638:10
c. came in with the middle classes	BELL 75:36
c. comes too late	SHAK 805:57
c. myself when	SURR 860:4
c. of thy worth and truth	SHAK 801:49
c. serves in a whirlwind	HOPK 429:92
C.'s in heaven	SHAK 764:43
c. to shift one's position	IRVI 447:61
c. ye my people	BIBLE 108:79
c. your bed	SHAK 777:18
C. yourself	PASC 668:94
dear husband for a c.	SMITH 830:32
hobbit-hole, and that means c.	TOLK 893:42
in comparative c.	KING 488:57
loves...of c. and despair	SHAK 803:87
Money is a c.	ANON 20:34
mutual society, help, and c.	BOOK 148:87
no c. like...having deserved it	SHER 817:92
no c., only anxiety	FRIS 351:84
not another c. like to this	SHAK 789:8
not ecstasy but it was c.	DICK 282:88
Nothing else will give you any c.	SCOTT 754:84
only c. about being a woman	STARK 843:21
receives c. like cold porridge	SHAK 804:18
seeketh in society c.	BACON 50:38
sees too deep for c.	FADI 329:7
sense of inward c.	AUBR 42:61
Society is no c.	SHAK 803:6
Such c. as do lusty young men	SHAK 765:68
tell you naught for your c.	CHES 220:80
This must my c. be	SHAK 764:34
Thou art all the c.	SHAK 803:2
willing to live in c.	DU 305:70
comfortable c. years allowed to man!	SASS 745:81
Exploring...is not c.	BUTL 185:91
palace more c.	HOOV 427:49
something more c.	HARL 398:37
think about a more c. one	WILD 943:43
When people are too c.	RICH 714:21
comforted Lord hath c. his people	BIBLE 109:91
refused to be c.	BIBLE 110:22
refused to be c.	BIBLE 93:39
comforter C., where, where	HOPK 429:90
comforters miserable c. are ye all	BIBLE 98:6
comforting c....to be the recipient	FOWL 345:64
comfortless c., and worn, and old	ROSS 726:39
comforts adversity is not without c.	BACON 51:65
c. we despise	SHAK 795:77
disregard for the sublime c.	SHIP 818:14
helpers fail and c.	LYTE 543:94
King of c.	VAUG 909:38
loves and c. should increase	SHAK 789:9
comic c. writers to have a hate figure	TOWN 895:69

encouragement of c. strips	UPDI 906:26
comical often think it's c.	GILB 369:52
comics C....great modern things	WARH 920:8
coming cold c. we had of it	ELIOT 318:17
c.! He is c.!	AYTO 48:12
going out and thy c. in	BIBLE 103:31
Welcome the c.	POPE 686:52
command at your c.	GRAV 382:16
basic c. of religion	TOYN 895:78
c. me any service	SHAK 774:28
c. of that vital sea	CHUR 226:97
c. what you will	AUGU 44:28
Had thine at their c.	WORD 960:15
singular c., I do not understand	AUDEN 44:27
The c. 'Thou shalt not kill'	JOHN 456:78
wide as his c.	DRYD 301:64
wisdom bears c.	MILT 607:83
commanded Have I not c. thee?	BIBLE 95:6
commanders c. of legions	JUVE 471:57
C....should die with troops	CHUR 225:93
commandment c. on the pulse of life?	SHAK 768:64
c. that states, 'Thou shalt fly'	CLEE 229:81
first and great c.	BIBLE 118:26
indivisibility, the first c.	ROTH 728:91
new c. I give unto you	BIBLE 123:50
Science knows only one c.	BREC 157:93
This is my c.	BIBLE 123:55
commandments Christian c.	KIER 485:6
c. in your face	SHAK 759:85
keep his c.	BIBLE 107:38
love me and keep my c.	BOOK 147:59
two great c. were	MACA 545:34
write poetical c.	BYRON 189:2
commands obedient to their c.	SIMO 822:79
commemorative cold c. eyes	ROSS 727:64
commendable silence is only c.	SHAK 769:72
commendation beautiful face is a dumb c.	PUBL 699:64
greater c.	DRYD 300:20
man's c. with woman	SHAK 786:14
commended highly c. of all	BUNY 174:81
comment C. is free	SCOTT 751:98
commentary c. on that cry	KAZA 474:51
proliferating c.	GRASS 382:13
commentators As learned c. view	SWIFT 862:62
C. quote economic studies	SAMU 741:2
commerce adventures...in c.	WEST 933:95
c....enhanced by success	TREV 896:10
form of c. and consumption	MARX 579:30
heaven fill with c.	TENN 871:17
In c. bygones are for ever bygones	JEVO 455:53
increase of riches and c.	HUME 438:4
In matters of c.	CANN 197:10
obstructed interstate c.	HOOV 427:54
poets of c.	GRAY 388:64
trade and c.	HALL 393:40
commercial among a c. one	FUSE 356:93
blend of the c. traveller	STAP 843:20
c. society	TREV 896:10
concern for c. viability	MAMET 563:26
phonograph...is not of any c. value	EDIS 312:53
safe haven from c. considerations	SAFER 737:16
commercials 30-second c.	DANF 261:27
commission c. you to carry out	GOER 374:57
Each bullet has got its c.	DIBD 276:31
commitment C. to the poor	JOHN 456:80
with a three-ocean c.	HAYW 403:29
committee C. is an animal	LECA 518:72
horse designed by a c.	ISSI 448:78
written by a c.	GRIS 389:75
commodities c. derive their...value	RICA 712:82
into the c. market	TYSON 904:9
levied upon c.	JOHN 460:74
commodity C. fetishism	TATE 867:42
c. of good names	SHAK 770:29
infinitely small amount of c.	JEVO 455:52
worker becomes...cheaper c.	MARX 578:25
Commodus accession of C.	GIBB 366:90
common call not thou c.	BIBLE 124:83
c. cry of curs	SHAK 799:98
c. good to all	SHAK 778:57
c. interest always will prevail	DRYD 302:85
c. is the commonplace	TENN 873:59
C. Law of England	HERB 413:50
c. people swarm	SHAK 760:11
c. property of the nation	TIMES 892:23
c. prudence, and c. sense	SMITH 830:46

concerns the c. weal	GEOR 364:54	non-Communist premier	BOHL 144:98	c. on the son of her womb?	BIBLE 109:89
Crime is c.	DOYLE 297:60	tremble at a c. revolution	MARX 579:34	c. to solve even a little	WILS 947:44
dream of a c. language	RICH 713:5	Vietnam took the c. road	NGUY 636:69	crumbs of c.	TUTU 901:23
he should not be so c.	WILS 947:42	would not even be a c.	ZHIV 970:10	heavenly c. in your hearts	DICK 281:74
insipid c. sense	SALI 740:89	**communists** looking…for C.	FOOT 342:80	his father saw him, and had c.	BIBLE 121:91
leapt straight past the c. cold	AYRES 48:9	theory of the C.	MARX 579:32	Jesu, thou art all c.	WESL 932:62
lose their c. sense	STEIN 845:71	**communities** c….slightly removed	COOP 246:85	live without real c.	WILS 947:45
loves not the c. people	SHAK 799:93	filthier and filthier c.	GARD 360:71	Mercy, c., and justice	WAITE 916:5
make it too c.	SHAK 772:74	half-civilized c.	BAGE 55:78	Samaritan…had c. on him	BIBLE 121:81
man of c. opinion	BAGE 55:80	**community** c. consisting of a master	BIER 134:82	sharp c. of the healer's art	ELIOT 320:64
man of great c. sense	SHAW 807:12	c. is a fictitious body	BENT 82:87	treat each other with c.	AKIH 10:12
nor lose the c. touch	KIPL 492:63	c. lacks goods	CHUR 225:71	**compassionate** to be generous and c.	THAT 881:51
Organizing around a c. interest	BLOOM 143:68	c. of Europe	GLAD 373:41	**compassions** c. fail not	BIBLE 110:26
praise that as c. sense	THOR 889:44	c. of thought	ADAMS 5:92	**compensations** c. for growing older	SKIN 825:49
speak as the c. people	ASCH 37:52	interests of the c.	TOCQ 892:30	**competition** Art…excludes all c.	FUSE 356:91
still be c., dear	RATT 707:79	interests of…the c.	RICA 712:83	c. between expert	KEYN 484:78
surpass C. revenge	MILT 602:63	involved as a c.	GINS 372:14	C. brings out the best	SARN 743:56
the man is a c. murderer	SAKI 739:65	member of a civilized c.	MILL 591:99	c. the laws of death	RUSK 733:99
those of c. sense	HUXL 443:10	no finer investment for any c.	CHUR 226:98	don't meet c.	REVS 711:67
Tom Paine's c. sense	ADAMS 5:3	not life that is not in c.	ELIOT 319:33	free c. of the market	RICA 712:81
trained and organized c. sense	HUXL 443:10	not of war…but of…c.	CHILD 222:16	free c. was wasteful	PUZO 701:6
way into the C. Market	WILS 948:64	part of the c. of Europe	SALI 740:90	law [of c.] may be sometimes hard	CARN 202:48
What [existentialists] have in c.	SART 744:71	rule of any modern c.	KEYN 485:83	tradition…Approves all forms of c.	CLOU 232:67
what we have in c.	CLIN 231:21	scientific c. thinks	KUHN 500:37	your only c. is idiots	MANK 565:73
commonalty dog to the c.	SHAK 798:87	well-conducted c.	CHIS 222:24	**complacence** thou My sole c.!	MILT 603:84
commonplace c. young man	GILB 369:45	**commuter** C.—one who spends his life	WHITE 935:47	**complacent** hauf o't smug, c.	SMITH 831:64
great minds in the c.	HUBB 434:98	**compact** c. of fire	SHAK 762:84	shake the c. pillars	BETH 87:13
Nature is c.	STEIN 845:72	**companies** busy c. of men	MARV 577:2	**complain** But do not c.	HAMM 394:58
never yawn or say a c. thing	KERO 483:53	great joint-stock c.	MILL 591:4	farmers…flourish and c.	CRAB 252:37
Nothing is so c.	HOLM 424:75	U.S.A. is a group of holding c.	DOSP 294:86	musn't c. too much	GREE 386:19
nothing so unnatural as the c.	DOYLE 297:53	**companion** dear c. of my soul	MIDD 590:73	Never c. and never explain	BALD 57:35
unassuming c. of Nature	WORD 959:97	found the c.	THOR 889:41	to whom to c.	FIRB 336:47
commons c., like an angry hive	SHAK 759:90	gave him a c.	VALE 907:5	**complainers** loudest c.	BURKE 175:8
Lords and C. of England	MILT 601:18	happiness of finding a c.	BERN 86:73	**complains** No one ever c.	SELF 756:10
common sense A sense of		ideal c. in bed	DAVI 265:37	**complaint** borne…without c.	ACHE 3:40
humour is…c.s.	JAMES 450:31	silent c., exacting and eternal	DELA 271:21	most fatal c. of all	HILT 418:65
won't take c. s. for an answer	DAWK 266:20	**companionable** c. as solitude	THOR 889:41	**complement** inevitable c.	SCHU 750:81
commonwealth c. in which work	SHAW 809:69	**companionless** Wandering c.	SHEL 816:66	mate with its c. of men	WRIG 962:60
C. is fixed and stable	BURKE 175:29	**companions** All her lovely c.	MOORE 618:3	**complete** And in herself c.	MILT 605:40
glorify God and benefit the C.	WENT 931:52	c. for middle age	BACON 51:75	articulate and c.	STEV 850:83
head of the C.	ACHE 2:33	keep pace with his c.	THOR 889:43	C. disillusionment	STEIN 845:64
service and conduct of the c.	BURKE 175:11	**company** Banish not…Harry's c.	SHAK 771:48	c. sentences	GASS 361:87
vision of the C.	MACM 556:63	because we have c.?	JARRY 452:93	Experience…is never c.	JAMES 450:43
commonwealths great c. collapse	HOPE 427:56	c. breaks up	CERV 211:46	made the pile c.	TENN 874:76
raise up c.	DRYD 301:69	c. of paper-blurrers	SIDN 820:58	most c. and free	STEV 851:31
communal experiment…in c. living	BOWL 153:2	c. of the like-minded	DELI 271:41	**completion** of socialism	MORR 620:52
we're such a c. society	SPIE 840:65	crowd is not c.	BACON 52:13	the c. of democracy	EAGL 309:4
communicate c. through sharing		enjoying their c.	RUSS 734:32	time available for its c.	PARK 665:38
information	BERN 86:82	frolicsome c. had begun	SCOTT 753:44	**complex** c. and irregular	SOLOW 833:3
c. with…emotions	ROTH 728:3	from mine own c.	SHAK 767:39	military-industrial c.	EISE 314:2
eliminate his ability to c.	SCHW 750:89	Good c., good wine, good welcome	SHAK 804:38	religious beliefs…simple or c.	DURK 308:30
Genuine poetry can c.	ELIOT 318:21	In c. with several other old ladies	DICK 282:85	**complexion** bad c.	GILB 368:38
power to c. with a third party	WOOLF 955:17	In such a jocund c.	WORD 960:26	c. of them all	SHAK 769:98
communication c. Of the dead	ELIOT 321:83	leave all this constant c.	DONNE 290:12	c. we were not to spoil	SCHR 749:63
evasion…rather than c.	JONES 465:21	live in c. with others	DELA 271:21	different c….than ourselves	CONR 243:27
In terms of c.	UMAS 905:2	man in a jail has…better c.	JOHN 460:88	gold c. dimmed	SHAK 800:37
public opinion and mass c.	MERT 589:56	My idea of good c.	AUST 47:87	thet depends on c.	LOWE 539:6
Thank you for your c.	ELLI 323:27	only c. whose assets all walk	MAYER 583:25	**complexities** All mere c.	YEATS 967:31
communications c. system	HAYEK 402:25	Our c. is too big	WILS 947:47	beyond our own c.	WILL 946:14
C. today puts a special	RUSK 732:79	provoked and have asked the c.	SNOW 832:76	**complexity** didn't grasp his own c.	ELLI 323:38
divine c.	AUBR 42:61	tell a man who boozes by the c.	BURT 181:71	possibility, c., and difficulty	TRIL 897:13
Evil c. corrupt	BIBLE 127:60	three is c. and two none	WILDE 941:99	reduce c. to simplicity	JAMES 451:65
communicator Great C.	ANON 26:83	to shine in c.	SWIFT 862:50	respect for the c. of learning	JOVA 469:13
communion C. of Saints	BOOK 146:3	Vandyke is of the c.	GAIN 357:10	Unthinkable c.	GIBS 367:15
communism beginning…of c.	HERZ 416:23	When c. comes	HUGH 434:8	**compliance** by a timely c.	FIEL 335:22
C….bores them	OROU 652:93	When c. comes	HUGH 434:9	c. with my wishes	CHUR 226:18
C. fits Germany	STAL 842:7	with all the c. of heaven	BOOK 147:70	tame and servile c.	WHIT 934:24
c. is a dead dog	SOLZ 833:7	worst of the c.	SWIFT 861:26	**complicated** any problem, however c.	ANDE 17:73
C. is like prohibition	ROGE 723:77	your bill of c.	SWIFT 861:30	arrived at in a c. manner	SAND 741:10
C. is the opiate	LUCE 541:57	**compare** c. to a stick and a string	JOHN 465:7	pattern more c.	ELIOT 320:68
c. versus capitalism	NGUY 636:68	C. with Caesars	SHAK 772:81	simple words,…in a c. way	DUFF 305:84
consistent opponent of C.	CHUR 225:90	Shall I c. thee	SHAK 800:37	Things become c.	MOYN 623:2
how good c. is!	MAO 568:24	**comparison** c. in point of beauty	MOORE 616:72	When a guy gets too c. he's unhappy	CHAN 213:81
Russian c. is the illegitimate child	ATTL 40:29	experience and c.	JOHN 463:73	**complications** mysteries and c.	GELL 363:32
socialism and c.	MORR 620:52	in c. to the infinite	PASC 667:85	one of the worst c.	AGNEW 9:96
spectre of c.	MARX 579:33	involuntary c. becomes a bore	HORN 430:25	piling up of c. of every sort	JAMES 451:57
USSR to reject C.	KHRU 485:90	read…partly for c.	SCHL 747:34	**complicity** our tribe's c.	HEAN 405:67
When we reach c.	ZHANG 969:6	**comparisons** C. are odorous	SHAK 774:48	**complies** He that c. against his will	BUTL 185:86
communist Catholic and the C.	ORWE 655:66	**compass** c. of his Canterbury Tales	DRYD 304:40	**compliment** empty c.	GILB 369:59
C. must grasp the truth	MAO 568:29	in that narrow c.	HUME 438:94	greater c. than to be loved	MACD 550:50
C. 'war of liberation'	MCNA 557:87	shorts in this c.?	MURR 627:80	take it as a c.	HAIG 391:14
Every c. has a fascist	SPARK 836:73	**compasses** took the golden c.	MILT 605:30	**compliments** c. reaching the proper	KIPL 489:69
fully-fledged c.	CAST 208:80	**compassion** bowels of c.	BIBLE 130:80	c. to the purist	CHAN 213:82
government of Vietnam is C.	GELL 363:36	character and c.	NEWM 635:52	**comply** If you don't c.	KELM 479:68
higher phase of c. society	MARX 579:43	c. and sacrifice	FAUL 331:46	**compose** Before I c. a piece	SATIE 746:4
In c. society	MARX 579:29	c. and sacrifice	FAUL 331:36	feel the urge to c.	BRAH 156:56
member of the C. Party	THOM 885:68	c. may become a justice	JONS 467:57	Never c. anything	HOLST 424:89

composed 1054

Whether you c. or act	DIDE 285:63	would seem to be well c.	GALB 357:23	bettering our c.	SMITH 827:84
write, c. or paint	GREE 386:25	concentrate c. to truth and liberty	SHEL 812:59	c....of the Working Class	CARL 201:22
composed c. as a conference report?	GRIS 389:75	concentrated c. and it nourishes you	DOVE 296:28	c. By which all mortal	MILT 599:79
c. too much	DVOR 308:42	concentrates c. his mind	JOHN 463:55	c. left to women	LEGU 520:11
c. wholly of constituents	RUSS 734:24	concentration c. camp is the final	MILL 593:43	c. of art	CONR 243:25
Cruel, but c. and bland	ARNO 35:2	open-ended stay in a c. camp	JOHN 457:3	c. of being human	ANOU 28:66
composer demands of a c.	HONE 425:15	When I visited c. camps	WHIT 937:79	c. of capital and population	MILL 591:94
limit to the...time a c.	LAMB 506:18	**concept** abstruse and even partial c.	MILL 571:1	c. of the cases, was supernatural	MILL 592:10
modern c. is a madman	HONE 425:12	c. of God	BALD 57:21	c. rather than a profession	GRAV 382:26
writer, the c., the artist	KENN 482:26	c., structure, and style	POUS 692:40	c. that things resound	MARI 571:82
composers advise all sensitive c.	WALT 920:97	**conception** false c. come true	MERT 589:54	c. upon which God hath given liberty	CURR 259:92
Not many c. have ideas	GERS 365:71	questions enlarge our c.	RUSS 734:23	economic c. has...improved	KRIS 499:14
works by contemporary c.	HEIF 407:12	responsibility does not end at c.	OBAMA 644:28	Equality of c. is incompatible	COOP 246:85
composing C. is not a profession	HONE 425:13	sorrow and c.	BIBLE 91:97	excellence of his physical c.	NIVEN 639:29
in c. a work	PASC 666:68	Yet her c. of God	STRA 856:39	fools decoyed into our c.	PEPYS 674:4
composition a style, not c.	MORT 621:72	**conceptions** All c. of God	WEIL 928:75	fugitives are of that c.	BACON 51:73
c. must be more accurate	JONS 468:96	**concepts** metaphysical c.	STEI 846:99	he knows his c.	PASC 667:89
c. of colours	THEO 882:79	mythical c., sun-gods and the like	FRYE 354:54	looking as cheerfully...in that c.	PEPYS 673:87
c....of tried medicines	BACON 50:41	up the stairs of his c.	STEI 845:80	Man's c.. Inconstancy	PASC 667:71
estimating my c.	AUST 46:70	**conceptual** c. art the idea	LEWI 527:76	movement and not a c.	TOYN 895:74
One c. is meagre	DIDE 285:76	**concern** c. not for your bodies	PLATO 681:43	perfect c. of slavery	ASTE 39:5
pure-painting c.	MALE 562:92	c. was speech	ELIOT 321:86	rises above the human c.	PAZ 671:48
compositions Read over your c.	JOHN 462:28	life and its largest c.	ARNO 36:35	towards the c. of music	PATER 668:10
composts Tomorrow c. today	STER 847:17	no c. for the common man	WILS 947:42	War is a c. of progress	RENAN 711:47
compound urban c.	MCLU 556:55	no c. with business	KIPL 489:78	whole human c.	HOPP 429:2
comprehensible world...is c.	EINS 314:87	no kind of c. with it	WHIS 934:22	**conditioned** I'm exhausted, or c.	PUIG 699:69
comprehension c. of the layman	GOWE 380:81	two things that c. them	JUVE 471:57	**conditions** Bad as our urban c.	HALD 392:22
devices of mere c.	HOLM 423:59	**concerned** being ultimately c.	TILL 891:15	c. that are unspiritual	MARX 578:24
comprehensions Wider c.	FERG 333:83	**concerns** first step that c. me	KENN 482:43	establish c.	UNIT 905:9
compression c. is the first grace	MOORE 617:78	futile his c.	SIMO 822:80	mirror of social c.	LIPP 531:40
compromise A good c.	OBAMA 643:18	**concert** Christmas c. by Pavarotti	BURKE 177:64	play under bad c.	KAUF 474:37
C. is a stalling	FRY 354:52	c. is dead	GOULD 379:72	social c. take recognizable	LIPP 531:41
C. makes a good	LOWE 539:15	shot fired in...a c.	STEN 847:3	they are only its c.	HEINE 407:16
C. used to mean	CHES 220:78	**concerts** don't write little c.	MERW 589:57	under c....unpropitious	ELIOT 320:67
English love of c.	CARD 198:41	**concessions** c. of the weak	BURKE 175:14	**condo** forcing them to go c.	OROU 652:95
every prudent act...founded on c.	BURKE 175:23	**conciet** glutted with c.	MARL 573:23	**conduct** C. is...our life	ARNO 36:35
idea of a c.	HUGH 436:47	newness, the democratic, c.	LAWR 513:49	c. of every private family	SMITH 827:85
would not tolerate c. on goals	DULL 306:88	**conclaves** Kingly c. stern and cold	SHEL 814:9	its National c.	PULI 699:71
compulsion c. doth in music lie	MILT 598:16	**conclusion** assume...powerful c.	SOLOW 833:4	judgements on political c.	NEW 634:41
freely grows in deep c.	SMITH 828:2	cannot come to any c.	SACK 737:12	My c. shrieks aloud for apology	BEER 73:78
Give you a reason on c.?	SHAK 771:46	c.: life is something	LEBO 517:59	nice C. of a clouded Cane	POPE 685:41
ne'er can be...happy by c.	COLE 235:32	c. must be very scientific	JAMES 452:77	observe a certain line of c.	MILL 591:2
stern hand of C.	THUR 891:95	c. no one has yet dared	NIET 638:93	one code of international c.	EISE 314:99
compulsions air all our c. meet	LARK 509:78	c. that sex is a sublimation	LODGE 534:98	secure the good c. of women	WOLL 953:87
c., the fantasies	LEGU 520:10	c. that they are élitist	LODGE 534:1	strange c.	ASTE 39:6
computer banks of every c.	GIBS 367:15	denoted a foregone c.	SHAK 790:28	**cone** country...is an inverted c.	JOHN 463:59
circuits of a digital c.	PIRS 679:89	economists...would not reach a c.	SHAW 811:32	sweet volcanic c.	LOWE 540:32
c. is a fast idiot	AMER 15:23	glorious c.	HUSS 440:39	treat nature by...the c.	CEZA 212:52
c. must be questioned	MUMF 625:39	impelled to the c.	JERO 454:38	**Coney Island** C. I. of the Mind	FERL 333:88
do not write on a c.	OROU 652:96	laugh together over so odd a c.	EDDI 311:26	**confection** c. of tried medicines	BACON 50:41
most extraordinary c. of all	KENN 481:17	Ninety-nine times, the c. is false	EINS 313:77	**confer** c. with thee somewhat	NASHE 632:91
Never trust a c.	WOZNI 962:58	other is a c.	JOHN 460:64	**conference** c. With the dead!	WEBS 927:59
no c. will ever ask	HOPP 429:4	Reasoning draws a c.	BACON 54:57	naked into the c. chamber	BEVAN 89:58
computer-age c.-a. journalists	MCFA 551:69	three days to reach its c.	STOP 856:22	No grand idea...born in a c.	FITZ 338:98
computers c. are...stupid	STER 847:14	what better c.	TATE 867:41	rather than hold three words' c.	SHAK 774:28
world market for...five c.	WATS 922:42	**conclusions** draw the correct c.	KISS 493:84	sales c. resembles a Passion play	SCRI 755:90
comrade c. with the wolf and owl	SHAK 792:2	Prime Minister reading out the c.	HESE 416:27	to hear our c.	SHAK 774:41
Never leave a fallen c.	ANON 27:20	reach their c. about life	KIER 485:99	**confess** cannot c. them	SHAW 807:18
stepping where his c. stood	SCOTT 752:26	wrong c. at which mankind arrive	PALM 661:67	C. yourself to heaven	SHAK 784:43
comrades blythe wi' C. dear	BURNS 178:89	wrong in its c.	REGAN 710:42	If we c. our sins	BIBLE 130:77
c. apparently find it hard	GORB 378:46	**concoct** c. oneself	DOYLE 297:75	truer than tongue c.	HOPK 428:69
help our French c.	KITC 494:98	**concord** c. of sweet sounds	SHAK 770:21	wiser world doth greater thee c.	CAREW 198:47
con great pains to c. it	SHAK 785:89	lover of c.	BOOK 146:39	**confessed** before the world c.	HOW 433:84
Thanks I must you c.	SHAK 791:81	oft in pleasing c. end	MILT 608:97	**confession** c....of its author	NIET 638:7
concave hell's c., and beyond	MILT 602:49	Sinews of c.	FORD 343:1	greatest c. of its failure	STEV 854:93
conceal duty...to c. his artifice	OGIL 648:5	**concrete** city is not a c. jungle	MORR 620:45	making my Easter c.	JOSE 469:7
Fate tried to c. him	HOLM 424:76	flower is the c. cloverleaf	MUMF 625:38	rage for c., autobiography	MANS 567:3
concealed utterly c. all	THOM 885:61	prams on c. balconies	BETJ 88:33	silence is your c.	EURI 328:60
concealment c., like a worm	SHAK 786:1	**concubine** c. or whore	HELO 408:53	sweetness of c.	FIRB 336:50
conceit all his c. taken out of him	HOLM 424:64	too good to be your c.	SHAK 760:12	**confide** c. freely in death	ANOU 28:62
As for c.	TROL 897:28	**concupiscence** wanderings of c.	BIBLE 112:76	seldom c. in those who are better	CAMUS 196:96
c. o' bein' richt	MACD 549:23	**concurrence** fortuitous c. of atoms	PALM 662:73	**confidence** a c. trick	WILS 947:40
C. spoils the finest genius	ALCO 12:41	**condamné** c. à être libre	SART 745:74	C. in an unfaithful man	BIBLE 105:94
in his own c.	GREE 386:33	**condemn** cannot c. it	DURK 308:29	fight with growing c.	CHUR 225:85
never forgive any c.	DRYD 304:43	c. it as an improbable fiction	SHAK 786:17	in quietness and in c.	BIBLE 108:73
only a c.	KAVA 474:48	thoughtless to c. them	BRON 161:61	Show your c.	GIUL 373:32
self and vain c.	SHAK 764:52	**condemnation** c. is the favourite	NIET 638:11	something like c.	GOOCH 378:44
so to his whole c.	SHAK 782:99	no c. to them which are in Christ	BIBLE 125:16	suaveness isn't born of c.	HYDE 444:22
conceited say he's c.	SALI 740:79	**condemned** behaviour which is c.	SPEN 837:10	unconditional c. of his people	WEI 927:66
very c. scurvy one	JONS 467:64	c. for what we are	FENT 332:61	**confident** c. I can do very well	JOHN 460:64
who is not c.?	TROL 897:28	c. to be free	SART 745:74	in this will I be c.	BIBLE 100:50
conceits Be not wise in your own c.	BIBLE 125:27	c. to repeat it	SANT 743:41	**confiding** c., the intimate	MACD 550:40
c. as clownage keeps	MARL 572:94	Grudge not...lest ye be c.	BIBLE 130:60	**confinement** c.'s lingering hour	BYRON 186:23
Some people...run to c.	BART 66:15	Prayers for the c. man	WEST 933:93	sentenced to solitary c.	WILL 945:98
conceive whatever we c. very clearly	DESC 274:97	**condensation** clever c.	PULI 699:72	**confirmation** c. of truth	MILT 600:11
conceived nothing...c. without God	SPIN 840:70	**condescend** c. to men of low estate	BIBLE 125:27	**conflagrations** c.....at Rome	AUGU 44:33
There is a man child c.	BIBLE 98:74	**condition** average c. of the people	MILL 591:97	**conflict** brought into c.	BRIG 159:16

console

c. of its elements	BYRON 189:84
lexicon of c. and drama	SAFI 737:17
Never in the field of human c.	CHUR 225:87
too weak the c. to support	SHAK 793:36
We are in armed c.	EDEN 311:32
conflicts internal c.	ROSS 725:35
conformity c. of the image	DIDE 285:61
reward for c.	BROWN 164:37
confounds not the deed C. us	SHAK 797:31
confrontation born of this c.	CAMUS 195:84
confront When you c. a problem	GIUL 373:34
confronts c. man with…choice	SART 744:70
confused the free	STEV 851:14
confusing c., disorienting	RICH 713:1
confusion all a c.	SCHL 747:36
C. now hath made his masterpiece	SHAK 797:41
c. of goals	EINS 313:82
C. on thy banners wait	GRAY 385:79
except my own c.	KERO 483:54
great blooming, buzzing c.	JAMES 451:67
let me never be put to c.	BIBLE 101:83
levee from a couch in some c.	CONG 241:73
confute how to c. him	SELD 756:8
congestion TB…that is the c.	ALLEN 14:85
Congo C., creeping through	LIND 530:18
congratulate sometimes c. ourselves	HAWT 401:99
congratulations C.…keep pouring	FREUD 350:56
congregation C. of Christ's flock	BOOK 147:77
Devil…hast the largest c.	DEFOE 269:69
landlord to the whole c.	ADDI 6:28
congress C. makes no progress	LIGNE 529:97
c. of stinks!	ROET 722:58
the job C. is doing	LENO 522:59
congressman easier…than…'C.'	GING 371:99
how to act like a C.	KENN 482:38
conjectural your audience is c.	ORWE 654:52
conjoined always c. together	HUME 438:95
conjunction epithalamic c.	ANDR 18:77
conjure c. up the blood	SHAK 775:74
conjuring c. trick with bones	JENK 454:31
conjuror level of the stage c.	MOORE 616:70
connect drive to c.	RICH 713:5
mystery of how they c. nouns	SAND 742:29
Only c.!	FORS 344:30
The web does not just c. machines	BERN 86:83
connecting digital technology	
makes c. possible	DOWD 296:33
connection cannot find any artistic c.	KLEE 494:1
no c. worth speaking of	GALS 358:47
connections expresses the sum of c.	MARX 579:38
connoisseur c. of tame excitement	MOORE 617:86
connoisseurs c. of bread and butter	MACD 550:39
conquer able to fight and c.	TROT 899:63
Antony should c. Antony	SHAK 795:81
cannot c. America	PITT 679:8
die here, and we will c.	BEE 73:60
easier to c. it	WALP 919:71
England that was wont to c.	SHAK 764:41
In this sign thou shalt c.	CONS 245:63
It's not the mountain we c.	HILL 418:62
resolve to c. or die	WASH 921:27
conquered c. and peopled	SEEL 756:2
C. people tend to be witty	BELL 77:83
God c.	JOHN 456:76
nation…perpetually to be c.	BURKE 175:15
Nothing can save the c.	VIRG 913:15
Romans c. the world	SWEE 861:9
same thing as the c.	ALEX 12:58
Thou hast c.	SWIN 864:99
will be c.	JOHN 464:98
conquering not c. but fighting well	COUB 248:20
worked too hard in c.	NAPO 630:48
conqueror commercial traveller…	
missionary…barbarian c.	STAP 843:20
Love is a cruel c.	LAFO 504:57
overcame her savage c.	HORA 430:16
proud foot of a c.	SHAK 768:66
conquerors born of the c.	WRIG 963:71
laurel, meed of mighty c.	SPEN 838:20
conquers Love c. all things	VIRG 914:25
ruling passion c. reason	POPE 686:67
conquest c. of an unknown country	HEDIN 406:4
c. of the earth	CONR 243:27
end and object of c.	ALEX 12:58
fanned by C.'s crimson wing	GRAY 385:79
nature of a c.	SHAK 773:93
never again seek…territory by c.	WILS 949:76
shameful c. of itself	SHAK 764:41
without threat of c.	RODO 721:51
conquests all the c.	SPEN 838:37
all thy c., glories, triumphs, spoils	SHAK 777:32
conquistador by temperament…c.	FREUD 350:55
conquistadores c. stole a page	MARTI 576:70
conscience binding on the c.	JOHN 456:73
catch the c. of the King	SHAK 782:5
c., above all liberties	MILT 600:6
c.…accomplishment of man's rest	BACON 51:88
c. ain't got no sense	TWAIN 903:66
c. ain't got no sense	TWAIN 903:67
c. always has	ROBI 718:91
c. clear my chief defence	DYER 309:50
c. does make cowards	SHAK 782:7
c. fools my wit!	JONS 467:53
C. has no more to do with gallantry	SHER 817:83
C. is a coward	GOLD 376:91
C. is but a word	SHAK 761:53
c. of the state	KING 487:33
C.: the inner voice	MENC 586:82
c. wakes despair	MILT 603:90
c. with injustice is corrupted	SHAK 759:91
dilemmas of c.	SNOW 832:75
exact a survey of his c.	DONNE 293:78
free c. from the paw	MILT 601:25
go against c.	LUTH 542:69
good digestion depends upon a good c.	DISR 287:17
good music and a clean c.	HIND 419:67
however strict their social c.	SMITH 829:20
In my c.…the baggage loves me	CONG 240:24
just as much c.	STOWE 856:29
keeper of his c.	DAVI 265:85
live with a good c.	SMITH 829:18
mortal sin on my c.	WILS 947:38
Neither c. nor sanity	MCNA 557:88
Nobody has any c.	HAWT 402:16
not burdening one's c.	WEIZ 928:78
O coward c.	SHAK 761:48
People talk about the c.	JAMES 450:50
policy sits above c.	SHAK 791:78
rule is a person's c.	LEE 518:88
Science without c.	RABE 703:6
siding champion c.	MILT 598:69
still and quiet c.	SHAK 805:51
sword with a clean c.	WILH 943:57
testimony of a good c.	KEMP 480:79
their c. as their King	TENN 877:56
the republic of c.	HEAN 405:77
to irritate your c.	OHEN 648:20
torn c. brings about	HUGO 437:79
umpire c., whom if	MILT 603:81
will not cut my c.	HELL 408:42
wound My c.	VAUG 909:35
You have a c.	ROTH 728:1
consciences c. about doing evil	MORE 618:17
c. of the citizens	JOHN 456:73
conscious always c. of an inferiority	JOHN 463:51
c. of an uncomfortable sensation	DICK 281:60
c. of their actions	SPIN 840:72
Doth seem half c.	WORD 957:72
first I was scarcely c.	RUSS 734:37
To become c.	SAINT 738:44
tyranny of c. thought	BEEC 73:70
consciously as we c. uncouple	PALT 662:79
consciousness African national c.	MACM 556:67
Allow but a little c.	ELIOT 319:40
a time of awakening c.	RICH 713:1
building…part of the American c.	BUSH 182:94
chamber of c.	JAMES 450:43
change of c.	GINS 372:14
C., her awful Mate	DICK 284:44
c. is a staging area	BELL 78:96
c. is the only form you need	SARO 744:58
c. of myself	KANT 473:19
c. of science	DEWEY 276:19
c. of the limits	NIEB 637:88
c. that I have exercised the powers	PEEL 672:67
C., then, does not appear	JAMES 451:66
Cosmic c.	BUCKE 172:38
created…national c.	WILS 949:79
divinity…place in the human c.	DURK 308:31
from the beginning of c. to the end	WOOLF 955:10
habit of one's c.	MALE 562:92
in our ordinary c.	MOND 612:98
lopped off…your c.	ORWE 653:19
moral c. of people	MAIL 559:41
morning comes to c.	ELIOT 317:71
multiplicity of agreeable c.	JOHN 461:12
one-eighth part c.	GERH 365:70
states of c.	MOORE 616:67
stream of thought, of c.	JAMES 451:66
sublime c. of striving	HUMB 438:93
consecration c., and…dream	WORD 961:28
consensus C. Terrorism	COUP 248:28
I am not a c. politician	THAT 882:77
consent approbation and c.	POWE 693:59
colonized people with their c.	SART 745:78
c. of all great men	RUSK 733:94
c. to the separation	GEOR 364:48
c.…under that Government	RAIN 705:37
engineering of c.	BERN 86:79
like enough to c.	SHAK 779:9
man without that other's c.	LINC 529:3
will ne'er c.	BYRON 189:95
consented Your father hath c.	SHAK 762:66
consenting between c. adults	NOZI 642:72
consequence as far as national c.	SCOTT 754:76
cause is the c.	FANON 329:13
c. of leaving one's home	LEBO 518:67
mistake subsequence for c.	JOHN 459:37
really a direct c.	PAST 668:4
trammel up the c.	SHAK 796:19
ultimate c.	MILL 593:43
consequences c. of changes	FRIE 351:68
damn the c.	MILN 596:27
In nature…only c.	VACH 907:1
In nature…there are c.	INGE 445:33
knowledge of c.	HOBB 420:98
of history and its c.	OBRI 645:62
social c. of their activities	HOBS 420:7
teach the c.	KISS 493:84
consequent c. to a time of war	HOBB 420:7
conservation C. of one resource	HERF 414:91
in favor of c.	TAFT 866:10
state…without the means of its c.	BURKE 176:35
conservatism barren thing this C.	DISR 287:27
c. and progress	TROL 897:29
C. discards Prescription	DISR 287:25
c. is based upon the idea	CHES 220:70
What is c.?	LINC 529:7
conservative banks were c.	THOM 885:69
called the C. party	CROK 255:13
C. Backbench MPs	BAKER 56:4
C.…enamoured of existing evils	BIER 134:70
C. government is…hypocrisy	DISR 288:38
C. ideal of freedom	MADAN 558:15
c. is a man	ROOS 724:10
C. Party at prayer	ROYD 730:31
leader of the C. Party	BEAV 71:25
leadership of the C. Party	HESE 416:28
make me c. when old	FROST 352:12
Metternich…was so c.	EVANS 328:66
most c. man in the world	BEVIN 90:65
Or else a little C.!	GILB 369:52
small c. majority	TYNAN 904:99
The Republic will be c.	THIE 883:97
the true C.	TENN 879:2
what's the point of being a C.	JOHN 457:98
conservatives c. and reactionaries	VIDAL 912:95
C., as being by the law	MILL 591:5
C. base their…approach	
to politics	HEATH 405:89
C. do not believe	HAIL 392:17
Life's better with the C.	ANON 25:37
terrible night for the C.	PORT 690:80
consequences the c. of their actions	MOORE 617:95
The law of unintended c.	FERG 333:81
conserve to c. it, we must love it	MONT 614:60
consider C. anything, only don't cry!	CARR 205:5
c. the end in everything	LAFO 504:56
considerable wish to appear c.	JOHN 462:23
considerate if he were wisely c.	STEV 852:53
consideration c. of characters	JOHN 462:44
others worthy of c.	BLOOM 142:63
turns on moral c.	NAPO 629:40
con-si-de-ra-tion For a c.	SCOTT 754:66
considerations dictated by military c.	MCCA 548:1
considering c. how well they sell	JOYCE 470:38
consistency foolish c.	EMER 324:54
Too much c. is as bad	HUXL 441:68
consolatory mind C. food can find	SMART 826:68
console be consoled as to c.	FRAN 347:99
generally c. them	STEV 852:44

consolidation

Knowledge...will not c. me — PASC 667:87
consolidation indissoluble c. — ROTH 728:91
consommé cyanide in the c. — WODE 952:43
consonants Only c. and vowels — RANS 707:73
shifting of vowels and c. — UNTE 905:11
thud of c. — BROY 169:88
consort But I c. with — KIPL 492:59
c. as they keep — MILT 598:58
conspiracies All professions are c. — SHAW 809:81
conspiracy Civilisation is a c. — BUCH 171:23
c. against the public — SMITH 827:81
c. is everything that ordinary life — DELI 271:42
c. of human beings — WELLS 930:21
c. to make you happy — UPDI 906:24
c. to oppress — DOUG 296:26
in a c. to under value them — JAMES 450:36
Indecency's c. of silence — SHAW 808:51
universal c. of silence — JAUR 452:98
vast right-wing c. — CLIN 231:26
conspirators All the c. — SHAK 778:57
C. have a logic — DELI 271:42
conspire stick'st not to c. — SHAK 800:35
constable Bible...c.'s handbook — KING 488:54
constabulary c. duty's to be done — GILB 368:42
constancy but c. in a good [cause] — BROW 165:59
C. alone is strange — ROCH 720:24
c. lives in realms above — COLE 235:34
c. of its vows — SHAW 808:33
no object worth its c.? — SHEL 816:66
constant c. as the Northern Star — SHAK 777:26
c. in a wondrous excellence — SHAK 802:75
C. you are — SHAK 771:43
more c. than a wife — RICK 715:28
No species remains c. — OVID 657:21
nothing in this world c. — SWIFT 861:24
one thing c. — JOUV 469:12
so c. to me — KEATS 476:89
To one thing c. never — SHAK 774:38
were man But c. — SHAK 759:73
Constantine walled by C. the Great — BAIL 55:87
Constantinople what is chaste in C. — FORD 342:90
constellation Los Angeles is a c. — MAIL 560:55
sets him in his c. — RILKE 715:40
constellations c. of data — GIBS 367:15
c. of feeling — DOUG 295:5
consternation returned in c. — SOME 833:10
constituencies elements in their c. — LIPP 531:42
go back to your c. — STEEL 844:36
constituency c. is the desperate — JACK 448:2
Every line in...budget has its own c. — WRIS 963:82
would not be in my c. — MENZ 587:20
constituents composed wholly of c. — RUSS 734:24
constitution abusing the best C. — FRAN 348:15
chief after of their c. — MORE 618:20
corresponding social c. — MARX 579:30
country has its own C. — MUNS 626:57
free c. — GIBB 366:91
In the name of the C. — STAL 842:4
Like the British c. — CARD 198:39
pale of the C. — GLAD 373:36
parchment of a c. — TROT 899:62
parliamentary C. is not favourable — DISR 288:63
part of an Englishman's c. — AUST 46:69
The C. has never greatly bothered — BIDD 133:52
to our ancient c. — SWIFT 862:43
words of the C. — KING 487:27
constitutionally C. I don't exist — EDIN 312:52
constitutions men look at C. — JEFF 454:28
most unlikely c. — DICK 282:92
political C., are not our Life — CARL 201:17
constraint c., and sad occasion dear — MILT 599:82
constraints c. aping marriage — UPDI 905:17
construct c. a decoration — TROL 897:21
constructed peace must be c. — UNES 905:8
rightly c. boy's life — TWAIN 902:46
construction c. of...bombs — EINS 313:78
lifelong c. — GOULD 379:73
who comprehended its c. — PALEY 661:57
consul born when I was c. — CICE 227:37
consult C. the genius — POPE 686:58
C....To seek another's approval — BIER 134:71
consultant you're a c. — ADAMS 6:10
consume Rot, and c. themselves — SHAK 762:82
consumed bush was not c. — BIBLE 93:51
c. by use — GILL 371:88
consumer A person who is capable — STEIN 845:77
c. isn't a moron — OGIL 648:6

c....is the king — SAMU 741:1
state for a potential c. — LURIE 542:67
consuming doubled their means of c. — MILL 591:96
consummation c....wished — TWAIN 902:63
consumption balance of...c. — MALT 563:23
birds...in a c. — WEBS 926:22
c. is polarized — ILLI 445:22
C. is the sole end — SMITH 828:88
c. of valuable goods — VEBL 910:46
form of commerce and c. — MARX 579:30
galloping c. — GAND 359:58
no remedy against this c. — SHAK 772:75
not increase its c. — KEYN 485:83
universal c. — ILLI 445:21
contact Fly hence, our c. fear! — ARNO 34:94
removed from c. with...life — PRIT 696:16
voters have no c. — PRICE 695:81
contagion breathes forth c. — TWAIN 902:63
c. from her sable wings — MARL 573:10
c. in the tears — DRYD 301:49
c. of the world's slow stain — SHEL 815:40
C. to this world — SHAK 783:30
c., when it has once made head — DICK 282:92
great danger of c. — WILD 943:48
Rot inwardly, and foul c. — MILT 599:89
contain stating what it is to c. — JOHN 460:64
contaminated c. by...an identity — HAZL 403:31
contaminates lack of love c. — GUNN 390:95
contemplating c....poetry — RICH 713:5
contemplation action, not by c. — BRON 160:51
Beneath thy c. — NEALE 632:7
best nurse c. — MILT 598:72
c. he and valour formed — MILT 604:99
c....more than his reading — AUBR 41:57
c. of created things — MILT 604:17
mind...in a rapt c. — ELIOT 320:53
sitting apart in silent c. — GRAND 381:97
sundry c. of my travels — SHAK 779:5
youngling in the c. of evil — MILT 600:10
contemporary c. and future society — MURP 627:77
works by c. composers — HEIF 407:12
contempt breeds c.—and children — TWAIN 903:75
c. and anger of his lip! — SHAK 786:11
C. and beggary hangs — SHAK 766:12
c. for an arrant shit — JOSE 469:7
c. for anything he didn't understand — WOOL 956:43
c. for my character and opinions — SHAW 807:14
C. for the poor — OCON 647:91
c. for the poor performances — RYLE 736:61
c. of a great man — FITZ 338:1
c. of shame — JOHN 460:83
excites their c. — REED 710:37
for c. too high — COWL 250:77
greatest c. for novels — FORD 343:94
held in c. by those — GOLD 376:83
hold writers in c. — BELL 77:81
in c. of chance happenings — RABE 704:20
inward and secret c. — BACON 51:80
not for such c. — SHAK 761:35
Object of c. — AUST 45:49
pour c. on all my pride — WATTS 922:46
so great and general a c. — PEPYS 673:84
treat you with c. — WHIT 938:15
weakness, no c. — MILT 608:3
contend what it is we have to c. for — PITT 680:11
contender could have been a c. — SCHU 749:70
content beautiful...have the least c. — FLAU 339:17
contain any c. — WEIL 928:76
c. myself with wishing — PITT 679:1
c., retirement — THOM 887:99
C.'s a kingdom — HEYW 417:42
c. thyself to be...good — ADDI 7:51
c. to be such a one — SIDN 820:57
c. with his common humanity — SHAW 809:89
draw upon c. — GOLD 376:90
emptying...of all form and c. — FANON 329:14
full flavour of their c. — MILL 593:56
land of lost c. — HOUS 431:52
learned...to be c. — BIBLE 128:6
Looking back, I am c. — STEV 850:4
Must make c. with his fortunes — SHAK 792:9
Nor that c. surpassing wealth — SHEL 812:68
Nothing less will c. me — BURKE 175:16
Poor and c. is rich — SHAK 789:20
religious, not so much by its c. — CUPI 258:85
soul hath her c. — SHAK 789:8
Strong and c. I travel — WHIT 937:1

contented c. sort of discontent — KEATS 476:8
scarce be a c. woman — ROCH 720:21
we are c. — SCHR 749:63
contentedness procurer of c. — WALT 920:92
contention brawling, c. — STUB 858:62
Let the long c. cease! — ARNO 35:24
contentment C. and fulfilment — TROL 898:58
enjoying, what c. find? — MILT 605:38
Preaches c. to that toad — KIPL 489:68
contents c. worn out — FRAN 348:7
contest c. between agreeable fancy — STEV 851:12
counted the cost of this c. — DICK 284:58
end a c. quicker — SHER 817:82
pissing c. with that skunk — EISE 314:97
contests What mighty c. rise — POPE 685:29
continence perversion known as c. — HUXL 441:55
what c. to forbear — MILT 600:5
continent blowing through this c. — MACM 556:67
c. a new nation — LINC 529:9
C., I do not believe...exists — COOK 245:65
c. of energetic mongrels — FISH 337:63
C. people have good food — MIKES 590:86
c.'s violent requiem — DUNC 307:9
C. will not suffer England — DISR 287:23
descended across the C. — CHUR 226:2
deserted c. which gave me birth — MELBA 584:44
every man is a piece of the c. — DONNE 293:68
in the presence of this c. — FITZ 338:86
like having a c. disappear — JARR 452:82
part of our European c. — TOLS 894:54
That means on our c. — LEAC 516:24
U.S.A. is the slice of a c. — DOSP 294:86
continentals c. think life is a game — MIKES 590:87
continents dotted with c. and islands — MUIR 624:26
less difficult to join both c. — BOLI 145:9
contingent c. and the unforeseen — FISH 337:62
nothing c. is granted — SPIN 840:71
continually c. with thee — BIBLE 101:86
continuance felicity and long c. — BACON 53:51
continue in this a quarter — SHAK 798:64
I intend to c. — THAT 881:71
we c....a barbarous traffic — PITT 679:10
continuity c. of civilization — ORWE 654:54
contraception If you won't have c. — OBRI 645:63
contraceptive The C. Problem — DALY 261:21
contraceptives little use for c. — SHAR 806:72
contract c....between those two — SMITH 827:80
c. theory in ritual form — NOVAK 641:64
Every law is a c. — SELD 756:7
Social C. is nothing more — WELLS 930:21
Society is indeed a c. — BURKE 176:45
verbal c. — GOLD 377:32
contracted happen to have c. it — JONES 465:20
more c. that power is — JOHN 463:59
contracts c. with the people — TRUM 899:83
Like all other c. — RICA 712:81
write enough to sign c. — GING 371:98
contradict c. myself? — WHIT 937:95
nobody to c. us — RADI 704:33
contradiction brook no c. — WEBS 927:25
c. in terms — SHAW 810:16
c., that New Orleans — MORT 621:72
fundamental c....between socialism — DENG 272:57
locked...in this impossible c. — EAGL 309:1
risings...on c. that they grow — EMPS 326:10
spirit of c. — MACL 554:25
Whoever fears c. — SAINT 738:45
Woman's at best a c. — POPE 688:16
contradictions c., of the grotesque — TZARA 904:17
reconcile these c. — CARL 199:73
contradictory holding two c. beliefs — ORWE 655:76
contrapuntist c. is only a post-horse — MOZA 623:6
contraries Without c. — BLAKE 139:94
contrary c. to nature, c. to life — HUXL 441:68
c. to that order — JOHN 456:73
Hail Mary, quite c.! — GREE 386:14
not c. to reason — HUME 438:99
On the c.! — IBSEN 444:10
contribution c. to reality — THOM 884:45
editor...accepts with joy the c. — CANN 196:6
Man's c. to human history — JIANG 455:57
contrition a devout act of c. — OBRI 646:74
contrivance c. enough — JOHN 460:88
c. to raise prices — SMITH 827:81
Sexually, Woman is Nature's c. — SHAW 808:29
control campaign for birth c. — MUNRO 625:48
C. is very important — FERG 332:75

C. over behavior	LEGU 520:13	convulsion wilful c.	STEV 854:91	Corinth Not everyone can sail to C.	ANON 20:19
c. that which he produces	NGUGI 636:67	convulsions groans and c.	STER 848:39	cork pop the c.	STEV 852:52
c. the meaning of words	DICK 277:37	in c. hurled	POPE 687:98	tossed like a c.	HUGH 436:50
history of arms c.	ADEL 8:61	Cook Illustrious C.	WENT 931:53	corked c. up for iver	ELIOT 315:23
in c. here	HAIG 391:13	cook C. is a little unnerved	BETJ 89:41	corkscrew Bring in…a c.	DICK 278:86
knows how to c. or direct	MUGG 623:11	c. was a good c.	SAKI 739:55	corkscrews crooked as c.	AUDEN 42:77
methods of c.	KEYN 484:77	good c. is like a sorceress	SCHI 747:23	Corky And C.'d protested	OATES 643:12
sceptre to c. the world	SHAK 760:22	'Tis an ill c.	SHAK 766:7	cormorant c. devouring time	SHAK 763:99
think you c. it	STEI 846:87	very uncommon c.	SAKI 739:65	Sat like a c.	MILT 604:95
we've lost a lot of c.	WOZNI 962:57	wanted to be a c.	DALI 261:12	corn amid the c.	HOOD 426:24
white people who were in c.	DAVIS 265:2	When you c.	BLANC 141:45	c. rigs are bonie	BURNS 177:88
wrong members in c.	ORWE 654:34	Cooke-ham Farewell (sweet C.-h.)	LANY 508:57	c. rigs are bonie	BURNS 178:90
controversy c. over capital	FISH 336:61	cookery c. do!	MERE 588:27	Golden c. for the stranger	WILDE 940:45
c. over freedom of speech	ORWE 655:67	cookie grandmother…like a c.	BAIL 55:86	golden ears of c.	HERR 415:14
great c. in antiquity	GERA 364:61	cooking C. is like love	VAN 908:23	graves…ploughed for c.	RED 709:19
convalescence c.…makes illness	SHAW 810:12	Good painting is like good c.	VLAM 914:36	In our sustaining c.	SHAK 793:19
convenience C. next suggested		offers succulent c.	POUND 691:8	meadows rich with c.	WHIT 938:22
elbow-chairs	COWP 251:10	Spare me from c.	PLATH 680:27	produce a bushel of C.	PETTY 676:45
convent c. for unloved women	BROY 169:91	cooks bad female c.	NIET 638:12	raise less c. and more hell	LEASE 517:49
convention books, c. and cliché	POUND 691:88	c., physicians, carpenters	SUN 860:96	there was c.	HERB 414:76
Social c. is irrelevant	PAGL 659:18	devil sends c.	FULL 355:84	two ears of c.	SWIFT 862:45
To the Lords of c.	SCOTT 754:82	not the c.	HARI 398:32	yellow like ripe c.	ROSS 726:50
conventional c. and orthodox way	KEYN 484:75	Skinny c. can't be trusted	ANON 26:95	Corneille C. is…a clipped hedge	JOHN 465:4
c. army loses	KISS 493:85	the Devil sends c.	GARR 360:80	Cornelius To you, C.	CATU 209:5
C. life and c. people	OBRI 645:66	Too many c.	ANON 22:71	corner a warm c. of hell	MCCA 547:71
c. way to rise above the c.	NABO 629:21	Whoso has sixpence…commands c.	CARL 200:91	buy one on a c.	DAY 267:32
proposal departing from c. lines	STAMP 842:10	cool chilli was something c.	THAC 880:21	drives into a c.	JOHN 464:84
conventionality C. is not morality	BRON 161:65	C. is hot	WASH 922:33	future…just around the c.	LESS 524:95
conventions c. of the present	LEWI 527:77	c. of the day	BIBLE 91:93	head stone of the c.	BIBLE 102:22
convergence c. of human lots	ELIOT 316:49	c. white dress	FIRB 336:50	House at Pooh C.	PARK 663:1
conversant c. with a Man's heart	POE 683:91	intellects vast and c.	WELLS 930:19	into every penetrable c.	MACA 544:16
conversation a great deal of c.	AUST 47:87	Keep c.	EMER 325:76	Joy shivers in the c.	ROBI 718:91
Among the Ibo the art of c.	ACHE 2:20	Keep c. but care	PYNCH 701:12	only one c. of the universe	HUXL 442:85
change people through c.	JAY 453:8	make government…c. again	OBAMA 643:22	pointed out one c. of a square	CONF 240:19
cheery c. and what-not	WODE 951:33	More than c. reason	SHAK 767:44	some c. of a foreign field	BROO 162:88
c. ends in a conspiracy	SMITH 827:81	cooled coal that must be c.	SHAK 762:85	spanked and stood in the c.	LEGU 520:17
c. I do acknowledge austere	BROW 164:43	C. a long age	KEATS 478:42	turn a c. jinkan	BURNS 177:84
C. is like playing tennis	LODGE 534:96	Coolibah shade of a C. tree	PATE 668:12	wake in a c.	KELM 479:70
C. is more often	JONES 465:21	Coolidge Nero fiddled, but C.	MENC 586:94	what lay round the c.	KAVA 474:50
C. is never easy for the British	BRAD 154:33	coomb stag in the Priory c.	DAVI 264:68	corners looking round more c.	MAND 565:64
c. of the blind	MOORE 616:73	Coonardoo C. they called it	PRIC 695:83	lounge at c. of the street	SPEN 837:96
c. wanders away from themselves	WILD 943:54	Cooper make Jilly C.…rich	BRAD 155:36	obscure c. in one's own mind	HUXL 443:11
c. with my best friend	LEWIS 526:48	rooting for Gary C.	BALD 57:23	planes and the c. of rooms	MALL 562:3
c. with the best men	DESC 274:92	cooperate C. on move one	RAPO 707:75	round earth's imagined c.	DONNE 292:50
different name for c.	STER 848:30	co-operating C. and so self-moving.	RYLE 736:61	Unregarded age in c. thrown	SHAK 778:69
difficult to go on with the c.	WODE 951:34	c.-o. in all that concerns	GEOR 364:54	corner-stones c.-s. of literary art	DUDEK 305:73
drown it by one's c.	WILDE 940:68	co-operation c.-o. in their mutual	NOVAK 641:64	cornfield o'er the green c.	SHAK 780:21
fitter for c. by 'em	WYCH 964:97	Government and c.-o.	RUSK 733:99	Cornpone C. and…Porkchop	ONAS 650:55
In private c.	CURT 259:98	coot haunts of c. and hern	TENN 876:37	cornucopia brown paper c.	DUNNE 307:19
intimate as any c.	STERN 847:18	cop c. beatin' up a guy	STEI 845:83	corollary C.—The history of science	SART 744:63
journalism…as an extension of c.	SAMP 741:97	Cope Hey, Johnnie C.	SKIR 825:51	coronation Bring c., and sops	SPEN 838:15
make his c. perfectly delightful	SMITH 831:57	Copernican universe is C.	PHIL 677:56	coroner like the c.'s inquest	CONG 241:54
materials for c.	JOHN 460:81	copier mere c. of nature	REYN 712:70	coronet bride of a ducal c.	DICK 280:25
politics…are a c.	OAKE 642:1	copies Make c., young man, many c.	INGR 446:41	coronets hearts are more than c.	TENN 871:10
stick on c.'s burrs	HOLM 423:61	coping c. with life	SPARK 835:63	corporal although this c. rind	MILT 599:78
support a flagging c.	HUNT 440:32	trigger the c. mechanism	WRIS 963:77	Uncle Toby, interrupting the c.	STER 848:45
conversational shallow c. ends	SASS 746:98	Copper When Lord C. was right	WAUGH 923:73	corporation C.…ingenious device	BIER 134:72
conversations c., and even a soliloquy	LINK 530:27	copper c. into gold	SENG 757:27	St Louis…arch of the c.	MAIL 560:55
converse hold high c.	THOM 887:4	Irishman is lined with c.	TWAIN 902:48	corporations c. and local boards	MILL 591:4
sweet c. of an innocent	KEATS 475:65	Copperfield that David C. kind of crap	SALI 739:71	great c.	GLEI 394:18
them and rational c.	WOLL 954:92	copperheads forgot the c.	SAND 742:17	great modern c.	JAY 453:1
conversion believed in sudden c.	FORS 344:26	coppers c. hot	ADE 7:59	corps effete c. of impudent snobs	AGNEW 9:94
converted Except ye be c.	BIBLE 118:10	old time 'c.'	COLL 237:64	corpse before me is its c.	MAZZ 583:30
sinners shall be c. unto thee	BIBLE 101:73	coppice love of field and c.	MACK 553:10	c. of the public credit	WEBS 926:15
convertible rogue…is still c.	EMER 325:99	copulate people who can c.	MACD 549:32	fingers of cold are c. fingers	LAWR 513:66
upholstery of a Packard c.	PERE 674:22	copulating two skeletons c.	BEEC 73:68	good wishes to the c.	BARR 65:84
convex Self-portrait in a C. Mirror	ASHB 37:57	copulation Birth, and c., and death	ELIOT 319:26	greeting a c. would give	BALD 57:26
conviction act out of religious c.	ECO 310:19	Let c. thrive	SHAK 793:21	hardly was the c. cold	STOP 855:15
author's c. on this day	POUND 692:17	Wit…is the unexpected c. of ideas	JOHN 459:54	I'll show you a c.	PUZO 701:7
best lack all c.	YEATS 966:24	copy all very well to c.	DEGAS 269:88	make a lovely c.	DICK 280:21
c. is to report that dialogue	KUNI 501:41	if you c. others	BERN 86:78	more complete than a c.	VIAN 911:71
c. that a hypothesis	MEDA 584:34	copying c. the answer out	KIER 485:99	resuscitated c.	JENK 454:31
damnable iteration…of earnest c.	STEAD 843:31	copyists shortened the labour of c.	CARL 200:89	surgeon dissects a c.	APOL 29:79
every c. begins as a whim	BROUN 163:19	copyrights Take away…their c.	TROL 898:54	corpses bivouac for c.	MUSS 627:88
I am a c. politician	THAT 882:77	coral bones are c. made	SHAK 803:16	c.…their unimportant look	DAVI 265:83
striking c. of the vanity	JOHN 459:53	India's c. strand	HEBER 406:1	mock the riddled c.	SASS 745:80
what is called c.	HUNT 439:18	Japonica Glistens like c.	REED 709:26	corpulence burdenous c. my love	DONNE 292:45
convictions c. are hills	FITZ 337:73	corbies twa c. making a mane	BALL 59:17	correct about to c. themselves	BRADY 155:53
C. are more dangerous	NIET 637:92	cord threefold c.	BIBLE 106:18	Are we c. to have changed	ASAHI 37:51
feelings and c.	MORI 619:36	Corde C. avoided cemeteries	BELL 78:93	blot out, c., insert	SWIFT 862:61
Stevenson's c.	LEHM 520:24	cordiale entente c.	LOUIS 537:73	do the perfectly c. thing	SHAW 810:4
convienient any c. time for	MITC 610:45	cords c. that hold India	CURZ 259:3	History is not politically c.	FERG 333:80
convince labouring to c.	JOHN 461:96	core compact c.	LENIN 521:37	moral is always c.	BART 66:21
persuading others, we c.	JUNI 471:48	heart and c. of ages	LOWE 539:96	not a c. deduction	KEYN 484:76
works harder to c. himself	FRAS 349:32	In my heart's c.	SHAK 783:22	Protocoligorically c.	SHER 818:8
convincing thought of c.	GOLD 377:17	red ball of fire at its c.	AGAWA 9:92	corrected C. and amended	FRAN 348:7
conviviality taper of c.	DICK 279:89	Corinna Come, my C., come	HERR 415:11	correcteth Lord loveth he c.	BIBLE 104:53

correction   1058

correction c. of private abuses	PEEL 672:66	soft, low, gentle c.	WODE 952:38	c. American means white	MORR 620:57
look you, under your c.	SHAK 775:77	coughing one c. and one not c.	SCHN 748:43	c. but for one flag	ROOS 725:23
correctitude feather-bed of c.	BENN 81:74	coughs C. and sneezes	ANON 24:24	c. called Technopolis	WINN 950:99
Corregio corregiescity of C.	STER 848:35	letting his c. fall	MORG 619:33	c.....disappointingly empty	BARN 64:64
correlative objective c.	ELIOT 317:90	coulda woulda, shoulda, c.	HOFF 422:27	c. evenly divided	VIDAL 912:95
correspondence c. was something like		council C. of Europe	BEVIN 90:67	c. far beyond the stars	VAUG 909:37
a duet	DONA 290:6	in danger of the c.	BIBLE 114:32	c. free otherwise than in name	MILL 591:4
corridors admit princes to the c.	DOUG 295:5	planned...In c. rooms apart	RICE 713:90	c. gentleman that never travelled	LASS 510:12
brain has C.	DICK 284:41	Sagest in the c.	DAVIS 266:8	c.....going to sleep	RENAN 711:47
c. of power	ALLEN 13:74	tongues of the French C.	SHAK 776:1	c. governed by a despot	JOHN 463:59
History has many...contrived c.	ELIOT 317:84	councillors As many c.	SALV 741:96	c. green	KEATS 478:42
corrupt a people generally c.	BURKE 175:26	councils In the c. of government	EISE 314:2	c. habit has me	SACK 737:10
appointment by the c. few	SHAW 808:37	counsel darkeneth c. by words	BIBLE 98:13	c. has its own Constitution	MUNS 626:57
Beauty...easy to c.	BACON 52:26	did c. spurn	VAUG 909:42	C. in the town	MART 576:78
c. my air	SHAK 799:98	Dost sometimes c. take	POPE 685:36	c. is the world	PAINE 660:36
daft or c.	FULL 355:77	follow this c. of Aristotle	ASCH 37:52	c. is too big for anyone	ATWO 41:37
should c. the world	TENN 878:85	guide me with thy c.	BIBLE 101:86	C. manners.	MUNRO 625:50
corrupted c. by money	GREE 386:7	his c. was not followed	BIBLE 96:48	c. needs to be united	JOHN 457:6
froth-c. lungs	OWEN 657:31	Who cannot give good c.?	BURT 181:81	c. of birds and trees	WRIG 963:70
corrupter power a c.	SHEL 812:51	counsels all good c.	BOOK 146:42	c. of defeat	PURDY 700:86
corruptible 'mongst things c.	MIDD 590:81	how mony c. sweet	BURNS 179:21	c. of the blind	WELLS 930:23
corruption c. in any government	BRUN 170:93	United thoughts and c.	MILT 601:37	c. of the mind	WHITE 935:52
C. is more than a poison	ECON 310:21	count 10 people who really c.	ANON 26:88	C. party	WHIT 937:83
c. of power	BRON 160:50	all men c. with you	KIPL 492:63	c. saves the difference	BAGE 54:71
C., the most infallible symptom	GIBB 366:93	nothing else to c.	EMER 325:97	c. so far lost to...self-importance	GEOR 363:47
gratify avarice, and extend c.	JOHN 460:86	they c. things carefully	WALE 917:28	c. so precipitously convoluted	JAMES 450:25
Louisianans don't tolerate c.	ANON 27:30	won the c.	SOMO 833:11	c.'s pride	GOLD 376:98
of dong and of c.!	CHAU 217:94	you will c. many friends	OVID 657:22	c. takes her place	EMMET 325:6
Stewed in c.	SHAK 784:42	counted refuse to be c.	DAVI 266:23	c. that is economically backward	TROT 899:67
suffer thine Holy One to see c.	BIBLE 99:36	countenance beautiful c.	BIBLE 96:35	c. then, tomorrow c. now	RICH 714:24
corruptions man's c.	OTWAY 656:94	chide God for making you that c.	SHAK 779:8	c. 'tis of centuries	CUMM 257:58
most pernicious C.	PRYN 698:62	c. more In sorrow than in anger	SHAK 780:44	c., 'tis of thee	SMITH 830:31
corruptly Were not derived c.	SHAK 769:95	c. was as the sun	BIBLE 131:88	c. to heel like a dog	LESS 523:91
corset c. is...a mutilation	VEBL 910:44	did the C. Divine	BLAKE 141:41	c. where death is	LORCA 537:59
Cory C., one calm summer	ROBI 718:82	dismal grew his c.	BALL 58:58	c. where the State is the Church	SHAW 809:69
Corydon Time, not C.	ARNO 36:13	help of his c.	BIBLE 100:64	C. will be called upon	HARD 396:91
cosine Brothers of the C.	ROOS 725:21	Look not on his c.	BIBLE 96:34	c. with a large foreign	RUSS 734:30
cosmetics c. and the silks	SEXT 758:48	Lord lift up his c. upon thee	BIBLE 94:79	Cry, the Beloved C.	PATON 699:27
factory, we make c.	REVS 712:68	merry heart maketh a cheerful c.	BIBLE 104:74	customs that his c. has evolved	POWE 693:59
cosmic bitter c. joke	GELL 363:33	ordinary human c.	LEAC 515:15	Cuts off the c. of Again	MUIR 623:15
born to make chaos c.	BEER 73:79	Thy c....thy mien	WORD 961:47	dear native c.	SWIFT 862:57
C. consciousness	BUCKE 172:38	counter All things c.	HOPK 428:73	defence of one's c.	HOMER 425:7
cosmology problem of c.	POPP 689:60	From c. or desk	YEATS 966:18	die but once to serve our c.!	ADDI 7:50
cosmos c. has forgiven you	MAIL 560:62	counties England has greater c.	CRIP 254:96	died to save their c.	CHES 221:5
push and pressure of the c.	JAMES 451:72	English c. like hunting-tunes	BENET 79:24	die fighting for his c.	HOMER 425:8
cossack c.'s whip	TROT 899:62	see the coloured c.	HOUS 431:44	die for my c.?	SITT 823:93
cost and counteth the c.	BIBLE 121:86	counting C. the slow heart beats	GRAV 382:30	die for your c.	GOLD 377:23
as though hate has no c.	SAND 742:25	countries c., art and lit.	LEWIS 527:58	die for your c.	PATT 670:31
c. of freedom	KENN 481:12	c. divided by a...language	SHAW 811:31	die...in my c.	MATAK 581:84
c. to freedom of opinion	SCHL 747:33	c. engaged in the war	LEES 519:4	different times in the same c.	RICA 712:79
counted the c. of this contest	DICK 284:58	c. have too much history	KING 487:42	division in a c. so small	DONO 293:81
greatest c., namely time	ANTI 29:75	C. that have soldiers in charge	MACK 554:16	done stranger things in that c.	THER 882:88
not apt to c. him	RUNY 731:57	differs in different c.	RICA 712:79	dresses, in every age and c.	LIN 529:2
that which dost c. me nothing	BIBLE 97:50	He...preferreth all c. before his own	OVER 656:11	duty to his c.	PEAC 671:53
costly C. thy habit	SHAK 781:52	in c. where capitalism	TROT 899:67	dying c.'s cries	GRAY 385:83
how c. summer was	SHAK 769:97	Ireland is one of the few c.	DANG 262:29	education...of this c.	DISR 288:62
costs C. merely register	KNIG 494:9	most prosperous c.	LEVI 525:26	egg production in this c.	CURR 259:96
Love c. us nothing	RICK 715:29	Music...language of all c.	ODETS 647:93	England...My c.!	COWP 251:13
subtract the c.	GATES 361:90	peace of all c.	ROOS 724:9	England's not a bad c.	DRAB 298:83
whatever it c. them	UPDI 906:22	series of fabulous c.	ORWE 654:55	England, this c. of ours	AUDEN 42:68
what everything really c.	SMITH 827:79	which of the two c.	GERA 364:61	English c. gentleman	WILDE 941:84
costume cardinal points of c.	MURR 627:80	Working men of all c.	MARX 579:34	enough room in your own c.	CORW 247:7
c. will be Indecent	LAVER 512:33	working populations of both c.	LOND 534:10	events outside their own c.	WILL 944:66
national, c. architecture	BIRD 136:11	country a c. that disagrees	RUMS 731:43	every c. but his own	GILB 369:61
cot paint the c.	CRAB 252:31	against any c. or doctrine	MARS 575:63	every c. except Germany	GREY 388:63
sheltered c.	GOLD 376:97	agreeable method of entering the c.	MACL 554:24	every c. in the world	KEEN 478:52
cottage before his c. door	SOUT 835:45	Alas, poor c.	SHAK 797:61	every c. ought to have a President	DOLE 290:99
no cheerful c. has blest my eyes	SCHAW 747:20	all in the same c.	KRAM 499:3	famous in this c. in seven days	HART 399:63
removed like a c.	BIBLE 108:66	allow this c. to be brought in	GEOR 364:52	fight for your c.	HOMER 425:7
Wherever there's a c. small	PARK 664:35	all their c.'s wishes blest!	COLL 237:71	films of one's own c.	ANDE 17:70
cottages march in c. of...weeds	MARL 572:3	almost every c. unpopular	MACA 544:21	first, best c. ever	GOLD 376:86
peace to the c.	CHAM 212:69	almost in the c.	WILS 947:39	fit c. for heroes to live in	LLOY 533:76
cottar stirk from a c.	SCOTT 753:37	America is a c. of young men	EMER 325:98	for C. and for Yale	THUR 890:88
cotton c. flowers of her dress	THOM 884:40	Anyone who loves his c.	GARI 360:73	foreign troop...in my c.	PITT 679:9
c. is high	HEYW 417:40	a political in this c.	TROL 898:46	for my c.	HALE 392:27
four c. ones	TRAV 895:88	around the c.	MACM 556:65	friends and c. are as nothing to that	JAMES 449:22
so are banks, so is c.	DICK 279:2	Art...will have a c.	APOL 29:84	from the heartland of the c.	SHUL 819:30
world wrapped up in...jeweller's c.	DICK 281:57	ask not what your c.	KENN 481:4	From yon far c. blows	HOUS 431:51
cotton-town Lancashire c.-t.	ORWE 653:14	betray my c.	FORS 345:46	game your c. loves	RICE 713:91
couch century of the psychiatrist's c.	MCLU 556:57	born in a half savage c.	POUND 691:99	gang should mismanage the c.	MARQ 575:61
c. for luxury	SHAK 781:65	Britain is a Morris Minor c.	ANON 26:84	God made the c.	COWP 251:11
hidden c.	GORD 378:53	bust up a c.	WARD 920:99	good for our c.	WILS 947:47
levee from a c.	CONG 241:73	call her a young c.	HOPE 427:57	good in the c.	WILDE 941:71
on a c. of straw	THOM 884:35	Canada...the only c. in the world	MCLU 556:58	greatest asset any c. can have	CHUR 225:73
There I c. when owls do cry	SHAK 804:32	cannot flourish in a c.	HUXL 442:94	grow up with the c.	GREE 385:97
when on my c. I lie	WORD 960:27	clein in the c.	FLEM 340:48	halved a c.	THOM 883:8
cough never let them c.	BARR 65:99	conquest of an unknown c.	HEDIN 406:4	has to understand the c.	LESS 523:89

heading into nut c.	KENN 482:30	sunlight falls across the c.	IHIM 445:19	the matter of c.	SONT 834:23
heart bleeds for his c.	JOHN 461:90	the past is another s.	WINT 950:17	to each of you, C.	RATH 707:76
history of every c.	CATH 208:84	the pride of my c. I sang	OBRU 646:75	void of c.	MAIL 560:52
hitherto unexplored c.	SHIP 818:15	the religion of the c.	SWIFT 863:77	Why, c., then	SHAK 760:18
How else can one govern a c.	DE 270:93	The worse the c.	HORN 430:24	With constant c.	JONS 466:43
how lovely our c. is	WORD 962:52	this c. safe to work in	THAT 881:52	without originality or moral c.	SHAW 807:12
how much wealth...in a c.	SIDG 819:32	This was my c.	BLUN 143:78	with the c. of their race	SULL 859:80
I can save this c.	PITT 679:3	to all the c. dear	GOLD 376:99	courageous C. and loyal to the tips	ACHE 3:43
If this c. is settled	STUA 858:58	to be had in the c.	HAZL 403:32	faith...creative and c.	CUPI 258:86
impossible to live in a c.	KEATS 476:81	to die for one's c.	HORA 430:10	couriers sightless c. of the air	SHAK 796:20
impress the people of this c.	PEEL 672:67	took away their c.	SHER 816:69	course c. already decided upon	BIER 134:71
index of this c.	MARC 570:57	totalitarianism in this c.	ORWE 655:68	c. of a dishonest life	FRAS 349:32
In every age and c.	GIBB 366:92	to your own c.	JOAN 455:59	c. of true love	SHAK 766:17
in every other c.	THOM 887:95	undiscovered c.	TWAIN 902:63	c. till I had ended	MUNDY 625:44
in love with a c.	LESS 524:2	United States is the only c.	ROGE 723:80	c. was unjustified	HIRO 419:73
In our c. the lie	SOLZ 833:6	unmapped c. within us	ELIOT 316:58	earth's diurnal c.	WORD 957:64
In the c. of the blind	ERAS 327:36	unsubduable c.	GILL 370:80	face forward his c.	ANON 22:74
in the c. places	STEV 854:85	virtues! they've undone his c.	ADDI 7:49	finish my earthly c.	BEET 74:4
In this c. it is considered a good thing	VOLT 914:32	vow to thee, my c.	SPRI 841:87	golf c. is the epitome	GIRA 372:24
In this c. it is rare	POWE 693:50	war rather than a c.	PILG 678:77	have finished my c.	BIBLE 129:30
In this c. poet-baiting	SITW 824:25	we shall liberate this c.	MAND 565:61	held in the true c.	CARL 201:26
in this happy c.	MORI 619:36	when our c. was born	INOU 446:49	played on a five inch c.	JONES 465:16
in whatever c.	PAZ 671:48	Where is the c., my friend?	ARGU 31:12	take the wrong c.	KENN 481:13
island C. of Japan	TOJO 893:41	who serves his c. best	HAYES 403:28	Take you a c.	DONNE 291:27
know something of his own c.	STER 848:43	Who slights his c. thus	INGR 446:36	There is no other c.	HUSS 440:39
Labour Governments in every c.	GREY 388:61	wild unexplored c.	LIVI 532:55	things take their c.	MACA 546:55
landlords of the c.	PARN 665:47	young c. is a real heritage	MANS 567:10	Time rolls his ceaseless c.	SCOTT 752:30
lavish streams to quench a c.'s thirst	POPE 686:68	Your c. is more precious	PLATO 681:47	courses in a series of c.	GOLD 375:81
law in any civilised c.	LEVIN 525:28	Your c. needs you!	ANON 24:6	miss out on any of the c.	RUSS 735:49
leads a c. such as Britain	THAT 881:68	countryman c. must have praise	BLYT 144:87	coursework Life isn't like c.	JOHN 457:92
leave his c. as good as he had found it	COBB 233:79	countrymen sacrifices of our fellow c.	EISE 314:8	court air of the c.	ETHE 327:48
legislature of this c.	PITT 679:10	steady his fellow c.	MURR 627:83	c. an amorous looking-glass	SHAK 760:32
lie abroad for the good of his c.	WOTT 962:54	countryside c. is the colour of a lion	BOWL 153:1	c. as an orphan	LEVA 525:17
life is a foreign c.	KERO 483:52	disappeared from the c.	MACL 555:41	c. he practised	DRYD 302:88
likes the c.	COWP 250:93	smiling and beautiful c.	DOYLE 297:59	c. is only as sound	LEE 519:90
literature of their c.	TROL 898:47	well-farmed c. was their favourite	TOLK 893:47	c. of kynge Arthure	MALO 563:11
looking out for your c.	COOL 246:82	counts grooves that c.	ANON 28:51	dreary length before the c.	DICK 281:56
love a sunburnt c.	MACK 553:10	county Emeralds big as half a c.	LAND 507:35	fill the c. with quarrels	SHAK 804:37
make...wreck of his c.	BIER 135:93	married with the C.	SHAK 766:6	in the c. a cloister	AELR 8:74
may our c. be always successful	ADAMS 5:4	couple fool...in every married c.	FIEL 335:27	Keeps his pale c.	SHEL 815:29
means nothing in this c.	GOLD 375:80	price paid for becoming a c.	COUP 248:35	kynges c., my brother	CHAU 217:80
mistress...little c. retreat	WYCH 964:94	couples happy c. in the face	STEV 852:35	taller...than any of his c.	SWIFT 862:42
more than one way to conquer a c.	CHAN 213:87	courage as good a c....father had	ELIZ 321:99	threshold of Jove's c.	MILT 598:62
my c. people	SENG 757:26	Be strong and of a good c.	BIBLE 95:6	Through the c.	WILDE 939:44
My c. right or wrong	CHES 220:54	c. and faith and zest	KENN 481:14	To the Tennis C.	PEPYS 674:97
my c. was confirmed to me	PENN 673:81	'C.!' he said	TENN 870:88	whole C. of Parliament	HENR 411:13
my people died to build this c.	ROBE 717:76	c. holds firm	ANON 20:29	courted c. by an Italian	HEPB 412:25
native c. was full	IRVI 447:56	C. in your own	GORD 378:52	courteous first, the Retort C.	SHAK 780:24
no better than any other c.	LEWIS 527:61	C. is a moral quality	MORAN 618:9	So c., so kind	SKEL 824:29
no choice here in the c.	BRON 161:57	C. is in the air	FROST 353:22	courtesan c. is a myth	FLAU 339:18
no instance of a c. having	SUN 859:89	C. is not simply one	LEWIS 526:47	when the c. farts	ANON 22:69
not have a c. to vote in	PANK 662:86	C. is the most important	KENN 482:40	courtesans crowd of c.	DUMAS 306:91
now they desire a better c.	BIBLE 129:41	c. mounteth with occasion	SHAK 768:52	courtesies c. that raise me	BROW 166:89
Of years, of c.	SHAK 788:92	c. never to submit or yield	MILT 602:38	small sweet c. of life	STER 849:56
One's c. is wherever one does well	ANON 20:21	c. of the Negro	PHIL 677:57	courtesy breeds patience and c.	MUIR 624:20
only Shake-scene in a c.	GREE 386:33	c. prove my title	SHAK 795:93	defence like elaborate c.	LUCAS 541:50
opportunity to serve our c.	SMITH 829:10	C., rashness, and rebellion	MARI 571:76	second time do such a c.	SHAK 772:64
or a home, or a c.	WILD 943:45	c. the greater	ANON 20:36	the greater c.	TENN 878:92
organized workers of the c.	SHIN 818:12	c. to change the things	NIEB 637:89	courthouse c. pacing up and down	LIND 530:20
our c., right or wrong	DECA 268:64	c. to follow the talent	JONG 466:29	court-huntsmen tell c.-h.	DONNE 291:25
our c. shall be victorious	PANK 662:86	c. to give you unqualified praise	STEI 846:85	courtier c. grave and serious	GILB 370:72
our dear c. had been free	DAVIS 266:8	c. to know	KANT 473:21	not the c.'s art	DRYD 302:88
our emancipated c.	MANS 567:94	c. to live out	MILL 594:69	courtings rhetorical c.	CLEV 230:93
our undiscovered c.	MANS 567:97	c. to love	TROL 897:24	courtliness c., and...fame	TENN 877:57
own France, a c.	MORL 619:40	c. to ride a horse	LEAC 515:7	courtly Be c. ay in clothing	DUNB 306:1
peace of each c.	JOHN 456:74	Develop enough c.	ANGE 19:67	courtmartialled c. in my absence	BEHAN 74:9
pension from his c.	RUSK 733:95	endurance, and c.	SCOTT 751:6	courts about her c. were seen	LAND 507:35
People in this c.	RICH 714:18	gently raised Their fainting c.	MILT 602:48	brawling c.	TENN 874:90
Pick out of every c.	LASS 510:11	get through our lives...with c.	BANKS 62:29	C. for Cowards were erected	BURNS 177:79
plant them...in his own c.	SOME 833:9	give me...the c.	BAUD 68:69	c. of Europe are a jungle	BOLT 145:14
politics of the c.	HAZL 403:45	history...is written in c.	BUSH 183:38	day in thy c.	BIBLE 101:90
problems of running a c.	THAT 881:55	home...saved by his c.	MACA 546:60	decision of the c.	LEAC 515:19
protect the c.	SUN 859:93	it is not man Made c.	POUND 692:24	forbidden by the c.	STIG 854:97
proudest c. under the sun	PARK 665:37	journey that required c.	MURP 626:76	not enough c.	HUMP 439:9
rooms of thy native c.	FULL 355:78	Kindness and c.	MUIR 624:20	courtship blindness of c.	LOWE 540:34
round the c. stirring up apathy	WHIT 936:76	manly c.	PEEL 672:68	brash c. of the muse	THOM 886:73
Saviour of 'is c.	KIPL 489:87	must have the c. to dare	DOST 294:90	C. to marriage	CONG 240:33
say to his c.	PARN 665:48	my C. and Skill	BUNY 174:83	c. was so much as thought on	LAMB 505:93
science knows no c.	PAST 668:4	Nature all c. me denyis	DUNB 306:5	cousin little c. is dead	RANS 706:67
service to his c.	SWIFT 862:45	Neither fear nor c. saves	ELIOT 317:85	cousins c., and his aunts!	GILB 368:33
shrink from the service of his c.	PAINE 660:29	never to let...your c. grow dim	CURZ 260:5	c. as the sands of the sea	SHAW 811:33
silence...seeps out over the c.	ACHE 2:34	on the c. and conduct	WASH 921:27	couth such a thing as too much c.	PERE 674:21
soon c. people forget	MORR 620:56	people who have the c.	MUSS 627:91	couturiers c. the last possessors	DIOR 287:4
soul of man is a far c.	THOM 883:2	Red Badge of C.	CRANE 253:71	covenant c. between me	BIBLE 92:13
spirit of our c.	CHEE 218:9	Screw your c.	SHAK 796:23	c. between me	BIBLE 92:21
stamp out literature in the c.	WAUGH 923:69	sheer c. and endurance	WAVE 925:2	c. from the beginning is	BIBLE 113:94
struggle for...my c.'s cause	OCON 646:83	Take c., my friend	READE 708:97	c. of our fathers?	BIBLE 112:62

Coventry

c. with death	BIBLE 108:70	would c. in the flame	JEFF 453:17	wealth that you never c.	TSON 900:8		
establish my c.	BIBLE 92:21	**crackling** c. of thorns under a pot	BIBLE 106:21	**creating** envisioning all without c.	GORO 379:66		
Coventry into a moral C.	PARN 665:46	generous with the c.	MACB 546:64	let us start c.	ANON 25:63		
cover c. of an old book	FRAN 348:7	**cracks** c. of other people's lives	WHAR 933:6	Shopping is Not C.	COUP 248:30		
C. your ass	SAFI 737:19	eighteen million c.	CLIN 231:31	**creation** all of your soul in c.!	HUGO 437:64		
I c. all	SAND 742:18	**cracky** joined with the Arabs, by c.!	ACHE 3:52	appropriate act of c.	FEIN 332:57		
on the c. of every issue	WAUGH 923:49	**cradle** c. of a new masterpiece	YEATS 966:13	Art is like C.	KLEE 494:4		
paste and c. to our bones	SHAK 764:51	c. of Spanish walnut	PLATH 681:36	artistic c. is modern life	WAGN 915:2		
they were just a c.	RAMOS 705:50	c. rocks above an abyss	NABO 628:3	Back of every c.	MILL 594:76		
time to run for c.	ASHD 37:66	c. to the grave	ANON 27:17	between human c.	MILL 594:71		
covering hair is given her for a c.	BIBLE 126:48	from the c. to the grave	SHEL 814:19	bless thee for our c.	BOOK 147:50		
covers c. are too close together	LEHM 520:25	hand that rocks the c.	WALL 918:52	blind fury of c.	SHAW 807:16		
covert c. from the tempest	BIBLE 108:75	high mountain c. in Pamere	ARNO 35:1	blot on the fair face of c.	BRON 161:62		
covertousness bereave him of his c.	MILT 600:16	In c. clothes our children	SHAK 770:26	c. first brought forth	MILT 607:71		
cover-up c.-u., or anything else	NIXON 640:35	Out of the c.	GRIF 388:67	c. of images	HOLL 423:51		
covet sin to c. honour	SHAK 776:87	Thou shalt not c.	BREC 157:90	c. of the heavens and the earth	KORAN 496:41		
Thou shalt not c.	BIBLE 94:66	**cradled** c. into poetry	SHEL 812:63	C.'s tears in shoulder blades	STEV 850:96		
Thou shalt not c.	CLOU 232:67	**cradles** bit the babies in the c.	BROW 167:16	deepest mysteries of c.	SHEL 811:47		
covetous Every c. and avaricious man	INNO 446:46	**craft** Between c. and credulity	BURKE 175:24	Did ever woman, since the c.	STER 847:21		
cow c. from a Lowland strath	SCOTT 753:37	cloakèd c. their store of skill	DYER 309:49	fairest of c.	MILT 606:51		
c. is of the bovine	NASH 630:54	continued with my c.	JAMES 451:58	from that equal c.	JEFF 453:19		
Kiss till the c. comes home	BEAU 71:16	c. be best to lerne?	LANG 508:50	horror of C.	HUGH 436:40		
Knowledge is a sacred c.	SZENT 865:30	C. is the handprint	ANON 27:36	inexhaustible fullness of c.	HUMB 438:93		
milk the c. of the world	WILB 939:34	c. so long	HIPP 419:69	jazz...process of c.	LIEB 529:96		
saddle fits a c.	STAL 842:7	c. so long to lerne	CHAU 216:57	Love all God's c.	DOST 294:94		
show me a c. who can earn	WINN 950:1	mere c. and cozenage	JONS 468:88	love C.'s final law	TENN 874:71		
steals a c. from a poor widow	SCOTT 753:37	writing a c.	PORT 690:73	love C.'s final law	TENN 874:80		
The Red C.	TRAV 896:93	**crafts** C. which require the most Time	CANT 197:13	morning of his c.	HUXL 442:90		
Truth, Sir, is a c.	JOHN 461:97	**craftsman** produce the perfect c.	VITR 914:29	participate in the c.	ROBBE 716:64		
you see a c. and think it's...better	FERG 333:76	**craftsmen** c. share a knowledge	SACK 737:9	parts of the C.	HALES 393:30		
Coward I love you—Noël C.	COWA 249:56	**crag** clasps the c.	TENN 875:4	present at the C.	EVANS 328:66		
coward Conscience is a c.	GOLD 376:91	**cragged** huge hill, C., and steep	DONNE 290:15	she is his new c.	STONE 855:11		
c. does it with a kiss	WILDE 942:17	**crags** among these barren c.	TENN 870:97	speak before you think c.'s [motto]	FORS 345:48		
c. in the presence of	STAN 842:11	**craigs** bizzing and mous to weet	FERG 333:86	spelled out the history of c.	FISKE 337:66		
c. in thine own esteem	SHAK 796:21	**cram** C. as much pleasure as you can		spilled...hate into his dearest c.	BURG 174:99		
Fore God I am no c.	TENN 878:95	into life	MACG 552:85	Spontaneous c.	HAWK 401:94		
gift of a c.	SHAK 785:81	**cramp** drugs cause c.	PARK 664:19	supreme c. of an era	BART 66:22		
coward just a c.	HEMI 410:81	**cranberries** man wrapping c.	DOLE 290:97	think more of the c.	GAUG 361:2		
The sea hates a c.!	ONEI 651:68	Rice, and a C. Tart	LEAR 516:33	through a limitless c.	HUXL 442:2		
This sanguine c.	SHAK 771:47	**crane** protection of the whooping c.	BRIN 159:25	tire of all c.	HOLM 424:70		
cowardice admit the c.	SHAW 807:28	Tall as a c.	SITW 823:8	took the whole of C.	HUGH 435:31		
C., as distinguished from panic	HEMI 410:82	**Cranford** here at C.	GASK 361:84	Vexing its own c.	WORD 957:73		
Nine times out of ten it is c.	SIDM 819:33	**crank** c. is a small engine	SHEE 811:40	warrants the c.	FIELD 335:11		
surest is c.	TWAIN 903:82	c. until the idea succeeds	TWAIN 903:81	whole c. groaneth	BIBLE 125:19		
cowardly c. way to score	PELE 672:74	serve...apprenticeship as a c.	BROUN 163:19	whole c. moves	TENN 875:3		
cowards conscience does make c.	SHAK 782:7	**crap** David Copperfield kind of c.	SALI 739:71	woman a mere after-thought in c.	STAN 843:17		
Courts for C. were erected	BURNS 177:79	**crape** saint in c. is twice	POPE 687:94	world was before the c.	BROW 165:67		
C. die many times	SHAK 777:21	**crash** the c. is coming	PARK 664:22	**creations** c. of a poet	SHEL 816:49		
fools and c. might sit safe	OTWAY 656:2	thoughts of the C.	THOM 885:69	human c. mechanical	LEGER 519:6		
goes to the heads of c.	MITC 610:43	**crave** mind forbids to c.	DYER 309:47	like all original c. of the human spirit	DYSON 309:60		
learn'd are c.	DRYD 301:62	the more you c.	POPE 688:22	**creative** a c. life	THARP 880:45		
Tho' c. flinch	CONN 242:84	**craved** c. no crumb	GILB 370:70	active and c. world	SPEN 837:12		
When c. mock the patriot's fate	INGR 446:36	**craves** c. wary walking	SHAK 776:15	always being c.	CANT 197:16		
coward-slave c.-s., we pass him by	BURNS 180:52	**craving** c. to risk death	FOWL 345:59	beautiful, c. and good	MING 608:8		
cowbind Green c.	SHEL 816:61	full as c.	DRYD 301:58	C. Endeavour lost	WAUGH 923:68		
cowboy last true c. in America	HEAT 406:96	**Crawford** best time...with Joan C.	DAVIS 265:96	c. gift	HOPK 429:97		
cowboys c. had lived for months	MCMU 557:83	**crawling** c. between heaven	SHAK 783:12	c. people hate mathematics	ISSI 448:76		
Cowdenknowes broom of C.	BALL 58:55	maybe she will do the c.	FAUL 331:45	c. talent...drained off	RICH 714:18		
Cowley Who now reads C.?	POPE 688:17	**crazed** c. with the spell	DELA 271:28	reading...highly c.	CARY 207:60		
cow pat humble violet under a c. p.	BARN 64:63	**crazy** all going to go c.	KRAM 499:3	satisfies the human c. instinct	QUEN 702:8		
cows Barrymore's acting till the c.	NATH 632:1	c. about cars	SALI 740:78	victim of c. suffering	KING 487:30		
cash c. to feed your pigs	ANDE 17:68	c. for love	BART 66:13	**creativity** angel of c. wrestling	LENG 521:36		
dance with you till the c.	MARX 578:17	C. Like A Fox	PERE 674:14	c. comes to an end	ROTH 727:76		
To be contented...that's for the c.	CHAN 214:4	edge of some c. cliff	SALI 740:81	C. in science	KOES 495:30		
cowshed smelling of the c.	THOM 884:35	grow a little c.	GOLD 375:78	dimensions of thought and c.	STEI 846:98		
cowslip C....like tethered foam	CRANE 253:66	I suppose all writers are c.	CHAN 213:94	keep that childlike c.	HIRS 419:77		
In a c.'s bell I lie	SHAK 804:32	Orr was c.	HELL 407:27	sex and c. are often seen	JONG 466:30		
I'th' bottom of a c.	SHAK 803:91	that's what is c.	JONAS 465:15	**creator** all-wise C.	HALES 393:30		
cowslip-banks sit on c.-b.	WALT 920:95	The people who are c. enough	ISAAC 447:66	c. from his work returned	MILT 605:32		
cowslips c., and kingcups	SPEN 838:15	unless I'm c.	HEMI 410:84	c. in the year 1902	MORT 621:72		
c. wan that hang	MILT 599:91	We are all born c.	BECK 72:45	C.'s power display	ADDI 7:40		
cow-woman c.-w. and the		would end by becoming c.	MAUP 583:17	endowed by their C.	STAN 842:12		
scum-woman	GRAND 381:97	**cream** cat to steal c.	SHAK 771:56	God, C. wise	MILT 606:64		
coxcomb c. ask two hundred guineas	RUSK 733:15	c. rises until it sours	PETER 675:37	greater glory of his C.	PIUS 680:20		
more consummate c.	WESL 932:70	queen of curds and c.	SHAK 799:21	my c., detest and spurn me	SHEL 812:48		
coxcombs some made c.	POPE 685:16	**cream-faced** c.-f. loon!	SHAK 798:68	Remember now thy C.	BIBLE 106:36		
cozenage town is full of c.	SHAK 762:91	**create** absence of the urge to c.	MAMET 563:31	served the creature more than the C.	BIBLE 125:3		
Crabbe With C. it may be difficult	BYRON 189:3	anything he might c.	MAMET 563:30	the C. is getting	ALLEN 13:81		
crabbedness not the result of mere c.	FADI 329:7	c. and keep quiet	FLAU 339:23	the C. made Italy	TWAIN 902:34		
crabs like wet c. in a basket	DURR 308:35	c., if it concerns poetry	HUGO 436:55	**creators** c. of odd volumes	LAMB 505:3		
roasted c. hiss in the bowl.	SHAK 763:28	c. in our minds the very things	ABER 1:5	**creature** c. driven by demons	FAUL 331:39		
crab-tree schoolboys...climb a c.-t.	ROCH 719:18	desire to c. something	PRIE 695:90	c. here Beast, bird, insect	MILT 604:8		
crack c. your cheeks!	SHAK 792:4	know, to kill and to c.	BAUD 69:86	c. of the common streets	DICK 281:73		
hear the mighty c.	POPE 687:98	To c. is...to destroy	CUMM 257:67	c.'s at his dirty work	POPE 687:99		
heaven's vault should c.	SHAK 793:37	to c. jazz	GILL 370:87	Dear is the helpless c.	BYRON 189:97		
no c. in a fortress	MILL 593:36	**created** C. half to rise	POPE 687:81	Deformèd c.	SPEN 838:23		
will sure c. both	SHAK 798:84	c. the poodle	THUR 891:97	Each c. of the world	ALAN 10:15		

crisis

entry	ref
every c. in a cave	SNYD 833:94
every c. shall be	MARL 573:25
God's first C.	BACON 53:45
imitator is a poor kind of c.	WHIS 934:21
in Christ, he is a new c.	BIBLE 127:70
kills a reasonable c.	MILT 600:99
lone lorn c.	DICK 280:37
Lovely c. in scarlet	GEOR 364:59
Man is a c. who	STEV 852:42
Man is a history-making c.	AUDEN 44:11
Man is the only c.	ORWE 654:46
No c. loves an empty space	MARV 578:8
no c. loves me	SHAK 761:51
No c. smarts so little	POPE 687:98
Not a c. was stirring	MOORE 616:60
proves, that every c.	SWIFT 863:65
ravished this fair c.	FIEL 335:22
served the c. more than the Creator	BIBLE 125:3
sigh of the oppressed c.	MARX 578:24
small c. of the night	AMIS 16:29
so good a c.	GALT 359:53
some new and wondrous c.	DARW 263:51
sort of c. that can't die	THER 882:90
thy c., to whom thou art bound	SHEL 812:48
Y'are the deed's c.	MIDD 590:80
creatures All c. great and small	ALEX 13:61
all c. here below	KEN 480:84
births of living c.	BACON 52:8
breastless c. under ground	ELIOT 317:77
countless joyful c. sing	KIER 486:7
c. give out a smell	LEES 519:2
c. in warmer countries	GUY 390:7
c….looked from pig to man	ORWE 654:50
c. of commanding sadness	LEE 519:98
c. there Live	MILT 605:36
disagree Of c. rational	MILT 603:67
distinguished from all other c.	ADDI 7:44
fair c. of an hour	KEATS 475:78
frustrated c. we were	MILL 594:63
home, you idle c.	SHAK 776:3
human c. breathe an atmosphere	DICK 282:92
lawful lords of earthly c.	DAVI 264:75
meanest of his c.	BROW 168:56
Men are very fragile c.	STEP 847:13
no better than c.	JOHN 462:40
obedience of c.	HOOK 424:39
orders and inferior c.	MILT 608:92
race of upstart c.	MILT 603:71
rarest of political c.	MCFA 551:64
shining c. of the chase	TENN 872:33
solidarity with other isolated c.	BELL 78:90
spiritual c. walk the earth	MILT 604:7
These Ibsen c.	ANON 23:97
widows…the most perverse c.	ADDI 6:33
worst sin towards our fellow c.	SHAW 807:98
credentials There are no c.	LLOY 532:69
credit corpse of the public c.	WEBS 926:15
c. cards cancelled	ANON 27:19
c. goes to the man	DARW 263:61
c. to a Trappist nun	SHAR 806:73
don't want my c. to look black	WEST 932:78
faces as thin as c. cards	AMIS 16:43
finally they c. the wrong person	BRYS 171:13
From your fair c.	FLET 341:61
get c. for anything	JOHN 458:19
impossible to c.	WILL 944:66
I will take the c. for	BEVIN 90:69
more c. than they deserved	REST 711:64
Of c. lost	JONS 468:87
physicians…take the c.	BURG 174:93
seek to take the c.	PARK 663:99
the c. of our…government	STEE 844:44
to give them c.	USTI 906:43
world will give thee c.	CHUR 224:56
creditors gaping c.	OTWAY 656:99
credulities c. of mankind	CONR 244:46
credulity Between craft and c.	BURKE 175:24
interest dictates and c. encourages	JOHN 460:84
present age is craving c.	DISR 288:48
credulous men are the most c.	POPE 686:57
creed c. and particular reality	MUNCH 625:42
c. of a second-rate man	BAGE 55:79
c. of different parties	TOCQ 892:30
c. which accepts	MILL 591:8
establishing your c.	BAGE 54:63
got the better of his c.	STER 848:32
need…shapes a human c.	CULL 257:47
Non-violence…last article of my c.	GAND 359:59
pagan suckled in a c. outworn	WORD 961:30
shrieked against his c.	TENN 874:71
shrieked against his c.	TENN 874:80
solemn c. with solemn sneer	BYRON 187:55
underlies every c.	BLAV 127:40
unionism is stronger than c.	LAWS 514:95
creeds dust of c. outworn	SHEL 814:12
keys of all the c.	TENN 874:66
our casual c.	ARNO 34:93
second of man's c.	LAWR 514:90
than in half the c.	TENN 874:92
creek here and there a c.	BYRON 189:6
creep C. into thy narrow bed	ARNO 35:24
Here! c.	HOPK 429:92
Men c., Not walk	WHIT 938:21
wealth will c. out	JOHN 463:61
creeper in Virginia c. drown	BETJ 88:29
creepers fellow c. on…planet	SAND 742:26
creeping any manner of c. thing	BIBLE 94:76
c. police state	GINS 372:14
things c. innumerable	BIBLE 102:13
creeps C. in this petty pace	SHAK 798:74
crème pupils are the c. de la c.	SPARK 836:67
crest glows on their c.	SCOTT 751:1
lapwing…another c.	TENN 871:11
red roses c. the caps	THOM 886:84
Cretan lied like a C.	HARDY 397:5
Cretans C. are always liars	BIBLE 129:31
Crete people of C.	SAKI 739:59
crevasse scream from a c.	GREE 386:9
crew c. is gambling in the forecastle	SHAW 810:9
We were a ghastly c.	COLE 235:17
crib angel in the c.	NEVE 634:31
If the c.'s on fire	GORE 379:61
cricket At least I am not playing c.!	POWYS 693:62
c. as organized loafing	TEMP 869:67
C. can be a bridge	ZIA 970:12
c. goes to the bone	ARLO 32:33
C. is a batsman's game	BENA 78:2
C. is a game of…stresses	ARLO 32:34
C. is baseball on valium	WILL 944:75
C. is…full of forlorn hopes	ORWE 654:44
c. is full of theorists	BOTH 152:80
c. is just another game	EDIN 312:50
C. is not illegal	ANNE 19:12
C. is the greatest game	WARN 921:11
C.? It civilises people	MUGA 623:7
c.—it's so very English	BERN 86:85
C., like the novel	ARLO 32:32
c. on the hearth	MILT 598:54
C. remains…the game of games	FOWL 346:65
'C.,' said Raffles	HORN 430:25
c.'s manly toil	BYRON 186:23
c. teams wiped out	STOP 855:16
c. tour in Australia	LARW 510:7
C….towards sentimentalism	CARD 198:42
C….was more than play	BLUN 143:82
c. was not made: it has 'grown'	CARD 198:39
C. weather	JOYCE 470:31
describing c. matches	THOM 884:23
elements are c.'s presiding geniuses	CARD 198:45
empty c. ground	SNOW 832:74
England are a good c. team	SMITH 828:97
English c….died at the Oval	ANON 23:92
English think c. is a game	MIKES 590:87
expressing itself in c.	JAMES 450:32
far more than a game, this c.	CARD 662:84
Golf is Fiji what c. is to America	SINGH 823:90
great advantage over c.	SHAW 810:27
Hail C.! glorious	LOVE 538:80
If Stalin had learned to play c.	DOWN 296:35
if there be c. in heaven	HOME 425:99
laws of c. tell of the English love	CARD 198:41
May C. continue to flourish	BRAD 155:47
never played at c.	MILL 592:12
play c. in the summer	KINN 488:62
playing c. for hard cash!	MITF 610:49
really keen c. fan	NORD 641:52
sound of the c. bats	JOYCE 470:19
Sphere of Influence'—the c. ball	ANON 23:94
The c. test	TEBB 869:64
theorist more than c.	TRUE 899:73
Village c. spread fast	TREV 896:5
when I hold a c. ball	UTTL 907:50
where the c. sings	YEATS 965:4
youths at c. did play	JOSE 469:9
cricketer c….by name John Small	EGAN 313:65
Cricklewood Midland, bound for C.	BETJ 88:28
cried say he c. out of sack	SHAK 775:69
Still it c. 'Sleep no more'	SHAK 797:35
when he c….children died	AUDEN 43:88
cries Everybody c.	STIPE 855:3
crime a C. in Progress	THOM 887:91
Arson…artificial c.	WELLS 930:28
Cambodia…was a c.	SHAW 811:39
commit any c. they like	DOST 294:89
conclusion…that almost all c.	WAUGH 923:66
coyness Lady were no c.	MARV 577:90
c. against humanity	JOHN 456:79
c….dodge…by secrecy	PULI 699:71
C….has its degrees	RACI 704:30
C. is common	DOYLE 297:60
C. is…socio-political	PACK 658:9
C. lies not in the deed	HELO 409:55
c. novel is not easy	JAMES 451:58
c. of being a young man	PITT 679:1
c. of stealing	TWAIN 902:45
c. pays	ALLEN 14:83
c. you haven't committed	POWE 693:47
end that stupid c.	SERV 757:37
help to cut the c. rate	WAUGH 923:51
lessen c. and reform the criminal	FRY 353:37
loved be with equal c.	SPEN 838:33
Murder is a unique c.	JAMES 451:59
Napoleon of c.	DOYLE 297:62
no c. like the present	WASH 922:34
No c.'s so great	CHUR 224:60
object from the c.	POPE 686:49
one guilt, one c.	MILT 605:54
promote intellectual c.	BIER 134:81
punishment fit the c.	GILB 370:66
right to commit nearly every c.	BENT 82:91
servitude…consequence of his c.	CURR 259:92
study of c.	MILL 594:77
the great c.	PACH 658:1
The more featureless…a c. is	DOYLE 297:50
tough on c.	BLAIR 138:49
tried…for a capital c.	JOHN 463:47
worst c.	WALC 916:18
Crimea C….Would Not Boil	TAYL 868:45
Crimean C. War is one	GUED 389:85
crimes All c. are safe	JOHN 459:43
All the poor c.	WEBS 926:29
C….are their own reward	FARQ 330:24
c. committed in the name of duty	SNOW 832:80
c. confined	GRAY 384:71
c. that shame mankind	NOON 641:50
detestation of the c.	PARN 665:46
How many c. are committed	CAMUS 196:98
our impudent c.	ELIOT 317:85
register of the c.	IRVI 447:55
Successful c. alone are justified	DRYD 302:1
virtues made or c.	DEFOE 269:73
worse c. than burning books	BROD 160:41
worst of c.	SHAW 809:70
criminal call it a c. thing	SOME 833:9
choose to count as c.	PACK 658:9
c. law is no use	SHAW 809:83
ends I think c.	KEYN 484:69
fixed in the favor of the c.	CAPO 197:21
lessen crime and reform the c.	FRY 353:37
When he got more c.	LONG 535:12
criminals Authors and uncaptured c.	LINK 530:25
misfits, looney tunes and squalid c.	REAG 708:8
These men too were c.	CLAV 229:77
crimson all c. barr'd	KEATS 476:4
bed Of c. joy	BLAKE 140:12
c….robin's breast	TENN 871:11
like the c. drops	SHAK 803:91
red like c.	BIBLE 107:50
cringe Cultural C.	PHIL 677:55
if you c. before her	FAUL 331:45
crinoline woman in a c.	LAVER 512:34
Cripps C. has a brilliant mind	ASQU 38:79
crises marked by an absence of c.	PECK 672:65
no libertarians in financial c.	KRUG 500:25
crisis any c. next week	KISS 494:91
any major c. of the capitalist system	EAGL 309:2
c. justifies permanent control	HUXL 442:94
c. of her experience	AUST 47:77
c. of understanding	WILL 944:72
C.? What c.?	CALL 193:31
each ball a potential c.	TREV 896:5

Crispian

exciting to have a real c.	THAT 881:59	go on feeding the c.	REAG 708:2
force the moment to its c.?	ELIOT 316:62	hen's egg don't turn into a c.	KING 488:53
how early…she can meet c.	PECK 672:65	How doth the little c.	CARR 203:64
In times of c.	BALZ 60:94	'You mean,'…'a c.'	NASH 631:70
patriot will, in this c.	PAINE 660:29	**crocodiles** wisdom of the c.	BACON 52:7
Poetry, surely, is in c.	SALI 740:84	**crocs** argosy of c. and dragons	AMIS 16:46
settlement of this c.	HUSS 440:37	**crocus** c. dress	JOYCE 470:32
the climate c. is real	GORE 379:63	c. lustres of the stars	CRANE 252:54
the c.…is past	POE 683:94	c. on a garbage heap	GARD 360:71
Crispian fought…upon Saint C.'s	SHAK 776:94	underfoot the violet, C.	MILT 604:8
Tomorrow is Saint C.	SHAK 776:89	**Cromwell** C., damned to…fame!	POPE 687:90
Upon Saint C.'s day	DRAY 298:95	C. said to the Long Parliament	AMERY 15:27
criteria need of outward c.	WITT 951:28	C.; the Philistine of genius	ARNO 36:38
criterion c.…to test the genuineness	AYER 48:5	C. took up arms	STAL 842:4
infallible c. of wisdom	BURKE 176:51	Some C. guiltless	GRAY 384:70
known by the c.	JEVO 455:52	**crook** are a C. or a Martyr	ROGE 723:75
critic a c. is a man who	TYNAN 904:4	by hook or by c.	MORE 618:10
A good drama c.	TYNAN 904:5	**crooked** c. be made straight	ELIOT 319:51
c. must attack the form	LAUT 512:29	c. fighting c. minds	MUIR 624:19
c. spits on what is done	HOOD 426:38	c. shall be made straight	BIBLE 108:79
c. when he cannot be an artist	FLAU 339:16	c. timber of humanity	KANT 473:22
c. who justly admires	BEER 74:94	c. winding ways	HERB 414:77
dramatic c. in the daytime	WODE 952:56	shortest line…may be the c. one	BREC 157:92
dramatic c. who is	NATH 632:3	**crop** A runnable stag, a kingly c.	DAVI 264:69
exposing them to the c.	BIER 135:84	**crops** among the gradual c.	SMITH 828:3
function of the c.	BELL 75:34	c. of love and hate	MUIR 624:24
good art c.	GREE 385:1	with increasing c.	SHAK 762:96
good c.…recognizes the adventures	FRAN 346:79	**croquet** good game of C.	REID 710:45
good writer is not…a good book c.	BISH 137:30	higher and dirtier c.-player	WOOL 956:47
in logic a great c.	BUTL 184:66	**cross** an ancient C.	YEATS 967:40
no c. can ignore	QUIL 702:15	bear your c. willingly	KEMP 480:81
novelist…his own most harsh c.	WILS 947:46	cling to the old rugged c.	BENN 80:42
role of the c.?	DIDE 285:68	C. alone has flown the wave	CRANE 252:52
role of the writer and c. divided	BRAD 155:37	c. be uncrossed	ELIOT 319:51
severe though not unfriendly c.	BAGE 54:70	c. is God's truth	BONH 146:22
To be a c.	BERR 87:3	c. of the Legion of Honour	TWAIN 902:47
Too nicely Jonson knew the c.'s part	COLL 237:69	c. the road	HAWK 401:91
truck, a producer or a c.	LEMM 521:32	C. to be Borne	SMITH 830:32
true c. ought to dwell	ADDI 6:32	endured the c.	BIBLE 129:43
critical c. period in matrimony	HERB 413:51	grace without the c.	BONH 146:23
stopped dead at the c. point	SOME 833:10	houses marked with a red c.	PEPYS 674:99
criticising brain stops c.	SLOAN 825:54	In the c. is salvation	KEMP 480:80
criticism As far as c. is concerned	VORS 915:55	let him now come down from the c.	BIBLE 119:46
cant of c.	STER 848:36	little marble c. below the town	HAYES 403:27
contemporary c. reads to me	CHES 221:7	orgasm has replaced the c.	MUGG 623:9
c. is ever inhibited by ignorance	MACM 556:70	shouldered high his voluntary C.	CAMP 194:56
c. is not a body	FRYE 354:53	sign of the C.	BOOK 147:77
C. is part of…democracy	CLIN 231:19	stone remains, and the c.	MACC 546:66
c. of administration	BAGE 54:66	survey the wondrous c.	WATTS 922:46
c.'s motto	FORS 345:48	taketh not his c.	BIBLE 116:73
definition of c.	ARNO 35:13	take up the c…and follow me	BIBLE 120:76
democracy…permits c.	FORS 345:47	take up his c. daily	BIBLE 120:76
dramatic c.…attempt to tattoo	BROWN 164:30	Upon the c.	SITW 823:11
father of English c.	JOHN 463:72	win the Holy C.	MALO 563:16
from science…is c.	RUSS 734:22	**cross-bow** With my c.-b. I shot	COLE 235:10
function of c.	DEWEY 276:20	**cross-breed** unhappy c.-b.	DISR 287:27
I have benefitted greatly from c.	RUMS 731:47	**crossed** c. in love	AUST 46:60
I love c.	COWA 249:62	**crosses** between the c.	MCCR 548:11
Impersonal c.…is like	NATH 632:2	nothing lives but c., cares, and griefs	SHAK 764:43
Poetry…a c. of life	ARNO 36:43	**cross-gartered** c.-g.…she detests	SHAK 786:5
To avoid c.	ANON 27:32	**crossness** make c. and dirt succeed	FORS 344:39
Writing c.	UPDI 906:25	**crossroads** c. of all the evil	GENET 363:40
criticisms most penetrating of c.	HUXL 441:66	mankind faces a c.	ALLEN 14:98
criticize Do not c. your Government	CHUR 226:19	**crossword** skill of a solved c. puzzle	SAND 742:36
criticized Being c.	TRUM 900:89	**crotch** c. of this fig-tree	PLATH 681:37
critic-pen Unboding c.-p.	TENN 872:28	**crouch** c., swivel, tug	OBRI 646:73
critics American c.…universities	ALBEE 11:28	make c. beneath his foot	BROW 169:75
ask anybody, particularly the c.	MATU 582:2	**crow** cock doth c.	BALL 60:83
c. all are ready made	BYRON 186:25	c. doth sing as sweetly	SHAK 770:24
C. are like eunuchs	BEHAN 74:12	c. loves his fledglings	MORE 618:11
c. called him a wheeler-dealer	MANC 564:49	c. Makes wing	SHAK 797:48
C. search for ages	USTI 906:43	dog bark at a c.	SHAK 773:21
gang of c.	VIAN 911:70	louder a cock can c.	TROL 898:37
Having the c. praise you	WALL 918:54	milk-white feather in a c.	CAMP 194:55
if I don't practise…the c. know	PADE 659:13	sun had risen to hear him c.	ELIOT 315:24
In c. hands, beware	BRAD 155:49	upstart c.	GREE 386:33
know who the c. are?	DISR 288:57	**crowbar** straightened out for a c.	HOLM 424:70
'mature' c.	WALK 917:34	**crowd** c. begins to pour in	ROST 727:70
more than all the writing of c.	DU 305:72	c. flowed over London Bridge	ELIOT 318:97
professional c., make me sick	HEMI 409:61	c. is not company	BACON 52:13
questioning among my c.	ARNO 35:10	c. laughs with you always	VIDOR 913:6
Tudor c. who wrote…Prayer Book	ACHE 2:28	c. of courtesans	DUMAS 306:91
Turned c. next	POPE 685:17	c. will always save Barabbas	COCT 233:86
what he thinks about c.	HAMP 395:76	c. without singeing someone's beard	LICH 528:89
critique both an homage and a c.	MOTH 622:86	faces in the c.	POUND 691:92
Crito C., we ought to offer	PLATO 682:57	Far from the madding c.'s	GRAY 384:72
crocodile appeaser…feeds a c.	CHUR 226:13	flock of sheep…make a c.	BEER 73:87

I saw a c.	WORD 960:24
jocosity catches the c.	MARQ 575:50
Out of the c. a mistress	SHEL 815:44
pale and anxious c.	WILDE 939:44
something about a c.	WALL 918:53
Will she pass in a c.	SWIFT 861:27
crowded marriage…was a bit c.	DIANA 276:24
crowds apprehensions come in c.	WORD 960:22
c., her beloved smoke	LAMB 505:79
enterprising firm that supplies c.	SIMP 822:82
talk with c.	KIPL 492:63
crow-flowers Of c.-f., nettles, daisies	SHAK 784:57
crown allegiance to one C.	GEOR 364:54
both divide the c.	DRYD 303:35
cause Against the c.	DRYD 302:75
c. enchased with pearl	MARL 572:98
c. enough to virtue	JONS 468:84
C. has made a purchase	WHIT 934:24
c. of a stranger	MOORE 617:1
c. of our life	SWIN 864:94
c. of sorrow	TENN 871:14
c. of twelve stars	BIBLE 131:9
Ere the King's c. shall fall	SCOTT 754:82
exchange it some day for a c.	BENN 80:42
farm to buy my c.	SHAK 776:99
fill me from the c. to the t.	SHAK 796:15
finest Colonies under the C.	STUA 856:37
from Ceasar's laurel c.	BLAKE 141:27
From the c. of his head	SHAK 774:42
fruition of an earthly c.	MARL 572:85
give thee a c. of life	BIBLE 131:91
hairy gold c.	KIPL 490:92
head that wears a c.	SHAK 772:85
impious hand to the C. of Thorns	BRON 161:65
influence of the C.	DUNN 307:22
King his c. and dignity	SHAK 759:98
Lion and the Unicorn…for the c.	CARR 205:15
Put on my c.	SHAK 795:92
Scepter and c. must tumble down	SHIR 819:20
set the c. upon a stock	HOWA 433:86
strike his father's c.	SHAK 775:62
to wear a c.	ELIZ 322:6
undoubted right of the c. of England	COVE 249:43
virtuous woman is a c.	BIBLE 104:66
wear that c.	HEYW 417:42
within the hollow c.	SHAK 764:52
Word climbs upward into Its c.	DUNC 307:10
worn the c.	BIBLE 113:90
crowned c. knot of fire	ELIOT 321:94
C. with rank fumitor	SHAK 793:19
crowning moment of the Queen's c.	DIMB 286:99
crowns Cast their c. before	BIBLE 131:98
climb soonest unto c.	SHAK 760:15
Give c. and pounds and guineas	HOUS 431:59
last act c. the play	QUAR 701:6
crows roused the ribald c.	SHAK 787:41
thought to keep out the c.	MILT 600:1
crow-toe c.-t., and pale gessamine	MILT 599:91
crucible America is God's C.	ZANG 969:1
cast a violet into a c.	SHEL 816:49
man in the c.	ELKIN 322:17
crucibles agony dancing in his c.	THOM 884:41
crucified choose who is to be c.	COCT 233:86
c. Jesus…picture of God	BAKER 56:3
not been c.?	USTI 906:45
was c., dead, and buried	BOOK 146:37
crucifixion c.…accuses human	BUTT 186:15
get in a whole C.	HUGH 435:25
crucify people would not even c. him	CARL 202:45
crudities c., doubts, and confusions	THOM 884:28
c. of his period	HAMER 393:46
cruel All c. people	WILL 945:21
bottom of the sea is c.	CRANE 252:53
c. brother will you betray	BALL 58:59
C., but composed and bland	ARNO 35:22
C. he looks	SHEL 814:7
c. men of Rome	SHAK 776:4
her c. sports	SPEN 839:60
no attack is too c.	MCCA 546:69
single men…are more c.	BACON 51:74
The man…was essentially c.	QUIL 702:15
crueller nothing c. or more vain	JONG 466:34
cruellest The c. lies	STEV 852:43
cruelty bar against your c.	LANY 508:56
C. is the law	HARDY 397:21
c. is the primary feeling	SADE 737:14
c. without incentive	JOHN 460:86

curlew

Hanging is too good…said Mr C.	BUNY 174:76	produce? The c. clock	WELL 929:93	c. of hot wine	SHAK 799:91
neither kindness or c.	ALBEE 11:21	rainbow and a c.'s song	DAVI 265:91	c. o' kindness	BURNS 178:6
top-full Of direst c.	SHAK 796:15	Responsive to the c.'s note	GRAY 383:55	c. runneth over	BIBLE 100:45
cruise all on our last c.	STEV 852:45	weather the c. likes	HARDY 397:29	death in the c.	BURNS 180:61
crumb craved no c.	GILB 370:70	cuckoo-echoing c.-e., bell-swarmèd	HOPK 428:78	Death's bitter c.	ABU 1:14
crumble the Rockies may c.	GERS 365:80	**cuckoos** Of owls and c., asses	MILT 601:21	Fill the c.	TENN 872:27
when I c., who will remember	DELA 271:29	**cucumber** c. is added to it	MACK 554:14	gold c. won by the worst horse	MASE 580:68
crumbled Hispanic world never c.	REYES 712:69	c. narrow	SITW 823:4	heaven in our c. has thrown	ROCH 719:14
crumbs c.…from the rich man's table	BIBLE 121:96	c. should be well sliced	JOHN 462:32	kiss but in the c.	JONS 467:75
c. of compassion	TUTU 901:23	**cucumbers** sun-beams out of c.	SWIFT 862:46	League and C. double	BUSBY 182:93
dogs eat of the c.	BIBLE 117:4	**cuddled** Who c. you when?	THOM 884:39	let this c. pass from me	BIBLE 119:42
not worthy…to gather up the c.	BOOK 147:72	**cue** With a twisted c.	GILB 370:67	life's enchanted c.	BYRON 187:47
crumpet C. Baking…Company	DICK 278:74	**cuff** Anything said off the c.	SKEL 825:39	my c. shall be full	BOOK 149:10
crumpets buttered scones and c.	ELIOT 317:87	**Cuinchy** C.…was a slaughter yard…	BLUN 137:14	no more personality than a paper c.	CHAN 213:86
crusade moral c., or it is nothing	WILS 948:62	**cuinsque** Mens c. is est	CICE 227:36	Perfect the c. as planned	BROW 168:61
Presidents start out pretending to		**cuisine** c. here in America	CHIR 222:22	remove this c. from me	BIBLE 122:5
run a c.	COOKE 245:72	**cully** Man was…Woman's c.	CONG 240:25	snow-water from a tin c.	SNYD 832:89
crusaders C. have multiplied	BERN 85:65	**culpable** How c. was he	HEAN 405:73	Socrates empties the c. of poison	FEUE 334:1
Crusades triumphs of the C.	RUNC 731:50	**culprit** Stirs the c.	DICK 283:29	still foul the c.	GREY 388:60
crush competition…I c. it	REVS 711:67	**culprits** better to choose the c.	PAGN 659:25	**Cup-a-Soup** let my kid eat C.-a.-S.	PALT 662:75
crust c. of an unfinished earth	KURA 501:42	**cult** c. is a religion with no	WOLFE 953:76	**cupboard** no c. should be barer	LLOY 532:70
Sleep in thy intellectual c.	WORD 957:67	c. of truth	PIER 677:66	wicked man in the bathroom c.	EWART 328:72
crutches Time goes on c.	SHAK 774:35	What's a c.?	ALTM 15:17	**cupboards** c. bursting with skeletons	ORWE 654:33
cry and a c. before	TENN 878:83	**cultivate** C. simplicity, Coleridge	LAMB 505:77	**Cupid** bolt of C. fell	SHAK 767:27
answer to 'Hi!' or to any loud c.	CARR 205:27	**cultivated** C. Underrated Nobleman	GILB 370:71	thrice cut C.'s bow-string	SHAK 774:43
Consider anything, only don't c.	CARR 205:5	**cultivation** structure of her c.	AUCH 42:64	winged C. painted blind	SHAK 767:19
c. I can no more	HOPK 429:88	**cultural** c. and historical role	SMITH 828:1	**cups** c. make any guilty men	JONS 467:70
c. in my bed	AGUS 9:98	C. Cringe	PHIL 677:55	c., That cheer but not inebriate	COWP 251:19
c. of Absence…in the heart	RANS 707:70	C. literacy is the oxygen	HIRS 419:74	in kitchen c.	STEV 849:66
c. or sing, justice must	MARIE 571:74	fight for c. space	NARO 630:53	in their flowing c.	SHAK 776:91
c. that was no more than a breath	CONR 243:30	personalities and c. traditions	WATS 922:41	pour not by c.	SPEN 839:50
c. that we are come	SHAK 793:27	physical and c. distance	VAN 908:12	**cur** 'bout the ears of the old c.	BUTL 185:74
C., the Beloved Country	PATON 669:27	**culture** all kinds of mental c.	MILL 591:94	**curate** average c. at home	FIRB 336:55
c. with you for only a day	VIDOR 913:6	America is…rooted in Negro C.	ROLL 723:90	shabby c. who has strayed	AUDEN 44:10
dying, if we could not c.	MAUP 583:17	arteriosclerosis of c.	MILL 594:92	sit upon the c.'s knee	CHES 221:1
empty compliment to c.	GILB 369:59	as some immense yeast c.	BOYD 153:11	**curates** abundant shower of c.	BRON 161:66
entire soul is a c.	KAZA 474:51	breasts, the hallmark of our c.	DONA 290:5	c. lean, and rectors fat	MACA 544:20
great c. in Egypt	BIBLE 93:60	Britain had a savage c.	BANDA 61:9	C., long dust, will come	BROO 162:93
heard my c.	BIBLE 100:61	Canada…enjoyed…French c.	COLO 238:80	**curb** use the snaffle and the c.	CAMP 194:51
hounds are in c.	SCOTT 752:33	courage in Chinese c.	MO 611:66	**curd** c. of ass's milk	POPE 688:5
If something makes you c.	CLIN 230:6	C.…acquainting…with the best	ARNO 36:32	soother than the creamy c.	KEATS 477:24
Need a body c.?	BURNS 180:55	c. and my language	KELM 479:69	**curds** concupiscent c.	STEV 849:66
new orphans c.	SHAK 797:60	C. is dead	ANON 25:63	queen of c. and cream	SHAK 799:21
no language but a c.	TENN 874:77	C. is the passion for sweetness	ARNO 36:33	**cure** as much for prevention as c.	GRAV 382:35
none to hear my c.	GILM 371:96	C. may…be described simply	ELIOT 321:95	be no more; sad c.	MILT 602:59
nor uttered c.	TENN 873:46	c. of modern painting	MOTH 622:86	cause or c.!	GOLD 376:88
not to be obliged to c.	BEAU 70:5	elaborate defence of c.	ARNO 36:31	c. except as a guillotine	LUCE 541:57
tears which I made her c.	RACI 704:28	evidence of a nation's c.	THUR 890:89	c. for it is occupation	SHAW 810:2
to c. it up	SWIFT 863:64	evolution of c.	LOOS 536:44	c. for this ill	KIPL 491:32
To c. to thee	HERB 414:79	excellence proper to c. itself	REYES 712:69	c. him for you	JUNG 471:47
What shall I c.?	BIBLE 108:79	flourishing c. in our land	MAO 569:94	c. of the id	ANON 24:10
your bald c.	PLATH 681:30	Football is…more central to our c.	GREER 387:46	c. the disease and kill the patient	BACON 52:15
crying all the way that wild high c.	MASE 580:69	genius of American c.	RODR 722:52	labour against our own c.	BROW 165:71
c. all the time	PRES 694:71	handprint of all c.	ANON 27:36	love's a malady without a c.	DRYD 304:50
then not hear it c.!	HERB 414:79	hear anyone talk of c.	JOHST 465:11	Love…the longest to c.	LABR 502:14
cryptograph experience is like a c.	SCHO 748:53	integral part of c.	GOULD 380:77	lunatic beyond all c.	WEBS 927:45
cryptology Maxim of c.	WRIS 963:80	marketers in our c.	GITL 373:31	no c. for this disease	BELL 76:59
crystal as much as a plant or a c.	EMER 324:66	men of c.	ARNO 36:28	no hope for a c.	AUST 46:65
C. sincerity	HOPK 428:66	Modern European c.	SUN 860:95	nothing…a little money will not c.	DURA 307:24
ego that can crack c.	CHEE 218:11	new ways…give a new c.	WERE 931:54	palliate what we cannot c.	JOHN 460:72
glass like unto c.	BIBLE 131:96	no c. of the earth	HOBB 420:2	sin the double c.	TOPL 894:61
hold my lady's head like a c.	HEAN 404:71	only place in our c.	STEI 846:94	there is no c.	HOME 425:97
crystalline his c. streams	SHEL 813:81	pursue C. in bands	WHAR 934:10	think they can c. them	VOLT 914:37
crystallization c.…in a poem	UPDI 906:27	sacred cow of American c.	HUGH 435:27	will c. epilepsy	THEO 882:80
crystals teeth of splintered c.?	BROW 168:54	sad fact about our c.	AUDEN 43:6	**cures** happy…in their c.	BACON 50:41
ten million little ice c.	SCHW 750:93	salvage Europe's c.	ADEN 8:62	If a lot of c. are suggested	CHEK 218:19
Cuba C. is always the best	GUIL 389:87	society and its c.	TRIL 897:18	seeker for c.	RICH 713:8
Havana, C.…high society	CABR 191:18	Speeches in our c.	GALB 357:27	**curfew** c. tolls the knell	GRAY 384:52
whirlpool of C.'s political crisis	CAST 208:80	Tigers…had c.	MACL 554:26	**curiales** Quot c., tot tyranni	SALV 741:96
Cubans when C. get together	LEZA 528:81	tools that go together with c.	REYES 712:69	**curiosities** c. would be quite forgot	AUBR 41:56
cube c. is the basis of architecture	MALL 562:3	unparalleled elsewhere in our c.	SHAP 805:68	**curiosity** c. about alien cultures	BOWL 153:3
divide a c. into two other c.s	FERM 333:94	various grades of c.	NIET 639:17	c. becomes a sin	FRAN 347:85
cubic Picasso paints…a c. shape?	MARC 569:51	vast intuitive c.	SHAF 758:53	c. is the life-blood	TREV 896:4
cubist pictures known…as C.	DAVIS 266:6	Versailles of American corporate c.	WOLFE 953:82	c. of an angel's stare	TATE 867:40
cubists C., or Octagonists	ROOS 725:21	**cultures** all c. of the earth	WEBER 925:12	die when c. goes	SWIFT 861:13
cubits c. this way and that	LAUR 511:22	curiosity about alien c.	BOWL 153:3	hungry c.	GREE 386:21
cubs ape his c.	MORE 618:11	**cumbersome** c. unwieldiness	DONNE 292:45	Love, c., freckles	PARK 664:12
Cuchulain Pearse summoned C.	YEATS 967:38	**cumulative** truly c. and progressive	SART 744:63	Newspapers always excite c.	LAMB 505:88
cuckoldom C. be a discredit	CONG 241:71	**cunning** c. known	POPE 687:95	'satiable c.	KIPL 491:36
cuckoo c. clock style	HEMI 409:59	c. men pass for wise	BACON 52:3	when one has lost all c.	WAUGH 924:97
C., jug-jug, pu-we	NASHE 632:93	need have much c.	BACON 53:28	**curious** c. in unnecessary matters	BIBLE 113:82
c.'s parting cry	ARNO 35:18	want of c. made me bold	SPEN 839:48	Never be c.	ACK 4:67
hear the pleasant c.	DAVI 265:92	what pleated c. hides	SHAK 792:87	What a c. shape it is!	WILDE 941:77
hedge-sparrow fed the c.	SHAK 792:92	**cup** Come fill up my c.	SCOTT 753:52	**curiouser** 'C. and c.!' cried Alice	CARR 203:63
Lhude sing c.!	ANON 21:43	c. is the new testament	BIBLE 126:49	**curl** Who had a little c.	LONG 536:40
merry c., messenger of Spring	SPEN 839:45	c. of bitterness	KING 487:29	**Curle** C.…has been writing letters	ARBU 30:3
One flew over the c.'s nest	KESEY 483:62	c. of full wine	FLET 341:58	**curlew** I could hear a c.	HEAN 405:77

curls

curls held c. to be effeminate — TWAIN 902:42
curragh got into...a c. — BEHAN 74:10
currency Beauty...form of c. — WOLF 952:62
  debauch the c. — KEYN 484:71
  new stamped with their c. — LAMB 505:93
  passed from c. — UPDI 906:36
current boats against the c. — FITZ 338:87
  c. to the source — FROST 352:7
  c. under sea — ELIOT 11:6
  giving a c. to the whole — HOPK 429:85
  misleading guide to c. affairs — KEYN 484:73
currents their c. turn awry — TWAIN 902:63
curriculum vitae c. v. of Civilization — ANDR 18:77
curry hotter than the c. — THAC 880:21
curs cast away upon c. — SHAK 778:62
  common cry of c. — SHAK 799:98
  like to village c. — SHAK 804:43
curse America as a black c. — MILL 593:58
  blessing, is to me a c. — MASS 581:79
  bless them that c. you — BIBLE 115:37
  common c. of mankind — SHAK 786:30
  c. be ended — ELIOT 319:51
  c. begins to act — SCHR 749:63
  c. God, and die — BIBLE 98:93
  c. I must send you — SIDN 820:59
  c. is come upon me — TENN 870:85
  C. not the king — BIBLE 106:33
  c. of children! — WEBS 926:21
  c. of Europe — SENI 757:30
  c. of hell upon the sleek — RANS 707:69
  c. of me and my nation — POUND 691:9
  c. of Scottish literature — MUIR 623:13
  C. on his virtues! — ADDI 7:49
  c. sound like a caress — FOOT 342:79
  C. the blasted, jelly-boned — LAWR 512:40
  c. thee to thy face — BIBLE 98:92
  c. upon your whunstane hearts — BURNS 177:72
  c. when one works for God — LIVI 532:55
  Empty C. — FRAN 348:13
  Ignorance is the c. — SHAK 760:99
  know how to c. — SHAK 803:13
  real c. of Eve — RHYS 712:72
  smite the earth a c. — BIBLE 112:66
  the c. has come upon us — OBRI 646:70
  the c. of a prose — STEP 847:12
  the c. of disobedience — OTWAY 656:98
cursed above all cattle — BIBLE 91:96
  c. is the ground for thy sake — BIBLE 91:98
  I who have c. — WALC 916:9
  We are c., Waldo — SCHR 749:62
curses C. are like young chickens — SOUT 835:50
  c....on each gashed head — SORL 834:33
  c. on my head? — MILT 607:75
cursing began c. the bloody bible — HEMI 409:63
  c. his staff — SASS 745:86
  I have set...blessing and c. — BIBLE 95:97
  proceedeth blessing and c. — BIBLE 130:57
curtain as if the c. never rose — DIDE 285:63
  cloud c. of the future — CARL 200:77
  c. call! — BARR 65:4
  c. was up — KAUF 474:37
  essay...must draw its c. round us — WOOLF 955:19
  prospectors who can't carry a c.? — DOUG 294:97
  slamming down his silly c. — SALI 740:86
  Thy hand...lets the c. fall — POPE 689:48
  When the final c. comes down — MAJOR 561:75
curtains Booze, of course, and then c. — AMIS 16:41
  bottoms of c. — STER 848:39
  c. are drawn with care — MONRO 612:4
  c., never meant to draw — POPE 686:69
  draw the c. — SHAN 805:62
  graves...like drawn c. — RALE 705:45
  Let fall the c. — COWP 251:19
  people...behind those clean lace c. — CHRI 223:36
  she...draws the c. back — OSBO 655:84
  shower c....great modern things — WARH 920:8
  Through windows, and through c. — DONNE 291:25
curtsey C. while you're thinking — CARR 204:91
curve c. of a blue bay — LOWE 539:1
curveship of the c. lend a myth — CRANE 253:58
Curzon met C. in Downing Street — BALD 57:26
cushion c. and soft Dean invite — POPE 686:61
cuspid c.'s last stand — PERE 674:19
cuss bloody town's a bloody c. — BLAIR 138:47
cussing c. and swearin' — STRA 856:38
custard every joke is...a c. pie — ORWE 654:39
custody in the c. of childhood — MISH 609:21

custom c.... of readers...pleased with a book — CONN 242:97
  c. has rendered necessary — DICK 278:63
  C. is the most certain — JONS 468:95
  C. reconciles us to everything — BURKE 175:7
  C. that is before all law — DANI 262:34
  justify a traditional c. — TWAIN 902:43
  lest one good c. — TENN 878:85
  Malay religion and c. — PANG 662:81
  more than c. has pronounced — BRON 161:61
  nor c. stale — SHAK 794:58
  Rather than c. — LEZA 528:81
  Render...c. to whom c. — BIBLE 126:30
  rule by c. not by force — LEGU 520:12
  tea and scandal...ancient c. — CONG 240:35
  till c. make it — SHAK 787:50
  'twill grow into a c. — WEBS 927:48
customer We start with the c. — BEZOS 90:73
customers raising up a people of c. — SMITH 828:87
  skinning your c. — KHRU 485:93
customs c. of his tribe — SHAW 807:10
  c....we hold sacred — ARON 36:48
  habits and c. of the people — RICA 712:79
  ill c. influence my very senses — ETHE 327:48
  laws and c....evolved — POWE 693:59
  such a part of our c. — ALME 14:10
  way to keep up old c. — BAGE 54:63
cut c. it off, and...kill it — POWE 693:54
  C. me to pieces — SHAK 799:6
  c. out of anything — THUR 891:7
  efforts to c. out 50,000 words — WOLFE 953:68
  most unkindest c. of all — SHAK 777:43
  pay me the c. — GOMEZ 377:39
  should have been c. — COWA 249:63
  soon c. off — BIBLE 101:94
cuts c. off twenty years of life — SHAK 777:30
cutting c....people off — FORD 343:13
cuttlefish like c. squirting out ink — ORWE 654:36
cutty sarks c. s. run in your mind — BURNS 179:31
cyberspace C....hallucination — GIBS 367:15
  C. is the funhouse mirror — STER 847:16
  C. is where you are — GIBS 367:16
cycle C. and epicycle, orb in orb — MILT 605:35
  decided to c. to India — MURP 626:73
  Life is a c. — MARC 569:52
cycle-clips c.-c. in awkward reverence — LARK 509:77
cycles know enough about business c. — BECK 71:35
cylinder C. in common fire engines — WATT 922:45
  treat nature by the c. — CEZA 212:52
cymbal talk but a tinkling c. — BACON 52:13
  tinkling c. — BIBLE 126:52
cymbals c. glorious — MAHO 559:34
Cymbry Mon Mam C. — FULL 355:79
cyme What rhubarb, c. — SHAK 798:72
Cymric Clear C. voices — BUNT 173:68
cynic C....A blackguard — BIER 134:73
cynical c. gestures of the poor — SPEN 837:96
  C. is the name we give — FRY 354:40
  I am not c. — WELD 928:91
cynicism better than the c. and...pessimism — WINF 950:97
  C. is an unpleasant way — HELL 408:39
  C. is humour in ill-health — WELLS 930:34
  C. is intellectual dandyism — MERE 588:34
  the worst c. — OATES 643:6
Cynthia round Of C.'s seat — MILT 597:34
cypress correct in c. wood — PARK 664:16
  c.-buss I plantit — YOUNG 968:53
  c. funeral — SPEN 838:20
  Nor waves the c. — TENN 873:49
Cyprian forsake her C. groves — DRYD 303:22
Cyril Nice one, C. — ANON 25:73
Cytherean thronèd C. be fallen — SWIN 864:1
Czechoslovakia dealing with C. — LLOY 533:79

D

dad fuck you up, your mum and d. — LARK 510:89
  girls in slacks remember d. — BETJ 88:35
  not everyone has a d. who talk to your d. — MILI 591:89 / BUSH 182:8
  that person is d. — FALU 329:11
Dada D. began not as — TZARA 904:19
  D. D. D., a howl — TZARA 904:17
  D. means nothing — TZARA 904:16
  mama of d. — FADI 329:5
daddy Are you lost d. — LARD 509:67

D., d., you bastard — PLATH 681:35
  knocked his D. down — HUGH 436:41
daemon divine d. is absolute — BELL 75:35
daffadillies d. fill their cups — MILT 599:91
daffadowndillies Strew me...with d. — SPEN 838:15
daffodil bed of d. sky — TENN 876:25
  shining d. dies — TENN 876:34
daffodils D....before the swallow — SHAK 799:19
  dances with the d. — WORD 960:27
  host, of golden d. — WORD 960:24
  what d. were for Wordsworth — LARK 510:98
daft ae...thinks the tither d. — SCOTT 754:72
  d. or corrupt — FULL 355:77
dagger d. drew and died — SHAK 768:48
  d....in the heart of France — QUIN 702:23
  d. which I see before me — SHAK 796:27
  Distress with d. keen — COLL 237:73
daggers d. in men's smiles — SHAK 797:42
  Give me the d. — SHAK 797:36
  laid their d. ready — SHAK 797:32
  speak d. to her — SHAK 783:31
daily cancer...growing d. — DEAN 267:40
  Yesterday, We had d. cleaning — REED 709:26
dainties never fed of the d. — SHAK 763:12
  spiced d., every one — KEATS 477:24
dais From high on the d. — VIRG 913:13
daises Meadows trim with d. — MILT 599:45
daisies covered...with violets and d.. — SHEL 815:26
  d., those pearled Arcturi — SHEL 816:60
  picking d. on the railway — WODE 952:37
  picks a posy of d. — THOM 884:35
Daisy Sweet D.! oft I talk to thee — WORD 959:97
daisy D. and Lily — SITW 823:10
  Not yellow like a d. — TRUMP 900:97
Dakotas D., I am for war — RED 709:19
  last bear, shot drinking in the D. — CRANE 253:60
Dalai Lama God...has created a D. L. — TUTU 901:27
dale through the lonely d. — BLAKE 139:92
  Through wood and d. — COLE 236:40
Dali D. is...disgusting — ORWE 655:82
Dalí D.'s importance for the Surrealists — SCHW 750:83
  D.'s nature to play Gilbert — RUSS 735:46
  When D. hallucinated — RUSS 735:47
dalliance primrose path of d. — SHAK 781:48
  silken d. in the wardrobe — SHAK 775:64
dam d. it up — ACHE 3:46
  leave the d. — SHAK 769:98
damage pay for the d. — STIG 854:97
Damascus travelled the road to D. — ASHD 37:64
damask Feed on her d. cheek — SHAK 786:1
dame dance in the old d. yet — MARQ 574:45
  La belle d. — KEATS 477:25
  La belle D. sans merci — KEATS 476:3
  sulky sullen d. — BURNS 179:19
  this looser d. did skill — SPEN 838:34
dames Ah! gentle d.! — BURNS 179:21
  laughing d. in who he did delight — BYRON 187:34
  O happy d. — SURR 860:3
  struts his d. before — MILT 597:44
dammed only saved by being d. — HOOD 426:27
damn d. by rule — OTWAY 656:95
  D. the torpedoes! — FARR 330:31
  D. you! — SHAW 807:8
  dear, I don't give a d. — MITC 610:46
  devil the black — SHAK 798:68
  Do I look like I give a d.? — CRAIG 252:50
  give a...d. who you sleep with — DAWK 267:25
  don't give a d. — SALI 740:76
  one d. thing over and over — MILL 592:28
  public doesn't give a d. — BEEC 73:67
  save those who d. them — HUGO 437:70
damnable d. degrees Of drinking — WEBS 926:18
  d. woman's trick — SHAW 807:20
  this d. war — ACHE 3:56
damnation blasted to eternal d.! — SHAW 810:14
  critical d. — WALT 920:97
  d. of almost everybody — INGE 445:31
  deep d. of his taking-off — SHAK 796:20
  which road leads to d. — DYSON 309:60
damnations Twenty-nine distinct d. — BROW 167:11
damned always those d. dishes — FREN 350:52
  among the d. already — SHAW 807:8
  And d. be him — SHAK 798:78
  Another d., thick, square book! — GLOU 374:51
  Beautiful and the D. — FITZ 337:77
  brandy of the d. — SHAW 807:23

darkness

Cromwell, d. to everlasting fame!	POPE 687:90
D. from here to eternity	KIPL 489:75
d. long, dark…dangerous way	GOLD 376:13
d. nice thing	WELL 929:3
If I were d.	KIPL 490:95
must be d. perpetually!	MARL 573:30
the desperate, the d.	JACK 448:2
damozel blessed d. leaned out	ROSS 726:49
damp poisonous d. of night	SHAK 795:75
dampness a slight d.	DE 268:53
damsel d. with a dulcimer	COLE 236:41
d. woll come to you anone	MALO 562:9
Dan from D. to Beersheba	STER 849:52
dance best d. e'er cam to the Land	BURNS 180:44
Can d. a little	ANON 24:15
Ceres will join in the d.	SITW 823:4
D., and Provençal song	KEATS 478:42
d. has begun	BETJ 88:25
d. in the old dame yet	MARQ 574:45
d. is a measured pace	BACON 49:30
d. is a poem	DIDE 285:62
D., little words	WORL 962:53
d. on this ball-floor	BLUN 143:76
d. round in a ring	FROST 353:17
d. round to all Eternity	FLET 340:50
d. the dullest beanbag	NOON 640:45
d. while you can	AUDEN 42:77
daughters of the year shall d.!	BLAKE 139:82
Drink and d.	PARK 664:15
face the music and d.	BERL 84:40
Learn then to d.	DAVI 264:75
Let's have a d.	SHAK 775:59
music…too far from the d.	POUND 692:17
returning lightly d.	THOM 885:64
spectral d., before the dawn	BROO 162:93
sprightly d.	WORD 960:25
teach an elephant to d.	MOSS 622:81
the d. and war	STEIN 845:70
the dancer from the d.	YEATS 966:27
the d. was long	DOWS 296:36
there is nothing to do but d.	ECO 310:17
There's no one way to d.	DEGEN 270:2
there the d. is	ELIOT 319:39
time to d.	BIBLE 105:14
To d. is to discover	SENG 757:29
walk…before they d.	POPE 688:23
When you do d.	SHAK 799:20
Will you, won't you…join the d.?	CARR 204:81
You expect to leave the d.	AGAS 9:83
danced d. down the street	KERO 483:53
d. his did	CUMM 258:69
d. with a man	FARJ 330:21
David d. before the Lord	BIBLE 96:43
ye have not d.	BIBLE 116:79
dancer Curled minion, d.	ARNO 34:96
How can we know the d.	YEATS 966:27
move…like a d.	ELIOT 321:87
Now, D.! Now, Prancer	MOORE 616:63
dancers d. dancing in tune	TENN 876:26
d. quick and quicker flew	BURNS 179:29
Like d. on the ropes	ETHE 327:42
dances doesn't think she d.	GILB 369:61
He capers, he d.	SHAK 773:9
dancing as d. is to walking	WAIN 915:4
Ask Nureyev to stop d.	KING 486:17
common sense, d.	JAMES 433:10
D. is a frenzy and a rage	DAVI 264:73
D. is a wonderful training	MORL 619:38
d. is love's proper exercise	DAVI 264:74
Hard times required furious d.	WALK 917:43
mature women, d.?	FRIEL 351:80
mourning into d.	BIBLE 100:51
pair Of d. pumps	MIDD 590:75
past our d. days	SHAK 765:73
stillness the d.	ELIOT 320:57
the d. floor	YEATS 967:32
very merry, d., drinking	DRYD 304:56
dancing-master manners of a d.-m.	JOHN 459:59
dandelions D. were either sweet	TRAV 896:93
Sheaves of drooping d.	BETJ 88:29
smell of the d.	COOKE 245:75
dandruff cure for d.	LUCE 541:57
dandy d. must aspire to be sublime	BAUD 69:82
dandyism Cynicism is intellectual d.	MERE 588:34
Dane never get rid of the D.	KIPL 492:65
Roman than a D.	SHAK 785:72
Dane-geld paying the D.-g.	KIPL 492:65
danger best way to avoid d.	ROCHE 719:3
bright face of d.	STEV 853:80
but what is d.?	HAWT 401:98
buzzard…is never…in d.	FAUL 331:44
d. in touching	BURNS 180:61
d. is always that he will not recognize	AUCH 42:63
d. is that gauge	LESS 524:94
D. knows full well	SHAK 777:23
d. of being torn with violence	ROSS 725:35
d. of coming back prodigies	AUST 46:73
d. of desire	SHAK 781:46
d. of its tricking the writer	SAND 742:35
D., the spur	CHAP 214:21
d. to all Christendom	INNO 446:48
d. to speak true	JONS 467:76
doctors are the greater d.	JONS 467:50
foresees d. and avoids it	KEYN 484:75
great d. of contagion	WILD 943:48
grouse are in no d.	EDIN 312:51
I realized there was a measure of d.	EARH 310:5
life from grief or d. free	JOHN 459:46
measure of d.	GREE 310:5
never be in d. of Popery	ADDI 7:35
no d. in sweetness and youth	ROCH 720:22
Out of this nettle d.	SHAK 771:42
Pleased with the d.	DRYD 301:71
political d.	GLAD 373:36
razor-edge of d.	WILD 943:45
rest in d. are	ETHE 327:42
run into any kind of d.	BOOK 146:40
The d. is past	POE 683:94
united under the threat of d.	DE 270:93
What d. will it be	SHAK 778:64
When in d., ponder	WAGN 915:3
would be in less d.	NASH 630:57
dangerous Caesar is more d.	SHAK 777:23
d. to climb a mountain	HAWT 401:98
d. to meet it alone	WHAR 934:10
d. to pay it off	SELL 756:16
delays are d.	DRYD 300:28
dirty, d. way	GOLD 376:13
Facility is a d. thing	SLOAN 825:54
generalizations are d.	DUMAS 306:92
have I something in me d.	SHAK 784:67
how d. everything is	STEIN 845:67
Mad, bad, and d. to know	LAMB 504:75
mad, then d.	BENN 79:33
makes it so d.	WILS 947:36
more d. is the abuse	BURKE 175:12
more d. than a mud-puddle	STEIN 845:59
most d. duo	SCAR 746:14
Nothing is more d.	ALAIN 10:14
Nothing is so d.	WILDE 942:11
potentially d.	JONES 465:20
Science becomes d.	SHAW 809:79
Sentiment was the more d.	GREE 386:7
sincerity is a d. thing	WILDE 940:59
some inquiries are too d.	SAGAN 737:24
such men are d.	SHAK 776:12
dangers appalling d. of family life	HUXL 441:73
d. thou canst make us scorn!	BURNS 179:27
limit the d. of this age	KENN 482:25
loved me for the d.	SHAK 788:95
perils and d. of this night	BOOK 146:43
Daniel D. come to judgement	SHAK 770:14
Dante D. makes me sick	VEGA 910:47
D. or Michelangelo	MULL 624:53
D. turned round violently	JOYCE 470:20
D., who loved well	BROW 160:63
dapper d. from your napper	COLL 237:63
dappled for d. things	HOPK 428:72
long d. grass	YEATS 965:10
dare art doesn't d. you	HUST 440:46
bear to live, or d. to die	POPE 687:87
d. lift a hand	JOHN 458:24
d. to eat a peach?	ELIOT 317:68
d., to slay Owen Roe O'Neil?	DAVIS 266:7
helps those who d.	VIRG 913:20
must have the courage to d.	DOST 294:90
Nobody'll d.	HUGH 434:9
They wouldn't d.	BARR 65:99
what others only d. to think	CHAR 215:28
dared d. to dream	OBAMA 644:41
never d. be radical	FROST 352:12
dares Who d., wins	ANON 24:21
daring d. of a moment's surrender	ELIOT 318:11
D. Young Man	SARO 744:57
dash of d.	SNOW 831:73
serious d. starts from within	WELTY 931:49
dark all aroun' in the d.	STEI 845:83
all before was d.	WENT 931:53
Between the d. and the daylight	LONG 536:34
blind man in a d. room	DARW 263:60
children fear to go in the d.	BACON 50:57
children talking…in the d.	DE 275:10
Climb to our proper d.	YEATS 967:38
colours will agree in the d.	BACON 50:61
come out after d.	WODE 952:56
d. and stormy night	BULW 173:63
D. as the Grave	LOWRY 541:44
D. as the world of man	SITW 823:11
d. backward and abyss of time?	SHAK 803:10
d. in light expos'd	MILT 607:84
D. is Light Enough	FRY 353:35
d.…Of night	YEATS 966:12
d. place where it leads	JONG 466:29
d. time of the year	ELIOT 318:17
d. was talking to the dead	MACN 558:6
d. with something more than night	CHAN 213:97
Death…drop from the d.	ROSE 725:33
don't be afraid of the d.	HAMM 394:65
drawing you fall over in the d.	HIRS 419:75
For d. hour or twain	SHAK 797:43
naked in the d. and cold	LEGU 520:8
never to refuse a drink after d.	MENC 586:96
night…like a great d. wing	RAND 706:57
O d. d. d.	ELIOT 320:57
one tunnel, d. and solitary	SABA 736:2
on that d. earth	TENN 877:61
Out in the d.	THOM 885:65
real d. night of the soul	FITZ 338:94
round from the d. and the light	SWIN 864:12
sinks his ship in the d.	CORN 247:6
the d. well	PRIC 695:83
very d., and no brightness	BIBLE 111:53
Walk behind me d. and d.	GRAV 382:19
ways that are d.	HARTE 400:42
we are for the d.	SHAK 795:89
what d. days seen.	SHAK 802:71
what in me is d. Illumine	MILT 601:31
when it was yet d.	BIBLE 123:64
With d. forgetting	DANI 262:31
work in the d.	JAMES 450:47
darken days d. round me	TENN 878:84
darkies colored people…replaced d.	FEIF 332:56
darkling here as on a d. plain	ARNO 33:67
darkness called you out of d.	BIBLE 130:67
cast away the works of d.	BOOK 147:51
cast out into outer d.	BIBLE 116:57
children of d.	BEND 78:14
d. again and a silence	LONG 536:37
d. and silence reign	LEAR 516:28
d. beautiful with thee	TENN 874:85
D. came down	THAC 880:26
d. comprehended it not	BIBLE 122:16
d. crumbles away	ROSE 725:30
d. falls at Thy behest	ELLE 322:19
D. falls like a wet sponge	ASHB 37:55
d. from light	BROW 169:63
d. he called Night	BIBLE 91:82
d. of the grave	MILL 592:27
d. ridged the riven dark	FREE 350:48
d. shall be the light	ELIOT 320:57
d. shot with lightning	OFAO 647:96
d.…sifts through your hand	ASHB 37:56
D. spreads his…wings	MILT 597:41
d. takes the edge off daylight	MOTI 622:88
d. visible Served only	MILT 601:35
d. was upon the face of the deep	BIBLE 90:80
Dawn on our d.	HEBER 406:98
day of the Lord be d.	BIBLE 111:53
design of d.	FROST 352:17
during the days of d.	PETA 675:36
first place of liquid d.	FRAME 346:76
Flags wearily through d.	SHEL 814:3
goeth in d.	BIBLE 112:68
Go out into the d.	HASK 400:81
he counteracts the powers of d.	SMART 826:62
Hell's d. under his feet	CARL 201:36
him who gropes painfully in d.	CARL 200:97
horror of outer d.	GORD 378:54
In that d. camaraderie	HUGH 435:35
in the d. and the cold	STEV 854:89
in the d. bind them	TOLK 893:45

darling

Is d., the fruit	SWIN 864:94
Lighten our d.	BOOK 146:43
Light out of d.!	MILT 607:71
light out of d.	DONNE 293:72
lots o' d.	MACD 549:28
make d. more visible	EDGE 311:41
men loved d.	BIBLE 122:26
minute of d.	RUSH 732:66
no d. but ignorance	SHAK 786:22
not d. but shadow	FRYE 354:57
Of d. till it smil'd	MILT 598:71
Of now done d.	HOPK 429:89
people that walked in d.	BIBLE 107:59
people which sat in d.	BIBLE 114:25
profounder the surrounding d.	HUXL 441:58
rear of d. thin	MILT 597:44
Ring out the d.	TENN 875:96
season of D.	DICK 282:94
seen in the d.	FRIE 351:75
shades of d.	DELA 271:33
Shares the d.	MILL 592:21
Surely the d. shall cover me	BIBLE 103:44
Swaddled with d.	ELIOT 317:83
sweeping through the d.	WORD 957:71
there's d.	SHAK 793:22
to d., on extended wings	STEV 849:71
torrent of d.	NOYES 642:70
turned around from d. to light	PLATO 682:65
two eternities of d.	NABO 628:3
universal d. buries all	POPE 628:48
Where there is d.	FRAN 347:99
darling bride and my d. to be?	BALL 59:65
Charlie he's my d.	BURNS 180:56
d. buds of May	SHAK 800:37
getting someone to call you d.	BARN 64:72
darlings d. of daytime!	KEND 480:85
darts fiery d. of the wicked	BIBLE 128:95
Darwinian D. principle	WILDE 940:60
dash d. away! Dash away!	MOORE 616:63
d. of daring	SNOW 831:73
d. of waves	ARNO 35:1
d. themselves to pieces	SHAK 761:38
data constellations of d.	GIBS 367:15
graphical representation of d.	GIBS 367:15
date all too short a d.	SHAK 800:37
arrive but at the d.	WALL 918:61
born...out of d.	POUND 691:99
d. which will live in infamy	ROOS 724:14
doubles your chances for a d.	ALLEN 14:88
merely a d. on a page	THOM 885:69
Name and d.	BUNT 173:66
out of d., obsolete	STEV 849:62
they d. from it	TWAIN 902:49
dated might become d. for a while	HAWES 401:86
dates blind d. are a way of life	EPST 327:34
ripping out the d.	LEAC 515:8
daughter begins to think of the d.	EDGE 311:47
dance like a plumber's d.	MIDD 590:71
d. and the Moor	SHAK 788:85
d. loved a man	SHAK 786:99
d. of a hundred Earls	TENN 871:9
d. of Earth and Water	SHEL 813:77
d. of the gods	TENN 869:75
d. of the Southern Cross	FRAN 348:23
d. to his blood	SHAK 769:90
Don't put your d. on the stage	COWA 249:54
Elderly, ugly d.	GILB 368:29
Filled her with a d.	MILT 597:42
Gigantic d. of the West	TENN 875:5
King o' Spain's d.	COLUM 238:89
kyngis d. of the londe	MALO 562:8
lost your d. to...men	FERRE 334:98
loves my d.	SHAK 799:23
loveth son or d.	BIBLE 116:73
marry My d. Jill	NASH 631:72
Nokomis bore a d.	LONG 535:28
Squire's own d.	GRAV 383:40
Thou art thy father's d.	SHAK 778:63
To my d. Leonora	WODE 952:44
youngest d. does not love thee	SHAK 792:85
daughters d. are inclined to love	MONT 613:13
d. of her daughter	SHAK 762:96
d. of Jerusalem	BIBLE 107:42
d. of musick shall be brought low	BIBLE 106:36
d. of the year shall dance!	BLAKE 139:82
Earth's heedless sons and d.	BLUN 143:75
love among the d.	BIBLE 107:40
outraging their wives and d.	GENG 363:43
sons and d. of Life's longing	GIBR 367:13
sons and your d. shall prophesy	BIBLE 111:48
wives and d. chaste	MOLI 611:74
Your d....will be married	WALP 919:75
Daumier one small Goya or a D.	AUDEN 42:75
dauntless d. in war	SCOTT 752:21
dauphin Daylight's d.	HOPK 428:76
David born this day in the city of D.	BIBLE 120:69
D. danced before the Lord	BIBLE 96:43
D. his ten thousands	BIBLE 96:40
D. was old and stricken in years	BIBLE 97:51
once in royal D.'s city	ALEX 13:63
Philistine said unto D.	BIBLE 96:39
upon the throne of D.	BIBLE 107:60
daVinci d. V. and the Renaissance	WELL 929:93
Davy D. Abominated gravy	BENT 82:1
dawn brown fog of a winter d.	ELIOT 318:97
d. broke like a face	SASS 745:82
d. comes up like thunder	KIPL 489:81
d. in the mountains	MURP 626:75
d. of intellectual enlightenment	CURZ 260:5
d. seem to be an alleviation	WILD 943:38
day doth d.	BALL 60:83
fight it at the d.	BALL 58:59
gathers God at d.	CRANE 253:70
grey d. breaking	MASE 580:50
grey d. of the morning after	ADE 7:59
I said to D.	THOM 886:82
I saw d. upon them	RAND 706:58
Lasses a-lilting before the d.	ELLI 322:25
magic of its d.	RUSS 735:42
Near the face of d.	MERE 587:24
No d.—no dusk	HOOD 426:36
peep of d.	GRAY 384:76
prays...that the d. may ripen	CARL 200:91
ray, and find no d.	MILT 603:74
redemption's happy d.	CASW 208:83
see by the d.'s early	CUMM 257:58
seen d. and sunset on moors	MASE 580:57
soft as the d.	THUR 890:75
spectral dance, before the d.	BROO 162:93
the white d.	SHEL 813:93
to reflect the d.	MACA 545:41
trees at d.	ARNO 34:77
dawning d. of the day	DONNE 293:72
daws For d. to peck at	SHAK 788:82
day a hard d.'s night	LENN 521:41
all I'd do all d.	SALI 740:81
all things all d. long	TENN 877:48
apple a d.	ANON 28:49
argue that I shall some d. die	LEAC 515:9
babbling, and remorseful d.	SHAK 759:93
better future and a brighter d.	SMUTS 831:70
bisy larke, messager of d.	CHAU 217:82
born on a d.	VALL 907:8
breaks the blank d.	TENN 873:63
bright d. is done	SHAK 795:89
bright d. that brings forth	SHAK 776:15
brings about the d.	SHAK 760:9
bring to the light of d.	FRIE 351:75
buried the d.	ELIOT 319:42
burn and rave at close of d.	THOM 884:27
But one d., one cold winter's d.	HOFF 422:32
by d. in a pillar of a cloud	BIBLE 93:62
By d. I shall be well	ARNO 34:73
By night or d.	WORD 959:5
cares, that infest the d.	LONG 535:23
centre, and enjoy bright d.	MILT 598:72
close of d.	YEATS 966:18
coldness of one particular d.	MOOD 615:53
committed unto him against that d.	BIBLE 129:26
compare thee to a summer's d.?	SHAK 800:37
course-compelling D.	PATM 669:21
damnable iteration d. after d.	STEAD 843:31
dawning of the d.	DONNE 293:72
d. and night shall not cease	BIBLE 92:11
d. and the way we met	SWIN 864:2
d. becomes more solemn and serene	SHEL 812:57
d. brought back my night	MILT 601:28
D. by d. make it new	POUND 692:27
d. cometh	BIBLE 112:65
d. consists of twenty-four hours	LECO 518:81
d. doth daw	BALL 60:83
d. for each of us	ANOU 28:66
d. he missed his loving bride	NASH 631:70
d. I can already remember	VALL 907:10
d. in April	SHAK 769:97
D. in Night	CRAS 253:78
d. in thy courts	BIBLE 101:90
d. I wish to be only a	NIET 638:96
d. joins the past eternity	BYRON 188:60
d. light such a candle	LATI 511:13
d. look ruefully on	STEV 853:81
d. may daw	BURNS 178:12
d....meant not to see	THAT 881:60
D., night...but in Britain?	SHAK 803:1
d. of his death	AUDEN 43:90
d. of their flight	MACA 545:37
d. of the Lord	BIBLE 130:76
d., Peace, plenty	NASHE 632:94
d.'s garish eye	MILT 598:58
d.'s hard work in thy life	LAWR 513:69
d. that I die	MCLE 554:22
d. thou gavest, Lord, is ended	ELLE 322:19
d. was lost, for art	LEWIS 527:73
d. we started to fight	ANON 26:94
d. when heaven was falling	HOUS 432:71
d. which the Lord hath made	BIBLE 102:22
d. will not follow night	TATE 867:41
d. you stop becoming	MILL 593:40
deal with all d. long	STEI 846:94
death will have his d.	SHAK 764:50
did just nothing all the d.	PRIOR 696:7
dim night of this immortal d.	SHEL 814:19
dog will have his d.	SHAK 784:68
Drunk many times a d.	SHAK 788:76
each d. is like a year	WILDE 942:85
end of a perfect d.	BOND 145:17
every blessèd d.	WILB 939:37
Every d., in every way	COUE 248:21
every d. is a life	ONEI 651:64
every d. Speaks a new scene	QUAR 701:6
every d. surmount a fear	EMER 325:92
every d. to be lost	JOHN 464:97
eye of d.	YEATS 966:28
far from the light of d.	ORAH 652:90
first d.	BIBLE 123:64
first d.	BIBLE 91:82
For a d. and a night	SWIN 864:12
for a year and a d.	LEAR 516:36
glorious d.	WORD 962:52
good d. to get out anything we want to bury	MOORE 616:71
Good morning to the d.	JONS 466:45
Good things of d.	SHAK 797:49
great d. of his wrath is come	BIBLE 131:2
grievance for the d.	MANS 567:4
Gwine to run all d.	FOST 345:53
Happy as the d. is long	RODR 722:52
have had my d.	TURN 901:21
have their d. and cease	TENN 873:56
heaven to gaudy d. denies	BYRON 189:80
hour or a d.	NASHE 632:90
ideal d. for football	SMITH 830:30
If it be a hot d.	SHAK 772:73
I have come to this d.	TAKU 866:13
in respect to this d.	DONNE 293:73
In the d., in the night	WHIT 938:9
It felt like a new d.	WINF 949:91
it sufficeth that the d. will end	SHAK 778:54
jocund d. Stands tiptoe	SHAK 766:2
journey take the whole long d.?	ROSS 726:45
Joy ruled the d.	DRYD 304:57
July's d. as short	SHAK 799:9
knell Of a spent d.	CRANE 253:70
knell of parting d.	GRAY 384:62
knowest not what a d. may bring	BIBLE 105:99
known a better d.	SCOTT 752:9
lamp of d.	DOUG 295:2
last d. as on the first	KLEE 494:4
last d. of 1943	HARD 396:93
lease...from d. to d.	ANOU 28:60
left alone with our d.	AUDEN 42:76
let the d. be time enough	DANI 262:31
Let the d. perish	BIBLE 98:94
light of common d.	WORD 959:8
live each d. as though one's last	AURE 45:47
live murmur of a summer's d.	ARNO 34:48
long glare of d.	SHEL 812:54
looking the whole d. long	ANON 23:2
make Perpetual d.	MARL 573:30
merry as the d. is long	SHAK 773:24
merry heart goes all the d.	SHAK 799:16

dead

midnight, and it is the d.'s	DONNE 291:29	warm precincts of the cheerful d.	GRAY 384:74	salad d.	SHAK 794:54
misery From this d.	MILT 606:63	Was the gradual d.	SPEN 837:94	seemed unto him but a few d.	BIBLE 93:34
morning after is the first d.	MACN 558:8	wealth abides...but for a d.	EURI 328:65	seven d. war	MUIR 624:23
morning shows the d.	MILT 607:77	Went the d. well?	ANON 24:25	siege of battering d.	SHAK 801:57
my d. was coming	RICH 714:14	when our d. was fair	HARDY 397:28	Six d. of the week it soils	LARK 509:79
myrie someris d.	CHAU 216:61	when will this long weary d.	SPEN 839:51	somewhat troublesome d.	FOST 345:52
needs every d.	WILD 943:47	world's great d.	MUIR 624:24	Talk of our enlightened d.	MANS 567:94
never finds the d.	SHAK 798:63	**daybreak** d. through the gateways	SASS 746:2	teach us to number our d.	BIBLE 101:95
news of the d.	LIPP 531:37	**daydreams** d.-d. of melancholy men	DRYD 299:11	Ten D. That Shook	REED 710:36
night of this worrisome d.	BERN 86:77	exotic d.	NABO 629:21	the d. dividing	SWIN 863:83
night shineth as the d.	BIBLE 103:44	other d.	HAMM 394:59	though fall'n on evil d.	MILT 605:27
no d. for me to look upon	SHAK 759:68	**day-labour** God exact d.-l.	MILT 601:26	three whole d. together	SUCK 858:72
no proper time of d.	HOOD 426:36	**daylight** Between the...d.	LONG 536:34	Time in hours, d., years	VAUG 909:39
Nor brought too long a d.	HOOD 426:22	buried by d.	PEPYS 674:2	walking for d., for months	ROBBE 716:63
not a second on the d.	COOK 245:64	darkness takes the edge off d.	MOTI 622:88	was a habit in those d.	ROGE 723:81
not going to have a good d.	LANCE 506:24	d. atheist	BEHAN 74:13	What are d. for?	LARK 509:72
not to me returns D.	MILT 506:24	d.-l. in the mind	ADDI 6:34	what dark d. seen.	SHAK 802:71
Now is come a darker d.	SHEL 812:65	kingdom of D.'s dauphin	HOPK 428:76	wi' her a' my simmer d.	SOUT 835:41
now is the d. of salvation	BIBLE 127:72	let in d. upon magic	BAGE 54:75	young d. of gathering flowers	PEAC 671:55
Now's the d.	BURNS 180:47	long and lone d.	SHEL 816:65	**day-spring** d.-s. born; here leave	MILT 607:81
obscure d. by d.	THOM 883:6	rule never to drink by d.	MENC 586:96	**day-star** d.-s. in the ocean bed	MILT 600:94
one d. as a lion	MUSS 627:90	see a church by d.	SHAK 773:25	**daytime** never met in the d.	THUR 891:9
one d....does not make a man	ARIS 31:20	When d. comes, comes in the light	CLOU 232:49	**deacons** jawbones of d.	THOM 884:47
One d. telleth another	BOOK 148:9	**days** All d. are nights	SHAK 801:50	**dead** Adonais—he is d.!	SHEL 815:27
one d., the light	MANS 567:3	Ancient of D.	SMITH 831:65	all d. men	BIBLE 93:61
One d. will flash	LERN 523:81	as the d. ran on	THUR 890:84	as good as d.	EINS 313:80
on the d. it is finished	ICHI 444:12	As thy d., so shall thy strength be	BIBLE 95:2	being d. is hard work	RILKE 715:38
On the Last D.	EWART 328:76	beauty can lie...in d.	FOWL 346:65	Bene they all d.	SPEN 838:37
ordinary d. in the modern world	PERCY 674:10	Beauty...in the house three d.	SHAW 808:34	better to be d.	NASH 630:61
or in the shortest d.	SURR 860:4	better than length of d.	AESC 8:79	Blessed are the d.	BIBLE 132:13
our long love's d.	MARV 577:90	brave d. of old	MACA 546:68	bring the d. to life	GRAV 382:23
passing of a d.	SPEN 838:33	burnt-out ends of smoky d.	ELIOT 317:70	brother was d., and is alive again	BIBLE 121:92
pause in the d.'s occupation	DE 275:11	came to the Ancient of d.	BIBLE 111:43	Bunny had been d. for several weeks	TARTT 867:33
pause in the d.'s occupations	LONG 536:34	Channel in the mad march d.	MASE 580:56	But he's d., but he's d.	DAVIS 266:8
perfect d. nor night	SHAK 760:7	count eternity in d.?	ROET 722:62	but in fact it is d.	MITF 610:58
Pleasures shorter than the d.	WALL 918:57	d. are as grass	BIBLE 102:10	By his d. smile	OWEN 657:33
present d. magazine	LOWE 540:39	d. are evil	BIBLE 128:91	Christ being raised from the d.	BIBLE 125:12
problems of our own d.	POEL 683:95	d. are swifter	BIBLE 98:98	Christ risen from the d.	BIBLE 127:57
rain it raineth every d.	SHAK 792:9	d. at the morn	BROW 167:9	Come not, when I am d.	TENN 873:53
rain it raineth every d.	SHAK 786:25	d. darken round me	TENN 878:84	Come up and be d.!	DICK 283:23
rising fogs prevail upon the d.	DRYD 300:44	d. go by, I remain	APOL 29:82	communication Of the d.	ELIOT 321:83
runs through the roughest d.	SHAK 796:10	d. grow short	ANDE 17:72	communism is a d. dog	SOLZ 833:7
said nothing all the d.	DONNE 292:43	d....like a wayward tune	YEATS 965:5	concert is d.	GOULD 379:72
second d., they took	NGU 636:66	d. of glory	PETA 675:36	conference With the d.!	WEBS 927:59
seek all d.	SHAK 769:73	d. of long ago	LIND 530:22	converse with the mighty d.	THOM 887:4
seest the twilight of such d.	SHAK 801:62	d....of my pilgrimage	BIBLE 93:48	Culture is d.	ANON 25:63
see this d. and live	SHAK 776:89	d. of my youth	SOUT 835:44	dark was talking to the d.	MACN 558:6
Seize the d.	HORA 429:6	d. short	ANDR 18:79	d. and gone	YEATS 966:17
shadows in a sunshine d.?	MARL 573:16	d. that are no more	TENN 872:41	d. and gone, lady	SHAK 784:48
So foul and fair a d.	SHAK 795:3	d. that are no more	TENN 872:42	d. and half alive	BETJ 88:14
soporific stew of every d.!	SARD 743:51	d. that are no more	TENN 872:43	D.! and so great	NERO 633:21
So tedious is this d.	SHAK 766:96	d. that are to try men's souls	WILS 949:77	d. and turned to clay	SHAK 784:65
speaks to you every d.	TOCQ 893:33	d. that have gone by	FLEC 340:36	d. are living	MACM 556:72
stand at the latter d.	BIBLE 98:8	d. that make us happy	MASE 580:66	d. are raised up	BIBLE 116:76
such a d. tomorrow as today	SHAK 799:7	d. were our mechanics	LEUP 525:14	d. bury their d.	BIBLE 116:60
sunny d.	GREE 385:2	d. when work was scrappy	CHES 221:2	d., but in the Elysian fields	DISR 288:64
support us all the d.	NEWM 635:46	death my d. should expiate	SHAK 800:40	d. come loupin' owre	MACD 549:20
Sweet d., so cool	HERB 414:80	dirk and drublie d.	DUNB 306:5	d. don't die	LAWR 513:64
tender eye of pitiful d.	SHAK 797:47	drawing d. out	SHAK 777:29	D. for a ducat, d.	SHAK 784:37
The busy d.	SHAK 787:41	E're half my d.	MILT 601:26	d. have come to take the living	DELI 272:43
the cool of the d.	ELIOT 319:25	Even as our d. do grow	SHAK 789:9	D. Heart of Australia	GREG 387:53
the d. you stop suffering	WILL 945:97	few the d. are that hold	MILL 593:40	d. know not any thing	BIBLE 106:26
The long d. wanes	TENN 870:2	fifteen or twenty d. longer	PERTH 675:31	d. level of provincial existence	ELIOT 315:34
The longest d.	STOWE 856:32	For forty d.	SITW 824:21	D., long dead	TENN 876:30
There's night and d., brother	BORR 151:69	for the rest of my d.	PLATH 681:38	d. man is the best fall guy	CHAN 213:92
the wave's intenser d.	SHEL 813:81	friends of other d.	ROBI 718:89	d. man without...the panoply	DAVI 265:83
third d. comes a frost	SHAK 805:52	full of d., riches, and honour	BIBLE 98:84	d. many times	PATER 668:9
this d.'s life as yours	EURI 328:53	genius of our d.	LARI 509:70	D. men are serious	FIND 336:44
this d. to find myself	TENN 877:69	glamour Of childish d.	LAWR 512:46	D. men never repent	DICK 278:66
this d. to the ending of the world	SHAK 776:92	glorious d.	GILB 369:53	d. might as well speak to the living	CATH 208:89
those who dwell in realms of d.	BLAKE 141:44	good d. speed and depart	MART 576:75	d. more than half	MILT 607:84
thousand years as one d.	BIBLE 130:75	Happy D. are Here Again	YELL 967:43	d. of winter	ELIOT 318:17
Three hours a d.	TROL 898:56	high, clear d.	CHAT 216:52	d. one lay moaning	SMITH 830:37
till our wedding d.	COLUM 238:88	if ever come perfect d.	LOWE 539:7	D. perfection, no more	TENN 875:14
time to call it a d.	COMD 239:93	In bygone d., Morag	LAUR 511:23	d. reign	ZOLA 970:16
Today's the d. the Teddy Bears	BRAT 157:79	In olden d. a glimpse	PORT 690:68	d. returning lightly	THOM 885:69
to fill our d.	KIPL 492:60	in the d. of villainy?	SHAK 771:55	d. shall be raised incorruptible	BIBLE 127:62
tomorrow is another d.	MITC 610:47	In the future d.	ROOS 724:13	d. shall not have died	LINC 529:9
true judgment d.	ANON 22:74	in these last d.	BIBLE 129:33	D. shepherd	SHAK 779:4
twelfth d. of my diet	PIER 677:69	in those d. ambition	LAGE 504:69	d. to sin	BIBLE 125:11
Underneath D.'s azure eyes	SHEL 812:64	Length of d. is in her right hand	BIBLE 104:55	d. which he slew at his death	BIBLE 96:20
unhappy d. too late	SHAK 764:48	live laborious d.	MILT 599:86	d., who will not fight	GREN 388:57
until polling d.	WHIT 937:84	Newgate in our schoolboy d.	DICK 277:39	D., your Majesty	DICK 281:74
up by break of d.	HERB 413:59	nights and down the d.	THOM 886:81	Death will come when thou art d.	SHEL 816:54
vehicle for the thought of our d.	FORD 343:93	number of my d.	BOOK 149:14	deeper insights to the d. belong	FERG 333:83
wake in the d. to find	LAWR 514:89	one of my well-looking d.	GOLD 376:10	democracy of the d.	CHES 220:69
wandering all d.	PRIOR 696:11	remember the d. of Old	MOORE 617:10	distance that the d. have gone	DICK 284:55

dead-born

dropping of the d. WILL 944:64
dry and d. SNYD 832:91
Either he's d. or my watch MARX 578:19
ended and d. GLAS 374:46
England mourns for her d. BINY 135:99
enough room...to bury your d. men CORW 247:7
fain to carry the d. PEPYS 674:2
fairy...falls down d. BARR 65:86
Faith without works is d. BIBLE 130:54
fear of the d. ACKR 3:62
fell as his feet as d. BIBLE 131:88
food that d. men eat DOBS 289:78
fool than to be d. STEV 852:46
for the d. remeid is none DUNB 306:4
found him with the d. WILDE 942:15
globe of d. THOM 883:8
healthy and wealthy and d. THUR 890:74
hear the D. March play KIPL 489:84
Heraclitus, they told me you were d. CORY 247:8
Here Vaughan lies d. SASS 746:1
heroic happy d. CUMM 257:59
her warrior is d. TENN 873:46
Hitler was d. SCHA 747:19
home among the d. SHEL 815:45
house where there was not one d. BIBLE 93:60
if this is pleasure we'd rather be d. COWA 249:45
if you were d. KNOB 495:12
imagined for the mighty d. KEATS 476:85
immortal spirit of the d. SPEN 837:12
in the den...nine d. men BALL 59:60
Joe, long d. SLES 825:52
judge the quick and the d. BOOK 146:37
just as easy for your d. to visit you BELL 78:93
just at this d. hour SHAK 780:29
kissed by the English d. OWEN 657:27
lain for a century d. TENN 876:28
lasting mansions of the d. CRAB 251:25
law hath not been d. SHAK 87:55
literature...very d. LEWIS 527:60
little cousin is d. RANS 706:67
live a life half d. MILT 607:86
liveth, and was d. BIBLE 131:89
living and the d. CIXO 227:42
Lycidas is d., d. ere MILT 599:82
main thing...is that he be d. HONE 425:15
make sure he was d. GOLD 77:28
make the d. live KNEL 494:8
marks our English d. KIPL 490:9
may be d. ground REED 709:28
might as well be bloody d. BLAIR 138:48
millions of the mouthless d. SORL 834:33
Mindful of the unhonoured d. GRAY 384:75
more to say when I am d. ROBI 718:88
most of 'em d. SASS 745:86
most of my friends are d. FENT 332:60
Most of the d. were poor THOM 83:2
Most people my age are d. STEN 847:10
Most poets are d. GRAV 383:36
mother...must be d. AUST 45:50
Naked and the D. MAIL 559:36
networks of d. speech STARK 843:23
not D., but feed the grass TATE 867:39
not for the d. HERN 414:92
not the one d. FROST 352:99
novel is d. DELI 271:39
Now thou art d. CAREW 198:48
of the happier d. TENN 877:62
only d. thing that THOM 885:59
only good Indian is a d. Indian SHER 816:68
Over my d. body KAUF 474:43
over the rich D.! BROO 162:90
pattern...Of d. and living ELIOT 320:68
praise the d. which are already d. BIBLE 106:16
Private Means is d. SMITH 830:42
quite for ever d.! CONG 241:53
raise the d. BIBLE 116:67
rather be d. HAMI 394:50
recently-d. fish ORWE 654:41
remember me before I'm d. BRAND 156:62
Remember me when I am d. DOUG 295:3
remind me of the d. SASS 745:91
rescue the d. IGNA 445:18
risen from the d. BIBLE 127:57
Sabbath of the d. MACL 555:31
salutation of the d. ROBI 718:89
savaged by a d. sheep HEAL 404:64
saw the d., small and great BIBLE 132:22

Sea shall give up her d. BOOK 149:39
She munched, half d. SMITH 828:3
She, she is d. DONNE 292:61
Shone round him o'er the d. HEMA 409:58
shrouded oft our martyred d. CONN 242:84
Some people are better off d. CHAN 213:88
Something was d. in each of us WILDE 942:19
soul so d. SCOTT 752:16
speak for sixty thousand d.! HUGH 436:49
still as the d. BLUN 143:73
stopped d. at the critical point SOME 833:10
strike me d. SHAK 795:80
The man is d.! WHIT 938:18
the president is d. ODON 647:94
The sleeping and the d. SHAK 797:36
they're a' d. ANON 23:84
This is the d. land ELIOT 317:95
thou being d. art God SWIN 864:1
though he were d., yet shall he live BIBLE 123:46
'tis Death is d. SHEL 815:41
to be said For being d. BENT 82:98
tombs of its illustrious d. HOWE 433:91
took their wages and are d. HOUS 432:71
to the d. we owe...truth VOLT 914:44
town...buried its d. SHAW 811:33
two d. and the other dying DOCH 289:80
two worlds, one d. ARNO 35:4
unheroic D. who fed the guns? SASS 746:99
until he's read...After that it's d. WAUGH 924:75
upon all the living and the d. JOYCE 470:18
useless to the d. RICH 713:98
vastly more ways of being d. DAWK 266:17
voice of the d. TENN 877:67
wakes or sleeps with the enduring d. SHEL 815:38
walking d. man ANON 27:26
was I d. before I was alive BROW 165:67
was living is now d. ELIOT 318:8
we are all d. KEYN 484:73
Weep me not d. DONNE 291:35
what we call d. is only changed CARL 201:7
When I am d. BELL 77:71
When I am d. ROSS 726:46
When I am d. and opened MARY 580:48
When I do not write...I'm d. CIXO 227:48
when she was d. GOLD 376:84
Why seek ye...among the d.? BIBLE 122:11
withered heart was d. SCOTT 752:11
with the departed d. SHEL 812:56
word is d. DICK 284:48
world of the d. FORS 345:43
you'll know you're d. WILL 945:97
youth stone d. SASS 745:85
dead-born fell d.-b. from the press HUME 439:8
deadliest endured the d. RUSK 733:18
deadlines I love d. ADAMS 4:81
deadliness d. of...purely scientific GILL 370:84
 recurring d. WILL 946:19
deadlock Holy D. HERB 412:47
deadly more d. in the long run TWAIN 902:36
Deadwood D. and Lost Mule Flat BENET 79:23
deaf At once is d. and loud SHEL 814:2
d. adder that stoppeth her ears BOOK 149:21
D.! Both d.! YEATS 967:42
d. hear BIBLE 16:76
d., how should they know SORL 834:33
d. to hear BIBLE 19:57
delightful period...if one was d. LARW 510:7
dialogue of the d. HOWE 433:87
ears of the d. shall be unstopped BIBLE 108:76
husband who may be d. OBRI 646:74
What d....murderer SHEL 815:37
deafanddumb language even d. CUMM 257:58
deafening silence was d. KARSH 473:32
Deal D. is a most villainous place COBB 233:76
faith-healer of D. ANON 24:13
deal d. with them constantly SHUL 819:24
ease some d. SHAK 760:25
Fair D. TRUM 899:77
good d. of a big-bug TWAIN 902:53
great d. has been lost WALL 918:50
New D. was ended by World War II MCGO 552:87
stand for the square d. ROOS 724:18
dealer agricultural implement d. MENC 587:16
dealers d. and collectors HAMM 394:60
dealing d. in facts, not realities GOLD 377:35
d. with a woman JACO 449:12
dealings d. with young men PO 683:79

dean the cushion and soft D. invite POPE 686:61
deans dowagers for d. TENN 872:31
dear Calm down, d. CAM 193:41
dangerously d. BYRON 188:78
d., I don't give a damn MITC 610:42
D. is the helpless creature BYRON 189:97
d., My no longer cherished MILL 592:22
d. to me as are the ruddy drops SHAK 777:19
d. to me as life SHAK 770:15
everything d. and valuable PITT 680:11
for earth too d. SHAK 765:74
My d. hands RACH 704:25
Plato is d. to me ARIS 32:30
that bread should be so d. HOOD 426:32
too d. for my possessing SHAK 802:22
dearer d. was the mother COLE 234:6
dearest d. thing he owed SHAK 796:11
d. to the world SHAK 804:22
dearheart Make up your mind d. OLIV 649:37
dearie kind D., O BURNS 180:46
o'er me and my D. BURNS 178:14
thinkin on my D. BURNS 178:13
death 25 years after his d. BEAV 1:28
absolute rest is d. PASC 667:72
after d. God knows ROSS 726:60
After the first d. THOM 883:19
After your d. people will write YEATS 965:2
all Life d. does end HOPK 429:92
allotted d. and hell MARL 574:31
all stories...end in d. HEMI 409:72
Angel of D. has been abroad BRIG 159:13
announcement of my d. BROD 160:34
Any man's d. diminishes me DONNE 293:69
Any woman's d. RICH 713:4
arise From d. DONNE 292:50
artist is in danger of d. HEMI 409:71
battles and d. GARI 360:73
beauty of life through d. LAUT 512:32
Be thou faithful unto d. BIBLE 131:91
Better passion and d. LAWR 513:53
better than the most glorious d. EURI 328:60
between life and d. WORD 960:20
Birth, and copulation, and d. ELIOT 319:26
blaze forth the d. of princes SHAK 777:20
bleeding to d. of time GRAV 382:30
body of this d.? BIBLE 125:15
bores them to d. OROU 652:93
bowl'd out by D.'s unerring ball EGAN 313:65
bridegroom in my d. SHAK 795:79
Brother to D. DANI 262:31
buffet you to d. WEBS 926:35
built your ship of d. LAWR 514:82
Calabria d. VIRG 914:24
Capital, where kingly D. SHEL 815:29
ceaseth only in d. HOBB 420:1
certain as d. and taxes DEFOE 269:81
Chairman...lying on his d. bed MIN 608:7
Christians deified in d. STAEL 841:96
'civilization'...is coupled with d. MILL 594:2
competition the Laws of D. RUSK 733:99
concerns himself with d. MANN 566:81
condemn you to d. CARR 203:65
consent to my own d. RODR 722:65
consideration of d.? STEV 852:52
could not stop for D. DICK 284:24
courting d. to be our friend PHIL 676:53
covenant with d. BIBLE 108:70
craving to risk d. FOWL 345:54
crushed him to d.! JOYCE 470:20
daily walk with d. WEBB 925:8
danger of violent d. HOBB 327:47
darker than d. or night SHEL 815:20
day of his d. AUDEN 43:90
dead, a living d. MILT 607:87
dead which he slew at his d. BIBLE 96:20
d. after life SPEN 838:28
D....a good for all BERN 86:77
d. and division SWIN 864:94
d. and I Am found eternal MILT 606:62
d. and I will coquette MARQ 574:45
d. and life attonce SPEN 839:40
D. and pain dominate LEVE 525:25
d. and taxes FRAN 348:19
d. and taxes MITC 610:45
d. and the sole d. BROW 169:63
d., a necessary end SHAK 777:22
D. approaches with little delay ORAH 652:90

death

D. at an early age	YUAN 969:67	D. tramples it to fragments	SHEL 815:43
d. being contrary to their principles	GALS 358:48	d....tyrant has in common	BROD 160:35
d. be not one stroke	MILT 606:63	d....under the power of language	CIXO 227:41
D. be not proud	DONNE 292:51	D. unfailing will strike the blow	CURR 259:91
d....can be done as easily	ALLEN 14:93	d. unloads thee	SHAK 787:65
D. cancels everything but truth	HAZL 403:46	D. was the only absolute	GREE 386:12
D. closes all	TENN 870:2	d. was there relief	MOOR 618:8
D. comes to everyone	BERG 83:25	d., where is thy sting?	BIBLE 127:63
D. cometh soon	MACA 545:45	d., where is thy sting?	BUNY 174:83
D. complete the same!	BROW 168:61	D. who comes at last	SCOTT 752:19
D. could drop	ROSE 725:33	d., who had the soldier singled	DOUG 295:4
D. destroys a man	FORS 344:31	D. will come when thou art dead	SHEL 816:54
D. devours all lovely things	MILL 592:21	d. will have his day	SHAK 764:50
d. had taken Mr Melchisedec	MERE 588:29	d. Will seize the doctor too	SHAK 803:8
d. had undone so many	ELIOT 318:97	d. without the responsibility	LEBO 517:58
d. has a useful function	LABR 502:21	defend to the d.	VOLT 915:50
D. has made	TENN 874:85	deflow'red, and now to d.	MILT 606:51
d. hath no more dominion	BIBLE 125:12	delivered my soul from d.	BIBLE 102:20
D. hath...several doors	WEBS 927:61	Desire is d.	SHAK 803:38
D. his court	SHAK 764:52	Desire paces Eternity...craving d.	DUNC 307:10
d. in childbirth	WELD 928:83	die the d.	BIBLE 13:94
d. in my hand	SHAK 760:23	done to d. by Lenin	CHUR 224:70
d. instead of 'human rights'	PEOP 673:83	do not see why d.	NABO 628:9
d. in the cup	BURNS 180:61	doomed to d.	DRYD 303:9
d. in the hunting	MORT 621:67	draw near unto the gates of d.	BIBLE 102:14
d. into the world	BIBLE 12:73	dull cold ear of D.?	GRAY 384:67
D. is a dialogue	DICK 284:46	either in nativity, chance, or d.	SHAK 773:13
D. is an acquired trait	ALLEN 14:90	end thereof are the ways of d.	BIBLE 104:70
D. is a name for beauty	LAYT 515:99	enormously improved by d.	SAKI 739:66
d. is as a lover's pinch	SHAK 795:94	ere her d., Ruffles her	TENN 878:88
D. is but a moment	SCHI 747:29	eternal: this is d.	LOWE 540:17
D....is certain to all	SHAK 772:86	Every soul shall taste of d.	KORAN 496:48
D. is...degrading punishment	BREN 158:99	Fear of d. and fear of life	MENC 587:6
D. is not an event in life	WITT 951:23	fear of something after d.	TWAIN 902:63
D....is nothing	DRYD 300:37	fed on the fullness of d.	SWIN 864:99
D. is nothing at all	HOLL 423:50	feet go down to d.	BIBLE 104:56
D. is not soft-mouthed	BROD 160:33	first day of our Jubilee is d.	BROW 165:63
D. is only for the mediocre	JARRY 452:94	For all the d., we...die unrehearsed	MURR 627:81
d. is the cure of all diseases	BROW 165:71	foretaste of d.	SCHO 749:60
D. is the end of life	TENN 870:91	frightened of d.	DONL 290:8
d. is the national spectacle	LORCA 537:59	from famine and d.	DARW 263:53
D. is the only mystery	SKEL 825:36	Glad to d.'s mystery	HOOD 426:34
D. is the only pure	LAWR 513:52	go on living even after d.	FRANK 348:3
D. is the remedy	CHAM 213:71	hand in hand to d.	ROSS 726:62
D. is the romantic	NOVA 642:65	hard at d.'s door	BOOK 149:34
D. is the supreme festival	BONH 146:25	I am become d.	OPPE 652:84
d. is to lose belief	DU 305:69	if ought but d. part thee and me	BIBLE 96:23
D. is to Poetry	ABSE 1:9	If people knew there'd be less d.	MALA 561:83
d. i' the other	SHAK 776:7	If they were drowning to d.	KROC 499:17
D. lays his icy hand	SHIR 819:20	I got a d. threat	BENN 80:40
D. lies dead	SWIN 864:71	In every parting...an image of d.	ELIOT 315:15
D. lies on her like	SHAK 766:9	in love with easeful D.	KEATS 478:46
d....like a cold abstraction	MILL 593:42	in most cases, a d. warrant	WHAR 933:9
D....like a gas bill	BURG 174:95	in that sleep of d.	SHAK 783:7
D., like the quintessence	BURG 174:2	in the arts of d.	SHAW 807:26
d. means little	CELI 211:37	in their d. they were not divided	BIBLE 96:42
d. my days should expiate	SHAK 800:40	In the ranks of D.	MOORE 618:2
D. never hurts. D. is sweet	ANOU 28:62	Into the jaws of D.	TENN 875:13
d....of a beautiful woman	POE 683:89	invincible in his d.	GIBB 366:94
d. of Domitian	GIBB 366:90	is not d. at watch	BLUN 143:75
d. of his fellow-creatures	FROU 353:27	isn't sex but d.	SONT 834:15
d. of his saints	BIBLE 102:21	Judge none blessed before his d.	BIBLE 13:91
d. of Nelson	SOUT 835:55	keep a league till d.	SHAK 765:58
d. of one so young	SPEN 837:4	keys of hell and of d.	BIBLE 131:89
d. of religion	WHIT 936:66	kisses after d.	TENN 872:43
d. of some of her	MASE 580:62	land of the shadow of d.	BIBLE 107:59
d. of the kindest owner	STOWE 856:28	last enemy...is d.	BIBLE 127:58
D....openeth the gate	BACON 50:60	law of d.	ANON 23:88
D. opens unknown doors	MASE 580:61	law of sin and d.	WESL 932:65
d. reveals the eminent	SHAW 808:52	Lead him to d.	ROCH 719:12
d. robs it of everything	VIEI 913:7	leads through d.	MANN 566:80
D.'s a great disguiser	SHAK 788:77	led all that way for Birth or D.?	ELIOT 318:18
'D.,' said Mark Staithes	HUXL 442:78	legions with the ways of D.	LIND 530:16
D.'s artifact	ABSE 1:8	let D. wreck all his rage	MILT 603:83
D.'s bitter cup	ABU 1:14	libraries of d.	DOMI 290:3
d.'s dark vale	SCOT 754:85	life after d.	DOCT 289:86
d.'s grey land	SASS 745:83	life, d., and that vast for-ever	KING 487:45
d. shall all the world subdue	SPEN 839:47	Life, the shadow of d.	SWIN 863:86
D. shall be no more	DONNE 292:52	life to d.	SHAK 772:91
d. shall have no dominion	THOM 883:7	life was d.	ROSS 726:59
D. should be a long	TZARA 904:15	lively form of d.	KYD 501:47
D.'s second self	SHAK 801:62	lost friends, some by d.	WOOLF 956:36
D.'s shadow at the door	BLUN 143:72	Love is strong as d.	BIBLE 107:49
D. stands above me	LAND 507:33	lovely and soothing d.	WHIT 938:9
d. the journey's end	DRYD 304:54	love...put it to a violent d.	ETHE 327:47
d. the worst of evils	HEINE 407:14	love thee better after d.	BROW 166:98
D. to life is crown	MILT 608:1	make d. proud	SHAK 795:85
masters the fear of d.	BACON 50:58		
matter of life and d.	SHAN 805:60		
May they walk in living d.	DAVIS 266:7		
Men fear d.	BACON 50:57		
men would take the d. sentence	LAWR 514:91		
midst of life we are in d.	BOOK 148:99		
misery, suffering and d.	HARD 396:93		
moment after d.	HAWT 401:99		
more beautiful than d.	WHIT 938:4		
more d. in it than Rubens	HUGH 435:25		
mortal taste Brought d.	MILT 601:29		
most uninspired form of d.	VALE 907:2		
mourned...not at his d.	MONT 614:37		
much of life and d.	SHEL 812:54		
much possessed by d.	ELIOT 317:77		
My name is D.	SOUT 835:56		
My relationship with d.	ALLEN 14:4		
my sister D.	FRAN 347:98		
mysterious East...silent like d.	CONR 244:35		
name that sat on him was D.	BIBLE 131:1		
nearness of d.	PAZ 671:48		
necessity of d.	HAWT 401:1		
neither d., nor life	BIBLE 125:22		
new terrors of D.	ARBU 30:3		
Night; perchance of D.	THOM 887:8		
no drinking after d.	FLET 340:53		
no lonelier man in d.	HEMI 409:72		
no more d.	BIBLE 125:12		
Nor shall d. brag	SHAK 800:37		
not d....which is terrible	FIEL 335:25		
nothing but d.	UNAM 905:3		
nothing...our own but d.	SHAK 764:51		
not so much afraid of d.	BROW 165:62		
obedient unto d.	BIBLE 128:97		
obey in life and in d.	BARTH 65:8		
Oh, world, Oh, d.?	SPEN 837:4		
one in love with d.	SHEL 815:26		
one medicine is D.	ABU 1:15		
On his d. bed poor Lubin	PRIOR 696:9		
only d. can stop it	HEMI 410:90		
only ending is d.	GRAY 383:41		
only nervousness or d.	LEBO 517:56		
Our own d. wish	PUZO 701:8		
owe God a d.	SHAK 772:88		
pale d. your vital twist shall sever	DAVI 264:75		
panoply of d.	DAVI 265:83		
Photography...flirting with d.	BERG 83:24		
plucked, for d. mature	MILT 606:68		
Poets after my d.	KEATS 476:82		
poor...whose d. interests no one	CELI 211:40		
power in the day of d.	BIBLE 106:24		
power of life and d.	BIBLE 12:79		
prepare as though for d.	MANS 567:9		
presence of the Red D.	POE 683:83		
quiet us in a d. so noble	MILT 608:3		
reflections on life and d.	HERN 414:92		
refusal of language is a d.	BART 66:24		
region and shadow of d.	BIBLE 114:25		
remedy for everything except d.	CERV 211:47		
rendezvous with D.	SEEG 755:99		
report of my d.	TWAIN 903:87		
riddles of birth and d.	FRYE 354:57		
room...we take up in d.	SHIR 819:16		
secret house of d.	SHAK 795:78		
seek D., or he not	MILT 606:65		
sense of d. is most	SHAK 788:66		
sentence of d. with a stay	CARS 206:34		
set before you life and d.	BIBLE 95:97		
sex and d.	CRON 256:29		
shadow of d.	BROW 166:83		
shew the Lord's d. till he come	BIBLE 126:49		
shot to d., with pearls?	WEBS 927:58		
since by man came d.	BIBLE 127:57		
six months' oblivion...newspaper d.	ADAMS 5:94		
sleep and d. differ	TRAH 895:83		
so many years of fearing d.	SHAK 777:30		
sorrow flouted at is double d.	SHAK 760:59		
soul beneath the ribs of d.	MANC 564:51		
spy sent...by the forces of d.	BOWL 153:99		
starving to d.	PLATH 681:37		
stories of the d. of kings	SHAK 764:52		
stream He met his d. in	DEVL 275:8		
studied in his d.	SHAK 796:11		
suffers upon d.	LABR 502:22		
swallow up d. in victory	BIBLE 108:67		
Swarm over, D.!	BETJ 88:20		
sway of d.	WORD 961:47		

deathbed 1070

talk of the d. of God	FACK 329:1	decay after first d.	SPEN 838:33	learn how to make d.	KISS 494:92
that stroke of d.	JOHN 464:76	All human things are subject to d.	DRYD 300:42	wartime d.	TRUM 900:87
theft with a fine, not d.	MORE 618:14	All things are in d.	HERB 413:69	decisive so grave and d.	STEV 852:38
The way to dusty d.	SHAK 798:74	always looked upon d.	MILL 594:79	deck boy stood on the burning d.	HEMA 409:58
this morning I signed my d. warrant	COLL 237:65	bring either d. or explosion	RUSS 734:34	d. of the Titanic	MORT 621:76
Though he is approaching d.	WILL 946:29	by a gentle d.	WESL 932:72	fall…on the d.	DAVI 264:65
thought of d. sits easy	WORD 958:90	d. of ability in the ruling class	ORWE 654:35	decks rose upon their d., and	
till d. us do part	BOOK 148:91	d. of Christianity	SAKI 739:51	he cried	TENN 879:99
Till life and d. remember	SWIN 863:80	d. of parts	CONG 241:58	turtle…'twixt plated d.	NASH 630:60
time and d. pinned human	FRAME 346:75	d. Of that colossal wreck	SHEL 816:86	declaration D. of Independence	KING 487:27
time come after d.	GINS 372:5	D. with imprecision	ELIOT 319:45	d. will inspire irony	GISC 373:29
'tis D. is dead	SHEL 815:41	falling to d.	WALP 918:65	declension D. looks from our land	RANS 706:68
to be carnally minded is d.	BIBLE 125:17	found its d.	COCK 233:81	fall with the d.	SMITH 827:82
To muddy d.	SHAK 784:58	Fretting for their d.	ROSE 725:32	declensions under a lot of d.	BURG 174:91
tragedies are finished by a d.	BYRON 190:13	inferno of insipidity and d.	LEWIS 527:75	decline preserve…from d.	STEU 849:60
translate thy life into d.	SHAK 780:17	introduced disease and d.	SHER 816:69	went into a bit of a d.	ADAMS 4:77
triumph over d. and sin	SPEN 839:43	less apt to d.	JOHN 460:68	writing the d. and fall	GIBB 366:23
triumph over d. and sin	SPEN 839:46	like to this d.	SPEN 839:47	declined answer me d.	SHAK 794:71
true knowledge only comes of d.	WHITE 935:52	many men's d.?	SPEN 839:60	declining d. age of a state	BACON 53:43
truly longed for d.	TENN 872:26	men d.	GOLD 376:98	decompose d. in a barrel of porter	DONL 290:9
ugly d. within my eyes	SHAK 761:40	pale court in beauty and d.	SHEL 815:29	decorations d.…of the embassy	MACI 553:3
Under the ribs of D.	MILT 599:77	The woods d.	TENN 877:60	d. over a void	YOUR 968:36
up the line to d.	SASS 745:84	decayed d. in his intellects	JOHN 464:87	such gaudy d.	MORE 618:21
valiant…taste of d. but once	SHAK 777:21	decaying we are but d.	HERR 415:11	decorative be d. and to do right!	FIRB 336:53
valley of D.	TENN 875:11	decays d. in the face	BEHN 75:25	decorum hunt D. down	BYRON 187:87
valley of D.	TENN 875:12	deceased name of the late d.	KIPL 490:99	sacrifices too much to d.	HAZL 403:31
valley of…d.	BIBLE 100:45	deceit by d. to breed offence	DYER 309:50	trousers of d.	LICH 528:85
vasty hall of d.	ARNO 34:86	kind without d.	DRYD 301:59	decoy fashion's brightest arts d.	GOLD 376:3
victory of sterility and d.	BELL 77:74	neither was any d. in his mouth	BIBLE 109:95	decrease I must d.	BIBLE 122:27
virtues carry with it life and d.	MARL 572:98	not up to small d.	HARTE 400:71	decree d. from Caesar Augustus	BIBLE 120:67
wages of sin is d.	BIBLE 125:13	shocked by honesty…few by d.	COWA 249:57	hot temper leaps o'er a cold d.	SHAK 769:76
walk with D.	TENN 873:51	deceitful blood-thirsty and d. man	BOOK 148:3	decrepit d. father takes delight	SHAK 801:49
wars and sudden d. do	HUGH 435:17	heart is d.	BIBLE 110:20	d., without being venerable	HAWT 402:10
wast not born for d.	KEATS 478:47	deceitfulness Cat of such d.	ELIOT 320:54	dedicated fanatically d. to…dogmas	PIRS 679:90
watch the night and d.	APOL 29:77	deceits d. are strong	MUIR 624:18	dedication d. of an artist	SPARK 836:78
welter of bloodshed and d.	LLOY 533:74	home to many d.	POUND 691:4	deduction as much d. as you please	DARW 263:59
what we fear of d.	SHAK 788:78	deceive d. and delude mankind	EPHO 326:22	logical d. from…hypotheses	EINS 314:89
When d. approached	GIBB 367:7	practise to d.!	SCOTT 752:24	not a correct d.	KEYN 484:76
who is stronger than d.?	HUGH 436:39	sweet to d. the deceiver	LAFO 504:54	deductions d. for the modern	BROW 166:89
whole world is frightened to d.!	SHER 818:10	deceived All children have to be d.	ISHI 448:75	Dee sands of D.	KING 487:43
Who owns all of space? D.	HUGH 436:39	Like a d. husband	SHAK 802:68	dee diddle, we take it, is d.	SWIN 864:18
Why fear d.?	FROH 351:87	deceiver sweet to deceive the d.	LAFO 504:54	deed A bloody d.	SHAK 784:38
with the rich in his d.	BIBLE 109:95	thou kind d.!	DRYD 301:60	blow the horrid d.	SHAK 796:74
women for escape from this d.	NIGH 639:21	deceivers Men were d.	SHAK 774:38	By thought, word, and d.	BOOK 147:67
worm of d.	GRAV 382:25	wicked race of d.	MILT 600:17	Crime lies not in the d.	HELO 409:55
worst friend and enemy is but D.	BROO 162:91	deceiving Seeing is d.	THUR 891:92	d. dying tongueless	SHAK 799:8
would burn you to d.!	MERM 588:47	December as short as D.	SHAK 799:9	d. I'll do before	SHAK 797:57
would like d.	MONT 613:20	D. when they wed	SHAK 780:12	d. without a name	SHAK 797:54
deathbed D. utterances	PLOUT 682:74	From May to D.	ANDE 17:72	defiant d.!	WHIT 937:97
death-dance d.-d. of our times	CHES 213:87	made D. June	TENN 874:93	dirty d.	SYNGE 865:24
death-doom Awaiting their d.-d.	WILDE 939:44	decencies content to dwell in d.	POPE 688:12	foul d. shall smell	SHAK 777:34
deathless d. friends	SASS 746:98	decency D. is indecency's conspiracy	SHAW 808:51	good d. in a naughty world	SHAK 770:52
sense of some d. shame	WEBS 926:26	d. of human beings	ORWE 653:24	living act, the undoubted d.	MELV 585:59
death-rate d.-r. meant…supply	SHAW 811:33	done in the name of 'd.'	LEWIS 527:66	may do the d.	KEATS 475:67
infantile d.-r.	HALD 392:22	fail to observe d. and discretion	BACON 49:22	my d. to my most painted word	SHAK 782:6
deaths d. column brought good	HAMER 393:45	ultimate d. of things	STEV 853:81	one good d. in all my life	SHAK 760:30
feigned d. to die.	DONNE 291:24	want of d.	DILL 286:96	right d. for the wrong reason	ELIOT 319:47
labouring masses to their d.	WEIL 928:76	with such spirit and d.	PITT 679:1	Th'attempt and not the d.	SHAK 797:31
many times before their d.	SHAK 777:21	decent d. godless people	ELIOT 319:32	there is no glory in the d.	READ 708:95
more d. than one must die.	WILDE 942:20	d. people live beyond their incomes	SAKI 739:63	water clears us of this d.	SHAK 797:38
ready for more d.	GREE 385:3	most d. nation	BUSH 182:98	whatever time the d. took place	ELIOT 320:54
death-warrant blood is my d.-w.	KEATS 478:49	no use to d. people	SHAW 809:83	Y'are the d.'s creature	MIDD 590:80
debasement d. of the human mind	CHAN 213:87	decentralization technology of d.	MURP 627:77	deeds better d. than words	SHAK 758:60
debate This leads to a d.	MACH 552:93	deception warfare is based on d.	SUN 859:88	D. are nothing	BALZ 61:3
debauch d. his friend's wife genteelly	BOSW 152:78	deceptions All are d.	WILS 947:44	d. determine us	ELIOT 315:21
d. the currency	KEYN 484:71	decide If I had to d.	GRAMM 381:93	d. left undone	STOWE 856:33
debauchery lead him into d. and sin	OFLA 647:98	You'll have to d.	DYLAN 309:52	D., not words	EDGE 311:49
debonair buxom, blithe, and d.	MILT 597:42	decided d. by a person's thoughts	KIM 486:12	d. of youth	SHAK 801:49
debris of a statue	YOUR 969:61	d. never to be afraid	KAVA 474:49	d. Shall be in water writ	BEAU 71:15
debt Ambition's d. is paid	SHAK 777:28	deciduous d. language	THOM 886:76	ends all other d.	SHAK 795:84
national d.	HAMI 394:47	deciphering philosophy is like the d.	SCHO 748:53	gentle mind by gentle d.	SPEN 839:58
old d. for a borrowing	DUNC 307:7	decision a d. to be made	PECK 672:63	Glorious d. are not embraced	PIUS 680:18
pay a d. to pleasure too?	ROCH 719:6	a very deliberate d.	POIN 684:99	good d. are gone	JANO 452:18
promise made is a d. unpaid	SERV 757:34	by d. more embroils	MILT 603:69	great d. were done	WHITE 936:59
debtors D. can't be leaders	IACO 444:3	come to a very important d.	MILNE 596:15	measure by thy d.	SHAK 801:60
debts D. are becoming	BALZ 61:8	d. makers face each other	SHUL 819:28	nameless in worthy d.	BROW 165:80
forgive us our d.	BIBLE 115:42	d. of the courts	LEAC 515:19	these unlucky d. relate	SHAK 790:51
our d., our care-full wives	SHAK 775:84	Drug misuse…is a d.	DICK 227:36	Words to the heat of d.	SHAK 796:29
pays all d.	SHAK 804:24	I made the d. long ago	RENO 711:51	worse d. worse suffering	MILT 603:90
unpaid d.	HALD 392:26	music that changed a man's d.	SCHN 748:44	wrong and d. malign	NOON 641:50
Words pay no d.	SHAK 787:34	never try to make a right d.	ONEI 651:74	years of noble d.	TENN 877:57
decade before this d. is out	KENN 481:5	right of ultimate d.	MUMF 625:39	deedy haven't been at all d.	COMP 239:7
d. or more of ruin	WIEN 939:29	specific d.	TUCH 901:11	deep beauty is only sin d.	SAKI 739:50
decadence absence…is d.	MAMET 563:31	This isn't about a lie…It's a d.	BLAIR 138:75	Black…Baltic d.	TENN 876:35
barbarism to d.	CLEM 230:89	wrong d. can make…miserable	DENN 273:73	clouds are d.	FREE 350:49
describe as 'Puritan d.'	SPEN 837:10	decisions d. are made beforehand	LEWI 527:76	commit his body to the d.	BOOK 149:39
decadent language grows d. too	VIDAL 912:4	d. to become mothers	FRIE 350:66	d. beyond d.	BETJ 89:46

D. calleth unto d.	BIBLE 100:65	**defended** d. by her armed sons	REDM 709:21	**delays** d. are dangerous	DRYD 300:28
d., yet clear	DENH 272:60	**defenders** surprising the d.	MANC 564:48	**delegate** When in trouble, d.	WAGN 915:3
dive into the bottom of the d.	SHAK 771:37	**defense** painting is…for attack and d.	PICA 677:60	**delete** government…has one button: d.	AI WEI 10:10
eye that sees too d.	FADI 329:7	strategy of d.	GALB 357:14	**delicate** d. death	WHIT 938:9
From the great d.	TENN 878:75	**defer** D., d.	GILB 369:62	rich and d. English language	WAUGH 924:1
heard the d. behind him	TENN 878:83	**defiance** act of wilful d.	SASS 745:79	sufficiently d.	KEYN 484:77
lowest d. a lower d.	MILT 604:92	bold d. with his prince	DRYD 302:75	The air is d.	SHAK 796:18
Not d. the Poet sees	ARNO 33:59	**defiant** before a d. deed	WHIT 937:97	**delicately** d. as possible	RUSS 734:26
remorseless d. Clos'd o'er	MILT 599:85	It is d.	READ 708:94	**delicates** fruits and princely d.	MARL 573:23
secrets of the d.	MILT 607:72	**deficiencies** d. of fortune	GOLD 376:90	**delicious** d. dinner of too much	JOHN 457:1
singularly d. young man	GILB 368:43	**deficiency** d. in the graces	JOHN 463:52	d., nourishing, and wholesome	SWIFT 862:58
so d. a measure does it have	HERA 412:35	**deficient** very d. in means	KISH 493:83	magic and d. power	WOOLF 955:27
thunders of the upper d.	TENN 869:71	**deficit** Olympics…d.	DRAP 298:89	wine…heavenly and d.	RABE 703:9
too d. for his hearers	GOLD 377:17	Park Avenue…trade d.	BART 66:30	With most d. poison	SHAK 794:53
Two voices…one is of the d.	STEP 847:11	**defile** neither shall ye d. yourselves	BIBLE 94:76	**delight** anyone's afflictions…source	
unfathomable d. forest	THOM 885:62	presumed to d.	DREN 299:2	of delight	LUCR 541:59
where the brook is d.	SHAK 759:88	**define** cannot d. the real problem	FEYN 334:6	bind another to its d.	BLAKE 140:10
wonders in the d.	BIBLE 102:15	d. her feelings in language	HARDY 397:6	calm in our d.	WORD 956:57
writers…do not seem so d.	LAND 506:27	d. jazz satisfactorily	KING 88:60	decrepit father takes d.	SHAK 801:47
deeper d. than did ever plummet	SHAK 804:31	ought to d. a man's income	HICKS 417:47	d. in simple things	KIPL 492:58
deeps d. are cold	HUGH 435:35	to d. is to eliminate	QUINE 702:21	d. is in the law of the Lord	BIBLE 99:25
deep-versed D.-v. in books	MILT 607:80	**defines** he who d. himself	LAO 508:61	d. of her husband	RANS 706:66
deer d. from the hill	SCOTT 753:37	**definite** d. maybe	GOLD 377:33	d. themselves in…peace	BIBLE 100:59
d., is in the wood of Hallaig	MACL 555:30	like d. form	STEV 851:30	D. thyself also in the Lord	BIBLE 100:58
d. sweeps by	SCOTT 752:33	no d. answers can	RUSS 734:23	do ill our sole d.	MILT 602:40
heart…chasing the d.	BURNS 179:15	**definition** d. of a free society	STEV 851:7	Energy is Eternal D.	BLAKE 139:95
time's d. is slain	MUIR 623:15	d. of a 'hero'	FIND 336:43	feelings of d.	WORD 961:34
where the d. and the antelope play	HIGL 418:54	d. of a horse	DICK 281:77	filled with such d.	SASS 745:92
Deever they're hangin' Danny D.	KIPL 489:84	d. of a specialist	MAYO 583:27	gift, my ever new d.	MILT 604:14
deface the image of man	IVAN 448:30	d. of happiness	KENN 482:29	give d. and hurt not	SHAK 804:25
defeat a refusal…to give in and		d. of utter waste	HUNT 438:18	go to't with d.	SHAK 795:74
admit d.	MEDA 584:36	d. of what a nurse	NIGH 639:24	harmony or true d.?	MILT 605:39
Champagne…in d.	POL 684:8	D.—Science is systematized	SART 744:63	high austerity to d.	FREE 350:49
country of d.	PURDY 700:86	incapable of any d.	MOORE 616:66	If you d. not in man	SHAK 782:91
In d.: defiance	CHUR 224:69	ultimate d. of this uniqueness	COUS 248:40	inordinate sensual d.	BAXT 69:94
In d. unbeatable	CHUR 226:14	want a d. of poetry	THOM 884:25	Love and d. are better teachers	DURER 307:26
laughing soldiers fought to their d.	FENT 332:60	**definitions** exact d. can be applied	QUIL 702:14	makes eating a d.	SUCK 858:68
pleasure of the d.	LACL 503:31	which…they call D.	HOBB 420:97	nursed by d.	LYLY 543:84
possibilities of d.	VICT 912:78	**deflationary** essentially a d. genius	MORR 620:47	Phantom of d.	WORD 960:19
scorn for d.	TWAIN 903:84	**deflowered** At last you are d.	COWA 249:56	simple human d.	BARB 63:46
snatching glory out of d.	PRIE 695:86	**deformed** how d. dost thou look!	SHAK 763:11	source of little visible d.	BRON 162:79
suffering a national d.	EDIN 312:49	None can be called d.	SHAK 786:21	succession of d.	SMART 826:68
through d. and humiliation	SMUTS 831:70	what a d. thief	SHAK 774:46	the fruit of your d.	SURR 860:3
victory turns into a d.	DE 268:47	**deformity** Art is significant d.	FRY 354:39	'Tis my d., alone in summer shade	WORD 958:91
we know we should d. you	KIPL 492:65	mine own d.	SHAK 761:34	to d.…paid thy utmost blessing	DELA 271:34
defeated destroyed but not d.	HEMI 410:87	**Degas** remember D.	PISS 679:98	Too bright for our infirm D.	DICK 284:47
Down with the d.	LIVY 532:61	**degenerate** creative protests to d.	KING 487:29	to teach and d.	SIDN 820:55
Down with the d.!	BREN 158:1	**degradation** breath of d.	BYRON 189:84	true spirit of d.	RUSS 734:25
History to the d.	AUDEN 42:76	children from utter d.	LOVE 538:89	unrest which men miscall d.	SHEL 815:40
meaning shows in the d.	MASE 580:67	consent to such d.	OCON 646:82	various objects of d.	MILT 607:84
you will never be d.	SUN 859:90	means of increasing her d.	STAN 842:15	what d. we…have	PEPYS 674:4
defect chief d. of Henry King	BELL 76:58	sense of intellectual d.	JAMES 450:24	What worlds d.	SPEN 838:26
d. of nature	FRAN 346:82	**degree** d. and a quality of trust	SHAP 805:68	**delighted** cruel, and d. in cruelty	QUIL 702:15
fatal d. of current principles	SIMON 821:74	d. of a person's intelligence	ALTH 15:15	d. particularly in quotations	SCHL 747:34
make d. perfection	SHAK 794:57	d. of certainty	RUSS 734:35	only too d. to have been born	STRA 856:37
some affliction or d.	BEER 74:90	d. of 'grand old man'	LEAC 516:24	primary object…to be d.	CECIL 210:24
that which depends on d.	ARIS 31:21	d. of serenity	NIEB 637:86	**delightful** d. to be a woman	SCHR 749:61
defective d. in its evidence	REGAN 710:42	didn't get a d.	DOWD 296:19	make his conversation perfectly d.	SMITH 831:57
defects all these d. came	WEBB 925:6	in however slight a d.	RYLE 736:61	society is wonderfully d.!	WILDE 941:90
by reason of her intellectual d.	WRIG 962:62	lady of beauty and high d.	RANS 706:66	two most d. things in it?	WALP 919:76
Mencken's d. were commonplace	MEYER 589:63	with d. dispense	JONS 467:73	**delights** all d. my fortune	JONS 466:47
defence awake endeavour for d.	SHAK 768:52	**degrees** 105 d. in Saigon	ANON 28:50	d. of a pantomime	DICK 278:73
cheap d. of nations	BURKE 176:41	arts are taught by d.	THEO 882:79	d. of the flesh castrate me	FUEN 354:59
conscience clear my chief d.	DYER 309:50	boil at different d.	EMER 325:95	d. Will vanish	MILT 604:2
d. against betrayal	WILL 945:87	by d. learn to work at all things	CARL 201:37	mind religiously affected d.	HOOK 427:41
d. like elaborate courtesy	LUCAS 541:50	Crime…has its d.	RACI 704:30	Of the d. of this world	TWAIN 903:92
d. of one's country	HOMER 425:7	d. of anger	EVANS 328:69	O love, for d.!	BIBLE 107:48
d. of the indefensible	ORWE 655:61	d. of communism and d.	NGUY 636:68	permissible d. of the soul	BACH 49:8
d. that will protect	SCHL 748:39	d. off east longitude	MUNDY 625:44	To scorn d., and live	MILT 599:86
die in d. of their rights	PITT 679:7	heal but by d.?	SHAK 789:15	violent d. have violent ends	SHAK 66:92
England's chief d.	PHIL 676:51	thirty d. below zero	MOOD 615:53	**delineation** d. of that which appeals	HUMB 438:92
greatest D. lay in the Art	ALBE 11:33	will name you the d.	SHAK 780:24	happiest d. of its varieties	AUST 46:83
Immodest words admit of no d.	DILL 286:96	**dehumanize** d., not just the slaves	MORR 620:58	**delinquencies** indulge in a few d.	ELIOT 315:16
In cases of d.	SHAK 775:72	**deities** d. of his own invention	PLATO 681:42	**delinquents** d. are frustrated actors	MULL 624:32
in her d.	GARI 360:72	**deity** believe in a personal d.	HAMM 394:54	**deliquescent** d. leaves of paper	ANDR 18:77
intelligent means of d.	KENT 483:49	D. and the Drains	STRA 856:39	**delirium** and one d. tremens	TWAIN 902:57
interpret my d.	THAT 881:50	d. when Cubans get together	LEZA 528:81	in such pleasant d.	ELIOT 315:19
make a pitiful d.	SIDN 820:52	doubted…the D.	WELLS 929:17	may attack you in d. tremens	OBRI 646:74
my rock…my d.	BIBLE 101:77	do not want to be…some d.	MAND 565:58	**delitabill** Storyss to rede ar d.	BARB 63:49
Never make a d.	CHAR 215:29	Half dust, half d.	BYRON 189:84	**deliver** come down to d. them	BIBLE 93:54
only d. is in offence	BALD 57:31	Prosperity…not a d.	COOL 246:80	let him d. him	BIBLE 99:42
tower of d.	ALCA 11:39	**Dekanahwideh** D., and…Chiefs	DEKA 270:7	sacrifice them all…to d. you	SHAK 770:15
defences and no d.	GOLD 375:77	**delay** D. and dirt are the realities	THER 882:94	who shall d. me	BIBLE 125:15
defend d. ourselves with guns	GOEB 374:53	reluctant amorous d.	MILT 600:1	**deliverance** songs of d.	BIBLE 100:55
d. to the death	VOLT 915:50	We safely may d.	BRON 161:60	**delivered** d. me from all my fears	BIBLE 100:55
d. us against nature	FREUD 350:57	why shou'd we d.?	WALL 918:57	**deliverer** No d. ever rose	MORG 619:34
let it d. itself	TOLS 893:62	**delayed** it has been d.	JOHN 460:63	**delivery** Punctual D. Company	DICK 278:74

dell

dell pure as the lily in the d. — LAUD 511:15
Delors UP YOURS D. — SUN 859:85
delph dresser filled with shining d. — COLUM 238:90
deluded Gods and men, we are all d. — SHEL 816:64
deluge After us the d. — POMP 684:11
delusion d. that macro-economics — HAYEK 402:26
  d. that one likes oneself — DIDI 286:79
  give up their liberties...under some d. — BURKE 175:33
  nothing...but that addled d. — ELIOT 315:41
  progress is utter d. — MILL 594:63
  Trial...will be a d. — DENM 273:72
  united by a d. — INGE 445:30
delusions mocked by d. — EMER 325:83
demagogue d. is a person — MARQ 575:61
demand d. disturbs the happy — BRON 161:68
  d. for their labour — STEU 849:60
  d. the time of the day — SHAK 770:27
  d. this...for the race — SCHR 749:65
  immeasurable or insolent d. — WALP 919:84
  we d. the excellence — REYES 712:69
demands d. of a composer — HONE 425:15
  d. that form the habit — TUCH 901:12
  spiritual d. — TAWN 868:43
De Maupassant beat Mr D. M. — HEMI 410:84
demeanour d. nobly bland — GILB 370:72
demesne private pagus or d. — AUDEN 44:15
demi-god magician is a d.-g. — MARL 573:22
demigods musicians are not d. — TURN 901:20
demi-monde d.-m. does not represent — DUMAS 306:91
democracies D. must try to find ways — THAT 881:62
  d. of the west — MASA 580:49
  not embraced by d. — PIUS 680:18
  tendency of d....to mediocrity — COOP 246:84
democracy bringing...d.to the Middle East — PINT 678:85
  crisis of Western d. — LIPP 530:35
  Criticism is part of...d. — CLIN 231:19
  d. and peace — WELL 929:93
  D. and proper drains — BETJ 88:22
  D.! Bah! — GINS 372:10
  D....by the uneducated — CHES 221:6
  d. is about just showing up — NADER 629:24
  d. is but a flickering candle — MACK 554:16
  d. is just a slogan — GORB 378:46
  D. is not a polite employer — HOOV 427:48
  D. is supposed to give — VIDAL 912:94
  d. is the best revenge — BHUT 90:79
  D. is the recurrent suspicion — WHITE 935:37
  D. is the theory — MENC 586:81
  d. is the worst form of Government — CHUR 226:4
  d.; it's the counting — STOP 855:17
  D. means government by discussion — ATTL 40:30
  D. means simply — WILDE 941:74
  d. must remain at home — BORAH 150:53
  d. of the dead — CHES 220:69
  D. substitutes election — SHAW 808:37
  d. was renewed in Scotland — DEWAR 276:17
  does not...have a functioning d. — CART 206:53
  duty of a d. — WHITE 935:35
  experience of d. is like...life — CART 206:47
  full-blooded and unconditional d. — GORB 378:48
  great arsenal of d. — ROOS 724:12
  grieved under a d. — HOBB 420:3
  ideal form of d. — BEUYS 89:49
  In a d. — FULB 355:62
  laboratories of d. — WHIT 937:85
  little less d. to save — ATKI 40:14
  Love of d. is love — MONT 614:41
  make d. stable — SKEL 824:32
  modern d. is a tyranny — MAIL 560:44
  never fought a war against a d. — OBAMA 644:37
  obstacle to d. — SCHU 750:81
  odyssey toward liberty, d. — MAIL 560:52
  our d. was — MACA 546:58
  political aspirant under d. — MENC 586:93
  Political d....in America — WHIT 938:11
  priestly offices in a d. — LIPP 531:37
  property-owning d. — SKEL 824:32
  put d. on hold for a while — LOVE 539:94
  Socialism is the completion of d. — EAGL 309:4
  stability at the expense of d. — RICE 713:84
  talk...about d. — ROOS 724:1
  Television has made...d. unbearable — PERES 674:23
  thanks to wine-less and d. — BROW 169:80
  trouble in modern d. — BEVE 90:61
  two cheers for d. — FORS 345:47
  uncrowned king of an educated d. — STEAD 843:32

voice, of the d. — STEAD 843:30
We are a d. — PULI 699:71
Why D. means — HUGH 435:11
world must be made safe for d. — WILS 949:83
worst thing I can say about d. — BEVAN 89:50
democrat Aristocrat, D., autocrat — TENN 876:20
  aristocrat is the d. ripe — EMER 325:82
  d. only on principle — TWAIN 903:88
  free man...and a D. — JOHN 458:10
democratic D. idea — BRYAN 170:97
  D. Intellect — DAVIE 264:70
  d. parliaments of tricks — WEBB 925:8
  denouncing liberal d. principles — AUNG 45:39
  Fig leaves of d. procedure — KENN 480:88
  ideals of a d....society — MAND 564:53
  market is so vulgarly d. — KRIS 499:15
  the D. pallbearer — FRIED 351:67
  The D. Party has succeeded — ONEI 651:81
  towards the d. powers — MASA 580:49
  whole new d. world — CARL 200:89
democrats D. are fleeing — SHEV 818:11
demography nothing to do with d. — BERG 83:26
demolished d. or rebuilt — BOOTH 150:49
demolition Slated for d. — ASHB 37:58
demon Celtic Demos rose a D. — TENN 879:5
demonic tends towards the d. — BAUD 69:78
demon-lover wailing for her d.-l. — COLE 236:37
demons artist...driven by d. — FAUL 331:39
demonstration logic of d. — NISB 639:27
  Spontaneous D. — ORWE 654:48
demoralize frighten people...and d. them — BENN 80:39
Demosthenes when D. spoke — OGIL 648:5
demur If I d. — HEAN 405:74
demurest D. of the tabby kind — GRAY 383:50
den beard the lion in his d. — SCOTT 752:23
  from the d. — SMART 826:67
  in the d....nine dead men — BALL 59:60
Deng revisionist clique of D. — JIANG 455:58
deniability some future d. — POIN 684:99
denial timid requests, invites d. — SENE 757:25
denied but half d. — BUTL 185:84
Denmark beard me in D.? — SHAK 782:95
  example of the king of D. — FACK 329:1
  look like a friend on D. — SHAK 780:34
  rotten in the state of D. — SHAK 781:59
  royal bed of D. — SHAK 781:65
  storks on the spires of D. — DOYLE 297:75
  throne of D. to thy father — SHAK 780:31
  villain dwelling in all D. — SHAK 781:68
denominator lowest common d. — JARR 452:90
  lowest common d. of human — CART 206:48
  no common d. — AUDEN 44:13
denote things which they d. — JOHN 460:68
dens d. of robbery and murder — NATI 632:4
dentist dread this like the d. — AUDEN 42:75
  like going to the d. — WILD 942:13
  smiling...like a clumsy d. — MANS 567:6
  sooner go to my d. — WAUGH 923:71
  talk like a d. when one isn't — WILDE 941:97
dentists adulteries of d. — WILD 943:51
  d. ride roughshod — PERE 674:19
denunciation d. of the young — SMITH 829:11
deny cannot but d. them — SHAW 807:18
  dare d. that the Third Estate — SIEY 820:62
  D. it to a king? — SHAK 772:85
  d. knowledge — KANT 473:25
  d. me thrice — BIBLE 119:41
  d. me thrice — BIBLE 122:6
  neither...palliate nor d. — PITT 679:1
  people d. that it is true — BRYS 171:13
  reason down or d. everything — EMER 325:77
denying to allure by d. — TROL 898:43
deoch-an-doris Just a wee d.-a.-d. — MORR 620:54
deodar smell of d. wood burning — CHAT 216:52
deodorant Success is a great d. — TAYL 868:53
depart D.,—be off — HOLM 424:77
  d. in God's name — JOAN 455:59
  D., I say — AMERY 15:27
  D., I say, and let us have done — CROM 255:22
  Let him d. — SHAK 776:88
  d. was a 'Roman' — LAWS 514:95
departing always arriving and d. — MILL 594:89
department d. of psychology — AYER 48:7
  d. stores...like museums — WARH 920:9
  fair sex is your d. — DOYLE 297:67
  material in every d. — BEAV 71:32
  not to a functionary or d. — STEAD 843:34

State D. — MCCA 547:84
departments public d. — DICK 282:83
department-store d.-s. state — CHAN 213:85
departure d. from this world — EMMET 325:6
  function is d. can depart — LISP 531:44
  grant them a fair d. — SHAK 769:81
  possible point of d. — WAGN 915:2
dependence d. of one fact — HOBB 420:98
  not subsist without D. — STEE 844:47
  total d. on the appreciation of others — CONN 242:1
dependencies colonies and wide d. — QUIL 702:13
deplore d. but was powerless — LEAC 515:16
  D. what is to be deplored — MORG 619:32
  though still I do d.? — DONNE 293:65
depository d. of power — DISR 287:29
depressed no one d. in this house — VICT 912:95
depression d., combined with — LURIE 542:67
  D. is when you lose — REAG 708:3
  d. when you lose yours — TRUM 899:86
deprivation D. is...daffodils — LARK 510:98
deprived needy, I was d. — FEIF 331:55
  violated and the d. — JORD 469:1
depriving chief means of d. them — HALL 393:40
de profundis D. P. clamavi ad te — BIBLE 133:38
Deptford famous in D. — DAVI 265:82
depth d. of her glowing breast — SHEL 815:22
  d. unfathomed no man knows — WESL 932:66
  in the d. be praise — NEWM 635:49
  love thee to the d. — BROW 166:97
depths d. of every heart — HAWT 402:12
  d. where thy marvels are manifest — GORD 378:53
  Out of the d. have I cried — BIBLE 103:39
  people...out of their d. — FITZ 338:92
  unfathomable d. of his...mind — COLE 236:53
  Up from the d. I have cried to thee — BIBLE 133:38
deputy books...may be read by d. — BACON 53:37
  if you and your d. will go back — ANDE 17:67
De Quincey Coleridge and D. Q. — THUR 891:94
Derby back streets of D. — CHRI 223:37
deride do not d. the fears — JORD 469:1
derision Lord shall have them in d. — BIBLE 99:27
  old days to d. — SWIN 864:94
derivative but what is only d. — MILT 601:24
  d. from this pure activity — LEWIS 527:65
descendants only chance for their d. — DAVI 264:72
descent claims of long d. — TENN 87:10
  no nobility of d. — POTT 690:84
describe do not d. it fitly — JAMES 451:66
  do nothing but d. — GRAY 384:60
  poet's business is not to d. — ABER 1:5
description d. of a happy state — LOCKE 534:92
  d. of the...Rhodes Scholar — MARA 569:45
  d. of the rising sun — SHER 818:2
  gay D. Aegypt glads — POPE 688:31
  It beggared all d. — SHAK 794:55
  picture that requires any d. — HOMER 425:11
  truth of d. and the sentiment — SCOTT 754:78
descriptions d. of scenery — LEVIN 525:29
Desdemona love the gentle D. — SHAK 788:87
  Othello subject D. — KOES 495:28
desert alone in the d. — SAINT 738:36
  arid d. of his mind — WEST 933:98
  call of the d. — STARK 843:23
  came through the d. — THOM 887:7
  Carlyle has led us all out into the d. — CLOU 232:46
  company of d. people — THES 882:96
  d. in a dry frigid weather — PIER 677:68
  D. Storm — SCHW 750:91
  d. were my dwelling-place — BYRON 188:69
  Down my d. rhyme — CRAIK 252:51
  Even in thy d. — BYRON 188:59
  every man after his d. — SHAK 782:98
  found him in a d. land — BIBLE 95:99
  garden...into a d. — YOUNG 968:51
  gardens of the D. — BRYA 170:3
  knowledge...areas of d. — CHAN 213:85
  legs of stone...in the d. — SHEL 813:85
  Nothing went unrewarded, but d. — DRYD 302:84
  pained d. lion — ARNO 34:97
  pain in the d. — MOOR 618:8
  power to make the world a d. — STEV 850:5
  shores, and d. wildernesses — MILT 598:68
  streams in the d. — BIBLE 108:76
  to say the d. is stingy — HEAT 406:94
  waste its sweetness on the d. air — GRAY 384:69
  went out into the d. — SITW 824:21
  Zuleika, on a d. island — BEER 73:80

destroyed

desertion treacherous d. of an ally	CHUR 224:70	naught for your d.	CHES 220:80	some divine d.	TENN 872:41
deserts D. are there	SACK 737:11	no longer d. happiness	SHAW 806:92	Symphony or give in to d.	ROY 730:30
d. of America	JOHN 460:86	nothing like wealth for dulling d.	MCGU 552:89	through darkness and d.	SHEL 814:7
d. of the heart	AUDEN 43:94	objects of d.	RICA 712:82	Where there is d.	FRAN 347:99
D. of vast eternity	MARV 577:91	one d. in life	SHAW 897:20	Where there is d.	THAT 881:54
Or his d. are small	MONT 615:50	questioning them was my mind's d.	BRID 158:10	winter of d.	DICK 282:94
Story is just just d.	ELKIN 322:17	raging d.	TWAIN 902:46	work…out of d.	BAUD 69:84
deserve advertising we d.	SAYE 746:11	restless d. of power	HOBB 420:1	despairer Too quick d.	ARNO 35:19
Something you…haven't to d.	FROST 352:93	singularity in d.	DONNE 293:77	desperado 'd.'…all over him	BIRD 135:7
deserved more credit than they d.	REST 711:64	strange d. to seek power	BACON 51:84	desperate a d. woman seeking applause	GREER 387:47
never have d. it	SATIE 746:6	this fond d.	ADDI 7:52	constituency is the d.	JACK 448:2
punished himself…if he d. it	ELIOT 315:29	To d. immortality	SCHO 748:55	d. act of men	READ 708:94
deserving d. to do it	GRAY 383:41	vain d. at last	ROSS 726:62	I am d. for change	OBAMA 645:55
lost without d.	SHAK 789:12	what I've tasted of d.	FROST 352:4	desperation hunger, poverty, d.	MARS 575:63
design according to the same d.	VIAN 911:73	what many men d.	SHAK 769:94	lives of quiet d.	THOR 888:25
any d. that you wish to give them	VAZD 910:43	Which of us has his d.?	THAC 880:30	despise comforts we d.	SHAK 795:77
characteristic of the d.	LEWO 528:78	yearning in d.	TENN 870:99	d. the uninitiated mob	HORA 430:9
d. career is a process of learning	BELL 76:48	youth pined away with d.	BLAKE 140:11	d. yourself too much	KAVA 474:48
d. of darkness	FROST 352:11	desired I have d. to go	HOPK 428:65	government I d.	KEYN 484:69
don't d. clothes, I d. dreams	LAUR 511:20	not one to be d.	TENN 871:9	live and d. writing	SMITH 830:40
ill d. is most ill	HESI 417:32	You who d. so much	CRANE 253:59	more things to admire…than to d.	CAMUS 196:89
only its d. The hand	MICH 590:66	desires all d. known	BOOK 147:58	they that d. me	BIBLE 96:24
when…dull there is a d.	STEE 844:41	all holy d.	BOOK 146:42	to hate and to d. myself	HAZL 404:50
designed deliberately d.	HAYEK 402:25	d. in the interest	RUSS 734:29	despised blind, d., and dying king	SHEL 812:70
d. to show those	KEIL 479:56	d. of the heart	AUDEN 42:77	certainly have d. Christ	GREE 386:23
designing d. for obsolescence	ISSI 448:77	give thee the d. of thine heart	BIBLE 100:58	d. and rejected of men	BIBLE 109:93
designs d. were strictly honourable	FIEL 335:25	He who d. and acts not	BLAKE 140:97	d. of the people	BIBLE 99:42
desirability d.…of telling lies	ORWE 655:67	increase Of my d.	SURR 860:98	despond Slough of D.	BUNY 173:73
desirable d.…be pretty	LAMB 508:92	infinite in its d.	NORR 641:57	despondency d. and madness	WORD 959:1
produce that anything is d.	MILL 592:9	lay lime to tangle her d.	SHAK 759:70	spread alarm and d.	PENI 673:80
desire admitted d. to dress	LIN 529:2	lopping off our d.	SWIFT 861:34	despot country governed by a d.	JOHN 463:59
all a wonder and a wild d.	BROW 169:72	means…to satisfy our d.	PREV 694:79	d. whom the wise ridicule and obey	BIER 134:78
animated by a sincere d.	PEEL 672:67	murder…than nurse unacted d.	BLAKE 140:3	despotism d. tempered by epigrams	CARL 201:11
ardently d. that our country	PANK 662:86	one's own transient d.	EINS 313:76	enemy to d.	GARI 360:72
arrows of d.!	BLAKE 141:42	outlived certain d.	WOOLF 956:36	handed over to a ruthless d.	ATTL 40:25
At Christmas I no more d.	SHAK 763:4	pimps for ill d.	DRYD 301:68	modern form of d.	MCCA 548:94
a' the learning I d.	BURNS 177:70	thoughtless youth…with vain d.	DRYD 303:11	dessert Cheese for d.	BRAC 154:19
bowls of fierce d.	CRAS 254:87	two d. toss about	ARNO 34:79	now she could eat d.	ALTH 15:13
bred by d.	LYLY 543:84	unrealistic goals and d.	LURIE 542:67	destination all signpost and no d.	KRON 500:20
bred in me a d.	MUNDY 625:44	desk but a d. to write upon	BUTL 185:77	a re-definition of our d.	OKRI 649:26
Can one d. too much	SHAK 779:11	d. is a dangerous place	ANON 26:87	Change is not a d.	GIUL 373:35
circling in his d.	FLAU 339:25	From counter or d.	YEATS 966:18	d. is never a place	MILL 594:89
crime is due to the repressed d.	WAUGH 923:66	votary of the d.	LAMB 505:99	physical d.	GRAT 382:14
danger of d.	SHAK 781:46	Desmond Wildly o'er D.	MCCA 547:75	destinies recognised, and robed as d.	LARK 509:78
d. for food and sex	TOOLE 894:59	desolate All is now d.…ambushed	MACA 544:18	destiny Anatomy is d.	FREUD 350:59
d.…is a tree of life	BIBLE 104:68	None are so d.	BYRON 187:37	by d., rather than choice	KENN 482:31
d.…is a tree of life	BIBLE 104:55	desolation D. Angels	KERO 483:57	cannot escape d.	ROBBE 716:60
d. is increased by the difficulty	WEBS 926:20	D. in immaculate public	ROET 722:55	character is d.	ELIOT 315:37
d. is, that the Almighty	BIBLE 98:10	Great d. of abomination	COBB 233:76	d. demands and keep	NAPO 629:39
d. more love and knowledge	SHAK 778:61	love in d. masked	SHEL 815:36	d. is to keep down	DOUG 294:97
d. not to be impinged upon	BERL 84:46	made a d. they called it a peace	BURG 174:91	d. obscure	GRAY 384:66
D. not to be rinsed with wine	HOPK 428:68	Magnificent d.	ALDR 12:55	d. to wear a skirt in all countries	IZZA 448:83
d. of beauty…has most	PATER 668:11	perfect d.	FIELD 335:11	escape his d.	PLATO 681:51
d. of bettering our condition	SMITH 827:84	witnesses to the d. of war	GEOR 364:49	great hour of d.	SASS 745:83
d. of satisfying a voracious appetite	FIEL 335:24	despair Be thine d.	GRAY 385:88	Hanging and marriage…go by d.	FARQ 330:25
D. paces Eternity	DUNC 307:10	birds…without d.	WEBS 926:22	Hanging and wiving goes by d.	SHAK 769:96
d. shall fail	BIBLE 106:36	conscience wakes d.	MILT 603:90	historic d. of the Irish	WAUGH 924:81
d. to be rich	BAGE 54:76	D., not feast on thee	HOPK 429:88	imagine a d.	FIED 334:10
d. to create something	PRIE 695:90	d. of crystal brilliance	MACN 557:94	man…looking for his own d.	SAINT 738:43
d. to do right	DICK 283:17	D. yawns	HUGO 437:80	measure up to their d.	APOL 29:83
d. to have all the fun	SAYE 746:7	dungeon of d.	CESA 211:50	naturally, it's d.	BAUD 69:77
d. to integrate into society	SARR 744:62	filled me with a kind of d.	KAVA 474:47	our d. is not written for us	OBAMA 644:29
d. to know	RUSS 734:29	final d.…supreme victory	WHIT 976:31	part of the d.	THOR 888:26
d. to know causes	HAZL 404:52	forerunner of d.	KENN 480:92	riddles of…future d.	FRYE 354:57
d. to make money	VAN 909:16	from d. Thus high	MILT 602:55	shears of d.?	SHAK 768:57
d. to objectify	MOORE 617:83	Giant D. had a wife	BUNY 174:77	stream of d.	SPEN 838:25
d. to take medicine	OSLER 656:88	Happiness…in savouring their d.	GENG 363:43	'Tis my d.	FORD 343:4
d. to touch the truth	PACH 658:1	hurries me back to d.	COWP 251:98	what I took to be our d.	LEWIS 526:48
d. to win	CONN 242:90	iron-clasped volume of d.	POE 683:91	who can deceive his d.	SPEN 838:38
d. what we do not have	LABR 502:18	It was begotten by D.	MARV 577:95	destroy chose to d. themselves	HOYLE 434:95
few things to d.	BACON 52:1	Look on my works…and d.	SHEL 813:86	D. his fib…in vain	POPE 687:99
flaming in d.	ROCH 719:5	loves…of comfort and d.	SHAK 803:87	d. ourselves due to atrophy	GELL 363:33
forced by d.	RICH 714:15	made D. a smilingness assume	BYRON 187:49	d. the law	BIBLE 114:30
Free from d.	LAO 508:60	my character I d. for	FLEM 340:47	d. the town	ANON 25:61
fruitless d.	BINY 135:3	My meer d.	VAUG 909:33	impatient to d.	JOHN 459:47
gave to the queen of Sheba all her d.	BIBLE 98:85	needst not then d.!	ARNO 33:70	the gods wish to d.	OATES 643:14
horizontal d.	SHAW 810:25	neither d. in the church	FACK 329:1	To create is…to d.	CUMM 257:50
If d. has become complicated	BARN 64:74	One path leads to d.	ALLEN 14:98	write to d.	ROBBE 717:66
impersonation of d.	BROO 163:10	perplexed, but not in d.	BIBLE 127:67	destroyed d. her man	SYNGE 865:22
Is it not strange that d.	SHAK 772:83	quality of his d.	CONN 243:17	d. your enemies	HUSS 441:57
is the prompting of d.	LEHM 520:12	racked with deep d.	MILT 602:39	everything…has been d.	FENT 332:60
lit my pinnacle d.	SASS 745:88	resolution from d.	MILT 602:42	man can be d.	HEMI 410:87
lost the d. to lead anyone	BEVE 90:61	ruin and d.	WIEN 939:29	many a good tall fellow had d.	SHAK 771:33
love beyond d.	ELIOT 321:89	Should all d.	SHAK 799:10	More dreams are d.	SKEL 825:45
man's d.	HABI 391:3	sign of d. in a woman	WILDE 942:10	more easily it is d.	JOHN 463:59
man's d. is for the woman	COLE 236:49	Slimness Of D.	NICH 636:73	once d., can never be supplied	GOLD 376:98
mixing Memory and d.	ELIOT 317:35	Snobbery…a form of d.	BROD 160:38	What's not d. by Time	BRAM 156:58

destroyer

destroyer D. and preserver	SHEL	813:13
Is my d.	THOM	883:3
Time the d.	ELIOT	320:74
destroys What nourishes me d. me	JOLIE	465:12
destruction dark angel of d.	LENG	521:36
d. of all justice	MORE	619:23
d. of human life	HARDY	396:98
d. of the whole world	HUME	483:99
d. that wasteth at noonday	BIBLE	102:96
D. with d. to destroy	MILT	606:65
for d. ice	FROST	352:4
going from us to be utter d.	BIBLE	112:74
Hell and d. are never full	BIBLE	105:4
most frightful form of d.	MACA	546:60
on the side of d.	KEYN	484:71
Pride goeth before d.	BIBLE	105:79
redeemeth thy life from d.	BIBLE	102:6
soul...startles at d.	ADDI	7:52
way, that leadeth to d.	BIBLE	115:52
Whose end is d.	BIBLE	128:3
destructive d. and often malign	MUGG	623:11
the most d. force	JONES	466:28
to the d. element submit yourself	CONR	244:32
desuetization d. of Scottish life	MACD	550:39
detachment strangest sense of d.	WELLS	930:20
detail become the slave of d.	RYDER	736:58
emotion, d. and image	BRAU	157:86
frittered away by d.	THOR	889:38
Retail is d.	SCHU	749:71
details deal with many d.	MILLS	595:8
d....of man and career	ELTON	323:42
particular features or d.	GOYA	380:82
detection D. is...an exact science	DOYLE	296:43
d. of...human woes	DEWEY	276:19
detainees condone torture of d.	RICE	713:86
detective d. novel...form of art	PRIT	696:16
Ladies' D. Agency	SMITH	828:94
writing a d. story	JAMES	451:58
determination d. of incident?	JAMES	450:45
determinism retrospective d.	BEND	78:12
deterrent credible d.	MCNA	712:90
d. would continue to deter	MACM	556:68
detest my creator, d. and spurn me	SHEL	812:48
detestation show him your d.	PARN	665:46
Detroit D. is a one-trade town	MAIL	560:55
deuce how the d. they ever could	BYRON	189:94
devaluation d. of the human	MARX	578:25
devastation d....at Rome	AUGU	44:33
developed all this will have to be d.	ISHE	447:68
development arrested our d.	MILL	595:96
continuous and healthy d.	PARS	666:56
creation, d. and being	HUMB	438:93
d. in the productive facilities	MARX	579:30
d. itself ceases	PEAR	671:56
d. of mankind	NIET	638:12
human history and cosmic d.	BELL	78:88
if we approve of the d.	BEND	78:12
limit of its d.	ANON	24:5
own way of d.	WILS	949:81
phases of its d.	ERNST	327:39
process of historical d.	ROBI	718:94
progressive d.	GORB	378:47
symptomatic of...arrested d.	DISCH	287:9
truism in technological d.	STER	847:15
device miracle of rare d.	COLE	236:39
devices d. still are overthrown	SHAK	783:24
devil any sort of d. and the deep		
blue sea	RATT	707:78
apology for the D.	BUTL	186:5
as though some poor d.	SKIN	825:48
break a man's spirit is d.'s work	SHAW	808:89
But the D. whoops	KIPL	490:98
can the D. speak true?	SHAK	796:8
children of the d.	TENN	878:96
cleft the D.'s foot	DONNE	291:23
cursèd d.	WEBS	926:38
D. always builds a chapel	DEFOE	269:69
d., as a roaring lion	BIBLE	130:73
d. be in my feet	SCOTT	753:53
d. cam fiddlin thro' the town	BURNS	180:43
d. can cite Scripture	SHAK	769:84
d. damn thee black	SHAK	798:68
d. dancing in me glorious	MASE	580:63
d. had done for the rest	STEV	852:59
D. himself cannot make	MELV	585:71
D. howling 'Ho'	SQUI	841:90
d. is dead!	READE	708:97

D. is forever grinning in upon me	MELV	585:72
D. is still at hand	DRYD	301:68
d. made himself a woman	HUGO	437:71
d....on the side of the learned	FRAN	347:85
D. out of hell!	JOYCE	470:20
d.'s awa wi' th' Exciseman	BURNS	180:43
d. sends cooks	FULL	385:84
d. sends cooks	GARR	360:80
d. should have all the good tunes	HILL	418:57
d.'s sooner raised	SHER	817:86
d.'s walking parody	CHES	220:50
d. taketh him up	BIBLE	114:24
d. understands Welsh	SHAK	771:52
d. will come, and Faustus	MARL	573:30
D. with d. damned	MILT	603:67
D. with perhaps	MUGG	623:10
d. won't turn them	SCOTT	754:77
envy of the d.	BIBLE	112:73
face the d.!	BURNS	179:27
favourable reference to the D.	CHUR	226:7
fears a painted d.	SHAK	797:36
fight...against...the d.	BOOK	148:77
given up believing in the d.	KNOX	495:19
give the d. his due	SHAK	771:32
go, poor d., get thee gone	STER	848:31
Half d. and half child	KIPL	491:20
heaviest stone that the d. can throw	HAZL	404:56
he counteracts the D.	SMART	826:63
how the D. they got there	POPE	687:1
If the d. doesn't exist	DOST	294:92
know he is a d.	ETHE	327:45
laughing d. in sneer	BYRON	188:75
May be the d.	SHAK	782:4
Nazarite conjured the d. into!	SHAK	769:82
old serpent, called the D.	BIBLE	132:10
opportunity for attacking the d.!	STEAD	844:35
plain to see, the D. walks	BETJ	89:40
politician is the d.'s quilted anvil	WEBS	927:50
poor d. has ended	BROW	168:37
Pope Fired in the D.'s belly	ANON	23:96
renounce the d. and all his works	BOOK	148:78
Resist the d., and he will flee	BIBLE	130:58
sacrifice...of the d.'s leavings	POPE	686:56
sacrifice them all...to this d.	SHAK	770:15
said the D.	WALL	917:47
saint when most I play the d.	SHAK	761:39
servant to the d.	SISS	823:92
serve the d. and his angels	WENT	931:52
shame the d.	SHAK	771:49
Tell us, pray, what d.	FORD	343:8
tempted of the d.	BIBLE	114:22
that d.'s madness—War	SERV	757:37
The d.!	ONEI	651:65
The d. Bush	HUSS	440:38
Till the D. whispered	KIPL	490:97
truth and shame the d.	LIPP	531:36
wiles of the d.	BIBLE	128:95
with you the d. will fly away	OCON	646:84
devil-born doubt is D.-b.	TENN	874:91
devildoms d. of Spain	TENN	878:95
devilish most D. thing	FLEM	340:43
devil-porter I'll d.-p. it no further	SHAK	797:39
devils casteth out d.	BIBLE	116:65
cast out d.	BIBLE	116:67
d. also believe	BIBLE	130:53
d. as tiles	LUTH	542:71
d. being offended	SHAK	789:6
d. to contest his vision	MAIL	560:46
foreign d. have made	ORAH	652:91
innumerable monsters and d.	LUTH	542:75
more d. than vast hell	SHAK	767:45
said they were d. incarnate	SHAK	775:69
devise what one man can d.	WRIS	963:80
Devon D., glorious D.	BOUL	152:91
devotee great d. of the Gospel	SHAW	807:9
devotees most d. arrive	UPDI	906:32
devotion d. and our prayers	FRIE	351:76
d. of the wind and seas	LANC	506:23
hate with greater d.	SHAK	799:94
intelligence that moves, d. is	DONNE	293:80
object of universal d.	IRVI	447:62
passion for abstracted d.	JOHN	461:13
promote my invisible d.	BROW	164:43
with evergreen d.	BIRN	136:20
devour seeking whom he may d.	BIBLE	130:73
shed tears when they would d.	BACON	52:7
devoured could have d. me	KARSH	472:24

has d. the infant child	HOUS	433:80
devourer Time the d.	OVID	657:20
dew as sunlight drinketh d.	TENN	869:76
As the d. of Hermon	BIBLE	103:40
continual d. of thy blessing	BOOK	146:41
Debauchee of D.	DICK	283:33
d. her orbs upon the green	SHAK	767:25
d. of heaven	FORD	343:99
d. on the mountain	SCOTT	752:32
Drop down d.	BIBLE	133:40
fades awa' like morning d.	BALL	60:79
fresh with blooming d.	MERE	587:24
honey wild, and manna d.	KEATS	476:2
in the d. of the morn	YEATS	965:9
meet the morning d.	ARNO	35:21
Orient d., Shed from	MARV	576:86
pastures...washed with d.	SASS	746:1
rained a ghastly d.	TENN	871:17
resolve itself into a d.	SHAK	780:37
roses washed in d.	MILT	597:42
sea of d.	FIELD	335:13
speech shall distil as the d.	BIBLE	95:98
wave glittered the d.	MANS	567:5
wet with the d. of heaven	BIBLE	111:40
who hath begotten the drops of d.?	BIBLE	99:16
your chains to earth like us	SHEL	813:74
dewdrop fragile d.	KEATS	475:66
globe as one great d.	MUIR	624:56
Starlight and d.	FOST	345:56
dewdrops seek some d. here	SHAK	767:25
showers and d. wet	ROSS	726:46
Dewey D. has no inner reserve	HOOV	427:53
dewfall d. at night	STEV	853:84
dew-like d.-l. steel	BRAU	157:86
dew-pearled hill-side's d.-p.	BROW	167:9
dews drinker of d.	DOYLE	297:75
night d. on still waters	TENN	870:89
dewy-feathered d.-f. Sleep	MILT	598:58
dhoti Mahatma's cotton d.	MURR	627:80
diabetes Politics is like having d.	JONES	465:20
diagnose able to d.	KEYN	484:71
diagnostician One finger...d.	OSLER	656:90
dial d.'s shady stealth	SHAK	801:65
needle on a d.	STEV	851:11
ride upon a d.'s point	SHAK	772:63
dialect d. I understand very little	PEPYS	673:96
purify the d. of the tribe	ELIOT	381:86
use of d. words	HARDY	397:11
dialogue And the d.!	CHAN	213:83
conviction is to report that d.	KUNI	501:41
Death is a d.	DICK	284:46
d. between client and architect	STERN	847:18
film script...without d.	MAMET	564:41
settlement through genuine d.	AUNG	45:40
unending d. between the present	CARR	202:51
dialogues d. with my Mother	WORD	958:81
dials carve out d.	SHAK	760:8
d. the signs	SHAK	770:27
diamond d. and safire bracelet	LOOS	536:52
d....has scarce any value in use	SMITH	827:78
find a d. or a pearl	VAN	908:20
immortal d.	HOPK	429:94
more of rough than polished d.	CHES	219:41
soul...like a rough d.	DEFOE	269:67
diamonds d. and rubies	MORE	618:25
D. are of most precious value	WEBS	926:42
d. in the smog of...Megalopolis	MAIL	560:55
give him d. back	GABOR	356:3
Goodness what beautiful d.!	WEST	933:84
graven with d. in letters plain	WYATT	963:88
put d. on the floor	RIVE	716:56
throat cut With d.?	WEBS	927:58
Diana awf'lly bad luck on D.	BETJ	89:44
break D.'s law	POPE	685:35
legs were such D. shows	HERR	415:8
diaries good girls keep d.	BANK	61:15
wrote in my d. about...meals	BUSH	182:95
diary life of every man is a d.	BARR	64:83
more important than...d.	SASS	746:94
Secret D. of Adrian Mole	TOWN	894:67
The d. will...tell people who you are	FOWL	346:66
dice A throw of the d.	MALL	562:2
d. of God	EMER	324:57
[God] does not play d.	EINS	313:75
God not only plays d.	HAWK	401:87
heraldic equivalent of...furry d.	ANON	27:13
If the iron d. roll	BETH	87:12

difference

dichotomy D. = operation	TYNAN 904:8
Dick D., I don't know how	NIXON 640:31
D. the shepherd blows	SHAK 763:27
Dickens D., Tolstoy, Hugo	LESS 523:93
D....unremitting humanity	BENN 80:50
D. was not the first	PRIT 696:19
rewritten by Charles D.	COOKE 245:73
Thackeray and D.	STEV 852:53
dickens what the d. his name is	SHAK 773:8
dictates d. of reason	DICK 282:3
dictation told at d. speed	AMIS 16:40
dictator I am not a d.	PINO 678:81
not a director, he's a d.	MONR 612:6
dictators d. nor the bureaucrats	ORWE 654:57
personal contact with the d.	CHAM 212:65
seen by d. as subversive	JONG 466:30
dictatorship class struggle...d.	MARX 579:31
decapitated him from the d.	POWE 693:52
d. is beginning	SHEV 818:11
establish a d.	ORWE 655:78
nakedness of Stalinist d.	KENN 480:88
Television has made d. impossible	PERES 674:23
dictatorships bringing down d.	OROU 652:95
dictionaries D. are like watches	JOHN 464:96
To make d. is dull work	JOHN 460:73
writer of d.	JOHN 460:67
writer of d.	JOHN 460:75
dictionary d. of popular usage	GREE 386:17
except in the d.	KIMB 486:13
father still reads the d.	SCAR 746:13
first time I ever made the d.	WEST 933:91
Like Webster's d.	BURKE 176:60
outside of a d.	LODGE 534:95
sensible as a d.!	CARR 204:92
set him upon his d.	STEV 852:53
the metre of the d.?	THOM 883:10
diddle d., we take it, is dee	SWIN 864:18
die After I d.	TOSC 894:64
all shall d.	SHAK 772:86
and let him d.	TENN 875:95
appetite may sicken and so d.	SHAK 785:77
appointed unto men once to d.	BIBLE 129:37
as in Adam all d.	BIBLE 127:57
asleep, or hearing, d.	SHAK 804:45
as natural to d.	BACON 50:59
bear to live, or dare to d.	POPE 687:87
Beauty lives though lilies d.	FLEC 340:31
before I d.	MARTI 576:71
believe in ideas and d. for them	ANOU 28:63
blithe earth d.	JEFF 453:12
Born but to d.	POPE 687:80
break it must d.	KIPL 490:7
but nobody wants to d.	LOUIS 538:76
but they d.	UPDI 906:34
but to d., and go we	SHAK 788:69
but to do and d.	TENN 875:12
can't d., along the coast	DICK 280:52
change, but I cannot d.	SHEL 813:77
content to d.	BROWN 164:28
Cowards d. many times	SHAK 777:21
Created to pretend we never d.	LARK 510:96
curse God, and d.	BIBLE 98:93
Death, thou shalt d.!	DONNE 292:52
d. after having lived this way	LABR 502:18
d. and be a riddance!	DICK 280:39
d. at the age of thirty-seven	WALT 920:97
d. but once to serve our country	ADDI 7:50
d. dishevelled and soft	LOWE 540:29
d. each time	HEMI 410:80
d. fighting for his country	HOMER 425:8
D. for adultery!	SHAK 793:21
d. for free	VALLE 907:7
d. for my country?	SITT 823:93
d. happy	FOX 346:70
d. if you let it loose	SHAW 809:88
d. in errancy	ABU 1:12
d. in exile	GREG 387:51
d. in harness	AMIS 16:33
d. in the Lord	BIBLE 132:13
d. is better than length of days	AESC 8:79
d. is cast	CAES 192:13
D.? I should say not	BARR 65:1
d. laughing	WEBS 926:35
d. on your feet	IBAR 444:5
d. or get kicked out	HOOV 427:48
d. so young	AUDEN 43:84
d. the death	BIBLE 113:94
d. when curiosity goes	SWIFT 861:13
d. while you're still productive	BROD 160:32
d. without having played	BORO 151:66
Don't d. of ignorance	ANON 26:97
Don't d. like I did	BEST 87:9
do or d.!	BURNS 180:48
do we not d.?	SHAK 769:1
Easy live and quiet d.	SCOTT 754:64
either love, or I must d.	FORD 343:4
Even if I d.	GAND 359:57
every man...born to d.	DRYD 304:54
Export or d.	ANON 24:22
Fall asleep, or hearing d.	SHAK 804:45
fated not to d.	DRYD 303:9
fear'st to d.?	SHAK 766:12
fight and d. for your country	GOLD 377:23
For all the death, we...d. unrehearsed	MURR 627:81
For another thing, they d. earlier	MENC 586:99
For thou must d.	HERB 414:80
for tomorrow we d.	BIBLE 127:59
For tomorrow we shall d.	PARK 664:15
God does not d.	HAMM 394:54
Good Americans, when they d.	APPL 30:92
good d. early	DEFOE 269:68
have the power to d.	TENN 877:62
hazard of the d.	SHAK 761:56
Hope I d. before	TOWN 895:70
hope that he will d.	EMER 325:86
I clasp them...because they d.	CORY 272:11
idea d. instead of you	LEWIS 527:64
If I d., avenge me	MUSS 627:89
if I shall d. here	MATAK 581:84
If I should d.	BROO 162:88
If it were now to d.	SHAK 789:8
I must d.	KEATS 478:49
in a month you've got to d.	GILB 369:59
in what peace a Christian can d.	ADDI 7:57
Is not born...does not d.	SITW 824:14
I, too, will d. by violence	MALC 562:90
I will d. in Paris	VALL 907:10
I will d. in peace	WOLFE 953:65
I will not have thee d.!	TENN 873:48
John Barleycorn should d.	BURNS 178:99
lerne to d. gladly	ANON 21:58
let it d. with thee	BIBLE 113:99
Let us determine to d. here	BEE 73:60
Live and Let D.	FLEM 340:40
live forever or d. in the attempt	HELL 407:26
live, I d.	LABE 501:3
love one man till I d.	HAMM 394:62
make a malefactor d. sweetly	DRYD 303:25
man can d. but once	SHAK 772:88
memory d. from the earth	SIDN 820:59
men to d.	BARK 63:54
most grand to d.	MASE 580:61
must men kill and d.?	SHEL 816:58
must needs d.	BIBLE 96:47
never can he d.	SPEN 839:40
not d. when the trees were green	CLARE 228:56
not made to d.	TENN 873:55
not so difficult to d.	BYRON 189:88
not that I'm afraid to d.	ALLEN 14:87
O, I d., Horatio!	SHAK 785:74
One should d.	PLATO 682:56
only d. once	MOLI 611:72
opponents eventually d.	PLAN 680:25
Or let me d.!	WORD 959:98
parting was to d.	TENN 874:93
people only d. at the last moment	CELI 211:39
pleasant thing to d. like this	BOUC 152:85
rather d. than not do so	BOUL 152:87
regret can d.!	TENN 874:87
religious system...can never really d.	SAKI 739:51
requested...that he might d.	BIBLE 97:66
resolve to conquer or d.	WASH 921:27
see my funeral before I d.	EDGE 311:38
smile can make one d.	SAINT 738:38
something he will d. for	KING 487:26
teach the rustic moralist to d.	GRAY 384:73
that I Must d.	DONNE 291:24
they only let Him d.	STUD 858:64
they say you d. twice	BANKS 62:31
those that do d.	SHAK 795:91
thou shalt surely d.	BIBLE 91:88
Thus will I d.	DYER 309:50
time to d.	BIBLE 105:14
to choose life and d.	LOWE 540:26
toddle safely home and d.	SASS 745:85
to d. for one's country	HORA 430:10
to d. in dust	SPEN 839:47
to d. is different	WHIT 937:91
to d. is gain	BIBLE 128:96
To d. is nothing	ANOU 28:67
To d., to sleep	SHAK 782:7
to d. upon a kiss	SHAK 791:52
To d. will be an awfully big adventure	BARR 65:87
To-morrow let us do or d.!	CAMP 194:67
to morrow we shall d.	BIBLE 108:65
To triumph, and to d.	GRAY 385:88
we d. in earnest	RALE 705:45
weep or she will d.	TENN 873:46
we shall d....'tis but the time	SHAK 777:29
we who are about to d.	ANON 20:22
What 'tis to d.	BEAU 71:14
when I came to d.	THOR 888:37
When I d.	DONL 290:9
When I d. people will say	COMP 239:5
Where thou diest, will I d.	BIBLE 96:23
Whether we live...or d.	BIBLE 126:33
why will ye d.	BIBLE 111:34
with us, or we d.	KEATS 476:86
wit may wander ere he d.	TENN 878:74
word...for which you d.	WEIL 928:76
would surely d.	HELL 408:33
Ye shall not surely d.	BIBLE 91:92
You and I ought not to d.	ADAMS 5:2
You know when I need to d.?	ARMS 32:43
died all summer settled there and d.	LARK 509:74
d. amidst your dying country's cries	GRAY 385:83
d. as he had lived	CLEM 229:85
d. As one that had been studied	SHAK 796:11
d....before his birth	THUR 891:8
D., has he?	LOUIS 537:72
d. to save us all	ALEX 13:64
friends who d.	SASS 745:89
Just before she d.	STEIN 845:75
like saying that the patient d.	JACO 449:9
Men have d. from time to time	SHAK 779:10
Mithridates, he d. old	HOUS 432:60
mother-in-law d.	JERO 454:39
my people d. to build this country	ROBE 717:76
question why we d.	KIPL 493:76
She should have d. hereafter	SHAK 798:74
sweet dove d.	KEATS 475:71
We came, we saw, he d.	CLIN 231:34
when a Forsyte d.	GALS 358:48
When I d.	JARR 452:83
would God I had d. for thee	BIBLE 97:49
Would to God we had d.	BIBLE 93:64
Yes. As I d.	HEMI 410:10
dies Breed never d.	BENN 80:46
d. among the mountains	WORD 958:90
d. married young	SHAK 766:10
each day d. with sleep	HOPK 429:92
erect...his own tomb ere he d.	SHAK 774:57
He that d.	SHAK 778:70
how a man d.	JOHN 462:19
kingdom where nobody d.	MILL 592:30
man marries, d., or turns Hindoo	SHEL 814:4
something in me d.	VIDAL 912:89
soul...languishes and d.	ROCH 720:25
spectre-thin, and d.	KEATS 475:75
that little flame which never d.	RENO 711:58
then he d.	KIPL 489:70
when the Poet d.	SCOTT 752:15
who d. fighting has increase	GREN 388:57
worm that never d.	BROO 163:2
diet adoption of vegetable d.	SHEL 812:53
d. unparalleled	DICK 278:75
Give it a d.	DONNE 292:45
gods will d. me with	SHAK 803:2
immortal d.	RALE 705:44
In D., Furniture and Dress	MAND 565:65
twelfth day of my d.	PIER 677:69
differ d. chiefly in the boldness	JEVO 455:54
d. from those of common sense	HUXL 443:10
difference biggest d....she was taller	FEIB 331:54
couldn't tell the d.	LENO 522:56
country saves the d.	BAGE 54:71
crucial d. between	NISB 639:27
d. between a dog and a man	TWAIN 903:73
d. between burning and gassing	SIHA 821:65
d. between most people	TUCH 901:13
d. between one young woman	SHAW 809:77

differences

d. between the most dissimilar	SMITH 827:77
d. between unethical and ethical	STEF 844:53
d. is…that of the living and the dead	CIXO 227:42
d. of 40,000 men	WELL 929:8
d. that makes a d.	BATE 68:54
don't make no d.	TWAIN 903:66
don't make no d.	TWAIN 903:67
love…Cares not for d.	DEKK 270:9
made all the d.	FROST 352:95
more d. within the sexes	COMP 239:4
only d. between us	BIRK 136:14
shade of d.	GREE 386:27
That's the d. between us	SHAW 810:26
The d. to me!	WORD 957:62
trust the very d.	JORD 469:2

differences cannot now end our d. — KENN 481:18
d. one finds among men	PASC 667:83
Jews and Arabs…settle their d.	AUST 47:99
little d. of speed	PRATT 694:68
National d. consist	NIET 639:17
open exchange of major d.	AUNG 45:40

different d. kinds of things sound — HONO 426:16
D. living is not living	SPEN 837:3
d. waters flow	HERA 412:33
do not feel greatly d.	BEAV 71:31
How d., how very d.	ANON 23:98
once you're hungry, you're d.	HUNT 439:17
saying something d.	HAVEL 401:85

differently One who has hope lives d. — BENE 79:22
they do things d. there — HART 400:76

difficult childhood…is just as d. — RILKE 715:37
D. do you call it	JOHN 464:1
d. not to write satire	JUVE 471:52
Endure what is d. to endure	HIRO 419:72
found d.; and left untried	CHES 220:77
living up to it that is d.	THAC 880:36
more d. from its rudeness	JOHN 463:63
others extremely d.	JOHN 464:85
still more d. question	GRAV 383:39
too d. for artists	SCHN 748:46
very d., maybe impossible	SOLOW 833:3
When a piece gets d.	SCHN 748:45
writing a good play is d.	PRIE 695:94

difficulties d. in providing — COMM 239:94
d. which have…amused philosophers	BERK 84:29
political and practical d.	KEYN 484:80

difficulty complexity, and d. — TRIL 897:13
if it had much d. — JOHN 463:70

diffidence and her name was D. — BUNY 174:77

dig d. and heap — ARNO 34:76
D. for Victory — DORAM 294:84
d. with it — HEAN 404:67

digamma simple d. in Homer — QUIL 702:16

digest inwardly d. them — BOOK 147:52
shall d. it — SHAK 770:9

digestion Few radicals have good d. — BUTL 186:7
good eater must have a good d. — DISR 287:17
man…think…about his d. — LEWIS 526:49
to facilitate d. — VOLT 914:47

diggeth d. a pit — BIBLE 106:31

digital d. technology makes connecting possible — DOWD 296:33

dignities by indignities…to d. — BACON 51:85
peace above all earthly d. — SHAK 805:51

dignity assumption of d. — GALT 359:56
confers d. on a picture	ALBE 11:31
declares his d.	MILT 604:5
d. and worth	UNIT 905:9
d. in tilling a field	WASH 921:22
d. or baseness of a person	CHRI 223:46
imperishable d. of man	CARL 200:86
love was of that d.	SHAK 781:63
Official d. tends to increase	HUXL 442:77
penumbra of somber d.	ATLAS 40:19
sense of…moral d.	CURZ 260:5
simple d. of a child	SAND 742:33
stark d. of entrance	WILL 946:9
to give it possibility, scope, even d.	MACL 555:43
walk with sincerity and d.	WAITE 916:6
with silent d.	GROS 389:80

Digressions D.…are the sunshine — STER 848:28

dildos delicate burdens of d. — SHAK 800:24

dilemmas d. of conscience — SNOW 832:75

dilettante d. looks only for pleasure — REDON 709:22
snowy-banded, d. — TENN 876:19

dilettantism bureaucracy and d. — WEBER 925:14

dilly-dally Don't d.-d. on the way — COLL 237:64

dilute d. it by voting for anyone	ONAS 650:53
dim d.…Of night	YEATS 966:12
Pinnacled in the intense inane	SHEL 814:18
so d. and they're so smart	ROTH 728:92
dime can you spare a d.?	HARB 396:87
still don't have a d.	FEIF 331:55
dimension extra d. of feeling	FOWL 345:61
dimensions certain d. of thought	STEI 846:98
d. of a man's self	LAMB 505:6
d. of a man's self	LAMB 505:8
Time has three d.	HOPK 429:85
dimes come here bright as d.	LOWE 540:29
diminished national dividend is d.	PIGOU 678:76
rights of every man are d.	KENN 481:19
what to make of a d. thing	FROST 352:97
diminution increase or d.	RICA 712:84
diminutive man is a d. to nothing	DONNE 293:66
dimples hair and d. is coming	MOORE 616:70
din louder still the d.	MACA 546:52
'mid the d. Of towns and cities	WORD 956:53
music's d.	GILB 368:40
will not be heard above the d.	READ 708:96
dine bulls and foxes d. very well	JUST 471:50
d. with some men	BENT 82:99
English would manage to meet and d.	JERR 455:49
heroes to d. with us	TROL 898:44
tempt me to d. with him	SWIFT 861:30
dined if one has not d. well	WOOLF 955:25
diner Dinner in the d.	GORD 378:56
philosophic d.-out	BROW 169:68
dinero Salud, D., Amor…y Tiempo	ANON 28:57
diners feeding the poop back to d.	COUP 248:29
laughing in the d.	SAND 742:15
locations such as d.	COUP 248:26
dines say something when he d.	HUNT 440:31
dingy fatally poor and d.	WHAR 933:5
dining thought of d.	GOLD 377:17
dinner After a good d.	WILDE 941:89
After d. to the Duke's house	PEPYS 673:95
At a d. party one should	MAUG 582:3
best number for a d. party	GULB 390:91
Burning d.	PIER 677:67
criticize after d.	MARX 579:29
delicious d. of too much	JOHN 457:1
D. in the diner	GORD 378:56
d. of herbs where love is	BIBLE 104:75
D. parties are for eating	FERB 332:72
d. party of more than two	MENC 587:8
D.…possessed…two dramatic features	POWE 693:44
expect if we haven't any d.	LEAR 517:43
expect our d.	SMITH 827:76
get it down onto the d. table	BONA 145:16
I managed at d.	RIDGE 715:33
mak our d. sweet	BALL 59:77
man should have d.	LEMAY 521:31
more business after d.	SWIFT 861:36
Music with d. is an insult	CHES 221:11
old friend for d.	TALLY 866:20
one cannot talk about after d.	WILDE 941:72
re-union d.	PARK 665:36
revolution is not a d. party	MAO 568:25
sinner…with no d.	RANS 707:73
three hours' march to d.	HAZL 403:40
too hungry for d. at eight	HART 400:67
whatever one had got for d.	RUSK 733:12
dinners all the d. are cooked	WOOLF 955:33
housewife's badly-cooked d.	BEET 74:7
more d. than appetites	CHAM 213:70
dinner-table dominate a…d.-t.	WILDE 941:93
dinosaurs like the bones of d.	RAND 706:58
dint d. of pity	SHAK 778:44
Diogenes would be D.	ALEX 12:57
Dionysus Christ follows D.	POUND 691:3
dip Leaning over…a lucky d.	DAY 267:38
diphtheria d. restored the status	HAMER 393:45
diploma d. is a lighted match	KOCH 495:23
diplomacy D.…patriotic art of lying	BIER 134:74
Megaphone d.	HOWE 433:87
Rolls Royce d.	ANON 26:84
superstition of an antiquated d.	CECIL 210:34
underrated aspects of d.	SHUL 819:22
When d. fails	CHEN 218:24
diplomat A d. these days	USTI 906:44
d. is a deaf Trappist	LECA 518:74
diplomatic D. problems	ACHE 2:26
putting out a d. boathook	CECIL 210:30
diplomatist salad…brilliant d.	WILDE 940:46

diplomats better that aged d.	AUST 47:98
D. and protocols are…good	PALM 661:68
D. lie to journalists	KRAUS 499:9
direction any sense of d.	WILS 947:38
blowing the new d. of Time	LAWR 512:45
d. of our fears	BERR 87:95
d. of society	TOCQ 892:26
d. of the right line	NEWT 635:57
d., which thou canst not see	POPE 687:79
going in the opposite d.	NICO 637:85
I have not settled in which d.	BEAV 71:31
lines running in every d.	ROSS 725:35
looking together in the same d.	SAINT 738:32
new d. to technological	SCHU 750:74
one positive pitch or d.	HOPK 429:85
our ways and our d.	THAT 881:53
precisely in the same d.	PEARY 671:60
step in the wrong d.	LEVA 525:16
directions moving in opposite d.	SMITH 831:58
not equally stupid in all d.	BELL 77:82
rode madly off in all d.	LEAC 515:14
director actor giving positive criticism to a d.	MULL 624:31
d. makes only one film in his life	RENO 711:52
no one but the d.	POLA 684:1
not a d., he's a dictator	MONR 612:6
telephone call from a d.	PORT 690:91
directors ideal board of d.	DOCH 289:27
direful something d. in the sound	AUST 46:78
dirge knell is rung…their d. is sung	COLL 237:72
dirt As ignorant as d.!	SHAK 790:47
Delay and d. are the realities	THER 882:44
d. doesn't get any worse	CRISP 255:4
d. kept breathing	ROET 722:58
d., or grubs, or worms	POPE 687:1
Huddled in d.	ROCH 719:12
If d. were trumps	LAMB 505:7
Instead of d. and poison	SWIFT 861:18
make crossness and d. succeed	FORS 344:39
mix sentences with d.	BRAU 157:83
out of the d.	ALTH 15:16
reputation for d.	THOR 889:49
turn to d.	SHAK 803:5
you should smell like d.	ATWO 41:53
dirty big words…about d. things	DOCT 289:82
d. son-of-a-bitch	STEI 845:82
D., ugly, disagreeable	DICK 281:73
d., wet hole	TOLK 893:42
the d. weekend	SMITH 828:1
this d., despicable little island	WALP 919:25
thugh d. is clein	FLEM 340:48
dirty-mindedness journalistic d.-m.	LAWR 513:74
disabled trade union for the d.	HEATH 405:84
disadvantage D. of being a hog	MORT 621:73
disagree when doctors d.	POPE 686:65
disagreeable not d. to him	JOHN 464:78
such a d. man	GILB 369:56
when she stoops to be d.	AUST 46:79
disagreement absence of d. testifies	MERT 589:55
disagrees a country that d.	RUMS 731:43
can't find anyone who d.	BENN 79:33
disappear like having a continent d.	JARR 452:82
want to d.	HUGO 437:5
disappointed haven't been d.	GRAMM 381:94
disappointing war is somewhat d.	GRIF 388:22
disappointment D. all I endeavour parents…sometimes a d.	HOPK 429:95
without a feeling of d.	POWE 693:42
disappointments hard work, d.	LAMB 505:88
disapprove d. of what you say	PEARY 671:59
something of which you d.	VOLT 915:50
disapproving Our capacity for d.	FIND 336:43
disarm d. the strong	DRAB 298:85
disarmament Iraq appears not to have come to a genuine acceptance…of…d.	FRAN 347:87
disaster a glimpse of such a d.	BLIX 142:59
audience was a d.	ORWE 653:24
d. until it is finally manifest	WILDE 941:82
genetic d.	MURP 626:74
loss is no d.	WELSH 930:41
meet with Triumph and D.	BISH 137:25
recent d. at Rome	KIPL 492:62
road to d.	AUGU 44:33
single…not such a fearful d.	LLOY 533:79
worst d. since my election	ZHANG 969:7
disasters children…notorious d.	BROWN 164:34
	EURI 328:64

day's d. in his morning face	GOLD 376:1	better part of valour is d.	SHAK 772:68	naked is the best d.	CONG 240:40
d. of the world	CONN 243:12	D. is the better part of Valerie	MCGO 552:77	disguised certainly very well d.	CHUR 226:1
make guilty of our d.	SHAK 792:89	d. that would have done credit	SHAR 806:73	d. as insoluble problems	GARD 360:70
the d. in your life are not the d.	MANT 568:21	fail to observe decency and d.	BACON 49:22	disguiser Death's a great d.	SHAK 788:77
disastrous d. and the unpalatable	GALB 357:18	now come to the years of d.	BOOK 148:82	disgust but as a d.	TZARA 904:19
d. Presidents and Prime Ministers	ONAS 650:52	reached the height of d.	BENN 81:74	d. is reason's proper response	PAGL 659:17
to win a war is as d. as to lose	CHRI 223:44	survives by d.	WILL 945:86	Loves die from d.	LABR 502:15
disbelief willing suspension of d.	COLE 236:44	That which love worst endures, d.	DONNE 292:45	Mummy, I'm sick with d.	BETJ 89:45
discerning Gives genius a better d.	GOLD 376:11	discrimination D. is a hellhound	KING 487:34	see…my body without d.	BAUD 68:69
discharge d. of any profession	JOHN 462:35	discussion after reasonable d.	CHUR 226:18	touch a newspaper without d.	BAUD 69:88
no d. in that war	BIBLE 106:24	Democracy means government by d.	ATTL 40:30	dish butter in a lordly d.	BIBLE 95:12
disciple d. is not above his master	BIBLE 116:70	d. of any subject	SHEL 812:50	discovery of a new d.	BRIL 159:18
d. who does not excel	LEON 522:73	opportunity cost of economic d.	GALB 357:22	d. fit for the gods	SHAK 776:17
disciples d. came to him	BIBLE 116:61	discussions hate d. of feminism	FREN 350:52	here's a d. I love not	SHAK 774:29
d. rebuked them	BIBLE 118:16	disdain d. the future now	KENN 481:21	some d. more sharply spiced	PATM 669:26
d. saw him walking on the sea	BIBLE 117:99	fall from her d.	KYD 501:47	dishclout Romeo's a d. to him	SHAK 766:6
followers of Jesus…his d.	JOHN 459:38	fortified with a strange d.	WEBS 927:55	dishes Are these the choice d.	GARR 360:80
gave it to the d.	BIBLE 119:40	gifts increased by d.	SURR 860:99	child will make two D.	SWIFT 862:59
hand toward his d.	BIBLE 117:89	little d. is not amiss	CONG 241:69	d. were ill-sorted	DRYD 304:43
know that ye are my d.	BIBLE 123:50	love or more d.	CAREW 199:59	do the bloody d.	JAMES 450:33
Likewise also said all the d.	BIBLE 119:41	What, my dear Lady D.!	SHAK 773:20	Home-made d. that drive	HOOD 426:28
nowadays has his d.	WILDE 940:54	disdainful d. wave of a white	ANGE 19:99	who does the d.	FREN 350:52
discipleship grace without d.	BONH 146:23	disease All writing is a d.	WILL 946:27	dishonour d. the vices	WILD 943:49
discipline d. of a monastery	AELR 8:74	artistic temperament is a d.	CHES 220:62	in d. stood	TENN 877:54
d. of humanity	BACON 51:74	biggest d. today	THER 882:81	dishonourable indecent and d.	HELL 408:41
d. of our holy Church	OCON 646:82	cause of my d.	SURR 860:98	dishwasher You emptied…the d.	MOORE 616:75
habit of d.	TUCH 901:12	cure the d. and kill the patient	BACON 52:15	disillusionment D. in living	STEIN 845:64
Life has no other d.	MILL 594:62	democratic d.	MILL 594:84	this age of d.?	SHIP 818:15
Nature's stern d.	DOBZ 289:79	desperate d.…dangerous remedy	FAWK 331:53	disillusionments d. in the lives	SAKI 739:54
scientist may find his d. severe	CORN 247:6	d. is incurable	CHEK 218:9	disinfectant Sunlight is the best d.	KENN 480:97
testifies to a developing d.	MERT 589:55	d. is incurable	SHAK 772:75	disintegrate People who d.	AUST 47:91
disciplines deeply biting of social d.	LAWR 514:93	d. will spread with…malignity	DICK 282:92	disinterested meant to be d., pure	SELF 756:10
disclosure a short story is always a d.	PRIT 696:24	d. you don't look forward to	MANK 565:70	dislike d.…at first sight	STEE 844:49
Discobbolos Till Mrs D. said	LEAR 516:34	Drug misuse is the only d.	DICK 277:36	like or d. them	FORS 334:34
discomfort d., fatigue, strain in large		elimination of some d.	SUTH 860:7	disliked d. by all his friends	WILDE 942:27
amounts	GELL 363:35	free from bad news and d.	BIOY 135:5	disloyalty not like subversion or d.	HELL 408:41
d. of…self-examination	PECK 672:62	Hypochondria is the only d.	ANON 26:77	dismal d. grew his countenance	BALL 58:58
disconnect d. it from the rest of them	FITZ 337:76	I have Bright's d.	PERE 674:13	dismay avoid us with d.	TOLK 893:47
discontent contented sort of d.	KEATS 476:8	introduced d. and decay	SHER 816:69	flies about in d.	KIER 485:5
divine d.	KING 488:55	Life is an incurable d.	COWL 250:74	dismayed Be not afraid nor d.	BIBLE 98:87
fruitful source of family d.	BEET 74:7	Life is a sexually transmitted d.	ANON 26:4	neither be thou d.	BIBLE 95:6
winter of our d.	SHAK 760:31	longer nurseth the d.	SHAK 803:88	dismissed fifty men d.?	SHAK 792:2
discontented hundred men d.	LOUI 537:67	name any d. after two guys	PUZO 701:9	dismount picking the place to d.	BALL 58:46
discontinuity d. within	ROTH 727:76	national d.	MCCU 549:13	Disney D. probably has the right idea	HITC 419:86
discord All d., harmony	POPE 687:79	no cure for this d.	BELL 76:59	disobedience campaign of civil d.	CHUR 225:79
dire effects from civil d.	ADDI 7:53	no d., bodily or mental	SHEL 812:53	curse of d.	OTWAY 656:98
Harmony in d.	HORA 430:15	Progress is a comfortable d.	CUMM 258:67	disorder last d. mortal	GOLD 376:84
Melodious d.	SHAK 762:87	rarer forms of d.	HARV 400:78	Post Traumatic Stress D.	SELL 756:16
Where there is d.	THAT 881:54	Red-and-gold d.	MUSC 627:86	sweet d. in the dress	HERR 416:17
discourage the composer	HEIF 407:12	remedy is worse than the d.	BACON 52:96	disorders common mental d.	GRAV 382:35
d. them from…attempts	STEV 852:44	scars of d.	MACA 545:36	disorientation stress and d.	TOFF 893:37
discouraged do not be d.	HEMI 410:89	shapes of foul d.	TENN 875:96	disorienting d., and painful	RICH 713:1
discourse Bid me d.	SHAK 762:83	strange d. of modern life	ARNO 34:94	disparities not for such large d.	KEYN 485:85
d. of the elders	BIBLE 113:86	suffering from the particular d.	JERO 454:38	disparity d. between things	ALBEE 11:23
d. was about hunting	PEPYS 673:96	Tedium is the worst d.	POMP 684:12	dispatch Spaniards' d.	ROCH 719:9
fittest for d.	DRYD 302:2	There is one d. which is widespread	MAIM 561:70	dispensation in the old d.	ELIOT 318:18
political or the scientific d.	LEGU 520:17	wasting d. of the frontal lobes	ALBEE 11:27	dispiriting cannot but be d.	SMITH 830:40
provisions for d.	AUST 45:51	while Nature cures the d.	VOLT 915:49	displaced I feel d. when I'm back in	
Read not to…find talk and d.	BACON 53:36	worse d., t'escape	JONS 467:50	America	HYNDE 444:23
subtle and sinewy to d.	MILT 601:18	diseased romantic d.	GOET 375:68	displacement d. is the rust	ANGE 18:83
discourses all d. but mine	JONS 467:61	When love grows d.	ETHE 327:47	displeasing which is not d.	LARO 510:1
discover anxious to d.	RUSS 734:35	diseases death is the cure of all d.	BROW 165:71	dispone for dede d.	DUNB 306:4
d. what we ourselves believe	GRANT 381:8	healeth all thy d.	BIBLE 102:6	disposes God d.	KEMP 480:76
Man…can only d.	PAINE 660:38	lists of fatal d.	HELL 407:29	disposition d. of the Working Class	CARL 201:22
often d. what will do	SMIL 827:72	painful, chronic d.	JONES 465:20	d. that I owe	SHAK 797:50
should not d.	GORD 378:53	remedy to all d.	BURT 181:83	goes so heavily with my d.	SHAK 782:88
To dance is to d.	SENG 757:29	scientific treatment for all d.	SHAW 809:80	his goatish d.	SHAK 792:89
discoverers They are ill d.	BACON 49:29	sneezes spread d.	ANON 24:24	liveliness of my d.	FRED 349:37
discoveries consequence of d.	BACON 50:45	subject to the same d.	SHAK 769:1	mild or choleric d.	ADDI 6:23
d. are made…in the dustbin	BENN 80:60	talk of d. is…entertainment	OSLER 656:91	strong d. in youth	POWE 693:42
d. made	FRAN 348:18	vulnerable to infectious d.	KOES 495:29	dispositions d.…loved in private	BURKE 175:11
more important than their d.	BRON 160:47	diseconomies hit d. of scale early	MCDO 550:14	d. of…mankind	BURKE 175:9
discovering Writing a poem is d.	FROST 353:18	disembodied d. and…murdered	SHAR 806:77	disproof d. is turned aimlessly aside	EDDI 311:26
discovery d. aside	MUNRO 625:49	disfigurement perceive their foul d.	MILT 598:63	disproven Nor yet d.	TENN 879:4
D. consists of seeing	SZENT 865:29	disgrace d. to the English nation	INNO 446:48	disputants d. put me in mind	ADDI 7:43
d. of some occult relation	JOHN 459:54	d. to the planet	STONE 855:10	disputation that's a feeling d.	SHAK 771:51
If scientists knew tomorrow's d.	ZUCK 970:20	d. to the playing fields	FRY 353:28	disputations d. of Plato	HONO 426:17
logic of d.	NISB 639:27	Even to a d.	SHAK 799:3	Doubtful d.	BIBLE 126:32
make room for d.	APOL 29:86	Peace without honour is not only a d.	CECIL 210:27	dispute D. it like a man	SHAK 798:62
medicinal d.	AYRES 48:9	retreats without fearing d.	SUN 859:93	Shakespeare–Bacon d.	GILB 370:75
moral d.…the object of every tale	CONR 244:42	disgraced dies rich…dies d.	CARN 202:47	disputes international d.	EISE 314:1
never made a d.	SMIL 827:72	d., impeached, and baffled	SHAK 764:30	lay your d. a' aside	SKIN 825:50
new theory…a d.	POPP 689:54	wrongfully d.	SHAK 801:58	left to their d.	MILT 605:35
portals of d.	JOYCE 470:27	You have d. yourselves	YEATS 966:13	traditional d. of philosophers	AYER 47:3
Scientific d. and…knowledge	PLAN 680:23	disgruntled if not actually d.	WODE 952:50	disquieted why art thou d. in me?	BIBLE 100:64
discreet whose ways are all d.	PARK 663:96	disguise better go in d.	BRAT 157:79	disquietude bone-ache d. of life	ALLEN 13:78
discretion attain years of d.	RUSK 733:9	d. of determined hostility	SHER 817:99	disregard d. for the sublime comforts	SHIP 818:14

dissatisfaction

dissatisfaction entire life in its flagrant d. — MILI 591:91
dissatisfaction well-modulated d. — TAAF 865:1
dissemble If you d. sometimes — BACON 52:20
dissembling killed by d. — LYLY 543:84
dissent d. is an act of faith — FULB 355:62
  in the name of d. — SNOW 832:80
  limit our expression of d. — MAMET 563:26
  Protestantism…is a sort of d. — BURKE 175:17
  successive waves of d. — SCHO 748:47
dissenter d. is every human being — MACL 555:38
dissidence d. of dissent — BURKE 175:17
dissident d. artist…d. government! — AI WEI 10:9
dissipated still keep looking so d. — BENC 78:8
dissipation d. of energy begin? — KELV 479:71
  year of art and d. — MOORE 616:68
dissociation d. of sensibility — ELIOT 317:93
dissolve I d. it in rain — SHEL 813:75
dissonance air with barbarous d. — MILT 599:76
dissonant No sound is d. — COLE 234:7
distance apparent from this d. — THUR 890:83
  At d. I forgive thee — MILT 608:95
  d. between your ears — JONES 465:16
  d. does not matter — DEFF 269:66
  d. lends enchantment to the view — CAMP 194:61
  d. that the dead have gone — DICK 284:55
  does not hold it at a d. — SENG 757:28
  emergency happening at a d. — BARZ 67:42
  for long d. after I hit it — TREV 896:9
  Freedom is only the d. — ZHAO 970:9
  In notes by d. made more sweet — COLL 238:78
  knack of judging a d. — REED 709:28
  love of grey-blue d. — MACK 553:10
  There's a hell of a d. — PARK 664:23
  time is the longest d. — WILL 945:80
  Tyranny of D. — BLAI 137:44
  viewed from a d. — SCHO 749:59
  worth of d. run — KIPL 492:63
distances decussated at equal d. — JOHN 460:76
  letting go of d. — STORR 856:26
distant We were d. — JOHN 457:5
distaste d. for fishing — STEI 846:84
distillation final d. of self — DELI 271:40
distinction d. among her companions — AUST 46:60
  d. between children and adults — BART 66:13
  d. between virtue and vice — JOHN 461:94
  d. in the intellectual powers — DARW 263:57
  few escape that d. — TWAIN 902:47
  great d. between the sexes — FOWL 345:61
  no useful d. can be made — GALB 357:16
  one pre-eminent d. — POTT 690:84
  only real d. — BELL 78:88
  pride of d. — SAND 742:25
  without reaching such d. — HUME 439:8
distinctions multiply d. — WORD 958:80
  trigger-fine d. — LOWE 540:33
distinguished be d. above the rest — HOMER 420:3
  d. by your enemies — HOOV 427:55
  d. thing! — JAMES 451:56
  more d. than the generality of mankind — BOSW 151:75
distorted facts and places were d. — PACH 658:1
distorts d., disfigures and destroys — FANON 329:14
distraction create some d. — HERN 414:92
distress Dear d., and joy allied — CULL 257:45
  D. with dagger keen — COLL 237:73
  happy at another's d. — LABR 502:25
  refuge from d. — WORD 961:38
  those who are in d. — VIRG 913:12
distresses insurmountable d. — JOHN 460:72
distressing most d. thing — HUXL 442:93
distribution arbitrary…d. — KEYN 484:82
  d., at fittest time — RUSK 733:97
  d. of uncertainty among economists — STEIN 845:78
  Laws…of D. — MILL 591:93
district ye can ramble over the d. — MCGO 551:74
districts d.…like squares of wheat — LARK 509:87
distrust d. a man that says — HAMM 395:71
  d. each other — BRAD 154:28
  d. of its own vision — JEFF 454:25
  have to d. each other — WILL 945:87
disturb d. the comfortable — BANKS 62:30
disturbances The Little D. of Man — PALEY 661:49
ditch both shall fall into the d. — BIBLE 117:3
  lay distracted in a d. — CRAS 254:88
ditches his windmills are d. — USTI 907:47
ditch-water drinking bottled d.-w. — SHAW 810:9
ditties Pipe to the spirit d. — KEATS 478:36
ditty played an ancient d. — KEATS 477:25

diversion merriment and d. — SMITH 827:81
  more fond of that d. — MELV 585:62
  turned a tax into a d. — STEE 844:44
diversity d. in the faculties of men — MADI 558:16
  infinite d. of movement — REDT 709:25
  reduction of…d. — HUXL 442:97
  world safe for d. — KENN 481:18
divide D. not nationally — STRA 857:44
  d. people into two groups — HAMP 395:74
  People sometimes d. others — SPEN 837:11
divided in…death…not d. — BIBLE 96:42
dividend national d. is diminished — PIGOU 678:76
  no d. from time's to-morrows — SASS 745:83
dividing line d. the state — GALB 357:19
divine all humanity d. — SHAW 809:69
  Could show me so d. — MARV 577:95
  d. and human history — GARC 359:67
  'd.' creation — MILL 594:71
  D. is everywhere — FRIE 351:74
  d. mystery in things — DOST 294:94
  double sacrilege on things d. — DRYD 303:8
  far-off d. event — TENN 875:8
  hand that made us is d. — ADDI 7:41
  image of the d. beauty — AQUI 30:95
  look d. as you advance — NASH 631:73
  lovely, Love D. — ROSS 726:48
  necessity of d. nature — SPIN 840:71
  political meetings…at a d. level — ACHE 2:26
  prohibition of d. — SHAK 803:97
  religion would still be holy and d. — BAUD 69:79
  Right D. of Kings — POPE 689:41
  some are fou o' love d. — BURNS 177:75
  soul so near d. — BRON 161:54
  to forgive, d. — POPE 685:25
divineness participation of d. — BACON 49:27
  voice of the people hath some d. — BACON 50:50
diviner glad d.'s theme — DRYD 302:77
divines Doubts 'mongst d. — SPEN 839:42
  little statesmen and philosophers and d. — EMER 324:54
divinest two d. things this world has — HUNT 439:22
divinity d. and in humanity — BACON 49:23
  d. has provided mortals — GERB 364:63
  d.…in…human consciousness — DURK 308:31
  d. in odd numbers — SHAK 773:13
  d. or school metaphysics — HUME 438:7
  d. that shapes our ends — SHAK 785:69
  d. that stirs within us — ADDI 7:52
  piece of d. in us — BROW 165:72
  Pure Accident, pure d. — OATES 643:7
  Seal of D. and Immortality — AUBR 42:61
  such d. doth hedge a king — SHAK 784:53
  What is d. — STEV 849:70
divinityship Plato…with all his d. — STER 848:41
division absurd d. into sexes — WAUGH 923:65
  alone in the third d. — NORTH 641:60
  d. in our…prosperous society — MACM 556:74
  d. is a thread — BUCH 171:22
  d. of labor…social functions — DURK 308:28
  d. of labour is nothing — MARX 578:27
  effects of the d. of labour — SMITH 827:75
  heated d. of opinion — TYNAN 904:99
  Irish experience…one of d. — DONO 293:81
  music of d. — RALE 705:45
  The deep d. — SWIN 864:13
divisions d. and precisions — ELIOT 317:72
divorce D. is the sign of knowledge — WILL 946:17
  D.…political — MONT 615:45
  lifelong relationship…d. will never — MORR 621:63
  with success come drugs, d. — HELL 407:31
divorced never wanted to get d. — PALT 662:78
  wouldn't want to be d. from — EPHR 326:24
Dixie whistle D. while humming — OBRI 646:71
dizzy I left the theatre, d. and pale — QUIR 703:27
DNA the salt of deoxyribose nucleic acid (D.) — WATS 922:40
do as they d. what I say — THAT 881:67
  capacity to d. — FAUL 331:38
  d. for your country — KENN 481:4
  Do not d. unto others — SHAW 808:59
  don't have to d. anything — FURT 356:90
  don't know what to d. — ERTZ 327:41
  d. or die! — BURNS 180:48
  d. the perfectly correct thing — SHAW 810:4
  d. what he got to d. — STEI 845:81
  d. what I please — FRED 349:41
  D. WHAT YOU WISH — RABE 704:17
  everything we d., we d. for the young — ELIZ 322:14

George—don't d. that — GREN 387:55
How Not To D. It — DICK 282:83
if we but know what to d. — EMER 324:49
isn't what I d., but how I d. it — WEST 933:92
know not…what I d. — SHAK 759:74
Let's D. It — BRAN 156:70
Love only what you d. — RICH 713:94
often discover what will d. — SMIL 827:2
That thou doest, d. quickly — BIBLE 123:49
This will never d. — JEFF 454:30
watch what they d. — LEVI 526:33
What sort of person would d. that…? — CAREY 199:65
will d. anything, Nerissa — SHAK 769:80
Doasyouwouldbedoneby Mrs D. — KING 488:51
docile warriors…prefer them d. — ANDR 18:77
docility d.…cardinal virtues — WOLL 954:89
  d. in the pupil — RYLE 736:61
  except d., obedience — WELD 928:83
dock bringing the judge…into the d. — ALGR 13:70
  dull, dark d. — GILB 369:64
  put you in the d. — ADAMS 5:7
  you may now leave the d. — ADAMS 5:8
docks No one on the d. — AMADO 15:21
doctor death Will seize the d. too — SHAK 803:8
  d. advised him not to — GREG 387:52
  D., d., what do you say — ROTH 728:81
  d. forbids me to play — WOOL 956:46
  d.…has mistaken his profession — SHAW 810:91
  D. is said also — MORT 621:75
  D. said that Death — WILDE 942:18
  don't accept any d. — VALLE 907:7
  drinks more than his own d. — BARA 63:40
  Even if the d. — STEV 852:54
  fee the d. for a nauseous draught — DRYD 304:48
  I am a D. — ALBEE 11:27
  interview with a d. — JAMES 450:24
  keeps the d. away — ANON 28:49
  man, not even a d. — NIGH 639:24
  O master d., he is past — MASS 581:77
  pass for a cathedral d. — JONS 466:48
  take off your clothes for the d. — CAUS 209:13
  thank God, D. — STAN 842:11
  The d. found — GOLD 376:84
doctors d. considering it doubtful — DICK 278:80
  d., judges…beadles — MARX 578:26
  d. of profound wisdom — DICK 278:63
  d. say this is no time — SHAK 763:29
  if you believe the d. — SALI 740:89
  Most of your d. — JONS 467:50
  We d. know — CUMM 258:68
  when d. disagree — POPE 686:65
doctrine against any country or d. — MARS 575:63
  d. of President Monroe — WILS 949:81
  d. of 'separate but equal' — WARR 921:12
  d. of those who desire — INGR 446:40
  d. shall drop as the rain — BIBLE 95:98
  d.…that each one should select — SHEL 815:44
  keep out evil d. — MILT 600:57
  Sa lyis thair ane d. wyse — HENR 411:18
  to church…not for the d. — POPE 685:23
  United States to the Monroe D. — ROOS 724:16
  what is alarming in the d. — SART 744:70
  women's eyes this d. — SHAK 763:19
  world more than d. — MILL 594:90
doctrines all d. plain and clear — BUTL 185:83
  d. and practice of Socialism — MORR 620:52
  d. chiefly vouched for — JAMES 452:77
  fundamental d. of Christianity — LAW 512:38
  seven great facts and d. — HUGEL 434:4
documentation the inadequacies of d. — BARN 64:76
dodge trying to d. it — TREE 896:1
Dodhead Jamie Telfer o' the fair D. — BALL 59:64
doe with the fallow d. — THOM 885:65
doers d.…not hearers only — BIBLE 130:50
  not of d. — HAZL 407:47
does He who can, d. — SHAW 808:39
  look for what she d. — GOET 375:59
dog A d.'s obeyed in office — SHAK 793:25
  always be a lost d. somewhere — ANOU 28:61
  Am I a d. — BIBLE 96:39
  Artist as a Young D. — THOM 883:15
  as though my d. has just died — WATE 922:36
  be a d., a monkey, or a bear — ROCH 719:10
  better than his d. — TENN 871:13
  Beware of the d.! — ANON 20:18
  circumcisèd d. — SHAK 790:51
  communism is a dead d. — SOLZ 833:7

doors

country to heel like a d.	LESS 523:91	what everyone is d.	HERB 412:42
D. eat d.	CUOMO 258:84	what they should be d.	FULL 355:68
d. goes, intently haphazard	LEVE 525:22	**doing-good** As for D.-g.	THOR 888:33
d. has a keener nose	SNYD 833:94	**doleful** dreamed a d. dream	BALL 59:60
d. is full of fleas	ACHE 3:54	**doll** d. in the d.'s house	DICK 283:25
d. is turned to his own vomit	BIBLE 130:74	**dollar** almighty d.	IRVI 447:62
d. licked me	SIMON 822:76	d. in another man's hands	OHEN 648:18
d. returneth to his vomit	BIBLE 105:96	life...printed on d. bills	ODETS 647:92
D. returns to his vomit	KIPL 493:79	one d., one vote	KRIS 499:15
d. that praised his fleas?	YEATS 966:15	thousand d. suit	ANON 27:24
d. to the commonalty	SHAK 798:87	**dollars** D. damn me	MELV 585:72
d. vacation at the taxidermist	PAGL 659:23	I feel like a thousand d.	OCON 647:90
d. will have his day	SHAK 764:50	leave him with two d.	WEST 933:88
every d. his day	KING 487:48	looks like a million d.	LINK 530:28
give them to a d.	SHAK 773:12	million d. to make a picture	TAYL 868:52
giving your heart to a d.	KIPL 492:60	poor race in a land of d.	DU 305:66
grin like a d.	BOOK 149:22	What's a thousand d.?	MARX 578:14
Holdfast is the only d.	SHAK 775:70	wuth eight hund'd d.	TWAIN 902:59
hot d. without the mustard	CHAR 216:47	**dolls** false pretences in	RUNY 731:60
I am his Highness' d.	POPE 689:49	**Dolores** splendid and sterile D.	SWIN 864:92
if a man bites a d.	BOGA 144:97	**dolorous** d. midland sea	SWIN 864:7
If I had a yaller d.	TWAIN 903:66	**dolphin-torn** That d.-t....sea	YEATS 967:32
I've been working like a d.	LENN 521:49	**domain** beasts of the intellectual d.	HOLM 424:62
just another d.	WILL 946:13	outside the d. of political	MARX 578:26
kill your d.	GREER 387:48	**Dombey** made for D. and Son	DICK 280:27
large, friendly d.	TOYN 895:73	**dome** blue d. of air	SHEL 813:77
Like a d., he hunts	TENN 871:15	D. is a lemon	TOYN 895:80
like a d. walking	JOHN 461:3	d. of the Pantheon	BRAM 156:57
living d. is better than a dead lion	BIBLE 106:26	Life, like a d.	SHEL 815:43
Love is a D. from Hell	BUKO 173:56	Millennium D. was intended to be	
Mine enemy's d.	SHAK 793:29	New Labour's Xanadu	RAWN 707:86
No d. can go as fast	FLAN 338:7	moonlit d.	YEATS 967:31
nothin' but a hound d.	PRES 694:71	Orchard, for a D.	DICK 283:35
not the lead d.	ANON 27:25	under the starry d.	MACN 558:99
paint...a d. as Picasso	MARC 569:51	**domes** d. and riggings and crooked	MORR 620:46
pancreatic ducts of d.	BANT 62:35	d. and statues, spires	LARK 509:84
pick up a starving d.	TWAIN 903:73	shape of d.	GILL 370:77
police d. of American fiction	FADI 329:7	Ships, towers, d.	WORD 959:3
portrait of a d. that I know	JOHN 465:3	**domestic** d. industry of women	GILM 371:93
Prevent the d. from barking	AUDEN 42:79	d. life	GIBB 366:92
rather have a man d.	FLEM 340:46	d. servants at home	MAUG 547:40
rather hear my d. bark	SHAK 773:21	great safeguard...of d. life	ELIOT 316:44
tail must wag the d.	KIPL 490:98	respectable d. establishment	BENN 80:44
Thou art a beaten d.	POUND 692:26	When d. servants are treated	SHAW 808:42
tongue like the tail of a d.	NASHE 632:97	**domesticate** To marry is to d.	STEV 852:41
work like a d.	SIMON 821:73	**domesticated** become d. too	GREE 386:15
dogged It's d. as does it	TROL 898:38	**domestic goddesses** I am allergic to d. g.	LETTE 524:9
dogma d. of the Ghost	RYLE 736:59	**dominant** d.'s persistence	BROW 167:30
dogmatic erect, elegant, d.	REST 711:62	**dominate** d. a...dinner-table	WILDE 941:93
dogmatism arrogant d.	WILS 948:71	**domination** d. by fat-minded men	ARNO 36:47
the greater the d.	OSLER 656:87	fought against white d.	MAND 564:53
dogs bang these d. of Seville	TENN 878:96	keeps male d. intact	WOLF 952:61
dancing d. and bears	HODG 421:23	military d. of Prussia	ASQU 38:84
dislike almost all d.	LEVIN 525:28	**dominion** death hath no more d.	BIBLE 125:12
d. barking idiotically through	MENC 587:17	death shall have no d.	THOM 883:7
d. called Spot	AMIS 16:44	d. of the sea	COVE 249:43
d. came and licked his sores	BIBLE 121:96	d., or empire above	KNOX 495:14
d. eat of the crumbs	BIBLE 117:7	d. over the works of thy hands	BIBLE 99:31
d. had eaten the upholstery	PERE 674:22	equal d. is given to woman	STAN 842:16
d. licked the blood of Naboth	BIBLE 97:69	never consent...to English d.	ANON 21:46
d. of Europe bark	AUDEN 43:93	To be given d. over another	MORR 621:60
d. shall drink him 'till they burst	POPE 686:68	women have d. over you	BIBLE 112:68
D. with broken legs	PATC 668:7	**dominions** increase in its d.	ADDI 6:21
Don't let's go to the d.	HERB 412:40	Majesty's d.	NORTH 641:58
fought the d.	BROW 167:16	**dominoes** d. outside a French café	WILDE 941:94
gaze of d.	CALV 193:35	row of d. set up	EISE 314:98
hates children and d.	FIEL 335:35	set of d.	TRAV 895:88
hates d. and babies	ROST 727:72	**dominus** Qualis d. talis est servus	PETR 676:44
holy unto the d.	BIBLE 115:49	**Domitian** death of D.	GIBB 366:90
hosses, d., and men	THAC 880:27	**done** as soon as I d. it	SAND 742:24
how it feels about d.	HAMP 395:76	discovers has to be d.	HUXL 442:86
keep parrots or puppy d.	CAMP 194:59	D. because we are too menny	HARDY 397:22
let slip the d. of war	SHAK 777:34	d. in their name	SNOW 832:87
like dancing d.	JOHN 462:40	d. it very well	JOHN 462:27
mad and hungry d.	MCKA 553:6	d. when 'tis d.	SHAK 796:19
Mad and Englishmen	COWA 249:50	I go, and it is d.	SHAK 796:29
'Orses and d. is some men's fancy	DICK 280:47	it is not what was d.	HELO 409:55
outlive her d.	WILL 945:84	Love...not what you have d.	RICH 713:94
show d. I breed	GRAV 382:31	So much has been d.	SHEL 811:47
sleep with d.	WEBS 926:34	that which is d....shall be d.	BIBLE 105:11
Throw physic to the d.	SHAK 798:71	that which they have d.	TENN 871:12
woman who is really kind to d.	BEER 73:83	things d. that he wants d.	SAMU 741:1
Dog-star D.-S. prancing	LAWR 513:56	What have I d. for you	HENL 411:7
The D.-S. rages!	POPE 687:97	what's been d. before them?	SKIN 825:50
doing d. it, actually d. it	KELM 479:67	What's d. is d.	SHAK 797:45
d. what is given us to do	ELIOT 315:33	When all is said and d.	SASS 746:94
No one...knows what they're d.	GERV 366:66	**Dong** D.!—the D.!	LEAR 516:28

Donne Anne D., Un-done	DONNE 292:48
doom and the d. assigned	TENN 876:36
crashing onwards irresistibly to d.	BOLD 145:5
d. is, to be sifted by the wind	BUNT 173:65
forfeit to a confined d.	SHAK 802:76
God would have changed his d.	CLEV 230:92
regardless of their d.	GRAY 383:47
scaffold and the d.	AYTO 48:12
the d. of man	JOHN 459:46
this black d.	ORAH 652:91
to the edge of d.	SHAK 802:80
tragedy, ecstasy, d.	ROTH 728:3
doomed d., conscripted, unvictorious	
ones?	SASS 746:99
d. to death	DRYD 303:9
Literature is d.	ORWE 655:69
story is ephemeral and d.	FAUL 331:35
dooms grandeur of the d.	KEATS 476:85
doomsayers D. have...their uses	WRIS 963:77
doomsday postpone d.	CAPO 197:21
Then is d. near	SHAK 782:84
Doon banks and braes o' bonie D.	BURNS 179:32
door an open d.	PALIN 661:59
another iron d.	SPEN 839:41
Armageddon will be at our d.	MACA 544:5
At the d. Dante turned	JOYCE 470:20
before his cottage d.	SOUT 835:45
big front d.	GILB 368:34
coming in at one d.	BEDE 72:59
Devil...holding the d. ajar	MELV 585:72
d. flew open	HOFF 422:34
d. has a creaking latch	POUND 691:8
d. of my flesh	BRID 158:10
d. of necessity	DEFOE 269:76
d. of the private whore	PARK 664:32
d. opens	GREE 385:5
d. out of the dungeon of self	MACD 550:46
d. to their own lives	AREN 31:10
d. we never opened	ELIOT 319:37
drive an angel from your d.	BLAKE 139:93
Drive out prejudices through the d.	FRED 349:39
exceed in interest a knock at the d.	LAMB 505:4
face...in a jar by the d.	LENN 522:51
Get up and bar the d.	BALL 59:62
grass beyond the d.	ROSS 726:54
hard at death's d.	BOOK 149:34
Holds fast the d.	CRAS 254:82
keep the d. of my lips	BIBLE 104:47
knocking at Preferment's d.	ARNO 34:89
Knocking on the moonlit d.	DELA 271:75
lamp beside the golden d.	LAZA 515:3
leaning on the john d.	OHARA 648:10
Lock the d., Lariston	HOGG 422:41
love shut his d. on me	SMITH 829:19
not being able to close his d.	STEN 847:5
off my d.!	POE 683:88
open d., and no man can shut it	BIBLE 131:93
opening and closing of a d.	SAND 742:20
over that same d. was likewise writ	SPEN 839:41
send them out of d.	BRAD 155:49
Shut close the d.	WORD 957:67
shut the d.	POPE 687:97
Shut the d. after you	EDGE 311:40
soldiers...round your d.	WILDE 940:45
stairs and a deal d.	DICK 277:57
stand at the d., and knock	BIBLE 131:95
steps outside my d.	HILL 418:64
trundle...through the d.	STEV 853:67
whining of a d.	DONNE 293:74
Will it knock on my d.	AUDEN 43:83
with the d. shut	WHAR 933:7
doorkeeper d. of a bordello	TOSC 894:64
rather be a d.	BIBLE 101:90
doorman d. discovered...his tasks	AREN 31:10
doors all the d. were shut	HUSS 440:37
bar thine adamantine d.	BLAKE 139:83
behind the d. of yesterday	HYDE 443:17
death hath...several d.	WEBS 927:61
Death opens unknown d.	MASE 580:61
d. are unlocked	WOZNI 962:55
d. of perception	BLAKE 140:4
d. shall be shut in the streets	BIBLE 106:36
d. upon a woman's wit	SHAK 780:13
D., where my heart	TENN 873:62
ears yielding like swinging d.	DOUG 295:5
fresh air should be...out of d.	MACA 544:17
Good clothes open all d.	FULL 355:85

doorstep

if there are no d.	MALA 561:84	from these dead d.	MELV 585:56	**drag** time did d. along	TWAIN 902:58
Let the d. be shut	SHAK 783:13	my d. are done	DRYD 303:11	**dragging** D. the whole sky	FROST 352:92
Life, within d.	HAWT 402:9	paint and have no d.	MICH 590:67	keeps d. me along	SEVI 758:42
little music out of d.	KEATS 476:96	**dough-baked** d.-b. prose	CAREW 198:49	**dragging** sagging, bagging and d.	PART 666:59
Men shut their d.	SHAK 791:76	**doughnut** the d. hole as a blank space	MURAK 626:58	**dragnet** swept like a d.-n.	DRYD 304:43
my d. are hateful	OTWAY 656:99	**doughnuts** coffee and d.	DAVI 265:84	**dragon** ant...in his d. world	POUND 692:24
nailed...the d. of Parliament	MUSS 627:88	**Douglas** doughty D.	BALL 58:51	d., a symbol	MOORE 617:85
pictures out of d.	SHAK 789:6	D. in his hall?	SCOTT 752:23	flagon with the d.	PANA 662:80
red cross upon the d.	PEPYS 674:99	**Doune** Look owre the castle D.	BALL 58:54	laid hold on the d.	BIBLE 132:21
shut d.	GIDE 367:21	**dove** Beside the springs of D.	WORD 957:62	Michael...fought against the d.	BIBLE 131:10
slamming d. and slopping water	MANS 567:95	burnished d.	TENN 871:11	**dragonfly** d. Hangs	ROSS 726:57
taxi-cab with both d. open	HUGH 434:7	d. came to him in the evening	BIBLE 92:10	**dragons** argosy of crocs and d.	AMIS 16:46
To live out of d.	STEV 851:31	d. complaining	DAY 267:37	Bores have succeeded to d.	DISR 287:18
To love is to...open d.	PAZ 671:47	d. descending breaks the air	ELIOT 321:90	d. of Laune and Lane	ORAH 652:90
Within d., or without	MILT 607:84	d. found no rest	BIBLE 92:9	habitation of d.	BIBLE 108:76
ye everlasting d.	BIBLE 100:47	gently as any sucking d.	SHAK 767:24	spleen of fiery d.	SHAK 761:54
doorstep worry on the d.	FIEL 335:28	Oh that I had wings like a d.!	BIBLE 101:75	**drain** d. him dry as hay	SHAK 795:1
dooryard in the d. bloom'd	WHIT 938:8	She is coming, my d.	TENN 876:28	From this foul d.	TOCQ 892:27
Dorcas D....full of good works	BIBLE 124:81	silly, harmless, household d.	DRYD 301:59	put it down the d.	HERB 412:45
Dorsey Tommy D. breathed	SINA 822:88	Spirit of God descending like a d.	BIBLE 114:21	**drains** Deity and the D.	STRA 856:39
dose double the d.	STOWE 856:31	sweet d. died	KEATS 475:71	**Drake** Hutton and Betsy D.	NIVEN 639:29
dossier preparation of the d.	GILL 371:90	wings like a d.	BOOK 149:19	**drake** neckyd lyke a d.	BERN 86:80
Dostoevsky D., and a dozen others	LESS 523:93	**dove-like** wings outspread D.-l.	MILT 601:31	**dram** Tak aff your d.!	BURNS 177:82
dote d. on his very absence	SHAK 769:81	**Dover** candle at D., to shew light	JOHN 461:2	**drama** A good d. critic	TYNAN 904:5
dots hurrying d. which are men	CUMM 257:51	chalk cliffs of D.	BALD 57:32	D. is a complete meal	IZZA 448:84
those damned d.	CHUR 224:66	dinner at D.	MACA 545:27	D. is action, sir	PIRA 679:88
double D., d., toil and trouble	SHAK 797:52	**doves** d.' eyes	BIBLE 107:45	D. is the third great form	HUGO 437:66
Global d. zero	ANON 26:96	harmless as d.	BIBLE 116:69	d.'s patrons give	JOHN 459:44
leading a d. life	WILDE 942:6	seats of them that sold d.	BIBLE 118:23	enemy of the ear in real d.	WILD 943:52
We will d. our emissions	OLEA 649:33	soft as the breast of d.	CORN 247:3	episode in a general d.	HARDY 397:13
double-bed deep peace of the d.-b.	CAMP 193:47	The moan of d.	TENN 873:52	exact past d.	PRIT 696:23
doubled found myself d. over	IGNA 445:17	**dovish** don't consider myself d.	SCHW 750:90	lexicon of conflict and d.	SAFI 737:17
doublet Lord Hamlet, with his d.	SHAK 781:72	**dowager** some sherry-crazed old d.	JOHN 457:97	marvel at the d.	SCRI 750:90
doublethink D. means the power	ORWE 655:76	**dowagers** d. for deans	TENN 872:31	Mistaken Identity is to D.	ABSE 1:9
doubt clouded with a d.	TENN 878:87	**dowdiness** beginning of d.	WILDE 941:91	mystical d. of the animal life	AMIS 16:44
curiosity, freckles, and d.	PARK 664:12	**dowdy** D...1 year after	LAVER 521:90	nodus of a d.	CARL 200:6
Decide this d. for me	COWP 250:84	**dower** ancient English d.	WORD 958:94	one character in literature or d.	PAGE 659:14
d. about...civilization	ORWE 654:54	Faith's transcendent d.	WORD 961:43	respond to a d.	MAMET 563:25
d. and to be ignorant	UNAM 905:6	for deathless d.	ROSS 726:57	talent for d.	VIDAL 912:82
d....cannot be removed	CARL 200:97	**dowered** d. with a sense of humour	SOME 833:10	Viewed as a d.	GRIF 388:66
D. everything at least once	LICH 528:93	**dowf** sae d. and weary	BURNS 180:45	**dramatic** d. criticism...tattoo	BROWN 164:30
d. His infinite goodness	WALL 917:45	**dowie** d. houms o' Yarrow	BALL 58:59	four head d. words	HART 400:70
D. is a necessary precondition	BART 66:17	d. houms o' Yarrow	BALL 59:60	modern era is d.	HUGO 436:52
d. is Devil-born	TENN 874:91	**down** brought d.	HAIL 302:18	thirty-seventh d. situation	JARRY 452:96
d. is in our passion	JAMES 450:47	death...done as easily lying d.	ALLEN 14:93	**drank** d. my ale	FARQ 330:27
d. of future foes	ELIZ 321:1	D., d. to hell	SHAK 760:19	d. without the provocation	SWIFT 826:49
D. thou the stars	SHAK 781:77	D. on your knees	SHAK 779:2	**drappie** d. in our e'e	BURNS 178:12
d. whether one may not	HAWT 402:13	D. she came and found a boat	TENN 870:86	**draught** for a d. of vintage!	KEATS 478:42
for her, d.	BALZ 61:98	D. with purists!	BAND 61:10	nauseous d.	DRYD 304:48
fouk wou'd hae a d. on	FERG 333:84	fear of letting people d.	WILK 944:62	nauseous d. of life	ROCH 719:14
he was prey to d.	CHAT 216:55	had me d.	GERS 365:78	**draughts** great d. of time	BERR 87:96
Horror and d. distract	MILT 603:89	He that is d. needs fear no fall	BUNY 174:82	peculiarly susceptible to d.	WILDE 942:7
I d. some foul play	SHAK 781:45	looked d. upon it in our old age?	SCHU 750:80	shallow d. intoxicate	POPE 685:19
imagine the least d.	DESC 274:94	never let you d.	WAUGH 923:54	**draughtsman** Dali is a good d.	ORWE 655:82
in d. to act or rest	POPE 687:80	nobody wants you to put it d.	RUCK 730:33	**draw** d. first, to cultivate the Spirit	MATI 581:93
itself and d. of itself	TILL 891:13	set me d. again	FROST 352:98	D. more and more often	PISS 679:98
Life is d.	UNAM 905:3	started at the top and worked d.	WELL 929:96	d. something every day	CENN 211:43
life of d.	BROW 168:39	this sucker could go d.	BUSH 183:43	d. upon content	GOLD 376:90
more faith in honest d.	TENN 874:92	what they knocked d.	FENT 332:59	d. what you see only in memory	DEGAS 269:88
new philosophy calls all in d.	DONNE 292:58	Why art thou cast d.	BIBLE 100:64	seemed to d. the same way	HIRS 419:77
no d. as to the elements	WHIT 936:71	wish to level d.	JOHN 461:1	Teaching people to d.	HOCK 421:16
prolonged neurotic d.	BARZ 67:42	**downfall** d. of the British Empire	CHUR 225:74	**drawback** d. of all sea-side places	DOUG 295:11
science teaches us to d.	BERN 85:70	**down-gyvèd** d.-g. to his ankle	SHAK 781:72	**drawbacks** everything has its d.	JERO 454:39
sunnier side of d.	TENN 879:4	**downhill** going d. ever since	SHAR 806:75	**drawer** Feminism...vegetable d.	PAGL 659:19
the good d. their own goodness	AUST 47:93	**Downing** from Germany to D. Street	CHAM 212:64	**drawers** d....of political cancer	ANON 26:9
though we oft d.	MILT 608:4	met Curzon in D. Street	BALD 57:26	**drawing** art of d.	LIEB 529:95
troubled with religious d.	CHES 221:1	**downpour** d. of apologies	BEER 73:78	D. is not the form	DEGAS 269:86
what you cannot d.	SKEL 825:37	**downs** carved upon her d.	HEAN 404:71	D. is only a necessary evil	HEIN 407:19
when all men d. you	KIPL 492:62	fair on the dewy d.	TENN 876:34	growing old in d. nothing up!	COWP 251:16
When in d.	BLASS 142:49	o'er unhabitable d.	SWIFT 863:63	three-dimensional d.	HIRS 419:75
When in d.	ITO 448:79	sun behind the D.	BETJ 89:40	**drawing-down** a d.-d. of blinds	OWEN 657:26
when in d., mumble	WAGN 915:3	**downsitting** knowest my d.	BIBLE 103:43	**drawing-room** magnificent in a d.-r.	THUR 890:62
When in d., shout	HARD 396:96	**downstairs** d. from their Ivory Towers	SMITH 829:21	Suez canal...through my d.-r.	EDEN 311:33
When in d., tell the truth	TWAIN 903:77	why did you kick me d.?	BICK 133:51	**drawl** quickest on the d.?	NEW 634:40
When in D.—Wash	GALL 358:38	**down-to-earth** people could be d.-t.-e.	SHUL 819:30	**drawling-master** D.-m....conger-eel	CARR 203:79
When in d., win	HOYLE 434:94	**downturns** market d. predicted	SAMU 741:2	**drayhorse** greatness is only the d.	PATC 668:6
Where there is d.	FRAN 347:99	**downwards** look no way but d.	BUNY 174:80	**dread** close your eyes with holy d.	COLE 236:42
Where there is d.	THAT 881:54	**dowry** your d. 'greed on	SHAK 762:66	d. of something after death	SHAK 782:7
Why do you d.	JONS 468:83	**dowser** d. and not a navvy	LEAV 517:54	every reason to d.	JORD 469:1
wisdom, dying in d.	LOWE 540:28	**Dowson** D....degenerates!	ONEI 651:70	greatest d. of all	BETJ 89:48
doubted cannot reasonably be d.	HUME 438:3	**dozen** d. times and he is great	JARR 452:84	secret d., and inward horror	ADDI 7:52
that they cannot be d.	HUXL 443:5	she has at least a d.	WILDE 941:76	silence...fills me with d.	PASC 667:75
doubter d. fights only with himself	GREE 386:27	**Dracula** night I finished D.	SAGE 738:29	walk in fear and d.	COLE 235:18
doubtful d. dreams of dreams	SWIN 864:97	**draft** d. an international agreement	TRUM 899:82	**dreadful** d. to look on	HAGG 391:9
doubts content to begin with d.	BACON 49:21	happy d. surpassed the image	DRYD 302:7	**dream** And d. about the great	YEATS 965:11
d. are traitors	SHAK 787:49	**drafted** didn't get d.	DOWD 296:29	as a d. doth flatter	SHAK 802:67
D. 'mongst divines	SPEN 839:42	**draftsman** d. of words	CUMM 258:73	as thou mightst in d.	SHEL 816:59

drink

Because thou must not d. ARNO 33:70
behold, it was d. BUNY 174:79
behold, it was a d. BIBLE 93:42
better to d....than to live PROU 697:39
consecration, and the poet's d. WORD 961:28
corresponds to our d. life MAMET 563:25
dared to d. OBAMA 644:41
deep d. of peace HUNT 439:28
draw nearer to d. CHIR 222:23
d. about the future HAMM 394:59
d. comes to an end GIRO 373:28
dreamed a dolefu' d. BALL 59:60
dreamed of was a d. ROSS 726:39
d. freely GAUG 361:3
d. my d.s away FLAN 338:6
d. of a common language RICH 713:3
d. of being dressed in Paris ANON 24:12
D. Of Electric Sheep? DICK 277:34
d. of Home FORD 343:9
d. of independent power JAY 453:99
d. of Jeannie FOST 345:55
d. of life JARR 452:83
d. of life SHEL 815:39
d. of money-bags SHAK 769:92
d. of revolution STOP 855:16
d. of social justice NGUY 636:69
d. of the soft look YEATS 965:7
d. that I am home again! FLEC 340:36
d. that they clarify HERN 414:92
d. things that never were SHAW 811:34
Everlasting peace is a d. MOLT 612:92
freshness of a d. WORD 959:5
glory and the d. WORD 959:7
golden d. of love and friendship DRYD 301:61
have had a d. past SHAK 767:43
held me like a d. WORD 958:77
If you can d. KIPL 492:62
I have a d. KING 486:25
I have a d. KING 487:31
In a d. SEXT 758:46
in a d. of passion SHAK 782:99
Liberals can d. MACL 556:50
life be but a d. PRIOR 696:13
Life is...a bad d. ONEI 651:64
Life is but a D. LI 528:82
Lives in a d. LENN 522:51
man that is born falls into a d. CONR 244:32
men d., but not equally LAWR 514:89
most blissful d. as a child SHIP 818:15
must we d. our d.s BISH 136:28
new pictures as in a d. MARC 569:48
old men's d.! DRYD 302:77
old men shall d. d.s BIBLE 111:48
one that hath a weary d. TENN 870:88
Out of a misty d. DOWS 296:37
perchance to d. SHAK 782:7
phantasma or a hideous d. SHAK 776:16
pictures come to me as if in a d. VAN 908:19
quiet sleep and a sweet d. MASE 580:52
shining and perishable d. DIDI 286:81
should not dare to d. MAND 565:59
silence to the d. ROSS 725:37
sister to the d. BAUD 68:68
Soft, I did but d. SHAK 761:48
something...to d. about FORD 343:12
So runs my d. TENN 874:77
Success he is the American D. LEGU 520:14
The more you d. PHEL 676:49
To d. is happiness HUGO 437:62
too old to d. HAMM 394:64
vanished like a d. CARL 201:33
waking from a troubled d. HAWT 401:99
We live, as we d. CONR 243:28
What happens to a d. deferred? HUGH 435:12
wrecks of a dissolving d. SHEL 816:57
dreamed at night he d. of it GREE 385:6
dreamer Beautiful d. FOST 345:56
Behold, this d. cometh BIBLE 93:38
d. of dreams BIBLE 95:92
poet and the d. KEATS 476:99
dreamers d. of the day LAWR 514:89
Soldiers are d. SASS 745:83
We have been the d. BEVAN 89:51
dreamest What d. thou, drunkard SKEL 824:31
dreaming boys are d. wicked THOM 884:33
D. like a love-adept SHEL 814:13
d. of a White Christmas BERL 84:41

d. spires ARNO 35:17
while d. before it GAUG 361:2
dreamlike a fact...so d. RICH 713:96
dreams according to his d. HUGO 437:83
advertising...dealt in...fugitive d. QUEN 702:8
armoured cars of d. BISH 136:27
awoke...from uneasy d. KAFKA 472:5
Big d. AGAS 9:85
books are either d. LOWE 539:97
City of perspiring d. RAPH 707:74
Come to me in my d. ARNO 34:72
different hopes, different d. CART 206:45
doubtful d. of d. SWIN 864:47
dreamer of d. BIBLE 95:92
D. and drives RODG 721:49
d., and our hopes POPP 689:62
d. are all egocentric WAUGH 924:93
d....are infanticiddle NASH 631:72
d. be tossed and blown HAMM 394:65
d. do show thee me SHAK 801:50
D. have only the pigmentation BARN 64:62
d. in pale battalions SORL 834:33
d. of a poet JOHN 460:71
d. of our childhood THOR 888:14
d. of perfection FAUL 331:43
d. of the participation NICH 636:71
d. that have stayed with me BRON 162:7
Fanatics have their d. KEATS 476:97
Full of sweet d. SHAK 765:72
had dreamed d. THOM 883:2
have no d. VREE 915:58
have only my d. YEATS 966:12
he hunts in d. TENN 871:15
help of d. WORD 961:35
he pulls the legs of his d. THOM 884:36
his summer d. SHEL 813:81
history of irresponsible d. POPP 689:63
hopes and d. of the Future FRAME 346:77
if empty d. so please HERR 415:2
in d. behold the Hebrides GALT 359:54
In my d. is a country SHAW 809:69
interpretation of d. FREUD 350:56
in that sleep of death what d. SHAK 782:7
I talk of d. SHAK 765:72
life together with your d. MOORE 616:59
Made holy by their d. GIBS 367:14
More d. are destroyed SKEL 825:45
never overstepped it save in d. FROST 352:2
Out of d., songs HERZL 416:27
Real are the d. of Gods KEATS 476:5
shadows and in d. STEV 849:70
steeple of my d. DEBU 268:59
substance of my d. SASS 745:88
such stuff As d. are made SHAK 804:28
talking about d. STERN 847:18
that I have bad d. SHAK 782:86
The quick D. SHEL 815:30
The way you haunt my d. GERS 365:76
treasured d. WORD 960:14
with their mothers in d. SOPH 834:32
dreamt d. I went to Manderley again DU 306:93
d. of in our philosophy SHAK 781:70
d. there was an Emperor SHAK 795:87
often d. of unhappiness SHAK 774:33
dreamtime easy Eden-d. WRIG 963:70
dreariness just to escape this d. PERCY 674:10
unredeemed d. of thought POE 683:80
dreary All seems d., savage SCHAW 747:20
dregs drain not to its d. the urn SHEL 816:58
d. of life DRYD 300:38
dreich kirkyairdielike and d. YOUNG 968:53
drenching in for a thorough d. BEER 73:78
dress begin to d. ourselves RICH 713:3
car has become an article of d. MCLU 556:55
cool white d. FIRB 336:50
cotton flowers of her d. THOM 884:40
crocus d. JOYCE 470:32
Diet, Furniture and D. MAND 565:65
d. according to your age DISR 288:69
d. and manners in England SHAW 806:94
d. by yellow candle-light STEV 853:63
D. is a form of visual art HOLL 423:51
d. is very independent GASK 361:84
d. me In borrowed robes? SHAK 796:9
d. of thought POPE 685:21
d....the badge of lost innocence PAINE 660:31
Fond Pride of D. FRAN 348:13

fop values himself upon his d. CHES 219:34
glory of man is his d. ANON 20:27
Heaven...how they d.! DICK 279:1
I'd like to d. the Queen VERS 911:63
in a last month's d. NASH 630:61
its mortal d. YEATS 966:26
make their d. a principal part HAZL 403:37
man cannot d. STER 848:48
noble youth did d. SHAK 772:80
no such thing as a moral d. CHUR 224:63
not a woman's d....a man's d. BOWIE 153:97
Peace, the human d. BLAKE 139:88
sweet disorder in the d. HERR 416:17
this fleshly d. VAUG 909:35
To d., to darn, to flower LEWIS 526:51
whose d. no one observes TROL 898:50
Women fond of d. DE 268:45
dressed All D. Up BURT 181:70
d. exactly like her NASH 631:84
d. for this short comedy RALE 705:45
d. in Paris ANON 24:12
good spirits...when he's well d. DICK 279:10
dresser d. filled with shining delph COLUM 238:90
dresses d. make a curious sound STEV 853:67
silk d. out of worms STEV 850:92
dressmaker ask for...your d. DACHE 260:1
drift d. is always towards barbarism REAG 709:16
twas Peter's d. SHEL 813:88
driftwood found out about the d.. ROSE 725:29
drill d. to the tooth of America CLIN 230:4
drill-sergeant d.-s. or animal trainer RYLE 736:61
drink abolition of strong d. MCGO 551:75
any little delicate thing to d. DICK 282:88
as oft as ye d. it BIBLE 126:49
be sure to d. it TAO 867:25
better to d. than to fight KING 488:56
careful not to d. HAMM 395:71
damn the d. they'll swally OBRI 646:70
D. a health to SYNGE 865:23
d. all the d. KEEN 478:52
D. and dance PARK 664:15
D. deep, or taste not POPE 685:19
d. for a living KERR 483:58
D.! for you know not FITZ 337:71
D....is stronger than unionism LAWS 514:95
d. life to the lees TENN 870:98
D. not the third glass HERB 413:55
d. one another's healths JERO 454:37
d. sooner than pray SHAK 771:38
d. takes the man LEWIS 527:63
D. this in remembrance BOOK 147:73
d. thy wine with a merry heart BIBLE 106:27
d. to her as long SHAK 785:82
D. to me, only JONS 467:75
d. to obliviate that decent actor FLYNN 341:64
d. unto one of these little ones BIBLE 116:74
d. when we are not thirsty BEAU 70:9
dripping blood our only d. ELIOT 320:65
drove me to d. FIEL 335:34
Eat, d., and love BYRON 190:29
every creature d. but I COWL 250:75
first d. on a Sunday morning MCCU 549:15
follow strong d. BIBLE 107:53
garments, heavy with their d. SHAK 784:58
go a week without a d. LEWIS 526:52
good as d. CHES 220:74
has taken to d. TARK 867:29
I am...a little in d. STEE 844:40
Let others d. thee freely HERR 415:7
let us eat and d. BIBLE 127:59
let us eat and d. BIBLE 108:65
Love...is not meat nor d. MILL 592:29
meaning is my meat and d. BROW 167:29
Nor any drop to d. COLE 235:13
not eat with you, d. with you SHAK 769:82
Now is the time to d. HORA 429:7
One more d. PARK 664:27
only one at the party with a d. ALLEN 13:80
rule never to d. by daylight MENC 586:96
spent $3m on d. DALY 261:20
taste d. once CABE 191:1
taste who always d. PRIOR 695:98
teach you to d. deep SHAK 780:41
That I might d. KEATS 478:42
The more you d. POPE 668:22
they gave me vinegar to d. BOOK 149:26
they take to it like d. HAZZ 404:61

– drinker –

think that I can d.	ANON 22:61	**drudge** harmless d.	JOHN 460:75	**dual** as antiquated as a d.	GOOCH 378:44
this calls for a d.	THUR 891:93	**drudgery** Makes d. divine	HERB 413:60	Everyone…holds d. citizenship	SONT 834:20
those who don't d.	KEIL 479:56	**drug** alleyways and d. fiends	LIND 530:16	**dualism** d. which now weighs	DEWEY 276:19
to eat and to d.	GUIL 389:87	D. misuse is not a disease	DICK 277:36	**Dublin** features of the D. style	KENN 481:20
too early for a d.?	GORD 378:57	Everything is a dangerous d.	CONN 243:10	served in all the pubs in D.	DONL 279:25
wants but little d. below	HOLM 423:60	most powerful d. used	KIPL 493:78	**ducat** Dead for a d., dead	SHAK 784:37
we d. too much tea	PRIE 695:88	Poetry's a mere d.	FARQ 330:22	**Duchess** D. of Malfi still	WEBS 927:60
We d. to thee	TENN 875:5	rape, sodomy and d. addiction	COOK 245:68	in the arms…of a D.	JOHN 463:64
what d. a man will have	MARQ 575:59	what purgative d.	SHAK 798:72	**duck** forgot to d.	DEMP 272:50
Whene'er you are inclin'd	BURNS 179:31	**drugging** not d., not robbing	PACK 659:11	forgot to d.	REAG 708:5
wittles and d. to me	DICK 280:47	**drugs** d. cause cramp	PARK 664:19	O dainty d.	SHAK 768:49
drinker first great…literary d.	THUR 891:94	Sex 'n' d. 'n' rock 'n' roll	DURY 308:40	**ducks** Four d. on a pond	ALLI 14:7
drinkers moderate d. both	SHAW 808:48	taken illegal d.	JOHN 457:88	**ducts** pancreatic d. of dog	BANT 62:35
drinking A d. man's someone	WILL 945:92	with success come d.	HELL 407:31	**due** give the devil his d.	SHAK 771:32
curse of the d. classes	WILDE 942:29	**druid** same old d. Time	ROSE 725:30	to every one his d.	JUST 471:51
damnable degrees Of d.	WEBS 926:18	**drum** Dumb as a d.	DICK 277:53	**duelling** My soul's a trampled d. ground	RICK 715:28
decided to stop d.	CONN 242:89	trumpet and the steady d.	MCCA 547:82	**dues** Render…to all their d.	BIBLE 126:30
D. in the morning	RABE 703:13	with his big brass d.	LIND 530:15	**duet** d. between a tuba and a piccolo	DONA 290:6
D. is the soldier's pleasure	DRYD 303:30	with two nightingales	AUDEN 42:79	d. of two nightingales	STEV 850:96
d. out of spittoons	HEMI 410:89	**Drumcliffe** In D. churchyard	YEATS 967:40	**dugs** old man with wrinkled d.	ELIOT 318:4
d….sobers us again	POPE 685:19	**drummer** hears a different d.	THOR 889:43	**Duke** will make the D. say	SHAK 767:23
D. the best tea	SNOW 832:74	**drums** are your d. a-beating yet?	SKIR 825:51	**duke** D. of Plaza-Toro!	GILB 370:71
D., to engender wit	ROCH 720:23	d. begin to roll	KIPL 489:86	D. takes a town	POMP 684:10
from robbing…next to d.	DE 274:85	Of guns, and d., and wounds	SHAK 771:33	everybody praised the D.	SOUT 835:47
give up smoking, d. and loving	FREUD 350:54	Still, like muffled d.	LONG 535:15	to the D.'s house	PEPYS 673:95
hae been merry d.	BURNS 178:89	trumpets, beat the d.!	MORE 619:27	with the D. in Flanders	LOWE 539:98
kept on d.	ROBI 718:86	**drunk** art of getting d.	JOHN 463:65	**dukes** drawing room full of d.	AUDEN 44:10
much d., little thinking	SWIFT 861:36	Be not d. with wine	BIBLE 128:92	**dulce** D. et decorum est	HORA 263:55
no d. after death	FLET 340:53	best audience…a little d.	BARK 63:55	D. et decorum est	OWEN 657:77
redfaced from eating and d.	ABBO 1:1	d. and asleep	STEV 850:78	pro patria, non 'd.'	POUND 691:4
red-hot with d.	SHAK 804:29	d. his fill	SCOTT 752:28	**dulcimer** damsel with a d.	COLE 236:41
there's nothing like d.	DIBD 276:30	D. many times a day	SHAK 788:76	**dull** But you are d.	MIDD 590:71
very merry, dancing, d.	DRYD 304:56	d. we like our art	LUCAS 541:53	d. and mean	WHIT 938:21
drinks couple of d. on a Saturday	FYFFE 356:96	d. with sight of power	KIPL 490:17	d., insipid thing is a billet-doux	ETHE 327:43
he d. no wine	SHAK 773:95	getting over a four-day d.	HELL 408:50	first requirement…be d.	ACHE 3:29
He that d. fast	FRAN 348:9	good d….a good bartender	BISH 137:30	found it so intolerably d.	DARW 263:55
drink-well Eat-well is d.-w.'s brother	FULL 355:82	got d. at onch	LONG 534:11	I am always deadly d.	BEER 73:76
drive d. and make love	MOSS 622:84	hasten to be d.	DRYD 304:47	In this d. world	SHAK 785:83
d. fast and furious	ABSE 1:10	I d. him to his bed	SHAK 794:62	Like a d. actor	SHAK 799:3
d. one from home	HOOD 426:28	Man…must get d.	BYRON 190:8	not stupid, but…very d.	BEAV 71:25
drivel Dilutes with d.	BYRON 187:33	My mother, d. or sober	CHES 220:54	recognize when he is d.	AUCH 42:63
when hearing this d.?	GERS 365:74	not genteel when he gets d.	BOSW 152:78	To make dictionaries is d. work	JOHN 460:73
drivelling occupy some d. reader	SARD 743:51	not so think as you d.	SQUI 841:91	**dullard** d.'s envy of brilliant men	BEER 73:81
driven writer is d. out far	HEMI 410:88	Of course I'm d.	RUSS 735:51	**dullest** d. person in the world	BENS 81:85
driver Do people…Wave at the d.	MCGO 522:80	Often and, and seldom sober	FULL 356:88	**dullness** cardinal sin is d.	CAPRA 198:33
hitting the d. so good	TREV 896:9	seen Wordsworth d.	HOUS 432:61	everyday life, with its…deadly d.	EINS 313:76
in the d.'s seat	BEAV 71:29	sober and come out d.	ABSE 1:11	invincible d.	JONS 467:66
drivers d. of negroes	JOHN 462:41	That which hath made them d.	SHAK 797:30	little d. spoils it	YOUR 968:57
driving like the d. of Jehu	BIBLE 97:77	this meeting is d.	DICK 277:56	reconciliation with d.	LOWE 540:35
dromedary d., two; Or else	NASH 631:66	very d. and very slovenly	WYCH 964:1	'tis a good d.	SHAK 803:12
drone d. of alliterations	BROY 169:88	way that a d. uses lamp-posts	LANG 507:40	**dumb** because the brutes are d.?	ELIOT 315:18
droop begin to d. and drowse	SHAK 797:48	**drunkard** d., my navigator	SEXT 758:44	cannot be absolutely d.	FORD 342:89
D. in a hundred A.B.C.'s	ELIOT 317:87	earth shall reel…like a d.	BIBLE 108:66	deaf to hear, and the d. to speak	BIBLE 119:57
fortunes Will ever after d.	SHAK 803:11	rolling English d.	CHES 221:93	D. as a drum	DICK 277:53
drop don't d. players	SHAN 805:61	take this d. for a god	SHAK 804:34	d., dark, dull, bitter belly-tension	GIBB 367:11
d. of a bucket	BIBLE 109:82	What dreamest thou, d.	SKEL 824:31	d. enough to turn it down	TAYL 868:52
d. of hatred in your soul	MUNRO 625:51	**drunkards** as d. sing and vomit	CARRA 202:58	D., inscrutable and grand	ARNO 35:2
d. serene hath quenched	MILT 603:74	have to become d. first	JONES 465:19	d. to say how hot	GRAV 382:17
Every d. of ink	WALP 919:67	miserly d.	WILD 943:49	Homage to plain d. luck	ACHE 3:51
last d. into that…glass	FITZ 337:83	**drunken** d. officer of British rule	WALC 916:5	if you cant be d.	OHARA 648:12
Nor any d. to drink	COLE 235:13	in one of my d. stupors	FORD 344:17	opposed to…a d. war	OBAMA 643:17
one d. in a limitless ocean	MITCH 609:31	not true that d. men cannot beget	YEATS 967:42	Our D. Friends	PARK 664:22
one d. of negro blood	HUGH 435:16	stagger like a d. man	BIBLE 102:16	So d. he can't fart	JOHN 458:16
One d. would save my soul	MARL 573:30	**drunkenness** anything so bad as d.	CHES 220:74	tongue of the d. sing	BIBLE 108:76
Raineth d. and staineth slop	POUND 691:91	d. expands	JAMES 451:71	**dump** What a d.!	COFF 234:91
That cordial d.	ROCH 719:14	D. is a joy reserved	CABE 191:4	**Dunblane** flower o' D.	TANN 867:24
droppeth d. as the gentle rain	SHAK 770:12	D. is his best virtue	SHAK 791:69	**Duncan** D. is in his grave	SHAK 797:46
dropping d. in a very rainy day	BIBLE 105:3	man that is given to d.	BIBLE 113:97	Hear it not, D.	SHAK 796:29
drops dear to me as are the ruddy d.	SHAK 777:19	time for d.	BAUD 68:73	wake D. with thy knocking	TWAIN 902:63
like d. of water	JOYCE 470:19	**drunks** d. and Americans	MOYN 623:4	**dunce** amiable d.	CLIF 230:97
These are gracious d.	SHAK 778:44	for two d.	TWAIN 902:57	because…you're a d.	JOHN 464:82
dross the rest is d.	POUND 692:23	**Drury** I did in D. Lane see	PEPYS 674:99	d. that has been sent to roam	COWP 251:6
drought Such thirst will argue d.	CAREW 198:46	**dry** d. brain in a d. season	ELIOT 317:86	D. the second reigns	POPE 688:29
droughts d. and flooding rains	MACK 553:10	hearts very d. and tough	HOOK 427:41	d. with wits	POPE 689:38
drove lifts a d. from a Sassenach	SCOTT 753:37	held out to d.	REAG 708:9	**dunces** A wit with d.	POPE 689:38
drown d. my book	SHAK 804:31	in a d. and thirsty land	BIBLE 101:78	d. are all…against him	SWIFT 861:32
drowned d. a blind bitch's puppies	SHAK 773:12	into a d. Martini	ANON 24:14	**Dundee** bonnet of Bonny D.	SCOTT 754:82
d. in the honey	HAWT 401:2	let us assemble, d., gray, spare	RANS 706:68	piper o' D.?	ANON 22:75
lies d. with us	HERR 415:11	Like giving d. birth	SIMP 822:83	stay langer in Bonny D.!	SCOTT 753:52
photograph…after I d.	ATWO 40:32	Sierras Will be d.	SNYD 832:91	**Dunfermline** king sits in D.	BALL 59:59
went and d. themselves	ANON 28:7	within the womb is d.	HOPE 427:57	**dung** better to sniff France's d.	HO 421:13
drowning a lot of people would be d.	COWE 249:67	Yankees, feeling very d.	ANON 24:9	floors of plaister, and the walls of d.	POPE 686:69
guardianship…against d.	PATR 669:29	**Dryad** light-winged D. of the trees	KEATS 478:41	more reeking the d.	INNO 446:47
like death by d.	FERB 332:71	**Dryden** D. fails to render him	ARNO 35:7	of d. and of corrupcioun!	CHAU 217:94
not waving but d.	SMITH 830:37	D., Pope, and all their school	ARNO 36:42	**dungeon** door out of the d. of self	MACD 550:26
drowns With too much labour d.	SHAK 763:97	Ev'n copious D.	POPE 688:20	d. flamed with light	WESL 931:57
drowsy dull ear of a d. man	SHAK 768:58	**dry-goods** churches and d.-g. stores	MCMU 557:82	d. horrible, on all sides	MILT 601:35

d. of despair	CESA 211:50
d. of self	CONN 243:15
Himself is his own d.	MILT 599:72
imprisonment! The D. of	MILT 607:87
Nor airless d.	SHAK 776:14
prisoner in his d.	FLAU 339:25
worse than chains, D.	MILT 607:84
dunghill cock crowing on its own d.	ALDI 12:48
This enormous d.	VOLT 914:43
Upon the d.	SHAK 793:15
Dunkirk from D. to Belgrade	DAVIS 266:9
the epic of D.	PRIE 695:86
Dunsinane do come to D.	TWAIN 902:63
duo most dangerous d.	SCAR 746:14
duodecimos humbler band of d.	CRAB 251:26
dupes If hopes were d.	CLOU 232:48
dusk each slow d.	OWEN 657:26
for a moment in the d.	BROW 167:10
In the d.	GILB 368:30
dust a handful of d.	TENN 876:30
But what is D.	SITW 824:18
chimney-sweepers, come to d.	SHAK 803:7
comprehended the d. of the earth	BIBLE 108:81
darkened with filthy d.	SPEN 838:30
dialogue between The Spirit and the D.	DICK 284:46
D. as we are	WORD 958:76
d. forbids the birds	SITW 823:6
D. in the air	ELIOT 321:84
d., in the cool tombs	SAND 742:17
d. of creeds outworn	SHEL 814:12
d. of the churchyard	DONNE 292:63
d. on the nettles	THOM 885:63
d. returneth to d. again	GORD 378:54
d. return to the earth	BIBLE 106:36
d. shall be the serpent's meat	BIBLE 110:10
d. shalt thou eat	BIBLE 91:96
d. thou art, and unto d.	BIBLE 91:99
d. to d.	BOOK 148:1
D. to the d.!	SHEL 815:38
d. would hear her	TENN 876:28
Ere Babylon was d.	SHEL 814:6
Excuse My D.	PARK 663:95
fear in a handful of d.	ELIOT 317:96
fine d.	KELM 479:67
first raised a d.	BERK 84:29
formed man out of the d.	BIBLE 91:86
frame was D.	DICK 284:50
glory smeared in d. and blood	SHAK 760:17
Guilty of d. and sin	HERB 413:65
Half d., half deity	BYRON 189:84
heat of life in the handful of d.	CONR 244:36
In that rich d. a richer d.	BROO 162:88
in the d. be equal made	SHIR 819:20
isn't just d.	MACA 544:10
leaves…turning to d.	ANON 20:32
like d. that is blown away	BIBLE 112:77
little d. of praise	TENN 874:86
noble father in the d.	SHAK 780:34
not without d. and heat	MILT 600:8
O'er English d.	MACA 546:54
pays us but with age and d.	RALE 705:47
piles of dry d.	GLAS 374:46
proud and angry d.	HOUS 432:65
provoke the silent d.	GRAY 384:67
recover once my d.	MONT 615:51
remembereth that we are d.	BIBLE 102:9
repent in d. and ashes	BIBLE 99:23
save from d.	SPEN 837:95
shouldst give d. a tongue	HERB 414:79
this unprofitable d.	WORD 957:67
Time, a maniac scattering d.	TENN 874:74
To die in d.	SPEN 839:47
vex the unhappy d.	TENN 873:53
we're only made out of d.	DICK 277:33
what a d. do I raise	BACON 53:42
what is this quintessence of d.	SHAK 782:89
when this d. falls	VAUG 909:36
You are not worth the d.	SHAK 793:18
dustbin d. upset in a high wind	GOLD 375:75
dustheap d. of history	TROT 899:67
dusty d. to the grave	STEV 852:40
Dutch D. may have their Holland	JOHN 458:24
fault of the D.	CANN 197:10
flowered once for D. sailors' eyes	FITZ 338:86
Dutchman icicle on a D.'s beard	SHAK 786:13
duties brace ourselves to our d.	CHUR 225:86
d. as King	EDWA 312:61
d. of the physician	OSLER 656:89
If I had no d.	JOHN 463:54
lowliest d. on herself	WORD 958:94
No d., only opportunities	ANON 26:2
Property has its d.	DRUM 299:8
duty absolved from all d.	PEAC 671:53
act…of d. and of justice	PITT 679:10
bounds of their d.	RICH 714:21
crimes committed in the name of d.	SNOW 832:80
declares that it is his d.	SHAW 807:11
done my d. as a man	TENN 879:99
do our d. as such	GLAD 210:33
Do the D. which lies nearest thee	CARL 200:97
do your d.	BADEN 54:58
d. as we understand it	LINC 529:8
d. in that state of life	BOOK 148:80
d. is to arouse the sleeper	BETH 87:13
d. laid down upon us by God	CARY 207:61
d. of a democracy	WHITE 935:35
d. of a journalist	STEAD 843:33
d. of an opposition	CHUR 224:67
d. of a serious biographer	TOYN 895:79
d. of being happy	STEV 852:51
d. of government	PAINE 660:32
d. of the writer	KENN 482:26
d., patriotism…clad	LLOY 533:72
d. that Mr Bulstrode rarely shrank	ELIOT 316:50
d. to have reported it	HELL 408:41
d. to the Queen	MARL 572:91
d. to try to prevent it	MILN 596:27
d….to wield the sword of France	DE 270:92
d., your reward, your destiny	HAMM 394:59
every man will do his d.	NELS 633:14
Every subject's d.	SHAK 775:82
fattening is the first d.	SPEKE 836:82
fiction…painful d.	WILDE 942:30
first d….is not to be poor	SHAW 809:70
first d. of a state	RUSK 733:9
first d. of the press	TIMES 892:23
first d. to serve society	JOHN 461:13
God, I have done my d.	NELS 633:16
health is a d.	SPEN 836:86
hold fast to d.	BARN 64:74
in d. both equally bound	STER 847:20
little d. and less love	SHAK 759:78
must do our d.	CECIL 210:33
my d. to have loved	TENN 877:59
one d. we owe to history	WILDE 940:56
one's d. to drown it	WILDE 940:68
our d. to follow	PALM 662:70
our only d.	GERG 365:67
perceive here a divided d.	SHAK 789:96
professional d. of the…agent	OGIL 648:5
religious sense of d.	DICK 283:17
Self-development is a higher d.	STAN 843:18
service is the common d.	ROCK 720:33
stage of d. run	KEN 480:83
stirring of d.	CURZ 260:5
terrible notions of d.	CLOU 232:58
tried to do his d.	MACA 544:9
urge thy d.	SHAK 778:50
whole d. of man	BIBLE 107:38
dwarf giant d., Dan Cupid	SHAK 763:9
dwarfish Upon a d. thief	SHAK 798:67
dwarfs D. standing on the shoulders	BERN 85:61
surrounded by d.	GELL 363:37
dwell at ease for aye to d.	TENN 870:94
D. I but in the suburbs	SHAK 777:18
means to d. therein	HERB 413:69
upon the logic…that you should d.	DOYLE 297:60
dwellers d. in different zones	DISR 288:34
dwelling d. place in all generations	BIBLE 101:92
thy humble d.	WESL 932:62
whimsical d.	CONG 241:68
Whose d. is the light	WORD 956:55
dwelling-place desert were my d.-p.	BYRON 188:69
How lovely is thy d.-p.	SCOT 755:87
dwellings how amiable are thy d.	BOOK 149:28
dwells In me there d.	TENN 877:52
dwindle d. into wife	CONG 241:75
Shall he d., peak, and pine	SHAK 795:1
dye behint yon auld fail d.	BALL 59:77
dying act of d.	JOHN 462:19
After d. has stopped	HOUS 431:41
An old, mad…and d. king	SHEL 812:70
behold you again in d.	STEV 854:88
blood with the thought of d.	MASE 580:69
born and d., d.	MISH 609:24
didn't mind d.	GLEN 374:49
d., and, behold, we live	BIBLE 127:73
d., bless the hand	DRYD 302:98
d., if we could not cry	MAUP 583:17
D., Is an art	PLATH 681:32
d. is merely to quit	OVID 657:21
d….is terrible	FIEL 335:26
d. man's room	STER 848:39
d. now and done for	BETJ 89:39
d. pray at the last	DILL 286:93
D's easy	MO 610:63
d. tongueless	SHAK 799:8
D., we live	BROW 169:83
habit of living indisposeth us for d.	BROW 165:75
Here am I, d.	POPE 689:50
hold his breath…without d.	ANTH 29:72
I am d.	WILDE 942:23
idea of d. is worse than d.	PROU 698:52
If this is d.	STRA 857:43
immortality…through not d.	ALLEN 14:91
in d. that we are born	FRAN 347:99
instead of d., he sings	BENC 78:11
It was in d.	THOM 886:75
living a little more or d.	MAIL 559:42
love to those of the d.	LOWRY 541:43
men that are d.	JEFF 453:15
so many ways of us d.	BAIN 55:92
We are d. continuously	PETR 676:42
worth fighting for, worth d.	MITC 610:39
Dylan Never mind D. and the Dead	MACG 552:84
dynamic a play is a d. thing	TYNAN 904:2
class people as static and d.	WAUGH 923:65
strong and d.	GAND 359:57
world is…in d. unbalance	BART 66:20
dynamite did and it is d.	TRUM 900:91
dynamo cannibal d.	GINS 372:6
dynasty not respect for a d.	LOUIS 538:74

E

eager less e….to marry	FALU 329:10
eagle as an e. toward heaven	BIBLE 105:90
E. has landed	ALDR 12:54
e. know what's in the pit	BLAKE 139:84
e. mewing her mighty youth	MILT 601:20
e. or the snake	KIPL 490:2
e. suffers little birds	SHAK 760:29
e. was killed by the arrow	KELL 479:66
Fearless the e.	MCCA 547:75
hooded e. among blinking owls	SHEL 547:75
like an e. in a dove-cot	SHAK 799:6
youth is renewed like the e.'s	BIBLE 102:6
eagles More rapid than e.	MOORE 616:63
mount up with wings as e.	BIBLE 109:85
swifter than e.	BIBLE 96:42
Where are the e.	ELIOT 317:87
Where his e. never flew	COWP 250:94
eaglet space, an e.'s wing	CRANE 253:62
ear age shall see the golden e.	POPE 686:62
artistic sense of eye or e.	WHIS 934:22
beat upon my whorled e.	HOPK 428:67
by the hearing of the e.	BIBLE 99:23
Christ in every e.	PATR 669:29
chuckle…from e. to e.	ELIOT 318:3
close at the e. of Eve	MILT 604:11
e. becomes more Irish	BYRON 190:17
e. for her music	DAY 267:35
e. is much enamoured	SHAK 767:36
e. is not sensitive enough	MAHL 559:33
e. of a merchant	NASHE 632:97
E.'s deep-sweet music	SHAK 762:87
enchant thine e.	SHAK 762:83
enemy of the e.	WILD 943:52
Even one e. is more	ROTH 728:87
flattery lost on poet's e.	SCOTT 752:14
flea in mine e.	NASHE 632:90
Give every man thine e.	SHAK 781:51
Good music…penetrates the e.	BEEC 73:64
Hark in thine e.	SHAK 793:24
have no e.	LAMB 505:96
heart was piercèd through the e.	SHAK 789:1
history's e., already listening	SAMU 741:99
hollow of thine e.	SHAK 766:1
horrid stillness first invades the e.	DRYD 299:67
In a believer's e.!	NEWT 636:65
In Reason's e. they all rejoice	ADDI 7:41

earl

Entry	Reference
in your husband's e.	GROM 389:77
Jacobites…give an e., give an e.	BURNS 179:37
jest's prosperity lies in the e.	SHAK 763:26
know not what into my e.	LAND 507:33
lark to shepherd's e.	SHAK 766:18
lend an e. to Plato	TENN 877:69
meant than meets the e.	MILT 598:56
Not to the sensual e.	KEATS 478:36
o'er my e. like the sweet sound	SHAK 785:77
Of eye, and e.	WORD 956:56
penetrated into the e. of man	FORS 344:25
pistol let off at the e.	LAMB 506:13
planted the e.	BIBLE 102:99
presented to the eye or e.	CRAB 252:43
purse out of your wife's e.	MORT 621:73
rich jewel in an Ethiope's e.	SHAK 765:74
Stop thine e. against the singer	SCOTT 754:64
telescope to his e.	SMITH 827:73
there reaches my e.	PAST 668:99
to the E. of Kings	POPE 688:29
tubes of the e.	WILL 946:22
Vexing the dull e.	SHAK 768:58
was all e.	MILT 599:77
whisper in her e.	WILB 939:34
whom he whispers in the e.	BROW 168:58
whose e. is a smoking tomb	GINS 372:6
world-deafened e.	ARNO 34:72

earl As far as the fourteenth e. HOME 425:94
e. and a knight of the garter ATTL 40:28
E. of Dudley and was beheaded MILLS 595:10
Oh I see said the E. ASHF 38:72
slain the E. of Murray BALL 58:53

Earls daughter of a hundred E. TENN 871:9

early always either too late or too e. SART 744:67
e. will I seek thee BIBLE 101:78
had it been e. JOHN 460:63
However monstrously e. SHIP 818:14
too e. for a drink? GORD 378:57
try to be e. DAY 267:29
vain for you to rise up e. BIBLE 103:36
Woe unto them that rise up e. BIBLE 107:53

earn e. it by enjoying such authority BERE 83:15
e. that I eat SHAK 779:89
e. your living WELD 928:85

earned Freedom…is e. CLIN 231:28

earnest impotence of being e. CANN 196:4
in good e. wish WILL 944:67
valuable or even e. THOR 888:32
we die in e. RALE 705:45

ear-pieces CIA agents with e.-p. TRUSS 900:3

ears and hedges e. SWIFT 862:55
blast of war…in our e. SHAK 775:74
bless our human e. MILT 597:35
Creep in our e. SHAK 770:18
distance between your e. JONES 465:16
dying has stopped the e. HOUS 431:41
e. fall off like figs THOM 884:41
e. he likes to bathe in sound BROWN 164:31
E. like bombs CAUS 209:14
e. like errant wings CHES 220:50
e. of every one…shall tingle BIBLE 96:27
e. of jet GRAY 383:51
e. of the deaf shall be unstopped BIBLE 108:76
e. that…hear one's secrets ONEI 651:63
e. that hear the soft rain RICK 714:27
e. to hear, let him hear BIBLE 116:78
e. to hear, let him hear BIBLE 119:53
e. yielding like swinging doors DOUG 295:5
eyes and hearts e. LYLY 543:84
fume of space foams in our e. CRANE 253:64
golden e. of corn HERR 415:14
Harrovian pricks up his e. ANON 23:89
He that hath e. to hear BIBLE 116:78
He that hath e. to hear BIBLE 119:53
if men had e. BYRON 190:27
In the porches of mine e. SHAK 781:64
lend me your e. SHAK 777:37
let thine e. be attentive BIBLE 103:39
make the fur Fly 'bout the e. BUTL 185:74
my e. drumming SAPP 743:49
never mentions Hell to e. polite POPE 686:61
noise of waters in my e. SHAK 761:40
Pour oil into their e. JONS 466:49
reaching the proper e. KIPL 489:69
Rome about your e. SHAK 799:2
seven thin e. BIBLE 93:42
shout about my e. CHES 220:51

Entry	Reference
That man's e. make	HUGH 434:7
thumbs vary…like e.	SHAW 810:23
To dying e.	TENN 872:43
two ambitious e.	JONS 466:48
up to the e. in love	STER 848:41
Walls have e.	ANON 24:23
Walls have e.	LINK 530:27
With ravished e.	DRYD 303:29

earth air, e., or sea MILT 607:72
alien planet is E. BALL 60:84
all cultures of the e. WEBER 925:12
All people that on e. SCOT 755:88
all the corners of the e. BOOK 149:30
all the e. o'erwhelm them SHAK 781:45
All the gold upon the e. PLATO 681:52
alone on e. BYRON 187:44
although the e. remove SCOT 755:86
any man that breathes on e. MARL 573:26
anything on e. can mend MANN 567:92
anywhere else on e. GURN 390:98
as if the e. had rolled WORD 957:71
As if this e.…were breathing COLE 236:38
at any time upon the e. WHIT 937:88
attempt to create heaven on e. BORO 151:67
back to e. as the doorkeeper TOSC 894:64
back to the nourishing e. SAND 742:23
beauty fed my common e. MASE 580:62
believe that the e. is flat DRIB 299:5
belonging as much to sky as to e. CARR 202:53
bleeding piece of e. SHAK 777:33
blithe e. die JEFF 453:12
Born for us on e. below CASW 208:83
bowels of the harmless e. SHAK 771:33
break e.'s sleep OWEN 658:38
bridal of the e. and sky HERB 414:80
brilliant light on e. HUSS 440:39
call heaven and e. to witness BIBLE 94:87
Canst work i'th' e. so fast? SHAK 781:69
Can the e. do to us BROW 166:94
care for no man on e. DICK 282:98
certain fathoms in the e. SHAK 804:31
Child on e. for me BETJ 88:36
clear, and the e. sure DONNE 291:18
clods and trampled e. MUIR 624:17
cloud Enveloping the E. COLE 235:30
comprehended the dust of the e. BIBLE 108:81
conquest of the e. CONR 243:27
cool flowery lap of e. ARNO 34:75
crawling between heaven and e.? SHAK 783:12
crust of an unfinished e. KURA 501:42
daughter of E. and Water SHEL 813:77
daughters of e. JOHN 460:68
did thee feel the e. move? HEMI 410:80
dominion…over all the e. BIBLE 91:84
earned here on e. THAT 881:56
e. abideth for ever BIBLE 105:9
e. able to sustain e. ASIM 38:78
e., and heav'n, and hell POPE 688:33
e. and the heaven fled away BIBLE 132:22
e.…Apparelled in celestial light WORD 959:5
e. as we now see it MACL 555:42
e. beneath her GORD 378:53
e. cares for her own ruins BINY 135:4
e. doth like a snake renew SHEL 816:57
E. felt the wound MILT 606:50
E. has waited ROSE 725:32
e. hath bubbles SHAK 796:7
E. hath not anything to show WORD 959:3
e. in an earthy bed TENN 876:28
e. in travail and in pain LONG 535:32
e. is but an echo of the spheres BYRON 190:27
e. is full of his glory BIBLE 107:54
e. is hell when NASHE 632:94
E. is here so kind JERR 455:46
e. is nobler than the world PRIE 695:85
e. is nothing very special HOYLE 434:95
e. is still going round the sun ORWE 654:57
e. is the Lord's BIBLE 126:47
e. its dower of river KEATS 476:87
E., lie heavily ROSS 726:43
e. must borrow its mirth WILC 939:43
e. of majesty SHAK 764:40
e. peopled as ever by the inept REPP 711:60
E. receive an honoured guest AUDEN 43:92
e. savage, e. broken COLUM 238:87
E.'s crammed with heaven BROW 166:3
e. self-balanced MILT 605:35

Entry	Reference
e. shall be full of the knowledge	BIBLE 108:62
e. shall reel to and fro	BIBLE 108:66
E.'s heedless sons	BLUN 143:75
E.'s shadows fly	SHEL 815:43
E. stood hard as iron	ROSS 726:47
e. the legend of the Gael	RUSS 735:42
E., thou bonnie	MACD 549:18
e. to e.	BOOK 148:1
e. to love	KIPL 491:47
e. was made for Dombey and Son	DICK 280:27
e. where cares abound	WORD 961:44
every man upon this e.	MACA 545:45
exalted in the e.	BIBLE 100:69
eyes…throughout the whole e.	BIBLE 98:86
feels the attraction of e.	LONG 536:38
fell to e.	HAMER 393:44
fell to e.	LONG 535:24
fifth part of the E.	FIELD 335:11
first man is of the e.	BIBLE 127:61
fixed upon the e.	MARL 572:96
for e. too dear	SHAK 765:74
For, heaven to e.	SHAK 772:64
foundations of the e.?	BIBLE 103:41
foundations of the e.?	BIBLE 109:84
From e.'s wide bounds	HOW 433:85
From sullen e.	SHAK 800:46
from which e., and grave	RALE 705:47
furniture of the e.	BERK 84:30
gazing on the e.	SHEL 816:46
get off the e.?	SAND 742:25
girdle round about the e.	SHAK 767:28
glance from heaven to e.	SHAK 767:45
globe of the e.	MUNDY 625:44
God…craves the e.	SEXT 758:52
God created the heaven and the e.	BIBLE 90:80
going to and fro in the e.	BIBLE 98:90
good men…make the e. wholesome	EMER 325:78
hallowed piece of e.	CLIN 230:3
happiest marriages on e.	DE 275:9
heaven and e. in…union	MILT 597:34
Heaven and e. shall pass away	BIBLE 188:30
Heaven in E.	CRAS 253:78
heaven on e.	FORD 343:1
heaven on e. I have won	SHAK 791:67
heav'n and e. hath made	SCOT 755:89
Hell as well as on e.	LEWIS 526:42
hell on e.	SHAW 807:13
Hold off the e.	SHAK 784:66
How on e. can you privatize	PAVL 670:39
inherit the e.	BIBLE 100:59
inherit the e.	BIBLE 114:27
in the deep-delved e.	KEATS 478:42
in the lowest parts of the e.	BIBLE 103:45
Johannesburg is needed upon the e.	PATON 669:28
judged the e. flat	UPDI 905:19
Judge of all the e.	BIBLE 92:22
kingly joys in e.	MARL 572:98
Kings are e.'s gods	SHAK 798:80
lap of e.	GRAY 384:77
last sound on the worthless e.	FAUL 331:47
let the e. be opened	BIBLE 128:96
lie with his mother e.?	SHAK 778:59
Lightly gentle e.	BEAU 67:13
little e., for charity	SHAK 775:23
longer than the e.	BIBLE 93:57
loose to play upon the e.	MILT 600:7
love…good tilled e.	TOLK 893:47
loves but half of E.	QUIL 702:9
low as where this e.	ROSS 726:51
make the e. my hell	SHAK 761:48
Man marks the e. with ruin	BYRON 188:71
meek shall inherit the e.	BIBLE 100:59
meek shall inherit the e.	BIRK 136:13
meek shall inherit the e.	DU 305:68
memory die from the e.	SIDN 820:59
Men are like the e.	SCHR 749:64
men call e.	MILT 598:62
men from the planet E.	ANON 25:69
men walk proudly through the e.	RAND 706:58
mingle our bloods…in the e.	SHAK 798:83
more nearer e.	SHAK 790:43
more things in heaven and e.	MAMET 564:36
more things in heaven and e.	SHAK 781:70
most beautiful things on e.	ISAA 447:63
most decent nation on…e.	BUSH 182:98
moved e. and hearth	TENN 870:2
much less grief on e.	BROD 160:40

echoes

must have a touch of e.	TENN 887:51	way of all the e.	BIBLE 97:52	Difficult or e.	MART 576:77
new heaven and a new e.	BIBLE 132:23	we are on the e.	SHAK 764:43	e.—terribly e.	SHAW 806:89
new heavens and a new e.	BIBLE 110:9	what on e. is the use of them	WILDE 941:96	If it were e.	HANKS 395:82
night close down on the e.	RAND 706:57	Wherewith to scorn the e.	MILT 606:55	Life is not e.	SAIF 738:30
no culture of the.	HOBB 420:2	While e.'s foundations stand	HOUS 432:78	Life is not meant to be e.	FRAS 349:29
none upon e. that I desire	BIBLE 101:86	whole e. as their memorial	PERI 675:24	take life e.	YEATS 965:3
no power on e.	BALD 57:31	whole face of the e.	PASC 667:74	too e. for children	SCHN 748:46
no such thing on e.	CHES 220:57	whole rainy, stony e.?	HUGH 436:38	eat all I had to e.	STEV 851:29
no supporter but the huge firm e.	SHAK 768:55	whole round e.	TENN 878:86	be able to e. less	PAVA 670:35
not in e. or time recoverable	PURDY 700:85	why e. loves e.	ANON 21:53	best place to e.	GUIL 389:87
nought…on the e. doth live	SHAK 766:87	Yours is the E.	KIPL 492:63	but I will not e. with you	SHAK 769:82
novelty on e., this fair defect	MILT 606:64	**earthling** alone in a way that no e.	COLL 237:66	buzzard…can e. anything	FAUL 331:44
Ocean and e.	WORD 961:36	**earthly** all e. things above	SPRI 841:87	couldn't e.	GREE 385:4
old in the e.	BRON 162:76	an e. song	TENN 874:81	do not e. for the good of living	EMER 324:70
ominously upon the e.	GRAV 382:21	e. immortality	FORD 343:1	earn that I e.	SHAK 779:89
on e. a vicious weed	DRYD 302:79	e. paragon	SHAK 803:4	e. all the food	KEEN 478:52
on e. do dwell	KETHE 483:67	ne'er touched e. faces	SHAK 800:36	e. and sleep and choose a wife	SASS 745:81
on e. I wait forlorn	ARNO 35:4	Off e. thingis nane may bettir be	DUNB 306:98	e. as much as a man	TRUTH 900:5
on e. no track	THOM 887:9	too well for any e. use	FROST 352:2	E., drink, and to be merry	BYRON 190:29
on that dark e.	TENN 877:61	**earthquake** e. swallows us	STEV 852:52	e.…drink, and to be merry	BIBLE 106:25
On the bare e. expos'd	DRYD 303:31	e. was really too much	LIGNE 529:98	e. in safety	SHAK 805:58
on the e. he strowèd	SPEN 839:61	e. were to engulf England	JERR 455:49	e. my ale	FARQ 330:27
oppressions of this e.	SHEL 812:62	haven't had an e. lately	MILNE 596:21	e. the power out of women	WEST 933:96
other nations of the e.	JAMES 450:36	Lord was not in the e.	BIBLE 97:67	e. thy bread with joy	BIBLE 106:27
our moment upon the e.	MANS 567:3	not smiling back—that's an e.	MILL 593:32	e. to live	MOLI 611:84
our room on this e.	GREN 388:58	shaken with an e.	ADDI 6:22	e.…with a glum urge	FISH 337:65
paleyce as ony on e.	MALO 562:9	starts with an e.	GOLD 377:31	e.…this do in remembrance	BIBLE 126:49
passenger on the spaceship, E.	FULL 355:72	takes an e. to remind us	KURA 501:42	hoping…he will e. you last	REAG 708:2
Peace on e. and mercy mild!	BEEC 73:65	the gloom of e.	SHEL 812:69	I did e.	BIBLE 91:95
peace upon the e.	MILT 597:32	to play golf during an e.	STAL 842:8	I e. what I see	CARR 203:70
pearled Arcturi of the e.	SHEL 816:60	win a war than…win an e.	RANK 705:64	kill, and e.	BIBLE 124:82
place among the nations of the e.	EMMET 325:6	**earthquakes** e.…bright weather	CARL 200:4	let us e. and drink	BIBLE 127:59
portion of the e.	NAIP 629:27	famines, and pestilences, and e.	BIBLE 118:29	let us e. and drink	BIBLE 108:65
present life of men on e.	BEDE 72:59	increases e.	SEDI 755:98	neither should he e.	BIBLE 129:16
rapture the e. and the seas	BRON 161:55	thought of e., and of wars	BYRON 189:94	Never e. at…Mom's	ALGR 13:68
regarded this e. with envious eyes	WELLS 930:19	**ease** Are you at e. now?	FLET 341:61	So I did sit and e.	HERB 413:66
returning him safely to e.	KENN 481:5	as in a doubtful e.	SURR 860:98	some wad e. that want it	ANON 22:82
revealed Not of e.	MILT 605:36	done with so much e.	DRYD 301:65	Take, e.: this is my body	BIBLE 126:49
round e.'s imagined corners	DONNE 292:50	E. after war	SPEN 838:28	Tell me what you e.	BRIL 159:17
salt of the e.	BIBLE 114:28	e. of body	SMITH 827:74	than e. China's all our lives	HO 421:13
salt of the e.	SHEL 814:3	e. some deal	SHAK 760:25	To e., to survive	STAN 843:19
Saviour Christ again to E.	MASE 580:64	for another gives its e.	BLAKE 140:9	**eaten** e. me out of house	SHAK 772:78
scatter them abroad…all the e.	BIBLE 92:15	health and perfect e.	DYER 309:50	has been e. by the bear	HOUS 433:80
scum of the e.	CHES 221:86	heart's first e.	DAY 267:37	never e. bread	KAIKO 472:11
scum of the e.…soldiers	WELL 929:99	hours of e.	SCOTT 752:25	**eater** good e. must be a good man	DISR 287:17
send peace on e.	BIBLE 116:72	ignoble e., and peaceful sloth	MILT 602:60	great e. of beef	SHAK 785:83
serious house on serious e.	LARK 509:78	interpose a little e.	MILT 599:92	Out of the e. came forth meat	BIBLE 95:15
shall move the e.	ARCH 30:8	Joys in another's loss of e.	BLAKE 140:10	**eating** Appetite comes with e.	RABE 703:11
shall not perish from the e.	LINC 529:9	man is most at e.	ALLS 14:8	e. paté	SMITH 831:61
shortest-lived profession on e.	ROGE 723:85	no longer at e. here	ELIOT 318:18	E. people is wrong!	FLAN 338:9
Silver out of the E. in Peru	PETTY 679:45	prodigal of e.?	DRYD 302:73	e. that's believing	THUR 891:92
Sing…all the e.	BIBLE 133:33	Studious of laborious e.	COWP 251:18	E. the air	SHAK 772:76
Six miles from e.	JARR 452:83	True e. in writing	POPE 685:24	for e., not mating	FERB 332:72
sleepers in that quiet e.	BRON 162:82	**easel** bread, and his e.	RYDER 736:57	good news is that he's e. less	JACO 449:9
small model of the barren e.	SHAK 764:51	**easier** e. to conquer it	WALP 919:71	It's like e. sushi	STOP 856:25
smell above the e.	SHAK 777:34	e. with practice	GREE 386:24	Lawful as e.	SHAK 800:32
smite the e. a curse	BIBLE 112:66	how much e.	HALI 393:33	loving alone is as dull as e. alone	WYCH 964:5
Spaceship E.	FULL 355:72	I am e. to be played on	SHAK 783:29	redfaced from e. and drinking	ABBO 1:1
spiritual creatures walk the e.	MILT 604:7	upon e. terms	JOHN 464:91	subject of e.	HUNT 440:32
Standing on e., not rapt	MILT 605:27	**easing** E. the spring	REED 709:27	While someone else is e.	AUDEN 42:80
strangers and pilgrims on the e.	BIBLE 129:40	**east** aristocracy of the E.	MAUG 582:9	**eats** e. up himself	SHAK 786:31
sun is coming down to e.	MERE 587:26	As far as the e. is from the west	BIBLE 102:8	Man is what he e.	FEUE 334:3
sun went around the e.	ARNO 36:46	chambers of the E.	BLAKE 139:78	way that he e. jelly beans	REAG 708:4
surface of the e.	SWIFT 862:44	determined to go E.	MAIL 560:67	Young misses whut e.	MITC 610:40
temples of the e.	DIDE 285:72	E. is E	KIPL 489:76	**eat-well** E.-w. is drink-well's brother	FULL 355:82
that e. lie light	WALL 918:58	e. wind made flesh	APPL 30:94	**eaves** sparrow in the e.	YEATS 965:6
the meek would inherit the e.	KEIL 479:61	e. wind presides over the west	MAO 563:95	upon her gilded e.	TENN 872:44
Things learned on e.	BROW 168:55	hold the gorgeous E. in fee	WORD 959:4	**ebb** ne'er e. to humble love	SHAK 790:29
this broad e. of ours	WHIT 938:12	Hunter of the E.	FITZ 337:68	**ebony** nine e. spikes	KING 488:57
this e. of ours	DE 273:81	inscrutability of the E.	STARK 843:25	**eccentricity** reputation for e.	SHAK 806:77
this green e.	WORD 956:56	lands of the E.	GILL 370:87	**ecclesiastical** interest in e.	WAUGH 923:60
thought about…the whole e.	BYRON 189:94	look the E. End in the face	ELIZ 322:15	**ecclesiologist** keen e.	BETJ 88:16
though the e. be removed	BIBLE 100:67	mysterious E., perfumed	CONR 244:35	**echo** all the church did e.	SHAK 762:72
three nights in the heart of the e.	BIBLE 117:86	politics in the E.	DISR 287:20	Art is dedicated e.	SANT 743:45
through heav'n and e.	MILT 603:88	sigh of the e. on my face	CONR 244:34	co-opted and obliterated e.	HEAN 405:79
through my lips to unawakened e.	SHEL 813:84	There is no silence in the E.	MAUG 582:7	e. began in some indescribable way	FORS 344:37
throw e. over your head	PASC 667:77	three kings into the e.	BURNS 178:99	E., sweetest nymph	MILT 598:70
Thy will be done in e.	BIBLE 115:42	tried to hustle the E.	KIPL 490:99	Scents, colours, and sounds e.	BAUD 65:20
Till e. and sky	KIPL 489:76	when the wind blew due E.	CARR 206:30	sound must seem an e.	POPE 685:24
tread on E.	ARNO 33:63	wind's in the e.	DICK 281:60	there reaches…the e.	PAST 668:99
treasures upon e.	BIBLE 115:43	**Easter** frome Candylmas untyll E.	MALO 563:14	waiting for the e.	MARQ 575:57
two paces of the vilest e.	SHAK 772:67	making my E. confession	JOSE 469:7	**echoes** all their e. mourn	MILT 599:84
uttermost part of the e.	BIBLE 124:70	**Eastern** save in E. clime	BURG 175:5	Dead e.! But I knew her body	CRANE 253:62
uttermost parts of the e.	BIBLE 117:87	**eastern** Come o'er the e. hills	BLAKE 139:80	e., dying, dying, dying	TENN 872:36
uttermost parts of the e.	BIBLE 99:28	**Eastertide** Wearing white for E.	HOUS 431:33	e., dying, dying, dying	TENN 872:39
wall as solid as the e.	BUCH 171:22	**Easthampstead** on E. Plain	KING 488:50	e. of fear	EVANS 328:69
way of all the e.	BIBLE 95:7	**easy** depending upon shock…is e.	PRIE 695:94	Our e. roll	TENN 872:40

eclipse 1086

eclipse
state-controlled manufactory of e. — DOUG 295:13
wild e. flying — TENN 872:38
eclipse earthquake and e. — SHEL 812:69
eclipses modus of lunar e. — POUND 691:98
ecological e. balance of the planet — SONT 834:16
economic accepted e. legends — GALB 357:17
an e. colony — TSON 900:7
chief source of e. insecurity — ELLW 323:39
cold metal of e. theory — SCHU 750:77
Commentators quote e. studies — SAMU 741:2
e. condition has…improved — KRIS 499:14
e. equivalent of the slave — WIEN 939:28
e. factors in society — GILM 371:92
e. ones are incomprehensible — HOME 425:95
E. policy is random — STEIN 845:79
e., political, and social life — LEWIS 526:53
e. services that it can render — DURK 308:27
e. status of women — GILM 371:91
e. substructure — FANON 329:13
e. value of…women — GILM 371:93
engineering an e. revival — LARD 509:66
essential form of e. speech — WRIS 963:81
forces of e. law — KEYN 484:71
industrial and e. status — SKEL 824:32
In e. terms — GLEI 374:48
more effective e. service — TAWN 868:43
much of e. theory — HICKS 418:49
normal e. system works — SALT 741:95
not the e. index — MARC 570:57
opportunity cost of e. discussion — GALB 357:22
take our e. blood pressure — WRIS 963:78
talented e. theorists — TOBIN 892:25
understand the e. system — ROBI 718:94
When I read e. documents — HOME 425:96
economical e. with the truth — ARMS 33:53
economically e. backward — TROT 899:67
economics basic law of e. — HARR 399:60
branch of e. — STIG 854:97
E. and art are strangers — CATH 208:95
E. as a positive science — FRIE 351:68
E. as if People Mattered — SCHU 750:73
E., if it is to be — JEVO 455:51
E. is all about…choices — DUES 305:82
E. is the science — ROBB 717:68
e. represents — LEVI 526:30
e. suggests that they — MISH 609:19
Enid Blyton of e. — HOLME 423:56
from the Principles of E. — KEYN 484:76
master of e. — HOLM 424:86
purpose of studying e. — ROBI 718:93
economies few factors help…e. — MCDO 550:44
two e. finally merged — WOLF 952:62
economist a one-handed e. — TRUM 900:90
death of a political e. — BAGE 54:64
e. is someone who — HELL 408:38
e. uses a complicated model — ADAMS 6:11
world's greatest e. — SCHU 750:76
economists among professional e. — HAYEK 403:26
a very large number of e. — GALB 357:23
classical e. — VINER 913:10
deceived by e. — ROBI 718:93
distribution of uncertainty among e. — STEIN 845:78
e., and…economic theorists — KNIG 494:10
e. are…disinclined to publish — CANN 196:6
e. hardly know enough — BECK 71:35
E. have the least influence — BLIN 142:53
e. need to abandon — KRUG 500:26
E. set themselves — KEYN 484:73
ideas of e. — KEYN 484:81
If all the e. in the world — SHAW 811:32
Sometimes e. give bad advice — KRUG 500:58
sophisters, e., and calculators — BURKE 176:40
economy arbitrary e. of nature — WOLL 954:89
Beauty…like any e. — WOLF 952:61
complex…as a modern e. — SOLOW 833:3
different schemes of e. — STEU 849:61
e. is based on planned obsolescence — STEV 849:62
E. is the art — SHAW 808:46
e. of a manufacture — BABB 48:1
e. of these people — SMOL 831:67
e., stupid! — ANON 27:14
her industry and e. — STAN 842:15
In art e. is always beauty — JAMES 451:52
in favour of general e. — EDEN 311:30
In the interests of e. — MAXT 583:18
its e. is in difficulty — WALE 917:29
No e. ever stands still — HARR 399:61

People want e. — IACO 444:1
performance of the American e. — STEIN 845:79
Political e. — RUSK 733:97
Political e. thus does — MARX 578:26
Political e. traces — BAGE 54:76
seeds of the spirit and e. — MARI 570:72
socialism and a market e. — DENG 272:57
working e. in the world — MARS 575:63
wrote 'Principles of Political E.' — BENT 82:2
ecstasies muddy e. of beer — CRAB 251:24
ecstasy bells of E. — GINS 372:13
e. of love — SHAK 781:73
e. Of sun-fed wine — NEIL 633:11
escape from circumstance to e. — BELL 75:33
immobility, e., and sleep — MARI 571:76
not e. but it was comfort — DICK 282:88
seraph-wings of e. — GRAY 385:90
think thereof without an e.? — BROW 165:54
What wild e.? — KEATS 478:35
ecstatic the e. and the bilious — ELIOT 315:17
ectoplasms Hollywood-movie e. — ELLI 323:35
Ector bare it forth unto syre E. — MALO 562:6
eczema Style…too often hides e. — CAMUS 196:93
eddy action's dizzying e. — ARNO 33:61
Eden birds of E. sang? — CULL 257:43
brooks of E. mazily murmuring — TENN 877:64
east of E. — BIBLE 92:6
easy E.-dreamtime — WRIG 963:70
E., demi-paradise — SHAK 764:40
E.'s green and gold — KIPL 490:97
E., shall enjoy their fill — MILT 604:4
E. took their solitary way — MILT 607:74
foot in E. — MUIR 624:22
garden eastwards in E. — BIBLE 91:87
out of the Garden of E. — MUGG 623:10
put him into the garden of E. — BIBLE 91:88
sent him forth from the garden of E. — BIBLE 91:1
when from E. we take — MACN 558:8
woe, With loss of E. — MILT 601:29
edge at the e. of Being — SPEN 837:97
e. of a new frontier — KENN 481:99
e. of some crazy cliff — SALI 740:81
e. of the stage — DIDE 285:63
e. of the world — SITW 824:22
e. to the superstitious tale — PRIT 696:15
Fills and trembles at the e. — ROET 722:57
hand…cutting e. of the mind — BRON 160:51
if they have a cutting e. — MURR 627:85
own folly, go over the e. — MOUN 622:93
push men over the e. — ROTH 727:78
edges octaves of its parallel e. — CUMM 257:51
Stain all your e. — SHAK 799:6
edify all things is not — BIBLE 126:46
Edina E.! Scotia's darling seat — BURNS 178:96
Edinburgh E. will not disagree — STEEL 844:38
It seemed to him a very E. thing — RANK 706:63
Ye E. Gentry! — BURNS 177:72
editing final e. down — DELI 271:40
products of e. — WALD 916:24
edition new e. of human nature — HAZL 403:48
new…more beautiful e. — FRAN 348:7
not in the latest e. — GREE 386:17
editor E.: a person employed — HUBB 434:1
e. is the uncrowned king — STEAD 843:32
e. must always be with the people — BENN 81:79
e. of an important magazine — CANN 196:6
e. of a village journal — MOOD 615:56
e. who cannot contemplate it — JOVA 469:13
Procrustes was an e. — SKEL 825:42
Show me a contented newspaper e. — CHRI 223:38
the one that the e. gives to the worms — MACH 552:90
Trust your e. — CHEE 218:12
editorial age of the e. chair — MCLU 556:57
This is the e. age — BENN 81:80
editors some newspaper e. — CHOP 223:34
true Church of England…in the E. — CARL 199:75
educability His whole e. — JAMES 451:69
educate e. the masses — OSLER 656:89
got to e. him first — SAKI 739:56
educated another sun to the e. — HERA 412:36
clothed, fed and e. — RUSK 733:9
'e.' people…come to the front — ORWE 653:12
government by the badly e. — CHES 221:6
instructed and amused…is e. — ATLAS 40:20
liberally e. person — BLOOM 142:63
never preach, but to the e. — AUST 46:70
stamps a man…as an e. gentleman — SHAW 809:71

that is e. — HAMI 394:49
thought highly e. — SNOW 832:76
uncrowned king of an e. democracy — STEAD 843:32
education American e. — ADAMS 5:96
apathy in e. — FORS 344:32
best kind of e. — BUCH 171:26
By e. most have been misled — DRYD 303:16
can't do with any more e. — WODE 952:49
e. and whisky the price it is — WAUGH 923:58
E. consists mainly — TWAIN 903:85
E….discloses to the wise — BIER 134:75
E. in science and technology — HUXL 442:97
E….in so much higher a degree — AUST 47:89
e. is a little too pedantic — CONG 241:48
E. is another sun — HERA 412:36
E. is a state-controlled — DOUG 395:13
E. is…hanging around — FROST 353:23
E. is…human — YOUS 969:66
E. is impossible without love — DESB 274:88
e….is mere sheep-herding — POUND 692:16
E. is the taming — BLOOM 143:64
E. is what remains — EINS 314:85
E. is what survives — SKIN 825:46
e. of the people — DISR 288:62
e. of the people — MILL 591:98
e. of the people — WHIT 934:25
e. produces no effect — WILDE 941:91
e. to eliminate the influence — MUSG 627:87
field of public e. — WARR 921:72
finished his e. till after — HAYD 402:23
good e….to sustain a failure — BELL 75:31
Harvard e. consists of what you learn — CONA 239:11
have no e. — SMOL 831:67
having no e. — SHAN 805:67
hope to agree about e. — RUSS 734:33
If you think e. is expensive — BOK 144:3
lacking any mathematical e. — HAYEK 403:26
man of any e. — JOHN 463:52
man's e. begins — ROUS 729:13
Marriage can wait, e. cannot — HOSS 430:31
Movies, and that is e. — ROGE 723:82
only accomplishment my e. — DRAB 298:79
part of every Englishman's e. — HUGH 436:46
priorities for Government…e., and e. — BLAIR 138:52
race between e. and catastrophe — WELLS 930:35
same relation to e. — HUBB 434:2
saw in my own e. — WEST 933:96
scramble themselves into a little e. — AUST 46:73
Soap and e. — TWAIN 902:36
So long as e. is not provided — DAVI 264:71
test and use of man's e. — BARZ 67:37
unblunted by formal e. — ANGE 18:85
value of a liberal e. — BREW 158:4
educational modern e. theorists — RUSS 734:32
political and e. status — SKEL 824:32
social and e. patterns — MCLU 556:56
educators priests and e. — NGU 636:66
Edward Prayer Book of E. VI — ACHE 2:28
proud E.'s army — WILL 947:31
proud E.'s power — BURNS 180:47
winding-sheet of E.'s race — GRAY 385:84
eel adder better than the e. — SHAK 762:75
funeral march of a fried e. — SHAW 810:24
eels small e. that left the deeper way — CRAB 252:42
topped with good, rich, broiled e. — KURO 501:43
Eeyore snowing still,' said E. — MILNE 596:21
effacement brought full e. — RANS 707:71
effanineffable ineffable effable E. — ELIOT 320:53
effect all that…despotism could e. — PITT 680:12
approaches the e. of painting — MICH 590:70
e. on other people — SART 744:64
instrument that has a good moral e. — ARIS 32:28
minimum effort for maximum e. — HIRST 419:78
Nature…a name for an e. — COWP 251:23
notion of cause and e. — HUME 438:55
poetry administers to the e. — SHEL 816:50
win an e. — UPDI 905:13
effective Being e. is more important — BECK 71:36
effects dire e. from civil discord — ADDI 7:53
e. deprave forever — BRON 161:72
e. of the division of labour — SMITH 827:75
grind out the true causes and e. — CARL 200:85
not in its taste, but its e. — FULB 355:43
slow preparation of e. — ELIOT 316:49
effectual any more e. way — TROL 897:34
effeminate held curls to be e. — TWAIN 902:42
efficiency competitive race for e. — ARNO 36:47

Elvis

e. and inefficiency	SHAW 809:68	
E....is measured	JAY 453:2	
Good architecture is...e. and beauty	HUXT 443:16	
industrial e. consists	ROBI 718:78	
Practical e. is common	ROOS 725:20	
efficient e. organization is one	STEA 843:29	
kept e. by the persistent absenteeism	SAMU 741:98	
Effie E. M. was a monster	LEE 519:97	
effigies e. of gods and goddesses	GILL 370:77	
effluence e. of bright essence increate	MILT 603:73	
effort e. to keep a party together	WILS 948:73	
e. very nearly killed her	BELL 77:63	
enjoyment of successful e.	SHIP 818:13	
Evil is done without e.	BAUD 69:77	
feeling that lures us on...to vain e.	CONR 244:36	
form of moral e.	LEAC 515:19	
main e....has been a critical e.	ARNO 35:8	
minimum e. for maximum effect	HIRST 419:78	
not the e. or the failure	EMPS 326:8	
only e. worth making	BOWL 153:6	
steadily decreasing amount of e.	SCHU 750:79	
team e. is a lot of people	WINN 950:5	
unusually obstinate e.	JAMES 451:63	
worth every e.	THES 882:96	
worth the e.	WINT 950:14	
years of e., hard work	PEARY 671:59	
efforts appreciate his e.	KENN 481:20	
e. to understand...nature	BUSH 184:50	
excuse to cease all e.	ANGE 19:94	
field for their e.	BRON 161:61	
effusion e. of...human blood	OCON 646:83	
effusions liveliest e. of wit	AUST 46:83	
egalitarian e....should be élitist	LODGE 534:1	
more e. than it wants	SWEE 861:10	
egg an e.'s way for making another e.	DAWK 267:26	
balancing an e. on a spoon	HILL 418:55	
bald as an e.	CHEE 218:10	
broody hen sitting on a china e.	FOOT 342:81	
e. heads are in one basket	ANON 25:47	
e. is full of meat	SHAK 766:93	
e. production in this country	CURR 259:96	
e.'s way of making another e.	BUTL 185:92	
hen's e. don't turn into a crocodile	KING 488:53	
It's very provoking...to be called an e.	CARR 205:7	
Killers from the e.	HUGH 435:33	
lay a tit's e.	MACD 550:42	
like eating an e.	KIPL 197:20	
No goose, no golden e.	TSON 900:8	
Remorse, the fatal e.	COWP 251:4	
See this e.	DIDE 285:72	
sitting on one addled e.	ELIOT 315:41	
to work on an e.	WELD 928:79	
when one is eating a demnition e.	DICK 278:82	
egghead way of the e. is hard	STEV 851:9	
eggheads E. are terrible Philistines	NABO 628:44	
E. of the world unite	STEV 851:8	
eggs all my e. in one bastard	PARK 638:15	
as a weasel sucks e.	SHAK 778:76	
boil e. in your shoes	LEAR 517:	
Do you like green e. and ham?	SEUSS 758:40	
helps scenery like ham and e.	TWAIN 902:37	
roast their e.	BACON 56:7	
ways to dress e.?	MOORE 618:7	
eglantine lush e.	SHEL 816:61	
ego e. that can crack crystal	CHEE 218:11	
have a bit of an e.	HOPK 428:62	
The e. is like a kid	ALLEN 13:82	
egocentric dreams are all e.	WAUGH 924:93	
ego-games religion without e.-g.	REED 710:35	
egomaniacs of neurotics, e.	MANK 566:75	
egos E....setting themselves apart	BUBER 171:20	
individual e., crazy for love	BART 66:13	
egotism Apology is only e.	HOLM 424:79	
dilemmas of conscience and e.	SNOW 832:75	
egotist E....person of low taste	BIER 134:76	
egregiously making him e. an ass	SHAK 789:10	
Egypt against all the firstborn of E.	SHAK 778:77	
ancient E. persisted	RUSS 734:34	
beauty in a brow of E.	SHAK 767:45	
broken reed, on E.	BIBLE 108:78	
brought thee out of...E.	BIBLE 94:66	
brought thee out of E.	BIBLE 101:87	
called my son out of E.	BIBLE 111:46	
can't judge E. by Aïda	FIRB 336:58	
died...in the land of E.	BIBLE 93:59	
good of the land of E.	BIBLE 93:46	
great cry in E.	BIBLE 93:60	

Jewish Queen of E.	TAYL 837:16	
not at war with E.	EDEN 311:32	
painting was brought to E.	VASA 909:27	
pass through the land of E.	BIBLE 93:59	
this bruised reed, even upon E.	BIBLE 98:82	
Egyptian as thou killedst the E.?	BIBLE 93:50	
imagined...ancient E. princess	CASS 207:71	
Egyptians E. were urgent upon the people	BIBLE 93:61	
E....worship an insect	DISR 288:45	
Eiffel stick them up your E. Tower	JAY 453:99	
eight Pieces of e.!	STEV 852:60	
eighteen E. is a good time	GOLD 375:77	
knew almost as much at e.	JOHN 461:99	
eighteenth E.-century houses	YEATS 966:18	
eighties vice of the E.	WOLFE 953:81	
any more than e. years	FRAN 349:29	
eighty At e.	BENN 80:58	
you are never e.	SEXT 758:46	
Eildon down by the E. Tree	BALL 59:74	
Einstein As E. once said	PERCY 619:33	
Let E. be!	SQUI 841:90	
eird Best thing in e.	HENR 411:20	
Eisenhower a second E.	SULL 859:76	
E....magic	WHITE 936:60	
elaborate suggests an e. hobby	PRIE 695:90	
Elaine Daintily alights E.	BETJ 89:37	
E. the fair	TENN 877:50	
elasticity maximum e. for our minds	BUTT 186:14	
elbow man demanding e. room	WAUGH 924:87	
seated e. to e.	GILL 370:79	
smokes on one e.	MORG 619:33	
elbow-chairs Convenience...e.-c.	COWP 251:10	
elbows Mr E. and Knees	ANON 24:40	
elder e. man not at all	BACON 51:76	
elderly care for the e.	FIELD 335:15	
e. man of 42	ASHF 37:93	
nightmare of e. white males	ABBO 1:1	
elders discourse of the e.	BIBLE 113:86	
listening to their e.	BALD 57:17	
Nat of oure e.	CHAU 217:89	
party taken over by the e.	FITZ 338:89	
eldritch e. light of sundown	DAY 267:37	
elect e., the elected	LOWE 540:29	
not...who you e.	THOM 887:92	
elected could have e. my chauffeur	KENN 482:55	
e. and anointed ones	WOLFE 953:75	
help them get e.	TAYL 868:54	
plebiscite e. generals	JUVE 471:57	
election 11.30pm on e. night	MOND 612:95	
acrimony of the last e.	DICK 279:2	
Democracy substitutes e.	SHAW 808:37	
e. but the making of	NEW 634:34	
e. by the incompetent many	SHAW 808:37	
e. is coming	ELIOT 315:40	
enthusiasm for the e.	WHIT 937:84	
fictitious e. results that elect a fictitious president	MOORE 617:93	
Labour Party's e. programme	SNOW 832:88	
worst disaster since my e.	BROWN 164:34	
elections leader who could...win e.	MCFA 551:64	
won the e.	SOMO 833:11	
electorate province of a despicable e.	PITT 679:2	
What the e. gives	BLAIR 138:54	
electors ever put before the e.	SNOW 832:88	
Electra Mourning becomes E.	ONEI 651:67	
electric Along the e. wires	AUST 47:96	
E. guitars are an abomination	SEGO 756:4	
E. Kool-Aid Acid Test	WOLFE 953:72	
married to an e. light	DIMA 286:98	
electrician practical e.	WELLS 929:17	
electricity E. is of two kinds	LEAC 515:12	
e. was dripping	THUR 890:68	
think that science is e.	GOUR 380:79	
electrons e. its personality	BRYS 171:14	
same number of e.	EDDI 311:27	
elegance e. is a state of mind	CASS 207:72	
E. is good taste	SNOW 831:73	
E. is not about being noticed	ARMA 32:37	
e. of Circe's hair	POUND 691:1	
her...un-American e.	SCHL 747:37	
outdone your e.	POUND 692:25	
elegancy e., facility...of poesy	SHAK 763:13	
elegant erect, e., dogmatic	REST 711:62	
Shakespeherian Rag...so e.	ELIOT 318:1	
elegy e. To crown thy hearse?	CAREW 198:48	
element can its native e.	MARV 576:86	
e. of fire is quite put out	DONNE 292:58	

e. within us	MURP 626:75	
Of all sweet sounds the life and e.!	COLE 235:30	
random e. in the world	EDDI 311:24	
to the destructive e. submit yourself	CONR 244:32	
yield their names to the e.	TATE 867:38	
elementary 'E.', said he	DOYLE 297:63	
elements among the e.	PLATH 681:30	
conflict of its e.	BYRON 189:84	
discordant e.	WORD 958:76	
e. and an angelic sprite	DONNE 292:56	
e. are cricket's presiding geniuses	CARD 198:45	
e. in their constituencies	LIPP 531:42	
e. in the record...evoked	WHIT 936:71	
e. of air and earth	SHAK 785:91	
framed out of four e.	MARL 572:99	
Men...defied The e.	WORD 961:42	
mirror of the universal e.	STEI 845:58	
our e., these piercing fires	MILT 602:61	
elephant E.'s Child	KIPL 491:36	
e. sings deep in the forest-maze	HUGH 436:42	
e. which brought us hither	MUNDY 625:43	
God...invented...the e.	PICA 677:62	
I'm ready for another e.	BUFF 172:49	
long noses like an e.	260:8	
masterpiece, an E.	DONNE 291:31	
shot an e. in my pyjamas	MARX 578:15	
sleeping with an e.	TRUD 899:71	
teach an e. to dance	MOSS 622:81	
thought he saw an E.	CARR 206:32	
elephants e. for want of towns	SWIFT 863:63	
True philosophers are like e.	FONT 342:76	
Women are like e.	FIEL 335:31	
elevation scoured us to an e.	LLOY 533:72	
elevator If you die in an e.	336:42	
eleventh about the e. hour he went	BIBLE 118:21	
elf deceiving e.	KEATS 478:48	
queen, an e. most fair	LAYA 515:98	
Elfland horns of E.	TENN 872:39	
Elginbrodde Martin E.	MACD 550:45	
Eli Let E. rejoice	SMART 826:60	
ran unto E.	BIBLE 96:25	
Elijah E....cast his mantle	BIBLE 97:68	
E....girded up his loins	BIBLE 97:65	
E. went up by a whirlwind	BIBLE 97:71	
send you E. the prophet	BIBLE 112:66	
spirit of E. doth rest on Elisha	BIBLE 97:72	
eliminate e. his ability	SCHW 750:89	
e. the unnecessary	HOFF 422:31	
To define is to e.	QUINE 702:21	
elimination e. of some disease	SUTH 860:7	
Eliot George E.'s husband	MORR 620:46	
How unpleasant to meet Mr E.!	ELIOT 319:49	
T. S. E.'s mother-in-law	BENN 80:56	
Elisha spirit of Elijah doth rest on E.	BIBLE 97:72	
elite sovereignty of an intellectual e.	ROCK 720:30	
élites right of colonial é.	ILLI 445:21	
Eliza So did take E.	JONS 468:81	
Elizabeth God save E.	ANON 22:66	
Queen E. owned silk stockings	SCHU 750:79	
saying...ascribed to Queen E.	ADDI 6:30	
Ellie So Tom went home with E.	KING 488:53	
elliptics glassy pinnacles correct e.	BISH 136:23	
elm tall e.'s shadow	THOM 885:54	
vine-prop e.	SPEN 838:20	
elms Behind the e.	PRIOR 696:6	
Beneath those rugged e.	GRAY 384:64	
e., Fade into dimness	ARNO 36:25	
immemorial e.	TENN 873:52	
elm-tree round the e.-t. bole	BROW 167:20	
elm-trees e.-t. in the...meadows	KING 487:47	
elopement as if you worked...an e.	DOYLE 296:43	
eloquence e. in speaking	MARIE 570:73	
e., native to famous wits	MILT 607:79	
E. should persuade	PASC 667:84	
more e. in a sugar touch	SHAK 776:1	
splendour of his e.	HUME 438:3	
Take e. and break its neck!	VERL 911:60	
True e. has no time for e.	PASC 666:67	
eloquent rich e., but he talks well	BEAV 71:25	
El Salvador peasants in E. S.	OROU 652:92	
else Who E. but Nelse?	ANON 25:64	
Elsinore wild and stormy steep, E.!	CAMP 194:66	
elusive Endings are e.	BART 66:16	
One's prime is e.	SPARK 836:68	
elves And the e. also	HERR 416:15	
spite of all the criticizing e.	CHUR 224:55	
Elvis E. ate America	BONO 146:29	

Elysian

finding E. on Mars	JOHN 457:90	
Elysian dead, but in the E. fields	DISR 288:64	
Elysium E. have ye known	KEATS 475:76	
emanation genius is a pure e.	HAZL 404:49	
emancipated more perfect when e.	WOLL 954:95	
emancipation e. of women	MILL 592:15	
internet, our greatest tool of e.	ASSAN 39:98	
understand by e.	GREER 387:42	
war for the e.	LLOY 533:74	
emancipator e….as a crank	BROUN 163:19	
embalmer triumph of the e.'s art	VIDAL 912:91	
embarrass failed to e. the claimant	STRA 857:42	
never e. my family	JOHN 457:88	
embarrassed e. by the words	HEMI 409:64	
embarrassment e. for those who benefit	MARI 571:85	
E. of Riches	ALLA 13:73	
embassies e.…were everywhere	HEAN 405:78	
embassy e. of a nation about to go into…liquidation	MACI 553:3	
embers dead man's e.	GRAV 382:23	
e. through the room	MILT 598:54	
O joy! that in our e.	WORD 959:9	
emblem e. of ignorance	ATAT 40:13	
emblems scarves and e.	BAIN 55:94	
embodiment Law is the true e.	GILB 369:50	
embody e. the Law	GILB 369:50	
embrace close clinging to e.	ROCH 719:5	
e. me she enclin'd	MILT 650:28	
e. of the Venus de Milo	DARIO 262:45	
endure, then pity, then e.	POPE 687:82	
I e. the purpose of God	TENN 876:36	
If I e. my rival	RACI 704:29	
none I think do there e.	MARV 577:92	
snug e. of the	TIME 892:20	
that may e.	SURR 860:3	
time to e.	BIBLE 105:14	
will be guarded by e.	LOWE 539:98	
embraced would have e. him	STAN 842:11	
embraces age in her e. passed	ROCH 720:25	
sleepy, soft e.	GORD 378:53	
embroidered e. cloths	YEATS 966:12	
embroideries Covered with e.	YEATS 966:16	
embroidery flower that sad e. wear	MILT 599:91	
emerald defile…the E. Isle	DREN 299:2	
e. eyes	GRAY 383:51	
e. twinkles in the grass	TENN 876:24	
see the E. Drop	RHYS 712:77	
emeralds E. big as half a county	LAND 507:35	
emergency compelled by e.	TROL 898:51	
e. happening at a distance	BARZ 67:42	
Microscopes…In an E.	DICK 283:32	
one e. following upon another	FISH 337:62	
Whatever the e.	GILB 368:32	
emigration e. is…necessity	MOOD 615:55	
eminence higher e. in whatever	DARW 263:57	
only chance of e.	SHAW 810:19	
raised To that bad e.	MILT 602:55	
eminent death reveals the e.	SHAW 808:52	
Emmanuel call his name E.	BIBLE 114:15	
emissions I love the smell of e.	PALIN 661:62	
We will double our e.	OLEA 649:33	
emotion coarse e. of mankind	ELIOT 316:52	
conveying an e.	HEPW 412:28	
degree of my aesthetic e.	BELL 75:34	
e. of art	ELIOT 317:88	
e. recollected in tranquillity	WORD 958:93	
expressing e. in the form of art	ELIOT 317:90	
for it is an e.	GOLD 375:79	
language concentrating e.	BRAU 157:86	
less bounding at e. new	ARNO 35:21	
morality touched with e.	ARNO 36:34	
plastic e. requires it	BOCC 144:90	
Poetry…an escape from e.	ELIOT 317:89	
Science…a source of strong e.	BARZ 67:39	
tranquillity remembered in e.	PARK 664:20	
undercurrent of e.	UPDI 906:37	
under stress of e.	POUND 692:37	
Undisciplined squads of e.	ELIOT 320:66	
emotional e. depth of woman	SCHR 749:66	
e. withdrawal in…overcrowding	COUP 248:33	
Humour…is e. chaos	THUR 891:98	
physical and e. sides	BURG 174:99	
emotionally e. I know she is better	LEWIS 527:61	
emotions basic human e.	ROTH 728:8	
e. as palpable and as true	HOLM 423:55	
e. entirely foreign	WHIS 934:22	
e. of the everydayness	STEI 845:58	

grounds for the noble e.	RUSK 733:89	
mother of our e.	KAND 473:16	
purgation of such e.	ARIS 31:23	
raised e. both of rage and fear	BYRON 188:75	
see his e. the sport	HARDY 396:3	
used his e. even a little	SAND 741:6	
world of the e.	COLE 236:56	
emparadised E. in one another's arms	MILT 604:4	
empathize Those who choose not to e.	ROWL 730:25	
empathy politician seeking e.	SAFI 737:21	
Emperor E. Caligula's Habits	LONG 534:11	
E. Claudius	LONG 535:12	
emperor dey makes you E.	ONEI 650:59	
dreamt there was an E.	SHAK 795:87	
e. of ice-cream	STEV 649:66	
revived and was an e.	SHAK 766:11	
emperors e. and kings	MARL 573:22	
Even e. cannot do it all	BREC 158:95	
emphasis e. is on the former	KUNI 501:40	
e. on what happens next	RUSK 732:79	
erotic e. upon it	UPDI 906:31	
empire all the rule, one e.	MILT 607:72	
arch Of the ranged e. fall	SHAK 794:44	
bounds of human E.	BACON 53:46	
bounds of human E.	BACON 50:52	
Britain has lost an E.	ACHE 2:33	
British E.	GEOR 364:54	
British E. and its Commonwealth	CHUR 225:86	
brooders…build the E.	OBRI 645:62	
downfall of the British E.	CHUR 225:74	
e. is…power in trust	DRYD 305:80	
e. must extend, so let extend	MILT 607:77	
e. wilderness of freight and rails	CRANE 253:61	
German E. arose?	HERZL 416:24	
good…for the E.	REDM 709:21	
government is…an E.	ONEI 650:58	
great e. and little minds	BURKE 175:22	
heavily thickening to e.	JEFF 453:10	
hold a vaster E.	MORR 620:50	
honour of the British E.	CHUR 225:93	
How beautiful…under the E.	DURR 308:34	
If the Austrian E. did not exist	PALA 660:47	
lead Britain and her fading e.	MANC 564:51	
liquidation of the British E.	CHUR 226:96	
Lo! they dread e., Chaos!	POPE 689:48	
loungers and idlers of the E.	DOYLE 296:38	
Mother E. stands splendidly isolated	FOST 345:52	
not…Roman or an E.	VOLT 914:40	
Pageant of E.	SITW 824:12	
play the old Glasgow E.	DODD 289:88	
To found a great E.	SMITH 828:87	
whole Moghul E. is in our power	CLIVE 231:39	
Without the E.	HUGH 436:50	
empires day of E. has come	CHAM 212:60	
don't seek e.	RUMS 731:45	
E. and old women	BACON 50:41	
faiths and e. gleam	SHEL 816:57	
ridiculous e. break like biscuits	FULL 355:75	
Vaster than e.	MARV 577:91	
empirical e. system to be refuted	POPP 689:52	
greatest number of e. facts	EINS 314:89	
empiricist e.…thinks he believes	SANT 743:44	
empiricists opposed camp of the e.	MERT 589:56	
employ e. their whole industry	SMITH 827:85	
employed mind is actually e.	JOHN 462:35	
so innocently e.	JOHN 462:34	
employee In a hierarchy every e.	PETER 675:37	
employees e. of the government	TOOLE 894:60	
love e. and	TSON 900:8	
employer not a polite e.	HOOV 427:48	
employers despise e.	TSON 900:8	
don't ask e.…to like blacks	BORO 151:68	
human e. quite literally	MUMF 625:39	
other side of their e.	DONO 293:82	
employment choosing for e.	SWIFT 862:47	
e. by authors of simile	NASH 631:81	
e. for his idle time	WALT 920:92	
e. jumps out the window	AGUI 9:97	
e. of the poor in roads	MALT 563:23	
engaged in his e.	GILB 368:42	
have to seek…gainful e.	ACHE 2:25	
Hunting is not a proper e.	ADDI 7:58	
lower e. of life	JOHN 460:67	
maintain continuous full e.	KEYN 484:77	
provide for full e.	KEYN 484:82	
Wants steady e. in Hollywood	DAVIS 265:94	
employs e. the whole mind	QUEN 702:8	

emptied You e.…the dishwasher	MOORE 616:75	
emptiness Swinburne is just e. to me	QUIL 702:17	
empty are e. sounds	JOHN 460:69	
Art for art's sake is an e. phrase	SAND 741:11	
carriage…went e., and e. it returned	CH 222:17	
country…disappointingly e.	BARN 64:64	
e. as paper	SCOTT 751:3	
e. of all human substance	SAINT 738:40	
his head be e.	SWIFT 861:21	
if e. dreams so please	HERR 415:2	
philosophy is virtually e.	AYER 45:89	
rich he hath sent e. away	BIBLE 120:66	
rich he hath sent e. away	BIBLE 133:43	
empty-hearted e.-h. whose low sound	SHAK 792:85	
empty-vaulted through the e.-v. night	MILT 598:71	
emulation pale and bloodless e.	SHAK 786:27	
emulsion feeling of e.	PERE 674:15	
enamoured e. of an ass	SHAK 767:42	
enchant e. thine ear	SHAK 762:83	
enchanted holy and e.	COLE 236:37	
enchanter ghosts from an e. fleeing	SHEL 813:79	
enchanting What music is more e.	SMITH 829:17	
enchantment distance lends e.	CAMP 194:61	
e.—what a great epoch	LARI 509:70	
enchilada He's the Big E.	EHRL 313:70	
enclosure what more magnificent e.	JOHN 458:29	
encomiast e. always knows	JOHN 463:73	
encounter free and open e.	MILT 650:57	
turf-dances of human e.	ALLEN 13:75	
encourage to e. the others	VOLT 914:32	
encouragement e. of comic strips	UPDI 906:26	
never-failing sympathy and e.	WODE 952:44	
encroachment gradual e. of ideas	KEYN 484:81	
encroachments e. on their property	GALS 358:48	
encyclopedia E. behind…world	LAMB 505:91	
like burning an e.	HAWK 401:90	
end all the economists…laid e. to e.	SHAW 811:32	
always treat humanity…as an e.	KANT 473:24	
around at the e. to know	KENN 482:44	
beginning, a muddle, and an e.	LARK 510:97	
beginning is assuredly the e.	WILL 946:14	
beginning is often the e.	ELIOT 321:92	
beginning of the e.	TALL 866:17	
Better Beast and know your e.	DEVL 275:8	
Better is the e. of a thing	BIBLE 106:22	
blessed the latter e. of Job	BIBLE 99:24	
came to an e. all wars	LLOY 533:75	
come to a bad e.	BEER 73:81	
consider the e. in everything	LAFO 504:56	
Consumption is the sole e.	SMITH 828:88	
death, a necessary e.	SHAK 777:22	
death…puts an e. to old age	LABR 502:21	
dream comes to an e.	GIRO 373:28	
e. a contest quicker	SHER 817:82	
e. and object of conquest	ALEX 12:58	
e. cannot justify the means	HUXL 442:79	
e. is bitter as wormwood	BIBLE 104:56	
e. is not yet	BIBLE 118:29	
e. may justify the means	TROT 899:69	
e. more than in the beginning	JONS 468:96	
e. of all our exploring	ELIOT 321:91	
e. of ane auld sang	OGIL 648:7	
e. of a perfect day	BOND 145:17	
e. of Britain	GAIT 357:13	
e. of everything we call life	WELLS 930:40	
e. of man is an action	CARL 200:95	
e. of May	HOUS 432:62	
e. of the beginning	CHUR 226:95	
e. of the fight	KIPL 490:99	
e. of this day's business	SHAK 778:54	
e. precedes the beginning	ELIOT 319:44	
e. thereof are the ways of death	BIBLE 104:70	
e. where 'e began	KIPL 490:14	
e., where I begun	DONNE 292:40	
e. which is a piece of propaganda	JOYCE 470:34	
e. which was no part	SMITH 828:86	
E. without audience	SHAK 762:89	
fight on until the e.	HAIG 392:15	
fresh, usual words to the e.	FORD 343:92	
go on till you come to the e.	CARR 204:85	
great e. comes slowly	DU 305:69	
great enterprises seldom e.	ELIZ 322:10	
In my beginning is my e.	ELIOT 320:56	
in the e., there was no e.	WHITE 935:50	
It hath no e.	SHAK 798:79	
laid e. to e.	PARK 663:82	
let me know mine e.	BOOK 149:14	

lies frae e. to e.	BURNS 177:73	Blind among e.	MILT 607:84	E. is Eternal Delight	BLAKE 139:95
Mankind must put an e. to war	KENN 481:9	bring our to justice	BUSH 182:15	E. is liberated matter	BRYS 171:17
means used to bring about the e.	WHIS 934:18	careful in the choice of his e.	WILDE 940:66	e. of a whole generation	THOM 886:88
minutes hasten to their e.	SHAK 801:56	destroyed your e.	HUSS 440:44	e. of mighty rivers	MILL 594:63
my e. is my beginning	MARY 579:47	distinguished by your e.	HOOV 427:55	e. stored up	GERS 365:71
no happy e. to it	HEMI 409:72	e. of freedom do not argue	INGE 445:28	every e. he may put forward	CURZ 259:3
not a means, it is an e.	ORWE 655:78	e. of truth than lies	NIET 637:92	Force is…an invisible e.	LEON 522:70
Now the e., I take it	MONT 613:22	e. to Ireland	EDGE 311:43	lakes of mental e.	GREER 387:45
only e. of writing	JOHN 460:80	forget to hate your e.	ROGE 723:87	managed to exude e.	SHAR 806:74
our being's e. and aim!	POPE 687:87	giving his e. the slip	STER 848:24	minimum expenditure of e.	WILS 948:53
poem…whose e. I knew	FROST 353:18	Happiness…conquering one's e.	GENG 363:43	reason and e.…are necessary	BLAKE 139:94
purpose is beyond the e.	ELIOT 321:82	If laws are their e.	BURKE 175:28	Science is an all-pervasive e.	BARZ 67:39
recurrent e. of the unending	ELIOT 321:85	inherited 100 per cent of his e.	BUSH 182:3	tempest, a redundant e.	WORD 957:73
see what the e. is	ANON 20:26	in the presence of mine e.	BIBLE 100:45	time and e. from	MORE 618:20
should make an e.	JONS 468:92	love your e.	BIBLE 115:37	Without passion, you don't have e.	TRUMP 900:99
simplicity of their e.	FUSE 356:92	make thine e. thy footstool	BIBLE 102:17	enfant terrible free to be an e. t.	SART 744:64
something ere the e.	TENN 870:2	many e. that know not	SHAK 804:43	engaged When a Forsyte was e.	GALS 358:48
sorrow without e.	AESC 8:79	mausoleums for his e.	LINK 530:26	engaging Sex is e.	JIANG 455:56
source and e.…of art	POPE 685:18	mine e. that trouble me	BOOK 149:15	engendered e. by honesty	MURP 627:77
speaking picture, with this e.	SIDN 820:55	naked to mine e.	SHAK 805:53	engine curious e.	WEBS 927:52
the e. of the way	PAST 668:98	no perpetual e.	PALM 662:70	greatest e. of temporary opinion	HAZL 403:41
there's an e. on't	JOHN 462:18	only e. accidentally	ROUS 729:17	great, growing e. of change	TOFF 893:38
think what may be the e.	WHYM 939:26	rescues your estate from your e.	BROU 163:16	in dirt, the reasoning e. lies	ROCH 719:12
this day to e. myself	TENN 877:69	scourge of his e.	GIBB 366:94	science is a two-handed e.	MONT 613:9
This is not the e. of anything	REAG 708:7	Shaw has no e.	WILDE 942:27	small e. that causes revolutions	SHEE 811:40
thoughts to an e.	SMITH 830:41	speak with the e. in the gate	BIBLE 103:37	steam…work the e.	WATT 922:45
triumphantly until the e.!	STEV 852:53	telling it gains you e.	RUIZ 730:39	this formidable e.	COOP 246:87
understood I their e.	BIBLE 101:85	through his e.	HUGH 435:18	throw herself in front of the e.	SHAW 807:20
unimproved e.	THOR 888:30	enemy afraid of his e.	PLUT 682:75	two-handed e. at the door	MILT 599:89
Waiting for the e.	EMPS 326:11	as the e. to Canada	MOOD 615:56	engineer glorified sanitary e.	STRA 856:39
War that will E. War	WELLS 930:30	death in no such terrible e.	BACON 50:58	engineering e. of consent	BERN 86:79
Whose e. is destruction	BIBLE 128:3	defense against the e.	PICA 677:60	engineers e. and physicists	KRUT 500:30
Wisdom begins at the e.	WEBS 927:43	despised the armed E.	ALBE 11:33	look out for e.	PAGN 660:27
endanger e. my soul gratis?	SHAK 773:4	e. and your friend	TWAIN 903:83	today are your e.	LEUP 525:14
endearment Terms of E.	MCMU 557:81	e. came and sowed tares	BIBLE 117:93	engines by our resistless e.	CARL 200:80
endears all the more e.	TENN 872:36	e. faints not	CLOU 232:47	e. based on mechanical	LEUP 525:14
endeavour awake e. for defence	SHAK 768:52	e.—for friendship's sake	BLAKE 141:39	e. to play a little on our own	BURKE 176:34
Creative E. lost	WAUGH 923:68	e. half a mile away	MUIR 624:16	so noiseless when the e. stopped	HEAN 405:77
disinterested e. to learn	ARNO 35:13	E. has been here	HOBB 420:5	England amuses the people of E.	JOHN 461:90
e. to find out	WELL 929:11	e. hath done this	BIBLE 117:94	any village in E.	TROL 897:35
e., wish, desire, or long for	SPIN 840:76	e. into a friend	KING 487:36	art-form…invented in E.	BEER 74:97
listlessness, nor mad e.	WORD 960:11	e. more mighty than he seems	SHAK 775:72	a town in the South of E.	ORWE 653:14
lost faith in individual e.	CARL 200:82	e. of clear language	ORWE 654:36	Be E. what she will	CHUR 224:61
Virtue…too painful an e.	POPE 688:12	e. of clear language	ORWE 655:63	between France and E.	JERR 455:48
endeavours e. are unlucky explorers	DOUG 295:6	e. of good art	CONN 242:99	bow was made in E.	DOYLE 297:49
e., in all branches of knowledge	ARNO 35:8	e. of liberty	ROOS 725:22	Church of E.	ROYD 730:31
ended e. by your inability	GONC 377:41	e. of life	SPEN 838:24	common law of E.	HERB 413:50
griefs are e.	SHAK 789:98	e. of the good	VOLT 914:42	continent will not suffer E.	DISR 287:23
no sooner was it e.	GLAS 374:46	e. of the human race	MILL 593:54	death of Nelson was felt in E.	SOUT 835:55
Endellion St E.…ring of bells	BETJ 88:31	e. reads the list of their names	WELL 929:98	deep, deep sleep of E.	ORWE 653:25
ending bread-sauce of the happy e.	JAMES 450:48	e. to despotism	GARI 360:72	defence of E.	BALD 57:32
got your happy e.	MILE 590:88	e. to human happiness	JOHN 464:85	describing E. in a phrase	ORWE 654:34
Never e., still beginning	DRYD 303:33	friends, what about all an e.	MULR 624:34	dress and manners in E.	SHAW 806:94
second act and the e.	ANON 26:1	great e. of clear language	ORWE 654:36	dull mercantile E.	BUCH 171:25
endings E. are elusive	BART 66:16	great e. of clear language	ORWE 655:63	earthquake were to engulf E.	JERR 455:49
endless e. and indestructible	WILL 946:21	hands of the e.	ANON 27:20	east longitude from E.	MUNDY 625:44
humility is e.	ELIOT 320:61	Have no e.	YEATS 966:29	E. and America	GREN 388:59
nowhere, and is e.	LARK 510:94	I am the e. you killed	OWEN 658:35	E. and America	SHAW 811:31
end of the world an e. o. t. w. party	HAWK 401:93	If thine e. be hungry	BIBLE 105:95	E. and Saint George!	SHAK 775:76
end-run trying to e.-r. him	REAG 708:99	invasion of a common e.	KITC 494:98	E. are a good cricket team	SMITH 828:97
ends actually deteriorated e.	HUXL 442:80	kill more…than the e.	BALD 57:31	E.…comfortable time-lag	WELLS 930:38
all the e. of the earth shall see	BIBLE 109:91	kisses of an e. are deceitful	BIBLE 105:2	E. does not love coalitions	DISR 288:43
burnt-out e. of smoky days	ELIOT 317:70	Know the e.	SUN 859:90	E. full of morons	WODE 952:57
But for his own e.	BEAU 71:22	last e.…is death	BIBLE 127:58	E. has greater counties	CRIP 254:96
constantly begins and e.	HAZL 403:35	man is e. to every man	HOBB 420:2	E. has saved herself	PITT 680:14
divinity that shapes our e.	SHAK 785:69	Man is not the e. of Man	PAINE 660:33	E.…in my childhood	ORWE 653:25
e. at half past five	EWART 328:73	Mine e.'s dog	SHAK 793:29	E. invented the phrase	BAGE 54:66
e. by our beginnings know	DENH 272:63	O mine e.?	BIBLE 97:69	E.…is a fen	WORD 958:94
e. I think criminal	KEYN 484:69	put an e. in their mouths	SHAK 789:13	E. is a garden	KIPL 492:67
from the e. of the earth	KIPL 489:76	Show me an e. of literature	HAMI 394:52	E. is a garden	KIPL 492:68
pursuing of the best e.	HUTC 441:48	sincere friend or a sincere e.	HUGO 437:58	E. is a great…nation	GARI 360:72
shallow conversational e.	SASS 746:98	speed toward the e.	HALS 393:43	E. is a nation	NAPO 630:47
violent delights have violent e.	SHAK 766:92	still the e.	BIBLE 99:30	E. is not ruined	PRIE 695:95
endurance e., and courage	SCOTT 751:6	strike the e.	PANK 662:84	E. is not the jewelled isle	ORWE 654:33
e., science, temper	LONS 536:42	sweet e., France	SIDN 820:47	E. is one of the greatest	PALM 662:74
serenity essential to e.	ACHE 3:40	The eye of the e.	WILD 943:52	E. is the mother of Parliaments	BRIG 159:15
sheer courage and e.	WAVE 925:2	Thinking is the great e. of perfection	CONR 244:48	E. is the paradise of women	FLOR 341:62
endure better to e. it	JOHN 460:80	unrelenting e.	WASH 921:27	E. is unrivalled for two things	DISR 289:76
cannot e. my Lady Tongue	SHAK 774:27	with the wrong e.	BRAD 155:44	E. mourns for her dead	BINY 135:99
e. passively	WILL 944:64	worst friend and e. is but Death	BROO 162:91	E., my E.?	HENL 411:7
e., then pity, then embrace	POPE 687:82	energies all the e. of his life	PIER 677:66	E. people have good table manners	MIKES 590:86
E. what is difficult to e.	HIRO 419:72	e. and skills	KEYN 484:78	E.'s chief defence	PHIL 676:51
life…difficult to e.	LABR 502:20	religious principles and e.	BERD 83:12	E.'s foreign policy	GLAD 373:39
man will not merely e.	FAUL 331:36	energy convert weaknesses…into		E. green and pleasant land	BLAKE 141:43
enemies Against his e.	SAINT 738:34	burnable e.	BELL 78:97	E. shall bide	KIPL 492:54
all e. under his feet	BIBLE 127:58	deprive the soul of its e.	BLOOM 143:64	E.'s mountains green?	BLAKE 141:40
all the e. that I hated	BUCH 171:38	dissipation of e. begin?	KELV 479:71	E.'s not a bad country	DRAB 298:83

England

English 1090

E.'s on the anvil	KIPL 493:80	suspended in favour of E.	SHAW 810:9	His E. reminds me of tattered	MENC 587:17
E.'s province stands	BURNS 179:41	symbol for E. is the Island	ATWO 41:38	In an E. lane	BROW 168:46
E.'s the one land, I know	BROO 162:94	ten thousand…men in E.	SHAK 775:86	in plain E.	JONS 467:64
E. still stands outside Europe	KEYN 484:72	that is for ever E.	BROO 162:88	in the E. language	THUR 890:88
E. that was wont to conquer	SHAK 764:41	That knuckle-end of E.	SMITH 830:53	in the E. ranks	WILL 944:64
E., their E.	MACD 550:53	the Church of E. begins	PRIE 695:93	judgments of the E. law	SYNGE 865:23
E., the system is benign	CRISP 255:8	There'll always be an E.	PARK 664:35	kissed by the E. dead	OWEN 657:27
E. will always be the sister	HUGO 437:59	things I've done for E.	BIRO 136:22	knowledge of literate E.…desert	CHAN 213:84
E. will have her neck wrung	CHUR 225:91	This E. never did	SHAK 768:66	lead the E. against the Armada	CUOMO 258:81
E., with all thy faults I love thee	COWP 251:13	this realm, this E.	SHAK 764:40	look back into E. history	PAXM 670:46
E. would have preferred the risk	CECIL 210:28	under the great seal of E.	PENN 673:81	made our E. tongue	SPEN 838:18
every actor in E.	GIEL 368:26	undoubted right of the crown of E.	COVE 249:43	man writing broken E.	NABO 628:2
except in E., of course	WAUGH 924:82	value on entry into E.	STEN 847:2	marks our E. dead	KIPL 490:79
eyes of all E.	WILL 944:67	way to ensure summer in E.	WALP 919:72	marrow in the E. tongue	SMART 826:61
fibres of E.	FORS 344:22	What do they know of E.	POWE 693:61	mobilized the E. language	MURR 627:83
for the honour of E.	CONG 241:57	What do you think about E.?	AUDEN 42:68	more martial air than the E.	HAYD 402:23
from E. her authors	TROL 898:54	Who dies if E. live?	KIPL 493:72	most beautiful words in the E.	JAMES 451:55
gentlemen in E. now abed	SHAK 776:94	who only E. know?	KIPL 490:94	muse is…of the E. strain	DRAY 298:91
Go anywhere in E.	SHAW 810:7	You that love E.	DAY 267:36	narrating E. virgins	UPDI 906:23
God's grace in E.	LATI 511:13	youth of E. are on fire	SHAK 775:64	never consent…to E. dominion	ANON 21:46
good society in E.	SHAW 810:6	**English** Africa and the E. tongue	WALC 916:9	No real E. gentleman	BAGE 54:64
government that E. can have	TROL 898:40	among the E. Poets	KEATS 476:82	no similar designation for the E.	PAXM 670:45
greatest mere village in E.	DEFOE 269:77	An E. home	TENN 870:96	Of the bold E.	JONS 467:51
Greece, Italy, and E. did adorn	DRYD 303:19	as E.…as a beefsteak	HAWT 402:18	old E. way	MACM 556:74
healthiest situation in E.	KING 488:50	beautifully the E. fight!	NAPO 630:42	only come from the E.	GORO 379:25
heard that E. Were busied	SHAK 775:71	Be friends, you E. fools	SHAK 775:83	O the E. Ascendancy	MACD 550:39
Heart of E.	DRAY 298:97	betwixt E. and Irish	STRA 857:44	pause to consider the E.	NASH 631:67
high road…to E.	JOHN 461:92	bought and sold for E. gold	BURNS 180:42	prefer his E. sloppy	SAYE 746:10
history of E.	MACA 545:42	Canada…E. government	COLO 238:80	principle of the E. law	DICK 281:72
history of E.	MACA 546:57	chased the E. out of France	LOUI 537:64	really nice E. people	SHAW 810:7
how can I help E.?	BROW 167:22	creating in every E. breast	MANC 564:51	reason the E. dislike them	MORL 619:40
hunt the Catholics from E.	LESL 523:88	cricket—it's so very E.	BERN 86:85	remains of the E. language	COUP 248:31
I am in E., everywhere	BROW 165:68	dominant facts in E. life	ORWE 654:35	rolling E. drunkard	CHES 221:93
in E. a particular bashfulness	ADDI 7:39	E. and in writing of oure tonge	CHAU 216:68	Roman-Saxon-Danish-Norman E.	DEFOE 269:71
In E., even the poorest	HEGEL 406:7	E. and not E.	HYDE 443:18	saved many an E. spinster	MITF 610:55
in E. is generally given	JOHN 460:77	E. are all right	WALE 917:28	Scots…hear the E. abused	PIUS 680:19
In E., justice is open to all	MATH 581:85	E. are best!	FLAN 338:11	scour these E. hence?	SHAK 798:72
in E. nobody goes to the theatre	AGATE 9:90	E. are born masters	VIDAL 912:99	seven feet of E. ground	HARO 398:40
In E., pop art	MACI 553:1	E. are funny and peculiar	CELI 211:41	she quite forgot…good E.	CARR 203:63
in E. seven halfpenny loaves	SHAK 759:95	E. are used to suffrage	CARL 201:28	somethin' he did against the E.	ANON 23:99
inhabitant of the North of E.	FORD 342:89	E. artists are…ruined	RUSK 733:13	speak E. and profanity	HOWE 433:90
In rural E., people live wrapped tight	CARR 202:55	E. children	GREER 387:43	success happens to an E. writer	AMIS 16:48
Into E., to drive a prey	BALL 58:51	E.…code of immorality	BRAD 154:22	sweet E. tongue	FLEC 340:30
Ireland gives E. her soldiers	MERE 588:39	E. conquered us	NAPO 630:43	talent of our E. nation	DRYD 302:96
I shall be in E.	PARK 663:91	E. counties like hunting-tunes	BENET 79:24	teach the E. how to talk	WILDE 942:19
kings of E.	GILB 368:39	E. country gentleman	WILDE 941:84	the E. and the bears	THOM 884:47
kynge borne of all E.	MALO 562:7	E. do add here and there	BEAU 70:10	the E. will penetrate	MACA 544:16
lie down…and think of E.	HILL 418:64	E. don't raise their voices	HELL 408:48	their E. God is not so dominant	CARR 202:52
live half our lives in E.	HYDE 443:19	E. have no respect	SHAW 780:61	they are Irish and he is pure E.	OBRI 645:61
loans of E. to foreign nations	BAGE 55:78	E. history is all about men	BRAD 154:26	thirst, which makes…the E. mad	DANTE 262:40
Lords and Commons of E.	MILT 601:18	E. in suzerainty over Scotland	GIBB 366:5	those pretty E. watercolourists	PISS 679:97
man who comes to E.	MANS 568:14	E. knew who they were	PAXM 670:44	trick of our E. nation	SHAK 772:74
Men of E.	SHEL 813:89	E. language	ROOS 725:23	under an E. heaven	BROO 162:89
my grave be E.	BROW 165:67	E. language readers	GISC 373:29	unlike being E.	FIED 334:10
My politics…is E.	DISR 287:32	E. life…is rather bland	PERE 674:21	usual sloppy E.	JOYCE 470:34
national sport of E.	TREE 896:1	E. love of compromise	CARD 198:41	wall up with our E. dead	SHAK 775:74
naturalist in E.	DARW 263:51	E.…maintain our grand talent	CARL 201:32	We be all good E. men	TENN 878:96
never merry world in E.	SHAK 759:94	E. manners	JARR 452:86	well of E. undefiled	SPEN 839:52
no amusements in E.	SMITH 831:62	E. may not always be the best writers	CHAN 213:79	when you can't think of the E.	CARR 204:94
no nation…less able to do harm to E.	BRIG 159:16	E. may not like music	BEEC 73:62	White as an angel is the E. child	BLAKE 139:87
no subject of E.	PITT 679:7	E. peer of the right sort	WODE 951:31	wish…so deeply rooted in the E.	BUTL 185:90
O E.! model to thy…greatness	SHAK 775:65	E. plays	GOET 375:58	with a strong E. accent	SAKI 739:52
Oh, to be in E.	BROW 167:20	E. poetry begins	FENT 332:62	**Englishman** as I am an E.	PITT 679:9
old E.'s roast beef	FIEL 335:19	E. poetry is not yet fit	OWEN 657:28	as thorough an E.	KING 488:49
old E.'s winding sheet	BLAKE 141:28	E. poets who grew up	ROET 722:61	being an E.	STAN 842:11
Old E. to adorn	KIPL 492:53	E. policy is to float lazily	CECIL 210:30	E.…afraid to feel	FORS 345:41
once even in E.	MORE 618:12	E. proletariat…more bourgeois	ENGE 326:12	E. among the under-dogs	WAUGH 924:82
organ-voice of E.	TENN 877:63	E. public school	WAUGH 923:67	E. as a guarantee	SHAW 809:66
Our E. is a garden	KIPL 492:67	E. seem to bid adieu	SMITH 830:46	E. does not joke	VERNE 911:62
Our E. is a garden	KIPL 492:68	E. ship, they say	LOND 534:10	E. does not travel to see Englishmen	STER 849:51
Parliament of E.	BAIL 55:89	E. should leave Scotland	HEFF 406:5	E.…flattered, is a lamb	CHAP 214:22
poison E. at her roots	BOTT 152:82	E. speaking audiences	WHAR 934:11	E. in the wrong	SHAW 807:97
poorest he that is in E.	RAIN 705:37	E. subject's sole prerogative	DRYD 302:6	E. is about to talk French	WODE 952:47
Prime Minister of E.	BUTL 184:59	E. talk is a quadrille	JAMES 450:49	E. is an island	NOVA 642:67
pulse-less lot that make up E.	LAWR 512:40	E. text is chaste	GIBB 366:3	E. is convinced of one thing	NASH 631:67
remain in union with E.	SCOTT 754:76	E. think cricket is a game	MIKES 590:87	E. never enjoys himself	HERB 413:52
respectable as the Church of E.	STEV 851:24	E. unofficial rose	BROO 162:92	E., sets foot on it	STEF 844:54
seeing a worse E.	JOHN 463:58	E. version of the touching melody	CARL 199:67	E.'s heaven-born privilege	ARNO 36:29
shower of curates…upon the north of E.	BRON 161:66	E. want to be there when she falls	CAMP 194:49	E.'s justification in India	CURZ 260:5
souls' prison we call E.	SHAW 810:8	E. winter	BYRON 190:23	E.'s never so natural	JAMES 450:39
Speak for E., Arthur!	AMERY 15:26	E. without an accent	BENC 78:5	E.…there only a week	FRAS 349:33
speech of E. has no name	BRYA 170:3	E.…polite by telling lies	BRAD 154:27	E. thinks he is moral	SHAW 807:25
stately homes of E.	COWA 249:55	European football without the E.	CHAR 216:47	E. was niver improved	DUNNE 307:20
stately homes of E.	HEMA 409:57	expression in E.	ARNO 35:14	genial E.	TENN 872:35
stately homos of E.	CRISP 255:6	find one E. book	ARNO 35:9	Give but an E. his whore	OTWAY 656:7
strength and the greatness of E.	CURZ 259:3	foreigners speak E.	CRISP 254:2	impossible for an E.	SHAW 810:93
strong arm of E.	PALM 662:72	God's patience and the King's E.	SHAK 773:1	last great E. is low	TENN 875:6

man, nay, even more, an E.	MORI 619:36	entangle e. those shall feed	WEBS 926:41	E. itself, and Vanity	MAND 565:65
No E. is ever fairly beaten	SHAW 810:15	entente e. cordiale	LOUIS 537:73	e. no man's happiness	SHAK 779:89
not one an E.	WALP 919:81	enter e. most intimately into	HUME 438:96	e. of brilliant men	BEER 73:81
one E. could beat three Frenchmen	ADDI 7:35	Let no-one e.	ANON 28:52	e. of great Caesar	SHAK 778:57
part of an E.'s constitution	AUST 46:69	save that they e.	WILL 946:8	e. of the devil	BIBLE 112:73
part of every E.'s education	HUGH 436:46	enterprise e. of martial kind	GILB 370:71	e. oft his shadow be	JONS 468:86
powerful image to your average E.	SMITH 828:1	for or against their e.	DICK 280:27	e. of those of others	RYLE 736:61
remains an E.!	GILB 368:35	hazard in the glorious e.	MILT 601:37	e. of thy happy lot	KEATS 478:41
Remember that you are an E.	RHOD 712:71	hold no brief for private e.	BURT 181:72	e. prevails	WALL 918:59
rights of an E.	JUNI 471:49	If E. is afoot	KEYN 484:74	From e., hatred, and malice	BOOK 146:47
takes off his hat to God's E.	SHAW 809:64	leave it to private e.	KEYN 484:80	he e. could obtain	SURR 860:99
the Irishman turned E.	OBRI 645:62	most important stage of any e.	PLATO 682:61	I shall never attain: E.	PARK 664:29
vain, ill-natured thing, an E.	DEFOE 269:70	nurse of…heroic e.	BURKE 176:41	mixture of e., vindictiveness	DISR 288:63
what an E. believes	SHAW 810:16	private e.	GALB 357:19	prisoners of e.	ILLI 445:23
Englishmen absurd nature of E.	PEPYS 673:92	steady stream of e.	KEYN 484:79	Too low for e.	COWL 250:77
damned mischievous E.	SCOTT 754:79	system of soft e.	ARNO 36:47	who is able to stand before e.?	BIBLE 105:1
Englishman does not travel to see E.	STER 849:51	there's more e.	YEATS 966:16	**enwrought** e. with golden	YEATS 966:12
E. act better than Frenchmen	BENN 81:63	**enterprises** e. that require	THOR 888:34	**ephemeral** not interested in the e.	WILD 943:51
E. are born gloaters	OBRI 645:62	great e. seldom end	ELIZ 322:10	story is e. and doomed	FAUL 331:35
E.…nervously excitable race	DAVI 264:72	**entertain** better to e. an idea	JARR 452:88	**Ephratah** Bethlehem, E.	BIBLE 111:55
E. never will be slaves	SHAW 807:24	**entertaining** more e. than…boats	STEV 851:23	**epic** classical era was e.	HUGO 436:52
find E. doing it	SHAW 807:97	we're not e.?	MOUR 623:95	the e. of Dunkirk	PRIE 695:86
first to his E.?	MILT 601:19	**entertainment** at an E. for Friends	SWIFT 862:59	thundrous E. lilted out	TENN 872:32
love of E.	THOM 885:55	craving e.; volatile	FERB 332:67	**epicure** the e. would say	SMITH 831:60
Mad dogs and E.	COWA 249:50	exotic and irrational e.	JOHN 464:75	**epidemic** Aids e.	WHITE 934:29
our very name as E.	PITT 680:11	proffered E.	TROL 897:31	living this e. every minute	KRAM 499:3
When two E. meet	JOHN 460:82	regard literature as e.	COND 240:14	**epidemics** Fashions…induced e.	SHAW 809:78
Englishwoman E. is so refined	SMITH 830:34	That's E.	DIETZ 286:89	**epididymis** psyches…tied to their e.	STEP 847:13
E.'s clothes	SITW 824:12	under the head of E.	BEAV 71:32	**epigram** Impelled to try an e.	PARK 663:99
Englishwomen better than E.	BENN 81:63	we've dominated e.	JOHN 457:7	purrs like an e.	MARQ 575:58
engraving E. then, is, in brief	RUSK 733:11	what lenten e.	SHAK 782:91	What is an E.	COLE 235:33
engulf chasm that threatens to e. him	BANN 62:33	**enthrall** Except You e. me	DONNE 292:55	**epigrams** Aphorisms and e.	DUDEK 305:73
enigma e. of the fever chart	ELIOT 320:64	Till they e. themselves	MILT 603:80	despotism tempered by e.	CARL 201:11
mystery inside an e.	CHUR 225:82	**enthralled** e. as I am	SHAK 800:26	**epigraph** for want of an e.	SIDN 820:59
enjoy did e. the music	JOHN 459:33	free, but to thyself e.	MILT 605:23	**epilepsy** will cure e.	THEO 882:80
do not e.	JULI 471:42	**enthroned** E. i'th' market-place	SHAK 794:56	**epilogue** good play needs no e.	SHAK 780:27
e. their triumph	HAMM 394:56	**enthusiasm** as e. would permit	GOSSE 379:69	**episcopalian** I am a E. just now	FLEM 340:48
here e. the shade	JONS 468:86	E. is nothing	MILL 594:76	**episode** e. in the life of a man	STAEL 841:92
highly taught and yet not to e.	ELIOT 316:54	e. turns to bitterness	ZATO 969:3	**epitaph** are no e. of that oak	DONNE 292:63
impossible to e. idling	JERO 454:35	fired with e.	LOMB 534:7	e. drear	KIPL 490:99
learnt to e. them	MORT 621:71	For sportswriters…it's the e.	FRAY 349:35	e. on the Kennedy administration	WHITE 936:59
liberty, that we'll e.	JONS 467:70	never to let your e. be soured	CURZ 260:5	e. to be my story	FROST 353:16
principal business of life is to e.	BUTL 185:96	Nothing great…without e.	EMER 324:64	Let no man write my e.	EMMET 325:6
enjoyed e. talking to her	SITW 824:14	Once we have made e. ridiculous	STAEL 841:95	that may be his e.	STEV 853:79
enjoying world…worth e.	DRYD 303:33	play with manic e.	LYTT 543:95	**epitaphs** nice derangement of e.	SHER 813:76
enjoyment done with e.	RUSK 732:81	poison of e. and superstition	SMITH 828:90	**epithalamic** e. conjunction	ANDR 18:77
essence of Toryism is e.	BAGE 54:63	rage and your e. for the election	WHIT 937:84	**epitome** all mankind's e.	DRYD 302:83
innocent e.	GILB 368:42	Whatever…my e. or impatience	SHIP 818:14	between an e. and a parody	ISAA 447:64
more ascetic reason than mere e.	STARK 843:22	**entire** e. and whole and perfect	SPRI 841:87	golf course is the e.	GIRA 372:24
receives as complete e.	HUME 438:3	entirety man in his e.	BECK 72:38	**epoch** civilization of one e.	CONN 243:11
retrospective e. of successful effort	SHIP 818:13	**entities** What are the fundamental e.	KUHN 500:37	e. of folly and shame	ZOLA 970:15
enjoys Englishman never e. himself	HERB 413:52	**entitlement** E. spending	ARMEY 32:39	e. unrivalled in world history	LARI 509:70
enlarge e., diminish, interline	SWIFT 862:62	**entity** not an animate e.	OBRI 645:65	great e. in our lives	MOOD 615:52
E. my life	JOHN 459:47	**entomologists** ready labelled as e.	STARK 843:22	most memorable e.	ADAMS 5:1
enlargement e. of the language	JOHN 460:70	**entrails** yearn to crush out their e.!	BRON 162:81	**equal** all are e., all are free	OBAMA 644:32
enlightenment herald of e.	BOOK 150:45	**entrance** e. to a quarrel	SHAK 781:50	all men are created e.	JEFF 453:19
intellectual e.	CURZ 260:5	From my first e. in	HERB 413:65	as men become more e.	TOCQ 892:31
literature…as transcendent e.	COND 240:14	grace the e. to Paradise	MICH 590:69	but which is e. to anything	LEAC 515:10
motto of e.	KANT 473:21	men have one e. into life	BIBLE 112:78	e. before a fish	HOOV 427:47
promises freedom or e.	SNYD 833:94	**entrances** e. of this world	BIBLE 112:69	e. dominion is given to woman	STAN 842:16
enmities e. between nations	KENN 481:18	exits and their e.	SHAK 779:80	e. rights of men and women	UNIT 905:9
enmity e. with joy	WORD 960:11	**entrepreneur** brain of a Yankee e.	ONET 651:82	e. to all things	GOLD 377:17
e. between thy seed	BIBLE 91:96	e. is no longer the bold	ROBI 718:92	E., unclassed, tribeless	SHEL 814:18
e. o'th' air	SHAK 792:2	**entrepreneurs** e. who have the guts	RODG 721:50	except that of being e. to us	TRIL 897:15
enormity e. of the task	ACHE 3:38	**entrepreneurship** E. can be learned	DRUC 299:6	in the dust be e. made	SHIR 819:20
enormous Like an e. yes	LARK 509:76	**entry** value on e. into England	STEN 847:2	maintenance of an e. number	SMITH 827:83
The E. Room was the greatest book	STEIN 845:62	**envelope** semi-transparent e.	WOOLF 955:10	men and women are created e.	STAN 842:12
enough E., if something from our hands	WORD 961:43	**envenomed** delusive and e. pleasure	BRON 161:72	more e. than others	ORWE 654:49
e., now, O Lord	BIBLE 97:66	**envies** e., all of them sad	AUDEN 43:3	never be completely e.	CUNN 259:76
first cries 'Hold, e.!'	SHAK 798:78	**envious** e. at the foolish	BIBLE 101:84	reason, is naturally e. in all men	DESC 274:93
if we only get e. of them	JAMES 451:64	silence e. tongues	SHAK 805:54	relatively e.	TOOLE 894:59
not e. jails	HUMP 439:9	**environment** e. and its teaching	LAWR 514:85	sees with e. eye, as God	POPE 686:73
poverty is never having e.	WYLIE 964:12	forced…through e. and pressures	FAUL 331:38	separate but e.	WARR 921:12
rainbow is e.	SHAN 805:59	humdrum issues like the e.	THAT 881:59	ta'en with e. thanks	SHAK 783:21
seen e. of one war	JEFF 454:24	luxury of a peacetime e.	TRUM 900:87	That all men are e.	HUXL 441:61
Two cheers are quite e.	FORS 345:42	moral e.	HAVEL 401:85	turn your thoughts to becoming his e.	CONF 240:18
enquire E., define, distinguish	ROCH 719:8	possible in his e.	RUSS 734:26	With e. mind	DRYD 304:54
enquiries e. about the UK climate	SAMU 741:3	product of my e.	NICH 636:78	You are everyone's e.	BIDEN 133:54
enrich how to e. a new nation	STIG 854:97	so well adjusted to his e.	JARR 452:85	**equality** apostles of e.	ARNO 36:28
ense calamus saevior e. patet	BURT 181:78	We accept…great inequality of e.	CARN 202:48	democracy is love of e.	MONT 614:41
enshrined e. in 10,000 indexes	ALLEN 13:76	**environmentalists** best thing you can		E. of condition is incompatible	COOP 246:85
ensigns ships and their e.	ROBE 717:71	do with e.	OLEA 649:32	E. of opportunity	KENN 481:18
enslave No woman shall ever e. me	SHAW 807:20	**envy** Death…extinguisheth e.	BACON 50:60	E. would be a heaven	TROL 898:49
enslaved either free or e.	GRIL 388:69	E. and calumny and hate and pain	SHEL 815:40	first e. is equity	HUGO 437:85
e. as farm stock	SHAW 809:87	E. and wrath shorten the life	BIBLE 113:3	freedom and e.	ROUS 729:12
ensnared beauty hath e. thee	SHAK 762:95	E. bark at thee	SPEN 837:14	general state of e.	JOHN 463:50
ensure e. summer in England	WALP 919:72	e.…is force t'admire!	DANI 262:32	Liberty, E., Adultery	BELL 77:84

equalize

Liberty, E., Fraternity!	LAMA 504:74	
majestic e. of laws	FRAN 347:89	
make some headway towards e.	FALU 329:12	
near e. is no e.	BLOOM 143:69	
never be complete e.	ANTH 29:74	
really great in favour of e.	SHAW 810:19	
equalize attempt to level...never e.	BURKE 176:37	
e. before the others have scored	BLAN 141:47	
equalized expectation is e.	ILLI 445:22	
equally comes e. to us all	DONNE 292:63	
henceforth be bestowed e.	SHAK 778:58	
not e. happy	JOHN 461:12	
equals 2 times 2 e. 13	LICH 528:86	
e., free from tyranny?	LANY 508:56	
far from being our e.	NAPO 630:43	
First among E.	ARCH 30:5	
little friendship...between e.	BACON 53:34	
Republic of e.	BABE 48:4	
equation e. that is the human heart	OROU 652:97	
e. will come out at last	MACN 558:3	
Equator disrespectfully of the E.!	SMITH 830:54	
equestrian e. classes	SHAW 810:6	
equilibrium functions... in e.	SPEN 836:87	
human psychic e.	MAMET 564:37	
point of e. will be known	JEVO 455:52	
equinoctial beams under the e.	BURT 181:85	
equipment e. by the truckload	WELL 929:95	
shabby e. always deteriorating	ELIOT 320:66	
survive with that e.	DAVIS 265:97	
equity first equality is e.	HUGO 437:85	
of all e. and justice	KNOX 495:14	
principles of e. and justice	PEEL 672:67	
equivalent musical e. of the towers	BEEC 73:66	
United Nations is not... internal e.	EDEN 311:31	
equivalents e. are given	WORD 962:50	
era dated a new e.	THOR 888:23	
ending of an historic e.	NEHRU 633:9	
new e. is upon us	MACA 544:5	
primitive e. was lyrical	HUGO 436:52	
eras buried under the shale of e.	RAND 706:58	
Erebus pit of lowest E.	WORD 961:35	
erect e., elegant, dogmatic	REST 711:62	
e....his own tomb	SHAK 774:57	
forms of virtue are e.	FUSE 356:94	
free man cannot long stand e.	WRIS 963:76	
Unless...he can E. himself	DANI 262:33	
erections E., Ejaculations	BUKO 173:55	
Erin when for E. dear we fall	SULL 859:80	
Ernest only really safe name is E.	WILDE 941:95	
erotic E. practices...diversified	BELL 78:95	
most e. part of the body	BART 66:25	
not more e. emphasis	UPDI 906:31	
err fools shall not e. therein	BIBLE 108:77	
Kings and Governments may e.	HERB 412:46	
Man will e.	GOET 375:62	
mortal, and may e.	SHIR 819:19	
most may e.	DRYD 302:86	
reas'ning but to e.	POPE 687:80	
they do not e.	SCOTT 752:15	
To e. is human	ANON 26:80	
To e. is human	POPE 685:25	
errancy die in e.	ABU 1:12	
errand in thy joyous e.	FITZ 337:72	
send the child a e.	DICK 279:19	
slightest e. now to the Antipodes	SHAK 774:28	
erred have e. exceedingly	BIBLE 96:41	
while I e.	GOET 375:72	
error commonest e. in politics	CECIL 210:31	
discharge from sin and e.	ELIOT 321:90	
E. is all around it	NICO 637:83	
E....never approached	METT 589:61	
e. of his way	BIBLE 130:63	
e.'s fenny bogs	ROCH 719:11	
e. to imagine the loudest	BURKE 175:8	
full of natural e.	PASC 667:70	
grave e. to believe	PISS 679:99	
judge of truth, in endless e.	POPE 687:81	
myopia makes all e. mortal	LOWE 540:33	
not a disease but an e. of judgement	DICK 277:6	
not wholly free from e.	VINER 913:10	
obstinacy, and of e.	POPP 689:63	
only one inborn e.	SCHO 749:58	
perpetuate an e. for ever	SCHO 748:55	
persistent leaning towards e.	CONR 244:40	
religion...so afraid of e.	SULL 859:75	
response to e. that counts	GIOV 372:16	
Where there is e.	THAT 881:54	
errors common e. of our life	SIDN 820:57	
containing the grossest e.	TOLS 894:53	
e. are volitional	JOYCE 470:27	
E., like straws	DRYD 301:46	
E. look so very ugly	ELIOT 315:16	
e. of the rich	CHES 220:60	
knowledge...mixed with our e.	POPP 689:62	
less e. of fact	GREE 386:20	
multitude of e.	DESC 275:98	
point out other people's e.	ELIOT 316:50	
reasoned e.	HUXL 443:9	
some female e.	POPE 685:33	
tares of spiritual e.	HOBB 420:5	
erudition e. and his historic impact	NISB 639:28	
eruptions Bimbo e.	WRIG 962:64	
Esaias spoken of by the prophet E.	BIBLE 114:18	
Esau E. despised his birthright	BIBLE 92:29	
E....is a hairy man	BIBLE 92:30	
E. sells his birthright	BIBLE 92:27	
E. was a cunning hunter	BIBLE 92:28	
escalating both sides e.	KENN 482:43	
escalator e. from the Social	HUXL 441:72	
Escalus thing to be tempted, E.	SHAK 787:51	
escape Author of the Whole e.	POPE 689:46	
from which he made his e.	MILL 594:80	
never quite e.	SMITH 828:98	
No man should e.	OPPE 652:87	
No one can e.	PLATO 681:51	
nothing to e. from	ELIOT 321:97	
Poetry...an e. from emotion	ELIOT 317:89	
poor...can hardly ever e.	FORS 344:28	
the word 'e.'	MUNRO 626:55	
women cannot e. it	GIBB 367:9	
writing as an e. from	WILL 945:95	
escapist e. fiction	GALB 357:26	
escarpments screes on her e.	HEAN 404:71	
eschew be the little turf-dances	ALLEN 13:75	
escort burning building without an e.	VAN 908:24	
Eskimo Hottentot and every E.	LEHR 520:27	
Esmé For E.	SALI 740:83	
esoteric e. matters	GOWE 380:81	
especial Sweet e. rural scene	HOPK 428:79	
espionage no place where e. is not	SUN 859:94	
espoused fairest, my e.	MILT 604:14	
essay e. on 'self-indulgence'	WAUGH 923:56	
good e....must draw its curtain	WOOLF 955:19	
Of seeming arms...a short e.	DRYD 304:47	
essays greatest of Man's e.	TOYN 895:75	
not much good at e.	BETJ 88:32	
essence effluence of bright e. increate	MILT 603:73	
e. and quintessence	LOWE 539:96	
e. of a book	NABO 628:15	
e. of an argument	SCHL 747:34	
e. of Christianity	WHIT 936:71	
e. of freedom	ASTE 39:5	
e. of inhumanity	SHAW 807:98	
e. of music is revelation	HEINE 407:16	
e. of real human love	ELIOT 315:27	
e. of technology	HEID 406:10	
e. of Toryism	BAGE 54:63	
e. of war is violence	MACA 545:38	
existence comes before e.	SART 744:71	
existence precedes e.?	SART 744:72	
glassy e., like an angry ape	SHAK 787:58	
poet gives us his e.	WOOLF 956:79	
poetry is the e.	STEV 850:93	
uncompounded is their e.	MILT 602:46	
very e. of phenomena	PAST 668:2	
with our mixed e.	BYRON 189:84	
essential e. oneness of mankind	STEI 845:58	
Secrecy is the first e.	RICH 714:20	
that something is e.	RENO 711:54	
what is e. is invisible	SAINT 738:37	
essentiality eternal and infinite e.	SPIN 841:83	
essentials e. of a...Prime Minister	WILS 948:72	
Essex fog on the E. marshes	DICK 281:55	
In E. seek them all	CRIP 254:96	
establishment found a handsome e.	DICK 282:89	
the American e.	TIME 892:20	
estate comfortable e. of widowhood	GAY 362:18	
e. of the realm	MACA 545:31	
Fallen from his high e.	DRYD 303:31	
fourth e. in the politics	HAZL 403:45	
grown to man's e.	STEV 853:66	
in low e. began	TENN 874:83	
ordered their e.	ALEX 13:62	
out of my e. the sum of £50,000	CHES 219:46	
relieving the human e.	DEWEY 276:19	
rescues your e. from your enemies	BROU 163:16	
they had his e.	DRYD 302:84	
estates live upon their own e.	EDGE 311:42	
O, that e., degrees, and offices	SHAK 769:95	
residents from raw e.	LARK 509:84	
esteem come to e. the universe	FONT 342:74	
coward in thine own e.	SHAK 796:21	
e. not of that obedience	MILT 600:15	
expressions of e. for Mr Boss	BAND 61:10	
far above him...my e.	DRYD 301:57	
higher e. among the gods	PLATO 681:47	
lessened my e. of a king	PEPYS 673:89	
object of love and e.	LAMB 505:94	
esteemed more e. in Russia	SNOW 832:81	
not with me e.	SHAK 770:15	
shall be lightly e.	BIBLE 96:24	
estimate know'st thy e.	SHAK 802:67	
estimation highest e. of learning	SIDN 820:52	
estranged e. from myself	HUGO 437:60	
esurientes E. implevit bonis	BIBLE 133:12	
eternal blasted to e. damnation!	SHAW 810:14	
Death and I Am found e.	MILT 606:63	
e. incognito	BARN 64:61	
e., inexorable lapse	STOWE 856:32	
e. monotony of passion	FLAU 339:21	
e. not ourselves	ARNO 36:36	
E. Passion!	ARNO 34:85	
e. reciprocity of tears	OWEN 658:40	
e. want of pence	TENN 872:28	
Hope springs e.	POPE 687:74	
idea alone is e.	FLAU 339:14	
no e. allies	PALM 662:70	
not for spreading e. truths	BLISS 142:57	
not so much e. vigilance	ORWE 653:16	
portion of the E.	SHEL 815:38	
Primary word addresses the e. Thou	BUBER 171:21	
prompts th' e. sigh	POPE 687:87	
society as something e.	ORWE 653:28	
summer is e.	GUY 390:7	
to be boy e.	SHAK 799:7	
trust was with the e.	MILT 602:57	
variations on the e. struggle	LIN 529:2	
eternities starlit with e. unknown	SASS 746:1	
eternity are from e.	HOUS 432:65	
As doth e.	KEATS 478:39	
at last e. changes him	MALL 562:1	
certain species of e.	SPIN 840:74	
circular e. may seem atrocious	BIOY 135:5	
dance round to all E.	FLET 340:50	
day joins the past e.	BYRON 188:60	
Deserts of vast e.	MARV 577:91	
Desire paces E.	DUNC 307:10	
e. in an hour	BLAKE 141:24	
E. is in love	BLAKE 140:98	
'E.' is there	DICK 284:52	
e....of life	ALLEN 13:78	
e. of nothing	RUSK 733:18	
E. of pleasures	FORD 343:1	
e. of print	WOOLF 955:20	
e. of thought	WORD 957:69	
E. shut in a span	CRAS 253:78	
E.! thou pleasing, dreadful thought!	ADDI 7:52	
E. was in our lips	SHAK 794:49	
E. was in that moment	CONG 240:28	
e. without a solecism	BROW 165:54	
feel a trace of e.	RILKE 715:38	
From Here to E.	JONES 465:18	
From here to e.	KIPL 489:57	
from the soul's e.	ROSS 726:55	
heirs of all e.	SHAK 763:99	
image of e.	BYRON 188:73	
in view of God and e.	CAVE 210:19	
is the e. that awaits you	THOM 886:77	
Lives in E.'s sunrise	BLAKE 140:6	
radiance of e.	CLAR 228:69	
saw E. the other night	VAUG 909:97	
shadows of e.	VAUG 909:34	
Silence is deep as E.	CARL 201:21	
silence of e.	STEV 852:76	
sing of Time or E.	TENN 877:63	
speculations of e. or infinitude	ADDI 7:36	
teacher affects e.	ADAMS 5:91	
Through all E. to Thee	ADDI 7:38	
thyself to all e.	ROSS 726:60	
To know e.?	ROET 722:62	
wander through e.	MILT 602:59	

everything

white radiance of E.	SHEL 815:43	part of the community of E.	CECIL 210:33	mists of e. lie	BETJ 88:27
Why didn't E. have this…age	KRAUS 499:6	part of the community of E.	SALI 740:90	morning wore to e.	TENN 873:60
ethereal blue e. sky	ADDI 7:40	Prince of E., should dare to invade	ELIZ 322:4	quiet-coloured end of e.	BROW 167:27
e. mountain	BENU 83:9	races of E. are melting	ZANG 969:1	rear cattle in the e.	MARX 579:29
etherized patient e. upon a table	ELIOT 316:60	regard for the liberties of E.	BRIG 159:14	shadow at e. rising to meet you	ELIOT 318:96
ethic e. is not an e.	KOHL 496:35	salvage E.'s culture	ADEN 8:62	Soup of the e.	CARR 204:82
ethical certain e. suspension	DIDI 286:84	save E. by her example	PITT 680:14	stronger scent towards e.	STAEL 842:97
e. reality of the individual	KIER 485:2	slain this year in E.	WALP 919:81	there morning and e.	RUSK 734:19
unethical and e. advertising	STEF 844:53	spectre is haunting E.	MARX 579:33	unique e.	WIMP 949:88
ethics can not conflict with e.	POIN 683:96	splendidly isolated in E.	FOST 345:52	welcome peaceful e. in	COWP 251:19
drew a system of e.	MACA 545:34	territories of E.	GOER 374:57	window in the autumn e.	MORG 619:31
E. are no more a part	STEV 850:91	that's old E.	RUMS 731:42	winter e. settles down	ELIOT 317:70
e., as a branch of knowledge	AYER 48:7	This going into E.	THOM 886:79	**evenings** known the e.	ELIOT 316:63
not aesthetics but e.	ROGE 722:68	Through E. to the Aetolian shore	ARNO 35:5	**event** Does arbitrate the e.	MILT 599:73
Ethiope rich jewel in an E.'s ear	SHAK 765:74	tomorrow in E.	GORD 378:57	enviable, boast-worthy, masculine e.	STEI 846:93
Ethiopian Can the E. change	BIBLE 110:19	torch of war in E.	HITL 420:92	e. at an obvious place	LIPP 531:39
ethnics I'm down with the e.	JOHN 457:95	travellers in E.	MELV 585:71	genuine imaginative e.	ROTH 728:90
Etna sight of E. at sunset	WAUGH 924:80	trip to E. would be superfluous	SAAR 736:1	greatest e.…that ever happened	FOX 346:68
Eton E. man…turns up his nose	ANON 23:89	valuation of E.	JAMES 450:34	horror…was the size of each e.	MAIL 560:56
feelings on leaving E.	CONN 242:5	**European** Britain…E. state	GAIT 357:13	importance of an historical e.	WHIT 937:82
holidays from E.	SITW 824:19	Britain will not be…in a E. war	DAILY 260:4	news is to signalize an e.	LIPP 531:41
on the playing-fields of E.	ORWE 654:35	centers of E. civilization	TOLS 894:54	no e. so commonplace	BUEC 172:42
playing fields of E.	WELL 929:13	colonisation by any E. powers	ADAMS 5:5	not a picture but an e.	ROSE 725:26
eucalypt tattered host of e.	ADAMS 4:73	E. football without the English	CHAR 216:47	outstanding e. was the doing	CARR 202:52
Euclid E. alone Has looked	MILL 592:26	E. harmonies	GILL 370:87	to celebrate the e.	JERR 455:49
fifth proposition of E.	DOYLE 296:43	E. philosophical tradition	WHIT 936:69	vertical in the tumultuous e.	CESA 211:51
liquid E.s in foolscaps of air	AVIS 47:1	E. societies…moneyed aristocracy	BLEST 142:52	**eventful** the past was not more e.	ORWE 654:31
eunuch between a e. and a snigger	FIRB 336:55	first time a E.…sets foot	STEF 844:54	**eventide** fast falls the e.	LYTE 543:94
kind of moral e.	SHEL 813:88	greater humanity than the E.	MCCA 547:87	**events** All strange and terrible e.	SHAK 795:77
prerogative of the e.	STOP 855:14	happy…is not a characteristic of a E.	CHAN 214:4	e., mostly unimportant	BIER 134:80
strain, Time's e.	HOPK 429:96	Latin America owes…to the E.	VASC 909:29	E., not books, should be forbid	MELV 585:75
time's e.	HOPK 429:93	Modern E. culture	SUN 860:95	e. of life	SARO 744:58
eunuched e. with formality	CLEV 230:95	not a E. thing	NOLAN 640:43	e. overlapping each other	DURR 308:35
eunuchs Critics are like e.	BEHAN 74:12	policy of E. integration	KOHL 496:34	In all the e. of life	HUME 438:97
e. are on strike	ROTH 728:5	Unlike the classical E.	SENG 757:28	irresistible march of e.	NAPO 629:39
e. of literature	HEMI 409:61	very low class among the E. states	GEOR 364:47	seek to fashion e.	NAPO 629:41
two or three e.	BIBLE 97:79	**Europeans** books written by E.	NAIP 629:28	three great e. for a person	LABR 502:22
Euphrates Nile or E.	GIBB 366:95	E. have scarcely visited any coast	JOHN 460:86	where there used to be e.	PIGL 678:75
eureka E., E.!	ARCH 31:9	hearten those E.	MURR 627:83	**eventualities** e. in the future	MURP 627:77
euro If the e. fails	MERK 588:43	**evangelical** but he is most e.	BEAV 71:25	**ever** But I go on for e.	TENN 876:38
Europe all over E.	GREY 388:62	**Evangelist** honour unto Luke E.	ROSS 726:61	fall asleep for e.	SASS 745:91
alterations on the map of E.	CHUR 224:68	**evaporate** automate—or e.!	MERR 588:48	For e. and e. by	TENN 876:20
best negotiators in E.	NELS 633:12	**evasion** attempt at deliberate e.	JONES 465:21	**evergreen** with e. devotion	BIRN 136:20
Better fifty years of E.	TENN 871:24	has not wit enough to invent an e.	CONG 241:59	**everlasting** damned to e. fame!	POPE 687:90
claim…to make in E.	HITL 420:94	**Eve** Adam and E. were dispossessed	BOUL 152:91	even from e. to e.	BIBLE 101:92
community of E.	GLAD 373:41	Adam and E. were turned out	MUGG 623:10	E. had not fixed	SHAK 780:37
courts of E. are a jungle	BOLT 145:14	Adam knew E.	BIBLE 92:2	with an e. love	BIBLE 110:21
curse of E.	SENI 757:30	all the fair daughters of E.	EDGE 311:34	**everlastingness** shoots of e.	VAUG 909:35
dogs of E. bark	AUDEN 43:93	child of our grandmother E.	SHAK 763:7	**evermore** Name Liveth for E.	KIPL 493:75
Don Quixotes of E.	COBD 233:80	close at the ear of E.	MILT 604:11	**Everton** If E. were playing	SHAN 805:62
England still stands outside E.	KEYN 484:72	E. ate Adam	HUGH 436:37	**everybody** E. but me	HUGH 435:11
E. and…the future	MARI 570:72	E. made Adam sin	MARG 570:63	E. cries	STIPE 855:3
E. catches cold	METT 589:58	E. miscarried of me	BROW 165:67	E. gets so much information	STEIN 845:71
E. from the thralldom	LLOY 533:74	E. the rites Mysterious	MILT 604:9	e. is as nasty as himself	SHAW 806:82
E. had arrived at a point	GREY 388:63	E., whose fault was only	LANY 508:55	E. lies about sex	SEIN 756:6
E. had plenty of art	BEHR 75:28	fallen sons of E.	CHES 221:91	I want to thank e.	STOCK 855:6
E. is a continent of	FISH 337:63	I span and E. span	GILM 371:95	Most e. in the world	WILD 943:39
E. is not a choice	SARK 743:54	meekest E.!	COLL 238:77	take care of e.	FULL 355:74
E. is our common home	BREZ 158:6	mother E., who tasted	LANY 508:53	think of e. else as native	STEIN 845:66
E. needs Russia	YELT 967:44	real curse of E.	RHYS 712:72	To e.'s prejudice	GILB 369:56
E. rock and sway	LLOY 533:72	son of Adam and of E.	PRIOR 695:99	What was e.'s business	SMUTS 831:71
E. should know	CONG 241:57	When Adam delved and E. span	BALL 58:49	when e. is somebody	HUTC 441:50
E. was rich	IRVI 447:56	When E. upon the first	HOOD 426:29	**everyday** E. young man!	GILB 369:45
E. without Greece	GISC 373:30	**eve** Be sudden—to E.	THOM 886:82	ordinary, e.-d. people	DRUC 299:7
ever another war in E.	BISM 137:36	from e. and morning	HOUS 431:49	**everydayness** e. of life	STEI 845:58
every Christian in Hitler's E.	FACK 329:1	stag at e. had drunk	SCOTT 752:28	**everyman** E., I will go with thee	ANON 21:57
Furnished as all E. is	FRAN 348:18	St. Agnes' E.	KEATS 477:14	**everyone** bow to e.	SKEL 825:43
glory of E. is extinguished	BURKE 176:40	were not sure, this e.	BROW 167:13	equally unsound to trust e.	SENE 752:2J
greatest in E. for Riches and Greatness	BAIL 55:87	**even** get e.	KENN 482:37	E. can master a grief	SHAK 774:44
guilty secrets of E.	DUNN 307:17	**evening** at e., casual flocks	STEV 849:71	E. feels it	TROL 898:55
hold the balance of E.	WILL 944:67	Come in the e.	DAVIS 266:12	E.…holds dual citizenship	SONT 834:20
If E. is wise and just	LAMA 504:74	couthy chiels at e. meet	FERG 333:86	E. o. is more or less mad	KIPL 489:71
If the euro fails then e. fails	MERK 588:43	delight in the e.	PRIOR 696:11	E. suddenly burst out singing	SASS 745:92
I long for E.	RIMB 715:42	descends the autumn e.	ARNO 36:25	e. will say	GILB 368:43
in E. nothing goes	ROTH 728:86	e. cup of tea	HOLM 424:85	stop e. from doing it	HERB 412:42
intellect of E.	ARNO 35:8	e. full of the linnet's wings	YEATS 965:4	**everything** against e. all the time	KENN 482:41
in the interest of E.	PALA 660:47	e. is spread out against the sky	ELIOT 316:60	beginning of e.	REAG 708:7
It broke E.	MORR 620:58	e. meal	BARL 63:56	boxing is e.	HEMI 410:97
last gentleman in E.	LEVE 525:21	e. quickens in the street	DE 275:11	Brains make e.	SHAW 807:4
leading journal of E.	HAZL 403:41	e. sees it close	LONG 535:19	devourer of e.	OVID 657:20
map of Africa lies in E.	BISM 137:37	e. the strange horses	MUIR 624:23	E. clever has been thought	GOET 375:64
more E., not less E.	MERK 588:44	go to and fro in the e.	BOOK 149:22	e. could be known and forgiven	GEE 362:28
nationalities of E.	ASQU 38:84	green chiffon e. gown	THAT 881:50	E.…endeavours to persist	SPIN 840:75
nations of E. and outside	LEES 519:4	It is a beauteous e.	WORD 959:96	e. except space and light	HEAT 406:94
noblest river in E.	ADDI 7:35	It was a summer e.	SOUT 835:45	e. had to swing	ELLI 322:22
no nation on the continent of E.	BRIG 159:16	Late at e., drinkin' the wine	BALL 58:59	E. has been discussed	ALEM 12:56
now afoot in E.	GUST 390:3	lengthen, and the e. comes	NEWM 635:46	E. has been done	INGR 446:39

everywhere

E. has been said	LABR 502:6	e. soul producing holy witness	SHAK 769:84	**evolution** birthday present from e.	DILL 286:91
E. has been written	FERN 334:97	e. to triumph	BURKE 176:58	e. of culture	LOOS 536:44
e. includes itself in power	SHAK 786:26	E., what is e.?	LAWR 513:63	gradual e. of the new order	WEBB 925:9
e. I never wanted	GARD 360:69	e. which I would not, that I do	BIBLE 125:14	method of e.	FISKE 337:66
e. in its place	BEET 74:8	e. wrangling with the e.	MUIR 624:19	**evolved** life e. out of...nothing	DAWK 266:18
e. is allowed	AMIS 16:53	expose the raw nerves of e.	CHUR 224:51	**ewe** e. obedient to the benders will	SPEN 838:20
E. is decided	KIM 486:12	Family!... the home of all social e.	STRI 827:94	one little e. lamb	BIBLE 96:45
e. is great	PASC 666:63	fear a day whose e. is upon the wing	KORAN 498:89	tupping your white e.	SHAK 788:84
e. matters	MCEW 551:62	fear nae e.	BURNS 179:27	**ewe-milking** lilting at our e.-m.	ELLI 322:25
E. presses on	STER 848:46	fear no e.	BIBLE 100:45	**ewes** Ca' the e. to the knowes	BURNS 180:51
e. that he can come by	SHAK 759:67	fear of one e.	BOIL 144:2	**exact** Nature is so e.	BARN 64:78
E. we see	TOML 894:56	few and e. have the days...been	BIBLE 93:48	**exaggerate** greatly e. the difference	SHAW 780:45
e. would be done far better	SIEY 820:62	forced into channels of e.	FAUL 331:38	**exaggeration** my death was an e.	TWAIN 903:87
good in e.	SHAK 778:66	for the good or e. side	LOWE 539:3	pitfalls of e.	TROL 898:53
how dangerous e. is	STEIN 845:67	free of e. done	KIPL 492:58	**exaggerations** except the e.	ADOR 8:72
If you love e.	DOST 294:94	goodness in things e.	SHAK 775:80	**exalt** praise him and e. him	BIBLE 133:41
it's about e. in particular	SPARK 836:74	good of e. shall produce	MILT 607:71	**exaltation** delight, the e.	RUSS 734:25
President...has to do e.	ASTU 39:12	Government...a necessary e.	PAINE 660:31	e. and horror	GRAV 382:27
real price of e.	SMITH 827:79	hurrying the day of the e.	STOWE 856:32	e. of the 'average'	WHITE 935:54
Sans teeth, sans eyes...sans e.	SHAK 779:83	Hypocrisy, the only e.	MILT 603:88	highest pitch of e.	BRIL 159:21
Science...knows e.	GOUR 380:79	If e. does not exist	PRIT 696:18	it is our just e.	PITT 680:12
seeing nothing as the sum of e.	DUDEK 305:80	If this is not e.	BUSH 183:21	solemn prayers for the great e.	COLU 238:91
spirit of youth in e.	SHAK 802:72	imagination...is e. from his youth	BIBLE 92:11	**exalted** e. in the earth	BIBLE 100:69
sure...that he knows e.	CARY 207:68	intrinsically e.	TUTU 901:24	he that humbleth himself shall be e.	BIBLE 121:2
take e. away from them	SOLZ 833:5	Is thine eye e.	BIBLE 118:22	scandal of an e. person's fall	CANM 196:3
thanks for e.	ATKI 40:15	knowing good and e.	BIBLE 91:92	**examination** method of careful e.	LEBO 517:59
there is time for e.	BOLD 145:5	knowledge of good and e.	CHEE 218:6	**examinations** E. are formidable	COLT 238:84
thinks he knows e.	SHAW 809:76	knowledge of good and e.	MILT 600:3	**example** annoyance of a good e.	TWAIN 903:74
time enough for e.	GUNN 390:94	knowledge of good and e.	MILT 600:5	don't set us a good e.	WILDE 941:96
wanting that have wanted e.	HAZL 404:54	Man is neither good nor e.	BALZ 61:6	E. is the school of mankind	BURKE 176:57
We cannot all do e.	VIRG 914:24	Men's e. manners	SHAK 805:56	E. moves the world	MILL 594:61
Where e. is bad	BRAD 155:42	mixture of e. in everything	COWP 251:9	e. of the king of Denmark	FACK 329:1
Winning isn't e.	PALM 661:65	no e. in the atom	STEV 850:5	learn only by e.	PREV 694:77
everywhere E. I see bliss	SHEL 812:49	non-existence as an e.	SCHO 748:54	living e. of natural selection	GOLD 375:76
e.—wherever you look	STEI 845:83	only one e., ignorance	SOCR 833:1	My great e.	DENH 272:60
What is e.	VINC 913:9	overcome e. with good	BIBLE 126:28	practical e.	WHIT 938:3
eves flies on summer e.	KEATS 478:45	Party is a political e.	BOLI 145:8	**ex ante** referred to as e. a.	MYRD 628:99
evidence before one has all the e.	DOYLE 296:39	passively accepts e.	KING 486:22	**exasperate** actions continued to e.	BULL 173:60
defective in its e.	REGAN 710:42	People are never so...evil as	ECO 310:19	**excavation** e. and of self-discovery	WALC 916:22
e. of our wisdom	TROL 897:26	perpetrates any e.	PLATO 682:58	**excel** thou shalt not e.	BIBLE 93:49
e. of supernatural beings	STEI 846:99	places where e. is impossible	GENET 363:40	**excellence** acute limited e.	FITZ 337:79
e. of things not seen	BIBLE 129:39	possible for e. to triumph	HAILE 392:16	along lines of e.	KENN 482:29
false views, if supported by some e.	DARW 263:56	practical solutions to...e.	GENET 363:39	constant in a wondrous e.	SHAK 802:75
ignore the absence of e.	VIDAL 912:92	predicted e. consequences	TROL 898:41	e....of the object	WORD 958:89
no e. from modern literature	BELL 77:81	preserve thee from all e.	BIBLE 103:31	e. proper to culture itself	REYES 712:69
opinion in the absence of e.	CRIC 254:92	punishment in itself is e.	BENT 82:89	ne'er will reach an e.	DRYD 300:27
presented in e.	PARK 664:33	Recompense to no man e.	BIBLE 125:27	nothing of e.	THUR 890:65
proportions his belief to the e.	HUME 438:6	represent poverty as no e.	JOHN 461:96	of the highest e.	RUSS 734:25
Some circumstantial e.	THOR 888:22	resist not e.	BIBLE 115:35	soul exhibiting e.	ARIS 31:20
still blind him to the e.	KOES 495:28	root of all e.	BIBLE 129:23	There shall not be e.	SMITH 828:4
theater is the primary e.	THUR 890:89	root of E., Avarice	MAND 565:65	**excellencies** dwell...upon e.	ADDI 6:32
evil accustomed to do e.	BIBLE 110:19	see himself as...good and e.	MAIL 560:53	**excellent** everything that's e.	GILB 369:50
a complex mixture of good and e.	MAIL 560:65	set in motion the forces of e.	CHES 219:33	e. if you were a village	STEIN 845:76
all else comes from the e.	RODR 722:52	Sufficient unto the day is the e.	BIBLE 115:46	E. wretch!	SHAK 789:16
All e. comes from this	GIRA 373:27	sun to rise on the e.	BIBLE 115:38	no one more fair and e.	SPEN 838:32
allow its e. effects to go on	BUCK 172:33	supernatural source of e.	CONR 244:45	**Excelsior** strange device, E.!	LONG 535:11
All partial e., universal good	POPE 687:79	teach...of moral e.	WORD 957:59	**exceptional** e. and insignificant	MAIL 560:53
all that we are e. in	SHAK 792:89	this e. in thy sight	BIBLE 101:71	people to see themselves as e.	PUTIN 700:99
an assured e.	DOMI 290:3	Those to whom e. is done	AUDEN 43:96	**exceptions** I never make e.	DOYLE 296:45
an unmitigated e.	LAWR 513:50	though fallen, and e. tongues	MILT 605:27	Science does not permit e.	BERN 85:67
being e., speak good things?	BIBLE 117:85	vice...lost half life e.	BURKE 176:41	**excess** behave in e. except	LACL 503:32
between good and e.	HUSS 440:38	Who knows what e. lurks	ATWO 41:46	Give me e. of it	SHAK 785:77
certainty of doing e.	BAUD 69:80	woman...author of e.	STAN 843:17	lover...dies from e.	BART 66:26
child comes to know e.	MITC 609:25	youngling in the contemplation of e.	MILT 600:10	Nothing in e.	ANON 20:20
Children...do not wish to suffer e.	LABR 502:23	**evils** all its threatening e.	WHIT 938:11	road of e.	BLAKE 130:90
clear the land of e.	KIPL 490:8	balls, from which many e. may arise	EDWA 312:56	that which depends on e.	ARIS 31:21
consciences about doing e.	MORE 618:17	cure for the e.	MACA 544:24	To some divine e.	COLL 238:75
constitute an axis of e.	BUSH 183:18	death the worst of e.	HEINE 407:14	**excesses** never regret one's e.	BANKS 62:25
days are e.	BIBLE 128:91	enamoured of existing e.	BIER 134:70	protection...from...e.	BLACK 137:40
deliver us from e.	BIBLE 115:42	entailed other e.	SUMN 859:81	**excessive** if it is not e.	HAMI 394:47
do not easily suspect e.	ABEL 1:2	e. arising from disturbance	MALT 563:23	welcome was not e.	USTI 907:49
Drawing is only a necessary e.	HEIN 407:19	e. mankind had to fear	ELIOT 315:31	**exchange** By just e. one for the other	SIDN 820:40
Every law is an e.	BERN 82:90	e. of capitalism	KINN 488:61	e. rate is only a statistic	KRUG 500:24
E. be to him that e. thinks	EDWA 312:58	e. that ye have committed	BIBLE 110:33	open e. of major differences	AUNG 45:40
E. draws...power from indecision	BENE 79:21	e....wrought by the technology	GABOR 356:2	thrilling mutual e.	THOM 886:79
e....face of total need	BURR 180:63	greatest of e.	PLATO 681:49	value in e.	SMITH 827:78
e. in this world	PECK 672:62	greatest of e.	SHAW 809:70	**exchanged** e. in addition	JEVO 455:52
e. intreated, or sent	NASHE 632:90	mother of all e.	RABE 704:21	**exchequer** Barons of the E.	WALP 919:66
E. is done without effort	BAUD 69:77	must expect new e.	BACON 52:9	**excise** E. A hateful tax	JOHN 460:74
e. is wrought by want	HOOD 426:35	necessary e.	JOHN 461:11	**Exciseman** deil's awa wi' th' E.	BURNS 180:43
E. news rides post	MILT 608:99	no rest from e.	PLATO 682:63	**excite** e. my amorous propensities	JOHN 459:51
e. of...a world wrapped up	DICK 281:57	Of two e. the lesser	KEMP 480:82	others which e. by their vigour	GAUG 361:47
e. of the day is sufficient	CARL 200:77	submit to the inevitable e.	TOCQ 892:28	**excitement** as a source of e.	HORN 430:25
E. one abstracted stood	MILT 606:48	Two e.—greed and faction	MORE 619:23	connoisseur of tame e.	MOORE 617:86
E. people...you never forget them	DAVIS 265:95	Two e., monstrous either one	RANS 707:70	enough aesthetic e. here	BART 66:15
E. ran like malaria	GREE 3865:6	worst Of e., and excessive	MILT 605:24	e. and gladness	BUEC 172:42
e. seek to bring forth good	MILT 602:41	**evocations** not e. but last choirs	STEV 850:85	jazz band can be used for artificial e.	BLISS 142:57

experience

special e. of a rumored resignation	SHUL 819:23
excites e. their contempt	REED 710:37
exciting e. life...outside	SABA 736:2
flute...is too e.	ARIS 32:28
found it less e.	GILB 370:71
look both moral and e.	FERB 332:69
exclude e....the working classes	GLAD 373:36
exclusive the most e. worms	PARK 664:16
exclusiveness civilization...of e.	EMER 325:83
excommunicated e. by the medieval	ANON 27:19
excommunication on pain of e.	INNO 446:48
excrement e. is his own	DONNE 290:13
excremental Whiteness is but an e.	MILT 600:10
excrucior sed fieri sentio et e.	CATU 209:11
excursion e. to another planet	BIRD 136:9
excursionist noisy Plebeian e.	CHES 219:49
excuse every man will plead	SELD 756:6
e. for never giving me anything	SHAW 810:98
e. for this war...color and race	DU 305:70
E. My Dust	PARK 663:95
use the rejection as an e.	ANGE 19:94
excuses avoid making e.	DAVI 264:79
Several e....less convincing	HUXL 441:62
execrable E. English Theatre	GOET 375:58
executed e. in this way every year	STEV 854:92
execution e. is a perfunctory affair	LEWI 527:76
e. of his plan	STEU 849:61
pardon after e.	SHAK 805:57
stay of e. for six years	CARS 206:34
stringent e.	GRANT 381:9
why the e. has not been	JOHN 460:64
executioner e.'s repentance	BENE 79:13
Lord High E.!	GILB 369:62
yet I am mine own e.	DONNE 293:67
executive half-creature of the e.	MANS 568:12
nominated by the e.	GIBB 366:91
weakest e. in the world	DISR 287:31
executives Damn the great e.	LEWIS 527:59
executor make you full e.	WEBS 926:32
exempt no more e. from saying	STER 848:45
exercise accountable for its e.	DISR 287:16
applies himself to labour and e.	CONF 240:22
dancing is love's proper e.	DAVI 264:74
e. for a research scientist	LORE 537:61
e. his invention	SMITH 828:89
E.? I get it on the golf course	SKEL 824:33
E. is bunk	FORD 343:97
e. of his own style	JONS 468:93
forgone all custom of e.	SHAK 782:88
his way of taking e.	DOUG 295:8
imaginative e.	VIDAL 912:84
manly Scottish e.	PENE 673:78
more...courage, than any other e.	PEEL 672:68
never taken any e.	TWAIN 904:95
only possible form of e.	WILDE 942:26
part of its beneficial e.	JAMES 450:41
pleasant e. of hope	WORD 960:23
rich advantage of good e.?	SHAK 768:63
sad mechanic e.	TENN 873:58
Squash—that's not e.	COWA 249:61
what e. is to the body	STEE 844:45
Whenever I feel like e.	HUTC 441:51
wise, for cure, on e. depend	DRYD 304:48
women...need e.	BRON 161:61
exercises delighting in such e.	POE 683:81
e. are unbloody battles	JOSE 469:10
e. in arrested development	SELF 756:11
preaching...most healthy e.	WESL 932:71
remove these e. from	STUB 858:60
running around doing e.	ARMS 33:52
exertion e. is too much for me	PEAC 671:52
forced on e.	AUST 47:88
keenest spur to e.	BENT 82:93
undergone severe e.	LIVI 532:55
exertions e. of a free people	PITT 680:12
saved herself by her e.	PITT 680:14
Exhall Dodging E.	ANON 24:32
exhausted e. as a great man	MILL 592:31
I'm e., or conditioned, or perverted	PUIG 699:69
exhibitionism Acting is...e.	OLIV 649:38
exhibitions seven historic e.	DUNL 307:13
exhilarated provident, fatigued, e.	MUNRO 625:52
exhilarating it's e. to be alive	RICH 713:1
exhilaration coffee has an e. about it	HOLM 424:85
feeling of e.	GREE 386:11
exile bind your sons to e.	KIPL 491:19
die in e.	GREG 387:51
e. has been to the Irish	WILDE 940:49
Fated to be an e.	VIRG 913:11
forget makes e. all the longer	WEIZ 928:78
kiss Long as my e.	SHAK 799:4
refuge for the e.	GARI 360:72
world is a place of e.	HUGH 434:6
exiles e. and invaders	ATWO 41:37
e. from our fathers' land	GALT 359:54
none save e. feel	AYTO 48:13
Paradise of e.	SHEL 812:61
exist A, B, C and D...already e.	SCHM 748:40
Constitutionally I don't e.	EDIN 312:52
Deeds...do not e.	BALZ 61:3
e., but are identical	FORS 344:37
e. in order to be happy	SCHO 749:58
e. with the nature I actually have	DESC 275:1
Facts do not cease to e.	HUXL 441:59
from the people...all must e.	DISR 287:16
he need not e.	DE 275:13
If evil does not e.	PRIT 696:18
making something e. by observing	BURR 181:68
nothing can e....without God	SPIN 840:70
nowhere does it e.	TEMP 869:69
right to e.	KELM 479:69
Sir, I e.!	CRANE 253:74
unable to e. as writers	SPEN 837:13
existence acquire a kind of material e.	MARX 579:41
art, that monopolizes one's whole e.	DUDEK 305:78
certain that e. is meaningful	HAMM 394:57
conceive any kind of e.	HUME 438:94
convince me of God's e.	NEWT 635:62
could not endure their e.	SHAW 809:74
dead level of provincial e.	ELIOT 315:34
diversity of e.	KENN 482:27
every evil...presupposes e.	SCHO 778:54
Every moment of one's e.	MAIL 559:42
e. and opportunity	TEMP 869:70
e. as a nation	PITT 680:11
e. comes before essence	SART 744:71
e. in the nature of things	FORD 342:87
e. is but a brief crack	NABO 628:3
e. of decent, serious British filth	OSBO 655:86
e. of me	WHIT 937:99
e. of students	NABO 628:7
e. of the things that are	PROT 697:32
e. only adds to our peril	MOUN 622:93
e. or...hope is gone	AUST 47:90
e. precedes essence?	SART 744:72
form only comes into e.	OLSON 650:47
God who let us prove his e.	BONH 146:21
harvesting from e.	NIET 638:97
historians...He tolerates their e.	BUTL 185:95
humanities in his very e.	ROLL 723:90
impossibility...proves to me his e.	LABR 503:29
Independent e.—so called	HUXL 441:72
intrinsic to human e.	ACK 4:66
justifies its own e.	WILDE 940:60
law of their e.	MILL 591:5
lead...an e.	THUR 890:66
Let us contemplate e.	DICK 279:13
main themes of our e.	WHITE 934:29
matter of fact or e.	HUME 438:7
miracle...of naked e.	HUXL 442:90
mysteriousness of e.	MALL 562:95
necessary to our easy e.	DICK 278:63
paint the e. of a d.	MARC 569:51
prove that the e. of classes	MARX 579:45
put out of e.	DICK 283:21
sordid perils of actual e.	WILDE 940:57
spheres of e.	ELIOT 320:79
system of e....with no eye	WIEN 939:30
threatens the very e. of life	SONT 834:16
unmaking so much e.	ANDR 18:76
world in which children have their e.	DICK 282:5
existentialism first principle of e.	SART 745:73
subsequent E.	KERO 483:56
exists man first of all e.	SART 744:72
Nothing e. except atoms	DEMO 272:48
exit E., pursued by a bear	SHAK 799:14
leave out e. through which	WAITE 916:6
exits e. and their entrances	SHAK 779:80
exorcism I need...an e.	COWE 247:79
exotic Cambridge...less e.	ANON 25:36
much to be said for e. marriages	BELL 77:85
exotics languish like e.	WOLL 954:90
expansion e. of the human race	SCHR 749:66
expansionist relax my e. measures	KEYN 484:77
Expatiate E. free o'er all this scene	POPE 686:70
expect a right to e.	TRUM 899:77
Could anyone e. less?	SHER 816:69
e. less of them	JOHN 464:91
e. the unexpected	HERA 412:37
takes longer than you e.	HOFS 422:35
expectancy Pick up bad habits of e.	LARK 509:71
expectation e. is equalized	ILLI 445:22
e. makes a blessing dear	SUCK 858:69
e. of getting what he wants	ORWE 653:12
e. of too great a happiness	FONT 342:77
E. whirls me round	SHAK 787:33
strain of e.	FIRB 336:54
trifle short of the wearer's e.	DICK 282:8
expectations to have great e.	ONEI 651:75
expected different from what one e.	KISS 494:90
e. a man should see	JOHN 463:51
For I had e. always	SPEN 837:95
no reasonable man could have e.	HERB 412:48
nothing is e. to happen	THER 882:87
expediency consistent e.	THOR 888:19
e. of different schemes	STEU 849:61
expedient all things are not e.	BIBLE 126:46
e. in the way of our thinking	JAMES 451:76
so pleasing an e.	STEE 844:44
strikes...not as an e.	ENGE 326:14
expedition abandoning the e.	DOUG 295:6
e. had now performed	SPEKE 836:81
We made an e.	PEAC 671:54
expel e. them from here	JOAN 455:59
expenditure annual e. nineteen nineteen six	DICK 280:43
e. of fortunes	PEARY 671:59
E. rises to meet income	PARK 665:41
general economy and particular e.	EDEN 311:30
was so much e. justified	SPEN 837:4
expense at the e. of the...masses	QUINE 702:22
cannot be achieved without e.	PIUS 680:18
e. damnable	CHES 219:48
one God...the e. of two?	CLOU 232:63
repay the trouble and e.	BELL 76:54
use alone that sanctifies e.	POPE 686:63
without incurring the e.	SHER 817:93
expenses for the funeral e.	JERO 454:39
expensive comes a little more e.	LEAC 515:12
everything...will get more e.	COUL 248:22
e....to be poor	BALD 57:18
Witnesses are e.	RACI 704:27
experience according to which we e. them	HEID 406:11
accumulated and organized the e.	HUXL 443:7
actual quality of e.	LEAV 517:50
act without benefit of e.	MILL 594:82
all e. is an arch	TENN 870:98
amateur e. of...nieces	RIDGE 715:30
a sense of mastery over e.	PAGE 659:15
belief...founded upon my e.	DOYLE 297:59
blissful visionary e.	HUXL 442:91
constantly amalgamating...e.	ELIOT 317:94
crisis of her e.	AUST 47:97
different sort of e.	BOWL 153:4
dirty nurse, E.	TENN 878:91
distinctive Irish e.	DONO 293:81
equality of e.	MILL 592:14
e. and comparison	JOHN 463:73
E. and history teach	HEGEL 406:8
e. and intuited knowledge	MO 611:67
e. and understanding of life	MILL 593:60
e. a story within	KAFKA 472:4
e. counts for everything	WILS 947:35
e. does not show that	KEYN 484:76
e. has left me with...belief	ORWE 653:24
E. has taught me	HOUS 432:74
e. is an arch	ADAMS 5:87
E. is...larger than language	RICH 714:10
e. is like a cryptogram	SCHO 748:53
E. is never limited	JAMES 450:43
E. is not what happens	HUXL 441:70
e...is the bitterest	CONF 240:16
E. is the child of Thought	DISR 287:15
E. is the name	WILDE 941:81
e. of being human	LEWO 528:79
e. of life	BEER 73:85
e. of mixed exaltation and horror	GRAV 382:27
e. of the ages	CONN 243:19
e....of the woman writer	WITT 951:30
E. shows...enterprises seldom end	ELIZ 322:10

experiences

e. to make me sad	SHAK 779:7
e. which led a former	JEVO 455:55
feast of e.	GOLD 375:81
from any human e.	JAMES 450:24
greatest...e. unknown to man	OGDEN 647:2
had the e. but missed the meaning	ELIOT 320:73
heavy with useless e.	RICH 713:95
I have e.: I have a wife	CONG 241:56
inner e. and inner feeling	LAWR 514:81
It's called e.	NOFZ 640:42
knowledge...by...e.	BACON 54:57
knowledge derived from e.	ELIOT 320:59
knowledge...recorded e.	CARL 201:14
learn in their own e.	SCHW 751:94
lessons of historical e.	KISS 493:84
light which e. gives	COLE 236:51
long e. of many generations	GLAD 373:39
many years of...sad e.	SACK 737:12
matters outside...everyday e.	CONR 244:47
Music is your own e.	PARK 663:93
No matter how vital e.	GLAS 374:46
old age and e.	ROCH 719:12
old e. to attain	MILT 598:60
one word, from e.	LOCKE 533:89
one year's e. 30 times	CARR 202:54
optimist...never had much e.	MARQ 575:49
philosophy teaching by e.	CARL 201:18
Some by e. find those words	CONG 240:31
store of e.	FRAME 346:77
stream of your e.	JAMES 451:74
substitute for a real e.	ALBEE 11:22
system to be refuted by e.	POPP 689:52
terminate in sensory e.	ELIOT 317:90
that hopeless wisdom of e.	ONEI 651:63
triumph of hope over e.	JOHN 462:21
try a new e.	SHAW 809:84
Twenty years e. as an actress	DAVIS 265:94
very little e. of self-government	EDIN 312:48
war...we don't have direct e.	DALL 261:18
When one does not e. it	SARR 744:61
women offer our e.	LEGU 520:15
world is diminished by the e.	SHAW 811:39
world...we don't have to e.	FRIS 351:82
worth a life's e.	HOLM 424:81
Your e. will be a lesson	AMIN 16:28
experiences categories in which e.	MANN 567:91
e. of life	NIEB 637:87
wisdom...after e.	PROU 698:44
experiment e....in communal living	BOWL 153:2
good e. lasts forever	KAPI 473:27
men of e.	BACON 50:44
Pure poetry is pure e.	SANT 743:48
reasoning to the test of e.	LAVO 512:35
wherever the e. has been fairly tried	SHEL 812:53
experimental All poetry is e.	STEV 850:90
e. reasoning concerning matter	HUME 438:7
experimentation spirit of e.	FRAN 348:18
experiments inquiries and e.	MENC 586:89
not necessarily...physical e.	CONN 243:18
expert An e. is someone	HEIS 407:24
became an e.'s art	RUDO 730:36
never trust an e.	MAMET 564:36
expertness unaccountable e.	THUR 890:65
experts divine right of e.	MACM 556:62
e. as stately and grand presidents	SUN 860:96
you should never trust e.	SALI 740:89
expiate death my days should e.	SHAK 800:40
something to e.; A pettiness	LAWR 513:60
expiring e., do foretell of him	SHAK 764:37
explain and which never e.	THOM 886:88
best way to e. it	CARR 204:88
e. to Her Majesty	KEMB 479:72
Never complain and never e.	BALD 57:35
You e. nothing, O poet	CLAU 229:71
explained painting...cannot be e.	RENO 711:54
Science has 'e.' nothing	HUXL 441:58
Shut up he e.	LARD 509:67
explainer Being the great e.	THOR 888:15
said he was a village e.	STEIN 845:76
explanation devil...is the only e.	KNOX 495:19
explain his e.	BYRON 189:89
no e. is necessary	SEAT 755:93
one failed e. after another	ROTH 728:98
saves tons of e.	SAKI 739:69
unless there is a verbal e.	COLE 234:4
explanations author's e.	MACL 555:36
explicable all things become e.	CLAU 229:71
explode Or does it e.?	HUGH 435:13
point where they e.	HENZE 412:24
exploit composed and high e.	MILT 602:58
e. of that gallant man	MILT 600:1
exploitation e. of their adult slave	GREER 387:43
exploiters against their capitalist e.	LENIN 521:39
exploiting a heavenly gift	QUIL 702:17
exploration e. was a...venture	THES 882:96
shall not cease from e.	ELIOT 321:91
explore happy nature to e.	POPE 687:83
irresistible need to e.	BRON 160:47
let us e. the stars	KENN 481:1
explorers endeavours are unlucky e.	DOUG 295:6
exploring E. is delightful	BUTL 185:91
explosion at the centre of an e.	ORWE 653:23
bring...decay or e.?	RUSS 734:34
hell of an e.	CATTO 209:4
export attempt to e. revolution	STAL 842:5
E. or die	ANON 24:22
expose don't let me e. myself	SCOTT 754:83
expositions e. of the doctrines	MORR 620:51
ex post referred to as e. p.	MYRD 628:99
exposure unseemly e. of mind	HAZL 404:58
expounder e. of our religious belief	SPEKE 836:81
ex-presidency directly to the e.-p.	MANN 566:90
ex-president define an e....is to eliminate	MANN 506:90
I'm a better e.-p.	CART 206:52
Express morons reading the E.	WODE 952:57
express e. in the small of the back	WODE 952:37
how e. and admirable	SHAK 782:89
little I can e.	NABO 628:12
never keen to e. themselves	BRAD 154:33
one's happiness to e.	MOORE 617:83
To e. yourself	AI WEI 10:8
expressed could no otherwise be e.	MONT 613:21
that which cannot be e. otherwise	DELI 272:46
expression define an e....is to eliminate	QUINE 702:21
desire for aesthetic e.	WAUGH 923:66
E., for me, does not reside	MATI 581:91
e. for the inner sound	KAND 472:15
e. in English	ARNO 35:14
e. in vain	HEMI 409:64
E. is the dress	POPE 685:21
e. is to the thought	FLAU 339:17
e. may often be called bald	ARNO 36:44
e. of a people reflected	ROCK 721:39
e. of falling gravely downstairs	CUMM 257:48
e. of human separateness	MILL 593:43
e. of life as growth	MILL 594:79
e. of our...state of mind	FEIN 332:57
e. of the will to power	PAZ 671:49
e. which the few desire	PARE 663:89
first man I heard use the e.	ELLI 322:22
gave her the e.	THUR 890:86
Italy is a geographical e.	METT 589:59
most perfect e. of scorn	SHAW 810:13
my effort is their self e.	THOM 883:12
official e. of civil society	MARX 579:30
others by their hunted e.	LEWIS 526:45
Perhaps it was the right e.	WATE 922:37
perpendicular e.	SHAW 810:25
right to any mode of e.	POUND 691:97
sufficient power of e.	CHES 220:62
supreme e. of the mediocrity	TROT 899:64
vulgar e. of the passion!	CONG 240:36
expressions e. of esteem for Mr Boss	BAND 61:10
feeling...about some religious e.	RABI 704:23
pure e. of feeling	AYER 48:6
expressly we are told e.	SWIFT 861:33
express-train e.-t. drew up there	THOM 885:51
exquisite e. and...unsatisfied	WILDE 940:69
extemporanea medley of e.	PARK 664:14
extemporizing e....grammatical sentences	JOHN 457:96
exterminate e. a nation	SPOCK 841:85
extermination weapons of mass e.	RUSS 734:38
external idea of an e. cause	SPIN 840:77
impressions of e. things	RUSK 733:70
extinct labelled 'E.'	KING 488:58
extinction doomed to e.	POUND 692:20
presage of e.	SCOTT 751:1
sure e. that we travel to	LARK 510:95
extinguish e. hell	REED 709:30
e. the light of my mind	CRUZ 256:40
extinguished assimilated...never e.	DOUG 296:25
Nature is...seldom e.	BACON 52:23
extra add some e., just for you	LARK 510:89
always pay it e.	CARR 205:11
extraction e. of surplus labour	MARX 579:40
extra-marital e.-m. relationships	ALLEN 14:97
extraordinary E. how potent	COWA 249:48
interested in the e.	HUBB 434:98
work of one e. man	HUBB 434:99
extras No e., no vacations	DICK 278:75
extravagance with e. goes...waste	DILL 286:92
extravagances look upon all his e.	STEV 851:26
extravagant e. and irrational	SWIFT 862:47
e. with his own	SALL 740:92
extreme politics of the e. centre	WELL 929:9
take things to an e.	KLEIN 494:6
extremes be whaur E. meet	MACD 549:23
E. meet	HOOD 426:26
two e. of passion	SHAK 793:36
woman did not fly to e.	CRISP 254:1
Women are all in e.	LABR 502:9
extremism E. in the defence	GOLD 377:20
extremities e. of her corollaries	OCON 646:84
leave the body and e.	SMOL 831:68
measured at the e.	JAY 453:2
extremity E. of griefs	SHAK 760:28
exuberance e. of his own verbosity	DISR 288:67
exultations friends are e.	WORD 960:46
eye Affection beaming in one e.	DICK 279:12
an e. simply	DOYLE 297:75
apple of his e.	BIBLE 112:59
apple of his e.	BIBLE 95:99
artistic sense of e. or ear	WHIS 934:22
as it were in the e.	MILT 600:99
ball as th' e. confin'd?	MILT 607:85
Bear welcome in your e.	SHAK 796:17
brought an e. for all	TENN 874:90
But with his leener e.	MARV 576:84
camera is an e. in the head	WELL 929:94
Care...in every old man's e.	SHAK 766:89
Cast a cold e.	YEATS 967:40
censor the gleam in my e.	LAUG 511:19
Christ in every e.	PATR 669:29
corner of your e.	NEW 634:35
curious hand or e.	LOVE 538:84
dark time the e.	ROET 722:63
drappie in our e.	BURNS 178:12
drown an e.	SHAK 801:47
drumlie grew his e.	BALL 58:58
every e. shall see him	BIBLE 131:86
e. did see Olivia	SHAK 785:79
e. diffused a quickening ray	WESL 931:57
e....ear...tongue of the people	STEAD 843:30
e. enthrallèd to thy shape	SHAK 767:36
e. for an e.	BIBLE 115:35
E. for e.	BIBLE 94:87
e. has permitted no change	HUGH 435:32
e. hath caught new pleasures	MILT 597:45
e. is the hammer	KAND 473:17
E. Nature's walks	POPE 686:71
e. never sees outlines	GOYA 380:82
e. of Almighty God	GLAD 373:38
e. of American man	BARR 64:81
e. of gods	WORD 962:48
e. of my understanding	JULI 470:40
e. of the big wind	MAIL 559:39
e. on the object	ARNO 35:7
e. on the prize	ANON 26:74
e. on the right hand	RUSH 732:77
e. that cannot be turned around	PLATO 682:65
e. that can open an oyster	WODE 952:52
e. that sees too deep	FADI 329:7
e. to e.	PEEL 672:68
e. to see nor tongue	LENT 522:60
e. was backward cast	SPEN 838:27
e....with thy nest	WORD 961:40
Fair nature's e., rise	MARL 573:30
ferlie he spied wi' his e.	BALL 59:74
fettered to her e.	LOVE 538:81
find a friend...close one e.	DOUG 295:14
Foley, I have only one e.	NELS 633:13
formed the e.	BIBLE 102:99
God finally caught his e.	KAUF 474:40
God with his mercyful e.	ANON 21:47
guide thee with mine e.	BIBLE 100:54
had but one e.	DICK 278:76
Half hidden from the e.!	WORD 957:62
harvest of a quiet e.	WORD 957:68
hath closèd Helen's e.	NASHE 632:95
hollow cheek or faded e.	TENN 873:48
horrid deed in every e.	SHAK 796:20

eyes

human e. could see	TENN 871:17	before the e. of the world	JOHN 456:81	Hath not a Jew e.?	SHAK 769:1
if thine e. offend thee	BIBLE 118:12	Behind the E. of God	DICK 284:44	have a pair of e.	DICK 277:57
if thy right e. offend thee	BIBLE 114:34	bodily hunger in his e.	SHAW 809:73	Her e. are homes	TENN 874:72
I have a good e., uncle	SHAK 773:25	brightness in their failing e.	BLUN 143:72	Her e., nose, mouth, skin	MCEW 551:58
in the twinkling of an e.	BIBLE 127:62	cast your e. on buildings	PEI 672:73	hid from our e.	SMITH 831:65
invisible to the e.	SAINT 738:37	cats with golden e.	SACK 737:11	His e. fixed	YEATS 967:37
In woman's e. the unanswerable	BYRON 188:78	cat with bright green e.	MONRO 612:4	His flashing e.	COLE 236:42
Is thine e. evil	BIBLE 118:22	censured by our e.	MARL 574:37	Histr'y ain't got e. to see	LAMM 506:20
Its e. is always open	TOCQ 892:30	Closed his e. in endless night	GRAY 385:90	hit a newspaper reader between the e.	BRIS 159:26
its e. is pasted.	MCCA 548:91	close my e.	HILL 418:64	I don't make music for e.	ADELE 8:60
judgement of the e.	LEON 523:79	cold commemorative e.	ROSS 727:64	if e. could penetrate	VIEI 913:7
less in this than meets the e.	BANK 61:11	Cortez when with eagle e.	KEATS 475:61	I have e. like a bullfrog	DAVIS 265:97
like a joyless e.	SHEL 816:66	cry our e. out	LLOYD 532:66	I lifted up mine e. again	BIBLE 112:58
long grey beard and glittering e.	COLE 234:8	dark e. darting light	BYRON 190:9	I looked into his e.	MCCA 547:70
looked into the e.	YEATS 966:28	darkness…no more assail mine e.	DELA 271:33	in our e.	MCCA 547:87
look into a human e.	MELV 585:69	death, come close mine e.	GIBB 367:7	in the world's e.	YEATS 966:16
may charm our e.	COLL 238:75	deign…to turn thine e.	JOHN 459:46	ladies, whose bright e.	MILT 597:47
mine e. seeth thee	BIBLE 99:23	delivered…mine e. from tears	BIBLE 102:20	large blue e., fair locks	BYRON 187:34
Monet is only an e.	CEZA 212:54	doors are hateful to my e.	OTWAY 656:99	Let waking e.	DANI 262:31
more than meets the e.	KIPL 492:67	downcast e.	WELD 928:83	lie heavily upon her e.	ROSS 726:43
mote that is in thy brother's e.	BIBLE 115:48	dwell in lovers' e.	SHAK 801:54	lift up mine e. unto the hills	BIBLE 103:31
nimble jugglers that deceive the e.	SHAK 762:91	dying e. were closed	POPE 685:46	light in a lady's e.	ANON 25:38
no e. to our convenience	WIEN 939:30	emerald e.	GRAY 383:51	long ere my e. had seen	WORD 961:47
no profaner e. may look	MILT 598:58	envious e.	WELLS 930:19	looked at me with shrewd e.	LAWR 513:69
No shape to feed each gazing e.	DYER 309:48	excited by…tone of their e.	WYETH 964:7	looks into the e. of a native	LESS 523:90
object seen, and e. that sees	WORD 958:89	e., and…forehead gaze	MARV 577:91	Love looks not with the e.	SHAK 767:19
objects seen by the e.	PIERO 678:72	e. are blurred	ADE 7:59	made one…Stretch one's E.	BELL 77:63
Of e., and ear	WORD 956:56	e. are lenses	DOUG 295:5	Make thy two e. like stars	SHAK 781:60
one e. may be very agreeable	SHER 817:74	e. are lodestars	SHAK 766:18	mask…shades our e.	DUNB 306:95
One e. was entirely gone	BIRD 135:7	e. are made the fool	SHAK 796:28	Meet in her aspect and her e.	BYRON 189:80
out of the corner of the e.	HOLL 423:52	e. are oddly made	HAMM 395:67	Mine e. are full of tears	SHAK 765:57
painted skin contents the e.?	SHAK 762:75	e. are quickened	GRAV 382:15	mine e. dazzle	WEBS 927:62
Pity the e.	MACL 555:29	e. are sentinels unto	MIDD 590:74	Mine e. do itch	SHAK 790:37
pleases the e.	TINT 892:24	e. are to rest upon	STEV 851:30	mine e. had seen it	BIBLE 97:56
poke in the e.	CARY 207:66	e. as wide as a football pool	CAUS 209:14	Mine e. have seen	HOWE 433:92
presented to the e. or ear	CRAB 252:43	e. at the full midday beam	MILT 601:20	mistress' e. are nothing	SHAK 773:51
roguish twinkle in his e.	THOM 887:5	e. can in another's e. read	ARNO 34:72	my daughter's e.	SHAK 799:23
Sail and sail, with unshut e.	ARNO 33:58	e. Darker than…pansies	TENN 871:5	my eyes are blinded	SAPP 743:49
see e. to e.	BIBLE 109:90	e. did see my substance	BIBLE 103:45	my e. looked back at me	RHYS 712:78
sees with equal e., as God	POPE 686:73	e. follow you about	ORWE 655:72	night has a thousand e.	BOUR 153:94
see with, not thro' the E.	BLAKE 141:29	e. have seen the glory	KING 487:35	Night hath a thousand e.	LYLY 543:87
see…with the spiritual e.	FRIE 351:75	e. have seen the King	BIBLE 107:55	no cheerful cottage has blest my e.	SCHAW 747:20
Set honour in one e.	SHAK 776:7	e. have seen thy salvation	BIBLE 120:70	not a friend to close his e.	DRYD 303:31
shuts up sorrow's e.	SHAK 767:39	e. might be shining for me	LAWR 514:88	not meant for human e.	MUIR 624:17
soft black e.	MOORE 618:6	e. more bright	YEATS 967:30	not put our e. out	TAYL 868:58
still-soliciting e.	SHAK 792:86	e. of all England	WILL 944:67	Not with his e.	SACK 737:10
such a wistful e.	WILDE 942:16	e. of all wait upon thee	BIBLE 104:48	Oedipus with his bloody, blinded e.	PAGE 659:14
suff'ring e. inverted Nature sees	POPE 686:60	e.…of an unsuccessful rapist	HEMI 410:91	Of e. again so royal	SHAK 795:95
tender e. of pitiful day	SHAK 797:47	e. of God and men	LESL 523:88	Oh e., no e.	KYD 501:49
that inward e.	WORD 960:27	e. of gold and bramble-dew	STEV 854:86	old Eben's e. were dim	ROBI 718:89
The e. is the enemy	WILD 943:52	e. of man are never satisfied	BIBLE 105:4	one whose subdued e.	SHAK 790:51
the e. of God	OLIV 649:41	e. of our mind	GREG 387:50	Only Have E. For You	DUBIN 304:62
through the e. of a needle	BIBLE 118:18	e. Of proud Adonis	MARL 574:34	only, with thine e.	JONS 467:75
watchful e.…of England	PALM 662:72	e. of the blind shall be opened	BIBLE 108:76	optics of these e. to behold felicity	BROW 165:63
what brightens the e.	WHIT 938:17	e. of the Lord run to and fro	BIBLE 98:86	optimist to open your e.	SAND 742:32
What immortal hand or e.	BLAKE 140:19	e. of them both were opened	BIBLE 91:93	Our e., upon one double string	DONNE 292:42
when first your e. I eyed	SHAK 802:74	e. of the Old World	MANS 567:97	our longing E. are turned	BLAKE 139:80
wink your e. at some…girl	MENC 586:85	e. of the world are upon you	EISE 314:92	over my neck and e.	STEV 851:29
with a threat'ning e.	SHAK 768:59	E. open on growing	REID 710:44	pair of sparkling e.	GILB 370:73
with e. serene	WORD 960:20	e. shall be opened	BIBLE 91:92	passion and party blind our e.	COLE 236:51
with sovereign e.	SHAK 801:48	e. so helpless and appealing	LERN 523:81	peep through their e.	SHAK 768:67
yellow to the jaundiced e.	POPE 685:26	E. still dazzled	LIND 530:17	Philistines…put out his e.	BIBLE 96:19
eyeball e.—like a bastion's mole	SMART 826:65	e., that roll in vain	MILT 603:74	pictures in our e. to get	DONNE 292:43
e. to e.	RUSK 732:78	e. the gazers strike	POPE 685:32	play the idiots in her e.	SHAK 787:36
eyeballs never to move his e.	AMIS 16:29	e., the glow-worm lend thee	HERR 416:15	quaint enameled e.	MILT 599:90
eye-beams Our e.-b. twisted	DONNE 292:42	E.…to study Flies?	POPE 689:46	quiet e.	STEV 854:85
eyefull E. Tower is devine	LOOS 536:51	e. were as a flame of fire	BIBLE 131:88	rape us with their e.	FREN 350:53
eyelashes lose our teeth and e.	LEAR 517:43	e. were blind with stars	HODG 421:21	set thine e. upon that which is not?	BIBLE 105:90
eyeless E. in Gaza at the mill	MILT 607:82	e. were deeper	ROSS 726:49	shall my sad e. again behold	LANY 508:58
Turn out that e. villain	SHAK 793:15	e. were green as leeks	SHAK 768:50	Sleep dwell upon thine e.	SHAK 766:86
eyelids close your e.	YEATS 965:11	face with blinking e.	SASS 745:82	Soft e. looked love to e.	BYRON 187:50
tired e. upon tired eyes	TENN 870:89	fiery e. are fixed	MARL 572:96	Stars scribble on our e.	CRANE 253:65
weigh my e. down	SHAK 772:84	flourish where you turn your e.	POPE 685:15	starveth in thy e.	SHAK 766:12
When she raises her e.	COLE 236:55	fortune and men's e.	SHAK 800:46	strike mine e.	JONS 467:60
With e. heavy and red	HOOD 426:30	frightened look in its e.	SITW 824:17	sun rose in your e.	MACC 548:8
eyes act their dream with open e.	LAWR 514:89	full of e. within	BIBLE 131:97	tears are in my e.	MASE 580:53
all tears from their e.	BIBLE 131:4	gather to the e.	TENN 872:41	tears for ever from his e.	MILT 600:95
all tears from their e.	BIBLE 132:24	Get thee glass e.	SHAK 793:26	tempts your wandering e.	GRAY 383:54
almost in his e.	MILT 600:15	glazed e. of a soldier dying	BISM 137:34	That girl's clear e.	THOM 885:61
amazes my e. as though	LOWE 539:1	glazed look that comes into their e.	WILD 943:54	that which was right in his own e.	BIBLE 96:21
amethyst e. of anemones	BRAS 156:77	Golden slumbers kiss your e.	DEKK 270:10	their pretty e. may roll	POPE 685:42
And all e. else	SHAK 800:29	good turns e. for e. have done	SHAK 800:46	they hurt our e.	UPDI 906:28
asked him with my e.	JOYCE 470:33	gray hazel e.	GUNT 390:97	Thine e. my pride	SIDN 820:51
assailed by e.	JAMES 451:67	great inspector, with a myriad e.	STEAD 843:34	thoughts have e.	LYLY 543:84
audience only look to their e.	SHAK 767:21	Had I your tongues and e.	SHAK 793:37	thou hast doves' e.	BIBLE 107:45
bat with tears in your e.	BRAD 155:45	happiness through another man's e.	SHAK 780:19	To celebrate her e.	GRAY 384:61
bees-winged e.?	BETJ 88:18	has e. of youth	SHAK 773:9	to the hills will lift mine e.	SCOT 755:89

eyeservice   1098

to these courteous e.   JONS 466:43
two grey e.   SHAK 785:90
two red e. that stare   RANS 707:72
ugly death within my e.   SHAK 761:40
Underneath Day's azure e.   SHEL 812:64
until you see the white of their e.   PUTN 700:2
unto dying e.   TENN 872:43
When absent from her e.   ROCH 720:25
wheresoe'er I turn my ravished e.   ADDI 6:16
where you turn your e.   POPE 685:15
windows of the e. of cats   DRAY 299:1
with bedroom e.   AUDEN 44:15
With e. up-raised   COLL 238:78
without lowering her e. and blushing   SARR 744:60
with two blered e.   LANG 489:96
wondering e. should appear   MOORE 616:62
write the beauty of your e.   SHAK 800:36
You have lovely e.   CHEK 218:18
young e. could see   NEIL 633:10
your e. had once   YEATS 965:7
youth's e. burned   ROSS 726:58
eyeservice Not with e.   BIBLE 128:94
eyesight e. has always been weak   GREG 387:52

F

Fabians civilization of the F.   INGE 445:29
man fallen among F.   LENIN 521:41
fable f., song, or fleeting shade   HERR 415:11
nocht but f.   BARB 63:49
vnder ane fenyeit f.   HENR 411:18
fables f. in the legend   BACON 51:78
old wives' f.   BIBLE 129:19
fabric f. of America   MCCA 547:82
f. of the heavens   MILT 605:35
monotonous f. of life   MILL 594:73
pull of a f. is governed   MOORE 617:88
face 50s f....60s f....70s f.   WATE 922:37
a beautiful f. is a dumb commendation   PUBL 699:64
acceptable f. of capitalism   HEATH 405:86
acceptable f. of capitalism   HEATH 405:87
Accustomed To Her F.   LERN 523:83
Am I in f. to-day?   GOLD 376:10
at their f. value   TAWN 868:43
autumnal f., her pieced beauty!   JONS 467:59
Before I knew thy f.   DONNE 291:33
before my f. the great increase   SURR 860:98
bend down my strange f.   SEXT 758:45
blot on the fair f. of creation   BRON 161:62
blow over the f.   AUBR 42:59
boot in the f., the brute   PLATH 681:34
boot stamping on a human f.   ORWE 655:77
born with a different f.?   BLAKE 140:23
bright f. of danger   STEV 853:80
cannot f. it steadily   ELIOT 320:75
canst not see my f.   BIBLE 94:75
cause his f. to shine upon us   BIBLE 101:80
chaos clapped on to my f.   WELLS 930:18
colors don't quite match your f.   ASHF 37:70
commandments in your f.   SHAK 759:85
Cover her f.   WEBS 927:62
curse thee to thy f.   BIBLE 98:92
dar'st not see my f.?   BEAU 71:21
decays in the f.   BEHN 75:25
Do thou amend thy f.   SHAK 771:54
draw a full f.   DRYD 303:24
each f. was turned   VIRG 913:13
earn the f. you have at fifty   CHAN 214:2
everybody's f. but their own   SWIFT 861:17
f. a British Government   TUCH 901:11
f....in a jar by the door   LENN 522:51
f....is so peculiarly unpleasant   SNOW 832:78
f....like a wedding-cake   AUDEN 44:24
f. ne'er shows   HERR 415:3
f. of American literature   PORT 690:75
f. of a moving-picture actor   MENC 587:16
f. of a saint   WELLS 930:33
F. of a traitor!   HUGO 437:68
f. of night is fair   TENN 876:34
f. of the world   LAUT 512:30
f. of Venus   BARR 65:98
f. softly made up   THAT 881:50
f. that launched a thousand ships   MARL 573:29
f. the man of the time   STEV 850:81
f. the music and dance   BERL 84:40
F. to f., silent   BROW 166:94
f. to the light   SASS 745:87

f. turned to the past   NARO 630:53
f. wearing the fixity   HARDY 397:18
f. with an undaunted tread   STEV 853:73
f. with blinking eyes   SASS 745:82
f. would be hardly observed   MONT 613:12
fall flat on your f.   THUR 890:77
False f. must hide   SHAK 796:25
famine in his f.   CHUR 224:52
Fanny Kelly's divine plain f.   LAMB 505:87
fell on his f.   BIBLE 119:42
filth returns in's f.   WEBS 926:28
first time...I saw your f.   MACC 548:8
garden in her f.   CAMP 195:76
gave his whole f. the expression   CUMM 257:48
give me a f.   JONS 467:60
glimpse of His bright f.   VAUG 909:34
God has given you one f.   SHAK 783:14
golden f. the meadows green   SHAK 801:48
good f. is a letter of recommendation   ADDI 6:30
hairy about the f.   SHAK 767:40
hand...goes over the f.   GARBO 359:64
Has he not a rogue's f.?   CONG 240:41
heart in's f.   SHAK 799:11
herds, of human f. divine   MILT 603:75
Her f. was lovely   SPEKE 836:82
Her fist of a f.   THOM 883:13
hides a smiling f.   COWP 250:87
hid the f.   DRYD 299:10
homely f.   GILB 368:38
honest, sonsie f.   BURNS 178:94
How my f., your flower   BROW 167:13
How unlike marble was that f.   KEATS 477:30
I have a grumpy f.   PINO 678:81
Intellectuals take apart her f.   SAINT 738:33
Jezebel...painted her f.   BIBLE 97:78
keeping your f. or your figure   CART 207:56
King's real. or his stamped f.   DONNE 291:27
kissed her...dainty f.   ASHF 38:76
like a f. full of character   MAUG 582:10
looked him honestly in the f.   DAVI 265:82
looking for the f.   YEATS 967:30
Look in my f.   ROSS 727:63
look on Helen's f. in hell   PARK 664:10
Look on her f.   POPE 685:33
look the East End in the f.   ELIZ 322:15
Lord spake unto Moses f. to f.   BIBLE 94:72
loss made one side of the f. repulsive   BIRD 135:7
love's f. May still seem love   SHAK 802:68
lying on his f.   THAC 880:26
make his f. shine upon thee   BIBLE 94:79
man has a black f.   EDWA 312:59
mannish manner of mind and f.   CARY 207:62
mark in every f. I meet   BLAKE 140:16
met him f. to f.   SULL 859:80
mind's construction in the f.   SHAK 796:12
mist on the sea's f.   MASE 580:50
monstrous carbuncle on the f.   CHAR 215:40
morning f.   GOLD 376:1
Moses hid his f.   BIBLE 93:53
most kiss-worthy f.   SIDN 820:49
my pilot f. to f.   TENN 879:6
never see my f. again   TENN 878:86
Newton with...silent f.   WORD 958:82
no f., only two profiles   ASQU 38:93
not recognize me by my f.   TROL 898:52
oft in my f.   SURR 860:97
oil to make his f. to shine   BIBLE 102:11
only f. I like to see   CAMP 194:52
on the f. of the globe   SMITH 830:50
painted f. of a savage   DICK 282:78
paint in the public's f.   RUSK 733:15
paradise...in his f.   DRYD 301:66
passions glowing in a human f.   MATI 581:91
people whom a fair f.   MAIL 560:68
Pity a human f.   BLAKE 139:88
plummet-measured f.   YEATS 967:38
poster with the enormous f.   ORWE 655:72
praised him to his f.   TENN 879:99
prayed for in our f.   BROW 166:99
proved to thy f.   SHAK 760:98
red in the f.   BENT 82:5
Royalty puts a human f.   RUNC 731:48
rude wind Blows in your f.   SHAK 793:18
sages have seen in thy f.   COWP 250:96
saw the f. of God   MARL 573:24
seeing his own f. in the glass   WILDE 940:63
Sex Life in Ancient Rome f.   AMIS 16:30

She has a lovely f.   TENN 870:87
shining morning f.   SHAK 779:81
sigh of the east on my f.   CONR 244:35
sing in the robber's f.   JUVE 471:56
smug suppressions of his f.   WELLS 930:22
stamping on someone's f.   OSBO 655:84
stand f. to f.   KIPL 489:76
staring me in the f.   THUR 890:91
straight in the f.   GILL 370:78
Strike heaven on the f.   SHAK 797:60
string to each side of its f.   LEAC 515:6
such a f. should bear   SHAK 763:98
such a February f.   SHAK 775:58
sullen cold Exhausted f.?   SASS 745:90
surgeon...responsible for this f.   CUOMO 258:79
tears run...down my f.   OBRI 646:72
that homely f.   WORD 959:97
the f. he deserves   ORWE 655:80
the huge massy f.   MACA 545:36
three have changed the whole f.   BACON 50:45
thy classic f.   POE 683:86
Thy f. is valanced   SHAK 782:95
torso which has no f.   YOUR 969:61
truth has such a f.   DRYD 303:10
turn away thy f.   SHAK 778:55
turning my f. towards home   PARK 663:91
unacceptable f. of capitalism   HEATH 405:86
unclouded f. of Truth   SCOTT 751:98
until you're blue in the f.   NEWM 634:43
upon the night's starred f.   KEATS 475:78
up to the f. of a nation   ROCK 721:39
Vice...familiar with her f.   POPE 687:82
view our inner f.   GREG 387:50
Visit her f. too roughly!   SHAK 780:39
way plain before my f.   BOOK 148:4
wear one f. to himself   HAWT 402:6
white f.   GIOV 372:20
whole f. of the earth   PASC 667:74
whole life shows in your f.   BACA 48:5
whole world in the f.   LONG 535:18
woman's f. with nature's own hand   SHAK 800:39
wounds are in his breast and f.   DAVIS 266:10
your changing f.   YEATS 965:7
Your f., my thane   SHAK 796:16
faces almost everywhere two f.   DRYD 300:34
among so many millions of f.   BROW 165:69
breathing in their f.   SHAK 804:29
clouds...silent f.   WORD 961:36
cover their f.   KNIG 494:10
f....a gallery of pictures   BACON 52:13
f. as thin as credit cards   AMIS 16:43
f. in the crowd   POUND 691:92
f. of most American women   FITZ 338:96
f. was that same immemorial look   LESS 524:93
foreign f.   SWIN 863:82
God...looks on shock-pried f.   EBER 310:11
hid...our f. from him   BIBLE 109:93
know the f. I shall see   ROSS 726:60
lords and owners of their f.   SHAK 802:69
make f.   JOHN 462:40
make f.   SCHN 748:45
men with ugly f.   MASE 580:68
Mild monastic f.   CLOU 232:61
most other people have f.   TOOLE 894:60
ne'er touched earthly f.   SHAK 800:35
plain men have rosy f.   STEV 854:85
probed their f.   ANGE 19:99
seen better f. in my time   SHAK 792:98
strange f., other minds   TENN 878:84
take their f. from 'em   PRIE 695:92
unidentifiable flying f.   MCGO 552:80
With f. new   LOWE 539:16
with vivid f.   YEATS 966:18
facilitates be admitted that it f. much   LACL 503:34
facility F. is a dangerous thing   SLOAN 825:54
fact a f....so dreamlike   RICH 713:96
apparent statements of f.   AYER 48:5
believe that any f.   VIDAL 912:84
by an ugly f.   HUXL 443:6
can't figure him out like a f.   SHUL 819:30
conceal from ourselves the f.   PASC 666:66
concerning matter of f.   HUME 439:7
dependence of one f.   HOBB 420:98
disagreeable f.   STEV 851:92
drinking at the fountain of f.   PIER 677:66
every f....has been examined   PEAR 671:56
evil comes from this f.   GIRA 373:27

faith

f. and fiction shouldn't be mixed	BOWEN	153:95
F. is stranger than fiction	GERV	365:82
f. is, you got to	WALK	917:38
f. of the artist	MAMET	563:30
f., propaganda, rumor	LIPP	531:37
f. that it is the…expression	PAZ	671:49
Frenchman is a f.	FRIE	351:72
grim f., however, is	PEAR	671:57
how to tell f. from fiction	MANT	568:15
important f. regarding Spaceship Earth	FULL	355:73
indispensable f. that Americans	JAMES	450:36
in one f. can all agree	CLOU	232:51
knife-edge of mere f.	RICH	713:95
knocking your head against a f.	HUXL	443:12
man's religion is the chief f.	CARL	201:30
Matters of F.	HUME	438:5
mixture of f. and truths	FRAME	346:76
national consciousness is a political f.	MACM	556:67
need only one f.	THOR	888:24
or records a f.	RUSK	732:82
pigmentation of f.	BARN	64:62
production of objective f.	MENC	586:3
reaching after f.	KEATS	475:75
Sit down before f.	HUXL	443:3
SPACE…the central f.	OLSON	624:74
The f. is	STEV	851:32
where the idea and the f. collided	MCIL	553:96
Womanhood is the great f.	STAN	842:13
faction by f. cry'd up	PRIOR	696:3
f. is the worst of all parties	BOLI	145:8
From f.; for none sure	MILT	602:56
made them a f.	MACA	546:56
no leader, f., party or 'class'	OAKE	642:2
Two evils—greed and f.	MORE	619:23
factions leaders of white-mouse f.	MACD	550:39
factitious tremble for something f.	CLOU	232:58
factor dominant f. in our society	ASIM	38:81
factories bombs are…in the f.	ORWE	654:57
dynamiting f.	TOLK	893:44
living f. of the soul	MAYA	583:22
poems…in the f. and fields	MACD	549:35
factory f. of books	SMITH	828:5
in the f., he serves a machine	MARX	579:42
In the f., we make	REVL	712:68
prefers…to a concrete f.	WALC	916:19
truck passing by a f.	CAGE	192:17
within the reach of f. girls	SCHU	750:79
facts abandoned the f.	WATE	922:35
all the f. are known	FORD	343:11
begin with a good body of f.	DARW	263:59
beings loaded up with f.	UNAM	905:7
bring to light the hidden f.	LIPP	531:41
deadlier f., not dreams	MELV	585:75
dominant f. in English life	ORWE	654:35
F. alone are wanted in life	DICK	281:75
f., and the general laws of nature	BURB	174:85
F. are cheels	BURNS	177:85
f. are f.	JAMES	451:64
F. are generally overesteemed	UPDI	905:19
F. are like	UPDI	906:28
f. are lost forever	MAIL	560:43
f. are sacred	SCOTT	751:98
F. are ventriloquist's dummies	HUXL	442:87
F. do not cease	HUXL	441:59
f. don't mean a thing	ONEI	651:69
f., not realities	GOLD	377:35
f. we know about a man	LAWR	513:57
F.…were distorted	PACH	658:1
f., with the specific	ROTH	728:90
False f. are highly injurious	DARW	263:56
government and report the f.	ROGE	723:86
greatest number of empirical f.	EINS	314:89
ignoring the f.	ADAMS	5:95
imperial gallons of f.	DICK	281:76
intelligent anticipation of the f.	CURZ	259:4
knowledge of relevant f.	JAY	453:2
manners, and even f.	TROL	898:53
not for the f. they elicited	INOU	446:50
obvious f. about grown-ups	JARR	452:91
outward with inward f.	ELIOT	315:21
Particular f. are never scientific	BERN	85:71
plainly evident f.	TOBIN	892:25
Religion…greatest of present f.	WHIT	936:65
rude f. at your feet	RABAN	703:4
Science is f.	POIN	683:97
seven great f.	HUGEL	434:4
severe f. of life	ELIOT	316:48
simultaneously the two f.	ORWE	655:82
small f., trends, or even politics	SCHI	747:22
the absence of f.	MANT	568:18
That's all the f.	ELIOT	319:26
the f. of life	PARK	664:33
trust to nothing but f.	LAVO	512:35
when the external f.…are given	ELIOT	317:90
world is the totality of f.	WITT	951:22
faculties according to his f.	BAKU	56:9
borne his f. so meek	SHAK	796:20
diversity in the f. of men	MADI	558:16
dull and half-dead f.	ALBEE	11:28
dull f. can comprehend	EINS	313:80
experience and of general f.	MILL	592:14
f. have departed	THUR	890:62
f. of the mind…benumbed	BROO	162:83
mind fully develops its f.	STAEL	841:93
need exercise for their f.	BRON	161:61
faculty f. of laughter	ADDI	7:44
f. of seeing	SPEN	837:7
how infinite in f.	SHAK	782:89
fad Psychoanalysis is a permanent f.	DE	274:14
fade f. as a leaf	BIBLE	110:7
f. away into the forest	KEATS	478:42
F. far away	KEATS	478:43
flourish or may f.	GOLD	376:98
just f. away	MACA	544:8
just f. away	MACA	544:9
Nothing of him that doth f.	SHAK	803:17
old soldiers…just f. away	MACA	544:8
faded She f.…in her little grey dress	WOOLF	955:24
She f., like a cloud	SHEL	815:31
fading f. in music	SHAK	769:2
faery relish in the f. power	KEATS	475:78
fags f. and cabbage-stumps	LAWR	513:74
fail all right if they f.	ZHOU	970:11
f. a bit less	NICK	637:82
f. as a woman	FRID	350:62
f. conventionally	KEYN	485:84
f. to find thee	TENN	877:70
greatness may not f.	TENN	879:3
Guaranteed never to f.	FORM	344:21
not ashamed to f.	JOHN	459:39
Others must f.	VIDAL	912:90
Screw your courage…we'll not f.	SHAK	796:3
system in which no one can f.	HUGH	435:27
Try again…F. again	BECK	72:52
what an artist does, is f.	BART	66:19
will not f. thee	BIBLE	95:5
failed one f. explanation	ROTH	728:98
failing f. just when…succeeding	REST	711:64
principal f. occurred in the sailing	CARR	206:30
fails if another f.	BROW	167:11
not what the f. to do	GOET	375:59
what you'll do if a plan f.	RICE	713:87
When State Magic f.	REED	710:34
failure can stand anything but f.	COMD	239:92
confession of its f.	STEV	854:93
either a f. or madman	HOLM	423:57
enables him to sustain a f.	BELL	75:31
f., in perpetual struggle	WHITE	935:51
f. is igniminious	MENC	586:93
f. of feeling	STEV	850:86
f., or misfortune, or imprudence	STOWE	856:28
f. to communicate	PRIT	696:21
f. to provide for	KEYN	484:82
grant me a f. like that!	GOUN	380:78
It's f. that gives…perspective	DEGEN	270:5
no fear of any f.	FAWC	331:52
nothing like the f. of a close friend	CAREY	199:64
not the effort or the f.	EMPS	326:8
political lives…end in f.	POWE	693:60
redeems from utter f.	FIELD	335:11
splendid f. to do the impossible	FAUL	331:43
triumph of f.	RYAN	736:54
What other people…call f.	WINF	949:94
With f. comes f.	HELL	407:31
Women can't forgive f.	CHEK	218:15
failures f. are almost as important	AGAS	9:86
f. are ultimately f.	MURD	626:64
fain Where f., f. I would sleep?	BALL	58:57
faineant A f. government	TROL	898:40
faint f. at best, the beams	POPE	688:36
f. in the day of adversity	BIBLE	105:92
f. in the light	TENN	876:25
Felt f.—and never dared uplift	SHEL	813:88
They f. on hill	TENN	872:40
faint-hearted Farewell, f.…king	SHAK	760:2
fainting F. in coils	CARR	203:79
fair a F. Deal	TRUM	899:77
all the rest, though f. and wise	SHEL	815:44
as f. a name	SHAK	776:10
black man or a f. man	ADDI	6:23
cheating is f.	FRY	353:29
come in for the f.	HOUS	431:46
Disguise f. nature	SHAK	775:74
f. and f., and twice so f.	PEELE	672:69
f. and free competition	RICA	712:81
f. art thou	BURNS	180:50
F., fat, and forty	SCOTT	754:70
f. friend, you never can be old	SHAK	802:74
F. is foul, and foul is f.	SHAK	795:97
f., my love	BIBLE	107:45
f. sex is your department	DOYLE	297:67
F. stood the wind for France	DRAY	298:94
f. terms and a villain's mind	SHAK	769:87
f., the chaste	SHAK	779:87
f. to everybody	APPL	30:90
f. words…in foulest letters?	SHAK	773:96
got by f. means or foul	ORWE	653:6
held to the f.	BURNS	178:3
How f. and how pleasant	BIBLE	107:48
how sweet and f.	WALL	918:55
if it prove f. weather	SUCK	858:72
in the f. and the market place	PARN	665:46
lot is fallen unto me in a f. ground	BOOK	148:8
Ludlow f.	HOUS	432:58
most divinely f.	TENN	869:75
never yet f. woman	SHAK	792:6
None but the brave deserves the f.	DRYD	303:28
no one more f. and excellent	SPEN	838:32
Nothing is f. or good alone	EMER	324:50
Outward be f.	CHUR	224:56
remained at 'set f.'	BENN	81:64
Say, lingering f.!	CRAS	254:83
settle what's right and f.	HUGH	436:47
so f. that they called him the lady	AUBR	42:58
The rose looks f.	SHAK	801:52
Though this was f.	BURNS	180:49
fair-and-square stole it f. a. s.	HAYA	402:21
fairies beginning of f.	BARR	65:85
f. at the bottom of our garden	FYLE	356:97
I don't believe in f.	BARR	65:86
large sale among the f.	HEMI	409:63
fairin thou'lt get thy f.!	BURNS	179:30
fairness Nocht is your f.	HENR	412:22
fairy Airy, f. Lilian	TENN	869:74
as if a passing f. had hiccuped	DICK	279:18
By f. hands their knell is rung	COLL	237:72
calls up the realms of f.	BYRON	190:18
Come not near our F. Queen	SHAK	767:31
f. kind of writing	DRYD	303:20
I mean by f. lamps	WOOD	953:9
moral tests and tasks set in f. tales	ELKIN	322:16
night-tripping f. had exchanged	SHAK	770:26
no one ever marries in a f. tale	KING	488:53
serve the F. Queen	SHAK	767:25
ugliest f. in the world	KING	488:51
fairy-godmother author's f. g.	LUCAS	541:54
fairy-gold We dealt in f.-g.	QUEN	702:8
fairyland childhood…f.-l.	BOGAN	144:94
everybody's got a F.	TRAV	896:90
faith add f., Add virtue, patience	MILT	607:72
America…was an object of f.	RABAN	703:4
author and finisher of our f.	BIBLE	129:43
basis of true f.	VIDAL	912:92
By f., and f. alone	TENN	873:54
comes i' f. full sail	CONG	241:64
died in f.	BIBLE	129:40
dissent is an act of f.	FULB	355:62
Draw near with f.	BOOK	147:65
dying for a f.	THAC	880:36
f., and…fire	ARNO	36:7
F.…belief without evidence	BIER	134:77
F. comprises	TILL	891:14
F. consists in believing	VOLT	914:41
f. finally free itself	CUPI	258:86
f. gives new light	TAYL	868:58
f., hope, charity	BIBLE	126:52
F., I have been a truant	SHAK	759:76
f. in fundamental human rights	UNIT	905:9
f. in the difficultest points	BROW	165:52
f. in the imperishable dignity of man	CARL	200:86

faithful

f. in the magic of official forms	WAUGH 924:88	f. over a few things	BIBLE 119:33	Followed f. lights	DRYD 303:11
F.' is a fine invention	DICK 283:32	f. to thee, Cynara!	DOWS 296:36	idle and most f. imposition	SHAK 789:12
f. I search for	SAND 741:11	give…a f. account of men	ELIOT 315:20	If she be f.	SHAK 789:23
F. is the state of	TILL 891:15	moderately f. wife	SHAW 808:48	In friendship f.	DRYD 302:74
f. is the substance of things	BIBLE 129:39	So f. in love	SCOTT 752:21	man who is f. to his friends	BERK 84:35
F., like a jackal	MELV 585:56	Translations…are seldom f.	CAMP 194:58	Ninety-nine times…is f.	EINS 313:77
F. may be defined briefly	MENC 586:87	**faithfulness** great is thy f.	BIBLE 110:26	origin of all f. science	HAZL 404:52
f. melteth into blood	SHAK 773:26	**faith-healer** f.-h. of Deal	ANON 24:13	prov'd true before, Prove f. again	BUTL 185:83
f. of a Tory	POWE 693:59	**faithless** Be not f., but believing	BIBLE 124:68	reject as if absolutely f.	DESC 274:94
f. of Christ	BOOK 148:77	**faiths** f. and empires gleam	SHEL 816:57	reject it as being f.	AYER 48:5
f., so that I could remove mountains	BIBLE 126:52	fanatically dedicated to…religious f.	PIRS 679:90	Ring out the f.	TENN 875:95
F.'s transcendent dower	WORD 961:43	men's f. are wafer-cakes	SHAK 775:70	they have committed f. report	SHAK 774:55
f. that right makes might	LINC 529:8	**fake** can't f. quality	BURR 181:66	thoughts dally with f. surmise	MILT 599:92
F., that's as well said	SWIFT 863:72	freedom…was…a f.	ORWE 653:22	true poet…from the f.	POUND 692:36
F….the Pierless Bridge	DICK 284:45	learned to f. that	GOLD 377:37	trying to think everything f.	DESC 274:95
f. unfaithful kept	TENN 877:54	Only something f. could work	HANKS 396:85	with love f.	YEATS 965:7
f.…we can make it	DICK 277:33	**fakest** survival of the f.	DOWD 296:31	**falsehood** category of truth and f.	AYER 48:8
f. without doubt	UNAM 905:3	**fakir** posing as a f.	CHUR 225:79	cuts f. like a knife	GURN 390:1
F. without works is dead	BIBLE 130:54	**falcon** be a f. and go free	DUNC 307:11	distinguishing truth from f.	DESC 274:93
For him, f.	BALZ 61:98	dapple-dawn-drawn f.	HOPK 428:76	f., cowardice, and poor descent	SHAK 759:69
fought for Queen and F.	TENN 879:99	f. cannot hear the falconer	YEATS 966:24	Let her and F. grapple	MILT 600:7
Found f. in me	DRAY 298:96	Gentle as f.	SKEL 824:29	strife of Truth with F.	LOWE 539:3
fright my f.	DRYD 303:11	**Falklands** F. held a mirror up	RABAN 703:1	to express lying or f.	SWIFT 862:48
future states…are left to f.	BYRON 190:13	F. thing…fight between two bald men	BORG 151:60	unfurnish'd Of f.	DRYD 301:59
genial f.	WORD 959:99	**fall** Another thing to f.	SHAK 787:51	what a goodly outside f. hath!	SHAK 769:84
gift of f.	JOHN 456:72	by dividing we f.	DICK 284:57	**falsehoods** f. to deceive the public	STEF 844:53
good fight of f.	BIBLE 129:24	Created…half to f.	POPE 687:81	f. which interest dictates	JOHN 460:84
have f. as a grain of mustard	BIBLE 118:9	dead man is the best f. guy	CHAN 213:92	**falseness** f. in all our impressions	RUSK 733:90
have kept the f.	BIBLE 129:30	decline and f.	GIBB 366:2	salutary pleasure in proving their f.	DARW 263:56
heresies…explosions of f.	BREN 158:97	despairing posture of his f.	POE 683:83	**falser** f. than vows made in wine	SHAK 779:3
impossibilities…for an active f.	BROW 165:51	dew shall weep thy f. tonight	HERB 414:80	**falsetto** curious f. voice	STRA 857:42
increase Catholic f.	VAZD 910:43	do not want to f.	HUGO 437:67	**falsifiable** statement…must be f.	POPP 689:61
In f. and hope	POPE 687:85	f., and not rise again	BIBLE 108:66	**falsity** regions of sin and f.	MILT 600:11
inmost f. is overthrown	SASS 746:97	f. flat on your face	THUR 890:77	**falter** hesitate and f. life away	ARNO 34:93
just shall live by f.	BIBLE 125:2	f. half in love	SALI 740:74	**fame** advances without coveting f.	SUN 859:93
kept f. with me	HARDY 397:30	f. of a prince	ANON 20:30	ancient and prophetic f.	MILT 602:62
lamp of f.	WORD 962:47	f. of the last civilization	READ 708:96	by verse seek f.	SIDN 820:51
life of doubt diversified by f.	BROW 168:39	f. out with those we love	TENN 872:36	claim to literary f.	BENN 80:56
like an arch, is f.	MILL 594:76	f. through the air	GOLD 375:74	Cromwell, damned to everlasting f.!	POPE 687:90
losing or regaining f.	FITZ 337:75	F. to thy prayers	SHAK 773:99	F. and rumour	JONS 467:56
lost f. in individual endeavour	CARL 200:82	fear no f.	BUNY 174:82	F. and tranquillity are two	MONT 614:25
make room for f.	KANT 473:25	great was the f. of it	BIBLE 116:56	f. can never heal	AYTO 48:13
man's f. in himself	SHAW 806:89	haughty spirit before a f.	BIBLE 105:79	f. did not delay	DRAY 298:95
may we bring f.	THAT 881:54	If he f. in	SHAK 771:35	F. is a food	DOBS 289:78
more f. in honest doubt	TENN 874:92	If only we might f.	ANON 24:27	F. is a powerful aphrodisiac	GREE 386:16
my cast-iron f.	STEV 853:81	If your ceiling should f. down	SMITH 828:96	F. is based on what people say	DUDEK 305:74
My f. shall wax	DANI 262:30	less likely to f.	GAY 362:14	f. is in the song	CARM 202:46
My staff of f.	RALE 705:44	Life is a horizontal f.	COCT 233:87	F. is no plant	MILT 599:87
necessary…he hold the Catholic F.	BOOK 146:44	meditated on the F.	BETJ 89:43	f. is shrewdly gored	SHAK 787:40
no f. in human perfectibility	POE 683:85	No paradise, no f.	SNYD 832:91	F. is the spur	MILT 599:86
no f. in physic	JONS 467:50	nowhere to f.	ALAN 10:17	f., of valour	MARL 572:3
no need for the f.	HOFF 421:24	pride comes before a f.	WELD 928:82	F.'s eternal beadroll	SPEN 839:52
Non-violence…first article of my f.	GAND 359:59	Rome alone can make Rome f.	BELL 76:42	F.'s luscious pot	RICK 715:29
not an amiable f.	CARL 201:24	should happen to f.	SCOTT 753:39	F. without…money	COUP 248:39
not f., but mere Philosophy	BROW 165:65	Soar not too high to f.	MASS 581:72	Farewel to a' our Scottish f.	BURNS 179:40
not found so great f.	BIBLE 116:57	some by virtue f.	SHAK 787:54	first alike in f.!	LOVE 538:80
O thou of little f.	BIBLE 117:1	take heed lest he f.	BIBLE 126:45	frailty hath thy f.	NASHE 632:92
O ye of little f.?	BIBLE 116:61	though free to f.	MILT 603:78	gate to good f.	BACON 50:60
reward your f. in us	SMITH 829:10	voices dying with a dying f.	ELIOT 316:63	general achieves f.	TS 900:6
Science…a f. as fanatical as any	BARZ 67:39	we f. and get crushed	DAY 267:28	genius…not to purchase f.	DRYD 301:45
sea of f.	ARNO 33:66	**fallacies** science is…exploded f.	RAND 706:54	great was his f.	EGAN 313:65
shield of f.	BIBLE 128:95	**fallacy** f.…about winning	BLAN 141:48	grow great in f.	DIBD 276:28
simple f. than Norman blood	TENN 871:10	f. of retrospective determinism	BEND 78:12	Let f., that all hunt	SHAK 763:99
stand fast in the f.	BIBLE 127:64	Pathetic F.	RUSK 733:90	live by f.	SPEN 839:49
still by f. he trod	LIND 530:17	principle…suspect some f.	DARW 263:59	Long life to thy f.	SCOTT 754:81
suspension of disbelief…poetic f.	COLE 236:44	**fallen** f. from grace	BIBLE 127:80	love and f. to nothingness so sink	KEATS 475:78
take thy word for f.	SHAK 798:84	Greece…though f., great!	BYRON 187:40	Man dreams of f.	TENN 877:46
test of our f.	LLOY 533:73	How are the mighty f.	BIBLE 96:42	no one shall work for f.	KIPL 490:15
there is no f.	KIER 485:1	How art thou f.	BIBLE 108:64	Physicians of the utmost f.	BELL 76:59
there is yet f.	ELIOT 320:57	**falling** feeling I'm f.	FERL 333:90	pursued f. always in the hope	STAEL 841:94
times of f. as best	SMITH 830:38	Part of a moon was f.	FROST 352:92	Rather use than f.	TENN 877:47
triumphs of f.	RUNC 731:50	without f. over	FREE 349:44	servants of f.	BACON 51:83
truth of our f.	JOHN 456:79	**fallows** Russet lawns and f. grey	MILT 597:45	that is f.	BERR 87:2
turning…people to our holy f.	COLU 239:91	**Falls** foaminess of the F.	SALA 739:70	the desire of f.	TENN 877:57
unshakeable f. in…enterprise	BURT 181:72	**false** Believe f. teachers	SHAK 803:98	verse the f. enrols	DONNE 292:45
walk by f., not by sight	BIBLE 127:69	be not f. to others	BACON 52:4	write for money or f.	MOORE 617:83
was of the f.	AMIS 16:36	Beware of f. prophets	BIBLE 115:53	**famed** As she is f. to do	KEATS 478:48
wears his f. but as the fashion	SHAK 773:17	Ere I am f. to you	OHAG 648:8	**familiar** Don't let us be f. or fond	CONG 241:74
When f. is lost	WHIT 938:18	every individuality is…a f. step	SCHO 748:55	F. in his mouth	SHAK 776:91
Where there is doubt, f.	FRAN 347:99	Everything is f.	BECK 72:48	**familiarity** F. breeds contempt	TWAIN 903:75
With Punic f.	SALL 740:94	f. definition of the situation	MERT 589:54	**families** All f. are silly	HOLL 423:53
with Thee in f.	HAMM 394:55	F. face must hide	SHAK 796:25	and there are f.	THAT 881:66
faithful Be thou f. unto death	BIBLE 131:91	f. gallop of verses	SHAK 779:90	begin our public affection in our f.	BURKE 176:49
called F. and True	BIBLE 132:19	f. ideas prevail as to woman	STAN 842:13	best-regulated f.	DICK 280:52
f. friend is the medicine	BIBLE 113:84	f. of heart	SHAK 802:78	branch of…antediluvian f.	CONG 240:46
f. in that which is least	BIBLE 121:95	f. sincere	POPE 687:95	but two f. in the world	CERV 211:48
		f. to any man	SHAK 781:54	F.! I hate you!	GIDE 367:21

fast

happy f. resemble each other	TOLS 894:51	hopeless f. feigned	TENN 872:43	farthing for a f. less	ADDI 7:56
in the best-regulated f.	NORTH 641:61	keep your f. free	HOUS 431:38	never pay a f.	CROM 255:21
Mothers of large f.	BELL 76:54	not expressed in f.	SHAK 781:52	threw in two mites, which make a f.	BIBLE 120:61
sensibility…from…large f.	COUP 248:33	now the f. passes by	HOUS 431:40	two sparrows sold for a f.?	BIBLE 116:71
setteth the solitary in f.	BIBLE 101:81	of most excellent f.	SHAK 784:63	farts the f. of blue-green algae	ACKER 3:58
family appalling dangers of f. life	HUXL 441:73	'Orses and dorgs is some men's f.	DICK 280:47	Three f. and a raspberry	BARB 63:47
beautiful f. talk	COMP 239:99	pleasing to the f.	ADDI 7:36	when the courtesan f.	ANON 22:69
be so in a f.?	ASTE 39:4	proud f. never taught	CRAB 251:24	fascinated f. by the form	JAMES 451:58
bread for the f.	LEWIS 526:54	unsound f. and self-contradictory	BACON 50:47	**fascination** f. of an ancient rite	SAND 742:33
brought up a large f.	GOLD 376:89	young man's f.	TENN 871:11	f. of one slowing down	GIBB 367:6
character of a f.	STER 848:26	**fangs** climes but nurse the cruellest f.	MELV 585:67	f. which draws me	HEDIN 406:4
conduct of every private f.	SMITH 827:85	**fans** between the F. and me	KING 488:56	maximum f. can continue	DIOR 286:3
each member of the f.	FRAME 346:77	fanclub with only two f.	HENRI 411:9	**fascism** Every communist has a f.	SPARK 836:73
every f. in America	JOHN 458:18	f. into their hand	BALL 59:71	Every woman adores a F.	PLATH 681:34
exceedingly clannish f.	SHAW 811:33	**fantasies** compulsions, the f.	LEGU 520:10	F. accepts the individual	MUSS 628:96
f. as an institution	MILLS 595:7	Mrs Forthby in his f.	SHAR 806:73	masked by the new macho f.	WHITE 934:27
f. denied both stories	SAKI 739:58	robbed of his f.	FONT 341:73	unless F. was defeated	SPEN 837:13
f. does not need to do	ROCK 720:28	Such shaping f.	SHAK 767:44	**Fascist** speak of the F. objective	ORWE 653:20
f. from sinking their property	MOOD 615:54	teach elegant f.	TOBIN 892:25	**Fascists** F. are sincere	DRIB 299:5
F. indivisibility	ROTH 728:91	thousand f. Begin	MILT 598:68	**fashion** as to its f. and material	HAWT 402:7
f. joke that when	ROTH 727:79	tree that f. had planted	HERZL 416:24	cannot long one f. entertain	DRAY 298:91
f. life is all the life she knows	SHAW 809:88	**fantastic** light f. round	MILT 598:66	dedicated follower of f.	DAVI 264:80
f.—that dear octopus	SMITH 828:98	more f. the world becomes	HUXL 441:58	deformed thief this f. is	SHAK 774:46
F.!… the home of all social evil	STRI 857:53	most f. and impracticable	SNOW 832:88	faith but as the f.	SHAK 773:17
f. traditions	IGNA 445:16	On the light f.	MILT 597:43	faithful…in my f.	DOWS 296:36
f. with the wrong members	ORWE 654:34	**fantasy** all f. and veneer	GALL 358:44	F…a despot	BIER 134:78
fine a f. he comes from	LEE 519:91	f. is…better than reality	LAGER 504:71	F. anticipates	CASS 207:72
fruitful source of f. discontent	BEET 74:7	nothing but vain f.	SHAK 765:72	f. as in it	TWAIN 901:30
incest holds the f. together	INNIS 446:45	substitute for the f.	ALBEE 11:22	f. a victim of me	MERT 589:53
influence…than that of our own f.	CHUR 224:50	suspicion, rumour, f.	RICH 713:95	F.—a word which knaves and fools	CHUR 224:53
insecurity…in a single-parent f.	ELLW 323:39	**far** Be it f. from me	BIBLE 96:24	F. can be bought	CHASE 216:51
member of the f.…is happier	FALU 329:11	Britain calls the F. East	MENZ 587:19	F. constantly begins and ends	HAZL 403:35
not lugged into F. Rows	WODE 952:39	F. may be sought	SKEL 824:29	F….guide of fools	CRAB 251:27
not of war…but of f.	CHILD 222:16	f. side of baldness	SMITH 829:16	F. is architecture	CHAN 214:3
organisation of the f.	MARX 579:30	how f. one can go too f.	COCT 233:84	F. is born by small facts	SCHI 747:22
other members of the f.	OZICK 658:42	No matter how f. away	SCEVE 746:17	F. is free speech	LURIE 542:66
Others have their f.	CATH 208:94	so near and yet so f.	TENN 874:94	F. is made to become unfashionable	CHAN 214:98
patriarchy's…institution is the f.	MILL 595:99	**farce** dreariness of his f.	WEBB 925:6	F. is more tyrannical at Paris	CHES 219:43
put your f. last	HUMP 439:10	F. is nearer tragedy	COLE 236:52	F. is only the attempt	HOLM 424:80
sell members of my f.	ANNE 20:16	f., melodrama, tragedy	SCHL 747:35	F. is something barbarous	SANT 743:40
study of f. portraits	DOYLE 297:65	second time as f.	BARN 64:70	F. is the image of an age	LAGE 504:70
stuffy Victorian f.	ORWE 654:33	the second as f.	MARX 579:36	F. is what one wears oneself	WILDE 942:12
tense and peculiar f.	BEER 74:99	wine was a f.	POWE 693:44	F….produces beautiful things	COCT 233:88
we, your blood f.	SPEN 836:83	**farcical** marriage is the most f.	BEAU 70:8	f.'s brightest arts	GOLD 376:3
when the F. dines alone	SWIFT 862:59	**fardels** who would f. bear	TWAIN 852:53	f. she detests	SHAK 786:5
Women leave the Royal F.	YORK 968:49	Who would these f. bear	SHAK 782:7	F. should be a game	QUANT 701:4
famine f. grew, and locusts came	THOM 883:9	**fare** F. thee well, great heart	SHAK 772:67	f. to go naked	MONT 613:12
f. in his face	CHUR 224:52	F. ye a' weel, ye bitches!	KAME 472:13	f. wears out more apparel	SHAK 774:47
F. is in thy cheeks	SHAK 766:12	F. you well	SHAK 778:61	fetch over a f.	JONS 466:44
f. was sore in the land	BIBLE 93:45	value not your bill of f.	SWIFT 861:32	for the f., I believe	SWIFT 863:68
Fire, Blood, and F.	HENR 411:12	**farewell** Ae f., and then for ever	BURNS 179:34	garment out of f.	SHAK 803:96
from f. and death	DARW 263:53	F., all joys	GIBB 367:7	highflyer at F.	DICK 283:15
Gaunt F. never shall approach	BYRON 190:20	F…degenerate king	SHAK 760:2	high Roman f.	SHAK 795:85
live with f.	JEFF 435:13	F., my friends	DUNC 307:6	independent of f.	GASK 361:84
not a f. of bread	BIBLE 111:54	F., my poor hands	RACH 704:25	intellectual f.	CONN 243:18
famines there shall be f.	BIBLE 118:29	F. sadness	ELUA 324:45	never cared for f.	BAIL 55:81
famous can't be f.…be notorious.	MAHA 559:29	F.—thou art too dear	SHAK 802:67	never out of f.	FULL 355:83
f. for being f.	ASHB 37:60	F….too lately known	DRYD 302:3	not for the f. of these times	SHAK 778:72
f. for fifteen minutes	WARH 920:7	no sadness of f.	TENN 879:6	Nothing else holds f.	SHAK 787:34
F. for his laugh	FLAU 339:28	This is f.	TOJO 893:41	One had as good be…out of the F.	CIBB 227:25
f. without ability	SHAW 807:99	Too-late, F.	ROSS 727:63	present f. is always handsome	FULL 356:87
f. witty saying	THUR 890:90	Without a solemn f.	MIDD 590:73	Quite out of f.	SHAK 787:38
found myself f.	BYRON 191:35	**Farish** Miss F.…in the way	WHAR 933:6	seek to f. events	NAPO 630:51
Let us now praise f. men	BIBLE 113:10	**farm** committed to a f.	THOR 888:31	strange f. of forsaking	WYATT 964:91
make f.	OATES 643:14	cultivated f.	GOLD 376:97	Style has gone out of f.	STRO 857:55
mark of many f. people	HELL 408:47	in a loft in Salt Lake F.	THOM 884:35	tell you the leading f.	RUSK 733:6
My uncle was f.	SPEN 837:9	language of f., city and love	ENGLE 326:16	the f. after the plague	PEPYS 674:3
that f. harmony	YEATS 965:6	sold my f.	SHAK 776:99	vain to mislike the current f.	FULL 355:86
'twas a f. victory	SOUT 835:47	When a man takes a f.	PARN 665:46	world reappear in one f.	MARX 579:36
You can get awful f.	HART 399:63	**farmer** f. without fields	PARK 665:42	world's new f.	SHAK 763:6
fan f. spread and streamers out	CONG 241:64	**farmers** embattled f. stood	EMER 324:48	worn-out poetical f.	ELIOT 320:58
with thy mystic f.	HERR 415:6	f. as they passed	MORG 619:31	**fashionable** f. female life	SPEKE 836:82
fanatic f. for the externality	LEWIS 527:72	f….well pleased with constant gain	CRAB 252:37	f. gentleman	ALSOP 15:12
f….great leader…just entering	BROUN 163:19	toil of the f.' wives	GARL 360:75	f. woman wears clothes	QUANT 701:3
fanatics F. have their dreams	KEATS 476:97	**farmhouse** damp front f.	THOM 884:47	For an idea ever to be f.	SANT 743:42
fancies f. about the things	HARR 399:54	**farms** fields of millions of f.	HOOV 427:42	**fashioned** F. so slenderly	HOOD 426:33
F. fond with gaudy	MILT 597:49	flocks and f. and heroes	VIRG 914:28	**fashions** best of our f.	VEBL 910:45
how many childish f.	SHIP 818:15	for him that f.	CRAB 252:30	f. all sins on him	WEBS 927:50
When you set your f. free	BROW 169:84	what f. are those?	HOUS 431:51	F….on only induced epidemics	SHAW 809:78
fanclub a lie with a f.	GASS 361:89	**farmyard** human society from the f.	SHAW 809:87	f. of gentlemen	ALSOP 15:12
Love is a f.	HENRI 411:9	louder…in its own f.	TROL 898:37	In Words, as F.	POPE 685:22
fancy agreeable f.	STEV 851:12	**farrago** of superlative nonsense	CHUR 224:65	know his nature and f.	BACON 53:33
call the Apollo a f. piece?	EMER 324:66	**fart** can't f. and chew gum	JOHN 458:16	laughs at the old f.	THOR 888:35
E'er F. you consult	FRAN 348:13	F. for the Bishop of Cork!	ANON 23:96	Old f. please me best	SHAK 762:69
f. cannot cheat so well	KEATS 478:48	f. in a gale of wind	BARN 64:63	to fit this year's f.	HELL 408:42
f. from a flower-bell	BROW 168:38	Love is the f.	SUCK 858:71	**fast** f. down, and…f. up	OWENS 658:41
f. of the mass of men	BAGE 54:68	**farther** the f. you get	PHEL 676:49	f., fiery, and true	DAVIS 266:9

faster

grew f. and furious	BURNS 179:29	meteor Ever hung my f.	MIDD 590:81	F. which is in heaven	BIBLE 115:55
He that drinks f.	FRAN 348:9	mock the patriot's f.	INGR 446:36	F. which is in heaven	BIBLE 117:89
More grievous...than a hermit's f.	KEATS 476:6	modern poet's f.	HOOD 426:38	F. which is in heaven give	
Move f. and break things	ZUCK 970:18	my life, my f.	TENN 876:28	good things	BIBLE 115:51
No dog can go as f.	FLAN 338:7	no armour against f.	SHIR 819:20	F. which is in heaven is perfect	BIBLE 115:39
one takes the music too f.	SAINT 739:49	no f. that cannot be surmounted	CAMUS 195:85	F. will come	TENN 872:37
poor, who will not f. in peace	CRAB 252:35	No gifts...have conquered f.	ARNO 33:60	f. worked with a horse-plough	HEAN 404:68
To be human...we must stand f.	BOLT 145:13	our pride, our folly, or our f.	DENH 272:61	Full fathom five thy f. lies	SHAK 803:16
faster Light thinks it travels f.	PRAT 694:64	Politics and the f. of mankind	CAMUS 195:81	glorify your F. which is in heaven	BIBLE 114:29
fasting between a fou man and a f.	SCOTT 754:71	power above The stars and f.	BUTL 185:88	God...an exalted f.	FREUD 350:60
f., for a good man's love	SHAK 779:2	proclaimed the f. that smote	ROBE 717:72	had a pig-headed f.	POUND 691:94
fasts come in f. divine!	HOPK 428:68	Read your f.	THOR 889:40	had it from my f.	SHAK 804:40
fat art waxen f.	BIBLE 95:1	scorn of f.	DRYD 301:56	Hath the rain a f.?	BIBLE 99:16
Butter merely makes us f.	GOER 374:56	stern hand of f.	LLOY 533:72	Have we not all one f.	BIBLE 112:62
Fair, f., and forty	SCOTT 754:70	the f. of peace	OBAMA 644:47	heavenly F. feedeth them	BIBLE 115:45
f. and flourishing	BIBLE 102:98	torrent of his f.?	JOHN 459:48	his f. saw him, and had compassion	BIBLE 121:91
f. and greasy citizens	SHAK 778:67	when f. summons	DRYD 300:42	Honour thy f. and thy mother	BIBLE 94:66
f. and grows old	SHAK 771:45	why should they know their f.?	GRAY 383:48	How like f.	BARR 65:4
f. man demanding elbow room	WAUGH 924:87	will...overruled by f.	MARL 574:37	I am like no f.	SHAK 760:20
f. of the land	BIBLE 93:46	won't triumph over his f.	KOES 495:28	inherited...melancholy from my f.	JOHN 462:30
f., oily man of God	THOM 887:5	**fates** F., we will know your pleasures	SHAK 777:29	it is I, your f.	BELL 75:30
I'd like to get f.	DIAZ 276:26	hostages to the f.	LUCAN 541:47	Labour is the F....of Wealth	PETTY 676:46
Imprisoned in every f. man	CONN 243:13	masters of their f.	SHAK 776:9	Lead us, Heavenly F.	EDME 312:55
maketh the bones f.	BIBLE 104:77	O f., come, come	SHAK 768:49	Like as a f. pitieth	BIBLE 102:9
men about me that are f.	SHAK 776:12	What f. impose	SHAK 760:14	Lord and F. of mankind	WHIT 938:24
no sex if you're f.	GIOV 372:18	wills and f....contrary run	SHAK 783:24	loveth f. or mother	BIBLE 116:73
November, he full gross and f.	SPEN 840:63	**fathead** F.-h. poet that nobody reads	CHES 221:8	lusts of the f. ye will do	BIBLE 123:42
Outside every f. man	AMIS 16:35	**fatheaded** f....wash-out of a cock-up	ANON 26:10	man leave his f. and his mother	BIBLE 91:90
resolved to grow f.	DRYD 299:17	**fatheads** famous f., old wives	MACD 550:39	mighty God, The everlasting F.	BIBLE 107:60
trouble is you get f.	BARN 64:65	**father** a f., that's what matters most	BROWN 164:24	murdered his mother and f.	LEVA 525:17
Who's your f. friend	BRUM 170:92	After the funeral, my f.	LAWR 513:69	My f. is deceased	MARL 573:13
fatal f. man	THAC 880:32	ascend unto my F.	BIBLE 124:66	My f. was a slave	ROBE 717:76
f. to good film-making	CHAN 213:89	ashamed to be my f.'s child!	SHAK 769:90	my f. wept	BLAKE 140:18
most f. complaint of all	HILT 418:65	ashes of his f.	MACA 545:45	My noble f.	SHAK 789:96
sincerity...absolutely f.	WILDE 940:59	As my poor f. used to say	HERB 412:43	Neither f. nor lover	ROET 722:60
fatality no exterior f.	SAINT 738:31	As the F. knoweth me	BIBLE 123:45	no man cometh unto the F.	BIBLE 123:53
fate A flame f. dares not move	PHIL 676:53	bed fell on my f.	THUR 890:67	O my F., if it be possible	BIBLE 119:42
and what I will is f.	MILT 605:29	better off dead...your wife and my f.	CHAN 213:88	one way to speak to my f.	SAINT 738:47
architect of his own f.	CLAU 229:73	born where my f. lived	SITT 923:93	one would want as a f.	WEST 933:99
bone to pick with F.	NASH 631:76	boy with his f.	IHIM 445:19	on the ground without your F.	BIBLE 116:71
books have their own f.	TERE 879:16	cannot have God for his f.	CYPR 260:8	Our F. which art in heaven	BIBLE 115:42
breathless on thy f.!	LONG 535:27	children of your F.	BIBLE 115:38	Our F. who art	PARRA 665:49
build that nation's f.	BLAKE 141:28	Church which prays 'Our F.'	BONH 145:21	person cannot choose his f.	FRIS 351:85
by warning to avoid his f.?	SPEN 838:38	decrepit f. takes delight	SHAK 801:49	Praise F., Son, and Holy Ghost	KEN 480:84
common f. has linked us	BREZ 158:6	Deny thy f.	SHAK 765:79	pray to thy F.	BIBLE 115:41
coughed, and called it f.	ROBI 718:86	draft-dodging f.	ROTH 727:74	proceedeth from the F. and Son	BOOK 147:62
curse my f.	SHAK 800:46	electrical display of God the F.	ONEI 651:66	record...of our mother and f.	FRAME 346:77
customary f. of new truths	HUXL 443:8	even as a f.	BIBLE 104:53	remembered dead f.	NICH 636:71
Far away be that f.!	OVID 657:13	f. before him	SYMI 865:19	resembled My f.	SHAK 797:32
f. as a nation	HOFS 422:39	f....did not have the time	CIXO 227:43	Seek for thy noble f.	SHAK 780:34
F. cannot harm me	SMITH 831:60	f. drove them out	LOUI 537:64	Singing to F., Son	HOW 433:85
f. carries in her other hand	LAWR 514:91	F.! f.! where are you going?	BLAKE 139:91	stopped loving my f.	NIN 639:26
f. decreed that the cloak	WEBER 925:11	F., forgive them	BIBLE 122:7	tenderness of a f.	MORE 618:14
F....goes as it must	ANON 20:28	f. gave him a box	MACN 558:9	Thou art thy f.'s daughter	SHAK 778:63
F. hath held sway	AESC 8:77	f. had a chain of dry cleaners	BENN 80:54	though her f. be very rich	SHAK 761:58
f. in what I cannot fear	ROET 722:59	f. had a daughter	SHAK 786:99	throne of Denmark to thy f.	SHAK 780:31
f. of human civilization	LOVE 538:90	f. hath chastised you with whips	BIBLE 97:58	Thus his f. wept	BIBLE 93:39
f. of poetry	WALC 916:21	F. in Heaven	KIER 485:5	time not to become a f.	WHITE 935:43
F. often preserves the undoomed	ANON 20:29	f., into thy hands	BIBLE 122:10	To be a successful f.	HEMI 410:95
f. of this country depends	DISR 288:62	F. is rather vulgar	DICK 282:91	'twill come to my f. anon	AUBR 42:59
f. of those who toil	JOHN 460:67	f. lived his soul	CUMM 258:65	What would f. say	MANS 567:8
f. of unborn millions	WASH 921:27	f. moved through dooms of love	CUMM 258:64	where's their f. live	THOM 884:37
f. so enviously debars	MARV 577:96	f., nor a mother	MARG 570:61	who my f. was	SEXT 758:50
F.'s such a shrewish thing	CHAP 214:18	f. of English criticism	JOHN 463:72	will of my F. which is in heaven	BIBLE 115:55
F., Time, Occasion, Chance	SHEL 814:16	f. of his people	GIBB 366:94	will of my F. which is in heaven	BIBLE 117:89
F. tried to conceal him	HOLM 424:76	f. of knowledge	HIPP 419:70	Wisdom's heavenly F.	WORD 962:49
F. wrote her a...tragedy	BEER 73:73	F. of lights	BIBLE 130:49	wise f. that knows	SHAK 769:88
fears his f. too much	MONT 615:50	f. of many nations	BIBLE 125:8	wise son heareth his f.'s instruction	BIBLE 104:67
fits for f.	DRYD 303:18	f. of our dramatic poets	DRYD 300:26	without f. bred	MILT 597:49
For all our children's f.	KIPL 493:71	F. of Peace	DODD 289:93	You are old, F. William	SOUT 835:43
forced by f.	DRYD 304:37	f. of psychoanalysis	GREER 387:41	Your f. hath consented	SHAK 762:66
foulness of their f.	SASS 746:99	f. of the child cried out	BIBLE 120:59	your f., whom you love, dies	STOP 855:15
full measure of thy f.	CRANE 253:63	f. of the fatherless	BIBLE 101:81	**fatherland** There we have the F.!	MANN 566:77
Happiness was my f.	RIMB 716:51	f. or my mother	STER 847:20	**fatherless** fields of the f.	BIBLE 105:91
has no ill f.	WALL 918:61	f. should be as a god	SHAK 766:16	for the f., and for the widow	BIBLE 95:35
I hold f.	FORD 343:6	f. sold me	BLAKE 139:90	visit the f. and widows	BIBLE 130:52
In case it tempted F.	MCGO 552:79	F., Son and Holy Ghost	MCLE 554:23	**fathers** common revolt against the f.	COWL 250:80
It's a complex f.	JAMES 450:34	f.'s sword he has girded	MOORE 618:2	f....are incurable	DAVI 264:72
Jove and F. require	POPE 688:29	f. still reads the dictionary	SCAR 746:13	f. brought forth upon	LINC 529:9
limits of a vulgar f.	GRAY 385:92	f., the chariot of Israel	BIBLE 97:71	f. had a Paris	HUGO 437:61
made weak by time and f.	TENN 870:2	F....thou hadst none	BRAD 155:49	f., provoke not your children	BIBLE 128:93
makers of our f.	POPP 698:56	f....throwing rocks at the stork	BREC 157:87	f. that begat us	BIBLE 113:10
master of his f.	TENN 876:41	f. used to say	MOORE 617:79	f. would never...have dreamed	MARC 569:48
master of my f.	HENL 411:6	f. was self-made	ATWO 41:47	glory of children are their f.	BIBLE 105:80
matter what f. befalls me	MILNE 596:25	f. watched him across	MARQ 574:43	God of our F.	MILT 608:92
meet my f.	YEATS 966:22	F. which is in heaven	BIBLE 114:29	Hast all our f. led	DODD 289:91
men cannot suspend their f.	DEFOE 269:68	F. which is in heaven	BIBLE 115:38	Instead of thy f.	BOOK 149:16

1103 — feather-bed

learned of their f.	BIBLE 113:86	Fortune, that f. fools		Pity is lost in rage and f.	CARL 201:10
men liking their f.	BRAD 154:26	willing to exchange…their f.	JONS 467:63	pleasant situation of having no f.	CUMM 257:49
My f. can have it	THOM 884:29	**fawn** f., crossed with a Buick	ANDR 18:77	poise of hope and f.	MILT 599:73
not better than my f.	BIBLE 97:66	**fawning** How like a f. publican	NICH 636:77	Render…f. to whom f.	BIBLE 126:30
Our f. have…provided	QUIL 702:13	**fawns** fallow f. invisible go	SHAK 769:83	salvation with f. and trembling	BIBLE 128:98
revolts against its f.	MUMF 625:35	**FBI** F. are powerless to act	THOM 885:65	self-examination with…f.	ICHI 445:13
scenes his f. loved	CULL 257:44	Texas, the F., and hunting trophies	HOOV 427:54	sense by…echoes of f.	EVANS 328:69
slept with his f.	BIBLE 97:59	**fear** abolition of poverty and f.	KENN 482:33	so long as they f.	ACCI 2:18
so did their f. to the false prophets	BIBLE 120:73	Ah F.! Ah frantic F.!	HOOV 427:43	strange that men should f.	SHAK 777:22
turn the heart of the f.	BIBLE 112:66	always a cause for f.	COLL 237:74	The f. that kills	WORD 959:2
visit the sins of the f.	BOOK 147:59	arming me from f.	CRIC 254:91	There is a lurking f.	SAGAN 737:24
We need f. to realize	OBAMA 644:28	As if his f. still followed	BRON 162:75	there is not a word of f.	LAND 507:33
fathom canst not f. it	TENN 869:73	blanched with f.	SPEN 838:27	those with an irrational f. of life	CONN 242:96
Full f. five	SHAK 803:16	by means of pity and f.	SHAK 797:50	'Tis time to f.	SHAK 798:82
them that sleep…many a f. deep	CAMP 194:66	care lost Went all his f.	ARIS 31:23	walk in f. and dread	COLE 235:18
fathoms certain f. in the earth	SHAK 804:31	concessions of f.	MILT 602:57	weakness to lament or f.	SHAK 760:18
fifty f. deep	BALL 59:72	contempt of f.	BURKE 175:14	Well-founded f.	WOOD 954:1
fatigue F. makes women talk	LEWIS 526:46	do it with no show of f.	JONS 466:43	what we f. of death	SHAK 788:70
f. of adjectives	BROY 169:88	editor…need f. nothing	SHAK 775:71	whom shall I f.?	BIBLE 100:49
lover…dies from…f.	BART 66:26	'ergophobia', meaning 'f. or hatred	BENN 81:79	whom shall I f.?	BIBLE 132:30
physical f. than the painter	LEON 522:67	of work'	TYNAN 904:1	who will not f.?	BIBLE 111:51
the f. of judging for themselves	SHER 817:98	every day surmount a f.	EMER 325:92	Why f. death?	FROH 351:87
fatigued chanced to be f.	FORS 344:37	every f. hides a wish	MAMET 564:45	with religion and f.	JONS 467:62
fatness covered with f.	BIBLE 95:1	fate in what I cannot f.	ROET 722:59	**feared** f. by Spain, by France	SIXT 824:26
f. of these pursy times	SHAK 784:44	f. a day whose evil is upon		is it better to be loved than f.	MACH 552:93
let your soul delight itself in f.	BIBLE 109:96	the wing	KORAN 498:89	they that f. the LORD	BIBLE 112:64
fattening f. is the first duty	SPEKE 836:82	f. and awe	WORD 961:35	**fearful** F. and hostile behavior	FULB 355:63
illegal, immoral or f.	WOOL 956:44	f. attends her not	SHAK 775:71	f. thing to fall into the hands	BIBLE 129:38
fatter f. man trying to close in	AMIS 16:35	f. before him	BIBLE 103:3	goodness never f.	SHAK 788:71
fatuity f. of idiots	SMITH 830:46	F….helps you to race longer and		O f. meditation!	SHAK 801:57
fatuous one term is as f. as another	ROOS 725:21	live longer	SENNA 757:31	Upon a f. summons	SHAK 780:30
fatuus Better an ignis f.	DICK 284:49	f. in a handful of dust	ELIOT 317:96	Why are ye f.	BIBLE 116:61
Faulkner read…Proust, F., Joyce	VARG 908:26	f. intensified the love	JACK 450:27	**fearing** f. to attempt	SHAK 787:49
fault clever to a f.	BROW 168:40	f. is a great teacher	IGNA 445:15	**fearless** But thou liv'st f.	HERR 415:3
Every man has his f.	SHAK 791:77	f. is f. itself	ROOS 724:6	F. minds climb	SHAK 760:15
f. being greater	LANY 508:56	F. is the great mover	BART 66:17	**fears** delivered me from all my f.	BIBLE 100:55
f.…is not in our stars	SHAK 776:9	f. it would make me conservative	FROST 352:12	direction of our f.	BERR 87:95
Faultless to a f.	BROW 169:74	f. no ill	SCOT 754:85	dispelled their f.	MILT 602:48
f. of our politicians	TROL 898:40	f. of being an absurdity	FIND 336:45	f. do make us traitors	SHAK 797:58
f. of the Dutch	CANN 197:10	f. of every man	JONS 468:92	f. may be liars	CLOU 232:48
f. though great, yet he	LANY 508:54	F. of Fifty	JONG 466:40	F., prejudices, misconceptions	LLOY 533:78
Find not f. with one another	KORAN 498:86	f. of finding something worse	BELL 77:61	f. shall be in the way	BIBLE 106:36
had only one f.	THUR 891:10	f. of letting people down	WILK 944:62	f. that I may cease to be	KEATS 475:77
He is all f.	TENN 877:51	f. of little men	ALLI 14:6	fifty hopes and f.	BROW 168:38
hide the f. I see	POPE 688:28	f. of one evil	BOIL 144:2	Humanity with all its f.	LONG 535:27
hint a f.	POPE 687:3	f. of Political economy	SELL 756:15	its joys and f.	BROW 960:13
His worst f.	SHAK 773:2	f. of something after death	TWAIN 902:63	leave us in pale f.	WEBS 926:21
least f. distorts it	YOUR 968:57	f. of suffering injustice	LARO 510:99	longer shivering under f.	MILT 606:65
never needs to admit a f.	BALZ 60:92	f. of the dead	ACKR 3:62	nightly f.	GRAY 385:80
no kind of f.	GILB 469:50	f. of the Lord is the beginning	BIBLE 102:19	no human f.	WORD 957:64
only f. is that I am alive	MAP 569:42	f. rationalized away	MAIL 560:52	nostalgic about old f.?	ACKR 3:63
suffer through no f. of their own	ELIZ 322:10	f. that the British electorate	WEBB 925:10	old f. about our sissiness	WHITE 934:27
Whose f.? Whose but his	MILT 503:78	f. that the Russian government	HERZ 416:23	producing f. and anxieties	KING 487:32
faultless Faultily f.	TENN 875:14	f. the birds of prey	SHAK 787:50	Prosperity is not without many f.	BACON 51:65
faults America has colossal f.	CUMM 258:60	f. thy nature	SHAK 796:13	secret…griefs and f.	BACON 51:67
blush at your f.	FLET 341:57	f. to hate	SHAK 765:59	To him that ever f.	SHAK 789:20
England…With all her f.	CHUR 224:61	f. toward me is taught	BIBLE 108:72	when f.…were rife	VAUG 909:38
England, with all thy f. I love thee	COWP 251:13	f.…we know not what	DRYD 300:37	Whoever f. contradiction	SAINT 738:45
f. it has not strength enough	GOLD 376:91	F. ye not therefore	BIBLE 116:71	Who f. to speak of Ninety-Eight?	INGR 446:36
f. of a Government	ROOS 710:38	first boredom, then f.	LARK 509:86	**feasibility** barest requirements of f.	MCEW 551:58
f. of the economic society	KEYN 484:82	flight and f.	MCCA 547:74	**feast** f. his neighbours	SHAK 776:89
fill you with the f. they had	LARK 510:89	Fly hence, our contact f.!	ARNO 34:94	f. is made for laughter	BIBLE 106:32
Jesus! with all thy f.	BUTL 186:11	for f.…never get out	WEBS 926:22	f. of experience	GOLD 375:81
Neebours' f. an folly	BURNS 178:92	Fostered…by f.	WORD 958:75	going to a f.	JONS 467:60
private school has all the f.	CONN 242:3	freedom from f.	ROOS 724:13	Goldsmith's fine f.	GARR 360:80
repair time's f.	MUIR 624:20	hate that which we often f.	SHAK 794:48	imagination of a f.	SHAK 764:36
Sum up my f., I pray	WEBS 926:29	haunts of horror and f.	TENN 876:33	improper mind is a perpetual f.	SMITH 829:15
to her f. a little blind	PRIOR 695:1	heart shall not f.	BIBLE 100:50	Liberty's a glorious f.!	BURNS 177:79
world of vile ill-favoured f.	SHAK 773:10	hope could have no f.	THOM 887:10	When I would make a f.	HARI 398:32
faun important senior f.	ANON 25:54	In f. begotten	GRAV 382:20	**feasting** f. with your ealdormen	BEDE 72:9
Faustus F., it is not half so fair	MARL 573:26	In Place of F.	BEVAN 89:54	**feasts** public f.…public rout	DAVI 264:78
F., leave this damnèd art	MARL 552:28	let thy wiseness f.	SHAK 784:67	**feat** difficult f. for a…male	PLATH 681:29
F. like a foggy mist	MARL 574:31	little with the f. of the Lord	BIBLE 104:75	empty f. to cheat	CLOU 232:66
F. may…save his soul!	MARL 573:30	Love mixed with f.	WEBS 927:51	**feather** Blade on the f.	CORY 247:12
favour Always take the f.	BALE 57:37	Mankind, f. your Lord	KORAN 496:50	each f.	HUGH 435:31
courtesan farts…as a f.	ANON 22:69	many things to f.	BACON 52:1	f. footed through	WAUGH 924:74
depend on…prince's f.	WEBS 927:49	masters the f. of death	BACON 50:58	f. to tickle the intellect	LAMB 506:13
F. is deceitful	BIBLE 105:8	Men f. death	BACON 50:57	f. will turn the scale	SHAK 788:74
f. to men of skill	BIBLE 106:29	mercy toward them that f. him	BIBLE 102:8	light as a f.	SPUR 841:89
feel so strongly in f.	BALC 56:12	Neither f. nor courage saves	ELIOT 317:85	milk-white f. in a crow	CAMP 194:55
never get f. for lacking skill	SIDN 820:59	never f., man	HOUS 433:83	never moults a f.!	DICK 279:89
odds be…in your f.	COLL 237:68	never negotiate out of f.	KENN 481:1	reach for my f. Boa	GINS 372:10
undoubtedly continue in f.	JANE 452:79	no f. of any failure	FAWC 331:52	snug as a f. mattress	ANGE 19:92
without her f.	JONS 468:89	No passion so effectually…than f.	BURKE 175:6	white owl's f.	ALLI 14:7
favourite f. has no friend!	GRAY 383:53	no want to them that f. him	BIBLE 100:56	winged with its own f.	KELL 479:66
which among my novels is my f.	ACHE 2:22	O believers, f. God	KORAN 497:63	wit's a f.	POPE 687:89
favours felt all its f.	COCK 233:81	perfect love casteth out f.	BIBLE 131:83	**feather-bed** f.-b. of correctitude	BENN 81:74

feathers

feathers beautified with our f.	GREE	386:33
bluejay in peacock f.	LAFO	504:58
brain of f.	POPE	688:35
cover thee with his f.	BIBLE	101:96
f. are more beautiful?	SHAK	762:75
f. will soon soak through	HOLM	424:64
'Hope' is the thing with f.	DICK	283:34
plumes her f.	MILT	598:72
sad Time his f. move!	SPEN	839:51
feature f. of the Rugby game	ANON	23:85
f. of this institution	DICK	279:2
immortal f. of loveliness	MILT	600:17
original f. of any religion	PAINE	660:35
show virtue her own f.	SHAK	783:19
features best f. of that…form	SHAW	810:27
commanding f.	HUNT	439:21
D…possessed…two dramatic f.	POWE	693:44
F. are an index	DICK	279:17
f. from behind the unreasoning	MELV	585:59
f. gets on your mind	LEAC	515:15
f. of clerical cut	ELIOT	319:49
many f. at the same time	HOMA	425:92
my f. rot away	WILB	939:38
One of the saddest f.	ECON	310:22
February not Puritanism but F.	KRUT	500:31
such a F. face	SHAK	775:58
fecundity what it is about f.	DILL	286:92
federal f. government	WILL	944:63
so poor a record…as the F. Reserve	FRIE	351:71
federation F. of the world	TENN	871:17
fee hold the gorgeous East in f.	WORD	959:4
set my life at a pin's f.	SHAK	781:58
soul moves in his f.	JONS	467:57
feeble resource of the f.	GIBB	366:96
weak and f. woman	ELIZ	321:4
feed f. he must and will	EMER	325:77
f. myself With…poison	SHAK	794:53
f. on him in thy heart	BOOK	147:73
throw a f. into her	RUNY	731:58
Will you still f. me	LENN	522:53
Feeder Mr F., B.A.	DICK	280:31
feeder doth choke the f.	SHAK	764:39
feeding starve with f.	SHAK	799:1
feel begins to f. unwell	KIPL	489:77
dislike what I fancy I f.	ANON	24:13
don't f. like going into it	SALI	739:71
don't know how to f.	KENN	480:94
Englishman…afraid to f.	FORS	345:41
f. good after	HEMI	409:70
f. hot and think cold	CARY	207:62
f. keenly and strongly	STAEL	842:99
f. not what they inspire	SHEL	816:53
f. with them	BENN	81:79
f. you've done something	HEMI	409:62
how you made them f.	ANGE	19:4
make him f. that way	TWAIN	902:61
No comfortable f.	HOOD	426:37
Now does he f.	SHAK	798:67
power…to make you f.	CONR	243:26
something more to do than f.	LAMB	504:76
that matters is whether you f. it	COLE	234:4
though you f. nothing	JULI	471:42
thow shalt nat f.	CHAU	216:58
women f. just as men f.	BRON	161:61
feeling All violent f.	RUSK	733:90
art must express a distinct f.	FRIE	351:78
barbarous f. of nationality	SENI	757:30
Certainty. F.. Joy	PASC	668:96
constellations of f.	DOUG	295:5
cruelty is the primary f.	SADE	737:14
extra dimension of f.	FOWL	345:61
failure of f.	STEV	850:86
f.….came as a…surprise	LESS	524:98
f. I'm falling	FERL	333:90
f. of all happiness	WORD	961:38
f. of emulsion	PERE	674:15
f. of Sunday	RHYS	712:76
f. of vengeance	DREN	299:2
F. teaches much more	DU	305:72
f. that here it is 11 o'clock	BRAN	156:67
f. that lures us on to joys	CONR	244:36
f. that you can't make it	POWE	693:55
f. which we derive from knowing	LAMB	505:94
f. you've been cheated?	ROTT	728:6
formal f. comes	DICK	284:36
generous and honest f.	BURKE	175:11
High mountains are a f.	BYRON	187:53

imprecision of f.	ELIOT	320:66
inner experience and inner f.	LAWR	514:81
keen vision and f.	ELIOT	316:51
lie down until the f. passes	HUTC	441:51
lonely f., but euphoric, too	CAMP	195:71
lost pulse of f.	ARNO	34:72
Love is not only a f.	BALZ	61:99
more true f.	JOWE	469:16
must not think that f. is everything	FLAU	339:15
Nor form, nor f.	WORD	957:66
not merely as f.	PLATH	681:29
obsessed by the f.	SPEN	837:13
profound f. of the power	NORTH	641:60
pure expressions of f.	AYER	48:6
purely personal F.	CUMM	257:50
that's a f. disputation	SHAK	771:51
true writers have experienced this f.	SARR	744:61
without a f. of disappointment	LAMB	505:88
feelings Aren't our best f.	BALZ	61:4
artist with true f.	FRIE	351:73
can't put them out of his f.	CARY	207:63
define her f. in language	HARDY	397:6
f. and convictions	MORI	619:36
f. of awe and respect	DICK	277:39
f. of human beings	JAMES	452:77
f. of liberty	PITT	679:5
f. of Sophia	AUST	45:48
f. on leaving Eton	CONN	242:5
f. prey upon us	AUST	47:88
f. these dull scenes produce	CRAB	252:43
f. you haven't really got	LAWR	513:75
get human f. right	HUTC	441:47
Irish f. and sensitivities	HAUG	401:84
keeping f. at bay	BROO	163:6
language of our f.	FRIE	351:76
no room for new f.	ELIOT	315:32
no spontaneous f.	ORWE	654:56
some of the uneasy f.	HUXL	443:4
feels f. it all as one	JAMES	451:67
fees answered, as they took their f.	BELL	76:59
f. are sufficient punishment	BAIL	55:85
very fat f.	BURG	174:92
feet aching hands and bleeding f.	ARNO	34:76
all enemies under his f.	BIBLE	127:58
all things under his f.	BIBLE	99:31
at a funeral and knew their f.	MAUG	582:5
beneath a monarch's f.	BURNS	178:96
black f. of the night	GILM	371:96
blooming round our f.	BETJ	89:42
both f. off the ground	JOHN	458:11
bound…about the f. of God	TENN	878:86
cloths under your f.	YEATS	966:12
credit…sprang upon its f.	WEBS	926:15
crowes f. be growen	CHAU	216:59
cutting off our f.	SWIFT	861:34
dapper from your napper to your f.	COLL	237:63
delivered…my f. from falling	BIBLE	102:20
die on your f.	IBAR	444:5
direct your f.	FIEL	335:28
down at her f.	TRAV	895:89
due f. never fail	MILT	598:59
exertions of your hands and f.	CONR	244:32
f. began to stutter	BURT	181:71
f. go down to death	BIBLE	104:56
f. in ancient time	BLAKE	141:40
f. like unto fine brass	BIBLE	131:88
f. of him that bringeth good tidings	BIBLE	109:90
f.….of iron and part of clay	BIBLE	111:38
f. of the aged	BIBLE	113:1
f. on the ground	FERL	333:90
f. planted firmly	ROOS	724:10
f. planted on level ground	GOHE	375:73
f. shod with the preparation	BIBLE	128:95
f. thy tribute bring	LYTE	543:93
f. were almost gone	BIBLE	101:84
fog comes on little cat f.	SAND	742:14
get a democracy on its f.	PULI	699:71
goat f. dance an antic hay	MARL	573:14
hear a horse's f.	KIPL	492:56
hear it through their f.	SOUSA	834:39
Hell's darkness under his f.	CARL	201:36
herb at your f.	TROL	897:34
I have deserted…sighing at your f.	CONG	241:72
Its f. were tied	KEATS	475:71
Keep Thou my f.	NEWM	635:45
lamp unto my f.	BIBLE	103:28
lantern to my f.	SHAK	759:87

leaves the marks of his f.	LEAC	515:8
let my f. spend…time	OWENS	658:41
like hinds' f.	BIBLE	99:39
little children…Round his f.	SHEL	812:71
little snow-white f.	YEATS	965:3
meet those dancing f.	DUBIN	304:59
moon under her f.	BIBLE	131:9
nearer than hands and f.	TENN	877:71
nice f. and plenty of money	ASHF	38:77
not on its f.	HEMP	410:99
of my f. and my nails	NERU	633:22
palms before my f.	CHES	220:51
pansy at my f.	WORD	959:7
polished with the tread of f.	DICK	279:1
room at your f.?	BALL	58:57
rude facts at your f.	RABAN	703:4
Scots lords at his f.	BALL	59:72
set my f. upon a rock	BIBLE	100:61
shake off the dust of your f.	BIBLE	116:68
shoes from off thy f.	BIBLE	93:52
shoes on your f.	BIBLE	93:59
shoes right off its f.	DICK	279:19
skull, and the f.	BIBLE	98:81
slippered f.	GRAH	381:91
swift pattering of naked f.	DOYLE	297:48
tempt with wand'ring f.	MILT	603:65
things before his f.	ENNI	326:17
through the head down to the f.	ANGE	19:90
thy holy f.	BLAKE	139:80
tremble under her f.	TENN	876:28
walks with aimless f.	TENN	874:76
What stranger's f.	HOUS	432:73
wind's f. shine	SWIN	863:88
feigning Most friendship is f.	SHAK	779:85
truest poetry is the most f.	SHAK	779:98
felicity Absent thee from f.	SHAK	785:73
bliss and sole f.	MARL	572:99
f. in such government a rarer thing	BACON	53:51
more f. on the far side	SMITH	829:16
none can boast sincere f.	DRYD	304:54
optics of these eyes to behold f.	BROW	165:63
Fell instant that he f.	SCOTT	752:26
stood, and f. who f.	MILT	603:79
fellers f….kick your bollocks	LOFT	534:1
fellow damned f.-feeling	MACD	550:40
f. ain't got a soul	STEI	845:83
f. of a good respect	SHAK	778:55
f. that is neither a wit…nor a fool	CONG	240:47
Hail f., well met	SWIFT	862:56
hard to be a good f.	WYCH	964:98
hook-nosed f. of Rome	SHAK	773:94
no f. in the firmament	SHAK	777:26
other f. just blinked	RUSK	732:78
perfect citizen may be a fine f.	DOUG	295:15
Promise to forget this f.	SHER	817:70
respect the other f.'s religion	MENC	586:5
That f. seems…to possess	JOHN	462:20
That's a brave f.	SHAK	799:93
this f. doesn't know	TRUM	899:81
touchy, testy, pleasant f.	ADDI	6:27
fellow-citizen As f.-c.	GILB	369:59
fellow-creature esteem with a f.-c.	LAMB	505:94
fellow-creatures torture…of his f.-c.	FROU	353:27
fellowmen majority of their f.	DU	305:70
fellow-men f.-m. can do little	EMER	325:99
one that loves his f.-m.	HUNT	439:29
fellow-rover laughing f.-r.	MASE	580:52
fellows Bark when their f. do	SHAK	804:43
f. of another college	LITT	531:47
f.….the flood could not wash away	CONG	240:46
f. were practising	JOYCE	470:19
level of his humble f.	HUXL	443:7
mighty fine f. nowadays	STEV	852:55
Nature hath framed strange f.	SHAK	768:67
Nay, droop not, f.	MASS	581:75
some o' them low f.	DICK	277:55
ten good f. and one good day	MILNE	596:25
Those grave f.	STEE	844:51
What should such f. as I do	SHAK	783:12
fellowship f. that they may never	MALO	563:11
he that hath f.	BIBLE	113:92
no f. with one that is mightier	BIBLE	113:93
pass through in His f.	SCHW	751:20
right hands of f.	BIBLE	127:78
felon When a f.'s not engaged	GILB	368:42
felt could not portray all I f.	HOLM	423:55
Genius is f.	DIDE	285:64

fifty

female adult American Negro f. ANGE 18:87
all f. life...unclean STAN 843:17
bad f. cooks NIET 638:12
cast on f. wits BRAD 155:50
child of our grandmother Eve, a f. SHAK 763:7
chosen and f. shall be homely KENN 480:91
Christ will perhaps be a f. NIGH 639:23
fashionable f. life SPEKE 836:82
f. emotions of aggression LESS 524:98
f. of the species KIPL 493:77
f. principle LEGU 520:12
f. worker is the slave CONN 243:22
images of f. beauty WOLF 952:60
lay down my life for the British f.? CLOU 232:57
male and f. created he them BIBLE 91:84
neither male nor f. BIBLE 127:79
our excess f. population WRIG 962:60
sea...is a mighty f. SEXT 758:49
Strengthen the f. mind WOLL 953:88
two and two...male and the f. BIBLE 92:8
unprotected f. travelling BUTL 185:1
vindictiveness of the f. CONN 243:8
What f. heart can gold despise? GRAY 383:52
whole f. line of ancestry EDGE 311:47
females imbecility in f. AUST 47:85
make no fuss about f. CAMPO 195:79
feminine beautiful f. tissue HARDY 397:15
distinctively f. HARDY 397:10
f. half of the world MERE 588:40
f. in the man KENT 483:50
Success is f. FAUL 331:45
tired of being the f. spouse DIAZ 276:26
who is her life, is f. PATM 669:22
femininity handicraft of f. OLIP 649:35
feminism 'beginning' of f. ROWB 729:18
brief flowerings of f. FALU 329:12
cardinal tenets of f. LYND 543:92
F. has become a...vegetable drawer PAGL 659:19
hate discussions of f. FREN 350:52
feminist f. writer WELD 928:87
I am a f. JORD 469:3
Virgin Mary...become a f. PUSSY 700:89
fen England...is a f. WORD 958:94
plashy f. WAUGH 924:74
fence Hussein...is the f. ANON 27:33
old mare might droop across a f. SMITH 828:3
fender propped on the f. GRAH 381:91
Fenianism guilty authors of F. ARNO 35:23
fennel box that f. Grows around RANS 707:72
fens of f. jargon? BAKER 56:7
reek o'th' rotten f. SHAK 799:98
ferlie f. he spied wi' his e'e BALL 59:74
fermentation requires long f. CAPO 197:27
fern sparkle out among the f. TENN 876:37
the f.-dark indifference LAWR 513:58
Ferrari If you have a f. MOUR 623:97
ferret-faced f.-f., white-eyed boys STEV 852:34
ferry row us o'er the f. CAMP 194:65
fertile ambrosial and f. THOR 888:21
f. pedant WALP 919:80
such a fix to be so f. NASH 630:60
fertilize f. the whole world TOCQ 892:27
fervent f. in spirit BIBLE 125:25
festal line of f. light ARNO 34:92
fester Lilies that f. SHAK 802:70
festina F. lente AUGU 45:37
festival cannot woo in f. terms SHAK 774:56
Death is the supreme F. BONH 146:25
night before some f. SHAK 766:96
Something like a f. ANGE 19:91
fetishism Commodity f. TATE 867:42
fettered so oft has f. me HERR 415:13
You are f. DICK 279:4
fetters bound him with f. of brass BIBLE 96:19
F. of gold are still f. ASTE 39:3
feud Fhairshon swore a f. AYTO 48:11
feudal anachronistic, f. institution ACHE 2:7
feuds f., and jealousies, and sorrows SASS 745:83
Forget all f. MACA 546:54
fever bred a f. THOM 883:9
enigma of the f. chart ELIOT 320:64
f. called 'Living' POE 683:94
life's fitful f. SHAK 797:46
Of chills and f. she died RANS 706:66
youth is bent by...wintry f. THOM 883:3
feverish over trembly and f. TWAIN 902:62
fever-trees set about with f.-t. KIPL 491:37

Février Janvier and F. NICH 636:70
few appointment by the corrupt f. SHAW 808:37
expression which the f. desire PARE 663:89
f. and evil have the days...been BIBLE 93:48
Gey f., and they're a' deid ANON 23:84
grinders cease because they are f. BIBLE 106:36
hated the ruling f. BENT 82:94
owed by so many, to so f. CHUR 225:87
There are so f. JONS 467:76
We f., we happy f. SHAK 776:92
where f. have been KENN 480:86
fez necessary to abolish the f. ATAT 40:13
Fhairshon F. swore a feud AYTO 48:11
fib Destroy his f....in vain POPE 687:99
fibre flesh and bone, f. and liquids ELLI 323:35
fibres f. of England FORS 344:22
fickle all men call thee f. SHAK 766:3
and f. is the South TENN 872:44
Whatever is f. HOPK 428:73
Woman is often f. FRAN 347:96
fiction AIDS is good for is f. WELD 928:81
All f. is for me WILS 947:40
best thing in f. WILDE 941:92
biography is ultimately f. MALA 562:88
But in a f. SHAK 782:99
condemn it as an improbable f. SHAK 786:17
don't make for very good f. TROL 898:58
escapist f. GALB 357:19
everyone writes f. KING 487:41
every 'I' and f. shouldn't be mixed WALC 916:15
fact and f. stranger than f. BOWEN 153:95
Fact is stranger than f. GERV 365:82
fascinating f. BANKS 62:28
f. is a necessity CHES 220:52
F. is life JAMES 450:30
f....makes justice PALEY 661:51
F. should render...morals FORD 343:94
great temple of f. UPDI 906:32
happiness ever been the subject of f.? UPDI 906:40
heroes and villains from f. AUDEN 44:17
in f. as in life AUCH 42:62
Isherwood became a f. BURU 182:90
money...to write f. WOOLF 955:26
more lies than...self-indulgent f. BYATT 186:17
newspapers...continuous f. BEVAN 90:59
not an easy country for a f.-writer UPDI 906:38
Poetry is a...piece of f. MENC 586:86
Poetry is the supreme f. STEV 849:65
Poetry is the supreme f. STEV 850:99
police dog of American f. FADI 329:7
predilection for genre f. DISCH 287:9
Science f., like Brazil DISCH 287:10
Stranger than f. BYRON 190:25
That is what f. means WILDE 941:4
The trouble with writing f. BANKS 62:27
to writing f. UPDI 906:25
traditional f. GALB 357:19
write f. and I'm told ROTH 728:92
wrote f. as if it were WILDE 942:30
fictions As a maker of f. LECA 518:78
Perhaps we are all f. GREE 386:26
Who says that f. only HERB 413:72
fictitious f. election results that
elect a f. president MOORE 617:93
fiddle F., we know, is diddle SWIN 864:18
good tune...on an old f. BUTL 185:2
hog that could f. ROCH 720:19
important beyond all this f. MOORE 617:77
Music...plays second f. to none ELLI 322:24
sell his f. BURNS 178:3
trissyllables are f. rhymes SMART 826:61
fiddle-de-dee French for f.-d.-d.? CARR 205:25
fiddler f., and consequently a rogue SWIFT 861:29
Fidele fair F.'s grassy tomb COLL 237:70
fidelity books...our f. to truth CONR 244:40
disparagements of his wife's f. SHAW 811:29
gossamer f. of mere Man POE 683:84
scrupulous f. to the truth CONR 244:47
stone f. They hardly meant LARK 509:81
fidget moved by little f. wheels SLES 825:52
fie F., fo, and fum SHAK 792:12
field as a flower of the f. BIBLE 102:10
be on the f. of play MILNE 596:25
beside a f. of grain PARK 664:35
big f. of rye SALI 740:14
death in the hunting f. MORT 621:67
dignity in tilling a f. WASH 921:22

every other f. has left nature MOND 612:97
f. for their efforts BRON 161:61
f. is full of shades THOM 886:84
f. of social organization MENC 586:89
Flodden's fatal f. SCOTT 752:27
Happy f. or mossy cavern KEATS 475:76
hill or f. or river TENN 872:40
In a f. by the river YEATS 965:3
In love's f. CRAS 254:86
It is that cricket f. POWYS 693:62
leave the whole f. HELL 407:30
left on the f. not a few DAVIS 266:9
like the brambles in a wild f. DIDE 285:10
love of f. and coppice MACK 553:10
man of the f. BIBLE 92:28
market, hearth and f. KIPL 493:70
on the f. and city THAC 880:26
on the f. of battle PAST 668:5
presence on the f. WELL 929:8
rushed into the f. BYRON 187:51
single f. WORD 959:7
single in the f. WORD 960:18
some corner of a foreign f. BROO 162:88
tills the f. TENN 877:60
What though the f. MILT 602:38
whether it's a f. WILD 943:45
you look in a f. FERG 333:76
Fields like...W. C. F. movies HAWES 401:86
say about W C F ROST 727:72
fields At Play In The F. MATT 582:99
blown f. or SWIN 864:4
blue f. of heaven KEATS 475:62
broken head in Cold Bath F. MACA 545:40
dead, but in the Elysian f. DISR 288:64
disgrace to the playing f. FRY 353:28
farmer without f. PARK 665:42
f. and flocks have charms CRAB 252:30
f. and the waters shout MERE 587:26
f. of amaranth LAND 507:32
f. of barley and of rye TENN 869:77
f. of millions of farms HOOV 427:42
f. that their fathers have tilled CHUR 225:90
f. that we have planted MUIR 624:24
f. where Troy once was OVID 657:15
fight in the f. CHUR 225:85
flowering of His f. TENN 878:79
flowerless f. of heaven SWIN 863:81
foreign f., from Dunkirk DAVIS 266:9
From the green f. WORD 957:72
In f. where roses fade HOUS 432:56
look on the f. BIBLE 122:29
Low over dim f. MERE 587:24
no definite...meaning in other f. SART 744:63
poems...in the factories and f. MACD 549:35
Poetic f. encompass me around ADDI 6:16
rush through the f. in trains CHES 221:8
sharp light the f. did lie FREE 350:48
Strawberry f. forever LENN 522:54
To f. where flies no...hail HOPK 428:65
unshorn f., boundless and beautiful BRYA 170:3
walk through the f. CORN 247:3
What f. SHEL 814:95
whispering of f. unsown OWEN 658:36
fiend Beneath is all the f.'s SHAK 793:22
dreadful f. of gods SPEN 839:54
f. for becoming a torrent LIGNE 529:98
F. walked up and down MILT 603:82
frightful f....behind him tread COLE 235:18
Like a f. hid in a cloud BLAKE 140:18
marble-hearted f. SHAK 792:94
fiends alleyways and drug f. LIND 530:16
f. that plague thee COLE 235:11
f. will snatch at it SHAK 790:49
fierce f. and bald SASS 745:84
That bright and f. TENN 872:44
fierceness cage if...any sign of f. CARB 198:36
swalloweth the ground with f. BIBLE 99:19
fiere my trusty f.! BURNS 178:7
Fife Thane of F. SHAK 798:66
fife Elephant, That practised on a f. CARR 206:32
fifth And he came f. JOYCE 470:26
f. of the people KENN 482:41
f. part of the Earth FIELD 335:11
plead the F. Amendment NIXON 640:35
The f. column MOLA 611:71
fifty At f. you have the choice CART 207:56
difficult thing is to have it at f. DEGAS 269:89

fig

Fear of F.		JONG 466:40
won't speak to me for f. minutes		DOYLE 297:55
fig an Olive, and a Turkey F.		BETH 87:10
don't care a f.!		LEAR 516:32
f. for those by law protected		BURNS 177:79
F. leaves of democratic		KENN 480:88
like a fat purple f.		PLATH 681:37
sewed f. leaves together		BIBLE 91:93
fight able to f. and conquer		TROT 899:63
a harder matter to f.		TENN 876:39
bear-like I must f.		SHAK 798:75
beautifully the English f.!		NAPO 630:42
believer will f. another		GREE 386:27
better to f. for the good		TENN 876:36
British won't f.		GALT 359:55
cannot f. against the future		GLAD 373:37
cannot f. for love		SHAK 767:29
can we f. with fifty-three?		TENN 878:95
clouds of the f.		KEY 483:68
cock won't f.		BEAV 71:26
couldn't begin to f.		TAYL 868:54
day we started to f.		ANON 26:94
Don't give up the f.		MARL 572:92
don't want to f.		HUNT 439:16
easier to f. for principles		STEV 850:2
f. and die for your country		GOLD 377:23
f. and f. again		GAIT 357:11
f. begins within himself		BROW 168:41
f. between two bald men		BORG 151:60
f. for freedom and truth		IBSEN 444:8
f. for mankind		SAINT 738:34
F. for our National Intelligence		CATT 209:3
f. for the right		CURZ 260:5
f. for your country		HOMER 425:5
f. in defence of one's country		HOMER 425:7
f. is bigger than life itself		KING 486:21
f. it out		GRANT 381:8
f. on the beaches		CHUR 225:85
f. on until the end		HAIG 392:15
F. the good f.		BIBLE 129:24
f. them, and pursue them		JOAN 455:59
fought a good f.		BIBLE 129:30
friendly kind of f.		STUB 858:61
Go I to f.		SHAK 764:33
great f. did win		SOUT 835:47
In the early years, you f.		DIDI 286:88
I shall f.		THAT 881:72
life be not a real f.		JAMES 451:70
lost, lost f., for the cause		CLOU 232:62
man...too proud to f.		WILS 949:78
man who runs away will f.		MENA 586:79
never a moment ceased the f.		TENN 878:97
no stomach to this f.		SHAK 776:88
not yet begun to f.		JONES 465:22
only the f. to recover		ELIOT 320:67
recalls...a f.		AMADO 15:21
those that fly, may f. again		BUTL 185:85
Those that I f.		YEATS 966:22
thou fought the better f.		MILT 605:21
To f. aloud		DICK 283:30
too frightened to f.		TALL 866:18
Ulster will f.		CHUR 224:64
we began this f.		GALS 358:51
We will f. them on the streets		HUSS 440:43
when you f.		HEMI 410:77
Wherever they's a f.		STEI 845:83
will not cease from mental f.		BLAKE 141:43
fighter clown, the boozer, the f.?		MAST 581:81
left to the f.'s honor		HEMI 409:71
no a bonny f.?		STEV 853:75
fighters nightmare f.		JARR 452:83
fighting f. against a superstitious		JAMES 450:34
f. amongst one and another		CLARK 228:63
f. for one thing—money		DEMP 272:51
F. is like champagne		MITC 610:43
F. still, and still destroying		DRYD 303:33
first twenty days of f.		CHUR 225:77
Football causeth f.		STUB 858:62
foremost f., fell		BYRON 187:51
formed through f.		MUSS 628:95
not conquering but f. well		COUB 248:20
period...between two periods of f.		BIER 135:86
tongue-tied's f.		HARR 399:56
twelve thousand f. men		SHAK 764:48
What are We f. for?		SERV 757:37
What is the use of f.		PANK 662:86
When there was any f.		GILB 370:71
when wilt thou leave f.		SHAK 772:82
who dies f. has increase		GREN 388:57
worth f. for, worth dying		MITC 610:39
fights f....best part of married life		WILD 943:41
f. historical		GILB 368:39
f. you on patriotic principles		SHAW 807:97
knows what he f. for		CROM 255:17
scuffles of great f.		SHAK 793:41
figs better than f.		SHAK 794:46
ears fall off like f.		THOM 884:41
fig-tree green f.-t. in the story		PLATH 681:37
Train up a f.-t.		DICK 280:33
figurative f....metaphorical God		DONNE 293:70
figure baby f. of the giant		SHAK 786:29
built about a mythical f.		HERB 413:50
can't f. him out		SHUL 819:30
f. in a country church		SWIFT 861:27
f. of Juno		BARR 65:98
f. which is as familiar to us		MACA 545:36
keeping your face or your f.		CART 207:56
masculine f. created by a woman		MENC 586:83
mourning f. walks		LIND 530:21
not a f. in the landscape		BRON 161:53
oblong angular f.		LEAC 515:10
passing away of a great f.		NEHRU 633:9
walk around a f.		ROSSO 727:69
figures f. fail you		ARLO 32:31
f. which do not exist for political		MARX 578:26
mystery is why we...collect these f.		BART 66:30
One composition...has many f.		DIDE 285:76
place occupied by the f.		MATI 581:91
prove anything by f.		CARL 201:23
traduce those f.		LEWIS 527:70
Fiji Golf is to F. what cricket is		
to America		SINGH 823:90
files foremost f. of time		TENN 871:22
filial untie the f. band		SCOTT 752:17
fill drunk his f.		SCOTT 752:28
I have big heels to f.		KENN 483:61
much less f. them		ISAA 447:65
fillets pink f.		MACB 546:64
fillip rest's not worth a f.		BYRON 190:29
film a f. of mine that wasn't the		
director's cut		ALTM 15:19
A good f. script		MAMET 564:41
average...f. star		HEPB 412:25
director makes only one f. in his life		RENO 712:22
earn a million dollars a f.		WINN 950:1
F. art has a greater influence		BALA 56:10
F. Industry...Monarchy		MAMET 564:39
f. is never really good		WELL 929:94
F. is the least realistic		MAMET 564:42
greatest f. in the world		COPP 246:1
I always direct the same f.		FELL 332:58
only a good f.		BENN 80:51
right place to f. it		GARD 360:68
would get the f. made		OLDM 649:30
filmmaker central fact about the f.		WELL 929:95
film-makers few great f.-m....might		
have been good novelists		RUSH 732:70
tell the younger f.-m.		SCOR 751:96
filmmaking no rules in f.		CAPRA 198:33
film-making F.-m. is...being God		GILL 371:89
fatal to good f.		CHAN 213:89
films best f. are the best because		POLA 684:1
f. of one's own country		ANDE 17:70
hope to build a house with my f.		FASS 330:32
most f. are about one guy with		
a gun		LOACH 533:83
output of f. was prodigious		NIVEN 639:29
paintings and f.		WARH 920:6
seldom go to f.		BERR 87:99
started off in f. as a king		MORL 620:42
worst f. were always bad		NORM 641:53
filth f. and the sordidness		DONO 293:82
f. returns in's face		WEBS 926:28
hairy American f.		OSBO 655:86
remove f. and foulness		ABEL 1:3
so is f.		FORS 344:37
filthy all together become f.		BIBLE 99:33
f., sturdy, unkillable infants		POUND 691:93
not greedy of f. lucre		BIBLE 129:18
righteousnesses are as f. rags		BIBLE 110:7
fin winks the gold f.		TENN 873:49
final f. pleasure left to man		SNOW 832:74
I must bring out my Late Night F.		BEAV 71:30
My Indecision is F.		EBER 310:13
not f. because we are infallible		JACK 449:7
When the f. curtain comes down		MAJOR 561:75
your f. answer?		TARR 867:32
finality F. is not the language		DISR 288:47
finance functions of national f.		CHUR 225:71
site, a brief and f.		ROGE 722:67
Finchley Catherine the Great of F.		HEAL 404:66
find cannot f. it myself		KAFKA 472:8
ere you f. them		SHAK 769:73
f. information upon it		JOHN 462:38
I will f. you		NEES 632:8
to f. where you are going		STEI 846:86
with men I f. Him not		TENN 878:79
finding f. myself everyday		GIRO 373:28
f. of limited use to backlash		FALU 329:11
find out f. o. what's in it		PELO 673:77
fine F. art is that in which		RUSK 733:92
f. wine leaves you with		AMER 15:24
May will be f. next year		HOUS 432:63
no one wants F. Artists		FULL 355:68
Old Cary Grant f.		GRANT 381:99
pop art and f. art		MACI 553:1
theft with a f., not death		MORE 618:14
think is particularly f.		JOHN 462:28
fineness no f. or accuracy		BELL 77:75
finer nothing could be f.		GORD 378:54
finery not bedizened with f.		TROL 897:21
finger bandaged f.		KIPL 493:79
Between my f. and my thumb		HEAN 404:67
chills the f. not a bit		NASH 631:77
clean f. nails		MORT 621:65
f. on the trigger		MACM 556:68
From the red gold keep thy f.		SCOTT 754:64
God's f. touched him		TENN 874:89
her choppy f. laying		SHAK 795:4
little f. shall be thicker		BIBLE 97:58
moving f. writes		FITZ 337:70
One f. in the...rectum		OSLER 656:90
pointed to with the f.		CICE 227:36
rugged f. to Heaven		LLOY 533:72
scratching of my f.		HUME 438:69
smile upon his f.'s end		SHAK 775:68
stick a f. into		SAFER 737:16
that lanky Yankee f.		CONN 242:83
Whose f....on the trigger?		DAILY 260:6
fingers came forth f. of a man's hand		BIBLE 111:41
cannot lick his own f.		SHAK 766:7
dead men's f. call them		SHAK 784:57
f. of cold are corpse f.		LAWR 513:66
forc'd f. rude		MILT 599:82
judged...by the hovering f.		ANON 25:38
Just as my f.		STEV 849:73
kissed The f.		BROW 166:70
loyal to the tips of his stubby f.		ACHE 3:49
my f. wandered idly		PROC 697:27
nimble f. are no more		SITW 824:20
separate as the f.		WASH 921:23
staining of white f.		LEWIS 527:66
time that we pulled our f. out		EDIN 312:49
Until the F. Begin to Bleed		BUKO 173:57
whose f. are ten armies		GINS 372:6
With f. weary and worn		HOOD 426:30
work of thy f.		BIBLE 99:31
world...slipping through your f.		SHAW 810:5
finger-stalls fit–less f.-s.		GILB 370:67
finish start together and f. together		BEEC 73:67
test...is that you f. it		BENN 81:70
work is the f.		PEARY 671:59
finished f. in the first 100 days		KENN 481:67
It is f.		BIBLE 123:62
what just f. happening		KESEY 483:65
finite f. number of heart-beats		ARMS 33:52
Infinite...bury under the F.		CARL 200:98
Finland too late with F.		LLOY 533:79
Finn book...called Huckleberry F.		HEMI 410:76
Finnegans F. Wake took...years		PRIE 695:90
Joyce's F. Wake		NICO 637:85
fir f. that weepeth still		SPEN 838:20
Instead of the thorn...the f. tree		BIBLE 109:2
fire Absence is to love what wind		
is to f.		BUSSY 184:55
adamantine chains and penal f.		MILT 601:33
against my f.		SHAK 793:29
a light f. runs beneath my skin		SAPP 743:49
am on f. and I drown		LABE 501:3
at their hearts the f.'s centre		SPEN 837:93
beast imbued with such immortal f.?		BYRON 187:39

fit

Beef and a sea-coal f.	OTWAY 656:7	
believe that f. warms	HUME 438:97	
brimstone and f.	BIBLE 92:23	
Bring me my chariot of f.!	BLAKE 141:42	
broad gate and the great f.	SHAK 791:71	
bush burned with f.	BIBLE 93:51	
Can a man take f. in his bosom	BIBLE 104:60	
can't stand f.?	GALS 358:51	
chariot of f.	BIBLE 97:71	
cloven tongues like as of f.	BIBLE 124:72	
compact of f.	SHAK 762:84	
crowned knot of f.	ELIOT 321:94	
different as…frost from f.	BRON 162:78	
Don't f. unless fired upon	PARK 664:34	
Doubt thou the stars are f.	SHAK 781:77	
dropping-wells of f.	TENN 874:88	
enjoyed setting f. to…thoughts	WOLFE 953:84	
equally inspired with eager f.	ROCH 719:5	
extinguishes candles and kindles f.	LARO 510:5	
eyes were as a flame of f.	BIBLE 131:88	
fell in the f.	GRAH 380:87	
fetch f. from hell	WEBS 926:39	
F. and fleet and candle-lighte	BALL 59:66	
F., Blood, and Famine	HENR 411:12	
F. burn, and cauldron bubble	SHAK 797:52	
f. can burn	DANI 262:30	
F.. God of Abraham	PASC 668:96	
f., is an excellent servant	COOP 246:87	
f. is quite put out	DONNE 292:58	
f. most pure	DONNE 291:18	
F. Next Time	BALD 57:22	
f. of soul	DICK 279:89	
f. of sacrifice	ROCK 720:33	
f. shall heat the deep	TENN 869:72	
f. was furry	SITW 823:9	
F. which Prometheus filch'd	BYRON 189:98	
glass mingled with f.	BIBLE 132:14	
God is a consuming f.	BIBLE 129:45	
hath given me f.	SHAK 797:30	
heap coals of f. upon his head	BIBLE 105:95	
heaped-up sods upon the f.	COLUM 238:90	
heart of f.	TENN 876:35	
help to quench the f.	PRIOR 696:12	
heretic that makes the f.	SHAK 799:13	
hold a f. in his hand	SHAK 764:36	
how great a matter a little f. kindleth	BIBLE 130:55	
If the cribs on f.	GORE 379:61	
immortal f.	AUDEN 43:99	
inspiration, 'sacred f.'	MOND 612:96	
it is a f.	PEELE 672:70	
kindle f. with snow	SHAK 759:65	
kindly f. was fled	SCOTT 752:11	
lake of f.	BIBLE 132:22	
let them go to the f.	BINY 135:3	
Like a cloud of f.	SHEL 813:91	
Lord was not in the f.	BIBLE 97:67	
melt in her own f.	SHAK 784:41	
Most sacred f.	SPEN 838:36	
more heat to the f.	ACK 4:68	
neighbour's house is on f.	BURKE 176:34	
nodding by the f.	YEATS 965:27	
no wind, but pentecostal f.	ELIOT 321:81	
O for a muse of f.	SHAK 775:61	
Oft f. is without smoke	SPEN 838:21	
on f. with the ships	ROBE 717:71	
or ashes of a f.	LEON 523:77	
Persons grouped around a f.	MCLU 556:56	
philosophy puts out the f.	VOLT 914:38	
pillar of f.	BIBLE 93:62	
played with f.	VAUG 909:42	
prepared to carry f.	PARN 665:47	
raptures were All air and f.	DRAY 299:98	
red ball of f.	AGAWA 9:92	
restored by that refining f.	ELIOT 321:87	
right Promethean f.	SHAK 763:19	
run through f. and water	SHAK 773:11	
set a house on f.	BACON 52:6	
set on f. of hell	BIBLE 130:56	
set the heart on f.	SHAK 762:85	
setting the…neighbourhood on f.	BLIN 142:56	
shadow cast by the light of a f.	VASA 909:27	
simple as a f.	YEATS 966:14	
sitting by the f.	FOX 346:71	
smoking his pipe over the f.	SHIP 818:14	
spark…of heavenly f.	DRYD 302:79	
spark o' Nature's f.	BURNS 177:70	
sparks of f., befriend thee	HERR 416:15	
steal F. from the mind	BYRON 187:47
stir the f.	COWP 251:19
substance of my dreams took f.	SASS 745:88
throw the entire book in the f.	SAND 741:8
till the very f. touched them	PEPYS 674:6
time is the f. that burns you	WILL 945:99
told him to f. away	TRUM 900:91
tongued with f.	ELIOT 321:83
trimmed its f.	ARNO 35:3
two irons in the f.	BEAU 71:13
unnumbered sparks…are all f.	SHAK 777:26
Upon a wheel of f.	SHAK 793:30
wabbling back to the F.	KIPL 493:79
when thou walkest through the f.	BIBLE 109:87
Where no wood is…the f. goeth out	BIBLE 105:98
while the f. burns the house down	WILL 945:4
wings break into f.	BROW 166:94
with a book by the f.	KIPL 491:32
with white f. laden	SHEL 813:76
world is an ever-living f.	HERA 412:34
world will end in f.	FROST 352:4
You don't f. God	KENN 482:34
youth of England are on f.	SHAK 775:64
fired after being f. at once or twice	BYRON 190:17
f. with enthusiasm	LOMB 534:7
when being f. at	USTI 906:46
You're f.!	TRUMP 900:98
firefly Life…a flash of a f.	HAGG 391:7
The f. wakens	TENN 873:49
fire-folk look at all the f.-f.	HOPK 428:75
firelit think of f. homes	SASS 745:83
fireplace sawed it into f. lengths	COWL 250:81
fires devastating or redeeming f.	GONC 241:70
hollow f. burn out	HOUS 433:83
Love…wastes in self-consuming f.	CONG 241:70
misled by wandering f.	DRYD 303:11
our elements, these piercing f.	MILT 602:61
veils her sacred f.	POPE 689:47
violent f. soon burn out	SHAK 764:37
when the f. are out	STEV 853:65
firing faced the f. squad	THUR 890:76
what to do after f.	REED 709:26
firm courage holds f.	ANON 20:29
enterprising f. that supplies crowds	SIMP 822:82
test of an army or a f.	JAY 453:2
'The f.'—a proud Victorian word	PRIT 696:25
firmament blood streams in the f.!	MARL 573:30
f. sheweth his handywork	BOOK 148:9
no fellow in the f.	SHAK 777:26
spacious f. on high	ADDI 7:40
firmness f. makes my circle just	DONNE 292:40
first as good as the f.	HEMI 409:69
as though for the f. time	SPEN 837:7
fattening is the f. duty	SPEKE 836:82
F. Among Equals	ARCH 30:5
f. and the last thing demanded	GOET 375:67
f. and wisest of them	MILT 607:78
f. argument that is brought against	STAMP 842:10
f., best country ever	GOLD 376:86
f. blow is half the battle	GOLD 377:14
f. by whom the New are try'd	POPE 685:22
f. class, and with children	BENC 78:3
f. day of the week cometh Mary	BIBLE 123:64
f. expounder of our religious belief	SPEKE 836:81
F. Lady has a white glove pulpit	REAG 708:98
f. powerful plain manifesto	SPEN 837:1
f. principle of existentialism	SART 745:73
f. prize in the lottery of life	RHOD 712:71
f. question must be	SPAR 836:80
f. scent you pour	HORA 427:91
f. time a European…sets foot	STEF 844:54
f. twenty years are the longest	SOUT 835:54
f. word on everything	HUGO 438:90
gained our f. objective	SASS 745:82
give it to the f. man	SCHR 749:61
isn't the f. step	KENN 482:43
knock over the f. one	EISE 314:98
legs so f.	FRAY 349:35
many that are f. shall be last	BIBLE 118:20
not the f.	HOUS 432:64
sung her f. and last	GIBB 367:7
that is the f. time	GERG 365:65
We were the f. that ever burst	COLE 235:11
you're a poet f.	SART 744:66
First Amendment the F. A.	
is…important if	FLYNT 341:65
firstborn f. in the land of Egypt	BIBLE 93:59
rail against all the f.	SHAK 778:77
first-born f.-b. of her daughters	LONG 535:28
first-class f.-c. man subsists on the matter	BELL 78:97
making f.-c. men	WHIT 938:11
First Class F. C. doesn't make you a f. c. person	DENCH 272:54
first-fruits f.-f. of them that slept	BIBLE 127:57
First Lady send the F. L.	CLIN 231:30
first-rate F.-r. School	WAUGH 923:53
powers of a f.-r. man	BAGE 55:79
test of a f.-r. work	BENN 81:70
fish a wet f.	GRIFF 388:68
Bill was a tropical f.	ANON 26:93
cars nose forward like f.	LOWE 540:25
drank like a f.	HEAN 405:72
equal before a f.	HOOV 427:47
F. are jumpin'	HEYW 417:40
F. don't applaud	HOPE 428:61
F. fiddle de-dee!	LEAR 516:39
f., for his Aunt Jobiska's	LEAR 516:41
F. got to swim	HAMM 394:62
F.…in depth of June	BROO 163:92
f. needs a bicycle	STEI 846:91
f. not with this melancholy	SHAK 768:71
f. say, they have their stream	BROO 163:99
f. that talks	DELA 271:30
f. would have bright mail	KEATS 476:87
how to f. for it	HERZ 416:21
human being and f. can coexist peacefully	BUSH 182:10
Ideas are like f.	LYNCH 543:89
if he ask a f.	BIBLE 115:51
island…surrounded by f.	BEVAN 89:52
kingdom of the f.	LOWE 540:23
knowledge…better than f.	WHIT 936:63
man may f. with the worm	SHAK 784:47
never lost a little f.	FIELD 335:14
no f. ye're buying	SCOTT 753:49
no more land, say f.	BROO 163:2
Phone for the f. knives	BETJ 89:41
piece of a broiled f.	BIBLE 122:14
poor pedestrian abilities of a f.	BURKE 176:63
put me in mind of the skuttle f.	ADDI 7:43
Salmon is the most stately f.	BERN 86:81
small 'Stute F.	KIPL 491:28
Thanks for All the F.	ADAMS 4:78
throws in a load of f.	MALA 562:87
To love is to be a f.	IGNA 445:18
Un-dish-cover the f.	CARR 205:23
Water too pure breeds no f.	MAO 569:38
What cat's averse to f.?	GRAY 383:52
Wise men f. here	STEL 846:1
would you rather be a f.	BURKE 176:61
fishbone monument sticks like a f.	LOWE 540:24
fisher f. of men	DOUG 295:8
fishermen believe that they are born f.	STEI 846:84
marks of f. on the beach	NAIP 629:28
fishers make you f. of men	BIBLE 114:26
fishery f. without nets	DEFOE 269:78
fishes f. and reptiles	BRYAN 170:98
f. first to shipping did impart	DRYD 299:15
five barley loaves, and two small f.	BIBLE 122:33
five loaves, and two f.	BIBLE 117:98
thousand men that f. gnawed	SHAK 761:40
uncommunicating muteness of f.	LAMB 505:1
welcomes little f. in	CARR 203:64
fishing angling or float f.	JOHN 465:7
distaste for f.	STEI 846:84
f. is a delusion	MARQ 575:62
F. is…a form of madness	HOME 425:97
go f. there	HALE 392:28
when he goes a-f.	WALT 920:90
fishpond That great f.	DEKK 270:11
fish-spawn as she is of f.-s.	HUGH 435:17
fission production of the f. bomb	FROMM 352:88
fist blows with the f.	MARI 571:76
Clasped in my f.	FORD 343:6
flower in a clenched f.	HOFF 421:25
Her f. of a face	THOM 883:13
impersonal f. fight	NATH 632:2
painted by a mailed f.	SITW 824:15
fists groan and shake their f.?	HOUS 433:81
fit Borrowed garments never f.	FULL 355:81
fell down in a sort of f.	EDGE 311:36
f. for the kingdom of God	BIBLE 120:77
f. of absence of mind	SEEL 756:2
F. only for barbarians	FULL 355:77

fits

Is this a f. time	STER	848:37
only f. for the slaves	FLET	340:51
only the F. survive	SERV	757:33
fits cope him in these sullen f.	SHAK	778:68
tortured into f.	ROBI	718:91
fitter F. for sickness	SHAK	759:77
fittest f. may also be the gentlest	DOBZ	289:79
necessary for survival of the f.	PALEY	661:52
survival of the f.	ROCK	720:31
survival of the f.	SPEN	836:87
five count f.-and-twenty	DICK	282:84
f. acts of Shakespeare's tragedy	FIELD	335:12
f. guys who hate you	STEN	847:7
f. reasons why men drink	ALDR	12:53
lives between f. bells	SLES	825:52
neither f. nor three	HOUS	432:70
that I have wedded f.!	CHAU	217:88
Two and two is f.	DOST	294:88
fix in a f. pretty soon	TRUTH	900:4
fixed arrest motion...and hold it f.	FAUL	331:42
f. it tonight	SNYD	832:92
f. place in the chain of being	EMER	324:66
fixity f. of a thoughtful child's	HARDY	397:18
fjord city...and the f.	MUNCH	625:41
flag beneath the British f.	JOHN	458:24
f....has not pledged its allegiance	BALD	57:23
f. is red, white and blue	JACK	448:4
f., the Stars and Stripes	ROOS	725:23
f. to April's breeze unfurled	EMER	324:48
f. was still there	KEY	483:68
keep the red f. flying	CONN	242:84
planted the British f. there	STUA	858:57
spare your country's f.	WHIT	938:23
The chequered f.	VETT	911:66
wave a red f.	GEOR	364:52
flagellation Squash...it's f.	COWA	249:61
flag-flapper Jelly-bellied F.-f.	KIPL	491:23
flagon f. with the dragon	PANA	662:80
flagpoles others climb f.	WEBB	925:8
flags F. are...cloth	ROY	730:28
F. wearily through darkness	SHEL	814:3
long white prayer f.	CHAT	216:52
mere discord of f.	GRAV	382:21
flail I wield the f.	SHEL	813:75
flakes f. burn in the sinking sun	SHEL	812:54
flame coal to kindle fleshly f.	SPEN	838:34
crack in the f.	JEFF	453:17
darkness shot with...purple f.	OFAO	647:96
feed his sacred f.	COLE	235:27
f. fate dares not move	PHIL	676:53
f. of incandescent terror	ELIOT	321:90
f. of life and love	LAWR	513:57
f. out like shining	HOPK	428:70
f. that lit the battle's wreck	HEMA	409:58
f. to qualify	SHAK	802:78
in a shapeless f.	DONNE	291:33
Jabberwock, with eyes of f.	CARR	204:90
Life, a Fury slinging f.	TENN	874:74
live f. will start	GRAV	382:23
Love is not a f.	MARG	570:69
malicious bloody f.	PEPYS	674:7
one burning f. together	TENN	870:86
plays around the f.!	GAY	362:15
sickly f.	CONG	241:70
sinking f. of hilarity	DICK	279:90
so full of subtil f.	BEAU	70:11
that little f. which never dies	RENO	711:58
tongues of f. are in-folded	ELIOT	321:94
whose f. creeps in	PEELE	672:70
with ethereal f.	BYRON	187:54
flames by her like thin f.	ROSS	726:52
Commit it then to the f.	HUME	438:7
f. but a lot of rubbish	MACD	550:42
f. from their large nostrils!	BLAKE	139:81
F. in the forehead	MILT	600:94
from those f. No light	MILT	601:35
on each hand the f.	MILT	602:43
warmth of shepherds' f.	MARL	572:3
world in f.	VOLT	914:38
world is in f. today	WITTE	950:19
flaming To f. youth	SHAK	784:41
Flanders armies swore terribly in F.	STER	848:34
In F. fields	MCCR	548:11
with the Duke in F.	LOWE	539:98
flap f. unfurled	YEATS	965:8
flapdragon swallowed than a f.	SHAK	763:21
flapped f. and fought	HODG	421:20

flash came by a lightning f.	WILS	948:51
f. that brings good fortune	RHYS	712:77
Life...a f. of a firefly	HAGG	391:7
Mirth is like a f. of lightning	ADDI	6:34
that seeming bang and f.	ORWE	653:23
flashes like f. of lightning	SCHO	748:52
objects recognised, In f.	WORD	958:85
occasional f. of silence	SMITH	831:57
saw the f.	SZIL	865:31
some f. of genius	BYRON	188:79
flask forty cents a f.	LEAC	515:7
flat back to the gentleman's f.	MANS	567:7
believe that the earth is f.	DRIB	299:5
fictional characters are f.	WAUGH	924:95
He is many times f.	DRYD	300:20
Strike f. the thick rotundity	SHAK	792:5
teach it round or f.	JOHN	458:20
theorists who declare...world is f.	CANN	196:6
Very f., Norfolk	COWA	249:47
flatten Age will f. a man	JONES	466:27
flatter abuse the King that f.	SHAK	798:81
F. the mountain tops	SHAK	801:48
Hope...dost thou f. me?	SIDN	820:48
flatterer f. does not have a good opinion	LABR	502:27
flattering nymphs with their f.	SITW	823:4
flattery care a bit for f.	MERE	588:35
care nothing for f.	CURZ	260:5
Dismiss...your f.	SHAK	762:86
f. is the bellows	SHAK	798:81
f. lost on poet's ear	SCOTT	752:14
f. of one's peers	LODGE	534:99
F. soothe...Death?	GRAY	384:67
guilt of f.	JOHN	463:73
Imitation is the sincerest form of f.	COLT	238:83
paid with f.	JOHN	460:78
questions...under the guise of f.	CHOP	223:34
school of f. and dissimulation	WENT	931:52
When f. soothes	DRYD	302:78
flatware look at f. catalogs	COUP	248:35
Flaubert a Tolstoy or a F.	WOLFE	953:83
His true Penelope was F.	POUND	691:1
shut up about F.	AMIS	16:42
flaunt got it, f. it	ANON	25:66
If you've got it, f. it	BROO	163:13
flavour faint f. of toast	TRAV	896:94
f. as hickory smoke	MUMF	625:40
full f. of their content	MILL	593:56
give f. to his tickled vanity	WEBB	925:6
high celestial f.	BYRON	190:11
ignorant of f.	FISH	337:65
spice...That gives it all its f.	COWP	251:15
flaw china jar receive a f.	POPE	685:35
fault of f.	GILB	369:50
flawed His f. heart	SHAK	793:36
I'm a f. character	ARMS	32:46
We are the f. ones	DELI	271:42
flaws beautiful f. in nature	WOLL	954:90
hundred thousand f.	SHAK	792:3
new kinds of f.	MINS	608:13
We all have f.	THUR	890:87
flax smoking f. shall he not quench	BIBLE	109:86
smoking f. shall he not quench	BIBLE	117:82
flayed saw a woman f.	SWIFT	861:22
flaying f. would be fair	HOUS	433:82
flea between a louse and a f.	JOHN	464:88
clog the foot of a f.	SHAK	786:15
English literature's performing f.	OCAS	646:80
f. in mine ear	NASHE	767:36
Mark but this f.	DONNE	291:36
naturalists observe, a f.	SWIFT	863:66
volume can ever be written on the f.	MELV	585:64
fleas dog is full of f.	ACHE	3:54
f. that tease	BELL	77:70
F....upon the body	LAND	506:28
praised his f.?	YEATS	966:15
rise with f.	WEBS	926:34
fled left his garment...and f.	BIBLE	93:41
lovers f. away	KEATS	477:37
fledglings crow loves his f.	MORE	618:11
flee They f. from me	WYATT	964:90
fleece f. was white as snow	HALE	392:29
forest f.	HOUS	431:47
won the Golden F.	BELL	76:14
fleet Arabian f.	GIBB	366:95
Beauteous the f.	SMART	826:66
Fire and f. and candle-lighte	BALL	59:54

f. of stars is anchored	FLEC	340:37
that is not also f.	THOM	885:59
Third F.'s sunken	HALS	393:43
took care of our f.	ADDI	7:35
who can be dull in F. Street	LAMB	505:78
whole f.'s lit up	WOOD	954:3
fleets Ten thousand f. sweep over	BYRON	188:71
flesh all f. shall see it together	BIBLE	108:79
All f. waxeth old	BIBLE	113:94
bloody f. our only food	ELIOT	320:65
bread and f. in the morning	BIBLE	97:60
delicate white human f.	FIEL	335:24
door of my f.	BRID	158:10
east wind made f.	APPL	30:94
empty boast of f.	HABI	391:2
errors of f.	THOM	885:72
feel new gods in the f.	LAWR	513:55
few blows are struck into f.	MAIL	560:47
f. and blood	THOR	888:25
f. and blood	THAC	880:21
f. and blood so cheap!	HOOD	426:32
f. and my heart faileth	BIBLE	101:86
f.; but in what shape	MILT	602:46
f. is as grass	BIBLE	130:65
f. is sad, alas!	MALL	562:96
f. is weak	BIBLE	119:43
f. longeth for thee	BIBLE	101:78
F. of f., Bone	MILT	606:52
f. of her f.	BINY	135:54
F. Of Hope	NICH	636:73
f. of mine might be	SWIN	863:88
f. of my f.	BIBLE	91:90
f. of thy dear Son	BOOK	147:72
f. profiteth nothing	BIBLE	123:37
f. sinks downward	SHAK	765:64
F. was the reason	DE	271:19
f. which walls	SHAK	764:52
f. without cares	CIXO	227:47
From this world-wearied f.	SHAK	766:14
give them an heart of f.	BIBLE	110:30
give us hearts o' f.!	OCAS	646:77
happit f. and blude	FERG	333:87
heart and my f. crieth out	BIBLE	101:88
hollow prison of my f.	SHAK	760:26
horror of the word 'f.'	RENO	711:55
huge hill of f.	SHAK	771:47
in my f. shall I see God	BIBLE	98:8
Is my somber f. and skin	CULL	257:45
joys are more to f. and blood	DRYD	303:15
Let's press the f.	JOHN	458:17
little f.	AURE	45:44
look like f. and blood	MOORE	616:70
maketh marks in the f.	BIBLE	113:2
make your f. creep	DICK	277:48
marriage makes man and wife one f.	CONG	240:37
material is our own f.	THOR	888:25
men are f. and blood	SHAK	777:26
more fatal than painted f.	MACN	557:94
Mrs Forthby in the f.	SHAR	806:73
Neither f. nor fleshless	ELIOT	319:49
not of f. and body	KEYN	484:72
outlive all f.	BYRON	189:82
pleasure of the f.	FUEN	354:59
poem...dream made f.	MILL	594:81
so much f....so much nimbleness	DEKK	270:13
Take thou thy pound of f.	SHAK	770:16
they shall be one f.	BIBLE	91:90
things of f.	BIBLE	125:17
this circle of f.	BROW	165:63
thorn in the f.	BIBLE	127:76
too solid f. would melt	SHAK	780:37
touch his bone and his f.	BIBLE	98:92
trees were surfaced like f.	LEE	519:98
vacations of the f.	TZARA	904:62
walk not after the f.	BIBLE	125:16
we are one, One f.	MILT	606:53
What case of f. and blood	ROCH	719:10
What's this f.?	WEBS	927:57
when we sat by the f. pots	BIBLE	93:64
Word was made f.	BIBLE	122:18
your despicable and rotten f.	MARQ	574:44
Fletcher gave Shakespeare and F. all	DENH	272:62
fleur f. de France as perdut	ANON	20:37
flew One f. over the cuckoo's nest	KESEY	483:62
something f. between me and the sun	BLUN	143:73
flexibility latter has f. of thought	PASC	666:62
flexible f. at all times	DIRK	287:6

flexitime F. is the essence of respect	PACK 658:7
flick bonded in their f. and flow	AVIS 47:1
flies As f. to wanton boys	SHAK 793:17
Dead f. cause the ointment	BIBLE 106:30
Eyes and Reason...to study F.	POPE 689:46
f. on summer eves	KEATS 478:45
f. when I pursue it	ELIZ 321:3
may catch small f.	SWIFT 861:23
Plague him with f.	SHAK 788:83
swarm like summer f.	SHAK 760:11
these summer f.	SHAK 763:24
Unfading moths, immortal f.	BROO 163:2
flight alarms of struggle and f.	ARNO 33:67
as immutable as those of f.	HEMI 410:83
day of their f.	MACA 545:37
Explores his solitary f.	MILT 603:68
f. is what they long for	WILL 945:85
f. of angels sing	SHAK 785:76
spread his aery f.	MILT 603:65
Swift be thine approaching f.	SHEL 816:54
Swift be thy f.!	SHEL 816:65
tiptoe for a f.	KEATS 475:63
flights four f. Thursday morning	WRIG 963:73
flighty f. as birds	DAY 267:38
flint snore upon the f.	SHAK 803:3
wait for the great f.	BIRN 136:19
Flintstones like relying on the F.	ARMEY 32:38
flip the rest is not worth a f.	BRON 161:62
flirtation bit of f. with missy	SPEKE 836:82
float English policy is to f. lazily	CECIL 210:30
F. like a butterfly	ALI 13:72
floating Artist of the F. World	ISHI 447:71
floats f. with the tide	HAZL 403:42
flock Christ's f.	BOOK 147:77
Fed the same f.	MILT 599:83
feed his f. like a shepherd	BIBLE 108:80
keeping watch over their f. by night	BIBLE 120:69
silent was the f.	KEATS 477:14
We are his f.	SCOT 755:88
flock-bed once a f.-b., but repaired	POPE 686:69
flocks fields and f. have charms	CRAB 252:30
f., or herds, of human	MILT 603:75
nibbling f. do stray	MILT 597:45
sang of f. and farms	VIRG 914:28
shepherds feed their f.	MARL 574:41
Flodden F.'s fatal field	SCOTT 752:27
flogging f. me constantly	TROL 898:52
flood across the f.	TENN 875:75
and takes the f.	TENN 878:88
broad f. behind	MACA 546:48
days that were before the f.	BIBLE 118:31
f. could not wash away	CONG 240:46
f. may bear me far	TENN 879:6
f. of remembrance	LAWR 512:46
f. that does not flow	SLES 825:52
not properly born, till f.	DICK 280:52
passage to the fallen f.	CRAB 252:42
rude bridge that arched the f.	EMER 324:48
taken at the f.	SHAK 778:48
telegraph poles above a f.	NICO 637:85
Thorough f., thorough fire	SHAK 767:25
tide...taken at the f.	BYRON 190:19
trees that yield to the f.	SOPH 834:28
years before the f.	MARV 577:90
floods f. of great waters	BIBLE 100:53
rain descended, and the f. came	BIBLE 115:56
serious storms and f.	SILV 821:72
floor beneath the watery f.	MILT 600:94
Clatter across the f.	MACC 546:65
f. under wages and a ceiling	WRIS 963:76
Look how the f. of heaven	SHAK 770:19
man has just waxed the f.	NASH 631:74
oiled his way around the f.	LERN 523:84
On the f. I am...at ease	POLL 684:2
put diamonds on the f.	RIVE 716:56
repeat that on the Golden F.!	HOUS 433:79
rose along the gusty f.	KEATS 477:26
swept the f.	GILB 368:34
three skips on the f.	BALL 59:62
trail...up the f.	STEV 853:67
women...kick the f.	OSBO 655:84
floors f. of memory	ELIOT 317:72
f. of plaister, and the walls of dung	POPE 686:69
f. of silent seas	ELIOT 316:64
flop Classics...prevent f.	WOOLF 956:37
f. in favour of your husband	DICK 282:97
f. is a f.	PAGL 659:18
flops F. are a part of life	RUSS 735:49
Flora if he had married F.	SCOTT 753:38
Tasting of F.	KEATS 478:42
floral F. fascism	INDE 445:24
Florence maid called F.?	SAKI 739:57
Rode past fair F.	KEATS 477:11
Flores At F. in the Azores	TENN 878:95
Florinda Her name is F.	SAKI 739:57
flotilla old f. lay	KIPL 489:81
flounder f., the air	ATWO 41:33
flour Finer than f., alive	ROET 722:56
flourish f. or may fade	GOLD 376:98
Human nature will not f.	HAWT 401:3
No more doth f.	SPEN 838:33
tidy and satisfactory f.	ELIZ 322:10
flourishing fat and f.	BIBLE 102:98
flow bonded in their flick and f.	AVIS 47:1
flower About the f. disguised	MARV 577:98
as a f. of the field	BIBLE 102:10
bar the f. away	ANON 21:42
bear no f.	SHEL 816:49
Beauty is but a f.	NASHE 632:96
blood-red f. of revolution	RAND 706:59
bloom upon a f.	THOM 885:63
blushing f. shall rise	POPE 685:15
bot ane faiding f.	HENR 412:22
Buddha...in the petals of a f.	PIRS 679:89
constellated f. that never sets	SHEL 816:60
creep from f. to f.	SHEL 812:55
drives the f.	THOM 883:3
fell upon a little western f.	SHAK 767:27
f. amang them a'	BALL 58:54
f. is born to blush unseen	GRAY 384:69
f. is the concrete cloverleaf	MUMF 625:38
f. of France is lost	ANON 20:37
f. of old age	DEMO 272:49
f. of Scotland	WILL 946:31
f. that sad embroidery wears	MILT 599:91
f. thereof falleth away	BIBLE 130:65
glory in the f.	WORD 960:12
grass withereth, the f. fadeth	BIBLE 108:79
held my f. in a clenched fist	HOFF 421:25
Here is the f. that you	MEIL 584:39
How my face, your f.	BROW 167:13
insect moves toward its f.	BALZ 61:1
learning lightly like a f.	TENN 875:2
look like the innocent f.	SHAK 796:17
loved a tree or f.	MOORE 618:6
lovelier f....was never sown	WORD 957:63
Man...cometh forth like a f.	BIBLE 98:5
meanest f. that blows	WORD 960:13
mysterious East, perfumed like a f.	CONR 244:35
nayles whitter than the lylye f.	CHAU 217:98
Nobody sees a f.	OKEE 648:23
orange f. perfumes the bower	SCOTT 754:69
pluck this f. safety	SHAK 771:42
Poetry...the f. of...experience	HUNT 439:25
same f. that smiles to day	HERR 415:12
see...heaven in a wild f.	BLAKE 140:24
seize the f.	BURNS 179:25
shakes the f. free	MANS 567:3
some gilded...f.	VAUG 909:34
stem of the contained f.	ROET 722:57
stronger than a f.	SHAK 801:57
sweetest f. for scent	SHEL 815:23
sweetest f. of all the field	SHAK 766:9
This midsummer f.	SKEL 824:29
this the noble f.	DONNE 293:63
to darn, to f. or knit	LEWIS 526:51
touch his f.	JONS 468:83
Wearing the white f.	TENN 876:40
white rose and bean f.	FRAME 346:75
whose fair f.	SHAK 786:97
ys the f. of chevalry	MALO 563:11
flower-bell fancy from a f.-b.	BROW 168:38
flowering f. of His fields	TENN 878:79
flowerings brief f. of feminism	FALU 329:12
flowerless f. fields of heaven	SWIN 863:81
f. rocks of hell	SITW 823:96
flowers And it won't be f.	AUDEN 42:70
azure moss and f.	SHEL 813:81
bees are assaulting...the f.	REED 709:27
better than a bunch of f.	CARY 207:66
blushing f.	POPE 685:15
brought...cannons rather than f.	PEOP 673:83
but as a bed of f.	DONNE 293:73
enjoy the spring f.	SU 858:65
fairest f.	WORD 962:48
Fair f. that are not gathered	SHAK 762:82
f. begotten	SWIN 863:83
f. come in stony places	MASE 580:68
F. of all hue	MILT 604:97
f. of the forest	COCK 233:81
f. of the forest	ELLI 322:25
f. the tenderness	OWEN 657:26
f. to strew Thy way	HERB 413:59
gathers its material from the f.	BACON 50:44
Gave...her f. to love	BROO 162:88
glass f. at Harvard	MOORE 617:79
ground with vernal f.	MILT 599:90
honey of all f.	NASHE 631:89
hundred f. blossom	MAO 569:34
immortal f. of poesy	MARL 572:2
into foam of f.	SWIN 863:88
intuitively in f.	RUNGE 731:53
leaves and f. do cover	WEBS 926:36
like f., a stronger scent	STAEL 842:97
love...as the f. do	RILKE 715:39
love to the f.	KEND 480:85
lusty song of fruits and f.	BLAKE 139:82
memories of f. and grass	ROBE 717:73
men bearing f.	SPARK 836:75
one which gathering f....fears a	DONNE 290:16
Our f. are merely—f.	POE 683:87
Overlook a space of f.	TENN 869:79
play with f.	SHAK 775:68
prairie f. lie low	LIND 530:22
sleeping f.	WORD 961:30
That f. would bloom	KEATS 476:87
the f. anew	PHIL 676:52
thy garden f.	JONS 467:72
to Barca f.	POPE 688:31
tomb-stones where f. should be	BLAKE 140:15
too soon for f.	DELA 271:35
Until the f. are fragrant	TOJO 893:41
Where have all the f. gone?	SEEG 755:1
With other f.	HERR 415:13
young days of gathering f.	PEAC 671:55
flowery cool f. lap of earth	ARNO 34:75
wakes me from my f. bed?	SHAK 767:35
flowing longer f., longer free	HERR 415:13
fluctuations mysterious f. of trade	ELIOT 315:31
fluffy But f., just f.	HERB 412:41
fluidity terrible f. of self-revelation	JAMES 451:53
fluids blood and other vital f.	STER 848:38
flush f. of a new-born sun	KIPL 490:97
flustered never f., never apathetic	AURE 45:47
flute brains upon the f.	BROW 169:82
f....is too exciting	ARIS 32:28
gauger played the f.	STEV 851:25
The sound of the f. will cure	THEO 882:80
flutes to the tune of f. kept stroke	SHAK 794:55
flutter f. far more, than leaves	CENN 211:44
fluttering f. to a bench	SACK 737:9
flux All is f., nothing is stationary	HERA 412:31
passing f. of immediate things	WHIT 936:65
fly as great a f. as Cassio	SHAK 789:7
cut off, and we f. away	BIBLE 101:94
f. in his hand	STER 848:31
f....may sting	JOHN 459:58
f. sat upon the axletree	BACON 53:42
I cannot f.	SHAK 798:75
Indoor f. casting	NASH 631:83
like a f. crawling	INGR 446:43
long-legged f.	YEATS 967:37
noise of a f.	DONNE 293:74
show the f. the way out	WITT 951:27
solitary f.!	GRAY 384:59
those that f., may fight again	BUTL 185:85
'Thou shalt.'	CLEE 229:81
unzipped f. caught in forever amber	COND 239:13
we cannot f.	EMPS 326:10
will f. no more	HOLM 424:64
wisdom made the f.	NASH 631:80
wouldn't hurt a f.	LEAC 515:23
fly-fishing F. f. may be...pleasant	JOHN 465:7
flying Armstrongs are f.	HOGG 422:41
f. in the face of presumptions	JAMES 450:41
f. through space forever	GAGA 356:8
growing, f., happening	REID 710:44
shot one bird f.	HEMI 409:69
foam Cowslip...like tethered f.	CRANE 253:66
f. on the river	SCOTT 752:32

foaminess

into f. of flowers	SWIN 863:88
wind…wild and dank with f.	KING 487:43
foaminess f. of the Falls	SALA 739:70
focus f. on the solution	TRUMP 900:1
Johnny, keep it out of f.	WILD 942:32
foe angry with my f.	BLAKE 140:17
Call no man f.	BENS 81:86
erect and manly f.	CANN 197:9
everyone's a f.	CLARE 228:51
find a f.	PARK 664:18
f. oft-times having the f. in sight	DONNE 291:19
furnace for your f.	SHAK 804:36
never made a f.	TENN 877:55
our sneaking f.	SITW 824:18
overcome but half his f.	MILT 602:51
perhaps a jealous f.	SHEL 815:45
wild unsated f.!	COLL 237:73
foes against the f.	SMART 826:65
doubt of future f.	ELIZ 321:1
f., and oh, my friends	MILL 592:19
judge a man by his f.	CONR 244:33
loins of these two f.	SHAK 765:65
neither f. nor loving friends	KIPL 492:63
new f. arise Threatening to	MILT 601:25
Set upon the f.!	SHAK 761:54
slay their f.	MACD 550:48
thirty thousand f.	MACA 546:48
Words…the great f. of reality	CONR 244:43
fog achievements…in a blessed, warm f.	CONR 244:49
A f., miss	DICK 281:58
brown f. of a winter dawn	ELIOT 318:97
f. comes on little cat feet	SAND 742:14
F. everywhere	DICK 281:55
f. is rising	DICK 284:56
Hover through the f.	SHAK 795:97
like a cold f.	ACHE 2:34
natural f. of the good man's mind	BROW 167:26
trying to sculpture f.	LEHM 520:23
fogeydom F. is the last bastion	THER 882:92
foggy f. day in London Town	GERS 365:78
fogs rising f. prevail upon the day	DRYD 300:44
foil golden f. all over them	SPEN 838:22
shining from shook f.	HOPK 428:70
foining f. o'nights	SHAK 772:82
fold f. after f., to the fainting air	SHEL 815:22
f. my tens	KAUF 474:38
if your name's above the f.	LANCE 506:24
Now I f. you down	SEXT 758:44
one f., and one shepherd	BIBLE 123:45
tangl'd in the f.	MILT 608:2
folders manila f. and mucilage	ROET 722:55
foliage love for Linton is like the f.	BRON 162:79
stillness of the buried f.	HOLM 423:55
Folies-Bergère F.-B. and looks at	STOC 855:7
folio whole volumes, in f.	SHAK 763:8
folios mighty f.…a lordly band	CRAB 251:26
folk All music is f. music	ARMS 33:49
f. begin to tak the gate	BURNS 179:18
F. music…fat people	DYLAN 309:58
f. to goon on pilgrimages	CHAU 217:70
f. wou'd hae a doubt on	FERG 333:84
itinerant f. artists	ROCK 721:40
just look at all the f.	LAUD 511:14
matches of the Southron f.	THOM 886:84
novels are strange f.	LUCAS 541:49
'the Big F.', as they call us	TOLK 893:47
trouble with a f. song	LAMB 506:19
Wee f., good f.	ALLI 14:6
we theatre f.	MANK 566:75
folks bunch of f. hoping	WALK 917:39
Don't let the old f. know	HERB 412:39
eat, good f.	PRIOR 696:7
F. don't like to have somebody	LEE 518:89
f. eat the stuff they raise	STEI 845:83
hand f. over to God's mercy	ELIOT 315:26
my f. were growing old	STEV 854:89
nor any of my f.	MITC 610:42
That's all f.!	FREL 350:51
We tortured some f.	OBAMA 645:54
What signifies't for f. to chide	SKIN 825:50
When f. git ole	HARR 399:50
where the old f. stay	FOST 345:54
follies charming f.	GILL 370:77
f. of this dull age	CAREW 198:46
f. which a man regrets most	ROWL 729:22
indulge in a few f.	PROU 697:41
point out to us our f.	TROL 897:26
Pour her exotic f. o'er the town	BYRON 187:28
pretty f. that themselves commit	SHAK 769:93
vices and f. of human kind	CONG 240:34
whose f. cease with their youth	PITT 679:1
follow f. me	GARI 360:73
f. thou me!	SCHW 751:94
he saith unto them, F. me	BIBLE 114:26
horrid thing to f.	JAMES 450:40
I f. the worse	OVID 657:19
In following him I f.	SHAK 788:81
Jesus said unto him, F. me	BIBLE 116:60
saith unto him, F. me	BIBLE 116:62
where few can f.	KENN 480:86
follower misguided f. climbs	ROCH 719:11
followers f. of Jesus	JOHN 459:38
vice promises to her f.	MILT 600:10
followship practising f.	THAT 881:74
folls Deal round to happy f.	BYRON 188:63
folly Age from f.	SHAK 794:51
All my joys to this are f.	BURT 181:74
brood of F.	MILT 597:49
curse of mankind, f. and ignorance	SHAK 786:30
darling F., Fickleness	MAND 565:65
epoch of f. and shame	ZOLA 970:16
Fashion, though F.'s child	CRAB 251:27
f.…has a certain stamp	GERH 365:69
f. him that is in reputation	BIBLE 106:30
f. in that of a great kingdom	SMITH 827:85
f. is not always f.	AUST 46:76
f. of 'Women's Rights'	VICT 912:76
f. to be wise	GRAY 383:48
fool returneth to his f.	BIBLE 105:96
in their f. not less blind	HOPE 427:56
knavery, and f. to excuse	CHUR 224:53
like f. shows	MILT 605:41
lovely woman stoops to f.	AUST 46:79
lovely woman stoops to f.	GOLD 376:93
make good their own f.	BACON 51:77
most loving, mere f.	SHAK 779:84
moved to f. by a noise	LAWR 514:92
Neebours' fauts an f.	BURNS 178:92
noise of f.	MILT 598:52
obstinacy of f.	STOWE 856:34
our pride, our f., or our fate	DENH 272:61
rather of their f.	ELIOT 320:60
shoot F. as it flies	POPE 686:71
such gratuitous f.	HUXL 441:71
too presumptuous f.	HARTE 400:74
uses his f. like a stalking-horse	SHAK 780:26
whirled into f. and vice	TENN 875:15
fond f. thing vainly invented	BOOK 150:41
F. without art	DRYD 301:59
never prove so f.	SHAK 791:75
rarity which I cannot but be f. of	ROCH 720:19
so f. of one another	SWIFT 861:26
Fonstein F.…advanced category	BELL 78:97
font in the porphyry f.	TENN 873:49
food America, bring your own f.	LEBO 518:66
and the f. a tragedy	POWE 693:44
As I do live by f.	SHAK 779:78
bloody flesh our only f.	ELIOT 320:65
Continent people have good f.	MIKES 590:86
desire for f. and sex	TOOLE 894:59
discovered that alcohol was a f.	WODE 952:40
don't want any f. that tastes white	WEST 932:78
enough f. for eight	MOLI 611:83
estimated even in f. and necessaries	RICA 712:79
every mouthful of f.	FORD 342:87
Fame is a f.	DOBS 289:78
fed by a different f.	DISR 288:34
fed with the same f.	SHAK 769:1
finds its f. in music	LILLO 529:1
f. and not fine words	MOLI 611:88
F. comes first	BREC 157:89
f. for worms!	FRAN 348:7
f. is love	SHEL 814:1
f. of love	SHAK 785:77
f. out of the earth	BIBLE 102:11
give them f. and shelter	JARR 452:89
glum urge for f. to fill us	FISH 337:65
Hard f. for Midas	SHAK 770:5
having f. and raiment	BIBLE 129:22
junk f.	GASS 361:86
knowledge is as f.	MILT 605:28
libraries are f.	TUCH 901:14
love of f.	SHAW 807:19
man in a jail has…better f.	JOHN 460:88
more delicate the f.	INNO 446:47
music, moody f.	SHAK 794:60
nourishing, and wholesome F.	SWIFT 862:58
perpetual struggle for room and f.	MALT 563:21
problem is f.	DONL 290:8
quantity of f. required	RICA 712:80
senses…supply Fresh f.	WORD 956:51
Sharing f.…an intimate act	FISH 337:64
ships to bear our f. away	WILDE 940:45
taste for…French f.	SCHL 747:37
think they're still getting real f.	COUP 248:29
Throwing away f.	FRAN 347:91
was there like f. or air	ROCK 720:29
what McDonalds is to f.	PILG 678:79
With eager feeding f.	SHAK 764:39
Women Whose Lives Are F.	OATES 643:8
fool A f., a f., I met a f.	SHAK 779:78
a f. never changes his mind	BRAN 156:72
Any f. can be brave	MITC 610:43
Any f. may write a…book	GRAY 385:96
any man is so very a f.	SHAK 761:58
appear a f., a blockhead, or a knave	DRYD 303:24
becomes a f. and a jester!	SHAK 773:99
Better a witty f.	SHAK 785:86
better to be a f.	STEV 852:84
blundering f. may	MORT 621:73
Busy old f.	DONNE 291:25
but in a f.'s cap	HOPK 428:66
can love like a f.	NASH 630:62
damn f. if he doesn't	FAUL 331:48
every f. in Buxton	RUSK 734:19
f. among fools	WILD 943:50
f. at the other	JOHN 465:7
f. consistent	POPE 687:95
f. doth think he is wise	SHAK 780:16
f. has a lot to teach	RABE 704:18
f. hath said in his heart	BIBLE 99:32
f. his whole life long	LUTH 542:76
F. in every man's mouth	BUNY 174:81
f.…in every married couple	FIEL 335:27
f., In power of others	MILT 607:84
f. in the eye of the world	CONG 240:47
f. is happy	POPE 687:83
f. is love that in your will	SHAK 801:55
F.: it is you who are pursued	SHAW 807:21
f. lies here	KIPL 490:99
f. o'th' other senses	SHAK 796:28
f. returneth to his folly	BIBLE 105:96
'F.,' said my muse to me	SIDN 820:44
f.'s bauble	CROM 256:23
f. some of the people	LINC 529:5
f.…that first invented kissing!	SWIFT 863:74
f. to make me merry	SHAK 779:7
f. too large for it	CHES 221:83
f. too many of the people	THUR 890:78
f. uttereth all his mind	BIBLE 105:5
f., who trusts a man	MARIE 571:75
greatest f. may ask more	COLT 238:84
have played the f.	BIBLE 96:41
He's a f. that marries	WYCH 964:3
human and makes me a f.	LEGU 520:18
I'd be a damn' f.	THOM 884:28
idle f.	FORD 343:5
Into a strumpet's f.	SHAK 794:42
knaves do work with, called a f.	BUTL 184:63
laughter of a f.	BIBLE 106:21
learned f. is more	MOLI 612:89
Let me play the f.	SHAK 768:69
like a musical f.	HUGH 434:10
little else than a f.	MCGO 551:75
Love's not time's f.	SHAK 802:80
make a f. of himself!	STEV 852:47
manage a f.	KIPL 489:70
man and wife make one f.	JONS 467:65
maxim is worthy of the f.	MACA 545:25
more of the f. than of the wise	BACON 50:91
Napoleon thinks that I am a f.	ALEX 12:59
No boasting like a f.	SHAK 797:57
Oh heav'nly f.	SIDN 820:49
patriot…a f.	DRYD 302:90
play the f.…in's own house	SHAK 783:13
power to do any damn f. thing	FULB 355:61
prove one's self a f.	HAWT 402:13
resolv'd to live a f.	BEAU 70:11
satisfy anyone but a damned f.	BART 66:15
'school' 'f.', a babbling rhyme	SHAK 774:56
smarts so little as a f.	POPE 687:98

foreboding

Socrates...than a f. satisfied	MILL 591:7	
surely f. a man	WHITE 935:40	
the more f. I	SHAK 778:74	
time to f. with politics	ROGE 723:83	
To please a f.	CONG 241:67	
What f. is not so wise	SHAK 763:15	
whether he is a wise man or a f.	BLAKE 141:33	
whosoever shall say, Thou f.	BIBLE 114:32	
works is a f.	MORL 620:43	
worship this dull f.	SHAK 804:34	
wretched, rash, intruding f.	SHAK 784:39	
foolery more hateful form of f.	BROW 169:68	
fooling always f. with something	WHITE 935:28	
foolish Better...than a f. wit	SHAK 785:86	
disguises from the f.	BIER 134:75	
envious of the f.	BIBLE 101:84	
f., fond old man	SHAK 793:31	
F. the man who trusts her	FRAN 347:96	
f. thing was but a toy	SHAK 786:25	
f. thing well done	JOHN 462:27	
Forgive our f. ways	WHIT 938:24	
God hath chosen the f. things	BIBLE 126:36	
I, being young and f.	YEATS 965:3	
likened unto a f. man	BIBLE 115:56	
never said a f. thing	ROCH 720:27	
not such a f. thing	ISHI 447:73	
old and f. king	BIBLE 106:19	
Only the f. are punished	MARG 570:64	
saying a f. thing	STER 848:45	
smallest f. act makes it idiotic	YOUR 968:57	
These F. Things	MARV 578:12	
foolishly don't think f.	JOHN 464:89	
foolishness age of f.	DICK 282:94	
f. of preaching	BIBLE 126:35	
fools all the f. in town	TWAIN 903:65	
Atheists, f., and madmen!	ONEI 651:70	
Be friends, you English f.	SHAK 775:83	
Beggared by f.	DRYD 302:84	
busy f. may be stopped	DONNE 291:19	
called the Paradise of F.	MILT 603:86	
exportation of f.	CONG 241:57	
Fashion...guide of f.	CRAB 251:27	
f. and cowards might sit safe	OTWAY 656:2	
F. are as like husbands	SHAK 786:6	
f. are in a...majority	IBSEN 444:7	
F. are my theme	BYRON 186:24	
f. by heavenly compulsion	SHAK 792:89	
F.! For I also had my hour	CHES 220:51	
f. rush in	POPE 685:28	
f. shall not err therein	BIBLE 108:77	
For...government let f. contest	POPE 687:84	
Fortune, that favours f.	JONS 467:63	
great stage of f.	SHAK 793:27	
I am two f.	DONNE 291:32	
If honest Nature made you f.	BURNS 177:68	
make f. of themselves about	SHAW 806:88	
many f. at a university	GERH 365:69	
marriage...leaves 'em still two f.	CONG 240:37	
more f. than wise	GIBB 367:7	
Nature meant but f.	POPE 685:16	
none but f. would keep	SHAK 787:64	
pair of credulous f.	SHIR 819:18	
people in the world are f.	WILD 943:48	
play the f. with the time	SHAK 772:79	
please the f.	DRYD 301:70	
poor f. decoyed	PEPYS 674:4	
proved plain f.	POPE 685:17	
secrets...must be kept...from f.	DRYD 299:16	
shoal of f. for tenders	CONG 241:64	
soldiers, mostly f.	BIER 134:80	
stalling between two f.	FRY 354:52	
suffer f. gladly	BIBLE 127:75	
the f. caught it	YEATS 966:16	
there are two kinds of f.	MORR 620:49	
Thus may poor f.	SHAK 803:98	
Tories remained f.	WALP 919:78	
traps for eager and clever f.	SNYD 833:94	
twenty-seven millions mostly f.	CARL 201:41	
virtue of f.	BACON 50:51	
What f. middle-class girls are	DRAB 298:81	
what f. these mortals be!	SHAK 767:38	
wise men follow f.	BACON 52:98	
With the flannelled f.	KIPL 492:49	
world is full up...of f. and knaves	BUCK 172:40	
foolscaps f. of air	AVIS 47:1	
foot And the Forty-second F.!	HOOD 426:20	
blood from head to f.	MACL 554:27	
breasts are under our f.	SHAW 807:20	
caught my f.	GROS 389:80	
cleft the Devil's f.	DONNE 291:23	
'eathen idol's f.	KIPL 489:82	
Englishman, sets f. on it	STEF 844:54	
espied his cloven f.	BALL 58:58	
f. and hand go cold	ANON 21:60	
f. for f.	BIBLE 94:67	
f. in Eden	MUIR 624:22	
f. is on my native heath	SCOTT 753:56	
f. less prompt	ARNO 35:21	
f. out of joint	BIBLE 105:94	
f. upon the stirrup	DELA 271:27	
from head to f.	TENN 874:66	
from head to f.	TENN 876:23	
from his head to his f.	MOORE 616:64	
his f. is guilty	BECK 72:38	
hold Creation in my f.	HUGH 435:31	
Leave not a f. of verse	POPE 689:39	
length of Prester John's f.	SHAK 774:28	
madly squeeze a right-hand f.	CARR 205:22	
make crouch beneath his f.	BROW 169:75	
never place their second f.	FONT 342:76	
no man's f. can pass	BOTT 152:82	
nor can f. feel	HOPK 428:70	
no rest for the sole of her f.	BIBLE 92:9	
One f. he centred	MILT 605:30	
One f. in Canada	GAY 362:9	
One f. in sea	SHAK 774:38	
One square f. less	BENC 78:6	
print of a man's naked f.	DEFOE 269:74	
proud f. of a conqueror	SHAK 768:66	
set her f. upon thy substance	BIBLE 113:88	
sole of his f.	SHAK 774:42	
speed of the f. race	YOUR 969:61	
stick out a f.	ADLER 8:67	
Th'inaudible and noiseless f.	SHAK 791:73	
trodden under f. of men	BIBLE 114:28	
trode her under f.	BIBLE 97:80	
walked with willing f.	STEV 851:25	
will not suffer thy f. to be moved	BIBLE 103:31	
wished myself on f.	MUNDY 625:43	
with shining f. shall pass	FITZ 337:72	
football All...I owe to f.	CAMUS 196:1	
base f. player	SHAK 792:90	
bewteis of the f.-b.	ANON 22:64	
College f.	GALL 358:37	
College f. is a sport	HUBB 434:2	
concentrate on f.	NICH 636:75	
concerning f. playing	STUB 858:61	
disregard for the rules of f.	ANON 23:85	
European f. without the English	CHAR 216:47	
F. causeth fighting	STUB 858:62	
f. field is a place	ROUS 729:8	
F. hooligans?	CLOU 232:68	
F....is a grand game	BADEN 54:59	
F. is all very well as a game	WILDE 942:25	
F. is like a religion	PELE 672:76	
F. is...more central to our culture	GREER 387:46	
f. is proposed at Christmas	ANON 23:89	
F....keep the coalminers off the streets	BRES 158:2	
f. magazines in their hands	BECK 71:34	
f. team is like a beautiful woman	WENG 931:50	
F.—the most exhilarating game	GOOD 378:45	
F. then was fighting sorrow	HOUS 431:42	
geriatric f. in the winter	KINN 488:62	
good of f.	TAYL 868:56	
ideal day for f.	SMITH 830:30	
In f. it is widely acknowledged	FRY 353:29	
kick it about all day like a f.	HOLM 424:68	
life is...a game of f.	SCOTT 753:39	
like a f. you do spurn me	SHAK 762:92	
married during the f. season?	SHAN 805:64	
more politics in f. than in politics	ERIK 327:38	
No f. player...within the City	ELIZ 321:2	
politics is like...a f. coach	MCCA 547:83	
seeing some sexy f.	GULL 390:93	
Some people think f.	SHAN 805:60	
talk about f. or women	BERL 85:51	
there be used F.-b., Golfe	JAME 449:19	
To watch a f. match	BARZ 67:42	
footballer no longer a f.	CRUY 256:37	
footballs street being full of f.	PEPYS 674:98	
footfalls F. echo in the memory	ELIOT 319:37	
foothold f. in the narrow strip of land	BAKER 56:4	
footing how...honesty, got f.	OTWAY 656:1	
lived on a friendly f.	LAMB 505:93	
foot-in-the-grave F.-i.-t.-g. young man!	GILB 369:48	
foot-landrakers joined with no f.-l.	SHAK 771:38	
footman eternal F. hold my coat	ELIOT 316:65	
footmen But of all f.	HAZL 404:55	
footnote greatness...soon be a f.	THAT 881:53	
footnotes series of f.	NABO 628:10	
series of f. to Plato	WHIT 936:69	
serried f. to man	GRASS 382:13	
footpath jog on, the f. way	SHAK 799:16	
footprint looking for a man's f.	BEER 73:80	
footprints f. of a gigantic hound!	DOYLE 297:64	
F. on the sands of time	LONG 535:16	
plaster casts of f.	PATE 669:14	
footsoles midwife slapped your f.	PLATH 681:30	
footsteps f. made no noise	DICK 279:95	
home his f....turned	SCOTT 752:16	
plants his f. in the sea	COWP 250:85	
poor slaves with weary f.	SHEL 815:45	
footstool make thine enemies thy f.	BIBLE 102:17	
fop f. in my heart	ETHE 327:48	
man of sense and a f.	CHES 219:34	
foppery f. of freedom	SHAK 787:48	
forbear F. to judge	SHAK 759:92	
forbid expressly to f. you	LOUI 537:65	
f. the King to keep it	INNO 466:48	
therefore I f. my tears	SHAK 784:59	
forbidden wicked and to be f.	STUB 858:60	
force alcohol is a...deadening f.	WEBB 925:7	
All governments use f.	PARE 663:89	
back her vote by physical f.	WRIG 962:62	
Better to use f.	SHUL 819:26	
combination of skill and f.	BURKE 176:38	
dedicated to f. and to beauty	RIMB 716:51	
disputes...settled by using f.	EISE 314:1	
envy...is f. t'admire!	DANI 262:32	
evil...is f. in the world	CHUR 224:51	
F. is the same throughout	LEON 522:70	
F. made the first slaves	ROUS 729:11	
f. maintaining...the world	DOST 294:91	
f. of honesty	SHAK 783:9	
f. of the bayonet!	MIRA 608:15	
f. that propels	KAND 472:14	
Life, f. and beauty	POPE 685:18	
lost faith...in natural f.	CARL 200:82	
May the f.	LUCAS 541:55	
motive f. impressed	NEWT 635:57	
No f. to win the victory	DYER 309:48	
no motion...no f.	WORD 957:64	
not by f. but by understanding	BRON 160:48	
not need to convince...by f.	WILS 949:78	
only f. capable	KING 487:36	
Other nations use 'f.'	WAUGH 924:77	
out by f. of arms	LOUI 537:64	
patience...achieve more than our f.	BURKE 176:47	
persuade gently, not by f.	PASC 667:84	
real revolutionary f.	OROU 652:95	
spent its novel f.	TENN 871:13	
supreme arbitrament of f.	CHUR 224:64	
The f. that through	THOM 883:3	
Tonality is a natural f.	HIND 419:66	
unofficial f.—the Baker Street	DOYLE 297:48	
use of f. alone is but temporary	BURKE 175:15	
Who overcomes By f.	MILT 602:51	
with an irresistible f.	HEDIN 406:4	
worth more than f. and rage	LAFO 504:53	
forced f.—by what?	FROMM 352:88	
f....into any...belief	RICH 714:15	
f. to like what you get	SHAW 808:56	
forces acknowledge the spiritual f.	MOORE 617:76	
balance of actual f.	NAPO 629:40	
centrifugal f. which are	NASH 631:85	
communicate with his f.	SCHW 750:89	
enhances the f. of the mind	PROU 698:58	
f., although small	MAO 568:26	
f. impressed thereon	NEWT 635:56	
f. which must bring	RUSS 734:34	
f. working in inverse order!	CARL 201:7	
modified aggregate of external f.	SPEN 835:67	
'targeted' by powerful f.	BELL 78:96	
Ford Jerome to F. Madox F.	COLE 234:2	
my friend F.	WILL 946:12	
Nixon...gave us General F.	ABZUG 2:17	
Our F....had been the first	HUXL 441:73	
ford bridge the f.	KIPL 490:8	
Fords swarming in F.	FERB 332:67	
fore at the f.	GILB 370:71	
foreboding I am filled with much f.	POWE 693:58	

forecast

with a deeper f. — FRAN 347:1
forecast even the weather f. — LODGE 534:94
prevents the events they f. — WRIS 963:77
forecastle crew is gambling in the f. — SHAW 810:9
forefathers f. had no other books — SHAK 759:98
genealogy of his f. — ECHE 310:14
Our f. would have died — OCON 646:82
recover it from all his f. — BUTL 186:12
rude f. of the hamlet — GRAY 384:64
simple f. would kill — MONT 613:17
Whatever our f. were — OVER 656:12
forefinger f. of all Time — TENN 872:32
f. of an alderman — SHAK 765:70
forehead Flames in the f. — MILT 600:94
He tapped his f. — CHRI 223:41
Love, knocking its blind f. — SAND 741:4
middle of her f. — LONG 536:40
Tap his f. first — WODE 951:36
with unbashful f. woo — SHAK 778:71
foreheads f. nobility is engraved — LAUT 511:27
foreign Armageddon is not a f. policy — ALBR 11:35
attacking the F. Secretary — BEVAN 89:57
courtly f. grace — TENN 879:99
defended...from f. invasion — REDM 709:21
do in f. affairs — JOHN 458:19
emancipating themselves from a f. — MAZZ 583:29
F. Secretary...naked — BEVAN 89:58
f. troop...in my country — PITT 679:9
in spite of...its f. propaganda — ORWE 654:37
knew a lot about f. affairs — REST 711:65
life is a f. country — KERO 483:52
loans...to f. nations — BAGE 53:44
No f. policy — KISS 493:88
past is a f. country — HART 400:76
portion of the f. world — WASH 922:31
sent into any f. wars — ROOS 724:11
speaking a f. language — WILD 943:36
The purpose of f. policy — ALBR 11:36
win the F. picture award — WILD 942:32
worst of the F....Office — CRIT 255:11
foreigner dagger which the f. left — QUIN 702:23
f. should in any respect — TROL 897:26
foreigners don't object to f. — WILD 943:36
f. always spell better — TWAIN 902:32
f. are fiends — MITF 610:54
f. could more easily — NGU 636:66
f. speak English — CRISP 254:2
forerunner f. of despair — KENN 480:92
foreseen What I had not f. — SPEN 837:94
foresight urge...to aftersight and f. — ELIOT 321:86
forest as a...hedge is to a f. — JOHN 465:4
behind it rose the f. — LONG 535:29
chose the f. path — FAWC 331:51
Dong through the f. goes — LEAR 516:29
even as the f. is — SHEL 813:83
flowers of the f. — COCK 233:82
flowers of the f. — ELLI 322:25
f. fleece — HOUS 431:47
F., where all must lose — THOM 885:62
f. with a golden track — LIND 530:18
Glimpse of the f. — SITW 823:4
into the f. dim — KEATS 478:42
lost to the f. — SCOTT 752:31
Marxism...like finding a map in a f. — CAST 208:80
met a fool i'th' f. — SHAK 779:78
paint a f. or a horse — MARC 569:49
redwood f. — GUTH 390:5
spark can start a f. fire — MAO 568:26
take a tree from the f. — SCOTT 753:37
the f.'s ferny floor — DELA 271:25
This is the f. primeval — LONG 535:25
thru the graveyard f. — PURDY 700:85
undulating tropical rain f. — BOYD 153:10
whole f. echoes — CARL 201:16
forests Among the f. — THOM 886:76
F. of middle-aged men — ABBO 1:1
f. of the night — BLAKE 140:19
f. where they roamed — SIGO 821:64
green days in f. — STEV 853:84
sole king of f. all — SPEN 838:20
foresworn Necessity will make us all f. — SHAK 763:5
foretaste f. of death — SCHO 749:60
foretold f. the rest — ELIOT 318:4
forever experiment lasts f. — KAPI 473:27
flying through space f. — GAGA 356:8
it lives f. — UPDI 906:30
talked on f. e. — HAZL 403:34

that vast f. — KING 487:45
The brave may not live f. — BRAN 156:71
forfeit f. of their name — HABI 391:3
forfended music of f. spheres — PATM 669:25
forget Best, to f.! — BROW 169:83
cause us to f. their existence — HAWT 402:12
either f. right away — BECK 72:42
far worse than to f. — BENU 83:10
f. because we must — ARNO 33:71
F. it, Jake — TOWNE 894:66
f. me not — GINS 372:7
f. so much — DAVI 264:76
f. that words — JOHN 460:68
f. to tell each other — HELL 408:44
f. yourself in the park? — TAYL 868:50
glad to have humanity f. — HOOV 427:46
going to f. the war — HEMI 409:65
if thou wilt, f. — ROSS 726:46
Lest we f.! — KIPL 490:16
Let us not f. — GAIT 357:12
lover who does not f. — BART 66:26
make one set of people f. — HUXL 442:82
never f. that a child — JUVE 471:59
people will f. — ANGE 19:4
Promise to f. this fellow — SHER 817:70
quite f. — KEATS 478:43
should both f. — SWIN 864:2
should f. it — HERR 415:97
teach us to f. our own — SHAK 798:85
yet will I not f. thee — BIBLE 109:89
forgetfulness to dumb F. a prey — GRAY 384:74
forgetting f. buries them — LABR 502:15
F. those things which are behind — BIBLE 128:2
sleep and a f. — WORD 959:8
world f., by the world forgot — POPE 686:50
forgive and to f. — SWIN 864:14
At distance I f. thee — MILT 608:95
do my people f. me? — RICH 713:9
F. and be happy — PRAT 694:67
f. me for not fulfilling some hopes — YELT 968:45
F. me, sir — KARSH 473:32
F., O Lord — FROST 353:19
F. the hero — WILB 939:35
f. them; for they know not — BIBLE 122:7
f. those sins — DONNE 293:65
God will f. me — HEINE 407:18
Good, to f. — BROW 169:83
one can f. anybody — WILDE 941:89
rarely...do they f. them — WILDE 941:88
sin against me, and I f. him? — BIBLE 118:14
to f., divine — POPE 685:25
forgiven f. all those who trespass — JOSE 469:7
healed, restored, f. — LYTE 543:93
neither can nor should be f. — SHAW 808:43
sins, which are many, are f. — BIBLE 120:75
forgiveness After..., what f.? — ELIOT 317:84
any person who asks for f. — CLIN 230:12
F. free of evil done — KIPL 492:58
F. of sins — BOOK 146:37
f. to the injured — DRYD 300:31
Mutual f. of each vice — BLAKE 140:5
there is always f. — BALZ 61:2
there is f. with thee — BIBLE 103:39
forgives neither f. you nor allows — SHAW 808:57
forgiving God's slim f. — BENE 79:13
forgot And she f. the stars — KEATS 477:12
f. for which he toiled — SHAK 800:44
f. to duck — DEMP 272:50
f. to duck — REAG 708:5
f. what things were called — ATWO 41:44
forgotten actress—never to be f. — DAVIS 265:95
always a f. thing — CHES 221:82
f. since their beauty — THOM 885:53
f. what it is like — JARR 452:91
I am all f. — SHAK 794:52
memory of them is f. — BIBLE 16:26
past is not f. — GRASS 382:11
what has been learnt has been f. — SKIN 825:46
what you have f. — FENT 332:59
fork a man with a f. — GALL 358:35
f. in his inexperienced hand — WELLS 930:25
forks pursued it with f. — CARR 206:31
forlorn on earth I wait f. — ARNO 35:4
form All is without f. and void — HAZL 404:60
All must love the human f. — BLAKE 139:89
Art is nothing without f. — FLAU 339:15
assume the f. of machinery — MARX 579:41

Beauty has only one f. — HUGO 436:51
both for power and f. — SPEN 838:32
but one f. — THOR 888:24
changing oftentimes its f. — WORD 958:86
critic must attack the f. — LAUT 512:29
does a human f. display — BLAKE 141:44
Drawing...the way of seeing the f. — DEGAS 269:86
emptying...of all f. and content — FANON 329:14
Every f. is individual — HEIN 407:21
every F. of being — WORD 961:40
experience In a different f. — ELIOT 320:73
favourite f. of revenge — NIET 638:11
feel the same way about f. and space — DAVIS 266:5
formal poetry perfect only in f. — SAND 742:36
f. as a tree has f. — POUND 692:34
f., colour and mood of a picture — FEIN 332:57
F. follows profit' — ROGE 722:66
f. of moral effort — LEAC 515:19
f. of our primitive ancestors — MILL 595:96
f. of the short story — SARO 744:58
f., so angel fair — BRON 161:54
f. that my style cannot discover — DARIO 262:45
hewed her lovely f. — MILT 600:17
highest f. of government — SPEN 836:90
Humanity in its basic f. — BARTH 66:9
in f. and moving — SHAK 782:89
let the f. of an object be what it may — CONS 245:60
Life is that the f. — MANN 566:78
like definite f. — STEV 851:14
Love, the human f. divine — BLAKE 139:88
Man found his f. — BERD 83:12
never make a god out of f. — KAND 472:15
no f. nor comeliness — BIBLE 109:93
Nor f., nor feeling — WORD 957:66
obituary in serial f. — CRISP 255:7
one loves only f. — OLSEN 650:47
outside to every f. — HEPW 412:29
pretty f. to the lips — DICK 282:91
relationships of color or f. — ROTH 728:3
significant f. — BELL 75:32
take thy f. — POE 683:88
than any other literary f. — DUDEK 305:73
Thanks to his bodily f. — REDT 709:25
The F. remains — WORD 961:42
theory in ritual f. — NOVAK 641:64
Thou, silent f. — KEATS 478:39
together in a f. called E — SCHM 748:40
visual f. of the 'otherness' — NOLAN 640:43
what the f. divine! — LAND 506:10
formal Wearing underwear is as f. — HEMI 410:96
formality eunuched with f. — CLEV 230:95
former f. are products of fortune — HELO 408:54
f. days were better — BIBLE 106:23
f. things are passed away — BIBLE 132:24
formidable less f. than...Genesis — ACHE 3:38
none more f. than man — SOPH 834:26
this f. kingdom — PITT 679:2
forms disguise...in a thousand f. — BEAU 70:7
Even f. and substances — WORD 958:85
f. of human knowledge — MANN 566:79
f. of virtue are erect — FUSE 356:94
f. that are lit up — GOYA 380:82
knell is rung, By f. unseen — COLL 237:72
magic of official f. — WAUGH 924:88
may not hope from outward f. to win — COLE 235:29
Mis-shapes the beauteous f. — WORD 957:59
same f. and the same language — FLAU 339:21
takes more f. — THUR 891:96
These beauteous f. — WORD 956:53
To create f. means: to live — MACKE 553:1
formula f., 'Term, holidays — LEWIS 526:48
relied on the classic f. — LARK 510:97
use the f. to say something — JAMES 451:58
fornication F.—but that was in — MARL 573:12
one fraud, the other f. — MATOS 582:95
forsake Even now f. me — SHAK 760:17
will not fail thee, nor f. thee — BIBLE 95:5
forsaken why hast thou f. me? — BIBLE 119:47
why hast thou f. me? — BIBLE 99:41
forsaking strange fashion of f. — WYATT 964:91
forsook true love has me f. — BALL 60:79
Forster F. never gets any further — MANS 567:67
same gods...and E M F. — DRAB 298:81
forsworn so sweetly were f. — SHAK 788:72
Forsyte When a F. was engaged — GALS 358:48
fort love may win The f. — CRAS 254:85
Forth rather like the F. Bridge — BRIT 159:28

forth Come f., Lazarus!	JOYCE	470:26
flying back and f.	PLATH	681:38
Forthby Mrs F. in the flesh	SHAR	806:73
fortissimo F. at last!	MAHL	559:32
fortitude virtue of adversity, is f.	BACON	51:63
fortnight I have been here a f.	PERTH	675:31
thought it out…for a f.	SAYE	746:8
fortress story of the unconquerable f.	SELZ	757:19
tear down a f.	LEUP	525:14
Theology, sir, is a f.	MILL	593:36
fortresses stone of our f.	FAVRE	331:50
fortunate Caesar…was f.	SHAK	777:36
So long as you are f.	OVID	657:22
fortune all else as F.'s	EURI	328:53
ambitious…needs to make his f.	LABR	502:17
arrows of outrageous f.	TWAIN	902:63
broker…takes your f.	WOOL	956:42
deficiencies of f.	GOLD	376:90
dramatic changes of f.	ORWE	654:44
flash that brings good f.	RHYS	712:77
former are products of f.	HELO	408:54
f. calls me to?	JONS	466:47
F. favours the brave	TERE	879:13
F….has made a mistress	DRYD	301:59
F. helps those who dare	VIRG	913:20
F. is merry	SHAK	778:46
F. knows We scorn her	SHAK	794:69
f. of my pleasant choice	SURR	860:3
F. on his damnèd quarry	SHAK	795:98
F.'s a right whore	WEBS	926:17
F.'s buffets and rewards	SHAK	783:21
f.'s dearest spite	SHAK	801:49
F., that favours fools	JONS	467:63
F. when she comes	HERR	415:3
F. wouldn't exist	ASTU	39:12
good f. of the affluent country	GALB	357:22
good f. to others	BIER	134:68
good man's f.	SHAK	792:99
had not the method of making a f.	GRAY	385:94
he shall see F.	BACON	52:25
hostages to f.	BACON	51:70
how does f. banter us	BOLI	145:7
In all adversity of f.	BOET	144:92
I've seen the smiling of F. beguiling	COCK	233:81
leads on to f.	SHAK	778:48
maker of his own f.	STEE	844:43
mock the good housewife F.	SHAK	778:58
mould of a man's f.	BACON	52:24
No…beauty without a f.	FARQ	330:30
not now in f.'s power	BUTL	185:75
not on f. pause	JONS	468:84
O fickle F.	COCK	233:82
O, f., f.	SHAK	766:3
On F.'s cap	SHAK	782:83
people of f. may naturally indulge	ELIOT	315:16
possession of a good f.	AUST	45:53
railed on Lady F.	SHAK	779:78
rascals who have had the good f.	STEN	847:6
risk of f., character	TWAIN	903:92
rob a lady of her f.	FIEL	335:25
ruined f. flout	DONNE	291:27
saddest sight that f.'s inequality exhibits	CARL	201:25
skittish F.'s hall	SHAK	787:36
slings and arrows of outrageous f.	SHAK	782:7
upon a plentiful f.	JOHN	461:96
When F. means to men most good	SHAK	768:59
Will f. never come	SHAK	773:96
young women of small f.	AUST	46:59
youth to f….unknown	GRAY	384:77
fortunes expenditure of f.	PEARY	671:59
F….come tumbling	BACON	50:39
f. sharpe adversitee	CHAU	216:63
f. Will ever after droop	SHAK	803:11
least rub in your f.	SHAK	804:41
Men in great f.	BACON	51:87
pride fell with my f.	SHAK	778:60
retrieve his f. by marriage	DICK	282:89
ruined f. are sure to stir	ARIS	32:17
fortune-teller juggler, and a f.-t.	SHAK	762:93
forty Between thirty and f.	BENN	81:74
Every man over f.	SHAW	808:54
Fair, fat, and f.	SCOTT	754:70
fasted f. days and f. nights	BIBLE	114:22
For f. days	SITW	824:21
to be f. years old	HOLM	424:84
what f. looks like	STEI	846:92
when you turn f.	SILVA	921:70
forty-five f.-f. minutes of…privacy	PARK	664:28
forty-three pass for f.-t.	GILB	368:30
forum f. of hate	SMITH	829:27
United Nations…is…a f.	OBRI	645:65
forward f. let us range	TENN	871:23
go f. to nature	GOTT	379:71
forwards F. in reverse	DUNN	307:15
life…must be lived f.	KIER	485:4
rapidly backwards and f.	REED	709:27
fosse sunken f. of her spine	HEAN	404:71
fossils f. of intention	PURDY	700:85
Language does not leave f.	BRAU	157:82
foster-child f.-c. of silence	KEATS	478:34
fou f. for weeks thegither	BURNS	179:22
we're nae that f.	BURNS	178:12
fought f. as they revelled	DAVIS	266:9
f. for our place	WILH	943:55
f. two draws with Stendhal	HEMI	410:84
f. with us upon Saint Crispin's day	SHAK	776:94
lads who f.	SASS	745:89
met and f. with outright	TENN	876:39
That f. and died for	WILL	946:31
'Tis better to have f. and lost	CLOU	232:54
what they f. each other for	SOUT	835:46
foul dead, by f. subtraction	RANS	706:67
doubt some f. play	SHAK	781:45
Fair is f., and f. is fair	SHAK	795:97
f. and pestilent congregation	SHAK	782:68
F. deeds will rise	SHAK	781:45
giving hand, though f.	SHAK	763:10
got by fair means or f.	ORWE	653:6
however f. within	CHUR	224:56
in the less, f. profanation	SHAK	787:59
Murder most f.	SHAK	781:61
nipped, and ways be f.	SHAK	763:27
still f. the cup	GREY	388:60
fouled Hath f. me	TENN	878:91
foulest fair words…in f. letters?	SHAK	773:96
foulness f. of their fate	SASS	746:99
no vicious blot, murder, or f.	SHAK	792:86
remove filth and f.	ABEL	1:3
found f. and lost again	ELIOT	320:67
f. Him in	TENN	878:79
f. myself	GRIL	388:71
f. you an argument	JOHN	464:94
Hast thou f. me	BIBLE	97:69
I f. it!	ARCH	31:9
if the ways be f.	JONS	467:67
lost, but now am f.	NEWT	635:63
To f. a great Empire	SMITH	828:87
foundation corner stone, a sure f.	BIBLE	108:71
destroyed the f. of the organization	EISE	314:1
end of our f. is…knowledge	BACON	53:46
end of our f. is…knowledge	BACON	50:52
f. of all good things	BURKE	176:50
f. of morals, Utility	MILL	591:8
f. of your ideas and phrases	LAUT	512:29
laid the f. of the earth	BIBLE	98:13
on the same f.	SWIFT	862:47
The Church's one f.	STONE	855:11
unassailable f.	ASQU	38:84
foundations again from the very f.	DESC	274:98
firmest f.	GLAD	373:39
f. of political liberty	WILS	949:83
laid the f. of the earth?	BIBLE	98:13
peaks, whose f.	LLOY	533:72
visible F. in Nature	PETTY	676:47
when earth's f. fled	HOUS	432:71
While earth's f. stand	HOUS	432:78
founder f. of civil society	ROUS	729:9
founders f. of a new colony	HAWT	402:4
fount f. of pride	CULL	257:45
fountain back to the burning f.	SHEL	815:38
broke into a f.	HARR	399:55
bubble on the f.	SCOTT	752:32
drinking at the f. of fact	PIER	677:66
F., never to be play'd	POPE	686:60
f. of all goodness	BOOK	148:97
f. of good sense	DRYD	304:41
f. of living waters	BIBLE	110:12
f. of the water of life	BIBLE	132:25
f. of vice as idleness	MONT	613:13
f. sealed	BIBLE	107:46
f. send forth at the same place	BIBLE	103:57
f., shade, and rill	MILT	599:83
f., spouting through his heir	POPE	686:68
Let the healing f. start	AUDEN	43:94
Let thy f. be blessed	BIBLE	104:57
long-abused sight at the f.	MILT	601:20
mighty f. momently was forced	COLE	236:38
pitcher be broken at the f.	BIBLE	106:36
rivulet and f.	GILB	368:36
Sang with a f.'s panache	DAY	267:38
summer-dried f.	SCOTT	752:31
voice rise like a f.	TENN	878:86
water in a f.	JOYCE	470:19
Fountainblues terrible case of the F.	HUXT	443:13
fountains Afric's sunny f.	HEBER	406:1
f. are within	COLE	235:29
f. fraught with tears	KYD	501:49
f. mingle with the river	SHEL	813:78
f. of timber	MUIR	624:25
in great f.	GALE	357:28
inscriptions on public f.	FLAU	339:29
two faithful f.	CRAS	254:81
What objects are the f.?	SHEL	814:95
writers, like clear f.	LAND	506:27
four F. be the things	PARK	664:12
two and two are f.	HOUS	432:70
fourscore F. and upward	SHAK	793:31
if…they be f. years	BIBLE	101:94
four-wheeled f.-w. part of him	JOHN	458:32
Fowey O the Harbour of F.	QUIL	702:11
fowl f., blinking at you	ELIOT	315:41
lord of the f.	COWP	250:76
small f. singis on the spray	DOUG	295:2
You elegant F.!	LEAR	516:36
fowler from the snare of the f.	BIBLE	101:96
fowlers Watchful as f.	OTWAY	656:99
fowls F. are to the kitchen	BRIL	159:19
f. of the air	BIBLE	115:45
f. of the air	BIBLE	124:82
fox beset the historical f.	HUXL	443:4
Crazy Like A F.	PERE	674:14
f. barks not when he would	SHAK	759:89
f. in the streets	MCCA	547:75
galloping after a f.	WILDE	941:84
kill a f. or the pheasant	SHAW	811:28
trusted like the f.	SHAK	772:62
Virginia f. hunt	WASH	922:28
working for 16th Century F.	RENO	711:53
foxes hands and f. dine very well	JUST	471:50
f. have holes	BIBLE	116:59
f….prolonging the lives	ELIOT	315:40
fox-hunting inferior forms of f.-h.	WAUGH	923:61
prefer f.-h.	HAIL	392:17
foxlike Or f. in the vine	TENN	873:51
foxy 70s face was f.	WATE	922:37
fragile essentially f.	BAIN	55:92
Men are very f.	STEP	847:13
fragments Death tramples it to f.	SHEL	815:43
f. I have shored	ELIOT	318:12
ideas, in f.	MILL	593:55
Live in f. no longer	FORS	344:30
fragrance f. was borne upon the breeze	DICK	279:18
Has she f.?	CAUL	209:12
Isles of f.	POPE	689:43
splendor and f.	ROCK	720:31
sweetest f. from the herb	TROL	897:34
frailties draw his f.	GRAY	384:78
frailty F., thy name is woman	SHAK	780:40
human f., folly, also crime	BYRON	190:1
human f. will have it so	ETHE	327:46
noblest f. of the mind	DRYD	299:12
frame all the human f. requires	BELL	76:60
another f. of things	TENN	877:68
an utterly exhausted f.	DOYLE	297:68
calm and heav'nly f.	COWP	250:88
f. of mind	FRIE	351:76
f. perish…in conquering pain	BYRON	188:64
f. was Dust	DICK	284:50
in his bodily f….his lowly origin	DARW	263:58
knoweth our f.	BIBLE	102:9
oddest f. of sense	SHAK	788:78
sensuous f.	TENN	874:74
solid f. of earth	WORD	960:36
spangled heavens, a shining f.	ADDI	7:40
this goodly f., the earth	SHAK	782:88
universal f. is without a mind	BACON	51:9
Whatever stirs this mortal f.	COLE	235:27
wield The mighty f.	MILT	605:35
framed have it f. and glazed	WALP	919:72
framework f. for a civilization	LECO	518:82
France always be the sister of F.	HUGO	437:59

Francesca

best soldiers F. ever had	PHIL 677:57	f. from guilt or pain	SHEL 814:18	controversy over f. of speech	ORWE 655:67
better to sniff F.'s dung	HO 421:13	f. from interest or prejudice	REES 710:38	cost of f. is always	KENN 481:12
between F. and England	JERR 455:48	f. from...nationalism	ORWE 654:51	cost to f. of opinion	SCHL 747:33
Cam ye ower frae F.?	ANON 22:77	f. lunch has still to be invented	GREE 387:38	could not give me f.	SHAK 794:51
chased the English out of F.	LOUI 537:64	F. man!	BAUD 68:62	does not come from f.	GIDE 368:24
dagger...in the heart of F.	QUIN 702:23	f. man cannot long stand erect	WRIS 963:76	dreaming of f.	SMITH 831:64
duty...to wield the sword of F.	DE 270:92	f. man thinks of nothing less	SPIN 841:80	easy to suppose in a time of f.	FRAS 349:30
fair stood the wind for F.	DRAY 298:94	f. nations are peaceful nations	BUSH 183:26	entrust the care of f.	EISE 314:96
fight in F.	CHUR 225:85	f. of the networks	STARK 843:23	Extreme f....to extreme slavery	PLATO 682:67
find your people in F.	JOAN 455:59	f. their minds of...rubbish	DUDEK 305:77	fight for f. and truth	IBSEN 444:8
five in F.	THER 882:91	f., therefore choose	SART 745:77	fit to use their f.	MACA 545:25
flower of F. is lost	ANON 20:37	f. to do whatever the Government	SHAW 807:24	foppery of f.	SHAK 787:48
follow them to F.	LESL 523:88	f. to wander where I liked	SHIP 818:15	f. and culture	MORE 618:20
F....a despotism...tempered	CARL 201:11	f. trade...blessings	MACA 544:21	f. and equality	ROUS 729:12
F., famed in all great arts	ARNO 33:65	f. world and the Communist	KENN 481:22	F. and WHISKY gang thegither	BURNS 177:82
F. had shown a light	TENN 879:5	give me the f. 'n' easy	GERS 365:74	F....cure of anarchy	BURKE 175:19
F. has lost a battle!	DE 270:91	he is f.	SOLZ 833:5	f. doth with degree	JONS 467:73
F. has more need of me	NAPO 630:41	I am a f. man	ARET 31:11	f. in my love	LOVE 538:82
F. in 1830	LOUIS 538:74	If the Son...shall make you f.	BIBLE 123:41	f. is a noble thing!	BARB 63:50
F. is adequately assured	ASQU 38:84	in the cause of the f.	BINY 135:99	f. is beautiful	BUSH 183:23
F. is revolutionary	LAMA 504:73	I was f. born	BIBLE 125:98	F. is never granted	CLIN 231:28
F., mother of arts	BELL 76:43	keep your fancy f.	HOUS 431:38	F. is not an ideal	STEV 851:13
Here lies F.	BISM 137:37	know our will is f.	JOHN 462:18	F. is only the distance	ZHAO 970:9
if Jack were President of F.	ONAS 650:49	let me gae f.	SCOTT 753:52	f. is slavery	ORWE 655:73
inadequate for getting to F.	KINN 488:63	live f. and uncommitted	THOR 888:36	f. is something people take	BALD 57:19
in F....play a set	SHAK 775:62	longer f.	HERR 415:13	f. is...supremely valuable	HUXL 442:45
In F., they study men	STAEL 842:1	lover bold and f.	CLEV 230:95	F. is the f. to say	ORWE 655:75
In F....words reign over ideas	SAND 741:5	lover...noble and f.?	EMER 324:67	F. is the right	MONT 614:43
insert...spirit of Christian F.	BOUR 152:93	makes the mind very f.	ELIOT 315:33	f. of choice	GITL 373:31
nineteenth-century F.	HELL 408:46	man is either f.	BARA 63:43	f. of choice	MILL 593:44
no concern to F.	WITTE 950:19	men naturally were born f.	MILT 601:23	F. of men under government	LOCKE 533:87
order...this matter better in F.	STER 849:50	mistaken in thinking themselves f.	SPIN 840:72	f. of my mind	MILT 599:78
own F., a country	MORL 619:40	most complete and f.	STEV 851:31	f. of religion	JEFF 454:26
singer in F.	SWIN 864:7	Mother of the F.	BENS 81:84	f. of speech	BLACK 137:41
sweet enemy, F.	SIDN 820:47	music is really a f. thing	COLE 234:3	f. of the press	TOCQ 892:28
swum from F.	MARL 573:13	neither bond nor f.	BIBLE 127:79	f. of the press and popular	MILL 591:4
the roads lead to F.	THOM 885:64	never do it for f.	LEDG 518:83	f. of the press in Britain	ORWE 653:22
Vive la F.!	DE 270:97	never shall be f.	DONNE 292:55	f. of those weakened	CESA 211:50
want to know what F. thinks	DE 270:98	Newspapers are born f.	SCOTT 751:4	F. shrieked	CAMP 194:62
we will become the F. of	ROMN 724:95	No f. man shall be taken or		f. to exploit	WIEN 939:29
You're thinking of Europe as		imprisoned	MAGN 559:26	f. to marry	WARR 921:13
Germany and F.	RUMS 731:42	No one can be perfectly f.	SPEN 836:84	F., what liberties...in thy name!	GEOR 364:57
Francesca F. di Rimini, miminy	GILB 369:46	no such thing as a f. lunch	FRIE 351:69	F. which in no other land	DRYD 302:6
Francis I think I'm St F. of Assisi	PARK 664:22	one who's not f.	AI WEI 10:5	gave him f. to choose	MILT 600:12
More than F. of Assisi	PACK 659:12	our dear country had been f.	DAVIS 266:8	give another joyous f.	SCEVE 746:16
St. F. de Sales	MCFA 551:69	people are as f. as they want	BALD 57:19	give you your name: F.	ELUA 324:44
frank f. to all beside	POPE 688:10	permanently half-slave and half-f.	LINC 529:4	greatest f.	BANN 62:34
Frankenstein media a F. monster	MUGG 623:11	place of f. speech	WENT 931:52	guarantee f.	TOCQ 893:34
soul of F.	SHEL 811:47	poet must be f.	SART 744:64	have a new birth of f.	LINC 529:9
frankincense gold, and f.	BIBLE 114:17	princes should be f.	SHAK 759:81	have so much more f.	JOHN 462:45
hill of F.	BIBLE 107:45	prisoners were left f. to choose	SHAW 808:33	History may be f.	ELIOT 321:88
Franklin body of Benjamin F.	FRAN 348:7	product of the f. mind	ORWE 653:30	honour, f. and curteisie	CHAU 217:71
frankness paragons of f.	WILL 945:2	pursuit...by f. men	WARR 921:13	I believe in f. of speech	MOUR 623:98
fraternity Liberty, Equality, F.!	LAMA 504:74	safer...than to be f.	KAFKA 472:6	if f. fall?	KIPL 493:72
fraud daily f., contempt	MILT 607:84	Shall the sex f.	HABI 391:3	illusions that restrict f.	FRYE 354:57
f. of the Christian system	PAINE 660:38	So f. we seem	BROW 168:44	invigorating air of f.	WOLL 954:90
one f., the other fornication	MATOS 582:95	So long as man remains f.	DOST 294:93	kept in their full f.	BAIL 55:89
Style is a f.	DE 271:18	someone to tell them they are f.	LAYT 515:2	Let the f. ring	SMITH 830:31
frauds to point at f.	RUSH 732:65	spirit, f. to choose	ROCH 719:10	live in f. and hell	MAIL 560:52
fray Fought was this noble f.	DRAY 298:95	struggling to be f.	SHAK 783:34	love of f.	GLAD 373:39
f. By which he reigns	MILT 603:69	Teach the f. man	AUDEN 43:94	manners, virtue, f., power	WORD 958:94
freckles love, curiosity, f.	PARK 664:12	Thou art f.	ARNO 33:62	must not confuse with f.	STEV 851:11
Freddy See F. before he sees you!	ANON 26:85	tied the f. And holy-day...spirit	LAMB 505:89	'Neath every one a f.	LOWE 539:16
Frederic Stay, F., stay!	GILB 368:41	to set me f.	STUA 858:59	None can love f. heartily	MILT 601:22
free advantage of not being f.	SNOW 832:81	to want to be f.	JONAS 465:15	nor even f. from pain	LAWR 513:55
A F. Man is he	HOBB 420:4	truth shall make you f.	BIBLE 123:40	out of servitude into f.	EMER 325:91
all are f.	OBAMA 644:32	uphold me with thy f. spirit	BIBLE 101:73	particular f. and a general orderliness	CARD 198:41
as a f. man	KENN 481:27	Was he f.?	AUDEN 43:86	perfect f.	HUGEL 434:4
be a falcon and go f.	DUNC 307:11	wholly slaves or wholly f.	DRYD 303:13	Perfect f. is reserved for the man	COLL 237:59
born f. as Caesar	SHAK 776:8	Who would be f.	BYRON 187:41	portal of f.	EISE 314:8
breed f. men?	HOPE 427:56	Writing f. verse	FROST 352:10	power of the hope of f.	BUCK 172:34
cleanly I myself can f.	DRAY 299:99	yearning to breathe f.	LAZA 515:3	prisoned birds must find in f.	SASS 745:92
Comment is f.	SCOTT 751:98	ye shall be f. indeed	BIBLE 123:41	promises f. or enlightenment	SNYD 833:94
condemned to be f.	SART 745:74	You who are f.	IGNA 445:18	questions of f.	JORD 468:49
either f. or enslaved	GRIL 388:69	**free-born** as only a f.-b. Briton	THAC 880:23	right action is f.	ELIOT 320:76
every people should be left f.	WILS 949:81	**freed** f. from his religion	SAINT 738:41	salvation of f.	STEV 851:10
exertions of a f. people	PITT 680:12	**freedom** and that is f.	MACA 544:24	satisfy our thirst for f.	KING 487:45
first people to demand f. speech	BISS 137:38	army...devoted to f.	LAWR 514:90	science...restricting human f.	BOOK 150:45
f. and clear from any image	SHAK 786:20	Art, Glory, F. fail	BYRON 187:43	so close to f.	TWAIN 902:62
f. and easy	STEV 851:14	bird that will live in f.	MEIL 584:38	supreme Festival on the road to f.	BONH 146:5
f. and equal association	ENGE 326:15	bondage which is f.'s self	SHEL 812:52	the f. to offend	RUSH 732:73
f., and f. they must remain	MILT 603:80	breathed the air of f.	WALE 917:27	there is no liberty or f.	NASHE 632:97
f. as nature first made man	DRYD 300:30	bringing f....to the Middle East	PINT 678:85	the secret of its f.	OAKE 642:2
f. as the road	HERB 414:75	cause of f.	SPEN 837:13	They lyve in f.	JAME 449:18
f., but to thyself enthralled	MILT 605:23	cherish f.	SCHI 747:31	To earn you f.	LAWR 514:88
f. competition of the market	RICA 712:81	conception of autonomy and f.	GEOR 364:54	unlimited idea of f.	BACH 49:11
f. constitution	GIBB 366:91	Conservative ideal of f.	MADAN 558:15	voice of f.	SHAR 805:69

friends

what f. really is	MITC 610:41	put F. on canvas	SCHW 750:83	to the category, old f.	MO 611:68
What's f. for?	ROET 722:62	trouble with F.	DODD 289:88	true f. and a good writer	WHITE 935:42
Where F. slowly broadens	TENN 872:29	**friars** barefooted f.	GIBB 366:2	Whenever a f. succeeds	VIDAL 912:89
whose service is perfect f.	BOOK 146:39	**Fribsbi** fatal man, Madame F.	THAC 880:32	when ye lose a f.	SCOTT 753:50
wind of nationalism and f.	BALD 57:33	**friction** f. of the whole machine	CLAU 229:75	Wherein my F. is Laid	LOWRY 541:44
With a great sum obtained I this f.	BIBLE 125:98	internal f. and strife	ROTH 728:91	Where is the country, my f.?	ARGU 31:12
zest for f.	KENN 481:14	produce the least f.	LEUP 525:15	Who's your fat f.	BRUM 170:92
freedom-for-all democracy and f.-f.-a.	MAIL 560:52	**Friday** call this F. good	ELIOT 320:65	wife for his f.	JOYCE 470:28
freedoms F. you'll not to me allow	BEHN 75:19	man F.	DEFOE 269:75	wish the author...was a terrific f.	SALI 739:72
upon four essential f.	ROOS 724:13	**friend** ain't no f. of mine	PRES 694:71	world is not thy f.	SHAK 766:12
freeman symbol of a f.'s power	BIER 135:93	America is a f. of each nation	OBAMA 644:33	worst f. and enemy is but Death	BROO 162:91
freemasonry bitter f.	BEER 73:82	angry with my f.	BLAKE 140:17	Yet, O my f.	TENN 873:48
freemen happy f., are the only slaves	MASS 581:79	as you choose a f.	DILL 286:95	Your f. the British soldier	SHAW 807:3
freer I feel strangely f.!	JOHN 457:4	A woman can become a man's f.	CHEK 218:17	**friendless** Omnipotent but f.	SHEL 814:14
free will cannot deprive...man		best f. I could ever have	KARL 473:29	**friendliness** friendship and got f.	MALA 561:82
of his f. w.	CONF 240:20	choose between...betraying my f.	FORS 345:46	**friendly** No matter how f.	TRUD 694:64
freeze f. thy young blood	SHAK 781:60	confide...in a f.	ANOU 28:62	**friends** 50 per cent of his f.	BUSH 182:3
freezing Between melting and f.	ELIOT 321:81	conversation with my best f.	LEWIS 526:48	All the f. that I loved	BUCH 171:28
freezings What f. have I felt	SHAK 802:71	courting death to be our f.	PHIL 676:53	an Entertainment for F.	SWIFT 862:59
frei Arbeit macht f.	ANON 24:20	enemy and your f.	TWAIN 903:83	Be f., you English fools	SHAK 775:83
freight Nation's F. Handler	SAND 741:13	enemy into a f.	KING 487:36	best f. hear no more of him?	SHEL 814:4
wilderness of f. and rails	CRANE 253:61	every f. we lose	POPE 686:64	better than f.	GERB 364:63
French as much Chinese as F.	FLAU 339:13	Everyone calls himself a f.	LAFO 504:59	cold and certain f.	HUGO 437:78
As the F. say	SMITH 830:55	fair f., you never can be old	SHAK 802:74	cut their f. to any shape	MERE 588:35
Englishman is about to talk F.	WODE 952:47	Faithful are the wounds of a f.	BIBLE 105:2	dear f. have to part?	BOND 145:17
F. are a logical people	MORL 619:40	faithful f. is the medicine	BIBLE 113:84	dear f., once more	SHAK 775:74
F. are nice people	MAZA 583:28	favourite has no f.!	GRAY 383:53	deathless f.	SASS 746:98
F. are polite	TWAIN 902:23	Forsake not an old f.	BIBLE 113:89	desires...to be f.	BETH 87:71
F. are wiser than they seem	BACON 52:11	for the f. of mankind	MOLI 611:81	disliked by all his f.	WILDE 942:27
F. Canadian Hinayana Buddhist	GINS 372:12	f. called Piggy	GOLD 375:74	don't trust him, we are f.	BREC 157:94
F. clothes and F. food	SCHL 747:37	f. in first habits of intimacy	LAMB 505:93	ensure his making f.	AUST 45:57
F....differs in nothing from prose	GRAY 383:49	f. in power is a f. lost	ADAMS 5:88	Farewell, my f.	DUNC 307:6
F. had a more martial air	HAYD 402:23	f. loveth at all times	BIBLE 105:81	few of his f.' houses	JOHN 464:86
F. is not a static language	HUGO 436:57	f. of man	COLL 237:73	foes, and oh, my f.	MILL 592:19
F. king, admittedly	MORL 620:42	f. of the negro assumes	FULL 355:66	For golden f. I had	HOUS 432:55
F. operas sung by Swedish	WHAR 934:11	f. of the oppressed	GARI 360:72	f. all united to puff	SWIN 864:11
F. Radicals...German	MARX 579:33	f. that sticketh closer than a brother	BIBLE 105:84	f., and native home	MILT 598:63
F. Revolution is merely the herald	BABE 48:4	f....the masterpiece of nature	EMER 324:60	f. are beginning to worry	EPST 327:34
F. she spak ful faire	CHAU 217:73	f. who can talk	ABU 1:13	f....are in cities	SNYD 832:89
F. want to attack	ANON 27:34	f. who loved perfection	SMITH 829:19	f. are true	BIER 134:79
F. will only be united	DE 270:93	God is the f. of silence	THER 882:84	f. begin to compliment him	IRVI 447:59
Germans classify...the F. arrange	CATH 208:91	good f. is someone who visits you	BRAD 154:32	f., but above all an enemy	MULR 624:34
get all the F.-f.	GORE 379:58	Good wine, a f.	ALDR 12:53	f. could only read the title	WOOLF 955:11
good because cooked by the F.	DOUG 295:7	hard to be...a good f.	WYCH 964:58	f. divide, never to meet	MIDD 590:73
help our F. comrades	KITC 494:98	He makes no f.	TENN 877:55	f. forsake me like a memory lost	CLARE 228:54
Imagine the Lord talking F.	DAY 267:30	I am the enemy...my f.	OWEN 658:35	F. love misery	JONG 466:37
improved her F.	GRAH 380:88	I paint a portrait I lose a f.	SARG 746:52	f. of other days	ROBI 718:89
look'd towards the F. coast	STER 848:43	kingdom with thy dearest f.	MARL 573:13	f. of the mammon	BIBLE 121:94
New Orleans...past the F. Quarter	MAIL 560:55	last best f.	SOUT 835:56	f. of totalitarianism	ORWE 655:68
not that the F. are not profound	BROO 163:15	lewd well natured f.	ROCH 720:23	F. part forever	BASHO 67:48
professor of F. letters	JOYCE 470:28	Little F. of all the World	KIPL 491:25	F., Romans, countrymen	SHAK 777:37
scrofulous F. novel	BROW 167:12	look like a f. on Denmark	SHAK 780:34	f. should drink	KEATS 476:95
serve the F. in place of a state religion	BIER 134:83	loss of a dear f.	SOUT 835:55	f. thou hast	SHAK 781:49
seventeen million F. women	GISC 373:29	lost F.!	WORD 961:47	F. To borrow my books	ROBI 718:83
Speak in F.	CARR 204:94	mine own familiar f.	BIBLE 100:62	f. who died	SASS 745:89
special task, as F. Canadians	BOUR 152:93	mistress or a f.	SHEL 815:44	f. with its grandfathers	MUMF 625:35
speech...precise as F.	QUIL 702:13	morn to night, my f.	ROSS 726:45	general has no f.	LEMAY 521:31
to men [I speak] F.	CHAR 215:38	most reliable f.	GRAMM 381:96	greet f. with a shrug	SPEN 837:96
tongues of the F. Council	SHAK 776:1	My best f. is myself	MORR 621:63	had been f. in youth	COLE 235:34
we die F.	WAUGH 924:89	myself shall be my f.	KYD 501:50	had many f.	GOET 375:72
We have F. quarrels	SHAK 775:83	no f. like a sister	ROSS 725:38	help from my f.	LENN 522:52
What are we learning F....for	OBRI 646:74	No F....so persists	DICK 284:52	honored by your f.	HOOV 427:55
What's the F. for fiddle-de-dee?	CARR 205:25	nor a f. to know me	STEV 853:83	judge a man...by his f.	CONR 244:33
wine...some are fond of F.	MASE 580:58	not a f. to close his eyes	DRYD 303:31	Keep your f. close	PACI 658:3
Frenchman	FRIE 351:72	nothing like the failure of a close f.	CAREY 199:64	lay down his f.	THOR 889:57
Frenchmen act better than F.	BENN 81:63	O f. unseen, unborn, unknown	FLEC 340:30	lay down his life for his f.	BIBLE 123:55
one Englishman could beat three F.	ADDI 7:35	O f. we have loved	CORN 247:4	leave your f. and go	HOUS 433:83
Frenchwomen F. better	BENN 81:63	old f. for dinner	TALLY 866:20	lend it not...to thy f.	SHAK 769:86
frenzy an old man's f.	YEATS 967:34	One chained f.	SHEL 815:45	literature have always been f.	LAFO 504:52
Dancing is a f. and a rage	DAVI 264:73	one damned good-natured f. or other	SHER 817:95	lost f., some by death	WOOLF 956:36
frequency tragedy...very fact of f.	ELIOT 316:52	One f. in a lifetime	ADAMS 5:92	love of old f.	PO 683:79
frère mon f.!	ELIOT 318:98	only way to have a f. is to be one	EMER 324:61	love of wicked f.	SHAK 765:59
fresh f. air and royalties	ASHF 38:73	O Sleep! the f. of Woe	SOUT 835:51	man that hath f.	BIBLE 105:84
f. and vigorous enough	WARD 920:2	quarrels...with a tiresome f.	BYRON 189:97	man who is false to his f.	BERK 84:35
F. as the air	JONS 467:72	save me, from the candid f.	CANN 197:9	misfortune of our best f.	LARO 510:1
f. colours deck the wanton prime	SPEN 838:39	say hello to my little f.	PACI 658:5	Money couldn't buy f.	MILL 595:2
how quick and f.	SHAK 785:78	sincere f. or a sincere enemy	HUGO 437:58	most of my f. are dead	FENT 332:60
So sad, so f.	TENN 872:42	'Strange f.,' I said	OWEN 657:34	mountains...to him were f.	BYRON 187:48
freshness f. of a dream	WORD 959:5	such a f., that one had need	COWP 251:3	never be f. again	VICT 912:77
fret Living, we f.	BROW 169:83	supreme f. to every individual	BAUD 69:87	old enough not to make f.	POUND 691:94
fretted so f. fast we are	BROW 168:44	Take courage, my f.	READE 708:97	old f.	GOLD 376:9
Freud F....dramatis personae	THOM 883:99	The boss is never your f.	APPEL 29:87	one code...for our f.	EISE 314:99
F. has often stated	RODG 721:49	think of him as a f.	SMITH 830:41	on the backs of his f.	HUGH 435:18
F. is the father	GREER 387:41	those who call them f.	TENN 878:86	organized workers...are our f.	SHIN 818:12
F. would have his revenge	DOCT 289:82	To find a f.	DOUG 295:14	our best f.	THOM 887:93
funny when F. died	JARR 452:82	to f. and foe alike	KENN 481:10	Our Dumb F.	PARK 664:22
If F. had worn a kilt	BURG 174:1	to have a f. takes time	OKEE 648:23	rich hath many f.	BIBLE 104:71

friendship

sad f. of Truth	MILT 600:17	Space—the final F.	RODD 721:44	thou art…a f.	AESC 9:82
some of their sad f.	DONNE 292:38	symbol for America is the F.	ATWO 41:38	**fugitives** f. are of that condition	BACON 51:73
soul rememb'ring my good f.	SHAK 764:45	**frontiers** cross the f. into Eternity	MELV 585:71	**fugue** hum a f.	GILB 368:40
tavern for his f.	DOUG 295:10	f. of the impossible	KILLY 486:8	**fugues** f. and symphonies	SASS 745:89
teaches beasts to know their f.	SHAK 799:90	**frost** cold climate, and f. and snow	SOUT 835:42	**fulfil** f. ourselves outside of [society]	SARR 744:62
tears of f.	DRYD 301:49	early f. to…flowerings of feminism	FALU 329:12	**fulfilled** f. a long time	BIBLE 112:76
tear to pieces…my f.?	BACON 53:53	it being a great f.	PEPYS 673:93	till all be f.	BIBLE 114:30
Those you make f.	SHAK 804:41	it being a great f.	PEPYS 674:98	**fulfilment** altered in f.	ELIOT 321:82
Thy f. are exultations	WORD 960:16	moonlight…like f.	THOM 885:54	Before f. is	BARK 63:53
together f. to keep	DRAY 298:92	So full of f.	SHAK 775:58	Contentment and f.	TROL 898:58
To my f. pictured within	ELGAR 314:11	tears Thaw not the f.	SHEL 815:27	f. only a step	LEGU 520:9
troops of f.	SHAK 798:69	The f. performs its secret ministry	COLE 235:23	**full** All then is f., possessing	POPE 686:47
truth loses you f.	RUIZ 730:39	third day comes a f.	SHAK 805:52	f. as craving…f. as vain	DRYD 301:58
Unmarried men are best f.	BACON 51:73	**frosts** f. are slain	SWIN 863:83	F. many a glorious morning	SHAK 801:48
We'll part good f.	WEBS 926:27	**froth** Life is mostly f.	GORD 378:52	f. of love and honesty	SHAK 789:17
we, my f.	WEBB 925:8	**frown** Actresses have to…f.	DENEU 272:52	f. stop…at the right place	BABEL 48:3
When I see my f. collapse	SKEL 824:33	communist has a fascist f.	SPARK 836:73	f. up years ago	WODE 952:49
Win F. and Influence People	CARN 202:49	f. and be perverse	SHAK 765:82	Hell ain't half f.	MCCA 547:76
with f. possessed	SHAK 800:46	f. of hatred	BYRON 188:75	lived his life to the f.	RAND 706:55
without f., without coin	SCOTT 753:51	persistent troubled f.	THUR 890:86	live it to the f.	SPARK 836:68
you will count many f.	OVID 657:22	**frowzy** pent up in f. lodgings	SMOL 831:69	Serenely f., the epicure would say	SMITH 831:60
friendship Agreements…true f.	CATI 208:97	**Froyd** So then Dr F. said	LOOS 536:54	so f. of unmannerly sadness	SHAK 769:78
beginning of a beautiful f.	WALL 918:63	**frozen** beautiful and f., I preserve you	ATWO 41:41	was na f.	BURNS 177:74
certain sort of f.	KING 488:56	sends the f.-ground-swell under it	FROST 352:90	What though…his commonplace	
cultivate your f.	JOHN 464:83	**frugal** what a f. man annually saves	SMITH 827:83	book be f.	SWIFT 861:21
dupe of f.	HAZL 440:50	wit…he was f. of it	DRYD 300:25	**fuller** Money…the true f.'s earth	GAY 362:17
Every long f., every old	LAMB 505:93	**fruit** also beareth f.	BIBLE 117:92	**fullers** f. and their wailing	ANON 20:25
F. and love	GRIL 388:70	And full of f.	HENR 411:61	**fullness** earth…and the f. thereof	BIBLE 100:46
f., books	THOM 887:99	autumn and the falling f.	LAWR 514:82	earth…and the f. thereof	BIBLE 126:47
f. in constant repair	JOHN 460:65	bears its f. and dies	STEV 850:77	filled with all the f. of God	BIBLE 127:88
F. is a disinterested commerce	GOLD 376:94	blooming ambrosial f.	MILT 604:96	**fullstoppers** f. and semicolonials	JOYCE 470:36
f. is never peaceful	SEVI 758:41	bringeth forth his f. in his season	BIBLE 99:25	**fumble** a day you f. through	WELSH 930:45
F. needs a certain parallelism	ADAMS 5:92	brought forth f.	BIBLE 117:90	f. with the sheets	SHAK 775:68
f. of the United States	GEOR 364:48	brought immortal f.	BIBLE 112:69	**fumbling** f. the flowers	REED 709:27
full joys of f.	CATH 208:94	delicate exotic f.	WILDE 941:1	**fume** captured f. of space	CRANE 253:64
golden dream of love and f.	DRYD 301:61	Forth reaching to the f.	MILT 606:50	**fumes** f. of tobacco and liquors	LEWIS 527:66
imputation of this idiot's f.!	NASHE 632:92	f. in old age	BIBLE 102:98	**fumitor** Crowned with rank f.	SHAK 793:19
In f. false	DRYD 302:74	f. of memory	CONR 244:51	**fun** Ain't we got f.	KAHN 472:9
Levin wanted f.	MALA 561:82	f. of our labour	MONT 613:11	Cancer can be rather f.	HALD 392:26
little f. in the world	BACON 53:34	f. Of that forbidden tree	MILT 601:29	do things for f.	STARK 843:22
Love and f. exclude one another	LABR 502:13	f. of the Spirit	BIBLE 125:17	for the f. of the thing	DOUG 295:8
more…ingenious than f.	LACL 503:36	globed f.	MACL 555:32	f. for…thick-skinned grown-ups	SHAW 807:18
Most f. is feigning	SHAK 779:85	green f. would swell	KEATS 476:87	F. is f. but no girl	LOOS 536:53
paltry f.…of mere Man	POE 683:84	Is darkness, the f.	SWIN 864:94	f. to believe them	BACH 49:14
sort of f. recognised	STEV 852:36	like ripe f. thou drop	MILT 606:68	f. where I've found it	KIPL 490:11
Time…strengthens f.	LABR 502:12	long for the f. at last	SHER 817:72	f. you think they had	JONG 466:35
when did f. take	SHAK 739:54	medlar being a f.	MACD 550:39	It's more f. to be a pirate	JOBS 455:61
wing of f.	DICK 279:89	O Autumn, laden with f.	BLAKE 139:82	make f. of people	GARC 359:65
wing of f.	DICK 279:90	ripest f. of all	MARL 572:99	mirth and f. grew fast	BURNS 179:29
woman's f. ever ends in love	GAY 362:12	tasting this fair f.	MILT 606:54	more f. to punt	SAYE 746:7
friendships F. begin with liking	ELIOT 316:59	the f. of your delight	SURR 860:3	most f.…without laughing	ALLEN 14:95
f.…invalidated by marriage	BUTL 185:99	To f. or shade	HERB 413:64	no reference to f.	HERB 413:49
fright f. my faith	DRYD 303:11	took of the f.	BIBLE 91:93	Sucking the f. out of life	OROU 652:99
in a hell of a f.	CARY 207:67	Too late for f.	DELA 271:35	watch a game, it's f.	HOPE 428:59
suaveness…it's born of f.	HYDE 444:22	venturing their necks for f.	ROCH 719:18	what…was all the f. for	BETJ 89:39
time's f. within me	WILB 939:39	With f. the vines	KEATS 477:32	**function** death has a useful f.	LABR 502:21
frightday f., shatterday	JOYCE 470:37	**fruitcake** it's f. weather!	CAPO 197:22	f. is to create…feeling of solidarity	DURK 308:27
frighten f. people and…demoralize them	BENN 80:39	**fruitcakes** Bring on the f.	PARR 666:53	f. of a writer	CONN 243:6
frightened f. look in its eyes	SITW 824:17	**fruitful** she'll be f.	SWIFT 862:79	f. of criticism	DEWEY 276:20
never more f.	VAN 908:51	**fruitfulness** f. and…enjoyment	NIET 638:97	f. of kings	LOUI 537:69
whole world is f. to death!	SHER 818:10	mellow f.	KEATS 477:32	f. of literature	TRIL 897:18
frightening manners are far more f.	JARR 452:86	**fruition** f.'s dull, and spoils	SUCK 858:69	f. of news	LIPP 531:41
nothing is really very f.	STEIN 845:67	**fruits** by their f. ye shall know them	BIBLE 115:54	f. of poetry	GRAV 382:21
Friuli blue F.'s mountains	BYRON 188:60	drop like the f. of the tree.	MERE 588:41	happiness is a by-product of f.	BURR 181:69
frivolity F. is sweet, at the right time	HORA 430:13	f. and princely delicates	MARL 573:23	own no other f.	SHAK 799:20
how precious is f.!	FORS 345:42	f. of Christian civilisation	BIRD 136:10	proper f. of women	ELIOT 315:36
frock complexion…and the white f.	SCHR 749:63	f. of knowledge	FREUD 350:61	pure f., and best power	WORD 958:89
dons a new street f.	NATH 632:98	f. of speaking art?	SIDN 820:39	society cannot f. properly	PARS 666:56
f. of frolic green	DRAY 298:90	gives to Zembla f.	POPE 688:31	special f. is departure	LISP 531:44
frock-coat man in a f. c.	LAVER 512:34	Here are f., flowers	VERL 911:58	the f. never dies	WORD 961:42
frocks f. are built in Paris	SAKI 739:52	immortal f. of joy and love	MILT 603:76	**functionary** not to a f.	STEAD 843:34
frog f. jumps in	BASHO 67:44	No f., no flowers	HOOD 426:37	**functioning** a f. democracy	CART 206:53
frogs All the night the f. go chuckle	MACG 551:71	Of f., and flowers	KEATS 477:20	f. out of ignorance	DENG 272:58
f. are decapitated	JAMES 452:77	twelve manner of f.	BIBLE 132:28	**functions** division of labor…social f.	DURK 308:28
frolic frock of f. green	DRAY 298:90	under their f. load	SPEN 838:39	expedition…performed its f.	SPEKE 836:81
wine can…Make the sage f.	POPE 686:51	**frustrated** never to be f.	BALL 58:48	f.…most nearly in equilibrium	SPEN 836:87
with a f. welcome took	TENN 870:2	**fry** F. me!	CARR 205:27	In her f. weary	MILT 607:90
frolicsome f. company had begun	SCOTT 753:44	marked among the f.	THOM 887:5	where it f. best	THAT 881:65
front All Quiet on the Western F.	REMA 710:46	**fuck** Fish f. in it	FIEL 335:36	**fund** for the maintenance	SMITH 827:83
f. page has nothing but	WARR 921:14	"F. it, it's in God's hands"	HOPK 428:64	**fundament** frigid upon the f.	NASH 631:77
I remember the f. door	POWE 693:55	f. you up, your mum and dad	LARK 510:89	**fundamental** f.…liberties	PITT 679:7
sit out f. and watch me	BARR 65:2	zipless f. is absolutely pure	JONG 466:31	f. postulate that there	MONOD 612:3
frontier edge of a new f.	KENN 481:99	**fucked** constantly getting f.	MAMET 564:40	f. question of philosophy	CAMUS 195:83
f. from the Atlantic to the Pacific	CHUR 225:80	**fudge** two-fifths sheer f.	LOWE 539:8	f. things apply	HUPF 440:35
f. of my Person	AUDEN 44:15	**fudging** f. and nudging	OWEN 657:23	**fundamentalism** F. is terrifying	DALAI 261:10
It is seldom at the f.	BENN 80:60	**fuel** bury their radioactive f.	LAMB 506:16	**funds** providing the f.	STEW 854:94
Rhine…is where our f. lies	BALD 57:32	**fugitive** f. and cloistered virtue	MILT 600:8	**funeral** After the f., my father	LAWR 513:69

gambler

at a f. and knew their feet	MAUG 582:5	fuss f. about sleeping together	WAUGH 923:71	**G**	
cypress f.	SPEN 838:20	make no f. about females	CAMPO 195:79	**Gael** legend of the G.	RUSS 735:42
for the f. expenses	JERO 454:39	without more f.	SPEN 837:1	**Gaelic** Michael read the G. scroll	RUSS 735:42
f. baked meats	SHAK 780:42	**fustian** whose f.'s so sublimely bad	POPE 687:2	**gaffe** a g. is when you tell the truth	BIDEN 133:55
f. marches around your heart	MILL 593:35	**futile** f. his concerns	SIMO 822:80	**gage** hope's true g.	RALE 705:44
F. marches to the grave	LONG 535:15	**future** a receding f.	THOM 886:77	**gags** no g., no chance	TODD 893:35
f. march of a fried eel	SHAW 810:24	arrow is pointing towards the f.	EDDI 311:24	**Gaia** G. grows angry	LOVE 538:92
f. sermon...which was long	BELL 77:65	better f. and a brighter day	SMUTS 831:70	**gaiety** eclipsed the g. of nations	JOHN 464:76
f. song	GIBB 366:94	Children have neither past nor f.	LABR 502:24	g., the intrigue and the anguish	SCHL 747:35
f. train which the bridegroom sees	CLOU 232:59	choose its own f.	KENN 481:18	**gain** farmers...with constant g.	CRAB 252:37
how to perform a f.	WILL 945:6	cloud curtain of the f.	CARL 200:77	g. and loss involved	PASC 667:78
low on his f. couch	GRAY 385:85	conceive extravagant hopes of the f.	BURKE 175:9	g. by marriage	DICK 282:89
or at a f.	TWAIN 902:52	concerned about our f.	RODO 721:51	g. I count but loss	WATTS 922:46
present is the f. of the past	CLARE 288:53	controls the f.	ORWE 655:74	his own g.	SMITH 828:86
see my f. before I die	EDGE 311:38	dipped into the f.	TENN 871:17	loss comes...from his g.	BROW 169:63
seen a costlier f.	TENN 877:66	disdain the f. now	KENN 481:21	love of g.	SOPH 834:25
showed up at his f.	GOLD 377:38	dream about the f.	HAMM 394:59	neither g. nor loss	ELIOT 320:67
two-thirds of the f.	LAWS 514:95	drowned the F.	THOM 885:11	neither g. nor loss of utility	JEVO 455:52
victory...celebrated with the f. rite	LAO 508:63	Europe and...the f.	MARI 570:72	no g.	ANON 24:31
funerals go to other men's f.	DAY 267:31	eventuality in the f.	MURP 627:77	no war for...material g.	CHUR 225:81
he does better f.	VIDAL 912:1	fight against the f.	GLAD 373:37	pursuit of g.	WEBER 925:12
steady supply of f.	SHAW 811:33	forbid...in the city in f.	EDWA 312:56	to g. applause	JOHN 459:55
fungus f. or a lichen	THOR 888:21	For the f. I cease	ORAH 652:90	to speculate is a g.	COUS 248:40
funhouse Cyberspace is the f. mirror	STER 847:16	From past and f.	ELIOT 320:76	weather that bringeth no g.	DEKK 270:8
funny Be f. on a golf course?	SILV 821:71	f. ain't what it used to be	ANON 26:91	what do you g.?	CRUZ 256:38
first f. thought	TRAV 896:91	f. generations	TOLS 894:54	what things were g. to me	BIBLE 128:1
f. as long as it is happening	ROGE 723:74	f....has a voice	OAKE 642:1	**gained** something is eternally g.	JAMES 451:70
f. is subversive	ORWE 654:39	f. has come to a full stop	ADIGA 8:66	**gains** Light g. make heavy purses	BACON 53:40
f. paper read backwards	WILL 945:96	f. in which our country	KENN 482:28	**gait** forced g. of a shuffling nag	SHAK 771:50
F. peculiar, or f. ha-ha?	HAY 402:19	f. is made of the same stuff	WEIL 928:71	**gaiters** All is gas and g.	DICK 279:87
f. when Freud died	JARR 452:82	f. is the man of statistics	HOLM 424:86	**gal** every boy and every g.	GILB 369:52
F. without being vulgar	GILB 370:74	f. of art	FLAU 339:17	slap-up g.	DICK 283:24
F. you should ask	CECIL 210:25	f. of humanity is uncertain	LEVI 525:26	**galaxy** bathe them in the g.	LOVE 538:87
knowing what's f. is one of them	AMIS 16:39	f.'s bright	ANON 27:37	g. is one of billions	BRAUN 157:81
less f. and lasts longer	ANOU 28:67	f. shock...disorientation	TOFF 893:37	glistening g. of childhood	MATT 582:17
Life was a f. thing	CRISP 255:5	F....That period of time	BIER 134:79	**gale** before the g.	SMART 826:66
those who say f. things	DODD 289:89	f. that will live up to my past	BENN 80:53	fart in a g. of wind	BARN 64:63
to write a really f. book	HEMI 409:60	they dreamed of	LESS 524:95	g., it plies the saplings	HOUS 431:47
fur dressed all in f.	MOORE 616:64	f. was a mystery	CHOP 233:31	war-cries...on the g.	MCCA 547:74
I'll make the f.	BUTL 185:74	f. while existing	NARO 630:53	**gales** cool g. shall fan the glade	POPE 685:15
furbelows little pleats and f.	SCHI 747:22	Germany was afraid of the f.	GREY 388:63	g. shall fan the glade	POPE 685:15
furies Break bitter f.	YEATS 967:32	great f. behind him	CART 206:41	**Galice** G. at Seint-Jame	CHAU 217:77
ye f. fell	SHAK 768:49	great f. behind him	MARA 569:46	**Galilean** Among the G. mountains	CRAS 254:81
furious grew fast and f.	BURNS 179:29	great soul in f.	EMER 325:89	G., thy dead shall go down	SWIN 864:1
furnace Heat not a f.	SHAK 804:36	happiness that the f. offers	DESB 274:89	O pale G.	SWIN 864:99
one great f. flamed	MILT 601:35	have seen the f.	STEF 844:55	**Galilee** like the Sea of G.	HOPK 429:85
thrown alive into the f.	BELL 78:92	hope increasingly in the f.	MAJOR 561:72	Ye men of G.	BIBLE 124:71
furnaces Your worship is your f.	BOTT 152:83	hopes and dreams of the F.	FRAME 346:77	**Galileo** like G. going before	
furnish f. forth the marriage tables	SHAK 780:42	hopes of f. years	LONG 535:35	the Inquisition	LIVI 532:57
f. the pictures	HEAR 405:83	I have seen the f.	TOYN 895:76	status of G.	GOULD 380:75
furnished F. as all Europe is	FRAN 348:18	in f. look upon me	KEMB 479:72	**gall** pigeon-livered and lack g.	SHAK 782:1
furnishings f. of each Was-land	FRAME 346:77	In the f. everybody	WARH 920:7	They gave me g. to eat	BOOK 149:26
furniture brain...with all the f.	DOYLE 297:58	lets the f. in	GREE 385:5	wormwood and the g.	BIBLE 110:25
Diet, F. and Dress	MAND 565:65	liberation From the f.	ELIOT 321:89	**gallant** g., civilized...people	ATTL 40:25
f. on the deck	MORT 621:76	nation...has no f.	AI WEI 10:7	He was a braw g.	BALL 58:54
f. that used to be in the salon	MACM 557:75	nations of the f.	CURZ 260:5	Sade, the g. marquis	RICK 715:28
nature's pride and richest f.!	MARL 572:96	no preparation for the f.	DISR 287:25	Where is this young g.	SHAK 778:59
No f. so charming	SMITH 830:51	one no longer believes in the f.	COUP 248:34	**gallantry** no more to do with g.	SHER 817:83
the f. inside his skull	BYATT 186:20	onward into its uncertain f.	HOFS 422:38	What men call g.	BYRON 817:83
useless and cumbersome f.	TREE 896:1	orgiastic f.	FITZ 338:87	**gallants** Travelled g.	SHAK 804:37
furrow Between the shafts and the f.	HEAN 404:68	past and f....conquered	ELIOT 320:79	**galleon** g. tossed upon cloudy seas	NOYES 642:70
leaves a shining f.	TENN 873:49	past and f. were comprehended	GEE 362:28	Stately as a g.	GREN 388:56
plough my own f.	ROSE 725:25	people who will run the f.	JONES 466:24	**galleries** g. of the house	MUNDY 625:43
furrows The sounding f.	TENN 870:2	picture of the f.	ORWE 655:77	**gallery** faces...a g. of pictures	BACON 52:13
furry fire was f.	SITW 823:9	preparing students for the f.	DEMI 272:47	g. in which the reporters sit	MACA 545:31
further I have seen f. than others	GELL 363:37	present in time f.	ELIOT 319:36	machine-gun to a shooting g.	OFAO 647:77
furtive f. tear	ROMA 723:92	present or any f. writer	MILL 591:95	Pit, box, and g.	POPE 687:98
look of f. shame	WODE 952:47	present, past and f. sees	BLAKE 140:8	**gallimaufry** g. or hodgepodge	SPEN 838:18
fury Allaying...their f.	SHAK 803:15	prophesying a fine f.	WILDE 940:50	**gallon** dying for $1.50 a g. oil	POWE 693:53
blind f. of creation	SHAW 807:16	Prudence...scans the f.	WORD 962:48	**gallons** imperial g. of facts	DICK 281:76
formless spawning f.	YEATS 967:38	Science creates the f.	ZUCK 970:20	**gallop** false g. of verses	SHAK 779:90
full of sound and f.	SHAK 798:74	security for the f.	TROL 897:29	G. about doing good	SMITH 830:45
f., and rage of mortal men	BURT 181:85	seen the f.	HALB 392:21	g. and g. about?	STEV 853:65
f., like a woman scorned	CONG 241:52	The f. belongs to the bridge-builders	MCAL 544:2	**galloped** g., Dirck g.	BROW 167:17
f. of aerial bombardment	EBER 310:11	the f. is happening to book selling	BEZOS 90:75	**gallowglass** Bonnought and g.	MCCA 547:74
f. of a patient man	DRYD 302:92	The f., Mr Gittes	TOWNE 894:65	**gallows** g. in my garden	CHES 221:3
f. of the winter	BEDE 72:59	too eager for the f.	LARK 509:71	High upon the g. tree	SULL 859:80
F. with th' abhorred shears	MILT 599:86	train of the f. to run over him	EISE 314:93	see nothing but the g.	BURKE 176:42
Great f., like great whisky	CAPO 197:27	will be in the f.	KIPL 493:79	world's going to be...one huge g.	BRAU 157:84
like a f. takest us out	BIBLE 113:13	wonderful f. beckoned	PLATH 681:37	**gallows-tree** Below the g.-t.	BURNS 178:2
no f. like an ex-wife	CONN 243:7	**futurelessness** so free of f.	COUP 248:32	Jack on the g.-t.!	SCOTT 753:21
sit and watch the f. pass	ROBE 717:73	**futurism** we establish F.	MARI 571:78	**galoshes** on his g. as he passes	LEAC 515:8
The f. and the mire	YEATS 967:31	**futurist** I am a f. today	OGDEN 647:99	**gals** No g., no gags	TODD 893:35
furze stepped...over the f.	SOME 833:10	**futurity** f. casts upon the present	SHEL 816:53	**galumphing** G. Goodness!	TRAV 896:72
fuse Each one of you is a f.	KOCH 495:23	no reference to f.	JOHN 463:54	**gambit** by ploy or g.	POTT 690:86
through the green f.	THOM 883:3	walk on into f.	THOR 889:40	**gambler** A g. is someone	TRUMP 900:96
fused f. together	GUST 390:3	**Fuzzy-Wuzzy** 'ere's to you, F.-W.	KIPL 489:89		

gambling

Show me a g.	PUZO 701:7
Time, that tireless g.	BAUD 68:67
whore and g.	BLAKE 141:28
gambling g. in human lives	DYSON 309:60
Inside every b....a g. streak	KORDA 498:97
spent...$3m on g.	DALY 261:20
women, g. and technicians	POMP 684:13
game Anybody on for a g.	SHAW 810:92
any g. in the world	TRUE 899:73
Art is a g.	PIER 677:70
Athalus, that made the g.	CHAU 216:56
Baseball is a Lockean g.	NOVAK 641:64
best g. in the world to watch	TREV 896:5
Bowls is a young man's g.	BRYA 170:1
continentals think life is a g.	MIKES 590:87
Cricket...is a manly g.	ANNE 19:12
cricket is just another g.	EDIN 312:50
Cricket is the greatest g.	WARN 921:11
Cricket...the g. of games	FOWL 346:65
enough to take up the g.	ROGE 723:87
far more than a g., this cricket	CARD 198:44
Fashion should be a g.	QUANT 701:4
food is love and g.	SHEL 814:1
Football...is a grand g.	BADEN 54:59
forbid...such g.	EDWA 312:56
fowlers when their g.	OTWAY 656:99
g. called Poohsticks	MILNE 596:24
g. for rough girls	WILDE 942:25
g....is never lost till won	CRAB 252:46
g. is so full of plot-interest	FRY 353:30
g. is too hard	JAMES 449:21
g. of catch-as-catch-can	FOOTE 342:83
g. of golf...played on a Sunday	LEAC 515:19
g. of life seriously	LEARY 517:47
g. of no use	BACON 50:37
g. of the most terrifying stresses	ARLO 32:34
g. your country loves	RICE 713:91
g....at which to be bad	MILNE 596:26
giving over of a g.	BEAU 71:14
golf g. went bad	TREV 896:7
good g. of Croquet	REID 710:45
great g. to see	SYNGE 865:22
how you played the g.	RICE 713:89
If you watch a g.	HOPE 428:59
inside g., cold, sure, undistracted	DELI 271:42
is surely his g.	ROUS 729:8
it is a good g.	HICKS 418:49
It's about the g.	DOUG 295:20
It's the g. that calls me	MILNE 596:25
kids playing some g.	SALI 740:81
killing the g. with this phoney mystique	BRES 158:2
know the g.	MCCA 547:83
Love is a g.	ROBBE 717:65
manly, British g.!	LOVE 538:80
more than a g.	HUGH 436:48
most exhilarating g.	GOOD 378:45
nature of my g.	JAGG 449:15
Never change a winning g.	TILD 891:12
no better than a g.	JAMES 451:70
nobly did he play the 'noble g.'	EGAN 313:65
no g. for the soft of sinew	WOOL 956:47
no hunter's g.	JEFF 453:17
parody is a g.	NABO 628:17
play with him at any g.	SHAK 794:59
Poetry...a mug's g.	ELIOT 319:29
poetry a pedant's g.	BUNT 173:68
present rules of the g.	ROOS 724:18
ruin your g. in no time	BOTH 152:80
Science...is not a g.	PAUL 670:34
Soccer is a man's g.	CHAR 216:48
Socratic method is not a g.	BEER 74:88
some g. on these lone heaths	HAZL 403:40
Soviet g. is chess	SHUL 819:25
take seriously a g.	STOP 856:22
The g.'s afoot	SHAK 775:75
They talk a good g.	BECK 71:35
things you can do in a baseball g.	STEN 847:8
time to win this g.	DRAKE 298:88
Truth is...the g. of the few	BERK 84:34
War's a bloody g.	SASS 745:93
war's a g.	COWP 251:20
What a polite g. tennis is	BARR 65:94
When's the g. itself	MARX 578:22
woman is his g.	TENN 872:33
gameboard steeplechase and g.	ELKIN 322:16
games best and loveliest of g.	CARD 198:43
bread and g.	JUVE 471:57
dread of g.!	BETJ 89:48
G. played with the ball	JEFF 454:29
I play no outdoor g.	WILDE 941:94
like an aptitude for g.	MORAN 618:9
Most g. are skin-deep	ARLO 32:33
or any sinful g.	HARTE 400:71
playing at children's g.	CHES 220:55
gamester sly g.	BEHN 75:19
gammon sucking pig and thick g.	MACB 546:64
world of g. and spinnage	DICK 280:50
gamut Hepburn runs the g.	PARK 663:6
Gandhi odious to see Mr G.	CHUR 225:79
gang Bush and his treacherous g.	HUSS 440:38
g. should mismanage the country	MARQ 575:61
Ganges by the Indian G.	MARV 577:90
gangrene smelly g. of professors	MARI 571:78
gangsterism g. is a...assimilation	DOCT 289:84
gangsters always acted like g.	KUBR 500:34
glorified g.	MACD 550:39
gaol snail...the world's thy g.	DONNE 292:46
who lie in g.	WILDE 942:21
gap Beyond the g. where	WILL 946:20
bridge the g. between the two	CHUR 225:71
duty is to bridge the g.	KISS 494:93
g. between brute power	COMM 239:95
g. in Christianity	FORS 345:51
g. in the hills	ANON 23:2
great g. between	SYNGE 865:24
made a g. in nature	SHAK 794:56
gaps g. even two can pass abreast	FROST 352:90
garb words clothed in reason's g.	MILT 602:60
garbage g. heap	GARD 360:71
G. in, g. out	ANON 25:43
garden alone in a g.	ROSSO 727:68
bleak rock...into a g.	YOUNG 968:51
Come into the g., Maud	TENN 876:25
England is a g.	KIPL 492:67
England is a g.	KIPL 492:68
everyone with a g.	DORAM 294:84
gallows in my g.	CHES 221:3
g. eastwards in Eden	BIBLE 91:87
g. hard by Heaven	BOUL 152:91
g. inclosed is my sister	BIBLE 107:46
g. in her face	CAMP 195:76
g. of cactus and sour grapes	MERR 589:49
G. of Love	BLAKE 140:14
g. of the world	MARV 578:10
g.'s umbrage mild	SMART 826:66
ghost of a g.	SWIN 864:16
Glory of the G.	KIPL 492:67
Glory of the G.	KIPL 492:68
God Almighty first planted a g.	BACON 53:30
God's Heart in a g.	GURN 390:98
God the first g. made	COWL 250:76
God walking in the g.	BIBLE 91:93
happy g. placed	MILT 603:76
have a g. of my own	MARV 577:89
I have the whole g.	HAMM 394:61
imperfection of my g.	MONT 613:20
into the g. to cut	FOOTE 342:83
jungles here are a well-kept g.	BOLT 145:14
like a...birdcage in a g.	WEBS 926:22
man and a woman in a g.	WILDE 941:83
Muses' g.	CAREW 198:51
Nothing grows in our g.	THOM 884:37
Our England is a g.	KIPL 492:67
Our England is a g.	KIPL 492:68
out of the G. of Eden	MUGG 632:10
playing down at the bottom of my g.	SHAN 805:62
rosebud g. of girls	TENN 876:27
Sensitive Plant in a g. grew	SHEL 815:21
we must cultivate our own g.	VOLT 914:34
gardener Adam was a g.	KIPL 493:69
Adam was a g.	SHAK 759:97
bad for God's g.	HARDY 397:19
supposing him to be the g.	BIBLE 124:66
gardeners g., ditchers	SHAK 784:60
goats to be g.	LOVE 538:93
which our wills are g.	SHAK 789:3
gardening G....most underrated	SHUL 819:22
gardens bodies are our g.	SHAK 789:3
Down by the salley g.	YEATS 965:3
g. of the Desert	BRYA 170:3
g. of the West	CONN 243:17
g., wine, and delicate	MONT 613:11
g. without sorrows	CIXO 227:47
in all of the neighbouring g.	REED 709:26
In his blue g.	FITZ 337:80
men Leaving the g.	LARK 509:82
ordered woods and g.	MACK 553:10
sweetest delight of g.	BROW 166:86
variety of g., meadows	MOORE 616:72
garden-state that happy g.-s.	MARV 577:6
gargling blood come g.	OWEN 657:31
garland immortal g. is to be	MILT 600:8
garlanded g. with carven imag'ries	KEATS 477:20
garlands crowning...with g.	COUB 248:19
Therewith fantastic g. did she make	SHAK 784:57
weave the g. of repose	MARV 577:1
you may gather g. there	SCOTT 753:34
garlic G. to mend her kissing	SHAK 799:22
garment caught him by his g.	BIBLE 93:41
City now doth like a g. wear	WORD 959:3
every new and eagerly expected g.	DICK 282:8
g. has looked very different	BONH 146:24
g. out of fashion	SHAK 803:96
g. that made skiing	ANON 25:46
Language is called the g. of thought	CARL 200:94
new cloth unto an old g.	BIBLE 116:64
Non-violence is not a g.	GAND 359:59
waxeth old as a g.	BIBLE 113:94
garments Borrowed g. never fit	FULL 355:81
g. too good For thee	CRAS 254:80
g. were always in patchez	NASH 631:65
Her g., heavy with their drink	SHAK 784:58
keepeth his g.	BIBLE 132:15
Kiss thy perfumed g.	BLAKE 139:80
part my g. among them	BIBLE 99:44
garners Hold like rich g.	KEATS 475:77
garret precious jewels into a g.	BACON 50:53
Garrick as evidently an actor as G.	WALP 919:70
garter earl and a knight of the g.	ATTL 40:28
George and G. dangling	POPE 686:69
garters girdles and g. to be bonds	BACON 51:72
thine own heir-apparent a g.!	SHAK 771:41
gas All is g. and gaiters	DICK 279:87
G. smells awful	PARK 664:19
where you put in the g.	TAYL 868:61
gaseous God...a g. vertebrate	HAEC 391:4
gases killing airs and g.	DICK 282:79
gash g. in its throat	HUGH 435:42
gaslamps light coming from g.	CASAL 207:69
gasp made one G. and Stretch one's Eyes	BELL 77:63
gassing burning and g. people	SIHA 821:65
gas station Russia is a g. s.	MCCA 547:73
gate A-sitting on a g.	CARR 205:21
by shutting the park g.	MILT 600:91
Captain of the G.	MACA 545:45
Death...openeth the g.	BACON 50:60
g. of bliss	CRAS 254:82
g. of paradise	SHAW 811:33
g. of the year	HASK 400:81
gazed upon the g.	BYRON 190:32
guards at the g.	SUN 860:96
here at the g. alone	TENN 876:25
hobbled...through the garden g.	SASS 745:81
house with the narrow g.	SHAK 791:71
Hun is at the g.	KIPL 493:71
lark at heaven g.	SHAK 803:93
matters not how strait the g.	HENL 411:6
passing through this G.	SASS 746:9
passion-flower at the g.	TENN 876:28
poor man at his g.	ALEX 13:62
watchful at his g.	DODD 289:92
wide is the g.	BIBLE 115:52
gates Come open your g.	SCOTT 753:52
g. of pearl and topaz	LAUR 511:22
g. of the world	HARDY 397:14
g....shall not be shut	BIBLE 132:27
g. to the glorious	FORS 344:24
heaven's g. she claps	LYLY 543:83
iron g. of life	MARV 577:94
Lift up your heads, O ye g.	BIBLE 100:47
Nor g. of steel so strong	SHAK 801:57
Open the temple g.	SPEN 839:22
shut the g. of mercy	GRAY 384:71
Sprouting...at area g.	ELIOT 317:76
Such are the G. of Paradise	BLAKE 140:5
Through g. of pearl	HOW 433:85
towards the g. of hell	MILT 603:68
gateways g. of the mind	SASS 746:2
g. to unexplored terrain	WILS 948:57
gather G. ye rose-buds	HERR 415:12
g. you out of the countries	BIBLE 110:33

go and g. them up?	BIBLE 117:94	soldiers, her g. too.	MERE 588:39	g. of Canada	MORR 620:47
gaucho really a g.	GUIR 389:89	too serious...to be left to g.	CLEM 229:84	g. of our days	LARI 509:70
gaudy one other g. night	SHAK 794:72	Whitehall g.	ASHD 37:66	g. of the place	POPE 686:58
rich not g.	SHAK 781:52	generation all a lost g.	STEIN 845:61	g. that could cut a Colossus	JOHN 464:92
gauge danger is that g.	LESS 524:94	energy of a whole g.	THOM 886:88	g. to correct them	TELL 869:66
gauger Master G. play	STEV 851:25	Every g. laughs	THOR 888:35	g. was too sullen	DRYD 300:24
Gaul G....is divided into three parts	CAES 192:11	Every g. revolts	MUMF 625:35	G. will never mount high	BROO 162:83
Gaullist G. only little by little	DE 270:95	every new idea...takes a g. or two	FEYN 334:6	Gives a better discerning	GOLD 376:11
gauntlet g. with a gift in't	BROW 166:99	every single g. gone	MACL 555:31	In every work of g.	EMER 324:51
take up the g.	BROW 165:47	evil and adulterous g.	BIBLE 117:86	interest to the fire of g.	LINC 529:6
gavottes birds sing g.	SITW 823:7	feminism divided my g.	LYND 543:92	in theory if g. had not proved	LESS 524:4
gay all the world was g.	POPE 685:34	for the next g. of men	LOWE 539:99	like many businessmen of g.	PUZO 701:6
assume everyone is g.	FIER 336:40	g. has come to know	TIME 891:18	lot of time to be a g.	STEIN 845:68
Being black is warm and g.	RHYS 712:73	G. x	COUP 248:23	man of g.	POUND 691:97
chimes ring out with a carol g.	BOND 145:17	grieved with this g.	BIBLE 102:2	men of g.	CONA 239:9
g. Description Aegypt glads	POPE 688:31	ills of an entire g.	ISHE 447:69	men of g.	DELA 271:20
G. gilded scenes	ADDI 6:16	in this g.	KENN 482:31	mind and g.	STEN 846:2
g. goodnight	YEATS 966:28	is a g. of men	HOMER 425:2	monotony of g.	HAZL 403:30
g. nature	SMART 826:68	meaning of the Lost G.	KERO 483:56	neither g. nor knowledge	JOHN 460:83
G. rich and Rich g.	ANON 22:78	men and women of this g.	LLOY 533:72	neurotic can...be a literary g.	AUCH 42:63
glass so g.	SPEN 839:57	men in every g.	MILL 594:75	no interest in anything but g.	LAGN 508:51
He has a g. appeal	COWA 249:52	My g. of Canadians	FULF 355:64	no man of g.	BEER 74:90
impiously g.	CRAB 251:28	new g....every 30 years	COWL 250:80	nothing to declare except my g.	WILDE 940:47
I think Jesus was a...g. man	JOHN 456:84	new g. grows up	PLAN 680:25	nourished all its g.	SMITH 831:64
It will be a g. world	READ 708:96	new g. of Americans	KENN 481:3	Philistine of g. in religion	ARNO 36:38
lay his g. caparisons apart	SHAK 794:71	new g. would take over	THOM 885:69	Political g.	HEGEL 406:9
lord and lady g.	SCOTT 752:10	O g. of vipers	BIBLE 117:85	some flashes of g.	BYRON 188:79
poet could not but be g.	WORD 960:26	O g. of vipers	BIBLE 114:20	stereotype of rejected g.	HUGH 435:23
verse again shall...make them g.	DRAY 298:93	one g. sacrificing for the next	MAYH 583:26	taking pains...said to be g.	ACHE 3:42
Gaza brought him down to G.	BIBLE 96:19	our g., though not indifferent	CECIL 210:28	talent instantly recognises g.	DOYLE 297:70
Eyeless in G. at the mill	MILT 607:82	poets of each g.	DAY 267:27	that is the way of g.	MANN 566:80
gaze fixed in steadfast g.	MILT 597:33	refuge from one g. to another	BOOK 149:29	the g. of the...press	BENN 81:82
g. of dogs	CALV 193:35	remind one g.	JEVO 455:55	thing demanded of g.	GOET 375:67
gone to g. on Cleopatra	SHAK 794:56	sad for my g.	SAINT 738:40	think like a g.	NABO 628:20
medium's g. is brief	IGNA 445:14	second g. has no time	BALD 56:14	Though taste, though g. bless	COLL 238:75
seal's wide spindrift g.	CRANE 252:55	Seldom is it given to one g.	SARN 743:55	Three-fifths of him g.	LOWE 539:8
shields him from the world's g.	WHITE 935:45	They lost a g!	NOON 640:47	to say I wasn't a g.	WEST 932:83
star of Truth...bade me g.	ARNO 35:3	third and fourth g....that hate me	BIBLE 94:66	true g. appears	SWIFT 861:32
gazed still they g.	GOLD 376:2	This g. shall not pass	BIBLE 118:30	true g. is...large general powers	JOHN 463:71
gazelle nursed a dear g.	MOORE 618:6	To my g.	AUDEN 44:20	vital g.	GOUR 380:79
gazers eyes the g. strike	POPE 685:32	unto this wicked g.	BIBLE 117:88	Work of Staggering G.	EGGE 313:66
gazes For him that g.	CRAB 252:30	With each g.	SCHR 749:66	works of a great g.	ADDI 7:55
Gazette I inclose the G.	STEE 844:39	ye are a chosen g.	BIBLE 130:67	geniuses cricket's presiding g.	CARD 198:45
Pall Mall G. is written	THAC 880:34	generations 10,000 generations	BENE 79:15	G. are the luckiest	AUDEN 44:14
gazing love does not consist in g.	SAINT 738:32	dwelling place in all g.	BIBLE 101:92	One of the greatest g....Shakespeare	WALP 919:68
gear Time's...chariot changing g.	LINK 530:30	future g.	TOLS 894:54	pretty good as far as g. go	WEST 932:80
women and g. are at the bottom	SCOTT 753:57	g. believe to have happened	WHIT 937:82	genocide g. is being carried out	JOHN 456:81
geek g. means you're willing to study	GATES 361:95	G. have trod	HOPK 428:70	genre writers choose the g.	JAMES 451:61
geese garrulous g.	WHITE 935:41	save succeeding g.	UNIT 905:9	genres these g. still hold	UPDI 906:26
G. are swans	ARNO 35:24	shadows upon two g.	LLOY 533:74	gent knight was...a valiant G.	EVEL 328:70
g. go south	WU 963:84	stolen g.	RUDD 730:34	genteel avoid is the 'shabby g.'	DISR 289:70
Like g. about the sky	AUDEN 43:81	through centuries of g.	MARQ 574:44	not g. when he gets drunk	BOSW 152:78
More g. than swans	GIBB 367:7	generosity luxury of g.	DICK 281:62	truly g.	HARDY 397:11
take their g. for swans	BROO 163:15	generous have more g. sentiments	JOHN 461:98	gentes G. and laitymen	JOYCE 470:36
wild g. lost in cloud	BASHO 67:48	to be g. and compassionate	THAT 881:51	gentile isolation to g. hostility	ROTH 728:91
Gehenna Down to G.	KIPL 489:74	genes selfish molecules known as g.	DAWK 266:15	Gentiles boasting as the G. use	KIPL 490:17
gem every tear a g.	SHEL 812:71	Wall St. g.	THOM 885:69	G.' Lord and King	AQUI 30:96
Full many a g.	GRAY 384:69	Genesis first chapter of G.	ACHE 3:38	G., which have not the law	BIBLE 125:4
g. of the western world	MOORE 617:1	G. was to be believed	SHAR 806:75	preach among the G.	BIBLE 127:87
treat it like a precious g.	PELE 672:76	Genet G. had been right	ANGE 19:99	gentility I expected kindness and g.	PERE 674:21
gendarme United States...global g.	MCNA 557:88	genetics G. is Important and Difficult	PARE 663:88	Money and g.	MITF 610:49
gender tired of the g. of things	SEXT 758:48	Geneva rules...from Rome or G.	BROW 164:45	Shabby g. has nothing	HOLM 424:73
to a kind and not to a g.	YOUR 968:55	Genghis g. Khan has arrived	THUR 891:21	What's g. worth	GALS 358:51
genealogy g. of his forefathers	ECHE 310:14	genitals very different attitude to g.	BURG 174:1	gentle As g. and as jocund	SHAK 764:33
general business of a g.	SUN 859:92	genius 25-year old g.	GREE 386:36	carry g. peace	SHAK 805:54
g. has no friends	LEMAY 521:31	absolute g. for malingering	PROU 698:47	Do not go g.	THOM 884:27
g. must know	REED 710:33	appearance of...greater g.	RUSS 734:27	g. and respectful ways	FENW 332:64
g.'s disdained	SHAK 786:27	attributes of g.	MOND 612:96	G. as falcon	SKEL 824:29
g. who advances	SUN 859:93	Bradman's batting g.	LARW 510:8	g. mind by g. deeds	SPEN 839:58
g. who does not believe	NATH 632:5	Celtic g.	ARNO 35:22	g., yet not dull	DENH 272:60
good for G. Motors	WILS 947:47	cocker up my g.	JONS 466:47	I have seen them g.	WYATT 964:90
imperator and great g.	SHAK 763:9	Conceit spoils the finest g.	ALCO 12:41	love, so g. in his view	SHAK 765:66
'Twas caviare to the g.	SHAK 782:46	destroy g. and art	HAZL 404:59	gentleman act the g.	TAFT 866:11
victorious g.	SUN 859:91	dispenses with the need for g.	GALB 357:20	ask the honourable g.	ROCHE 719:2
generalization g. can establish science	BERN 85:71	each...be considered a g.	BERG 83:21	attire for a g.	SHAR 806:72
generalizations can be no g.	FISH 337:62	Every age has a...universal g.	DRYD 300:18	back to the g.'s flat	MANS 567:7
g. are dangerous	DUMAS 306:92	everything but g. and virtue	HAZL 403:46	beautiful woman...qualities of a g.	LABR 502:8
g. of science sweep	HUXL 442:2	G. and regularity are utter Enemies	GAIN 356:9	chance of becoming a g. in it	LAMM 506:21
tentatively accepted g.	FRIE 351:68	g. for painting, poetry, music	EMER 325:87	fashionable g.	ALSOP 15:12
generals bite some of my other g.	GEOR 363:46	g. found respectable?	BROW 166:2	g. an' scholar	BURNS 177:80
g. are in my coach	MARL 572:91	g. is an enormous littleness	PATC 668:6	g. is an attorney	JOHN 462:22
g. of his day	WELL 929:98	g. is enough	ARET 31:11	g....loves to hear himself talk	SHAK 766:91
G., right-wing politicians	STEI 846:93	G. is felt	DIDE 285:64	g. on whom I built	SHAK 796:12
like dead g.	TUCH 901:10	G. is one per cent inspiration	EDIS 312:54	g. poet	JOYCE 470:25
most people and G.	TUCH 901:13	g. lies in taking...ordinary people	BANKS 62:28	g. to be the best dressed	TROL 898:77
plebiscite elected g.	JUVE 471:57	g. makes no mistakes	JOYCE 470:27	Gladstone...never a g.	DISR 288:63
Russia has two g.	NICH 636:70	g....not to purchase fame	DRYD 301:45	He's a g.	SHAW 810:94

gentleman-drover

honourable g. caught the Whigs	DISR 288:37	G. and Garter dangling	POPE 686:69	like g. from an enchanter fleeing	SHEL 813:79
honourable g.'s poodle	LLOY 532:68	G.—don't do that	GREN 387:55	rain Is full of g.	MILL 592:23
I am a g.	SHAW 807:22	G. Ill...consecrated obstruction	BAGE 54:74	**ghoul** g. of literature	DELI 271:39
king...cannot make a g.	BURKE 176:53	G. the Third	BENT 82:4	**giant** As when a g. dies	SHAK 788:66
last g. in Europe	LEVE 525:21	G. who discovered that alcohol	WODE 952:40	chalk g.	HEAN 404:71
legal g. who rescues your estate	BROU 163:16	great G. weighs twenty stone	BYRON 190:20	G. Despair had a wife	BUNY 174:77
lovely g.!	SHAK 766:6	King G.'s glorious days	GILB 369:53	g. girls that have no secret	SPEN 837:2
man was apparently a g.	RIDGE 715:31	**George Bush** G. B. doesn't care	WEST 932:77	g. refreshed with wine	BOOK 149:27
no g. could...give offence	ROCHE 719:99	**George W. Bush** The rest...were G. W. B.	BRYS 171:19	G.'s Causeway worth seeing?	JOHN 463:68
No real English g.	BAGE 54:64	**Georgian** G. Silver goes	MACM 557:75	lies a sleeping.	NAPO 629:38
Once a g.	DICK 282:93	**geranium** madman shakes a dead g.	ELIOT 317:73	like a g.'s robe	SHAK 798:67
reputability to the g. of leisure	VEBL 910:46	**Géricault** G. corpses, or Picasso	LIPP 530:34	'This is I, the g..'	MAST 581:83
serving a great g.	ISHI 447:72	**germ** very g. and first upgrowth	KING 488:55	To have a g.'s strength	SHAK 787:57
So this g. said a girl	LOOS 536:46	**German** G. Empire arose?	HERZL 416:24	upon the body of a g.	LAND 506:28
stamps a man...as an educated g.	SHAW 809:71	G. memory was like...tongue	BURU 182:92	**giantism** To go for g.	SCHU 750:74
that which you call a G.	CROM 255:17	G. people will turn	LENIN 521:39	**giants** G. in physical power	CARL 200:84
this venerable old g.	LEAC 516:24	G. police spies	MARX 579:33	g., the sons of Anak	BIBLE 94:80
too pedantic for a g.	CONG 241:48	G. text of French operas	WHAR 934:11	like precocious g.	PEAR 671:57
true breeding of a g.	BYRON 190:14	like G. opera	WAUGH 924:79	standing on the shoulders of g.	BERN 85:61
unable to describe a g.	TROL 898:57	saw a G. soldier	STRA 857:42	**Gibraltar** G. may tumble	GERS 365:80
use of a g. in travelling	LOWE 539:95	Should the G. people lay down	GOEB 374:54	**giddy** g., shallow, humorous youth	SHAK 775:71
When a g. is disposed	SHAK 803:90	two literatures [French and G.]	ARNO 35:8	**Gideon** sword of the Lord, and of G.	BIBLE 95:13
Who was then a g.	BALL 58:49	under G. influence	GOER 374:57	**gier-eagle** G. the g.-e.	SMART 826:65
gentleman-drover he...is a g.-d.	SCOTT 753:37	wee, wee G. lairdie!	CUNN 258:75	**gift** Beauty is the lover's g.	CONG 241:63
gentlemen American g. are the best	LOOS 536:52	**Germans** Beastly to the G.	COWA 249:58	cause of this fair g.	SHAK 802:67
ask you g.	RODR 722:54	G....are going to pay	GEDD 362:26	chance g. of nature	MORAN 618:9
creates good g.	MUGA 623:7	G. classify...the French arrange	CATH 208:91	creative g.	HOPK 429:27
difficult to behave like g.	MACK 554:15	I hate not G.	THOM 885:15	destroying her g. by maiming	BACON 53:54
G. do not take soup	CURZ 260:7	let the G. win the war	MILE 590:88	Every good g....is from above	BIBLE 130:49
g. in England now abed	SHAK 776:94	problem of the Sudeten G.	HITL 420:95	exploiting a heavenly g.	QUIL 702:17
g....in the same Lobby	PALM 662:73	**Germany** Communism fits G.	STAL 842:7	for a New Year's g.	SHAK 773:12
G. know that fresh air	MACA 544:17	country is at war with G.	CHAM 212:66	gauntlet with a g. in't	BROW 166:99
g....possess only strength and valour	BRON 161:62	every country except G.	GREY 388:63	g. half understood	ELIOT 320:78
G. Prefer Blondes	LOOS 536:45	from G. to Downing Street	CHAM 212:64	g. of a coward	SHAK 785:81
G.-rankers out on the spree	KIPL 489:75	G. has become a menace	ROOS 725:22	g. of God is eternal life	BIBLE 125:13
G....seem to remember blondes	LOOS 536:47	in G., books	STAEL 842:1	g. of tears	SWIN 863:85
G., you can't fight in here	KUBR 500:33	Islam is part of G.	MERK 588:45	g. of vanity and pride	GRIL 388:70
Hard pounding this, g.	WELL 929:1	ruined cities of G.	ORWE 654:54	g. or trust	MCCA 547:90
ladies and g., last night	NATH 632:1	You're thinking of Europe as		Heav'n's last best g.	MILT 604:14
male officers are g.	CADOR 191:9	G. and France	RUMS 731:42	love is the g. of oneself!	ANOU 28:68
most of the g.	WAUGH 923:52	**germinates** g. and gestates by itself	HUST 440:46	love, or g., which is	MILT 600:15
no ancient g. but gardeners	SHAK 784:60	**germs** Trap the g.	ANON 24:24	Madness if g.	PALEY 661:54
no salvation for g.	MOLI 611:73	**Gershwin** G. died last week	OHARA 648:11	make the g. rich	TROL 898:42
patriots...not to forget we are g.	BURKE 175:11	G. keeps pounding on tin	GERS 365:74	music is a g. and a burden	SIMO 822:78
since g. came up.	SHAK 759:94	**Gerty** G....taken up...concerts	WHAR 933:5	naught her priceless g.	PATM 669:15
spoken of themselves as g.	WAUGH 923:57	**gessamine** crow-toe, and pale g.	MILT 599:91	only g. is a portion of thyself	EMER 324:71
Tea...Is a g.	CHES 221:88	**gesture** army without parade or g.	LAWR 514:90	other than the g. of life	KOSI 499:2
'Then, g.,' said Redgauntlet	SCOTT 754:73	never make a fine g.	BERN 86:86	problem without a g.	BACH 49:12
two very civil g.	SHER 817:96	**gestures** cynical g. of the poor	SPEN 837:96	speech, that supremely human g.	MATH 581:28
When G. can see	DICK 283:32	parody...invades all g.	PIGL 678:75	When God hands you a g.	CAPO 197:25
while the G. go by!	KIPL 492:50	**get** away inwardly	HERZ 416:22	**gifted** divinely g. man	TENN 874:83
written by g. for g.	THAC 880:34	G. up, g. up for shame	HERR 415:9	g. individuals manage to do both	SAKI 739:63
gentleness all...through my g.	WYATT 964:90	time to g.	BIBLE 105:14	young, g. and black	HANS 396:86
Crist...we claym of him oure g.	CHAU 217:89	will never g. it	WEAT 925:5	**gift horse** Always look a g. h.	RABE 703:12
G....cardinal virtues	WOLL 954:89	**getting** g. over a four-day drunk	HELL 408:50	**gifts** cannot recall their g.	TENN 877:61
g. of heaven	WORD 959:96	Let's be g. at them	GRACE 380:83	countless g. of love	WINK 950:98
gentles It's weel wi' you g.	SCOTT 753:50	with all thy g. get understanding	BIBLE 104:54	diversities of g.	BIBLE 126:51
gentlest fittest may also be the g.	DOBZ 289:79	**get up** We g. u. in the morning	DENCH 272:53	even when bearing g.	VIRG 913:14
gentlewoman cut out for a G.	SWIFT 863:68	**Gettysburg** G. address was so short	HEMI 410:83	For your g.	WEBS 926:32
talk so like a waiting g.	SHAK 771:33	**gewgaw** This g. world	DRYD 301:51	g. may henceforth be bestowed	SHAK 778:58
gently persuade g., not by force	PASC 667:84	**ghastly** grave is g.	ANON 20:35	give good g. unto your children	BIBLE 115:51
gentry Ye Enbrugh G.!	BURNS 177:72	more g. a business	HARDY 397:25	great g. with one hand	SNOW 832:79
genuine place for the g.	MOORE 617:77	**ghetto** idea of an arts g.	HARR 399:58	man's work or his own g.	MILT 601:28
genuineness g. of apparent statements	AYER 48:5	radio is a g. of good taste	KEIL 479:55	No g. from chance	ARNO 33:60
G. only thrives in the dark	HUXL 441:57	**ghost** Ay, thou poor g.	SHAK 781:66	offer g. to people one knew	DE 268:49
geographers So g., in Afric-maps	SWIFT 863:63	bowling of a g.	THOM 886:84	presented unto him g.	BIBLE 114:17
geography different from G.	BENT 82:97	cease to be a g.	PAZ 671:47	rarer g. than gold	BROO 162:90
g. of one's own nature	BOWL 153:6	dogma of the G.	RYLE 736:59	received g. for men	BIBLE 101:82
like trying to stop G.	MONT 614:34	Father, Son and Holy G.	MCLE 554:23	received g. for men	BOOK 149:25
too much g.	KING 487:42	gave up the g.	BIBLE 120:62	Rich g. wax poor	SHAK 783:8
geologists G. are never at a loss	BRYS 171:18	gave up the g.	BIBLE 122:10	Rich men deal g.	SHAK 791:83
geology reduced easily to basic g.	HILL 418:59	g. from the tomb	SHEL 813:77	Spend not then his g.	JONS 467:56
geometrician God is a g.	PLATO 682:68	g. of a garden	SWIN 864:16	stars were the g.	MACC 548:8
géométrie Vanité de la g.	FRED 349:40	g. of a great house	LEVE 525:23	whose heavenly g.	SURR 860:99
Geometry G. is that part	NEWT 635:40	g. of wind	WILL 946:22	Win her with g.	SHAK 759:66
geometry does not know his g.	ANON 28:52	g. stories...for ghosts	ALDI 12:49	**Gilbert** G. had a baddish streak	QUIL 702:15
g. in the humming of the strings	PYTH 701:16	g. will walk	BROW 168:46	G. to someone else's Sullivan	RUSS 735:46
G. is not true	PIRS 679:93	given up the g.	BIBLE 98:31	laid down by G. and Sullivan	HUTC 441:50
G. is to sculpture	APOL 29:80	mind full of g.	MANS 567:95	**gild** g. the blade if you will	QUIN 702:22
G....the only science	HOBB 420:97	peacock like a g.	TENN 873:49	verse again shall g.	DRAY 298:93
g. was degraded	MACA 545:43	The g. of Roger Casement	YEATS 967:35	**gilded** vegetables too g.	GIRA 372:26
Night G.	KENN 480:89	thought to please my g.	MENC 586:85	**gilding** g. of setting sun	GARL 360:75
no 'royal road' to g.	EUCL 328:51	yielded up the g.	BIBLE 119:48	**gile** thai er ful of g.	MINOT 608:9
Geordie Jingling G.	SCOTT 754:67	**ghosts** ambushed with g.	MACA 544:18	**Gilead** balm in G.	BIBLE 110:18
George Amelia was praying for G.	THAC 880:26	g. of beauty glide	POPE 688:15	**gillyflowers** With g.	SPEN 838:15
England and Saint G.!	SHAK 775:76	haunted by the g.	SHAK 764:52	**gimble** Did gyre and g.	CARR 204:89
fair Saint G.	SHAK 761:54	I sought for g.	SHEL 812:56	**gimcrack** how g. a place	LAUR 511:22

global

gin for a g. and for a snare	BIBLE 107:58
G. and chicken helpless	BARK 63:52
G. by pailfuls	SCOTT 753:43
G. was mother's milk	SHAW 810:99
Of all the g. joints	EPST 327:26
proper union of g. and vermouth	DE 275:9
receptacle for Gilbey's g.	CHEE 218:8
sooner we can get out the g.	REED 710:32
ginger empty g. ale bottles	THUR 890:65
Nutmegs and g.	ANON 22:68
Gipper win…one for the G.	GIPP 372:21
gipsy Time, you old g. man	HODG 421:19
giraffe God…invented the g.	PICA 677:62
Swelling to maculate g.	ELIOT 317:80
giraffes G.!—a People	CAMP 194:57
man who believes in g.	MITC 609:27
return the g. to the zoo	NASH 631:86
gird g. up the loins of your mind	BIBLE 130:64
girders Rumbling under blackened g.	BETJ 88:28
girdle At her own g.	WEBS 926:23
folds of a bright g.	ARNO 33:66
g. round about the earth	SHAK 767:28
g. when your hips stick	NASH 631:82
leathern g. about his loins	BIBLE 114:19
Off with that g.	DONNE 291:19
the g. do the gods inherit	SHAK 793:22
girdles g. and garters to be bonds	BACON 51:72
girl a…g. born into…poverty	OBAMA 644:48
Boy Meets G. in Winnipeg	MACL 555:49
can't get no g. reaction	JAGG 449:13
dark g. I couldn't play with	WRIG 963:70
do a g. in	ELIOT 319:27
doubt whether any g.	TROL 897:30
first rock at a g. like I	LOOS 536:55
forget myself with that g.	TAYL 868:50
Fun is fun but no g.	LOOS 536:53
g. in our town	ANON 23:87
g. I saw was myself	RHYS 712:78
g. likes to be crossed in love	AUST 46:60
g.…marries a literary man	CHEE 218:7
g. must marry for love	GABOR 356:4
g. solid with yearning	LOWE 540:38
g. throwing a ball	WOOLF 955:23
g. to miss out on any	RUSS 735:49
g.…turned into a chimpanzee	PERE 674:17
g., unschooled, unpractisèd	SHAK 770:6
g., who's danced with the Prince	FARJ 330:21
g. whose cheeks	NASH 630:58
g. who was a lady	LOOS 536:50
g. with big boobs	KING 486:18
Give me a g.	SPARK 836:69
great mountainous sports g.	BETJ 88:21
Home is the g.'s prison	SHAW 808:53
I am a material g.	MADO 558:19
I'm not a g.	MANS 567:96
like a chorus g.'s tights	LAWR 514:87
Look like a g.	SIMON 821:73
maddest fantasticalest g.	DEKK 270:13
nice g. should only fall	SPARK 836:72
Oh, she's a splendid g.	HUXL 441:74
Poor Little Rich G.	COWA 249:44
pretty g. is like a melody	BERL 84:37
quite loved by a g.	TROL 898:42
Since I was a little g.	ROTH 727:77
So this gentleman said a g.	LOOS 537:46
There's a Burma g.	KIPL 489:80
There was a little g.	LONG 536:40
What can you expect of a g.	WHAR 934:12
where the g. smiled before	WHIT 938:17
wink your eye at some…g.	MENC 586:85
young g.'s skin	RENO 711:55
young g. stood beside	NEIL 633:10
girlfriend going to visit our g. f.	MAMET 564:43
girl-graduates sweet g.-g.	TENN 872:31
girlie here and tell me, g.	NASH 631:76
girls all the g.…were laid	PARK 663:8
Always be civil to the g.	MITF 610:55
Anyone who marries three g.	STEIN 845:74
Dancing…training for g.	MORL 619:38
different part of your heart with g.	AMIS 17:62
For coloured g.	SHAN 805:59
from the g. I want	BERL 85:57
game for rough g.	WILDE 942:25
giant g. that have no secret	SPEN 837:2
g. aren't ignorant	COOP 246:89
G. aren't like that	AMIS 16:31
G. are so queer	ALCO 12:44
g. in slacks remember dad	BETJ 88:35
g. so constantly do this	TROL 897:31
g. suffered during this month	BERR 87:3
g. think that they can do so	TROL 898:45
g.' thin laughter	RICK 714:27
g. were no longer to be treated	LEE 519:98
g. with wax faces	WILD 943:44
Golden lads and g.	SHAK 803:7
good g. keep diaries	BANK 61:15
It was the g. I liked	BAIL 55:81
lads for the g.	HOUS 431:46
lovely, gifted g.	GRAV 382:32
make passes At g.	PARK 664:17
Many g. have not the advantage	FLEM 340:44
mean g. on Twitter	PAGL 659:24
men and g. came and went	FITZ 337:80
mill g. clumping	ORWE 653:9
Most plain g. are virtuous	ANGE 19:88
No g.…no chance	ANON 24:26
other g. and boys	STEV 853:66
pallor of g.' brows	OWEN 657:26
process whereby American g. turn	HAMP 395:75
robust, dynamic g.	WODE 952:42
rose-lipt g.	HOUS 432:56
save women and g.	WEBB 925:7
Secrets with g.…are never valued	CRAB 252:48
thing about g.	SALI 740:74
to g. and boys	HORA 430:9
Treaties are like g.	DE 270:94
trouble with g.	SALI 740:79
twelve little g. in two straight lines	BEME 78:98
two g. had me buried!	MANS 567:83
What do g. do	ALCO 12:45
What fools middle-class g. are	DRAB 298:81
what some g. marry	ROWL 729:19
where g. might be sent	AUST 46:73
within the reach of factory g.	SCHU 750:79
Gittes The future, Mr G.	TOWNE 894:65
give G., and it shall be given	BIBLE 120:74
G. it up! G. it up!	KAFKA 472:8
g. what you command	AUGU 44:28
If she g. aught	WEBS 926:17
It's best to g.	ROTH 728:97
more blessed to g. than to receive	BIBLE 125:96
giver God loveth a cheerful g.	BIBLE 127:74
givers when g. prove unkind	SHAK 783:8
giving in g. that we receive	FRAN 347:43
giving in tired of g. i.	PARKS 665:45
glaciers rock inlaid with azure g.	BENU 83:9
glad g. grace	YEATS 965:7
g. mad brother's name	SWIN 864:15
g. of another death	ELIOT 318:18
g. when they said unto me	BIBLE 103:32
g. with all my heart	DRAY 299:99
g. you like adverbs	JAMES 451:54
heart was g.	FOX 346:71
just g. to see me	WEST 933:89
glade cool gales shall fan the g.	POPE 685:15
in the bee-loud g.	YEATS 965:4
gladiators G. fight, or die, in flow'rs	POPE 686:60
gladness excitement and g.	BUEC 172:42
girded me with g.	BIBLE 100:51
half with melancholy, half with g.	LUGO 542:62
in heill wes and g.	DUNB 306:3
poets…begin in g.	WORD 959:1
serve the Lord with g.	BIBLE 102:4
serve the Lord with g.	BOOK 133:33
stale is their g.	HARP 398:41
Teach me half the g.	SHEL 814:99
Without g. availis no tresour	DUNB 306:99
Gladstone G., like Richelieu	DISR 288:65
Like G. speaking to Victoria	MANC 564:52
Mr G. read Homer	CHUR 225:75
unprincipled maniac G.	DISR 288:63
Glamis G. hath murdered sleep	SHAK 797:35
glamour G.…makes a man ask	DACHE 260:1
g. Of childish days	LAWR 512:46
g. of poetry	GARL 360:75
insolvency spelt g.	STOP 855:16
smiling g. girls	MACI 553:98
glamour-studded g.-s. 1950s	YEATS 966:27
glance O brightening g.	YEATS 966:27
snatch a g.	WORD 961:32
wherever his g. falls	JOHN 456:75
whose g. was glum	GILB 370:70
glances Expressive g.	GILB 369:55
mystical grammar of amorous g.	CLEV 230:93
piercing g. into the life	MOORE 617:76
glands smaller adrenal g.	MENC 587:10
glare g. of the pressing present	STUA 857:76
jaded with the rush and g.	ARNO 34:72
long g. of day	SHEL 812:54
protect you from the g.	COWA 249:51
Glasgow cleanse the G. slums	GIBB 366:5
G., the sort of…city	GRAY 383:43
I belong to G.	FYFFE 356:96
play the old G. Empire	DODD 289:88
glass an excuse for a g.	SHER 817:90
beholding his natural face in a g.	BIBLE 130:50
division is…a sheet of g.	BUCH 171:22
dome of many-coloured g.	SHEL 815:43
drank rapidly a g. of water	CUMM 257:59
Drink not the third g.	HERB 413:55
duller than dusty g.	TAKU 866:12
Enjoy another g.	ANON 20:26
fill your g. with us	INGR 446:36
Get thee g. eyes	SHAK 793:26
g. held up to the face	ROCK 721:39
G. is a thing in disguise	CAREY 199:62
g. is falling hour by hour	MACN 557:98
g. mingled with fire	BIBLE 132:14
g. of Guinness	GREE 385:2
g. shall not persuade me	SHAK 800:40
g. so gay	SPEN 839:57
g. was between us	RHYS 712:78
g. will not do you…service	ASTE 39:1
g. will show thee	SHAK 801:65
grief with a g.	SWIN 863:85
hairshirts, pinks and g.	LOWE 540:34
He was indeed the g.	SHAK 792:80
if we had g. winders	DICK 280:22
let him hate you through the g.	BLUN 143:76
made mouths in a g.	SHAK 792:6
magic house of g.	ROBE 717:73
New g. skyscrapers	TALE 866:15
No g. of ours was never raised	HEAN 405:74
Pride is his own g.	SHAK 786:31
Satire is a sort of g.	SWIFT 861:17
sea of g.	BIBLE 131:96
sea of g.	BIBLE 132:14
see its hopes as in a g.	MARV 577:99
Something of g. about her	MACN 557:94
stand before the g.	SCHR 749:63
swift sandy g.	HEYW 417:43
talent, g., and some cracked ice	BARR 65:3
tap and sigh Upon the g.	MILL 592:23
that there crystal g.	FITZ 337:83
Thou art thy mother's g.	SHAK 800:33
through a g., darkly	BIBLE 126:52
till I set you up a g.	SHAK 784:36
turn down an empty g.	FITZ 337:72
Unless it was an empty g.	LOWRY 541:41
Venus, take my votive g.	PRIOR 696:5
glassblower gifted g. of language	HERS 416:20
glass ceiling shatter this…g. c.	CLIN 231:31
glasses Fill all the g. there	COWL 250:75
girls who wear g.	PARK 664:17
set wet g. on them	ROBI 718:83
Women…as looking-g.	WOOLF 955:27
gleam add the g.	WORD 961:28
spent lights quiver and g.	ARNO 33:57
visionary g.	WORD 959:7
gleams sunbeams…convex g.	SHEL 813:77
glee counterfeited g.	GOLD 376:1
girlish g.	GILB 369:63
songs of pleasant g.	BLAKE 139:85
this night wi' mirth and g.	SKIN 825:50
glen Down the rushy g.	ALLI 14:6
g. with one thin stream	DEVL 275:8
your wee bit hill and g.	WILL 946:31
glens purple g. replying	TENN 872:39
glibness brilliant g. of the Berlitz-school	FIRB 336:56
glimpse clothing affords a g.	BART 66:25
first g. of the building	POE 683:80
g. of…freedom	BANN 62:34
G. of the forest	SITW 823:4
In olden days a g. of stocking	PORT 690:68
glimpses g.…less forlorn	WORD 961:30
glisters Nor all that g. gold	GRAY 383:54
gloaming calm simmer g.	TANN 867:24
Roamin' in the g.	LAUD 511:16
gloaters Englishmen are born g.	OBRI 647:62
global G. double zero	ANON 26:96
g. village of tomorrow	GATES 361:93

globe

world in the image of a g. village	MCLU 556:54	going to g.!	DUNC 307:6	When things g. wrong	OBRI 646:68
globe All that tread The g.	BRYA 170:2	good man's g.	KEMP 480:79	when you do g.	HOPK 428:63
g. as one great dewdrop	MUIR 624:26	gown of g.	RALE 705:44	when you have to g. there	FROST 352:93
g. of dead	THOM 883:8	great and sudden g.	DE 275:9	whither thou goest, I will g.	BIBLE 96:23
g. of the earth	MUNDY 625:44	greater g. of His Creator	PIUS 680:20	will not let thee g.	BIBLE 93:36
great g. itself	SHAK 804:27	heaven and earth are full of thy g.	BOOK 147:70	Will ye g. wi' me	BALL 59:65
In this distracted g.	SHAK 781:66	heavens declare the g. of God	BOOK 148:9	**goal** achieving the g.	KENN 481:5
on the face of the g.	SMITH 830:50	hope of g.	BOOK 147:50	colour is the g.	HEIN 407:19
rattle of a g.	DRYD 301:51	in g. and in joy	WORD 959:1	final g. of ill	TENN 874:75
survive on this g.	TRUM 899:82	In God 'tis g.	DRYD 302:79	g. in the World Cup	RAMS 706:52
globes little g. extent	MARV 576:86	joy and their g. must be	ABEL 1:4	g. of art is almost divine	HUGO 436:55
gloom amid the encircling g.	NEWM 635:45	King of g., King of peace	HERB 413:68	g. of every system of law	ROUS 729:12
Brooding o'er the g.	MERE 587:23	King of G. wore	MARV 577:98	g. of our actions	MORE 619:22
g. of clouds	ADDI 6:34	known a. in it all	MILL 592:18	g. of the anti-abortion forces	LEGU 520:13
g. pervaded my spirit	POE 683:80	Land of Hope and G.	BENS 81:84	g. on these journeys	THES 882:96
Lamps for my g.	SASS 746:98	like thy g., Titan	SHEL 815:20	g. that supplies the political magic	SCHL 748:39
light to counterfeit a g.	MILT 598:54	Lo now my g.	SHAK 760:17	grave is not its g.	LONG 535:14
see them through the g.	WILDE 940:44	looks on war as all g.	SHER 818:9	imagines that it has reached its g.	SHAW 809:79
glooms Welcome, kindred g.!	THOM 887:3	mellow g. of the Attic stage	ARNO 33:64	life...had a g.	HAMM 394:57
glories g. of our blood and state	SHIR 819:20	Not as our g.	WORD 958:79	Of your g. as it ghosts	MOTI 622:89
g. of the human	GOULD 380:77	party...may retain its g.	GAIT 357:11	reach the g.	HUXL 443:5
those weaker g.	VAUG 909:34	paths of g. lead but to the grave	GRAY 384:66	scored a g. from the halfway line	WILK 944:61
glorious As g. to this night	SHAK 765:78	power, and the g.	BIBLE 115:42	stood to keep the g.	HOUS 431:42
came back g.	PRIE 695:86	prince of g. died	WATTS 922:46	Till yon g. be won	GORD 378:52
gates to the g.	FORS 344:24	radiancy of g.	NEALE 632:7	Try for a g. that's reasonable	ZATO 969:3
G., Galumphing Goodness!	TRAV 896:92	sea Of g.	BYRON 188:60	**goalkeepers** nation of g.	STOP 856:56
g. land of ours	FERB 332:66	seen the g.	KING 487:35	**goals** confusion of g.	EINS 313:82
g. nothing did I see	DONNE 291:33	set the g. above the heavens	BIBLE 99:30	dedicated to...dogmas or g.	PIRS 679:90
g. sense of words	ACHE 2:28	shew me thy g.	BIBLE 94:74	muddied oafs at the g.	KIPL 492:49
G. the northern lights	SMART 826:67	short of the g. of God	BIBLE 125:6	'theories' and 'g.'	KIPL 492:49
g. thing	GILB 368:37	snatching g. out of defeat	PRIE 695:86	would not tolerate compromise on g.	DULL 306:88
G. things are spoken	BIBLE 101:91	some desperate g.	OWEN 657:31	**goat** g. feet dance an antic hay	MARL 573:14
g. to be a human boy!	DICK 281:66	Son of man shall come in his g.	BIBLE 119:35	g., on which the lot fell	BIBLE 94:77
more g. to them that see it	ELIZ 322:6	spread, my sons, your g.	POPE 689:39	**goats** better than sheep or g.	TENN 878:86
Mud! Mud! G. mud!	FLAN 338:8	sun that was Munster's g.	ORAH 652:91	g. on the left	BIBLE 119:35
What a g. morning	ADAMS 5:9	there is no g. in the deed	READ 708:95	g. to be gardeners	LOVE 538:93
words sacred, g. and sacrifice	HEMI 409:64	There's g. for you!	CARR 205:14	hair is as a flock of g.	BIBLE 107:45
write your g. name	SPEN 839:47	this g., this fair luminous mist	COLE 235:31	Not for Cadwallader and all his g.	SHAK 776:97
glory after the g. hath he sent	BIBLE 112:59	though not indifferent to g.	CECIL 210:28	**goblets** g. for a dish of wood	SHAK 764:54
afterward receive me to g.	BIBLE 101:86	Thy g. flames from sun and star	HOLM 424:82	**goblin** g. Honour	CAREW 198:56
Art, G., Freedom fail	BYRON 187:43	to thy name give g.	BIBLE 133:35	spirit of health or g. damned	SHAK 781:57
beheld his g.	BIBLE 122:18	unreveal'd g. of Nature	SHIP 818:15	That hobnailed g.	SITW 823:5
boredom, and the horror, and the g.	ELIOT 319:30	Unto him be g. in the church	BIBLE 128:89	**God** abandoned a belief in G.	STEV 850:93
clouds of g.	WORD 959:8	virtue...sum of g.	MARL 572:3	abide with my Creator G.	CLARE 228:55
clouds of his own g.	GREE 385:3	waste of g.	STUD 858:63	a cheap version of being G.	GILL 371:89
crowned him with g. and honour	BIBLE 99:31	What Price G.?	ANDE 17:71	Adversary of G. and man	MILT 603:68
days of g.	PETA 675:36	Where is the antique g.	SPEN 838:37	afraid to look upon G.	BIBLE 93:53
days of our g.	BYRON 190:30	Who is this King of g.?	BIBLE 100:47	after death G. knows	ROSS 726:60
dying G. smiles	BYRON 188:58	whose g. is in their shame	BIBLE 128:3	Ah G., for a man	TENN 876:20
earth is full of his g.	BIBLE 107:54	Why in the name of G.	KEATS 477:10	air out of G.'s own presence	WILS 949:75
external g. in the room	AUBR 42:61	Yet I g.	JONS 466:46	all belongs to G., the Lord of	
eyes have seen the g.	HOWE 433:92	Your great g.	PERI 675:25	all Being	KORAN 497:60
Fareweel our ancient g.	BURNS 179:40	**gloss** glistering g. darkened	SPEN 838:30	All conceptions of G.	WEIL 928:75
full meridian of my g.	SHAK 805:50	**glove** hand of steel in a velvet g.	WOOL 956:40	All G.'s Chillum got Rhythm	KAHN 472:10
game is about g.	BLAN 141:48	mailed fist in a cotton g.	SITW 824:15	allow G. to penetrate	WEIL 928:73
give him g.	HOPK 429:86	play'd at the g.	BALL 58:54	Almighty G., give us grace	BOOK 147:51
g. a bubble	SHEL 812:51	white g. pulpit	REAG 708:98	Almighty G., the fountain	BOOK 148:97
g. and good of Art	BROW 169:79	**gloves** capitalism with the g. off	STOP 855:18	Almighty G., unto whom all hearts	BOOK 147:58
g. and the dream	WORD 959:7	people in g. and such	CHES 221:8	America is G.'s Crucible	ZANG 969:1
G. be to God	HOPK 428:72	through the fields in g.	CORN 247:3	And G.'s bell	YEATS 965:8
G. be to the Father	BOOK 146:35	wearing g. more often	ANDE 17:69	as G. granted it	QUIL 702:10
g. in large coins	HUGO 437:74	with his g. on	THUR 890:86	as G. is my witness	MITC 610:42
g. in the flower	WORD 960:12	**glow** a purple g.	YEATS 965:4	As if we were G.'s spies	SHAK 793:33
g. in the piling up	JAMES 451:57	g. more...than blaze of branch	ELIOT 321:81	asks G. only for peace	BONH 145:21
G. is to God	BUEC 172:41	**glow-worm** eyes, the g.-w. lend thee	HERR 416:15	as the angels of G.	BIBLE 118:25
g., jest, and riddle	POPE 687:81	**glutton** g. of wordes	LANG 507:45	as though G. made both	SCHR 749:63
g., laud and honour	NEALE 632:6	More g. than priest	PARK 663:2	attracted by G.	INGE 445:27
g., like the phoenix	BYRON 187:30	**gluttony** G. demands a heavy tribute	INNO 446:47	Behind the Eyes of G.	DICK 284:44
g. next to thee	MILT 603:83	like adultery or g.	MAUG 582:6	believe in G. the Father Almighty	BOOK 146:31
g. not their own	WORD 958:85	rode loathsome G.	SPEN 838:23	Be merciful unto me, O G.	BOOK 149:20
g. of a dawn	MURP 626:75	**glycosuria** isolate...to relieve g.	BANT 62:35	Be not as those who forgot G.	KORAN 498:88
g....of a dream	WORD 959:5	**gnat** strain at a g.	BIBLE 118:27	best thing G. invents	BROW 167:28
g. of Europe is extinguished	BURKE 176:40	**gnomes** little g. in Zurich	WILS 948:59	better than to gaze upon G.	MELV 585:69
g. of everything	WHITE 935:41	**go** cannot, cannot g.	BRON 161:73	better to have no opinion of G.	BACON 52:87
g. of God	BLAKE 140:2	G. along and get along	RAYB 708:91	bit like G. confessing	LOEN 534:3
g. of God is man	ANON 20:27	G., and the Lord be with thee	BIBLE 96:37	bitter to G. to follow	SWIN 864:98
g. of Ronald	WARR 921:20	G. directly—see what she's doing	PUNCH 699:79	Blow, thou wind of G.!	KING 487:44
g. of the Lord is risen	BIBLE 110:5	G., girl	SHAK 762:70	bound...about the feet of G.	TENN 878:86
g. of the Lord shall be revealed	BIBLE 108:79	G., g., g., said the bird	ELIOT 319:38	bush afire with G.	BROW 166:3
g. of the Lord shone	BIBLE 120:69	g. in there with all they've got	GIPP 372:21	but for the grace of G., goes G.	CHUR 226:20
g. of the resistance	LACL 503:31	g. with so much still to say	BART 67:31	By G. I mean a being	SPIN 841:83
g. of the world passes	KEMP 479:75	I g., I g.—look how I g.	SHAK 767:37	'By G.,' quod he	CHAU 217:95
g. of thy people Israel	BIBLE 120:70	know not how to g. out	BIBLE 97:53	by searching find out G.?	BIBLE 98:1
g. that shall be revealed	BOOK 147:57	know not why you g.	FITZ 337:71	By the livin' G.	KIPL 490:91
g. that was Greece	POE 683:86	Led g.!	KIPL 491:38	call in, and invite G.	DONNE 293:74
G., the grape, love, gold	BYRON 190:8	Let my people g.	BIBLE 93:57	calling heads that G. exists	PASC 667:78
G. to Man in the highest	SWIN 864:10	One to come, and one to g.	CARR 205:18	cannot serve G. and mammon	BIBLE 115:44

God

church to G.	BYRON	191:37
closer walk with G.	COWP	250:88
community...lived in praise of G.	ELIOT	319:33
conceal G. and reveal	THOM	886:78
contumely to G.	KNOX	495:14
dazzled by the ways of G.	LIND	530:17
dearer...than that son of G.?	AIDAN	10:1
depend, under G.	WASH	921:27
desired...even G.	CHES	220:76
dice of G.	EMER	324:57
die for G.'s eternal truth	BROWN	164:28
direct G....a literal G.	DONNE	293:70
disbelieve in G.	ORWE	653:7
does not have to believe in G.	KRUT	500:29
don't believe in the Hebrew G.	MACG	552:86
Draw nigh to G.	BIBLE	130:58
effect, Whose cause is G.	COWP	251:23
embrace the purpose of G.	TENN	876:36
endowed with the idea of G.	DESC	275:1
enter into the kingdom of G.	BIBLE	118:18
eternal G. is thy refuge	BIBLE	95:3
Even if G. did not exist	BAUD	69:79
ever found G. in church?	WALK	917:39
except G., man is a diminutive	DONNE	293:66
eye of Almighty G.	GLAD	373:38
eye of G.	OLIV	649:41
eyes of G. and men	LESL	523:88
facts and doctrines concerning G.	HUGEL	434:4
fair sunlight of G.	MACD	550:46
Fall into the hands of G.	TENN	879:98
far more certain than G.	GREE	386:12
Fear G.	BIBLE	130:68
Fear G.	BORR	151:70
Fear G., and keep his commandments	BIBLE	107:38
Fear G.. Honour the King	KITC	494:98
final proof of G.'s omnipotence	DE	275:13
first sense...of G.	AUBR	42:61
fit for the kingdom of G.	BIBLE	120:77
Fore G. I am no coward	TENN	878:95
For G., for Country	THUR	890:88
For G. so loved the world	BIBLE	122:25
For G.'s sake	SHAK	764:52
For G.'s sake	STEV	852:47
For those who believe in G.	SEAT	755:93
"Fuck it, it's in G.'s hands"	HOPK	428:64
further from G.	ANDR	18:80
gathered...in the sight of G.	BOOK	148:84
gave G. one year	ALMO	15:11
Gentle G., if I wrote	PARK	664:24
glorify G. and benefit	WENT	931:52
Glory be to G.	HOPK	428:72
glory is to G.	BUEC	172:41
glory of G.	BLAKE	140:2
glory of G. is man	ANON	20:27
G....a gaseous vertebrate	HAEC	391:4
G. Almighty first planted a garden	BACON	53:30
G. and sinners reconciled	WESL	931:58
G. answers sharp	BROW	166:99
G. appears and G. is light	BLAKE	141:44
G. be merciful unto us	BIBLE	101:80
G. bless America	ANON	24:9
G. blessed the seventh day	BIBLE	91:85
G. bless our good and gracious King	ROCH	720:27
G. bless the child	HOLI	423:47
G. bless us every one!	DICK	279:5
G. blew	ANON	22:65
G. cannot alter the past	BUTL	185:95
G. cannot grant so much	DRYD	302:91
G. caused a deep sleep	BIBLE	91:90
G. comes to thee	DONNE	293:72
G. confirms those who believe with the firm word	KORAN	497:70
G. could have made a better berry	BUTL	186:13
G. created man	VALE	907:5
G., Creator wise	MILT	606:64
G....destroys their mind	DRYD	303:18
G. disposes	KEMP	480:76
G. does not die	HAMM	394:54
G. does not live in buildings	SACKS	736:5
G. erects a house of prayer	DEFOE	269:69
G. exact day-labour	MILT	601:26
G. finally caught his eye	KAUF	474:40
G. forbid	BIBLE	125:5
G. forbid	BIBLE	125:11
G. forbid that I should	GOET	375:70
G. for Harry!	SHAK	775:76
G. from everlasting	BOOK	149:29

G. fulfils himself	TENN	878:85
G. gave [Adam] reason	MILT	600:12
G. gave him the light	MACA	544:9
G. gave the increase	BIBLE	126:37
G. gives all men	KIPL	491:47
G. gives him	RYDER	736:57
G. gives us to see...right	LINC	529:11
G. grant me a failure	GOUN	380:78
G. grant that we may	MARY	579:46
G. had never spoken anything but	DAY	267:30
G. had wanted us to bend over	RIVE	716:56
G. ha' mercy	KIPL	489:75
G. has a few of us	BROW	168:58
G....has a responsibility	DAWK	266:22
G. has given knowledge	MARIE	571:73
G. has given us...license	MORE	618:14
G. has given you one face	SHAK	769:79
G. has instituted in our time	GUIB	389:86
G. has us...on loan	FERRE	334:78
G. has written all the books	BUTL	186:5
G. hath chosen the foolish things	BIBLE	126:36
G. hath given liberty	CURR	259:92
G. hath shut up all light	RALE	705:46
G. have mercy	RANS	707:73
G. having given us indoors	MACA	544:17
G. heard before creating the world	FERN	334:97
G. help me; amen	LUTH	542:68
G. hez sed so plump	LOWE	539:5
G. Himself is simple	UPDI	906:41
G. in His wisdom	NASH	631:80
G. in Man	CRAS	253:78
G. in Three Persons	HEBER	406:2
G. is a consuming fire	BIBLE	129:45
G. is a geometrician	PLATO	682:68
G. is a little tribal G.	BURR	181:64
G. is All-knowing, All-aware	KORAN	498:87
G. is a man	GIRA	373:27
G. is...another artist	PICA	677:62
G. is a Spirit	BIBLE	122:28
G....is a verb	FULL	355:69
G. is beginning to resemble	HUXL	442:1
G. is dead	NIET	638:94
G. is decreeing to begin	MILT	601:19
G. is gone up with a merry noise	BOOK	149:18
G. is good to Israel	BIBLE	101:84
G. is his own interpreter	COWP	250:86
G. is love	BIBLE	130:81
G. is love	KIER	486:7
G. is love	LEE	518:85
G. is no respecter of persons	BIBLE	124:84
G. is not a Christian	TUTU	901:27
G. is not a man	BIBLE	94:84
G. is not ashamed to be called	BIBLE	129:41
G. is not mocked	BIBLE	127:82
G. is on everyone's side	ANOU	28:69
G. is on the side	VOLT	914:45
G. is our refuge	SCOT	755:86
G. is our refuge and strength	BIBLE	100:67
G. is present in it	BUEC	172:42
G. is registered to vote	WALL	917:44
G....is so great	HOPK	429:86
G. is subtle	EINS	313:74
G....is sweetly informal	OZICK	658:42
G. is the Light of the heavens	KORAN	498:78
G. is the perfect poet	BROW	167:8
G. is the strength of my heart	BIBLE	101:86
G. is the tangential point	JARRY	452:95
G. is thy law	MILT	604:6
G. is with us!	WESL	932:73
G. knows where	MORT	621:70
G. loves not the aggressors	KORAN	496:43
G. loveth a cheerful giver	BIBLE	127:74
G. made and eaten all day	BROW	167:23
G. made him	SHAK	769:79
G. made himself a man	HUGO	437:71
G. made the country	COWP	251:11
G. made thee perfect	MILT	604:18
G. made the integers	KRON	499:18
G. made them, high or lowly	ALEX	13:62
G....make me able to pay	PEPYS	673:86
G. moves in a mysterious way	COWP	250:85
G. must think	KNOX	495:18
G. never made...for man to mend	DRYD	304:48
G. not only plays dice.	HAWK	401:87
G. of Abraham	PASC	668:96
G. of love!	DODD	289:93
G. of Love...Beteth his wynges	CHAU	217:90

G. of our Fathers	MILT	608:92
G. of things as they are!	KIPL	490:15
G. on his side	DYLAN	309:52
G. only, she for G. in him	MILT	604:99
G. ordered motion	VAUG	909:40
G. owns heaven	SEXT	758:52
G. passes through the thicket	JOHN	456:75
G. personally responsible	CHAP	215:24
G. planted a garden	BIBLE	91:87
G. recognizes I will do that	CART	206:46
G. rest his soul	SMITH	830:42
G.'s a good man	SHAK	774:50
G. said...I am that I am	BIBLE	93:55
G. save Elizabeth	ANON	22:66
G. save me from...adventures	BYRON	191:38
G. save me from being 'nice'	LAWR	513:71
G. save thee, ancient Mariner!	COLE	235:10
G. save the king	BIBLE	96:31
G. save the king	SHAK	765:55
'G. save the Queen'	KIPL	491:22
'G. save the Queen'	WHIT	937:84
G. saw that it was good	BIBLE	91:83
G. sends meat	FULL	355:84
G. send thee good ale	ANON	21:60
G.'s eternal store	MILT	605:30
G.'s finger touched him	TENN	874:89
G.'s first Creature	BACON	53:53
G. shall be my hope	SHAK	759:87
G. shall help her	BIBLE	100:68
G. shall supply all your need	BIBLE	128:8
G. shall wipe away all tears	BIBLE	131:4
G. shall wipe away all tears	BIBLE	132:24
G. shed His grace	BATES	68:53
G.'s in His heaven	BROW	169:23
G.'s police	CHIS	222:24
G.'s querulous calling	HUGH	436:37
G.'s the theme	SMART	826:67
G. summons to the Abode of Peace	KORAN	497:66
G. tells me how	TOSC	894:63
G. tempers the wind	STER	849:58
G. that made the world	BIBLE	125:92
G. that maketh men to be	BOOK	149:23
G., the best maker	SHAK	776:2
G. the first garden made	COWL	250:76
G. their severance ruled	ARNO	34:82
G. the Omnipotent!	ELLE	322:18
G. therefore let him free	MILT	600:15
G. the soul	POPE	687:78
G. thi makere	CHAU	216:67
G. to send us a merry meeting	LANC	506:23
G. to trust in	MARG	570:61
G. unmakes but to remake the soul	BROW	169:78
G. was good on the physical	BURG	174:99
G. was sick	VALL	907:8
G., we know you are in charge	TUTU	901:28
G., who does whatever pleases him	WESL	932:71
G., who is able to prevail	WALT	920:88
G. who is all-forgiving	SMITH	828:3
G. who is her life	PATM	669:22
G., who is our home	WORD	959:8
G. who kills us	YOUR	968:59
G. who let us prove	BONH	146:27
G. who Looks after	KIPL	492:52
G. who made him	KIPL	493:69
G. who made thee mighty	BENS	81:84
G. will forgive me	HEINE	407:18
G. will provide himself a lamb	BIBLE	92:26
G. will recognize his own	ARNA	33:54
G. with his mercyful iye	ANON	21:47
G. won't, and we can't mend it	CLOU	232:51
G....would give a...damn	DAWK	267:25
G. wouldn't be homophobic	TUTU	901:29
G. would have changed his doom	CLEV	230:92
G. wrongs not men anything	KORAN	497:67
go to your G.	KIPL	489:88
greatest good...knowledge of G.	SPIN	841:79
Great G.!	SCOTT	751:5
Great G.!	STEN	847:4
ground G.'s-Acre	LONG	535:22
Had I but served my G.	SHAK	805:53
hand folks over to G.'s mercy	ELIOT	315:26
hand of G.	BIBLE	112:74
hand of G.	HASK	400:81
hand of G.	MARA	569:43
hath not one G. created us?	BIBLE	112:62
Have G. to be his guide	BUNY	174:82
heavens declare the glory of G.	BOOK	148:9

hear the voice of G.	ANGE 19:9	My G. and King	HERB 413:58	thank G.?	THOM 884:38
hidden love of G.	WESL 932:66	My G. must have my best	HERB 414:84	thank G., Doctor	STAN 842:11
holy Lamb of G.	BLAKE 141:40	my G. what an eye!	CEZA 212:54	thank G. for my sanguine	MURP 626:74
honest G. is the noblest work	INGE 445:32	my G., why hast thou forsaken me?	BIBLE 119:47	thank G. that he has spared me	BELL 76:57
honour of G.	BACH 49:8	my G., why hast thou forsaken me?	BIBLE 99:41	that is really your G.	LUTH 542:74
hope thou in G.	BIBLE 100:64	My Lord and my G.	BIBLE 124:68	The G. of the Old Testament	DAWK 266:19
household of G.	BIBLE 127:86	my spirit hath rejoiced in G.	BIBLE 120:66	their English G. is not so dominant	CARR 202:56
how can he love G.	BIBLE 131:84	my spirit hath rejoiced in G.	BIBLE 133:42	There G. is dwelling too	BLAKE 139:89
How could G.	LOUI 537:68	Nature is G.	WALK 917:41	There is no G.	BIBLE 99:32
how dwelleth the love of G. in him?	BIBLE 130:80	nature of G.	WHIT 936:71	There is no G.	CLOU 232:52
How odd Of G.	EWER 329:77	neither doth G. respect any person	BIBLE 96:47	there is no G.!	ONEI 650:61
I am a G.	SHEL 814:11	noblest work of G.	POPE 687:89	thinks little of G.	PLUT 682:75
I am G., and King, and Law	SHEL 813:73	noble work of G.	BURNS 177:76	this man was the Son of G.	BIBLE 120:62
I came, I saw, G. conquered	JOHN 456:76	no power but of G.	BIBLE 126:29	Those who know G.	PATM 669:23
if a G. there be	SWIN 864:9	not afraid of G.	POPE 688:27	Those who marry G.	GREE 386:15
If G. be for us	BIBLE 125:21	not…a supremely good G.	DESC 275:99	Those whom G. hath joined	BOOK 148:94
if G. choose	BROW 166:98	not G., is greater	WHIT 937:94	thou art G.	BIBLE 101:92
If G. did not exist	VOLT 915:48	Not only is there no G.	ALLEN 14:84	Thou shalt have one G. only	CLOU 232:63
If G. had meant us to have group sex	BRAD 154:29	not that we loved G.	BIBLE 130:82	three-personed G.	DONNE 292:54
If G.…has any validity	BALD 57:21	not three G.s: but one G.	BOOK 146:45	through darkness up to G.	TENN 874:79
If, knowing G.	TENN 878:86	not yet G.	THOR 888:16	Thus G. and nature linked	POPE 687:86
if there was a G.	FRY 354:41	now with G.	WALT 920:93	thy G. my G.	BIBLE 96:23
if this manifest G. enlightens men	CYRA 260:12	obedience to G.	DAVI 266:13	To G. belong the Names Most	
ignorance G. winked at	BIBLE 125:94	O believers, fear G.	KORAN 497:53	Beautiful	KORAN 497:64
image of man created by G.	IVAN 448:80	obey G. rather than men	BIBLE 124:76	To G. I speak Spanish	CHAR 215:38
imitate G.	FLAU 339:23	observed by Yours faithfully, G.	ANON 24:11	to G. Or to each other	MILT 606:58
immortal, invisible, G.	SMITH 831:65	O Christ, O G.	HOPK 428:69	To The Unknown G.	BIBLE 125:91
impulse which G. has	CRUZ 256:40	O city of G.	BIBLE 101:91	To whom…will ye liken G.?	BIBLE 109:83
Inclines to think there is a G.	CLOU 232:53	Of all G.'s works	SPEN 838:32	trust G.	BROW 168:59
indurate heart against G.	KNOX 495:15	O G. in Heaven	ANON 21:56	trust in G.	DENN 273:73
infants are trying to spell G.	ROBI 718:87	O G. of battles	SHAK 775:85	trust in G.	SMITH 830:52
in favour with G. and man	BIBLE 120:71	O G. of Bethel!	DODD 289:91	unknown to anyone but G.	PLATO 681:45
In G. 'tis glory	DRYD 302:79	O G.! Put back	JONES 465:17	Unlike G. the artist	PERCY 674:11
in my flesh shall I see G.	BIBLE 98:8	Oh G.! that man	MELV 585:68	unto G. the things that are G.'s	BIBLE 118:24
in science there exists no G.	STEI 846:99	Oh, G.! that men would see	BRAC 154:20	up to Nature's G.	POPE 687:91
intellectual love of G.	SPIN 841:82	oily man of G.	THOM 887:5	Verb is G.	HUGO 437:75
interpret G.'s will	RUNC 731:49	old abusing of G.'s patience	SHAK 773:1	Very G. of very G.	BOOK 147:61
in the minds of G.	GREE 386:26	O Lord my G., I hope	STUA 858:59	vindicate the ways of G. to man	POPE 686:71
In the name of G., go!	AMERY 15:27	O my G., Take the gentle path	HERB 414:85	vision of the holiness of G.	BLOOM 143:65
Invisible, except to G. alone	MILT 603:88	One G., one law	TENN 875:3	voice of G.	ALCU 12:46
Is G. by definition indifferent	EBER 310:12	One man with G.	KNOX 495:16	voice of G.	POPE 688:18
It is G. who splits the grain	KORAN 497:59	one that would circumvent G.	SHAK 784:61	wait at G.'s right hand	GURN 390:2
It is not necessary to invoke G.	HAWK 401:94	Only G., my dear	YEATS 967:33	walking…and praising G.	BIBLE 124:74
I would to G.	SHAK 770:29	only make a sacrifice to G.	POPE 686:56	was G. out there	LEIS 520:28
jealous G.	BIBLE 94:66	only men could serve G.	STEI 846:93	waste of G.	STUD 858:63
jealous G.	BIBLE 95:89	order of G. and of nature	MANN 567:93	weigh your G. and you	KIPL 491:21
Jesus never claims to be G.	ROBI 718:96	Our G., our help	WATTS 923:48	We need to find G.	THER 882:84
Just are the ways of G.	MILT 607:89	out of the mouth of G.	BIBLE 114:22	Whatever is, is in G.	SPIN 840:70
just die, G. willing	RULFO 731:40	owe G. a death	SHAK 772:88	What G. abandoned	HOUS 432:72
justify G.'s ways to man	HOUS 432:57	paltered with Eternal G.	TENN 875:10	What G. hath cleansed	BIBLE 124:83
justify the ways of G. to men	MILT 601:31	person to worship G.	ROOS 724:13	what G. hath given us	TAYL 868:52
Just what G. would do	WOOL 956:49	play only Bach in praising G.	BARTH 66:12	what G. would have done	KAUF 474:39
kick in the pants to G.	MILL 593:52	pleased G. hitherto to bestow	HOBB 420:97	What hath G. wrought!	BIBLE 94:85
kills the image of G.	MILT 600:99	Praise belongs to G.	KORAN 496:38	what is a mind without G.?	PRAT 694:66
kingdom of G. is within you	BIBLE 121:99	Praise G., from whom	KEN 480:84	What therefore G. hath joined	BIBLE 118:15
know that I am G.	BOOK 149:17	prepare to meet thy G.	BIBLE 111:52	What was good for G.'s birds	HARDY 397:19
know the mind of G.	HAWK 401:88	presume not G. to scan	POPE 687:80	When G. at first made man	HERB 414:82
label men for G.	THOM 886:85	prey I G. that non	CHAU 216:68	When G. hands you a gift	CAPO 197:25
laboratory of G.	WILL 945:88	prime work of G.	MILT 607:84	When G. hath made	TENN 874:76
Lamb of G., I come!	ELLI 323:26	Prompt me, G.	THOM 886:74	Where G.'s presence is no longer	STEI 846:98
lay wrestling with…my G.	HOPK 429:89	prove G. statistically	GALL 358:46	Where is now thy G.?	BOOK 149:15
leap up to my G.!	MARL 573:30	prove that G. does not exist	LABR 503:29	White people…deal more with G.	GIOV 372:19
lend a myth to G.	CRANE 253:58	pure in heart…shall see G.	BIBLE 114:27	whose G. is their belly	BIBLE 128:3
let me be awake, my G.!	COLE 235:22	Put your trust in G.	BLAC 137:42	Who trusted G.	TENN 874:71
light…the shadow of G.	BROW 166:83	reason and the will of G.	ARNO 36:27	Who trusted G.	TENN 874:80
like a G. in pain	KEATS 477:17	reason, it is playing G.	LEGU 520:17	why G. created women?	WALL 917:45
living G. who made all things	FOX 346:71	recognize G. without Jesus	PASC 667:91	wild G. of the world	JEFF 453:15
Lord G. made them all	ALEX 13:61	remembered my G.!	SOUT 835:44	will of G.	JOHN 456:79
Lord G. of Hosts	KIPL 490:16	reserved only for G.	BACON 49:31	wind thrashes G.	HUID 438:91
Lord G. of Sabaoth	BOOK 146:36	riddles of…the purposes of G.	FRYE 354:57	with G. all things are possible	BIBLE 118:19
Lord G., we ha' paid	KIPL 490:10	rouse G. to relent	EBER 310:11	with G.'s favour	WALT 919:87
Lord is G. indeed	SCOT 755:88	Rowing Toward G.	SEXT 758:51	words which he of G.	LANY 508:55
Lord thy G. am a jealous G.	BOOK 147:59	same G. which worketh all in all	BIBLE 126:51	Word was with G.	BIBLE 122:15
Lord thy G. is a jealous G.	BIBLE 95:89	same relation to G.	UPDI 906:21	works of G. in heav'n	MILT 607:72
love of Man, and in praise of G.	THOM 884:28	saw the face of G.	MARL 573:24	worship of G.	WHIT 936:66
love the Lord Thy G.	BIBLE 118:26	saw the Spirit of G.	BIBLE 114:21	worship Sunday, not G.	BLYT 144:88
madness…to believe oneself to be G.	FOUC 345:58	security…in our relationship with G.	EDDI 311:26	worship the Lord thy G.	BIBLE 114:24
man G. hates	DOWL 296:34	sees…as G. of all	POPE 686:73	would G. this flesh	SWIN 863:88
man's bedevilment and G.'s	HOUS 432:68	Servant of G., well done	MILT 605:21	Would to G. that we were dead	WILDE 940:45
man's distinctive mark…Not G.'s	BROW 169:64	servant of the Living G.	SMART 826:62	ye believe in G.	BIBLE 123:51
Man's word is G. in man	TENN 878:72	shalt not tempt the Lord thy G.	BIBLE 114:23	Yellow G. forever gazes down	HAYES 403:27
may G. help us	BETH 87:12	sinning against G.	BOTHA 152:79	Yet her conception of G.	STRA 856:39
may G. set me there	JOAN 455:60	sufficiency is of G.	BIBLE 127:65	You don't fire G.	KENN 482:37
May G. wither up their hearts!	DAVIS 266:7	suppose even G. was born	LOWE 540:28	Zion, city of our G.!	NEWT 636:64
men that G. made mad	CHES 220:81	sword without G.'s authority	LUTH 542:72	**god** Assumes the g.	DRYD 303:29
mercy o' my soul, Lord G.	MACD 550:45	talk of the death of G.	FACK 329:1	before the g. of science	KING 487:32
more just than G.?	BIBLE 98:96	Teach me, my G. and King	HERB 413:61	beneficent but implacable g.	LECO 518:81

gongs

could have been a g.	CHRI 223:45	makes G. by the dozen	MONT 614:28	rarer gifts than g.	BROO 162:90
Cry aloud: for he is a g.	BIBLE 97:62	man who would argue with the g.	MAIL 560:46	religion of g.	BAGE 54:69
cyclical economic g.	CUOMO 258:80	masculine invisibility makes g.	DUNN 307:14	sand and ruin and g.	SWIN 864:7
deem himself a g., or beast	POPE 687:80	men that strove with g.	TENN 870:2	Silver and g. have I none	BIBLE 124:73
either a g. or a wolf	WEBS 926:31	nature of the g.?	SHAK 760:21	street of the city was pure g.	BIBLE 132:26
extemporal g. of rhyme	SHAK 763:8	no other g. before me	BIBLE 94:66	There is g.	SHAK 794:63
g. going thro' his world	BROW 167:10	Now g., stand up for bastards!	SHAK 792:88	think g. that is brass	SPEN 839:57
g. is not so glorious	MARL 572:98	one day become g.	MILL 594:67	Thou gaudy g.	SHAK 770:5
g. of contemporary man's	MONT 613:9	only g. should speak	ROET 722:61	tipped with g. for this	JONS 467:58
g. self-slain	SWIN 864:17	Real are the dreams of G.	KEATS 476:5	travell'd in the realms of g.	KEATS 475:60
if g. be pleased	EDWA 312:57	reflected in its g.	SCHI 747:24	wear g. on your hair	BALL 59:73
immortal g. of harmony	BEET 74:1	respect the same g. as themselves	DRAB 298:81	Wedges of g., great ouches	SHAK 761:40
never a g.	WOOL 956:48	Sees G. with Daemons	POPE 688:33	What is bettre than g.?	CHAU 217:96
never make a g. out of form	KAND 472:15	Shall g. be said to thump	THOM 883:11	what's become of all the g.	BROW 168:32
next to of course g.	CUMM 257:58	shall not go after other g.	BIBLE 95:89	What use…the g. place	FRAME 346:75
Now the melancholy g.	SHAK 786:98	sinned against my g.	FORD 343:94	When g. becomes her object!	SHAK 773:97
presents the g. unshorn	HERR 415:9	superior to the G.	CATU 209:9	With g.…cover ev'ry part	POPE 685:20
thank we all our G.	WINK 950:98	tempest of the g.	MARL 572:3	**golden** cats with g. eyes	SACK 737:11
the g. pursuing	SWIN 863:84	the g. wish to destroy	OATES 643:12	circle of the g. year	TENN 872:30
to be like a g.	CATU 209:9	The g. themselves	TENN 877:61	g. age in all the arts	VIDAL 912:97
told me of my g.	BRID 158:10	The g. thought otherwise	VIRG 913:16	g. and silver	YEATS 966:12
to the g. he worships	THOR 888:25	there are innumerable g.	BURR 181:64	g. bowl be broken	BIBLE 106:36
treat it like a g.	PELE 672:76	These be thy g., O Israel	BIBLE 94:69	g. cadence of poesy	SHAK 763:13
triangles had made a g.	MONT 614:38	these that were G.	SWIN 864:1	g. ear	POPE 686:62
turning into a g.	VESP 911:65	utterance of the early G.	KEATS 477:31	g. foil all over them	SPEN 838:22
wild beast, or a g.	BACON 52:12	What men or G. are these?	KEATS 478:35	G. lads and girls	SHAK 803:7
Yblessed be g.	CHAU 217:88	what the g. had given him	BEER 74:90	g. rules for an orchestra	BEEC 73:67
God-conditioned G.-c. forms	MANN 566:79	When G. were young	THOM 885:49	g. years return	SHEL 816:57
goddess blind g. in the lottery	ASTU 39:12	When men make g.	ONEI 650:61	In the g. lightning	SHEL 813:92
Chaste g.	ROMA 723:91	whom the g. love dies young	MENA 586:78	Kissing with g. face	SHAK 801:48
g. is better than no g.	WARN 921:10	Whom the g. wish to destroy	CONN 242:98	poets only deliver a g.	SIDN 820:54
G. of the Battle	BARK 63:54	will of the g.	AESC 8:77	west to the G. Gate	KIPL 493:73
G. sage and holy	MILT 598:50	ye g., you make the weak	SHAK 776:14	**golden age** there is always a g. a.	OZICK 658:43
never saw a g. go	SHAK 802:83	ye shall be as g.	BIBLE 91:92	**golden-calf** g.-c. of self-love	CARL 201:13
godfather always a g.	WOOL 956:48	your g. or your vegetables	GIRA 373:26	**Goldengrove** Over G. unleaving?	HOPK 428:80
God-gifted G.-g. organ-voice	TENN 877:69	**Goebbels** inferno depicted by Dr G.	ORWE 654:33	**golden-haired** young Apollo, g.-h.	CORN 247:2
god-given g.-g. (though not to me)	PALEY 661:54	**going** g. out and thy coming in	BIBLE 103:31	**Goldsmith** G. tells us	AUST 46:79
godhead Buddha, the G.	PIRS 679:89	lead by g.	KESEY 483:66	Here lies Nolly G.	GARR 360:79
g. in which all life is human	SHAW 809:69	long and loath at g.	RANS 707:70	Swift is more Irish than G.	OBRI 645:61
godless decent g. people	ELIOT 319:32	**goings** established my g.	BIBLE 100:61	**goldsmith** not in g.'s ware	MIDD 590:71
God-like G.-l. erect, with native	MILT 604:98	**gold** All the g. upon the earth	PLATO 681:52	**Goldwyn** You talk of art Mr G.	SHAW 810:26
godlike anything G. about God	MILL 594:72	apples of g. in pictures of silver	BIBLE 105:93	**golf** American people than G. has	ROGE 723:75
dictates of his g. mind	OTWAY 656:94	Beauty…like the g. standard	WOLF 952:61	Be funny on a g. course?	SILV 821:71
endurance is g.	LONG 535:26	blood mixed with wasted g.	KING 488:59	better he plays g.	WELLS 930:32
one of their g. qualities	MENC 587:9	bought and sold for English g.	BURNS 180:42	Fute-ball, G., or uther sik	JAME 449:19
god-like g.-l. hours	WORD 958:83	bow of burning g.!	BLAKE 141:42	get it on the g. course	SKEL 824:33
godliness Cleanliness is next to G.	DICK 282:2	burned g. was his colour	CHAU 217:98	g. course is the epitome	GIRA 372:24
continual g.	BOOK 147:56	but litel g. in cofre	CHAU 217:75	g. game went bad	TREV 896:7
exercise which withdraweth from g.	STUB 858:60	chain of g.	SCOTT 753:46	G. is a game	JONES 465:16
In cheerful g.	WORD 958:94	colour in Australia is g.	STRE 857:51	G. is a good walk spoiled	TWAIN 904:96
godmother Cinderella's Fairy G.	DIOR 287:4	copper into g.	SENG 757:27	G. is a sport for white men	WOODS 954:7
gods against all the g. of Egypt	BIBLE 93:59	covered in g. paint	BANKS 62:32	G. is in the interest	TAFT 866:11
alien people clutching their g.	ELIOT 318:18	differs from g.	SHEL 816:46	G. is like life	CLIN 230:13
Allotted by the G.	TENN 877:69	envelopeḋ with g.	SPEN 838:30	G. is not…a fair game	NICK 637:81
angels would be g.	POPE 687:76	eyes of g. and bramble-dew	STEV 854:86	G. is so popular	MILNE 596:26
As flies…are we to th' g.	SHAK 793:17	Fetters of g.	ASTE 39:3	G. is to Fiji what cricket is to America	SINGH 823:90
By the nine g. he swore	MACA 545:44	fly to India for g.	MARL 573:19	G.…makes me so damned angry	GEOR 364:53
Concerning the g.	PROT 697:34	fly to India for g.	MARL 573:23	g. may be played on a Sunday	LEAC 515:19
daughter of the g.	TENN 869:75	From the red g. keep thy finger	SCOTT 754:64	g.…way of playing marbles	CHES 221:12
dish fit for the g.	SHAK 776:17	gild refined g.	SHAK 768:62	great game of g.	CROS 256:32
do not know much about g.	ELIOT 320:70	Glory, the grape, love, g.	BYRON 190:8	intrepid hunters of g. balls	SMITH 828:4
dreadful fiend of g.	SPEN 839:44	g., and frankincense, and myrrh	BIBLE 114:17	mind off everything like g.	ROGE 723:87
effigies of g. and goddesses	GILL 370:77	g. and silver	SHAK 768:56	picking up the wrong g. ball	LEMM 521:34
even the g. themselves struggle	SCHI 747:32	g. and silver	SHAK 803:5	playing g. during a war	BUSH 183:44
eye of g.	WORD 962:48	g. and silver becks me	SHAK 768:56	Playing polo is like…to play g.	STAL 842:8
feel new g. in the flesh	LAWR 513:55	g. an' velvet	ANON 23:87	thousand lost g. balls	ELIOT 319:32
fit love for g.	MILT 606:49	G.. Cadillac G.	TRUMP 900:97	unforgiving as g. greens	ELKIN 322:16
Give, you g.	DRYD 301:51	g. doth more than either	KYD 501:48	when one is playing g.	LYND 543:91
G. and men, we are all deluded	SHEL 816:64	G. is the gift	GRIL 388:70	work at it, it's g.	HOPE 428:59
g. are absent	MACN 558:99	g. wes changyd in to lede	ANON 21:44	**golfer** Actually, I am a g.	MATU 582:2
g. are come down to us	BIBLE 124:85	green tigering the g.	HUGH 435:33	gymnast and g., soldered together	BRYA 170:99
g. are just	SHAK 793:34	Gross g. from them runs	MARL 574:40	make a g. out of him	HAGEN 391:5
g., employed to	LOWE 540:33	head was of fine g.	BIBLE 111:38	**Goliath** Nobody roots for G.	CHAM 212:68
g. had made thee poetical	SHAK 779:97	He who hath the g.	ANON 26:11	**Gomorrah** rained upon…G.	BIBLE 92:23
g. recognized by the state	PLATO 681:42	If g. ruste	CHAU 217:78	**gondola** What else is like the g.?	CLOU 232:50
G., that wanton in the air	LOVE 538:81	Like g. to airy thinness beat	DONNE 292:39	you have swam in a g.	SHAK 779:8
g. there morning	RUSK 734:19	must be propped with g.	MAST 581:82	**gone** all is g.	HOOD 426:38
g. will diet me with	SHAK 803:2	narrowing lust of g.	TENN 875:96	And they are g.	KEATS 477:27
higher esteem among the g.	PLATO 681:47	never have too much g.	MORE 618:15	dead and g.	YEATS 966:17
In Mexico the g. ruled	COND 239:12	never owned his g.	LAFO 504:60	dead and g., lady	SHAK 784:48
inspired by the g. inside	SAINT 738:41	next, my g.!	JONS 466:45	g., and for ever!	SCOTT 752:32
joy reserved for the G.	CABE 191:4	Nor all that glisters g.	GRAY 383:54	g. without a word?	SHAK 758:60
Kings are earth's g.	SHAK 798:80	patens of bright g.	SHAK 770:19	Now thou art g.	MILT 599:84
knowledge from the g.	WILS 948:51	property turns sand to g.	YOUNG 968:51	Or that when I am g.	LOVE 538:83
Land of lost g.	BYRON 187:42	provoketh thieves sooner than g.	SHAK 778:67	They're all g. now	SYNGE 865:21
like G. together	TENN 870:92	pure g. flows	TOCQ 892:27	you'll find you've g.	HOPK 428:63
looks…dare the g.	MARL 572:96	rain of g.	DAY 267:37	**gongs** struck regularly, like g.	COWA 249:49

gong-tormented

gong-tormented g.-t. sea	YEATS 967:32
good a complex mixture of g. and evil	MAIL 560:65
aim at some g.	ARIS 31:19
all men's g.	TENN 872:30
all men's g.	TENN 879:5
All partial evil, universal g.	POPE 687:79
all things work together for g.	BIBLE 125:20
and when she was g.	LONG 536:40
Anybody can be g. in the country	WILDE 941:71
Any g. thing	GREL 387:54
art for the sake of the g.	SAND 741:11
Be a g. man	SCOTT 754:84
beautiful, creative and g.	MING 608:8
because they are so g.	TROL 898:44
because we deem it g.	SPIN 840:76
being really g. all the time	WILDE 942:6
Beneath the g. how far	GRAY 385:92
better to be g. than to be ugly	WILDE 940:70
between g. and evil	HUSS 440:38
but to be g.	STEV 852:41
can't make it g….make it look g.	GATES 361:17
common g. to all	SHAK 778:57
constitutes its highest g.	RUSS 734:23
content…to be obscurely g.	ADDI 7:51
Do all the g. you can	WESL 932:68
does not do much g.	GILM 371:97
do him little g.	JOHN 461:93
dull prospect of a distant g.	DRYD 303:15
enemy of the g.	VOLT 914:42
every evil, like every g.	SCHO 748:54
every g. and excellent thing	WILD 943:45
Every soul pursues the g.	PLATO 682:64
evil seek to bring forth g.	MILT 602:41
evil turn to g.	MILT 607:71
For g. ye are and bad	TENN 878:77
for the general G.	WELLS 930:21
for the g. or evil side	LOWE 539:3
Gallop about doing g.	SMITH 830:45
General G. is the plea	BLAKE 141:31
glory and of Art	BROW 169:79
God saw that it was g.	BIBLE 91:83
God-willing, I will make g.	HITL 420:94
g. almost kill a man as kill	MILT 600:99
g. and bad of every land	BAIL 55:88
g., and had no power to see	LANY 508:53
g. and ill together	SHAK 791:68
g. both going and coming back	FROST 352:98
G., but not religious-good	HARDY 396:1
G. company, g. wine, g. welcome	SHAK 804:38
g. Compensate bad in man	BROW 169:76
g. day to get out anything we want to bury	MOORE 616:71
g. die early	DEFOE 269:68
G. done anywhere is g.	ANGE 19:3
g. ended happily	WILDE 941:4
g. fast bowler	TRUE 899:74
g. For which to strive	MILT 602:56
g. for your legs	SCHU 749:72
G., great and joyous	SHEL 815:20
G. grows with her	SHAK 805:58
g. guy with a gun	LAPI 508:59
g. honest and painful	PEPYS 673:88
g. in everything	SHAK 778:66
g. is always a product of art	BAUD 69:77
G. isn't the word	GILB 370:76
g. man to do nothing	BURKE 176:58
g. men starve	DRYD 302:4
g. must associate	BURKE 175:10
g. never will be our task	MILT 602:40
g. news baits	MILT 608:99
g. of the land of Egypt	BIBLE 93:46
g. of the people	CICE 227:29
g. or they were bad	TRAV 896:93
G., pleasure, ease, content	POPE 687:87
g. that I would I do not	BIBLE 125:14
G. Time was Had By All	SMITH 830:33
G., to forgive	BROW 169:83
g. to know the worst	BRAD 155:42
g. to some man	SHAW 807:6
g. to talk	HOSK 430:27
g. turns out to be	ARIS 31:20
g. we oft might win	SHAK 787:49
greatest of the mind	SPIN 841:79
great harm and great g.	HESI 417:33
great instrument of moral g.	SHEL 816:50
greed…is g.	DOUG 295:16
hear all the g. things said about ye	BOUC 152:85
hear more g.	HAZL 403:38
heav'n sees g.	MILT 599:78
He wos wery g. to me	DICK 281:64
hold fast that which is g.	BIBLE 129:15
if we were very g.	FULF 355:64
If ye think g.	BIBLE 112:61
If you're g. at something	LEDG 518:83
intuitive knowledge of G.	SPIN 841:81
It does g. though	JULI 471:42
It is always g.	BEAU 71:13
it must be g.	HOCK 421:14
it would be a g. idea	GAND 359:61
kills the very g.	HEMI 409:66
knowing g. and evil	BIBLE 91:92
knowing the g.	GRIS 389:76
knowledge of g. and evil	MILT 600:3
knowledge of g. and evil	MILT 600:5
Knowledge of g. bought dear	MILT 604:96
learning things that are g.	HERN 415:94
'Leave…while you're looking g..'	LOOS 536:48
lies precisely the greatest g.	ROUS 729:12
lives not three g. men	SHAK 771:45
make bad g.	SHAK 788:73
Man is neither g. nor evil	BALZ 61:6
men most g.	SHAK 768:59
more harm than g.	SNOW 832:85
never had it so g.	MACM 556:65
never known much g. done	SMITH 828:86
noble type of g.	LONG 536:33
no for ony g. or ill	BURNS 177:71
no g. in arguing	LOWE 539:14
none that doeth g.	BIBLE 99:33
none that doeth g.	BOOK 148:7
not g. enough	GALS 358:49
not g. enough yourself	TROL 897:33
nothing either g. or bad	SHAK 782:85
nothing g. to be had	HAZL 403:32
Nothing is fair or g. alone	EMER 324:50
nothing so bad or so g.	SHAW 807:97
not necessary…that the world is g.	CONR 244:39
not quite so g.	GALT 359:53
only one g., knowledge	SOCR 833:1
only read what is truly g.	STEIN 845:73
only time it isn't g. for you	HEMI 410:77
overcome evil with g.	BIBLE 126:28
O ye wha are sae g.	BURNS 178:92
preferred to be g.	SALL 740:93
remained Stupidly g.	MILT 606:48
rise on the evil and on the g.	BIBLE 115:38
shall he not make it g.?	BIBLE 94:84
shall not want any g. thing	BIBLE 100:56
sick one gets of being 'g.'	JAMES 450:23
single thing that is g.	GALL 358:39
some g. thing comes tomorrow	SHAK 772:92
some special g. doth give	SHAK 766:87
something g. about someone	LONG 536:41
still rich in genial g.	WORD 959:99
strong antipathy of g. to bad	POPE 688:26
suffer for the G.	KIER 485:3
teach…of g.	WORD 957:59
tell someone how g.	KNUD 495:21
That is indeed very g.	HOUS 433:79
That was very g. of him	KAUN 474:46
the g. doubt their own goodness	AUST 47:93
The g. want power	SHEL 814:10
the national g.	PANK 662:86
They love the G.	BROO 162:96
think something is g. or bad	STEV 851:11
To believe in 'the greater g.'	DIDI 286:84
too much of a g. thing?	SHAK 779:11
what g. came of it	SOUT 835:47
What's the g. of a home	GROS 389:79
what we like is not necessarily g.	BELL 75:37
what were g. to be done	SHAK 769:75
what you feel g. after	HEMI 409:70
When I'm g.	WEST 933:86
When I'm g., I can be really g.	DETT 275:5
When it sounds g., it is g.	ELLI 322:21
where g. men rest	FLEC 340:31
whoso hath this world's g.	BIBLE 130:80
ye're just no a g. man	KELM 479:70
You're g., you're real g.	HUST 440:45
You're only g. if	FORD 343:14
goodbye as you wave me g.	PARR 665:50
G. Mr Zanuck	RENO 711:53
G. to All That	GRAV 382:18
good-for-nothing g.-f.-n. woman	SHAW 808:62
Good Friday soldest him on G. F.	SHAK 771:31
good-looking all the men are g.-l.	KEIL 479:53
goodly g. to look to	BIBLE 96:35
goodman g. of the house	BIBLE 118:32
good-morning G.-m.; g.-m.!	SASS 745:86
good-morrow bade g.-m.	KEATS 476:89
good-mother almost as bad, g.-m.	SHAK 784:38
good-nature keep her g.-n.	SCOTT 754:76
goodness all my g. pass before thee	BIBLE 94:75
crownest the year with thy g.	BIBLE 101:79
distinguished from ordinary g.	STOWE 856:27
fountain of all g.	BOOK 148:97
Galumphing G.!	TRAV 896:92
g. and mercy shall follow me	BIBLE 100:45
g. infinite, g. immense!	MILT 607:71
g. in things evil	SHAK 775:80
g. never fearful	SHAK 788:71
g. of your mechanics	MOORE 617:81
G. what beautiful diamonds!	WEST 933:84
I don't think g. is	MCCA 547:79
If g. lead him not	HERB 414:83
odor…from g. tainted	THOR 888:28
The powerful g. want	SHEL 814:10
Wealth does not bring g.	PLATO 681:43
goodnight gay g.	YEATS 966:28
G.-n. Ensured release	HOUS 432:72
say g.-n. till it be morrow	SHAK 766:85
till our last g.	PEAC 671:55
goods all my g. to feed the poor	BIBLE 126:52
Bill of G.	MORR 620:53
boat…had the g. of a house	PEPYS 674:8
community lacks g.	CHUR 225:71
consumption of valuable g.	VEBL 910:46
g. and trappings of your life	MOORE 616:59
g. do not spontaneously present	ECON 310:22
g….procured by labour	RICA 712:82
g….produced jointly with bads	BOUL 152:90
Labour does not only create g.	MARX 578:25
power of purchasing other g.	SMITH 827:78
with all my worldly g.	BOOK 148:93
good-tempered g.-t….young woman	AUST 45:49
goose every g. a swan	KING 487:48
g. because you like pâté	LINK 530:31
No g., no golden egg	TSON 900:8
on the ground at G. Green	KINN 488:64
goosecap g. and…no judgement	NASHE 632:91
goose-hiss dumb g.-h. of the wives	THOM 884:39
goosie Ridin' on a g.?	ANON 22:77
Gorbachev G. has 100…advisers	GORB 378:50
I like Mr G.	THAT 881:61
gore g. no more, they bellow	LIND 530:23
mayn't be human g.	DICK 279:96
gored fame is shrewdly g.	SHAK 787:40
tossed and g. several persons	BOSW 152:76
gorge into the narrow g., unseen	WILL 946:20
My g. rises at it	SHAK 784:63
gorgon taught his g. destinies to sing	CAMP 194:56
gorgonised G. me from head	TENN 876:23
gorry by g. by jingo by gee	CUMM 257:58
gory Never shake Thy g. locks	SHAK 797:49
gospel based on the G.	JOHN 456:80
Christian g. is the knowledge	NIEB 637:87
G. of Getting On	SHAW 807:9
light of the g.	JOHN 460:90
preached a G.	TENN 879:5
preach the g.	BIBLE 120:63
receptive to the g.	RUET 730:37
spirit of the g.	JOHN 456:72
wolves whose g.	MILT 601:25
gospels canonical g. do not record	FORS 345:51
teachings of the G.	KHRU 485:95
gossip Blood sport…in the g. columns	INGH 446:34
G. is a sort of smoke	ELIOT 316:56
G. is the opiate	JONG 466:33
juicy piece of g.	HELL 408:42
pines are g. pines	FLEC 340:35
roving woman gives rise to g.	ANON 20:33
gossiping telling jokes or g.	CABR 191:8
got g. him.	ATWO 41:50
gothic G. cathedrals…supreme creation	BART 66:62
G. structure, the impenetrable	EDGE 311:29
old one of G. windows	KORN 498:99
gout chide my palsy, or my g.	DONNE 291:27
govern administer is to g.	MIRA 608:16
have to g. afterwards	HUGH 435:18
He that would g. others	MASS 580:51
intellect will always g.	WOLL 953:85

Right...of Kings to g.	POPE 689:41	meddling with the g.	LEST 524:8	God shed his g.	BATES 68:53
Those that g. most	SELD 756:9	monarchy...intelligible g.	BAGE 54:73	G. be unto you	BIBLE 131:85
you g. in prose	CUOMO 258:77	most important job in G.	GARN 360:77	g. beyond recognition	REID 710:44
governance g. of Ronald Reagan	BAKER 56:8	no art which one g.	SMITH 828:91	g. did much more abound	BIBLE 125:10
governed g. by no other sway	MONT 615:49	no British g. should be brought	MACM 556:69	G. from that g.	LANY 508:57
g. by the mob	GREN 388:59	No G. can be long secure	DISR 287:24	G. is given of God	CLOU 232:45
g. by the pull	MOORE 617:88	no g. can stand	CONF 240:21	g. is sufficient for thee	BIBLE 127:77
one of the most g. people	EDIN 312:48	no g., church, corporation	OAKE 642:2	g. of accuracy	LOWE 540:38
governess woman who cannot be a g.	OLIP 649:35	No g. has the right	BROWN 164:35	g. of its external	VIEI 913:7
governesses If neither g. or mothers	DAVI 264:71	No g. is going to take from me	MACL 554:27	g. of our Lord Jesus Christ	BIBLE 132:29
government 25 years of Labour g.	BEVAN 89:51	not one that g. can indulge in	RENO 711:50	g. of Terpsichore	BARR 65:98
a dissident g.!	AI WEI 10:9	only good g....is a bad one	CARY 207:67	g. under pressure	HEMI 409:67
administration of the g.	SWIFT 862:43	only two kinds of g.	DAFOE 260:3	g. us in the disgrace	SHAK 763:99
against every G. on earth	JEFF 454:23	operations of g.	RUNC 731:48	g. was short	PRIOR 696:8
agencies of central g.	HUXL 442:94	prepare for g.	STEEL 844:46	grows eke greater g.	SPEN 838:29
All forms of g. fall	LEWIS 526:54	pretend to obey a G.	RUSS 735:38	had at least the g.	BENT 82:5
all g....founded on compromise	BURKE 175:23	prying meddlesome G.	MACA 546:55	If I am not in g.	JOAN 455:60
all g. without the consent	SWIFT 861:38	relations of a weak G.	REED 710:37	into g. againe	FLET 341:60
all of them branches of g.	MILL 591:4	republican model of g.	WASH 922:29	inward and spiritual g.	BOOK 148:81
ANC is a G. in waiting	MAND 564:54	revolution than a g.	MARC 569:53	it is not man...made g.	POUND 692:24
art of g.	SHAW 808:36	see the g. get out of the war	HELL 407:30	lend her g.	TENN 870:87
ask me what a free g. is	BURKE 175:27	sister is given to g.	DICK 282:4	life itself is g.	BUEC 172:42
At the head of the G.	PETA 675:36	so pleased to be in the G.	BAXT 69:92	means of g.	BOOK 147:50
best politics is good g.	STEV 851:19	stability to a popular G.	WHIT 934:25	motions all accompanied with g.	DRYD 301:66
British g. and...colonial population	SCHL 747:33	studied as a branch of g.	JAY 453:1	nature and the living g.	POPE 685:20
Canada...enjoyed: English g.	COLO 238:80	take from such G.	PAINE 660:34	Never mind my g., lassie	SCOTT 754:61
checks and balances in g.	ANON 26:92	The foundation of the g.	SUN 860:96	novel...it's a g.	MAIL 560:62
corruption in any g.	BRUN 170:93	The g. computer	AI WEI 10:10	Observe his honour, or his g.	DONNE 291:27
Democracy...g. by the uneducated	CHES 221:6	The object of g.	BEVE 90:62	O mickle is the powerful g.	SHAK 766:87
Democracy means g. by discussion	ATTL 40:30	three main priorities for G.	BLAIR 138:52	pity g. obtain	SIDN 820:43
Do not criticize your G.	CHUR 226:19	two ideas of g.	BRYAN 170:97	something of a g.	WORD 959:97
duty of g.	PAINE 660:32	want of g. is any new kind of g.	HOBB 420:3	such a lovely g.	SIDN 820:49
employees of the g.	TOOLE 894:60	whatever the G. and public allow	SHAW 807:24	sweet attractive g.	MILT 604:99
Every line in the g.'s budget	WRIS 963:82	What your g. believes	KENN 482:32	tabernacles of thy g.	SCOT 755:87
every man...under a G.	RAIN 705:37	who understands g.	TRUM 899:85	To win her g.	MILT 597:47
expect from his G.	TRUM 899:77	wish the G. would put a tax	SITW 824:16	unbought g. of life	BURKE 176:41
face a British G.	TUCH 901:11	worst form of G.	CHUR 226:4	what g. he throws	FLEC 340:33
faineant g.	TROL 898:40	would be great in our little g.	ROCH 719:18	wordy of a g.	BURNS 178:94
false system of g.	PAINE 660:33	You should not trust g.	CLEGG 229:83	**graces** deficiency in the g.	JOHN 463:52
faults of a G.	ROOS 724:7	**governmental** g. machinery	SPEN 836:89	G....not...natives of Great Britain	CHES 219:41
fear that the Russian g.	HERZ 416:23	**governments** All g. use force	PARE 663:89	g. slighted, blossom on the tomb	CRAB 252:39
federal g. does basically	WILL 944:63	climates, council, g.	TENN 870:98	no time for the fine g.	SMITH 828:2
feeble g.	JOHN 459:40	G. care for...security of property	PANK 662:84	number all your g.	SHAK 800:36
first object of g.	MADI 558:16	g. have never learned anything	HEGEL 406:8	**gracious** Oh, my G., Glorious	TRAV 896:92
form of native g.	ONEI 650:58	G. need...shepherds	VOLT 914:46	**grades** various g. of culture	NIET 639:17
Freedom of men under g.	LOCKE 533:87	Kings and G. may err	HERB 412:46	**gradual** Was the g. day	SPEN 837:94
frightening views of g.	INOU 446:50	most despotic of infidel G.	BYRON 187:31	**gradualness** inevitability of g.	WEBB 925:10
G....contrivance of human wisdom	BURKE 176:39	Most g. lie to each other	GATES 361:99	**graduate** g. from Canada	FULF 355:64
giving money to the G.	HERB 412:45	nothing new in Third World g.	AUNG 45:39	than to be a g.	HARDY 397:20
G. and co-operation	RUSK 733:99	not to form g.	KING 486:19	**graft** opportunity for g.	BIRNS 136:21
g. and report the facts	ROGE 723:86	strong mutually antagonistic g.	WAUGH 923:72	**Grafton** Hungry G.	ANON 24:32
g. and the people	MILL 591:92	**governor** advising the...g. of Florida	BUSH 182:96	**grain** amber waves of g.	BATES 67:53
G....a necessary evil	PAINE 660:31	Can't afford them, G.	SHAW 810:97	beside a field of g.	PARK 666:13
G. cannot endure...half-slave	LINC 529:4	G. of the Bank of England	HOWE 433:88	Divine...in a g. of sand	FRIE 351:74
g. doesn't work	OROU 652:94	G. of the Bank of England	KORDA 498:97	full ripened g.	KEATS 475:77
g. funding for...comic strips	UPDI 906:26	G. was strong upon	WILDE 942:18	g. of sense	DRYD 302:4
G. has no other end	LOCKE 533:85	I'd be a terrific g.	CLIN 231:23	guano and on g.	TENN 872:35
g. I despise	KEYN 484:69	moved beyond words to be your g.	SCHW 750:87	Rot half a g. a day	SHAK 790:46
g. is far funnier than we are	BUCH 171:31	**Governor-General** save the G.-G.	WHIT 937:84	the g. and hammer	HEAN 405:79
G. is like everything	MONT 614:40	**governors** whereof ye are the g.	MILT 601:18	well meant for g.	TENN 873:59
G. looks with favour	BALF 58:39	**governs** see how well she g.	SIXT 824:26	which g. will grow	SHAK 796:5
g. may...withdraw...troops	REDM 709:21	**gowd** man's the g.	BURNS 180:52	**grains** two g. of wheat	SHAK 769:73
G....must fall	DRYD 302:87	**gowk** be a conceited g.	HOGG 422:42	**grammar** don't want to talk g.	SHAW 810:95
g. of a woman	BACON 53:51	**gown** dressed in a new g.	HUME 438:3	down to posterity talking bad g.	DISR 289:73
g. of laws	ADAMS 5:98	ease a heart Like a satin g.	PARK 663:97	erecting a g. school	SHAK 759:98
g. of the people	LINC 529:9	for an almsman's g.	SHAK 764:54	g. is to the art of the writer	APOL 29:80
G. of the strongest interests	CALH 192:24	g. and mossy cell	MILT 598:60	kings must bow to g.	MOLI 611:87
G. of which Harrow	BALD 57:36	g. of glory	RALE 705:44	mystical g. of amorous glances	CLEV 230:93
g....reflections on human nature	MADI 558:17	wrap me in a g.	HERB 413:62	never made a mistake in g.	SAND 742:24
G. regulation	GREEN 387:39	**gowns** priests in black g.	BLAKE 140:15	Once the g. has been learnt	BAIN 55:90
g. representatives in the affairs	NICH 636:71	**Goya** one small G.	AUDEN 42:75	readers must take such g.	MACA 545:33
g. shall be upon his shoulder	BIBLE 107:60	**Gracchi** Who can bear the G.	JUVE 471:53	Religious law is like...g.	SACKS 736:4
g. subsidized commission	KRUT 500:30	**grab** G. a mop.	OBAMA 644:36	To be loose with g.	EDWA 313:64
g. subsidy	ANON 27:17	**grace** Amazing G.! How sweet	NEWT 635:63	Why care for g.	WARD 920:3
g. which imprisons any	THOR 888:17	Being and Ideal G.	BROW 166:97	With g., and nonsense	GOLD 376:11
g. without newspapers	JEFF 453:20	better deeds...to g. it	SHAK 758:60	**grammars** What sairs your G.	BURNS 177:68
greatest blessings which a g.	MACA 544:21	but for the g. of God, goes God	CHUR 226:20	**grammatical** a series of g. English	
having looked to g. for bread	BURKE 176:54	by g. divine	WORD 961:46	sentences	JOHN 457:96
help from a g. agency	STEIN 845:77	by the g. of God I am	BIBLE 127:55	**gramophone** puts a record on the g.	ELIOT 318:5
highest form of g.	SPEN 836:90	Cheap g. is g. without discipleship	BONH 146:23	**granaries** guard our master's g.	WILDE 940:45
husband, like a g.	BALZ 60:92	deprived me of your g. and favour	SHAK 792:86	**grand** but never g.	HEAT 406:95
influence of the g.	REES 710:38	divine g. cleansed...me	ABEL 1:3	g., the barbarous, the savage	DIDE 285:66
In the councils of g.	EISE 314:2	except through g.	PASC 667:70	petal down the G. Canyon	MARQ 575:57
kept in sober g.	SPEN 838:32	fallen from g.	BIBLE 127:80	the g. manner	POUS 692:49
land of settled g.	TENN 872:29	for heaven's g. and boon	KEATS 477:21	**grandchild** little g. Wilhelmine	SOUT 835:45
live under one form of g.	JOHN 462:24	full of g. and truth	BIBLE 122:18	**grandeur** baldness full of g.	ARNO 36:44
machinery of G.	MONT 613:8	glad g.	YEATS 965:7	g. in this view of life	DARW 263:53

grandfather

Entry	Reference
g. of the dooms	KEATS 476:85
g. that was Rome	POE 683:86
G....with a disdainful smile	GRAY 384:66
little bit of g. is gone	ANON 25:49
old Scotia's g.	BURNS 177:76
sort of g. creeps into it	MENC 587:17
with the g. of God	HOPK 428:70
grandfather who his g. is	WALC 916:11
grandfathers friends with its g.	MUMF 625:35
grandma g.'s maiden name	BERE 83:13
grandmama dear G. died	GEOR 364:50
grandmother child of our g. Eve	SHAK 763:7
day my g. exploded	BANKS 62:20
g. actually smelled like a cookie	BAIL 55:86
have become a g.	THAT 881:69
look...back to the g.	EDGE 312:47
may not marry his G.	BOOK 150:44
sell his g.	GRANT 381:2
grandmothers careful g.	DICK 278:63
grandsire heard my g. say	SHAK 760:28
your g. cut his throat	SWIFT 862:40
grandstands retire to the g.	GERG 365:67
granite monoliths made of g.	MENC 587:15
Of shadowy g.	TENN 870:89
Grannie G. remarked	FRAN 348:22
Grant Old Cary G. fine	GRANT 381:99
granted as God g. it	QUIL 702:10
taking things for g.	HUXL 442:88
grape blood of g.	BLAKE 139:82
Glory, the g., love, gold	BYRON 190:8
no g. that's kindly ripe	SUCK 858:70
peel me a g.	WEST 933:87
grapes sour g. and ashes	ASHF 38:75
where the g. of wrath	HOWE 433:92
grapeshot car...seems to ride on g.	MARI 571:77
whiff of g.	CARL 200:5
graphical g. representation of data	GIBS 367:15
grapple G. them to thy soul	SHAK 781:49
grasp should exceed his g.	BROW 168:45
grass a blade of g. stuck	WODE 952:38
books...like green g.	WELTY 931:47
burn the old g.	POL 684:6
causeth the g. to grow	BIBLE 102:11
dappled g.	YEATS 965:10
days are as g.	BIBLE 102:10
destroy a blade of g.	BOTT 152:82
eateth g. as an ox	BIBLE 99:20
eat g. as oxen	BIBLE 111:40
emerald twinkles in the g.	TENN 876:24
fall on g.	MARV 577:4
g., and a hare sitting up	LAWR 513:47
G. and trees wither	WU 963:84
g. grew longer	LEE 519:98
g. grows on the weirs	YEATS 965:3
g. is singing	ELIOT 318:10
g. is soft as...doves	CORN 247:3
g., it grew as scant	BROW 168:34
g., so springlike	ABSE 1:7
g. will grow in the streets	HOOV 427:42
g. withereth	BIBLE 130:65
g. withereth	BIBLE 108:79
g. withereth, the flower fadeth	BIBLE 108:79
green g. above me	ROSS 726:46
greenness of the g.	MARV 577:99
happy as the g. was green	THOM 883:17
heard by snakes in the g.	MO 610:63
hearing the g. grow	ELIOT 316:51
I am the g.	SAND 742:18
indicates that...g. is green	STEP 847:11
isn't g. to graze a cow	BETJ 88:20
kissed the lovely g.	BROO 162:84
know the g. beyond	ROSS 726:54
moonlight lying on the g.	THOM 885:54
not Dead, but feed the g.	TATE 867:39
only beautiful if it has good g.	BUTL 185:89
Pigeons on the g.	STEIN 845:63
Please Walk on the G.	THOM 887:94
rustling of the g.	WORD 960:22
sallower than g.	SAPP 743:49
showers upon the g.	BIBLE 95:98
snake lurks in the g.	VIRG 913:22
soft wind breathing through the g.	BRON 162:82
splendour in the g.	WORD 960:12
star-scattered on the g.	FITZ 337:72
the g. polyanthus cheques	SMART 826:64
thin g. clothed them	THOM 885:70
two blades of g.	SWIFT 862:45
wan g. sea	SITW 823:10
grass-growing silent g.-g. mood	MELV 585:72
grasshopper afraid as a g.?	BIBLE 99:18
g. shall be a burden	BIBLE 106:36
grasshoppers g. with triumphing	ROBE 717:72
in our own sight as g.	BIBLE 94:80
grateful g. at last for a little thing	TENN 876:33
g. to the CLF	STEW 854:94
none more g.	WORD 957:72
revolution must be g.	LEGU 520:16
gratification g. of your wishes	SHEL 811:45
gratify g. some people	TWAIN 903:90
gratis endanger my soul g.?	SHAK 773:4
gratitude g. is a species	JOHN 459:52
G. looks to the past	LEWIS 526:43
vulgar g. to you	DICK 281:62
gratuitous prophecy is the most g.	ELIOT 316:47
grave Alcestis from the g.	MILT 601:27
amaranth on this side of the g.	LAND 507:32
A Page, a g.	POPE 689:39
bed...the cold, cold g.	BALL 58:57
birth astride of a g.	BECK 72:46
bring down my gray hairs...to the g.	BIBLE 93:44
broken-hearted woman tends the g.	HAYES 403:27
cold in the dreary g.!	BRON 162:76
cradle to the g.	ANON 27:17
cradle to the g.	BREC 157:90
Dark as the G.	LOWRY 541:44
darkness of the g.	MILL 592:27
dig the g. and let me	STEV 853:62
Duncan is in his g.	SHAK 797:46
dusty to the g.	STEV 852:40
even the g. yawns for him	TREE 896:98
foolish tears upon my g.	TENN 873:62
from the cradle to the g.	SHEL 814:19
Funeral marches to the g.	LONG 535:15
gift of a g.	SHAK 785:81
go down into the g....mourning	BIBLE 93:39
g. and serious	GILB 370:72
g. is ghastly	ANON 20:35
g. is not its goal	LONG 535:14
g. keeps bodies	DONNE 292:62
g. of Christianity	ELIOT 319:35
g.'s a fine and private	MARV 577:92
g.'s narrowness	GRAV 382:19
G. where is thy Victory?	BUNY 174:83
g., where is thy victory?	BIBLE 127:63
heaped its g.	CRANE 252:52
humours, whether g. or mellow	ADDI 6:27
in the cold g. leave	WEBS 926:21
in the dark and silent g.	RALE 705:47
jealousy is cruel as the g.	BIBLE 107:49
large kingdom for a little g.	SHAK 764:54
learned the secrets of the g.	PATER 668:9
Longfellow's g. or the glass	MOORE 617:79
lower me into the g.	LEE 519:94
made his g. with the wicked	BIBLE 109:95
made me a g. so rough	TENN 876:32
Marriage is the g. or tomb of wit	CAVE 210:20
mysterious East...dark like a g.	CONR 244:35
No repose...but in the g.	SCOTT 754:83
now in his colde g.	CHAU 217:85
no work...in the g.	BIBLE 106:28
O'Leary on the g.	YEATS 966:17
on that g. where English oak	HARTE 400:74
on the way to the g.	CRISP 255:5
Over this damp g.	ROET 722:60
paths of glory lead but to the g.	GRAY 384:66
Peace is in the g.	SHEL 814:11
pompous in the g.	BROW 166:81
profound as the g.	ADAMS 5:94
put on the g. of Gomer Owen	THOM 884:35
receive no letters in the g.	JOHN 464:99
she is in her g.	WORD 957:62
sinking into the g.	WESL 932:72
So pleasant this side of the g.	DIBD 276:30
sunk into the g.	JOHN 460:69
take me out o'th' g.	SHAK 793:30
that dark inn—the G.!	SCOTT 753:40
this side of the g.	PITT 680:11
thy humble g. adorned	POPE 686:46
till we go into the g.	SMITH 827:84
travelling towards the g.	WORD 958:74
Upon his mother's g.?	WORD 957:65
vast and wandering g.	TENN 873:61
Victorious o'er the g.	DODD 289:93
vortex of our g.	CRANE 252:55
within the g.'s brink	ANON 21:53
Without a g., unkindled	BYRON 188:72
gravemakers ditchers, and g.	SHAK 784:60
graves Arise from their g.	BLAKE 140:11
bloody hands and hospitable g.	CORW 247:7
climbs into their g. married	WILD 943:39
filled with g.	BLAKE 140:15
find ourselves dishonourable g.	SHAK 776:9
g. of the best soldiers	PHIL 677:57
g. of the martyrs	STEV 854:87
g. of the martyrs	STEV 854:88
g. that hide us	RALE 705:45
g. were opened	BIBLE 119:48
g. will give thee memory	SHAK 801:65
here about the g.	STEV 854:87
never went near the g. of his parents	BELL 78:93
Over the tumbled g.	ELIOT 318:10
sacred g. to be ploughed	RED 709:59
tears shed over g.	STOWE 856:33
gravestones Black village of g.	HUGH 436:43
graveyard thru the g. forest	PURDY 700:85
gravity governed by g.	MOORE 617:88
impulsive g. of head	POPE 688:37
natural force, like g.	HIND 419:66
Playing in musicked g.	AVIS 47:1
gravy No g. and no grub	RANS 707:72
Sir Humphrey Davy Abominated g.	BENT 82:1
slip with the g.	MACB 546:64
graze Could neither g. nor pierce	SHAK 790:33
grazes vacuum cleaner g.	RAINE 705:38
Graziano G. speaks...of nothing	SHAK 769:73
grease slides by on g.	LOWE 540:25
greasy fat and g. citizens	SHAK 778:67
g. Limpopo River	KIPL 491:37
great A being...rudely g.	POPE 687:87
All things both g. and small	COLE 235:20
anyone among the g. men	INGR 446:38
dream about the g.	YEATS 965:11
far above the g.	GRAY 385:92
fears of being g.	TENN 879:3
g. and almost only comfort	STARK 843:21
g. is thy faithfulness	BIBLE 110:26
G. men are not always wise	BIBLE 98:11
g. men have...elements of comicality	JENK 454:33
g. men have their poor relations	DICK 281:70
g. men...in politics	ELTON 323:42
G. men may jest	SHAK 787:59
g. minds in the commonplace	HUBB 434:98
G. To do that thing	SHAK 795:86
g. was his fame	EGAN 313:65
he is always g.	DRYD 300:20
He is truly g.	KEMP 479:47
how g. a matter a little fire kindleth	BIBLE 130:55
How indigent the g.!	GRAY 384:57
in order to be g.	HOPK 429:99
leave g. things undone	GLAS 374:44
Madness in g. ones	SHAK 783:17
makes every man feel g.	CHES 220:64
Man is only truly g.	DISR 287:30
Minds that are g.	JONS 468:84
never produces anything g.	REYN 712:70
Nothing g....without enthusiasm	EMER 324:64
Nothing g....without g. men	DE 270:90
qualities in a g. King	RICH 714:19
really g. in favour of equality	SHAW 810:19
some g. man	HOOV 427:45
ten g. artists	GREE 385:1
that Caesar might be g.!	CAMP 194:63
the g. crime	PACH 658:1
the g. have kindness	POPE 688:4
this g....kingdom	PITT 679:2
those who were truly g.	SPEN 837:92
Thou wouldst be g.	SHAK 796:14
To be g.	EMER 324:55
We live in the g. indoors	RAINE 705:38
when the One G. Scorer comes	RICE 713:89
works of a g. genius	ADDI 7:55
world's g. men	HOLM 424:71
would be g. in our little government	ROCH 719:16
Great Britain G. B. calls the Far East	MENZ 587:19
G. B. is going to make war	BETH 87:11
imperial might of G. B.	STEW 854:95
Metropolis of G.-B.	BAIL 55:87
Russia and G. B.	CECIL 210:34
greater Four things g. than all	KIPL 490:93
g., broader and fuller life	DU 305:69
g. cannot be thought	ANSE 29:71

ground

lesser life shall be as the g.	GORD 378:54
Something made g. by ourselves	ANGE 19:96
the g. the differences	PASC 667:83
greatest as well as the g. He	RAIN 705:37
g. thing in the world	FORS 344:33
I am the g.!	ALI 13:71
least…control the g.	WORD 956:52
nation's art is g.	HOPP 429:1
the g. country on earth	OBAMA 644:42
great-grandmothers g.-g. dread	BATT 68:56
great-great-grandchildren our g.-g.g., when they learn	PRIE 695:86
great-great-grandfather in any one's g.-g.-g.	SOME 833:9
greatness certain g. in her	ELIOT 316:55
far-off touch of g.	TENN 877:52
glory and its g.	GAIT 357:11
greatest in Europe for Riches and G.	BAIL 55:87
g. is a-ripening	SHAK 805:52
g. of the British Nation	ADDI 7:35
g. thrust upon him	CANN 196:5
highest point of all my g.	SHAK 805:50
himself attain g.	POE 683:93
Man's unhappiness…comes of his g.	CARL 200:98
Men…who have g. within them	CAMUS 195:81
moment of my g. flicker	ELIOT 316:65
our g. as a nation	THAT 881:53
some achieve g.	SHAK 786:4
strength and the g. of England	CURZ 259:3
great-rooted g.-r. blossomer	YEATS 966:27
Greece Athens, the eye of G.	MILT 607:79
Captive G.	HORA 430:16
Europe without G.	GISC 373:30
Fair G.! sad relic	BYRON 187:40
glory that was G.	POE 683:86
G., Italy, and England did adorn	DRYD 303:19
G. might still be free	BYRON 190:15
summoned G. to arms	MARL 572:4
greed G. begins where poverty ends	BALZ 61:7
g.…is good	DOUG 295:16
g. is only one of them	VAN 905:16
politics of g.	ARMEY 32:39
socially commendable form of g.	SCHW 750:82
writer's g. is appalling	BALD 56:56
greedy Be not g. to add money	BIBLE 112:71
G. for the belongings of others	SALL 740:92
not g. of filthy lucre	BIBLE 129:18
thank goodness, I am g.	PUNCH 699:81
Greek By dint o' G.	BURNS 177:69
G. and Roman poets	PRIOR 696:13
G. of today is essentially	MILL 594:66
he could speak G.	BUTL 184:65
imitator of G. forms	MACKE 553:9
neither G. nor Jew	BIBLE 128:11
neither Jew nor G.	BIBLE 127:79
ne of G.	SPEN 839:42
poets who grew up on G.	ROET 722:61
questioned him in G.	CARR 206:33
say a word against G.	SHAW 809:71
small Latin, and less G.	JONS 468:79
talk of knowing G.	WOOLF 955:16
Things in G. are not read	ANON 21:41
Greeks ethnic connection between the G. and me	MICH 589:64
G. Had a Word for It	AKINS 10:13
G.…hiding behind their columns	DE 271:18
I fear the G.	VIRG 913:14
make way, the G.	PROP 697:31
superiority of the G.	FUSE 356:92
with cannibals, And Trojan G."	SHAK 772:81
green believed in the g. light	FITZ 338:87
cakes…looked g. with worry	FIRB 336:54
fairest shepherd on our g.	PEELE 672:69
fresh and g. they look	THAC 880:21
frock of frolic g.	DRAY 298:90
golden face the meadows g.	SHAK 801:48
g. and yellow melancholy	SHAK 786:2
G. cowbind	SHEL 816:61
g. earth's end	MILT 599:80
g. flash that brings good fortune	RHYS 712:77
G. how I love you g.	LORCA 537:58
g. in judgement	SHAK 794:54
G. only on the banner	BROD 160:36
g. thought in a g. shade	MARV 577:2
honey set in a g. bowl	SMITH 828:99
In pastures g.	SCOT 754:85
In thy g. lap	GRAY 385:89
June…in g. leaves	SPEN 839:62
laid him on the g.	BALL 58:53
leaves are g.	ANON 20:32
leaves are g.	ANON 22:66
Make it a g. peace	DARN 263:49
margent g.	MILT 598:70
passport's g.	HEAN 405:74
sees a g. light everywhere	SCHW 751:95
smooth-shaven g.	MILT 598:53
sported on the g.	SOUT 835:45
What use…the g. river	FRAME 346:75
Where I used to play on the g.	BLAKE 140:14
whiten the g. plains	SHEL 813:75
greenery-yallery g.-y., Grovesnor	GILB 369:48
green-eyed g.-e. monster	SHAK 789:19
greengrocers lying in the rain outside g.	BRAD 154:25
Greenland G.'s icy mountains	HEBER 406:1
greens g.…that screeeeeeam	CARRA 202:57
healing g.	ABSE 1:7
Greensleeves to the tune of 'G.'	SHAK 773:14
greenstone lighting up the g. years	IHIM 445:19
greenwood in the good g.	SCOTT 752:33
Under the g. tree	SHAK 778:75
greet it gars me g.	BURNS 179:21
greeted expect to be g. with smiles	BROO 163:8
greeting g. a corpse would give	BALD 57:26
grenadiers Pensions and G.	STER 848:37
Grenville Sir Richard G. lay	TENN 873:75
Greta G. woods are green	SCOTT 753:34
grey among g.…houses	YEATS 966:18
black and g.	GREE 386:29
death's g. land	SASS 745:83
few locks…are g.	SOUT 835:43
g. twilight	YEATS 965:9
head grown g. in vain	SHEL 815:40
in her little g. dress	WOOLF 955:24
instead of the general g.	MILL 593:40
Into their g.	FREE 350:49
old and g.	YEATS 965:7
question of it being g.	TRAV 896:93
turn those amber locks to g.	DRAY 298:93
two horrible shades of g.	THOR 889:54
withered weak and g.	MILT 607:68
grey-bearded g.-b. and wrinkled	HAWT 402:10
greybeards g. call divine	SHAK 760:20
grey-green great g.-g., greasy	KIPL 491:37
greyhound g.…heeded lyke a snake	BERN 86:80
greyhounds stand like g.	SHAK 775:75
greyness Bright g.	GUNT 390:97
gridiron act a g.	CLIVE 231:38
grief acquainted with g.	BIBLE 109:93
As is my g.	SHAK 764:53
between g. and nothing	FAUL 330:33
bore within their breasts the g.	AYTO 48:13
bottom of my g.?	SHAK 766:5
bravery of his g.	SHAK 785:70
Each substance of a g.	SHAK 764:42
foundation of g.	HUGO 437:80
Fretting the enemy	SPEN 838:24
g. and sin of idleness	MELV 585:53
G. fills the room	SHAK 768:57
g. flieth to it	BACON 50:58
G. for a while is blind	SHEL 814:8
g. forgotten	SWIN 863:83
G. is a species of idleness	JOHN 462:26
G. is carried off by the wings	LAFO 504:64
G. is itself a med'cine	COWP 251:99
g. is proud	SHAK 768:54
g. itself be mortal	SHEL 815:34
G. never mended	DICK 277:38
g. of heart	SHAK 804:45
g. of heart	SHAK 804:47
g. returns with the revolving year	SHEL 815:32
G. turns out to be	DIDI 286:85
g.…upon the heels of pleasure	CONG 240:30
g. with a glass	SWIN 863:85
heard g. named the eldest	WEBS 926:37
in much wisdom is much g.	BIBLE 105:12
life from g. or danger free	JOHN 459:46
long g. and pain	TENN 876:29
make less the depth of g.	SHAK 760:6
master a g.	SHAK 774:47
much less g. on earth	BROD 160:40
My g.'s so great	SHAK 768:55
No man can cause more g.	FAUL 330:34
nor g. bitterness	LYLY 543:86
Oh my g.	SYNGE 865:25
or grey g.	SWIN 864:4
Pale G. and pleasing Pain	GRAY 385:87
particular g. Is of so	SHAK 788:89
part my g. have eas'd	MILT 607:84
pitch of g.	HOPK 429:90
quickened so with g.	GRAV 382:15
silent manliness of g.	GOLD 376:6
Smiling at g.	SHAK 786:2
sounds of g. and mourning	DICK 279:95
spends a bootless g.	SHAK 789:90
That g. for which the senses	WORD 956:51
the g. I feel	TENN 873:58
The theme…is g., sheer g.	GOLD 375:79
Thine be the g.	AYTO 48:10
Till g. did tell me roundly	HERB 413:63
wish to drown your g.	MCGO 551:74
with a mother's g.	TRUTH 900:5
griefs Extremity of g.	SHAK 760:28
[Friendship]…cutteth g. in half	BACON 52:14
g. are ended	SHAK 789:98
g. which bow	ARNO 33:63
oldest g. of summer	RICK 714:27
tales of others' g.	SHAK 798:85
grievance g. for the day	MANS 567:4
grievances not magnifying g.	RIDGE 715:32
redress of real g.	PEEL 672:66
grieve Nor joy nor g. too much	DRYD 304:54
thou leavest me to g.	SHEL 812:59
We will g. not	WORD 960:12
grieves gay nature g.	SMART 826:68
g. that menial needs	HYDE 443:21
grieving Margaret, are you g.	HOPK 428:80
thought it died of g.	KEATS 475:71
grievous most g. to him	TROL 898:39
grills As long as mixed g.	JANE 452:79
grim brow so g.	ELIOT 319:49
the g.…to prove himself	PAGL 659:18
grin g. and fine intelligence	NEW 634:34
G. Will Win	ANON 26:75
How cheerfully he seems to g.	CARR 203:64
it vanished…ending with the g.	CARR 203:69
malevolent aged g.	HUGH 435:33
Nature wears one universal g.	FIEL 335:20
with a lipless g.	ELIOT 317:77
grind g. in the prison house	BIBLE 96:19
g. the faces of the poor?	BIBLE 107:52
life is one demd horrid g.!	DICK 279:88
grinders forty teeth…twenty-four g.	DICK 281:77
g. cease because they are few	BIBLE 106:36
gringo According to a g.	GUIL 389:87
grip g. down and begin	WILL 946:9
holding a people in its g.	FANON 330:14
holds us in an iron g.	FRID 350:62
in their dead g.	TUCH 901:10
groan Condemned alike to g.	GRAY 383:48
hear each other g.	KEATS 478:43
thousands counted every g.	ARNO 35:5
with bubbling g.	BYRON 188:72
groaneth all that which g. to be so	HERB 413:57
groans g. and convulsions	STER 848:39
g. of love	LOWRY 541:43
Warring sighs and g.	BURNS 179:34
grocer g. puts a pound weight	SPEN 837:9
Grogan as old mother G. said	JOYCE 470:23
Gromboolian great G. plain	LEAR 516:28
grooves in the g. that those who rob	CONN 243:20
what's in the g.	ANON 28:51
grope g. about in the labyrinth	SCHO 748:52
gross Not g. to sink	SHAK 762:84
November, he full g. and fat	SPEN 840:63
grossness measureless g.	WHIT 938:12
vice…losing all its g.	BURKE 176:41
Grosvenor G. Gallery	GILB 369:48
grotesque became a g.	ANDE 18:75
fashions strike us as g.	VEBL 910:45
from the g. to the horrible	DOYLE 297:73
grots cage like g.	SITW 823:7
ground at length it stands the g.	DRYD 302:93
both feet off the g.	JOHN 458:11
can't keep on the g.	TRAV 896:91
clearing g. a little	LOCKE 533:88
Close by the g.	SHAK 774:41
commit his body to the g.	BOOK 148:1
cursed is the g. for thy sake	BIBLE 91:98
dead g. in between	REED 709:28
dewy g.	WORD 961:44
Exiled to the g.	BAUD 68:59

grounds

feet planted on level g. — GOHE 375:73
fertile g. he caused to grow — MILT 604:96
found a watch upon the g. — PALEY 661:57
generally loses g. — STEV 851:17
good for the g. — SCHU 749:72
g. is like a beautiful woman — SNOW 832:84
g. itself is falling — FERL 333:90
g. with vernal flowers — MILT 599:90
grow upon a spot of g. — SWIFT 862:45
If that plane leaves the g. — EPST 327:30
In his own g. — POPE 685:43
inlay Broidered the g. — MILT 604:8
kamikaze g. staff — PARK 665:36
knit hands, and beat the g. — MILT 598:66
know you by your g. — BLUN 143:74
leaves…fall to the g. — ANON 20:32
let us sit upon the g. — SHAK 764:52
little time on the g. — OWENS 658:41
lot is fallen unto me in a fair g. — BOOK 148:8
lying on the g. — ALAN 10:17
Marching o'er the metric g. — CRAIK 252:51
most at ease on the g. — ALLS 14:8
on the g. at Goose Green — KINN 488:64
place…is holy g. — BIBLE 93:52
Resources left in the g. are saved — BRODY 160:44
second foot on the g. — FONT 342:76
seven feet of English g. — HARO 398:43
spilled it on the g. — BIBLE 93:40
Stand your g. — PARK 664:34
stone falls to the g. — THOR 889:45
swalloweth the g. — BIBLE 99:19
tears have overflowed his g.? — DONNE 291:28
that never left the g. — LOWE 540:28
their burthen to the g. — TENN 877:60
they plopped to the g. — PLATH 681:37
till the g. from whence he was taken — BIBLE 91:1
till thou return to the g. — BIBLE 91:99
tread on classic g. — ADDI 6:16
unhurried G. swell — ELIOT 320:72
when he has reached g. — JOHN 460:63
when he hit the g. — HUGH 436:41
when I was on the g. — SIMON 822:76
grounds beautify their g. — MALT 563:23
noble g. for the noble — RUSK 733:89
group characterizes…minority g. — MAIL 560:53
g. of other people — ROSSO 727:68
g. of the unwilling — HARK 398:35
nation or g. — RUNC 731:49
only exploited g. in the world — JONG 466:39
place in any political g. — HELL 408:42
sobs from among the g. — DICK 279:95
groupies don't get g. — STIPE 855:4
groups divide people into two g. — HAMP 395:74
g. of inflexible political persuasion — WILS 948:71
g. who question that status — MAMET 563:27
marginal g. who — RUET 730:37
split into two polar g. — SNOW 832:77
grouse g. are in no danger — EDIN 312:51
grove deep windings of the g. — BEAT 70:2
G. nods at g., each a mirror — POPE 686:60
meadow, g., and stream — WORD 959:5
While in a g. I sate — WORD 957:60
grovelled he g. before him — THAC 880:23
groves g. of their academy — BURKE 176:42
o'er shady g. they hover — WEBS 926:36
will seek the g. — ROSS 726:53
grow For sure then I should g. — HERB 413:64
g. for ever — TENN 872:40
How do poems g.? — WARR 921:18
isn't going to g. — WHITE 935:48
its radiance would g. — RAND 706:59
more we g. in numbers — TERT 879:18
my wrath did g. — BLAKE 140:17
some skin on to g. — KHRU 485:93
which grain will g. — SHAK 796:5
grow'd I 'spect I g. — STOWE 856:30
growing ever grew anything worth g. — SAND 742:25
g., bodily that is — THOM 886:73
g., flying, happening — REID 710:44
G. old is like being…penalised — POWE 693:47
g.…when ye're sleeping — SCOTT 753:60
growing up I wasn't good At g. up — FANT 330:16
growl sit and g. — JOHN 464:84
grown now g. up to riper age — BRON 161:59
grown-up g.-u. people's feet — STEV 853:63
Lillian as a g.-u. — FEIB 331:54
take seriously…g.-u. women — STEI 846:94

grown-ups obvious facts about g.-u. — JARR 452:91
ordinary thick-skinned g.-u. — SHAW 807:18
grows box that fennel G. around — RANS 707:72
g. daily worse and worse — SPEN 839:55
What g. by the words? — SIDN 820:39
growth birth and g.…are ubiquitous — DILL 286:92
children of a larger g. — DRYD 301:58
expression of life as g. — MILL 594:79
for the g. of any and everything — STUA 858:58
g. in the individual — SMIL 827:69
g. is a leap in the dark — MILL 594:82
g. of this nation — GAND 359:57
growths sun-searched g. — ROSS 726:57
grow up country safe to g. u. in — THAT 881:52
g. u. to be Prime Minister — RICH 714:26
grub No gravy and no g. — RANS 707:73
old ones, g. — SHAW 806:64
poor g., poor pay — LOND 534:10
sphere of use…in the g. state — DOUG 294:97
grudge g. against the children — BIBLE 94:78
G. not one against another — BIBLE 130:60
took it as a personal g. — OHEN 648:18
grudges all their ancient g. — WAUGH 924:81
don't hold no g. — KENN 483:47
Grundy What will Mrs G. say? — MORT 621:77
grunt every twitch and g. — TRUD 899:71
gruntled far from being g. — WODE 952:50
guarantee beauty is a g. of happiness — PROU 698:50
each will g. all — LEES 519:4
Englishman as a g. — SHAW 809:66
guaranteed g. never to fail — FORM 344:21
guard Alice is marrying one of the g. — MILNE 595:12
g. against…unwarranted influence — EISE 314:2
g. of the world proletarian army — LENIN 521:39
Made good g. for itself — SHAK 794:73
Those that I g. — YEATS 966:22
guarded G. by timeless principalities — GRAV 382:25
guardian g. angels sung this strain — THOM 887:97
my g. angel — BENE 79:18
guardianship Christ for my g. — PATR 669:29
guards Brigade of G. — MACM 556:73
g. at the gate — SUN 860:96
G. die but do not surrender — CAMB 193:36
Up g. and at them — WELL 929:2
guardsman g.'s cut and thrust differ — HUXL 443:10
guerdon fair g. when we hope — MILT 599:86
guerre mais ce n'est pas la g. — BOSQ 151:73
guerrilla cardinal maxims of g. war — KISS 493:85
Insurrection—by means of g. bands — MAZZ 583:29
guess g. about what is seen — SAND 742:21
venture A g. — REED 709:28
you can perhaps g. why — SEVI 758:42
guesses only hints and g. — ELIOT 320:78
secrets everybody g. — SHAW 807:7
supporting their g. by argument — BAGE 54:77
guest as a g. thanks his host — DILL 286:93
awaited the expected g. — ELIOT 318:4
Earth receive an honoured g. — AUDEN 43:92
g. of one's time — KENN 480:87
remembrance of a g. that tarrieth — BIBLE 112:77
speed the parting g. — POPE 686:52
guests g. should praise it — HARI 398:32
Jews are hosts, and not g. — SACH 736:3
the g. star-scattered — FITZ 337:72
two great classes: hosts and g. — BEER 74:92
Unbidden g. — SHAK 759:75
what…other g. thought of him — SKIN 825:48
guidance act under the g. of reason — SPIN 840:78
g. have I sought — WORD 962:49
guide be thy g. — ANON 21:57
except some man should g. me? — BIBLE 124:79
g. informed him later — NASH 631:70
g. of life — HUME 438:1
g. thee with mine eye — BIBLE 100:54
Have God to be his g. — BUNY 174:82
infallible critical g. — AUDEN 43:7
None need a g. — POPE 688:37
place within them as a g. — MILT 603:81
probability…very g. of life — BUTL 184:57
without a g.…I…work — ARET 31:11
guides Ye blind g. — BIBLE 118:27
Guildford G.…the most agreeable — COBB 233:77
guile g. of a cobra — WOOL 956:47
Of g., of hate, of envy — MILT 606:48
packed with g. — BROO 162:95
guillotine cure except as a g. — LUCE 541:57
guilt blood with g. is bought — SHEL 814:9

blushing…a sign of g. — CONG 241:60
difference between politics and g. — CLIN 230:6
free from g. or pain — SHEL 814:18
g. and power — TOPL 894:61
G. in his heart — CHUR 224:52
g. of dissimulation — SCOTT 754:67
g. of flattery — JOHN 463:73
industry is g. — RUSK 733:10
one g., one crime — MILT 606:54
sense of g., which he denies — LESS 523:90
servitude…the punishment of his g. — CURR 259:92
she trembles with g. — OCON 646:84
suspicious of g. in myself — HELL 408:49
What art can wash her g. — GOLD 376:93
guiltier G. than him they try — SHAK 787:52
guiltless Lord will not hold him g. — BIBLE 94:66
guilty 100 per cent not g. — SIMP 822:86
better that ten g. persons escape — BLAC 137:43
cups make any g. men — JONS 467:70
feel somehow g. — GRASS 382:12
Find me but g. — WEBS 926:27
g. never escape unscathed — BAIL 55:85
g. of corrupting…the young — PLATO 681:42
G. of dust and sin — HERB 413:65
g. spice to this recreation — WAUGH 924:78
g. when they read — VIDAL 912:96
his foot is g. — BECK 72:38
innocent while g. — BELL 78:94
like a g. thing surprised — WORD 960:10
make g. of our disasters the sun — SHAK 792:89
rich, deep, and g. — CHAN 214:7
started like a g. thing — SHAK 780:30
when one loves a g. person? — CYRA 260:10
guinea but the g.'s stamp — BURNS 180:52
force of the g. — RUSK 733:96
g. pigs in the laboratory of God — WILL 945:88
jingling of the g. — TENN 871:16
guinea-coast G.-c. slavery — MELV 585:70
guineas g. for flinging a pot of paint — RUSK 733:15
twenty g. per annum — DICK 278:75
Guinevere delyverd hys doughtir G. — MALO 562:6
syght of queene G. — MALO 562:8
Guinness G. on a sunny day — GREE 385:2
guise no newe g. that it nas old — CHAU 217:81
guitar sang to a small g. — LEAR 516:35
What seems to pass for g. — POP 684:14
will break their g. — MIRO 608:17
You have a blue g. — STEV 850:80
guitars boys with bright red g. — HENRI 411:8
corpses, or Picasso g. — LIPP 530:34
gulf across the g. of space — WELLS 930:19
g. of mutual incomprehension — SNOW 832:77
G. War was like teenage sex — HARK 398:34
peace and civil order in the G. — ELIZ 322:10
social that divides him — MARX 579:35
teeming g. — WHIT 938:10
there is a great g. fixed — BIBLE 121:98
turning of the G. crisis — HUSS 440:37
walking on a string across a g. — DAVI 264:65
widening g. between the rich — COUP 248:27
gulfs g. will wash us down — TENN 870:2
gull g. sees farthest — BACH 49:10
g.'s way and the whale's way — MASE 580:52
image of the Great G. — BACH 49:11
gull-marked shining g.-m. mud — LARK 509:84
gulls does not even require g. — KEYN 484:17
gum can't fart and chew g. — JOHN 458:16
gun a g. can only kill — YOUS 969:65
bad guy….good guy with a g. — LAPI 508:59
double-barrelled g. and pointers — KING 488:50
draw her g. — WHITE 935:46
give up my g. — HEST 417:35
Great G. of Athlone — ANON 23:96
g. gives you the body — THOR 889:47
How can a ballpoint fight with a g. — MUGA 623:8
likes to shoot his g. — COBA 232:25
Maxim G. — BELL 76:56
more likely to kill… than the g. — LEVI 526:32
nice guy if you have a g. — KOCH 495:22
no g., but I can spit — AUDEN 44:15
out of the barrel of a g. — MAO 568:25
state where g. control — SIMP 822:84
gunfire g.…sounded unreal — USTI 906:46
Gunga Din than I am, G. D.! — KIPL 490:60
gunner And the g. said — TENN 879:98
gunpowder g. and printer's ink — KRAUS 499:10
g. ran out of the heels — FOOTE 342:83

halls

printing, g. and the magnet	BACON	50:45
guns but for these vile g.	SHAK	771:33
defend ourselves with g. not butter	GOEB	374:53
G. aren't lawful	PARK	664:19
g. begin to rattle	BARK	63:54
g. begin to shoot	KIPL	489:87
G. don't kill people	MOORE	617:96
heard amid the g.	MCCR	548:11
hundred men with g.	PUZO	701:5
loaded g. with boys	CRAB	252:48
monstrous anger of the g.	OWEN	657:25
more powerful than g.	BENN	80:38
not found any smoking g.	BLIX	142:58
Of g., and drums, and wounds	SHAK	771:33
rather have butter or g.?	GOER	374:56
slaught'rin g.	BURNS	178:91
spring-g. in the realm	LOWE	539:2
unheroic Dead who fed the g.?	SASS	746:99
when the g. begin	SASS	745:83
gunshot g. is the perfect way	KENN	482:35
gust g. he hath in quarrelling	SHAK	785:81
gusts explanation of our g.	ELIOT	316:58
Gutenburg G. made everybody	MCLU	556:61
gut-feel g.-f. of the 55-year old	GREE	386:36
guts g. of a butterfly	CAPO	197:30
I'll lug the g.	SHAK	784:46
gutter born in the g.	KIPL	491:23
I lay down in the g.	BURT	181:71
straight into the g.	SMITH	829:21
We are all in the g.	WILDE	941:78
gutterals world of g.	STEV	849:68
guy Ah! County G.	SCOTT	754:69
average g. who could carry a tune	CROS	256:33
cop beatin' up a g.	STEI	846:83
dresses like a g.	GILB	369:61
g. that plays the kettle drums	SALI	740:80
kind of g. that wouldn't talk	SALI	740:75
nice g. if you have a gun	KOCH	495:22
no matter how nice a g.	SALI	740:79
optimist is a g.	MARQ	575:49
snatching a hard g.	RUNY	731:56
guys five g. who hate you	STEN	847:7
g. using false pretences	RUNY	731:60
name any disease after two g.	PUZO	701:9
Nice g. finish last	DURO	308:32
unmarried g. in New York suck	BUSH	184:52
gwine G. to run all night	FOST	345:53
Gyges G. of Lydia	VASA	909:27
gymnasium g. of the mind	LENIN	521:42
life's g.	WHIT	938:11
gymnast g. and golfer, soldered	BRYA	170:99
Gyn/Ecologists recommended by G.	DALY	261:21
Gypsies fat of rendered Jews and G.	VONN	915:51
gypsy Two-wheeled g. queen	DYLAN	309:55
vagrant g. life	MASE	580:52
gyre Did g. and gimble	CARR	204:89
turning in the widening g.	YEATS	966:24

H

habeas corpus protection of the h. c.	JEFF	454:26
habit because it was a h.	ROGE	723:81
becomes a h.	LOMB	534:8
breed a h. in a man!	SHAK	759:72
Costly h.	SHAK	781:52
country h. has me	SACK	737:10
gentlemen are in the h.	PALM	662:73
Getting to be a H. with Me	DUBIN	304:60
good h. makes a child a man	WEBS	926:24
h. cannot be tossed	TWAIN	904:98
h., custom and education	SMITH	827:77
h. in writing articles	FEYN	334:5
h. of civilisation	WEST	933:94
h....of correcting things	BRADY	155:53
h. of discipline	TUCH	901:12
h. of disgruntled men	TOLK	893:44
h. of profound reflection	CONR	244:48
h. of revelation	SKEL	825:44
H....the test of truth	CRAB	252:41
instinct; the h. is already old	LAWR	513:67
in the h. of flogging	TROL	898:52
monster that devours everything: h.	BALZ	60:90
order breeds h.	ADAMS	5:90
remnants of such a beautiful h.	ALME	15:10
shook the h. off	WORD	958:88
taste of lies...a h.	GELL	363:34
Television has spread the h.	SCHL	748:38
habitat native h. was hot water	ANON	26:93
habitation Deep-founded h.	BLAKE	139:83
God in his holy h.	BIBLE	101:81
h. for bears and wolves	SCHAW	747:20
h. of dragons	BIBLE	108:76
Lord...thy h.	BIBLE	102:97
none doth build a stately h.	HERB	413:69
world Of destined h.	MILT	605:33
habitations brick shops and h.	THOR	889:52
miles of human h.	CONR	244:50
receive you into everlasting h.	BIBLE	121:94
habitis prelatis in h. clericall	DUNB	306:2
habits each other's h., thoughts	DISR	288:34
first h. of intimacy	LAMB	505:93
h. and customs of the people	RICA	712:79
h. are geared towards	LIVE	531:51
h. of metaphoric thought	FRYE	354:54
h. of peace and patience	WALT	920:92
Pick up bad h. of expectancy	LARK	509:71
superficial h. of 'good citizenship'	WAUGH	924:81
habitual that which has become h.	ARIS	32:29
Habsburg H. monarchy	TAAF	865:1
hackles of tan with henna h.	STEV	849:72
hackneyed h. jokes from Miller	BYRON	187:25
hades phonographs of h. in the brain	CRANE	253:69
haemophilia kind of psychological h.	CURR	259:90
haft change the h. if you please	QUIN	703:23
hag h. obscene, and grisly phantom	BEAT	72:2
you...equiangular old h.!	OCON	646:84
haggard h. and careworn	WODE	952:43
h. and lank	GILB	369:48
Haggards the H. Ride no more	STEP	847:12
haggis Gie her a H.!	BURNS	178:95
haggling still h. at the price	GRAV	382:33
hags secret, black, and midnight h.	SHAK	797:54
ha-ha Funny peculiar, or funny h.-h.?	HAY	402:19
hail beaten dog beneath the h.	POUND	692:26
H. Caesar, we...salute you	ANON	20:22
H. fellow, well met	SWIFT	862:56
H. Mary, quite contrary!	GREE	386:14
H. nothing full of nothing	HEMI	409:68
h. shall sweep away the refuge	BIBLE	108:71
H. to the Chief	SCOTT	752:29
lashing h.	SHEL	813:75
say a H. Mary for you	JOYCE	470:17
such a h. of words	JONS	467:57
Where falls not h.	TENN	878:87
Hailsham Lord H. said	MONT	613:8
hair backward by the h.	BROW	166:92
braided her yellow h.	BALL	59:73
braid to bind your h.	SCOTT	753:46
ceases to alter...her h.	AUST	47:97
dressing their h.	SMOL	831:67
each particular h. to stand on end	SHAK	781:60
elegance of Circe's h.	POUND	691:1
fair h. gently waved	THAT	881:50
fictions only and false h.	HERB	413:72
for the colour of his h.	HOUS	433:81
h. a glory like a saint	KEATS	477:21
h. and dimples is coming	MOORE	616:70
h. and harpstring of gold	SWIN	864:98
h. as white as gin	CAUS	209:15
h. has become very white	CARR	203:66
h. is as a flock of goats	BIBLE	107:45
h. More black than ashbuds	TENN	871:5
h. off the Great Cham's beard	SHAK	774:28
h. that lay along	ROSS	726:50
h. 'twixt south and southwest side	BUTL	184:66
his floating h.!	COLE	236:42
hoary h.	GRAY	385:81
If a man have long h.	BIBLE	126:48
if my h. do but tickle	SHAK	767:40
in politics...with that h.	ASTOR	39:11
in their golden h.	TENN	872:31
I rise with my red h.	PLATH	681:33
kame my h.	BALL	60:79
lass wi' tousled h.	MACD	549:21
letters...serve one to pin up one's h.	CONG	241:65
light brown h.	FOST	345:55
lodestone of live h.	MACN	557:94
long h....is a glory to her	BIBLE	126:48
long, limp h.	DAVIS	265:97
loosen your h.	YEATS	965:11
loses his h.	DIAZ	276:26
man of your head and h.	JONS	467:62
must sugar my h.	CARR	204:83
My h. has been in training	SHER	817:73
never hurt a h. of him	STUD	858:64
no more that shining h.	LOVE	538:84
not hurt a h.	STER	848:39
one strangling golden h.	ROSS	726:58
pin up your h.	CONG	241:66
reft the jewels from her h.	HYDE	443:21
ruddy limbs and flourishing h.	BLAKE	139:81
scant as h. in leprosy	BROW	168:34
smoothes her h.	ELIOT	318:5
snow-white h. who has kept out	LEAC	516:24
space...laid on her h.	CRANE	253:62
stars in her h.	ROSS	726:49
such a head of h.	HOUS	433:82
tangles of Neaera's h.?	MILT	599:86
Thy hyacinth h.	POE	683:86
watching myself brush my h.	RHYS	712:78
wear gowd on your h.	BALL	59:67
weave the sunlight in your h.	ELIOT	317:74
When I lie tangled in her h.	LOVE	538:81
Wi' ribbons in her h.	BALL	59:67
woman, with such h.	BROW	168:32
you have lovely h.	CHEK	218:16
your yellow h.	YEATS	967:33
haircut rather bad h.	MCCA	547:87
hairs bring down my gray h.	BIBLE	93:44
few, sad, last grey h.	KEATS	478:43
five grey h.	DONNE	291:27
Had all his h.	SHAK	790:47
h. of your head are all numbered	BIBLE	116:71
h. were grown like eagles' feathers	BIBLE	111:40
h. were white like wool	BIBLE	131:88
How ill white h. becomes	SHAK	773:99
If h. be wires	SHAK	802:83
when my h. be grey	SURR	860:4
hairy Esau...is a h. man	BIBLE	92:30
h. American filth	OSBO	655:86
Haiti Go to H. and stand	PHIL	677:57
hale You are h., Father William	SOUT	835:43
half advantage...is h. the victory	DRAKE	298:87
fall h. in love	SALI	740:74
H. of them don't know	QUINN	703:24
h. of the nation is mad	SMOL	831:66
h. o't smug, complacent	SMITH	831:64
h. the battle	GOLD	377:14
h. the people are right	WHITE	935:37
h. was not told me	BIBLE	97:56
image of myself and dearer h.	MILT	604:15
live with only h. a heart	WILS	947:45
longest h. of your life	SOUT	835:54
loves but h. of Earth	QUIL	702:9
No, but h. a one	JONS	467:65
not told even the h.	POLO	684:5
The ae h. of the warld	SCOTT	754:72
to be thought h. so good	WHIT	938:25
half-baked attractive to the h.-b.	FORS	344:26
half-believers h.-b. in our...creeds	ARNO	34:93
half-brother America, thou h.-b.	BAIL	55:88
half-creature h.-c. of the Senate	MANS	568:12
half-dark From h.-d. to h.-d.	POUND	692:18
half-hour h.-o. to Aberdour	BALL	59:72
half-hung with mat h.-h.	POPE	686:69
half-light and the h.-l.	YEATS	966:12
half-naked striding h.-n. up the steps	CHUR	225:79
half-traitor never be h.-t.	HUGO	437:58
half-truths speak no more than h.-t.	LINK	530:27
half-workers women Must be h.-w.?	SHAK	803:94
Hall I have seen...Thomas H.	SMART	826:60
filled Douglas in his h.?	SCOTT	752:23
filled our h. like	RIVA	716:53
grey assembly h.	MUSS	627:88
H. or Terrace	LEAR	516:29
hire a h.	BELL	78:93
I knew that sullen h.	OWEN	657:33
kindest in the h.	DAVIS	266:8
logs into the h.	SHAK	763:27
skittish Fortune's h.	SHAK	787:36
sparrow should fly...into the h.	BEDE	72:59
vasty h. of death	ARNO	34:86
waited in our tutor's h.	BYRON	186:23
wealth of h. and bower	WORD	958:94
Halliag will go down to H.	MACL	555:31
hallmark h. of our culture	DONA	290:5
hallowed H. be thy name	BIBLE	115:42
halls Amphitrite's destined h.	SHEL	812:64
blood-bedecked h. of their revel	POE	683:83
h. of the White House	JOHN	457:96
through Tara's h.	MOORE	618:4

hallucinated

hallucinated when Dalí h. RUSS 735:47
hallucination A consensual h. GIBS 367:15
hallways along these same h. ROBBE 716:63
  enclosed h. GIDE 367:21
halo jealousy with a h. WELLS 930:31
  Life...is a luminous h. WOOLF 955:10
  What...Is a h.? FRY 353:32
halt h. ye between two opinions? BIBLE 97:61
  make it h. behind her SHAK 804:26
halcyon first h. period WALT 920:97
ham Do you like green eggs and h.? SEUSS 758:40
  helps scenery like h. and eggs TWAIN 902:37
Hambledonians last of H. EGAN 313:65
hambre La mejor salsa...el h. CERV 211:45
hamburger like ordering a h. COWE 249:68
hamburgers future and it is h. HALB 392:21
Hamelin H. town's in Brunswick BROW 167:15
Hamilton [H.] smote the rock WEBS 926:15
  Marie H.'s to the kirk gane BALL 59:67
Hamlet Could H. have been written GRIS 389:75
  get Tree to recite H. GILB 370:75
  H. is so much paper and ink PRIE 695:84
  H. Prince of Denmark EVEL 328:71
  H. with no rehearsal than TV golf LEMM 521:33
  Lord H., with his doublet SHAK 781:72
  No! I am not Prince H. ELIOT 316:66
hammer an also dropped h. RUSK 733:17
  beating as hard as my h. SCOTT 753:50
  eye is the h. KAND 473:17
  hit my thumb with a h. AMIS 16:38
  never killed...with a h. SEDA 755:96
  the grain and h. HEAN 405:79
  thunderous h. shall drive thee BLAKE 141:33
  took an h. in her hand BIBLE 95:11
  with the h. she smote Sisera BIBLE 95:12
hammers hear the h. ring KIPL 493:80
hammock safety-net, not a h. ANON 27:31
  slept in a h. SAKI 739:58
  slow movement of a tropical h. CHOC 222:25
hammock-shroud heavy-shotted h.-s. TENN 873:61
Hampton-court servant...got to H.-c. STEE 844:39
hand admire my sleight of h. BUTL 185:81
  beloved h. is laid ARNO 34:72
  bishops eat from my h. DUPL 307:23
  bite the h. that fed them BURKE 176:54
  bless the h. that gave the blow DRYD 302:98
  bringing me up by h. DICK 282:6
  by whose h....people still are fed DODD 289:91
  came forth fingers of a man's h. BIBLE 111:41
  cap in h. the day SMITH 831:64
  Clean from my h.? SHAK 797:37
  cravens my weak h. SHAK 803:97
  curious engine, your white h. WEBS 927:52
  darkness...sifts through your h. ASHB 37:56
  death in my h. SHAK 760:23
  Devil is still at h. DRYD 301:68
  disdainful wave of a white woman's h. ANGE 19:99
  Don't let the h. fall SLOAN 825:54
  end...is close at h. WELLS 930:40
  Even there shall thy h. lead me BIBLE 103:44
  Eve's fair h., as from a...book LANY 508:55
  eye on the right h. RUSH 732:97
  fans into their h. BALL 59:71
  fate carries in her other h. LAWR 514:91
  fearful h. in felling quake DONNE 290:16
  fear thy skinny h.! COLE 235:14
  Fed with cold and usurous h.? BLAKE 140:13
  flame...one holds in the h. MARG 570:69
  fly in his h. STER 848:31
  foot and h. go cold ANON 21:60
  fork in his inexperienced h. WELLS 930:25
  Give me thy h. SHAK 766:13
  giving h., though foul SHAK 763:10
  great gifts with one h. SNOW 832:79
  h....cutting edge of the mind BRON 160:15
  h. for h. BIBLE 94:67
  h. from day to day MACN 557:98
  h....goes over the face GARBO 359:64
  h. in all things WASH 921:23
  h. in h., on the edge LEAR 516:38
  h. in h. to death ROSS 726:62
  h. in h. to hell SHAK 761:53
  h. in h. with Plenty TENN 873:51
  h. in h. with wand'ring MILT 607:74
  h.-in-h. even with the vow SHAK 781:63
  h. in too many pies MENC 586:89
  handle toward my h.? SHAK 796:27

h. more instrumental to the mouth SHAK 780:31
h. of God BIBLE 112:74
h. of God MARA 569:43
h. of Heaven WORD 962:50
h. of steel in a velvet glove WOOL 956:40
h. on the throat of Venice TOME 894:55
h. so various MILT 608:92
h. that follows intellect MICH 590:65
h. that holds dominion THOM 883:9
h. that kings Have lipped SHAK 794:63
h. that made us is divine ADDI 7:41
h. that rocks the cradle WALL 918:52
h. that signed the paper THOM 883:8
h. that writ it SHAK 801:61
h., the head RUSK 733:92
h. under his head YEATS 967:37
h. wherewith I write BROW 166:96
h. will be against every man BIBLE 92:19
hard h. of...need OTWAY 656:98
Have still the upper h. COWA 249:55
have the use...but of my left h. MILT 600:97
held her in his golden h. GEE 362:28
hold a fire in his h. SHAK 764:36
holden me by my right h. BIBLE 101:86
if they want a h. GERS 365:74
if thy right h. offend thee BIBLE 115:34
infinity in the palm of your h. BLAKE 141:24
In his h. are all the corners BOOK 149:30
in his h. a spade SPEN 839:61
in the palm of my h. JULI 470:40
In this close h. of love BROW 166:95
in thy h. a withered spray ARNO 34:91
Into thine h. I commit my spirit BIBLE 100:52
invisible h. of some...god CUOMO 258:80
Jesus stretched forth his h. BIBLE 117:1
join h. in h. DICK 284:57
keep the Classics at h. WOOLF 956:37
Keep your left h. high ONEI 651:80
kissed her slender h. TENN 876:22
kissed h. and by the h. led BLAKE 139:92
kissing your h. LOOS 536:52
kiss thy h. to bid adieu STER 848:46
laid her snow-white h. YEATS 965:3
laid thine h. upon me BIBLE 103:43
lay his h. on his heart STRA 857:45
lays his h. on his heart BEER 73:78
lays his icy h. on kings SHIR 819:20
led by an invisible h. SMITH 828:86
left h. is my thinking h. HEPW 412:30
lest he put forth his h. BIBLE 91:1
let not man have the upper h. BOOK 148:6
let not thy left h. know BIBLE 115:40
Let your h. slip MACB 546:64
lilies in her h. ROSS 726:49
little cloud...like a man's h. BIBLE 97:64
made by h. which feels HEPW 412:28
magic h. of chance KEATS 475:78
makes...with the things at h. PERCY 674:11
make your h. so unsteady CENN 211:44
man with heart, head, h. TENN 876:20
mine...the painter's h. WORD 961:28
Moses held up his h. BIBLE 94:65
murd'rous h. a drowsy bench protect CRAB 252:34
my h. a needle better fits BRAD 155:50
my hat, and h. BROW 164:43
My times be in Thy h.! BROW 168:61
Nature's own h. painted SHAK 800:39
nectar from his h. MARL 574:36
of one whose h. SHAK 790:51
Old Hodge stays not his h. RANS 707:72
on each h. the flames MILT 602:43
openest thine h. BIBLE 104:48
other h. full of seas HYDE 443:19
other h. held a weapon BIBLE 98:88
Our times are in His h. BROW 168:59
Poetry is an extra h. MITC 609:28
poor man's h. WORD 960:15
pure h. can touch a newspaper BAUD 69:88
put forth thine h. now BIBLE 98:92
put his h. by the hole BIBLE 107:47
put your h. into the h. of God HASK 400:81
quality...made...by the human h. CATH 208:92
rare fine h. at that MANS 567:98
rash h. in evil hour MILT 606:50
regard the h. of the clock LECO 518:81
right h. of the Majesty BIBLE 129:33
sandwich in her h. DICK 277:42

shake your h. and help you LOFT 534:4
show her the back of your h. FAUL 331:45
Sit thou at my right h. BIBLE 102:17
soon as I get hold of a h. FITZ 337:76
stand on either h. MACA 545:46
stern h. of Compulsion THUR 891:95
stern h. of fate LLOY 533:72
supplication of a dead man's h. ELIOT 318:14
tennis-girl's h.! BETJ 88:25
the kindlier h. TENN 875:96
there's a h., my trusty fiere! BURNS 178:7
this is my lady's h. SHAK 786:3
this unworthy h.! CRAN 253:76
thrust my h. into his side BIBLE 124:67
Thy h., great Anarch! POPE 689:48
till I have a good h. SWIFT 863:78
time is now near at h. WASH 921:27
tiny h. is frozen GIAC 366:89
touch of a vanished h. TENN 871:4
waiting for a h. TENN 873:62
walking close at h. CARR 204:99
wander h. in h. NOYES 642:69
waters in the hollow of his h. BIBLE 108:81
What immortal h. or eye BLAKE 140:19
what mortal h. SCOTT 752:17
Whatsoever thy h. findeth BIBLE 106:23
what strong h. can hold SHAK 801:57
with as delicate a h. BUTL 184:69
with automatic h. ELIOT 318:5
Women...tricks by sleight of h. CONG 240:45
work of an Almighty h. ADDI 7:40
written...with mine own h. BIBLE 127:84
wrote it with a second h. SPEN 839:47
Your h., your tongue SHAK 796:17
handbag hitting it with her h. CRIT 255:11
handbook Bible as...a constable's h. KING 488:54
handclasp h.'s a little stronger CHAP 214:12
handcuffs with the h. on his wrist? HOUS 433:81
Handel H. is so great and so simple BUTL 186:6
  wisdom; H. sings it EMER 325:93
handful fear in a h. of dust ELIOT 318:96
  give the barest h. KIPL 491:23
  h. of grey ashes CORY 247:9
handicraft primitive and original h. OLIP 649:35
handicrafts manufacture and in h. MARX 579:42
handiwork sheweth his h. BOOK 148:9
handkerchief feels like a damp h. MACK 554:14
  germs in your h. ANON 24:24
  without wetting his h. LASS 511:12
handkerchiefs in the house wi' h. SCOTT 753:50
  waistcoats and moral pocket h. DICK 277:54
handle h. toward my hand? SHAK 796:74
  h. which fits them all HOLM 424:69
handles no h. to a horse LEAC 515:6
handmaid h. of the Lord BIBLE 120:65
  h. to religion BACON 50:34
  nature's h. art DRYD 299:15
  Riches are a good h. BACON 50:49
handmaiden low estate of his h. BIBLE 120:66
handmaidens five h., whose names ROSS 726:53
  War has three h. HENR 411:12
handprint h. of all culture ANON 27:36
handrails color I want those h. TRUMP 900:97
hands aching h. and bleeding feet ARNO 34:76
  additional number of productive h. SMITH 827:83
  a lot of intelligence in her h. WAITS 916:7
  And then take h. SHAK 803:14
  and with clean h. WILH 943:57
  Art to fold her h. ROSS 726:47
  Beneath the bleeding h. ELIOT 320:64
  big h. and big feet HAGEN 391:5
  bind the h. of...rogues OTWAY 656:2
  blood and wine were on his h. WILDE 942:15
  both grasp h. STAN 842:11
  both h. in the pocket SATIE 746:5
  By fairy h. their knell is rung COLL 237:72
  By foreign h. thy dying eyes POPE 685:46
  Cease to use your h. ORWE 653:19
  cheap seats clap their h. LENN 521:43
  clasping his h. together SCOTT 754:73
  clean h. GALS 358:51
  coarse warty h. DONO 293:82
  cold immortal h. SWIN 864:96
  Come; let us squeeze h. MELV 585:66
  dirty h., the nails bitten MACA 545:36
  dollar in another man's h. OHEN 648:16
  done with the brain, not the h. MICH 590:67

happy

Droops on the little h.	MILNE 596:13	H. my Hat is Home	JERO 454:44	h. of his humble home	GLAD 373:38
education...should be in State h.	MILL 591:98	h. no longer on me	SHAK 795:75	h. of knowing	FRAN 348:18
engraft our h.	DONNE 292:43	H. on thy walls	JONS 467:72	h. of the common man	BEVE 90:62
exertions of your h. and feet	CONR 244:32	h. them on the horns	SHAK 799:89	h. of the greatest number	BENT 82:88
Farewell, my poor h.	RACH 704:25	H. thyself	SHAK 771:41	h. of the next w.	BROW 165:74
Father, into thy h.	BIBLE 122:10	let him h. there	EHRL 313:71	h. or blessedness of man	SPIN 841:81
flabby h.	GILB 369:60	to have done is to h.	SHAK 787:38	h. that the future offers	DESB 274:89
folding of the h. to sleep	BIBLE 104:59	handdog shifty, h. look	WODE 952:47	h. through another man's eyes	SHAK 780:19
fortune...with both h. full	SHAK 773:96	hanged got myself burned or h.	JERO 454:43	h. too swiftly flies	GRAY 383:48
free heart from its own h.!	CRAS 254:84	h. for stealing horses	HALI 393:34	H. was my fate	RIMB 716:51
greet you with bloody h.	CORW 247:7	h., if some eternal villain	SHAK 790:36	however uncertain of giving h.	AUST 46:59
h. are blue	LEAR 516:31	h. in a fortnight	JOHN 463:55	independent h.	WORD 961:38
h. employed in work	STEU 849:60	I'll be h.	SHAK 771:39	In love, h. is abnormal	PROU 697:40
h. guiding where I stumble	SASS 746:98	we shall be h.	CROM 255:19	jealous possessions of h.	GIDE 367:21
h. his office on ourselves	MILT 606:65	hanging H. and marriage...go by destiny	FARQ 330:25	lifetime of the h.!	SHAW 807:13
h. of the enemy	ANON 27:20	H. and wiving goes by destiny	SHAK 769:96	lives in sin and looks for h.	BUNY 174:84
h. of the living God	BIBLE 129:38	h. for the colour that it is	HOUS 433:82	longing for h.	CAMUS 195:84
H. of the surgeon	MAP 569:40	H. is too good for him	BUNY 174:70	lost h. and lasting pain	MILT 601:34
h. of those who implement	SHUL 819:27	h. on with one hand	HYDE 443:19	magic lore of h.	RIMB 716:48
H. that led me to the limelight	HEAN 405:75	nane the waur o' a h.	MACQ 558:12	Man's h.	GIDE 368:94
h. themselves do reach	MARV 577:4	plain piece of work, a bare h.	DRYD 303:25	meaning...We can assign to h.	ELIOT 320:73
H. up! Don't shoot!	ANON 28:47	they're h. Danny Deever	KIPL 498:84	money does not bring h.	LACL 503:34
h. upon their hearts	HOUS 432:66	word got out about my h.	BUSH 183:45	nearly like h.	GREE 385:4
hath no h.?	BIBLE 109:88	hangman like having the h.	WALL 918:54	no h. within this circle of flesh	BROW 165:63
Hath not a Jew h., organs	SHAK 769:1	little h. dare not shoot	SHAK 774:43	no longer desire h.	SHAW 806:92
heart and h. and voices	WINK 950:98	naked to the h.'s noose	HOUS 431:37	not his own h.	SAINT 738:43
heavens are the work of thy h.	BIBLE 102:5	hangover a bad reputation is like a h.	PRES 694:75	Oh H.! our...end and aim!	POPE 687:87
his restless h.	PRIT 696:17	what a h. is like	KEIL 479:56	paint the memory of h.	SAIF 738:30
Holding the h. at midnight	GERS 365:79	hangs h. before her all the year	TENN 869:81	Perfect h., by princes sought	CHAP 214:17
h....that would light the world	MILL 593:94	hangups everybody else's h.	BRAU 157:84	private h. of the nation	JOHN 461:16
in his h. the print of the nails	BIBLE 124:67	hanky panky no h. in the Tardis	BAKER 56:99	procures the greatest h.	HUTC 441:49
Into thy h. I commend	BOOK 149:11	Hannibal how to gain a victory, H.	MARH 570:71	promised...either peace or h.	LEBON 517:55
keep my h. from picking	BOOK 148:79	Hanover By famous H. city	BROW 167:15	pursuit of h.	JEFF 453:19
knit h., and beat the ground	MILT 598:66	Hansard H. is history's ear	SAMU 741:99	pursuit of h.	STAN 842:12
language that...spits on its h.	SAND 742:31	happen Can't H. Here	LEWIS 527:62	science...can give no h.	POIN 683:96
large and sinewy h.	LONG 535:17	Can't is the cancer of h.	SHEEN 811:42	seemed to teach that h.	HARDY 397:13
License my roving h.	DONNE 291:20	even if it didn't h.	KESEY 483:63	seize more of h.	ANON 21:49
lift not h. of prayer	TENN 878:86	h. later to h.	NICH 636:74	Simply seek h.	PECK 672:64
made with our h.	SWIN 864:12	too much seems to h.	COUP 248:25	somebody else's h.	HUXL 441:52
man's fortune is in his own h.	BACON 52:24	Whatever must h. ultimately	KISS 494:95	so much h. is produced	JOHN 462:43
man's h. empty	WALC 916:46	what shouldn't h. doesn't h.	BLAIR 138:72	sorceress who dispenses h.	SCHI 747:23
murders sticking on his h.	SHAK 798:67	You think it will never h.	AUST 47:95	sound off about h.	ICHI 444:11
nearer than h. and feet	TENN 878:71	happened fact that it had h. elsewhere	FOWL 345:64	such a short-liv'd h.	BEHN 75:26
not into the h. of Spain	TENN 859:98	reminiscences of what never h.	SAKI 739:53	To dream is h.	HUGO 437:62
only one of the h. tends to get quoted	BLIN 142:54	'that h. to me!'	SEDA 755:97	too happy in thine h.	KEATS 478:41
prize-fighters shaking h.	MENC 586:97	happenings contempt of chance h.	RABE 704:20	Virtue is simply h.	BURR 181:69
puny h. Of heroes	COWP 251:20	happens not what h. to a man	HUXL 441:70	what is commonly called h.	SCHO 748:51
right h. of fellowship	BIBLE 127:78	When something h. to me	KENN 480:94	where...We find our h.	WORD 958:87
rise and shake h. with me	SPEKE 836:82	happier four times h. than the rest	RABE 704:19	white man's h.	DOUG 296:24
Rose-bloom fell on her h.	KEATS 477:21	member of the family...is h.	FALU 329:11	happy Adults talk about being h.	WINT 950:7
seem thus washing her h.	SHAK 798:64	happiest best and h. moments	SHEL 816:52	all be as h. as kings	STEV 853:70
Shake h. forever	DRAY 299:99	h. Africans in the world	SMITH 829:7	all the while I was quite h.	GIOV 372:17
shook h. with Reputation	WEBS 927:64	h. moment of the happy man	SCHO 749:57	all who are h.	JOHN 461:12
shook h. with time	FORD 343:2	H. when he is trying	LEHM 520:23	Anyone h. in this age	FULL 355:77
slipping from our h.	LOWE 540:36	h. women...have no history	ELIOT 315:35	bread-sauce of the h. ending	JAMES 450:48
Soon my h., on the sunken fosse	HEAN 404:71	happiness accustomed, in...h.	WHAR 933:6	conspiracy to make you h.	UPDI 906:24
soul clap its h.	YEATS 966:26	annual expenditure...result h.	DICK 280:43	die h.	FOX 346:70
Strength without h.	SWIN 863:86	banquet of h.	HUGO 437:63	difficult...to be h. with someone!	LABR 502:16
stretch forth thy h.	BIBLE 124:69	bat is a symbol of h.	LAWR 513:48	duty of being h.	STEV 852:51
such small h.	CUMM 258:61	beauty is a guarantee of h.	PROU 698:50	Eisenhower...makes people h.	WHITE 936:60
Take h. and dance there	BROW 168:38	beginnings of the people's h.	STRA 857:45	exist in order to be h.	SCHO 749:58
temples made with h.	BIBLE 125:92	best recipe for h.	AUST 46:68	feel really h.	KEIL 479:63
thin h. of the poor	WILDE 940:45	consume h. without producing it	SHAW 806:87	Forgive and be h.	PRAT 694:67
thought it out with both h.	SAYE 746:8	definition of h.	KENN 482:29	Getting up...does not make you h.	RABE 704:13
through most jewellers' h.	WEBS 926:42	does more for the h. of mankind	BRIL 159:18	happiest moment of the h. man	SCHO 749:57
tides of men into my h.	LAWR 514:88	dower Of inward h.	WORD 958:94	h. as the grass was green	THOM 883:17
toil of brain, or toil of h.	MELV 585:53	enemy to human h.	JOHN 464:85	H. Days are Here Again	YELL 967:43
washed his h. before the multitude	BIBLE 119:45	envy no man's h.	SHAK 779:89	h. families resemble each other	TOLS 894:51
washes his h.	SHAK 771:44	full measure of h.	OBAMA 644:32	H., h., h., pair!	DRYD 303:28
wash your h. and pray	KIPL 493:69	Greatest H. Principle	MILL 591:8	h....is not a characteristic	CHAN 214:4
what h. you would hold!	LAMB 505:7	greatest obstacle to h.	FONT 342:77	H. is the country	AGATE 9:88
will these h. ne'er be clean?	SHAK 798:66	H. consists in the multiplicity	JOHN 461:12	H. is the man	BIBLE 103:37
with crooked h.	TENN 875:4	H. engulfs our strength	BALZ 60:95	H. is the man	BIBLE 133:34
with h. blood stained	ORTE 652:2	h. ever been the subject of fiction?	UPDI 906:40	H. is the man	BIBLE 104:55
work of his h.	LOCKE 533:86	H. in marriage	AUST 45:55	H. is the man that findeth wisdom	BIBLE 104:55
work with your own h.	BIBLE 128:14	H. is always a work of art	YOUR 968:57	h. land	GOLD 376:7
world's great h.	HUNT 439:23	h. is assured	BIER 134:79	H....like Ulysses	BELL 76:44
wringing their h.	WALP 919:82	H. is full of strife	ANOU 28:64	h. man inevitably confines	HAWT 402:11
handsaw know a hawk from a h.	SHAK 782:93	H. is healthy for the body	PROU 698:58	h. much of the time	PECK 672:64
handsome as h. as my sister	KING 488:51	H. is like coke	HUXL 441:67	H. those early days	VAUG 909:34
Looks h. in three hundred pounds	SHAK 773:10	H. is no laughing matter	WHAT 934:16	h. through science	POIN 683:96
once h. and tall as you	ELIOT 318:7	H. is pretty simple	BROWN 164:39	H. till I woke again	HOUS 432:59
present fashion is always h.	FULL 356:87	H. lies in conquering one's enemies	GENG 363:43	h. time when one is in misery	DANTE 262:38
handy-dandy change...and h.-d.	SHAK 793:24	H. Makes up in Height	FROST 353:14	h....we are not over-h.	SHAK 782:83
hang all h. together	FRAN 348:17	H. mankind can gain	DRYD 299:14	h. who have called thee so	SOUT 835:51
as much as the half of a h.	OBRU 646:75	h. of an individual	JOHN 462:24	have been very h.	ATTL 40:27
cowslips wan that h.	MILT 599:91	h. of finding a companion	BERN 86:73	How h. I could be	GAY 362:22

Happy Isles

human race was most h.	GIBB 366:90	h. limped trembling	KEATS 477:14	**Harrovian** H. pricks up his ears	ANON 23:89
if life is…h.	LABR 502:20	o'er the timid h.!	THOM 887:2	**Harrow** H. would not be ashamed	BALD 57:36
If the prisoner is h.	SHAW 808:33	start a h.!	SHAK 771:36	**harrow** beneath the h. knows	KIPL 489:68
If you are as h.	BUCH 171:29	**hare-bells** heath and h.-b.	BRON 162:82	H. the house of the dead	AUDEN 42:66
in nothing else so h.	SHAK 764:45	**hare-brained** every h.-b. nut	SAFER 737:16	h. up thy soul	SHAK 781:60
I've had a h. life	HAZL 404:53	**harem** like eunuchs in a h.	BEHAN 74:12	**Harry** Banish not…H.'s company	SHAK 771:48
I were but little h.	SHAK 774:30	**hares** h. have no time to read	BROO 163:4	England breed again…a King H.?	DRAY 298:95
keep me h. all the day	STEV 853:68	little hunted h.	HODG 421:23	grunted H. to Jack	SASS 745:86
Let us all be h.	WARD 920:1	**hark** H.! ah, the Nightingale!	ARNO 34:84	Know what I mean, H.?	BRUNO 170:95
look these h. couples	STEV 852:35	H., h., the lark	SHAK 803:93	little touch of H.	SHAK 775:79
make men h.	POPE 688:22	H.! how all the welkin rings	WESL 931:58	**Harry Potter** an eighth H. P. book	RADC 704:32
Marriages would…be as h.	JOHN 462:44	H. in thine ear	SHAK 793:24	**harsh** seem h., impertinent	JONS 467:61
no h. end to it	HEMI 409:72	**Harlem** like…a son of H.	OBRI 645:62	**harshness** h. which resides in your heart	LABE 501:1
none should be h.	JOHN 463:50	**harlot** h.'s cheek	SHAK 782:6	no h. gives offence	POPE 685:24
no one can be perfectly h.	SPEN 836:84	h.'s cry from street	BLAKE 141:28	**Hart** one H. that you will not leave	HART 399:64
nor as h. as one hopes	LARO 510:2	he that cleaveth to h.	BIBLE 113:98	**hart** As the h. panteth	BIBLE 100:63
not a h. one	GILB 368:42	Portia is Brutus' h.	SHAK 777:18	**Harvard** chair at H. or Princeton	MENC 586:89
not a h. prospect	THOM 887:91	prerogative of the h.	BALD 57:30	didn't go to H.	JOHN 458:19
now to be most h.	SHAK 789:8	**harlots** Mother Of H.	BIBLE 132:17	glass flowers at H.	MOORE 617:79
one of those h. places	THOR 889:53	**Harlow** t is silent, as in H.	ASQU 38:92	graduate of H. or not	JOHN 458:27
one of those h. souls	SHEL 814:3	**harm** does h. to my wit	SHAK 785:83	H. education consists of what	CONA 239:11
one should feel h.	SARR 744:61	does men great h.	HESI 417:33	Yale College and my H.	MELV 585:57
only one thing to make me h.	HAZL 404:54	does no h.	GILM 371:97	**harvest** And it is h.	RANS 706:68
prevent me being h.	ANOU 28:61	don't think it does any h.	THOM 883:14	continual spring, and h.	SPEN 838:39
remote from the h..	AUDEN 43:1	Fate cannot h. me	SMITH 831:60	h. is past	BIBLE 110:17
shame…from being h.	LABR 502:25	fear we'll come to h.	BALL 59:70	h. of a quiet eye	WORD 957:68
so few h. marriages	ASTE 39:6	good provoke to h.	SHAK 788:73	laughs with a h.	JERR 455:46
so few marriages are h.	SWIFT 861:35	How can it h. you	CRUZ 256:38	Raymond like the H. Moon	FARJ 330:20
so h. as to sigh for	BEAU 70:12	in his sleep he does little h.	SHAK 791:69	seedtime and h.	BIBLE 92:11
So, I'm h. tonight	KING 487:35	may do great h.	SHAW 809:82	sheaves in h.	DONNE 293:72
someone, somewhere, may be h.	MENC 586:1	more h. than good	SNOW 832:85	When thou cuttest down thine h.	BIBLE 95:93
strangely h. with myself	IGNA 445:17	no h. to retool our imaginations	WELD 928:81	white already to h.	BIBLE 122:29
think themselves h.	BACON 51:86	Shall h. Macbeth	SHAK 797:55	**harvested** heart has been h.	BAUD 68:63
This is the h. warrior	READ 708:93	h. You do to others	WALK 917:42	**harvesting** h. from existence	NIET 638:97
thy h. strain?	SHEL 814:95	Whoop, do me no h., good man	SHAK 800:24	**harvests** bad h., and…fluctuations	ELIOT 315:31
too h. in thine happiness	KEATS 478:41	**harmful** may be more h.	HUXL 443:9	h. bury all his pride has planned	POPE 686:62
twentieth will be h.	HUGO 438:87	who say it is h.	CRUZ 256:40	**hash** product is a final h.	MELV 585:72
unfurnish'd Of falsehood to be h.	DRYD 301:59	**harming** perpetual h. of somebody	FORD 342:87	**hashish** puffed h.…didn't inhale	RICH 714:25
Was he h.?	AUDEN 43:86	**harmless** book is not h.	ELIOT 319:34	**hasta** H. la vista, baby	SCHW 750:86
When I am h. I live	SMITH 830:40	h. and even beneficial	SHAW 809:82	**haste** Do nothing in h.	WHYM 939:26
whether you are h. or not	SHAW 810:2	h. as doves	BIBLE 116:69	eat it in h.	BIBLE 93:59
Which of us is h.	THAC 880:30	**harmonies** European h.	GILL 370:87	h. now to my setting	SHAK 805:50
wretched…once to have been h.	BOET 144:92	h. are concealed from me	FISH 337:62	life and light, with envious h.	ROCH 720:25
Happy Isles touch the H. I.	TENN 871:2	h. of the body	BERN 86:74	make what h. I can to be gone	CROM 256:24
harbour a voyage and not a h.	TOYN 895:74	inventor of h.	TENN 877:63	Married in h.	CONG 240:30
h. and neighbour wood	THOM 883:20	tranquil h.	GAUG 361:1	marry in h.	CABE 191:3
h. without ships	DEFOE 269:78	tumult of thy mighty h.	SHEL 813:83	Men love in h.	BYRON 190:22
looking over h. and city	SAND 742:14	**harmony** All discord, h., not		repent in h.	CONG 240:31
O the H. of Fowey	QUIL 702:11	understood	POPE 687:79	send them out of the land in h.	BIBLE 93:61
rain over the dwindling h.	THOM 883:21	body's h.	POPE 689:42	shall not make h.	BIBLE 108:71
hard game is too h.	JAMES 449:21	h. comes…as a shock	RAINE 705:42	such h. to be doing	STEV 852:56
gave me the h. shoulder	HENRI 411:10	h.…comes to heal	WORD 956:51	**hasty** let not thine heart be h.	BIBLE 106:20
h. and practical man	HOYLE 434:95	h. for the honour of God	BACH 49:8	man is ever h.	KORAN 497:73
h. on His Majesty's Opposition	HOBH 420:6	H.! H.!	SCHO 748:48	need na start awa sae h.	BURNS 177:77
'H.,' replied the Dodger	DICK 278:67	h. In autumn	SHEL 812:57	**hasty-pudding** sweets of h.-p.	BARL 63:56
h. rhyme	SHAK 774:56	h. in discord	HORA 427:11	**hat** All h. and no cattle	CONN 242:82
H. times require furious dancing	WALK 917:43	h. or true delight?	MILT 605:39	as is the h. of a soldier	HERB 414:90
h. to be room-mates	SALI 740:76	immortal god of h.	BEET 74:1	Beneath her torn h.	WHIT 938:19
h. to be sought out	HERA 412:37	in h. with the sentiments of an assassin	BIER 134:59	can't think without his h.	BECK 72:40
It's supposed to be h.	HANKS 395:82	knew such h. alone	MILT 597:34	coat and top h.	LAVER 512:34
no success without h. work	SOPH 834:30	Like h. in music	WORD 958:76	fashion of his h.	SHAK 773:17
powerful h. thing	CONN 243:23	may we bring h.	THAT 881:54	from whose h.	KIPL 491:35
read very h.	JOHN 461:99	ninefold h.	MILT 597:35	get your h.	FIEL 335:28
Ruling is h.	MART 576:82	notions of law and h.	THOR 888:24	Hang my H. is Home	JERO 454:44
The woman is so h.	TENN 872:34	other h. of prose	DRYD 304:38	instinctively raise my h.	TREE 896:99
when the times were not h.	EMER 325:96	ravish like enchanting h.	SHAK 763:6	Irishman takes off his h.	SHAW 809:64
where a heart is h.	SHAK 762:86	Sentimentally…disposed to h.	LAMB 505:94	Mistook his Wife for a H.	SACKS 737:6
hardcover Europe…a h. book	DELI 271:37	that famous h.	YEATS 965:6	Mr Pickwick's h. rolled	DICK 277:47
harden H. not your heart	BIBLE 102:2	untaught h. of spring	GRAY 383:55	my knee, my h.	BROW 164:43
harder they would be h. to them	TROL 898:36	what hope of h.?	SHAK 759:86	No h. upon his head	SHAK 781:72
hardest h. thing to bear	JUVE 471:54	**harms** bars a thousand h.	SHAK 761:57	nothing so characteristic as its h.	HOLM 424:88
h. thing to do	HEMI 410:75	**harness** die in h.	AMIS 16:33	puttin' on my top h.	BERL 84:39
The h. negotiation	ADAMS 4:84	joints of the h.	BIBLE 97:70	Queen to get away with a h.	LOOS 536:49
hardhearted more cruel and h.	BACON 51:74	**Harold** a masseur called H.	WOOD 954:99	silk h. on a Bradford millionaire	ELIOT 318:4
hard-hearts nature…makes		**harp** h., his sole remaining joy	SCOTT 752:9	still in straw h. and sandals	BASHO 67:43
these h.-h.	SHAK 792:13	h. that once through	MOORE 618:4	stone in my straw h.	STEV 851:29
hardship experience nothing but h.	BELL 76:46	No h.…could so cheerily play	CAMP 194:60	Swept off his tall h.	GRAV 383:40
meet any h.	KENN 481:3	played everything but the h.	BARR 65:5	The Cat in the H.	SEUSS 758:38
teacheth him wholesome h.	LASS 510:12	wild h. slung behind	MOORE 618:2	The way you wear your h.	GERS 365:75
hardships disappointments, h.	PEARY 671:59	**Harper** H. smiled, well pleased	SCOTT 752:14	Under the black h.	HEMI 410:91
h. of an emigrant's life	MOOD 615:52	**harps** h. upon the willows	BIBLE 103:42	where he laid his h.	JOHN 464:87
very bottom of h.	DU 305:66	**harpstring** hair and h. of gold	SWIN 864:98	**hatches** h. and…Rain!	KEATS 476:81
hard working it's h. w.—and that's me	KOCH 495:25	**harpy** conference with this h.	SHAK 774:28	**hatchet** with my little h.	WASH 921:24
Hardy either 29 or Thomas H.	PARK 664:30	**harried** h. man I think I be!	BALL 59:64	**hate** All men h. the wretched	SHEL 812:48
Kiss me, H.	NELS 633:15	**Harris** the present Mrs H.	THUR 890:64	an act of h.	BLANC 141:45
hare covers…the h. and the hunter	PATC 668:6	**Harrison** if Rex H. doesn't	GRANT 381:98	as though h. has no cost	SAND 742:25
grass, and a h. sitting up?	LAWR 513:47	to see…H. hanged	PEPYS 673:87	Boys' h. was dangerous	MUNRO 625:47

head

crops of love and h.	MUIR 624:24	h. is not…mere crabbedness	FADI 329:7	chicken whose h. has	MITF 610:58
deadly h. have pierced so deep	MILT 604:94	h. of progress and civilization	ATAT 40:13	curses heaped on each gashed h.?	SORL 834:33
do good to them that h. you	BIBLE 115:37	H. of the bourgeois	FLAU 339:24	curses on my h.?	MILT 607:75
Each sequestered in its h.	AUDEN 43:93	h….the longest pleasure	BYRON 190:22	Cut Scandal's h. off	SHER 817:86
even the h. of sins	SURR 860:2	heartbreak, h. blind	NOON 641:50	cuts off his h.	SHAW 807:97
Families! I h. you!	GIDE 367:21	Ideas are born from h.	GENET 363:41	dusty thudding in his h.	AMIS 16:29
fear to h.	SHAK 765:59	love to h. turned	CONG 241:52	each wat'ry h.	BYRON 187:33
five guys who h. you	STEN 847:7	no h. or bitterness towards anyone	CAVE 210:19	eye in th. h. of a poet	WELL 929:94
free to love or h.	SART 744:64	people…have…in common…h. and		face for turning its h.	LEAC 515:6
glance of supernatural h.	BYRON 190:32	humour	PRYOR 699:63	Fan her h.	CARR 205:24
God…spilled his own h.	BURG 174:99	sport…is…bound up with h.	ORWE 655:81	from h. to foot	TENN 874:66
h. a fellow whom pride	JOHN 464:84	stalled ox and h. therewith	BIBLE 104:75	from h. to foot	TENN 876:23
h. all that don't love me	FARQ 330:23	Where there is h.	FRAN 347:99	from his h. to his foot	MOORE 616:64
h. all the people	HAMM 395:67	hatreds systematic organization of h.	ADAMS 5:86	From the crown of his h.	SHAK 774:42
h. American simplicity	JAMES 451:57	hats h., as in Victorian days	SITW 824:12	frost which binds so dear a h.!	SHEL 815:27
h. and character assassination	SMITH 829:27	offensive h., defensive h.	WHIT 936:74	get his h. kicked off	KHRU 485:95
h. and death	SHEL 816:58	other one's h.	LINK 530:28	get it through his h.	TRUM 900:89
h. being told How It Is	GALL 358:43	hatter mad as a h.	ELIOT 319:52	get one's h. cut off	CARR 205:2
h. discussions of feminism	FREN 350:52	haughtily h. he lifts his nose	SWIFT 862:52	good grey h.	TENN 875:7
h. in a woman	SHAW 807:5	haughtiness h. of soul	ADDI 7:46	Go up, thou bald h.	BIBLE 97:73
H. is always more clairvoyant	LACL 503:36	haughty Children are h., disdainful	LABR 502:23	hair of thy h.	STER 848:31
h. is hardly to be hidden	CARL 199:72	h. scorn which mocked the smart	ARNO 35:5	hang his h., and view the lazy tide	CRAB 252:42
h. liberality	SIDM 819:33	haunches on silent h.	SAND 742:14	h., and the heart	RUSK 733:92
h. me as much as you love me	BECK 72:54	haunt exempt from public h.	SHAK 778:66	h. belongs to a body	ROSSO 727:68
h. that which we often fear	SHAK 794:48	favourite h.	TOLK 893:47	h. bit off	SHAK 792:92
h. the idea of causes	FORS 345:46	My h….my song	WORD 961:35	h. drooping as he increased	WHITE 935:50
h. them if I can	ANON 20:23	haunting-look h.-l. to me	CONG 240:41	h. fantastically carved upon it	SHAK 772:90
h. the one, and love the other	BIBLE 115:44	haunts h. of coot and hern	TENN 876:37	h. for high politics	MERE 588:40
h. walking	SMOL 831:67	h….where the dead walls rear	BYRON 188:65	h. grown grey in vain	SHEL 815:40
h. with greater devotion	SHAK 799:94	haute h. couture is one of the last	DIOR 287:4	h. is as full of quarrels	SHAK 766:93
haughty Juno's unrelenting h.	DRYD 304:37	Havana H., Cuba…high society	CABR 191:8	h. is bloody but unbowed	HENL 411:5
have I not reason to h.	HAZL 404:50	Our man in H.	GREE 386:13	h. is not more native	SHAK 780:31
h….Iberian peninsula has inspired	BOLI 145:9	have Be thankful for what you h.	WINF 950:96	h. is not oval but round	NABO 628:18
how I h. you!	RIMB 715:43	To h. and to hold	BOOK 148:91	h….little use without my shoulders	CARR 203:62
how many people h. me	BAN 62:36	haven h. from sophistications	POUND 691:8	h….of myself	DEKK 270:15
h….pain accompanied by the idea	SPIN 840:77	h. under the hill	TENN 871:4	h. of the human infant	SCHR 749:66
I h. and I love.	CATU 209:11	inviolate h.	ROTH 728:91	h. of the Protestant interest	WILL 944:67
implacable in h.	DRYD 302:74	safe h. from commercial	SAFER 737:16	h. of your lov'd Lycidas?	MILT 599:85
know enough of h.	FROST 352:4	Safe into the h. guide	WESL 931:59	h. she bowed, Stooping	MILT 598:53
let him h. you through the glass	BLUN 143:76	havens in the h. dumb	HOPK 428:65	heap coals of fire upon his h.	BIBLE 105:95
Let them h.	ACCI 2:18	haves H. and the Havenots	CERV 231:41	Heaven's splendour over his h.	CARL 201:36
love and h….are necessary	BLAKE 139:94	h. of give	CUMM 258:64	Here rest his h.	GRAY 384:77
murd'rous h.	SHAK 800:35	havoc Cry 'h.!'	SHAK 777:34	hings his h.	BURNS 180:52
never h. a song	BERL 84:43	Strokes of h. unselve	HOPK 428:79	his h. be empty	SWIFT 861:21
not to h. him now	RACI 704:26	what h. must we make?	HUME 438:7	hold in one's h.	ORWE 655:82
not to weep…nor to h. them	SPIN 840:69	Hawaii instead of the H. air route	ROCK 720:36	hold my lady's h.	HEAN 404:71
Of guile, of h., of envy	MILT 606:48	hawk bold as a h.	THUR 890:75	Hold your h. up high	HAMM 394:65
or in h.	STEV 852:35	h. encumbered with his hood	BYRON 189:89	House of Lords in his own h.	LLOY 533:78
owe no man h.	SHAK 779:89	h., his hound, and his lady fair	BALL 59:77	How shall your houseless h.	SHAK 792:11
People must learn to h.	MAND 565:56	h. of the tower	SKEL 824:29	If you can keep your h.	KIPL 492:62
Politicians neither love nor h.	DRYD 302:76	h. remembers him	JEFF 453:15	I'll eat my h.	DICK 278:69
power to love, or h.	MARL 574:37	kill a man than a h.	JEFF 453:16	impulsive gravity of h.	POPE 688:37
religion to make us h.	SWIFT 861:31	know a h. from a handsaw	SHAK 782:93	Israel's h. forlorn	LAZA 515:4
scarcely h. any one	HAZL 403:39	managed h.	SCOTT 753:46	Jezebel…tired her h.	BIBLE 97:78
study of revenge, immortal h.	MILT 602:38	hawkish don't consider myself h.	SCHW 750:90	just come into my h.	LEAR 516:34
Take away this murtherin' h.	OCAS 646:77	hawks h. will stoop to lure	KYD 501:47	knocking your h. against a fact	HUXL 443:12
they all do h. him	SHAK 804:23	hawthorn h. bush a sweeter shade	SHAK 760:10	lain Under my h.	MILL 592:23
time to h.	BIBLE 106:14	when h. buds appear	SHAK 766:18	Lay your sleeping h.	AUDEN 43:95
what I h. myself most	LEAV 517:54	hay drain him dry as h.	SHAK 795:1	learned lumbers in his h.	POPE 685:27
women highly hold in h.	SHAK 759:69	Good h., sweet hay	SHAK 767:41	letting my h. go round	HERZ 416:22
worst sin…is not to h.	SHAW 807:98	live on h.	HILL 418:56	lifted up his h. a little	THAC 880:39
hated h. iniquity	GREG 387:51	mowers in the h.	MUIR 624:16	lighted rooms Inside your h.	LARK 510:92
loved well because he h.	BROW 168:53	muir-men win their h.	BALL 58:51	like a dropsical h.	SMOL 831:68
never h. a man	GABOR 356:3	hay-harvest h.-h. breeze	CORY 247:12	man of your h. and hair	JONS 467:62
never more h.	ELLI 323:36	haystack search a h. for a needle	JACK 449:8	mechanical in h.	CARL 200:82
Or being h.	KIPL 492:62	hazard all is on the h.	SHAK 778:52	monstrous h. and sickening cry	CHES 220:50
Vice…to be h.	POPE 687:82	father's crown into the h.	SHAK 775:62	murderous angels in his h.	DEVL 275:8
hateful h. heresies	SPEN 839:42	h. of the die	SHAK 761:56	my h. is a map	FIEL 335:18
more h. form of foolery	BROW 169:68	hazards two occupational h.	CRIT 255:10	No hat upon his h.	SHAK 781:72
my doors are h.	OTWAY 656:99	hazelnut chariot is an empty h.	SHAK 765:71	normal humble h.	HERB 414:90
The self is h.	PASC 667:82	Hazlitt ape to H., to Lamb	STEV 853:77	nowhere yet to rest my h.	ARNO 35:4
hater join the h.	GORD 378:54	we cannot write like H.	STEV 852:55	off the top of your h.	NEW 634:35
hates h. children and dogs	FIEL 335:35	head aircraft slope above his h.	FULL 355:75	Off with her h.!	CARR 203:73
h. them for it	SHAW 806:82	and hidden her h.	SWIN 864:1	Off with his h.	SHAK 761:43
Nothing h. him more or envies him	FAUL 331:44	anointest my h. with oil	BIBLE 100:45	one small h. could carry all	GOLD 376:2
hating Loving not, h. not	BROW 169:66	an unusually large-sized h.	MOORE 617:94	On my defenceless h.	MILT 606:63
hatless H., I take off	LARK 509:77	apples drop about my h.	MARV 577:4	on my h. be it	BALC 56:12
hatred all your h. now on me?	SHAK 761:82	At his h. a grass-green turf	SHAK 784:46	Orion standing on his h.	LAWR 513:56
common h. of its neighbours	INGE 445:30	At the h. of the Government	PETA 675:36	ostrich, with its h. in the sand	WILS 949:80
'ergophobia', meaning 'fear or h. of		Blood and revenge…in my h.	SHAK 760:23	over h. and ears in it	STER 848:41
work'	TYNAN 904:2	blood from h. to foot	MACL 554:27	painting in which the h.	MOTH 622:86
From envy, h., and malice	BOOK 146:47	bloody ice on bloody h.	BLAIR 138:48	parboiled h. upon a stake	MONT 615:51
frown of h.	BYRON 188:75	book and a h. collide	LICH 528:87	pensive h.	MILT 599:91
h. for the Tory Party	BEVAN 89:53	brains go to his h.	ASQU 38:91	perishing never entered my h.	DOUG 294:98
H. is always a sin	MUNRO 625:51	bullet through his h.	ROBI 718:82	pops its h. into the shop	FOOTE 342:83
h. is a tonic	BALZ 60:96	busk my h.	BALL 60:79	precious jewel in his h.	SHAK 778:65
H. is generalized	DUDEK 305:79	but for your good h.	ELIZ 322:5	punching people in the h.	LEON 522:65

headache

put things out of his h. — CARY 207:63
Raindrops Keep Fallin' on my H. — DAVID 264:63
raise his fiery h. — WILL 946:26
repairs his drooping h. — MILT 600:94
room at your h. — BALL 58:57
roses at my h. — ROSS 726:46
round my fallen h. — TENN 873:53
Say nowt...talk your h. off — CLOU 232:69
Scotch tongue in your h. — SCOTT 754:61
Scratched his h. — ROBI 718:86
sever h. from body — WEBS 926:27
sex rears its ugly h. — ALLI 14:5
shall bruise thy h. — BIBLE 91:96
sharp tongue in your h. — PERE 674:20
Shoot...this old grey h. — WHIT 938:23
should have his h. examined — GOLD 377:26
singing about her h. — GRAV 383:40
smote off his h. — BIBLE 95:12
Socialist after he is forty...no h. — WILL 947:33
so much music in my h. — RAVEL 707:83
such a h. of hair — HOUS 433:82
suddenly bowed his h. — JOYCE 470:20
their h. the prow — DRYD 299:15
thou hast anointed my h. with oil — BOOK 149:10
through the h. down to the feet — ANGE 19:90
throw earth over your h. — PASC 667:77
Thy h., thy sovereign — SHAK 762:78
Tomorrow's vengeance on the h. — SHAK 761:52
tremendous world in my h. — HEWE 417:37
tumble h. over heels — KING 488:52
turns no more his h. — COLE 235:8
two ideas in her h. — LINK 530:28
under his h. — YEATS 967:37
Uneasy lies the h. — SHAK 772:85
Upon his own rebellious h. — MILT 603:77
violet's reclining h. — DONNE 292:41
we as h., and you as members — HENR 411:13
wheels go over my h. — TENN 876:30
where to lay his h. — BIBLE 116:59
Whose h. proud fancy never taught — CRAB 251:24
with your 'ayrick h. of 'air — KIPL 489:89
Words the h. does not shape — ANON 21:58
would shake his h. and say — LEAC 515:18
you incessantly stand on your h. — CARR 203:66
headache dismal h. — GILB 369:54
headaches problems...We call them h. — ACHE 3:45
sex is good for h. — WILB 939:42
headgear h. worn by the...world — ATAT 40:13
heading h. into nut country — KENN 482:30
headland All night, this h. — WILB 939:40
some bold h. — WORD 961:36
headlines H. pass — SKEL 825:38
newspaper needs...in its h. — PULI 699:72
headlong H. themselves they threw — MILT 605:26
h., wild uncertain thee? — DONNE 290:12
sons Hurled h. — MILT 602:64
headmistress h. of a certain age — JAMES 450:26
headpiece H. filled with straw — ELIOT 318:13
headpieces h. stuffed with straw — MACD 550:39
heads calling h. that God exists — PASC 667:78
can't mess with people's h. — HEND 411:4
carve h. upon cherry-stones — JOHN 464:92
cut off the h. of people — PEPYS 674:3
egg h. in one basket — ANON 25:47
goes to the h. of cowards — MITC 610:24
hardly miss their h. — SHAW 810:20
h. are green — LEAR 516:31
h....beneath their shoulders — SHAK 788:93
H., h.—take care of your h. — DICK 277:42
h. pass out — BERR 87:96
h. replete with thoughts — COWP 251:21
hover in their restless h. — MARL 572:2
Hung their h. — SHAK 804:45
keep their own h. — MUMF 625:39
lose their h. — FITZ 338:92
old h. on your young shoulders — SPARK 836:67
Reared...their flourished h. — MILT 604:8
sugarplums danced in their h. — MOORE 616:61
tall men had ever very empty h. — BACON 50:53
Tossing their h. — WORD 960:25
vulgar h. that look asquint — BROW 164:44
with h. on their shoulders — JAMES 452:77
wooden h. may be [inherited] — CONK 242:79
write plays in our h. — MAMET 564:43
headstone h. s. of the corner — BIBLE 102:22
headstones H. stagger — BERR 87:96
h. yield their names — TATE 867:38

milestones into h. — LOWE 539:16
headstrong h., moody, murmuring — DRYD 301:67
headway women...make some h. — FALU 329:12
heal balm to h. their wounds — SHAK 760:16
fame can never h. — AYTO 48:13
Physician, h. thyself — BIBLE 120:72
time to h. — BIBLE 105:14
What wound did ever h. — SHAK 789:15
healed h. by the same means — SHAK 769:1
with his stripes we are h. — BIBLE 109:94
healer compassion of the h.'s art — ELIOT 320:62
time is no h. — ELIOT 320:75
healing h. in his wings — BIBLE 112:65
leaves of the tree...h. of the nations — BIBLE 132:28
not heroics but h. — HARD 396:94
of the most High cometh h. — BIBLE 113:8
health Christian that is in h. — LAW 512:37
disliked hearing about h. — MITF 610:52
Drink a h. to — SYNGE 865:23
drink his h. with three cheers — EDGE 311:36
good to preserve the h. of Man — BYRD 186:21
great deal better for the h. — STEV 851:23
H. and an able body — FLET 341:59
h. and plenty cheered — GOLD 376:96
h. of his wife — CONN 243:14
H., Wealth, Love...and Time — ANON 28:57
His h., his honour — BLUN 143:79
hunt in fields, for h. — DRYD 304:48
implies an idea of h. — TRIL 897:14
in h. wes and gladnes — DUNB 306:3
in sickness and in h. — BOOK 148:89
in sickness and in h. — BOOK 148:90
in sickness and in h. — BOOK 148:91
interest of good h. — TAFT 866:11
lack of h. in the body — PLATO 681:50
no h. in us — BOOK 146:32
nor hope nor h. — SHEL 812:68
Only do always in h. — SIGI 821:63
people in the soundest h. — DICK 282:92
preservation of h. — SPEN 836:86
psychological h. — PECK 672:65
save men of indifferent h. — DOUG 295:12
saving h. among all nations — BIBLE 101:80
Say that h. and wealth — HUNT 440:30
simple beauty and rustic h. — WHIT 938:19
spirit of h. — SHAK 781:57
When you have both it's h. — DONL 290:8
healths drink one another's h. — JERO 454:37
healthy classical period was h. — GOET 375:68
Happiness is h. for the body — PROU 698:58
If you are h. — FORD 343:97
makes a male h. — THUR 890:74
heap all is a knot, a h. — JONS 468:97
dig and h. — ARNO 34:76
garbage h. — GARD 360:71
H. high the...platter — MACB 546:64
rude h. together hurl'd — MARV 578:9
heaped H. for two days — KHAY 485:86
hear can't h. what they say? — SMITH 829:17
Come on and h. — BERL 84:36
deaf to h. — BIBLE 119:57
Do not let me h. — ELIOT 320:60
ears to h., let him h. — BIBLE 119:53
ears to h., let him h. — BIBLE 116:78
h. it through their feet — SOUSA 834:39
H., O Israel — BIBLE 95:88
h. the soft rain — RICK 715:27
If you really want to h. — SALI 739:71
I h. you, I will come — HOUS 431:45
I shall h. in heaven — BEET 74:6
It startled him just to h. — RAMOS 705:50
much to h. and see — SKEL 824:27
neither see nor h. — JOHN 459:33
one you cannot h. — NORTH 641:60
power...to make you h. — CONR 243:26
public only gets to h. — STEIN 845:78
something we cannot h. — SCOTT 751:3
then not h. it crying! — HERB 414:79
unto you that h. shall more be given — BIBLE 119:54
what they h., they repeat! — SITW 823:2
what they wanted to h. — SHAR 806:76
heard Ain't H. Nothin' Yet — JOLS 465:13
every man that h. him — JONS 468:92
fall of...civilization will not be h. — READ 708:91
generally h. — GILB 370:69
have ye not h.? — BIBLE 109:84
I h. no longer — TENN 876:19

My God, I h. this day — HERB 413:69
never have been h. of — HAZL 404:49
Oon ere it h. — CHAU 216:64
the more h. — WILD 943:52
We had h. them — HEMI 409:64
hearers Be ye doers...not h. only — BIBLE 130:50
maiming it to suit her h. — BACON 53:54
move h. to h. — FRAS 349:32
too deep for his h. — GOLD 377:17
hearing Fall asleep, or h. die — SHAK 804:47
mentioned in your h. — AUST 46:62
hearings h. are just like a s. — NIXON 640:30
h. will be remembered — INOU 446:50
hearse h. presently arrived — LAWS 514:95
h. where Lycid lies — MILT 599:91
In an h. she rode — SMART 826:59
laid in doleful h.? — SPEN 838:37
Why does a h. horse snicker — SAND 742:19
heart A broken h. — SEDA 755:94
abundance of the h. — BIBLE 117:85
actor in his h. believes — WELL 929:97
a different part of your h. — AMIS 17:62
adultery with her already in his h. — BIBLE 114:33
affectations rise up in his h. — DIDE 285:78
after Heaven's own h. — DRYD 301:64
after leaving my h. on the screen — QUIR 703:27
age should show your h. — MARV 577:91
always knew in my h. — HOPK 429:98
Ancient person of my h. — ROCH 720:26
and the h. is sick — TENN 874:74
artists try to break your h. — RAUS 707:81
as the h. grows older — HOPK 428:81
As well as want of h.! — HOOD 426:35
At h. I knew — THES 882:96
a trickling of h. — PATC 668:6
Batter my h. — DONNE 292:54
beak from out my h. — POE 683:88
beanbag of a h. — NOON 640:45
Because it is my H. — OATES 643:10
bind the h. of man! — GILM 371:95
bitter...because it is my h. — CRANE 253:72
Blessed are the pure in h. — WHAR 934:13
blue and white Wednesday h. — HATT 400:82
books are novels at h. — RABAN 703:3
breaks the h. — MACD 549:38
broken and a contrite h. — BIBLE 101:74
broken h. lies here — MACA 546:54
bullet through his h. — THAC 880:26
Bury my h. at Wounded Knee — BENET 79:26
'Calais' lying in my h. — MARY 580:40
Calls my h. to be his own — BRID 158:9
calm sunshine of the h. — CONS 244:58
captain's h. — SHAK 793:41
carried in the h. of none — KISS 493:88
cathedrals in my h. — SASS 745:88
change of h. — AUDEN 42:66
Christ in the h. — PATR 670:29
Cloe...wants a h. — POPE 688:11
commune with your own h. — BIBLE 99:29
conversant with a Man's h. — POE 683:87
corrupt the h. — BYRON 187:28
Create in me a clean h. — BIBLE 101:73
cry of Absence...in the h. — RANS 707:70
dagger...in the h. of France — QUIN 703:23
darkness of man's h. — GOLD 375:74
Dead H. of Australia — GREG 387:53
depths of every h. — HAWT 402:12
deserts of the h. — AUDEN 43:94
desires of the h. — AUDEN 42:77
desperateness of man's h.! — BUNY 173:72
dialogues with my Mother's h. — WORD 958:81
Did not our h. burn — BIBLE 122:13
directly to the h. — POE 683:84
Don't search...for my h. — BAUD 68:64
dried up your h. — FLAU 339:12
drink thy wine with a merry h. — BIBLE 106:27
ease a h. Like a satin gown — PARK 663:69
entered into my h. — HOLM 423:55
Enter every trembling h. — WESL 932:62
every Russian's inmost h. — PUSH 700:88
fade from my h. — MOORE 617:99
false h. doth know — SHAK 796:25
Fare thee well, great h. — SHAK 772:67
feed on him in thy h. — BOOK 147:73
felt my h. strangely warmed — WESL 932:65
figure of my h. — SHAK 788:82
finite number of h.-beats — ARMS 33:52

heart

flesh and my h. faileth	BIBLE 101:86	h. shall not fear	BIBLE 100:50	man after his own h.	BIBLE 96:32
fop in my h.	ETHE 327:48	h.'s in the Highlands	BURNS 179:15	man's h. is small	KIPL 491:47
for such a kind h.	SHAK 773:11	h.'s so full of joy	DRYD 301:54	man with h., head, hand	TENN 876:20
foul…shop of the h.	YEATS 967:36	h.'s stalled motor	MAYA 583:23	mean to a tired h.	BOND 145:17
free, the larger h.	TENN 875:96	h.…that of a little child	THAC 880:39	mechanical in…h.	CARL 200:82
from my h. the strings do break	CAMP 195:73	h. that swells	DRYD 301:56	meek and lowly in h.	BIBLE 116:81
full h. Remains in use	SHAK 794:50	h. that watches and receives	WORD 957:59	Mercy has a human h.	BLAKE 139:88
funeral marches around your h.	MILL 593:35	h. that with every year grows dim	CONR 244:36	merry h. doeth good	BIBLE 105:82
gambled my h. and lost	RIVE 716:55	h. the keener	ANON 20:36	merry h. goes all the day	SHAK 799:16
gay clothes, a merry h.	WEBS 926:29	h. untravelled	GOLD 376:85	merry h. maketh a cheerful	BIBLE 104:74
give thee the desires of thine h.	BIBLE 100:58	h. was free	WESL 931:57	merry h. with small possessioun	HENR 411:20
give them an h. of flesh	BIBLE 110:30	h. was glad	FOX 346:71	mind and in the h.	LARO 510:6
give them one h.	BIBLE 110:30	h. was one of those	BYRON 189:86	mind, h.…not myself	WELTY 930:46
giving your h. to a dog	KIPL 492:60	h. was to thy rudder	SHAK 794:68	more native to the h.	SHAK 780:31
glad with all my h.	DRAY 299:99	h. was used to beat	TENN 873:62	mother's h. is an abyss	BALZ 61:2
great flint…singing into his h.	BIRN 136:19	h. which beats only for you	VERL 911:58	much against my h.	PATM 669:20
grief of h.	SHAK 804:45	h. why do you pound	APOL 29:77	much it grieved my h.	WORD 957:61
grief of h.	SHAK 804:47	h. will break in twa	NAIR 629:34	Must my h. grow sick	CULL 257:46
Guilt in his h.	CHUR 224:52	h.…with thy nest	WORD 961:44	My h. has made its mind up	COPE 246:95
Harden not your h.	BIBLE 102:2	h. with usury to such scenes?	LAMB 505:79	my h. is a handful of dust	TENN 876:30
harshness which resides in your h.	LABE 501:1	heaven-entreated h.	CRAS 254:82	my h. is glad	ANON 22:72
has ached with a h.!	SWIN 864:93	heavenly and hidden h.	BUEC 172:42	My h. leaps up	WORD 959:98
haven't he h.	GRAH 380:97	hedgehog of the h.	LOWE 541:34	my h. remembers how!	STEV 854:87
haven't the h. to take a minute	CARA 198:35	His flawed h.	SHAK 793:36	My h. would hear her	TENN 876:28
have the h. to stay	BUTL 185:87	history…begins in the h.	CATH 208:84	my old bitter h.	ORAH 652:91
h. aches	KEATS 478:41	holiness of the h.'s affections	KEATS 475:73	nation…had the lion h.	CHUR 226:12
h., all mad with misery	SHAK 760:26	Hope deferred maketh the h. sick	BIBLE 104:68	naughtiness of thine h.	BIBLE 96:36
h. and core of ages	LOWE 539:96	How irksome…to my h.!	SHAK 759:86	nearly breaks my h.	JERO 454:40
h. and mind of America	BARZ 67:40	human h. is slightly left of centre	FRYE 354:58	no iron can stab the h.	BABEL 48:3
h. and my flesh crieth out	BIBLE 101:88	humble and a contrite h.	KIPL 490:16	No nearer the h. than the lip	ANON 21:58
h. and stomach of a king	ELIZ 321:4	hurt you to the h.	TWAIN 903:83	No pitying h.	GRAY 385:85
h. as big as Waterloo Station	AGATE 9:91	index to the h.	DICK 279:17	not in the h. or in the saliva	ARGU 31:12
h. as sound as a bell	SHAK 774:43	indurate h. against God	KNOX 495:15	not my h.	JONS 467:60
h. be full of the spring?	SWIN 863:79	in his painted h.	KEATS 477:18	not really bad at h.	BELL 77:64
h. blackening	JEFF 453:12	in his private h.	TWAIN 903:80	not wear your h. on your sleeve	WEBS 927:65
h. bleeds for his country	JOHN 461:90	In its secret h.	SMITH 831:64	not your h. away	HOUS 431:38
h. broken even more surely	LESS 524:2	in my h. his iron arrow	SPEN 838:26	ocean or the human h.?	LAUT 511:26
h. but one	BOUR 153:94	In my h.'s core	SHAK 783:22	oft…my h. to ache	BLAKE 141:39
h. dies within me	SCHAW 747:20	in our h. we know	WORD 960:14	O my little h.!	SHAK 763:9
h. distrusting asks	GOLD 376:3	Into my h. an air	HOUS 431:51	one body and one h.	DOUG 295:4
h. either breaks or boldens	BALZ 60:94	into the bell of her h.	THOM 884:40	Only with the h.	SAINT 738:37
h. enough to begin to live	STEV 852:53	into the h. of man	SWIFT 862:47	open a window into one's h.	MELBA 584:44
h. grown cold	SHEL 815:40	into the world with your h.	SHEL 812:50	Open not thine h.	BIBLE 113:87
h. has been harvested	BAUD 68:63	In your h.	GOLD 377:21	opens the h. and lungs	STER 848:38
h. has its reasons	PASC 667:80	Irishman's h. is nothing	SHAW 809:63	Open your h.	BROW 168:47
h. hath ne'er within him burned	SCOTT 752:16	Is your h. at rest?	FLET 341:61	O pure of h.	COLE 235:31
h. in a case o' gowd	BALL 60:80	Keep the free h.	CRAS 254:84	O tiger's h.	SHAK 760:3
h. in hiding	HOPK 428:77	kid…about her h. condition?	SILV 821:71	Out-worn h.	YEATS 965:9
h. in's face	SHAK 799:11	king's h. is in the hand	BIBLE 105:86	own the h. and stool	COLUM 238:90
h. into my mouth	SHAK 791:84	know in my h. of h.s	STARK 843:22	pageant of his bleeding h.	ARNO 35:5
H. Is A Lonely Hunter	MCCU 549:12	knowledge of the h.	JOHN 462:5	passionate h. of the poet	TENN 875:15
H. Is A Lonely Hunter	SHARP 806:70	know my h.	BIBLE 104:46	Pass on, weak h.	TENN 873:53
h. is deceitful	BIBLE 110:20	know not the h.	SHAK 800:43	Pitee…in gentil h.	CHAU 217:83
h. is Highland	GALT 359:54	land of their h.'s hope	DAVIS 266:9	place that's broken my h.	BAUG 69:91
h. is in the coffin	SHAK 777:40	language of the h.	POPE 688:7	poor man's h.	WORD 958:81
h. is in their boots	CHES 221:90	larger was his h.	DRYD 302:88	Pourest thy full h.	SHEL 813:90
h. is in the right place	LIVI 532:55	laughing h.'s long peace	BROO 162:91	Praise…can freeze the h.	BUCK 172:36
h. is like wax	BIBLE 99:43	lay his hand on his h.	STRA 857:45	Presume not on thy h.	SHAK 800:41
h. knocked in its cage	GREE 386:22	lays his hand on his h.	BEER 73:78	Pride leaves the h.	GAUT 361:6
h. leap in my breast	SAPP 743:49	Left my H. in San Francisco	CROSS 256:34	produces a sadness of h.	MORSE 621:64
h. less bounding	ARNO 35:21	Let every h. exult with joy	DODD 289:90	quickening of the h.	AUDEN 42:72
'h.' lies much lower	LICH 528:88	let not thine h. be hasty	BIBLE 106:25	red red vitals of his h.	RANS 707:69
h. lies plain	ARNO 34:72	Let not your h. be troubled	BIBLE 123:54	Religion's in the h.	JERR 455:45
h. lingered so far	MOOD 615:32	Let not your h. be troubled	BIBLE 123:51	removed their h. far from me	BIBLE 108:72
h. love till now?	SHAK 765:75	Lift up your h.	WESL 932:61	revolting and a rebellious h.	BIBLE 110:14
h. never knows the colour of the skin	GEOR 364:56	light h. lives long	SHAK 763:22	Rise in the h.	TENN 872:41
h. of a brute like you	PLATH 681:34	like a h. in reserve	CESA 211:51	road to the h.	BALZ 61:1
h. of a man	ROUS 729:15	Like music on my h.	COLE 235:19	roaming with a hungry h.	TENN 870:98
h. of a man…lodged in a woman	CONG 241:68	listened at his h.	FROST 352:99	round his h. one…hair	ROSS 726:58
H. of England	DRAY 298:97	little body with a mighty h.	SHAK 775:65	ruddy drops that warm my h.	GRAY 385:83
h. of fire	TENN 876:35	Little skill, a little h.	ROSS 727:66	Sacred H. o' Jesus	OCAS 646:77
h. of lead	POPE 688:35	live in my h.	HAMM 394:64	sad, good Christian at her h.	POPE 688:9
h. of man…dignity	TATE 867:41	live with only half a h.	WILS 947:45	safe within its central h.	WHIT 938:12
h. of man go together	RUSK 733:92	lock your h. away	DEPP 273:79	said to H., 'How goes it?'	BELL 77:67
h. of man has long been sore	HOUS 432:70	long let your h. be strong	LAUD 511:17	sank down Into my h.	WORD 958:77
h. of our island	FORS 344:22	look in thy h., and write	SIDN 820:44	seat…in the h.	GAND 359:60
h. of standing	EMPS 326:10	loosed our h. in tears	ARNO 34:75	see my h.…without disgust	BAUD 68:69
h. of the city	MOYN 623:1	Lord looketh on the h.	BIBLE 96:34	see what breeds about her h.	SHAK 792:13
h. of the North is dead	LAWR 513:66	lotion of the h.	PARK 665:43	self-destruction enter the h.	CHEE 218:5
h. of woman	SHAK 777:25	Lourd on my h.	MACD 549:33	sensations…felt along the h.	WORD 956:53
h. on your sleeve	THAT 881:65	love which is inside his h.	LAWR 513:57	set the h. on fire	SHAK 762:85
h. responsive swells	BYRON 188:76	love you with all my h.	ROCH 719:4	sick at h.	SHAK 780:28
h.'s beatin' rhythm	BERRY 87:94	Made of a h.	HERB 413:56	sickening of the h.	POE 683:80
h.'s deep-sore wounding	SHAK 762:87	made tender to the h.	PROU 698:48	Sink h. and voice	NEALE 632:7
h.'s first ease	DAY 267:37	Mad with much h.	DONNE 291:17	sleeps on his own h.	WORD 957:68
h. shall break	SHAK 792:3	make this h. rejoice or ache	COWP 250:84	some h. did break	TENN 873:60
h. Shall break into	SHAK 792:3	malpractice of h.	CLOU 232:58	souls Of the pure in h.	RANS 707:72

heart-ache

spring of love gushed from my h.	COLE 235:16	Content in the…cell of their h.	BOGAN 144:93	white h. of this revolution	WILS 948:61
stone of the h.	YEATS 966:20	curse upon your whunstane h.	BURNS 177:72	**heath** foot is on my native h.	SCOTT 753:56
straightest road to a man's h.	FERN 334:96	day with…brave h.	CLIN 230:1	Land of brown h.	SCOTT 752:17
strings…in the human h.	DICK 279:98	dealt in hides, but never in h.	DICK 280:28	likewise a wind on the h.	BORR 151:69
struggle…fill a human h.	CAMUS 195:86	devices and desires of our own h.	BOOK 146:32	moths fluttering among the h.	BRON 162:82
stuffed roast h.	JOYCE 470:29	enthroned in the h. of kings	SHAK 770:13	**Heathcliff** Nelly, I am H.	BRON 162:79
take from them all…hardness of h.	BOOK 147:53	ever grow in our h.	JOHN 456:82	**heathen** break the h.	TENN 877:56
take their h. in one hand	BILL 135:97	evil lurks in the h. of men?	ATWO 41:46	h. in 'is blindness	KIPL 490:13
temples th'upright h. and pure	MILT 601:31	eyes and h. ears	LYLY 543:84	h. in 'is blindness	KIPL 490:14
than a h. untainted?	SHAK 759:91	free h., free foreheads	TENN 870:2	exalted among the h.	BIBLE 100:69
Thanks to the human h.	WORD 960:13	given our h. away	WORD 961:30	h. Chinee is peculiar	HARTE 400:72
that mighty h. is lying still!	WORD 959:3	hands upon their h.	HOUS 432:66	h. for thine inheritance	BIBLE 99:28
That the bruised h.	SHAK 789:1	harden not your h.	BOOK 149:31	h. in the carnal part	POPE 688:9
the fart Of every h.	SUCK 858:71	H. after them tangled	MILT 607:76	h. so furiously rage	BOOK 148:2
the human h.	OROU 652:97	h. all rocky	BYRON 188:64	In h., Turk or Jew	BLAKE 139:89
them whose h. is perfect	BIBLE 98:86	h. and hands and voices	WINK 950:98	in soul a h.	DICK 281:73
there will your h. be also	BIBLE 115:43	H. and minds	ANON 25:53	Why do the h. rage	BIBLE 99:26
The tears fall in my h.	VERL 911:57	h. are more than coronets	TENN 871:10	**heather** pore benighted h.	KIPL 489:89
the waters of the h.	THOM 883:4	h. are yearning	FORD 343:9	pu'd the h. green	BALL 59:60
thoughts, and h. enlarges	MILT 605:42	h. be frolic	GREE 386:32	sweet as the h.	LAUD 511:15
thou hast my h.	PRIOR 696:10	h. of men…have melted	SHAK 765:60	tumble on the h.	SCOTT 753:39
through a broken h.	WILDE 942:22	h., though stout	LONG 535:15	whare the h. grows	BURNS 180:51
Thy rebuke hath broken my h.	BOOK 149:26	h. very dry and tough	HOOK 427:41	**heaths** some game on these lone h.	HAZL 403:40
tiger's h.	GREE 386:33	H. wound up with love	SPEN 837:5	**heats** give your h. to	SHAK 804:41
to each loving h. how near!	HOLM 424:82	Heaven in our h.	NIGH 639:20	h. which my veins fill	DONNE 291:28
Toyshop of their h.	POPE 685:31	heavenly compassion in your h.	DICK 281:74	**heaven** accusing…h.	CAMUS 196:95
tragic h.	BENET 79:27	if our h. were beating	SCOTT 753:50	after H.'s own heart	DRYD 301:64
triumph of the h.	ADDI 7:35	In h. at peace	BROO 162:89	airs from h.	SHAK 781:57
true love hath my h.	SIDN 820:40	in our h. either to marry	STEV 851:32	All this, and h. too!	HENRY 411:14
trust not the h. of that man	CARL 200:1	in the gentlest h.	SPEN 838:35	all we know of h.	DICK 284:53
truths of the h.	FAUL 331:35	in the imagination of their h.	BIBLE 120:66	and approving H.	THOM 887:99
turn the h. of the fathers	BIBLE 112:66	keep your h. and minds	BIBLE 128:4	an impossible h.	OKRI 649:27
united in one h.	WALT 919:87	keep your h. and minds	BOOK 147:75	any thing that is in h. above	BIBLE 94:66
United to a h. like thine	BRON 161:54	lighten our own h.	SHAK 775:59	are the brain of h.	MERE 588:37
unpack my h. with words	SHAK 782:2	Lord pondereth the h.	BIBLE 105:87	as high as h.	BIBLE 98:1
unquiet h. and brain	TENN 873:58	May God wither up their h.!	DAVIS 266:7	as near to h.	GILB 368:28
utmost passion of her h.	HAWT 402:5	modern life…palsied h.	ARNO 34:94	as the h. is high	BIBLE 102:8
Vacant h., and hand, and eye	SCOTT 754:64	Of finite h. that yearn	BROW 168:50	at h.'s command	THOM 887:97
Vengeance is in my h.	SHAK 760:23	Our h. are broken	GIUL 373:33	awful rainbow once in h.	KEATS 477:9
verses from my h.	MARTI 576:71	our h. are great	TENN 876:42	beteem the winds of h.	SHAK 780:39
visit my sad h.	SHAK 777:19	Our h., unrisen	WILK 943:60	blue fields of h.	KEATS 475:62
walk in the ways of thine h.	BIBLE 106:35	our h. were fulfilled	SWIN 864:12	breath of H. fresh-blowing	MILT 607:81
weather in the h.	RICH 713:93	O, you hard h.	SHAK 776:4	brightest h. of invention	SHAK 775:61
were my dear h.-strings	SHAK 789:22	queen in people's h.	DIANA 276:25	build haunted h.	STEV 849:65
whan every lusty h.	MALO 563:14	sing to find your h.	FLEC 340:31	But was a race of h.	SHAK 794:49
Whatever your h.	LUTH 542:74	song for thinking h.	WORD 958:91	By h., I do love	SHAK 763:14
What female h. can gold despise?	GRAY 383:52	steel my soldiers' h.	SHAK 775:85	By h., methinks it were	SHAK 771:37
where a h. is hard	SHAK 762:86	still can pierce our h.	MUIR 624:22	call h. and earth to witness	BIBLE 94:87
where my h. is turning	FOST 345:54	stout h. and stout swords	BIRK 136:12	choir of h.	BERK 84:30
Where the h. lies	BROW 168:51	sweetness…inspired their h.	MARL 572:2	climb…Toward h.	FROST 352:98
wine that maketh glad the h.	BIBLE 102:11	take away our h. o' stone	OCAS 646:77	Comfort's in h.	SHAK 764:43
with a hopeful h.	LAWR 513:73	take them with our h.	NEWM 634:42	Confess yourself to h.	SHAK 784:43
withered h. was dead	SCOTT 752:11	tempts your…heedless h.	GRAY 383:54	conquer H. also	CARL 200:84
with its h. cut out	STEG 844:56	thousand h. are great	SHAK 761:54	contains or h., or hell	WEBS 927:44
With rue my h. is laden	HOUS 432:55	thousand h. beat happily	BYRON 187:50	crawling between h. and earth?	SHAK 783:12
woman touches another's h.	LACL 503:39	touching their h.	TROL 897:34	day when h. was falling	HOUS 432:71
word have I hid in mine h.	BIBLE 103:25	two h. beating each to each!	BROW 167:24	dew of h.	FORD 343:99
wound my h.	VERL 910:55	undeveloped h.	FORS 344:40	Did h. look on	SHAK 798:62
heart-ache h. and the…shocks	SHAK 783:7	unto whom all h. be open	BOOK 147:58	don't believe in h.	GALL 358:32
heart attack the occasional h. a.	CHEN 218:22	Where men with Splendid H.	BROO 162:94	Down from the verge of h.	MILT 605:26
heartbeats slow h.	GRAV 382:30	with beating h.	STOWE 856:28	Down on your knees…thank h.	SHAK 779:2
heartbreak feel the h.	GIBS 367:14	wore at their h.	SPEN 837:93	earth and the h. fled away	BIBLE 132:22
h.-b. in the heart of things?	GIBS 367:14	wot's hidden in each other's h.	DICK 280:22	Earth's crammed with h.	BROW 166:3
h., hatred blind	NOON 641:50	**heartstring** intelligencer's h.	WEBS 927:49	Elijah went up…into h.	BIBLE 97:71
H. Hotel	PRES 694:72	**heartstrings** playeth with your h.	LYLY 543:86	enter into the kingdom of h.	BIBLE 115:55
heart-easing tell the most h.-e. things	KEATS 475:69	sweep across our h.	WILS 949:75	enter into the kingdom of h.	BIBLE 118:10
heartening h. and the strong reply	EMPS 326:10	**hearty** h. old man	SOUT 805:96	enter into the kingdom of h.	BIBLE 114:31
hearth as from an unextinguished h.	SHEL 813:84	**heat** ally the h.	BLAKE 139:81	Equality would be a h.	TROL 898:49
By this still h.	TENN 870:97	bear…the h.	ARNO 34:76	eternal joys of h.	MARL 573:24
cricket on the h.	MILT 598:54	but he gat no h.	BIBLE 97:51	Even if h. were real	LAUR 511:22
drive hunger from the h.	LLOY 532:71	can't stand the h.	TRUM 899:80	ever-moving spheres of h.	MARL 573:30
h. of television	NEW 634:38	false of h.	SHAK 802:78	every purpose under the h.	BIBLE 105:14
moved earth and h.	TENN 871:2	fantastic summer's h.?	SHAK 764:36	every star that h.	MILT 598:60
hearth-fire h.-f. and the home-acre	KIPL 492:55	h. full of coldness	LYLY 543:84	exile Hath emptied h.	MILT 602:50
heartiness h. that compels belief	TWAIN 902:33	H. not a furnace	CONR 244:36	eye of h. shines	SHAK 800:37
heartland from the h. of the country	SHUL 819:30	h. of life	ETHE 327:43	eye of h. to garnish	SHAK 768:62
heartless appallingly h. thing to do	MANS 567:8	h. of the business is over!	SHAK 803:7	fallen from h.	BIBLE 108:64
heartlessness the h. of human beings	OKRI 649:25	h. o'th' sun	SHAK 803:7	fame in h. Err not	MILT 602:62
heart-of-gold bawcock and a h.-o.-g.	SHAK 775:81	In my limbs their former h.?	HERR 415:1	farther off from h.	HOOD 426:23
hearts all that human h. endure	GOLD 376:88	in temperate h.	SURR 860:4	Fire…filch'd for us from H.	BYRON 189:98
any trace of it in their h.	REDON 709:24	more h. to the fire	ACK 4:68	flowerless fields of h.	SWIN 863:81
apply our h. unto wisdom	BIBLE 101:95	not without dust and h.	MILT 600:8	for h.'s grace and boon	KEATS 477:21
broke the h.	WAUGH 924:81	of h. or cold	HUME 438:96	For, h. to earth	SHAK 772:64
cannot find it in our h.	GELL 363:36	stirs up the Native H.	PENE 673:78	from h. he came	STONE 855:11
carry in their h.	LLOY 533:72	transmit h. slowly	WATT 922:45	From plots and treasons H. preserve	DRYD 302:91
clasp we to our h.	ROSS 726:57	trellises Of the h.	SITW 823:1	gazing up into h.?	BIBLE 124:71
Combine your h. in one	SHAK 776:4	voice of high midsummer's h.	ROBE 717:72	gentle rain from h.	SHAK 770:12

heels

glance from h. to earth	SHAK 767:45	lawyer's dream of h.	BUTL 186:12	tricks before high h.	SHAK 787:58
glorify your Father which is in h.	BIBLE 114:29	leave to h.	JOHN 459:49	trouble deaf h.	SHAK 800:46
God created the h. and the earth	BIBLE 90:80	leaving mercy to h.	FIEL 335:23	under an English h.	BROO 162:89
God owns h.	SEXT 758:52	loftiest star of unascended h.	SHEL 814:18	up to the chin in h.	MIDD 590:78
going direct to H.	DICK 282:94	long or short permit to h.	MILT 607:69	wants to go to h.	LOUIS 538:76
going to h.	GAIN 357:10	looked up to h.	IHIM 445:20	war in h.	BIBLE 131:10
gold bar of H.	ROSS 726:49	Look how the floor of h.	SHAK 770:19	watered h. with their tears	BLAKE 140:20
hand of H.	WORD 962:50	looks do menace h.	MARL 572:96	weariness of climbing h.	SHEL 816:66
he ascended into h.	BOOK 146:37	mathematics of the city of h.	BROW 166:85	we shall practise in h.	BROW 168:55
h. above her	GORD 378:53	may be h.	BROW 167:25	what's a h. for?	BROW 168:45
h. admits no jest	FORD 343:3	meted out h. with the span	BIBLE 108:81	when h. shall be stripped off	KORAN 498:91
h. And calculate the stars	MILT 605:35	mind and thoughts travelled to h.	BLAKE 141:35	who art in H.	PARRA 665:49
h. and earth disturbed	SURR 860:98	more things in h. and earth	MAMET 564:36	Whom have I in h.	BIBLE 101:86
h. and earth hath made	SCOT 755:89	more things in h. and earth	SHAK 781:70	will hurl my soul from h.	SHAK 790:49
h. and earth in...union	MILT 597:34	My idea of h.	SMITH 831:61	windows of h.	BIBLE 112:63
H. and earth shall pass away	BIBLE 118:30	nerar h. blis	HENR 411:16	winds of h. mix for ever	SHEL 813:78
H. and Home	WORD 961:45	never be Saints in H.	BROW 165:61	wingèd messenger of h.	SHAK 765:78
h. be in these lips	MARL 573:29	never to h. go	SHAK 783:35	wing wherewith we fly to h.	SHAK 760:99
H. born child	MILT 597:31	new h. and a new earth	BIBLE 132:23	with all the company of h.	BOOK 147:70
H. doth with us	SHAK 787:47	O all you host of h.!	SHAK 781:66	without a thought of H. or Hell	BROW 165:64
h. endures	HOUS 432:78	offence...smells to h.	SHAK 783:32	world, to our native h.	MILT 606:60
h. fill with commerce	TENN 871:17	offspring of H. first-born	MILT 603:73	Yes, H. is thine	POE 683:87
h. forbids us certain	MOLI 611:77	o h. fool	SIDN 820:49	heavenly exploiting a h. gift	QUIL 702:17
h. had made her such	SHAK 788:94	O h., were man	SHAK 759:73	h. touches ne'er touched	SHAK 800:36
h. hath my empty words	SHAK 787:62	Order is h.'s first law	POPE 687:88	H. weather	JOYCE 470:31
H....how they dress!	DICK 279:1	O then h. mocks itself!	SHAK 789:23	heavens as the h. are higher	BIBLE 109:98
H. in Earth	CRAS 253:78	others have to hope for h.	SLOAN 825:55	chase our imagination to the h.	HUME 438:94
h. in hell's despair	BLAKE 140:9	Our Father which art in h.	BIBLE 115:42	clothed with the h.	TRAH 895:85
h. in our cup has thrown	ROCH 719:14	patch up thine old body for h.?	SHAK 772:82	create new h.	BIBLE 110:9
H. in our hearts	NIGH 639:20	pavilion of H. is bare	SHEL 813:77	descend from the h.	VERL 910:56
H. is for thee	MILT 605:36	Pennies don't fall from h.	THAT 881:56	eternal in the h.	BIBLE 127:68
H. is free From clouds	BYRON 188:60	Pennies from H.	BURKE 176:59	fabric of the h.	MILT 605:35
h. is like to a grain of mustard	BIBLE 117:95	peopled highest h.	MILT 606:64	From yon blue h.	TENN 871:10
h. is like unto a merchant	BIBLE 117:96	pleasure they enjoy in H.	MARL 572:98	Good h., your divine nature	PEACE 671:50
H. is not a place	BACH 49:9	power of H.	MOORE 617:85	h. are the work of thy hands	BIBLE 102:5
H. itself would stoop	MILT 599:81	Prompted...by h. and hell	SHAK 782:2	h. declare the glory of God	BOOK 148:9
h. keeps souls	DONNE 292:62	Puts all H. in a rage	BLAKE 141:25	h.' embroidered cloths	YEATS 966:12
h. lies about us	WORD 959:8	regard of H. on all	MILT 604:5	h. free from strife	CORY 247:10
H. of hell, a hell of h.	MILT 602:44	remedies...we ascribe to h.	SHAK 791:58	h. rain odours on you	SHAK 786:8
h. on earth	FORD 343:1	renounce...attempt to create h.	BORO 151:67	h. themselves blaze forth	SHAK 777:20
h. on earth I have won	SHAK 791:67	ring in H.'s street	MASE 580:64	h. were opened unto him	BIBLE 114:21
h. planted us to please	MARV 578:10	ring the bells of h.	HODG 421:23	in the h. write	SPEN 839:47
h....points out an hereafter	ADDI 7:52	Road to H.	BALL 59:75	O Thou that in the h. does dwell!	BURNS 177:71
h.'s cherubin, horsed	SHAK 796:20	rugged finger to H.	LLOY 533:72	Out-glares the H. Osiris	HERR 415:5
H.'s deep organ blow	MILT 597:35	sabill all the h. arrayis	DUNB 306:5	Pure as the naked h.	WORD 958:94
H. sends us fine meat	GARR 360:80	Satan as lightning fall from h.	BIBLE 120:79	rideth upon the h.	BIBLE 101:81
h. sent us Soda Water	CHES 221:89	Save wings, for h.	KEATS 477:21	Since the h. have shaped	SHAK 760:20
h.'s gates she claps	LYLY 543:83	saw h. opened	BIBLE 124:82	sitteth in the h.	BIBLE 99:27
H.'s great lamps do dive	CAMP 195:72	saw h. opened	BIBLE 132:19	spangled h., a shining frame	ADDI 7:40
H.'s light forever shines	SHEL 815:43	send more souls to H.	BENN 81:81	starry h. above	THOM 887:6
H. smiles	SHEL 816:57	shall not enter...kingdom of h.	BIBLE 118:10	starry h. above me	KANT 473:26
H.'s splendour over his head	CARL 201:36	silence in h.	BIBLE 131:5	Study is like the h.'	SHAK 763:1
h.'s vault should crack	SHAK 793:37	silent summer h.	TENN 878:95	The h. forbid	SHAK 789:9
h.'s wide pathless way	MILT 598:53	singing till his h. fills	MERE 588:31	though the h. may fall	WATS 922:44
h.'s zone glistering	DONNE 291:19	sing...of H.	HERR 415:98	When I consider thy h.	BIBLE 99:31
H. the judicious...spectator	RALE 705:45	sinned against h.	BIBLE 121:90	heaviness I am full of h.	BOOK 149:26
h. to gaudy day denies	BYRON 189:80	sinned against h.	BIBLE 121:91	heavy hot as molten lead, and as h.	SHAK 772:65
h. we have below	ADDI 6:15	slip from h. at night	FROST 352:3	ld man, and h.	BIBLE 96:29
h. without stars	SANT 743:47	smile of h.	SHAK 804:46	light wife doth make a h. husband	SHAK 770:25
hell as well as h.	HUXL 442:91	son of H.'s eternal King	MILT 596:30	Sob, h. world	AUDEN 43:1
hell I suffer seems a h.	MILT 604:92	sons of h.	JOHN 460:68	Weigh them: it is as h.	SHAK 776:10
hell, than seven in h.	MILT 602:45	soul may but ascend to h.	MARL 574:31	heavy-shotted His h.-s. hammock	TENN 873:61
hell that is not h.	MARL 573:25	soul, the King of H.	LYTE 543:93	Hebraism H. and Hellenism	ARNO 36:30
help me h.	FIRB 336:53	spark from h.	ARNO 34:91	Hebrew few odd words in H.	DAY 267:30
Home is h.	NASH 630:65	spark from h.	ARNO 34:93	H. of the H.s	BIBLE 128:99
house as nigh h.	MORE 619:24	spark from h.!	ARNO 34:93	Hebrides behold the H.	GALT 359:54
how far away H. is	RULFO 731:40	star fall from h.	BIBLE 131:6	seas colder than the H.	FLEC 340:37
husbandry in h.	SHAK 796:26	stored vengeances of h. fall	SHAK 792:1	heck doing a h. of a job	BUSH 183:35
If I ascend up into h.	BIBLE 103:44	Strike h. on the face	SHAK 797:60	Hector struggles of H.	HONO 426:17
If not to h., then hand	SHAK 761:53	subtle master under h.	TENN 877:57	Hecuba For H.! What's H. to him	SHAK 782:99
if there be cricket in h.	HOME 425:99	summons thee to h.	SHAK 797:29	hedge in the warm h.	SHEL 816:61
If there is a h. it's...already filled	DUDEK 305:68	sweet breath of h.	WORD 957:73	whoso breaketh an h.	BIBLE 106:31
I have sinned against h.	BIBLE 121:90	Thank H.! the crisis	POE 683:94	hedge-fund h.-f. managers...into...	
I have sinned against h.	BIBLE 121:91	the h. above	STEV 853:83	cage fights	PARR 666:54
I look up to h.	SMART 826:60	theirs is the kingdom of h.	BIBLE 114:27	hedgehog h. of the heart	LOWE 540:34
Imagine there's no h.	LENN 521:46	The quincunx of h.	BROW 166:84	hedgehogs Thorny h., be not seen	SHAK 767:31
immanacl'd, while h.	MILT 599:78	thinks that up in h.	CULL 257:42	hedges and h. ears	SWIFT 862:55
in at H.'s gate	BLAKE 141:32	think'st thou h.	MARL 573:26	hedge-sparrow h.-s. fed the cuckoo	SHAK 792:92
In h. no single star	THOM 887:9	thirtieth year to h.	THOM 883:20	heed take h. lest he fall	BIBLE 126:45
inherit h.'s graces	SHAK 802:69	thorny way to h.	SHAK 781:48	heel From h. to throat	YEATS 966:16
I shall hear in h.	BEET 74:6	thought raised to h.	LESS 524:5	In the h. of	KIPL 490:2
Is it any better in H.	WILL 946:12	thrones in h.	RUSK 732:85	lifted up his h. against me	BOOK 100:62
it were not h., if	SUCK 858:69	through h. and earth	MILT 597:34	long thrust of his h.	HUGH 435:30
jolly h. above	STEV 853:82	to be young was very h.!	WORD 960:23	on the boldest h.	CRANE 253:67
keys of the kingdom of h.	BIBLE 117:6	top of h. doth hold	MILT 598:75	shalt bruise his h.	BIBLE 91:96
kingdom of h. is at hand	BIBLE 114:18	top of it reached to h.	BIBLE 93:32	well-apparell'd April on the h.	SHAK 765:68
lark at h. gate	SHAK 803:93	treasure in h.	BIBLE 118:17	heels At his h. a stone	SHAK 784:48

Heffalump

double-crossing of a pair of h.	HART 399:66	having harrowed h.	SPEN 839:43	There is h. as well	HUXL 442:91
grief...treads upon the h. of pleasure	CONG 240:30	having harrowed h.	SPEN 839:46	there must be h.	BROW 167:25
grow out at h.	SHAK 792:99	heaven in h.'s despair	BLAKE 140:9	There's a h. of a distance	PARK 664:23
gunpowder ran out of the h.	FOOTE 342:83	heav'n of h., a h. of heav'n	MILT 602:44	There's h.	SHAK 793:22
I have big h. to fill	KERRY 483:61	he descended into h.	BOOK 146:37	'To h. with ye!' says she	STRO 857:54
lighten...our wives' h.	SHAK 775:59	H. a fury, like a woman scorned	CONG 241:52	too cold for h.	SHAK 797:39
like champagne or high h.	BENN 81:66	H. ain't half full	MCCA 547:76	towards the gates of h.	MILT 603:68
reclining back upon my h.	WORD 957:71	H. and destruction are never full	BIBLE 105:4	walked eye-deep in h.	POUND 691:4
Heffalump H., a Horrible H.	MILNE 596:18	H. as well as on earth	LEWIS 526:42	war...is all h.	SHER 818:9
Hegel H. says somewhere	MARX 579:36	h. at the time	WILD 942:33	ways of saying 'To h. with you'	FENW 332:64
heifer plowed with my h.	BIBLE 95:16	h. delivered up the dead	BIBLE 132:22	warm corner of h.	MCCA 547:71
heigh H. ho, h. ho	MOREY 619:28	h. followed with him	BIBLE 131:1	we stood in H.	OWEN 657:33
With h.-ho	SHAK 792:9	H. grant what Love	MILT 598:55	What is h.?	ELIOT 321:97
height arms is equal to his h.	LEON 523:76	H. hath no limits	MARL 573:25	when H. shall be set blazing	KORAN 498:91
climbed up a h.	SUN 859:92	h. in heaven's despite	BLAKE 140:10	whole body...cast into h.	BIBLE 115:34
father moved through depths of h.	CUMM 258:64	H. is a city	SHEL 813:87	whose entrance leads to H.	MILT 599:74
Happiness Makes up in H.	FROST 353:14	H. is being trapped	JOHN 458:22	Why, this is h.	MARL 573:24
Holiest in the h.	NEWM 635:49	H. is full of musical amateurs	SHAW 807:23	wilt not leave my soul in h.	BIBLE 99:36
kindred spider to that h.	FROST 352:11	H. is murky	SHAK 798:65	with h. are we at agreement	BIBLE 108:70
love will be seen at its h.	FORS 344:30	H. is other people	SART 744:69	without a thought of Heaven or H.	BROW 165:64
None can usurp this h.	KEATS 476:98	H....is to no longer love	BERN 85:60	write about h.	FIEN 336:38
performed...to such an h.	DRYD 300:24	h. itself breathes out	SHAK 783:30	write of H.	HERR 415:98
The trees are the right h.	ROMN 724:97	H. itself cannot encroach	BAUD 68:58	**Hellenism** Hebraism and H.	ARNO 26:73
heights brood on the towering h.	LEAR 516:28	h. lay about him	GREE 385:3	**Hellespontus** over H. swam	SPEN 839:61
struggle...towards the h.	CAMUS 195:86	H. lies about us	MITC 609:25	**hellfire** eyes to be cast into h. f.	BIBLE 118:12
heinous what h. sin	SHAK 769:90	h. make crooked	SHAK 760:20	in danger of h. f.	BIBLE 114:32
heir h. of all things	BIBLE 129:33	h.; myself am h.	MILT 604:92	**hellhound** Discrimination is a h.	KING 487:34
h. to an inheritance	OAKE 642:4	h. of a good universe	CUMM 258:68	h. is always a h.	WODE 952:51
I am the h. to Blair	CAM 193:37	h. of an explosion	CATTO 209:4	**hellish** whole of the H. nation	SITW 823:97
I the h. of all the ages	TENN 871:22	h. of an opening	REAG 709:15	**hello** Come say h.	PACI 658:5
never comes but brings an h.	SHAK 798:86	h. on earth	SHAW 807:13	H. sadness	ELUA 324:45
sole h. of the whole world	TRAH 895:85	h.'s concave, and beyond	MILT 602:49	**helm** at the h. of our country	HOOV 427:45
son of memory, great h.	MILT 597:39	H.'s darkness under his feet	CARL 201:36	**helmet** h. and the h.-feather	TENN 870:84
spouting through his h.	POPE 686:68	h. should bar the way	NOYES 642:71	h. of salvation	BIBLE 128:95
you are his h.	STOP 855:15	h., than serve in heav'n	MILT 602:45	saw the h. and the plume	TENN 870:85
heiress American h.	MCCA 547:86	h. they made unmade	MORG 619:34	**help** and h. there's none	HODG 421:22
heirs children; they have h.	NEWM 635:53	h. within him, for within him h.	MILT 603:89	another to h. him up	BIBLE 106:17
if children, then h.	BIBLE 125:18	her steps take hold on h.	BIBLE 104:56	best way to h. the poor	HANC 395:77
held H. we fall to rise	BROW 169:85	holiday...excursion to h.	PRIE 695:86	can't h. people against their will	FREE 349:46
I'm being h. out to dry	REAG 708:9	hot from h.	SHAK 777:34	encumbers him with h.?	JOHN 460:63
Helen hath closèd H.'s eye	NASHE 632:96	hotter name Than any in h.	SHAK 798:76	from whence cometh my h.	BIBLE 103:31
H., did Homer never see	JONS 468:85	how the h. I ever got here	TRUM 899:76	give them h.	GELL 363:36
H., make me immortal	MARL 573:29	If Hitler invaded H.	CHUR 226:7	h. and support of the woman I love	EDWA 312:61
H.'s beauty in a brow	SHAK 767:45	I'm neurotic as h.	PLATH 681:38	H., angels!	SHAK 783:34
H., whose beauty summoned	MARL 572:4	I myself am h.	LOWE 540:22	h. from a government agency	STEIN 845:77
look on H.'s face in hell	PARK 664:10	In h. they'll roast thee	BURNS 179:30	h. him to do it	HALI 393:32
Past ruined Ilion H. lives	LAND 507:29	injured lover's h.	MILT 604:16	h. me heaven	FIRB 336:5
where H. lies	BALL 59:63	in the interests of H.	FORS 344:39	h. of any ally	GARI 360:72
Helena dross that is not H.	MARL 573:29	Into the mouth of H.	TENN 875:13	h. of his countenance	BIBLE 100:64
Helicon watered our houses in H.	CHAP 214:19	keys of h. and of death	BIBLE 131:89	h. our French comrades	KITC 494:98
hell allotted death and h.	MARL 574:31	lead apes in h.	SHAK 761:62	h. thou my unbelief	FORS 345:45
all the tribes of h.	SHAK 789:4	leadest to the gates of h.	BIBLE 112:79	How shall I h. you	HOUS 431:50
all we need of h.	DICK 284:53	liar gone to burning h.	SHAK 790:45	I get by with a little h.	LENN 522:52
America...may be going to H.	CUMM 258:60	like Christianity without h.	BORM 151:62	look on and h.	LAWR 513:64
And shall I couple h.?	SHAK 781:66	like that in Milton's h.	NERV 633:24	make him an h. meet for him	BIBLE 91:89
ane to heaven, an' ten to h.	BURNS 177:71	live in freedom and h.	MAIL 560:52	mutual h....as often as warfare	DOBZ 289:79
art as black as h.	SHAK 803:88	look on Helen's face in h.	PARK 664:10	mutual society, h., and comfort	BOOK 148:87
A tolerable h. is better	OKRI 649:27	Love is a Dog from H.	BUKO 173:56	no h. for it	AUBER 41:55
believe myself to be in h.	RIMB 716:50	make my bed in h.	BIBLE 103:44	seeking h. from none	GORD 378:52
blasts from h.	SHAK 781:57	make the earth my h.	SHAK 761:45	Since there's no h.	DRAY 299:99
Came not all h. broke loose?	MILT 604:13	man who lives in h.	GALL 358:32	there is no h. in them	BOOK 149:38
cannot commit evil in h.	GENET 363:40	married to h.	SHAK 761:58	they cannot h. him	SHAK 791:60
carried H. about with him	GREE 385:6	more devils than vast h.	SHAK 767:45	very present h. in trouble	BIBLE 100:67
characters of h. to trace	GRAY 385:84	never give them h.	TRUM 899:84	where no one can h. him	HEMI 410:88
charm thy soul to h.	MARL 573:28	never know where the h. you are	SALI 740:73	who can h. it?	ETHE 327:46
childhood prolonged...h.	BOGAN 144:94	never married, and that's his h.	BURT 181:80	without the h. of the air	ETHE 327:47
claim in h. Précédence	MILT 602:56	never mentions H. to ears polite	POPE 686:61	**helper** mother's little h.	JAGG 449:14
contains or heaven, or h.	WEBS 927:44	night seems termless h.	THOM 887:7	**helpers** h. fail and comforts	LYTE 543:94
curse of h. upon the sleek	RANS 707:69	No h. below us	LENN 521:46	**helping** h. every feeble neighbour	GORD 378:52
deeper than h.	BIBLE 98:1	Oh H.!	SNYD 832:91	**helpless** H., naked, piping loud	BLAKE 140:18
Descent into H.	LESS 524:99	out of h. leads up to light	MILT 603:66	Must h. man	JOHN 459:48
Devil Fired into H.	ANON 23:96	passed a h. of time	SHAK 802:82	**hem** h. of Nature's shift	SHEL 813:88
Down, down to h.	SHAK 760:19	paving stones for H.	KING 488:59	**Hemingway** back to H.'s work	COWL 250:82
earth, and heav'n, and h.	POPE 688:33	people who are scared of h.	TYSON 904:14	H., remarks are not literature	STEIN 845:62
earth is h. when	NASHE 632:94	Pequod packing off to h.	LOWE 540:19	marriage to Ernest H.	BARR 64:82
England...the h. of horses	FLOR 341:62	Pope told us all to go to h.	OBRI 646:69	**hemisphere** crystals...in a h.	SCHW 750:93
extinguish h.	REED 709:30	Prompted...by heaven in h.	SHAK 782:2	gilding the eastern h.	SHER 818:2
fetch fire from h.	WEBS 926:39	Quiet to quick bosoms is a h.	BYRON 187:52	In the western h.	ROOS 724:16
flowerless rocks of h.	SITW 823:96	readiest way to H.?	ROCH 720:20	western to the eastern h.	PEARY 671:60
focus...on reducing the h.	BORO 151:67	riches grow in h.	MILT 602:53	**hemlock** h. I had drunk	KEATS 478:41
foul h. within	SHAK 802:81	road to h. is paved	ROTH 728:85	**hen** h. is only an egg's way	BUTL 185:92
gates of h. shall not prevail	BIBLE 117:6	save more from H.	BENN 81:81	nought worth a h.	DUNB 305:91
good...definition of h.	SHAW 810:3	set on fire of h.	BIBLE 130:56	Royal Commission is a broody h.	FOOT 342:81
go to h. like lambs	CHES 221:90	sounds frae h.	FERG 333:85	Two Owls and a H.	LEAR 516:74
Go to h. Yours sincerely	ELLI 323:27	special place in h. for women	ALBR 11:34	**hence** going h....coming hither	SHAK 793:32
great painter of American h.	ALLEN 13:78	tell them the truth and they think		**Hendrix** H. could do so much better	COST 247:16
hand in hand to h.	SHAK 761:53	it's h.	KEANE 475:55	H. had both	POP 685:14

hill

hen-pecked have they not h.-p. BYRON 189:90
Henry H. the Eighth Took a thuctheththion BENT 82:3
H. VIII....ideal MACK 554:18
without strict doubt a Hoorah H. RUNY 731:61
hens h. to moor-cocks call YEATS 966:19
Hepburn H. runs the gamut PARK 663:6
Heraclitus H., they told me CORY 247:8
herald perfectest h. of joy SHAK 774:30
Revolution is merely the h. BABE 48:4
heraldic h. equivalent of...furry dice ANON 27:13
heraldry boast of h. GRAY 384:66
heralds Nobles and h. PRIOR 695:99
herb dew-bespangling h. and tree HERR 415:10
h. for the service of man BIBLE 102:11
h. that sips the dew MILT 598:60
light on such another h. SHAK 791:70
small rain upon the tender h. BIBLE 95:98
some single h. or tree MARV 577:1
herbs dinner of h. where love is BIBLE 104:75
greatest among h. BIBLE 117:95
In plants, h., stones SHAK 766:87
spinneys of murdering h. THOM 884:41
Hercules character like Samson, H. SIEG 820:60
Let H. himself SHAK 784:68
herd h. instinct in the individual NIET 638:95
more numerous was the h. DRYD 302:82
resigns momentarily from the h. MACL 555:38
unique to the level of the h. MILL 594:84
herds h., of human face divine MILT 603:75
here From H. To Eternity JONES 465:18
H. am I BIBLE 96:25
H. am I; send me BIBLE 107:55
h. and now HAMM 394:59
h. and now cease to matter ELIOT 320:69
h. it is at last JAMES 451:56
H. we are again! GRIM 388:72
one-tenth H. and Now SWIFT 861:12
We're h., We're queer ANON 26:8
Where is h.? FRYE 354:55
would...never happen h. FOWL 346:64
hereafter heaven...points out an h. ADDI 7:52
hereditary peers, and they are h. LLOY 533:78
heresies begin as h. HUXL 443:8
hateful h. SPEN 839:42
h....explosions of faith BREN 158:97
h. perish not with their authors BROW 165:49
most interesting ideas are h. SONT 834:19
heresy ancient saying is no h. SHAK 769:96
this hidden h. RAHN 705:36
what an Englishman believes be h.? SHAW 810:16
widespread modern h. DRIB 299:5
heretic h. that makes the fire SHAK 799:13
lawyer and politician and a h. MENC 586:89
revolutionary ends as...a h. CAMUS 196:92
heretics burning of the h. WELD 928:83
heritage British have more h. than is good BRYS 170:6
children are an h. BIBLE 103:37
goodly h. BIBLE 99:35
I have a goodly h. BOOK 148:8
proud of our ancient h. KENN 481:3
thy true h. POUND 692:23
young country is a real h. MANS 567:10
hermaphrodites Nor even h. LAUT 511:27
hermit dwell a h. anywhere LOWE 539:12
In habite an h. unholy LANG 507:44
hermitage Find out the peaceful h. MILT 598:60
palace for a h. SHAK 764:54
That for a h. LOVE 538:82
Hermon As the dew of H. BIBLE 103:40
hern haunts of coot and h. TENN 876:37
hero American history as a great h. MENC 586:95
Being a h. is about ROGE 723:85
be your own h. WINT 950:12
conquering h. comes! MORE 619:27
definition of a 'h.' FIND 336:43
Every h. becomes a bore EMER 325:79
Forgive the h. WILB 939:35
h. from his prison AYTO 48:12
h. is a man who would argue MAIL 560:46
h. is a sneaking piece SCOTT 753:38
h. of his own life story BARTH 65:6
h. perish, or a sparrow fall POPE 686:73
H., Venus' nun MARL 574:35
memory of an h. GIBB 366:94
no such thing as a h. MO 611:69

one murder...millions a h. PORT 690:77
Show me a h. FITZ 338:99
Show me a h. PUZO 701:7
to his very valet seemed a h. BYRON 189:85
truth about its h. CHES 220:61
who aspires to be a h. JOHN 463:66
Herod Oh, for an hour of H.! HOPE 427:58
heroes become statesmen and h. WARD 920:99
cowards as quickly as of h. MITC 610:43
fit country for h. to live in LLOY 533:76
h. and heroines will have to change WELD 928:81
h. and villains from fiction AUDEN 44:17
h. of three recent novels BROY 169:89
h. to dine with us TROL 898:44
h. were made RUSS 735:43
I'll follow the h. ORAH 652:90
land that has need of h. BREC 157:91
land that has no h. BREC 157:91
men...want to be h. WINT 950:10
past h. of production LOWE 540:39
puny hands Of h. COWP 251:20
risk of being h. BOLT 145:13
sang of...farms and h. VIRG 914:28
speed glum h. SASS 745:84
This book is not about h. OWEN 657:28
Weird h. THOM 886:87
heroic h., or epic ROUA 729:7
How h. to be able to JAMES 449:21
obstacle to being h. HAWT 402:13
of h. hearts TENN 871:2
our Ministry is not h. CECIL 210:28
persons of h. stature AMIS 17:55
running something much less h. COOKE 245:72
heroine When a h. goes mad SHER 818:4
heroines h. will have to change WELD 928:81
start with plain h. FITZ 338:2
heroism h. is to resist the doubt HAWT 402:13
h. of Johnson STEV 852:53
not the kind of h. they enjoy WINT 950:10
Unnatural vices...fathered by our h. ELIOT 317:85
heron h. priested shore THOM 883:20
reminded me of a h. BANKS 62:17
herring A plague o' these pickle h.! SHAK 785:88
roast thee like a h.! BURNS 179:30
herrings as pilchards are to h. SHAK 786:6
'New h., new!' NASHE 631:88
Herzog thought Moses H. BELL 77:78
hesitate h. and falter life away ARNO 34:93
h. dislike POPE 688:3
hesitates He who h. THUR 890:85
hesitation H. increases in relation HEMI 410:94
least h. changes it YOUR 968:57
hest broke your h. to say so! SHAK 804:22
Heston H. thinks America should arm its teachers RUSH 732:71
heterosexual no sensitive h. MAIL 559:40
hew h. blocks with a razor POPE 686:53
h. him as a carcass SHAK 776:17
hey With a h., and a ho. SHAK 780:21
heyday h. in the blood SHAK 784:40
hibakusha H., atomic victims GEE 362:27
hibernation long h. GRAV 382:25
people live in h. OHARA 648:14
Hibernia H.'s Land JOHN 459:42
hick Sticks nix h. pix ANON 24:17
hickory flavor as h. smoke MUMF 625:40
hid Where truth is h. SHAK 782:78
hidden h. even as a strange tongue DURER 307:25
H. in wonder SCOTT 751:3
the h. persuaders PACK 658:8
this h. heresy RAHN 705:36
hide False face must h. SHAK 796:25
h. his two ambitious ears JONS 466:48
h. is sure to flatten 'em BELL 76:53
h. myself in T. TOPL 894:61
of a rhinoceros BARR 65:98
h. us from the face BIBLE 131:2
run, but he can't h. LOUIS 538:75
wrapped in a woman's h.! SHAK 760:3
hideous always seemed...quite h. BAUD 69:83
hated because they are h. RUSS 734:28
h. when...in a child SHAK 792:94
hides H. from himself JOHN 459:47
often dealt in h. DICK 280:28
hiding Because he's h. BUSH 183:31
heart in h. HOPK 428:77

h. place from the wind BIBLE 108:75
Thou art my h. place BIBLE 100:53
waters shall overflow the h. place BIBLE 108:71
hiechts down frae its auld h. SMITH 831:64
hierarchy In a h. every employee PETER 675:37
Nature admits no h. FRY 354:48
Hierocles like the pedant in H. JOHN 461:9
hieroglyphs Words...are but dead h. MILL 594:88
hierophants Poets are the h. SHEL 816:53
high ascended on h. BIBLE 101:82
being h. and solitary YEATS 966:14
between the h. and low SIDN 820:46
Chancellor in his H. Court DICK 281:55
for contempt too h. COWL 250:77
h. and lifted up BIBLE 107:54
h. heels are most agreeable SWIFT 862:43
h. in poor countries SMITH 827:82
h. Roman fashion SHAK 795:85
I get h. with a little help LENN 522:52
return from H. Mass MACA 553:17
setteth me upon my h. places BIBLE 99:39
stayed in the h. room SPEN 837:6
tabernacles of the most H. BIBLE 100:68
Way up h. HARB 396:90
highballs Three h. and I think PARK 664:22
higher capable of h. things FORS 345:42
Swifter, h., stronger ANON 23:3
highest h. form of government SPEN 836:90
h. point of all my greatness SHAK 805:50
sees farthest who sees h. BACH 49:10
highflyer h. at Fashion DICK 283:15
highland between lowland and h. SWIN 864:16
heart is H. GALT 359:54
prescribed H. manner BURG 174:1
solitary H. Lass WORD 960:18
Highlander no H. need...shame SCOTT 753:37
highlanders Twelve H. and a bagpipe ANON 28:53
highlands chieftain to the H. CAMP 194:65
de-Tibetanization of the H. MACD 550:39
gang to the H. wi' me? BALL 59:65
heart's in the H. BURNS 179:15
In the h. STEV 854:85
in the Scottish H. STEV 851:27
Ye H. and ye Lawlands BALL 58:53
high-minded I am not h.-m. BOOK 149:35
high street The h. s. is where ROGE 722:69
high-water h.-w. mark of my youth THUR 890:67
The h.-w. mark...of...literature ORWE 653:18
highway broad h. of the world SHEL 815:45
h. for our God BIBLE 108:79
h. shall be there BIBLE 108:77
make seas our smooth h. CARL 200:80
highwayman h. came riding NOYES 642:70
highways happy h. HOUS 431:52
spacious h. of books SAND 742:34
hijackers starve...the h. THAT 881:62
hilarity h. was like a scream GREE 386:9
sinking flame of h. DICK 279:90
Hilary I like H. PAGL 659:20
hill All, all, are sleeping on the h. MAST 581:81
as it trundles down the h. TROL 898:46
Behind the cloud-topped h. POPE 687:75
city that is set on an h. BIBLE 114:29
climbed a h. as light fell short HODG 421:20
deer from the h. SCOTT 753:37
dwell in thy holy h.? BIBLE 99:34
flung us on the windy h. BROO 162:84
God's h. BOOK 149:24
green h. far away ALEX 13:64
haven under the h. TENN 871:4
h. of beans GARN 360:78
h. of beans in this crazy world EPST 327:29
h. of frankincense BIBLE 107:45
h. or field or river TENN 872:40
h. will not come to Mahomet BACON 52:92
huge h., Cragged, and steep DONNE 290:15
huge h. of flesh SHAK 771:47
hunter home from the h. STEV 853:62
hunts on a lonely h. SHARP 806:70
meadow and the h. ROBE 717:73
o'er the h. the eastern star BURNS 180:45
Over h., over dale SHAK 767:25
rolls down a h. TAKU 866:13
round it was, upon a h. STEV 855:7
Shepherd, from the h. ARNO 34:87
sit upon a h. SHAK 760:8

hillbilly

sleep upon his h.	LIND 530:21	To a h.	TUCH 901:14	h. of a battle	WELL 929:6
stood upon that silent h.	HODG 421:21	When I meet a h.	ELTON 323:42	h. of all hitherto…society	MARX 579:31
topped the neighbouring h.	GOLD 376:97	historians ancient Spanish h.	ECHE 310:14	h. of America	ADAMS 5:1
upon the self-same h.	MILT 599:83	Dali's importance…for art h.	SCHW 750:83	h. of bat and ball	ARLO 32:31
walk up on a windy h.	TYSON 904:9	Future h. will	MUGG 623:11	h. of City architecture	JOHN 458:31
what was at the other side of the h.	WELL 929:11	God cannot alter the past, h. can	BUTL 185:95	h. of England	MACA 545:42
yon high, high h.	BALL 59:60	h. left blanks in their writings	POUND 691:11	h. of England	MACA 546:57
your wee bit h. and glen	WILL 946:31	H. repeat each other	GUED 389:84	h. of every country	CATH 208:84
hillbilly sing like a h.	WILL 944:70	H. spend their lives	HOPE 427:56	h. of Mr. Blackman	NGU 636:66
Hillborough Haunted H.	ANON 24:32	h. will allocate the responsibility	HIRO 419:73	h. of publicity	LEAV 517:51
hills around the h. no more	LIND 530:23	**historical** cultural and h. role		h. of science	POPP 689:63
blue remembered h.	HOUS 431:51	fights h.	SMITH 828:1	h. of science	SART 744:63
convictions are h.	FITZ 337:73	H. Overdosing	GILB 368:39	h. of…scientific work	TOLS 894:54
could show you h.	CARR 204:92	H. Slumming	COUP 248:25	h. of the affections	IRVI 447:58
daft and happy h.	THOM 884:47	imply h. dependency	COUP 248:26	h. of the different intonations	BORG 150:56
fight in the h.	CHUR 225:85	importance of an h. event	MURP 627:77	h. of the human race	HARL 398:36
gap in the h.	ANON 23:2	It is a h. truth	WHIT 937:82	h. of the human spirit	ARNO 36:32
harp-shaped h.	THOM 884:47	lessons of h. experience	ANGE 19:89	h. of the land	LONG 535:33
h. and towers	MUIR 623:14	process of h. development	KISS 493:84	h. of the Victorian age	STRA 856:36
h. are alive	HAMM 395:68	to h. materials	ROBI 718:94	h. of the world	GIBB 366:90
h. in a balance?	BIBLE 108:81	**histories** H. make men wise	STIN 854:1	h. of this country	MACM 556:65
h. of the Chankly Bore	LEAR 516:28	I only believe in h.	BACON 53:39	h., real solemn h.	AUST 46:84
H. of the North, rejoice	OAKL 643:5	soon as h. are properly told	PASC 677:92	H. repeats itself	GUED 389:84
h. shall break forth	BIBLE 109:1	true h. contain instruction	WHIT 937:89	H. shows that	STAL 842:6
H. tell each other	BLAKE 139:80	**history** all of his potted h.	BRON 161:56	H. shows us no example	WEBB 925:9
h. were no harder	THOM 885:70	American h. as a great hero	LEVIN 525:29	H. teaches us	EBAN 310:8
hoary h. are seen	POPE 688:31	Antiquities are h. defaced	MENC 586:95	H. teaches us	KENN 481:18
lift up mine eyes unto the h.	BIBLE 103:31	Art is h.'s nostalgia	BACON 49:26	H. teaches us these lessons	ASHD 37:68
lost beyond the h.	HYDE 443:17	bad jokes of h.	WALC 916:19	H., this old…lying woman	MAUP 582:12
Low h., rich fields, calm rivers	CRIP 254:96	Before h. is written down	GUED 389:84	h.…through the kitchen window	CHILD 222:16
name to the reverberate h.	SHAK 785:91	Beneath every h., another h.	BUSH 183:38	H. to the defeated	AUDEN 37:62
Nkongsamba was built on seven h.	BOYD 153:10	cancer of human h.	MANT 568:19	h. whither are you spinning?	GRAY 384:6
o'er vales and h.	WORD 960:24	collective opinion…can make h.	SONT 834:16	H. will absolve me	CAST 208:77
on the frozen h.	TENN 878:83	color h. to achieve that objective	SAFI 737:22	H. will not judge this kindly	ASHCR 37:62
Over the h.	THOM 884:37	contribution to human h.	MCNA 557:92	Human h.…a race	WELLS 930:35
Over the h. and far away	GAY 362:19	conveying a whole h.	JIANG 455:57	hypochondriacs of h.	AGNEW 9:95
Over the h. and far away	STEV 851:25	country which has no h.	PRIT 696:23	If men could learn from h.	COLE 236:51
range of shadeless h.	ROBE 717:72	dangerous moment in human h.	AGATE 9:88	if you read your h.	OROU 652:92
reclined on the h.	TENN 870:92	deriving from a h.	BELL 78:88	in spite of H.	WALC 917:21
silence in the h.	TENN 873:65	disasters of English h.	TOOLE 894:58	iron laws of h.	EAGL 309:2
strength of the h. is his also	BOOK 149:30	discerned in h. a plot	WAUGH 923:59	journalism…as an extension of h.	SAMP 741:97
sunset on moors and windy h.	MASE 580:57	distinguishing h. from old movie	FISH 337:62	just as h. is rushing by	ADLER 8:67
to the h. will lift mine eyes	SCOT 755:89	divine and human h.	BAKER 56:8	keep h. and theology apart	WELLS 930:36
upon our clouded h.?	BLAKE 141:41	Does h. repeat itself	GARC 359:67	knowledge…product of h.	CARL 201:14
whole sky…to the h.	FROST 352:92	do more to shape h.	BARN 64:70	know of our h.	NAIP 629:28
Why hop ye so, ye high h.?	BOOK 149:24	dustheap of h.	TAYL 868:46	large scale in h.	INGE 445:29
hill-side h.-s.'s dew-pearled	BROW 167:9	duty we owe to h.	TROT 899:61	lessons of h.	HUXL 442:96
hilt gyrdyll aboute the h.	MALO 563:15	English h. is all about men	WILDE 940:56	lies down on the tracks of h.	EISE 314:93
himself better pleased with h.	JOHN 463:62	entire h. of science	BRAD 154:26	life's h.	HOOD 426:34
better than he understands h.	HUGO 437:77	epoch unrivalled in world h.	RAND 706:54	look back into English h.	PAXM 670:46
fell in love with h.	POWE 693:43	exceeds an infamous h.	LARI 509:70	magic moment in American h.	WHITE 936:59
fights only with h.	GREE 386:27	footnote in the h. books	BROW 165:80	make more h. than they can consume	SAKI 739:59
loves nothing but h.	SOUT 835:53	funny pages of the h. books	THAT 881:53	More than at any other time in h.	ALLEN 14:98
loving h. better than all	COLE 236:46	Hansard is h.'s ear	DEAN 267:39	much prefer h.	TOLK 893:46
Nothing resembles him less than h.	DIDE 285:71	happiest women…have no h.	SAMU 741:99	myth rather than h.	FIED 334:10
reads only what is…within h.	PROU 698:61	H. admits no rules	ELIOT 315:35	never learned anything from h.	HEGEL 406:8
walking into h.	THUR 890:83	H.…An account, mostly false	MITCH 609:33	nine-tenths a h. lesson	SWIFT 861:12
hind as the loving h.	BIBLE 104:57	H., at least	BIER 134:80	no h. of art	WERE 931:55
h. that would be mated	SHAK 791:55	H.…badly constructed concert hall	MACA 545:29	no h.; only biography	EMER 324:58
Hindoo marries, dies, or turns H.	SHEL 814:4	H. does not long entrust	MACL 555:40	not burdened with a h.	THOR 889:53
hindrances legal and material h.	WOLF 952:60	H. does not provide	EISE 314:96	Not written on by h.	SCOTT 751:3
hinds feet like h.' feet	BIBLE 99:39	H. gets thicker	KRIS 499:13	novel of mankind, not the h.	GAUT 362:5
Soft maids and village h.	COLL 237:70	H. had achieved a happy ending	TAYL 868:49	Of h. and its consequences	OBRI 645:62
hindsight at the very best, 20-20 h.	PIRS 679:94	H. has many cunning passages	MCCA 548:93	our h., our idealistic pretensions	OBRI 645:65
H. is always twenty-twenty	WILD 943:37	H.…is a nightmare	ELIOT 317:84	Our whole h. inclines	MASA 580:49
h. proves us wrong	MCNA 557:93	H. is…a tableau	JOYCE 470:24	out of life into h.	CHUR 225:74
hint h. a fault	POPE 688:3	H. is a tale of efforts	VOLT 914:39	pain of h. words contain	WALC 916:12
hints only h. and guesses	ELIOT 320:78	H. is condemned…to lies	KISS 494:90	Painters of h.	KNEL 494:8
hip h. hooray and bally hoo	DUBIN 304:64	H. is hard to know	FRAN 347:82	parody had completely replaced h.	PIGL 678:75
H. is the sophistication	MAIL 559:37	H. is littered with the wars	THOM 886:88	people without h.	ELIOT 321:93
smote them h. and thigh	BIBLE 96:17	H. is more or less bunk	POWE 693:57	Political h. is far too criminal	AUDEN 44:17
hip-hop H.-h. is a perfect mix	JAY 453:7	H. is not a science	FORD 343:95	political or constitutional h.	JAY 453:1
Hippocrene blushful H.	KEATS 478:42	H. is not merciful	FRAN 347:86	problems of biography, of h.	MILLS 595:6
H. is somewhat drouthy	BYRON 189:3	H. is not politically correct	NEW 634:41	Psychology has…a short h.	EBBI 310:9
hippopotamus shoot the H.	BELL 76:53	H. isn't through with me	FERG 333:80	reading of the h. of thought	MERT 589:55
hips girdle when your h. stick	NASH 631:82	H. is on our side	MARC 570:55	Read no h.	DISR 287:19
hire ask employers to h.	BORO 151:68	H. is past politics	KHRU 485:91	repeat h.	ILLI 445:21
hireling h., and not the shepherd	BIBLE 123:45	H. is philosophy	FREE 350:47	resuscitate, if it concerns h.	HUGO 436:55
h. of the Ministry	OCON 646:82	H. is the endless repetition	CARL 201:18	reverberates through men's h.	KOES 495:31
Pay given to state h.	JOHN 460:79	H. is the essence of…biographies	DURR 308:38	sailed through American h.	MENC 587:15
Hispanic H. world never crumbled	REYES 712:69	H. is the myth	CARL 201:15	Science…opposed to h.	BORN 151:65
historian first be an h.	HARR 398:42	H.…is the struggle between love	MILL 594:85	skies of h. hurrying	SASS 746:96
first requisite of the h.	STRA 856:36	H. is written for the victors	BENE 79:14	sleep and a sense of h.	WILS 948:72
h. is often only a journalist	KRAUS 499:8	H. may be servitude	DREX 299:4	so vain that he wants to figure in h.	DISR 288:63
h. must have a third quality	FORS 345:43	H. must not be written with bias	ELIOT 321:80	study of military h.	CLAU 229:75
I will be a h.	OGDEN 647:99	H. never exactly repeats itself	BETJ 88:34	takes a great deal of h.	JAMES 450:35
Only one safe rule for the h.	FISH 337:62	H. never stops	DEAN 267:42	the h. of the world	POPP 689:57
			MONT 614:34		

There is no h. of mankind	POPP 689:57	H. on, h. on!	ANON 26:94	h. place of the tabernacles	BIBLE 100:68
those who study h.	TAYL 868:48	H. them cheap	HOPK 429:91	h. rest, and peace	NEWM 635:46
thousand years of h.	GAIT 357:13	H. then my sword	SHAK 778:55	h. Satan	DAMI 261:22
Throughout h.	HAILE 392:16	like to h. it back	SEVI 758:42	h. thing to see	BLAKE 140:13
thy lips my h.	SIDN 820:51	put democracy on h.	LOVE 539:94	h. unto the dogs	BIBLE 140:13
till h. is no longer made	PEAR 671:56	To have and to h.	BOOK 148:91	Made h. by their dreams	GIBS 367:14
too much h.	KING 488:42	undermine her h. on life	FORS 344:37	Nothing but h., pure, and clear	HERB 413:57
trample over their h.	STREE 858:49	**Holden Caulfield** There's no more to H. C.	SALI 740:87	place...is h. ground	BIBLE 93:52
understand a science...know its h.	COMTE 239:8	**Holding** bowler's H.	JOHN 465:9	proofs of h. writ	SHAK 789:24
uses h. to develop theory	STIN 854:1	**holding** not good at h. my tongue	MURD 626:71	religion would still be h. and divine	BAUD 69:79
war h....simple one	WODE 952:54	**hole** decayed h. among the mountains	ELIOT 318:10	Sabbath...making it h.	WALK 917:37
War makes rattling good h.	HARDY 397:27	dry, bare, sandy h.	TOLK 893:42	Sae pious and sae h.	BURNS 178:92
way of indicating how h.	MALA 561:85	flame creeps in at every h.	PEELE 672:70	suffer thine H. One	BIBLE 99:36
We make h.	REAG 708:10	h. in the ground	TOLK 893:42	thy h. feet	BLAKE 139:80
What is h., in fact	IRVI 447:55	h. in the subconscious	HALE 392:28	touch of h. bread	SHAK 779:1
What will H. say?	SHAW 807:2	h. that allows the mouse in	JACO 449:10	**holy-day** free And h.-d....spirit	LAMB 505:89
whole of contemporary h.	ROY 730:27	kick a h. in a stained glass window	CHAN 213:76	**Holy Ghost** Because the H. G.	HOPK 428:71
Who owns h.?	NEW 634:33	Might stop a h.	SHAK 784:65	blasphemy against the H. G.	BIBLE 117:84
You appear before h.	CLEM 229:86	not enough...to be h.	BRAT 157:78	but by the H. G.	BIBLE 126:50
hit A h., a very palpable h.	SHAK 785:71	sphere into an inaccessible h.	CHUR 226:17	filled with the H. G.	BIBLE 125:72
can't think and h.	BERRA 87:92	**holes** into a bag with h.	BIBLE 111:57	Have ye received the H. G.?	BIBLE 125:95
get there; h. it	RANJ 706:61	**holiday** His first h.	BOUC 152:86	H. G. is come upon you	BIBLE 124:70
h. a ball further	PRIE 695:95	h. steamers made an excursion	PRIE 695:86	I believe in the H. G.	BOOK 146:31
h. at all if it can be avoided	ROOS 724:19	in a h. humour	SHAK 780:9	I believe in the H. G.	BOOK 147:62
h. that stride and keep it	SAND 742:34	perpetual h. is a good...definition	SHAW 810:3	John Wesley and the H. G.	MENC 587:14
hither transported h. and thither	OVID 657:21	regular h. to them	DICK 278:61	pretending to...gifts of the H. G.	BUTL 184:58
Hitler at least H. was mad	LIVI 532:59	Roman h.	BYRON 188:66	temple of the H. G.	BIBLE 126:39
cable H. and kick him	GOLD 377:24	two years in H. Inns	MOND 612:94	who was conceived by the H. G.	BOOK 146:37
destruction of H.	CHUR 226:7	**holidays** h. from Eton	SITW 824:19	**Holy Grail** see the H. G.	MALO 563:13
every Christian in H.'s Europe	FACK 329:1	h....interfere with one's work	EDWA 312:62	There lies the H. G.	MACA 544:4
German Chancellor, Herr H.	CHAM 212:63	H....learning experience	OGDEN 647:2	**Holy See** insult to the H. S.	INNO 446:48
grew up scared of H.	BAIL 55:82	Term, h., term, h.	LEWIS 526:48	**Holy Spirit** H. S....invisible	TAYL 868:59
Herr H. and Signor Mussolini	HALI 393:33	**holier** h. lot to be unknown	HOPK 428:83	inspiration of thy H. S.	BOOK 147:58
H. attacked the Jews	NIEM 637:91	h. than thou	BIBLE 110:8	**holy-water** h.-w. death	MCGO 552:76
H. had already found	ROBI 718:95	In h. shapes	SHAK 791:81	**homage** both an h. and a critique	MOTH 622:86
H.'s gas chambers	MEIR 584:41	**holiness** beauty of h.	BIBLE 102:3	h. of a tear	BYRON 187:37
H. showed surprising loyalty	BULL 173:59	h. of always being the injured party	ANGE 19:94	H. to plain dumb luck	ACHE 3:51
H. was a Jeanne d'Arc	POUND 692:22	mind is bent to h.	SHAK 759:84	involuntarily pay h.	POTT 690:84
H. was dead	SCHA 747:19	vision of the h. of God	BLOOM 143:65	**home** advocating for H. Rule	MCGO 551:75
H...missed the bus	CHAM 212:67	way of h.	BIBLE 108:77	against books the H. Secretary	WAUGH 923:69
Like kissing H.	CURT 259:1	**Holland** Dutch may have their H.	JOHN 458:24	A h. filled with nothing	ATWO 41:51
marches with H.	CHUR 225:90	H....lies so low	HOOD 426:27	airs have brought me h.	POE 683:86
people H. never understood	BULL 173:60	**hollow** Down to the h.	FLAN 338:8	ALL parts and none are h.	MAIL 560:67
Was not H. a paper tiger	MAO 569:33	h., heartless, mirthless	THUR 891:96	always a bad sign, at h.	MITF 610:57
When I go to see Herr H.	HEND 410:2	h. of thine ear	SHAK 766:1	and I am far from h.	NEWM 635:45
hits go to see h.	JOUR 469:11	waters in the h. of his hand	BIBLE 108:81	and returning h.	BUCH 171:29
hive angry h. of bees	SHAK 759:90	We are the h. men	ELIOT 318:13	Are they being...too much at h.?	COLE 234:2
bitter h. to grope for honey	SPEN 839:48	**hollow-headed** h.-h. mediocrity	MENC 587:16	At h., whispering	OWEN 658:36
h. for the honey-bee	YEATS 965:4	**hollowness** h. disappoints at the time	BRON 161:72	At h., you always have to be	MACM 556:66
in the h. of home	MACN 558:99	Reverb no h.	SHAK 792:85	best country ever is, at h.	GOLD 376:86
hives fill our h. with honey	SWIFT 861:18	**hollows** bowery h. crowed	TENN 878:87	blest by suns of h.	BROO 162:88
hoard Our h. is little	TENN 876:42	**Hollywood** America gets H.	JONG 466:38	both h. runs and strike outs	RODG 721:50
To h. is...villainous	RABE 704:15	Americans...considered H.	MAMET 564:34	call the cattle h.	KING 487:43
Hoare Samuel H. was the pygmiest	BOOT 150:49	average H. film star	HEPB 412:25	came h., h. to a lie	POUND 691:4
hoary h. hills are seen	POPE 688:31	every actor in H.	GIEL 368:26	Can't Go H. Again	WOLFE 953:71
Hobbes H. clearly proves	SWIFT 863:65	Hooray for H.	MERC 587:22	cart with the h. packed	COLL 237:64
hobbit in the ground there lived a h.	TOLK 893:42	Inside this H. playboy	FLYNN 341:64	chickens have come h. to roost	MAMET 564:32
hobbit-hole h.-h....comfort	TOLK 893:42	I should not have been invited to H.	CHAN 213:80	children who leave h.	SLOVO 826:56
hobbits H. are an unobtrusive	TOLK 893:47	last...anyone cares about in H.	STREE 857:48	Comes h. again	SHAK 802:67
hobby suggests an elaborate h.	PRIE 695:90	not very keen on H.	COWA 249:65	consequence of leaving one's h.	LEBO 518:67
hobby-horse man rides his H.-H.	STER 848:23	vote for H. as a Republican	WALL 917:44	could have stayed h.	CLIN 231:22
hobgoblin h. of little minds	EMER 324:54	Wants steady employment in H.	DAVIS 265:94	domestic servants at h.	MAUG 582:11
hobnailed That h. goblin	SITW 823:5	**holme** carver h.	SPEN 838:20	dream of going 'h.'	PARK 665:37
hobo-trekkers H.-t. that forever	CRANE 253:61	**Holmes** H. remarked, impatiently	DOYLE 297:69	dream of H.	FORD 343:9
hock sipped at the weak h.	BETJ 88:18	John Clellon H.	KERO 483:56	dream that I am h. again!	FLEC 340:36
hockey mom a h. m. and a pit bull	PALIN 661:58	To Sherlock H. she is always	DOYLE 297:56	drive one from h.	HOOD 426:28
hodgepodge h. of all other speeches	SPEN 838:18	**Holocaust** truth of the H.	WEIZ 928:78	dunce that has been kept at h.	COWP 251:6
hoe But to take a large h.	KIPL 491:32	**holsters** inside of his h.	SHAW 806:84	E.T. phone h.	MATH 581:89
tickle her with a h.	JERR 455:46	**holy** be h....with impunity?	RACI 704:31	everything off and went h.	SZIL 865:45
Hofstadter H.'s Law	HOFS 422:35	called the H. Roman Empire	VOLT 914:40	Family!... the h. of all social evil	STRI 857:53
hog disadvantage of being a h.	MORT 621:73	cased up, like a h. relic	WEBS 927:53	feel ashamed of h.	DICK 282:7
H. Butcher for the World	SAND 741:13	coming to that h. room	DONNE 293:64	field, or a h.	WILD 943:45
h. that could fiddle	ROCH 720:19	discipline of our h. Church	OCON 646:82	friends, and native h.	MILT 598:63
mere h. at his trough	HUNT 440:30	give solemn thanks to the H. Trinity	COLU 239:91	gat him h. to his house	BIBLE 97:48
put lipstick on a h.	RICH 714:13	great source of the h. river	SPEKE 836:81	get h. from work	PARKS 665:44
talk h. and hominy	FERB 332:68	h. alliance to exorcise	MARX 579:33	give me a h.	HIGL 418:54
hogamus H., higamous	JAMES 452:78	h. and enchanted	COLE 236:37	God, who is our h.	WORD 959:8
hogs Fattenin' h. ain't in luck	HARR 399:49	H. Catholic and Apostolic	TEMP 869:69	Hang my Hat is H.	JERO 454:44
fatting h. of late	SPEN 840:63	H. Deadlock	HERB 412:47	Heaven and H.	WORD 961:45
let it not be like h.	MCKA 553:6	H., divine, good	MILT 606:51	hills of h.!	STEV 854:88
Holbein H. of Jell-O ads	ADLER 8:68	h.; for I am h.	BIBLE 94:76	h. among the dead	SHEL 815:45
hold first cries 'H., enough!'	SHAK 798:78	H., h., h.	BIBLE 131:97	h. and put a bullet	ROBI 718:82
He who will h. another down	ACH 2:24	H., h., h.	BOOK 147:70	'h.'—a real life	MANS 576:96
h. down one thing	BELL 77:75	H., h., h., is the Lord	BIBLE 107:54	h. his footsteps...turned	SCOTT 752:16
h. fast that which is good	BIBLE 129:15	H., H., H.! Lord God Almighty!	HEBER 406:2	h., in a flood of tears	DICK 278:58
H. fast the form of sound words	BIBLE 129:27	h. hush	STEV 849:69	H. is heaven	NASH 630:65
H., h., my heart	SHAK 781:66	h. nation	BIBLE 130:67	H. is the girl's prison	SHAW 808:53

home-acre

H. is the place	FROST 352:93
H. is where one starts from	ELIOT 320:68
H. I would go	OTWAY 656:99
H. James	HILL 418:63
H. life as we understand it	SHAW 809:85
h. life of our own dear Queen	ANON 23:98
H. of lost causes	ARNO 35:12
h. of the brave?	KEY 484:68
h. of the scorpion	SNYD 832:91
h. of the weird	LAWS 514:94
h....saved by his courage	MACA 546:60
H.'s h.	ARBU 30:2
H. they brought	TENN 873:46
h. to...Jews, Muslims and Christians	CLIN 230:3
h., you idle creature	SHAK 776:3
House is not a H.	ADLER 8:71
humble h.	GLAD 373:38
husbands to stay at h.	ELIOT 315:36
I can get all that at h.	COOK 245:68
if they go from h.	GASK 361:84
in my bosom, and at h.	JONS 467:74
in the hive of h.	MACN 558:99
into the h.—where it belongs	HITC 419:84
isn't much to write h. about	HYDE 443:20
it never is at h.	COWP 250:91
keep the Sabbath...staying at H.	DICK 284:35
Kiss till the cow comes h.	BEAU 71:16
last night the cows came h.	NATH 632:1
live at h., quiet, confined	AUST 47:88
lov'd at h., rever'd abroad	BURNS 177:76
luminous h. of waters	ARNO 35:1
Lurching to...'H. sweet H.'	SASS 745:80
man who thinks to found a h.	DOUG 295:10
merely ready to go h.	KAIKO 472:12
merriest when they are from h.	SHAK 775:63
milk comes frozen h.	SHAK 763:27
My h. policy? I wage war	CLEM 229:87
national h. for the Jews	BALF 58:39
never felt myself from h.	BOSW 152:77
never to attempt to make at h.	SMITH 827:85
Next to a letter from h.	DOOL 294:83
not a thing remains at h.	BELLI 76:47
not yet gone h.	THUR 890:62
ocean...was his h.	BYRON 187:48
our eternal h.	WATTS 923:48
out of house and h.	SHAK 772:78
problems of running a h.	THAT 881:55
refuge from h. life	SHAW 806:95
Rowing h. to haven	MASE 580:55
small places, close to h.	ROOS 724:2
snail...is at h.	DONNE 292:46
sons, her h., her food	NATI 632:4
stay at h. and help	WINT 950:10
stay at h., my noble lord	BALL 59:59
Stay h. and cause no trouble	AESC 9:80
They should go back h.	BLUN 143:84
thou art my h.	PRIOR 696:11
till the cows come h.	MARX 578:17
toddle safely h. and die	SASS 745:85
to go h. in the dark	OHEN 648:21
to the mountains is going h.	MUIR 624:25
turning my face towards h.	PARK 663:91
unconquerable...the American h.	SELZ 757:19
was just that I was leaving h.	STEV 854:89
welcome h. to me!	BURNS 178:4
What's the good of a h.	GROS 389:79
When I was at h.	SHAK 778:74
when mum stays h.	FALU 329:11
who gives a child a h.	MASE 580:64
woman's true position in the h.	STAN 842:13
women are to stay at h.	WEST 933:95
you can't go h. again	BRYS 170:5
You will be h. before	WILH 943:56
home-acre hearth-fire and the h.-a.	KIPL 492:55
homecoming h. of...companions	HOMER 425:9
home-fires Keep the H.-f. burning	FORD 343:9
home-keeping H.-k. youth	SHAK 758:55
homeland h. is sweet to him	HUGH 434:6
live in his h.	BELL 76:44
PLO is a h.	NEW 634:36
homeless fine for the h.	VAN 908:22
h. and self-forgetful	WHIT 936:71
h. by choice	SOUT 835:53
h. man in a thousand dollar suit	ANON 27:24
h., tempest-tossed	LAZA 515:3
homely female shall be h.	KENN 480:91
h. slighted Shepherd's trade	MILT 599:86

home-made H.-m. dishes	HOOD 426:28
Homer a simple digamma in H.	QUIL 702:16
blind H. sing to me?	MARL 573:27
Helen, did H. never see	JONS 468:85
H....chronicled the siege of Troy	CUOMO 258:81
H. invariably composes	ARNO 35:7
H....Never existed.	FLAU 339:28
in H. then H. knew	SWIFT 862:62
Mr Gladstone read H.	CHUR 225:75
never read a line of H.	MILL 594:66
Shakespeare was the H.	DRYD 300:26
when the worthy H. nods	HORA 430:21
homes firelit h., clean beds and wives	SASS 745:83
h. of silent prayer	TENN 874:72
stately h. of England	COWA 249:55
stately h. of England	HEMA 409:57
homesteads carry fire...into your h.	PARN 665:47
homeward Look h. Angel	MILT 600:93
sent him h. tae think again	WILL 947:31
homewards Most roads lead men h.	MASE 580:59
homey taste of lies was h.	GELL 363:34
hominy Mrs H....slowly up it	DICK 280:23
talk hog and h.	FERB 332:68
homme h. n'est rien d'autre	SART 745:73
h. n'est rien d'autre	SART 745:75
homo Ecce h.	BIBLE 133:47
h. sapiens, a vertebrate mammal	CARB 198:36
neotenic ape, species h. sapiens	ALDI 23:11
homophobic God wouldn't be h.	TUTU 901:29
homos stately h. of England	CRISP 255:6
homosexuality H. was the badge	EAGL 309:1
preoccupied with his latent h.	MAIL 559:40
honest any h. man's	GILB 368:42
both h. and intelligent	ORWE 655:66
for h. Poverty	BURNS 180:52
good h. and painful	PEPYS 673:88
hated...when I tried to be h.	ELLI 323:36
h. God	INGE 445:32
h. man's the noble work of GOD	BURNS 177:76
h. men and bonny lasses	BURNS 179:20
h., old-fashioned Boarding-school	AUST 46:73
h., sonsie face	BURNS 178:94
hope to remain h.	HOWE 434:93
in a general h. thought	SHAK 778:57
like an h. man	SHAK 774:36
looking for an h. man	DIOG 286:2
man who lies...is an h. man	SAFI 737:20
moderately h. man	SHAW 808:48
most of us are h. all the time	MATH 581:88
not h....but he is most evangelical	BEAV 71:25
not naturally h.	SHAK 800:28
obscure things that are h.	BIBLE 112:76
one of the few h. people	FITZ 337:81
people...are least h.	AUST 46:64
To be h.	SHAK 782:79
whatsoever things are h.	BIBLE 128:5
world's grown h.	SHAK 782:84
writer overwhelmingly h.	MOORE 617:87
write straight h. prose	HEMI 410:75
honestly deal with each other h.	CHAN 213:90
honesty Art, whose h. must work	RIDI 715:34
brings more h. and care	WEBB 925:8
full of love and h.	SHAK 789:17
h. be no puritan	SHAK 791:59
H. coupled to beauty	SHAK 779:99
h. is a good thing	MARQ 575:53
h. is his	SHAK 791:77
h. is not to be based	RUSK 733:8
H. was a cheat	OTWAY 656:2
it lacks h.	YEATS 967:35
most important thing...is h.	GOLD 377:37
people are shocked by h.	COWA 249:57
perilous to a man's h.	TROL 898:42
so rich as h.	SHAK 791:64
that damn'd...quality call'd h.	OTWAY 656:1
transform h. from what it is	SHAK 783:9
Wisdom without h.	JONS 468:88
writers...have a terrible h.	CHAN 213:94
honey Believe me, h.	TUCK 901:15
bitter hive to grope for h.	SPEN 839:48
buzzes in the h. there	THOM 884:40
Come Back...Huck H.!	FIED 334:9
drowned in the h.	HAWT 401:2
eat my peas with h.	NASH 631:87
fill our hives with h.	SWIFT 861:18
flowing with milk and h.	BIBLE 93:54
h., and plenty of money	LEAR 516:35

h. a sauce to sugar	SHAK 779:99
h. of all flowers	NASHE 631:89
h. of poison-flowers	TENN 875:16
h. pot for every scholar	SAFER 737:16
h. wild, and manna dew	KEATS 476:2
how can I be h. now?	OLSEN 650:44
in my mouth sweet as h.	BIBLE 131:8
is there h. still for tea?	BROO 162:97
locusts and wild h.	BIBLE 114:19
milk and h. blessed	NEALE 632:7
Money...sweeter than H.	FRAN 348:11
Pedigree of H.	DICK 284:51
Reach me a rose, h.	FITZ 337:83
scoop of pure h.	SMITH 801:57
summer's h. breath	SHAK 828:99
sweeter than h.	BIBLE 103:27
honey-bee hive for the h.-b.	YEATS 965:4
honeycomb gave him...an h.	BIBLE 122:14
lips...drop as an h.	BIBLE 104:56
honey-dew he on h.-d. hath fed	COLE 236:42
honeymoon H.'s over...get married	EPST 327:32
Hong Kong buildings of H. K.	BOOTH 150:50
honour All h.'s mimic	DONNE 291:26
as an h. to Shakespeare	JONS 468:90
Can H.'s voice provoke	GRAY 384:67
Cavalier who loves h.	SCOTT 754:82
chastity of h.	BURKE 176:41
Chief who in h. advances!	SCOTT 752:29
clear h....purchased by the merit	SHAK 769:95
crowned him with glory and h.	BIBLE 99:31
for the h. of England	CONG 241:57
fount whence h. springs	MARL 572:1
from the book of h. razèd	SHAK 800:44
full of days, riches, and h.	BIBLE 98:84
Giving h. unto the wife	BIBLE 130:70
glory, laud and h.	NEALE 632:6
goblin H. which the world adores	CAREW 198:56
had the h. to be	TILL 891:16
he was valiant, I h. him	SHAK 777:36
his h. and his quality taken	BLUN 143:79
His h. rooted	TENN 877:54
H. all men	BIBLE 130:68
h. and good actions	BACON 52:16
h. aspireth to it	BACON 50:58
H. but an empty bubble	DRYD 303:33
h. cuts falsehood	GURN 390:1
h. did but jest	GREE 386:31
h., duty, patriotism	LLOY 533:72
h., fredom and curteisie	CHAU 217:71
h., her reputation, and her person	GOTT 379:70
h. is a private station	ADDI 7:51
H. is like a match	PAGN 659:26
h. is my life	SHAK 764:32
H. is not the exclusive property	HOOV 427:51
h., it is no longer peace	RUSS 735:45
h. lies in killing men	MARG 570:67
h., love, obedience	SHAK 798:69
h. May privilege more sins	SHIR 819:17
h. of God	BACH 49:8
h. of the British Empire	CHUR 225:93
H. pricks me on	SHAK 771:59
h. turn to dust	MARV 577:92
h. unto Luke Evangelist	ROSS 726:61
h. would thee do	SHAK 775:55
how I do h. thee!	SHAK 770:14
hurt that H. feels	TENN 871:56
If I lose mine h.	SHAK 794:65
If your h. disna ken	SCOTT 753:52
in her left hand riches and h.	BIBLE 104:55
It is not for me, Your H.	BIRK 136:15
Jealous in h.	SHAK 779:82
Keeps h. bright	SHAK 787:38
leave not a stain in h.	BIBLE 113:7
left to the fighter's h.	HEMI 409:71
Legion of H.	TWAIN 902:47
louder he talked of his h.	EMER 325:90
Loved I not h. more	LOVE 538:86
mace of h.	MANC 564:51
make one vessel unto h.	BIBLE 125:23
no spark of h. bides	SHAK 760:2
Observe his h.	DONNE 291:27
Of power, of h.	MARL 573:21
once stood for h.	WHITE 934:28
only h. and life...spared	FRAN 347:95
peace, I hope, with h.	DISR 288:66
Peace without h.	CECIL 210:27
pension list...a roll of h.	CLEV 230:91

horse

pluck bright h.	SHAK 771:37	h. never comes That comes to all	MILT 601:35	To sympathy with h. and fears	SHEL 814:94
prophet is not without h.	BIBLE 117:97	h. of glory	BOOK 147:50	vanity of human h.	JOHN 459:53
Render…h. to whom h.	BIBLE 126:30	h. of instant results	SCHL 748:38	**hoping** go truly h. to find adventure	HEAT 406:93
reputation for wisdom and h.	BIBLE 106:30	h. of science	INGE 445:31	h….someone will make things right	REAG 708:2
Set h. in one eye	SHAK 776:7	h. of winning her love	STAEL 841:94	**Hopper** Do you know, Mr H.	WILDE 941:77
signed with their h.	SPEN 837:93	h., once crushed	ARNO 35:21	H. is the great painter	ALLEN 13:78
sin to covet h.	SHAK 776:87	h. on God is founded	BRID 158:9	**hoppy** H., Croppy, Droppy	ELLIS 323:28
some smatch of h.	SHAK 778:55	H. sleeps in our bones	PIER 677:71	**hop-yards** for what were h.-y. meant	HOUS 432:57
staff of h. for mine age	SHAK 760:22	h. so transcendent	LAWR 514:90	**Horace** Virgil and H.	DRYD 300:40
stain her h., or…brocade	POPE 685:35	H. springs eternal	POPE 687:74	**Horatio** more things…H.	SHAK 781:70
symbol of national h.	KRUG 500:24	h.'s true gage	RALE 705:44	O, I die, H.	SHAK 785:74
them that h. me I will h.	BIBLE 96:24	h. that he will die	EMER 325:86	**Horatius** H. kept the bridge	MACA 546:50
this journey…and the h. thereof	EDWA 312:57	h. thou in God	BIBLE 100:64	out spake brave H.	MACA 545:45
To h. his own words	TENN 877:56	h. to get one every 30 years	SIMON 822:77	stood brave H.	MACA 546:48
Upon my h.	PARK 664:32	h. to joy is little less	SHAK 764:44	**horde** language of the h.	MALL 562:99
when h. dies	WHIT 938:18	h….unwilling to be fed	WORD 959:2	Society is now one polished h.	BYRON 190:24
with native h. clad	MILT 604:98	H. ushers in a Revolution	CARL 200:4	**horizon** always somebody else's h.!	GRAH 381:90
with wealth and h. blest	DRYD 302:73	H. withering fled	BYRON 188:75	h. of daily environment	EINS 313:76
honourable Brutus is an h. man	SHAK 777:37	Idle to h.	REED 709:30	multiplying on the sold h.	WALC 916:17
designs were strictly h.	FIEL 335:25	if…h. should e'er decline	WORD 962:47	narrow h. of bourgeois	MARX 579:43
intentions are perfectly h.	SHAW 809:66	I h. in thee	STUA 858:59	neither h., cloud, nor sound	CARR 202:53
most h.…was to steal	RABE 703:7	illusions that…limit h.	FRYE 354:57	pressing up over the h.	TIME 891:18
surrender…was as h. as resistance	ANGE 18:86	in the store we sell h.	REVS 712:68	workhouse from the h.	LLOY 532:71
true and h. wife	SHAK 777:19	in trembling h. repose	GRAY 384:78	**horizons** h. come	HUGH 435:30
whatever is sweet, and h.	MELV 585:61	Is it too much to h.	REDM 709:21	sorrow's h. are vague	MCMU 557:85
honoured but h. of them all	TENN 870:98	Land of H. and Glory	BENS 81:84	**horizontal** h. desire	SHAW 810:25
H. and bless'd be	SCOTT 752:29	land of their heart's h.	DAVIS 266:9	your position would be h.	OHARA 648:13
h. by your friends	HOOV 427:55	lined himself with h.	SHAK 772:76	**horn** blind H.'s hate	KIPL 493:73
More h. in the breach	SHAK 781:56	living h. rose in me	FOX 346:71	h., the h., the lusty h.	SHAK 780:15
honouring wirschep and great h.	DUNB 306:98	Love without h.	GRAV 383:40	hunter's h. is ringing	SCOTT 752:33
honours bears his blushing h.	SHAK 805:52	Maybe all one can do is h.	MILL 593:48	if we can pick up a h.	FREE 349:44
neither h. nor wages	GARI 360:73	may be brought to h.	TROL 898:39	it won't come out of your h.	PARK 663:93
talk of high h.	TS 900:6	may we bring h.	THAT 881:54	keys of a postboy's h.	BENET 79:24
hood him that wears a h.	ANON 22:61	miserable have…only h.	SHAK 787:63	Poured thro' the mellow h.	COLL 238:78
racing car whose h.	MARI 571:77	must run with h.	ZATO 969:2	'scorn' 'h.', a hard rhyme	SHAK 774:56
wear the h.	DUNC 307:11	Nature to his h. has giv'n	POPE 687:75	small but sullen h.	COLL 238:76
Hoo-doo H.-d….unorganized	REED 710:35	no h. of finding ourselves	MILL 594:64	wreathèd h.	WORD 961:30
hoods gaudy h. and linings!	DICK 279:1	nor h. nor health	SHEL 812:68	**Hornby** my H. and my Barlow	THOM 886:84
hoofs plunging h. were gone	DELA 271:27	no very lively h.	SMITH 831:63	**hornets** wasps and h. break through	SWIFT 861:23
hook button, h., and lace	LOWE 539:98	one more rich h.	SHAK 800:46	**Hornie** Auld H., Satan, Nick	BURNS 177:83
by h. or by crook	MORE 618:10	One who has h.	BENE 79:22	**hornpipes** h. and strathspeys	BURNS 180:44
draw out leviathan with an h.?	BIBLE 99:22	only h. of creating something	FLAU 339:22	**horns** got to draw in their h.	LEMAY 521:30
head down on the h.	JUST 471:50	others have to h. for heaven	SLOAN 825:55	h. of cockled snails	SHAK 763:16
Not a h. in all my breast	VAUG 909:38	Our h. for years to come	WATTS 923:48	h. of Elfland	TENN 872:39
hooker the local h.	PART 666:60	place where sanity and h.	ROUS 729:8	keeping clear of her h.	SZENT 865:30
hookers played so many h.	MACL 554:19	poise of h. and fear	MILT 599:73	Morning on the silver h.	TENN 873:51
hook-nosed h.-n. fellow of Rome	SHAK 773:94	power of the h. of freedom	BUCK 172:34	on the h. o'th' moon	SHAK 799:89
hooks baited h. shall tangle	WYATT 963:87	Rootless h.	BINY 135:3	pulled in their h.	JUVE 471:57
With silken lines, and silver h.	DONNE 292:37	Some blessed H.	HARDY 397:23	taking the bull by both h.	ASHF 38:76
hooligans Football h.?	CLOU 232:68	spring of h.	DICK 282:94	With its h. through mist	THOM 883:21
hoops pot shall have ten h.	SHAK 759:95	strength and my h. is perished	BIBLE 110:25	**horny-handed** H.-h. sons of toil	SALI 740:88
with h. of steel	SHAK 781:49	The absence of h.	OBAMA 644:38	**horrible** grotesque to the h.	DOYLE 297:73
hooray Dear Mrs A, H., h.	COWA 249:56	this pleasing h.	ADDI 7:52	It is h., yet fascinating	DOYLE 297:68
H. for Hollywood	MERC 587:22	Through love, through h.	WORD 961:43	people were so h.	AMIS 16:37
hooter because the h. hoots	CHES 221:90	triumph of h.	JOHN 462:21	to not feel any, that is h.	VIAN 911:72
Hoover H. with a smile	ONEI 651:79	True h. is swift	SHAK 761:46	**horribly** h. in love with her	SHAK 774:40
hop H. forty paces	SHAK 794:57	unconquerable h.	ARNO 34:95	**horrid** h. malicious bloody flame	PEPYS 674:7
hope Abandon all h.	DANTE 262:37	wait without h.	ELIOT 320:57	h. thing, a very h. thing	BUTL 184:58
against h. believed in h.	BIBLE 125:8	Whatever h. is yours	OWEN 658:34	h. thing to follow	JAMES 450:40
belief and h. had gone	RUSS 735:42	what h. of harmony?	SHAK 759:86	was bad, she was h.	LONG 536:40
Can something, h.	HOPK 429:88	what was dead was H.	WILDE 942:19	**horror** beauty…watch it only full of h.	VIEI 913:7
do not h. to turn	ELIOT 318:22	What…we may gain from h.	MILT 602:42	boredom, and the h., and the glory	ELIOT 319:30
exercise of h.	WORD 960:23	Where there is despair, h.	FRAN 347:99	define your own h. journey	GELL 363:35
fair guerdon when we h.	MILT 599:86	who can h.	WALL 918:59	haunts of h. and fear	TENN 876:33
faith, h. charity	BIBLE 126:52	wish for what I faintly h.	DRYD 299:11	H. and doubt distract	MILT 603:89
feeble H. could ne'er	MARV 577:95	woes which H. thinks infinite	SHEL 815:20	h….for a whole nation	WHAR 933:2
Flesh Of H..	NICH 636:73	**hopeful** To be h. in an artistic sense	CONR 244:39	h. of civil war	HOMER 425:6
fruitful h. of nourishment	SPEN 839:61	**hopelessness** h. of knowing	LEAC 515:15	h. of Creation	HUGH 436:40
gathers her most vital h.	MELV 585:56	**hopes** airy h.	WORD 961:39	h. of outer darkness	GORD 378:54
God shall be my h.	SHAK 759:87	all h. to disappear	GILB 368:38	h. of the Twentieth Century	MAIL 560:56
high h. of adventure	WHIT 936:66	clues, h., and fears	LIPP 531:37	H., tyrant of the throbbing breast	GRAY 385:87
high uplifted beyond h.	MILT 602:55	Cricket is…full of forlorn h.	ORWE 654:44	I have a h. of the word	RENO 711:55
H., art thou true	SIDN 820:48	day with h.	CLIN 230:1	in the midst of h.	ANGE 18:82
h. could have no fear	THOM 887:10	different yearnings, different h.	CART 206:45	no imagination…no h.	DOYLE 296:40
H. deferred maketh the heart sick	BIBLE 104:68	fifty h. and fears	BROW 168:38	one expanding h. in American life	MAIL 560:52
H., for a season	CAMP 194:62	fondest h. decay	MOORE 618:6	secret dread, and inward h.	ADDI 7:72
h. for the best	SMITH 830:52	forgive me for not fulfilling some h.	YELT 968:45	The h.! The h.!	CONR 243:30
h. full of immortality	BIBLE 112:74	h. and dreams of the Future	FRAME 346:77	**horrors** Congenial h., hail!	THOM 887:3
H. guides us by her star	BRON 161:69	h. and h. to open	SHAK 802:81	I have supped full with h.	SHAK 798:73
H. has often caused	SOPH 834:25	h. and prayers of liberty-loving people	EISE 314:92	**horse** Always look a gift h.	RABE 703:12
h. in Christ	BIBLE 127:56	h. of future years	LONG 535:27	behold a pale h.	BIBLE 131:1
H. is a good breakfast	BACON 50:54	How strangely h. delude men	MASS 581:78	behold a white h.	BIBLE 132:19
H. is the bedrock	OBAMA 643:23	If h. were dupes	CLOU 232:48	between a rider and his h.	SURT 860:6
H. is the power of being cheerful	CHES 220:59	late on h. depended	SHAK 789:98	Be ye not as the h.	BIBLE 100:54
'H.' is the thing with feathers	DICK 283:34	nor as happy as one h.	LARO 510:2	camel is a h.	ISSI 448:78
h., love of finished years	ROSS 725:37	shipwrecking all their h.	MOOD 615:54	courage to ride a h.	LEAC 515:6
H. may vanish	SHEL 816:55	tender leaves of h.	SHAK 805:54	cup won by the worst h.	MASE 580:68

horseback

Entry	Reference
dearer than his h.	TENN 871:13
definition of a h.	DICK 281:77
duchess-faced h.	THOM 884:47
even do for a h.	NIGH 639:24
flung himself upon his h.	LEAC 515:14
fond of a h.	HALI 393:31
for want of a h.	FRAN 348:14
Give me another h.!	SHAK 761:48
given the h. strength?	BIBLE 99:18
Go not my h. the better	SHAK 797:43
hear a h.'s feet	KIPL 492:56
h. came spurring in	MACA 546:52
h. drench to bring 'em off	LAMB 505:86
h. in the silence champed the grasses	DELA 271:25
h. is drawn by the cart	KIPL 490:98
h. on the mountain	LORCA 537:58
H. riding is a perfect comparison with singing	PAVA 670:36
kingdom for a h.!	SHAK 761:55
leene was his h. as is a rake	CHAU 217:74
never heard no h. sing	ARMS 33:49
never look at another h.	MARX 578:20
no handles to a h.	LEAC 515:6
No h.'s cry was that	ARNO 34:97
nothing but talk of his h.	SHAK 769:77
One h. endeavoured to climb	SOME 833:10
One stiff blind h.	BROW 168:34
paint a forest or a h.	MARC 569:49
part man, part h.'s ass	ACHE 2:35
rather have a goddam h.	SALI 740:78
ridden the passions…magnificent h.	BROY 169:87
sightless h.	WALEY 917:31
sting a stately h.	JOHN 459:58
strong as a farm h.	LEE 519:97
The h. loves the hound	SURT 860:5
The h. that comes	YEATS 966:19
Then hey for boot and h.	KING 488:48
thrown from his h.	ANON 22:74
to my h.[I speak]German	CHAR 215:38
tried to milk the h.	BUSH 183:47
true as truest h.	SHAK 767:34
two men ride of a h.	SHAK 774:50
where's the bloody h.?	CAMP 194:51
Why does a hearse h. snicker	SAND 742:19
horseback as long as I live on h.	BIRD 136:8
horse-backbreaker this h.-b.	SHAK 771:47
horseguards can be in the H.	RATT 707:79
horsehair settee of the h. sea!	SITW 823:94
horse-hoof A h.-h. slides	YEATS 966:19
horseless-carriage h.-c….a luxury	ANON 23:1
horseman H., pass by!	YEATS 967:40
world's greatest h.	SCHU 750:76
horsemen apocalyptic h. in the air	MARC 569:48
chariot of Israel, and the h. thereof	BIBLE 97:71
horse-plough worked with a h.-p.	HEAN 404:68
horsepond celibacy is…a muddy h.	PEAC 671:51
horse-racing makes h. r….stable	STEI 846:89
horses as fed h. in the morning	BIBLE 110:13
best carriage h.	TROL 898:46
Bring on the empty h.!	CURT 259:2
But so are h.	GILM 371:92
cannot ride two h.	MAXT 583:19
Come saddle my h.	SCOTT 753:52
Don't Spare the H.	HILL 418:63
England…the hell of h.	FLOR 341:62
evening the strange h.	MUIR 624:23
frighten the h.	CAMP 194:48
generally given to h.	JOHN 460:77
hanged for stealing h.	HALI 393:34
heaven…filled—with h.	DUDEK 305:75
h. of instruction	BLAKE 140:1
h. o' Kansas	KIPL 491:18
h. who had never seen a man	BRIN 159:24
hurdling the meter like tired h.	BROY 169:88
in h., dawgs, and men	THAC 880:27
love of h.	FIND 336:45
never know what Trojan h.	BEVIN 90:66
H. and dorgs is some men's fancy	DICK 280:47
what they value in their h.	EMER 325:84
wild white h. play	ARNO 33:56
Women and H.	KIPL 490:93
horticulture You can lead a h.	PARK 664:26
hosanna Glorious h.	SMART 826:67
hosannas Made sweet h. ring	NEALE 632:6
hose put a h. in their mouth	KROC 499:17
hospital I was in h. once	BECK 72:53
Randolph Churchill went into h.	WAUGH 924:99
hospitality old Irish h.	EDGE 311:37
overwhelmed by the h.	BUSH 182:97
h., of golden daffodils	WORD 960:24
as a guest thanks his h.	DILL 286:93
Guarded…as by an h.	BYRON 189:6
met a h., and quelled it	PEAC 671:54
O all you h. of heaven!	SHAK 781:66
soundless-clapping h.	THOM 884:84
streams in the countless h.	HOW 433:85
tattered h. of eucalypt	ADAMS 4:73
Though an h. should encamp	BIBLE 100:50
under the h.	PARK 664:27
hostage h. to hostage-takers	INOU 446:51
other guy is called a h.	IACO 444:3
hostages Freeing h. is like	WAITE 916:6
h. to fortune	BACON 51:70
h. to the fates	LUCAN 541:47
hostile cannot let…rogue nations hold this nation h.	BUSH 182:15
Fearful and h. behavior	FULB 355:63
morally h.	THUB 890:60
regarded…as a h. regime	BUSH 183:17
hostilities prevent a resumption of h.	EDEN 311:31
hostility the disguise of determined h.	SHER 817:99
hosts God of H., be with us	KIPL 490:16
Lord of H., to me!	SCOT 755:87
two great classes: h. and guests	BEER 74:92
university where…the Jews are h.	SACH 736:3
hot armed h. dog thefts	TOOLE 894:59
beat the iron while it is h.	DRYD 304:36
Can one go upon h. coals	BIBLE 104:60
Cool is h.	WASH 922:33
don't understand too h.	SALI 740:73
feel h. and think cold	CARY 207:62
for your foe so h.	SHAK 804:36
H. and rebellious liquors	SHAK 778:71
H. as any hottentot	SITW 823:95
h. as molten lead	SHAK 772:65
h. as the steam	WATT 922:45
h. from hell	SHAK 777:34
h. temper leaps o'er a cold decree	SHAK 769:76
how h. the day is	GRAV 382:17
If it be a h. day	SHAK 772:73
while the strike is h.	ANON 26:7
hot-bloods h.-b. between fourteen	SHAK 774:46
hotel great advantage of a h.	SHAW 806:95
man comes into a great h.	MILL 593:37
open to all—like the Ritz H.	MATH 581:85
small clerk of some h.	MANS 567:1
hotel-keepers Swiss are inspired h.-k.	MONT 613:17
that h.-k. continue	TROL 897:27
hotels all stuck over with large brown h.	HEMI 409:59
h. will…have disappeared	LEVIN 525:29
Hotspur H. of the North	SHAK 771:44
Hottentot H. and every Eskimo	LEHR 520:27
might as well have been H.	LAWR 513:69
hottentot Hot as any h.	SITW 823:95
hotter call'st thyself a h. name	SHAK 798:76
houms dowie h. o' Yarrow	BALL 59:59
dowie h. o' Yarrow	BALL 59:60
hound footprints of a gigantic h.!	DOYLE 297:64
hawk, his h., and his lady fair	BALL 59:77
mettled h.	SCOTT 753:46
slepyng h. to wake	CHAU 216:60
The horse loves the h.	SURT 860:5
hounding World, in h. me	CRUZ 256:38
hounds carcass fit for h.	SHAK 776:78
h. are in cry	SCOTT 752:33
keep…any racehorse or pack of h.	CHES 219:46
like fell and cruel h.	SHAK 785:79
When the h. of spring	SWIN 863:82
hour arrival of an h.	SHAK 772:63
At such an h. the sinners	RUNY 732:62
Awaits alike th' inevitable h.	GRAY 384:66
awful quarters of an h.!	ROSS 727:67
books of the h.	RUSK 733:3
but one bare h. to live	MARL 573:30
child's a plaything for an h.	LAMB 505:82
companioned inarticulate h.	ROSS 726:57
dead deathless h.	ROSS 726:55
Do not expect again a phoenix h.	DAY 267:37
during that h.…I forgot	ATWO 41:44
eternity in an h.	BLAKE 141:24
falling h. by h.	MACN 558:98
For dark h. or twain	SHAK 797:43
from childhood's h.	MOORE 618:6
great h. of destiny	SASS 745:83
h. ago since it was nine	SHAK 779:78
h. approaches Tam maun ride	BURNS 179:26
h. be but A year	MARL 573:30
h. for getting up	SHIP 818:14
h. is not far off	LENIN 521:39
h. is upon her again	GIBB 367:9
h. of my death	KEATS 476:94
h. Of thoughtless youth	WORD 956:55
h. or a day	NASHE 632:90
h.'s come, but not the man	SCOTT 753:58
h. when earth's foundations fled	HOUS 432:71
How many makes the h.	SHAK 760:9
humblest h. is when he compares	BARR 64:83
I also had my h.	CHES 220:51
I Have known the lightning's h.	DAY 267:35
its h. come round	YEATS 966:25
just at this dead h.	SHAK 780:29
known as the Children's H.	LONG 536:34
meaning of this happy h.	KLEE 494:3
mine h. is not yet come	BIBLE 122:21
Not an h. more nor less	SHAK 793:31
nothing can bring back the h.	WORD 960:12
now's the h.	BURNS 180:47
Of a ship's h.	SLES 825:52
Of thee one h.	DONNE 292:44
Oh, for an h. of Herod!	HOPE 427:58
pause…known as the cocktail h.	DE 275:11
rash hand in evil h.	MILT 606:50
ring out the h.	APOL 29:82
serve the future h.	WORD 961:43
Some luckless h.	BURNS 177:84
take an h.'s leisure	STARK 843:24
the h. is nigh	SCOTT 754:69
their finest h.	CHUR 225:86
This is the exquisite h.	VERL 910:56
Time and the h. runs	SHAK 796:10
to serve the h.	TENN 875:10
to the h. its solitude	STEV 850:79
uncertain h. before the morning	ELIOT 321:85
watch at that midnight h.	LEAR 516:29
weight of the superincumbent h.	SHEL 815:36
world's best moment is a calm h.	ABU 1:13
world-without-end h.	SHAK 801:55
hour-glass still as the h.-g.	ROSS 726:56
hours best…in a couple of h.	WEST 933:90
crime…The h. are good	ALLEN 14:83
ever-rolling silent h.	PEAC 671:58
few h. in life more agreeable	JAMES 450:38
few h. of giving his enemies	STER 848:24
fruitless h., but neither	MILT 606:56
glare Of the interminable h.	ARNO 34:72
golden H., on angel wings	BURNS 178:11
hath not known his god-like h.	WORD 958:83
h. are made for men	RABE 704:16
h., days, months…rags of time	DONNE 291:25
h. of weariness	WORD 956:53
h. they know not how to employ	MONT 613:13
h. were cups of sack	SHAK 770:27
h. will take care of themselves	CHES 219:37
How slowly do the h.	SPEN 839:51
I was in Tennessee 24 h.	RAY 708:88
march of only a few h.	PEARY 671:60
sweetest h. that e'er I spend	BURNS 177:66
talk its pensive h. away	BRON 161:72
the darksome h.	GOET 375:61
The pitiless h.	THOM 887:7
three and a half h. long	CHAP 215:25
Three h. a day	TROL 898:56
tide of h.	YEATS 965:8
time card office h.	BAND 61:10
Time in h., days, years	VAUG 909:39
Upon the h. and times	SHAK 801:55
Work eight h.	PICK 677:64
house About the lilting h.	THOM 883:17
allegations…repeated outside the H.	PROF 697:28
All my h.	JONS 467:55
approbation of this H.	WALP 919:83
as for me and my h.	BIBLE 95:10
bawdy h. is to a cathedral	MENC 586:91
boat…had the goods of a h.	PEPYS 674:8
brawling woman in a wide h.	BIBLE 105:88
built his h. upon a rock	BIBLE 115:56
called a woman in my own h.	WAUGH 924:76
clean someone's h.	THER 882:83
corrupt and servile H. of Commons	SHER 818:6
dark h. and a whip	SHAK 779:96
Dark h., by which	TENN 873:62

depart out of that h. or city	BIBLE 116:68	play the fool...in's own h.	SHAK 783:13	person who knows 'h.'	RAVI 707:85
doll in the doll's h.	DICK 283:25	regulates the size of the h.	LECO 518:81	**Howard** Then sware Lord Thomas H.	TENN 878:95
dwell in the h. of the Lord	BIBLE 100:45	return into my h.	BIBLE 117:88	**how-de-do** Here's a h.-d.-d.!	GILB 370:65
dwell in the h. of the Lord	BIBLE 100:50	secret h. of death	SHAK 795:78	**Howell** H. & James young man	GILB 369:48
even in the h. of worship	PARN 665:46	serious h. on serious earth	LARK 509:78	however The word 'h.' is like an imp	MANT 568:20
Except the Lord build the h.	BIBLE 103:36	set a h. on fire	BACON 52:6	**howl** H., h., h., h.!	SHAK 793:37
far from the club h.	LINK 530:24	seven pillared worthy h.	LAWR 514:88	New widows h.	SHAK 797:60
From Bauhaus to Our H.	WOLFE 953:77	sharing the h. with a disembodied	SHAR 806:77	**howling** h. commercial success	GREE 386:23
full h.	MACA 544:13	sit in the h. wi' handkerchers	SCOTT 753:50	**howls** h. on for more	SHEL 814:2
galleries of the h.	MUNDY 625:43	snail...Carrying his own h.	DONNE 292:46	**hub** h. of the solar system	HOLM 424:70
gat him home to his h.	BIBLE 97:48	sneak into the h. in her train	LAMB 505:93	**hubris** H. clobbered by Nemesis	ALDI 12:52
ghost of a great h.	LEVE 525:23	sparrow hath found an h.	BIBLE 101:88	**Hudson** Close by the H.	HUGH 435:22
go into the h. of the Lord	BIBLE 103:32	Speaker of the H.	GARN 360:77	**hue** innermost idea of this h.	MELV 585:61
gone tiptoe in this h.	MILL 593:35	still more honourable H.	ROCHE 719:2	most lily-white of h.	SHAK 767:34
great h. of our humanity	DUNC 307:12	talking about building a h.	STERN 847:18	native h. of resolution	SHAK 783:7
great h. of Tarquin	MACA 545:44	tell you your h. is burning	MUNRO 625:50	of dazzling h.	KEATS 476:4
Harrow h. of the dead	AUDEN 42:66	Tenants of the h.	ELIOT 317:86	**hues** all one's favourite h.	DOYLE 297:75
hauf-way h.	MACD 549:23	thief breaks into my h.	PAINE 660:30	Rainbow...left thee all her lovely h.	DAVI 265:89
H....a place of free speech	WENT 931:52	this is no my ain h.	ANON 22:73	**huffing** h. of hyphenated words	BROY 169:88
h. as nigh heaven	MORE 619:24	to clean h.	THUR 891:95	**huffy** Not h., or stuffy	HERB 412:41
H. at Pooh Corner	PARK 663:1	to the Duke's h.	PEPYS 673:95	**hugged** h. the offender, and forgave	DRYD 304:46
H. Beautiful is...lousy	PARK 663:4	Unless the Lord has built the h.	BIBLE 133:37	**hulk** stoop-shouldered h.	TIME 891:18
h....become a den of robbers	BIBLE 110:16	venal H. of Peers	SHER 818:6	**hum** h. a fugue	GILB 368:40
h. divided against itself	LINC 529:4	What h. more stately	HERB 413:69	h. of either army	SHAK 775:78
h. fell upon the lords	BIBLE 96:20	when all through the h.	MOORE 616:60	H. Of human cities	BYRON 187:53
h. in the world	RYBC 736:55	Wisdom hath builded her h.	BIBLE 104:61	mist and h.	ARNO 34:99
H. is not a Home	ADLER 8:71	women in the h.	GILM 371:92	pilgrim borne in heedless h.	COLL 238:76
H. is pleased to direct me	LENT 522:60	young and inexperienced h.	JERO 454:42	**human** accusing...the h. race	CAMUS 196:95
h. not made with hands	BIBLE 127:68	You take my h.	SHAK 770:17	all female life, animal and h.	STAN 843:17
H. of Lords	WELL 929:9	**housed** h., clothed, fed	RUSK 733:9	All h. life is there	NEWS 635:54
H. of Lords, an illusion	STOP 855:14	**household** a great actor or a h. word?	OLIV 649:37	All h. things are subject to decay	DRYD 300:42
H. of Lords in his own head	LLOY 533:78	Her h. to me	HERB 413:64	All must love the h. form	BLAKE 139:89
H. of Lords is a model	FIELD 335:15	h. features her person	PRIOR 696:3	all that h. hearts endure	GOLD 376:88
H. of Lords is like a glass	ATTL 40:31	h. of God	BIBLE 127:86	All that is h.	GIBB 366:97
H. of Lords must be the only		keep thy h. the Church	BOOK 147:56	all the months of h. birth	MASE 580:62
institution	SAMU 741:98	My name...is h. word	ASHB 37:60	animals could be made h.	HEINE 407:15
H. of peers	GILB 369:53	not a member of the h.	KENN 480:87	application of h. ingenuity	NUTT 642:75
h. rose like magic	HARG 398:31	our names...as h. words	SHAK 776:91	articulate h. relationships	VIDAL 912:82
h. that has got over	JERO 454:42	put his h. in order	BIBLE 97:48	as h. eye could see	TENN 871:17
h. to be broken up	BIBLE 119:32	real centre of the h.	SHAW 810:7	awing the h. mind	JEFF 454:25
h. was filled with smoke	BIBLE 107:54	woman, than to study h.	MILT 606:46	basic h. emotions	ROTH 728:3
h. wherein our Life is led	CARL 201:11	Yiddish is a h. tongue	OZICK 658:42	become h. is art	NOVA 642:68
h. where I was born	HOOD 426:22	**housekeeper** a man marries his h.	PIGOU 678:76	Being h., she must	KIPL 491:24
h. where there was not one dead	BIBLE 93:60	h. think she's a householder	WILD 943:40	belief in h. liberty	MACL 555:45
h., which I have hallowed	BIBLE 97:54	**housekeeping** H. ain't no joke	ALCO 12:42	believe in taking h. life	NATH 632:3
h. with the narrow gate	SHAK 791:71	**housemaid** If I'd been a h.	MELBA 584:46	between h. creation	MILL 594:71
I can see Russia from my h.!	FEY 334:4	nice to the second h.	JAMES 450:50	bless our h. ears	MILT 597:35
imprison the child in her h.	WHITE 935:49	**housemaids** damp souls of h.	ELIOT 317:76	boot stamping on a h. face	ORWE 655:77
In my Father's h. are many mansions	BIBLE 123:52	**houses** big h. sat in...propinquity	GILL 370:79	bounds of h. Empire	BACON 50:52
in the h. of bondage	MACA 545:24	calling of selling h.	LEWIS 527:56	bounds of h. Empire	BACON 53:46
In the h. of Life	THUR 890:66	cry in strangers' h.	MANS 567:7	breathes with h. breath	TENN 872:26
invisibly all over the h.	THUR 890:68	Eighteenth-century h.	YEATS 966:18	But h. creatures' lives!	HOOD 426:31
jewel of our h.	SHAK 791:66	few of his friends' h.	JOHN 464:86	but it's greater to be h.	ROGE 723:84
just moved into the chicken h.	MACA 544:12	going on inside their h.	ALME 14:10	call the sciences h. invention	PAINE 660:38
Killing the Angel in the H.	WOOLF 956:35	h. are made of stones	POIN 683:97	cancer of h. history	SONT 834:16
labor of keeping h.	MCCA 548:96	h. deserve to be burnt	WELLS 930:28	can no longer bear to be h.	BECK 72:67
Leader of the H. of Commons	DISR 288:45	h. just as big	SMITH 829:20	care for far more than h. life	PANK 662:84
live in a h. on fire	WILL 945:4	h. marked with a red cross	PEPYS 674:99	chaos of h. experience	MACL 555:47
Looking around the H.	THOR 889:58	h. there wear verandahs	MURR 627:79	chords in the h. mind	DICK 281:67
love the H. of Commons so passionately	CHAN 214:8	h. without books	LESS 524:3	city is...a h. zoo	MORR 620:45
luck about a h.	YEATS 967:35	live in the h. they build	STEI 846:83	civilized h. life	TRUM 899:82
magic h. of glass	ROBE 717:73	narrow streets, old h.	THOR 889:50	collection...of h. knowledge	KENN 481:11
Majesty entered the H.	RUSH 732:77	not the h.	FENT 332:59	condition of being h.	ANOU 28:66
'Make my h. your inn.'	MOORE 617:80	pigeons...loath to leave their h.	PEPYS 674:6	condition of the h. race	GIBB 366:90
man...in the way in the h.	GASK 361:85	plague o' both your h.	SHAK 766:94	considerers of h. things	MILT 600:14
man's h. is his castle	COKE 234:97	round their golden h.	TENN 870:92	constituting of h. virtue	MILT 600:1
Marriage is not a h.	ATWO 41:35	sandstone apartment h.	CHEE 218:4	contribution to h. history	JIANG 455:2
meanest member of the H.	HENR 411:13	sensible to build h.	KEYN 484:80	could be the whole h. condition	HOPP 429:2
Members of this H.	BAXT 69:93	seven o'clock from the h.	REED 709:28	death instead of 'h. rights'	PEOP 673:83
mind to sell his h.	SWIFT 862:39	staying in their h.	PEPYS 674:6	degraded h. life	MARX 579:37
mistress of every h.	MILL 592:16	studios, and in the workers' h.	MAYA 583:22	destiny of the h. race	THOR 888:26
moat defensive to a h.	SHAK 764:40	The trees and the h.	THOM 887:6	destruction of h. life	HARDY 396:98
moderately healthy h.	SHAW 808:48	the very h. seem asleep	WORD 959:3	devaluation of h. world	MARX 578:25
neighbour's h. is on fire	BURKE 176:34	towns or h. raised by poetry	COWL 250:72	development of h. destinies	FISH 337:62
no one depressed in this h.	VICT 912:78	ugly h. stand	MILL 592:20	does a h. form display	BLAKE 141:44
not just the person who fills a h.	MITCH 609:34	unessential h. began to melt	FITZ 338:86	do h. rights begin	ROOS 724:2
offered his h. to sale	JOHN 461:9	**housetops** lowered o'er our h.	TWAIN 903:63	Education...is human	YOUS 969:66
office of the White H.	MENC 586:2	**housewife** busy h. ply her evening care	GRAY 384:65	enemy of the h. race	MILL 593:54
Oh, to have a little h.!	COLUM 238:90	h.'s badly-cooked dinners	BEET 74:7	escapes from h. life	YOUR 968:55
old h. carried an assurance	ACHE 2:29	Many a h.	GREER 387:44	essence of real h. love	ELIOT 315:27
one-man H. of Commons	MANC 564:52	mock the good h. Fortune	SHAK 778:58	establishment of h. activity	MARX 578:27
One need not be a H.	DICK 284:41	scholar or a complete h.	PLATH 680:28	every h. has a finite number	ARMS 33:52
on the front porch of the h.	LANCE 506:24	the h. that's thrifty	SHER 817:90	experience of being h.	LEWO 528:79
out of h. and home	SHAK 772:78	**housework** help with the h.	WINT 950:10	fight for their own h. rights	PANK 662:85
out of the h. of the Lord	BIBLE 103:23	no need to do any h.	CRISP 255:4	forget the h. race	BYRON 188:69
Peace be to this h.	BIBLE 120:78	**Houston** oil depletion...makes H.	MAIL 560:55	For insight into h. affairs	DYSON 309:59
Peace be to this h.	BOOK 148:96	**how** H. you?	GRANT 381:99	form of h. reason	LEVI 526:36

human being

forms of h. knowledge	MANN 566:79	Poetry...through h. language	MALL 562:95	straight honest prose on h. b.	HEMI 410:75
frightened by my h. impossibility	ANDR 18:76	point the highest that h.	MILT 601:18	too dangerous for h. b.	SAGAN 737:24
from any h. experience	JAMES 450:24	portions of the h. anatomy	HELP 409:56	treated as h. b.	SHAW 808:42
From what h. ill	WILD 943:38	possible for a h. creature	SMITH 828:89	Unlike h. b., computers possess	STER 847:14
get h. feelings right	HUTC 441:47	power of the h. intellect	LEWIS 527:65	vulnerable h. b.	TURN 901:20
giving life in h. fashion	REDON 709:23	promotion of the h. race	WEST 933:95	humane h....are not the leaders	CONR 244:44
godhead in which all life is h.	SHAW 809:69	propels the h. spirit	KAND 472:14	H., but not human	CUMM 258:72
greatest thing a h. soul	RUSK 733:14	pump all his h. weaknesses	MENC 566:84	humaneness h. and awe	WILS 947:44
greatness of the h. soul	ROCK 720:33	reaches of a h. wit	MARL 572:2	humanistic My theme is always h.	WILS 947:43
herds, of h. face divine	MILT 603:75	records of the h. spirit	MACL 555:37	humanitarian man...not first a h.	FAUL 331:46
histories...of h. life	POPP 689:57	redressing h. wrongs	TENN 877:56	humanitarianism h. of...high order	LOOS 536:56
history of the h. race	HARL 398:36	relation between the h. tongue	WAXM 925:4	humanities exemplified the h.	ROLL 723:90
Hope...in the h. breast	POPE 687:74	replacement of h. forces	MARX 579:41	produced...by the h.	STEA 843:28
horse is at least h.	SALI 740:78	Royalty puts a h. face	RUNC 731:48	humanity all h. divine	SHAW 809:69
h. activity that takes	TRIL 897:13	sacrifice h. life to figures	WEIL 928:74	always treat h....as an end	KANT 473:24
h. affairs would never improve	ORWE 653:7	satisfies the h. creative instinct	QUEN 702:8	breed apart from the rest of h.	MANK 566:75
h. being and h. can coexist peacefully	BUSH 182:10	science of arresting h. intelligence	LEAC 515:20	conscience of h.	JOHN 456:78
H. blunders usually	TAYL 868:46	sense of h. sight	MILT 598:50	content with his common h.	SHAW 809:89
h. body is sacred	WHIT 937:98	skins fewer than any other h.	CURR 259:90	crooked timber of h.	KANT 473:22
h. creation mechanical	LEGER 519:6	Socialism...is only H.	CONN 243:21	discipline of h.	BACON 51:74
h. desire for food	TOOLE 894:59	Somewhere...form of a h. being	WOOLF 956:38	distresses of h.?	JOHN 460:72
Humane, but not h.	CUMM 258:72	speech, that supremely h. gift	MATH 581:86	divinity and in h.	BACON 49:23
h. employers quite literally	MUMF 625:39	springs of the h. character	HAMI 394:48	dualism...weighs h. down	DEWEY 276:19
h. enterprise	GOULD 380:76	state of h. improvement	MILL 591:94	future of h. is uncertain	LEVI 525:26
h. experience is actively offered	WILL 944:73	strange mutability of h. affairs	DICK 277:43	glad to have h. forget	HOOV 427:46
h. history	GARC 359:67	stream of h. industry	TOCQ 892:27	great house of our h.	DUNC 307:12
H. history...a race	WELLS 930:35	studies h. behaviour	ROBB 717:68	H....a superhuman undertaking	GIRA 372:23
h. intellectual tradition	GOULD 380:77	tension all h. energies	MUSS 627:91	h. attains...complete development	TOCQ 892:27
h. kind Cannot bear...reality	ELIOT 319:38	terms of the h. awareness	LEAV 517:52	H. does not pass through phases	LEWIS 526:40
H. life is but a series	NABO 628:10	The h. crisis	WILL 944:72	h., frendlynesse	MALO 563:17
h. offspring	MILT 604:10	The H. Zoo	MORR 620:44	H. i love you	CUMM 257:55
h. or domestic life second	MANN 567:93	ticking...of the h. timepiece	ASLET 38:83	H. in its basic form	BARTH 66:9
h. plane	GILL 370:83	To be h....we must stand fast	BOLT 145:13	H. is best described as inhumanity	CONR 244:54
h. progress	GARI 360:72	To err is h.	LICH 528:90	H. is just a work in progress	WILL 945:88
h. psychic equilibrium	MAMET 564:37	To err is h.	POPE 685:25	H. with all its fears	LONG 535:27
h. race commit suicide	ADAMS 5:85	too impersonally h.	HARDY 397:10	I hate 'H.'	CAMP 194:59
h. race has...potential for idiocy	ONET 651:82	To step aside is h.	BURNS 178:93	knowledge belongs to h.	PAST 668:4
h. race...playing at children's games	CHES 220:55	triumph of h. reason	HAWK 401:88	Lies are essential to h.	PROU 698:55
h. species, according to...theory	LAMB 505:2	truth, as h. truth	LEGU 520:15	music of h.	WORD 956:55
h. species is	MILL 595:96	turf-dances of h. encounter	ALLEN 13:75	no h. before...yourself	GARV 360:83
h. spirit is immortal	MURP 626:75	universe of h. subjectivity	SART 745:76	out of h.'s reach	COWP 251:97
H. temperaments	LUCAS 541:53	utmost bound of h. thought	TENN 870:99	particular illusion on h.	MAUP 583:15
If h. souls did never	KEATS 476:87	Utopia of h. virtue	HAWT 402:4	Passion is all of h.	BALZ 61:5
imagination makes me h.	LEGU 520:18	vanity of h. hopes	JOHN 459:53	perfection does not recognize h.	WOOD 954:2
imitative side of h. behavior	MCCA 548:99	very h. events	WATS 922:41	popular h. is treason	ADDI 7:49
immeasurable h. misery	HARD 396:93	vices and follies of h. kind	CONG 240:34	raw nerve ends of h.	ANON 27:18
important a h. activity	MONT 613:9	Whites...are only h.	BIKO 135:94	rediscover their h.	TUTU 901:22
improvisation of h. existence	MCCU 549:14	human being category of h. b.	ASIM 38:80	salvation of h.	MENC 587:13
increase in h. misery	HARR 398:43	disgusting h. b.	ORWE 655:82	save h. from lapsing back	HUGH 435:19
influence on h. life	MULL 624:33	dissenter is every h. b.	MACL 555:38	snow, and fire h.	RUSK 732:85
inherent in the h. situation	GREE 386:25	every h. b. has	CARL 201:29	spark of h. can tolerate	RUSS 734:38
interesting and h. fellow	ROGE 723:76	Every h. b. is born	OAKE 642:4	teaches us that h.	RUNGE 731:51
key to h. warmth	ISHI 448:73	h. b. dissatisfied	MILL 591:7	through the latter, to serving h.	ISHI 447:72
known by the h. mind	PAGE 659:16	h. b. who is not myself	WELTY 930:46	truth of our h.	JOHN 456:79
Larger than h.	TENN 878:83	intelligent h. b.	ROTH 728:89	unremitting h.	BENN 80:50
laugh at h. actions	SPIN 840:69	native and sees the h. b.	LESS 523:90	used for the benefit of h.	WIEN 939:29
limits of h. knowledge	NIEB 637:88	No h. b. can give orders	SAND 741:9	what h., reason, and justice, tells me	BURKE 175:18
look into a h. eye	MELV 585:69	no sane h. b.	HUXL 441:61	humankind highest bliss of h.	KEATS 475:65
man to tell how h.	MILT 605:37	tourist is an ugly h. b.	KINC 486:15	H. can...be divided	HOLUB 425:71
many h. relationships	WEBB 925:6	Truth...makes him or her a h. b.	SAINT 738:46	H. is reflected	SCHI 747:24
mayn't be h. gore	DICK 279:96	human beings apes and h. b.	LORE 537:62	laughter is the basis of h.	RABE 703:8
Mercy has a h. heart	BLAKE 139:88	capacity of h. b.	MENC 587:8	the basic nature of h.	GATES 361:98
moon...is not h.	SCOTT 751:2	civilized h. b. are flying	ORWE 654:32	human nature best in h. n.	WHIT 936:71
necessary to h. existence	BLAKE 139:94	complexity of h. b.	WILS 947:44	conquered h. n.	DICK 278:77
necessary to the h. mind	REES 710:38	considers all these h. b.	STOWE 856:26	constituting of h. n.	MILT 600:1
no h. claim can be of...significance	OATES 643:11	decency of h. b.	ORWE 653:24	crucifixion...accuses h. n.	BUTT 186:15
No perfect solution...in h. affairs	BERL 84:48	feelings of h. b.	JAMES 452:77	disappointed in h. n.	DONL 290:10
nor...will the h. race	PLATO 682:63	heartlessness of h. b.	OKRI 649:25	government...reflections on h. n.	MADI 558:17
not, as a h. type...a success	OBRI 645:62	h. b. and animals	MOOR 618:8	great ignorance of h. n.	JOHN 463:73
nothing that is h. alien	TERE 879:12	H. b. are good at many things	ATTE 40:23	highest type of h. n.	SPEN 836:90
nothing to distinguish h. society	SHAW 809:87	H. b. are perhaps	VAN 908:15	h. n. is finer	KEATS 476:80
not meant for h. eyes	MUIR 624:17	h. b. cannot become fully human	HUXL 442:95	H. n. is the same	TWAIN 903:84
objects of h. reason	HUME 438:5	H. b....go on being	MISH 609:24	H. n. will not flourish	HAWT 401:3
ocean or the h. heart?	LAUT 511:26	H. b....have always hesitated	HARDY 397:7	infirmities of h. n. will allow	MACK 554:18
Of all h. struggles	SHAW 807:17	h. b. have an infinite capacity	HUXL 442:88	new edition of h. n.	HAZL 403:48
one h. sound	THOM 886:76	h. b. such perfect bliss	LAYT 515:1	noblest production of h. n.	ADDI 6:26
ordinary h. countenance	LEAC 515:15	h. b. they ought to leave	HEIN 407:20	observer of h. n.	DICK 277:43
other sets of people are h.	HUXL 442:82	h. b. want to be good	ORWE 654:40	part of h. n. to hate a man	TACI 865:3
own-goal scored by the h. race	ANNE 19:14	h. b. will live and progress	DU 305:69	salty quality of h. n.	ARLO 32:32
partly of h. institution	MILL 591:93	kindness that h. b. do not lose	LEGU 520:8	shame to h. n.	HOUS 433:82
passion in the h. soul	LILLO 529:1	last sound...will be two h.	FAUL 331:47	sovereign good of h. n.	BACON 50:56
passions glowing in a h. face	MATI 581:91	live among h. b. or not	WILD 943:50	There is in h. n.	BACON 51:91
paucity of h. pleasures	JOHN 465:5	machines...promoting the h. b.	PRIE 695:89	thorough knowledge of h. n.	AUST 46:83
people are only h.	COMP 239:97	man who does not believe in h. b.	CAST 208:79	Treatise of H. N.	HUME 439:8
people being more than h.	AMIS 17:55	normal state of h. b.	MILL 591:96	weakness of h. n.	MACA 546:53
perversity of the h. mind	TROL 898:39	number of h. b. involved	HUXL 442:84	human rights despotic regimes trample
pleasures of h. intercourse	MOORE 616:67	previously amusing h. b.	COUP 248:35	h. r.	CHEN 218:23

1148

Hussein

fundamental h. r.	UNIT 905:9	he that cometh to me shall never h.	BIBLE 122:34	h. one till one sweats	HALD 392:26
separate from h. r.	CLIN 231:24	H. allows no choice	AUDEN 43:97	h. that Honour feels	TENN 871:16
undoing of those h. r.	KENN 481:3	H. and love	FRAN 346:81	I h. her	RIMB 716:49
humans But then, so are h.	LYND 543:90	h. for recognition and money	SELF 756:10	it will do no h.	SHAK 791:59
cats and h....symptotic?	ANON 24:30	H. is the best sauce	CERV 211:45	never h. a hair of him	STUD 858:64
h....categorized as vermin	CAREY 199:61	h. no more	BIBLE 131:4	Nothing doth more h.	BACON 52:3
Slough...isn't fit for h.	BETJ 88:20	h., thirst...and death	GARI 360:73	shall not h. nor destroy	BIBLE 108:62
Humber Of H. would complain	MARV 577:90	idle if h. didn't pinch him	ELIOT 316:43	shall not h. nor destroy	BIBLE 110:10
humble He that is h. ever shall	BUNY 174:82	kill this whole assembly with h.	BIBLE 93:64	stomach that they mayn't h.	LAMB 505:86
h. and aloof	BETJ 88:15	O sacred h.	SPEN 839:53	they had never h. us	GELL 363:36
h. people of Cambodia	SIHA 821:66	perish with h.!	BIBLE 121:90	what you said h. me	LIBE 528:83
Man is not meant to be h.	TYSON 904:13	perpetual h. to be beautiful	RHYS 712:72	Wrath brings...gravest h.	EURI 328:62
mother is...a very h. person	DICK 280:44	present to plese' with H.	LANG 508:48	**hurting** instead of h.	HUME 438:4
ne'er ebb to h. love	SHAK 790:29	suffered thee to h.	BIBLE 95:90	You are h. be!	KIPL 491:38
no normal h. man can help	HERB 414:90	**hungred** h., and ye gave me meat	BIBLE 119:36	**husband** at all times your faithful h.	STEE 844:40
thy h. dwelling	WESL 932:62	**hungry** ate when we were not h.	SWIFT 862:49	attempting to cuckold a h..	JONG 466:31
use such names and be not h.?	SASS 746:98	feed the h. on statistics	LLOY 532:67	back of her h.'s newspaper	GREER 387:44
we are so very h.	DICK 280:45	fight so h. people can eat	STEI 846:83	Chaste to her h.	POPE 688:10
Wisdom is h.	COWP 251:22	filled the h. with good things	BIBLE 120:66	dear h. for a comfort	SMITH 830:32
humbler has gi'vn...an h. heav'n	POPE 687:75	filled the h. with good things	BIBLE 133:43	Dear h.! I take shame	MOOD 615:52
h. after it is done	SHAK 799:99	I am not h.	PUNCH 699:81	delight of her h.	RANS 706:66
humbly h. do beseech you	SHAK 789:21	if ever thou art h.	KIPL 490:5	established for the h. and wife	MONT 615:45
humbug lie to and h. themselves	WELLS 930:21	If thine enemy be h.	BIBLE 105:95	finding a h. for one's mistress	COOP 246:90
humbugs most artists and all h.	CONN 242:4	known what it was like to be h.	LARD 509:68	flop in favour of your h.	DICK 282:97
humdrum dealing with h. issues	THAT 881:59	lean and h. look	SHAK 776:12	Get thee a good h.	SHAK 791:57
just as h. a marriage	GREE 386:15	never going to be h. again	MITC 610:42	good works in her h.	MILT 606:46
humiliation except the course of h.	HUSS 440:39	once you're h., you're different	HUNT 439:17	hands of the h.	ADAMS 4:71
sense by...shades of h.	EVANS 328:69	rare and h.	STEV 316:54	has an ideal h.	TARK 867:31
through defeat and h.	SMUTS 831:70	small h. shivering self	ELIOT 316:54	h. and a happy home	PLATH 681:37
valley of H.	BUNY 174:74	**Huns** H....chanted a funeral song	GIBB 366:94	h. be a man	LAMB 505:93
With publicity comes h.	JANO 452:81	**hunt** h., and vote, and raise the price	BYRON 191:34	h. frae the wife despises!	BURNS 179:31
humiliations sensitive boy's h.	SHAW 807:18	h. in fields, for health	DRYD 304:48	h. held her upright	SMITH 828:3
humility Before Thee in h.	HAMM 394:55	H., shoot, and fight	BRON 161:62	H., I come	SHAK 795:93
haven't is to h.	BAIN 55:93	people who h.	SHAW 810:10	h. is a whole-time job	BENN 81:67
wisdom of h.	ELIOT 320:61	To H. an 'assault'	CRAN 253:75	h. is thy lord	SHAK 762:78
humorist know I was a h.	JERO 454:43	You will see H.	SHEL 814:3	h. is torn from her	NATI 632:4
humorists difficulty with h.	UPDI 905:13	**hunter** between the h. and his prey	ZHAO 970:9	h. is what is left of the lover	ROWL 729:21
H. are not happy men	CONN 242:2	covers...the hare and the h.	PATC 668:6	h., like a government	BALZ 60:92
not an easy time for h.	BUCH 171:31	Esau was a cunning h.	BIBLE 92:28	h. pays for all	DUNB 306:1
humorous 'tis no marvel, he is so h.	SHAK 771:52	Heart Is A Lonely H.	MCCU 549:12	h....shall rule over thee	BIBLE 91:97
humour A sense of h.	JAMES 450:31	Heart Is A Lonely H.	SHARP 806:70	h. wears a mask	MARI 571:83
dowered with a sense of h.	SOME 833:10	h. home from the hill	STEV 853:62	if she loses her h.	EURI 328:55
effusions of wit and h.	AUST 46:83	H. of the East	FITZ 337:68	If your h. is a bore	BELL 77:85
have a good sense of h.	SALI 740:76	h.'s horn is ringing	SCOTT 752:33	in her h.'s heart	SHAK 785:96
h. in ill-health	WELLS 930:34	h.'s javelin in his side	ARNO 34:97	in your h.'s ear	GROM 389:77
H....is emotional chaos	THUR 891:98	Man is the h.	TENN 872:33	is it well with thy h.?	BIBLE 97:74
h., its music	ROLL 723:90	mighty h. before the Lord	BIBLE 92:14	life her h. makes for her	ELIOT 316:53
h. of a scholar	BACON 53:35	Miss Joan H. Dunn	BETJ 88:25	light wife doth make a heavy h.	SHAK 770:25
in a holiday h.	SHAK 779:9	no h.'s game	JEFF 453:17	Like a deceived h.	SHAK 802:68
lack of a sterner kind of h.	WEBB 925:6	rings no h.'s shout	SIGO 821:64	makes a bad h.	EMER 325:87
malignity...in a piece of h.	STEE 844:51	without ever becoming h.	MARX 579:29	man...makes the best h.	NORR 641:56
no h. to marry	DEKK 270:14	**hunters** intrepid h. of golf balls	SMITH 828:4	most indulgent h.	DICK 282:88
no sense of h.	ALBEE 11:25	**hunting** call h. one of them	JOHN 465:5	must have a h.	SHAK 761:62
people...have...in common...hatred		discourse was about h.	PEPYS 673:96	My H. and I	ELIZ 322:9
and h.	PRYOR 699:63	English counties like h.-tunes	BENET 79:24	Never trust a h. too far	ROWL 729:20
sufficient sense of h.	HALD 392:26	hound is to the h. gane	BALL 59:77	nothing but his being my h.	CONG 241:49
warn't in a good h.	TWAIN 902:55	h. he loved	SHAK 762:81	send me no h.	SHAK 773:23
woman in this h. wooed?	SHAK 761:36	H. is not a proper employment	ADDI 7:58	so ill bred as to love a h.	WYCH 964:92
humours h. of the whole English	DRYD 304:40	H. the author, painter and musician	SITW 824:25	So may my h.	SHAK 788:80
h., whether grave or mellow	ADDI 6:27	I went in. wild	OWEN 658:34	to vote for one's h.	ONAS 650:53
in all h. sportively I range	DRAY 298:91	passion for h.	DICK 278:68	to yourself, that h.	JAMES 449:22
hump camel has a single h.	NASH 631:66	tuckt up she a h. goes	HERR 415:8	unbelieving h. is sanctified	BIBLE 126:41
camel's h.	KIPL 491:31	we must have h.	JOHN 458:23	We have to...grimace for a h.	OBRI 646:74
husband who may...have a h.	OBRI 646:74	**hunting-frock** cashier the h.-f.	SHER 817:73	**husbandry** h. in heaven	SHAK 796:26
without a positive h.	THAC 880:21	**hunting-grounds** h.-g. for the poetic	ELIOT 316:46	**husbands** bad h....good wives	BACON 51:77
humph H. yourself!	KIPL 491:34	**Huntlie** lay on H. bank	BALL 59:74	Chumps...make the best h.	WODE 951:36
Hun H. is at the gate	KIPL 493:71	**hunts** he h. in dreams	TENN 871:15	divine right of h.	WOLL 954:91
hundred As long as one h....remain	ANON 21:46	**hurled** Atoms or systems into ruin h.	POPE 686:73	doan nover ketch h.	MITC 610:40
be all one a h. years hence	EMER 325:76	Swift to be h.	HOOD 426:34	Fools are as like h.	SHAK 786:6
dying of a h. good symptoms	POPE 689:50	**hurly-burly** h.-b. of the chaise	CAMP 193:47	h. lie snoring in bed	MORE 618:18
h. judges have declared	QUIL 702:12	**hurrah** The Last H.	OCON 647:85	H., love your wives	BIBLE 128:12
h. pound on't	SHAK 803:89	**hurricane** America is a h.	MAIL 559:39	h. to stay at home	ELIOT 315:36
h. years later	FAUL 331:42	crazy-eyed H. blowing	KIPL 491:45	Let h. know Their wives	SHAK 790:38
Rode the six h.	TENN 875:11	heard there was a h. on the way	FISH 336:60	reformed rakes make the best h.	BRON 161:57
Rode the six h.	TENN 875:12	Irish h., a flat calm	BOWEN 153:96	some women govern their h.	WOLL 953:85
Rode the six h.	TENN 875:13	Let the h. drag the pieces	HUID 438:91	When h....breathe their last	POPE 685:40
steal more than a h. men	PUZO 701:5	**hurricanoes** You cataracts and h.	SHAK 792:4	women...succeed in spite of their h.	LEE 519:1
trade a h. contemporary readers	KOES 495:27	**hurroosh** h. that follows	CRIT 255:10	**hush** A brooding h.	THOM 887:9
hundredth h. time I am right	EINS 313:77	**hurry** H. slowly	AUGU 45:37	h. with the setting moon	TENN 876:26
hung who ne'er h. there	HOPK 429:91	Liberals in a h.	SAINT 738:48	somebody ought to have said 'h.'	CAMP 193:46
Hungarian not enough to be H.	KORDA 498:98	modern life...sick h.	ARNO 34:94	**hushed** h. and anxious hours	HOOV 427:45
Hungary sons of H.	GILB 369:57	senseless h.	WORD 961:32	**hushed-up** like wrongs h.-u.	OWEN 658:39
hunger against h., poverty	MARS 575:63	So who's in a h.?	BENC 78:9	**husk** h. of meaning	ELIOT 321:82
bodily h. in his eyes	SHAW 809:73	there will be no special h.	HEMI 409:66	**Hussein** deflecting America's anger	
drive h. from the hearth	LLOY 532:71	**hurt** done the lover mortal h.	DOUG 295:4	from Bin Laden to Saddam H.	LECA 518:79
Fainting forms, h. stricken	WILDE 940:45	give delight and h. not	SHAK 804:25	H. isn't just sitting	ANON 27:33
fed your h. like an endless task	CRANE 253:59	helped and h. us	MILL 593:34	not going after Saddam H.	SCHW 750:89

hussies

hussies h. in your beds — SHAK 789:6
hustle tried to h. the East — KIPL 490:99
hut Love in a h. — KEATS 476:6
hyacinth h. with rich inlay — MILT 604:8
  Thy h. hair — POE 683:86
hyacinths h. and biscuits — SAND 742:22
Hyades rainy H. vext the dim sea — TENN 870:98
hybreds h. and lubberds! — JOYCE 470:36
hydrogen h. bomb — FROMM 352:88
hyena wolf, the h., and the skunk? — BRYAN 170:98
hyenas H. have integrity — FRAN 349:28
hygiene H. is the corruption — MENC 586:90
  h. of older people — SMITH 829:11
hymns brought home to me by the h. — LAWR 514:85
  Singing h. unbidden — SHEL 814:94
  Sing on, with h. uproarious — BETJ 88:15
  sings h. at heaven's gate — SHAK 800:46
hyperbole encourage unedifying h. — DUNN 307:17
  scarcely h. to say — CLIVE 231:39
  speaking in perpetual h. — BACON 51:81
hyperboles Three-piled h. — SHAK 763:24
hyphenate Everybody else has to h. — MORR 620:57
hypochondria H. is the only disease — ANON 26:77
hypochondriacs h. of history — AGNEW 9:45
hypocrisy H. is a tribute — LARO 510:4
  H. is the most difficult…vice — MAUG 582:6
  H., the only evil — MILT 603:88
  m-m-making the world safe for h. — WOLFE 953:67
  old-fashioned American h. — GALL 358:37
  organized h. — DISR 288:38
  That would be h. — WILDE 942:6
  the Pharisees' h. — PAST 668:98
hypocrite first bolt-hole of the h. — BRAGG 156:54
  h. lecteur! — ELIOT 318:98
  H. reader — BAUD 68:57
  liar that's also a h. — WILL 945:83
  No man is a h. — JOHN 464:95
  The good thing about being a h. — ALDA 12:47
hypocrites cant of h. — STER 848:36
  h. austerely talk — MILT 604:9
  h….in the synagogues — BIBLE 115:40
  scribes and Pharisees, h.! — BIBLE 118:28
  tongue and soul…be h. — SHAK 783:31
  ye h., ye can discern — BIBLE 117:5
hypotheses smallest number of h. — EINS 314:89
hypothesis character…to an h.? — STER 848:26
  conviction that a h. — MEDA 584:34
  discard a pet h. — LORE 537:61
  endeavour to construct a h. — HARDY 397:7
  nature of an h. — STER 848:33
  slaying of a beautiful h. — HUXL 443:6
hyssop Purge me with h. — BIBLE 101:72
  sprinkle me with h. — BIBLE 132:31
Hyssopps H. of the Glen — ASHF 38:74
hysteria therapy of h. — FREUD 350:56
hysterics blind h. of the Celt — TENN 875:97

I

iacta I. est alea — CAES 192:13
Iago I.'s soliloquy — COLE 236:54
  yet the pity of it, I. — SHAK 790:31
iambics In keen i. — DRYD 301:45
Iban The I., when they decide — OHAN 648:9
Ibo Among the I.…conversation — ACHE 2:20
Ibsen Nietzsche, I.…madmen! — ONEI 651:70
  These I. creatures — ANON 23:97
ice bloody i. on bloody head — BLAIR 138:48
  cracked i. crunching — STEV 850:96
  Glitt'ring with i. — POPE 688:31
  good to break the i. — BACON 52:2
  hot i. and wondrous…snow — SHAK 768:46
  i. age ended years ago — ZHAO 969:8
  I. formed on the butler — WODE 952:55
  i. of its own indifference — ROOS 724:7
  i. on a hot stove — FROST 353:13
  i. was in the blood — PIER 677:68
  may not dissolve the i. — SURR 860:4
  skating on very thin i. — CAMP 194:49
  skating over thin i. — EMER 324:62
  sunny pleasure-dome with caves of i.! — COLE 236:39
  talent, a glass, and some cracked i. — BARR 65:3
  To curl on the i. — PENE 673:78
  To smooth the i. — SHAK 768:62
  world will end…in i. — FROST 352:4
iceberg All tip and no i. — KEAT 475:57
  portent of an i. — BROW 168:54

The i. rises — BISH 136:23
icebergs like i. in the ocean — GERH 365:70
icecaps blue i. on the mountains — CHAT 216:52
ice-cream emperor of i.-c. — STEV 849:67
  enjoy your i.-c. — WILD 943:42
Iceman The I. Cometh — ONEI 651:72
ice pick Baby LeRoy with an i. p. — ROST 727:72
ices after tea and cakes and i. — ELIOT 316:62
ice-scratched I.-s. slabs — SNYD 832:91
ichor perspiration was but i. — BYRON 191:32
icicle hang like an i. — SHAK 786:13
icicles When i. hang by the wall — SHAK 763:27
  White night of i. — MALL 562:98
  Why are there i. everywhere? — ZHAO 969:8
iciness an i., a sinking — POE 683:80
icing i. that detracts from the cake — AUCH 42:64
id cure of the i. — ANON 24:10
Ida I.'s shady brow — BLAKE 139:78
idea absurd is the fundamental i. — CAMUS 195:82
  Alligators have the right i. — MACD 550:54
  always gone in for the i. that — WILS 947:35
  Between the i. And the reality — ELIOT 318:15
  charge that an i. is radical — GALB 357:14
  controlling i. that holds us — FRID 350:62
  Dying for an i. — LEWIS 527:64
  endowed with the i. of God — DESC 275:1
  entertain an i. — JARR 452:88
  every new i….takes a generation — FEYN 334:6
  failure is not in the i. — MCGO 552:87
  first i. was not our own — STEV 850:82
  For an i. ever to be fashionable — SANT 743:42
  general i., of course — LEAC 515:21
  good i. but it won't work — ROGE 723:77
  had the wrong i. first — FEYN 334:5
  Hang your i. on a peg — BRIS 159:27
  hate the i. of causes — FORS 345:46
  his every i. rationalized — PIER 677:66
  i. alone is eternal — FLAU 339:14
  i.-bound in the past — LAWR 513:51
  i. for which I can live — KIER 485:98
  i….has still not been said enough — DELA 271:20
  i. of an external cause — SPIN 840:77
  i. of a system — GEOR 364:54
  i. of death saves him — FORS 344:31
  i. of dying is worse — PROU 698:52
  i. of elder wisdom — UPDI 906:36
  i. of liberty — SPIN 840:72
  i. of weapons — RUSS 734:38
  i. or concept — LEWI 527:76
  i. that they are going to live — DAVIS 265:93
  innermost i. of this hue — MELV 585:61
  it would be a good i. — GAND 359:61
  let the i. soak in — MILL 594:68
  new i….close to insanity — MILL 593:38
  nice place, inside an i. — MCIL 553:96
  No grand i. was ever born — FITZ 338:98
  Nothing is more dangerous than an i. — ALAIN 10:14
  possess but one i. — JOHN 462:20
  sacrificed…for…an i. — MILL 595:94
  shoot his like in the name of an i. — BROD 160:40
  slightest i. what they should be doing — FULL 355:68
  teach the young i. — THOM 887:98
  the i. of death must be born — MACH 552:91
  The man with a new i. — TWAIN 903:81
  to whom the i. first occurs — DARW 263:61
  Whatever is…perceived is an i. — BERK 84:30
  What redeems it is an i. only — CONR 243:27
  when a politician does get an i. — MARQ 575:54
ideal American is an i. — FRIE 351:72
  an i. view of the world — NAIP 629:31
  An i. wife — TARK 867:31
  boy's i. of a manly career — DISR 287:33
  Christian i. has not been tried — CHES 220:77
  Conservative i. of freedom — MADAN 558:15
  Freedom is not an i. — STEV 851:13
  i. day for football — SMITH 830:30
  i. which I hope to live for — MAND 564:53
  i. would be to belong to none — DUDEK 305:76
  ideas, or on an i. — LAWR 513:50
  my song has an i. — CHOC 222:25
  nearer today to the i. — HOOV 427:43
  not charmed with the i. of life — MILL 591:96
  Religion…ultimate i. — WHIT 936:65
  softly sleeps the calm I. — DICK 280:24
idealism grips with so-called i. — MENC 587:11
  i. is not uncommon — ROOS 725:20
  I. is the noble toga — HUXL 442:98

idealistic America…only i. nation — WILS 949:87
  our i. pretensions — OBRI 645:64
idealists I. are very apt to walk — SMITH 829:21
idealized i. into powerlessness — JONG 466:39
idealizer Sorrow, the great i. — LOWE 539:13
ideals A society that has no i. — AI WEI 10:35
  forever hallowed by the i. — EISE 314:8
  i. and visions to the past — KENN 481:21
  i. of a democratic…society — MAND 564:53
  i….painters' techniques — RENO 711:57
  men without i. — CAMUS 195:81
  tell the i. of a nation — DOUG 295:9
  white man's superior i. — VASC 909:29
ideas addiction…to the i. — GALB 357:15
  alter and exchange our i. — BERN 85:68
  believe in i. and die for them — ANOU 28:63
  borrowed i. — CALL 192:27
  cemetery of dead i. — UNAM 905:5
  dreams that have…changed my i. — BRON 162:77
  false i. prevail as to woman's — STAN 842:13
  find really marvellous i. — LEON 523:77
  foundation of your i. and phrases — LAUT 512:29
  founded not upon visionary i. — GLAD 373:39
  great i. are hogwash — NABO 628:15
  Great people talk about i. — LEBO 517:63
  i. about the native — LESS 523:89
  I. are born from hatred — GENET 363:41
  I. are like fish — LYNCH 543:89
  I. are more powerful than guns — BENN 80:56
  i. begin to destroy sex in America — DOCT 289:82
  i. get cloath'd — STER 848:48
  i. must be as broad as Nature — DOYLE 296:42
  i. of economists — KEYN 484:81
  i., or on an ideal — LAWR 513:50
  i. take their beginnings — LOCKE 533:90
  Innate i. are in every man — BLAKE 141:37
  isolate him, and his i. disintegrate — DIDE 285:78
  live in the mind, in i. — MILL 593:55
  machine for transmission of i. — BOWL 153:99
  most interesting i. — SONT 834:19
  new i. or fresh outlooks — MACK 553:5
  no i. and the ability — KRAUS 499:7
  no i. but in things — WILL 946:16
  Not many composers have i. — GERS 365:71
  of nasty i. — SWIFT 862:52
  our i. that make us — UNAM 905:4
  People find i. a bore — POUND 692:19
  publishing of his i. — KAZIN 474:52
  realm of i. — MILL 593:38
  Relations of I. — HUME 438:5
  share no one's i. — TURG 901:18
  signs of i. — JOHN 460:68
  two i. are more inseparable — SMITH 830:48
  two i. in her head — LINK 530:28
  two i. of government — BRYAN 170:97
  two opposed i. in the mind — FITZ 338:93
  unexpected copulation of i. — JOHN 459:54
  vehicle for conveying i. — MACB 546:63
  where good i. go to die — OBAMA 643:26
  without any i. — LOCKE 533:89
  words reign over i. — SAND 741:5
identical exist, but are i. — FORS 344:37
identity live without an i. — MCLU 556:58
  losing their own i. — BENE 79:81
  mistaking…similarity for real i. — PALM 661:67
  questions of freedom and i. — JORD 468:99
  sense of personal i. — STEV 852:50
  short circuit in his i. — ROTH 727:72
ideological i., or the abstract — ROTH 728:90
ideologies i. and inventions — SONT 834:16
  not to have i. — HOFS 422:39
ideology an i. that is warlike — OBRI 645:64
  more important than i. — NEWM 635:52
  single i. for 70 years — YELT 967:44
ides Beware the i. of March — SHAK 776:5
idiocy facilitate the infection of i. — BIER 134:81
  human…potential for i. — ONET 651:82
idioms licentious i. — JOHN 459:57
  long words and exhausted i. — ORWE 654:36
idiot artist, like the i. — SITW 824:22
  computer is a fast i. — AMER 15:23
  good loser…an i. — DURO 308:33
  i. who praises — GILB 369:61
  law is…a i. — DICK 278:72
  possibly an i. — DALI 261:14
  tale Told by an i. — SHAK 798:74
idiotism hundred new titles of i. — NASHE 631:88

ns of this i. God winked at

Entry	Reference
idiots fatuity of i.	SMITH 830:46
I. are always in favour	SHAW 810:19
play the i. in her eyes	SHAK 787:36
village i., policemen	MACD 550:39
your only competition is i.	MANK 565:73
idle all be i. if we could	JOHN 463:48
all the day i.?	BIBLE 118:21
As i. as a painted ship	COLE 235:12
be not i.	BURT 182:89
happiest when I am i.	WARD 920:2
I. to hope	REED 709:30
If you are i.	JOHN 463:69
many a one who would be i.	ELIOT 316:43
merely the art of the i.	INGR 446:40
most i. and unprofitable	GIBB 366:98
Most 'scruciating i.	KIPL 491:33
Reputation is an i....imposition	SHAK 789:12
such i. fellows as I	AUBR 41:56
idleness faculty for i.	STEV 852:50
grief and sin of i.	MELV 585:53
Grief is a species of i.	JOHN 462:26
I., which is often becoming	STEV 852:40
pains and penalties of i.	POPE 689:45
reading is not i.	SPEN 837:12
idlers loungers and i. of the Empire	DOYLE 296:38
idling enjoy i. thoroughly	JERO 454:35
idol ancient i., on his base again	BROW 168:38
celestial and my soul's i.	SHAK 781:76
'eathen i.'s foot	KIPL 489:82
God...would be an i.	BONH 146:27
i. to offend the national religion	BENT 82:91
natural i. of the Anglo-Saxon	BAGE 54:69
one-eyed yellow i.	HAYES 403:27
plaything and their i.	SHEL 811:46
idolatry contemporary man's i.	MONT 613:19
on this side i.	JONS 468:90
organization of i.	SHAW 808:36
stubbornness is as iniquity and i.	BIBLE 96:33
idols i. of consumption'	LOWE 540:39
like old i.	BOTT 152:83
if 'i.' is the only peacemaker	SHAK 780:25
Iffucan Chieftain I. of Azcan	STEV 849:72
ignis fatuus Reason, an i. f.	ROCH 719:11
ignoble made i. talk	TENN 877:55
ignominious so acute, so i.	SHAW 807:18
ignorance acknowledge our own i.	HAZL 404:52
Alike in i.	POPE 687:80
between the i. and poverty	WALP 918:65
blind and naked I.	TENN 877:48
but i. of evil	MITC 609:25
child of i.	BACON 51:90
consistent with the i.	ORWE 655:67
criticism is ever inhibited by i.	MACM 556:70
curse of mankind, folly and i.	SHAK 786:30
Don't die of i.	ANON 26:97
dull pastures of her i.	SMITH 828:3
education...expensive—try i.	BOK 144:3
from knowledge i.	BROW 169:63
functioning out of i.	DENG 272:58
great i. of human nature	JOHN 463:73
I. is as much the fountain	MONT 613:13
i. is bliss	GRAY 383:48
I. is like a delicate exotic fruit	WILDE 941:1
i. is never better than knowledge	FERMI 334:95
I. is not innocence	BROW 169:81
i. is strength	ORWE 655:73
I. is the curse	SHAK 760:99
i. is the first requisite	STRA 856:36
I. is the mother of all evils	RABE 704:21
I., madam, pure i.	JOHN 460:61
i. of alternatives	ANGE 18:84
i. of morality	PASC 667:87
i. of our own i.	BUTL 186:8
I. of the law	SELD 756:8
in i. sedate	JOHN 459:48
in i., to refrain	BERN 85:70
It was a childish i.	HOOD 426:23
make us wish for i.?	DENH 272:59
night of our natural i.	HOBB 420:5
no darkness but i.	SHAK 786:22
no sin but i.	MARL 572:7
only one evil, i.	SOCR 833:1
opinion breeds i.	HIPP 419:70
O thou monster i.	SHAK 763:11
our i. must...be infinite	POPP 690:86
scope and structure of our i.	PYNCH 701:13
take from them all i.	BOOK 147:53
The greater the i.	OSLER 656:87
times of this i. God winked at	BIBLE 125:94
true source of our i.	POPP 690:65
uncertainty? Even i.	NIET 638:6
Until you understand a writer's i.	COLE 236:43
wake from i.	JOHN 459:41
where i. prevails	DOUG 296:26
ignorant Be not i. of any thing	BIBLE 113:83
doubt and to be i.	UNAM 905:6
foolish than an i. fool	MOLI 612:89
girls aren't i.	COOP 246:89
i. and unpolished people	DICK 283:17
i. in spite of their age	PITT 679:1
i. of all the rules of art	ADDI 7:55
i. of each other's habits	DISR 288:34
i. of the causes	SPIN 840:72
i. of what he's most assured	SHAK 787:28
i., only on different subjects	ROGE 723:72
many i. men are sure	DARR 263:50
Men i. of letters	SAND 743:39
right of the i. man	CARL 201:26
stupid and i.	SMITH 828:89
Then I should be i.	GREG 387:52
we are i. of	SWIFT 861:33
we are utterly i.	BEDE 72:59
We live i.	ABU 1:12
ignore First they i. you	BENN 79:33
i. him	BIEL 134:57
ignored because they are i.	HUXL 441:59
Ike I like I.	ANON 24:28
Iliad as in the I. itself	ARNO 35:9
something greater than the I.	PROP 697:31
Ilion Past ruined I. Helen lives	LAND 507:29
Ilium topless towers of I.?	MARL 573:29
ill all the measureless i.	TENN 875:16
ash for nothing i.	SPEN 838:20
British Bourgeoisie...if it is i.	SITW 824:17
cure for this i.	KIPL 491:32
do i. our sole delight	MILT 602:40
fear no i.	SCOT 755:85
good and i. together	SHAK 791:68
How i. white hairs becomes	SHAK 793:39
i. and old and terrified	BETJ 89:39
i. design is most i.	HESI 417:32
I. fares the land	GOLD 376:98
I. is the weather	DEKK 270:8
looking i. prevail?	SUCK 858:66
Love worketh no i.	BIBLE 126:31
never risk being i.	GIEL 368:25
no for nony gude or i.	BURNS 177:71
only half there when I am i.	LAWR 512:44
so i. bred as to love a husband	WYCH 964:92
some desperate i.	JONS 468:87
some i. a-brewing	SHAK 769:92
speak i. of any man	JOHN 462:22
speak i. of the i.	HAZL 404:57
though she's not really i.	JAGG 449:14
'Tis an i. cook	SHAK 766:7
to rail at the i.	TENN 876:36
warn you not to fall i.	KINN 488:65
We are all i.	TRIL 897:14
We fell morally i.	HAVEL 401:85
woman coloured i.	SHAK 803:87
ill-born amphibious i.-b. mob	DEFOE 269:70
ill-dresssed ill-kept, and i.-d.	SHAK 464:90
illegal Cricket is not i.	ANNE 19:12
i., immoral or fattening	WOOL 956:44
means that it is not i.	NIXON 640:39
taken i. drugs	JOHN 457:88
ill-fame clearer of i.-f.	AUST 46:79
ill-favoured poor virgin...an i.-f. thing	SHAK 780:22
ill-fed it is i.-f., ill-killed	JOHN 464:90
ill-health humour in i.-h.	WELLS 930:31
illiberality ignoble i.	NASHE 632:90
illimitable the i. inane	TENN 877:68
Illingworth Lord I.	WILDE 941:83
Lord I.	WILDE 941:85
Lord I.	WILDE 941:90
Illinois I....in hibernation	OHARA 648:14
illiteracy i. level of our children	BUSH 183:27
illiterate i. know how to count	BACON 53:55
to i. him, I say	SHER 817:70
ill-nature just so much i.-n.	SCOTT 754:76
ill-natured vain, i.-n. thing	DEFOE 269:70
illness I. is the night-side	SONT 834:20
i. should attend it	SHAK 796:14
I....tyrant has in common	BROD 160:35
i. was also my antidote	ARMS 32:42
like the treatment of an i.	WITT 951:26
lingering i. Is over	POE 683:94
Living is an i.	CHAM 213:71
makes i. worth while	SHAW 810:12
mental i. of the United States	ATWO 41:36
no i....it cannot counterfeit	PROU 698:47
illnesses not from their i.	MOLI 612:90
three new i. brought by Christ	GAUT 361:4
ills All the i. of mankind	DUDEK 305:76
i. of an entire generation	ISHE 447:69
marvelling sweetly on her i.	RANS 706:66
No sense...of i. to come	GRAY 383:47
O'er a' the i. o' life	BURNS 179:2
quack, long versed in human i.	CRAB 252:34
what i. the scholar's life assail	JOHN 459:46
ill-shapen creatures at first are i.-s.	BACON 52:8
ill-spent sign of an i.-s. youth	SPEN 837:91
illume Better...Than no i. at all	DICK 284:49
illuminate i. his subject's life work	TOYN 895:79
illuminated not enough to be i.	JOHN 456:72
illumination Painters...produce i.	DELA 271:23
support rather than i.	LANG 507:40
illumine what in me is dark I.	MILT 601:31
illumined i. by the steady radiance	HAMM 394:54
illusion an i. to which	STOP 855:14
consecrated...to i.	BYRON 191:37
great poetry gives the i.	ELIOT 318:19
i. that the eternal blessed life	TOLS 894:54
Limits...are...an illusion	JORD 469:5
nothing but sophistry and i.	HUME 439:7
not to foster the i.	GOWE 380:80
particular i. on humanity	MAUP 583:15
sheer i. to think	WEBER 925:14
web of our grand i.	PAGE 659:15
illusions books...contain...our i.	CONR 244:40
discard i.	GORB 378:49
friend of flattering i.	CONR 244:37
i. that restrict freedom	FRYE 354:57
i. that they have generated	MOUN 622:93
lost all his i.	HOLM 424:64
illustrate i. and simplify	HOME 425:96
illustration i. of character?	JAMES 450:45
illustrious Children, to be i.	NEME 633:17
Illyria drink in I.	SHAK 785:82
Ilsley looks on I. downs	ARNO 35:16
image any graven i.	BIBLE 94:66
conformity of the i. with the thing	DIDE 285:61
created him in his own i.	DOST 294:92
cried in a whisper at some i.	CONR 243:30
dull red i. of the moon	WORD 958:86
emotion, detail and i.	BRAU 157:86
Every painted i.	BERG 83:27
express i. of his person	BIBLE 129:33
Fashion is the i. of an age	LAGE 504:70
fleeting i. of a shade	SHEL 815:25
i. in her mind	DRYD 302:7
i. of life	ANOU 28:60
i. of myself	AUDEN 44:12
i. of myself and dearer half	MILT 604:15
i. of offence	SHAK 786:20
i. of the divine beauty	AQUI 30:51
i. of the King	TENN 878:77
i. of those...mountain peaks	LLOY 533:72
I. that...gleamed	WORD 957:70
i. we have already made	PROU 698:57
In every parting...an i. of death	ELIOT 315:14
in the i. of God made he man	BIBLE 92:12
living i. to all ages	NASHE 632:90
made them...like their own i.	PATC 668:8
man's i.	YEATS 965:6
Met his own i.	SHEL 814:6
powerful i. to...Englishman	SMITH 828:1
reconstituted in the i.	RODO 721:51
Scattered his Maker's i.	DRYD 301:64
scorn for our i.	SHAK 783:19
she marks her i.	POPE 688:33
Technology is not an i.	PAZ 671:49
to the i., not to the man	PRICE 695:81
visual i. of ourselves	LAWR 513:67
world in its own i.	NIET 638:8
imagery antics and wild i.	SPEN 838:30
rhythm, i., sweep	NOON 640:45
images Fair trains of i.	WORD 961:34
Here the stone i.	ELIOT 318:14
i. of Nature were...present to him	DRYD 300:20
i....remote from each other	JOHN 459:54

imaginary 1152

infinite i. of itself	LEON 523:78	**immigrants** all i. to this place	ATWO 41:37	more beloved for the i.	RUSK 733:87
novel is…philosophy put into i.	CAMUS 196:2	children of i.	RUSS 734:30	**imperial** enslaves you on i. principles	SHAW 807:97
Those i. that yet…beget	YEATS 967:32	**immoral** All art is i.	WILDE 940:58	**imperialism** i. would be razed	MAO 568:32
traditional stories and i.	FRYE 354:4	illegal, i. or fattening	WOOL 956:44	US i.	MAO 569:33
translate pulsations into i.	RICH 713:99	i. is what you feel bad after	HEMI 409:70	When i. feels weak	CHAV 217:2
imaginary the i. and the real	STEF 844:52	moral or an i. book	WILDE 940:62	**imperialistic** We're not i.	RUMS 731:45
imagination act of a writer's i.	WELTY 930:46	not considered i., or even bad form	CECIL 210:26	**imperialists** i. brought…cannons	PEOP 673:83
An Irishman's i.	SHAW 808:62	people looked on it as i.	GALS 358:50	**impermanence** beautied with i.	SCOTT 751:1
anyone of i. must feel	SHIP 818:15	self-assertion as i.	KURO 501:44	**impersonation** i. of desire	BROO 163:10
appeals most strongly to the i.	HUMB 438:92	**immorality** i. is what they dislike	WHIT 936:72	**impertinent** Ask an i. question	BRON 160:52
atrophy of the i.	GELL 363:33	old i. condoned	SHAW 811:37	**impinged** desire not to be i. upon	BERL 84:46
by reason of corrupt i.	BURT 181:87	rigid code of i.	BRAD 154:22	**impious** i. men bear sway	ADDI 7:51
chase our i. to the heavens	HUME 438:94	smacks of levity, i. almost	STARK 843:22	**implacable** i. in hate	DRYD 302:74
computer…has no i.	AMER 15:23	**immortal** Being a thing i.	SHAK 781:58	**implanted** God has i. in me	CRUZ 256:40
depends only upon the force of i.	DRYD 303:20	cold i. hands	SWIN 864:96	**implausible** no matter how i.	SHAR 806:76
enrich our intellectual i.	RUSS 734:23	dim night of this i. day	SHEL 814:19	**implication** idiomatical kind of i.	STER 848:41
For those who have no i.	CELI 211:37	grow i. as they quote	YOUNG 968:54	**implore** I adore thee, i. thee	STUA 858:59
goading of the i.	POE 683:80	His biting is i.	SHAK 795:91	**importance** attach too much i.	RUSS 734:32
great instrument…is the i.	SHEL 816:50	human spirit is i.	MURP 626:75	diminish the i. [of newspapers]	TOCQ 893:34
help of a powerful i.	HERZ 416:22	i.…because he has a soul	FAUL 331:36	don't learn the i.	YOUS 969:64
History…succeed in it…through the i.	FRAN 347:86	i. diamond	HOPK 429:94	inverse ratio to the i.	HUXL 442:77
how abhorred my i. is!	SHAK 784:63	i. diet	RALE 705:44	little of his own i.	GREE 386:18
hunting-grounds for the poetic i.	ELIOT 316:46	i. god of harmony	BEET 74:1	**important** i. while they're doing it	MITC 609:38
i. created the world	BAUD 69:76	I., invisible, God	SMITH 831:65	little things are infinitely the most i.	DOYLE 297:52
I. is the queen	BAUD 69:75	i. longings in me	SHAK 795:92	living well…most i.	PLATO 681:46
I. is the voice	MILL 594:72	i. part of myself	SHAK 789:11	look i. and to say	KIPL 492:65
i. makes me human	LEGU 520:18	i. spirit of the dead	SPEN 837:12	more i. than keeping a good diary	SASS 746:94
i. of a boy	KEATS 476:83	i. youth to mortal maids	LAND 507:29	most i. of all the lessons	HUXL 442:96
i. of man is evil from his youth	BIBLE 92:11	lifting…into i. sunlight	CUMM 257:51	most i. single thing	JOVA 469:43
I. should be integrated with life	DUDEK 305:78	long i. dream	KEATS 476:5	most i. thing in acting	GOLD 377:37
i. soars, as a voice	WILL 946:20	Sire of an i. strain	SHEL 815:28	most i. thing in life	PASC 667:86
i. the rudder	KEATS 475:72	son who…would make you i.	MARQ 574:44	most i. thing in the world	SHAW 806:79
Liberty of the i.	CONR 244:38	taken an i. wound	FROST 353:25	Paintin's not i.	MOSES 622:78
men without i.	PROU 698:54	This little steamer…is i.	PRIE 695:86	Personal relations are the i. thing	FORS 344:29
mysterious power of i.	HOLM 423:59	What i. hand or eye	BLAKE 140:19	seen to be so i.	JAMES 451:75
no i.…no horror	DOYLE 296:40	**immortality** angling for i.	HUXL 442:83	think that's pretty i.	KING 486:23
nothing but his i.	SHAW 809:63	belief in i.	DOST 294:91	to be i.	JOBS 455:62
Politics mixed with the i.	STEN 847:3	cannot bear the sight of your i.	MARQ 574:44	**importation** i. of all foreign wines	SMITH 827:85
power of i.	FEUE 334:2	earthly i.	FORD 343:1	**importune** too proud to i.	GRAY 385:94
property of the i.	WALC 916:14	hope full of i.	BIBLE 112:74	**imposition** idle and most false i.	SHAK 789:12
Propinquity had brought I.	YEATS 967:41	i.…through not dying	ALLEN 14:91	**impossibility** frightened by my human i.	ANDR 18:76
protein of our cultural i.	HUGH 435:21	I.…to such as are fit for it	EMER 325:89	i.…to prove that God does not exist	LABR 503:29
save those that have no i.?	SHAW 810:18	just Ourselves—And I.	DICK 284:42	Upon i.	MARV 577:95
schools for the i.	GIRA 372:25	longing after i.?	ADDI 7:52	**impossible** beings which are i.	REDON 709:23
see only…figments of their i.	ELLI 323:35	milk's leap toward i.	FADI 329:6	certain because it is i.	TERT 880:19
suspend the functioning of the i.	HEMI 410:82	millions long for i.	ERTZ 327:41	frontiers of the i.	KILLY 486:8
sweeten my i.	SHAK 793:22	no i., no soul or mind	STEI 846:99	i. that any beholder	SIDN 820:57
The secret of survival is…i.	BAN 62:39	only cruel i.	TENN 877:60	i. to find out who was…leaking	REAG 709:14
travel…engages the i.	CELI 211:36	permanence, for i.	NUTT 642:75	i.…to open his mouth	SHAW 810:93
triumph of i. over intelligence	WILL 944:77	Seal of Divinity and I.	AUBR 42:61	i. to repeat in one period	RENO 711:57
Under the force of the i.	ACK 4:65	To desire i.	SCHO 748:55	i.…will be done	CALO 193:34
truth of the i.	KEATS 475:73	**immortals** battles with the i.	HOMER 425:1	Loving your neighbour…bloody i.	CLEE 229:81
Were it not for i.	JOHN 463:64	Francis Parkman and other i.	PRIAL 695:80	nothing shall be i. unto you	BIBLE 118:9
whispering chambers of I.	DICK 280:24	President of the I.	HARDY 397:16	one can't believe i. things	CARR 205:6
woman indulges her i.	NATH 632:98	verbal portraits…of the i.	CHUR 224:50	Only the i. is worth the effort	WINT 950:14
imaginations jumbled…in our i.	AUST 46:61	**immunity** shield of congressional i.	SMITH 829:27	peaceful revolution i.	KENN 481:10
perish through their own i.	BOOK 148:5	Sleep demands…guilty i.	BARN 64:61	scientist…states that something is i.	CLAR 228:68
imaginative genuine i. event	ROTH 728:90	**immutable** Few things are as i.	GALB 357:15	splendid failure to do the i.	FAUL 331:43
richness of i. resource	WILDE 940:50	laws of prose writing are as i.	HEMI 410:83	think on things i.	DRYD 299:11
the truly i.…analytic	POE 683:82	perfect, not i.	MILT 604:18	very difficult, maybe i.	SOLOW 833:3
imagine i. a boot stamping	ORWE 655:77	**imp** i. coiled beneath your chair	MANT 568:20	when you have eliminated the i.	DOYLE 297:46
i. a destiny	FIED 334:10	i. of fame	SHAK 775:81	wish it were i.	JOHN 464:1
Try to i.	THUR 890:90	**impact** historic i. upon the social	NISB 639:28	works at the i.	STEI 846:90
young men can possibly i.	SMITH 829:16	judgement that makes an i.	LEAV 517:53	**imposters** treat those two i.	KIPL 492:62
imagined i., not recalled?	LOWE 540:37	**impartial** i. in thought as well	WILS 949:77	**impotence** cases of wrongdoing or i.	ROOS 724:16
imbecility i., extravagance and		**impartiality** I. is an acquired taste	RIFK 715:35	i. of being earnest	CANN 196:4
political hysteria	CHUR 224:65	Protestantism is i. I shall make none	COBB 233:74	wasn't i. that led me in to a reclusive	
i. in females	AUST 47:85	**impassioned** i., at the birth	ERNST 327:39	existence	ROTH 728:94
reduce women of a certain age to i.	BROO 163:10	**impatience** time…ticking with i.	RAINE 705:40	**impotent** An i. people	THOM 885:71
sneaking piece of i.	SCOTT 753:38	Whatever…my enthusiasm or i.	SHIP 818:14	i. as a beached whale	TIME 891:19
imbrown golden ear I. the slope	POPE 686:62	**impatient** i. as the wind	WORD 961:33	**impoverishment** increase…in i.	HARR 398:43
imitate i. the action of the tiger	SHAK 775:74	i. to see him	SMITH 830:41	**imprecision** Decay with i.	ELIOT 319:45
never failed to i. them	BALD 57:17	so i. of inferiority	JOHN 459:52	i. of feeling	ELIOT 320:66
imitated Genius…is not i.	DIDE 285:64	**impeachment** i. against William		**impress** marked with their own i.	WOOLF 955:18
who has not i.?	INGR 446:38	Jefferson Clinton	ANON 27:40	**impression** change…the received i.	PRICE 695:82
imitation Comedy is an i.	SIDN 820:57	**impediment** know cause or just i.	BOOK 148:83	conveyed much the same i.	SIMON 822:75
I. is more interesting	STEIN 845:72	**impediments** free of all i.	MARP 574:42	figure to receive an i.	ROSSO 727:49
i.…is the easiest	CONF 240:16	**impenetrable** what is i.…really exists	EINS 313:80	first i. pleases	TINT 892:24
I. is the sincerest form of flattery	COLT 238:83	**imperfect** abhor the i.	CURZ 260:5	i. is of a slightly	NICO 637:84
Poetry…is an art of i.	SIDN 820:55	I describe i. characters	BRON 161:67	i. you produce	ROSSO 727:49
servile i. thrown away	CAREW 198:51	i. is all our knowledge!	DONNE 293:75	naive i. of the scene	MONET 612:99
What is the beauty of i.?	DIDE 285:61	perfect use of an i. medium	WILDE 940:64	novel is an i.	HARDY 397:17
imitator i. is a poor kind of creature	WHIS 934:21	thereby be i. in all	PLATH 680:28	produce an i. on the reader	BENN 81:76
Immanuel call his name I.	BIBLE 107:57	**imperfection** hold on to my i.	FRAN 347:84	produces a false i.	WILDE 941:97
immensity I. cloistered	DONNE 292:49	still I find Some i.	WORD 958:74	**impressionable** girl at an i. age	SPARK 836:69
in that enormous i.	BRAUN 157:81	**imperfections** dwell rather upon…i.	ADDI 6:32	**impressions** falseness in all our i.	RUSK 733:90
immigrant i. hordes…keep…country alive	DOCT 289:85	means of seeing one's i.	NIEB 637:87	few true i.	BELL 78:91

individual

imbued with two deep i.	PAST 668:4	
most striking of all the i.	MACM 556:67	
occupation and change...weaken i.	AUST 47:88	
one hundred times more i.	LEGER 520:7	
weaving and unweaving of false i.	ELIOT 315:14	
imprison i. the child in her house	WHITE 935:49	
Take me to You, i. me	DONNE 292:55	
imprisoned i. some, and beheaded	STAL 842:4	
No free man shall be taken or i.	MAGN 559:26	
Which i. you	HUGH 436:45	
imprisonment i.! The Dungeon of	MILT 607:87	
morality of i.	SHAK 787:48	
on pain of i.	EDWA 312:56	
upon pain of i.	ELIZ 321:2	
improbabilities adding to the i.	HAWT 402:16	
improbable occurrence of the i.	MENC 586:87	
improbity guards against i.	BENT 82:93	
impromptu preparing his i. speeches	BIRK 136:18	
improper conceal something i.	FLAU 339:29	
impropriety I. is the soul of wit	MAUG 582:4	
no i....with Miss Keeler	PROF 697:28	
without i.	GILB 369:54	
improve can't i. something	TUTU 901:24	
done to i. it	KEIL 479:54	
i. the means for achieving	HUXL 442:80	
improved Englishman was niver i.	DUNNE 307:20	
enormously i. by death	SAKI 739:66	
i. her French	GRAH 380:88	
i. out of all knowledge	SITW 824:12	
lives would be...i.	SMITH 828:95	
improvement i. in the productive	SMITH 827:75	
in its gradual i.	THOR 888:26	
only i. she could detect	ALTH 15:13	
or i. than population	MILL 591:97	
improvements no i....introduced	ANON 24:5	
improving an i., an advancing	DONNE 293:77	
certain of i.	HUXL 442:85	
improvisation i. of human existence	MCCU 549:14	
impudence much of Cockney i.	RUSK 733:15	
starve for want of i.	DRYD 302:4	
impudent i. mountebank who sold pills	ADDI 6:22	
silly things...in an i. way	AUST 46:76	
impulse i. from a vernal wood	WORD 957:59	
i. of the moment	AUST 45:56	
i. to acquisition	WEBER 925:12	
i. to punish is powerful	NIET 638:5	
i. to write a novel	WILS 947:41	
i. without purpose	BIER 135:92	
narrative i. is always with us	COOV 246:91	
natural i. which God	CRUZ 256:40	
owes all its onward i.	HAWT 402:11	
rooted in the sexual i.	SCHO 748:56	
their wonted i. give	COLE 235:28	
impulses manipulation of his own i.	MILL 594:71	
impunity holy...with i.?	RACI 704:31	
with strict i.	TATE 867:38	
impure To the Puritan all things are i.	LAWR 514:83	
impurity bring i. much rather	MILT 600:8	
imputation of this idiot	NASHE 632:92	
inability historic i. in Britain	HAUG 401:84	
i. to cross the street	WOOLF 956:36	
i. to put on your socks	GONC 377:41	
inaccuracy little i. sometimes saves	SAKI 739:69	
inaction i. of those who could	HAILE 392:16	
inadequate i. for getting to France	KINN 488:63	
inane Pinnacled dim in the intense i.	SHEL 814:18	
inanimate stupidity of the i.	STER 847:14	
inanition surrounded by a vast i.	JOHN 457:89	
inanity folly and i.	STOWE 856:34	
inarticulate I., arctic	SCOTT 751:3	
raid on the i.	ELIOT 320:66	
inattention same i. is discovered	JOHN 464:87	
inbreeding sick with i.	THOM 885:71	
Inca sensuous and elegant I.	DARIO 262:44	
Who was our first I.?	GARC 360:67	
incantation overlay of priestly i.	GALB 357:24	
incantations Whispering lunar i.	ELIOT 317:72	
incapacitated man who is not...i.	GLAD 373:36	
incapacity is worse	JEFF 453:14	
incarnate Jesus Christ, living and i.	BONH 146:23	
world is order i.	MILL 594:70	
incarnation gift...is I.	ELIOT 320:78	
i. of this verse	SHEL 813:84	
nearest thing in i. to...God	OLIV 649:41	
incense morning i.	BARL 63:56	
Orchid—breathing i.	BASHO 67:47	
stupefying i.-smoke	BROW 167:23	
incentive cruelty without i.	JOHN 460:86
incentives might reduce i.	KRUG 500:23
inceptions multiplying of former i.	DONNE 293:77
incest i. holds the family together	INNIS 446:45
luxury and damnèd i.	SHAK 781:65
inch cubic i. of some stars	MACC 546:67
every i. a king	SHAK 793:20
Not an i. of our territory	FAVRE 331:50
inch-rule his own i.-r. of taste	ADAMS 5:89
incident Body-line was not an i.	JAMES 450:32
determination of i.	JAMES 450:45
incidental wifehood...but i.	STAN 842:13
incidents i. well linked	COWP 250:89
incisions Underneath their fine i.	DICK 283:29
incite do not rear children, you i.	JARR 452:89
incivility sabbath-breaking...to i.	DE 274:85
inclination i. leads him	JOHN 461:93
do not check their i.	MONT 613:13
door of i.	DEFOE 269:76
general i. of all mankind	HOBB 420:1
i. of my nature	ELIZ 321:98
who have no i. for either	LESS 524:6
wicked i. in most people	JOHN 464:87
inclinations highest i. of a man	LONS 536:42
multitude of perverse i.	SHAR 806:73
our i. daily alter	ETHE 327:46
include I. me out	GOLD 377:34
incognito eternal i.	BARN 64:61
income Annual i. twenty pounds	DICK 280:43
as a source of i.	KEMB 479:72
define a man's i.	HICKS 417:47
good i. is of no avail	SMITH 829:14
I. Tax return has made i.	ROGE 723:75
in favour of inequality of i.	SHAW 810:19
large i. is the best recipe	AUST 46:68
lottery...yields public i.	QUINE 702:22
real i. is increased	KEYN 485:83
real i. of the community	KEYN 484:80
rises to meet i.	PARK 665:41
that sort of i. bracket	MORL 620:42
incomes inequalities of i. and wealth	KEYN 485:85
live beyond their i.	SAKI 739:63
incompetence not i. but war	PIER 677:67
rise to his level of i.	PETER 675:37
incompetent election by the i. many	SHAW 808:37
i. as the average male	CUNN 258:76
i. swine	SASS 745:86
tax on pianos for the i.	SITW 824:16
incomplete i. self	GASS 361:87
judge yourself i.	NERVO 634:40
incomprehension gulf of mutual i.	SNOW 832:77
inconsistencies searches out any i.	RUSS 734:22
inconsistency I. on the part of pastors	FRAN 347:92
inconstancy I., boredom, anxiety	PASC 667:71
infidelity is not i.	LACL 503:37
Man with that i. was born	BEHN 75:26
nothing...constant, but i.	SWIFT 861:24
inconstant i., uncertain, unknown	LOCKE 533:87
incontinence turpitude of i.	SCOTT 754:67
inconvenience adventure is...i.	CHES 220:73
i. is often considerable	AUST 46:77
not made without i.	JOHN 460:66
inconveniences free...of all i.	MARP 574:42
i. attend play-going	TYNAN 904:1
inconvenient cause may be i.	BENN 81:66
i. to be poor	COWP 251:1
incorruptible seagreen I.	CARL 201:97
increase another man's price i.	WILS 948:68
God gave the i.	BIBLE 126:37
He must i.	BIBLE 122:27
i. in inverse ratio	HUXL 442:77
i. of riches and commerce	HUME 438:4
not i. its consumption	KEYN 485:83
without either i. or diminution	RICA 713:84
increases What judgement I had i.	DRYD 304:38
incredulity epoch of i.	DICK 282:94
increments i. of noise	BYATT 186:18
indebted I. and discharged	MILT 604:91
thing I'm i. to her for	FIEL 335:34
indecency I.'s conspiracy of silence	SHAW 808:51
indecent I....10 years before	LAVER 512:33
i. behaviour	WAUGH 923:52
inhuman and i. and dishonorable	HELL 408:41
name itself as i.	SPEN 837:10
to assume such i. postures	WILDE 942:28
indecision Evil draws its power from i.	BENE 79:21
My I. is Final	EBER 310:13
indefensible defence of the i.	ORWE 655:61
defending...i.	CHES 220:59
indemnity Double I.	CAIN 192:21
independence chief virtue...is its i.	SCOTT 751:99
for our i.	PITT 680:11
new electronic i.	MCLU 556:54
war for i.	SCHL 747:33
willing to grant America i.	GEOR 363:47
independent Britain as an i.	
European state	GAIT 357:13
free and i. condition	ADAMS 5:5
I. existence—so called	HUXL 441:72
i. of the vagaries	ACHE 2:30
We are...the only i. newspaper	MURD 626:70
indestructible endless and i.	WILL 946:21
We, i.!	GRASS 382:13
indeterminate Science rejects the i.	BERN 85:69
index i. of a feeling mind	CRAB 252:47
i. of output per capita	MISH 609:19
i. of this country	MARC 570:57
i. to the heart	DICK 279:17
man the i. of that book	DONNE 293:79
marble i. of a mind	WORD 958:82
true i. of a man's character	CONN 243:14
indexes enshrined in 10,000 i.	ALLEN 13:76
Wall Street i. predicted	SAMU 741:2
India decided to cycle to I.	MURP 626:73
Englishman's justification in I.	CURZ 260:5
fly to I. for gold	MARL 573:19
fly to I. for gold	MARL 573:23
From I.'s coral strand	HEBER 406:1
gone to I.	YEATS 967:35
in twentieth-century I.	FRIE 351:70
loss of I.	CHUR 225:74
money in I.	KIPL 491:27
Nothing in I. is identifiable	FORS 344:36
pitched battles in I.	MACA 545:40
realize what I. is	CURZ 259:3
So far I like I.	MAIL 561:69
Indian history of the I. Ocean	NAIP 629:28
likely to be an I.	HEAT 406:96
Like the base I.	SHAK 790:51
Lo! the poor I.	POPE 687:75
only good I.	SHER 816:68
poetry...in the legendary I.	DARIO 262:44
Shadow...an old I. name	AMIS 16:44
treated like an I. widow	MITF 610:55
Indians I. are you	BALD 57:23
I., if we last another twenty years	MCMU 557:82
I. singing the...requiem	DUNC 307:9
reading Neville Cardus to the I.	THOM 884:23
Indies carry the wealth of the I.	JOHN 463:60
indifference heresy in the form of i.	RAHN 705:36
i., a physical i.	LAWR 513:54
i. of those	HAILE 392:16
i.—the fern-dark i.	LAWR 513:58
pass over youth in dull i.	CONG 241:61
serene i.	WILL 944:66
superb i. to mortal	STEV 852:53
there shall be i.	SMITH 828:4
indifferent delayed till I am i.	JOHN 460:63
i....at the birth of his work	ERNST 327:39
i. judge	SIDN 820:46
Is God by definition i.	EBER 310:12
worst sin...to be i.	SHAW 807:98
indifferentism rather than i.	NIGH 639:20
indifferently look on both i.	SHAK 776:77
indigenous intrinsic, i., something	MORR 621:59
indigent How i. the great!	GRAY 384:57
indigestion morale and high i.	MURK 626:72
indignation Moral i.	WELLS 930:31
noble and terrific i.	LESS 524:93
wrath and i. against us	BOOK 147:67
indignations books...contain...our i.	CONR 244:40
indignities by i....to dignities	BACON 51:85
i. real and imagined	WHITE 935:96
indignity God...spared me the i.	BELL 76:57
held himself free from i.	PALM 662:72
ultimate i. is to be given	KUHN 500:36
indirection sense by i.	EVANS 328:69
indiscretion cliché and an i.	MACM 556:64
i. without temptation	BIER 135:92
indispensable temptation of being thought i.	ATWO 41:49
individual and every i.	TRUM 899:77
And the i. withers	TENN 871:20
bestowed on the i.	MCCA 547:90

individualism

Entry	Reference
capacity for i. enterprise	WAVE 925:2
debased of style, not i.	MAIL 560:52
definition of an i.	KOES 495:26
difficult...for the i.	HAYEK 402:24
economic liberties of the i.	KRIS 499:13
ethical reality of the i.	KIER 485:2
Every form is i.	HEIN 407:21
Every i....intends only	SMITH 828:86
faith in i. enterprise	BURT 181:72
feeling i. appeared weak	BELL 78:90
for a private i. or for a city	PLATO 682:67
force...the i. to believe	PENF 673:79
growth in the i.	SMIL 827:69
happiness of an i.	JOHN 462:24
herd instinct in the i.	NIET 638:95
idea...extinguished in i. minds	DURK 308:31
immortality for the i.	SCHO 748:55
i., and only the	NABO 628:14
i. features are portrayed	HUMB 438:92
i. integrity	GREEN 387:39
i. is a minority	ELLI 323:37
i. is no longer to be sovereign	DOUG 295:23
i. men and women	THAT 881:66
i. opinions are not colorful	SAFI 737:22
i. profit without i. responsibility	BIER 134:72
Insists I too am an i.	LARK 509:73
law [of competition]...hard for the i.	CARN 202:48
life style...destructive of the i.	HARV 400:79
moral i. courage in Chinese	MO 611:66
no i. can recollect the order	WELL 929:6
of the ignorant i.	KEYN 484:78
only done by one i.	MACH 553:94
oppressed or obscure i.	HAZL 403:43
ordinary in the i.	MANN 566:87
the autonomous i.	ORWE 653:30
the i. and...the state	PLATO 681:43
wanted to be an i.	GULL 390:92
what any i. thinks	PETE 675:39
work of the i.	SIKO 821:68
individualism aberrations of i.	SMALL 826:58
American system of rugged i.	HOOV 427:44
individuality i. is...special error	SCHO 748:55
I....the aim of political liberty	COOP 246:86
i....the weakness of our race	DELA 271:21
men without i. have no taste	BENN 81:75
individuals gifted i. manage	SAKI 739:63
hostile behavior...to i.	FULB 355:63
i. are always right	VIAN 911:69
I. pass like shadows	BURKE 175:29
i. when they make up	KEYN 484:76
negotiation between i.	MUNCH 625:42
not consist of i.	MARX 579:38
satisfactory to i. inside	BIOY 135:5
set of atomic i.	NOVAK 641:64
worth of the i. composing	MILL 591:6
Indochina jungles of I.	MCGO 552:87
passed in I.	GREE 386:10
indoctrination substituting i.	PETE 676:39
indoor Done with i. complaints	WHIT 937:1
indoors We live in the great i.	RAINE 705:38
indubitable absolutely i.	DESC 274:94
inducement if...i. were offered	KING 488:56
indulge i. in a few follies	PROU 697:41
naturally i. in a few delinquencies	ELIOT 315:16
not one that government can i. in	RENO 711:50
indulgence i. encourages us	COWP 251:9
i. to sit in a room	HELL 408:40
kind protection and i.	STOWE 856:28
indulgences i....never change	BEAU 70:7
industrial advanced i. society	HAYEK 402:25
i. and economic status	SKEL 824:32
i. balance sheets	WEIL 928:74
i. worker would sooner have...£5	BLYT 144:87
new i. revolution	WIEN 939:29
The I. Revolution	TOYN 895:71
industrially they who rule i.	CONN 243:19
industrious man who...is i.	DICK 281:54
industry British i.	HEATH 405:86
Captains of I.	CARL 201:38
employ their whole i.	SMITH 827:85
grip upon i.	TAWN 868:43
her i. and economy	STAN 842:15
I am an i.	CRUY 256:37
I. and all the virtues	HUXL 441:64
i. and intuition	WILS 947:44
i. can't take you	UPDI 905:15
i. that...needs better people	DRUC 299:7

Entry	Reference
Life without i.	RUSK 733:10
literary i. would not exist	LESS 524:1
Ministers of I.	MAND 565:65
re-equipping of British i.	BEVE 90:63
stream of human i.	TOCQ 892:27
subsidy to the high technology i.	CHOM 222:28
there is no place for i.	HOBB 420:2
War is the national i.	MIRA 608:14
whole field to private i.	HELL 407:30
inedible i. raised to the unspeakable	BASK 67:50
ineffable as an i. mystery	SCHW 751:94
i. effable	ELIOT 320:53
ineffective i. from close up	SCHO 749:59
inefficiency efficiency and i.	SHAW 809:68
inept earth peopled as ever by the i.	REPP 711:60
inequalities significant i. of incomes	KEYN 485:85
inequality great i. of environment	CARN 202:48
in favour of i. of income	SHAW 810:19
saddest sight...fortune's i. exhibits	CARL 201:25
inevitable arguing with the i.	LOWE 539:14
foresee the i.	ASIM 38:79
have a suspicion it's i.	LEAC 516:25
how i. the i. was	EAGL 309:3
i. the Titanic was going to set sail	HAGUE 391:10
violent revolution i.	KENN 481:10
inexhaustible what is i. is benevolent	FRYE 354:57
inexpressible expressing the i.	HUXL 441:69
infallible i. criterion of wisdom	BURKE 176:51
i. symptom	GIBB 366:93
not final because we are i.	JACK 449:7
infamous acting...unlawfull, i.	PRYN 699:62
infamy I.! I.!	ROTH 724:14
old lies and new i.	POUND 691:4
infancy about him in his i.	GREE 385:3
dug a spring in i.	BRON 161:59
Heaven...in our i.	WORD 959:8
i. of our poetry	DRYD 304:39
In unexperienc'd i.	TRAH 895:81
Irish...in the i. of the race	OFAO 647:96
lies about us in our i.	MITC 609:25
Women are from their very I.	ASTE 39:2
infant an i. of three	RANS 706:66
describe the i. phenomenon	DICK 278:83
head of the human i.	SCHR 749:66
i. breaks its rattle	SADE 737:14
i. crying for the light	TENN 874:77
i. whose middle	NASH 631:77
Sooner murder an i.	BLAKE 140:3
to a little i.	BACON 50:59
infantile i. death-rate	HALD 392:22
infants filthy, sturdy, unkillable i.	POUND 691:93
i. are trying to spell God	ROBI 718:87
Sustenance for their helpless I.	SWIFT 862:57
infect she would i. to the North Star	SHAK 773:27
infected come i. back	WILB 939:38
infection difficult to stay a moral i.	DICK 282:92
facilitate the i. of idiocy	BIER 134:81
for fear of the i.	PEPYS 674:3
i. and the hand of war	SHAK 764:40
i. of politics	BRON 160:50
i. of the common sky	GRAV 382:21
new risks of i.	WEIZ 928:78
infelicity her i....years too many	WEBS 927:62
inference i....watch...had a maker	PALEY 661:57
inferior becomes the i.	GREE 386:18
i. to most civilised ages	CARL 200:83
not to be i. ...nature	PERI 675:25
Switzerland as an i.	SMITH 830:47
Titles...are disgraced by the i.	SHAW 808:41
inferiority always conscious of an i.	JOHN 463:51
lie of their i.	KING 487:34
preserved from a state of i.	GEOR 364:47
say he has an i. complex	SALI 740:79
inferno i. depicted by Dr Goebbels	ORWE 654:33
moronic i.	BELL 77:87
moronic i. of insipidity	LEWIS 527:75
infidelity I. does not consist	PAINE 660:39
i. is not inconstancy	LACL 503:37
infield No reason why the i.	SHAW 811:29
infinite being absolutely i.	SPIN 841:83
Canna see the i.	MACD 549:30
everything would appear...i.	BLAKE 140:4
for both are i.	SHAK 766:84
Her I. variety	SHAK 794:58
his passion is I.	PARK 664:13
how i. in faculty	SHAK 782:89
in comparison to the i.	PASC 667:85

Entry	Reference
i. can never meet	MARV 577:96
i. choice	GITL 373:31
i. diversity of movement	REDT 709:25
i. number of possibilities	GREE 386:22
man and the i.!	MACD 549:24
striving toward the i.	HUMB 438:93
there is an I. in him	CARL 200:98
To feel the i.	STAEL 842:3
zero and the i.	JARRY 452:95
infinitely i. large and i. small	LEVI 525:26
i. small amount of commodity	JEVO 455:52
infinities arise...you numberless i.	DONNE 292:50
infinitive split an i....stay split	CHAN 213:82
split i. is always wrong	THUR 891:5
infinitude speculations of eternity or i.	ADDI 7:36
infinity i. in the palm of your hand	BLAKE 141:24
infirm I. of purpose!	SHAK 797:36
Minstrel was i. and old	SCOTT 752:9
infirmities i. of old age	WESL 932:71
infirmity feblit with i.	DUNB 306:3
i. of noble mind	MILT 599:86
prop To our i.	WORD 958:79
inflammation i. of the sentence	THUR 890:91
inflation Having a little i.	HEND 410:1
not just i....or stagnation	MACL 556:51
Rising prices...do not cause i.	WRIS 963:63
Steel prices cause i.	BLOU 143:71
inflexible i. political persuasion	WILS 948:71
inflict i. myself on the public	MORL 620:42
influence auspicious star, whose i.	SHAK 803:11
books that i. us	FORS 345:50
bright eyes Rain i.	MILT 597:47
British 'Sphere of I.'	ANON 23:94
clothes possess an i.	ALCO 12:43
direct i. upon the soul	KAND 473:17
Film art has a greater i.	BALA 56:10
guard against...unwarranted i.	EISE 314:2
i. of a government	REES 710:38
i. of a nation	BENN 79:31
i. of...Milton and Dryden	ELIOT 317:93
i....of our own family	CHUR 224:50
i. of the Crown	DUNN 307:22
i. them from within	JOHN 456:72
i. which is moved not	SHEL 816:93
no i. on the future value	JEVO 455:53
often malign i.	MUGG 623:11
save...from its i.	WEBB 925:7
think I can i. them slightly	THOM 884:26
two points of i.	ARNO 36:30
where his i. stops	ADAMS 5:91
influences i. them in proportion	TOCQ 892:32
intellectual i.	KEYN 484:81
thousand i. constantly press	ORWE 653:11
influenza call it i. if ye like	BENN 81:65
information armed with the same i.	MISH 609:20
branch of the i. business	WRIS 963:79
dispersed i.	HAYEK 402:25
Everybody gets so much i.	STEIN 845:71
find i. upon it	JOHN 462:38
haphazard heap of i.	TOLS 894:53
I. is any difference	BATE 68:54
I. is a beacon	LEVI 526:31
I....necessary to the human mind	REES 710:38
i. vegetable, animal and mineral	GILB 368:39
knowledge...lost in i.?	ELIOT 319:31
maximum amount of i.	WILS 948:53
money is just another form of i.	WRIS 963:81
not by giving new i.	WITT 951:22
only ask for i.	DICK 280:48
pure i.	GOULD 380:76
read partly for i.	SCHL 747:34
Withholding i. from someone	KLINE 494:7
woman of...little i.	AUST 45:54
informed but far better i.	BIRK 136:16
desire to be i.	BROW 165:46
informer i....cannot be a soldier	FLAU 339:16
informing i. them narrowly	GALB 357:22
ingenious i. are always fanciful	POE 683:82
no matter how i.	KISS 493:88
ingots back with i. bows	SHAK 787:65
i., like in each respect	MARL 574:37
ingrateful for the multitude to be i.	SHAK 799:95
On her i. top!	SHAK 792:1
ingratitude As man's i.	SHAK 779:84
buried by i.	LYLY 543:84
I. is monstrous	SHAK 799:95
I., more strong than traitors' arms	SHAK 777:43

I., thou marble-hearted fiend	SHAK 792:94
ingredients the very i. of virtue	MILT 600:13
ingress i. into the world	LONG 536:36
inhabitant i. of the North of England	FORD 342:89
ordinary i. is incomprehensible	STARK 843:25
inhabitants i. not...grow old	CONN 243:12
i. of different planets	DISR 288:34
i. of myth	FIED 334:10
landscape and its i.	UPDI 906:37
shared among its i.	SIDG 819:32
such uncomely i.	WALP 918:64
inhale as if she would i. them	FIRB 336:57
but I didn't i.	RICH 714:25
didn't i.	DOWD 296:29
To i. Paris	HUGO 437:82.
inherent i. in the human situation	GREE 386:25
inherit all which it i.	SHAK 804:27
inheritance care for its literary i.	ELIOT 319:28
Has had a like i.	YEATS 967:35
have our i.	SMITH 828:4
heathen for thine i.	BIBLE 99:28
heir to an i.	OAKE 642:4
how my i. was proceeding	HAMER 393:45
spending my children's i.	ANON 27:29
inherited he...i. nothing	JACK 448:5
inheritor succeed as his i.	SHAK 798:86
inheritors i. of an old civilization	REYES 712:69
inhibition I. is no good provider	HESI 417:33
inhibitions cultivate a few i.	LOOS 536:54
inhuman artists...want to become i.	APOL 29:78
i. and indecent and dishonorable	HELL 408:41
i. in its materialism	WILS 947:43
inhumanity essence of i.	SHAW 807:98
Humanity is best described as i.	CONR 244:54
i. of a boa constrictor	WOOL 956:47
Man's i. to Man	BURNS 177:86
refuses to remember the i.	WEIZ 928:78
rewarded with i.	ROLL 723:90
iniquities bruised for our i.	BIBLE 109:94
forgiveth all thine i.	BIBLE 102:6
If thou, Lord, shouldest mark i.	BIBLE 103:39
rewarded us according to our i.	BIBLE 102:7
iniquity hated i.	GREG 387:51
infamous seminary of i.	CHES 219:46
i. is taken away	BIBLE 107:55
shapen in i.	BIBLE 101:71
stubbornness is as i.	BIBLE 96:33
tongue is...a world of i.	BIBLE 130:56
visiting the i. of the fathers	BIBLE 94:66
initiation i. into a new state	ELIOT 315:25
injured always being the i. party	ANGE 19:94
forgiveness to the i.	DRYD 300:31
injuries i. sustained in his native town	ANON 23:88
poisons and awkward i.	ANOU 28:62
take revenge for slight i.	MACH 552:92
injurious highly i. to the poor	HALL 393:40
injury height without sustaining i.	LEON 522:71
i. is much sooner forgotten	CHES 219:36
i. would vex a very saint	SHAK 762:70
members from i. and molestation	MILL 591:2
Where there is i.	FRAN 347:99
injustice cruel i. if you deny it	CARL 201:29
fear of suffering i.	LARO 510:99
grave i. to bees	ORWE 653:20
I. anywhere is a threat	KING 486:24
i. of taking a speck for the whole	EDGE 311:45
I....prevents my doing it	BUTL 186:4
neutral in situations of i.	TUTU 901:26
nothing so finely perceived...as i.	DICK 282:5
protect him against i.	PALM 662:72
superior to i.	PLATO 682:60
injustices i. are sanctioned	FRAN 347:87
ink 12 ounces of paper and i.	MORL 619:39
a better teacher than i.	FRY 354:49
black i. in white milk	MUNRO 625:51
brain that i. may character	SHAK 802:77
buy i. by the barrel	KIRK 493:81
cuttlefish squirting out i.	ORWE 654:36
Every drop of i.	WALP 919:67
gunpowder and printer's i.	KRAUS 499:10
Hamlet is so much paper and i.	PRIE 695:84
hath not drunk i.	SHAK 763:12
I....A villainous compound	BIER 134:81
i....tempered with love's sighs	SHAK 763:18
medium is printer's i.	KRAUS 499:6
mix...water with their i.	GOET 375:66
Rorschach i. blots	LICH 528:94
spend time and i.	GALS 358:49
win...By blood or i.	BYRON 189:70
inmate who is...the i.	CONA 239:10
inn best in every i.	STEV 851:26
brought him to an i.	BIBLE 121:81
Do you remember an I.	BELL 77:70
In the worst i.'s worst room	POPE 686:69
no room for them in the i.	BIBLE 120:68
that dark i.—the Grave!	SCOTT 753:40
world's an i.	DRYD 304:54
inn-door up to the old i.-d.	NOYES 642:70
inner i. process	WITT 951:28
strengthened...in the i. man	BIBLE 127:88
innings life was like his i.	EGAN 313:65
Innisfree go to I.	YEATS 965:4
innocence ceremony of i. is drowned	YEATS 966:24
end of i.	GOLD 375:74
first state of i.	BEHN 75:23
Ignorance is not i.	BROW 169:81
i. and even the right	RODR 722:52
I. ends when one is stripped	DIDI 286:79
I. is a science of the sublime	CIXO 228:49
i. should be bold	MASS 581:75
I. thy Sister dear!	MARV 577:2
lost their i.	GREER 387:43
Never such i.	LARK 509:82
purity and place and i.	MILT 604:9
Some final i.	SPEN 837:95
spurious i.	BELL 78:94
though conscious of your i.	JOHN 463:47
wanting to hold onto i.	WILS 947:35
worthy of the joy of i.	OFLA 647:98
innocency state of i. Adam fell	SHAK 771:55
innocent 'baby', an i. rhyme	SHAK 774:56
But who is i.?	WORD 961:46
Can one be i.	CYRA 260:10
essential self is i.	UPDI 906:30
guilty until...proved i.	ORWE 655:79
i. as strawberries	THOM 883:16
i. of the charge	ARCH 30:6
look like the i. flower	SHAK 796:17
one i. suffer	BLAC 137:43
sleep'—the i. sleep	SHAK 797:34
sores on i. tongues	OWEN 657:31
The i. and the beautiful	YEATS 966:29
to hurt i. people	HELL 408:41
innocents We are...the i.	DELI 271:42
innovate I....or evaporate!	MERR 588:48
To i. is not to reform	BURKE 176:55
innovation Fashion...produces i.	SANT 743:40
I. most of the time	SCHM 748:40
innovations ill-shapen, so are all i.	BACON 52:8
innovator time is the greatest i.	BACON 52:9
inns i. of Molten Blue	DICK 283:33
two years in Holiday I.	MOND 612:94
innuendoes beauty of i.	STEV 850:74
in-office i.-o. attitudes and behavior	COUP 248:28
inquest like the Coroner's I.	CONG 241:54
inquire i. in his temple	BIBLE 100:50
I. often	PENN 673:82
not to i. why or whither	WILD 943:42
inquiries invited his i.	MENC 586:89
religious i.	GIBB 366:99
some i. are too dangerous	SAGAN 737:24
inquiry every i....is thought to aim	ARIS 31:19
i. of truth	BACON 50:56
result of a critical i.	RUSS 734:22
Inquisition like Galileo going	
before the I.	LIVI 532:57
inquisition I....from the pulpit	WELD 928:83
To these I. dogs	TENN 878:95
inquisitiveness tribalism and i.	ALDI 12:51
inquisitors severe i.	BACON 51:74
inroad i. on the discipline	OCON 646:82
insane among the i.	DE 268:45
Man is quite i.	MONT 614:28
insanity new idea...close to i.	MILL 593:38
prelude to i.	WAUGH 923:60
So with sanity and i.	MELV 585:76
inscription i. on public fountains	FLAU 339:29
inscriptions In lapidary i.	JOHN 462:42
inscrutability i. of the East	STARK 843:25
inscrutable i. singular name	ELIOT 320:53
i. to the last	THUR 890:76
insect Egyptians came to	
worship an i.	DISR 288:45
i. moves toward its flower	BALZ 61:1
i. youth are on the wing	GRAY 384:58
into a gigantic i.	KAFKA 472:5
one is but an i.	JOHN 459:58
insects dancing i.	WORD 961:41
Fabulous the i.	WILK 943:59
I. are what neurosis	AMIS 16:54
keep down microscopic i.	DOUG 294:97
insecurity source of economic i.	ELLW 323:39
inseparable found i.	HUME 438:95
i. part	GAND 359:60
inside i. and an outside	HEPW 412:29
i. and strength were philosophy	SIDN 820:53
i. the tent pissing out	JOHN 458:14
insides rest of a person's i.	TWAIN 903:66
insight For i. into human affairs	DYSON 309:59
if it only added judgement to i.	FORS 344:33
I. have gained from poker	MAMET 564:35
moment's i.	HOLM 424:81
most revolutionary i. of all	JONG 466:30
read...partly for i.	SCHL 747:34
insights deeper i. to the dead belong	FERG 333:83
i. of the Jewish prophets	NIEB 637:87
perceptions and i.	KISS 494:92
insignificance Men thin away to i.	HARDY 397:4
without losing their i.	BAXT 69:93
insignificant as i. as possible	GALT 359:56
obvious and i.	JAMES 451:75
see themselves at both exceptional and i.	MAIL 567:51
insincerity enemy of clear language is i.	ORWE 655:63
enemy of clear language is i.	ORWE 654:36
insipid He is many times flat, i.	DRYD 300:20
i. thing is a billet-doux	ETHE 327:43
Simplicity...is wholly i.	HOGA 422:40
insipidity inferno of i. and decay	LEWIS 527:26
insolence is not invective	DISR 288:42
i. of wealth	JOHN 463:61
lazy i. of a shoe salesman	PERE 674:18
supports with i.	JOHN 460:78
insolencies i. of other Turks	BUTL 184:62
insoluble political ones are i.	HOME 425:95
science leads only to the i.	DISR 288:53
insolvency i. spelt glamour	HAMI 394:51
insomnia febrile i., mortal leaps	MARI 571:76
ideal i.	JOYCE 470:35
inspector An I. Calls	PRIE 695:87
great i., with a myriad eyes	STEAD 843:34
inspiration Genius is one per cent i.	EDIS 312:54
hierophants of an unapprehended i.	SHEL 816:53
My sole i.	PORT 690:71
scripture is given by i.	BIBLE 129:28
temperamental i.	MOND 612:96
inspire feel not what they i.	SHEL 816:53
i. free hearts	KENN 481:14
i. hopeless passion	THAC 880:32
your selves i. These...works	POPE 688:29
inspired i. by the gods inside	SAINT 738:41
inspirer poet is more the i.	ELUA 324:43
instalment last i. missing	CRISP 255:7
instant at that i.	KARSH 474:32
Before me at this i.	SHAK 792:98
be i. in season	BIBLE 129:29
i. that he fell	SCOTT 752:26
Life changes in the i.	DIDI 286:86
perish in the very i.	GRAY 383:44
instinct delicacy of poetic i.	WILDE 940:50
i. for being unhappy	SAKI 739:60
i. for contentment	KRIS 499:14
i. for not ruining...vision	BLUN 143:80
i. of mankind	TAWN 868:43
i.; the habit is already old	LAWR 517:47
i. told him that the best liar	BUTL 185:98
intimate with him by i.	AUST 46:69
Love has its own i.	BALZ 61:1
maternal i.	FRID 350:62
natural i. to abjure man	HARDY 397:8
nerve and i. is clamouring	LESS 523:92
rather of i. than of practice	REED 710:33
satisfies the human creative i.	QUEN 702:8
sublimation of the work i.	LODGE 534:98
what the i....can conceive	PICA 677:59
what we believe upon i.	BRAD 155:41
womanly i. that clothes possess	ALCO 12:51
instinctively what you know i.	BELL 76:48
instincts atheism is against...our i.	BURKE 176:44
born with i. and abilities	BALZ 61:6
High i.	WORD 960:10
i. already catered for	BENN 80:44

institution

only trust our own i.	LAFO 503:47
true to your i.,' was his motto	LAWR 512:39
institution cannot see an i.	CRIT 255:11
deep stake...in such a glorious i.	BURKE 175:21
family as an i.	MILLS 595:7
feature of this i.	DICK 279:2
i. of the throne	ACHE 2:7
Is an i. always	JARR 452:90
It's an i.	HUGH 436:48
no major i. in the US	FRIE 351:71
only i. in the world	SAMU 741:98
partly of human i.	MILL 591:93
such as are in the i.	EMER 312:29
institutions destroy i.	WHIT 938:5
free i. can exist	MARS 575:63
i. are framed	TREV 896:10
i., civil and ecclesiastical	PEEL 672:66
i. presuppose a Supreme Being	DOUG 295:22
most licentious of human i.	SHAW 808:32
old i. entirely reformed	MACH 553:94
take the i. and liberties	POWE 693:59
walls of i.	ROET 722:56
instruct amuse and i.	UPDI 906:26
i. thee and teach thee	BIBLE 100:54
instructed i. and amused	ATLAS 40:20
instruction all the i. and knowledge	JAY 453:2
All true histories contain i.	BRON 161:56
horses of i.	BLAKE 140:1
i. in righteousness	BIBLE 129:28
i. without talent	VITR 914:29
no i. book came with it	FULL 355:73
instructions Bloody i.	SHAK 796:19
literature is the operating i.	LE GU 520:19
instructive something i.	KHOM 485:89
instrument great i. of moral good	SHEL 816:50
I am an i.	RICH 713:99
i. might be less	JOHN 460:68
i. of chase	WELLS 930:25
i. of Your peace	FRAN 347:99
i. plays itself	BACH 49:7
i. that has a good moral effect	ARIS 32:28
i. with which each learns	PLATO 682:65
more perfect i. of the soul	PIUS 680:20
most sensitive i. known to man	BEEC 73:71
old one-stringed i.	RANJ 706:60
painting...an i. of war	PICA 677:60
Polling is merely an i.	GALL 358:45
Prosperity is only an i.	COOL 246:80
supersensitive...i.	ERNST 327:40
The book...a kind of optical i.	PROU 698:61
tune the i. here at the door	DONNE 293:64
instruments all the i. agree	AUDEN 43:90
fit i. to make slaves	PITT 679:5
Furnished...with nice i.	FRAN 348:18
i. ill-adapted for the purpose	CHUR 226:17
i. of labour	MARX 579:41
i. of vengeance	DONO 293:82
I. of War	ALBE 11:33
i., strung to a vast precision	CRANE 253:60
i. to plague us	SHAK 793:64
lofty i. of war	SHAK 772:64
man, and not his i.	MO 611:67
insufferable Oxford...has made me i.	BEER 73:77
insufferables sovereign of i.	BIER 134:58
insult His presence here...an i.	RED 709:19
i. of each other's presence	ISHE 447:70
i. of each shabby skirt	DONO 293:82
i. to the Holy See	INNO 446:48
i....to the cook	CHES 221:11
much sooner forgotten than an i.	CHES 219:36
prolonged i.	MILL 593:52
ring of a really original i.	CARR 203:60
standing i. to sportsmen	FRY 353:28
who do not understand studied i.	GALL 358:40
insulted i....in our old age?	SCHU 750:80
possible for me to get i.	DAVIS 266:3
when somebody i. Caruso	LOUIS 538:79
insults Clothes are our...visible i.	CART 206:36
insurance for their i. money	DOYLE 296:44
tongue at the i.	MARQ 574:46
insurrection I....guerrilla bands	MAZZ 583:29
intangible O world i.	THOM 886:83
integrate desire i. into society	SARR 744:62
integrity Hyenas have i.	FRAN 349:28
i. of her honour	GOTT 379:70
i. of the Irish nation	REDM 709:21
national i.	WILS 949:76

still retain thine i.?	BIBLE 98:93
strictest i.	WASH 921:26
intellect Democratic I.	DAVIE 264:70
feather to tickle the i.	LAMB 506:13
i. of Europe	ARNO 35:8
i. will always govern	WOLL 953:85
march of i.	SOUT 835:58
merely great i.	THOM 885:48
Our meddling i.	WORD 957:59
power of the human i.	LEWIS 527:65
put on i.	BLAKE 141:33
revenge of the i. upon art	SONT 834:13
scorched my i. into a cinder	CARL 199:71
so-called things of the i.	LISP 531:45
to perfect...the i. or reason	SPIN 841:81
What i., what calculation	YEATS 967:38
intellects decayed in his i.	JOHN 465:87
i. vast and cool	WELLS 930:19
powerful of human i.	MACA 545:41
intellectual beasts of the i. domain	HOLM 424:62
by reason of her i. defects	WRIG 962:62
chief distinction in the i. powers	DARW 263:57
dash of i. curiosity	WEBB 928:6
Disinterested i.	TREV 896:4
end to purely i. intercourse	WRIG 962:63
great i. talents	TOCQ 892:26
i. attraction	HICKS 418:49
i. capacity	SCHR 749:66
i. fashion	CONN 243:18
i. life of our century	ARNO 35:12
i. life of...western society	SNOW 832:77
i. love of God	SPIN 841:82
I.: someone whose mind watches	CAMUS 195:80
most i. of all ages	BENN 81:80
passage to the i. World	STER 848:40
promote i. crime	BIER 134:81
Tears may be i.	BELL 79:92
The i....flower of the bourgeoisie	BOGAN 144:95
then an i.	HOOK 427:40
word 'I.' suggests	AUDEN 43:98
ye lords of ladies i.	BYRON 189:90
intellectually I....America	LEWIS 527:61
I....people never wash	DUDEK 305:77
intellectuals characterize...as i.	AGNEW 9:94
I. can tell themselves anything	HELL 408:46
I....no longer see the smile	SAINT 738:33
opiate of the i.	LUCE 541:57
intelligence bewitchment of our i.	WITT 951:20
Book learning, or i.	BYRNE 186:22
degree of a person's i.	ALTH 15:15
elaborate...waste of human i.	CHAN 213:96
explain school to a higher i.?	MATH 581:90
Fight for our National I.	CATT 209:3
grin and fine i.	NEW 634:34
have i. and yet not understand	LISP 531:45
i. and necessity	ANGE 18:85
i. in the winds	HOLM 423:55
i. of a respectable agricultural	MENC 587:16
i. that moves	DONNE 293:80
men started at the i.	SOUT 835:55
morning and evening with i.	JOHN 460:81
most correct i.	TIMES 892:23
Oh i., flaming solitude	GORO 379:66
Poetry must resist the i.	STEV 850:89
powers of i.	LYND 543:92
public subsidy of i.	QUINE 702:22
science of arresting human i.	LEAC 515:20
test of a first-rate i.	FITZ 338:93
triumph of imagination over i.	WILL 944:77
Truths discovered by i.	FRAN 347:83
works of thought and i.	PAST 668:4
intelligent attacked many an i.	MAIM 561:70
best audience is i.	BARK 63:55
both honest and i.	ORWE 655:66
first rule of i. tinkering	EHRL 313:69
i....are not the leaders	CONR 244:44
i. Mr Toad	GRAH 381:92
no i. woman	MUNRO 625:48
not a very i. means	KENT 483:49
not my business to do i. work	RUMS 731:46
not...quite i. enough	HUXL 441:71
room-mates...if they're i.	SALI 740:76
Shakespeherian Rag...So i.	ELIOT 318:1
The more i. one is	PASC 667:83
too old and i.	BRAD 154:34
intend i. to prejudice the past	WHIT 936:75
since what I well i.	SHAK 792:86

intensions geometric i.	LEGER 519:6
intensity i. of perception	WILL 946:24
passionate i.	YEATS 966:24
texture and i.	THOM 884:44
intensiveness i. as stricture	BURKE 176:63
intent prick the sides of my i.	SHAK 796:20
intention appreciate the i.	TROL 897:31
fossils of i.	PURDY 700:85
in the doer's i.	HELO 409:55
no i. of rearranging	MORT 621:76
no part of his i.	SMITH 828:86
plain i.	HERB 413:73
intentions act...with such i.	PEEL 672:66
express their i.	LESS 524:94
i. are perfectly honourable	SHAW 809:66
prince whose i. were pure	JOSE 469:8
intents i. wicked or charitable	SHAK 781:57
interchange ennobling i.	WORD 958:89
intercourse i. of touch	WORD 958:81
i. with foreign nations	DECA 268:64
i. with the natives	PARK 663:91
living forms and social i.	HOLM 424:80
nations; between whom there is no i.	DISR 288:34
oxygen of social i.	HIRS 419:74
pleasures of human i.	MOORE 616:67
purely intellectual i.	WRIG 962:63
Sexual i. began	LARK 509:88
synonym for i.	DWOR 308:46
interest ability nor i.	MORE 618:10
allurement of private i.	STEU 849:61
an i., a point of view	POPP 689:59
an i. in life	PALEY 661:52
By pursuing his own i.	SMITH 828:86
case...not entirely devoid of i.	DOYLE 297:54
common i. always will prevail	DRYD 302:85
common i. is...part of democracy	BLOOM 143:68
derives its collective i.	HUMB 438:92
falsehoods which i. dictates	JOHN 460:84
free from i. or prejudice	REES 710:38
fuel of i. to the fire	LINC 529:6
gentle lack of i.	LISP 531:45
i. in life does not lie	WOOLF 955:17
i. of the community	BENT 82:87
little in it to i.	THOR 889:50
no i. in anything but genius	LAGN 508:51
no i. whatever	MACL 554:26
operates in the public i.	KEYN 484:76
public i. may	LIPP 531:43
regard to their own i.	SMITH 827:76
sustain a uniform degree of i.	BOWL 153:5
want of any other i.	VOLT 914:47
what sustains i.	JIANG 455:56
interested he was i.	VIDAL 913:5
i. in music	SIMO 822:78
more i. in himself than in me	BIER 134:76
more i. in yourself	GIDE 367:19
interesting hardly be made i.	TROL 898:55
He was i.	VIDAL 913:5
Imitation is more i.	STEIN 845:72
i. as a wall can be	SHAW 810:42
law of the newspaper is to be i.	DANA 261:26
mildly i. ...frankly i.	BRYS 171:16
more i. than being yourself	GIEL 368:27
most i. ideas	SONT 834:19
that it be i.	JAMES 450:42
time fails to find them i.	MASE 580:70
interests harming their true i.	MONT 614:39
i. are by no means the same	SMITH 827:80
i. coincide with the state's	MUSS 628:96
i. of...the community	RICA 712:83
in the i. of Hell	FORS 344:39
Man's earthly i....held up	CARL 200:92
matters thus bearing on her i.	PALM 662:75
opportunity as against material i.	WILS 949:75
Our i. are eternal	PALM 662:70
power of vested i.	KEYN 484:81
pursue their respective i.	JEVO 455:54
uniformity of i.	MADI 558:16
watch over our i.	LLOY 532:68
interference trophy to magisterial i.	ANON 23:88
interfolds leaden i. are bright	FREE 350:49
interim i. is Like a phantasma	SHAK 776:16
interjection life is but an i.	BYRON 190:26
interline enlarge, diminish, i.	SWIFT 862:61
interlude Strange i.!	ONEI 651:66
interludes our lives are...dark i.	ONEI 651:66
Internet I. has taken shape	GLEI 374:48

iron

I. is becoming the town square	GATES 361:93	I., Nature's child	SIDN 820:44	I.'s dead	YEATS 966:17
Thanks to the i.	HART 399:65	i. of a mouse!	DISN 287:14	I. still continues poor?	BERK 84:33
the I. changes everything	GATES 361:92	i. of gunpowder	KRAUS 499:10	last British Prime Minister with	
The I.'s completely over.	PRIN 695:97	i. of the landscape painter	FUSE 356:59	jurisdiction in I.	ADAMS 4:82
The I....offers immense possibilities	FRAN 347:94	i. or true artistry	POUND 692:25	mad I. hurt you	AUDEN 43:91
The i., our greatest tool	ASSAN 39:98	no i. as to stories	BYRON 188:79	message of peace to I.	ARNO 35:23
TV and the I. are good	COUP 248:37	poem is a test of i.	KEATS 475:72	met in the streets of I.	OBRI 646:70
interpretation i. for...convenience	WIEN 939:30	their own i. shall furnish	HOBB 420:2	name of I. is mentioned	SMITH 830:46
I. is the revenge of the intellect	SONT 834:13	trim i.	HERB 413:73	never met anyone in I.	FRAS 349:33
i. of dreams	FREUD 350:56	Without i.	WILL 946:18	soup in I.	WAUGH 923:55
other i. is nonsense	GALL 358:45	**inventions** half ashamed of those i.	MACA 545:43	Think—what I have got for I.?	COLL 237:65
their i. is...ethical	ORWE 654:44	ideologies and i.	SONT 834:16	Though I. starve	BYRON 190:20
what is lost in i.	FROST 353:26	i. have endowed material forces	MARX 579:37	violence in Northern I.	OROU 652:92
interpreter God is his own i.	COWP 250:86	i. have no other apparent purpose	MENC 587:8	west of the Romans	CHRI 223:43
I don't know which is the i.	SHER 817:96	Our i. are wont	THOR 888:30	withdraw...troops from I.	REDM 709:21
soul...has an i.	BRON 161:63	rules for odd i.	SHAK 762:69	**iris** I. all hues, roses	MILT 604:8
interrupted when I was i.	CONN 243:23	we read the i. of others	MANG 565:68	I. of the West	BYRON 188:60
intersection old lady at a busy i.	ACHE 3:44	What excellent i.	AUGU 44:32	livelier i.	TENN 871:11
intersections i. within a society	MILLS 595:6	**inventive** manipulation of the i.	LEWIS 527:65	**irises** better than I.	HAMM 394:61
interstices between the i.	JOHN 460:76	**inventor** i. of harmonies	TENN 877:63	**Irish** answer to the I. Question	SELL 756:14
interstellar vacant i. spaces	ELIOT 320:62	**inventory** i. of unfinished thinking	RAND 706:55	as I. as Black Americans are African	GELD 362:30
interval during the i.	TYNAN 904:99	**inversions** all sorts of semantic i.	MAMET 564:32	becoming like the I. Census	MACR 558:14
i. betwixt one passion and another	STER 849:54	**invertebrates** belly-wriggling i.	LAWR 512:40	Ben Hur translated into I.	STEW 854:95
make a lucid i.	DRYD 300:44	**investigation** careful i. of cases	HARV 400:78	betwixt English and I.	STRA 857:44
intervals during his sober i.	LAMB 506:9	sphere of natural i.	HUMB 438:92	chiefs of the I. Brigade	DAVIS 266:9
enough fine i.	STEV 851:27	sufficiently careful i.	GALB 357:14	cross the river by an I. bridge	STEW 854:96
interveners lessons for the i.	ASHD 37:68	**investigations** obscurity of our i.	SCHO 748:52	distinctive I. experience	DONO 293:81
interview after an i. with a doctor	JAMES 450:24	**investigator** i. to pretend	LEWO 528:79	Dress British, look I.	KOFF 496:32
I once said in an i.	MCCA 548:2	**investment** i. in the quickest time	ROGE 722:66	ear becomes more I.	BYRON 190:17
interviewer i. asked me	MCCA 548:98	i. over its whole life	KEYN 484:78	exile has been to the I.	WILDE 940:49
interweaving complex, vital i.	PLATH 681:29	no finer i. for any community	CHUR 226:98	helpless in her I. hand	BARK 63:52
intestine dark i.	HUGH 436:37	**investor** average private i.	KEYN 484:78	He was a black I. type	PRIE 695:91
tapeworm in an i.	GOLD 375:76	**invidiousness** in sheer i.	ACHE 2:22	historic destiny of the I.	WAUGH 924:81
intimacy avoid any i.	KITC 494:98	**invincible** both sides were i.	SWIFT 861:38	integrity of the I. nation	REDM 709:21
determine i.	AUST 45:52	i. dullness	JONS 467:66	involved in the I. situation	OBRI 645:61
i. of a surgeon's scalpel	ANGE 19:98	Love i. in battle	SOPH 834:29	I. are in the same...position	OROU 652:92
no shore, no i.	SCOTT 751:2	no i. armies	STAL 842:6	I. [are] Paddies or Micks	PAXM 670:45
intimate art, i., heroic	ROUA 729:7	**inviolable** clutching the i. shade	ARNO 34:95	I. are the niggers of Europe	DOYLE 298:76
confiding, the i.	MACD 550:40	i. in the eye of Almighty God	GLAD 373:38	I. feelings and sensitivities	HAUG 401:84
i. as any conversation	STERN 847:18	**invisibility** This masculine I.	DUNN 307:14	I. hurricane, a flat calm	BOWEN 153:96
Sharing food...an i. act	FISH 337:64	**invisible** Clothes make the poor i.	HARR 398:44	I. melts into the tune	CARL 199:67
intonations history of the different i.	BORG 150:56	Fortune...she is not i.	BACON 52:25	I. people are too well off	SHAW 809:67
intoxicated exposes himself		I am an i. man	ELLI 323:35	I. question	FRAS 349:33
when he is i.	JOHN 463:65	immense; at times i.	MOORE 617:85	Let the I. vessel lie	AUDEN 43:92
intoxication best of Life is but i.	BYRON 190:8	i. man was...invisible to himself	ELLI 323:48	Look at the I.!	BUCH 171:25
not in the delicious i.	HUXL 442:80	led by an I. hand	SMITH 828:86	miserable I. Catholic childhood	MCCO 548:9
intricacies No pleasing I. intervene	POPE 686:60	limping i. down to	THOM 884:31	No blithe I. lad was so happy	CAMP 194:60
intrigue clannishness, routine and i.	JAUR 452:98	no i. means of support	BUCH 171:27	No modern I. writer	ORWE 654:51
Everything is done by i.	HUGO 437:72	Reputation...made him i.	WEBS 927:54	old I. hospitality	EDGE 311:37
intrigues I. half-gathered	CRAB 252:40	skuttle fish...becomes i.	ADDI 7:43	one of our little I. boats	BEHAN 74:10
introduce allow me to i. myself	JAGG 449:15	things visible and i.	BOOK 147:60	President of I. descent	KENN 481:20
introduced i. to the Aged	DICK 283:9	what is essential is i.	SAINT 739:37	Shakespeare was an I. Catholic	ONEI 651:69
introduction one is an i.	JOHN 460:64	Women...are i. people	FRIE 350:65	symbol of I. art	JOYCE 470:22
intuition by pure soul-i.	LAWR 513:57	**invocation** i. of the Muse	GRAV 382:27	teach...the I. how to listen	WILDE 942:13
human i., human autonomy	MUMF 625:39	more like an i.	LEZA 528:81	teach the I. to drink beer	EDGE 311:39
i. and compassion	WILS 947:44	**invulnerable** I. nothings	SHEL 815:39	The I. and the Jews have a psychosis	BEHAN 74:14
invade dare to i....my realm	ELIZ 322:4	**inward** from the outside i.	FRIE 351:75	those of the I. nation	PARN 665:47
very uncivilised to i.	HUNT 440:33	**Ionian** under I. skies	SHEL 816:47	To marry the I.	DONL 290:7
invader won from her proud i.	MOORE 617:1	**IOUs** guy holding the I.	IACO 444:3	turn to early I. literature	OFAO 647:96
invaders exiles and i.	ATWO 41:37	**IQ** IQ had been two points lower	TREV 896:8	Upon the I. shore	BURNS 180:59
invasion defended...from foreign i.	REDM 709:21	**IRA** deal with the I. or the British		was an I. rat	SHAK 779:91
defend the realm against i.	PHIL 676:51	government	PAIS 660:43	We I....that ancient sect	YEATS 967:38
i. of a common enemy	KITC 494:98	We dislike the I.	OBRI 645:64	what the I. people wanted	DE 275:7
not an i. of Vietnam	NIXON 640:34	**Iraq** crime...against I. and humanity	HUSS 440:41	**Irish-American** leader is an I.-A.	WILDE 940:49
invective insolence is not i.	DISR 288:42	invasion on I.	GORE 379:59	**Irishman** I. is lined with copper	TWAIN 902:48
invent choose—that is to say, i.	SART 745:77	I. appears not to have come to a		I.'s heart is nothing	SHAW 809:63
God...necessary to i. him	VOLT 915:48	genuine acceptance...of...disarmament	BLIX 142:59	I.'s imagination	SHAW 808:62
I just i.	FULL 355:70	I. is...a situation where	OBAMA 643:20	I. turned Englishman	OBRI 645:62
i. because you enjoy it	WILS 947:48	I. probably has no weapons of mass		I. would kill a negro	FREE 349:45
reason properly can i.	LESS 524:6	destruction	COOK 245:70	poor silly-clever I.	SHAW 809:64
writer does not need to i.	PROU 698:60	no cutting and running in I.	BLAIR 138:66	**Irishmen** I. born brooders	OBRI 645:62
invented Everything...has been i.	DUELL 305:81	rid I. of these killers	BUSH 183:28	**Irishness** I. is not...question of birth	OBRI 645:61
fond thing vainly i.	BOOK 150:41	the problem in I. today	BLAIR 138:65	**Irishy** more I. than is necessary	TWAIN 903:69
If...born...were being i.	DOYLE 297:75	weapons of mass destruction...in I.	BLIX 142:60	**irksome** harsh, impertinent, and i.	JONS 467:61
i. to make fun	GARC 359:65	**Iraqi** I. is really not whacky	ACHE 3:52	How i. is this music	SHAK 759:86
i. what I conceived	HUXL 443:4	**ire** 'shinning' arouses his i.	ANON 23:89	**iron** An i. man	SHAK 772:91
lazy people...i. the wheel	WALE 917:30	**Ireland** advantages of I.	SAKI 739:44	another i. door	SPEN 839:41
invention brightest heaven of i.	SHAK 775:61	Consider I.	DISR 287:31	Any old i.	COLL 237:63
call the sciences human i.	PAINE 660:38	do nothing...for I.	FREE 349:46	beat the I. while it is hot	DRYD 304:36
Ceremony is an i.	LAMB 505:94	enemies to I.	EDGE 311:43	bend thy pillars with thine i. car	BLAKE 139:83
deities of his own i.	PLATO 681:42	future government of I.	CHUR 224:65	break them with a rod of i.	BIBLE 99:28
exercise his i.	SMITH 828:89	'God save I.'	SULL 859:80	but he has i. teeth	GROM 389:78
'Faith' is a fine i.	DICK 283:32	great Gaels of I.	CHES 220:81	carcass seemed to be made of i.	MENC 587:15
fresh i. planted	CAREW 198:51	I. and...for the United Kingdom	LLOY 533:77	cloak should become an i. cage	WEBER 925:11
genuine i. in the realm	MILL 593:38	I. gives England her soldiers	MERE 588:39	Don't i.	ANON 26:27
greatest I. since the novel	MEAD 583:32	I. is one of the few countries	DANG 262:29	hard as i. bloody bars	GALL 358:44
i., hearing not my tongue	SHAK 787:62	I. never was contented	LAND 507:35	If the i. dice roll	BETH 87:12

iron-grey

in my heart his i. arrow — SPEN 838:26
i. and blood — BISM 137:32
i. coat all overgrown — SPEN 838:30
i. curtain has descended — CHUR 226:2
i. curtain would at once descend — GOEB 374:54
i. entered into his soul — BOOK 149:33
I. Lady of the Western World? — THAT 881:50
legs of i. — BIBLE 111:38
meddles with cold i.! — BUTL 185:73
men of i. — ALBA 11:20
no i. can stab the heart — BABEL 48:3
Nor i. bars a cage — LOVE 538:82
nor strong links of i. — SHAK 776:14
rule them with a rod of i. — BIBLE 131:92
shod with i. — DICK 281:77
sound of i. on stone — DELA 271:27
touch of i. about you — THAT 881:68
what shall i. do? — CHAU 217:78
iron-grey colour of my soul is i.-g. — DEBU 268:59
ironically answers were meant i. — TRIL 897:12
dogmatic, and i. witty — REST 711:62
ironing if you do your own i. — STREE 857:50
ironmongery warlike i. — GILB 369:57
irons two i. in the fire — BEAU 71:13
irony calculated i. — ELIOT 316:49
inspire i. — GISC 373:29
you can't help but consider i. — BEAT 70:99
irradiation Intense i. of a mind — SHEL 814:3
irrational i. is rational — STEV 850:84
something deep and i. — WILS 947:36
irrationality almost medieval i. — INDE 445:24
irrecoverable advantage...lost is i. — DRAKE 298:87
irregularity i. in Nature — THOR 888:24
natural world is full of i. — BOYD 154:13
irrelevance said...with apparent i. — SOME 833:9
irreplaceable essentially i. — GIDE 368:22
irresistible changes...be thus i. — JOHN 460:72
theatre is i. — ARNO 36:39
irresponsible better to be i. — CHUR 226:8
irreverence New York, thy name is i. — HUXT 443:15
irreverent unless you are i. — MAIL 560:45
irritates Perfection i. — AUCH 42:62
is Whatever i., i. in God — SPIN 840:70
Isaac God of I. — PASC 668:96
I., whom thou lovest — BIBLE 92:25
Isabel Anchors on I. — SHAK 787:62
Isabella I. forbid me to — FLEM 340:49
Isaiah consults the prophet I. — CROM 255:14
Isherwood I....not...in Berlin — BURU 182:90
Ishmael Call me I. — MELV 585:54
shalt call his name I. — BIBLE 92:19
Isis careful search that I. — MILT 600:17
Islam America is not...at war with I. — OBAMA 644:35
I. is part of Germany — MERK 588:45
Is-land furnishings of...each I.-l. — FRAME 346:77
island air of the Enchanted I. — MERE 587:26
an i. in the West Indies — ONEI 650:58
as an inland i. — SWIN 864:16
cast my lot in an i.? — DICK 282:96
defend our i. — CHUR 225:85
down by the i. crags — TENN 879:1
Englishman is an i. — NOVA 642:67
heart of our i. — FORS 344:22
i. of the pests — MACA 544:20
i. rock in space — CIAR 226:22
larger the i. of knowledge — MACI 553:4
lone shieling of the misty i. — GALT 359:54
memory of an offshore i. — THAT 881:53
mistress of half an i. — SIXT 824:26
No man is an i. — DONNE 293:68
old i. here that flowered — FITZ 338:86
symbol for England is the I. — ATWO 41:38
this dirty, despicable little i. — WALP 919:75
whole i. was shaken — ADDI 6:22
Zuleika, on a desert i. — BEER 73:80
islands Among the smaller i. — GERA 364:61
dotted with continents and i. — MUIR 624:26
Highlands and I. — MACD 550:39
i. of light — WOOLF 956:34
mirror...to our own i. — RABAN 703:1
one of those i. — MANS 567:97
people and their favourite i. — AUDEN 42:74
see these i. — WALC 916:13
island-valley i.-v. of Avilion — TENN 878:87
isle an i. so long unknown — MARV 578:11
An i. under Ionian skies — SHEL 816:47
a pumice i. — SHEL 813:81
called the I. of Man — GERA 364:61
chimeras and enchanted i. — MILT 599:74
dear and happy I. — MARV 578:10
England is not the jewelled i. — ORWE 654:33
ere he arrive The happy i. — MILT 603:65
Fairest I. — DRYD 303:22
i. is full of noises — SHAK 804:25
ship, an i., a sickle moon — FLEC 340:28
shores of this happy I. — GLAD 373:39
silent i. imbowers — TENN 869:79
this sceptred i. — SHAK 764:40
isles fished by obstinate i. — POUND 691:1
I. of fragrance — POPE 689:43
taketh up the i. — BIBLE 109:82
Venice...thron'd on her hundred i.! — BYRON 188:58
islets acini degenerate leaving I. — BANT 62:35
Islington from I. to Marybone — BLAKE 141:30
isolated splendidly i. in Europe — FOST 345:52
isolation mute chandeliered i. — CAPO 197:29
personal i. to gentile — ROTH 728:91
Israel bring you into the land of I. — BIBLE 110:33
chariot of I. — BIBLE 97:78
glory of thy people I. — BIBLE 120:70
God is good to I. — BIBLE 101:84
Hear, O I. — BIBLE 95:88
If he be the King of I. — BIBLE 119:46
if I. were to put down its arms — NETAN 634:28
In I. it's enough — ROTH 728:87
I. loved Joseph — BIBLE 93:37
I. shall be a proverb — BIBLE 97:54
I.'s head forlorn — LAZA 515:4
I.'s monarch — DRYD 301:64
judgment of the children of I. — BIBLE 94:68
lost sheep of the house of I. — BIBLE 116:66
no king in I. — BIBLE 96:21
no, not in I. — BIBLE 116:57
of the stock of I. — BIBLE 128:99
Palestinians in I. — OROU 652:92
ruler in I. — BIBLE 111:55
smote the king of I. — BIBLE 97:70
there is a prophet in I. — BIBLE 97:75
These be thy gods, O I. — BIBLE 94:69
When I. was a child — BIBLE 111:46
issue great i. between the free world — KENN 481:22
i. of that darling Plea — FLET 340:50
poverty, as an i. — KRUG 500:22
issues i. and the highest authorities — SHUL 819:28
truth about important i. — LEWO 528:79
isthmus this i. of a middle state — POPE 687:80
Italia I.! oh I. — BYRON 188:61
Italian cursed be the I. — GARI 360:72
expensive I. pictures — BERE 83:15
I. character has to — MUSS 628:95
speech...dulcet as I. — QUIL 702:13
to women [I speak] I. — CHAR 215:38
italics I. provide a wonderful advantage — BEAT 70:99
Italy Berlusconi is unfit to lead I. — ECON 310:23
evoke the soul of I. — MAZZ 583:30
from I. that we launch — MARI 571:78
graved inside of it, 'I.' — BROW 168:47
Greece, I., and England did adorn — DRYD 303:19
I....garden of the world — BYRON 188:59
I. is a geographical expression — METT 589:59
made I. from designs — TWAIN 902:34
not been in I. — JOHN 463:51
opera houses in I. — JOHN 459:33
Paradise of exiles, I.! — SHEL 812:61
ruined by residence in I. — RUSK 733:13
Troy and reach I. — VIRG 913:11
itch disease...an i. — MUSC 627:86
i. all over — TWAIN 902:52
i. but a kind of colourable right — LEST 524:8
i. of praise? — CAREW 198:46
Mine eyes do i. — SHAK 790:37
poetry is like having an i. — WARR 921:17
poor i. of your opinion — SHAK 798:88
item any i. of the agenda — PARK 665:39
iteration damnable i. day after day — STEAD 843:31
i. of nuptials — CONG 241:76
Ithaka I. always in your mind — CAVA 210:17
itself Forever be I. again — GINS 372:13
i. and doubt of I. — TILL 891:14
itsy I. bitsy...Bikini — VANCE 908:11
Itylus half assured for I. — SWIN 863:82
ivory cargo of i., And apes — MASE 580:55
downstairs from their I. Towers — SMITH 829:21
i. on which I work — AUST 46:80
i. sun — PIER 677:68
ivy creeping i. clings to wood — COWP 251:5
dead walls...Their i. mantles — BYRON 188:65
like i. round a sapling — SHER 817:89
myrtle and i. of sweet — BYRON 190:30
myrtles brown, with i. — MILT 599:82
pluck an i. branch for me — ROSS 726:40
ivy-mantled yonder i.-m. tower — GRAY 384:63

J

Jabberwock Beware the J., my son! — CARR 204:89
Jack grunted Harry to J. — SASS 745:86
if J. were President — ONAS 650:49
J....a charming name — WILDE 941:95
J.—I'm all right! — BONE 145:19
J. on the gallows-tree! — SCOTT 753:42
one vote—for J. — ONAS 650:53
sack-and-sugar J.? — SHAK 770:31
The days of you and J. — ONAS 650:52
This J., joke — HOPK 429:94
jack j. in the box — ELKIN 322:17
When I kissed the j. — SHAK 803:89
jackal Faith, like a j. — MELV 585:56
jackassonance derided as j. — UNTE 905:11
jackdaws mixed-media j. — BACON 53:52
Pig, and some green J. — LEAR 516:33
jacket Green j., red cap — ALLI 14:6
jack-in-a-box bounced up like a j. — HUGH 436:41
jack-knife Just a j.-k. has Macheath — BREC 157:88
Jacob God of J. — PASC 668:96
J. awaked out of his sleep — BIBLE 93:33
J. served seven years for Rachel — BIBLE 93:34
J. was a plain man — BIBLE 92:28
sold his birthright unto J. — BIBLE 92:29
wrestled...as the Angel did with J. — WALT 920:88
Jacobean J....translated the Bible — ACHE 2:28
Jacobites either J. or became Whigs — WALP 919:78
Ye J. by name — BURNS 179:37
jade Let the galled j. wince — SHAK 783:28
jaded j. with the rush and glare — ARNO 34:72
jades hollow pampered j. of Asia — SHAK 772:81
pampered j. of Asia — MARL 572:6
Jael J....took a nail — BIBLE 95:11
Jaguar park one J. and drive away — HAGUE 391:12
jaguar said Painted J. — KIPL 491:40
Jah by his name J. — BIBLE 101:81
jail being in a j. — JOHN 460:88
farm or the county j. — THOR 888:36
kept out of j. till eighty — LEAC 526:12
patron and his j. — JOHN 459:46
jailer brutal j. is strict — DELA 271:21
j. of your murderer — HUGH 436:45
to free...the j. as well — OBAMA 645:51
jails not enough j. — HUMP 439:9
Jake Forget it, J. — TOWNE 894:66
jake If everything is simply j. — DONL 290:8
jam rule is, j. to-morrow — CARR 205:3
jamais j. triste archy j. triste — MARQ 575:52
James Henry J. wrote fiction — WILDE 942:30
J. II, and the old Pretender — GUED 389:83
name is Truthful J. — HARTE 400:71
read all of Henry J. — THUR 891:4
take Eliza, and our J.! — JONS 468:81
William J. could almost hear — LOWE 540:24
work of Henry J. — GUED 389:83
Jane got used to being called J. — SAKI 739:57
J., J., — SITW 823:8
Whatever Happened to Baby J.? — DAVIS 265:96
jangling I have long been j. — OTWAY 656:9
j. around gently — PAIGE 660:28
Janissaries forced to hire J. — BUTL 184:62
January Blasts of J. — SHAK 799:18
Janus by two-headed J. — SHAK 768:67
J. glance of...significant eye — BYRON 188:63
J. of poets — DRYD 300:34
J.-type figure — NARO 630:53
see myself as the J. — BRAD 155:40
Janvier J. and Février — NICH 636:70
Japan Empire of J. — ROOS 724:14
ensure J.'s self-preservation — HIRO 419:71
island country of J. — TOJO 893:41
J. is like the black hole — UMAS 905:2
J. offers as much novelty — BIRD 136:9
J.'s manufacturing base — TSON 900:7
next week in J. — THER 882:91
Japanese J....have a saying — MORR 620:49

job

J. have perfected good manners	THER 882:89	
J....rarely commit a solecism in taste	BIRD 136:11	
J. see self-assertion	KURO 501:44	
J. should have no concern	KIPL 489:78	
J. young man	GILB 369:46	
japonica J. Glistens like coral	REED 709:26	
jar amid the city's j.	ARNO 34:74	
Carry moonbeams home in a j.	BURKE 176:61	
china j. receive a flaw	POPE 685:35	
face...in a j. by the door	LENN 522:51	
placed a J. in Tennessee	STEV 849:64	
scent you pour in a j.	HORA 430:14	
When such strings j.	SHAK 759:86	
jargon fens of j.?	BAKER 56:7	
Jarndyce J. and J. still drags	DICK 281:56	
jasper What is bettre than j.?	CHAU 217:96	
jaundice good for the j.	SMART 826:60	
javelin hunter's j. in his side	ARNO 34:97	
jaw j. is better than...war	CHUR 226:11	
zebra stripes along his j.	ELIOT 317:80	
jawbone With the j. of an ass	BIBLE 96:18	
jaws finger their j. in painful	CIAR 226:23	
gently smiling j.!	CARR 203:64	
Into the j. of Death	TENN 875:13	
j. that bite	CARR 204:89	
ponderous and marble j.	TWAIN 903:63	
stand at the j. of the cave	AMIS 16:45	
jay j. more precious than the lark	SHAK 762:75	
jays overstocked with j.	OHEN 648:19	
jazz amateur j. musician	LYTT 543:95	
define j. satisfactorily	KING 488:60	
difference between classical...and j.	PREV 694:76	
j....artificial excitement	BLISS 142:57	
J. came to America...in chains	WHIT 937:78	
J. has always been	JONES 466:23	
J. is an impure art	MELLY 584:50	
J. is a small word	TEAL 868:62	
J. is the result of...energy	GERS 365:72	
J. music has haunted America	HOLM 423:58	
J. musicians are	TURN 901:20	
J. musicians have some outlaw	ZWER 970:21	
J. performance centers	LIEB 529:96	
J. will endure	SOUSA 834:39	
New Orleans is the cradle of j.	MORT 621:72	
Though the J. Age continued	FITZ 338:89	
to create j.	GILL 370:87	
jealous Art is a j. mistress	EMER 325:87	
J. in honour	SHAK 779:82	
J. souls will not be answered	SHAK 790:30	
Lord thy God is a j. God	BIBLE 95:89	
perhaps a j. foe	SHEL 815:45	
jealousy ear of j.	BIBLE 112:72	
j. can no more...lose sight	ELIOT 315:30	
J. is all the fun	JONG 466:35	
j. is cruel as the grave	BIBLE 107:49	
j....the green-eyed monster	SHAK 789:19	
j. to the bride	BARR 65:84	
j. with a halo	WELLS 930:31	
Love...is full of j.	SHAK 758:63	
Nor j. Was understood	MILT 604:16	
Poetry...no more...than j.	WYCH 964:3	
quiet resting from all j.	BEAU 71:14	
tyrant J.	DRYD 303:27	
weaned by j.	LYLY 543:84	
Jeannie dream of J.	FOST 345:55	
jeering j. at everything	PEPYS 673:92	
jeers in the midst of j.	BAUD 68:59	
Jeeves J. coughed...like a sheep	WODE 952:39	
Jefferson when Thomas J. dined alone	KENN 481:11	
Jehu driving of J.	BIBLE 97:77	
Jellicoe J. was the only man	CHUR 225:73	
jellies j. soother than the creamy	KEATS 477:24	
jelly Out, vile j.!	SHAK 793:14	
jelly beans way that he eats j. b.	REAG 708:4	
jelly-bellied J.-b. Flag-flapper	KIPL 491:23	
jellyfish little uproar as a j.	WODE 951:35	
Jemuel Let J. rejoice	SMART 826:60	
je-ne-sais-quoi j.-n.-s.-q. young man	GILB 369:46	
Jenny J. kissed me	HUNT 439:30	
Jeoffry my cat J.	SMART 826:62	
Jericho from Jerusalem to J.	BIBLE 120:80	
jerk turned with a sudden j.	KAFKA 472:8	
jerkin with a buff j.?	SHAK 770:28	
jerks bring me up by j.	DICK 282:6	
jeroboams bad vats and j.	THOM 884:41	
Jerome Said J. K. J. to Ford Madox	COLE 234:2	
jerseys striped j. of one colour	ANON 23:91	

Jerusalem Built in J.'s wall	BLAKE 141:32	
certain man went down from J.	BIBLE 120:80	
daughters of J.	BIBLE 107:42	
from the east to J.	BIBLE 114:16	
hadde she been at J.	CHAU 217:77	
holy city, new J.	BIBLE 132:23	
J. the golden	NEALE 632:7	
Pray for the peace of J.	BIBLE 103:33	
Sing through all J.	CASW 208:83	
snare to the inhabitants of J.	BIBLE 107:58	
Speak ye comfortably to J.	BIBLE 108:77	
there J.'s pillars stood	BLAKE 141:30	
Till we have built J.	BLAKE 141:43	
To measure J.	BIBLE 112:71	
was J. builded here?	BLAKE 141:41	
waste places of J.	BIBLE 109:91	
jessamine casement j. stirred	TENN 876:26	
Jesse rod out of the stem of J.	BIBLE 108:61	
Jessie J., the flower o' Dunblane	TANN 867:24	
jest fellow of infinite j.	SHAK 784:63	
glory, j., and riddle	POPE 687:81	
heaven admits no j.	FORD 343:3	
He had his j.	DRYD 302:84	
honour did but j.	GREE 386:31	
j.'s prosperity lies in the ear	SHAK 763:26	
jocund as to j.	SHAK 764:33	
Life is a j.	GAY 362:11	
that's no j.	RALE 705:45	
they do but j., poison in j.	SHAK 783:26	
use myself in j.	DONNE 291:24	
very good j.	WEBS 926:40	
whole wit in a j.	BEAU 70:11	
jester becomes a fool and j.!	SHAK 773:99	
Jesu J., lover of my soul	WESL 931:59	
J., thou art all compassion	WESL 932:62	
Jesus all one in Christ J.	BIBLE 127:79	
around when J. Christ	JAGG 449:15	
black people with J.	GIOV 372:19	
call his name J.	BIBLE 113:14	
come, Lord J.	BIBLE 132:29	
crucified J....picture of God	BAKER 56:3	
dear Lord J., set me free	STUA 858:59	
followers of J.	JOHN 459:38	
for all cometh of J.	LYDG 543:79	
grace without J. Christ	BONH 146:23	
greatest Jew since J. Christ	ROBB 717:67	
If J. Christ were to come today	CARL 202:45	
I think J. was...gay	JOHN 456:84	
J. and a nameless ape	MACD 549:29	
J. Christ her little child	ALEX 13:63	
J. Christ is a Democrat	WALL 917:44	
J. Christ...Word of God	BARTH 65:8	
J. cried with a loud voice	BIBLE 119:47	
J., here we are	HILL 418:61	
J....I love thee still	BUTL 186:11	
J. increased in wisdom	BIBLE 120:71	
J. led up of the Spirit	BIBLE 114:22	
J., meek and mild	WESL 931:60	
J. never claims to be God	ROBI 718:96	
J. of Nazareth was the most scientific man	EDDY 311:29	
J. said	KEIL 479:61	
J. saw it, he was much displeased	BIBLE 120:60	
J. shall reign where'er	WATTS 923:47	
J. stretched forth his hand	BIBLE 117:1	
J. the author and finisher	BIBLE 129:43	
J., the very thought of Thee	CASW 208:81	
J., 'tis such a vulgar expression	CONG 240:36	
J. took bread	BIBLE 119:40	
J....took bread	BIBLE 126:49	
J. was a moderniser	BLAIR 138:60	
J. went into the temple of God	BIBLE 118:23	
J. went unto them	BIBLE 117:99	
J. wept	BIBLE 123:47	
J. wept	HUGO 438:89	
J., when he had cried again	BIBLE 119:48	
J., when he was baptized	BIBLE 114:21	
John seeth J.	BIBLE 122:19	
more popular than J. Christ	LENN 521:44	
No man can say that J.	BIBLE 126:50	
none but J. heard	TRUTH 900:5	
recognize God without J.	PASC 667:91	
Sacred Heart o' J.	OCAS 646:77	
Stand Up For J.!	DUFF 305:83	
sweet reasonableness of J.	ARNO 36:37	
sweet the name of J.	NEWT 636:65	
thing that J. really would've liked	SALI 740:80	

When J. came to Birmingham	STUD 858:64	
When J. heard it, he marvelled	BIBLE 116:57	
when J. was born in Bethlehem	BIBLE 114:17	
wrong to...blame J.	BENN 79:30	
Jesus Christ I am the J.C. of politics	BERL 85:53	
Jesuses trained seals, creeping J.	MACD 550:39	
Jew eke most lovely J.	SHAK 767:34	
greatest J. since Jesus Christ	ROBB 717:67	
Hath not a J. eyes?	SHAK 769:1	
I'm not really a J....Just J.-ish	MILL 595:95	
In heathen, Turk or J.	BLAKE 139:89	
J. is only the name	MILL 593:42	
J. of Tarsus	BIBLE 125:97	
like an...assimilated J.	OBRI 645:62	
makes you a normal J.	ROTH 728:88	
neither Greek nor J.	BIBLE 128:11	
neither J. nor Greek	BIBLE 127:79	
States...the J. among the nations	FERB 332:67	
take my leave of the J.	SHAK 767:64	
jewel chastity's the j.	SHAK 791:66	
For your sake, j.	SHAK 789:97	
has yet one j. left	MILT 600:16	
j. in a...chest.	SHAK 764:32	
j. [judged] by the light	ANON 25:38	
j. of the kingdom	SUN 859:93	
j. that we find	SHAK 787:53	
precious j. in his head	SHAK 778:65	
rich j. in an Ethiope's ear	SHAK 765:74	
time's best j.	SHAK 801:57	
jewelled j. mass of millinery	TENN 875:17	
jewellers through most j.' hands	WEBS 926:42	
jewellery Don't ever wear artistic j.	COLE 236:57	
jewelry gigantic chunk of costume j.	LAUR 511:22	
hang on to her j.	LOOS 536:50	
rest...can rattle your j.	LENN 521:43	
jewels capital bosom to hang j. upon	DICK 282:86	
Dumb J....move a woman's mind	SHAK 759:66	
Health and...body are two j.	FLET 341:59	
j. five-words-long	TENN 872:32	
j. for a set of beads	SHAK 764:54	
precious j. into a garret	BACON 50:53	
reft the j. from her hair	HYDE 443:21	
unvalued j.	SHAK 761:40	
With gold and j. cover	POPE 685:20	
jewel-sea love her j.-s.	MACK 553:10	
Jewish insights of the J. prophets	NIEB 637:87	
J. family has an inviolate	ROTH 728:91	
J.. I don't work out	RIVE 716:56	
J. Puritan of the middle	NEME 633:19	
J. Queen of Egypt	TAYL 868:51	
solution of the J. question	GOER 374:57	
Jews All men are J.	MALA 561:85	
don't ask employers...to like...J.	BORO 151:68	
fat of rendered J. and Gypsies	VONN 915:51	
Have mercy upon all J.	BOOK 147:53	
Hitler attacked the J.	NIEM 637:91	
J., a headstrong...race	DRYD 301:67	
J. and Arabs should settle	AUST 47:99	
J. in Palestine	OROU 652:92	
J. lived by...insight	SACKS 736:5	
J. which believeth not	BIBLE 124:88	
King of the J.	BIBLE 114:16	
King of the J.	BIBLE 123:60	
national home for the J.	BALF 58:39	
noticed that J. shout?	ROTH 728:87	
The Irish and the J. have a psychosis	BEHAN 74:14	
the last J. to die without standing up	MEIR 581:37	
To choose The J.	EWER 329:77	
university where...the J. are hosts	SACH 736:3	
What captivity was to the J.	WILDE 940:49	
Jezebel J....painted her face	BIBLE 97:78	
jib cut of his j.	DOUG 295:23	
jilt cruel j. to me	MORSE 621:64	
jingle must j. in his ears	WOLL 954:89	
jingles trifles and j.	BACON 52:22	
jingling one j. padlock	POPE 689:40	
Jingo by J. if we do	HUNT 439:16	
J. K. Rowling if J. K. R. had been born	HIGH 418:53	
jo For auld lang syne, my j.	BURNS 178:76	
John Anderson my j.	BURNS 179:16	
Joan If J. of Arc had been born play Saint J.	SIMON 822:75 / THOR 889:48	
Job All books are the Book of J.	ELKIN 322:16	
blessed the latter end of J.	BIBLE 99:24	
J. open his mouth in vain	BIBLE 98:12	
poor as J.	SHAK 772:72	
job $60 GI j.	EISE 314:4	

Jobiska

difficultest j. a man can do	DAVI 264:64	if a j. were a charity auction	MCIL 553:95	robbed upon a j.	STEV 851:26
doing a heck of a j.	BUSH 183:35	If we live inside a bad j.	RABAN 703:2	soul of a j. is liberty	MARP 574:42
finish the j.	CHUR 225:89	j.'s a very serious thing	CHUR 224:58	such a long j.	ELIOT 318:17
hard j. of using reason	WILS 947:44	many a j. had he	GOLD 376:1	To j. is better than to arrive	WELD 928:84
How would you like a j.	PLAN 680:26	our only j.	BARR 65:91	visible portions of the j.	STARK 843:24
husband is a whole-time j.	BENN 81:67	**jokes** bad j. of history	GUED 389:85	well this j. be his	EDWA 312:57
If they will only do their j.	SELZ 757:20	civil servant doesn't make j.	IONE 447:52	Whenever I prepare for a j.	MANS 567:9
It's a man's j.	AESC 9:80	difference of taste in j.	ELIOT 316:57	when the j.'s over	HOUS 431:36
j., as I see it	MACD 550:42	don't make j.	ROGE 723:86	worst time…to take a j.	ANDR 18:79
j. is likely to be ill-done	KEYN 484:79	hackneyed j. from Miller	BYRON 187:25	**journeys** Do not plan long j.	AUGU 45:35
j. of the nurture of children	PALEY 661:53	Krishna's j. may be vapid	FORS 345:51	j. through the valley	LEE 519:98
Keeping up…a full-time j.	CRISP 254:88	my little j. on Thee	FROST 353:19	successive j. run	WATTS 923:47
loneliest j. in the world	BALD 57:29	no j.…no chance	ANON 24:26	who was driven far j.	HOMER 425:9
loses his j.	TRUM 899:86	no more j. in Music-halls	SASS 745:80	word of worse j.	WOOD 954:1
lost the j.	JOYCE 470:26	shouldn't make j.	CARR 204:95	**journey-work** j.-w. of the stars	WHIT 937:92
man who wants to do a good j.	ELIOT 320:55	telling j. back there	KAUF 474:41	**Jove** if J. stray	SHAK 798:80
most improper j.	TOLK 893:43	telling j. or gossiping	CABR 191:8	J. and Fate require	POPE 688:29
Nae harder j. to mortals	MACD 549:25	The best j.	HUMP 439:11	J. might have sipped	MARL 574:36
neighbour loses his j.	REAG 708:3	**joking** My way of j.	SHAW 809:65	J.'s dread clamours	SHAK 790:27
only doing my j. if they do	WHIT 937:83	**jollier** j. than the people	LUCAS 541:48	Now J. in his next commodity	SHAK 786:7
our j. to make women unhappy	PUCK 699:67	**jolly** If I was very ragged and very j.	DICK 279:10	threshold of J.'s court	MILT 598:62
second most important j.	GARN 360:77	**jolly-rogered** and the j.-r. sea	THOM 884:33	**jow** j. or ring	FERG 333:85
since he has lost his j.	MORG 619:33	**Jonas** sign of the prophet J.	BIBLE 117:86	**joy** amidst that j. and uproar	CAMP 194:66
social order…my j. to preserve	FRAN 347:87	**Jonathan** distressed for…J.	BIBLE 96:42	an ace of j. up his sleeve	ONDA 650:50
to do the j. too long	SWIFT 862:40	**Joneses** Keeping up with the J.	CRISP 254:98	at enmity with j.	WORD 960:11
whether my j. is a j.	KNIG 494:10	**jonquils** land-locked pools of j.	BETJ 88:26	at the expense of j.	FORS 344:27
will always have a j.	RAVI 707:85	**Jonson** Ben J. his best piece of poetry	JONS 467:77	bed Of crimson j.	BLAKE 140:12
Jobiska Aunt J. made him drink	LEAR 516:39	In Spenser, and in J., Art	DENH 272:62	better…to weep at j.	SHAK 773:16
Aunt J.'s Runcible Cat	LEAR 516:41	J. was the Virgil	DRYD 300:26	binds to himself a j.	BLAKE 140:6
jobs climbing into j.	REST 711:64	O rare Ben J.	JONS 468:82	Break forth into j.	BIBLE 109:91
fewer the j. worth doing	JAY 453:3	Too nicely J. knew the critic's part	COLL 237:69	Certainty. Feeling. J.	PASC 668:96
j. that pay more than others	WILL 945:5	**Jordan** draw up J. into his mouth	BIBLE 99:21	Dear distress, and j. allied	CULL 257:45
Mine is one of the j.	WEAT 925:5	I call him J.	WINT 950:8	doubt…exiles my present j.	ELIZ 321:1
woman…not the top j.	THAT 880:46	j. running through it	HOPK 429:85	eat thy bread with j.	BIBLE 106:27
You work three j.?	BUSH 183:32	**jostle** rough sense of the daily j.	DELI 271:42	enter thou into the j. of thy lord	BIBLE 119:33
Jock J., when ye hae naething	SCOTT 753:60	**jot** j. of former love retain	DRAY 299:99	good tidings of great j.	BIBLE 120:69
stop yer tickling, J.!	LAUD 511:14	**jouissance** naught but j.	GREE 386:32	go out with j.	BIBLE 109:1
tears…For J. of Hazeldean	SCOTT 753:45	**journal** editor of a village j.	MOOD 615:56	greater j. than love itself	PROU 698:49
Wi' J. of Hazeldean	SCOTT 753:47	keep up a daily j.	STARR 843:27	harp, his sole remaining j.	SCOTT 752:9
jocosity j. catches the crowd	MARQ 575:50	leading j. of Europe	HAZL 403:41	heart's so full of j.	DRYD 301:54
jocund As gentle and as j.	SHAK 764:33	**journalism** bent and twisted j.	AITK 10:2	Hope to j. is little less	SHAK 764:34
j. day Stands tiptoe	SHAK 766:2	context of…j.	THOM 887:89	if this be j.	GOLD 376:3
Joe J., long dead	SLES 825:52	crisis in j.	LIPP 530:35	in glory and in j.	WORD 959:1
Say it ain't so, J.	ANON 24:8	higher law in j.	LIPP 531:36	in J. and woe	SURR 860:98
jog As we j. on	STER 848:22	j.…as an extension of history	SAMP 741:97	is no j. but calm!	TENN 870:90
J. on, j. on	SHAK 799:16	J. largely consists in saying	CHES 221:97	it is a j. to enjoy what is good	GOET 375:60
jogging J. is for people	WOOD 954:98	j.…read once	CONN 242:95	J. always came after pain	APOL 29:81
J. is very beneficial	SCHU 749:72	Modern j.	WILDE 940:60	J. and function of poetry	THOM 884:24
Johannesburg No second J.	PATON 669:28	root of debunking j.	THAT 881:75	J. and their glory must be	ABEL 1:4
John I J. saw the holy city	BIBLE 132:3	**journalist** Any daily j. will tell you	ORWE 654:42	j. at last	GUY 390:7
J. Brown is stowed	NASH 631:75	duty of a j.	STEAD 843:33	j. delights in j.	SHAK 800:34
J. had his raiment of camel's hair	BIBLE 114:19	functions of the modern j.	CURZ 259:4	j.…From the green fields	WORD 957:72
J., like J.	FARJ 330:20	historian is often only a j.	KRAUS 499:8	j. he gave me	AUDEN 44:20
J. seeth Jesus	BIBLE 122:19	j. exists…as the publicity agent	ORWE 653:6	J., I did lock thee up	HERB 414:81
J. to the seven churches	BIBLE 131:85	j. is hardly an authority	DAFOE 260:2	j. in the presence of the angels	BIBLE 121:88
notorious domesticity for J.	WILDE 941:95	life of the j.	GIBB 367:8	J. is fleeting	KENN 480:92
shew J. again those things	BIBLE 116:76	making of a j.	KRAUS 499:7	j. of elevated thoughts	WORD 956:55
unto the multitudes concerning J.	BIBLE 116:77	Never trust a j.	COPE 246:97	j. of heav'n…come down	WESL 932:62
why…name your baby 'J.'	GOLD 377:29	**journalists** Diplomats lie to j.	KRAUS 499:9	j. of living speech	SPEN 838:26
john leaning on the j. door	OHARA 648:10	[j.] must report only what is true	HUMP 439:15	j. of the artist	MILL 594:71
Johnny Here's J!	NICH 636:76	J.…require some protection	BLACK 137:40	j. of the whole earth	BIBLE 100:70
Little J. Head-in-Air	HOFF 422:33	J. say a thing	BENN 81:68	j. of thy salvation	BIBLE 101:73
not despair For J. Head-in-Air	PUDN 699:68	**journals** articles…in scientific j.	FEYN 334:5	j. of working	KIPL 490:15
sleeps as sound As J. Underground	PUDN 699:68	Of all j.	TIMES 892:22	j. past j. calls out	SHAK 766:99
Johnson heroism of J.	STEV 852:53	**journey** A Long Day's J.	ONEI 651:71	j. ruled the day	DRYD 304:57
J. approached a…position	MANC 564:48	begin a j. on Sundays	SWIFT 863:73	j. shivers in the corner	ROBI 718:91
J.'s morality	HAWT 402:18	Business at the end of its j.	LLOYD 532:64	j. that the day has brought	BOND 145:17
J. went through three years	WHITE 935:56	day's j. into the wilderness	BIBLE 97:66	j. they were making	ROBE 717:71
that great man, Dr J.	WESL 932:72	death the j.'s end	DRYD 304:54	j. to his mighty heart	KIPL 490:97
You are a philosopher, Dr J.	EDWA 312:63	define your own horror j.	GELL 363:35	know of no j.	FIRB 336:50
Johnsonian subtlety of J. strategy	MANC 564:49	dreariest and the longest j.	SHEL 815:45	Labour without j.	RUSK 730:17
joined j. with no foot-landrakers	SHAK 771:38	heavy riches but a j.	SHAK 787:65	Let every heart exult with j.	DODD 289:90
joiner imagination of a lodge j.	MENC 587:16	he who…has taken a wondrous j.	BELL 76:44	Like an unbodied j.	SHEL 813:92
j. with j.	HESI 417:31	intellectual j.	MILLS 595:6	love and j. that fights	MANS 567:96
joint manacled with j. or limb	MILT 602:46	j. from London	TALB 866:14	Man was made for J. and Woe	BLAKE 141:26
The time was out of j.	STRA 856:17	j. in my head	SHAK 800:45	moment of j. is…harder to get	PO 683:78
together every j. and member	MILT 601:17	j. is like a marriage	STEI 846:87	My scrip of j.	RALE 705:44
jointed It is nothing j.; it flows	JAMES 451:62	j. of life	DICK 283:17	no j. in pouring out one's sins	FIRB 336:51
joints between the j. of the harness	BIBLE 97:70	j. of our life	DANTE 262:36	Nor j. nor grieve too much	DRYD 304:54
fettle your fine j.	SHAK 766:4	j. on, till you come	LAUD 511:17	not an obligation but a j.	KILLY 486:8
j. are stiff	SHAK 766:9	j. ov life	BILL 135:97	now 'tis little j.	HOOD 426:23
joke bitter cosmic j.	GELL 363:33	j.'s end, here is my butt	SHAK 790:48	oil of j. for mourning	BIBLE 110:6
Every j. I make	RIVE 716:58	j. take the whole long day?	ROSS 726:45	O j.! that in our embers	WORD 959:9
every j. is…a custard pie	ORWE 654:39	j. that required courage	MURP 626:76	passages of j.	JOHN 459:47
family j. that when	ROTH 727:79	j. towards oblivion	LAWR 514:82	perfectest herald of j.	SHAK 774:30
funniest j. in the world	SHAW 809:65	Nothing for my J. Now	ANGE 19:2	perfect j. therein I find	DYER 309:47
Housekeeping ain't no j.	ALCO 12:42	pursuing, or he is in a j.	BIBLE 97:62	planet, all j. gone	LOWE 540:32

promise of untrammeled j.	HOLM 423:58	O wise young j.	SHAK 770:14	lukewarm parsnip j.	WOOL 956:45
reap in j.	BIBLE 103:35	readers may j. my books	HOBS 421:9	nor half so full of j.	SUCK 858:70
running stream of sparkling j.	DICK 281:66	sober as a J.	FIEL 335:21	runnel of j.	RANS 706:68
Scarce any j.	SHAK 800:31	Who made thee a prince and a j.	BIBLE 93:50	whether there is enough j.	GEDD 362:26
secret of j.	WALK 917:40	You wags that j.	OTWAY 656:95	**juices** Keep the j. flowing	PAIGE 660:28
shall run mad with j.	MIDD 590:77	**judged** j. by our peers	BALZ 60:93	sexual j. flow toward a painting	FUEN 354:59
sheer j. of felicitous statement	SCHL 747:34	j. by the colour	KING 487:25	**juke** j. box's blowin' a fuse	BERRY 87:94
short-haired j. and roughness	SNYD 833:95	j....through her toilette	DE 268:46	**Julia** in silks my J. goes	HERR 416:16
snatch a fearful j.	GRAY 383:46	that you are j.	HARDY 397:12	thought of Donna J.'s eyes	BYRON 189:94
sons of God shouted for j.	BIBLE 98:14	**judgement** Aaron shall bear the j.	BIBLE 94:68	**Julian** remembered poor J.	HEMI 410:78
taste is now of j.	MILT 604:2	after this the j.	BIBLE 129:17	**Juliet** east, and J. is the sun	SHAK 765:77
There's not a j.	BYRON 189:81	better j. making	SHAK 802:67	J. and her Romeo	SHAK 766:15
Thine be ilka j. and treasure	BURNS 179:36	biases the j.	DOYLE 296:39	Unless philosophy can make a J.	SHAK 766:98
Thou Child of j.	WORD 959:6	conformity of our j.	DIDE 285:61	**July** born on the fourth of J.	COHAN 234:93
Uninterrupted j., unrivalled love	MILT 603:76	criterion of wisdom to vulgar j.	BURKE 176:51	J.'s day as short	SHAK 799:9
vehicle of j.	HOOV 427:46	Daniel come to j.	SHAK 770:14	second day of J. 1776	ADAMS 5:1
Where I in lust and j.	SURR 860:1	Do not wait for the last j.	CAMUS 196:97	winter—ending in J.	BYRON 190:23
Where there is sadness, j.	FRAN 347:99	expect a j.	DICK 281:59	**Jumblies** lands where the J. live	LEAR 516:31
joyance With my clear keen j.	SHEL 814:96	God will bring thee into j.	BIBLE 106:35	**jump** decide which way to j.	BOYC 153:7
joy-bells Makes j.-b. ring	MASE 580:64	goosecap and hast no j.	NASHE 632:81	J. her, and thump her	SHAK 800:24
Joyce clumsy olla putrida James J.	LAWR 513:74	greater j. shewn in deviating	ADDI 7:55	j. the life to come	SHAK 796:19
J.'s Finnegans Wake	NICO 637:85	great J. seat	KIPL 489:76	j. with common spirits	SHAK 769:94
J. was a synthesizer	BECK 72:51	green in j.	SHAK 794:54	**jumping** j. over the moon	RAMS 706:51
read...Proust, Faulkner, J.	VARG 908:26	He j. brings	OAKL 643:5	**June** It was late J.	THOM 885:51
joyful a j. Song I'll raise	ADDI 7:38	if it only added j. to insight	FORS 344:33	Jolly J., arrayed	SPEN 839:62
All Christendom ought to feel j.	COLU 239:91	in danger of the j.	BIBLE 114:32	J. for beauty's heightening	ARNO 35:17
be j. in the Lord	BOOK 149:32	j. faileth me	KNOX 495:15	made December J.	TENN 874:93
j. with swift movement	ANON 20:31	j. fouk wou'd hae a doubt on	FERG 333:84	newly sprung in J.	BURNS 180:50
make a j. noise	BIBLE 102:1	j. frame By her...standard	POPE 685:18	rare as a day in J.	LOWE 539:7
joys All my j. to this are folly	BURT 181:74	j. is a mere lottery	DRYD 300:22	**jungle** art world is a j.	HAMM 394:60
all that's precious in our j.	STER 849:59	j. is...subject to affection	JOHN 463:73	city is not a concrete j.	MORR 620:45
blinding with briars my j.	BLAKE 140:15	j. Of all mankind	SCHI 747:21	courts of Europe are a j.	BOLT 145:14
buy the j. o'er dear	BURNS 179:31	j. of the great whore	BIBLE 132:16	dangerous to explore a j.	HAWT 401:98
feeling that lures us on to j.	CONR 244:36	j. that makes an impact	LEAV 517:53	J. star or j. track	CULL 257:43
fleeting j. Of Paradise	MILT 606:62	j. that yourself arise	SHAK 801:54	law of the j.	JUMB 471:43
[Friendship] redoubleth j.	BACON 52:14	j. what they see	MIDD 590:74	Law of the j.	KIPL 490:4
hide our j. no longer	SHAK 787:41	j. with this generation	BIBLE 117:87	Law of the j.	KIPL 490:7
homely j.	GRAY 384:66	last j. of mankind	FRYE 354:53	Mumbo-Jumbo is dead in the j.	LIND 530:19
its j., and fears	WORD 960:13	Last J.'s fire must cure this place	BROW 168:33	New York is a j.	AMIS 16:46
j. await us there	NEALE 632:7	Men of business have a solid j.	BAGE 54:77	wise primitive in a giant j.	MAIL 559:37
j. in another's loss of ease	BLAKE 140:10	men of j. frame	MARL 573:9	**jungles** lost...in the j. of Indochina	MCGO 552:87
j. of marriage	FORD 343:1	Moral j.	NIET 638:11	**juniper** sat down under a J. tree	BIBLE 97:66
j. of parents	BACON 51:68	neither do the aged understand j.	BIBLE 98:11	white leopards sat under a j.-tree	ELIOT 319:25
present j....to flesh and blood	DRYD 303:15	not a disease but an error of j.	DICK 277:36	**junk** j. food	GASS 361:86
profanation of our j.	DONNE 292:38	notoriously unsound in j.	HOLM 424:65	**junkyards** j. of secular carpentry	ROSE 725:34
Repeating only j. above	LOVE 538:87	O j.! thou art fled	SHAK 777:39	**Juno** figure of J.	BARR 65:98
rich man's j. increase	GOLD 376:4	on whose j. they	TUCH 901:13	haughty J.'s unrelenting hate	DRYD 304:37
should we defer our j.?	JONS 467:56	people's j. always true	DRYD 302:86	**Jupiter** By J., an angel	SHAK 803:4
sole part of all these j.	MILT 604:3	possessing j.	KEYN 484:78	J. from above	OVID 657:14
Some unknown j. there be	TRAH 895:82	power of j.	HARD 396:95	temple of J.	GIBB 366:2
Time, which takes...our j.	RALE 705:47	put in the breastplate of j.	BIBLE 94:68	**juries** j. fill their stomachs	SYNGE 865:23
vain deluding J.	MILT 597:49	reserve thy j.	SHAK 781:51	**jurisprudence** American j.	CAPO 197:21
voice less loud, through its j.	BROW 167:24	spirit and j. equal	MILT 601:87	**jury** acquitted by a Limerick j.	ADAMS 5:8
jubilate J. Deo, omnis terra	BIBLE 133:33	still have j. here	SHAK 796:19	I'll be judge, I'll be j.	CARR 203:65
jubilation extraordinary sense of j.	GREE 386:22	till J. Tide	KIPL 492:54	j. is only as sound	LEE 519:90
Jubilee first day of our J. is death	BROW 165:63	Too many...pass j.	TRUM 900:87	j. passing on the prisoner's life	SHAK 787:52
Jubjub Beware the J. bird	CARR 204:89	true j. day	ANON 22:74	lawyer trying to pick a smart j.	BAIL 55:84
Judas Damned below J.	COWP 250:83	vulgar...capacities do make a j.	BACON 49:22	Press is the living J.	BENN 81:78
J. Iscariot, went unto the chief priests	BIBLE 119:39	wait till J. break	DICK 284:43	Trial by j.	DENM 273:72
J. who writes the biography	WILDE 940:54	What j. I had increases	DRYD 304:38	tried before a j.	JOHN 463:47
So J. did to Christ	SHAK 765:55	would not give his j. rashly	ADDI 6:29	**jury-men** that j.-m. may dine	POPE 685:38
Whether J....Had God on his side	DYLAN 309:52	**judgements** Delivers brawling j.	TENN 877:48	**just** and I should be j.	HERB 411:55
judge after a time they j. them	WILDE 941:88	j. below our own	BROW 165:46	Be j., my lovely swain	BEHN 75:19
bringing the j....into the dock	ALGR 13:70	j. of the English law	SYNGE 865:23	cause is j.	DICK 284:58
decided by the j.	JOHN 462:29	j. on political conduct	NEW 634:41	Give it because it is j.	LLOY 533:77
Forbear to j.	SHAK 759:92	moral j. do not say anything	AYER 48:6	gods are j.	SHAK 793:34
Here comes the j.	MARK 571:89	obstinate, ridiculous j.	MORE 618:12	How j., how bountiful	WORD 962:19
History may j. my politics	HOBS 421:9	sentinels unto our j.	MIDD 590:74	it is our j. exaltation	PITT 680:12
I'll be j., I'll be jury	CARR 203:65	**judges** doctors, j....beadles	MARX 578:26	j....are not the leaders	CONR 244:44
indifferent j.	SIDN 820:46	hundred j. have declared	QUIL 702:12	j., gentle, wise	SHEL 814:18
in righteousness he doth j.	BIBLE 132:19	hungry j.	POPE 685:38	j. people...are happier than unjust	PLATO 682:59
j. a man by his foes	CONR 244:33	j. thronging thickly	WILDE 939:44	j. shall live by faith	BIBLE 125:2
j. a man more certainly	HUGO 437:83	threw me in front of the J.	BETJ 89:45	rather be British than j.	PAIS 660:42
j. and the brother are one	WILS 949:75	When j. steal themselves	SHAK 787:60	sendeth rain on the j.	BIBLE 115:38
j. how wide the limits stand	GOLD 376:4	**judging** j. others according to	LAFO 504:63	Shall mortal man be more j.	BIBLE 98:96
j. I carried within me	CARP 202:50	j. the values of things	JEVO 455:53	soul of the j.	STAEL 842:44
j. in the legal and moral sense	DEWEY 276:20	knack of j. a distance	REED 709:28	Thou art indeed j., Lord	HOPK 429:95
j. is not supposed to know	PARK 664:33	the fatigue of j. for themselves	SHER 817:98	thou art j.	TENN 873:55
j. less harshly	BRAC 154:20	**judicious** happy condition of j.	MELV 585:71	whatsoever things are j.	BIBLE 128:5
J. not, that ye be not judged	BIBLE 115:47	Heaven the j....spectator	RALE 705:45	**justice** act...of duty and of j.	PITT 679:10
J. not the play	QUAR 701:6	**jug** j., j., j., tereu	LYLY 543:82	ain't the shop for j.	DICK 278:71
J. of all the earth	BIBLE 92:22	Pap took the j.	TWAIN 902:57	bring our enemies to j.	BUSH 182:16
J. of the widows	BIBLE 101:81	w'en it git loose fum de j.	HARR 399:47	destruction of all j.	MORE 619:23
j. of truth, in endless error	POPE 687:81	**Juggins** you J.!	PUNCH 700:83	Die he must, and j. must	MILT 603:82
j. rarely	PENN 673:82	**juggler** perceive a j.'s sleight	BUTL 185:81	do j. to my character	EMMET 325:6
j. standeth before the door	BIBLE 130:60	**jugglers** nimble j. that deceive the eye	SHAK 762:91	dream of social j.	NGUY 636:69
make us a king to j. us	BIBLE 96:30	**juice** j. of deliberate, journalistic	LAWR 513:74	Equal and exact j.	JEFF 454:26

justification

firm belief in the j. of our cause — WASH 921:26
have ravished j. — WEBS 926:30
humanity, reason, and j., tells me — BURKE 175:18
Injustice anywhere is a threat to j. — KING 486:24
j. and mercy are reconciled — WILS 949:75
J. is being allowed to do — BUTL 186:4
J. is doing one's work — PLATO 682:62
J. is such a fine thing — LESA 523:87
J. is superior — PLATO 682:60
J. is the constant — JUST 471:51
J. is the means — FRAN 347:87
J. is truth — DISR 288:41
j. must be carried out — MARIE 571:74
j., or happiness or prosperity — CURZ 260:5
J. should consider — HELO 409:55
J. should not only be done — HEWA 417:36
'J.' was done — HARDY 397:16
Let j. be done — FERD 332:73
Let j. be done — MANS 568:13
Let j. be done — WATS 922:44
Literature...makes j. — PALEY 661:51
love of j. in most men — LARO 510:99
may become a j. — JONS 467:68
Mercy...and j. come from God — WAITE 916:5
no business with the j. — JOHN 462:29
of all equity and j. — KNOX 495:14
Poetic j., with her lifted scale — POPE 688:30
Posterity will do j. to...Gladstone — DISR 288:63
price of j. is eternal publicity — BENN 81:73
principles of equity and j. — PEEL 672:67
Publicity is the very soul of j. — BENT 82:93
pursuit of j. — GOLD 377:20
quicker Than j., judge or vicar — SHER 817:82
Revenge is a kind of wild j. — BACON 50:62
rule of distributive j. — HOMA 425:93
seldom has j. enough to accuse — GOLD 376:91
small things and in j. — SOPH 834:27
temper so J. with mercy — MILT 606:57
Thwackum was for doing j. — FIEL 335:23
To no man will we...deny...j. — MAGN 559:27
treat the films...with less than j. — ANDE 17:70
under which j. — UNIT 905:9
when I show j. — SHAK 787:56
When mercy seasons j. — SHAK 770:13
Where j. grows — SPEN 838:29
Where j. is denied — DOUG 296:26
which is the j. — SHAK 793:24
justification Englishman's j. in India — CURZ 260:5
j. in every line — CONR 243:25
social and psychological j. — KEYN 485:85
justifications power j. would go on — STEI 846:93
justified half as good as j. — BUTL 185:84
justifies that j. the end — TROT 899:69
justify end cannot j. the means — HUXL 442:79
'j.' and affirm...beliefs — ELLI 323:36
the less there is to j. — TWAIN 902:43
justifying better j. themselves — SZASZ 865:27
justitia Fiat j. — FERD 332:73
Fiat j. — WATS 922:44
Fiat j., pereat coelum — ADAMS 5:4
jutty No j., frieze — SHAK 796:18
juvescence j. of the year — ELIOT 317:83
juxtaposition Allah...and J. — CLOU 232:60

K

Kaa thou art hungry, O K. — KIPL 490:5
Kalashnikovs didn't have K. — BONO 146:28
kaleidoscope it's like a beautiful k. — COLE 234:5
kamikaze the k. ground staff — PARK 665:36
kangaroo K., K.! — FIELD 335:11
kangaroos little k. flying about — WILDE 941:77
Kansas farmers of K. — LEASE 517:49
horses o' K. think — KIPL 491:18
nights in K. City close early — MAIL 560:55
Kasper Old K.'s work was done — SOUT 835:45
Kate angel is like you, K. — SHAK 776:98
kiss me, K. — SHAK 762:67
kiss me, K. — SHAK 762:80
sometimes K. the curst — SHAK 761:65
Swear me, K. — SHAK 771:53
witchcraft in your lips, K. — SHAK 776:1
Kathmandu to the north of K. — HAYES 403:27
Kean K. is original — COLE 236:45
There is in K. — HAZL 403:30
keel Set k. to breakers — POUND 691:10
keener grows k. with constant use — IRVI 447:57

keep k., and pass, and turn again — EMER 325:85
k. our people in — KENN 481:23
k. the salary — GOMEZ 377:39
k. things like this — HUGH 435:52
love to k. it by me — JERO 454:40
may God k. me there — JOAN 455:60
time to k. — BIBLE 106:14
To k. him...two — DOUG 295:14
we must k....promises — OBAMA 644:49
you can k. the lot — JAY 453:99
keeper Am I my brother's k.? — BIBLE 92:3
first lost k. — SEXT 758:44
k. of his conscience...k. of the stone — DAVI 265:85
Lord is thy k. — BIBLE 103:31
keepers k. of the house shall tremble — BIBLE 106:36
keeps gave it us for k. — AYRES 48:9
keepsake rope for a k. — TWAIN 903:78
Kelly Fanny K.'s divine plain face — LAMB 505:87
Kemble Mr K. sacrifices too much — HAZL 403:31
Kennedy epitaph on the K. — WHITE 936:59
Mrs K. is going to marry — JOHN 457:4
you're no Jack K. — BENT 82:8
Kennedys we K., we eat Rockefellers — KENN 482:45
Who killed the K.? — JAGG 449:16
kennel whips to k. The renegade — RANS 707:72
Kensal Paradise by way of K. — CHES 221:95
Kent everyone knows K. — DICK 277:45
K. and Christendom — WYATT 963:86
Kentish courts of K. Town — BETJ 88:29
fog on the K. heights — DICK 281:55
kept married women are k. women — SMITH 829:22
kerchiefed k. in a comely cloud — MILT 598:57
Kern to K. or Cole Porter — GERS 365:74
kernel Haldis the k., sueit — HENR 411:18
k. is boredom — GELL 363:35
k. scarcely compensates...cracking — BRON 161:56
kernels meagre hill of k. — RANS 706:68
Kerouac not even Mr K. — CAPO 197:19
Ketch as Jack K.'s wife said — DRYD 303:25
kettle different k. of fish — SHAR 806:73
guy that plays the k. drums — SALI 740:80
how agree the k. — BIBLE 113:93
Polly put the k. on — DICK 279:97
speech is like a cracked k. — FLAU 339:20
Kew his Highness' dog at K. — POPE 689:49
K. in lilac-time — NOYES 642:69
key easy k., Dost open life — DRYD 301:60
Getting into the k. of C sharp — BUTL 185:1
k. is Russian national interest — CHUR 225:82
k. of knowledge — BIBLE 121:82
k. of the bottomless pit — BIBLE 131:6
k. to human warmth — ISHI 448:73
looking for the k. — BENN 80:43
out of k. with his time — POUND 691:99
smile is often the k. — SAINT 738:38
the k., the minor k., to existence — BLIX 142:62
Turn the k. deftly — KEATS 476:91
keyboard Color is the k. — KAND 473:17
song along the k. — OHARA 648:10
keyhole age has a k. — MCCA 548:91
out at the k — SHAK 780:13
Keynes cure...before K. — ROBI 718:95
keys enter the names and hand
 the k. — MANS 567:1
fingers on these k. — STEV 849:73
k. of all the creeds — TENN 874:66
k. of hell and of death — BIBLE 131:89
k. of Paradise — DE 273:82
k. of the kingdom of heaven — BIBLE 117:6
k. of the...liquor store — BALL 58:47
Over the noisy k. — PROC 697:27
keystone night's black arch the k.-s. — BURNS 179:26
KGB a former K. man — PUTIN 700:91
khaki gentleman in K. — KIPL 491:22
zephyr and k. shorts — BETJ 88:21
Khan In Xanadu did Kubla K. — COLE 236:36
kick If I can k. them four years — CHAR 216:49
I get no k. from champagne — PORT 690:67
k. against the pricks — BIBLE 124:80
k. it about all day — HOLM 424:68
k. you out — WAUGH 923:54
sold...for 'one and a k.' — FORM 344:21
watch...hirelings k. a ball — PRIE 695:84
kicked die or get k. out — HOOV 427:48
get his head k. off — KHRU 485:95
kicking k. and screaming — STEV 851:15
kid Here's looking at you, k. — EPST 327:28

leopard shall lie down with the k. — BIBLE 108:62
The ego is like a k. — ALLEN 13:82
when you have a k. — HEMI 410:95
When you're a k. — ALBEE 11:22
kiddies You k. have crumpled — BETJ 89:41
kidnapped realize that I'm k. — ALLEN 14:92
kidney most unscrupulous k. — FRY 353:28
kidneys liked grilled mutton k. — JOYCE 470:29
kids cooking breakfast...for my k. — SCHR 749:67
don't have any k. yourself — LARK 510:90
help with the housework and the k. — WINT 950:10
How many k. did you kill — ANON 25:55
K. from Kilburn — WIGG 939:32
k. playing some game — SALI 740:81
way k. laugh when they're hungry — STEI 846:83
Kilburn Kids from K. — WIGG 939:32
Kildare broke a window in K. — JOYCE 470:31
kill almost k. a man as k. — MILT 600:99
Americans k. people — MOORE 617:96
As k. a king — SHAK 784:38
canst thou k. me — DONNE 292:51
cure the disease and k. the patient — BACON 52:15
How many kids did you k. — ANON 25:55
intendest thou to k. me — BIBLE 93:50
I will k. you — NEES 632:8
k. all the lawyers — SHAK 759:56
k. a man than a hawk — JEFF 453:16
k., and eat — BIBLE 124:82
k. a wife with kindness — SHAK 762:73
k. my mother — BOYD 154:12
k. sick people — MARL 573:11
k. them all — ARNA 33:54
k. us for their sport — SHAK 793:17
k. your dog — GREER 387:48
know, to k. and to create — BAUD 69:86
mettle enough...to k. care — SHAK 774:54
must men k. and die? — SHEL 816:58
My k. shall be thy k. — KIPL 490:5
never k. for sport — FROU 353:27
no approaches, but to k. — JONS 468:87
No sportsman wants to k. a fox — SHAW 811:28
not catastrophes...k. us — WOOLF 955:12
simply has to go out and k. — LEAC 515:23
The command 'Thou shalt not k.' — JOHN 456:78
Thou shalt not k. — BIBLE 94:66
Thou shalt not k. — CLOU 232:64
time to k. — BIBLE 105:14
to be professional, but to k. him — TYSON 904:12
To wit, I k. thee — SHAK 780:17
will not actually k. him — BERR 87:4
word for which you k. — WEIL 928:76
you can k. anyone — PACI 658:4
killed don't mind your being k. — KITC 494:99
effort very nearly k. her — BELL 77:63
I would prefer to be k. — STOP 856:24
k. all the day long — BIBLE 100:66
k. in no time — DICK 278:63
k. not thee — SHAK 778:56
kiss thee ere I k. thee — SHAK 791:52
Who k. the Kennedys? — JAGG 449:16
would each have k. the other — KING 488:56
killer k. with the ball — LARW 510:8
lover and k. are mingled — DOUG 295:4
killers K. from the egg — HUGH 435:33
Killiecrankie braes o' K. — BURNS 179:17
killing if war did not include k. — ANGE 19:91
K. care and grief — SHAK 804:45
K. care and grief — SHAK 804:47
kills cancer often k. — HALD 392:26
it k. me — HOPK 429:93
k. life within himself — SAINT 738:45
k. me some six or seven dozen — SHAK 771:44
k. the very good — HEMI 409:66
Life always k. you — COUP 248:38
that k. and pains not? — SHAK 795:90
Time k. us — SITW 824:24
time quietly k. them — BOUC 152:84
waste remains and k. — EMPS 326:8
kilt k., the lava-lava — MURR 627:80
kin little more than k. — SHAK 780:32
makes the whole world k. — SHAK 787:39
Religion and art...close k. — CATH 208:95
kin and kith own k. a. k. — NASH 630:57
kind children k. and natural — SHAK 775:65
Earth is here so k. — JERR 455:46
euerich in his k. — JAME 449:18
finish...among k. people — BEET 74:4

kings

for such a k. heart	SHAK 773:11
for the maiming of his k.	MACG 551:71
I am one with my k.	TENN 876:36
isolating him from his k.	PARN 665:46
K. is my love today	SHAK 802:75
k. its caressing	COCK 233:81
k. without deceit	DRYD 301:59
more than kin and less than k.	SHAK 780:32
one of their own k.	KORDA 498:97
people will always be k.	SASS 745:87
romantic poet…no other k.	FROST 352:9
should be pretty of its k.	LAMB 505:92
so constant…so k.	KEATS 476:89
So courteous, so k.	SKEL 824:29
to a k. and not to a gender	YOUR 968:55
woman who is really k. to dogs	BEER 73:83
your lack of k.	COLUM 238:88
kinder k. to the brutes	ELIOT 315:18
kindergarten kind of k.	ROBI 718:87
Kindle library consists of a K.	LIVE 531:54
kindness acts Of k.	WORD 956:54
cup o' k.	BURNS 178:6
husband's k. when it comes	BACON 51:77
I expected k. and gentility	PERE 674:21
kill a wife with k.	SHAK 762:73
K. and courage	MUIR 624:20
K. in another's trouble	GORD 378:52
K. is worth more than beauty	ARRAS 37:50
k. of strangers	WILL 945:82
k. that human beings do not lose	LEGU 520:8
k. that I can show	GREL 387:54
little bit of plain, ordinary k.	BUCH 171:30
Melting through k.	ROCH 719:5
milk of human k.	SHAK 796:13
neither k. or cruelty	ALBEE 11:21
place your k. there	ROCH 719:17
sheer k. and affection	TROL 897:31
the great have k.	POPE 688:4
thought of you with k.	PEAC 671:55
value on spontaneous k.	JOHN 464:83
kindred k. spider	FROST 352:11
kindreds all k. of the earth shall wail	BIBLE 131:86
all nations, and k.	BIBLE 131:3
kinds divided into two k.	HUME 438:5
Knowledge is of two k.	JOHN 462:38
There are two k.	SAINT 739:49
two k. of audience	SCHN 748:43
two k. of Methodists	ELIOT 315:17
two k. of mind	PASC 666:62
kine home-bred k.	WORD 960:14
King abuse the K.	SHAK 798:81
abusing…the best k.	FRAN 348:15
a' for our rightfu' k.	BURNS 180:57
am I sent for to a k.	SHAK 764:55
Authority forgets a dying k.	TENN 878:82
balm from an anointed k.	SHAK 764:47
beat the K. ninety-nine times	CROM 255:19
be the favourite of a k.?	MARL 573:13
between the k. and the people	SELD 756:7
blind, despised, and dying k.	SHEL 812:70
bold K. of Sweden	LESL 523:88
born K. of the Jews?	BIBLE 114:16
Carle, now the K.'s come!	SCOTT 754:68
catch the conscience of the K.	SHAK 782:5
chief defect of Henry K.	BELL 76:58
could a Don K. happen	KING 486:20
Willie K. made up like Philip	NICO 637:84
king Better to be k.	DE 273:67
consumer…is the k.	SAMU 741:1
contrary to the k.	SHAK 759:98
Creston Clarke played K. Lear	FIELD 335:12
Curse not the k.	BIBLE 106:33
Deny it to a k.?	SHAK 772:85
did a k. to death	THOM 883:8
editor is the uncrowned k.	STEAD 843:32
England breed again…a K. Harry?	DRAY 298:95
every inch a k.	SHAK 793:20
example of the k. of Denmark	FACK 329:1
executed the k.	STAL 842:4
Exempt from awe…the k.	SHEL 814:18
faint-hearted and degenerate k.	SHAK 760:2
follow the k.	TENN 878:93
forbid on behalf of the K.	EDWA 312:56
forced from the K.	INNO 446:48
found in the k. a monk	AELR 8:74
Gentiles' Lord and K.	AQUI 30:96
Glory to the K. of k.s	WESL 931:58
God bless our good and gracious K.	ROCH 720:27
God save the K.	ANON 24:9
God save the K.	BIBLE 96:31
God's patience and the K.'s English	SHAK 773:1
go in unto the k.	BIBLE 98:89
hath not offended the k.	MORE 619:26
heart and stomach of a k.	ELIZ 321:4
Here lies a k.	CAREW 198:52
Honour the k.	BIBLE 130:68
If he be the K. of Israel	BIBLE 119:46
If the k. loves music	MENC 586:80
image of the K.	TENN 878:77
impossible for the K.	PEPYS 673:90
In sleep a k.	SHAK 802:67
is the year's pleasant k.	NASHE 632:93
kill a k. and marry	SHAK 784:38
k. borne of all Englond	MALO 562:7
K. George's glorious days	GILB 369:53
K. has no dignity	MORE 618:16
k. is always a k.	WOLL 954:92
k. is strongest	BIBLE 112:67
K. Lodgreaunce delyverd	MALO 562:10
k. may make a nobleman	BURKE 176:53
k. of codpieces	SHAK 763:9
K. of comforts, K. of life	VAUG 909:38
K. of glory, K. of peace	HERB 413:68
K. of Glory wore	MARV 577:98
k. of infinite space	SHAK 782:86
K. of K.s	BIBLE 132:20
K. of the Jews	BIBLE 123:60
K. of the Jews	BIBLE 114:16
k. of the world	CAME 193:43
K. of the world shall raise us	BIBLE 113:13
K. o' Spain's daughter	COLUM 238:89
K.'s a bawcock	SHAK 775:81
K. said 'Butter, eh?'	MILNE 596:14
K. shall answer and say unto them	BIBLE 119:37
k.'s heart is in the hand	BIBLE 105:86
K. sits in Dunfermline	BALL 59:69
K.'s name is a tower	SHAK 761:47
K.'s real, or his stamped face	DONNE 291:27
k.'s torch throws its light	CYRA 260:12
k. thought mair o' Marie	BALL 59:67
k. was much moved	BIBLE 97:49
K., who ordainest Great winds	ELLE 322:18
k. who wants to maintain	MORE 618:15
lad that's born to be k.	BOUL 152:92
lessened my esteem of a k.	PEPYS 673:86
Let a k. recall	ERAS 327:37
like a tyrant or k.	PASC 667:84
looking for a k.	MACD 550:48
Lord Lion K.-at-arms!	SCOTT 752:20
make us a k. to judge us	BIBLE 96:30
Man Who Would be K.	KIPL 489:72
mortal temples of a k.	SHAK 764:52
my crowned K.	HOWA 433:86
My dead k.!	JOYCE 470:20
My God and K.	HERB 413:58
name the k. would give it	PENN 673:81
no k. in Israel	BIBLE 96:21
not so glorious as a k.	MARL 572:98
old and foolish k.	BIBLE 106:19
once and future k.	MALO 563:16
one-eyed man is k.	ERAS 327:36
one-eyed man is k.	WELLS 930:23
O worship the K.	GRANT 381:5
Ozymandias, k. of k.s	SHEL 813:86
passions of a K.	HUGO 437:69
priests ruled, the k. interpreted	COND 239:12
profits that an idle k.	TENN 870:97
qualities in a K.	RICH 714:19
Quhen Alysaunder oure k.	ANON 21:44
quietly along the K.'s highway	STER 848:23
Reagan…hell of a k.	ONEI 651:77
receive honour of the k.	BIBLE 113:8
Rejoice, the Lord is K.!	WESL 931:61
ruthless K.!	GRAY 385:79
saw the K. play at tennis	PEPYS 679:97
Say 'Pardon', k.	SHAK 765:61
served my K.	SHAK 805:53
singeing of the K. of Spain's beard	DRAKE 298:86
smote the k. of Israel	BIBLE 97:70
soldier of the K.	KITC 494:98
sole k. of forests all	SPEN 838:20
son of Heaven's eternal K.	MILT 596:30
soul, the K. of Heaven	LYTE 543:93
started off in films as a k.	MORL 620:42
still am I K. of those	SHAK 765:56
subject's duty is the K.'s	SHAK 775:82
substitute shines brightly as a k.	SHAK 770:23
such a plain K.	SHAK 776:99
such divinity doth hedge a k.	SHAK 784:53
supports his k. on loyal principles	SHAW 807:97
Tartars made them a K.	POLO 684:4
Teach me, my God and K.	HERB 413:61
Thee, Redeemer, K.	NEALE 632:6
The K. dropp'd a tear	BLAKE 141:38
The K. makes no distinction	STRA 857:44
The K. to Oxford sent a troop	BROW 166:87
the K. will ride	DONNE 291:25
To be a K.	ELIZ 322:6
To be a Pirate K.	GILB 368:37
To be k.	SHAK 796:6
to have blown up the K.	HOBY 421:11
To reverence the K.	TENN 877:56
to see the K. beheaded	PEPYS 673:87
To the K.'s Theatre	PEPYS 673:91
Upon the K.	SHAK 775:84
Wha…hae we got for a K.	CUNN 258:75
What must the K. do now?	SHAK 764:54
when we had a k.	SCOTT 753:59
Who…is a k. indeed	CHAP 214:16
Who is this K. of glory?	BIBLE 100:47
with a k.'s son my childish	SURR 860:1
worm that hath eat of a k.	SHAK 784:47
kingdom best walls of this k.	COVE 249:43
Childhood is the k.	MILL 592:30
children of the k.	BIBLE 116:58
Content's a k.	HEYW 417:42
folly in that of a great k.	SMITH 827:85
God hath numbered thy k.	BIBLE 111:42
His k. stretch	WATTS 923:47
if a k. be divided against itself	BIBLE 119:52
jewel of the k.	SUN 859:93
k. against k.	BIBLE 118:29
k. for a horse!	SHAK 761:55
k. for it was too small	SHAK 772:67
k. has ever been so	MONT 614:36
k. is as wide as the universe	FLAU 339:26
k. of God is within you	BIBLE 121:99
k. of the well	SONT 834:20
k. shall not continue	BIBLE 96:32
large k. for a little grave	SHAK 764:54
mind to me a k. is	DYER 309:47
My k., safeliest when with one man	DONNE 291:20
one end of the k. to the other	WEBB 925:10
palaces in K. come	MASE 580:64
people of this k.	LOUI 537:63
re-establishment of the laws of the k.	BLOOM 143:66
share the k. with	MARL 573:13
this formidable k.	PITT 679:2
Thy k. come	BIBLE 115:42
vegetating k.	LOWE 540:23
when thou comest into thy k.	BIBLE 122:8
yet thy k. shall pass	SWIN 864:1
kingdoms acquiring new k.	MORE 618:10
children of former k.	BACON 52:21
How many k.	PASC 667:76
kissed away K.	SHAK 794:66
returned to…these K.	ELIOT 318:18
sheweth him all the k. of the world	BIBLE 114:24
kinged England…is so idly k.	SHAK 775:71
kingfisher After the k.'s wing	ELIOT 319:43
kings accounted poet k.	KEATS 475:69
all be as happy as k.	STEV 853:70
axe to fell k.	BUNT 173:69
breath of k.	BURNS 177:76
But not of k.	MARL 573:13
captains and the k. depart	KIPL 490:16
change my state with k.'	SHAK 800:46
divine right of k.	MACM 556:62
enthroned in the hearts of k.	SHAK 770:13
function of k.	LOUI 537:64
great k. and fine cities	CATU 209:10
hand that k. Have lipped	SHAK 794:63
K. and Desperate Men	KRON 500:19
K. and Governments may err	HERB 412:46
K. are earth's gods	SHAK 798:80
K.…began their reigns	GARC 360:67
k. break faith	SHAK 768:53
k. can cause or cure	GOLD 376:88
K. for such a tomb	MILT 597:40
k. is mostly rapscallions	TWAIN 903:64
K. may be blest	BURNS 179:24

Kinnock

k. must bow to grammar — MOLI 611:87
k. of the earth stand up — BOOK 148:2
k. shall shut their mouths — BIBLE 109:92
K. should not p. — COWP 251:20
k. that fear their subjects' treachery? — SHAK 760:10
k. to mount guard — CARL 200:91
K. will be tyrants from policy — BURKE 176:43
k., with standards — MOORE 617:1
know the K. of England — GILB 368:39
lays his icy hand on k. — SHIR 819:20
Many k. have sat down — BIBLE 113:90
Might first made k. — MARL 573:8
palaces of k. are built — PAINE 660:31
pale k., and princes — KEATS 476:3
Physicians are like k. — WEBS 927:63
powerful K. and...Queens — DONNE 293:73
power of k. and magistrates — MILT 601:24
pride of k. — POPE 686:70
Punctuality...of k. — LOUI 537:71
raise up commonwealths and ruin k. — DRYD 301:69
security which k. are fighting for — SMITH 827:74
Some men are born k. — SHAW 810:17
statue of one of our k. — APPL 30:90
stories of the death of k. — SHAK 764:52
such is the breath of k. — SHAK 764:35
than that of most k. — HOOV 427:49
three k. into the east — BURNS 178:99
throne of k. — SHAK 764:40
to the Ear of K. — POPE 688:29
Until philosophers rule as k. — PLATO 682:63
Walk with K. — KIPL 492:63
War is the trade of k. — DRYD 303:21
what are k. — MARL 573:16
Kinnock K. has travelled the road — ASHD 37:64
Kipling a sort of gutless K. — ORWE 653:18
the boys, principally K. — HEMI 409:63
kirk or market — STEV 852:50
Marie Hamilton's to the k. gane — BALL 59:67
Kirkconnell On fair K. lea! — BALL 59:63
kirtle kilted her green k. — BALL 59:73
kiss about to k. your hand — GILB 370:72
Ae fond k. — BURNS 179:34
Anger's self I needs must k. — SIDN 820:49
best part of love is the k. — MANN 566:88
bluest veins to k. — SHAK 794:63
body k. a body — BURNS 180:55
can no more keep...a k. there — DE 275:12
clung to a k. — BYRON 190:9
cup...leaped to k. me — FLET 341:58
did never k. and greet? — KEATS 476:87
drew with one long k. — TENN 869:76
envied to share — GRAY 384:65
first k. is magic — CHAN 213:91
glowing k. had won — HOOD 426:24
heralded by a k. — DARIO 263:45
I tried to k. her — RHYS 712:78
k. again with tears! — TENN 872:36
k. but in the cup — JONS 467:75
k. her and mix her with me — SWIN 864:5
k. his dirty shoe — SHAK 775:81
k. is still a k. — HUPF 440:35
k. Long as my exile — SHAK 799:4
K. me as if you made — BROW 167:13
K. me, Hardy — NELS 633:15
k. me once again — JONS 468:83
k. my ass in Macy's window — JOHN 458:15
k. my parchèd lips — SHAK 768:65
k. thee ere I killed thee — SHAK 791:52
k. thy hand to bid adieu — STER 848:46
K. till the cow comes home — BEAU 71:16
k. you take is better — SHAK 787:42
let us k. and part — DRAY 299:99
make me immortal with a k.! — MARL 573:29
rough male k. of blankets — BROO 162:86
Salute...with an holy k. — BIBLE 126:34
saw you take his k. — PATM 669:17
took the k. sedately — TENN 876:22
visit with a wandering k. — CAREW 198:54
when tyrants seems to k. — SHAK 798:82
When women k. — MENC 586:97
whisper it in the k. — ONEI 651:63
With this k. I wed thee — HEYW 417:44
kissed had I wist, before I k. — BALL 60:80
how he k. me — JOYCE 470:33
Jenny k. me — HUNT 439:30
k. away Kingdoms and provinces — SHAK 794:66
k. by a man — KIPL 489:73

k. by the English dead — OWEN 657:27
k. her once by the pig-sty — THOM 884:35
k. her violently — ASHF 38:76
k. it and then fled — SHEL 816:59
When first we k. — BRID 158:8
When I k. the jack — SHAK 803:89
kisses Are not your k....filthy a-wastin' Christian k. — KIPL 489:82
couches and k. — THOM 884:40
forgotten my k. — SWIN 864:3
how many k. — CATU 209:7
k. of an enemy are deceitful — BIBLE 105:2
littered with remembered k. — MACN 558:2
More than k. — DONNE 292:47
numbering of k. — CLEV 230:93
Of many thousand k. — SHAK 795:82
remembered k. — TENN 872:43
Stolen k. much completer — HUNT 439:24
understand thy k. — SHAK 771:51
kissing constant click and k. — BETJ 89:38
fool...that first invented k.! — SWIFT 863:74
Garlic to mend her k. — SHAK 799:22
I wasn't k. her — MARX 578:13
K. don't last — MERE 588:27
k. had to stop? — BROW 167:31
k. is as full of sanctity — SHAK 779:1
K. with golden face — SHAK 801:48
Like k. Hitler — CURT 259:1
lip...it was made For k. — SHAK 761:35
lipped, and trembled k. — SHAK 794:63
overeagerly k. women — PACK 659:11
Kissinger if Mr K. is a great writer — ANON 27:22
Nixon and K. began — PILG 678:78
kiss-worthy most k.-w. face — SIDN 820:46
kitchen better get out of the k. — TRUM 899:80
Eat in the k. — HUGH 434:8
Fowls are to the k. — BRIL 159:19
history...through the k. window — CHILD 222:16
in k. cups — STEV 849:66
k. in the right place — JOHN 458:27
lack of reason in the k. — NIET 638:12
make my k. — STEV 854:84
mischief in the k. — THUR 891:94
Out of the k., to stew — ONEI 651:75
perpetually clean k. — BUKO 172:53
send me to eat in the k. — HUGH 434:8
Kitchener K....a great poster. — ASQU 38:87
kitchens talked of warm k. — GRAH 381:91
kites k. to whet their beaks — RANS 707:69
kitten trouble with a k. — NASH 631:69
kittle place Ca'd the K. Housie? — ANON 22:77
knack k. of judging a distance — REED 709:28
Technology...the k. of so arranging — FRIS 351:82
knave k. a k. or half a slave — INGR 446:36
he's an arrant k. — SHAK 781:68
K. of Hearts — CARR 204:84
my quaint k. — WEBS 926:35
knavery k. and folly to excuse — CHUR 224:53
religion, k., and change — BEHN 75:18
knaves Bold k. thrive — DRYD 302:4
K. and Knavery — ANON 23:96
rulers, mostly k. — BIER 134:80
to conclude, they are lying k.! — SHAK 774:55
world is made up...of fools and k. — BUCK 172:40
knavish either k. or childish — JOHN 463:67
knee A little aboon her k. — BALL 59:73
and bend my k. — SHAK 765:55
child upon her k. — TENN 873:47
civility of my k. — BROW 164:43
every k. should bow — BIBLE 128:97
k. which contains all the speed — YOUR 969:61
nobleman...cap and k. — WEBS 927:48
on bended k. — STUA 858:59
Sitting on a wise man's k. — HUXL 442:87
sit upon the curate's k. — CHES 221:1
woman is as young as her k. — QUANT 701:5
knee-cap soul started at the k.-c. — LEWIS 527:71
kneel k. still with one little cheek — SCHR 749:63
K. to nobody — SKEL 825:43
knees body between your k. — CORY 247:12
climb upon his k. — GRAY 384:65
creeps rustling to her k. — KEATS 477:22
Down on your k. — SHAK 779:2
just on its k. — HEMP 410:99
live on your k. — IBAR 444:5
Mr Elbows and K. — ANON 26:99
not in the k. — JERR 455:45

Sweeney spreads his k. — ELIOT 317:80
upon my k. every morning — SHAK 773:23
work is done upon his k. — KIPL 493:69
knell for it is a k. — SHAK 797:29
k. Of a spent day — CRANE 253:70
k. of parting day — GRAY 384:62
sound strikes like a rising k.! — BYRON 187:50
knew Adam k. Eve — BIBLE 92:2
I k. him, Horatio — SHAK 784:63
k. almost as much at eighteen — JOHN 461:99
k. a lot about foreign affairs — REST 711:65
k. too well — FROST 352:2
that he nothing k. — MILT 607:78
those who k. Him not — SCHW 751:94
knickers k....of crêpe-de-chine — MACN 557:97
wearing calico k. — JAMES 450:26
knife carved upon it with a k. — SHAK 772:90
crumbling...under the k.-e. — RICH 713:95
cuts as keen as a k. — BAUG 69:91
gave her a dull paring k. — BRID 158:11
I had a k. and two forks — RIDGE 715:33
keeps 'em on the k. — NASH 631:87
k. is lost in it — SHEL 814:5
k. through a layer cake — MILL 593:45
sharpness like a clasping k. — BROW 166:95
smylere with the k. — CHAU 217:84
strike with our spirit's k. — SHEL 815:39
Surgeons...take the k.! — DICK 283:29
War to the k. — PALA 661:40
wind's like a whetted k. — MASE 580:52
knight gentle k. was pricking — SPEN 838:19
k. at arms — KEATS 476:1
K. had made a sudden pause — CARR 205:20
K. in the triumph — ADDI 7:35
k. of the garter — ATTL 40:28
k. to be their wooer — BALL 58:52
k. was...a valiant Gent — EVEL 328:70
name of ony k. — MALO 563:12
never was k. like...Lochinvar — SCOTT 752:21
new-slain k. — BALL 59:77
parfit gentil k. — CHAU 217:72
Poor K.! — NABO 628:2
red-cross k. — TENN 869:83
seyde that on k. — MALO 563:11
shortest k. of the year — RICH 714:14
knight-errant masquerading k.-e. — PARN 665:47
knighthood k. as...accomplishment — NAIP 629:29
never accept a k. — KENN 482:39
knights k. and barons bold — MILT 597:47
K. of the Isosceles Triangle — ROOS 725:21
k. used in those days — CAXT 210:22
order of k. — GUIB 389:86
Red-Branch K. to danger — MOORE 617:1
knit to darn, to flower or k. — LEWIS 526:51
knits k. me to thy rugged strand! — SCOTT 752:17
knitter beautiful little k. — SITW 824:14
knitting as if it were k. — GLAS 374:45
woman still at her k. — PLATH 681:36
knock k., and it shall be opened — BIBLE 115:50
k., breathe, shine, and...mend — DONNE 292:54
k. over the first one — EISE 314:98
none will hear the postman's k. — AUDEN 42:72
right to k. him down — JOHN 464:77
stand at the door, and k. — BIBLE 131:95
knocked be the bastard off! — HILL 418:60
knocker Tie up the k. — POPE 687:97
knocks nature k. them all flat — RENO 711:54
What really k. me out — SALI 739:72
knot bomb the k. off a tree — JENS 454:34
certain k. of peace — SIDN 820:46
crowned k. of fire — ELIOT 321:94
k. be unknotted — ELIOT 319:51
political k. that would not yield — BIER 134:65
then all is k. — JONS 468:97
know all ye need to k. — KEATS 478:40
already k. the answer — JONG 466:52
As I k. more of mankind — JOHN 464:91
Be still, and k. — BIBLE 100:69
by their fruits ye shall k. them — BIBLE 115:54
can be said to k. — RUSS 734:35
courage to k. — KANT 473:21
do not k. who or what I am — SELL 756:17
don't k. where you are — GROS 389:81
Dost thou k. me? — SHAK 793:60
full up with the things they k. — HERN 415:94
general must k. — REED 710:33
greatest virtue...is to k. God — SPIN 841:79

labour

hate any one that we k.	HAZL	403:39
How did they k.?	PARK	663:5
I do not k. myself	GOET	375:70
I k. it well, your mishap	HEINE	407:17
I k. not	HAND	395:79
I k. thee well	SHAK	793:28
K. all that there is to be knowed	GRAH	381:92
k. I'm right	GOLD	377:21
k. more than you think	SPOCK	841:84
K. most of the rooms	FULL	355:78
k. nothing whatever about you	DOYLE	297:66
k. that they're going on	ASSAN	39:95
k. thee not, old man	SHAK	773:99
k., to kill and to create	BAUD	69:86
k. what to do with it	WALP	919:71
k. what we are	SHAK	784:49
k. without learning	INGR	446:40
leader…must k. that he knows	RAND	706:56
Let him not k.!	SHAK	790:26
let's learn not to k.	CRUZ	256:39
Mistress, k. yourself	SHAK	779:2
must k. where you are	STEI	846:86
never k. what's hit you	KENN	482:35
no one knows what he doesn't k.	CARY	207:68
not stand to k. any more	MUNRO	625:49
O that a man might k.	SHAK	778:54
other half don't k. they don't k.	QUINN	703:24
people k. what the land k.s	SAND	742:28
pity those I do not k.	SHAK	787:56
place thereof shall k. it no more	BIBLE	102:10
reading might make her k.	SIDN	820:43
report on what I k.	FRIS	351:81
Scientists k. so much	SHAP	805:68
something that you k.	HEMI	410:74
the more we k.	HUXL	441:58
thought to k. this	BIBLE	101:85
We don't k. where that money	REAG	708:11
what I do k. I k. better	AGATE	9:89
what should they k. of England	KIPL	490:94
what thou dost not k.	SHAK	771:43
what you do not k.	ELIOT	320:63
When will the world k.	WALP	919:76
Yet I k. her for	SHAK	805:48
You k. I k. you k.	GUNN	390:95
knowes Ca' the yowes to the k.	BURNS	180:51
knoweth be as one that k.	BIBLE	113:6
know-how American k.-h.	COLO	238:80
knowing art of k. what to overlook	JAMES	451:68
k. there was no corner	KAVA	474:50
k. what will be known	FRAN	348:41
k. who we are is k.	MILL	593:42
lust of k.	FLEC	340:32
precisely in k. its limits	KANT	473:20
knowledge After such k., what forgiveness?	ELIOT	317:84
all branches of k.	ARNO	35:8
all k. and wonder	BACON	49:19
all k. is human	POPP	689:62
all k.…my province	BACON	49:16
any addition to k.	DONNE	293:77
a pound of k.	WESL	932:74
because they lead to the k.	JONG	466:30
best mode of k.	SENG	757:29
Bitter is the k.	BAUD	68:70
blocked up the way to k.	BERK	84:29
by words without k.?	BIBLE	98:13
Can k. have no bound	DENH	272:59
carry k. with him	JOHN	463:60
chapter of k. is very short	CHES	219:44
civilizations that abandon the quest for k.	LOVE	538:91
climbing after k.	MARL	572:99
collection…of human k.	KENN	481:11
craftsmen share a k.	SACK	737:9
deny k.	KANT	473:25
dissemble sometimes your k.	BACON	52:20
enlightenment in all spheres of k.	BOOK	150:45
ethics, as a branch of k.	AYER	48:7
evergreen tree of diabolical k.	SHER	817:72
ever to have pure k.	PLATO	682:55
exactly of their own k.	MONT	613:10
experience and intuited k.	MO	611:67
father of k.	HIPP	419:70
forms of human k.	MANN	566:79
for want of better K.	PATE	669:13
from k. ignorance	BROW	169:63
fruits of k.	FREUD	350:61
genius of k.	GOUR	380:79
God has given k.	MARIE	571:73
greatest good…is the k. of God	SPIN	841:79
ignorance is never better than k.	FERMI	334:95
imperfect is all our k.!	DONNE	293:75
impersonation…of secret k.	BROO	163:10
improved out of all k.	SITW	824:12
inner reserve of k.	HOOV	427:53
intuitive k. of God	SPIN	841:81
jazz, if one has the k.	MORT	621:72
key of k.	BIBLE	121:84
K. advances by steps	MACA	545:28
k. and is not rejected	RUSS	734:36
k. and love of God	BOOK	147:75
k. and survey of vice	MILT	600:11
K. and timber shouldn't	HOLM	424:72
k. as collective k.	SHAP	805:68
k.…at the center of true religiousness	EINS	313:80
k. belongs to humanity	PAST	668:4
k. can only be finite	POPP	690:65
k. combined with that of other	GALB	357:20
K. comes, but wisdom	TENN	871:20
k. derived from experience	ELIOT	320:59
k.…did ne'er unroll	GRAY	384:68
K. dwells in heads	COWP	251:21
k. for the sake of understanding	BUSH	184:51
k. from the gods	WILS	948:51
k. increaseth sorrow	BIBLE	105:12
k. in her presence	MILT	605:41
K. is a polite word	CUMM	258:70
K. is a sacred cow	SZENT	865:30
k. is as food	MILT	605:28
k. is bought in the market	CLOU	232:45
K. is of two kinds	JOHN	462:38
k. is, ourselves to know	POPE	687:92
K. is power	BACON	49:17
K. is proud	COWP	251:22
K.…keep any better than fish.	WHIT	936:63
k.…lost in information?	ELIOT	319:31
k. might become more clear	LANY	508:55
K. might pity win	SIDN	820:43
k. of causes	BACON	53:46
k. of causes	BACON	50:52
k. of good and evil	MILT	600:3
k. of good and evil	MILT	600:5
k. of its giant strength	NORR	641:57
k. of literate English…desert	CHAN	213:84
k. of man is as the waters	BACON	49:28
k. of oneself	MILL	594:77
k. of the Bible, Shakespeare	WAUGH	924:98
k. of the boundless skies	BYRON	189:94
k. of the heart	JOHN	462:25
k. of the stars	EDDI	311:25
k. originates in…experience	MAO	568:27
k.…recorded experience	CARL	201:14
k. shall be increased	BIBLE	111:44
k.…shall vanish away	BIBLE	126:52
k. that he lived in vain	BYRON	187:49
k. that since perfection	NIEB	637:87
k. that the soul	PATM	669:22
k. that you can have is inexhaustible	FRYE	354:57
k. that you'll grow out of it	DAY	267:33
K. the wing	SHAK	760:99
K.…will not console me	PASC	667:87
Language and k.	SULL	859:79
larger the island of k.	MACI	553:4
Let k. grow	TENN	873:57
lies in the way to k.	LOCKE	533:88
limits of human k.	NIEB	637:88
love of Christ, which passeth k.	BIBLE	128:88
materials of reason and k.	LOCKE	533:89
men naturally desire k.	ARIS	31:17
more love and k. of you	SHAK	778:61
multiplieth words without k.	BIBLE	98:12
no k. of myself	KANT	473:19
no k. when the day was done	KEATS	477:12
nor k.…in the grave	BIBLE	106:28
not be lessened by the k.	HUXL	443:7
Of k. there is no satiety	BACON	49:35
one who speaks, without k.	BIER	134:77
only one good, k.	SOCR	833:1
opinion…is but k.	MILT	600:4
ourselves, and our k.	POPP	689:60
Out-topping k.	ARNO	33:62
possession of k.	POPP	689:55
presupposition of the k.	HEID	406:11
progress of human k.	FRAN	348:18
province of k. to speak	HOLM	424:83
Science is k. arranged	BURB	174:85
Science is organized k.	SPEN	836:85
Science is systematized positive k.	SART	744:63
scientific k. have been achieved	PLAN	680:23
seek for k. and wisdom	SHEL	811:45
sign of k. in our time	WILL	946:17
small advances in k.	PROU	698:46
sociologists of k.	MERT	589:56
Sorrow is k.	BYRON	189:83
Such k. is too wonderful	BIBLE	103:43
Such k. is too wonderful	BOOK	149:36
The most important k.	BUFO	172:52
things that are preventing k.	PROT	697:34
third kind of k.	SPIN	841:82
thorough k. of human nature	AUST	46:83
through their union can k. arise	KANT	473:18
time to close the five parts of k.	BROW	166:84
to follow k.	TENN	870:99
too much k.	POPE	687:80
tree of k.	BYRON	189:83
tree of k.	BYRON	189:98
Tree of K. grew fast	MILT	604:96
true antithesis to k.	DE	273:83
true k. only comes of death	WHITE	935:52
two modes of acquiring k.	BACON	54:57
Why seek for k.	EDGE	311:41
win k. of the causes	VIRG	914:27
without k. of the same	LEON	523:79
known be k., and not know	COLT	238:85
Canada only needs to be k.	HOPK	429:99
Have ye not k.?	BIBLE	109:84
k. them all already, k. them all	ELIOT	316:63
must have k. me	TROL	898:52
not meant 'to be k.'	SAGAN	737:24
She's very k.	MIRR	609:18
than to be k.	HOPK	428:83
there are k. knowns	RUMS	731:41
till I am k.	JOHN	460:63
knows going one k. not where	MASE	580:54
He k. nothing	SHAW	809:76
nobody k. what they're talking about	CLEE	229:82
no one…k. what they're doing	GERV	366:86
person who k. 'how'	RAVI	707:85
what no one k. about you	DELI	272:44
Knox Lady K.…irrelevance	SOME	833:9
see John K. in Paradise	PARK	664:10
knuckle-end That K.-e. of England	SMITH	830:53
knuckleheads young people are k.	OBAMA	645:60
Köhln K., a town of monks	COLE	236:50
Ko-Ko If K.-K. tells us true	GILB	369:59
Koran interpretation of the K.	GIBB	366:95
Korea dust that is settling in K.	MACA	544:10
shall go to K.	EISE	314:94
Kosciusko as K. fell!	CAMP	194:62
Kosovo K. is not a part of Serbia	MILO	596:28
stop ethnic cleansing in K.	BLAIR	138:61
Kraken the K. sleepeth	TENN	869:71
Krazy ball made of K. Putty	LODGE	534:96
Krieg K. findet immer einen Ausweg	BREC	158:96
Krishna K.'s jokes may be vapid	FORS	345:51
Kruger finished killing K.	KIPL	491:22
kurrajong Under a k.	NEIL	633:11
Kurtz Mistah K.—he dead	CONR	243:31
kuwaiting We're k.	ANON	26:5
Kyle lad was born in K.	BURNS	178:97
Kyrie K. eleison	ANON	21:56

L

label l. our toys good and bad	DYSON	309:60
rag of a l. to cover himself	HUXL	443:4
labelling L. makes the invisible visible	STEIN	846:96
labials heavenly l.	STEV	849:68
labor onward march of l.	LEWIS	526:53
laboratories Outside their l.	PAST	668:5
states are the l. of democracy	WHIT	937:85
laboratory Give me an l.…	PERE	674:17
hissing l. of his wishes	THOM	884:41
l. of God	WILL	945:88
We cannot haul…generations into the l.	BENE	79:15
laborious rising unto place is l.	BACON	51:85
Studious of l. ease	COWP	251:18
Labour only leaders L. loves	HARR	399:52
labour 25 years of L. Government	BEVAN	89:51
all ye that l.	BIBLE	116:81
applies himself to l. and exercise	CONF	240:22
as much of a l. to write	HUXL	441:63

laboured

Britain with a L. Government	WILS 948:67
British L. movement…strikes	ENGE 326:14
calamity of a L. Government	HESE 416:29
Chinese cheap l.	HARTE 400:73
common wages of l.	SMITH 827:80
daily l. to pursue	WESL 932:63
demand for their l.	STEU 849:60
dignify the l.	CRANE 253:59
division of l.	BABB 48:1
division of l. is nothing	MARX 578:27
division of l….social functions	DURK 308:28
don't let L. ruin it	ANON 25:37
do ye not l. and toil	BIBLE 112:68
Ease and alternate l.	THOM 887:99
example of unproductive l.	GRAY 383:44
extraction of surplus l.	MARX 579:40
fruit of our l.	MONT 613:11
Give us l.	SCHR 749:65
good reward for their l.	BIBLE 106:17
I in l. lie	DONNE 291:19
In all l. there is profit	BIBLE 104:72
In l. and trouble…more dignified	CHES 219:49
instruments of l.	MARX 579:41
intellectual l. (of science)	HUMB 438:93
l. and wages first	MANN 567:93
L. does not only create goods	MARX 578:25
l. going upstairs	MUNDY 625:43
L. government	GEOR 364:50
L. Governments in every country	GREY 388:61
l. in his vocation	SHAK 770:30
l. in the deep mid-ocean	TENN 870:93
l. in vain	BIBLE 103:36
L. isn't working	ANON 26:81
L. is the Father…of Wealth	PETTY 676:46
L. is the Party of law and order	BLAIR 138:49
l. leader	MCFA 551:64
l. movement was truly religious	WOLFE 953:79
L. of an age in piled stones	MILT 597:39
l. of his body	LOCKE 533:86
l. of keeping house	MCCA 548:96
l. of women	GILM 371:92
l. once spent	JEVO 455:53
L. Party is a moral crusade	WILS 948:65
L. Party's election programme	SNOW 832:88
L. Party, when…entrusted with power	WEBB 925:10
l. required to obtain…goods	RICA 712:82
l.-time necessary to reproduce	MARX 579:39
l….to pervert that end	MILT 602:41
l. until the evening	BIBLE 102:12
l. was the first p.	SMITH 827:79
l. weariness	LYLY 543:86
l. we delight in	SHAK 797:40
l. which he taketh under the sun?	BIBLE 105:9
L. without joy	RUSK 733:7
last l. that thou and I shall waste	WYATT 964:49
little effect after much l.?	AUST 46:80
many still must l. for the one	BYRON 188:74
more l. in hewing	JOHN 463:63
mountains are in l.	HORA 430:19
natural price of l.	RICA 712:79
natural price of l.	RICA 712:84
no time to l.	ROGE 723:83
performed much of the l.	STAN 842:15
performing any kind of l.	WARD 920:2
productive powers of l.	SMITH 827:75
product of mental l.	MARX 579:39
rest rather than l.	RICH 714:21
role of l. in society	NEVI 634:32
sacrifice of more and more l.	RICA 712:80
shortened the l. of copyists	CARL 200:89
Six days thou shalt l.	BIBLE 94:66
society do not want his l.	MALT 563:22
they that live l.	BIBLE 112:69
this waye to l.	ANON 21:40
To learn and l.	BOOK 148:80
true success is to l.	STEV 852:48
understood…the natural price of l.	RICA 712:82
With too much l. drowns	SHAK 763:97
yet is their strength l.	BIBLE 101:94
laboured l. to it without the reward	SCOTT 751:5
labourer employed as an under-l.	LOCKE 533:86
king's torch throws its light upon a l.	CYRA 260:12
l. is worthy of his hire	BIBLE 120:78
l. or a tradesman	LAW 512:37
l. to take his pension	RUSK 733:95
labourers enable the l….to subsist	RICA 712:84
take that of L.' Unions	RUSK 733:16
too many L. to cultivate the Lands	CANT 197:12
labouring A l. man that is given	BIBLE 113:97
l. swain	GOLD 376:96
Sleep is sweet to the l. man	BUNY 174:78
labours Children sweeten l.	BACON 51:69
from their l. rest	HOW 433:84
notice…of my l.	JOHN 460:63
One thousand l.	LABE 253:4
share of the l. and sacrifices	MILL 591:2
uncessant l. see	MARV 577:1
laburnums L., dropping-wells	TENN 874:88
labyrinth dreamt I was in the l.	MUIR 624:18
is in the l.	ROBBE 716:62
l. of our life	SCHO 748:52
peopled l. of walls	SHEL 812:64
labyrinthine down the l. ways	THOM 886:81
lace button, hook, and l.	LOWE 539:98
Lachlan I met him, down the L.	PATE 669:13
lack l. of many a thing	SHAK 801:47
l. their sacred poet	HORA 430:12
lacked If I l. any thing	HERB 413:65
lacrosse I thought l. was	WILL 944:74
lad brisk and a bonnie l.	ANON 22:72
l. does not care for	JOHN 461:14
l. of life	SHAK 775:81
l. that's born to be king	BOUL 152:92
l. was born in Kyle	BURNS 178:97
many a lightfoot l.	HOUS 432:55
myself a sterling l.	HOUS 432:59
Up, l.	HOUS 431:36
When I was a l.	GILB 368:34
ladder bottom of a l.	EGGE 313:68
can't climb…without a l.	ZATO 969:3
climb the l. of success	SCHW 750:88
kick away the l.	SUN 859:92
l. set up on the earth	BIBLE 93:32
Now that my l.'s gone	YEATS 967:36
raise a l. without a wall	HONE 425:14
rounds of society's l.	MOORE 616:68
with lantern and with l.	STEV 853:72
laden heart is l.	HOUS 432:55
ladies art that helps old l.	OLDE 649:29
by act of God, we are l.	CADOR 191:9
Cambridge l….furnished souls	CUMM 257:53
chic old blue-haired l.	CAPO 197:29
delectable lusty l.	DUNB 306:2
Good l., help to fill	SURR 860:3
good night, sweet l.	SHAK 784:49
keep us from scaring the l.	MCMU 557:82
l….admitted on special days	WARN 921:10
l. and gentlemen, last night	NATH 632:1
l. apparently rolled along	HUXL 441:65
l. in very high positions	AMIN 16:28
L., just a little more virginity	TREE 896:97
l. that must be wooed	CAMP 195:74
l., whose bright eyes	MILT 597:47
l., yield to love	LYLY 543:86
lang may the l. sit	BALL 59:71
lion among l.	SHAK 767:33
old l. in tennis shoes	MOSK 622:80
old l. of both sexes	DICK 282:85
remember the l.	ADAMS 4:71
Sigh no more, l.	SHAK 774:38
worth any number of old l.	FAUL 331:41
ye lords of l. intellectual	BYRON 189:90
young l. spend their time	SWIFT 861:35
lads Golden l. and girls	SHAK 803:7
l. are far away	FORD 343:9
l. in their hundreds	HOUS 431:46
l. who fought	SASS 745:89
Then strip l.	SCOTT 753:39
three wild l. were we	SCOTT 753:43
Two l. that thought	SHAK 799:7
lady accomplished l.	SHAK 786:8
act like a l.	SIMON 821:73
behaved like a perfect l.	TRAV 896:93
cannot endure my L. Tongue	SHAK 774:29
certain little l. comes by	GAY 362:25
Come, l., let not this	MARL 572:95
coyness L. were no crime	MARV 577:90
dreamt my l. came	SHAK 766:11
Fair l., will you any?	LYLY 543:84
for the love of a l.!	GILB 370:70
girl who was a l.	LOOS 536:50
hawk, his hound, and his l. fair	BALL 59:77
Here lies a l. of beauty	RANS 706:66
hold my l.'s head	HEAN 404:71
l. as thou art	SHAK 771:53
l. from the provinces	GILB 369:61
L. in the wig	DICK 280:24
L., l., should you meet	PARK 663:96
l. novelist	GILB 369:61
l. of Christ's College	AUBR 42:58
L. of my own	WORD 957:63
L. of Shalott	TENN 869:79
L. of Shalott	TENN 869:82
L. of Shalott	TENN 870:85
L. of Shalott	TENN 870:86
L. of Shalott	TENN 870:87
L. of the Lake	MALO 562:9
L. of the West Country	DELA 271:29
l. protests too much	SHAK 783:25
L.'s not for Burning	FRY 353:31
l. that's known as Lou	SERV 757:35
l. wants to be dressed	NASH 631:84
l. was not seen!	SCOTT 753:47
l. who found out	ROSE 725:29
L. with a Lamp	LONG 535:33
L. would be Queen	POPE 688:14
L. you deserve this state	MARV 577:91
like a dying l.	SHEL 816:67
lord and l. gay	SCOTT 752:10
lovely l., garmented in light	SHEL 815:24
Lydia The Tattooed L.	HARB 396:89
make a sweet l. sad	SHAK 786:32
manners of a l.	FRAN 348:22
No l. closer	SHAK 771:43
no rhyme to 'l.'	SHAK 774:56
not exactly a l.	RIDGE 715:31
Of many a l.	SPEN 838:23
O lang will his l.	BALL 58:54
old l. at a busy intersection	ACHE 3:44
quarrel for a l.	HALI 393:39
San Francisco is a l.	MAIL 560:55
saw a l. bright	BALL 59:74
talk like a l.	SHAW 810:95
the l. is a tramp	HART 400:67
'Twas a good l.	SHAK 791:70
When a l.'s in the case	GAY 362:13
wrong to strike a l.	THUR 891:5
You are the body, l.	SCEVE 746:18
lag with some l.	HOMA 425:93
lain l. for ages and will lie	TENN 869:72
l. with their mothers	SOPH 834:32
lair silence round about his l.	KEATS 477:28
laird l. o' Cockpen	NAIR 629:32
lifts a drove from a Sassenach l.	SCOTT 753:37
laity conspiracies against the l.	SHAW 809:81
tell the l. of our love	DONNE 292:38
laitymen Gentes and l.	JOYCE 470:36
lake beside a cold l.	SCOTT 751:2
bosom of the l.	TENN 873:49
daffodils…beside the l.	WORD 960:24
glitter like a l.	BYRON 190:6
l. am in the l.	ATWO 41:32
l. I saw bass-viols	LEVE 525:23
l. is the great source	SPEKE 836:81
l. of fire	BIBLE 132:22
Maker, in that crimson l.	MONT 615:51
Marriage may…be a stormy l.	PEAC 671:51
middle of a stormy l.	EISE 314:6
real pitch l.	HUXL 442:76
Round the Mareotic L.	YEATS 967:39
lakes grass is green, l. damp	STEP 847:11
L., mountains, and rivers	AUST 46:61
shakes across the l.	TENN 872:38
Some people swim l.	WEBB 925:8
songs in its l.	SCOTT 751:3
lakeside by the l.	SCHW 751:94
lamb ape to Hazlitt, to L.	STEV 853:77
Behold the L. of God	BIBLE 122:19
brought as a l. to the slaughter	BIBLE 109:94
Did he who made the L. make thee?	BLAKE 140:20
Englishman…flattered, is a l.	CHAP 214:22
God will provide himself a l.	BIBLE 92:26
holy L. of God	BLAKE 141:40
L. of God	CASW 208:83
L. of God, I come!	ELLI 323:26
l. shall be without blemish	BIBLE 93:58
leads me to the L.!	COWP 250:88
Little l., who made thee?	BLAKE 139:86
Maria, to the shorn l.	STER 849:58
Mary had a little l.	HALE 392:29
one little ewe l.	BIBLE 96:45

language

Pipe a song about a l.!	BLAKE 139:85	in a strange l.?	BIBLE 103:42	workman in the l.	LLOY 532:71
washed in the blood of the L.	LIND 530:15	in the l. of the living	BIBLE 102:20	would be a grand l.	FREE 349:45
washed in the blood of the L.?	LIND 530:16	l. and ocean without rest	MILT 601:26	wrong throughout the l.	MUIR 623:14
when he would steal the l.	SHAK 759:89	l. and the mind	NGU 636:66	Your l., your wealth	JAY 453:99
wolf also shall dwell with the l.	BIBLE 108:62	l. flowing with milk and honey	BIBLE 93:54	**landing** l. a man on the moon	KENN 481:5
wolf and the l. shall feed together	BIBLE 110:10	l. God gave to Andy Stewart	SMITH 828:4	**landlady** l. of a boarding-house	LEAC 515:10
wolf and the l....united	ARIS 31:16	l. God gave to Cain	CART 207:55	**landlord** architecture...for the l.	WRIG 962:66
lambs gather the l. with his arm	BIBLE 108:80	l. is the only thing	MITC 610:39	interest of the l.	RICA 712:83
go to hell like l.	CHES 221:90	l. lies desolate and stripped	ADAMS 4:73	l. does not intend to repair	ADAMS 5:6
l. end up head down	JUST 471:50	l. may be said to be discovered	STEF 844:54	l. to the whole congregation	ADDI 6:28
poor little l.	KIPL 489:75	l. may vary more	FROST 352:8	**landlords** before the l. of the country	PARN 665:47
lame l. man leap as an hart	BIBLE 108:76	L. of brown heath	SCOTT 752:17	l. and persons of property	MALT 563:23
l. man who keeps the right road	BACON 50:48	l. of Calvin	SMITH 830:53	**landmark** Remove not the old l.	BIBLE 105:91
l. walk	BIBLE 116:76	l. of cattle and sheep	LAWS 514:96	removeth his neighbour's l.	BIBLE 95:95
made l. by...spite	SHAK 801:49	l. of hope and glory	BENS 81:84	**landmarks** l. that are scarcely more	HUBB 434:3
Science without religion is l.	EINS 313:79	l. of light and revelation	CLIN 230:3	nomads, on a plain with few l.	MCMU 557:85
lament childish weakness to l.	SHAK 760:18	l. of lost content	HOUS 431:52	**landmined** l. and unforgiving	ELKIN 322:16
l. of the poets	THOM 886:76	l. of lost gods	BYRON 187:42	**lands** different from things in other l.	LAWS 514:94
l. the past	BURKE 175:9	l. of Nod	BIBLE 92:6	envy of less happier l.	SHAK 764:40
naught other to l.	PATM 669:19	L. of Nod at last	STEV 853:74	forsake me, and of all my l.	SHAK 760:17
lamentation l., and bitter weeping	BIBLE 110:22	L. of our birth	KIPL 492:57	l. are the mother	PETTY 676:46
lamented ye have not l.	BIBLE 116:79	l. of sand and ruin	SWIN 864:7	l. beyond the sea	WORD 958:92
Lammas It fell about the L. tide	BALL 58:51	l. of settled government	TENN 872:29	l. where the Jumblies live	LEAR 516:31
It was upon a L. night	BURNS 177:88	l. of the free	KEY 484:68	satisfies the poor in other l.	HEGEL 406:7
lamp dying l., a falling shower	SHEL 815:36	l. of their heart's hope	DAVIS 266:9	sold your own l.	SHAK 779:6
Eternal l. of love!	HERR 415:5	l. of the pilgrims'	CUMM 257:58	songs of other l.	EVANS 328:68
Lady with a L.	LONG 535:33	l. o' the leal	NAIR 629:33	Where are our l.?	SITT 823:93
l. beside the golden door	LAZA 515:3	l. stares at the sun	SCOTT 751:2	**landscape** art of l.	RUNGE 731:52
l. light dull and sickly	WILDE 939:44	l. that has need of heroes	BREC 157:91	Burning like a sunlit l.	MACD 550:41
l. of day	DOUG 295:2	l. that has no heroes	BREC 157:91	half the l. is unavailable	DOUG 295:11
l. of faith	WORD 962:47	l. that I heard of	HARB 396:90	implacability of the l.	NOLAN 640:43
l. unto my feet	BIBLE 103:28	l. wherein thou art a stranger	BIBLE 92:21	invention of the l. painter	FUSE 356:95
l. was dark	MACN 558:6	L. where my fathers died	SMITH 830:31	l. and its inhabitants	UPDI 906:37
smell of the l.	HERR 415:7	l. where the Bong-tree	LEAR 516:36	l. broken into	LEGER 519:7
smell too strong of the l.	STER 848:29	laughing Ceres re-assume the l.	POPE 686:62	L. is to American painting	HUGH 435:24
sovran vital l.	MILT 603:74	length and breadth of the l.	MOOD 615:56	l. round it measures	MILT 597:45
To keep a l. burning	THER 882:82	light across the l.?	TENN 872:30	l. to a blind man's eye	WORD 956:53
lamppost asking a l. how it feels	HAMP 395:76	Lilacs out of the dead l.	ELIOT 317:95	shaper of the l.	BRON 161:53
leaning on a l.	GAY 362:25	little wrong in the l.	MENC 586:80	the beauty of l.	HILL 418:59
lampposts way that a drunk uses l.	LANG 507:40	love-sick l. that mourns for thee	BLAKE 139:80	**landscapes** fades the glimmering l.	GRAY 384:62
lamps I mean by fairy l.	WOOD 954:3	loving the l.	MOORE 618:7	if l. were sold	STEV 851:30
l. are going out	GREY 388:62	made our l. a tomb	ORAH 652:91	l. of seas full of fish	CIXO 227:47
l. are guttering low	HOUS 433:83	Maker's image through the l.	DRYD 301:64	Someone said of his l.	HAZL 404:60
l., by whose dear light	MARV 577:97	Marched into their l.	AYTO 48:11	**landslide** Republican l. on Nov 8	CUOMO 258:83
L. for my gloom	SASS 746:98	mist and hum of that low l.	ARNO 34:99	**lane** country l.	PARK 664:35
l. that shone o'er fair women	BYRON 187:50	my own, my native l.!	SCOTT 752:16	dragons of Laune and L.	ORAH 652:90
lampshade a Nazi l.	PLATH 681:31	nakedness of the l..	BIBLE 93:43	In an English l.	BROW 168:46
Lancashire In a L. cotton-town	ORWE 653:14	narrow strip of l.	BAKER 56:4	l. was made	DICK 280:23
typical sound of L.	ORWE 653:9	Oh, thou dear l.	SCHAW 747:20	walk down the l.	FREED 349:42
Lancelot at that tyme sir L.	MALO 563:12	once-loved l.	WRIG 963:77	**lanes** green and shaded l.	MACK 553:10
bold Sir L.	TENN 869:83	Only the weathering l.	SNYD 832:91	**language** abstruseness in their l.	GOWE 380:81
L. mused a little space	TENN 870:87	Past is a strange l.	THOM 885:50	American l.	ADAMS 5:96
Not L., nor another	TENN 877:59	Peace is...more precious than...l.	SADAT 737:13	any l. you choose	GILB 369:54
which I found in L.	TENN 877:58	people know what the l. knows	SAND 742:28	Bad l. or abuse	GILB 368:32
lances Shall be our l.	GILB 369:55	pocket of my l.	FRAME 346:75	beyond the l. of the living	ELIOT 321:83
lancet veins...to invite the l.	SHER 817:81	pointed toward the l.	TENN 870:88	beyond the range of l.	REID 710:44
land across the other l.	MUIR 624:24	poor race in a l. of dollars	DU 305:66	braver in another l.	BROO 163:7
all that travel by l.	SWIFT 863:73	Praise the sports of the l.	REID 710:45	cash, everyone knows your l.	ADIGA 8:64
America...heroic, sentimental l.	RABAN 703:4	publishes to every l.	ADDI 7:40	certain mistress of l.	JONS 468:95
away into the silent l.	ROSS 726:41	rich fruitful l.	BLAKE 140:13	Color and bite permeate a l.	SAFI 737:18
best dance e'er cam to the L.	BURNS 180:44	rural virtues leave the l.	GOLD 376:7	confound the l. of all the earth	BIBLE 92:15
best people never l.	MACN 558:7	security of the l.	COVE 249:43	constantly changing l. of politics	SAFI 737:17
brought me in to possess this l.	BIBLE 95:91	She was our l.	FROST 353:15	conveyed...in the best chosen l.	AUST 46:83
by l. and sea	WORD 960:21	Silence ruled this l.	DARK 263:47	countries divided by a common l.	SHAW 811:31
by sea as by l.	GILB 368:28	sun rose and set on their l.	SITT 823:93	deciduous l.	THOM 886:76
clear the l. of evil	KIPL 490:8	than ever before in any l.	HOOV 427:43	define her feelings in l.	HARDY 397:6
clung...to the l.	MOOD 615:52	The l. of my fathers	THOM 884:29	don't use whatever l.	KELM 479:68
cut off Israel out of the l.	BIBLE 97:54	the law of the l.	MAGN 559:26	dramatic words in the English l.	HART 400:70
darkness of the l.	TENN 875:96	there was no l. left	IHIM 445:20	dream of a common l.	RICH 713:5
death's grey l.	SASS 745:83	think of my own native l.	COWP 251:98	enemy of clear l.	ORWE 654:36
doghter of the l. of Camylarde	MALO 562:8	This is the dead l.	ELIOT 318:14	enemy of clear l.	ORWE 655:63
England's green and pleasant l.	BLAKE 141:43	This l. is your l.	GUTH 390:5	English l. is nobody's...property	WALC 916:14
exact survey of the l.	DONNE 293:78	Thou on the l.	SCOTT 753:43	English l. readers	GISC 373:29
exiles from our fathers' l.	GALT 359:54	Thus fares the l.	GOLD 376:5	enlargement of the l.	JOHN 460:70
famine was sore in the l.	BIBLE 93:45	town surrounded by l.	MOORE 616:72	ere we learn the l.	THOR 888:14
fat of the l.	BIBLE 93:46	traveller from an antique l.	SHEL 813:85	every l. even deafanddumb	CUMM 257:58
flourishing culture in our l.	MAO 569:34	truth is a pathless l.	KRIS 499:11	Experience is...larger than l.	RICH 714:10
glorious l. above the sky	HILL 418:56	unto a l. that I will shew thee	BIBLE 92:16	Finality is not the l. of politics	DISR 288:47
glorious l. of ours	FERB 332:66	want to build a better l.	CHRI 223:36	fine flow of l.	RIDGE 715:31
good and bad of every l.	BAIL 55:88	want to free this l.	MARI 571:78	French is not a static l.	HUGO 436:57
happy l.	GOLD 376:4	westward...the l. is bright	CLOU 232:49	from one l. to another	SHEL 816:49
harsh l.'s red and green	HYDE 443:21	what shall this l. produce?	RANS 706:68	fumbling with...English l.	WAUGH 921:7
his hands prepared the dry l.	BOOK 149:30	wide brown l. for me	MACK 553:10	gifted glassblower of l.	HERS 416:20
history of the l.	LONG 535:33	windy sea of l.	MILT 602:85	Great literature is simply l.	POUND 691:12
Ill fares the l.	GOLD 376:98	with my native l.	TENN 876:36	greed wrapped in the l. of love	ARMEY 32:39
in a blatant l.	TENN 876:20	Woe to that l.	SHAK 761:41	inaccessible...except...their l.	FRAME 346:77
in a dry and thirsty l.	BIBLE 101:78	woman is a foreign l.	PATM 669:18	in a room with the English l.	HUTC 441:47

languages

in the English l.	THUR 890:88	universal l.: love, music and sports	MOSES 622:79	lasting more l. than bronze	HORA 430:11
lack of a whole l.	MUIR 623:13	wit in all l.	DRYD 300:19	latch door has a creaking l.	POUND 691:8
l. all nations understand	BEHN 74:17	woman speaks eighteen l.	PARK 663:7	press down the l.	WORD 957:67
L. and knowledge	SULL 859:79	langue au pouvoir de la l.	CIXO 227:41	late always either too l. or too early	SART 744:67
l. an opera is sung in	APPL 30:91	languish l. like exotics	WOLL 954:90	comfort comes too l.	SHAK 805:57
l. concentrating emotion	BRAU 157:86	Relieve my l.	DANI 262:31	coming l. to a performance	ZOLO 970:17
L. does not leave fossils	BRAU 157:82	languor L. cannot be	SHEL 814:96	Dread of being l.!	BETJ 89:48
l. grows decadent, too	VIDAL 912:4	pain or l.	WORD 962:47	five minutes too l.	COWL 250:79
L. grows out of life	SULL 859:78	languors lilies and l. of virtue	SWIN 864:91	L. have I loved you	AUGU 44:27
l. has said that reason	MACL 555:28	lank haggard and l. young man	GILB 369:48	long choosing, and beginning l.	MILT 605:43
l. have the right	KELM 479:69	lanky that l. Yankee finger	CONN 242:83	make sure of not being l.	KIER 486:6
l. he was the lodesterre	LYDG 542:78	lantern Hang a l. on your problem	MATT 582:96	people who are l.	LUCAS 541:48
L. in art	PINT 678:86	hast no l.	JONS 467:71	sit up l.	BIBLE 103:36
L. is a form	LEVI 526:36	l. of Aristotle's brain	RALE 705:46	soon or l.	THOM 885:62
L. is a skin	BART 66:27	l. on the stern	COLE 236:51	unhappy day too l.	SHAK 764:48
L. is only the instrument	JOHN 460:68	with l. and with ladder	STEV 853:72	wakest too l.	SKEL 824:31
L. is the flesh-garment	CARL 200:94	lanterns jaunty gilded l.	GILL 370:77	we have come too l.	LABR 502:6
L. is using us to talk	MATH 581:87	Laocoön L....made different?	EMER 324:66	later l. than you think	SERV 757:36
l. of our feelings	FRIE 351:76	lap brooks, On whose fresh l.	MILT 599:90	Latin Don't quote l.	WELL 929:12
l. of the age	GRAY 383:49	cool flowery l. of earth	ARNO 34:75	from the L. e, 'out'	LEAC 515:22
l. of the heart	POPE 688:7	drop Into thy mother's l.	MILT 606:68	L. America owes its being	VASC 909:29
l. of the horde	MALL 562:99	In thy green l.	GRAY 385:89	L.. Man's natural language	FLAU 339:29
l. that can serve our purposes	MACD 550:41	lap-dogs l.-d....shake	POPE 685:30	more fanatical official than a L.	HAZZ 404:61
l. that is not ours	WITT 951:30	lapidary In l. inscriptions	JOHN 462:42	ne yet of L.	SPEN 839:42
L. was not powerful enough	DICK 278:83	laps tumbling into some men's l.	BACON 50:39	small L., and less Greek	JONS 468:79
l., which is what you use	MERW 589:57	lapse l. of moments is ever	STOWE 856:32	speech as...dignified as L.	QUIL 702:13
law is like the grammar of l.	SACKS 736:4	l. of one lesser	CANM 196:3	Latin America state of emergency has	
learned l.	GIBB 366:3	lapwing Beatrice like a l. runs	SHAK 774:41	existed in L. A.	DEBR 268:56
Life is a foreign l.	MORL 619:37	wanton l.	TENN 871:11	latitude wishes to claim a certain l.	HAWT 402:7
life...under the power of l.	CIXO 227:41	lard as fed with l.	SPEN 840:63	Latium arts into rustic L.	HORA 430:16
Man's natural l.	FLAU 339:29	large l. as life	CARR 205:19	latrine mouth...used as a l.	AMIS 16:29
mobilized the English l.	KENN 481:15	small thing...made l.	TWAIN 903:71	latter l. stems from virtue	HELO 409:54
mobilized the English l.	MURR 627:83	Lariston Lock the door, L.	HOGG 422:41	lattice cried through the l.	BIBLE 95:12
more learning in their [Chinese] l.	JOHN 463:63	lark bisy l., messager of day	CHAU 217:82	laudanum abuse...like l.	STOWE 856:31
most beautiful words in the...l.	JAMES 451:55	jay more precious than the l.	SHAK 762:75	laudate L. Dominum, omnes gentes	BIBLE 133:36
Murky l.	JONG 466:41	l. at break of day arising	SHAK 800:46	laugh And l. as I pass	SHEL 813:75
Music is the universal l.	LONG 535:13	l. at heaven gate	SHAK 803:93	Anything awful makes me l.	LAMB 505:83
must re-invent l.	IRIG 447:54	l....sightless song	TENN 875:99	arms hang down to l.	ELIOT 317:80
My l. fails!	BELL 77:62	l.'s on the wing	BROW 167:9	But I l.	HUGH 434:8
my l. is plain	HARTE 400:72	More tuneable than l.	SHAK 766:18	Dinna mak' me l.	LAUD 511:14
natural l. of all religions	STAEL 842:2	nightingale, and not the l.	SHAK 766:1	do we not l.?	SHAK 769:1
neither speech nor l.	BOOK 148:9	sing as sweetly as the l.	SHAK 770:24	Famous for his l.	FLAU 339:28
no l. but a cry	TENN 874:77	Waked by the l.	SHAK 787:41	heard...a meaning l.	EWART 328:72
No respect for their l.	SHAW 810:93	larks Four L. and a Wren	LEAR 516:27	if I l. at any mortal thing	BYRON 190:16
not...a question of...blood or l.	OBRI 645:61	hear the l. so high	HOUS 431:44	If we didn't l.	LLOYD 532:66
no word in their l.	SWIFT 862:48	imprisoned l.	GRAV 383:40	knows how to l. at himself	MACL 554:20
Numbers...universal l.	WEST 933:93	l....singing the same five notes	CATH 208:85	l. all of the time	LOOS 536:53
obligated to its l.	BROD 160:42	larkspur The l. listens	TENN 876:28	l. and lie	PARK 664:15
Only where there is l.	RICH 713:97	lash bear de l. as well	TRUTH 900:5	l. at all you trembled at	COWP 251:7
our l. fails	WALL 918:59	Why dost thou l. that whore?	SHAK 793:25	l. at him before	NATH 632:99
our l. grows	WALL 918:60	lashes make the l. dark	YEATS 967:30	l. at human actions	SPIN 840:69
Ours is a precarious l.	THUR 891:99	lass A l. unparalleled	SHAK 795:95	l. at...l. with	SPEN 837:11
people...of an hard l.	BIBLE 110:29	Drink to the l.	SHER 817:90	l. broke into a thousand pieces	BARR 65:85
Poetry happens because of l.	OLIV 649:36	every l. a queen	KING 488:48	l., heart	YEATS 965:9
Poetry...through human l.	MALL 562:95	it came with a l.	JAME 449:20	l. is the best pesticide	NABO 628:19
Political l.	ORWE 655:65	l. wi' tousled hair	MACD 549:21	l. like a squadron of cavalry	WODE 952:42
pure rhetoric of a l.	STEV 850:85	lover and his l.	SHAK 780:21	l. like parrots	SHAK 768:45
refine our l.	JOHN 459:57	my bonie l.	BURNS 178:8	l. me to scorn	BIBLE 99:42
refusal of l. is a death	BART 66:24	my bonie l.	BURNS 180:50	l. No man to scorn	BIBLE 113:85
remains of the English l.	COUP 248:31	solitary Highland L.	WORD 960:18	l. of superiority	GREE 386:28
room for but one l.	ROOS 725:23	lasses honest men and bonny l.	BURNS 179:20	l. on that particular day	TRAV 896:91
same forms and the same l.	FLAU 339:21	L. a-lilting before the dawn	ELLI 322:25	l. to scorn	SHAK 780:15
Slang is a l.	SAND 742:31	lassie Bony l. will ye go	BURNS 178:1	l. uproariously in youth	BROO 162:96
sociologists...I do not speak their l.	DYSON 309:59	love a l., a bonnie	LAUD 511:15	L. where we must	POPE 686:71
sophisticated use of l.	KUNI 501:40	love she's but a l.	BURNS 178:14	l. with me, or at me	STER 848:22
sorry when any l. is lost	JOHN 462:31	Never mind my grace, l.	SCOTT 754:61	lips that l. and hide	SWIN 863:84
speak the same foreign l.	WILD 943:36	service to my bonie l.	BURNS 178:8	man cannot make him l.	SHAK 773:95
strange l. all I know	LAND 507:33	wae my l. by my side	LAUD 511:16	more ridiculous than a ridiculous l.	CATU 209:8
suicides have a special l.	SEXT 758:47	last childhood does not l.	AMIS 17:61	not a thing to l. to scorn	SHAK 780:15
sure in l. strange she said	KEATS 476:2	cobbler stick to his l.	APEL 29:71	nothing more unbecoming...to l.	CONG 240:36
taught her l.	SHAK 803:13	great thing is to l.	HEMI 410:74	Poetry is what makes me l.	THOM 884:25
The l. plain	COWP 250:89	here it is at l.	JAMES 451:56	quick to l. at everything	BEAU 70:5
They are, after all, a l.	BANKS 61:17	l. best friend	SOUT 835:56	sitteth in the heavens shall l.	BIBLE 99:27
unvisionary l. of farm, city and love	ENGLE 326:16	l. of all he was seen of me	BIBLE 127:55	the ability to l.	HUMP 439:12
use in measured l.	TENN 873:58	l. of all the Bards	SCOTT 752:9	those whom I love...make me l.	AUDEN 44:13
Words are...from a defunct l.	CIXO 227:46	l. one is as good	HEMI 409:69	way people look and l.	WOOLF 955:12
world understands my l.	HAYDN 402:22	l. person to say anything	SAKI 739:68	laughed Full well they l.	GOLD 376:1
writers...make their l. convey more	CONN 242:4	l. shall be first	BIBLE 118:20	I l. him out of patience	SHAK 794:62
languages dictate the l. in which	BALL 60:86	l. shall be first	BIBLE 188:22	l. and suffered at my side	SASS 745:89
Do you know L.	CARR 205:25	l. to lay the Old aside	POPE 685:22	speck ter be l. at	HARR 399:50
exchanged...in our respective l.	COOK 245:67	l....will go over very quickly	EISE 314:98	When he l.	AUDEN 43:88
Fluent in all the l.	CURN 259:88	l. word on nothing	HUGO 438:90	laughing boughs do l. blossoms bear	SPEN 838:39
instructed in all l., living and dead	DICK 278:55	One of the l.	UPDI 906:23	cannot forbear l.	PEPYS 673:92
three hundred l. are spoken	LIVI 532:60	put your family l.	HUMP 439:10	l. in the diners	SAND 742:15
three or four l.	SHAK 785:80	She is the l. of lands	HOPE 427:57	L., quaffing, and unthinking	DRYD 304:56
thunder In such lovely l.	LAWR 514:79	sung her first and l.	GIBB 367:7	most fun...without l.	ALLEN 14:95
two l. in Canada	SAINT 738:47	the l. act crowns the play	QUAR 701:6	so filled with L. Gas	TRAV 896:91

laws

waked herself with l.	SHAK 774:33
when I am l. at anyone	BEER 73:76
laughing stock l. s. of children	SIDN 820:52
laughs crowd l. with you always	VIDOR 913:6
get l. without falling	WISD 950:10
he l. longest who l. last	MASE 580:65
he who l. last	ALEX 12:59
irritating l.	GILB 369:60
l. with a harvest	JERR 455:46
world l. with you	WILC 939:43
laughter alone with his l.	KAFKA 472:8
better to write of l.	RABE 703:8
bitterness in our l.	EMER 325:83
faculty of l.	ADDI 7:44
feast is made for l.	BIBLE 106:32
girls' thin l.	RICK 715:27
'Homeric l.'	FLAU 339:28
illiberal and so ill-bred, as audible l.	CHES 219:40
inexhaustible source of l.	TOLS 894:54
kind of l. people laugh at	MCIL 553:95
l. at their quaint opinions	MILT 605:35
L. is a reward	CHAN 214:5
L. is pleasant	PEAC 671:52
l., It is mad	BIBLE 105:13
L. need not be cut out	THUR 891:7
l. of a fool	BIBLE 106:21
Let us have…mirth and l.	BYRON 190:7
listens to your sweet l.	CATU 209:9
love and l.	GORD 378:54
no time for mirth and l.	ADE 7:59
Our sincerest l.	SHEL 814:97
peals of l.…round thee	POPE 687:98
produce l.	JOHN 462:40
scattered l. in the rear	KAUF 474:41
seismic with l.	BARK 63:52
senators burst with l.	AUDEN 43:88
The l. of man	THUR 891:96
turns herself to l.	SPEN 839:44
under running l.	THOM 886:81
weeping and with l.	MACA 546:50
With mirth and l.	SHAK 768:69
laundries Land of l.	BETJ 88:28
laundry any first-class l.	LEAC 515:21
goes into the l.	KIPL 492:50
Laune dragons of L. and Lane	ORAH 652:90
Laura if L. had been Petrach's wife	BYRON 190:12
Rose-cheeked L.	CAMP 195:75
laurel l. for the perfect prime	ROSS 726:40
l., meed of mighty conquerors	SPEN 838:20
laurels l. to paeans	CICE 227:35
'Tis sweet to win…one's l.	BYRON 189:97
worth all your l.	BYRON 190:30
ye l., and once more	MILT 599:82
lava walk on the l.…while it was cooling	PATE 669:14
lavatory men-servants' l.	WAUGH 923:70
lavender L. water tinged with pink	LEAR 516:39
Lavinian Italy, at its L. shore	VIRG 913:11
law above the l.	CAM 193:40
All things, by a l. divine	SHEL 813:78
almost a l.	WELLS 930:32
Angel, it's a l. of nature	LACL 503:38
basic l. of economics	HARR 399:60
bondage known to our l.	MILL 592:16
both the l. and the gospel	JONS 468:89
break Diana's l.	POPE 685:35
breeds without the L.	KIPL 491:17
brilliance is needed in the l.	MORT 621:65
business of the l.	MACL 555:43
care for your l.	TRUM 900:94
come to destroy the l.	BIBLE 114:30
Conservatives, as being by the l.	MILL 591:5
Creation's final l.	TENN 874:71
Creation's final l.	TENN 874:80
criminal l. is no use	SHAW 809:83
Custom that is before all l.	DANI 262:34
dinna ken muckle about the l.	SCOTT 753:59
Every l. is a contract	SELD 756:7
Every l. is an evil	BENT 82:90
first is l.	DRYD 303:12
fulfilled the l.	BIBLE 126:30
game within the view of the l.	LEAC 515:19
goal of every system of l.	ROUS 729:12
God is thy l.	MILT 604:6
God's l. thet fetters	LOWE 539:6
good of the people is the chief l.	CICE 227:29
hang all the l. and the prophets	BIBLE 118:26
he whom l. calls yours	DRYD 301:57
higher l. in journalism	LIPP 530:36
Hofstadter's L.	HOFS 422:35
Ignorance of the l.	SELD 756:8
in his l. doth he meditate	BIBLE 99:25
internal equivalent of…rule of l.	EDEN 311:31
invariable l. of the newspaper	DANA 261:26
it is of no force in l.	COKE 234:95
judgments of the English l.	SYNGE 865:23
keepeth the l., happy is he	BIBLE 105:6
Keep ye the l.	KIPL 490:8
know the l. since I have spent	MILI 591:91
l. that needs to change	CAM 193:42
l. cannot make a man love	KING 486:23
l. has very wisely given	JOHN 461:6
l. hath not been dead	SHAK 787:55
l. is a ass	DICK 278:72
L. is a bottomless pit	ARBU 30:1
L. is naturally founded	MONT 614:39
l. is such an ass	CHAP 215:23
l. is the most powerful	GIRA 372:25
L. is the true embodiment	GILB 369:50
l. not supported by the people	HUMP 439:9
l. of academic life	LODGE 534:99
l. [of competition]…hard	CARN 202:48
l. of death	ANON 23:88
l. of God	MARG 570:67
l. of love	SCEVE 746:16
l. of Moses is harsh	MORE 618:14
l. of nature	HOOK 427:39
L. of the jungle	JUMB 471:43
L. of the jungle	KIPL 490:7
L. of the jungle	KIPL 490:4
l. of the musical world	WHAR 934:11
L. of the Yukon	SERV 757:33
l. pervading all nature	HARDY 397:21
l. seems like a sort of maze	MORT 621:66
l.'s their will	SHAK 798:80
l. to weed it out	BACON 50:62
l. unto themselves	BIBLE 125:4
l.…like a…black cobweb	WEBS 926:41
love is liberty, and nature, l.	POPE 686:87
love is the fulfilling of the l.	BIBLE 126:31
love thy l.	BIBLE 103:30
Men…have L. for their god	PLATO 681:48
moral l. within	KANT 473:26
mysterious l., true source	MILT 604:10
nine points of the l.	ANON 22:70
nine-tenths of the l. of chivalry	SAYE 746:7
no l. if we were to invoke one code	EISE 314:99
no l. to prevent us	SHAW 807:20
No man can point to any l.	DOUG 296:27
no right to transgress the l.	DOST 294:89
nor the world's l.	SHAK 766:12
not according to the l.	BIBLE 98:89
one l., one element	TENN 875:3
Order is heaven's first l.	POPE 687:88
Party of l. and order	BLAIR 138:49
People crushed by l.	BURKE 175:28
prayers for the observers of his l.	BACON 52:92
president…incapable of enforcing the l.	MARC 569:54
principle of the English l.	DICK 281:72
prisoners…I'll find them l.	MACQ 558:13
Prisons are built with stones of L.	BLAKE 140:99
prohibited by l.	LEVIN 525:28
protection of the English l.	MANS 568:14
purlieus of the l.	TENN 874:90
Raped by…alien l.	WRIG 963:71
rational study of the l.	HOLM 424:86
rebellion against the existing l.	SHAW 809:86
religions established by l.	PAINE 660:35
Religious l. is like…grammar	SACKS 736:4
rigid l. pursues	JOHN 459:43
rule by l. and rule by whim	DOUG 295:21
saved me from the l. of sin	WESL 932:65
scarecrow of the l.	SHAK 787:50
shatterday till the fear of the L.	JOYCE 470:37
should become a universal l.	KANT 473:23
simple that has lost its l.	LOWE 540:30
So long as the l. considers	STOWE 856:28
sources of international l.	UNIT 905:9
sufficient to keep His L.	CRUZ 256:40
suppressed by federal l.	HOOV 427:46
Take the moral l.	STEV 849:65
that is the l.	BAUD 68:67
the l. of the land	MAGN 559:26
The l. of the survival	SUMN 859:82
The l.'s delay	TWAIN 902:63
The l. of unintended consequences	FERG 333:81
those by l. protected	BURNS 177:79
truant in the l.	SHAK 759:76
usual l. of nature	HARV 400:78
very good l. for all that	SCOTT 753:42
violated any l.	LOVE 538:89
we're l. reformers	HUMP 439:13
What l. have I broken?	SITT 823:93
where no l.…no transgression	BIBLE 125:7
whole of the L.	CROW 256:36
Who to himself is l.	CHAP 214:16
windward of the l.	CHUR 224:57
windy side of the l.	SHAK 786:18
Would it be a reasonable l.	SMITH 827:85
lawbreakers We're not l.	HUMP 439:13
law-courts regard the l. c.	INGR 446:37
lawful All things are l. for me	BIBLE 126:46
L. as eating	SHAK 800:32
not l. for me to do	BIBLE 118:22
lawless Tribeless, l., homeless	HOMER 425:6
lawlessness l. of something simple	LOWE 540:30
lawn chocolate can't mow the l.	BROW 167:7
l. about the shoulders	HERR 416:17
L. as white as driven snow	SHAK 800:25
l. tennis…and Handel's Messiah	SHAW 810:27
L. Tennyson	JOYCE 470:25
Out on the l. I lie	AUDEN 43:92
rivulets…through the l.	TENN 873:52
to rake the l.	UPDI 906:28
twice a saint in l.	POPE 687:94
vomit on somebody's…l.	BOYD 153:10
wet bird-haunted English l.	ARNO 34:77
lawns fair with orchard l.	TENN 878:87
l. and avenues	KIPL 492:67
level green l.	GILL 370:79
mowers on suburban l.	RICK 714:27
Russet l. and fallows grey	MILT 597:45
satyrs grazing on the l.	MARL 573:14
law-religions feature of all l.-r.	PAINE 660:35
Lawrence D H L.'s 'Kangaroo'	STEW 854:94
D. H. L. was right	GIBB 367:11
keep D.H. L. poor	BRAD 155:36
laws all the l. of Nature	THOR 888:24
as for Thy l.	HERB 413:60
Bad l. are the worst sort of tyranny	BURKE 175:31
bad or obnoxious l.	GRANT 381:9
base l. of servitude	DRYD 300:30
brain may devise l.	SHAK 769:76
customs…are the l. of nature	SHAW 807:10
do anything the l. permit	MONT 614:43
dole unequal l.	TENN 870:97
drama's l.	JOHN 459:44
eluded L.	JOHN 459:40
enforces, and breaks l.	LEGU 520:12
except general l. of nature	HUGO 436:53
explained by a few simple l.	BROWN 164:33
Farewell, Love, and all thy l.	WYATT 963:87
good l. should make	JONS 469:52
government of l.	ADAMS 5:98
If there are…iron l. of history	EAGL 309:2
In their l.…one clause	RABE 704:17
l. and customs…evolved	POWE 693:59
l. and sets mantraps	LOWE 539:2
L. are like cobwebs	SWIFT 861:23
L.…are not our Life	CARL 201:17
l. bound in calf	DOSP 294:86
L. grind the poor	GOLD 376:87
l. of God, the l. of man	HOUS 432:67
l. of God will be suspended	SHAW 810:9
L. of Nature cannot account	MILL 592:10
l. of possibility	REDON 709:23
L. of Production	MILL 591:93
l. of prose writing	HEMI 410:83
l. of space and time	CORY 247:11
l. of the fallen world	BLOOM 143:66
l. or kings can cause	GOLD 376:88
l.…silent in time of war	CICE 227:30
l. were made to be	NORTH 641:59
l. were then most sure	MARL 573:8
majestic equality of l.	FRAN 347:89
makers, and their l. approve	DRYD 303:17
more we know of the l.	HARDY 397:25
neither the l. made	JOHN 456:73
new code of l.	ADAMS 4:71
No doubt there are l.	HEINE 407:16
not governed by the same l.	DISR 288:34

lawsuits

nothing in the l. of value	MILL 591:95	L....do the right things	BENN 81:83	of the opinion with the l.	CONG 240:23
nothing to do with the l.	HORS 430:26	l. of white-mouse faction	MACD 550:39	one thing we l.	READ 708:95
of breach of l.	SURR 860:2	l. who make them suffer	SIHA 821:66	who has l. well how to obey	KEMP 480:77
offended...thy holy l.	BOOK 146:32	only l. Labour loves	HARR 399:52	**learning** accuse him to have wanted l.	DRYD 300:20
one of my l. of Physics	OATES 643:7	scrupulous...are not the l.	CONR 244:44	a' the l. I desire	BURNS 177:70
rape us with...their l.	FREN 350:53	**leadership** men do not approach to l.	BEVE 90:61	attain good l.	ASCH 37:53
skulked behind the l.	DRYD 302:75	not practising l.	THAT 881:74	Beauty and the lust for l.	BEER 73:84
Technology breaks the l.	OGDEN 648:3	put forward for the l.	HESE 416:28	better than l. a lot of things	HERN 415:94
things the l. of life	RUSK 733:99	Reagan...wasn't without l. ability	ONEI 651:77	can't be alwayth a l.	DICK 282:82
Useless l. weaken	MONT 615:46	stuff of political l.	WILS 948:73	complexity of l.	JOVA 469:13
Where l. end	PITT 679:6	**leading** can't tell who's l.	SNAG 831:72	design career is a process of l.	BELL 76:48
whether L. be right	WILDE 942:21	L. School, First-rate School	WAUGH 923:53	Hibernian l.	ROCH 719:9
who writes the nation's l.	PERE 674:17	l. the Conservatives	HESE 416:29	highest estimation of l.	SIDN 820:52
women themselves help to make l.	ANTH 29:74	with most of his l. ladies	NIVEN 639:29	just enough of l. to misquote	BYRON 187:25
lawsuits L. make poverty	ANON 21:55	**leads** dark place where it l.	JONG 466:29	know without l.	INGR 446:40
lawyer client is fain to hire a l.	BUTL 184:62	**leaf** Are you the l.	YEATS 966:27	l. and blundering will live on	SAND 742:23
I am only a l.	BIRK 136:17	aspes l. she gan to quake	CHAU 216:62	l. is...dangerous	POPE 685:19
important attribute of a l.	KENN 482:40	burning l.; prithee	MILL 592:18	L., that cobweb of the brain	BUTL 185:76
l. and politician and a heretic	MENC 586:89	I were like the l.	SWIN 864:4	l. what not to say	BAIN 55:90
l. could not have been heard	JONS 467:55	last red l.	TENN 873:64	let all l. in	ANON 21:58
l. has no business	JOHN 462:29	l. also shall not wither	BIBLE 99:25	light of l.	RALE 705:46
l. interprets the truth	GIRA 372:25	l. of grass is no less than	WHIT 937:92	lost in their collected l.	HAWT 401:2
l.'s dream of heaven	BUTL 186:12	l. still in October	FLET 341:54	men with book l.	RAMOS 705:50
l.'s truth is not Truth	THOR 888:19	l. that lies rotting	CARL 201:7	more l. in their [Chinese] language	JOHN 463:63
l....swallowed up with business	WALT 920:95	l., the bud, the flower	SPEN 838:33	much l. doth make thee mad	BIBLE 125:99
l. trying to pick a smart jury	BAIL 55:84	Love every l.	DOST 294:94	Of such deep l.	SPEN 839:42
l. with a briefcase can steal	PUZO 701:5	night that numbers the l.	STEV 850:96	on scraps of l. doat	YOUNG 968:54
not, what a l. tells me I may do	BURKE 175:18	November's l. is red	SCOTT 752:18	O this l.	SHAK 761:61
seditious Middle Temple l.	CHUR 225:79	olive l. pluckt off	BIBLE 92:10	process of l. is accompanied	WILD 943:53
trial with a l.	THOM 887:91	outline of l.	WILL 946:9	Reading is the basics for all l.	BUSH 182:7
When a l. cashes in?	SAND 742:19	the sere, the yellow l.	SHAK 798:69	tough time l. how	KENN 482:38
lawyers coachload of l.	HUNT 439:18	Where the dead l. fell	KEATS 477:29	Wear your l., like your watch	CHES 219:39
How l. make work	OATES 643:13	**league** believe in a L. system	ATTL 40:24	where l. may be...impossible	OAKE 642:2
kill all the l.	SHAK 759:96	devotion to this great L. of Nations	CHAM 212:57	**learnt** smash...everything he had l.	ORTE 652:2
l. find out...Litigious men	DONNE 291:28	hadna sailed a l., a l.	BALL 58:58	what has been l. has been forgotten	SKIN 825:46
l. who don't care	RENO 711:49	Half a l. onward	TENN 875:11	**leas** In lusty l. at liberty	WYATT 963:85
Poor l....dear	WHIS 934:23	keep a l. till death	SHAK 765:58	**lease** l. for a year	ANOU 28:60
Woe unto you, l.!	BIBLE 121:84	L. and Cup double	BUSBY 182:93	summer's l.	SHAK 800:37
lay from her melodious l.	SHAK 784:58	L. of Nations	MACD 550:59	without any predictable l.	KOSI 699:2
l. it on so thick	BUTL 185:97	L. of Nations with an absolute	LEES 519:4	**leash** Mankind Under The L.	DISCH 287:8
L. on, Macduff	SHAK 798:78	smaller but older l.	CHAM 212:57	**least** l. of all saints	BIBLE 127:87
unpremeditated l.	SCOTT 752:10	**leaking** who was doing the l.	REAG 709:14	Where the l....control	WORD 956:52
layman comprehension of the l.	GOWE 380:81	**leal** land o' the l.	NAIR 629:33	**leather** case me in l.	SHAK 762:92
lays constructing tribal l.	KIPL 490:3	**lean** dying lady, l. and pale	SHEL 816:67	Gave up...his l., wax and all	EGAN 313:65
Lazarus certain beggar named L.	BIBLE 121:96	l. and hungry look	SHAK 776:12	l....to a shoemaker	WAUGH 924:84
Come forth, L.!	JOYCE 470:26	L. In	SAND 742:37	little bit of l.	MITF 610:50
l. in his bosom	BIBLE 121:97	l. over too far	THUR 890:77	real l. ball	UTTL 907:50
lazy ignominiously l.	SAND 743:39	**leap** giant l. forward	ARMS 33:51	**leave** For who would l.	JOHN 459:42
L. and silly	SITW 823:10	it were an easy l.	SHAK 771:37	I don't want to l. Manhattan	KOCH 495:24
l., long, lascivious reign	DEFOE 269:72	l. over the rude facts	RABAN 703:4	l. her far away	KEATS 476:89
l. people...invented the wheel	WALE 917:30	**leaping** l., and praising God	BIBLE 124:74	l. out of the definition	KING 488:60
responsibility...to be l.	PALEY 661:56	**leaps** moves in mighty l.	AYRES 48:9	l. some skin on	KHRU 485:93
LBJ All the Way with L.	HOLT 424:90	**Lear** King l....closest you can get	BUEC 172:41	not l. in San Francisco	HART 399:64
Hey, hey, L.!	ANON 25:55	**lea-rig** meet thee on the l.-r.	BURNS 180:46	shall be happy to l.	BAUD 68:68
lea On fair Kirkconnell l.!	BALL 59:63	**learn** can't l. architecture	JOHN 458:30	take my l. of the Jew	SHAK 769:89
On yonder l.	BURNS 180:60	constantly l. more	SOLO 833:2	will take my l. of you	SHAK 782:82
The sun has left the l.	SCOTT 754:69	enough...know how to l.	ADAMS 5:93	will ye l. me thus?	HERB 414:84
this pleasant l.	WORD 961:30	for life...that we l.	SENE 757:24	**leaves** amongst the shady l.	SPEN 839:39
lead don't l. by pointing	KESEY 483:66	From all I can l.	GALS 358:47	Autumn fills thy lap with l.	COLL 238:77
Go down like lumps of l.	HODG 421:22	it is up to us to l.	RABAN 703:2	before the l. have fallen	WILH 943:56
gold wes changyd in to l.	ANON 21:44	l. all the Law	KIPL 490:4	between The sleeping l.	COWP 251:12
heart of l.	POPE 688:35	L. even from Novels	WELLS 930:24	burning of the l.	BINY 135:2
hot as molten l.	SHAK 772:65	l. how we began this war	PRIE 695:86	covered up in l.	KEATS 478:45
l. from the back	MAND 565:60	l. in suffering	SHEL 812:63	crowned with calm l.	SWIN 864:96
L. us, Heavenly Father	EDME 312:55	l. so little	DAVI 264:76	dazzling through the l.	TENN 869:83
looked to the other to take the l.	SMUTS 831:71	l. to love by loving	HUXL 442:86	deliquescent l. of paper	ANDR 18:77
not the l. dog	ANON 27:25	l. to pray	HERB 414:89	Falls like the l. in October	FULL 356:88
pound in l. to your marriage	MIDD 590:71	l. what not to play	GILL 370:85	famous harmony of l.	YEATS 965:6
scald like molten l.	SHAK 793:30	l. while they teach	SENE 757:23	flutter far more, than l. do	CENN 211:44
leaden if I use the l. ones	BELL 76:53	l....who He is	SCHW 751:94	fond of handling the l.	SHER 817:72
leader commons...want their l.	SHAK 759:90	let's l. not to know	CRUZ 256:39	golden dead l.	LEVE 525:23
fanatic is a great l....just entering	BROUN 163:19	men do not l. very much	HUXL 442:96	June...in green l.	SPEN 839:62
first practical l.	WILDE 940:49	Parents l. a lot	SPARK 835:63	laughing l. of the tree	SWIN 863:84
l. cut from whipcord	MANC 564:47	she may l.	SHAK 770:6	l. and flowers do cover	WEBS 926:36
l. of the Conservative Party	BEAV 71:25	To l. and labour	BOOK 148:30	l. are green	ANON 20:32
L. of the Opposition	DISR 288:63	We live and l.	POMF 684:9	l. are green	ANON 22:66
No l. deserves	WEI 927:66	We live and l.	TILM 891:17	l. dead Are driven	SHEL 813:79
no l., faction, party or 'class'	OAKE 642:2	what you l....not studying	CONA 239:11	l. grow on the tree	YEATS 965:3
One realm, one people, one l.	ANON 24:16	Where there is much to l.	MILT 600:4	l. of myrtle	MARL 574:41
rarest...a Labor l.	MCFA 551:64	you shall l. nothing	HUXL 443:3	l. of the tree...for the healing of	
such a man was L. of the House	DISR 288:45	**learned** devil...on the side of the l.	FRAN 347:85	the nations	BIBLE 132:28
The l. must know	RAND 706:56	Entrepreneurship can be l.	DRUC 299:6	l. to a tree	KEATS 476:79
young, bald L. of the Opposition	KINN 488:66	For I have l.	WORD 956:55	Like that of l.	HOMER 425:2
leaders believe in magical l.	NEWM 635:52	l. are cowards	DRYD 301:62	lisp of l.	SWIN 863:82
choose our l. on...basis of their		L. men...do many times fail	BACON 49:22	long l. cover me	SWIN 863:88
reading	BROD 160:40	l....to be content	BIBLE 128:6	noise among the l.	KEATS 475:62
continue being l. in the world	IACO 444:3	marries...hasn't l. much	STEIN 845:74	only l. me fifty more	HOUS 431:34

letters

on Severn snow the l.	HOUS 431:47	foundation of…l.	BENT 82:88	**leopard** l. his spots?	BIBLE 110:19
past…like the l. of a book	WOOLF 955:11	frame its l. upon…justice	PEEL 672:67	l. on a branch-strained	MOORE 617:89
sewed fig l. together	BIBLE 91:93	L.'s sov'reign pow'rs	BURNS 178:96	l. shall lie down with the kid	BIBLE 108:62
Shatter your l.	MILT 599:82	strength to influence l.	MURR 627:84	whiff of a snow l.	CHAT 216:52
shows his hoar l.	SHAK 784:57	**legislative** important l. actions	JEVO 455:55	**leopards** Lions make l. tame	SHAK 764:31
spear through the dead l.	MANS 567:3	l. power	GIBB 366:91	three white l.	ELIOT 319:25
Tawny are the l.	RANS 706:68	**legislators** unacknowledged l.	SHEL 816:53	**leper** if he were a l. of old	PARN 665:46
tender l. of hopes	SHAK 805:52	**legislature** constitution of the l.	MILL 591:4	**lepers** cleanse the l.	BIBLE 116:67
the falling l.	SMART 826:68	interference of the l.	RICA 712:81	l. are cleansed	BIBLE 116:76
The riverbed…half full of l.	HEAN 405:76	l. of this country	PITT 679:10	**leprosy** not l. or tuberculosis	THER 882:81
those barren l.	WORD 957:57	l. was animated by a sincere desire	PEEL 672:67	scant as hair in l.	BROW 168:34
thou among the l.	KEATS 478:43	**Legree** makes L. a bachelor	CHES 219:32	**LeRoy** Baby L. with an ice pick	ROST 727:72
to some, l. free to all	MILT 604:9	**legs** animal with four back l.	LECA 518:72	**Lesbia** L. with her sparrow	MILL 592:21
Uneasily the l. fall	PURDY 700:85	asure were his l.	CHAU 217:98	My sweetest L.	CAMP 195:72
What if my l. are falling	SHEL 813:83	chess with arms and l.	BARZ 67:41	**lesbians** performed on l.	TYNAN 904:8
yellow drifts Of withered l.	ARNO 36:25	could never have stood upon his l.	DICK 279:7	**less** do more with l.	FULL 355:74
yellow l., or none	SHAK 801:62	Dogs with broken l.	PATC 668:7	expect l. of them	JOHN 464:91
leave-taking It is not worth l.-t.	SHAK 795:94	Four l. good	ORWE 654:47	in the l., foul profanation	SHAK 787:59
leaving Dear World, I am l.	SAND 742:38	good for your l.	SCHU 749:72	l. a man knows, the more sure he is	CARY 207:68
his life…the l. of it	SHAK 796:11	he pulls the l. of his dreams	THOM 884:36	l. in this than meets the eye	BANK 61:11
L. reminds us	FORD 343:12	His l. bestrid the ocean	SHAK 795:88	L. is a bore	VENT 910:53
prevent them from l.	KENN 481:23	His l., perhaps, were shorter	STRA 856:40	l. is more	PART 666:57
leavings sacrifice…of the devil's l.	POPE 686:56	l. go first	FRAY 349:35	l. than 'arf o' that	KIPL 489:90
Lebanon cedared L.	KEATS 477:24	l. ungainly huddled	SASS 745:90	l. than themselves	TESS 880:20
Irish…as the Shiites in L.	OROU 652:92	l. were such Diana shows	HERR 415:8	Not a Penny L.	ARCH 30:4
Leben L. ist Nur ein Moment	SCHI 747:29	more to marriage than four bare l.	DAVI 265:81	The l. seen	WILD 943:52
Mehr als das L.	SCHI 747:31	no l.…no chance	ANON 24:26	The l. there was to see	DELI 272:45
lechery L., l., still	SHAK 787:44	not for your bad l.	ELIZ 322:5	You mean you can't take l.	CARR 203:72
lecteur hypocrite l.!	ELIOT 318:98	open my l.	HILL 418:64	**lesser** l. life shall be as the greater	GORD 378:54
lecture classic l.	TENN 872:32	recuvver the use of his l.	DICK 278:80	Of two evils the l. should	KEMP 480:82
twilight from the l.	STEV 850:84	same old l.	GIRO 373:28	**lesson** final l. in…despair	POE 683:91
lecturers l. shouldn't be wasted	ZELD 969:4	see my l. when I take my boots off	DICK 280:36	l. of life	EMER 325:92
lectures comes to hear your l.	BRAD 154:32	slimy things did crawl with l.	COLE 235:13	l. to all of us men	AMIN 16:28
l. & my poetry	BERR 87:3	strongest l. in Pontefract	BETJ 89:42	l. to be learned	MILL 594:86
lecturing experience of popular l.	HUXL 443:11	two perfectly good l.	ROOS 724:10	l. we learn from life	FORD 342:87
lederhosen Metaphysical l.	ENRI 326:21	Two vast and trunkless l.	SHEL 813:85	mankind at least one l.	MUMF 625:36
lee between windward and l.	SWIN 864:16	uglier a man's l. are	WELLS 930:32	No l. seems to be so deeply inculcated	SALI 740:89
dragons of Laune…and L.	ORAH 652:90	under his huge l.	SHAK 776:9	paradoxical l.	GLEI 374:48
leek l. is the asparagus	FRAN 347:88	walking on its hinder l.	JOHN 461:3	profited by the l.	PALM 661:69
leeks eyes were green as l.	SHAK 768:50	walls of spiders' l.	DRAY 299:1	Satire is a l.	NABO 628:17
leer assent with civil l.	POPE 687:3	Wooden l. are not inherited	CONK 242:79	still harder l.!	PORT 690:79
fascinating l.	GILB 369:56	you have between your l.	BEEC 73:71	**lessons** first l.	GREER 387:43
lees l. left by Bismarck	GREY 388:60	**Leibniz** L. never married	FONT 342:78	give l. to the public	DIDE 285:68
le Fey third sister, Morgan l. F.	MALO 562:3	**leisure** At l. married	CONG 240:31	history, what l. it might teach us!	COLE 236:51
left better to be l. than never…loved	CONG 241:62	better pastime for their l.	WELLS 930:37	learn'd l. from	WHIT 938:15
Keep your l. hand high	ONEI 651:80	disguised l. are regarded	MISH 609:19	l.…lessen from day to day	CARR 203:77
l. hand is my thinking hand	HEPW 412:30	Increased means and increased l.	DISR 288:59	l. of historical experience	KISS 493:84
l. the room	GROS 389:80	iron…polish it at l.	DRYD 304:36	l. they might have drawn	HEGEL 406:8
Let them be l.	HOPK 429:84	l. answers l.	SHAK 788:79	most important of all the l.	HUXL 442:96
liberal middle class will shift to the l.	EAGL 309:2	l. of study	GERB 365:64	your l. never be forgotten	WALL 918:50
not allowing his l. wing to see	ASQU 38:94	l. ruined great kings	CATU 209:10	**lethargy** l. hath seized him	MASS 581:77
slightly l. of centre	FRYE 354:58	l. to bother about	SHAW 810:2	**Lethe** if no L. flows beneath	RANS 707:71
The L. doesn't even have	BERL 85:54	live at more l.	MONT 613:22	L.-wards had sunk	KEATS 478:41
left behind half its people are l. b.	CLIN 231:33	Men…detest at l.	BYRON 190:22	**Lethean** drunken of things L.	SWIN 864:99
left-guard play l.-g. for the Colts	BRES 158:2	monotony, work or l.	POMP 684:12	**letter** deal by speech than by l.	BACON 53:31
leg here I leave my second l.	HOOD 426:20	repeat at l.	CABE 191:3	good face is a l. of recommendation	ADDI 6:30
literary man—with a wooden l.	DICK 283:14	repent at l.	CONG 240:30	had a l. from her	LEVE 525:20
sell his wooden l.	DICK 279:19	reputability to the gentleman of l.	VEBL 910:46	if this l. speed	SHAK 792:88
which l. went after which	CRAS 254:88	take an hour's l.	STARK 843:24	I had written him a l.	PATE 669:13
legacy I left a l. of shame	MADO 558:18	wisdom…by opportunity of l.	BIBLE 113:9	l. from his wife	CARR 206:32
No l. is so rich	SHAK 791:64	**LeMay** Bombs away with Curtis L.	ANON 25:59	l. killeth, but the spirit giveth life	BIBLE 127:65
legal hasn't exactly got a l. mind	BETJ 88:32	**lemon** in a squeezing of a l.	GOLD 376:12	lone l. from a young man	BERR 87:2
judge in the l. and moral sense	DEWEY 276:20	squeezed as a l. is squeezed	GEDD 362:26	made this l. longer	PASC 668:95
l. and material hindrances	WOLF 952:60	the Dome is a l.	TOYN 895:80	Next to a l. from home	DOOL 294:83
l. and moral responsibility	HAYD 402:23	with a slice of l.	FLEM 340:42	See what a large l.	BIBLE 127:84
l. gentleman who rescues your estate	BROU 163:16	**lend** If thou wilt l. this money	SHAK 769:86	thou unnecessary l.	SHAK 792:97
plethora of l. requirements	BIRNS 136:21	L. less than thou owest	SHAK 792:91	uncertain process of l.-writing	ELIOT 315:14
legality taint of l.	KNOX 495:17	**lender** Neither a borrower nor a l. be	SHAK 781:53	you received…a l. from me	STEE 844:39
legend bloody tough being a l.	ATKI 40:17	**lendeth** l. unto the Lord	BIBLE 105:85	**lettering** stripped of its l.	FRAN 348:7
fables in the l.	BACON 51:78	**length** drags its dreary l.	DICK 281:56	**letters** all l.…should be free and easy	OSBO 655:83
I'm now a l.	BOLT 145:15	nothing…but my body's l.	SHAK 760:17	allured to l.	STEE 844:50
l. of the Gael	RUSS 735:42	of fabulously reptilian l.	LEWIS 527:68	answer 20,000 l. a year	CART 207:57
past exudes l.	MALA 562:88	poem of immeasurable l.	POUND 691:96	faint gold l.	UTTL 907:50
legends accepted economic l.	GALB 357:17	thou giv'st line, and l.	VAUG 909:38	fair words…in foulest l.?	SHAK 773:96
aged l. say	ROSS 726:61	thumbs vary in l.	SHAW 810:23	graven with diamonds in l. plain	WYATT 963:88
legion aunts and uncles were l.	SHAW 811:33	What it Lacks in L.	FROST 353:14	l. at the end of an address	DOSP 294:86
L.: for we are many	BIBLE 119:55	**Lenin** done to death by L.	CHUR 224:70	l. mingle souls	DONNE 292:47
L. of Honour	TWAIN 902:47	L. was right	KEYN 484:71	l., soft interpreters	PRIOR 696:2
l. of the unremarked	SAFI 737:22	L.…would say the same	ZHIV 970:10	like individual l.	UPDI 906:28
refuse the L. d'Honneur	SATIE 746:6	ought to remain of L.	RODC 721:43	like to write l.?	HEMI 409:62
legions give me back my l.	AUGU 45:36	**lenses** eyes are l.	DOUG 295:5	Men ignorant of l.	SAND 743:39
l. with the ways of Death	LIND 530:16	**lenten** L. is come with love	ANON 21:45	nat the L. space	CHAU 216:66
puissant l., whose exile	MILT 602:50	what l. entertainment	SHAK 782:91	Nobody knows how to write l.	CONG 241:65
leg-irons with tinkling l.-i.	WALC 916:17	**lentils** pottage of l.	BIBLE 92:29	no more exempt…than a man of l.	STER 848:45
legislate If civil authorities l.	JOHN 456:73	**lentil-soup** L-s. colors	HUGH 435:20	Pause awhile from l.	JOHN 459:46
l. to make the well-to-do	BRYAN 170:97	**Leonora** L., L., How the word rolls	CRAIK 252:51	pin up your hair with…l.?	CONG 241:66
legislation a good piece of l.	OBAMA 643:18	To my daughter L.	WODE 952:44	pray you, in your l.	SHAK 790:51

lettuce

publishes his l.	WHITE 935:45
sayings are generally like women's l.	HAZL 404:51
Scottish life and l.	MACD 550:39
shall receive no l.	JOHN 464:99
writing l. to every body	ARBU 30:3
lettuce allegories are so much l.	GINS 371:4
Leucon Let Eli rejoice with L.	SMART 826:60
levee Chevy to the l.	MCLE 554:22
l. from a couch	CONG 241:73
level dead l. of provincial existence	ELIOT 315:34
l. of the light	FORD 343:94
l. to which it belongs	HAMM 394:56
meetings…held at a divine l.	ACHE 2:26
ranks of life…upon a l.	SMITH 827:74
Those who attempt to l.	BURKE 176:37
wish to l. down	JOHN 461:1
levellers l. wish to level	JOHN 461:1
leviathan draw out l. with an hook?	BIBLE 99:22
there is that l.	BIBLE 102:13
Lévi-Strauss diagnosed by L.-S.	VAN 908:12
levitate People also claim…to l.	BOWL 153:5
levity smacks of l., immorality almost	STARK 843:22
lewd l. fellows of the baser sort	BIBLE 124:88
l. well natured friend	ROCH 720:23
lewdness aspect of l. in Liverpool	FORD 342:90
Lewis Daniel Day L. has what	GIEL 368:26
Mr L.'s pictures	SITW 824:15
lexicographer L. A writer of dictionaries	JOHN 460:75
l. can only hope	JOHN 460:67
wake a l.	JOHN 460:71
lexicography lost in l.	JOHN 460:68
lexicon international l.	GORB 378:47
l. of conflict and drama	SAFI 737:17
liabilities no longer l. but assets	SCHL 747:37
liability clarity is a great l.	BALF 58:42
liable l. To read in the Bible	HEYW 417:41
liaison hypothetical l.	NATH 632:98
l. is almost always pardonable	GRAV 382:28
liar as a Prime Minister I cannot be a l.	BERL 85:52
best l. is he who makes	BUTL 185:98
every man a l.	BIBLE 125:5
exceptionally good l.	JERO 454:41
He was not a l.	LAUT 511:25
I am the Club L.	SAKI 739:67
l. gone to burning hell	SHAK 790:45
Love is always a l.	RUIZ 730:38
man who tells the truth…is a l.	SAFI 737:20
only thing worse than a l.	WILL 945:83
picturesque l.	TWAIN 903:70
proved l.	HAIL 392:18
liars all cheats and l.	JONES 465:21
All men are l.	BIBLE 102:20
Cretans are always l.	BIBLE 129:31
fears may be l.	CLOU 232:48
lecherous l.	WILD 943:49
l. in old clothes	MARQ 575:62
l. in public places	POUND 691:4
l. need to have good memories	QUIN 703:25
l. ought to have good memories	SIDN 819:34
l. out of the American people	ROGE 723:75
libel excessive wealth a l.	SHEL 812:51
limitations those of l.	THUR 891:2
that wholesale l.	PARK 663:8
writs for l. and slander	PROF 697:28
liberal either a little L.	GILB 369:52
l.…conservative…arrested	WOLFE 953:80
l. democratic principles	AUNG 45:39
l.…tells other people	BARA 63:42
l.…wishes to replace them	BIER 134:70
sector of the l. middle class	EAGL 309:2
value of a l. education	BREW 158:4
We who are l.	TRIL 897:15
liberalism l. has been tried	MCGO 552:87
liberality hate l.	SIDM 819:33
liberalization l. of prices	PAVL 670:39
liberal-minded gentle; l.-m., great	TENN 875:2
Liberals L. can dream	MACL 556:50
L. in a hurry	SAINT 738:48
not mind the L.	WHIT 937:83
liberate we shall l. this country	MAND 565:61
liberated l. from a small…self	ELIOT 316:54
liberation between further l.	GINS 372:14
Communist 'war of l.'	MCNA 557:87
For l.—not less of love	ELIOT 321:89
l. of both body and mind	BANN 62:34
trumpet for Women's L.	LESS 524:98

Women's L. is just a lot of foolishness	MEIR 584:42
Women's l. is the l.	KENT 483:50
liberationists Woman's L.	LOOS 536:57
libert Pour te nommer L.	ELUA 324:44
libertarians no l. in financial crises	KRUG 500:25
libertas L. et natale solum	SWIFT 862:41
liberties conscience, above all l.	MILT 600:6
essential maxim of your l.	PITT 679:7
Freedom, what l.…in thy name!	GEOR 364:57
people never give up their l.	BURKE 175:33
repressed the economic l.	KRIS 499:13
take the institutions and l.	POWE 693:59
libertine puffed and reckless l.	SHAK 781:48
liberty belief in human l.	MACL 555:45
blaze of truth and l.	MACA 544:24
blessings of l.	BUSH 183:29
can be no effective l.	BELL 75:37
cause of a single life is l.	BACON 51:72
certainly destroys l.	JOHN 464:85
conceived in l.	LINC 529:9
concentrate to truth and l.	SHEL 812:59
condition…God hath given l.	CURR 259:92
constitutional l.	GIBB 366:93
contend for their l.	HALI 393:38
defence of l.	GOLD 377:20
desiren l.	CHAU 217:91
desire…to lose l.	BACON 51:84
Enjoy such l.	LOVE 538:82
every law is an infraction of l.	BENT 82:90
feelings of l.	PITT 679:5
for our l.	PITT 680:11
foundations of political l.	WILS 949:83
Give me the l. to know	MILT 600:6
greater license…to obtain l.	COOP 246:87
idea of l.	SPIN 840:72
If l. means anything	ORWE 654:45
if l. of thought perishes	ORWE 655:69
Individuality…the aim of political l.	COOP 246:86
Know no such l.	LOVE 538:81
lakkith l.!	JAME 449:18
let us have our l. again	LANY 508:56
l. against tyranny	ROOS 725:22
l., and the pursuit of happiness	JEFF 453:19
l.…cannot flourish	HUXL 442:94
l. cannot long exist	BURKE 175:26
l.…conceived by current opinion	MCCA 547:90
L., Equality, Adultery	BELL 77:84
L., Equality, Fraternity!	LAMA 504:74
L. is l.	BERL 84:45
L. is…working or starving	JOHN 461:89
L. lends us her wings	BRON 161:69
L. means responsibility	SHAW 808:38
L.…mother of virtue	WOLL 954:90
L.…must be limited	BURKE 175:25
l. of the press	JOHN 461:16
l. of the press	JUNI 471:49
l. of the press	SHER 818:6
L.'s a glorious feast!	BURNS 177:79
L.'s exquisite pain	BROW 166:91
L.'s in every blow	BURNS 180:48
l. that the citizen enjoys	SPEN 836:89
l., that we'll enjoy	JONS 467:70
l. to follow my own will	LOCKE 533:87
l. to go abroad for ayre	PEPYS 674:2
life, l., and the pursuit of happiness	STAN 842:12
light, of l., and of learning	DISR 288:60
long odyssey toward l.	MAIL 560:52
love of l.	HAZL 403:36
lusty leas at l.	WYATT 963:85
men are to wait for l.	MACA 545:25
notion of l.	JOHN 461:90
prefer poverty with l.	PITT 679:7
price of l. is…dirt	ORWE 653:17
proclaim l. to the captives	BIBLE 110:6
recipients of the boon of l.	MAMET 563:29
recovering his l.	GALT 359:56
rules of ancient l.	MILT 601:21
sacred fire of l.	WASH 922:29
settle our true l.	MONT 614:23
so easy as l.	ASTE 39:3
soul of a journey is l.	MARP 574:42
spirit of l.	HAND 395:78
survival and success of l.	KENN 481:3
Sweet land of l.	SMITH 830:31
taking place a l. in going astray	ELIOT 315:16
there is no l. or freedom	NASHE 632:97
thy chosen music, L.!	WORD 961:31

thy l. into bondage	SHAK 780:17
tree of l. must be refreshed	JEFF 454:22
voices of l. be mute?	CUMM 257:59
walking…with the Statue of L.	CONR 244:53
When love is l.	POPE 686:47
Wine gives you l.	WYCH 964:99
yelps for l.	JOHN 462:41
liberty-loving prayers of l.-l. people	EISE 314:92
librarians l. are keepers	MACL 555:37
libraries l. are food	TUCH 901:14
L. are reservoirs of strength	GREER 387:45
l. of death	DOMI 290:3
l., querulous criticisms	WHIT 937:1
When we run over l.	HUME 438:7
library a circulating l. in a town	SHER 817:72
cloister without a l.	GEOF 363:44
damned l. of yours!	ONEI 651:70
l. consists of a Kindle	LIVE 531:54
lumber room of his l.	DOYLE 297:58
replaced the l. pass	LODGE 534:97
smell of the l.	ACKR 3:60
than a public l.	JOHN 459:53
turn over half a l.	JOHN 462:36
libre condamné à être l.	SART 745:74
No vers is l.	ELIOT 320:55
Vive le Québec l.!	DE 270:97
libretto l. that should never	THOM 888:12
Libya first triumph over L.	PLUT 682:76
licence love not freedom, but l.	MILT 601:22
scientist is given l.	LISP 531:44
servitude and extreme l.	TOCQ 892:28
TV l.	THOM 888:11
license accord greater l.	COOP 246:87
licensing l. and prohibiting	MILT 600:97
licentious l. passages	GIBB 366:3
Marriage is the most l.	SHAW 808:32
licentiousness satisfy luxury and l.	MORE 618:19
lichen fungus or a l.	THOR 888:21
lick so good you'll want to l. them	JOBS 455:63
licker L. talks mighty loud	HARR 399:47
licorice l. fields at Pontefract	BETJ 89:42
lid down came the l.	LEWIS 527:73
I dips me l.	DENN 273:74
lids lift their heavy l.	PATM 669:16
with thy vailèd l.	SHAK 780:34
lie A cause is a l.	GASS 361:89
Art is a l.	PICA 677:63
believe a l.	TAYL 868:58
big l. is no worse	ORWE 655:68
cannot tell a l.	WASH 921:25
couldn't tell a l.	LENO 522:56
Don't l.	SZIL 865:32
Dost thou l. so low?	SHAK 777:32
every word she writes is a l.	MCCA 548:2
fall victim to a big l.	HITL 420:91
honest man sent to l. abroad	WOTT 962:54
I mean, you l.	SWIFT 863:67
isn't told a l.	KIPL 492:56
know to be a l.	HAMP 395:74
led to believe a l.	BLAKE 141:29
l. can travel halfway round the world	CALL 192:29
L. Circumstantial	SHAK 780:23
l. down alone	HOUS 432:76
l. down until the feeling passes	HUTC 441:51
l. follows by post	BERE 83:16
l. has become…a pillar	SOLZ 833:6
l.…is a beautiful twilight	CAMUS 196:99
l. is an abomination	STEV 850:1
l. is the handle	HOLM 424:69
L. not one to another	BIBLE 128:11
l. of their inferiority	KING 487:34
L. soft, sleep hard	MIDD 590:72
l. that I repeated	ARMS 32:46
l. to and humbug themselves	WELLS 930:21
l. where I am and sleep	SHIP 818:44
l. which is all a l.	TENN 876:39
l. will go round the world	SPUR 841:89
l. with his mother earth?	SHAK 778:59
l. with me	BIBLE 93:41
l. without moving	RHYS 712:74
l. with your legs ungainly	SASS 745:70
loves to l. with me	SHAK 778:75
makes me down to l.	SCOT 754:58
misleading impression, not a l.	ARMS 33:53
Most governments lie	GATES 361:99
Nature admits no l.	CARL 201:40
not a man, that he should l.	BIBLE 94:84

life

old L.: Dulce et decorum est	OWEN 657:31	appeal to the l. of Christ	WHIT 936:71	Does thy l. destroy	BLAKE 140:12
Parliaments are the great l.	POBE 683:77	a précis of l.	FRIEL 351:79	domestic l.	GIBB 366:92
rather l. in the woollen	SHAK 773:23	Architecture is the…mirror of l.	PEI 672:73	dominant facts in English l.	ORWE 654:35
remedies oft in ourselves do l.	SHAK 791:58	arena to which he devoted his l.	LEHM 520:24	done it all my l.	NASH 631:87
rule and dare not l.	TENN 876:20	Art is only a means to l.	MILL 594:78	don't want…more in your l.	RHYS 712:74
Science…is the great l.	GOUR 380:79	as though my very l.	JORD 469:3	Doth the winged l. destroy	BLAKE 140:6
sixth, the L. with Circumstance	SHAK 780:24	At fifteen l. had taught me	ANGE 18:86	Do you believe in the l. to come?	BECK 72:49
Soul of my l.	HERR 415:5	Bankrupt of l.	DRYD 302:73	dream of l.	JARR 452:83
telling a big l. about you	TRUM 899:78	beauty of l. through death	LAUT 512:32	dream of l.	SHEL 815:39
the silence is a l.	YEVT 968:47	believe in l.!	DU 305:69	dregs of l.	DRYD 300:38
This isn't about a l.	BLAIR 138:75	believe in taking human l.	NATH 632:3	dress according to…your object in l.	DISR 288:69
truth of God into a l.	BIBLE 125:3	be Queen for l.	POPE 688:14	drink l. to the lees	TENN 870:98
Violence is a l.	JOHN 456:79	best of L. is but intoxication	BYRON 190:8	Each stage in l.	MACH 552:90
what is a l.?	BYRON 190:21	best part of married l.	WILD 943:41	easy key, Dost open l.	DRYD 301:60
What's the good of a l.	GREE 386:30	better standards of l.	UNIT 905:9	end of everything we call l.	WELLS 930:40
When he speaketh a l.	BIBLE 123:42	better to dream your l.	PROU 697:39	endows our l. with authenticity	MALL 562:95
when you come to l. here	SCOTT 754:84	better to enjoy l.	JOHN 460:80	enemy of l.	SPEN 838:24
When you tell a l.	HOSS 430:29	between l. and death	WORD 960:20	English l.…is rather bland	PERE 674:21
you have to l.	JUNCK 471:45	birthday of my l.	ROSS 725:36	Enlarge my l.	JOHN 459:47
lied to women l. like a Cretan	HARDY 397:5	bitter moments of l.	POWYS 693:62	entire l. in its flagrant disregard	MILI 591:91
lies all propaganda is l.	ORWE 654:38	bitterness of l.!	CARR 206:32	Envy and wrath shorten the l.	BIBLE 113:3
Autobiographies tell more l.	BYATT 186:17	blind dates are a way of l.	EPST 327:34	eternal blessed l.	TOLS 894:54
dashed and brewed with l.	DRYD 301:70	blood-thirsty clinging to l.	ARNO 35:11	events of l.	SARO 744:58
desirability…of telling l.	ORWE 655:67	bone-ache disquietude of l.	ALLEN 13:78	ever burnt in my l.	GONC 377:40
don't deal in l.	KIPL 492:62	Book of L.	WILDE 945:8	ever saw in your l.	WELL 929:3
English are polite by telling l.	BRAD 154:27	books echoing the l.	WILL 946:22	everyday l., with its drab…dullness	EINS 313:76
Everybody l. about sex	SEIN 756:6	Books make sense of l.	BARN 64:68	everydayness of l.	STEI 845:58
few more l. eat into the seed	MAIL 559:38	books, they are the l.	LOWE 539:96	every day of your l.	LEE 519:91
here he l.	STEV 853:62	born to eternal l.	FRAN 347:99	Every l. has a Scheherazadesworth	BARTH 65:7
Here l. Nolly Goldsmith	GARR 360:79	bottom of l.	WASH 921:22	every morning of your l.	POWE 693:51
History is condemned…to l.	FRAN 347:82	breathed into his nostrils…breath of l.	BIBLE 91:86	every part of human l.	MACA 546:55
History, sir, will tell l.	SHAW 807:2	breath of l.	YEATS 966:28	everything that meets us in l.	MARC 570:59
how would l. resist passions?	DIDE 285:60	brevity of human l.	PROT 697:34	everything that ordinary l. is not	DELI 271:42
L. and Literature	LAFO 504:52	brings about a disconnected l.	HUGO 437:79	except my l., my l., my l.	SHAK 782:82
L. are essential to humanity	PROU 698:55	bring the dead to l.	GRAV 382:23	except with l.	SPEN 837:8
l. are invented	BRAQ 156:76	brisking about the l.	SMART 826:63	exchange a l. of kind protection	STOWE 856:28
l., damned l. and statistics	DISR 289:74	broke up their…habits of l.	SHER 816:69	experience and understanding of l.	MILL 593:60
l.…from the loudspeakers	ORWE 654:57	business of l.	WELL 929:11	experience it in this l.	WILL 944:71
l. one who meant well	STEV 853:79	but once in my l.	SAND 742:24	experience of democracy is like…l.	CART 206:47
L. That Are My Life	ELLI 323:34	By my l.	SHAK 786:3	experience of l.	BEER 73:85
l., thinking it is the truth	SAFI 737:20	calamity of so long l.	TWAIN 902:63	experiences of l.	NIEB 637:87
make l. sound truthful	ORWE 655:65	care for far more than human l.	PANK 662:84	expression of l. as growth	MILL 594:79
Matilda told such Dreadful L.	BELL 77:63	careless of the single l.	TENN 874:78	Facts alone are wanted in l.	DICK 281:75
more readily swallow l. than truth	GELL 363:34	cause of a single l. is liberty	BACON 51:72	facts of l.	PARK 664:33
old men's l.	POUND 691:4	cessation of individual l.	HUXL 443:7	failed promises of American l.	GILL 370:78
one of the social l.	IBSEN 444:7	chain I forged in l.	DICK 279:4	family l. is all the l. she knows	SHAW 809:88
Our l. reveal as much as…truths	COET 233:90	change…we see in l.	FROST 352:89	fashionable female l.	SPEKE 836:82
Plain l. are dangerous	SAYE 746:9	Chaos often breeds l.	ADAMS 5:90	Fear of death and fear of l.	MENC 587:6
Some books are l.	BURNS 177:73	choice, becomes a way of l.	MILL 593:44	fear of l.!	ONEI 651:62
some of them l.	MANT 568:17	choose l.	BIBLE 95:97	feeling and l. must depart	MOORE 617:99
sweep away the refuge of l.	BIBLE 108:71	cities, throbbed the true l.	NORR 641:57	felt the pricks of l.	HARDY 397:18
telling l. and selling socks	MERW 589:57	citizen of l.	SASS 745:81	fences for his l.	RICK 715:28
tell me no more unnecessary l.	ADAMS 5:7	civilized human l.	TRUM 899:82	fever of l. is over	NEWM 635:46
The cruellest l.	STEV 852:43	cold as l.	RHYS 712:75	Fiction is l.	JAMES 450:30
truth to cover l.	CONG 240:40	comes late in l.	JERR 455:47	Fie upon this quiet l.!	SHAK 771:44
When the l. are all told	MCCA 547:78	common errors of our l.	SIDN 820:57	fight is bigger than l. itself	KING 486:21
lieutenant died…like a second l.	CLEM 229:85	compensate for too little l.	BURG 174:94	filled his l. with bitterness	TWAIN 902:42
life access to a better l.…denied	ANGE 19:94	conclusions about l.	KIER 485:99	findeth his l. shall lose it	BIBLE 116:73
a creative l.	THARP 880:45	consumed by the l. process	MCCA 548:96	first prize in the lottery of l.	RHOD 712:71
advances through l.	JOHN 460:65	continentals think l. is a game	MIKES 590:87	flame of l. and love	LAWR 513:57
afraid of l.	STEV 851:32	contrary to l.	HUXL 441:68	Flops are a part of l.'s	RUSS 735:49
Alcohol…makes l. bearable	SHAW 809:74	cool sequestered vale of l.	GRAY 384:72	flower of a blameless l.	TENN 876:40
a l. lived for music	PAVA 670:37	coping with l.	SPARK 835:63	fool his whole l. long	LUTH 542:76
all female l.…unclean	STAN 843:17	corresponds to our dream l.	MAMET 563:25	for l.…that we learn	SENE 757:24
all his l.…in the wrong	ROCH 719:12	course of a dishonest l.	FRAS 349:32	for the l. in them	THOM 885:60
All human l. is there	NEWS 635:54	course to take in l.	KURO 501:44	for the rest of your l.	JARR 452:88
all human l. is there!	JAMES 450:37	crown of our l.	SWIN 864:94	fought for l.	SPEN 837:93
all L. death does end	HOPK 429:92	cut off from real l.	CROS 256:35	fountain of the water of l.	BIBLE 132:25
all my l.	JOHN 456:95	cuts off twenty years of l.	SHAK 777:30	fountains of l.	MUIR 624:25
all my l.	JOHN 462:30	dangers of family l.	HUXL 441:73	freezes up the heat of l.	SHAK 766:8
all the blessings of this l.	BOOK 147:50	day's hard work in thy l.	LAWR 513:69	friends for his l.	THOR 889:57
all the emergencies of l.	FORS 344:27	dearly love in your l.	TROL 898:44	from books…and not from l.	POUND 691:88
all the energies of his l.	PIER 677:66	dear to me as l.	SHAK 770:15	game of l. seriously	LEARY 517:47
amend my l.	SHAK 771:54	dear to me as light and l.	BURNS 178:11	gift of God is eternal l.	BIBLE 125:13
American l.	MAIL 560:52	death after l.	SPEN 838:28	give for his l.	BIBLE 98:92
American l.	MCCA 547:88	death and l. attonce	SPEN 839:40	give l. everything you've got	YOST 968:50
American way of l.	MENC 587:13	Death is not an event in l.	WITT 951:23	give thee a crown of l.	BIBLE 131:91
American writer…acquires a new l.	AMIS 16:48	Death to l. is crown	MILT 608:1	giveth his l. for the sheep	BIBLE 123:45
America's cultural l.	ROCK 721:40	dedicated my l.	MAND 564:53	Give to me the l.	STEV 853:82
A missed l.	HEINE 407:17	destruction of human l.	HARDY 396:98	giving l.…to beings	REDON 709:23
and for her l. he died	STONE 855:11	devoted the best years of his l.	BIRK 136:18	glorious in his l.	GIBB 366:94
And the l. everlasting	BOOK 146:31	differ as to the ends of l.	RUSS 734:33	godhead in which all l. is human	SHAW 809:69
And this our l.	SHAK 778:66	different ranks of l.	SMITH 827:74	God's opinion that l. should go on	SAND 742:30
an essential part of l.	AUST 47:94	difficulties in providing for…l.	COMM 239:94	goes through l. with…expectation	ORWE 653:12
animal thirst for l.	BANKS 62:22	diminish my l.	RENO 711:51	Golf is like l.	CLIN 230:13
Anythin' for a quiet l.	DICK 278:62	discovered the secret of l.	CRICK 254:94	good a material…to build a l. from	CAREY 199:62
A planned l.	BACA 49:6	does not care that l.	HYDE 443:21	Good l. be now my task	DRYD 303:11

life

good l. is a main argument	JONS 468:88	King of l.	VAUG 909:38	L. is a pure flame	BROW 166:82
good man's l.	WORD 956:54	know that l. is difficult	PECK 672:61	L. is a screen	HUGO 437:76
goods and trappings of your l.	MOORE 616:59	labyrinth of our l.	SCHO 748:52	L. is a sexually transmitted disease	ANON 26:4
go on forgetting all your l.	FENT 332:59	large as l.	CARR 205:19	L. is as tedious	SHAK 768:58
go through l.	THOR 889:55	last of l.	BROW 168:59	L. is a struggle	KEIL 479:63
government for every rise in l.	MILL 591:4	later l. renew	SPEN 839:47	L....is boring	BERR 87:97
grandeur in this view of l.	DARW 263:53	latter years of her l.	THUR 890:68	L. is brief	CARM 202:46
great art is great l.	WRIG 962:65	law of academic l.	LODGE 534:99	L. is but a day	KEATS 475:66
great fact in her l.	STAN 842:13	Laws...are not our L.	CARL 201:17	L. is but a Dream	LI 528:82
great ignorance of...human l.	JOHN 463:73	lay down his l. for his friends	BIBLE 123:55	L. is but a moment	SCHI 747:29
great l. if you don't weaken	BUCH 171:24	leading a good l.	SASS 746:94	L. is but an interjection	BYRON 190:26
great, powerful souls love l.	HEINE 407:13	least unpleasant state of l.	BERN 86:73	L. is but the joy of delusion	KORAN 496:48
great safeguard...of domestic l.	ELIOT 316:44	lengthens l.	SHAK 761:57	L. is changed	MUIR 624:22
great spectacle of l.	ELIOT 316:54	lengthen thy L.	FRAN 348:8	L. is colour and warmth	GREN 388:57
grow out of your l.	WARR 921:18	lesson of l.	EMER 325:92	L. is determined for us	ELIOT 315:33
guide of l.	HUME 438:1	lesson we learn from l.	FORD 342:87	L. is doubt	UNAM 905:3
Half our l. is spent	ROGE 723:79	Let l. be short	SHAK 776:95	L....is far from gay	LEAR 517:42
hath a l. to live	RAIN 705:37	Let l. go on in it	TOLS 893:50	L. is first boredom	LARK 509:86
have a right notion of l.	MONT 613:11	let l. in	CRAS 254:85	L. is frittered away	THOR 889:38
have everlasting l.	BIBLE 122:25	liberal education...makes l.	BREW 158:4	L. is just one damned thing	HUBB 434:97
healthy l. is hardly	PECK 672:65	lie in wait for thine own l.	BIBLE 113:96	L. is like playing a violin solo	BUTL 185:94
healthy state of political l.	MILL 591:1	Lies That Are My L.	ELLI 323:34	L. is made up of marble	HAWT 402:8
he is tired of l.	JOHN 463:56	l. according to reason	ARIS 31:22	L. is made up of sobs	OHEN 648:15
Here one is in Later L.	MERR 589:49	l. after death	DOCT 289:86	L. is making us abandon	GORB 378:49
hero of his own l. story	BARTH 65:6	L. always kills you	COUP 248:38	L. is mostly froth	GORD 378:52
his dull l.	BEAU 70:11	L., a Fury slinging flame	TENN 874:74	L. is nobler	SHAW 806:92
His l. was gentle	SHAK 778:57	l. and light, with envious haste	ROCH 720:25	L. is not a theme park	BRAND 156:65
histories of...human l.	POPP 689:57	l. and never managed	MURD 626:67	L. is not easy	SAIF 738:30
Home l. as we understand it	SHAW 809:85	L. and these lips	SHAK 766:9	L. is not having been	NASH 631:74
honour is my l.	SHAK 764:32	L. as a Man	ROTH 728:83	L. is not hurrying	THOM 886:77
hope not l. from grief or danger free	JOHN 459:46	L., as it is called	MILL 594:83	L. is not just to be alive	MART 576:76
hope...Was my l. also	OWEN 658:34	l. as narration	MANN 566:79	L. is not meant to be easy	FRAS 349:34
How...rushing l. can...seem	SWIFT 861:14	L....a solitary cell	ONEI 650:60	L. is not worth living	PLATO 681:44
how to invent his own l.	ROBBE 717:64	l. at the ocean bottom	HECHT 406:3	L. isn't all beer and skittles	HUGH 436:46
Human l. is but a series	NABO 628:10	l. be but a dream	PRIOR 696:13	L. isn't like coursework	JOHN 457:92
human or domestic l. second	MANN 567:93	L. becomes miserable	BAUD 68:63	L. is one damn thing	MILL 592:28
I am the resurrection, and the l.	BIBLE 123:46	L., being weary	SHAK 776:14	L. is one demd horrid grind!	DICK 279:88
If A is success in l.	EINS 314:86	l. be not a real fight	JAMES 451:70	L. is one-tenth Here	SWIFT 861:12
If in this l. only we have hope	BIBLE 127:56	l. beyond l.	MILT 600:2	L. is rather like a tin of sardines	BENN 80:43
I first in my l....did see people	PEPYS 673:1	l. can be perfectly satisfying	MUNRO 626:54	L. is real, l.	LONG 535:14
If l. is miserable	LABR 502:20	l. can little more supply	POPE 686:70	L. is short and bothersome	LABR 502:19
If l. was always like that	JOYCE 470:31	l. changes in the instant	DIDI 286:86	L. is so beautiful	MACH 552:91
if l. was bitter	SWIN 864:14	L.. Consider the alternative	MCLU 556:59	L. is something to do	LEBO 517:59
If you don't love l.	CLARK 228:60	l. contained an infinite number	GREE 386:22	L. is that the form	MANN 566:78
if your l. should become clouded	OVID 657:22	L. creates order	SAINT 738:39	L. is the greatest of blessings	HEINE 407:14
illusion of a view of l.	ELIOT 318:19	l. depends on your power	SCAR 746:13	L. is the other way	LODGE 534:93
image of l.	ANOU 28:60	l. devouring itself	GOUR 380:79	L....is the proper binge	CHILD 222:15
important thing in l.	HAIL 392:17	l. does not imitate art	ALLEN 14:2	L. is thorny	COLE 235:34
impressions...what we call l.	BELL 78:91	l. doesn't make sense	LYNCH 543:48	L. is too precious	ELIOT 315:14
in anyone's l. span	DIDI 286:80	l. endured and known	SASS 746:97	L. is too short	LOWE 540:33
in every...boy's l.	TWAIN 902:46	l. every nerve and instinct	LESS 523:92	L. is too short	SCOTT 751:8
in fiction as in l.	AUCH 42:62	l. evolved out of...nothing	DAWK 266:18	L. is very sweet, brother	BORR 151:69
influence on human l.	MULL 624:33	L., force and beauty	POPE 685:18	L. is washed in the speechless real	BARZ 67:38
infused l....into the daily newspaper	BENN 81:82	l. for evermore	BIBLE 103:40	L. it pretends to build on	PRIT 696:16
In him was l.	BIBLE 122:16	l. for l.	BIBLE 94:67	L. itself going on	WOOLF 956:34
in l. as it is in ways	BACON 50:40	l., good, bad, or peculiar	PALEY 661:52	L. itself is a mystery	MORT 621:69
In l....in tears	WEBS 926:21	l....had a goal	HAMM 394:57	L. itself is but the shadow	BROW 166:83
in l. people will take	TROL 897:33	L. has its tail	FERL 333:92	L. itself requireth	HOOK 427:40
in married l.	WILDE 941:99	L. has no other discipline	MILL 594:62	L. itself...was enough	WOOLF 955:15
inside our own skins, for l.!	WILL 945:98	l. has no subject matter	DAVIS 266:6	L. I've been working	MOTH 622:87
intellectual l....of western society	SNOW 832:77	l. has taught us	SAINT 738:32	L., Joy, Empire and Victory	SHEL 815:20
interest in l. does not lie	WOOLF 955:11	l. hath had some smatch of honour	SHAK 778:55	L. levels all men	SHAW 808:52
In the arts of l.	SHAW 807:26	l. her husband makes for her	ELIOT 316:53	L., liberty, and...happiness	STAN 842:12
in the cross is l.	KEMP 480:80	l. hovers like a star	BYRON 190:28	L., like a dome	SHEL 815:43
In the house of L.	THUR 890:66	L. imitates Art far more	WILDE 940:61	L....lived in pleasant thought	WORD 959:99
In the midst of l.	BOOK 148:99	l. in another l.	ELIOT 315:27	L....lost in living?	ELIOT 319:31
In the pride of l.	WILDE 940:44	l. in a race	MERE 588:41	L. loves the liver	ANGE 19:95
In the prime of your l.	RICH 713:95	l. in the movie business	MAMET 564:40	L. makes no...statement	LAWR 513:59
In this l.	WINT 950:12	l. in the village began	LEE 519:96	L....makes us suffer	ANOU 28:62
In this l. he laughs	MASE 580:65	l. is 6 to 5 against	RUNY 731:59	l. may be prolonged	SHAK 803:8
iron gates of l.	MARV 577:94	L. is...a bad dream	ONEI 651:64	l. may change	SHEL 816:55
I saw my l. branching out	PLATH 681:37	L....is a beautiful thing	BURT 181:73	l. must be understood	KIER 485:4
isn't l. a terrible thing	THOM 884:38	L. is a cycle	MARC 569:52	l. of a man	MORG 619:30
is the first rule in l.	MELBA 584:45	L....is a dreary business	PERCY 674:10	l. of every man	MUIR 624:21
It may be l.	HERB 413:53	L. is a foreign country	KERO 483:52	l. of every man is a diary	BARR 64:83
it moves again since it is l.	FAUL 331:42	L. is a foreign language	MORL 619:37	l. of happiness	MUNRO 626:53
it was L. I hated	GALL 358:43	L. is...a game of football	SCOTT 753:39	l. of man	BACON 53:49
it were a happy l.	SHAK 760:8	L. is a glorious cycle of song	PARK 664:14	l. of man, solitary	HOBB 420:2
It would be l.	DICK 284:40	L. is a great surprise	NABO 628:9	l. of men is painful	EURI 328:58
I've had a happy l.	HAZL 404:53	L. is a horizontal fall	COCT 233:87	l. of sensations	KEATS 475:74
I was wasting my l.	BUFF 172:46	L. is a jest	GAY 362:11	l. of strict obedience	DOST 294:89
journey of l.	DICK 283:17	L. is all memory	WILL 945:3	l. of such simple...races	MAIL 560:68
journey of our l.	DANTE 262:36	L....is a luminous halo	WOOLF 955:10	l. of the journalist	GIBB 367:8
jump the l. to come	SHAK 796:19	L. is a malady	ABU 1:15	l. of the modern hardback	MORT 621:68
jurney ov l.	BILL 135:97	L. is a maze	CONN 243:9	l. of the poet is the l.	NERV 634:9
keep the tree of l.	BIBLE 91:1	L. is an incurable disease	COWL 250:74	l. of this Administration	KENN 481:2
kills l. within himself	SAINT 738:45	l. is a process of burning	WILL 945:99	l. o'th' building	SHAK 797:41

life

l. passed among pictures	WHIS 934:19	lusty plesand l.	DUNB 306:97	one expanding horror in American l.	MAIL 560:52
l. pasturing freely	THOR 888:27	made l. my common stake	VAUG 909:42	one good deed in all my l.	SHAK 760:30
l....printed on dollar bills	ODETS 647:92	Mad from l.'s history	HOOD 426:34	one l. to lose	HALE 392:27
l. ran gaily as the sparkling Thames	ARNO 34:94	make a successful l.	TEMP 869:70	one of the lords Of l.	LAWR 513:60
l. rose over it all	FOX 346:71	make l....one grand, sweet song	KING 487:45	one of the worst things about l.	POWE 693:49
l. runs on, the road	LOWE 539:16	make your l. interesting	DICK 279:15	one passion of my l.	GOOD 385:40
l.'s a pain	DAVI 264:77	making l. meaningful	WARR 921:16	one regret in l.	ALLEN 14:89
L.'s battle is a conquest	MASE 580:67	making the most of l.	SHAW 808:46	only honour and l....spared	FRAN 347:95
L.'s better with the Conservatives	ANON 25:37	Man's love is of man's l.	AMIS 16:31	on Nature, and on Human L.	WORD 961:34
L.'s business...the terrible choice	BROW 169:76	man the living sepulchre of l.	CLARE 228:53	Ordinary l. bypassed me	OBRI 645:66
L.'s but a walking shadow	SHAK 798:74	Mantua brought me l.	VIRG 914:28	other than the gift of l.	KOSI 499:2
l.'s common way	WORD 958:94	man whose l. is spent	SMITH 828:89	O thou lord of l.	HOPK 429:96
L.'s early cup	SHEL 815:37	Married l. requires shared mystery	FORD 343:11	our l. makes its leap	UPDI 906:31
l.'s fitful fever	SHAK 797:46	married to a single l.	CRAS 253:79	outer l. of telegrams and anger	FORS 344:29
L.'s gymnasium	WHIT 938:11	material forces with intellectual l.	MARX 579:37	out of l. into history	CHUR 225:74
L. shapes the face you have at thirty	CHAN 214:2	matter of l. and death	SHAN 805:60	own individual l.	GEOR 364:54
l. should serve up its feast	GOLD 375:81	meanest l. is better	EURI 328:61	owns my l.	RODR 722:54
L.'s longing for itself	GIBR 367:13	measured out my l.	ELIOT 316:63	Pagans deified l.	STAEL 841:96
l....so astonishingly cheap	DILL 286:92	meddling...in my private l.	WILL 945:1	parallelism of l.	ADAMS 5:92
l. so fast doth fly	DAVI 264:76	meditation not of death but of l.	SPIN 841:80	pardon that man's l.	SHAK 793:21
l. so short	CHAU 216:57	me for him, l. for l.	MILT 603:83	passing on the prisoner's l.	SHAK 787:52
l. so short	HIPP 419:69	memoirs of his l.	ARBU 30:3	passion and the l.	COLE 235:29
L.'s paradise	FORD 343:1	men have one entrance into l.	BIBLE 112:78	pass my whole l.	DICK 282:95
L.'s single lesson	PYNCH 701:11	mine for l.	SPARK 836:69	People say that l. is the thing	SMITH 829:24
l. starts new	BACH 49:15	Mistakes are a fact of l.	GIOV 372:45	period in one's l.	LARW 510:7
L.'s too short for chess	BYRON 191:36	Modern l., too, is often	HEMI 410:77	person concerns himself with l.	MANN 566:81
l. that I have	MARKS 572:90	modern l. would lack	WILB 939:38	piercing glances into the l.	MOORE 617:76
l. that I have chosen	HOMER 425:10	moments in his l.	MACL 555:38	place where I've lived my l.	BAUG 54:27
L., the shadow of death	SWIN 863:86	monotonous fabric of l.	MILL 594:73	play is l.	SHAW 809:69
l., the soul of reading	STER 848:28	moral l. of man	WILDE 940:64	Poetry...a criticism of l.	ARNO 36:43
L., the Universe and Everything	ADAMS 4:76	More than l.	SCHI 747:31	Poetry is a way of taking l.	FROST 353:20
L., to be sure	HOUS 432:77	most beautiful adventure in l.	FROH 351:87	poetry, no less than in l.	ARNO 36:40
L. today is junglelike	WILS 947:43	Most glorious Lord of L.!	SPEN 839:43	possibilities of l.	LEAV 517:52
l. to death	SHAK 772:91	Most glorious Lord of L.!	SPEN 839:46	power of l. and death	BIBLE 112:79
l. to give	KIPL 493:72	most important thing in l.	COUB 248:20	Practically a third of my l. is over	ALLEN 14:1
L....too short to stuff a mushroom	CONR 244:52	most important thing in l.	PASC 667:86	Praise l., it deserves praise	JEFF 453:18
l....under the power of language	CIXO 227:41	motion, which is l.	FAUL 331:42	prescribes for us a joyous l.	MORE 619:22
L. was a funny thing	CRISP 255:5	mourning for my l.	CHEK 218:14	preservation of l.	JEFF 453:19
l. was a strange one	HOLL 423:52	Much l. cannot be affected	ACHE 3:40	preservation of l.	LEGU 520:13
l. was death	ROSS 726:59	much of l. and death	SHEL 812:54	prices of l.	GURN 390:1
l. was like a box of chocolates	HANKS 395:83	muddy pond of daily l.	HERZ 416:21	principal business of l. is to enjoy	BUTL 185:96
l. was like his innings	EGAN 313:65	Music is l.	NIEL 637:90	principle in l. with me	SHAW 806:96
l. was married to it	TOML 894:57	my l. for the British female?	CLOU 232:57	private l....determined by...public l.	ELIOT 315:39
l. was one round of activity	LEAC 515:16	My l. has crept so long	TENN 876:33	problems which beset our l.?	MAMET 564:38
L. was pain	MOOR 618:8	my l., my fate	TENN 876:24	promise of what l. ought to be	COOKE 245:74
L. was simple before	HOPP 429:3	mystery is its l.	BAGE 54:75	pulse of l.?	SHAK 768:64
l., which is a work of art	MILL 594:81	mystery of l.	WHITE 935:51	quality of l. deteriorates	LEVI 525:26
l., within doors	HAWT 402:9	My way of l.	SHAK 798:69	questions of contemporary l.	JORD 468:99
l. without industry	RUSK 733:10	My whole l.	DRYD 301:61	real happiness of l.	MORE 618:20
l. without literature	ABRAM 1:6	nauseous draught of l.	ROCH 719:14	Real l. seems to have no plots.	COMP 239:1
l. without theory	DISR 287:19	Nay, take my l. and all	SHAK 770:17	real purpose of l.	SCHO 748:55
l. would always be too large	RIMB 716:51	necessaries of l.	HALL 393:40	Reason thus with l.	SHAK 787:64
l. wouldn't turn out...like literature	BARN 64:75	neither death, nor l.	BIBLE 125:22	redeemeth thy l. from destruction	BIBLE 102:6
L. would ring the bells	GINS 372:13	never in one's l.	STARK 843:24	reflections on l. and death	HERN 414:92
l. yields nothing further to recall	BYRON 189:98	new era in his l.	THOR 888:23	refuge from home l.	SHAW 806:95
light of a whole l. dies	BOUR 153:94	new l. begins	HERZ 416:26	righteous, and sober l.	BOOK 146:33
light of l.	BIBLE 123:39	night-side of l.	SONT 834:20	right order of l.	TAWN 868:44
light of my l.	NABO 628:4	no green l. shoots	BOTT 152:82	risk of maiming it for l.	SHAW 808:43
lines and l. are free	HERB 414:75	no inside l. of any sort	LAWR 513:54	road is l.	KERO 483:55
Listen to your l.	BUEC 172:42	no l. so happy	WALT 920:95	road of l.	GARL 360:74
Literature is based not on l.	STEV 850:88	No l. that breathes	TENN 872:26	romantic principle of l.	NOVA 642:65
little l....rounded with a sleep	SHAK 804:28	no l. that can be recaptured	MALA 562:80	round out anybody's l.	HAMM 395:72
live a good l.	HALD 392:25	nomad's l. enthralls	MAIL 560:67	sacrifice human l. to figures	WEIL 928:74
live a l. half dead	MILT 607:86	no more...healthy l.	SCHR 749:63	saddest l. is that of a political	MENC 586:93
live a miserable l.	BEET 74:2	no sorrow more intense than...l.	DARIO 263:46	sanctity of l.	SCHL 747:33
lived her normal l.	SABA 736:2	not a L. at all	GLAD 373:43	saved my l.	SHAK 772:68
lived his l. to the full	RAND 706:55	not by what is, in this l.	HARDY 397:12	save his l. shall lose it	BIBLE 118:8
live my l. over again	PAVA 670:35	not charmed with the ideal of l.	MILL 591:96	saw l. steadily	ARNO 33:64
live the good l.	WADD 915:1	nothing half so sweet in l.	MOORE 618:5	scenes of our l.	SCHO 749:59
lodestar of his l.	PARK 663:96	Nothing in his l.	SHAK 796:11	Scottish l. and letters	MACD 550:39
longer linked with l.	MELV 585:58	Nothing would give up l.	ROET 722:58	sea of l.	ARNO 34:81
longest half of your l.	SOUT 835:54	Not many sounds in l.	LAMB 505:4	secret of l.	CUMM 254:94
Long l. to Nanki-Poo	GILB 369:59	not one l....destroyed	TENN 874:76	Seek not...immortal l.	PIND 678:80
Long l. to you—till then!	GILB 369:59	no transcendent themes in l.	FORD 343:10	sell him a whole new l.	MORL 619:39
long littleness of l.	CORN 247:2	no wealth but l.	RUSK 733:2	serving in a state of l.	ATTL 40:27
Lose l.	GREE 386:12	now they want my l.	KRUG 500:21	set before you l. and death	BIBLE 95:97
lose L....to discover victory	APOL 29:86	obey in l. and in death	BARTH 65:8	set my l. at a pin's fee	SHAK 761:56
loses her husband...loses her l.	EURI 328:55	O Death in L.	TENN 872:43	severe facts of l.	ELIOT 316:48
loss of l.	PEARY 671:59	O'er a' the ills o' l.	BURNS 179:24	sheltered l....a daring l.	WELTY 931:49
love is the best thing in l.	MANN 566:88	Of all sweet sounds the l. and element!	COLE 235:30	she...who l. eternal gave?	BYRON 187:39
love long l.	SHAK 794:46	of inconsistencies: L.	TZARA 904:17	should l. all labour be?	TENN 870:91
love of l. is necessary	JOHN 459:56	Of mortal l. the leaf	SPEN 838:33	since my l. began	COWA 249:46
lover of l.	GORD 378:54	of my whole l.	GIBB 366:98	single page from our l.	SAND 741:8
love sport because I love l.	YEVT 968:46	Oh l., no l.	KYD 501:49	sketchy understanding of l. itself	CRICK 254:95
love thy l., nor hate	MILT 607:69	once in her l.	SPARK 836:72	Slave, I have set my l.	SHAK 761:56
lower employments of l.	JOHN 460:67	one desire in l.	SHAW 807:20	sleep...through l.	ALBEE 11:29
lower form of l.	THER 882:90	one evil, to deny l.	LAWR 513:76	slits the thin-spun l.	MILT 599:86

life-blood

small sweet courtesies of l.	STER 849:56	unified vision of l.	WILS 947:41	all the l. they wish	COWP 251:12
Smiles, tears, of all my l.	BROW 166:98	Unless you stake your l.	HEIS 407:23	angels, progeny of l.	MILT 604:19
Social l. is mutual	MUNCH 625:42	used by l. for its own purposes	MERR 589:50	answered l. to l.	ELIOT 319:43
so in everyday l.	THOM 886:78	Variety's the spice of l.	COWP 251:15	as l. fell short	HODG 421:20
so long as you have your l.	JAMES 451:51	very meaninglessness of l.	KUBR 500:35	bathe the world in l.	WORD 961:36
soon and for the rest of your l.	EPST 327:30	virtues carry with it l. and death	MARL 572:98	beauty from the l. retir'd	WALL 918:56
So on the ocean of l.	LONG 536:37	vision...of all ordinary human l.	ELIOT 316:51	believed in the green l.	FITZ 338:87
sort of l.	GREE 386:20	voyage of their l.	SHAK 778:48	Beneath thy lingering l.	COLL 238:77
sound...which tells of l.	COLE 234:7	walls about our l.	SHAK 764:52	big red l. goes on	PLAN 680:26
space of l. between	KEATS 476:83	wastes part of his l.	JOHN 459:55	birth to the world's l.	SHAK 789:5
spends his l....riding	WHITE 935:47	way of l.	GOER 374:55	blasted with excess of l.	GRAY 385:90
spy sent into l.	BOWL 153:99	way, which leadeth unto l.	BIBLE 115:52	bring nothing to l.	SOCR 833:96
Squat on my l.?	LARK 509:79	Wealth cannot make a l.	HERR 415:4	bring to the l. of day	FRIE 351:75
squirming l. underneath	WHITE 934:29	web of our l.	SHAK 791:68	burning and a shining l.	BIBLE 122:31
stand aside from l.	COMP 239:3	well-written l. is almost as rare	CARL 201:19	But soft, what l.	SHAK 765:77
stately ship of l.	KENN 481:14	we're all selling l.	CHER 219:29	by l. Of moon	WORD 958:82
still be a long l.	YUAN 969:67	whatever time of your l.	SPARK 836:68	candle for warmth or l.	MCLU 556:56
still calm of l.	ADAMS 4:72	what have I been doing all my l.	LAMB 505:79	Casting a dim religious l.	MILT 598:59
storm of l.	WESL 931:59	What is L.?	HAGG 391:7	celestial l.	WORD 959:5
story of a woman's l.	STAEL 841:92	What is our l.?	RALE 705:45	circumfused...with l. divine	WORD 958:85
strong almost as l.	MUIR 624:18	What is this l.	DAVI 265:90	Clear arias of l.	DAY 267:36
struggling for his own l.	HOMER 425:9	What is your l.?	BIBLE 130:59	contend with growing l.	SHAK 760:7
struggling for l.	JOHN 460:63	what l. has taught me	MANS 567:9	correct incidence of l.	ALBE 11:32
stuff of l. to knit me	HOUS 431:49	what l. honestly and deeply means	JAMES 451:72	crack of l. between	NABO 628:3
subject's l. work	TOYN 895:79	What l....if...not l. together?	ELIOT 319:33	Cry as the wild l. passes	LEAR 516:29
Sucking the fun out of l.	OROU 652:99	what matters in your l.	RUSH 732:64	danced by the l. of the moon	LEAR 516:38
Superstition is the poetry of l.	GOET 375:65	What signifies the l. o' man	BURNS 177:67	dark in l. expos'd	MILT 607:84
sweets of l.	CONG 241:61	What wondrous l.	MARV 577:4	Dark is L. Enough	FRY 353:35
sweet, sweet is this human l.	CORY 247:10	wheel of l.	STER 848:38	Darkness from l.	BROW 169:63
take away my l.	BIBLE 97:66	when l. is hard	VIRG 914:26	darkness shall be the l.	ELIOT 320:57
take l. easy	YEATS 965:3	When l. looks black	OBRI 646:68	dawn's early l.	KEY 483:68
take my l. from thee	KIPL 490:5	wherever you go in l.	MORR 620:46	Dear as the l.	GRAY 385:83
taken me all my l.	GILL 370:85	whether l. is or is not worth living	CAMUS 195:83	dear to me as l. and life	BURNS 178:11
takest us out of this present l.	BIBLE 113:13	while his l. lingered on	HOOV 427:45	deriving l. from each other	BERL 84:49
tender words as l. ebbed	WHIT 936:71	whole l. shows in your face	BACA 48:5	dungeon flamed with l.	WESL 931:57
that brings l.	STOWE 856:27	whole l. was spent riding	BLAN 141:46	eldritch l. of sundown	DAY 267:37
That I., a very rebel to my will	SHAK 795:75	whose l. in low estate	TENN 874:83	entrance of thy words giveth l.	BIBLE 103:29
That's my l.	HERB 412:44	Wine is as good as l.	BIBLE 113:5	every ray of God's l.	DOST 294:94
that they might have l.	BIBLE 123:44	without...any practical part of l.	ADDI 6:24	everything except space and l.	HEAT 406:94
that which makes l. worth living	ELIOT 321:95	Without music, l.	NIET 639:16	face to the l.	SASS 745:87
theatre of man's l.	BACON 49:31	woman's whole l.	IRVI 447:58	far from the l. of day	ORAH 652:90
there is no rock bottom to l.	MILL 593:32	words into l.	SENG 757:27	fierce l. which beats	TENN 876:40
the way, the truth, and the l.	BIBLE 123:53	world of material l.	ARNO 35:22	'Forward, the L. Brigade!'	TENN 875:12
things of daily l.	RUSS 734:21	worrisome day that one calls l.	BERN 86:77	from far thy beauteous l.	WESL 932:66
things the laws of l.	RUSK 733:99	worst of prison l.	STEN 847:5	from fidelity to the l.	RODR 722:52
think about a better l.	WILD 943:43	worth a l.'s experience	HOLM 424:81	from those flames No l.	MILT 601:35
think it that 'New L.!'	DICK 283:31	yet been brought to l.	TOYN 895:75	Give me a l.	HASK 400:81
Think of this l.	SHAK 776:8	you risk your l. for it	VAN 908:20	gives a lovely l.	MILL 592:19
this day's l. as yours	EURI 328:53	life-blood l.-b. of a master spirit	MILT 600:2	God called the l. Day	BIBLE 91:82
This was l.—my l.	FRAN 348:21	life-chances l.-c. of the young	MUSG 627:87	golden and silver l.	YEATS 966:12
thorns of l.	SHEL 813:82	life-efficiency l.-e. and adaptability	MUMF 625:39	Hail holy L.	MILT 603:73
those with an irrational fear of l.	CONN 242:96	lifeguard l. duties	COW 249:67	hands...that would l. the world	MILL 593:34
thread from l.'s frayed mantle	ABU 1:16	life-insurance detest l.-i. agents	LEAC 515:9	happy realms of l.	MILT 601:36
threatened its l. with a railway-share	CARR 206:31	life-jacket French for l.-j.	BARN 64:67	Heaven's l. forever shines	SHEL 815:43
threatens the very existence of l.	SONT 834:16	lifeless l. as the piles of dry dust	GLAS 374:46	hours of l. return	ARNO 34:76
threaten to invade my waking l.	ROBBE 717:66	L. in appearance	WILL 946:8	how my l. is spent	MILT 601:26
three-fourths of our l.	ARNO 36:35	life-like not l.-l.; it is alive	CECIL 210:23	I am black...bereaved of l.	BLAKE 139:87
throughout the rest of l.	ORWE 654:55	lifelong l. relationship...divorce will		I am the l. of the world	BIBLE 123:39
thy dissolute l.	SURR 860:2	never	MORR 621:63	infant crying for the l.	TENN 874:77
Till l. and death remember	SWIN 863:80	life-long l.-l. lock	GILB 369:64	In l. inaccessible	SMITH 831:65
time in a man's l.	MALA 561:84	life-sentence escape the l.-s.	LAWR 514:91	into his marvellous l.	BIBLE 130:67
time in everybody's l.	WILD 943:50	l.-s. in the dungeon of self	CONN 243:15	jewel [judged] by the l.	ANON 25:38
time is eating away my l.	BAUD 68:61	life-style considers your whole l.-s.	THOM 887:91	lamps, by whose dear l.	MARV 577:97
time...medium of l.	MANN 566:84	life-support financial system...on l. s.	SOROS 834:35	land of l.	CLIN 230:3
time of l. is short	SHAK 772:63	kept on a l.-s. system	HARR 399:58	last l. has gone	THOM 885:54
time of this mortal l.	BOOK 147:51	lifetime During my l.	MAND 564:53	laws...of l. and shade	CAPO 197:24
'Tis from high l.	POPE 687:94	gather sense...for a whole l.	RILKE 715:36	Lead, kindly L.	NEWM 635:45
to be spiritually minded is l.	BIBLE 125:17	in our l.	GREY 388:62	leave a l....before was dark	WENT 931:53
to breathe were l.	TENN 870:98	In the l. of one person	HORN 430:23	Let there be l.	BIBLE 91:81
to choose l. and d.	LOWE 540:26	l. of happiness!	SHAW 807:13	Let there be l.	MACD 549:28
too far back...in anybody's l.	AMIS 16:53	l. of standing out	JARR 452:84	Let there be l.!	SHEL 816:56
too far out all my l.	SMITH 830:37	l. on this planet	KENN 481:2	level of the l.	FORD 343:94
tournament of l.	NORM 641:54	locked for a l. in this impossible		life and l., with envious haste	ROCH 720:25
tragedy of l. is not that man loses	BROUN 163:18	contradiction	EAGL 309:1	l. after l. well used	MILT 603:81
translate thy l. into death	SHAK 780:17	Love...once a l.	PATM 669:16	l. and shadow never stand still	WEST 932:95
tree of knowledge is not that of L.	BYRON 189:83	Once in a l.	ELIOT 319:27	l., and will aspire	SHAK 762:84
tried to live his l. by it	ANDE 18:75	prosperity...never had in my l.	MACM 556:65	l. at the end	LOWE 540:36
troubled with her lonely l.	PEPYS 673:94	theater has died in my l.	MILL 593:47	l. beyond compare	NEALE 632:7
turn to poetry to interpret l.	ARNO 36:41	too late all my l.-t.!	COWL 250:79	l. breaks where	THOM 883:4
Twice in your l.	FITZ 338:5	twice in our l.	UNIT 905:9	L. dies before thy...word	POPE 689:48
two paths in l.	MANN 566:80	lift L. her with care	HOOD 426:33	l. dissolved in star-showers	SHEL 812:67
two things to aim at in l.	SMITH 829:12	opposite the l. shaft	ORWE 655:72	l. falls and fills	ROET 722:57
unbought grace of l.	BURKE 176:41	lifting inside work with no heavy l.	DOLE 290:95	l. fantastic round	MILT 598:66
unconscious unity with l.	MILL 594:80	ligate L. ducts of dog	BANT 62:35	l. gleams an instant	BECK 72:46
undermine her hold on l.	FORS 344:37	light against the dying of the l.	THOM 884:27	l. heart lives long	SHAK 763:22
unexamined l.	PLATO 681:44	air pollution and...artificial l.	MATT 582:1	l. in manners	ASCH 37:54
unexamined l. is not worth living	SOCR 833:99	a l. to all men	TENN 879:5	l. in the white mackerel sky	BISH 136:26

Lin

l. in the window	SPEN	837:6
l. is braying	SITW	823:99
l. is in the soul	MILT	607:85
l. is still	ELIOT	319:43
l. of learning	RALE	705:46
l. of my mind	CRUZ	256:40
l. of setting suns	WORD	956:55
l. of Terewth	DICK	281:68
l. of the bright world dies	BOUR	153:94
l. of the gospel	JOHN	460:86
l. of the world	BIBLE	114:29
l. of the world	BIBLE	123:39
l. of thought	SHEL	814:94
l. out for the territory	TWAIN	903:68
L. out of darkness!	MILT	607:71
l. out of darkness	DONNE	293:72
l. ranged in the non-space	GIBS	367:15
l., shade and perspective	CONS	245:60
l., she said, not of the sky	NEIL	633:10
l. shineth in darkness	BIBLE	122:16
l. that is love	KEND	480:85
l. that she loves	TENN	876:25
L. thickens	SHAK	797:48
l. thinks it travels faster	PRAT	694:64
l. to counterfeit a gloom	MILT	598:54
l. to lighten the Gentiles	BIBLE	120:70
l. to see that duty	MACA	544:9
l. to shine upon the road	COWP	250:88
l. unto my path	BIBLE	103:28
l. which experience gives	COLE	236:51
l. wife doth make a heavy husband	SHAK	770:25
l. within his own clear breast	MILT	599:72
L. wrestling…incessantly with l.	CRANE	253:56
like a shaft of l.	TENN	872:30
line of festal l.	ARNO	34:92
lived l. in the spring	ARNO	33:69
long l. shakes	TENN	872:38
Lord is my l.	BIBLE	100:49
lord of l.	DOUG	295:2
lost to l. for evermore	BYRON	188:76
lovely lady, garmented in l.	SHEL	815:24
making them see the l.	PLAN	680:25
married to an electric l.	DIMA	286:98
mellowed to that tender l.	BYRON	189:80
men loved darkness rather than l.	BIBLE	122:26
More l.!	GOET	375:71
morning l. creaks down again	SITW	823:8
mosquitoey summer night l.	ASHB	37:59
naked l. bulb	WILL	945:81
Night, the shadow of l.	SWIN	863:86
noose of l.	FITZ	337:68
Not l. them for themselves	SHAK	787:47
Of night and l.	YEATS	966:12
one day, the l.	MANS	567:3
On the l. fantastic	MILT	597:43
out of hell leads up to l.	MILT	603:66
passed away in colder l.	PEAC	671:55
passion for sweetness and l.	ARNO	36:83
poem is…a l. by which	WARR	921:16
poets…set their own inimitable l.	POUND	692:38
Prince of L.	MILT	597:32
pure and endless l.	VAUG	909:39
put out the l.	SHAK	790:39
quality of fiery aery l.	MACD	550:41
radiant l., though sun	MILT	598:72
realms of l.	GURN	390:2
reft the sonne his l.	CHAU	217:92
remember while the l.	SWIN	864:95
restore the l.	DANI	262:31
river of crystal l.	FIELD	335:13
round from the dark and the l.	SWIN	864:12
saw great l.	BIBLE	114:25
season of L.	DICK	282:94
second place of air and l.	FRAME	346:76
seen a great l.	BIBLE	107:59
sees a green l. everywhere	SCHW	751:95
severity of perfect l.	TENN	877:58
sharp l. the fields did lie	FREE	350:48
shed such l. before	MUNRO	626:53
shew l. at Calais	JOHN	461:2
slaked the l. with blood	TENN	879:5
so airy and l. a quality	SHAK	782:87
Some true, some l.	TENN	878:77
such scant l.	WHAR	933:6
sweetness and l.	SWIFT	861:18
that earth lie l.	WALL	918:58
That was the true L.	BIBLE	122:17
the frosty l.	TENN	875:95
The l. that loses	SWIN	863:83
The l. that never was	WORD	961:28
themes in a new l.	LUCAS	541:56
This l., this glory	COLE	235:31
To l. thee thither	WEBS	926:39
turned around from darkness to l.	PLATO	682:65
unchanged, and universal l.	POPE	685:18
University should be a place of l.	DISR	288:60
waited for the l.	ROBI	718:82
when my l. is low	TENN	874:74
where sweetness and l. failed	FORS	344:39
Where there is darkness, l.	FRAN	347:99
with a l. behind her!	GILB	368:30
within…all l. was contained	MARTI	576:70
world of l.	VAUG	909:41
lightbulbs recklessly inserted l.	KENN	480:95
lighten l. our own hearts	SHAK	775:59
l. the tax burden	QUINE	702:22
lightest l. that wear most of it	SHAK	770:4
light-headed l.-h., variable men	STEV	852:38
light-hearted l.-h. way…he seduces	POMP	684:10
lighthouse Keeping a l.-h. with his eyes	CAMP	194:57
sitivation at the l.	DICK	278:62
lighting Bring in the bottled l.	DICK	278:86
through its own internal l. blind	SHEL	814:3
lightning beheld Satan as l.	BIBLE	120:79
brilliance of a l. storm	FLAU	339:19
came by a l. flash	WILS	948:51
different as a moonbeam from l.	BRON	162:78
I Have known the l.'s hour	DAY	267:35
In the golden l.	SHEL	813:92
In thunder, l., or in rain?	SHAK	795:96
L. rods have had it better	NEW	634:39
like flashes of l.	SCHO	748:52
loosed the fatal l.	HOWE	433:92
Mirth is like a flash of l.	ADDI	6:34
O at l. and lashed rod	HOPK	428:69
rather be a l. rod	KESEY	483:64
reading Shakespeare by flashes of l.	COLE	236:45
struck by l.	ORWE	653:23
struck by l. five or six times	JARR	452:84
thunder and l. of Desert Storm	SCHW	750:91
tree On fire by l.	BYRON	187:54
light-o'-love watching his luck…his l.-o.-l.	SERV	757:35
lights always knew the l. were on	STARR	843:27
an all-the-l.-on man	REED	709:31
broken l. of thee	TENN	873:56
carnival l.	GREE	386:22
Father of l.	BIBLE	130:49
Followed false l.	DRYD	303:11
l. around the shore	ROSS	726:54
l. begin to twinkle	TENN	870:2
name Zimmermann in bright l.?	MERM	588:47
spent l. quiver and gleam	ARNO	33:57
There will be l. everywhere	READ	708:96
though the l.	HAWT	402:12
turn on the l.	GUIM	389:88
Turn up the l.	OHEN	648:21
two l. of Christendom	PIUS	680:17
like as she is, I do not l. her	SHAK	773:22
Besides, I l. you not	SHAK	779:3
does not mean that you l. him	CHUR	226:9
Do I not l. that	TAYL	868:57
don't l. something	GREE	385:99
get what you l.	SHAW	808:56
If we are l. you	SHAK	769:1
l. enough to consent	SHAK	779:9
l. it or not	THOM	887:93
l. or dislike them	FORS	344:34
more l. my own	HOPK	429:98
nothing…made me l. him less	CONG	241:49
shall not look upon his l. again	SHAK	780:43
What I l. about Clive	BENT	82:98
what is l. the?	BYRON	188:59
whether I l. it	VAUG	909:31
Whether you l. it not	KHRU	485:91
woman whom you do not l.	ANOU	28:58
liked l. by only four people	HOCK	421:14
like-minded company of the l.-m.	DELI	271:41
likeness any l. of any thing	BIBLE	94:66
l. and correct incidence of light	ALBE	11:32
translate beauty into his l.	SHAK	783:9
likes Agreements in l. and dislikes	CATI	208:97
everyone l. you except yourself	BROWN	164:37
liking Friendships begin with l.	ELIOT	316:59
Thy lust and l.	SKEL	824:31
lilacs l. last…bloom'd	WHIT	938:8
L. out of the dead land	ELIOT	317:95
lilac-time Kew in l.-t.	NOYES	642:69
Lilian Airy, fairy L.	TENN	869:74
lilies And a few l. blow	HOPK	428:65
Beauty lives though l. die	FLEC	340:31
Consider the l. of the field	BIBLE	115:45
feedeth among the l.	BIBLE	107:44
l. and languors of virtue	SWIN	864:91
l. in her hand	ROSS	726:49
l. of ambition	DOUG	295:6
L. that fester	SHAK	802:70
L. without, roses	MARV	576:88
peacocks and l.	RUSK	732:84
put thy pale, lost l. out of mind	DOWS	296:36
roses overgrown, And l.	MARV	577:89
Ye L. male!	CRAB	252:40
Lillabullero half a dozen bars of L.	STER	848:27
Lillian L. as a grown-up	FEIB	331:54
L., you should have stayed a virgin	CART	207:54
Lilliput Swiftian L.	MCCA	548:92
lilting l. at our yowe-milking	ELLI	322:25
lily Daisy and L.	SITW	823:10
How sweet the L. grows	HEBER	406:99
l. all her sweetness	TENN	873:49
l. of the valleys	BIBLE	107:40
pure as the l. in the dell	LAUD	511:15
splendid…glows the l.	FLEC	340:33
The l. whispers	TENN	876:28
to paint the l.	SHAK	768:62
lily-handed l.-h. baronet he	TENN	872:35
lily-silvered l.-s. values	POPE	689:43
lily-white l.-w. reserve	HOLM	423:58
limb bestow on every airth a l.	MONT	615:51
gathering up l. by l.	MILT	600:17
manacled with joint or l.	MILT	602:46
one l. to another	HERB	413:70
limbo l. large and broad	MILT	603:86
limbs decent l. composed	POPE	685:46
don't start measuring her l.	PICA	677:59
ere their l. grew stiff	CONN	242:84
In my l. their former heat?	HERR	415:1
l. may issue	MARL	574:31
l. that fester	ABSE	1:7
l. were old	SCOTT	752:11
lower l. in pants	NASH	631:73
mighty l. asleep	SWIN	864:13
movements of the l.	LEON	522:74
repose for l.	SHAK	800:45
ruddy l. and flourishing hair	BLAKE	139:81
upon the tender l.	WALL	918:58
lime lay l. to tangle her desires	SHAK	759:70
walked through the l.	SOME	833:10
limèd l. soul	SHAK	783:34
limelight led me to the l.	HEAN	405:75
Limerick acquitted by a L. jury	ADAMS	5:8
limestone On l. quarried near	YEATS	967:40
limit l. of its development	ANON	24:5
l. the dangers	KENN	482:25
l. the human spirit	HAWK	401:92
l. to his ambitions	RICH	714:26
l. to the…time a composer	LAMB	506:18
sky is the l.	SHUL	819:30
limitations Argue for your l.	BACH	49:13
I think I've found my l.	BUSH	183:37
only l. those of libel	THUR	891:27
poetry reminds him of his l.	KENN	482:27
limited Experience is never l.	JAMES	450:43
In l. professions	SHAK	791:81
Liberty too must be l.	BURKE	175:25
limits in knowing its l.	KANT	473:20
l.,…are…just an illusion	JORD	469:5
l. of all possible sense-experience	AYER	48:4
l. of expansion	SCHR	749:66
pushing against the l.	DAWK	267:23
small imperfect l.	HEAN	404:69
wants have no l.	FLAU	339:26
within ancient l.	HAWT	402:11
witness our own l.	THOR	888:27
limner-laureate l.-l. of the beauty	ALLEN	13:78
limousine All we want is a l.	MACN	557:97
One perfect l.	PARK	664:11
Limpopo greasy L. River	KIPL	491:37
L. of swamped Ninth Avenue	AMIS	16:46
limps l. once she sees someone	MONT	614:35
Lin young Tam L. is there	BALL	59:73

Lincoln 1178

Lincoln L.'s bedroom! — ONAS 650:51
  reservoir from which L. also drew — ACHE 2:28
  When Abraham L. was shovelled — SAND 742:17
Lindsay gang wi' me, Lizzy L — BALL 59:65
line all along the l. — WEBB 925:7
  cancel half a l. — FITZ 337:70
  cannot be a new l. — WILL 946:19
  Choose thou whatever suits the l. — COLE 235:26
  direction of the right l. — NEWT 635:57
  end of the l. — MILL 593:47
  fight it out on this l. — GRANT 381:8
  Haven't I heard that l. before? — SHER 818:3
  justification in every l. — CONR 243:25
  l. dividing the state — GALB 357:19
  l. of least resistance — AMERY 15:25
  l. where man leaves off — FROST 352:2
  measuring l. in his hand — BIBLE 112:58
  motion in a right l. — NEWT 635:56
lion l. hath roared — BIBLE 111:51
  l. in the way — BIBLE 105:97
  L. looked at Alice — CARR 205:17
  l. shall eat straw — BIBLE 110:10
  l. shall eat straw like the ox — BIBLE 108:62
  living dog is better than a dead l. — BIBLE 106:26
  looketh upon a l. — BIBLE 112:68
  nation…had the l. heart — CHUR 226:12
  one day as a l. — MUSS 627:90
  out of the paw of the l. — BIBLE 96:37
  pained desert l. — ARNO 34:97
  still a living l. — SOLZ 833:7
  Strong is the l. — SMART 826:65
  To rouse a l. — SHAK 771:36
  unicorn and l. wild — SHAK 762:96
  winged L.'s marble piles — BYRON 188:58
  would be mated by the l. — SHAK 791:55
  wrath of the l. — BLAKE 140:2
lion-like L.-l., in full-mouthed — CRAIK 252:51
lions like l. to the roaring slaughter — CUMM 257:59
  L. make leopards tame — SHAK 764:31
  Rise like l. — SHEL 813:74
  stronger than l. — BIBLE 96:42
  throne was supported by l. — BACON 51:67
  young l. do lack — BIBLE 100:56
lip contempt and anger of his l.! — SHAK 786:11
  He bit his l. — PERE 674:16
  l. Of his world — DAY 267:38
  No nearer the heart than the l. — ANON 21:58
  shoot out the l. — BIBLE 99:42
  Teach not thy l. — SHAK 761:35
  what moistens the l. — WHIT 938:17
lipped l., and trembled kissing — SHAK 794:63
lips And soft as l. — SWIN 863:84
  at the touching of the l. — TENN 871:12
  coming from the l. of another — CARP 202:50
  Eternity was in our l. — SHAK 794:49
  far more red than her l. — SHAK 802:83
  From my l. would flow — SHEL 814:99
  hands and our l. — SWIN 864:12
  keep the door of my l. — BIBLE 104:47
  kent her be her caller l. — SOUT 835:40
  kissed her l. with such a…smack — SHAK 762:72
  kiss my parched l. — SHAK 768:65
  kiss that is placed on my l. — DARIO 263:45
  lay upon thy l. — SHAK 795:82
  let me put my l. to it — DICK 279:16
  Life and these l. — SHAK 766:9
  life with kisses in my l. — SHAK 766:11
  l. are like a thread of scarlet — BIBLE 107:45
  l. are not yet unsealed — BALD 57:34
  l., as sunlight drinketh dew — TENN 869:76
  l. espous'd — HERR 415:7
  l. more scarlet — YEATS 967:30
  l. of a strange woman — BIBLE 104:56
  l. suck forth my soul — MARL 573:29
  l. that are for others — TENN 872:43
  man of unclean l. — BIBLE 107:55
  never come out of a ladys l. — FLEM 340:45
  On a poet's l. — SHEL 814:13
  open thou my l. — BIBLE 101:74
  playing about his l. — THUR 890:76
  pretty form to the l. — DICK 282:91
  put my l. together—and blow — FURT 356:90
  Read my l. — BUSH 182:99
  Red l. are not so red — OWEN 657:27
  rosy l. and cheeks — SHAK 802:80
  round their narrow l. — ROSS 726:59
  steal immortal blessing from her l. — SHAK 766:97

  sulky l. were shaped for sin — BETJ 89:42
  take thy l. away — SHAK 788:72
  through my l. to unawakened earth — SHEL 813:84
  thy l. my history — SIDN 820:51
  Truth sits upon the l. — ARNO 34:98
  two l., indifferent red — SHAK 785:90
  Upon her skinny l. — SHAK 795:4
  Watch my l. — BLUN 143:83
  What l. my l. have kissed — MILL 592:23
  witchcraft in your l. — SHAK 776:1
  with stammering l. — BIBLE 108:69
  with their l. do honour me — BIBLE 108:72
lipstick got on too much l. — NASH 631:82
  put l. on a hog — RICH 714:13
  putting l. on the Venus de Milo — PICK 677:65
liquefaction That l. of her clothes — HERR 416:16
liquid Cats, no less l. — TESS 880:20
  first place of l. darkness — FRAME 346:76
  let their l. siftings fall — ELIOT 317:81
  l. Euclids in foolscaps of air — AVIS 47:1
  l. had no time — GREE 385:4
  l. which rots braces — MORT 621:75
liquidation l. of the British Empire — CHUR 226:96
  nation about to go into voluntary l. — MACI 553:3
liquids l., all one's favourite hues — DOYLE 297:75
liquor bring it home in l. — DICK 279:19
  bumper of good l. — SHER 817:82
  Good l., I stoutly maintain — GOLD 369:61
  Here's yet some l. left — SHAK 785:72
  lads for the l. are there — HOUS 431:46
  licensed l. traffic — TWAIN 903:76
  l. for boys — JOHN 463:66
  L. is one way out — WILL 945:94
  l. is quicker — NASH 630:59
  l. is the only mechanical relief — HEMI 410:77
  L.…sidestepping necessity — FADI 329:4
  Livelier l. than the Muse — HOUS 432:57
  some such…spiritual l. — BYRON 191:32
  world's largest l. store — BALL 58:47
liquorice allsorts that L.A. of things — BOYLE 154:17
liquors fumes of tobacco and l. — LEWIS 527:66
  Hot and rebellious l. — SHAK 778:71
lisp Look you l. — SHAK 779:8
list enemy reads the l. — WELL 929:98
  got a little l. — GILB 369:61
  l. of subscribers — JOHN 464:81
listen don't l. to writers talking — HELL 408:45
  If an actor reads…I hardly l. — SALI 740:77
  l. carefully indeed — TRUM 900:88
  l. to others — GRANT 381:1
  L. to them moan — RAMS 706:52
  l. to what I'm saying — MARL 572:93
  l. to what others say — HOLM 424:72
  l. when I am unhappy — SMITH 830:40
  l. without meeting — TOCQ 892:30
  l.…you don't hear — NYE 642:76
  people l. to you — SNOW 832:81
  privilege of wisdom to l. — HOLM 424:83
  rather l. than work — BOYD 153:9
  teach me now to l. — HEAN 405:79
  wonderful to l. to — HARDY 396:2
listener give a picture to the l. — COLT 238:86
  modern…l.…is…overloaded — BELL 78:96
  resistance in your l. — MILL 595:93
listening Children…never…good at l. — WYLIE 964:10
  L.…that mistresses offer — ANON 27:27
  nobody's l. — WELLS 930:37
  subdue themselves to 'l.-in' — JOHAN 456:70
  The secret to talking is l. — WORD 960:11
  seek repose In l. — WORD 958:74
lists collected l. of fatal diseases — HELL 407:29
lit not see them l. again — GREY 388:62
  whole fleet's l. up — WOOD 954:3
literacy Cultural l. is the oxygen — HIRS 419:74
literal money stays l. — DWOR 308:44
literary care for its l. inheritance — ELIOT 319:28
  claim to l. fame — BENN 80:56
  fully mature l. tradition — FRYE 354:54
  l. education did not fit — BURG 175:4
  l. industry would not exist — LESS 524:1
  l. intellectuals at one pole — SNOW 832:77
  l. man—with a wooden leg — DICK 283:14
  L. Review under my editorship — WAUGH 923:49
  l. work — JOHN 460:64
  lowest class is l. footmen — HAZL 404:55
  more…than any other l. form — DUDEK 305:73

  neurotic can…be a l. genius — AUCH 42:63
  Never l. attempt was more — HUME 439:8
  parole of l. men — JOHN 464:80
  viewing them as a l. performance — WHIT 938:16
  when she marries a l. man — CHEE 218:7
  l. with the l., I am Impelled — PARK 663:99
literature All modern American l. — HEMI 410:76
  All the rest is l. — VALE 907:4
  art and l. are left — LEWIS 527:58
  Bad l. — GIDE 368:23
  base of all l. — GIRA 372:22
  camp-following eunuchs of l. — HEMI 409:61
  classics are only primitive l. — LEAC 515:17
  curse of Scottish l. — MUIR 623:13
  edge of the chair of L. — THUR 890:66
  English l.'s performing flea — OCAS 646:80
  English poetic l. — GRAV 383:36
  every other branch of classical l. — DICK 278:75
  Everything else is mere l. — VERL 911:61
  face of American l. — PORT 690:75
  function of l. — TRIL 897:18
  ghoul of l. — DELI 271:39
  Great l. is simply language — POUND 691:12
  had been formed by l. — LESS 523:93
  lies and l. — LAFO 504:52
  Life without l. — ABRAM 1:6
  Life wouldn't turn out…like L. — BARN 64:75
  l. clear and cold and pure — LEWIS 527:60
  l.…gives no man a sinecure — POUND 691:17
  L. happens at the level of the sentence — RUSH 732:76
  L. has a lot to answer for — LIVE 531:52
  l. has tended to exalt — MARI 571:76
  L. is…about having sex — LODGE 534:93
  L. is a human apocalypse — FRYE 354:53
  L. is a luxury — CHES 220:52
  L. is a power line — CURT 259:97
  L. is based not on life — STEV 850:88
  L. is conscious mythology — FRYE 354:54
  L. is doomed — ORWE 655:69
  L.…is lonely — MOORE 616:73
  'l.' is more pluralistic now — MORR 620:55
  L. is news — POUND 692:15
  L. is not an abstract science — QUIL 702:14
  L. is strewn with the wreckage — WOOLF 955:29
  L. is the art of writing — CONN 242:95
  L. is the operating instructions — LE GU 520:19
  L. is the orchestration — WILD 943:46
  L.…makes justice — PALEY 661:51
  l. of their country — TROL 898:47
  l. seeks to communicate power — DE 273:83
  L. was the best plaything — GARC 359:65
  l. would be greatly — NASH 631:81
  mark…of Socialist l. — ORWE 653:18
  mars good l. — TWAIN 904:97
  men who have failed in l. and art — DISR 288:57
  metaphysics…fantastic l. — BORG 150:55
  moratorium on l. talk — ROTH 728:95
  Movies are more likely than l. to reach deep feelings — MAIL 560:64
  muse of modern l. — SONT 834:14
  neither created nor supplanted l. — BAUD 68:71
  no evidence from modern l. — BELL 77:81
  one character in l. or drama — PAGE 659:14
  Our l. is a substitute for religion — ELIOT 318:20
  people which ceases to produce l. — ELIOT 319:28
  people who have read good l. — HAYA 402:40
  Philistine of genius in l. — ARNO 36:38
  prettiest love stories in all l. — PARK 663:99
  produce a little l. — JAMES 450:35
  regard l. as entertainment — COND 240:14
  remarks are not l. — STEIN 845:62
  science fiction is the apocalyptic l. — BALL 60:85
  Show me an enemy of l. — HAMI 394:52
  stamp out l. — WAUGH 923:69
  the locks of l. — TENN 879:10
  The only authentic l. — CRON 256:28
  Three-fourths of philosophy and l. — SNYD 833:94
  Today's l.: prescriptions — KRAUS 499:5
  true lover of l. — SOUT 835:52
  truly black l. — MORR 620:59
  turn to early Irish l. — OFAO 647:96
  tweed through twentieth-century l. — BENN 80:46
  used l. as an ornament — VARG 908:26
  what is going to happen to l. — PRIT 696:17
literatures Of these two l. — ARNO 35:8
litigation l. takes the place of sex — VIDAL 912:93
little Austria is a l. world — HEBB 406:97

living

But wants that l. strong	HOLM 423:60	
here a l., and there a l.	BIBLE 108:69	
He was born with l.	JACK 448:5	
how l. the mind is	JOHN 462:35	
knows so l....accomplishes	MCFA 551:70	
Let all the l. poets	SMITH 830:36	
l. along with the great	WILS 949:81	
l. body with a mighty heart	SHAK 775:65	
l. inaccuracy sometimes saves	SAKI 739:69	
L. Johnny Head-in-Air	HOFF 422:33	
l. minds are interested	HUBB 434:98	
l. things	GIBS 367:14	
l. things...the most important	DOYLE 297:52	
l. tiny boy	SHAK 786:25	
l. to say	SKEL 824:27	
l. with the fear of the Lord	BIBLE 104:75	
never lost a l. fish	FIELD 335:14	
Only the l. people pay taxes	HELM 408:52	
Poor L. Rich Girl	COWA 249:44	
There is our l. bungalow	REAG 709:13	
There's l. to relate	CARR 205:21	
those who had l. to say	BEER 74:89	
tried a l.	STEV 853:79	
within a l. room	SMITH 830:35	
With l. here to do or see	WORD 959:97	
works of a l. genius	ADDI 7:55	
littleness genius is an enormous l.	PATC 668:6	
Little Piney axe on the L. P.	RED 709:19	
live all but one—shall l.	SHAK 783:15	
bear to l., or dare to die	POPE 687:87	
Begins to l. That day	DICK 284:48	
begin to l. in the present	CHEK 218:20	
better to dream...than to l.	PROU 697:39	
better to l. quietly	ELIOT 315:14	
but one bare hour to l.	MARL 573:30	
But thou l. fearless	HERR 415:3	
cannot l. with you	DICK 284:40	
cannot l. with you—or without	MART 576:77	
Come l. with me	DONNE 292:37	
create traditions...not to l.	MARC 569:50	
Days are where we l.	LARK 509:72	
decided to l. forever	HELL 407:26	
desires to l. long	SWIFT 862:51	
Did ever so long l.	SHAK 800:31	
does not l. long	HOMER 425:1	
do not l. to experience death	WITT 951:23	
Do you want to l. forever?	DALY 261:19	
Dying, we l.	BROW 169:83	
Easy l. and quiet die	SCOTT 754:64	
evil manners l. in brass	SHAK 805:56	
forgets to l.	LABR 502:22	
For to me to l. is Christ	BIBLE 128:96	
For what do we l.	AUST 46:63	
hath a life to l.	RAIN 705:37	
hath but a short time to l.	BOOK 148:98	
home to l. with you	JARR 452:88	
How can men bear...to l.	CORN 247:4	
how long I have to l.	BOOK 149:14	
how to l. democracy	ROOS 724:1	
how to l. well	GERB 364:62	
how to l. well	THAC 880:28	
idea for which I can l.	KIER 485:98	
If I'd known I was gonna l.	BLAKE 139:76	
If we l. inside a bad joke	RABAN 703:2	
If you l. long enough	DE 268:47	
inability to l.	GONC 377:41	
in him we l., and move	BIBLE 125:93	
I should bid thee l.	TENN 873:48	
isn't fit to l.	KING 487:26	
It is best to l.	SOPH 834:32	
let us l. and love	CAMP 195:72	
Let us l., my Lesbia	CATU 209:6	
lief not be, as l. to be	SHAK 776:8	
l. according to the same design	VIAN 911:73	
l. a good life	HALD 392:25	
l. all you can	JAMES 451:51	
l. a long time	AUBER 41:55	
L. always in this paradisal now	KHAY 485:57	
l. among human beings or not	WILD 943:50	
l. among wicked people	RICH 714:12	
L. and Let Die	FLEM 340:40	
L. and lie reclined	TENN 870:92	
l. as if it were the first time	BIOY 135:4	
l. as long as you may	SOUT 835:34	
'I.' as to...be lived	MERR 589:50	
l. at the pitch	EBER 310:10	
l. beyond their incomes	SAKI 739:63	
l. by fame	SPEN 839:47	
l. by robbing the rich	SHAW 807:22	
l. by trade	RUSK 733:16	
l. by what they know	HAMP 395:74	
l. dangerously	NIET 638:97	
l. deliberately	THOR 888:37	
l. each day as though one's last	AURE 45:47	
l. for months without	WARD 920:2	
l. for years	AUDEN 43:84	
l. free	JONS 466:47	
l. free and uncommitted	THOR 888:36	
l. half our lives in England	HYDE 443:19	
l., I die	LABE 501:3	
L. in fragments no longer	FORS 344:30	
l. in love	SIDN 820:59	
l. in the Middle Ages	SMITH 830:38	
l. in you...when you are absent	SCEVE 746:17	
l. it to the full	SPARK 836:68	
l. like our names	WALC 916:12	
l. may we	DUNB 306:4	
l. no longer by thinking	SHAK 780:20	
l. no longer in monument	SHAK 774:57	
l. not in myself	BYRON 187:53	
l. on horseback	BIRD 136:8	
l. on your knees	IBAR 444:5	
l. the rest of our lives	HERZ 416:26	
l. the time that a match	STEV 852:52	
l. to be 150	DAVIS 265:93	
l. under one form	JOHN 462:24	
l. upon soup and bouille	SMOL 831:67	
l. very happily	JOHN 461:96	
l. we as merry as the day	SHAK 773:24	
l. where the idea and the fact collided	MCIL 553:96	
l. with a good conscience	SMITH 829:18	
l. with famine	JEFF 453:13	
l. within our means	WARD 920:1	
l. without killing	MILL 594:68	
l. with scarlet Majors	SASS 745:84	
l. with the objective of being happy	FRANK 348:4	
L. you, or are you aught	SHAK 795:4	
Man cannot l.	GILL 370:83	
married people l. longer?	FIEL 335:32	
minute by minute they l.	YEATS 966:19	
mortal man may l.	SHAK 760:9	
must please to l.	JOHN 459:44	
Nay, but to l.	SHAK 784:42	
no more to l.	SWIN 864:14	
None would l. past years	DRYD 300:38	
nothing to l. for	GERV 366:85	
nought...on the earth doth l.	SHAK 766:87	
one day l. in a nation	KING 486:25	
one month you have to l.	GILB 369:59	
ones who are mad to l.	KERO 483:53	
only people...who really l.	SLOAN 825:55	
people will l. on	SAND 742:23	
religion...anything but l. for it	COLT 238:81	
society in which they l.	JAMES 451:58	
So longe mote ye l.	CHAU 216:59	
someone you can stand to l. with	TROL 898:60	
So shall I l.	SHAK 802:68	
So wise...do never l. long	SHAK 761:42	
tell...stories in order to l.	DIDI 286:82	
They l. in fredome	JAME 449:18	
Thus did they l.	LOVE 538:87	
Thus do I l.	DYER 309:50	
To l. is like to love	BUTL 186:9	
To l. with thee	RALE 705:43	
We l. and learn	POMF 684:9	
We l. and learn	TILM 891:17	
We l., as we dream	CONR 243:28	
We l. ignorant	ABU 1:12	
We l. in the great indoors	RAINE 705:38	
When I am happy I l.	SMITH 830:40	
when you l. with a person	FORD 342:89	
where most people l.	GRAY 383:43	
Whether we l....or die	BIBLE 126:33	
Who l. under the shadow	SPEN 837:99	
would you l. for ever?	FRED 349:38	
Yif thou wolte l. frely	ANON 21:51	
You might as well l.	PARK 664:19	
lived died as he had l.	CLEM 229:85	
discover that I had not l.	THOR 889:37	
Had he l., Had he l.	DAVIS 266:8	
Had it l. long	MARV 576:88	
Had we l.	SCOTT 751:6	
I have l., beyond my means	WILDE 942:23	
l. before Agamemnon's time	HORA 430:12	
l. long enough	SAND 742:38	
l. more than people who cannot	HAYA 402:20	
l. to be carried in a basket	SHAK 773:12	
Mary l. by wondering	KAVA 474:50	
must be l. forwards	KIER 485:4	
tell me roundly, that I l.	HERB 413:63	
while you l. it	GLAS 374:46	
livelihood read and work for a l.	MONT 613:13	
seek a l. elsewhere	CANT 197:12	
work for their honest l.	SWIFT 862:57	
liveliness a certain l. of mind	RABE 704:20	
l. of my disposition	FRED 349:37	
liver blood in his l.	SHAK 786:15	
end up with cirrhosis of the l.	EAGL 309:1	
I ate his l.	TALLY 866:19	
Life loves the l.	ANGE 19:95	
l. slices fried	JOYCE 470:29	
Liverpool aspect of lewdness in L.	FORD 342:90	
folk that live in L.	CHES 221:90	
L. and L. reserves	SHAN 805:65	
young men from L.	BAIN 55:94	
lives all their l....they'll have to rush	DUNN 307:15	
but dying l.	SPEN 839:40	
But human creatures' l.!	HOOD 426:31	
conceive of our l. as narratives	LEHM 520:21	
cracks of other people's l.	WHAR 933:6	
door to their own l.	AREN 31:10	
even terror of their l.	SHAR 806:70	
Even though our l. wander	PROU 698:56	
events in our l.	WELTY 931:48	
every detail of our l.	WAVE 925:2	
Every instant of L.	GIDE 368:22	
fatal climax with their l.	SASS 745:83	
gambling in human l.	DYSON 309:60	
going on with their own l.	KRAM 499:3	
has happened in our l.	MUNRO 626:53	
He l., he wakes	SHEL 815:41	
he who lives more l.	WILDE 942:20	
how he l.	JOHN 462:19	
idle l.	WORD 961:32	
impoverish our l.	SCHU 750:80	
in their l. fought for life	SPEN 837:93	
lead people to give their l.	EINS 313:76	
light heart l. long	SHAK 763:22	
lived many l.	SLES 825:52	
L. and Loves of a She-Devil	WELD 928:80	
l. cease to be illumined	HAMM 394:54	
l. have been given to find	MACD 550:41	
l. not three good men	SHAK 771:45	
L. of great men	LONG 535:16	
l. of men and women	HOOV 427:43	
l. of quiet desperation	THOR 888:29	
l. of the medieval saints	SAKI 739:54	
looking to other l. for answers	BRAU 157:80	
Man l. by science	JAMES 451:62	
man l. well	KIPL 489:77	
Most people spend...their l.	LABR 502:26	
music of men's l.	SHAK 765:63	
ninety l. have been taken away	MCGO 551:73	
no fish ye're buying—it's men's l.	SCOTT 753:49	
Not a moment of your l.	BLUN 143:74	
obstructed by the l. of Christians	JOHN 460:86	
of all l.	STEV 851:31	
other Annapurnas in the l. of men	HERZ 416:26	
our l. are...dark interludes	ONEI 651:66	
our l. resemble the stuff of...novels	AUST 47:92	
Our l....shall end	PHIL 679:53	
our l. would grow together	SWIN 864:4	
political l....end in failure	POWE 693:60	
poor l. we lead	NIGH 639:21	
pounces upon it and l.	MILL 593:59	
quintessence of their l.	LOWE 539:96	
repeat in the l. of the millions	WILD 943:51	
rest of their l.	TREE 896:1	
some l. duller	TAKU 866:12	
statements about the world and our l.	BOYD 154:14	
their jumpsome l.	KIPL 491:43	
Upon the King...our l.	SHAK 775:84	
waking moment of their l.	KING 487:34	
Where nothing l. but crosses	SHAK 764:43	
Women Whose L. Are Food	OATES 643:8	
writers' l.	GIBB 367:14	
liveth l., and was dead	BIBLE 131:89	
living act of l. had been enjoyable	BOWL 153:4	
'alternative' modes of l.	SELF 756:11	
Are you yet l.?	SHAK 773:20	
be considerate to the l.	VOLT 914:44	

living-room

Begin by l.	ANOU 28:67	both loved and l.	MIDD 590:76	with your l. girded	BIBLE 93:59
better than l. badly?	CRIT 255:12	loathing deepest l. to the stomach	SHAK 767:32	loitered l. my life away	HAZL 404:54
beyond the language of the l.	ELIOT 321:83	l. of the tragedies of the past	PAIS 660:46	loiterers Liege of all l.	SHAK 763:9
bodies of the l.	SPEN 837:12	loathsome Exercise is l.	TWAIN 904:95	Lolita L., light of my life	NABO 628:4
by l. well	JONS 468:88	l. mask has fallen	SHEL 814:18	loll l. on velvet and satin	FRAN 348:23
catch the Manners l.	POPE 686:71	loaves five barley l.	BIBLE 122:33	Lombardy waveless plain of L.	SHEL 812:64
cut off out of the land of the l.	BIBLE 109:95	five l., and two fishes	BIBLE 117:98	London All of L. littered	MACN 558:2
dead might as well speak to the l.	CATH 208:89	l. sold for a penny	SHAK 759:95	art, in L.	DRYD 300:35
difference is...that of the l.	CIXO 227:42	metaphor...provides two l.	MALA 562:87	As L. is to Paddington	CANN 196:7
Different l. is not l.	SPEN 837:3	lob nothing but a l.	RUNY 731:61	at once removed...to L.	ANON 23:88
Disillusionment in l.	STEIN 845:64	lobbies l. during the interval	TYNAN 904:99	best built city...L. excepted	DEFOE 269:79
do not eat for the good of l.	EMER 324:70	lobby gentlemen...in the same L.	PALM 662:73	best club in L.	DICK 283:22
drink for a l.	KERR 483:58	go into the l. against us	BALD 57:34	Cam ye doun by L.?	ANON 22:77
equal dominion...over every l. thing	STAN 842:16	lobes disease of the frontal l.	ALBEE 11:27	crowd flowed over L. Bridge	ELIOT 318:97
fever called 'L.'	POE 683:94	lobster 'Tis the voice of the l.	CARR 204:83	dependence of L. on Washington	BENN 79:32
get mine own l.	BOOK 148:80	local little l. difficulties	MACM 556:63	do not live in L.	RICH 714:12
good l. and good poetry	LUCAS 541:52	l. thing called Christianity	HARDY 397:26	far from L.!	NOYES 642:69
in the land of the l.	BIBLE 102:20	location worst possible l. in the world	ACHE 3:56	foggy day in L. Town	GERS 365:78
it's l. that's hard	MO 610:64	locations visiting l. such as diners	COUP 248:26	gazed at the L. skies	BETJ 88:18
l. a little more or dying	MAIL 559:42	loch bonnie banks o' L. Lomond	ANON 22:79	Hell is...much like L.	SHEL 813:87
l. and dying at once	KUNI 501:41	Lochinvar O, young l.	SCOTT 752:21	If a man bring to L.	PETTY 676:45
L. and partly l.	ELIOT 319:46	lock crying at the l.	MILL 595:98	impressions...since I left L.	MACM 556:67
l. are dead	MACM 556:72	Joy, I did l. thee up	HERB 414:81	it's still 1938 in L.	MIDL 590:83
l. dead man	SHAK 762:93	life-long l.	GILB 369:64	journey from L.	TALB 866:14
l. dog is better than a dead lion	BIBLE 106:26	L. the door, Lariston	HOGG 422:41	L. Bridge was a greater piece of work	ADDI 7:35
l. in sin	HERB 412:39	l. your heart away	DEPP 273:79	L., hast thou accused	SURR 860:2
L. is abnormal	IONE 447:53	twisting that l.	STER 848:46	L. is a modern Babylon	DISR 288:42
L. is an illness	CHAM 213:71	why l. him in?	SHAW 808:33	L. is enchanting	WOOLF 955:22
l. is made...by selling	WILD 943:47	locked l., letter'd, braw brass-collar	BURNS 177:80	L....Metropolis of Great-Britain	BAIL 55:87
l. know No bounds?	SHIR 819:16	locket l. around his neck	SOME 833:10	L. money-dealers	BAGE 55:78
L. next to love	TRUD 899:71	locks drowned honour by the l.	SHAK 771:37	L. spread out in the sun	LARK 509:87
l. stood motionless	WILL 944:64	few l. which are left	SOUT 835:43	L., that great cesspool	DOYLE 296:38
L., we fret	BROW 169:83	knotty and combinèd l.	SHAK 781:60	L., that great sea	SHEL 814:2
l. well...most important	PLATO 681:46	l. were like the raven	BURNS 179:16	L., thou art of townes	DUNB 306:2
l. which are yet alive	BIBLE 106:16	Never shake Thy gory l.	SHAK 797:49	longer to elect a Mayor for L.	WATE 922:32
long habit of l.	BROW 165:75	shaking her invincible l.	MILT 601:20	lowest and vilest alleys in L.	DOYLE 297:59
man to earn his own l.	MORE 618:13	turn those amber l. to grey	DRAY 298:93	man in L.	GALT 359:53
miserable beyond all l. things	SHEL 812:48	locomotion purposes of human l.	DOUG 295:11	many MPs never see the L.	LIVI 532:56
New York...'l.' there	DIDI 286:81	locomotive l....more efficient	CANN 196:6	must have a L. audience	AUST 46:70
no l. with thee	ADDI 6:27	More powerful than a l.!	SIEG 820:61	my Acquaintance in L.	SWIFT 862:58
no pleasure i' l.	ELIOT 315:23	rails are to a l.	RIVE 716:54	No foteball player...within...L.	ELIZ 321:2
partnership not only between...l.	BURKE 176:45	up to the approaching l.	KAFKA 472:4	out into the streets of L.	HICKS 417:45
pattern...Of dead and l.	ELIOT 320:68	were never no l.	GINS 372:7	rainy Sunday in L.	DE 273:81
prospect of l. in it	JAY 453:5	locomotives l. travelling twice as fast	ANON 23:86	rather live in lively L.	EWART 328:74
realize Art in l. forms	HOLM 424:80	where the l. sing	LIND 530:22	reach the length o' L.	SCOTT 753:59
repetition of the wrong way of l.	DURR 308:38	Loc Suilig steed by L. S.	MCCA 547:74	scarce go to L.	LASS 511:12
scale of l. must be reduced	CHUR 225:72	locust l. blossoms	WILL 946:23	stagecoach from L. to Oxford	HAZL 403:38
still a l. lion	SOLZ 833:7	years that the l. hath eaten	BIBLE 111:47	this is a L. particular	DICK 281:58
sure of l. forever	HAWT 401:1	locusts famine grew, and l. came	THOM 883:9	tired of L.	JOHN 463:56
they must hate to work for a l.	ROWL 729:19	meat was l.	BIBLE 114:19	tumble...from L. to York	KING 488:52
tired of l.	WHITE 935:39	lodestar his wife Is the l.	PARK 663:96	tumbler of L. Water	SMITH 830:50
upon all the l. and the dead	JOYCE 470:18	lodesterre language he was the l.	LYDG 542:78	would have sold L.	RICH 714:11
was l. is now dead	ELIOT 318:8	lodge where thou lodgest, I will l.	BIBLE 96:23	Londonmania L. was now stronger	EDGE 311:46
wasted his substance with riotous l.	BIBLE 121:89	lodging give us a safe l.	NEWM 635:46	lone L., l., and l. I stand	GILM 371:96
who l. had no note	GIBB 367:7	l., wife, and children	DICK 280:47	lonelier l. than any spinster	GREER 387:44
Why seek ye the l. among the dead?	BIBLE 122:11	lodgings fair lightsome l.	WEBS 927:45	no l. man in death	HEMI 409:72
world...does not owe us a l.	EDIN 312:49	pent up in frowzy l.	SMOL 831:69	loneliest l. game of all	ARLO 32:34
living-room comfort of the l. r.	MCLU 556:40	loft in a l. in Salt Lake Farm	THOM 884:35	loneliness All that bowery l.	TENN 877:64
Livingstone 'Dr L., I presume?'	STAN 842:11	loftiness l. of thought	DRYD 303:19	gift of l.	WALK 917:33
wouldn't vote for Ken L.	SCAR 746:15	log big rotting l.	WHITE 934:29	If a cloud knew l.	RICH 713:9
Lloyd L. George could not see a belt	ASQU 38:89	Blackened l. and stump	LAWS 514:97	intensifying his l.	BELL 78:90
L. George spoke	BENN 81:69	logic as it isn't it ain't. That's l.	CARR 204:97	L. is not being alone	BERE 83:14
lo L., thro' her works	SMART 826:68	By a kind of perverted l.	FANON 330:14	L. of the Long Distance Runner	SILL 821:69
load for her the heavier l.	BALZ 61:98	Conspirators have a l.	DELI 271:42	Man's l. is but his fear	ONEI 651:62
how to l. and bless	KEATS 477:32	Her l. was a combination	TOOLE 894:58	lonely All the l. people	LENN 522:51
like a heavy l.	HUGH 435:13	kind of internal l.	HONE 425:14	are not l.	WEBB 925:8
l. of sorrow	SHAK 774:52	l. and rhetoric	BACON 53:39	I was a child and very l.	RHYS 712:78
taking home a 'l.'	BURT 181:71	L. doesn't apply to	MINS 608:12	oft, in l. rooms	WORD 956:53
under their fruits l.	SPEN 839:39	L. is rare	DOYLE 297:60	the end of l. street	PRES 694:72
loaded dice of God are always l.	EMER 324:57	l. of discovery	NISB 639:27	to be l. as an artist	THOM 883:14
loads ploughs and borne our l.	MUIR 624:22	l.'s chiefest end?	MARL 573:20	long by ten words...too l.	SHAK 768:47
loaf half a l....better than no bread	CHES 220:78	logical fears...and remains l.	SAINT 738:45	how l. this is going to take	KEIL 479:57
loafed to have l. and lost	THUR 890:80	l. deduction from...hypotheses	EINS 314:89	I l. for Europe	RIMB 715:42
loafing cricket as organized l.	TEMP 869:67	never met a steadily l. person	GELL 363:32	It's l....but it's very, very beautiful	CARR 205:20
loam Men are but gilded l.	SHAK 764:32	straightforward l. manner	WATS 922:41	kiss L. as my exile	SHAK 799:4
rife as the l. Of prairies	CRANE 253:66	logicians If we may believe our l.	ADDI 7:44	live as l. as you may	SOUT 835:54
loan brief l. of his own body	CABE 191:2	logic-mill Philosophers...sort of L.-m.	CARL 200:85	l. and loath at going	RANS 707:70
God has us...on l.	FERRE 334:98	logs pile the l.	POUND 692:27	l., dark, boggy, dirty	GOLD 376:13
memories on l.	FRAME 346:77	Tom bears l.	SHAK 763:27	L. run is a misleading guide	KEYN 484:73
they would still give you a l.	KNOB 495:12	loins Elijah...girded up his l.	BIBLE 97:65	l. run, the easiest	MILL 594:86
loaning moaning on ilka green l.	ELLI 322:25	fire of my l.	NABO 628:4	Lord, how l.?	BIBLE 107:56
loans effect of the new l. of England	BAGE 55:77	forth the fatal l.	SHAK 765:65	merry as the day is l.	SHAK 773:24
loath l. to cast away my speech	SHAK 785:89	Gird up now thy l.	BIBLE 98:13	night is l.	SHAK 798:63
long and l. at going	RANS 707:70	gird up the l. of your mind	BIBLE 130:64	shame will be too l.	SHAK 776:95
shall l. yourselves	BIBLE 111:33	leathern girdle about his l.	BIBLE 114:19	So L., and Thanks	ADAMS 4:78
loathe l. to rin an' chase thee	BURNS 177:77	l. girt about with truth	BIBLE 128:95	stay the way they are very l.	FORD 343:15
loathed and l. him	TWAIN 902:40	thicker than my father's l.	BIBLE 97:58	thou art l., and lank, and brown	COLE 235:14

lords

too l. and too loud	WAUGH 924:79	loose dare let l.	JONS 467:51	L. said unto my L.	BIBLE 102:17
Too l. a sacrifice	YEATS 966:20	To be l. with grammar	EDWA 313:64	L., save us: we perish	BIBLE 116:61
way is l.	SENE 757:22	loosed l. a little season	BIBLE 132:21	L.'s command	GURN 390:2
long-distance L. d. Runner	SILL 821:69	looted museum to be l.	RAINE 705:41	L.'s First Word	FARJ 330:20
longed L. for him.	ATWO 41:50	lopped l. off…your consciousness	ORWE 653:19	L.! since thou knowest	MONT 615:51
longer made this letter l.	PASC 668:95	**lord** abomination unto the L.	STEV 850:1	L.'s my shepherd	SCOT 754:85
takes l. than you expect	HOFS 422:35	Am an attendant l.	ELIOT 316:66	L. spake unto Moses face to face	BIBLE 94:72
longevity confuse l. with merit	WOGAN 952:58	behold the beauty of the L.	BIBLE 100:50	L. survives the rainbow	LOWE 540:20
Patience and l.	LAFO 504:53	Bless the L., O my soul	BIBLE 102:6	L.! Thou knowest how busy	ASTL 39:8
long-haired consort with l.-h. things	KIPL 492:59	But My L.	MAND 564:53	L. thy God is a jealous God	BIBLE 95:89
longing hopeless l. of the day	ARNO 34:73	coming of the L.	HOWE 433:92	L. thy God is with thee	BIBLE 95:6
l. after immortality?	ADDI 7:52	coming of the L.	KING 487:35	L. was not in the wind	BIBLE 97:67
l. to move the stars	FLAU 339:20	Commit thy way unto the L.	BIBLE 100:58	L. watch between me and thee	BIBLE 93:35
longings Immortal l. in me	SHAK 795:92	David danced before the L.	BIBLE 96:43	L., what fools	SHAK 767:38
Longinus L. o'er a Bottle	BYRON 189:2	day of the L.	BIBLE 130:33	L., with me abide	LYTE 543:94
longitude l. with no platitude?	FRY 353:33	day thou gavest, L., is ended	ELLE 322:19	L. with the sound of the trump	BOOK 149:18
long-legged l.-l. moor-hens	YEATS 966:19	dear L. was crucified	ALEX 13:64	made by the L. Chancellor	JOHN 462:44
longs l. for everything	SHAK 759:67	dwell in the house of the L.	BIBLE 100:45	magnify the L.	BIBLE 120:66
long-term superior l.-t. forecasts	KEYN 484:75	dwell in the house of the L.	BIBLE 100:50	magnify the L.	BIBLE 133:42
loo l. paper gets thicker	MITF 610:57	Each of himself was l.	OTWAY 656:94	mak me l. and king	HENR 411:16
look Always l. a gift horse	RABE 703:12	enter thou into the joy of thy l.	BIBLE 119:33	Man is ungrateful to his L.	KORAN 498:94
at a comedy we only l.	HUXL 442:89	every man thanks the L.	SCHR 749:61	Mankind, fear your L.	KORAN 496:50
at least make it l. good	GATES 361:97	Except the L. build the house	BIBLE 103:36	Most glorious L. of Life!	SPEN 839:43
better'n you l.	TWAIN 902:39	eyes of the L.	BIBLE 98:86	Most glorious L. of Life!	SPEN 839:46
can now l. forward	GOOCH 378:44	fall into the hands of the L.	BIBLE 112:81	My help cometh from the L.	BIBLE 103:31
corpses…their unimportant l.	DAVI 265:83	Forgive, O L.	FROST 353:19	My L. and my God	BIBLE 124:68
does not l. at it	SENG 757:28	Gain, be my l.	SHAK 768:53	My L., one thing is certain	MACI 553:98
don't l. for the first two years	HEMI 410:95	Gentiles' L. and King	AQUI 30:96	Nocht is your famous l.	HENR 412:22
don't like the l. of it	BARR 65:93	Go, and the L. be with thee	BIBLE 96:37	nor the servant above his l.	BIBLE 116:70
Don't l. forward	WILL 945:97	good l., deliver us!	NASHE 632:95	O L. our L.	BIBLE 99:30
don't l. where they're going	SALI 740:81	great and dreadful day of the L.	BIBLE 112:66	O merciful L.	BOOK 147:72
every kind l. adds a link	ROCH 720:22	Great is the L.	BIBLE 100:70	Our L. gave them good bodies	VAZD 910:43
get a good l.	GIBB 367:6	If the L. be God, follow him	BIBLE 97:61	Our L.….said	SHEEN 811:44
Give me a l.	JONS 467:60	If the L. will	BIBLE 130:59	owned him for their L.	POLO 684:4
glazed l. that comes into their eyes	WILD 943:54	if thou come to serve the L.	BIBLE 112:80	Possibly not, My L.	BIRK 136:16
how I l. when I do and say it	WEST 933:92	Imagine the L. talking French	DAY 267:30	Praise the L.	FORGY 344:19
I will l. for you	NEES 632:8	In The Fields Of The L.	MATT 582:99	Prepare ye the way of the L.	BIBLE 108:79
lean and hungry l.	SHAK 776:12	I will repay, saith the L.	BIBLE 126:27	Rejoice, the L. is King!	WESL 931:61
Let him l. to his bond	SHAK 769:99	know that I am the L.	BIBLE 110:33	sae the L. be thankit	ANON 22:82
like to l. at them	FIEL 335:31	know that I am the L.	BIBLE 111:37	safety cometh from the L.	SCOT 755:89
L. at little Johnny there	HOFF 422:33	let men know we serve the L.!	KIPL 490:8	said with tears, L., I believe	BIBLE 120:59
L. at the stars!	HOPK 428:75	L. also of the sabbath	BIBLE 119:51	sapient sutlers of the L.	ELIOT 317:79
L. back, and smile	SCOTT 753:36	L. among wits	JOHN 459:60	shalt not tempt the L. thy God	BIBLE 114:23
l. both ways	EDDI 311:25	L. and Father of mankind	WHIT 938:24	Sing to the L.	KETHE 483:67
l. for him rather than themselves	WINT 950:9	L. and giver of life	BOOK 147:62	Sing to the L.	SCOT 755:88
l. for what she does	GOET 375:59	l. and lady gay	SCOTT 752:10	sought the L.	BIBLE 100:55
L. like a girl	SIMON 821:73	L. bless thee, and keep thee	BIBLE 94:79	Speak, L.	BIBLE 96:26
L. not thou on beauty's	SCOTT 754:64	L. called Samuel	BIBLE 96:25	stay at hame, my noble l.	BALL 59:59
l. on Helen's face in hell	PARK 664:10	l. commended the unjust steward	BIBLE 121:93	Surely the L. is in this place	BIBLE 93:33
l. says maybe	HUGO 437:68	L. he is God	BIBLE 102:4	sword of the L.	BIBLE 95:13
L. thy last on all things lovely	DELA 271:34	L., forgive me	CULL 257:47	taste and see that the L. is good	BIBLE 100:56
l. upon every day	JOHN 464:97	L. gave, and the L. hath taken away	BIBLE 98:91	the fear and nurture of the L.	BOOK 148:86
love or l. at later	SEXT 758:44	L.! give me the strength	BAUD 68:69	The L. shall raise me up	RALE 705:47
not l. back	HAMM 394:59	L. God of Sabaoth	BOOK 146:36	theme of L. of the Flies is grief	GOLD 375:79
not much to l. at	SALI 740:74	L. has decreed you shall not serve		The name of the L.	BIBLE 94:66
one longing ling'ring l. behind?	GRAY 384:74	any but Him	KORAN 497:74	The name of the L.	BIBLE 97:55
Only a l. and a voice	LONG 536:37	L. Hailsham said	MONT 613:24	The name of the L.	BIBLE 105:83
shall not l. upon his like again	SHAK 780:43	L. hath spared our lives	TENN 879:98	The name of the L.	BIBLE 98:91
sit and l. at it for hours	JERO 454:40	L., have mercy on us!	NASHE 632:96	The name of the L.	BIBLE 103:23
teaching people to l.	HOCK 421:16	L. he is God	BIBLE 102:4	The name of the L.	BIBLE 99:40
the soft l.	YEATS 965:7	L. High Executioner!	GILB 369:62	the word of the L.	BIBLE 122:6
We l. before and after	SHEL 814:97	L., how long?	BIBLE 107:56	the Words of my L.	KORAN 498:76
You could l. it up	STEN 847:10	L., I am not worthy	BIBLE 116:57	they that feared the L.	BIBLE 112:64
looked Alexander l. o' this fashion	SHAK 784:64	L. I disbelieve	FORS 345:45	they that fear the L.	BIBLE 113:84
l. up to heaven	IHIM 445:20	L., I do fear Thou'st	MILL 592:18	Thou art indeed just, L.	HOPK 429:95
no sooner l. but they loved	SHAK 780:18	L. is a man of war	BIBLE 93:63	thou, O L., art more	TENN 873:56
seen but not l. at	JOHNS 457:86	L. is my light	BIBLE 100:49	thy l., thy life, thy keeper	SHAK 762:78
She l. at me	JARR 452:87	l. it…above their betters	OTWAY 656:2	trust in the L.	BIBLE 103:34
looker-on My soul…a patient l.-o.	QUAR 701:6	L. looketh on the heart	BIBLE 96:34	trust in the L.	BIBLE 104:52
looking l. round…corners	MAND 565:64	looks after drunks	MOYN 623:4	waited patiently for the L.	BIBLE 100:61
never thought of l. up	GRAND 381:97	L., L., how subject we old men	SHAK 772:89	we are the L.'s	BIBLE 126:33
looking-glass court an amorous l.-g.	SHAK 761:32	L. mighty in battle	BIBLE 100:47	what hour your L. doth come	BIBLE 118:32
cracked l.-g. of a servant	JOYCE 470:22	L. of all being	HOLM 424:82	Who art thou, L.?	BIBLE 124:80
There is no l.-g. here	RHYS 712:78	L. of all power and might	BOOK 147:54	Who is on the L.'s side?	BIBLE 94:71
Women…as l.-g.	WOOLF 955:27	L. of all, the greater was the shame	LANY 508:54	whom the L. loveth	BIBLE 104:53
looks searched with saucy l.	SHAK 763:1	L. of all things	POPE 687:81	wild beasts and L. man	MUIR 624:27
Stolen l. are nice	HUNT 439:24	l. of fat prize-oxen	TENN 872:35	will serve the L.	BIBLE 95:10
what every actor…wants: l.	GIEL 368:24	l. of folded arms	SHAK 763:9	wist not that the L. was departed	BIBLE 96:19
look up l. u. at the stars	HAWK 401:97	L. of hosts, to me!	SCOT 755:87	woman, dear my l.	SHAK 789:18
loom left the l.	TENN 870:85	L. of Lords	BIBLE 132:20	worship the L. thy God	BIBLE 114:24
loomp poor in a l. is bad	TENN 878:90	L. of lycht	DOUG 295:2	Ye servants of the L.	DODD 289:92
looms passage through these l.	VAUG 909:40	L. of Malacca	TOME 894:55	**lordly** butter in a l. dish	BIBLE 95:12
loon By a love-lorn l.	GILB 370:70	l. of the fowl	COWP 250:96	**lords** admiring the House of L.	BAGE 54:70
cream-faced l.!	SHAK 798:68	L. on my hert	MACD 549:33	Dead, my l. and gentlemen	DICK 281:74
looney misfits, l. tunes…criminals	REAG 708:8	L. our God is one L.	BIBLE 95:88	For the L.	SHEL 813:89
loopholes l. for an unorthodox	ORWE 653:22	L. pondereth the hearts	BIBLE 105:87	Government was creaking. My L.	MONT 613:8
neat, through l.	TESS 880:37	L., put beneath Thy special care	BETJ 88:22	lawful l. of earthly creatures	DAVI 264:75
		L. Ronald said nothing	LEAC 515:14		

lordship

L. and Commons of England		MILT 601:18
l. and owners of their faces		SHAK 802:69
L. are lordliest		MILT 608:98
l., a spacious world		MILT 606:60
l., barons, and many goodly knyght		DUNB 306:2
L. is the British Outer Mongolia		BENN 79:29
l. may flourish		GOLD 376:98
naked majesty seemed l. of all		MILT 604:98
one of the l. Of life		LAWR 513:60
Princes and l….the breath of kings		BURNS 177:76
To the L. of convention		SCOTT 754:82
ye l. of ladies intellectual		BYRON 189:90
lordship I should your l.		SHAK 786:99
point out to your l.		ADAMS 4:74
lore In our l.		ROTH 728:91
l. of arms		ANON 21:50
Sweet is the l.		WORD 957:59
Loren Sophia L. is not a citizen		GRAMM 381:95
Los Angeles L. A. is a constellation		MAIL 560:55
transport in L. A.		LEBO 518:65
lose even if you l., you win		WIES 939:31
if he l. he makes a swanlike end		SHAK 769:2
If I do l. thee		SHAK 787:64
if you l. you l. nothing		PASC 667:78
l. all…sacrifice them all		SHAK 770:15
l. an oath		SHAK 763:15
l. mine honour, I l. myself		SHAK 794:65
l. your own soul		SHAW 810:5
may even win if we l.		DOLE 290:1
nothing much to l.		HOUS 432:77
nothing to l. but our aitches		ORWE 653:21
one life to l.		HALE 392:27
on the right side and l.		GALB 357:21
play well and l.		FULL 356:89
time to l.		BIBLE 106:14
to l. both		WILDE 941:2
To l….really to l.		APOL 29:21
whatever we l.		CUMM 258:71
loser he came out the l.		RAMOS 705:50
I'll show you a l.		PUZO 701:7
neither party l.		SHAK 773:93
show me a good l.		DURO 308:33
losers all are l.		CHAM 212:61
what they leave out is the l.		DREX 299:4
Without l.		STEN 847:9
loses neighbour l. his job		REAG 708:3
losing always change a l. one		TILD 891:12
art of l. isn't hard to master		BISH 137:29
loss black as our l.		SITW 823:11
gain and l. involved		PASC 667:78
learn about l.		DE 273:69
l. feels bad		AGAS 9:84
l. comes…from his gain		BROW 169:63
l. of a dear friend		SOUT 835:55
l. of a worm?		SIDN 820:41
neither gain nor l.		ELIOT 320:67
neither gain nor l. of utility		JEVO 455:52
no one knoweth the l. or gain		GORD 378:54
reports that I took the l. badly		DOLE 290:96
those I counted l. for Christ		BIBLE 128:1
lost all a l. generation		STEIN 845:61
every day to be l.		JOHN 464:97
go after that which is l.		BIBLE 121:87
Hath l. me in your liking		SHAK 792:86
If we l. them		HAGG 391:9
I shall be l.		BLAKE 139:91
lambs who've l. our way		KIPL 489:75
l. all his illusions		HOLM 424:64
l. all my mirth		SHAK 782:88
l. beyond the hills		HYDE 443:17
l., but now am found		NEWT 635:63
l. by not being vice		WALP 919:79
l. happiness and lasting pain		MILT 601:34
l. him surely		SYNGE 865:25
l. indeed		GREER 387:42
l. in their collected learning		HAWT 401:2
l. in the miles		SCOTT 751:3
L.! l.! l.!		SCOTT 752:13
l. my reputation		SHAK 789:11
l. the job		JOYCE 470:26
L. til all pride		SMITH 831:64
l. without deserving		SHAK 789:12
l. your ability		GONC 377:41
never completely l.		SCHI 747:28
no love l. between us		GOLD 377:15
none of them is l.		BIBLE 123:58
not that you won or l.		RICE 713:89

on whom nothing is l.!		JAMES 450:44
Poetry is what is l.		FROST 353:26
Praising what is l.		SHAK 791:72
principles…are irrevocably l.		GIBB 366:91
recover what has been l.		ELIOT 320:67
something is l.		THOM 886:74
They l. a generation		NOON 640:47
'Tis better to have fought and l.		CLOU 232:54
to have loafed and l.		THUR 890:80
to have loved and l.		TENN 874:69
to ourselves were l.		DRYD 301:55
we are l.!		PYRR 701:15
we've l. a lot of control		WOZNI 962:57
We l.		MAJOR 561:76
we l. our way		NEWS 635:55
What one gives…is forever l.		DESB 274:90
woman that deliberates is l.		ADDI 7:48
you're in the woods and…l.		DEGEN 270:3
Lot like l.'s wife		MOOD 615:52
Remember L.'s wife		BIBLE 121:1
lot got a l. of what it takes		DUBIN 304:61
l. is fallen unto me		BOOK 148:8
Not milder is the general l.		ARNO 33:61
policeman's l.		GILB 368:42
uneasy l. at best		ELIOT 316:54
weary l. is thine		SCOTT 753:35
wish to ease his l.		TOLS 894:52
lotion l. of the heart		PARK 665:43
lots cast l. upon my vesture		BIBLE 99:44
stealthy convergence of human l.		ELIOT 316:49
lottery blind goddess in the l.		ASTU 39:12
first prize in the l. of life		RHOD 712:71
judgement is a mere l.		DRYD 300:22
state l. as a public subsidy		QUINE 702:22
lotus l. position at her yoga class		SHAR 806:74
Lou lady that's known as L.		SERV 757:35
loud l., you're too old		NUGE 642:73
too long and too l.		WAUGH 924:79
louder l. he talked of his honour		EMER 325:90
music like Wagner, only l.		GOLD 377:27
loudspeakers lies are…from the l.		ORWE 654:57
Louis L., I think		WALL 918:63
St L….golden arch		MAIL 560:55
Louisianans L. don't tolerate		ANON 27:30
loungers l. and idlers of the Empire		DOYLE 296:38
louse between a l. and a flea		JOHN 464:88
l. in the locks of literature		TENN 879:10
lousy had a l. personality		SALI 740:75
it was kind of l.		THUR 891:10
what my l. childhood was like		SALI 739:71
louts oafish l. remember Mum		BETJ 88:35
Louvre L. is the book		CEZA 212:53
love Absence is to l. what wind is to fire		BUSSY 184:55
absurdity of being in l.		LACL 503:30
acts…of l.		WORD 956:54
admire, And l. thee		HERR 415:7
Anyone who falls in l.		MURAK 626:61
Alcohol is like l.		CHAN 213:91
all for l.		DIBD 276:29
all for l.		SPEN 838:31
All l., all liking		HERR 415:11
All must l. the human form		BLAKE 139:89
All this to l.		ROCH 719:6
almost l. you		HEAN 404:70
almost l. you again		SNYD 833:95
a missed l.!		HEINE 407:17
am like to l. three more		SUCK 858:72
an old l. straitened him		TENN 877:54
an ounce of l.		WESL 932:74
An oyster may be crossed in l.!		SHER 818:5
ape the magnanimity of l.		MERE 588:30
arms of my true l.		TENN 876:29
as though you l. him		BLUN 143:76
As woman's l.		SHAK 783:23
attract Thy l., not thy subjection		MILT 606:59
banner over me was l.		BIBLE 107:41
beauty and l. lay bare		SHEL 815:22
before we can l. it much		HOLM 424:78
beggary in the l.		SHAK 794:43
being in l.		OATES 643:15
better to l. a woman		HARDY 397:20
bind my l.		HERR 415:13
Black l.		GIOV 372:17
bring back the things we l.		CHAT 216:52
bringeth it to his l.		BIBLE 112:68
brotherly l.		WELL 929:93

burdenous…my l. had grown		DONNE 292:45
business that we l.		SHAK 795:74
but not for l.		SHAK 779:10
but sworn my l.		SHAK 765:79
By heaven, I do l.		SHAK 763:14
by the force of l.		WHITE 935:42
Call me but l.		SHAK 765:81
cannot fight for l.		SHAK 767:29
cannot l. any one of them		BEER 74:94
cannot l. a woman so well		ELIOT 316:55
cannot make a life, but L.		HERR 415:4
cannot make a man l.		KING 486:25
cannot think well, l. well		WOOLF 955:25
cannot write of l.		BELL 76:46
cantons of contemnèd l.		SHAK 785:91
cocktail is to…wine as rape is to l.		CLAU 229:72
Come…and be my l.		DONNE 292:37
comely in nothing but l.		BACON 51:81
come unto my l.?		SPEN 839:51
connubial l. refused		MILT 604:9
Cooking is like l.		VAN 908:23
could not l.		LOVE 538:86
countless gifts of l.		WINK 950:98
courage to l.		TROL 897:24
course of true l.		SHAK 766:1
crazy for l.		BART 66:13
crops of l. and hate		MUIR 624:24
crossed in l.		AUST 46:60
cruel madness of l.		TENN 875:16
daily possibility of l. dying		GREE 386:12
dance of l.		SENG 757:29
dark secret l.		BLAKE 140:12
dear and only l.		MONT 615:49
dearly l. in your life		TROL 898:44
deep as first l.		TENN 872:43
deep l. for women		HAGG 391:9
dinner of herbs where l. is		BIBLE 104:75
distinguish you in l.		ROCH 719:17
does not l. these dead		SHAK 792:85
do not fall in l. with me		SHAK 779:3
dooms of l.		CUMM 258:64
dream of l. survives…houses		CHEE 218:4
drive and make l.		MOSS 622:84
duteous l.		WORD 962:29
Eat, drink, and l.		BYRON 190:29
ecstasy of l.		SHAK 781:73
Education is impossible without l.		DESB 274:88
either l., or I must die		FORD 343:4
essence of real human l.		ELIOT 315:27
Eternal lamp of l.!		HERR 415:5
Eternity is in l.		BLAKE 140:4
every morning is the l.		KEBLE 478:51
evil of those whom we l.		ABEL 1:2
exponent of free l.		DOCT 289:82
express my l.		SHAK 802:77
eyes That feed my l.		ROCH 720:25
fail at mother l.		FRID 350:62
failures in l.		MURD 626:64
fall half in l.		SALI 740:74
falling in and out of l.		NIVEN 639:29
fall in l. as quickly as possible		ACHE 2:36
fall in l. once		SPARK 836:72
fall in l. with a city		MORR 620:56
fall in l. with the world		WALC 916:21
fall out with those we l.		TENN 872:36
Farewell, L., and all thy laws		WYATT 963:39
fasting, for a good man's l.		SHAK 779:2
fault was only too much l.		LANY 508:55
favor mother l.		BRIN 159:25
fear intensified the l.		JACK 450:27
feeling that lures us on…to l.		CONR 244:36
fell in l. with himself		POWE 693:43
Filled with her l.		DONNE 291:17
filled with l.		ROCH 719:5
first l.'s impassioned blindness		PEAC 671:55
first two l. the third		WAXM 925:4
fit l. for gods		MILT 606:47
fitter for me to l.		ROCH 719:16
flame of life and l.		LAWR 513:57
food is l.		SHEL 814:1
food of l.		SHAK 785:77
fool of l.		HAZL 404:50
For liberation—not less of l.		ELIOT 321:20
For L.'s sake		JONS 468:83
for L. thou wakest not		FERG 333:83
for the l. he had to her		BIBLE 93:34
for the l. of a ladye!		GILB 370:70

love

For thy sweet l. remembered	SHAK 800:46	In this close hand of l.	BROW 166:95	l. in a golden bowl	BLAKE 139:84
for your l. to her	SHAK 761:62	Is first and passionate l.	BYRON 189:98	L. in a hut	KEATS 476:6
freedom in my l.	LOVE 538:82	Is l. a tender thing?	SHAK 765:69	l. in desolation masked	SHEL 815:36
free to l. or hate	SART 744:64	I wish I were in l. again	HART 399:66	l. in public	DRYD 301:54
Friendship l.	GRIL 388:70	jot of former l. retain	DRAY 299:99	l. in shadow best is made	JONS 468:86
From Russia with L.	FLEM 340:41	Kind is my l. today	SHAK 802:75	l. in summer's wonderland	NOYES 642:69
fruit of the Spirit is l.	BIBLE 127:81	know by l.	PATM 669:24	L. interests me more	LAUR 511:24
full of l. and honesty	SHAK 789:17	knowledge and l. of God	BOOK 147:75	L. invincible in battle	SOPH 834:29
Garden of L.	BLAKE 140:14	lack of l. contaminates	GUNN 390:95	L. is a boy	BUTL 185:78
Give me more l.	CAREW 199:59	lack of l. from l.	BROW 169:63	L. is a cruel conqueror	LAFO 504:57
give orders to l.	SAND 741:9	Lassie l. best	BURNS 178:9	L. is a Dog from Hell	BUKO 173:56
give them your l.	GIBR 367:13	late remorse of l.	BYRON 188:64	L. is a fanclub	HENRI 411:9
give us thine own eternal l.!	OCAS 646:77	law of l.	SCEVE 746:16	L. is a game	ROBBE 717:65
Glory, the grape, l., gold	BYRON 190:8	learn to l. by loving	HUXL 442:86	L. is a human emotion	BAKER 56:99
God is l.	BIBLE 130:81	left thy first l.	BIBLE 131:90	L. is always a liar	RUIZ 730:38
God is l.	KIER 486:7	Lenten is come with l.	ANON 21:45	l. is a mystery	LAFO 504:67
God is l.	LEE 518:85	Lerne to l.	LANG 508:50	L. is an abstract noun	AMIS 17:59
God of l.!	DODD 289:93	less skill to l.	SKEL 825:40	L. is a payment	DUNC 307:7
God of L….Beteth his wynges	CHAU 217:90	let me l.	DONNE 291:7	l. is as a fever	SHAK 803:88
golden dream of l. and friendship	DRYD 301:61	let me sow l.	FRAN 347:99	L. is a spirit	SHAK 762:84
got to l. one man	HAMM 394:62	let us live and l.	CAMP 195:72	L. is a universal migraine	GRAV 382:34
grace Which l. makes	WORD 959:97	let us l.!	CATU 209:6	L. is a very papithatick thing	FLEM 340:49
Greater l. hath	THOR 889:57	Linked in l. so dear	MILT 606:54	L. is blind	SHAK 769:93
Greater l. hath no man	BIBLE 123:55	little duty and less l.	SHAK 759:78	l. is come to me	ROSS 725:36
Greater l. than this	JOYCE 470:28	lived to l.	DESB 274:91	L. is ever rewarded	BACON 51:80
great, powerful souls l. life	HEINE 407:13	live in l.	SIDN 820:59	l. is for the particular	DUDEK 305:79
greed wrapped in the language of l.	ARMEY 32:39	live with me and be my l.	MARL 574:41	L….is full of jealousy	SHAK 758:63
groans of l.	LOWRY 541:43	long-liv'd as present l.	WALL 918:61	L. is here to stay	GERS 365:80
Hail, wedded l.	MILT 604:10	looking for is perfect l.	WELD 928:86	L. is just a system	BARN 64:72
hate that don't l. me	FARQ 330:23	looks breed l.	MARL 572:98	L. is like a child	SHAK 759:67
hate me as much as you l. me	BECK 72:54	lost the world for l.	DRYD 304:52	L. is like any other luxury	TROL 898:48
hate the one, and l. the other	BIBLE 115:44	l. a bright particular star	SHAK 791:54	L. is like the measles	JERO 454:36
hath business, and makes l.	DONNE 291:34	L. and the inability to.	BENE 79:14	L. is merely a madness	SHAK 779:96
Have I forgot, my only L.	BRON 162:76	L., all alike, no season knows	DONNE 291:25	l. is more cruel than lust	SWIN 864:94
have you left the ancient l.	BLAKE 139:79	L. all God's creation	DOST 294:94	L. is most nearly itself	ELIOT 320:69
Health, Wealth, and Time	ANON 28:57	l. all my characters	WELTY 930:67	L. is mutually feeding each other	HEAD 404:62
Hearts wound up with l.	SPEN 837:5	l. among the daughters	BIBLE 107:40	L. is not a flame	MARG 570:69
Hell grant what L.	MILT 598:55	l., an abject intercourse	GOLD 376:94	L. is nothing else than	SPIN 840:77
Hell…is to no longer l.	BERN 85:60	L. and delight are better teachers	DURER 307:26	L. is not l.	SHAK 802:80
help and support of the woman I l.	EDWA 312:61	L., and do what you like	AUGU 44:31	L….is not meat nor drink	MILL 592:29
Herein is l.	BIBLE 130:82	L. and friendship exclude	LABR 502:13	L. is not only a feeling	BALZ 61:99
hidden l. of God	WESL 932:66	l. and hate…are necessary	BLAKE 139:94	l. is not secure	CHES 221:82
his l. made mine	DRYD 301:57	l. and honour and pity	FAUL 331:35	L. is of a birth	MARV 577:95
His strange l. still admire	DONNE 292:53	l. and joy that fights	MANS 567:96	L. is off sae mekill mycht	BARB 63:51
honeying and making l.	SHAK 784:42	l. and laughter	GORD 378:54	L. is of the valley	TENN 873:51
hope nor l.	STEV 853:83	l. and marriage rarely can combine	BYRON 190:11	L. is only one of many	JOHN 461:10
hope of winning her l.	STAEL 841:94	l. and murder will out	CONG 240:39	L. is secured by good nature	ROCH 720:22
horribly in l. with her	SHAK 774:40	l. and mutual honour	MILT 605:34	L. is space and time	PROU 698:48
How dare he make l. to me	KRAS 499:4	l. and no sex if you're fat	GIOV 372:18	L. is strong as death	BIBLE 107:49
How do I l. thee?	BROW 166:97	L. and scandal	FIEL 335:17	L. is that common tone	WILL 946:26
how dwelleth the l. of God in him?	BIBLE 130:80	l., and she be fair!	KEATS 478:37	L. is the answer	MOORE 616:74
how to l. himself	SHAK 789:2	l. and toil	KIPL 492:57	l. is the best thing in life	MANN 566:88
Humanity i l. you	CUMM 257:55	l. a quarrel	ETHE 327:44	L. is the delusion	MENC 586:98
Hunger and l.	FRAN 346:81	l. as deep	SHAK 766:84	L. is the extremely	MURD 626:65
I behold, in l.	STEV 850:77	l. at first sight	GRANT 381:4	L. is the fart	SUCK 858:71
I do not l. thee, Dr Fell	BROWN 164:40	l. a wench	SHIR 819:17	l. is the fulfilling of the law	BIBLE 126:31
I do not l. you, Sabidius	MART 576:73	l. a womman that she woot it nought	CHAU 216:58	L. is the gift of oneself!	ANOU 28:68
I fell in l….at once	THOM 884:26	L. bade me welcome	HERB 417:65	L. is the only force	KING 487:36
If l. be a god	LYLY 543:85	l. betwixt us two?	COWL 250:73	L. is the story	STAEL 841:94
If l. be treasure	OTWAY 656:4	l. be younger than thyself	SHAK 786:97	L. is the whole	CUMM 258:65
If l. remains	BROW 168:46	l. but only her!	BYRON 188:69	L., knocking its blind forehead	SAND 741:4
If l. were all	COWA 249:46	L. came down at Christmas	ROSS 726:48	l. leans through geranium windows	LEE 519:95
if l. were what the rose is	SWIN 864:4	l. can claim no place	ANDR 18:78	L. long life	SHAK 794:46
if my l. were in my armes	ANON 21:59	l. can do with a twined thread	BURT 181:85	L. looks not with the eyes	SHAK 767:19
If thou beest l., begone	BEAU 71:21	l.…can never go wrong	PARK 664:14	L. [looks] to the present	LEWIS 526:43
If thou must l. me	BROW 166:93	l. carries within itself	NERVO 634:27	L. means not ever	SEGAL 756:3
If two people l. each other	HEMI 409:72	L. ceases to be a pleasure	BEHN 75:21	l. men too little	BURKE 176:68
If you don't l. life	CLARK 228:60	l., cherish, and to obey	BOOK 148:92	L. mixed with fear	WEBS 927:51
I had definitely fallen in l.	BENU 83:9	l. colour the most	RUSK 732:86	l. not a gaping pig	SHAK 770:10
I l. all waste	SHEL 812:60	L. comforteth…like sunshine	SHAK 762:88	l. not man less	BYRON 188:70
I l. metaphor	GASS 361:86	L. conquers all things	VIRG 914:26	l. of art for its own sake	PATER 668:11
I l. not hollow cheek	TENN 873:48	L. costs us nothing	RICK 715:29	l. of Christ, which passeth	BIBLE 128:88
immortal L.	TENN 873:54	l. Creation's final law	TENN 874:74	l. of country	HOWE 433:91
Imperious l. hath highest	SPEN 838:35	L. Creation's final law	TENN 874:80	L. of democracy is l.	MONT 614:41
impure l. for cities	CASAL 207:69	L., curiosity, freckles	PARK 664:12	l. of earth	MERE 588:38
in business, politics…l.	WHIT 938:13	loved as to l.	FRAN 347:99	l. of Englishmen	THOM 885:55
in l. as in sport	GRAV 382:29	l. divine…excelling	WESL 932:62	L. of finished years	ROSS 725:37
In l., happiness is abnormal	PROU 697:40	l. does not consist in gazing	SAINT 738:32	l. of food	SHAW 807:19
In l.'s field	CRAS 254:86	l. endures no tie	DRYD 304:51	l. of freedom	GLAD 373:39
in l. with a beautiful blonde	FIEL 335:34	l. everything that's old	GOLD 376:9	l. of horses	FIND 336:45
in l. with a cold climate	SOUT 835:42	l., excludes all competition	FUSE 356:91	l. of justice in most men	LARO 510:99
in l. with a country	LESS 524:2	l. for Linton is like the foliage	BRON 162:79	l. of liberty	HAZL 403:36
in l. with American names	BENET 79:23	l., frendshyp, cowardyse	MALO 563:17	l. of life is necessary	JOHN 459:56
in l. with easeful Death	KEATS 478:46	L. give me more such nights	HERR 415:2	l. of man	JEFF 453:11
in l. with my bed	SHAK 758:59	l. has always mixed	LAFA 503:42	l.…of man and woman	PAINE 660:29
in l. with seventeen million	GISC 373:29	L. has its own instinct	BALZ 61:1	l. of money is the root	BIBLE 129:23
intellectual l. of God	SPIN 841:82	l. he laughed to scorn	SHAK 762:81	l. of old friends	PO 683:79

love

l. of our neighbour	MACD 550:46	l. will live in my heart	HAMM 394:64	Ovid, the soft philosopher of l.	DRYD 303:26
L. of Peace, and lonely musing	COLL 238:79	L. will vanquish someday	LABE 501:1	Pains of l.	DRYD 300:29
l. of pleasure	POPE 688:13	L. without hope	GRAV 383:40	party we l.	GAIT 357:11
l. of posterity	HAWT 401:1	L. wol nat been constreyned	CHAU 217:90	passing the l. of women	BIBLE 96:42
l. of spiders	WHITE 935:41	l....would at once be dried up	DOST 294:91	penitence from l.?	POPE 686:49
l. of the people	BURKE 175:21	l. you more than one	JOHN 464:83	people who have no l.	SHAW 806:90
l. of truth	GOET 375:67	l. your majesty	SHAK 791:84	perfect l. casteth out fear	BIBLE 131:83
l. of truth and right	TENN 875:96	L., you shall perfect for me	HEAN 404:69	physic of l.	CLEV 230:93
l. of wicked friends	SHAK 765:59	l. you till the ocean	AUDEN 43:81	planet of L. is on high	TENN 876:25
l. one another	BIBLE 123:50	l. you've been dreaming of	LAUD 511:17	Poetry in l. is no more to be	WYCH 964:4
l. one another	BIBLE 130:81	l. you with all my heart	ROCH 719:4	Politicians neither l. nor hate	DRYD 302:76
l. one another	BIBLE 123:55	loyal sport of l.	ANON 21:50	power above...to manage l.	BUTL 185:88
l. one another	BIBLE 126:30	make l. at any time	BEAU 70:9	power and his l.	GRANT 381:5
l. one another or die	AUDEN 43:97	make l. in a canoe	BERT 87:5	power Of unreflecting l.	KEATS 475:78
l. one maiden only	TENN 877:57	Make l., not war	ANON 25:50	power to hurt us that we l.	BEAU 71:19
l. only means one thing	BENN 81:62	make l. to every woman	KEEN 478:52	power to l., or hate	MARL 574:37
L. only what you do	RICH 713:94	make l. with a woman	ANOU 28:58	Pride leaves...the moment l. enters	GAUT 361:6
l., or gift, which is	MILT 600:15	make us l. one another	SWIFT 861:31	purple with l.'s wound	SHAK 767:27
l. or look at later	SEXT 758:44	making l. is child's play	MITF 610:51	Quhome that ye l.	HENR 411:21
l., patriotism and the like	WHIS 934:22	Making l. is the sovereign	LEBO 518:70	reason is identical with l.	MACL 555:28
l. prove likewise variable	SHAK 765:83	man is fallen in l.	STER 848:41	rebuke is better than secret l.	BIBLE 105:2
L. refines The thoughts	MILT 605:42	Man's l. is of man's life	AMIS 16:31	regain L. once possessed	MILT 608:96
L. repulsed	SHEL 816:55	Man's l. is of man's life	BYRON 189:1	remembrance of my former l.	SHAK 759:64
l. respects no blood	DEKK 270:9	man to be in l.	MORL 619:41	reservoir of l.	BAUD 69:87
L. [ruled] the night	DRYD 304:57	man who any woman might l.	BIRD 135:6	Revolution is like a l. story	AL-AS 10:19
L.'s a bird that will	MEIL 584:38	Marilyn...every man's l. affair	MAIL 560:58	rogue gives you L. Powders	LAMB 505:54
I....sae ill to win	BALL 60:80	marriage without l.	CLARK 228:62	rooted and grounded in l.	BIBLE 127:88
l.'s a malady without a cure	DRYD 304:50	marriage without l.	ZHANG 969:6	rose of l.	SPEN 838:33
L. sang to us	SWIN 864:12	marry for l.	GABOR 356:4	sacrifice L. to pity	GRAV 382:33
l.'s a noble madness	DRYD 301:50	Maybe that's what l. is	ATWO 41:54	said, 'I l. thee true'	KEATS 476:2
l. says humming	MAYA 583:23	me and my true l.	ANON 22:79	seem to disregard l.	HUNT 439:21
L.'s but the frailty of the mind	CONG 241:70	measure of l.	LEWIN 526:39	seldom find him making l.	DRYD 300:24
L. seeketh not itself to please	BLAKE 140:9	medicines to make me l. him	SHAK 771:39	separate us from the l. of God	BIBLE 125:22
L. seeketh only self to please	BLAKE 140:10	Men l. in haste	BYRON 190:22	service of my l.	SPRI 841:87
L. set you going	PLATH 681:30	message of peace, l. and sympathy	WHIT 936:71	sex with someone I l.	ALLEN 14:96
l.'s face May still seem love	SHAK 802:68	might not sing of L.?	SCOTT 752:11	shalt l. thy neighbour	BIBLE 94:78
L.'s feeling is more	SHAK 763:16	mile or two from my first l.	VAUG 909:34	shalt l. thy neighbour	BIBLE 118:26
l. Shakespeare	DRYD 300:26	ministers of L.	COLE 235:27	shalt l. thy neighbour	BIBLE 115:37
L. shall come	GRAV 382:16	Moderate sorrow Fits vulgar l.	DRYD 301:52	shows of l. to other men	SHAK 776:6
l. shall in my verse	SHAK 800:38	money can't buy me l.	LENN 521:48	silence was the song of l.	ROSS 726:57
l. shall live	SPEN 839:47	monstruosity in l.	SHAK 787:35	since perfection is l.	NIEB 637:87
l. she's but a lassie	BURNS 178:14	more anxious to please than to l.	SAND 741:46	sing the l. of danger	MARI 571:76
l. should appear instantaneously	FLAU 339:19	more l. and knowledge of you	SHAK 778:61	so charming...I must l. him	ETHE 327:45
l. shut his door on me	SMITH 829:19	more of l. than of matrimony	GOLD 376:92	So faithful in l.	SCOTT 752:21
l. slights	BACON 50:58	Music is L. in search	LANI 508:52	soft interpreters of l.	PRIOR 696:2
L.'s like the measles	JERR 455:45	must undertake to l. myself	JORD 469:3	So is my l.	SHAK 801:64
L., so gentle in his view	SHAK 765:66	my l. and I did meet	BETJ 89:42	some are fou o' l. divine	BURNS 177:75
l. sought is good	SHAK 786:12	my l. and I did meet	YEATS 965:3	Something...that doesn't l. a wall	FROST 352:90
l. sprung from my...hate!	SHAK 765:76	My l. and I would lie	HOUS 431:44	something you l.	ANGE 19:6
l.'s sad satiety	SHEL 814:96	My l. has died	BALL 58:50	sonnets and courtly l.	GALL 358:44
l.'s the noblest frailty	DRYD 299:12	My L. in her attire	ANON 22:67	sooner allured by l.	ASCH 37:53
l. such a complication	JAMES 451:60	my L.'s like a red, red rose	BURNS 180:50	sorrow of true l.	THOM 885:66
l. supports his reign	SMART 826:68	necessity of l.	ANGE 19:93	so true l. should do	SHAK 758:60
l.'s young dream	MOORE 618:5	needs must l. the highest	TENN 877:59	spirit...of power, and of l.	BIBLE 129:25
L. taught me	GREE 386:31	Need we say it was not l.	MILL 592:22	sports of l.	JONS 467:56
l. that dare not speak	DOUG 294:95	ne'er ebb to humble l.	SHAK 790:29	spring of l.	COLE 235:16
L., that doth reign and live	SURR 860:97	never been in l.	STEV 852:35	Stay away from the ones you l.	TARTT 867:37
l. that endures	SWIN 863:86	never doubt I l.	SHAK 782:77	stricken with most obstinate l.	SIDN 820:37
l. that I have	MARKS 572:90	Never, my l., repent.	PATM 669:11	strive for perfection is to kill l.	WOOD 954:2
l. that loves a scarlet coat	HOOD 426:21	Never pain to tell thy l.	BLAKE 140:7	strong l. shielding	GORD 378:53
l. that moves the sun	DANTE 262:42	never told her l.	SHAK 758:56	subject but eternal l.	SHEL 814:16
L. the Beloved Republic	FORS 345:47	nexus of all l. and money and power	DIDI 286:81	supreme pleasure of l.	BAUD 69:80
l. thee in prose	PRIOR 696:10	no go my honey l.	MACN 557:98	Sweetest l. I do not go	DONNE 291:24
L., the human form divine	BLAKE 139:88	no l. lost between us	GOLD 377:15	Sweet lovers l. the spring	SHAK 780:21
l. the Lord thy God	BIBLE 95:88	no more bear to lose sight...than l.	ELIOT 315:30	symptom of true l.	HUGO 437:86
l. the Lord thy God	BIBLE 118:26	none other I can l.	TENN 877:53	Take them, L.	BROW 168:51
l. the lovely bully	SHAK 775:81	Not Death, but L.	BROW 166:92	teach the world new l.	PHIL 676:53
l. them—against my will	ANON 20:23	not from reason but from l.	GIDE 367:20	tell me the truth about l.	AUDEN 43:83
l. the noise it makes	BEEC 73:62	Nothing in l.	SHAK 798:67	tell the laity of our l.	DONNE 292:38
L., the reeling midnight through	PARK 664:15	not in l. with Mopsa	SHAK 800:26	tempered with l.'s sighs	SHAK 763:18
l. the things we l.	FROST 352:96	Not l., but the astonishment	REID 710:44	temple gates unto my l.	SPEN 839:49
l. to cope him in these sullen fits	SHAK 778:68	not to travel but to l.	AUGU 45:35	that l. may never cease	HERB 413:68
l. to hatred turned	CONG 241:52	Nought so of l.	SPEN 838:34	that we may perfectly l. thee	BOOK 147:58
l. to lie o' both sides	DEKK 270:14	Now with his l.	CHAU 217:85	the life I l.	STEV 853:82
l. to me was wonderful	BIBLE 96:42	object of l. and esteem	LAMB 505:94	The more I l....I quarrel	MARG 570:62
l. to the flowers	KEND 480:85	objects of reverence and l.	CARL 199:73	then they dream of l.	SHAK 765:71
l. to wander in that golden maze	DRYD 299:11	Older than l.	SCOTT 751:3	There is no l.	AUDEN 43:3
L., unperceived	TENN 871:5	O L., O fire!	TENN 869:76	The wise want l.	SHEL 814:10
l. upon the honest square	BEHN 75:19	O lyric l.	BROW 169:72	They l. for it	TENN 872:63
L. wakes men, once	PATM 669:16	O mighty l.!	HERB 413:71	thine inestimable l.	BOOK 147:50
l. was not in their looks	MILT 606:58	one in l. with death	SHEL 815:26	think of one's absent l.	TROL 897:30
l. was of that dignity	SHAK 781:63	One wakes only to the touch of l.	CIXO 227:47	this l. of ours is immoderate	BURT 181:84
l. was passion's essence	BYRON 187:54	one who gives me her l.	CAMPO 195:79	this l. of the land	MITC 610:39
l. which doth us bind	MARV 577:96	only queer people...don't l.	BROWN 164:15	this spring of l.	SHAK 758:58
L. which strikes suddenly	LABR 502:14	or successful without l.	TROL 898:55	this word, 'l.'	SHAK 760:20
l. will be seen at its height	FORS 344:30	O spirit of l.	SHAK 785:78	those whom they want to l.	FORS 344:28
l. will change in growing old	BRID 158:8	over-shoes in l.	SHAK 758:56	thoughts of l.	TENN 871:11

thousands…that l. me	BOOK	147:59
Through l., through hope	WORD	961:43
Thus did they l.	LOVE	538:87
till l. have all his rites	SHAK	774:35
time of our l. and pride	SU	858:65
time to l.	BIBLE	106:14
Time…weakens l.	LABR	502:12
'Tis l. in l.	SUCK	858:67
to be wroth with one we l.	COLE	235:34
to conserve it, we must l. it	MONT	614:40
to dissemble your l.	BICK	133:51
To live is like to l.	BUTL	186:9
To l., and bear	SHEL	815:20
to l. and to be wise	BACON	50:36
to l. and to cherish	BOOK	148:91
To l. is to be a fish	IGNA	445:18
touch of l.	SHAK	759:65
tragedy, l. and heroism	LEWIS	527:57
true l. hath my heart	SIDN	820:40
two Milwaukeeans in l.	HECHT	406:3
Uninterrupted joy, unrivalled l.	MILT	603:76
universal languages: l., music and sports	MOSES	622:79
unselfish and self-sacrificing l.	POE	683:84
unspoken l.	MORG	619:30
Unutterable l.	WORD	961:36
us that trade in l.	SHAK	794:60
vain in verse my l. to show	SIDN	820:43
vanity, sets l. a task	HUNT	439:27
vegetable l. should grow	MARV	577:91
visible world seems formed in l.	MELV	585:60
voice falls as they say l.	LARK	509:76
wait without l.	ELIOT	320:57
war, as in l.	NAPO	630:45
warrior that is rapt with l.	MARL	572:3
War springs from the l.	RUNC	731:49
was sick, in l.	POPE	687:93
we are always in l.	PASC	666:66
we don't accomplish our l.	RILKE	715:39
we l. thee best	TENN	875:5
we who were strong in l.	WORD	960:23
What is commonly called l.	FIEL	335:24
what is denied to l.	WILL	946:21
What is l.	SHAK	785:93
What l.?	SHEL	814:95
What l. he must have lost	SMITH	828:5
What l. I bore to thee	WORD	958:92
what manner of l.	BIBLE	130:79
What one gives in l.	DESB	274:90
what thing is l.	PEELE	672:70
What will survive of us is l.	LARK	509:81
when I l. thee not	SHAK	789:16
when I was in l. with you	HOUS	431:39
When l. grows diseased	ETHE	327:47
When l. is done	BOUR	153:94
When l. is liberty	POPE	686:47
Where I and my l. wont to gae	BALL	60:79
Where mercy, L. and Pity dwell	BLAKE	139:89
where there is no l.	BACON	52:13
which men call L.	SPEN	838:36
Whose l. is given	PARK	664:10
who's injured by my l.?	DONNE	291:28
wilder shores of l.	BLAN	141:46
will not be long, L.	COLUM	238:88
with an everlasting l.	BIBLE	110:21
with L. and Squalor	SALI	740:83
with l. false	YEATS	965:7
woman's friendship ever ends in l.	GAY	362:12
woman wakes to l.	TENN	877:46
Women…l. completely	BAIN	55:96
Women's l. is for their men	EURI	328:56
Women will l. her	SHAK	800:30
wondrous miracle did L. devise	DAVI	264:74
write of your l. affairs	YEATS	965:2
written for the l. of Man	THOM	884:28
wrong for me to l. my own?	SITT	823:93
yet His l. observes	AUDEN	43:2
yet to see the one she should l.	LABR	502:11
yield, that l. may win	CRAS	254:85
yield to l., ladies	LYLY	543:86
you and l. are still my argument	SHAK	801:63
you'll l. Mogadishu	HEMP	410:98
'You must sit down,' says L.	HERB	413:66
young things that marry for l.	SHAW	809:84
Youth means l.	BROW	169:71
love-adept Dreaming like a l.-a.	SHEL	814:13
love-broker no l.-b. in the world	SHAK	786:14
loved Alas! that all we l. of him	SHEL	815:34
As Caesar l. me	SHAK	777:36
beautiful only when she is l.	EPST	327:32
Be l. like Nature!	COLE	235:25
both l. and loathed	MIDD	590:76
Dante, who l. well	BROW	168:53
daughter l. a man	SHAK	786:99
didn't come…to be l.	GRAMM	381:94
each l. one blotted	BYRON	187:44
for she l. much	BIBLE	120:75
greater compliment than to be l.	MACD	550:50
Had we never l. sae kindly	BURNS	179:35
I have l.	SUCK	858:72
l. even the tears	RACI	704:28
l l. him too much	RACI	704:26
is it better to be l. than feared	MACH	552:93
Late have I l. you	AUGU	44:27
l. her against reason	DICK	283:10
l. me for the dangers	SHAK	788:95
l. most living things	THOM	885:60
l. not at first sight?	MARL	574:37
l. not at first sight?	SHAK	779:4
l. righteousness	GREG	387:51
l. thee once	AYTO	48:10
l. the man	JONS	468:90
l. to be changing	DRAY	298:96
many l. your moments	YEATS	965:7
never been more l.	ELLI	323:36
no sooner looked but they l.	SHAK	780:18
Now thou hast l. me	DONNE	291:22
self and the l. one	PHIL	677:56
Sir, you and I have l.	SHAK	794:52
skill…to be l.	SKEL	825:40
thirst to be l.	RHYS	712:72
to be l. needs only to be seen	DRYD	303:10
to have l. and lost	TENN	874:69
To have l., to have thought	ARNO	33:69
Twice or thrice had I l. thee	DONNE	291:33
We l., sir	BROW	169:67
what thou and I Did, till we l.?	DONNE	291:21
love-in-idleness maidens call it l.-i.-i.	SHAK	767:27
loveliness Its l. increases	KEATS	476:84
l. to living youth denied	WORD	962:47
portion of the l.	SHEL	815:42
lovelorn advice to the l.	LEBO	518:69
love-lorn By a l.-l. loon	GILB	370:70
lovely Her face was l.	SPEKE	836:82
How l. is thy dwelling-place	SCOT	755:87
In Claude's landscape all is l.	CONS	244:58
Look thy last on all things l.	DELA	271:34
more l. and more temperate	SHAK	800:37
once he made more l.	SHEL	815:42
whatsoever things are l.	BIBLE	128:5
woods are l., dark and deep	FROST	352:5
love-making l.-m., or wooing of it	BACON	50:56
love-quarrels L.-q. oft in pleasing	MILT	605:87
lover all affliction taught a l.	POPE	686:49
As to a l.'s bed	SHAK	795:79
Beauty is the l.'s gift	CONG	241:63
death is as a l.'s pinch	SHAK	795:94
dividing l. and l.	SWIN	863:83
ex-wife looking for a new l.	CONN	243:7
fause L. staw my rose	BURNS	179:33
fond l.?	SUCK	858:66
Give me a l. bold and free	CLEV	230:95
hard to be…a l. of women	WYCH	964:98
Have I a l.	EMER	324:67
Having a l. isn't much	HYDE	443:20
husband is what is left of the l.	ROWL	729:21
injured l.'s hell	MILT	604:16
l. and his lass	SHAK	780:21
l. and killer are mingled	DOUG	295:4
l., and the poet	SHAK	767:45
l. chosen	GRAV	382:28
l.…of angling	WALT	920:92
l. of life	GORD	378:54
l. of men, the sea	SWIN	864:5
l. of the meadows	WORD	956:56
l.'s bad reputation	NAPO	630:46
l.'s quarrel with the world	FROST	353:16
l. who does not forget	BART	66:26
maner of l. spryngith	MALO	563:14
mankind love a l.	EMER	324:59
Neither father nor l.	ROET	722:60
place her l. as high as she	BALZ	60:89
Scratch a l.	PARK	664:18
sighed as a l.	GIBB	366:1
sweeter…will be the word l.	HELO	408:53
true l. of literature	SOUT	835:52
weary l.	GORD	378:53
Who can deceive a l.?	VIRG	913:18
woman loves her l.	BYRON	190:10
world's greatest l.	SCHU	750:76
Your passionate l.	STEE	844:39
lovers Catherine had…l.	WEST	933:90
Journeys end in l.	SHAK	785:92
L. and madmen	SHAK	767:44
l. be virtuous	LYLY	543:85
L. be war and tak gude heid	HENR	411:21
l. cannot see	SHAK	769:93
l. fled away	KEATS	477:27
l. lately wed	TENN	869:82
l. of the picturesque	MCGO	551:74
l. old are l and she	BROW	168:47
l.' perjury	DRYD	304:51
l. were all untrue	DRYD	304:58
me and the apparent l.	REED	709:28
Mirrors are the perfect l.	ATWO	41:40
Mitterrand has 100 l.	GORB	378:50
sleepless l.…awake	POPE	685:30
star-crossed l.	SHAK	765:65
Though l. be lost	THOM	883:7
time becometh l. best	DRAY	298:92
to thy motions l.' seasons run?	DONNE	291:25
track for l. on the printed snow	CAREW	198:54
loves Anyone who l. his country	GARI	360:73
For who l. me must	TENN	877:51
from their l. receive	KEATS	477:16
game your country l.	RICE	713:91
He l. us not	SHAK	797:59
kills the thing he l.	WILDE	942:17
Let him that l. me	SHAK	795:80
Life and l. of a She-Devil	WELD	928:87
l. and comforts should increase	SHAK	789:9
l. but half of Earth	QUIL	702:9
L. die from disgust	LABR	502:15
l. me dearly	KEATS	476:89
l., must I remember them?	APOL	29:81
l. my daughter	SHAK	799:23
l. nothing but himself	SOUT	835:53
l. the horror	HOMER	425:6
l. to lie with me	SHAK	778:75
man swear he l. me	SHAK	773:21
one that l. his fellow-men	HUNT	439:29
pettiness ruins the greatest l.	ANOU	28:59
Seat of pleasures, and of l.	DRYD	303:22
true l. without suspicion	SPEN	839:39
Two l. I have	SHAK	803:87
when no one l. us	STAEL	842:98
whose l. I prize	SHAK	799:98
love-sick l.-s. land that mourns	BLAKE	139:80
love songs l. s. written…by God	CONR	244:55
lovest What thou l. well	POUND	692:23
love stories collaborations are l. s.	THARP	880:44
love-story as if you worked a l.-s.	DOYLE	296:43
loveth He prayeth well, who l. well	COLE	235:20
Lord l. he chasteneth	BIBLE	129:44
l. father or mother	BIBLE	116:73
love-whispering L.-w. woods	POPE	689:44
loving but the astonishment of l.	REID	710:44
discharge for l. one	MATL	582:94
For l., and for saying so	DONNE	291:32
give up smoking, drinking and l.	FREUD	350:54
Hated wickedness that hinders l.	BROW	168:53
l. alone is as dull as eating alone	WYCH	964:5
L. in truth	SIDN	820:43
L. not, hating not	BROW	169:66
L. your neighbour as…yourself	CLEE	229:81
most l., mere folly	SHAK	779:85
privilege…of l. longest	AUST	47:90
So l. to my mother	SHAK	780:39
stop l. ourselves	STAEL	842:98
loving-kindness crowneth…l. k.	BIBLE	102:6
low between the high and l.	SIDN	820:46
Dost thou lie so l.?	SHAK	777:32
en Brer Fox, he lay l.	HARR	398:45
had me l.	GERS	365:78
He that is l.	BUNY	174:82
Holland…lies so l.	HOOD	426:27
l. in rich…countries	SMITH	827:82
Sweet and l.	TENN	872:37
Too l. for envy	COWL	250:77
lowbrow l., a bit of a murderer	MILL	595:94
lowcut l., belongings on show	JOYCE	470:32

Lowells   1186

Lowells L. talk to the Cabots   BOSS 151:74
lower gittin a little l. ever since   BILL 135:95
   if the l. orders don't   WILDE 941:96
   l. middle classes!   GILB 369:49
   no longer l. classes   TOCQ 892:26
low flying a l. f. person   KEAT 475:59
lowing grazes over the carpet, l.   RAINE 705:38
lowland between l. and highland   SWIN 864:16
   Ye Highlands and ye L.   BALL 58:53
low-pay l.-p., low-prestige   COUP 248:24
loy blow of a l.   SYNGE 865:24
loyal l. sport of love   ANON 21:50
   l. to the tips of his stubby fingers   ACHE 3:43
   supports his king on l. principles   SHAW 807:97
loyalties above all other l.   JAMES 449:22
   Home of...impossible l.   ARNO 35:12
loyalty applauded...his l.   HATT 400:82
   done by intrigue, not by l.   HUGO 437:72
   I want l.   JOHN 458:15
   love and l.   RUNC 731:49
   l. and order   GLAD 373:39
   l. to the United States   ROOS 725:23
   l. to the world organization?   CHUR 226:3
   l. we all feel   GREE 386:8
lucasta L. might I crave   LOVE 538:83
lucid l., inescapable rhythms   STEV 850:75
   make a l. interval   DRYD 300:44
lucidity I have a terrible l.   VAN 908:19
Lucifer L., son of the morning!   BIBLE 108:64
luck always just my l.   PARK 664:11
   belief in l.   OATES 643:6
   Fattenin' hogs ain't in l.   HARR 399:49
   Homage to plain dumb l.   ACHE 3:51
   I never had bad l.   TRUM 899:79
   L. is a dividend of sweat   KROC 499:16
   L. is what happens when   BRAN 156:73
   l. o' the prize   BURNS 180:43
   l. to be called upon   CHUR 226:12
   man...down on his l.   DAVI 265:84
   more l....than any other game   ARLO 32:34
   no l. about a house   YEATS 967:35
   Oedipus he had the l.   HUGH 436:41
   of that natural l.   SHAK 794:59
   such a thing as l.   MAMET 564:35
   Was there ever man had such l.?   SHAK 803:89
   watching his l.   SERV 757:35
   when he's unhappy—his l. runs out   CHAN 213:81
   Wish me l., as you wave   PARR 665:50
   worst l. any man could have   HEMI 410:81
   your faltering l.   CIAR 226:22
luckier to die is different...and l.   WHIT 937:91
luckiest l. of mortals   AUDEN 44:14
lucky Do I feel l.   EAST 310:6
   if we are too l.   JONG 466:37
   L. is the man   EURI 328:64
   My L. Star   FREED 349:43
lucrative most l. of its branches   PAINE 660:34
lucre not greedy of filthy l.   BIBLE 129:18
Lucy When L. ceased to be   WORD 957:62
ludicrous dignity becomes l.   GALT 359:56
   rogue alive to the l.   EMER 325:99
Ludlow L. fair   HOUS 432:58
   to L. come   HOUS 431:46
luely O l., I cam she in   SOUT 835:40
   Sae l., I cam she in   SOUT 835:41
lug I'll l. the guts   SHAK 784:46
luggage Empty l. may be easier   NEW 634:37
   look after the l.   LOWE 539:95
luggies jaups in l.   BURNS 178:95
lukewarm thou art l.   BIBLE 131:94
lullaby dreamy l.!   GILB 369:58
   L. of Broadway   DUBIN 304:64
   Once in a l.   HARB 396:90
   Rock them, rock them, l.   DEKK 270:10
lullay l., l., like a child   SKEL 824:30
lullings l. and the relishes of it   HERB 413:67
lumber l. of the schools   SWIFT 861:16
   l. room of his library   DOYLE 297:58
luminous l. home of waters   ARNO 35:1
lump l. of clotted nonsense   DRYD 300:36
   L. the whole thing!   TWAIN 902:34
   ugly l.   KIPL 491:31
lumps Go down like l. of lead   HODG 421:22
lunar Held in a l. synthesis   ELIOT 317:72
lunatic all in l. asylums   CHES 220:67
   as though I were in a l. asylum   CONA 239:10
   certified a l.   CROS 256:35

engagingly l. about Ralph   USTI 907:47
   l., the lover   SHAK 767:45
lunatics if any l. were at large   ELIOT 316:44
   L. are sincere   DRIB 299:5
lunch free l. has still to be invented   GREE 387:38
   long-range planning is l.   OGDEN 648:4
   L. is for wimps   DOUG 295:18
   naked l. is natural   GINS 371:4
   no such thing as a free l.   FRIE 351:69
   When he sat down to l.   LONG 535:11
   wish the meeting...as the l.   CHRI 224:48
luncheon do not take soup at l.   CURZ 260:7
   l. with a city friend   BELL 77:72
lunch time Every l. t.   HAMER 393:45
lung have a l. removed   WAUGH 924:99
   our left l.   GAND 359:58
lungs air ungainly in our new l.   ATWO 41:33
   opens the heart and l.   STER 848:38
   using your l. all the time   LEAC 515:13
lure swimming towards the l.   HEAN 405:72
   wherever you may l. it   KAFKA 472:4
luscious Fame's l. pot   RICK 715:29
lush L., calm and voluptuous   BAUD 68:65
lust avarice, l. and ambition   LEWIS 526:43
   Beauty and the l. for learning   BEER 73:84
   hutch of tasty l.   HOPK 428:68
   looked on a lot of women with l.   CART 206:46
   looketh on a woman to l. after her   BIBLE 114:33
   love is more cruel than l.   SWIN 864:94
   L. carries her sharp whip   WEBS 926:23
   l. of knowing   FLEC 340:32
   l. of the goat   BLAKE 140:2
   same rule applies for l.   MONT 614:44
   Thy l. and liking   SKEL 824:31
   weigh their pleasure by their l.   DYER 309:49
   women's unnatural, unsatiable l.   BURT 181:86
lustre exceeding l. and the pure   SHEL 814:3
   l. in its sky   SHEL 812:57
   l. of it will never appear   DEFOE 269:67
   l. of midday to objects   MOORE 616:62
   Where is thy l. now?   SHAK 793:14
lusts of the father ye will do   BIBLE 123:42
   prince's appetite And serve his l.   MASS 581:76
   Thou hotly l.   SHAK 793:25
   to satisfy men's carnal l.   BOOK 148:85
lusty am strong and l.   SHAK 778:71
   In l. leas at liberty   WYATT 963:85
   l. song of fruits   BLAKE 139:82
   l. young men   SHAK 765:68
lute As her l. doth live   CAMP 195:73
   little rift within the l.   TENN 877:44
   l. its tones   KEATS 476:87
   My l., awake!   WYATT 964:89
   pleasing of a l.   SHAK 761:32
   with his l. made trees   SHAK 804:44
lute-resounding l.-r. waves   POPE 689:44
Luther L.; the Philistine of genius   ARNO 36:38
Lutheran spleeny L.   SHAK 805:48
luxuries distinction...between l.   GALB 357:16
   l. That modern life   WILB 939:38
   l. to brood over in my walks   KEATS 476:94
luxury l. betrayed   GOLD 376:5
   couch for l.   SHAK 781:65
   every l. was lavished on you   ORTON 652:4
   'horseless-carriage' is at present a l.   ANON 23:1
   Love is like any other l.   TROL 898:48
   l. of a peacetime environment   TRUM 900:87
   l. of doing good   CRAB 252:45
   l. the accomplished sofa   COWP 251:10
   satisfy l. and licentiousness   MORE 618:19
   style is the only real l.   ARMA 32:36
   whilst L. Employed   MAND 565:65
Lycid hearse where L. lies   MILT 599:91
Lycidas head of your lov'd L.   MILT 599:85
   L. is dead, dead ere   MILT 599:82
   L. your sorrow   MILT 600:94
Lydia L. The Tattooed Lady   HARB 396:89
lying l. for one's country   BIER 134:74
   One of you is l.   PARK 664:13
   putting away l.   BIBLE 128:90
   smallest amount of l.   BUTL 185:98
   subject...to this vice of l.!   SHAK 772:89
   We've been l. so long   STEI 846:92
   you can tell when a man is l.   BOHL 144:99
lynching keep him from l. me   KING 486:23
Lyndon L. gave me that instead   ROCK 720:36
lynx sharp as any l.   SITW 823:95

Lyons coming hither from L.   WALP 918:64
lyre Make me thy l.   SHEL 813:83
   many-chorded l.   RANJ 706:60
   my l. has a soul   CHOC 222:25
   remembered tone of a mute l.   BYRON 188:64
lyric a'e gowden l.   MACD 549:34
   O l. love   BROW 169:72
lyrical primitive era was l.   HUGO 436:52
lyricism sick of cautious l.   BAND 61:10

M

ma Look M.   CAGN 192:19
   M.'s out, Pa's out   FLAN 338:10
Mabel Nay, M., nay!   GILB 368:41
macadam made of melting m.   AMIS 16:46
Macaulay cocksure...as Tom M.   MELB 584:47
   M., Gibbon, Tolstoy   PRIAL 695:80
   memory of M.   BARR 65:98
   Philistine, Lord M.   ARNO 35:15
   young M. or Ruskin   BARB 63:45
Macavity M., M....no one like M.   ELIOT 320:54
Macbeth Little Nell and Lady M.   WOOL 956:40
   M. does murder sleep   SHAK 797:2
   M. shall sleep no more   SHAK 797:35
   M. slurping your soup?   PAGE 659:14
   My name's M.   SHAK 798:76
   Shall harm M.   SHAK 797:55
McDonalds what M. is to food   PILG 678:79
Macduff Lay on, M.   SHAK 798:78
   M. was from his mother's womb   SHAK 798:77
mace fool's bauble—the M.   CROM 256:23
   m. of honor   MANC 564:51
   m. to knock down the passengers   BENT 82:91
macerations Made way for m.   POUND 691:3
MacGregor name is M.!   SCOTT 753:56
   Selwyn M., the nicest boy   SPARK 835:64
Macheath Just a jack-knife has M.   BREC 157:88
Machiavellian rare tricks of a M.   WEBS 926:35
machine A reading m.   LOWE 539:9
   automatic m.   WIEN 939:28
   body is a m. for living   TOLS 893:50
   depressing the keys of the m.   BIER 135:88
   friction of the whole m.   CLAU 229:75
   Ghost in the M.   RYLE 736:59
   m. for transmission of ideas   BOWL 153:99
   m.-gun to a shooting gallery   OFAO 647:97
   m. is running away with him   WILH 943:58
   m. slipping from   LOWE 540:36
   m. that makes the art   LEWI 527:76
   m., the m. is necessary   MILL 593:32
   m., the railway   NIET 638:93
   man...a minutely set, ingenious m.   BLIX 142:61
   [man] is a universal m.   REDT 709:25
   muskets and m. guns   MUSS 628:92
   not a man, you're a m.   SHAW 806:86
   One m. can do the work   HUBB 434:99
   Prayers...on an adding m.   WEST 933:93
   pulse of the m.   WORD 960:20
   pulverizing m.   BACON 53:52
machine-gunned wall and m.-g.   TAYL 868:56
machinery Age of M.   CARL 200:79
   assume the form of m.   MARX 579:41
   by chemistry and m.   SHAW 807:26
   governmental m. that he lives under   SPEN 836:89
   m. of Government   MONT 613:8
   mind is pure m.   GINS 372:6
   primitive m. and primitive music   LEAC 515:17
   read somewhere that m.   MARI 571:80
   warfare of men and m.   WOLFE 953:70
   whole m. of the state   ENGE 326:15
machines begin with sewing m.   PAGN 660:27
   m. and to be chosen   LEUP 525:15
   M. are worshipped   RUSS 734:28
   m. devised by mankind   BORE 150:54
   m....do not make men...happier   DE 267:43
   m. for making more m.   BOTT 152:83
   m. we worship   PRIE 695:89
   problem is not whether m. think   SKIN 825:47
   We are survival m.   DAWK 266:15
machismo m. reeks of violence   WHITE 934:28
macho the new m. fascism   WHITE 934:27
mackerel light in the white m. sky   BISH 136:26
mackintosh trademark Gannex m.   MCFA 551:66
Macmillan M. comes back   WILS 948:60
   M. held his party together   ASQU 38:94
   M. was canonized   WILS 948:73

mail

Macmorris Captain M., I think — SHAK 775:77
Macon In M.…'Where do you go — BERE 83:13
macro-economics delusion that m.-e. — HAYEK 402:26
maculate Swelling to m. giraffe — ELIOT 317:80
mad All poets are m. — BURT 181:76
  As m. as the vexed sea — SHAK 793:19
  bolshevism run m. — SNOW 832:88
  but m. north-north-west — SHAK 782:93
  Dear Madam, You are stark m. — ROCH 719:16
  Don't get m. — KENN 482:37
  for me are the m. ones — KERO 483:53
  grave of M. Carew — HAYES 403:27
  griefs would make men m. — SHAK 760:28
  half of the nation is m. — SMOL 831:66
  heart, all m. with misery — SHAK 760:26
  he is m. is he? — GEOR 363:46
  He made me m. — SHAK 771:33
  heroically m. — DRYD 302:94
  How sad and bad and m. — BROW 169:67
  If she be m. — SHAK 788:78
  If you fear making anyone m. — CART 206:48
  laughter, It is m. — BIBLE 105:13
  let me not be m. — SHAK 792:96
  M. about the boy — COWA 249:52
  m. all my life — JOHN 462:30
  m. and hungry dogs — MCKA 553:6
  m. as a hatter — ELIOT 319:52
  M., bad, and dangerous to know — LAMB 504:75
  M. from life's history — HOOD 426:34
  m. if they behold a cat — SHAK 770:10
  madness without being m. — LISP 531:45
  m., or very tired — LOWE 539:1
  M. with much heart — DONNE 291:17
  Mahdi pretends to be half m. — CECIL 210:32
  men that God made m. — CHES 220:81
  Men will always be m. — VOLT 914:37
  more or less m. — KIPL 489:71
  much learning doth make thee m. — BIBLE 125:99
  not poetry, but prose run m. — POPE 687:2
  now run m. — JONS 468:87
  O Fool, I shall go m.! — SHAK 792:3
  pleasure…In being m. — DRYD 302:97
  saint run m. — POPE 688:25
  shall run m. with joy — MIDD 590:77
  some believed him m. — BEAT 70:1
  talk themselves m. — SHAK 774:34
  that she was going m. — LESS 524:96
  there the men are as m. — SHAK 784:62
  these two may run m. — SHAK 787:43
  they say you are m. — BENN 79:33
  those people will be going m. — RAMS 706:52
  Though they go m. — THOM 883:7
  way guys yell when they're m. — STEI 846:83
  will think me m. — DRYD 301:54
madam Dear Sir or M. — ELLI 323:27
  Do not blame me, m. — LABE 501:4
  M., if you don't — WALL 918:62
  M., there are fifty thousand men — WALP 919:81
  M., you have bereft me — SHAK 770:7
  Seems, m.? Nay, it is — SHAK 780:35
madame M. Bovary — MCCA 548:98
maddening more m. as he goes on — QUIL 702:17
madder Nothing can make me m. — RENO 711:49
maddest m. of all — VOLT 914:37
made All things were m. by him — BIBLE 122:15
  Do you know who m. you? — STOWE 856:30
  everything has been m. — FERN 334:97
  fearfully and wonderfully m. — BIBLE 103:45
  land was m. for you and me — GUTH 390:5
  m. at one stroke — FRAN 348:1
  m. by the Lord Chancellor — JOHN 462:44
  no straight thing can ever be m. — KANT 473:22
  when or you or I are m. — HERR 415:11
Madeira cup of M. — SHAK 771:31
  We're from M. — SHAW 806:93
madhouse How…in the m.? — POUND 692:29
Madison M. Square Garden — AUCH 42:65
madman angel and a m. — THOM 883:12
  dream of a m. — SHAW 809:69
  either a failure or m. — HOLM 423:57
  m. bum and angel — GINS 372:5
  m. in his padded cell — NABO 628:6
  m. shakes a dead geranium — ELIOT 317:73
  modern composer is a m. — HONE 425:12
  That is the m. — SHAK 767:45
madmen as m. do — SHAK 779:96
  Atheists, fools, and m.! — ONEI 651:70

discourse as m.'s are — SHAK 803:88
Lovers and m. — SHAK 767:44
M. in authority — KEYN 484:81
none but m. know! — DRYD 302:97
They were m. — RENO 711:58
worst of m. — POPE 688:25
madness Ambition…man's m. — WEBS 927:45
  a moment of m. — DAVI 265:88
  blessing like experiencing m. — LISP 531:45
  cells of m. — TENN 876:33
  close to m. — ALCU 12:46
  cruel m. of love — TENN 875:16
  Don't hide the m. — GINS 371:4
  escape the m. — GREE 386:25
  fine m. still he did retain — DRAY 299:98
  form of m. — HOME 425:97
  Great wits…to m. near allied — DRYD 301:72
  harmless m. — HONE 425:13
  in an age of m. — BELL 77:77
  in the end despondency and m. — WORD 959:1
  Ireland has her m. — AUDEN 43:91
  Love is merely a m. — SHAK 779:96
  love's a noble m. — DRYD 301:50
  m. hath the oddest frame — SHAK 788:78
  M. in great ones — SHAK 783:17
  m. is a final distillation of self — DELI 271:40
  M. is a gift — PALEY 661:54
  m.…to believe oneself to be God — FOUC 345:58
  moon-struck m. — MILT 606:67
  Much M. is divinest Sense — DICK 284:37
  pitch that is near m. — EBER 310:10
  rouse the sacred m. — HERR 415:6
  Such harmonious m. — SHEL 814:99
  that devil's m.—War — SERV 757:37
  that way m. lies — SHAK 792:10
  there is a woe that is m. — MELV 585:63
  The rest is m. — JAMES 450:47
  Though this be m. — SHAK 782:81
  very midsummer m. — SHAK 786:16
  wits are sure to m. near allied — DRYD 301:72
  work like m. on the brain — COLE 235:34
madonna a M.–whore complex — THER 882:85
  I saw a M. — PARK 664:32
  motorcycle black m. — DYLAN 309:55
  moustache on a m. — VENT 910:52
madonnas m. and shameless nudes — MALE 562:92
Madras bars of M., Oregon — SNYD 833:95
madrigals birds sing m. — MARL 574:41
maestro Music, M., Please — MAGI 559:25
magazine air of a fashion m. — WAUGH 924:86
  editor of an important m. — CANN 196:6
  m. heroes — LOWE 540:39
  photographer without a m. — PARK 665:42
magazines girlie m. and TV — UPDI 906:26
Magdalen M. College — GIBB 366:98
  M., Margaret and Rosalys — ROSS 726:53
Maggie M.'s home-made remedy — FORM 344:21
maggot full of m. ostentation — SHAK 763:24
  know how to make a m. — MONT 614:28
  m.…born i' the rotten cheese — ELIOT 315:22
maggots make a speech to m. — CELI 211:38
magic All I have of m. wand — HARR 397:57
  argosies of m. sails — TENN 871:17
  ersatz m. from the real thing — BYATT 186:19
  goal that supplies the political m. — SCHL 748:39
  If this be m. — SHAK 800:32
  indistinguishable from m. — CLAR 228:67
  It was m. — GILL 370:86
  kind of m. and trickery — WILS 947:40
  let in daylight upon m. — BAGE 54:75
  like m. in a pint bottle — DICK 282:88
  m. and delicious power — WOOLF 955:27
  m. in American politics — WHITE 936:60
  m. lore of happiness — RIMB 716:48
  m. moment in American history — WHITE 936:59
  m. of its dawn — RUSS 735:42
  m. of manners — ALCO 12:43
  m. of official forms — WAUGH 924:88
  m. sound to me — BYRON 190:18
  m., that will charm thy soul — MARL 573:28
  mistook m. for medicine — SZASZ 865:26
  no great m. — GRAV 382:23
  practice of m. — HAYEK 403:26
  science…succeeded where m. failed — BRON 160:48
  the m. of words — PAGL 659:21
  This rough m. — SHAK 804:30
  We do not need m. — ROWL 730:26

When State M. fails — REED 710:34
Words divested of their m. — MILL 594:88
magical M. music never leaves — BEEC 73:64
  moments of m. accident — THOM 884:44
  most m. moment in the theater — CRON 256:31
  sight…most m. — BART 66:23
  using the word 'm.' — JOBS 455:66
magician m. is a demi-god — MARL 573:22
magicians m. sawn in half — STOP 855:16
magistrate commandment of the M. — BOOK 150:43
  elderly and ignorant m. — RUSS 735:39
magistrates power of kings and m. — MILT 601:24
  sovereigns and m. — LUTH 542:72
Magna Carta [M. C.] has been forced — INNO 446:48
magnet accrete things…like a m. — HOLM 423:59
  printing, gunpowder and the m. — BACON 50:45
magnetism animal m. drew thee — BRON 161:71
magnificat M. anima mea — BIBLE 133:42
magnificence m. is of a different — MONT 613:11
  m. of the buildings we burnt — ELGIN 315:13
magnificent feel m. in…suit — HERB 414:90
  M. Ambersons — TARK 867:30
  m., but it isn't war — BOSQ 151:73
  M. desolation — ALDR 12:55
  M. magpiety — ANON 25:58
  Mute and m. — DRYD 302:5
magnifique m., mais ce n'est pas — BOSQ 151:73
magnifying not m. grievances — RIDGE 715:32
magpie swollen m. in a fitful sun — POUND 692:26
magpiety Magnificent m. — ANON 25:58
Mahatma Ghandi since M. G. died — PUTIN 700:95
Mahdi M. pretends to be half mad — CECIL 210:32
Mahler Beethoven and M. — COPL 246:99
mahogany red m. book-case — BETJ 88:19
Mahomet hill will not come to M. — BACON 52:92
  revelation of M. — GIBB 366:95
Mahoun wife cries, auld M. — BURNS 180:43
maid Be good, sweet m. — KING 487:45
  Being an old m. — FERB 332:71
  chariest m. is prodigal enough — SHAK 781:47
  Come down, O m. — TENN 873:50
  fair m. you would win me — CAMP 194:68
  he makes the m. to answer — SHAK 800:24
  I'm just an awkward old m. — RENO 711:48
  In a vision…an Abyssinian m. — COLE 236:41
  I would not die a m. — CAMP 195:78
  like a moth, the simple m. — GAY 362:15
  m. called Florence? — SAKI 739:97
  m. not vendible — SHAK 769:72
  m. no Whitson-ale — SUCK 858:70
  m. so tender, fair — SHAK 788:88
  m. whom there were none to praise — WORD 957:62
  man with a m. — KIPL 490:2
  meekest m. of the three — HENR 411:12
  passion for a m. — TENN 877:57
  weary lot is thine, fair m. — SCOTT 753:35
  wedded m.…virgin mother — MILT 597:30
  Widowed wife, and married m. — SCOTT 754:74
maiden A m. never bold — SHAK 788:92
  love one m. only — TENN 877:57
  M., and mistress — SWIN 863:81
  m. of bashful fifteen — SHER 817:90
  man, a m., and a tre — ANON 21:54
  many a rose-lipt m. — HOUS 432:55
  Marrying left your m. name — LARK 509:80
  not one m. here — GILB 368:38
  pursued a m. — SHEL 816:64
  That orbèd m. — SHEL 813:76
  the m. hid — SWIN 863:84
maidenhead Or else their m. — BALL 59:73
maidens forbid you, m. a' — BALL 59:73
  m. call it love-in-idleness — SHAK 767:27
  m., watching said — TENN 873:46
  to the fairest of all m. — LAYA 515:98
  What m. loth? — KEATS 478:35
  young fair m. — STEV 854:85
maids Immortal youth to mortal m. — LAND 507:29
  m. are full of longing thoughts — CAMP 195:77
  M. are May — SHAK 780:12
  M. as we are — SHAK 778:64
  m. come forth — HARDY 397:29
  m. dance in a ring — NASHE 632:93
  Old m. like the houseless — BRON 161:68
  Soft m. and village hinds — COLL 237:70
  Three little m. — GILB 368:19
maid-servants M.-s., I hear people — CARL 202:43
mail like a rusty m. — SHAK 787:38

mails

m. it to people	WILL 944:63	m. quality	HOPK 429:97
Night M. crossing the border	AUDEN 42:71	m. who enforces order	LEGU 520:12
the multitudes in m.	SMART 826:66	more deadly than the m.	KIPL 493:77
mails two weeks' delayed m.	KIPL 492:52	neither m. nor female	BIBLE 127:79
main every man...part of the m.	DONNE 293:68	no reason for the existence of the m.	WEST 933:1
hushed the stormy m.	GRAY 385:82	rough m. kiss of blankets	BROO 162:86
owre the friendly m.	NAIR 629:34	self-worship of the m.	MILL 592:17
Maine inhabitant of...the State of M.	FORD 342:89	weapon of the m.	CONN 243:8
mainstream gladly enter the m.	COEN 233:89	Ye Lilies m.!	CRAB 252:40
main-travelled m.-t. road	GARL 360:74	**malefactor** make a m. die sweetly	DRYD 303:25
Maisie Proud M. is in the wood	SCOTT 754:62	**males** Nothing but m.	SHAK 796:24
maize with Plenty in the m.	TENN 873:51	six...left...all m.	BENN 80:47
majestic m. river floated on	ARNO 34:99	**malevolent** something m.	CATH 208:90
Majesty his M. hath determined	SWIFT 862:43	thought a m. speech	JONS 468:90
M. entered the House	RUSH 732:77	**Malfi** Duchess of M. still	WEBS 927:60
M.'s dominions	NORTH 641:58	**malice** crabbed m.	DISR 288:46
May it please your M.	LENT 122:60	From envy, hatred, and m.	BOOK 146:47
majesty appears to Your M.'s slave	KISH 493:83	m. in my breath	SHAK 799:92
as his m. is	BIBLE 112:81	M. is of a low stature	HALI 393:36
Beauty's princely m.	SHAK 759:75	m. mingled with a little wit	DRYD 303:14
certain alienated m.	EMER 324:51	m. toward none	LINC 529:11
Dead, your M.	DICK 281:74	the wildest m.	SITW 823:3
explain to Her M.	KEMB 479:72	worst your m. can	DRYD 301:57
first in loftiness...next in m.	DRYD 303:19	**malicious** God is...not m.	EINS 313:74
his M.'s Opposition	HOBH 420:6	horrid m. bloody flame	PEPYS 674:7
love your m.	SHAK 791:84	**malignity** m. and rapidity	DICK 282:92
naked m. seemed lords of all	MILT 604:98	motiveless m.	COLE 236:54
paucity...imparts m.	ALBE 11:31	the m. of a lie	STEE 844:51
right hand of the m.	BIBLE 129:33	**malingering** absolute genius for m.	PROU 698:47
sight so touching in its m.	WORD 959:3	**malleable** speech as m. and pliant	QUIL 702:13
suddenly recognised by His M.	FREUD 350:56	**malpractice** m. of heart	CLOU 232:58
major All poets who...are m.	WHITE 935:33	**malt** m. does more than Milton	HOUS 432:57
books m. or minor	SAND 742:34	**maltworms** purple-hued m.	SHAK 771:38
major-general modern M.-G.	GILB 368:39	**Malvernian** That old M. brother	BETJ 88:21
majority big enough m.	TWAIN 903:65	**mama** M. may have	HOLI 423:47
don't believe in black m. rule	SMITH 829:8	m. of dada	FADI 329:5
Government of the absolute m.	CALH 192:24	**mamas** Red-Hot M.	TUCK 901:16
m....happen to like	WHIT 936:72	**mamby-pambies** outing for m.-p.	CHAR 216:48
m. never has right	IBSEN 444:7	**mammal** You are...a vertebrate m.	CARB 198:36
m....the best repartee	DISR 288:39	**mammon** cannot serve God and m.	BIBLE 115:44
no m., no government	OAKE 642:2	friends of the m.	BIBLE 121:94
One man with God is always a m.	KNOX 495:16	pale M. pine amidst his store	POPE 686:68
poverty, ignorance...of the m.	DU 305:70	**man** Account me m.	MILT 603:83
Putting a m. together	DOLE 290:97	all animals, except m., know	BUTL 185:96
small conservative m.	TYNAN 904:99	all that may become a m.	SHAK 796:22
majors live with scarlet M.	SASS 745:84	All visible objects, m.	MELV 585:59
make cannot m. a man love	KING 486:23	almost kill a m. as kill	MILT 600:99
cost him more to m.	SMITH 827:85	always a m.'s shadow	JARR 452:90
Every joke I m.	RIVE 716:58	an all-the-lights-on m.	REED 709:31
may not quite m. it	YOST 968:50	And ah for a m.	TENN 876:21
Scotsman on the m.	BARR 65:89	and all that makes m.	TENN 877:57
What you see is what you m.	OKRI 649:28	an educated m.	HEAN 405:73
maker appealing directly to my M.	BRAH 156:56	Angry Young M.	PAUL 670:32
best m. of all marriages	SHAK 776:2	An iron m.	SHAK 772:91
God thi m.	CHAU 216:67	an old m. young	TENN 871:6
hope to meet my M.	CORN 247:5	any m. is so very a fool	SHAK 761:58
M., in that crimson lake	MONT 615:51	Any m.'s death diminishes me	DONNE 293:69
m. of heaven and earth	BOOK 146:37	any m. that breathes on earth	MARL 573:26
m. of his own fortune	STEE 844:43	any m. whatsoever	TARK 867:29
M. of the stars and sea	BETJ 88:36	anything said, ask a m.	THAT 881:48
ready to meet my m.	CHUR 226:6	ape in m.	MCCA 548:99
Scattered his M.'s image	DRYD 301:64	apparel oft proclaims the m.	SHAK 781:52
serve therewith my M.	MILT 601:26	architectural m.-milliner	RUSK 733:6
shall a man be more pure than his m.	BIBLE 98:96	arms and the m.	ANON 20:25
striveth with his M.!	BIBLE 109:88	Arms, and the m. I sing	DRYD 304:37
the watch...had a m.	PALEY 661:57	Art...absorbs the m.	FUSE 356:91
makers m. of our fate	POPP 689:56	artist m. and the mother woman	SHAW 807:17
T'abhor the m.	DRYD 303:17	as artist and as m.	THUR 891:6
making process of m. something else	HUXL 441:67	as good as life to a m.	BIBLE 113:5
somebody who is obsessed by M.	CUMM 257:57	as if you were a simple m.	PARRA 665:49
mal Honi soit qui m. y pense	EDWA 312:58	As m.'s ingratitude	SHAK 779:84
Malacca Whoever is Lord of M.	TOME 894:55	as much as a m.	TROL 898:56
maladies all the m. of stinking states	JOHN 459:40	as much as a m.	TRUTH 900:5
call all sorts of m....by one name	CARL 199:69	Athwart m.'s noses	SHAK 765:70
malady Life is a m.	ABU 1:15	average m. sees woman	MUIR 624:28
love's a m. without a cure	DRYD 304:50	A was a m.	SHAK 780:43
malaria like m. in his veins	GREE 386:6	battle of m. with m.	WEBER 925:13
Malay M. Peninsula...climate	SWET 861:11	Be a good m.	SCOTT 754:84
M. religion and custom	PANG 662:81	before m. knew how to sin	BEHN 75:23
Malaysia in M. 1937	THER 882:91	Behold the m.	BIBLE 133:47
male chosen and m. shall go forth	KENN 480:91	being more than m.	RUSS 734:25
Especially the m. of the species	LAWR 513:77	better angel is a m.	SHAK 803:87
incompetent as the average m.	CUNN 258:76	better m. than I am	KIPL 490:91
keeps m. domination intact	WOLF 952:61	between a m. and a woman	GIBB 367:11
makes a m. healthy	THUR 890:74	between m. and wife	ANDR 18:78
m. and female created he them	BIBLE 91:84	bind the heart of m.!	GILM 371:95
m. officers are gentlemen	CADOR 191:9	Books and the m. I sing	POPE 688:29
Both m. and bird and beast	COLE 235:20		
bread to a m.	LEWIS 526:54		
breed a habit in a m.!	SHAK 759:72		
bring a m. peace	BOOK 149:13		
busy m. who can keep up	STARR 843:27		
call m. a little world	DONNE 293:66		
call up my m.	SCOTT 753:52		
Can a M. be a Christian	HARD 396:92		
cannot be abrogated by m.	SUMN 859:82		
cannot make a m. love	KING 486:23		
can throw at a m.	HAZL 404:56		
care for no m. on earth	DICK 282:98		
Care...in every old m.'s eye	SHAK 766:89		
care-wearied m.	WHIT 938:17		
celebration of m.	THOM 884:24		
century of the common m.	ROUS 729:8		
century of the common m.	WALL 918:51		
Chancery Lane young m.	GILB 369:47		
child...in the debased, degraded m.	ELIOT 315:27		
Child is father of the M.	WORD 959:98		
civilized m....into a savage	TOCQ 892:27		
clever chiel', m.	MACQ 558:12		
cold charities of m. to m.	CRAB 252:33		
coloured m.	MACI 553:2		
comfortable years allowed to m.!	SASS 745:81		
comfort to each m.	ANON 20:24		
coming together of a m. and wife	STOP 855:13		
commonplace young m.	GILB 369:45		
confronts m. with...choice	SART 744:70		
conservative is a m.	ROOS 724:10		
contemporary m.'s idolatry	MONT 613:9		
conversant with a M.'s heart	POE 683:91		
covetous m. all his treasure	MILT 600:16		
create m. in our image	BIBLE 91:84		
creative nature of m.	MILL 594:80		
crime of being a young m.	PITT 679:1		
cultured modern m.	RODC 721:43		
Dark as the world of m.	SITW 823:11		
darkness of m.'s heart	GOLD 375:74		
dat m. of mine	HAMM 394:62		
dead m. leave to think!	SHAK 766:11		
dead m.'s embers	GRAV 382:23		
Dealing with a m.	JACO 449:12		
dear and valuable to m.	PITT 680:11		
Death destroys a m.	FORS 344:31		
deface the image of m.	IVAN 448:80		
degree of 'grand old m.'	LEAC 516:24		
Desiring this m.'s art	SHAK 800:46		
desperateness of m.'s heart!	BUNY 173:72		
dimensions of a m.'s self	LAMB 505:6		
dimensions of a m.'s self	LAMB 505:8		
Dispute it like a m.	SHAK 798:62		
distinguishes m. from animals	OSLER 656:88		
divinely gifted m.	TENN 874:83		
double minded m. is unstable	BIBLE 129:48		
dream past the wit of m.	SHAK 767:43		
drinking m. is never less	LAMB 506:9		
drive a m. out of his wits	ALCO 12:44		
dull ear of a drowsy m.	SHAK 768:58		
dying m.'s room	STER 848:39		
Each m. has his Jew	MILL 593:42		
each m. is alone	BERG 83:20		
Each m. is the architect	CLAU 229:73		
Ech m. for hymself	CHAU 217:80		
effect of travel on a m.	LIVI 532:55		
elderly m. of 42	ASHF 37:69		
employment for a thinking m.	ADDI 7:58		
Enclosing every thin m.	WAUGH 924:87		
end of m.'s motion	BACON 51:88		
episode in the life of a m.	STAEL 841:92		
ever tasted M.?	KIPL 491:87		
every great m. nowadays	WILDE 940:54		
every m. against his brother	BIBLE 112:62		
every m. a liar	BIBLE 125:5		
every m. and nation	LOWE 539:3		
Every m. at every moment	BAUD 69:85		
every m....born to die	DRYD 304:54		
Every m. has a right	JOHN 464:77		
Every m. has his fault	SHAK 791:77		
every m. is enemy to every m.	HOBB 420:2		
Every m. is not a proper champion	BROW 165:47		
Every m. is the maker	STEE 844:43		
every m. is two men	BORG 151:58		
Every m. is wanted	EMER 324:72		
every m. must play a part	SHAK 768:68		
every m. of every nation	THAC 880:36		
Every m. over forty	SHAW 808:54		

man 1189

every m. reclaimed his own property	BUTL 186:12	hate a m. you have hurt	TACI 865:3	looking for an honest m.	DIOG 286:2
every m. shall eat	SHAK 805:58	heaping obligations on a m.	SHAW 807:20	Look out for this m.'s music	PARRY 666:55
Every m.'s own reason	BROW 165:48	heart of a m.	ROUS 729:15	love freedom...but good m.	MILT 601:22
every m. straight before him	BIBLE 95:8	heart of a m....lodged in a woman	CONG 241:68	love is a thing below a m.	STER 848:41
every m....under a Government	RAIN 705:37	heart of m. go together	RUSK 733:92	love not m. less	BYRON 188:70
Every m. who is high up	BARR 65:91	hearty old m.	SOUT 835:43	love of m.	JEFF 453:11
every m. will do his duty	NELS 633:14	hero is a m.	MAIL 560:46	lowly m.	WHIT 936:71
every m., woman and child	GOLD 377:25	holy m. to crysten hym	MALO 562:6	make a deal with one m.	DWOR 308:45
every m. would lay his hand	STRA 857:45	honest m.'s	GILB 368:42	make a m. appear a fool	DRYD 303:24
Every moment dies a m.	TENN 872:27	honest m.'s the noblest	POPE 687:89	make a m. blessed and happy	ARIS 31:20
everyone has sat except a m.	CUMM 258:66	honest m.'s the noble work	BURNS 177:76	make a m. by standing a sheep	BEER 73:87
Every time I leave the old m.	OCON 647:90	honest m. who married	GOLD 376:89	make a monkey of a m.	BENC 78:4
Every true m.'s apparel	SHAK 788:75	hour's come, but not the m.	SCOTT 753:58	make me bearded like a m.!	DICK 284:54
Every unjust m.	PLATO 681:53	how a m. dies	JOHN 462:19	make me mistress to the m.	POPE 686:48
Every wise m.'s son	SHAK 785:92	However vast a m.'s spirit	PASC 666:64	makes a m. stand straight	HELL 408:43
exploit of that gallant m.	MILT 600:1	how hard it is to become a m.	CARP 202:50	making of m.	SWIN 863:85
eye of American m.	BARR 64:81	How many roads must a m. walk	DYLAN 309:51	m. about whom all is forgotten	BENT 82:6
facts we know about a m.	LAWR 513:57	husband a m.	LAMB 505:93	m. a child	SHAK 762:96
false to any m.	SHAK 781:54	hyest thyng that m. may kepe	CHAU 217:93	m. after his own heart	BIBLE 96:32
fancy of m. has painted	LOCKE 533:89	I am a free m.	ARET 31:11	manage a clever m.	KIPL 489:70
fasting, for a good m.'s love	SHAK 779:2	I am a m.	SHAK 792:7	m. a little pope of perfection	LAWR 513:49
Fathers, what is m.!	MILT 608:92	I am a m.	TERE 879:12	m. alone can keep that peace	CHUR 226:99
fear of every m.	JONS 468:92	I am a sincere m.	MARTI 576:71	m. alone does m. betray	ROCH 719:13
feminine in the m.	KENT 483:50	if a m. bites a dog	BOGA 144:97	m. alone in a room	HUTC 441:47
final pleasure left to m.	SNOW 832:74	If a m. does not make	JOHN 460:65	m. also has his moral	LICH 528:85
find a m.	PASC 666:69	If a m. do not erect	SHAK 774:57	M. always desires...happiness	ANON 21:49
fine m. who...knows nothing	EISE 314:6	If a m. have a tent	LEON 522:71	M....always to be blest	POPE 687:74
first-class fightin' m.	KIPL 489:89	If a m. have long hair	BIBLE 126:48	m., a madyn, and a tre	ANON 21:54
first enterprising m.	RUDO 730:35	If a m. look sharply	BACON 52:25	m. and a woman in a garden	WILDE 941:83
first m. I heard use the expression	ELLI 322:22	If a m. should spit	WEBS 926:28	m. and a woman looking at a girl	WOOLF 955:23
first m. is of the earth	BIBLE 127:61	If a m. were called	GIBB 366:90	m. and his wine's sae bewitching!	BURNS 180:61
fog of the good m.'s mind	BROW 167:26	If a m. were sure of living	HAWT 401:1	m. and his work existed	MEYER 589:63
follies which a m. regrets most	ROWL 729:22	If a m. write little	BACON 53:38	m., and not his instruments	MO 611:67
foolish, fond old m.	SHAK 793:31	if any m. be in Christ	BIBLE 127:70	m. and the infinite!	MACD 549:24
Foolish the m. who trusts her	FRAN 347:96	If any m. will come after me	BIBLE 120:76	m. and the intention	LEON 522:74
fool, who trusts a m.	MARIE 571:75	If m. were anything	DONNE 292:59	m. and wife make one fool	JONS 467:65
For a m. to admit a distaste	STEI 846:84	If m. were robbed	FONT 341:73	M. appears to be the missing link	LORE 537:62
For he owes not any m.	LONG 535:18	if the Queen were a m.	VICT 912:77	m. at the wheel	MARI 571:76
For m. will be blotted out	JEFF 453:12	If this young m.	GILB 368:43	m. bears beliefs	EMER 325:88
formed m. out of the dust	BIBLE 91:86	If you delight not in m.	SHAK 782:91	M., being reasonable	BYRON 190:8
For tribal m. space	MCLU 556:52	If you hate a m.	CARL 199:72	M. be my metaphor	THOM 883:5
Free m.!	BAUD 68:62	If you would work any m.	BACON 53:33	m. [']s body both for power	SPEN 838:32
free m.	JOHN 458:10	Ignorance...excuses no m.	SELD 756:8	m. booste of conning	LYDG 542:79
free m. thinks of nothing less	SPIN 841:80	I got my m.	GERS 365:73	m. born in America	OLSEN 650:45
friend of m.	COLL 237:73	immense new powers on m.	CHUR 226:5	m. by nothing is so well bewrayed	SPEN 839:58
fury of a patient m.	DRYD 302:92	imperishable dignity of m.	CARL 200:86	m. can be a parent	MUIR 624:29
gave m. speech	SHEL 814:15	Imprisoned in every fat m.	CONN 243:13	m. can become famous	SHAW 807:99
Get a new m.!	SHAK 804:21	in a young m. is timidity	HUGO 437:86	m. can be destroyed	HEMI 410:87
ghastly to every m.	ANON 20:35	inclinations of a m.	LONS 536:42	m. can be so innocently employed	JOHN 462:34
Give a m. the secure possession	YOUNG 968:51	inestimable privilege of m.	SHEL 812:50	m. can die but once	SHAK 772:88
Give every m. thine ear	SHAK 781:51	in favour with God and m.	BIBLE 120:71	m. can never elevate his mistress	BALZ 60:89
give it to the first m.	SCHR 749:61	injured no m.'s reputation	LOVE 538:89	M....can not be happy	POIN 683:96
Give me a m.	HAGEN 391:5	Innate ideas are in every m.	BLAKE 141:37	m. cannot be too careful	WILDE 940:66
Give me that m.	SHAK 783:22	in spirit she is a m.	GOTT 379:70	m. cannot choose but pay	PATM 669:15
give the white m. nothing else	WALK 917:38	interrupt a m.	STER 848:21	m. cannot dress	STER 848:48
giving m. dominion over woman	STAN 843:16	in the image of God made he m.	BIBLE 92:12	m. cannot...hold another	FULL 355:66
glory of God is m.	ANON 20:27	in truth the m.	POPE 687:93	M. cannot live	GILL 370:83
God created m.	VALE 907:5	in youth m. is...depraved	MITC 609:25	M. cannot live without seeking	BERL 84:47
God hath given liberty to m.	CURR 259:92	I saw an aged, aged m.	CARR 205:21	m. cannot make him laugh	SHAK 773:75
God in M.	CRAS 253:78	is m. an ape or an angel?	DISR 288:50	M. cannot make principles	PAINE 660:38
God is a m.	GIRA 373:27	It profits a m. nothing	BOLT 145:12	m. ceases to be a beginner	COLL 237:60
God is not a m.	BIBLE 94:84	It's a m.'s job	AESC 9:80	M. comes and tills	TENN 877:60
God made himself a m.	HUGO 437:71	Japanese young m.	GILB 369:46	m. comes around to needing	FULL 355:70
God, M., Destiny	MILL 593:52	Jewish m. with parents	ROTH 727:80	m. comes into a great hotel	MILL 593:37
God never rose...for m. to mend	DRYD 304:48	join together this m.	BOOK 148:84	m. couldn't wear a moustache	HOOV 427:25
good eater must be a good m.	DISR 287:17	justify God's ways to m.	HOUS 432:57	M. delights not me	SHAK 782:90
good habit makes a child a m.	WEBS 926:24	kill a m. than a hawk	JEFF 453:16	m. desires to live long	SWIFT 862:51
good m.'s glory	KEMP 480:79	know thee not, old m.	SHAK 773:99	m. die better	MACA 545:45
good to preserve the health of M.	BYRD 186:21	labouring m. that is given	BIBLE 113:97	m. does not attain	GOULD 380:75
good to some m.	SHAW 807:6	large-hearted m.	BROW 166:88	m. does not keep pace	THOR 889:43
gossamer fidelity of mere M.	POE 683:84	last strands of m.	HOPK 429:88	M. does not live by bread alone	GILL 370:84
Go West, young m.	SOULE 834:38	laws of m.	HOUS 432:67	m. does what he likes	GILL 370:81
Greater love hath no m.	BIBLE 123:55	less m. has to do with...death	MELV 585:58	m. doth not live by bread only	BIBLE 95:90
greatest m. in the world	TRUM 900:88	let him pass for a m.	SHAK 769:79	m. doth seek a triple perfection	HOOK 427:40
great m. walking down the street	COPL 246:99	let not m. have the upper hand	BOOK 148:6	m....down on his luck	DAVI 265:84
guess what a m.	MORL 619:38	Life as a M.	ROTH 728:83	M. dreams of fame	TENN 877:46
had made her such a m.	SHAK 788:94	life of a m....heroic poem	CARL 201:20	m. enough for a woman	DEKK 270:15
haggard and lank young m.	GILB 369:48	life of every m.	MUIR 624:21	m....even more, an Englishman	MORI 619:36
half a m. to suffer	LAWR 512:44	life of m.	BACON 53:49	m. fallen among Fabians	LENIN 521:41
happiness of m.	PAINE 660:39	like a m....chasing rainbows	WODE 952:53	m. feels instinctively	LOWE 539:11
happiness or blessedness of m.	SPIN 841:81	like an honest m.	SHAK 774:36	m. feel so lonely, alien	LAWR 513:56
happiness through another m.'s eyes	SHAK 780:19	Like master like m.	PETR 676:44	m. feels that...in woman	WRIG 962:63
Happy is the m.	BIBLE 104:55	like unto the Son of m.	BIBLE 131:88	m. first of all exists	SART 744:72
Happy is the m.	BIBLE 133:34	line where m. leaves off	FROST 352:2	M. for all seasons	BOLT 145:11
Happy is the m.	BIBLE 103:37	Little m., little m.!	ELIZ 322:7	m. found his form	BERD 83:12
harried m. I think I be!	BALL 59:64	lonely m. is a lonesome thing	CHEE 218:8	m. Friday	DEFOE 269:75
hate a m. who swallows it	LAMB 505:90	looked from pig to m.	ORWE 654:50	m. gets into the ring	MAIL 560:59

man 1190

m. God hates	DOWL 296:34	M. is what he eats	FEUE 334:3	m. should have dinner	LEMAY 521:31
m. goes in for politics	ROGE 723:83	M. is who he is	SAINT 738:42	m. should importune me	MONT 613:21
M. goeth forth unto his work	BIBLE 102:12	m. keeps another person's secret	LABR 502:10	m. should know something	STER 848:43
m. goeth to his long home	BIBLE 106:36	m. knows he is to be hanged	JOHN 463:55	m. should never be ashamed	POPE 686:54
m. got to do	STEI 845:81	m. knows that he is miserable	PASC 667:89	m. should never think that	TROL 897:33
M. hands on misery to m.	LARK 510:90	m. lay down his wife	JOYCE 470:28	m. shouldn't fool with booze	FAUL 331:48
m. has a House of Lords	LLOY 533:78	m. lies late	MORG 619:33	m. should rejoice in his own works	BIBLE 106:15
m. has a property	LOCKE 533:86	M....little lower than the angells	BILL 135:95	m. should think	MORE 618:11
m. has created him	DOST 294:92	M. lives by science as well	JAMES 451:62	m.'s image	YEATS 965:6
m. has just waxed the floor	NASH 631:74	m. lives well	KIPL 489:77	M.'s inhumanity to M.	BURNS 177:86
m. hasn't discovered	KING 487:26	m. looketh on the outward	BIBLE 96:34	M.'s loneliness is but his fear	ONEI 651:62
m. has one hundred dollars	WEST 933:88	m....loyal to his club	WHITE 935:34	M.'s love is...a thing apart	BYRON 189:1
m. has to prove himself	PAGL 659:18	m. made the rest	KRON 499:18	M.'s love is of m.'s life	AMIS 16:31
m. has two irons	BEAU 71:13	m. made the town	COWP 251:11	M.'s lovely...power	LOWE 540:26
m. hates to be moved	LAWR 514:92	M....makes of himself	SART 745:73	m.'s natural language	FLAU 339:29
M. hath his daily work	MILT 604:5	M. marks the earth with ruin	BYRON 188:71	m.'s natural qualities	SHER 817:91
M....held only by the slightest	EDGE 311:35	m. married is...marred	SHAK 791:62	m. so various	DRYD 302:83
M., her last work	TENN 874:80	m. marries his housekeeper	PIGOU 678:76	m.'s power of selection	DARW 263:52
m. he was to all the country	GOLD 376:99	m. may be born a poet	SASS 746:3	m.'s reach should exceed	BROW 168:45
m. hurling himself at...chaos	POUND 692:31	m. may be brought to hope	TROL 898:39	m.'s strength is but little	SIMO 822:80
m. in a frock coat	LAVER 512:34	m. may fish with the worm	SHAK 784:47	M. stands face to face	CAMUS 195:84
m. in a large check suit	WELLS 930:29	M. may not marry his Grandmother	BOOK 150:44	m.'s the gowd	BURNS 180:52
m. in all the world's	SHAK 763:6	m. may write	JOHN 459:50	m....successful with his children	EURI 328:64
M. (in good earnest)	MONT 613:18	m....mere complexities	YEATS 967:31	m.'s unhappiness	PASC 667:73
m. in higher rank	RUSK 733:95	m. must be sacrificed	LOWE 539:99	m. swear he loves me	SHAK 773:21
m. in his entirety	BECK 72:38	m. must have a rare recipe	LAMB 505:78	M.'s word is God in m.	TENN 878:72
m. in London	GALT 359:53	Manners makyth m.	WILL 944:65	m.'s work or his own gifts	MILT 601:26
m. in the crucible	ELKIN 322:17	M....never have attempted	THOM 888:12	m.'s worth something	BROW 168:41
M. in the highest	SWIN 864:10	m. nor angel can discern	MILT 603:88	m. takes a drink	LEWIS 527:63
m. in the smoker	SAND 742:15	m., not even a doctor	NIGH 639:24	m. taketh his sword	BIBLE 112:68
m. in the street	BALD 57:31	m. of clay, son	MILT 606:45	m. talks loudly against religion	STER 848:32
m....in the way in the house	GASK 361:85	m. of...comprehensive nature	DRYD 304:40	m. telling the truth	JONES 466:23
m. invents nothing	SHAW 807:26	m. of genius	BEER 74:90	m. that could look no way	BUNY 174:80
M. is a bungler	SHAW 807:27	m. of genius	POUND 691:97	m. that Fortune's buffets	SHAK 783:21
m. is a common murderer	SAKI 739:65	m. of giant stature	NEHRU 633:9	m. that gets drunk	MCGO 551:75
M. is a creature who	STEV 852:42	m. of good character	SHAW 810:96	m. that hails you Tom or Jack	COWP 251:3
M. is a history-making creature	AUDEN 44:11	m. of great common sense	SHAW 807:12	m. that hath friends	BIBLE 105:84
M. is all symmetry	HERB 413:70	m. of great worth	POLO 684:4	m. that hath no music	SHAK 770:21
M. is a noble animal	BROW 166:81	m. of independent means	MENC 586:89	m. that is born	TWAIN 902:38
M. is a rope, fastened	NIET 638:1	m. of many ways	HOMER 425:9	m. that is born falls into a dream	CONR 244:32
M. is a singular creature	BRON 161:53	m. of my name	NAPO 630:52	M. that is born of a woman	BOOK 148:98
M. is a tool-using animal	CARL 200:90	m. of paradoxes	ROUS 729:14	m. that meddles with cold iron!	BUTL 185:73
M. is a torch borne in the wind	CHAP 214:15	m. of science	PIER 677:66	m. that men like	NORR 641:56
M. is a useless passion	SART 744:68	m. of sense and a fop	CHES 219:34	m. that says when	HAMM 395:71
m. is a wolf	PLAU 682:69	m. of sorrow who wins	LAO 508:64	m. that will nocht quhen he may	HENR 411:17
M. is become as one of us	BIBLE 91:1	m. of substance, of flesh and bone	ELLI 323:35	m. the index of that book	DONNE 293:79
M. is born free	ROUS 729:10	m. of the present	HOLM 424:86	m. the living sepulchre	CLARE 228:53
M. is born to live in society	DIDE 285:78	m. of wealth and taste	JAGG 449:15	m. there walked without a mate	MARV 577:6
m. is born unto trouble	BIBLE 98:97	m. of yearning thought	ROSS 727:65	m. the wonderful	BYRON 189:94
m. is bound to rebel against	IBSEN 444:7	m. o'independent mind	SMITH 831:64	m. to be in love	MORL 611:91
M. is by his constitution	BURKE 176:44	m. on the flying trapeze	LEYB 528:80	m. to create his own meaning	KUBR 500:35
M. is condemned	SART 745:74	m. on the flying trapeze	SARO 744:57	m. to do nothing	BURKE 176:58
M. is distinguished	ADDI 7:44	M. On the moon	BAKER 56:6	m. to earn his own living	MORE 618:11
m. is either free	BARA 63:43	m. or a woman	WELTY 931:46	m. to han ben in prosperitee	CHAU 216:63
M. is essentially the imitative	JAMES 451:69	M....political animal	ARIS 31:25	m. to know that he is his own	MONT 614:24
m. is ever hasty	KORAN 497:73	m. possesses nothing certainly	CABE 191:2	M. to M. the warld o'er	BURNS 180:54
m. is in substance	HUXL 443:7	M. proposes	KEMP 480:76	m....too proud to fight	WILS 949:78
m. is killing time	LOWE 540:27	m....proud and yet a wretched thing	DAVI 264:77	m. to reduce women...to imbecility	BROO 163:10
m. is like a phonograph	SHAW 809:89	m., proud a m.	SHAK 787:58	m. to tell how human	MILT 605:37
M. is m. and master	TENN 876:41	m. reaches old age	MAO 568:31	m. under authority	BIBLE 116:57
m. is most at ease	ALLS 14:8	m.'s affection	GILB 368:38	M., unlike any other thing	STEI 845:80
M. is neither angel nor beast	PASC 667:88	m.'s a fool to look	MOODY 615:57	m....up against Nature	GABOR 356:1
M. is neither good nor evil	BALZ 61:6	m.'s a m.	BURNS 180:53	m. wants but little	HOLM 423:60
M. is no other	SART 745:75	m. says he likes a woman	HEPB 412:26	m. wants to murder a tiger	SHAW 808:61
M. is nothing but a subject	PASC 667:70	m. says what he knows	ROUS 729:16	m. wants what a woman has—sex	DWOR 308:43
M. is not meant to be humble	TYSON 904:13	m.'s behaviour...harmless	SHAW 809:82	m. was apparently a gentleman	RIDGE 715:31
M. is...not more happy	POE 683:85	m.'s boots	MACC 546:65	M. was by Nature Woman's cully	CONG 240:55
m. is not 'taking'	JONG 466:31	m.'s commendation with woman	SHAK 786:14	M. was made for Joy and Woe	BLAKE 141:26
M. is not the enemy of M.	PAINE 660:33	M.'s condition. Inconstancy	PASC 667:71	m. wastes part of his life	JOHN 459:55
M....is of few days	BIBLE 98:5	M.'s contribution to human history	JIANG 455:57	m. way out there in the blue	MILL 593:32
M. is one world	HERB 413:71	m.'s corruptions	OTWAY 656:94	m. who any woman might love	BIRD 135:6
M. is only a reed	PASC 667:81	m.'s critical actions	ELIOT 315:21	m. who believes in giraffes	MITC 609:27
M. is only truly great	DISR 287:30	m.'s decision on how to vote	SCHN 748:44	m. who boasts	MENC 586:88
M. is...over-complicated	POUND 692:20	m.'s desire is for the woman	COLE 236:49	m. who can dominate	WILDE 941:93
M. is polygamous	JAMES 452:78	m.'s dying	MANN 566:83	m. who can reason	LESS 524:6
M. is quite insane	MONT 614:28	m....searches for recognition	MANN 566:87	m. who cares no more	SOUT 835:53
m. is something that	NIET 638:99	m.'s education begins	ROUS 729:13	m. who comes to England	MANS 568:14
M. is still	KENN 481:17	m.'s failures	WARR 921:14	m. who conducts himself well	DICK 281:54
m. is strong before he is moral	FAUL 331:18	m.'s fall made manifest	MILL 594:85	m. who didn't wax	KIPL 489:17
m. is the being who wills	SCHI 747:25	m.'s first disobedience	MILT 601:29	M. Who Died Twice	ROBI 718:90
M. is the hunter	TENN 872:33	m.'s gotta do what a m.'s	LADD 503:41	m. who...dies among	WORD 958:90
M. is the measure of all things	PROT 697:32	m.'s got to figure	LOUIS 538:77	m. who dies rich	CARN 202:47
M. is the Only Animal	TWAIN 903:79	m. shall be as an hiding place	BIBLE 108:75	m. who does not believe in human	CAST 208:79
M. is the only creature	ORWE 654:46	m. shall be known in his children	BIBLE 113:91	m. who does not return	SHAW 808:57
M. is the only one	FROU 353:27	M. shall not live by bread alone	BIBLE 114:22	m. who doesn't love oysters	SAKI 739:60
M. is the shuttle	VAUG 909:40	M.'s happiness	GIDE 368:24	m. who goes to a psychiatrist	GOLD 377:26
M. is ungrateful to his Lord	KORAN 498:94	m.'s heart good to hear	SHAK 767:23	m. who has acted	EMER 325:81

man

m. who has lived many years	HEMI 409:72	most fantastical odd m. alive	ROCH 719:17	old m....had so much blood	SHAK 798:65
m. who has murdered	LEVA 525:17	most married m.	WARD 920:4	old m. in a hurry	CHUR 224:65
m. who has no office	SHAW 806:81	mother's life made me a m.	MASE 580:62	old m. of Thermopylae	LEAR 517:46
m. who has quarrelled	PEAC 671:53	mould of a m.'s fortune	BACON 52:24	old m. puffed into sight	TIME 891:18
m. who has seen the world	MACA 545:26	must believe in m.	KRUT 500:29	old m. with a shotgun	TWAIN 902:54
m. who hates dogs	ROST 727:72	Must helpless m.	JOHN 459:48	Ol' M. River	HAMM 394:63
m. who hears the voice	SHAR 805:69	m....walks across his century	LEAC 515:8	once a m. has conceived it	STER 848:33
m. who is born	MALT 563:22	m....who is neither tarnished	CHAN 213:78	one bullet...kills a m.	SPEN 837:4
m. who is false to his friends	BERK 84:35	my fellow m.—my brother	BAUD 68:57	one-eyed m.	WELLS 930:23
m. who knows the price of everything	WILDE 941:80	My old m.	COLL 237:64	one m. for every seven women	BERN 85:65
m. who lay with a beast	HELL 408:33	myth of m.'s capacity	WARR 921:16	One m. in a thousand	KIPL 492:64
m. who lies	SAFI 737:20	natural instinct to abjure m.	HARDY 397:8	one m. in his time	SHAK 779:80
m. who listens to Reason	SHAW 808:50	nature first made m.	DRYD 300:30	One m. is as good	JOWE 469:15
m. who lives alone	BUKO 172:53	nature must produce a m.	HUME 438:2	one m. picked out of ten thousand	SHAK 782:79
m. who lives by his own work	COLL 237:59	nature of a m.	STEI 846:88	One m. shall have one vote	CART 207:58
m. who makes every m. feel small	CHES 220:64	Neither a wise m. nor a brave m.	EISE 314:93	One m. that has a mind	SHAW 810:21
m. who makes no mistakes	PHEL 676:48	never an Angry Young M.	AMIS 16:38	one m. to remember	RUNY 732:63
M. who Mistook his Wife	SACKS 737:6	never hated a m.	GABOR 356:3	One m. with God	KNOX 495:16
m. whom the city sets up	SOPH 834:27	never mentioned a m.	POUND 691:7	Only m. behaves with such	HUXL 441:71
m. who nearly becomes Prime Minister	BUTL 184:59	never saw a m. who looked	WILDE 942:16	Only m. delights	AQUI 30:98
m. who never ate bacon	HATT 400:82	never yet met a m.	ROGE 723:76	only m. I knew	FOOT 342:79
m. who never missed an occasion	SHAW 811:35	new tribunal...the educated m.'s!	BROW 169:77	only repelled by m.	INGE 445:27
m. who never...travelled to heaven	BLAKE 141:35	nice m.	SWIFT 862:52	On M., on Nature	WORD 961:34
m. who offers a bribe	GREE 386:18	night out for m. or beast	FIEL 335:30	ony m. can be's	MACD 549:26
m. who owns up to arthritis	NASH 630:61	noblest work of m.	INGE 445:32	Or can be, than is M.?	HERB 413:69
m. who paints only...surface	WHIS 934:21	noble young m.	ROCHE 719:99	ordinary working m.	ORWE 653:16
M. who publishes his letters	WHITE 935:45	no concern for the common m.	WILS 947:42	Our m. in Havana	GREE 386:13
m. who runs away will fight	MENA 586:79	No free m. shall be taken or imprisoned	MAGN 559:26	out of the mouth...defileth a m.	BIBLE 117:2
m., who's danced with a girl	FARJ 330:21	No m. at all	SYNGE 865:20	Outside every fat m.	AMIS 16:35
m. whose God is in the skies	SHAW 808:44	No m. but a blockhead	JOHN 463:49	owe no m. hate	SHAK 779:89
m. whose life is spent	SMITH 828:89	No m. can know where he is going	ANGE 19:89	O wretched state of m.	SIDN 820:36
m. whose second thoughts	BARR 65:90	No m. can say that Jesus	BIBLE 126:50	Parliament of m.	TENN 871:17
m. who should loose me	LOWE 539:98	No m. can serve two masters	BIBLE 115:44	part m., part horse's ass	ACHE 2:35
m. who sits gazing	CATU 209:9	no m. can teach himself	SHAW 810:93	penetrated into the ear of m.	FORS 344:25
m. who sits in the outer office	MENC 586:2	No m. can tickle himself	BACON 53:47	people arose as one m.	BIBLE 96:22
m. who stood at the gate	HASK 400:81	No m....can wear one face	HAWT 402:6	Peter chose from m. to hide	CRAB 252:42
m. who thinks to found a home	DOUG 295:10	No m....can write	FAUL 331:46	phasing out the white m.	WALK 917:36
m. who trusts nobody	MACM 556:71	no m....could bear it	SHAW 807:13	phenomenon of m.	ALLS 14:9
m. who wants to do a good job	ELIOT 320:55	no m. could head me	TRUTH 900:5	philosophy inclineth M.'s mind	BACON 51:79
m. who was alleged	MACM 557:77	No m. does	WILDE 941:3	plain blunt m.	SHAK 778:45
m. who was not content	GLAS 374:44	no m. ever learned to tame	MEIL 584:38	play the m.	TAFT 866:11
M. who Would be King	KIPL 489:72	No m. has a right	PARN 665:48	poor a thing is m.!	DANI 262:33
m. who would not give his judgement	ADDI 6:29	no m. hath any quarrel	SHAK 786:20	poor m.'s Parnassus	EMER 325:1
m. will begin with certainties	BACON 49:21	No m. is an island	DONNE 293:68	poor m.'s wealth	SIDN 820:46
M. will err	GOET 375:62	No m. is good enough	LINC 529:3	power of m.	SHAK 797:55
m. willing to work	CARL 201:25	no m. is well pleased	JOHN 460:62	power of m.'s concentrated efforts	BUSH 184:50
m. will not merely endure	FAUL 331:36	no m. knoweth of his sepulchre	BIBLE 116:64	praise any m.	SHAK 794:64
m. will so live as to show	LAW 512:38	no m. knows	DELA 271:24	privilege of the fighting m.	STRA 856:38
m. with a bellyful	MILL 593:54	No m. likes to see	HARDY 396:3	problems which the m.	KRUT 500:30
m. with all his noble qualities	DARW 263:58	No m. putteth a piece	BIBLE 116:64	productive facilities of m.	MARX 579:30
m. with a maid	KIPL 490:2	No m., who knows nothing else	ARNO 36:31	proper study of mankind is m.	POPE 687:80
m. with bodily hunger	SHAW 809:73	No m. would set a word	MILL 594:69	proper study of mankind is m.	RABI 704:23
m. with heart, head	TENN 876:20	no more exempt...of letters	STER 848:45	propriety of civilized m.	MUIR 624:27
M., with his Satan	SNYD 832:91	no more...than a m. can have a baby	DRAP 298:89	put off the old m.	BIBLE 128:11
M. with murderous angels	DEVL 275:8	non-commissioned m.!	KIPL 490:14	quiet m. is here to stay	SMITH 829:6
m. without principles	FORD 342:88	none more formidable than m.	SOPH 834:26	rather have a m. dog	FLEM 340:46
m....without some vision	LAWR 514:81	no passion in the mind of m.	BACON 50:58	real needs of m.	SCHU 750:74
m., with soul so dead	SCOTT 752:16	no reasonable m.	HERB 412:48	reasonable m. adapts himself	SHAW 808:49
m. would be given a chance	ROST 727:70	normal humble m.	HERB 414:90	reason no m. knows	MARL 574:37
m. writing...English	NABO 628:2	Noselessness of M.	CHES 221:92	reasons...unknown to m.	LEVI 526:36
M., you have a son	MARQ 574:44	no shame for a m. to die	HOMER 425:8	reflecting the figure of m.	WOOLF 955:27
Marilyn...every m.'s love affair	MAIL 560:58	not a m., but—a cloud	MAYA 583:21	refresh the mind of m.	SHAK 762:68
marriage on the part of a m.	DICK 282:89	not a m. dare lift	JOHN 458:24	relationship between m. and m.	ROUS 729:17
married to a m. called John	WILDE 941:95	not...a m. of science	FREUD 350:55	remember one m. saw	BROW 168:48
mask has fallen, the m. remains	SHEL 814:18	not a m. to act hastily	SHAW 809:66	revealed as the m.	PARN 665:47
masterpiece of m.	MONT 614:32	not a m., you're a machine	SHAW 806:86	revive the stature of m.	CHUR 225:81
masters of different bits of m.	LAWR 514:84	not be a married m.?	KRAS 499:4	rich m. in his castle	ALEX 13:62
met a great m.	THAC 880:23	not good that the m. should be alone	BIBLE 91:89	Ridley, and play the m.	LATI 511:13
mildest mannered m.	BYRON 190:14	nothing makes a m. suspect	BACON 52:19	rights of one m.	KENN 481:19
military m. who	MOUN 622:93	nothing more unbecoming a m.	CONG 240:36	Ring in the valiant m.	TENN 875:96
mind of m.	MARL 573:22	not the m. we have to change	PRICE 695:82	robbed m. of everything	SOLZ 833:5
mind of m.	WORD 956:55	not the perfect m.	DOUG 295:15	rule of another m.	LOCKE 533:87
miseries that m. has inflicted	IRVI 447:55	not what happens to a m.	HUXL 441:70	sabbath was made for m.	BIBLE 119:51
Misery acquaints a m.	SHAK 804:20	Nowher so bisy a m.	CHAU 217:76	sadder and wiser m.	COLE 235:21
moderately honest m.	SHAW 808:48	No white m. ever had the blues	LEAD 516:26	savage individual m.	WELLS 930:21
Modern m. lives	LEGER 519:6	no wise m. believes	PLATO 682:58	saving one m. at a time	BUKO 173:54
Modern m. registers	LEGER 520:7	No young m. appeared	HAYD 402:23	say it was the same m.?	LOCKE 534:91
moral life of m.	WILDE 940:64	obstinate love to a young m.	SIDN 820:37	scan your brother M.	BURNS 178:93
more apparel than the m.	SHAK 774:47	o'er all this scene of m.	POPE 686:70	scenes where m. hath never trod	CLARE 228:55
more efficient...than any that m.	HAYEK 402:25	of all 'rights of m.'	CARL 201:26	scribble, to a m.	POPE 688:19
more flesh than another m.	SHAK 771:55	Of m. or worm	MILT 607:84	second of m.'s creeds	LAWR 514:90
more potent than any other m.	STEAD 843:31	Of m.'s bedevilment	HOUS 432:68	see a m.—not a colour	STEV 851:16
more right to be obeyed than m.	JOHN 456:73	Of some new race called M.	MILT 602:62	sell a m. a book	MORL 619:39
more than any m. in all Venice	SHAK 769:73	Oh God! that m.	MELV 585:68	separates a m. from a woman	ROBBE 716:61
more things m. is ashamed of	SHAW 807:15	old m. broken	SHAK 805:55	serried footnotes to m.	GRASS 382:13
More worth than any m.	SHAK 800:30	Old m.!...difficult to die	BYRON 189:88	servant of m.	SHAW 809:86
mortal m. may live	SHAK 760:9			shake a m.'s faith	SHAW 806:89

manage

Shall mortal m. be more just	BIBLE 98:96
shew thyself a m.	BIBLE 97:52
sick m. must think	LEWIS 526:49
sick m.'s passport	MARL 573:10
since by m. came death	BIBLE 127:57
sit by and see the blind m.	WALEY 917:31
sit on a m.'s back	TOLS 894:52
slave themselves to m.'s desire	HABI 391:3
small m. can be	MILL 592:31
smith a mighty m.	LONG 535:17
so becomes a m.	SHAK 775:74
Soccer is a m.'s game	CHAR 216:48
solace to m. giffis	BARB 63:50
sole nexus of m. to m.	CARL 201:27
solitary child and solitary m.	ACKR 3:62
So long as m. remains free	DOST 294:93
some great m.	HOOV 427:45
Son of m. shall come in his glory	BIBLE 119:35
sorrow…for a vulgar m.	DRYD 301:52
So this is m.	TATE 867:41
soul of m.	AUBR 42:61
soul of this m.	SHAK 791:63
sovereign'st thing that any m.	SKEL 824:27
spake on that ancient m.	COLE 235:9
span of a m.'s…arms	LEON 523:76
special kind of m.	GILL 370:82
spirit of m. is a good adversary	WILL 945:99
sportsman is a m. who	LEAC 515:23
stamps a m. at once	SHAW 809:71
state of m.	SHAK 805:52
still at least a m.	SCOTT 753:51
straightest road to a m.'s heart	FERN 334:96
strange prodigious creatures, M.	ROCH 719:10
strange what a m. may do	THAC 880:37
strengthened…in the inner m.	BIBLE 127:88
strips a m. of everything	HAZL 403:46
strong m. after sleep	MILT 601:20
strong m. exults in his…ability	POE 683:81
stupid m. is doing something	SHAW 807:11
such a degradation of m.?	BRYAN 170:98
such a disagreeable m.	GILB 369:56
such another m.!	SHAK 795:87
Such was their awe of m.	MILT 604:8
superiority of one m.'s opinion	JAMES 450:46
surely fool a m.	WHITE 935:40
system…makes m. its appendix	FROMM 352:88
Take up the White M.'s burden	KIPL 491:19
teach a wise m.	RABE 704:18
Teach the free m.	AUDEN 43:94
thanks of m. and woman	PAINE 660:29
That m.'s silence	HARDY 396:2
That which once united m.	BOLD 145:5
The greater m.	TENN 878:92
their murdered m.	KEATS 477:11
The Little Disturbances of M.	PALEY 661:49
The m. is dead!	WHIT 938:18
Then a m. will say it	ANCO 17:66
The Reasonable M.	HERB 413:50
therefore the state of m.	MILT 600:5
There is a m. child conceived	BIBLE 98:94
There's not a m. That lives	WORD 958:83
There was an old m.	QUIL 702:16
There was once a m.	KNOX 495:18
thing civilized by M.	MERE 587:25
thinking m.'s television	HAMP 395:73
think like a m.	SIMON 821:73
thin m. inside every fat m.	ORWE 653:26
This m., Comrades	GROM 389:78
This was a m.	SHAK 778:57
Thou art the m.	BIBLE 96:46
Thou madest m.	TENN 873:55
till m. ceases to be	PEAR 671:56
time in a m.'s life	MALA 561:84
time of a m. or woman	WHIT 937:99
tired of being a m.	NERU 633:22
tireless m. of Marshall	ROBI 718:92
'Tis no sin for a m.	SHAK 770:30
To be a poor m.	DU 305:66
To cheat a m. is nothing	GAY 362:21
Toil is m.'s allotment	MELV 585:53
To no m. will we…deny…justice	MAGN 559:27
totality of m., sense	MARI 571:81
to the image, not to the m.	PRICE 695:81
to the last m.	HAIG 392:15
touches this touches a m.	WHIT 938:6
truth in no m.	BEAU 71:22
two civilizers of m.	DISR 288:59
two things no m.	MOSS 622:84
type of m.	TOYN 895:77
understand a m. better	HUGO 437:77
used car from this m.?	ANON 25:41
Use every m.	SHAK 782:98
'Vain m.,' said she	SPEN 839:47
value of a m.	ANON 26:76
value, or worth of a m.	HOBB 420:99
Victory switches from m. to m.	HOMER 425:4
vilify a great m.	POE 683:93
vindicate the ways of God to m.	POPE 686:71
walking dead m.	ANON 27:26
wants to buy a m.	MCCA 547:86
War is to m.	MUSS 628:94
was a self-made m.	HELL 407:25
was a spare m.	AUBR 42:58
Wash That M.	HAMM 395:66
Was m. made stupid	EBER 310:12
wasn't the m. who could do it	JOHN 457:6
Was there a m. dismayed?	TENN 875:12
Was there ever m. had such luck?	SHAK 803:89
watching a m.	BYATT 186:16
wears m.'s smudge	HOPK 428:70
wed a fair young m.	CAMP 195:77
what a frugal m. annually saves	SMITH 827:83
what a m. does with his solitariness	WHIT 936:68
what a m. would like to be true	BACON 50:43
What a piece of work is a m.!	SHAK 782:89
what drink a m. will have	MARQ 575:59
Whatever each m. can…do	BURKE 176:38
What is great in m.	NIET 638:2
What is m.	BLIX 142:61
What is m. in nature?	PASC 667:85
What is m., that thou art mindful	BIBLE 99:31
What m. has made of m.	WORD 957:61
what m. is there of you	BIBLE 115:51
What manner of m. is this	BIBLE 116:61
What m. that sees	SPEN 839:60
What m. thinks of changing	TROL 897:11
what m. will do any good	TROL 897:28
what one m. can devise	WRIS 963:80
whatsoever a m. soweth	BIBLE 127:82
When a m. marries	SHEL 814:4
when a m. should marry?	BACON 51:76
When a m. takes a farm	PARN 665:46
When God at first made m.	HERB 414:82
When I was a young m.	SCHU 750:76
When the military m. approaches	SHAW 808:30
Where m. has manned the trenches	MACG 551:71
where no m. has gone before	RODD 721:45
Where's the m. could ease	PARK 663:97
whether a m. is good or evil	BLAKE 141:33
white m. in Africa	LESS 523:90
whole duty of m.	BIBLE 107:38
whore-master m.	SHAK 792:89
Who's master, who's m.	SWIFT 862:56
Whoso would be a m.	EMER 324:53
wicked m. in the bathroom	EWART 328:72
wife full of words to a quiet m.	BIBLE 113:1
wise m. knows himself to be a fool	SHAK 780:16
within this learned m.	MARL 574:33
wit of m.	WARN 921:11
woman a m. loves	STEV 851:31
woman be more like a m.?	LERN 523:85
woman needs a m.	STEI 846:91
woman…sees much more than a m.	MILL 592:14
woman…to be the toy of m.	WOLL 954:89
woman to hold a m.	SPARK 835:62
Woman to m.	WEBS 926:31
wonderous and fearful in m.	MELV 585:65
working m. into a passive role	ORWE 653:11
work of one extraordinary m.	HUBB 434:99
world an honest m.	LICH 528:91
worm, and no m.	BIBLE 99:42
worst luck any m. could have	HEMI 410:81
Would this m.…ask why?	AUDEN 43:4
wrong m. the woman	HARDY 397:15
Yet each m. kills	WILDE 942:17
You'll be a M., my son!	KIPL 492:63
young m. at the age of twenty-three	DAMR 261:23
young m. cleanse his way?	BIBLE 103:24
young m. will be wiser	TENN 878:74
manage by those who m. it	JOHN 463:70
m. a clever man	KIPL 489:70
m. without butter	GOEB 374:53
managed world is disgracefully m.	FIRB 336:47
management m. can only be properly	JAY 453:1
m. of external things	CARL 200:83
Reagan…lacked m….skills	ONEI 651:77
manager Want To See The M.	BURR 181:65
managers M.…do things right	BENN 81:83
m. to run their concerns	ROBI 718:92
Manchester M.…mere village	DEFOE 269:77
man-cub m.-c. is a m.-c.	KIPL 490:4
Mandalay Come you back to M.	KIPL 489:81
come you back to M.!	KIPL 489:80
M. has its name	MAUG 582:8
Mandarin great yellow M.	CHES 221:87
M. style	CONN 242:4
Mandelson M.…can skulk in broad daylight	HOGG 423:46
Manderley went to M. again	DU 306:93
mandrake child a m. root	DONNE 291:23
manger laid him in a m.	BIBLE 120:68
m. for his bed	ALEX 13:63
Mother, the Child and the bare m.	WHIT 936:71
wrapped in the rude m.	MILT 597:31
mangle immense pecuniary M.	DICK 282:95
Manhattan I don't want to leave M.	KOCH 495:24
in M.'s Town	HUGH 435:22
mast-hemm'd M.	WHIT 937:2
middle-management of M.	AMIS 16:43
statistics for M. Island	BART 66:30
manhood envied beginning of m.	STEI 846:93
envy men their m.	PANK 662:87
gives m. more approbation	SHAK 786:59
linger in m.	THOR 888:14
M. a struggle	DISR 287:26
m. is cast Down	LAWR 512:46
m., long misled	DRYD 303:11
m.'s beauty	WILDE 940:44
nobility of m.	HUXL 443:7
manhoods hold their m. cheap	SHAK 776:94
mania Composing…is a m.	HONE 425:13
m. for sentences	FLAU 339:12
maniacal mirthless, m.	THUR 891:96
manifest disaster until it is finally m.	MURP 626:74
It was m. to me	TROL 897:35
manifestation teabreaks and…m.	MISH 609:19
manifestations see only the m.	LAO 508:60
manifesto first powerful plain m.	SPEN 837:1
rely on some political m.	JOHN 456:80
upsetting incendiary m.	MARI 571:78
man-in-the-street To the m.	AUDEN 43:98
manipulation m. of…impulses	MILL 594:71
m. of the inventive	LEWIS 527:65
science…system of m.	BOOK 150:45
Manitoba climate of M.	ANON 23:93
mankind All the ills of m.	DUDEK 305:76
an apple damn'd m.	OTWAY 656:96
As I know more of m.	JOHN 464:91
benefit of m.	MACL 554:27
bestow on m.	HOBB 420:97
careless of m.	TENN 870:92
coarse emotion of m.	ELIOT 316:52
common curse of m.	SHAK 786:30
common duty of m.	ROCK 720:33
conclusions at which m. arrive	PALM 661:67
crimes that shame m.	NOON 641:50
deceive and delude m.	EPHO 326:22
deserve better of m.	SWIFT 862:45
destroy in m. the belief	DOST 294:91
development of m.	NIET 638:12
drug used by m.	KIPL 493:78
essential oneness of m.	STEI 845:58
evils m. had to fear	ELIOT 315:31
Example is the school of m.	BURKE 176:57
existence of m. in its power	ADAMS 5:85
Father of m.	WHIT 938:24
fight for m.	SAINT 738:34
for the friend of m.	MOLI 611:81
furnishing m. with the two	SWIFT 861:52
general inclination of all m.	HOBB 420:1
generality of m.	BOSW 151:75
giant leap forward for m.	ARMS 33:51
greatest of m.	DRYD 301:57
great mass of m.	HALL 393:40
half of m. died	MAO 568:32
happiness m. can gain	DRYD 299:14
How beauteous m. is!	SHAK 804:33
I am involved in m.	DONNE 293:69
instinct of m.	TAWN 868:43
judgement Of all m.	SCHI 747:27
last judgment of m.	FRYE 354:53

marks

Entry	Reference
machines devised by m.	BORE 150:54
m. at least one lesson	MUMF 625:36
m. does not bother	WHIT 936:64
m. faces a crossroads	ALLEN 14:98
M., fear your Lord	KORAN 496:50
m. from superfluous ornament	LOOS 536:43
m. is divisible into two great classes	BEER 74:92
M. is resilient	HELL 408:34
m. love a lover	EMER 324:59
m. minus one	MILL 591:3
M. must put an end to war	KENN 481:9
m. rules its women	CATO 208:98
m.'s concern is charity	POPE 687:85
M. Under The Leash	DISCH 287:8
m., We have created you male and female	KORAN 498:87
M. won	KHRU 485:94
mass massacre of m.	RUSS 735:38
mass of m. understand it	BAGE 54:73
miseries or credulities of m.	CONR 244:46
motto of m.	LAFO 503:50
my words among m.	SHEL 813:84
Nature has in store for m.	FERMI 334:95
novel of m.	GAUT 361:5
only the wisest of m.	SMITH 829:12
only two Of m.	MILT 603:76
peace for all m.	ANON 25:69
principles of m.	WILS 949:81
progress of m.	SART 744:63
proper study of m. is man	POPE 687:80
proper study of m. is science	RABI 704:23
ride m.	EMER 324:73
shut the gates of mercy on m.	GRAY 384:71
significance for m.	KRAUS 499:10
small step for m.	BROD 160:39
spark that moves m.	SIKO 821:68
Spectator of m.	ADDI 6:24
study of m. is books	HUXL 441:53
Survey m.	JOHN 459:45
tenth of m.	SHAK 799:10
There is no history of m.	POPP 689:57
Three quarters of m.	COTM 247:18
tragedy of m.	WILS 947:36
universal language of m.	LONG 535:13
untold sorrow to m.	UNIT 905:9
war that has ever scourged m.	LLOY 533:75
wisest, brightest, meanest of m.	POPE 687:90
manliness sense of m.	CURZ 260:5
silent m. of grief	GOLD 376:6
manly boy's ideal of a m. career	DISR 287:33
bullies you on m. principles	SHAW 807:97
glorious m. pleasures	WYCH 964:1
man-made Aids in a m.-m. disease	WEST 932:76
manna M. and dates	KEATS 477:24
m., which thou knewest not	BIBLE 95:90
tongue Dropped m.	MILT 602:58
We loathe our m.	DRYD 302:99
manner extraordinary m.	STOP 855:15
m. rude and wild	BELL 76:51
m. which will make	NICH 636:74
poetry is written in a m.	POUND 691:88
to the m. born	SHAK 781:56
treated in…unemotional m.	DOYLE 296:43
urbanity of m.	CHES 221:87
mannerly M. Margery	SKEL 824:24
manners bewrayed…by his m.	SPEN 839:58
blessed with such happy m.	AUST 45:57
catch the M. living	POPE 686:71
cities of men and m.	TENN 870:98
corrupt good m.	BIBLE 127:60
Country m.	MUNRO 625:50
describe morals, m.	TROL 898:53
dress and m. in England	SHAW 806:94
have books for good m.	SHAK 780:24
health and good m.	TAFT 866:11
in divers m.	BIBLE 129:33
Japanese have perfected good m.	THER 882:89
Leave off first for m.' sake	BIBLE 113:4
light in m.	ASCH 37:54
magic of m.	ALCO 12:43
m. and religion of	MONT 613:10
m. are far more frightening	JARR 452:86
M. makyth man	WILL 944:65
m. of a dancing master	JOHN 459:59
m. of a lady	FRAN 348:22
m.…of the whole English nation	DRYD 304:40
M.…the need of the plain	WAUGH 924:92
m., virtue, freedom, power	WORD 958:94
Men's evil m.	SHAK 805:56
Men's m. ne'er were viler	JONS 467:69
music marreth men's m.	GALE 357:29
not to his m.	SHAK 769:90
ordered by different m.	DISR 288:34
perfectly good m.	VAND 908:14
Scientists have odious m.	TWAIN 903:93
soften m., but corrupt the heart	BYRON 187:28
teach you better m.	PALM 661:69
Manning manned by M.	BROW 169:70
mannish m. manner of mind	CARY 207:62
manor He that purchases a m.	DONNE 293:78
manservant clothing of a m.	HUGO 437:69
mansion careless of its m. new	MARV 576:86
Jove's court My m. is	MILT 598:62
modest m.	GOLD 376:99
mansionry By his loved m.	SHAK 796:18
mansions Build…stately m.	HOLM 424:67
In my Father's house are many m.	BIBLE 123:52
lasting m. of the dead	CRAB 251:25
mantelpiece remained on the m.	MACN 558:9
mantle Elijah…cast his m.	BIBLE 97:68
m. o' green	TANN 867:24
thread from life's frayed m.	ABU 1:14
Thy m. good	SHAK 768:49
twitched his m. blue	MILT 600:96
mantles their rings or green m.	BALL 59:2
mantraps laws and sets m.	LOWE 539:2
Mantua M. brought me life	VIRG 914:28
manual the owner's m.	CRON 256:28
manufacture economy of a m.	BABB 48:1
m. and in handicrafts	MARX 579:42
manufactures greater part of m.	HALL 393:40
manufacturing m. base	TSON 900:7
m. profits are lowered	RICA 712:80
persists in m. an article	HONE 425:12
manunkind this busy monster, m.	CUMM 258:67
manure civilization…the m.	CONN 243:11
m., lime, piled against	ROET 722:58
natural m.	JEFF 454:22
smell of m.	WHITE 935:41
smelt a lot of mule m.	WILL 944:70
manuscript chopped the m.	COWL 250:81
manuscripts Lenin's m.	MAO 569:37
many Done because we are too m.	HARDY 397:22
election by the incompetent m.	SHAW 808:37
m. be called, but few chosen	BIBLE 118:22
M. things are formidable	SOPH 834:26
not m. of your nation	SHAK 775:77
so much been owed by so m.	CHUR 225:87
the m. change and pass	SHEL 815:43
many-headed m.-h. monster	POPE 688:21
many-maned M.-m. scud-thumper	UPDI 905:14
map Agatha has found it on the m.	WILDE 941:77
creating in the mind a m.	SPEN 837:3
false m. of the world	ORWE 654:55
m. of the world shows no country	WINN 950:99
Marxism…m. in a forest	CAST 208:80
my head is a m.	FIEL 335:18
nor to make a m.	THES 882:96
on any m. of the world	ROOS 724:2
Roll up that m.	PITT 680:13
Sorrow…cannot be rolled up like a m.	CH 222:18
tide across a m.	LOWE 540:38
maple m. seldom inward sound	SPEN 838:20
maps all the m. change	LEGU 520:15
Geography is about M.	BENT 82:97
relief M. of…unhappiness	FITZ 338:96
the m. are spread	YEATS 967:37
mar did not make, and cannot m.	ARNO 34:74
Maradona with a ball M. could	PLAT 681:39
Marathon From M. to Waterloo	GILB 368:39
mountains look on M.	BYRON 190:15
trivial skirmish fought near M.	GRAV 382:24
marble Forget thyself to m.	MILT 598:51
Glowed on the m.	ELIOT 318:99
hammering m. instead	THOR 888:25
How unlike m. was that face	KEATS 477:30
made up of m. and mud	HAWT 402:8
m. block doth not confine	MICH 590:66
m. to retain	BYRON 189:86
modelled in m.	BIRD 135:7
Not m. nor the gilded	SHAK 801:53
ponderous and m. jaws	TWAIN 903:63
portrait in m.	BERN 86:87
The pure m. air	MILT 603:87
this in m.	BEAU 71:15
winged Lion's m. piles	BYRON 188:58
marble-hearted m.-h. fiend	SHAK 792:94
marbles golf…playing m.	CHES 221:12
M. of the dancing floor	YEATS 967:32
put away their rattles, m.	MORE 619:21
where they played m.	KIPL 491:23
March ashbuds in the front of M.	TENN 871:5
beware the ides of M.	SHAK 776:5
Channel in the mad M. days	MASE 580:56
droghte of M.	CHAU 217:69
M. is the month	KEIL 479:56
sturdy M. with brows	SPEN 839:61
winds of M.	SHAK 799:19
march m. of a nation	PARN 665:48
m. of intellect	SOUT 835:58
m. of only a few hours	PEARY 671:60
m. of stupidity	DELI 271:38
mare old m. might droop	SMITH 828:3
remember Tam o' Shanter's m.	BURNS 179:31
son of a m.	AIDAN 10:1
Though Patience be a tired m.	SHAK 775:66
Tom Pearce, lend me your grey m.	BALL 60:81
Mareotic Round the M. Lake	YEATS 967:39
Margaret As Merry M.	SKEL 824:29
It is M. you mourn for	HOPK 428:82
M., are you grieving	HOPK 428:80
M.…at her happiest confronting political dragons	MAJOR 561:77
marge page having an ample m.	TENN 877:49
Margery Mannerly M.	SKEL 824:28
margin m. is too narrow	FERM 333:94
m. of a bay	WORD 960:25
meander through a meadow of m.	SHER 817:87
vanishes over the m.	TENN 879:8
whose m. fades	TENN 870:98
marginality epitomized m.	ECON 310:20
margins work in the m.	DELI 271:39
Marie I am M. of Roumania	PARK 664:14
king in M. Antoinette	MORL 620:42
marijuana experimented with m.	CLIN 230:99
marinated I am well m.	OLSEN 650:44
mariner It is an ancient M.	COLE 234:8
M. hath his will	COLE 234:9
mariners m. had fabled news	LOWE 540:18
My m.	TENN 870:2
not yet self-determined by White M.	ONEI 650:58
rest ye, brother m.	TENN 870:93
marital m. problem	KEIL 479:60
mark If you would hit the m.	LONG 536:38
m. of high civilisation	BERL 84:46
m.…of the beast	BIBLE 132:11
m. of the mint	CHES 221:2
m. of the philosopher	SOCR 833:97
m. upon Cain	BIBLE 92:5
press toward the m.	BIBLE 128:2
Progress, man's distinctive m.	BROW 169:64
Some m. of virtue	SHAK 770:3
this m. I saw	SHEL 813:73
marked in M. Harborough	CHES 221:10
She m. thee there	POPE 689:45
market black m. universities	ZELD 969:4
commodities m.	TYSON 904:9
free competition of the m.	RICA 712:81
In m., hearth and field	KIPL 493:70
kirk or m.	STEV 852:50
knowledge is bought in the m.	CLOU 232:45
m. is so vulgarly democratic	KRIS 499:15
no way…can buck the m.	THAT 881:73
offering them on the m.	PAVL 670:39
price that the m. sets	FRIE 351:70
studies alleging that m. downturns	SAMU 741:2
which we call the m.	HAYEK 402:25
You can't beat the m.	BART 66:29
market-days m.-d. are wearing late	BURNS 179:18
marketing M.…feeding the poop	COUP 248:29
market-place in the fair and the m. p.	PARN 665:46
market research Did…Bell do any m. r.?	ISAAC 447:67
markets m. work perfectly	KRUG 500:26
M. are…in state of…flux	SOROS 834:34
markings treasured for their m.	RAINE 705:39
marks indelible m. of that mould	SCHR 749:66
leaves the m. of his feet	LEAC 515:8
M. of weakness, m. of woe	BLAKE 140:98
m. the first place	PARK 663:1
Signor Benedick. Nobody m. you	SHAK 773:19

marksmen

- terrible m. of the beast — HARDY 397:11
- **marksmen** Men, you are all m. — PUTN 700:2
- **Marlbro** M.'s mighty soul — ADDI 6:18
- **marlet** temple-haunting m. — SHAK 796:18
- **Marlowe** M., bathed in…springs — DRAY 299:98
- **marriage** blessings of m. — SHAW 808:33
  - comedies are ended by a m. — BYRON 190:13
  - constraints aping m. — UPDI 905:17
  - Courtship to m. — CONG 240:33
  - definition of m. — BRAD 154:28
  - definition of m. — SMITH 831:58
  - every m. is different — BERG 83:25
  - fall in with the m.-procession? — CLOU 232:59
  - friendly footing before m. — LAMB 505:93
  - friendships…invalidated by m. — BUTL 185:99
  - furnish forth the m. tables — SHAK 780:42
  - getting over a 4-year m. — HELL 408:50
  - Hanging and m.…go by destiny — FARQ 330:25
  - Happiness in m. — AUST 45:55
  - Hasty m. — SHAK 760:13
  - if m. be such a blessed state — ASTE 39:6
  - impersonal m. — NATH 632:2
  - In m., a man becomes slack — STEV 852:33
  - Is not m. an open question — EMER 325:75
  - journey is like a m. — STEI 846:87
  - joys of m. — FORD 343:1
  - just as humdrum a m. — GREE 386:15
  - lease it…m. in the United States — DWOR 308:43
  - many different sorts of m. — SHAW 809:84
  - M.…a community — BIER 134:82
  - m. and death — SWIN 864:94
  - m. and prostitution — DWOR 308:45
  - M. can wait, education cannot — HOSS 430:31
  - m. dois him mell — DUNB 306:97
  - m. had always been her object — AUST 46:59
  - M. has many pains — JOHN 460:87
  - M. is a bribe — WILD 943:40
  - M. is a matter — SHAK 759:82
  - M. is a state — MARG 570:68
  - M. is a step so grave — STEV 852:38
  - M. is a wonderful invention — CONN 242:87
  - M. is honourable — CONG 241:71
  - M. is like life in this — STEV 852:39
  - M. is not a house — ATWO 41:35
  - M. is popular — SHAW 808:40
  - M. is supposed to be a partnership — BENN 80:59
  - M. is terrifying — STEV 852:32
  - M. is the grave or tomb of wit — CAVE 210:20
  - m. is the most farcical — BEAU 70:8
  - M. is the most licentious — SHAW 808:32
  - M. is the only chance — NIGH 639:22
  - m. is to morality — TWAIN 903:76
  - M. is a triumph of imagination — WILL 944:77
  - m. its alarms — LAFO 504:55
  - M. may often be a stormy lake — PEAC 671:51
  - m. of birds — MOORE 616:73
  - m.…of mind and body — FOWL 346:65
  - m. of true minds — SHAK 802:80
  - M.…only actual bondage — MILL 592:16
  - m. on the part of a man — DICK 282:89
  - m.…prostitution to one man — CART 206:39
  - M. should always combat — BALZ 60:90
  - m. to Ernest Hemingway — BARR 64:82
  - m. without love — CLARK 228:62
  - m. without love — ZHANG 969:6
  - m. with your mother! — SOPH 834:32
  - marrying and giving in m. — BIBLE 118:31
  - merry as a m. bell — BYRON 187:50
  - m.…leaves…still two fools — CONG 240:37
  - monotony of m. — GIBB 367:11
  - more to m. than four bare legs — DAVI 265:81
  - nor are given in m. — SWIFT 861:33
  - not fit for m. — BERG 84:28
  - not mount the m. bed — JONS 467:62
  - opposite to m. — SHAK 788:88
  - pound in lead to your m. — MIDD 590:71
  - prevents a bad m. — SHAK 785:85
  - problem of a satisfactory m. — MILLS 595:7
  - rob…by way of m. — FIEL 335:25
  - So that is m. — WOOLF 955:23
  - take m. at its lowest — STEV 852:36
  - three of us in this m. — DIANA 276:24
  - universal in the institution of m. — MACK 553:8
  - Virginity…Compared with m. — MARL 574:18
  - vow…made to her in m. — SHAK 781:63
  - was m. ever out of fashion? — BUTL 185:82
  - What do you think of m.? — WEBS 927:44
- will not contain itself within…m. — BURT 181:84
- woman…a subject in m. — STAN 843:17
- woman dictates before m. — ELIOT 316:45
- **marriages** best maker of all m. — SHAK 776:2
- m. Lasting a little while longer — LARK 509:82
- m., where both or one is an artist — SPARK 836:79
- m. with other men — TROL 897:31
- M. would in general — JOHN 462:44
- much to be said for exotic m. — BELL 77:85
- no more m. — SHAK 783:15
- one might say of most modern m. — MACK 554:13
- one of the happiest m. — DE 275:9
- so few m. are happy — SWIFT 861:35
- unhappy m.…brains — WODE 951:36
- **married** all right when he's m. — BRON 161:57
- anes we m. be! — BALL 58:56
- as if we had been m. — CONG 241:74
- At leisure m. — CONG 240:31
- best part of m. life — WILD 943:41
- but a week m. — SHAK 774:34
- characters when they are m. — TROL 898:45
- climbs into their graves m. — WILD 943:39
- cut his throat before he m. — SWIFT 862:40
- dance ere we are m. — SHAK 775:59
- fool…in every m. couple — FIEL 335:27
- he that is m. careth — BIBLE 126:42
- honest man who m. — GOLD 376:89
- if ever we had been m.? — GAY 362:16
- if he had m. Flora — SCOTT 753:38
- imprudently m. the barber — FOOTE 342:83
- in m. life — WILDE 941:99
- Leibniz never m. — FONT 342:78
- life was m. to it — TOML 894:57
- man m. is…marred — SHAK 791:62
- m. and endowed the public — BACON 51:70
- m. any one of them — WILDE 942:31
- m. beneath me — ASTOR 39:10
- M.…chaste, and twenty-three — BYRON 189:91
- m. during the football season? — SHAN 805:64
- M. impossible men? — GRAV 382:32
- M. in haste — CONG 240:30
- M. life requires shared mystery — FORD 343:11
- m. or a bachelor — ADDI 6:23
- m. past redemption — DRYD 300:33
- m. people live longer? — FIEL 335:32
- m. to Americans — WALP 919:75
- m. to an electric light — DIMA 286:98
- m. to an Englishman — HEPB 412:25
- m. to a single life — CRAS 253:79
- m. to a sponge — SHAK 769:80
- m. to a wife — SHAK 770:15
- m. to hell? — SHAK 761:58
- m. to Mrs Wadman — STER 848:42
- m. woman is a slave — BALZ 60:91
- M. women are kept women — SMITH 829:22
- most m. man — WARD 920:4
- Next to being m. — AUST 46:60
- not well m. that lives m. long — SHAK 766:10
- One was never m. — BURT 181:80
- rather than queen and m.! — ELIZ 321:98
- Reader, I m. him — BRON 161:64
- result of being unhappily m. — PARK 665:40
- staying m. and playing snooker — REAR 709:18
- those that are m. already — SHAK 783:15
- time to get m. — EPST 327:33
- To me she's m. — SHAK 762:71
- Trade Unionism of the m.? — SHAW 808:31
- we m. people — PEPYS 674:4
- when a m. man doth woo — DONNE 291:34
- **marries** Anyone who m. three girls — STEIN 845:74
- man m. his housekeeper — PIGOU 678:76
- When a man m. — SHEL 814:4
- with man who m. — STEV 852:37
- **marrow** beauty of m. — SITW 823:4
- stay at hame, my m. — BALL 59:59
- winsome M.! — WORD 960:14
- **marry** advice…about to m. — PUNCH 699:73
- better to m. than to burn — BIBLE 126:40
- careful not to m. ladies — AMIN 16:28
- Doänt thou m. for munny — TENN 878:89
- easy to m. a rich woman — THAC 880:33
- For one thing, they m. later — MENC 586:99
- freedom to m. — WARR 921:13
- if you do not m. Mr Collins — AUST 46:58
- in the resurrection they neither m. — BIBLE 118:25
- I will m. you — SHAK 762:66
- less eager…to m. — FALU 329:10
- m. for love — GABOR 356:4
- m. for purely selfish reasons — BROO 163:3
- m. his wife's mother — EDGE 311:47
- m. in haste — CABE 191:3
- M. me and I'll never — MARX 578:20
- m. thee…to be rid of thee — CONG 240:32
- m. whom she likes — THAC 880:22
- m. with his brother — SHAK 784:38
- may not m. his Grandmother — BOOK 150:44
- Mrs Kennedy is going to m. — JOHN 457:4
- Never m. a man — EPHR 326:24
- no humour in m. — DEKK 270:14
- no sane woman would m. — BIRD 135:6
- no woman should m. a teetotaller — STEV 852:37
- Poets should never m. — GONNE 377:42
- taken in when they m. — AUST 46:64
- they neither m. — SWIFT 861:33
- Those who m. God — GREE 386:15
- To m. is to domesticate — STEV 852:41
- to m. or not to m. — STEV 851:32
- what some girls m. — ROWL 729:19
- when a man should m.? — BACON 51:76
- When you m.…grab a chump — WODE 951:36
- why young women should m. — JOHN 462:45
- women m. indiscriminately — STEV 852:34
- young things that m. for love — SHAW 809:84
- **marrying** the act of m. for money — MAIL 560:63
- **Mars** Science may carry us to M. — REPP 711:60
- this seat of M. — SHAK 764:40
- visitor from M. contemplating — LAVER 512:34
- **Marshall** tireless man of M. — ROBI 718:92
- **marshes** fog on the Essex m. — DICK 281:55
- **Marston** Dancing M. — ANON 24:32
- **Martha** M. and Jasmine smiled — LESS 524:95
- M. was cumbered about much — BIBLE 121:83
- **martial** enterprise of m. kind — GILB 370:71
- more m. air than the English — HAYD 402:23
- valiant and m. — BACON 52:17
- **martian** M. met me — ANDR 18:76
- **Martin** M. like a flying bird — FARJ 330:20
- Mr Raymond M., beyond question — KIPL 491:23
- **martini** into a dry M. — ANON 24:14
- keep a m. in the refrigerator — DE 275:12
- **martinis** dry M. did the work — ADE 7:59
- **Martin Luther King** so M. L. K. could walk — JAY 453:6
- **martyr** Crook or a M. — ROGE 723:75
- Hitler…was a m. — POUND 692:22
- I'm a m. to music — THOM 884:32
- m. of the people — CHAR 215:31
- the m.'s gore — SMART 826:67
- **martyrdom** M. is the test — JOHN 464:77
- M.…the only way — SHAW 807:99
- m. to live — BROW 165:74
- **martyr-men** Books are written by m.-m. — CARL 201:29
- **martyrs** blood of all the m. — IVAN 448:80
- m. or reformers—or both — CHAR 215:28
- the graves of the m. — STEV 854:87
- the graves of the m. — STEV 854:87
- When atheism wants m. — SADE 737:15
- **marvel** a strange man is a m. — SYNGE 865:24
- m. and a mystery — LONG 536:39
- m. at the drama — SCRI 755:90
- m. more and more — BELL 76:52
- Match me such m. — BURG 175:5
- that's no m. — SHAK 773:95
- 'tis no m. — SHAK 771:52
- **marvelling** m. sweetly on her ills — RANS 706:66
- **marvellous** America…m.…land — RABAN 703:4
- repositories of the m. — DIOR 287:4
- **Marx** cold metal…in M.'s pages — SCHU 750:77
- illegitimate child of Karl M. — ATTL 40:29
- M. is a case in point — GALB 357:25
- M.'s erudition — NISB 639:28
- Moneybags of M. — ROBI 718:92
- wrong to blame M. — BENN 79:30
- you have Dr M. — HESS 417:34
- **Marxism** cowardly M. — GOER 374:55
- Discovering M.…finding a map — CAST 208:80
- M. is, above all — TROT 899:68
- M. is at the root — THAT 881:75
- prophecy, that M. survives — NISB 639:28
- **Marxist** I am not a M. — MARX 579:44
- **Marxists** sociologists are akin to M. — ARON 37:49
- **Mary** born of the Virgin M. — BOOK 146:37
- cometh M. Magdalene early — BIBLE 123:64
- Good work, M. — PARK 664:9

matrimony

Hail M., quite contrary!	GREE 386:14	Has a new m.	SHAK 804:21	strike a m.	AMIS 16:45
Jesus saith unto her, M.	BIBLE 124:66	himself to be my m.	TUTU 901:23	**matchboxes** substitute...empty m.	DOUG 295:7
M....call the cattle home	KING 487:43	In order to become the m.	DE 270:99	**matches** as m. in the rough	DICK 279:19
M., God has chosen thee	KORAN 496:45	insufferable m.	JEFF 453:11	extravagant a m.	GILB 370:67
M. had a little lamb	HALE 392:29	Like m. like man	PETR 676:44	have to have a box of m.	HOME 425:96
M. hath chosen that good part	BIBLE 121:83	man...becomes a m. in that science	COLL 237:60	little I repair to the m.	THOM 886:84
M. said, Behold the handmaid	BIBLE 120:65	Man...is m. of everything	MILL 594:74	playing with a box of m.	HARL 398:36
M. said, My soul doth magnify	BIBLE 120:66	Man is the m. of things	SWIN 864:10	With that stick of m.	MAND 565:61
M. was that mother mild	ALEX 13:63	marvel thy m. hath not	SHAK 763:21	**mate** Among the beasts no m.	MILT 605:42
passion for the name of 'M.'	BYRON 190:18	m. a grief	SHAK 774:44	Consciousness, her awful M.	DICK 284:44
sweet Highland M.	BURNS 178:11	m., a mistress and two slaves	BIER 134:82	lady's ta'en another m.	BALL 60:77
Where the lady M. is	ROSS 726:53	m. minds of all nations	TWAIN 903:72	man there walked without a m.	MARV 577:6
young child with M. his mother	BIBLE 114:17	m.-mistress of my passion	SHAK 800:39	m. with its complement of men	WRIG 962:60
Marybone from Islington to M.	BLAKE 141:30	M. morality	NIET 638:13	Not...one solitary m.	EGAN 313:65
masculine adoption of the m.	GREER 387:42	m. of himself	MASS 580:71	people should m. for life	ALLEN 14:97
dignified as Latin, m.	QUIL 702:13	m. of his fate	TENN 876:41	shearing m. who wrote it	PATE 669:13
enviable, boast-worthy, m. event	STEI 846:93	m. of his trade	DRAY 299:1	**mated** But we was badly m.	STRO 857:54
feminine spouse to the m. animal	DIAZ 276:26	m. or servant of the state	KING 487:33	**material** basic m. a writer works with	CATH 208:93
m. for a woman to be melancholy	WOLL 954:89	M.: records prove the title	ARLO 32:31	body and m. substance	CARL 201:33
m. in the woman	KENT 483:50	maxim of every prudent m.	SMITH 827:85	Corridors—surpassing M. Place	DICK 284:41
m. values that prevail	WOOLF 955:30	no more subtle m.	TENN 877:57	endowed m. forces with	MARX 579:37
say she has a m. mind	FULL 355:67	not make dreams your m.	KIPL 492:62	external m. things	LOCKE 533:90
sombre-suited m. world	WARN 921:10	O divine M.	FRAN 347:99	From a m. and spiritual terrain	FULL 355:77
This m. invisibility	DUNN 307:14	Oh my divine m.!	HUGO 437:65	gathers its m. from the flowers	BACON 50:44
mask husband wears a m.	MARI 571:83	old clothes know who's m.	SHER 817:73	good a m....to build a life from	CAREY 199:62
loathsome m. has fallen	SHEL 814:18	O m. doctor, he is past	MASS 581:77	good m. for poetry	WILL 946:30
m. like Castlereagh	SHEL 812:72	only the m. shall praise	KIPL 490:15	living in a m. world	MADO 558:19
m. of a vulgar soul	MAUG 582:10	Our m. Caesar	YEATS 967:37	make it m....interesting	BEAV 71:32
m. of prevailing morals	BEAU 70:7	poet is a m. of the quotidian	PRIT 696:23	march of m. ugliness	WHITE 935:54
monkey's m. reveals the monkey	BASHO 67:45	press...a terrible m.	COOP 246:87	m....and the moral	DEWEY 276:19
No m. like open truth	CONG 240:40	Rabboni; which is to say, M.	BIBLE 124:66	m. is our own flesh	THOR 888:25
obliged to throw off the m.	PARN 665:47	slave has but one m.	LABR 502:17	m. position of the worker	MARX 579:35
pluck the m. from...face of the Pharisee	BRON 161:65	village m. taught his little school	GOLD 376:1	moral or a m. one	ARNO 35:7
profound loves the m.	NIET 638:9	when I hae a gude m.	SCOTT 753:53	Nothing is m. in space	ROSSO 727:69
thousand-year-old m.	ROSE 725:28	which is to be m.	CARR 205:10	only objects in the m. universe	FORS 345:44
We wear the m. that grins	DUNB 306:95	Who's m., who's man	SWIFT 862:56	so many people...for m. benefits	COLU 239:91
masked love in desolation m.	SHEL 815:36	Without a m....I...work	ARET 31:11	universe...as a m. system	PAGE 659:16
masks are but as pasteboard m.	MELV 585:59	work of the m.	LEON 522:66	world of m. life	ARNO 35:22
trying on gas-m.	CHAM 212:62	world with her divine M.	MILT 600:17	**materialism** deteriorate into m.	MOLT 612:92
masochism spirit of national m.	AGNEW 9:94	**mastered** m. whatever was	LOWE 539:9	inhuman in its m.	WILS 947:43
masonry bind...into the social m.	WELLS 930:21	only athletic sport I m.	JERR 455:50	**materialist** m. of all great religions	TEMP 869:68
masons professionals, like...m.	EICH 313:72	**masterpiece** cradle of a new m.	YEATS 966:13	**materials** action...essential m.?	CARL 201:14
masquerade miss a m.	POPE 685:35	driven to create a m.	SELF 756:10	m. for conversation	JOHN 460:81
truth in m.	BYRON 190:21	friend...the m. of nature	EMER 324:60	m. of reason and knowledge	LOCKE 533:89
masquerading m. knight-errant	PARN 665:47	function...is to produce a m.	CONN 243:6	raw m. out of which	TEMP 869:70
mass blessed mutter of the m.	BROW 167:23	great and glorious m.	MONT 614:32	sculptor can use twenty different m.	BOCC 144:90
broad m. of a nation	HITL 420:91	knows, at first sight, a m.	POUND 691:6	she begins to gather the m.	OCON 647:89
Chaos, a rough unordered m.	OVID 657:16	m. of art has...a fixed place	EMER 324:66	**maternity** m. to women	MUSS 628:94
from its m. Walls	BYRON 188:67	Nature's great m.	DONNE 291:31	woman...cursed in her m.	STAN 843:17
go to M. every day	BELL 76:57	no m. can be anything	MARI 571:76	**mates** thuctheththion of m.	BENT 82:3
haven't been to m. for years	WILS 947:38	now hath made his m.	SHAK 797:41	very popular among his m.	EWART 328:75
malicious...crapulous m.	ADAMS 5:3	obscure unfinished m.	NABO 628:10	**math** m. is quite straightforward	GATES 361:90
m. of the nation	TWAIN 903:72	**masterpieces** creation of genuine m.	DALI 261:16	M. was my worst subject	TRIL 897:12
ocean's liquid m.	WORD 961:36	m. having one-night stands	RAUS 707:80	**Mathematica** Principia M.	RUSS 734:37
opium for every conceivable m.	KENN 480:93	**masters** any of those m.	MCCU 549:15	**mathematical** m. concepts	GIBS 367:15
The m. of men	THOR 888:29	beasts are our m.	FLET 341:56	m. elegance	GREE 386:36
We were one m.	DRYD 301:55	copying the m.	INGR 446:41	m. or philosophical author	WHIT 936:62
massacre mass m. of mankind	RUSS 735:38	fall from their m.' table	BIBLE 117:4	Moriarty of m. celebrity	DOYLE 297:62
not as sudden as a m.	TWAIN 902:36	made lunch of m.	MORR 620:58	must be a m. science	JEVO 455:51
Massermann M., the cat man	ANON 24:30	m. at the moment	SHAW 811:36	one m., the other...intuitive	PASC 666:62
masses anything said about the m.	PRIE 695:92	m. of different bits of man	LAWR 514:84	The m. is that evident aspect	HEID 406:11
art of the m.	HALL 393:41	m. of their fates	SHAK 776:9	**mathematician** m. is a blind man	DARW 263:60
back the m.	GLAD 373:40	m.' thoughts	MARL 572:2	trifles in which a m.	MACA 545:43
benighted m. of wishful thinkers	QUINE 702:22	new m.	HALI 393:38	**mathematicians** m....cabbages	BOYD 154:13
bow ye m.!	GILB 369:49	not m. of our own affections	ETHE 327:46	**mathematics** All science requires m.	BACON 53:55
Carving is interrelated m.	HEPW 412:28	Old M.: how well they understood	AUDEN 42:80	Angling...like m.	WALT 920:89
educate the m.	OSLER 656:89	people are the m.	BURKE 175:30	Between the penis and m.	CELI 211:35
gathered itself...into m.	CARL 200:81	Power of new M.	ALBE 11:33	creative people hate m.	ISSI 448:76
Government...exasperates the m.	REED 710:37	relations with their m.	MILL 592:13	extensive use of m.	HAYEK 402:26
intelligence of the great m.	MENC 586:92	serve two m.	BIBLE 115:44	laws of m....are not certain	EINS 314:90
make the m. prosperous	BRYAN 170:97	The people are the m.	BLAIR 138:54	m. as surely as in poetry	RUSS 734:25
m. yearning to breathe	LAZA 515:3	Unmarried men...best m.	BACON 51:73	M. is the door	BACON 53:56
paper which the m. call money	ANDR 18:77	**mastery** Love...constreyned by m.	CHAU 217:90	M. is thought moving	WHIT 936:67
philosopher should judge the m.	CYRA 260:11	m. of the thing!	HOPK 428:77	m., orthography, geometry	DICK 278:75
The m. are wrong	VIAN 911:69	m. of vocabulary and syntax	SAYE 746:10	M. possesses not only truth	RUSS 734:20
tumult of the m.	ALCU 12:46	**mast-hemm'd** m.-h. Manhattan	WHIT 937:2	no one ignorant of m.	PLATO 681:40
wide support of the m.	LENIN 521:37	**mastiff** trusty m. that is to watch	LLOY 532:68	of flight, of m., of physics	HEMI 410:83
masseur m. called Harold	WOOD 954:99	**mastodons** calling to Aunt like m.	WODE 952:39	order and mystical m.	BROW 166:85
Massey M. won't be satisfied	KAUF 474:35	**masturbation** Don't knock m.	ALLEN 14:96	secret of success in m.	LEHR 520:26
mast bends the gallant m.	CUNN 258:74	M. is the thinking man's television	HAMP 395:73	ugly m.	HARDY 396:97
master belonging to the m.	STOWE 856:28	**mat** foot in the m.	GROS 389:80	Vanity of m.!	FRED 349:40
brave m. was no more	MACA 546:60	worst room, with m. half-hung	POPE 686:69	ways to teach m.	NEWM 634:43
condemned by a faceless m.	PAZ 671:47	**match** burnt m. skating in a urinal	CRANE 253:69	**maths** M. is the purest science	BROW 167:6
disciple is not above his m.	BIBLE 116:70	diploma is a lighted m.	KOCH 493:69	**Matilda** a-waltzing M. with me	PATE 669:12
does not excel his m.	LEON 522:73	Honour is like a m.	PAGN 659:26	M. told such Dreadful Lies	BELL 77:63
do not M. or Campbell me	SCOTT 753:56	m. flickers	STEV 852:52	**mating** for eating, not m.	FERB 332:72
great M. so to sympathize	MILT 597:31	m. its military strength	KENN 482:28	**matrimony** argument in favour of m.	AUST 46:81

matron

critical period in m.	HERB 413:51	From M. to December	ANDE 17:72	no m. city	BIBLE 125:97
holy estate of M.	BOOK 148:89	Maids are M.	SHAK 780:12	people who m. everything	HOSS 430:30
holy estate of M.	BOOK 148:90	M.'s new-fangled shows	SHAK 763:4	too m. to be your queen	SHAK 760:12
in holy M.	BOOK 148:83	M. will be fine next year	HOUS 432:63	woman of m. understanding	AUST 45:54
in holy M.	BOOK 148:84	mid-m.'s eldest child	KEATS 478:45	**meaner** m. things To low ambition	POPE 686:70
m....was also a legalized way of committing assault	EMEC 324:46	moonlight-coloured m.	SHEL 816:61	She must take m. things	ELIOT 316:42
more of love than of m.	GOLD 376:92	nightingale when M. is past	CAREW 199:57	**meanest** wisest, brightest, m.	POPE 687:90
not be joined together in holy M.	BOOK 148:83	that the moneth of M.	MALO 563:14	**meaning** control the m. of words	DICK 277:37
respectable as that of m.	TROL 897:22	wife left you in M.	NORD 641:52	experience but missed the m.	ELIOT 320:73
safest in m....a little aversion	SHER 817:71	world is white with M.	TENN 878:75	Free from all m.	DRYD 302:94
Without thinking...of men or m.	AUST 46:59	**maybe** definite m.	GOLD 377:33	Has no m.	SNYD 832:90
matron sober-suited m.	SHAK 766:95	**May-day** M.-d. freshness amidst	MORR 620:51	husk of m.	ELIOT 321:82
worn m. smiles	WHIT 938:17	**Maying** let's go a M.	HERR 415:11	Is there a m. to music?	COPL 246:98
matrons stout m.	GILL 370:79	**mayonnaise** M....One of the sauces	BIER 134:83	it lacks m.	PAZ 671:49
matter Does it m.?	SASS 745:87	**mayor** longer to elect a M. for London	WATE 922:38	language charged with m.	POUND 691:12
doesn't so much m. what you do	JAMES 451:51	lord m. of Birmingham	LLOY 533:80	man to create his own m.	KUBR 500:35
Energy is liberated m.	BRYS 171:17	my Lord M. commands	PEPYS 674:2	m. is my meat and drink	BROW 167:29
few things m. at all	BALF 58:43	tart who has...married the m.	BAXT 69:92	m., not to find yours	RUSK 733:4
here and now cease to m.	ELIOT 320:69	**maypole** where's the M. in the Strand	BRAM 156:58	m. of the Lost Generation	KERO 483:56
here's no great m.	ELIOT 316:65	**May-poles** sing of M.-p.	HERR 415:99	never mistake pattern for m.	BANKS 62:26
if it is it doesn't m.!	GILB 370:69	**maze** A mighty m.!	POPE 686:70	no definite and unquestionable m.	SART 744:63
is no 'living m.'	MONOD 612:2	every m. of quick	TENN 875:98	precise m. of a word	BAND 61:10
least m. dear to Him	AUDEN 43:2	law seems like a sort of m.	MORT 621:66	Religion...gives m. to all	WHIT 936:65
living and non-living m.	PAGE 659:16	Life is a m.	CONN 243:9	richest without m.	RUSK 732:82
Marriage is a m.	SHAK 759:82	Philosophy to him was...a m.	SANT 743:43	to some faint m. make pretence	DRYD 300:44
m. is the scaffolding	THOM 886:78	the m. of schools	POPE 685:16	true m. of religion	ARNO 36:34
m. of life and death	SHAN 805:60	through the watery m.	MARV 578:11	**meaningless** creative world...m.	SPEN 837:12
More m. with less art	SHAK 781:75	wander in that golden m.	DRYD 299:11	half of what she wrote would be m.	CHAN 213:84
no rights in this m.	ROET 722:60	**MCC** where the M. ends	PRIE 695:93	**meaninglessness** very m. of life	KUBR 500:35
no subject m.	DAVIS 266:6	**McCarthyism** M. is Americanism	MCCA 547:85	**meanings** let my m. show	CAMP 194:55
not the m. of the work	GLAS 374:44	**McGrew** dangerous Dan M.	SERV 757:35	Minding our m.	AUDEN 43:2
obscurity of the m.	PROT 697:34	**Mcjob** M....no-future job	COUP 248:24	two m. packed up into one word	CARR 205:12
order...this m. better	STER 849:50	**McLuhan** M. put a telescope	SMITH 827:73	VALUE...has two different m.	SMITH 827:78
removing the m. of sin	MILT 600:14	**McNamara** M.'s war	MCNA 557:86	war...an openness about the m.	DALL 261:18
some arduous and difficult m.	SIDN 820:35	**McTavish** Against the clan M.	AYTO 48:11	wrestle...words and m.	ELIOT 320:58
straightforward a m.	RUSK 733:95	**me** gone up and met m.	HOFF 422:26	**meanness** land of m.	BYRON 187:32
subsists on the m. he destroys	BELL 78:97	I most delight in M.	CAMP 194:52	vice of m.	THOM 887:95
that great renovator of m.	OVID 657:21	M., evidently	HUGH 436:39	**meannesses** assorted m.	GILL 370:78
then he's full of m.	SHAK 778:68	not with m. is against m.	BIBLE 117:83	**means** best ends by the best m.	HUTC 441:48
thet's wots the m. with you	SHAW 809:67	see m. bat	GRACE 380:84	by defective m.	WILL 946:13
this high m.	WORD 962:49	soul is never required of m.	SMITH 830:43	doubled their m. of consuming	MILL 591:96
throat of well-printed m.	MORR 620:51	'that happened to m.!'	SEDA 755:97	end may justify the m.	TROT 899:69
Vain m. is worse	BACON 49:24	trouble with m.	SALI 740:77	good...By all the m.	WESL 932:68
when all the m.'s spent	DANI 262:30	**meadow** a m. of margin	SHER 817:87	grant...that my m. may lie	COWL 250:77
Why, what's the m.	SHAK 775:58	Burn-mill m.	WORD 960:14	honestly and deeply m.	JAMES 451:72
matter-of-fact m.-o.-f. young man	GILB 369:45	By the stream and o'er the m.	BLAKE 139:86	improve the m.	HUXL 442:80
matters m. just as little	SHAW 807:28	in m. or plain	SWIN 863:82	Increased m. and increased leisure	DISR 288:59
m. not how a man dies	JOHN 462:19	m., grove, and stream	WORD 959:5	m. employed determine the nature	HUXL 442:79
m. outside...everyday experience	CONR 244:47	painted m., or a purling stream	ADDI 6:17	m. nothing in this country	GOLD 375:80
questions about the greater m.	ARIS 31:18	Winter scourged the m.	ROBE 717:73	m. of grace	BOOK 147:50
read strange m.	SHAK 796:16	**meadows** among green aits and m.	DICK 281:55	m. of increasing her degradation	STAN 842:15
suspect his taste in higher m.	LAMB 505:90	by-path m.	STEV 852:40	m. of procuring respect	JOHN 463:46
What can I do that m.?	SPEN 837:99	enamelled m. with filigree hedges	WALP 919:66	m. of rising in the world	JOHN 462:39
what m. in your life	RUSH 732:64	Fair these broad m.	GALT 359:54	m....to satisfy our desires	PREV 694:79
Matthew saw a man, named M.	BIBLE 116:62	floor the m. with cement	MACL 555:41	m. which have never yet been tried	BACON 50:47
Sir M. left the room	LINK 530:26	golden face the m. green	SHAK 801:48	never simply as a m.	KANT 473:24
mattress cold porridge on a damp m.	BRID 159:12	Golden lie the m.	MERE 587:26	No one m. all he says	ADAMS 5:97
gasping on a little flock m.	DICK 278:63	lover of the m.	WORD 956:56	Perfections of m.	EINS 313:82
snug as a feather m.	ANGE 19:92	m. fresh and gay	MARV 577:99	persons of small m.	ELIOT 315:16
mature have in our m. years	TROL 897:32	m. runnels	KEATS 476:17	Power is not a m.	ORWE 655:78
m. imagination of a man	KEATS 476:83	M. trim with daisies	MILT 597:45	report what he m.	ANON 25:52
m. poets steal	ELIOT 317:92	undulating green m.	HUXL 442:76	Sceptical scrutiny is the m.	SAGAN 737:26
maturity wisdoms of m.	LIVE 531:50	Up from the m.	WHIT 938:22	take the m. whereby I live	SHAK 770:17
Maud M. is not seventeen	TENN 876:22	variety of gardens, m.	MOORE 616:72	took away...their m. of support	SHER 816:69
maul not afraid...of a 'm.'	ANON 23:89	**meadowsweet** timothy-tops and m.	ROBE 717:72	unapproachable by any other m.	LEAV 517:50
maunder Let her m. and mumble	CARL 200:2	**meagre** m. hill of kernels	RANS 706:68	uniformity of their m.	FUSE 356:92
mausoleum mouth...as its m.	AMIS 16:29	One composition is m.	DIDE 285:76	We call that a man's m.	DONNE 293:78
mausoleums m. for his enemies	LINK 530:26	**meal** Breakfast is the one m.	VAND 908:14	**meant** it's what I m.	VAUG 909:31
mavis m. and merle are singing	SCOTT 752:33	can't fake...a good m.	BURR 181:66	m. than meets the ear	MILT 598:56
mawkishness thence proceeds m.	KEATS 476:83	evening m.	BARL 63:56	said what I m.	STEV 850:4
maws feed the m.	KEYN 484:78	m. was large	PRIOR 696:8	**Meany** M. could run for President	DOLE 290:94
maxim essential m. of your liberties	PITT 679:7	Salad is not a m.	LEBO 517:60	**measles** Love is like the m.	JERO 454:36
grounded m. So rife	MILT 608:93	**meals** cooking three m. a day	PLATH 680:27	Love iz like the m.	BILL 135:98
M. Gun	BELL 76:56	good m. that I...am wearing	BUSH 182:95	Love's like the m.	JERR 455:47
m. is worthy of the fool	MACA 545:25	keep with you at m.	SHAK 777:18	**measure** beyond m. astonished	BIBLE 119:57
m. of every prudent master	SMITH 827:85	lessen thy M.	FRAN 348:8	full m. of their fate	CRANE 253:65
so useless as a general m.	MACA 545:26	**mealy** M. boys, and beef-faced boys	DICK 278:70	good m., pressed down	BIBLE 120:74
will that my m.	KANT 473:23	**mean** abhor...the m.	CURZ 260:5	Man is the m. of all things	PROT 697:32
maxims cardinal m. of guerrilla war	KISS 493:85	a bunch of m. girls	PAGL 659:24	m. and choice	JOHN 459:49
m., of self-justification	EDGE 311:34	dull and m.	WHIT 938:21	m. by thy deeds	SHAK 801:60
maximum m. of temptation	SHAW 808:40	family talk, m. and worried	COMP 239:99	m. of love	LEWIN 526:39
May 21st M.—a glorious day	WORD 962:52	Happy the golden m.!	MASS 581:79	m. of public support	TIMES 892:22
airiest M.?	GRAV 382:21	I m. what I say	CARR 203:70	m. of the universe	SHEL 814:15
at least the seventh of M.	TROL 897:23	improved m.	THOR 888:30	m. shadows	HUBB 434:3
darling buds of M.	SHAK 800:37	m. between nothing and everything	PASC 667:18	m. still for m.	SHAK 788:79
end of M.	HOUS 432:62	m. between two vices	ARIS 31:21	m. up to their destiny	APOL 29:83
		meanly admires m. things	THAC 880:31	modernness is the m. of merit	EMER 325:80

move in m.	ELIOT 321:87	**medicine** art of m. consists of	VOLT 915:49	preaching point is not a m. point	THER 882:83
No one had any m.	PERK 675:27	By m. life may be	SHAK 803:8	since our last m.?	OTWAY 656:5
number, weigh and m.	HALES 393:30	complete dispensary of m.	GRAV 382:35	this m. is drunk	DICK 277:56
Number, Weight, or M.	PETTY 676:47	driven into m.	MILL 595:97	wish the m. had been as good	CHRI 224:48
Shrunk to this little m.?	SHAK 777:32	educate…not to take m.	OSLER 656:89	with the purpose of the m.	LEZA 528:81
There is a m. in things	HORA 430:22	Find that M. (if you can)	HERR 415:1	**meetings** summit m.	ACHE 2:26
To the beat of the m.	POUND 692:18	Grief is itself a m.	COWP 251:99	**megalomania** American m.	JOHN 458:26
with what m. ye mete	BIBLE 115:47	Hygiene is the corruption of m.	MENC 586:90	M.…the occupational disease	HOBS 421:8
with what m. ye mete	BIBLE 119:54	Like m., the test of its value	FULB 355:62	**megaphone** m. of big type	MAST 581:83
measured m. at the extremities	JAY 453:2	m.…distinguishes man	OSLER 656:88	**Meistersinger** M.…set breath	CRANE 253:67
m. by his worth	SHAK 798:79	M. Hat	BENET 79:23	**melancholy** day-dreams of m. men	DRYD 299:11
measurement ghostly errors of m.	HUBB 434:3	M. is a noble profession	ROLL 723:89	green and yellow m.	SHAK 786:2
measurements terms of m.	MYRD 628:99	m. of life	BIBLE 113:84	half with m.	LUGO 542:62
measures Better than all m.	SHEL 814:98	merry heart doeth good like a m.	BIBLE 105:82	Hence loathèd M.	MILT 597:41
In buskined m. move	GRAY 385:87	miserable have no other m.	SHAK 787:63	inherited a vile m.	JOHN 462:30
not changed my m.	ANNE 19:13	mistook magic for m.	SZASZ 865:26	less given to m.	SIDN 820:35
relax my expansionist m.	KEYN 484:77	one m. is Death	ABU 1:15	Like some m. watchman	APOL 29:77
measuring art of m.	NEWT 635:60	patent m. advertisement	JERO 454:38	little of the m. element	SHAK 774:33
measuring-rod m.-r. of distance	RILKE 715:40	proper practice of m.	HARV 400:78	masculine for a woman to be m.	WOLL 954:89
meat Anger's my m.	SHAK 799:1	single coin to m.	VALLE 907:7	M. marked him for her own	GRAY 384:77
bread and m.	STEV 851:29	The longer I practise m.	BENN 80:48	m., nodding pines	SCHAW 747:20
eat but little m.	ANON 22:61	**medicines** confection of tried m.	BACON 50:41	m. of mine own	SHAK 779:5
egg is full of m.	SHAK 766:93	die from meet of m.	MOLI 612:90	m. seems to be fortified	WEBS 927:55
gallant appetite for M.	PENE 673:78	m. for the health	AUGU 44:32	m. truth	DICK 281:70
God sends m.	FULL 355:84	m. to make me love him	SHAK 771:39	M., Whose saintly visage	MILT 598:50
Heaven sends us fine m.	GARR 360:80	**medicos** m. marvelling…on her ills	RANS 706:66	Methinks is m.	LOWE 539:4
if one eat my m.	DONNE 290:13	**mediocre** Death is only for the m.	JARRY 452:94	mistress of true m.	SHAK 795:75
little of solid m. for men	DRYD 304:43	gilded tomb of a m. talent	SMITH 829:23	Moping m. and moon-struck	MILT 606:67
Love…is not m. nor drink	MILL 592:29	high church for the true m.	MAIL 560:48	musical, most m.!	MILT 598:52
meaning is my m. and drink	BROW 167:29	hire m. people	MURP 627:78	Naught so sweet as m.	BURT 181:74
m., and cursed the bread	ROBI 718:82	Titles distinguish the m.	SHAW 808:41	Nothing is so poor and m.	SANT 743:46
m. in due season	BIBLE 104:48	use of m. people	STEV 852:44	Pale M. sate retired	COLL 238:78
m. in due season	BIBLE 102:13	**mediocrities** surrounded by m.	MACM 557:76	pleasing fit of m.	MILT 599:75
m. is savory	EMER 324:70	**mediocrity** forces satisfied m.	RENAN 711:47	rare recipe for m.	LAMB 505:78
m. it feeds on	SHAK 789:19	hollow-headed m.	MENC 587:16	regress…a m. thing	BACON 51:85
milk, and not of strong m.	BIBLE 129:35	m.…always at its best	BEER 74:96	Solitude and m.	CART 206:37
no stomach for such m.	DOBS 289:78	M. knows nothing higher	DOYLE 297:70	suck m. out of a song	SHAK 778:76
nothing was done with the m.	HEMI 409:64	m. of the apparatus	TROT 899:64	Sunday…heavy, m.	RHYS 712:76
Out-did the m.	HERR 416:18	tendency of democracies…to m.	COOP 246:84	taught me…to be m.	SHAK 763:14
Out of the eater came forth m.	BIBLE 95:15	**meditate** in his law doth he m.	BIBLE 99:25	'Tis m., and a fearful sign	BYRON 190:11
plate of m.	MACB 546:63	**meditation** cat in profound m.	ELIOT 320:53	Virginity, mysticism, m.!	GAUT 361:4
poor the remnant m.	PRIOR 696:8	He that…neglects m.	CONF 240:22	**Melbourne** M. sure is the right place	GARD 360:68
Some hae m.	ANON 22:82	m.…is the noblest	CONF 240:16	**Melchizedek** after the order of M.	BIBLE 102:18
soul abhorreth all manner of m.	BIBLE 102:14	m. not of death but of life	SPIN 841:80	**Melissa** M. is her nom de guerre	GRAY 384:61
taste my m.	HERB 413:66	O fearful m.!	SHAK 801:57	**mellow** humours, whether grave or m.	ADDI 6:52
there may be m. in mine house	BIBLE 112:63	sage in m. found	SHEL 812:68	m. glory of the Attic stage	ARNO 33:64
There's the m. eaters and there's us	HYNDE 444:24	stimulus and object of our m.	MANN 566:76	m. lin-lan-lone	TENN 879:7
'Tis not the m.	SUCK 858:68	testimonies are my m.	BIBLE 103:26	**mellows** temper never m. with age	IRVI 447:57
Upon what m.	SHAK 776:11	**meditations** little story of m.	STEIN 845:62	**melodies** Heard m. are sweet	KEATS 478:36
why are they made out of m.?	BRAND 156:59	**Mediterranean** blue M.	SHEL 813:81	**melodious** M. discord	SHAK 762:87
Why not 'm.'	RENO 711:55	circling movement in the M.	CHUR 226:97	**melodist** think of a good m.	MOZA 623:6
meat-fly Thackeray settled like a m.-f.	RUSK 733:12	taken from the M.	SHAF 758:53	**melody** at pleasure stint their m.	SHAK 760:29
meats Avoid fried m.	PAIGE 660:28	**medium** call it a m.	ACE 2:19	blund'ring kind of m.	DRYD 302:94
funeral baked m.	SHAK 780:42	m. is the message	MCLU 556:53	Drink! it is m.	NEIL 633:11
m. for the throat	AUGU 44:32	m. of a false system	PAINE 660:33	From ancient m. have ceased	BLAKE 139:78
mechanical Caxtons are m. birds	RAINE 705:39	m.'s gaze is brief	IGNA 445:14	luve's like the m.	BURNS 180:50
M. Age	CARL 200:79	perfect use of an imperfect m.	WILDE 940:64	M. is the very essence	MOZA 623:6
m. in head and in the heart	CARL 200:82	refracting m. of a symbol system	HUXL 442:97	m. lingers on	BERL 84:38
the m.…and the moral	DEWEY 276:19	visible self as its m.	HOLL 423:51	pretty girl is like a m.	BERL 84:37
mechanics days were our m.	LEUP 525:14	**mediums** all m. of art	PISS 679:99	the storm-clouds thundrous m.	STEP 847:11
goodness of your m.	MOORE 617:81	**medlar** m. being a fruit	MACD 550:39	You're a m. from a symphony	PORT 690:70
part of universal m.	NEWT 635:60	**meed** of mighty conquerors	SPEN 838:20	**melons** raiser of huge m.	TENN 872:35
mechanism effective braking m.	WILL 944:78	**meek** Blessed are the m.	BIBLE 114:27	Stumbling on m.	MARV 577:4
efficient m. for digesting	HAYEK 402:25	brave and m. with thirty bob a week	DAVI 264:64	**Melrose** view fair M. aright	SCOTT 752:12
m. of perception	SNYD 832:93	gentle, tame, and m.	WYATT 964:90	**melt** let us m., and make no noise	DONNE 292:38
m.…that can force the mind	PENF 673:79	good tidings unto the m.	BIBLE 110:6	m. in her own fire	SHAK 784:41
our skill in M.	CARL 200:83	Jesus, m. and mild	WESL 931:60	**melting** Between m. and freezing	ELIOT 321:81
medal m. for killing two men	MATL 582:94	m. and gentle	SHAK 777:33	great M. Pot	ZANG 969:1
medals no m. on my chest	EISE 314:4	m. and lowly in heart	BIBLE 116:81	ride on its own m.	FROST 353:13
nothing to do with m.	BELL 78:88	m. shall inherit the earth	BIBLE 100:59	United States is…the great m. pot	MARS 575:65
meddle and muddle	DERBY 274:86	m. shall inherit the earth	BIRK 136:13	**Melville** M. who split the atom	LODGE 534:95
Wha daur m. wi' me?	ANON 28:54	m. shall inherit the earth	DU 305:68	**member** accept me as a m.	MARX 578:21
meddlers free from m.	SUMN 859:83	the m. would inherit the earth	KEIL 479:61	characterizes a m.	MAIL 560:53
meddling Justice is…not m.	PLATO 682:62	**meekest** chosen the m. maid	HENR 411:12	each m. of the family	FRAME 346:77
Medea like to have M. for dinner?	PAGE 659:14	**meet** charming thing to m.	JAMES 450:40	lowest and poorest m.	MORI 619:36
media favourite m. catchphrase	THAT 881:58	don't m. competition	REVS 711:67	m. of a civilized community	MILL 591:99
m. a Frankenstein	MUGG 623:11	I shall m. my fate	YEATS 966:22	m. of the choir	LOOS 536:55
m. have, indeed, provided	MUGG 623:10	m. and right so to do	BOOK 147:69	m. of the Communist Party	THOM 885:68
M. people should have long noses	DALAI 260:8	m. them at Philippi	SHAK 778:49	m. of the family…is happier	FALU 329:11
No matter how many m.	CHRI 223:39	never the twain shall m.	KIPL 489:76	not a m. of the household	KENN 480:87
today's m.…hunts in a pack	BLAIR 138:74	prepare to m. thy God	BIBLE 111:52	recognize the honourable M.	CHUR 226:9
medical already had m. attention	SIMON 822:76	When shall we the three m. again?	SHAK 795:96	together every joint and m.	MILT 601:17
county m. society	SUTH 860:7	When two Englishmen m.	JOHN 460:82	You choose a M. indeed	BURKE 175:13
m. men all over the world	CARL 199:69	**meeting** British want…another m.	ANON 27:34	**members** acquainted with…m.	WHITE 935:34
well in advance of m. thought	WODE 952:40	God to send us a merry m.	LANC 506:22	disenfranchising a m.	LYND 543:92
Medici Miniver loved the M.	ROBI 718:85	m. place of the peoples	BARN 64:59	m. from injury and molestation	MILL 591:2
medicinal M. discovery	AYRES 48:9	m. that did not take place	HESE 416:27	m. of our secret service	FOOT 342:80

memoir

M. of this House	BAXT 69:93	All m. are brothers	POWE 693:45	faithful account of m. and things	ELIOT 315:20
m. one of another	BIBLE 128:90	all m. are created equal	JEFF 453:19	Famous m. have the whole earth	PERI 675:24
most vile m.	ABEL 1:3	all m. are created equal	LINC 529:9	fancy of the mass of m.	BAGE 54:68
one of thy m. should perish	BIBLE 114:34	all m. are equal	HUXL 441:61	fashions m. with true nobility	MARL 572:3
persistent absenteeism of its m.	SAMU 741:98	All m. are Jews	MALA 561:85	favours of these m.	SHAK 765:55
persons who are considered…its m.	BENT 82:87	All m. are liars	BIBLE 102:20	fear of little m.	ALLI 14:6
sell m. of my family	ANNE 20:16	all m. are lonely	MCCU 549:13	fifty m. and women	BROW 168:51
we as head, and you as m.	HENR 411:13	all m. are Noah's sons	WILB 939:35	fifty thousand m. slain	WALP 919:81
memoir unconscious of	NIET 638:7	all m. are rapists	FREN 350:53	finds too late that m. betray	GOLD 376:93
memoirs diary, his friends' m.	RODC 721:43	all m. at sea	GOLD 375:78	first-class m.	WHIT 938:11
m. of his life	ARBU 30:3	all m. call thee fickle	SHAK 766:3	fisher of m., and of women	DOUG 295:8
memoranda capital of m.	WHITE 935:38	all m. die from	MOLI 612:90	Forests of middle-aged m.	ABBO 1:1
memorandum m.…not to inform	ACHE 3:47	All m. hate the wretched	SHEL 812:48	form Christian m.	ARNO 36:45
memorial M. from the soul	ROSS 726:55	all m. have one entrance	BIBLE 112:78	For the m. it's better	WELD 928:83
m. more lasting	HORA 430:11	All m. that are ruined	BURKE 176:56	for the next generation of m.	LOWE 539:99
whole earth as their m.	PERI 675:24	all m. then did virtue call	SPEN 839:56	for us m. and for our salvation	BOOK 147:61
memories a few transcendent m.	WHITE 934:31	all m. would be tyrants	ADAMS 4:71	Freedom of m. under government	LOCKE 533:87
Liars need…m.	QUIN 703:25	all save m. of indifferent health	DOUG 295:12	fruits…accessible to m.	FREUD 350:61
Liars ought to have good m.	SIDN 819:34	all things to all m.	BIBLE 126:43	furnished well with m.	SHAK 777:26
m. are card-indexes	CONN 243:16	all thinking m. are interested	POPP 689:60	fury, and rage of mortal m.	BURT 181:85
M. are not shackles	BENN 80:45	America is a country of young m.	EMER 325:98	gallant m. danced	WHITE 936:59
M. are what warm you up	MURAK 626:62	among all m., good and bad	PEPYS 673:84	generation of m.	HOMER 425:2
m. come to you genuinely virgin	ORWE 654:31	among m. of understanding	PLATO 681:47	generosity of m.	MARI 571:85
m. of flowers and grass	ROBE 717:73	Among new m.	TENN 878:84	God, And justifiable to m.	MILT 607:89
m. of truths	FRAME 346:76	and go like m.	STEV 853:73	Gods and m., we are all deluded	SHEL 816:64
m. on loan	FRAME 346:77	And makes m. mad	SHAK 790:43	Good m. made evil	MUIR 624:19
more m. than if I were	BAUD 68:66	apparition, sole of m.	SHEL 814:6	government…not of m.	ADAMS 5:98
not your m. which haunt	FENT 332:59	argument with m. a woman	MILT 608:94	greatest m. that ever lived	MACA 545:35
our m. insist on cherishing	ONEI 651:65	as cheap as other m.	PEPYS 673:90	Great m. are almost always bad m.	ACTON 4:69
our m. remain in one place	PROU 698:56	asked m. for votes	WEST 933:97	great m. have…elements of comicality	JENK 454:33
these m. grow	TATE 867:39	asketh m. to have?	CHAU 217:85	great m.…in politics	ELTON 323:42
what m. do you have	GARC 360:67	ask m. who have loved them	TROL 897:31	Great m. may jest	SHAK 787:59
memory burden of m.	BERG 83:22	As long as m. are m.	TAWN 868:44	great m. of the past	DESB 274:88
dies from…strain of m.	BART 66:26	best-laid schemes o' Mice an' M.	BURNS 177:78	griefs of private m.	MARL 573:15
draw what you see only in m.	DEGAS 269:88	best leading m.	TAYL 868:55	griefs would make m. mad	SHAK 760:28
floors of m.	ELIOT 317:72	best m. of past centuries	DESC 274:92	half my m. are sick	TENN 878:95
Footfalls echo in the m.	ELIOT 319:37	betray more m.	SHAK 790:39	happy m. that have the power	TENN 877:62
For my name and m.	BACON 53:44	better m. than we	KIPL 492:68	hearts of m.…have melted	SHAK 765:60
friends forsake me like a m. lost	CLARE 228:54	Beware of m.	SPARK 836:75	honest m. and bonny lasses	BURNS 179:20
fruit of m.	CONR 244:51	Bloody m. are like bloody buses	COPE 246:94	honour lies in killing m.	MARG 570:67
happiest m.	GREE 386:10	boastful m. so oft abashed	SPEN 838:37	hosses, dawgs, and m.	THAC 880:27
happiness…in my m.	DESB 274:89	bodies of unburied m.	WEBS 926:36	How can m. bear…to live	CORN 247:4
honour his m.	JONS 468:90	Books are written…for all m.	CARL 201:29	how imprudently m. engage	ASTE 39:6
injury is fresh in my m.	NASHE 632:90	Brave m. are a city's strongest tower	ALCA 11:39	How strangely hopes delude m.	MASS 581:78
In m. everything seems	WILL 945:79	brave m., living and dead	LINC 529:10	how subject we old m.	SHAK 772:89
Life is all m.	WILL 945:3	breed free m.?	HOPE 427:56	How vainly m. themselves	MARV 577:1
m. be left in oblivion	EMMET 325:6	breed of m.	SHAK 764:40	Humorists are not happy m.	CONN 242:2
m. die from the earth	SIDN 820:59	brotherhood of m.-at-wars	PAZ 671:48	hundred m. discontented	LOUI 537:67
m. from the past	THOM 883:1	brutes m., and m. divine	PATM 669:15	hurrying dots which are m.	CUMM 257:51
m. holds a seat	SHAK 781:66	busy companies of m.	MARV 577:2	I don't hate m.	WINT 950:10
m., hope, love	ROSS 725:37	busy hum of m.	MILT 597:47	I eat m. like air	PLATH 681:15
m. is fair and bright	VAUG 909:41	but given the way of m.	NIET 638:94	If all m. are born free	ASTE 39:5
m. is going	JOHN 464:87	But while m. slept	BIBLE 117:93	If m. cease to believe	MILL 594:67
m. of all that	GERS 365:75	by pains m. come to greater pains	BACON 51:85	If m. could learn from history	COLE 236:51
m. of an offshore island	THAT 881:53	By this shall all m. know	BIBLE 123:50	If m. knew how women	OHEN 648:16
m. of Macaulay	BARR 65:98	called the book M. Without Women	HEMI 409:63	If m. were angels	MADI 558:17
m. of them is forgotten	BIBLE 106:26	cannot fight…as m. may do	SHAK 767:29	if m. withheld their praise	SHEEN 811:44
m. refuses such orderliness	LIVE 531:51	cannot learn m. from books	DISR 287:15	incompatible by m.?	LEWIS 526:51
m. that only works backwards	CARR 205:4	cause that wit is in other m.	SHAK 772:70	In France, they study m.	STAEL 842:1
m. the only plot	WALC 916:16	challenge all the m. alive	ANON 22:83	insecure and intimidated m.	LIPP 531:42
Midnight shakes the m.	ELIOT 317:73	cheerful ways of m.	MILT 603:75	insinuate…into m.'s affections	CAVE 210:21
mixing M. and desire	ELIOT 317:95	chiefly made by m.	HARDY 397:6	In societies where m.	AUNG 45:41
need have a great m.	BACON 53:38	clerkes been noght wisest m.	CHAU 217:87	In the hands of m.	DWOR 308:44
No m. of my friends	SASS 745:89	clever m. at Oxford	GRAH 381:92	in the likeness of m.	BIBLE 124:85
No woman should have a m.	WILDE 941:91	closest m. ever come to childbearing	MAIL 560:49	in the likeness of m.	BIBLE 128:97
only in m. that we are the same	DIDE 285:69	Columbus and his m.	WILB 939:38	Is there no way for m. to be	SHAK 803:94
paint the m. of happiness	SAIF 738:30	common to all…conditions of m.	WEBER 925:12	justice to all m.	JEFF 454:26
Pluck from the m.	SHAK 798:70	common wonder of all m.	BROW 165:69	justify the ways of God to m.	MILT 601:31
point…devoid of m.	DIDI 286:80	consent of all great m.	RUSK 733:94	killed the m. who held it	PEAC 671:54
quits the m. with difficulty	BEEC 73:64	cunning m. pass for wise	BACON 52:3	Kings and Desperate M.	KRON 500:19
sever the roots of m.	THOM 885:69	Dead m. are serious	FIND 336:44	Land of…godlike m.!	BYRON 187:42
stay in a man's m.	KIPL 492:51	dealings with young m.	PO 683:79	Learned m.…do many times fail	BACON 49:22
Thanks For The M.	ROBIN 718:77	depends upon that of m.	GILM 371:91	lesson to all of us m.	AMIN 16:28
the imperfections of m.	BARN 64:76	difference of 40,000 m.	WELL 929:8	Let m. tremble	HAWT 402:5
This is the use of m.	ELIOT 321:89	diversity in the faculties of m.	MADI 558:16	Let us now praise famous m.	BIBLE 113:10
throng into my m.	MILT 598:68	domination by fat-minded m.	ARNO 36:47	Liberty…most m. dread it	SHAW 808:38
vanish out of m.	THOR 888:14	doon m., if I sooth	CHAU 217:91	Life levels all m.	SHAW 808:52
vibrates in the m.	SHEL 816:63	Do other m., for they would do you	DICK 279:14	life of m. is painful	EURI 328:58
wakes the bitter m.	MILT 603:90	dreadful fiend of gods and m.	SPEN 839:54	Like all young m.	SHAW 809:77
weakened by unfaithful m.	ISAA 447:63	droop m. and beasts	NASHE 632:94	like I like my m.	DEGEN 270:6
men absurd to argue m.	NEWM 634:44	drowned more m. than Neptune	FULL 355:80	Like m. we'll face the…pack	MCKA 553:7
A few honest m.	CROM 255:16	enables m. to produce more	GILM 371:92	lips of dying m.	ARNO 34:98
affairs of m. rest still uncertain	SHAK 778:53	Eve upon the first of M.	HOOD 426:29	Lives of great m.	LONG 535:15
airplanes…do not make m.…happier	DE 267:43	evil lurks in the hearts of m.	ATWO 41:46	lost 30,000 m.	WELL 929:3
a' is done that m. can do	BURNS 180:58	except in the minds of m.	READ 708:96	lot of hard-faced m.	BALD 57:25
all are m.	GRAY 383:48	eyes of God and m.	LESL 523:88	love m. too little	BURKE 176:48
All except the best m.	LEWIS 526:50	failed to inspire sympathy in m.	BEER 73:83	love of gain to ruin m.	SOPH 834:25

men

love of justice in most m.	LARO 510:99	m. in the habits of women	CHAR 215:32	m. who really believe in themselves	CHES 220:67
Love wakes m., once	PATM 669:16	m....in their old age	POPE 686:56	m. who say yes, lie	MELV 585:71
lusty young m.	SHAK 765:68	m. into their chief providers	MILLS 595:7	M. Whose Lives Are Money	OATES 643:8
make m. happy	POPE 688:24	m. it hurt when it fell	DONNE 292:63	m. who want to become inhuman	APOL 29:78
makes m. ridiculous	JUVE 471:54	m. kill the fat swine	ANON 20:40	m. will boast of knowledge	LANY 508:55
maketh m. to be of one mind	BOOK 149:23	m. know so little of m.	DU 305:67	m. will...do it for pay	MELV 585:77
make you fishers of m.	BIBLE 114:26	M. learn while they teach	SENE 757:23	m. wish to hear no stories	BERN 85:72
management of m.	MERE 588:40	M. Leaving the gardens	LARK 509:82	m. with book learning	RAMOS 705:50
man that m. like	NORR 641:56	m. liked to put me down	OKEE 649:24	m. with broken souls	PATC 668:7
Many m. have pride	BALZ 61:97	m., like satyrs grazing	MARL 573:14	m. without ideals	CAMUS 195:81
many m.'s decay	SPEN 839:60	m. liking their fathers	BRAD 154:26	m. without imagination	PROU 698:54
Many m. would hardly miss	SHAW 810:20	m. loved darkness	BIBLE 122:26	M. with secrets	DELI 271:41
Married impossible m.?	GRAV 382:32	M. love in haste	BYRON 190:22	m. with sisters dear	HOOD 426:31
medal for killing two m.	MATL 582:94	m. may come	TENN 876:38	m. with the muck-rakes	ROOS 724:17
m. about me that are fat	SHAK 776:12	M. might as well project	LARD 508:65	m. with ugly faces	MASE 580:68
m. agree to be of one mind	BACON 50:50	m. mispronounce it	MORL 619:37	m., women, and clergymen	SMITH 830:55
m. all so good for nothing	AUST 46:84	M. most good	SHAK 768:59	M. would be angels	POPE 687:76
m. always try to make virtues	MENC 587:6	M. multiply like Mice	CANT 197:14	m. would take the death sentence	LAWR 514:91
m. and dogs shall drink him	POPE 686:68	M. must endure	SHAK 793:32	m. write in place lite	CHAU 216:66
m. and girls came and went	FITZ 337:80	M. must learn now	SHAK 791:78	M., you are all marksmen	PUTN 700:2
m. and nations behave wisely	EBAN 310:8	M. must needs abide	SHAK 760:14	more animated beings than...m.	SMITH 830:50
m. and women are created equal	STAN 842:12	m. must walk	POPE 688:23	more I admire m.	LEVIN 525:28
m. and women are not so...enslaved	SHAW 809:87	M., my brothers	TENN 871:17	Most wretched m.	SHEL 812:63
m. and women laughing	SAND 742:15	m. naturally desire knowledge	ARIS 31:17	music of m.'s lives	SHAK 765:63
m. and women merely players	SHAK 779:80	M. not afraid of God	POPE 688:27	music marreth m.'s manners	GALE 357:29
m. and women of this generation	LLOY 533:72	m. of any other class	LODGE 534:2	must judge m.	LICH 528:28
M. are April	SHAK 780:12	M. of business	BAGE 54:77	must m. kill and die?	SHEL 816:58
M. are as chancy as children	KIPL 491:26	m. of culture	ARNO 36:28	name all the m.	MCCA 547:84
M. are born makers	WALC 916:18	M. of England	SHEL 813:89	Nearly all our best m. are dead!	PUNCH 699:82
M. are but children	DRYD 301:58	m. of experiment	BACON 50:44	Noble m. in the quiet of morning	DUNC 307:9
M. are but gilded loam	SHAK 764:32	m. of genius	DELA 271:20	No m. who knows aught	MILT 603:67
m....are discriminated against	MEIR 584:42	m. of iron	ALBA 11:20	not dreams of doting m.?	MELV 585:75
M. are equal before a fish	HOOV 427:47	m. of judgement frame	MARL 573:9	nothing noble-minded m.	KINC 486:14
m. are good-looking	KEIL 479:53	m. of like passions	BIBLE 124:86	not into the hands of m.	BIBLE 112:81
M. are grown mechanical in head	CARL 200:82	m. of measured merriment	LEWIS 527:59	not permit thirty m.	WHITE 934:26
M. are like the earth	SCHR 749:64	m. of our time	MACA 544:22	obey God rather than m.	BIBLE 124:76
M. are lived over again	BROW 165:50	M. of power	FOOT 342:82	of all m. most miserable	BIBLE 127:56
m. are merriest	SHAK 775:63	m. of science	MILL 593:51	of war I have slain m.	SHAK 788:86
M. are mistaken	SPIN 840:72	M. of sound sense	PLATO 681:48	Old m. and comets	SWIFT 862:53
M. are nearly always willing	CAES 192:12	m. of the hour	HAMM 394:56	Old m. forget	SHAK 776:90
M. are never so good	MACK 554:17	m. of the present age	OVER 656:12	only m. like thee are fit	OTWAY 656:9
m. are not hanged	HALI 393:34	m. of the West	WEIL 927:69	O shame to m.!	MILT 603:67
M. are not made for hours	RABE 704:16	m. of the world	DICK 278:59	other m. are tempted	BUTL 185:80
m. aren't attracted to me	LEE 518:84	m. only become great	DE 270:90	pacific—and all his m.	KEATS 475:61
M. are rewarded	SZASZ 865:27	M. out of servitude	EMER 325:91	port, for m.	JOHN 463:66
m. are so romantic	WELD 928:86	M. reverence one another	THOR 888:47	powerful m. in our society	BELL 77:81
m. are still	MACN 558:99	M. see objects	FOWL 345:61	present life of m. on earth	BEDE 72:59
M. are the Brahmin	STAN 842:14	M. seldom make passes	PARK 664:77	presumed to be what m.	LIPP 531:43
M. are the only animals	MENC 587:9	M.'s evil manners	SHAK 805:56	primitive m. are...credulous	POPE 686:57
M. are to wait for liberty	MACA 545:25	M. should be either treated	MACH 552:92	problem is...whether m. do	SKIN 825:47
M. are very fragile	STEP 847:13	m. should have a...feeling	LAUR 511:24	pursuit...by free m.	WARR 921:13
m. as angels without feminine	MILT 606:64	M. should put an enemy	SHAK 789:13	push m. over the edge	ROTH 727:78
M. at sometime were masters	SHAK 776:9	M. shut their doors	SHAK 791:76	quit you like m.	BIBLE 127:64
m. at whiles are sober	HOUS 432:66	m. sit and hear	KEATS 478:43	quit yourselves like m.	BIBLE 96:28
m. call earth	MILT 598:62	M.'s manners	JONS 467:69	rank of devoutly religious m.	EINS 313:80
m. cannot suspend their fate	DEFOE 269:68	M., some to business	POPE 688:14	reality on which m. can act	LIPP 531:41
m. can tell me things	MITC 609:38	m. so old as we	SHAK 765:67	reason m. are greater than animals	ELLI 323:32
m....capable of every wickedness	CONR 244:45	m....spread it around	BAIN 55:96	reason why m. lived	LOWE 539:96
m. creep, Not walk	WHIT 938:21	M. started at the intelligence	SOUT 835:55	reputation of m.	MONT 613:13
m. dare trust themselves	SHAK 791:74	m....succeed through the help of their wives	LEE 519:1	resident in m.	SHAK 760:20
m. decay	GOLD 376:98	m.'s watch upon the world	MACL 555:37	reverberates through m.'s history	KOES 495:31
m. do not learn very much	HUXL 442:96	M. talk of killing time	BOUC 152:84	Rich m. deal gifts	SHAK 791:83
M. don't and can't	RUSK 733:16	m. that are dying	JEFF 453:15	rich m. rule the law	GOLD 376:87
M. don't know women	TROL 898:36	m. that God made mad	CHES 220:81	rights as m., as free m.	PITT 679:7
m. dream, but not equally	LAWR 514:89	m. that make a city	NICI 637:80	robot mice and robot m.	BRAD 155:39
M....employ their reason	WOLL 953:86	m. that strove with gods	TENN 870:2	sardine m. crammed in	MACN 557:96
M. enter local politics	PARK 665:40	m. that women marry	LONG 536:39	say best m. are moulded	SHAK 788:80
m....expect brick	ASTE 39:2	m., their rights and nothing more	ANTH 29:73	see m. as trees, walking	BIBLE 119:58
M. fear death	BACON 50:57	M.! The only animal	LAWR 513:61	Sensible m. are all the same religion	DISR 289:71
m. feel a little more secure	MORE 618:17	m. there are love not a gaping pig	SHAK 770:10	sent ten thousand m. to battle	SITT 823:93
m. first make slaves	DOUG 296:27	m. thin away to insignificance	HARDY 397:4	short-lived weak animals m.	MONT 613:11
m. from the planet Earth	ANON 25:69	m. too profoundly convinced	READ 708:94	should make m. atheists	CAREW 198:56
m. from whom my ways begin	BLUN 143:74	m. to take their exits	WEBS 927:61	show m. energetically	GRAY 383:41
m. have a much better time	MENC 586:99	m. trying to be writers	JONES 465:19	shows of love to other m.	SHAK 776:6
M. have died from time to time	SHAK 779:10	m. walk proudly through the earth	RAND 706:56	sinewy brown m.	PRIE 695:95
M. have every advantage	AUST 47:89	M. were deceivers	SHAK 774:38	single m....more charitable	BACON 51:74
m. have lost their reason!	SHAK 777:39	M. were only capable	MILL 594:68	So long as m. can breathe	SHAK 800:37
m. have their price	WALP 919:85	m. were the answer	BARN 64:69	So long as m. worship	HUXL 442:81
M. ignorant of letters	SAND 743:39	m. who are as various as the sands	FORS 344:40	so many kinds of awful m.	COPE 246:93
m. ill at ease	HAWT 402:11	m. who are not historians	FORS 345:43	Some m. are born kings	SHAW 810:17
m. in appetite	BACON 53:32	m. who argues by increments	BYATT 186:18	Some m. creep in	SHAK 787:36
m. in a smoke-filled room	SIMP 822:85	m. who borrow	LAMB 505:2	some m. who have their heads	HERN 415:94
m. in brotherhood	NOON 641:50	m. who'd want to flee	HARM 398:38	something true about m.	JAMES 451:58
m. in considerable number	MILL 592:15	m. who had never seen a horse	BRIN 159:24	som m. say in many partys	MALO 563:16
M. in great fortunes	BACON 51:87	m. who have minded	WOOLF 955:29	sound as the m. who make it	LEE 519:90
M. in great place	BACON 51:83	m. who live with	NIEB 637:86	Strong bronzed m.	CULL 257:43
				stuffed shirts, hollow m.	MACD 550:39

menace

substance of m.	SWIN 864:9	
take a minute from the m.	CARA 198:35	
taking ordinary m.	GALB 357:20	
tale which holdeth...old m.	SIDN 820:56	
talked about by m.	PERI 675:25	
tall m. had ever very empty heads	BACON 50:53	
ten thousand of those m.	SHAK 775:86	
the purgatory of m.	FLOR 341:62	
There the m. are as mad	SHAK 784:62	
these m. paid their shillings	PRIE 695:84	
think as wise m.	ASCH 37:52	
thou hast m.	SHAK 760:98	
thousand m. that fishes gnawed	SHAK 761:40	
three m. I admired most	MCLE 554:23	
tide in the affairs of m.	SHAK 778:48	
tides of m. into my hands	LAWR 514:88	
'Tis all m.'s office	SHAK 774:52	
'Tis no shame for m.	SHIR 819:17	
toil in other m.'s extremes	KYD 501:51	
to m. [I speak] French	CHAR 215:38	
torment, kill and damn m.	MARG 570:63	
transform M. into Monsters	FORD 343:8	
travelled among unknown m.	WORD 958:92	
truthful towards m.	HARDY 397:5	
trying to do with eight m.	ROBI 718:78	
twelve thousand fighting m.	SHAK 764:48	
twice as well as m.	WHIT 938:25	
two m. look out	LANG 507:43	
two m. stand together	WAVE 925:2	
Two m. who differ	RUSS 734:33	
two strong m.	KIPL 489:76	
understanding better than other m.	DRYD 300:39	
Unmarried m. are best friends	BACON 51:73	
unmarried or childless m.	BACON 51:70	
upon two generations of m.	LLOY 533:74	
vain, unnecessary things are m.	ROCH 719:15	
vast majority o' m.	MACD 549:23	
vexes public m.	TENN 872:28	
voices elected me of all m.	LEE 519:98	
war between m. and women	THUR 890:69	
war...between m. and women	LYND 543:92	
war is obsolete or m. are	FULL 355:71	
wasteful of promising young m.	HUGH 435:17	
way to meet other queer m.	MCKE 554:11	
weak and miserable m.	CHOM 222:26	
We are selfish m.	WORD 958:94	
We are the hollow m.	ELIOT 318:13	
Weary m., what reap ye?	WILDE 940:45	
we've got the m.	HUNT 439:16	
What all m. should avoid	DISR 289:70	
What are m. to rocks	AUST 46:61	
what many m. desire	SHAK 769:94	
What m. or Gods are these?	KEATS 478:35	
when all m. shall speak well	BIBLE 120:73	
When m. make gods	ONEI 650:61	
When m. reach...50	TEKA 869:65	
when shall English m.	DRAY 298:95	
where good m. rest	FLEC 340:31	
where m. May read	SHAK 796:16	
which all m. knew!	TENN 875:7	
which m. call Love	SPEN 838:36	
While m. are rolling round	WEST 933:95	
white m. cheat black m.	LEE 519:91	
Who, of m., can tell	KEATS 476:87	
Wine and women will make m.	BIBLE 113:98	
wise m. do not say	MART 576:72	
Wise m. fish here	STEL 846:1	
wisest of m. in all ages	STER 848:23	
wisest of you m.	PLATO 681:41	
With four-and-twenty m.	AYTO 48:11	
with m.'s blood	KING 488:59	
With m. this is impossible	BIBLE 118:19	
Without thinking highly...of m.	AUST 46:59	
Women...behave like m.	MACK 554:15	
women...envy m.	PANK 662:87	
Working m. of all countries	MARX 579:34	
Would m....distil it out	SHAK 775:80	
Wrath brings mortal m....hurt	EURI 328:62	
Yes, Sir, many m.	JOHN 461:91	
Yesterday's m.	ANON 25:71	
you are m. of stones	SHAK 793:37	
Young m. mend not their sight	DONNE 293:76	
young m.'s vision	DRYD 302:77	
young m. think it is	HOUS 432:77	
menace against every form of m.	ROTH 728:91	
m. of aggression	ASQU 38:84	
public m.	BURG 174:89	

men-children Bring forth m.-c.	SHAK 796:24	
Mencken M.'s defects	MEYER 589:63	
mend Garlic to m. her kissing	SHAK 799:22	
God won't, and we can't m. it	CLOU 232:51	
mendacities Better m.	POUND 691:2	
mendacity M. is a system	WILL 945:94	
mene M., M., Tekel, Upharsin	BIBLE 111:42	
menopause going through the m.	WALT 919:86	
menpleasers with eyeservice, as m.	BIBLE 128:94	
Mensch M. ist das Wesen	SCHI 747:25	
M. ist, was er isst	FEUE 334:3	
menstrual m. years are vestigial	LEGU 520:11	
menstruation m....enviable	STEI 846:93	
mental sort of m. rebellion	ORWE 654:39	
mentality Australians inherited the British m.	PACK 659:10	
mentally m....deadening force	WEBB 925:7	
mentation forms of m.	KOES 495:29	
mention recourse to the m. of it	JOHN 464:78	
menu and then I saw the m.	WESK 931:50	
full m. of rights	TUTU 901:23	
part of life's m.	RUSS 735:49	
Menuhin first choice...M.	ADLER 8:70	
mercantile dull m. England	BUCH 171:25	
Mercaptan M. went on to preach	HUXL 441:55	
Mercator M.'s North Poles	CARR 205:29	
Mercedes-Benz buy me a M.-B.	JOPL 468:98	
merchandise mechanical arts and m.	BACON 53:43	
merchant ear of a m.	NASHE 632:97	
heaven is like unto a m.	BIBLE 117:96	
What m.'s ships have my sighs	DONNE 291:28	
merchants m. full of sybstaunce and myght	DUNB 306:2	
m....intent on profit	PIUS 680:18	
m., who mind little	MONT 613:10	
mercies All occasions invite his m.	DONNE 293:72	
church is of m.	DONNE 293:71	
tender m.	BIBLE 102:6	
thy faithful m. crown	WESL 932:62	
merciful Blessed are the m.	BIBLE 114:27	
Draw near...in being m.	SHAK 760:21	
God be m. unto us	BIBLE 101:80	
merciless sunlight streaming m.	ATWO 41:33	
time is a m. thing	WILL 945:99	
mercury M. with a Pitchfork	BRAU 157:85	
mercy at the m. of the reflexes	BALD 56:15	
easy in the m. of his means	THOM 883:18	
entirely and helplessly at his m.	SHAW 807:20	
God ha' m.	KIPL 489:75	
God have m.	RANS 707:73	
goodness and m. shall follow me	BIBLE 100:45	
hand folks over to God's m.	ELIOT 315:26	
have m., and not sacrifice	BIBLE 116:63	
Have m. upon all Jews	BOOK 147:53	
have m. upon us	BOOK 146:46	
in wrath remember m.	BIBLE 111:56	
justice and m. are reconciled	WILS 949:75	
La belle dame sans m.	KEATS 477:25	
Large and without m.	OLSEN 650:45	
leaving m. to heaven	FIEL 335:23	
'Lord have m. upon us'	PEPYS 674:99	
merciful...shall obtain m.	BIBLE 114:27	
M., compassion, and justice	WAITE 916:5	
m. endureth for ever	BIBLE 103:41	
M. has a human heart	BLAKE 139:88	
m. is on them that fear him	BIBLE 120:66	
m. show to me	POPE 688:28	
M. sighed farewell!	BYRON 188:75	
m. to forgive	DRYD 303:12	
most tender m. is neglect	CRAB 252:34	
Mother of M.	ROBI 718:81	
new law of m.	MORE 618:14	
Nothing emboldens sin...as m.	SHAK 791:79	
Peace on earth and m. mild	WESL 931:58	
Peace on earth and m. mild!	BEEC 73:65	
plenteous in m.	BIBLE 102:7	
property is always to have m.	BOOK 147:72	
quality of m. is not strained	SHAK 770:12	
shewed m. on him	BIBLE 121:82	
shewing m. unto thousands	BIBLE 94:66	
shew m. unto thousands in them	BOOK 147:59	
shut the gates of m.	GRAY 384:71	
so great is his m.	BIBLE 102:8	
so is his m.	BIBLE 112:81	
still at the m. of words	THOM 884:26	
temper so Justice with m.	MILT 606:57	
When m. seasons justice	SHAK 770:13	

Where m., Love and Pity dwell	BLAKE 139:89	
Meredith M. is a prose Browning	WILDE 940:55	
mergers m.-and-acquisitions	GLEI 374:48	
meridian full m. of my glory	SHAK 805:50	
merit confuse longevity with m.	WOGAN 952:58	
greatest m. for the public	BACON 51:70	
herein consisted his m.	MILT 600:15	
How he esteems your m.	COWP 251:3	
irrespective of any possible m.	WAUGH 923:50	
M. and good works	BACON 51:88	
m. of both sexes	LABR 502:8	
m. of the wearer!	SHAK 769:95	
m. wins the soul	POPE 685:42	
modernness is the measure of m.	EMER 325:80	
of rewarding m.	SWIFT 862:47	
oft got without m.	SHAK 789:12	
positive m. of enjoying	RUSS 734:32	
merits m. of a classification	MILL 592:11	
seek his m. to disclose	GRAY 384:78	
meritus m., 'so he ought to be'	LEAC 515:22	
Merkel public image of M.	FARA 330:18	
merle mavis and m. are singing	SCOTT 752:33	
Merlin child was delyvered unto M.	MALO 562:6	
unto M., and the Table Rounde	MALO 562:10	
mermaid Choicer...M. Tavern?	KEATS 475:76	
Done at the M.!	BEAU 70:17	
m....tolled my son to shipwreck	DEKK 270:12	
mermaids heard the m. singing	ELIOT 318:11	
merriest men are m.	SHAK 775:63	
merrily M., m. shall I live now	SHAK 804:32	
merriment damn...measured m.	LEWIS 527:59	
even for m. and diversion	SMITH 827:81	
Frame your mind to...m.	SHAK 761:57	
it is no m.	KORAN 498:93	
merry As M. Margaret	SKEL 824:29	
began to be m.	BIBLE 121:91	
eat...drink, and to be m.	BIBLE 106:25	
fool to make me m.	SHAK 779:7	
Fortune is m.	SHAK 778:46	
keep our Christmas m. still	SCOTT 752:22	
Let us be m.	CURR 259:91	
meet that we should make m.	BIBLE 121:92	
m. as a marriage bell	BYRON 187:50	
m. as the day is long	SHAK 773:24	
m. cuckoo, messenger of Spring	SPEN 839:45	
m. heart goes all the day	SHAK 799:16	
m. heart maketh a cheerful	BIBLE 104:74	
M. it is in the good greenwood	SCOTT 752:23	
m. songs of peace	SHAK 805:58	
never m. when I hear	SHAK 770:20	
to be m. best becomes you	SHAK 734:31	
very m., dancing, drinking	DRYD 304:56	
wine maketh m.	BIBLE 106:32	
Meshach Shadrach, M.	BIBLE 111:39	
mess don't m. with it	WALL 918:62	
general m. of...feeling	ELIOT 320:66	
God...has made an awful m.	BURR 181:64	
Here's another fine m.	HARDY 396:99	
it's best not to m. with us	PUTIN 700:99	
let other people clean up the m.	FITZ 338:85	
m. of pottage	BIBLE 92:27	
the world is a m.	ALBR 11:38	
unspeakable idiotic m.	ORWE 653:28	
what we can make of the m.	ELIOT 319:50	
message may your m. be heard	WALL 918:75	
medium is the m.	MCLU 556:53	
m. came...for me	PENI 673:80	
m. of fear	MCCA 547:81	
m. of peace to Ireland	ARNO 35:23	
m. to the businessmen	CURR 259:94	
Send them a m.	ANON 25:72	
the m. came	AUST 47:96	
will never deliver the m.	MILL 593:37	
messages m. go quicker to the brain	SPARK 836:66	
messenger Anglo-Saxon M.	CARR 205:16	
m. of Satan	BIBLE 129:74	
m. of Spring	SPEN 839:45	
says, I am a m.	MILL 593:37	
winged m. of heaven	SHAK 765:78	
messing m. about in boats	GRAH 380:89	
m. with people's heads	HEND 411:4	
mess-makers pioneers...m.-m.	PIRS 679:92	
met way we m.	SWIN 864:2	
when We innocently m.	JONS 467:70	
metal breed for barren m.	SHAK 769:86	
cold m. of economic theory	SCHU 750:77	
forests of m.	THOM 886:76	

milk

metaphor All slang is m. authors of simile and m. CHES 220:53
authors of simile and m. NASH 631:81
branch-strained m. MOORE 617:89
Cricket...the great m. FOWL 346:65
I love m. GASS 361:86
I love m. MALA 562:87
Man be my m. THOM 883:5
No m. reinvents...nurture PALEY 661:53
Science is all m. LEARY 517:48
through m. to reconcile WILL 946:11
whaling a universal m. LODGE 534:95
metaphoric habits of m. thought FRYE 354:54
metaphorical deeper than m. sense CARL 200:84
metaphors abuse of m. PALM 661:67
Curling with m. HERB 413:73
didn't have m. in my day TRUE 899:75
handful of m. BORG 150:56
m. by which it is most naturally JAMES 451:66
sweet phrases, lovely m. HERB 414:84
metaphysic high As m. wit can fly BUTL 184:68
metaphysical M. lederhosen ENRI 326:21
M. questions and reflections HERN 414:92
metaphysics divinity or school m. HUME 438:7
Explaining m. to the nation BYRON 189:89
m. is a branch of fantastic literature BORG 150:55
M. is the finding of bad reasons BRAD 155:41
M. means nothing but JAMES 451:63
science of m. MENC 587:8
small portion of m. PLAN 680:22
meteor cloud-encircled m. of the air SHEL 814:3
m. Ever hung my fate MIDD 590:81
slides the silent m. TENN 873:49
Streamed, like a m. GRAY 385:81
methinks lady protests too much, m. SHAK 783:25
method All m. is imperfect NICO 637:83
anything other than...general m.! BAUD 68:72
genius has invented a m. RUSS 734:27
had a certain m. RUSS 734:37
M. acting? BARR 65:3
m. and secret...of Jesus ARNO 36:37
m. of assisting...pure science CONA 239:9
no objection to this m. STER 848:29
our m. of questioning HEIS 407:22
people and the m. RYLE 736:60
scientific m. has always been PIRS 679:94
there is m. in't SHAK 782:81
true m. of warfare MAZZ 583:29
You know my m. DOYLE 297:47
You know my m. DOYLE 297:51
Methodist insufferable as a M. MENC 587:18
Methodists two kinds of M. ELIOT 315:17
methods institution of m. UNIT 905:9
m. are outdated and incorrect ANON 25:44
m. differ from those HUXL 443:10
m. of control KEYN 484:77
other m. to stop them KISH 493:83
rule-of-thumb m. MARX 579:41
theory and m. of revolution MAO 568:27
You know my m. DOYLE 297:47
Methuselah days of M. BIBLE 92:7
metre hurdling the m. like tired horses BROY 169:88
m. of the dictionary? THOM 883:10
Time is the m. WALC 916:16
metres not m., but...argument EMER 324:69
Two m., or a little more ROBBE 716:61
Metro Win a M.! PRIV 696:26
metropolis art is born of the m. POUND 691:89
M. of Great-Britain BAIL 55:87
Metternich M....so conservative EVANS 328:66
mettle m. enough in thee SHAK 774:54
undaunted m. should compose SHAK 796:24
mettlesome m. women ANDR 18:77
mew cat will m. SHAK 784:68
Mexican If I were a M. CORW 247:7
Mexico In M. the gods ruled COND 239:12
Poor M., so far from God DIAZ 276:27
Micawber never will desert Mr M. DICK 280:42
mice as long as it catches m. DENG 272:56
best-laid schemes o' M. an' Men BURNS 177:78
Men multiply like M. CANT 197:14
robot m. and robot men BRAD 155:39
Michael M....against the dragon BIBLE 131:10
M. read the Gaelic scroll RUSS 735:42
Michelangelo Dante or M. MULL 624:33
If M. were a heterosexual BROWN 164:36
women...Talking of M. ELIOT 316:61
mickle O m. is the powerful grace SHAK 766:87

microbe M. is so very small BELL 76:55
microcosm m. of little world BROW 165:72
microphone paid for this m. REAG 708:12
microscopes magnifyin' gas m. DICK 277:57
M. are prudent DICK 283:32
Microsoft M. were a car MURR 627:82
Midas Hard food for M. SHAK 770:5
midday walks under the m. sun MILT 599:72
middle honeyed m. of the night KEATS 477:16
In the m. ages JERO 454:43
live in the M. Ages SMITH 830:38
m.-management of Manhattan AMIS 16:43
m. of the journey of our life DANTE 262:36
moist his m.! NASH 631:72
nuclear power in the m. ages LAMB 506:16
politics the m. way ADAMS 5:99
reconnected with the angry m.? ANON 27:28
royal family in the m. ages HALD 392:22
safely by the m. way OVID 657:17
Secret sits in the m. FROST 353:17
middle-age companions for m. a. BACON 51:75
frightening thing about m. a. DAY 267:33
mere m. a. snuffs out HUGH 435:17
m. a. of a state BACON 53:43
misspent youth and m. a. THUR 891:4
pleasures of m. a. POUND 692:14
middle-aged m.-a. man can't UPDI 906:27
nine m.-a. couples THOM 886:76
The M.-A. Man THUR 890:70
middle class great English m. c. ARNO 35:11
M. C. was quite prepared BELL 77:62
m.-c. woman LURIE 542:65
provincial, resolutely m.-c. MCFA 551:65
Puritan of the m. c. NEME 633:19
symbol of an emerging m.-c. Briton MCFA 551:67
true m.-c. unit SHAW 808:40
up agen m.-c. morality SHAW 810:98
We of the sinking m. c. ORWE 653:21
What fools m.-c. girls are DRAB 288:81
world is full of m.-c. people SHAR 806:78
middle classes lower m. c. GILB 369:49
Middle East America's dependence
on oil from the M. E. KERRY 483:59
bringing freedom...to the M. E. PINT 678:85
here in the M. E. RICE 713:85
progress in the M. E. BLAIR 138:63
Middlemarch M....grown up WOOLF 955:21
middles m. are nowhere to be found BART 66:16
Middlesex All M. is ugly COBB 233:75
midge lightly skims the m. BETJ 88:27
like a fretful m. ROSS 726:51
mid-heaven prancing in m.-h. LAWR 513:56
Midland M., bound for Cricklewood BETJ 88:28
midlands living in the M. BELL 77:68
south...north and m. MACM 556:74
midnight Cerberus and blackest m. MILT 597:41
gathered at m. KEATS 476:90
heard the chimes at m. SHAK 772:87
Holding hands at m. GERS 365:79
If you wake at m. KIPL 492:56
Love, the reeling m. through PARK 664:15
m., in our little town LIND 530:20
m. in the silence BROW 169:84
m. never come MARL 573:30
m.'s all a-glimmer YEATS 965:4
M. shakes the memory ELIOT 317:73
m. with no pain KEATS 478:46
mock the m. bell SHAK 794:72
roused themselves at m. TROL 898:35
shadow of the m. hour BYRON 188:65
stroke of m. ceases HOUS 432:76
'Tis m., falls the lamp-light WILDE 939:44
troubled m. and the noon's repose ELIOT 317:75
midst there am I in the m. of them BIBLE 118:13
through the m. JONS 468:96
midstream has to stop in m. BAND 61:10
midsummer high M. pomps ARNO 35:19
saw M. Night's Dream PEPYS 673:91
This m. flower SKEL 824:29
very m. madness SHAK 786:16
Midwest a baby in the M. MOORE 617:94
midwife fairies' m. SHAK 765:70
m. slapped your footsoles PLATH 681:30
revolution was our m. INOU 446:49
so far like the m. SOCR 833:96
midwinter M. Spring ELIOT 321:80
mien monster of so frightful m. POPE 687:82

rapture of thy m. WORD 962:47
might as our m. lessens ANON 20:36
danced...with all his m. BIBLE 96:43
do it with thy m. BIBLE 106:28
duty past thy m. SHAK 778:50
faith that right makes m. LINC 529:8
famoused for m. SHAK 800:44
M. first made kings MARL 573:48
Not by m., nor by power BIBLE 112:60
O tell of his m. GRANT 381:6
sovereign sway...dissolved by m.? DRYD 302:86
unbelief...no source of m. MACD 550:49
mightier m. and richer than thyself BIBLE 113:93
mightily levis mirry...levis m. DUNB 306:99
mighty God who made thee m. BENS 81:84
How are the m. fallen BIBLE 96:42
little body with a m. heart SHAK 775:65
Look on my works, ye M. SHEL 813:86
m. things from small beginnings DRYD 299:15
more m. than he seems SHAK 775:72
some have called thee M. DONNE 292:51
the brave, the m. WORD 961:42
with his m. talk SYNGE 865:24
migraine Love is a universal m. GRAV 382:34
Major Earl M. E.'s Grendorter! SHAW 809:75
mild m. or choleric disposition ADDI 6:23
milder Not m. is the general lot ARNO 33:61
mile braces at a distance of a m. MORT 621:75
compel thee to go a m. BIBLE 115:36
enemy half a m. away MUIR 624:16
mile-a sad tires in a m.-a. SHAK 799:16
miles end of evening smiles, M. BROW 167:27
first m. of the brief march PEARY 671:60
had gone m. away HEAN 405:72
Looking down for m. SNYD 832:89
lost in the m. SCOTT 751:17
m. of human habitations CONR 244:50
m. to go before I sleep FROST 352:5
Six m. from earth JARR 452:83
Thousands of m. of wheat RICH 714:23
twenty m. a day? MARL 572:6
two m. more and then we rest! BRON 161:60
milestones m. into headstones LOWE 539:16
milieu writer from the m. ROTH 727:76
militant m. ceases to be m. MORR 620:52
military among a m. one, trophies FUSE 356:93
close my m. career MACA 544:9
defeat...lost m. campaign EDIN 312:49
defiance of m. authority SASS 745:79
hold the m. mind TUCH 901:10
m. and nuclear sense WALE 917:29
m. society TREV 896:10
m. struggle may frankly be regarded SCHL 747:33
m. success will have achieved ELIZ 322:10
m. system...subsidy CHOM 222:28
m. take positions KENN 482:44
M. Two-Step GREN 388:56
overseas m. commitments FERG 333:77
political and the other m. MCNA 557:91
race has no m. purpose MOUN 622:93
species of m. instinct HAYD 402:23
study of m. history CLAU 229:75
thralldom of a m. caste LLOY 533:74
When the m. man approaches SHAW 808:30
military-industrial m.-i. complex EISE 314:2
milk black ink in white m. MUNRO 625:51
child drinking a bowl of m. SAND 742:33
crudded m. WEBS 927:57
curd of ass's m. POPE 688:5
drunk the m. of Paradise COLE 236:42
end is moo, the other, m. NASH 630:54
find a trout in the m. THOR 888:22
flowing with m. and honey BIBLE 93:59
for water...brought him m. BIBLE 95:12
Gin was mother's m. SHAW 810:99
gone to the m. bull JOHN 461:97
how we can m. her SZENT 865:30
hubbies moaned in M. Wood THOM 884:39
m. and ale SKEL 824:29
m. and honey blessed NEALE 632:7
m., and not of strong meat BIBLE 129:35
m. and sperm of kindness MELV 585:66
m. and the yoghurt MORT 621:68
m. and toast and honey MITC 609:36
m. comes frozen home SHAK 763:27
m. in an old breast MANS 567:96
m. of human kindness SHAK 796:13

milk-white

Entry	Ref
m.'s leap toward immortality	FADI 329:6
m. the cow of the world	WILB 939:34
m. the horse	BUSH 183:47
putting m. into babies	CHUR 226:98
sincere m. of the word	BIBLE 130:66
sucked such m.	YEATS 967:35
this m.-soup men call domestic bliss	PATM 669:26
milk-white m.-w.; now, purple	SHAK 767:27
milky called the M. Way	MARTI 576:70
Far as the solar walk, or m. way	POPE 687:75
m. sky	YEATS 965:6
stars…on the m. way	WORD 960:25
Mill John Stuart M.…effort of will	BENT 82:2
mill busy m.	GOLD 376:97
Gaza at the m. with slaves	MILT 607:82
God's m. grinds slow	HERB 414:88
sallow for m.	SPEN 838:20
stomach is a m.	HUNT 440:34
mill-dams bonnie m.-d. o' Binnorie	BALL 58:52
millennium century and m.	LEVI 525:26
M. Dome was intended to be New Labour's Xanadu	RAWN 707:86
millinery jewelled mass of m.	TENN 875:17
million a m. is made by producing	WILD 943:47
a m. to one	COWE 249:66
looked like a m. dollars	CART 206:42
m. dollars to make a picture	TAYL 868:52
multitude of one m.	KOES 495:26
patent double m.	DICK 277:57
turn-up in a m.	BEVIN 90:68
millionaire billionaire instead of a m.	WATE 922:39
I am a m.	SHAW 809:72
If you want to be a m.	BRAN 156:74
Who wants to be a m.?	PORT 690:72
millionaires m. and bums taste	MARQ 575:48
m. love a baked apple	FIRB 336:48
millions 'as m. at 'ome	KIPL 490:92
M. drew up before	NEW 634:38
m. long for immortality	ERTZ 327:41
m. of the mouthless dead	SORL 834:33
m. which it is…sucking up	COBB 233:75
probably been m. of earths	HOYLE 434:95
repeat in the lives of the m.	WILD 943:51
There are m. to be grabbed	MANK 565:73
Three m. of people	PITT 679:5
What m. died	CAMP 194:63
mills dark Satanic m.?	BLAKE 141:41
m. of God grind slowly	LOGAU 534:5
millstone bosom is actually a m.	GREER 387:40
m.…into the sea	BIBLE 132:18
m. were hanged about his neck	BIBLE 118:11
Tradition…can be as much a m.	MACI 553:99
millstones m.…about your neck	DAVI 264:65
M. around our neck	DISR 289:75
tears…Turned to m.	SHEL 812:71
mill-wheel millstone as a m.-w.	MACI 553:99
Milton like that in M.'s hell	NERV 633:24
malt does more than M.	HOUS 432:57
M., a name to resound	TENN 877:63
M.! thou shouldst be living	WORD 958:94
M.…was a genius	JOHN 464:92
Some mute inglorious M.	GRAY 384:70
Thou shalt believe in M.	BYRON 189:3
Milwaukeeans two M. in love	HECHT 406:3
mime m. can be a bridge between	MARC 569:52
mimic All honour's m.	DONNE 291:26
mimsy All m. were the borogoves	CARR 204:89
mince m., and slices of quince	LEAR 516:38
mincing M. poetry	SHAK 771:50
mind agree to be of one m.	BACON 50:50
all in the m.	WOLFE 953:66
altered the colour of my m.	BRON 162:77
A man's m.	TROL 898:51
ambitious m. Will covet more	MILT 602:56
A m. thinking	WOOLF 956:34
And to my m.	SHAK 781:56
angling…rest to his m.	WALT 920:92
arid desert of his m.	WEST 933:98
assail his m. another while	MARL 573:17
attracted to me by my m.	LEE 518:84
attractive to the half-baked m.	FORS 344:26
author's m.	GAUG 361:3
awing the human m.	JEFF 454:25
A Woman seldom Writes her M.	STEE 844:48
beauty of thy m.	SHAK 801:60
best marriage…of m. and body	FOWL 346:65
blessedness is…satisfaction of m.	SPIN 841:81
Boston is a state of m.	APPL 30:93
breast, and quiet m.	LOVE 538:85
brilliant m.	ASQU 38:90
broad of M.	BETJ 88:16
calming influence on the m.	MATI 581:92
Calm of m., all passion	MILT 608:5
calm the troubled m.	CONG 241:77
certain liveliness of m.	RABE 704:20
certain unsoundness of m.	MACA 544:23
chaos of the m.	SNYD 832:91
chords in the human m.	DICK 281:67
Clarity of m. results in	PASC 666:65
classical m. at work	PIRS 679:95
clear, attentive m.	SNYD 832:90
clear your m. of cant	JOHN 464:89
concentrates his m. wonderfully	JOHN 463:55
Coney Island of the M.	FERL 333:88
conjunction of the m.	MARV 577:96
consistency is as bad for the m.	HUXL 441:68
constant still in m.	MACA 546:48
contracts the m.	THER 882:86
contradictory beliefs in one's m.	ORWE 655:76
converse of an innocent m.	KEATS 475:65
corners in one's own m.	HUXL 443:11
corridors into the m.	DOUG 295:5
corrupt and befool the m.	BAXT 69:94
couldn't make up my m.	PLATH 681:37
country of the m.	WHITE 935:52
creating in the m. a map	SPEN 837:3
crooked my m. to answer	SHAK 760:20
culture of the m.	MORE 618:20
cutty sarks run in your m.	BURNS 179:31
debasement of the human m.	CHAN 213:87
depths of his own oceanic m.	COLE 236:53
dictates of his godlike m.	OTWAY 656:94
does not m. his belly	JOHN 461:4
don't m. not being President	KENN 480:96
dribble your m. out	ELIOT 315:23
elegance is a state of m.	CASS 207:72
employs the whole m.	QUEN 702:8
enter into the m.…not myself	WELTY 930:46
exist out of the m.	BERK 84:31
extreme thoughts…in his m.	DIDE 285:78
face should bear a wicked m.	SHAK 763:98
facility for m. games	COUP 248:33
fair terms and a villain's m.	SHAK 769:87
Farewell the tranquil m.	SHAK 790:27
favours only the prepared m.	PAST 668:1
features gets on your m.	LEAC 515:15
feeble powers of my m.	SIDN 820:35
fit of absence of m.	SEEL 756:2
fog of the good man's m.	BROW 167:26
frailty of the m.	CONG 241:70
frame of m.	FRIE 351:76
Frame your m. to mirth	SHAK 761:57
freedom of my m.	MILT 599:78
gateways of the m.	SASS 746:2
gentle m. by gentle deeds	SPEN 839:58
gird up the loins of your m.	BIBLE 130:64
God…destroys their m.	DRYD 303:18
greatest good of the m.	SPIN 841:79
greatness of m.	MARC 570:59
green sickness of the m.	CLEV 230:94
gymnasium of the m.	LENIN 521:42
hand…cutting edge of the m.	BRON 160:51
has a vulgar m.	LEWIS 526:44
having an open m.	PRAT 694:63
having it affect his m.	HOOV 427:53
heart and m. of America	BARZ 67:40
His m. moves	YEATS 967:37
hold the military m.	TUCH 901:10
hold the m. in place	MILL 593:40
homeland of the m.	NEW 634:2
If I am out of my m.	BELL 77:78
If the ocean was pure m.	PRAT 694:66
ignis fatuus in the m.	ROCH 719:11
image in her m.	DRYD 302:7
impotence of m.	MILT 607:83
improper m. is a perpetual feast	SMITH 829:15
index of a feeling m.	CRAB 252:47
Indian, whose untutored m.	POPE 687:75
infirmity of noble m.	MILT 599:86
in one's m. a…map	ORWE 654:55
Intense irradiation of a m.	SHEL 814:3
interwoven with the highest m.	AGAS 9:87
In youth open your m.	ANON 21:58
Ithaka always in your m.	CAVA 210:17
Jealousy…tyrant of the m.!	DRYD 303:27
Keep violence in the m.	ALDI 12:50
known by the human m.	PAGE 659:16
know the m. of a woman	LAWR 513:70
know the m. of God	HAWK 401:88
lack of a whole m.	MUIR 623:13
land and the m.	NGU 636:66
leaves by m.'s imprint	SHAK 801:65
Let this m. be in you	BIBLE 128:97
liberation of both body and m.	BANN 62:34
light of my m.	CRUZ 256:40
lingers in the m.	LARO 510:6
Little subconscious m.	ONEI 651:73
live in the m., in ideas	MILL 593:55
long in your m.	HOLM 424:72
Love looks…with the m.	SHAK 767:19
made up my m.	LLOY 532:70
maintain a quiet m.	DYER 309:49
makes the m. very free	ELIOT 315:33
Make up your m. dearheart	OLIV 649:37
man but changed his m.	POPE 687:93
mannish manner of m.	CARY 207:62
man o'independent m.	SMITH 831:64
man's unconquerable m.	WORD 960:16
masterpiece of art…in the m.	EMER 324:66
measure what the m.	MILT 605:28
might…be said to possess a m.	ELLI 323:35
m. against speculation	RUSS 734:23
m. and genius	STEN 847:2
m. be afterwards applied	THEO 882:79
m. By owing owes not	MILT 604:91
m. can make Substance	BYRON 189:82
m. can weave itself	LOWE 539:12
m. charged with an eager purpose	ELIOT 315:32
m. doth serve for all	DYER 309:48
m.…fixed on the horizon	EINS 313:76
m. for ever Voyaging	WORD 958:82
m. full of ghosts	MANS 567:95
m. fully develops its faculties	STAEL 841:93
m. has a thousand eyes	BOUR 153:94
m.…in a rapt contemplation	ELIOT 320:53
m. is actually employed	JOHN 462:35
m. is a museum	RAINE 705:41
m. is bent to holiness	SHAK 759:84
m. is clouded	TENN 878:87
m. is its own place	MILT 602:44
m. is maturing late	NASH 631:76
m. is…more self-reliant	LIVI 532:55
m. is not a bed	AGATE 9:89
m. is pure machinery	GINS 372:6
m. is ta'en up wi'	NAIR 629:32
m. is the least of possessions	WHITE 935:54
m. is the true self	CICE 227:36
m. makes us	GRIL 388:69
m. may loose its force	BYRON 188:64
m. may rest on the intuition	BACON 54:57
m. o'er all the world	MILT 607:77
m. off everything like golf	ROGE 723:87
m. of large general powers	JOHN 463:71
m. of man	MARL 573:22
m. of man	WORD 956:55
m. of Ronald Reagan	NOON 640:44
m. or body grieved	CAMP 195:77
m. or body to prefer	POPE 687:80
m. religiously affected	HOOK 427:41
m.'s construction in the face	SHAK 796:12
m. shuttles and reminds	ROTH 727:75
m. skating circles	FROST 353:24
m. that has seen, and suffered	CARL 199:74
m. that went into	GLAS 374:44
m. to me a kingdom is	DYER 309:47
m. to prance	JOHN 461:17
m. was less difficult to develop	AUST 45:54
m. was like a many-legged, wingless insect	UPDI 906:39
m. was once the true	MARV 577:99
m. was too wide for a professor	MENC 586:89
m. watches itself	CAMUS 195:80
m. with all your toys	MILT 597:49
m. with arts improve	DONNE 291:27
minister to a m. diseased	SHAK 798:70
mirrored themselves in my m.	ELIOT 315:20
miserable state of m.	BACON 52:1
most personal state of m.	FEIN 332:57
move a woman's m.	SHAK 759:66
Music affects the human m.	KHOM 485:89
necessary to the human m.	REES 710:38

Mirabeau

Entry	Ref
never brought to m.?	BURNS 178:5
noble m. is here o'erthrown!	SHAK 783:16
no blemish but the m.	SHAK 786:21
noblest frailty of the m.	DRYD 299:12
no grayness in the m.	GUNT 390:97
non-space of the m.	GIBS 367:15
no passion in the m. of man	BACON 50:58
not astound The virtuous m.	MILT 598:69
not be sound…in body or m.	LLOY 532:69
nothing unbends the m. like them	GAY 362:20
not in my perfect m.	SHAK 793:31
not m. its being buried	HOPK 429:93
not yet of Percy's m.	SHAK 771:44
of a m.…that they cannot help	SHAK 791:60
Of any good m.	JONS 467:76
Of my own m.	THOM 886:81
one-dimensional m.	RUSS 735:40
One man that has a m.	SHAW 810:21
O the m., m. has mountains	HOPK 429:91
our better m.	ARNO 35:23
our rightful m.	WHIT 938:24
out of his m.	SHAR 806:78
padlock—on her m.	PRIOR 695:1
peace of m.	SMITH 827:74
pendulum of the m.	JUNG 471:46
perversity of the human m.	TROL 898:39
philosophy inclineth Man's m.	BACON 51:79
plastic state of m.	CARRA 202:58
pleasure in the exercise of the m.	BARZ 67:37
poet represents the m.	STEV 850:95
poet's m. is perfectly equipped	ELIOT 317:94
pollen from one to another m.	LOWE 539:10
pray to have a sound m.	JUVE 471:58
presence of m.	LIVI 532:55
prodigious quantity of m.	TWAIN 901:31
product of the free m.	ORWE 653:30
proud m., a crafty wit	KNOX 495:15
putting the m. to sleep	SLOAN 825:54
Put your brilliant m. to work	ONAS 650:49
raise and erect the m.	BACON 49:27
Reading is to the m.	STEE 844:45
reconstruction of the m.	RICH 713:99
refresh the m. of man	SHAK 762:68
relationship between the m.	HEPW 412:28
robs the m. of all its powers	BURKE 175:6
sacred city of the m.	CAMP 194:54
Sa dois the m. that is ay diligent	HENR 411:19
same m. animating them all	BROWN 164:33
satisfied with her lover's m.	TROL 897:30
say she has a masculine m.	FULL 355:67
scientific attitude of the m.	RUSS 734:29
scientific m. does not	LEVI 526:37
scorn…our m.	BAST 67:51
Scots accent of the m.	STEV 853:76
see in my m. a noble	MILT 601:20
shackled the enquiring m.	HOPE 427:56
short neck denotes a good m.	SPARK 836:66
sorcerers that change the m.	SHAK 762:91
sorrow which enhances…the m.	PROU 698:58
sound m. in a sound body	LOCKE 534:92
spirit…of a sound m.	BIBLE 129:25
stamp no character on the m.	JEFF 454:29
state of m. from which it springs	DURK 308:29
steal Fire from the m.	BYRON 187:47
stock my m.	CRUZ 256:38
suffered to relax his m.	MACA 545:43
suppose the m. to be	LOCKE 533:89
sweetest music to a woeful m.	SIDN 820:42
thanks to his m.	REDT 709:25
That m. and soul	TENN 873:57
The m. continues free	PENF 673:79
The m. is a mill	MAMET 564:44
The poem in the m.	THOM 886:75
the poet's m.	TENN 869:73
there grows in the m.	WILL 946:23
thinks his m.…more clever	MAIM 561:70
To the noble m.	SHAK 783:8
touching a new m.	STEV 850:77
tumours of a troubl'd m.	MILT 607:88
two kinds of m.	PASC 666:62
Two things fill the m.	KANT 473:26
unbent her m. afterwards	LAMB 505:98
undermine the simple m.	BIBLE 112:76
universal frame is without a m.	BACON 51:78
Unless…new m.	WILL 946:19
unseemly exposure of m.	HAZL 404:57
until reeled the m.	GIBBS 367:12

Entry	Ref
urge the m. to aftersight	
Venice will linger in your m.	
very unusual m.	
warriors of Eternal M.	
whatever in my m.	
white m.	
Whitman's m. to be more like	
whose m. is stayed on thee	
with a quiet m.	
With equal m.	
within thy m. rehearse	
words echo…in your m.	
work my m.	
work of body or m.	
you put me in m. on't	
Your m. now, moldering	
minded m. what they were about	
minds add to our m.	
begin in the m. of men	
best m. in the world	
born in the m. of a few	
Cambridge…comfortable m.	
change m.	
change the m. of others	
cloaks for untidy m.	
corrupting the m. of the young	
Danger, the spur of all great m.	
discrimination of our m.	
dusty recesses of their m.	
except in the m. of men	
extinguished in individual m.	
fairly developed m.	
far from their nasty little m.	
Fearless m. climb	
free their m. of…rubbish	
from the closed m. of the many	
great empire and little m.	
great m. in the commonplace	
happiest and best m.	
have aspiring m.	
Hearts and m.	
hobgoblin of little m.	
hunger of ambitious m.	
image…in the m. of others	
infirm and baby m.	
in the m. of God	
keep your hearts and m.	
keep your hearts and m.	
Little things affect little m.	
live…close to great m.	
marriage of true m.	
maximum elasticity for our m.	
m., and muses on	
m. and soules of men	
m. grown crooked	
m. innocent and quiet	
M. like beds	
m. of American women	
m. so impatient	
M. still passion-ridden	
M. that are great	
m. that are to our m.	
mislead their weak m.	
model the m. of his subjects	
most thoughtful m.	
Nothing issues from their m.	
nurse and tutor of eccentric m.	
one thing on their m.	
operations of our own m.	
paid to have dirty m.	
power to cloud men's m.	
praise effect in mighty m.	
Publishers can get their m.	
question…potential parents' m.	
Reason enslaves all whose m.	
reflection of your own m.	
Regimented m. cannot grasp	
self-pleasing and humorous m.	
strange faces, other m.	
such relationships as our m.	
Superstition…religion of feeble m.	
take them with our m.	
tenderness of patient m.	
thousand m. the same thought	
virtue of weak m.	
want of congenial m.	
whose m. he learned of	

Ref
ELIOT 321:86
MORR 620:46
WHIT 936:64
RUSS 735:42
MORR 620:52
GIOV 372:20
HOPK 429:98
BIBLE 108:68
BOOK 147:55
DRYD 304:54
TENN 872:25
ELIOT 319:37
SHAK 800:45
MILT 604:5
SHER 818:3
RICH 713:95
STER 847:20
CRUZ 256:39
UNES 905:8
ACHE 3:56
KISS 493:88
CUMM 257:53
KING 486:19
SAFI 737:18
MOND 612:96
PLATO 681:42
CHAP 214:21
STEV 851:11
LAWR 514:89
READ 708:96
DURK 308:31
FORS 344:40
DEBU 268:61
SHAK 760:15
DUDEK 305:77
ROBB 716:59
BURKE 175:22
HUBB 434:98
SHEL 816:52
MARL 572:99
ANON 25:53
EMER 324:54
SPEN 839:53
AUDEN 44:12
COWP 251:20
GREE 386:26
BIBLE 128:4
BOOK 147:75
DISR 288:35
BUCH 171:26
SHAK 802:80
BUTT 186:14
MARL 572:2
PRYN 698:62
MUIR 624:19
LOVE 538:82
WILL 946:15
FRIE 350:64
JOHN 459:52
LIND 530:16
JONS 468:84
WELLS 930:19
SAYE 746:10
STEU 849:61
RUSK 732:86
WOOLF 955:18
LAWS 514:19
EVANS 328:69
LOCKE 533:90
TREV 895:12
BAKER 56:8
DRYD 302:78
LECA 518:76
SCHU 750:80
SHAW 808:50
ASTE 39:1
AUNG 45:40
BACON 51:72
TENN 878:84
LEBON 517:55
BURKE 176:46
NEWM 634:42
OWEN 657:26
TOCQ 892:32
DRYD 299:13
MOOD 615:52
HOMER 425:9

Entry	Ref
Women never have young m.	DELA 271:36
writers could live in their own m.	BRAD 155:35
mine m. my own past	MANT 568:23
You go Uruguay…I'll go m.	MARX 578:16
mineral vegetable, animal and m.	GILB 368:39
minerals M. grow, plants grow	LINN 530:33
miners m. poured to war	MACA 546:51
m. sweat their guts out	ORWE 653:10
Minerva brains of M.	BARR 65:98
mine-sweeper captain of a m.-s.	CATTO 209:4
mineworkers Union of M.	MACM 556:73
mingle m. it with the love of others	SHAW 806:90
m. our bloods together	SHAK 798:83
miniature life in m.	ONEI 651:64
mining snakeskin-titles of m.-claims	BENET 79:23
minion Curled m.	ARNO 34:96
Mistress m., you	SHAK 766:4
morning's m.	HOPK 428:76
minister As a M.	TAAF 865:1
fair spirit for my m.	BYRON 188:69
first M. in history	HOWE 433:89
give the M. a venal House of Peers	SHER 818:6
King's First M.	CHUR 226:96
M. said it wald dee	YOUNG 968:53
m. the like to you	SHAK 758:62
m. to a mind diseased	SHAK 798:70
old Barnet, the m.'s man	HOGG 422:42
quotes from the…Prime M.	MCFA 551:68
safety of a M.	WALP 919:83
Yes, M.! No, M.!	CROS 256:35
ministerial regular m. majorities	WHIT 934:24
ministering m. angel thou!	SCOTT 752:25
ministers changed my M.	ANNE 19:13
confirmed by the Council of M.	FREUD 350:56
Foreign M. were called	ACHE 2:26
hard on His Majesty's M.	HOBH 420:6
how much my M. talk	THAT 881:67
M. fully design	MACA 545:27
M. of Industry	MAND 565:65
m. of Love	COLE 235:27
m. of the new testament	BIBLE 127:65
M. of thought	SHEL 815:30
m. to consult the public good	SWIFT 862:47
my actions are my M.	CHAR 215:34
permit his M. to serve him	RICH 714:19
ministration gentle m. of science	ARNO 35:23
ministries has made many m.	BAGE 54:67
ministry hireling of the M.	OCON 646:82
Miniver M. loved the Medici	ROBI 718:85
minnows this Triton of the m.?	SHAK 799:96
minor books major or m.	SAND 742:34
minorities m. who…suffer	ELIZ 322:10
we are all m. now	THOR 889:58
minority individual is a m.	ELLI 323:37
member of a m. group	MAIL 560:53
minstrel Ethereal m.!	WORD 961:44
fuller m. in. of	TENN 875:96
M. was infirm and old	SCOTT 752:9
wandering m.	GILB 369:58
minstrel-boy M.-b. to the war	MOORE 618:2
mint helps the m. and the thyme	VERL 911:61
mark of the m.	CHES 221:2
minute both in the same m.	KEATS 476:94
Changes at the Last M.	PALEY 661:50
do something phoney every m.	SALI 740:77
Even in a m.!	SHAK 785:78
fill the unforgiving m.	KIPL 492:63
Let there pass A m.	LOWE 540:17
m. bit of…Feeling	CUMM 257:50
M. by m. they change	YEATS 966:19
m. of darkness	RUSH 732:66
speak more in a m.	SHAK 766:91
sucker born every m.	BARN 64:79
take a m. from the men	CARA 198:35
minutes and m. capons	SHAK 770:27
forty-five m. of…privacy	PARK 664:28
how slowly m. roll	ROCH 720:25
m. hasten to their end	SHAK 801:56
m. how they run	SHAK 760:9
precious m. waste	SHAK 801:65
seem to do it every 10 m.	FULB 355:61
take care of the m.	CHES 219:37
Twenty three and a quarter m.	MITF 610:56
was fifteen m. before	TWAIN 902:62
watched for ten m.	SZIL 865:31
minx This m., of course	SITW 823:95
Mirabeau Under M. Bridge	APOL 29:81

miracle

miracle m. in me	DANI 262:30
m. is not the breaking of…laws	BLOOM 143:66
m., moment by moment	HUXL 442:90
m. of a kind of internal logic	HONE 425:14
m. of rare device	COLE 236:39
m. of the lit bush	THOM 886:77
no greater m.?	MARL 573:20
power of m.	FEUE 334:2
prays for a m.	TURG 901:19
sort of walking m.	PLATH 681:31
therein works a m. in nature	SHAK 770:4
to be rich…it's a m.	CONN 242:81
unless this m. have might	SHAK 801:57
wondrous m. did Love devise	DAVI 264:74
miracles civilization works its m.	TOCQ 892:27
m. are ceased	COWL 250:72
one believes, then m. occur	MILL 594:76
we…are little m. of self-reference	HOFS 422:36
miraculous m. becomes the norm	MILL 594:65
reduce the m. to the mundane	DIDI 286:81
mirages m. are… miracles	HOFS 422:36
Miranda Admired M.!	SHAK 804:22
mire Sow returns to her M.	KIPL 493:79
The fury and the m.	YEATS 967:31
wallowing in the m.	BIBLE 130:74
mirror Art is…a m.	PIER 677:70
as in a m., we perceive	MARL 572:2
bevelled edge of a sunlit m.	ABSE 1:8
Cyberspace is the funhouse m.	STER 847:16
each a m. of the other	POPE 686:60
Each creature…a m.	ALAN 10:15
Falklands held a m. up.	RABAN 703:1
From m. after m.	YEATS 967:30
gilt-framed drawing room m.	ROCK 721:39
Hold…the m. up to nature	SHAK 783:19
like a m. which copies	LEON 523:79
live and sleep in front of a m.	BAUD 69:82
m. cracked from side	TENN 870:85
m. of and a connection	MILL 595:99
m. of the soul	QUIN 702:19
moving through a m. clear	TENN 869:81
news is not a m.	LIPP 531:40
not have a rear-view m.	MURR 627:82
oppose a m.	JONS 466:43
Photography was conceived as a m.	STEI 845:58
prince is like a m.	CHAR 215:37
scripture…like a m.	GREG 387:50
Self-portrait in a Convex M.	ASHB 37:57
world is the m.	MILL 593:57
mirrored m. themselves in my mind	ELIOT 315:20
mirrors Better m. than yours	JEFF 453:17
blaming m. for being untrue	LAFO 503:49
cell whose walls are m.	ONEI 650:60
live without m.	ATWO 41:42
M. are the perfect lovers	ATWO 41:40
m. of the gigantic shadows	SHEL 816:53
m. of the sea	FLEC 340:38
sexual pull towards m.	COND 240:15
women have walked past m.	ALLEN 13:77
mirth all resort of m.	MILT 598:54
commended m.	BIBLE 106:25
earth must borrow its m.	WILC 939:43
Frame your mind to m.	SHAK 761:57
he is all m.	SHAK 774:42
Him serve with m.	SCOT 755:88
lost all my m.	SHAK 782:88
m. and fun grew fast	BURNS 179:29
M. cannot move	SHAK 763:25
m. hath present laughter	SHAK 785:93
M. is short and transient	ADDI 6:34
m. of the billow	CALL 193:32
m. that has no bitter springs	KIPL 492:58
m., What doeth it?	BIBLE 105:13
no time for m. and laughter	ADE 7:59
Our m. the music	RALE 705:45
red with m.	SHAK 799:17
Religion does not banish m.	WALT 920:96
so much wit, and m.	ADDI 6:42
sunburnt m.!	KEATS 478:42
swim in m., and fancy	MILT 606:55
this night wi' m. and glee	SKIN 825:50
With m. and laughter	SHAK 768:69
mirthless heartless, m., maniacal	THUR 891:96
misanthropy compounded of m.	MACA 545:34
Racism…a form of m.?	BROD 160:37
misbehave Even if I m.	ANON 27:17
miscarriage disgraced by m.	JOHN 460:67

success and m.	JOHN 460:69
mischief All punishment is m.	BENT 82:89
at the bottom of a' the m.	SCOTT 753:57
Comet, that bodes M.	MAKIN 561:80
evil…working visible m.	CHUR 224:51
if any m. follow	BIBLE 94:67
if m. befall him	BIBLE 93:44
mean m. and break a foul gap	SHAK 800:24
minds…gratified with m.	COWP 251:20
mourn a m. that is past	SHAK 789:98
seem like a bit of m.	THUR 891:94
mischiefs intolerable M.	PRYN 698:62
misconception prejudices, m.	LLOY 533:78
misconduct prodigality and m.	SMITH 827:83
misdeed planning any m.	JUVE 471:59
miserable arise and make them m.	HUXL 442:81
Heaven Knows I'm M. Now	MORR 621:17
If life is m.	LABR 502:20
If you are m.	LAUT 512:28
Life becomes m.	BAUD 68:63
life of the artist sufficiently m.	BELL 75:35
live a m. life	BEET 74:2
making others m.	LABR 502:26
man knows that he is m.	PASC 667:89
m. beyond all living things	SHEL 812:48
m. have no other medicine	SHAK 787:63
m. Irish Catholic childhood	MCCO 548:9
m. people on earth	CELI 211:39
m. sinners	BOOK 146:46
m. state of mind	BACON 52:1
moral once we are m.	PROU 698:43
of all men most m.	BIBLE 127:56
one thing is certain too, I'm m.	MACI 553:98
secret of being m.	SHAW 810:2
she is even more m.	FARA 330:18
through life absolutely m.	THOR 889:55
wrong decision can make me very m.	DENN 273:73
miseries ambitions…on the m.	CONR 244:46
bound in shallows and in m.	SHAK 778:48
m. of the world	KEATS 476:98
misery affluent m.	GARD 360:71
Amid…the m. of nations	PITT 680:12
annual expenditure…result m.	DICK 280:43
can only mean a common m.	COOP 246:85
departure is taken for m.	BIBLE 112:74
Friends love m.	JONG 466:37
greatest m. is a battle	WELL 929:5
heart, all mad with m.	SHAK 760:26
hopeless m. and toil	STOWE 856:28
Man hands on m.	LARK 510:90
Man…is full of m.	BOOK 148:98
mine affliction and my m.	BIBLE 110:25
M. acquaints a man	SHAK 804:20
m. From this day	MILT 606:63
m. of being it	DRAB 298:80
m. of us, that are born great	WEBS 927:47
m. peculiar to the young	LESS 523:92
moral restraint, vice and m.	MALT 563:20
nothing but pure m.	JOHN 464:77
Oppressed…with m.	CRAB 252:43
pain is perfect m.	MILT 605:24
perfect in their m.	MILT 598:63
poverty, vice, and m.	SUMN 859:81
privileges of m.	DONO 293:82
purchased by the black man's m.	DOUG 296:24
supreme In m.	MILT 604:93
when one is in m.	DANTE 262:38
Who finds himself, loses his m.	ARNO 34:78
misfits m. and precocious children	MANK 566:75
strangest collection of m.	REAG 708:8
misfortune m. extinguishes	BALZ 60:95
m. of an old man	CARY 207:63
m. of our best friends	LARO 510:1
m. to ourselves	BIER 134:68
m. to see all his plans	JOSE 469:8
m.…to be born a woman	EDGE 311:41
regarded as a m.	WILDE 941:2
sour m.'s book	SHAK 766:13
misfortunes boils and many other M.	FLEM 340:44
heaped with so huge m.	SPEN 838:26
history is…crimes and m.	VOLT 914:39
laugh at the m. of others	HUMP 439:12
m. more bitter	BACON 51:69
strong enough to bear the m.	LARO 510:3
talks of his m.	JOHN 464:78
misgivings Blank m.	WORD 960:10
mishap know it well, your m.	HEINE 407:17

mislead m. their weak minds	SAYE 746:10
m. the public	ASQU 38:86
misleading generate m. thoughts	SPEN 836:88
m. guide to current affairs	KEYN 484:73
misnomer ever was a m.	TELL 869:60
This town's a m.	QUIL 702:16
mispronounce men m. it	MORL 619:37
misquote enough of learning to m.	BYRON 187:25
misrepresentation degree of m.	ELIOT 315:14
power of steady m.	DARW 263:54
way to escape m.	LEAV 517:53
misrepresented Science…is m.	GOUR 380:79
miss could not m. 'em	SHAK 797:32
I m. you	HUGO 437:60
little m.	HUME 438:3
missed A m. life, a m. love!	HEINE 407:17
sure she'd not be m.	GILB 369:61
who never would be m.	GILB 369:60
missiles bombs and m. lie…buried	RAND 706:58
missing M. so much and so much?	CORN 247:3
years of m. each other	RICH 713:6
you start m. everyone	SALI 740:82
mission claim the m. workers	RUNY 732:62
Complete the m.	ANON 27:20
m. each time he went up	HELL 407:26
m. of science will be completed	PEAR 671:56
never have a m.	DICK 281:71
What'er ere is m.	WORD 957:72
missionary I would eat a m.	WILB 939:33
more of a m. than a politician	CART 206:51
Mississippi into M. Bay	KIPL 493:73
missy bit of flirtation with m.	SPEKE 836:82
mist clearing a m.	THOM 883:1
Faustus like a foggy m.	MARL 574:31
Mantled in m.	AUDEN 43:1
m. and hum	ARNO 34:99
m. of time	THAT 881:53
m. on the sea's face	MASE 580:50
rank m. they draw	MILT 599:89
this fair luminous m.	COLE 235:31
mistake Among all forms of m.	ELIOT 316:47
Anything you make a m. about	BEVIN 90:69
Cambodia was not a m.	SHAW 811:39
Every great m. has a halfway	BUCK 172:35
every time you make a m.	PLAN 680:26
it's a m. not to	JAMES 451:51
life would be a m.	NIET 639:16
make a m.	STEV 849:63
Many a sweet m. doth lie	TRAH 895:81
m. to confound strangeness	DOYLE 296:41
m. to theorize before…evidence	DOYLE 296:39
Murder is always a m.	WILDE 941:72
never made a m.	SMIL 827:72
never made a m. in grammar	SAND 742:24
never make the same m.	COPE 246:93
see the m. you've made	ISHI 448:74
shall be no m.	WELL 929:14
under a m.	SWIFT 863:67
Worst damnfool m.	GARN 360:77
worst m. I made	POUND 692:30
Your best teacher is your last m.	NADER 629:27
mistaken M. Identity is to Drama	ABSE 1:7
M. in its assumptions	REGAN 710:42
must needs be m.	SWIFT 862:41
not likely that everybody is m.	DESC 274:93
possible you may be m.	CROM 255:20
thou wilt not often be m.	PENN 673:82
mistakenly to be…m. understood	WINT 950:13
mistakes America makes…m.	CUMM 258:60
causes so many m.	HELL 408:44
everyone makes some m.	TINT 892:24
genius makes no m.	JOYCE 470:27
knows some of the worst m.	HEIS 407:24
learn from our m.	POPP 689:63
learn from previous m.	MURP 627:77
M. are a fact of life	GIOV 372:16
name everyone gives to their m.	WILDE 941:81
not see our own m.	TELL 869:66
physician can bury his m.	WRIG 962:67
result of m. which arrested	MILL 595:96
the man who makes no m.	PHEL 676:48
those who do nothing…make no m.	CONR 243:24
to make m.	THAT 881:54
too many wrong m.	BERRA 87:90
whatever m. it…may condone	WEBB 925:10
mister-ectomy M.-e.…solution	DALY 261:21
mistier and round him, m.	THOM 885:52

money

mistress Art is a jealous m.	EMER 325:87
become a man's friend...next a m.	CHEK 218:17
certain m. of language	JONS 468:95
finding a husband for one's m.	COOP 246:90
Fortune...has made a m.	DRYD 301:59
good handmaid, but the worst m.	BACON 50:49
good understanding with a new m.	ETHE 327:44
have no beautiful m.	BELL 76:46
Maiden, and m.	SWIN 863:81
make me m. to the man	POPE 686:48
man can never elevate his m.	BALZ 60:89
m. is nude	KILP 486:11
M., know yourself	SHAK 779:2
m....little country retreat	WYCH 964:94
m. of every house	MILL 592:16
m. of half an island	SIXT 824:26
m. of true melancholy	SHAK 795:75
m. when she walks	SHAK 802:83
Music is my m.	ELLI 322:24
Nature...virtuous m.	BEHN 75:24
never have a m. as beautiful	ARLT 32:35
No casual m.	TENN 874:82
O m. mine	SHAK 785:92
Out of the crowd a m.	SHEL 815:44
Power is my m.	NAPO 630:48
proved but a mean m.	JONS 468:89
smiling m. to many	MORSE 621:64
teeming m.	POPE 688:10
mistresses Listening...m. offer	WYLIE 964:10
M. are like books	WYCH 964:97
my little m.	RIMB 715:43
Wives are young men's m.	BACON 53:75
mistrusted m. by those who pay	GOLD 376:83
mists m. of evening lie	BETJ 88:27
misunderestimate new word for our press corps: m.	BUSH 182:13
misunderstanding m. by marketers	GITL 373:31
misunderstood being m.	COCT 233:85
have m. what I said	GREE 386:34
neglected and m.	RABAN 703:1
so universally m.	MADO 558:21
To be great is to be m.	EMER 324:55
misused How often m. words	SPEN 836:88
Mithridates half M.	MACA 546:53
M., he died old	HOUS 432:60
Mitterrand M. has 100 lovers	GORB 378:50
Mitty M., the undefeated	THUR 890:76
mixture creative m. of both games	SHUL 819:85
m. of evil in everything	COWP 251:9
m. of fact and truths	FRAME 346:76
revolting m.	STEV 851:29
mixtures study of the m.	THEO 882:79
moan Listen to them m.	RAMS 706:52
twa corbies making a m.	BALL 59:57
moaning m. on ilka green loaning	ELLI 322:25
moat m. defensive to a house	SHAK 764:40
mob amphibious ill-born m.	DEFOE 269:70
best...to do what the m. do	DICK 277:49
bibblebabbling m.	LEWIS 526:53
despise the uninitiated m.	HORA 430:9
governed by the m.	GREN 388:59
m. of scribbling women	HAWT 402:14
nose of a m. is...imagination	POE 683:92
presence of such a m.	STAN 842:11
whisper to a m.	HUNT 439:20
mobile M....and more affable	DAVIS 265:94
mobility contributes...to our m.	STEV 851:11
mobilized m. the English language	KENN 481:15
mock m. the air with idle state	GRAY 385:79
m. the good housewife Fortune	SHAK 778:58
m. the midnight bell	SHAK 794:72
m. the riddled corpses	SASS 745:80
m. the time	SHAK 796:25
Pray do not m.	SHAK 793:31
sit in the clouds and m. us	SHAK 772:79
to muddy or m.	PALEY 661:53
mocked God is not m.	BIBLE 127:82
smiles...As if he m. himself	SHAK 776:13
mockery In monumental m.	SHAK 787:58
Trial...will be...a m.	DENM 273:72
mockingbird sin to kill a m.	LEE 518:87
Moctezuma poetry in...great M.	DARIO 262:44
mode any m. of expression	POUND 691:97
any m. to abolish war	PAINE 660:34
broke up their m. of living	SHER 816:69
m. of interestedness	UPDI 907:29
m. of talking	JOHN 464:89

m. of their times	DAY 267:27
model 1910 m. has a string	LEAC 515:6
draw anything in the m. line	BRON 161:37
House of Lords is a m.	FIELD 335:15
m. for the New Woman	WARN 921:10
m. of all the catastrophes	SONT 834:21
m. our political systems	HAMI 394:48
m. the minds of his subjects	STEU 849:61
m. to thy inward greatness	SHAK 775:65
not the M. boy	TWAIN 902:40
pattern on which to m. themselves	CHAR 215:37
small m. of the barren e.	SHAK 764:51
take as your m.	ALBE 11:32
very m.	GILB 368:39
without a m....I...work	ARET 31:11
modelling go after the m. like a fly	INGR 446:43
models Children...have no other m.	BALD 57:17
m. destroy genius	HAZL 404:59
not with women but with m.	BUSH 184:53
writers...find their own m.	COWL 250:80
moderate be in nothing so m.	JEFF 453:11
uncompromising but m.	WELL 929:9
under a m. weight of prose	LAND 507:36
moderation astonished...own m.!	CLIVE 231:40
easier than perfect m.	AUGU 44:30
I am still for m.	ANNE 19:13
Let your m. be known	BIBLE 128:4
m. in m.	ANGE 19:7
m. in the pursuit of justice	GOLD 377:20
m. in war is imbecility	MACA 545:38
playful m. in politics	HUNT 439:20
modern being too m.	WILDE 942:11
cultured m. man	RODC 722:43
destructive influence of...m. culture	BENE 79:17
m. art tends towards	BAUD 69:78
m. Churchman	WAUGH 923:64
m. craze for regulating	WAVE 925:2
m. democracy is a tyranny	MAIL 560:44
m. era is dramatic	HUGO 436:52
M. European culture	SUN 860:95
m. hardback writer	MORT 621:68
m. life would lack	WILB 939:38
m. Major-General	GILB 368:39
M. poets mix	GOET 375:66
m. science and technology	GALB 357:20
muse of m. literature	SONT 834:14
My music is not m.	SCHO 748:49
not be either m. nor art	ROSE 725:28
our m. technic shows	OPPE 652:88
point of departure...is m. life	WAGN 915:2
Science is to the m.	DISR 287:28
this filthy m. tide	YEATS 967:38
traditional work at a m. pace	BUFO 172:51
triumph of m. science	WAUGH 924:99
waste of m. tenements	THOR 890:51
moderniser Jesus was a m.	BLAIR 138:60
modernity frauds of m.	WAUGH 924:81
modernness Perpetual m.	EMER 325:80
modes of thinking are different	JOHN 464:70
modest M.? My word, no	REED 709:31
modesty charm of all power is m.	ALCO 12:41
maintain a becoming m.	BOUL 152:88
time to cultivate m.	SITW 824:13
modicum of alacrity	RYLE 736:61
modish the more m.	SWIFT 863:69
modus m. of lunar eclipses	POUND 691:98
Mogadishu went to M.	HEMP 410:98
Moghul M. Empire is in our power	CLIVE 231:35
mold work of...curious m.	SPEN 838:30
Mole Diary of Adrian M.	TOWN 894:67
mole like a bastion's m.	SMART 826:65
On her left breast A m.	SHAK 803:91
Well said, old m.	SHAK 781:69
wilt thou go ask the m.?	BLAKE 139:84
molecule not a single m. of my body	DIDE 285:69
molecules preserve the selfish m.	DAWK 266:15
molestation injury and m.	MILL 591:2
Molière advances...since M.	PROU 698:46
the French M.	DUVA 308:41
Moloch M....is pure machinery	GINS 372:6
mome m. raths outgrabe	CARR 204:89
moment at the last m.	GUIM 389:88
awful daring of a m.'s surrender	ELIOT 318:11
carefully choose one's m.	BECK 72:50
Consider every m. past	ABU 1:16
dangerous m. in human history	BELL 78:88
Eternity was in that m.	CONG 240:28

Every great mistake has a halfway m.	BUCK 172:35
Every m. dies a man	TENN 872:27
Every m. is a golden one	MILL 594:62
exact m. at which	WELL 929:6
force the m. to its crisis?	ELIOT 316:62
happiest m. of the happy man	SCHO 749:57
Life is but a m.	SCHI 747:29
masters at the m.	SHAW 811:36
m. after death	HAWT 401:99
m. of joy is...harder to get	PO 683:78
m. of my greatness flicker	ELIOT 316:65
m.'s insight	HOLM 424:81
m.'s ornament	WORD 960:19
m. when curiosity becomes a sin	FRAN 348:85
m. white	BURNS 179:25
naked m. in politics	GERG 365:66
No more distressing m.	TUCH 901:11
Not for a m.	WORD 961:29
of no m. to the happiness	JOHN 462:24
one m. in childhood	GREE 385:5
people only die at the last m.	CELI 211:39
present m. that goes by	WILL 945:3
public of the m.	LUCAS 541:56
rejoice for a m.	YUAN 969:67
stands m. by m.	WILD 943:45
state of mind at that particular m.	FEIN 332:57
suspension of disbelief for the m.	COLE 236:44
there is only the unattended M.	ELIOT 320:77
what is seen during a m.	SAND 742:21
world's best m. is a calm hour	ABU 1:13
worry and terror of the m.	MORR 620:51
momentariness delight in m.	GRAV 382:19
moments all m. are key m.	BUEC 172:42
best and happiest m.	SHEL 816:52
bitter m. of life	POWYS 693:62
bright m. illuminate our path	SCHO 748:52
brilliant frozen m.	LIVE 531:50
designed a bench in a few m.	BELL 76:49
highest quality to your m.	ANON 26:89
m. of vision	BLUN 143:80
pattern Of timeless m.	ELIOT 321:93
pressing present m.	STUA 857:56
quality to your m.	PATER 668:11
such m. really mean	MUNRO 626:53
There are no ordinary m.	MILL 595:5
Wagner has good m.	ROSS 727:67
worst m. into money	DONL 290:11
Mona Lisa lotta cats copy the M. L.	ARMS 33:50
M. L. of the vegetable world	HUGH 435:26
M. L. painted by a child?	GRIS 389:75
M. L. seem an open book	LEAC 515:15
Monan danced the...on M.'s rill	SCOTT 752:28
monarch beneath a m.'s feet	BURNS 178:96
invades authors like a m.	DRYD 300:21
Israel's m.	DRYD 301:64
merry M., scandalous and poor	ROCH 719:7
modern constitutional M. exists no longer by right	HOGG 423:45
m. of all I survey	COWP 250:96
m. of the sea	GILB 368:33
self-worship of the m.	MILL 592:17
With a m.'s voice	SHAK 777:34
With ravished ears The m. hears	DRYD 303:29
monarchies All the four M.	DONNE 293:73
m. end by poverty	MONT 615:42
monarchs m. to choose favourites	SWIFT 862:47
when fate summons, m. must obey	DRYD 300:42
monarchy discontented under m.	HOBB 420:3
Film Industry is the American M.	MAMET 564:39
Habsburg m.	TAAF 865:1
m....intelligible government	BAGE 54:73
Than purest m.	MONT 615:49
monasteries some join m.	WEBB 925:8
monastery discipline of a m.	AELR 8:74
Protective M. of Aesthetic Truth	MAMET 564:34
Monday Arriving M.	SWAN 861:8
fell a-bleeding on Black M.	SHAK 769:78
left Calais on M.	MACA 545:27
worked M....fired Wednesday	ALGR 13:69
Monet M. is only an eye	CEZA 212:54
money America had plenty of m.	BEHR 75:28
America is so m.-hungry	TYSON 904:10
Aphorisms...more for your...m.	DUDEK 305:72
art...pursued with a view to m.	BUTL 186:3
ask for my m. back	HUXL 442:76
athlete cannot run with m.	ZATO 969:2
authors...talking about m.	PRIT 696:20

moneybag

Ayatollah's m. to support	NORTH 641:63	m. you save	LARK 510:93	that efficient m.	PUZO 701:6
Beauty…became m.	WOLF 952:62	most m. on a style	MING 608:8	**monosyllabic** nothing so m.	FRY 353:34
blame someone…for making m.	ORWE 654:43	Much discussion of m.	GALB 357:24	**monotonous** becomes m.	TROL 897:30
borrowed time, borrowed m.	CALL 192:27	never been able to dominate m.	JOHN 457:7	m., and wearisome	THOR 889:51
borrow m. from people	WILL 944:63	nexus of all love and m. and power	DIDI 286:81	**monotony** articulate m.	STEP 847:11
borrow m. off them	TWAIN 903:93	nice feet and plenty of m.	ASHF 38:77	certain m. of genius	HAZL 403:30
borrow the m.	WARD 920:1	no m. in poetry	GRAV 383:37	eternal m. of passion	FLAU 339:21
Brass M.	ANON 23:96	no m. in your purse	SHAK 778:73	m. of a watery surface	MOORE 616:77
can be young without m.	WILL 945:91	no one shall work for m.	KIPL 490:15	m. of marriage	GIBB 367:11
clever enough to get all that m.	CHES 221:96	nothing…a little m. will not cure	DURA 307:24	m., work or leisure	POMP 684:12
come to applaud their m.	HIRS 419:76	nothing left but m. and power	STAEL 841:95	**Monroe** doctrine of President M.	WILS 949:81
corrupted by m.	GREE 386:7	original purchase m.	SMITH 827:79	making a picture with Marilyn M.	WILD 942:33
cost me much m.	PEPYS 673:86	paper which the masses call m.	ANDR 18:77	Marilyn M. who was blonde	MAIL 560:58
desire to make m.	VAN 908:16	poet can earn much more m.	AUDEN 43:6	United States to the M. Doctrine	ROOS 724:16
divided from…courtesans…by m.	DUMAS 306:91	poisoning…for their insurance m.	DOYLE 296:44	**monsieur** m., for methinks	SHAK 767:40
don't like m., actually	LOUIS 538:78	possession of m.	KIPL 491:27	**monster** art should be a m.	TZARA 904:14
Either your m.	WALK 917:38	power and m. and fine robes	WELD 928:83	capital is become an overgrown m.	SMOL 831:68
enough to get m. from it	LEAC 515:20	power of m. is…male power	DWOR 308:44	Effie M. was a m.	LEE 519:97
except for m.	JOHN 463:49	press…eagerly to pay m.	STEE 844:44	Frankenstein m.	MUGG 623:11
Fame without…m.	COUP 248:39	Prince calls in the good old m.	LAMB 505:93	IS, the whited m.	LOWE 540:18
feeling they've wasted their m.	OLIV 649:42	put your m. in trust	HOLM 424:66	jealousy…the green-eyed m.	SHAK 789:19
for…such sums of m.	SCHAW 747:20	rattle of the m. box	LABO 501:5	make a m. of the multitude	SHAK 799:95
giving m. to the Government	HERB 412:45	ready m.	GRAMM 381:96	many-headed m. of the pit	POPE 688:21
goä wheer m. is!	TENN 878:89	religion of m.	GAUT 361:7	m. that devours everything	BALZ 60:90
God would do if he had the m.	WOOL 956:49	retreated back into their m.	FITZ 338:85	m. was indeed the best	KARL 473:28
greatest possible amount of m.	WEBER 925:12	rub up against m.	RUNY 731:55	m., which the Blatant beast men call	SPEN 839:54
greedy to add m. to m.	BIBLE 112:71	runs into real m.	DIRK 287:7	O thou m. ignorance	SHAK 763:11
happened to be a lot of m.	MERR 589:51	Sex is like m.	UPDI 905:18	the m. there's no gagging	SHER 817:86
hard to be…a lover of m.	WYCH 964:98	share out the little m.	MONT 613:17	this busy m., manunkind	CUMM 258:67
hath no m.	BIBLE 109:96	side with plenty of m.	ANOU 28:69	Vice is a m.	POPE 687:82
haven't got the m., so we've got to think	RUSH 735:53	sixty-three ways to find the m.	RABE 703:7	**monster-breeding** m.-b. breast	POPE 688:33
his private parts, his m.	BUTL 186:10	spent all the m.	JOHN 464:81	**monsters** enable real m.	ROWL 730:25
honey, and plenty of m.	LEAR 516:35	spent some of my own m.	KENN 482:38	m. and devils	LUTH 542:75
hunger for recognition and m.	SELF 756:10	state…master of m.	BEVE 90:64	nocturnal m. that threaten	ROBBE 717:62
if he'd had the m.	KAUF 474:39	take no m. of me	SHAK 800:26	stay out of politics or become m.	GINS 372:11
If m. go before	SHAK 773:5	take the favour over the m.	BALE 57:37	transform Men into M.	FORD 343:8
If thou wilt lend this m.	SHAK 769:86	tells you it is not a m. problem	CLIN 230:2	vile, unlovable, morbid m.	ANON 23:97
If you can…count your m.	GETTY 366:87	the act of marrying for m.	MAIL 560:63	**monstrous** all that is m.	GOLD 375:78
innocently employed…in getting m.	JOHN 462:34	The ascent of m.	FERG 333:79	Ingratitude is m.	SHAK 799:95
In the absence of m.	BALC 56:11	Time is m.	FRAN 348:12	m. with politics	GINS 372:11
It's not about the m.	DOUG 295:20	unlimited m.	CICE 227:32	seem a m. thing	FORD 342:90
leg for any m.	DICK 279:19	voice is full of m.	FITZ 337:84	Two evils, m. either one	RANS 707:70
licence to print m.	THOM 888:11	voter who uses his m.	SAMU 741:1	**Montana** M. skies seemed deeper	MCMU 557:83
little m., but not much	BEAV 71:35	We're in the m.	DUBIN 304:61	**Mont Blanc** M. B. yet gleams	SHEL 812:54
lost m. by underestimating	MENC 586:92	we've got the m. too!	HUNT 439:16	**Monte Testaceo** its own M. T.	CLOU 232:55
love of m. is the root	BIBLE 129:23	We want our m. back	OBAMA 644:40	**Montgomery** gie's a sang, M. cry'd	SKIN 825:50
Make all the m.	SHAK 789:4	What m. is better bestowed	THAC 880:38	Robert M.'s genius	MACA 545:33
makes the current m.	JONS 468:95	what m. will do	PEPYS 674:9	**month** April is the cruellest m.	ELIOT 317:95
make the white people…some m.	DAVIS 265:2	what to do with their m.	BARA 63:42	beginning of a new m. or year	MANN 566:82
making m. at the same time	BENN 81:81	when m. rolled in	HUGH 435:15	hesitates about a m.	STEV 852:34
man's reputashun outlasts his m.	BILL 135:96	when you don't have any m.	DONL 290:8	m. that God designed	KEIL 479:56
marry for m. and comfort	SHAW 809:84	where that m. came from	REAG 708:11	old man in a dry m.	ELIOT 317:82
Men Whose Lives Are M.	OATES 643:8	With the m. I spent	KENN 482:36	one m. you have to live	GILB 369:59
m. and a room of her own	WOOLF 955:26	with the m. of the people	WHIT 934:24	stand to in a m.	SHAK 766:91
M. and gentility	MITF 610:49	women who have the most m.	GILM 371:93	this is the m.	MILT 596:30
m. answereth all things	BIBLE 106:32	worst moments into m.	DONL 290:11	**months** all the m. of human birth	MASE 580:62
m. appears to vary	HUXL 442:99	write for m. or fame	MOORE 617:83	few m. obliterate	BUNT 173:66
m. can't buy me love	LENN 521:48	Yes, they have more m.	HEMI 410:78	first six m.	TRUM 899:76
m. controls opinion	ORWE 653:22	You pays your m.	PUNCH 699:74	for m., for years	ROBBE 716:63
M. couldn't buy friends	MILL 595:2	You talk of art…I think of m.	SHAW 810:26	go for m. on end	ORWE 653:14
m. does not bring happiness	LACL 503:34	**moneybag** Aristocracy of the M.	CARL 201:12	of the m. and stars	SWIN 863:81
M. does not smell	VESP 911:66	**money-bags** dream of m.-b.	SHAK 769:92	seven m. since she is gone	MILL 593:35
m. from the pockets of the people	SMITH 828:91	**money-changers** tables of the m.	BIBLE 118:23	think for m.	EINS 313:77
m. has a power above	BUTL 185:88	**moneys** my m. and my usances	SHAK 769:85	**Monticelso** M.: How!	WEBS 926:30
m. has dissolved more worries	BLEST 142:52	**Mongolia** British Outer M.	BENN 79:29	**Montmorenci** steep Of M.	KEATS 475:66
M. is a comfort	ANON 20:34	**mongrels** continent of energetic m.	FISH 337:63	**Montparnasse** not rest quiet in M.	BENET 79:26
M. is a good soldier	SHAK 773:6	**monitor** sad m. scorning	CALL 193:32	**Montreal** M. Olympics	DRAP 298:89
M. is a kind of poetry	STEV 850:97	**monk** a very political old m.	MURD 626:69	**monument** Builds his m. mockingly	JEFF 453:12
M. is better than poverty	ALLEN 14:94	found in the king a m.	AELR 8:74	built thyself a livelong m.	MILT 597:39
M. is how we keep the score	CHAP 214:13	m. throwing himself	MAP 569:41	like patience on a m.	SHAK 786:2
m. is just…information	WRIS 963:81	**monkey** make a m. of a man	BENC 78:4	live no longer in m.	SHAK 774:57
M. is like muck	BACON 52:95	m.'s mask reveals the m.	BASHO 67:45	m. of English prose	ELIOT 319:35
m. is made	SOROS 834:34	M. with lollipop paws	LEAR 516:33	m. of old Irish hospitality	EDGE 311:17
m. is the standard	MORE 618:19	never look long upon a M.	CONG 241:50	m. sticks like a fishbone	LOWE 540:24
M.…is the true fuller's earth	GAY 362:17	no reason to attack the m.	BEVAN 89:57	m. to the man who did it	APPL 30:90
M. manipulators and speculators	MAMET 564:39	**monkeys** Cats and m.	JAMES 450:37	not trying to make a m.	HARR 399:59
M. never sleeps	DOUG 295:17	gave a million m. typewriters	HART 399:65	only m. left of R.	BELL 76:41
m. on de bob-tail nag	FOST 345:53	**monks** m.…lathy lot of thkunkth	BENT 82:3	only m. the asphalt road	ELIOT 319:32
M.'s a horrid thing	JAMES 450:40	m.…naturally have a weak stomach	BERN 85:62	sonnet is a moment's m.	ROSS 726:55
M. speaks sense	BEHN 74:17	town of m. and bones	COLE 236:50	**monumental** buried in those	
m.…Spend it, spend it	SHAK 773:7	**monogamous** Woman m.	JAMES 452:78	m. arms	WALL 918:58
M.…sweeter than Honey	FRAN 348:11	**monoliths** m. made of granite	MENC 587:15	**monuments** nor the gilded m.	SHAK 801:53
M.…that purchased that manor?	DONNE 293:78	**monomania** m. of accounting	WEIL 928:74	**mood** In vacant or in pensive m.	WORD 960:27
M.…the most important thing	SHAW 806:79	**monopoly** best of all m. profits	HICKS 417:46	life's business…a summer m.	WORD 959:99
M.…was exactly like sex	BALD 57:20	M. is Business	LLOYD 532:64	m. will give us anything	SHAK 778:46
m. was not scarce?	EMER 325:96	M. power must be abused	SIMO 822:81	silent grass-growing m.	MELV 585:72
m. you bet on him	FLAN 338:7	newspaper is…a m.	SCOTT 751:98	that sweet m.	WORD 957:60

moods envy not in any m.	TENN 874:68	slow tyranny of m.	CRANE 253:57	without originality or m. courage	SHAW 807:12
ever...changing m.	VIRG 913:19	the m.-coloured may	SHEL 816:61	**morale** greatest m. builder	DOOL 294:83
moon an affair with the m.	STER 849:53	things smoother than m.	SCOTT 751:2	Low m. and high	MURK 626:72
and the m. was full	TENN 878:81	visit it by the pale m.	SCOTT 752:12	threat to m.	ROBB 716:59
apples of the m.	YEATS 965:10	Watch for me by m.	NOYES 642:71	**moralist** Poor m.!	GRAY 384:59
ask for the m.	ROBI 718:79	while there's m. and music	BERL 84:40	teach the rustic m. to die	GRAY 384:73
beneath a waning m.	COLE 236:37	with a northern m.	SOUT 835:42	**morality** All...about m.	CAMUS 196:1
Beneath the visiting m.	SHAK 795:84	**moonlit** m. cedar what a burst	ARNO 34:84	British public...fits of m.	MACA 545:30
brilliant m.	YEATS 965:6	m. dome	YEATS 967:31	cities for our best m.	AUST 46:66
broad m. rose circling into sight	BYRON 190:9	**moons** Till m. shall wax	WATTS 923:47	Cleopatra's m.	LAUT 512:29
calm...As is the crescent m.	WORD 957:57	**moonshine** m. that are gilded	DRAY 299:1	Conventionality is not m.	BRON 161:65
carry the m. in my pocket?	BROW 168:37	Transcendental m.	CARL 201:42	corruption of medicine by m.	MENC 586:90
cold o' the m.	BROW 169:65	**moon-struck** m.-s. madness	MILT 606:64	Dr Johnson's m.	HAWT 402:18
corners of the M.	MILT 599:80	**Moor** daughter and M.	SHAK 788:85	Goodbye, m.!	HERB 412:43
course of one revolving m.	DRYD 302:83	make the M. thank me	SHAK 789:10	ignorance of m.	PASC 667:87
danced by the light of the m.	LEAR 516:38	M. is of a free...nature	SHAK 789:5	marriage is to m.	TWAIN 903:76
danced the m.	SCOTT 752:28	noble M. whom our	SHAK 790:33	m. and slave m.	NIET 638:13
Daughter of the M.	LONG 535:29	**moor** moonlight over the purple m.	NOYES 642:70	M. is herd instinct	NIET 638:95
dull red image of the m.	WORD 958:86	**moorcocks** hens to m. call	YEATS 966:19	M. is nothing other	THRA 889:59
empty when the m. is full	BUTL 184:69	**Moore** muse of M.	BYRON 189:3	m. of imprisonment	SHAK 787:48
even the m. is frightened	SHER 818:10	trouble with M.	FRY 354:38	M....represents	LEVI 526:30
from the dying m.	TENN 872:37	**moor-hens** long-legged m.-h.	YEATS 966:19	m. touched with emotion	ARNO 36:34
honour from the pale-faced m.	SHAK 771:37	**Moorish** under the M. wall	JOYCE 470:33	M. Weighs heavily	KEATS 475:64
How many miles the m. might	BYRON 189:94	**moors** blows the wind on the m.	STEV 854:87	M. which is based on ideas	LAWR 513:50
hush with the setting m.	TENN 876:26	sunset on m. and windy hills	MASE 580:57	No rule of general m.	SART 745:77
I didn't go to the m.	WILL 945:80	**moose** a m. is a cow drawn by a		periodical fits of m.	MACA 545:30
if the m.'s a balloon	CUMM 257:56	three-year-old	BRYS 170:8	personal and national m.	SHAW 806:79
jumping over the m.	RAMS 706:51	**mop** Grab a m.	OBAMA 644:36	qualities essential for the artist: m.	DIDE 285:75
landing a man on the m.	KENN 481:5	**moping** merryman m. mum	GILB 370:70	serious attack upon m.	ORWE 654:39
lovely m.—she lifted	FREE 350:50	**Moppsikon** M. Floppsikon bear	LEAR 517:45	so-called new m.	SHAW 811:37
Man on the m.	BAKER 56:6	**Mopsa** not in love with M.	SHAK 800:25	such a thing as physical m.	SPEN 836:86
melodious cats under the m.	HUXL 442:75	**moral** afraid of losing your m. sense	STEIN 845:59	sure it is bad m.	SKEL 825:34
m. and stars are set	STEV 853:64	All reform except a m. one	CARL 202:44	true m. has no time for m.	PASC 666:67
m. and the stars	MACC 548:8	building...to point to a m.	CASS 207:74	unawares M. expires	POPE 689:47
m....in her silver shoon	DELA 271:31	contaminated m. environment	HAVEL 401:85	up agen middle-class m.	SHAW 810:98
m. is up	BYRON 188:60	degeneration of his m. being	STEV 852:33	What is m.	WHIT 936:72
m. of moons	DICK 281:68	difficult to stay a m. infection	DICK 282:92	**moralizing** aestheticizing or m.	CABR 191:8
m. on the breast	MOORE 616:62	don't have a m. plan	CRON 256:26	**morally** M., spiritually	MILL 594:63
m. on this cloud sea	SCOTT 751:2	Englishman thinks he is m.	SHAW 807:25	**morals** also true in m.	FONT 342:75
m. or favouring stars	WORD 958:82	Everything's got a m.	CARR 203:74	art and m.	MURD 626:65
m.'s unclouded light	BURNS 178:88	gain m. detachment	VAN 908:12	attempts to describe m.	TROL 898:53
m. under her feet	BIBLE 131:9	great instrument of m. good	SHEL 816:50	food comes first, then m.	BREC 157:89
m. was a ghostly	NOYES 642:70	high m. tests and tasks	ELKIN 322:16	foundation of m.	BENT 82:88
m. was overhead	TENN 869:82	His m. pleases	POPE 688:17	foundation of m., Utility	MILL 591:8
m....which thou hast ordained	BIBLE 99:30	instrument that has a good m. effect	ARIS 32:28	greatest teacher of m.	HOOV 427:52
mortals call the M.	SHEL 813:76	intellect, m. activity	NIGH 639:19	Have you no m., man?	SHAW 810:97
never gazed the m.	SHAK 799:23	into a m. Coventry	PARN 665:46	mask of prevailing m.	BEAU 70:7
new m. hangs	THOM 885:57	judge in the legal and m. sense	DEWEY 276:20	m....blind obedience to words of	
nor the m. by night	BIBLE 103:31	kind of m. eunuch	SHEL 813:88	command	ELLIS 323:30
O more than m.	DONNE 291:35	League...grows in m. courage	MACD 550:51	m. of a baboon	CAPO 197:30
only a paper m.	HARB 396:88	legal and m. responsibility	HAYD 402:23	teach the m. of a whore	JOHN 459:59
on the horns o'th' m.	SHAK 799:89	Let us be m.	DICK 279:13	what m.!	CICE 227:38
O swear not by the m.	SHAK 765:83	live beyond his m. means	TOYN 895:77	**moratorium** m. on literature talk	ROTH 728:95
Part of a m.	FROST 352:92	look both m. and exciting	FERB 332:69	**Mordor** In the Land of M.	TOLK 893:45
project a voyage to the m.	LARD 508:65	lower m. quality	HARDY 397:7	**more** do m. with less	FULL 355:74
Raymond like the Harvest M.	FARJ 330:20	man is strong before he is m.	FAUL 331:38	Is there m. m.	ROCH 719:6
saucer like some full m.	MONRO 612:5	mean by a m. society	THAT 881:51	I think m. is m.	PART 666:57
saw the new m.	BALL 59:70	m. activity which disentangles	POE 683:81	It's very easy to take m. than nothing	CARR 203:72
Scotland kens beneath the m.	FERG 333:86	m. and social progress	MILL 591:94	less is m.	PART 666:57
set foot upon the m.	ANON 25:69	m. character...was full of promise	DICK 279:11	M. is vulgar	SPARK 836:70
shone the wintry m.	KEATS 477:22	m. consciousness of people	MAIL 559:41	M. will mean worse	AMIS 16:34
slow m. climbs	TENN 870:2	m. crusade, or it is nothing	WILS 948:62	Not a Penny m.	ARCH 30:4
sun and m. Were in	MILT 598:72	m. discovery...the object of every tale	CONR 244:42	Please, sir, I want some m.	DICK 278:64
sung to the m.	GILB 370:70	m. effort is required to get rid of it	MACM 556:74	the m. heard	WILD 943:52
sun, m., and stars, brother	BORR 151:69	M. indignation	WELLS 930:31	**mores** O m.	CICE 227:38
sun provides the m.	ANAX 17:65	m. in it will be banished	TWAIN 902:50	**Morgan** M. liked to imagine	BOYD 153:11
the m. and the sun...in silence	THER 882:84	m. is always correct	BART 66:21	**morganatic** m. alliance	HARD 396:91
The M. is a splendid object	MOORE 617:97	m. is what you feel good after	HEMI 409:70	**Moriarty** Ex-Professor M.	DOYLE 297:62
under the sun and m.	GOLD 375:78	m. judgements do not say anything	AYER 48:6	**Morison** Ye are na Mary M.	BURNS 180:49
Unique things about the m.	LUGO 542:62	m. law within	KANT 473:26	**morn** approach of ev'n or m.	MILT 603:75
unmask her beauty to the m.	SHAK 781:47	m. life of man	WILDE 940:64	civil-suited M.	MILT 598:57
wandering m., Riding	MILT 598:53	m. necessity of acting together	MILL 591:92	days at the m.	BROW 167:9
we are the m.	SCHR 749:64	m. of all this	SAYE 746:11	dew of the m.	YEATS 965:9
wind up the sun and m.	BYRON 190:31	m. once we are miserable	PROU 698:43	Each new m.	SHAK 797:6
moonbeam different as a m.	BRON 162:78	m. or a material one	ARNO 35:7	ever-blessed m.	CASW 208:83
m....all the light they wish	COWP 251:12	m. or an immoral book	WILDE 940:62	Fair laughs the m.	GRAY 385:86
moonbeams Carry m. home	BURKE 176:61	m. or physical devastation	WALK 917:40	golden light of m.	HOOD 426:24
moonlight braw bricht m. nicht	MORR 620:54	m. restraint, vice and misery	MALT 563:20	healthy breath of m.	KEATS 477:28
except this m.	THOM 885:54	no one can be perfectly m.	SPEN 836:84	He rose the morrow m.	COLE 235:21
hating m.	STEI 846:84	no such thing as a m. dress	CHUR 224:63	incense-breathing M.	GRAY 384:64
How sweet the m.	SHAK 770:18	not just a m. category	SOLZ 833:6	long before the m.	DICK 283:31
Ill met by m.	SHAK 767:56	physics, chemistry...become m.	DEWEY 276:19	m. not walking	LYLY 543:5
In the faint m.	ELIOT 318:10	picayune compared to the m. effect	DURK 308:27	m. of youth	WORD 961:42
m. and the starlight	LONG 535:28	quality of m. behaviour	HUXL 442:84	new m. she saw not	KEATS 477:12
m. hung upon the lifted oars	MANS 567:5	read a novel...from m.	OCON 647:88	No m.—no noon	HOOD 426:36
m. over the purple moor	NOYES 642:70	shelf life of the m. causes	IGNA 445:14	old Autumn in the misty m.	HOOD 426:18
seen the bush by m.	LAWS 514:97	story with a m.	OHEN 648:20	peeping in at m.	HOOD 426:22

morning

rouse before the m.	TENN 872:27	morrow He rose the m. morn	COLE 235:21	mother another to talk to my m.	SAINT 738:47
When the bedabbled m.	HERR 415:14	no thought for the m.	BIBLE 115:46	artist man and the m. woman	SHAW 807:17
morning all in one m.	DONNE 293:78	say good-night till it be m.	SHAK 766:85	because I had a m.	CAMP 195:77
always three o'clock in the m.	FITZ 338:94	watching for the m.	GOET 375:61	Behold thy m.!	BIBLE 123:61
amid the dews of m.	HOUS 432:73	mortal all m. things doth sway	SPEN 839:60	church for his m.	CYPR 260:8
awoke one m.	BYRON 191:35	beyond a m.'s share	MARV 578:7	dangerous fondness of his m.	LASS 510:12
beauty of the m.	WORD 959:3	creating a m. of a clay of mud	KORAN 497:71	dear M., the Church is cold	BLAKE 140:21
below zero that m.	MOOD 615:53	every m. sin	WILS 947:38	dialogues with my M.'s heart	WORD 958:81
breeze of the m. moves	TENN 876:25	febrile insomnia, m. leaps	MARI 571:76	disclaim her for a m.	GIBB 366:98
caught this m. m.'s minion	HOPK 428:76	gathers all things m.	SWIN 864:96	Don't tell my m.	HERB 412:39
Christian...up early in the m.	LAW 512:37	gentle m., sing again	SHAK 767:36	drop Into thy m.'s lap	MILT 606:68
come in the m.	DAVIS 266:12	grief itself be m.!	SHEL 815:34	fail at m. love	FRID 350:62
cooking breakfast this m.	SCHR 749:67	grows on m. soil	MILT 599:87	faith in M. Church	FITZ 337:75
Early in the m.	HEBER 406:2	Immortal youth to m. maids	LAND 507:29	father, nor a m.	MARG 570:61
eleven in the m.	SHAW 809:74	its m. dress	YEATS 966:26	father or my m.	STER 847:20
eleven o'clock this m.	LLOY 533:75	last disorder m.	GOLD 376:84	For m. will be there	HERB 412:40
first drink on a Sunday m.	MCCU 549:15	m. frailty must subsist	MILT 599:79	for the m.'s sake	COLE 234:6
from eve and m.	HOUS 431:49	m. limitation that set	STEV 852:53	France, m. of arts	BELL 76:43
Full many a glorious m.	SHAK 801:48	m. millions live alone	ARNO 34:81	from his m.'s womb	SHAK 798:77
ful misty m.	CHAU 216:61	m. taste Brought death	MILT 601:29	from our m.'s arms	WINK 950:98
gang to the coals i' the m.	SKIR 825:51	m. thing so to immortalise	SPEN 839:47	Gin was m.'s milk	SHAW 810:98
Getting up in the m.	RABE 704:13	myopia makes all error m.	LOWE 540:33	Good Luck's M.	AESC 9:81
get up in the m.!	NIXON 640:31	presume you're m.	SHIR 819:19	great sweet m.	SWIN 864:5
Good m. to the day	JONS 466:45	purest treasure m. times afford	SHAK 764:32	Greece, m. of arts	MILT 607:79
great m. of the world	SHEL 815:33	raised a m. to the skies	DRYD 303:35	had no m.	GREER 387:41
happy m. Seeing Roo	MILNE 596:23	safe I sing with m. voice	MILT 605:27	Honour thy father and thy m.	BIBLE 94:66
Here of a Sunday m.	HOUS 431:44	Shall m. man be more just	BIBLE 98:96	I'm not M. Teresa	TYSON 904:11
hunt in the m., fish	MARX 579:29	shuffled off this m. coil	SHAK 783:7	kid my best friend's m.	SILV 821:71
If they take you in the m.	BALD 57:24	Surely m. man	SWIFT 861:25	kill my m.	BOYD 154:12
in the m., It will be foul	BIBLE 117:5	tend on m. thoughts	SHAK 796:15	lands are the M.	PETTY 676:46
Late one m.	KAIKO 472:12	To make us m.	MARV 578:10	lie with his m. earth?	SHAK 778:59
laugh of the m.	CALL 193:32	mortality m. has whispered to them	LEVE 525:25	look sharp at the m.	EDGE 312:47
Lucifer, son of the m.!	BIBLE 108:64	Old m., the ruins	BROW 165:73	loveth father or m.	BIBLE 116:73
make us sad next m.	JONS 467:70	smell its own m.	TATE 867:41	marriage with your m.!	SOPH 834:32
m. after	ADE 7:59	mortals Composing m.	AUDEN 43:99	might be your m., your brother	HOCK 421:14
m. after is the first day	MACN 558:8	divinity has provided m.	GERB 364:63	more precious...than your m.	PLATO 681:47
m. again in America	ANON 26:86	greatest good that m. know	ADDI 6:15	M. always told me	RICH 714:14
m. comes to consciousness	ELIOT 317:71	luckiest of m.	AUDEN 44:14	m. and I...so long together	GAY 362:6
m. cup of coffee	HOLM 424:85	m. call the Moon	SHEL 813:76	m. and my brethren!	BIBLE 117:89
M. has broken	FARJ 330:19	M., give thanks and sing	WESL 932:61	M.-Bush that bore you!	LAWS 514:97
m. incense	BARL 63:56	m. name attorneys	MACA 544:20	m. died...I was very young	BLAKE 139:90
M. in the bowl of night	FITZ 337:68	M. that would follow	MILT 599:87	m. died today	CAMUS 196:87
m. it is when love	LEE 519:95	m. their afflictions spell	PHIL 677:54	M. Empire stands splendidly isolated	FOST 345:52
m. light creaks down again	SITW 823:8	m. who ring bells	MANN 566:82	m. Eve, who tasted	LANY 508:53
m. of his creation	HUXL 442:90	Nae harder job to m.	MACD 549:25	m. for her children	BINY 135:99
M. on the silver horns	TENN 873:51	necessary for m. to be worn	EURI 328:59	m. is...a very umble person	DICK 280:44
M.'s at seven	BROW 167:9	not in m. to command success	ADDI 7:45	m. I see in myself	FRID 350:63
m. sees some task	LONG 535:19	novelist is, like all m.	NABO 628:13	M. Knows Best	FERB 332:65
m. shows the day	MILT 607:77	only m., even...superior species	VINER 913:10	m. laid her baby	ALEX 13:63
m. stars sang together	BIBLE 98:14	these unhappy m.	JOHN 460:67	m. lived the latter years	THUR 890:68
Never glad confident m. again!	BROW 167:19	what fools these m. be!	SHAK 767:38	m., m., mak my bed	BALL 58:50
Never m. wore	TENN 873:60	mortar Lies are the m. that bind	WELLS 930:21	m....must be dead	AUST 45:50
new every m.	BIBLE 110:26	without m. laid	SPEN 838:22	m. of all evils	RABE 704:21
New every m. is the love	KEBLE 478:51	mortify to m. a wit	POPE 688:21	M. Of Harlots	BIBLE 132:17
On the same bloody m.	SCOTT 753:40	mosaic between, and wrought M.	MILT 604:8	M. of Mercy	ROBI 718:81
quiet of m.	DUNC 307:9	pictures in rough m.	SCHO 749:59	m. of months	SWIN 863:82
regaled every m.	JOHN 460:81	Moscow Do not march on M.	MONT 615:47	m. of our emotions	KAND 473:16
shadow at m. striding behind	ELIOT 317:96	M....what surge	PUSH 700:88	M. of the Free	BENS 81:84
shining m. face	SHAK 779:81	Moses as I was with M.	BIBLE 95:5	M. of Wales	DAVIS 265:94
shores of m.	ATWO 41:33	law of M. is harsh	MORE 618:14	M. o' mine	FULL 355:79
singing each m. out of each night	CUMM 258:64	Lord spake unto M. face to face	BIBLE 94:72	M., she alas is poor	KIPL 490:95
sons of the m.	HEBER 406:98	M. held up his hand	BIBLE 94:65	m.'s heart is an abyss	BRAD 155:49
spend every m....writing	POWE 693:51	M. hid his face	BIBLE 93:53		BALZ 61:2
splendid in the m.	FLEC 340:33	M. the servant of the Lord died	BIBLE 95:4	m.'s life made me a man	MASE 580:62
start so early in the m.	LEBO 518:68	our M.	BLOOM 143:70	m.'s little helper	JAGG 449:14
there m. and evening	RUSK 734:19	the people of M.	KORAN 497:62	m.'s yearning	ELIOT 315:27
the veils of the m.	YEATS 965:4	turning aside like M.	THOM 886:77	m. taught me as a boy	BERR 87:98
uncertain hour before the m.	ELIOT 321:85	mosquito like the bite of a m.	OHEN 648:20	m. thinks Vietnam is somewhere	ANON 25:6
upon my knees every m.	SHAK 773:23	m. and sandfly	DOUG 294:97	M. to dozens	HERB 412:44
waking him in the m.	MANS 567:4	stung him like a m.	SITW 823:2	m. was constructed by others	ATWO 41:7
was a Chelsea m.	MITC 609:36	tried to fall asleep with a m.	WHIT 937:87	m. who talks about her own children	DISR 288:61
wear on to a m.	STOWE 856:32	mosquitoey m. summer night light	ASHB 37:59	m. will never see you again	AUST 46:58
We this m. have done	PARK 663:91	moss azure m.	SHEL 813:81	m. would have loved it!	MACA 544:13
What a glorious m.	ADAMS 5:9	wait beneath the m.	TOJO 893:41	murdered his m. and father	LEVA 525:17
When m. gilds the skies	CASW 208:82	whole world for a m.	BARB 63:46	My m. bore me	BLAKE 139:87
when you wake in the m.	SAND 742:32	mosses as the m. that glow	MERE 588:41	My m., drunk or sober	CHES 220:54
morning-after rather grisly m.-a.	HUXL 442:80	mote m. that is in thy brother's eye	BIBLE 115:48	My m. groaned!	BLAKE 140:18
morning-mist m.-m. picnic	FRAME 346:75	motel [Poetry] in every m.	BROD 160:43	Naked came I out of my m.'s womb	BIBLE 98:91
mornings music o' m.	SHAK 803:92	motels M. can be big	HEAT 406:95	Old M. Wit	DENH 272:62
Mornington M. Crescent	HARG 398:31	motes air is not so full of m.	DONNE 293:71	one's m. is a virgin	JARRY 452:96
Morocco we're M. bound	BURKE 176:60	gay m. that people	MILT 598:49	record...of our m. and father	FRAME 346:77
moron consumer isn't a m.	OGIL 648:6	moth How, like a m.	GAY 362:15	rest, on m.'s breast	TENN 872:37
morons England full of m.	WODE 952:57	I felt like a m.	ONAS 650:50	seeks his m. once more	WHIT 938:17
morose temper, naturally m.	DISR 288:46	m. and rust doth corrupt	BIBLE 115:43	Silence is become his m. tongue	GOLD 376:95
morphemes m. and phonemes	THOM 886:76	m.'s kiss, first!	BROW 167:12	sin, my m. told me	MUNRO 625:51
morris Britain is a M. Minor country	ANON 26:84	steered the white m.	FROST 352:11	So loving to my m.	SHAK 780:39
Whitsun m. dance	SHAK 775:71	moth-eaten m.-e. musical brocade	LARK 510:96	the m. who one day chose	MCGO 552:81

Thou art thy m.'s glass SHAK 800:33
thought of my m. MUNRO 625:48
to his m. brought BLAKE 139:92
universal m. CHES 220:79
Upon his m.'s grave? WORD 957:65
wedded maid...virgin m. MILT 597:30
wife's fidelity and his m.'s respectability SHAW 811:29
writer has to rob his m. FAUL 331:41
mother-death sea is m.-d. SEXT 758:49
Mother Goose M. G., Cinderella, and...hooker PART 666:60
motherhood M....joyous...act FRIE 350:66
wifehood and m. are but incidental STAN 842:13
mothering naughty m. arms THOM 884:79
mother-in-law m.-i.-l....over a cliff VENA 910:49
T. S. Eliot's m.-i.-l. BENN 80:56
when his m.-i.-l. died JERO 454:39
mother-love denouncing m.-l. STEI 846:84
mothers decisions to become m. FRIE 350:66
If m. ruled the world FIELD 335:16
If neither governesses or m. know DAVI 264:71
keep the m. in a state of coma DAVI 264:72
men with m. and wives! HOOD 426:31
m. bring us into the world SCHR 749:62
M. of large families BELL 76:54
m. to help them ALCO 12:45
Our m.' wombs RALE 705:45
Pale m., wherefore weeping? WILDE 940:45
These M., instead of SWIFT 862:57
think back through our m. WOOLF 955:31
women become like their m. WILDE 941:3
mother-wits veins of rhyming m.-w. MARL 572:94
moths candle to the m. WEBB 925:6
cheaper...but the m. get into it LEAC 515:12
like m. among the whisperings FITZ 337:80
m. fluttering among the heath BRON 162:82
Unfading m., immortal flies BROO 163:2
motion acting...And the first m. SHAK 776:16
aim...is to arrest m. FAUL 331:42
alteration of m. NEWT 635:57
At worst, one is in m. GUNN 390:96
backward m. toward the source FROST 352:7
Between the m. And the act ELIOT 318:15
breath And everlasting m. WORD 957:69
constant m. WILL 944:64
Devoid of sense and m. MILT 602:59
end of man's m. BACON 51:88
eternal m. WORD 959:96
God ordered m. VAUG 909:40
in his m. like an angel SHAK 770:19
men a forward m. love VAUG 909:36
m. in a right line NEWT 635:56
no m. has she now WORD 957:64
only while...in m. NABO 628:1
poetry of m.! GRAH 380:90
rapid line of m. WORD 957:71
Unshaked of m. SHAK 777:26
motionless living stood m. WILL 944:64
motions causes, and secret m. BACON 53:46
causes, and secret m. BACON 50:52
m. all accompanied with grace DRYD 301:66
m. of the viewless winds WORD 958:84
secret m. of things BACON 53:46
secret m. of things BACON 50:52
So delicate his m. be BRID 158:8
to thy m. lovers' seasons run? DONNE 291:25
two weeping m. CRAS 254:81
motivated ideologically m. KIM 486:12
motivation if you must have m. COWA 249:59
love—outlaw m. ZWER 970:21
motive m. for recording GREE 386:21
m. in this narrative TWAIN 902:50
m. of many Socialists ORWE 653:17
run the paper...with no other m. BEAV 71:27
secret of the absent-minded BELL 78:94
motives at the...bottom of their m. ORWE 654:60
attribution of false m. BALD 57:35
no corrupt or interested m. PEEL 672:67
no man who knows my m. EMMET 325:6
One of the strongest m. EINS 313:76
motor before the m. car THOM 884:47
heart's stalled m. MAYA 583:23
Money...in m. racing nowadays CHAP 214:13
m....is the reader CURT 259:97
M. racing is dangerous HAWT 401:98
right is only a m. hand HEPW 412:30
motorcycle m. black madonna DYLAN 309:55

powerful m.-c. USTI 907:47
motors good for General M. WILS 947:47
motorway outside lane of a m. BOYC 153:7
motto criticism's m. FORS 345:48
jamais triste that is my m. MARQ 575:52
Let their m. be:—Hunt, shoot BRON 161:62
m. of everyone DORAM 294:84
m. of mankind LAFO 503:50
Nixon's m. COUS 248:41
that's the m. HARD 396:96
true to your instincts...was his m. LAWR 512:39
With this for m. TENN 877:47
woman's m. STAN 843:18
mottoes m. on sundials POUND 691:1
mould as through a m. SCHR 749:66
broke the m. ARIO 31:13
lips the m. falls close ROSS 726:59
settles in the m. JEFF 453:10
through the m. MANS 567:3
mouldering m. like wedding-cake RICH 713:95
Moulmein By the old M. Pagoda KIPL 489:80
M. is situated KIPL 489:79
moulting when they're m. NASH 630:55
mount never climbed M. Fuji MORR 620:49
O Oisin, m. by me YEATS 965:5
There is a high m. STUA 858:57
mountain 'assault' on the m. CRAN 253:75
bare m. tops are bald ARNO 36:41
Buddha...at the top of a m. PIRS 679:89
chilly and inhospitable m. KENN 480:86
climbed my last political m. WALL 918:49
dangerous to climb a m. HAWT 401:98
dew on the m. SCOTT 752:32
Doing time is like climbing a m. DEAN 267:41
ethereal m. BENU 83:9
every m. and hill shall be made low BIBLE 108:79
Flatter the m. tops SHAK 801:48
from his m. walls TENN 875:4
get me to the m. of myrrh BIBLE 107:45
gone on the m. SCOTT 752:31
heaping m. on m. CARL 200:84
high m. cradle in Pamere ARNO 35:1
horse on the m. LORCA 537:58
in m. exploration SHIP 818:13
It's not the m. we conquer HILL 418:62
Land of the m. SCOTT 752:17
light atop the m. POUND 692:38
m. and a national shrine MUMF 625:37
m. of his holiness BIBLE 100:70
m. outline varies THOR 888:24
m. revealing its geologic MILL 593:45
m. which is of no use for sheep BUTL 185:89
mowing down m. ranges MILL 594:63
mysterious m....called reality MAIL 560:66
one m., one sea, one river BURT 181:79
purple m. majesties BATES 67:53
ragged m. ranges MACK 553:10
river jumps over the m. AUDEN 43:81
robes the m. in its azure hue CAMP 194:61
rocky m. GILB 368:36
say unto this m. BIBLE 118:9
somebody has shifted the m. LEVIN 525:29
stood on more m. tops THOR 889:55
Tching prayed on the m. POUND 692:27
there stands One m. BROW 167:10
Throng from each m.-pass! MCCA 547:74
Up the airy m. ALLI 14:6
wires that span the m. stream CRANE 253:60
yonder m. height TENN 873:50
mountain-daisy to this m.-d. WORD 962:51
mountaineer On, every m. MCCA 547:74
mountainous great m. sports girl BETJ 88:21
mountains Among the Galilean m. CRAS 254:81
Before the m. were brought forth BIBLE 101:92
Before the m. were brought forth BOOK 149:29
blue Friuli's m. BYRON 188:60
blue icecaps on the m. CHAT 216:52
born and dies among the m. WORD 958:90
dawn in the m. MURP 626:75
decayed hole among the m. ELIOT 318:10
England's m. green? BLAKE 141:40
faith, so that I could remove m. BIBLE 126:52
grass is green...m. steep STEP 847:11
Greenland's icy m. HEBER 406:1
High m. are a feeling BYRON 187:53
How beautiful upon the m. BIBLE 109:90
intellects, like the tops of m. MACA 545:41

mind has m. HOPK 429:91
m. are stern teachers TILM 891:17
M. are the beginning RUSK 733:91
m. be carried into the...sea BIBLE 100:67
m. by the winter sea TENN 878:80
M. divide us GALT 359:54
m. look on Marathon BYRON 190:15
M. of whimsy ROCH 719:11
M. on whose...breast MILT 597:45
m....shall break forth BIBLE 109:1
m....to him were friends BYRON 187:48
m. were there HERZ 416:25
remove m., and make seas CARL 200:80
said to the m....Fall on us BIBLE 131:2
shadow of the blue m. MELBA 584:44
skill to move m. HOFF 421:24
There are new m. LEGU 520:15
to the m. is going home MUIR 624:25
true call...of the m. STARK 843:23
voices...One of the m. WORD 961:31
weighed the m. in scales BIBLE 108:81
What are men to rocks and m.? AUST 46:61
when the m. shall be set moving KORAN 498:91
Woods, or steepy m. MARL 574:41
mountainside along the m. WORD 959:1
every m. SMITH 830:31
mountain-spring Rivers and m.-s. OAKL 643:5
mountain-stream in the fall of m.-s. BEAT 72:2
m.-s. that ends LOWE 539:4
mountain-top as on a m.-t. HUXL 443:7
been to the m. t. KING 487:35
mountaintops misty m. SHAK 766:2
mountain-tops m. t. that freeze SHAK 804:44
mountebank impudent m. who sold pills ADDI 6:22
mere anatomy, a m. SHAK 762:93
story of a m. and his zany WALP 919:77
mountebanks M....imitate LEWIS 527:70
mounted always well m. HALI 393:31
Mountjoy M. began to move MACA 546:60
mourn Blessed are they that m. BIBLE 114:27
countless thousands m.! BURNS 177:86
Margaret you m. for HOPK 428:82
m. a mischief that is past SHAK 789:98
m. with ever-returning spring WHIT 938:8
secure, and now can never m. SHEL 815:40
time enough to m. DANI 262:31
time to m. BIBLE 106:14
mourned m. unto you BIBLE 116:79
mourners let the m. come AUDEN 42:79
m. go about the streets BIBLE 106:36
mournful M. and Never-ending POE 683:90
mourning in such very deep m. AUST 45:49
M. becomes Electra ONEI 651:67
m. for my life CHEK 218:14
m. into dancing BIBLE 100:51
M. is a hard business MALA 561:83
mourns m. when many leave OWEN 658:40
one m. alone BERG 83:25
mouse absurd little m. HORA 430:19
catch a m. or two (for form's sake) GRAY 385:93
invention of a m.! DISN 287:14
leave room for the m. SAKI 739:68
m. in a mousehole EISE 314:10
m. sticks in his sharp paw ANON 20:31
not even a m. MOORE 616:60
not the m. who is the thief JACO 449:10
way a m. waltzes WHITE 935:44
mouse-trap baiting a m.-t. SAKI 739:68
The M. SHAK 783:27
moustache Big chap with a small m. WODE 952:52
couldn't wear a m. like that HOOV 427:53
didn't wax his m. KIPL 489:73
drawing a m. on a madonna VENT 910:52
worn a m. SIMON 822:75
moustaches Nothing...except m. BROD 160:36
mouth Christ in the m. PATR 670:29
doth become the m. as well SHAK 776:10
draw near me with their m. BIBLE 108:72
Even in the cannon's m. SHAK 779:82
Familiar in his m. SHAK 776:91
for an Englishman to open his m. SHAW 810:93
gift horse in the m. RABE 703:12
hand more instrumental to the m. SHAK 780:31
have not found the m. ACHE 2:21
heart into my m. SHAK 791:84
In his m. are Lies WELLS 930:22
in my m. sweet as honey BIBLE 131:8

mouthful

Into the m. of Hell	TENN 875:13
just whispering in her m.	MARX 578:13
keep your m. shut	DE 273:68
keep your m. shut	ITO 448:79
laugh…before he opens his m.	NATH 632:99
m. and my breasts	SEXT 758:48
m. do crush their wine	MARV 577:4
m. is smoother than oil	BIBLE 114:56
m. it, as many of your players do	SHAK 783:18
m. must be held in	BIBLE 100:54
m. of a hog to eat	NASHE 632:97
m. of the cannon	RUSK 732:80
m. shall shew forth thy praise	BIBLE 101:74
m. so prim	ELIOT 319:49
m.…used as a latrine	AMIS 16:29
No M. And I Must Scream	ELLI 323:31
no m. to put it in	DICK 277:42
opened not his m.	BIBLE 109:94
open thy m. wide	BIBLE 101:87
out of his m. went a…sword	BIBLE 131:8
Out of the same m. proceedeth	BIBLE 130:57
Pain is…a creature without a m.	WINT 950:15
purple-stained m.	KEATS 478:42
put a hose in their m.	KROC 499:17
put my words in thy m.	BIBLE 110:11
put one into her m.	THAC 880:21
rash with thy m.	BIBLE 106:20
satisfieth thy m. with good things	BIBLE 102:6
Set a watch…before my m.	BIBLE 104:47
slap-dash down in the m.	CONG 240:29
strawberries at the m. of their pot	ELIZ 322:8
tail in its m.	FERL 333:92
that which goeth into the m.	BIBLE 117:2
The boy's m.	TWAIN 903:69
When the m. says yes	HUGO 437:68
wine will burn our m.	EMER 325:83
with an open m.	STEV 851:20
with its tail in its m.	HOOD 426:26
z is keeping your m. shut	EINS 314:86
mouthful every m. of food	FORD 342:87
m. of air	YEATS 966:11
mouthless millions of the m. dead	SORL 834:33
mouth-organ Menuhin on the m.-o.	ADLER 8:70
mouths bizzing craigs and m. to weet	FERG 333:86
Blind m.! that scarce	MILT 599:88
from your smoky m.	MARL 574:31
made m. in a glass	SHAK 792:6
m. Of wisest men	MILT 608:93
'Pardon' for kings' m.	SHAK 765:61
put an enemy in their m.	SHAK 789:13
speaking truth, to m. like mine	BROW 169:79
move America is always on the m.	CUMM 258:60
feel the earth m.?	HEMI 410:80
if it made its own m.	JARR 452:87
in him we live, and m.	BIBLE 125:93
m. his hearers	FRAS 349:32
Sometimes you m. publicly	BAKER 56:2
moveables to my chattels and my m.	SHAK 775:70
moved Being m. is what collecting	ANNE 20:15
do not like being m.	CLOU 232:58
m. by what is not unusual	ELIOT 316:52
m., not only as an author	GRASS 382:17
not m. with concord	SHAK 770:21
shall not be m.	BIBLE 100:68
movement aggressive m.	MARI 571:76
infinite diversity of m.	REDT 709:25
joyful with swift m.	ANON 20:31
neither arrest nor m.	ELIOT 319:39
Never confuse m. with action	HEMI 410:93
only m.…dropping of the dead	WILL 944:64
Our m. took a grip	GOER 374:55
Our nature consists in m.	PASC 667:72
slow m. of clouds	DAY 267:36
ticking m. of the human timepiece	ASLET 38:83
movements m. of human thought	BENN 81:81
m. of the limbs	LEON 522:74
natural and ordinary m.	FONT 342:75
physical m.	GALS 358:49
mover Fear is the great m.	BART 66:17
moves it m. again since it is life	FAUL 331:42
Nevertheless, it m.	GALI 357:30
movie can't wait till the m. comes out	JACK 448:6
cheats of the m. screen	MAIL 559:38
Life in the m. business	MAMET 564:40
Making a m. is like	ALTM 15:20
m.-makers…put more reality	HECHT 406:3
m., this is the way to do it	LANE 507:39

old m. plots	BAKER 56:8
only a m. could be seen	KESEY 483:65
same m. could be seen	JORD 469:6
movies Adding sound to m.	PICK 677:65
Good. m. make you care	KAEL 472:2
lesson in how not to write for the m.	CHAN 213:83
like pornographic m.	ROGE 723:88
M. are more likely…to reach deep feelings	MAIL 560:64
Thanks to the m.	USTI 906:46
the basic appeal of m.	KAEL 472:1
thing that can kill the M.	ROGE 723:82
trot down to the m.	WILD 943:44
violence in m.	TARA 867:26
W. C. Fields m.	HAWES 401:86
moving always already m.	HEID 406:11
face of a m.-picture actor	MENC 587:16
in form and m.	SHAK 782:89
lie without m.	RHYS 712:74
privilege of always m.	LEWIS 526:40
mowers m. in the hay	MUIR 624:16
Mowgli M. answered	KIPL 490:5
mown often as we are m. down	TERT 879:18
Mozart en famille they play M.	BARTH 66:12
sonatas of M.	SCHN 748:46
MP Being an MP feeds your vanity	PARR 666:52
goings-on of an unlucky MP	CRIT 255:10
MPs many M. never see the London	LIVI 532:56
Mr Bean M. B., creating chaos	CABLE 191:7
Mr Right M. R's coming	WINF 950:95
much how m. unexpected, by so m.	SHAK 768:52
know how m.…haven't got m.	MARC 570:58
m. I want which most men have	DYER 309:47
m. to hear and see	SKEL 824:27
no man is wanted m.	EMER 324:72
muck in lovely m. I've lain	HOUS 432:59
Money is like m.	BACON 52:95
sing 'em m.	MELBA 584:43
when to stop raking the m.	ROOS 724:17
muckle M. he made o' that	MACQ 558:11
muckrake with a m. in his hand	BUNY 174:80
mud blades pricked the m.	BROW 168:34
clouds, or m. or like places	LEON 523:77
cover the universe with m.	FORS 344:39
gaping mussels, left upon the m.	CRAB 252:42
he was just all m.	TWAIN 902:56
He who slings m.	STEV 851:17
hold another down in the m.	ACH 2:24
made up of marble and m.	HAWT 402:8
more dangerous than a m.-puddle	STEIN 845:59
M.! M.! Glorious m.!	FLAN 338:8
pure clay of time's m.	MALA 562:88
Science is angling in the m.	HUXL 442:83
sees the m., and…the stars	LANG 507:43
shining gull-marked m.	LARK 509:84
stream that ends in m.	LOWE 539:4
muddied The people m.	SHAK 784:52
muddle Ah, Rachel, aw a m.!	DICK 282:81
beginning, a m., and an end	LARK 510:97
intellectual m. early	MURD 626:67
meddle and m.	DERBY 274:86
solve…the m. with humaneness	WILS 947:44
muddy to m. or mock	PALEY 661:53
muffin Hot M.…Company	DICK 278:74
mug Poetry…a m.'s game	ELIOT 319:29
muir-men m.-m. win their hay	BALL 58:51
mulberry tarrying in m. shade	SHAK 768:48
mule m. of politics	DISR 287:27
not as the horse, or as the m.	BIBLE 100:54
Sicilian m. was to me	GLAD 373:42
smelt a lot of m. manure	WILL 944:70
mules m.…accustomed to burdens	RICH 714:21
multifarious another of the m. ways	SITW 824:24
multiplication m. of the fittest	SPEN 836:87
multiplied m. itself in broad ways	REYES 712:69
multiply be fruitful and m.	BIBLE 91:84
multitude another to the m.	HAWT 402:6
by reason of this great m.	BIBLE 98:87
cover the m. of sins	BIBLE 130:71
for the m. to be ingrateful	SHAK 799:95
From an exemplary m.	VIAN 911:74
hide a m. of sins	BIBLE 130:63
m. of one million	KOES 495:26
m. of perverse inclinations	SHAR 806:73
M. too familiar	LEST 524:8
m., which no man could number	BIBLE 131:3
sprung in affluent m.	TWAIN 903:72

stupidity of the m.	BAUD 68:71
washed his hands before the m.	BIBLE 119:45
multitudes I contain m.	WHIT 937:95
rank me with the barbarous m.	SHAK 769:94
seeing the m., he went up	BIBLE 114:27
Weeping, weeping m.	ELIOT 317:87
mum fuck you up, your m.	LARK 510:89
merryman moping m.	GILB 370:70
M., the Persil-user	BETJ 89:40
oafish louts remember M.	BETJ 88:35
when m. stays home	FALU 329:11
mumble Let her maunder and m.	CARL 200:2
m. with great coherence	GREE 386:34
when in doubt, m.	WAGN 915:3
mummies make the m. dance	LIND 530:14
mummy had his M.'s leave	KIPL 491:30
M., I'm sick with disgust	BETJ 89:45
Never being able to say 'M' again	WILL 944:69
munched And m., and m., and m.	SHAK 795:99
mundane miraculous to the m.	DIDI 286:81
mundus pereat m.	FERD 332:73
Munster sun that was M.'s glory	ORAH 652:91
mural purest…is the m.	OROZ 652:1
murals m. on the wall	BETJ 89:43
murder anyone meditating m.	FISH 336:61
brought back m. into the home	HITC 419:82
call it m.	MAXT 583:18
commit rape, m.	BARN 64:61
dens of robbery and m.	NATI 632:4
hard to tell it fr'm m.	DUNNE 307:19
in five years…ready to commit m.	DAMR 261:23
love and m. will out	CONG 240:39
Macbeth does m. sleep	SHAK 797:34
man indulges himself in m.	DE 274:85
man wants to m. a tiger	SHAW 808:92
met M. on the way	SHEL 812:72
Most sacreligious m.	SHAK 797:41
m. and to ravish	AYTO 48:11
M. doesn't round out	HAMM 395:72
m., hate, vertue	MALO 563:17
m., homicide	STUB 858:62
M. is always a mistake	WILDE 941:72
M. is a unique crime	JAMES 451:59
M. most foul	SHAK 781:61
M.…One of the Fine Arts	DE 273:84
m. shrieks out	WEBS 927:56
M., though it have no tongue	SHAK 782:3
m. to dissect	WORD 957:59
M. wol out	CHAU 217:99
no vicious blot, m.	SHAK 792:86
one m. made a villain	PORT 690:87
rape and m.	NOON 641:50
scymitars, wi' m. crusted	BURNS 179:28
Sooner m. an infant	BLAKE 140:3
took m. out of the Venetian vase	CHAN 213:95
Treason and m.	SHAK 775:67
warfare, terror, m.	WELL 929:93
war, I call it m.	LOWE 539:5
war…I think it m.	PAINE 660:30
murdered all that I had m.	SHAK 761:52
except the m.'s	HAMM 395:72
Glamis hath m. sleep	SHAK 797:35
m. them 0–0	SHAN 805:66
one a m. self	ROSS 726:60
recently m. woman	SHAR 806:77
their m. man	KEATS 477:17
murderèd son of the dear m.	SHAK 782:2
murderer jailer of your m.	HUGH 436:45
m. for a fancy prose	NABO 628:5
m. from the beginning	BIBLE 123:42
m., to be a politician	MILL 595:94
sometimes the m.'s	HAMM 395:72
the man is a common m.	SAKI 739:65
you must bear his m.	YEATS 967:22
murderers M.! Stop murdering	BRAND 156:66
of whores and m.	WEBS 926:28
murdering Murderers! Stop m.	BRAND 156:66
murderous m. hate	SHAK 800:35
murders m. sticking on his hands	SHAK 798:67
murk only adds to the m.	MILL 594:91
murky M. language	JONG 466:41
murmur live m. of a summer's day	ARNO 34:48
m. about his name	RUSK 733:42
m. among the zealots	HUME 439:8
m., soon replies	MILT 601:26
murmurings noise of m.	BIBLE 112:72
murmurs In hollow m. died away	COLL 238:79

musicians

muscle m. of my nation	FRAN 348:23	
not extra m.	TRUE 899:74	
take the m. from bone	ELIOT 319:48	
muscles call his m. into action	POE 683:81	
girls with the m. of a welter-weight	WODE 952:42	
m. of his brawny arms	LONG 535:17	
relax your m.	MOSS 622:83	
She had the rippling m.	PERE 674:18	
muscular His Christianity was m.	DISR 288:68	
muse brash courtship of the m.	THOM 886:73	
'Fool,' said my M. to me	SIDN 820:44	
invocation of the M.	GRAV 382:27	
Let my M.	HERR 415:7	
Livelier liquor than the M.	HOUS 432:57	
loving a foreign m.	BENET 79:25	
meditate the thankless m.	MILT 599:86	
M. invoked	SWIFT 862:61	
m. is...of the English strain	DRAY 298:91	
m. of Moore	BYRON 189:3	
M. shall sit, and think	GRAY 384:56	
O for a m. of fire	SHAK 775:61	
Perversity is the m.	SONT 834:14	
provokes the snarling m.	JOHN 459:43	
same soil as the M.	UNTE 905:11	
shelter, and even m.	TUCH 901:14	
spelt by the unlettered m.	GRAY 384:73	
Tell me, M.	HOMER 425:9	
The tenth M.	TROL 897:20	
trivial people should m. and thunder	LAWR 514:79	
Who loves not...the heavenly m.	DOWL 296:34	
Why does my M. only speak	SMITH 830:40	
muses Among the M.	WYATT 963:86	
M.' garden	CAREW 198:51	
m. gave their full consent	LANY 508:57	
M. in striped trousers	ORWE 654:53	
M. sing of happy swains	CRAB 252:29	
priest of the M.	HORA 430:9	
sweet M. of the Light	RUSK 734:19	
who brings The Smithfield M.	POPE 688:29	
museum in the South Kensington M.	KING 488:58	
marble m. of the soul	RODR 722:53	
mind is the m.	RAINE 705:41	
m. of antiquities	ENGE 326:15	
You're the Louvr' M.	PORT 690:70	
museums art m. to worship dead works	MAYA 583:22	
department stores...like m.	WARH 920:9	
free her from the numberless m.	MARI 571:78	
In all m. throughout the world	PATE 669:14	
mush m. and slush	OWEN 657:23	
mushroom I am...a m.	FORD 343:99	
Life...too short to stuff a m.	CONR 244:52	
m. which has poisoned	MILL 593:58	
mushrooms m., thriving only in the dark	ALBR 11:37	
Patriots...like m.	WALP 919:84	
music advised to give her m.	SHAK 803:92	
after the m. had finished	HELP 409:56	
a life lived for m.	PAVA 670:37	
All m. is folk m.	ARMS 33:49	
Appalling Popularity of M.	LAMB 506:17	
as Beethoven was born for m.	PELE 672:75	
Beer, tobacco, and m.	MANN 566:77	
Bells, the poor man's only m.	COLE 235:24	
Birds warbling all the m.	COWP 251:12	
British m....perpetual promise	BEEC 73:69	
by that m....embrace	SHAK 772:64	
Canned m....audible wallpaper	COOKE 245:76	
century...deserves its own m.	DEBU 282:22	
city is built to m.	TENN 878:94	
compulsion doth in m. lie	MILT 598:61	
consume it in m.	MONT 613:11	
creation of m. is...natural	COLE 234:3	
daughters of m. shall be brought low	BIBLE 106:36	
day the m. died	MCLE 554:21	
day the m. died	MACL 554:23	
did enjoy the m.	JOHN 459:33	
doesn't want new m.	HONE 425:15	
Do not take up m.	BOUL 152:87	
Don't just move to the m.	MARL 572:93	
don't know anything about m.	BEER 73:86	
ear for her m.	DAY 267:36	
Ear's deep-sweet m.	SHAK 762:87	
English may not like m.	BEEC 73:62	
essence of m.	MOZA 623:6	
ethereal m.	GALL 358:44	
everything seems to happen to m.	WILL 945:79	
existence like a piece of m.	MACB 546:63	
face the m. and dance	BERL 84:40	
finds its food in m.	LILLO 529:1	
function of m. is to release us	BEEC 73:70	
good m. and a clean conscience	HIND 419:67	
Good m....penetrates the ear	BEEC 73:64	
go twang, and you've got m.	VICI 912:75	
heard the m.'s din	GILB 368:40	
how he wants this m. played	TOSC 894:63	
How irksome is this m.	SHAK 759:86	
how our m. should be played	GILL 370:86	
how potent cheap m. is	COWA 249:48	
How sour sweet m. is	SHAK 765:63	
How sweet his m.!	WORD 957:58	
humour, its m.	ROLL 723:90	
I am the number one... in m.	WEST 932:72	
I don't know anything about m.	PRES 694:74	
I don't make m. for eyes	ADELE 8:60	
If m. be the food of love	SHAK 785:77	
If one hears bad m.	WILDE 940:68	
If that was m.	FAURE 331:49	
If the king loves m.	MENC 586:80	
I got m.	GERS 365:73	
I'm a martyr to m.	THOM 884:32	
inexpressible is m.	HUXL 441:69	
In sweet m. is such art	SHAK 804:45	
In sweet m. is such art	SHAK 804:47	
Is there a meaning to m.?	COPL 246:98	
It's just m.	PARK 663:92	
jazz m. is a style	MORT 621:72	
learn a sense of m.	JOHN 458:30	
Let m. sound	SHAK 769:2	
let the sounds of m.	SHAK 769:18	
lights, the m., and revelry	HAWT 402:12	
Like harmony in m.	WORD 958:76	
Like m. on my heart	COLE 235:19	
like Wagner's m. better	WILDE 940:67	
little m. in the name Jack	WILDE 941:95	
little m. out of doors	KEATS 476:96	
live entirely in my m.	BEET 74:2	
Look out for this man's m.	PARRY 666:55	
make the m. mute	TENN 877:44	
man that hath no m.	SHAK 770:21	
man who can read m.	BEEC 73:61	
May make one m.	TENN 873:57	
M....all your cares beguile	DRYD 303:23	
M. alone with sudden charms	CONG 241:77	
M. and women I...give way to	PEPYS 674:5	
m. begins to atrophy	POUND 692:17	
m. can't be heard	MACL 555:40	
m. crept by me	SHAK 803:15	
m. feedeth that disposition	BACON 53:48	
m. from a farther room	ELIOT 316:63	
m. from the sounds	MCCA 547:82	
m....greater than its performance	PREV 694:76	
m. has a taste	GRIEG 388:65	
m. hath a far more pleasing sound	SHAK 802:83	
M. hath charms to soothe	CONG 241:51	
M. helps not the toothache	HERB 414:87	
m. he made with us	SWIN 864:12	
m. in its roar	BYRON 188:70	
m. in the air	ELGAR 314:12	
m. in the sighing of a reed	BYRON 190:27	
m. in the spacings of the spheres	PYTH 701:16	
m. is a gift and a burden	SIMO 822:78	
M. is feeling	STEV 849:73	
M. is life	NIEL 637:90	
M. is Love in search	LANI 508:52	
M. is my mistress	ELLI 322:24	
M. is no different from opium	KHOM 485:89	
M. is the art of sounds	BUSO 184:54	
M. is the best means	AUDEN 44:21	
m. is the brandy	SHAW 807:23	
M. is the great cheer-up...language	ODETS 647:93	
M. is the poor man's Parnassus	EMER 325:1	
M. is the universal language	LONG 535:13	
m. is universal	GILL 370:87	
M. is your own experience	PARK 663:93	
M., Maestro, Please	MAGI 559:25	
m. marreth men's manners	GALE 357:29	
M. might tame and civilize	GAY 362:23	
m.—m., moody food	SHAK 794:60	
M. of Broadway	GERS 365:74	
m. of forfended spheres	PATM 669:25	
m. of his own vain tongue	SHAK 763:6	
m. of its trees	ARNO 34:77	
M. oft hath such a charm	SHAK 788:73	
m. on diverse subjects	VIAN 911:74	
m. piercing that solitude	THOM 885:53	
M. says nothing to the reason	BURG 174:3	
m. she learned in bed	WILM 947:34	
m. soars within the...lark	BROW 166:1	
m. that changed a man's decision	SCHN 748:44	
M. that expresses...nothing	BART 67:32	
M. that gentlier	TENN 870:89	
m. that I care to hear	HOPK 428:67	
m. that I don't take to in	COST 247:16	
M., the greatest good	ADDI 6:15	
m. the least disagreeable	JOHN 465:6	
M. to hear	SHAK 800:34	
M. was invented to deceive	EPHO 326:22	
M. when soft voices	SHEL 816:63	
M. with dinner is an insult	CHES 221:11	
m....with its voluptuous swell	BYRON 187:50	
m., yearning like a God	KEATS 477:17	
My m. is best understood	STRA 857:46	
My m. is like anchovies	MANI 565:69	
My m. is not modern	SCHO 748:49	
New m.?	ELLI 322:23	
night...filled with m.	LONG 535:23	
no m. in the nightingale	SHAK 759:68	
not for the doctrine, but the m.	POPE 685:23	
old good m.	HAWES 401:86	
one takes the m. too fast	SAINT 739:49	
opera...is to m.	MENC 586:91	
Our mirth the m.	RALE 705:45	
piece for orchestra without m.	RAVEL 707:83	
Poetry is m.	ANGE 19:1	
Poetry must be read as m.	POUND 691:95	
Pop m. is the classical m. of now	MCCA 548:3	
primitive m. and primitive medicine	LEAC 515:17	
reactions to art or to m.	COLE 234:4	
serious about this m.	ZWER 970:21	
set to more or less lascivious m.	MENC 586:86	
shall be made Thy M.	DONNE 293:64	
so much m. in my head	RAVEL 707:83	
soul of m. shed	MOORE 618:4	
sound of m.	HAMM 395:68	
spare...patience towards...m. or art	GLEN 374:50	
still, sad m.	WORD 956:75	
stop when there's no more m.	ARMS 32:47	
strong m. in the soul	COLE 235:31	
struck one chord of the m.	PROC 697:27	
sweetest m. to a woeful mind	SIDN 820:42	
sweet m. is such art	SHAK 804:45	
sweet m. is such art	SHAK 804:47	
taught me...to face the m.	HEAN 405:79	
that's what m.'s all about	HEND 411:4	
the noise of classical m.	HOLL 423:54	
theorizing about m.	HEINE 407:16	
thou hast thy m. too	KEATS 478:33	
thy beauty's Silent m.	CAMP 195:75	
thy chosen m.	WORD 961:31	
time is the medium of m.	MANN 566:84	
to write American m.	THOM 888:13	
To write m. is to raise a ladder	HONE 425:14	
universal languages: love, m. and sports	MOSES 622:79	
Wagner's m. is better	TWAIN 904:94	
well set to m.	ADDI 6:25	
we provide the m.	STOK 855:9	
What m. is more enchanting	SMITH 829:17	
when I hear sweet m.	SHAK 770:20	
when you listen to m.	GAUG 361:3	
Who loves not m.	DOWL 296:34	
Why is Schoenberg's M. so Hard	BERG 83:17	
why m. was ordained!	SHAK 762:68	
Without m., life	NIET 639:16	
worth expressing in m.	DELI 272:46	
write m. like Wagner	GOLD 377:27	
Your lordship...is fond of m.	SHER 817:84	
musical happier still is that m.	AGATE 9:88	
Hell is full of m. amateurs	SHAW 807:23	
no rules...of m. composition	SHAW 810:23	
Which is more m.	CAGE 192:17	
musicals m....about...1950's	MACI 553:98	
music-halls no more jokes in M.-h.	SASS 745:80	
musician amateur jazz m.	LYTT 543:95	
main thing a m. would like to do	COLT 238:86	
no one but a professional m.	BUTL 184:16	
rather bitter British m.	WILM 947:34	
resources of a m.	MORR 620:59	
You could be a great m.	DAVIS 265:31	
musicians appear...To all m.	AUDEN 43:99	
Jazz m. are	TURN 901:20	
M. don't retire	ARMS 32:47	

musicked

m. listen to see who	MING 608:8	divine m. in things	DOST 294:94	these vain weak n.	SHAK 765:62
M. paint their pictures	STOK 855:9	do not have to solve all m.	HERN 414:92	upsetting of a bag of n.	RUSK 733:17
M. wrestle everywhere	DICK 283:31	fathomless m.	BUEC 172:42	**naïve** Our people are not n.	REYES 712:69
older m. like me	FREE 349:44	lose myself in a m.	BROW 165:53	**naked** blind and n. Ignorance	TENN 877:48
thousand poor m.	VAUG 909:32	love is a m.	LAFO 504:67	clothe my n. villainy	SHAK 761:39
'tis not we m. know	BROW 168:58	Married life requires shared m.	FORD 343:11	enterprise in walking n.	YEATS 966:16
musicked Playing in m. gravity	AVIS 47:1	M., Babylon The Great	BIBLE 132:17	Helpless, n., piping loud	BLAKE 140:18
musicologist m....can read music	BEEC 73:61	m. behind knowledge	FRYE 354:57	knew that they were n.	BIBLE 91:93
musing Love of Peace, and lonely m.	COLL 238:79	m. is its life	BAGE 54:75	lest he walk n.	BIBLE 132:15
M. on roses	RAND 706:57	m. is why we even collect these figures	BART 66:30	N. and stone-like	FREE 350:48
musk m. of the rose is blown	TENN 876:25	m. of life	WHITE 935:51	N. and the Dead	MAIL 559:36
muskets m. and machine guns	MUSS 628:92	m....Of the glorious Body	AQUI 30:96	N., and ye clothed me	BIBLE 119:36
musk-rose m.-r., full	KEATS 478:45	m. of things	SHAK 793:33	N. came I out of my mother's womb	BIBLE 98:91
violet, The m.-r.	MILT 599:91	m. of words	WORD 958:84	n. in the dark and cold	LEGU 520:8
musk-roses sweet m.-r.	SHAK 767:30	m. to the world	LONG 536:39	n. into the conference chamber	BEVAN 89:58
Muslim the number of M. Americans	OBAMA 644:34	m. which defies solution	MORT 621:69	n. is the best disguise	CONG 240:40
Muslims the m...Jews, M.	CLIN 230:3	Out of silence m. comes	DARK 263:47	n. lunch is natural	GINS 371:4
mussel And the m. pooled	THOM 883:20	realise the m.	LAO 508:60	n. man covered in gold	BANKS 62:32
mussels gaping m.	CRAB 252:42	remain a m. to us	RUNGE 731:53	n. moment in politics	GERG 365:66
Mussolini Hitler...loyalty to M.	BULL 173:59	riddle wrapped inside a m.	CHUR 225:82	N. she lay	ROCH 719:5
M. had been at Oxford	HALI 393:33	separates us from the m.	HUGO 437:76	n. shingles of the world	ARNO 33:66
must All other things m.	SCHI 747:25	shew you a m.	BIBLE 127:62	n. to mine enemies	SHAK 805:53
'M.' is not to be used to princes!	ELIZ 322:7	Some m. should be left	WILL 945:89	n. to the hangman's noose	HOUS 431:37
rather than when you m.	SHUL 819:26	space was the uncontrollable m.	MCLU 556:52	Poetry is a n. woman	FERL 333:93
mustard have faith as a grain of m.	BIBLE 118:9	ultimate m. of nature	PLAN 680:24	poets have to go n.	SART 744:64
heaven is like to a grain of m.	BIBLE 117:95	verbs and the m.	SAND 742:29	Poor n. wretches	SHAK 792:11
hot dog without the m.	CHAR 216:47	voice, a m.	WORD 958:95	Th' have left thee n., Lord	CRAS 254:80
sowed in youth a m. seed	BRON 161:59	Women. They are a complete m.	HAWK 371:86	wallow n. in December snow	SHAK 764:36
mutability m. in them doth play	SPEN 839:40	**mystic** how a m. shape did move	BROW 166:92	When a was n.	SHAK 772:90
Nought may endure but M.	SHEL 812:58	m. way	GILB 368:43	whore may be n.	KILP 486:11
strange m. of human affairs	DICK 277:43	white samite, m., wonderful	TENN 878:73	Who told thee that thou wast n.?	BIBLE 91:94
mutations through all its m.	TRIL 897:18	with thy m. fan	HERR 415:6	With n. foot, stalking	WYATT 964:90
mute long since m.	KEATS 477:25	**mystical** most beautiful...the m.	EINS 313:80	**nakedness** n., an art stripped	MOTH 622:85
make the music m.	TENN 877:44	m. drama of the animal life	AMIS 16:44	n. of Stalinist dictatorship	KENN 480:88
M. and magnificent	DRYD 302:5	**mysticism** m., melancholy!	GAUT 361:4	n. of the land	BIBLE 93:43
m. on Tara's walls	MOORE 618:4	**mystification** intensify by m.	WHITE 935:36	n. of woman	BLAKE 140:2
use those languages, or we remain m.	BALL 60:86	**mystique** phoney m.	BRES 158:2	not in utter n.	WORD 959:8
voices of liberty be m.?	CUMM 257:59	**myth** courtesan is a m.	FLAU 339:18	**name** another n. more free	POPE 686:48
mutilation corset is...a m.	VEBL 910:44	History is the m., the true m.	MILL 594:85	answered to his n.	THAC 880:39
mutton kill their own m.	EDGE 311:42	inscrutability of the East is...a m.	STARK 843:25	as its n. imported	THAC 880:21
mutual gulf of m. incomprehension	SNOW 832:77	lend a m. to G.	CRANE 253:58	as my poor n. rehearse	SHAK 801:61
m. objective to allow	STEV 851:16	modern m. of psychoanalysis	THOM 883:99	bless his holy n.	BIBLE 102:6
muzzle m. of the revolver	GREE 386:22	m. before the m. began	STEV 850:83	brother's n.	SWIN 864:15
shalt not m. the ox	BIBLE 95:94	M. deals in false universals	CART 206:38	called thee by thy n.	BIBLE 109:87
my-lorded and m.-l. him	THAC 880:23	m. rather than history	FIED 334:10	called them by n.	MOORE 616:63
myopia means to treat m.	PRATT 694:68	m. that if you're liked	HOCK 421:14	ches, so was his n.	CHAU 216:56
m. makes all error mortal	LOWE 540:33	M., whereof I sing	CRANE 253:67	cometh in the n. of the Lord	BIBLE 103:23
myriad inspector, with a m. eyes	STEAD 843:34	poem...is a little m.	WARR 921:16	dare not speak its n.	DOUG 294:95
There died a m.	POUND 691:5	sceptred m. to hold	RUSS 735:44	Death is a n. for beauty	LAYT 515:99
myriads outshine M. though bright	MILT 601:36	starting point is m.	FRAME 346:76	deed without a n.	SHAK 797:54
myrrh get me to the mountain of m.	BIBLE 107:45	thing itself and not the m.	RICH 713:2	different n. for conversation	STER 848:30
gold, and frankincense, and m.	BIBLE 114:17	**mythical** built about a m. figure	HERB 413:50	done in their n.	SNOW 832:87
m. sweet bleeding	SPEN 838:20	The m. America	RABAN 703:4	done in the n. of 'decency'	LEWIS 527:66
myrtle instead of the brier...the m.	BIBLE 109:2	**mythologies** Artists make m.	KAP 473:28	ease, content! whate'er thy n.	POPE 687:87
leaves of m.	MARL 574:41	old m.	YEATS 966:16	Every n. is a tune	MOORE 617:82
m. and ivy	BYRON 190:30	**mythology** Literature is conscious m.	FRYE 340:54	extraordinary n. to give a maid!	SAKI 739:57
sails thro' m. bow'rs	POPE 686:60	m. of self	STEV 850:76	followed in its n.	CRANE 252:52
secure all the m. and turkey	AUST 46:68			forfeit of their n.	HABI 391:3
myrtles m. brown, with ivy	MILT 599:82	**N**		forgotten your n.	SWIN 864:3
myself being always with m.	GIRO 373:28	**nabobs** nattering n.	AGNEW 9:95	for his own n.'s sake	SCOT 755:85
can't even tell it m.	GREE 386:30	**Naboth** dogs licked the blood of N.	BIBLE 97:69	For my n. and memory	BACON 53:44
consciousness of m.	KANT 473:19	**nace** N. Novels that is	WELLS 930:24	Forth in thy n.	WESL 932:63
cry for m....cry for all	AGUS 9:98	**nag** bob-tail n.	FOST 345:53	Freedom, what liberties...in thy n.	GEOR 364:57
estranged from m.	HUGO 437:60	forced gait of a shuffling n.	SHAK 771:50	give you your n.	ELUA 324:44
girl I saw was m.	RHYS 712:78	**Nagasaki** even in the ruins of N.	BRON 160:46	good n. is seldom got	WYCH 964:93
I did it all m.	MILL 595:3	**Naiad** N. airs have brought me home	POE 683:86	good n. it is	DICK 277:50
In awe of...m.	SHAK 776:8	**nail** breadth of my n.	SWIFT 862:42	great N. we praise	SMITH 831:65
in order to save m.	HELL 408:41	Dick...blows his n.	SHAK 763:27	Guess her n.	ANON 23:87
into what I call m.	HUME 438:96	for want of a n.	FRAN 348:14	Halloo your n.	SHAK 785:91
lose mine honour, I lose m.	SHAK 794:65	n. by strength	SHAK 759:64	hallowed thy fair n.	SHAK 802:77
My best friend is m.	MORR 621:63	put her hand to the n.	BIBLE 95:12	hast not denied my n.	BIBLE 131:93
never...see m. perform live	WEST 932:81	smote the n. into his temples	BIBLE 95:11	have you lose that n.	MASS 581:80
quite m. again	HOUS 431:40	**nails** a person's n.	MCEW 551:61	He has no other n.	WINT 950:8
searched for m. across time	CIXO 227:45	'As n.,' added Charley	DICK 278:67	He that is without n.	SCOTT 753:51
too busy thinking about m.	SITW 824:13	beauty with my n.	SHAK 759:85	hope you guess my n.	JAGG 449:15
mysteries childlike m.	JAUR 452:98	blouse out and her n. grimed	MANS 567:95	hotter n. Than any in hell	SHAK 798:76
deepest m. of creation	SHEL 812:47	blowing of his n.	SHAK 760:7	house...hallowed for my n.	BIBLE 97:54
display her secret m.	HARV 400:78	half a dozen pounds of n.	CONR 244:50	how excellent is thy n.	BIBLE 99:30
m. and complications	GELL 363:32	in his hands the print of the n.	BIBLE 124:67	I am become a n.	TENN 870:98
understand all m.	BIBLE 126:52	naebody's n. can reach	SCOTT 753:59	if your n.'s above the fold	LANCE 506:22
mysterious m. and marvelous	THOR 888:21	n. bitten and pared	MACA 545:36	inscrutable singular n.	ELIOT 320:53
something m.. Find it.	MAUP 583:16	n. like birds' claws	BIBLE 111:40	in the n. of duty and obedience	SNOW 832:80
mystery as an ineffable m.	SCHW 751:94	n. whitter than the lylye flour	CHAU 217:98	In the n. of the Constitution	STAL 842:4
at the...bottom...lies a m.	ORWE 654:60	nineteen hundred and forty n.	SITW 823:11	Jack...a charming n.	WILDE 941:95
confound strangeness with m.	DOYLE 296:41	of my feet and my n.	NERU 633:22	Jew is only the n.	MILL 593:42
Death is the only m.	SKEL 825:36	sellin' tinpinny n.	DUNNE 307:19	kept them in thy n.	BIBLE 123:58
death's m.	HOOD 426:34			killing time Is only the n.	SITW 824:24

nation

known by the n. of perseverance	STER 848:25	what the dickens his n. is	SHAK 773:8	arm the n.	MANC 564:51
laud and magnify thy glorious N.	BOOK 147:70	what was done in his n.	BENN 79:30	as a n. taste-blind	FISH 337:65
lesser than my n.	SHAK 764:53	when somebody says your n.	BANKS 62:31	as a n., we don't dress well	SHAW 806:94
Let me not n.	SHAK 790:39	Why should that n. be sounded	SHAK 776:10	asset for one n.	RUNC 731:49
liberal shepherds give a grosser n.	SHAK 784:57	With a n. like yours	CARR 205:8	be a n. of shopkeepers	PUNCH 699:75
local habitation and a n.	SHAK 768:45	without a n.	SCHW 751:94	bedrooms of the n.	TRUD 899:70
lose the n. of action	TWAIN 903:63	write against your n.	RICE 713:89	best serves his n.	KENN 482:26
lose The n. of King	SHAK 764:54	write your glorious n.	SPEN 839:47	Better one suffer, than a n. grieve	DRYD 302:81
magnify thy holy N.	BOOK 147:58	Yossarian? Is that his n.?	HELL 407:28	bind up the n.'s wounds	LINC 529:11
Man by a scribbled n.	THOM 883:9	your n. moves, Leonora	CRAIK 252:51	British are an aggressive n.	ABSE 1:10
man of my n.	NAPO 630:52	nameless n. in worthy deeds	BROW 165:80	broad mass of a n.	HITL 420:91
Marrying left your maiden n.	LARK 509:80	names American n.	BENET 79:23	build that n.'s fate	BLAKE 141:28
mentioned your n.	DOYLE 297:66	Called him soft n.	KEATS 478:46	common property of the n.	TIMES 892:23
more common than the n. friend	LAFO 504:59	called them by wrong n.	BROW 168:42	continent a new n.	LINC 529:9
much less his n.?	WALC 916:11	calleth them all by their n.	BIBLE 104:49	credit of n.	CONG 241:57
murmur about his n.	RUSK 733:94	cat must have Three Different N.	ELIOT 319:52	curse of me and my n.	POUND 691:9
My n....a household word	ASHB 37:60	commodity of good n.	SHAK 770:29	darlings of our n.	SHAK 788:88
My n. is Death	SOUT 835:56	enter the n. and hand the keys	MANS 567:1	doing it to a whole n.	SIHA 821:65
My n. is on the building	FORD 343:98	five handmaidens, whose n.	ROSS 726:53	engaged in n. building	GARV 360:82
My n. is Ozymandias	SHEL 813:86	forgets words as one forgets n.	WAUGH 924:94	every man and n.	LOWE 539:3
n. all the men	MCCA 547:84	For your n.	WEBS 926:28	every man of every n.	THAC 880:36
N. and date	BUNT 173:66	given their n. up to her	JONS 468:89	existence as a n.	PITT 680:11
n. any disease after two guys	PUZO 701:9	Home of...unpopular n.	ARNO 35:12	Explaining metaphysics to the n.	BYRON 189:89
n. everyone gives	WILDE 941:81	How can they use such n.	SASS 746:98	exterminate a n.	SPOCK 841:85
n. flows on for ever	SASS 746:1	live like our n.	WALC 916:12	fate as a n.	HOFS 422:39
n. for problems...headaches	ACHE 3:45	live so long in our n.	BROW 165:77	fetishism...God of this n.	TATE 867:42
n....in honor of my father	PENN 673:81	lost all the n.	JOHN 464:81	fourth-class n.	JAY 453:5
n. in man and woman	SHAK 789:18	men's n. On sand	MILT 598:68	general synod of the n.	BAIL 55:89
n. is MacGregor!	SCOTT 753:56	men whose n. you never knew	ARLO 32:31	government of a n.	SUN 860:96
n. is Might-have-been	ROSS 727:63	n....associated...with racehorses	SAKI 739:54	great and powerful n.	GARI 360:72
n. is on your waters	SIGO 821:64	n. in print	CHES 221:2	great n. betrayed	INOU 456:51
n. is Truthful James	HARTE 400:71	n. of dogs	AMIS 16:44	half of the n. is mad	SMOL 831:66
n. not bound to anything	WINT 950:8	n. of those who in their lives	SPEN 837:93	happiness of the n.	JOHN 461:16
n. of an Australian be equal	PARK 665:37	n. to be mentioned	AUST 46:62	history of our n.	TOOLE 894:58
n. of Ireland is mentioned	SMITH 830:46	our n....as household words	SHAK 776:91	holy n.	BIBLE 130:67
n. of pictures produces	MORSE 621:64	spare the grossness of the n.	DRYD 303:24	in any one n.	HUME 438:4
n. of royalty	LABO 501:5	what are in but air?	COLE 235:26	influence of a n.	BENN 79:31
n. of the beast	BIBLE 132:11	naming n. of parts	REED 709:26	inspired the n.	CHUR 226:12
n. of the late deceased	KIPL 490:99	Nanda N. Devi Basin	SHIP 818:15	integrity of the Irish n.	REDM 709:21
n. of the Lord thy God in vain	BIBLE 94:66	Nanki-Poo Long life to N.-P.	GILB 369:59	I want to talk to a n.	PULI 699:70
n. of wife seems more blessed	HELO 408:53	nanny n. seemed to be extinct	HOGG 423:44	little war for a great n.	WELL 929:10
n. shall be called Wonderful	BIBLE 107:60	Nantucket spewed N. bones	LOWE 540:19	living Jury of the N.	BENN 81:81
n. to be put forward	HESE 416:28	nap short n. at sermon	ADDI 6:28	lowest rank of every n.	JOHN 461:89
n. upon the strand	SPEN 839:47	Naples now N. holds me	VIRG 914:28	make war on a kindred n.	BETH 87:11
n. was invented by novelists	WELLS 930:29	See N. and die?	DEBR 268:57	most decent n.	BUSH 182:98
n. was small	EGAN 313:65	Napoleon Maybe N. was wrong	STOP 856:20	muscle of my n.	FRAN 348:23
n. were John D Smith IV	ROCK 720:34	N. did not manoeuvre	WELL 929:4	n. about to go into...liquidation	MACI 553:3
n. which is above every n.	BIBLE 128:97	N. had commanded	ORWE 654:48	n....against n.	BIBLE 118:29
Nature is but a n.	COWP 251:23	N. learned from the mistakes	TAYL 868:48	n....against n.	BIBLE 107:51
New York, thy n. is irreverence	HUXT 443:15	N. of crime	DOYLE 297:62	n. being so right	WILS 949:78
none under n. under heaven	BIBLE 124:75	N. thinks that I am a fool	ALEX 12:59	n. blesses what undoes it	HUGO 431:7
No one...has just one n.	AMADO 15:21	signs of N.'s greatness	UNSE 905:10	n. has always been committed	KENN 481:3
object behind that n.	SPEN 837:10	wanted to be N.	DALI 261:12	n. heaps its scorn	LAZA 515:4
one whose n. was writ in water	KEATS 478:50	Napoleons Caesars and N.	HUXL 442:81	n. is a rainbow	JACK 448:3
only a woman in n.	GOTT 379:70	napper from your n. to your feet	COLL 237:63	n. is a society united	INGE 445:30
our very n. as Englishmen	PITT 680:11	narcissistically reflecting...n.	TALE 866:15	n. is not governed	BURKE 175:15
pass my n. in large letters	TREE 896:99	narcotics Like dull n.	TENN 873:58	n. is the universality	MAZZ 583:31
People you know, yet can't quite n.	LARK 510:92	narration life as n.	MANN 566:79	n. not slow and dull	MILT 601:18
Puritan decadence regards the n.	SPEN 837:10	time is the medium of n.	MANN 566:84	n. of gentlemen	MUGA 623:7
ravished with the whistling of a n.	POPE 687:90	narrative construct a n. for ourselves	AUST 47:91	n. of shopkeepers	NAPO 630:47
refuse thy n.	SHAK 765:79	motive in this n.	TWAIN 902:50	n. of shopkeepers	SMITH 828:87
remember the n. of the Lord	BIBLE 99:40	n. impulse is always with us	COOV 246:91	n. of shopkeepers	STOP 856:20
shade of a great n.	LUCAN 541:46	no longer...fiction...only n.	DOCT 289:83	n. of violence	JORD 469:1
someone wants to know my n.	MONT 614:35	narratives conceive of our lives as n.	LEHM 520:21	n. ruled by swine	THOM 887:90
sons acclaim you glorious n.	CUMM 257:58	narrow bestride the n. world	SHAK 776:9	n....run by an old man	BROD 160:35
spell my n. right	COHAN 234:94	cucumber n.	SITW 823:4	n. seems to slouch onward	HOFS 422:38
stranger...calls you by your first n.	KUHN 500:36	margin is too n.	FERM 333:94	n.'s experience and his vision	KISS 494:93
strong n. of the Trinity	ALEX 13:65	n. straight channels	RANJ 706:60	N.'s Freight Handler	SAND 741:13
sweet the n. of Jesus	NEWT 636:65	path...sometimes 'tis too n.	DRYD 301:48	n. shall rise against n.	BIBLE 118:29
terror of his n.	BEAU 71:20	straight and n. as a tomb	SMITH 830:35	n. should commit itself	KENN 481:5
that n. for the last four centuries	WEIL 927:69	narrow-necked as with n.-n. bottles	POPE 686:55	n. suspects...regular ministerial	WHIT 934:24
Their N. Liveth	KIPL 493:75	narrow-souled It is with n.-s. people	POPE 686:55	n.'s whole scale of living	CHUR 225:72
their n. liveth for evermore	BIBLE 113:11	Nasticreechia N. Krorluppia	LEAR 517:44	n. talking to itself	MILL 593:39
thought of his n.	ELIOT 320:53	nastier anything n. to say	SAYE 746:8	n., to remain healthy	MUSS 628:61
thy n. in high account	SCOTT 752:20	Blood...a great deal n.	SOME 833:9	n. to the policy	ROOS 724:5
thy n. is woman	SHAK 780:40	nasty everybody is as n. as himself	SHAW 806:82	n. was ever blessed with	FRAN 348:15
Thy n., O Jesu	HOW 433:84	far from their n. little minds	DEBU 268:61	n....without a sense of beauty	WHAR 933:2
To n. the unnamable	RUSH 732:65	how n. the n. people are	POWE 693:49	needed to constitute a n.?	SIEY 820:62
to that n. my courage	SHAK 795:93	n....reflects my personality	OLEA 649:31	nobility of descent in a n.	POTT 690:84
to thy n. give glory	BIBLE 133:35	of n. ideas	SWIFT 862:52	nobody...or I'm a n.	WALC 916:10
under any other n.	DOYLE 297:56	Something n. in the woodshed	GIBB 367:10	our greatness as a n.	THAT 881:53
underfoot her honest n.	SPEN 838:34	Zip that turns n.	CHRI 223:42	parcel of rogues in a n.	BURNS 179:40
weak witness of thy n.	MILT 597:39	nation affairs of the n.	AMERY 15:27	parcel of rogues in a n.!	BURNS 179:41
wealth and a good n.	WALT 919:87	American n. will speak	ROOS 724:15	personification of the n.	PAST 668:4
What is thy n.?	BIBLE 119:55	America...only instance of n.	WILS 949:87	puissant n. rousing herself	MILT 601:20
What is your n.?	SHAK 804:22	any n. where Christianity	SWIFT 863:77	realm, n., or city	KNOX 495:14
What's in a n.?	SHAK 765:80	any other n. may be its workshop	CHAM 212:59	reform a n.	CARL 200:87

national

rich and lazy n.	KIPL 492:65	n. into a new-made artificial state	POWE 693:59	art continue to follow n.	MOND 612:97
service of this n.	GAND 359:57	n. large and small	UNIT 905:9	art is the perfection of n.	BROW 165:57
social life of our n.	LEWIS 526:53	n. of Europe and outside	LEES 519:4	as broad as N....to interpret N.	DOYLE 296:42
tell the ideals of a n.	DOUG 295:9	n. of the future	CURZ 260:5	at once as N.'s self	BROW 168:38
that we are a n. of amateurs	ROSE 725:24	n. that have prospered and declined	LARD 509:66	attracted by God, or by N.	INGE 445:27
the n. that...dared to dream	OBAMA 644:41	N. touch at their summits	BAGE 54:72	back to n.	GOTT 379:71
the one indispensable—or was it indisposable?—n.	VIDAL 912:2	n. which spoiled you	BIBLE 112:59	beautiful flaws in n.	WOLL 954:90
things that matter for a n.	LLOY 533:72	N. would do well	COWP 251:20	betwixt N. and Art	PRIOR 696:10
thinking in terms of n. states	ADEN 8:62	not living n. but dead states	CHAM 212:57	blank Of n.'s work	MILT 603:75
to enrich a new n.	STIG 854:97	no very good symptom...of n.	CARL 199:76	bold and adventurous piece of n.	BROW 165:56
To every n. a term	KORAN 497:61	often that n. learn	KISS 493:84	by their n. intent on profit	PIUS 680:18
trade union for the n.	HEATH 405:84	other n. of the earth	JAMES 450:36	by their n., mess-makers	PIRS 679:92
train for war...a n.	WILS 949:84	peace...with all n.	LINC 529:11	cannot command N.	BACON 50:46
Type of a coming n.	LAWS 514:96	place among the n. of the earth	EMMET 326:6	chance gift of n.	MORAN 618:9
up to the face of a n.	ROCK 721:39	Praise the Lord, all n.	BIBLE 133:36	chance or n.'s changing	SHAK 800:37
We have, as a n.	MAMET 563:26	Spaniards and other n.	GARC 359:67	child...sweetest thing in n.	LAMB 505:92
What ish my n.?	SHAK 775:77	system of British n.	GEOR 364:54	come to n. with your theories	RENO 711:54
what our N. stands for	BETJ 88:22	the pedigrees of n.	JOHN 462:31	commonplace of N.	WORD 959:97
what stupid age or n.	BUTL 185:82	To belong to other n.	GILB 368:35	Consistency is contrary to n.	HUXL 441:68
whole of the Hellish n.	SITW 823:97	two n. have been at war	VOLT 914:36	Constant, in N. were inconstancy	COWL 250:71
who writes the n.'s laws	PERE 674:17	war between civilised n.	GOOCH 378:44	control the forces of n.	BUSH 184:50
will make of thee a great n.	BIBLE 92:16	whether civilized n. can restore	SMALL 826:58	convulsion of brute n.	STEV 854:91
wise n. preserves its records	HOWE 433:91	wickedness of these n.	BIBLE 95:91	creative n. Of man	MILL 594:80
With a n., as with a boxer	ACHE 3:55	wonder of hostile n.	MACA 545:43	customs...are the laws of n.	SHAW 807:10
Youth of the n.	DISR 288:36	**native** aren't n. to a place	LAMM 506:21	defect of n.	FRAN 347:32
national African n. consciousness	MACM 556:67	can its n. element	MARV 576:86	defend us against n.	FREUD 350:57
German N. Socialism	GOER 374:55	considerable in his n. place	JOHN 462:23	despite her n.	GOTT 379:70
n. capacity for individual enterprise	WAVE 925:2	dear n. country	SWIFT 862:57	determine the n. of the ends	HUXL 442:79
n. costume...architecture, or...art	BIRD 136:11	emptying the n.'s brain	FANON 330:14	Disguise fair n.	SHAK 775:74
N. Debt is a very Good thing	SELL 756:15	foot is on my n. heath	SCOTT 753:56	do by n. the things...in the law	BIBLE 125:4
n. dividend is diminished	PIGOU 678:76	form of n. government	ONEI 650:58	ever seen in Art or N.	WAUGH 924:80
our n. slogans	THUR 891:93	ideas about the n.	LESS 523:89	except his own n.	MILL 594:74
policeman in the N. Gallery	WHIS 934:19	looks into the eyes of a n.	LESS 523:90	existence in the n. of things	FORD 342:87
rock of the n. resources	WEBS 926:15	My n. heath	OHAG 648:8	exist with the n. I actually have	DESC 275:1
suffering a n. defeat	EDIN 312:49	N. always means people	STEIN 845:66	Eye N.'s walks	POPE 686:71
think little of the n. interest	WILL 944:66	n. of Ashbourn, Derbyshire	ANON 23:88	fair defect Of n.	MILT 606:64
nationalism also took...their n.	GOER 374:55	status of 'n.'	SART 745:78	Fair n.'s eye, rise	MARL 573:30
Canadian n. was systematically	INNIS 446:44	though I am n. here	SHAK 781:56	fear thy n.	SHAK 796:13
Current n. is merely	ILLI 445:21	**natives** bulk of your n.	SWIFT 862:44	First follow n.	POPE 685:18
dangerous being n.	RUNC 731:49	intercourse with the n.	PARK 663:91	floodgate and o'erbearing n.	SHAK 788:89
free from...n.	ORWE 654:51	**nativity** in n., chance, or death	SHAK 773:13	forces of N.	MARX 579:41
N., and its chum, patriotism	DUNN 307:17	out of love with your n.	SHAK 779:8	For n., heartless, witless n.	HOUS 432:73
N. is a silly cock	ALDI 12:48	**NATO** 15 representatives...in N.	MACM 556:68	fortress built by n.	SHAK 764:40
n....seen as a noble thing	BAKER 56:5	Serbs out, N. in, refugees back	ROBE 717:75	free as n. first made man	DRYD 300:30
somewhat blatant n.	RUSS 734:30	**natural** causes of n. things	NEWT 635:58	friend...the masterpiece of n.	EMER 324:60
wind of n. and freedom	BALD 57:33	culture of n. sciences	SUN 860:95	gay n. grieves	SMART 826:68
nationalities smaller n.	ASQU 38:84	double addition, and n. supernatural	HUGEL 434:4	general laws of n.	BURB 174:85
nationality barbarous feeling of n.	SENI 757:30	Home life...is no more n.	SHAW 809:85	general laws of n.	HUGO 436:53
Other people have a n.	BEHAN 74:14	in the n. way	KIPL 492:60	geography of one's own n.	BOWL 153:6
nations advantageous...to n.	PAINE 660:34	know so much about the n. world	SHAP 805:68	good gifts of n.	SHAK 785:80
all n., and kindreds	BIBLE 131:3	large as life and twice as n.!	CARR 205:19	Great n.'s second course	TWAIN 902:63
Amid...the misery of n.	PITT 680:12	living example of n. selection	GOLD 375:76	grossness of procreative n.	PAGL 659:17
among 50 n.	TRUM 899:82	lost faith...in n. force	CARL 200:82	hand of N.	GIBB 367:9
before him shall be gathered all n.	BIBLE 119:35	most n. way of approach	WEIL 928:73	happy n. to explore	POPE 687:83
both rich and poor n.	ILLI 445:22	naked lunch is n.	GINS 371:4	hem of N.'s shift	SHEL 813:88
cheap defence of n.	BURKE 176:41	n. and ordinary movements	FONT 342:75	Hold...the mirror up to n.	SHAK 783:19
civilized n. of the world	PEARY 671:59	n. language of all religions	STAEL 842:2	How quickly n. falls	SHAK 773:97
day of small n. has passed away	CHAM 212:60	N. rights is simple nonsense	BENT 82:92	husband n.'s riches	SHAK 802:69
dazzle and bewilder n.	MACA 544:24	n. science accumulates new riches	ALEM 12:56	If honest N. made you fools	BURNS 177:68
dead n. never rise again	LONG 535:32	n., simple, affecting	GOLD 377:18	If N. had not befriended us	CAVE 210:21
deceive the n. no more	BIBLE 132:21	n. to please	DRYD 301:65	images of N. were...present to him	DRYD 300:20
different n. should do	MONT 614:39	n., wholesome...English people	SHAW 810:7	imagination, n. itself is changed	ACK 4:65
enmities between n.	KENN 481:18	never so n.	JAMES 450:39	inclination of my n.	ELIZ 321:98
fierce contending n.	ADDI 7:53	new art to them is n.	DAVI 264:75	informed by the light of n.	BACON 49:28
free n. are peaceful n.	BUSH 183:26	not n. in an age	YEATS 966:14	In N.'s presence stood	WORD 958:88
great n. have always acted	KUBR 500:34	not n. to have come from there	STEIN 845:69	in n. the only ending	GRAY 383:41
happiest n., have no history	ELIOT 315:35	of that n. luck	SHAK 794:59	In n. there are no rewards	VACH 907:1
hostile behavior...to n.	FULB 355:63	said something n.	HILL 418:61	In n. there's no blemish	SHAK 786:25
intercourse with foreign n.	DECA 268:64	something...more than n.	SHAK 782:92	insight into the n.	HALES 393:30
Jew among the n.	FERB 332:67	wants the n. touch	SHAK 797:79	interpreted n. as freely	GIRA 372:25
king to judge us like all the n.	BIBLE 96:30	war is n.	STALL 842:9	In the n. of things	SPIN 840:71
language all n. understand	BEHN 74:17	was his n. self	TWAIN 902:55	Invention, N.'s child	SIDN 820:44
League of n.	MACD 550:51	what is n. cannot touch me	ETHE 327:48	irrelevant thing in n.	LAMB 506:12
leave it to...foreign n.	BACON 53:44	When we see a n. style	PASC 666:69	Is there any cause in n.	SHAK 792:13
leaves of the tree...for the healing of the n.	BIBLE 132:28	wildly n. and primitive	THOR 888:21	It can't be N.	CHUR 224:62
Levitical degrees between n.	ROCHE 719:1	Woman is n.	BAUD 69:81	it is its n.	TOLS 893:50
living n. wait	AUDEN 43:93	**naturalist** n. in England	DARW 263:51	know his n. and fashions	BACON 53:33
loans...to foreign n.	BAGE 55:78	**naturalists** N. observe, a flea	SWIFT 863:58	law of n.	HOOK 427:39
master minds of all n.	TWAIN 903:72	**nature** Abandon yourself to N.	RABE 704:22	law pervading all n.	HARDY 397:21
men and n. behave wisely	EBAN 310:8	absurd n. of Englishmen	PEPYS 673:92	Laws of N. cannot account	MILL 592:10
most bourgeois of all n.	ENGE 326:12	All n. is but art	POPE 687:79	lay on n.	SHAK 788:70
n. and governments have never	HEGEL 406:8	All N. was degraded	BLAKE 141:38	leaving light of n.	ROCH 719:11
n. are as a drop	BIBLE 109:82	all the laws of N.	THOR 888:24	let N. take her course	MILL 592:10
n.; between whom...no intercourse	DISR 288:34	almost a force of n.	WHITE 936:23	like N., half reveal	TENN 873:58
n. desirous of emancipating	MAZZ 583:29	Angel, it's a law of n.	LACL 503:38	lines in n.	GOYA 380:82
		arbitrary economy of n.	WOLL 954:89	Little we see in n.	WORD 961:30

necessity

lore which N. brings	WORD 957:59	N. that heard such sound	MILT 597:34	woman…N.'s agreeable blunders	COWL 250:78
love is liberty, and n., law	POPE 686:47	N. that is above all art	DANI 262:34	workings of n.	AQUI 30:99
made a gap in n.	SHAK 794:56	N. was as strongly bricked out	DICK 282:79	works of N. are…simple	BORE 150:54
Man has wrested from n.	STEV 850:5	N. wears one universal grin	FIEL 335:20	writer…an outcast by n.	BARN 64:66
Man masters n.	BRON 160:48	N. wept, thinking she	MARL 574:35	your divine n. is always free	PEACE 671:50
man of…comprehensive n.	DRYD 304:40	n. within me seems	MILT 607:90	youth…is n.'s priest	WORD 959:8
man…outdoes N. herself	SHAW 807:26	n. yearned to a.	WHITE 935:56	**natures** alien to their n.	HAZZ 404:61
man's n. runs to	BACON 50:62	n. yet remembers	WORD 959:9	n. that are mute!	MERE 588:31
man…up against N.	GABOR 356:1	necessary n. of a political	TROL 898:46	Pleasures of worse n.	MASS 581:74
Man was by N. woman's cully	CONG 240:25	never have enough of n.	THOR 888:27	subsists…in all n.	WORD 961:40
may delight N.	CAREW 198:55	never trifle with n.	AGAS 9:87	**naught** falling into n.?	ADDI 7:52
mere copier of n.	REYN 712:70	noble n.…treats with simplicity	ARNO 35:10	haif n. quhen he wald	HENR 411:17
more than Wisdom, Art, or N.	HERR 415:6	not beauty because it is not n.	CONS 244:57	n. but jouissance	GREE 386:32
Mute N. mourns her worshipper	SCOTT 752:15	odious vermin that n.	SWIFT 862:44	wear out to n.	SHAK 793:23
N. admits no hierarchy	FRY 354:48	Old Mother Wit, and N.	DENH 272:62	**naughtiness** bewitching of n.	BIBLE 112:76
N. admits no lie	CARL 201:40	O N.! we are thine	WORD 961:46	n. of thine heart	BIBLE 96:36
N. all curage me denyis	DUNB 306:5	One of n.'s Balkans	CURR 259:89	**naval** n. and air forces	ROOS 724:14
N. always does contrive	GILB 369:52	On Man, on N.	WORD 961:34	n. combat	GIBB 366:93
N. can decree	BYRON 188:59	order of God and of n.	MANN 567:93	**nave** make a n. of it	STEV 849:65
n. cannot be fooled	FEYN 334:43	order of n.	FONT 342:74	walk down the n. of his abbey	HOME 425:98
n.…careless as it is bountiful	DILL 286:92	O ruined piece of n.	SHAK 793:23	**navel** soul…ended at the n.	LEWIS 527:71
n. could never be intended	TAYL 868:58	our mortal n.	WORD 960:10	steam comes…her n.	THOM 884:41
n. could no farther go	DRYD 303:19	Our n. consists	PASC 667:72	**navies** nations' airy n.	TENN 871:17
N. does not endure	RABE 704:14	painter…must take n.	MALL 562:97	**navigation** employ steam n.	LARD 508:65
N. does not make jumps	LINN 530:32	physicians…leave it to N.	BURG 174:92	**navigation lady** the n. l. wasn't speaking	LETT 524:13
N. does require	SHAK 805:49	poetical n.	WHIT 937:88	**navigator** drunkard, my n.	SEXT 758:69
n. from her seat Sighing	MILT 606:50	presented to us by N.	LAVO 512:35	**navvy** dowser and not a n.	LEAV 517:54
N. gives you the face	CHAN 214:2	primary feeling that n. imprints in us	SADE 737:14	**navy** England's chief defence…the n.	PHIL 676:51
N. has given women	JOHN 461:6	pure mortal n.	CARL 200:83	join the n.	JOBS 455:61
n. hates a vacuum	WILL 945:93	renovator of matter N.	OVID 657:71	n. nothing but rotten timber	BURKE 175:21
n. hath framed strange fellows	SHAK 768:67	representations of general n.	JOHN 461:8	N. will run the blockade	ANDE 17:67
n. having intended greatness	ELIOT 316:55	repugnant to n.	KNOX 495:11	one-and-a-half ocean n.	HAYW 403:29
n. herself prescribes	MORE 619:22	rich in n.'s store	FORD 343:7	put at the head of the n.	CARS 206:35
N. I loved…next to N.	LAND 507:34	scientist does not study n.	POIN 683:98	Queen's n.	GILB 368:33
N. in him was almost lost in Art	COLL 237:69	scream passing through n.	MUNCH 625:41	Queen's N.	GILB 368:34
n. in hir corages	CHAU 217:70	secured by good n. and truth	ROCH 720:22	**nay** N., Mabel, n.!	GILB 368:41
N. in some partial…shape	POPE 689:46	See how n.…grows in silence	THER 882:84	yea be yea; and your n., n.	BIBLE 130:61
N. is a social category	LUKA 542:63	Sexually, Woman is N.'s contrivance	SHAW 808:29	**Nazareth** any good…out of N.?	BIBLE 122:20
N. is as wasteful	HUGH 435:17	she in spite of n.	SHAK 788:92	**Nazarite** your prophet the N.	SHAK 769:82
N. is but a name	COWP 251:23	Simple N. is the most harmless	BEHN 75:24	**Nazi** a N. lampshade	PLATH 681:21
N. is commonplace	STEIN 845:72	simple N. to his hope has giv'n	POPE 687:75	give him the N. salute	HEND 410:2
N. is God	WALK 917:41	singing is delightful to n.	BYRD 186:21	**Nazidom** fights on against N.	CHUR 225:90
N. is not a temple	TURG 901:17	sketch from n.	CONS 244:59	**Neaera** tangles of N.'s hair?	MILT 599:86
N. is nowhere accustomed	HARV 400:78	spark o' N.'s fire	BURNS 177:70	**near** as n. to heaven	GILB 368:28
N. is often hidden	BACON 52:23	spectacle of n.	ROUS 729:15	come not to me	BIBLE 110:8
N. is so exact	BARN 64:78	state of war by n.	SWIFT 863:65	so n. and yet so far	TENN 874:94
n. is That I incline	MILT 599:73	struggles and strives against n.	INNO 446:46	**nearer** draw a little n.	BRAC 154:20
n. is the art of God	BROW 165:58	subtlety of n.	BACON 50:42	n. by not keeping still	GUNN 390:96
N. is to be taken as she is	WHIS 934:20	suff'ring eye inverted N. sees	POPE 686:60	**nearness** n. of death	PAZ 671:48
N. made him	ARIO 31:13	teach us the n. of the ties	PLATO 682:66	**neat** n. as a furled umbrella	EMERY 325:2
N. meant but fools	POPE 685:16	the basic n. of humankind	GATES 361:98	n., clean, shaved and sober	CHAN 213:73
N. meant me A wife	DRYD 301:59	therein works a miracle in n.	SHAK 770:4	Still to be n.	JONS 469:60
n. might stand up	SHAK 778:57	thou and n. can so gently part	SHAK 795:94	You look n.	COLL 237:63
n. must produce a man	HUME 438:2	thro' N., up to N.'s God	POPE 687:91	**Nebraska** skies of Texas or N.	MCMU 557:83
N.…nothing without…purpose	ARIS 31:26	Thus God and n. linked	POPE 687:86	**Nebuchadnezzar** N.…was driven	BIBLE 111:39
n. of a conquest	SHAK 773:93	To look on n.	WORD 956:55	**necessaries** required three n.	JONS 468:93
n. of a man	STEI 846:88	too much after n.	GAUG 361:2	**necessary** absolutely n.	JOHN 460:83
n. of an hypothesis	STER 848:33	to see in paintings bits of n.	MALE 562:92	love of life is n.	JOHN 459:56
n. of a river	BACON 49:25	to sin our biased n. leans	DRYD 301:68	n. for mortals to be worn	EURI 328:59
n. of a theory	POPP 689:58	touch of n.	SHAK 787:39	n. not to change	FALK 329:9
n. of God	WHIT 936:71	trace The naked N.	POPE 685:20	n. to the human mind	REES 710:38
n. of my game	JAGG 449:15	travellers and wanderers by n.	FERB 332:67	no explanation is n.	SEAT 755:93
n. of politics	POWE 693:60	treat n. by the cylinder	CEZA 212:52	No more things…than is n.	OCCAM 646:81
n. of reason to perceive things	SPIN 840:74	true n. of poetry	RICH 713:5	Notes are often n.	JOHN 461:11
n. of the gods?	SHAK 760:21	true n. of the 'otherness'	NOLAN 640:43	slavery…so n.	ASTE 39:5
n. of the sickness	SHAK 786:28	ultimate mystery of n.	PLAN 680:24	so that the n. may speak	HOFF 422:31
n. of the Universe	HARDY 397:25	Unerring n., still divinely bright	POPE 685:18	that unnoticed and that n.	ATWO 41:43
N., red in tooth and claw	TENN 874:71	unrevealed glory of N.	SHIP 818:15	The superfluous, a very n. thing	VOLT 914:31
N., red in tooth and claw	TENN 874:80	Verse hath a middle n.	DONNE 292:62	whatever language is n.	KELM 479:68
N. remains	WHIT 938:13	violates the order of n.	HERO 415:95	**necessities** art of our n.	SHAK 792:8
N. repents she made her	DEKK 270:12	visible Foundations in N.	PETTY 676:47	distinction…luxuries and n.	GALB 357:16
N.'s darling	GRAY 385:89	voice the word 'n.'	REDON 709:24	earliest practical n.	HAWT 402:4
N.'s great masterpiece	DONNE 291:31	Vows can't change n.	BROW 169:71	n. call out…virtues	ADAMS 4:72
n.'s handmaid art	DRYD 299:15	war of n.	DARW 263:53	simple n. of human life	COMM 239:94
n.'s infinite book of secrecy	SHAK 794:45	war with rude N.	CARL 200:80	**necessity** chain of strong n.?	SPEN 838:25
n.'s law to change	ROCH 720:24	weakest in n.	PASC 667:81	door of n.	DEFOE 269:76
N.'s only interest	WELD 928:89	Whatever N. has in store	FERMI 334:95	Europe is…a n.	SARK 743:54
n. so preposterously to err	SHAK 788:90	What is man in n.?	PASC 667:85	fold Of dire n.	MILT 608:2
n.'s own hand painted	SHAK 800:39	what n. itselfe cant endure	FLEM 340:43	hard n. of bringing the judge	ALGR 13:70
N.'s scheme of colour	STRE 857:51	whatsoever abysses N. leads	HUXL 443:3	intelligence not a n.	ANGE 18:85
n.'s state, where all have right	DRYD 302:87	what you have been given by n.	PERI 675:25	Liquor…sidestepping n.	FADI 329:4
N.'s stern discipline	DOBZ 289:79	when n. is so beautiful	VAN 908:19	N. and chance Approach	MILT 605:27
N. still is fair	BYRON 187:43	where man leaves off and n. starts	FROST 352:2	n. has induced…greater license	COOP 246:87
n.'s truth is primary	THOM 886:72	while N. cures the disease	VOLT 915:49	n. invented stools	COWP 251:10
N.'s way of telling you	ANON 25:39	Whose body, N. is	POPE 687:78	N. never made a good bargain	FRAN 348:10
N. teaches beasts	SHAK 799:90	Wise n. did never put her…jewels	BACON 50:53	N. never makes prostitution	WOLL 954:94
N. that framed us	MARL 572:99	wished to copy n.	CEZA 212:55	n. of divine nature	SPIN 840:71

neck

n. of doing so — GERH 365:68
n. of making things plain — HUXL 443:11
n. of stealing — MORE 618:13
N.'s sharp pinch! — SHAK 792:2
N. will make us all forsworn — SHAK 763:5
nothing stronger than N. — EURI 328:54
strong n. of time — SHAK 794:50
sworn...To grim n. — SHAK 765:58
neck clothed his n. with thunder? — BIBLE 99:18
eloquence and break its n.! — VERL 911:60
had but one n.! — CALI 192:26
his n. brake, and he died — BIBLE 96:29
left his straight n. — ROSS 726:58
locket around his n. — SOME 833:10
millstone around a woman's n. — GREER 387:40
millstones...about your n. — DAVI 264:65
Millstones around our n. — DISR 289:75
millstone were hanged about his n. — BIBLE 118:11
n. God made for other use — HOUS 431:37
n. is like the tower — BIBLE 107:45
n. like an ostrich — DAVIS 265:97
one n., one chin — SHAK 785:90
one washes one's n. — BARN 64:60
over my n. and eyes — STEV 851:29
rain on the n. — COOKE 245:75
short n. denotes a good mind — SPARK 836:66
Some chicken, some n.! — CHUR 225:91
sticks its n. out — ANON 27:16
took the bride about the n. — SHAK 762:72
you've got a pretty n. — WALL 918:54
necklaces with our n. — MAND 565:61
necks venturing their n. for fruit — ROCH 719:18
necktie left my n. God knows where — HOUS 432:58
necromancy grete clerke of n. — MALO 562:5
nectar as butterflies sipping n. — ELIOT 315:19
lie beside their n. — TENN 870:92
n. from his hand — MARL 574:36
nectarine n., and curious peach — MARV 577:4
need Deserted at his utmost n. — DRYD 303:31
evil...face of total n. — BURR 180:63
God shall supply all your n. — BIBLE 128:8
hand of a vexatious n. — OTWAY 656:98
human n. and...silence — CAMUS 195:84
human n. continues to grow — COMM 239:95
In thy most n. — ANON 21:57
Lord, forgive me if my n. — CULL 257:47
most n. of blessing — SHAK 797:33
N. and oppression starveth — SHAK 766:12
n. for a well-defined personal space — COUP 248:33
n. to look within — SNYD 832:93
n. was the sorest — SCOTT 752:31
no n. for the faith — HOFF 421:24
seeth his brother have n. — BIBLE 130:80
Will you still n. me — LENN 522:53
worse n. for them — SHEL 814:10
needed makes it feel n. — SCHU 749:72
needing n. what I've invented — FULL 355:70
needle my hand n. better fits — BRAD 155:50
n. and the pen — LEWIS 526:51
n. is not worth the search — JACK 449:8
phonograph n. — GOLD 377:22
Plying her n. and thread — HOOD 426:30
reading of a n. — STEV 851:11
shove...with a red-hot n. — WODE 952:41
that poor little n....of femininity — OLIP 649:35
through the eye of a n. — BIBLE 118:10
needs according to his n. — BAKU 56:9
each according to his n.! — MARX 579:43
menial. n. and base — HYDE 443:21
must n. die — BIBLE 96:47
primary n. — GABOR 356:2
real n. of man — SCHU 750:74
tools, the ideals, the n. — RENO 711:57
needy provider for a n. man — HESI 417:33
wasn't poor, I was n. — FEIF 331:55
negation affirmation from n. — THUR 891:99
negative All satisfaction...always n. — SCHO 748:51
Electricity...positive and n. — LEAC 515:12
Great N. — ROCH 719:8
it was also n. — SNOW 832:76
N. Capability — KEATS 475:75
negativism nattering nabobs of n. — AGNEW 9:95
neglect easy to n....the truth — CORN 247:6
most tender mercy is n. — CRAB 252:34
n. God and his Angels — DONNE 293:74
punished for n. — JOHN 460:67
sweet n. more taketh me — JONS 467:60

neglected n. and misunderstood — RABAN 703:1
negotiate If we are to n. — BISM 137:35
n....into the Common Market — WILS 948:64
never no n. out of fear — KENN 481:1
negotiation n. and society — MUNCH 625:42
The hardest n. — ADAMS 4:84
negotiations opened n. — KISH 493:83
negotiators Agreement...by the n. — SHUL 819:27
best n. in Europe — NELS 633:12
negro all her n. train — SMART 826:59
America is...rooted in N. culture — ROLL 723:90
American N. female — ANGE 18:87
American N. problem — BALD 56:13
average N. could never hope to go — DAVIS 265:3
courage of the N. — PHIL 677:57
every Irishman would kill a n. — FREE 349:45
friend of the N. assumes — FULL 355:66
n. either didn't get in the pot — MARS 575:65
N. or saint — HOLM 423:57
N....was never looked at — BALD 56:19
One drop—you are a N.! — HUGH 435:16
The past of...the N. — OBRI 645:62
negroes Afro-American...replaced N. — FEIF 332:56
bronze N. breathe — LOWE 540:24
drivers of n. — JOHN 462:41
gnaws at n. — KING 487:34
infant n. in the West Indies — DICK 277:54
neighbour covet thy n.'s wife — BIBLE 94:66
false witness against thy n. — BIBLE 94:66
guinea in your n.'s pocket — RUSK 733:96
into the n. room — SHAK 784:46
look his n. in the face — STEV 851:16
love thy n. — BIBLE 94:78
love thy n. — BIBLE 118:26
love thy n. — BIBLE 115:37
love thy n. as thyself — BIBLE 94:78
love thy n. as thyself — BIBLE 118:26
Loving your n. as much as yourself — CLEE 229:81
n. loses his job — REAG 708:3
n. loses his job — TRUM 899:86
policy of the good n. — ROOS 724:5
removeth his n.'s landmark — BIBLE 95:95
stare...at our unintroduced n. — ELIOT 316:49
to hate your n. — MACA 545:34
Whenever our n.'s house is on fire — BURKE 176:34
wrest the ball from your n. — ANON 23:91
neighbourhood everyone in the n. — WHAR 933:9
n. kids — WILL 945:95
neighbourly like to be n. — HALI 393:32
neighbours advantage over their n. — SMITH 827:85
as the n. described them — MIN 608:6
commerce of all its n. — HUME 438:4
common hatred of its n. — INGE 445:30
drouthy n....meet — BURNS 179:18
feast his n. — SHAK 776:89
merry songs...to all his n. — SHAK 805:58
Sane people did what their n. did — ELIOT 316:44
sport for our n. — AUST 46:63
neighed n. after his neighbour's wife — BIBLE 110:13
Nell Little N. and Lady Macbeth — WOOL 956:40
Nelly Let not poor N. starve — CHAR 215:35
Nelson death of N. — SOUT 835:55
N. confides that every man — NELS 633:14
nemesis Hubris clobbered by N. — ALDI 12:52
neon something like n. signs — UREY 906:42
neotenic achievement for the n. ape — ALDI 12:51
nephew n....propounded 'Oysters' — DICK 279:9
Neptune more men than N. — FULL 355:80
Nerissa will do anything, N. — SHAK 769:80
Nero N. fiddled, but Coolidge — MENC 586:94
nerve Anatomised in every n. — JONS 466:43
a tough combo: n. and restraint — SULL 859:77
every n. a man may strain — CURZ 259:3
n. and instinct is clamouring — LESS 523:92
n. o'er which do creep — SHEL 812:62
raw n. ends of humanity — ANON 27:18
nerves but it quiets my n. — LOUIS 538:78
n. out of the job in hand — MANS 567:95
n. prick and tingle — TENN 874:74
N. sit ceremonious — DICK 284:36
quiver from the average n. — WHITE 935:54
nerve-shaken n.-s., over-civilized — MUIR 624:25
nervos N. belli — CICE 227:32
nervous came the turn of the n. system — RAMO 705:49
'native' is a n. condition — SART 745:78
n. tics — UPDI 906:33
take your n. system seriously — LEARY 517:47

nest brood over a full n. — ELIOT 315:41
It's like building a n. — OCON 647:89
long since my n. is made — TENN 873:45
n. of singing birds — JOHN 459:36
n. upon the dewy ground — WORD 961:44
One flew over the cuckoo's n. — KESEY 483:62
swallow a n. for herself — BIBLE 101:88
nest-egg not a n.-e. person — JOHN 456:83
nestling N. me everywhere — HOPK 429:87
net admiration...crosses the n. — BARR 65:94
bring her to the n. — KING 486:18
goodness make the n. — SHAK 789:14
just get rid of the n. — HUGH 435:27
N.. Anything reticulated — JOHN 460:76
over the n. in a different shape — LODGE 534:96
stick it in the n. — SHAN 805:63
tennis with the n. down — FROST 352:10
Whizzing them over the n. — BETJ 88:21
nets fishery without n. — DEFOE 269:78
n. of wrong — YEATS 965:9
tangled in amorous n. — MILT 607:76
time in making n. — SWIFT 861:35
nettle Out of this n. danger — SHAK 771:42
nettles dust on the n. — THOM 885:63
network indispensable n. — GLEI 374:48
networks n. of dead speech — STARK 843:23
neuroses store their moldy n. — PAGL 659:19
neurosis N. has...genius — PROU 698:47
N. is the way of — TILL 891:13
what n. would sound like — AMIS 16:54
neurotic character...described as n. — PAGE 659:14
I'm n. as hell — PLATH 681:38
Makes cats n. — ANON 24:30
n. builds castles — ANON 24:19
n. can...be a literary genius — AUCH 42:63
person as n. — SZASZ 865:28
prolonged n. doubt — BARZ 67:42
the n. classes — SHAW 810:6
neurotics gatherings of n. — MANK 566:75
neutral n. in situations of injustice — TUTU 901:26
United States must be n. — WILS 949:77
neutrality Armed n. is ineffectual — WILS 949:82
overwhelmingly for a policy of n. — BORAH 150:53
neutralizing n....newspapers — TOCQ 892:29
never could n. tell why — GILB 368:31
everything I n. wanted — GARD 360:69
N. again — ANON 25:42
n., n. use — GILB 368:32
N.'s a hard call — VENA 910:50
N. take advice from anybody. — ALTM 15:18
N. to have lived — YEATS 966:28
This will n. do — JEFF 454:30
You think it will n. happen — AUST 47:95
never-ending n.-e. Remembrance — POE 683:90
nevermore Quoth the raven, 'N.' — POE 683:88
never-never in the N.-N. — GUNN 390:94
Radio is a n-n. land — SAFER 737:16
never-sere ivy n.-s. — MILT 599:82
new against the n. and untried — LINC 529:7
all things are become n. — BIBLE 127:70
brook the n. — FERG 333:87
discovery of the 'n.'? — INGR 446:39
draw n. mischief on — SHAK 789:98
feel comfortable in the n. — MO 611:65
find the old in the n. — MANN 566:87
I make all things n. — BIBLE 132:24
It felt like a n. day — WINF 949:91
making something n. — GILL 370:86
n. and original plan — GILB 369:51
N. Deal for the American people — ROOS 724:4
N. Deal was ended by World War II — MCGO 552:87
n. every morning — BIBLE 110:26
n. heaven and a n. earth — BIBLE 132:23
N. to me — TRAH 895:84
Nothing...Which is not n. — FLET 341:60
not make a n. acquaintance — JOHN 464:97
put on the n. man — BIBLE 128:11
ring in the n. — TENN 875:95
Shock of the N. — DUNL 307:13
something impossibly n. — THARP 880:42
something n. to look forward to — FORD 343:12
the n. will grow — POL 684:6
things n. and curious — CUMM 257:51
New Age signs of a N. A. coming? — SMITH 830:25
new born pity, like a...n.-b. babe — SHAK 796:20
use of a n.-b. child? — FRAN 348:20
New England brought against N. E. — KRUT 500:31

night

Newfoundland Quoyle steered away to N.	PROU 697:38	other half doesn't read n.	VIDAL 912:98	black as the hour of n.	OBRI 646:68
Newgate gaze on the exterior of N.	DICK 277:39	Rage...writing columns for n.	BRES 158:3	black bat, n.	TENN 876:25
kind of N. calendar	IRVI 447:55	to please n.	THOM 885:55	black feet of the n.	GILM 371:96
New Jersey learned in N. J.	BALD 56:15	world mirrored in the n.	LESS 524:97	borrower of the n.	SHAK 797:43
New Labour N. L. brand has been badly contaminated	GOULD 379:74	**New Testament** blessing of the 'N. T.'	BACON 51:64	bowl of n.	FITZ 337:68
N. L.'s Xanadu	RAWN 707:86	blood of the N. T.	BIBLE 119:40	braw bricht moonlicht n.	MORR 620:54
saw 'N. L.' conceived	GALL 358:41	Could the N. T. have	GRIS 389:75	brother, in one n.	LUMI 542:64
Newman new-manned By N.	BROW 169:70	ministers of the N. T.	BIBLE 127:65	brothers...in the unending n.	MACL 555:42
Newmarket N., that infamous	CHES 219:46	N. T. had not proved in time	GREE 386:23	bucking ranches of the n.	THOM 884:33
newness conditioned to respect n.	UPDI 906:22	N. T. in my blood	BIBLE 126:49	But peaceful was the n.	MILT 597:32
n., the democratic conceit	LAWR 513:49	**Newton** N. with his prism	WORD 958:82	by and by black n.	SHAK 801:62
New Orleans Hoo-doo...in N. O.	REED 710:35	Shakespeare or Sir Isaac N.	FERG 333:84	by n. in a pillar of fire	BIBLE 93:62
N. O. is unremarkable	MAIL 560:55	**newts** N. and blindworms	SHAK 767:31	By n. or day	WORD 959:5
news always n. to somebody	KAVA 474:49	**New Year** on this day of N. Y.	POUND 692:17	calmest and most stillest n.	SHAK 772:85
a newspaper needs in its n.	PULI 699:72	**New York** a kind of N. Y.	USTI 907:48	cheek of n.	SHAK 765:74
brought bitter n. to hear	CORY 247:8	all the churches or chapels in N. Y.	BENN 81:81	Closed his eyes in endless n.	GRAY 385:90
cold roads...cold n.	SCOTT 754:75	an aviary...called N. Y.	OHEN 648:19	closes Saturday n.	KAUF 474:36
dog bites a man, that is not n.	BOGAN 144:97	In N. Y. people don't	JOUR 469:11	Come, civil n.	SHAK 766:95
Evil n. rides post	MILT 608:99	little trip to N.Y.	OHARA 648:13	come from n....go into n.	FOWL 345:59
free from bad n. and disease	BIOY 135:5	N. Y. is a jungle	AMIS 16:46	come like a thief in the n.	POE 683:83
get n....from objective sources	BUSH 183:25	N. Y. Island	GUTH 390:5	comes at n. to die	ARNO 34:97
good n. is that he's eating less	JACO 449:9	N. Y. is not the cultural centre	BELL 77:86	Come, seeling n.	SHAK 797:87
good n. yet to hear	CHES 221:95	N. Y. is one of the capitals	MAIL 560:55	coming for us that n.	BALD 57:24
literature is n.	POUND 692:15	N. Y. is the meeting place	BARN 64:59	dark and stormy n.	BULW 173:63
mariners had fabled n.	LOWE 540:18	N. Y. Pop artists	LIPP 530:34	darker than death or n.	SHEL 815:20
master passion is the love of n.	CRAB 252:36	N. Y. State will decertify him	CUOMO 258:79	darkness he called N.	BIBLE 91:82
media for the dissemination of n.	CHRI 223:39	N. Y. theater has died	MILL 593:47	dark n. of tyranny	MURR 627:83
n....and nothing but the n.	DANA 261:25	N. Y., thy name is irreverence	HUXT 443:15	day and a n.	SWIN 820:84
n. is not a mirror	LIPP 531:40	N. Y. was no mere city	DIDI 286:81	day and n. shall not cease	BIBLE 92:11
n. of the day	LIPP 531:37	When it's three o'clock in N. Y.	MIDL 590:83	day brought back my n.	MILT 601:28
n. or no n. to be	LEST 524:8	**New Yorkers** busy N. Y. take time	OKEE 648:23	Day in N.	CRAS 253:78
n. when there is no n.	ORWE 654:42	**New Zealand** I was born in N. Z.	MANS 567:10	Day's Journey into N.	ONEI 651:69
n....would have made me sick	SHAK 772:69	**next** What time's the n. swan?	SLEZ 825:53	day will not follow n.	TATE 867:41
not...different enough to make n.	SAFI 737:22	**nexus** n. of all love and money	DIDI 286:81	death's dateless n.	SHAK 801:47
only n. until he's read it	WAUGH 924:75	**NHS** N. is quite like heaven	HALD 392:26	dim n. of this immortal day	SHEL 814:19
primary office is the gathering of N.	SCOTT 751:98	**Nicaraguan** N. resistance	NORTH 641:63	do the same things every n.	OSBO 655:84
suckers for good n.	STEV 851:12	**nice** All the n. people	SPARK 836:71	dream by n. in the dusty recesses	LAWR 514:89
Tell Tchaikovsky the n.	BERRY 87:94	be sae n. wi' Robin	BURNS 178:97	dreaming n. will hide	SHAK 787:41
The function of n.	LIPP 531:41	But they sounded n.	RAMOS 706:50	dying in the n.	TENN 875:95
The more abhorrent a n. item	FOWL 345:64	change is always n.	EURI 328:63	earned a n.'s repose	LONG 535:19
today is no longer n.	RUSK 732:79	don't try to make things n.!	IVES 448:82	ending of interminable n.	ELIOT 321:85
to get the n. to you	TWAIN 903:83	how nasty the n. people	POWE 693:49	ensnared thee to this n.	SHAK 762:95
uncovers the run of the n.	LIPP 531:39	I'm a n. guy	HOFF 422:28	every n. at tea-time	STEV 853:72
What's the n.?	SHAK 782:84	Makes of no vile hold	SHAK 768:60	every n. to sit	ROCH 720:23
when I see the evening n.	CLIN 230:7	n. girl should only fall	SPARK 836:72	Every n., whisper 'Peace'	GROM 389:77
New South Wales govern N. S. W.	BELL 77:62	N. guys finish last	DURO 308:32	face of n. is fair	TENN 876:34
newspaper art of n. paragraphing	MARQ 575:58	n. man	SWIFT 862:52	forests of the n.	BLAKE 140:19
daily n....greatest organ	BENN 81:81	N. people	FRAN 349:27	foul womb of n.	SHAK 775:78
even from a small provincial n.	WODE 952:46	n. to the second housemaid	JAMES 450:50	gentle into that good n.	THOM 884:27
every word in...my n. must be clear	CHRI 223:36	someone wants to be n. to me	PUIG 699:69	genuine n. admits no ray	DRYD 300:44
good n., I suppose	MILL 593:39	Too n. for a statesman	GOLD 377:17	get up at n.	STEV 853:63
hit a n. reader between the eyes	BRIS 159:26	**nicety** sift...with the utmost n.	STEE 844:51	gloomiest n. will wear on	STOWE 856:32
invariable law of the n.	DANA 261:26	**niche** Madonna Standing in a n.	PARK 664:32	going to be a bumpy n.	MANK 565:74
I will show you a bad n.	CHRI 223:38	**Nicholas** St. N. soon would be there	MOORE 616:61	Good n., ladies, good n.	SHAK 784:50
n. is...a monopoly	SCOTT 751:98	**Nick** Satan, N., or Clootie	BURNS 177:83	Good n., sweet prince	SHAK 785:76
n. is an adviser	TOCQ 893:33	**nickel** if it doesn't make a n.	GOLD 377:25	Gwine to run all n.	FOST 345:53
n. represents an association	TOCQ 892:31	**nickname** Everybody has a n.	AMADO 15:21	hard day's n.	LENN 521:49
n.'s one and only aim	ORWE 653:6	n. is the heaviest stone	HAZL 404:56	Harry in the n.	SHAK 775:79
oblivion amounts to n. death	ADAMS 5:94	only one...that ain't got a n.	DICK 277:50	haunts you n. and day	BERL 84:37
Once n. touches a story	MAIL 560:43	**niece** hitting the n. of a bishop	ORWE 653:14	If he fall in, good n.	SHAK 771:35
One of the virtues...of a n.	SCOTT 751:99	**nieces** carrying of n.	RIDGE 715:30	in endless n.	HERR 415:11
Only a n. can place	TOCQ 892:32	**Nietzsche** I'm the black, basketball-playing N.	ONEAL 650:57	infant crying in the n.	TENN 874:77
person employed by a n.	HUBB 434:1	N....fools, and madmen!	ONEI 651:70	in the long n.	SURR 860:4
reaches the n. office	LIPP 531:37	**Nigel** dogs called N.	AMIS 16:44	in the n., to all, to each	WHIT 938:9
Reading someone else's n.	BRAD 154:23	**Nigeria** I am a daughter of N.	EMEC 324:47	invisible worm...flies in the n.	BLAKE 140:12
stamp of a n.	KRAUS 499:6	**nigger** blue-gum N. to sing me blues	BENET 79:25	I often wish the n.	HOOD 426:22
subsist without a n.	JOHN 460:81	humble myself to a n.	TWAIN 902:61	I saw n. close down	RAND 706:57
the only independent n.	MURD 626:70	just a red n.	WALC 916:10	Let n. come	APOL 29:82
touch a n. without disgust	BAUD 69:88	**niggers** 'twixt de n. of de Souf	TRUTH 900:4	Let no n. Seal thy sense	DELA 271:34
What a n. needs	PULI 699:72	**nigh** Draw n. to God	BIBLE 130:58	long n. settling in	MILL 593:58
newspapers believe all you read in n.	MACA 544:14	**night** 11.30pm on election n.	MOND 612:95	loud even in the dead of n.	SHAK 785:91
importance (of n.)	TOCQ 893:34	ability to get a good n.'s sleep	WILS 948:70	Love [ruled] the n.	DRYD 304:57
I read the n. avidly	BEVAN 90:59	acquainted with the n.	FROST 352:6	middle of the n.	CARR 204:98
lies from the print of n.	MAIL 559:38	ain't a fit n. out	FIEL 335:30	middle of the n.	KEATS 477:16
My approach to n.	CHRI 223:40	All n. has the casement	TENN 876:26	middle of the n.	THOM 885:69
neutralising the effects of n.	TOCQ 892:29	All n. long in the dark	STEV 853:65	middle of the n.	THUR 891:95
N. always excite curiosity	LAMB 505:88	All n., this headland	WILB 930:47	middle of the n.	TWAIN 902:63
n. and dogeared historybooks	DOSP 294:86	all of n.'s pathways	AGUS 9:92	moonless n. in the small town	THOM 884:31
N. are born free	SCOTT 751:4	All the grey n.	DELA 271:32	moon Walks the n.	DELA 271:31
n....are the most villainous	SHER 817:94	al the n. with open ye	CHAU 217:70	morn to n., my friend	ROSS 726:45
N. have degenerated	WILDE 940:51	armies clash by n.	ARNO 33:67	mosquitoey summer n. light	ASHB 37:79
N....inevitably reflect	LIPP 531:38	as a watch in the n.	BIBLE 101:93	museum to be looted at n.	RAINE 705:41
n....querulous and bellicose	MENC 586:84	As glorious to this n.	SHAK 765:78	ne'er forget that happy n.	BURNS 178:90
n. without a government	JEFF 453:20	ask of thee, belovèd N.	SHEL 816:54	N. and day on me she cries	BALL 593:9
not n. in the ordinary acceptance	BALD 57:30	Awoke one n.	HUNT 439:28	n. before Christmas	MOORE 616:60
				n. before some festival	SHAK 766:96
				n. Darkens the streets	MILT 602:47

night-clubbing

n. doth summon all to sleep?	DRAY 298:92	wide womb of uncreated n.	MILT 602:59	nobility destroy the pretended n.	BOCC 144:90
n....filled with music	LONG 535:23	will not last the n.	MILT 592:19	fashions men with true n.	MARL 572:3
N. Geometry	KENN 480:89	witching time of n.	SHAK 783:30	New n. is but the act of power	BACON 52:93
n. has a thousand eyes	BOUR 153:94	with us perpetual n.	JONS 467:56	N. brings obligations	LEVIS 526:35
N. hath a thousand eyes	LYLY 543:87	wonderful Southern n.-sky	LAWR 513:56	n. is of great use	BAGE 54:69
n. is beginning to lower	LONG 536:34	world's last n.?	DONNE 292:57	no n. of descent	POTT 690:84
n. is dark, and I am	NEWM 635:45	Would the n. were come	SHAK 781:45	pain is the one n.	BAUD 68:58
n. is darkening round me	BRON 161:73	write through the n.	PATC 668:7	seal of n. those people	MUSS 627:91
n. is long	SHAK 798:63	night-clubbing for n.-c. souses	GERS 365:74	with n. and tranquillity	SHAK 771:38
n. of our natural ignorance	HOBB 420:5	nightfall After n., I wouldn't leave V.S.N.	VAN 908:24	noble all were n., save Nobility	BYRON 187:36
n. of this worrisome day	BERN 86:77		WALC 916:23	fredome is a n. thing!	BARB 63:50
n. once more	BECK 72:46	night-gown in his n.-g.	MILL 595:98	How n. in reason	SHAK 782:89
n.'s black agents	SHAK 797:48	night-gowns seven flannel n.-g.	TRAV 895:88	I know n. accents	STEV 850:75
n.'s black arm	BURNS 179:26	nightingale an 'twere any n.	SHAK 767:24	My n. father	SHAK 789:96
N.'s candles are burnt out	SHAK 766:2	bright n. amorous	SWIN 863:82	n. and the slave	SCOTT 753:40
n. shineth as the day	BIBLE 103:44	for the sake of Miss N.	STRA 856:38	n....are not the leaders	CONR 244:44
n.'s lodging of their wives	WEBS 927:48	Hark! ah, the N.!	ARNO 34:84	n. grounds for the n.	RUSK 733:89
n. that numbers the leaf	STEV 850:96	little brown n.	HARDY 397:29	n., historically fair	LERN 523:85
n. that wins	SWIN 863:83	n., and not the lark	SHAK 766:1	N. men in the quiet of morning	DUNC 307:9
n., the shadow of light	SWIN 863:86	N. begins its song	COLE 235:25	n. mind is here o'erthrown!	SHAK 783:16
n. time I shall not forget	SWIN 864:95	n. does sit so late	MARV 577:97	n. race and brave	SIGO 821:64
n. to do with sleep?	MILT 598:65	n. when May is past	CAREW 199:57	n. to be good	TENN 871:10
n. when choice was any more	DIDI 286:80	no music in the n.	SHAK 759:68	no good at being n.	EPST 327:29
n. will more than pay	ARNO 34:73	'tis the ravished n.	LYLY 543:82	position where they may be n.	KAZIN 474:53
N., with all her negro train	SMART 826:59	nightingales duet of two n.	STEV 850:96	silence is most n.	SWIN 863:87
n. with different stars	SACK 737:11	nightmare History...is a n.	JOYCE 470:24	thou art n. and nude	SWIN 863:90
nothing but the n.	HOUS 433:83	n. of elderly white males	ABBO 1:1	To the n. mind	SHAK 783:8
Of n. and light	YEATS 966:12	n. of the dark	AUDEN 43:93	Was n. man	TENN 877:55
one calm summer n.	ROBI 718:82	nightmares horrible n.	WEST 933:98	What's brave, what's n.	SHAK 795:58
one n. certifieth another	BOOK 148:9	n. of many	RODO 721:51	noble-hearted swung the n.-h. three	SULL 859:80
one other gaudy n.	SHAK 794:72	night-raven n.-r. sings	MILT 597:41	nobleman Cultivated Underrated N.	GILB 370:71
only for a n. and away	WYCH 964:94	nights All days are n.	SHAK 801:50	king may make a n.	BURKE 176:53
on the n. before	SHIP 818:14	dogs barking...through endless n.	MENC 587:17	n. from surfeiting of his parents	LASS 510:12
out-soared the shadow of our n.	SHEL 815:40	fled Him, down the n.	THOM 886:81	noblemen N....cap and knee	WEBS 927:48
perfect day nor n.	SHAK 760:7	long, long wintry n.	LEAR 516:28	nobleness allied with perfect n.	ARNO 35:9
poisonous damp of n.	SHAK 795:75	long n. after Samhain	OBRI 646:70	That n. made simple	YEATS 966:14
politician...late at n.	WHITE 936:57	Love give me more such n.	HERR 415:2	nobler earth is n. than the world	PRIE 695:85
poor souls who dwell in n.	BLAKE 141:44	n. in Kansas City	MAIL 560:55	life is n.	SHAW 806:92
progresses...day and n.	MONT 614:34	n. not sufficing to do it in	PEPYS 674:2	nobles luxurious N.	JOHN 459:40
raised many of them in one n.	WALP 919:84	night-side Illness is the n.-s.	SONT 834:20	N. and heralds	PRIOR 695:99
real dark n. of the soul	FITZ 338:94	night-tripping n.-t. fairy	SHAK 770:26	noblesse n. and of chivalry	SPEN 837:14
reign of chaos and old N.	MILT 602:49	night-wind breath of the n.-w.	ARNO 33:66	nobody either I'm n.	WALC 916:10
returned on the previous n.	BULL 173:58	nihilism n. of technology	PAZ 671:49	I care for n., not I	BICK 133:49
Revel the n.	SHAK 773:98	Nile banks of the N.	SHER 817:77	Kneel to n.	SKEL 825:43
sat by n.	SCOTT 751:2	down the N....as Cleopatra	BROWN 164:29	more space where n. is	STEIN 845:65
saw Eternity the other n.	VAUG 909:39	more impassable than the N.	GIBB 366:95	n. agrees with you	STEIN 845:64
see another Saturday n.	MCNA 557:89	old father N.	SPEKE 836:81	N., as I knows on	STOWE 856:30
sense of a long last n.	MAIL 560:50	sources of the N.	ELIOT 316:46	N. can be exactly like me	BANK 61:16
seye as it was n.!	CHAU 217:92	waters of the N.	CARR 203:64	N. can say a word against Greek	SHAW 809:71
shades of n.	LONG 535:21	Nilus pretty worth Of N.	SHAK 795:90	N. comes, n. goes	BECK 72:39
shadow of the silent n.	MARL 573:10	nimble n. fingers are no more n.	SITW 824:20	N. has any conscience	HAWT 402:16
Ships that pass in the n.	LONG 536:37	nimbleness so much n.	DEKK 270:13	N. holds a good opinion	TROL 897:28
silence of the n.	ROSS 725:37	Nimrod N. the mighty hunter	BIBLE 92:14	n. is anybody	HUTC 441:50
sinning of the n. before	RUNY 732:62	nine hour ago since it was n.	SHAK 779:79	n. knows what they are talking about	CLEE 229:82
sleep one ever-during n.	CAMP 195:72	n. points of the law	ANON 22:70	N. rules safely	KEMP 480:77
slept the n. away	PRIOR 696:7	nineteen doesn't mean n.	BENN 81:62	n.'s around—n. big	SALI 740:81
small creature of the n.	AMIS 16:29	n. hundred and forty nails	SITW 823:11	N. shoots Santa Claus	SMITH 828:92
Some n. you'll fail	BROW 168:48	nineteenth n. century is great	HUGO 438:87	n. tells me anything	GALS 358:47
something more than n.	CHAN 213:97	Nineveh Quinquireme of N.	MASE 580:55	n. wants to read	TWAIN 903:89
something of the n. in him	WIDD 939:27	ninth about the n. hour Jesus cried	BIBLE 119:47	proved to be n.'s business	SMUTS 831:71
son of the sable N.	DANI 262:31	Limpopo of swamped N. Avenue	AMIS 16:46	someone gave a war & N. came?	GINS 372:13
Spirit of N.!	SHEL 816:65	nipple bites its nurse's n.	SADE 737:14	where n. knows us?	GASK 361:84
studying all the summer n.	MARV 577:97	Nixon If Richard N. was second-rate	HELL 407:32	nod Affects to n.	DRYD 303:29
Tender is the N.	FITZ 338:91	N.'s motto	COUS 248:41	dwelt in the land of N.	BIBLE 92:6
Tender is the N.	KEATS 478:44	Richard N. self-impeached	ABZUG 2:17	Land of N. at last	STEV 853:74
that n. I knew	SZIL 865:31	What N....began	PILG 678:78	n. on the parterre	POPE 686:62
That n., that year	HOPK 429:89	Nkongsamba N. was built	BOYD 153:10	nods Grove n. at grove	POPE 686:60
The City is of N.	THOM 887:7	no land of the omnipotent N.	BOLD 144:4	when the worthy Homer n.	HORA 430:21
The City is of N.	THOM 887:8	n. is just as short as...God	YOUR 969:60	nodus n. of a drama	CARL 200:6
there shall be no n. there	BIBLE 132:27	n. one else can	PITT 679:3	noise argues by increments of n.	BYATT 186:18
There's n. and day, brother	BORR 151:69	n. one ever sent me	PARK 664:11	barbarous n. environs me	MILT 601:21
thief in the n.	BIBLE 130:76	N. sun—n. moon!	HOOD 426:36	cannot be found in n.	THER 882:84
This ae n., this ae n.	BALL 59:66	N. warmth, n. cheerfulness	HOOD 426:37	emit a n. of any kind	MONT 613:8
This n. shall thy soul	SMITH 830:43	Oh, n., n., n.	SMITH 830:37	great n. in the city	EDWA 312:56
this n. wi' mirth and glee	SKIN 825:50	rebel...says n.	CAMUS 196:90	happy n. to hear	HOUS 431:43
thoughts that come in the n.	HEAT 406:92	say n. when they mean yes	ALCO 12:44	if neurosis could make a n.	AMIS 16:54
through the empty-vaulted n.	MILT 598:71	sound is 'n.'	KOH 496:33	is no n., nothing	MILL 593:37
torment of the n.'s untruth	DANI 262:31	That woman...can't say N.	PARK 663:7	let us melt, and make no n.	DONNE 292:38
upon the n.'s starred face	KEATS 475:78	The everlasting N.	CARL 200:96	little noiseless n.	KEATS 475:62
walks in beauty like the n.	BYRON 189:80	We say n., and we are the state	WRIG 963:72	loud n. at one end	KNOX 495:20
watch the coming of the n.	MATT 582:1	Noah all men are N.'s sons	WILB 939:35	love the n. it makes	BEEC 73:62
watch the n. and death	APOL 29:71	N. entered into the ark	BIBLE 118:31	make a joyful n.	BIBLE 102:1
western sky in the n.	WHIT 938:8	N. he often said to his wife	CHES 221:85	make least n.	SELD 756:9
What he sall ken this n.	MACD 549:31	two and two unto N.	BIBLE 92:8	make n. enough	SHAK 780:14
while the n. is gathering g.	BRON 161:74	won't start with N.'s Ark	ECHE 310:14	more n. they make in pouring	POPE 686:55
white moth thither in the n.?	FROST 352:11	Nobel N. is just another prize	HEAN 405:80	most sublime n.	FORS 344:25
White n. of icicles	MALL 562:98	worth the N. Prize	FEYN 334:7	moved to folly by a n.	LAWR 514:92

never valued till they make a n. CRAB 252:48
n. machines AMIS 16:46
n. of a fly DONNE 293:74
n. of battle rolled TENN 878:80
Nursed amid her n. LAMB 505:79
that kind of background n.? HOWE 433:88
the n. of classical music HOLL 423:54
wild n. of prattling visitants WEBS 927:45
noiseless Th'inaudible and n. foot SHAK 791:73
noises isle is full of n. SHAK 804:25
n. of America CUMM 257:51
Of all n. JOHN 465:6
painting of sounds, n. and smells CARRA 202:57
noisy when it is brash or n. AUDEN 44:16
Nokomis N. bore a daughter LONG 535:28
Noll for shortness called N. GARR 360:79
nomad n.'s life enthralls MAIL 560:67
nomadism test of n. LAWR 514:93
nomads sorrowing are n. MCMU 557:85
nomination decide the n. DAUG 264:62
non N. nobis, Domine BIBLE 133:35
non-being avoiding n.-b. TILL 891:13
non-combatant no fury like a n.-c. MONT 613:15
nonconformist man must be a n. EMER 324:53
N. conscience WILDE 941:79
nonconformity n....in America MCCA 548:93
none better than n. JOHN 464:96
n. but Antony SHAK 795:81
n. should be happy JOHN 463:50
non-existence n.-e. as an evil SCHO 748:54
n.-e. of the things that are not PROT 697:32
non-necessity n.-n. of it HARDY 397:25
nonsense author...talking n. WHIT 936:62
between sense and n. JUNG 471:46
export revolution is n. STAL 842:5
farrago of superlative n. CHUR 224:65
grammar, and n., and learning GOLD 376:11
infernal n. GILB 368:40
lump of clotted n. DRYD 300:36
may call it "n." CARR 204:92
memorable n. SANT 743:48
Music...closely structured n. BURG 174:3
music that is not n. ADDI 6:25
n. upon stilts BENT 82:92
other interpretation is n. GALL 358:45
perfect republics are a perfect n. FOWL 345:59
Protestations...perfect n. COBB 233:74
say nothing, or talk n. HUXL 442:87
secondary showbiz n. AMIS 16:47
sense from n. THUR 891:99
sounds like n., my dear SCOTT 753:42
winnowed from deep n. SAGAN 737:26
wish you'd stop yer n. LAUD 511:14
non-space n.-s. of the mind GIBS 367:15
non-violence N.-v....first article
of my faith GAND 359:59
N.-v. is not a garment GAND 359:60
noon as the sun at n. DONNE 293:72
from the fiery n. KEATS 477:28
liquid n. GRAY 384:58
midnight and the n.'s repose ELIOT 317:75
near her highest n. MILT 598:53
n. a purple glow YEATS 965:4
Rise not till n. PRIOR 696:13
the shameless n. TENN 871:8
turned white at n. MCMU 557:83
When n. is past SHEL 812:57
noonday wasteth at n. BIBLE 102:96
noose naked to the hangman's n. HOUS 431:37
n. of light FITZ 337:68
nooses N. give PARK 664:19
Norfolk bear him up the N. sky BETJ 88:19
Very flat, N. COWA 249:47
norm miraculous becomes the n. MILL 594:65
when homosexuality was the n. PROU 698:45
normal I don't know what n. is HARRY 399:62
n. economic system works SALT 741:95
that is the n. thing HEND 410:2
normalcy not nostrums but n. HARD 396:94
Norman N. arrow and sword WILL 944:64
N. blood TENN 871:10
north Entreat the n. SHAK 768:65
Far East is to us the near n. MENZ 587:19
heart of the N. is dead LAWR 513:66
Hills of the N., rejoice OAKL 643:5
in the N. long since TENN 873:45
likeness of the N. RODO 721:51

proceed n. of the 38th parallel MARS 575:64
sailed into the n. SHAK 786:13
school that I went to in the n. WILS 948:58
Spring to the N. MACD 549:33
talk slid n. KIPL 490:93
tender is the N. TENN 872:44
travelling due n. PEARY 671:60
unripened beauties of the n. ADDI 7:45
women at de N. TRUTH 900:4
North America N. A. colonization
underpants in N. A. MURR 627:80
Northcliffe blame someone like N. ORWE 654:43
northern constant as the N. Star SHAK 777:26
Glorious the n. lights SMART 826:67
with a n. moonlight SOUT 835:42
Northern Ireland violence in N. I. OROU 652:92
north-north-west but mad n.-n.-w. SHAK 782:93
North Pole N. P. out of my system PEARY 671:59
North Sea oil rig in the N. S. HEATH 405:87
North Star infect to the N. S. SHAK 773:27
Northumberland species of N. SCOTT 754:76
north-west N.-w. passage STER 848:40
Norway ten in the N. THER 882:91
nose assiduously picking his n. FIRB 336:51
Cleopatra's n.: if it had been shorter PASC 667:74
dog has a keener n. SNYD 833:94
Dong with a Luminous N.! LEAR 516:29
Entuned in his n. CHAU 217:73
haughtily he lifts his n. SWIFT 862:54
He had no n. CUMM 257:48
Marian's n. looks red SHAK 763:28
noise with its n. AMIS 16:54
n. fell a-bleeding on Black Monday SHAK 769:91
N., n., jolly red n. ANON 22:68
n. of a mob is...imagination POE 683:92
n. would not...have grown LAUT 512:30
not a n. at all WELLS 930:18
picking his n. with his toe BOYC 153:8
picking my n. AUDEN 43:83
ring at the end of his n. LEAR 516:36
same old n. GIRO 373:28
thirty inches from my n. AUDEN 44:15
To see...in front of one's n. ORWE 654:30
nosegay smelling his n. SITW 823:7
noselessness N. of Man CHES 221:92
noses blowing of n. STER 848:39
haven't got no n. CHES 221:91
slightly flatter n. than ourselves CONR 243:27
nostalgia N. IS A Weapon COUP 248:36
nostalgic n. about old fears? ACKR 3:63
when we're n. SONT 834:18
nostrils breathed into his n. BIBLE 91:86
flames from his large n.! BLAKE 139:81
glory of his n. is terrible BIBLE 99:18
own breath in our own n. MACD 550:46
nostrum never-failing n. BYRON 187:31
note and sound his n. WILL 946:26
keeps warm her n. CAREW 199:57
Lady, make a n. PARK 664:13
turn his merry n. SHAK 778:54
Tu-whit, tu-whoo!—a merry n. SHAK 763:27
Twenty Volume Suicide N. BARA 63:41
without a stir or n. THOM 887:9
Wrapped up in a five-pound n. LEAR 516:35
notebook Armed with a n. NEW 634:34
notes Bach on the wrong n. PROK 697:29
cheap and the n. LUCAS 541:51
dark n. rose everywhere HARR 399:55
In n. by distance made more sweet COLL 238:78
larks...singing the same five n. CATH 208:85
looking for the pretty n. PARK 663:92
million dollars...in well-used n. CART 206:42
n. are few! BLAKE 139:79
N. are often necessary JOHN 461:94
n. I handle no better SCHN 748:41
n. of the bell-birds KEND 480:85
right n. at the right t. BACH 49:7
sing Such n. MILT 598:55
suicide n. PLOUT 682:74
tearing up £5 n. HEATH 405:91
There are only twelve n. HIND 419:68
These rough n. SCOTT 751:6
thousand blended n. WORD 957:60
two n. a song DAVI 265:92
wrong n. are right IVES 448:43
nothing A home filled with n. ATWO 41:51
Ain't Heard N. Yet JOLS 465:13

artist...makes something of the n. PERCY 674:11
be responsible for n. PITT 679:4
Between grief and n. FAUL 330:33
Between the penis...there's n. CELI 211:35
brought n. into this world BIBLE 129:22
by doing n. MCEW 551:63
cannot get something for n. HARR 399:60
do n....for Ireland FREE 349:46
don't know n. DICK 281:65
doth n. but talk of his horse SHAK 769:77
Either Caesar or n. BORG 151:61
elsewhere they say n. HUXL 442:87
expects n. from society SAND 741:7
Hail n. full of n. HEMI 409:68
having n., and yet possessing all BIBLE 127:73
he...inherited n. JACK 449:5
He knows n. SHAW 809:76
He's done n. HOPE 428:60
I am not n. PESS 675:34
I have said n. RAVEL 707:83
I know n. GALS 358:47
I never heard n. about it PUZO 701:9
infinite deal of n. SHAK 769:73
I shall say n. YEATS 965:2
Is it n. to you BIBLE 110:24
life evolved out of...n. DAWK 266:18
like to say n. SOPH 834:31
Live Well on N. THAC 880:28
long for n. SPIN 840:76
lose n. again for ever GREE 386:12
Man is n. but a subject PASC 667:70
Man invents n. SHAW 807:26
means n. in this country GOLD 375:80
moral crusade, or it is n. WILS 948:62
n. at all to say SAINT 738:33
n. but his imagination SHAW 809:63
N. but males SHAK 796:24
n....but my body's length SHAK 760:17
n. but our own red blood YEATS 966:21
n. but the highest quality PATER 668:11
n....by which so much happiness JOHN 462:43
N. can be created from n. LUCR 541:58
N. can be done without it SIEY 821:62
n. can be said to be certain FRAN 348:19
N. can please many JOHN 461:8
n. either good or bad SHAK 782:85
N. for my Journey Now ANGE 19:2
n. for n. 'ere PUNCH 699:77
n. for reward SPEN 838:31
n. good to be had HAZL 403:32
N. happens, nobody comes BECK 72:39
N. has changed since HUGH 435:32
N. has raised more questioning ARNO 35:10
n. he cannot do KIM 486:12
N. in comparison to the infinite PASC 667:85
N. in excess ANON 20:20
n. in his life SHAK 796:11
n. in particular GILB 369:53
N. in the world is single SHEL 813:78
n. in thy purse BIBLE 113:96
N. is easier to say TERE 879:14
n. is made with n. INGR 446:38
n. is really very frightening STEIN 845:67
N. is wasted, n. is in vain HERB 413:54
n. left remarkable SHAK 795:84
N., like something LARK 509:75
n. mattered, n. was lost GEE 362:28
n. matters AMIS 16:53
N. matters very much BALF 58:43
n. much to lose HOUS 432:77
n. much to worry about HERR 416:19
N. of him that doth fade SHAK 803:17
N. really wrong with him HILT 418:65
N. remains of it all WOOLF 955:33
n. to do with the laws HORS 430:26
n. to live for GERV 366:85
n. to offer anybody KERO 483:54
n. to say, say n. COLT 238:82
n. to say...that is poetry CAGE 192:18
n. will remain HOUS 431:40
now I'm n. GINS 372:8
Now we know n. CORN 247:4
on whom n. is lost! JAMES 450:44
pictures of n. HAZL 404:60
reason knows n. PASC 667:80
say n., do n., be n. ANON 27:32
Science...knows n. GOUR 380:79

nothingness

seeing n. as the sum of everything	DUDEK 305:80
sees n. within him	FRIE 351:77
sit around so much doing n.	STEIN 845:68
that which dost cost me n.	BIBLE 97:50
thenceforth good for n.	BIBLE 114:28
there is n.	BECK 72:48
there is n.—absolutely n.	GRAH 380:89
There is n. to it	BACH 49:7
There's n. behind it!	WARH 920:6
there was n. before	HEMI 410:76
they that starve with n.	SHAK 769:74
those who do n....make no mistakes	CONR 243:24
those who had n.	BEER 74:89
thought n. of her writing	SITW 824:14
though you feel n.	JULI 471:42
To do n. and get something	DISR 287:33
To say n. is out here	HEAT 406:94
to whom such things are n.	SOPH 834:32
we can talk of n.	TROL 897:25
wise For saying n.	SHAK 768:70
writing is n.	HEMI 410:97
you shall learn n.	HUXL 443:3
Youth...forgives itself n.	SHAW 808:55
nothingness never Pass into n.	KEATS 476:84
old, split N.	FERN 334:97
nothings Invulnerable n.	SHEL 815:39
notice n. makes me feel sick	WODE 952:46
n. which you have been pleased	JOHN 460:63
Over the piano was printed a n.	WILDE 940:48
without my n.	HOMER 425:10
noticed hardly n. how it came	KHAY 485:88
notion a great n.	STEE 844:44
foolish n.	BURNS 177:87
give up every preconceived n.	HUXL 443:3
n. of cause and effect	HUME 438:95
n. that geometry was degraded	MACA 545:43
outworn n.	THUR 891:5
what a silly n.!	KING 488:53
notions counter to their narrow n.	STEV 854:92
notorious can't be famous...be n.	MAHA 559:29
Notre Dame turrets Of N. D.	MAHO 559:34
Nottingham N. lace of the curtains	BETJ 88:18
nought N. may endure but Mutability	SHEL 812:58
n. so vile	SHAK 766:87
when that my hap is n.	SURR 860:4
noun beyond its n.	REID 710:44
God...is a verb not a n.	FULL 355:69
Love is an abstract n.	AMIS 17:59
n. and a verb	SHAK 760:98
nouns how they connect n.	SAND 742:29
We are not n.	FRY 354:51
nourish n. a blind life	TENN 878:86
nourished grow and be n.	RAND 706:59
nourishes What n. me destroys me	JOLIE 465:12
nourishing back to the n. earth	SAND 742:23
nourishment as n. to wind	MILT 605:28
fruitful hope of n.	SPEN 839:61
proper n.	STER 848:33
without n. and support	SMOL 831:68
Novalis 'Character' says N.	ELIOT 315:37
novel admitted that a n.	TROL 898:55
aesthetic debate about the n.	BRAD 155:37
American n.	HUGH 435:24
atom of the traditional n.	LODGE 534:95
Australian n. is not...dreary	WHITE 935:55
because a n.'s invented	POWE 693:48
cannot care for in a n.	TROL 898:44
Cricket, like the n.	ARLO 32:32
crime n. is not easy	JAMES 451:58
given away by a n.	KEATS 476:93
greatest invention since the n.	MEAD 583:32
had he professed to be writing a N.	HAWT 402:7
impulse to write a n.	WILS 947:41
in the morning room reading a n.	WAUGH 924:78
liberated the n.	SPARK 836:77
modern n. has been many things	BRAD 155:36
notion of a British n.	BUFO 172:50
n. and art would be useless	BALZ 61:5
n....a Protestant form of art	ORWE 630:7
n. for the old stable ego	LAWR 512:42
n. is absolutely the only vehicle	FORD 343:93
n. is an impression	HARDY 397:17
n. is a static thing	TYNAN 904:2
n. is balanced between...impressions	BELL 78:91
n. is dead	DELI 271:39
n. is serious, the n.	NEME 633:19
n. of mankind	GAUT 361:5
n....philosophy put into images	CAMUS 196:2
n. tells a story	FORS 344:38
n. was not a trumpet	LESS 524:98
obligation to which...hold a n.	JAMES 450:42
Oh! it is only a n.!	AUST 46:83
project a serial n.	STEV 852:53
read a n....for the moral	OCON 647:88
scrofulous French n.	BROW 167:12
television has killed the n.	FRAN 348:26
When a n. comes	MAIL 560:62
Writing a n.	GREE 386:24
Writing a n.	SPARK 836:76
novelist admire you more as a n.	COOP 246:88
A n. could...run a country	TOIB 893:40
being a n., I consider	LAWR 514:84
characteristic of the really great n.	BENN 80:61
Jane Austen...only n. I know	BANKS 62:28
lady n.	GILB 369:61
made me a n.	GREE 386:21
most precious possession of a n.	CONR 244:38
No poet or n. wishes	AUDEN 43:9
n....does not have the right	FLAU 339:23
n....his own most harsh critic	WILS 947:46
n. is banging on his typewriter	COLL 237:62
n. is, like all mortals	NABO 628:13
popular n.'s trade	BURG 175:4
novelistic beginning of a n. affair	MANN 566:85
novelists n. for most n.	ROTH 728:90
few great film-makers...might have been good n.	RUSH 732:70
major n. who count	LEAV 517:52
N....are also children	DE 275:10
Phelps calls Medlar N.	MACD 550:39
novels all n....deal with character	WOOLF 955:14
books are n. at heart	RABAN 703:3
cultivation sits on her n.	AUCH 42:64
do not read n.	VIDAL 912:96
few English n. for grown up	WOOLF 955:21
heroes of three recent n.	BROY 169:89
Learn even from N.	WELLS 930:24
n. are about certain minorities	ELLI 323:37
n. is banging on his typewriter	COLL 237:62
n. written with a purpose	FORD 343:94
Readers of n.	LUCAS 541:49
reading all the n. you can	HUGH 435:19
which among my n. is my favourite	ACHE 2:22
novelty charm of n.	FLAU 339:21
Japan offers as much n.	BIRD 136:9
novel-writer woman...n.-w.	OLIP 649:35
November N., he full gross	SPEN 840:63
N.'s sky is chill	SCOTT 752:18
On the 5th N.	HOBY 421:11
these N. skies	FREE 350:49
now all is always n.	ELIOT 319:44
fierce urgency of n.	KING 487:28
here and n. cease to matter	ELIOT 320:69
Live always in this paradisal n.	KHAY 485:87
must be a great soul n.	EMER 325:89
n. is the day of salvation	BIBLE 127:72
N. is the time to drink	HORA 429:7
N. what?	SARO 744:59
nowadays many left like him n.	WAUGH 923:58
nowhere From n. we came	HAGG 391:7
in other words, n.	JARRY 452:92
n. to fall	ALAN 10:17
you're n.	GROS 389:81
nowt Say n.	CLOU 232:69
nozzle hits the exit n.	SCHW 750:93
nuance No colour, only n.!	VERL 911:59
n. in an ideological difference	COND 239:12
nubbly Nice but n.	KIPL 491:28
nuclear AIDS, cancer, n. war	MAMET 564:38
ancestors had discovered n. power	LAMB 506:16
military and n. sense	WALE 917:29
n. arms race	MOUN 622:93
n. reaction in uranium	EINS 313:78
n. war survivors	COUP 248:31
so-called independent n. weapons	BENN 79:32
nude Bare like n.	SPEN 837:2
mistress is n.	KILP 486:11
n. and antique	SWIN 863:90
nudes madonnas and shameless n.	MALE 562:92
nudging fudging and n.	OWEN 657:23
nudism lyrical bit about n.	JOYCE 470:39
nudist becomes a n.	WHITE 935:45
nugget n. of the human condition	ACKE 3:57
nuisance n. for the few people	CHES 220:55
pleasant n. in not being able to walk	DARW 263:51
positive n. to you	HOLST 424:89
nuisances pestilential n.	GILB 369:60
nuke a bad guy with a n.	PALIN 661:64
nukes they have n.	OROU 652:98
null splendidly n.	TENN 875:14
number best n. for a dinner party	GULB 390:91
big positive n.	GATES 361:90
called the wrong n.	THUR 890:72
cousins...without n.	SHAW 811:33
express myself in Terms of N.	PETTY 676:47
finite n. of heart-beats	ARMS 33:52
ghost with a n.	PAZ 671:47
increase their n.	TOCQ 892:29
n. all your graces	SHAK 800:36
n. of syllables	SAND 742:36
n. of the beast	BIBLE 132:11
n. of the stars	BIBLE 104:49
n., weigh and measure	HALES 393:30
n. who can write	MACD 549:32
On this next n.	LENN 521:43
teach us to n. our days	BIBLE 101:95
number one n. o....in music	WEST 932:79
numbers better than n.	CROM 255:16
brings home full n.	SHAK 773:13
By n. here from shame	JOHN 459:43
divinity in odd n.	SHAK 773:13
gadgets...fill your head with n.	PRIN 695:97
greatest happiness for the greatest n.	HUTC 441:49
hours their n. spend!	SPEN 839:51
more we grow in n.	TERT 879:18
no safety in n.	THUR 890:73
N....universal language	WEST 933:93
n. which could call	COWL 250:72
politics of n.	TANA 867:22
write the beauty...in fresh n.	SHAK 800:36
numbness drowsy n. pains	KEATS 478:41
numerous more n. formerly	TOLK 893:47
nun credit to a Trappist n.	SHAR 806:73
Hero, Venus' n.	MARL 574:35
quiet as a n.	WORD 959:96
nunc N. dimittis	BIBLE 133:44
N. est bibendum	HORA 429:7
nunnery Get thee to a n.	SHAK 783:10
Get thee to a n.	TWAIN 903:63
n. Of thy chaste breast	LOVE 538:85
put to scole in a n.	MALO 562:5
nuptials iteration of n.	CONG 241:76
Nureyev Ask N. to stop dancing	KING 486:17
nurse best n. contemplation	MILT 599:72
Chinese n. with green trousers	MANS 567:96
definition of what a n.	NIGH 639:24
dirty n., Experience	TENN 878:91
keep a hold of N.	BELL 77:61
Nature's soft n.	SHAK 772:84
n. and tutor of eccentric minds	LAWS 514:94
n. for a poetic child!	SCOTT 752:17
n. of manly sentiment	BURKE 176:41
n. of ninety years	TENN 873:47
priest continues what the n. began	DRYD 303:16
nursery light in the night n.	MACN 558:99
nurses old men's n.	BACON 51:75
to be n. and pianists	ROTH 727:77
nursing n. the unconquerable hope	ARNO 34:45
nursling n. of the sky	SHEL 813:77
Ocean's n., Venice	SHEL 812:64
nurture job of the n. of children	PALEY 661:53
nut cracking the n.	BRON 161:56
every hare-brained n.	SAFER 737:16
heading into n. country	KENN 482:30
n. schell, thocht it be hard	HENR 411:18
nut-brown spicy n.-b. ale	MILT 597:46
nutlike hard, brown, n. word	BART 66:15
nutmegs N. and ginger	ANON 22:68
nutrition People in n.	DAVIS 265:93
nuts fearful...would go n.	CUMM 257:49
where the n. come from	DISCH 287:10
where the n. come from	THOM 883:98
nutshell bounded in a n.	SHAK 782:86
Nyasaland bring Stonehenge to N.	BANDA 61:9
nymph Echo, sweetest n.	MILT 598:70
n. shall break Diana's law	POPE 685:35
rose like a n.	SHEL 815:22
nymphs n. with their flattering	SITW 823:4
Where were ye N.	MILT 599:85
Ye N. that reign o'er sewers and sinks	COLE 236:50

O

oak ashes of an o.	DONNE	292:63
builder o., sole king	SPEN	838:20
charms to…bend a knotted o.	CONG	241:51
English o. and holly	HARTE	400:74
fells the hardest-timbered o.	SHAK	760:5
O., and Ash, and Thorn	KIPL	492:53
O., and Ash, and Thorn	KIPL	492:54
o.'s thick branches	GRAY	383:56
plant an o. in a flower-pot	BRON	162:80
wedges cleave the hardest o.	KYD	501:47
win the palm, the o.	MARV	577:1
Oakland having come from O.	STEIN	845:69
oaks Beneath our o. hast slept	BLAKE	139:81
oak-tree When the o.-t. is fallen	CARL	201:16
O altitudo reason to an O. a.!	BROW	165:53
oar wind and wave and o.	TENN	870:93
oars like a ship with the o. lifted	MANS	567:3
The o. were silver	SHAK	794:55
oat-cakes o.-c. and sulphur	SMITH	830:53
oath A terrible o.	SHAK	786:19
forced to swear an o.	MARG	570:70
good mouth-filling o.	SHAK	771:53
He who cheats with an o.	PLUT	682:75
If ever I utter an o. again	SHAW	810:14
lose an o.	SHAK	763:15
man is not upon o.	JOHN	462:42
neither by any other o.	BIBLE	130:61
not ask thine o.	SHAK	798:84
since I took the o.	MACA	544:8
sin to keep a sinful o.	SHAK	760:1
sworn a solemn o.	BURNS	178:99
trust man on his o.	SHAK	791:75
oaths for o. are straws	SHAK	775:70
o. are but words	BUTL	185:79
standers-by to curtail his o.	SHAK	803:90
'Tis not the many o.	SHAK	791:65
oats O. A grain…given to horses	JOHN	460:77
OBE O. stands for Old Big 'Ead	CLOU	232:70
obedience end to blind o.	WOLL	953:88
except docility, o.	WELD	928:83
infuses…that liberal o.	BURKE	175:21
in the name of duty and o.	SNOW	832:80
life of strict o.	DOST	294:89
O.…is Good Luck's mother	AESC	9:81
o. of creatures	HOOK	427:39
o. to God	DAVI	266:13
swift in all o.	KIPL	490:8
truth in no man, nor o.	BEAU	71:22
obedient o. to their commands	SIMO	822:79
o. unto death	BIBLE	128:97
obey easy enough to o.	TUCH	901:12
love, cherish, and to o.	BOOK	148:92
o. God rather than men	BIBLE	124:76
One must o. the man	SOPH	834:27
That can so well o.	MARV	576:85
to o. is better than sacrifice	BIBLE	96:33
to those who o. Him	SCHW	751:94
who has learned well how to o.	KEMP	480:77
wise ridicule and o.	BIER	134:78
obeyed God has more right to be o.	JOHN	456:73
o. as a son	GIBB	366:1
She who must be o.	HAGG	391:8
when to be o.	HAWT	402:13
obituaries look at the o.	MOORE	617:98
obituary autobiography is an o.	CRISP	255:7
object America…an o. of faith	RABAN	703:4
B-b-british o.	MALO	563:18
chosen o., a definite task	POPP	689:59
desperately insignificant o.	DAVI	265:83
distinguish himself from an o.	SENG	757:28
end and o. of conquest	ALEX	12:58
'express' an o.	ROSE	725:26
eye on the o.	ARNO	35:7
let the form of an o. be what it may	CONS	245:60
most exalted o.	DARW	263:53
no o. worth its constancy?	SHEL	816:66
o. all sublime	GILB	370:66
o. behind that name	SPEN	837:10
o. from the crime	POPE	686:49
o.…is less discernible	LEGER	519:7
o. of aesthetic appreciation	BARR	64:81
O. of C.	AUST	45:49
o. of interest	RUSK	732:79
o. of love and esteem	LAMB	505:94
o. of universal devotion	IRVI	447:62
o. of war is not to die	PATT	670:31
o. quite forgotten	SHAK	759:64
o. seen, and eye that sees	WORD	958:89
o. strange and high	MARV	577:95
o. to seeing on the screen	GOLD	377:30
Picasso studies an o.	APOL	29:79
poem…is a physical o.	MACB	546:63
saddest o. in civilization	STEV	854:93
see the o. as in itself	ARNO	35:8
set before him a provoking o.	MILT	600:49
sex o.	GIOV	372:18
stimulus and o. of our meditation	MANN	566:76
utility of some particular o.	SMITH	827:78
When gold becomes her o.	SHAK	773:97
why should…your team o.?	HEND	410:2
woman into a sex o.	MORG	619:35
objection no o. to this method	STER	848:29
objectionable O. in action	GOET	375:58
objections o. to this proposition	HOBH	420:6
objective achieve that o.	MCNA	557:92
final o. is not	LIEB	529:96
gained our first o.	SASS	745:82
o. by pretending	LEWO	528:79
o. correlative	ELIOT	317:70
o. was the world	DULL	306:88
production of o. fact	MENC	586:3
speak of the Fascist o.	ORWE	653:20
objectives limited o. he has now	OCON	647:88
objectivity slivers and shreds of o.	CUPI	258:86
objects All visible o., man	MELV	585:59
arranging any set of o.	MILL	592:11
Artists don't make o.	KAP	473:28
bad poet dwells…in a world of o.	ELIOT	317:91
Caring too much for o.	TARTT	867:36
credit ordinary and visible o.	BROW	165:52
enjoyment of beautiful o.	MOORE	616:67
extracted from many o.	SHAK	779:5
forward the o. which we have	PLATO	682:66
lose sight of their o.	ELIOT	315:30
lustre of midday to o.	MOORE	616:62
Men see o.	FOWL	345:61
o. as I think them	PICA	677:61
o. of desire	RICA	712:82
o. of human reason	HUME	438:5
o. of Sensation	LOCKE	533:90
o. recognised, In flashes	WORD	958:85
o. seen by the eye	PIERO	678:72
One by one the o.	WILL	946:9
only o. in the material universe	FORS	345:44
ornament from utilitarian o.	LOOS	536:44
secure those important o.	PITT	679:10
too visible as sex o.	FRIE	350:65
try to forget what o.	MONET	612:99
obligated o. to Russia	BROD	160:42
obligation acknowledge no o.	GIBB	366:78
because o. is a pain	JOHN	459:52
not an o. but a joy	KILLY	486:8
o. of a more scrupulous fidelity	CONR	244:47
o. to become the servant	SHAW	809:86
o. to which…we may hold a n.	JAMES	450:42
pile o. on o.	CHAM	215:57
politics is an o.	ROGE	723:83
sense of o.	CRANE	253:74
obligations honourable o.	CHUR	225:80
Nobility brings o.	LEVIS	526:35
o. arising	UNIT	905:9
o. of man	CAMUS	196:1
trick of heaping o.	SHAW	807:20
obliging civil and o. young woman	AUST	45:49
obliviate drink to o.	FLYNN	341:64
oblivion Alms for o.	SHAK	787:37
cold o.	SHEL	815:44
memory be left in o.	EMMET	325:6
o. amounts to newspaper death	ADAMS	5:94
O, my o. is a very Antony	SHAK	794:32
Second childishness and mere o.	SHAK	779:83
oblivious one who is o. of you	OATES	643:15
oblong o. of pink	MONET	612:99
obloquy greatest o. i' th' world	SHAK	791:66
speechless o.	BYRON	188:63
obnoxious o. to each carping tongue	BRAD	155:50
obscene anachronistic is o.	BART	66:28
pictures of o. books!	ARLT	32:35
obscenity o., a depraved act	CHOM	222:26
O. is a cleansing process	MILL	594:91
o. is what happens	RUSS	735:73
Sex and o. are not synonymous	BREN	158:50
obscurantist He's a pre-Copernican o.	KEAT	475:58
obscure getting more o.	THOM	883:6
he who sits o.	SHEL	814:3
through the palpable o.	MILT	603:65
obscurity afraid of losing my o.	HUXL	441:57
o. of a learned language	GIBB	366:3
o. of our investigations	SCHO	748:52
o. of the matter	PROT	697:34
rest in o. and peace!	EMMET	325:6
obsequies celebrates his o.	SCOTT	752:15
tear to grace his o.	GRAY	385:85
obsequiousness O. is glorified	CHAO	214:9
observance breach than the o.	SHAK	781:56
o. of trifles	DOYLE	297:51
observation from personal o.	WILS	947:36
Let o. with extensive	JOHN	459:45
O. is always selective	POPP	689:59
product of that simple o.	BEHR	75:28
road of experiment and o.	LAVO	512:35
Scientific o. is always a viewing	HUXL	442:97
sense and o.	WORD	961:40
things…worth their o.	ADDI	6:32
Where o. is concerned	PAST	668:1
observations pure o. alone	POPP	689:58
what o. would lead him	AYER	48:5
observe never can o. anything	HUME	438:96
O. how system into system runs	POPE	686:72
o.…just by watching	BERRA	87:91
o. the best speakers	JONS	468:93
You see, but you do not o.	DOYLE	297:57
observed exists until…it is o.	BURR	181:68
o. by Yours faithfully, God	ANON	24:11
o. with sufficient closeness	TROL	898:39
observer every o. necessarily suffers	ORWE	655:67
keen o. of life	AUDEN	43:98
o. of human nature	DICK	277:43
social position of the o.	MANN	567:91
obsessed o. by the feeling	SPEN	837:13
obsolescence designing for o.	ISSI	448:77
obsolete Either war is o.	FULL	355:71
out of date, o.	STEV	849:62
obstacle Bureaucracy is not an o.	SCHU	750:81
gameboard and o. course	ELKIN	322:16
greatest o. to being heroic	HAWT	402:13
greatest o. to happiness	FONT	342:77
obstacle-racing sport…is o.-r.	TREE	896:1
obstacles all of civilization's o.	SAND	741:4
raining down o.	MANC	564:48
obstinacy o., and of error	POPP	689:63
O. in a bad cause	BROW	165:59
o. in a bad one	STER	848:25
obstinate not because he is o.	BLOOM	142:63
stricken with most o. love	SIDN	820:37
obstructed o. interstate commerce	HOOV	427:54
obstruction consecrated o.	BAGE	54:74
obtain o. the largest measure	TIMES	892:22
o. the reputation	TROL	898:47
obviating o. of all future wars	FORD	343:94
obvious afraid of the deafeningly o.	KAVA	474:49
analysis of the o.	WHIT	936:64
occasion constraint, and sad o. dear	MILT	599:82
courage mounteth with o.	SHAK	768:52
every possible o.	LYTT	543:95
had frequent o. to test…friendship	POE	683:84
man who never missed an o.	SHAW	811:1
nations, and on this o.	ROCHE	719:1
no o. to exert his understanding	SMITH	828:89
o., catalyst, or tripwire	ACKE	5:37
O., Chance, and Change?	SHEL	814:16
o. is not merely	NEHRU	633:9
occasions All o. invite his mercies	DONNE	293:72
august o. of the state	FROST	353:21
crowds for all o.	SIMP	822:82
feeling…on rare o.	FERL	333:90
o. and causes why	SHAK	776:96
o. such as these	MURP	626:74
Prose on certain o.	LAND	507:36
occult some o. relation	JOHN	459:54
occupation continual o. and change	AUST	47:88
cure for it is o.	SHAW	810:2
Every o.…is…absurd	QUEN	702:8
golfer…my real o.	MATU	582:17
no housewifery, nor…earthly o.	SMOL	831:67
not quite the o. of an adult	OLIV	649:38
pause in the day's o.	DE	271:7
pause in the day's o.	LONG	536:34
Sport…is an o.	PIUS	680:20

occupations

occupations imaginable o.	THUR 890:84
worse o. in this world	STER 849:57
occurred never o. to him	GARC 359:65
ocean at the bottom of the o.	RAND 706:58
butterfly poised on a pigtailed o.	SITW 823:96
crossed an o.	NICH 636:72
dark unfathomed caves of o.	GRAY 384:69
day-star in the o. bed	MILT 600:94
eye that sees on the o.	MACL 555:29
from o.'s farthest coast	HOW 433:85
His legs bestrid the o.	SHAK 795:88
icebergs in the o.	GERH 365:70
If the o. was pure mind	PRAT 694:66
land and o. without rest	MILT 601:26
lavished the o. on you in vain	BORG 151:57
life at the o. bottom	HECHT 406:3
Neptune's o. wash this blood	SHAK 797:37
new joys to the mild o.	MILT 597:32
O. and earth	WORD 961:36
one drop in a limitless o.	MITCH 609:31
o. for orient pearl	MARL 573:19
o. for orient pearl	MARL 573:23
o. is flat again	KEYN 484:73
o. of truth lay all	NEWT 635:61
o. or the human heart?	LAUT 511:26
o. protesting against separation	GRAT 382:14
O. racing is like standing	HEATH 405:91
O.'s child, and then his queen	SHEL 812:65
O.'s nursling, Venice	SHEL 812:64
o....was his home	BYRON 187:48
one-and-a-half o. navy	HAYW 403:29
On one side lay the O.	TENN 878:81
outstretch'd o. glitter	BYRON 190:6
painted ship Upon a painted o.	COLE 235:12
pores of the o. and shores	SHEL 813:77
rivers with the o.	SHEL 813:78
round o.	WORD 956:55
sky...Spread like a rosy o.	BYRON 190:9
So on the o. of life	LONG 536:37
till the o. Is folded	AUDEN 43:81
Tweed rins to the o.	BURNS 179:41
oceans Portable and compendious o.	CRAS 254:81
octaves o. of its parallel edges	CUMM 257:51
octavos o. fill a spacious plain	CRAB 251:26
October Falls the leaves in O.	FULL 356:88
fifteenth of O. 1764	GIBB 366:2
funny...month, O.	NORD 641:52
leaf still in O.	FLET 341:54
O.'s strife	GURN 390:1
octopus o. is soft	ARNO 36:47
odd cure of the id by the o.	ANON 24:10
divinity in o. numbers	SHAK 773:13
o. old ends, stol'n	SHAK 761:39
people's voice is o.	POPE 688:18
something o. about women	BENN 80:49
odds beats thee 'gainst the o.	SHAK 794:59
face the o.	HOUS 432:68
May the o. be	COLL 237:68
the o. of you winning	COWE 249:66
ode O. on a Grecian Urn	FAUL 331:41
odes quoted o.	TENN 872:32
odi O. et amo	CATU 209:11
odium He lived in the o.	BENT 82:1
odorous Comparisons are o.	SHAK 774:48
odour no o. so bad	THOR 888:28
o. of sanctity	WALL 917:46
o. of wine	RABE 703:9
principle of its colour and o.	SHEL 816:49
Stealing and giving o.	SHAK 785:77
sweet o....doth in it live	SHAK 801:52
odours dirt and ill o.	THOR 889:49
gentle o. led my steps	SHEL 816:59
phoenix...Exhales her o.	BYRON 187:30
probed...their o.	ANGE 19:99
puff of wind...laden with strange o.	CONR 244:34
Odysseus Like O., the President	KEYN 484:70
odyssey long o. toward liberty	MAIL 560:52
Oedipus O....dripping	PAGE 659:14
O. he had the luck	HUGH 436:41
O. triumph over gravity	KOES 495:28
reason is his best O.	BROW 165:48
Oedipuses peculiar family, the O.	BEER 74:99
off if honour prick me o.	SHAK 771:59
Want To Get O.	ANON 25:45
offal barrow of butcher's o.	SHAK 773:12
offence After o. returning	MILT 608:82
by deceit to breed o.	DYER 309:50
forgave the o.	DRYD 304:46
greatest o. against virtue	HAZL 404:57
image of o.	SHAK 786:20
like to give o.	FROST 352:91
mean to give o.	ROCHE 719:99
never resented for an o.	SWIFT 861:20
no harshness gives o.	POPE 685:24
O, my o. is rank!	SHAK 783:32
only defence is in o.	BALD 57:31
Shipton 'assault'...a criminal o.	CRAN 253:75
sour o.	SHAK 786:32
What dire o....springs	POPE 685:29
whatsoever o. or injury	HENR 411:13
offences more o. at my beck	SHAK 783:11
offend nothing shall o. them	BIBLE 103:30
o., when 'tis let loose	SUCK 858:71
the freedom to o.	RUSH 732:73
to o. somebody	FLYNT 341:65
offended I have o. reputation	SHAK 794:67
Just because you're o.	GERV 366:84
no one is consciously o.	ELIOT 319:34
no right...not to be o.	RUSH 732:74
This hath o.!	CRAN 253:76
we are sharply o.	TWAIN 903:80
offender hugged the o.	DRYD 304:46
offenders society o.	GILB 369:60
offensive It may sound o.	STEV 851:29
someone else is being o.	BROO 163:5
taking the o.	PENI 673:80
offer intend to o.	KENN 481:99
nothing to o. anybody	KERO 483:54
o. he can't refuse	PUZO 701:4
power to o....love	SHAW 806:90
offering delightest not in burnt o.	BIBLE 101:74
lamb for a burnt o.	BIBLE 92:26
o. too little	CANN 197:10
offerings burnt o.	BIBLE 93:33
burnt o.	BIBLE 97:50
delight in burnt o.	BIBLE 97:50
offers when most she o. blows	SHAK 794:69
office A dog's obeyed in o.	SHAK 793:25
By o. boys for o. boys	SALI 740:91
don't have power...have o.	TODD 893:36
Each in his o. wait	DODD 289:92
eternal villain...to get some o.	SHAK 790:36
fill a high o.	LOUI 537:67
gainful employment...not...public o.	ACHE 2:25
high officials leave o.	KISS 494:92
in which the o. is held	HUXL 442:77
man who has no o.	SHAW 806:81
never pretend to any other o.	HUME 438:98
never seen an o.	STEV 851:23
not going to be in o.	MOND 612:95
o. boy	GILB 368:34
o. of respiration	DICK 278:63
o. of the White House	MENC 586:2
o. sanctifies the holder	ACTON 4:69
o. to be new stamped	LAMB 505:93
o. was his pirate ship	LEWIS 527:57
primary o. is the gathering of News	SCOTT 751:98
raised taxes before he took o.	DOLE 290:98
reaches the newspaper o.	LIPP 531:31
seven years in o.	GISC 373:29
So clear in his great o.	SHAK 796:20
they have once won o.	GALB 357:15
'Tis all men's o.	SHAK 774:52
vote somebody into o.	GERG 365:67
way out of elective o.	HOOV 427:48
officer British o.	PANG 662:81
officers o. and fellow-rankers said	SMITH 830:42
offices ants to harvest o.	DONNE 291:25
go back to your o.	ANDE 17:67
good o. that sex can discharge	WOOLF 955:32
great o....give social prestige	BAGE 54:71
official more fanatical o.	HAZZ 404:61
The o. world	SNOW 832:75
officials high o. leave office	KISS 494:92
o. are the servants	GOWE 380:80
o. working in offices	WEBER 925:14
set of bigmouthed o.	DOSP 294:86
off-key sing...a little o.	MILL 593:52
sing o. k.	GERS 365:76
offspring human o.	MILT 604:10
o. of Heav'n first-born	MILT 603:73
o. of journalistic realism	WHITE 935:55
would not care about his o.	HAWT 401:1
often written so o.	GERG 365:65
oil America's dependence on o.	KERRY 483:59
anointest my head with o.	BIBLE 100:45
go out to an o. rig	HEATH 405:87
how much o....with one's vinegar	WILDE 940:46
in him we see O.	GOLD 377:16
keep putting o. in it	THER 882:82
mix like O. and Vinegar	GAIN 356:9
mouth is smoother than o.	BIBLE 104:56
o. can is mightier than the sword	DIRK 287:5
o. depletion...makes Houston	MAIL 560:55
o. to make his face to shine	BIBLE 102:11
Pour o. into their ears	JONS 466:49
Some people find o.	GETTY 366:88
thou hast anointed my head with o.	BOOK 149:10
Warren's blackin', or Rowland's o.	DICK 277:55
where you put in the o.	TAYL 868:61
why o. painting was invented	DE 271:19
wine...sweeter...than o.	RABE 703:9
oily o. man of God	THOM 887:5
ointment Dead flies cause the o.	BIBLE 106:30
like the precious o.	BIBLE 103:40
Oisin O O.	YEATS 965:5
Wanderings of O.	WILDE 940:50
okie O. use' ta mean	STEI 845:82
Oklahoma Okie...from O.	STEI 845:82
old adherence to the o. and tried	LINC 529:7
A human being is o.	FITZ 338:4
And she, being o.	SMITH 828:3
appeared o. unto me	BIBLE 110:21
appeared, to have been of o.	SPEN 838:30
As an o. soldier	SHAW 807:28
As you are o. and reverend	SHAK 792:93
beauty so o. and so new	AUGU 44:27
Behold, thou art o.	BIBLE 96:30
Being an o. maid	FERB 332:71
being o. is having lighted rooms	LARK 510:92
be she o.	SWIFT 863:76
boredom makes you o.	CAST 207:75
born o. and ugly?	DICK 279:99
brook the o.	FERG 333:87
buried in a good o. age	BIBLE 92:18
can't be o. without it	WILL 945:91
chancèd in the times of o.	SHAK 760:27
chilly and grown o.	BROW 168:32
country safe to grow o. in	THAT 881:52
crown of o. men	BIBLE 105:80
die before I get o.	TOWN 895:70
die or grow o.	MONT 613:11
fat and grows o.	SHAK 771:45
find the o. in the new	MANN 566:82
folks git o. en strucken	HARR 399:50
foolish, fond o. man	SHAK 793:31
growing o. in drawing nothing up!	COWP 251:16
Grow o. along with me	BROW 168:59
how subject we o. men	SHAK 772:89
I am just o.	WELD 928:91
If you're going to get o.	STEG 844:57
I grow o....I grow o.	ELIOT 316:67
ill and o. and terrified	BETJ 89:37
I'm just an awkward o. maid	RENO 711:48
insecurity in America...growing o.	ELLW 323:39
know thee not, o. man	SHAK 773:99
Long be it ere thou grow o.	ROCH 720:26
love everything that's o.	GOLD 376:9
make me conservative when o.	FROST 352:12
more virtue than o. men	JOHN 461:98
never can be o.	SHAK 802:74
never too o.	THOR 889:48
no fashion for the o.	CHAN 214:1
no man would be o.	SWIFT 862:51
now am not too o.	BLUN 143:79
now am o.	BIBLE 100:60
o. and stricken in years	BIBLE 97:51
O. and young	STEV 852:45
o. fashioned	ALLEN 14:97
o., For a dream's sake	ROSS 726:39
o. have reminiscences	SAKI 739:53
o. heads on your young shoulders	SPARK 836:67
o. immorality condoned	SHAW 811:37
o., mad...dying king	SHEL 812:70
o. man, and heavy	BIBLE 96:29
o. man broken	SHAK 805:55
o. man does not care for	JOHN 461:54
o. man in a dry month	ELIOT 317:82
O. Man with a beard	LEAR 516:27
o. man with wrinkled dugs	ELIOT 318:4
o. man young	TENN 871:6

opinion

o. men shall dream	BIBLE 111:48	**old woman** an o. w.'s touch	ENRI 326:19
o. [might as well speak] to the young	CATH 208:89	**Old World** eyes of the O. W.	MANS 567:97
O. people are scary	SMITH 829:28	**O'Leary** with O. in the grave	YEATS 966:17
o. people are square	SHAF 758:54	**oligarchy** always an o. that governs	PARE 663:89
o. people make so many journeys	BLYT 144:89	call it o.	HOBB 420:3
o. ways are the safest	COKE 234:96	**olive** an O., and a Turkey Fig	BETH 87:10
our land, it is o.	RANS 706:68	children like o. plants	BIBLE 103:28
persuade you, young and o.	PLATO 681:43	fruitful o.	SPEN 838:20
put off the o. man	BIBLE 128:11	o. leaf pluckt off	BIBLE 92:10
redress the balance of the O.	CANN 197:11	Stretched under the o. trees	SPEN 837:4
remember the days of O.	MOORE 617:1	**Oliver** difficulty in inducing O.	DICK 278:63
Ring out the o.	TENN 875:95	**olives** acquired taste, like o.	RIFK 715:35
same o. nose	GIRO 373:28	**Olivet** brows of O.	TENN 874:70
Say I'm growing o.	HUNT 440:30	**Olympic** O. games	COUB 248:20
she is not yet so o.	SHAK 770:6	O. weight lifter	NIGH 639:18
socialize the cost of growing o.	HEWE 417:38	**Olympics** Montreal O.	DRAP 298:89
Some day before I'm o.!	KIPL 491:39	**omega** Alpha and O.	BIBLE 131:87
suppose an o. man decayed	JOHN 464:87	**omen** One o. is best of all	HOMER 425:5
Tell me the o., o. story	HANK 395:81	**ominous** is o.	SANT 743:42
tell when one is getting o.	EDWA 312:62	**omission** art of o.	LIEB 529:95
The o....talk to themselves	ONEI 651:63	glaring sin of o.	OSLER 656:90
the o. will go on	WILL 946:19	**omissions** O. are not accidents	MOORE 617:84
think he is growing o.	IRVI 447:59	O. are not accidents	MOORE 617:90
Though I look o.	SHAK 778:71	o. of a Government	ROOS 724:7
times begin to wax o.	BIBLE 112:70	**omit** o. to paint that which he sees	FRIE 351:77
'Tis well an o. age is out	DRYD 304:58	**omnibuses** run up the steps of o.	WOOLF 955:12
to be forty years o.	HOLM 424:84	**omnipotence** final proof of God's o.	DE 275:13
too o. and intelligent	BRAD 154:34	honour, and o.	MARL 573:21
too o. to dream	HAMM 394:64	**omnipotent** God the O.	ELLE 322:18
warn you not to get o.	KINN 488:65	O. but friendless	SHEL 814:14
We are o., we are o.	SMITH 830:39	Power, which seems o.	SHEL 815:20
we grow o.	TENN 872:30	**omniscience** his specialism is o.	DOYLE 297:71
whats the use of being o.	OHARA 648:12	**Omnium** Duke of O.	TROL 898:57
when he is o., he will not depart	BIBLE 105:89	**Onan** O....spilled it on the ground	BIBLE 93:40
when they get to feeling o.	BROO 162:96	**Onassis** going to marry...O.!	JOHN 457:4
when thou shalt be o.	BIBLE 124:69	**once** O. upon a time	KING 487:46
When you are o.	YEATS 965:7	**once-bitten** happily for the o.-b.	HOME 425:97
when you are o. sit	DICK 280:33	**ondulous** lifting with a great o. stride	CUMM 257:51
you and I are o.	TENN 870:2	**one** dial but o.	SHAK 783:15
You get o.	KEIL 479:64	all o.—shall live	BIBLE 127:79
youth, before I waxèd o.	SPEN 839:48	all o. in Christ Jesus	GREE 385:2
old age cold and forlorn o. a.	STEV 832:52	At o. with the O.	FLET 340:50
death...puts an end to o. a.	LABR 502:21	being o. and not two	FROST 353:19
died in a good o. a.	BIBLE 98:84	forgive Thy great big o.	SHAK 776:2
first sign of o. a.	HICKS 417:45	hearts in o., your realms in o.	POTT 690:85
flower of o. a.	DEMO 272:49	how to be o. up	BRAD 155:51
fruit in o. a.	BIBLE 102:98	If ever two were o.	CARR 204:86
infirmities of o. a.	WESL 932:71	it ought to be Number O.	EMER 325:76
looked down upon in our o. a.?	SCHU 750:80	it will be all o.	SHAK 769:81
man reaches o. a.	MAO 568:31	not o. among them	SPEN 837:4
men...in their o. a.	POPE 686:56	o. bullet in ten thousand	DUMAS 306:89
o. a., accident, sickness	LLOY 532:71	o. for all	SHAW 809:69
o. a. and experience	ROCH 719:12	o. in three	SHAK 769:75
O. A. a regret	DISR 287:26	o. of the twenty	INGE 445:25
O. a. hath yet his honour	TENN 870:2	only o. to make a quarrel	BIBLE 96:22
o. a. is always fifteen years older	BARU 67:35	people arose as o. man	PHIL 676:53
O. a. is...a massacre	ROTH 728:96	souls in o. shall grow	SHEL 815:43
O. a. is second childhood	ARIS 31:15	The O. remains	ALEX 13:65
O. a....it's the only disease	MANK 565:70	Three in O.	BIBLE 106:17
O. A. may come after you	WHIT 938:14	Two are better than o.	HOUS 431:38
o. a. of cards	POPE 688:15	**one-and-twenty** When I was o.-a.-t.	DOLE 290:97
O. a. should burn and rave	THOM 884:27	**one-armed** o.-a. man	RUSS 735:40
should accompany o. a.	SHAK 798:69	**one-dimensional** o.-d. mind	ERAS 327:36
son of his o. a.	BIBLE 93:37	**one-eyed** o.-e. man is king	WELLS 930:23
The best armour of o. a.	MUNG 625:45	o.-e. man is king	TRUM 900:90
Oldcastle Sweet Jack O.	SHAK 771:48	**one-handed** a o.-h. economist	DAVIS 266:7
older As I get o.	FERL 333:92	**O'Neil** slay Owen Roe O.?	MANC 564:52
As I grow o.	SOLO 833:2	**one-man** o.-m. House of Commons	STEI 845:58
As we get o.	REED 709:29	**oneness** essential o. of mankind	RAUS 707:80
As we grow o.	ELIOT 320:68	**one-night** o.-n. stands in collectors'	SONT 834:20
enjoy getting o.?	CHER 218:27	**onerous** more o. citizenship	MONT 615:46
growing o. has served no purpose	RILKE 715:37	**ones** weaken the necessary o.	DIDI 286:79
grow o. and o.	SAYE 746:12	**oneself** delusion that one likes o.	ELIOT 321:97
I get sillier as I get o.	DENCH 272:55	Hell is o.	BERL 84:46
man as he grows o.	STEI 846:88	left to o.	ANOU 28:68
O. than love	SCOTT 751:3	love is the gift of o.!	SPIN 840:78
O. than the time of chronometers	ELIOT 320:72	what is useful to o.	RANJ 706:60
The o. I get	FRID 350:63	**one-stringed** old o.-s. instrument	MAIL 560:55
was so much o. then	DYLAN 309:53	**one-trade** Detroit is a o.-t. town	EDDI 311:22
oldest o. hath borne most	SHAK 793:40	**one-way** o.-w. property of time	SMITH 831:59
old-fashioned apt to grow o.-f.	WILDE 942:11	**onion** Let o. atoms lurk	SHAK 794:47
be always o.-f.	SANT 743:42	tears live in an o.	KING 486:20
make these products o.-f.	STEV 849:62	**only** o. in America	SHAW 806:88
o.-f. Boarding-school	AUST 46:73	o. things that are true	WHIT 937:91
o.-f. Virginia fox hunt	WASH 922:28	**onward** o. and outward	NABO 628:13
Old Testament O. T. makes	STAN 843:17	**ooze** present than in the o.	SHAK 786:98
Prosperity...blessing of the O. T.	BACON 51:64	**opal** mind is a very o.	PALIN 661:59
		open an o. door	PULI 699:71
get these things out in the o.	PULI 699:71		
getting out into the o.	KELM 479:67		
having an o. mind	PRAT 694:63		
keep the store o. nights	KAUF 474:42		
Never lay yourself o.	HUNT 439:19		
o. door, and no man can shut it	BIBLE 131:93		
o. thy mouth wide	BIBLE 101:87		
whole nation out in the o.?	SIHA 821:65		
open-minded We should be o.	DAWK 267:24		
opening Eyes...go on o.	REID 710:44		
hell of an o.	REAG 709:15		
No better o. anywhere	DICK 281:54		
o. and closing of a door	SAND 742:21		
opening-night o.-n. audience	HIRS 419:76		
opera born for o. buffa	ROSS 727:66		
first rule in o.	MELBA 584:45		
I am like an o. singer	MEAT 584:33		
language an o. is sung in	APPL 30:91		
like German o.	WAUGH 924:79		
No good o. plot	AUDEN 43:5		
o....composed by God	CARD 198:40		
o. isn't what it used to be	COWA 249:53		
o....is to music	MENC 586:91		
O. is where a guy gets stabbed	BENC 78:11		
poor man's o.	HUXL 442:92		
Some of the o. houses	JOHN 459:33		
to the o. one goes either	VOLT 914:47		
opera-glasses O. to view...take o.-g.	RIDGE 715:32		
operas French o. sung by Swedish	WHAR 934:11		
operating literature is the o. instructions	LE GU 520:19		
operation military-style o.	CRAN 253:75		
o. of separating	JOHN 458:32		
refused an o.	GREG 387:52		
operations diversities of o.	BIBLE 126:51		
field of o.	BELL 78:96		
o. of government	RUNC 731:48		
o. of our own minds	LOCKE 533:90		
performing a few simple o.	SMITH 828:89		
operator dial the o.	TREV 896:9		
operators billions of legitimate o.	GIBS 367:15		
Ophelia most beautified O.	SHAK 781:76		
much of water hast thou, poor O.	SHAK 784:29		
soft you, the fair O.	TWAIN 903:63		
Ophir Nineveh from distant O.	MASE 580:55		
opiate Communism is the o.	LUCE 541:57		
emptied some dull o.	KEATS 478:41		
o. of the oppressed	JONG 466:33		
opinion almost of o.	MONT 613:11		
better to have no o. of God	BACON 52:97		
Busy o.	FORD 343:5		
client asks his o.	JOHN 462:29		
collective o....can make history	SAFI 737:22		
combat...with particular o.	DRYD 300:39		
cost to freedom of o.	SCHL 747:33		
current o.	MCCA 547:90		
Do not despise my o.	LEON 523:77		
drift of public o.	DAFOE 260:2		
engine of temporary o.	HAZL 403:41		
everything else is o.	DEMO 272:48		
flatterer does not have a good o.	LABR 502:27		
fool gudgeon, this o.	SHAK 768:71		
form a clear o.	BONH 146:26		
gave it for his o.	SWIFT 862:45		
give him my o.	DICK 281:69		
God's o. that life should go on	SAND 742:30		
guided by o. polls	THAT 881:74		
have his every o. regenerated	PIER 677:66		
heated division of o.	TYNAN 904:99		
high in Mr Podsnap's o.	DICK 283:18		
instrument for gauging public o.	GALL 358:45		
laughter at their quaint o.	MILT 605:35		
low o. of himself	TROL 897:28		
mankind...of one o.	MILL 591:3		
man of common o.	BAGE 55:80		
money controls o.	ORWE 653:22		
north of my lady's o.	SHAK 786:13		
offer him an o.	SPEN 837:9		
of his own o. still	BUTL 185:86		
o. with the learned	CONG 240:23		
o. breeds ignorance	HIPP 419:70		
o. in good men	MILT 600:4		
o. in the absence of evidence	CRIC 254:92		
o. is about a woman	JAMES 450:46		
o. of himself, having once risen	BENN 81:64		
o. of our best friends	MARG 570:68		
o. of Winston Churchill	ELTON 323:42		
organization of public o.	LIPP 531:38		

opinions

Party is organized o.	DISR 288:49
poor itch of your o.	SHAK 798:88
Prejudice...vagrant o.	BIER 135:90
public o. will sweep them away	PULI 699:71
reason the o. of others	WOOLF 955:29
recurring again to Plato's o.	STER 848:41
scorching world's o.	FLET 341:61
was ever of the o.	GOLD 376:89
whole climate of o.	AUDEN 43:89
wolf remains of a different o.	INGE 445:25
opinions as many o. as...people	TERE 879:15
borrow other men's o.	BACON 51:86
confirm and establish our o.	BROW 165:46
contempt for my character and o.	SHAW 807:14
don't care to give o.	HERN 414:93
his o. and fancies	HARR 399:54
How long halt ye between two o.?	BIBLE 97:61
I have...strong o.	BUSH 182:2
Men...bad as their o.	MACK 554:17
men who have no o.	CHES 220:63
one truth, and many o.	KURZ 501:46
o. that they...entertain	PALM 662:73
o. were not acted on	ELIOT 316:44
private parts...and his religious o.	BUTL 186:10
Stiff in o.	DRYD 302:83
takes no notice of their o.	CROM 255:18
think his own o.	MORE 618:11
those who have certain o.	STEIN 845:78
what their o. make of them	LICH 528:92
wish to spread those o.	BUTL 185:90
Women were expected to have weak o.	ELIOT 316:44
opium against art, as against o.	RODC 721:43
antidote against the o. of time	BROW 165:79
help of o. or alcohol	HERZ 416:22
It is the o. of the people	MARX 578:24
just, subtle, and mighty o.!	DE 273:82
Music is no different from o.	KHOM 485:89
o. for every conceivable mass	KENN 480:93
o. has left the happiest memory	GREE 386:10
o. of the West	FRAN 346:80
opium-dose Bible as...an o.-d.	KING 488:54
opponent an o. cannot be...honest	ORWE 655:66
sound to his o. bitter	MILNE 595:11
tries to best his o.	PAUL 670:34
opponents pushed back...by their o.	PANK 662:83
trip, hack and push their o.	FRY 353:28
truth...convincing its o.	PLAN 680:25
opportunist rather be an o. and float	BALF 58:44
opportunities equal o.	MAND 564:53
No duties, only o.	ANON 26:2
o....thicker than anywhere else	BALD 56:14
series of great o.	GARD 360:70
wise man will make more o.	BACON 53:41
woman with fair o.	THAC 880:22
opportunity age of right and o.	WILS 949:75
build a society of o.	MAJOR 561:72
Equality of o.	KENN 481:16
existence and o.	TEMP 869:70
giving you the o.	DICK 281:62
improving the present o.	WILL 944:67
Know thine o.	PITT 680:16
least o. invades it	NICO 637:83
let slip an o.	SHAW 811:35
maximum of o.	SHAW 808:40
not time or o.	AUST 45:52
o. accorded him since Adam	MUGG 623:10
o. as against material interests	WILS 949:76
o. cost of economic discussion	GALB 357:22
o. for attacking the devil!	STEAD 844:35
o. for graft	BIRNS 136:21
O. makes a thief	BACON 49:18
o. to rise again	SARN 743:55
o. to serve our country	SMITH 829:10
scarcity of o.	ANGE 19:88
strong seducer, o.!	DRYD 300:32
substantial equality of o.	ROOS 724:18
unfettered o.	MADAN 558:15
when preparation meets o.	BRAN 156:73
opposed o. may beware of thee	SHAK 781:50
opposite in justice and in its o.	SOPH 834:27
o. of talking	LEBO 518:64
opposition duty of an O.	CHUR 224:67
formidable O.	DISR 287:24
Her Majesty's O.	BAGE 54:66
His Majesty's O.	HOBH 420:6
Prime Minister or Leader of the O.	DISR 288:63
war of eternal o.	LYND 543:92

We need an o.	MAHA 559:30
when it has a strong o.	SWEE 861:10
young, bald Leader of the O.	KINN 488:66
oppositions riven by a dozen o.	ROSS 725:35
oppress o., rob, and degrade them	DOUG 296:26
oppressed Christ comes to the o.	RUET 730:37
friend of the o.	GARI 360:72
opiate of the o.	JONG 466:33
o. can find...safety	ANGE 19:94
o., who wanted strength	WORD 960:15
past of the o. people	FANON 330:14
oppression Need and o. starveth	SHAK 766:12
often a mechanical o.	HEMI 410:77
o. he may heretofore have suffered	MANS 568:14
proud o. will not hear me	OTWAY 656:97
To make o. bitter	SHAK 782:1
oppressions o. of this earth	SHEL 812:62
oppressor confront the o.	MAKW 561:81
day o' the O. is ended	KIPL 490:18
revolutionary ends as an o.	CAMUS 196:92
The o.'s wrong	TWAIN 902:63
oppressors we may have our o.	PUIG 699:69
Oprah I go on O. and sob	LETT 524:12
optical o. flecks	UPDI 906:33
o. form of thought	HUGO 436:56
optimism as agreeable as o.	BENN 81:72
optimist have to be an o.	SAND 742:32
last o. left in Colombia	GARC 359:66
o. after it, he knows too little	TWAIN 903:91
o. is a guy	MARQ 575:49
o. proclaims that we live in the best	CABE 191:6
o....sees a green light everywhere	SCHW 751:95
optimistic If I was not o.	OUD 656:10
make us o. or	UNAM 905:4
O. lies have...therapeutic value	SHAW 810:91
options discuss your o. afterwards	SHAN 805:63
opulent o. calm of angelfish	ALLEN 13:74
oracle pronounces as an o.	WESL 932:70
oracles o. are dumb	MILT 597:37
o. of God	BIBLE 129:35
orange clockwork o.	BURG 174:87
Orangeman Pocket of a Stout O.	ANON 23:96
oranges bowl of o., too	MITC 609:36
coffee and o.	STEV 849:69
orator An o. is a good man	CATO 209:99
greatest o., who triumphs	HUME 438:3
no o. as Brutus is	SHAK 778:45
oratory Poetry...not as o.	POUND 691:95
orb Cycle and epicycle, o. in o.	MILT 605:35
monthly changes in her circled o.	SHAK 765:83
There's not the smallest o.	SHAK 770:19
orbit o. the earth	FOLL 341:72
most beautiful sight in o.	SCHW 750:93
orbits circled in their o.	DICK 280:27
orbs dew her o. upon the green	SHAK 767:25
o., Or dim suffusion veiled	MILT 603:74
orchard fair with o. lawns	TENN 878:87
hath thy o. fruit	JONS 467:72
O., for a Dome	DICK 284:35
orchards Not all do o. please	VIRG 913:23
orchestra for o. without music	RAVEL 707:84
golden rules for an o.	BEEC 73:67
plays the kettle drums in the o.	SALI 740:80
separates you from the o.	DIDE 285:63
orchestrated Three farts...o.	BARB 63:47
orchestration o. of platitudes	WILD 943:46
orchid O.—breathing incense	BASHO 67:47
ordeal of meeting me	CHUR 226:6
worst possible o.	BERR 87:4
order all in o. stand	CRAB 251:26
And o., truth, and beauty range	SMART 826:64
arranged them in alphabetical o.	HELL 407:29
been a rock of o.	METT 589:60
benevolence of the passive o.	MERE 588:32
change the social o.	FRAN 347:87
colours assembled in a certain o.	DENIS 273:71
decently and in o.	BIBLE 127:54
establishing a world o.	EISE 314:1
explain to our sense of o.	HARDY 397:15
fairest o. in the world	HERA 412:38
forces working in inverse o.!	CARL 201:7
Good o. is the foundation	BURKE 176:50
loyalty and o.	GLAD 373:39
new o. from the old	WEBB 920:67
old o. changeth	TENN 878:85
ordainer of o.	BROW 166:85
o. breeds habit	ADAMS 5:90

o. does not create life	SAINT 738:39
O. is heaven's first law	POPE 687:88
o. of Melchizedek	BIBLE 102:18
o. of nature	FONT 342:74
o. of the acts	PAST 668:98
o. our lives more rationally	LECO 518:81
possess internal o.	FORS 345:44
precise idea of o.	BERN 86:75
preponderantly geometric o.	LEGER 519:6
recollect the o. in which	WELL 929:6
re-establish peace and civil o.	ELIZ 322:10
reminders of o.	GREER 387:45
sense of o.	ORWE 653:17
significance to ourselves...find...o.	WELTY 931:48
society, social o.	MUNCH 625:42
some sort of o.	GREE 386:21
some sort of o. (or beauty)	POUND 692:31
subversion of good o.	KNOX 495:14
sudden light that shows new o.	CORN 247:6
values o. without constraint	LEGU 520:12
vast o. of the universe	PAGE 659:16
where all is o. and beauty	BAUD 68:65
words in their best o.	COLE 236:48
world has not to be put in o.	MILL 594:70
ordered You o. I obeyed	BERN 85:65
orderliness freedom and a general o.	CARD 198:41
orders Almighty's o. to perform	ADDI 6:19
'E don't obey no o.	KIPL 490:13
give o. to love	SAND 741:9
Gordon should be under my o.	CROM 255:14
in all his tinted o.	FIRB 336:52
lower o. are seen unfavourably	CHES 219:49
o. and inferior creatures	MILT 608:92
organisation...of o.	MARX 579:30
Reasonable o. are	TUCH 901:12
willing to follow his o.	BIBLE 133:34
ordinary all o. people	CHEK 218:16
divided into 'o.' and 'extraordinary'	DOST 294:89
I find the...the o. much more satisfying	RAUS 707:81
o. affairs of o. people	GOWE 380:81
o. in the individual	MANN 566:87
O. life bypassed me	OBRI 645:66
o. man and woman	ATTL 40:26
o. people through o. situations	BANKS 62:28
o. wine just leaves	AMER 15:24
taking o. men	GALB 357:20
There are no o. moments	MILL 595:5
warn you not to be o.	KINN 488:65
work of fifty o. men	HUBB 434:99
ore slaves that dig the golden o.	CRAB 252:32
organ Heaven's deep o. blow	MILT 597:33
Seated one day at the o.	PROC 697:27
With most miraculous o.	SHAK 782:3
organ-grinder o. g. is present	BEVAN 89:57
organism o. is preparing to rest	MAMET 564:38
over-complicated o.	POUND 692:20
organization appropriate o.	GALB 357:20
bigger the o.	JAY 453:3
destroyed the foundation of the o.	EISE 314:1
efficient o. is one in which	STEA 843:29
o. for pleasure	JOHN 458:29
O. is alien to their natures	HAZZ 404:61
o. is the greatest morale builder	DOOL 294:83
o. of idolatry	SHAW 808:36
o. of public opinion	LIPP 531:58
systematic o. of hatreds	ADAMS 5:86
organizations part in the various o.	JOHN 456:72
organized highly o. part of it	GALB 357:17
o. for that	TOLS 893:50
organizing nations need o. principles	CLIN 231:37
organs given us all more o.	BRAD 154:27
inner o. of beasts	JOYCE 470:29
take your sense o. seriously	LEARY 517:47
that o. that piss	LAYT 515:1
orgasm like a really bad o.	GAGA 356:6
o. has replaced the cross	MUGG 623:9
orgy need an o., once	NASH 630:65
Orient O. dew, Shed from	MARV 576:86
slow revenge of the O.	PRIE 695:88
oriental Tea, although an O.	CHES 221:58
you are an O.	FORS 344:34
orientation from the o. of a few	ROBB 716:59
origin account for their own o.	MILL 592:10
indelible stamp of his lowly o.	DARW 263:58
Philosophy...has no other o.	SOCR 833:97
takes its o. from emotion	WORD 958:90
original curse Their frail o.	MILT 603:64

paces

greatest o. practical example	WHIT 938:3	O., damned spot	SHAK 798:65	Ovid O., the soft philosopher	DRYD 303:26
great O. proclaim	ADDI 7:40	O., vile jelly!	SHAK 793:14	ovum Via o. cranium	STEV 851:9
in order to imitate the o.	BERN 86:87	relevance…for what it leaves o.	FERL 333:91	owe O. no man any thing	BIBLE 126:30
line up to see the o.	ARMS 33:50	wit is o.	SHAK 774:49	o. no man hate	SHAK 779:89
new and o. plan	GILB 369:51	outcast writer…an o. by nature	BARN 64:66	o. nothing to Women's Lib	THAT 880:47
She's the o. good time	DAVIS 265:98	outcome o. of the struggle	ANGE 18:87	Owen grave of Gomer O.	THOM 884:35
things counter, o., spare	HOPK 428:73	outcomes History admits…only o.	MITCH 609:23	owl blind as any noonday o.	TENN 878:78
thought is like o. sin	LEBO 517:62	out-compete countries…will o.-c. us	OBAMA 644:39	comrade with the wolf and o.	SHAK 792:2
thought is often o.	HOLM 424:63	outdated methods are o.	ANON 25:44	moping o.	GRAY 384:64
originality All my o. consists	REDON 709:23	outdoor I play no o. games	WILDE 941:94	of the white o. sweeping	MERE 587:23
Artistic o. has only	NABO 628:16	out-educate countries who o.-e. us	OBAMA 644:39	O., and a useful Cart	LEAR 516:33
o.…manner of thinking	MAUP 582:13	outfits bareleg o.	MURR 627:80	O. and the Pussy-Cat	LEAR 516:35
result is his o.	ROTH 727:76	outlaw attacks from o. states	REAG 708:8	o., for all his feathers	KEATS 477:14
without o. or moral courage	SHAW 807:12	Jazz musicians have some o.	ZWER 970:21	singing o.	ROCH 720:19
originals o. from whence all	LOCKE 533:90	wandering o. of his…mind	BYRON 187:46	sings the staring o.	SHAK 763:27
Orion loose the bands of O.?	BIBLE 99:17	outline drew his own o.	VASA 909:27	white o.'s feather	ALLI 14:6
O. standing on his head	LAWR 513:56	mountain o. varies	THOR 888:24	owlish describe myself as o.	SCHW 750:90
orisons his morning o.	SMART 826:63	outlines eye never sees o.	GOYA 380:82	owls castle brown as o.	THOM 883:21
their hasty o.	OWEN 657:25	outlive I o. you	SEXT 758:45	hooded eagle among blinking o.	SHEL 814:3
Orkney In bloody O.	BLAIR 138:47	many years o. performance?	SHAK 772:83	Of o. and cuckoos, asses	MILT 601:21
In bloody O.	BLAIR 138:48	outlook Writers of comedy have o.	THUR 891:1	Two O. and a Hen	LEAR 516:27
Orlando Run, run, O.	SHAK 779:87	outrage do o. to its…unity	HOMA 425:92	Who brings o. to Athens?	ARIS 31:14
Orleans who are besieging O.	JOAN 455:59	Satire is moral o.	ROTH 728:84	own call my o.	DRYD 302:3
ornament esteem'st the o. of life	SHAK 796:21	outrageous don't know how to be o.	LEMMY 521:35	crisis…we can call our o.	SALI 740:84
mankind from superfluous o.	LOOS 536:43	outside England…o. Europe	KEYN 484:72	prefer to o. slot machines	TRUMP 900:96
moment's o.	WORD 960:19	from the o. inwards	FRIE 351:75	what isn't one's o.	PLATO 682:62
old o. of his cheek	SHAK 774:45	Give me the o. of all things	LEWIS 527:72	what you o.	ELIOT 320:63
o. from utilitarian objects	LOOS 536:44	I am just going o.	OATES 643:16	wouldn't want to o. one	FIEL 335:31
o. which truth doth give	SHAK 801:51	o. pissing in	JOHN 458:14	own-alone All by my o.-a. self	HARR 399:51
respecting all o.	RUSK 732:81	o. to every form	HEPW 412:29	owner rather o. be	DONNE 292:44
used literature as an o.	VARG 908:26	people who live o.	SABA 736:2	owners sons of former slave o.	KING 487:31
ornamentation building without o.	SANT 743:47	watch…from the o.	WELLS 930:20	ownership importance of social o.	STRA 856:35
ornaments hide with o. their…art	POPE 685:20	we can get o. ourselves	RABI 704:23	its source of power: o.	KINN 488:61
orphan carried by an o. boy	SCOTT 752:9	outsider can an o. understand	KAFKA 472:4	own-goal AIDS…a classic o.-g.	ANNE 19:14
court as an o.	LEVA 525:17	outsiders imagined by o.	WATS 922:41	owns Who o. all of space?	HUGH 436:38
widow and his o.	LINC 529:11	o. do not understand	MUNRO 625:52	ox Baby in an ox's stall?	BETJ 88:36
orphans Mostly o.' tears	BRAND 156:61	war against the o.	GARI 360:73	eateth grass as an ox	BIBLE 99:20
new o. cry	SHAK 797:60	outstanding o. men become fewer	TOCQ 892:26	shalt not muzzle the ox	BIBLE 95:94
Orpheus O. with his lute made trees	SHAK 804:44	outstrip o. all praise	SHAK 804:26	stalled ox and hatred therewith	BIBLE 104:75
soul of O. sing	MILT 598:55	outward inevitably turns o.	UPDI 906:29	oxen eat grass as o.	BIBLE 111:40
orthodox certainly not o.	STRA 856:39	man looketh on the o. appearance	BIBLE 96:34	o. frae the furrowed field	BURNS 180:45
orthodoxy 'o.'…no longer means	CHES 220:56	need of o. criteria	WITT 951:28	Oxenford Clerk ther was of O.	CHAU 217:74
O. or My-doxy	CARL 201:8	onward and o.	WHIT 937:91	Oxford clever men at O.	GRAH 381:92
unimpeachable o.	RAHN 705:36	virtue on his o. parts	SHAK 770:3	either O. or Cambridge	SNAG 831:72
orthography now is he turned o.	SHAK 774:36	outworn free itself from all that is o.	CUPI 258:86	Mussolini had been at O.	HALI 393:13
Orwell episode out of George O.	COOKE 245:73	out-worn o.-w. heart	YEATS 965:9	O.…has made me insufferable	BEER 73:77
O. told us we would	MAMET 564:32	Oval English cricket…died at the O.	ANON 23:92	O.…more attractive than Cambridge	BAED 54:61
Oscar assume that O. said it	PARK 663:99	Oval Office what happened		poetry, which is in O. made	DRYD 300:35
Oscars pick out stage actors at the O.	MCKE 554:12	inside this O. O.	BUSH 183:46	schools of O.	GIBB 366:95
Walk two O. behind	WARR 921:15	ovation Arrange o.	SWAN 860:8	stagecoach from London to O.	HAZL 403:38
Osiris mangled body of O.	MILT 600:17	oven burn as an o.	BIBLE 112:65	The King to O. sent a troop of horse	BROW 166:87
Out-glares the Heav'ns O.	HERR 415:5	ovens gassing people in o.	SIHA 821:65	to found at O. a chair	ARNO 35:23
ostrich America cannot be an o.	WILS 949:80	over It ain't o. 'til it's o.	BERRA 87:93	University of O.	GIBB 366:98
neck like an o.	DAVIS 265:97	never get o. it	FROST 353:25	Oxfordshire all the birds Of O.	THOM 885:52
Othello O. subject Desdemona	KOES 495:28	O. after o.	JOYCE 470:31	oxlips o. and the nodding violet	SHAK 767:30
something like it in O.	SHER 818:43	O. my dead body	KAUF 474:43	Oxtail university of O.	JOYCE 470:28
other think there is no o.	SCHR 749:64	O.paid, o.fed, o.sexed, and o. here	TRIN 897:19	Oxus O., forgetting the bright speed	ARNO 35:1
Were she o. than she is	SHAK 773:22	they think it's all o.	WOLS 954:97	oxygen o. of publicity	THAT 881:62
otherness quintessence of o.	BURG 174:2	overalls pantheon of boots and o.	DUNN 307:14	o. of social intercourse	HIRS 419:74
visual form of the 'o.'	NOLAN 640:43	overboard propose to throw us	MANN 566:79	oyster An o. may be crossed in love!	SHER 818:5
others alone among o.	SAINT 738:36	throw the occasional man o.	GILM 371:97	bold Man that first ate an O.	SWIFT 863:71
Do not do unto o.	SHAW 808:59	overcoat meaning…only its o.	CAREY 199:63	eye that can open an o.	WODE 952:52
liberty is the love of o.	HAZL 403:36	put on your o.	LOWE 539:14	No o. ever profited	THUR 890:81
love of o.	SHAW 806:90	overcoats never taken off their o.	THUR 890:66	o. of the old school	DICK 281:63
more pleasing to o.	JOHN 463:62	overcrowding situations of o.	COUP 248:33	sympathetic unselfishness of an o.	SAKI 739:62
o. were only my wives	GUIT 389:90	over-dressed If you are o.-d.	RICE 713:88	world's mine o.	SHAK 773:3
pity o. had to leave	KINN 488:64	oversteemed Facts are generally o.	UPDI 905:19	you can't enjoy an o.	CLARK 228:60
The harm…you do to o.	WALK 917:42	overflow Clancy, of the O.	PATE 669:13	oyster-knife sneer…like an o.-k.	ANNAN 19:11
otters glistening like wet o.	JOHN 457:99	spontaneous o.	WORD 958:93	oysters But by no means unlike o.	DICK 279:9
ought It is, but hadn't o. to be	HARTE 400:75	overlook knowing what to o.	JAMES 451:68	eat my o.	SWIFT 863:76
o. to flow through	KIPL 489:79	overpaid all that they are being o. for	SELZ 757:20	man who doesn't love o.	SAKI 739:60
what o. to be	HOMA 425:93	O., overfed, oversexed, and over here	TRIN 897:20	Poverty and o.…seem to go	DICK 277:52
what you o. to do	SART 745:77	overpower She can o., astonish	HUNT 439:21	Ozymandias My name is O.	SHEL 813:86
ounce o. of Silver out of the Earth	PETTY 676:45	overrated three most o. things	KENN 482:33		
ourselves advance a step beyond o.	HUME 438:94	override she will o. you	FAUL 331:45	**p**	
do not talk of o.	TROL 897:25	overrule threaten to o. him	PAXM 670:43		
how to get rid of o.	HORN 430:23	oversexed Overpaid, overfed, o., and		pa Don't beat me, pa!	JOYCE 470:17
interplay between nature and o.	HEIS 407:22	over here	TRIN 897:19	Ma's out, Pa's out	FLAN 338:87
no hope of finding o.	MILL 594:64	over-shoes o.-s. in love	SHAK 758:56	pace bloody thoughts with violent p.	SHAK 790:29
O. to end o.	SHAK 795:76	oversights mistakes and o.	MURP 627:77	dance is a measured p.	BACON 49:30
power is the love of o.	HAZL 403:36	oversimplification O. is now	BERG 83:18	jogging justling p.	MUNDY 625:43
stop loving o.	STAEL 842:98	over-simplification systematic o.-s.	POPP 690:66	know how to p. themselves	DIOR 286:3
vainly conceal from o.	PASC 666:66	overstate Don't o. your…achievements	BLIN 142:55	not keep p.	THOR 889:43
we conquer but o.	HILL 418:62	overstepped never o. it	FROST 352:2	one p. ahead of myself	MCGO 552:78
out fall not o. by the way	BIBLE 93:47	overstocked aviary o. with jays	OHEN 648:19	p. of science	FROMM 352:88
I don't have to go o.	SMITH 829:25	overthrow think'st thou dost o.	DONNE 292:51	paces Hop forty p.	SHAK 794:57
Let me o.!	ATWO 41:34	over-well love is given o.-w.	PARK 664:10	three p. through the room	TENN 870:85

paciencia

Time travels in divers p.	SHAK 779:95
paciencia p. y barajar	CERV 211:49
Pacific Atlantic to the P.	CHUR 225:80
star'd at the p.	KEATS 475:61
Pacioli heard of Fra Luca P.	MULL 624:33
pack changed the form of the p.	TROT 899:65
face the murderous cowardly p.	MCKA 553:7
God! I will p., and take a train	BROO 162:94
revenged on the whole p.	SHAK 786:24
soldier's p. is not so heavy	EISE 314:95
with rifle and p.	SASS 745:86
packages internationally marketed p.	ILLI 445:21
Packard upholstery of a P.	PERE 674:22
pack-horses Shall p.-h.	SHAK 772:81
pact I make a p. with you	POUND 691:94
pad dolor of p.	ROET 722:55
Paddington As London is to P.	CANN 196:7
paddle leave to p.	KIPL 491:30
paddles 'ear their p. chunkin'	KIPL 489:81
padlock clap your p.	PRIOR 695:1
one jingling p. on the mind	POPE 689:40
pads writing p., notebooks	RODC 721:43
Padua wive it wealthily in P.	SHAK 761:60
paeans laurels to p.	CICE 227:35
paga Non si p., non si p.	FO 341:66
pagan animals (p., I regret to say)	DICK 279:9
p. suckled in a creed	WORD 961:30
pagans example of the ancient p.	GUIB 389:86
P. deified life	STAEL 841:96
wild p. at the cash register	CHER 219:43
page A P., a Grave	POPE 689:39
blotted from life's p.	BYRON 187:44
cannot tear out a single p.	SAND 741:8
father struggled through half a p.	LAWR 513:69
looks well enough on the p.	BUNT 173:67
on a beautiful quarto p.	SHER 817:87
one sweet p.	PATM 669:16
p. having an ample marge	TENN 877:49
pictures for the p. atone	POPE 688:34
Rule 1, on p. 1	MONT 615:47
sports p. records	WARR 921:14
stole a p. from the Universe!	MARTI 576:70
when you looked at the front p.	CHRI 223:40
pageant like this insubstantial p.	SHAK 804:27
P. of Empire	SITW 824:12
p. of his bleeding heart	ARNO 35:5
pages funny p. of the history books	DEAN 267:39
read the first 2 p.	JOYCE 470:34
pagoda old Moulmein P.	KIPL 489:79
pagus private p. or demesne	AUDEN 44:15
paid Ambition's debt is p.	SHAK 777:28
being p. in or p. out	HUXL 442:99
getting what you haven't p. for	WHAR 933:8
more women are p.	FALU 329:10
p. for a woman	GREE 386:18
p. for this microphone	REAG 708:12
p. the prices of life	GURN 390:1
p. with a smile	SAINT 738:38
p. with flattery	JOHN 460:78
these men p. their shillings	PRIE 695:48
you p. us more	HAMM 395:70
pail milk comes frozen home in p.	SHAK 763:27
pails ice crunching in p.	STEV 850:96
pain After great p.	DICK 284:36
alternations of p.	WILD 943:53
always in p.	BELL 76:46
and all the p.	SWIN 863:82
boredom and p. of it	BUEC 172:42
cause of all this p.	JULI 471:41
clenched on a round p.	THOM 883:13
delight in physics p.	SHAK 797:40
drama of p.	HARDY 397:13
draw thy breath in p.	SHAK 785:73
earth in travail and in p.	LONG 535:32
ease after p.	MILT 599:79
equal ease unto my p.	CAREW 199:59
Eternal P.!	ARNO 34:85
first feel p. yourself	HORA 430:18
forgets the p.	JEFF 453:18
forget the wandering and p.	FLEC 340:36
for quhome ye suffer p.	HENR 411:21
frame perish...in conquering p.	BYRON 188:64
hark—what p.!	ARNO 34:84
Infinite passion, and the p.	BROW 168:50
inflict p. upon oneself	MERE 588:32
Joy always came after p.	APOL 29:81
know the p.	WALC 916:12
lack the thing should rid my p.	SURR 860:98
Liberty's exquisite p.	BROW 166:91
life's a p.	DAVI 264:77
like a God in p.	KEATS 477:17
long grief and p.	TENN 876:29
lost happiness and lasting p.	MILT 601:34
midnight with no p.	KEATS 478:46
most intolerable p.	SHAW 808:45
narcotics, numbing p.	TENN 873:58
neither...any more p.	BIBLE 132:24
no greater p. than to remember	DANTE 262:38
no living thing to suffer p.	SHEL 814:8
no p. is greater than...being alive	DARIO 263:46
No p.—no gain	ANON 24:31
nor even freedom from p.	LAWR 513:55
obligation is a p.	JOHN 459:52
Oh p.! Oh p.!	BAUD 68:61
on p. of imprisonment	EDWA 312:56
Our Lady of P.	SWIN 864:92
owes its pleasure to another's p.	COWP 251:17
p. accompanied by the idea	SPIN 840:77
p. and anguish wring the brow	SCOTT 752:25
p. full of pleasantness	LYLY 543:84
p. in the desert	MOOR 618:8
p. in the soul	HAMM 394:59
P. is...a maimed creature	WINT 950:15
p. is dreadful	CATU 209:11
P. is inevitable	MURAK 626:63
p. isn't real	ANON 24:13
p. is perfect misery	MILT 605:24
p. is the one nobility	BAUD 68:58
p. is worse	JEFF 453:14
p. of particular circumstances	CART 206:38
p....of their thorns	BERN 86:76
p. or languor	WORD 962:47
p. or pleasure	HUME 438:96
p. than paralysis!	NIGH 639:20
p. that the artist feels	REDON 709:22
Pale Grief and pleasing P.	GRAY 385:87
pleasure of my p.	SIDN 820:43
rest from p.	DRYD 299:14
startle this dull p.	COLE 235:28
studies or his usual p.?	SHAK 762:68
sufferance of your friendly p.	KYD 501:47
Superflux of p.	SWIN 863:89
Sweet is pleasure after p.	DRYD 303:30
tender for another's p.	GRAY 383:48
Though full of p.	MILT 602:59
threshold of p.	GELL 363:35
travaileth in p.	BIBLE 125:19
turns to pleasing p.	SPEN 839:40
unforgotten p.	ROSS 727:62
upon p. of imprisonment	ELIZ 321:2
wicked to deserve such p.	BROW 168:35
with a sob of p.	JOYCE 470:20
with ceaseless p.	GOLD 376:85
without one p.	TENN 877:70
With some p. is fraught	SHEL 814:97
world without our p.	LANY 508:56
would not give Him p.	STUD 858:64
painch P., tripe, or thairm	BURNS 178:94
Paine Tom P.'s common sense	ADAMS 5:3
painful as p. as the other	BACON 50:59
confusing, disorienting, and p.	RICH 713:1
good honest and p.	PEPYS 673:88
growing up is p.	ANGE 18:83
life of men is p.	EURI 328:58
p. warrior	SHAK 800:44
too p. for me	BIBLE 101:85
painkiller P. X and P. Y	VIDAL 912:94
pains at p. to attract	JOHN 464:83
Beauty p.	HAAS 391:1
by p. men come to greater p.	BACON 51:85
great p. to con it	SHAK 785:89
infinite capacity for taking p.	ACHE 3:42
Luff...all p. makis lycht	BARB 63:51
made my p. his prey	SPEN 839:47
many the p. he suffered	HOMER 425:9
Marriage has many p.	JOHN 460:87
Muses never knew their p.	CRAB 252:29
one thousand scathing p.	LABE 501:4
p. and penalties of idleness	POPE 689:45
p. a world of kisses	SHAK 788:94
P. of love	DRYD 300:29
p. the immortal spirit must endure	ARNO 33:63
pleasure in poetic p.	COWP 251:14
sympathize with people's p.	HUXL 441:52
that kills and p. not?	SHAK 795:90
too much p. to think	HUME 438:97
paint artist should not only p.	FRIE 351:77
cheeks are covered with p.	NASH 630:58
do not p.	GAUG 361:2
flinging a pot of p.	RUSK 733:15
I p. a portrait I lose a friend	SARG 743:52
keep her in p. and powder	NIMI 639:25
P. as they spoke in Sparta	DIDE 285:77
p. the living	KNEL 494:8
p. the memory of happiness	SAIF 738:30
showed the p.	DRYD 299:10
those who p. 'em truest	ADDI 6:20
worth more than the price of the p.	VAN 908:21
painted best picture that was ever p.	HEMI 410:92
have p. a picture	HOMER 425:11
Mona Lisa by. by a club?	GRIS 389:75
p. skin contents the eye?	SHAK 762:75
painter A p. can leave you with nothing	JAMES 450:29
appear to one American p.	ROSE 725:26
best woman p.	OKEE 649:24
canvas is to the p.	BRIL 159:19
Every good p.	DALI 261:16
for the p., style is...vision	PROU 698:59
great p. of American hell	ALLEN 13:78
He that would be a p.	DURER 307:26
I am a p.	KLEE 494:3
invention of the landscape p.	FUSE 356:95
makes not a p.	WHIS 934:19
mine...the p.'s hand	WORD 961:28
not a great sculptor or p.	RUSK 733:88
p. carries the whole	MOTH 622:86
p. has two chief objects	LEON 522:74
p. only needs brushes	WINN 950:3
p. pursues his with greater	LEON 522:67
p. sketches A visible world	AUDEN 42:78
p. who draws by practice	LEON 523:79
picture-p. is indistinguishable	LEWIS 527:58
some great p.	SHEL 812:69
subject is to the p.	RIVE 716:54
Telling a p.	MALL 562:97
tools...or the p.' techniques	RENO 711:57
to say to the p.	WHIS 934:20
very great p. said to me	SITW 824:15
painters P....dissipated	BLAKE 141:34
P. of history	KNEL 494:8
p. speak with works	CARR 202:59
p., thus unskilled to trace	POPE 685:20
P. who are not colourists	DELA 271:23
sculptors and p.	THOR 888:25
painting Abstract p....confronts	POLL 684:3
Art of P.	BLAKE 141:36
art of p. cannot be truly judged	DURER 307:25
bridle and rudder of p.	LEON 523:75
culture of modern p.	MOTH 622:86
difference between p. and sculpture	LEON 522:67
excellent p.	ALBE 11:32
Good p. is like good cooking	VLAM 914:30
grasped what p. could be	MONET 612:1
I feel...part of the p.	POLL 684:2
Landscape p. to American p.	HUGH 435:24
of poetry than...of p.	STEV 850:94
P. and Punctuality	GAIN 356:9
P....art of protecting	BIER 135:84
P. has been a smiling	MORSE 621:64
p. is done with the brain	MICH 590:67
p....is essentially a flat surface	DENIS 273:71
p. is merely the image	CELL 211:4
p. is not done to decorate	PICA 677:60
P. is poetry which is seen	LEON 522:69
P. is...representation	PIERO 678:72
p. of sounds, noises and smells	CARRA 202:57
p., poetry, music, architecture	EMER 325:87
p. should be considered excellent	MICH 590:70
P.'s not important	MOSES 622:78
p. that is an act	ROSE 725:27
p....the presence of absence	BERG 83:27
p. was brought to Egypt	VASA 909:37
p. which cannot be explained	RENO 711:54
produce illumination and not p.	DELA 271:23
purest...form of p.	OROZ 652:1
reason for p.	WYETH 964:7
sense of music or of p.	JOHN 458:30
sexual juices flow toward a p.	FUEN 354:59
to achieve this total p.	CARRA 202:57
walks around a p.	ROSSO 727:69

pardon

when you are moved by a p.	ANNE 20:15	
when you look at p.	GAUG 361:3	
paintings accept p. and sculptures	CHUR 224:50	
all the allegorical p.	JOHN 465:30	
In judging p.	TINT 892:24	
my p. do not sell	VAN 908:21	
Novels are like p.	DIDI 286:87	
P. are Rorschach	LICH 528:94	
p....exist only to illustrate the text	WOLFE 953:74	
poor lawyers, like poor p.	WHIS 934:23	
surface of my p.	WARH 920:6	
to see in p. bits of nature	MALE 562:92	
paints artist with true feelings p.	FRIE 351:73	
pair gentle p., ye little think	MILT 604:2	
Happy, happy, happy, p.!	DRYD 303:28	
p. of credulous fools	SHIR 819:18	
p. of sparkling eyes	GILB 370:73	
pairs like proverbs, they occur in p.	SIMON 821:74	
pal Me p....does the toff	DENN 273:74	
palace chalice from the p.	PANA 662:80	
hazards of the P. of Varieties	CRIT 255:10	
in at the p. door	DICK 277:43	
in the p....a monastery	AELR 8:74	
in the p. walk	TENN 873:49	
left her p. bare	HYDE 443:21	
Love in a p.	KEATS 476:6	
p. and a prison on each hand	BYRON 188:58	
p. built of squared brick	SPEN 838:22	
p. built upon the sand	MILL 592:20	
p. fit for you and me	STEV 853:84	
p. more comfortable	HOOV 427:49	
p. of the soul	WEBS 926:38	
p. of wisdom	BLAKE 139:96	
princely p. willed me to indite	LANY 508:57	
purple-lined p.	KEATS 476:7	
room of the p.	SITW 823:3	
thine own p.	DONNE 292:46	
palaces gorgeous p.	SHAK 804:27	
iron p. of Art	HUGH 435:22	
old p.	SHEL 813:81	
p. in Kingdom come	MASE 580:64	
p. of kings are built	PAINE 660:31	
thy p. and tow'rs	BURNS 178:96	
palate carries the p. to its highest	BRIL 159:21	
gave to his p.	JOYCE 470:29	
Glide o'er my p.	BARL 63:56	
man's heart is through his p.	FERN 334:96	
P., the hutch of tasty lust	HOPK 428:68	
steps down the p.	NABO 628:4	
palates p. both for sweet and sour	SHAK 790:38	
pale Art thou p. for weariness	SHEL 816:66	
I left the theatre, dizzy and p.	QUIR 703:27	
In p. contented sort	KEATS 476:8	
in sorrow p.	BLAKE 139:92	
P., beyond porch	SWIN 864:96	
p. of the Constitution	GLAD 373:36	
p., unripened beauties	ADDI 7:47	
started...and turned p.	SOUT 835:55	
Why so p. and wan	SUCK 858:66	
Palenke poetry...in P. and Uatlán	DARIO 262:44	
Palestine establishment in P.	BALF 58:39	
haven in sunny P.	MASE 580:55	
Jews in P.	OROU 652:92	
Palestinian P. peace movement	ANON 27:23	
Palestinians P. in Israel	OROU 652:92	
P., PLO is a homeland	NEW 634:36	
palfrey p. fresh and fair	SCOTT 753:46	
pall pallor...shall be their p.	OWEN 657:26	
would p. a little	THUR 890:84	
pallbearer being the Democratic p.	FRIED 351:67	
Palladium P. of the civil	JUNI 471:49	
palliate p. what we cannot cure	JOHN 460:72	
palliative sleep...a p.	CHAM 213:71	
pallid p. and thin young man	GILB 369:48	
P., unshaved and thirsty	SASS 745:82	
Palliser Mr P. was one of those	TROL 897:29	
P., Duke of Omnium	TROL 898:57	
Pall Mall P. M. Gazette is written	THAC 880:34	
pallor of girls' brows	OWEN 657:26	
palm where the p. tree grows	MARTI 576:71	
wind is in the p. tree	KIPL 489:80	
win the p., the oak	MARV 577:1	
palm-oil proverbs are the p.-o.	ACHE 2:20	
palms in their hands	BIBLE 131:3	
the p. of her hands	BIBLE 98:81	
palooka sobbed the panting p.	PERE 674:13	
palpable very p. hit	SHAK 785:71	

palsy chide my p., or my gout	DONNE 291:27	
p. shakes a few	KEATS 478:43	
strucken wid de p.	HARR 399:50	
paltry man is but a p. thing	YEATS 966:36	
Pam P., I adore you, P.	BETJ 88:21	
Pamere high mountain cradle in P.	ARNO 35:1	
pan fish that talks In the frying p.	DELA 271:30	
panacea suffrage...is their p.	CARL 201:28	
panache Sang with a fountain's p.	DAY 267:38	
Panama Vietnam...near P.	ANON 25:65	
pancake know how that p. feels	WRIG 963:69	
pancreatic p. ducts of dog	BANT 62:35	
pandemic AIDS p....own-goal	ANNE 19:14	
pandemonium p., the high capital	MILT 602:54	
pandering p. to the public taste	BEAV 71:33	
Pandora If you open that P.'s box	BEVIN 90:66	
pane cheek...against the p.	SCHR 749:63	
tap at the p.	BROW 167:24	
panegyrics Coarse p.	GRAY 384:61	
panes diamonded with p.	KEATS 477:20	
pangs More p. will	HOPK 429:90	
quietus which his p. might take	TWAIN 902:63	
panic Don't P.	ADAMS 4:75	
made me p. most	WHITE 935:54	
p. in which the passenger is kept	HAZL 403:44	
What a p.'s in thy breastie!	BURNS 177:77	
Panjandrum Grand P. himself	FOOTE 342:83	
panoply p. of death	DAVI 265:83	
pansies p.; that's for thoughts	SHAK 784:55	
pansy p. at my feet	WORD 959:7	
pink, and the p.	MILT 599:91	
pant I p., I sink	SHEL 816:48	
Pantagruelism P. is...liveliness	RABE 704:20	
pantheon dome of the P.	BRAM 156:57	
p. of boots and overalls	DUNN 307:14	
panther muscles of a p.	PERE 674:18	
sofa upholstered in p. skin	PLOM 682:73	
pantomime delights of a p.	DICK 278:73	
in p. the puppets fumbling	WHITE 935:38	
pantry stow'd his p.	BURNS 177:72	
pants chair...judged by one's p.	ANON 25:38	
in fast thick p. were breathing	COLE 236:38	
kick in the p. to God	MILL 593:52	
lower limbs in p.	NASH 631:73	
secret of life in your p.	CUMM 257:55	
Stretch p.	ANON 25:46	
Pap P. warn't in a good humor	TWAIN 902:55	
papa P....gives a pretty form	DICK 282:91	
p. may have	HOLI 423:47	
paper 12 ounces of p. and ink	MORL 619:39	
crawling over a piece of p.	INGR 446:43	
deliquescent leaves of p.	ANDR 18:77	
empty as p.	SCOTT 751:3	
few sheets of p.	ARET 31:11	
figures which look well on p.	WEIL 928:74	
good manners to read the p.	VAND 908:14	
grey p. with blunt type!	BROW 167:12	
Hamlet is so much p. and ink	PRIE 695:84	
hand that signed the p.	THOM 883:8	
hath not eat p.	SHAK 763:12	
here is the p. that bears his name	CHAM 212:63	
I had the p.	HEMI 409:65	
It is a commercial p.	HAZL 403:42	
just for a scrap of p.	BETH 87:11	
keepers of print and p.	MACL 555:37	
look at the p.	DE 268:54	
loo p. gets thicker	MITF 610:57	
needs only a typewriter and p.	WINN 950:3	
only a p. moon	HARB 396:88	
on passive p.	POPE 689:39	
p. allegories but ill comprehended	MELV 585:73	
P. blushes not	MIDD 590:79	
p. it's written on	GOLD 377:32	
puppets...with their slips of p.	WHITE 935:38	
reactionaries are p. tigers	MAO 569:33	
run the p.	BEAV 71:27	
sheet of green p.	ATWO 41:34	
talking on p.	BAIN 55:90	
unpleasant'st words...blotted p.	SHAK 770:8	
We set down on p.	TRUM 899:82	
when...this p. appears dull	STEE 844:41	
white p., void of all	LOCKE 533:89	
word down on p.	MILL 594:69	
Your eight-page p.	MAST 581:83	
paperback America as the p. version	DELI 271:97	
paper-blurrers company of p.-b.	SIDN 820:58	
paper-mill thou hast built a p.-m.	SHAK 760:98	

papers He's got my p.	PINT 678:82	
what I read in the p.	ROGE 723:71	
paper-weight pad and p.-w.	ROET 722:55	
paperweights never at a loss for p.	BRYS 171:18	
paperwork keep the p. down	ORTON 653:5	
papist between Protestant and P.	STRA 857:44	
P. have no right to complain!	OBRI 645:63	
paprika splash of p.	VREE 915:56	
parables end up writing p.	BERG 83:23	
many things unto them in p.	BIBLE 117:90	
parachute jumping out of a p.	MACL 554:24	
What color is your p.?	BOLL 145:10	
parade army without p. or gesture	LAWR 514:90	
solemnised with pomp and p.	ADAMS 5:1	
paradise be with me in p.	BIBLE 122:8	
blessed and admit me to P.	ROSS 727:66	
blundered into P.	THOM 886:85	
built upon the bowers of p.	PAINE 660:31	
called the P. of Fools	MILT 603:86	
cheapened p.	PATM 669:15	
Cheese for dessert...like P. Lost	BRAC 154:19	
closest you can get this side of P.	BUEC 172:41	
drunk the milk of P.	COLE 236:42	
England is the p. of women	FLOR 341:62	
fleeting joys Of P.	MILT 606:62	
gate of p.	SHAW 811:33	
grace the entrance to P.	MICH 590:69	
heavenly p. is that place	CAMP 195:76	
In P. of all things	MILT 604:10	
keys of P.	DE 273:82	
lay on nature is a p.	SHAK 788:70	
Life's p.	FORD 343:1	
Lost Angel of a ruined P.!	SHEL 815:31	
my dying place was P.	BROW 165:67	
No p., no fall	SNYD 832:91	
P. by way of Kensal Green	CHES 221:95	
p. for a sect	KEATS 476:97	
p....in his face	DRYD 301:66	
P. of exiles	SHEL 812:61	
p. of four seas	MARV 578:10	
P. shall be the refuge	KORAN 498:90	
possess A p. within	MILT 607:72	
see John Knox in P.	PARK 664:10	
serpent...in P.	HUGH 436:37	
spindrift gaze toward p.	CRANE 252:55	
Such are the Gates of P.	BLAKE 140:5	
They paved p.	MITC 609:37	
when P. shall be brought nigh	KORAN 498:90	
wilderness is p.	FITZ 337:69	
win a p.?	SHAK 763:15	
wreck of P.	SHEL 816:47	
paradises Two p. 'twere in one	MARV 578:7	
paradox p. of high religion	NIEB 637:87	
paradoxes man of p.	ROUS 729:14	
paragon earthly p.	SHAK 803:4	
p. of animals!	SHAK 782:89	
paragons p. of frankness	WILL 945:2	
paragraph canvas a sentence or p.	MOTH 622:87	
most beautiful prose p.	BLOOM 143:67	
paragraphing art of newspaper p.	MARQ 575:58	
paragraphs hardening of the p.	THUR 890:91	
parallel north of the 38th p.	MARS 575:64	
speaks...of things without p.	BIER 134:77	
there is no p. term	BERG 83:18	
parallelism Friendship needs...p.	ADAMS 5:92	
parallelogram landlady...is a p.	LEAC 515:10	
paralyse p. it by encumbering	TOLS 894:50	
paralysis pain than p.!	NIGH 639:20	
paramedics run for the p.	SKEL 824:33	
paramour her lusty p.	MILT 597:31	
many a p.	SPEN 838:33	
paramours willow worn of forlorn p.	SPEN 838:20	
Worn of p.	SPEN 838:15	
paranoia P's the garlic in life's kitchen	PYNCH 701:14	
paraphrase soul in p.	HERB 414:78	
the classics in p.!	POUND 691:2	
parasite not born a p.	FRAN 348:23	
parasols What various p.!	DICK 279:1	
parcel p. of rogues	BURNS 179:41	
p. of rogues	BURNS 180:42	
parcels deals it in small p.	WEBS 926:17	
parched p. ground...a pool	BIBLE 105:79	
parchment p. of a constitution	TROT 899:62	
pard freckled like a p.	KEATS 476:4	
pard-like p.-l. Spirit, beautiful	SHEL 815:36	
pardon beseech you of your p.	SHAK 789:21	
bitter to thee, p.	SWIN 864:14	

pardonable

cannot help nor p.	AUDEN 42:76	Cromwell said to the Long P.	AMERY 15:27
I p. that man's life	SHAK 793:21	dissolved P.	STAL 842:4
ne'er p., who have done the wrong	DRYD 300:31	enables P. to do things	SHAW 809:74
O p. me	SHAK 777:33	in a 21st-century p.	ASHD 37:67
p. after execution	SHAK 805:57	In the last P.	JOWE 469:14
P. me boy	GORD 378:55	Kiss my P.!	PEPYS 673:84
p. not that	SHAK 770:17	majorities in P.	WHIT 934:24
Say 'P.', king	SHAK 765:55	mockery to call it a P. House	WENT 931:52
Where there is injury, p.	FRAN 347:99	nailed...the doors of P.	MUSS 627:88
pardonable almost always p.	GRAV 382:28	P. is a deliberative assembly	BURKE 175:13
pardoning in p. that we are	FRAN 347:99	P. must lay the burden equally	CHUR 225:72
parent child whose p. is unkent	SPEN 837:14	P. of England	BAIL 55:89
man can be a p.	MUIR 624:29	P. of man	TENN 871:17
p. who could see his boy	LEAC 515:18	P. speaking through reporters	CARL 201:41
successful p....raises a child	EPHR 326:23	People in P.	WILL 944:66
To lose one p.	WILDE 941:2	Scottish P....hereby reconvened	EWING 329:78
parents appalled by our p.	JONG 466:42	set up an entire Scottish P.	WATE 922:38
avoid having p.	CRISP 255:55	There shall be a Scottish P.	DEWAR 276:16
be good to p.	KORAN 497:74	two-thirds majority in P.	FREUD 350:56
best friends and p.	MARG 570:68	**parliamentarian** pleasure for a p.	CRIT 255:10
born...with ready-made p.	FRAME 346:77	**parliaments** democratic p. of tricks	WEBB 925:8
cannot get subsistence from his p.	MALT 563:22	England is the mother of P.	BRIG 159:15
children inter their p.	HERO 415:95	P. are the great lie	POBE 683:77
how my p. were occupied	SALI 739:71	**parlour** perfumed p. snake	DUNNE 307:21
influence of p.	MUSG 627:87	**parlours** farmhouse p.	THOM 884:47
In mine it was the p.	SLOVO 826:56	**Parma** P....should dare to invade	ELIZ 321:4
Jewish man with p.	ROTH 727:80	**parmacity** p. for an inward bruise	SHAK 771:33
joys of p.	BACON 51:68	**Parnassus** poor man's P.	EMER 325:1
loving their p.	WILDE 941:88	to climb P.	BURNS 177:69
nobleman from surfeiting of his p.	LASS 510:12	**Parnell** Poor P.!	JOYCE 470:20
No one understands their p.	FRIS 351:83	**parodies** P. and caricatures	HUXL 441:66
Of p. good	SHAK 775:81	**parody** between an epitome and a p.	ISAA 447:64
P. are the bones	DOUG 295:19	p. is a game	NABO 628:17
p. can't take you	UPDI 905:15	p....replaced history	PIGL 678:75
p. don't have to say	MORE 619:21	**parole** p. of literary men	JOHN 464:80
p. kept me from children	SPEN 837:98	**parrot** Sick as a p.	ANON 26:79
P. learn a lot	SPARK 835:63	this p. what I have purchased	CLEE 229:79
p. lived like	MIN 608:6	with a p. and five companions	HEYE 417:39
p....realize that I'm kidnapped	ALLEN 14:92	**parrots** keep p. or puppy dogs	CAMP 194:59
p....sometimes a disappointment	POWE 693:41	laugh like p.	SHAK 768:67
p. were created for	NASH 630:64	**Parsee** There lived a P.	KIPL 491:35
p. won't slight you	COLUM 238:88	**parsimonious** Nothing...more p.	SMOL 831:67
question...in many potential p.	SCHU 750:80	**parsimony** beggarly p. and ignoble	NASHE 632:90
stranger to one of your p.	AUST 46:58	Capitals are increased by p.	SMITH 827:83
two first p.	MILT 603:76	**parsley** P. Is gharsely	NASH 631:79
web do p. weave	NASH 631:71	**parsnip** lukewarm p. juice	WOOL 956:45
Pariahs women the P.	STAN 842:14	**parson** different cause, says p. Sly	PRIOR 696:9
Paris As far as P.	JONS 466:44	drowns the p.'s saw	SHAK 763:28
dressed in P.	ANON 24:12	If P. lost his senses	HODG 421:23
Fashion is more tyrannical at P.	CHES 219:43	p. owned his skill	GOLD 376:2
frocks are built in P.	SAKI 739:52	**part** bids me play my p.	SPEN 839:44
good Americans die they go to P.	WILDE 941:85	every man must play a p.	SHAK 768:68
in P., I remained a Canadian	RICH 714:25	every prudent p.	POPE 688:11
I will die in P.	VALL 907:10	fifth p. of the Earth	FIELD 335:11
Nothing can compare to P.	DESC 275:2	forgot my p.	SHAK 799:3
old house in P.	BEME 78:98	however and whenever we p.	DICK 279:6
Outside of P.	MOLI 611:73	know in p....prophesy in p.	BIBLE 126:52
P. is a beast of a city	HAZL 403:44	let us kiss and p.	DRAY 299:99
P. is a city where	WHITE 934:30	lose a p. of ourselves	POPE 686:64
P. made of stone	HUGO 437:61	no p. of his intention	SMITH 828:86
P. preserves the soul	HUGO 437:82	no p. with lads	SASS 745:89
plant our religion in P.	LESL 523:88	Not a tolerable woman's p.	AUST 46:67
When P. sneezes	METT 589:58	p. of all that I have met	TENN 870:98
when they die, go to P.	APPL 30:92	P. of a moon	FROST 352:92
parish all the world as my p.	WESL 932:67	p. on better terms	OTWAY 656:9
consent of every butcher in the p.	SHER 817:80	p. with their brightest hour	HELL 408:47
p. of rich women	AUDEN 43:91	play its...rational p.	LEWIS 526:53
pension from his p.	RUSK 733:95	principal p. of themselves	HAZL 403:37
Paris Hilton all of the attention	GORE 379:62	see the inmost p. of you	SHAK 784:36
is on P. H.		Sir, you and I must p.	SHAK 794:52
Park as Mungo P. once had to do	GALT 359:56	Some p. of us	SKEL 825:35
park All I need...is a p.	CHAP 214:11	take your own p.	BORR 151:70
don't want to come out to the p.	BERRA 86:89	thou and nature can so gently p.	SHAK 795:94
gentleman's p. is my aversion	CONS 244:57	we ourselves are p. of nature	PLAN 680:24
Over p., over pale	SHAK 767:25	what we can p. with	FORD 343:12
P. Avenue...trade deficit	BART 66:30	white...yet a p. of me	HUGH 435:14
Then over the p.	PEPYS 673:93	will more willingly p. withal	SHAK 782:82
Parker Charlie P....always filled	KAVA 474:47	**parted** measured swords, and p.	SHAK 780:23
When I first heard Charlie P.	GILL 370:86	the way we p.	SWIN 864:2
Parkinson's With P., it's like	FOX 346:82	**parterre** nod on the p.	POPE 686:62
parks mountain p. and reservations	MUIR 624:25	**Parthenon** though it were the P.	LOWE 539:1
p., my walks, my manors	SHAK 760:17	**Parthenons** miniature P.	GILL 370:77
They're p....not wildernesses	RABAN 703:5	**particel** every p. and utensil	SHAK 785:90
parliament are on this P.	WILL 944:67	**participant** point of view of p.	GALL 358:39
as in the time of P.	HENR 411:13	**participate** everybody is invited to p.	SCRI 755:90
began our P.	HOBY 421:11	p. in a tragedy	HUXL 442:89
create a modern P.	CONN 242:85	**participation** dreams of the p.	NICH 636:71

particle catching every air-borne p.	JAMES 450:43
pushing young p.	GILB 369:48
particular Every p. Thou	BUBER 171:21
it's about everything in p.	SPARK 836:74
p. and universal	BERG 83:23
p. expenditure	EDEN 311:30
So singular in each p.	SHAK 799:20
particulars must do it in Minute P.	BLAKE 141:31
out of p.	WILL 946:13
parties both p. nobly are subdued	SHAK 773:93
contract...between those two p.	SMITH 827:80
cowardly, middle-class p.	GOER 374:55
creed of different p.	TOCQ 892:30
Dinner p. are for eating	FERB 332:72
Things must be done by p.	DISR 288:63
without the p.	JOHN 462:44
parting at our p.	JONS 467:70
Every p. is a foretaste	SCHO 749:60
In every p....an image of death	ELIOT 315:15
P. is all we know	DICK 284:53
P. is such sweet sorrow	SHAK 766:85
true love p.	THOM 885:66
partitions thin p. do their bands	DRYD 301:72
partner look for a perfect p.	WELD 928:86
Sole p. and sole part	MILT 604:3
partnership P....between...living	BURKE 176:45
parts All p. and none are home	MAIL 560:67
better p. must dance...forever	DAVI 264:75
consist of the fewest p.	LEUP 525:15
decay of p.	CONG 241:58
directed to contrary p.	NEWT 635:59
divided into three p.	NORTH 641:60
first rule...is to save all the p.	EHRL 313:69
Gaul...is divided into three p.	CAES 192:11
How p. relate to the p.	POPE 689:22
in his time plays many p.	SHAK 779:80
p. answering p.	POPE 686:59
p. may be transported	OVID 657:21
p. of one stupendous whole	POPE 687:78
p. remaining as they were	MILT 598:63
p. that people skip	LEON 522:62
three p. iced over	ARNO 34:83
woman must have fine p.	GAY 362:21
party advantage of the stronger p.	THRA 889:59
At a dinner p. one should	MAUG 582:3
blame it on the other p.	ANON 26:80
child ought to be of the p.	AUST 45:51
children's p. taken over by the elders	FITZ 338:89
communist p.	MCCA 547:51
Conservatives...the stupidest p.	MILL 591:15
each p. is worse	ROGE 723:73
effort to keep a p. together	WILS 948:73
expression of the p. line	GINS 372:15
great p. ought not to	HAIL 392:18
Heard there was a p.	LILL 529:99
holiness of always being the injured p.	ANGE 19:94
If I'd seen me at a p.	HOFF 422:26
It ain't a p.	SHEEN 811:43
'Let's p.!'	WILL 944:76
Labour is the P. of law and order	BLAIR 138:49
Macmillan held his p. together	ASQU 38:94
neither p. loser	SHAK 773:93
only one at the p. with a drink	ALLEN 13:86
only p. with clear policies	THAT 881:71
P. is a political evil	BOLI 145:8
p. is organized opinion	DISR 288:49
p. of order or stability	MILL 591:1
p. of political zombies	WILS 948:71
P. on, dude	MYERS 628:97
P. platforms are contracts	TRUM 899:83
P. slogan	ORWE 655:74
p. we love	GAIT 357:19
passion and p. blind our eyes	COLE 236:51
property of any political p.	HOOV 427:51
same is true of a p.	MAO 568:21
serves his p. best	HAYES 403:28
The p.'s over	COMD 239:93
The sooner every p. breaks up	AUST 46:75
third p. who stands	TAYL 868:59
pasarán No p.!	IBAR 444:5
pass all ye that p. by?	BIBLE 110:21
aspirations that never come to p.	SAKI 739:53
in a gleaming p.	TENN 870:89
it will p. with a lass	JAME 449:20
neither can they p. to us	BIBLE 121:98
p. for a cathedral doctor	JONS 466:48
p. for forty-three	GILB 368:30

pathetic

p. through this world — GREL 387:54
replaced the library p. — LODGE 534:97
They shall not p. — PETA 675:35
passage afraid, reading this p. now — FENT 332:60
confessional p….that didn't stink — SALI 740:85
dispute the p. with you — WHIT 938:15
long black p. up to bed — STEV 853:73
meet with a p. — JOHN 462:28
p. in my throat — SHAK 785:82
p. of good style — FORD 343:92
p. through these looms — VAUG 909:40
p. to the intellectual world — STER 848:40
p. which we did not take — ELIOT 319:37
slow p. to the fallen flood — CRAB 252:42
Your last high p. — CIAR 226:22
passages cite p. is to pull — MOORE 617:91
History has many cunning p. — ELIOT 317:84
p. of Ulysses — MILL 593:56
shall not lose our p. — DONNE 291:18
shuts up all the p. — JOHN 459:47
unmagical p. come closest — THOM 884:44
passageway moving through my p. — SABA 736:2
passageways smell of steaks in p. — ELIOT 317:70
passed all have p. away — SIGO 821:64
passenger p. on the spaceship, Earth — FULL 355:72
passengers Wave at the p. — MCGO 552:80
passes hands…move towards the p. — HEAN 404:71
Men seldom make p. — PARK 664:17
passing-bells p.-b. for these who die — OWEN 657:25
passion Better p. and death — LAWR 513:53
betwixt one p. and another — STER 849:54
Calm of mind, all p. — MILT 608:5
capable of one great p. — PASC 666:64
clarity of p. — PASC 666:65
conference resembles a P. play — SCRI 755:90
connect the prose and the p. — FORS 344:30
Death…conclusion of a great p. — LAWR 513:52
desolate and sick of an old p. — DOWS 296:36
destructive p. — BURT 181:84
eternal monotony of p. — FLAU 339:21
Eternal P.! — ARNO 34:85
extremes of p., joy and grief — SHAK 793:36
held in holy p. — MILT 598:51
he vows his p. — PARK 664:13
Infinite p., and the pain — BROW 168:50
In her first p. — BYRON 190:10
in love with himself…a p. — POWE 693:43
inspire hopeless p. — THAC 880:32
Into a tow'ring p. — SHAK 785:70
led by her p. — CAMP 195:73
life? a play of p. — RALE 705:45
lingering and consumptive p. — ETHE 327:47
lov'd with such transcendent p. — DRYD 301:52
love was p.'s essence — BYRON 187:54
Man is a useless p. — SART 744:68
man…not p.'s slave — SHAK 783:22
master-mistress of my p. — SHAK 800:39
master p. is the love of news — CRAB 252:36
Minds still p.-ridden — LIND 530:16
no p. in the mind of man — BACON 50:58
No p. so effectually robs the mind — BURKE 175:60
one p. of my life — GOOD 378:45
or in any other high p. — STEV 852:35
p. and party blind our eyes — COLE 236:51
p. and the life — COLE 235:29
P. and the power to roam — BYRON 187:48
p. could not shake — SHAK 790:33
p. for abstracted devotion — JOHN 461:13
p. for any woman — RIVE 716:55
p. for hunting — DICK 278:68
p. for sweetness and light — ARNO 36:33
p. for the name of 'Mary' — BYRON 190:18
P., intellect, moral activity — NIGH 639:19
p. in the human soul — LILLO 529:1
P. is all of humanity — BALZ 61:5
p. is one which interests — TROL 898:55
p. is our task — JAMES 450:47
p. of the brain — BURT 181:87
poetic p….has most — PATER 668:11
ruling p. conquers reason — POPE 686:67
Search then the Ruling P. — POPE 687:95
their fury and my p. — SHAK 803:15
utmost p. of her heart — HAWT 402:5
vulgar expression of the p.! — CONG 240:36
weary, and drowsy p. — WEBS 926:20
when his p. shall have spent — TENN 871:13
Without p., you don't have energy — TRUMP 900:99

passionate beautiful p. body — SWIN 864:93
p. desire to create — PRIE 695:90
p. heart of the poet — TENN 875:15
passion-flower p.-f. at the gate — TENN 876:28
passionless but man P.? — SHEL 814:18
P. bride — TENN 877:70
passions governs the p. — HUME 438:3
Man…when he acts from the p. — DISR 287:30
men of like p. — BIBLE 124:86
moderator of p. — WALT 920:92
most violent of all the p. — LAFA 503:45
not his reason, but his p. — STER 848:32
only one of many p. — JOHN 461:10
P. can lead me on — LAFA 503:44
P. destroy more prejudices — DIDE 285:60
p. of a king — HUGO 437:69
ridden the p. as if…horse — BROY 169:87
slave of the p. — HUME 438:98
taming…of the soul's raw p. — BLOOM 143:64
To know that there are p. — VIAN 911:72
to move the p. — DRYD 300:24
tragedy paints the p. — HUGO 437:66
two favourite p. — LACL 503:31
various ruling p. — POPE 688:13
passion-winged P.-w. Ministers — SHEL 815:30
passive p., receptive side — SPEN 837:12
Patience is p. — FITZ 338:3
passivity people are reduced to p. — GITL 373:31
passkeys words are the p. to our souls — ACKER 3:59
Passover it is the Lord's p. — BIBLE 93:59
passport man's p. in her…beak — MARL 573:10
p. is sometimes asked for — BAED 54:60
p.'s green — HEAN 405:74
unwrinkled brows in p. offices — STARK 843:22
use only the good p. — SONT 834:20
warmonger put on my p. — BYRON 191:39
past always praising the p. — SMITH 830:38
A man's p. keeps growing ancient? — GARC 360:67
an imagined p. — THOM 886:77
arrow points towards the p. — EDDI 311:24
art of the p. — LEWI 527:77
atone for our p. — CHEK 218:20
back ceaselessly into the p. — FITZ 338:87
burthened too much with the p. — HAWT 402:18
cannot do without the p. — POEL 683:95
changed…to p. Without a word — LARK 509:82
Children have neither p. nor future — LABR 502:24
cut off from the p. — THOM 883:1
dismiss the p. with a smile — LESS 523:91
drowned…the P. — THOM 885:50
economy that belonged to the p. — MARI 570:72
escaping from the burden of the p. — YELT 967:44
face turned to the p. — NARO 630:53
feel the presence of the p. — PEI 672:73
From p. and future — ELIOT 320:76
future as well as the p. — ELIOT 321:89
future contained in time p. — ELIOT 319:36
future that will live up to my p. — BENN 80:53
give you back the p. — HAMM 394:59
glories of the p. — HOWE 433:91
God cannot alter the p. — BUTL 185:95
Gratitude looks to the p. — LEWIS 526:43
greatest secrets of the p. — FAWC 331:51
great men of the p. — DESB 274:88
History is p. politics — FREE 350:47
inherited the p. — ACKR 3:64
intend to prejudge the p. — WHIT 936:75
journeys into the p. — BLYT 144:89
learn from the p. — KISS 493:84
Leave thy low-vaulted p. — HOLM 424:67
Many a woman has a p. — WILDE 941:76
mine my own p. — MANT 568:23
mistakes of the p. — TAYL 868:48
nation cannot face its p. — AI WEI 10:7
never pity the p. — FOWL 345:60
one do with the p.? — MURD 626:66
only a movie of the p. — KESEY 483:65
ooze of the p. — NABO 628:16
others, p. and present — NABO 628:16
p. and future…conquered — ELIOT 321:79
p. and future were comprehended — GEE 362:28
p. exudes legend — MALA 562:88
p….has a voice — OAKE 642:1
p. is a bucket of ashes — SAND 742:16
p. is a foreign country — HART 400:76
P. is a strange land — THOM 885:50

p. is just the same — SASS 745:93
p. is not forgotten — GRASS 382:11
p. is the only dead — THOM 885:59
p….is…too explosive — OBRI 645:62
p….like the leaves of a book — WOOLF 955:11
p. of the oppressed people — FANON 330:14
p. redress…p. care — SHAK 764:46
p. was nothing to her — CHOP 223:31
p. was not more eventful — ORWE 654:31
p., with its crimes — CHUR 225:90
p. would have been washed away — NAIP 629:28
pencils of the p. — STERN 847:19
present is the funeral of the p. — CLARE 228:53
present, p. and future sees — BLAKE 140:8
Psychology has a long p. — EBBI 310:9
quarrels of the p. — MCCA 548:93
remember what is p. — HALI 393:37
Repent what's p. — SHAK 784:43
scraps of the p. — GREE 386:21
something rather absurd about the p. — BEER 73:74
such great writers in the p. — HEMI 410:88
the p. is another country — WINT 950:17
Those who cannot remember the p. — SANT 743:41
tragedies of the p. — PAIS 660:46
visions to the p. — KENN 481:21
weary of the p. — SHEL 816:58
weep like a child for the p. — LAWR 512:46
What calls back the p. — WHIT 938:17
When it comes to the p. — KING 487:41
When remedies are p. — SHAK 789:98
Who controls the p. — ORWE 655:74
paste p. and cover to our bones — SHAK 764:51
Pasteur work such as P.'s — ROST 727:70
pastime ancient…forgotten p. — SCOTT 753:44
better p. for their leisure — WELLS 930:37
fellowly sport or p. — STUB 858:61
joyous birds make their p. — SPEN 839:39
ruin any p. under the sun — MITF 610:49
pastimes Proust of p. — FOWL 346:65
pastoral Cold P.! — KEATS 478:39
working classes…p. decorations — WAUGH 924:96
pastors as some ungracious p. do — SHAK 781:48
pasture dewy p., dewy trees — TENN 870:96
people of his p. — BOOK 149:30
pastures dull p. of her ignorance — SMITH 828:3
In p. green — SCOT 754:85
lie down in green p. — BIBLE 100:45
p. of the spirit — SASS 746:1
Pipe me to p. still — HOPK 428:67
pleasant p. seen? — BLAKE 141:40
woods, and p. new — MILT 600:96
patch any p. left of us — POUND 691:98
p. up thine old body — SHAK 772:82
patches thing of shreds and p. — GILB 369:58
pate drunkard, drowsy p.? — SKEL 824:31
p. of a politician — SHAK 784:61
pâté eating p. de foie gras — SMITH 831:61
patens p. of bright gold — SHAK 770:19
patent p. system…added — LINC 529:6
so my p. back — SHAK 802:67
paterfamilias p. worth his salt — ACHE 2:22
path cannot approach it by any p. — KRIS 499:11
chose the forest p. — FAWC 331:51
compassest my p. — BIBLE 103:43
dark is his p. — GRANT 381:6
farther down our particular p. — FORS 345:50
Guide us in the straight p. — KORAN 496:38
midst the twilight p. — COLL 238:76
moments illuminate our p. — SCHO 748:52
Never follow anyone else's p. — DEGEN 270:3
One p. leads to despair — ALLEN 14:98
Our p. emerges for a while — DOWS 296:37
p. and process taken — LIEB 529:3
p. is scarcely opened — ROST 727:70
P. of Wickedness — BALL 59:75
p. that leads to the truth — HUXL 443:5
p. up and down is…the same — HERA 412:32
p. we shall never choose — KENN 481:12
primrose p. of dalliance — SHAK 781:48
straight p. was lost — DANTE 262:36
Take the gentle p. — HERB 414:85
travelling along every p. — HERA 412:35
Virtue's his p. — DRYD 301:48
walking along a p. — MUNCH 625:41
pathetic Love is a very p. thing — FLEM 340:49
shocking, but not p. — HUGH 435:34
too p. for the feelings — AUST 45:48

pathless

pathless P. and dangerous — ROCH 719:11
pathological physiological or p. — UNAM 905:4
pathos gulf of years and p. — MARQ 574:43
  P., piety, courage — FORS 344:37
paths all her p. are peace — BIBLE 104:55
  away from the p. of violence — JOHN 456:79
  direct thy p. — BIBLE 104:52
  grubbing weeds from gravel p. — KIPL 492:68
  make his p. straight — BIBLE 114:18
  p. drop fatness — BIBLE 101:79
  p. of righteousness — BIBLE 100:45
  p. of righteousness — SCOT 755:85
  p. of the Spirit — MATI 581:93
  two p. in life — MANN 566:80
pathway strew your p. — HOLM 423:61
pathways all of night's p. — AGUS 9:98
patience Be riche in p. — DUNB 306:99
  breeds p. and courtesy — MUIR 624:20
  dying With a little p. — ELIOT 318:8
  habits of peace and p. — WALT 920:92
  Hence hath flowed P. — WORD 962:49
  how long will you abuse our p. — CICE 227:28
  I laughed him out of p. — SHAK 794:62
  In your p. possess — BIBLE 122:4
  less p. than a wolf's — TATE 867:41
  like p. on a monument — SHAK 786:2
  men's office to speak p. — SHAK 774:52
  old abusing of God's p. — SHAK 773:1
  other people's p. — UPDI 905:16
  overturns All p. — MILT 605:24
  P. and longevity — LAFO 504:53
  p., and shuffle the cards — CERV 211:49
  p. He stands waiting — LOGAU 534:5
  P. is a virtue — ANON 21:48
  P. is passive — FITZ 338:3
  P....minor form of despair — BIER 135:85
  p. of the general public — KRUG 500:22
  p., temperance, add love — MILT 607:72
  p. will achieve more than our force — BURKE 176:47
  seek you help in p. and prayer — KORAN 496:40
  they that ha' not p.! — SHAK 789:15
  Though P. be a tired mare — SHAK 775:66
  wives take a pride in their p. — BACON 51:77
patient amusing the p. — VOLT 915:49
  cure the disease and kill the p. — BACON 52:15
  fury of a p. man — DRYD 302:92
  like saying that the p. died — JACO 449:9
  most p. people grow weary — STEV 851:27
  My soul...a p. looker-on — QUAR 701:6
  p. endurance is godlike — LONG 535:26
  p. etherized upon a table — ELIOT 316:60
  p. in spirit is better — BIBLE 106:22
  p. is no longer here — ELIOT 320:75
  p., not a brawler — BIBLE 129:18
  poor as Job...but not so p. — SHAK 772:72
  tenderness of p. minds — OWEN 657:26
  vet can't catch his p. — HERR 416:19
patients Be careful then, p. — VALLE 907:7
  prescriptions written by p. — KRAUS 499:5
patio start laying his own p. — SELF 756:10
patois I write in a...broken-down p. — CHAN 213:82
patria Pro p. mori — OWEN 657:31
  pro p., non 'dulce' — POUND 691:4
patriarch the murderous p. — BLUN 143:73
patriarchal p. unit within a p. whole — MILL 595:99
patriarchy P.'s...institution — MILL 595:99
patrician rise of a p. — TIME 892:20
  Say great P.! — POPE 688:29
  This is the P. — DONNE 293:63
Patrick Wearing, by St. P.'s bounty — LAND 507:35
patrimony fair p. That I must leave — MILT 606:63
patriot is he a p. for me? — FRAN 347:97
  no p. would think of saying — CHES 220:54
  p....a fool — DRYD 302:90
  sunshine p. will...shrink — PAINE 660:29
patriotic fights you on p. principles — SHAW 807:97
  p. Old Man — ANON 23:88
patriotism British p. — BALF 57:38
  duty, p....clad — LLOY 533:72
  encouraged now as p. — TOLK 893:44
  Nationalism, and its chum, p. — DUNN 307:17
  P. in Vietnam — NGUY 636:69
  P. is a lively sense — ALDI 12:48
  P. is being convinced — APPEL 29:89
  P. is easy to understand in America — COOL 246:82
  p. is not enough — CAVE 210:19
  P. is the last refuge — JOHN 462:37

P....last refuge of the scoundrel — BRAGG 156:54
p. that has nerved women — PANK 662:86
spring of p. — CURZ 260:5
patriots blood of p. and tyrants — JEFF 454:22
  For what were...country p. born? — BYRON 191:34
  p....not to forget we are gentlemen — BURKE 175:11
  P. spring up like mushrooms — WALP 919:84
patron Is not a P. — JOHN 460:63
  p. and the jail — JOHN 459:46
  P.. Commonly a wretch — JOHN 460:78
  p. of some thirty charities — TENN 872:35
  p. saint of journalists — MCFA 551:69
patroness celestial p., who deigns — MILT 605:43
patrons drama's p. give — JOHN 459:44
patsies often p. for the ruling classes — HELL 408:46
patter rifles...Can p. out — OWEN 657:25
pattering swift p. of naked feet — DOYLE 297:48
pattern Here such a p. is — MILL 592:18
  history is a p. — ELIOT 321:93
  In a p. called a war — LOWE 539:98
  in a strong p. — SMITH 828:2
  in history...a predetermined p. — FISH 337:62
  never mistake p. for meaning — BANKS 62:26
  p. for the future of the world — CHUR 225:80
  p. more complicated — ELIOT 320:68
  p. of elaborate writing — DRYD 300:26
  p. on which to model themselves — CHAR 215:37
  slavery to a p. — NIN 639:29
  such a coarse p. — HARDY 397:15
patterns assent to p. of limited — NOVAK 641:64
  Christ! What are p. for? — LOWE 539:98
  short...if one follows p. — SENE 757:22
  social and educational p. — MCLU 556:56
  Those are old p. — STUA 857:56
pattle Wi' murd'ring p.! — BURNS 177:77
paucity of human pleasures — JOHN 465:5
  p. of its reverberation — MAIL 560:56
  p. of restraints — SPEN 836:89
  p. of words imparts majesty — ALBE 11:31
pauperism increasing p. — WOOL 955:9
pause buck doesn't even p. here — REGAN 710:40
  easy to forget to p. — ELIZ 322:13
  eine kleine p. — FERR 334:99
  Must give us p. — SHAK 783:7
  must p. till it come back — SHAK 777:40
  not enough to be p. — BRAT 157:78
  p....for an angel to pass — FIRB 336:46
  p. in the day's occupation — DE 275:11
  then there's a p. — BENN 79:33
pauses p. between the notes — SCHN 748:41
Pavarotti Christmas concert by P. — BURKE 177:64
pavement shoe along the p. — TRAV 895:89
  walking along a nice wide p. — JACO 449:12
pavements crammed...p. of gold — LAUR 511:22
  p. fang'd with murderous stones — COLE 236:50
pavilion of Heaven is bare — SHEL 813:77
paving quarry of p. stones for Hell — KING 488:59
paw free conscience from the p. — MILT 601:25
  grim wolf with privy p. — MILT 599:89
  out of the p. of the lion — BIBLE 96:37
  sticks in his sharp p. — ANON 20:31
Pawnees P., lying low — LIND 530:23
paws Monkey with lollipop p. — LEAR 516:33
pax P. Britannia takes a bit — CARY 207:61
  P. Romana — BURG 174:91
  P. Vobis — BIBLE 133:45
pay and for what p.? — RUSK 733:5
  as big as they can p. for — SMITH 829:20
  cannot p. too dearly — LESA 523:87
  dangerous to p. it off — SELL 756:15
  Death...gas bill one can't p. — BURG 174:95
  do what you p. them to do — WALD 916:26
  jobs that p. more than others — WILL 945:5
  men will...do it for p. — MELV 585:77
  Not a penny off the p. — COOK 245:64
  p. any price — KENN 481:3
  p. for one by one! — KIPL 490:1
  P. given to state hireling — JOHN 460:78
  p. me the cut — GOMEZ 377:39
  p. you this exorbitant charge — KEMB 479:72
  poor grub, poor p. — LOND 534:10
  think of your p. packet — COWA 249:59
  unless they can p. a lot — RUBE 730:32
  We won't p., we won't p. — FO 341:66
  wonders what's to p. — HOUS 432:69
payment cash p....nexus of man — CARL 201:27
  love is a p. — DUNC 307:7

Peabury Lady P. — WAUGH 924:78
peace abundance of p. — BIBLE 100:59
  agree on a genuine p. — KENN 481:18
  all her paths are p. — BIBLE 104:55
  asks God only for p. — BONH 145:21
  as we to keep the p. — SHAK 765:67
  at p. you think about — WILD 943:43
  author of p. — BOOK 146:39
  bodies are buried in p. — BIBLE 113:11
  Bomb brought p. — CHUR 226:99
  bring a man p. — BOOK 149:13
  brings p. and good will — LLOY 533:77
  bring white p. — LIND 530:21
  but in p. Hung over — KEATS 477:12
  carry gentle p. — SHAK 805:54
  certain knot of p. — SIDN 820:46
  chastisement of our p. — BIBLE 109:94
  craving p. — WORD 961:38
  Cricket for p. — ZIA 970:12
  deathless and painless p. — HUGH 436:42
  deep p. of the double-bed — CAMP 193:47
  defences of p. — UNES 905:8
  demands and keep p. — NAPO 629:39
  democracy and p. — WELL 929:93
  each of those words signifies p. — LAMA 504:74
  enter into you in p. — MURD 626:66
  Everlasting p. is a dream — MOLT 612:92
  Father of P. — DODD 289:93
  find p. in...desert travel — THES 882:56
  for ever hold his p. — BOOK 148:88
  give p. a chance — LENN 521:45
  Give p. in our time — BOOK 146:38
  give thee p. — BIBLE 94:79
  God's p. betide the souls — RANS 707:72
  good arts of p. — MORE 618:10
  good p. would never have won — CHUR 225:76
  good war makes a good p. — HERB 414:86
  government in p. and in war — BEVE 90:62
  habits of p. and patience — WALT 920:92
  hard and bitter p. — KENN 481:3
  haunt of ancient P. — TENN 870:96
  hold their p. — BIBLE 122:13
  holy rest, and p. — NEWM 635:46
  honey p. in old poems — JEFF 453:12
  if one wishes to travel in p. — STARK 843:22
  Imperishable p. — HOUS 432:78
  inglorious arts of p. — MARV 576:83
  In hearts at p. — BROO 162:89
  In His will is our p. — DANTE 262:41
  in p. and...in war — MONT 614:39
  In p., children inter their parents — HERO 415:95
  In p.: goodwill — CHUR 224:69
  instrument of Your p. — FRAN 347:99
  In the arts of p. — SHAW 807:27
  in Thee in p. — HAMM 394:55
  in what p. a Christian can die — ADDI 7:57
  keep him in perfect p. — BIBLE 108:68
  King of glory, King of p. — HERB 413:68
  led forth with p. — BIBLE 109:1
  Let him who desires p. — VEGE 910:48
  lettest thou thy servant depart in p. — BIBLE 133:44
  lettest thou thy servant depart in p. — BIBLE 120:70
  let us make p. — CROM 255:19
  live together in p. — UNIT 905:9
  Love of P., and lonely musing — COLL 238:79
  made a desolation they called it a p. — BURG 174:91
  made a separate p. — HEMI 409:65
  Make it a green p. — DARN 263:49
  means of preserving p. — WASH 922:30
  merry songs of p. — SHAK 805:58
  message of p., love — WHIT 936:71
  more p. and it is the holier — HOPK 428:83
  more potent advocates of p. — GEOR 364:49
  never...a bad p. — FRAN 348:16
  no better p.-keepers — PALM 661:68
  no p....to the wicked — BIBLE 110:4
  Nor for my p. — JONS 467:74
  Nor p. within nor calm around — SHEL 812:68
  no such thing as inner p. — LEBO 517:56
  not a p. treaty — FOCH 341:68
  Nothing can bring you p. — EMER 324:56
  now do hold their p. — SURR 860:98
  Now we have to win the p. — CLEM 230:90
  Palestinian p. movement — ANON 27:23
  p. above all earthly dignities — SHAK 805:51
  p. among our peoples — KIPL 490:8
  p. and propagation — WALP 919:76

p. and rest can never dwell	MILT	601:35
P....a period of cheating	BIER	135:86
P. be to this house	BIBLE	120:78
P. be to this house	BOOK	148:96
p. betrayed us	MUIR	624:19
P. be unto you	BIBLE	133:45
P. cannot be built on exclusion	ADAMS	4:83
p. cannot be maintained	RUSS	735:45
P.; come away	TENN	874:81
p. comes dropping slow	YEATS	965:4
P., Enjoyment, Love and Pleasure!	BURNS	179:36
p. for our time	CHAM	212:64
peaceful sloth, Not p.	MILT	602:60
p. has been broken	ROOS	724:9
p. hath her victories	MILT	601:25
p. have they which love thy law	BIBLE	103:30
p., I hope, with honour	DISR	288:66
P. I leave with you	BIBLE	123:54
p. in Shelley's mind	SHEL	816:62
p. in thy breast	SHAK	766:86
P. is in the grave	SHEL	814:11
P. is...more precious than...land	SADAT	737:13
p. is of the nature	SHAK	773:93
P. is poor reading	HARDY	397:27
P. its ten thousands	PORT	690:78
P. makes plenty	ANON	21:55
P. nor beauty	LAWR	513:55
p. of each country	JOHN	456:74
p. of God, which passeth	BIBLE	128:4
p. of God, which passeth	BOOK	147:75
p. of mind	SMITH	827:74
P. on earth and mercy mild	BEEC	73:65
P. on earth and mercy mild	WESL	931:58
p....on the tested foundations	WILS	949:83
P., p.; when there is no p.	BIBLE	110:15
p. talks	ALBR	11:37
P., the human dress	BLAKE	139:88
p. there's nothing	SHAK	775:74
P. to corrupt no less	MILT	607:70
p. to hers is small	CRIP	254:96
p. to him that is far off	BIBLE	109:3
p. to Ireland	ARNO	35:23
p. to the cottages	CHAM	212:69
p. to thy soul	SCOTT	754:81
p. to you which were afar off	BIBLE	127:85
p. which the world cannot give	BOOK	146:42
P. without honour	CECIL	210:27
piping time of p.	SHAK	761:34
Policemen...keepers of the p.	MAMET	563:27
poor, who will not fast in p.	CRAB	252:35
power, p. and healing	MATT	582:1
Pray for the p. of Jerusalem	BIBLE	103:33
Prince of P.	BIBLE	107:60
probabilities of p. or war	PALM	662:74
programme of the world's p.	WILS	949:85
promised...either is p. or happiness	LEBON	517:5
publisheth p.	BIBLE	109:90
re-establish p. and civil order	ELIZ	322:10
rest in obscurity and p.!	EMMET	325:6
Rest in soft p.	JONS	467:77
send p. on earth	BIBLE	116:72
shall the Great P. be established	DEKA	270:7
should kneel for p.	SHAK	762:79
soft phrase of p.	SHAK	788:91
Stalin...lover of p.	NEHRU	633:9
take chances for p.	DULL	306:87
the fate of p.	OBAMA	644:47
there abides a p. of thine	ARNO	34:74
they are in p.	BIBLE	112:74
they love p. and quiet	TOLK	893:47
thing fall down in p.	MAYB	583:24
though not its p.	GRAV	382:19
though sorrowing, yet in p.	MILT	606:66
thousand years of p.	TENN	875:95
time of p.	BIBLE	106:14
Universal p. is declared	ELIOT	315:40
universal p. lie	TENN	872:30
waging of p.	ELIZ	322:12
War is p.	ORWE	655:73
war is preferable to a shameful p.	TACI	866:6
war yield to p.	CICE	227:35
We came in p.	ANON	25:69
weeds of p....triumphs	MILT	597:47
we prepare...for p.	PEAR	671:67
What hast thou to do with p.?	BIBLE	97:76
When there was p.	AUDEN	43:85
whisper 'P.'	GROM	389:77
wilderness and they call it p.	TACI	865:2
workshop for world p.	HARR	399:59
peaceful free nations are p. nations	BUSH	183:26
friendship is never p.	SEVI	758:41
On every p. home	KIPL	493:70
p. revolution impossible	KENN	481:10
What...made her p.	YEATS	966:14
peace-keepers no better p.-k.	PALM	661:68
peacemaker 'if' is the only p.	SHAK	780:25
peacemakers Blessed are the p.	BIBLE	114:27
peacetime p. environment	TRUM	900:87
where they're living it's p.	KRAM	499:3
peach better than an insipid p.	HUNT	439:26
dare to eat a p.?	ELIOT	317:68
nectarine, and curious p.	MARV	577:4
peacock bluejay in p. feathers	LAFO	504:58
droops the milk-white p.	TENN	873:49
Eyed like a p.	KEATS	476:4
pride of the p.	BLAKE	140:2
peacocks p. and lilies	RUSK	732:84
p. strutting by	KIPL	492:67
peak 17,000-foot p.	BENU	83:9
upon a p. in Darien	KEATS	475:61
peaked my career has just p.	FIRTH	336:59
peaks great p. we had forgotten	LLOY	533:72
Sundered by p.	TU	900:9
peal widest p. for years	HODG	421:23
peals p. of laughter...round thee	POPE	687:98
peanut P. butter has survived	KEIL	479:54
the showmanship of a p.	COWE	249:69
peanuts more salted p. consumed	SPIL	840:68
pea-pod povere peple tho p.-p.	LANG	508:48
pear know the taste of a p.	MAO	568:27
p. on top of two toothpicks	ACHE	2:32
pearl crown enchased with p.	MARL	572:98
find a diamond or a p.	VAN	908:20
gates of p. and topaz	LAUR	511:22
great ouches, heaps of p.	SHAK	761:40
ocean for orient p.	MARL	573:25
ocean for orient p.	MARL	573:23
p. in every cowslip's ear	SHAK	767:25
profited from its p.	THUR	890:81
tears to p. he turned	MARL	574:39
threw a p. away	SHAK	790:51
pearls Give p. away	HOUS	431:38
p. by the seashore	MORE	618:21
Scatter thy p.	BLAKE	139:80
search for p.	DRYD	301:46
seeking goodly p.	BIBLE	117:96
shot to death, with p.?	WEBS	927:58
Pearse P. summoned Cuchulain	YEATS	967:38
peartree glassy p.	HOPK	428:74
peas eat my p. with honey	NASH	631:87
Here are sweet p.	KEATS	475:63
peasant p. and a philosopher	JOHN	461:12
thankful I am a p.	FRAN	348:23
peasantry bold p.	GOLD	376:98
p. its pack animal	TROT	899:65
peasants changed from p.	WAUGH	924:47
p. in El Salvador	OROU	652:92
p. now Resign their pipes	CRAB	252:29
p. should be killed	LUTH	542:72
peason beans and p. put within	ANON	20:40
pebble p. or a prettier shell	NEWT	635:61
p. Ruttled in dry ground	JEFF	453:18
Pebworth Piping P.	ANON	24:32
pecker p. in my pocket	JOHN	458:15
Peckham classes within classes in P.	SPARK	836:65
peculiar Funny p., or funny ha-ha?	HAY	402:19
p. people	BIBLE	130:68
pecuniam p. infinitam	CICE	227:32
pecuniary immense p. Mangle	DICK	282:95
pedagogic for p. and other purposes	GALB	357:23
pedal large gas p.	MURR	627:82
pedant fertile p.	WALP	919:80
like the p. in Hierocles	JOHN	461:9
poetry a p.'s game	BUNT	173:68
pedantic too p. for a gentleman	CONG	241:48
pedants P. may cry out loud	GONZ	378:43
pederast [Music] a p. might hum	PROU	698:53
pedestalled p. in triumph?	BROW	169:75
pedigree P. of Honey	DICK	284:51
religious ties...social p.	WOLFE	953:78
pedigrees p. of nations	JOHN	462:31
pedlar looked like a p.	MOORE	616:64
pee P., po, belly, bum, drawers	FLAN	338:10
peel p. me a grape	WEST	933:87
peep p. and botanize	WORD	957:65
p. through their eyes	SHAK	768:67
treason can but p.	SHAK	784:53
peeping p. Tom of the sciences	BISH	137:31
peepshow ticket for the p.	MACN	557:97
peer English p. of the right sort	WODE	951:31
Lycidas...not left his p.	MILT	599:82
Peerless P.	ROCH	720:20
peerage were I to be offered a p.	CHAN	214:8
You should study the P.	WILDE	941:92
peers flattery of one's p.	LODGE	534:99
House of p.	GILB	369:53
judged by our p.	BALZ	60:93
Of Satan and his p.	MILT	602:54
p., and they are hereditary	LLOY	533:78
peevish something p. that way	SHAK	773:2
temper...has become licentiously p.	DISR	288:46
Virginity is p., proud, idle	SHAK	791:56
peeweets the p. crying	STEV	854:48
peg Hang your idea on a p.	BRIS	159:27
Pegasus thought it P.	KEATS	475:68
peignoir Complacencies of the p.	STEV	849:69
Pele I was not the White P.	BEST	87:8
pellet p. with the poison	PANA	662:80
pelt wear my p. tanned	MIDD	590:74
pelting p. of this pitiless storm	SHAK	792:11
pen altar, sword and p.	WORD	958:94
Before my p. has gleaned	KEATS	475:67
Biting my truant p.	SIDN	820:44
could use the sword and p.	LAND	507:35
Devise wit, write p.	SHAK	763:8
drop of ink in my p.	WALP	919:67
far less brilliant p. than mine	BEER	73:75
garden with your p.	CAMP	194:53
hung up my p.	SIMON	822:77
needle and the p.	LEWIS	526:51
Never durst poet touch a p.	SHAK	763:18
one p. can change the world	YOUS	969:62
p. but also with a blue pencil	LUCAS	541:54
p. has been in their hands	AUST	47:89
p. is mightier than the sword	BULW	173:64
p. is worse than the sword	BURT	181:78
p. refusing to draw anything	BRON	161:67
poet's p. all scorn	BRAD	155:50
poet's p. Turns them to shapes	SHAK	768:45
prevents his holding a p.	DICK	278:80
sad words of tongue or p.	WHIT	938:20
squat p. rests	HEAN	404:67
This p.'s all I have	HARR	399:57
With such acts fill a p.	DRAY	298:95
words of tongue and p.	HARTE	400:75
penal blood...on your p. code	BYRON	187:31
this planet is used as a p. colony	HITCH	419:88
penalties pains and p. of idleness	POPE	689:45
penalty in the p. area	SHAN	805:63
lines marking a p. area	FRY	353:28
p. is...cowardly	PELE	672:74
pence Take care of the p.	LOWN	540:40
pencil coloured p. long enough	CHES	220:75
dips His p.	SHEL	812:69
drew your p. from you	TENN	871:5
pen but also with a blue p.	LUCAS	541:54
p. drew whate'er her soul designed	DRYD	302:27
pencils inexorable sadness of p.	ROET	722:55
p. of the past	STERN	847:19
pendulum p. of the mind	JUNG	471:46
p. swinging up and down	COLUM	238:90
Penelope His true P.	POUND	691:1
penetrate music...will p.	SHAK	803:92
p. some thick skull	SARD	743:51
penguin In the P. book	HEAN	405:75
young p. lies screaming?	EWART	328:74
penis p. and mathematics	CELI	211:35
president's p. was on everyone's mind	ROTH	728:93
pennies P. don't fall from heaven	THAT	881:56
P. from Heaven	BURKE	176:59
Pennsylvania by the name of P.	PENN	673:26
penny Germans...pay every p.	GEDD	362:26
loaves sold for a p.	SHAK	759:95
Not a p. off the pay	COOK	245:64
not give one p.	CATU	209:6
one p. plain	STEV	851:30
pens p. that ever poets held	MARL	572:2
Penshurst Thou art not, P.	JONS	467:71
pension labourer to take his p.	RUSK	733:95
p. list...a roll of honour	CLEV	230:91
P.. Pay given	JOHN	460:79

pensioners 1232

pensioners cowslips tall her p. be SHAK 767:25
trade union for p. and children HEATH 405:84
pensions P. and Grenadiers STER 848:37
p. and other boring TOWN 895:68
Pentecost day of P. was fully come BIBLE 124:72
pentecostal no wind, but p. fire ELIOT 321:81
penthouse Hang upon his p. lid SHAK 795:1
penumbra p. of somber dignity ATLAS 40:19
penuries sheave…to fill all p. DONNE 293:72
penury Chill P. GRAY 384:68
ragged p. of shade ADAMS 4:73
talk…tendeth only to p. BIBLE 104:72
people 10,000 p. looking for 10 p. ANON 26:88
18,000 p. boo PLAN 680:26
advice to p. today LEARY 517:47
after p. who interest me KERO 483:53
ageing college p. NABO 628:7
ain't twelve hundred p. KIPL 490:96
all country p., in the world SENG 757:26
All cruel p. WILL 945:2
all nations…and p. BIBLE 131:3
All p. that on earth SCOT 755:88
All the nice p. SPARK 836:71
all the p. I'd hoped were dead BOGA 144:96
Alps and their p. RUSK 732:85
American p. GERG 365:65
American p.…were like him REST 711:66
Among a p. generally corrupt BURKE 175:26
Artists are the only p. SLOAN 825:55
as long as p. hear it SOUSA 834:39
August for the p. AUDEN 42:74
average condition of the p. MILL 591:97
balance to the p. ANON 26:92
bearable by millions of p. SHAW 809:74
beat my p. to pieces BIBLE 107:52
Before we were her p. FROST 353:15
before you were born to p. LEBO 517:62
believe that p. accept THAT 881:57
Be nice to p. on your MIZN 610:60
best p. never land MACN 558:7
between the king and the p. SELD 756:7
Black p. possess the secret of joy WALK 917:40
black p. with Jesus GIOV 372:19
brings out…the worst in p. SARN 743:56
buckler of the p.'s cause DRYD 302:75
burning and gassing p. SIHA 821:65
but ye are the p. BIBLE 98:2
by all p. believed VINC 913:9
by the p., and for the p. LINC 529:5
Can make good p. SHAK 804:38
cannot prevent p. from thinking SCHI 747:26
can't help p. against their will FREE 349:46
causes public, p. to feel…downcast MCGO 551:72
certain sick p. are said to do LAMB 505:99
character of its p. HOPP 429:1
Church [is] the p. SHAW 809:69
circumcised p. GIBB 366:95
city where most p. live GRAY 383:43
civilized and democratic p. ATTL 40:25
classes of p. GARL 360:74
class of p. WARD 920:99
clever, well-informed p. AUST 47:87
colonialism forces the p. FANON 330:15
common p. know what they MENC 586:81
common p. swarm SHAK 760:11
confident that the unfortunate p. WELLS 930:37
Conquered p. tend to be witty BELL 77:83
contracts with the p. TRUM 899:83
control the p. DICK 277:37
country p. forget MORR 620:56
Cricket? It civilises p. MUGA 623:7
Cultured p. practise self-examination ICHI 445:13
DEAL…full of filthy-looking p. COBB 233:76
decent godless p. ELIOT 319:32
decent p. live beyond their incomes SAKI 739:63
desire of our two p. CHAM 212:63
different p., different beliefs CART 206:43
different sorts of p. SHAW 809:84
do my p. forgive me? RICH 713:9
don't think I understand p. FORS 344:34
drawn between him and the p. HARD 396:91
Eating p. is wrong! FLAN 338:9
economy of these p. SMOL 831:67
education of the p. DISR 288:62
education of the p. MILL 591:98
effect on other p. SART 744:64
enslaved and stubborn p. MORE 618:14

every p. should be left free WILS 949:81
excellent p. never go there SAKI 739:64
exertions of a free p. PITT 680:12
express purpose of letting p. in DICK 277:39
eye…ear…tongue of the p. STEAD 843:30
far into other p. AMIS 16:94
father of his p. GIBB 366:94
fight so hungry p. can eat STEI 846:83
folk music…fat p. DYLAN 309:58
fool some of the p. LINC 529:5
for many p. in the West SOLZ 833:7
French are a logical p. MORL 619:40
from the p., and for the p. DISR 287:16
from the p. to the common good MILT 601:24
get p. into a position KAZIN 474:53
get p. to call me Newt GING 371:99
good of the p. CICE 227:29
good…To all the p. WESL 932:68
government and the p. MILL 591:92
government can confer on a p. MACA 544:21
govern the p. LOUI 537:63
great many p. TAFT 866:10
great masses of the plain p. MENC 586:92
Great p. talk about ideas LEBO 517:63
habits and customs of the p. RICA 712:79
half the p. are right WHITE 935:34
hard to meet new p. LEMM 521:34
hate p. and children CAMP 194:59
hate p. who play bridge MAUG 582:5
hath such p. in't! SHAK 804:33
Hell is other p. SART 744:69
hire mediocre p. MURP 627:78
hits where the other p. are LARD 509:69
holding a p. in its grip FANON 330:14
How many p. ASIM 38:78
humble p. of Cambodia SIHA 821:66
Hundreds of p. can talk RUSK 733:14
If by the p.…multitude DRYD 300:22
If p. could deal…honestly CHAN 213:90
If p. knew there'd be less death MALA 561:83
Imagine all the p. LENN 521:46
In America few p. will trust MAIL 560:45
induce p. to buy them STEV 849:62
industry that…needs better p. DRUC 299:7
investigator to pretend that p. LEWO 528:79
It is for the p. OROZ 652:1
jokes upon the American p. MENC 586:95
keen city…filled with pretty p. CUMM 257:56
Let my p. go BIBLE 93:57
Let the p. praise thee BIBLE 101:80
Liars out of the American p. ROGE 723:75
life and times of a p. ROCK 721:40
live among wicked p. RICH 714:12
look after our p. SCOTT 751:7
losing p. you love OATES 643:9
lot of p. doing what I say WINN 950:5
lot of p. under you ANON 27:32
love of the p. BURKE 175:21
make fun of p. GARC 359:65
make one set of p. forget HUXL 442:82
make p. believe WILS 947:40
makes p. happy WHITE 936:60
many p. in the world KENN 481:22
mark of many famous p. HELL 408:47
married p. live longer? FIEL 335:32
martyr of the p. CHAR 215:31
materialistic p. MCCA 547:86
money from the pockets of the p. SMITH 828:91
moral consciousness of p. MAIL 559:41
more than a p. lover LARK 510:91
more than p. could afford LEWIS 527:56
Most p. are relieved TUCH 901:13
most p. are wrong KURZ 501:46
most p. in most places LEGU 520:14
Most p. my age STEN 847:10
Most p. sell their souls SMITH 829:18
Most p. spend…their lives LABR 502:26
motivating p. MCDO 550:44
mouths of fallible p. BENN 80:55
my p. died to build this country ROBE 717:76
New Deal for the American p. ROOS 724:3
no use to decent p. SHAW 809:83
no vision, the p. perish BIBLE 105:6
number of p. have tried KERR 483:58
Observing these p. MAUG 582:11
Of all the clever p. round me CAMP 194:52
of the p. by the p. for the p. WILDE 941:74

o my p. OLSEN 650:46
one million p.…a small sum DENG 272:58
one of the few honest p. FITZ 337:81
one of the p. took one ANDE 18:75
One realm, one p., one leader ANON 24:16
only ordinary p. asked MO 611:69
Only the little p. pay taxes HELM 408:52
opium of the p. MARX 578:24
Other p.'s babies HERB 412:44
ought to class p. as static WAUGH 923:65
Our p. are not naive REYES 712:69
our p. can build Angkor Wat POL 684:7
over-civilized p. MUIR 624:25
parts that p. skip LEON 522:62
p.…contemplate writing GERA 364:60
peculiar p. BIBLE 130:67
p.…abusing the best Constitution FRAN 348:15
p. according to their abilities MAIN 561:71
p., after fifty VIDAL 912:93
p. all exulting WHIT 938:7
p. always say GOTT 379:71
p. and I have come to an agreement FRED 349:41
p. and the method RYLE 736:60
p., and the sheep of his pasture BIBLE 102:4
p. and the stones WILL 946:11
p. answered him not a word BIBLE 97:51
p. are all too clean LINK 530:29
p. are entitled to JEFF 454:23
p. are fanatically dedicated PIRS 679:90
p. are frequenting MACL 555:31
p. are hostile CRISP 255:8
p. are like portmanteaux MANS 567:2
p. are mostly rational ADAMS 6:12
p. are nice and polite MAHA 559:28
P. are not as smart as bugs WHITE 935:44
P. are not fallen angels LAWR 512:43
p. are not so unpolished MONT 613:11
p. are only human COMP 239:97
p. are paying attention SONT 834:22
p. are reduced to passivity GITL 373:31
p. are shocked by honesty COWA 249:57
p. are the masters BURKE 175:30
p. are too stupid by three-quarters MAJOR 561:74
p. are travellers FERB 332:67
p. arose as one man BIBLE 96:22
p. believe that they have rights HEGEL 406:7
p. between twenty and forty FAUL 331:38
p. brought up in…slums WAUGH 923:67
p. came to theirs HODG 421:23
p. can be poor OCON 647:91
p. can claim America ROLL 723:90
p. change and forget HELL 408:44
p. contend for their liberty HALI 393:38
p. could be down-to-earth SHUL 819:30
p. could neither see JOHN 459:33
p. do actually desire it MILL 592:9
p. do not change VIAN 911:68
P. don't choose their careers DOSP 294:87
p. don't go to the theater JOUR 469:11
P. don't…like…beautiful DEBU 268:61
P. don't resent having nothing COMP 239:98
p.…don't trust their reactions COLE 234:44
P. do what you pay WALD 916:26
P. find ideas a bore POUND 692:19
p. free from routine LINK 530:25
p. getting into a state GALS 358:49
p. have spoken FITT 337:67
p. I hate HART 400:67
p. in nutrition DAVIS 265:93
p. in portraits are thinking LIVE 531:48
P. in Power PATC 668:8
p. in the back streets of Derby CHRI 223:37
p. in the world are fools WILD 943:48
P. in this country RICH 714:70
p. know what the land knows SAND 742:28
P. listen to you SNOW 832:81
P. live within winter MUNRO 625:52
p. look at the sea FROST 352:8
p. love junk food GASS 361:86
p. may be made to follow CONF 240:17
p. may complain WEBER 925:14
P. must learn to hate MAND 565:56
P.…must not be bartered WILS 949:60
P. must not do things for fun HERB 413:49
P. mutht be amuthed DICK 282:82
p. never fail to amaze WINF 949:93
p. never give up their liberties BURKE 175:33

perfection

p. not spoken about	GEE 362:27	
p. of all sorts	APOL 29:83	
p. of a strange speech	BIBLE 110:29	
p. of Crete	SAKI 739:59	
p. of his pasture	BOOK 149:30	
p. of South Africa	SMUTS 831:70	
P. of the same trade	SMITH 827:81	
P. of the world, unite	MAO 569:36	
p. of this country	PEEL 672:67	
p. of whom we know nothing	CHAM 212:62	
p. on their way towards God	WINT 950:9	
p. on whom nothing is lost!	JAMES 450:44	
p. ought to be free	MACA 545:25	
p. out of work	EVANS 328:69	
p. overlaid with taxes	BACON 52:17	
p. say the president	MARC 569:54	
p. seem to be divided	DOST 294:89	
p.'s flag is deepest red	CONN 242:84	
p. should mate for life	ALLEN 14:97	
p. sinned against	COMP 239:6	
p. sliding with their skates	PEPYS 673:93	
p. sometimes divide others	SPEN 837:11	
p. starved for self-definition	BURNS 177:65	
P. struggled on for years	WHAR 934:9	
p. supplied with electric light	MCLU 556:56	
p.'s voice is odd	POPE 688:18	
p.'s wery scarce	DICK 277:38	
P. will always talk	GAGA 356:7	
p.'s wrongs his own	DRYD 302:85	
p. taut for war	THOM 885:70	
p. that do err in their heart	BIBLE 102:2	
p. that on earth	KETHE 483:67	
p. that walked in darkness	BIBLE 107:59	
p. that want to try a new experience	SHAW 809:84	
p. to complexify them	MOYN 623:2	
p. trying to convince themselves	SNYD 833:94	
p. until they set the basket	NASH 631:86	
p. want a sense of purpose	MACM 557:78	
P. want economy	IACO 444:1	
p. were a kind of solution	CAVA 210:16	
p. were so horrible	AMIS 16:37	
p. which ceases to care	ELIOT 319:28	
P. who are always praising	SMITH 830:38	
p. who are late	LUCAS 541:48	
p. who are moral or immoral	CHUR 224:63	
p. who are paid to have attitudes	HEMI 409:61	
p. who are too busy	WAUGH 924:90	
p. who belong somewhere else	STEIN 845:66	
p. who called the Milky Way	MARTI 576:70	
p. who can copulate	MACD 549:32	
p. who can't get along	GRAY 383:42	
p. who dare not assert	MUMF 625:39	
p. who do not hear the sound	MAIL 559:39	
p. who have been persecuted	KISS 494:96	
p. who have flabby hands	GILB 369:60	
p. who have no love	SHAW 806:90	
p. who have read	HAYA 402:20	
p. who have the courage	MUSS 627:91	
p. who hire them	NEW 634:33	
p. who hunt	SHAW 810:10	
P. who leave their own time	MASE 580:70	
p. who live outside	SABA 736:2	
p. whom a fair face	MAIL 560:68	
P. who never get carried away	FORB 342:84	
p. who never trouble	STARK 843:25	
P. who obtain power	VIDAL 912:87	
p. who shoot grouse	EDIN 312:51	
p. who want to do nothing	DODD 289:87	
p. wave at trains	MCGO 552:80	
p. who were not as obsessed	LESS 524:97	
p. who will run the future	JONES 466:24	
p. will always be kind	SASS 745:87	
P. will do anything	PERCY 674:10	
p. will live on	SAND 742:23	
p. will more readily swallow lies	GELL 363:34	
p. wish to be settled	EMER 324:63	
p. without business	DEFOE 269:78	
p. without history	ELIOT 321:93	
p. would rather sleep	ALBEE 11:29	
p. you have seen	MURR 627:84	
P. you know	LARK 510:92	
persuade...half the p.	GAIT 357:12	
photographing p.	EISE 314:9	
platypus and p.	THUR 891:97	
please all of the p.	CONN 243:23	
pleasure of pleasing inferior p.	CLOU 232:56	
poetry ignores most p.	MITC 609:26	
poor little street-bred p.	KIPL 490:94	
Poor p. staying	PEPYS 674:6	
power over p.	SOLZ 833:5	
Power to the p.	ANON 25:67	
prayers of liberty-loving p.	EISE 314:92	
Pray, good p., be civil	GWYN 391:8	
present at gatherings of p.	SNOW 832:76	
problems of three little p.	EPST 327:29	
proud conceited ignorant p.	ANON 22:81	
p....shows that I communicate	ROTH 728:3	
punching p. in the head	LEON 522:65	
Quiet p. avoid the question	DICK 279:2	
raising up a p. of customers	SMITH 828:87	
really nice English p.	SHAW 810:7	
rebellious p.	REED 710:37	
religion of these p.	MONT 613:10	
representatives of the p.	WHIT 934:24	
resented by thousands more p.	ROCK 720:28	
Respected p. are only rascals	STEN 847:6	
sacrifice other p. without blushing	SHAW 808:58	
self-help created among working p.	SMIL 827:71	
shame more p. don't switch	PIRS 679:91	
showing other p. where to dig	LEAV 517:54	
slam at the p.	FITZ 338:97	
smiles of the p.	MARC 570:57	
snake about to devour p.	NIXON 640:30	
society in which what p. fulfil	MAJOR 561:72	
so long as the right p. get shot	EAST 310:7	
so many p.	GALS 358:50	
so many p. showed up	GOLD 377:38	
some p. a bit behind	VARE 908:25	
Some p. find oil	GETTY 366:88	
Some p. read too much	MENC 586:4	
Some p. swim lakes	WEBB 925:8	
Some p. think football	SHAN 805:60	
Soviet p.	GORB 378:48	
speak as the common p.	ASCH 37:52	
stiffnecked p.	BIBLE 94:70	
struggle of the African p.	MAND 564:53	
submitted...to the whole p.	STEAD 843:34	
suicide kills two p.	MILL 593:41	
Superior p. never make	MOORE 617:79	
supported by...the British p.	LAW 512:36	
Take most p.	SALI 740:78	
tell p. what they do not want	ORWE 654:45	
tell p. you are	THAT 882:78	
tells other p. what to do	BARA 63:42	
TELL THE P.!	CHRI 223:39	
The p. are the masters	BLAIR 138:54	
The p. die so	PEPYS 674:2	
The p. muddied	SHAK 784:54	
These p. are good	VAZD 910:43	
These p....do not read books	WORD 961:32	
things p. had once held against her	SCHL 747:37	
thy p. shall be my p.	BIBLE 96:23	
till p. behave themselves	KING 488:51	
time changes p.	PROU 698:57	
too many of the p.	THUR 890:78	
Trees're always a relief, after p.	MITCH 609:75	
trivial p. should muse and thunder	LAWR 514:79	
two p. miserable instead of four	BUTL 185:93	
two sorts of p.	SHAW 809:68	
two types of p.	PASC 667:90	
unconditional confidence of his p.	WEI 927:66	
united p.	PARK 665:37	
very ancient p.	TOLK 893:47	
Very Decent to P.	ROTH 727:7	
very few p. come this way	LEAR 517:42	
views of the p.	GALL 358:45	
voice of the p.	ALCU 12:54	
voice of the p.	BACON 50:50	
voice of the p.	PITT 679:4	
voices of young p.	SMITH 829:17	
Waldo is one of those p.	SAKI 739:66	
way p. look and laugh	WOOLF 955:12	
We are a religious p.	DOUG 295:22	
we are the p.	WRIG 963:72	
What kind of p.	CHUR 225:92	
what other p. wear	WILDE 942:12	
what p. have got against	HOPE 428:60	
what p. say of us	SMITH 829:13	
what the p. think it so	BURKE 175:27	
When p. are too comfortable	RICH 717:21	
When p. do not respect us	TWAIN 903:80	
when you bore p.	KISS 494:94	
wherever I find your p.	JOAN 455:59	
whether just p....are happier	PLATO 682:59	
whole world is bereft of p.	LAMA 504:72	
willing to see p. sacrificed	MILL 595:94	
will of the p.	PARE 663:89	
Win Friends and Influence P.	CARN 202:49	
without other p. hearing	WILDE 940:67	
Women...are invisible p.	FRIE 350:65	
Words can keep p. apart	MARC 569:52	
world empty of p.	LAWR 513:47	
world is full of middle-class p.	SHAR 806:78	
you too are p.	SAND 742:26	
peopled earth p. as ever by the inept	REPP 711:60	
p. half the world	SEEL 756:2	
peoples meeting place of the p.	BARN 64:59	
new-caught, sullen p.	KIPL 491:20	
other p.' Kings	GARC 360:67	
peace among our p.	KIPL 490:8	
silent p.	KIPL 491:21	
We the P.	UNIT 905:9	
pepper a little P. or Salt	SWIFT 862:59	
cucumber...dressed with p.	JOHN 462:32	
pepper-pot p.-p. breast of thrush?	FRAME 346:75	
Pequod P. packing off to hell	LOWE 540:10	
perceive nature of reason to p. things	SPIN 840:74	
p. their foul disfigurement	MILT 598:63	
perceived being is to be p.	BERK 84:30	
percent Six p. unemployment	PASS 668:97	
perception doors of p.	BLAKE 140:4	
dullest p. always	THOR 889:44	
intensity of p.	WILL 946:24	
Japanese...destitute of p.	BIRD 136:11	
mechanism of p.	SNYD 832:93	
outside a central p.	DELI 271:39	
p. that something ought to be done	WELLS 930:38	
reeducation of p.	DEWEY 276:20	
some particular p. or other	HUME 438:96	
perceptions but those p.	HUME 438:94	
p. and insights	KISS 494:92	
perch p., and not their terror	SHAK 787:50	
percussion Like a P. Instrument	BUKO 173:57	
Percy not yet of P.'s mind	SHAK 771:44	
perdition ante-chamber of p.	SHAW 811:33	
path to p.	ACK 4:67	
P. catch my soul	SHAK 789:16	
P. catch my soul	SHER 818:3	
Science...is the soul's p.	RABE 703:6	
son of p.	BIBLE 123:58	
To bottomless p.	MILT 601:33	
perestroika Russian word 'p.'	GORB 378:47	
perfect be thou p.	BIBLE 92:20	
Be ye therefore p.	BIBLE 115:39	
Can a man be p.	FORS 345:51	
constant, he were p.!	SHAK 759:73	
end of a p. day	BOND 145:17	
formal poetry p. only in form	SAND 742:36	
giving up being p.	QUIN 702:20	
God...had created a p. world	SHAR 806:75	
grow more p. when emancipated	WOLL 954:95	
gunshot is the p. way	KENN 482:35	
Heaven is being p.	BACH 49:9	
I am not a p. man	OBAMA 644:27	
If thou wilt be p.	BIBLE 118:17	
most p. expression of scorn	SHAW 810:13	
most p. of Swiss clockmakers	STRA 857:47	
no knowledge comes to be p.	DONNE 293:77	
None of us are p.	WILDE 942:7	
no one is p.	MAIN 561:71	
Nothing is more p.	VIAN 911:71	
not in my p. mind	SHAK 793:31	
One p. limousine	PARK 664:11	
p. as much as we can	SPIN 841:81	
p. condition of slavery	ASTE 39:5	
p. in a short time	BIBLE 112:76	
p. republics are a p. nonsense	FOWL 345:59	
P. the cup as planned	BROW 168:61	
p. use of an imperfect medium	WILDE 940:64	
strength is made p. in weakness	BIBLE 127:77	
them whose heart is p.	BIBLE 98:86	
thought p. by every body	AUST 46:72	
three inches long, p.	HUGH 435:33	
union is p.	DICK 284:58	
We're not all p.	PIZZ 680:21	
when that which is p. is come	BIBLE 126:52	
would be the p. friend	SMITH 829:19	
perfectability no faith in human p.	POE 683:85	
perfection achieved p.	HUGH 434:6	
achieved some sort of p.	HOYLE 434:95	
Almighty unto p.?	BIBLE 98:1	

perfectionist

Entry	Reference
a placid p. unattainable	STRA 856:36
confess p. so could err	SHAK 788:92
Dead p., no more	TENN 875:14
dreams of p.	FAUL 331:43
friend who loved p.	SMITH 829:19
got to be p. for me	MELBA 584:16
make defect p.	SHAK 794:57
man a little pope of p.	LAWR 513:49
Nestles the seed p.	WHIT 938:12
p. does not recognize humanity	WOOD 954:2
p. in a new kind of art	RUNGE 731:52
P. irritates	AUCH 42:62
P., of a kind	AUDEN 43:87
p. of behaviour	CHRI 223:46
p. of character	AURE 45:47
p. of the human race	INGE 445:31
Pictures of p.	AUST 46:82
pursuit of p.	ARNO 36:27
Right p.	SHAK 801:58
seek a triple p.	HOOK 427:40
since p. is love	NIEB 637:87
Thinking is the great enemy of p.	CONR 244:48
through Art...realise our p.	WILDE 940:57
What's come to p. perishes	BROW 168:55
perfectionist I am not a p.	HOFF 422:28
perfidious P. wretch!	TREI 896:2
perfidy petty p.	BYRON 188:63
performance any p. is discussable	BURKE 176:63
been all words, And no p.	MASS 581:73
brilliance in the p.	HEMI 409:71
Britain's comparative p.	MISH 609:19
coming late to a p.	ZOLO 970:17
full of promise, but of no p.	DICK 279:11
instant of the p.	GRAY 383:44
jazz p. centers	LIEB 529:96
literary p.	WHIT 938:16
many years outlive p.?	SHAK 772:83
music...greater than its p.	PREV 694:76
p. of the American economy	STEIN 845:79
p. of the life of man	MUIR 624:21
p. of the task itself	SHIP 818:13
resulting p.	GALB 357:20
so poor a record of p.	FRIE 351:71
the p. everything	HUNT 439:26
performances intellectual p.	YOUR 968:56
poor p. of others	RYLE 736:61
performed be p. with tact	JOHN 458:32
perfume all p. yes	JOYCE 470:33
like p. on a whore	ASSAN 39:96
p. is itself a wind	WILL 946:23
p. of a thousand roses	BERN 86:76
wear coffee as a p.	VAN 908:17
perfumes ...are chafed	WEBS 926:19
p. is there more delight	SHAK 802:83
Pergo P. Park knew me	LEVE 525:23
peril at his p. further go	HERB 413:57
At the p. of its soul	SCOTT 751:98
perilous no position more p.	TROL 898:42
perils feeling that lures us on...to p.	CONR 244:36
p. and dangers of this night	BOOK 146:43
p. do environ	BUTL 185:73
smile at p. past!	SCOTT 753:36
sordid p. of actual existence	WILDE 940:57
through the p. of winter	TROL 897:23
period during this p.	THUR 890:83
from an early p.	MACA 546:58
lived in any other p.	HAZL 404:49
p. in one's life	LARW 510:7
p. in question	MYRD 628:99
p. not to be judged	LEVI 525:25
p. of cheating	BIER 135:86
p., once past	RUNGE 731:51
persist for a long p.	RUSS 734:34
repeat in one p.	RENO 711:57
periodical governs the p. press	TROL 897:20
periods Art of all p.	RUNGE 731:51
really had two p.	NABO 628:2
periphery you most inimitable p.	OCON 646:84
periphrastic p. study	ELIOT 320:58
perish All things p.	KEMP 480:78
hero p., or a sparrow fall	POPE 686:73
If I had to p. twice	FROST 352:4
if I p., I p.	BIBLE 98:89
p. in the very instant	GRAY 383:44
shall p. unconsoled	LANG 507:41
those that offer resistance p.	SOPH 834:28
perishing p. never entered my head	DOUG 294:98
periwigs fashion...as to p.	PEPYS 674:3
perjuries Jupiter...laughs at lovers' p.	OVID 657:14
perjury lovers' p.	DRYD 304:51
permanent cheerfulness fixed and p.	ADDI 6:34
less p. than thought	BUNT 173:65
P. crisis justifies p. control	HUXL 442:94
p., like the things	JOHN 460:68
The word p.	FRAME 346:78
very small extent p.	NIET 639:17
pernicious most p. race	SWIFT 862:44
Perón see Eva P. as either	MADO 558:20
perpendicular p. expression	SHAW 810:25
perpetual light...seemed p.	SPEN 837:6
no p. enemies	PALM 662:70
p. holiday is a good...definition	SHAW 810:3
p. hunger to be beautiful	RHYS 712:72
steady and p. serenity	ADDI 7:35
'Tis with us p. night	JONS 467:56
perpetuate helps to p. it	KING 486:22
p. an error for ever	SCHO 748:55
perpetuated So they are p.	GALB 357:17
perpetuating contrivance for p.	SHAW 808:29
perplex wildness to p. the scene	POPE 686:60
perplexed p., but not in despair	BIBLE 127:67
perplexities obvious p.	ARIS 31:18
perplexity listlessness from vain p.	WORD 958:74
perquisites scorn of irregular p.	WAUGH 923:57
persecute Why p. we him	BIBLE 98:9
persecuted because he is p.	GOULD 380:75
born...of the p.	WRIG 963:71
most legally p. man	BERL 85:55
p. for righteousness' sake	BIBLE 114:27
persecution P. is a bad...way to plant religion	BROW 165:60
P. is not an original feature	PAINE 660:35
p. of the transvestite	WHITE 934:27
P. produced its natural effect	MACA 546:56
some degree of p.	SWIFT 863:77
persecutions greatest of all p.	PASC 668:93
perseverance by the name of p.	STER 848:25
P., dear my lord	SHAK 787:38
p. is...hard work	GING 371:3
Persian p. pussy from over the sea	MARQ 575:51
Persians Truth-loving P.	GRAV 382:24
Persil Mum, the P.-user	BETJ 89:40
persist p. in its own being	SPIN 840:75
person advantage to take of a p.	MANS 567:8
aggravates an earnest p.	MELV 585:74
altered her p.	SWIFT 861:22
Ancient P., for whom I	ROCH 720:26
another p. in America	NORTH 641:62
being in love with a p.	LESS 524:2
but as a p.	GRASS 382:12
can a p. see rightly	SAINT 738:37
classify a p.	SZASZ 865:28
demagogue is a p.	MARQ 575:61
dullest p. in the world	BENS 81:85
explain it to the average p.	FEYN 334:7
For her own p.	SHAK 794:55
his breath and p.	WALL 917:46
household features her p.	PRIOR 696:3
judged as done against our p.	HENR 411:13
last p. to say anything	SAKI 739:68
lifetime of one p.	HORN 430:23
most pleasing p. in all the world	LABR 502:8
My idea of an agreeable p.	DISR 288:58
never met a steadily logical p.	GELL 363:32
no more a p.	AUDEN 43:89
no p. can be a poet	MACA 544:23
no sane p. would do	SHAW 809:74
not a political p.	HELL 408:42
not at all the sort of p.	CARL 199:68
not a well-rounded p.	BELL 77:82
not just the p. who fills a house	MITCH 609:34
old p. of Ware	LEAR 517:45
one p. were of the contrary opinion	MILL 591:3
only in memory...same p.	DIDE 285:69
only thing...is an uninterested p.	CHES 220:57
p. bearing his share of the labours	MILL 591:2
p. born who is so unlucky	MARQ 575:55
p. can be fully involved	MANN 566:86
p. can be truly affectionate	PREV 694:78
p. cannot choose his father	FRIS 351:85
p. concerns himself with life	MANN 566:81
p. freed from his religion	SAINT 738:41
P. from Porlock	SMITH 830:41
p. seldom falls sick	EMER 325:86
p. should be mourned	MONT 614:37
p. to worship God	ROOS 724:13
p. up early...is a Christian	LAW 512:37
p. we were yesterday	UPDI 906:34
p. who expects nothing from society	SAND 741:7
p. who fenced in...land	ROUS 729:9
p. who has used his emotions	SAND 741:6
p. who is capable of choosing	STEIN 845:77
p. who is not	RUSK 733:88
p. who knows 'how'	RAVI 707:85
p. who likes sports	MENC 587:12
p. who lives for today	BELL 76:45
p. who reads or thinks	YOUR 968:55
poet is a p.	FROST 352:9
politician is a p.	LLOY 533:81
species of p.	WAUGH 923:64
the only p. I know	MONR 621:7
This is a low flying p.	KEAT 475:59
three great events for a p.	LABR 502:22
Time, the world and the p.	CIXO 227:44
umblest p. going	DICK 280:44
unhappy p. seeks out another	MARG 570:65
unmusical p.	HENZE 412:23
when you live with a p.	FORD 342:89
wish to absorb this p.	MAMET 563:30
worse than killing a p.	LAUR 511:23
wretched p.'s feelings	MARI 571:87
personal ourselves and least p.	MANS 567:3
p. and national morality	SHAW 806:70
p. aspect of a thing	RICH 714:17
P. relations are the important thing	FORS 344:29
transcend the painfully p.	SART 744:65
Vengeance is a p. reaction	RENO 711:50
personalities all great events and p.	MARX 579:36
original displaced p.	MANK 566:75
People who disintegrate as p.	AUST 47:91
p. and cultural traditions	WATS 922:41
trivial p. decomposing	WOOLF 955:20
personality discontinuity within his p.	ROTH 727:76
had a lousy p.	SALI 740:75
no more p. than a paper cup	CHAN 213:86
P. is an unbroken series	FITZ 337:78
P. Tithe: A price paid	COUP 248:35
Poetry...an escape from p.	ELIOT 317:89
persons civilized p. are willing	DU 305:70
congratulation that p.	MILL 591:96
divers paces with divers p.	SHAK 779:95
God is no respecter of p.	BIBLE 124:84
great p....borrow	BACON 51:86
interested in things, not in p.	CURIE 259:87
neither p. nor property will be safe	DOUG 296:26
Ordinary p. do not perceive	PASC 667:83
P....entering into relation	BUBER 171:20
p. of small means	ELIOT 315:16
p. using parties as tools	DISR 288:63
p. who are accused	DENM 273:72
p. who are considered...its members	BENT 82:87
p. whom you cannot care for	TROL 898:44
resentment towards p.	NEWM 635:48
some have done in their p.	BROW 165:77
which private p.	ROUS 729:17
perspective everything in p.	CEZA 212:52
light, shade and p.	CONS 245:60
lovely thing this p.	UCCE 904:1
P. is the bridle	LEON 523:75
p. of a subway tunnel	TOOLE 894:58
reality seen from the p. of reason	PAGE 659:16
scenic p. suits it	HUGO 436:56
Writing has laws of p.	CAPO 197:24
perspiration Genius is...p.	EDIS 312:54
p. was but ichor	BYRON 191:32
persuade p. gently, not by force	PASC 667:84
p....half the people	GAIT 357:12
p. others to do what we want	ALBR 11:36
trying to p. you	PLATO 681:43
persuaded p. that God hath shut	RALE 705:46
persuaders hidden p. into the code	KOES 495:29
the hidden p.	PACK 658:8
persuading By p. others	JUNI 471:48
persuasion lexicon of...p.	SAFI 737:17
not faith but p.	BROW 165:52
P. is the resource of the feeble	GIBB 366:96
persuasiveness personal p.	QUIL 702:14
Peru Silver out of the Earth in P.	PETTY 676:27
peruked p. sea whose swell	SITW 823:96
perverse frown and be p.	SHAK 765:82
multitude of p. inclinations	SHAR 806:73

physical

widows...the most p. creatures	ADDI 6:33	p. has been so compelling	WHITE 934:29
perversion last great p.	FOWL 345:59	present or past p.	PEAR 671:56
melancholy sexual p.	HUXL 441:55	recurring p.	FALU 329:12
War...the universal p.	RAE 705:35	**phial** take the p. cleanly	DOYLE 297:75
perversity P. is the muse	SONT 834:14	**Philadelphia** P....like dull diamonds	MAIL 560:55
p. of the human mind	TROL 898:39	**philanthropy** p. and symphony	WHAR 933:5
Sexual P. in Chicago	MAMET 563:24	**Philip** Let us march against P.	OGIL 648:5
perverted I'm exhausted...or p.	PUIG 699:69	Willie King made up like P.	NICO 637:84
pessimism P....as agreeable	BENN 81:72	**Philippi** meet them at P.	SHAK 778:49
p....regurgitated throughout Washington	WINF 950:97	**Philippines** In the P., there are	COWA 249:51
pessimist p. before 48	TWAIN 903:91	**Philistine** apostle of the P.	ARNO 35:15
p. fears this is true	CABE 191:6	P. of genius in religion	ARNO 36:38
p. sees only the red	SCHW 751:55	P. said unto David	BIBLE 96:39
what a p. is?	SHAW 806:82	**Philistines** angelic revenges on the P.	ARNO 35:23
pessimistic optimistic or p.	UNAM 905:4	Barbarians, P., and Populace	ARNO 36:26
'p.' about broadcasting	WELLS 930:37	Eggheads are terrible P.	NABO 628:18
pesticide laugh is the best p.	NABO 628:19	Let me alone with the P.	BIBLE 96:20
pestilence noisome p.	BIBLE 101:96	P. be upon thee	BIBLE 96:19
purged the air of p.	SHAK 785:79	P. took him, and put out his eyes	BIBLE 96:19
sooner caught than the p.	SHAK 773:18	**Philistinism** P.!...we have not	ARNO 35:14
who desires...breeds p.	BLAKE 140:97	**Phillis** P., why shou'd	WALL 918:57
winter, plague and p.	NASHE 632:95	**philosopher** define a p.	DAWK 266:20
pestilences famines, and p.	BIBLE 118:29	For every p.	SPAR 836:80
pests Rumour is of all p. the swiftest	VIRG 913:17	he was a p.	CHAU 217:75
petal dropping a rose p.	MARQ 575:57	man of science is a poor p.	EINS 314:83
sleeps the crimson p.	TENN 873:49	mark of the p.	SOCR 833:97
petals Buddha...in the p. of a flower	PIRS 679:89	No p. now looks	WEBB 925:9
P. on a wet, black bough	POUND 691:92	nothing so absurd...said by some p.	CICE 227:33
pursed Its p. up	BROW 167:13	Ovid, the soft p. of love	DRYD 303:26
softer falls Than p.	TENN 870:89	peasant and a p.	JOHN 461:12
Peter other disciple did outrun P.	BIBLE 124:65	P.!—a fingering slave	WORD 957:65
P., and upon this rock	BIBLE 117:6	p. and a common street porter	SMITH 827:77
P. chose from man to hide	CRAB 252:42	p., and the poet	LAWR 514:84
P. like a piper's tune	FARJ 330:20	p. should judge the masses	CYRA 260:11
P. remembered the word of the Lord	BIBLE 122:6	p.'s treatment of a question	WITT 951:26
P. said unto him	BIBLE 119:41	properly to be called a p.	PIER 677:66
P.'s drift	SHEL 813:88	prove the weeping p.	SHAK 769:78
Saint P....pattered with his keys	BYRON 190:32	saying of an ancient p.	ADDI 6:30
Where P. is...is the Church	AMBR 15:22	There was never yet p.	SHAK 774:53
wholly in P. Pan ever since	TYNAN 904:3	You are a p., Dr Johnson	EDWA 312:63
Peterkin Quoth little P.	SOUT 835:47	**philosophers** amused p.	BERK 84:29
petition circulating a p.	STEG 844:56	economists and political p.	KEYN 484:81
petitioners save me...from my p.	DRYD 302:91	God of Jacob, not of the p.	PASC 668:96
Petrarch I do not...copy P.	ARET 31:11	little statesmen and p. and divines	EMER 324:54
petrifactions p. of a plodding brain	BYRON 187:22	or p. can judge	THOM 885:55
petrol matches on a p. dump	HARL 398:36	p. have not maintained	SWIFT 862:47
petticoat P. said to the Chemise	PARK 663:94	p....interpreted the world	MARX 579:28
turned out of the realm in my p.	ELIZ 321:99	P....stand among us	CARL 200:85
petticoats perpendicular in p.!	OCON 646:84	p. to teach him	CARL 200:91
red-flannel p.	THOM 884:47	traditional disputes of p.	AYER 47:3
pettiness p. of those who should carry them	BREC 158:95	True p. are like elephants	FONT 342:76
p. ruins the greatest loves	ANOU 28:59	Until p. rule as kings	PLATO 682:63
something to expiate; A p.	LAWR 513:60	**philosophic** p. diner-out	BROW 169:68
petulance p. is not sarcasm	DISR 288:42	p. republic of Mr de Valera	STEW 854:95
pewter No p. and no pub	RANS 707:73	the p. mind	SMART 826:68
phagocytes stimulate the p.	SHAW 809:80	**philosophical** European p.	WHIT 936:92
phallic P. and ambrosial	POUND 691:3	mathematical or p. author	WHIT 936:62
phantasma Like a p.	SHAK 776:16	one p. problem	POPP 689:60
phantom hag obscene, and grisly p.	BEAT 70:2	one truly serious p. problem	CAMUS 195:83
p. beings loaded up with facts	UNAM 905:7	p. problem has the form	WITT 951:25
P. of delight	WORD 960:19	p., the ideological	ROTH 728:90
phantoms p. an unprofitable strife	SHEL 815:39	**philosophies** all p. shall fail	CHES 221:83
Pharaoh P. awoke	BIBLE 93:42	point their blind P.	ROCH 719:8
P. rose up in the night	BIBLE 93:60	**philosophizing** p. or aestheticizing	CABR 191:8
Pharisee pluck the mask from...face of the P.	BRON 161:65	**philosophy** aim in p.	WITT 951:27
Pharisees P. said, He casteth out	BIBLE 116:65	angel...tell...his p.	LICH 528:86
righteousness of the scribes and P.	BIBLE 114:31	any p. in thee, shepherd?	SHAK 779:88
the P.' hypocrisy	PAST 668:98	characteristic of p.	RUSS 734:22
when he saw many of the P.	BIBLE 114:20	compound of poetry and p.	MACA 545:29
Woe unto you, scribes and P.	BIBLE 118:28	destroy more prejudices than p.	DIDE 285:60
phase p. in a continuing process	ROBI 718:94	dreamt of in our p.	SHAK 781:70
p. of...life	PEAR 671:56	from plumbing to p.	LAUG 511:18
phases Humanity does not pass through p.	LEWIS 526:40	Hang up p.!	SHAK 766:98
p. in the development	MARX 579:45	Histories make...natural p., deep	BACON 53:39
p. of its development	ERNST 327:39	History is p.	CARL 201:18
Phelps P. calls Medlar Novelists	MACD 550:39	if p. could find it out	SHAK 782:92
phenomena economic p.	FRIE 351:68	in knowing its limits that p. consists	KANT 473:20
very essence of p.	PAST 668:2	inside and strength were p.	SIDN 820:53
phenomenon Crime...not a natural p.	PACK 658:9	interest of p.	POPP 689:60
describe the infant p.	DICK 278:83	mere touch of cold p.?	KEATS 477:9
describe the opposite p.	BERG 83:18	moral p....handmaid to religion	BACON 50:34
Felicitous p.!	MOORE 617:85	new p. calls all in doubt	DONNE 292:50
one actual p.	THOR 888:24	Nice p.	FORD 343:3
		not confounded p.	PIRA 679:88
		not faith, but mere P.	BROW 165:65
		Not p., after all	BEER 74:91
		p. has hitherto been	NIET 638:7

P....has no other origin	SOCR 833:97
P., if it cannot	RUSS 734:21
p. inclineth Man's mind	BACON 51:79
P.! In whose light	NERV 633:24
P. is a battle against the bewitchment	WITT 951:24
p. is like the deciphering	SCHO 748:53
p. is this tyrannical	NIET 638:8
p. is to be studied	RUSS 734:23
P....kind of charcoal appetite	CLEV 230:94
p. of the pig trough	WEIG 927:67
p. puts out the fire	VOLT 914:38
P....route of many roads	BIER 135:87
P.! the lumber of	SWIFT 861:16
P. to him was...a maze	SANT 743:43
P. was wrong	RANS 707:71
p. which is so important	JAMES 451:72
p. will be replaced by poetry	ARNO 36:41
Plain women...to be faced with p.	ELIOT 316:48
political power and p.	PLATO 682:63
science...blind without p.	AYER 48:8
spoil you through p.	BIBLE 128:9
that's my p.	WILD 943:42
Three-fourths of p.	SNYD 833:94
true business of p.	BACON 50:44
truth in p.	DIDE 285:61
universe which p. contemplates	RUSS 734:23
what is p.?	SPAR 836:80
years of analytical p.	HARDY 397:15
Phlebas Consider P.	ELIOT 318:7
Phoebus golden P. never be beheld	SHAK 795:95
P. gins arise	SHAK 803:93
phoenix Do not expect...p. hour	DAY 267:37
P. builds her spicy nest	CAREW 199:58
p. midst her fires	BYRON 187:30
phone answer the p.	THUR 890:72
call him up on the p.	SALI 740:72
p. for the fish knives	BETJ 89:41
pick up their p.	WHITE 935:38
put the p. down thoughtfully	SHAR 806:77
phonemes morphemes and p.	THOM 886:78
phoney going to do something p.	SALI 740:77
phonograph man is like a p.	SHAW 809:89
p....is not of any commercial value	EDIS 312:53
vaccinated with a p. needle	GOLD 377:22
phonographs p. of hades	CRANE 253:69
phosphorescence rubbing a	MACD 550:46
photo look like your passport p.	GORE 379:64
photograph like flames around a p.	HOLL 423:52
p....after I drowned	ATWO 40:32
p. and be photographed!	RODC 721:43
p. of the Pope	ANON 27:16
signed of the Kaiser	WAUGH 923:70
the world looks like the p.	HOCK 421:17
took the p.	KARSH 474:32
photographer p. without a magazine	PARK 665:42
photographing p. people	EISE 314:9
photographs p., of the immortals	CHUR 224:50
p. taken of him at work	RODC 721:43
use p....literally	BACON 53:52
photography If p. is allowed	BAUD 68:71
P. is truth	GODA 374:52
P....stops the flow of life	BERG 83:24
p. takes on an authority	BAIL 55:83
P. was conceived as a mirror	STEI 845:58
phrase beauty...in one tiny p.	FOWL 346:65
empty p.	SAND 741:11
I find the p. in Shakespeare	SCOTT 754:81
that's an ill p.	SHAK 781:76
phrases Farewell, sweet p.	HERB 414:84
foundation of your ideas and p.	LAUT 512:29
p. in his brain	SHAK 763:6
ready-wrapped p.	HILL 418:59
Taffeta p., silken terms	SHAK 763:24
wealth of steaming p.	SCHU 750:77
physic In poison there is p.	SHAK 772:69
no faith in p.	JONS 467:50
Throw p. to the dogs	SHAK 798:71
physics P. is...a search for...simplicity	BRYS 171:15
physical adding daily to our p. ease	STEV 851:11
affliction...either p. or spiritual	BEER 74:90
emotions that are so lightly called p.	COLE 236:56
endurance, p. and mental	WAVE 925:9
Knowledge of p. science	PASC 667:87
most representative, the p. scientists	SNOW 832:77
p. and cultural distance	VAN 908:12
p. and emotional sides	BURG 174:99
p. pleasure	WAUGH 923:71

physically

p. vigour	SCHR 749:66	p. of the future	ORWE 655:77	P. on the grass	STEIN 845:63
relaxation from p. fatigue	MATI 581:92	p. on the wall	JOHN 458:18	**pig-headed** had a p.-h. father	POUND 691:94
rendering of the p. man	OPPE 652:85	p. that is beautiful	FRAN 348:5	**piglet** cried P., 'a Heffalump	MILNE 596:18
such a thing as p. morality	SPEN 836:86	p. that requires any description	HOMER 425:11	**pigmentation** only the p.	BARN 64:62
takes the p. out on whores	FROST 352:9	p. the afterlife	UPDI 906:33	**pigmies** embassage to the p.	SHAK 774:28
physically developing a lad p.	BADEN 54:59	plane of the p.	PIERO 678:72	**pigs** as much right…as p. have to fly	CARR 203:76
p.…deadening force	WEBB 925:7	rhythm, form…mood of a p.	FEIN 332:57	as naturally as p. squeak	BUTL 184:65
physician As if you would call a p.	BACON 52:15	speaking p., with this end	SIDN 820:55	cash cows to feed your p.	ANDE 17:68
died last night of my p.	PRIOR 696:4	the more successful the p.	HITC 419:85	p. are upwardly-mobile	THOM 887:90
duties of the p.	OSLER 656:89	to make a good p.	VAN 908:20	solid p. would disdain	ROCH 719:18
Honour a p.	BIBLE 113:8	Turkey carpet bears to a p.	MACA 545:32	whether p. have wings	CARR 204:1
is there no p. there?	BIBLE 110:18	win the foreign p. award	WILD 942:32	**pig-sty** kissed her once by the p.-s.	THOM 884:35
no need of the p.	BIBLE 119:50	**pictures** actress in motion p.	DAVIS 265:94	**pigtailed** butterfly…on a p. ocean	SITW 823:96
p. and chemist are soldiers	PAST 668:5	all his p. faded	BLAKE 141:38	**pike** P., three inches long	HUGH 435:33
P. art thou?	WORD 957:65	apples of gold in p. of silver	BIBLE 105:93	The great p. lies	BLUN 143:73
p. can bury his mistakes	WRIG 962:67	Are but as p.	SHAK 797:36	**Pilate** jesting P.	BACON 50:55
P., heal thyself	BIBLE 120:72	book…without p.	CARR 203:61	Made damn sure that P.	JAGG 449:15
p. to my love	SHAK 803:88	cutting all the p. out!	BELL 76:50	P. saith…What is truth?	BIBLE 123:59
They that be whole need not a p.	BIBLE 116:63	enjoy p. because	MORT 621:71	suffered under Pontius P.	BOOK 146:7
Time is the great p.	DISR 287:21	expensive Italian p.	BERE 83:15	the good thief than P.?	BROW 165:80
physicians He and his p.	SHAK 791:60	faces…a gallery of p.	BACON 52:13	When P. saw that	BIBLE 119:45
It is incident to p.	JOHN 459:37	fighting tooth and nail for p.	HAMM 394:60	**pilchards** as p. are to herrings	SHAK 786:6
Keep away from p.	BURG 174:92	furnish the p.	HEAR 405:83	**pile** standst an ancient p.	JONS 467:71
more happy…than learned p.	BACON 50:41	life passed among p.	WHIS 934:19	**pilgrim** p. borne in heedless hum	COLL 238:76
P. are like kings	WEBS 927:63	looking at p.	HAZL 404:54	p. of the sky!	WORD 961:44
P. of the utmost fame	BELL 76:59	Mr Lewis's p.	SITW 824:15	p. soul in you	YEATS 965:7
unless the p. are vigilant	SUTH 860:7	name of p. produces	MORSE 621:64	talk about their P. blood	LOWE 539:4
physicists p. could create a worm	KRUT 500:30	or paint little p.	MERW 589:57	**pilgrimage** I'll take my p.	RALE 705:44
p. have changed our world	SNOW 832:82	paint their p. on silence	STOK 855:9	shall succeed me in my P.	BUNY 174:83
physics delight in p. pain	SHAK 797:40	people…who understand p.	KIPL 490:96	songs beguile your p.	FLEC 340:31
P.…the first of the natural sciences	CRIC 254:90	p. are the love stories	LAUR 511:24	through this weary p.	DODD 289:91
resort to p. and chemistry	MENC 587:7	p. come to me as if in a dream	VAN 908:19	years of my p.	BIBLE 93:48
science is either p.	RUTH 735:52	p. for the page atone	POPE 688:34	**pilgrimages** folk to goon on p.	CHAU 217:70
Theoretical p. forces atomic	FROMM 352:88	p. in our eyes to get	DONNE 292:43	**pilgrims** land of the p.	CUMM 257:58
When p., chemistry, biology	DEWEY 276:19	p. in rough mosaic	SCHO 749:59	Land of the p.' pride	SMITH 830:31
physiological p. or pathological	UNAM 905:4	p. of nothing	HAZL 404:60	Like p. to th'appointed place	DRYD 304:54
physiologists Some p. will have it	HUNT 440:34	p. of obscene books!	ARLT 32:35	p., passynge to and fro	CHAU 217:86
pianist do not shoot the p.	WILDE 940:48	P. of perfection	AUST 46:82	strangers and p. on the earth	BIBLE 129:40
pianists no better than many p.	SCHN 748:41	p. which are so contrived	ORWE 655:72	**pill** little yellow p.	JAGG 449:14
to be nurses and p.	ROTH 727:77	p. with cameras	NEWM 634:72	**pillar** compound pulsing p.	UPDI 906:31
piano cat…walking over the p.	MERI 588:42	stand before the new p.	MARC 569:48	p. of a cloud	BIBLE 93:62
he may sit on the p.	WHIS 934:20	weep before my p.	ROTH 728:3	p. of salt	BIBLE 92:24
Over the p. was printed a notice	WILDE 940:48	when we're nostalgic we take p.	SONT 834:18	p. of the State	SOLZ 833:6
P.…a parlour utensil	BIER 135:88	**pie** every joke is…a custard p.	ORWE 654:39	sat by a p. alone	TENN 875:18
p. is a percussion instrument	JOEL 455:68	he was put into a p.	POTT 690:82	triple p. of the world	SHAK 794:42
Play the P. drunk	BUKO 173:57	If they see p. in the sky	BONA 145:16	**pillars** antic p. massy proof	MILT 598:59
soul is the p.	KAND 473:17	p. in the sky when you die	HILL 418:56	bend thy p. with thine iron car	BLAKE 139:83
virtuoso…can sit on the p.	MALL 562:97	**piece** Before I compose a p.	SATIE 746:4	builded over with p. of gold	BLAKE 141:30
What are we learning…the p. for	OBRI 646:74	p. of a big one	STEI 845:83	hewn out her seven p.	BIBLE 104:61
pianos put a tax on p.	SITW 824:16	reform that little p. too	MILLS 595:8	Of polished p.	JONS 467:91
Silence the p.	AUDEN 42:79	When a p. gets difficult	SCHN 748:45	Pylons, those p.	SPEN 837:2
Picasso corpses, or P. guitars	LIPP 530:34	**piece-meal** She is dying p.-m.	POUND 691:93	shake the complacent p.	BETH 87:13
paint…a dog as P.	MARC 569:51	**pieces** dash themselves to p.	SHAK 761:38	strong p. and pregnant supporters	BAIL 55:89
P. studies an object	APOL 29:79	laugh broke into a thousand p.	BARR 65:85	**pillow** finds the down p. hard	SHAK 803:3
P. was drawing	NEVE 634:31	p., and scattered them	MILT 600:17	From my p., looking forth	WORD 958:82
picayune economic services…are p.	DURK 308:27	P. of eight!	STEV 852:60	p. on a bed	DONNE 292:41
piccolo duet between a tuba and a p.	DONA 290:6	'Tis all in p.	DONNE 292:60	**pillows** two p. at my head	STEV 853:68
pick Everybody wants you to p.	RUCK 730:33	took her to p.	CONG 241:55	**pills** Beecham's P. are just the thing	BEEC 73:65
p., pack, pock, puck	JOYCE 470:19	Who can I tear to p.	BACON 53:53	gave me bitter p.	SHAK 726:82
pick-axes take up p.-a. and sticks	HO 421:12	**pie-crust** promises and p.-c.	SWIFT 863:75	mountebank who sold p.	ADDI 6:22
picked p. out of ten thousand	SHAK 782:79	**pier** effusive welcome of the p.	AUDEN 42:74	**pilot** my p. face to face	TENN 879:6
pickle Don't p. me away as done	CARR 202:52	**pierced** p. to the soul	SHAK 764:30	**pimple** p.…of American literature	PORT 690:75
pick-purse no p.-p. of another's wit	SIDN 820:50	**Pierian** pun is P.	UNTE 905:11	**pimps** p. for ill desires	DRYD 301:68
picnic morning-mist p.	FRAME 346:75	taste not the P. spring	POPE 685:19	white men dressed like black p.	WOODS 954:7
p. tables…great modern things	WARH 920:8	**pies** Bellamy's veal p.	PITT 680:15	**pin** every p. she takes out	JOYCE 470:30
Teddy Bears have their p.	BRAT 157:79	hand in too many p.	MENC 585:89	p.…punctures my skin	ANON 24:13
Picninnies P.…the Joblillies	FOOTE 342:83	**piety** Bound…by natural p.	WORD 959:98	set my life at a p.'s fee	SHAK 781:64
picture arrangement of my p. is	MATI 581:91	fear of life become p.	MENC 587:6	stand as straight as a p.	CAUS 209:13
best p. that was ever painted	HEMI 410:92	p. nor wit	FITZ 337:70	wi' a siller p.	BALL 60:80
confers dignity on a p.	ALBE 11:31	weaker sex, to p. more prone	ALEX 13:66	with a little p.	SHAK 764:52
Each creature…a p.	ALAN 10:15	**piffle** p. before the wind	ASHF 38:72	**Pinafore** that infernal nonsense P.	GILB 368:40
forget that I have ever seen a p.	CONS 244:59	**pig** Dear P., are you willing	LEAR 516:37	well-bred Captain of the P.	GILB 368:32
give a p. to the listener	COLT 238:86	it's still a p.	RICH 714:13	**pinch** death is as a lover's p.	SHAK 795:94
Last P. Show	MCMU 557:80	looked from p. to man	ORWE 654:50	Necessity's sharp p.!	SHAK 792:2
make a p. of reality	LIPP 531:41	love not a gaping p.	SHAK 770:10	With…a p. of salt	PLIN 682:47
making a p. with Marilyn	WILD 942:33	philosophy of the p. trough	WEIG 927:67	**pine** black and gloomy p.-trees	LONG 535:29
million dollars to make a p.	TAYL 868:52	P., and some green Jack-daws	LEAR 516:33	bless'd be the evergreen P.!	SCOTT 752:29
never see the whole p.	MANN 566:79	got up and slowly walked away	BURT 181:70	Learn about a p. tree	BASHO 67:49
not a p. but an event	ROSE 725:26	p. on Sunday	TRUM 899:81	pale Mammon p. amidst his store	POPE 686:68
One p. is worth	BARN 63:57	p. satisfied	MILL 591:7	p. for what is not	SHEL 814:97
only accurate p. of God	BAKER 56:3	sucking and thick gammon	MACB 546:64	raiser…of p.	TENN 872:35
paint my p. truly like me	CROM 255:21	**pigeon-livered** But I am p.-l.	SHAK 782:1	sailing p., the cedar proud	SPEN 838:20
p. about the terrors of life	HECHT 406:3	**pigeons** break onetwo…p.…	CUMM 257:54	spray of Western p.!	HARTE 400:24
p. cannot express	BACON 52:28	casual flocks of p.	STEV 849:71	stood close against a p. tree	THOM 883:71
p. is finished meter	WHIS 934:18	mate for life, like p.	ALLEN 14:97	uproot the tallest p.	DEKA 270:7
p. is only an approximation	MOTH 622:87	p.…hovered about the windows	PEPYS 674:6	**pineapple** the very p. of politeness	SHER 817:75
p. of me, the me that is seen	LAWR 513:16			**pines** melancholy, nodding p.	SCHAW 747:20

plain

p. are gossip p.		FLEC 340:35
pinions p. from flight		SWIN 864:12
pink girl's skin that is p.		RENO 711:55
grey or perhaps p.		TRAV 896:93
p. and purple columbine		SPEN 838:15
p., and the pansy		MILT 599:91
pinko-grey white…really p.-g.		FORS 334:35
pinnace p., like a fluttered bird		TENN 878:95
send out any p. to seek me		LANC 506:23
pinnacle p. of sacrifice		LLOY 533:72
pinnacled lit my p. desire		SASS 745:88
pinnacles glassy p. correct elliptics		BISH 136:23
p. of the Serenissima		MORR 620:46
pint fetch to me a p. o' wine		BURNS 178:8
p. of plain		OBRI 646:68
pints P. and quarts of Ludlow beer		HOUS 432:58
pioneer not belittling…p. men		FERB 332:66
p. a new way		SHEL 811:47
pioneers One thing about p.		PIRS 679:92
P. and all		SHAK 790:27
pious In p. times		DRYD 301:63
p. man prays without speaking		FRIE 351:73
Sae p. and sae holy		BURNS 178:92
pipe easier to be played on than a p.?		SHAK 783:29
his p. and my yowes		BALL 58:55
P. a song about a lamb!		BLAKE 139:85
P. with solemn interposing puff		COWP 250:90
puff of the p.		COOKE 245:75
sit placidly smoking his p.		SHIP 818:14
The earliest p.		TENN 872:43
through a p. and exhaled in a pun		LAMB 506:15
tune thy jolly voice to my fresh p.		BLAKE 139:82
piped p. unto you		BIBLE 116:79
piper Peter like a p.'s tune		FARJ 330:20
p. loud and louder blew		BURNS 179:29
p. o' Dundee?		ANON 22:75
pipers five-and-thirty p.		AYTO 48:11
pipes bird-like p.		STEP 847:11
boast their peasants' p.		CRAB 252:29
P. of wretched straw		MILT 599:89
What p. and timbrels?		KEATS 478:35
ye soft p., play on		KEATS 478:36
pipe-smoking p.-s. northerner		MCFA 551:67
piping Helpless, naked, p. loud		BLAKE 140:18
pips squeezed—until the p. squeak		GEDD 362:26
piqued always p. myself		HALI 393:31
piracies p. should not again		TWAIN 902:45
pirate more fun to be a p.		JOBS 455:61
Smith…an over-dressed p.		LEAC 515:15
To be a P. King		GILB 368:37
pirates p., preachers		SYNGE 865:23
piss pitcher of warm p.		GARN 360:78
pissed being p. off		ATWO 41:54
pissing inside the tent out		JOHN 458:14
p. contest with that skunk		EISE 314:97
pistol P. let off at the ear		LAMB 506:13
pistols carry p. and cartridges		SHAW 806:84
mortals who…fire off p.		MANN 566:82
pistons black statement of p.		SPEN 837:1
pit after them to the bottomless p.		MILT 605:26
cast him into the bottomless p.		BIBLE 132:21
diggeth a p.		BIBLE 106:31
eagle know what's in the p.		BLAKE 139:84
key of the bottomless p.		BIBLE 131:6
Law is a bottomless p.		ARBU 30:1
many-headed monster of the p.		POPE 688:21
out of an horrible p.		BIBLE 100:61
P., box, and gallery		POPE 687:98
The darkest p.		WORD 961:35
there is the sulphurous p.		SHAK 793:22
To your black p.		BURNS 177:84
pit bull a hockey mom and a p. b.		PALIN 661:58
pitch drove him into such a p.		CRAS 254:88
He that toucheth p.		BIBLE 113:92
Imagination to that p.		YEATS 967:41
one positive p. or direction		HOPK 429:85
people on the p.		WOLS 954:97
Pitched past p. of grief		HOPK 429:90
p. that is near madness		EBER 310:10
roller, p., and stumps		LANG 507:41
turn her virtue into p.		SHAK 789:14
word is 'P. and pay'		SHAK 775:70
pitcher p. be broken at the fountain		BIBLE 106:36
p. of warm piss		GARN 360:78
pitches p. thudding into gloves		RICE 713:91
pitchfork Mercury with a P.		BRAU 157:85
thrown on with a p.		SWIFT 863:68

pitfalls p. of exaggeration		TROL 898:53
pith all the p. is in the postscript		HAZL 404:51
pities what a thousand p. then		HOOD 426:29
pit-ponies wretched, blind, p.		HODG 421:23
Pitt P. is to Addington		CANN 196:7
Pittsburgh P. has lost…triangle		MAIL 560:55
pity avoid the feeling of p.		COMP 239:5
by means of p. and fear		ARIS 31:23
childish wave of p.		BETJ 88:29
dint of p.		SHAK 778:44
endure, then p., then embrace		POPE 687:82
Kind p. chokes my spleen		DONNE 290:14
Knowledge might p. win		SIDN 820:43
Let p. teach thee		SHAK 765:61
looked for some to have p.		BOOK 149:26
loved her that she did p. them		SHAK 788:95
move the stars to p.		FLAU 339:20
never p. the past		FOWL 345:60
none to p. him		SYNGE 865:22
no p. sitting in the clouds		SHAK 766:5
one can p. them		WILDE 941:73
P. a human face		BLAKE 139:88
p. hath been balm		SHAK 760:16
P.…in gentil herte		CHAU 217:83
P. is lost in rage		CARL 201:10
p., like a…new-born		SHAK 796:20
p., love, patriotism		WHIS 934:22
p. my simplicity		WESL 931:60
p. never ceases to be shown		DRYD 302:85
p. to ill-humour		GRAV 382:33
p. upon the poor		BIBLE 105:85
p.…weakens our weaknesses		BALZ 60:96
Then cherish p.		BLAKE 139:93
The Poetry is in the p.		OWEN 657:29
'tis p. she's a whore		FORD 343:7
What a p.		SMITH 831:62
What a p. is it		ADDI 7:50
Where mercy, Love and P. dwell		BLAKE 139:89
with p. to dispense		SHAK 791:78
Yet show some p.		SHAK 787:56
pitying shrieks to p. heav'n		POPE 685:40
pix Sticks nix hick p.		ANON 24:17
placate p., appease, bribe		LIPP 531:42
place accent of the p.		LARO 510:6
advantage of time and p.		DRAKE 298:87
all other things give p.		GAY 362:13
All rising to great p.		BACON 51:82
an awful p.		SCOTT 751:5
An open p. it was		WORD 958:86
any given time or p.		WHIT 936:72
aren't native to a p.		LAMM 506:21
at some p. or other		PALEY 661:57
bestow you in some better p.		SHAK 759:77
bodies measure out their p.		MARV 578:8
bourne of time and p.		TENN 879:6
bruised in a new p.		IRVI 447:61
buried in so sweet a p.		SHEL 815:26
cares no more for one p.		SOUT 835:53
choose Their p. of rest		MILT 607:74
citizens of that other p.		SONT 834:20
colours…thick on every p.		DRYD 299:10
cultural and historical role of the p.		SMITH 828:1
destination is never a p.		MILL 594:89
do not very much like the p.		PERTH 675:31
event at an obvious p.		LIPP 531:39
feel…the spirit of a p.		PEI 672:73
fine and private p.		MARV 577:92
fixed p. in the chain of being		EMER 324:66
flaming bounds of p. and time		GRAY 385:90
fought for our p.		WILH 943:55
genius of the p.		POPE 686:58
get you a p.		DONNE 291:27
give p. to better		SHAK 778:47
grown and take our p.		KIPL 492:57
Have No P. To Go		WHIT 937:81
how he arrived at his present p.		ANGE 19:89
I go to prepare a p. for you		BIBLE 123:52
know the p. for the first time		ELIOT 321:91
leaving the poor old p.		BAUG 69:91
left a p. to stand on		PURDY 700:87
love can claim no p.		ANDR 18:78
mark our p.		MCCR 548:11
mind is its own p.		MILT 602:44
No P. to Go		BURT 181:71
no respect of p., persons, nor time		SHAK 785:94
not ask for a p.…in the world		BRON 161:68

no third p. in't		WEBS 927:44
not know the p.		MUIR 624:18
p. as kind as it is green		MOORE 617:82
p. for everything		BEET 74:8
p. for me		ANON 27:17
p. for self-presentation		RYBC 736:56
p. for the genuine		MOORE 617:77
P. I can Hang my Hat		JERO 454:44
p. that is uniquely		MOORE 616:59
p. there is an unspoken		MORG 619:30
p. thereof shall know it no more		BIBLE 102:10
p.…to have large spiritual adventures		DAVI 265:86
p. where a story ended		ELIOT 321:84
p. where bulls		JUST 471:50
p. where success comes		KIMB 486:13
p. where the spirit is		JOHN 458:29
p. where…We find our happiness		WORD 958:87
p. where woman never smiled		CLARE 228:55
reign in this horrible p.		COWP 250:96
right p. to film it		GARD 360:68
savage p.!		COLE 236:37
stands upon a slipp'ry p.		SHAK 768:60
takes p. in your absence		RUSH 732:64
that's the only p.		SCOTT 754:83
that we were in his p.		ROBI 718:82
toward the Third P.		FRAME 346:76
tragic a p. this world		LYND 543:91
true p. for a just man		THOR 888:17
understood this p.		VAUG 909:34
Upon the p. beneath		SHAK 770:12
What am I doing in this p.		RHYS 712:78
what better p. to learn?		WILM 947:34
what can be thy p.		POUND 692:25
What use…the gold p.		FRAME 346:75
will not stay in p.		ELIOT 319:45
places change p., and handy-dandy		SHAK 793:24
exactly in the right p.		BUTL 185:97
flowers come in stony p.		MASE 580:68
good…In all the p.		WESL 932:68
hunger for foreign p.		MCCU 549:13
I love…solitary p.		SHEL 812:60
immaculate public p.		ROET 722:55
in proper p.		SWIFT 861:37
living in different p.		SPEN 837:3
New p. you will not find		CAVA 210:18
only leave our p.		MIRA 608:15
p. shall be hell		MARL 573:25
p. were distorted		PACH 658:1
quietest p. Under the sun		HOUS 432:54
secret p.		GORD 378:53
see broken p. as long		MITC 610:46
small p., close to home		ROOS 724:2
warm lift-up p.		HEAN 407:52
plagiarism P. is the base		GIRA 372:2
plagiarize P.…only be sure		LEHR 520:26
plagiarizing responsible for p. me		NABO 628:8
plague after the p. is done		PEPYS 674:3
Ay, a p. on't		JONS 467:53
instruments to p. us		SHAK 793:34
malignity and rapidity of the p.		DICK 282:92
p. o' both your houses		SHAK 766:94
p. upon't		SHAK 771:40
slaughter of p., pestilence		SHAW 807:26
that's his p.		BURT 181:80
What a p. have I		SHAK 770:28
winter, p. and pestilence		NASHE 632:95
plagues cause of p. is sin		WHITE 936:61
two main p.		BURT 181:77
plaid chameleon on p.		HOOV 427:50
plaidie p. to the angry airt		BURNS 180:60
plain above the fruited p.		BATES 68:53
as on a darkling p.		ARNO 33:67
eagle sweeps over the p.		MCCA 547:75
from foggy mount and marshy p.		BYRON 187:33
gleamed Upon the glassy p.		WORD 957:70
great Gromboolian p.		LEAR 516:28
heavens above that p.		THOM 887:6
Jacks…more than usually p.		WILDE 941:95
language is p.		HARTE 400:72
loveliest village of the p.		GOLD 376:96
Manners…need of the p.		WAUGH 924:92
Most p. girls are virtuous		ANGE 19:88
nomads, on a p.		MCMU 557:85
no p. women on television		FORD 342:86
octavos fill a spacious p.		CRAB 251:26
p. blunt man		SHAK 778:45
p. facts		THOM 886:78

plainness 1238

p. single vow	SHAK 791:65
P. women...faced with philosophy	ELIOT 316:48
pricking on the p.	SPEN 838:19
speak p. and to the purpose	SHAK 774:36
such a p. king	SHAK 776:99
waveless p. of Lombardy	SHEL 812:64
plainness perfect p. of speech	ARNO 35:9
Your p. and your shortness	SHAK 762:76
plains land of sweeping p.	MACK 553:10
the green p.	SHEL 813:75
plan any p. for stopping it	PERK 675:27
don't have a moral p.	CRON 256:26
execution of his p.	STEU 849:61
if a p. fails	RICE 713:87
isn't a very good p.	THAT 881:65
new and original p.	GILB 369:51
not without a p.	POPE 686:70
p. of attack	SASS 745:86
p. that we arrive here	VAZD 910:43
postulate that there is no p.	MONOD 612:3
rogue is outlining a treacherous p.	FRAS 349:32
save it, save the p.	NIXON 640:35
planarian cross-eyed p.	THER 882:90
plane If that p. leaves the ground	EPST 327:30
inclined p. of little vessels	DICK 281:76
landing by p.	MACL 554:24
p. of the picture	PIERO 678:72
p. with the general	NATH 632:3
We travel by p.	CHEE 218:9
planes p. which advance	GOYA 380:82
vertical and horizontal p.	MALL 562:3
planet After one look at this p.	BURR 181:65
alien p. is Earth	BALL 60:84
As the p. globalizes	OGDEN 647:1
Capitalism is destroying the p.	ROY 730:29
creepers on a commodious p.	SAND 742:26
disgrace to the p.	STONE 855:10
ecological balance of the p.	SONT 834:16
excursion to another p.	BIRD 136:9
Given the state of the p.	CAREY 199:61
her in her cooling p.	EMPS 326:9
lifetime on this p.	KENN 481:2
loyal to his club than to his p.	WHITE 935:34
men from the p. Earth	ANON 25:69
nobody on the p.	GILL 370:86
not born under a rhyming p.	SHAK 774:56
Out of the Silent P.	LEWIS 526:41
Pity the p.	LOWE 540:32
p. is used as a penal colony	HITCH 419:88
p. of Love is on high	TENN 876:25
p. swims into his ken	KEATS 475:61
points about this p.	MACA 544:16
pushed around by a p.	PEACE 671:50
wandering p.'s course	MARL 572:99
planetary obedience of p. influence	SHAK 792:89
planets blowing up p.	SHAW 811:38
inhabitants of different p.	DISR 288:34
mind can...people p.	BYRON 189:82
Shall such high p.	SIDN 820:41
stars and p. circled	DICK 280:27
use of the sun and the p.	LEAC 515:11
What other p. circle other suns	POPE 686:72
plank thick as a p.	DIANA 276:23
planks piled against slippery p.	ROET 722:58
planned A p. life	BACA 49:6
planner p. made lots of them	HOYLE 434:95
planners acting like socialist p.	GLEI 374:78
planning all p. and decisions	LEWI 527:76
my idea of long-range p.	OGDEN 648:4
p. any misdeed	JUVE 471:59
the more difficult p. becomes	HAYEK 402:2
plans all his p. collapse	JOSE 469:8
drew their p. against us	WELLS 930:19
felonious little p.	GILB 368:42
finest p. have always been spoiled	BREC 158:95
hurled Their hopeful p.	HOUS 432:64
no place for women's p.	AESC 9:40
p. for remedying...human estate	DEWEY 276:19
plant as much as a p. or a crystal	EMER 324:66
fame is no p.	MILT 599:87
grow up...as a tender p.	BIBLE 109:93
I'd have been a p. somewhere	TREV 896:8
p. must spring again	SHEL 816:49
p. where savages are	BACON 52:22
Sensitive P. in a garden grew	SHEL 815:21
those who p. cabbages	RABE 704:19
time to p.	BIBLE 105:14

plantations new p....the children	BACON 52:21
planted I have p.	BIBLE 126:37
p. and replanted	HAWT 401:3
p. on level ground	GOHE 375:73
plants best subjects...animals and p.	HEIN 407:20
love the p.	DOST 294:94
Minerals grow, p. grow	LINN 530:33
talk to the p.	CHAR 215:41
to collect p.	THES 882:96
plashes horse p. within it	YEATS 966:19
plaster Paris made of p.	HUGO 437:61
plastering beautied with p. art	SHAK 782:6
plastic constellation of p.	MAIL 560:55
pictorial or p. art	TZARA 904:18
p. surgeon...responsible	CUOMO 258:79
plastic bag wet fish in a p. b.	GRIFF 388:68
platan p. round	SPEN 838:20
plate fed from a mashed p.	SMITH 828:3
ice-cream while it's on your p.	WILD 943:42
p. of meat	MACB 546:63
silver p. on a coffin	CURR 259:93
plates p. and cups washed	WOOLF 955:33
platform On the p....policeman	STEW 854:95
platforms Party p. are contracts	TRUM 899:83
platinum bullets made of p.	BELL 76:53
platitude Applause...echo of a p.	BIER 134:64
longitude with no p.?	FRY 353:33
p. is simply a truth	BALD 57:27
stroke a p. until it purrs	MARQ 575:58
platitudes orchestration of p.	WILD 943:46
slaughter of a thousand p.	ORTE 652:2
Plato disputations of P.	HONO 426:17
lend an ear to P.	TENN 877:69
P. divined in theory	WHIT 936:70
P....in the body of his work	SIDN 820:53
P. is dear to me	ARIS 32:30
P., thou reason'st well!	ADDI 7:38
recurring again to P.'s opinion	STER 848:41
series of footnotes to P.	WHIT 936:69
platypus poodle, the p. and people	THUR 891:97
play admiration of each other's p.	BARR 65:94
author of the p.	GILB 370:75
band begins to p.	KIPL 489:85
Better than a p.	CHAR 215:33
boys in their happy p.	SCHR 749:63
boys late at their p.!	ARNO 36:25
Close the p.	KAUF 474:42
done your work and may go p.	ASTL 39:9
do not p. things as they are	STEV 850:80
Everything that heard him p.	SHAK 804:45
for fair p.	ROOS 724:18
Forsake thy books, and mateless p.	BRON 161:74
good p. needs no epilogue	SHAK 780:27
holdeth children from p.	SIDN 820:56
Judge not the p.	QUAR 701:6
learn what not to p.	GILL 370:85
life? a p. of passion	RALE 705:45
loved your p.	ANON 26:1
made to p. therein	BIBLE 102:13
Marry, our p. is	SHAK 767:20
mend My wretched p.	MANN 567:92
most insipid, ridiculous p.	PEPYS 673:91
Mr Puff's p. within a p.	SHER 818:3
nothing to do with fair p.	ORWE 655:81
Not only will I not p.	GRANT 381:98
our p. is played out	THAC 880:30
perfectly dreadful p.	BANK 61:14
p. a creative mixture	SHUL 819:25
p. a thing quickly	MOZA 623:5
P. ball!	RICE 713:88
p., I remember, pleased not	SHAK 782:96
p. is a dynamic thing	TYNAN 904:2
p. is life	SHAW 809:69
P. it!	EPST 327:27
p. it over again and p.	LAMB 506:19
p. left a taste of...parsnip	WOOL 956:45
p. lousy	PARK 663:4
p....never really takes on	HART 400:69
p....some ten words long	SHAK 768:47
p.'s the thing	SHAK 782:5
p. that after you've been	KEIL 479:57
p. the fools with the time	SHAK 772:79
p. under bad conditions	KAUF 474:37
p. well and lose	FULL 356:89
p. with him at any game	SHAK 794:59
p. without a woman	KYD 501:52
rest of the p.	PASC 667:77

Shakespeare set his p. writing aside	CUOMO 258:81
spoils the p. much more	SUCK 858:69
The action of the p.	ONEI 650:58
The p. is over	AUGU 45:38
The p. was a great success	WILDE 941:82
thing I didn't like about...the p.	PARK 663:3
unless the p. is stopped	KEMB 479:73
usually the p. itself	TYNAN 904:1
What do you call the p.?	SHAK 783:27
what's the p.?	BOOTH 150:47
will not let my p. run	DENN 273:75
witty prologue to a very dull p.	CONG 240:33
woman's part in the p.	AUST 46:67
writing a good p. is difficult	PRIE 695:94
y is p.	EINS 314:86
youths at cricks did p.	JOSE 469:9
playboy expected me to be a p.	FLYNN 341:63
Inside this Hollywood p.	FLYNN 341:64
P. of the Western World	SYNGE 865:25
played easier to be p. on	SHAK 783:29
how you p. the game	RICE 713:89
My music...is merely badly p.	SCHO 748:49
p. an ancient ditty	KEATS 477:25
p. on a five inch course	JONES 465:16
p. the way I would	KAVA 474:47
p. with both hands	SATIE 746:5
player as he a P. were	SPEN 839:62
not monstrous that this p. here	SHAK 782:99
raped...nothing a p.	MCEN 550:57
say to the p.	WHIS 934:20
walking shadow, a poor p.	SHAK 798:74
whatever the other p. did	RAPO 707:75
wrapped in a p.'s hide	GREE 386:33
players don't drop p.	SHAN 805:61
entertainment the p. shall receive	SHAK 782:91
I and the rest of the p.	QUIN 702:18
little black book with two p. in	CHAR 216:49
men and women merely p.	SHAK 779:80
mouth it, as many of your p. do	SHAK 783:18
p. have often mentioned	JONS 468:90
p. not to be too good	NICH 636:75
P., Sir!	JOHN 462:40
p. think of a football	PELE 672:76
too cold for the p.	SMITH 830:30
Will you see the p.	SHAK 782:97
playfield p. of Satan	NABO 628:11
play-going p.-g. in any large city	TYNAN 904:1
playing ask me to stop p.	KING 486:17
staying married and p. snooker	REAR 709:18
playing-fields p.-f. of Eton	ORWE 654:35
play-poets Profession of P.-p.	PRYN 698:62
plays Absurdist p....in No Man's Land	ADAM 4:70
All p. are about decay	MAMET 564:37
cause of sin are p.	WHITE 936:61
don't want to see p. about rape	COOK 245:68
English p.	GOET 375:58
Leave writing p.	DRYD 301:45
old p....disgust this refined age	EVEL 328:71
p. are suited to incoherent argument	BENN 80:55
p. can define a moment	HYTN 444:25
The proof is in his p.	ONEI 651:69
tremendous stage on which it p.	RABI 704:23
women's parts in p.	CHAR 215:32
write p. in our heads	MAMET 564:43
PlayStation part of the P. generation	CHAR 216:44
plaything literature was the best p.	GARC 359:65
p. and their idol	SHEL 811:46
sensualists...want...a p.	WOLL 954:88
plaything-house little p.-h.	WALP 919:66
playthings choice of p.	KIPL 491:26
playwright some p. was forever	SALI 740:86
Plaza-Toro Duke of P.-T.!	GILB 370:71
plea beauty hold a p.	SHAK 801:57
issue of that darling P.	FLET 340:50
without one p.	ELLI 323:26
plead But when I p.	SPEN 839:44
so what I p. is just	HOPK 429:95
pleasant be p. to Russia	PUTIN 700:98
fallen unto me in p. places	BIBLE 99:35
How fair and how p.	BIBLE 107:48
how p., Lord, they be!	SCOT 755:55
Laughter is p.	PEAC 671:52
make myself as p. as I can	GILB 369:56
more glorious...than it is p.	ELIZ 322:6
of our p. vices	SHAK 793:3
p. and clean work	RUSK 733:5
p. or bitter	MART 576:77

p. situation, and yet nothing p.	DEFOE 269:78	p. is not enhanced	AUST 46:77	**plenitude** carries within itself its own p.	NERVO 634:27
wine leaves you with something p.	AMER 15:24	P. is…the least fallible	AUDEN 43:7	**plenty** health and p. cheered	GOLD 376:96
pleasantness pain full of p.	LYLY 543:84	p. of believing what we see	SHEL 812:60	here is God's p.	DRYD 304:42
please Art cannot be made…to p.	DEGAS 269:87	p. of hearing 'em rattle a little	FARQ 330:29	just had p.	BURNS 177:74
can p. many, and p. long	JOHN 461:8	p. of my pain	SIDN 820:43	p. has made me poor	OVID 657:18
hard thing to p. all of the people	CONN 243:23	p. of not being surpassed	HALI 393:31	P. makes pride	ANON 21:55
more anxious to p.	SAND 741:6	p. of pleasing inferior people	CLOU 232:56	Where P. smiles	CRAB 252:32
must p. to live	JOHN 459:44	p. of the defeat	LACL 503:31	**pleonasm** fashion…is a p.	CHAN 241:1
natural to p.	DRYD 301:65	p. of the fleeting year!	SHAK 802:71	**plethora** p. of legal requirements	BIRNS 136:21
not p. but thank you	DILL 286:93	p. of the flesh	FUEN 354:59	**plight** eke the heavy p.	SURR 860:3
P. DO NOT TOUCH	PRAT 694:65	P.'s a sin	BYRON 189:99	**Pliny** According to P.	VASA 909:27
say what they p.	FRED 349:41	p.…to hear the English abused	PIUS 680:19	**plodder** always the p.	POUND 692:35
thinking what they p.	SCHI 747:26	p. working for 16th Century Fox	RENO 711:53	**plodders** Small have continual p.	SHAK 763:2
those whom I wished to p.	JOHN 460:69	poet's p. is to withhold…meaning	WHITE 935:36	**plop** I don't want to make p. art	WHITE 937:80
who would not wish to p. her!	GRAY 384:61	prolonging the keenest p.	SHAW 808:45	tug, pull and p.	OBRI 646:73
without saying 'p.'	SITW 823:97	pursuit of p.	PROU 698:55	**plot** beginning of a p.	LEHM 520:22
pleased All seemed well p.	MILT 604:20	rare and simple p.	DRAB 298:80	discerned in history a p.	FISH 337:62
makes a man better p.	JOHN 463:62	recompense is a p.	JOHN 459:52	Her p. hath many changes	QUAR 701:6
p. not the million	SHAK 782:96	Refrain from the unholy p.	BELL 76:50	In some melodious p.	KEATS 478:41
P. to meet you	JAGG 449:15	rule…to give p.	MOLI 611:76	knew the p. before	SUCK 858:69
pleasing art of p.	HAZL 403:33	sadistic p. in…violence	ORWE 655:81	new p. in the cemetery	DAY 267:32
p. fit of melancholy	MILT 599:75	salutary p. in proving their falseness	DARW 263:59	No good opera p.	AUDEN 43:5
p. himself is almost sure	MOORE 617:87	seldom peruses a book with p.	ADDI 6:23	p. and rhyme	LOWE 540:37
pleasurable even the most p.	THUR 890:84	sometime do p. bring	SURR 860:98	p. in it will be shot	TWAIN 902:50
pleasure antithesis…is not p.	DE 273:83	some to p. take	POPE 688:14	p. thickens	BUCK 172:39
at p. stint their melody	SHAK 760:29	Some weigh their p.	DYER 309:49	p. was to have blown up	HOBY 421:11
be his good will and p.	LANC 506:23	sort of p. in thinking	ORWE 653:7	p.…where these memories grow	TATE 867:39
Beware of over-great p.	FULL 355:65	stock of harmless p.	JOHN 464:76	**plot-interest** game is so full of p.-i.	FRY 353:30
Business first; p. afterwards	THAC 880:41	study of present p.?	MONT 613:11	**plots** From p. and treasons	DRYD 302:91
cannot write of p.	BELL 76:46	suburbs Of your good p.?	SHAK 777:18	P.…are necessary things	DRYD 301:69
Compassed round by p.	WORD 961:38	supreme p. of love	BAUD 69:80	p. come from	MORT 621:70
Cram as much p. as you can into life	MACG 552:85	sweated out of golden p.	VALL 907:9	p. from old novels	BYRON 188:79
descended at p.	MOORE 616:68	Sweet is p. after pain	DRYD 303:30	preventing or contriving p.	WALT 920:95
dilettante looks only for p.	REDON 709:22	takes p. in it	POIN 683:98	Real life seems to have no p.	COMP 239:1
entrancing p. of	WILDE 941:95	try a little p.	BAGE 54:63	spoil her simple p.	HOLME 423:56
Excess of p.	BAXT 69:94	Unlawful p.…is delusive	BRON 161:72	**plotting** p. some new reformation	DRYD 302:96
fatal egg by p. laid	COWP 251:4	Variety is the soul of p.	BEHN 74:15	**plough** Following his p.	WORD 959:1
final p. left to man	SNOW 832:74	weight of p.	WORD 958:77	plod behind the p.	CRAB 252:29
fine p. is not to do	HOPK 429:93	Were it but to p. you	HERR 415:1	p.…doth rent?	DONNE 290:16
forced…your p.	WEBS 926:30	What p. lives in height?	TENN 873:50	P.…twin to the Sword	COLUM 238:87
forms of p. undulate	FUSE 356:94	what p. would be left him?	FONT 341:74	put his hand to the p.	BIBLE 120:77
for thy p. they…were created	BIBLE 131:98	when of p. she doth sing	CAMP 195:73	wherefore p.	SHEL 813:89
Good, p., ease, content	POPE 687:87	When there is p.	EGGE 313:67	**ploughman** cheer the p.	SHAK 762:96
good p. of God	WESL 932:71	which give little or no p.	MILL 591:96	p. homeward plods	GRAY 384:62
greatest amount of p.	SHIP 818:13	without one p.	TENN 877:70	the p. of bulls	PROP 697:30
greatest p. I know	LAMB 506:14	Words…intense p.	WAUGH 924:84	tither was a p.'s collie	BURNS 177:81
green p.	SWIN 864:4	would have been my p.	TENN 877:59	**ploughs** greatest of his p.	CURZ 260:5
grief…treads upon the heels of p.	CONG 240:30	would it p. me	WEBS 927:58	p. and borne our loads	MUIR 624:22
hatred…the longest p.	BYRON 190:22	**pleasure-dome** stately p.-d.	COLE 236:36	**ploughshare** Soldiers of the p.	RUSK 733:98
if this is p. we'd rather be dead	COWA 249:45	**pleasure-house** lordly p.-h.	TENN 870:64	**ploughshares** p. into swords	BIBLE 111:49
impression of p.	BACON 49:19	**pleasures** cares and p.	GIBB 366:92	swords into p.	BIBLE 107:51
invented any new sensual p.	FLAU 339:18	celibacy has no p.	JOHN 460:87	**plover** wind sweep and the p. cry	TENN 873:53
know the ways of P.	HERB 413:67	Eternity of p.	FORD 343:1	**plowed** p., and planted	TRUTH 900:5
leave…an intangible residuum of p.	CATH 208:96	eye hath caught new p.	MILT 597:45	**ploy** by p. or gambit	POTT 690:86
lonely p.	KENN 480:86	Fates, we will know your p.	SHAK 777:29	**pluck** And p.…The…apples	YEATS 965:10
Love ceases to be a p.	BEHN 75:21	forbids us certain p.	MOLI 611:77	p. it out, and cast it from thee	BIBLE 118:12
major vice and greatest p.	HEMI 410:90	glorious manly p.	WYCH 964:1	p. it out, and cast it from thee	BIBLE 114:34
married any one of them with p.	WILDE 942:31	hypocrite in his p.	JOHN 464:95	**plucked** p. the cigar out	KARSH 473:32
Much p., then from thee	DONNE 292:51	more I see P. about	MILT 605:44	**plum** with the later p.	JONS 467:72
must give you p.	KILLY 486:8	not with their p.	HUXL 441:52	**plumber** dance like a p.'s daughter	MIDD 590:71
no p. i' living	ELIOT 315:23	of all the sweet p. Known	REID 710:45	p. on weekends	ALLEN 14:84
no p. in the death of the wicked	BIBLE 111:34	paucity of human p.	JOHN 465:5	**plumbing** from p. to philosophy	LAUG 511:18
not in p.	DRYD 299:14	p. are like poppies spread	BURNS 179:25	**plum-cake** Some gave them p.-c.	CARR 205:15
Not sunk in carnal p.	MILT 605:42	p. in a long immortal dream	KEATS 476:5	**plume** blast-beruffled p.	HARDY 397:23
now we love p.	ETHE 327:46	p. in the world	CORY 247:13	danced on a p. of words	DAY 267:38
of p. complain	ROCH 720:22	p., of a free world	LURIE 542:66	Ruffles her pure cold p.	TENN 878:88
only safe p. for a parliamentarian	CRIT 255:10	p. of middle age	POUND 692:14	Sir P., of Amber Snuff-box	POPE 685:41
only sensual p. without vice	JOHN 465:2	p. of the other	AUST 46:74	**plummet** deeper than did ever p.	SHAK 804:31
organization for p.	JOHN 458:29	P. of worse natures	MASS 581:74	**plump** danger is to meet it p.	ROCHE 719:3
other words, p.	MORE 619:22	p. round about us	MILT 600:13	p. Venetian, fat, and lusty	FLET 341:58
owes its p. to another's pain	COWP 251:17	P. shorter than p.	WALL 918:57	so round, so p., so soft	SUCK 858:70
painful p. turns	SPEN 839:40	p. which my thoughts	LANY 508:58	**plunder** cannot separately p. a third	BIER 134:62
pay a debt to p. too?	ROCH 719:6	purest of human p.	BACON 53:30	**plundering** p.…at Rome	AUGU 44:33
physical p.	WAUGH 923:71	Seat of p.	DRYD 303:22	**plural** Incorrigibly p.	MACN 559:95
p. accompanied by the idea	SPIN 840:77	sucked on country p., childishly?	DONNE 291:21	**pluralism** P.—that is, the conception	BERL 84:49
p. and pain	GORD 378:54	sweeter…Than all other p.	DRYD 300:29	**plures** Abiit ad p.	PETR 676:43
p. at his own successes	RYLE 736:61	tear our p.	MARV 577:94	**plutography** p.…vice	WOLFE 953:81
P. at the helm	GRAY 385:86	These pretty p.	RALE 705:43	**plutonium** p. blonde	SCAR 746:14
p. can be the beginning of beauty	PROU 698:50	we will some new p. prove	DONNE 292:37	**Plymouth** land on P. Rock	MALC 562:91
p. in a sensual sty	MILT 598:63	will all the p. prove	MARL 574:41	**pneumatic** Wonderfully p.	HUXL 441:74
p.…In being mad	DRYD 302:97	**pleats** little p. and furbelows	SCHI 747:22	**Pobble** P. who has no toes	LEAR 516:39
p. in poetic pains	COWP 251:14	**plebeian** this the P. bran	DONNE 293:63	**pocket** both hands in the p.	SATIE 746:3
p. in the exercise of the mind	BARZ 67:37	**plebiscite** p. elected generals	JUVE 471:57	carry the moon in my p.?	BROW 168:37
p. in the pathless woods	BYRON 188:70	**plectrum** luminous p. of books	BELLI 76:47	guinea…in p.	RUSK 733:96
p. in what yet remain	DRYD 300:38	**pledge** p. to thee	KIPL 492:57	hands…in each other's p.	BIER 134:62
P. is a thief to business	DEFOE 269:80	p. with mine	JONS 467:75	no longer in your p.	SOLZ 833:5
p. is momentary	CHES 219:48	**Pleiades** sweet influences of P.	BIBLE 99:77	pecker in my p.	JOHN 458:15

pocketbook

pocketbook
- piece of brick in his p. — SWIFT 862:39
- p. of my land — FRAME 346:75
- poison in one p. — MACA 546:53
- pound...in your p. — WILS 948:66
- smile I could feel in my hip p. — CHAN 213:77
- would not scruple to pick a p. — DENN 273:76
- **pocketbook** not their p. — KENN 481:99
- **pocket-money** furnished with p.-m. — DICK 278:75
- **pockets** money from the p. of the people — SMITH 828:91
- rare in our p. — CHES 221:2
- turn their p. out — SPEN 837:96
- young man feels his p. — HOUS 432:69
- **pods** p. went pop on the broom — DAVI 264:68
- **Podsnap** Mr P. settled that — DICK 283:21
- Mr P. was well to do — DICK 283:18
- **Poe** P.!...and degenerates! — ONEI 651:70
- P....nonstop literary drinker — THUR 891:94
- P., with his raven — LOWE 539:8
- those who haunted...P. — ELLI 323:35
- **poem** A...p. should have — FENT 332:63
- a p. to escape — MANT 568:22
- best way to read [a p.] — NEW 634:35
- chryselephantine p. — POUND 691:96
- dance is a p. — DIDE 285:62
- does not like a p. — VIDAL 912:86
- elaborate polished p. — NASHE 632:90
- epic p., and the science — MENC 587:8
- form of the p. — SARO 744:58
- goes on in a p. — UPDI 906:27
- good p. is a contribution — THOM 884:45
- good p. is like a bouillon cube — DOVE 296:28
- haven't written the p. yet — BORG 151:57
- I could never begin a p. — MCGO 552:79
- Let the p. speak — PAGL 659:22
- life of a man...is a heroic p. — CARL 201:20
- made one p.'s period — MARL 572:2
- married to a p. — KEATS 476:93
- metre-making...makes a p. — EMER 324:69
- never started a p. — FROST 353:18
- only the p. comes near — DUDEK 305:73
- p. can be improved — MACL 555:36
- p....dream made flesh — MILL 594:81
- p. full of space and reverie — BAUD 69:89
- p. has a material existence — MACB 546:63
- p....is a little myth — WARR 921:16
- p. is a test of invention — KEATS 475:72
- p. is never finished — VALE 907:3
- p. is...the most primitive — KUNI 501:40
- p. must ride — FROST 353:13
- P. should be palpable — MACL 555:32
- p. should be wordless — MACL 555:33
- p. should not mean — MACL 555:34
- read a political p. — NEME 633:20
- right reader of a good p. — FROST 353:25
- The best p. is that — THOM 884:44
- The p. in the rock — THOM 886:75
- United States...greatest p. — WHIT 937:88
- vices nor...virtues further the p. — DUNC 307:8
- What is a p. — WARR 921:19
- writing a p. — WASH 921:22
- **poems** Anon...wrote so many p. — WOOLF 955:28
- any p. to the greater glory — WARR 921:20
- he is possessed by many p. — WILL 946:29
- honey peace in old p. — JEFF 453:12
- How do p. grow? — WARR 921:18
- I write p. — SART 744:65
- Naming me the fifty p. — BROW 168:51
- p. amount to so little — RILKE 715:36
- p. spoken in the factories — MACD 549:35
- Some p. have form — POUND 692:34
- These p., with all their crudities — THOM 884:28
- turn to stones and p. — DYSON 309:59
- understood Yeats's p. — SAKI 739:58
- We all write p. — FOWL 345:63
- **poesy** call p. vinum daemonum — BACON 49:33
- elegancy, facility...of p. — SHAK 763:13
- Myself in p. — KEATS 475:67
- **poet** accounted p. kings — KEATS 475:69
- another fig was a famous p. — PLATH 681:37
- as a p....not born yet — THOM 886:73
- bad p. dwells...in a world of objects — ELIOT 317:11
- because I was a p. — BROW 166:89
- becoming the first modern p. — LEVE 525:18
- better p. than Porson — HOUS 432:61
- business of a comic p. — CONG 240:34
- Byron is only great as a p. — GOET 375:69
- consecration, and the p.'s dream — WORD 961:28
- creations of a p. — SHEL 816:49
- decided to be a p. — TOWN 895:68
- don't have to suffer to be a p. — CIAR 226:24
- dreams of a p. — JOHN 460:71
- each p. took the color he needed — GALE 357:28
- essential advantage for a p. — ELIOT 319:30
- Every P. his own Aristotle — BYRON 189:2
- every p., in his kind — SWIFT 863:66
- Every p. knows — UNTE 905:11
- eye in the head of a p. — WELL 929:94
- Fat-head p. that nobody reads — CHES 221:8
- flattery lost on p.'s ear — SCOTT 752:14
- gentleman p. — JOYCE 470:25
- God is the perfect p. — BROW 167:8
- good p. is someone — JARR 452:84
- If a p. is anybody — CUMM 257:57
- Is this the great p. — GARR 360:80
- I was a p. — FLEC 340:30
- let the p. be a p. — PALEY 661:55
- Like a P. hidden — SHEL 814:94
- madness...should possess a p.'s brain — DRAY 299:98
- man may be born a p. — SASS 746:3
- matter made for famous p.'s verse — SPEN 838:37
- more correct p. — DRYD 300:25
- Never durst p. touch a pen — SHAK 763:18
- no other English p. seemed — AUDEN 44:20
- no person can be a p. — MACA 544:23
- no p. ever interpreted nature — GIRA 372:25
- No p. is ever completely lost — ACKR 3:61
- No p. or novelist wishes — AUDEN 44:9
- Not deep the P. sees — ARNO 33:59
- obviously a p. — DALI 261:14
- Oh Virgil! Oh p.! — HUGO 437:65
- On a p.'s lips — SHEL 814:13
- once more a p. — GRAV 382:25
- passionate heart of the p. — TENN 875:15
- p. and the dreamer — KEATS 476:99
- p. can earn much more money — AUDEN 43:6
- p. can...warn — OWEN 657:30
- p. could not but be gay — WORD 960:26
- p. emerges from morphemes — THOM 886:78
- p. gives us his essence — WOOLF 956:39
- p. is allowed the stride — SAND 742:34
- p. is a master of the quotidian — PRIT 696:54
- p. is a person — FROST 352:9
- p. is a unique being — VIAN 911:74
- P. is like that prince — BAUD 68:59
- p. is more the inspirer — ELUA 324:43
- p. is the life of everyone — NERV 634:26
- p. is the true fire-stealer — RIMB 715:45
- p. is the unsatisfied child — GRAV 383:39
- p. knows himself — MARI 571:82
- p. like an acrobat — FERL 333:89
- p. lives as long as his lines — BOLD 145:6
- p. makes silk dresses — STEV 850:92
- p. must be free — SART 744:64
- p. named Clough — SWIN 864:11
- p. reminds men of their uniqueness — COUS 248:40
- p. represents the mind — STEV 850:95
- p.'s business is not to describe — ABER 1:5
- p.'s feverish blood — ARNO 34:79
- P.'s food — SHEL 814:1
- p. shares with other artists — SPEN 837:7
- p.'s inward pride — DAY 267:35
- p.'s mind is perfectly equipped — ELIOT 317:94
- p.'s pen all scorn — BRAD 155:50
- p....spewed up — DRYD 300:36
- p.'s pleasure is to withhold — WHITE 935:36
- p.'s work...To name — RUSH 732:65
- p....used as a barometer — TRIL 897:17
- priest, warrior, p. — BAUD 69:86
- rank of every p. is well known — AUDEN 43:84
- rarely what the p. wants — NEME 633:20
- responsibility of the p. — PALEY 661:55
- responsibility of the p. — PALEY 661:54
- role of the p. to look — PRIT 696:22
- say the perfect thing to the p. — MUNRO 626:56
- something about a p. — THUR 891:8
- Spare the p. — COWP 251:2
- their sacred p. — HORA 430:12
- The p. as well — JEFF 453:12
- the p. is watching a fly — COLL 237:62
- The...scientist thinks like a p. — WILS 948:56
- This is truth the p. sings — TENN 871:14
- This p. lies — SHAK 800:36
- Thy skill to p. — SHEL 814:98
- To be a p. — GRAV 382:26
- true p. that you are! — BROW 168:48
- true p....trusts himself — POUND 692:36
- war p. — GURN 390:1
- What is a modern p.'s fate? — HOOD 426:38
- what the p. does — GINS 372:15
- when the P. dies — SCOTT 752:15
- When you're a p. — SART 744:66
- worst tragedy for a p. — COCT 233:85
- You explain nothing, O p. — CLAU 229:71
- **poet-baiting** In this country p.-b. — SITW 824:25
- **poetic** delicacy of p. instinct — WILDE 940:50
- English p. literature — GRAV 383:36
- nurse for a p. child! — SCOTT 752:17
- P. fields encompass me around — ADDI 6:16
- P. justice, with her lifted scale — POPE 688:30
- short-circuit — SENG 757:27
- subtlest and most p. — FOWL 346:65
- suspension of disbelief...p. faith — COLE 236:44
- the less p. are its morals — DIDE 285:65
- **poetical** fullest p. nature — WHIT 937:88
- gods had made thee p. — SHAK 779:97
- Smith, the name is so p. — CHES 220:58
- worn-out p. fashion — ELIOT 320:58
- **poetry** all metaphor is p. — CHES 220:53
- All p. is experimental — STEV 850:90
- almost than the finest p. — LAWR 514:85
- Angling is somewhat like p. — WALT 920:91
- art of p. — MACL 555:47
- Ben Jonson his best piece of p. — JONS 467:77
- butter nor shoes nor p. — LEWIS 527:56
- compound of p. and philosophy — MACA 545:29
- cradled into p. — SHEL 812:63
- create, if it concerns p. — HUGO 436:51
- Death is to P. — ABSE 1:9
- elements of our p. — MARI 571:76
- Emptied of its p. — AUDEN 43:92
- English p. begins — FENT 332:62
- English p. is not yet fit — OWEN 657:28
- even bad p. has relevance — FERL 333:19
- fate of p. — WALC 916:21
- fine graces of p. — SMITH 828:22
- force from widowed p. — CAREW 198:48
- formal p. perfect only in form — SAND 742:36
- function of p. — GRAV 382:27
- Genuine p. can communicate — ELIOT 318:21
- glamor of p. — GARL 360:75
- good living and good p. — LUCAS 541:52
- good material for p. — WILL 946:30
- good p. is forged slowly — DOUG 294:96
- grand style arises in p. — ARNO 35:10
- great p. gives the illusion — ELIOT 318:19
- If there is p. in our America — DARIO 262:44
- infancy of our p. — DRYD 304:39
- In whining p. — DONNE 291:32
- joy and function of p. — THOM 884:24
- lectures & my p. — BERR 87:3
- made p. a pedant's game — BUNT 173:68
- made p. seem word-bound — KAVA 474:47
- mathematics as surely as in p. — RUSS 734:25
- Mincing p. — SHAK 771:50
- Money is a kind of p. — STEV 850:97
- more rhyme there is in p. — SAND 742:35
- never the language of p. — GRAY 383:49
- No good p. is written — POUND 691:88
- no money in p. — GRAV 383:37
- no more a part of p. — STEV 850:90
- nothing to say...that is p. — CAGE 192:18
- not p., but prose run mad — POPE 687:2
- one perfect expression, p. — MALL 562:93
- or can even enjoy p. — MACA 544:23
- over into its basic p. — LEVE 525:23
- Painting is p. which is seen — LEON 522:69
- people ignore most p. — MITC 609:26
- pitiful defence of poor p. — SIDN 820:62
- P....a criticism of life — ARNO 36:50
- p. administers to the effect — SHEL 816:50
- p. and boxing — JAY 453:7
- p. and tragedy, love — LEWIS 527:57
- P....an escape from emotion — ELIOT 317:89
- p....as you please — BAUD 68:73
- p. begins to atrophy — POUND 692:17
- p. by young writers — WILDE 940:50
- p. can communicate — LEAV 517:50
- P. cannot take sides — SPEN 837:8
- p. comes not as naturally — KEATS 476:79
- p. consists largely in the instinct — BLUN 143:80

policy

p. different from all…arts MERW 589:57
p. does not swing from the branches CHOC 222:25
P. happens because of life OLIV 649:36
p. he invented was easy AUDEN 43:87
p. in a bottle FADI 329:8
P. in love is no more to be avoided WYCH 964:4
P. in this latter age JONS 468:89
p. is a game ROBBE 717:65
P. is a means of redemption STEV 850:87
P. is a naked woman FERL 333:93
P.…is an art of imitation SIDN 820:55
P. is an expression MALL 562:95
P. is an extra hand MITC 609:28
P. is a…piece of fiction MENC 586:86
P. is a record SHEL 816:52
P. is a rich…whistle STEV 850:96
P. is a way of taking life FROST 353:20
P.…is capable of saving us RICH 714:16
p. is conceived…in the soul ARNO 36:42
p. is kept on a life-support HARR 399:58
P. is man's rebellion CABE 191:5
P. is music ANGE 19:1
P. is not a career ELIOT 319:29
P. is not an expression GINS 372:15
P. is…overflow of…feelings WORD 958:93
P.…is perfection's sweat WALC 916:20
P. is the achievement SAND 742:22
P. is the art of understanding MACL 555:46
p. is the essence STEV 850:93
P. is the honey NASHE 631:89
P. is the impish attempt to paint…wind BODE 144:91
P. is the natural language STAEL 842:2
P. is the opening and closing SAND 742:21
P. is the supreme fiction STEV 849:65
P. is the supreme fiction STEV 850:99
P. is to prose WAIN 915:4
P. is what is lost FROST 353:26
P. is when some…fall short BENT 82:95
p.…makes justice PALEY 661:51
p. makes nothing happen AUDEN 43:91
P. makes things happen NEME 633:20
P. must be all well written POUND 691:90
P. must be read as music POUND 691:95
P. must resist STEV 850:89
P. needs something DIDE 285:66
p., no less than in life ARNO 36:40
p. of motion! GRAH 380:90
p. of our aspirations CUOMO 258:82
p. of the will? BALZ 61:4
p. on the air ORWE 654:53
P. proceeds from the totality MARI 571:81
p. reminds him of his limitations KENN 482:27
P.'s a mere drug FARQ 330:22
P. should be composed LAUT 512:31
p. should improve your life ASHB 37:61
p. sinks and swoons under LAND 507:36
p. strays into my memory HOUS 432:74
P.'s unnat'ral DICK 277:55
P., surely, is a crisis SALI 740:84
p. = the best words COLE 236:48
P.…the flower of any kind of experience HUNT 439:25
P.—tries to tell you about a vision ENGLE 326:16
p., which is in Oxford made DRYD 300:35
P. will no longer keep step RIMB 716:46
Polar star of p. KEATS 475:72
primal thing in p. BEER 74:91
process of p. WALC 916:22
prose, but not p. THOM 885:48
publicity rather than of p. LEAV 517:51
Pure p. is pure experiment SANT 743:48
reclaim these things—p., rock'n'roll, political activism SMITH 829:29
repeat p. as well as other folk CARR 205:13
say the perfect thing…about his p. MUNRO 626:56
She that with p. is won BUTL 185:77
skin…depended most on p. SIDN 820:53
slee p. nocht ta'en is DOUG 294:99
Superstition is the p. of life GOET 375:65
teenagers…read us their p. STIPE 855:4
the dead art of p. POUND 691:99
The P. is in the pity OWEN 677:67
the p. of Lord Byron MACA 545:34
There P. shall tune JOHN 459:41
To see clearly is p. RUSK 733:14
towns or houses raised by p. COWL 250:72
true nature of p. RICH 713:5

truest p. is the most feigning SHAK 779:98
turn to p. to interpret life ARNO 36:41
urge to write p. WARR 921:17
want a definition of p. THOM 884:25
What is p.? RUSK 733:89
when we read his p. ACKR 3:61
without the help of p. WAUGH 924:83
Writing a book of p. MARQ 575:57
writing bears…to p. MACA 545:32
writing fiction and p. UPDI 906:25
You campaign in p. CUOMO 258:77
poets Aeson had (as P. fain) HERR 415:1
All p. are mad BURT 181:76
among the English P. KEATS 476:82
Artists and p. ANON 27:18
because of other p. OLIV 649:36
behalf of all p. SIDN 820:59
cause of p. SPEN 837:13
English p. who grew up ROET 722:61
enterprising p. SHER 818:99
father of our dramatic p. DRYD 300:26
Fortunately for p. HILL 418:59
Great p. seldom make bricks POUND 692:38
Immature p. imitate ELIOT 317:92
Janus of p. DRYD 300:34
lament of the p. THOM 886:76
Like dancers…poor p. fare ETHE 327:42
little p. be gathered SMITH 830:36
Love is a boy, by p. styled BUTL 185:78
madmen! And your p.! ONEI 651:70
major p., in the sense LEAV 517:52
Modern p. mix GOET 375:66
Most p. are dead GRAV 383:36
most powerful p. of the century ELIOT 317:93
ought to leave to p. HEIN 407:20
pains…only p. know COWP 251:14
pensive p. painful vigils keep POPE 688:32
pens that ever p. held MARL 572:2
P.…are literal-minded men MACL 555:44
P. are the hierophants SHEL 816:53
p.…at the White House WHITE 936:59
P. do not go mad CHES 220:66
p. get a quizzical ahem FULL 355:76
p.…if you copy others BERN 86:78
p. in our youth WORD 959:1
P.! Madness is a gift PALEY 661:54
P. may boast WALL 918:59
p. of commerce GRAY 388:64
p. of each generation DAY 267:27
P. of the proud old lineage FLEC 340:31
p. only deliver a golden SIDN 820:54
P. paint with words CARR 202:59
p.…reading from their own works WHITE 935:33
P. sage SPEN 838:20
P. should never marry GONNE 377:42
p. should stay out of politics GINS 372:11
p. sometimes have to seem FROST 352:1
P.…unskilled to trace POPE 685:20
p.…write in words FOWL 345:63
sights as youthful p. MILT 597:48
sung by aged p. MITC 609:25
Three p. in an age SWIFT 862:60
Three p., in three distant ages DRYD 303:19
translunary things…the first p. had DRAY 299:98
what makes men p. or sages CHAR 215:28
what would be theft in other p. DRYD 300:21
Poggio P.'s, where people go DURR 308:37
poignance p.…of life ALLEN 13:78
poignant few sorrows, however p. SMITH 829:14
most p. sights JOHN 457:2
poinsettia p. meadows of her tides CRANE 252:54
point balanced p. of view SPEN 837:9
bring it up to a certain p. JAMES 450:50
creeping on from p. to p. TENN 871:18
feel I had gained a p. DICK 279:10
from the distant p. KAFKA 472:4
from the vantage p. PASS 668:97
highest p. of all my greatness SHAK 805:50
interest, a p. of view POPP 689:59
It is at the remotest p. JAY 453:2
mad on one p. KIPL 489:71
missed the p. completely ELIOT 321:96
one fixed p. in a changing age DOYLE 297:72
particular results at that p. THOR 888:24
p. free in time DIDI 286:80
p. of highest perfection RUNGE 731:52
p. of view is not the same RENO 711:57

p. on a sheet of green paper ATWO 41:34
p. out to us our follies TROL 897:26
p. the highest that human MILT 601:18
reached the p. KLEE 494:1
still p. of the turning world ELIOT 319:39
still p. of the turning world ELIOT 319:43
tangential p. of zero JARRY 452:95
pointers double-barrelled gun and p. KING 483:66
pointing don't lead by p. KESEY 483:66
points kindred p. WORD 961:45
superior attentions in little p. LAMB 505:94
the p. about this planet MACA 544:16
Poirot Hercule P. looked down CHRI 223:43
poison antidotes are p. SHAK 791:82
Corruption is more than a p. ECON 310:21
deal in p. with thee SHAK 780:17
Do it not with p. SHAK 790:32
guardianship…against p. PATR 669:29
has drunk p. SHEL 815:37
If you p. us SHAK 769:1
In p. there is physic SHAK 772:69
instead of dirt and p. SWIFT 861:18
I would p. him TWAIN 903:66
pellet with the p. PANA 662:80
p. cruelly tortures BRON 161:72
p. in jest SHAK 783:26
p. in one pocket MACA 546:53
p. of enthusiasm and superstition SMITH 828:90
p. the whole blood stream fills EMPS 326:8
potent p. quite o'ercrows SHAK 785:74
Socrates empties the cup of p. FEUE 334:1
strongest p. ever known BLAKE 141:27
they slew with p. DAVIS 266:7
venomous as the p. of a serpent BOOK 149:21
With its sickening p. LARK 509:79
With most delicious p. SHAK 794:53
poisoner That old p. DEBU 268:60
poison-flowers honey of p.-f. TENN 875:16
poisoning hanged for p. DOYLE 296:44
perish from Brie-cheese p. ADLER 8:69
poisons Life…with its p. ANOU 28:62
poke p. poor Billy GRAH 380:87
poker insight I have gained from p. MAMET 564:35
rigidity of a p. MACM 557:77
Soviet game is chess…ours is p. SHUL 819:25
The p. player learns MAMET 564:36
Pol Pot completed PILG 678:78
Poland takes place in P. JARRY 452:92
too late with P. LLOY 533:79
polar split into two p. groups SNOW 832:77
polarities as angels, not p. RICH 713:7
pole serpent of brass…upon a p. BIBLE 94:82
Suspended…between p. and tropic ELIOT 321:80
top of the greasy p. DISR 288:52
poles move between the quiet p. MARL 573:22
police German p. spies MARX 579:33
God's p. CHIS 222:24
international p. power ROOS 724:16
P. action must be to separate EDEN 311:31
p. are prowling ORWE 654:57
p. can pick him up DOUG 295:23
p. dog of American fiction FADI 329:7
p. state GINS 372:14
Reading…among p. officers ORTON 653:5
recognised by the p. STEV 852:36
policeman p. in the National WHIS 934:19
p. of normal proportions STEW 854:95
p.'s lot is not a happy one GILB 368:42
terrorist and the p.…from the same basket CONR 244:41
would not do for a p. NIGH 639:24
policemen how young the p. look HICKS 417:45
not enough p. HUMP 439:9
P. so cherish their status MAMET 563:27
repressed sadists…become p. CONN 242:96
village idiots, p. MACD 550:39
policies carcasses of old p. CECIL 210:31
only party with clear p. THAT 881:71
p., nor stratagems MILT 600:9
policy active p. is best advanced BAKER 56:2
agreement with government p. HOWE 433:89
best p. to speak JERO 454:41
British p. ROCH 719:9
conforms to the party p. BEAV 71:25
Economic p. is random STEIN 845:7
either on religion or p. RUSK 733:8
England's foreign p. GLAD 373:39

polished

Entry	Ref
English p. is to float lazily	CECIL 210:30
field of world p.	ROOS 724:5
foreign p. of the noble Earl	DERBY 274:86
From great defects of p.	HOPE 427:56
indispensable act of p.	PITT 679:10
least influence on p.	BLIN 142:53
Making foreign p.	ROGE 723:88
No foreign p.	KISS 493:88
our true p.	WASH 922:31
p.? I wage war	CLEM 229:87
p. sits above conscience	SHAK 791:78
p. to keep all the nationalities	TAAF 865:1
tyrants from p.	BURKE 176:43
Wisdom and p. dictate	NAPO 629:39
polished p. up the handle	GILB 368:32
p. with the tread of feet	DICK 279:1
soul…must be p.	DEFOE 269:67
polite English are p. by telling lies	BRAD 154:27
imbues his p. things	TWAIN 902:33
never mentions Hell to ears p.	POPE 686:61
not a p. employer	HOOV 427:48
The French are p.	TWAIN 902:33
What a p. game tennis is	BARR 65:94
politeness ceremonious p.	TWAIN 902:33
Punctuality is the p.	LOUI 537:71
politic they are p.	WEBS 926:20
'Twere p. to do the like	YEATS 966:15
political addiction of p. groups	GALB 357:15
a very p. old monk	MURD 626:69
binary p. arena	LEHM 520:24
Britain's New P. Order	MITC 609:29
circulates p. life	TOCQ 892:30
climbed my last p. mountain	WALL 918:49
confronting p. dragons	MAJOR 561:77
Divorce…has a great p.	MONT 615:45
foundations of p. liberty	WILS 949:83
frightened by 'p.' sermons	BARTH 66:11
goal that supplies the p. magic	SCHL 748:39
half your p. life	THAT 881:59
lucky…discovered a p. theory	CAST 208:80
making man a p. animal	ARIS 31:26
model our p. systems	HAMI 394:48
My p. opinions	TOLK 893:43
national consciousness is a p. fact	MACM 556:67
not a p. person	HELL 408:42
particular p. conditions	MARX 579:30
points clearly to a p. career	SHAW 809:76
P. action is of second rank	MANN 566:89
p. ammunition runs low	STEV 850:6
p. and educational status	SKEL 824:32
p. and practical difficulties	KEYN 484:80
p. and social conditions	MARS 575:63
p. and the other military	MCNA 557:91
p. animal can be defined	STEG 844:56
p. aspirant under democracy	MENC 586:93
p. cancer	ANON 26:9
p. consequences	MANS 568:13
p. danger	GLAD 373:36
P. democracy…in America	WHIT 938:11
P. economy thus does	MARX 578:26
P. economy traces	BAGE 54:76
P. genius	HEGEL 406:9
p. gentlemen drape over	HUXL 442:98
p. in this country	TROL 898:46
p. meetings…at a divine level	ACHE 2:26
p. noncommitment	VAN 908:12
p. ones are insoluble	HOME 425:95
p. or constitutional history	JAY 453:1
p. or religious faiths	PIRS 679:90
p. point of view	WHIT 934:25
p. power grows out of the barrel	MAO 568:29
p. question is…a painful sight	LODGE 534:2
p. struggle	HAIL 392:17
p. zombies	WILS 948:71
reclaim these things—poetry, rock'n'roll, p. activism	SMITH 829:29
single p. argument left	THAT 881:63
stuff of p. leadership	WILS 948:73
Tears…can never be p.	BELL 78:92
third-rate p. wheel-horse	MENC 587:16
We are not a p. party	MAND 564:54
politically History is not p. correct	FERG 333:80
rule industrially…rule p.	CONN 243:19
politician At home, you always have to be p.	MACM 556:66
consummate British p.	MCFA 551:67
I am not a…p. I am a…p.	THAT 882:77

Entry	Ref
lawyer and p. and a heretic	MENC 586:89
like a scurvy p.	SHAK 793:26
more of a missionary than a p.	CART 206:51
murderer, to be a p.	MILL 595:94
No man can be a p.	HARR 398:42
pate of a p.	SHAK 784:61
p. is a man	TRUM 899:85
p. is an arse	CUMM 258:66
p. is a person	LLOY 533:81
p. is a statesman who	STEV 851:20
p. is the devil's quilted anvil	WEBS 927:50
p. is trained	MURR 627:85
p.…on a street corner	WHITE 936:57
p. poses as the servant	DE 270:99
p. rises on the backs	HUGH 435:18
p. seeking empathy	SAFI 737:21
prefer to have a p.	WILS 947:37
the kind of p.	STEV 851:21
when a p. does get an idea	MARQ 575:54
politicians All p. are like crazed wasps	JOHN 457:94
always impress p.	HAYEK 403:26
fault of our p.	TROL 898:40
Few p. are good at taking the high ground	MAND 565:62
If the answer is more p.	MAJOR 561:79
Natural p. are skilled actors	MARA 569:45
one of those p.	TROL 897:29
Outer Mongolia for retired p.	BENN 79:29
p. and scientists were lazier	WAUGH 924:90
P. are neither bad nor good	EICH 313:72
P. are the same all over	KHRU 485:92
p.…enormous sexual pull	COND 240:15
P.…entitled to change their minds	HATT 400:83
p. have had to listen	FITT 337:67
p.…hold writers in contempt	BELL 77:81
P. neither love nor hate	DRYD 302:76
p. of our time	MACA 545:25
p. or philosophers	THOM 885:55
P. use statistics	LANG 507:40
race of p. put together	SWIFT 862:45
revolution to get the p. out	CAST 208:78
sense of purpose…not…from their p.	MACM 557:78
Successful p.	LIPP 531:42
too important to be left to the p.	DE 270:1
Two p.' rotten bladders	WEBS 927:49
what p. are up to	HUMP 439:14
wind instead of the p.	WADD 915:1
politics American p.	GRAMM 381:96
American p.	WHITE 936:60
an important component of p.	OROU 652:99
any more about p.	TRUM 899:81
axiom of p.	TOCQ 892:29
Beauty…determined by p.	WOLF 952:61
best p. is good government	STEV 851:19
boundaries between p. and art	DANG 262:29
choice in p.	THOR 889:54
commonest error in p.	CECIL 210:31
constantly changing language of p.	SAFI 737:17
contact I have had with p.	HEMI 410:86
cross current of world p.	HUGH 436:50
democracy…is to p.	PILG 678:79
didn't come into p. to change the Labour Party	BLAIR 138:51
difference between p. and guilt	CLIN 230:6
Don't be 'practical' in p.	CONN 243:20
England is unrivalled for…p.	DISR 289:76
Finality is not the language of p.	DISR 288:47
get on in p.	BAKER 56:4
great men…in p.	ELTON 323:42
History is past p.	FREE 350:47
infection of p.	BRON 160:50
In p.…anything said	THAT 881:48
In p., madame	MULR 624:34
In p.…retreat is honorable	MCCA 548:1
Like art and p.	DOCT 289:84
long experience of p.	MACM 556:70
making p. a spectator sport	GERG 365:67
man goes in for p.	ROGE 723:83
matter of modern p.	ARNO 35:22
Men enter local p.	PARK 665:40
mistaken zeal in p.	JUNI 471:48
mixed with p. and p.	LAFA 503:42
more p. in football than in p.	ERIK 327:38
more than our p. and our laws	DEWAR 276:18
mule of p.	DISR 287:27
My p.…is England	DISR 287:32
naked moment in p.	GERG 365:66
nature of p.	POWE 693:60

Entry	Ref
never get on in p.	ASTOR 39:11
no true friends in p.	CLARK 228:57
observe about this p. thing	ROGE 723:73
people who want to get on in p.	DEED 269:65
Philistine of genius in…p.	ARNO 36:38
playful moderation in p.	HUNT 439:20
poets should stay out of p.	GINS 372:11
P. and the fate of mankind	CAMUS 195:81
P. are much discussed	DICK 279:2
P. are now nothing more	JOHN 462:39
P., as a practice	ADAMS 5:86
p. as a profession	HOWE 434:93
P. come from man	WAITE 916:5
P. determine who has the power	KRUG 500:27
P. has got to be…fun	CLARK 228:58
p. in the East	DISR 287:20
P. is a blood sport	BEVAN 90:60
P. is a thing	AMIS 16:32
P. is just like show business	REAG 709:15
P. is like…a football coach	MCCA 547:83
P. is like having diabetes	JONES 465:20
P. is not an exact science	BISM 137:33
P. is not the art of the possible	GALB 357:18
P. is perhaps the only profession	STEV 852:58
P. is the art of preventing	VALE 907:6
P. is the art of the possible	BUTL 184:60
P. is the skilled use	PEAR 671:58
P. is too important	DE 270:1
P. is war	MAO 568:28
P. make you think	CAST 207:75
P. mixed with the imagination	STEN 847:3
p. of greed	ARMEY 32:39
p. of numbers	TANA 867:22
p. of the country	HAZL 403:45
p. of the extreme centre	WELL 929:9
p. stops at the water's edge	CLIN 231:32
p. than men of any other class	LODGE 534:2
p. the middle way	ADAMS 5:99
Practical p. consists in	ADAMS 5:95
secret springs of p.	TOCQ 892:30
sex is just p.	BRAD 154:31
society…think much about p.	LEWIS 526:49
some scheme of p.	MONT 613:11
South Africa, renowned…For p.	CAMP 194:50
sphere of practical p.	KING 488:58
the Jesus Christ of p.	BERL 85:53
the p. of our society	OAKE 642:1
There are times in p.	GALB 357:21
to blame…is p.	ANON 26:80
view of history…not of war and p.	CHILD 222:16
volunteer to go into p.	LEE 519:92
War…the continuation of p.	CLAU 229:76
week is a long time in p.	WILS 948:63
what p. is all about	TRUM 900:89
what there is in business, p.	WHIT 938:13
Without alienation…no p.	MILL 593:46
World-p. stepped in	LEWIS 527:73
You will find in p.	BALD 57:35
polkadot Yellow P. Bikini	VANCE 908:11
polkadots One week he's in p.-d.	DAVI 264:80
Poll talked like poor P.	GARR 360:79
poll p. results	GALL 358:45
pollen p. from one to another mind	LOWE 539:10
polling P. is merely an instrument	GALL 358:45
polls P.…for strippers…and skiers	PALIN 661:61
polluter the world's biggest p.	BUSH 183:42
pollution air p. and…artificial light	MATT 582:1
p.—environmental problem	BOUL 152:90
universal p.	ILLI 445:21
pollutions p. of a great…city	DICK 281:55
Polly Hullo, P., my love	THOM 884:39
Mr P.	WELLS 930:27
polo Playing p. is like…golf	STAL 842:8
polyanthus grass the p. cheques	SMART 826:64
polyester P.…most valuable word	ANON 26:12
polygamous Man is p.	JAMES 452:78
polygamy chaste p.	CAREW 199:60
p. was made a sin	DRYD 301:63
pomegranate sings on yon p. tree	SHAK 766:1
temples are like a piece of a p.	BIBLE 107:45
pommy called a p. bastard	CHAR 216:45
pomp grinning at his p.	SHAK 764:52
No princely p.	DYER 309:48
p. of power	GRAY 384:66
p. of the superfluous causes	NEWT 635:58
solemnised with p. and parade	ADAMS 5:1
Pompeius P.…his first triumph	PLUT 682:76

portion

Pompey Knew you not P.?	SHAK 776:4
pomps high Midsummer p.	ARNO 35:19
p. and vanity	BOOK 148:78
pond An old p.	BASHO 67:44
Four ducks on a p.	ALLI 14:7
have their stream and p.	BROO 163:99
In the p. beside the meadow	MACG 551:71
muddy p. of daily life	HERZ 416:21
ponder When in danger, p.	WAGN 915:3
poniards She speaks p.	SHAK 773:27
ponies p. have swallowed their bits	BETJ 89:44
Pontefract licorice fields at P.	BETJ 89:42
poodle bulldog into a Reagan	STEEL 844:37
created the p.	THUR 891:97
honourable gentleman's p.	LLOY 532:68
Pooh happy morning Being P.	MILNE 596:23
House at P. Corner	PARK 663:1
'I ought to say,' explained P.	MILNE 596:19
pooh P., p. to you	GILB 369:43
Poohsticks game called P.	MILNE 596:24
pool In a great p. a swan's nest	SHAK 803:1
Leaning over…a rock p.	DAY 267:33
rears from off the p.	MILT 602:43
pools Where the p. are bright	HOGG 422:43
poop feeding the p. back to diners	COUP 248:29
p. was beaten gold	SHAK 794:55
poops high on the p. of the ships	ROBE 717:71
poor annals of the p.	GRAY 384:66
a p. church for the p.	FRAN 347:90
as a p. woman	THAC 880:33
As for the virtuous p.	WILDE 941:73
asparagus of the p.	FRAN 347:88
backward steward for the p.	POPE 686:68
being p.	YEATS 966:12
being so p.	BLUN 143:72
Bells, the p. man's only music	COLE 235:24
bestow all my goods to feed the p.	BIBLE 126:52
best way to help the p.	HANC 395:77
Better is a p. and a wise child	BIBLE 106:19
Blessed are the p. in spirit	BIBLE 114:27
brings him into the world p.	INNO 446:46
children of the p.	DICK 281:61
Clothes make the p. invisible	HARR 398:44
Commitment to the p.	JOHN 456:80
cynical gestures of the p.	SPEN 837:96
destruction of the p. is their poverty	BIBLE 104:63
distance between the rich and the p.	CARL 200:81
don't leave out the p.	ZELD 969:4
Employed a Million of the P.	MAND 565:65
expensive…to be p.	BALD 57:18
Farewell, my p. hands	RACH 704:25
fatally p. and dingy	WHAR 933:5
first duty…is not to be p.	SHAW 809:70
Four spectres haunt the p.	LLOY 532:71
Give me your tired, your p.	LAZA 515:3
grind the faces of the p.?	BIBLE 107:52
gulf between the rich and the p.	COUP 248:27
high and low, rich and p.	MORI 619:36
high in p. countries	SMITH 827:82
houseless and unemployed p.	BRON 161:68
How p. are they	SHAK 789:15
If thou art rich, thou'rt p.	SHAK 787:65
If you're p.	MART 576:79
inconvenient to be p.	COWP 251:1
keep D.H. Lawrence p.	BRAD 155:36
kisses the p. last	SHAK 795:82
knew…that he was p.	DICK 284:50
Laws grind the p.	GOLD 376:87
life of the journalist is p.	GIBB 367:8
live by robbing the p.	SHAW 807:22
merry Monarch, scandalous and p.	ROCH 719:7
more p. than you think	MEIJ 584:37
murmuring p., who will not fast	CRAB 252:35
nice people were p.	SPARK 836:71
Nothing is so p. and melancholy	SANT 743:46
one of the undeserving p.	SHAW 810:98
Peace is p. reading	HARDY 397:27
pitiful defence of p. poetry	SIDN 820:52
pity upon the p.	BIBLE 105:85
plenty has made me p.	OVID 657:18
p. always with you	BIBLE 119:38
p. always have with you	BIBLE 123:48
P. and content is rich	SHAK 789:20
p. and the weary predominate	GARL 360:74
p. are to be proud!	SHAK 786:9
p. as Job	SHAK 772:72
p. cannot always reach	FORS 344:28
p. for a' that!	BURNS 180:52
p. get children	KAHN 472:9
p. have no right	RUSK 733:1
p.…have occasion for	HALL 393:40
p. have the gospel preached	BIBLE 116:76
p. in a loomp is bad	TENN 878:90
p. in spirit	SPARK 836:91
p. Ireland still continues p.?	BERK 84:33
p. is hated	BIBLE 104:71
P. Little Rich Girl	COWA 249:44
p. man at his gate	ALEX 13:62
p. man had nothing	BIBLE 96:45
p. man's opera	HUXL 442:92
p. man's Parnassus	EMER 325:1
p. man's wealth	SIDN 820:46
P. naked wretches	SHAK 792:11
p.'s decay	GOLD 376:4
p. silly-clever Irishman	SHAW 809:64
p. Sir Patrick	EDGE 311:36
p. slaves with weary footsteps	SHEL 815:45
p. to do him reverence	SHAK 777:41
p. virgin…an ill-favoured thing	SHAK 780:22
p.…whose death interests no one	CELI 211:40
p., yet making many rich	BIBLE 127:73
rich and I've been p.	TUCK 901:15
Rich And The P.	DISR 288:34
Rich gifts wax p.	SHAK 783:8
rich should become p.	ARIS 32:27
so p. a record of performance	FRIE 351:71
the p. are our equals	TRIL 897:15
the p. dream all their lives	ADIGA 8:63
The p. sleep little	OTWAY 656:8
thin hands of the p.	WILDE 940:45
Though very p.	GOLD 376:8
thousand p. musicians	VAUG 909:32
Thus may p. fools	SHAK 803:98
To be a p. man	DU 305:66
Too p. for a bribe	GRAY 385:94
to this day is every scholar p.	MARL 574:40
tragedy…not that men are p.	DU 305:67
unkillable infants of the very p.	POUND 691:93
used to think I was p.	FEIF 331:55
wealth…makes them doubly p.	CRAB 252:89
When that the p. have cried	SHAK 777:38
poorer for richer for p.	BOOK 148:91
poorest p. he that is in England	RAIN 705:37
p. of people believe	HEGEL 406:7
poorhouse p. in an automobile	ROGE 723:80
pop p. art and fine art	MACI 553:1
P. art is the inedible	BASK 67:50
P. artists did images	WARH 920:8
P. music…classical music of now	MCCA 548:3
popcorn Everything else is mere p.	BELL 78:88
pope ay, or a p.!	HARDY 397:20
Depicting the P.	FRAN 347:93
Dryden, P., and all their school	ARNO 36:42
elected a President, not a P.	STRE 857:52
man a little p. of perfection	LAWR 513:49
not you who are p.	BERN 85:64
photograph of the P.	ANON 27:15
P. and Tsar, Metternich	MARX 579:33
P. composes with his eye	ARNO 35:7
P. is quite satisfied	MICH 590:65
P. should surrender…authority	WYCL 964:6
P. told us all to go to hell	OBRI 646:69
popery never be in danger of P.	ADDI 7:35
popes P. and Popery	ANON 23:96
popinjay Came the great P.	SITW 823:7
poplar p. never dry	SPEN 838:20
poplars white p. fluttering	CHAT 216:52
poppet no go my p.	MACN 557:98
poppies Flanders fields the p.	MCCR 548:11
pleasures are like p. spread	BURNS 179:25
Poppins Mary P. looked down	TRAV 895:89
poppy Not p. nor mandragora	SHAK 789:25
poppycock this is p.	JOHN 458:27
pops p. of Sillery	GILB 369:55
populace Barbarians…and P.	ARNO 36:26
factious P.	JOHN 459:40
give the name of P.	ARNO 36:29
popular Marriage is p.	SHAW 808:40
Nothing can render them p.	SWIFT 863:77
over-great pleasure in being p.	FULL 355:65
p. humanity is treason	ADDI 7:49
P. in our time	HUGH 435:23
very p. among his mates	EWART 328:75
why soap operas are…so p.	STEI 846:94
popularity Appalling P. of Music	LAMB 506:17
no easy p.	THAT 881:57
P.? It is glory	HUGO 437:74
population capital and p.	MILL 591:94
control the p. without…Herod?	OBRI 645:63
foreign p. must endeavour	RUSS 734:30
full half of the p.	MORE 618:18
immediate checks to p.	MALT 563:20
Ireland…a starving p.	DISR 287:31
only talked of p.	GOLD 376:89
P. EXPLOSION	BRUN 170:94
P.…increases in geometrical ratio	MALT 563:19
p. provides a subsidy	CHOM 222:28
segment of our p.	TRUM 899:77
populations moving whole p.	MILL 594:63
privileged p.	SONT 834:21
working p. of both countries	LOND 534:10
populous p. and smoky city	SHEL 813:87
p. railway town	THOR 889:52
porcelain rogue in p.	MERE 588:33
porch beyond p. and portal	SWIN 864:96
he'll be on your p.	JOHN 458:12
on the front p. of the house	LANCE 506:24
To the top of the p.!	MOORE 616:63
porches In the p. of mine ears	SHAK 781:64
porcupine dry birth to a p.	SIMP 822:83
key is to be a p.	MATT 582:97
like fucking a p.	MIZN 610:61
quill from a p.	MOORE 617:91
quills upon the fretful p.	SHAK 781:60
pore charm from every p.	LERN 523:84
pores came through the p.	GREE 385:4
p. of the ocean and shores	SHEL 813:77
pork Yes, to smell p.	SHAK 769:82
porkchop Uncle…and his Little P.	ONAS 650:55
Porlock a person on business from P.	COLE 235:35
Person from P.	SMITH 830:41
pornography give p. a bad name	BARN 63:58
P.…attempt to insult sex	LAWR 514:80
p. is really about	SONT 834:15
p. only adds to the murk	MILL 594:91
P.…vice of the Seventies	WOLFE 953:81
porphyry and polished p.	SMART 826:64
porpoise lively p. in a strong tide	DICK 277:47
p.…treading on my tail	CARR 203:80
porpoises sporting like p.	SITW 823:98
porridge lines falling like cold p.	BRID 159:12
receives comfort like cold p.	SHAK 804:18
sand in the p.	COWA 249:45
venomous p.	THOM 884:41
Porsches friends all drive P.	JOPL 468:98
Porson better poet than P.	HOUS 432:61
port brother…who drinks p.	BARR 65:55
p. after stormy seas	SPEN 838:28
p., for men	JOHN 463:66
p. is near	WHIT 938:7
p. without trade	DEFOE 269:78
ship in p. is safe	HOPP 429:5
Still bent to make some p.	ARNO 34:80
the little p.	TENN 877:66
There lies the p.	TENN 870:2
portal beyond porch and p.	SWIN 864:96
p. of freedom	EISE 314:8
well-marked front p.	UPDI 906:32
portals p. of discovery	JOYCE 470:27
portent p. of an iceberg	BROW 168:54
Self-parody is the first p.	MCMU 557:84
This is the best p.	HOMER 425:7
Porter to Kern or Cole P.	GERS 365:74
porter Ultimate P.	MANS 567:2
porter all p. and skittles	DICK 278:61
decompose in a barrel of p.	DONL 290:9
definition…for a p.	NIGH 639:24
mug of p. in the long nights	OBRI 646:70
philosopher and…p.	SMITH 827:77
Portia P. is Brutus' harlot	SHAK 777:18
porticos spitting on p.	NERU 633:23
portion no claim…to the smallest p.	MALT 563:22
only gift is a p. of thyself	EMER 324:71
p. for ever	BIBLE 101:86
p. is so small Of…pain	MILT 602:56
p. of the earth	NAIP 629:27
p. of the Eternal	SHEL 815:38
p. of the loveliness	SHEL 815:42
right to a fair p.	BURKE 176:38
That best p. of…life	WORD 956:54
that is his p.	BIBLE 106:15

portmanteau

that p. of the ball	POPE 688:36
the curse...all your p.	OTWAY 656:98
portmanteau p....two meanings	CARR 205:12
portmanteaux people are like p.	MANS 567:2
portrait do not paint a p.	DALI 261:13
I paint a p. I lose a friend	SARG 743:52
make a p.	ROSSO 727:68
p. in marble	BERN 86:87
p. of a dog that I know	JOHN 465:3
p. of a trout	HUGH 435:25
P. of the Artist	THOM 883:15
two styles of p. painting	DICK 278:78
portraits accept the verbal p.	CHUR 224:50
oil p., etchings	RODC 721:43
people in p. are thinking	LIVE 531:48
p. I paint of women	LAUR 511:24
study of family p.	DOYLE 297:65
portray could not p. all I felt	HOLM 423:55
Portuguese assurance, typically P.	ACHE 2:29
pose combine a p. imperious	GILB 370:72
posies thousand fragrant p.	MARL 574:41
posing P. is a performing art	SCHW 750:84
position at the cost of his social p.	MARX 579:35
Every p. must be held	HAIG 392:15
get people into a p.	KAZIN 474:53
high p., but not a safe one	BERN 85:63
if not impossible p.	LEWO 528:79
in a p. to instruct us	PEOP 673:83
lucidly justifying his p.	AMERY 15:25
mathematical is this fundamental p.	HEID 406:11
no p. more perilous	TROL 898:42
only one p. for an artist	THOM 884:43
p. at the summit of the world	PEARY 671:60
p....epitomized marginality	ECON 310:20
p., I'd have done the same	NIXON 640:39
p. of the artists of Wales	THOM 884:43
p. ridiculous	CHES 219:48
rose to his p.	TROT 899:64
Whatever its p. or character	SCOTT 751:99
positions military take p.	KENN 482:44
ridiculous p.	DANF 261:27
positive All satisfaction...never p.	SCHO 748:51
P....Mistaken at the top of one's voice	BIER 135:89
something p. and precious	PRIT 696:21
possess not enough to p. her	LACL 503:35
possessed limited in order to be p.	BURKE 175:25
p. by what is not	LEGU 520:10
p. with murd'rous hate	SHAK 800:35
possessing P. what one loves	PROU 698:49
too dear for my p.	SHAK 802:67
possession everlasting p.	BIBLE 92:21
in the glad p.	JONS 466:46
merry hart with small p.	HENR 411:20
p. intended to last	THUC 890:61
P. is nine points	ANON 22:70
p. is the final good	WHIT 936:65
p. of a bourgeois aristocracy	ENGE 326:12
p. of that object conveys	SMITH 827:78
secure p. of a bleak work	YOUNG 968:51
possessions concern not for...p.	PLATO 681:43
for he had great p.	BIBLE 118:17
jealous p.	GIDE 367:21
mind is the least of p.	WHITE 935:54
possessor libel on its p.	SHEL 812:51
not profitable to its p.	MARQ 575:53
possibilities p. of life	LEAV 517:52
short of their inherent p.	MUMF 625:36
To believe only in p.	BROW 165:65
You are your p.	WINF 949:92
possibility How great a P.	CARL 200:2
laws of p.	REDON 709:23
life...to give it p.	MACL 555:43
objective p.	WEBER 925:12
p. of anybody getting me out	BRAD 155:48
p. of human happiness	ERNST 327:40
Religion...a remote p.	WHIT 936:65
Violent, vivid and of infinite p.	EBER 310:10
possible art of the p.	GALB 357:18
if a thing is p.	CALO 193:34
no explanation is p.	SEAT 755:93
Politics is the art of the p.	BUTL 184:60
p. is one of the provinces	BAUD 69:75
scientist states that something is p.	CLAR 228:68
thank all those who made this p.	ANDR 18:81
wasn't p. for me or anyone	KAVA 474:47
where all things are p.	OBAMA 644:30
possum Honourable P.	BERR 87:99
post boats...near the winning p.	COKE 234:98
Lie follows by p.	BERE 83:16
may not quit the p.	TENN 877:69
p. of honour	ADDI 7:51
stalked through the P. Office	YEATS 967:38
postal cheque and the p. order	AUDEN 42:71
desire to take p. courses	BRAD 154:21
postboy keys of a p.'s horn	BENET 79:24
postcard and a p. album	TRAV 895:88
postcards have a set of p. printed	ELLI 323:27
post-chaise driving briskly in a p.-c.	JOHN 463:54
poster Kitchener...a great p.	ASQU 38:87
live up to one's p.	TREE 896:99
p. on the student's wall	VETT 911:67
p. with the enormous face	ORWE 655:72
posterior protecting his p.	SAFI 737:19
posterity fear of vexing p.!	ROCHE 719:2
footprints preserved for p.	PATE 669:14
love of p.	HAWT 401:1
People will not look forward to p.	BURKE 176:36
p. be after him	CROM 255:19
P. do something for us	ADDI 7:54
P. stands cursed	MILT 606:63
p. talking bad grammar	DISR 289:73
P. will do justice to...Gladstone	DISR 288:63
protecting his posterior from p.	SAFI 737:19
Thy p. shall sway	COWP 250:94
To evoke p.	GRAV 382:22
To invoke one's p.	CELI 211:38
trustees of P.	DISR 288:36
posters P. of the sea and land	SHAK 795:2
post-feminism no such thing as p.-f.	STEIN 846:95
post-horse contrapuntist...p.	MOZA 623:6
postman hear the p.'s knock	AUDEN 42:72
The P. Always Rings Twice	CAIN 192:20
postmodern p....Australia	NARO 630:53
postpone p. no more	WHIT 937:1
postponement Life...one long p.	MILL 594:83
posts sprinkle all the p.	SPEN 839:50
postscript pith is in the p.	HAZL 404:51
seldom Writes...but in her P.	STEE 844:48
postulate lay down as a p.	WEIL 928:75
p. of objectivity	MONOD 612:3
Postumus Oh, my P., P.	HORA 430:8
posture died each in the despairing p.	POE 683:83
postures indecent p.	WILDE 942:28
post-war awash in p.-w. testosterone	SCHR 749:68
posy picks a p. of daisies	THOM 884:35
pot don't make them in the one p.	JOYCE 470:23
Fame's luscious p.	RICK 715:29
great Melting P.	ZANG 969:1
Joan doth keel the p.	SHAK 763:27
melting p. never worked	MORR 620:55
not a melting p.	CART 206:45
strawberries at the mouth of their p.	ELIZ 322:8
three-hooped p.	SHAK 759:95
potato any more than a p.	HAWT 401:3
no more bounce than a boiled p.	PORT 690:76
p. candidate	ANON 27:21
You say P.	GERS 365:77
potatoes Let the sky rain p.	SHAK 773:14
Papa, p., poultry, prunes	DICK 282:91
potent more p. than any other man	STEAD 843:31
potential both as chaos and as p.	POUND 692:31
p. for the disastrous rise	EISE 314:2
potentialities puritanical p.	LEWIS 527:66
potions p. have I drunk of siren tears	SHAK 802:81
Potomac All quiet along the P.	MCCL 548:7
potsherd Let the p. strive	BIBLE 109:88
p. to scrape himself	BIBLE 98:93
pottage bread and p. of lentiles	BIBLE 92:29
mess of p.	BIBLE 92:27
Potter Harry P. was a highly unusual boy	ROWL 729:24
potter Hath not the p. power	BIBLE 125:23
like a p.'s vessel	BIBLE 99:28
P. and clay endure	BROW 168:60
P. is piqued with p.	HESI 417:31
poultry A p. matter	MARX 578:14
foxes...prolonging the lives of the p.	ELIOT 315:40
I hate pudgy p.	PERD 674:12
Pound in Ezra P.'s term	MACD 550:39
pound Christian on a P. a Week?	HARD 396:92
give thee a silver p.	CAMP 194:65
grocer puts a p. weight	SPEN 837:9
hundred p. on't	SHAK 803:89
pound P. a week and his keep	LAWS 514:96
p....in your pocket	WILS 948:65
Take thou thy p. of flesh	SHAK 770:16
two thousand p. in lead	MIDD 590:71
who will p. longest	WELL 929:1
pounds Fifty p.!	LAWR 513:69
p. will take care	LOWN 540:40
three hundred p. a year!	SHAK 773:10
weight in p., shillings	MILNE 596:22
pour p. on him all we can	HERB 414:82
poverty abolition of p.	HOOV 427:43
against hunger, p., desperation	MARS 575:63
America has mitigated p.	WOOL 955:9
amidst its p. and squalor	ARNO 36:29
best-dressed p.	HARR 398:44
between the ignorance and p.	WALP 918:65
born into the bleakest p.	OBAMA 644:48
destruction of the poor is their p.	BIBLE 104:63
Greed begins where p. ends	BALZ 61:7
hardest thing to bear in p.	JUVE 471:54
hated p.	JOHN 459:43
inhibition attaches to p.	HESI 417:33
In honoured p. thy voice	SHEL 812:59
In p., hunger, and dirt	HOOD 426:30
marry the Irish...look for p.	DONL 290:7
monarchies end by p.	MONT 614:42
Money is better than p.	ALLEN 14:94
no...crime so shameful as p.	FARQ 330:23
P. and oysters...seem to go	DICK 277:52
P. has a home in Africa	HEAD 404:63
p., ignorance and disease	DU 305:70
P. is a great enemy	JOHN 464:85
P. is...blamed on anyone	OCON 647:91
P. isn't being broke	WYLIE 964:12
P. makes peace	ANON 21:55
p. of blackness	DANG 262:28
p.'s catching	BEHN 74:16
prefer p. with liberty	PITT 679:7
represent p. as no evil	JOHN 461:96
So shall thy p. come	BIBLE 104:59
struggled with p.	BALD 57:18
terrible reality of p.	LEGU 520:14
there for honest P.	BURNS 180:52
trouble with p.	KRUG 500:22
upon p., vice, and misery	SUMN 859:81
where p. is enforced	DOUG 296:26
worst of crimes is p.	SHAW 809:70
pow blessings on your frosty p.	BURNS 179:16
powder keep her in paint and p.	NIMI 639:25
keep your p. dry	BLAC 137:42
take a p. and they are gone	ACHE 3:45
powdered Still to be p.	JONS 467:60
powders P. and liquids	DOYLE 297:75
rogue gives you Love P.	LAMB 505:86
power above thy p.	BIBLE 113:93
according to the p. that worketh	BIBLE 128:89
add reach to p.	ACHE 3:55
all p. is a trust	DISR 287:16
Almighty p. Hurled	MILT 601:33
antithesis...is not pleasure, but p.	DE 273:83
apt words have p.	MILT 607:88
awful shadow of some unseen P.	SHEL 812:55
beauty...hath strange p.	MILT 608:96
because they confer p.	RUSS 734:28
because we had p.	BENET 79:28
best in his p.	TROL 898:41
Black p.	ANON 25:57
brute p. and human need	COMM 239:95
certainty of p.	DAY 267:35
changing it is within our p.	REAG 708:10
charm of all p. is modesty	ALCO 12:41
conceal the p. of the atom	COLE 234:1
conceive a dominant p.	HARDY 397:7
constructs p. structures	LEGU 520:12
corridors of p.	ALLEN 13:74
corruption of p.	BRON 160:50
cowards...sit safe in p.	OTWAY 656:2
Creator's p. display	ADDI 7:67
cult...religion with no political p.	WOLFE 953:76
defy P., which seems omnipotent	SHEL 815:20
delightful and delighting p.	MITF 610:50
depository of p.	DISR 287:29
descriptive p....literary style	PULI 699:72
Desire of p.	DRYD 302:79
desire of p. after p.	HOBB 420:1
desire to seek p.	BACON 51:84
devil hath p.	SHAK 782:4
differences of speed And p.	PRATT 694:68
drape over their will to p.	HUXL 442:98

praise

dream of independent p.	JAY 453:99	p. of asking questions	RUSS 734:21	welcome, thou dread p.!	BYRON 188:65
drunk with sight of p.	KIPL 490:17	p. of beauty	SHAK 783:9	what sustains interest…is p.	JIANG 455:56
During my tenure of p.	PEEL 672:67	p. of Christianity	WHIT 936:70	When p. corrupts	KENN 482:27
earthly p. doth then show	SHAK 770:13	p. of holding…beliefs	ORWE 655:76	When p. leads man	KENN 482:27
eat the p. out of women	WEST 933:96	p. of its own	BACON 50:44	who will come to p.	SHEV 818:11
Eternal God of p.	TENN 875:10	p. of judging well	DESC 274:93	will to p. must increase	LEGU 520:9
excessive love for the balance of p.	BRIG 159:14	p. of kings and magistrates	MILT 601:24	With barefaced p.	SHAK 797:44
existence of mankind in its p.	ADAMS 5:85	p. of life and death	BIBLE 112:79	women breached the p. structure	WOLF 952:62
expression of the will to p.	PAZ 671:49	p. of man	SHAK 797:55	ye shall receive p.	BIBLE 124:70
fealty to those in p.	MAMET 564:39	p. of many	SHEL 812:54	You don't have p. if	TODD 893:36
feel herself a source of p.	BROO 163:10	p., Of many ways to die	MILT 606:65	powerful evil spirit…supremely p.	DESC 275:99
fool, In p. of others	MILT 607:84	p. of miracle	FEUE 334:2	'It's p.,' he said	HUGH 435:16
Force is a spiritual p.	LEON 522:70	p. of money is…male p.	DWOR 308:44	more p. conclusion	SOLOW 833:4
fourth p….into two p.s	FERM 333:94	P. of new Masters	ALBE 11:33	More p. than a locomotive!	SIEG 820:61
friend in p. is a friend lost	ADAMS 5:88	p. of newspapers	TOCQ 892:31	p. hard thing	CONN 243:23
full of p.	TENN 875:2	p. of purchasing other goods	SMITH 827:78	p. men in our society	BELL 77:81
gauge of their real p.	LESS 524:94	p. of reasoned speech	ARIS 31:26	preparedness makes us p.	GOER 374:56
given women so much p.	JOHN 461:6	p. of science	SHAP 805:68	republic has been much more p.	ADDI 6:21
God…loved the People in P.	PATC 668:8	p. of Solidarity	WALE 917:27	this p.…kingdom	PITT 679:2
good, and had no p. to see	LANY 508:53	p. of solitude	NORTH 641:60	two most p. poets	ELIOT 317:93
guessing p.	BAGE 54:77	p. of steady misrepresentation	DARW 263:54	wealthier or more p.	HELO 409:54
guilt and p.	TOPL 894:61	p. of temptation	TROL 897:32	powerless any other world p.	THUB 890:60
have the p. to die	TENN 877:62	p. of the hope of freedom	BUCK 172:34	FBI are p. to act	HOOV 427:67
history of political p.	POPP 689:57	p. of the human intellect	LEWIS 527:65	p. to be born	ARNO 35:4
hold on to p. until then	WANG 920:98	p. of the will	MORAN 618:9	powerlessness idealized into p.	JONG 466:39
if he had the p.	MILL 591:3	p. of the written word	CONR 243:26	resurrection…is always p.	WILL 944:71
its source of p.	KINN 488:61	p. or respect in the world	BAGE 54:76	powers all rest my p. defy	DONNE 291:19
Knowledge is p.	BACON 49:17	p. over people	SOLZ 833:5	all th' ethereal p.	MILT 607:72
lawful p. is still superior	DRYD 302:93	p. over women	LEGU 520:13	distinction in the intellectual p.	DARW 263:57
legislative p.	GIBB 366:91	p., peace and healing	MATT 582:1	exercised the p. committed to me	PEEL 672:67
legislative p. vested	LOCKE 533:87	P. requires that one do	SART 744:64	explore unknown p.	SHEL 812:47
Literature is a p. line	CURT 259:97	P. tends to corrupt	ACTON 4:69	feeble p. of my mind	SIDN 820:35
love of p.	HAZL 403:36	p. that can make us truthful	BONH 146:22	full use of your p.	KENN 482:29
magic and delicious p.	WOOLF 955:27	p. that created	THUR 891:97	greatest p. of the world	PALM 662:74
making our p. credible	KENN 481:6	p. that I have on you	SHAK 803:9	immense new p. on man	CHUR 226:5
manners, virtue, freedom, p.	WORD 958:94	p. to add or detract	LINC 529:10	Legislation's sov'reign p.	BURNS 178:96
mans body both for p.	SPEN 838:32	p. to ask for love	SHAW 806:90	mind of large general p.	JOHN 463:71
man's p. of selection	DARW 263:52	P. To chasten and subdue	WORD 956:55	p. of intelligence	LYND 543:92
means most within our p.	MALT 563:23	p. to cloud men's minds	BAKER 56:8	p. of old Europe	MARX 579:33
measure the p.	MACC 546:67	p. to communicate	WOOLF 955:17	p. of the state	GIBB 366:92
Men of p.	FOOT 342:82	p. to do any damn fool thing	FULB 355:61	p. that be are ordained	BIBLE 126:29
microscopes of hextra p.	DICK 278:57	p. to do me harm	SHAK 790:67	productive p. of labour	SMITH 827:75
mind…when it attacks p.	STAEL 841:93	p. to end it	SASS 745:79	prostitute all their p.!	FORS 345:42
Moghul Empire is in our p.	CLIVE 231:39	P.…to him who dares	DOST 294:90	rise of misplaced p.	EISE 314:2
Monopoly p. must be abused	SIMO 822:81	p. to hurt and will	SHAK 802:69	towards the democratic p.	MASA 580:49
more contracted that p. is	JOHN 463:59	p. to learn	PLATO 682:65	vital p. wither	WILB 939:38
most p. to hurt us	BEAU 71:19	p. To live, and act	WORD 961:43	we lay waste our p.	WORD 961:30
must climb to p.	TAWN 868:43	p. to love, or hate	MARL 574:37	with large p. and privileges	PENN 673:81
name is in p.	NAPO 630:52	p. to make dance	NOON 640:45	ye heavenly p.	GOET 375:61
Never lacks p. to dismiss itself	SHAK 776:14	p. to make the world a desert	STEV 850:5	pox p. of her autumnal face	JONS 467:59
New nobility is but the act of p.	BACON 52:93	p. to master words	SCAR 746:13	practical as p. as the theory	OPPE 652:88
nexus of all love and money and p.	DIDI 286:81	p. to shake me	WORD 960:22	by p. achievements	TAWN 868:43
no hope but from p.	BURKE 175:28	P. to the people	ANON 21:30	Don't be 'p.' in politics	CONN 243:20
no man…hath p. over the spirit	BIBLE 106:24	p. to touch our senses	MILT 597:35	For most p. purposes	UPDI 905:19
none can call our p. to account?	SHAK 798:65	p. we embody	JORD 469:2	hard and p. man	HOYLE 434:95
no p. game	JONG 466:31	p. with our purpose	KENN 482:28	might have a p. use	UREY 906:42
no p. on earth	BALD 57:31	p. without responsibility	BALD 57:30	original p. example	WHIT 938:3
Not by might, nor by p.	BIBLE 112:60	present possessors of p.	BURKE 175:9	seeks after immediate p. utility	HELM 408:51
nothing left but money and p.	STAEL 841:95	proletariat can take p.	TROT 899:67	practice bloody or murmuring p.	STUB 858:61
Now we have shown our p.	SHAK 799:99	proud Edward's p.	BURNS 180:47	doctrines and p. of Socialism	MORR 620:51
obedience is ever sought for by p.	WOLL 954:88	pure function, and best p.	WORD 958:89	easier with p.	GREE 386:24
Of p., of honour	MARL 573:21	Repentance…want of p. to sin	DRYD 304:53	no p. without art	PROT 697:33
Passion and the p. to roam	BYRON 187:48	responsibility without p.	STOP 855:14	offending both legal and natural p.	STOP 855:15
People who obtain p.	VIDAL 912:87	satisfying exercise Of p.	MACB 546:62	Politics, as a p.	ADAMS 5:86
political p. and philosophy	PLATO 682:63	self-limited writers have a p.	WOOLF 955:18	p.…be greatly simplified	CARL 199:69
Politics determine who has the p.	KRUG 500:27	self-sufficing p. of Solitude	WORD 958:78	proved them wrong in p.	LESS 524:4
pomp of p.	GRAY 384:66	sheer joyous p. of song	BEER 74:91	rather of instinct than of p.	REED 710:33
p. a corrupter	SHEL 812:51	slow-chapped p.	MARV 577:93	respiration—a troublesome p.	DICK 278:63
p. and his love	GRANT 381:5	some P. the giftie gie us	BURNS 177:87	something which works in p.	HELL 408:38
p. and money and fine robes	WELD 928:83	spirit…of p., and of love	BIBLE 129:25	stoop from speculation to p.	MACA 545:43
p. and spirit of America	NORR 641:57	spiritual will to p.	NIET 638:8	trainer…knows in his p.	RYLE 736:61
p., and the glory	BIBLE 115:42	still and solemn p.	SHEL 812:54	practices consists of p. of this kind	HEATH 405:86
P. and War	KIPL 490:93	such unlimited p.	ADAMS 4:71	no place for restrictive p.	WILS 948:61
p. attractive shines	MARL 572:98	that diffusion of p.	OAKE 642:2	practise p. to deceive!	SCOTT 752:24
p. can be…applied	LEUP 525:15	That false secondary p.	WORD 958:80	practiser frequent p. of…angling	WALT 920:92
p. can be rightfully exercised	MILL 591:99	the balance of p.	PALM 662:74	practising p. long shies	JOYCE 470:19
p. can get people	KAZIN 474:53	The good want p.	SHEL 814:10	practitioners art for p. and readers	LEAV 517:52
p. divine	WORD 962:47	The greater the p.	BURKE 175:12	many p. make a living	SUTH 860:7
p. divine…wash the river Rhine?	COLE 236:50	The press has enormous p.	TOCQ 892:30	prætorian P. here, p. there	SCOTT 753:48
P. Girt round with weakness	SHEL 815:36	This beautiful and beauty-making p.	COLE 235:31	prairie p. flowers lie low	LIND 530:22
p. in small things	SOPH 834:27	Thy p. to save	DODD 289:93	prairies rife as the loam Of p.	CRANE 253:66
P. into will	SHAK 786:26	ungodly in great p.	BOOK 149:13	speech of England…The P.	BRYA 170:9
P. is my mistress	NAPO 630:48	United States as an independent p.	GEOR 364:48	praise all other p. is shame	SIDN 820:51
P. is not a means	ORWE 655:78	use of his p.	HOBB 420:99	community…lived in p. of God	ELIOT 319:33
P. is the ultimate aphrodisiac	KISS 493:86	vast amounts of p. could be released	EINS 313:78	counterpoise to unintelligent p.	WAUGH 924:85
p. justifications would go on	STEI 846:93	Visionary p.	WORD 958:84	countryman must have p.	BLYT 144:87
p. of all true art	EINS 313:80	weakening of the royal p.	INNO 446:48	courage to give you unqualified p.	STEI 846:85

praised 1246

Damn with faint p.	POPE 687:3	people's p.	DRYD 302:77	**predict** model to p....anything	ADAMS 6:11
garment of p.	BIBLE 110:6	P. Book of Edward VI	ACHE 2:28	**predicting** better at p. events	STOP 856:23
girded with p.	GRANT 381:5	p., observance, discipline	ELIOT 320:78	**prediction** regardless of p.	RICH 713:93
Give them not p.	SORL 834:33	p. of a righteous man	BIBLE 130:62	**predilection** p. for genre fiction	DISCH 287:9
giving hand...shall have fair p.	SHAK 763:10	Shakespeare and a p. book	BAIN 55:95	p....is with us	AUDEN 43:2
guests should p. it	HARI 398:32	Thy wish nor p.	VAUG 909:33	**pre-eminence** keep...the p.	BIBLE 113:7
Heedless o' p.	MACD 549:27	wing and a p.	ADAM 6:13	**preface** P. to a...Suicide Note	BARA 63:41
His p. forth tell	KETHE 483:67	wish for p.	BERN 85:59	**prefer** Did not p. You	DRAY 298:96
His p. forth tell	SCOT 755:88	wish her gratefu' p.	BURNS 178:95	p. the destruction	HUME 438:99
if men withheld their p.	SHEEN 811:44	**prayers** added vexation of p.	TWAIN 902:41	**preference** P. and prejudice creep in	HILL 418:59
In deeper reverence p.	WHIT 938:24	Christopher Robin is saying his p.	MILNE 596:13	p. which it is forced	LAMB 505:94
In p. of what another's said	YEATS 966:15	devotion and our p.	FRIE 351:76	with p. and aversion	SHER 817:71
itch of p.?	CAREW 198:46	Fall to thy p.	SHAK 773:99	work: if not by p.	BAUD 69:84
knowledge and her p.	MILT 604:6	Forgets her p.	SITW 823:97	**preferment** knocking at P.'s door	ARNO 34:87
let all the people p. thee	BIBLE 101:80	Knelt down with angry p.	HODG 421:23	**pregnancy** avoid p....mathematics	MENC 587:7
let the song of p. be sung	POTT 690:81	know whose p.	KIPL 490:95	**pregnant** finish...without getting p.	ANON 26:98
little dust of p.	TENN 874:86	not very addicted to p.	ASHF 38:71	like being a little p.	HEND 410:1
mouth shall shew forth thy p.	BIBLE 101:74	P. for the condemned man	WEST 933:93	Like finding oneself p.	ACHE 2:36
Never p. a sister	KIPL 489:69	p. for the observers of his law	BACON 52:92	mad'st it p.	MILT 601:31
only the master shall p.	KIPL 490:15	p. of liberty-loving people	EISE 314:92	strong pillars and p. supporters	BAIL 55:89
outstrip all p.	SHAK 804:26	p. of the church, to preserve	SWIFT 863:73	trying to stay half p.	BOHL 144:98
paint 'em truest p. 'em most	ADDI 6:20	p. they dare not speak aloud	WILDE 940:44	**prejudice** Borat...lets people...expose	
p. any man	SHAK 794:64	set it in my p.	SHAK 804:22	their own p.	BARON 64:80
P....can freeze the heart	BUCK 172:36	solemn p. for the great exaltation	COLU 239:91	critic...without p.	NATH 632:3
p. effect in mighty minds	DRYD 302:78	sudden on some p.	BROW 166:99	free from interest or p.	REES 710:38
P. for the singing!	FARJ 330:19	yet like p. divine	SHAK 802:77	let no p....asperse them	EMMET 325:6
P. God, from whom	KEN 480:84	**prayeth** He p. well	COLE 235:20	Preference and p. creep in	HILL 418:59
P. him	HOPK 428:73	**praying** No p., it spoils business	OTWAY 656:6	p. runs in favour of two	DICK 278:76
p. him and exalt him	BIBLE 133:41	**prays** never trust a person who p.	KING 487:40	P....vagrant opinion	BIER 135:90
P. life, it deserves p.	JEFF 453:18	Whatever a man p.	TURG 901:19	Race p....a shadow	BUCK 172:33
p. should sing	LYTE 543:93	**preach** could never p.	AUST 46:70	suburban p. of anti-Semitism	POUND 692:30
P. the Lord	FORGY 344:19	p. among the Gentiles	BIBLE 127:87	the p....run in favour of two	SHER 817:74
P. the sports of the land	REID 710:45	p. good tidings unto the meek	BIBLE 110:6	To everybody's p.	GILB 369:56
P. to the Holiest	NEWM 635:49	P. not because you have to say	WHAT 934:15	Travel is fatal to p.	TWAIN 902:35
pudding against empty p.	POPE 688:30	p. the discovery of the 'new'?	INGR 446:39	We call it p.	CRIC 254:92
sing the p.	MARV 578:11	P. the word	BIBLE 129:29	**prejudices** Drive out p.	FRED 349:39
so long as it's unqualified p.	COWA 249:62	**preacher** as the P. saith	HARDY 397:25	employ their reason to justify p.	WOLL 953:86
song in thy p.	BURNS 178:10	village p.'s modest mansion	GOLD 376:99	honest p....of a true Englishman	ADDI 7:35
Teach the free man how to p.	AUDEN 43:94	**preachers** don't believe in p.	BENE 79:13	our errors, our p., our dreams	POPP 689:62
the p. of his holy Name	BOOK 148:86	pirates, p.	SYNGE 865:23	paradoxes than of p.	ROUS 729:14
this rich p.	SHAK 802:66	**preaching** Christian p.	BARTH 66:11	Passions destroy more p.	DIDE 285:60
unmerited p.	JOHN 463:73	foolishness of p.	BIBLE 126:35	p., misconceptions	LLOY 553:78
utter all thy P.	ADDI 7:38	gone about p.	JERO 454:43	**prelates** p. in habitis clericall	DUNB 306:2
without hope of p.	JOHN 460:67	p....one of the most healthy exercises	WESL 932:71	**prelude** p. to insanity	WAUGH 923:60
praised more in him to be p.	JONS 468:91	p. point is not a meeting point	THER 882:83	p. to resurrection	WILL 944:71
p. him to his face	TENN 879:99	woman's p. is like a dog	JOHN 461:3	**preludes** p. to that eternal separation	STER 848:46
p. the living God	FOX 346:71	**preamble** Pardon my long p.	LAWR 514:87	**premium** greater p. on temperament	BRAD 155:46
praises high p. of God	BIBLE 104:50	**precautions** take some elementary p.	LEVIN 525:29	**prentices** schoolboys, and sour p.	DONNE 291:25
sing p. lustily	BOOK 149:12	take the necessary p.	CRISP 255:3	**preoccupation** chief p. to avoid	LESS 523:90
praising doing one's p. for oneself	BUTL 185:97	took p. against it	GALS 358:48	one constant p.	RUSS 734:35
P. all alike, is p. none	GAY 362:10	**precedence** battle for p.	SITW 824:12	**preparation** complete lack of p.	WAVE 925:3
P. what is lost	SHAK 791:72	believe I take p.	SAKI 739:67	no p. for the future	DISR 287:25
walking, and leaping, and p. God	BIBLE 124:74	claim in hell P.	MILT 602:56	no p. is thought necessary	STEV 852:58
when I am p. anyone	BEER 73:76	**precedency** p. between a louse	JOHN 464:88	when p. meets opportunity	BRAN 156:73
pram enemy of good art...the p.	CONN 242:99	**precedent** From p. to p.	TENN 872:29	**preparations** all the p. with regard to	GOER 374:57
prams p. on concrete balconies	BETJ 88:33	**precedents** there are no p.	DEBU 268:63	**prepare** p. for government	STEEL 844:36
prance mind to p.	JOHN 461:17	**precept** carry p. to the highest	BYRON 189:2	p. to meet thy God	BIBLE 111:52
prater pert, prim P.	CHUR 224:52	Let your p. be, Be Easy	STEE 844:46	p. to shed them now	SHAK 777:42
pray drink sooner than p.	SHAK 771:38	p. must be upon p.	BIBLE 108:69	**prepared** Be P.	BADEN 54:58
dying p. at the last	DILL 286:93	true business p.	DICK 279:14	**preparedness** p. makes us powerful	GOER 374:56
fold her hands and p.	ROSS 726:61	very little p. and practice	EDGE 311:34	**preposterous** p. troop of sons	SOME 833:9
learn to p.	HERB 414:89	**preceptor** artist...p. of his time	BETH 88:13	**Pre-Raphaelite** decorated by a P.-R.	BEER 74:98
nor p. with you	SHAK 769:82	**precepts** if one follows p.	SENE 757:22	**prerogative** first is law, the last p.	DRYD 303:12
P. do not mock.	SHAK 793:31	**precincts** warm p. of the cheerful day	GRAY 384:74	p. of the eunuch	STOP 855:14
p. exclusively of others	WAUGH 924:93	**precious** all p. in God's sight	JACK 448:3	**presage** p. of extinction	SCOTT 751:1
p. for my soul	TENN 878:86	all that's p. in our joys	STER 849:59	**presagers** dumb p.	SHAK 800:42
p. for you	SMITH 831:63	how p. is frivolity!	FORS 345:42	**Presbyterian** P. at Kercaldy	FLEM 340:48
P. God our greatness	TENN 879:3	Life is too p.	ELIOT 315:14	**Presbyterians** regarded by strict P.	THOM 887:96
P. inwardly	JULI 471:42	make vile things p.	SHAK 792:8	**prescription** discards P.	DISR 287:25
P., love, remember	SHAK 784:55	most p. to me	SHAK 798:62	**prescriptions** according to her p.	MORE 619:22
'P., my dear'	STER 847:21	my P., my P.?	TOLK 893:49	p. are not kept	SHAK 803:88
p. thee then	HUNT 439:29	P. in the sight of the Lord	BIBLE 102:21	p. written by patients	KRAUS 499:5
p. to have a sound mind	JUVE 471:58	something positive and p.	PRIT 696:21	rules and p.	NISB 639:27
p. to thy Father	BIBLE 115:41	Thy words are too p.	SHAK 778:62	**presence** castellated, shimmering p.	MORR 620:46
p. we have the wisdom	ALLEN 14:98	**precipice** On the summit of the p.	HOLM 423:55	Cast me not...from thy p.	BIBLE 101:73
p. you do not fall in love	SHAK 779:3	**precise** too p. in every part	HERR 416:17	come before his p. with a song	BOOK 149:32
wash your hands and p.	KIPL 493:69	**precisely** Thinking p.	SOLOW 833:3	come before his p. with thanksgiving	BIBLE 102:1
Watch and p.	BIBLE 119:43	**precision** p. unapproachable	LEAV 517:50	feel the p. of the past	PEI 672:73
When I would p. and think	SHAK 787:62	strung to a vast p.	CRANE 253:60	from whose unseen p.	SHEL 813:79
prayer Conservative Party at p.	ROYD 730:31	**precisions** divisions and p.	ELIOT 317:72	His p. here is...an insult	RED 709:19
fruitless p.	TENN 874:80	**precondition** p. to meaningful action	BART 66:17	horror that her p. excites	GRAV 382:27
given to p.	SHAK 773:2	**pre-Copernican** He's a p.-C.		If thy p. go not with me	BIBLE 94:73
God erects a house of p.	DEFOE 269:69	obscurantist	KEAT 475:58	insult of each other's p.	ISHE 447:50
homes of silent p.	TENN 874:72	**predecessors** shoulders of their p.	RUSS 734:27	majestic p.	HUNT 439:21
house of p.	BIBLE 118:23	steal from their p.	POUND 692:38	not often let their p. be known	DU 305:68
More things are wrought by p.	TENN 878:86	**predestination** Social P. Room	HUXL 441:72	p. of a bad historian	ELTON 323:42
most perfect p.	LESS 524:5	**predestined** everything is p.	HAWK 401:91	p. of absence	BERG 83:27

prick

p. of the cherished child — ELIOT 315:27
p. of the Red Death — POE 683:83
Where God's p. is no longer — STEI 846:98
whither shall I flee from thy p.? — BIBLE 103:44
present afraid of the p. — GREY 388:63
alcohol made the p. enough — GEE 362:28
bitter birthday p. — DILL 286:91
Children…live in the p. — LABR 502:24
conventions of the p. — LEWI 527:77
dialogue between the p. and the past — CARR 202:51
die…when you are…p. — SCEVE 746:17
except for the one p. moment — WILL 945:3
finding myself at p. — MUNDY 625:44
Forsytes were p. — GALS 358:48
For the p. at any rate — ROSE 725:25
future…same stuff as the p. — WEIL 928:71
futurity casts upon the p. — SHEL 816:53
gave it me…for an un-birthday p. — CARR 205:9
give this p. to her dear — LANY 508:55
It is the p. that counts — CELI 211:38
love [looks] to the p. — LEWIS 526:43
man of the p. — HOLM 424:86
men of the p. age — OVER 656:12
more eventful than the p. — ORWE 654:31
no crime like the p. — WASH 922:34
no redress for the p. — DISR 287:25
not live in the p. — THOM 883:1
others, past and p. — NABO 628:16
Piers this p. to plese — LANG 508:48
politics in p. history — FREE 350:47
p. alone was significant — CHOP 223:31
p. at the Creation — EVANS 328:66
p. at their marriages — TROL 897:31
p.…growth out of the past — WHIT 938:10
p.…has a voice — OAKE 642:1
p. in time future — ELIOT 319:36
p. is an age of talkers — HAZL 403:47
p. is an important time — CARL 200:78
p. is burthened too much — HAWT 402:15
p. is the funeral of the past — CLARE 228:53
p. or any future writer — MILL 591:95
p., past and future sees — BLAKE 140:8
p. than in the ooze — NABO 628:13
p. things…as they are — FRED 349:36
shows the world its p. — BETH 87:13
think we're in the p. — KESEY 483:65
this p. were the world's last night? — DONNE 292:57
who controls the p. — ORWE 655:74
presentation mode of p. — SCOTT 751:98
under the p. of that — SHAK 780:26
presents Christmas without any p. — ALCO 12:40
coincided as p. — MURP 626:73
P., I often say — LAMB 505:97
preservation p., and distribution — RUSK 733:97
p. of health — SPEN 836:86
p. of property — LOCKE 533:85
times of p. — SHAK 805:49
preservative pleasantest p. from want — AUST 46:59
preserve frozen, I p. you — ATWO 41:41
p. it from putrefaction — JOHN 464:93
p. thy body and soul — BOOK 147:73
p. thy body and soul — BOOK 147:74
p. thy soul — BIBLE 103:31
preserver Destroyer and p. — SHEL 813:80
time the p. — ELIOT 320:74
presidency cancer…close to the p. — DEAN 267:40
P. provides some happiness — KENN 482:29
question of the P. — DICK 279:2
what does he think the P. is? — EISE 314:7
president advising the former P. — BUSH 182:96
all the P.'s men — KISS 493:87
another Democratic P. — CART 206:49
any boy may become p. — STEV 851:22
any P. of Irish descent — KENN 481:20
bank p. finish the script — EPST 327:35
Being p. is like — TRUM 900:92
capable of choosing a p. — STEIN 845:77
does not speak well of you as a p. — PETE 676:40
don't mind not being P. — KENN 480:96
elected P., not a Pope — STRE 857:52
elected Vice-P. — GARN 360:77
every country ought to have a P. — DOLE 290:99
Every US p. has to have a war — GORB 378:51
fictitious election results that elect a fictitious p. — MOORE 617:93
George Meany could run for P. — DOLE 290:94
him that is the p. — SPEN 837:14
hoping to hear the P. sneeze — MENC 586:2
I can't stop being P. — CLIN 230:5
if Jack were P. of France — ONAS 650:49
If the P. has a bully pulpit — REAG 708:98
If you want to be vice-p. — BRADY 155:52
I'm a better ex-president than…p. — CART 206:52
I was sleeping with the P. — REAG 708:1
make a fine p. — MACA 544:11
Mr Clinton…is our first black P. — MILL 593:50
Mr P., I speak for sixty thousand — HUGH 436:49
Mr P., the p. is dead — ODON 647:94
never…bothered any wartime P. — BIDD 133:52
not to ask the P. — POIN 684:99
Oh, Mr P., do not let — KNOX 495:17
one's husband for a P. — ONAS 650:52
one thing to be said about being P. — EISE 314:5
only have one vice p. — ROGE 722:70
P. bears the burden — KENN 481:53
P. can't get to — GORE 379:58
P. Clinton returned today — DOWD 296:29
P.…has to do everything — ASTU 39:12
P. is a walking dead man — ANON 27:26
p. is incapable of enforcing the law — MARC 569:54
P. looked wiser — KEYN 484:70
P. of the Immortals — HARDY 397:16
P. of the United States — UPDI 905:20
P. Robbins was so well — JARR 452:85
P. should not wear emblems — MCAL 543:1
p.'s penis was on everyone's mind — ROTH 728:93
P.'s vision — SCHL 748:39
P. will go down in history — DOLE 290:98
Running a cemetery…like being P. — ANON 27:27
running for p. — CLOO 232:43
security around the American P. — MAIL 560:61
skills that a P. needs — ONEI 651:77
slept more than any other P. — MENC 586:94
sometimes name the p.? — TANA 867:23
terrific p. — CLIN 231:23
The P. hears a hundred — TRUM 900:88
to the P., not his wife — REGAN 710:41
When a p.…pays attention when the p. does it — GALL 358:45 / NIXON 640:39
presidents disastrous P. — ONAS 650:52
do with all the vice p. — ROGE 722:70
making of our p. — NEW 634:34
p. and ministers — SUN 860:96
P.…pretending to run a crusade — COOKE 245:22
press As for the p. — TOCQ 892:28
competitive p. knows — RUSK 732:79
controversy over freedom…of the p. — ORWE 655:67
fell dead-born from the p. — HUME 439:8
first duty of the p. — TIMES 892:23
freedom of the p. — JEFF 454:26
freedom of the p. in Britain — ORWE 653:22
free p. compels them to bend — MILL 591:92
give up my p.-clippings agency — WODE 952:46
governs the periodical p. — TROL 897:20
inform p. home Christmas — WRIG 963:73
Let's p. the flesh — JOHN 458:17
liberty of the p. — JOHN 461:16
liberty of the p. — JUNI 471:49
liberty of the p. — SHER 818:6
more reliable than the p. — ORWE 654:37
p.…above the law — CAM 193:40
p.…an excellent servant — COOP 246:87
P. freedom — CAM 193:40
P. is at once the eye — STEAD 843:30
P. is the living Jury — BENN 81:81
P. was squared — BELL 77:62
ridicule them in the p. — PULI 699:17
Supposing the p. — LEST 524:8
The p. has enormous power — TOCQ 892:30
The p., the machine wouldn't…rely on the p. — NIET 638:93 / HITCH 420:89
pressure economic blood p. — WRIS 963:78
grace under p. — HEMI 409:67
P. is…the shadow of…opportunity — JOHN 458:21
pressure-cooker p.-c. on simmer — SHAR 806:74
prestige authority and p. — BERE 83:15
great offices…give social p. — BAGE 54:71
presume p. not God to scan — POPE 687:80
p. you're mortal — SHIR 819:19
presumed no more things…be p. — OCCAM 646:81
presumption amused by its p. — THUR 890:71
height of p. — BRAUN 157:81

presumptions in the face of p. — JAMES 450:41
presupposition fundamental p. — HEID 406:11
pretences false p. on dolls — RUNY 731:60
pretend I can't… — PALT 662:76
others p. and don't care — KIPL 490:96
p. to be more stupid — STARK 843:21
why p. that he is? — SHAW 808:33
pretender fight for the P. — SWIFT 862:57
Old P. — GUED 389:83
pretending whoever…you're p. to be — BARN 64:71
pretension p. is nothing — HUNT 439:26
pretensions p. of final truth — NIEB 637:88
undeniable p. as civilisation — PITT 679:10
pretentiousness ugly twin, p. — KUSH 501:45
pretext the rest is only a p. — ELTIT 323:40
pretexts Tyrants seldom want p. — BURKE 176:52
pretty All my p. ones? — SHAK 798:62
Every time they do something p. — SALI 740:74
Leave the p. women — PROU 698:54
p. and picturesque use — HARDY 397:11
p. as an airport — ADAMS 4:79
p., but is it Art? — KIPL 490:97
p. can get away with anything — WAUGH 924:92
p. follies that themselves commit — SHAK 769:93
p. to see what money — PEPYS 674:9
sex object if you're p. — GIOV 372:18
These p. pleasures — RALE 705:43
too successful or too p. — JONG 465:14
Whether you are p. or not — SEXT 758:45
Why shouldn't art be p.? — RENO 711:59
prevenience adorableness and his p. — HUGEL 434:4
prevent knowing how to p. them — RUSS 735:41
p. them from leaving — KENN 481:23
prevention as much for p. as cure — GRAV 382:35
prey alone bent on his p. — MILT 603:85
between the hunter and his p. — ZHAO 970:9
destined p. — SHAW 807:21
expects his evening p. — GRAY 385:86
fear the birds of p. — SHAK 787:50
fleas on him p. — SWIFT 863:66
Into England, to drive a p. — BALL 58:51
lord…yet a p. to all — POPE 687:81
made my pains his p. — SPEN 839:47
soon must be his p. — SHEL 812:65
preys to their p. do rouse — SHAK 797:48
Priam P.'s sons of Troy — SURR 860:5
price another man's p. increase — WILS 948:68
a p. for our values — OBAMA 643:21
at a p. far dearer — SCHAW 747:20
Blood, all p. excelling — AQUI 30:96
buy it of thee at a p. — BIBLE 97:50
couldn't name its p. — GREE 386:7
dear at any p. — WHIS 934:23
give me my p. — BIBLE 112:61
haggling at the p. — GRAV 382:33
If blood be the p. — KIPL 490:10
men have their p. — WALP 919:85
natural p. of labour — RICA 712:79
natural p. of labour — RICA 712:84
pay any p. to get it — IACO 444:1
p. he has to pay — HUXL 441:71
p. is far above rubies — BIBLE 105:7
p.…is poverty, ignorance and disease — DU 305:70
p. of everything…value of nothing — WILDE 941:80
p. of liberty is…dirt — ORWE 653:13
p. of raw produce — RICA 712:80
p. on the Washington Monument? — KENN 482:46
p. paid for becoming a couple — COUP 248:35
p. that the market sets — FRIE 351:70
p. was quite reasonable — MERR 589:51
p. will probably fall — ANON 23:1
real p. of everything — SMITH 827:79
sex is the p. — FRY 354:50
sold at a reasonable p. — AUST 46:73
the natural p. of the other — PETTY 676:45
What P. Glory? — ANDE 17:71
worth more than the p. of the paint — VAN 908:21
worth of a man, is…his p. — HOBB 420:99
prices ceiling over p. — WRIS 963:76
contrivance to raise p. — SMITH 827:81
liberalization of p. — PAVL 670:39
p. will be…different — LEVIN 525:29
reduce the rise in p. — HEATH 405:85
Rising p.…do not cause inflation — WRIS 963:81
prick If you p. us — SHAK 769:1
it is a p. — PEELE 672:70
pain…after the p. — BERN 86:76

pricking

p. the sides of my intent	SHAK 796:20	**primary** cruelty is the p. feeling	SADE 737:14	put not your trust in p.	BOOK 149:38
When the p. stands up	ROTH 728:82	p. requirement for a writer	STAEL 842:99	She's all states, and all p.	DONNE 291:26
pricking By the p. of my thumbs	SHAK 797:53	p. word addresses the eternal Thou	BUBER 171:21	though p. rage	ANON 22:63
p. on the plain	SPEN 838:19	**primative** wildly natural and p.	THOR 888:21	you that are p. born	DAVI 264:75
prickly p. to the smooth	MACD 550:40	**prime** dead ere his p.	MILT 599:82	**princess** ancient Egyptian p.	CASS 207:71
pricks Honour p. me on	SHAK 771:59	fresh colours deck the wanton p.	SPEN 839:39	great p.	FORD 343:1
hundred p. against one	MIZN 610:61	gathered in their p.	SHAK 762:82	p. among the provinces	BIBLE 110:23
kick against the p.	BIBLE 124:80	In the p. of your life	RICH 713:95	the peoples' p.	BLAIR 138:56
p. like thorn	SHAK 765:69	lovely April of her p.	SHAK 800:33	**Princeton** chair at Harvard or P.	MENC 586:89
pride appeals to their p.	KENN 481:99	One's p. is elusive	SPARK 836:68	**principalities** timeless p.	GRAV 382:25
As a matter of racial p.	FEIF 332:56	**Prime Minister** as a P.M. I cannot		**principle** active p. of Wealth	PETTY 676:46
blot upon my p.	SHAK 764:40	be a liar	BERL 85:52	advocates no great p.	HAZL 403:43
breath of degradation and of p.	BYRON 189:84	best P. M. we've got	BUTL 184:61	aesthetic p. of our times	ROGE 722:66
bursting with p.	JOSE 469:7	essentials of a successful P. M.	WILS 948:72	an active P.	WORD 961:40
country's p.	GOLD 376:98	every p. m. ... since		called this p. ... Natural Selection	DARW 263:52
cowardice and false p.	STAN 842:11	Balfour ... died unhappy	HAIL 392:20	Cats seem to go on the p.	KRUT 500:32
coy condescension, modest p.	MILT 604:1	grow up to be P. M.	RICH 714:26	Conservatism ... shrinks from P.	DISR 287:25
Fond P. of Dress	FRAN 348:13	I forget I'm P. M.	BLAIR 138:55	does everything on p.	SHAW 807:97
fosters national p.	HOWE 433:91	last British P. M. with jurisdiction		facts and not ... a p.	DARW 263:59
fount of p.	CULL 257:45	in Ireland	ADAMS 4:82	female p.	LEGU 520:12
harvests bury all his p. has planned	POPE 686:62	man who nearly becomes P. M.	BUTL 184:59	first p. of existentialism	SART 745:73
He that is low no p.	BUNY 174:82	My chances of being PM	JOHN 457:90	formal p. of its colour	SHEL 816:49
In the p. of life	WILDE 940:44	next P. M. but three	BELL 77:62	Greatest Happiness P.	MILL 591:8
know thy p.	BIBLE 96:36	P. M. is the loneliest job	BALD 57:29	identifying oneself with a p.	HEGEL 406:9
Many men have p.	BALZ 61:97	P. M. or Leader of the Opposition	DISR 288:63	It has no other p.	HAZL 403:42
nature's p. and richest furniture!	MARL 572:96	P. M. reading out the conclusions	HESE 416:27	on p., not by instinct	TWAIN 903:82
odious P.	MAND 565:65	that the P. M.'s advisers are responsible		p. in life with me	SHAW 806:96
poet's inward p.	DAY 267:35	is absurd	FOLL 341:70	p. laid down by Gilbert	HUTC 441:50
P. comes before a fall	WELD 928:82	unknown P. M.	ASQU 38:85	p. of the English law	DICK 281:72
p. fell with my fortunes	SHAK 778:60	would not want to be P. M.	THAT 880:46	p. which ... gives us a firm Rock	BUTT 186:14
P. goeth before destruction	BIBLE 105:79	**Prime Ministers** disastrous ... P. m.	ONAS 650:52	p. which prompts to save	SMITH 827:84
p. in having given up his p.	SALI 740:85	**primetime** doesn't help ... when p. TV	QUAY 702:7	rebels from p.	BURKE 176:43
P. is his own glass	SHAK 786:31	**primeval** p. ooze to the stars	VIDAL 912:88	romantic p. of life	NOVA 642:65
P. leaves the heart	GAUT 361:6	This is the forest p.	LONG 535:25	Self-determination ... imperative p.	WILS 949:86
P. makes lawsuits	ANON 21:55	**primitive** comprehend ... p. forms	EINS 313:80	sensibility of p.	BURKE 176:41
p. of distinction	SAND 742:25	most p. and most sophisticated	KUNI 501:40	snob ... on p.	SHAW 809:90
p. of kings	POPE 686:70	p. era was lyrical	HUGO 436:52	tenth time, lack of p.	SIDM 819:33
p. of people in their ... trade	PRIT 696:25	p. form of cricket ... Tip-and-Run	SHAW 810:27	**principles** acceptance of p.	UNIT 905:9
p. of race or spirit	SMITH 831:64	p. men are ... credulous	POPE 686:57	action of religious p.	BERD 83:12
p. of the peacock	BLAKE 140:2	p. music and p. medicine	LEAC 515:17	based on mechanical p.	LEUP 525:14
p., or cowardice	JOHN 464:84	radicals who seem p.	WOLFE 953:73	betrayed the p.	INOU 446:51
P. still is aiming	POPE 687:76	wise p. in a giant jungle	MAIL 559:37	civilization with sound p.	JOHN 456:72
p. struck out new sparkles	DRYD 303:11	**primrose** P. Hill and Saint John's Wood	BLAKE 141:30	contrary to their p.	GALS 358:48
p. which causes thirst	DANTE 262:40	p. path of dalliance	SHAK 781:48	current p. of administration	SIMON 821:74
rank p., and haughtiness of soul	ADDI 7:46	p. that forsaken dies	MILT 599:91	denouncing liberal democratic p.	AUNG 45:39
Ring out false p.	TENN 875:96	p. way	SHAK 797:39	easier to fight for p.	STEV 850:2
soul that perished in his p.	WORD 959:1	**primroses** Wan as p.	KEATS 476:90	fights you on patriotic p.	SHAW 807:97
spite of P.	POPE 687:79	**prince** Advise the p.	ELIOT 316:66	Great nations need organizing p.	CLIN 231:37
Such is our p.	DENH 272:61	bold defiance with his p.	DRYD 302:75	happily arrogating those p.	MAMET 563:28
take p. in the words	KENN 481:24	danced with the P. of Wales	FARJ 330:21	if you surrender all your p.	TODD 893:36
the great and their p.	YEATS 966:11	Dread p. of plackets	SHAK 763:9	man of fixed and unbending p.	DIRK 287:6
the p. of my country I sang	OBRU 646:75	fall of a p.	ANON 20:30	man without p.	FORD 342:88
Thine eyes my p.	SIDN 820:51	Good night, sweet p.	SHAK 785:76	morally acting on the highest p.	SHAW 809:82
time of our love and p.	SU 858:65	Here lies a p.	JOSE 469:8	mythical stories become structural p.	FRYE 354:54
too much weakness for the stoic's p.	POPE 687:80	His Weariness the P.	FIRB 336:52	Politicians ... when they adjust their p.	HATT 400:24
What argufies p. and ambition?	DIBD 276:31	preservation of the P. and State	WENT 931:52	p. are the same	JOHN 464:79
will her p. deflower	SPEN 838:33	P. calls in the good old money	LAMB 505:93	p. around my neck	BALF 58:44
priest both the p. and clerk?	SHAK 765:55	p. is like a mirror	CHAR 215:37	p. employed in science	RUSS 734:22
came down a certain p.	BIBLE 121:80	P. of Europe, should dare to invade	ELIZ 322:4	p. form the bright constellation	JEFF 454:26
Churches built to please the P.	BURNS 177:79	p. of glory died	WATTS 922:46	p. of a free constitution	GIBB 366:91
Delicate-handed p. intone	TENN 876:19	P. of Light	MILT 597:32	p. of equity and justice	PEEL 672:67
parish p. rebuked him	OFLA 647:98	p. of the clouds	BAUD 68:59	p. of mankind	WILS 949:81
p. begets children	SMITH 830:49	p. of the devils	BIBLE 116:65	p. which at first lead to scepticism	BERK 84:32
p. continues what the nurse began	DRYD 303:16	P., thou art sad	SHAK 775:60	putting our p. into execution	WEBB 925:10
p. is given permission	LISP 531:44	safer for a p. to be feared	MACH 553:93	round certain p.	TOCQ 892:30
p. is the worshipper	SHAW 809:69	soothe the p.'s appetite	MASS 581:76	when the p. dissolve	MILL 593:40
p. of the Muses	HORA 430:9	soul of a p.	LOCKE 533:91	wrote 'P. of Political Economy'	BENT 82:2
p., warrior, poet	BAUD 69:86	Sweet p., I come	MARL 573:13	**print** definite ... in p.	COMP 239:2
rid me of this turbulent p.?	HENR 411:11	under the rank of a p.	KING 488:53	eternity of p.	WOOLF 955:20
Thou art a p. for ever	BIBLE 102:18	Were you with these, my p.	ADDI 7:47	keepers of p. and paper	MACL 555:37
why he was a p.	WINT 950:6	Who made thee a p.	BIBLE 93:50	love a ballad in p.	SHAK 800:27
youth ... is nature's p.	WORD 959:4	**Prince Charles** P. C.'s right to marry	INGH 446:35	names in p.	CHES 221:2
priestcraft ere p. did begin	DRYD 301:63	**princedoms** p., virtues, powers	MILT 604:19	p. of a man's naked foot	DEFOE 269:74
p. into a great religious	LEWIS 527:65	**princes** admit p. to the corridors	DOUG 295:5	put them into p.	LESS 524:98
priesthood arcane p.	GOULD 380:77	blaze forth the death of p.	SHAK 777:20	we quarrel in p.	SHAK 780:24
one or another kind of p.	MILL 593:38	make p. in all lands	BOOK 149:16	when they see them in p.	KRAUS 499:75
royal p.	BIBLE 130:67	'must' is not to be used to p.!	ELIZ 322:7	**printed** chaff is p.	HUBB 434:1
priests invention of theologians or p.	NIEB 637:87	Of p. shall outlive	SHAK 801:53	developed, carefully p., fixed	ISHE 447:68
p. and educators	NGU 636:66	pale kings, and p.	KEATS 476:3	**printing** invented the art of p.	CARL 200:89
p. are only men	BROW 169:71	Perfect happiness, by p. sought	CHAP 214:17	p., gunpowder and the magnet	BACON 50:45
p. in black gowns	BLAKE 140:15	power ... shines in p.' eyes!	MARL 572:98	restrained from p.	JOHN 461:16
p. interpreted and interposed	COND 239:12	P. and lords may flourish	GOLD 376:98	**Prior** once was Matthew P.	PRIOR 695:99
P., princes, women	POPE 687:95	P. and lords ... the breath of kings	BURNS 177:76	**priority** without the reward of p.	SCOTT 751:5
p. very dear to the people	TROL 898:35	p. apply themselves	MORE 618:10	**priory** stag in the P. coomb	DAVI 264:68
p. were infinitely more attentive	FITZ 337:75	p. my ancestors followed	ORAH 652:90	**Prism** Charity, dear Miss P.	WILDE 942:7
seize our p.	ANON 21:56	p. should be free	SHAK 759:81	**prism** Newton with his p.	WORD 958:82
women nor with p.	SOUT 835:49	p. to know their true interest	SWIFT 862:47	**prison** endure torture in p.	PANK 662:86

professions

good friend...visits you...in p.	BRAD 154:32	
hero from his p.	AYTO 48:12	
his dwelling, and a p.	WEBS 926:41	
hollow p. of my flesh	SHAK 760:26	
Home is the girl's p.	SHAW 808:53	
impenetrable barriers of our p.	EDGE 311:41	
in p., and ye came unto me	BIBLE 119:36	
opening of the p.	BIBLE 110:6	
palace and a p. on each hand	BYRON 188:58	
pestilential p.	GILB 369:64	
portion as the site of a p.	HAWT 402:4	
P., dungeons, blessed places	GENET 363:40	
p. is to live without mirrors	ATWO 41:42	
p. of his days	AUDEN 43:94	
public school...at home in p.	WAUGH 923:67	
put me in p.	ONDA 650:56	
So cruel p. how could	SURR 860:1	
souls' p. we call England	SHAW 810:8	
Stone walls do not a p. make	LOVE 538:82	
taking him to p.	HOUS 433:81	
true place...also a p.	THOR 888:17	
What is a ship but a p.?	BURT 181:82	
worst of p. life	STEN 847:5	
prisoned p. birds must find	SASS 745:92	
prisoner free not just the p.	OBAMA 645:51	
passing on the p.'s life	SHAK 787:52	
p. in his dungeon	FLAU 339:25	
p.'s release	SIDN 820:46	
sculpture is the p.	THOM 886:78	
your being taken p.	KITC 494:99	
prisoners p., be not despairit	ANON 22:63	
p., handcuffed two	LESS 524:93	
p....I'll find them law	MACQ 558:13	
p. of addiction	ILLI 445:23	
p. out of captivity	BOOK 149:23	
p. were left free to choose	SHAW 808:33	
p. whom they hide	HAWT 402:12	
Queen Victoria treats her p.	WILDE 942:14	
stand p. at the bar	WILDE 940:44	
which p. call the sky	WILDE 942:16	
prison-house grind in the p. h.	BIBLE 96:19	
secrets of the p.-h.	MOOD 615:54	
Shades of the p.-h.	WORD 959:8	
prisons disastrous policy in the p.	KENN 480:98	
P. are built with stones	BLAKE 140:99	
privacy a world where there's no p.	SNOW 832:86	
P. is a privilege not granted	LAUR 511:21	
undisturbed p.	PARK 664:28	
private allurement of p. interest	STEU 849:61	
am to become a p. citizen	EISE 314:3	
better that we stay p. people	SART 744:64	
his p. parts, his money	BUTL 186:10	
hold no brief for p. enterprise	BURT 181:72	
in his p. heart	TWAIN 903:80	
making the p. world public	GINS 372:15	
matter of p. gain	OROZ 652:1	
meddling too much in my p. life	WILL 945:1	
p. animosities	WILL 944:66	
p. enterprise	GALB 357:19	
P. faces in public places	AUDEN 42:67	
p. life...by...public life	ELIOT 315:39	
P. Means is dead	SMITH 830:42	
p. silence in which we live	PRIT 696:21	
p. sports the stews would blush	MASS 581:74	
public good P. respects	MILT 608:93	
She's p. to herself	BEAU 70:12	
takes no p. road	POPE 687:91	
privations hardships, p.	PEARY 671:59	
physical p. philosophically	MOOD 615:52	
privatization P. must come after	PAVL 670:39	
privatize p. the cost of childhood	HEWE 417:38	
privilege heaven-born p.	ARNO 36:29	
inestimable p. of man	SHEL 812:50	
most cherished p.	STRA 856:38	
p. I claim for my own sex	AUST 47:90	
p. of always moving	LEWIS 526:40	
p. of wisdom to listen	HOLM 424:83	
to maintain this p.	DU 305:70	
privileged certain p. few	OROZ 652:1	
not from its p. classes	TWAIN 903:72	
They were p. children	BROO 163:8	
Third Estate...without the p. classes?	SIEY 820:62	
privileges one of the p.	LURIE 542:66	
p. of misery	DONO 293:82	
p. on the basis of a physical characteristic	BOTHA 152:79	
with large powers and p.	PENN 673:81	
prize eye on the p.	ANON 26:94	
lawful p.	GRAY 383:54	
Let old Timotheus yield the p.	DRYD 303:35	
looks to gain the p.	MARL 572:98	
luck o' the p.	BURNS 180:43	
Nobel is just another p.	HEAN 405:80	
one receiveth the p.?	BIBLE 126:44	
p. of half a crown	WAUGH 923:66	
p. of the high calling	BIBLE 128:2	
P. Of wit or arms	MILT 597:47	
p. we sought is won	WHIT 938:7	
prize-fighters p.-f. shaking hands	MENC 586:97	
prizes be given to them	SMITH 830:96	
world continues to offer glittering p.	BIRK 136:12	
probability p. is the very guide of life	BUTL 184:57	
problem American Negro p.	BALD 56:13	
a point of view, a p.	POPP 689:59	
confront a p.	GIUL 373:34	
dearly loved difficult p.	ANON 20:31	
Hang a lantern on your p.	MATT 582:96	
have yet to see any p.	ANDE 17:73	
it is not a money p.	CLIN 230:2	
main p. of the actor?	OLIV 649:42	
marital p.	KEIL 479:60	
obvious that there's no real p.	FEYN 334:6	
one philosophical p.	POPP 689:60	
one truly serious philosophical p.	CAMUS 195:83	
only concrete p. I know	CAMUS 196:88	
philosophical p. has the form	WITT 951:25	
p. for the invisible man	ELLI 323:38	
p. in making our power	KENN 481:6	
p. is food	DONL 290:8	
p. is not style but quality	ROGE 722:68	
p. is not whether machines think	SKIN 825:47	
p. is their subjugation	THOM 883:12	
p. lay buried	FRIE 350:64	
p. of race and color	DU 305:70	
p. of the Sudeten Germans	HITL 420:95	
p. of the twentieth century	DU 304:65	
p. of when and where	TOLS 894:54	
p. was to make unfamiliar	CONR 244:47	
p. without a gift	BACH 49:12	
p. with the US economy	KRUG 500:23	
prospect of tackling an unsolved p.	SHIP 818:13	
social p. of the twentieth century	SMALL 826:58	
social p. solved	MACD 549:34	
solution to the p.	LEMAY 521:30	
Solving a p. is hard enough	LEVI 526:34	
they can't see the p.	CHES 221:9	
three-pipe p.	DOYLE 297:55	
you're part of the p.	CLEA 229:78	
problematic lives are at their most p.	DE 268:51	
problems all kinds of p.	PARRA 665:49	
architectural p. of our own day	POEL 683:95	
Diplomatic p. used to be discussed	ACHE 2:82	
do not choose our p.	FROMM 352:88	
his p. in living	SZASZ 865:28	
insoluble p.	GARD 360:70	
methodological p.	LEWO 528:78	
No p. can be solved	BURR 181:67	
p. are solved...by arranging	WITT 951:24	
p....may be inevitable	ASIM 38:79	
p. of biography, of history	MILLS 595:6	
p. of three little people	EPST 327:29	
p. that we are facing	PAVL 670:41	
p. which the man	KRUT 500:30	
p. with your main character	ANON 26:1	
Science...with p.	POPP 689:64	
show people the p.	GATES 361:94	
so many couples are having p.	CART 207:57	
two kinds of Arctic p.	STEF 844:52	
two p. in my life	HOME 425:95	
procedure p. that spells much	DOUG 295:21	
procedures set p. and expressions	BAND 61:10	
proceeds p. of human sweat	FRAN 348:23	
with a good conscience on the p.	SMITH 829:18	
process inner p.	WITT 951:28	
malpractice...and illegitimate p.	CLOU 232:58	
Obscenity is a cleansing p.	MILL 594:91	
painful p. of Unthinking	CUMM 257:50	
path and p. taken	LIEB 529:96	
phase in a continuing p.	ROBI 718:94	
p. of learning	WILD 943:53	
p. should be effected	RUSS 734:30	
take the energy p. seriously	LEARY 517:47	
The first p. in art	THEO 882:79	
too considered a p.	BARN 64:70	
uncertain p. of letter-writing	ELIOT 315:14	
procession p. of one	DICK 280:23	
proclaiming p. as I go	PLATO 681:43	
proclamations p....slapped up	HEMI 409:64	
procrastination incivility and p.	DE 274:85	
p. is the art	MARQ 574:47	
procreation main road of p.	WAUGH 923:62	
Procrustes P. was an editor	SKEL 825:42	
proctors prudes for p.	TENN 872:31	
procurator p. Pontius Pilate	TACI 866:7	
prodigal chariest maid is p. enough	SHAK 781:47	
how p. the soul	SHAK 781:55	
p. of ease?	DRYD 302:73	
prodigality diminished by p.	SMITH 827:83	
prodigies danger of coming back p.	AUST 46:73	
thousand horrid P.	JOHN 459:60	
prodigy normal child and not as a p.	BARB 63:45	
produce price of raw p.	RICA 712:80	
p. and consumption	MALT 563:23	
p. something cheap	GILL 371:88	
p. without working	INGR 446:40	
what shall this land p.?	RANS 706:68	
producer truck, a p. or a critic	LEMM 521:32	
producers association of the p.	ENGE 326:15	
produces never p. anything great	REYN 712:70	
product a p. of my environment	NICH 636:78	
artist...p....of his time	BETH 88:13	
infinitesimal fraction of a p.	CARL 200:99	
p. of a scoffer's pen	WORD 961:37	
p. of mental labour	MARX 579:40	
p. of the untalented	CAPP 197:32	
production development in p.	MARX 579:30	
development of p.	MARX 579:45	
end and purpose of all p.	SMITH 828:88	
labour-time...for its original p.	MARX 579:39	
Laws of P.	MILL 591:93	
noblest p. of human nature	ADDI 6:26	
past heroes of p.	LOWE 540:39	
p. of objective fact	MENC 586:3	
p. of surplus-value	MARX 579:40	
p. of the higher animals	DARW 263:53	
simply in the p.	RUSK 733:97	
society that will organize p.	ENGE 326:15	
the means of p.	STRA 856:35	
productivity increase p.	HEATH 405:85	
national p.	WRIS 963:80	
products brings out the best in p.	SARN 743:56	
do not choose our p.	FROMM 352:88	
make good p.	STEV 849:62	
p. of all the colonies	SITW 824:12	
p. of editing	WALD 916:24	
profanation in the less, foul p.	SHAK 787:59	
p. of our joys	DONNE 292:38	
profane Coldly p.	CRAB 251:28	
profaneness Avoid, P.; come not here	HERB 413:57	
profanity speak English and p.	HOWE 433:90	
utter p. to show how exciting it was	CHRI 223:40	
profession adopt politics as a p.	HOWE 434:93	
branches of a new p.	TROL 898:47	
choose a p.	PASC 667:86	
Composing is not a p.	HONE 425:13	
cowards by p.	DRYD 301:62	
discharge of any p.	JOHN 462:35	
doctor who...has mistaken his p.	SHAW 810:91	
general scandal of my p.	BROW 164:42	
hold up Adam's p.	SHAK 784:60	
honourable p.	GREE 386:19	
in any other p....offensive	WAUGH 924:85	
Medicine is a noble p.	ROLL 723:89	
only p. for which no	STEV 852:58	
practice of his own p.	JOHN 456:72	
p....consists of bringing truths	HENZE 412:24	
p. of book writing	STEI 846:89	
P. of Play-poets...unlawfull	PRYN 698:62	
put into a 'p.'	BETJ 88:32	
rather than a p.	GRAV 382:26	
shortest-lived p. on earth	ROGE 723:85	
take the place of every p.	MARI 571:80	
You have always a p.	AUST 47:88	
professional being a p. writer	ROST 727:73	
distinguishes...from the p.	LYTT 543:95	
maws of the p.	KEYN 484:78	
p. duty of the advertising agent	OGIL 648:5	
p. players are soccer slaves	CHAR 216:46	
professionals between expert p.	KEYN 484:78	
Politicians...are p.	EICH 313:72	
professions All p. are conspiracies	SHAW 809:81	

professor

go forth unto p.	KENN 480:91
In limited p.	SHAK 791:81
let in some of all p.	SHAK 797:39
Politics...whatever its p.	ADAMS 5:86
p. which are full	THOR 888:33
way of their own p.	JONS 468:89
professor called a p. emeritus	LEAC 515:22
mind...too wide for a p.	MENC 586:89
non-Jewish p.	TILL 891:16
P. Twist could not	NASH 631:70
Zarathustra, sometime regius p.	JOYCE 470:28
professors American p.	LEWIS 527:60
conscientious p. thereof	PAINE 660:32
Respectable P. of the Dismal Science	CARL 201:39
smelly gangrene of p.	MARI 571:78
profiles infinite number of p.	THOR 888:24
two p. clapped together	ASQU 38:93
profit I despise p.	OLIV 649:39
In all labour there is p.	BIBLE 104:72
merchants...intent on p.	PIUS 680:18
my p. had I known	TENN 877:59
my p. on't	SHAK 803:13
p. of capital rises	MARX 579:35
p. without individual responsibility	BIER 134:72
rate of p.	SMITH 827:82
refreshment and p.	COLU 239:91
such p. he of envy	SURR 860:99
Thieves out, p. in!	ANON 20:24
What p. hath a man	BIBLE 105:9
profits best of all monopoly p.	HICKS 417:46
civilization and p.	COOL 245:77
natural tendency of p.	RICA 712:80
status and p. of war	TREV 896:10
profound French are not p.	BROO 163:15
p., evocative and universal	NUTT 642:75
p. loves the mask	NIET 638:9
turbid look the most p.	LAND 506:27
profundity misty p.	WHIT 936:62
through the vast p.	MILT 605:30
programme Labour...election p.	SNOW 832:88
p. of the world's peace	WILS 949:85
terrorist's p.	JONAS 465:14
programming scrutinize the p.	MUMF 625:39
progress any measure of its p.	PERK 675:27
Congress makes no p.	LIGNE 529:97
conservatism and p.	TROL 897:29
Conservatism...disavows P.	DISR 287:25
Conservative ideal of...p.	MADAN 558:15
dependent for p.	RUSS 734:27
Donald Trump is the price of p.	KRUG 500:23
encouraging the p. of science	JEFF 454:25
essential to mutual p.	WASH 921:23
essential to the future p. of the race	CARN 202:48
great p. in the world	HALI 393:31
history of p.	MACA 545:42
history of p.	MACA 546:57
human beings will live and p.	DU 305:69
human p.	GARI 360:72
injurious to the p. of science	DARW 263:56
its p. cannot but be slow	JOHN 460:86
moral and social p.	MILL 591:94
party of p. or reform	MILL 591:1
present stage of human p.	HOOV 427:46
p. depends on the unreasonable	SHAW 808:49
p. has no definite...meaning	SART 744:63
P. is a comfortable disease	CUMM 258:67
p.—is always revolutionary	POPP 689:54
p. is utter delusion	MILL 594:63
P., man's distinctive mark	BROW 169:64
p. of human knowledge	FRAN 348:18
p. of society and wealth	RICA 712:80
p. through the world	LONG 536:36
promote social p.	UNIT 905:9
same each time with p.	BENN 79:33
scientific and technical p.	JOHN 456:72
since Social P. began	KIPL 493:79
sing the p.	DONNE 291:30
skin of p.	SOYI 835:59
social p.	JOHN 456:74
speak...about making p.	POPP 689:63
swell a p.	ELIOT 316:66
thanking the God of P.	LEWIS 527:55
turtle...makes p.	ANON 27:16
War is a condition of p.	RENAN 711:47
When one hears of p.	SKEL 825:41
progression by gradual p.	ARIS 31:18
p. of exploded fallacies	RAND 706:54
Without contraries is no p.	BLAKE 139:94
progressive liberal and p.	TRIL 897:15
p. who is prudent	JOHN 458:11
truly cumulative and p.	SART 744:63
prohibiting licensing and p.	MILT 600:7
prohibition Communism is like p.	ROGE 723:77
p. so divine	SHAK 803:97
project p....for...shopkeepers	SMITH 828:87
p. for extracting sun-beams	SWIFT 862:46
projected it's what's p.	PRICE 695:82
projections other figures...p.	ELIOT 321:97
pro-jobs cannot be p.-j.	TSON 900:8
proletarians p. have nothing to lose	MARX 579:34
proletariat dictatorship of the p.	MARX 579:45
English p....more bourgeois	ENGE 326:12
p. can take power	TROT 899:67
the true p.	BLIX 142:62
prologue foolish thing...long p.	BIBLE 113:12
witty p. to a very dull play	CONG 240:33
prolonged War is being deliberately p.	SASS 745:79
prom libel on a Yale p.	PARK 663:8
Prometheus Fire which P. filch'd	BYRON 189:98
promiscuity emotional p.	MAIL 560:51
sexuality and p.	WYLIE 964:11
promise against reason, against p.	DICK 283:13
appalling p.	AUDEN 43:2
black p. of untrammeled joy	HOLM 423:58
Eating the air on p.	SHAK 772:76
full of p., but of no performance	DICK 279:11
full of youthful p.	IRVI 447:56
gaudy p. of what life ought to be	COOKE 245:74
p. kept, And a child	NEME 633:18
p. made is a debt unpaid	SERV 751:41
p. none relies on	ROCH 720:27
p. of fair weather	DICK 280:27
p. of pneumatic bliss	ELIOT 317:78
p. of their early years	POWE 693:41
p. to build a bridge	KHRU 485:92
state of perpetual p.	BEEC 73:69
promised p. to do when you are sick	SIGI 821:63
seen the p. land	KING 487:35
promises Don't ask me for p.	SHAW 806:83
failed p. of American life	GILL 370:78
keep the p. we've...made	OBAMA 644:49
not a set of p.	KENN 481:99
not having received the p.	BIBLE 129:40
P. and pie-crust	SWIFT 863:75
p. to keep	FROST 352:5
Wealth...made up largely of p.	POUND 692:39
young man of p.	BALF 58:41
promissory one long p. note	BEEC 73:69
signing a p. note	KING 487:27
promontory seems to me a sterile p.	SHAK 782:88
See one p.	BURT 181:79
promote he will p. himself	DUGO 305:86
promotion p. of the human race	WEST 933:95
sweat but for p.	SHAK 778:72
prompt I meant to be p.	DAY 267:29
pronounce frame to p. it right	BIBLE 95:14
p. it Vinchy	TWAIN 902:32
proof absence of any other p.	NEWT 635:62
admirable p. of this	FERM 333:94
exist as living p.	THOM 886:87
final p. of God's omnipotence	DE 275:13
flawless p. of the existence of God	EDDI 311:26
no need of formal p.	BOYD 154:14
p. that only men	STEI 846:93
p. through the night	KEY 484:68
The p. is in his plays	ONEI 651:69
tyrannous and rough in p.	SHAK 765:66
written for...narrative, not of p.	QUIN 703:26
proofs purist who reads your p.	CHAN 213:82
prop Science...a p.	WORD 958:79
you do take the p.	SHAK 770:17
propaganda all p. is lies	ORWE 654:38
engines of p.	BALD 57:30
full of p.	ACHE 3:54
in spite of...its foreign p.	ORWE 654:37
piece of p. in favour	JOYCE 470:34
p. arm of the American Dream	HASK 400:80
p., rumor, suspicion	LIPP 531:37
strikes...not as a means of p.	ENGE 326:14
to...catapult the p.	BUSH 183:33
propagandist p.'s purpose	HUXL 442:82
propagandists cleverest p. extant	BUCH 171:25
propagation peace and p.	WALP 919:76
Was all our p.	DONNE 292:43
propensities excite my amorous p.	JOHN 459:51
side of their natural p.	BURKE 176:56
propensity hereditary p.	EDGE 311:34
p. for being poor	AUST 46:81
property Abolition of private p.	MARX 579:32
any object of p.	BENT 82:91
bourgeois p. is...revolutionary	OROU 652:95
character, person, or p.	LOVE 538:89
civilization...of p., of fences	EMER 325:83
common p. of the nation	TIMES 892:23
consider himself as public p.	JEFF 454:27
destroys my p.	PAINE 660:30
every man reclaimed his own p.	BUTL 186:12
family from sinking their p.	MOOD 615:54
for our p.	PITT 680:11
Happiness...in taking their p.	GENG 363:43
landlords and persons of p.	MALT 563:25
magic of P.	YOUNG 968:51
misapplied is a'body's p.	MACD 549:22
neither persons nor p. will be safe	DOUG 296:26
one-way p. of time	EDDI 311:24
on their p.	GALS 358:48
preservation of p.	LOCKE 533:85
P. has its duties	DRUM 299:8
p. in his person	LOCKE 533:86
P. is theft	PROU 697:35
P. like incest	INNIS 446:45
p. of any political party	HOOV 427:51
p. of the rich	RUSK 733:1
rights of p. originate	MADI 558:16
sanctity of life and p.	SCHL 747:33
security of p.	PANK 662:84
Thieves respect p.	CHES 220:72
violent p. fordoes itself	SHAK 781:73
property-owning p.-o. democracy	SKEL 824:32
prophecies verification of...p.	TROL 898:41
prophecy art united with p.	NISB 639:28
p., and religion, all in one	RUSK 733:14
p. is the most gratuitous	ELIOT 316:47
self-fulfilling p. is	MERT 589:54
though I have the gift of p.	BIBLE 126:52
trumpet of a p.!	SHEL 813:84
urn Of bitter p.	SHEL 816:58
verses and the p.	WALL 918:59
prophesy hang out and p.	PALEY 661:56
P. upon these bones	BIBLE 111:37
who can but p.?	BIBLE 111:51
prophet banner of the P.	BROD 160:36
happen to a p.	HUXL 442:93
I am no p.	ELIOT 316:65
If there arise among you a p.	BIBLE 95:92
Juxtaposition his p.	CLOU 232:60
loathing Was p. to the rest	MIDD 590:81
Methinks I am a p.	SHAK 764:3
more than a p.	BIBLE 116:77
p. is not without honour	BIBLE 117:97
there is a p. in Israel	BIBLE 97:75
What-you-may-call-it is his p.	DICK 280:35
your p. the Nazarite	SHAK 769:82
prophetic like p. strain	MILT 598:60
O my p. soul!	SHAK 781:62
prophets Beware of false p.	BIBLE 115:53
destroy the law, or the p.	BIBLE 114:30
films of one's own country like the p.	ANDE 17:70
hang all the law and the p.	BIBLE 128:26
persecuted they the p.	BIBLE 114:27
so did their fathers to the false p.	BIBLE 120:73
spake by the P.	BOOK 147:62
prophilaxis wise course of p.	SILVA 821:70
propinquity P. had brought	YEATS 967:41
self-congratulatory p.	GILL 370:79
proportion bills! That's out of p.	LARK 509:79
in equal p. to age	HEMI 410:94
in inverse p. to the sum	PARK 665:39
innate sense of p.	HONE 425:14
no p. kept	SHAK 765:63
sense of wholesome p.	POWYS 693:62
soul refines...in p.	MARI 571:88
strangeness in the p.	BACON 53:29
proportions distorted...p.	MILL 592:13
exact p.	HALES 393:30
Fashion...is a matter of p.	CHAN 214:3
Full of p., one limb to another	HERB 413:70
p. are easily determined	HEIN 407:15
p., everything has its share	MATI 581:91
proposal every new p.	STAMP 842:10
propose We p. it, we massage it	CUOMO 258:78

psychology

proposes Man p., but God disposes — KEMP 480:76
proposition no longer a tenable p. — STEI 846:98
  p. that all men are created — LINC 529:9
  p. that two times two — LICH 528:93
  p. which it purports to express — AYER 48:5
  p. which we can understand — RUSS 734:24
  self-evident p. — MACA 545:25
  thinks over that p. — KIER 485:4
propositions central p....are these — HUXL 443:5
  p. would sound like — LICH 528:86
  truth of P. — HOBB 420:96
proprietor hotel without a p. — MANS 567:1
propriety despaired, with more p. — WEBS 926:33
  p. of thoughts and words — DRYD 300:41
proscription punished by p. — CHES 219:43
prose condescend to p. — BYRON 189:2
  connect the p. and the passion — FORS 344:30
  dough-baked p. — CAREW 198:49
  fancy p. style — NABO 628:5
  for discourse and nearest p. — DRYD 302:2
  Gertrude Stein's p. song — LEWIS 527:68
  Good p. is like a window — ORWE 654:59
  In p., the worst thing — ORWE 655:64
  laws of p. writing — HEMI 410:83
  love thee in p. — PRIOR 696:10
  'monument of English p.' — ELIOT 319:35
  most beautiful p. paragraph — BLOOM 143:67
  never pin up my hair with p. — CONG 241:66
  not poetry, but p. run mad — POPE 687:2
  other harmony of p. — DRYD 304:38
  Poetry is to p. — WAIN 915:4
  produce great p. — THOM 885:48
  P. books are the show dogs — GRAV 382:31
  P. is when all the lines — BENT 82:95
  p. of the realities — CUOMO 258:82
  P. on certain occasions — LAND 507:36
  p. takes the mould of the body — WOOLF 956:39
  P. = words in their best order — COLE 236:48
  shut me up in P. — DICK 284:38
  speaking p. for forty years — MOLI 611:86
  straight honest p. — HEMI 410:75
  translate aphorisms into...p. — FRYE 354:56
  unattempted yet in p. or rhyme — MILT 601:30
  well written as p. — POUND 691:90
  you govern in p. — CUOMO 258:77
prosecution attention in the p. — WASH 921:26
  p. of any undertaking — JOHN 459:56
prospect dull p. of a distant good — DRYD 303:15
  hold out a p. for nations — PITT 680:12
  noblest p. — JOHN 461:92
  p. from the watershed — STARK 843:24
  p. of a brighter day — WORD 962:49
  p. of another campaign — JOHN 457:3
  p. of belief — SHAK 796:5
  p. of reigning — JAY 453:5
  p. of tackling an unsolved problem — SHIP 818:13
  which...has the happier p. — PLATO 681:45
prospectors unoffending p. — DOUG 294:97
prospects few pleasanter p. — HAWT 402:9
  gilded scenes and shining p. rise — ADDI 6:16
  Wide and undetermined p. — ADDI 7:36
prosper keep it may p. — KIPL 490:7
  p. that love thee — BIBLE 103:33
  Treason doth never p. — HARI 398:33
prosperity Grit riches and p. — BROWN 164:41
  jest's p. lies in the ear — SHAK 763:26
  man to han ben in p. — CHAU 216:63
  man who can stand p. — CARL 201:35
  No, for p. — BERL 84:44
  P. is not without many fears — BACON 51:65
  P. is only an instrument — COOL 246:80
  P. is the blessing — BACON 51:64
  p. of the wicked — BIBLE 101:84
  p. will leak through — BRYAN 170:97
  rise with the p. — SMITH 827:82
  state of p. — MACM 556:65
  virtue of p. — BACON 51:63
  Without publicity...no p. — ZELD 969:5
prostitute p. all their powers! — FORS 345:42
prostituted most p. being — BAUD 69:87
prostitutes p. if they do — MILL 595:1
  small nations like p. — KUBR 500:34
  thoughts are my p. — DIDE 285:70
prostitution marriage and p. — DWOR 308:45
  Necessity never makes p. — WOLL 954:94
  P.. Selling one's body — MACK 554:13
  rent it (p.) — DWOR 308:43

protagonists lost...even to the p. — MAIL 560:43
protect Americans...p. their children — ACH 2:23
protection it is not even a p. — STEV 851:13
  Journalists...require some p. — BLACK 137:40
  life of kind p. — STOWE 856:28
  receives the p. of society — MILL 591:2
protections p. against temptation — TWAIN 903:82
protein p. of...imagination — HUGH 435:21
proteins not getting the right p. — CART 207:57
protest First I p. — DOUG 294:99
  men p. and disapprove — CATU 209:6
  strongest p. against selfishness — GOOD 378:45
protestant armed P. Ulsterman — REDM 709:21
  attacked...P. church — NIEM 637:91
  between P. and Papist — STRA 857:44
  care at one time for the p. interest — BRIG 159:14
  free p. assemblies — BAIL 55:89
  head of the P. interest — WILL 944:67
  P....can only go to his solicitor — DISR 288:54
  P. form of art — ORWE 653:30
  P. religion...like a gentlemen's club — WARN 921:10
  P. whore — GWYN 391:8
Protestantism P....is...dissent — BURKE 175:17
Protestants P. can be expected — WILS 947:38
  rouse the P. in France — LESL 523:88
  White P. who live in the center — MAIL 559:39
protestations P. of impartiality — COBB 233:74
protests creative p. to degenerate — KING 487:29
  The lady p. too much — SHAK 783:25
Proteus P. rising from the sea — WORD 961:30
protocoligorically P. correct — SHER 818:8
protocols p. are very good things — PALM 661:68
protons P. give an atom its identity — BRYS 171:14
  p. in the universe — EDDI 311:27
prototypes Spanish....our p. — ECHE 310:14
protracted life p. is p. woe — JOHN 459:47
  p. my work — JOHN 460:69
proud all the p. — BIBLE 112:65
  better than the p. in spirit — BIBLE 106:22
  but he's vengeance p. — SHAK 799:93
  Death be not p. — DONNE 292:51
  He that is p. — SHAK 786:31
  how little are the p. — GRAY 384:57
  how you use p. words — SAND 742:20
  I am p. of my country — OBAMA 645:56
  I am still p. to be who I am — ZIDA 970:13
  I have no p. looks — BOOK 149:35
  instruct my sorrows to be p. — SHAK 768:54
  make death p. — SHAK 795:85
  man...a p. and yet a wretched thing — DAVI 264:77
  man, p. man — SHAK 787:58
  man...too p. to fight — WILS 949:78
  poor are to be p.! — SHAK 786:9
  p. and disdainful — THUR 890:76
  p. an' he's great — NAIR 629:32
  P., art thou met? — MILT 605:22
  p. conceited ignorant people — ANON 22:81
  p. foot of a conqueror — SHAK 768:66
  p. of one another — CONG 241:74
  p. of the position of the bungalow — WILS 947:39
  p. of your contempt — SHAW 807:14
  p., revengeful, ambitious — SHAK 783:11
  p. that I am an Australian — FRAN 348:23
  p. to tell their sons — ARLO 32:31
  remember how p. you were — YEATS 965:2
  so p., so witty, and so wise — ROCH 719:12
  too p. for a wit — GOLD 377:17
  too p. to importune — GRAY 385:94
  very p. and great — STEV 853:66
  Why were they p.? — KEATS 477:10
  with p. people — SURR 860:4
  Yes, I am p. — POPE 688:27
proud-pied p.-p. April — SHAK 802:72
Proust P. Can Change Your Life — DE 268:50
  P. of pastimes — FOWL 346:65
  read...P., Faulkner, Joyce — VARG 908:26
prove determined to p. — WHITE 935:55
  P. all things — BIBLE 129:15
  p. God statistically — GALL 358:46
  p. him with hard questions — BIBLE 97:55
  p. one's self a fool — HAWT 402:3
  p. the weeping philosopher — SHAK 769:78
  wakening and uprising p. — KEBLE 478:51
proved O, that it could be p. — SHAK 770:26
  That which was to be p. — EUCL 328:50
Provence In P. called — KEATS 477:25
  Than you found it in P.? — WILL 946:12

proverb according to her own p. — SCOTT 754:76
  have a p. down here — SAKI 739:68
  Israel shall be a p. and a byword — BIBLE 97:54
  Italian p. succinctly puts it — HUXL 442:92
  Know that famous p.? — ROTH 728:82
  Spanish p. says — JOHN 463:60
proverbs breaker of p. — SHAK 771:32
  like p., they occur in pairs — SIMON 821:74
  p. are the palm-oil — ACHE 2:20
proves this p. I'm not alone — HIRST 419:81
providence assert Eternal P. — MILT 601:31
  Behind a frowning p. — COWP 250:87
  fathom the inscrutable workings of P. — BIRK 136:15
  go the way that P. — HITL 420:93
  popular one is P. — TWAIN 903:86
  P. Out of our evil — MILT 602:41
  P. their guide — MILT 607:74
  P. would have cast my lot — DICK 282:96
  purposes of P. — UPDI 906:20
  Tempest thy p. — MILT 608:92
  whatever Divine P. permitted — DANA 261:24
provident watchful, p., fatigued — MUNRO 625:52
  Women...are p. instead — BOGAN 144:93
provider bad husband and an ill p. — EMER 325:87
  good p. for a needy man — HESI 417:33
providers men into their chief p. — MILLS 595:7
province all knowledge...my p. — BACON 49:16
  p. of a despicable electorate — PITT 679:2
provinces lady from the p. — GILB 369:61
  obeyed in their several p. — MARL 573:22
  princess among the p. — BIBLE 110:23
  p. must not be bartered — WILS 949:86
  p. of the froth — BAUD 69:75
provincialism taken in...p. — HUXL 441:54
proving nothing worthy p. — TENN 879:4
provision p. for...young women — AUST 46:59
  provisions p. for discourse — AUST 45:51
provocation as in the p. — BIBLE 102:2
  what p. I have had? — POPE 688:26
provoke I like to p. — MADO 559:22
prow round about the p. she wrote — TENN 870:86
  their head the p. — DRYD 299:73
prowess Dutch p. — ROCH 719:9
prowl spirits...began to p. around — ADAMS 4:80
Prudence P. dwells in dark abodes — WORD 962:48
  P. is the other woman — ANON 27:39
prudence age of p. — ELIOT 318:11
  effect of p. on rascality — SHAW 808:47
  I hate to see p. clinging — SHER 817:89
  p. in the conduct — SMITH 827:85
prudent progressive who is p. — JOHN 458:11
  p. for a purpose — BROWN 163:22
  p. to gain the whole world — SHAW 810:5
prudes p. for proctors — TENN 872:31
  women p. if they don't — MILL 595:1
pruninghooks p. into spears — BIBLE 111:49
  spears into p. — BIBLE 107:51
Prussia military domination of P. — ASQU 38:84
  national industry of P. — MIRA 608:14
  P. was hatched from — NAPO 630:49
psalm practising the hundredth p. — BYRON 191:33
  rolled the p. — TENN 874:80
  the echo of a p. — PAST 668:99
psalmist Death, as the P. saith — SHAK 772:86
psalms shew ourselves glad...with p. — BOOK 149:36
  the melody of p. — HOOK 427:41
psyche human p. and butterfat — WAXM 925:4
psyches p....tied to their epididymis — STEP 847:13
psychiatrist man who goes to a p. — GOLD 377:26
  p. is a man who goes — STOC 855:7
psychiatrists P. classify a person — SZASZ 865:28
psychiatry branch of p. — ASLET 38:82
psychic human p. equilibrium — MAMET 564:37
  use p. bullets — MAIL 560:47
psychoanalysis father of p. — GREER 387:41
  In p. nothing is true — ADOR 8:72
  modern myth of p. — THOM 883:99
  pay for their own p. — EPHR 326:23
  P. is a permanent fad — DE 275:14
  what sex and p. are — HUGH 435:25
psychoanalytic p. therapy — FREUD 350:56
psychologists p....in the study — MERT 589:56
psychology department of p. and sociology — AYER 48:7
  no use for p. — SING 823:89
  P. has a long past — EBBI 310:9
  The word 'p.' — SARR 744:60

psychosis

Entry	Reference
When my daughter needs p.	ANON 25:35
psychosis The Irish...have a p.	BEHAN 74:14
psychotic castles...a p. lives in them	ANON 24:19
p. if he makes others	SZASZ 865:28
Ptolemaic Copernican, not P.	PHIL 677:56
pub No pewter and no p.	RANS 707:73
puberty American at p.	WAUGH 924:89
pubic P. hair...substitute for wit	PRIE 695:94
public a person who prays in p.	KING 487:40
as if I were a p. meeting	VICT 912:80
because the p. praised	BROW 166:89
British p.	MACA 545:30
conspiracy against the p.	SMITH 827:81
consult the p. good	SWIFT 862:47
contented section of the p.	HUGO 437:84
corpse of the p. credit	WEBS 926:15
decent chap never lets his p. down	FLYNN 341:63
dresses for p. appearances	ONAS 650:49
falsehoods to deceive the p.	STEF 844:53
field of p. education	WARR 921:12
give lessons to the p.	DIDE 285:68
gulls amongst the p.	KEYN 484:78
I and the p. know	AUDEN 43:96
inflict myself on the p.	MORL 620:43
keeping the p. informed	PULI 699:71
liars in p. places	POUND 691:4
loudest complainers for the p.	BURKE 175:8
love in p.	DRYD 301:54
make ourselves p.	NASHE 631:88
making the private world p.	GINS 372:15
man assumes a p. trust	JEFF 454:27
married and endowed the p.	BACON 51:70
mass of p. wrongs	KYD 501:49
measure of p. support	TIMES 892:22
minds of the general p.	BALA 56:10
mislead the p.	ASQU 38:86
more than a p. calamity	SOUT 835:55
naked p. person...ridiculous	SART 744:64
paint in the p.'s face	RUSK 733:15
patience of the general p.	KRUG 500:22
Policemen...protectors of the p.	MAMET 563:27
private life...by a wider p. life	ELIOT 315:39
progressive causes in the p. eye	SIMP 822:82
p. consensus that Donald Trump	KRUG 500:23
p. detriment of the latter	LYTT 543:95
p. dislikes one of my...covers	ROCK 721:42
p....divided into two parts	RAY 708:87
p. does not always know	DIDE 285:67
p. doesn't give a damn	BEEC 73:67
p. doesn't want new music	HONE 425:15
p. faces in private places	AUDEN 42:67
p. falls for this	HAIL 392:19
p. good Private respects	MILT 608:93
p. health measures	SUTH 860:7
p. interest is	LIPP 531:43
p. is an old woman	CARL 200:3
p. man lays his hand	BEER 73:78
P. Mercury should not have my Vote	LEST 524:8
p. needs permit	MORE 618:20
p. of the moment	LUCAS 541:56
p. only gets to hear	STEIN 845:78
p. subsidy of intelligence	QUINE 702:22
p....thinks...there may be something in it	CANN 196:6
p., though dull	SWIN 864:31
reality...over p. relations	FEYN 334:8
roads and p. works	MALT 563:23
servants of the p.	GOWE 380:80
sound of p. scorn	MILT 606:61
speaks to you...of p. affairs	TOCQ 893:33
spotlight of p. life	FOST 345:57
strike against the p. safety	COOL 245:78
that gives it to the p.	VALE 907:3
that incredible thing, a p.	CRAW 254:89
trade for the p. good	SMITH 828:86
tribunal of p. opinion	TOCQ 892:30
true to the p.	BERK 84:35
vexes p. men	TENN 872:28
Well, British P.	BROW 169:69
whatever the...p. allow	SHAW 807:24
Whatever they may be in p. life	FREN 350:53
write for yourself and have no p.	CONN 242:92
public-address station p.-a. system	JAMES 450:26
publican How like a fawning p.	SHAK 769:83
publicists use to backlash p.	FALU 329:11
publicity history of p.	LEAV 517:51
oxygen of p.	THAT 881:62
price of justice is eternal p.	BENN 81:73
p. agent of big business	ORWE 653:6
P. is the very soul of justice	BENT 82:93
Without p....no prosperity	ZELD 969:5
With p. comes humiliation	JANO 452:81
publicly Sometimes you move p.	BAKER 56:2
public-school English p. s.	WAUGH 923:67
p.-s. system all over	WAUGH 923:54
publish ask a superior to p.	HOPK 428:83
I'll p., right or wrong	BYRON 186:24
P. and be damned.	WELL 929:15
p....what you actually did	FEYN 334:5
published never have been p.	MACL 555:36
publisher Barabbas was a p.	CAMP 194:69
had a p. shot	UNSE 905:10
p., to take writers seriously	POWE 693:50
Xerox makes everybody a p.	MCLU 556:61
publishers fear...become p.	CONN 242:96
P. can get their minds	LECA 518:76
publishing important...in p.	JOVA 469:13
p. of his ideas	KAZIN 474:52
pubs served in all the p. in Dublin	DONL 290:9
pudding cold, black suet-p.	LEWIS 527:68
p. against empty praise	POPE 688:30
Puddin-race Chieftain o' the P.-r.!	BURNS 178:94
puddle wonderful	CUMM 257:52
superficial as a p. in the sunlight	LEAC 515:15
puddling p. in a tub continually	PERTH 675:31
pudenda vile members...called 'p.'	ABEL 1:3
puff friends all united to p.	SWIN 864:11
pipe with solemn interposing p.	COWP 250:90
the p. oblique, or p. by implication	SHER 817:97
puffed get one's self p.	TROL 898:47
puffing P. is of various sorts	SHER 817:97
puff-paste fantastical p.-p.	WEBS 927:57
puffs p. from the hookah-mouth	KIPL 490:93
Pugh Mr P. minces among bad vats	THOM 884:41
pull they p. me back in	PACI 658:6
tug, p. and plop	OBRI 646:73
pulp become so much p.	CAMP 193:44
If P. Fiction had been set	GRANT 381:3
pulpit If the President has a bully p.	REAG 708:98
Inquisition fulminating from the p.	WELD 928:83
pulsations translate p. into images	RICH 713:99
pulse feeling a woman's p.	STER 849:57
lost p. of feeling	ARNO 34:72
p. of life?	SHAK 768:64
p. of the machine	WORD 960:20
scene before him beat like a p.	AMIS 16:29
pulse-less p. lot...England	LAWR 512:40
pulses feeling of p. the physic of love	CLEV 230:93
pumice Beside a p. isle	SHEL 813:81
polished with dry p.?	CATU 209:5
pumpkin like the rich P. pie	WHIT 938:17
pun p. is Pierian	UNTE 905:11
so vile a p.	DENN 273:76
through a pipe and exhaled in a p.	LAMB 506:15
punctual p. rape of every...day	WILB 939:37
punctuality Painting and P.	GAIN 356:9
P. is the politeness	LOUI 537:71
P. is the vice	PATR 670:30
P....virtue of the bored	WAUGH 924:91
punctuation dropped p. marks	WEST 933:98
mix...the sun with p.	BRAU 157:83
Zero Tolerance Approach to P.	TRUSS 900:2
Punic With P. faith	SALL 740:94
punish impulse to p. is powerful	NIET 638:5
P. a body	DRYD 302:73
p. everyone who deserved it	ELIOT 315:29
punished p. not for what they do	SZASZ 865:27
punishment All p. is mischief	BENT 82:89
Death is...degrading to p.	BREN 158:99
fees are sufficient p.	BAIL 55:85
marked out for p.	BUCH 171:28
p. fit the crime	GILB 370:60
p. is greater than I can bear	BIBLE 92:4
P. is not for revenge	FRY 353:37
seek to convert by p.	MILL 594:77
servitude...the p. of his guilt	CURR 259:92
Some p. seems preparing	FRAN 348:15
take a lot of p. to write	HEMI 409:60
punishments charged with p.	HENL 411:6
neither rewards nor p.	INGE 445:33
Severe and terrible p.	MORE 618:13
punk Well do you p.?	EAST 310:6
punt more fun to p.	SAYE 746:7
slow p. swings round	ARNO 34:90
punters p. don't want to sleep	CURT 259:99
pupil p. is too young	RYLE 736:61
pupils p. are the crème de la crème	SPARK 836:65
p. might demonstrate	GIBB 366:95
teacher who does not equip his p.	PETE 675:39
puppets box and a P. show	THAC 880:30
p....with their slips of paper	WHITE 935:38
puppies drowned a blind bitch's p.	SHAK 773:12
puppy p.'s insolent yelp	ANON 21:58
purchase More in the cunning p.	JONS 466:46
water...will p. scarce any thing	SMITH 827:78
purchased see 'tis p. by the weight	SHAK 770:4
purchasers to encourage p.	SWIFT 862:39
pure Be warm, but p.	BYRON 187:26
blank virtue, not a p.	MILT 600:10
Blessed are the p. in heart	BIBLE 114:27
ever to have p. knowledge	PLATO 682:55
in gudis be p.	DUNB 306:99
know nothing, p. and simple	WILL 946:14
Live p., speak true	TENN 878:93
meant to be disinterested, p.	SELF 756:10
more p. than his maker?	BIBLE 98:96
Nothing but holy, p., and clear	HERB 413:57
only you are p.	VALL 907:9
O p. of heart	COLE 235:31
prince whose intentions were p.	JOSE 469:8
p. air and water	REES 710:38
p. as the driven slush	BANK 61:13
p. science can flourish	STEA 843:28
souls Of the p. in heart	RANS 707:72
temples th'upright heart and p.	MILT 601:31
truth is rarely p.	WILDE 941:98
Unto the p. all things are p.	BIBLE 129:32
whatsoever things are p.	BIBLE 128:5
zipless fuck is absolutely p.	JONG 466:31
purest p. and most thoughtful	RUSK 732:86
purgation p. of such emotions	ARIS 31:23
purgatory England...p. of men	FLOR 341:62
no other p. but a woman	BEAU 71:17
those that deny p.	WEBS 927:44
purge Every book is like a p.	DU 306:94
P. me with hyssop	BIBLE 101:72
purify p. the dialect of the tribe	ELIOT 321:86
purists Down with p.!	BAND 61:10
puritan describe as 'P. decadence'	SPEN 837:10
honesty be no p.	SHAK 791:59
P. hated bear-baiting	MACA 546:59
P. of the middle class	NEME 633:19
To the P. all things are impure	LAWR 514:83
puritanism not P. but February	KRUT 500:31
P. names the behaviour	SPEN 837:10
P.. The haunting fear	MENC 586:1
purity preserve unblemished p.	ABEL 1:3
P. of race does not exist	FISH 337:63
purling p. stream	ADDI 6:17
purple Before, milk-white; now, p.	SHAK 767:27
pink and p. columbine	SPEN 838:15
P. haze is in my brain	HEND 411:3
p. wardrobe of thy side	CRAS 254:80
So cool a p.	KEATS 476:88
with reverend p.	JONS 466:48
purpose art achieves a p.	CONS 245:62
As if all this had some p.	SARD 743:51
before this p. cool	SHAK 797:57
called according to his p.	BIBLE 125:20
can cite Scripture for his p.	SHAK 769:84
devoted to a nobler p.	CURZ 259:3
end and p. of all production	SMITH 828:88
except for a noble p.	HERB 413:52
God, for some strong p.	SHAK 765:60
human autonomy, human p.	MUMF 625:39
impulse without p.	BIER 135:92
know how to live to p.	MONT 614:32
mind charged with an eager p.	ELIOT 321:78
Nature...nothing without some p.	ARIS 31:26
novels written with a p.	FORD 343:94
old p. done up in aspic	LAWR 513:53
one increasing p. runs	TENN 871:19
power with our p.	KENN 482:28
p. and determination	KENN 481:27
p. breaks...when it is fulfilled	ELIOT 321:82
p. of art	GOULD 379:73
p. so ravenous	LAWR 514:90
p. was less firm	MOOD 615:52
real p. of life	SCHO 748:55
set p. and...exhausted frame	DOYLE 297:68
speak plain and to the p.	SHAK 774:36
system which has no p.	FROMM 352:88

questioning

unconquerable p. shall be realized — LAMB 505:84
without any practical p. — PLAN 680:23
yoke-devils sworn to either's p. — SHAK 775:67
purposes Can execute their airy p. — MILT 602:46
  p. to which it is instrumental — MILL 592:11
  put it to useful p. — ACHE 3:46
  riddles of…the p. of God — FRYE 354:57
purring p. of contented cats — GRAH 381:91
purse as thy p. can buy — SHAK 781:52
  carrying a very heavy p. — ASCH 37:54
  consult your P. — FRAN 348:13
  consumption of the p. — SHAK 772:75
  no money in your p. — SHAK 778:73
  nothing in thy p. — BIBLE 113:96
  p. is the mirror — QUIN 702:19
  silk p. out of your wife's — MORT 621:73
  steals my p. steals trash — SHAK 789:18
purses Light gains make heavy p. — BACON 53:40
pursue fight them, and p. them — JOAN 455:59
pursued only the p., the pursuing — FITZ 337:82
  want to be p. by it — KAFKA 472:4
  you who are p. — SHAW 807:21
pursuer you are the p. — SHAW 807:21
pursuit every action and p. — ARIS 31:19
  p. of happiness — WARR 921:13
  p. of pleasure — PROU 698:55
  p. of sanity — BELL 77:77
  p. of truth — DESC 274:94
  p.…without any practical purpose — PLAN 680:23
  spare no p. — DICK 282:92
  What mad p.? — KEATS 478:35
pursuits dress according to…your p. — DISR 288:69
  engaged in congenial p. — MOOD 615:52
pursy fatness of these p. times — SHAK 784:44
push p. may send him over it — SITW 824:22
  total p. and pressure — JAMES 451:72
pussy Owl and the P.-Cat — LEAR 516:35
  persian P. from over the sea — MARQ 575:51
  P. said to the Owl — LEAR 516:36
put to your family last — HUMP 439:10
Putin drive P. away — PUSSY 700:89
putrefaction preserve it from p. — JOHN 464:93
puzzle Don't p. me — STER 848:44
  p. all the wise — DRYD 301:70
puzzling But what's p. you — JAGG 449:15
pygmies like retarded p. — PEAR 671:57
  Of all the p. — BOOT 150:49
  p.…content to have our paper — MELV 585:73
pyjamas shot an elephant in my p. — MARX 578:15
pylons P., those pillars — SPEN 837:2
Pym Mr P. used to sit — RUSH 732:77
pyramid society has resembled a p. — NAPO 630:50
  star-y-pointing p.? — MILT 597:39
  unquestionable, like a p. — ORWE 653:28
pyramids p. of sweetmeats — DRYD 304:43
  summit of these p. — NAPO 629:37
Pyramus Death of P. and Thisbe — SHAK 767:20
  Most radiant P. — SHAK 767:34
  scene of young P. — SHAK 768:46
Pyrenees tease in the High P. — BELL 77:70
Pythagoras never…since P.' time — SHAK 779:91
  P.' metempsychosis — MARL 574:32
python shoes are made of p. — MACN 557:97

Q

quack potent q., long versed — CRAB 252:34
quad always about in the Q. — ANON 24:11
  no-one about in the Q. — KNOX 495:18
quadrille q. in a sentry box — JAMES 450:49
quaffing q., and unthinking — DRYD 304:56
quails we long for q. — DRYD 302:99
quaint Q.…50 years after — LAVER 512:33
Quaker But I knaw'd a Q. feller — TENN 878:89
quaking eat thy bread with q. — BIBLE 110:31
qualifications only q. I…respect — JAMES 451:54
qualities a man's natural q. — SHER 817:91
  endued with such q. — ELIZ 321:99
  herbs…and their true q. — SHAK 766:87
  man with all his noble q. — DARW 263:58
  one of their godlike q. — MENC 587:9
  q. essential for the artist — DIDE 285:75
  q. in a great King — RICH 714:19
  q.…of a leader — BEAV 71:25
  q. which he does not possess — JOHN 459:55
  two q. in the world — SHAW 809:68
quality can't fake q. — BURR 181:66

certain q. of magnanimity — STOWE 856:27
Courage is a moral q. — MORAN 618:9
degree and a q. of trust — SHAP 805:68
highest q. to your moments — PATER 668:11
his honour and his q. taken — BLUN 143:79
historian must have a third q. — FORS 345:43
male q. — HOPK 429:97
q. of a smile — SAINT 738:38
q. of his despair — CONN 243:17
q. of mercy is not strained — SHAK 770:12
q. of things made…by the human — CATH 208:92
q. which we assert — MOORE 616:66
Rage is the only q. — BRES 158:3
salty q. of human nature — ARLO 32:32
so airy and light a q. — SHAK 782:87
some good q. to recommend — STRA 857:41
some other means of reckoning q. — CARD 198:43
trespass on Q. Street — LASKY 510:10
true fixed and resting q. — SHAK 777:26
unbecoming a man of q. — CONG 240:36
with the q. — TWAIN 902:52
Quangle Q.-Wangle Quee — LEAR 517:42
quantitative triumph of the q. method — BELL 77:74
quantities Q. defined in terms — MYRD 628:99
quantity prodigious q. of mind — TWAIN 901:31
  q. of delicate…flesh — FIEL 335:24
  reasoning concerning q. — HUME 438:7
  treasure…so trivial in q. — BRON 161:56
quantum theory q. t. has been of little practical value — DISKI 287:12
Quarles Mr Q.…susceptible — HUXL 441:65
  Q. is saved by beauties — POPE 688:34
quarrel entrance to a q. — SHAK 781:50
  hath his q. just — SHAK 759:91
  I won't q. with my Bread — SWIFT 863:70
  love a q. — ETHE 327:44
  lover's q. with the world — FROST 353:16
  no man hath any q. — SHAK 786:20
  only one to make a q. — INGE 445:25
  q. for a lady — HALI 393:39
  q. in a far away country — CHAM 212:62
  q. with its society — TRIL 897:18
  sudden, and quick in q. — SHAK 779:82
  The more I love…I q. — MARG 570:62
  the q. is a very pretty q. — SHER 817:79
  we q. in print — SHAK 780:24
quarreling q. about…going — FAUL 331:47
quarreller He's a great q. — SHAK 785:81
quarrels head is as full of q. — SHAK 766:93
  Litigious men, which q. move — DONNE 291:28
  petty q. — WILL 944:66
  q., talk, and tailors — SHAK 804:37
  sometimes sweet to have our q. — BYRON 189:97
  We have French q. — SHAK 775:83
quarry Fortune on his damnèd q. — SHAK 795:98
  just a q. of paving stones — KING 488:59
  marked down q. — SHAW 807:21
quarter fore or hind Q. — SWIFT 862:59
  only for the remaining q. — NAPO 629:40
quartos perverted by q. — MACA 544:22
  q. their well-ordered ranks maintain — CRAB 251:26
quay meets her on the q. — STRO 857:54
quean flaunting extravagant q. — SHER 817:90
Quebec independent Q. — DESC 275:3
  see the surrender of Q. — MONT 614:33
  Vive le Q.! — DE 270:97
  written those lines than take Q. — WOLFE 953:64
queen ambassador that beds a q. — CLEV 230:96
  be q. for life — POPE 688:14
  dropp'd a tear into the Q.'s ear — BLAKE 141:38
  duty to the Q. — MARL 572:91
  Elizabeth, our noble q. — ANON 22:66
  every lass a q. — KING 488:48
  flame-sceptred Irish q. — HYDE 443:21
  fought for Q. and Faith — TENN 879:99
  gliding like a q. — SPEN 837:1
  'God save the Q.' — WHIT 937:84
  grace a summer q. — SCOTT 753:34
  Great Q. in her regalia — GAY 362:9
  home life of our own dear Q. — ANON 23:98
  I am your anointed q. — ELIZ 321:99
  I'd like to dress the Q. — VERS 911:63
  if the Q. were a man — VICT 912:77
  I have been to the Q. — GLAD 373:42
  Jewish Q. of Egypt — TAYL 868:51
  laughing q. — HUNT 439:23
  made in the days of Q. Bess — SWIFT 863:68

moment of the Q.'s crowning — DIMB 286:99
No scandal about Q. Elizabeth — SHER 818:1
Ocean's child, and then his q. — SHEL 812:65
q., an elf most fair — LAYA 515:98
q. had four Maries — BALL 59:68
q. in bondage — SHAK 759:89
q. in people's hearts — DIANA 276:25
q. of curds and cream — SHAK 799:21
Q. of Hearts — CARR 204:84
q. of the south — BIBLE 117:87
q. of the truth — BAUD 69:75
Q. rose of the rosebud — TENN 879:27
Q. to get away with a hat — LOOS 536:49
rather than q. and married! — ELIZ 321:98
ruler of the Q.'s Navee — GILB 368:33
ruler of the Q.'s Navee — GILB 368:34
Solomon gave to the q. of Sheba — BIBLE 98:85
sung 'God save the Q.' — KIPL 491:22
too mean to be your q. — SHAK 760:12
To toast The Q. — HEAN 405:74
Two-wheeled gypsy q. — DYLAN 309:55
was the Q.'s luve — BALL 58:54
would not be a q. — SHAK 804:42
queenly being Q. in her own room — WHAR 933:7
queens all the beautiful Q. — DONNE 293:73
  all your acts are q. — SHAK 799:20
  Q. have died young — NASHE 632:96
Queensland gone to Q. droving — PATE 669:13
queer all the world is q. — OWEN 657:24
  begin to cut up q. — MOODY 615:57
  q. shoulder — GINS 372:9
  Scotland! a q. country — BORR 151:72
  Technology…is a q. thing — SNOW 832:79
  The only q. people…don't love — BROWN 164:35
  We're here, We're q. — ANON 26:8
queerer q. than we suppose — HALD 392:23
quench q. the fire of love — SHAK 759:65
quenched What hath q. them — SHAK 797:30
quest bless the q. — CRANE 253:59
  persistent and…critical q. for truth — POPP 689:55
  q. of the Sankgreall — MALO 563:13
  Religion…hopeless q. — WHIT 936:65
  winding q. — VAUG 909:40
question almost be a q. — TROL 897:32
  approaches every q. — STEV 851:20
  Ask an impertinent q. — BRON 160:52
  ask the hard q. — AUDEN 42:69
  ask themselves the q. constantly — FANON 330:15
  ask yourself a q. — EAST 310:6
  avoid the q. of the Presidency — DICK 279:2
  consideration of any q. — TROL 898:46
  contempt of q. her hand — SHAK 786:3
  difficult q. — GRAV 383:39
  first q. is 'What's your business?' — BERE 83:13
  first q. must be — SPAR 836:80
  Great Q. Of…Life — ADAMS 4:76
  interrupt…with such a silly q.? — STER 848:21
  Irish q. — FRAS 349:33
  Irish secretly changed the q. — SELL 756:14
  mere asking of a q. — FORS 344:36
  no q. of it being grey — TRAV 896:93
  Others abide our q. — ARNO 33:62
  other stock q. — STRA 857:42
  philosopher's treatment of a q. — WITT 951:27
  political q. is…a painful sight — LODGE 534:2
  q.…in…parents' minds — SCHU 750:80
  q. is absurd — AUDEN 43:86
  Q. not, but live — GORD 378:72
  q. that he frames — FROST 352:97
  q. whether…worth seeing — WALP 918:65
  refuse to answer that q. — ASHCR 37:63
  right answer to the wrong q. — CHRI 224:49
  right q. to ask — RUSK 732:81
  silent q.—'Is this all?' — FRIE 350:64
  still the q. of what — JENK 454:31
  style is not a q. of technique — PROU 698:59
  That is the Irish Q. — DISR 287:31
  That man may q.? — SHAK 795:4
  the q. as to whether we are winning — RUMS 731:44
  thinking about any significant q. — BELL 77:81
  though I q. others — SOCR 833:96
  up to the q. of bread — LEWIS 526:51
  what is the q.? — STEIN 845:75
  Who—or what—put the q. — HAMM 394:57
  will ever ask a new q. — HOPP 694:7
  without having asked any clear q. — CAMUS 196:94
questioning sweetly q. — HERB 413:65

questionings

questionings Those obstinate q. — WORD 959:10
question-mark gigantic q. m. — AGAWA 9:92
questions advice...on all q. — PANG 662:81
  all q. are open — BELL 75:37
  answers...ask the right q. — LEVI 526:37
  answer so many q. — RUSS 734:21
  answers to economic q. — ROBI 718:93
  answers to its q. — RUSS 734:23
  answer to all the q. of men — YOUR 969:60
  ask me the most ridiculous q. — EVANS 328:67
  bring out the crucial q. — BONH 146:26
  ever so many q. — KIPL 491:36
  firm answers to q. — KUHN 500:37
  great q. of our day — BISM 137:32
  little q. from women — ROTH 727:78
  men...weren't even one of the q. — BARN 64:69
  prove him with hard q. — BIBLE 97:55
  q. about the greater matters — ARIS 31:18
  q. and reflections on life — HERN 414:92
  q., not answers — LECA 518:73
  q. of contemporary life — JORD 468:99
  q. that deeply concern us — PAGE 659:16
  q. that we do not know — MACL 555:35
  q. the distempered part — ELIOT 320:64
  q. which some newspaper editors — CHOP 223:34
  Science...asks hard q. — CHOM 222:29
  settler of all the great q. — DISR 288:63
  substituting unimportant q. — BOUL 152:89
  successive answers to q. — PAST 668:2
  Them that asks no q. — KIPL 492:56
  three most important q. — BRAH 156:56
quick How q....life can...seem — SWIFT 861:14
  judge the q. and the dead — BOOK 146:37
  q. in wit — ASCH 37:54
  sudden, and q. in quarrel — SHAK 779:82
  words are q. and vain — SHEL 814:8
quickening q. of the heart — AUDEN 42:72
quicker time passes q. — ALLEN 14:3
quickly play a thing q. — MOZA 623:5
quickness sickness...cured by q. — CAMP 195:77
quiddities in thy quips and thy q.? — SHAK 770:28
quiet All Q. on the Western Front — REMA 710:46
  choose one's moment and keep q. — BECK 72:50
  create and keep q. — FLAU 339:23
  Fie upon this q. life! — SHAK 771:44
  q. life — HICKS 417:46
  q. man is here to stay — SMITH 829:6
  q. moments in q. places — GRIS 389:76
  q. of morning — DUNC 307:9
  scallop-shell of q. — RALE 705:44
  still and q. conscience — SHAK 805:51
  Study to be q. — BIBLE 128:14
  where the world is q. — SWIN 864:97
quiet-coloured q.-c. end of evening — BROW 167:27
quietest q. places Under the sun — HOUS 432:54
quietness in q. and in confidence — BIBLE 108:73
  possess ourselves in...much q. — WALT 920:95
  unravished bride of q. — KEATS 478:34
quietude in that q. you might hear — ANGE 19:9
quill q. from a porcupine — MOORE 617:91
  sucks his substance...through a q. — LAMB 505:99
  With a goose q. — ARET 31:11
quills q. upon the fretful porcupine — SHAK 781:60
quilt America is more like a q. — JACK 448:3
  never folded my own q. — PU 700:3
quince mince, and slices of q. — LEAR 516:38
quincunx The q. of heaven runs low — BROW 166:84
Quinquireme Q. of Nineveh — MASE 580:55
quintessence heavenly q. — MARL 572:2
  q. of all sciences — NASHE 631:89
  q. of their lives — LOWE 539:96
  what is this q. of dust? — SHAK 782:89
quip second, the Q. Modest — SHAK 780:24
quips What, in thy q. — SHAK 770:28
quit learn to q. — LOMB 534:8
  q. because I am not a quitter — NIXON 640:32
  q. until I get run over — LEMM 521:32
  q. yourselves like men — BIBLE 96:28
quitter I am not a q. — NIXON 640:32
quiver man that hath his q. full — BIBLE 103:37
  raise a q. — WHITE 935:54
  spent lights q. and gleam — ARNO 33:57
Quixote Don Q. of Europe — COBD 233:80
quixotic Q. quality — USTI 907:47
quo Q. vadis — BIBLE 133:46
quotation Every q. contributes — JOHN 460:70
  q. is a national vice — WAUGH 924:83

quotations ability to think in q. — DRAB 298:79
  Classical q. is the parole — JOHN 464:80
  delighted particularly in q. — SCHL 747:34
  q. from the Bible — LAWR 513:74
  q. from the Bible, Browning — MCFA 551:68
  q. in Latin — FLAU 339:29
  recommend him by select q. — JOHN 461:9
quote grow immortal as they q. — YOUNG 968:54
  not...q. a line of Shakespeare — CAREY 199:66
  q. the fights historical — GILB 368:39
quotes q. from the shortstop — MCFA 551:68
quotidian poet is a master of the q. — PRIT 696:23

R

rabbits r. ruled by stoats — ORWE 653:20
rabble r. of the filthy...infants — POUND 691:93
Rabboni R.; which is to say, Master — BIBLE 124:66
Raca say to his brother, R. — BIBLE 114:32
race adroit and joyless r. — WAUGH 924:81
  antennae of the r. — POUND 692:28
  Art among a religious r. — FUSE 356:93
  avoid a competitive r. — ARNO 36:47
  brave, generous, humorous, talented,
    warm-hearted — BUCH 171:25
  But was a r. of heaven — SHAK 794:49
  colonel comes from Brian's r. — DAVIS 266:10
  courage of their r. — SULL 859:80
  demand this...for the r. — SCHR 749:65
  destiny of the human r. — THOR 888:26
  Englishmen...nervously excitable r. — DAVI 264:72
  entire r. passes through — SCHR 749:66
  hearted r. — BUCH 171:25
  ills...spring from belonging to a r. — DUDEK 305:76
  intent on my own r. — STEV 854:90
  Irish...in the infancy of the r. — OFAO 647:96
  Jews...murmuring r. — DRYD 301:67
  law [of competition]...for the r. — CARN 202:48
  like the rest of my r.? — BLAKE 140:23
  men and women with our r. — KIPL 492:57
  my second r. — VAUG 909:34
  noble r. and brave — SIGO 821:64
  No r. can prosper — WASH 921:22
  northern r. — CHUR 224:52
  nuclear arms r. — MOUN 622:93
  Of some new r. called Man — MILT 602:62
  perpetuate their r. — RICA 713:84
  poor r. in a land of dollars — DU 305:66
  pride of r. or spirit — SMITH 831:64
  problem of r. and color — DU 305:70
  Purity of r. does not exist — FISH 337:63
  quiet, pilfering, unprotected r. — CLARE 228:52
  r. between education — WELLS 930:35
  r. is not to the swift — BIBLE 106:29
  r. is to the swift — DAVI 264:66
  r. of glory run — MILT 607:91
  r. of upstart creatures — MILT 603:71
  R. prejudice...a shadow — BUCK 172:33
  r. that is set before us — BIBLE 129:43
  r. which has become self-conscious — LAWR 513:51
  rear my dusky r. — TENN 871:21
  simple r.! — SCOTT 752:14
  slinks out of the r. — MILT 600:8
  Swift was the r. — DRYD 302:89
  they which run in a r. — BIBLE 126:44
  unbodied joy whose r. — SHEL 813:92
  unto a savage r. — TENN 870:97
  what avails the sceptred r.! — LAND 506:26
  white r. does not really think — STEIN 845:66
  white r. is the cancer — SONT 834:16
race horse think of a fine r. h. — MOZA 623:6
racehorse keep...any r. — CHES 219:46
racehorses associated...with r. — SAKI 739:54
races after they have won a few r. — DIOR 286:3
  appointed you r. and tribes — KORAN 498:87
  Brings forth its r. — LONG 535:32
  composed of two distinct r. — LAMB 505:2
  glory of rulers or of r. — BEVE 90:62
  so-called white r. — FORS 344:35
  war of r. — MUIR 624:27
  worst horse at the r. — MASE 580:68
Rachel R. weeping for her children — BIBLE 110:22
  seven years for R. — BIBLE 93:34
racial As a matter of r. pride — FEIF 332:56
  r. antipathies...of the Old World — BORAH 150:53
racing Ocean r. is like standing — HEATH 405:91
  r. car whose hood — MARI 571:77

rack Leave not a r. behind — SHAK 804:27
  stretched on the r. — POPE 689:45
racket job or a r. — KNIG 494:10
  ruins the whole r. — LOOS 536:57
  whar dar is so much r. — TRUTH 900:4
rackets matched our r. to these balls — SHAK 775:62
Rackrent Sir Patrick R. lived — EDGE 311:37
racquets boxing with r. — BARR 65:96
radiance fountain itself of heavenly r. — MILT 601:20
  its r. would grow — RAND 706:59
  white r. of Eternity — SHEL 815:43
radiant cherry blossoms...r. — ANON 24:27
radical charge that an idea is r. — GALB 357:14
  never dared be r. — FROST 352:12
  R. chic — WOLFE 953:73
  r. is a man — ROOS 724:10
radicalism feeling...R. cannot allay — CHES 219:49
radicals Few r. have good digestion — BUTL 186:7
  French R. and German — MARX 579:33
radio BBC R. is a never-never land — SAFER 737:16
  Down for a new r. — SNYD 832:93
  everything you hear on the r. — MANK 565:72
  largely on television and r. — HUMP 439:14
  Public r. is a ghetto — KEIL 479:55
  than ever existed in r. — SARN 743:55
radioactive bury their r. fuel — LAMB 506:16
radish like a forked r. — SHAK 772:90
Raffles 'Cricket,' said R. — HORN 430:25
raft Come Back To The R. — FIED 334:9
  put to sea on a wooden r. — HEYE 417:39
rag that Shakespearian r. — BUCK 171:32
  the charisma of a damp r. — FARA 330:17
rage Dancing is a frenzy and a r. — DAVI 264:73
  fury, and r. of mortal men — BURT 181:85
  let Death wreck all his r. — MILT 603:83
  Maintain your r. — WHIT 937:84
  no r., like love to hatred turned — CONG 241:52
  Pity is lost in r. and fear — CARL 201:10
  R. is the only quality — BRES 158:3
  r. of Caliban — WILDE 940:63
  r. of will — DYER 309:49
  R., r. against the dying — THOM 884:27
  repressed their noble r. — GRAY 384:68
  Strong without r. — DENH 272:60
  such an immodest r. — CAREW 198:46
  void of noble r. — TENN 874:68
  Why do the heathen r. — BIBLE 99:26
  with hard-favoured r. — SHAK 775:77
  worth more than force and r. — LAFO 504:53
ragged a r. virtue — OTWAY 656:3
  If I was very r. and very jolly — DICK 279:22
raggedness looped and windowed r. — SHAK 792:11
rags no scandal like r. — FARQ 330:28
  r., and hags, and hideous wenches — COLE 236:50
  r. of time — DONNE 291:25
  righteousnesses are as filthy r. — BIBLE 110:7
  rows of disgusting old r. — LAWR 513:62
  You had better be in r. — DISR 289:70
rag-time Lurching to r.-t. tunes — SASS 745:80
raid r. on the inarticulate — ELIOT 320:66
rail never...any body else to r. at me — CONG 240:24
  r. against all the firstborn — SHAK 778:77
  r. at the ill — TENN 876:36
railed r. on Lady Fortune — SHAK 779:78
railroad r....you blasted its rocks — RUSK 734:19
  ride on the r. — THOR 889:39
railroads country of r. — CHEE 218:9
  Player with R. — SAND 741:13
rails r. are to a locomotive — RIVE 716:54
  r. into the Grand Stand — SOME 833:10
  wilderness of freight and r. — CRANE 253:61
railway climax to the r. age — TAYL 868:42
  picking daisies on the r. — WODE 952:37
  populous r. town — THOR 889:52
  read out over a r. station — JAMES 450:32
  threatened its life with a r.-share — CARR 206:31
raiment having food and r. — BIBLE 129:22
  parted his r., and cast lots — BIBLE 122:7
  thieves, which stripped him of his r. — BIBLE 121:80
rain after the r....never a stain — SHEL 813:77
  as the r. cometh down — BIBLE 109:99
  As the r. over the town — VERL 911:57
  cloud which had outwept its r. — SHEL 815:31
  columns of the old r. forest — AMIS 16:46
  continually wetted with r. — STEV 852:17
  dissolve it in r. — SHEL 813:75
  doctrine shall drop as the r. — BIBLE 95:98

drees the wind and r.	SMITH 831:64	rampallion r., you fustilarian!	SHAK 772:77
droppeth as the gentle r.	SHAK 770:12	ramparts O'er the r.	KEY 484:68
Dull roots with spring r.	ELIOT 317:95	rams fat of r.	BIBLE 96:33
fall like r.	AUDEN 42:70	**Ramsgate** visit to R.	CHES 219:49
flat calm with drizzling r.	BOWEN 153:96	ran didn't know how it r.	TAYL 868:61
glazed with r. water	WILL 946:10	door flew open, in he r.	HOFF 422:34
hail, or r., or any snow	TENN 878:87	r. a hundred years	HOLM 424:74
Hath the r. a father?	BIBLE 99:16	r. away with me	WILH 943:58
I saw r. falling	STEV 854:90	r. both together	BIBLE 124:65
It can r. for 100 days	WAUGH 923:50	**random** Economic policy is r.	STEIN 845:79
left Him in the r.	STUD 858:64	heap of r. sweepings	HERA 412:38
let there also be r.	HOME 425:99	r. element in the world	EDDI 311:24
Let the sky r. potatoes	SHAK 773:14	**Rangers** R. and Celtic had both lost	DODD 289:88
like a drop of r.	BYRON 188:72	**ranges** Something lost behind the R.	KIPL 491:44
like sunshine after r.	SHAK 762:88	**ranging** for that I was r.	DRAY 298:96
like wet sidewalks cause r.	BLOU 143:71	**Rangoon** from R. to Mandalay?	KIPL 489:81
lying in the r. outside greengrocers	BRAD 154:25	**rank** elevate his mistress to his r.	BALZ 60:89
nor the clouds return after the r.	BIBLE 106:36	holds on his r.	SHAK 777:26
not even the r.	CUMM 258:61	keep no r. nor station	LOWE 540:21
old man...waiting for r.	ELIOT 317:82	lowest r. of every nation	JOHN 461:89
Only the r. never tires	HUGH 436:44	man in higher r.	RUSK 733:95
Pale r. over	THOM 883:21	O, my offence is r.!	SHAK 783:32
politician...in the r.	WHITE 936:57	Political action is of second r.	MANN 566:89
r. also filleth the pools	BIBLE 101:89	r. is but the guinea's stamp	BURNS 180:52
r. Is full of ghosts	MILL 592:23	r. of devoutly religious men	EINS 313:50
r. is over and gone	BIBLE 107:43	r. pride, and haughtiness of soul	ADDI 7:46
r. of bombs	WHITE 935:53	**rankles** r....with Louisa	WHAR 933:8
r. of gold	DAY 267:37	**ranks** different r. of life	SMITH 827:74
r....of the failing stars	RICK 715:27	even the r. of Tuscany	MACA 546:49
r. on my bicycle	LEE 519:98	In the r. of death	MOORE 618:2
r. on the neck	COOKE 245:75	well-ordered r. maintain	CRAB 251:26
R., r., and sun!	TENN 878:74	**ransomed** R., healed, restored	LYTE 543:93
R.! R.! R.!	KEATS 476:81	**ransoming** this world's r.	AQUI 30:96
r. will come and wash	DE 273:66	**rape** cocktail...as r. is to love	CLAU 229:72
ripple of r.	SWIN 863:82	commit r., murder	BARN 64:61
send my roots r.	HOPK 429:96	don't want to see plays about r.	COOK 245:68
singin' in the r.	FREED 349:42	man...can steal it (r.)	DWOR 308:43
smalle r. downe can r.?	ANON 21:59	principle of procrastinated r.	PRIT 696:14
sound of abundance of r.	BIBLE 97:63	r. and murder	NOON 641:50
stand out here in the r.	BRADY 155:52	r.! a r.!	WEBS 926:30
Still falls the R.	SITW 823:11	r. of every blessèd day	WILB 939:37
sun and the r. are flying	STEV 854:87	**raped** R. by rum	WRIG 963:71
through the drizzling r.	TENN 873:63	**rapes** holy r. upon our will	CAREW 198:50
to command the r.	PEPYS 673:89	If there are armed r.	TOOLE 894:59
tomorrow...acid r.	WYLIE 964:8	**Raphael** R. paints wisdom	EMER 325:93
volleying r.	ARNO 35:18	**Raphaels** talked of their R.	GOLD 377:19
Weather and r.	KIPL 492:61	**rapid** progress...will be r.	FRAN 348:18
wedding-cake left out in the r.	AUDEN 44:24	R. Reaction Force	ANON 27:35
wind and the r.	SHAK 792:9	**rapids** while shooting the r.	HILL 418:55
wind and the r.	SHAK 786:25	**rapist** unsuccessful r.	HEMI 410:91
rainbow and the r. drawn	STEV 854:90	**rapists** all men are r.	FREN 350:53
another hue Unto the r.	SHAK 768:62	**rapscallions** kings is mostly r.	TWAIN 903:64
awful r. once in heaven	KEATS 477:9	**rapture** first fine careless r.!	BROW 167:21
light as the r.	HARR 399:55	love, and r.'s due	ROCH 719:6
nation is a r.	JACK 448:3	r. on the lonely shore	BYRON 188:70
r. and a cuckoo's song	DAVI 265:91	still r. of thy mien	WORD 962:47
R. gave thee birth	DAVI 265:89	**raptures** frantic with thy r.	HERR 415:6
r. in the sky!	TENN 878:74	r. and roses of vice	SWIN 864:91
r. is enuf	SHAN 805:59	r. were All air and fire	DRAY 299:98
r. of his will	LOWE 540:20	**rare** as r. things will, it vanished	BROW 168:52
simple blessing of a r.	ABSE 1:8	Logic is r.	DOYLE 297:60
Somewhere over the R.	HARB 396:90	Nothing is thought r.	FLET 341:60
when I behold A r.	WORD 959:98	O r. Ben Jonson	JONS 468:82
Who in the r. can draw	MELV 585:76	r....after the fall of a prince	ANON 20:30
rainbows like a man...chasing r.	WODE 952:53	r. as a day in June	LOWE 539:7
r. gave them promise	DICK 280:27	r....to take writers seriously	POWE 693:50
raindrops fresh as the r. on a statue's	WALC 916:20	**rarest** r. of all women	SHAK 800:30
R. Keep Fallin' on my Head	DAVID 264:63	**rarity** r....I cannot but be fond of	ROCH 720:19
rainfall in r. at morning	STEV 854:84	**rascal** r. have not given me medicines	SHAK 771:39
rainforest burning the r.	STING 855:2	rather be called a r.	JOHN 463:52
rainmakers sweating r.	AMIS 16:46	stretch-mouthed r.	SHAK 800:24
rains droughts and flooding r.	MACK 553:10	**rascality** effect of prudence on r.	SHAW 808:47
Every time it r.	BURKE 176:59	shocked by its r.	MENC 587:11
winter's r. and ruins	SWIN 863:83	**rascals** r. use me!	DENN 273:75
raise Still r. for good	JOHN 459:49	R., would you live for ever?	FRED 349:18
The Lord shall r. me up	RALE 705:47	Respected people are only r.	STEN 847:6
raisin like a r. in the sun?	HUGH 435:12	**rash** Be not r.	BIBLE 106:20
rake leene was his hors as is a r.	CHAU 217:74	look rather r. my dear	ASHF 37:70
woman is at heart a r.	POPE 688:14	not splenative and r.	SHAK 784:67
rakes reformed r....husbands	BRON 161:57	r. of...American filth	OSBO 655:86
rally language designed to r.	SAFI 737:18	**raspberry** Three farts and a r.	BARB 63:47
ram old black r. Is tupping	SHAK 788:84	**rat** Droll r., they would	ROSE 725:31
rode upon a r.	SPEN 839:61	How now, a r.?	SHAK 784:37
we often have to r. it	CUOMO 258:78	like a r. without a tail	SHAK 795:99
Ramah voice was heard in R.	BIBLE 110:22	Never r. on your friends	DE 273:68
ramble joins me in my R.	DICK 284:52	ship...associated with the giant r.	DOYLE 297:74
The social r. ain't restful	PAIGE 660:28	Taylled lyke a r.	BERN 86:50
tyranny of 'the r. race'	THOM 886:87
used to be the r. race	HOUL 431:32
was an Irish r.	SHAK 779:91
rate r. of profit	SMITH 827:82
wages...above their actual r.	SMITH 827:80
ratio increases in geometrical r.	MALT 563:19
inverse r. to the importance	HUXL 442:77
inverse r. to the number	HUXL 442:84
rational assuming that everyone is r.	KRUG 500:26
disagree Of creatures r.	MILT 603:67
fully r., fully men	BERL 84:49
hostile behavior is not r.	FULB 355:63
irrational is r.	STEV 850:84
people are mostly r.	ADAMS 6:12
process of a r. mind	HELL 407:27
rationality Appeals to r.	MELL 584:49
rats nearness of r.	WHITE 935:41
rattle care for the child's r.	JOHN 461:14
infant breaks its r.	SADE 737:14
pleasure of hearing 'em r. a little	FARQ 330:29
r. of a globe	DRYD 301:51
r. of the bones	ELIOT 318:3
silencer on its r.	ACHE 3:49
spoilt his nice new r.	CARR 204:96
stuttering rifles' rapid r.	OWEN 657:25
woman...the toy of man, his r.	WOLL 954:89
rattles put away their r., marbles	MORE 619:21
rattlesnake r. with a silencer	ACHE 3:49
thought he saw a r.	CARR 206:33
Ravel R. toward the end of La Valse	LAMB 506:18
ravelled not r. and perplexed	JONS 468:97
raven locks were like the r.	BURNS 179:16
Poe, with his r.	LOWE 539:8
Quoth the r.	POE 683:88
sad presaging r.	MARL 573:10
smoothing the r. down	MILT 603:74
ravens Beast r. in its own avidity?	EBER 310:12
doth the r. feed	SHAK 778:70
r. brought him bread	BIBLE 97:60
three r. sat on a tree	BALL 59:76
ravish except You r. me	DONNE 292:55
murder and to r.	AYTO 48:11
r. like enchanting harmony	SHAK 763:6
ravished r. always with her love	BIBLE 104:57
r. this fair creature	FIEL 335:22
r. with the whistling of a name	POPE 687:90
ravishing dear r. thing	BEHN 75:22
raw price of r. produce	RICA 712:80
r. nerve ends of humanity	ANON 27:18
ray down with a flaming r.	BOND 151:48
every r. of God's light	DOST 294:94
eye diffused a quickening r.	WESL 931:57
genuine night admits no r.	DRYD 300:44
r. from the infinite source	HUXL 443:7
r. of rays	DICK 281:68
To find thy piercing r.	MILT 603:74
ray-gun President R.-G.	SCAR 746:14
Raymond R. like the Harvest Moon	FARJ 330:20
rays last r. of feeling	MOORE 617:99
splendour borrows all her r.	POPE 686:63
razor hew blocks with a r.	POPE 686:63
r. ceases to act	HOUS 432:74
r. that threatens the throat	ANGE 18:83
razor-edge r.-e. of danger	WILD 943:45
razors R. pain you	PARK 664:19
RCA windows of the R. Building	THUR 890:84
reach add r. to power	ACHE 3:55
daring beyond our r.	DELI 271:42
He disdains all things above his r.	OVER 656:11
meaner things are within her r.	ELIOT 316:42
out of humanity's r.	COWP 251:97
Religion...beyond all r.	WHIT 936:65
resources...within your r.	PIND 678:80
truth...beyond our r.	POPP 689:62
within the r. of factory girls	SCHU 750:79
reaching without any irritable r.	KEATS 475:75
reacting Acting is r.	DEPP 273:80
reaction habit of instant r.	SCHL 748:58
opposed an equal r.	NEWT 635:59
Vengeance is a personal r.	RENO 711:50
reactionaries conservatives and r.	VIDAL 912:95
r. are paper tigers	MAO 569:33
reactionary r. is a somnambulist	ROOS 724:10
read advised him not to r.	GREG 387:52
books were r.	BELL 77:71
cannot or will not r.	HAYA 402:20
go r. with thee	SHAK 760:27

reader 1256

hares have no time to r.	BROO 163:4	R. it, however	MOORE 617:77	**reality shows** Thank God for r. s.	CLOO 231:41
haven't r. any of your books	JOYCE 470:38	r. of a white man's chuckle	ANGE 19:99	**realization** makes this r. bearable	NIEB 637:87
how it should be r.	FENT 332:63	r., writing and 'rithmetic	DICK 280:47	r. that to be sporting	SKIN 825:49
if he r. little	BACON 53:38	so much eager r.	BELLI 76:47	r. that we have denied…reality	PAGE 659:15
If you only r. the books	MURAK 626:59	soul of r.	STER 848:28	With this r. we turn	HERZ 416:26
I r., and sigh, and wish	HERB 413:64	substitute for r. it	BURG 174:93	**realize** dare you to r. it	HUST 440:46
little I can r.	SHAK 794:45	the endlessness of r.	MANG 565:66	**realm** better to improve his r.	ERAS 327:37
man ought to r.	JOHN 461:93	time is spent in r.	JOHN 462:36	corrupted the youth of the r.	SHAK 759:98
never loved to r.	LEE 518:86	worse crime…is not r. them	BROD 160:41	estate of the r.	MACA 545:31
never r. so far	SHAK 762:68	**reads** One r. books	KEIL 479:59	in na place of the R.	JAME 449:19
no time to r.	BROO 163:4	r. Incessantly	MILT 607:80	In the r. of science	STEI 846:99
only r. what is truly good	STEIN 845:73	The man who never r.	MART 576:81	invade the borders of my r.	ELIZ 322:4
Pick up and r.	AUGU 44:26	**ready** books…or which we are r.	FORS 345:50	One r., one people, one leader	ANON 24:16
Pleasure might cause her r.	SIDN 820:43	jobs before they were r.	REST 711:64	provided this r.	QUIL 702:13
r. about the war	HEMI 409:65	merely r. to go home	KAIKO 472:12	ready to defend the r.	PHIL 676:51
r. a novel…gravest sins	WAUGH 924:78	Rapid Reaction Force to be r.	ANON 27:35	r., nation, or city	KNOX 495:14
r., mark, learn, and inwardly digest	BOOK 147:52	R. writing makes	JONS 468:94	r. of free song	LOWE 539:2
R. not to contradict and confute	BACON 53:36	**Reagan** bulldog into a R. poodle	STEEL 844:37	r. of ideas	MILL 593:38
r. only the kind	KAFKA 472:3	glory of Ronald and Nancy R.	WARR 921:20	r. of the Spirit	MATI 581:93
R. over your compositions	JOHN 462:28	governance of Ronald R.	BAKER 56:8	this r., this England	SHAK 764:40
r. partly for information	SCHL 747:34	had it better than Nancy R.	NEW 634:39	turned out of the r. in my petticoat	ELIZ 321:99
R. somewhat seldomer	BROW 168:40	mind of Ronald R.	NOON 640:44	**realms** constancy lives in r. above	COLE 235:34
r. strange matters	SHAK 796:16	President R. is a rhetorical roundheels	SAFI 737:21	existed in different r.	MEYER 589:63
r. that stuff by myself	SALI 740:77	R.…hell of a king	ONEI 651:77	great Anna! whom three r. obey	POPE 685:36
r. the best authors	JONS 468:93	to R. the main fact was a vision	SHUL 819:30	happy r. of light	MILT 601:36
r. the first 2 pages	JOYCE 470:34	**real** any less r. and true	SHAW 806:88	hearts in one, your r. in one	SHAK 776:2
r. very hard	JOHN 461:99	imaginary are the most r.	STEF 844:52	travell'd in the r. of gold	KEATS 475:60
slowly r.	YEATS 965:7	other than oneself is r.	MURD 626:65	unreal r. of the canals	MCCA 548:92
Stand still, traveller, and r.!	ANON 28:56	r., honest…Boarding-school	AUST 46:73	whatever r. to see	GOLD 376:85
teach a child to r.	BUSH 181:1	r. price of everything	SMITH 827:79	**reap** r. where he hath sown	KIPL 490:8
things I once r.	SNYD 832:89	r. truths and made-up truths	BARRY 65:97	that shall he also r.	BIBLE 127:82
this is why we r.	MANG 565:67	Religion…something which is r.	WHIT 936:65	**reapers** r., reaping early	TENN 869:80
wants to have r.	TWAIN 903:89	the climate crisis is r.	GORE 379:63	**reaping** r. something new	TENN 871:17
We are what we r.	MANG 565:66	**realism** dislike of R.	WILDE 940:63	**rear** Americans do not r. children	JARR 452:89
What do you r., my lord?	SHAK 782:80	offspring of journalistic r.	WHITE 935:55	r. of your affection	SHAK 781:46
What people r. most of the time	CRIT 255:9	**realities** facts, not r.	GOLD 377:35	surprising the defenders from the r.	MANC 564:48
when you r.	GAUG 361:3	prose of the r.	CUOMO 258:82	**reascend** fail to r. Self-raised	MILT 602:50
where I r. and rhyme	WYATT 963:86	**reality** absolute r.	HUGO 436:54	**reason** act under the guidance of r.	SPIN 840:78
Who'll r. that sort of thing?	PERS 675:30	aspect of r.	HART 400:69	asked one another the r.	SHAK 780:18
writes as fast as they can r.	HAZL 403:48	awesome r. to Rent Day	ANGE 19:97	atheism…against…our r.	BURKE 176:44
reader anyone finishing…great r.	ANON 27:22	Between the idea And the r.	ELIOT 318:15	before reaching the age of r.	SADE 737:14
average r. read a novel	OCON 647:88	bring them back to r.	KLEIN 494:6	believing what r. cannot	VOLT 914:41
breaks it gently to the r.	BIER 134:69	Cannot bear very much r.	ELIOT 319:38	beyond all r.	HAMM 394:47
Far from neglecting him [the r.]	ROBBE 717:64	can't face r. nor deal with it	SHAW 808:62	Blotting out r.	GRAV 382:34
Gutenburg made everybody a r.	MCLU 556:61	choice is not between dream and r.	BANKS 62:19	boundaries our r.	RODO 722:51
In reality, each r. reads	PROU 698:61	circumstantial r. is	UPDI 906:28	but a woman's r.	SHAK 758:57
motor…is the r.	CURT 259:97	consecrated to r.	BYRON 191:37	cleverness and r.	STOWE 856:34
not say so to the r.	LAUT 512:28	contribution to r.	THOM 884:45	dark of r. grows	BETJ 89:47
not to inform the r.	ACHE 3:47	covered the world of r.	MILL 593:51	dictates of r., religion, and morality	DICK 282:2
one r. in a hundred years	KOES 495:27	craftsmen…have held R. down	SACK 737:9	disgust is r.'s proper response	PAGL 659:17
produce an impression on the r.	BENN 81:76	creed and particular r.	MUNCH 625:42	Eyes And R.…to study Flies?	POPE 689:67
r.…does not view	ROBBE 716:62	destroys the discovery of r.	KRIS 499:12	find out the r. for it	LECA 518:73
r. is important to me	NABO 628:14	discovery of r.	MURD 626:65	form of human r.	LEVI 526:36
r. must conclude	STARR 843:27	do not refer to r.	EINS 314:90	for some specific r.	RUSS 734:36
r. seldom peruses a book	ADDI 6:23	ethical r. of the individual	KIER 485:2	Give you a r. on compulsion?	SHAK 771:46
reception of the r.	TERE 879:16	Fantasy is…better than r.	LAGER 504:71	God gave [Adam] r.	MILT 600:12
right r. of a good poem	FROST 353:25	In r., killing time	SITW 824:24	governments…founded on r.	PARE 663:89
That ideal r.	JOYCE 470:35	In r., who am I?	FANON 330:15	great r. to be sad	SHAK 779:40
Will you be a r.	THOR 889:40	make a picture of r.	LIPP 531:41	hearing all manner of r.?	MILT 600:11
readers addresses each of its r.	TOCQ 892:31	make r. bearable	PROU 697:41	How noble in r.	SHAK 782:82
art for practitioners and r.	LEAV 517:52	manipulation of r.	DICK 277:37	Human r. won	KHRU 485:94
imprinted on the minds of his r.	BOLD 145:6	more r. into a picture	HECHT 406:3	if it be against r.	COKE 234:95
poets…give their r. sleep	POPE 688:32	mugged by r.	ADEL 8:61	ignorance, his r. such	POPE 687:80
r. better to enjoy life	JOHN 460:80	mysterious mountain…called r.	MAIL 560:66	in erring R.'s spite	POPE 687:79
r. how to read them	RUSH 732:68	politicians…recreating r.	MARA 569:45	In R.'s ear they all rejoice	ADDI 7:41
r. who are pleased with a book	CONN 242:97	R.…doesn't go away	DICK 277:35	It is not, therefore, r.	HUME 438:1
r. will find it very French	GISC 373:29	r.…is unendurable	CONN 243:10	kills r. itself	MILT 600:99
so few good r.	VIDAL 912:3	R. is what I see	BURG 174:98	lack of r. in the kitchen	NIET 638:12
to which so many of my r. belong	CHES 220:55	r.…over public relations	FEYN 334:8	Let's r. with the worst	SHAK 778:53
reading A book you finish r.	MITCH 609:30	'r.' transcending the limits	AYER 48:4	let us r. together	BIBLE 107:50
As the art of r.	JAMES 451:68	r. was no less wonderful	SHIP 818:15	live in a world ruined by R.	MAMET 564:33
careful r. between the lines	MARA 569:44	regulate imagination by r.	JOHN 465:8	longing…for r.	CAMUS 195:84
choose…leaders on the basis of…r.	BROD 160:40	remove all traces of r.	PICA 677:58	lost everything except his r.	CHES 220:65
contemplation…more than his r.	AUBR 41:57	rhetoric passed for r.	BENT 82:7	loved her against r.	DICK 283:10
finish r. one	GERA 364:60	salt of r.	BELL 77:69	man who can r.	LESS 524:6
inclined to love r.	MONT 613:13	Science provides a vision of r.	PAGE 659:16	man who listens to R.	SHAW 808:50
I prefer r.	SMITH 829:24	sense of ultimate r.	BELL 75:32	materials of r. and knowledge	LOCKE 533:89
no taste for r.	SMOL 831:67	speaks about r.	POPP 689:61	men have lost their r.!	SHAK 777:39
not to pretend that r. is…passive	CARY 207:60	straining against r.	MCCA 548:93	more ascetic r. than…enjoyment	STARK 843:22
Peace is poor r.	HARDY 397:27	taming of r.	UPDI 906:35	More than cool r.	SHAK 767:22
Promiscuous r. is necessary	MILT 600:1	terrible r. of poverty	LEGU 520:14	Music says nothing to the r.	BURG 174:3
r. all the novels	HUGH 435:19	thoughts have any relation to r.	CHES 220:68	nature of r. to perceive things	SPIN 840:74
r. books	HAZL 404:54	tourist in other people's r.	SONT 834:17	not contrary to r.	HUME 438:7
r. is not idleness	SPEN 837:12	upon which r. is written	MILT 593:53	not from r. but from love	GIDE 367:20
R. isn't an occupation	ORTON 653:5	way of operating on r.	PAZ 671:49	not his r., but his passions	STER 848:32
R. is the basics for all learning	BUSH 182:7	we eat r. sandwiches	GINS 371:4	not to r. why	TENN 875:12
R. is to the mind	STEE 844:45	Words…the great foes of r.	CONR 244:43	Now tell me the r.	SOUT 835:43

reflection

objects of human r.	HUME 438:5	between sycophancy and r.	BAKER 56:4	**recreation** guilty spice to this r.	WAUGH 924:78
Only r. can convince us	BELL 75:37	Courage, rashness, and r.	MARI 571:76	play or r.	STUB 858:61
produces innovation without r.	SANT 743:40	If r. was the certain consequence	MANS 568:13	**recruiting** r. field for the militant	WRIG 962:60
prose which knows no r.	STEP 847:12	I incite this meeting to r.	PANK 662:84	**rector** accident happened to the r.	TROL 898:35
pursue my r. to an O altitudo!	BROW 165:53	little r. now and then	JEFF 454:21	An ancestor was r.	YEATS 967:40
reality…from the perspective of r.	PAGE 659:16	r. against being what he is	CABE 191:5	**rectors** curates lean, and r. fat	MACA 544:20
r. against reading!	SHAK 763:3	R. against tyrants	DAVI 266:13	**rectum** portion of the r.	BELLI 76:47
r. and energy…are necessary	BLAKE 139:94	r. is as the sin of witchcraft	BIBLE 96:33	**recur** things do not occur; they r.	BENN 80:58
r. and the will of God	ARNO 36:27	R. lay in his way	SHAK 771:57	**recycling** One sort of believes in r.	WELD 928:90
R., an ignis fatuus	ROCH 719:11	Twelve Highlanders…make a r.	ANON 28:53	**red** An Admiral r.	SITW 823:96
r. doth buckle and bow	BACON 49:27	women are in furious secret r.	SHAW 809:86	crimson r., blood r., wine r.	GALE 357:28
r. down or deny everything	EMER 325:77	**rebellious** for the r. also	BIBLE 101:82	fiction…printed in r. ink	BOWEN 153:95
r. for being	FRAN 347:84	Hot and r. liquors	SHAK 778:71	keep the r. flag flying.	CONN 242:84
r. for being a professional	ROST 727:73	r. dwell in a dry land	BIBLE 101:81	November's leaf is r.	SCOTT 752:18
r. for having children	RUSS 735:41	r. people	REED 710:37	pessimist sees only the r.	SCHW 751:95
r. for my rhyme	SPEN 840:64	revolting and a r. heart	BIBLE 110:14	r. in the face	BENT 82:5
r. for rejecting them	RUSS 734:22	**rebelliousness** centuries of r.	PRIE 695:91	r. like crimson	BIBLE 107:50
r. I escaped	DOUG 294:98	**rebels** Cheering a rout of r.	SHAK 772:91	R. lips are not so r.	OWEN 657:27
r. is best and pleasantest	ARIS 31:22	r. from principle	BURKE 176:43	r. r. vitals of his heart	RANS 707:69
r. is equally cogent	GASK 361:84	**reboot** update and r. itself	FERG 333:82	r. wheel barrow	WILL 946:10
r. I should be the same?	AYTO 48:10	'…we might have to r.'	ALLEN 13:81	r. with mirth	SHAK 799:17
r. is identical with love	MACL 555:28	**rebuke** Open r. is better	BIBLE 105:2	rose is r.	ANON 22:66
r., is naturally equal in all men	DESC 274:93	r. of his people shall he take away	BIBLE 108:67	tawdry yellow strove with dirty r.	POPE 686:69
r. is not the subversion	STEV 851:10	scorner heareth not r.	BIBLE 104:67	[The R. Flag] is the funeral march	SHAW 810:24
R. is…the slave of the passions	HUME 438:98	Thy r. hath broken my heart	BOOK 149:26	The r. rose cries	TENN 876:28
r. knows nothing	PASC 667:80	**recant** will not r. anything	LUTH 542:69	took their r. straight	ACHE 3:37
r. of the strongest	LAFO 503:48	**receipt** Applause is a r.	SCHN 748:42	two r. eyes that stare	RANS 707:72
r. so many people	GOLD 377:38	**receive** in giving that we r.	FRAN 347:99	unnatural r. and black	DICK 282:2
r. straightens it out	LAFO 504:65	more blessed to give than to r.	BIBLE 125:96	When in doubt wear r.	BLASS 142:49
R. thus with life	SHAK 787:64	r. no letters in the grave	JOHN 464:99	**red-branch** R.-B. Knights	MOORE 617:1
R. to rule	DRYD 303:12	skill to give as…to r.	QUIL 702:14	**redecorating** my temple needs r.	RIVE 716:57
R. to rule all	AURE 45:44	those who r. it	GOLD 376:83	**redeemed** Fear not: for I have r. thee	BIBLE 109:87
r. why I loved him	MONT 613:21	whosoever shall not r. you	BIBLE 116:68	not r. from time	ELIOT 321:93
r. with one another	MOLI 612:91	**reception** meets with a better r.	JOHN 461:95	**redeemer** know that my r. liveth	BIBLE 98:8
Respect and r.	SHAK 762:94	r. of the reader	TERE 879:16	**re-definition** a r.-d. of our destination	OKRI 649:26
rest may r. and welcome	BROW 168:58	**receptive** r. to beautiful things	DE 268:51	**redemption** life's r.	STEV 850:93
right deed for the wrong r.	ELIOT 319:47	**recesses** dusty r. of their minds	LAWR 514:89	married past r.	DRYD 300:33
ruling passion conquers r.	POPE 686:72	**recession** R. is when your neighbour	REAG 708:3	Our great r.	MILT 597:30
Science…distrusts pure r.	MENC 586:3	r. when your neighbour	TRUM 899:86	Poetry is a means of r.	STEV 850:87
there is r. to hope	JOHN 460:86	**recessions** four out of the last five r.	SAMU 741:2	secret of r.	WEIZ 928:78
There's r. good	JONS 467:69	**recipe** best r. for happiness	AUST 46:68	**redfaced** r. from eating and drinking	ABBO 1:1
To express yourself needs a r.	AI WEI 10:8	man must have a rare r.	LAMB 505:18	**Redgauntlet** 'Then…' said R.	SCOTT 752:75
to perfect…the intellect or r.	SPIN 841:81	**recipes** r. that are always successful	VALE 907:4	**red-haired** R.-H. Man's Wife	CARL 199:67
triumph of human r.	HAWK 401:88	**recipient** comforting…to be the r.	FOWL 345:64	**red-hot** Last of the R.-H.	TUCK 901:16
vaster r.	THOM 886:72	**reciprocity** eternal r. of tears	OWEN 658:40	r.-h. with drinking	SHAK 804:29
voice of r. is stifled	BURKE 175:24	**reciproque** rewarded…with the r.	BACON 51:80	**rediscover** r. their humanity	TUTU 901:22
war…for such a stupid r.	MARY 579:46	**recklessly** r. inserted lightbulbs	KENN 480:95	**redress** no r. for the present	DISR 287:25
what humanity, r.…tells me	BURKE 175:18	**reckon** if you could tell how to r.	SHAK 775:83	r. of real grievances	PEEL 672:66
what's the r.?	HARI 398:33	**reckoning** much at your own r.	TROL 897:33	Things past r.	SHAK 764:46
where we go is r.	PATC 668:6	**re-clothe** r.-c. us in our rightful mind	WHIT 938:24	**reds** R.…that shouuuuuuurt	CARRA 202:57
with how little r.	JOHN 459:38	**recognition** books…deserve r.	VIAN 911:70	**reed** And night this toppling r.	BLUN 143:73
without the use of r.	LEON 523:79	cannot force a r.	KISS 493:84	bruised r. shall he not break	BIBLE 117:82
words clothed in r.'s garb	MILT 602:60	displaced by the r.	WAGN 915:2	bruised r. shall he not break	BIBLE 109:86
worse appear The better r.	MILT 602:58	grace beyond r.	REID 710:44	clasped a r.	SHEL 816:64
reasonable Man, being r.	BYRON 190:8	hunger for r. and money	SELF 756:10	Man is only a r.	PASC 667:81
no r. man could have expected	HERB 412:48	**recognize** as if I should r. it	DOYLE 297:66	r. shaken with the wind	BIBLE 116:77
r. man adapts himself	SHAW 808:49	not r. me by my face	TROL 898:52	sighing of a r.	BYRON 190:27
right than be r.	NASH 631:78	r. the honourable Member	CHUR 226:9	staff of this broken r.	BIBLE 108:78
The R. Man	HERB 413:50	r. your prime	SPARK 836:68	staff of this bruised r.	BIBLE 98:82
reasonableness sweet r. of Jesus	ARNO 36:37	**recollect** does not r. where	JOHN 464:87	**reeducation** r. of perception	DEWEY 276:20
reasoning contain any abstract r.	HUME 438:7	r. all the little events	WELL 929:6	**reefs** collection of r., rocks	MORT 621:66
knowledge…by r.	BACON 54:57	We must r.	PITT 680:11	**Reekie** Auld R.!	FERG 333:86
r. and belief…essential materials?	CARL 201:14	**recollection** alas! r. at hand	COWP 251:98	**reel** beheaded in the third r.	MILLS 595:10
r. comes down to…feeling	PASC 667:79	**recommendation** letter of r.	ADDI 6:30	earth shall r. to and fro	BIBLE 108:66
r. to the test of experiment	LAVO 512:35	**recommendations** opposite r.	SIMON 822:74	r. to and fro	BIBLE 108:65
What has R. to do with…Painting	BLAKE 141:36	**recompense** r. is a pleasure	JOHN 459:52	r. to and fro	BIBLE 102:16
reasons bad r. for what we believe	BRAD 155:41	**reconcilement** never can true r.	MILT 604:94	**re-elected** don't know how to get r.-e.	JUNCK 471:44
born, And he had r.	ROBI 718:84	**reconciliation** r. with dullness	LOWE 540:35	**reeling** Love, the r. midnight through	PARK 664:15
five r. why men drink	ALDR 12:53	**record** artistic r. created	ROCK 721:40	**reels** threesome r.…foursome r.	BURNS 180:44
function…to make r. for husbands	ELIOT 315:36	dreadful r. of sin	DOYLE 297:59	**refer** r. to Rule 1	ITO 448:79
Good r. must…give place	SHAK 778:47	I think that's the r.	THOM 884:30	**reference** favourable r. to the Devil	CHUR 226:7
heart has its r.	PASC 667:80	Poetry is a r.	SHEL 816:52	no r. to fun in any Act	HERB 413:49
r. are as two grains of wheat	SHAK 769:73	puts a r. on the gramophone	ELIOT 318:5	**references** R. upon request	DAVIS 265:94
r. for making war	FRED 349:37	r. is fragmentary	WHIT 936:71	**refine** correct, insert, r.	SWIFT 862:61
r. that I quit going to the theatre	SALI 740:86	r. of his triumphant passage	KENN 481:14	r. our language	JOHN 459:57
Strong r. make strange actions	SHAK 768:61	r.…of our mother and father	FRAME 346:47	**refined** Englishwoman is so r.	SMITH 830:34
there are no r.	MO 611:68	searched the r. for years	MENC 586:92	more r., restricted, ceremonial	REAG 708:98
two very cogent r.	JOHN 464:81	set down the following r.	FRAME 346:76	R. himself to soul	DRYD 304:44
rebel bound to r. against	IBSEN 444:1	to r. what you want	HOLI 423:48	**refinement** r. on the principle	BURKE 175:17
boy is a r. and an anarch	MILL 594:87	**recording** r., not thinking	ISHE 447:16	**reflect** gave Leibniz time to r.	FONT 342:78
Nobody wants to feel they're *not* a r.	CRIC 254:93	**records** half-a-dozen r.	SHAW 809:89	r. that what people may say	SMITH 829:13
r.…turning into an autocrat	DURR 308:36	r. for both home runs	RODG 721:50	**reflection** after long r.	GALL 358:39
Showed like a r.'s whore	SHAK 795:98	r. of the human spirit	MACL 555:37	buildings…the r. of society	PEI 672:73
very r. to my will	SHAK 795:75	r. prove the title good	ARLO 32:31	habit of profound r.	CONR 244:48
What is a r.?	CAMUS 196:90	wise nation preserves its r.	HOWE 433:91	humiliating r.	FERN 334:96
rebelled or him who hath r.	MILT 605:23	**recover** r. what has been lost	ELIOT 320:67	Mental r. is…more interesting	PIRS 679:91
rebellion a sort of mental r.	ORWE 654:39	seldom or ever r.	SHAK 795:91		

reflections

objects of R.	LOCKE	533:90
probably a r.	HOPP	429:2
r. of your own minds	ASTE	39:1
truth of a r.	MONT	613:12
reflections Mortifying R.	CONG	241:50
reflex r. of a star	WORD	957:70
reflexes r....caused in other people	BALD	56:15
reform All r. except a moral one	CARL	202:44
Beginning r.	WELL	929:7
party of progress or r.	MILL	591:1
r. a world	CARL	200:87
r. the old man	TWAIN	902:54
r. this little piece	MILLS	595:8
spirit of the R. Bill	PEEL	672:66
To innovate is not to r.	BURKE	176:55
reformation plotting some new r.	DRYD	302:96
reforming of R. itself	MILT	601:19
reformers All R., however strict	SMITH	829:20
drifting social r.	STRA	856:35
martyrs or r.—or both	CHAR	215:28
R. are going into hiding	SHEV	818:11
we're law r.	HUMP	439:13
refrain still remember the r.	MACA	544:8
with a happy r.	FREED	349:42
refreshment R. after toil	MILT	599:79
refrigerator keep a martini in the r.	DE	275:12
refrigerators r....great modern	WARH	920:8
refudiate Peaceful Muslims, pls r.	PALIN	661:60
refuge eternal God is thy r.	BIBLE	95:3
God is our r.	SCOT	755:86
God is our r. and strength	BIBLE	100:67
last r. of a scoundrel	JOHN	462:37
Lord, which is my r.	BIBLE	102:97
Paradise shall be the r.	KORAN	498:90
r. from distress	WORD	961:38
r. from home life	SHAW	806:95
r. open to every man	BABE	48:4
safe r. for the exile	GARI	360:72
so easy to take r. in	IBSEN	444:9
thou hast been our r.	BOOK	149:29
thy wings shall be my r.	BOOK	149:20
refugees Serbs out, Nato in, r. back	ROBE	717:75
refusal Every known class of r.	SOME	833:10
every r. to act	REED	710:37
r. of language is a death	BART	66:24
refuse an offer he can't r.	PUZO	701:4
I r. to become a seeker	RICH	713:8
I r. to send anyone else	RANK	706:64
large r. bin	BAIN	55:95
mind will very generally r.	TROL	898:51
no just government should r.	JEFF	454:23
people r. to see me	ELLI	323:35
r. in respect of our child	BIBLE	112:71
r. to answer that question	ASHCR	37:63
refute r. it thus	JOHN	461:5
regalia Great Queen in her r.	GAY	362:9
regard have as great a r. for religion	OCAS	646:79
r. the law courts	INGR	446:37
r. to their own interest	SMITH	827:76
Should be without r.	SHAK	797:45
Unconditional positive r.	ROGE	722:65
Victorian r. for the pride of people	PRIT	696:25
without r. to your happiness	PECK	672:64
regeneration r....into a new state	ELIOT	315:25
Regent's Park in the sun, in R. P.	WOOLF	955:15
regime in love...a political r.	LESS	524:2
we enter a new r.	DOUG	295:23
regiment breasts for r.	MARL	572:99
kings, when r. is gone	MARL	573:16
led his r. from behind	GILB	370:71
Monstrous R. of Women	KNOX	495:13
r.'s in 'ollow square	KIPL	489:84
region airy r. thrilling	MILT	597:34
r. is facing a deep abyss	HUSS	440:37
r. where 'twas born	MARV	576:86
regions r. mild of calm and...air	MILT	598:62
r. of sin and falsity	MILT	600:11
r. of sorrow, doleful shades	MILT	601:35
unknown r. preserved	ELIOT	316:46
views...the r. of the sky	ENNI	326:17
register r. of the crimes and miseries	IRVI	447:55
regress r. is...downfall	BACON	51:85
regret at last and vain r.	ROSS	726:62
If that plane leaves...you'll r. it	EPST	327:30
Old Age a r.	DISR	287:26
one r. in life	ALLEN	14:89
One should never r.	BANKS	62:25

only possible r. I have	BORO	151:66
only r. in the theatre	BARR	65:2
r. can die!	TENN	879:87
r. that I have but one	HALE	392:27
r. very much that	HOMER	425:11
said goodbye to without r.	HARD	396:93
seldom spoken with greater r.	BALD	57:34
the most destructive force...? R.	JONES	466:28
those who do not r.	PUTIN	700:93
wild with all r.	TENN	872:43
regrets Do I have r.?	CLIN	230:17
end up with the right r.	MILL	593:48
follies which a man r. most	ROWL	729:22
I can't say I have any r.	ARMS	32:45
regular icily r.	TENN	875:14
regularity Genius and r.	GAIN	356:9
regulation The R. Act	WILDE	942:18
regulations cannot frame r.	HAWT	401:98
rehabilitation sad, refusing r.	KIRK	493:82
rehearsal Comedy of 'The R.'	JOHN	464:93
rehearsed if I had r. you	YEATS	966:23
Reich greater part of the R.	GOEB	374:54
reign called upon some day to r.	HARD	396:91
coined in some r.	LAMB	505:93
dead r.	ZOLA	970:16
govern is to r.	MIRA	608:16
lazy, long, lascivious r.	DEFOE	269:72
Omnipotent but friendship is to r.	SHEL	814:41
r. had here its last	MILT	597:34
r. in this horrible place	COWP	250:96
r. of chaos and old Night	MILT	602:49
reigning r. over a fourth-class nation	JAY	453:5
reigns arrangement into three r.	GUED	389:83
Dunce the second r.	POPE	688:29
reincarnated If I were r.	FAUL	331:44
reindeer Can R. Fly?	HIGH	418:51
sleigh, and eight tiny r.	MOORE	616:62
reinforcement r. of the State	CAMUS	196:91
reins try the r.	BIBLE	110:20
reinvent r. himself	BURU	182:90
reject those who r. you	WHIT	938:15
rejected despised and r. of men	BIBLE	109:93
rejection concise, slighting r. slip	HELL	408:35
eventual r.	LEBO	517:59
use the r. as an excuse	ANGE	19:94
rejoice before Him, and r.	KETHE	483:67
before him and r.	SCOT	755:88
fortunate, I r. at it	SHAK	777:36
I r. that America has resisted	PITT	679:5
R., and be exceeding glad	BIBLE	114:27
r. and be glad	BIBLE	102:22
r. for a moment	YUAN	969:67
R. in the Lord alway	BIBLE	128:4
R., O young man	BIBLE	106:35
R.! R.! R.!	HEATH	405:88
R., the Lord is King!	WESL	931:61
R. with them that do r.	BIBLE	125:26
that wanted to r.	SURR	860:3
rejoicing come again with r.	BIBLE	103:35
related men to whom they are r.	GILM	371:91
relation mental r. with a woman	LAWR	513:70
nobody like a r.	THAC	880:24
No cold r. is a zealous citizen	BURKE	176:49
poor r. is the most irrelevant	LAMB	506:12
some occult r.	JOHN	459:54
relations altering the old r.	CARL	200:81
even one's own r.	WILDE	941:89
great men have their poor r.	DICK	281:70
memory...all its clear r.	ELIOT	317:72
r. of...Government and...people	REED	710:37
unreasonably large stock of r.	SHAW	811:33
whatever their r. with men	FREN	350:53
relationship a r. with Ms Lewinsky	CLIN	230:95
if we have that r.	EDDI	311:26
lifelong r....divorce will never	MORR	621:63
outside this work r.	MARX	578:26
r. between man and man	ROUS	729:17
remains of the 'special r.'	BENN	79:32
special r.	CHUR	226:13
special r. with the United States	ACHE	2:33
their mutual association and r.	PLATO	682:66
women see the r. between objects	FOWL	345:61
relationships don't spend...in r.	BRAD	154:25
extra-marital r.	ALLEN	14:97
r. of color or form	ROTH	728:3
such r. as our minds	LEBON	517:55
sum of connections and r.	MARX	579:38

relative set out...In a r. way	BULL	173:58
Success is R.	ELIOT	319:50
relatives people your r. hate	HAMM	395:67
We're down to blood r.	MCCA	547:72
relativism R. implies...indifference	VAN	908:12
relaxation form of r. to me	HAMM	394:60
release illusory r.	UPDI	906:35
inescapable, imperative need for r.	FEIN	332:57
prisoner's r.	SIDN	820:46
relic cased up, like a holy r.	WEBS	927:53
rob the r.	DRYD	303:8
sad r. of departed worth!	BYRON	187:40
relics hallowed r.	MILT	597:39
R. from the past	CHEE	218:4
relief approaches the effect of r.	MICH	590:70
certain r. in change	IRVI	447:61
experience r. when one returns	COUP	248:26
for the r. of the body	RICH	713:99
For this r. much thanks	SHAK	780:28
great r. to reach this	SKIN	825:49
liquor is the only mechanical r.	HEMI	410:77
r. and depth	GOYA	380:82
sleep provides r.	CHAM	213:71
religion all the r. I want	HALD	392:25
anger about r.	HALI	393:39
any r., by any sect	KRIS	499:11
Art and R....two roads	BELL	75:33
As to r.	PAINE	660:32
as well as in r.	JUNI	471:48
As with the Christian r.	ORWE	653:15
basic command of r.	TOYN	895:78
belief imposed by r.	KRIS	499:12
black face and a different r.	EDWA	312:59
broken down by Age, Sex, and R.	MACR	558:14
brothels with bricks of R.	BLAKE	140:89
can't talk r. to a man	SHAW	809:73
Christianity...man's r.	WELD	928:83
Christianity was the r.	SWIFT	863:77
cult is a r. with no...power	WOLFE	953:76
do the same by their r.	DICK	282:2
drunk on whiskey or r.	MENC	586:4
each r. only one of the seven colours	BLAV	142:51
either on r. or policy	RUSK	733:8
established as a r.	LEWIS	527:66
Football is like a r.	PELE	672:76
For my r.	BROW	164:42
freed from his r.	SAINT	738:41
freedom of r.	JEFF	454:26
handmaid to r.	BACON	50:34
happens by accident...becomes a r.	WRIS	963:74
hearing about r. even more	MITF	610:52
Hoo-doo...was an unorganized r.	REED	710:35
If r. is about truth	SULL	859:75
If r. is only a garment	BONH	146:24
if R. were intended	BUTL	185:70
in both science and r.	SAGAN	737:26
indirect way to plant r.	BROW	165:60
In matters of r....I never give any advice	CHES	219:45
in the Roman Catholic r.	TROL	897:35
late to trust the old r.	LOWE	540:28
leave him for r.	SPARK	835:62
life smashes r.	NERU	633:23
literature is a substitute for r.	ELIOT	318:20
Malay r. and custom	PANG	662:81
manners and r.	MONT	613:10
man's r. is the chief fact	CARL	201:30
man talks loudly against r.	STER	848:32
Men will wrangle for r.	COLT	238:81
My r. and my art	JOHN	456:85
no reason to bring r. into it	OCAS	646:79
not impossibilities enough in r.	BROW	165:51
of any r., or party or profession	COLE	236:53
One r. is as true as another	BURT	181:48
original feature of any r.	PAINE	660:35
paradox of high r.	NIEB	637:87
Philistine of genius in r.	ARNO	36:36
philosophy bringeth...to r.	BACON	51:79
plant our r. in Paris	LESL	523:88
prophecy, and r., all in one	RUSK	733:14
Pure r. and undefiled	BIBLE	130:52
reject me on account of my r.	BELL	76:57
R. and art...from the same root	CATH	208:95
R. blushing veils	POPE	689:47
r. but a childish toy	MARL	572:7
R. Caesar never knew	COWP	250:94
R. does not banish mirth	WALT	920:96

representative

r. has had its day	BENN 81:81
r., history…would be useless	BALZ 61:5
R. is far more acute than science	FORS 344:33
R. is for people…scared of hell	TYSON 904:14
R. is something which stands	WHIT 936:65
R. is the sigh	MARX 578:24
r. is to do good.	PAINE 660:36
R. is what a man does	WHIT 936:68
r. is whatever…most interested in	BARR 65:92
r., knavery, and change	BEHN 75:18
r. most prevalent in our northern	BURKE 175:17
r.…not simply morality	ARNO 36:34
r. of gold	BAGE 54:69
r. of money	GAUT 361:7
r. of science	LEWIS 527:65
R.'s in the heart	JERR 455:45
r. to make us hate	SWIFT 861:31
R.…tragedy of mankind	WILS 947:36
r.…true remedy for superstition	BURKE 175:19
r.…will be replaced by poetry	ARNO 36:41
r. without science is blind	EINS 313:79
r. would still be holy and divine	BAUD 69:79
respect the other fellow's r.	MENC 586:5
revolution of 1789 is her political r.	LAMA 504:73
rules of my r. from Rome	BROW 165:45
rum and true r.	BYRON 189:5
Self-righteousness is not r.	BRON 161:65
Sensible men are all the same r.	DISR 289:71
serve the French in place of a state r.	BIER 134:83
snare to R.	TAYL 868:58
standard of r., intelligence, and virtue	SMIL 827:71
Superstition…r. of feeble minds	BURKE 176:46
That is my r.	SHAW 809:72
'Theosophy' is the essence of all r.	BLAV 142:50
this man's r. is vain	BIBLE 130:51
true r. of America	MAIL 560:60
truly bad effects of r.	DAWK 266:21
when r. was strong	SZASZ 865:26
wisest r.	HAIL 392:17
with r. and fear	JONS 467:62
religions knit and break r.	SHAK 791:80
natural language of all r.	STAEL 842:2
of all great r.	TEMP 869:68
R. are kept alive by heresies	BREN 158:97
religious act out of r. conviction	ECO 310:19
All known r. beliefs	DURK 308:30
Art among a r. race	FUSE 356:93
belief is made r.	CUPI 258:85
be virtuous—be r.	SCOTT 754:84
Casting a dim r. light	MILT 598:59
commit…to any r. belief	WAUGH 923:64
decline of r. belief	FREUD 350:61
feeling…about some r. expressions	RABI 704:23
first expounder of our r. belief	SPEKE 836:81
hope I will be r. again	FLEM 340:47
labour movement was truly r.	WOLFE 953:79
Man…a r. animal	BURKE 176:44
natural r. sense	LAWR 514:86
private parts…and his r. opinions	BUTL 186:10
r. inquiries	GIBB 366:99
R. law is like…grammar	SACKS 736:4
r. system…green Chartreuse	SAKI 739:51
r. ties…social pedigree	WOLFE 953:78
R. tolerance	ROMN 723:94
same r. experience	ROTH 728:3
seem to be r.	BIBLE 130:51
take an almost r. view	HOYLE 434:95
troubled with r. doubt	CHES 221:1
virtually r. prophecy	NISB 639:28
We are a r. people	DOUG 295:22
religious-good Good, but not r.-g.	HARDY 396:1
religiously follows r. the new	THOR 888:35
religiousness center of true r.	EINS 313:80
reliques religious race produces r.	FUSE 356:93
relish some r. of the saltness	SHAK 772:71
relishes lullings and the r. of it	HERB 413:67
reluctantly r., unexpectedly	MORT 621:70
rely wouldn't…r. on the press	HITCH 420:89
remain but the rocks in.	HERB 413:54
days go by, I r.	APOL 29:82
nothing will r.	HOUS 431:40
'Shall r.?'	SHAK 799:96
so r. ignorant	GREG 387:52
south of us r.	JOHN 458:24
remains cut up what r.	KIPL 489:88
r. an Englishman!	GILB 368:35
remake Myself I must r.	YEATS 967:34
remark can't stand…rude r.	WILL 945:81
fowl, blinking at you without r.	ELIOT 315:41
Which I wish to r.	HARTE 400:72
remarkable nothing left r.	SHAK 795:84
r. thing about Shakespeare	GRAV 383:38
to wish to be r.	HOLM 424:75
remarks r. are not literature	STEIN 845:62
remedies encumbering it with r.	TOLS 894:50
not apply new r.	BACON 52:9
prescribes the r.	MOLI 612:91
r. oft in ourselves	SHAK 791:58
When r. are past	SHAK 789:98
remedy Auntie Maggie's…r.	FORM 344:21
Death is the r.	CHAM 213:71
desperate…dangerous r.	FAWK 331:53
for the deid r. is none	DUNB 306:4
know not how to r.	KYD 501:51
no r. against this consumption	SHAK 772:75
r. for everything except death	CERV 211:47
r. is worse than the disease	BACON 52:96
sought the r.	SHAK 780:18
Things without all r.	SHAK 797:45
What is the r.?	SHAK 786:28
remember Ah yes! I r. it well	LERN 523:82
cannot but r. such things	SHAK 798:62
cannot r. anyone ever asking	REAR 709:17
day I can already r.	VALL 907:10
if thou wilt, r.	ROSS 726:46
I r., I r., The fir trees	HOOD 426:23
I r., I r., The house	HOOD 426:22
I r. watching myself	RHYS 712:78
must r. this	HUPF 440:35
never r. whether it snowed	THOM 884:46
r. Degas	PISS 679:98
R. First to possess his books	SHAK 804:23
r. me before I'm dead	BRAND 156:62
R. me when I am gone	ROSS 726:41
R. that you are an Englishman	RHOD 712:71
R. thee?	SHAK 781:66
R. the rights	GLAD 373:38
r. what is past	HALI 393:37
thou r. and I forget	SWIN 863:80
To r. is far worse	BENU 83:10
who I r. he was	SEXT 758:50
Who will r.	SASS 746:99
wrong people r. Vietnam	HERR 415:97
ye want to r.	KELM 479:70
remembered Campbell-Bannerman is	
r. chiefly	BENT 82:6
it's about being r.	ARMA 32:37
names…freshly r.	SHAK 776:91
r.…for the invention of a mouse!	DISN 287:14
r. poor Julian	HEMI 410:78
surest way not to be r.	MAIL 560:54
tranquillity r. in emotion	PARK 664:20
remembrance book of r. was written	BIBLE 112:64
first…to my I ever saw	PEPYS 674:99
flood of r.	LAWR 512:46
Makes the r. dear	SHAK 791:72
Mournful and never-ending R.	POE 683:90
My r. is very free	SHAK 786:20
r. of things past	SHAK 801:47
rosemary, that's for r.	SHAK 784:55
this do in r. of me	BIBLE 126:49
reminiscences old have r.	SAKI 739:53
R. make one feel	SHAW 806:80
some of your grosser r.	WOOL 956:41
remission Without…no r.	BIBLE 129:36
remnants r. of such a beautiful habit	ALME 15:10
remodified We can be r., changed	DOUG 296:25
remonstrance all complaint and r.	MACA 546:55
remorse hottentot, without r.!	SITW 823:95
r., my worm	RIMB 716:51
R., the fatal egg	COWP 251:4
What says Monsieur R.?	SHAK 770:31
with as little r.	SHAK 773:12
remorseless treacherous and r.	SHAW 807:17
remote inconceivably r.	WELLS 930:20
removed cannot be r., but abideth	BIBLE 103:34
It ought to be r.	BEEC 73:63
r. from contact with…life	PRIT 696:16
r. from the sphere	KING 488:58
remuneration r. for…footballer	ANON 23:95
renaissance antiquity and its R.	KLEE 494:1
Leonardo da Vinci and the R.	WELL 929:93
r. is a logical link	MASA 580:49
R. was simply the green end	FOWL 345:62
rend time to r.	BIBLE 106:14
render perfumes…more they r.	WEBS 926:19
r. to every one his due	JUST 471:51
rendezvous r. with Death	SEEG 755:99
renegade whips to kennel The r.	RANS 707:72
renewal Boston…Urban R.	MAIL 560:55
renovator that great r. of matter	OVID 657:21
renown high r., riches, and royaltie	DUNB 306:2
Some, for r., on scraps	YOUNG 968:54
rent like r. and wages	SMITH 827:82
r. everything	KOSI 499:2
r. out my room	ALLEN 14:92
r. we pay	GREN 388:58
to go on paying the r.	TURN 901:20
Rentacrowd R. Ltd.	SIMP 822:82
rent-day awesome reality to R. D.	ANGE 19:97
rentiers indistinguishable from r.	ROBI 718:92
renunciation act of r.	MORAN 618:9
beautiful things made by r.	DEGAS 269:85
repair friendship in constant r.	JOHN 460:65
reparation never make r.	JAMES 451:59
repartee majority…the best r.	DISR 288:39
repeal method to secure the r.	GRANT 381:9
repeat condemned to r. it	SANT 743:41
does no harm to r.	LESS 524:1
r. in one period	RENO 711:57
shall have to r. that	HOUS 433:79
those things that r. and r.	WILD 943:51
what they hear, they r.!	SITW 823:2
repel retard what we cannot r.	JOHN 460:72
repelled r. in r. by those	REDON 709:24
only r. by man	INGE 445:27
repent all men every where to r.	BIBLE 125:94
Dead men never r.	DICK 278:66
It doth r. me	SHEL 814:8
r. at leisure	CONG 240:30
r. in dust and ashes	BIBLE 99:23
r. in haste	CONG 240:31
r. it from my very soul	SHAK 760:30
R. what's past	SHAK 784:43
R. ye: for the kingdom of heaven	BIBLE 114:18
when one cannot r.?	SHAK 783:33
repentance R. is the virtue of weak	DRYD 299:13
R.…want of power to sin	DRYD 304:53
sinners to r.	BIBLE 116:63
sinners to r.	BIBLE 119:50
Try what r. can	SHAK 783:33
repetition r. of the wrong way	DURR 308:38
repetitions use not vain r.	BIBLE 115:41
replace One technology doesn't r. another	FRY 354:46
reply heartening and the strong r.	EMPS 326:10
not to make r.	TENN 875:12
sportive kind of r.	GRAY 384:59
third, the R. Churlish	SHAK 780:24
report composed as a conference r.?	GRIS 389:75
good r. maketh the bones fat	BIBLE 104:77
not too proud to r.	DANA 261:24
r. of an aspect	LIPP 531:40
r. of my death	TWAIN 903:87
r. of valour	SHAK 786:14
r. on what I know	FRIS 351:81
r. what he means	ANON 25:52
the right to r. events	ORWE 655:67
they have committed false r.	SHAK 774:55
Who hath believed our r.?	BIBLE 109:93
reporters gallery in which the r. sit	MACA 545:31
reports daily r. are submitted	STEAD 843:34
r., films, phonograph records?	RODC 721:43
r. that I took the loss badly	DOLE 290:96
repose appreciate the charm of r.	LIVI 532:55
give thy r. To the wet sea-boy	SHAK 772:85
hushed in grim r.	GRAY 385:86
In Claude's landscape all is…r.	CONS 244:58
No r. for Sir Walter	SCOTT 754:83
r. implicitly on	JEFF 454:25
r. is taboo'd	GILB 369:54
r. of a pacific station	ADAMS 4:72
seek r. In listlessness	WORD 958:74
sigh for thy r.	WESL 932:66
repositories r. of the marvellous	DIOR 287:4
representation Taxation without r.	OTIS 656:92
Tragedy is…a r.	ARIS 31:23
without r.	TOYN 895:72
representations just r. of general	JOHN 461:8
representative being your r.	BELL 76:57
most r., the physical scientists	SNOW 832:77
r. of wealth	MILL 591:96

representatives

representatives r. of the people — WHIT 934:24
repressed being persecuted and r. — ROLL 723:90
repression r. of the high hope — WHIT 936:66
reproach common r. is true — SOCR 833:96
  common term of r. — BERG 83:18
  escape r. — JOHN 460:67
  lexicon of...ridicule and r. — SAFI 737:17
reproduce cannot be expected to r. — HOLM 424:85
reproduction Strangelove R. — COUP 248:34
reptile of the fish and r. — LOWE 540:23
reptiles fishes and r. — BRYAN 170:98
  poisonous r. — GERA 364:61
republic architects of our r. — KING 487:27
  At its birth, the r. — LAMA 504:74
  despair of the R.! — WHAR 933:2
  How beautiful the R. was — DURR 308:34
  Love the Beloved R. — FORS 345:47
  rarely happens that a r. — MACH 553:94
  r. has been much more powerful — ADDI 6:21
  R. has no need for scientists — COFF 234:92
  r. of conscience — HEAN 405:77
  R. of equals — BABE 48:4
  The R. will be conservative — THIE 883:97
  true R. — ANTH 29:73
republican on r. principles — SHAW 807:97
  R. form of government — SPEN 836:90
  R. landslide on Nov 8 — CUOMO 258:83
  The R. Party — STEV 851:15
  unaware that baseball was a R. sport — ROBB 717:70
  vote for Hollywood as a R. — WALL 917:44
Republicans If R. will stop — STEV 850:3
  its members are now R. — ONEI 651:81
  R....get elected — OROU 652:94
republics Large r. seem — PALM 662:71
  Mischiefes to Churches, to R. — PRYN 698:62
  perfect r. are a perfect nonsense — FOWL 345:59
  R. end by wealth — MONT 614:42
repugnance historical r. to woman — PAGL 659:17
repulsion Attraction and r. — BLAKE 139:94
reputation At ev'ry word a r. dies — POPE 685:37
  bad r. is like a hangover — PRES 694:75
  better for the r. — KEYN 485:84
  dignity has descended over his r. — ATLAS 40:19
  her scandalous r. — SITW 823:97
  I have offended r. — SHAK 794:67
  injured no man's r. — LOVE 538:89
  lover's bad r. — NAPO 630:46
  made himself of no r. — BIBLE 128:97
  man's r. outlasts his munny — BILL 135:96
  purest treasure...Is spotless r. — SHAK 764:32
  r. for being difficult — MATT 582:97
  r. for eccentricity — SHAR 806:77
  r. for honesty — JONS 468:88
  r. for wisdom and honour — BIBLE 106:30
  R. is an idle...imposition — SHAK 789:12
  r. is at stake — SHAK 787:40
  r. of five-and-twenty — DRYD 299:17
  r. of having read — THUR 891:4
  r. of understanding — DRYD 300:39
  R., r., r.! — SHAK 789:11
  Seeking the bubble r. — SHAK 779:82
  shook hands with R. — WEBS 927:54
  so high a public r. — FRIE 351:71
  the r. of benevolence — SHER 817:93
  unenviable r. — THOR 889:49
  Until you've lost your r. — MITC 610:41
  women as the r. of men — MONT 613:13
  wrecks a woman's r. — COLE 236:57
  your r. will take care of itself — SUGAR 859:73
reputations murdered r. of the week — CONG 241:54
  true fuller's earth for r. — GAY 362:17
request r. for my resignation — DARM 263:48
  r....at my departure — EMMET 325:6
requests let your r. be made known — BIBLE 128:4
  timid r., invites denial — SENE 757:25
requiem continent's violent r. — DUNC 307:9
required r. neither genius nor knowledge — JOHN 460:83
  that which is r. of him — GILL 370:81
requirement first r. of a statesman — ACHE 3:39
  primary r. for a writer — STAEL 842:99
requirements meet the barest r. — MCEW 551:28
  unfortunate r. — SHAR 806:73
requisite It is r. from time to time — JEVO 455:55
requite lest he r. thee — BIBLE 113:87
rescue come to our r. — YOUR 968:59

rescuers had to r. themselves — TIME 892:21
  r. the dead — IGNA 445:18
  To r. our children — JORD 469:2
rescuers r. had to rescue themselves — TIME 892:21
research design of scientific r. — LEWO 528:78
  Effective r. scarcely begins — KUHN 500:37
  supply plenty of r. — FALU 329:11
researches no end to our r. — MONT 614:30
  r. in original sin — PLOM 682:73
resemblance r. to World War II — BARR 64:82
resemble r. her to thee — WALL 918:55
  we will r. you in that — SHAK 769:1
resent r....unless...biased — VORS 915:55
resentment r. and...the whip — LESS 523:90
  r. towards persons — NEWM 635:48
reservation stick us on a r. — MCMU 557:82
reservations mountain parks and r. — MUIR 624:25
reserve kindness in r. — POPE 688:4
  r. inventory of...thinking — RAND 706:55
reserves it was Rochdale r. — SHAN 805:64
reservoir inexhaustible r. of love — BAUD 69:87
  r. on Forty-second Street — AUCH 42:65
  r., to keep and spare — POPE 686:68
  words drawn from the special r. — ACHE 2:28
reservoirs r. of strength — GREER 387:45
residence Ireland as a place of r. — SAKI 739:64
  ruined by r. in Italy — RUSK 733:13
residencies Inns are not r. — MOORE 617:80
residents r. from raw estates — LARK 509:84
resignation admire their r. — MACD 549:17
  first request for my r. — DARM 263:48
  Please accept my r. — MARX 578:21
  r. is active — FITZ 338:3
  special excitement of a rumored r. — SHUL 819:23
  with courage and r., both — BANKS 62:29
resigned r....in full agreement — HOWE 433:89
resist It boots not to r. — SHAK 760:14
  r. everything except temptation — WILDE 941:75
  r. only what is inevitable — MILL 594:90
  R. the devil, and he will flee — BIBLE 130:58
  respect only those who r. me — DE 270:96
resistance Americans...r. — TRIL 897:17
  glory of the r. — LACL 503:31
  length of r. to which Ulster — LAW 512:36
  line of least r. — AMERY 15:25
  passive r. — MELV 584:74
  refinement on the principle of r. — BURKE 175:17
  r. in your listener — MILL 595:93
  salvation along the lines of least r. — FORD 342:88
  support the Nicaraguan r. — NORTH 641:63
  surrender...was as honorable as r. — ANGE 18:86
  those that offer r. — SOPH 834:28
resisted when it ought to be r. — HAWT 402:13
resolution could reach that great r. — BROW 165:64
  native hue of r. — SHAK 783:7
  native hue of r. — TWAIN 902:63
  r. from despair — MILT 602:42
  thought and r. — TROL 897:32
resolutions great and mighty r. — BUTL 185:72
resolve fixed r. not to quit — MORAN 618:9
  R. not to be poor — JOHN 464:85
  R. to be thyself — ARNO 34:78
resolved inwardly r. — TWAIN 902:45
resonance r. of his solitude — CONN 243:17
resort various bustle of r. — MILT 599:72
resource r. of the feeble — GIBB 366:96
  sacrifice of another r. — HERF 414:91
  the world's most underused r. — CLIN 231:35
resources between scarce r. — ROBB 717:68
  confident of its own r. — LIVI 532:55
  R. left in the ground are saved — BRODY 160:44
  r....within your reach — PIND 678:80
  services of our r. — FRIE 351:70
  you have no Inner R. — BERR 87:98
respect due r. — STEE 844:44
  English have no r. — SHAW 810:93
  Failure to r. — BENE 79:16
  feelings of awe and r. — DICK 277:39
  fellow of a poet — SHAK 778:55
  first claim on your r. — JUVE 471:59
  guarded only by neighbourly r. — CHUR 225:80
  hold them in r. — SAND 742:26
  How I did r. you — TROL 898:36
  how much I should r. myself — JAMES 450:23
  means of procuring r. — JOHN 463:46
  neither doth God r. any person — BIBLE 96:47
  no r. of place, persons, nor time — SHAK 785:94

On both sides more r. — SHAK 799:97
only qualifications I really much r. — JAMES 451:54
poor but deserving of r. — OCON 647:91
R. and reason — SHAK 762:94
r. for anything — LOUIS 538:74
r. for the living symbol — LABO 501:5
r. if not enthusiastic acceptance — ANGE 18:87
r. must give us pause — TWAIN 902:63
r. only those who resist me — DE 270:96
that faint word, r.! — DRYD 301:53
treat him with priestly r. — OFLA 647:98
Treat people with r. — OBAMA 645:53
When people do not r. us — TWAIN 903:80
without losing one's r. — SAKI 739:61
respectability R. is a very good thing — STEV 851:24
  save a shred of its r. — READ 708:94
  wife's fidelity and his mother's r. — SHAW 811:29
respectable cannot make him r. — EMER 325:77
  easy and r. — TROL 897:22
  except to appear r. — STEV 852:57
  from Madeira, but perfectly r. — SHAW 806:93
  genius found r.? — BROW 166:2
  highly r. — GILB 369:47
  more r. he is — SHAW 807:15
  those who aren't r. — SAKI 739:63
respected R. people are only rascals — STEN 847:6
  r....through her toilette — DE 268:46
respectful gentle and r. ways — FENW 332:64
respiration it was artificial r. — BURG 174:88
response disgust is reason's proper r. — PAGL 659:17
  r. is to the image — PRICE 695:81
  r. to error that counts — GIOV 372:16
  r. will be adequate — FULL 355:74
responsibility allocate the r. — HIRO 419:73
  artist's first r. is to himself — DAVIS 265:1
  burden of r. — EDWA 312:61
  death without the r. — LEBO 517:58
  don't have the sole r. — DENN 273:73
  equality of r. — KENN 481:16
  heavy burden of r. — EDWA 312:61
  legal and moral r. — HAYD 402:23
  Liberty means r. — SHAW 808:38
  no sense of r. — KNOX 495:20
  power without r. — BALD 57:30
  profit without individual r. — BIER 134:72
  r. does not end at conception — OBAMA 644:28
  r. of society — PALEY 661:55
  r. of the poet — PALEY 661:55
  r. of the poet — PALEY 661:56
  r. of the writer — ALGR 13:70
  r. without power — STOP 855:14
  sense of collective r. — ALDI 12:48
  shunning r. — WEIZ 928:78
  writer have a social r.? — NABO 629:22
  writer's only r. — FAUL 331:40
responsible Being r., I will direct — PITT 679:4
  r. and wrong — CHUR 226:8
rest absolute r. is death — PASC 667:72
  accomplishment of man's r. — BACON 51:88
  all r. my powers defy — DONNE 291:19
  astonish the r. — TWAIN 903:90
  command me to my r. — DRAY 298:92
  die or r. at last! — SHEL 816:58
  distinguished above the r. — HOMER 425:3
  dove found no r. — BIBLE 92:9
  far, far better r. that I go to — DICK 282:1
  fly away, and be at r. — BIBLE 101:75
  give thee r. — BIBLE 94:73
  God...ordained no r. — VAUG 909:40
  ill a-brewing towards my r. — SHAK 769:22
  In returning and r. shall ye be saved — BIBLE 108:73
  in which to r. — GUNN 390:96
  Is your heart at r.? — FLET 341:61
  long long ago at r. — CORY 247:9
  needful hours of r.? — DRYD 302:73
  no r. from evils — PLATO 682:63
  Nothing is easier...than r. — ADAMS 5:94
  One needs more r. — WAUGH 923:63
  playing, to our latest r. — RALE 705:45
  r. from pain — DRYD 299:14
  r. from their labours — BIBLE 132:13
  r. in danger are — ETHE 327:42
  r. in obscurity and peace! — EMMET 325:6
  r. not day and night — BIBLE 131:97
  r. of them ever got here — TRUM 899:76
  r. rather than labour — RICH 714:21
  r. us here...relating tales — SHAK 798:85

rhetoric

seeking r., and findeth none	BIBLE 117:88
shall not r. quiet in Montparnasse	BENET 79:26
should not enter into my r.	BIBLE 102:2
Sleep and r.	TENN 872:37
weary be at r.	BIBLE 98:95
Where's the r. of me?	ROBI 718:80
will not let them r.	KEATS 476:98
restaurant always went right to a r.	LARD 509:68
restaurants don't go to r.	WINN 950:4
preoccupying myself with...r.	SELF 756:12
rested better r. than ordinarily	HEYE 417:39
resting-place find the necessary r.-p.	KIER 485:44
restless his r. hands	PRIT 696:17
its people...moving, shifting, r.	FERB 332:67
R., he rolls	ROCH 719:7
restoration not revolution but r.	HARD 396:94
worst of a revolution is a r.	FOX 346:69
restoratives No r.	FORD 343:1
restrain it is not possible to r. them	RICH 714:21
restraint a tough combo: nerve and r.	SULL 859:77
free from this r.	CONG 241:78
praise the firm r.	CAMP 194:51
suffer from too rigid a r.	BRON 161:61
with our moral r.	KENN 482:28
would that r. upon us	JOHN 461:16
restraints paucity of r.	SPEN 836:89
restrictions r. on woman	FULL 355:66
restructuring whole world needs r.	GORB 378:47
result accomplished the r.	ACHE 3:41
how small a realized R.	CARL 200:2
our r. is vitiated	THOR 888:24
r. is the battle won or lost	WELL 929:6
r. looked rather like the Forth Bridge	BRIT 159:28
r. of my upbringing	DYSON 309:59
r. of the energy stored	GERS 365:72
satisfied with that r.	SCHW 750:89
secure and lasting r.	DESC 275:98
results hope of instant r.	SCHL 748:38
how many dangerous r.	LOUI 537:65
poll r.	GALL 358:45
r. dies with the worker	LEON 522:68
r. of thought and resolution	TROL 897:32
resurrection by man came also the r.	BIBLE 127:57
foretaste of r.	SCHO 749:60
I am the r., and the life	BIBLE 123:46
in the r. they neither marry	BIBLE 118:25
prelude to r.	WILL 944:71
reclaimed...property at the r.	BUTL 186:12
r. is rare	ADAMS 5:94
r. of the body	BOOK 149:39
R. to eternal life	BOOK 146:37
resuscitate r., if it concerns history	HUGO 436:55
resuscitated I wouldn't mind being r.	BERL 85:56
retail R. is detail	SCHU 749:71
retard r. what we cannot repel	JOHN 460:72
reticence R., in three volumes	GLAD 373:43
retire being young until you r.	LARK 510:93
don't r. in this business	MITC 610:48
r., and in retiring draw	MILT 607:76
r....from who's who to who's that	WRIS 963:75
r. to the grandstands	GERG 365:67
sign for him to r.	DISR 288:55
want to r. at 50	KINN 488:62
retirement must be no r.	HAIG 392:15
short r. urges sweet return	MILT 606:47
retiring r. at high speed	HALS 393:43
retort first, the R. Courteous	SHAK 780:24
retreat If I r., kill me	MUSS 627:89
into which one can r.	ORWE 654:55
mistress...little country r.	WYCH 964:94
principle solitude and r.	MONT 614:32
r....in his own soul	AURE 45:45
r. into advance	ROOS 724:6
retrograde r. if it does not advance	GIBB 366:97
retrospect dark unfathom'd r.	WHIT 938:10
in r....all a blur	SCHL 747:36
we live in r.	HAZL 403:47
return alas! we r.	FORS 344:24
came through and...shall r.	MACA 544:3
day of their r.	MACA 545:37
r. no more	SWIFT 861:19
shall not r. unto me void	BIBLE 109:99
returnable children...are not r.	CRISP 254:99
returned r. from battle	HOMER 425:1
returning In r....shall ye be saved	BIBLE 108:73
r. him safely to earth	KENN 481:5
R. were as tedious	SHAK 797:31
returns gives the basest r.	INNO 446:47
reunion every r. a foretaste	SCHO 749:60
re-union r.-u. dinner	PARK 665:36
reveal r. the appalling dangers	HUXL 441:73
something to r.	THOM 885:61
revealed People...are merely r.	ENRI 326:20
those things which are r.	BIBLE 95:96
reveals Being president...r. who you are	OBAMA 645:57
revel blood-bedecked halls of their r.	POE 683:83
R. the night	SHAK 773:98
revelation continuous thread of r.	WELTY 931:48
essence of music is r.	HEINE 407:16
few weeks ago I had a r.	STEIN 845:79
habit of r.	SKEL 825:44
inspired by divine r.	BACON 49:28
land of light and r.	CLIN 230:3
lies in its r. in act	WHIT 936:70
man's r. to man	FRYE 354:53
r. of character in a play	WILL 945:89
r. of Jesus Christ	BIBLE 130:64
r. of Mahomet	GIBB 366:95
r. of the nature of God	WHIT 936:71
r. of the sexual goings-on	CRIT 255:10
r. of Thought	EMER 325:91
revelations extraordinary r.	BUTL 184:58
heaven...measured as R. says	LAUR 511:22
It ends with R.	WILDE 941:83
sounded like the book of R.	JAMES 450:26
revelled fought as they r.	DAVIS 266:9
revellers one by one dropped the r.	POE 683:83
revelry sound of r. by night	BYRON 187:50
revenge Blood and r....in my head	SHAK 760:23
blows and r. for me!	SHAK 760:6
Caesar's spirit, ranging for r.	SHAK 777:34
capable and wide r.	SHAK 790:29
democracy is the best r.	BHUT 90:79
favourite form of r.	NIET 638:11
first blood shed in r.	PEPYS 673:87
Freud would have his r.	DOCT 289:82
General Ford as his r.	ABZUG 2:17
harbour any thoughts of r.	JOSE 469:7
in r. I took her to pieces	CONG 241:55
kiss...sweet as my r.!	SHAK 799:4
little R. herself	TENN 879:1
On desperate r.	MILT 603:77
permanent...had its own kind of r.	FRAME 346:78
Prompted to my r.	SHAK 782:2
Punishment is not for r.	FRY 353:37
R. is a kind of wild justice	BACON 50:62
r. of the intellect upon art	SONT 834:13
R. triumphs over death	BACON 50:58
shall we not r.?	SHAK 769:1
slow r. of the Orient	PRIE 695:88
species of r.	JOHN 459:52
study of r., immortal hate	MILT 602:38
surpass Common r.	MILT 602:63
Sweet is r.	BYRON 189:96
Voting's the best r.	OBAMA 644:45
revenged on a wretch wilt thou be r.?	SIDN 820:41
r. on the whole pack	SHAK 786:24
revenges angelic r. on the Philistines	ARNO 35:23
time brings in his r.	SHAK 786:23
will have such r. on you both	SHAK 792:3
revenue abundant streams of r.	WEBS 926:15
reverberation paucity of its r.	MAIL 560:56
Revere ride of Paul R.	LONG 536:35
reverence cycle-clips in awkward r.	LARK 509:77
In deeper r. praise	WHIT 938:24
little more r., please	SARG 743:53
objects of r. and love	CARL 199:73
poor to do him r.	SHAK 777:41
r. in us dwell	TENN 873:57
with sanctimonious r.	JEFF 454:28
reverend As you are old and r.	SHAK 792:93
reverends Right R. and Wrong R.	DICK 281:74
reverie poem full of space and r.	BAUD 69:89
reveries r. so airy	COWP 251:16
reverse Forwards in r.	DUNN 307:15
produce the r. of happiness	MILL 592:8
sleep, and shall again r.	SPEN 838:37
review I have your r. before me	REGER 710:43
r. of institutions	PEEL 672:66
reviewers chorus of indolent r.	TENN 877:65
metropolitan r.	BEER 74:89
reviewing devote myself to r.	NICO 637:85
reviews r. are mostly for people who still read	WILL 947:32
r. that were good	HELL 408:36
revisionist r. clique of Deng	JIANG 455:58
revival engineering an economic r.	LARD 509:66
revive r. thy work	BIBLE 111:13
revolt Is this a r.?	LOUI 537:70
nature falls into r.	SHAK 773:97
of the old r. from Awe	MERE 588:37
seduced them to that foul r.?	MILT 601:32
sign of a r.	EAGL 309:1
writers...join in a common r.	COWL 250:80
revolting r. and a rebellious heart	BIBLE 110:14
revolution any true r.	SWIFT 861:13
attempt to export r.	STAL 842:5
beginning r.	WELL 929:7
blood-red flower of r.	RAND 706:59
children of the r.	LEGU 520:16
dream of r.	STOP 855:16
Gracchi deploring r.?	JUVE 471:53
Hope ushers in a R.	CARL 200:4
new industrial r.	WIEN 939:29
No, sir, it's a r.	LOUI 537:70
not the leaders of a r.	CONR 244:44
r. has been stolen	JIANG 455:58
r. in America	LINK 530:29
r. in how writers write	WELD 928:81
R. is like a love story	AL-AS 10:19
r. is not a dinner party	MAO 568:25
r. itself is a game	ROBBE 717:65
r. of 1789 is her political religion	LAMA 504:73
r. than a government	MARC 569:53
r. to get the politicians out	CAST 208:78
r. was our midwife	INOU 446:49
r. where love is not allowed	ANGE 19:93
safeguard a r.	ORWE 655:78
some kind of cultural r.	GINS 372:14
sun of the socialist r.	LENIN 521:39
The Industrial R.	TOYN 895:71
theory and methods of r.	MAO 568:27
the R. may...devour	VERG 910:54
tremble at a communist r.	MARX 579:34
Universal suffrage is counter-r.	PROU 697:36
violent r. inevitable	KENN 481:10
what the Russian R. can become	ONET 651:82
white heat of this r.	WILS 948:61
worst of a r.	FOX 346:69
revolutionaries May r. said	ROBBE 717:65
Most r. are...Tories	ORWE 653:29
revolutionary either a r. or you're not	STOP 856:19
most r. insight	JONG 466:30
not believe...not a r.	CAST 208:79
r. ends as an oppressor	CAMUS 196:92
revolutionists organisations of r.	LENIN 521:37
views of the r.	SCHL 747:33
revolutions main cause of r.	INGE 445:29
modern r. have ended	CAMUS 196:91
R. have never lightened the burden	SHAW 808:35
R....start with enthusiasm	SOROS 834:36
roses out of r.	RAND 706:57
small engine that causes r.	SHEE 811:40
sure to stir up r.	ARIS 32:27
revolver instead of a r.	STEW 854:25
r. into my right ear	GREE 386:22
r. ready to hand	STEV 851:29
reward Crimes...are their own r.	FARQ 330:24
fruit of the womb is his r.	BIBLE 103:37
good r. for their labour	BIBLE 106:17
in no wise lose his r.	BIBLE 116:74
nothing for r.	SPEN 838:31
only r. of virtue is virtue	EMER 324:61
only r. one should offer	RENO 711:56
r. for conformity	BROWN 164:37
r. of a thing well done	EMER 324:68
R. that young man	DUGO 305:86
r. your faith in us	SMITH 829:10
right of his r.	MILT 600:15
without the r. of priority	SCOTT 751:5
rewarded r. and punished	SZASZ 865:27
r. with a smile	SAINT 738:38
rewarder who now will be my R.	BUNY 174:83
rewards Fortune's buffets and r.	SHAK 783:21
multitude of r.	PATR 669:29
neither r. nor punishments	INGE 445:33
r. for being sane	AMIS 16:39
world its veterans r.	POPE 688:15
rewrite owe to history is to r. it	WILDE 940:56
Reykjavik in touch with R.	WHITE 935:38
rhetoric fearful about...their own r.	OBRI 645:65

rhetorical

logic and r.	BACON 53:39	Poor Little R. Girl	COWA 249:44	riddance die and be a r.!	DICK 280:39
r. passed for reality	BENT 82:7	poor, yet making many r.	BIBLE 127:73	riddle could not...expound the r.	BIBLE 95:15
rhetorical artlessly r.	BISH 136:23	property of the r.	RUSK 733:1	glory, jest, and r.	POPE 687:81
rhetorician sophistical r.	DISR 288:67	r. and delicate English language	WAUGH 924:1	had not found out my r.	BIBLE 95:16
Rhine R....Doth wash your city	COLE 236:50	R. And The Poor	DISR 288:34	How still the R. lies!	DICK 283:28
R....is where our frontier lies	BALD 57:32	r....are different from you and me	FITZ 338:88	r. wrapped inside a mystery	CHUR 225:82
The R. is not more impassable	GIBB 366:95	r. are the scum	CHES 221:86	**ride** being taken for a r.	JOSE 469:7
rhino like the White R.	BENN 80:47	r. because you are white	FANON 329:13	It's been an excellent r.	ARMS 22:5
rhinoceros hide of a r.	BARR 65:98	r. boys—this is the problem	CAPEL 197:17	mount by me and r.	YEATS 965:5
Rhodesia black...rule ever in R.	SMITH 829:8	r. don't have children	NEWM 635:53	ticket to r.	LENN 522:50
rhubarb r. words	SIDN 820:45	r. get r.	KAHN 472:9	two men r. of a horse	SHAK 774:50
What r., cyme	SHAK 798:72	R. gifts wax poor	SHAK 783:8	we r. them down	TENN 872:33
rhyme All r., and scrawl	POPE 688:19	r. hath many friends	BIBLE 104:71	**rider** between a r. and his horse	SURT 860:6
Down my desert r.	CRAIK 252:51	r. he hath sent empty away	BIBLE 120:66	good r. may often be thrown	ANON 22:74
forty long years of good r.	OBRU 646:75	r. he hath sent empty away	BIBLE 133:43	r. hanging like a locket	SOME 833:10
love...hath taught me to r.	SHAK 763:14	r. in apparel	TROL 897:21	steed That knows his r.	BYRON 187:45
more r. there is in poetry	SAND 742:35	r. in nature's store	FORD 343:7	The r., the birds	YEATS 966:19
names in many a musèd r.	KEATS 478:46	r. is better	TUCK 901:15	the r. was lost	FRAN 348:14
no r. to 'lady'	SHAK 774:56	r. man in his castle	ALEX 13:62	**riders** r. on the earth together	MACL 555:42
outlive this powerful r.	SHAK 801:53	r. man's joys increase	GOLD 376:4	**ridicule** wise r. and obey	BIER 134:78
plot and r.	LOWE 540:37	r. man's wealth is his strong city	BIBLE 104:63	**ridiculous** fine sense of the r.	ALBEE 11:25
poet...climbs on r.	FERL 333:89	r. man to enter into the kingdom	BIBLE 118:18	made r. by friends	BIER 134:63
reason for my r.	SPEN 840:64	r. man told me recently	BARA 63:42	makes men r.	JUVE 471:54
R. is the rock	DRYD 302:95	R. men deal gifts	SHAK 791:83	most r. and scornful sort	SIDN 820:57
r. the rudder is of verses	BUTL 185:71	r. men rule the law	GOLD 376:87	R....20 years after	LAVER 512:33
unattempted yet in prose or r.	MILT 601:30	r. not gaudy	SHAK 781:52	step above the r.	PAINE 660:40
where I read and r.	WYATT 963:86	R. people, God bless us	CLIN 231:29	To the R.	GRAH 380:85
rhymes Different r.	BROD 160:30	R. people spend...money	GATES 361:96	we have made enthusiasm r.	STAEL 841:95
ring out my mournful r.	TENN 875:96	r. should become poor	ARIS 32:27	**riding** keep on r.	TRUM 900:92
rhyming drasty r. is nat worth	CHAU 217:95	r. society too r.	TAWN 868:44	**Ridley** good comfort Master R.	LATI 511:13
not born under a r. planet	SHAK 774:56	r. with forty pounds a year	GOLD 376:99	**rife** r. as the loam Of prairies	CRANE 253:66
r., ranting, raving billie	BURNS 177:81	r. with suspicion	RICH 713:95	**rifle** a r....had gone off	ORWE 653:23
rhythm All God's Chillum got R.	KAHN 472:10	R. with the spoils of time	GRAY 384:68	Let him who has a r.	HO 421:12
all things have a r.	MAMET 564:35	robbing the r.	SHAW 807:22	r. all the breathing spring	COLL 237:70
I got r.	GERS 365:73	shall not be r.	BIBLE 113:97	roll to your r.	KIPL 489:88
language restored to its essential r.	MALL 562:95	There was a certain r. man	BIBLE 121:96	with r. and pack	SASS 745:86
r. brings about a poetic short-circuit	SENG 757:27	the r. he hath sent empty away	BIBLE 120:66	**rifles** stuttering r.' rapid rattle	OWEN 657:25
r....of a picture	FEIN 332:57	the r. he hath sent empty away	BIBLE 133:43	**rift** little r. within the lute	TENN 877:44
rhythms lucid, inescapable r.	STEV 850:75	The very r. are different	HEMI 410:78	**rig** Tato, R. and Scunge	MURR 627:80
Rialto In the R. you have rated me	SHAK 769:85	this r. praise	SHAK 802:66	**Rigby** Eleanor R. picks up the rice	LENN 522:51
ribald roused the r. crows	SHAK 787:41	though her father be very r.	SHAK 761:58	**right** absolute and unlimited r.	BENT 82:91
riband for a r. to stick in his coat	BROW 167:18	to strike it r.	HEAN 405:79	age of r. and opportunity	WILS 949:75
ribbon blue r. of the turf	DISR 288:44	we'll be wondrous r.	OTWAY 656:4	All's r. with the world	BROW 167:9
like a soldier's r.	ABSE 1:8	what do the r. dream of?	ADIGA 8:63	Always do r.	TWAIN 903:90
ribbons bondage of certain r.	SHAK 800:26	widening gulf between the r.	COUP 248:27	as much r....as pigs have to fly	CARR 203:76
fluttering of r.	DICK 279:1	with the r. in his death	BIBLE 109:95	be decorative and to do r.!	FIRB 336:53
none of your r. and bells	MARQ 575:51	**Richard** on the head of R.	SHAK 761:52	belief which may be r.	FORS 344:26
Wi' r. in her hair	BALL 59:67	To put down R.	SHAK 771:34	better to be approximately r.	BUFF 172:44
ribs soul beneath the r. of death	MANC 564:51	**Richardson** one letter of R.'s	JOHN 462:25	beyond doubt that they are r.	VAN 908:15
through the flinty r.	SHAK 765:62	**Richelieu** Gladstone, like R.	DISR 288:65	boldly speak in r.	OTWAY 656:97
took one of his r.	BIBLE 91:90	**richer** for r. for poorer	BOOK 148:91	born to set it r.!	SHAK 781:71
yerked him here, under the r.	SHAK 788:86	for which I am r.	SHAK 792:86	Brotherhood of the R. Stuff	WOLFE 953:75
Ribstone Pippin Right as a R. P.!	BELL 77:67	get r. and r.	GARD 360:71	desire to do r.	DICK 283:17
rice R., and a Cranberry Tart	LEAR 516:33	mightier and r. than thyself	BIBLE 113:93	D. H. Lawrence was r.	GIBB 367:11
r. in a church	LENN 522:51	**riches** according to his r. in glory	BIBLE 128:8	discussion of any subject is a r.	SHEL 812:50
They gave us our r. bowl	QIAN 701:2	bear'st thy heavy r.	SHAK 787:65	divine r. of husbands	WOLL 954:91
rich acute shortage of r. people	WILS 948:74	count our r.	PREV 694:79	doesn't mean you're r.	GERV 366:84
All I am or was is r.	MAY 583:20	deceitfulness of r.	BIBLE 117:91	Do the r. thing	FOX 346:73
Beauty too r. for use	SHAK 765:74	Embarrassment of R.	ALLA 13:73	editor...will always be r.	BENN 81:79
Be r. in patience	DUNB 306:99	full of days, r., and honour	BIBLE 98:84	every man did that which was r.	BIBLE 96:21
best of the r.	SPARK 836:71	greatest in Europe for R.	BAIL 55:87	exclusively in the r.	HUXL 441:60
both r. and poor nations	ILLI 445:22	Grit r. and prosperity	BROWN 164:41	fight for the r.	CURZ 260:5
consumed almost wholly by...the r.	HALL 393:40	hire old r.	CHAU 217:89	Give it because it is r.	LLOY 533:77
curse not the r.	BIBLE 106:33	increase of r. and commerce	HUME 438:4	great r. of an excessive wrong	BROW 169:73
demand disturbs...the r.	BRON 161:68	infinite r. in a little room	MARL 573:9	have the r. to exist	KELM 479:69
desire to be r.	BAGE 54:76	in her left hand r.	BIBLE 104:55	her r. to...opinions	PALM 662:74
distance between the r. and the poor	CARL 200:81	natural science accumulates new r.	ALEM 12:74	hundredth time I am r.	EINS 313:77
equality of laws forbids the r.	FRAN 347:89	R. are a good handmaid	BACON 50:49	I did what I thought was r.	BLAIR 138:73
errors of the r.	CHES 220:60	R. are for spending	BACON 52:16	If the young fellow is r.	QUIN 702:18
Gay r. and R. gay	ANON 22:78	r. certainly make themselves wings	BIBLE 105:90	if two wrongs don't make a r.	COUS 248:41
gift r. by delaying it	TROL 898:43	r. fineless is as poor	SHAK 789:20	irresponsible and r.	CHUR 226:8
high and low, r. and poor	MORI 619:36	r. grow in hell	MILT 602:53	itch but a kind of colourable r.	LEST 524:8
If thou art r.	SHAK 787:65	r. to men of understanding	BIBLE 106:29	it isn't enough to be r.	OATES 643:12
I'm only r. because	SOROS 834:37	r. where is my deserving?	SHAK 802:67	Judge of all the earth do r.	BIBLE 92:22
Into something r. and strange	SHAK 803:17	r. will leave us sick	EMER 325:83	know I'm r.	GOLD 377:21
I's r. now	TWAIN 902:59	unsearchable r. of Christ	BIBLE 127:87	legal r. to say what you like	ORWE 653:22
Just because you're r.	SEIB 756:5	world's r., which dispersèd lie	HERB 414:82	Lenin was r.	KEYN 484:71
Let him be r. and weary	HERB 414:83	**richness** all in a rush With r.	HOPK 428:74	Let's do it r.	PEI 672:71
low in r....countries	SMITH 827:82	r.; his double action	HUGEL 434:4	majority never has r.	IBSEN 444:7
making Gay r.	JOHN 463:74	r....of existence	KENN 482:27	may she always be in the r.	DECA 268:64
man who dies r.	CARN 202:97	**rickshaw** no go the r.	MACN 557:97	meet and r. so to do	BOOK 147:69
marry a r. woman	THAC 880:33	**Rico** is this the end of R.	ROBI 718:81	must also be r.	GOULD 380:75
No legacy is so r.	SHAK 791:64	**rid** harder it is to get r.	TWAIN 902:43	My country r. or wrong	CHES 220:54
not a sin to be r.	CONN 242:81	how to get r. of ourselves	HORN 430:23	nation being so r.	WILS 949:78
not really a r. man	GETTY 366:87	idea of getting r. of it	JERO 454:40	nature's state, where all have r.	DRYD 302:87
One composition...is r.	DIDE 285:76	r. of Paul Revere	LONG 536:35	neither r. nor safe	LUTH 542:69
Poor and content is r.	SHAK 789:20	time we got r. of Him	BALD 57:21	never try to make a r. decision	ONEI 651:74

rivulet

Next to being r. — HUXL 443:12
no claim of r. — MALT 563:22
No government has the r. — BROWN 164:35
no more r. to…happiness — SHAW 806:87
no r. to strike — COOL 245:78
no r. to transgress the law — DOST 294:89
not between r. and wrong — JUNG 471:46
novelist…does not have the r. — FLAU 339:23
one thing we did r. — ANON 26:94
on the r. side — GALB 357:21
people who hunt are the r. people — SHAW 810:10
petty r. or wrong — THOM 885:55
quite r. too — GREY 388:61
r. action is freedom — ELIOT 320:76
r. angle is necessary — MALL 562:3
R. as a Ribstone Pippin! — BELL 77:67
R. Divine of Kings — POPE 689:41
r. in his own eyes — BIBLE 105:87
r. in his own eyes — BIBLE 96:21
r. is not what someone gives you — CLARK 228:64
r. is only a motor hand — HEPW 412:30
r. is retreating — FOCH 341:67
r. not to understand — CALV 193:35
r. now is wrong — SPEN 839:56
r. out of wrong — JONS 467:67
R. perfection — SHAK 801:58
r. place to film it — GARD 360:68
r. to a fair portion — BURKE 176:38
r. to hear what other…human — CARL 201:29
r. to the property — RUSK 733:1
r. to utter what he thinks — JOHN 464:77
saddling of the r. to a child — SHAW 809:86
secure of private r. — DRYD 302:86
settle what's r. and fair — HUGH 436:47
Sit thou at my r. hand — BIBLE 102:17
solve it r. or wrong — WATS 922:43
someone will make things r. — REAG 708:2
sometimes in the r. — DRYD 300:22
steal someone's r. to the truth — HOSS 430:29
Still in thy r. hand — SHAK 805:54
successful or otherwise, always r. — ADAMS 5:4
sure that it is r. — HAND 395:78
take from me my r. to speak — MACL 554:27
There is no r. in the world — RUSH 732:74
'the r.' is only the expedient — JAMES 451:76
the r. thing — BLAIR 138:71
the r. to report events — ORWE 655:67
the r. to tell people — ORWE 654:45
the r. way — DE 273:70
They can't all be r. — DRIB 299:5
things…will not come r. — OBRI 646:68
though r. were worsted — BROW 169:85
to be proved r. — HUXL 442:93
to get things r. — RYLE 736:61
turn'd him r. and round about — BURNS 180:59
Ulster will be r. — CHUR 224:64
undoubted r. of the crown — COVE 249:43
way which seemeth r. — BIBLE 104:70
What didn't go r.? — BUSH 183:36
whatever be his r. to it — STEV 853:78
what his r. wing was doing — ASQU 38:94
when ye turn to the r. hand — BIBLE 108:74
whether you do r. — TWAIN 903:66
whether you do r. — TWAIN 903:67
wrong and r. — YEATS 965:9
wrong because not all was r. — CRAB 252:44
wrong notes are r. — IVES 448:82
young and perhaps he is r. — MAHL 559:33
righted none that could be r. — JONAS 465:14
righteous came not to call the r. — BIBLE 119:50
I have seen the r. forsaken — BLUN 143:79
not come to call the r. — BIBLE 116:63
not seen the r. forsaken — BIBLE 100:60
r. runneth into it — BIBLE 105:83
r. with impunity? — RACI 704:31
souls of the r. — BIBLE 112:74
righteousness breastplate of r. — BIBLE 128:95
eternal…makes for r. — ARNO 36:36
feareth him, and worketh r. — BIBLE 124:84
For my r. the Lord hath brought — BIBLE 95:91
hunger and thirst after r. — BIBLE 114:27
kingdom of God, and his r. — BIBLE 115:46
let the clouds rain down r. — BIBLE 133:40
loved r. — GREG 387:51
paths of r. — BIBLE 100:45
paths of r. — SCOT 755:85
r. shall exceed the r. of the scribes — BIBLE 114:31

Sun of r. arise — BIBLE 112:65
things that we think are our r. — BUTT 186:15
what r. really is — ARNO 36:37
worketh r. — BIBLE 124:84
worketh r. — BIBLE 99:34
righteousnesses r. are as filthy rags — BIBLE 110:7
rights all a talkin' 'bout r. — TRUTH 900:4
backlash against women's r. — FALU 329:12
believe that they have r. — HEGEL 406:7
bill of r. — JEFF 454:23
certain inalienable r. — STAN 842:12
death instead of 'human r.' — PEOP 673:83
die in defence of their r. — PITT 679:7
discuss women's r. — CLIN 231:24
exercise the r. of children — COWP 251:9
fight for their own human r. — PANK 662:85
full menu of r. — TUTU 901:23
Human r., national integrity — WILS 949:76
Let woman share the r. — WOLL 954:95
maintenance of established r. — PEEL 672:66
men, their r. and nothing more — ANTH 29:73
Natural r. is simple nonsense — BENT 82:92
of all 'r. of man' — CARL 201:26
Our r. are being infringed — BERN 86:84
Property has…its r. — DRUM 299:8
r. inherent and inalienable — JEFF 453:19
r. of an Englishman — JUNI 471:49
r. of every man — KENN 481:19
r. of every other nation — PARN 665:47
r. of the individual — CHUR 225:81
r….of the laboring man — BAER 54:62
r. of the savage — GLAD 373:38
r. of the smaller nationalities — ASQU 38:84
r….on…basis of a physical — BOTHA 152:79
Stand up for your r. — MARL 572:92
the r. of the people — SUN 860:96
trenching on another's r. — BRON 161:72
vital personal r. — WARR 921:13
rill By cool Siloam's shady r. — HEBER 406:99
danced the moon on Monan's r. — SCOTT 752:28
gushing of a r. — BYRON 190:27
the descending r. — SMART 826:64
Rimbauds always chasing R. — PARK 664:21
ring clear, clean r. of…insult — CARR 203:60
dance round in a r. — FROST 353:17
fantastic r., Round — BROW 168:38
forms a r. — SCHR 749:66
four walls and a r. — HEAN 404:69
get me in any r. with Mr Tolstoy — HEMI 410:84
great r. of…light — VAUG 909:39
his luminous r. — TENN 870:95
jow or r. — FERG 333:85
man gets into the r. — MAIL 560:59
One R. to rule them all — TOLK 893:45
R. out the want — TENN 875:96
R. out, wild bells — TENN 875:95
This pretty r. — SCHR 749:61
unconquered in a r. — CHES 221:99
what shall we do for a r.? — LEAR 516:36
willing to sell…Your r.? — LEAR 516:37
with this r. I thee wed — BOOK 148:93
ringmaster r. has altered — ASHD 37:65
rings r., and things — SHAK 762:67
their r. of green mantles — BALL 59:73
Rio roll to R. — KIPL 491:39
riot blaze of r. cannot last — SHAK 764:37
He didn't r. — TEBB 869:63
ripe we r. and r. — SHAK 779:79
ripeness R. is all — EMPS 326:9
R. is all — SHAK 793:32
ripped Untimely r. — SHAK 798:77
ripples the infernal r. — POUND 691:98
rise but stoop to r. — MASS 581:72
Created half to r. — POPE 687:81
Early to r. — THUR 890:74
One man's wage r. — WILS 948:68
opportunity to r. again — SARN 743:55
R., take up thy bed — BIBLE 122:30
R. up, my love — BIBLE 107:43
Some r. by sin — SHAK 787:54
risen He is not here, but is r. — BIBLE 122:11
rising constantly r. at four — WESL 932:71
means of r. in the world — JOHN 462:39
ways of the bird r. — REID 710:44
risings r….on contradiction — EMPS 326:10
risk Artists r. it all — MART 575:69
England…preferred the r. — CECIL 210:28

increases in relation to r. — HEMI 410:94
r. of becoming a subordinate species — SCOTT 754:76
r. of being heroes — BOLT 145:13
r. of maiming it for life — SHAW 808:43
The biggest r….not taking any r. — ZUCK 970:19
Without r. there is no faith — KIER 485:1
risks one of the r. that he takes — STEV 851:22
suffering, and some r. — PEARY 671:59
rite fascination of an ancient r. — SAND 742:33
newer r. is here — AQUI 30:97
victory…celebrated with the funeral r. — LAO 508:63
rites body of organized r. — LEWIS 527:66
till love have all his r. — SHAK 774:35
ritual part of the Texas r. — FERB 332:68
rival If I embrace my r. — RACI 704:29
rivalry r. of aim — ADAMS 5:92
r.; sane and healthy — NORR 641:57
tendencies to r., jealousy — JAMES 451:69
rivals r. rail — JOHN 459:39
river air moves like a r. — LEON 522:72
Alph, the sacred r. — COLE 236:36
bread I dip in the r. — STEV 853:82
can't argue with a r. — ACHE 3:46
cross the r. by an Irish bridge — STEW 854:96
drinketh up a r. — BIBLE 99:21
either side the r. lie — TENN 869:77
foam on the r. — SCOTT 752:32
fog down the r. — DICK 281:55
fountains mingle with the r. — SHEL 813:78
great source of the holy r. — SPEKE 836:81
hill or field or r. — TENN 872:40
In a field by the r. — YEATS 965:43
listening to a r. — HEAN 405:76
majestic r. floated on — ARNO 34:99
nature of a r. — BACON 49:25
not so much like any r. — HOPK 429:85
Ol' Man R. — HAMM 394:63
On a tree by a r. — GILB 370:68
one great winding r. — RANJ 706:60
pure r. of water of life — BIBLE 132:28
r….a strong brown god — ELIOT 320:70
r. glideth at his own sweet will — WORD 959:3
r. is within us — ELIOT 320:71
r. jumps over the mountain — AUDEN 43:81
r. of crystal light — FIELD 335:13
'r.' or a 'stream' are the metaphors — JAMES 451:66
r. remains unchanged — KIRK 493:82
r.'s slow presence — LARK 509:84
R. Tiber foaming with much blood — POWE 693:58
r. winding clearly — TENN 869:80
salmon from the r. — SCOTT 753:37
Sleepless as the r. — CRANE 253:58
snow falls in the r. — BURNS 179:25
Thames…the noblest r. — ADDI 7:35
up the mouth of a r. — KIPL 489:79
Up the r. and o'er the lea — HOGG 402:43
wanted to give him a r. name — WINT 950:8
waters Of the R. Lee — MAHO 559:35
What use the green r. — FRAME 346:75
where there is no r. — KHRU 485:92
where the r. plunges — WILL 946:20
white flows the r. — STEV 854:84
world's greatest r. — DOSP 294:86
riverbed cold fog over a r. b. — ACHE 2:34
The r., dried-up — HEAN 405:76
river-rounded rook-racked, r.-r. — HOPK 428:78
rivers All the r. run into the sea — BIBLE 105:10
as the r. of water: he turneth it — BIBLE 105:86
brooks, and r. wide — MILT 597:45
By shallow r. — MARL 574:41
By the r. of Babylon — BIBLE 103:42
energy of mighty r. — MILL 594:63
R. and mountain-spring — OAKL 643:5
R. and seas…to float their ships — DICK 280:27
R. are damp — PARK 664:19
r. flowing through it — JAMES 450:25
r. of water in a dry place — BIBLE 108:75
R. ran reid — DOUG 294:1
r….shall not overflow thee — BIBLE 109:87
step into the same r. — HERA 412:33
timber and irrigating r. — MUIR 624:25
washed by the r. — BROO 162:88
when r. are swollen — SOPH 834:28
river-slaying r.-s. as something worse — LAUR 511:23
rivets r….that join'd us — DRYD 301:55
rivulet neat r. of text — SHER 817:87
Skipping r. — GILB 368:36

rivulets 1264

rivulets Myriads of r. — TENN 873:52
road and the r. below me — STEV 853:83
  artists took to the r. — ROCK 721:40
  Before us lay a painful r. — WORD 962:49
  cross the r. — HAWK 401:91
  drive the r. — KIPL 490:8
  endless r. you tread — HOUS 433:83
  every r. I wandered by — HOUS 431:53
  Golden R. to Samarkand — FLEC 340:32
  Help me down Cemetery R. — LARK 509:85
  high r....to England — JOHN 461:92
  horse...from the r. — YEATS 966:19
  however long and hard the r. — CHUR 225:83
  lame man who keeps the right r. — BACON 50:48
  layer cake or a r. — MILL 593:45
  life runs on, the r. — LOWE 539:16
  light to shine upon the r. — COWP 250:88
  look ahead up the white r. — ELIOT 318:9
  main r. of procreation — WAUGH 923:62
  make the whole r. — DEAN 267:39
  merry r., a mazy r. — CHES 221:94
  no expeditious r. — THOM 886:85
  no 'royal r.' to geometry — EUCL 328:51
  on a lonesome r. — COLE 235:18
  only monument the asphalt r. — ELIOT 319:32
  out on the r. — MASE 580:54
  right on to the end of the r. — LAUD 511:17
  r. along which — TAWN 868:43
  r. is life — KERO 483:55
  r. leads me forth — MASE 580:59
  r. leads me seawards — MASE 580:60
  r. is the light — GRANT 381:6
  r. lies long and straight — STEV 852:40
  r. of excess — BLAKE 139:96
  r. of experiment and observation — LAVO 512:35
  r. of life — GARL 360:74
  r. runs by — TENN 869:77
  r. that we did not take — HUSS 440:37
  r. to a knowledge of the stars — EDDI 311:25
  R. to Heaven — BALL 59:75
  r. to hell is paved — ROTH 728:85
  r. to suns — SCOTT 751:2
  r. to the heart — BALZ 61:1
  r. to wealth — TROL 897:22
  r. was a ribbon — NOYES 642:70
  r. wind up-hill — ROSS 726:45
  rolling English r. — CHES 221:93
  shut the r. through the woods — KIPL 492:61
  straightest r. to a man's heart — FERN 334:96
  surpassed on the r. — HALI 393:31
  takes no private r. — POPE 687:91
  The beaten R. — SHEL 815:45
  the middle of the r. — BEVAN 89:55
  travel any r. a second time — IBN 444:6
  travel the open r. — WHIT 937:1
  turn of the r. — FAWC 331:51
  upon the r. — MCCA 547:76
  various cause the same wild r. — SCOTT 753:40
  watched the ads...not the r. — NASH 631:75
  which r. leads to damnation — DYSON 309:60
  Words spoken on the r. — MO 610:63
  ye'll tak the high r. — ANON 22:79
  yon braid, braid r. — BALL 59:75
road-maps book of r. m. — STEI 846:86
roads All r. lead to Rome — LAFO 504:68
  Came through cold r. — SCOTT 754:75
  dangerous to cross main r. — HAWT 401:98
  employment of the poor in r. — MALT 563:23
  How many r. must a man — DYLAN 309:51
  lawless r. Ran wrong — MUIR 623:14
  Most r. lead men homewards — MASE 580:59
  Now all the r. lead — THOM 885:64
  r. by which men escape — BELL 75:33
  r. leading from nowhere — BIER 135:87
  r. that turning always — MUIR 623:15
  r., the railways, the banks — MILL 591:4
  thousand r. lead to Rome — ALAN 10:18
  three r. to ruin — POMP 684:13
  Two r. diverged in a wood — FROST 352:95
  wet, winding r. — COLUM 238:89
roadside must show him on the r. — PARN 665:46
roadway by the r. poplar-lined — MACG 551:71
roam power to r. — BYRON 187:48
  Where'er I r. — GOLD 376:85
  where'er we r. — GOLD 376:86
roar called upon to give the r. — CHUR 226:12
  Let him r. again — SHAK 767:23
  melancholy, long, withdrawing r. — ARNO 33:66

r. Of...pained desert lion — ARNO 34:97
r....on the other side of silence — ELIOT 316:51
that unmoving r.! — WILL 946:20
roars r. of infuriated spectators — ORWE 655:81
roast r. beef of England — FIEL 335:19
rob peace to thy soul, R. Burns! — SCOTT 754:81
  r. a lady of her fortune — FIEL 335:25
  r., murder, and commit — SHAK 773:98
  slays More than you r. — SHAK 791:82
  those who r. you — CONN 243:20
  time I began to r. — SITW 823:5
robbed He that is r. — SHAK 790:26
  r. man of everything — SOLZ 833:5
  sooner or later be r. — STEV 851:26
  The r. that smiles — SHAK 789:99
  We wuz r.! — JACO 449:11
robber sing in the r.'s face — JUVE 471:56
robbers den of r. in your eyes? — BIBLE 110:16
robbery dens of r. and murder — NATI 632:4
  just a cover for r. — RAMOS 706:50
  r. to be equal with God — BIBLE 128:97
  Thieves for their r. — SHAK 787:60
robbing not drugging, not r. — PACK 659:11
  r. the rich — SHAW 807:22
  think little of r. — DE 274:85
Robbins President R. was so well — JARR 452:85
robe Bring forth the best r. — BIBLE 121:91
  falling...like a r. — FLAU 335:10
  Give me my r. — SHAK 795:92
  like a giant's r. — SHAK 798:67
  r. is the light — GRANT 381:6
robes all her r. are gone — ANON 22:67
  dress me In borrowed r.? — SHAK 796:9
  impatient child that hath new r. — SHAK 766:96
  R. loosely flowing — JONS 467:60
  R., Tato, Rig — MURR 627:80
  washed their r. — BIBLE 131:4
  Winter...rudely rends thy r. — COLL 238:77
robin be sae nice wi' R. — BURNS 178:97
  Call for the r.-red-breast — WEBS 926:36
  Rantin' rovin' R. — BURNS 178:98
  r. red breast in a cage — BLAKE 141:25
  Sweet R. sits on the bush — SCOTT 754:63
robot r. mice and r. men — BRAD 155:39
  r. vehicles blindly programmed — DAWK 266:15
robots not using these r. — ANGLE 19:10
  technically efficient r. — CALL 192:28
  work of r. — GOULD 380:76
robs r. himself that spends — SHAK 789:99
  r. you on business principles — SHAW 807:97
robust too much attainted...to be r. — HOFS 422:38
Rochdale take my wife to see R. — SHAN 805:64
Rochefoucauld Duke of R.-Liancourt — LOUI 537:70
rock been a r. of order — METT 589:60
  blue-black tooth of sheer r. — BENU 83:9
  cut a Colossus from a r. — JOHN 464:92
  don't have a r. voice — MEAT 584:33
  first r. at a girl like I — LOOS 536:55
  go first, r. and roll or Christianity — LENN 521:44
  It's Only R. and Roll — JAGG 449:17
  made himself the r. — SCHO 748:41
  more women in the r. scene — HARV 400:77
  my r. and my salvation — BIBLE 101:77
  principle which...gives us a firm R. — BUTT 186:14
  prisoner of the hard r. — THOM 886:78
  reclaim these things—poetry, r.'n'roll, political activism — SMITH 829:29
  Rhyme is the r. — DRYD 302:95
  r. a quarter of a million miles up — BAKER 56:6
  R. of Ages — TOPL 894:61
  r. of offence — BIBLE 107:58
  r. of the national resources — WEBS 926:15
  r. that is higher than I — BIBLE 101:76
  Safe upon solid r. — MILL 592:20
  secure possession of a bleak r. — YOUNG 968:51
  set my feet upon a r. — BIBLE 100:61
  Sex 'n' drugs 'n' r. 'n' roll — DURY 308:40
  shadow of a great r. — BIBLE 108:75
  The poem is the r. — THOM 886:75
  three very simple r. and roll reasons — GELD 362:29
  truth is the uncharted r. — CORN 247:6
rocked they r. the system — ROBI 718:97
Rockefellers eat R. for breakfast — KENN 482:45
rocket he rose like a r. — PAINE 660:37
  r.'s red glare — KEY 484:68
rockets r. used by the barbarians — KISH 493:83
Rockies the R. may crumble — GERS 365:80

rocking-chair always has the r.-c. — ROBI 718:91
rocking-horse about upon a r. h. — KEATS 475:68
rocks begin to twinkle from the r. — TENN 870:2
  but the r. remain — HERB 413:54
  change the r. of Scotland — JOHN 459:42
  charms...To soften r. — CONG 241:51
  father...throwing r. at the stork — BREC 157:87
  flowerless r. of hell — SITW 823:96
  Guarded by shoals and r. — BYRON 189:6
  heaven but the r. — RUSK 732:85
  hitting...bottles with small r. — THUR 890:65
  Love...resembles the eternal r. — BRON 162:79
  miraculously glide past the r. — CUOMO 258:80
  older than the r. — PATER 668:9
  railroad...you blasted its r. — RUSK 734:19
  rifted r. whose entrance leads — MILT 599:74
  r. melt wi' the sun — BURNS 180:50
  steering...for the r. — GILM 371:97
  Such uncouth r. — WALP 918:64
  walled round with r. — SWIN 864:16
  What are men to r. — AUST 46:61
  will sit upon the r. — MARL 574:41
  With r., and stones and trees — WORD 957:64
Rockwell Norman R., the Brueghel — ADLER 8:68
rod chief a r. — POPE 687:89
  enforced by the r. — SPEKE 836:82
  r. and staff me comfort still — SCOT 755:85
  r. and thy staff — BIBLE 100:45
  r. out of the stem of Jesse — BIBLE 108:61
  rule them with a r. of iron — BIBLE 131:92
  spare the r., and spoil the child — BUTL 185:78
  spareth his r. — BIBLE 104:69
  steel r. runs right through — ANGE 19:90
  The r. of Aaron — BIBLE 94:81
  Throw away thy r. — HERB 414:28
  wisdom be put in a silver r. — BLAKE 139:84
rode Then she r. forth — TENN 871:7
roe following the r. — BURNS 179:55
  loving hind and pleasant r. — BIBLE 104:57
roes breasts are like two young r. — BIBLE 107:45
Roger Sir R. is landlord — ADDI 6:28
  steal from Samuel R. — BYRON 189:3
rogue 100,100 thalers a r. — LICH 528:91
  bewitched with the r.'s company — SHAK 771:39
  busy and insinuating r. — SHAK 790:36
  easy it is to call r. — DRYD 303:24
  fiddler, and consequently a r. — SWIFT 861:29
  Has he not a r.'s face? — CONG 240:41
  O, what a r. and peasant slave — SHAK 782:45
  r. alive to the ludicrous — EMER 325:99
  r. gives you Love Powders — LAMB 505:85
  r. in porcelain — MERE 588:33
  r. is outlining a treacherous plan — FRAS 349:32
  wasna he a r. — ANON 22:75
rogues bold deserving r. — OTWAY 656:2
  parcel of r. — BURNS 179:41
  parcel of r. — BURNS 180:42
  r. slighted me into the river — SHAK 773:12
  you dissentrious r. — SHAK 798:88
Roland Child R. to the dark tower — SHAK 792:12
role How do you approach a r.? — EVANS 328:67
  masculine r. — GREER 387:42
  play the r. of watchmaker — DAWK 266:16
  r. is...filling vacuums — CART 206:50
  r. of the poet to look — PRIT 696:22
  subside into the r. — STRA 856:35
  time that occupies the same r. — MCLU 556:52
  You have played out your r. — TROT 899:61
roll R. darkling down — JOHN 459:48
  r. us shoreward soon — TENN 870:88
roller basic white and with a r. — BROWN 164:36
rolling r. down the street — IGNA 445:17
Rolls Royce R. R. diplomacy — ANON 26:84
roman Before the R. came to Rye — CHES 221:95
  challenges: the R. Catholic — MACM 556:73
  departed was a 'R.' — LAWS 514:95
  fabulous yellow r. candles — KERO 483:53
  Greek and R. poets — PRIOR 696:13
  heard the snobbish R. say — BEER 74:93
  high R. fashion — SHAK 795:85
  I am a R. citizen — CICE 227:34
  in the R. Catholic religion — TROL 897:35
  Like the R., I seem to see — POWE 693:58
  Make way, R. writers — PROP 697:31
  more an antique R. — SHAK 785:72
  noblest R. of them all — SHAK 778:57
  not...holy, or R. — VOLT 914:40

roses

R. holiday	BYRON 188:66	
since the R. colonists	HYDE 443:19	
the R., in days of old	PALM 662:72	
To-day the R. and his trouble	HOUS 431:48	
Would that the R. people	CALI 192:26	
romance calls his work a R.	HAWT 402:7	
chiaroscuro of r.	MAUG 582:8	
cloudy symbols of a high r.	KEATS 475:78	
fine r.	FIEL 335:29	
not a little given to r.	EVEL 328:70	
There's r. for you!	MORR 620:46	
Utopian and revolutionary r.	WEBB 923:9	
while there's...love and r.	BERL 84:40	
romances are like r. read	SUCK 858:69	
no more need of r.	WHIT 937:89	
Romans Friends, R., countrymen	SHAK 777:37	
poverty of the present R.	WALP 918:65	
R. call it stoicism	ADDI 7:46	
R. conquered the world	SWEE 861:9	
west of Ireland, the R. had never	CHRI 223:43	
romantic defining a r. poet	FROST 352:9	
Men are so r.	WELD 928:86	
New York...an infinitely r. notion	DIDI 286:81	
R....100 years after	LAVER 512:33	
r. awe of them	HEMI 410:78	
r. diseased	GOET 375:68	
r. interest in our own sex	CONN 243:18	
R. Ireland's dead	YEATS 966:11	
romanticism all else is grandiose r.	BUKO 173:54	
tinge it with r.	DOYLE 296:43	
Rome All roads lead to R.	LAFO 504:68	
ascribed to the augurs of R.	KNIG 494:10	
At R. she hadde been	CHAU 217:77	
Bishop of R. hath no jurisdiction	BOOK 150:42	
Burn, with Athens and with R.	CAMP 194:54	
cruel men of R.	SHAK 776:4	
deliberating in R.	LIVY 532:62	
founded before the City of R.	BAIL 55:87	
grandeur that was R.	POE 683:86	
hook-nosed fellow of R.	SHAK 773:94	
Humorists...burn while R. fiddles	CONN 242:2	
irreverential word of R.?	HAWT 402:7	
It was at R.	GIBB 366:2	
Let R. in Tiber melt	SHAK 794:44	
Like R., Nkongsamba was built	BOYD 153:10	
O lucky R.	CICE 227:37	
Only R. can resemble R.	BELL 76:42	
on my way to R.	WAUGH 924:99	
out of R.	GARI 360:73	
recent disaster at R.	AUGU 44:33	
R.!...city of the soul	BYRON 188:62	
R. immortal	GURN 390:1	
R. is but a wilderness	SHAK 760:24	
R....is like its own Monte Testaceo	CLOU 232:55	
R....only monument left of R.	BELL 76:41	
R. shall perish	COWP 250:95	
R. shall stand	BYRON 188:68	
R.'s just a city	BURG 174:90	
R. to chase the Antichrist	LESL 523:88	
rules of my religion from R.	BROW 165:45	
see R. while it yet exists	WALP 918:65	
serve not R.	KIPL 493:70	
Sex Life in Ancient R. face	AMIS 16:30	
shake your R.	SHAK 799:2	
that I loved R. more	SHAK 777:35	
thousand roads lead to R.	ALAN 10:18	
Three nuncios from R.	MACA 545:27	
Romeo Juliet and her R.	SHAK 766:15	
never will be R.	SHAK 765:81	
O R., R.	SHAK 765:79	
roof artist needs but a r.	RYDER 736:57	
Beneath my shady r.	BLAKE 139:82	
Blown through the r.	THOM 885:72	
can't live under the same r.	MONT 614:25	
cat on a hot tin r.	WILL 945:90	
corrugated tin r.	BEEC 73:68	
good umbrella but a poor r.	LOWE 539:15	
He has restored the r.!	BETJ 88:15	
high embowèd r.	MILT 598:59	
majestical r.	SHAK 782:88	
prefers a thatched r.	WALC 916:19	
r., instead of slats	DRAY 299:1	
r. in words deceiving	MILT 597:37	
r. of gold	JONS 467:71	
tiles on the r.	LUTH 542:71	
twigs into a leaky r.	RUDO 730:35	
weeks of watching the r. leak	SNYD 832:92	
roofs abjure all r.	SHAK 792:2	
over the r. of the world	WHIT 937:96	
r. of this distracted City	CARL 200:6	
Shake not thy r.	BLAKE 139:83	
slate r. in sun	DAY 267:38	
rooks r...came home	HODG 421:20	
The r. are blown about	TENN 873:64	
rooky Makes wing to th' r. wood	SHAK 797:48	
room although the r. grows chilly	GRAH 380:87	
always r. at the top	WEBS 926:16	
being Queenly in her own r.	WHAR 933:7	
Books do furnish a r.	POWE 693:46	
coming to that holy r.	DONNE 293:64	
dark r. where I began	MASE 580:62	
dog in a very small r.	TOYN 895:73	
dying man's r.	STER 848:39	
embers through the r.	MILT 598:54	
enough r. in your own country	CORW 247:7	
flung himself from the r.	LEAC 515:14	
framed...in a comfortable r.	WALP 919:72	
Grief fills the r.	SHAK 768:57	
Here in this r.	STEV 849:73	
How little r.	SHIR 819:16	
infinite riches in a little r.	MARL 573:9	
in the morning r. reading	WAUGH 924:78	
into the neighbour r.	SHAK 784:46	
leave r. for the mouse	SAKI 739:68	
left the r.	GROS 389:80	
lights in the r.	GUIM 389:88	
make r. for discovery	APOL 29:86	
make r. for faith	KANT 473:25	
man in a jail has more r.	JOHN 460:88	
men in a smoke-filled r.	SIMP 822:85	
Minister's r. is like a padded cell	CROS 256:35	
music from a farther r.	ELIOT 316:63	
no r. for new feelings	ELIOT 315:32	
no r. in his workshop	FAUL 331:35	
not r....to swing a cat	SMOL 831:69	
only slipped away into the next r.	HOLL 423:50	
our r. on this earth	GREN 388:58	
Paces about her r. again	ELIOT 318:5	
parents...rent out my r.	ALLEN 14:92	
perpetual struggle for r. and food	MALT 563:21	
retired to my r.	STER 849:51	
r. at your head	BALL 58:57	
r. full of good air	LEAC 515:13	
r. in the west for wolves	BABB 48:2	
r. in this country	ROOS 725:23	
r. of her own	WOOLF 955:26	
r. of the palace	SITW 823:3	
r. or on the street	ROSSO 727:68	
r. to recognize him	BUEC 172:42	
r. to swing a cat	DICK 281:53	
R. with a View	FORS 344:23	
silence in the r.	KINS 488:67	
Sir Matthew left the r.	LINK 530:26	
sit in the same r. with me	PARK 664:24	
Social Predestination R.	HUXL 441:72	
stayed in the high r.	SPEN 837:6	
stay quietly in his r.	PASC 667:73	
that r.'s upper end	SPEN 839:41	
took up a great deal of r.	WHAR 933:47	
vilest earth Is r. enough	SHAK 772:67	
within a little r.	SMITH 830:35	
you shall keep your r.	STEV 854:84	
room-mates hard to be r.-m.	SALI 740:76	
rooms close-pent r.	WEBS 927:45	
Know most of the r.	FULL 355:78	
lighted r. Inside your head	LARK 510:92	
Other Voices, Other R.	CAPO 197:18	
People fill their r.	TREE 896:1	
planes and the corners of r.	MALL 562:3	
shimmering in r.	WODE 951:35	
Roosevelt answer that I will give...R.	CHUR 225:89	
R.'s spare tire	GARN 360:77	
R. will...go down into American	MENC 586:95	
roost come home to r.	SOUT 835:50	
rooster Charm never made a r.	ACHE 3:53	
Hongry r. don't cackle	HARR 399:48	
root March hath perced to the r.	CHAU 217:69	
neither r. nor branch	BIBLE 112:65	
nips his r.	SHAK 805:52	
r. of all evil	BIBLE 129:23	
r. of all genuine growth	SMIL 827:69	
r. of the matter is found in me?	BIBLE 98:9	
r. of the old one	NICH 636:72	
r. of the social unrest	LECO 518:80	
r. out of a dry ground	BIBLE 109:93	
rooted thicker and more deeply r.	ROTH 728:2	
rootholds nourishing earth for r.	SAND 742:23	
roots blasts the r. of trees	THOM 883:3	
Dull r. with spring rain	ELIOT 317:95	
r. here and there	MERE 588:41	
r. of relish sweet	KEATS 476:2	
R. ripe as old bait	ROET 722:58	
r. that can be pulled up	ELIOT 316:59	
send my r. rain	HOPK 429:96	
world withering at the r.	MILL 593:58	
rope buy a piece of the r.	TWAIN 903:78	
child skips r.	WHITE 935:44	
Man is a r., fastened	NIET 638:1	
suspicious even...piece of r.	DALAI 260:7	
ropes Like dancers on the r.	ETHE 327:42	
Rorschach R. ink blots	LICH 528:94	
rortie This r. wretched city	SMITH 831:64	
Rosa Parks R. P. sat	JAY 453:6	
rose all-willowed and white r.	FRAME 346:75	
Al night by the r.	ANON 21:42	
American Beauty r.	ROCK 720:31	
colour like the red r.	SHAK 767:34	
compare the cheeks...to a r.	DALI 261:14	
dropping a r. petal down	MARQ 575:57	
dumb to tell the crooked r.	THOM 883:3	
fause Luver staw my r.	BURNS 179:33	
fire and the r. are one	ELIOT 321:94	
go as deep as a r.'s	SWIN 864:94	
Go happy r.	HERR 415:13	
Go, lovely r.	WALL 918:55	
have plucked thy r.	SHAK 790:40	
know the colour r.	ABSE 1:7	
last r. of summer	MOORE 618:3	
like a full-blown r.	KEATS 477:18	
make a right R. Tree	YEATS 966:21	
musk of the r. is blown	TENN 876:25	
no more desire a r.	SHAK 763:4	
One perfect r.	PARK 664:17	
O r., thou art sick!	BLAKE 140:12	
Queen r. of the rosebud	TENN 876:27	
raise up the ghost of a r.	BROW 166:86	
Reach me a r., honey	FITZ 337:83	
red, red r.	BURNS 180:50	
R. is a r. is a r.	STEIN 845:60	
r. is red	ANON 22:66	
r. like a nymph	SHEL 815:22	
R. of all R.s	YEATS 965:8	
r. of all the world	MACD 549:38	
r. of love	SPEN 838:33	
r. of Sharon	BIBLE 107:40	
r. Of youth	SHAK 794:70	
r.'s scent is bitterness	THOM 886:80	
Roves back the r.	DELA 271:24	
summer r.	GRAV 382:17	
supplication to the r.	FLEC 340:33	
that sweet lovely r.	SHAK 771:34	
That which we call a r.	SHAK 765:80	
The red r. cries	TENN 876:28	
The r. looks fair	SHAK 801:52	
though a r. should shut	KEATS 477:23	
thought that wants to be a r.	DARIO 263:45	
tiger sniffs the r.	SASS 746:95	
vernal bloom, or summer's r.	MILT 603:75	
Viva la, the R. shall fade	DAVIS 266:11	
what the r. is	SWIN 864:4	
without thorn the r.	MILT 604:97	
Rosebery [Lord R.]...never missed an occasion	SHAW 811:35	
rose-bloom R.-b. fell on her hands	KEATS 477:21	
rosebud r. garden of girls	TENN 876:27	
touch the r., and it fell	PHIL 677:54	
rosebuds r. in their perfumed bed	CAREW 198:54	
rose-buds Gather ye r.-b.	HERR 415:12	
rose-garden door...Into the r.-g.	ELIOT 319:37	
rosemary r., that's for remembrance	SHAK 784:55	
rose-red r.-r. city	BURG 175:5	
roses days of wine and r.	DOWS 296:37	
fields where r. fade	HOUS 432:56	
flung r.	DOWS 296:36	
For women are as r.	SHAK 786:97	
garden...with r.	MARV 577:89	
Into the blowing r.	MARV 576:86	
Lilies without, r.	MARV 576:88	
make the beds of r.	MARL 574:41	
not a bed of r.	STEV 852:39	
perfume of a thousand r.	BERN 86:76	

Ross

petals from blown r.	TENN 870:89	r. priesthood	BIBLE 130:67	gold maketh the r.	ANON 26:11
raptures and r. of vice	SWIN 864:91	stand so highly in our estate r.	HENR 411:13	greatest r. of all	MOLI 611:76
red r. there may blow	THOM 886:84	Women leave the R. Family	YORK 968:49	knowledge of how to r.	TOCQ 892:26
r. and revolutions	RAND 706:59	**royalties** fresh air and r.	ASHF 38:73	No r. of general morality	SART 745:77
r. at my head	ROSS 726:46	**royalty** r. is to be reverenced	BAGE 54:75	one absolute r.	HEMI 410:95
r. for the flush of youth	ROSS 726:40	R. puts a human face	RUNC 731:48	one guiding r.	HUXL 443:5
r., r., all the way	BROW 168:36	the r. of virtue	POTT 690:84	One Ring to r. them all	TOLK 893:45
r. washed in dew	MILT 597:42	**rub** Ay, there's the r.	SHAK 783:7	one r. that should never be broken	CHRI 223:39
seen r. damasked	SHAK 802:83	least r. in your fortunes	SHAK 804:41	one who can r.	TENN 876:20
Ross Down...to R. Lake	SNYD 832:93	r. my language against another	BART 66:27	perpetuate authoritarian r.	AUNG 45:39
Rosseau mock on, Voltaire R.	BLAKE 140:22	**rubbish** cast as r. to the void	TENN 874:76	Reason to r.	DRYD 303:12
Rossetti R....without principles	FORD 342:88	flame but a lot of r.	MACD 550:42	rich men r. the law	GOLD 376:87
rot R., and consume themselves	SHAK 762:82	r. of centuries	DUDEK 305:77	ruin or to r. the state	DRYD 302:74
R. inwardly, and foul contagion	MILT 599:89	r. that lies in the way	LOCKE 533:88	R. 1: Be cautious	ITO 448:79
shapes of r.	PURDY 700:85	r. was sent to Stockport	ANON 28:55	R. 1, on page 1	MONT 615:47
we r. and r.	SHAK 779:79	somewhere among the r.	JERR 455:49	r....assumes that players intend to trip	FRY 353:28
rotarians R. in space!	VIDAL 912:85	**Rubens** more death in it than R.	HUGH 435:25	r. by custom not by force	LEGU 520:12
rote cage of routine and r.	PLATH 680:27	**rubies** diamonds and r.	MORE 618:21	r. by law and r. by whim	DOUG 295:21
judge by r.	OTWAY 656:95	price is far above r.	BIBLE 105:7	r. for bargains	DICK 279:14
Rothermere papers...by Lord R.	BALD 57:30	Shouldst r. find	MARV 577:90	r. is...Do anything you can	BROUN 163:20
rotten goodly apple r. at the heart	SHAK 769:84	Those be r., fairy favours	SHAK 767:25	r. is, jam to-morrow	CARR 205:3
r. in the state of Denmark	SHAK 781:59	wisdom...more precious than r.	BIBLE 104:55	r. never to drink by daylight	MENC 586:96
small choice in r. apples	SHAK 761:59	**ruby** natural r. of your cheeks	SHAK 797:50	r. never to look into a newspaper	SHER 817:94
rottenness r. in his bones	BIBLE 104:66	r. and amethyst eyes	BRAS 156:77	R. No.1...R. No.2	BUFF 172:47
r. of our civilization	READ 708:94	**rudder** bridle and r. of painting	LEON 523:75	r. of another man	LOCKE 533:87
rotters miserable sodding r.	LAWR 512:40	heart was to thy r.	SHAK 794:68	r. of distributive justice	HOMA 425:93
rotundity thick r. o' th' world	SHAK 792:5	rhyme the r. is of verses	BUTL 185:71	r. of safety	WHIT 936:66
rouge wore far too much r.	WILDE 942:10	Their tail the r.	DRYD 299:15	r. of wealth	BAGE 54:69
rough And what r. beast	YEATS 966:25	**ruddy** r....and goodly to look to	BIBLE 96:35	R. that Love is ever rewarded	BACON 51:80
children who were r.	SPEN 837:98	r. limbs and flourishing hair	BLAKE 139:81	r. that may serve for a statesman	CHAR 215:29
I am r.	SHAK 761:63	**rude** first r. sketch	KIPL 490:97	safe r. to apply	WHIT 936:62
If they want r.	BURKE 176:62	let's talk r.	FLAN 338:10	same r. applies for lust	MONT 614:44
love...so tyrannous and r.	SHAK 765:66	manner r. and wild	BELL 76:51	same r. will hold	POPE 685:22
real music...is r.	DAY 267:28	rather r. and wild	BELL 77:64	standing r. to live by	ASTE 39:5
r. and ready man	BROW 168:40	r. facts at your feet	RABAN 703:4	standing r. to live by	LOCKE 533:87
R. winds do shake	SHAK 800:37	when people are r.	FITZ 338:97	take it as a general r.	DESC 274:97
Too r., Too rude, too boist'rous	SHAK 765:69	**rudeness** difficult from its r.	JOHN 463:63	that's not a regular r.	CARR 204:86
rough-hew R.-h. them how we will	SHAK 785:69	indistinguishable from r.	THER 882:89	they who r. industrially	CONN 243:19
Roughing It writing R. I.	MOOD 615:56	offensive act of theatrical r.	ZOLO 970:17	we r. all mankind	CATO 208:98
roughness short-haired joy and r.	SNYD 833:95	**Rudge** raven, like Barnaby R.	LOWE 539:8	**ruled** Art of Being R.	LEWIS 527:74
roughnesses remark all these r.	CROM 255:21	**rudiments** after the r. of the world	BIBLE 128:9	world is r. by little else	KEYN 484:81
rough-tongued lifted, r.-t. bled	LARK 509:73	**Rudyards** R. cease from kipling	STEP 847:12	**ruler** make the r. over many things	BIBLE 119:33
round act of walking r. him	BEER 74:95	**Rudy Giuliani** R.G.—...9/11	BIDEN 133:53	resemble not a r.	HUXL 442:1
Am I so r. with you	SHAK 762:92	**rue** press the r. for wine!	SCOTT 753:35	r. in Israel	BIBLE 111:55
As r. as the world	SITW 823:98	**ruffian** r. stern, and soldier good	SCOTT 753:37	R. of the Queen's Navee	GILB 368:33
body was as r.	SPEKE 836:82	**rug** upon a r. mingle	STEV 849:69	R. of the Queen's Navee	GILB 368:34
Cricket...presents men in the r.	ARLO 32:32	**Rugby** feature of the R. game	ANON 23:85	**rulers** events...brought about by r.	BIER 134:80
Glasgow...going r. and r.	FYFFE 356:96	turns up his nose at R.	ANON 23:89	government...not the glory of r.	BEVE 90:62
other way r.	GOWE 380:80	**rugged** It's r., it's hard working	KOCH 495:25	r. take counsel...against the Lord	BOOK 148:2
r. and full at evening	HOLM 424:68	**rugs** lined with tiger r.	MACN 557:97	**rules** depending not on r.	JOHN 463:92
r. it was, upon a hill	STEV 849:64	**ruin** Atoms or systems into r. hurled	POPE 686:73	deviating from the r. of art	ADDI 2:54
r. of bells	SLES 825:52	countries...going fastest to r.	SMITH 827:82	disregard of all r.	ORWE 655:81
teach it r. or flat	JOHN 458:20	don't let Labour r. it	ANON 25:37	following the r.	SEDA 755:95
unto Merlion, and the Table R.	MALO 562:10	God to r. has designed	DRYD 303:18	follow the r. until I go against them	FRAN 348:6
With visible motion her diurnal r.!	WORD 957:71	hideous r. and combustion down	MILT 601:33	golden r. for an orchestra	BEEC 73:67
roundabouts What's lost upon the r.	CHAL 212:56	hides the r. that it feeds upon	COWP 251:5	No r., however wise	RUSS 734:31
roundheels Reagan is a rhetorical r.	SAFI 737:21	invented his own r.	WEBS 926:33	no r. in filmmaking	CAPRA 198:33
rounds priests...walking their r.	BLAKE 140:15	love of gain to r. men	SOPH 834:25	no r....of musical composition	SHAW 810:23
Roupell by the late Mr Charles R.	SPEN 837:91	Man marks the earth with r.	BYRON 188:71	not even by my own r.	WILL 946:25
rouse If anything might r. him	OWEN 658:37	r. and despair	WIEN 939:29	present r. of the game	ROOS 724:18
r. before the morn	TENN 872:27	r. or to rule the state	DRYD 302:74	rearrange the r. to suit yourself	CAPO 197:24
Rousseau Imagine R., Voltaire	HESS 417:34	R. seize thee	GRAY 385:79	R. and models destroy genius	HAZL 404:59
R. said...he was only trying	HAZL 403:44	r.—yet what r.!	BYRON 188:67	r. and prescriptions	NISB 639:27
Voltaire, R....fools, and madmen!	ONEI 651:70	three roads to r.	POMP 684:13	r. are so ill-defined	ORWE 654:44
rout feasts where meet a public r.	DAVI 264:78	**ruined** England is not r.	PRIE 695:95	r. comedy can tolerate	THUR 891:2
route r. towards the unknown	HUGO 438:88	O r. piece of nature	SHAK 793:23	r. for odd inventions	SHAK 762:69
routine people free from r.	LINK 530:25	r. by Chinese cheap labour	HARTE 400:73	r. made poetry a pedant's game	BUNT 173:68
relentless cage of r.	PLATH 680:27	r. in a conventional...way	KEYN 484:75	r. of ancient liberty	MILT 601:21
rove she may r. as well	BEHN 75:19	r. the whole estate and kingdom	HOBY 421:11	r. of strict secrecy	LENIN 521:37
roving r. woman gives rise to gossip	ANON 20:43	r. your perfectly dreadful play	BANK 61:14	sex r. for myself	SALI 740:73
row canst boast a r.	JONS 467:71	**ruins** familiar r., began to cry	NEME 633:18	there are no golden r.	SHAW 808:60
frightful, appalling r.	OBRI 646:69	fragments...shored against my r.	ELIOT 318:12	There are no r. or models	HUGO 436:53
r. of dominoes set up	EISE 314:98	mortality, the r. of forgotten times	BROW 165:73	the r. of the game	BLAIR 138:70
R. upon r.	TATE 867:38	open space among the r.	SHEL 815:26	the universe...governed by r.	PAGE 659:16
sitting in the last r.	KAUF 474:34	r. of the Capitol	GIBB 366:2	two cents for all your fancy r.	BUCH 171:30
rowdies round up us old r.	MCMU 557:82	**Ruislip** Gaily into R. Gardens	BETJ 89:37	**ruling** decay of...the r. class	ORWE 654:35
rows not lugged into Family R.	WODE 952:39	**rule** abide by majority r.	LEE 518:88	R. is hard.	MART 576:82
ranged in more frequented r.	CRAB 251:26	acting under the unanimity r.	MACM 556:68	r. passion conquers reason	POPE 686:67
r. and r. of empty seats	OLIV 649:40	bedspreads according to r.	LEVE 525:25	sports for the old r. classes	HOBS 421:10
royal every r. verdict	WHIT 934:24	be each man's r.	TENN 872:30	**rum** A day without a morning r.	WELSH 930:45
member of the R. Family called Ena	WOOD 954:99	been one to write by r.	WILL 946:25	bottle of r.!	STEV 852:59
no 'r. road' to geometry	EUCL 328:51	best fitted to r.	GILM 371:94	Raped by r.	WRIG 963:71
Of eyes again so r.	SHAK 795:95	damn by r.	OTWAY 656:95	r. and true religion	BYRON 189:5
r. bed of Denmark	SHAK 781:65	exception disproves the r.	DOYLE 296:45	r., Romanism, and rebellion	BURC 174:86
R. Commission is a broody hen	FOOT 342:81	first r. of intelligent tinkering	EHRL 313:69	what a R. Go everything is	WELLS 930:26
r. corpses	GILL 370:77	fundamental psychological r.	KEYN 485:83	**rummy** chappie is r.	WODE 951:35
r. family in the middle ages	HALD 392:22	golden r.	LICH 528:92	**rumour** Fame and r.	JONS 467:56

Saguntum

Entry	Ref
R. is of all pests the swiftest	VIRG 913:17
suspicion, r., fantasy	RICH 713:95
rump contempt is the R. come to	PEPYS 673:84
run A novelist could…r. a country	TOIB 893:40
born to r.	SPRI 841:88
'Don't r., walk'	JOHAN 456:71
many shall r. to and fro	BIBLE 111:44
minutes how they r.	SHAK 760:9
no way to r.	OBAMA 644:42
or r. it down	SWIFT 863:64
r. after it and bring it back	BARR 65:93
r., and not be weary	BIBLE 109:85
r. before it	KAFKA 472:4
r., but he can't hide	LOUIS 538:75
R., r., Orlando	SHAK 779:87
r., that ye may obtain	BIBLE 126:44
r. with patience the race	BIBLE 129:43
Still as they r.	GRAY 383:46
stumble that r. fast	SHAK 766:90
What Makes Sammy R.?	SCHU 749:69
While I do r. upon it	SHAK 778:55
would have r. to him	STAN 842:11
would r.	GRAMM 381:93
runagates letteth the r. continue	BOOK 149:23
runaway a r. train	SPIEL 840:67
runic full of r. tales	FLEC 340:35
runner lame man…outstrips the r.	BACON 50:48
Loneliness of the Long Distance R.	SILL 821:69
running Avoid r. at all times	PAIGE 660:28
first sprightly r. could not give	DRYD 300:38
it takes all the r. you can do	CARR 204:93
r. for president	CLOO 231:43
r. people down is considered sport	FOST 345:57
r.…the greatest freedom	BANN 62:34
US aggressors and all their r. dogs	MAO 569:36
with me r. after it	IGNA 445:17
running-horse loves a r.-h.	SHIR 819:17
run-stealers r.-s. flicker to and fro	THOM 886:84
runway curlew high above the r.	HEAN 405:77
Rupee chapter on the fall of the R.	WILDE 942:5
rupture possibility of a r.	SCOTT 754:76
rural all urban and r. sounds	LAMB 505:4
in a r. spot!	HUNT 439:22
r. virtues	GOLD 376:7
sly shade of a R. Dean	BROO 162:93
Sweet especial r. scene	HOPK 428:79
Rus R. in urbe	MART 576:78
rush all their lives…they'll have to r.	DUNN 307:15
As we r.	THOM 887:6
jaded with the r. and glare	ARNO 34:72
r. into the secret house	SHAK 795:78
rushes Green grow the r., O	BURNS 177:66
rushing r. of the larger worlds	DICK 281:57
Ruskin young Macaulay or R.	BARB 63:45
Russell foreign policy of…R.	DERBY 274:86
Russia action of R.	CHUR 225:82
antagonism between R.	CECIL 210:34
be pleasant to R.	PUTIN 700:98
cause that interests R.	WITTE 950:19
Europe needs R.	YELT 967:44
For us in R.	SOLZ 833:7
From R. with Love	FLEM 340:41
Here lies R.	BISM 137:37
I can see R. from my house!	FEY 334:4
more esteemed in R.	SNOW 832:81
no nation…less able…than R.	BRIG 159:16
R. has two generals	NICH 636:70
R. is a gas station	MCCA 547:21
R. is my home	BROD 160:42
twentieth-century R. and America	HELL 408:46
Russian An intelligent R.	MUNS 626:57
every R.'s inmost heart	PUSH 700:88
R. imbues	TWAIN 902:33
R. soldiers standing on the threshold	CHUR 225:90
R. word 'perestroika'	GORB 378:47
what the R. Revolution can become	ONET 651:82
Russians cannon, the R. flinched	RUSK 732:80
R.…such a beating!	VICT 912:77
when he says he understands R.	BOHL 144:99
rust moth and r. doth corrupt	BIBLE 115:43
overgrown with r.	SPEN 838:30
r. on the razor	ANGE 18:83
scrap and r.	SAND 742:15
to r. unburnished	TENN 870:98
rustic r. murmur of their bourg	TENN 876:43
rustics Amazed the gazing r.	GOLD 376:2
rustling r. of the grass	WORD 960:22
rusty Weapons grow r. if unused	HICKS 417:48
rut state of r.	GALS 358:49
Ruth entrepreneurs…like Babe R.	RODG 721:50
Who is this 'Babe' R.?	SHAW 811:30
ruthless r. if he is a good one	FAUL 331:40
ruttled R. in dry ground	JEFF 453:18
Ryanair R. will never fly the Atlantic	OLEA 649:34
rye boys was drinkin' whiskey and r.	MCLE 554:22
catcher in the r.	SALI 740:81
Comin thro' the r.	BURNS 180:55
get a drink of r.	ANON 24:9

S

Entry	Ref
Sabaoth Lord God of S.	BOOK 146:36
sabbath exercises from the S.	STUB 858:60
keep the S. going to Church	DICK 283:35
observe the S.	WALK 917:37
On the last S. day of 1879	MCGO 551:73
Remember the s. day	BIBLE 94:66
S. of the dead	MACL 555:31
s. was made for man	BIBLE 119:51
sabbath-breaking drinking and s.-b.	DE 274:85
sabbaths Those endless s.	ABEL 1:4
sack back us or s. us	CALL 193:30
hours were cups of s.	SHAK 770:27
say he cried out of s.	SHAK 775:69
sackcloth put off my s.	BIBLE 95:8
sacrament This great S.	AQUI 30:97
sacramental it is s.	SPEN 837:12
sacred Alph, the s. river	COLE 226:36
beliefs…we hold s.	ARON 36:48
classification of…profane and s.	DURK 308:30
facts are s.	SCOTT 751:98
feed his s. flame	COLE 235:27
followed by a s. song	BELL 77:65
If anything is s.	WHIT 937:98
Most s. fire	SPEN 838:36
O s. hunger	SPEN 839:53
s. cow of American culture	HUGH 435:27
s. graves to be ploughed	RED 709:19
S. Heart o' Jesus	OCAS 646:77
slavery…so s.	ASTE 39:5
too s. to be touched	JEFF 454:28
veils her s. fires	POPE 689:47
words s., glorious and sacrifice	HEMI 409:64
sacredness nothing of a s. of war	BONH 145:21
sacrilegious Most s. murder	SHAK 797:41
sacrifice fire of s.	ROCK 720:33
further human s.	OBRI 645:64
have mercy, and not s.	BIBLE 116:63
how Irishly you s.	GRAV 382:33
hush of ancient s.	STEV 849:69
only make a s. to God	POPE 686:56
perfect, and sufficient s.	BOOK 147:71
pinnacle of s.	LLOY 533:72
present your bodies a living s.	BIBLE 125:24
readiness to s. for others	LLOY 533:73
s. human life to figures	WEIL 928:74
s. instead of more security	KENN 481:99
s. of another resource	HERF 414:91
s. of more and more labour	RICA 712:80
to obey is better than s.	BIBLE 96:33
Too long a s.	YEATS 966:20
unpitied s. in a contemptible struggle	BURKE 175:10
without some s.	KOHL 496:35
sacrificed De profundis of the S.	KIER 486:7
spent and s.	SWIN 864:8
sacrifices s. of God…broken spirit	BIBLE 101:74
s. of our fellow countrymen	EISE 314:8
s. were like the stock-yards	HEMI 409:64
share of the labours and s.	MILL 591:2
sacrilege double s. on things divine	DRYD 303:8
sad being white is cold and s.	RHYS 712:73
day…more or less s.	ANOU 28:66
experience to make me s.	SHAK 779:7
great reason to be s.	SHAK 779:6
griefs…seem less s.	RICK 714:27
How s. and bad and mad	BROW 169:67
How slowly does s. Time	SPEN 839:51
make a sweet lady s.	SHAK 786:32
make us s. next morning	JONS 467:70
More s. are these	HARTE 400:75
need to be a little s.	DE 268:52
remember and be s.	ROSS 726:42
s. and strange	TENN 872:43
s. as going to work	ANOU 28:58
s. bad…brother's name	SWIN 864:15
s. for my generation	SAINT 738:40
s. obscure sequestered state	BROW 169:78
s., sour, sober beverage	BYRON 190:11
s. tale's best for winter	SHAK 799:12
s. tires in a mile-a	SHAK 799:16
s. vicissitude of things	STER 848:49
s. words of tongue or pen	WHIT 938:20
say I'm s.	HUNT 440:30
She is never s.	SHAK 774:33
sisterhood with s. experience	WELD 928:82
so deliciously aged and s.	SHAW 806:80
something s. about the boy	COWA 249:52
So s., so fresh	TENN 872:42
So s., so strange	TENN 872:43
visit my s. heart	SHAK 777:19
who were never s.	HARP 398:41
why sae s. gang ye O?	BALL 59:61
saddest s. are, 'It might have been,'	HARTE 400:75
saddle s. fits a cow	STAL 842:7
shone the s. leather	TENN 870:84
Things are in the s.	EMER 324:73
Sadducees Pharisees and S.	BIBLE 114:20
Sade S., the gallant marquis	RICK 715:28
sadism long act of s.	LECA 518:77
sadists s.…become policemen	CONN 242:96
sadness angling…a diverter of s.	WALT 920:92
Hello s.	ELUA 324:45
no s. of farewell	TENN 879:6
s., as the Preacher saith	HARDY 397:25
s. makes no approaches	JONS 468:87
s. of the women's movement	ANGE 19:93
so full of unmannerly s.	SHAK 769:78
Sweet though in s.	SHEL 813:83
unpleasing s.	WORD 961:34
Where there is s.	FRAN 347:99
safe choice…irregular but s.	WEST 933:70
he, who servilely creeps…Is s.	DRYD 300:27
in me you are s.	ATWO 41:41
Is it s. here?	WOLF 952:63
make everything s.	HAWT 401:98
neither right nor s.	LUTH 542:69
S. with his wound	SASS 745:81
ship in port is s.	HOPP 429:5
thought it was s.	ANON 26:78
world be made fit and s.	WILS 949:85
world s. for diversity	KENN 481:18
safeguard great s. of society	ELIOT 316:44
s. a revolution	ORWE 655:78
s. of the West	WORD 959:4
safeguards surrounded with such s.	THOR 889:56
safely You will go most s.	OVID 657:17
safer s. than a known way	HASK 400:81
s. to be in chains	KAFKA 472:5
safety 15 fingers on the s. catch	MACM 556:68
concern for one's s.	HELL 407:27
eat in s.	SHAK 805:58
greatest assurances of s.	ACHE 3:55
no s. in numbers	THUR 890:73
pluck this flower s.	SHAK 771:42
provide…for our own s.	PITT 680:12
s. cometh from the Lord	SCOT 755:89
s. in the state of victimization	ANGE 19:94
s. is in our speed	EMER 324:62
source of my light and my s.	BIBLE 132:50
strike against the public s.	COOL 245:78
string and s. pins	ACHE 3:48
take off the s. catch	JOHST 465:11
safety-net Welfare should be a s.-n.	ANON 27:31
safire diamond and s. bracelet	LOOS 536:52
sagas Stars scribble…the frosty s.	CRANE 253:65
sage Goddess s. and holy	MILT 598:50
mony lengthen'd s. advices	BURNS 179:21
more hateful…The social s.'s	BROW 169:68
s. feels too small for life	CHES 221:83
s. in meditation found	SHEL 812:68
venerable s.	WORD 961:40
wine can…Make the s. frolic	POPE 686:51
sages as witches and s.	SMITH 830:38
dozing s. drop the drowsy strain	COWP 250:90
s. have seen in thy face?	COWP 250:96
teach you more…than all the s.	WORD 957:59
what makes men poets or s.	CHAR 215:28
what the s. spoke	YEATS 967:39
sagging s., bagging and dragging	PART 666:59
sags Maybe it just s.	HUGH 435:13
Saguntum S. was captured	LIVY 532:62

Sahara

Sahara crawling across the S. — BENN 80:57
said everything has been s. — FERN 334:97
everything has been s. — LABR 502:6
I'll stand by what I s. — ROMN 724:98
S. I to myself—s. I — GILB 369:51
so very little s. — CHUR 224:54
thing well s. — DRYD 300:19
Well s., old mole — SHAK 781:69
What can be s. at all — WITT 951:20
what is not worth being s. — BEAU 70:4
When all is s. and done — SASS 746:94
Saigon 105 degrees in S. — ANON 28:50
sail globed like a full s. strung — HEAN 404:68
Had chosen thus to fling his s. — HARDY 397:23
Not everyone can s. to Corinth — ANON 20:19
S. and s., with unshut eye — ARNO 33:58
s. in a yot — QUIL 702:11
sea-mark of my utmost s. — SHAK 790:48
white and rustling s. — CUNN 258:74
white s.'s shaking — MASE 580:50
sailing best thing I find in s. — BELL 77:69
s. proudly down the years — PRIE 695:86
sailor an old s. — STEV 850:78
home is the s. — STEV 853:62
no man will be a s. — JOHN 460:88
part of me as of the s. — MAIL 560:67
s.'s wife had chestnuts — SHAK 795:99
the s. tells stories of the winds — PROP 697:30
sailors men s. should be tinkering — MELV 585:62
sails fancy is the s. — KEATS 475:72
had spread their s. — ROBE 717:71
Purple is the s. — SHAK 794:55
s. are now hoisting — PARK 663:91
s. with the stream — HAZL 403:42
Silver s. all out of the west — TENN 872:37
thought-woven s. — YEATS 965:8
To the white dipping s. — MASE 580:60
we our s. advance — DRAY 298:94
Saimear squadrons in S.'s — MCCA 547:74
saint become a s. without God? — CAMUS 196:88
Be neither s. nor sophist-led — ARNO 33:68
converting Abe into a plaster s. — MENC 587:14
face of a s. — WELLS 930:33
hair a glory like a s. — KEATS 477:21
Hitler was...a very s. — POUND 692:22
injury would vex a very s. — SHAK 762:70
no s. was ever silent — PASC 668:93
patron s. of journalists — MCFA 551:69
Primrose Hill and S. John's Wood — BLAKE 141:30
S....dead sinner revised — BIER 135:91
s. in crape is twice — POPE 687:94
s. run mad — POPE 688:25
s., the scientist — LAWR 514:84
s. when most I play the devil — SHAK 761:39
saw my late espoused S. — MILT 601:27
shoulders of the....s. — WEBER 925:11
'twould a s. provoke! — POPE 687:96
saintliness s. in my view — STOWE 856:27
saints bodies of the s. which slept arose — BIBLE 119:48
choir of his s. — DONNE 293:64
Communion of S. — BOOK 146:37
death of his s. — BIBLE 102:21
entertain him all the s. — MILT 600:95
fellow citizens with the s. — BIBLE 127:86
For all the S. — HOW 433:84
jest with s. — SHAK 787:59
Klee-drawn s. — WILK 943:59
least of all s. — BIBLE 127:87
lives of the medieval s. — SAKI 739:54
lose With my lost S. — BROW 166:98
never be S. in Heaven — BROW 165:61
s. aware of their own sinfulness — BLOOM 143:65
S. in your injuries — SHAK 789:6
s. may do the same things — BUTL 185:80
S. should always be judged — ORWE 655:79
s. smiled gravely — LIND 530:15
Thousand thousand S. attending — WESL 932:64
Vermin-eaten s. — LIND 530:16
ways the s. have trod — STUD 858:63
We are not s. — BECK 72:44
We need s. without cassocks — ANON 27:44
saintship s. of an anchorite — BYRON 187:34
sake Except for love's s. — BROW 166:93
for the s. of Miss Nightingale — STRA 856:38
salad Our Garrick's a s. — GOLD 377:16
s. days — SHAK 794:54
S. is not a meal — LEBO 517:60
To make a good s. — WILDE 940:46
salad dressing s. d. is out-grossing my films — NEWM 635:51
salads combination s. are popular — JANE 452:79
pick a thousand s. — SHAK 791:70
salary keep the s. — GOMEZ 377:39
s. of a beneficed clergyman — WAUGH 923:64
their s. depends upon — GORE 379:61
sale America is up for s. — TSON 900:7
books...their s. forbid — MELV 585:75
large s. among the fairies — HEMI 409:63
sales s. conference...Passion play — SCRI 755:90
Take the s. — GATES 361:90
salesman lazy insolence of a shoe s. — PERE 674:18
s. is got to dream, boy — MILL 593:33
Willie was a s. — MILL 593:32
Salisbury Lord S....spokesman — CHAM 212:58
S. and myself have brought you peace — DISR 288:66
saliva not in the heart or in the s. — ARGU 31:12
salley Down by the s. gardens — YEATS 965:3
sallow s. for the mill — SPEN 838:20
Sally S. said I was a sacrilegious — SALI 740:80
sally I make a sudden s. — TENN 876:32
salmon s. from the river — SCOTT 753:37
S. is the most stately fish — BERN 86:81
s. sing in the street — AUDEN 43:81
salmonella egg...infected with s. — CURR 259:96
salon s. for his agents — BYRON 191:37
used to be in the s. — MACM 557:75
saloon s. make a woman bare of all — NATI 632:4
saloons Solomon of s. — BROW 169:68
salsa La mejor s. del mundo — CERV 211:45
salt eating an egg without s. — KIPL 489:73
little Pepper or S. — SWIFT 862:59
loft in S. Lake Farm — THOM 884:35
pale spectrum of the s. — BROW 166:89
pillar of s. — BIBLE 92:24
s. of reality — BELL 77:69
s. of tears — KAIKO 472:11
s. of the earth — BIBLE 114:28
s. of the earth — SHEL 814:3
s. tides seawards flow — ARNO 33:56
s. weed sways in the stream — ARNO 33:57
speech...seasoned with s. — BIBLE 128:13
unplumbed, s., estranging sea — ARNO 34:82
With...a pinch of s. — PLIN 682:71
salt-caked s.-c. smoke-stack — MASE 580:56
Salteena Mr S....marched up to bed — ASHF 38:71
Mr S. was an elderly man — ASHF 37:69
Salter Mr S.'s side — WAUGH 923:73
saltness s. of time — SHAK 772:71
vinegar, sugar, and s. agree — GOLD 377:16
saltpetre villainous s. — SHAK 771:33
salty s. quality of human nature — ARLO 32:32
salud S., Dinero, Amor...y Tiempo — ANON 28:57
salus S. populi — CICE 227:29
salutation s. of the dead — ROBI 718:89
what manner of s. — BIBLE 120:64
salute give him the Nazi s. — HEND 410:2
S....with an holy kiss — BIBLE 126:34
saluted s. her on the by — JONS 468:89
salvaged ships have been s. — HALS 393:43
salvation all things necessary to s. — BOOK 150:40
bottle of s. — RALE 705:44
Christ alone for s. — WESL 932:65
come unto me for thy s. — BHAG 90:78
confuse it with the S. Army — ASHB 37:61
eyes have seen thy s. — BIBLE 120:70
for us men and for our s. — BOOK 147:61
from him cometh my s. — BIBLE 101:77
helmet of s. — BIBLE 128:95
In bumf lay s. — WAUGH 924:88
In the cross is s. — KEMP 480:80
Lord is my light and my s. — BIBLE 100:49
Neither is there s. in any other — BIBLE 124:75
new way of gaining s. — GUIB 389:86
no s. for gentlemen — MOLI 611:73
no s. outside the church — CYPR 260:9
now is the day of s. — BIBLE 127:72
provide for their s. — VAZD 910:43
s. along the lines of least resistance — FORD 342:88
s. of a few — INGE 445:31
s. of freedom — STEV 851:10
s. of our God — BIBLE 109:91
s. of our own souls — JOHN 461:13
strength of our s. — BOOK 149:30
Visit us with thy s. — WESL 932:62

wedded to S. — AESC 9:81
wells of s. — BIBLE 108:63
Work out your own s. — BIBLE 128:98
salve S. to thy sores — MILT 607:88
Sam S. the Gonoph says — RUNY 731:59
Samarcand From silken S. — KEATS 477:24
Samaritan S....had compassion — BIBLE 121:81
Samarkand Golden Road to S. — FLEC 340:32
same kings...are seldom the s. — SHAW 810:17
Lately things don't seem the s. — HEND 411:3
make sure they are not the s. — PICK 677:64
past is just the s. — SASS 745:93
path up and down is one and the s. — HERA 413:32
Politicians are the s. — KHRU 485:92
reason I should be the s.? — AYTO 48:10
s. yesterday, and to day — BIBLE 129:47
Two things are always the s. — STEIN 845:70
sameness spotted wolf of s. — SOYI 835:59
sames s. of am — CUMM 258:64
Samhain the long nights after S. — OBRI 646:70
samite Clothed in white s. — TENN 878:73
Sammy What Makes S. Run? — SCHU 749:69
Samothrace Victory of S. — MARI 571:77
Samsa S. awoke one morning — KAFKA 472:5
Samson character like S., Hercules — SIEG 820:60
Philistines be upon thee, S. — BIBLE 96:19
S. said, Let me die — BIBLE 96:20
Samuel Lord called S. — BIBLE 96:25
sanctify s. yourselves — BIBLE 94:76
sanction pile...s. on s. — CHAM 212:57
sanctity kissing is as full of s. — SHAK 779:1
odour of s. — WALL 917:46
s....in the state of victimization — ANGE 19:94
s. of life — GLAD 373:38
s. of life and property — SCHL 747:33
sanctuary inner s. of the Nanda — SHIP 818:15
shall be for a s. — BIBLE 107:58
three classes which need s. — BALF 57:28
Until I went into the s. — BIBLE 101:85
sand as a snowdrift on the s. — KHAY 485:86
as tough a rope of s. — BUTL 184:69
cathedrals In the s. — GIDE 367:18
colour of s. — ASHB 37:56
die upon the s. — ARNO 34:97
Divine...in a grain of s. — FRIE 351:74
edge of the s. — LEAR 516:38
every grain of s. — DOST 294:94
gasped upon the s. — MARL 573:13
I on the s. — SCOTT 753:43
no bigger than a grain of s. — CHEE 218:5
ostrich, with its head in the s. — WILS 949:80
palace built upon the s. — MILL 592:20
print...plain to be seen in the s. — DEFOE 269:78
property turns s. to gold — YOUNG 968:51
s. and ruin and gold — SWIN 864:7
s. dunes the wind lifted — PIER 677:68
s. in the porridge — COWA 249:45
see a world in a grain of s. — BLAKE 140:24
Such quantities of s. — CARR 204:99
throw the s. against the wind — BLAKE 140:22
waste of white barren s. — SCHAW 747:20
write in s. — WALL 918:60
sandal massive s. set on stone — MILL 592:26
sandals still in straw hat and s. — BASHO 67:46
Sanders a bed...Clerk S. said — BALL 58:56
sandfly mosquito and s. — DOUG 294:97
sands Come unto these yellow s. — SHAK 803:14
cousins as the s. of the sea — SHAW 811:33
Footprints on the s. of time — LONG 535:16
golden s., and crystal brooks — DONNE 292:37
lone and level s. — SHEL 813:86
men's names On s. — MILT 598:86
men who are as various as the s. — FORS 344:40
s. of Africa — JOHN 460:86
s. of Dee — KING 487:43
s. o' life shall run — BURNS 180:50
smoothed down like silly s. — BUNT 173:65
steer too nigh the s. — DRYD 301:71
vision of the crowded, howling s. — CHES 219:49
sand-strewn S.-s. caverns — ARNO 33:57
sandwich raw-onion s. — BARN 64:70
sandwiches other...eating s. — DICK 277:42
we eat reality s. — GINS 371:4
sane above all, of s. vitality — LUCAS 541:52
Mahdi...is very s. — CECIL 210:32
no s. person would do — SHAW 809:74
rewards for being s. — AMIS 16:39

scarcity

s. balance of values POUND 692:21
S....did what their neighbours ELIOT 316:44
Show me a s. man JUNG 471:47
they shall be s. THOM 883:7
San Francisco Heart in S. F. CROSS 256:34
not leave in S. F. HART 399:64
S. F. is a lady MAIL 560:55
sang s. and wallowed THOM 884:47
s. his didn't CUMM 258:69
s. themselves to sleep HODG 421:20
sanitary glorified s. engineer STRA 856:39
sanity fight...to bring back s. GAIT 357:11
Neither conscience nor s. MCNA 557:88
place where s. and hope ROUS 729:8
pursuit of s. BELL 77:77
restore themselves to s. SMALL 826:58
So with s. and insanity MELV 585:76
There ain't no S. Claus MARX 578:18
sans S. teeth, s. eyes, s. taste SHAK 779:83
San Salvador bells off S. S. CRANE 252:54
sanspareil Cricket...the s. FOWL 346:65
Santa S.'s grotto lies not in icy Lapland HIGH 418:52
Santa Claus Nobody shoots S. C. SMITH 828:92
sap s. flows up through our arms RILKE 715:39
soul's s. quivers ELIOT 321:81
sapient s. sutlers of the Lord ELIOT 317:79
saplings gale, it plies the s. HOUS 431:47
sapphire s. melts into the sea TENN 876:24
sapphire-blaze throne, the s.-b. GRAY 385:90
Sappho Call me S., Call me Chloris COLE 235:36
Dark S. BYRON 187:39
Sara S. could commit adultery CARY 207:64
Sarajevo lost, for art, at S. LEWIS 527:73
sarcasm Never use s. on players FERG 332:74
petulance is not s. DISR 288:42
sardines Life...like a tin of s. BENN 80:43
sark S. rins o'er the Solway sands BURNS 179:41
sashes nice new s. GRAH 380:87
Sassenach drove from a S. laird SCOTT 753:37
sat s. down on the right hand BIBLE 129:33
you have s. too long here CROM 255:22
Satan beheld S. as lightning BIBLE 120:79
called the Devil, and S. BIBLE 132:10
diligence of S. BUNY 173:72
Get thee behind me, S. BIBLE 118:7
Get thee hence, S. BIBLE 114:24
like a blond S. HAMM 395:69
Lord said unto S. BIBLE 98:90
Man, with his S. SNYD 832:91
messenger of S. BIBLE 127:76
Of S. and his peers MILT 602:54
other toward S. BAUD 69:85
playfield of S. NABO 628:11
S. exalted sat MILT 602:55
s. has not geven me boils FLEM 340:44
S., Nick, or Clootie BURNS 177:83
S. with thoughts inflamed MILT 603:68
satchel schoolboy with his s. SHAK 779:81
satiated rather die s. than slim PIER 677:69
satiety love's sad s. SHEL 814:96
Of knowledge there is no s. BACON 50:35
s. is a blunt...passion WEBS 926:20
satin allowed to wear black s. WHAR 934:12
ease a heart Like a s. gown PARK 663:97
heroine...goes into white s. SHER 818:4
loll on velvet and s. FRAN 348:23
Silk an' s. ANON 23:87
satire British...gluttons for s. LODGE 534:94
difficult not to write s. JUVE 471:52
let s. be my song BYRON 186:24
s., being levelled at all SWIFT 861:20
s. costs a lot! RICK 715:29
S. is a lesson NABO 628:17
S. is a sort of glass SWIFT 861:17
S. is dependent on strong beliefs BROO 163:9
S. is moral outrage ROTH 728:84
S. or sense, alas! POPE 688:5
satiric have the s. temperament BEER 73:76
satisfaction All s....never positive SCHO 748:51
cannot render s. MIDD 590:73
can't get no s. JAGG 449:13
s. of human needs NUTT 642:75
What's the s. HORN 430:25
won a s. and a triumph WOLFE 953:69
satisfied and we must be s. SYNGE 865:20
eyes of man are never s. BIBLE 105:4
forces s. mediocrity RENAN 711:47

having it, is s.? THAC 880:30
kisses...to make me fully s. CATU 209:7
Massey won't be s. KAUF 474:35
may be equally s. JOHN 461:12
s. with her lover's mind TROL 897:30
s. with that result SCHW 750:89
way to be s. BAGE 54:63
satisfy delights of art s. me FUEN 354:59
none of these finally s. WHIT 938:13
s. our thirst for freedom KING 487:29
those who are hardest to s. DESC 274:93
saturated too s. with it DURK 308:29
Saturday couple of drinks on a S. FYFFE 356:96
date on S. night ALLEN 14:88
Glasgow Empire on a S. night DODD 289:88
see another S. night MCNA 557:89
Saturdays passionately, on...S. SHER 817:84
Saturn the Revolution may, like S. VERG 910:54
saturn Sat gray-haired S. KEATS 477:28
while S. whirls TENN 870:95
satyrs men, like s. grazing MARL 573:14
Where the s. are chattering SITW 823:4
sauce honey a s. to sugar SHAK 779:99
Hunger...best s. in the world CERV 211:45
saucepans ghosts of s. MANS 567:95
saucer s. like some full moon MONRO 612:5
saucy no be half sae s. BURNS 179:14
Saul S. and Jonathan were lovely BIBLE 96:42
S. hath slain his thousands BIBLE 96:40
S., S., why persecutest thou me? BIBLE 124:80
whose name was S. BIBLE 124:78
sausage tin of Bologna s. STEV 851:29
savage civilized man...into a s. TOCQ 892:27
manner in which a s. wields HUXL 443:10
not a genuine foreign-grown s. DICK 281:73
painted face of a s. DICK 282:78
removed from the s. state COOP 246:85
rights of the s. GLAD 373:38
s. individual man WELLS 930:21
s. man...does man betray ROCH 719:13
s. place! COLE 236:37
s. servility slides by LOWE 540:25
subtle, but s. CAPO 197:26
take some s. woman TENN 871:21
unto a s. race TENN 870:97
wild...the noble s. ran DRYD 300:30
savaged s. by a dead sheep HEAL 404:64
We s. them GELL 363:36
savage-pictures s.-p. fill their gaps SWIFT 863:63
savages plant where s. are BACON 52:22
Savannah In S....drink? BERE 83:13
savannahs s. grew lonely as the sea HARR 399:55
savant Buddhist Beat Catholic s. GINS 372:12
save bit to s. humanity HUGH 435:19
destroy the town to s. it ANON 25:61
himself he cannot s. BIBLE 119:46
I can s. this country PITT 679:3
need not exist in order to s. us DE 275:13
nothing will s. the Governor WHIT 937:84
principle which prompts to s. SMITH 827:84
s. a shred of its respectability READ 708:94
s. everything that anyone else DOWD 296:30
S. something ANON 26:90
s. those that have no imagination? SHAW 810:18
s. those who damn them HUGO 437:70
s. us from the power JORD 469:2
saved is sometimes s. THUR 890:85
name...whereby we must be s. BIBLE 124:75
only s. by being dammed HOOD 426:27
s. the sum of things HOUS 432:72
we are not s. BIBLE 110:17
what must I do to be s.? BIBLE 124:87
Whosoever will be s. BOOK 146:44
Who then can be s.? BIBLE 118:19
saviour a s. spring to life BIBLE 133:40
Between the role of s. YOUR 968:58
God my S. BIBLE 120:66
God my S. BIBLE 133:42
Hark...The S. comes DODD 289:90
Hide me, O my S. WESL 931:59
in the city of David a S. BIBLE 120:69
S. of 'is country KIPL 489:87
s. or assassin MURP 627:77
words our S. Christ saith BOOK 147:68
savour if the salt have lost his s. BIBLE 114:28
s. like unto a blessed field HERR 415:14
stinking s. BIBLE 106:30

very homely household s. BYRON 190:11
with your sweet s. BIBLE 110:33
savoury meat is s. EMER 324:70
saw find thy s. of might SHAK 779:4
We came, we s., he died CLIN 231:34
sawdust S. and spangles CARD 198:38
sawed-off as a s.-o. shotgun PARK 664:31
Sawyer Tom S. he says the same TWAIN 903:66
saxophone s. is the embodied spirit BENN 81:77
s. was...his key to the world HOLM 423:57
say can s. only one thing at a time HOMA 427:71
don't have to s. anything FURT 356:90
don't listen to what people s. LEVI 526:33
have something to s. WHAT 934:15
I have so much more to s. RAVEL 707:83
isn't what I s., but how I s. it WEST 933:92
little to s. SOPH 834:31
little to s. nothing SKEL 824:27
many things to s. unto you BIBLE 123:56
mean everything they s. HOSS 430:30
must s. something but not much REAG 708:9
nothing at all to s. SAINT 738:13
Nothing is easier to s. TERE 879:14
nothing to s. BALF 58:42
nothing to s., s. nothing COLT 238:82
not moved to s. something HUNT 440:31
O s., can you see KEY 483:68
relevance for what it does not s. FERL 333:93
s. nothing, do nothing, be nothing ANON 27:32
S. not soft things SORL 834:33
s. the perfectly correct thing SHAW 810:4
s. what they please FRED 349:41
s. what you have to s. WELL 929:12
so much still to s. BART 67:31
that's what I shall s.! GILB 369:44
you should s. what you mean CARR 203:77
saying ancient s. is no heresy SHAK 769:96
do now remember a s. SHAK 780:16
famous witty s. THUR 890:90
lest a s. learnt TENN 877:61
s. of an ancient philosopher ADDI 6:30
thinking it and not s. it NOON 640:46
This is a faithful s. BIBLE 129:17
used to s. something different HAVEL 401:85
sayings heareth these s. of mine BIBLE 115:56
s. are generally like women's letters HAZL 404:51
says Don't report what he s. ANON 23:52
Who is it that s. most SHAK 802:66
scabs Make yourselves s.? SHAK 798:88
scaffold content to die...on the s. BROWN 164:28
s. and the doom AYTO 48:12
whether on the s. high SULL 859:80
scaffolding s. of spirit THOM 886:78
There is no s. HONE 425:14
scald s. and viper through her THOM 884:41
tears Do s. like molten lead SHAK 793:30
scale judicious, the s. is MILT 605:42
On every golden s.! CARR 203:64
Poetic justice, with her lifted s. POPE 688:30
s. doesn't matter DONO 293:81
Scotland in true s. MACD 549:30
something on the s. of the grand DIDE 285:66
scales cannot balance tragedy in the s. BENET 79:27
weighed the mountains in s. BIBLE 108:81
scallop-shell s.-s. of quiet RALE 705:44
scalpel intimacy of a surgeon's s. ANGE 19:98
scan presume not God to s. POPE 687:80
scandal Cut S.'s head off SHER 817:86
divided...by public s. DUMAS 306:91
Love and s. FIEL 335:17
No s. about Queen Elizabeth SHER 818:1
no s. like rags FARQ 330:28
Retired to their tea and s. CONG 240:35
s....gives offence MOLI 611:78
s. is often worse than the sin MARG 570:66
s. of...exalted person's fall CANM 196:3
scandalous Monarch, s. and poor ROCH 719:7
poor s. HEAN 404:70
scapegoat let him go for a s. BIBLE 94:77
scapegoats s. for our blunders TWAIN 903:86
they are the classic s. WHITE 934:27
scar far from cliff and s. TENN 872:39
scarce money was not s. EMER 325:96
s. a thing but is MIDD 590:76
scarcity by the influence of s. ROBB 717:68
from their s. and from...labour RICA 712:82
s. of opportunity ANGE 19:88

scarecrow

scarecrow s. of the law	SHAK 787:50
scared s. or too sulky	RYLE 736:61
scarf S. up the tender eye	SHAK 797:47
scarlet bind this line of s. thread	BIBLE 95:7
lips more s.	YEATS 967:30
live with s. Majors	SASS 745:84
Lovely creature in s.	GEOR 364:59
raise the s. standard	CONN 242:84
s. coat	WILDE 942:15
sins were s.	BELL 77:71
though your sins be as s.	BIBLE 107:50
scars My Marks and S. I carry	BUNY 174:83
scarred who carry our s.	GEE 362:27
s. that never felt a wound	SHAK 765:77
sleeve and show his s.	SHAK 776:90
scarves present them with s.	BAIN 55:94
scary If I know anything, I know s.	KING 487:39
Old people are s.	SMITH 829:28
scatter s. and gather	HERA 412:33
s. up and down	SHAK 759:90
scattered God blew and they were s.	ANON 22:65
scene Act One, S. One	HART 400:70
ask to see The distant s.	NEWM 635:45
breath, a little s.	SHAK 764:52
every day Speaks a new s.	QUAR 701:6
lofty s. be acted over	SHAK 777:31
naive impression of the s.	MONET 612:99
Of what s.	SHEL 815:35
preside o'er the s.	TANN 867:24
start a s. or two	ELIOT 316:66
Supporting…Unto the S.	DICK 284:45
Sweet especial rural s.	HOPK 428:79
this s. of man	POPE 686:70
Upon that memorable s.	MARV 576:84
waste his destined s.	COLL 237:73
wildness to perplex the s.	POPE 686:60
scenery chew up the s.	PARK 663:2
end of all natural s.	RUSK 733:91
helps s. like ham and eggs	TWAIN 902:37
lovely descriptions of s.	BELL 75:40
S. is fine	KEATS 476:80
s. was beautiful	WOOL 956:50
scenes behind your s.	JOHN 459:51
feelings these dull s. produce	CRAB 252:43
From s. like these	BURNS 177:76
heart with usury to such s.	LAMB 505:79
s. his fathers loved	CULL 257:44
s. of our life	SCHO 749:59
s. where man hath never trod	CLARE 228:55
seldom…making love in any of his s.	DRYD 300:24
synthesizing the s.	MARA 569:45
scent first s. you pour	HORA 430:14
How hot the s. is	GRAV 382:17
s.…locust blossoms	WILL 946:23
s. of unwashed bodies	ACKR 3:60
s. survives their close	THOM 886:80
stronger s. towards evening	STAEL 842:97
sweetest flower for s.	SHEL 815:23
scents render Their pleasing s.	WEBS 926:19
sceptic knowledge for the s. side	POPE 687:80
scepticism if we start from s.	RUSS 734:36
preserve our s.	HUME 451:9
principles which at first lead to s.	BERK 84:32
sceptre and crown…tumble down	SHIR 819:20
s. as an emblem of royalty	BENT 82:91
s. for a palmer's…staff	SHAK 764:55
s. so fantastically borne	SHAK 775:71
s. to control the world	SHAK 760:22
sceptreless S., free…but man	SHEL 814:18
schedule s. is already full	KISS 494:91
Scheherazadesworth S. of stories	BARTH 65:7
Scheisskopf S. had the facts	HELL 407:28
scheme assist this detestable s.	MACA 545:27
interpret it as a rational s.	ROBI 718:94
s. by which the nations	LEES 519:4
s. of merriment	JOHN 460:85
Socialists can s.	MACL 556:50
stoical s. of supplying	SWIFT 861:34
schemes best-laid s. o' Mice	BURNS 177:78
expediency of different s.	STEU 849:61
s. for persuading monarchs	SWIFT 862:47
schizophrenia Canada is paranoid s.	ATWO 41:36
schizophrenic experience…is…s.	WITT 951:30
schmuck S. for a lifetime	DE 273:67
Schoenberg Why is S.'s Music	BERG 83:17
scholar better s. than Wordsworth	HOUS 432:61
gentleman an' s.	BURNS 177:80
humour of a s.	BACON 53:35
Like a dull s.	STEV 850:77
my honest s.	WALT 920:95
never be a complete s.	PLATH 680:28
s.'s life	JOHN 459:55
to this day is every s. poor	MARL 574:40
Zip, I am such a s.!	RODG 721:49
scholars nor its great s. great men	HOLM 424:71
philosophers and s.	PASC 668:96
scholarship boys or s. candidates	LITT 531:47
school aim of the s. of business	DEMI 272:47
at s. or college	STEV 852:50
Example is the s. of mankind	BURKE 176:57
explain s. to a higher intelligence?	MATH 581:90
for life, not for s.	SENE 757:24
get the feeling…you're not in s.	BRAN 156:67
growth of the Skyscraper S.	JOHN 458:26
kiddie in s.	NASH 630:62
no rhyme…for 's.'	SHAK 774:56
oyster of the old s.	DICK 281:63
playing fields of a public s.	FRY 353:28
private s. has all the faults	CONN 242:3
s. boys or scholarship	LITT 531:47
S. is where you go	UPDI 905:15
s. of flattery and dissimulation	WENT 931:52
s. that I went to in the north	WILS 948:58
s.…with tomorrow inside	AKERS 10:11
taught his little s.	GOLD 376:1
Three little maids from s.	GILB 369:63
till he's been to a good s.	SAKI 739:56
till we leave s.	LEWIS 526:48
truck passing by a music s.?	CAGE 192:17
went to s. without any boots	BULM 173:61
schoolboy Not the s. heat	TENN 875:97
what every s. knows	SWIFT 862:52
whining is with my satchel	SHAK 779:81
schoolboys go chide Late s.	DONNE 291:25
like s.	KIER 485:99
s. who…climb a crab-tree	ROCH 719:18
schoolchildren What all s. learn	AUDEN 43:96
schoolgirl Pert as a s.	GILB 369:63
schooling finish my s. without	ANON 26:98
s. any actress needs	GING 371:98
school-inspector s.-i. of average	KING 488:52
schoolman s.'s subtle art	POPE 688:7
schoolmaster s.'s answer	GRAV 383:39
you'll be becoming a s.	WAUGH 923:52
schoolmasters all the s. you can	CHIS 222:24
Let s. puzzle their brain	GOLD 376:11
schools class s.…into four grades	WAUGH 923:53
endeavour, through its s.	RUSS 734:30
hundred s. of thought	MAO 569:34
in the maze of s.	POPE 685:16
lumber of the s.	SWIFT 861:16
s. are not much good	DRUC 299:6
s. for the imagination	GIRA 372:25
s. of Oxford	GIBB 366:95
s. of theology…are to be overturned	DIDE 285:72
Tedium…in s.	POMP 684:12
wait for s. to be built	QABO 701:1
schooner was the s. Hesperus	LONG 535:20
Schopenhauer S.…madmen!	ONEI 651:70
Schubert not Bach or S.	MCCU 549:15
sciatic cure epilepsy and s. gout.	THEO 882:80
science Advertising…as the s.	LEAC 515:20
aim of s. is always	JAMES 451:65
All s. is cosmology	POPP 689:60
All s. requires mathematics	BACON 53:55
an art and not a s.	MO 611:67
and s. weak	SZASZ 865:26
application of natural s.	MARX 579:41
Art and S. cannot exist	BLAKE 141:31
a serious interest…in s.	PYKE 701:10
beams of S. fall	POPE 688:36
by s. as well as bread	JAMES 451:62
can s. flourish	PARS 666:56
consciousness of s.	DEWEY 276:19
create a whole s.	ROST 727:70
Creativity in s.	KOES 495:30
Detection is…an exact s.	DOYLE 296:43
early successes of s.	HUXL 442:80
Economics as a positive s.	FRIE 351:68
Economics is the s.	ROBB 717:68
Enough of s.	WORD 957:9
express themselves…upon the s.	MAIM 561:70
Fair S. frowned not	GRAY 384:77
find in art and s.	HALD 392:35
from s., is criticism	RUSS 734:22
Furnished…with Academies of S.	FRAN 348:18
generalizations of s. sweep	HUXL 442:2
give their lives to art and s.	EINS 313:76
god of s.	KING 487:32
grand aim of all s.	EINS 314:89
great man of s.	KING 488:53
great tragedy of S.	HUXL 443:5
hardest s. to forget	POPE 686:49
higher parts of his s.	MACA 545:43
History is not a s.	FRAN 347:86
history of s. reaches Alan Turing	HODG 421:18
history of s. shows	DARW 263:54
hope of s.	INGE 445:31
human s. is at a loss	CHOM 222:27
I am called s.	FLAU 339:26
if it is to be a s.	JEVO 455:51
if s. is feared	POIN 683:92
important to the cause of s.	AGAS 9:58
in both s. and religion	SAGAN 737:26
In everything that relates to s.	LAMB 505:91
injurious to the progress of s.	DARW 263:56
In s., the best precept	BERN 85:68
In s. the credit goes	DARW 263:61
in s.…we can get outside ourselves	RABI 704:23
in the pursuit of s.	HELM 408:51
In the realm of s.	STEI 846:99
Knowledge of physical s.	PASC 667:87
lasting result in s.	DESC 275:98
latest refinements of s.	CHUR 226:94
Learn the ABC of s.	PAVL 670:38
Literature is not an abstract s.	QUIL 702:14
man of s. is a poor philosopher	EINS 314:83
men of s.	MILL 593:51
method of assisting…pure s.	CONA 239:9
modern s. and technics	MUMF 625:36
modern s. and technology	GALB 357:20
name of s. for a…bogus purpose	WHIT 936:73
Natural s. does not simply describe	HEIS 407:22
No s.…immune to the infection	BRON 160:50
not…a man of s.	FREUD 350:55
only applications of s.	PAST 668:3
only generalization can establish s.	BERN 85:91
only s. that it hath pleased God	HOBB 420:97
only the instrument of s.	JOHN 460:68
origin of all s.	HAZL 404:52
or studying some s.	MONT 613:11
pace of s.	FROMM 352:88
Plain women…investigated by s.	ELIOT 316:44
Politics is not an exact s.	BISM 137:33
potentialities of s.	LEWIS 527:66
professors of the Dismal S.	CARL 201:39
progress in s.	POPP 689:54
progress of s.	JEFF 454:25
proud S.	POPE 687:75
Religion is far more acute than s.	FORS 344:33
reunite…world through s.	ARNO 35:23
S., after all, is only an expression	BUTL 186:8
S.…aggregate of all the recipes	VALE 907:4
s.—always stands far below	MARX 579:39
s. and common sense are wrong	MAMET 564:36
S. and technology…are unpredictable	DYSON 309:60
S. and technology multiply	BALL 60:86
S. appears but what in truth she is	WORD 958:79
S. becomes dangerous	SHAW 809:79
s. begins to concern itself	KLEE 494:2
S. bestowed immense new powers	CHUR 226:5
s.…blind without philosophy	AYER 48:8
S. cannot exist	PLAN 680:22
S. cannot solve…mystery	PLAN 680:24
S. can only state what is	EINS 313:81
s. consists in originating	WILS 948:63
S. creates the future	ZUCK 970:20
S. does not permit exceptions	BERN 85:76
s.…explained by a few simple laws	BROWN 164:33
S. fiction is no more…for scientists	ALDI 12:49
S. fiction is the apocalyptic literature	BALL 60:85
S. fiction, like Brazil	DISCH 287:10
S. fiction writers foresee	ASIM 38:79
S.…full of mistakes	TELL 869:66
S. had married the wilderness	FERB 332:70
S. has, as its whole purpose	OPPE 652:85
S. has…a system of principles	PAINE 660:50
S. has 'explained' nothing	HUXL 441:58
S. has nothing to be ashamed of	BRON 160:46
S. has promised us truth	LEBON 517:55
S.…instrumental system	BOOK 150:45

S. in the modern world	CHES 220:60	peeping Tom of the s.	BISH 137:31	take no s.	DAVI 264:75
S. is a cemetery	UNAM 905:5	progress of the arts and the s.	MAO 569:34	Teach not thy lip such s.	SHAK 761:35
S. is all metaphor	LEARY 517:48	quintessence of all s.	NASHE 631:89	think foul s.	ELIZ 321:4
S. is an all-pervasive energy	BARZ 67:39	servant of the s.	BAUD 68:71	thou canst make us s.!	BURNS 179:27
S. is analytical	GILL 370:84	study of all these s.	PLATO 682:66	With haughty s.	ARNO 35:5
S. is an integral part	GOULD 380:77	**scientific** all that is purely s.	GILL 370:84	**scorner** s. heareth not rebuke	BIBLE 104:67
S. is a search for truth	PAUL 670:34	articles published in s. journals	FEYN 334:5	s. of the ground!	SHEL 814:98
s. is a two-handed engine	MONT 613:9	before it became s., cricket	TREV 896:5	**scornful** most ridiculous and s. sort	SIDN 820:57
S. is a way of thinking	SAGAN 737:25	but A s. fact:	WILDE 942:18	sitteth in the seat of the s.	BIBLE 99:25
s. is either physics	RUTH 735:52	conclusion must be very s.	JAMES 452:77	**scorpion** home of the s.	SNYD 832:91
s. is…exploded fallacies	RAND 706:54	dread s. truth	POIN 683:96	S. so wishes	SMITH 830:44
S. is facts	POIN 683:97	Every s. statement	POPP 689:53	**scorpions** chastise you with s.	BIBLE 97:58
s. is inherently neither a potential for good nor for evil	SEAB 755:91	how deeper and more s.	BERR 87:3	Those two s.	OPPE 652:89
s. is intimately integrated	PARS 666:56	new s. truth	ORTE 652:2	**Scot** Had Cain been S.	CLEV 230:92
S. [is] knowledge of the truth	HOBB 420:96	replaced by 'the s. method'	BORN 151:64	S. come from Scotland	LOUI 537:63
S. is not everything	OPPE 652:86	s. and technical progress	JOHN 456:72	**Scotch** queerer set of people than the S.	BORR 151:72
S. is nothing but trained	HUXL 443:10	s. attitude implies	MONOD 612:3	show you have a S. tongue	SCOTT 754:61
s. is not just any similarity	WILS 948:52	s. attitude of mind	RUSS 734:29	**Scotia** old S.'s grandeur	BURNS 177:76
s. is organized knowledge	SPEN 836:85	S. discovery and…knowledge	PLAN 680:23	S.'s darling seat	BURNS 178:96
S.…is really anti-intellectual	MENC 586:3	S. discovery consists	WIEN 939:30	**Scotland** canna S. see wha yet	MACD 549:30
s. is said to be useful	HARDY 396:98	s. mind does not	LEVI 526:37	claret and burgundy in S.?	SMITH 827:85
S. is systematized positive knowledge	SART 744:63	s. revolution	WILS 948:61	dead bird of s.	MACL 555:29
S. is the father of knowledge	HIPP 419:70	s. statement speaks	POPP 689:61	democracy was renewed in S.	DEWAR 276:17
S. is the great antidote	SMITH 828:90	s. treatment for all diseases	SHAW 809:80	English in suzerainty over S.	GIBB 366:5
S. is the knowledge of	HOBB 420:98	s. validity of psychoanalysis	THOM 883:99	English should leave S.	HEFF 406:5
S. is the only truth	GOUR 380:79	technique are s.	RUSS 734:34	fair S.'s spear	SCOTT 752:27
S. is the reduction	HUXL 442:97	**scientist** But a s.?	SELF 756:10	flower of S.	WILL 946:31
S. is to the modern	DISR 287:28	Dissent…native activity of the s.	BRON 160:45	hideous about S.	WELSH 930:42
S. is triumphant	COMM 239:94	exercise for a research s.	LORE 537:61	inferior sort of S.	SMITH 830:47
S. is voiceless	WEIL 928:70	give any s….better advice	MEDA 584:34	in S. afore ye	ANON 22:9
s. I worshipped	LIND 530:13	I'm just an old mad s.	PERE 674:17	in S. supports the people	JOHN 460:77
s. knows no country	PAST 668:4	Nothing leads the s.	ROST 727:71	'In S.,' Tavish muttered	NEVI 634:32
s. knows only one commandment	BREC 157:93	s. does not study nature	POIN 683:98	in S. translated into a virtue	THOM 887:95
s. leads only to the insoluble	DISR 288:53	s. is given license	LISP 531:44	left fair S.'s strand	BURNS 180:57
S. may be described	POPP 690:66	s. is trying to expand	HALD 392:25	multiform, infinite S. small?	MACD 550:43
s. may carry us to Mars	REPP 711:60	s. may find his discipline severe	CORN 247:6	new voice of S.	CONN 242:86
s. may have the existence of mankind	ADAMS 5:85	s. should remove the word 'impossible'	REEVE 710:39	no harm in wishing S.	SCOTT 754:76
S. might almost be redefined	BOUL 152:89	s. soon discovers	MEDA 584:35	Scot come from S.	LOUI 537:63
S. moves, but slowly	TENN 871:18	s. states…something is possible	CLAR 228:68	S.! a queer country	BORR 151:72
s. must be understood	GOULD 380:76	social s. is in a difficult	LEWO 528:79	S. for the Strand?	JOHN 459:42
s. of the sublime	CIXO 228:49	The…s. thinks like a poet	WILS 948:58	S. is not wholly surrounded by the sea	MACD 549:36
S.…opposed to history	BORN 151:65	took her for a Christian S.	MITF 610:52	S. kens beneath the moon	FERG 333:86
S. proceeds by…answers	PAST 668:2	**scientists** 90 per cent of all the s	MACK 553:5	S., land of the omnipotent No	BOLD 144:4
S. provides a vision of reality	PAGE 659:16	Curse the s.	COOK 245:66	S.'s much vaunted partnership	EWING 329:79
s. reassures	BRAQ 156:75	Good s. often possess	MEDA 584:36	S.'s rightful heritage	CONN 242:85
S. rejects the indeterminate	BERN 85:69	incredulity at the illiteracy of s.	SNOW 832:76	S. wants nae skinking ware	BURNS 178:95
S. robs men of wisdom	UNAM 905:7	no more written for s.	ALDI 12:49	Seeing S.	JOHN 463:58
S. says the first word	HUGO 438:90	politicians and s. were lazier	WAUGH 924:90	Stands S. where it did?	SHAK 797:61
[S.] seldom proceeds	WATS 922:41	Republic has no need for s.	COFF 234:92	state that S.'s in	MACD 549:33
S. talks about…simple things	CHOM 222:29	s. have in their briefcases	KHRU 485:96	Succour S., and remede	ANON 21:44
s. the successors	RUSS 734:27	S. have odious manners	TWAIN 903:93	white rose of S.	MACD 549:38
S., which cuts its way through	HERZ 416:21	s.…hold writers in contempt	BELL 77:81	**Scots** S. accent of the mind	STEV 853:76
s. will appear incomplete	ARNO 36:41	S. know so much	SHAP 805:68	S. are Jocks	PAXM 670:45
s. without conscience	RABE 703:6	S. should be on tap	CHUR 226:15	S.…hear the English abused	PIUS 680:19
S. without religion is lame	EINS 313:79	s. who talk	WEIL 928:70	S. lords at his feet	BALL 59:72
S.…with problems	POPP 689:64	socially responsible s.	HOBS 420:7	S., wha hae	BURNS 180:47
s. would be more appealing	LEVI 526:38	society of s. is more important	BRON 160:47	S. Wha Ha'evers	MACD 550:39
sense and the world of s.	RUSS 734:37	**scimitars** s., wi' murder crusted	BURNS 179:28	six or seven dozen of S.	SHAK 771:54
Sociology is the s. of talk	KNIG 494:11	**scissor-man** red-legged s.-m.	HOFF 422:34	upon the S. with a Vengeance	FLET 340:50
task of s. can never end	PEAR 671:56	**scoffer** product of a s.'s pen	WORD 961:37	**Scotsman** S. on the make	BARR 65:89
the man of s.	PIER 677:66	**scold** or be she s.	SWIFT 863:76	S. with a grievance	WODE 952:48
the man of s.	POPP 689:55	**scones** buttered s. and crumpets	ELIOT 317:87	**Scottish** any of at least three S. seasons	RANK 706:62
think that s. can do anything	RAY 708:87	**scoop** s. of pure honey	SMITH 828:99	Fareweel to a' our S. fame	BURNS 179:40
thorugh his s. soothy	LANG 508:49	**scope** unaware of the s.	PYNCH 701:13	S. land and skies	GIBB 366:4
today hidden by s.!	NIET 639:14	**score** Chaos is the s.	MILL 593:53	S. life and letters	MACD 550:39
To pursue s. is not to disparage	BUSH 184:49	I will not go, without the s.	MAJOR 561:78	S. Parliament…hereby reconvened	EWING 329:78
touch of s., even bogus s.	PRIT 696:15	Money is how we keep the s.	CHAP 214:13	settled will of the S. people	SMITH 829:79
triumph of modern s.	WAUGH 924:99	**scoreboard** s. is an ass	CARD 198:43	set up an entire S. Parliament	WATE 922:38
True s. teaches	UNAM 905:6	**scorer** when the One Great S. comes	RICE 713:89	sulky S. spirit	SCOTT 754:77
True s. teaches us	BERN 85:70	**scorn** Fortune knows We s. her	SHAK 794:69	There shall be a S. Parliament	DEWAR 276:16
understand a s.	COMTE 239:8	laugh me to s.	BIBLE 99:42	**scoundrel** Every man…is a s.	SHAW 808:54
unexpected nature of s.	WOLP 954:96	Laugh no man to s.	BIBLE 113:85	last refuge of a s.	JOHN 462:37
very power of s.	SHAP 805:68	Laugh to s.	SHAK 797:55	last refuge of a s.	BRAGG 156:54
we lost s.	WEIL 927:69	little s. is alluring	CONG 241:69	morally behaving like a s.	SHAW 809:82
What counts…in s.	CHAR 215:27	love…the present s.	BEHN 75:26	plea of hers, hypocrite, and flatterer	BLAKE 141:31
What is called s. today	TOLS 894:53	nation heaps its s.	LAZA 515:4	**scoundrels** corporation-paid s.	LEWIS 526:53
What is s.?	HUXL 442:83	not a thing to laugh to s.	SHAK 780:15	**scour** s. these English hence?	SHAK 798:72
what s. has to teach us here	BRON 160:47	O, what a deal of s.	SHAK 786:11	**scout** Girl S. in uniform	APPEL 29:88
What we gain by s.	HARDY 397:25	s. and a mockery to call it	WENT 931:52	**Scrabble** Playing bop is like playing S.	ELLI 322:20
world of thought and s.	ARNO 35:22	s. for defeat	TWAIN 903:84	**scramble** days…into a wild s.	ANGE 19:97
		s. her own image	SHAK 783:19	**scrap** coaches shall be s.	SAND 742:15
sciences advanced in the Arts and S.	HAZL 403:47	's.' 'horn', a hard rhyme	SHAK 774:56	just for a s. of paper	BETH 87:11
Books must follow s.	BACON 53:50	s. of fate	DRYD 301:56	**scratch** all you can do is s. it	BEEC 73:71
call the s. human invention	PAINE 660:38	s. to change my state	SHAK 800:46	Art of S.	RUSK 733:11
culture of natural s.	SUN 860:95	self-respecting s.	WAUGH 923:57	quick sharp s.	BROW 167:24
door and key to the s.	BACON 53:56	suffice to wail their s.	DANI 262:31	**scrawl** s., and scribble	POPE 688:19
no such things as applied s.	PAST 668:3	surmounted by s.	CAMUS 195:85	**scream** I'll s. and s. and s.	CROM 255:15

screams

Entry	Reference
No Mouth And I Must S.	ELLI 323:31
s. from a crevasse	GREE 386:9
sensed a s. passing	MUNCH 625:41
to get wounded one needs the s.	ELTIT 323:40
screams I could hear his s. continually	BECK 72:53
lots of s. but little wool	PUTIN 700:97
screech-owls Drawn by s.-o.	SMART 826:59
screen leaving my heart on the s.	QUIR 703:27
Life is a s.	HUGO 437:76
No safety s. stands between	SHUL 819:28
seeing on the s.	GOLD 377:30
screens Philippines…lovely s.	COWA 249:51
with its s. and nodules	CESA 211:51
screes s. on her escarpments	HEAN 404:71
screw Don't s. around	CURR 259:95
S. It	BRAN 318:6
s.-top wine	AMIS 17:60
S. your courage	SHAK 796:23
screwed s. it up real good	NIXON 640:38
screwing gave up s. around	LODGE 534:98
screwy s. visions	BELL 77:84
scribblative arts babblative and s.	SOUT 835:57
scribble Always s., s., s.!	GLOU 374:51
scrawl, and s.	POPE 688:19
scribblement all his s.	DISR 288:65
scribes righteousness of the s.	BIBLE 114:31
Woe unto you, s. and Pharisees	BIBLE 114:31
scrimmage 'maul' or 's.'	ANON 23:89
scrip My s. of joy	RALE 705:44
script bank president finish the s.	EPST 327:35
no such thing as a good s.	BENN 80:51
Whatever your s. is like	CURT 259:99
Worst s. I've ever	MULL 624:30
scripture as the S. says	TWAIN 902:38
devil can cite S.	SHAK 769:84
Holy S. containeth	BOOK 150:40
s. is given by inspiration	BIBLE 129:28
s. is placed before the eyes	GREG 387:50
S. is silent	BROW 164:45
S. moveth us	BOOK 146:31
scriptures Search the s.	BIBLE 122:32
while he opened to us the s.?	BIBLE 122:13
scrivener notched and cropt s.	LAMB 505:99
scroll Michael read the Gaelic s.	RUSS 735:42
scrotumtightening s. sea	JOYCE 470:21
scruple not s. to pick a pocket	DENN 273:76
scrupulous s.…are not the leaders	CONR 244:44
scrutiny Sceptical s. is the means	SAGAN 737:26
scud-thumper Many-maned s.-t.	UPDI 905:14
scuffles s. of great fights	SHAK 793:41
scullion Away, you s.	SHAK 772:77
scullions contentment with noisy s.	STEV 852:34
sculptor I was a.	HIRS 419:75
not a great s. or painter	RUSK 733:88
s. can use twenty different materials	BOCC 144:90
s. pursues his work	LEON 522:67
sculptors We are all s.	THOR 888:25
sculpture difference between painting and s.	LEON 211:42
difference between…s.	CELL 522:67
Geometry is to s.	APOL 29:80
In s., did ever anybody call	EMER 324:66
like that of s.	RUSS 734:20
mediocre s.	ALBE 11:32
might call it moral s.	MERE 588:35
music or s.	MACB 546:63
S. in stone	MOORE 616:70
s. is the prisoner	THOM 886:78
sculptured s. Ann is seventy	THOM 883:13
sculptures accept paintings and s.	CHUR 224:50
scum Okie means you're s.	STEI 845:82
rich are the s.	CHES 221:86
s. of the earth as…soldiers	WELL 929:99
wash all this s. off	DE 273:66
scurvy like a s. politician	SHAK 793:26
very conceited s. one	JONS 467:64
scythe poor crooked s. and spade	SHIR 819:20
s.'s keen edge	SHAK 763:99
Scythian S. shepherd	MARL 572:96
sea all men at s.	GOLD 375:78
All the rivers run into the s.	BIBLE 105:10
always ourselves we find in the s.	CUMM 258:71
am wholly at s.	CARS 206:35
any sort of devil and the deep blue s.	RATT 707:78
anything more the s. can do	SYNGE 865:21
As mad as the vexed s.	SHAK 793:19
as the waters cover the s.	BIBLE 108:62
Beneath is spread like a green s.	SHEL 812:64
beyond it the s.	ANON 23:2
blue days at s.	STEV 854:84
bosom of the s.	SHAK 759:93
bottom of the s.	SHAK 761:40
bottom of the s. is cruel	CRANE 252:53
boundless as the s.	SHAK 766:84
broader than the s.	BIBLE 98:1
by land and s.	WORD 960:21
by s. as by land	GILB 368:28
Calm is the s.	SURR 860:98
changing s.	STEP 847:11
cherish the s.	BAUD 68:62
Copper sun or scarlet s.	CULL 257:43
crowed with summer s.	TENN 878:87
current under s.	ELIOT 318:6
dark…serpent-haunted s.	FLEC 340:34
disciples saw him walking on the s.	BIBLE 117:99
dolorous midland s.	SWIN 864:7
dominion of the s.	COVE 249:43
Down to a sunless s.	COLE 236:36
drowned in the depth of the s.	BIBLE 118:11
eastward to the s.	KIPL 489:80
far over the summer s.	TENN 878:97
fed our s.	KIPL 490:9
fishingboat-bobbing s.	THOM 884:31
flat s. sunk	MILT 598:72
forth on the godly s.	POUND 691:10
France and England is—the s.	JERR 455:48
From s. to shining s.	BATES 68:53
From s. to shining s.	HUXT 443:14
From the centre…to the s.	COWP 250:96
garden fronts the s.	SWIN 864:16
gazed upon the glittering s.	BYRON 190:9
gaze into s. or sky	MELV 585:69
go down to the s. in ships	BIBLE 102:15
gong-tormented s.	YEATS 967:32
great and wide s.	BIBLE 102:13
grey stones, O S.!	TENN 871:3
hate…broader than the s.	BOLI 145:9
home from s.	STEV 853:62
hyaline, the glassy s.	MILT 605:33
if we gang to s.	BALL 59:70
in the abysmal s.	TENN 869:71
Into that silent s.	COLE 235:11
jolly-rogered s.	THOM 884:33
keen s. wind	STEV 854:90
let him go to s.	HERB 414:89
like any river or any s.	HOPK 429:85
like sunrise from the s.	SHEL 816:56
London, that great s.	SHEL 814:2
lonely as the s.	HARR 399:55
lonely s. and the sky	MASE 580:50
lover of men, the s.	SWIN 864:5
love the s.	WALC 916:10
man that is born…falls into the s.	CONR 244:32
Marathon looks on the s.	BYRON 190:15
Mediterranean…that vital s.	CHUR 226:97
mirrors of the s.	FLEC 340:38
monarch of the s.	GILB 368:33
moon on this cloud s.	SCOTT 751:77
More hideous…Than the s.-monster	SHAK 792:94
more steady than an ebbing s.	FORD 343:6
mountains by the winter s.	TENN 878:80
not wholly surrounded by the s.	MACD 549:36
One foot in s.	SHAK 774:38
out of the swing of the s.	HOPK 428:65
over a cardboard s.	HARB 396:88
people look at the s.	FROST 352:8
persian pussy from over the s.	MARQ 575:51
perukèd s. whose swell	SITW 823:96
plants his footsteps in the s.	COWP 250:85
Posters of the s. and land	SHAK 795:2
Pussy-Cat went to s.	LEAR 516:35
put to s. on a wooden raft	HEYE 417:39
quiet, as under the s.	MERE 588:41
rebuked the winds and the s.	BIBLE 116:61
Receiveth as the s.	SHAK 785:78
rough rude s.	SHAK 764:47
sailed the wintry s.	LONG 535:20
sailing in the open s.	UPDI 906:25
sail upon the s.	BIBLE 112:68
sang in my chains like the s.	THOM 883:18
sapphire melts into the s.	TENN 876:24
s. escaping With the sun	RIMB 716:47
s. gave up the dead	BIBLE 132:22
s. is all about us	ELIOT 320:71
s. is a teacher	BELL 77:69
s. is his, and he made it	BOOK 149:30
s. is mother-death	SEXT 758:49
s. is the universal sewer	COUS 249:42
s. itself floweth in your	TRAH 895:85
s. of dew	FIELD 335:13
s. of faith	ARNO 33:66
s. of glass	BIBLE 131:96
s. of glass	BIBLE 132:14
s. of glass mingled with fire	BIBLE 132:14
s. of life	ARNO 34:81
s. of sorrows deep	SPEN 838:26
s. protesting against union	GRAT 382:14
s. rises higher	CHES 220:80
S. shall give up her dead	BOOK 149:39
s. that bares her bosom	WORD 961:30
s. was ever loved	TOML 894:57
s. would fold me	GORD 378:53
see nothing but s.	BACON 49:29
sent them o'er the s.	BALL 60:82
settee of the horsehair s.!	SITW 823:94
shine along the s.	SWIN 863:88
shining Big-S.-Water	LONG 535:29
ship on the s.	LORCA 537:58
sink through the s.	THOM 883:7
smiling s.	WORD 961:29
snotgreen s.	JOYCE 470:21
squires ride slowly towards the s.	CHES 221:3
stillness of the central s.	TENN 875:1
stone set in the silver s.	SHAK 764:40
sun was shining on the s.	CARR 204:98
Sussex by the s.!	KIPL 492:48
that immortal s.	WORD 960:11
The breeze is on the s.	SCOTT 754:69
there was no more s.	BIBLE 132:23
The s. hates a coward!	ONEI 651:68
The s.! The s.!	XENO 965:1
they went to s. in a Sieve	LEAR 516:30
they were on that s.	ROBE 717:71
to look at the s.	UPDI 906:28
tossing s. of clouds	BENU 83:9
true call of…the s.	STARK 843:23
universal as s. sickness	SHAW 807:28
unplumbed, salt, estranging s.	ARNO 34:82
Upon the slimy s.	COLE 235:13
uttermost parts of the s.	BIBLE 103:44
Vaulting the s.	CRANE 253:58
vext the dim s.	TENN 870:98
voice…like the s.	WORD 958:94
voice of the s.	CHOP 223:30
voices…one is of the s.	WORD 961:31
wander from s. to s.	BIBLE 111:54
wan grass s.	SITW 823:10
went to s. in a sieve	LEAR 516:30
wet sheet and a flowing s.	CUNN 258:74
Where no s. runs	THOM 883:4
Who hath desired the S.?	KIPL 491:45
why the s. is boiling hot	CARR 204:1
will not find another s.	CAVA 210:18
wind had sprung from the s.	THOM 883:1
Wind of the western s.	TENN 872:37
windy s. of land	MILT 603:85
world's tempestuous s.	EDME 312:55
wrecks will surface over the s.	EWART 328:76
wrinkled s. beneath him	TENN 875:4
yacht on the s.	REID 710:78
sea-boy repose To the wet s.-b.	SHAK 772:85
sea-change But doth suffer a s.-c.	SHAK 803:17
sea-down at the s.-d.'s edge	SWIN 864:16
sea-fogs s.-f. lap and cling	KIPL 491:46
sea-green s.-g. Incorruptible	CARL 201:9
seagull s. is…unlimited…freedom	BACH 49:11
seagulls s. follow a trawler	CANT 197:15
seal heard a s. bark!	THUR 890:63
opened the seventh s.	BIBLE 131:5
s. is set	BYRON 188:65
S. of Divinity and Immortality	AUBR 42:61
s. of nobility those people	MUSS 627:91
s. of the weakness of our race	DELA 271:21
s.'s wide spindrift gaze	CRANE 252:55
under the great s. of England	PENN 673:81
sealing-wax like sticks of s.-w.	DICK 279:7
seals faint aroma of performing s.	HART 399:66
loose the s. thereof?	BIBLE 131:99
trained s., creeping Jesuses	MACD 550:39
seam touch of the s.	UTTL 907:50
seamen s. made reply	TENN 879:98

seeds

Seamus Yours truly, S.	HEAN 405:75
search needle is not worth the s.	JACK 449:8
not worth the s.	SHAK 769:73
Science is a s. for truth	PAUL 670:34
S. me, O God	BIBLE 104:46
s. so painful and so long	ROCH 719:12
S. the scriptures	BIBLE 122:32
seas dark broad s.	TENN 870:2
devotion of the wind and s.	LANC 506:23
down the salt s.	KIPL 492:66
Draw not up s.	DONNE 291:35
fight on the s. and oceans	CHUR 225:85
floors of silent s.	ELIOT 316:64
For the s.' worth	SHAK 788:87
landscapes of s. full of fish	CIXO 227:47
make s. our smooth highway	CARL 200:80
must down to the s.	MASE 580:50
must down to the s.	MASE 580:51
must down to the s.	MASE 580:52
On desperate s.	POE 683:86
other hand full of s.	HYDE 443:19
paradise of four s.	MARV 578:10
port after stormy s.	SPEN 838:28
rapture the earth and the s.	BRON 161:55
Rivers and s....to float their ships	DICK 280:27
s. colder than the Hebrides	FLEC 340:37
s. roll over	HERB 413:54
strange s. of Thought	WORD 958:82
Till a' the s. gang dry	BURNS 180:50
tossed upon cloudy s.	NOYES 642:70
traversed the s.	WILB 939:38
waste of s.	GALT 359:54
sea-sand ribbed s.-s.	COLE 235:14
seashell raise a s. to one's ear	DE 268:54
seashore pearls by the s.	MORE 618:21
playing on the s.	NEWT 635:61
sea-side drawback of all s.-s. places	DOUG 295:11
season be instant in s.	BIBLE 129:29
buy himself a s. ticket	ASHD 37:64
disturb your s. due	MILT 599:82
dry brain in a dry s.	ELIOT 317:86
every s. she hath dressings	ANON 22:6
for a s., Let us be merry	CURR 259:91
from that time unto this s.	SPEN 840:64
In a somer s.	LANG 507:44
in due s. we shall reap	BIBLE 127:83
loosed a little s.	BIBLE 132:21
meat in due s.	BIBLE 104:48
meat in due s.	BIBLE 102:13
Midwinter Spring is its own s.	ELIOT 321:80
nice sickly s.	DICK 278:65
Praise out of s.	BUCK 172:36
s. of calm weather	WORD 960:11
s. of love and laughter	GORD 378:54
S. of mists	KEATS 477:32
s. of snows and sins	SWIN 863:83
s. ticket on the line	AMERY 15:25
s. was the airiest May?	GRAV 382:21
stay the due s.	JONS 467:62
terrible beyond any s.	MACA 545:37
this fine s.	WORD 962:52
To every thing there is a s.	BIBLE 105:14
was no s. then for her	MILT 597:31
willing for a s.	BIBLE 122:31
Will there never come a s.	STEP 847:12
word spoken in due s.	BIBLE 104:76
seasoned till they are s.	HOLM 424:72
seasons All times are his s.	DONNE 293:72
assailed the s.	ROBI 718:84
As the swift s. roll	HOLM 424:67
changing s.	WHITE 935:41
her changing s.	THOM 886:72
Man for all s.	BOLT 145:11
not for you to know...the s.	BIBLE 124:70
returning s. bring	PHIL 676:52
s. never change	GUY 390:7
S. return	REED 709:29
s. such as these?	SHAK 792:11
to thy motions lovers' s. run?	DONNE 291:25
seat and built his s.	SURR 860:97
another world, the happy s.	MILT 602:62
before you take your s.	STEV 853:72
castle hath a pleasant s.	SHAK 796:18
Fasten your s. belts	MANK 565:74
fell from off the s. backward	BIBLE 96:29
from her wild sequestered s.	COLL 238:78
got to save your s.	ANON 26:3
providing he was in the driver's s.	BEAV 71:29
regain the blissful s.	MILT 601:29
repossess their native s.	MILT 602:50
round of Cynthia's s.	MILT 597:34
Scotia's darling s.	BURNS 178:96
s. of this sensation	HOUS 432:75
seated looked wiser when he was s.	KEYN 484:70
Seaton Marie S., and Mari Beaton	BALL 59:68
seats cheap s. clap their hands	LENN 521:43
fixed in our s.	STEE 844:49
rows of empty s.	OLIV 649:40
with three empty s.	HUNT 439:18
seawards road leads me s.	MASE 580:60
sea-water salt s.-w. passes by	TENN 873:65
seaworms huge s. in his sleep	TENN 869:72
Seckler Dorothy S. has noted	LIPP 530:34
second a s. Eisenhower	SULL 859:76
asking 'Who came s.?'	REAR 709:17
blinding split s.	FOWL 346:65
here I leave my s. leg	HOOD 426:20
not a s. on the day	COOK 245:64
one year we came s.	PAIS 660:41
S. childishness and mere oblivion	SHAK 779:83
s. spring	PHIL 676:52
split s. when it can be recalled	BUCK 172:35
The s. best's	YEATS 966:73
travel any road a s. time	IBN 444:6
wrote it with a s. hand	SPEN 839:47
second-best s.-b. is anything but	LESS 524:96
second-rate creed of a s.-r. man	BAGE 55:79
If Richard Nixon was s.-r.	HELL 407:32
secrecy crime...vice...by s.	PULI 699:71
for s. No lady closer	SHAK 771:43
live off s.	MOYN 623:3
nature's infinite book of s.	SHAK 794:45
S. is the first essential	RICH 714:20
s. with which they pursue	JEVO 455:54
secret alms may be in s.	BIBLE 115:40
always a s. singing	SAND 742:19
book...of my s. soul	SHAK 785:84
bread eaten in s.	BIBLE 104:62
ceases to be a s.	BEHN 75:21
Father which is in s.	BIBLE 115:41
giant girls that have no s.	SPEN 837:2
in my soul that tender s. dwells	BYRON 188:76
in s. sin	CHUR 224:56
joys of parents are s.	BACON 51:68
keeps a s. like a child	HUGO 437:81
keep the mistakes s.	MOYN 623:3
know that's a s.	CONG 240:43
man keeps another person's s.	LABR 502:10
members of our s. service	FOOT 342:80
method and s....of Jesus	ARNO 36:37
no s. better kept	SHAW 807:7
no s. so close	SURT 860:6
one s. thing s. in American life...racism	CISN 227:40
s. for harvesting	NIET 638:97
s. house of death	SHAK 795:78
s. of being miserable	SHAW 810:2
s. of decorating	TROL 897:21
s. of life	CUMM 257:55
s. of managing a ball club	STEN 847:7
s. of redemption	WEIZ 928:78
s. of success in mathematics	LEHR 520:26
S. sits in the middle	FROST 353:17
s. things belong unto the Lord	BIBLE 95:96
That is the ancient s.	PRAT 694:67
There's no s.	VUKO 915:59
The S. Diary of Adrian	TOWN 894:67
when I was made in s.	BIBLE 104:45
whole s. would be out	WILL 945:7
secretaries s....have an advantage	ROCK 720:32
secretary revelation and told my s.	STEIN 845:79
S. of State	MCCA 547:84
s.'s diary	RODC 721:43
secretion isolate the internal s.	BANT 62:35
secretly go s. hoping they won't	HEAT 406:93
So s....they went	OWEN 658:39
secrets ears that...hear one's s.	ONEI 651:63
from whom no s. are hid	BOOK 147:58
greatest s. of the past	FAWC 331:51
guilty s. of Europe	DUNN 307:16
learned s. of the grave	PATER 668:9
Men with s.	DELI 271:41
s. are edged tools	DRYD 299:15
S....Are never valued	CRAB 252:48
s. of his trade	ORWE 654:42
s. of the prison-house	MOOD 615:54
tell you all her s.	SNOW 832:84
walls...sharers of s.	AMMI 17:63
sect any religion, by any s.	KRIS 499:11
attached to that great s.	SHEL 815:40
Christ...leader of the s.	TACI 866:7
found them a s.	MACA 546:56
Irish...that ancient s.	YEATS 967:38
loving his own s....better	COLE 236:46
paradise for a s.	KEATS 476:97
sad-coloured s.	HOOD 426:25
sects diversity of s.	SPEN 839:42
secure No Government can be long s.	DISR 287:24
s., and now can never mourn	SHEL 815:40
security beggar...possesses that s.	SMITH 827:74
being on social s.	WELD 928:85
from s. into something malevolent	CATH 208:90
live without other s.	HOBB 420:2
lost...a lovely feeling of s.	CHAT 216:53
peace and s.	UNIT 905:99
sacrifice instead of more s.	KENN 481:99
s. and peace	MACD 550:51
s. around the American President	MAIL 560:61
S. can only be obtained	LEES 519:4
s. for the future	TROL 897:29
s....in our relationship with God	EDDI 311:26
s. of property	PANK 662:84
s. of the land	COVE 249:43
s. to persons who are accused	DENM 273:72
sedate s., sober, silent	HOOD 426:25
sedately took the kiss s.	TENN 876:22
try to walk s.	STEV 853:71
sedge s. has wither'd	KEATS 476:1
seditions surest way to prevent s.	BACON 52:94
seduce s., bamboozle	LIPP 531:42
seducer Thou strong s.	DRYD 300:32
seduction ethical or social s.	BEVAN 89:53
persuade her to give it away (s.)	DWOR 308:43
see cannot s., and in the third	NORTH 641:60
complain we cannot s.	BERK 84:29
day...meant not to s.	THAT 881:60
few...learn to s.	OKRI 649:24
Helen, did Homer never s.	JONS 468:85
In all things Thee to s.	HERB 413:61
I s. what I eat	CARR 203:70
I was blind, now I s.	BIBLE 123:43
lovers cannot s.	SHAK 769:93
much to hear and s.	SKEL 824:27
neither s. nor hear	JOHN 459:33
never...s. myself perform live	WEST 932:81
not that I did not s.	HOLM 423:55
pleasure of believing what we s.	SHEL 812:60
power...to make you s.	CONR 243:26
s. and hear and understand	HEMI 410:74
s. better than I do	GOYA 380:82
S. one...s. all	BURT 181:79
s. them as they are	JOHN 465:8
s. things, and you say, 'Why?'	SHAW 811:34
s. this day and live	SHAK 776:89
still can't s.	HUGH 435:11
stream...we s. ourselves in	FROST 352:7
The less there was to s.	DELI 272:45
what we do not s.	SHAK 787:53
what we s. is life	WARR 921:16
What you s. is what you make	OKRI 649:28
won't even go to s. it	GRANT 381:98
yet I s. thee still	SHAK 796:27
You s., but you do not observe	DOYLE 297:57
seed bearing precious s.	BIBLE 103:35
blood...is the s.	TERT 879:18
carrying your s.	MARQ 575:44
democrat...gone to s.	EMER 325:82
enmity between thy s. and her s.	BIBLE 91:96
few more lies eat into the s.	MAIL 559:38
Nestles the s. perfection	WHIT 938:12
nor his s. begging bread	BIBLE 100:60
received s. among the thorns	BIBLE 117:91
received s. into the good ground	BIBLE 117:92
s. its harvest	KEATS 476:87
s. of knowledge	BACON 49:19
s. should not be his	BIBLE 93:40
sowed in youth a mustard s.	BRON 161:59
spring again from its s.	SHEL 816:49
thy s. may live	BIBLE 95:97
weed...of celestial s.	DRYD 302:79
seeds colonization planted the s.	MARI 570:72
in a bag all sorts of s.	SPEN 839:61

seedtime

s. of time	SHAK 796:5	thy s. present	SPEN 837:14	s. his grandmother	GRANT 381:2
some s. fell by the wayside	BIBLE 117:90	to thine own s. be true	SHAK 781:54	**selling** lives by s. something	STEV 853:78
seedtime s. and harvest	BIBLE 92:11	was his natural s.	TWAIN 902:55	**selves** Anger and tenderness: my s.	RICH 713:7
seed-time Fair s.-t.	WORD 958:75	weave my s. into the sense	HERB 414:74	many…hundreds of s.?	MANS 561:1
seeing better at believing than at s.	SANT 743:44	Wisdom's s. Oft seeks	MILT 598:72	nor is it our s.	UPDI 906:33
faculty of s. things	SPEN 837:7	write for the public and have no s.	CONN 242:92	s. conditional	UPDI 906:34
gave up s. years ago	JOHN 459:33	**self-absorbed** sign of the s.-a.	RYBC 736:56	stronger, riskier s.	MORR 620:56
Not 'S. is Believing'	WOLFE 953:74	**self-assertion** Japanese see s.-a.	KURO 501:44	the particularity of s.	TRIL 897:18
point is the s.	REID 710:44	**self-assured** s.-a. who strut	HAMM 394:56	**semantic** s. inversions	MAMET 564:32
S. is deceiving	THUR 891:92	**self-awareness** highest state of s.-a.	LARD 509:66	**semblable** mon s.	ELIOT 318:98
s. on the screen	GOLD 377:30	**self-complacency** s.-c. brought	WEBB 925:6	**semblance** bore S. of worth	MILT 602:48
s. what Adam had seen	HUXL 442:90	**self-condeming** neither s.-c.	MILT 606:56	**semicolon** not enough…to be s.	BRAT 157:78
s. what everybody has seen	SZENT 865:29	**self-confession** Christ…the s.-c.	FEUE 334:1	**semicolony** to be s.	BRAT 157:78
way of s. is also a way of not s.	BURKE 176:63	**self-conscious** most s.-c. people	JAMES 450:36	**seminars** girls suffered…so did my s.	BERR 87:3
way of s. them	RUSK 733:93	race which has become s.-c.	LAWR 513:51	**sempiternal** S. though sodden	ELIOT 321:80
Worth s.?	JOHN 463:68	**self-consciousness** writer's s.-c.	UPDI 906:29	**Sempronius** we'll do more, S.	ADDI 7:45
seek do not s. to understand	ANSE 29:70	**self-consumer** s.-c. of my woes	CLARE 228:54	**senate** half-creature of the S.	MANS 568:12
may not so much s.	FRAN 347:99	**self-contain'd** placid and s.-c.	WHIT 937:93	S. becomes the wife	TAYL 868:54
not need to s. out	TOCQ 893:33	**self-contradiction** poet is a s.-c.	FROST 352:7	tuned in the US S.	BRIN 159:23
s. all day	SHAK 769:73	**self-control** s.-c….courage	PEEL 672:68	**senator** Korea, S.…American blood	MACA 544:10
s., and ye shall find	BIBLE 115:50	**self-definition** starved for s.-d.	BURNS 177:65	Time is the 101st S.	DODD 289:87
S. ye the Lord	BIBLE 109:97	**self-denial** S.-d. is not a virtue	SHAW 808:47	United States S.	JOHN 458:10
To strive, to s.	TENN 871:2	**self-destruction** beginnings of s.-d.	CHEE 218:5	**senators** group of s.	DAUG 263:62
Who s., who hope, who love	SIDN 820:51	**self-determination** S.-d. is not	WILS 949:86	s. burst with laughter	AUDEN 43:88
seeker s. for cures	RICH 713:8	**self-development** s.-d. is…duty	STAN 843:18	**send** I refuse to s. anyone else	RANK 706:64
seemed s. well pleased, all s.	MILT 604:20	**self-devotion** saved by his…s.-d.	MACA 546:60	not about to s. American boys	JOHN 458:13
seems know not 's.'	SHAK 780:35	**self-discovery** s.-d.	WALC 916:22	s. in the First Lady	CLIN 231:30
seen as I done it I s. it	SAND 742:24	**self-division** man in s.-d.!	SIDN 820:36	time for you to s. it back	JACK 448:1
cannot be s. and sung	ISAA 447:63	**self-esteem** s.-e. is sacrosanct	HUGH 435:27	Whom shall I s.	BIBLE 107:55
God whom he hath not s.?	BIBLE 131:84	wiping out his s.-e.	MARI 571:87	**senility** the prime of s.	OTOO 656:93
if it's s. through	GREE 386:30	**self-examination** practise s.-e.	ICHI 445:13	**senior** s. years are reached	RAND 706:55
I've sometimes s.	RIMB 715:41	significant s.-e.	PECK 672:62	**sennights** Weary s. nine times nine	SHAK 795:1
much have I s.	TENN 870:98	**self-fashioned** s.-f. chains of slavery	MANS 567:94	**sensation** delightful s.	FERB 332:71
not having a	JOHN 463:51	**self-flagellation** for s.-f. solely	CAPO 197:25	objects of S.	LOCKE 533:90
s. enough of one war	JEFF 454:24	**self-fulfilling** s.-f. prophecy	MERT 589:54	seat of this s.	HOUS 432:75
s. for what one is	DRAB 298:80	**self-government** experience of s.-g.	EDIN 312:48	s. is the same	HEMI 409:69
s. to be done	HEWA 417:36	**self-help** healthy spirit of s.-h.	SMIL 827:71	s. of a short, sharp shock	GILB 369:64
s. to want…certainly never get	WEAT 925:5	spirit of s.-h.	SMIL 827:69	**sensational** somewhat too s.	WILDE 942:5
The less s.	WILD 943:52	**self-image** crippled s.-i.	THOM 887:90	**sensations** life of s.	KEATS 475:74
Things that are s.	JOHNS 457:86	**self-indulgence** essay on 's.-i.'	WAUGH 923:56	penultimate s.	GALS 358:49
things that I have s.	POLO 684:5	**self-interest** enlightened s.-i.	KEYN 484:76	secret of their s.	MACKE 553:9
to be loved needs only to be s.	DRYD 303:10	**selfish** s. molecules known as genes	DAWK 266:15	s. sweet	WORD 956:53
vanity of being s.	SMOL 831:67	s. propriety of civilized man	MUIR 624:27	truth of my own s.	CONR 244:47
what is s. during a moment	SAND 742:21	slack and s.	STEV 852:33	**sense** afraid of losing your moral s.	STEIN 845:45
where they cannot be s.	HAWK 401:87	**selfishness** a cheerleader for s.	ONEI 651:79	any s. of direction	WILS 947:38
sees s. is truly seen	SNYD 832:90	dross of s.	ROCK 720:33	art of making s.	MACL 555:47
thinks he believes only what he s.	SANT 743:44	S. must always be forgiven	AUST 46:65	beauty to my s. shall run	DONNE 291:18
segment s. of our population	TRUM 899:77	strongest protest against s.	GOOD 378:45	Bereaving s., but endless	MILT 606:63
segregation S. now, s. tomorrow	WALL 917:48	**self-justification** habit…of s.-j.	EDGE 311:34	Bestow a purer s.	MALL 562:99
Seine flows the S.	APOL 29:81	**self-love** golden-calf of s.-l.	CARL 201:13	between s. and nonsense	JUNG 471:46
seismograph Collage…a s.	ERNST 327:40	life depends upon s.-l.	JORD 469:3	bring men back to common s.	BERK 84:32
lightning rod than a s.	KESEY 483:64	s.-l. and social be the same	POPE 687:86	common s., and relatively	MORT 621:65
seize S. the day	HORA 429:6	s.-l. is always the beginning	MANN 566:85	common s. tells us	NABO 628:3
seldom s. look at them	MORT 621:71	S.-l., my liege	SHAK 775:73	creeps after s.	DRYD 300:27
select not to a s. committee	PULI 699:70	S.-l.…often unrequited	POWE 693:43	Decking the s.	HERB 413:73
selection called this…Natural S.	DARW 263:52	**self-lovers** nature of extreme s.-l.	BACON 52:6	deep s. of…shame	WEBS 926:26
S. is the invention	FUSE 356:95	**self-made** was a s.-m. man	HELL 407:25	Devoid of s. and motion	MILT 602:59
selective even more s.	GREE 386:20	**self-neglecting** vile a sin As s.-n.	SHAK 775:73	don't need so much s.	HERN 415:94
Observation is always s.	POPP 689:59	**self-parody** S.-p. is the first portent	MCMU 557:84	each other and with the s.	KUHN 500:37
selects s. and omits	STRA 856:36	**self-pity** S.-p.…is as snug	ANGE 19:92	echo to the s.	POPE 685:24
self All by my own-alone s.	HARR 399:51	**self-portrait** S.-p. in a Convex Mirror	ASHB 37:57	established s. it is socially nil	LAWR 513:54
Am I your s.	SHAK 777:18	**self-presentation** place for s.-p.	RYBC 736:56	fiction…has to make s.	BANKS 62:27
Anger's s. I needs must kiss	SIDN 820:49	**self-preservation** ensure Japan's s.-p.	HIRO 419:71	fine s. of the ridiculous	ALBEE 11:25
at once as Nature's s.	BROW 168:38	**self-raised** fail to reascend s.-r.	MILT 602:50	fountain of good s.	DRYD 304:41
Dearer than s.	BYRON 187:37	**self-reference** little miracles of s.-r.	HOFS 422:36	free of s. and restriction	HEAT 406:92
door out of the dungeon of s.	MACD 550:46	**self-removed** must be s.-r.	MANS 567:94	glorious s. of words	ACHE 2:28
dungeon of s.	CONN 243:15	**self-respect** Being an MP…starves		Good s. is the most fairly	DESC 274:93
fictitious s.	CHOP 223:32	your s.-r.	PARR 666:52	If that s. is lost	EMER 325:99
final distillation of s.	DELI 271:40	self-love and s.-r.	JORD 469:3	in a two-fold s.	MILL 594:81
for its absolute s.	WORD 961:38	S.-r.…comes to us	GRIS 389:76	integrated s.	THUR 891:97
greater to one than one's s.	WHIT 937:94	**self-restraint** promotes s.-r.	TAFT 866:11	it is not s.	CHUR 224:62
high authority of the s.	TRIL 897:18	**self-revelation** fluidity of s.-r.	JAMES 451:53	It is not tricks of s.	WILB 939:39
incomplete s.	GASS 361:87	**self-righteousnes** S.-r. is not religion	BRON 161:65	life doesn't make s.	LYNCH 543:88
knowledge of the s.	KANT 473:19	**self-sacrifice** higher duty than s.-s.	STAN 843:18	lose the sin, yet keep the s.	POPE 686:49
live without the s.	ATWO 41:42	s.-s. as the sensible course	KURO 501:44	lost s. of Victorian regard	PRIT 696:25
look within and examine		S.-s. enables us to sacrifice	SHAW 808:58	man of s. and a fop	CHES 219:34
your own s.	CONF 240:18	**self-schooled** s.-s., self-scanned	ARNO 33:63	Men of sound s.	PLATO 681:48
mysterious belief in a s.	MANS 567:3	**self-seeking** in a less s.-s. age	CECIL 210:28	more or less dumb s.	JAMES 451:72
s. as the window	UPDI 906:33	**self-slain** god s.-s.	SWIN 864:17	Much S.—the starkest Madness	DICK 284:37
s. cannot be escaped	BART 66:18	**self-slaughter** Against s.-s.	SHAK 803:97	none in her s.	BEHN 75:25
s.…epicentre of the solar system	PHIL 677:56	canon 'gainst s.-s.!	SHAK 780:37	oddest frame of s.	SHAK 788:78
s. is now the sacred cow	HUGH 435:27	**self-sufficing** reasoning, s.-s. thing	WORD 957:66	one…of s. forlorn	COLE 235:21
s. persists like a dying star	ROET 722:64	**self-worship** s.-w. of the monarch	MILL 592:17	poor toper whose untutored s.	CRAB 251:24
small hungry shivering s.	ELIOT 316:54	**sell** as if it were to s.	HERB 413:73	religious s. of duty	DICK 283:17
that's your own s.	HUXL 442:85	buy with you, s. with you	SHAK 769:82	rough s. of the daily jostle	DELI 271:42
The essential s.	UPDI 906:30	how well they s.	JOYCE 470:38	Seal thy s. in deathly slumber	DELA 271:34
The s. is hateful	PASC 667:82	no man might buy or s.	BIBLE 132:11	s. and observation	WORD 961:40

s. and outward things	WORD 959:10	
s. by indirection, degrees of anger	EVANS 328:69	
s. from nonsense	THUR 891:99	
s. is mocked in every thing	DAVI 264:77	
s. of a long last night	MAIL 560:50	
s. of being more	RUSS 734:25	
s. of intellectual degradation	JAMES 450:24	
s. of taste	BALL 60:88	
's.' of what is going on	BART 66:14	
s. of wonder	SOCR 833:97	
s. sublime	WORD 956:55	
Shadwell never deviates into s.	DRYD 300:44	
shamefaced s.	MORE 619:21	
splendour borrows…from s.	POPE 686:63	
Still follow s.	POPE 686:56	
Take care of the s.	CARR 203:75	
That it enchants my s.	SHAK 787:33	
That the s. aches	SHAK 790:34	
the ground s. necessary	WILL 945:6	
the s. faints	SHEL 813:81	
Through s. and nonsense	DRYD 302:94	
to curb the s.	DRYD 304:44	
Touch…most demystifying of all s.	BART 66:23	
use only Arguments of S.	PETTY 676:47	
using good s.	LOUI 537:69	
want of s.	DILL 286:96	
weave my self into the s.	HERB 414:74	
without any sign of common s.	CHIR 222:23	
without one grain of s.	DRYD 302:4	
work upon the vulgar with fine s.	POPE 686:53	
world of s. and the world	RUSS 734:37	
sense-experience limits of…s.-e.	AYER 48:4	
senseless worse than s. things!	SHAK 776:4	
senses assault on the s.	MCCA 547:88	
colour to that of the S.	MATI 581:93	
come to my s.	GRAMM 381:93	
disagreeable to all the s.	DICK 281:73	
extensions of our s.	STEV 851:11	
five s. within whose pentagon	BERG 83:20	
fool o'th' other s.	SHAK 796:28	
ill customs influence my very s.	ETHE 327:48	
Let s. rule	SHAK 775:70	
makes the s. rough	SHAK 759:79	
Parson lost his s.	HODG 421:23	
power to touch our s.	MILT 597:35	
s. can think nothing	KANT 473:18	
stuck to all my s.	MITC 609:36	
subtlety of the s.	BACON 50:42	
there are only five s.	PATM 669:23	
the s. still supply	WORD 956:51	
Unto our gentle s.	SHAK 796:18	
use of the s. and hands	DARW 263:57	
sensibilities as the s. decline	STOWE 856:31	
middle-class people of nice s.	SHAR 806:78	
one's own fine s.	HELL 408:49	
sensibility Dear s.!	STER 849:69	
dissociation of s.	ELIOT 317:93	
Experience…an immense s.	JAMES 450:43	
multisibling s.	COUP 248:33	
self-confession of human s.	FEUE 334:1	
s. of a male adolescent	AUDEN 44:20	
s. of principle	BURKE 176:41	
s. transformed into intelligence	GOUR 380:79	
sensible Extremely s.	STEW 854:96	
no s. man directly challenges	MACM 556:73	
s. as a dictionary	CARR 204:92	
S. men are all the same religion	DISR 289:71	
silly things…done by s. people	AUST 46:76	
sing when they are feeling s.	AUDEN 43:5	
sensitive s. boy's humiliations	SHAW 807:17	
s. man understands	FRIE 351:73	
S. Plant in a garden grew	SHEL 815:21	
sensitivities Irish feelings and s.	HAUG 401:84	
sensual first a s.	HOOK 427:40	
inordinate s. delight	BAXT 69:94	
music and s. matters	KHOM 485:89	
only s. pleasure without vice	JOHN 465:2	
sensualists tyrants and s.	WOLL 954:88	
sensuality s.…into sexual vanity	WEBB 925:6	
sent Who s. you to me—God?	PUCC 699:66	
sentence canvas a s. or paragraph	MOTH 622:87	
declared meaning of a spoken s.	CAREY 199:63	
hit…reader…with your first s.	BRIS 159:26	
if this is slavery, give me a life s.	CHAR 216:46	
judges soon the s. sign	POPE 685:38	
Literature…at the level of a s.	RUSH 732:76	
most important…the English s.	JOVA 469:13	
pronounced a more rounded s.	JOHN 464:93
pull of the s.	MOORE 619:88
S. first—verdict afterwards	CARR 204:87
s. is a sound	FROST 352:94
s. is factually significant	AYER 48:5
s. structure	THUR 890:91
single s. in a routine article	MEYER 589:63
The s. is the greatest invention	BAN 62:38
sentences Backward ran s.	GIBBS 367:12
complete s.	GASS 361:87
cutting…people off after two s.	FORD 343:13
grammatical English s.	JOHN 457:96
in a world of truncated s.	FIEN 336:37
mania for s.	FLAU 339:12
mix s. with dirt	BRAU 157:83
Mr. Blackman in three s.	NGU 636:66
s., the structure	MORR 621:59
S. which simply express moral	AYER 48:6
silences between s.	LIND 529:12
sentiment corrupted by s.	GREE 386:7
nurse of manly s.	BURKE 176:41
rich in s.	TENN 872:32
s. jointly dictate	RODO 722:51
s. which I feel strongly	SCOTT 754:81
those who have no s.	MAIL 560:51
truth of description and the s.	SCOTT 754:78
sentimental America…s. land	RABAN 703:4
corrupt art is the s.	PISS 679:96
getting more s. as I get older	CART 206:40
sentimentalism inclined against s.	CARD 198:42
S. is the working off	LAWR 513:75
sentimentality S. is a failure	STEV 850:86
S. is the emotional promiscuity	MAIL 560:51
Sledgehammer!	KENT 483:51
sentimentering no time to be s.	TWAIN 902:60
sentiments beautiful s.	GIDE 368:23
s. in the world	LOWE 539:11
Them's my s.!	THAC 880:25
sentry quadrille in a s. box	JAMES 450:49
stands a wingèd s.	VAUG 909:37
separated now we're s.	STRO 857:54
separately all hang s.	FRAN 348:17
separateness his weakness and his s.	BELL 78:90
separation consent to the s.	GEOR 364:48
preludes to that eternal s.	STER 848:46
protesting against s.	GRAT 382:14
s. breeds…regrets	CH 222:19
Six degrees of s.	GUARE 389:82
sepòlchered s. in such pomp	MILT 597:40
September cool S. morn	WHIT 938:22
sing in S.	KEND 480:85
When you reach S.	ANDE 17:72
sepulchre came first to the s.	BIBLE 124:65
man the living s.	CLARE 228:53
no man knoweth of his s.	BIBLE 95:4
stone taken away from the s.	BIBLE 123:64
sepulchres like unto whited s.	BIBLE 118:28
sequence events…happen in a s.	WELTY 931:48
sequential s., but memory	LIVE 531:51
sequestered Each s. in its hate	AUDEN 43:93
one of those s. spots	HARDY 397:14
Serbia I'm the Ayatollah Khomeini of S.	MILO 596:29
Kosovo is not a part of S.	MILO 596:28
Serbs S. out, Nato in, refugees back	ROBE 717:75
S. will follow me	MILO 596:29
sere fall'n into the s.	SHAK 798:69
serene more solemn and s.	SHEL 812:57
Serengeti six…left in the S.	BENN 80:47
Serenissima pinnacles of the S.	MORR 620:46
serenity complaints…undermine the s.	ACHE 3:40
steady and perpetual s.	ADDI 7:34
serf hands of a s.	HYDE 443:21
serfdom abolish s. from above	ALEX 13:60
serial obituary in s. form	CRISP 255:7
serial killer Unless you're a s. k.	DEGEN 270:4
series in a s. of courses	GOLD 375:81
s. of great opportunities	GARD 360:70
s. of undertakings	SART 745:75
serious Comedy is a very s. thing	GARR 360:81
Dead men are s.	FIND 336:44
from s. things	THOR 888:30
Make…the s. smile	POPE 686:51
more s. than I should be	SIDN 820:35
much more s. than that	SHAN 805:60
Of all s. things	BEAU 70:8
position is s.	KEYN 484:79
s. attempt to do it	WELLS 930:38
s. reading	WELLS 930:24
tell when one is getting old and s.	EDWA 312:62
the s. and the smirk	DICK 278:78
think of something s.	TRAV 896:91
When it becomes s.	JUNCK 471:45
you are not s.	RIMB 715:44
You cannot be s.!	MCEN 550:56
seriousness wallowing in low s.	BELL 78:89
sermon funeral s.	BELL 77:65
painful s.	PEPYS 673:88
preach a brilliant s.	HUXL 441:55
rejected the S. on the Mount	BRAD 155:43
short nap at s.	ADDI 6:28
whole of her s.	FORS 344:30
sermons frightened by 'political' s.	BARTH 66:11
S. and soda water the day after	BYRON 190:7
S. in stones	SHAK 778:66
serpent dust shall be the s.'s meat	BIBLE 110:10
find the s. old	MARV 577:98
old s., called the Devil	BIBLE 132:10
s. beguiled me	BIBLE 91:95
s. did not seduce Eve	HUGH 436:37
s. of brass	BIBLE 94:82
s. shall bite him	BIBLE 106:31
s. to sting you	SHEL 811:45
s. under't	SHAK 796:17
s. was more subtil	BIBLE 91:91
sharper than a s.'s tooth	SHAK 792:95
Time like a s.	CRANE 253:62
venomous as the poison of a s.	BOOK 149:21
will he give him a s.?	BIBLE 115:51
serpent-haunted s.-h. sea	FLEC 340:34
serpents s. of explosive breath	MARI 571:77
wise as s.	BIBLE 116:69
servant act of the s.	LEON 522:66
bid your s. once adieu	SHAK 801:55
cast ye the unprofitable s.	BIBLE 119:34
clever s.	JEFF 453:11
good and faithful s.	BIBLE 119:33
he is the s. of the Living God	SMART 826:62
looking-glass of a s.	JOYCE 470:22
Lord, thy s. rears	HERB 413:56
never leave to be Your humble s.	ROCH 719:16
nor the s. above his lord	BIBLE 116:70
now lettest thou thy s.	BIBLE 133:44
now lettest thou thy s.	BIBLE 120:70
obligation to become the s.	SHAW 809:86
politician poses as the s.	DE 270:99
press…is an excellent s.	COOP 246:87
public s. who make it	NEW 634:33
S. of God, well done	MILT 605:21
s. of the sciences	BAUD 68:71
s. or has business	LAW 512:37
s. shall be healed	BIBLE 116:57
s. to be bred at an University	CONG 241:48
s. to the devil	SISS 823:92
s. with this clause	HERB 413:60
services of a menial s.	GRAY 383:44
Speak, Lord; for thy s. heareth	BIBLE 96:26
took upon him the form of a s.	BIBLE 128:97
wakes them himself, or sends his s.	ADDI 6:28
when ye hae a gude s.	SCOTT 753:53
whose s. I am	LENT 522:60
writer or a good public s.	MACM 557:79
servants as one of thy hired s.	BIBLE 121:90
domestic s. at home	MAUG 582:11
Give unto thy s. that peace	BOOK 146:42
reveal Himself to his s.	MILT 601:19
S. accumulate the privileges	DONO 293:82
s. of the public	GOWE 380:80
s. of the sovereign	BACON 51:83
Unmarried men…best s.	BACON 51:73
We are the s. of the people	BLAIR 138:54
When domestic s. are treated	SHAW 808:42
workmen and menial s.	MALT 563:23
Ye s. of the Lord	DODD 289:92
serve Choose you…whom ye will s.	BIBLE 95:10
Him s. with fear	KETHE 483:67
s. and obey them	HUME 438:98
Thee only we s.	KORAN 496:38
serves S. to say thus	SHAK 772:92
service abdicated the s. of it	PITT 679:4
any s. to the world's end?	SHAK 774:28
arrived in my s. already christened	SAKI 739:57
century of active s.	MOUN 622:93
did more s. than he	GOLD 376:89
do you…much s.	ASTE 39:1

serviceable

do you that last good s.	ROCH 720:21
essential s. to his country	SWIFT 862:45
If I last in this s.	SHAK 762:92
in purer lives thy s. find	WHIT 938:24
in the s. the scum	WELL 929:99
no-future job in the s. sector	COUP 248:24
point to his years of s.	ISHI 447:72
reward for equally good s.	ROOS 724:18
s. and the greater glory	PIUS 680:20
s., as to the Lord	BIBLE 128:94
s. is the common duty	ROCK 720:33
s. of my love	SPRI 841:87
s. of this nation	GAND 359:57
s. to my bonie lassie	BURNS 178:8
s. we render to others	GREN 388:58
shrink from the s. of his country	PAINE 660:29
soong the s. dyvyne	CHAU 217:73
whose s. is perfect freedom	BOOK 146:39
serviceable s. villain	SHAK 793:28
serviceman do not call a s.	BRIN 159:23
services commands Our s. a while	SHAK 794:50
if his s. are not recognised	DUGO 305:86
Nor s. to do	SHAK 801:55
price...on the s.	FRIE 351:70
s. of a menial servant	GRAY 383:44
serviettes crumpled the s.	BETJ 89:41
servile s. minds into terror	TZARA 904:18
servility slave in base s.	SHAK 759:81
serving s. the client	JOHN 458:28
servitude base laws of s.	DRYD 300:30
History may be s.	ELIOT 321:88
out of s. into freedom	EMER 325:91
s. and extreme licence	TOCQ 892:28
s. still can pierce	MUIR 624:22
s....the consequence of his crime	CURR 259:92
s....To serve th' unwise	MILT 605:23
sesquipedalian S. blackguard	CLOU 232:44
sessions s. of sweet silent thought	SHAK 801:47
set by God's grace, play a s.	SHAK 775:62
s. down This	ELIOT 318:15
turn on your s.	BRIN 159:23
Virtue is...best plain s.	BACON 52:27
Setebos S., S., and S.!	BROW 169:65
settee Lady Venus on the s.	SITW 823:94
setting Had elsewhere its s.	WORD 959:8
haste now to my s.	SHAK 805:50
s. which influences it	ROSSO 727:8
settle Don't s.	JOBS 455:64
helped to s. this glorious land	FERB 332:66
less will you s. for one	KIPL 490:11
settlement political s. of this crisis	HUSS 440:37
s. through genuine dialogue	AUNG 45:40
settler maintained by the s.	SART 745:78
settlers When old s. say	LESS 523:89
seven hewn out her s. pillars	BIBLE 104:61
Jacob served s. years	BIBLE 93:34
s. great facts and doctrines	HUGEL 434:4
seventy times s.	BIBLE 118:14
seventh God blessed the s. day	BIBLE 91:85
opened the s. seal	BIBLE 131:5
seventies vice of the S.	WOLFE 953:81
seventy To be s. years young	HOLM 424:84
seventy-seven At s.-s. it is time	JOHN 462:33
severance God their s. ruled	ARNO 34:82
severe intentionally a little too s.	KIER 485:6
s. he was and stern to view	GOLD 376:1
severest s. writers of this s. age	DRYD 300:40
severity pure s. of perfect light	TENN 877:58
simplicity or with s.	ARNO 35:10
Summer...with its usual s.	COLE 236:47
Severn from the S. to the Tyne!	KIPL 493:80
on S. snow the leaves	HOUS 431:47
the S. fills	TENN 873:65
Seville dogs of S.	TENN 878:96
sew time to s.	BIBLE 106:14
Sewell S. & Cross young man	GILB 369:48
sewer filthy s. pure gold flows	TOCQ 892:27
sea is the universal s.	COUS 249:42
trip through a s.	MIZN 610:62
sewers Ye Nymphs that reign o'er s.	COLE 236:50
sex accident of s.	GILM 371:94
broken down by Age, S.	MACR 558:14
call you darling after s.	BARN 64:72
can either s. assume	MILT 602:46
cardinal virtues of the s.	WOLL 954:89
complete example of her s.	RUSS 735:48
desire for food and s.	TOOLE 894:59
destroy s. in America	DOCT 289:82
difference is not that of s. or age	CIXO 227:42
eclipses and predominates...her s.	DOYLE 297:56
equal, as their s. not equal	MILT 604:99
Everybody lies about s.	SEIN 756:6
Every city has a s. and age	BERG 83:26
fair s. is your department	DOYLE 297:67
Gulf War was like teenage s.	HARK 398:34
have s. with me	BERL 85:58
his authority and her s.	WOLL 954:92
If God had meant...group s.	BRAD 154:29
if S-E-X ever rears its ugly head	AYCK 47:2
In the s. war	CONN 243:8
isn't s. but death	SONT 834:15
Literature is...about having s.	LODGE 534:93
litigation takes the place of s.	VIDAL 912:93
money buys women, s., status	DWOR 308:44
Money...was exactly like s.	BALD 57:20
offices that s. can discharge for s.	WOOLF 955:32
one s. from another	THUR 891:99
Pornography...attempt to insult s.	LAWR 514:80
practically conceal its s.	NASH 630:60
privilege...for my own s.	AUST 47:90
Redeem the age and s.	PHIL 676:53
riding high on s. and self-esteem	HOLL 423:52
romantic interest in our own s.	CONN 243:18
run after by the other s.	SHAW 809:84
s. and creativity are often	JONG 466:30
s. and death	CRON 256:29
S. and obscenity are not synonymous	BREN 158:98
S. had never before asserted	HARDY 397:10
S....I really don't understand	SALI 740:73
S. is engaging	JIANG 455:56
s. is good for headaches	WILB 939:42
s. is just politics	BRAD 154:31
S. is like money	UPDI 905:18
s. is the price	FRY 354:50
S. Life in Ancient Rome face	AMIS 16:30
S. 'n' drugs 'n' rock 'n' roll	DURY 308:40
s. object	GIOV 372:18
s. rears its ugly 'ead	ALLI 14:5
s. should be so simple	JAMES 451:60
S....single-crop farming	BELL 78:95
S. suppressed will go berserk	EWART 328:75
s. was something no woman	MUNRO 625:48
S.! What is that but life	CHER 219:29
s. without smiling	FRY 354:44
s. with someone I love	ALLEN 14:96
Shall the s. free	HABI 391:3
She gave him s.	HEPB 412:27
soft, unhappy s.	BEHN 75:27
talk on 'S. and Civics'	BETJ 89:43
too visible as s. objects	FRIE 350:65
weaker s., to piety more prone	ALEX 13:66
what s. and psychoanalysis are	HUGH 435:24
When you have money, it's s.	DONL 290:8
woman into a s. object	MORG 619:35
Women complain about s.	LAND 506:25
word s. in capital letters	WAUGH 923:49
sexes absurd division into s.	WAUGH 923:65
great distinction between the s.	FOWL 352:24
intellectual powers of the two s.	DARW 263:57
merit of both s.	LABR 502:8
more difference within the s.	COMP 239:4
old ladies of both s.	DICK 282:85
there are three s.	SMITH 830:55
wiser...of the two s.	GIBB 366:27
wives of both s.	MACD 550:39
sexologist kind of German s.	DOCT 289:82
sexophones s. wailed like...cats	HUXL 442:75
sexual felt s. urgings	COND 240:15
man cares most for s. intercourse	TWAIN 903:92
rooted in the s. impulse	SCHO 748:56
S. Etiquette	LOCH 533:85
s. juices flow toward a painting	FUEN 354:59
s. relations with that woman	CLIN 230:9
sublimated...into s. activity	BRAD 154:21
sexuality s. and promiscuity	WYLIE 964:11
s....suddenly recognised	FREUD 350:56
women's horrifying s.	MILL 593:49
sexy seeing some s. football	GULL 390:93
shabby If I were s.	WHAR 933:3
S. gentility has nothing	HOLM 424:73
shackles garters to be bonds and s.	BACON 51:72
Memories are not s.	BENN 80:45
s. of an old love	TENN 877:54
shad-blow s.-b., flaked	CRANE 253:66
shade alone in summer s.	WORD 958:91
Amaryllis in the s.	MILT 599:86
broader browner s.	GRAY 383:56
clutching the inviolable s.	ARNO 34:95
enjoy the s.	JONS 468:86
fleeting image of a s.	SHEL 815:25
fountain, s., and rill	MILT 599:83
his steadfast s.	TENN 870:95
laws...of light and s.	CAPO 197:24
light, s. and perspective	CONS 245:60
Lord is thy s. upon thy right hand	BIBLE 103:31
No s., no shine	HOOD 426:37
ragged penury of s.	ADAMS 4:73
returned that s.	KEATS 476:98
s. is on the brightest wing	SITW 823:6
s. of a great name	LUCAN 541:46
S. off the trees	CORY 247:12
shall crowd into a s.	POPE 685:15
sitting in the s.	KIPL 492:68
sit under the s. of it	DICK 280:33
Spring...with rustling s.	SEEG 755:99
Summer-house, that knows no s.	POPE 686:60
throw no one into the s.	BULOW 173:62
Under the s. of a Coolibah	PATE 669:12
variable as the s.	SCOTT 752:25
Within its s. we'll live	CONN 242:84
shades Alcestis rises from the s.	LAND 507:29
luminous s.	GORD 378:53
preparing for bed with the s. up	STARR 843:27
regions of sorrow, doleful s.	MILT 601:35
s. and wanton winds	MILT 599:90
s. of darkness	DELA 271:33
s. of humiliation	EVANS 328:69
shadow ancient s. and twilights	RUSS 735:43
awful s. of some unseen Power	SHEL 812:55
but a s.'s s.	SHAK 782:87
care is like my s.	ELIZ 321:3
days on the earth are as a s.	BIBLE 98:83
dream...of a s.	CHAP 214:15
Falls the s.	ELIOT 318:15
hair and my s.	NERU 633:22
have to vanquish his s.	NIET 638:94
I am your s.	SCEVE 746:18
I have a little s.	STEV 853:69
land of the s. of death	BIBLE 107:59
Life's but a walking s.	SHAK 798:74
light and s. never stand still	WEST 932:75
love in s. best is made	JONS 468:86
Man...fleeth also as a s.	BIBLE 98:5
merest s. line	THUR 891:99
neither s. of turning	BIBLE 130:49
No s. walks behind me	JOHN 457:4
not darkness but s.	FRYE 354:57
out-soared the s. of our night	SHEL 815:40
s. at morning striding behind	ELIOT 317:96
s. cast by the light of a fire	VASA 909:27
s. of a great rock.	BIBLE 108:75
S. of annoyance	SHEL 814:96
s. of cloud	YEATS 966:19
s. of the midnight hour	BYRON 188:65
s. of the silent night	MARL 573:10
s. over the colored	BUCK 172:33
s. shortened in the sun	JARR 452:90
S. That Comes in Sight	AMIS 16:44
s. that runs across the grass	HAGG 391:7
s. white as stone	ROET 722:62
spy my s.	SHAK 761:34
star-shaped s.	WORD 962:51
swan and s.	WORD 960:14
tall elm's s.	THOM 885:54
The S. cloaked	TENN 874:66
Time...a vast s.	VAUG 909:39
under the s. of thy wings	BIBLE 100:57
under the s. of thy wings	BIBLE 99:37
under the s. of war	SPEN 837:99
with the s. of his wings	SHAK 760:29
you have got a s.	FLET 341:67
shadowless Stand s. like Silence	HOOD 426:18
shadows Cats...than their s.	TESS 880:20
colour of s.	WALC 916:17
Each substance...hath twenty s.	SHAK 764:42
Earth's s. fly	SHEL 815:43
fills the s.	SWIN 863:82
half sick of s.	TENN 869:82
illustrate all s.	DONNE 293:72
individuals pass like s.	BURKE 175:29
live to trace Their s.	KEATS 475:78

shelves

make the s. visible	NERV 633:24
measure s.	HUBB 434:3
mirrors of the gigantic s.	SHEL 816:53
s. among s.	UPDI 905:19
s. have offended	SHAK 768:51
s. in a sunshine day?	MARL 573:16
s., not substantial things	SHIR 819:20
s. of eternity	VAUG 909:34
S. of the world appear	TENN 869:81
s. upon two generations	LLOY 533:74
shapes, and beckoning	MILT 598:68
silent s. and in dreams?	STEV 849:70
sleepers and the s.	WHIT 938:10
their s. deep	YEATS 965:7
the well in the s.	PRIC 695:83
Types and s. have their ending	AQUI 30:97
very s. of the clouds	WORD 960:22
what is time but s.	SASS 746:96
where the S. lie	TOLK 893:45
shadow-sister your s.-s.	WRIG 963:70
Shadrach S., Meshach	BIBLE 111:39
Shadwell S. never deviates	DRYD 300:44
S....of all my sons	DRYD 300:43
shafts Between the s. and the furrow	HEAN 404:68
birch for s.	SPEN 838:20
shake seems to s. the spheres	DRYD 303:29
s. a man's faith	SHAW 806:89
s. off its apathy	RENAN 711:47
s. your Rome	SHAK 799:2
the rousing s.	POPE 685:30
shaken S. and not stirred	FLEM 340:42
Shakespeare as wise...As S.	FERG 333:84
closest you can get to S.	BUEC 172:41
compare [Jonson] with S.	DRYD 300:25
complete S. and a prayer book	BAIN 55:95
dig up S. and dig up Bacon	GILB 370:75
five acts of S.'s tragedy	FIELD 335:12
gave S. and Fletcher all	DENH 272:62
good enough for S.'s day	VICT 912:79
honour to S.	JONS 468:90
I find the phrase in S.	SCOTT 754:81
I hear S. think	CALL 193:33
knowledge of the Bible, S. and Wisden	WAUGH 924:98
not...quote a line of S.	CAREY 199:66
read S. I am struck	LAWR 514:79
remarkable thing about S.	GRAV 383:38
s. and i are often low browed	MARQ 575:50
S. by flashes of lightning	COLE 236:45
S....eye of God	OLIV 649:41
S. for his honoured bones	MILT 597:39
S....had the largest and most comprehensive soul	DRYD 300:20
S. is the great genius of the drama	BENN 81:82
S. made use of it first	SHER 818:3
S. one gets acquainted with	AUST 46:69
S. set his play writing aside	CUOMO 258:81
S.'s much-quoted passage	ORWE 654:33
S.'s name...stands absurdly too high	BYRON 188:79
S....wanted taste	WALP 919:68
S. was an Irish Catholic	ONEI 651:69
S. was the Homer	DRYD 300:26
S....weak in chemistry	WELLS 930:17
S....is...a forest	JOHN 465:4
souls most fed with S.'s flame	CHES 221:99
special reservoir...fed by S.	ACHE 2:28
Stratford trades on S.	BURG 174:90
The English have S.	DUVA 308:41
three good sets of S.	ONEI 651:70
tried...to read S.	DARW 263:55
Whaur's yer Wullie S. noo?	ANON 22:80
Shakespearian That S. rag	BUCK 171:32
shall His absolute 's.'?	SHAK 799:96
shallow s. conversational ends	SASS 746:98
shallows bound in s. and in miseries	SHAK 778:48
small eels...within the s. play	CRAB 252:42
Shalott beside remote S.	TENN 869:83
Lady of S.	TENN 869:79
Lady of S.	TENN 869:82
Lady of S.	TENN 869:85
Lady of S.	TENN 869:86
Lady of S.	TENN 869:87
shame all other praise is s.	SIDN 820:51
contempt of s.	JOHN 460:83
epoch of folly and s.	ZOLA 970:16
greater was the s.	LANY 508:54
hangs his head for s.?	INGR 446:36
I left a legacy of s.	MADO 558:18

look of furtive s.	WODE 952:47
neither sin nor s.	ROCHE 719:1
neither sin nor s.	STER 849:53
noble s.	KING 488:55
no love...no s.	SHAW 806:90
no s. for a man to die	HOMER 425:8
race of s.	MILT 607:91
sense of...deathless s.	WEBS 926:26
s....from being happy at another's distress	LABR 502:25
S. is the most violent	LAFA 503:45
S. of the versifying tribe!	GRAY 384:60
s. on you	ARMS 32:48
s. or censure free	JOHN 459:43
s. the devil	SHAK 771:49
s. will be too long	SHAK 776:95
'Tis no s. for men	SHIR 819:17
whose glory is in their s.	BIBLE 128:3
shameful s. conquest of itself	SHAK 764:41
vile members...called 'pudenda' ['s.']	ABEL 1:3
shameless S....5 years before	LAVER 512:33
shamrock S. shine for ever new!	DAVIS 266:11
shandeism True S....opens the heart	STER 848:38
Shandon bells of S.	MAHO 559:35
Shannon green banks of S.	CAMP 194:60
shape art thou, execrable s.?	MILT 603:70
assume a pleasing s.	SHAK 782:4
com'st in such a questionable s.	SHAK 781:57
exact colour and s.	MONET 612:99
eyes have drawn thy s.	SHAK 800:43
flesh; but in what s. they	MILT 602:46
good s. for more sinning	RUNY 732:62
gordian s. of dazzling hue	KEATS 476:4
in the s. of a woman	RICH 713:99
let it keep one s.	SHAK 787:50
might be any s.	CARR 205:8
most rational s.	WEBER 925:13
nobler s. erect and tall	MILT 604:98
No s. to feed each gazing eye	DYER 309:48
O Attic s.!	KEATS 478:38
over the net in a different s.	LODGE 534:96
s. of things to come	WELLS 930:39
share the selfsame s.	MACD 549:29
some partial narrow s.	POPE 689:46
stereotyped s. assumed	LIPP 531:39
what s. it will take	SHEV 818:11
who's in worse s. than	MONR 612:7
shaper s. of the landscape	BRON 161:53
shapes full of s. is fancy	SHAK 785:78
horrid s., and shrieks	MILT 597:41
immortal s. Of bright	MILT 598:62
In holier s.	SHAK 791:81
s., and beckoning shadows	MILT 598:68
s. of rot	PURDY 700:85
Turns them to s.	SHAK 768:45
share biggest snouts...largest s.	WEIG 927:87
s. the insult	ISHE 447:70
to her s....errors fall	POPE 685:33
shareholder large s.	TANA 867:23
shareholders mass of inert s.	ROBI 718:92
shares sell its s.	DRUC 299:7
sharing a kind of s.	FRY 354:47
not of war...but of...s.	CHILD 222:16
S. a bed and a future	FADI 329:2
shark oppose the man-eating s.	BRIN 159:25
s. has pretty teeth, dear	BREC 157:88
sharks swimming with the s.	FORD 344:16
Sharon rose of S.	BIBLE 107:40
sharp s. as any lynx	SITW 823:95
s. be the weather	SCOTT 753:39
short, s. shock	WHIT 936:77
so s. the conquerynge	CHAU 216:57
sharper s. than any two-edged sword	BIBLE 129:34
s. than a serpent's tooth	SHAK 792:95
sharpest s. men in argument	HOLM 424:65
shatterday frightday, s.	JOYCE 470:37
shave buy you more than a s.	LARK 510:93
rides back to s. again	WHITE 935:47
To s. the beard is a sin	IVAN 448:80
shaving when I am s. of a morning	HOUS 432:72
Shaw S. has no enemies	WILDE 942:27
shay wonderful one-hoss s.	HOLM 424:74
she great S.-who-must-be-obeyed	HEAL 404:66
S. who must be obeyed	HAGG 391:8
sheaf forgot a s. in the field	BIBLE 95:93
shears Fury with th' abhorred s.	MILT 599:86
resembles a pair of s.	SMITH 831:58

s. of destiny?	SHAK 768:64
sheath never s. the sword	ASQU 38:84
you s.	SHAK 771:47
sheaves bringing his s.	BIBLE 103:35
s. in harvest	DONNE 293:72
Sheba queen of S.	BIBLE 97:55
queen of S.	BIBLE 98:85
Solomon gave to the queen of S.	BIBLE 98:85
she-bear s.-b. coming up the street	FOOTE 342:83
shedding Without s. of blood	BIBLE 129:36
She-Devil Loves of a S.-D.	WELD 928:80
she-elephant great S.-e.	HEAL 404:66
sheep All we like s. have gone astray	BIBLE 109:94
an old half-witted s.	STEP 847:11
as a s. before her shearers	BIBLE 109:94
as s. going astray	BIBLE 130:69
come to you in s.'s clothing	BIBLE 115:53
counted as s. for the slaughter	BIBLE 100:66
Dream Of Electric S.?	DICK 277:34
erred and strayed...like lost s.	BOOK 146:32
giveth his life for the s.	BIBLE 123:45
go rather to the lost s.	BIBLE 116:66
having an hundred s.	BIBLE 121:87
hundred years as a s.	MUSS 627:90
hungry s. look up	MILT 599:89
land of cattle and s.	LAWS 514:96
like a s. with a blade of grass	WODE 952:38
little black s.	KIPL 489:75
lying in bed counting s.	SIEG 820:60
men better than s.	TENN 878:86
mountain s. are sweeter	PEAC 671:54
mountain which is of no use for s.	BUTL 185:89
nation of panicked s.	THOM 887:90
prize-oxen and of s.	BIBLE 872:35
sameness of s.	WHITE 935:41
savaged by a dead s.	HEAL 404:66
s. go to a slaughter-house	MACD 549:17
s. he doth us take	SCOT 755:88
s. in s.'s clothing	GOSSE 379:68
s. in the midst of wolves	BIBLE 116:69
s. of his hand	BOOK 149:30
s. on his right hand	BIBLE 119:35
s. out of the window	WELD 928:87
shepherds looking on their seely s.	SHAK 760:10
shrouds as I a s. were	LANG 507:44
standing a s. on its hind-legs	BEER 73:87
strange that s.'s guts	SHAK 774:37
teeth are like a flock of s.	BIBLE 107:45
the shepherd his s.	PROP 697:30
useless for the s. to pass	INGE 445:25
with not many black s.	ORWE 654:33
sheep-bells s.-b. and the ship-bells	KIPL 491:46
sheepfold let the wolf into the s.!	HEAL 446:42
sheep-herding mere s.-h.	POUND 692:16
sheep-hook how to hold A s.-h.	MILT 599:88
sheepskins well down among the s.	STEV 851:29
sheet causes, the balance s.	MO 611:68
great s. knit at the four corners	BIBLE 124:82
old England's winding s.	BLAKE 141:28
wet s. and a flowing sea	CUNN 258:74
sheets brother popped...into his s.	STOP 855:15
fumble with the s.	SHAK 775:68
Sheffield reminded him of S. United	HATT 400:82
shelf deepens like a coastal s.	LARK 510:90
Life...Behind the S.	DICK 284:40
stuffed ones on a s.	POUND 692:19
take the phial cleanly from its s.	DOYLE 297:75
shelf-life s. l. of the moral causes	IGNA 445:01
s. l. somewhere between	TRIL 897:11
shell dry s. on the beach	DU 306:94
pebble or a prettier s.	NEWT 635:61
s. of his victim	ANNAN 19:11
s....of meaning	ELIOT 321:82
skin and s. of things	VAUG 909:33
Within thy airy s.	MILT 598:70
Shelley did you once see S. plain	BROW 168:43
Like S. and like Baudelaire	ISHE 447:69
peace in S.'s mind	SHEL 816:62
What S. shrilled	SASS 746:98
shells not the s. and rockets	KISH 493:83
shelter no s. but in a fool's cap	HOPK 428:66
Our s. from the stormy blast	WATTS 923:85
running for the s.	JAGG 449:14
s., and even muse	TUCH 901:14
s. thee, I'd s. thee	BURNS 180:67
s., warmth and accommodation	NUTT 642:75
shelves symmetry of s.	LAMB 505:3

shepherd

shepherd any philosophy in thee, s.? SHAK 779:88
as a s. divideth his sheep BIBLE 119:35
Dead s. SHAK 779:4
Dick the s. blows SHAK 763:27
feed his flock like a s. BIBLE 108:80
finding herself at S.'s Bush BUTL 185:1
homely slighted S.'s trade MILT 599:86
I am the good s. BIBLE 123:45
Lord is my s. BIBLE 100:45
Lord's my s. SCOT 754:85
power by which our S. rose DODD 289:93
Scythian s. MARL 572:96
S. and Bishop of your souls BIBLE 130:69
S., from the hill ARNO 34:87
s., thee the woods MILT 599:84
star that bids the s. MILT 598:64
the fairest s. PEELE 672:69
the s. his sheep PROP 697:30
truth in every s.'s tongue RALE 705:43
shepherds liberal s. SHAK 784:57
s. abiding in the field BIBLE 120:69
s. and butchers VOLT 914:46
s. feed their flocks MARL 574:41
s. looking on their seely sheep SHAK 760:10
s., weep no more MILT 600:94
warmth of s.' flames MARL 572:3
What time the s. SHAK 760:7
sherry have a sweet s. BENN 80:52
mischief...with the cooking s. THUR 891:94
unattainable soda and s. SALA 739:70
very fond of brown s. CHES 221:7
sherry-crazed some s.-c....dowager JOHN 457:97
Shibboleth Say now S. BIBLE 95:14
shield broken was her s. SCOTT 752:27
lady in his s. TENN 869:83
Our S. and Defender GRANT 381:5
our sword and our s. HUGH 436:50
s. me with shining breast GORD 378:53
s. of congressional immunity SMITH 829:27
s. of faith BIBLE 128:95
s. ourselves from the sordid perils WILDE 940:57
trusty s. and weapon LUTH 542:73
truth shall be thy s. BIBLE 102:96
where the s. and spear SPEN 838:37
why should you want to s. him? SAKI 739:65
shift let me s. for myself MORE 619:25
shifty s., hangdog look WODE 952:47
Shiites Irish...as the S. in Lebanon OROU 652:92
shilling kindly drop a s. KIPL 491:22
willing to sell for one s. LEAR 516:37
shillings these men paid their s. PRIE 695:84
weight in pounds, s. MILNE 596:22
shimmering s. into rooms WODE 951:35
shine Arise, s. BIBLE 110:5
can give me a s. GORD 378:55
every one doth s. SHAK 777:26
No one could s. his shoes ISAA 447:65
not to s. in use! TENN 870:98
sun...shall s. on me SHAK 764:34
To see him s. so brisk SHAK 771:33
shingles naked s. of the world ARNO 33:66
shining see it s. plain HOUS 431:52
shinning those who do not allow 's.' ANON 23:89
shins not afraid of his s. ANON 23:89
ship aloe...like a s. MANS 567:5
As idle as a painted s. COLE 235:12
being in a s. JOHN 460:88
built your s. of death LAWR 514:82
English s., they say LOND 534:10
Matilda Briggs...was a s. DOYLE 293:74
mildest...That ever scuttled s. BYRON 190:14
Of a s.'s hour SLES 825:52
office was his pirate s. LEWIS 527:57
O S. of State LONG 535:27
sail this new s. of mine? BALL 59:69
s., an isle, a sickle moon FLEC 340:38
s. has weather'd every rack WHIT 938:7
s. in port is safe HOPP 429:5
s. is always referred NIMI 639:25
S. me somewhere KIPL 489:83
s. [of state] will be saved CUOMO 258:80
s. on the sea LORCA 537:58
s.'s upon the sea KIPL 490:2
s. would not travel due West! CARR 206:30
Sink me the s. TENN 879:98
steel s. loaded with monoliths MENC 587:15
Swimming full upon the s. BROW 168:54

swimming toward a sinking s. YARB 965:1
tall s. and a star to steer MASE 580:50
The s.'s ignored BISH 136:23
truth...sinks his s. CORN 247:6
went down to the s. POUND 691:10
whale s. was my Yale College MELV 585:57
What is a s. but a prison? BURT 181:82
ship-bells sheep-bells and the s.-b. KIPL 491:46
shipping fishes first to s. did impart DRYD 299:15
tiers of s. DICK 281:55
ships as s. on the foam KIPL 490:92
boats or s. came near LEAR 516:40
down to the sea in s. BIBLE 102:15
drew a thousand s. MARL 572:4
face that launched a thousand s. MARL 573:29
fleet of British s. NELS 633:12
harbour without s. DEFOE 269:78
My experience of s. BRAD 154:24
my s. are out of gear TENN 878:95
my thoughts on white s. COLUM 238:89
nor its s. empty of men NICI 637:80
old s. sail like swans FLEC 340:31
railways, magnificent s. LARI 509:70
Rivers and seas...to float their s. DICK 280:27
s. and stars and isles FLEC 340:31
S. that pass in the night LONG 536:37
S., towers, domes WORD 959:3
something wrong with our bloody s. BEAT 70:5
stately s. are twirled and spun HODG 421:22
stately s. go on TENN 871:4
Stately s. to bear our food WILDE 940:45
sunken and damaged s. HALS 393:43
There go the s. BIBLE 102:13
Thracian s. and the foreign SWIN 863:82
We've got the s. HUNT 439:16
What merchant's s. have my sighs DONNE 291:28
with the moving s. SWIN 864:6
Shipton S. 'assault' CRAN 253:75
shipwreck like s. CATH 208:90
mermaid...tolled my son to s. DEKK 270:12
s. of time BACON 49:26
shipwrecking s. all their hopes MOOD 615:54
shire s. which we...may call DRAY 298:97
shires Round both the s. HOUS 431:43
shirt sang the 'Song of the S.' HOOD 426:30
s. or collar ever comes back LEAC 515:21
shirts stuffed s., hollow men MACD 550:39
than the coarse s. THOM 885:70
shit contempt for an arrant s. JOSE 469:7
give a s. what happens NIXON 640:35
look and feel like s. AMIS 16:52
whatta you do when you s.? CARU 207:59
shivering s. and sighing PARK 664:13
shivering-sweet s.-s. to the touch? CORN 247:3
shivers broken to s. BIBLE 131:92
shoals Guarded by s. and rocks BYRON 189:6
shock depending upon s. tactics PRIE 695:94
harmony comes...as a s. RAINE 705:42
s. around the age of five BALD 57:23
S. of the New DUNL 307:13
short, sharp s. GILB 369:64
short, sharp s. WHIT 936:77
The plan is called 's. and awe' ANON 27:42
shocking glimpse of stocking...s. PORT 690:68
s., but not pathetic HUGH 435:34
shock-pried s.-p. faces EBER 310:11
shocks thousand natural s. SHAK 783:7
shod s. with iron DICK 281:77
shoe blaming his s. BECK 72:38
Chinese woman's foot fits her s. SCHR 749:63
for want of a s. FRAN 348:14
Into a left-hand s. CARR 205:22
lazy insolence of a s. salesman PERE 674:18
Sailed off in a wooden s. FIELD 335:13
smiled at the s. TRAV 895:89
shoemaker leather...to a s. WAUGH 924:84
shoes blue suede s. PERK 675:26
boil eggs in your s. LEAR 517:46
butter nor s. nor poetry LEWIS 527:56
drunk its little s. DICK 278:19
Give a girl the right s. MIDL 590:84
I can buy a new pair of s. CHAR 216:50
make his own s. SMITH 827:85
mind it wipes its s. THOM 884:34
most s. wins ANON 27:41
never even...tied my s. PU 701:3
No one could shine his s. ISAA 447:65

old ladies in tennis s. MOSK 622:80
pinching of thin s. DICK 279:1
put off thy s. BIBLE 93:52
s.—and ships—and sealing-wax CARR 204:1
s. are made of python MACN 557:97
s....expensive and too small BAIN 55:91
s. on your feet BIBLE 93:59
tips of his patent-leather s. CHRI 223:43
when we want s. SWIFT 861:34
Wooden S. ANON 23:96
shoeshine on a smile and a s. MILL 593:32
shoestring careless s. HERR 416:1
runs it into a s. WOOL 956:42
shoon moon...in her silver s. DELA 271:31
shoot ask him to s. around you GOLD 377:24
Do not s. MALO 563:18
do not s. the pianist WILDE 940:48
environmentalists...s. them OLEA 649:32
guns begin to s. KIPL 489:87
Hands up! Don't s! ANON 28:47
idea how to s. THOM 887:98
just need to s. straight GOLD 377:23
s. his like in the name of an idea BROD 160:40
S., if you must WHIT 938:23
s. me in my absence BEHAN 74:9
s. them down WHITE 935:46
shout and they s. INGE 445:28
When we're afraid we s. SONT 834:18
shooting always helps my s. HEMI 410:77
Nothing wrong with s. EAST 310:7
shoots s. of everlastingness VAUG 909:35
shop ain't the s. for justice DICK 278:71
foul rag-and-bone s. YEATS 967:34
pops its head into the s. FOOTE 342:83
talking s. in Strasbourg BEVIN 90:67
shopkeepers be a nation of s. PUNCH 699:75
nation of s. NAPO 630:47
nation of s. SMITH 828:87
nation of s. STOP 856:20
shoplift My advice...is to s. JONES 466:25
shopping S. is Not Creating COUP 248:30
watch the s. channel COUP 249:35
shopping list absurd s. l. TROL 898:59
shops hideous brick s. THOR 889:52
men that run the s. LEWIS 527:59
s. curiously low THOR 889:50
sordid little s. LESS 524:95
shopworn word...has become so s. RENO 711:55
shore beat on the rocky s. LEAR 516:28
Bequeath us no earthly s. CRANE 252:55
broad sandy s. BYRON 189:6
children sport upon the s. WORD 960:11
control...Stops with the s. BYRON 188:71
here is no s. SCOTT 751:2
hugging the s. UPDI 906:25
I linger on the s. TENN 871:20
left the Trojan s. DRYD 304:37
lights around the s. ROSS 726:54
(more stony than a s.) WILL 946:15
one on s. SHAK 774:38
print...on the s. DEFOE 269:74
rapture on the lonely s. BYRON 188:70
reedy s. GIBB 367:7
refuse of your teeming s. LAZA 515:3
s. of Gitche Gumee LONG 535:29
s. of the wan grass sea SITW 823:10
S. of the wide world KEATS 475:78
small eels that left...For the warm s. CRAB 252:42
some false impossible s. ARNO 34:80
stretch from s. to s. WATTS 923:47
This embattled s. EISE 314:18
towards the pebbled s. SHAK 801:56
unknown and silent s. LAMB 505:80
Upon the Irish s. BURNS 180:59
waves upon the s. SHEL 812:67
shoreline longer the s. of wonder MACI 553:1
shores bade betwixt their s. ARNO 34:82
Desolate s. KEATS 475:70
glide past the rocks to safer s. CUOMO 258:80
many leave these s. OWEN 658:40
s., and desert wildernesses MILT 598:68
s. of morning ATWO 41:33
s. of this happy isle GLAD 373:39
To s. by the wash YEATS 965:5
wilder s. of love BLAN 141:46
short all too s. a date SHAK 800:37
as s. as December SHAK 799:9

sight

Gettysburg address was so s.	HEMI 410:83	S. me a sane man	JUNG 471:47	the s. may have liberty	PEPYS 674:2
Let life be s.	SHAK 776:95	that within which passeth s.	SHAK 780:36	they that are s.	BIBLE 116:63
Life is s. and bothersome	LABR 502:19	the s. does not go on	PAGL 659:18	they that are s.	BIBLE 119:50
Life is too s.	SCOTT 751:8	What wealth the s....had brought	WORD 960:26	when he is s.	JOHN 464:86
nasty, brutish and s.	HOBB 420:2	**showbiz** secondary s. nonsense	AMIS 75:27	When I was s.	SHAK 758:62
not so s. as sweet	SHAK 765:61	**show-business** s.-b. with blood	BELA 75:29	When I was s.	STEV 853:68
poor, nasty, brutish and s.	GIBB 367:8	**showdown** begun the great s.	HUSS 440:38	**sickening** s. of the heart	POE 683:80
s....if one follows patterns	SENE 757:22	**shower** abundant s. of curates	BRON 161:66	**sickness** breed a bloodless s.	CAMP 195:77
s. neck denotes a good mind	SPARK 836:66	dying lamp, a falling s.	SHEL 815:36	Fitter for s.	SHAK 759:77
s. one ready for my own	FROST 353:16	in sun and s.	WORD 957:63	green s. of the mind	CLEV 230:94
s., sharp shock	GILB 369:64	like standing under a cold s.	HEATH 405:91	in s. and in health	BOOK 148:89
s., sharp shock	WHIT 936:77	pierced with softest s.	KYD 501:47	in s. and in health	BOOK 148:90
s. story is always a disclosure	PRIT 696:24	Pope in the s.	ANON 27:15	in s. and in health	BOOK 148:91
time of life is s.	SHAK 772:65	s. of all my days	THOM 884:22	nature of the s.	SHAK 786:28
shortage acute s. of rich people	WILS 948:74	sweetness of a s.	THOM 885:63	s., and unemployment	LLOY 532:71
s. of coal and...of fish	BEVAN 89:52	turf such the honeyed s.	MILT 599:90	s. enlarges the dimensions	LAMB 505:6
short-circuit poetic s.-c.	SENG 757:27	with a sudden s.	VALL 907:10	s. enlarges the dimensions	LAMB 505:8
shortcut s. c. to everything	MILL 594:86	**showers** Aegypt glads with s.	POPE 688:31	trublit now with gret s.	DUNB 306:3
shortcuts but I know the s.	RULFO 731:40	s. betumble the chestnut spikes	HARDY 397:29	universal s.	TRIL 897:14
shortest s. knight of the year	RICH 714:14	Small s. last long	SHAK 764:38	**Sidcup** If only I could get...to S.!	PINT 678:82
s. line between two points	BREC 157:92	Spring shall pour his s.	COLL 238:77	**side** Back and s. go bare	ANON 21:60
s. way to do many things	SMIL 827:70	**showery** S., Flowery, Bowery	ELLIS 323:28	ever strong upon the stronger s.	HAZL 403:43
short-haired s.-h. joy and roughness	SNYD 833:95	**showgirl** out-of-work s.	CHAN 213:74	From thy riven s.	TOPL 894:61
shortness spend that s. basely	SHAK 772:63	**showing up** democracy is about...s. u.	NADER 629:24	go by thy s.	ANON 21:57
Your plainness and your s.	SHAK 762:76	**showing-up** Eighty percent...is s.-u.	ALLEN 14:99	move over to the other s.	REED 710:33
shorts s. and washing themselves	LINK 530:29	**showmanship** the s. of a peanut	COWE 249:69	on the right s.	GALB 357:21
s. in this compass?	MURR 627:80	**shows** May's new-fangled s.	SHAK 763:4	on the s. of the underdog	PALEY 661:51
shot long shot...a very long s.!	DOYLE 297:61	**shrapnel** defensive hats, and s.	WHIT 936:74	purple wardrobe of thy s.	CRAS 254:80
Major Strasser has been s.	EPST 327:31	**shred** save a s. of its respectability	READ 708:94	spear pierced his s.	BIBLE 123:63
marvellously good s.	COWA 249:64	**shreds** s. of objectivity	CUPI 258:86	suffered at my s.	SASS 745:89
never s. anything	SITW 824:21	thing of s. and patches	GILB 369:58	this s. of the grave	PITT 680:11
Out of the s....of desire	SHAK 781:46	**shrew** taming the savage s.	FERB 332:70	this s. the tomb	BYRON 187:49
plot in it will be s.	TWAIN 902:50	**shriek** bat With short shrill s.	COLL 238:76	through a s. door	UPDI 906:32
s. an arrow	HAMER 393:44	**shrieks** louder s. to pitying heav'n	POPE 685:40	thrust my hand into his s.	BIBLE 124:67
s. at for sixpence	DIBD 276:28	**shrimp** s. of an author	GRAY 385:95	turn always one s.	SCHR 749:64
s. fired in...a concert	STEN 847:1	until a s. learns to whistle	KHRU 485:90	Walk on the Wild S.	ALGR 13:67
s. from one of the batteries	MACA 546:60	**shrine** deface the s.!	DRYD 303:8	Who is on my s.?	BIBLE 97:79
s. heard around the world	EMER 324:48	erect our national s.	FORS 344:22	Who is on the Lord's s.?	BIBLE 94:71
s. one bird flying	HEMI 409:69	mountain and a national s.	MUMF 625:37	with Ate by his s.	SHAK 777:34
s. to death, with pearls?	WEBS 927:58	United Nations...a s.	OBRI 645:65	**sides** houseless heads and unfed s.	SHAK 792:11
used to be a big s.	WALD 916:25	**shrines** like vapour over s.	BROW 166:90	much might be said on both s.	ADDI 6:29
volley of words...quickly s. off	SHAK 758:61	**shrivelling** s. away into nothingness	KELM 479:67	On both s. more respect	SHAK 799:97
when it pained most, I s.	HAAS 391:1	**Shropshire** brother in S.	BARR 65:95	Poetry cannot take s.	SPEN 837:8
shotgun as a sawed-off s.	PARK 664:31	**shroud** s. Of thoughts	BYRON 188:57	prick the s. of my intent	SHAK 796:20
old man with a s.	TWAIN 902:54	starched pleats of a s.	LEVE 525:25	room at your twa s.	BALL 58:57
shots but of the best s.	VOLT 914:45	stiff dishonoured s.	ELIOT 317:81	to take s.	RUSH 732:65
shoulda woulda, s. coulda	HOFF 422:27	**shrouds** s. are put on us	SCHR 749:62	work from the four s.	POLL 684:2
shoulder on my leaning s.	YEATS 965:3	**Shrovetide** far back as S.	ANON 23:88	would have three s.	MONT 614:38
queer s.	GINS 372:9	**shrub-ruster** s.-r., sky-mocker	UPDI 905:14	**sidewalks** like wet s. cause rain	BLOU 143:71
shifted it to another s.	SHAW 808:75	**shrug** borne it with a patient s.	SHAK 769:85	**sideways** step s. into a parallel universe	WELSH 930:47
S. the sky	HOUS 432:65	s. of shoulder	SPEN 837:96	**side-whiskers** by growing s.-w.	WELLS 930:33
shrug of s.	SPEN 837:96	**shucks** Church ain't s.	TWAIN 902:44	**siege** chronicled the s. of Troy	CUOMO 258:81
stand s. to s.	TALE 866:15	**shut** I wish he had just s. up	QUIL 702:17	fallen by S. into the Power	ALBE 11:33
stands on any s.	SHAK 792:98	who was...leaking and s. them up	REAG 709:14	**Sierras** S. Will be dry	SNYD 832:91
tears in s. blades	STEV 850:96	**shutter** camera with its s. open	ISHE 447:68	**sieve** in a s. I'll thither sail	SHAK 795:99
shoulders burdens on the broadest s.	LLOY 532:70	not clicking the s.	EISE 314:9	Our S. ain't big	LEAR 516:32
City of the Big S.	SAND 741:13	**shutters** close the s. fast	COWP 251:19	sifted in my private s.	CAMPO 195:79
grow beneath their s.	SHAK 788:93	we'd need keep the s. up	DICK 280:22	they went to sea in a s.	LEAR 516:30
head...little use without my s.	CARR 203:62	**shuttle** Man is the s.	VAUG 909:40	they went to sea in a s.	LEAR 516:31
lie on the s. of the...saint	WEBER 925:11	swifter than a weaver's s.	BIBLE 96:42	Washington is a s.	REAG 709:14
old heads on your young s.	SPARK 836:67	Welcome to s. diplomacy!	SISCO 823:91	went to sea in a s.	LEAR 516:30
s. globed	HEAN 404:68	**shuttles** s. again and rejoins	ROTH 727:75	**siftings** let their liquid s. fall	ELIOT 317:81
s. held the sky suspended	HOUS 432:72	**shy** I am terribly s.	CHAN 214:6	**sigh** long-drawn s.	WALL 917:45
s. of their predecessors	RUSS 734:27	s. of 'the Big Folk'	TOLK 893:47	not spare a s.	HOPK 428:81
Square your s.	HOUS 433:83	**Sicilian** S. mule has come to me	GLAD 373:42	prompts th' eternal s.	POPE 687:29
standing on the s. of giants	BERN 85:61	S. Muses, let us sing	VIRG 913:23	shall I ever s. and pine?	HERB 414:75
shout rings no hunter's s.	SIGO 821:64	**sick** Dante makes me s.	VEGA 910:47	s. for thy repose	WESL 932:66
s. and they shoot	INGE 445:28	from my s. bed	LEE 519:94	S., heart	YEATS 965:9
shouted with a great s.	BIBLE 95:8	get s. or die	HOOV 427:48	s. is just a s.	HUPF 440:35
s. that tore hell's	MILT 602:49	half my men are s.	TENN 878:95	s. of the east on my face	CONR 244:34
S. with the largest	DICK 277:49	Heal the s.	BIBLE 116:67	s. still for the dark	LOWE 540:23
Silent;—hardly a s.	ARNO 36:25	heart is s.	TENN 874:74	so happy as to s. for	BEAU 70:12
When in doubt, s.	HARD 396:96	Hope deferred maketh the heart s.	BIBLE 104:68	telling this with a s.	FROST 352:95
shouting heavens fill with s.	TENN 871:17	How s. one gets of being 'good'	JAMES 450:23	when I s.	SPEN 839:44
S. is not a substitute	STEV 851:10	if you are s.	FORD 343:97	**sighed** even s. offensively	GERH 365:68
thunder of the captains, and the s.	BIBLE 99:19	kingdom of the s.	SONT 834:20	no sooner loved but they s.	SHAK 780:18
tumult and the s. dies	KIPL 490:16	news...would have made me s.	SHAK 772:9	Or s. and looked	THOM 887:1
shouts let me hear thy s.	WORD 959:6	person seldom falls s.	EMER 325:86	S. and looked, and s. again	DRYD 303:34
shovel s. also	KIPL 491:32	promised to do when you are s.	SIGI 821:63	s. as a lover	GIBB 366:1
S. them under	SAND 742:18	riches will leave us s.	EMER 325:83	**sighing** Shivering and s.	PARK 664:13
show backers of the s.	HIRS 419:76	s. and wicked	AUST 46:82	**sighs** Before my s. did dry it	HERB 414:76
do it with no s. of fear	SHAK 775:71	s., and ye visited me	BIBLE 119:36	heaving copious s.	CHEE 218:27
in his simple s.	SHAK 759:88	S. as a parrot	ANON 26:79	ships have my s. drowned?	DONNE 291:28
Last Picture S.	MCMU 557:80	s. at heart	SHAK 780:28	Warring and groans	BURNS 179:34
mock the time with fairest s.	SHAK 796:25	s. of both	JOHN 463:53	**sight** all Wonders in one s.!	CRAS 253:78
No Business Like S. Business	BERL 84:42	s. that surfeit with too much	SHAK 769:74	at first s., a masterpiece	POUND 691:6
really a weird s.	LAWR 513:16	thcream until I'm s.	CROM 255:15	Beauty...at first s.	SHAW 808:34

sigh-tempests

blind the wisest s.	SPEN 839:57
can no more bear to lose s.	ELIOT 315:30
can to s. or thought	MILT 606:51
Charms strike the s.	POPE 685:42
dislike...at first s.	STEE 844:49
Does lecher in my s.	SHAK 793:21
ere he drove out of s.	MOORE 616:65
fell in love...at first s.	POWE 693:43
gleamed upon my s.	WORD 960:19
keen discriminating s.	CANN 197:8
keeps it out of s.	BREC 157:88
long-abused s. at the fountain	MILT 601:20
losing your s.?	SASS 745:87
lost s.	KISS 493:85
many a vanished s.	SHAK 801:47
most beautiful s. in orbit	SCHW 750:93
never to admit them in your s.	AUST 46:62
saddest s. that fortune's inequality	CARL 201:25
sad s. to me	PEPYS 674:99
sense of human s.	MILT 598:50
s....most magical	BART 66:23
s. of Proteus	WORD 961:30
s. of you alone	ROSSO 727:68
s. so touching in its majesty	WORD 959:3
s. to make an old man	TENN 871:6
s. To such a tender ball	MILT 607:85
someliest in s.	DUNB 306:2
sweep him from my s.	SHAK 797:44
thousand years in thy s.	BIBLE 101:93
trees of noblest kind for s.	MILT 604:96
walk by faith, not by s.	BIBLE 127:69
What a s. it were	JONS 468:81
with the blessing of s.	HOLM 423:55
wonderful s.	MACA 544:13
Young men mend not their s.	DONNE 293:76
sigh-tempests nor s.-t. move	DONNE 292:38
sights behold such s.	SHAK 797:50
come to such s. colder	HOPK 428:81
discover s. of woe	MILT 601:35
few more impressive s.	BARR 65:89
most poignant s.	JOHN 457:2
power of many s.	SHEL 812:54
seen some strange s.	HOUS 432:61
s. as youthful poets	MILT 597:48
sounds and smells And s.	BETJ 89:47
sign And it is a good s.	PARN 665:47
In this s. thou shalt conquer	CONS 245:63
it is a bad s.	SARR 744:61
know him by this s.	SWIFT 861:32
might be the s. of something	JENK 454:31
never give out my zodiac s.	PEACE 671:50
outward and visible s.	BOOK 148:81
s. for him to retire	DISR 288:55
s. of an ill-spent youth	SPEN 837:91
s. of an unconscious act	MOND 612:98
s. of the Cross	BOOK 147:77
s. of the self-absorbed	RYBC 736:56
s. or a wonder	BIBLE 95:92
s. that silence heaves	KEATS 475:62
signal Only a s. shown	LONG 536:37
really do not see the s.	NELS 633:13
signal-elm s.-e., that looks on	ARNO 35:16
signals receives s.	UMAS 905:2
significance literal s.	AYER 48:4
significations s. of their words	HOBB 420:97
signify What does it s.	GASK 361:84
signifying S. nothing	SHAK 798:74
signpost all s. and no destination	KRON 500:20
signs merely conventional s.!	CARR 205:29
S. are taken for wonders	ELIOT 317:83
s. might be permanent	JOHN 460:68
s. of a New Age coming?	SMITH 830:39
s. of our own time	CARL 200:78
something like neon s.	UREY 906:42
silence After s.	HUXL 441:69
all in s....stand	CRAB 251:26
answered best with s.	JONS 467:52
Be checked for s.	SHAK 791:53
charity of its s.	EMMET 325:6
conspiracy of s.	JAUR 452:98
darkness again and a s.	LONG 536:37
darkness and s. reign	LEAR 516:28
die in s.	PLATO 682:56
earth...in that eternal s.	MACL 555:42
Elected S., sing to me	HOPK 428:67
eternal s.	WORD 960:11
eternal s. of these...spaces	PASC 667:75
even s., is spray-gunned?	OLSEN 650:46
foster-child of s.	KEATS 478:34
God is the friend of s.	THER 882:84
grand talent pour le s.	CARL 201:32
great beauty of s.	CHAP 214:10
heart...trembles into s.	BYRON 188:76
Indecency's conspiracy of s.	SHAW 808:51
in that s. we the tempest fear	DRYD 299:9
land stares...in a huge s.	SCOTT 751:3
Learning to lie with s.	BYRON 188:93
midnight in that s.	BROW 169:84
most magical moment...is a s.	CRON 256:31
moves upon s.	YEATS 967:37
No voice, but oh! the s. sank	COLE 235:19
occasional flashes of s.	SMITH 831:57
often told in s.	STEV 852:43
pink, spread s.	CARR 202:53
private s. in which we live	PRIT 696:21
roar...on the other side of s.	ELIOT 316:51
sign that s. heaves	KEATS 475:62
s....does not necessarily brood	ELIOT 315:41
s. envious tongues	SHAK 805:54
s. has a sound	KOH 496:33
s. in heaven	BIBLE 131:5
s. in the hills	TENN 873:65
s. in the room	KINS 488:67
s. in the White House	ACHE 2:34
S. is become his mother tongue	GOLD 376:95
s. is most noble till the end	SWIN 863:87
s. is only commendable	SHAK 769:72
S. is the greatest of all persecutions	PASC 668:93
S. is the most perfect expression	SHAW 810:13
S. is the perfectest herald	SHAK 774:30
S. is the virtue of fools	BACON 50:51
s. is your confession	EURI 328:60
s. makes a woman beautiful	SOPH 834:24
S. more musical	ROSS 726:44
s. most offends me	SHAK 774:31
s. of eternity	STEV 852:56
s. of the night	ROSS 725:37
s. of the voice of justice	HAILE 392:16
S. round about his lair	KEATS 477:28
S. ruled this land	DARK 263:47
s. sounds no worse	HOUS 431:41
s. surged softly backward	DELA 271:27
s., told me truths	THOM 885:53
s. until any voice is heard	LEZA 528:81
s. was deafening	KARSH 474:32
small change of s.	MERE 588:28
soft grey s.	JOYCE 470:19
solemn s.	GILB 369:64
Sorrow and s. are strong	LONG 535:26
sounds of s.	DOWD 296:32
speak by s.	PATM 669:24
Stand shadowless like S.	HOOD 426:18
stones of s.	HEAN 404:70
Sunset and s.!	COLUM 238:87
That man's s.	HARDY 396:2
There is no s. in the East	MAUG 582:7
There is s.	BLUN 143:74
The rest is s.	SHAK 785:75
the s. is a lie	YEVT 968:47
thought bullets would s. us	YOUS 969:63
threatened to s. Father Fahrt	OBRI 646:69
Till a s. fell	TENN 876:26
time to keep s.	BIBLE 106:14
'Tis visible s.	ROSS 726:56
true call...is their s.	STARK 843:23
Under all speech there lies a s.	CARL 201:21
upon the wings Of s.	MILT 598:71
widening slowly s. all	TENN 877:44
Wildness and s. disappeared	MACL 555:41
you provide the s.	STOK 855:9
silencer rattlesnake with a s.	ACHE 3:49
silences s. between sentences	LIND 529:12
Success is in the s.	CARM 202:46
silencing no more be justified in s.	MILL 591:3
silent infinite spaces Are still s.	EBER 310:11
in the dark and s. grave	RALE 705:47
kingfisher's wing...is s.	ELIOT 319:43
not enough...to be s.	BRAT 157:78
Out of the S. Planet	LEWIS 526:41
should not be s.	MARIE 571:73
S.;—hardly a shout	ARNO 36:25
s. majority of my fellow Americans	NIXON 640:33
s. manliness of grief	GOLD 376:6
s. sullen peoples	KIPL 491:21
s. was the flock	KEATS 477:14
thereof one must be s.	WITT 951:20
They fell s.	VIRG 913:13
Thou, s. form	KEATS 478:39
t is s., as in Harlow	ASQU 38:92
ways of...keeping s.	WEIZ 928:78
silhouette s. of a brooding soul	SAND 741:12
the s. of greatness	TIME 891:18
silica more dangerous than s.	ROET 722:56
silk blue-shadowed s.	STEV 849:73
S. an' satin	ANON 23:87
s. dresses out of worms	STEV 850:92
s. stockings...within the reach	SCHU 750:79
s. suit	PEPYS 673:86
s., too often hides eczema	CAMUS 196:93
skein of s.	JONS 468:97
that thing of s.	POPE 688:5
silks rainbow s. and satins!	DICK 279:1
When as in s. my Julia goes	HERR 416:16
silkworm Heaven—of s.	MOORE 617:85
sillier I get s. as I get older	DENCH 272:55
silly All families are s.	HOLL 423:53
Lazy and s.	SITW 823:10
s. things do cease to be s.	AUST 46:76
so young and so s.	SPEN 837:4
You were s. like us	AUDEN 43:91
silly-clever poor s.-c. Irishman	SHAW 809:64
Siloam By cool S.'s shady rill	HEBER 406:99
silver apples of gold in pictures of s.	BIBLE 105:93
better than the merchandise of s.	BIBLE 104:55
Between their s. bars!	FLEC 340:38
breast and his arms of s.	BIBLE 111:38
fill it in a s. tassie	BURNS 178:8
Georgian S. goes	MACM 557:75
give thee a s. pound	CAMP 194:65
gold and s.	SHAK 768:56
gold and s.	SHAK 803:5
gold and s. becks me	SHAK 768:56
golden and s.	YEATS 966:12
Just for a handful of s.	BROW 167:18
no s. lining...without its cloud	STER 847:15
S. and gold have I none	BIBLE 124:73
s. cord be loosed	BIBLE 106:36
S. out of the Earth in Peru	PETTY 676:45
S. sails all out of the west	TENN 872:37
s. thimble lies cold	SITW 824:20
s. waves of thy sweet singing	SHEL 814:17
that s. sphere	SHEL 813:93
There's a s. lining	FORD 343:9
thirty pieces of s.	BIBLE 112:61
thirty pieces of s.	BIBLE 119:39
what woman having ten pieces of s.	BIBLE 121:88
Silvia S. in the night	SHAK 759:68
Who is S.?	SHAK 759:71
Simeon S.-quiet evensong	LEVE 525:23
similar s. to independent...states	JAY 453:1
similarity science is not just any s.	WILS 948:52
simile authors of s. and metaphor	NASH 631:81
simple as s. as possible	EINS 314:91
beliefs...whether s. or complex	DURK 308:30
business is very s.	GATES 361:90
God Himself is s.	UPDI 906:41
good and s.	VAZD 910:43
Happiness is pretty s.	BROWN 164:39
Life was s.	HOPP 429:3
nature...runs on such s. things	FONT 342:74
no vice so s.	SHAK 770:3
pure and s., beyond	WILL 946:14
s. great ones gone	TENN 876:20
s. question	GRAV 383:39
S. truth	SHAK 801:59
s. words,...in a complicated way	DUFF 305:84
spoil her s. plots	HOLME 423:54
the situation is not as s.	FOLL 341:71
Truth is too s.	SAND 741:10
truth...never s.	WILDE 941:98
understanding unto the s.	BIBLE 103:79
whether they be wise or s.	SCHW 751:94
simples compounded of many s.	SHAK 779:5
simpleton revolutionary s.	LEWIS 527:67
simplicities totalitarian s.	LYND 543:92
simplicity Cultivate s., Coleridge	LAMB 505:77
die out for want of s.	POUND 692:20
hate American s.	JAMES 451:57
Her bygone s.	HARDY 397:9
makes s. a grace	JONS 467:60
miscalled s.	SHAK 801:59

sins

Physics is…a search for s.	BRYS 171:15
reduce complexity to s.	JAMES 451:65
s. cannot endure for long	DELA 271:22
s. of their end	FUSE 356:92
s. of this clause of Catch-22	HELL 407:27
s. or with severity	ARNO 35:10
S., without variety	HOGA 422:40
Success…founded on s.	BEAV 71:33
simplification s. of the human	FORS 344:39
simplified my life is much s.	CHUR 226:7
simplifies s. and clarifies	STRA 856:36
simplify ability to s.	HOFF 422:31
s. the points to myself	HOME 425:96
simply play it s.	CHEK 218:16
simulacrum sun itself is but the dark s.	BROW 166:83
simulation A good s., be it…myth	PAGE 659:15
simultaneity long sweetness of the s.	ASHB 37:59
sin All manner of s.	BIBLE 117:84
All s. tends to be addictive	AUDEN 44:18
almost a s. of abstinence	DRYD 304:44
as a carnal s.	THOM 887:74
beauty is only s. deep	SAKI 739:50
before man knew how to s.	BEHN 75:23
bellows blows up s.	SHAK 798:81
Can cunning s. cover	SHAK 774:51
cause of plagues is s.	WHITE 936:61
curiosity becomes a s.	FRAN 347:85
discharge from s. and error	ELIOT 321:90
dreadful record of s.	DOYLE 297:59
eldest child of s.	WEBS 926:37
Eve made Adam s.	MARG 570:63
every mortal s.	WILS 947:38
Excepting Original S.	CAMP 194:68
fat cats…without s.	PECK 672:62
fight…against s.	BOOK 148:77
filth that attends conviction for s.	BUNY 174:73
glaring s. of omission	OSLER 656:90
grief and s. of idleness	MELV 585:53
Guilty of dust and s.	HERB 413:65
hate, vertue, and s.	MALO 563:17
Hatred is always a s.	MUNRO 625:51
He that is without s.	BIBLE 123:38
He that lives in s.	BUNY 174:84
hold it half a s.	TENN 873:58
how oft shall my brother s.	BIBLE 118:14
If any man s.	BIBLE 130:78
If it be a s.	SHAK 776:87
If we say that we have no s.	BIBLE 130:77
imagine to remove s.	MILT 600:14
in s. did my mother conceive me	BIBLE 101:71
Is it s. To rush	SHAK 795:78
law of s. and death	WESL 932:65
lead him into debauchery and s.	OFLA 647:98
living in s.	HERB 412:39
lose the s., yet keep the sense	POPE 686:49
more unpopular forms of s.	BRIN 159:25
most inhibited s. in the canon	SHAK 791:56
neither s. nor shame	ROCHE 719:1
neither s. nor shame	STER 849:53
no s. but ignorance	MARL 572:7
no s. but to be rich	SHAK 768:53
not a s. to be rich	CONN 242:81
Nothing emboldens s. so much	SHAK 791:79
not so vile a s.	SHAK 775:73
only one real s.	LESS 524:96
palace of sweet s.	KEATS 476:7
patched with s.	SHAK 785:87
polygamy was made a s.	DRYD 301:63
real s. against life	PORT 690:74
regions of s. and falsity	MILT 600:11
Repentance…want of power to s.	DRYD 304:53
researches in original s.	PLOM 682:73
Ring out…the s.	TENN 875:96
scandal is…worse than the s.	MARG 570:66
several s. to every sense	VAUG 909:35
Shall we continue in s.	BIBLE 125:11
s. and inconvenience	WALK 917:35
s. and nothing more	SEXT 758:43
S. has many tools	HOLM 424:69
S. if thou wilt	CHUR 224:56
s. in private is not to s.	MOLI 611:78
s. is ever before me	BIBLE 100:71
s. is the cause	JULI 471:41
s., my soul. Lo-lee-ta	NABO 628:4
sinner and s. boldly	LUTH 542:70
s. of whisky	SPARK 835:64
s. purged	BIBLE 107:55
S.'s rotten trunk	COWP 251:5
s. the double cure	TOPL 894:61
s. to keep a sinful oath	SHAK 760:1
s. to kill a mockingbird	LEE 518:87
s. to swear unto s.	SHAK 760:1
s. until I blow up!	THOM 884:42
s. which doth so easily beset us	BIBLE 129:43
s. which preaches virtue	MARI 571:86
s. will find you out	BIBLE 94:86
s. With statisticians	AUDEN 44:23
s. ye go by two and two	KIPL 490:1
Some rise by s.	SHAK 787:54
sometimes s. is a pleasure	BYRON 189:99
Stand in awe, and s. not	BIBLE 99:29
sulky lips were shaped for s.	BETJ 89:42
Sure it is no s.	SHAK 788:68
taketh away the s. of the world	BIBLE 122:19
that I might not s.	BIBLE 103:25
That noble S.	MAND 565:65
this ambrosial s.	BYRON 189:98
'Tis no s. for a man	SHAK 770:30
To shave the beard is a s.	IVAN 448:80
to s. our biased nature leans	DRYD 301:68
triumph over death and s.	SPEN 839:43
triumph over death and s.	SPEN 839:46
unconsciousness of s.	CHES 221:87
wages of s. is death	BIBLE 125:13
what heinous s.	SHAK 769:90
Where s. abounded	BIBLE 125:10
Wilt thou forgive that s.	DONNE 293:65
world, to offer for their s.	MARV 576:87
worst s. towards our fellow creatures	SHAW 807:98
Sinatra ask S. to stop singing	KING 486:17
S.'s voice was highly valued	FRIE 351:70
sincere I am s.	SHAW 809:66
s. friend or a s. enemy	HUGO 437:58
sincerely Go to hell. Yours s.	ELLI 323:27
sincerity A little s. is a dangerous belief in their s.	WILDE 940:59
belief in their s.	TWAIN 902:33
Crystal s.	HOPK 428:66
S. is all that counts	DRIB 299:5
test of your s.	BENN 81:70
walk with s. and dignity	WAITE 916:6
sinecure gives no man a s.	POUND 691:7
sinew Bracing brain and s.	KING 487:44
sinews lay s. upon you	BIBLE 111:37
s., grow not instant old	SHAK 781:66
S. of concord	FORD 343:1
s. of war	CICE 227:32
Stiffen the s.	SHAK 775:74
sinewy s. brown men	PRIE 695:95
sinfulness saints aware of their own s.	BLOOM 143:65
sing allow them to s. and to write	MAZA 583:28
Bow themselves when he did s.	SHAK 804:44
Can't act. Can't s.	ANON 24:15
charmingly sweet you s.!	LEAR 516:36
crow doth s. as sweetly	SHAK 770:24
cry or s., justice must	MARIE 571:74
in ev'ry corner s.	HERB 413:58
Let me s. of thee	HUXT 443:14
let us s. unto the Lord	BIBLE 102:1
let us s. unto the Lord	BOOK 149:30
might not s. of Love?	SCOTT 752:11
people do not s.	AUDEN 43:5
S….Booh to you—	GILB 369:44
s., alang wi' me	SKIN 825:50
s….a little off-key	MILL 593:52
s. both high and low	SHAK 785:92
s. giving opinions	HERN 415:93
s. in September	KEND 480:85
s. in the choir	KINN 488:62
S. joyfully to God	BIBLE 133:33
s. like a hillbilly	WILL 944:70
s. myself	WHIT 937:90
s. of brooks	HERR 415:99
s….of Heaven	HERR 415:98
s. of Time or Eternity	TENN 877:63
S. on, with hymns	BETJ 88:15
S. to the Lord	SCOT 755:88
S. unto the Lord a new song	BOOK 149:12
suffers little birds to s.	SHAK 760:29
that in me s. no more	MILL 592:25
That s., and singing	MILT 600:95
The way you s. off key	GERS 365:76
What are you going to s.?	MELBA 584:43
whereat I weep and s.	SURR 860:98
work goes on merrily, when folks s.	BICK 133:50
Yanks began to s.	ANON 24:9
Singapore S. you don't volunteer	LEE 519:92
singe That it do s.	SHAK 804:36
singeing s. of…Spain's beard	DRAKE 298:86
singer aboriginal…s. of America electric s.?	CHOC 222:25
electric s.?	SEGO 756:4
I am like an opera s.	MEAT 584:33
none hear Beside the s.	LAND 507:30
Stop thine ear against the s.	SCOTT 754:64
There lived a s.	SWIN 864:7
singers have known s.	HERN 414:93
not the work of other s.	SINA 822:88
singing ask Sinatra to stop s.	KING 486:17
burst out s.	SASS 745:92
come before his presence with s.	BIBLE 102:4
delight in s., tho' none hear	LAND 507:30
Horse riding is a perfect comparison with s.	PAVA 670:36
Praise for the s.!	FARJ 330:19
silver waves of thy sweet s.	SHEL 814:17
s. aloud	SHAK 793:19
s. each morning out of each night	CUMM 258:64
s. in the rain	FREED 349:42
s. in the wilderness	FITZ 337:69
S. is delightful to nature	BYRD 186:21
S. is like going to a party	CHER 218:28
S., it's the same thing	CARU 207:59
S. so rarely	SCOTT 754:63
s. still dost soar	SHEL 813:91
sweeter than s.	KEND 480:85
single become a s. war	GUST 390:3
beggar-woman and s.	ELIZ 321:98
come not s. spies	SHAK 784:51
continued s.	GOLD 376:89
Nothing in the world is s.	SHEL 813:78
s. in the field	WORD 960:18
s. man in possession	AUST 45:53
s….not such a fearful disaster	ZHANG 969:7
single-parent s.-p. family	ELLW 323:39
sings instead of dying, he s.	BENC 78:11
waking till she s.	LYLY 543:83
singular Is it not s.	TROL 898:47
So s. in each particular	SHAK 799:20
singularity affect a s. in that article	SHER 817:74
s. in a desire	DONNE 293:77
S. is almost invariably a clue	DOYLE 297:50
things s. abhors most, s. and vulgarity	HAZL 403:35
sinister derk and straucht and s.	YOUNG 968:53
s., the malignant	MACD 550:40
sink good night, or s. or swim	SHAK 771:35
Not gross to s.	SHAK 762:84
s. her, split her in twain!	TENN 879:98
sinkhole Hollywood…a s.	MAMET 564:34
sinking kind of alacrity in s.	SHAK 773:12
s., a sickening of the heart	POE 683:80
s. middle class	ORWE 663:1
swimming toward a s. ship	YARB 965:1
sinned all have s.	BIBLE 125:6
have s. [Sind]	NAPI 629:36
More s. against	SHAK 792:7
people s. against	COMP 239:6
s. against my gods	FORD 343:94
would have s. incessantly	ROBI 718:85
sinner converteth the s.	BIBLE 130:63
dead s. revised and edited	BIER 135:91
make of…her a s.	CONG 241:78
please my ghost, forgive some s.	MENC 586:85
s. and sin boldly	LUTH 542:70
s….with no dinner	RANS 707:73
who is that young s.	HOUS 433:81
sinners believe themselves to be s. combination s.	PASC 667:90
combination s.	WILD 943:49
for favoured s. slain	WESL 932:64
for we are s. all	SHAK 759:92
God and s. reconciled	WESL 931:58
miserable s.	BOOK 146:46
s. before the Lord	BIBLE 92:17
s.; of whom I am chief	BIBLE 129:17
s. on this part of Broadway	RUNY 732:62
s. shall be converted unto thee	BIBLE 101:73
s. to repentance	BIBLE 116:63
s. to repentance	BIBLE 119:50
standeth in the way of s.	BIBLE 99:25
While we were yet s.	BIBLE 125:9
Why do s.' ways prosper?	HOPK 429:95
wouldst thou be a breeder of s.?	SHAK 783:10
sins believes anyone s. willingly	PLATO 682:58

Sioux

confess our manifold s.	BOOK 146:31	Teach us to s. still	ELIOT 319:24	lacking s. of a sonnet	SIDN 820:59
cover the multitude of s.	BIBLE 130:71	Though I s. down now	DISR 287:22	less s. to love	SKEL 825:40
executor To all my s.	WEBS 926:32	we s. down and weep	WALP 919:73	Little s., a little heart	ROSS 727:66
fashions all s. on him	WEBS 927:50	You must s. down	HERB 413:66	men—the s.	ROOS 724:12
Forgiveness of s.	BOOK 146:31	**sitting** s. in the last row	KAUF 474:34	my Courage and S.	BUNY 174:83
from the bondage of s.	BHAG 90:78	strut s. down	REST 711:63	no s. involved	DIMA 286:97
hate of s. that grow	SURR 860:2	**situation** Beautiful for s.	BIBLE 100:70	S. comes so slow	DAVI 264:76
hath not dealt with us after our s.	BIBLE 102:7	conscious of an uncomfortable s.	DICK 281:60	s. is measured today	ROGE 722:66
hide a multitude of s.	BIBLE 130:63	faith that even in this lousy s.	DICK 277:33	s. of a solved crossword puzzle	SAND 742:36
manifold s. and wickedness	BOOK 146:31	false definition of the s.	MERT 589:54	s. to move mountains	HOFF 421:24
manifold s. and wickedness	BOOK 147:67	find yourself in an odd s.	HEYE 417:39	store of s.	DYER 309:49
no rules...Only s.	CAPRA 198:33	only improvement...in her s.	ALTH 15:13	Thy s. to poet	SHEL 814:98
not the constant thought of their s.	BLOOM 143:65	pleasant s. of having no fear	CUMM 257:49	use all your s.	CROM 255:21
oldest s. the newest kind of ways?	SHAK 773:98	quarrelling about its relative s.	AUST 46:61	wounded by its own s.	KELL 479:66
Other s. only speak	WEBS 927:56	s. at the lighthouse	DICK 278:62	**skilled** s. in the practice	JOHN 456:72
pouring out one's s.	FIRB 336:51	s. excellent, I am attacking	FOCH 341:67	**skills** Reagan...lacked...s.	ONEI 651:77
present us with all other s.	WEBS 926:38	The healthiest s. in England	KING 488:50	s. that mistresses offer	WYLIE 964:50
privilege more s.	SHIR 819:17	the s. is not as simple	FOLL 341:71	unemployed...not have the s.	CALL 192:28
propitiation for our s.	BIBLE 130:82	thirty-seventh dramatic s.	JARRY 452:96	**skin** after my s. worms destroy	BIBLE 98:8
save his people from their s.	BIBLE 113:14	vanity of person and of s.	AUST 47:86	Can the Ethiopian change his s.	BIBLE 110:19
season of snows and s.	SWIN 836:83	**situations** comparable s.	KISS 493:84	color of one's s.	BALD 56:15
shed...for the remission of s.	BIBLE 119:40	s....make them witty	DIDE 284:59	colour of his s.	MAND 565:56
s. are attempts to fill voids	WEIL 928:72	**Sitwells** S. belong to the history	LEAV 517:51	colour of his s.	MANS 568:14
s. of my youth	BIBLE 100:48	**six** hold you s. to four	ROCH 719:4	except his bare s.	WHITE 935:45
s. of the whole world	BOOK 147:71	Rode the s. hundred	TENN 875:11	his electrical s.	SMART 826:63
s. that I had never committed	WILDE 940:53	Rode the s. hundred	TENN 875:12	Is my somber flesh and s.	CULL 257:45
s. were scarlet	BELL 77:71	Rode the s. hundred	TENN 875:13	Language is a s.	BART 66:27
s., which are many	BIBLE 120:75	s. hundred threescore and s.	BIBLE 132:11	leave some s. on	KHRU 485:93
taken away my s.	WESL 932:65	S. inches is perfectly adequate	SPARK 836:70	never knows the colour of the s.	GEOR 364:56
though your s. be as scarlet	BIBLE 107:50	S. percent unemployment	PASS 668:97	painted s. contents the eye?	SHAK 762:75
thy s. Do run	WEBS 926:39	twelve nights when I was s.	THOM 884:46	pin...punctures my s.	ANON 24:13
visit the s. of the fathers	BOOK 147:59	**sixpence** precious little for s.	PUNCH 699:77	scar that whiter s.	SHAK 790:39
weep for her s.	CARY 207:64	shot at for s.	DIBD 276:28	s. and shell of things	VAUG 909:33
Ye that...repent you of your s.	BOOK 147:66	Whoso has s. is sovereign	CARL 200:91	s. black or white	WELTY 930:46
Sioux S. owned the world	SITT 823:93	**sixth** don't go to the s.	KENN 482:43	s. bristles so	HOUS 432:74
sip can't be tasted in a s.!	DICK 279:91	wonder that is the s. sense	LAWR 514:86	s....depended most on poetry	SIDN 820:53
sipped s. no sup	GILB 370:70	**sixty** Now that I am s.	UPDI 906:36	S. for s.	BIBLE 98:92
sir Dear S. or Madam	ELLI 323:27	s. staring me in the face	THUR 890:91	s. is a different shade	HAMM 395:67
sire from the s. the son shall hear	SCOTT 752:27	When I'm s. four	LENN 522:53	s. of my teeth	BIBLE 98:7
S. of an immortal strain	SHEL 815:28	**size** actual s. of man	SCHU 750:71	s. of progress	SOYI 835:59
siren potions have I drunk of s. tears	SHAK 802:81	s. of sums of money	HUXL 442:96	skull beneath the s.	ELIOT 317:77
sirens S. Dear me! s.	DICK 279:9	s....of the human head	SCHR 759:66	sofa upholstered in panther s.	PLOM 682:73
sires Land of my s.!	SCOTT 753:17	upon one of ordinary s.	LAND 506:28	sweated through his apostolic s.	BYRON 190:32
Sisera mother of S. looked out	BIBLE 95:12	**skates** climbing...wearing roller s.	DEAN 267:41	take the s. from the arm	ELIOT 319:48
sissiness old fears about our s.	WHITE 934:27	**skating** mind s. circles	FROST 353:24	walking miracle, my s.	PLATH 681:31
sissy called a s. by the neighborhood kids	WILL 945:95	s. over thin ice	EMER 324:62	What I like is s.	RENO 711:55
sister always be the s. of France	HUGO 437:59	**Skegness** S. is so bracing	ANON 24:4	**skin-deep** Most games are s.-d.	ARLO 32:33
as handsome as my s.	KING 488:51	**skein** s. of silk	JONS 468:97	**skinning** s. your customers	KHRU 485:93
Bless you, S.	BEHAN 74:11	**skeleton** carcass And a s.	TRAH 895:83	**skinny** Nothing tastes as good as s. feels	MOSS 622:82
dear S.!...death's bride	WORD 961:47	**skeletons** bursting with s.	ORWE 654:33	S. cooks can't be trusted	ANON 26:95
garden inclosed is my s.	BIBLE 107:46	two s. copulating	BEEC 73:68	**skins** black s. don't chafe	LOWE 539:6
gentler s. Woman	BURNS 178:93	**skelp** s. across her backside	ANON 25:35	confinement inside our own s.	WILL 945:98
Innocence thy S. dear!	MARV 577:2	**sketch** first rude s.	KIPL 490:97	covered with the s. of bats	DRAY 299:1
marrying our own s.	ROCHE 719:1	s. from nature	CONS 244:59	lower classes had such white s.	CURZ 260:6
my s. Death	FRAN 347:98	**sketches** s. should prove	MOOD 615:54	sisters under their s.!	KIPL 490:12
no friend like a s.	ROSS 725:38	strong, manly, spirited s.	AUST 46:80	s. fewer than any other human	CURR 259:90
Nor a s., nor a brother	MARG 570:61	**skew** take the truth and just s. it	PARV 666:61	**skipper** get a skeely s.	BALL 59:69
O s. swallow	SWIN 863:79	**ski** cardinal s. badly	JOHN 456:77	**skipping** art of s.	JAMES 451:68
praise a s. to a s.	KIPL 489:69	**skies** beautiful for spacious s.	BATES 67:53	S. rivulet	GILB 368:36
s. hath left me to serve alone?	BIBLE 121:83	beneath the sodden s.	MUIR 624:17	**skips** three s. on the floor	BALL 59:62
s. is given to government	DICK 282:4	blown about the s.	TENN 873:64	**skirmish** trivial s.	GRAV 382:24
S. of the Stars	PATM 669:21	Can I expound the s.?	DICK 283:28	**skirt** blessings of a good thick s.	KING 488:57
s. to the dream	BAUD 68:68	cloudless climes and starry s.	BYRON 189:80	destiny to wear a s. in all countries	IZZA 448:83
third s., Morgan le Fey	MALO 562:5	dark and the empty s.	MACC 548:8	insult of each shabby s.	DONO 293:28
trying to violate your s.	STRA 857:42	Deserts...and different s.	SACK 737:11	likes a woman in a s.	HEPB 412:26
your shadow-s.	WRIG 963:70	God is in the s.	SHAW 808:44	shortening or lengthening of a s.	SCHI 747:22
sisterhood sense of s.	WELD 928:82	knowledge of the boundless s.	BYRON 189:94	**skittish** s. Fortune's hall	SHAK 787:36
sisters brave and battered s.	PRIE 695:86	look, look up at the s.!	HOPK 428:75	whiffling, s., snappish	HAZL 403:44
bunches of clingy sob s.	PAGL 659:19	love of...dim s.	MACK 553:10	**skittishness** merry-go-round of s.	HARDY 396:3
men with s. dear	HOOD 426:31	raised a mortal to the s.	DRYD 303:35	**skittles** all porter and s.	DICK 278:45
s., and his cousins	GILB 368:33	s. are not cloudy	HIGL 418:54	Life isn't all beer and s.	HUGH 436:46
s. under their skins!	KIPL 490:12	s. are painted with unnumbered	SHAK 777:26	not all Beer and S.	STEV 853:81
twa s. in a bower	BALL 58:52	s. of history hurrying	SASS 746:95	**Skottes** War yit with the S.	MINOT 608:90
weird s. hand in hand	SHAK 795:2	s. of Texas or Nebraska	MCMU 557:83	**skulduggery** skunkoil s.	MACD 550:39
Sistine S....painted basic white	BROWN 164:36	these November s.	FREE 350:49	**skulked** s. behind the laws	DRYD 302:75
Sisyphus imagine that S. is happy	CAMUS 195:86	though the s. may fall	MANS 568:13	**skull** had not such a s.	SWIN 864:11
sit cannot s. on it	INGE 445:26	under Ionian s.	SHEL 816:47	hidden auditorium of his s.	STER 757:32
has the time to s. down	HUGO 437:84	watcher of the s.	KEATS 475:60	no more of her than the s.	BIBLE 98:81,
nobody can tell you when to s. down	EISE 314:5	When morning gilds the s.	CASW 208:82	penetrate some thick s.	SARD 743:51
s. around so much doing nothing	STEIN 845:68	**skiing** garment that made s.	ANON 25:46	s. beneath the skin	ELIOT 317:77
s. back hoping that some day	REAG 708:2	S. is a battle	KILLY 486:8	s. that housed white angels	SASS 746:2
S. down before fact	HUXL 443:3	**skill** art is not...merely a s.	FRIE 351:76	the furniture inside his s.	BYATT 186:20
s. down with trouble	GLAS 374:45	combination of s. and force	BURKE 176:38	well-dressed s.	VIEI 913:7
s. right here by me	LONG 536:41	depends on...the author's s.	QUIL 702:14	**Skullion** S. had little use	SHAR 806:70
s. thou a patient looker-on	QUAR 701:6	drowns for want of s.	SHAK 763:97	**skunk** blaming a s. for stinking	ORWE 654:43
s. up and take notice	BENN 80:54	favour to men of s.	BIBLE 106:29	pissing contest with that s.	EISE 314:97
		greater part of the s., dexterity	SMITH 827:75	wolf, the hyena, and the s.?	BRYAN 170:98

sleep

skuttle put me in mind of the s. fish	ADDI 7:43	tops of s.	GILL 370:77	escapes s. except by a...revolution	LACL 503:40
sky About us in the s.	HOUS 431:44	**slab** Beneath this s.	NASH 631:75	Extreme freedom...to extreme s.	PLATO 682:67
above, the vaulted s.	CLARE 228:55	**slabs** Ice-scratched s.	SNYD 832:91	freedom is s.	ORWE 655:73
Above us only s.	LENN 521:46	**slack** observing me grow s.	HERB 413:65	nothing so dreadful as voluntary s.	DICK 284:58
and in the s.	MCCR 548:11	**slacks** girls in s. remember dad	BETJ 88:35	perfect condition of s.	ASTE 39:5
bed of daffodil s.	TENN 876:25	**slag** measureless grossness and the s.	WHIT 938:12	perished in hopeless s.	OCON 646:82
belonging as much to s. as to earth	CARR 202:53	**slag-heap** post-industrial s.-h.	DRAB 298:83	S. broke the world	MORR 620:58
blue ethereal s.	ADDI 7:40	**slain** he...that's s.	BUTL 185:85	S.'s a thing thet depends	LOWE 539:6
blue s. of spring	ALLI 14:7	O s. and spent	SWIN 864:8	s. to a pattern	NIN 639:26
boats were tossed S.-high	LOWE 540:18	s. the Earl of Murray	BALL 58:53	s. was originally established	DOUG 296:27
Brain...wider than the S.	DICK 284:39	s. think he is s.	EMER 325:85	S....weed that grows	BURKE 175:20
bridal of the earth and s.	HERB 414:80	s. this year in Europe	WALP 919:81	sold off into s.	TRUTH 900:5
bright reversion in the s.	POPE 685:44	**Slaka** In S., sex is just politics	BRAD 154:31	soon as they got out of s.	WALK 917:38
clean the s.	ELIOT 319:48	**slam** not a s. at you	FITZ 338:97	state of S.	GILL 370:81
close against the s.	HOOD 426:23	**slamming** s. down his silly curtain	SALI 740:86	thought s. tolerable	UPDI 905:19
color of the s.	CRANE 253:73	**slander** civic s.	TENN 875:96	worst possible kind of s.	BARA 63:44
common s.	GRAV 382:21	devised this s.	SHAK 790:36	**slaves** all women are born s.	ASTE 39:5
die in yon rich s.	TENN 872:40	one to s. you	TWAIN 903:83	asking s. what was going on	ALME 14:10
Dragging the whole s.	FROST 352:92	s.'s venomed spear	SHAK 764:30	barbarous traffic in s.	PITT 679:5
evening is spread out against the s.	ELIOT 316:60	S. Valentine With falsehood	SHAK 759:69	Britons never will be s.	THOM 887:97
flaming from th' ethereal s.	MILT 601:33	To speak no s.	TENN 877:56	Englishmen never will be s.	SHAW 807:24
forehead of the morning s.	MILT 600:94	writs for libel and s.	PROF 697:28	Force made the first s.	ROUS 729:11
from yon azure s.	WORD 957:72	**slanders** secondarily they are s.	SHAK 774:55	freemen or s.	WASH 921:27
gaze into sea or s.	MELV 585:69	**slang** All s. is metaphor	CHES 220:53	Gaza at the mill with s.	MILT 607:82
Give me the clear blue s.	HAZL 403:40	S. is a language	SAND 742:31	happy freemen, are the only s.	MASS 581:79
glorious land above the s.	HILL 418:56	S. is vigorous and apt	GALS 358:52	impart to wives and s.	DRYD 301:64
great bowl of the s.	MCMU 557:83	s....was...out of date	GREE 386:17	intercourse between tyrants and s.	GOLD 376:94
held the s. suspended	HOUS 432:72	**slant** Truth...tell it s.	DICK 284:47	martyred s. of Time	BAUD 68:73
hollowing out the s.	BETJ 89:46	**slap-dash** s.-d. down in the mouth	CONG 240:29	only fit for the s.	FLET 340:51
Is a golden s.	HAMM 394:65	**slaps** if someone s. you	KHRU 485:95	our posterity made s.	CROM 255:19
isolation of the s.	STEV 849:71	**slate** split in soft s.	BUNT 173:66	poor s. with weary footsteps	SHEL 815:45
keen city in the s.	CUMM 257:56	write his thoughts upon a s.	HOOD 426:38	professional players are soccer s.	CHAR 216:46
Let the s. rain potatoes	SHAK 773:14	**slats** roof, instead of s.	DRAY 299:1	remain no legal s.	MILL 592:16
light, she said, not of the s.	NEIL 633:10	**slaughter** counted as sheep for the s.	BIBLE 100:66	ruling them like s.	SHEL 814:18
lonely sea and the s.	MASE 580:50	Cuinchy...was a s. yard	BLUN 143:77	S. and Slavery	ANON 23:96
lustre in its s.	SHEL 812:57	face such s.	WALC 916:9	s. that dig the golden ore	CRAB 252:32
meet the s.	TENN 869:77	'I am going to s. you'	TRAV 895:86	s. we'll ever be	DAVIS 266:8
milky s.	YEATS 965:6	like lions to the roaring s.	CUMM 257:59	sons of former s.	KING 487:31
no bright sign in the s.	HUSS 440:39	one who delights in s.	LAO 508:62	soul of the s.	GILL 370:87
No more to use the s.	JEFF 453:13	perpetrators of Tuesday's s.	SONT 834:23	two kinds of s.	ILLI 445:23
no s. could squeak through	PLATH 681:34	s. of a thousand platitudes	ORTE 652:2	tyrants...only want s.	WOLL 953:88
November's s. is chill	SCOTT 752:18	s. of plague, pestilence and famine	SHAW 807:26	voluntarily to submit to be s.	PITT 679:5
nursling of the s.	SHEL 813:77	s. will ensue	CONG 240:26	wholly s. or wholly free	DRYD 303:13
obstacles...from the s.	MANC 564:48	wade through s. to a throne	GRAY 384:71	women into darling little s.	MILLS 595:7
purest s. with brightness	SPEN 838:22	war and mutual s.	MILT 605:25	**Slavs** cause of the S.	WITTE 950:19
rainbow in the s.	WORD 959:98	**slaughterhouse** sheep go to a s.-h.	MACD 549:17	**slay** Though he s. me, yet will I trust	BIBLE 98:4
rainbow in the s.!	TENN 878:74	s. thoughts	SHAK 798:73	**slayer** red s. think he slays	EMER 325:85
sent him down the s.	CORY 247:8	soul's s.	WEBS 926:38	**slaying** s. of a beautiful hypothesis	HUXL 443:6
Shoulder the s., my lad	HOUS 432:65	**slaughtering** s. one another	GUIB 389:86	**slays** s. More than you rob	SHAK 791:82
s. cannot have two suns	CHIA 222:13	**slaughters** S. a thousand waiting	SHAK 799:8	**sleave** ravelled s. of care	SHAK 797:34
s. changes when they are wives	SHAK 780:12	**slave** act a s. to limit	SHAK 787:35	**sledgehammer** S. sentimentality	KENT 483:51
s. grows darker	CHES 220:80	adult s.	GREER 387:43	**sleek** curse...upon the s. upstart	RANS 707:69
s. is darkening like a stain	AUDEN 42:70	Being your s.	SHAK 801:55	**sleeket** Wee, s., cowrin, tim'rous	BURNS 177:77
s. is red	BIBLE 117:5	Be not the s. of words	CARL 200:93	**sleek-headed** S.-h. men	SHAK 776:12
s. is the limit	SHUL 819:30	economic equivalent of the s.	WIEN 939:28	**sleep** ability to get a good night's s.	WILS 948:70
s., Never before so beautiful	WORD 958:77	greatest of mankind...my s.	DRYD 301:57	afford much comfort in s.	BROW 166:86
s. no height above him	ATWO 41:34	gross plodding s.	WEBS 926:35	awaked out of his s.	BIBLE 93:33
s. snivels green snot	MITS 610:59	has been s. to thousands	SHAK 789:18	azure-lidded s.	KEATS 477:24
s....Spread like a rosy ocean	BYRON 190:9	made them s. masters	MORR 620:58	battening...in his s.	TENN 869:72
stared into the s.	HODG 421:21	man...not passion's s.	SHAK 783:22	bleary eyed for lack of s.	DAUG 263:62
starry s.	GERS 365:79	married woman is a s.	BALZ 60:91	borders of s.	THOM 885:62
star...shining in the s.	WORD 957:62	My father was a s.	ROBE 717:76	break earth's s.	OWEN 658:38
Sunset divides the s.	BYRON 188:60	noble and the s.	SCOTT 753:40	Caged in its s.	SMITH 831:64
there a glimpse of mystic s.	LAWS 514:97	peasant s. am I	SHAK 782:99	calf won't get much s.	ALLEN 14:86
The Sheltering S.	BOWL 153:98	permanently half-s. and half-free	LINC 529:4	Care-charming s.	FLET 340:52
the s. acutest at its vanishing	STEV 850:79	Philosopher!—a fingering s.	WORD 957:65	Cervantes usually puts me to s.	GONZ 378:43
th'eternal spheres and lamping s.	SPEN 838:36	s. has but one master	LABR 502:17	closes soft in s.	STEP 847:11
thread loosened from the s.	ROSS 726:57	S., I have set my life	SHAK 761:56	Come s., O s.	SIDN 820:46
to the wild s.	TENN 875:95	s. in base servility	SHAK 759:81	country...going to s.	RENAN 711:47
triple-towered s.	DAY 267:37	s. morality	NIET 638:13	deep, deep s. of England	ORWE 653:25
true as the s.	KIPL 490:7	s. of some defunct economist	KEYN 484:81	deep House of Commons s.	CHAN 214:7
turrets split the s.	LAND 507:35	s. of the author's mind	GAUG 361:3	dewy-feathered S.	MILT 598:58
under the benign s.	BRON 162:82	s. of the passions	HUME 438:98	doen they only s.	SPEN 838:37
views...the regions of the s.	ENNI 326:17	S. to no sect	POPE 687:91	dreamless, uninvaded s.	TENN 869:71
walking down the s.	GILM 371:96	S. to Prodigality	MAND 565:65	each day dies with s.	HOPK 429:92
western s. in the night	WHIT 938:8	Some cogging, cozening s.	SHAK 790:36	endless—as s.	WILL 946:20
wheeling s.	SNYD 832:91	This yellow s.	SHAK 791:80	full of s.	YEATS 965:7
which prisoners call the s.	WILDE 942:16	Throw duty s.	SHAK 793:15	get a good night's s.	KEEN 478:52
wide and starry s.	STEV 853:62	victim and s. of his action	EMER 325:81	giveth his beloved s.	BIBLE 103:36
will across the s. in stars	LAWR 514:88	worker is the s. of capitalist society	CONN 243:22	go s. if I can	SHAK 778:77
wonderful Southern night-s.	LAWR 513:56	Your Majesty's s.	KISH 493:83	grinning in their s.	LAWR 513:62
yon twelve-winded s.	HOUS 431:49	**slavery** administration of s.	STOWE 856:28	have a nice, quiet s.	CHAM 212:64
Skye over the sea to S.	BOUL 152:92	because they impose s.	RUSS 734:28	haven't been to s. for	WAUGH 923:63
sky-mocker s.-m., rave!	UPDI 905:14	Chains and S.!	BURNS 180:47	immobility, ecstasy, and s.	MARI 570:77
skyscraper growth of the S. School	JOHN 458:26	chains of s.	GRIL 388:69	inhibitions and get some s.	LOOS 536:54
skyscrapers about four s. behind	JOHN 459:35	cowardice perpetuated s.	ROUS 729:11	in his cunning s.	THOM 884:35
New glass s.	TALE 866:15	definition of s.	SWIFT 862:38	in his s. he does little harm	SHAK 791:69

sleeper

In s., afraid	ROET 722:64	never sad but when she s.	SHAK 774:33	s. did my spirit seal	WORD 957:64
in s. old palaces	SHEL 813:81	**sleep-time** silence of the s.-t.	BROW 169:84	s. is more sweet	TENN 870:98
I shall s.	SWIN 864:6	**sleepwalker** assurance of a s.	HITL 420:93	softer than s.	KEND 480:85
I s. like a baby too	POWE 693:56	**sleepy** not s. and…no place	DYLAN 309:57	**slumbers** Golden s. kiss your eyes	DEKK 270:10
lack of s.	GOLD 375:77	**sleeve** ace of joy up his s.	ONDA 650:56	unquiet s.	BRON 162:82
lasting s.	BEAU 71:14	heart on your s.	THAT 881:65	**slums** gay intimacy of the s.	WAUGH 923:67
let me s. a little	MACN 558:1	heart upon my s.	SHAK 788:82	**slush** mush and s.	OWEN 657:23
let me s. alway	COLE 235:22	lacy s. with a bottle of vitriol	WOOL 956:40	pure as the driven s.	BANK 61:13
Lie soft, s. hard	MIDD 590:72	not wear your heart on your s.	WEBS 927:65	**slut** be she s.	SWIFT 863:76
lie where I am and s., s., s.	SHIP 818:14	strip his s.	SHAK 776:90	**smack** some s. of age in you	SHAK 772:71
like unwilling s.	KEATS 475:64	**sleeves** language that rolls up its s.	SAND 742:31	**Small** Here lies…John S.	EGAN 313:65
miles to go before I s.	FROST 352:5	s. rolled	MCCA 547:84	**small** All things both great and s.	COLE 235:20
more in your life except to s.	RHYS 712:74	**sleigh** s., and eight tiny reindeer	MOORE 616:62	design…in a thing so s.	FROST 352:11
Murders the innocent s.	TWAIN 902:63	sprang to his s.	MOORE 616:65	division in a country so s.	DONO 293:81
never s. with anyone	ALGR 13:68	**sleight** admire his s. of hand	BUTL 185:81	do s. things well	GLAS 374:44
night doth summon all to s.?	DRAY 298:92	**slender** kissed her s. hand	TENN 876:22	Man is s.	SCHU 750:74
night to do with s.?	MILT 598:65	**slept** and he s.	TENN 874:89	Microbe is so very s.	BELL 76:55
of Night, but not of S.	THOM 887:7	But while men s.	BIBLE 117:93	S. is Beautiful	SCHU 750:73
One short s. past	DONNE 292:52	s. with his fathers	BIBLE 97:59	S. is Beautiful	SCHU 750:74
O partial s.	SHAK 772:85	**slew** as he was ambitious, I s. him	SHAK 777:36	S. is the worth	WALL 918:55
O s., O gentle s.	SHAK 772:84	dead which he s. at his death	BIBLE 96:20	s. thing…made large	TWAIN 903:71
O S.! the friend of Woe	SOUT 835:51	Who s. them?	SITT 823:93	so s. a thing	ARNO 33:69
O, such another s.	SHAK 795:87	**slice** people want a larger s.	CRIP 254:97	still s. voice	BIBLE 97:67
poets…give their readers s.	POPE 688:32	**sliced** they'd come up s.	TREV 896:7	**smallest** in the s. room of my house	REGER 710:43
poor Indian's s.	KEATS 475:66	**slide** We can s. it	REED 709:27	**small-talk** s.-t. flows from lip	CRAB 252:40
putting the mind to s.	SLOAN 825:54	**sliding** hear time s. past you	RHYS 712:74	**small-talking** s.-t. world	FRY 353:33
quiet s. and a sweet dream	MASE 580:52	**slight** s. all that do	FARQ 330:23	**small-town** s.-t. bourgeois at heart	NABO 629:21
rounded with a s.	SHAK 804:28	**Slightly** S. in Peter Pan	TYNAN 904:3	**smart** Even s. girls do it	SALI 740:79
sang themselves to s.	HODG 421:20	**slime** slimier s.!	BROO 163:1	if we were…very s.	FULF 355:64
shall not all s.	BIBLE 127:62	**slimness** S. Of Despair	NICH 636:73	not s. enough to hide it	REST 711:61
S. after toil	SPEN 838:28	**slimy** s. things did crawl with legs	COLE 235:13	One is s.	GORB 378:50
s. and a forgetting	WORD 959:8	thousand thousand s. things	COLE 235:15	scorn which mocked the s.	ARNO 35:5
s. and a sense of history	WILS 948:72	**slings** and arrows	SHAK 782:97	surety…shall s.	BIBLE 104:65
s. and death differ	TRAH 895:83	**slinkiness** hint of Bacall's s.?	ALLEN 13:77	Wherever s. people work	WOZNI 962:55
S. and rest	TENN 872:37	**slip** gave us all the s.?	BROW 167:14	**smarter** S. than…his colleagues	REST 711:61
S. demands…guilty immunity	BARN 64:61	giving his enemies the s.	STER 848:24	s. than you are	BART 66:29
s. dwell upon thine eyes	SHAK 766:86	s. into something more comfortable	HARL 398:37	Some are s. than others	MARC 570:56
s. Full of sweet dreams	KEATS 476:84	**slippery** real world…is s.	DAY 267:28	thought themselves s.	ATTL 40:47
s. I can get nane	BURNS 178:13	standing is s.	BACON 51:85	**smarts** tyrannizeth in the bitter s.	SPEN 838:35
s. in security	AUNG 45:42	stands upon a s. place	SHAK 768:60	**smeddun** the s. tane	SMITH 831:64
S. is death without	LEBO 517:58	woman's brain: vague, s.	RICH 714:17	**smell** creatures give out a s.	LEES 519:2
S. is sweet to the labouring man	BUNY 174:78	words are s.	ADAMS 5:97	oozy s.	TOLK 893:42
S. is when all the unsorted shuts	GOLD 375:29	**slips** like greyhounds in the s.	SHAK 775:75	shares man's s.	HOPK 428:70
S. no more	SHAK 797:34	**slithy** 'S.' means 'lithe and slimy'	CARR 205:12	s. far worse than weeds	SHAK 802:70
S. no more	SHAK 797:35	**slivers** last s. and shreds of objectivity	CUPI 258:86	s. of steaks	ELIOT 317:70
s. out-of-doors	BIRD 136:8	**sloeblack** s., slow, black	THOM 884:31	s. so sweet	SHAK 771:33
s. provides relief	CHAM 213:71	**slog** with a s. to square leg	JOYCE 470:19	s. the blood of a British man	SHAK 792:12
s. shall neither night nor day	SHAK 795:1	**slogan** democracy is just a s.	GORB 378:46	s. too strong of the lamp	STER 848:29
S., son of the sable Night	DANI 262:31	s. than a genuine goal	LEGU 520:13	sweet keen s.	ROSS 726:54
S., that sometimes shuts	SHAK 767:39	**slogans** our national s.	THUR 891:93	the s. of it	UTTL 907:50
s.…through life	ALBEE 11:29	s.…confused with solutions	BENT 82:7	What a lovely s.	SMITH 827:73
S. to wake	BROW 169:85	**slogged** s. up to Arras	SASS 745:86	would s. as sweet	SHAK 765:80
s. under bridges	FRAN 347:89	**slope** golden ear Imbrown the s.	POPE 686:62	Yes, to s. pork	SHAK 769:82
s. upon ale	FARQ 330:27	That s. through darkness	TENN 874:79	you should s. like dirt	ATWO 41:53
s. when you ain't sleepy	TWAIN 902:52	**slopes** butler's upper s.	WODE 952:55	**smells** faint stale s. of beer	ELIOT 317:71
S. will come when thou art fled	SHEL 816:54	**sloppy** prefer their English s.	SAYE 746:10	measured out by sounds and s.	BETJ 89:47
s. with dogs	WEBS 962:34	**slot** plays s. machines	TRUMP 900:96	painting of sounds, noises and s.	CARRA 202:57
s. with women we do not love	DIDE 285:73	**sloth** ignoble ease, and peaceful s.	MILT 602:60	still s. of sulphur	CHAV 217:3
softer than s.	TENN 870:96	too much time in studies is s.	BACON 53:35	tell me it s. like roses	JOHN 458:51
Still it cried 'S. no more'	SHAK 797:35	when resty is s.	SHAK 803:3	**smelt** And s. so? Pah!	SHAK 784:64
stop it from going to s.	RUSH 732:65	**slothful** Not s. in business	BIBLE 125:25	**smile** by his s., I knew	OWEN 657:33
such as s. o'nights	SHAK 776:12	s. man saith	BIBLE 105:97	Cambridge people rarely s.	BROO 162:95
The poor s. little	OTWAY 656:8	**Slough** friendly bombs…fall on S.	BETJ 88:20	dismiss the past with a s.	LESS 523:91
think of them that s.	CAMP 194:66	**slough** S. of Despond	BUNY 173:73	every fascist a communist s.	SPARK 836:73
Thou art inclined to s.	SHAK 803:12	**slovenly** very drunk and very s.	WYCH 964:1	faint fleeting s.	THUR 890:76
time enough to s.	HOUS 431:36	**slow** but ain't it s.?	HERB 413:53	has a nice s.	GROM 389:78
To die, to s.	SHAK 782:7	clock is always s.	SERV 757:36	heaven-revealing s.	WORD 961:47
together out of s.	MARI 571:82	come he s., or come he fast	SCOTT 752:19	if I s. it happens	TRAV 896:91
wake to s.	ROET 722:59	drinks fast, pays s.	FRAN 348:9	last fading s.	HUXL 442:99
waking from its s.	KIER 485:4	each s. dusk	OWEN 657:26	make a s. go on all fours	MACA 545:39
when you s. you remind me	SASS 745:91	grinds s., but sure	HERB 414:87	of that human s.	HUGO 438:89
Where fain, fain I would s.?	BALL 58:57	s. of speech	BIBLE 93:56	on a s. and a shoeshine	MILL 593:32
Yet a little s.	BIBLE 104:59	takes the music…too s.	SAINT 739:49	should forget and s.	ROSS 726:42
sleeper duty is to arouse the s.	BETH 87:13	telling you to s. down	ANON 25:39	simply watch her s.	SAINT 738:33
never a quiet s.?	TENN 876:32	**slowing** s. down to get a good look	GIBB 367:6	s. and s. and be a villain	SHAK 781:67
sleepers in the diners and s.	SAND 742:15	**slowly** Hurry s.	AUGU 45:37	s. at perils past!	SCOTT 753:36
s. in that quiet earth	BRON 162:82	much easier…than to play it s.	MOZA 623:5	s. at the claims	TENN 871:10
sleepest Thou s. too long	SKEL 824:30	Wisely and s.	SHAK 766:90	s. I could feel in my hip pocket	CHAN 213:77
sleepeth s., and must be wakened	BIBLE 97:62	**sluggard** Go to the ant, thou s.	BIBLE 104:58	s. is often the key	SAINT 738:38
sleeping except s. and resting	TWAIN 904:95	**slugs** silver trails of inebriated s.	JAMES 450:25	s. of heaven	SHAK 804:46
growing…when ye're s.	SCOTT 753:60	**sluice** Grand S., and a high steeple	ANON 22:87	S. or sigh	BARK 63:54
I was s. with the President	REAG 708:99	stop beside the opening s.	CRAB 252:43	So thou would'st s.	MARL 573:13
The s. and the dead	SHAK 797:36	**sluicing** browsing and s.	WODE 951:33	vain tribute of a s.	SCOTT 752:14
wake s., and sleep	MONT 614:29	**slum** if you've seen one city s.	AGNEW 9:19	way your s. just beams	GERS 365:17
sleepless S. as the river	CRANE 253:58	not s. in the country	HALD 392:22	where the s. dwells a little longer	CHAP 214:12
S. with cold	ROSS 727:64	**slumber** neither s. nor sleep	BIBLE 103:31	with a heavenly s.	KIER 485:4
sleeps Money never s.	DOUG 295:17	Seal thy sense in deathly s.	DELA 271:34	**smiled** At me you s.	TENN 871:9

s. with…spontaneity	ACHE	2:31
soldiers he s. at	SASS	745:86
smiler s. with the knyf	CHAU	217:84
smiles charmed it with s.	CARR	206:31
daggers in men's s.	SHAK	797:42
expect to be greeted with s.	BROO	163:8
men with careful s.	LEWIS	527:59
Nae mair your s. can cheer me	COCK	233:82
Seldom he s.	SHAK	776:13
S. awake you when you rise	DEKK	270:30
s. of the people	MARC	570:57
S., tears, of all my life!	BROW	166:98
Their s., Wan as primroses	KEATS	476:90
The robbed that s.	SHAK	789:99
smiling Sex without s.	FRY	354:44
S. at grief	SHAK	786:2
villain with a s. cheek	SHAK	769:84
smilingness a s. assume	BYRON	187:49
smirk serious and the s.	DICK	278:78
s. with his wife	MARI	571:83
smite s. once, and s. no more	MILT	599:89
Smith calling him S.	HOLM	424:76
F E S. is very clever	ASQU	38:91
name were John D S. IV	ROCK	720:34
S.…an over-dressed pirate	LEAC	515:15
S., the name is so poetical	CHES	220:58
smith s. a mighty man	LONG	535:17
Smithfield who brings The S. Muses	POPE	688:29
smithy village s. stands	LONG	535:17
smitten be s. against the other	BIBLE	113:93
may be s., and die	BIBLE	96:44
s. me these three times?	BIBLE	94:83
smog diamonds in the s.	MAIL	560:55
smoke Above the s. and stir	MILT	598:62
blind with s.	SASS	745:82
crowds, her beloved s.	LAMB	505:79
don't s.	CURR	259:95
flavor as hickory s.	MUMF	625:40
Gossip is a sort of s.	ELIOT	316:56
house was filled with s.	BIBLE	107:54
middle page you said: 'Holy s.'	CHRI	223:40
occasionally emitting s.	WHITE	936:58
Oft fire is without s.	SPEN	838:21
or a man who does not s.	STEV	852:37
s. of their torment ascendeth	BIBLE	132:12
s. out at the chimney	SHAK	780:13
smudge of s.	TIME	891:18
smoke-filled men in a s.-f. room	SIMP	822:85
s.-f. room in some hotel	DAUG	263:62
smoker bad taste of the s.	ELIOT	316:56
man in the s.	SAND	742:15
smokes noises…throbbed with s.	CUMM	257:51
smoke-stack salt-caked s.-s.	MASE	580:56
smoking give up s., drinking and loving	FREUD	350:54
not found any s. guns	BLIX	142:58
seed her first a-s.	KIPL	489:82
sit placidly s. his pipe	SHIP	818:14
s. flax shall he not quench	BIBLE	117:82
s. flax shall he not quench	BIBLE	109:86
smooth I am a s. man	BIBLE	92:30
prickly to the s.	MACD	550:40
S. runs the water	SHAK	759:88
true love never did run s.	SHAK	766:17
smudge wears man's s.	HOPK	428:70
Smudges wasn't it naughty of S.	BETJ	89:45
smug hauf o' ts., complacent	SMITH	831:64
s. suppressions of his face	WELLS	930:22
snaffle use the s. and the curb	CAMP	194:51
snail s.'s on the thorn	BROW	167:9
s., which everywhere doth roam	DONNE	292:46
snails horns of cockled s.	SHAK	763:16
snake earth doth like a s. renew	SHEL	816:57
gathering flowers…fears a s.?	DONNE	290:16
greyhound…heeded lyke a s.	BERN	86:80
Like an uneasy s.	WORD	958:86
Once bitten by a s.	DALAI	260:7
perfumed parlor s.	DUNNE	307:21
s. about to devour people	NIXON	640:30
s. lurks in the grass	VIRG	913:22
snake-oil back on the s.-o. standard	VONN	915:53
snakes heard by s. in the grass	MO	610:63
s. with double tongue	SHAK	767:31
snakeskin s.-titles of mining-claims	BENET	79:23
snapper-up s.-u. of…trifles	SHAK	789:75
snare from the s. of the fowler	BIBLE	101:96
I saw the s.	TENN	871:9

s. to Religion	TAYL	868:58
s. to the inhabitants of Jerusalem	BIBLE	107:58
Trial…will be…a s.	DENM	273:72
wha can avoid the fell s.?	BURNS	180:61
snarling s. all before I came	SHAK	761:37
snatched s. from our hands	YOUS	969:64
snaw-wreaths s.-w. in thaw	NAIR	629:33
sneaking 's.'…not to his taste	ANON	23:89
s. piece of imbecility	SCOTT	753:38
sneer celebrated s.	GILB	369:56
s.…like an oyster-knife	ANNAN	19:11
solemn creed with solemn s.	BYRON	187:55
teach the rest to s.	POPE	687:3
sneering without s., teach the rest	POPE	687:3
sneeze it's like having a good s.	LAWR	512:41
sneezed given cocaine but I s.	JOHN	457:93
sneezes beat him when he s.	CARR	203:68
Coughs and s.	ANON	24:24
snigger between a eunuch and a s. entertaining s.	FIRB	336:55
	GILB	369:56
snob admires mean things is a S.	THAC	880:31
s.…on principle	SHAW	809:90
snobbery S.…a form of despair	BROD	160:38
S. with Violence	BENN	80:46
snobs effete corps of impudent s.	AGNEW	9:94
snooker Billiards is very similar to s.	DAVIS	266:4
staying married and playing s.	REAR	709:18
snore s. upon the flint	SHAK	803:3
snorting S. and sporting	SITW	823:98
snot sky snivels green s.	MITS	610:59
snotgreen s. sea	JOYCE	470:21
snout as wise a s. on	FERG	333:84
snouts get your s. in the trough	WEIG	927:68
snow beautiful in their s.	RUSK	732:85
bells, across the s.	TENN	875:75
birds sit brooding in the s.	SHAK	763:28
chaste as unsunned s.	SHAK	803:95
cold climate, and frost and s.	SOUT	835:42
dark over the s.	THOM	885:65
deep s. piled above	BRON	162:76
few acres of s.	VOLT	914:36
hail, or rain, or any s.	TENN	878:87
Hidden in wonder and s.	SCOTT	751:3
ice and wondrous…black s.	SHAK	768:46
icicles and bitter s.!	MALL	562:78
If s. be white	SHAK	802:83
kindle fire with s.	SHAK	759:65
last streak of s.	TENN	875:98
locks are like the s.	BURNS	179:16
made whiter than s.	BIBLE	132:31
'mid s. and ice	LONG	535:21
new-fallen s.	MOORE	616:62
pale virgin shrouded in s.	BLAKE	140:11
pink bonbon stuffed with s.	DEBU	268:62
See amid the winter's s.	CASW	208:83
sleigh bells in the s.	BERL	84:41
s. falling faintly	JOYCE	470:18
s. falls in the river	BURNS	179:25
S. fell, the trees stood	NEME	633:18
S. had fallen, s. on s.	ROSS	726:47
S. has begun to fall	DUNN	307:16
S. in May's new-fangled shows	SHAK	763:4
wallow naked in December s.	SHAK	764:36
white as driven s.	SHAK	800:25
white as s.	BIBLE	131:88
white as s.	BIBLE	107:50
whiter skin of hers than s.	SHAK	790:39
whiter than s.	BIBLE	101:72
whiter than s.	BIBLE	132:31
snowdrift as a s. on the sand	KHAY	485:86
snow-leopard like a s.-l. waiting	LAWR	513:66
snows frigid as their s.	BYRON	187:33
season of s. and sins	SWIN	863:83
where are last year's s.?	VILL	913:8
snowstorm watching a s.	ROTH	727:79
snow-water Drinking cold s.-w.	SNYD	832:89
snow-white little s.-w. feet	YEATS	965:33
s.-w. trunk	FROST	352:98
snowy, Flowy, Blowy	ELLIS	323:28
snuff only took s.	GOLD	377:19
s., tobacker, and sleep	DICK	280:47
snuff-box of Amber S.-b.	POPE	685:41
soap S. and education	TWAIN	902:36
What! no s.?	FOOTE	342:83
why s. operas are…so popular	STEI	846:94
soap-boxes keep getting up on s.-b.	LOOS	536:57
soap opera It's like a s. o.	CAMP	194:70

soar s. where he is sitting now	SHEL	815:37
soaring s. ever singest	SHEL	813:91
s. human boy!	DICK	281:66
sob S., heavy world	AUDEN	43:1
sober at least not s.	JOHN	462:30
be s., and hope to the end	BIBLE	130:64
Be s., be vigilant	BIBLE	130:73
during his s. intervals	LAMB	506:9
go to bed s.	FLET	341:54
if they were quite s.	SHAW	809:74
kept in s. government	SPEN	838:32
man must stay s.	DAY	267:28
men at whiles are s.	HOUS	432:66
Merely s.	BANKS	62:18
My mother, drunk or s.	CHES	220:54
Often drunk, and seldom s.	FULL	356:88
one-third s.	BURT	181:71
or when both were s.	THUR	891:9
sedate, s., silent	HOOD	426:25
s. and come out drunk	ABSE	1:11
s. as a Judge	FIEL	335:21
stuff when I'm s.	RUSS	735:51
Wordsworth drunk and Porson s.	HOUS	432:61
sober-suited s.-s. matron	SHAK	766:95
sobriety liquor traffic is to s.	TWAIN	903:76
S. diminishes	JAMES	451:71
sobs life is made up of s.	OHEN	648:15
s. from among the group	DICK	279:95
soccer I was born for s.	PELE	672:75
professional players are s. slaves	CHAR	216:46
S. is a man's game	CHAR	216:48
s., of all sports	ROUS	729:8
world's best s. teams	CALI	192:25
sociable To one not s.	SHAK	803:6
social at the cost of his s. position	MARX	579:35
being on s. security	WELD	928:85
commit A s. science	AUDEN	44:23
corresponding s. constitution	MARX	579:30
fitting for the s. scientist	BOUL	152:88
how to apply s. theory	STIN	854:1
impact upon the s. sciences	NISB	639:28
importance of s. ownership	STRA	856:35
moral and s. progress	MILL	591:94
more hateful…The s. sage's	BROW	169:68
No s. study	MILLS	595:6
political and s. conditions	MARS	575:63
political, and s. life	LEWIS	526:53
self-love and s. be the same	POPE	687:86
since S. Progress began	KIPL	493:79
s. and educational patterns	MCLU	556:56
s. consequences of their activities	HOBS	420:7
S. Contract is nothing more	WELLS	930:21
s. fabric would fly asunder	SHAW	808:53
s. phenomenon	GOULD	380:76
s. position of the observer	MANN	567:91
s. problem of the twentieth century	SMALL	826:58
s. problem solved	MACD	549:34
s. progress	JOHN	456:74
S. scientists could supply	FALU	329:11
society, s. order	MUNCH	625:42
things that are purely s.	WASH	921:23
without s. advance	HARR	398:43
works in the s. sciences	NISB	639:27
socialising better off not s.	WALK	917:32
socialism creeping s.-libertarianism	GINS	372:14
doctrines and practice of S.	MORR	620:51
identify modern s.	WILS	948:65
meaning of s.	GOER	374:55
nothing in S. that…will not cure	DURA	307:24
proceed to the building of s.	LENIN	520:67
restating our s.	WILS	948:61
s. and a market economy	DENG	272:57
s. and communism	MORR	620:52
s. comes through the door	AGUI	9:97
S. does not mean much	ORWE	653:16
S. is neither Protestant nor Catholic	CONN	243:21
S. is the completion of democracy	EAGL	309:4
s. works	WILS	948:54
While there's capitalism, there'll be s.	MILI	591:90
This is not s.	SNOW	832:88
worst advertisement for S.	ORWE	653:15
socialist America's leading s.	ECON	320:53
main business of s. parties	KING	486:19
mark…of S. literature	ORWE	653:18
S. before he is forty	WILL	947:33
S. papers…came out	MORR	620:51
s. society	NOZI	642:72

socialists

solid workingman's s.	MCFA 551:66	s. do not want his labour	MALT 563:22	Say not s. things	SORL 834:33
sun of the s. revolution	LENIN 521:39	s. has resembled a pyramid	NAPO 630:50	wanted your s. verges	HENRI 411:10
The secular s. machine	GING 371:1	s. here would be quite civilised	WILDE 942:13	softly but never hit s.	ROOS 724:19
world could become s.	MAO 568:32	s. in which they live	JAMES 451:58	Soho Perambulate in glamorous S.	HUGH 435:22
socialists If s. lose sight	STRA 856:35	s. in which thought	RUSS 734:34	**soil** don't fight war on our s.	DALL 261:18
motive of many S.	ORWE 653:17	S. is all but rude	MARV 577:3	Foul as their s.	BYRON 187:33
S. are Liberals	SAINT 738:48	s. is an organized conspiracy	DOUG 296:26	grows on mortal s.	MILT 599:87
S. can scheme	MACL 556:50	S. is composed of two large classes	CHAM 213:70	portion of the virgin s.	HAWT 402:4
socialize s. the cost of growing old	HEWL 417:38	s. is full of women	WILDE 942:9	same s. as the Muse	UNTE 905:11
social mobility s. m. now means	HARM 398:39	S. is indeed a contract	BURKE 176:45	same worn-out s.	HAWT 401:3
social security more important than s. s.	WHIT 937:86	S. is no comfort	SHAK 803:6	s. Is bare now	HOPK 428:70
societies marriage in most s.	DWOR 308:43	S. is now one polished horde	BYRON 190:24	s. may best Deserve	MILT 602:53
s. which...cannot sustain	MO 611:66	S. needs first of all	SUMN 859:83	s. of his shallow cares!	BRON 162:80
troops, and sweet s.	MILT 600:95	S. offenders	GILB 369:60	texture of the s.	SMITH 828:2
society advanced industrial s.	HAYEK 402:25	S. requires...retrieve his fortunes	DICK 282:89	**soils** Six days of the week it s.	LARK 509:79
All classes of s.	JEVO 455:54	S. should not ask anything	SAND 741:7	**sojourner** discontented s.	WORD 957:72
altering the shape of s.	ORWE 653:29	s. that admires	LECA 518:75	**sojourners** s. and passing subjects	MUIR 624:20
A s. that has no ideals	AI WEI 10:3	s. that repressed	KRIS 499:13	**solace** s. to man giffis	BARB 63:50
as s. develops, its mythical stories	FRYE 354:54	s. that will organize production	ENGE 326:15	**solar** hub of the s. system	HOLM 424:70
avenue of assimilation into s.	DOCT 289:84	s....they had emigrated	MO 611:65	self...epicentre of the s. system	PHIL 677:56
Bourgeois s. is infected	WEIL 928:74	s., where none intrudes	BYRON 188:70	**sold** s. and again s.	SAND 742:23
build a s. of opportunity	MAJOR 561:72	s....which is riven	ROSS 725:35	s. my farm	SHAK 776:99
buildings...the reflection of s.	PEI 672:73	s., with all its...skill and force	BURKE 176:38	s. your own lands	SHAK 779:6
carrying on in s.	PAIGE 660:28	s. women never serve chilli	RAYB 708:90	think I've s. myself	CARL 199:70
certain types of s.	PARS 666:56	solitude sometimes is best s.	MILT 606:47	would have s. London	RICH 714:11
classless s.	MARX 579:45	suppose s. is wonderfully	WILDE 941:90	**soldier** always tell an old s.	SHAW 806:84
cling together In one s.	WORD 958:76	temptation to see all of s.	LEWO 528:79	As an old s.	SHAW 807:28
comparatively prosperous s.	MACM 556:74	the politics of our s.	OAKE 642:1	as is the hat of a s.	HERB 414:90
contemporary and future s.	MURP 627:77	There is such a thing as s.	CAM 193:38	'A s.,' cried my Uncle Toby	STER 848:34
declension, of the s.	SMITH 827:82	truth in the s.	KING 487:34	assumed the s.	WASH 921:25
definition of a free s.	STEV 851:7	two classes in good s.	SHAW 810:6	Ben Battle was a s. bold	HOOD 426:19
democratic and free s.	MAND 564:53	unequals what s.	MILT 605:39	British s. can stand up to anything	SHAW 807:3
desire to integrate into s.	SARR 744:62	value judgments about the s.	VAN 908:12	Christ's faithful s.	BOOK 147:77
direction of s.	TOCQ 892:26	very fabric of s.	JOHN 456:79	Come you back, you British s.	KIPL 489:80
dominant factor in our s.	ASIM 38:80	well adjusted members of s.	CALL 192:28	death, who had the s. singled	DOUG 295:4
economic factors in s.	GILM 371:92	well-being of s.	ROOS 724:17	Drinking is the s.'s pleasure	DRYD 303:30
every one of that s.	LOCKE 533:87	we're such a communal s.	SPIE 840:65	Every British and French s. killed	CHUR 224:70
existing basis of s.	KEYN 484:71	We want a s. in which	THAT 881:51	For a s. I listed	DIBD 276:28
faults of the economic s.	KEYN 484:82	where s. comes into itself	ROGE 722:69	German s. trying to violate	STRA 857:42
first duty to serve s.	JOHN 461:13	working s.	TREV 896:10	glazed eyes of a s. dying	BISM 137:34
founder of civil s.	ROUS 729:9	**sociologist** according to a s.	UNSE 905:10	go to your Gawd like a s.	KIPL 489:88
greater pest to s.	MACA 546:55	was a s.	MURD 626:67	honest man and a s.	SHAK 774:36
great safeguard of s.	ELIOT 316:44	**sociologists** s. are akin to Marxists	ARON 37:49	informer when he cannot be a s.	FLAU 339:16
Havana, Cuba...high s.	CABR 191:8	s. of knowledge	MERT 589:56	like a s.'s ribbon	ABSE 1:8
higher phase of communist s.	MARX 579:43	**sociology** department of...s.	AYER 48:7	Money is a good s.	SHAK 773:6
If the idea of s. were extinguished	DURK 308:31	s....attaches the adjective 'arbitrary'	ARON 36:48	never expect a s. to think	SHAW 807:1
In a consumer s.	ILLI 445:23	S. is...about why they don't have	DUES 305:82	Not though the s. knew	TENN 875:12
In communist s.	MARX 579:29	S. is a new science	GOWE 380:81	ruffian stern, and s. good	SCOTT 753:40
In our s. this person	MAMET 563:30	S. is the science of talk	KNIG 494:11	s. of the King	KITC 494:98
intellectual life...of western s.	SNOW 832:77	s., it is as an art	NISB 639:28	s.'s life is terribly hard	MILNE 595:12
intersections within a s.	MILLS 595:68	S. seems to have missed	VAN 908:13	s.'s pack is not so heavy	EISE 314:95
In the affluent s.	GALB 357:16	S. was born	SMALL 826:57	s. wears a badge	READ 708:95
just as s. ought to be	MORR 620:55	What is it about s.	BAKER 56:7	sound of the white s.'s axe	RED 709:19
knowledge of the s. it serves	CASS 207:73	**sockets** candles burn their s.	HOUS 432:69	summer s. and the sunshine patriot	PAINE 660:29
looking closely at s.	TRIL 897:16	**socks** inability to put on your s.	GONC 377:41	the s. lists his wounds	PROP 697:30
loss of s. in which	MOOD 615:52	s. are loners	COPE 246:96	Unknown S.	ASQU 38:85
Man is born to live in s.	DIDE 285:78	s. compelled one's attention	SAKI 739:61	very poor s.	SHAW 806:85
Man seeketh in s.	BACON 50:38	s. on the altar	NERU 633:23	would himself have been a s.	SHAK 771:33
member of s.	MORI 619:36	telling lies and selling s.	MERW 589:57	**soldiers** best s. France ever had	PHIL 677:60
mirror of our own s.	STER 847:16	women who wear ankle s.	BENN 80:49	black s. to death	LOWE 540:26
modern ardor to improve s.	SMALL 826:57	**Socrates** be S. dissatisfied	MILL 591:7	changed from peasants and s.	WAUGH 924:81
mutual s., help, and comfort	BOOK 148:87	realized, like S.	PLATO 681:41	common s.	WELL 929:99
negotiation and s.	MUNCH 625:42	S. empties the cup of poison	FEUE 334:1	Countries that have s. in charge	MACK 554:16
no Arts; no Letters; no S.	HOBB 420:2	S. in every classroom	GRIS 389:74	if you believe the s.	SALI 740:89
noble s. for providing	DICK 277:54	S. is guilty	PLATO 681:42	ladder behind s.	SUN 859:92
no importance...to s.	NABO 628:40	**Socratic** S. method is not a game	BEER 74:88	laughing s. fought to their defeat	FENT 332:60
no one in our s. is allowed	OAKE 642:2	**sod** prairies' dreaming s.	CRANE 253:58	make his s. fight	SUN 859:91
no such thing as s.	THAT 881:66	stands fixed to the s.	WILL 944:64	men like s. may not quit	TENN 877:69
nothing to distinguish human s.	SHAW 809:87	withered in the s.?	BRON 161:59	old s. never die	MACA 544:8
pervading all nature and s.	HARDY 397:21	**soda** heaven sent us S. Water	CHES 221:89	physician and chemist are s.	PAST 668:5
place in s.	NIGH 639:19	Sermons and s. water	BYRON 190:7	proud array of s.	WILDE 940:45
play a much larger part in s.	SNOW 832:81	unattainable s. and sherry	SALA 739:70	S. are citizens	SASS 745:83
poor s.	TAWN 868:44	**sodden** s. towards sundown	ELIOT 321:80	s. drilling in Berlin	MORI 619:38
powerful men in our s.	BELL 77:81	**sodium** having discovered s.	BENT 82:1	S. find wars	DONNE 291:28
progress of s. and wealth	RICA 712:80	**Sodom** men of S. were wicked	BIBLE 92:17	s. he smiled at	SASS 745:86
promotes that of the s.	SMITH 828:86	rained upon S. and upon Gomorrah	BIBLE 92:23	S., I'm getting out	GARI 360:73
quarrel with its s.	TRIL 897:18	**sodomy** rape, s. and drug addiction	COOK 245:68	s., mostly fools	BIER 134:80
radical vision of s.	WALK 917:33	**sods** flaming s., the snivelling	LAWR 512:40	s....of the Irish Brigade	DAVIS 266:9
receives the protection of s.	MILL 591:2	heaped-up s. upon the fire	COLUM 238:90	s. of the ploughshare	RUSK 733:98
responsibility of s.	PALEY 661:55	**sofa** fainted alternately on the s.	AUST 45:48	S., think that	NAPO 629:37
role of labour in s.	NEVI 634:32	luxury the accomplished s.	COWP 251:10	steel my s.' hearts	SHAK 775:85
rounds of s.'s ladder	MOORE 616:68	s., chair or a hot-water bottle	SMITH 830:32	**sole** no rest for the s. of her foot	BIBLE 92:9
sick s. must think	LEWIS 526:49	s. upholstered in panther skin	PLOM 682:73	s. cause of...unhappiness	PASC 667:73
socialist s.	NOZI 642:72	wheel the s. round	COWP 251:9	s. evidence...possible	MILL 592:9
s. as something eternal	ORWE 653:28	**soft** cushion and s. Dean invite	POPE 686:61	s. of his foot	SHAK 774:42
S. became my...bride	WORD 961:39	Her voice was ever s.	SHAK 793:38	**solecism** eternity without a s.	BROW 165:54
s. distributes itself	ARNO 36:26	meets me s. and supple	FLET 341:58	Japanese...rarely commit a s.	BIRD 136:11

songs

solemn more s. and serene — SHEL 812:57
s. creed with s. sneer — BYRON 187:55
s. gladness even crowned — TENN 874:70
s. slope of mighty limbs — SWIN 864:13
solicitor can only go to his s. — DISR 288:54
solicitors accountants and s. — TAYL 868:56
solid not s. at all, but a liquid — CAREY 199:62
only s....reformation — CARL 200:87
s. pudding against empty praise — POPE 688:30
something s. and concrete — KELM 479:67
solidarity create...a feeling of s. — DURK 308:27
power of S. — WALE 917:27
s. with other isolated creatures — BELL 78:90
solidity an appearance of s. — ORWE 655:65
s. of a water buffalo — PERE 674:18
solids surfaces and s. — PIERO 678:72
soliloquy conversation, and even a s. — LINK 530:27
Iago's... — COLE 236:54
solitariness man does with his s. — WHIT 936:68
solitary Be not s. — BURT 182:89
Be not s. — JOHN 463:69
for each man a s. cell — ONEI 650:60
high and s. — YEATS 966:14
How doth the city sit s. — BIBLE 110:23
one tunnel, dark and s. — SABA 736:2
Only s. men know the full joys — CATH 208:94
sentenced to s. confinement — WILL 945:98
setteth the s. in families — BIBLE 101:81
s. child and s. man — ACKR 3:62
s. laugh — GREE 386:28
the life of man, s. — HOBB 420:2
till I am s. — JOHN 460:63
To wander s. there — MARV 578:7
solitude a healthy appetite for s. — SELF 756:13
bliss of s. — WORD 960:27
companionable as s. — THOR 889:41
endure our own s. — PRIT 696:21
feel his s. more keenly — VALE 907:5
flaming s. — GORO 379:66
groaned from s. — LEE 519:98
In blissful s. — MILT 603:76
inviolate s. — ROBE 717:74
music piercing that s. — THOM 885:53
Musing in s. — WORD 961:34
one to s. — ARNO 34:79
O S.! where are the charms — COWP 250:96
power of s. — NORTH 641:60
principle s. and retreat — MONT 613:23
resonance of his s. — CONN 243:17
self-sufficing power of S. — WORD 958:78
single moment's s. — WILDE 941:95
soft like S.'s — SHEL 812:66
S. is the playfield — NABO 628:11
S. is un-American — JONG 466:32
S. restores the harmonies — BERN 86:74
s. sometimes is best society — MILT 606:47
s. What happiness — MILT 605:38
sweet retired s. — MILT 598:72
total is of s. — BRON 161:60
to the hour its s. — STEV 850:79
To this delicious s. — MARV 577:3
Whosoever is delighted in s. — BACON 52:12
solo in a s. game — SERV 757:35
Solomon even S. in all his glory — BIBLE 115:45
fame of S. — BIBLE 97:55
greater than S. is here — BIBLE 117:87
S. gave to the queen of Sheba — BIBLE 98:85
S. his son reigned in his stead — BIBLE 98:84
S. loved many strange women — BIBLE 97:57
S. of saloons — BROW 169:68
S. says — KIPL 492:64
S.'s throne was supported by lions — BACON 51:67
song of songs, which is S.'s — BIBLE 107:39
wisest of men...not excepting S. — STER 848:23
solution crowding towards s. — CARL 200:6
focus on the s. — TRUMP 900:1
incapable of purely private s. — MILLS 595:7
It isn't that they can't see the s. — CHES 221:9
mystery which defies s. — MORT 621:69
No perfect s....possible — BERL 84:48
people were a kind of s. — CAVA 210:16
s. for...habitual accidents — BENC 78:7
s. to the problem — LEMAY 521:30
total s. of the Jewish question — GOER 374:57
You're either part of the s. — CLEA 229:78
solutions employed in seeking s. — KUHN 500:37
inevitable, s. are not — ASIM 38:79

practical s. to the problems of evil — GENET 363:39
show people the s. — GATES 361:94
slogans...confused with s. — BENT 82:7
s. lead to more problems — BURR 181:67
solve confront a problem, you begin to s. — GIUL 373:34
mystery we all s. — SKEL 825:36
problems...the United States can s. — CLIN 231:36
S. it quickly — WATS 922:43
solving S. a problem is hard enough — LEVI 526:34
Solway Sark rins o'er the S. sands — BURNS 179:41
Somalia years to get S. not on its feet — HEMP 410:99
sombre penumbra of s. dignity — ATLAS 40:19
sombrero sunbonnet as well as the s. — FERB 332:66
some S. people find oil — GETTY 366:88
s. should be unhappy — JOHN 463:50
somebody could have been s. — SCHU 749:70
S. was telling jokes — KAUF 474:41
someone mind that s. else is — KENN 480:96
living s. else's life — JOBS 455:65
S.—or Something — HAMM 394:57
somersault one complete s. — IGNA 445:17
Somerset in the records of S. House — BIRK 136:13
S. House young man — GILB 369:47
something always start with s. — PICA 677:58
artist...makes s. of the nothing — PERCY 674:11
cannot get s. for nothing — HARR 399:60
feel you've done s. — HEMI 409:62
I...thinking this, was s. — DESC 274:95
say s. about me — COHAN 234:94
s. flew between me and the sun — BLUN 143:78
S. is rotten — SHAK 781:59
s. more comfortable — HARL 398:37
S. nasty in the woodshed — GIBB 367:10
s. ought to be said — CARL 201:22
S. there had been — HYDE 443:17
To do nothing and get s. — DISR 287:33
sometime come up s. — WEST 933:85
sometimes S. I sits and thinks — PUNCH 700:84
somewhere once belonged s. — STEIN 845:66
somnambulist reactionary is a s. — ROOS 724:10
son bring forth a s. — BIBLE 113:14
bring forth a s. — BIBLE 114:15
brought forth her firstborn s. — BIBLE 120:68
by this s. of York — SHAK 760:31
dirty s. of a bitch — STEI 845:82
divide a father from his s. — MARQ 574:43
Father, S. and Holy Ghost — MCLE 554:23
from the Father and S. — BOOK 147:62
from the sire the s. shall hear — SCOTT 752:27
gave his only begotten S. — BIBLE 122:25
hateth his s. — BIBLE 104:69
if his s. ask bread — BIBLE 115:51
if the s. of peace be there — BIBLE 120:78
If the S....shall make you free — BIBLE 123:40
if thou be the S. of God — BIBLE 114:22
into the grave unto my s. — BIBLE 93:39
loveth s. or daughter — BIBLE 116:73
man of clay, s. — MILT 606:45
Man, you have a s. — MARQ 574:44
no more worthy to be called thy s. — BIBLE 121:90
no more worthy to be called thy s. — BIBLE 121:91
obeyed as s. — GIBB 366:1
O my s. Absalom — BIBLE 97:49
one like the S. of man — BIBLE 111:43
only s. Isaac — BIBLE 92:25
renounce me for a s. — GIBB 366:98
s. in whom he delighteth — BIBLE 104:53
s. of a carpenter — GREE 386:23
s. of a mare — AIDAN 10:1
S. of a whore — ROCH 720:20
s. of Heaven's eternal King — MILT 596:30
s. of his old age — BIBLE 93:37
S. of man be three days — BIBLE 117:86
S. of man hath not where — BIBLE 116:59
S. of man is Lord — BIBLE 119:51
S. of man shall come in his glory — BIBLE 119:35
s. of memory, great heir — MILT 597:39
s. of the dear murderèd — SHAK 782:2
s. shall not go down — BIBLE 93:44
Strong S. of God — TENN 873:54
tell you, s. of mine — NOON 641:50
This is my beloved S. — BIBLE 114:21
This is my s. — TENN 870:1
this man was the S. of God — BIBLE 120:62
Thou art my S. — BIBLE 99:28
unfeathered two-legged thing, a s. — DRYD 302:73
unto us a s. is given — BIBLE 107:60

virgin shall conceive, and bear a s. — BIBLE 107:57
wed ye to my youngest s. — SCOTT 753:45
wise s. heareth his father — BIBLE 104:67
Woman, behold thy s.! — BIBLE 123:61
worst s. of a bitch — PARK 664:32
younger s. gathered all together — BIBLE 121:89
sonatas s. of Mozart — SCHN 748:46
song acquaints His soul with s. — BROW 169:82
As easily as s. — ROSE 725:33
A s. belongs to no man — DOYLE 298:77
Assist our s. — GURN 390:2
awake for sake of S.! — FERG 333:83
breeze of s. — TENN 874:86
carcase of an old s. — THOM 885:71
come before his presence with a s. — BOOK 149:32
Come, gie's a s. — SKIN 825:50
Dance, and Provençal s. — KEATS 478:42
every voice be s.! — DODD 289:90
fame is in the s. — CARM 202:46
followed by a sacred s. — BELL 77:65
For if such holy s. — MILT 597:36
For I have a s. to sing — GILB 370:70
funeral s. — GIBB 366:94
Glorious the s. — SMART 826:67
How shall we sing the Lord's s. — BIBLE 103:42
human existence as a s. unfinished — MCCU 549:14
I have made my s. — YEATS 966:16
joyful S. I'll raise — ADDI 7:38
lark...sightless s. — TENN 875:99
let satire be my s. — BYRON 186:24
let the s. of praise be sung — POTT 690:81
life is a...cycle of s. — PARK 664:14
more musical than any s. — ROSS 726:44
my s. has an ideal — CHOC 222:25
new unhallowed s. — DAVI 264:66
no horse sing a s. — ARMS 33:49
One grand, sweet s. — KING 487:45
our s. shall rise to Thee — HEBER 406:2
picnic of s. — FRAME 346:75
play a s. for me — DYLAN 309:57
poets...seldom sing a new s. — DAY 267:27
rainbow and a cuckoo's s. — DAVI 265:91
realm of free s. — LOWE 539:2
region of my s. — WORD 961:35
run softly till I end my s. — ELIOT 318:3
sang the 'S. of the Shirt' — HOOD 426:30
sheer joyous power of s. — BEER 74:91
she whispered a s. — OHARA 648:10
silence was the s. of love — ROSS 726:57
Sing to the Lord a new s. — BIBLE 132:32
Sing unto the Lord a new s. — BOOK 149:12
s. about a whore-house — GUTH 390:6
s. for thinking hearts — WORD 958:91
s. in thy praise — BURNS 178:10
s. is ended — BERL 84:38
s. of canaries — NASH 630:55
s. of songs — BIBLE 107:39
s. Should make all Nature lovelier — COLE 235:25
s. that echoes cheerly — TENN 869:80
s. that has sold half a million — BERL 84:43
suck melancholy out of a s. — SHAK 778:76
swallow-flights of s. — TENN 874:73
sweet silver s. — HAMM 394:65
teach in s. — SHEL 812:63
that's my kind of s. — HERN 414:93
the burthen of his s. — BICK 133:49
the s. of woe — TENN 874:81
this subject for heroic s. — MILT 605:43
thow be, or elles s. — CHAU 216:68
thrush...sings each s. twice over — BROW 167:21
Time is our tedious s. — MILT 597:38
trouble with a folk s. — LAMB 506:19
two notes a s. — DAVI 265:92
weigh this s. — YEATS 965:11
wheel's kick and the wind's s. — MASE 580:50
when this s. is sung — WYATT 964:89
Without a s. — PRES 694:73
woman, wine and s. — LUTH 542:76
Wrote one s. — BROW 168:57
songs all their s. are sad — CHES 220:81
am singing s. — HORA 430:9
ballads, and snatches — GILB 369:58
best of trades, to make s. — BELL 77:66
I will sing no more s. — OBRU 646:65
lean and flashy s. — MILT 599:89
love s. for maids — SHAK 800:24
matchless s. does meditate — MARV 577:97

sonnet

merry s. of peace	SHAK	805:58
Our sweetest s. are those	SHEL	814:97
Out of dreams, s.	HERZL	416:24
Piping s. of pleasant glee	BLAKE	139:85
Sing no sad s.	ROSS	726:46
s. are like your...parents	BONO	146:30
s., ballattis, and of playis	DUNB	306:5
s. beguile your pilgrimage	FLEC	340:31
s. I had	GURN	390:99
s. in its lakes	SCOTT	751:3
s. of deliverance	BIBLE	100:53
s. of other lands	EVANS	328:68
s. of the May-time	KEND	480:85
s. they have sung	HAMM	395:68
s. weren't theirs any more	COST	247:17
thy voice did weave S.	SHEL	812:59
Where are the s. of Spring?	KEATS	478:33
sonnet lacking skill of a s.	SIDN	820:59
s. is a moment's monument	ROSS	726:55
sure I shall turn s.	SHAK	763:8
sonnets By wailful s.	SHAK	759:70
s. and courtly love	GALL	358:44
would have written s. all his life?	BYRON	190:12
sonofabitch other s. dies for his	PATT	670:31
sons advent of twin s.	HAMER	393:45
called the s. of God	BIBLE	130:79
Come on you s. of bitches!	DALY	261:19
defended by her armed s.	REDM	709:21
delight in ungodly s.	BIBLE	113:95
doughty s. of Hungary	GILB	369:57
Earth's heedless s.	BLUN	143:75
faithless s. betrayed	MOORE	617:1
fallen s. of Eve	CHES	221:91
forth the s. Of Belial	MILT	602:47
Go, bind your s. to exile	KIPL	491:19
Horny-handed s. of toil	SALI	740:88
May all your s. be bishops	BEHAN	74:11
preposterous troop of s.	SOME	833:9
robbed of her s.	NATI	632:4
Shadwell...of all my s.	DRYD	300:43
s. acclaim you glorious name	CUMM	257:58
s. and daughters of Life's longing	GIBR	367:13
s. and your daughters shall prophesy	BIBLE	111:48
s. Hurled headlong	MILT	602:64
s. of former slaves	KING	487:25
s. of God shouted for joy	BIBLE	98:14
s. Of great and mighty resolutions	BUTL	185:72
S. of Men once think	POPE	689:46
s. of the morning	HEBER	406:98
s. of toil	CECIL	210:29
s. walk not in thy ways	BIBLE	96:30
s. will have a Paris	HUGO	437:61
spread, my s., your glory	POPE	689:39
That I must leave ye, s.	MILT	606:63
three stout and stalwart s.	BALL	60:82
Why thus torment us poor s. of day?	COCK	233:82
wife, I have s.	LUCAN	541:47
sonsie honest, s. face	BURNS	178:94
soon come s., s.!	SHEL	816:54
s. or late	THOM	885:62
We got in too s.	HARK	398:34
sooner cometh s. or later	GORD	378:54
I'd s., except the penalties	JEFF	453:16
soot in s. I sleep	BLAKE	139:87
tarnished with ashes and s.	MOORE	616:64
sooth Good s., she is	SHAK	799:21
soothed s. and solaced	BACON	53:54
soothsayers s....interpret	WHITE	936:58
Sophia existence of St S.	BYRON	191:73
feelings of S.	AUST	45:48
sophisticated most s.	KUNI	501:40
sophistication Hip is the s.	MAIL	559:37
s. for a woman	THUR	890:62
sophistications haven from s.	POUND	691:8
sophist-led Be neither saint nor s.-l.	ARNO	33:68
sophistry land...of s.	BYRON	187:32
nothing but s. and illusion	HUME	438:7
s., cleaves close	COWP	251:5
soporific s. stew of every day!	SARD	743:51
sopranos beneath all these s.	KIER	486:7
sops s. in wine	SPEN	838:15
Sorbonne one day at the S.	STEV	850:84
sorcerers Dark-working s.	SHAK	762:91
sorceress good cook is like a s.	SCHI	747:23
sorcery sullen s. and mad lineaments	BLUN	143:77
sore No wily wit to salve a s.	DYER	309:48
worm sucking an envenomed s.?	DONNE	290:16
sores dogs came and licked his s.	BIBLE	121:96
Salve to thy s.	MILT	607:88
vile, incurable s.	OWEN	657:31
sorrow bring down...with s.	BIBLE	93:44
crown of s.	TENN	871:14
days in s. without end	AESC	8:79
Football then was fighting s.	HOUS	431:42
full of s.	KEATS	478:43
full of s. and spite	COMP	239:99
full of s. and travail	BIBLE	112:69
headed for s.	SZIL	865:31
if she doth of s. speak	CAMP	195:73
in s. pale	BLAKE	139:92
in s. shalt thou eat of it	BIBLE	91:98
in s. thou shalt bring forth	BIBLE	91:97
knowledge increaseth s.	BIBLE	105:12
labour and s.	BIBLE	101:94
Labour without s.	RUSK	733:7
laughter and s.	TOLS	894:54
load of s.	SHAK	774:52
Lycidas your s.	MILT	600:94
man of s. who wins	LAO	508:64
mix with my s.	LUGO	542:62
Moderate s. Fits vulgar love	DRYD	301:52
more In s. than in anger	SHAK	780:44
more s. than they could bear	REST	711:64
much s. shall it sup	BARK	63:53
no s. more intense	DARIO	263:46
not aggravate the s.	TROL	897:31
Nought but vast S.	DELA	271:32
One s. never comes	SHAK	798:86
O S., wilt thou live	TENN	874:82
Parting is such sweet s.	SHAK	766:85
Pluck...a rooted s.	SHAK	798:70
restored, and s. end	SHAK	801:47
see if there be any s.	BIBLE	110:24
she gaed wi' s.	BALL	59:60
shuts up s.'s eye	SHAK	767:39
S. and silence are strong	LONG	535:26
S. comes as in a circle	CH	222:18
S. flouted at s.	SHAK	760:25
S. is knowledge	BYRON	189:83
S. is tranquillity	PARK	664:20
s. leave awhile to tutor	SHAK	764:55
s. never comes too late	GRAY	383:48
s. of true love	THOM	885:66
s.'s horizons are vague	MCMU	557:85
S., the great idealizer	LOWE	539:13
s. to him sell	DUNB	306:97
s. unforeseen and scarcely feared	PHIL	677:54
S. was all my soul	HERB	413:63
s. was too sore laid on	SHAK	800:31
s. which enhances...the mind	PROU	698:58
Sudden s.	SHAK	772:92
there is only s.	WHAR	934:14
There is s. enough	KIPL	492:60
tomorrow's s.	KHAY	485:87
To S., I bade	KEATS	476:89
untold s. to mankind	UNIT	905:9
water this s.	SHAK	794:47
when I s. most	TENN	874:69
with s. new sustain	SPEN	839:40
Your cause of s.	SHAK	798:79
sorrowing though s., yet in peace	MILT	606:66
sorrows costly in our s.!	STER	849:59
eat the bread of s.	BIBLE	103:36
few s., however poignant	SMITH	829:14
gardens without s.	CIXO	227:47
Half the s. of women	ELIOT	315:38
Here I and s. sit	SHAK	768:55
instruct my s. to be proud	SHAK	768:54
man of s.	BIBLE	109:93
new s. Strike heaven	SHAK	797:60
sea of s. deep	SPEN	838:26
s. of your...face	YEATS	965:7
When s. come	SHAK	784:51
world's great s.	RUSS	735:43
sorry chief word...seems to be 's.'	BARR	65:94
having to say you're s.	SEGAL	756:3
I am truly s.	BENE	79:19
we say s.	RUDD	730:34
wild thing S. for itself	LAWR	514:78
sort any s. rather than no s.	POUND	691:9
smiles in such a s.	SHAK	776:13
What s. of person...?	CAREY	199:65
sot without them He's but a s.	SHAK	804:23
sought I s. you and I found myself	GRIL	388:71

Love s. is good — SHAK 786:12

soul acquaints His s. with song — BROW 169:82
adventures of his own s. — FRAN 346:79
affirming the affirmations of the s. — EMER 324:74
At the peril of its s. — SCOTT 751:98
Awake my s. — KEN 480:83
beaming my s. — POPE 689:42
bequeath my s. to God — BACON 53:44
birth of your brave s. — CRAS 254:83
bitterness of his s. — BIBLE 113:85
Body and s. — JORD 468:99
bones and s.'s delivery — DONNE 292:51
book...of my secret s. — SHAK 785:84
bottom of one's s. not to care — LAWR 513:58
boundaries of the s. — HERA 412:35
Brevity is the s. of lingerie — PARK 663:94
bright s. of the sad year — NASHE 632:94
built my s. — TENN 870:94
by pure s.-intuition — LAWR 513:57
Calm s. of all things! — ARNO 34:74
came with music in his s. — NEVE 634:31
captain of my s. — HENL 411:6
Casket of My s. — KEATS 476:91
celestial and my s.'s idol — SHAK 781:76
chamber of my s. — SHAR 805:69
Christe receive thy s. — BALL 59:66
clothing for the s. divine — BLAKE 141:26
colour of my s. is iron-grey — DEBU 268:27
courageous s. that dares and defies — CHOP 223:33
creative s. — WORD 958:88
damned of body and s. — KIPL 490:95
dark s., and foul thoughts — MILT 598:72
dear companion of my s. — MIDD 590:73
devil and thee about thy s. — SHAK 770:31
dignity of s. and character — CARL 200:83
dividing asunder of s. and spirit — BIBLE 129:34
drop of hatred in your s. — MUNRO 625:51
Dull would he be of s. — WORD 959:3
endanger my s. gratis? — SHAK 773:4
entire s. is a cry — KAZA 474:51
Every s. pursues the good — PLATO 682:64
everything that I have in my s. — BROD 160:42
evoke the s. of Italy — MAZZ 583:30
Fair seed-time had my s. — WORD 958:75
father lived his s. — CUMM 258:65
Faustus may...save his s.! — MARL 573:30
fellow ain't got a s. — STEI 845:83
fire of s. — DICK 279:89
force his s. — SHAK 782:99
for my s., what can it do — SHAK 781:58
freed my s. — BERN 85:66
from the author's s. — HUXL 441:63
from the s. itself must issue forth — COLE 235:30
genial current of the s. — GRAY 384:68
Give not thy s. unto a woman — BIBLE 113:88
glad at s. — SHAK 789:97
God rest his s. — SMITH 830:42
God the s. — POPE 687:78
Grapple them to thy s. — SHAK 781:49
greatest thing a human s. — RUSK 733:14
greatness of s. — STOWE 856:27
greatness of the human s. — ROCK 720:33
half conceal the S. within — TENN 873:58
harmonical and ingenious s. — AUBR 42:58
harmonies...of the s. — BERN 86:74
harrow up thy s. — SHAK 781:60
haughtiness of s. — ADDI 7:46
height My s. can reach — BROW 166:97
'he' or 'him' of the s. — PATM 669:22
he who would be a great s. — EMER 325:89
His s. proud Science never taught — POPE 687:75
Hope...perches in the s. — DICK 283:34
how prodigal the s. — SHAK 781:55
I am black...my s. is white — BLAKE 139:87
I...am, with all my s. — STEE 844:39
immortal...because he has a s. — FAUL 331:36
Impropriety is the s. of wit — MAUG 582:4
In a great s. — PASC 666:63
in exchange for his s.? — BIBLE 118:8
influence upon the s. — KAND 473:17
in my s. am free — LOVE 538:82
in my s. that tender secret dwells — BYRON 188:76
in s. a heathen — DICK 281:73
inspire my s. — BARL 63:56
intention of his s. — LEON 522:74
Involve all of your s. — HUGO 437:64
iron entered into his s. — BOOK 149:33

souls

Is my s.'s pleasure	KEATS 475:65	save a s. from death	BIBLE 130:63	subject's s. is his own	SHAK 775:82
Is the eternal truth man's fighting s.	EBER 310:12	save thy secret s.	GRAY 385:80	taming...the s.'s raw passions	BLOOM 143:64
it is the cause, my s.	SHAK 790:39	Science...is the s.'s perdition	RABE 703:6	taught my s. to fancy aught	VAUG 909:34
Jesu, lover of my s.	WESL 931:59	sea speaks to the s.	CHOP 223:30	That mind and s.	TENN 873:57
largest and most comprehensive s.	DRYD 300:20	Seek not, my s.	PIND 678:80	that my s. knoweth right well	BOOK 149:37
Let man's s. be a sphere	DONNE 293:80	Selling one's body to keep one's s.	MACK 554:13	then shall a s. know what it has produced	KORAN 498:91
light is in the s.	MILT 607:85	sent my s. abroad	COLE 235:28	The s. shrinks	WILB 939:37
like a s. pursued	ROBE 717:74	silhouette of a brooding s.	SAND 741:12	This night shall thy s.	SMITH 830:43
lips suck forth my s.	MARL 573:29	sleepless s. that perished	WORD 959:1	this night thy s. shall be required	BIBLE 121:85
living factories of the s.	MAYA 583:22	smooth-rubbed s.	WORD 957:66	thistle, O my s.	MACD 549:27
lose your own s.	SHAW 810:6	some s. of goodness	SHAK 775:80	Thou art a s. in bliss	SHAK 793:30
love...with all thy s.	BIBLE 95:88	so panteth my s. after thee	BIBLE 100:63	Till then, sit still, my s.	SHAK 781:45
love...with all thy s.	BIBLE 118:26	Sorrow was all my s.	HERB 413:63	Tommy 'ow's yer s.?	KIPL 489:86
magic, that will charm thy s.	MARL 573:28	s. abhorred all...meat	BOOK 149:34	tongue and s....be hypocrites	SHAK 783:31
man who doesn't love...has got a s.	SAKI 739:60	s. abhorreth all manner of meat	BIBLE 102:14	true attribute of the s.	STAEL 842:3
man with an immortal s.	BRYAN 170:98	s. and God laugh together	EDDI 311:26	unless S. clap	YEATS 966:26
marble museum of the s.	RODR 722:53	s. beneath the ribs of death	MANC 564:51	Variety is the s. of pleasure	BEHN 74:15
Marlbro's mighty s.	ADDI 6:18	s. by itself	PLATO 682:55	what benefit to the s.	HONO 426:17
mask of a vulgar s.	MAUG 582:10	s. doth magnify the Lord	BIBLE 120:66	whate'er her s. designed	DRYD 302:7
May his pernicious s.	SHAK 790:46	s. doth magnify the Lord	BIBLE 133:42	What of s. was left	BROW 167:31
may my s. be blasted	SHAW 810:14	s. exhibiting excellence	ARIS 31:20	What's was his	WORD 961:36
Memorial from the S.'s	ROSS 726:55	s....has an interpreter	BRON 161:63	Whose s. was sad	GILB 370:70
mercy o' my s.	MACD 550:45	s. has to itself decreed	KEATS 475:67	Why shrinks the s.	ADDI 7:52
merit wins the s.	POPE 685:42	s. has wings	DELA 271:21	will hurl my s. from heaven	SHAK 790:49
might create a s.	MILT 599:77	s. hath her content	SHAK 789:8	With consistency a great s.	EMER 324:54
mind and the s. together	NGU 636:66	s. he doth restore again	SCOT 754:85	with unshaken s.	FEUE 334:1
mirror of the s.	QUIN 702:19	s. in agony	SHAK 763:25	yet my s. drew back	HERB 413:65
mockery o' his s.	MACD 549:26	s. in paraphrase	HERB 414:78	young man's s.	HOUS 431:42
most offending s. alive	SHAK 776:87	S. is all but out of me	MILL 592:18	your s....my sorrow	LUGO 542:62
Mount, mount, my s.	SHAK 765:64	s. is an enchanted boat	SHEL 814:17	**soul-destroying** prison so s.-d.	WAUGH 923:67
must return to the s.	ISAA 447:63	s. is awakened	BRON 161:55	**soulless** sapless, s., beginningless	RUSK 733:18
my gazing s.	VAUG 909:34	s. is forfeit	MACN 558:99	**soul-making** vale of s.-m.	KEATS 476:92
my lyre has a s.	CHOC 222:25	s. is in a ferment	KEATS 476:83	**souls** About their blessed s.	KIPL 492:59
My s. doth magnify the Lord	BIBLE 120:66	s. is not more than the body	WHIT 937:94	All great, powerful s. love life	HEINE 407:13
My s. doth magnify the Lord	BIBLE 133:42	s. keeps a singin' the blues	BERRY 87:94	bind our s. with secular chains	MILT 601:25
My s.'s a trampled duelling ground	RICK 715:28	s....languishes and dies	ROCH 720:25	boundless, as we wish our s. to be	SHEL 812:60
My s.; sit thou	QUAR 701:6	s. leading the way	GUIR 389:89	coast where s. are lost	ANON 22:81
My s., there is a country	VAUG 909:37	s....like a rough diamond	DEFOE 269:67	contented your s.	KIPL 492:49
my s. trusteth in thee	BOOK 149:20	s., like lightning	HERB 415:6	damp s. of housemaids	ELIOT 317:76
my whole s. through	TENN 869:76	s. longeth, yea, even fainteth	BIBLE 101:88	days that are to try men's s.	WILS 949:77
narrow For his vast s.	DRYD 301:48	s. may but ascend to heaven	MARL 574:31	find rest unto your s.	BIBLE 116:81
nevere no s. ysaved	LANG 508:49	s. more bent To serve	MILT 601:26	fine wire around our s.	STEV 851:11
never thought...a s. could ache	VAUG 909:42	s. moves in his fee	JONS 467:57	fright the s.	SHAK 760:32
new light to the s.	TAYL 868:58	s. of a journey is liberty	MARP 574:42	God's peace betide the s.	RANS 707:72
No coward s.	BRON 162:75	S. of all the rest	MILT 607:72	hale s. out of men's bodies?	SHAK 774:37
No...gentleman, in his secret s.	BAGE 54:64	S. of A New Machine	KIDD 485:97	heaven keeps s.	DONNE 292:62
nor the prophetic s.	SHAK 802:76	s. of a prince	LOCKE 533:91	highest welfare of your s.	PLATO 681:43
no s. will pity me	SHAK 761:51	s. of Frankenstein	SHEL 811:47	human s. did never kiss	KEATS 476:87
not spoken of the s..	LONG 535:14	s. of her beauty	SHEL 815:22	immortal s. to sieve through!	MELV 585:68
of ev'ry art the s.	POPE 686:59	s. of its own	SCOTT 751:97	Jealous s. will not be answered	SHAK 790:30
oh s. desired?	LABE 510:2	s. of man	AUBR 42:61	jewel of their s.	SHAK 789:18
O limèd s.	SHAK 783:34	s. of man is a far country	THOM 883:2	join both countries' s.	BOLI 145:9
O my prophetic s.!	SHAK 781:62	s. of music shed	MOORE 618:4	letters mingle s.	DONNE 292:47
only thou can'st raise the meeting s.!	COLL 238:75	S. of my lie	HERR 415:5	live in furnished s.	CUMM 257:53
Oppressed the s.!	CRAB 252:43	s. of Orpheus sing	MILT 598:55	men with broken s.	PATC 668:6
pain in the s.	HAMM 394:59	S. of patched	STER 848:28	mindes and s. of men	PRYN 698:62
palace of the s.	WEBS 926:38	S. of the Age!	JONS 468:78	Most people sell their s.	SMITH 829:18
Paris preserves the s.	HUGO 437:82	s. of the just	STAEL 842:97	numberless infinities Of s.	DONNE 292:50
passion in the human s.	LILLO 529:1	s. of the slaves	GILL 370:87	one of those happy s.	SHEL 814:3
Perdition catch my s.	SHAK 789:16	s. of the whole Past Time	CARL 201:33	only in men's s.	STEV 850:5
Perdition catch my s.	SHER 818:3	s. of this man	SHAK 791:63	our s. that cannot be embraced	CAREW 198:53
permissible delights of the s.	BACH 49:8	s. of wit	SHAK 781:74	our twin s. in one	PHIL 676:53
Pierced to the s.	SHAK 764:30	s.-power frail	LIND 530:16	pious s. in the workplace	CHER 219:30
pilgrim s. in you	YEATS 965:7	s.' prison we call England	SHAW 810:8	poor misguided s.	LANG 507:41
poetry...composed in the s.	ARNO 36:42	s. refines itself	MARI 571:88	poor s. who dwell in night	BLAKE 141:44
Poured thro'...her pensive s.	COLL 238:78	s. rememb'ring my good friends	SHAK 764:45	possess ye your s.	BIBLE 122:4
pouring forth thy s.	KEATS 478:46	s. should fly from me	MARL 574:32	salvation of our own s.	JOHN 461:13
Praise, my s.	LYTE 543:93	s. so dead	SCOTT 752:16	send more s. to Heaven	BENN 81:81
pray for my s.	TENN 878:86	s. so near divine	BRON 161:54	Shepherd and Bishop of your s.	BIBLE 130:69
prepare thy s. for temptation	BIBLE 112:80	s.'s quiet	FORD 343:1	s. departed but the shadows	BROW 166:83
present in everyone's s.	PLATO 682:65	s.'s sap quivers	ELIOT 321:81	s. most fed with Shakespeare	CHES 221:99
preserve thy s.	BIBLE 103:31	s. started at the knee-cap	LEWIS 527:71	s. mounting up to God	ROSS 726:52
prided itself...on its s.	LYND 543:92	s. swooned slowly	JOYCE 470:18	s. negotiate there	DONNE 292:43
profits a man nothing to give his s.	BOLT 145:12	s. that is not healthy	PLATO 681:50	s. of all that I had murdered	SHAK 761:52
progress of a deathless s.	DONNE 291:30	s. that rises with us	WORD 959:8	S. of Poets dead	KEATS 475:76
rap and knock and enter in our s.	BROW 168:38	s. that through me ran	WORD 957:61	s. of the brave	CLOU 232:62
real dark night of the s.	FITZ 338:94	s....the eternity of thought	WORD 927:69	s. of the righteous	BIBLE 112:74
Refined himself to s.	DRYD 304:44	s. thirsteth for God	BIBLE 100:63	s.' path	MARTI 576:70
remake the s.	BROW 169:78	s. thirsteth for thee	BIBLE 101:78	s. that have toiled	TENN 870:62
repent it from my very s.	SHAK 760:30	S., thou hast much goods	BIBLE 121:85	s. undaunted to their doom	SULL 859:80
restoreth my s.	BIBLE 100:45	s. waiteth upon God	BIBLE 101:77	s. washed	BOOK 147:72
retreat...in his own s.	AURE 45:45	s. was like a star	WORD 958:94	s., whose faculties	MARL 572:99
Revolving in his altered s.	DRYD 300:32	s. within the house	SHAK 785:91	sweat and blood and s.	FRAN 348:23
roll from s. to s.	TENN 872:40	Stole many a man's s. and faith	JAGG 449:15	the sizes of enemy s.	HOFS 422:37
Rome...city of the s.	BYRON 188:62	story of the s.	RUSS 735:42	the s.' sorrow	
sacred story of the s.'s delight	LANY 508:57	strikes more of a panic to the s.	MELV 585:61	times that try men's s.	PAINE 660:29
said to my s., be still	ELIOT 320:57	strong music in the s.	COLE 235:31	to be able to touch s.	THER 882:84

soul-sides

two s....are one	DONNE 292:39
two s. stand up erect	BROW 166:94
Upon the King...our s.	SHAK 775:84
when s. each other draw	POPE 686:47
whisper to their s.	DONNE 292:38
yet barbarous s.	MELV 585:52
Young s....as unsympathetic	ELIOT 315:19
soul-sides boasts two s-s.	BROW 168:56
sound Adding s. to movies	PICK 677:65
all is not s.	JONS 467:60
all s. and successful...morality	SHAW 806:79
deeper than did ever plummet s.	SHAK 804:31
delightful s.	SHEL 814:98
dull, unvaried, sad'ning s.	CRAB 252:43
ears he likes to bathe in s.	BROWN 164:31
empty-hearted whose low s.	SHAK 792:85
expression for the inner s.	KAND 472:15
full of s. and fury	SHAK 798:74
Hark, the glad s.!	DODD 289:90
hollow s. is heard	LICH 528:87
individual s. Insists	LARK 509:73
last s. on the worthless earth	FAUL 331:47
let the s. of music	SHAK 770:18
Lion-like, in full-mouthed s.	CRAIK 252:51
maple seldom inward s.	SPEN 838:20
most persistent s.	KOES 495:31
No s. is dissonant	COLE 234:7
not very s.	SMOL 831:66
sentence is a s.	FROST 352:94
sighing s., the lights	ROSS 726:54
Silence has a s.	KOH 496:33
S., and sweet airs	SHAK 804:25
's.' banker, alas!	KEYN 484:75
s. diffuses itself in circles	LEON 523:78
s. his breathing kept	SHEL 814:13
s. is forced	BLAKE 139:79
s. is gone out into all lands	BOOK 148:9
s. mind in a s. body	JUVE 471:57
s. must seem an echo	POPE 685:24
s. of abundance of rain	BIBLE 97:63
s. of a great amen	PROC 697:27
s. of drubbing and sobbing	SMITH 830:39
S. of Surprise	BALL 60:87
s. of the cricket bats	JOYCE 470:19
s. of the white soldier's axe	RED 709:19
s. of water's murmuring	SHEL 816:59
s. strikes like a rising knell!	BYRON 187:50
s., substantial flesh and blood	ELIOT 320:65
s. That saved a wretch	NEWT 635:63
s. together harmoniously	HONO 426:16
Sweet is every s.	TENN 873:52
sweet s....upon a bank of violets	SHAK 785:77
thinking have been s.	WELLS 930:40
thund'ring s.	GOLD 376:2
twelve great shocks of s.	TENN 871:4
typical s. of Lancashire	ORWE 653:9
what surge that s. can start	PUSH 700:88
wound...with a sinful s.	VAUG 909:35
soundbites can't speak in s.	CLAR 229:70
sounded But they s. nice	RAMOS 705:50
s. like the book of Revelations	JAMES 450:26
sounds better than it s.	TWAIN 904:94
concord of sweet s.	SHAK 770:21
doggerel of s.	RUSK 733:18
empty s.	JOHN 460:69
measured out by s.	BETJ 89:47
Music is the art of s.	BUSO 184:54
Not many s. in life	LAMB 505:4
Of all sweet s. the life and element!	COLE 235:30
painting of s., noises and smells	CARRA 202:57
power of...many s.	SHEL 812:54
Scents, colours, and s.	BAUD 68:56
self-same s.	STEV 849:57
s. frae hell	FERG 333:85
s. of silence	DOWD 296:32
s. of their voices	ANGE 19:99
s. which oft have raised me	COLE 235:28
s. will take care of themselves	CARR 203:75
When it s. good	ELLI 322:21
soup Beautiful S.	CARR 204:82
Gentlemen do not take s.	CURZ 260:7
in a world of s.	GALL 358:95
live upon s. and bouille	SMOL 831:67
Macbeth slurping your s.	PAGE 659:14
never let his s. get cold	HOFF 422:32
s. in Ireland	WAUGH 923:55
speak of his own s.	TARA 867:28

steam of the social s.	ACKR 3:60
thick giblet s.	JOYCE 470:29
soupkitchener Sao long, aol s.!	SHAW 809:75
sour fathers have eaten s. grapes	BIBLE 110:32
garden of cactus and s. grapes	MERR 589:49
gotta take the s.	GOLD 377:36
How s. sweet music is	SHAK 765:63
mixture of the sweet and the s.	LAFO 504:55
s. grapes and ashes	ASHF 38:75
s. misfortune's book	SHAK 766:13
s. offence	SHAK 786:32
sweet or s.	TRAV 896:93
source as a s. of income	KEMB 479:72
backward motion toward the s.	FROST 352:7
chief s. of economic insecurity	ELLW 323:39
great s. of the holy river	SPEKE 836:81
inexhaustible s. of laughter	TOLS 894:54
s. and end...of art	POPE 685:18
s....beyond all reason	HAMM 394:54
S. inexhausted of all	STER 849:59
s. of practically every good title	HEMI 409:63
sources from the most remote of s.	HEAT 406:95
invisible s. and echoes	HARR 399:55
s. of the Nile	ELIOT 316:46
ultimate s. of knowledge	POPP 689:62
sours world of sweets and s.	POE 683:87
souses night-clubbing s.	GERS 365:74
south a town in the S. of England	ORWE 653:14
fickle is the S.	TENN 872:44
full of the warm S.	KEATS 478:42
In the S., the war	TWAIN 902:49
must s. of us remain	JOHN 458:24
niggers of de S.	TRUTH 900:4
s., where there is no autumn	LAWR 513:66
The S. is avenged!	BOOTH 150:46
the S. is hardly Christ-centred	OCON 647:87
travelling due s.	PEARY 671:60
wanton in the S.	TENN 873:45
South Africa people of S. A.	SMUTS 831:70
S. A., renowned...For politics	CAMP 194:50
victory for all the people of S. A.	MAND 564:55
When I left S. A.	WOODS 954:4
South America flow through S. A.	KIPL 489:79
southern acquire the S. knack	STEV 853:76
daughter of the S. Cross	FRAN 348:23
S. Black girl	ANGE 18:83
S. Cross insignificantly mixed	LAWR 513:56
southerners S. can never resist	MITC 610:44
Southey S....so quaint	BYRON 189:3
South Pacific mask from the S. P.	ROSE 725:28
south-wind s.-w. rushing warm	TENN 871:17
sovereign bandy civilities with my s.	JOHN 461:15
called by my s.	PITT 679:4
Five s. fingers taxed	THOM 883:8
good service to his s.	SUN 859:93
individual is no longer to be s.	DOUG 295:23
servants of the s.	BACON 51:83
s., accompanied by all the army	GRAY 383:44
S. of cities	DUNB 306:2
s. of insufferables	BIER 134:58
s. of sighs and groans	SHAK 763:9
s. sway...dissolved by might?	DRYD 302:86
Whoso has sixpence is s.	CARL 200:91
with s. eye	SHAK 801:48
sovereignest s. thing that any man	SKEL 824:27
telling me the s. thing on earth	SHAK 771:33
sovereigns s. and magistrates	LUTH 542:72
we...its s.	BYRON 189:84
sovereignty challenge...no s.	LANY 508:56
If absolute s. be not necessary	ASTE 39:4
the supranational s.	ROCK 720:30
soviet all-eclipsing S. world	THUB 890:60
bully...S. Union	HAIG 391:14
Civil war...in the S. Union	PAVL 670:40
going on in the S. Union	GORB 378:47
S. game is chess	SHUL 819:25
S. Republic needs an army	TROT 899:63
S. Union remains a superpower	WALE 917:29
S. Union would be of enormous extent	GOEB 374:54
twenty years ago in the S. Union	THER 882:91
Soviets S. sought not...the sun	DULL 306:87
S....would occupy...Europe	GOEB 374:54
Soviet Union collapse of the S. U. was a...disaster	PUTIN 700:92
those who do not regret the collapse of the S. U.	PUTIN 700:93

sow S. returns to her Mire	KIPL 493:79
s. that was washed	BIBLE 130:74
What s. ye?	WILDE 940:45
sower s. went forth to sow	BIBLE 117:90
soweth whatsoever a man s.	BIBLE 127:82
sown reap where he hath s.	KIPL 490:8
s. the tares of spiritual errors	HOBB 420:5
space across the gulf of s.	WELLS 930:19
any visitor from outer s.	BURR 181:65
Architecture...how to waste s.	JOHN 459:34
atoms and empty s.	DEMO 272:48
beyond S. and Time	BROO 163:1
bodies in s.	MANN 566:84
camembert of time and s.	DALI 261:15
captured fume of s.	CRANE 253:64
cemetery is an open s.	SHEL 815:26
everything except s. and light	HEAT 406:94
feel the same way about form and s.	DAVIS 266:5
flying through s.	MUIR 624:26
flying through s. forever	GAGA 356:8
gleaming cantos of unvanquished s.	CRANE 253:65
inner s....is the real subject	BALL 60:85
island rock in s.	CIAR 226:22
king of infinite s.	SHAK 782:86
Lancelot mused a little s.	TENN 870:87
laws of s. and time	CORY 247:21
Love is s. and time	PROU 698:48
more s. where nobody is	STEIN 845:65
need for a well-defined personal s.	COUP 248:33
no analogue in s.	EDDI 311:24
No creature loves an empty s.	MARV 578:8
Nothing is material in s.	ROSSO 727:69
o' s. at aince	MACD 549:20
out of time, out of s.	WELLS 930:20
pleasure of enclosed s.	JOHN 458:29
poem full of s. and reverie	BAUD 69:89
puzzles me more than time and s.	LAMB 505:81
Rotarians in s.!	VIDAL 912:85
shining s.	GRAV 382:19
smallest s. of calmness	BEDE 72:59
s. in which to reproduce	ROSE 725:26
S. isn't remote	HOYLE 434:96
s....laid on her hair	CRANE 253:62
s. not to dwell in	GIRA 372:24
s. of life between	KEATS 476:83
S....the central fact	OLSEN 650:45
S.—the final frontier	RODD 721:44
start of s.	SCOTT 751:2
vacancy which occupies the s.	TOOLE 894:60
spaces figures...empty s. around	MATI 581:91
infinite s. Are still silent	EBER 310:11
silence of these infinite s.	PASC 667:75
s. between the houses	FENT 332:59
s. between the stars	HENRI 411:8
s. swarming with erotic bodies	CIXO 227:47
vacant interstellar s.	ELIOT 320:62
spaceship passenger on the s., Earth	FULL 355:72
S.-s. and time machines	KOES 495:28
trying to launch a homemade s.	FAUL 331:47
spacings s. of the spheres	PYTH 701:16
spade call a s. a s.	BURT 181:75
glad...never seen a s.	WILDE 942:8
poor crooked scythe and s.	SHIR 819:20
s. he also hent	SPEN 839:61
s. is never so merely a s.	FRY 353:24
truth calls s. a s.!	BROW 169:80
Write with your s.	CAMP 194:53
spades Let s. be trumps!	POPE 685:29
spaghetti feeding on booze and s.	LEWIS 527:58
you see I owe to s.	LOREN 537:60
Spain devildoms of S.	TENN 878:95
feared by S., by France	SIXT 824:26
In S., the priests ruled	COND 239:12
King o' S.'s daughter	COLUM 238:38
not into the hands of S.	TENN 879:98
not only S....will...have refreshment	COLU 238:91
Pretender in S.	SWIFT 862:57
singeing of the King of S.'s beard	DRAKE 298:86
slow old tunes of S.	MASE 580:57
S. gets bullfights	JONG 466:52
S. is the only country	LORCA 537:59
S.! renown'd, romantic land!	BYRON 187:38
S....should dare to invade	ELIZ 321:4
war in S. is over	MUSS 628:95
spam wanted steak...offered s.	MALA 561:82
span Contract into a s.	HERB 414:82
Eternity shut in a s.	CRAS 253:78

spell

flung the s. on even wing — CRANE 253:67
I s. and Eve s. — GILM 371:95
Less than a s. — BACON 53:49
life's...but a s. — DAVI 264:77
should reach the s. — SASS 745:81
spangled s. heavens, a shining frame — ADDI 7:40
Unpin that s. breastplate — DONNE 291:19
spangles Sawdust and s. — CARD 198:38
stars were so many s. — ARNO 36:46
Spaniard S. brought to America — MARI 570:72
S. have his Spain — JOHN 458:24
Spaniards S. and other nations — GARC 359:67
S. seem wiser than they are — BACON 52:11
thrash the S. too — DRAKE 298:88
spaniel s. on those principles — LLOY 532:69
Spanish after the S. Empire fell — REYES 712:69
ancient S. historians of America — ECHE 310:14
fond of S. wine — MASE 580:57
S. ships of war at sea! — TENN 878:95
speech...sonorous as S. — QUIL 702:13
To God I speak S. — CHAR 215:38
spanner fished...with a s. — BETJ 89:44
spare can you s. a dime? — HARB 396:87
power...is to s. you — SHAK 803:9
was a s. man — AUBR 42:58
spark no s. of honour bides — SHAK 760:2
single s. can start a...fire — MAO 568:26
s. from heaven — ARNO 34:91
s. from heaven! — ARNO 34:93
s....of heavenly fire — DRYD 302:79
s. of humanity can tolerate — RUSS 734:38
s. of inextinguishable thought — SHEL 816:51
s. o' Nature's fire — BURNS 177:70
s. that moves mankind — SIKO 821:68
tiny s. of energy — MACC 546:67
sparkles Alive with s. — KEATS 476:88
pride struck out new s. — DRYD 303:11
sparkling s. eyes — GILB 370:73
sparks Ashes and s., my words — SHEL 813:84
as the s. fly upward — BIBLE 98:97
like s. among the stubble — BIBLE 112:75
painted with unnumbered s. — SHAK 777:26
s. that are like wit — SHAK 774:39
sparrow brawling of a s. — YEATS 965:6
hero perish, or a s. fall — POPE 686:73
providently caters for the s. — SHAK 778:70
s. hath found an house — BIBLE 101:38
s. should fly swiftly — BEDE 72:59
sparrows Lesbia with her s. — MILL 592:21
two s. sold for a farthing? — BIBLE 116:71
Sparta Paint as they spoke in S. — DIDE 285:77
Spartans tell the S. — SIMO 822:79
spasm emotional s. — BEVAN 89:58
spate Riveris ran reid on s. — DOUG 294:1
speak danger to s. true — JONS 467:76
do not care to s. ill — JOHN 462:22
how to s. well — GERB 364:62
it be you who s. — THOM 886:74
it cannot s. — SHAK 758:60
Murder...will s. — SHAK 782:3
Never s. more clearly — BAKER 56:1
Let the poem s. — PAGL 659:22
province of knowledge to s. — HOLM 424:83
regret...that it cannot s.! — CARR 206:33
s. daggers to her — SHAK 783:31
s. for sixty thousand dead! — HUGH 436:49
S. less than thou knowest — SHAK 792:91
S., Lord — BIBLE 96:26
s. more in a minute — SHAK 766:91
s. no more than is set down — SHAK 783:20
S. not when the people listens — SCOTT 754:64
s. now, and I will answer — HOUS 431:50
s. plain and to the purpose — SHAK 774:36
s. sooner than drink — SHAK 771:38
S. then to me — SHAK 796:5
S. the speech — SHAK 783:18
S. to Him — TENN 877:71
S. what we feel — SHAK 793:40
s. when he is spoken to — STEV 853:64
s. when she is unhappy? — SMITH 830:40
Think before you s. — FORS 345:48
time to s. — BIBLE 105:14
To s. and purpose not — SHAK 792:86
When I think, I must s. — SHAK 779:93
When you s., sweet — SHAK 799:20
whereof one cannot s. — WITT 951:20
won't s. to me for fifty minutes — DOYLE 297:55

speaker By your leave, Mr S. — RUSH 732:77
Mr S., I think — ROCHE 719:99
s., and the schoolmaster — DICK 281:76
s. at a meeting — SUTH 860:7
s. is not to be trusted — EUDA 328:52
S. of the House — GARN 360:77
What, Mr S.! — ROCHE 719:2
speakers observe the best s. — JONS 468:93
speakest howsome'er thou s. — SHAK 770:9
speaking before s., before — ROUS 729:13
ill s. between a fou man — SCOTT 754:71
it is I, your father, s. — BELL 75:30
prays without s. — FRIE 351:73
speaks every day S. a new scene — QUAR 701:6
She s. poniards — SHAK 773:27
s. holiday — SHAK 773:9
s. to us the same word — SCHW 751:94
spear boomerang No more s. — NOON 641:51
Bring me my s.! — BLAKE 141:42
cutteth the s. in sunder — BIBLE 100:69
deadly s. rests — ANON 20:30
fair Scotland's s. — SCOTT 752:27
knappeth the s. — BOOK 149:17
slander's venomed s. — SHAK 764:30
s. pierced his side — BIBLE 123:63
s. through the dead leaves — MANS 567:3
where the shield and s. — SPEN 838:37
spearmen stubborn s. — SCOTT 752:26
spears pruninghooks into s. — BIBLE 111:49
s. into pruninghooks — BIBLE 107:51
stars threw down their s. — BLAKE 140:20
spec Just 'on s.', addressed as follows — PATE 669:13
special earth is nothing very s. — HOYLE 434:95
I think I'm a s. one — MOUR 623:94
something s. about a poet — FROST 352:9
s. kind of man — GILL 370:82
still want to be s. — GRAY 383:42
specialist definition of a s. — MAYO 583:27
specialists All other men are s. — DOYLE 297:71
specialized s. but equally ordinary — GALB 357:20
s. form of art — PRIT 696:16
specials You can't trust the 's.' — COLL 237:64
species belonged to different s. — LAVER 512:34
certain s. of eternity — SPIN 840:74
Especially the male of the s. — LAWR 513:77
female of the s. — KIPL 493:77
human s., according to...theory — LAMB 505:2
human s....result of mistakes — MILL 595:96
No s. remains constant — OVID 657:47
of a superior s. — VINER 913:10
one of the s. — ADDI 6:24
particular intelligent s. — HOYLE 434:95
s. of military instinct — HAYD 402:23
s. of person — WAUGH 923:64
subordinate s. of Northumberland — SCOTT 754:76
specific apply to s. subjects — HUGO 436:53
comes forth the grand s. — BYRON 187:31
committing itself to anything s. — LODGE 534:94
facts, with the s. — ROTH 728:90
specimens s., the lilies of ambition — DOUG 295:6
speck taking a s. for the whole — EDGE 311:45
speckled S. and white...and brown! — COLUM 238:90
spectacle duller s. this earth of ours — DE 273:81
great s. of life — ELIOT 316:54
national s. — LORCA 537:59
no s. so ridiculous — MACA 545:30
s. of nature — ROUS 729:15
s. that is now unfolding — CHUR 225:90
s. unto the world — BIBLE 126:38
spectacles gray-framed s. — GUNT 390:97
lewd, ungodly S. — PRYN 698:62
s. of books — DRYD 300:20
using old men's s. — DONNE 293:76
spectacular really a s. sight — SCHW 750:93
spectator artist is a s. — ERNST 327:39
atrocious to the s. — BIOY 135:5
participant or s. — GALL 358:39
S. of mankind — ADDI 6:24
s. sport — GERG 365:67
think no more of the s. — DIDE 285:63
spectators actors or s.? — SHEL 815:35
gave pleasure to the s. — MACA 546:59
roars of infuriated s. — ORWE 655:81
too cold for the s. — SMITH 830:30
spectre s. is haunting Europe — MARX 579:33
spectres Four s. haunt the poor — LLOY 532:71
spectrum like the white ray of the s. — BLAV 142:51

speculate to s. is a gain — COUS 248:40
speculation from this top Of s. — MILT 607:73
mind against s. — RUSS 734:23
watches the s. — DICK 279:15
speculations s. of eternity or infinitude — ADDI 7:36
s. of lasting tranquillity — HAMI 394:48
speculator investor and s. — KEYN 484:78
speculators manipulators and s. — MAMET 564:39
S. may do no harm — KEYN 484:79
speech after-dinner s. — WAUGH 924:83
as it does in one's s. — LARO 510:6
begin my s....'My husband and I' — ELIZ 322:9
concern was s. — ELIOT 321:86
controversy over freedom of s. — ORWE 655:67
deal by s. than by letter — BACON 53:31
era of free s. is closing — ORWE 653:22
essential form of economic s. — WRIS 963:81
Fashion is free s. — LURIE 542:66
first people to demand free s. — BISS 137:38
freedom of s. — MOUR 623:98
freedom of s. — ROOS 724:13
freedom of s. means — BLACK 137:41
free s., free passes — BETJ 88:22
gave man s. — SHEL 814:15
given to extravagant s. and gestures — FERB 332:67
highest sense of human s. — STEV 852:52
integrity, plain s. — RODR 722:52
intelligible and rational s. — HUXL 443:7
joy of living s. — SPEN 838:26
killed...and make a s. — AUBR 42:60
learn the s. of the place — STEV 850:81
Let thy s. be short — BIBLE 113:6
loath to cast away my s. — SHAK 785:89
make a s. to maggots — CELI 211:38
neither s. nor language — BOOK 148:9
networks of dead s. — STARK 843:73
never taxed for s. — SHAK 791:53
people of a strange s. — BIBLE 110:29
perfect plainness of s. — ARNO 35:9
political s. and writing — ORWE 655:61
power of reasoned s. — ARIS 31:26
Rude am I in my s. — SHAK 788:91
slow of s. — BIBLE 93:56
Speak the s. — SHAK 783:18
s. as...dignified as Latin — QUIL 702:13
s. be alway with grace — BIBLE 128:13
s. in that victorious brow — ARNO 33:63
s. is admirable — EUDA 328:52
s. is comely — BIBLE 107:45
s. is like a cracked kettle — FLAU 339:20
S. is often barren — ELIOT 315:41
s. is poetry: cadence — NOON 640:45
S. is the small change — MERE 588:28
s. of England has no name — BRYA 170:3
s. shall distil as the dew — BIBLE 95:98
s., that supremely human gift — MATH 581:86
s. they have resolved not to make — ELIOT 315:38
s. was rather like being savaged — HEAL 404:64
such is the s. — AELI 8:73
Thought could wed itself with S. — TENN 874:67
Under all s. there lies a silence — CARL 201:21
U.S.A. is the s. of the people — DOSP 294:86
verse is a measured s. — BACON 49:30
visible s....of the democracy — STEAD 843:30
what the dead had no s. for — ELIOT 321:83
speeches cannot be solved by s. — BISM 137:32
hodgepodge of all other s. — SPEN 838:18
leave it to men's charitable s. — BACON 53:44
preparing his impromptu s. — BIRK 136:18
S. in our culture — GALB 357:27
s. were prepared with...genius — ACHE 3:42
tries on s. — CURT 259:98
speed beauty of s. — MARI 571:76
beauty of s. — MARI 571:77
forgetting the bright s. — ARNO 35:1
Full s. ahead — FARR 330:31
high s. toward the enemy — HALS 393:43
knee which contains all the s. — YOUR 969:61
little differences of s. — PRATT 694:68
riding at breakneck s. — BLAN 141:46
safety is in our s. — EMER 324:62
s. was far faster than light — BULL 173:58
told at dictation s. — AMIS 16:40
with s. I cannot render — MIDD 590:73
speedboat bailing out of a s. — CAMP 193:44
spell sit and rightly s. — MILT 598:60
s. better than they pronounce — TWAIN 902:32

spells

s. it so abominably	SHAW 810:93	as the s. moves him	SART 744:64	S. gave them utterance	BIBLE 124:72
s. my name right	COHAN 234:94	be filled with the S.	BIBLE 128:92	S. grew robust	DICK 284:50
s. of far Arabia	DELA 271:28	blood and s. together	MARI 571:81	s. hath rejoiced in God	BIBLE 120:66
tyrant s. has bound me	BRON 161:73	born of the S.	BIBLE 122:24	s. hath rejoiced in God	BIBLE 133:42
went Thy s. through him	ROSS 726:58	break a man's s.	SHAW 806:89	s. I have seen	SHAK 782:4
spells s. into the spongy air	MILT 598:67	broken s. drieth the bones	BIBLE 105:82	s. in a loyal breast	SHAK 764:32
spend s., and s., and s.!	NICH 637:79	'Brutus' will start a s.	SHAK 776:10	s. indeed is willing	BIBLE 119:43
S. it, s. it; s. more	SHAK 773:7	by my s., saith the Lord	BIBLE 112:60	s. in which it was done	HELO 409:55
S. not then his gifts	JONS 467:56	cabined ample S.	ARNO 34:86	s. is cuddled	JOHN 458:29
s. the rest of my life	JERO 454:42	Caesar's s., ranging	SHAK 777:34	s. is soaring	BRON 161:55
whatever you have, s. less	JOHN 464:85	chiefly thou O s.	MILT 601:31	S. of adoption	BIBLE 125:18
spending cut s. after he left office	DOLE 290:98	clear s. doth raise	MILT 599:86	s. of an Australian	FRAN 348:22
s. my children's inheritance	ANON 27:29	commit my s.	BIBLE 100:52	S. of Australia	FIELD 335:11
spendthrift true s.	GUIL 389:87	disembodied s.	WHAR 933:4	s. of Elijah doth rest on Elisha	BIBLE 97:72
Spens Sir Patrick S.	BALL 59:69	diversities of gifts, but the same S.	BIBLE 126:51	s. of experimentation	FRAN 348:18
Sir Patrick S.	BALL 59:70	dividing asunder of soul and s.	BIBLE 129:34	s. of health	SHAK 781:57
Spenser gentle S. fondly led	LAND 507:31	do the same things by The s.	BUTL 185:80	s. of her s.	BINY 135:99
Immortal S., no frailty	NASHE 632:92	evil s….does his utmost to deceive	DESC 275:99	s. of liberty	HAND 395:78
In S., and in Jonson, Art	DENH 272:62	exasperated s. Proceeds	ELIOT 321:87	s. of man is a good adversary	WILL 945:99
spent s. some of my own money	KENN 482:38	fair s. for my minister	BYRON 188:69	S. of Night!	SHEL 816:65
s. your years and…s. yourself	BORG 150:57	feel…the s. of a place	PEI 672:73	s. of our City	GIUL 373:33
sperm drop of s.	JIANG 455:57	fervent in s.	BIBLE 125:25	s. of our country	CHEE 218:9
milk and s. of kindness	MELV 585:66	fruit of the S.	BIBLE 127:81	s. of self-help	SMIL 827:69
spew s. thee out of my mouth	BIBLE 131:94	full of the Great S.	MARTI 576:70	s. of self-help	SMIL 827:71
sphere British 'S. of Influence'	ANON 23:94	genial s. droop	MILT 607:90	S. of the Age	HAZL 404:49
direct an uncontrollable s.	CHUR 226:17	gentlier on the s. lies	TENN 870:89	S. of the Age	VIDAL 912:84
drown me in thy s.	DONNE 291:35	gloom pervaded my s.	POE 683:80	S. of the Lord God is upon me	BIBLE 110:6
fit our s.	SCHR 749:63	greatness of your s.	ROCH 719:17	s. of the Reform Bill	PEEL 672:66
gladdened once our humble s.	BRON 161:54	Hail to thee, blithe S.	SHEL 813:90	s. of wisdom and understanding	BIBLE 108:61
Let man's soul be a s.	DONNE 293:80	hath not One s. to command	SHAK 804:23	s. of youth in everything	SHAK 802:72
nobody has one exclusive s.	MARX 579:29	haughty s. before a fall	BIBLE 105:79	s. shall return unto God	BIBLE 106:36
soul of every s.	HOLM 424:82	healthy s. of self-help	SMIL 827:71	s. that now resists	PITT 679:7
s. of complete abstraction	WHIT 936:67	history of the human s.	ARNO 36:32	s. within it is tough	WAVE 925:2
s. of leisure time	LOWE 540:39	However vast a man's s.	PASC 666:64	S. with S. can meet	TENN 877:71
s. With centric	MILT 605:35	human s. is immortal	MURP 626:75	Stirs the dumb s.	ELIOT 321:81
than the moon's s.	SHAK 767:25	I commend my s.	BOOK 149:11	strike with our s.'s knife	SHEL 815:39
treat nature by…the s.	CEZA 212:52	immortal s. grows like harmony	WORD 958:76	sulky Scottish s.	SCOTT 754:77
spheres amongst th'eternal s.	SPEN 838:36	immortal s. must endure	ARNO 33:63	sword of the S.	BIBLE 128:95
Driven by the s.	VAUG 909:39	immortal s. of the dead	SPEN 837:12	take not thy holy s. from me	BIBLE 101:73
echo of the s.	BYRON 190:27	indifference to…soul or s.	LAWR 513:54	the s. leaves his mortal body	BHAG 90:77
moving as the restless s.	MARL 572:99	ingenious, and piercing s.	MILT 601:18	the S. wanders on to a new body	BHAG 90:76
music in the spacings of the s.	PYTH 701:16	In one s. meet	SHEL 813:78	things of the S.	BIBLE 125:17
Ring out, ye crystal s.	MILT 597:35	in s. she is a man	GOTT 379:70	this body did contain a s.	SHAK 772:67
seems to shake the s.	DRYD 303:29	in the S. on the Lord's day	BIBLE 133:87	This grey s.	TENN 870:99
s. of existence	ELIOT 320:79	into thy hands I commend my s.	BIBLE 122:10	to thee my true s.?	SHAK 802:77
s. were formed in fright	MELV 585:60	is the abstract s.	KAND 472:14	to the strength of s.	SHAK 776:14
start from their s.	SHAK 781:60	It is a s.; and they cried out	BIBLE 117:99	true s. of delight	RUSS 734:25
spice Variety's the s. of life	COWP 251:15	It is the s. that quickeneth	BIBLE 123:37	unclean s. is gone out of a man	BIBLE 117:88
spider foul black cobweb to a s.	WEBS 926:41	Jesus led up of the S.	BIBLE 114:22	uphold me with thy free s.	BIBLE 101:73
S., s., spin	MACN 558:1	kill the s. here	MAIL 560:47	Whither shall I go from thy s.?	BIBLE 103:44
s.'s touch, how exquisitely fine	POPE 687:77	leap into s.	UPDI 906:31	Wild S., which art moving	SHEL 813:90
What brought the kindred s.	FROST 352:11	let my s.…rejoice	WORD 961:47	Wisdom and S. of the universe!	WORD 957:69
Spider-Man He's not S.-M.	OBAMA 645:59	letter killeth, but the s. giveth life	BIBLE 127:86	with a joyful s.	TENN 879:99
spiders like s. across the stars	KERO 483:53	life-blood of a master s.	MILT 600:2	with such a s. and decency	PITT 679:1
love of s.	WHITE 935:41	like all…creations of the human s.	DYSON 309:60	worser s. a woman	SHAK 803:87
reasoners resemble s.	BACON 50:44	Long my imprisoned s. lay	WESL 931:57	worship him in s. and in truth	BIBLE 122:28
walls of s.' legs	DRAY 299:1	Love is a s.	SHAK 762:84	**spirits** aerial s. live inspher'd	MILT 598:62
spider-web kind of huge s.-w.	JAMES 450:43	my s. hath rejoiced in God	BIBLE 120:66	angling…a cheerer of his s.	WALT 920:92
spies As if we were God's s.	SHAK 793:33	my s. hath rejoiced in God	BIBLE 133:42	By our own s. are we deified	WORD 959:1
come not single s.	SHAK 784:51	never approached my s.	METT 589:61	Come, you s.	SHAK 796:15
German police s.	MARX 579:33	no man…hath power over the s.	BIBLE 106:24	disposition of the s.	BACON 53:48
subtle s.	FREE 350:49	not given us the s. of fear	BIBLE 129:25	For S. when they please	MILT 602:46
Ye are s.	BIBLE 93:43	not to disparage things of the s.	BUSH 184:49	freeing s.	FLAU 339:26
spikes sitting on nine ebony s.	KING 488:57	nought…so much the s. calms	BYRON 189:5	frost-bound-blood, and s.	HERR 415:6
s. and loops	UPDI 906:28	o'ercrows my s.	SHAK 785:74	good s. and good temper	DICK 279:10
spin whether it would take s.	HOME 425:98	Of s. so still	SHAK 788:92	great and solemn s.	HUMB 438:93
spinach it's s.…the hell with it	WHITE 935:43	on my s. make a music, too	STEV 849:73	jump with common s.	SHAK 769:94
spin-doctors s.-d. in spin clinics	BENN 79:35	pard-like S., beautiful and swift	SHEL 815:36	Kate's s. sank to the very bottom	ADAMS 4:80
spindrift seal's wide s. gaze	CRANE 252:55	pastures of the s.	SASS 746:1	like two s.	SHAK 803:85
spine chill down the s.	COOKE 245:75	patient in s. is better	BIBLE 106:22	making the most of good s.	HARDY 397:4
Sits on its craggy s.	SMITH 831:64	poor in s.	SPARK 836:71	on their softened s. sink	BYRON 188:64
sunken fosse of her s.	HEAN 404:71	pour out my s.	BIBLE 111:48	s. fetch me what I	MARL 573:23
spinnage world of gammon and s.	DICK 280:50	power and s. of America	NORR 641:57	s. have forgot	ARNO 33:61
spinning-wheel losing the s. w.	GAND 359:58	pride of race or s.	SMITH 831:64	s. in heaven	RUSK 732:83
spinster live to hear myself called s.	SHER 817:80	pure s. shall flow	SHEL 815:38	s. masculine, create	MILT 606:64
lonelier than any s.	GREER 387:44	put a new s. within you	BIBLE 110:30	s. of our ancestors	RED 709:19
saved many an English s.	MITF 610:55	question thee concerning the S.	KORAN 497:75	s. of the wise	SHAK 772:79
slightly bearded s.	NICO 637:84	realm of the S.	MATI 581:93	S. of well-shot woodcock	BETJ 88:19
spinsters insisted upon by s.	DALY 261:21	renew a right s. within me	BIBLE 101:73	s. rushed together	TENN 871:12
spires dreaming s.	ARNO 35:16	scaffolding of s.	THOM 886:78	stillness where our s. walk	SASS 746:97
slope their pointing s.	MILT 602:43	seeds of the s. and economy	MARI 570:72	two kindred s. flee	KEATS 475:65
s. and cranes cluster	LARK 509:84	s. and judgement equal	MILT 607:80	widowhood…keeps up a wife's s.	GAY 362:18
storks on the s. of Denmark	DOYLE 297:75	S. and the Dust	DICK 284:46	**spiritual** acknowledge the s. forces	MOORE 617:20
What s., what farms	HOUS 431:51	s. burning but unbent	BYRON 188:77	affliction…either physical or s.	BEER 74:90
Ye distant s.	GRAY 383:45	s. capable of compassion	FAUL 331:36	Force is a s. power	LEON 522:70
spirit adventure of the s.	WHIT 936:66	s. could remain tinged	LOWE 540:31	From a material and s. terrain	FULL 355:77
angry s.'s yell	BEAT 70:2	s., free to choose	ROCH 719:10	large s. adventures	DAVI 265:86

squire

lastly a s. and divine — HOOK 427:40
man with detestable s. qualities — BUKO 172:53
our only s. task — MALL 562:95
see...with the s. eye — FRIE 351:75
s. demands — TAWN 868:43
sustain them through any s. — WALK 917:40
spiritually Morally, s. — MILL 594:63
s. limited on those — NIET 638:11
spit distaff, or the s.? — LEWIS 526:51
gob of s. in the face — MILL 593:52
never s. white again — SHAK 772:73
s. against the wind — WEBS 926:28
spite beating myself for s. — SIDN 820:44
fortune's dearest s. — SHAK 801:49
O curs'd s. — SHAK 781:71
slander and the s. — TENN 875:96
s. of Pride, in erring Reason's s. — POPE 687:79
spit-spot s.-s. into bed — TRAV 895:87
spittoons drinking out of s. — HEMI 410:86
obsolete as s. — BLACK 137:39
spleen Kind pity chokes my s. — DONNE 290:14
s. of fiery dragons — SHAK 761:54
splenative not s. and rash — SHAK 784:67
splendid Oh, she's a s. girl — HUXL 441:74
s. and a happy land — GOLD 376:4
s. and sterile Dolores — SWIN 864:92
splendour Heaven's s. over his head — CARL 201:36
not be content with...present s. — CARL 200:77
Pavilioned in s. — GRANT 381:15
s. borrows all her rays from sense — POPE 686:63
s. in the grass — WORD 960:12
s. of a sudden thought — BROW 169:62
s. of his mid-day beams — HERR 415:5
sun...in his first s. — WORD 959:3
splinters teeth like s. — CAUS 209:14
Spode Roderick S.? — WODE 952:52
spoil Beware lest any man s. you — BIBLE 128:9
complexion we were not to s. — SCHR 749:63
s. our own — JERO 454:37
spoiled You can't get s. — STREE 857:50
spoils loaded with s. — CARL 200:80
s. of time — GRAY 384:68
spoken Glorious things are s. — BIBLE 101:91
have s. it — GRIS 389:76
people not s. about — GEE 362:27
s. lightly of my deathless friends — SASS 746:98
spokesmen find their own...s. — COWL 250:80
sponge Darkness falls like a wet s. — ASHB 37:55
married to a s. — SHAK 769:80
Sponge Bob Square Pants S. B. S. P. is more important — WHIT 937:86
spontaneity s. of a mechanical tiger — ACHE 2:31
spoof forecast...some kind of s. — LODGE 534:94
spook s....who haunted...Poe — ELLI 323:35
spoon ate with a runcible s. — LEAR 516:38
balancing an egg on a s. — HILL 418:55
blindly searching the s. — SMITH 828:4
traces of the...gold s. — DICK 282:80
Why doesn't he use a s.? — DE 275:6
spoons faster we counted our s. — EMER 325:90
let us count our s. — JOHN 461:94
measured out my life with coffee s. — ELIOT 316:63
s. and the pots — SEXT 758:48
when you want his s.? — HORN 430:25
world locks up its s. — SHAW 808:30
sport Detested s. — COWP 251:17
ended his s. with Tess — HARDY 397:16
fellowly s. or pastime — STUB 858:61
good enough s. — HORN 430:25
idea of a contact s. was chess — HUGH 435:29
in love as in s. — GRAV 382:29
In no s....more humiliated — MAIL 560:59
kill us for their s. — SHAK 793:17
love s. because I love life — YEVT 968:46
loyal s. of love — ANON 21:50
made skiing a spectator s. — ANON 25:46
make her more s. — MONT 614:27
national s. of England — TREE 896:1
never kill for s. — FROU 353:27
no such s. as s. by s. — SHAK 763:23
only athletic s. I mastered — JERR 455:50
Our s., our studies, and our souls — BYRON 186:23
Politics is a blood s. — BEVAN 90:60
running people down considered s. — FOST 345:57
spectator s. — GERG 365:67
s. for our neighbours — AUST 46:63
S....is an occupation — PIUS 680:20

s....is war minus the shooting — ORWE 655:81
s. of a merry-go-round — HARDY 396:3
s. that bears the same relation — HUBB 434:2
submits to them in s. — EDGE 311:35
Summer loves to s. — COLL 238:77
that makes the s. — SUCK 858:67
traditional and popular s. — SITW 824:25
sporting realization that to be s. — SKIN 825:49
Snorting and s. like porpoises — SITW 823:39
sports axiom of s. — FRAY 349:35
First of all S.! — LOVE 538:80
hate all s. as rabidly — MENC 587:12
her cruel s. — SPEN 839:60
lawfullest of s. — BAXT 69:94
No outdoor s. can be — AI WEI 10:6
Organised outdoor s. — HOBS 421:10
Praise the s. of the land — REID 710:45
private s. the stews would blush — MASS 581:74
simple s. — TENN 874:90
soccer, of all s. — ROUS 729:8
S. do not build character — BROUN 163:21
s. pages are strictly — NASH 631:53
turn to the s. section — WARR 921:14
universal languages: love, music and s. — MOSES 622:79
uther sik unprofitable s. — JAME 449:19
We've dominated s. — JOHN 457:7
sportsman he was never...A S. — SITW 824:21
No s. wants to kill — SHAW 811:28
s. is a man who — LEAC 515:23
sportsmanship S....the Church — HOOV 427:52
sportsmen standing insult to s. — FRY 353:28
sportswriters s....enthusiasm — FRAY 349:35
sportswriting thing that s. teaches — FORD 343:10
Sporus Let S. tremble — POPE 688:5
spot come to this hallowed s. — KING 487:28
dear the schoolboy s. — BYRON 189:97
dogs called S. — AMIS 16:44
firm s. on which to stand — ARCH 30:8
hit the sorest s. — CHES 219:32
only one bright s. — TOLK 893:44
Out, damned s. — SHAK 798:65
pleasanter s. you never spied — BROW 167:15
s. acclaimed by savant — HUGH 435:22
s....at the back of the head — WOOLF 955:32
s....it can take out — GAY 362:17
s. which no vicissitude — WORD 961:23
stir of this dim s. — MILT 598:62
there is no s. in thee — BIBLE 107:45
tied to the s. by some...creature — DARW 263:51
trouble finding the sensitive s. — LACL 503:39
spotlight s. of public life — FOST 345:57
spots leopard his s.? — BIBLE 110:19
making my s. ache — KIPL 491:40
sequestered s. — HARDY 397:14
spouse Adam from his fair s. — MILT 604:9
sister, my s. — BIBLE 107:46
s. is in despair — PRIOR 696:9
tired of being the feminine s. — DIAZ 276:26
spray in thy hand a withered s. — ARNO 34:91
small fowlys singis on the s. — DOUG 295:2
s. of Western pine! — HARTE 400:74
toss in the s. — ARNO 33:56
spray-gunned even silence, is s.-g.? — OLSEN 650:46
spread not good except it be s. — BACON 52:95
sprig s. of bays — SWIFT 862:60
spring absent in the s. — SHAK 802:72
Bare Winter...changed to S. — SHEL 816:59
bear waiting for s. — PIER 677:71
blue sky of s. — ALLI 14:7
buffalos of the s. — LIND 530:22
can S. be far behind? — SHEL 813:84
cherry blossoms in the s. — ANON 24:27
chilly fingered s. — KEATS 474:90
colds a forward s. remove? — DONNE 291:28
continual s., and harvest — SPEN 838:39
Cowslip...bloomed that s. — CRANE 253:66
darling of the S. — WORD 958:95
dazed s. approaches — WILL 946:8
dug a s. in infancy — BRON 161:59
Easing the s. — REED 709:27
enjoy the s. flowers — SU 858:65
ever-returning s. — WHIT 938:8
every winter change to s. — TENN 874:77
found in the s. to follow? — SWIN 863:79
from my native s. — DRYD 301:56
honeyed s. — GRAY 384:58

In the S. a livelier iris — TENN 871:11
It is s., moonless night — THOM 884:31
less quick to s. again — ARNO 35:21
like a man taking his last s. — BANN 62:33
lived light in the s. — ARNO 33:69
messenger of S. — SPEN 839:45
Midwinter S. is its own season — ELIOT 321:80
only the certain s. — BINY 15:4
play'd a s., and danc'd it round — BURNS 178:2
rifle all the breathing s. — COLL 237:70
second s. — PHIL 676:52
seen...with his vision, S. — SACK 737:10
severest winter...the s. — COWP 251:8
songs of S.? — KEATS 478:33
S. is nature's way of — WILL 944:76
s. of love — COLE 235:71
S. shall pour his showers — COLL 238:77
s. summer autumn winter — CUMM 258:69
S., the sweet s. — NASHE 632:93
S. to the North — MACD 549:33
s. when the world is puddle wonderful — CUMM 257:52
Sweet lovers love the s. — SHAK 780:21
taste not the Pierian s. — POPE 685:19
the s. begins — SWIN 863:83
thou have no s. — DONNE 293:72
untaught harmony of s. — GRAY 383:55
When S. comes round — SEEG 755:99
When the hounds of s. — SWIN 863:82
when their game will s. — OTWAY 656:99
when the s. comes — GIBB 367:9
wind that breathes the s. — MILT 597:42
year's at the s. — BROW 167:9
springing Praise for them s. — FARJ 330:19
springs Beside the s. of Dove — WORD 957:62
fifty s. are little room — HOUS 431:35
four wanton s. — SHAK 764:35
from the people...all s. — DISR 287:16
Hope s. eternal — POPE 687:74
Marlowe, bathed in the Thespian s. — DRAY 299:98
no bitter s. — KIPL 492:58
s. to catch woodcocks — SHAK 781:55
take from seventy s. a score — HOUS 431:34
weaker s. of the human character — HAMI 394:48
Where s. not fail — HOPK 428:65
springtime In s.-t....ring-time — SHAK 780:21
s. of America's cultural — ROCK 721:40
sprinkle So shall he s. many nations — BIBLE 109:92
sprite elements and an angelic s. — DONNE 292:56
spur Danger, the s. — CHAP 214:21
have no s. — SHAK 796:20
keenest s. to exertion — BENT 82:93
spurn s. me hence...s. me hither — SHAK 762:92
spurred always be booted and s. — MONT 613:19
spurs suffre hym...to wynne his s. — EDWA 312:57
spurt blue s. of a lighted match — BROW 167:24
spy Here's none to s. — JONS 468:83
not to play the s. — TOYN 895:79
s. ring — MCCA 547:84
s. sent into life — BOWL 153:99
S. who Came in — LECA 518:71
th'infected s. — POPE 685:26
spying S. on other people's lives — ALME 14:10
squabble s. in your back-yard — SYNGE 865:24
squadrons side of the big s. — BUSSY 184:56
s. in Saimear's — MCCA 547:74
squads Undisciplined s. of emotion — ELIOT 320:66
squalid misfits...and s. criminals — REAG 708:8
s. wretchedness — BYRON 187:31
squalor amidst its poverty and s. — ARNO 36:29
with Love and S. — SALI 740:83
square broke a British s.! — KIPL 489:89
grows a glimmering s. — TENN 872:43
here is a little s. of blue — MONET 612:99
honest, so thoroughly s. — LERN 523:85
old people are s. — SHAF 758:54
pointed out one corner of a s. — CONF 240:19
run quite out of s. — SPEN 839:55
slog to s. leg — JOYCE 470:31
thin trees in a city s. — LOWE 539:1
squares about the flowering s. — TENN 875:98
squash S. is boxing — BARR 65:96
S....it's flagellation — COWA 249:61
squeaks Thin s. of radio static — CRANE 253:60
squeeze s. ourselves universally — MELV 585:66
squeezing in a s. of a lemon — GOLD 376:12
squire S.'s own daughter — GRAV 383:40

squires s. ride slowly towards the sea — CHES 221:98
squirrel joiner s. or old grub — SHAK 765:71
  s.'s heart beat — ELIOT 316:51
stab I saw him s. and s. again — READ 708:92
  noble Caesar saw him s. — SHAK 777:43
  s. me in the back — LAMP 506:22
  wound and s. us — KAFKA 472:3
stability s. or enlargement — JOHN 460:70
  s. to a popular Government — WHIT 934:25
  the United States, pursued s. — RICE 713:85
stables s. are the real centre — SHAW 810:7
stack s. or the barn door — MILT 597:44
stadiums listen, at the s. — ABSE 1:10
staff break my s. — SHAK 804:31
  cursing his s. — SASS 745:86
  kamikaze ground s. — PARK 665:36
  My s. of faith — RALE 705:44
  rod and s. me comfort still — SCOT 754:85
  rod and thy s. — BIBLE 100:45
  s. in your hand — BIBLE 93:59
  s. of honour for mine age — SHAK 760:22
  s. of this broken reed — BIBLE 108:78
  s. of this bruised reed — BIBLE 98:82
staffers We're down to…paid s. — MCCA 547:72
staffocracy 's.' has been created — SHUL 819:29
stag s. at eve had drunk — SCOTT 752:28
  s. in the Priory coomb — DAVI 264:68
  s. of warrant — DAVI 264:69
stage actor everywhere but…s. — CHES 219:47
  All the world's a s. — SHAK 779:80
  As large as is the s. — JONS 466:43
  before we go quite off this s.? — POPE 686:64
  daily s. of duty — KEN 480:83
  Don't put your daughter on the s. — COWA 249:54
  edge of the s. — DIDE 285:63
  final s. — GARD 360:71
  frets his hour upon the s. — SHAK 798:74
  great s. of fools — SHAK 793:27
  mellow glory of the Attic s. — ARNO 33:64
  musty breezes of a bare s. — HART 400:69
  On the s. he was natural — GOLD 377:18
  On the s. of the universe — LAFO 504:61
  played upon a s. — SHAK 786:17
  putting up a s. set — WAITE 916:6
  science…has this tremendous s. — RABI 704:23
  Self-pity in its early s. — ANGE 19:92
  s. but echoes back — JOHN 459:44
  s. of wisdom — SKIN 825:49
  s. where every man must play — SHAK 768:68
  s. where truth calls spade a spade! — BROW 169:80
  time to get off the s. — MAJOR 561:75
  to know the people…on the s. — PAGE 659:14
  United Nations…is…a s. — OBRI 645:65
  Where's the s. — BOOTH 150:47
  wonder of our s.! — JONS 468:78
stagecoach s. from London to Oxford — HAZL 403:38
  travelling in a s. — IRVI 447:61
stagecoaches twice as fast as s.? — ANON 23:86
stages constantly in their early s. — SHUL 819:24
stagflation sort of s. situation — MACL 556:51
staggered drinking have you s. — WEBS 926:18
stagnate freedom to s. — STEV 851:13
stagnation not just inflation…or s. — MACL 556:51
  too absolute a s. — BRON 161:61
stain after the rain…never a s. — SHEL 813:77
  as with no s. — SHEL 815:31
  bright s. on the vision — GRAV 382:34
  sky is darkening like a s. — AUDEN 42:70
  S. all your edges — SHAK 799:6
  s….it can take out — GAY 362:17
  s. like a wound — BURKE 176:41
  s. the stiff dishonoured shroud — ELIOT 317:81
  world's slow s. — SHEL 815:40
stains Innumerable of s. — KEATS 477:20
stair highest pavement of the s. — ELIOT 317:74
  one pair of s. by the waterside — PEPYS 674:6
  rising…by a winding s. — BACON 51:82
  structure in a winding s.? — HERB 413:72
staircase S. wit — DIDE 285:74
  steps of a s. — MALL 562:3
stairs Fallen Down S. — MORT 621:74
  naked feet upon the s. — DOYLE 297:48
  pushed her down the s. — DAVIS 265:96
  rat-riddled s.? — BROW 168:37
  see through a flight o' s. — DICK 277:57
  Up s. and doun s. — MILL 595:98
  up the s. of his concepts — STEI 845:80

stake burnt at the s. — SMITH 830:38
  made life my common s. — VAUG 909:42
  parboiled head upon a s. — MONT 615:51
  reputation is at s. — SHAK 787:40
  s….in such a glorious institution — BURKE 175:21
  tied me to a s. — SHAK 798:75
  Unless you s. your life — HEIS 407:23
  what it is we have at s. — PITT 680:11
stale frizzled, s. and small — LOWE 540:21
  nor custom s. — SHAK 794:58
  s., a garment out of fashion — SHAK 803:96
  s. is their gladness — HARP 398:41
  Winter…hangs on until it is s. — CATH 208:88
Stalin from S. to Mr Bean — CABLE 191:17
  If S. had learned…cricket — DOWN 296:35
  S….lover of peace — NEHRU 636:9
  that S. himself rose — TROT 899:64
Stalinist nakedness of S. dictatorship — KENN 480:88
stalk With martial s. — SHAK 780:29
stalking It's only s. if — RODD 721:47
  s. in my chamber — WYATT 964:90
stalking-horse folly like a s.-h. — SHAK 780:26
Stalky this was S.'s contribution — KIPL 491:23
stalling a s. between two fools — FRY 354:52
stallion black s. on a field of snow — CAMP 194:55
  watersmooth-silver-…s. — CUMM 257:54
stallions bared teeth of s. — CRANE 253:66
stalls Tank come down the s. — SASS 745:80
stalwart three stout and s. sons — BALL 60:82
stamina lowering a man's s. — DOUG 294:98
stamp but the guinea's s. — BURNS 180:52
  indelible s. of his lowly origin — DARW 263:58
  physics or s. collecting — RUTH 735:52
  s. collection waits — BETJ 88:19
  s. makes the current money — JONS 468:95
  s. of his authority — LAMB 505:93
  s. of university training — GERH 365:69
stand able to s. before thee — BIBLE 95:5
  By uniting we s. — DICK 284:57
  climb the rails into the Grand S. — SOME 833:10
  cuspid's last s. — PERE 674:19
  firm spot on which to s. — ARCH 30:8
  having done all, to s. — BIBLE 128:95
  If she can s. it, I can — EPST 327:27
  light and shadow never s. still — WEST 932:75
  makes a man s. straight — HELL 408:43
  no time to s. — DAVI 265:90
  not s. for — WAUGH 924:76
  someone you can s. to live with — TROL 898:60
  s. a year or two — BURNS 178:14
  s. by what I said — ROMN 724:98
  s. like greyhounds — SHAK 775:75
  S. still, traveller, and read! — ANON 28:56
  s. up for yourself — ANGE 19:5
  S. Up! S. Up For Jesus! — DUFF 305:83
  s. up to anything — SHAW 807:3
  therefore I hope to s. — WALP 919:83
  They that s. high — SHAK 761:38
  who shall be able to s.? — BIBLE 131:2
standard advancing s. of religion — SMIL 827:71
  her just s. — POPE 685:18
  raise the scarlet s. — CONN 242:84
  s. of…Red Hugh — MCCA 547:74
  Truth is its own s. — SPIN 840:73
standardized he is s.; transformed — DOUG 295:11
standards Advance our s.! — SHAK 761:54
  s. by which he lived — CHRI 223:43
  s. of green unfurled — MOORE 617:1
standers-by not for any s.-b. — SHAK 803:90
standing heart of s. — EMPS 326:10
  like to write s. up — HEMI 410:85
  s. is slippery — BACON 51:85
  s. on the edge — SALI 740:81
  tired with s. — DONNE 291:19
standoffish Are they being s. — COLE 234:2
standpoint s. of what it attains — BURKE 176:63
stands No economy ever s. still — HARR 399:61
  s. an instant in the sun — HYDE 443:21
  s….for something younger — FIRB 336:49
  strengthen whilst one s. — ROSS 725:38
Stanford S. Rivers lost me — LEVE 525:23
staple s. of his argument — SHAK 763:20
Stapleford osier-beds, S. Abbots — LEVE 525:23
star about its chilling s. — BERR 87:96
  Being a s. has made it possible — DAVIS 265:3
  birth to a dancing s. — NIET 638:3
  catch a falling s. — DONNE 291:23

constant as the Northern S. — SHAK 777:26
curb a runaway young s. — BYRON 190:31
discovery of a s. — BRIL 159:18
don't want to sleep with the s. — CURT 259:99
dusk lit by one large s. — MERE 587:23
every s. that heaven — MILT 598:60
eve's one s. — KEATS 477:28
Fair as a s. — WORD 957:62
grapples with his evil s. — TENN 874:83
great s. early droop'd — WHIT 938:8
height, and at the s. — MERE 588:37
Hitch your wagon to a s. — EMER 325:94
Hope guides us by her s. — BRON 161:69
In heaven no single s. — THOM 887:9
in his separate s. — KIPL 490:15
Jungle s. in a jungle track — CULL 257:43
Knew you, and named a s.! — BROW 168:48
life hovers like a s. — BYRON 190:28
like a sinking s. — TENN 870:99
loftiest s. of unascended heaven — SHEL 814:18
love a bright particular s. — SHAK 791:54
merely the s.' tennis-balls — WEBS 927:64
most auspicious s. — SHAK 803:11
My Lucky S. — FREED 349:43
No one ever leaves a s. — WILD 942:34
not one s. of all — FROST 352:3
o'er the hill the eastern s. — BURNS 180:45
on the charge of a s.! — SHAK 792:89
our life's s. — WORD 959:8
Polar s. of poetry — KEATS 475:72
put on the yellow s. — FACK 329:1
reflex of a s. — WORD 957:70
self persists like a dying s. — ROET 722:64
soul was like a s. — WORD 958:94
S. and angels — ROSS 726:48
s. fall from heaven — BIBLE 131:5
s. in the east — BIBLE 114:16
S. kissing s. — CRANE 253:56
s. of deathless and painless peace — HUGH 436:42
s. of stars — DICK 281:68
s. that bids the shepherd — MILT 599:64
s. to every wand'ring — SHAK 802:80
swart s. sparely looks — MILT 599:74
tall ship and a s. to steer — MASE 580:50
twinkle of a fading s. — ELIOT 318:14
when the white s. hovers — MERE 587:24
white s. of Truth — ARNO 35:3
would you like to swing on a s. — BURKE 176:61
stardom s….gave me everything — GARD 360:94
stare frozen s….at…neighbour — ELIOT 316:49
no time to stand and s.? — DAVI 265:90
stony British s. — TENN 876:23
two red eyes that s. — RANS 707:72
When I do s. — SHAK 793:21
with one bold s. — ELIOT 318:4
Stark or Molly S.'s a widow — STARK 843:26
stark tranced woman, bound and s. — FREE 350:48
We are s. naught all — FLET 341:55
starlight And s. wood — SHEL 812:56
Into the frosty s. — ARNO 34:99
moonlight and the s. — LONG 535:28
S. and dewdrop — FOST 345:56
starlit s. or a moonlit dome — YEATS 967:31
s. with eternities unknown — SASS 746:1
starry sky — GERS 365:79
stars almost immense, with s. — MILT 605:35
Among the scattered s. — WORD 956:57
And she forgot the s. — KEATS 477:12
and the s. came out — TENN 878:97
as the s. are slow — THOM 885:65
as the s. for ever and ever — BIBLE 111:44
Beneath the s. — MIDD 590:81
broad stripes and bright s. — KEY 483:68
came forth to see the s. — DANTE 262:39
champagne and the s. — FITZ 337:80
chilly s. I can forgo — CORY 247:10
Continuous as the s. — WORD 960:25
crocus lustres of the s. — CRANE 252:54
crowned with the s. — TRAH 895:85
crown of twelve s. — BIBLE 131:9
cubic inch of some s. — MACC 546:67
Doubt thou the s. are fire — SHAK 781:77
eyes were blind with s. — HODG 421:21
Far beyond the s. — VAUG 909:37
fault…is not in our s. — SHAK 776:9
fiercer than s. — BRAS 156:77
flag, the S. and Stripes — ROOS 725:23

statistics

fleet of s. is anchored	FLEC 340:37	weapon is s.	STEV 854:92
have the s.	ROBI 718:79	**starve** bury whom he helped to s.	POPE 688:4
heaven And calculate the s.	MILT 605:35	s. with feeding	SHAK 799:1
heaven without s.	SANT 743:47	they that s. with nothing	SHAK 761:38
He treated the s. as	CONR 244:55	**starveling** 'Sblood, you s.	SHAK 771:47
high time we relit the s.	APOL 29:85	**starving** disdain if they were not s.	ROCH 719:18
How strange the s.	SCOTT 751:1	truly affectionate when he is s.?	PREV 694:78
imitate the s. celestial	DAVI 264:75	**StarWars** a S. W. civilization	WILS 948:55
in his right hand seven s.	BIBLE 131:88	**state** assist the S.	PITT 679:4
journey-work of the s.	WHIT 937:92	august occasions of the s.	FROST 353:21
just as he do	BELL 78:97	bestowed...by the s.	MCCA 547:90
knowledge of the s.	EDDI 311:25	between S. and S.	ROUS 729:17
let us explore the s.	KENN 481:1	beweep my outcast s.	SHAK 800:46
like never-ending s.	BETJ 89:46	body continues in its s.	NEWT 635:56
Look at the s.!	HOPK 428:75	Boston is a s. of mind	APPL 30:93
looker at s.	DOYLE 297:75	California, the department-store s.	CHAN 213:85
look up at the s.	HAWK 401:97	cannot...miss it in my weak s.	COMP 239:99
men...dream of the s.	ELLI 323:32	desirable mental s.	LURIE 542:67
moon and s. are set	STEV 853:65	difference of birth or s.?	DEKK 270:9
moon and the s.	MACC 548:8	discumbered Atlas of the s.	COWP 250:92
moon or favouring s.	WORD 952:82	dividing the s. from...private	GALB 357:19
More s. than...heaven	DIETZ 286:90	economy of a s.	RUSK 733:97
morning s. sang together	BIBLE 98:14	Fascist...'beehive s.'	ORWE 653:20
move the s. to pity	FLAU 339:20	first duty of a s.	RUSK 733:9
new-bathed s.	ARNO 35:1	general S. education	MILL 591:98
night with different s.	SACK 737:11	glories and my s. depose	SHAK 765:56
number of the s.	BIBLE 104:49	glories of our blood and s.	SHIR 819:20
Of all the western s.	TENN 870:2	gods recognized by the s.	PLATO 681:42
of the months and s.	SWIN 863:81	Government, even in its best s.	PAINE 660:31
opposition to the s.	MARV 577:96	greatest asset...head of s. can have	WILS 948:70
Owl looked up to the S.	LEAR 516:35	happy s. in this world	LOCKE 534:92
power above The s. and fate	BUTL 185:88	healthy s. of political life	MILL 591:1
primeval ooze to the s.	VIDAL 912:88	highest s. of self-awareness	LARD 509:66
rain...of the failing s.	RICK 714:27	his nature to live in a s.	ARIS 31:25
sees the mud, and one the s.	LANG 507:43	I am the S.	LOUI 537:66
seven s. go squawking	AUDEN 43:81	if marriage be such a blessed s.	ASTE 39:6
shining of the s.	TENN 878:79	independent European s.	GAIT 357:13
shooting s. attend thee	HERR 416:15	individual and...the s.	PLATO 681:43
Sister of the s.	PATM 669:21	initiation into a new s.	ELIOT 315:25
spaces between the s.	HENRI 411:8	interests coincide with the s.'s	MUSS 628:96
splendid s.	FLEC 340:82	In that s. I came, return	VAUG 909:36
s. all singing and shining	MUIR 624:26	in whatsoever s. I am	BIBLE 128:6
s. and planets circled	DICK 280:27	living symbol of the s.	LABO 501:5
s. are dead	AUDEN 42:76	meetings have caused in my S.	LOUI 537:65
s. came otherwise	BROW 169:65	mental s.	MANN 566:89
s., democratically inconspicuous	LAWR 513:56	mock the air with idle s.	GRAY 385:79
s. in her hair	ROSS 726:49	naked s.	MCCA 548:96
s. in our galaxy	BRAUN 157:81	new-made artificial s.	POWE 693:59
s. move still, time runs	MARL 573:30	no such thing as the S.	AUDEN 43:97
S. scribble on our eyes	CRANE 253:65	Nothing doth more hurt in a s.	BACON 52:3
S., s., And all eyes else	SHAK 800:29	not necessary to the s.	ASTE 39:4
s. that have a different birth	SHEL 816:66	not the same as the s.	CAM 193:38
s. that reigned at my nativity	MARL 574:31	Oh happy s.!	POPE 686:47
s. Thou knew'st by name	MILT 607:72	O Ship of S.!	LONG 535:27
s. threw down their spears	BLAKE 140:20	Our s. cannot be severed	MILT 606:53
s. to flight	FITZ 337:68	O wretched s. of man	SIDN 820:36
s. were going out	CLAR 228:66	pillar of the S.	SOLZ 833:6
s. were so many spangles	ARNO 36:46	police s.	GINS 372:14
s. were suddenly for	LEE 519:98	portentous, and a thing of s.	LIND 530:20
s., which thou hast ordained	BIBLE 99:31	powers of the s.	GIBB 366:62
s. with deep amaze	MILT 597:33	reinforcement of the S.	CAMUS 196:91
strives to touch the s.	SPEN 838:16	ruin or to rule the s.	DRYD 302:74
sun, moon, and s., brother	BORR 151:69	sad obscure sequestered s.	BROW 169:78
to you, you chaste s.	SHAK 790:39	Scoffing his s.	SHAK 764:52
who didst the s....know	ARNO 33:63	Secrecy...in the affairs of S.	RICH 714:20
will across the sky in s.	LAWR 514:88	servant of the s.	KING 487:33
yoke of inauspicious s.	SHAK 766:14	servants of the sovereign or s.	BACON 51:83
star-shine and s.-s. at night	STEV 853:84	ship [of s.] will be saved	CUOMO 258:80
star-showers light dissolved in s.-s.	SHEL 812:67	s....called the Holy Roman Empire	VOLT 914:40
star-spangled s.-s. banner	KEY 483:68	s., condition, or degree	MILT 605:36
start end is where we s. from	ELIOT 321:92	S. Department	MCCA 547:84
forgiven you...so that you can s.	MAIL 560:62	s. has no place	TRUD 899:70
Nature got the s.	DENH 272:62	s. Is kingly	MILT 601:26
s. again, somewhere else	MAJOR 561:73	S. is responsible	THAT 881:51
s. of space	SCOTT 751:2	S. is the Church	SHAW 809:69
s. together and finish t.	BEEC 73:67	s. lottery as a public subsidy	QUINE 702:22
Straining upon the s.	SHAK 775:75	s. manifested by a specific syndrome	SELYE 756:18
To make a s.	WILL 946:13	s....master of money	BEVE 90:64
started s. like a guilty thing	SHAK 780:30	s. of innocency Adam fell	SHAK 771:55
s. out very quiet	HEMI 410:84	s. of man	SHAK 805:52
starter Few thought he was even a s.	ATTL 40:28	s. of rut	GALS 358:49
starting consternation to the s.-point	SOME 833:10	s. of war by nature	SWIFT 863:65
startled It s. him just to hear	RAMOS 705:50	s....takes no notice	CROM 255:18
starts buck s. here	GREE 386:35	s. where gun control	SIMP 822:84
everything by s.	DRYD 302:83	s....withers away	ENGE 326:13
s. with an earthquake	GOLD 377:31	s. without...some change	BURKE 176:35
starvation degradation and s.	LOVE 538:89	s. won't bother us anymore	MAO 568:24
storms of s.	SHAK 805:55		
That s. is a s. of Slavery	GILL 370:81		
The more the s. 'plans'	HAYEK 402:24		
things o' the S.	NAIR 629:32		
this isthmus of a middle s.	POPE 687:80		
To preserve a trading s.	STEU 849:60		
vital importance to the s.	SUN 859:87		
voter...pernicious to the S.	WRIG 962:62		
we are the s.	WRIG 963:72		
When S. Magic fails	REED 710:34		
Where Venice sate in s.	BYRON 188:58		
whole machinery of the s.	ENGE 326:15		
whole worl's in a s.	OCAS 646:76		
With wealth your s....improve	DONNE 291:27		
women do not count in the S.	DAVI 266:13		
worst s. of affairs	KLEE 494:2		
worth of the S.	MILL 591:6		
youth of a s.	BACON 53:43		
state-controlled s.-c....echoes	DOUG 295:13		
stately grow great and s.	STEV 853:71		
more s. and admirable	WHIT 937:2		
one of the s. homos	CRISP 255:6		
she is tall and s.	TENN 876:22		
S. as a galleon	GREN 388:56		
s. homes of England	COWA 249:95		
statement Every scientific s.	POPP 689:53		
general s. is like a cheque	POUND 691:13		
least cheering s.	LEBO 516:61		
no s. which refers to a 'reality'	AYER 48:4		
scientific s. speaks	POPP 689:53		
sheer joy of felicitous s.	SCHL 747:34		
s. and a metaphorical way	MALA 561:85		
s. as an act of wilful defiance	SASS 745:79		
statements apparent s. of fact	AYER 48:5		
states attacks from outlaw s.	REAG 708:8		
Have more s. perished	HOPE 427:56		
independent or semi-independent s.	JAY 453:1		
In s. unborn	SHAK 777:31		
She's all s.	DONNE 291:26		
s. of consciousness	MOORE 616:67		
stinking s.	JOHN 459:40		
thinking in terms of nation s.	ADEN 8:62		
statesman abroad, you almost feel...as s.	MACM 556:66		
agree with him, he is a s.	LLOY 533:81		
business of a s.	STEU 849:61		
constitutional s. is in general	BAGE 55:80		
definition of a constitutional s.	BAGE 55:79		
first requirement of a s.	ACHE 3:39		
politician is a s. who	STEV 851:20		
rule...for a s., a courtier, or a lover	CHAR 215:29		
s....enamoured of existing evils	BIER 134:70		
speculative s.	ADDI 6:24		
s. is a politician who	TRUM 899:85		
s. is preventing...plots	WALT 920:95		
s.'s duty is to bridge	KISS 494:93		
Too nice for a s.	GOLD 377:17		
statesmanship You call that s.	BEVAN 89:58		
statesmen adored by little s.	EMER 324:54		
Among modern s.	CHES 220:78		
become s. and heroes	WARD 920:99		
some are born s.	SHAW 810:17		
s....ignore at their peril	WILS 949:86		
s. of Europe	TAYL 868:47		
s....take on a science fictional way	ASIM 38:81		
static A novel is a s. thing	TYNAN 904:2		
class people as s. and dynamic	WAUGH 923:51		
French...will never become s.	HUGO 436:57		
Thin squeaks of radio s.	CRANE 253:64		
station Eternity...as of a s.	DICK 284:52		
honour is a private s.	ADDI 7:51		
keep no rank nor s.	LOWE 540:21		
towers of St Pancras S.	BEEC 73:66		
Worked on Middleton's s.	LAWS 514:96		
stationary All is flux, nothing is s.	HERA 412:31		
stations train passes through s.	LEWIS 526:40		
statistic exchange rate is only a s.	KRUG 500:24		
statisticians sin With s.	AUDEN 44:23		
statistics feed the hungry on s.	LLOY 532:67		
lies, damned lies and s.	DISR 289:74		
man of s.	HOLM 424:86		
only tables and s.	OPPE 652:85		
Politicians use s.	LANG 507:40		
seemingly inanimate of s.	MAMET 564:35		
S. are designed	DISKI 287:11		
S. are the triumph	BELL 77:74		
s. for Manhattan Island	BART 66:30		

statue

unless s. lie — CUMM 258:62
statue s. inside every block — ORWE 653:26
s. of one of our kings — APPL 30:90
s.'s brow — WALC 916:20
walk around a s. — ROSSO 727:69
walking...with the S. of Liberty — CONR 244:53
statues like sepulchral s. — DONNE 292:43
Trees cut to S. — POPE 686:60
With s. on the terraces — KIPL 492:67
stature add one cubit unto his s.? — BIBLE 115:45
increased in s. — WHITE 935:50
Jesus increased in wisdom and s. — BIBLE 120:71
Look not...on the height of his s. — BIBLE 96:34
Malice is of a low s. — HALI 393:36
man of giant s. — NEHRU 633:9
mighty s. — MILT 602:43
persons of heroic s. — AMIS 17:55
status Bureaucracy defends the s. quo — PETER 675:38
economic s. of women — GILM 371:91
industrial and economic s. — SKEL 824:32
Policemen so cherish their s. — MAMET 563:27
restored the s. quo — HAMER 393:45
restored the s. quo — SQUI 841:90
s. and profits of war — TREV 896:10
s. of a cathedral — RODR 722:53
s. of Galileo — GOULD 380:75
s. of 'native' — SART 745:78
the quo has lost its s. — PETER 675:38
statute A s. is written to entrap meaning — MANT 568:22
statutes s. or usages therein obtaining — MILL 591:93
staves aspen good for s. — SPEN 838:20
comest to me with s.? — BIBLE 96:39
stay My s., my guide, and lantern — SHAK 759:87
poor man's s. — WORD 960:15
S., Frederic, s.! — GILB 368:41
s. in a concentration camp — JOHN 457:3
things don't s. the way they are — FORD 343:15
Will you not s. — HODG 421:19
Yet will not s. — GRAV 382:16
stay away S. a. from the ones you love — TARTT 867:37
stays Old Hodge s. not his hand — RANS 707:72
stay up s. u. later — BUSH 183:48
steadiness s., self-control...courage — PEEL 672:68
steady s. how you hold your weapon — SIMP 822:84
s. and perpetual serenity — ADDI 6:34
s. and stolid-y — GILB 369:45
steak s. spread with butter — KURO 501:43
wanted s. and they offered spam — MALA 561:82
steaks smell of s. — ELIOT 317:70
steal most honourable...was to s. — RABE 703:7
poets...beg, borrow, or s. — POUND 692:87
silently s. away — KAUF 474:38
s. bread — FRAN 347:89
S. me a while — SHAK 767:39
s. my Basil-pot away — KEATS 477:13
s. us from ourselves — DRYD 301:60
Thou shalt not s. — BIBLE 94:66
Thou shalt not s. — CLOU 232:66
When judges s. themselves — SHAK 787:60
stealth a s. bomber — BENN 80:37
steam powers of s. — WATT 922:45
s. comes...navel — THOM 884:41
s. of the social soup — ACKR 3:60
steamer This little s....is immortal — PRIE 695:86
steamers all you Big S. — KIPL 492:66
Daily the s. sidle up — AUDEN 42:74
steed s. and the shrill trump — SHAK 790:27
s. by Loc Suilig — MCCA 547:74
s. was the best — SCOTT 752:21
waves bound...as a s. — BYRON 187:45
steeds curb thy fierce s. — BLAKE 139:81
mounting barbèd s. — SHAK 760:32
steel dew-like s. — BRAU 157:86
Give them the cold s. — ARMI 32:40
hand of s. in a velvet glove — WOOL 956:40
him they feared to meet with s. — DAVIS 266:7
locomotive of s. — KAFKA 472:4
Meistersinger...set breath in s. — CRANE 253:67
red line tipped with s. — RUSS 735:50
s. my soldiers' hearts — SHAK 775:85
S. prices cause inflation — BLOU 143:71
s. rod runs right through — ANGE 19:90
though locked up in s. — SHAK 759:91
with hoops of s. — SHAK 781:49
wounded surgeon plies the s. — ELIOT 320:64
steel-true S.-t. and blade-straight — STEV 854:86
Steemie S. lecturing — SCOTT 754:67

steep s. and thorny way — SHAK 781:48
steeple Grand Sluice, and a high s. — ANON 22:81
in his own religious s. — CAMP 194:57
in s. hing — FERG 333:85
s. of my dreams — DEBU 268:59
steeplechase s. and gameboard — ELKIN 322:16
steeples In s. far and near — HOUS 431:43
Till you have drenched our s. — SHAK 792:4
steering s. full speed ahead — GILM 371:97
Stein Gertrude S. said — STEIN 845:62
Gertrude S.'s prose song — LEWIS 527:68
Stella S., think not that I — SIDN 820:51
stem s. of the contained flower — ROET 722:57
stems gold is on the pine-s. — MERE 587:26
stench s. of appeasement — THAT 881:70
stenches two and seventy s. — COLE 236:50
Stendhal fought two draws with S. — HEMI 410:84
step but one s. from...the horrible — DOYLE 297:73
dare not take a s. — SHAW 807:20
every individuality is...a false s. — SCHO 748:55
first s. that counts — DEFF 269:66
get up a s. that ain't there — JACO 449:12
isn't the first s. — KENN 482:43
look well to each s. — WHYM 939:26
must go nowhere, s. out — LEWIS 527:67
new theory...a...s. forward — POPP 689:53
One S. Forward — LENIN 521:38
small s. for a man — ARMS 33:51
small s. for mankind — BROD 160:39
s. in the wrong direction — LEVA 525:16
s....into a parallel universe — WELSH 930:44
varies with every s. — THOR 888:24
step-dame fled s.-d. Study's blows — SIDN 820:44
step-parents s.-p....disappointment — POWE 693:41
stepping s. where his comrade — SCOTT 752:26
steps by backward s. — VAUG 909:36
gentle odours led my s. — SHEL 816:59
s. down the palate — NABO 628:4
s. had well nigh slipped — BIBLE 101:84
s. of a staircase — MALL 562:3
s. take hold on hell — BIBLE 104:56
treading the s. already marked — SHEL 811:47
stereotype s. of rejected genius — HUGH 435:23
stereotypes abandon established s. — GORB 378:40
All s. turn out to be true — CRON 256:27
sterile seems to me a s. promontory — SHAK 782:88
splendid and s. Dolores — SWIN 864:92
Truths discovered...are s. — FRAN 347:83
sterility victory of s. — BELL 77:74
stern Kingly conclaves s. and cold — SHEL 814:9
lantern on the s. — COLE 236:51
solitary and most s. — YEATS 966:14
s., obdurate, flinty, rough — SHAK 760:4
sterner s. stuff — SHAK 777:38
Stevenson S.'s convictions — LEHM 520:24
stew soporific s. of every day! — SARD 743:51
steward backward s. for the poor — POPE 686:68
lord commended the unjust s. — BIBLE 116:50
Stewart land God gave to Andy S. — SMITH 828:4
stewing no matter how much s. — CURT 259:99
stewpan others again that it is a s. — HUNT 440:34
stews Of s. and brothels only knew — HERB 414:84
private sports the s. would blush — MASS 581:74
St Francis I'm S. F. of Assisi — PARK 664:22
stick coat upon a s. — YEATS 966:26
fell like the s. — PAINE 660:37
give me my s.. I'll face it — LEAC 516:25
heard his s. thumping — MANS 567:8
scratched with a s. — KIPL 490:97
Speak softly and carry a big s. — ROOS 724:15
s. and a string — JOHN 465:7
s. I am about to cut — BENT 82:91
water curves a s. — LAFO 504:65
sticking-place courage to the s.-p. — SHAK 796:23
sticks like s. of sealing-wax — DICK 279:7
Nothing s. to him — SCHR 749:67
S. nix hick pix — ANON 24:17
take up pick-axes and s. — HO 421:12
stiffen S. the sinews — SHAK 775:74
time to s. — ORWE 654:41
stiffnecked s. people — BIBLE 94:70
stile-a merrily hent the s.-a. — SHAK 799:16
still America...isn't standing s. — CUMM 258:60
Be s., and know — BIBLE 100:69
commune...and be s. — BIBLE 99:29
No economy ever stands s. — HARR 399:61
not keeping s. — GUNN 390:96

said to my soul, be s. — ELIOT 320:57
s. and quiet conscience — SHAK 805:51
S. falls the Rain — SITW 823:11
s. small voice — BIBLE 97:67
Sunday...standing s. — RHYS 712:76
they liked me 's.' — DICK 284:38
stillness air a solemn s. holds — GRAY 384:62
horrid s. first invades the ear — DRYD 299:9
sense of rapacious s. — BANKS 62:21
solemn s. of the buried foliage — HOLM 423:55
s. can outlast — SASS 746:96
s. in the midst of chaos — BELL 77:80
s. where our spirits walk — SASS 746:97
that s. ultimately best — CRANE 253:59
stilts nonsense upon s. — BENT 82:92
stimulus s. and object — MANN 566:76
sting care not who they s. — SHAK 759:90
death, where is thy s.? — BIBLE 127:63
it is a s. — PEELE 672:70
s. a stately horse — JOHN 459:59
s. like a bee — ALI 13:72
that inwardly doth s. — SURR 860:98
stings s. in their tails — BIBLE 131:7
stink earth shall have a foul s. — ANON 21:53
stinker Outrageous S. — KIPL 491:23
stinks stenches...and several s.! — COLE 236:50
stint at pleasure s. their melody — SHAK 760:29
stipple s. leaves with sun — SACK 737:10
stir s. not up, nor awake my love — BIBLE 107:42
stirk s. from a cottar — SCOTT 753:37
stirks They gang in S. — BURNS 177:69
stirred Shaken and not s. — FLEM 340:42
S. for a bird — HOPK 428:77
stirrup foot upon the s. — DELA 271:27
sprang to the s. — BROW 167:17
stirrup-pump simple s.-p. — REED 709:30
stitch S.! s.! s.! — HOOD 426:30
St John Awake, my S. J.! — POPE 686:70
Rev S. J. Froude put the phone down — SHAR 806:77
St Louis three girls from S. L. — STEIN 845:74
St Mary still S. M.'s Lake — WORD 960:14
stoats rabbits ruled by s. — ORWE 653:20
stock column of s. quotations — DOSP 294:86
enslaved as farm s. — SHAW 809:87
fight for that s. — HOWA 433:86
impoverished the public s. — JOHN 464:76
waste its s. — CRUZ 256:38
stocking glimpse of s. — PORT 690:68
stockings come to her in yellow s. — SHAK 786:5
for the silk s. — JOHN 459:51
her last...pair of s. — CHAN 213:74
his s. fouled — SHAK 781:72
pinking of thin s. — DICK 279:1
Queen Elizabeth owned silk s. — SCHU 750:79
s. were hung — MOORE 616:61
stock market the s. m. is closed — LENO 522:58
Stockport rubbish was sent to S. — ANON 28:55
stocks feet...hurt in the s. — BOOK 149:33
reads 'storks' for 's.' — FREUD 350:58
s. were sold — BELL 77:62
stoic Every S. was a S. — EMER 324:52
weakness for the s.'s pride — POPE 687:80
with a s. calm — SOME 833:10
stoicism Romans call it s. — ADDI 7:46
Stoics Let the S. say what they please — EMER 324:70
stole s. it fair and square — HAYA 402:32
wonder where you s. 'em — SWIFT 862:41
stolen horses may not be s. — HALI 393:34
not wanting what is s. — SHAK 790:26
revolution has been s. — JIANG 455:58
s. generations — RUDD 730:34
S., s., be your apples — HUNT 439:24
S. waters are sweet — BIBLE 104:62
They'll say it's s. — BRAD 155:50
stolid steady and s.-y — GILB 369:45
stolidity cinder of s. — CARL 199:71
stomach A bit of a s. — HITCH 419:87
adventures on a drained s. — BYRON 191:38
army marches on its s. — NAPO 630:44
bring 'em off your s. — LAMB 505:86
but a s., gentlemen, a s. — HUNT 440:34
deepest loathing to the s. — SHAK 767:32
good s. to a feast — WEBS 926:29
Had s. for 'em all — SHAK 790:67
healthy s. is...conservative — BUTL 186:7
heart and s. of a king — ELIZ 321:4
If your s. disputes you — PAIGE 660:28

St Paul — 1297

in his s. more animated beings — SMITH 830:50
little wine for thy s.'s sake — BIBLE 129:21
naturally have a weak s. — BERN 85:62
no s. for such meat — DOBS 289:78
no s. to this fight — SHAK 776:88
pit of the s. — HOUS 432:75
soul, or a s. — SAKI 739:60
s. is not good — ANON 22:61
s. sets us to work — ELIOT 316:43
s. thinks her throat is cut — RUNY 731:58
when you have a s. ache — GORO 379:67
stomachs juries fill their s. — SYNGE 865:23
St Omer old man of S. O. — QUIL 702:16
stone At his heels a s. — SHAK 784:48
blessed is the hard s. — DARIO 263:46
bomb them into the S. Age — LEMAY 521:30
carved in s. — TENN 875:18
chipping away at a s. — ALTM 15:20
creeping ivy clings to…s. — COWP 251:5
cruelties of the S. Age — CHUR 226:94
Here the s. images — ELIOT 318:14
hurl a s. at — MOOD 615:56
inside every block of s. — ORWE 653:26
keeper of the s. — DAVI 265:85
lay s. on s. — ARNO 34:76
Leave not…a foot of s. — POPE 689:39
let him first cast a s. — BIBLE 123:38
Like a s. — TAKU 866:13
lonely man…a s., a bone, a stick — CHEE 218:8
massive sandal set on s. — MILL 592:26
naked s. — WORD 962:51
nickname is the heaviest s. — HAZL 404:56
no bigger than an agate s. — SHAK 765:70
no s. unturned — SHAR 806:71
Paris made of s. — HUGO 437:61
Saturn, quiet as a s. — KEATS 477:28
Sculpture in s. — MOORE 616:70
see and imitate…in s. — CUMM 257:50
seventy years of s. — THOM 883:13
shadow white as s. — ROET 722:62
sound of iron on s. — DELA 271:27
s. and earth is closer to the truth — HEAT 406:94
s. besmeared with sluttish time — SHAK 801:51
s. commemorates…Ellis — ANON 23:85
s. falls to the ground — THOR 889:45
s. fidelity They hardly meant — LARK 509:81
s. flung into the water — LEON 523:78
s. in my straw hat — STEV 851:29
s. of our fortresses — FAVRE 331:50
s. of stumbling — BIBLE 107:58
s. of the heart — YEATS 966:20
s. remains, and the cross — MACC 546:66
s. set in the silver sea — SHAK 764:40
s. taken away from the sepulchre — BIBLE 123:64
s. than with an axe — JOHN 463:3
s. that puts the stars to flight — FITZ 337:68
s. the twenty-first — BROW 169:66
S. walls do not a prison — LOVE 538:82
s. was cut out without hands — BIBLE 111:38
s. which the builders refused — BIBLE 102:22
swerd of this s. — MALO 562:7
sword…out of the s. — MUNRO 625:47
take away our hearts o' s. — OCAS 646:77
take the s. from the s. — ELIOT 319:48
themselves as s. — SHAK 802:69
The s.'s in the midst — YEATS 966:19
things of bronze and s. — RUNY 732:63
trunkless legs of s. — SHEL 813:85
turn you like them to s. — TATE 867:40
understanding of the S. Age — ARMEY 32:38
violet by a mossy s. — WORD 957:62
Virtue is like a rich s. — BACON 52:27
water upon the s. — STEAD 843:31
Wedding-Guest sat on a s. — COLE 234:9
weight which is the s. — HEPW 412:28
will he give him a s.? — BIBLE 115:51
written of me on my s. — FROST 353:16
Stonehenge bring S. to Nyasaland — BANDA 61:9
like a monogrammed S. — RIVA 716:53
stone-like Naked and s.-l. — FREE 350:48
stones could aye peeble them wi' s. — SCOTT 753:59
five smooth s. out of the brook — BIBLE 96:38
houses are made of s. — POIN 683:97
Inestimable s. — SHAK 761:40
on thy cold grey s. — TENN 871:3
pavements fang'd with murderous s. — COLE 236:50
pavement s. are polished — DICK 279:1

people and the s. — WILL 946:11
picked up with s. — FROST 352:3
raise a cone of s. — STUA 858:57
reconcile ourselves to the s. — MACD 549:37
red As the stained s. — OWEN 657:27
Sermons in s. — SHAK 778:66
s. be made bread — BIBLE 114:22
s. have stood for a thousand years — JEFF 453:12
s. into the Theban wall — COWL 250:72
s. of silence — HEAN 404:70
s. with little water drops — SHAK 762:96
s. would cry out — SHEEN 811:44
s. would immediately cry out — BIBLE 122:3
storm-sculptured s. — SASS 746:96
threw words like s. — SPEN 837:98
throwing s. at autocracy — AI WEI 10:6
time to cast away s. — BIBLE 105:14
will move s. — SHAK 767:21
With rocks, and s. and trees — WORD 957:64
you are men of s. — SHAK 793:37
stonewall want you all to s. — NIXON 640:35
stood Freely stood s. who s. — MILT 603:79
somebody s. up — OBAMA 643:25
s. upon that silent hill — HODG 421:21
stool on his rickety s. — HUGH 434:10
own the hearth and s. — COLUM 238:90
stools necessity invented s. — COWP 251:10
stoop dares to s. — DOST 294:90
grief…makes his owner s. — SHAK 768:54
jewel…we s. and take — SHAK 787:53
stoops lovely woman s. to folly — GOLD 376:93
stop ask me to s. playing — KING 486:17
nobody's gonna s. them — BERRA 86:89
one approaches your s. — COPE 246:94
S. and consider! — KEATS 475:66
s. everyone from doing it — HERB 412:42
S. murdering — BRAND 156:66
S. The World — ANON 25:45
Time…Must have a s. — SHAK 772:66
You can't s. it — WILL 946:27
stop-light sees only the red s.-l. — SCHW 751:95
store as large as s. — HERB 414:75
from great s. — KIPL 491:23
in the s. we sell hope — REVS 712:68
keep the s. open nights — KAUF 474:42
Laid up in s. for me — TRAH 895:82
no wealthy s. — DYER 309:48
pale Mammon pine amidst his s. — POPE 686:68
rich in nature's s. — FORD 343:7
s. of experience — FRAME 346:77
s. of skill — DYER 309:49
those who…behold her s. — CRAB 252:32
vast s. which the busy — LOCKE 533:89
Whatever Nature has in s. — FERMI 334:95
Who's minding the s.? — REAG 708:6
stored lay s. in me — RICH 713:8
stores department s.…museums — WARH 920:9
stories added to his s. — STEIN 845:62
all s.…end in death — HEMI 409:73
believe of my own s. — IRVI 447:60
copious s., oftentimes begun — SHAK 762:89
dead men never bring awkward s. — DICK 278:66
family denied both s. — SAKI 739:58
make up your own s. — WADD 915:1
mythical s. become structural — FRYE 354:54
new s. are born from old — RUSH 732:67
no invention as to s. — BYRON 188:79
pictures are the love s. — LAUR 511:24
s.…about the great and powerful — BERN 85:72
Sad s. are chaced — SHAK 760:27
Scheherazadesworth of s. — BARTH 65:7
s. And not by his blows — LAFO 504:57
s. of the death of kings — SHAK 764:52
S. to rede ar delitabill — BARB 63:49
tell ourselves s. — DIDI 286:82
there are no answers, just s. — KEIL 479:64
there are only two or three human s. — CATH 208:85
turn to s. and poems — DYSON 309:59
stork throwing rocks at the s. — BREC 157:87
storks reads 's.' for 'stocks' — FREUD 350:58
s. on the spires of Denmark — DOYLE 297:75
storm At the end of the s. — HAMM 394:65
brows like gathering s. — BURNS 179:19
colour if the s. — RYDER 736:58
did na mind the s. — BURNS 179:23
driven away with the s. — BIBLE 112:77
fled away into the s. — KEATS 477:27

full of frost, of s. and cloudiness? — SHAK 775:58
infinite s. of beauty — MUIR 624:26
In the howling s. — BLAKE 140:12
pelting of this pitiless s. — SHAK 792:11
Rides…and directs the s. — ADDI 6:19
rides upon the s. — COWP 250:85
S. and stress — KAUF 474:45
s. is long past — KEYN 484:73
s. is up — SHAK 778:52
s. of life — WESL 931:59
swell before s. — KIPL 491:45
wings of the s. — GRANT 381:6
storm-clouds s.-c. brood — LEAR 516:28
the s.-c. thundrous melody — STEP 847:11
storms broken in on by the s. — ADAMS 5:6
explanation of our gusts and s. — ELIOT 316:58
haunts the s. — BAUD 68:59
He sought the s. — DRYD 301:71
raging s. movis us to shake — ANON 22:63
serious s. and floods — SILV 821:72
s. of state — SHAK 805:55
sudden s. are short — SHAK 764:38
weathered the severest s. — KENN 481:14
Where no s. come — HOPK 428:65
storm-sculptured s.-s. stones — SASS 746:96
stormy dark and s. night — BULW 173:63
s. and altogether warlike — LUTH 542:75
S., husky, brawling — SAND 741:13
story advantage…in telling their s. — AUST 47:89
any s. is ephemeral — FAUL 331:35
building…to tell a s. — CASS 207:74
epitaph to be my s. — FROST 353:16
Every fine s. must leave…pleasure — CATH 208:96
fool in the old s. — MACA 545:25
form of the short s. — SARO 744:58
gallous s. — SYNGE 865:24
going to tell a true s. — ECHE 310:14
green fig-tree in the s. — PLATH 681:37
Here then will we begin the s. — BIBLE 113:12
how he had started a s. — HEMI 410:78
involved in a s. — MANN 566:86
means to write one s. — BARR 64:83
Never was a s. — SHAK 766:15
no matter how implausible your s. — SHAR 806:76
No s. comes from nowhere — RUSH 732:70
not trying to tell a s. — WOOLF 956:34
novel tells a s. — FORS 344:38
Once a newspaper touches a s. — MAIL 560:43
On the Beach is a s. — GARD 360:68
our own s. — THUR 890:75
place where a s. ended — ELIOT 321:84
present moments in the s. — STUA 857:56
sacred s. of the soul's delight — LANY 508:57
Still is the s. told — MACA 546:50
s. books had been written by people — WELTY 931:47
s. for which the world — DOYLE 297:74
S. is just just deserts — ELKIN 322:17
s. of a mountebank and his zany — WALP 919:77
s. of an ape — HARL 398:36
s. of a woman's life — STAEL 841:92
s. of Colonel Chapman's — WAVE 925:3
s. of the soul — RUSS 735:42
s. of the unconquerable fortress — SELZ 757:19
s. shall the good man teach — SHAK 776:92
s. with a moral — OHEN 648:20
s. within yourself — KAFKA 472:4
summits old in s. — TENN 872:38
'Tell me a s.' — CONR 244:56
Tell me the old, old s. — HANK 395:81
tells a s. or records — RUSH 732:82
tell this s. as much — NORTH 641:62
The art of telling a s. — RUSH 732:75
this s. is unreal — PACH 658:1
To tell my s. — SHAK 785:73
truly be an extraordinary s. — STIPE 855:5
whatever s. you want — KELM 479:68
'what is all this s. about?' — STER 848:47
What we want is a s. — GOLD 377:31
when a scandalous s. is believed — SHER 817:92
story-teller no true s.-t. — HEMI 409:73
stout s. and resolute little man — WELLS 930:29
three s. and stalwart sons — BALL 60:82
stove ice on a hot s. — FROST 353:13
Stowe Mrs. S. did not hit — CHES 219:32
St Pancras towers of S. P. — BEEC 73:66
St Paul didn't quite build S. P.'s — THOR 889:55
I am designing S. P.'s — BENT 82:99

straight

pray for you at S. P.'s	SMITH 831:63	Economics and art are s.	CATH 208:95	danced down the s.	KERO 483:53
straight crooked be made s.	ELIOT 319:51	entertain s.	BIBLE 129:46	don't do it in the s.	CAMP 194:48
don't need to be 's.' to fight	GOLD 377:23	kindness of s.	WILL 945:82	drab s.	GREE 386:22
every man s. before him	BIBLE 95:8	loved s. and bread	LEE 519:98	evening quickens in the s.	DE 275:11
however s. or winding	THOM 885:62	shall we s. be	TU 900:9	Forty-Second S.	DUBIN 304:59
makes a man stand s.	HELL 408:43	s. and pilgrims on the earth	BIBLE 129:40	great man walking down the s.	COPL 246:99
make s. in the desert	BIBLE 108:79	s. before thee	BIBLE 98:83	harlot's cry from s. to s.	BLAKE 141:28
narrow s. channels	RANJ 706:60	s. honoured, and by s.	POPE 685:46	inability to cross the s.	WOOLF 956:36
no s. thing can ever	KANT 473:22	s. to flight and fear	MCCA 547:74	lamp-post at the corner of the s.	GAY 362:25
nothing ever ran quite s.	GALS 358:50	s. to themselves	BACON 51:87	long s. roars	TENN 875:1
sets you all s. again	HUXL 443:12	ye are no more s.	BIBLE 127:86	long unlovely s.	TENN 873:62
s. and narrow as a tomb	SMITH 830:35	**strangle** it is to s. him	RACI 704:29	looking in the s.	KIPL 492:56
took their red s.	ACHE 3:37	S. her in her bed	SHAK 790:32	once walked down a s.	KIPL 492:51
straightfaced S. in his cunning	THOM 884:36	**strangling** s. in a string	HOUS 431:37	On the bald s.	TENN 873:63
strain Big Bow-wow s.	SCOTT 754:78	**Strasbourg** S.—the Council	BEVIN 90:67	Out into the s. I ran	MASE 580:63
dozing sages drop the drowsy s.	COWP 250:90	**Strasser** Major S. has been shot	EPST 327:31	passed down the s.	STUD 858:64
muse is…of the English s.	DRAY 298:91	**stratagems** policies, nor s.	MILT 600:9	past me in the s.	STEV 853:63
s. of expectation	FIRB 336:54	**strategists** lesson here for s.	GLEI 374:48	politician…on a s. corner	WHITE 936:57
s. on the affections	ELIOT 316:57	**strategy** s. of defense	GALB 357:14	posting up the s.	STEV 853:72
That s. again	SHAK 785:77	subtlety of Johnsonian s.	MANC 564:49	pulled to the side of the s.	STEI 846:86
untarnished by its s.!	LOWE 540:31	**Stratford** scole of S. atte Bowe	CHAU 217:73	ring in Heaven's s.	MASE 580:64
straits echoing s. between us	ARNO 34:81	S. trades on Shakespeare	BURG 174:90	room on the s.	ROSSO 727:68
in s. a present aid	SCOT 755:86	**strath** cow from a Lowland s.	SCOTT 753:37	salmon sing in the s.	AUDEN 43:81
strand Come sailing to the s.!	BALL 59:71	**strathspeys** hornpipes and s.	BURNS 180:44	sawdust-trampled s.	ELIOT 317:71
knits me to thy rugged s.!	SCOTT 752:17	**Strato** I prithee, S.	SHAK 778:55	she-bear coming up the s.	FOOTE 342:83
left fair Scotland's s.	BURNS 180:57	**Strauss** symphony by S.	PORT 690:70	s. being full of footballs	PEPYS 674:85
name upon the s.	SPEN 839:47	waltz must be S.'s!	GERS 365:74	s. of the city was pure gold	BIBLE 132:26
Scotland for the S.?	JOHN 459:42	**Stravinsky** no new music since S.	ELLI 322:23	such a sunny s.	DICK 279:1
wandering on a foreign s.	SCOTT 752:16	**straw** couch of s.	THOM 884:35	sunny side of the s.	FIEL 335:28
where's the Maypole in the S.	BRAM 156:58	expect brick where they afford no s.	ASTE 39:2	the middle of the s.	FOX 346:74
strands lost s. and weave	MCCA 547:82	Headpiece filled with s.	ELIOT 318:13	through the public s.	SHAK 794:57
these last s. of man	HOPK 429:88	headpieces stuffed with s.	MACD 550:39	wander through each charter'd s.	BLAKE 140:16
strange acquaints a man with s.		Oft stumbles at a s.	SPEN 838:16	when they met on the s.	KNIG 494:10
bedfellows	SHAK 804:20	once a flock-bed, but repaired with s.	POPE 686:69	wouldn't cross the s. for it	JONAS 465:15
All s. and terrible events	SHAK 795:77	Pipes of wretched s.	MILT 599:89	**streets** beg in the s.	FRAN 347:89
Constancy alone is s.	ROCH 720:24	sleep on s.	CHEE 218:12	Beside grain-scattered s.	LARK 509:84
foul, s., and unnatural	SHAK 781:61	still in s. hat and sandals	BASHO 67:46	creature of the common s.	DICK 281:73
How s. it seems, and new	BROW 168:43	s. for a bedding	BELL 77:70	Down these mean s. a man must go	CHAN 213:78
How s. the stars	SCOTT 751:1	Where is this s.	SHAK 792:8	fox in the s.	MCCA 547:75
in a s. land?	BIBLE 103:42	**strawberries** innocent as s.	THOM 883:16	game to keep the coalminers off the s.	BRES 158:2
Into something rich and s.	SHAK 803:17	**strawberry** Like s. wives	ELIZ 322:8	good-for-nothing woman on the s.	SHAW 808:62
Let us be very s.	CONG 241:74	S. fields forever	LENN 522:54	in the s., in the trams	MAYA 583:22
read s. matters	SHAK 796:16	**straws** Errors, like s.	DRYD 301:46	in the s. of the town	PARN 665:46
Solomon loved many s. women	BIBLE 97:57	**stray** never taught to s.	POPE 687:75	into the s.	ANON 25:68
So sad, so s.	TENN 872:43	with me you'd fondly s.	GAY 362:19	Martian met me in the s.	ANDR 18:76
S. all, and New	TRAH 895:84	**streak** Gilbert had a baddish s.	QUIL 702:15	night Darkens the s.	MILT 602:47
s. instruments	GERS 365:71	s. of yellow	MONET 612:99	not the s. that exist	FENT 332:59
s. land, most s.	THOM 885:50	**stream** Against the s.	FROST 352:7	principal s. are the fairest	DEFOE 269:79
s. man is a marvel	SYNGE 865:24	bosom of the s.	SHEL 816:59	prowling the s.	JANO 452:80
s. one that summer	HOLL 423:52	By the s. and o'er the mead	BLAKE 139:86	s. of a hundred cities	HOOV 427:42
s. that men should fear	SHAK 777:22	cloud on the s.	YEATS 966:19	s. o' the toon?	MACD 549:35
s. that sheep's guts	SHAK 774:37	dark-lit s.	THOM 885:56	s. were dark with something more	CHAN 213:94
You make me s.	SHAK 797:50	eves by haunted s.	MILT 597:48	town of narrow s.	THOR 889:50
Strangelove S. Reproduction	COUP 248:34	glen with one thin s.	DEVL 275:8	uttereth her voice in the s.	BIBLE 104:51
strangeness confound s.	DOYLE 296:41	have their s. and pond	BROO 163:99	wandering in the s. below	HUGH 435:22
no…beauty that hath not some s.	BACON 53:29	leaves in the glassy s.	SHAK 784:57	**strength** all the necessary s.	GOLD 375:77
s. and wonder lying	RUSS 734:21	make thy s.	DENH 272:60	As thy days, so shall thy s. be	BIBLE 95:2
stranger A S. here	TRAH 895:84	meadow, grove, and s.	WORD 959:5	by reason of s.	BIBLE 101:94
bedpan by a s.	KUHN 500:36	mountain-s. that ends	LOWE 539:4	deemed Equal in s.	MILT 602:57
crown of a s.	MOORE 617:1	painted meadow, or a purling s.	ADDI 6:17	devoured all our s.	LAWR 514:90
for the s.	BIBLE 95:93	paint with tinted s.	CONS 245:61	for thou hast a little s.	BIBLE 131:93
From the wiles of a s.	NASH 630:57	passed many a straunge s.	CHAU 217:77	gentleman…possess only s.	BRON 161:62
Golden corn for the s.	WILDE 940:45	poison the whole blood s. fills	EMPS 326:8	give me the s.	BAUD 68:69
Go, s., and tell the Spartans	SIMO 822:79	river bed where no s. runs	ACHE 2:34	God is our refuge and s.	BIBLE 100:67
I, a s. and afraid	HOUS 432:68	rowing against the s.	SCOTT 754:65	God is the s. of my heart	BIBLE 101:86
I'm a s. here	PESS 675:33	running s. of sparkling joy	DICK 281:66	go from s. to s.	BIBLE 101:51
land wherein thou art a s.	BIBLE 92:21	salt weed sways in the s.	ARNO 33:57	Happiness engulfs our s.	BALZ 60:95
name we give to that s.	MILL 593:42	steady s. of enterprise	KEYN 484:79	ignorance is s.	ORWE 655:73
never love a s.	BENS 81:86	s. bears us	JONS 468:96	inadult'rate s.	HERR 415:7
No s. to trouble	VIRG 913:12	s., confined in narrow bound	CRAB 252:43	in quietness…shall be your s.	BIBLE 108:73
s., and ye took me in	BIBLE 119:36	s. of destiny	SPEN 838:25	inside and s. were philosophy	SIDN 820:53
S., pause and ask thyself	DICK 283:26	s. of human industry	TOCQ 892:27	knowledge of its giant s.	NORR 641:57
s. strayed into…their valleys	MONT 613:17	s. of thought, of consciousness	JAMES 451:66	man's s. is but little	SIMO 822:80
s. that is within thy gates	BIBLE 94:66	s. of your experience	JAMES 451:74	military s. with our moral restraint	KENN 482:28
s. to one of your parents	AUST 46:58	sunlight on a s.	ROSS 725:37	misdoubt her s.	MILT 600:7
S., unless with bedroom eyes	AUDEN 44:15	Trailing in the cool s.	ARNO 34:90	name is a tower of s.	SHAK 761:47
surety for a s.	BIBLE 104:65	wires that span the mountain s.	CRANE 253:60	no s. in unbelief	MACD 550:54
this emotion is a s.	EINS 313:80	**streamers** fan spread and s. out	CONG 241:64	not now that s.	TENN 870:2
What s.'s feet may find	HOUS 432:73	**streams** abundant s. of revenue	WEBS 926:15	not s. enough to prevent	GOLD 376:91
when a s. looks at it	FAUL 331:42	golden run the s.	MERE 587:26	not the s. to choose	CHEE 218:6
who is the smiling s.	CAUS 209:15	lavish s. to quench a country's thirst	POPE 686:68	oppressed, who wanted s.	WORD 960:15
world becomes s.	ELIOT 320:68	love of…Brown s.	MACK 553:10	outlive Thy youth, thy s.	MILT 606:68
strangers agreeable to s.	SHAW 808:62	mix'd, As meeting s.	DRYD 301:55	pleasure of the flesh robs s.	FUEN 354:52
bought by faceless s.	WRIG 963:71	s. in the desert	BIBLE 108:76	present s. and best security	TROL 897:29
Closest of S.	WASH 922:32	these silver s.	WALT 920:95	refuge and our s.	SCOT 755:86
cry in s.' houses	MANS 567:7	winds and s.	GIBS 367:14	rejoiceth in his s.	BIBLE 99:18
desire we may be better s.	SHAK 779:94	**street** clumping down the cobbled s.	ORWE 653:9	roll all our s.	MARV 577:94

shewed s. with his arm	BIBLE 120:66	tied by th' s.	SHAK 794:68	s. for...my country's cause	OCON 646:83
size of...its industrial s.	BENN 79:31	When such s. jar	SHAK 759:86	s. for survival	ROTH 727:74
S. and beauty	DEMO 272:49	**strip** Then s. lads	SCOTT 753:39	s....towards the heights	CAMUS 195:86
s. and my hope is perished	BIBLE 110:25	**stripe** s. for s.	BIBLE 94:67	s. won by survivors	ANGE 18:87
s. and the greatness of England	CURZ 259:3	**stripes** broad s. and bright stars	KEY 483:68	thirty years of s.	LOOS 536:43
s. and weakness of human nature	MACA 546:53	cut his s. away	KIPL 489:84	To see...needs a constant s.	ORWE 654:58
s. is made perfect in weakness	BIBLE 127:77	next week he's in s.	DAVI 264:80	unpitied sacrifice in a	
s. is small	BIBLE 105:92	red and white s.	HATT 400:82	contemptible s.	BURKE 175:10
s. lined with tenderness	ANGE 18:85	with his s. we are healed	BIBLE 109:94	variations on the eternal s.	LIN 529:2
s. might have refused	LANY 508:54	**stripling** muzzled s.	STEP 847:12	What s. to escape?	KEATS 478:35
s. nor the will	WALE 917:29	**strive** To s., to seek	TENN 870:2	**struggles** hope for our political s.	ROBBE 717:65
s. of five	BETJ 88:21	We must s.	NADER 629:23	Of all human s.	SHAW 807:17
s. of our salvation	BOOK 149:30	**strives** s. for nothing so incessantly	DOST 294:93	s. and strives against nature	INNO 446:46
s. that is almost frightening	ANGE 19:90	**striving** rather than to arrive	HILL 418:58	s. of Hector	HONO 426:17
s. to force the moment	ELIOT 316:62	s. evermore for these	GREN 388:57	**strumpet** Into a s.'s fool	SHAK 794:42
s. to harvest your fruit	MURR 627:84	**stroke** made at one s.	FRAN 348:5	**strut** s. sitting down	REST 711:63
S. without hands to smite	SWIN 863:86	s. of death is as a lover's pinch	SHAK 795:94	**struts** s. and frets his hour	SHAK 798:74
than would their own s.	HOBB 420:2	s. of midnight ceases	HOUS 432:76	**Stuart** S. or Nassau go	PRIOR 695:99
tower of s.	TENN 875:8	that s. of death	JOHN 464:76	**Stuarts** went out...with the S.	DISR 289:72
triumphant conviction of s.	CONR 244:36	This would, at a s.	HEATH 405:85	**stubble** like sparks among the s.	BIBLE 112:75
what is s. without	MILT 607:83	to the tune of flutes kept s.	SHAK 794:55	**stubbornness** s. is as iniquity	BIBLE 96:33
what s. I have's mine	SHAK 804:35	**strokes** better than bad s.	SHAK 778:51	**stucco** s. houses	BETJ 88:29
which by his s. and wit	HOBB 420:4	Many s....with a little axe	SHAK 760:5	**student** s. merely	THOR 889:40
with my utmost s.	VAUG 909:38	**strong** advantage, of s. people	BONH 146:26	s. must remember	AGAS 9:86
would but fain his s. renew	HERR 415:1	all the women are s.	KEIL 479:53	S. of our sweet English tongue	FLEC 340:30
strengths make my s.	JONS 467:74	am s. and lusty	SHAK 778:71	**students** s. on campus	NABO 628:7
stress in times of s.	ORWE 653:12	battle to the s.	BIBLE 106:29	teach s. how business is conducted	DEMI 272:47
Storm and s.	KAUF 474:45	battle to the s.	DAVI 264:70	**studied** s. as a branch of government	JAY 453:1
s. and disorientation	TOFF 893:37	Be s. and of a good courage	BIBLE 95:6	s. in his death	SHAK 796:11
S. is the state	SELYE 756:18	Be s., and quit yourselves	BIBLE 96:28	**studies** After his s.	SHAK 762:68
under s. of emotion	POUND 692:37	be thou s. therefore	BIBLE 97:52	air of delightful s.	MILT 600:98
stresses s. of accent	SAND 742:36	Come; and s. within us	KING 487:44	He that in his s. wholly applies	CONF 240:22
stretch S. pants	ANON 25:46	conquest for the s.	MASE 580:67	inclines...to some particular s.	DRYD 300:18
stricken s. with most obstinate love	SIDN 820:37	disarm the s.	FRAN 347:87	s. in which the work that results dies	LEON 522:68
strictly It's s. business	PACI 658:2	ever s. upon the stronger side	HAZL 403:43	too much time in s. is sloth	BACON 53:35
stricture intensiveness as s.	BURKE 176:63	every s. woman	FULL 355:67	**studio** go to my s. every day	GUST 390:4
stride poet is allowed the s.	SAND 742:34	grow s.	HUGH 434:8	s. is a torture area	LIBE 528:84
put the batter off his s.	SHAW 811:29	irrational and s. within us	WILS 947:36	**studious** s. for their bellies	SAND 743:39
strife dull and endless s.	WORD 957:58	let the weak say, I am s.	BIBLE 111:49	S. of laborious ease	COWP 251:18
Happiness is full of s.	ANOU 28:64	man is s. before he is moral	FAUL 331:38	S. to please	JOHN 459:39
hear the silver s.	DICK 283:31	many are s. at the broken places	HEMI 409:66	There s. let me sit	THOM 887:4
heavens free from s.	CORY 247:10	Men's actions are less s.	EMER 325:81	**study** dry air of the s.	HART 400:69
In Place of S.	CAST 208:76	minds are not s. enough	SHAW 808:50	fled step-dame S.'s blows	SIDN 820:44
internal friction and s.	ROTH 728:91	more s. than traitors' arms	SHAK 777:43	leisure of s.	GERB 364:64
madding crowd's ignoble s.	GRAY 384:72	only the S. shall thrive	SERV 757:33	most uncreative subject you can s.	ISSI 448:76
may be but sturt or s.	DUNB 306:97	out of the s. came forth sweetness	BIBLE 95:15	my first s. to obtain	WALP 919:83
none was worth my s.	LAND 507:34	pain is worse to the s.	JEFF 453:14	No social s.	MILLS 595:6
no s. can grow up there	MILT 602:56	quit you like men, be s.	BIBLE 127:64	periphrastic s.	ELIOT 320:58
no talebearer, the s. ceaseth	BIBLE 105:98	s. and dynamic	GAND 359:57	proper s. of mankind	HUXL 441:53
on the verge of s.	CORN 247:2	s. enough to bear the misfortunes	LARO 510:3	proper s. of mankind is man	POPE 687:80
pleasures with rough s.	MARV 577:94	s. impulsive gravity of head	POPE 688:37	proper s. of mankind is science	RABI 704:23
put an end To s.	BYRON 189:97	S. is the lion	SMART 826:65	result of previous s.	AUST 45:56
root of s.?	SURR 860:2	S. without rage	DENH 272:60	s. distinct from science	RUSS 734:22
some to public s.	POPE 688:14	too s....to succumb	HOFS 422:38	S. is a weariness of the flesh	BIBLE 107:37
S. discorde and waistis wanis	ANON 22:64	wants that little s.	HOLM 423:60	S. is like the heavens	SHAK 763:1
the stern s.	SCOTT 752:27	**stronger** at least the s.	GIBB 366:92	s. of all these sciences	PLATO 682:66
The s. is o'er	POTT 690:81	nothing s. than Necessity	EURI 328:53	s. of crime	MILL 594:77
With phantoms an unprofitable s.	SHEL 815:39	s. by every thing you see, hear	STER 848:33	s. of how to live well	GERB 364:62
strike afraid to s.	POPE 687:3	Swifter, higher, s.	ANON 23:3	s. of present pleasure	MONT 613:11
By and by it will s.	SHAK 804:19	unofficial magic becomes s.	REED 710:34	s. of public opinion	MERT 589:56
General S. has taught the		who is s. than death?	HUGH 436:39	s. them	GIBS 367:17
working classes	BALF 58:40	**strongest** reason of the s.	LAFO 503:48	S. to be quiet	BIBLE 128:14
If you s. a child	SHAW 808:43	**stronghold** s. our God is still	LUTH 542:73	**studying** still s. verbs	SAND 742:29
I s. out three of them	BOIL 144:1	**strongholds** s. of...hypocrisy	GALL 358:37	what you learn...while...not s.	CONA 239:11
no right to s.	COOL 245:78	**strong-men** s.-m....rolled into one	SIEG 820:60	**stuff** Ambition...sterner s.	SHAK 777:38
organise a formidable s.	HICKS 417:48	**structuralism** theme defeats s.	GOLD 375:79	Brotherhood of the Right S.	WOLFE 935:75
S. and sink and split	SHAW 810:9	**structure** concept, s., and style	POUS 692:40	folks eat the s. they raise	STEI 845:83
s. it out	JOHN 462:28	glittering s. of her cultivation	AUCH 42:64	It is frivolous s.	FORS 345:42
s. sooner than speak	SHAK 771:38	kind of democratic s.	MO 611:66	Nobody will see the s. again	HERB 412:45
s. with our spirit's knife	SHEL 815:39	scope and s. of our ignorance	PYNCH 701:13	s. that will do the trick	FORM 344:21
that loves me s. me dead	SHAK 795:80	s. of traditional stories	FRYE 354:54	such s. As dreams are made	SHAK 804:28
while the s. is hot	ANON 26:7	style and s.	NABO 628:15	**stumble** hands guiding where I s.	SASS 746:98
strikers longstaff sixpenny s.	SHAK 771:38	whole social s.	PARS 666:56	s. that run fast	SHAK 766:90
s. couldn't score in a brothel	DOCH 289:81	**structures** repairs its great public s.	HOWE 433:91	**stumbling** stone of s.	BIBLE 107:58
strikes narrow circle of s.	ENGE 326:14	Those blessed s.	LOWE 540:37	**stump** Blackened log and s.	LAWS 514:97
string chewing little bits of s.	BELL 76:58	**struggle** alarms of s. and flight	ARNO 33:67	**stumps** roller, pitch, and s.	LANG 507:41
dullis on the s.	HENR 411:19	as if it was quite a s.	FERB 332:69	**stunned** like one that hath been s.	COLE 235:21
end of the golden s.	BLAKE 141:32	delightful...after you cease to s.	FERB 332:71	**stunt** s. our ambitions	SCHU 750:80
held together with s.	ACHE 3:48	living is a s.	WILD 943:45	**stupendous** parts of one s. whole	POPE 687:78
Our eyes, upon one double s.	DONNE 292:42	Manhood a s.	DISR 287:26	**stupid** better the actor the more s.	CAPO 197:31
strangling in a s.	HOUS 431:37	not the triumph but the s.	COUB 248:20	economy, s.!	ANON 27:14
s. along with you	DUBIN 304:63	perpetual s. for room and food	MALT 563:21	If someone was s. enough	TAYL 868:52
s. to each side of its face	LEAC 515:6	Say not the s. naught availeth	CLOU 232:47	more s. one becomes	MAO 569:39
walking on a s. across a gulf	DAVI 264:65	s. against the impossible	HEDIN 406:4	not s., but...very dull	BEAV 71:25
warbled to the s.	MILT 598:55	s. between a set purpose	DOYLE 297:68	people are too s. by three-quarters	MAJOR 561:74
strings humming of the s.	PYTH 701:16	s. between the artist man	SHAW 807:17	pretend to be more s.	STARK 843:21
s....in the human heart	DICK 279:98	s. for form only as long	KAND 472:15	s. about some things	BELL 77:82

stupidity

s. and ignorant — SMITH 828:89
s. enough to want it — CHES 212:96
s. man is doing something — SHAW 807:11
s., or sulky — HUNT 440:31
s. people — COUP 248:37
Was man made s. — EBER 310:12
stupidity America—your s. — SNYD 833:95
confirmed in full s. — DRYD 300:43
intellect, a sweet s. — LISP 531:45
march of s. — DELI 271:38
profound s. of the inanimate — STER 847:14
struggle in vain against s. — SCHI 747:32
s. of the multitude — BAUD 68:71
the s. of its...propaganda — ORWE 654:37
stupors one of my drunken s. — FORD 344:17
sturdy filthy, s., unkillable infants — POUND 691:93
sturt may be but s. or stryfe — DUNB 306:97
stutter feet began to s. — BURT 181:71
sty No better than a s.? — SHAK 795:83
Over the nasty s. — SHAK 784:42
pleasure in a sensual s. — MILT 598:63
style called this s. the Mandarin s. — CONN 242:4
colouring and his s. — VASA 909:28
concept, structure, and s. — POUS 692:40
debased of s., not individual — MAIL 560:52
Dressed in s., brand new tile — COLL 237:63
exercise of his own s. — JONS 468:93
eye on his s. — ARNO 35:7
first grace of s. — MOORE 617:78
form that my s. cannot discover — DARIO 262:45
forward in the old s. — WELL 929:4
game is about...doing things in s. — BLAN 141:48
'give s.' to one's character — NIET 638:98
God...but for s. — PICA 677:62
height of his own towering s. — CHES 221:84
inflated is...euphemism — ORWE 655:62
killed...in a high s. — AUBR 42:60
Latin...Spoils your s. — FLAU 339:29
Let others worry...about s. — ARET 31:11
most money on a s. — MING 608:8
Neither action nor s. — ACHE 3:41
newspaper needs...literary s. — PULI 699:72
Not their s. to say — NYE 642:76
one must first acquire a s. — SAINT 738:44
particularly high-class s. — WAUGH 924:74
passage of good s. — FORD 343:92
process of adopting a new life s. — COWL 250:80
Salad...is a s. — LEBO 517:60
sense of s. — GREE 386:19
So is his s. — GIBB 367:8
s. and structure — NABO 628:15
S. has gone out of fashion — STRO 857:55
S. is a fraud — DE 271:18
S. is beginning — NICH 636:74
s. is not a question of technique — PROU 698:59
S. is the dress of thoughts — CHES 219:42
s. is the only real luxury — ARMA 32:36
s., not compositions — MORT 621:72
s. of writing — THOR 889:45
S. one must possess — CHASE 216:51
s. purely his own — THOR 888:25
s. should be as a skein — JONS 468:97
S....too often hides eczema — CAMUS 196:93
that was the MGM s. — LEIS 520:28
true definition of s. — SWIFT 861:37
uninhibited was his s. — MEYER 589:63
what na s. — BURNS 178:97
what s. is to an artist — BUEC 172:41
When we see a natural s. — PASC 666:69
words—noble, the grand s. — ARNO 35:10
styles Different s. for...climes — BROD 160:30
two s. of portrait painting — DICK 278:78
styling S. is designing — ISSI 448:77
suaveness s. isn't born of confidence — HYDE 444:22
subconscious hole in the s. — HALE 392:28
Little s. mind, say I — ONEI 651:73
subdue attempt to s. — GILL 370:80
s. one single man — SWIFT 861:38
subject black because of its s. — MORR 620:59
British s., in whatever land — PALM 662:72
clicking with the s. — EISE 314:9
discussion of any s. — SHEL 812:50
do the same s. over again — DEGAS 269:84
elegantly adapted to the s. — DRYD 300:41
Every s.'s duty — SHAK 775:82
fickle, and unstable s. — MONT 613:18
individual s. — HORS 430:26

I never s. myself to hours — RABE 704:16
interested...not in its s. — SANT 743:46
introduce the s. of eating — HUNT 440:32
know a s. ourselves — JOHN 462:38
look like the s. — DALI 261:13
Math was my worst s. — TRIL 897:12
no s. of England — PITT 679:7
no such thing...as an uninteresting s. — CHES 220:57
see how the s. quakes! — SHAK 793:21
serious s. — ARNO 35:10
Spare...for his s.'s sake — COWP 251:2
Stick to your s. — CATO 209:1
s....concept, structure — POUS 692:40
s. full of natural error — PASC 666:70
s. is to the painter — RIVE 716:54
s. matter of the artist — WILDE 940:64
s. that should never — THOM 888:12
s. to the judgement — SCHI 747:27
s....to this vice of lying! — SHAK 772:89
theory of the s. is complete — MILL 591:95
this s. for heroic song — MILT 605:43
woman...for his s. in marriage — STAN 843:17
worst mistakes...in his s. — HEIS 407:24
subjection As to woman's s. — STAN 842:16
attract Thy love, not thy s. — MILT 606:59
subjective begin from the s. — SART 744:48
subjectivity universe of human s. — SART 745:76
subject-matter nobility of s.-m. — WILDE 940:50
subjects best s. for artists — HEIN 407:20
ignorant, only on different s. — ROGE 723:72
model the minds of his s. — STEU 849:61
pray To several s. — SHAK 787:62
prosperous and happy s. — MORE 618:16
sojourners and passing s. — MUIR 624:20
S. choose me — MOORE 617:89
s. for a pair of...saints — SHAK 764:54
Talk about those s. — HOLM 424:72
tyrant has in common with his s. — BROD 160:35
Unmarried men...not always best s. — BACON 51:73
were their s. wise — COWP 251:20
sublimation s. of the work instinct — LODGE 534:98
sublime dandy must aspire to be s. — BAUD 69:82
Howls the s. — DICK 280:24
object all s. — GILB 370:66
science of the s. — CIXO 228:49
short from the S. — GRAH 380:85
step above the s. — PAINE 660:40
s. position, but not a secure one — BERN 85:63
s., there yet lurks — MELV 585:61
'the s.' In the old sense — POUND 691:99
torture into aught of the s. — POE 683:80
submerged s. beneath the surface — GERH 365:70
submission coy s., modest pride — MILT 604:1
have an appetite for s. — ELIOT 316:45
starving them into s. — MANC 564:48
submissive Remember to be s. — AESC 9:82
subordinate all other ends are s. — PIUS 680:20
subsequence s. for consequence — JOHN 459:37
subsidy government s. — ANON 27:17
public s. of intelligence — QUINE 702:22
subsist enable the labourers...to s. — RICA 712:84
S...increases in arithmetical ratio — MALT 563:19
unlimited Means of S. — CANT 197:14
withdraw my means of s. — STEV 854:92
substance body and s. of his works — COLE 236:53
change of s. — MANN 566:78
Charisma without s. — CAMP 193:45
decision-making, not s. — KISS 494:92
Each s. of a grief — SHAK 764:42
empty of all human s. — SAINT 738:40
is the s. of men — SWIN 864:9
man of s. — ELLI 323:35
merchauntis full of s. — DUNB 306:2
My s. was not hid from thee — BIBLE 102:45
one s. with the Father — BOOK 147:61
one that sucks his s. — LAMB 505:99
renews and varies its s. — OVID 657:21
set her foot upon thy s. — BIBLE 113:88
s. consisting in infinite attributes — SPIN 841:83
s. of my dreams — SASS 745:88
suck out the very s. — RABE 704:1
summed with all his s. — CHAP 214:15
wasted his s. with riotous living — BIBLE 121:89
worth, not s. — MILT 602:48
substances Even forms and s. — WORD 958:85
substitute adequate s. for wit — PRIE 695:94

applied to some God s. — RUNC 731:49
bloodless s. for life — STEV 852:49
excellent and nutritious s. — DOUG 295:7
in creating a s. — PAGE 659:15
most flawless proof...is no s. — EDDI 311:26
no s. for talent — HUXL 441:64
no s. for victory — MACA 544:7
offer abuse as a s. — GALL 358:40
Shouting is not a s. — STEV 851:10
s. for a real experience — ALBEE 11:22
s. shines brightly as a king — SHAK 770:23
test is a mere s. — MUSS 627:91
substructure economic s. — FANON 329:13
subterfuge s. for hiding something — CALAS 192:22
subtle almost invariably s. — STRA 857:41
God is s. — EINS 313:74
know not well the s. ways — EMER 325:85
schoolman's s. art — POPE 688:7
serpent was more s. — BIBLE 91:91
s., but savage — CAPO 197:26
subtlest s. and most poetic — FOWL 346:65
subtleties I do not deal with s. — BIRK 136:17
s., not made to rule — MILT 607:83
subtlety brother came with s. — BIBLE 92:31
s. of nature — BACON 50:42
subtraction that's s. — WEST 933:88
suburban mowers on s. lawns — RICK 714:27
s. prejudice of anti-Semitism — POUND 692:30
suburbs Chekhov of the s. — LEON 522:61
Dwell I but in the s. — SHAK 777:18
subversion do not like s. or disloyalty — HELL 408:41
subversive funny as s. — ORWE 654:39
seen by dictators as s. — JONG 466:30
subway perspective of a s. tunnel — TOOLE 894:58
succedaneum Science...a s. — WORD 958:79
succeed all right if the talks s. — ZHOU 970:11
If at first you don't s. — HICK 418:50
not enough to s. — VIDAL 912:90
s. as his inheritor — SHAK 798:86
s. unconventionally — KEYN 485:84
succeeded only thing we haven't s. in — HUXL 442:78
succeeding just when they were s. — REST 711:64
success a million miles away from s. — BROWN 164:27
any chance of s. — KISS 493:88
argue...after...your technical s. — OPPE 651:83
climb the ladder of s. — SCHW 750:88
Eighty percent of s. — ALLEN 14:99
For an actress to be a s. — BARR 65:98
gained for the universe by s. — JAMES 451:70
harness of their s. — HAMM 394:56
hope of s. — SMITH 831:63
howling commercial s. — GREE 386:23
If A is s. in life — EINS 314:86
it deifies s. — TWAIN 903:84
judge the level of s. — BROWN 164:38
May all s. — GILB 369:57
no s. without hard work — SOPH 834:30
not in mortals to command s. — ADDI 7:45
not solved by s. — WHITE 935:51
owed his lack of s. to nobody — HELL 407:25
perspective on s. — DEGEN 270:5
religion...is S. — BARR 65:92
S. and failure are both difficult — HELL 407:31
s. and miscarriage — JOHN 460:69
s. comes before work — KIMB 486:13
s. four flights — WRIG 963:79
s. happens to an English writer — AMIS 16:48
S. hath made me — JONS 467:54
s. hide its emptiness — HAMM 394:59
S. in Circuit lies — DICK 284:47
S., instead of — MILL 593:44
s. in war — CHUR 225:88
S. is a great deodorant — TAYL 868:53
S. is counted sweetest — DICK 283:27
S. is disgraceful — MENC 586:93
S. is feminine — FAUL 331:45
S. is in the silences — CARM 202:46
S. isn't everything — HELL 408:40
S. is relative — ELIOT 319:50
S. is the American Dream — LEGU 520:14
S. never depended on pandering — BEAV 71:33
The play makes a great s. — WILDE 941:82
triumphant with far-ranging s. — COMM 239:94
true s. is to labour — STEV 852:48
vanquished by his own s. — SCHI 747:30
With his surcease s. — SHAK 796:19
successes important...as his s. — AGAS 9:86

sun

pleasure at his own s.	RYLE 736:61	
successful He who is s. is good	ECO 310:15	
Horrible as s. artists	JONG 466:34	
no matter how s.	JOHN 458:19	
or s. without love	TROL 898:55	
S. crimes alone are justified	DRYD 302:1	
s. in business	GILL 371:88	
s. person is a sinner	ECO 310:15	
The more s. the villain	HITC 419:85	
To be a s. father	HEMI 410:95	
too lucky or too s.	JONG 466:30	
succession interminable s.	EINS 313:76	
s. and Horatio Alger in one	MAMET 564:39	
successor science the s.	RUSS 734:27	
succinct try hard to be s.	HORA 430:17	
succour for s. flee	SPEN 837:14	
succumb Too…resourceful to s.	HOFS 422:38	
suck s. melancholy out of a song	SHAK 778:76	
s. out the very substance	RABE 703:10	
sucker Never Give a S.	FIEL 335:33	
s. born every minute	BARN 64:79	
this s. could go down	BUSH 183:43	
suckers green s. of youth	SHER 817:89	
sucklings mouth of babes and s.	BIBLE 99:30	
sucks s. us all up	SEXT 758:49	
Where the bee s., there suck I	SHAK 804:32	
Sudan at your 'ome in the S.	KIPL 489:89	
sudden all of a s. it hits me	SIEG 820:60	
s., and quick in quarrel	SHAK 779:82	
s. with summer	SCOTT 751:3	
suede blue s. shoes	PERK 675:26	
Suez somewhere east of S.	KIPL 489:83	
S. canal…flowing through	EDEN 311:33	
suffer Better one s.	DRYD 302:81	
better to s. than to die	LAFO 503:50	
But doth s. a sea-change	SHAK 803:17	
does not the woman always s.	BALZ 61:98	
don't have to s. to be a poet	CIAR 226:24	
have courage to s.	TROL 897:24	
if he makes others s.	SZASZ 865:28	
if so be that we s. with him	BIBLE 125:18	
leaders who make them s.	SIHA 821:66	
Life…makes us s.	ANOU 28:62	
make them s. before I pack…in	CHAR 216:49	
prepared to s. for it	BENN 81:66	
s. for the Good	KIER 485:3	
s. from the strangest sense	WELLS 930:20	
S. her self	WALL 918:56	
s. hym…to wynne his spurres	EDWA 312:57	
s. in one's whole self	LAWR 512:44	
S. me to come to thee	WESL 931:60	
s. through no fault of their own	ELIZ 322:10	
s. what is difficult to s.	HIRO 419:72	
voice of those who s.	CESA 211:50	
sufferance s. is the badge	SHAK 769:85	
suffered greatly, have s. greatly	TENN 870:98	
He who has s. much	ANON 20:38	
s. at my side	SASS 747:89	
s. in his spirit	HOMER 425:9	
s….the neurotic ills	ISHE 447:69	
women s. in the…United States	FRIE 350:64	
You have s. grievously	BENE 79:19	
sufferers We have been the s.	BEVAN 89:51	
suffering About s.…never wrong	AUDEN 42:80	
any 'artist' must have…s.	DISKI 287:13	
by s. even animals could	HEINE 407:15	
Deep, unspeakable s.	ELIOT 315:25	
Doing or s.	MILT 602:40	
Give us back our s.	NIGH 639:20	
good time for s.	GOLD 375:77	
learn in s.	SHEL 812:63	
likely to lead to s.	BERL 84:48	
loved by the s. many	BENT 82:94	
s., and some risks	PEARY 671:59	
s. from galloping consumption	GAND 359:58	
s. from the particular disease	JERO 454:38	
S. is intrinsic	ACK 4:66	
S. is optional	MURAK 626:83	
s., the agony, the tender words	WHIT 936:71	
tell of their s.	ACHE 2:21	
the day you stop s.	WILL 945:97	
To each his s.	GRAY 383:48	
victim of creative s.	KING 487:30	
You can't avoid s.	COOP 246:89	
suffers every observer necessarily s.	ORWE 655:67	
If there is one who s.	AI WEI 10:5	
one who does, not s. wrong	SHEL 814:7	

suffice ice…would s.	FROST 352:4	
sufficiency An elegant s.	THOM 887:99	
s. is of God	BIBLE 127:65	
sufficient S. to have stood	MILT 603:78	
Suffolk S. used to worship Sunday	BLYT 144:88	
suffrage English are used to s.	CARL 201:28	
Universal s. is counter-revolution	PROU 697:36	
universal s. prevails	PARE 663:89	
suffragists militant s.	WRIG 962:60	
sugar against a pound of s.	SPEN 837:9	
honey a sauce to s.	SHAK 779:99	
more eloquence in a s. touch	SHAK 776:1	
suggestion s., by the imagination	RUSK 733:89	
suggestions absorb whispered s.	KOES 495:29	
suicide a s. bomber	BENN 80:37	
depression, neurosis and s.	HELL 407:31	
except the s.	HEMI 409:72	
excessive tolerance of s.	DURK 308:29	
girls who have considered s.	SHAN 805:59	
human race commit s.	ADAMS 5:85	
not even s.	STEV 852:41	
s. 25 years after his death	BEAV 71:28	
s. is a great source	NIET 638:10	
s. is not a very intelligent	KENT 483:49	
S. is the role you write	ROTH 728:99	
s. kills two people	MILL 593:41	
s. notes	PLOUT 682:74	
S.: that mysterious route	HUGO 438:88	
Twenty Volume S. Note	BARA 63:41	
upright, or to commit s.	MISH 609:23	
war…it is s.	MACD 550:52	
who have considered s.	WEBB 925:8	
suicides s. have a special language	SEXT 758:47	
suit A silk s.	PEPYS 673:86	
fresh s. of bright white linen	HERB 414:90	
man in a large check s.	WELLS 930:29	
thousand dollar s.	ANON 27:24	
suitcases s. are much better	SALI 740:76	
suitor think that you are Ann's s.	SHAW 807:21	
suits customary s. of solemn	TWAIN 902:63	
middle-aged men in dark s.	ABBO 1:1	
s. of woe	SHAK 780:36	
wear strange s.	SHAK 779:8	
sulky s. Scottish spirit	SCOTT 754:77	
sullen cope him in these s. fits	SHAK 778:68	
genius was too s.	DRYD 300:24	
I knew that s. hall	OWEN 657:33	
s. cold Exhausted face?	SASS 745:90	
Sullivan Gilbert to someone else's S.	RUSS 735:46	
sulphur oat-cakes and s.	SMITH 830:53	
Puffed its s.	BETJ 88:28	
still smells of s.	CHAV 217:3	
Sultan S.'s turret	FITZ 337:68	
sultans Both S. of Swat	LARD 509:69	
sultry where the climate's s.	BYRON 189:92	
sum final s. never balances	MO 611:68	
proportion to the s. involved	PARK 665:39	
rolling up the s.	WILL 946:13	
s. and substance, of capitalist	MARX 579:40	
s. of all the choices gone before?	DIDI 286:80	
s. of the interests of…members	BENT 82:87	
the s. of all matter is constant	OVID 657:21	
worked out the s. for themselves	KIER 485:99	
Sumatra giant rat of S.	DOYLE 297:74	
summer after many a s.	TENN 877:60	
all s. settled there and died	LARK 509:74	
All through that s.	MUIR 624:16	
chords of s.	DAY 267:36	
dark s. dawns	TENN 872:43	
dead long s. days	BYRON 189:6	
dream On s. eves	MILT 597:48	
fantastic s.'s heat?	SHAK 764:36	
grace a s. queen	SCOTT 753:37	
guest of s.	SHAK 796:18	
how costly s. was	SHAK 769:97	
if it takes all s.	GRANT 381:8	
In s., quite the other way	STEV 853:63	
It was a s. evening	SOUT 835:45	
last rose of s.	MOORE 618:3	
last s. of its kind	HOLL 423:52	
like a s. birdcage	WEBS 926:22	
Like s. tempest	TENN 873:47	
live murmur of a s.'s day	ARNO 34:88	
love in s.'s wonderland	NOYES 642:69	
Made glorious s.	SHAK 760:31	
mosquitoey s. night light	ASHB 37:59	
no s. progress	ANDR 18:79	

oldest griefs of s.	RICK 714:27	
one swallow does not make a s.	ARIS 31:20	
reasonable s. weather	WAUGH 923:50	
same winter and s.	SHAK 769:1	
silent s. heaven	TENN 878:95	
Singest of s.	KEATS 478:41	
studying all the s. night	MARV 577:97	
sudden with s.	SCOTT 751:3	
S. afternoon—s. afternoon	JAMES 451:55	
s. all the year round	ORWE 653:27	
s. droops, droop men	NASHE 632:94	
S. in Winter	CRAS 253:78	
s. is ended	BIBLE 110:17	
s. is eternal	GUY 390:7	
S. is icumen in	ANON 21:43	
S. loves to sport	COLL 238:77	
s. out of winter	DONNE 293:72	
s. sang in me	MILL 592:25	
s.'s lease	SHAK 800:37	
s. soldier and the sunshine patriot	PAINE 660:29	
s. winds that creep	SHEL 812:55	
S.…with its usual severity	COLE 236:47	
sunlight of your s. day	ARLO 32:31	
thou, O S.	BLAKE 139:81	
thro endless s. days	DICK 283:33	
through the s. is not heard	SHEL 812:57	
through the s. suns	RICE 713:91	
waken from his s. dreams	SHEL 813:81	
way to ensure s. in England	WALP 919:72	
winter's big with s.	SACK 737:8	
summer-dried s.-d. fountain	SCOTT 752:31	
summer-fruits Beauty is as s.-f.	BACON 52:26	
summer-gale sun and s.-g.	GRAY 385:89	
summer-house S.-h.…no shade	POPE 686:60	
summers ninety s. had Death	EGAN 313:65	
raw inclement s.	SWIFT 862:46	
So many s. dry	SHAK 800:31	
thousand s. are over	SWIN 863:79	
summertime In s. in Bredon	HOUS 431:43	
summit ascend to its s.	PAVL 670:38	
at the s. of the world	PEARY 671:60	
made to foot on its s.	NAPO 630:50	
somebody thought of the s. meetings	ACHE 2:26	
s. of these pyramids	NAPO 629:37	
summits Nations touch at their s.	BAGE 54:72	
snowy s. old	TENN 872:38	
summons s. thee to heaven	SHAK 796:29	
Upon a fearful s.	SHAK 780:30	
when fate s., monarchs must obey	DRYD 300:42	
sums size of s. of money	HUXL 442:99	
sun After the greatest clouds, the s.	ALAN 10:16	
against a setting s.	SHAK 791:76	
Aldershot s.	BETJ 88:24	
all the s. that shines?	SHAK 803:1	
And I will sing of the s.	POUND 691:87	
And the s. went down	TENN 874:97	
apples of the s.	YEATS 965:10	
as the s. at noon	DONNE 293:72	
beauty of the s.	SHAK 758:58	
before you let the s. in	THOM 884:34	
beneath the S.	KIPL 492:53	
between me and the s.	BLUN 143:78	
black cloud carries the s. away	ELIOT 319:42	
blessed s. himself	SHAK 770:27	
Born of the s.	SPEN 837:93	
bosom-friend of the maturing s.	KEATS 477:32	
Bright as the s., her eyes	POPE 685:32	
broad s. Is sinking down	WORD 959:96	
Busy old fool, unruly s.	DONNE 291:25	
cannot make our s.	MARV 577:94	
chambers of the s.	BLAKE 139:78	
Close to the s.	TENN 875:4	
cock who thought the s. had risen	ELIOT 315:24	
Copper s. or scarlet sea	CULL 257:43	
countenance was as the s.	BIBLE 131:88	
Cricket…worship in the summer s.	BLUN 143:82	
dawn upon them like the s.	RAND 706:58	
description of the rising s.	SHER 818:2	
Doubt that the s. doth move	SHAK 781:77	
earth is still going round the s.	ORWE 654:57	
Education is another s.	HERA 412:36	
enjoyed the s.	ARNO 33:69	
eyes are nothing like the s.	SHAK 802:83	
flakes burn in the sinking s.	SHEL 812:54	
flush of a new-born s.	KIPL 490:97	
from the searching s.	RALE 705:45	
glory flames from s. and star	HOLM 424:82	

sunbeams

going down of the s.	BINY 135:1	s. shines bright on Loch Lomond	ANON 22:79	remember through the summer s.	RICE 713:91
Go out in the midday s.	COWA 249:50	s. that lights the ages	CASAL 207:69	road to s.	SCOTT 751:2
heat of the s.	WHITE 935:41	s. that warms you	SHAK 764:34	sky cannot have two s.	CHIA 222:13
heavens' glorious s.	SHAK 763:1	s. was darkened	BIBLE 122:9	S. that set may rise	JONS 467:56
he beheld the s.	WORD 961:36	s. was shining on the sea	CARR 204:98	What other planets circle other s.	POPE 686:72
in s. and shower	WORD 957:63	s. was up, they were scorched	BIBLE 117:90	**sunset** sail beyond the s.	TENN 870:2
in the s., in Regent's Park	WOOLF 955:15	s. went around the earth	ARNO 36:46	seen dawn and s. on moors	MASE 580:57
IT'S THE S. WOT WON IT	SUN 859:86	s. will not rise	HOMER 425:10	shadow that…loses itself in the s.	HAGG 391:7
ivory s.	PIER 677:68	sweetheart of the s.	HOOD 426:24	sight of Etna at s.	WAUGH 924:80
kiss of the s.	GURN 390:98	The kind old s.	OWEN 658:37	slow, exquisite coming on of s.	COOKE 245:75
labour which he taketh under the s.?	BIBLE 105:9	the s.…has gone down	ORAH 652:91	sulphur to the s.	BETJ 88:28
land stares at the s.	SCOTT 751:3	The s. has left the lea	SCOTT 754:69	S. and silence!	COLUM 238:87
Laughed in the s.	BROO 162:84	the s. loves him	SMART 826:63	S. divides the sky	BYRON 188:60
like a raisin in the s.?	HUGH 435:12	the s. will rise	HANKS 395:84	s. fadeth in the west	SHAK 801:62
little window where the s.	HOOD 426:22	tired the s. with talking	CORY 247:8	urine dump at s.	SCHW 750:93
live by an invisible s.	BROW 166:82	too much i' th' s.	SHAK 780:33	**sunset-touch** there's a s.-t.	BROW 168:38
London spread out in the s.	LARK 509:87	to the rime-ringed s.	KIPL 493:73	**sunshades** Sit around under s.	JOYCE 470:31
love that moves the s.	DANTE 262:42	under the s. and moon	GOLD 375:78	**sunshine** calm s. of the heart	CONS 244:58
love to all men 'neath the s.!	KIPL 492:58	unwearied s. from day to day	ADDI 7:40	Digressions…are the s.	STER 848:28
maketh his s. to rise	BIBLE 115:38	upon the quickening s.	DONNE 291:18	into adventure and s.	FORS 344:24
meet the s. upon the upland lawn	GRAY 384:76	upper boulders in the s.	FROST 352:90	Love comforteth…like s.	SHAK 762:88
mix…the s. with punctuation	BRAU 157:83	use of the s. and the planets	LEAC 515:11	Scotsman…and a ray of s.	WODE 952:48
Move him into the s.	OWEN 658:36	Vermeer gave to the s.'s	LOWE 540:38	shadows in a s. day?	MARL 573:16
neither shall the s. light on them	BIBLE 131:4	walks under the midday s.	MILT 598:72	s. patriot will…shrink	PAINE 660:29
Never did s. more beautifully steep	WORD 959:3	wanton with the s.	MILT 597:31	the thunder and the s.	TENN 870:2
no homage unto the s.	BROW 165:72	watch the s. set again	RHYS 712:77	**sup** s. upon myself	SHAK 765:57
no new thing under the s.	BIBLE 105:11	We make guilty…the s.	SHAK 792:89	s. with him, and he with me	BIBLE 131:95
No s.—no moon!	HOOD 426:36	When the s. goes down	BOND 145:17	**superficiality** discussed as s.	BURKE 176:63
not a place in the s.	DULL 306:88	When the s. shall be darkened	KORAN 498:91	**superfluous** s. in me to point out	ADAMS 4:74
observations of the s.	STUA 858:57	where'er the s.	WATTS 923:47	s. to demand the time	SHAK 770:27
on which the s. never sets	NORTH 641:58	where no s. shines	THOM 883:4	The s., a very necessary thing	VOLT 914:31
our own place in the s.	BULOW 173:62	Wherever there is s.	BEAU 71:20	trip to Europe would be s.	SAAR 736:1
our place in the s.	WILH 943:55	While the s.…be not darkened	BIBLE 106:36	**superflux** S. of pain	SWIN 863:89
Our s. is one of 100 billion	BRAUN 157:81	wind up the s. and moon	BYRON 190:31	**superhuman** s. undertaking	GIRA 372:23
over the fjord—the s.	MUNCH 625:41	With the dying s.	BOUR 153:94	**superincumbent** s. hour	SHEL 815:36
pleasures Known under the s.	REID 710:45	with the s.	KEN 480:83	**superior** ask a s. to publish	HOPK 428:83
proudest country under the s.	PARK 665:37	with the s. to match	BROW 169:65	A s. pilot uses…s. judgement	BORM 151:63
Quick-glancing to the s.	GRAY 384:58	woman clothed with the s.	BIBLE 131:9	Justice is s.	PLATO 682:60
quietest places Under the s.	HOUS 431:54	worlds…circle round the s.	DICK 281:57	lawful power is still s.	DRYD 302:93
Rain, rain, and s.!	TENN 878:74	**sunbeams** extracting s.-b.	SWIFT 862:46	of the feudal s.	MILL 592:17
rays of the s.	KIPL 491:35	fatuous s. toil	OWEN 658:38	relieved to find a s.	TUCH 901:13
robbed even the s.	MCMU 557:83	motes that people the s.	MILT 597:49	rise s. to all considerations	STEV 851:24
ruin any pastime under the s.	MITF 610:49	s. dart through them	SHEL 812:54	s. creation	HARD 396:91
sea escaping With the s.	RIMB 716:47	**sunbonnet** s. as well as the sombrero	FERB 332:62	s. persons can remain s.	ORWE 653:10
see the s. the other way round?	BISH 136:27	**Sunday** feeling of s.	RHYS 712:76	s. to all…despotism	PITT 680:12
setting s.	GARL 360:75	first drink on a S. morning	MCCU 549:15	s. to any imaginative exercise	VIDAL 912:84
shadow in the s.	ELIZ 321:3	first S. in a new chariot	CONG 241:74	that is sick Of his s.	SHAK 786:27
shadow in the s.	SHAK 761:64	golf may be played on a S.	LEAC 515:19	Titles…embarrass the s.	SHAW 808:41
sitting in the s.	SOUT 835:45	Here of a S. morning	HOUS 431:44	**superiority** laugh of s.	GREE 386:28
softe was the s.	LANG 507:44	married o' S.	SHAK 762:67	s. of one man's opinion	JAMES 450:46
stand out of my s.	DIOG 286:1	rainy S. in London	DE 273:81	s. of the Greeks	FUSE 356:92
stands an instant in the s.	HYDE 443:21	smelt like S. afternoons	THOM 884:47	**superiors** counsels of their s.	LEST 524:8
stipple leaves with s.	SACK 737:10	than a pig on S.	TRUM 899:81	**superlatives** s.…worn shoddy	FITZ 338:2
s. and moon Were in	MILT 598:72	worship S., not God	BLYT 144:88	**superman** between animal and S.	NIET 638:1
s. and summer-gale	GRAY 385:89	**sundial** I am a s.	BELL 77:73	teach you the S.	NIET 638:99
s. and the rain are flying	STEV 854:87	**sundials** mottoes on s.	POUND 691:1	the Pope as a sort of S.	FRAN 347:93
s. behind the Downs	BETJ 89:10	**sundown** eldritch light of s.	DAY 267:37	**supernatural** by s. means	HOOK 427:40
s. came dazzling	TENN 869:83	sodden towards s.	ELIOT 321:80	cases, was s.	MILL 592:10
s. climbs slow	CLOU 232:49	s. makes them mournful	BLUN 143:72	evidence of s. beings	STEI 846:99
s. comes up with a word	CURN 259:88	**sundry** s. contemplation	SHAK 779:5	s. source of evil	CONR 244:45
s. could not be reproduced	CEZA 212:55	**sunflower** s., weary of time	BLAKE 140:11	**superpower** resources of a s.	SHAR 805:69
s. delights to peep	SHAK 800:43	S., you were a s.	GINS 372:7	s. in the military and nuclear sense	WALE 917:29
s. doth parch the green	SURR 860:4	**sung** not worth being said is s.	BEAU 70:4	**supersensitive** s.…instrument	ERNST 327:40
s. farthest off	ANDR 18:79	s. her first and last	GIBB 367:7	**supersize** make our wages s.!	ANON 28:46
s. go down upon your wrath	BIBLE 128:90	s. of Border chivalry	SCOTT 752:9	**superstition** In all s. wise men	BACON 52:98
s. has gane down	TANN 867:24	**sun-girt** S.-g. city, thou hast been	SHEL 812:65	poison of enthusiasm and s.	SMITH 828:90
s. has gone in	SMITH 829:25	**sun-gods** s.-g. and the like	FRYE 354:54	religion…true remedy for s.	BURKE 175:19
s. has gone to rest	LAUD 511:16	**sunlight** brooks the s. worse	JONS 468:86	s. in avoiding s.	BACON 52:99
s. has left the sky	STEV 853:72	fair s. of God	MACD 550:46	S. is the poetry of life	GOET 375:65
s. hums down	THOM 884:40	S. falls across the country	IHIM 445:19	S. is the religion of feeble minds	BURKE 176:46
s. is coming down to earth	MERE 587:26	S. is the best disinfectant	KENN 480:97	s. of an antiquated diplomacy	CECIL 210:34
s. is daily new and old	SHAK 801:64	s. of your summer day	ARLO 32:31	s. sets the…world in flames	VOLT 914:42
s. is going down	SMITH 830:39	s. on a stream	ROSS 725:37	**superstitions** end as s.	HUXL 443:8
s. is lost	DONNE 292:58	s. streaming merciless	ATWO 41:33	town whence s. comes	LESL 523:88
s. itself is but the dark simulacrum	BROW 166:83	superficial as a puddle in the s.	LEAC 515:15	**superstitious** edge to the s. tale	PRIT 696:15
s. loste his hewe	CHAU 217:92	upwards into hard s.	CUMM 257:51	men of Athens…ye are too s.	BIBLE 124:91
s., moon, and stars, brother	BORR 151:69	weave the s. in your hair	ELIOT 317:74	must be benighted and s.	JAMES 452:77
S. of righteousness arise	BIBLE 112:65	will be s. later	MACN 558:3	**superstructure** dubiousness of…s.	DESC 274:32
s. of suns	DICK 281:68	**sunny** s. pleasure-dome	COLE 236:39	economic substructure is also a s.	FANON 329:13
s. of the socialist revolution	LENIN 521:39	s. side of the street	FIEL 335:28	**superwoman** I am not s.	BLAIR 137:45
s.…on the…Australian bush	LAWS 514:94	**sunrise** Life starts new, every s.	BACH 49:15	S. is the adversary	STEIN 846:99
s. poured in like butterscotch	MITC 609:36	like s. from the sea	SHEL 816:56	**supped** I have s. full with horrors	SHAK 798:73
s. provides the moon	ANAX 17:65	Lives in Eternity's s.	BLAKE 140:6	**supper** After s. Pap took the jug	TWAIN 902:57
s. Rises upon a world	HUGH 435:36	s. Brings back the brightness	BLUN 143:72	Hope…is a bad s.	BACON 50:54
s. rose and set on their land	SITT 823:93	**suns** gleam of a million…s.?	TENN 879:9	know s.'s ready	STEI 845:83
s. rose in your eyes	MACC 548:8	light of setting s.	WORD 956:55	**supple** meets me soft and s.	FLET 341:58
s. shall not smite thee	BIBLE 103:31	process of the s.	TENN 871:19	**suppliant** thus the s. prays	JOHN 459:47

supplication s. of a dead man's hand — ELIOT 318:14
s. to the rose — FLEC 340:33
supplications voice of my s. — BIBLE 103:39
supply promise of s. — SHAK 772:76
see that the s. is not tainted — SCOTT 751:98
steady s. of funerals — SHAW 811:33
support ask for your s. — NIXON 640:33
help and s. of the woman I love — EDWA 312:61
mutually s. one another — PARS 666:56
no invisible means of s. — BUCH 171:27
prepared to s. them — LAW 512:36
s. a flagging conversation — HUNT 440:32
s. blowing up planets — SHAW 811:38
s. my cat — GRAV 382:31
s. rather than illumination — LANG 507:40
to have everybody's s. — OLLI 650:43
what is low raise and s. — MILT 601:31
without nourishment and s. — SMOL 831:68
supporter no s. but the...earth — SHAK 768:55
supporters pregnant s. — BAIL 55:89
suppress easy to...s. the truth — CORN 247:6
s. one's vanity — JAMES 449:21
suppressed could not be generally s. — HOOV 427:46
must be s. — DENG 272:58
suppression no...accuracy of s. — BELL 77:75
supreme presuppose a S. Being — DOUG 295:22
sure Be s. your sin will find you out — BIBLE 94:86
grinds slow, but s. — HERB 414:88
hateth suretiship is s. — BIBLE 104:65
make s. he was dead — GOLD 377:38
uncomfortable with not being s. — PERRY 675:29
surety s. for a stranger — BIBLE 104:65
surface crawl upon the s. — SWIFT 862:44
Errors...upon the s. flow — DRYD 301:46
in the lake...under the s. — ATWO 40:32
just below the s. — RUSS 734:21
mind...looks dingy on the s. — PIRS 679:95
monotony of a watery s. — MOORE 616:72
painting...is essentially a flat s. — DENIS 273:71
s. of articulate apprehension — GERH 365:70
thrown On the smooth s. — WORD 962:51
surfaces painterly s. — POPE 686:51
representation of s. and solids — PIERO 678:72
surfeit s. of the sweetest things — SHAK 767:32
s. with too much — SHAK 769:74
surge s....In every Russian's...heart! — PUSH 700:88
surgeon abilities of a brain s. — BRES 158:2
Hand of the s. — MAP 569:40
intimacy of a s.'s scalpel — ANGE 19:98
Picasso studies...like a s. dissects — APOL 29:79
plastic s....responsible for this face — CUOMO 258:79
poor s. hurts one person at a time — BOYER 154:38
way a s. operates — WHITE 935:44
wounded s. plies the steel — ELIOT 320:64
surgeons S. must be very careful — DICK 283:29
surgical s. war — ASHD 37:66
surpassed pleasure of not being s. — HALI 393:31
surplus-value production of s.-v. — MARX 579:40
surprise perchance, with strange s. — THOM 886:85
Sound of S. — BALL 60:87
sure of a big s. — BRAT 157:79
s. them out of — KIPL 491:43
Truth's superb s. — DICK 284:47
surprised Don't be s. — HEAN 405:74
s. by joy — WORD 961:33
s. they had remembered — PRIT 696:17
s. to find it done at all — JOHN 461:3
surprises S. are foolish things — AUST 46:77
surrealism I am s. — DALI 261:17
surrealists Dali's...for the S. — SCHW 750:83
surrender daring of a moment's s. — ELIOT 318:11
Guards...do not s. — CAMB 193:36
never s. — CHUR 225:85
path of s. — KENN 481:12
see the s. of Quebec — MONT 614:33
shall never s. — CHUR 225:85
s....was as honorable as resistance — ANGE 18:86
unconditional and immediate s. — GRANT 381:7
worst thing...is s. — ORWE 655:64
surrendered never s. before — NORM 641:55
Surrey full S. twilight! — BETJ 88:25
surrounded I am s. by dwarfs — GELL 363:37
surroundings see only my s. — ELLI 323:35
surveillance keep me under s. — WANG 920:98
survey exact s. of the land — DONNE 293:78
S. mankind — JOHN 459:45
s. of all the world — SHAK 772:66

survival insures the s. of the fittest — CARN 202:48
necessary for s. of the fittest — PALEY 661:52
struggle for s. — ROTH 727:74
s. had depended on...reading — ANGE 19:99
s. of the fittest — SPEN 836:87
s. of the fittest — SUMN 859:82
s. of the vulgarest — WILDE 940:60
The secret of s. — BAN 62:39
We are s. machines — DAWK 266:15
survive Can capitalism s.? — SCHU 750:78
continue to s. — TRUM 899:82
fitted to s. — GOLD 375:76
s. with that equipment — DAVIS 265:97
those will s. whose functions — SPEN 836:87
To eat, to s. — STAN 843:19
survived Peanut butter has s. — KEIL 479:54
they who s. fought and drank — DAVIS 266:9
survivor lone s. — ANON 27:20
survivors are relentless s. — BUCK 172:37
more the s.' affair — MANN 566:83
nuclear war s. — COUP 248:31
struggle won by s. — ANGE 18:87
sushi It's like eating s. — STOP 856:25
suspect no matter how s. — VIDAL 912:84
nothing makes a man s. — BACON 52:19
suspects Round up the usual s. — EPST 327:31
suspend s. my audience's power — HARD 396:95
s. the functioning of the imagination — HEMI 410:82
suspended Illinois...s. animation — OHARA 648:14
s. in me — ATWO 41:41
s. my religious inquiries — GIBB 366:99
suspenders must not forget the S. — KIPL 491:29
suspense more s., more dramatic torque — LANE 507:38
suspension willing s. of disbelief — COLE 236:44
suspicion banish squint s. — MILT 599:73
Caesar's wife must be above s. — CAES 192:15
Democracy is the recurrent s. — WHITE 935:37
have a s. it's inevitable — LEAC 516:25
rich with s. — RICH 713:96
s. that electricity — THUR 890:68
true loves without s. — SPEN 838:39
suspicions S. amongst thoughts — BACON 52:18
suspicious more s. of adjectives — SAND 742:29
Sussex bury my body in S. grass — BENET 79:26
S. by the sea! — KIPL 491:48
S. countryside — GRANT 381:3
sustenance S. for their helpless — SWIFT 862:57
sutlers sapient s. of the Lord — ELIOT 317:79
swaddled S. with darkness — ELIOT 317:83
swaddling-clothes him in s. c. — BIBLE 120:68
swagman once was a s. camped — PATE 668:12
swain Be just, my lovely s. — BEHN 75:19
labouring s. — GOLD 376:96
no better than a homely s. — SHAK 760:8
with my dear s. — BALL 58:55
swains all our s. commend her? — SHAK 759:71
Muses sing of happy s. — CRAB 252:29
swallow Daffodils...before the s. — SHAK 799:19
flies with s.' wings — SHAK 761:46
one s. does not make a summer — ARIS 31:20
O sister s. — SWIN 863:79
O tell her, S. — TENN 872:44
O tell her, S. — TENN 873:45
s. a nest for herself — BIBLE 101:88
s. twitt'ring — GRAY 384:64
s. up death in victory — BIBLE 108:67
swallowed or be s. — TRUM 900:92
swallow-flights Short s.-f. of song — TENN 874:73
swallows passage of s. — WHITE 935:41
swam think you have s. in a gondola — SHAK 779:8
swamps bellowing across the...s. — WODE 952:39
swan dies the s. — TENN 877:60
every goose a s. — KING 487:48
full-breasted s. — TENN 878:88
great pool a s.'s nest — SHAK 803:1
like a sleeping s. — SHEL 814:17
silver s. — GIBB 367:7
s. on...St Mary's Lake — WORD 960:14
Sweet S. of Avon! — JONS 468:81
wild s. of a world — JEFF 453:17
swan-bosomed s.-b. tree — SITW 823:10
Swanee down upon the S. River — FOST 345:54
swanlike he makes a s. end — SHAK 769:2
swans Chuzzlewit suggested 'S.' — DICK 279:9
old ships sail like s. — FLEC 340:39
s. are geese — ARNO 35:24
take their geese for s. — BROO 163:15

swarm S. over, Death! — BETJ 88:20
swarming s. in Fords, in ocean liners — FERB 332:67
swastika Not God but a s. — PLATH 681:34
sway How fit he is to s. — MARV 576:85
s. of death — WORD 961:47
swaying S. to and fro — HUGH 434:10
swear conscience...to s. by — STOWE 856:29
gentlemen is disposed to s. — SHAK 803:90
man s. he loves me — SHAK 773:21
O s. not by the moon — SHAK 765:83
sin to s. unto a sin — SHAK 760:1
S. me, Kate — SHAK 762:67
S. not — BIBLE 130:61
s. to the Lord — HUGH 435:11
swearing cussin' and s. — STRA 856:38
take me up for s. — SHAK 803:89
swears Hardly ever s. a big, big D— — GILB 368:32
sweat In the rank s. — SHAK 784:42
In the s. of thy face — BIBLE 91:99
Luck is a dividend of s. — KROC 499:16
miners s. their guts out — ORWE 653:10
none will s. but for promotion — SHAK 778:72
perfection's s. — WALC 916:20
s. and blood and tears — DOUG 294:96
s. of my brow — FRAN 348:23
s. of one's brow — LIVI 532:55
s. pours down me — SAPP 743:49
wet through with s. — GREE 385:4
wet with honest s. — LONG 535:18
sweating s. it out again — GREE 385:4
sweats the bloody s. — WILDE 942:20
Sweden bold King of S. — LESL 523:88
Swedish sung by S. artists — WHAR 934:11
sweep need of making a clean s. — DESC 274:98
s. him from my sight — SHAK 797:44
sweepings heap of random s. — HERA 412:38
sweeps Who s. a room — HERB 413:60
sweet All is not s. — JONS 467:60
buried in so s. a place — SHEL 815:26
day...never came so s. — SHAK 769:97
dead thing that smells s. — THOM 885:59
Death is s. — ANOU 28:62
For thy s. love remembered — SHAK 800:46
Heard melodies are s. — KEATS 478:36
how it was s.! — BROW 169:67
How sour s. music is — SHAK 765:63
how s. and fair — WALL 918:55
How s. are thy words — BIBLE 103:27
How s. the lily grows — HEBER 406:99
How s. the moonlight — SHAK 770:18
if s., give thanks — SWIN 864:14
in my mouth s. as honey — BIBLE 131:8
make a s. lady sad — SHAK 786:32
mixture of the s. and the sour — LAFO 504:55
my own, my s. — TENN 876:28
Naught so s. as melancholy — BURT 181:74
not so short as s. — SHAK 765:61
not so s. now — SHAK 785:77
shady leaves, their s. above — SPEN 838:39
So s. love seemed — BRID 158:8
So s., the sense faints — SHEL 813:81
Stolen waters are s. — BIBLE 104:62
S. and low — TENN 872:37
s. and seemly thing — HORA 430:10
s. as those — TENN 872:43
s. enemy, France — SIDN 820:47
s. full of bitterness — LYLY 543:84
S. is pleasure after pain — DRYD 303:30
S. is revenge — BYRON 189:96
s. music is such art — SHAK 804:45
s. music is such art — SHAK 804:47
s. odour...doth in it live — SHAK 801:52
s. or sour — TRAV 896:93
s. pea, that has run wild — STEV 850:96
s., s. is this human life — CORY 247:10
s. though in sadness — SHEL 813:83
Tell me not, S. — LOVE 538:85
That s. bondage — SHEL 812:52
'Tis s. to win — BYRON 189:97
would smell as s. — SHAK 765:80
sweet-apple Just as the s.-a. reddens — SAPP 743:53
sweeteners best s. of tea — FIEL 335:17
sweetest s. flower for scent — SHEL 815:23
s. music to a woeful mind — SIDN 820:42
s. way to me — KIPL 490:2
sweetheart Like the s. of the sun — HOOD 426:24
s. ran away with an actor — WINC 949:89

sweetmeats

sweetmeats pyramids of s. — DRYD 304:43
sweetness cannot write of s. — BELL 76:46
  long s. of the simultaneity — ASHB 37:59
  Love…is s. — WEBS 927:51
  no danger in s. and youth — ROCH 720:22
  out of the strong came forth s. — BIBLE 95:15
  passion for s. and light — ARNO 36:33
  s. and light — ARNO 36:27
  s. and light — SWIFT 861:18
  s. fell from the air — MACL 555:41
  s. fills the breast — CASW 208:81
  s. never breedeth satiety — LYLY 543:86
  s. of confession — FIRB 336:50
  waste its s. on the desert air — GRAY 384:69
  where s. and light failed — FORS 344:39
sweets brought'st Thy s. along — HERB 413:59
  only safe pleasure…boiled s. — CRIT 255:10
  sing the s. I know — BARL 63:56
  Stolen s. are always sweeter — HUNT 439:24
  Stolen s. are best — CIBB 227:27
  S. into your list — HUNT 439:30
  s. of Burn-mill — WORD 960:14
  s. of life — CONG 241:61
  S. with s. war not — SHAK 800:34
  world of s. and sours — POE 683:87
swell And go to ev'ry s. affair — PORT 690:72
  bones on the thrashed s. — LOWE 540:19
  burnish, sprout, and s. — HERB 413:73
  music…with its voluptuous s. — BYRON 187:50
  peruked sea whose s. — SITW 823:96
  unhurried Ground s. — ELIOT 320:72
  Where the green s. is — HOPK 428:65
  with its mighty s. — KEATS 475:70
swelling s. into bombast — DRYD 300:20
swerve s. neither to the right — CURZ 260:5
swerving most unnoble s. — SHAK 794:67
Swift S. is more Irish than Goldsmith — OBRI 645:61
swift race is not to the s. — BIBLE 106:29
  race is to the s. — DAVI 264:66
  S. was the race — DRYD 302:89
  True hope is s. — SHAK 761:46
  With s., slow — HOPK 428:73
  swifter S., higher, stronger — ANON 23:3
Swiftian S. Lilliput — MCCA 548:92
swim good night, or sink or s. — SHAK 771:35
  s. to the Bermudas — WEBS 927:49
swimmer excellence as a s. — BURKE 176:63
  Like an unpractised s. — SHAK 763:97
swimming pool s. p. is…more likely to kill — LEVI 526:32
Swinburne S.…degenerates! — ONEI 651:70
  S. is just emptiness to me — QUIL 702:17
swindler as if I were a s. — LAWR 513:69
swindles as all truly great s. are — OHEN 648:17
swine husks that the s. did eat — BIBLE 121:90
  incompetent s. — SASS 745:86
  men kill the fat s. — ANON 20:40
  nation ruled by s. — THOM 887:90
  on a filthy s. — SPEN 838:23
  pearls before s. — BIBLE 115:49
  s. to show you — ALBEE 11:26
swine-drunk for he will be s.-d. — SHAK 791:69
swines blasted, jelly-boned s. — LAWR 512:40
swing if it ain't got that s. — ELLI 322:22
  if it ain't got that s. — MILLS 595:9
swinger s. of birches — FROST 352:98
swinging keep s. after the music — HELP 409:56
swings we pulls up on the s.! — CHAL 212:63
swiped s. all the good ones — HEMI 409:63
Swiss operated by the S. — USTI 907:48
  S. are inspired hotel-keepers — MONT 613:17
  S. clockmakers — STRA 857:47
switch We turned the s. — SZIL 865:31
Switzerland look upon S. — SMITH 830:47
  S.…had brotherly love — WELL 929:93
  S. is a small, steep country — HEMI 409:59
swivel crouch, s., tug — OBRI 646:73
swollen udder a s. wobble — RAINE 705:38
  when rivers are s. — SOPH 834:28
swoop take away all at one s. — WEBS 926:17
sword altar, s. and pen — WORD 958:94
  Arthur's s. snatched — MUNRO 625:47
  brave man with a s. — WILDE 942:17
  came not to send peace, but a s. — BIBLE 116:72
  carry fire and s. — PARN 665:47
  caution of a s. — CLEV 230:96
  China asked for a s. — BRID 158:11

could use the s. and pen — LAND 507:35
duty…to wield the s. of France — DE 270:92
fallen by the edge of the s. — BIBLE 113:2
father's s. he has girded — MOORE 618:2
flaming s. — BIBLE 91:1
gave them a s. — NIXON 640:39
Hold then my s. — SHAK 778:55
is that your s., or — WEST 933:89
It is at once our s. — HUGH 436:50
let him who has a s. — HO 421:12
lightnings Thy s. — ELLE 322:17
man taketh his s. — BIBLE 112:68
may gyff you that s. — MALO 562:9
My S., I give to him — BUNY 174:83
Negro's s. — PHIL 677:57
never sheath the s. — ASQU 38:84
Norman arrow and s. — WILL 944:64
Nor shall my s. sleep — BLAKE 141:43
oil can is mightier than the s. — DIRK 287:5
oyster…with s. will open — SHAK 773:3
peasants take up the s. — LUTH 542:72
pen is mightier than the s. — BULW 173:64
pen is worse than the s. — BURT 181:78
Plough…twin to the S. — COLUM 238:87
pulleth oute this s. — MALO 562:7
sharper than any two-edged s. — BIBLE 129:34
soldiers of the s. — RUSK 733:98
s. against s. — SHAK 794:71
s. has won in half a year — MOLT 612:93
s. of the Lord — BIBLE 95:13
s. of the Spirit — BIBLE 128:95
s. shall perish with the s. — BIBLE 119:44
threw the s. as farre — MALO 563:15
Turning the word to s. — SHAK 772:91
two-edged s. — WIEN 939:29
two-edged s. in their hand — BIBLE 104:56
watery if not flaming s. — MARV 578:10
We draw the s. — WILH 943:57
Wounds inflicted by the s. — RICH 714:22
sword-belt s.-b. upside down — LAWR 513:56
sword-pen raise my s.-p. — BURG 174:87
swords beat their s. into plowshares — BIBLE 107:51
  Beat your plowshares into s. — BIBLE 111:49
  so we measured s. — SHAK 780:23
  stout hearts and stout s. — BIRK 136:12
  s., our law — SHAK 761:53
  sworn I am s. brother — SHAK 765:58
  s. to action — SASS 745:83
sycophancy between s. and rebellion — BAKER 56:4
sycophants surrounded by s. — HARD 396:91
syllable first s. of…advice — THOR 888:32
  last s. of recorded time — SHAK 798:74
syllables number of s. — SAND 742:36
symbiosis s. of architecture — MURP 627:77
symbol education on the s. level — HUXL 442:97
  In China the bat is a s. — LAWR 513:48
  respect for the living s. — LABO 501:5
  see nothing without a visible s. — BAGE 54:68
  s. for America — ATWO 41:38
  s. of an emerging middle-class — MCFA 551:67
  s. of Irish art — JOYCE 470:22
  s. of national honor — KRUG 500:24
  s. of the power — MOORE 617:85
  what it is the s. of — JENK 454:31
symbolism handles s. rather like — NIGH 639:18
symbols cloudy s. of a high romance — KEATS 475:78
  let us know…as s. do — MACC 546:66
  s. effortlessly shared — UPDI 906:37
symmetry frame thy fearful s.? — BLAKE 140:19
  Man is all s. — HERB 413:70
  S. is boredom — HUGO 437:80
sympathetic s. unselfishness — SAKI 739:62
sympathies cosmopolitan s. — ROSE 725:31
sympathy a lot of s. with him — KINN 488:66
  awakened my maternal s. — PERE 674:16
  failed to inspire s. in men — BEER 73:83
  God-damned s. — WOOL 956:41
  never-failing s. and encouragement — WODE 952:44
  no intercourse and no s. — DISR 288:34
  s. for the selfish — MUIR 624:27
  s. with freedom — GLAD 373:39
  tea and s. — ANDE 18:74
  To s. with hopes and fears — SHEL 814:94
  writer…universal in s. — BARN 64:66
symphonies five sweet s. — ROSS 726:53
  fugues and s. have brought — SASS 745:89
symphony consort to th'angelic s. — MILT 597:35

orchestrating a s. of unhappiness — ROCK 720:35
philanthropy and s. concerts — WHAR 933:5
s. must be like the world — MAHL 559:31
write a s. like that — DAMR 261:23
write his Ninth S. — ROY 730:30
You're a melody from a s. — PORT 690:70
symptom first s. of true love — HUGO 437:86
  infallible s. — GIBB 366:93
  s. of a deficient vitality — STEV 852:50
  s. of…emotional disturbances — VAN 908:16
symptoms hundred good s. — POPE 689:50
  s. are similar — BANKS 62:18
syndrome manifested by…s. — SELYE 756:72
Synge persons…out of S.'s plays — OBRI 646:70
synod general s. of the nation — BAIL 55:89
synonym Violation is a s. — DWOR 308:46
syntax mastery of vocabulary and s. — SAYE 746:10
  shackled by the rules of s. — MACA 545:33
  S. and vocabulary — MATH 581:87
synthesis Held in a lunar s. — ELIOT 317:72
  s. of forty-six years — STEIN 845:79
  s. of hyacinths and biscuits — SAND 742:22
synthesizer Joyce was a s. — BECK 72:51
syphilis manage to avoid s. — SILVA 821:70
Syrian On arrival at a S. port — BAED 54:60
syrops lucent s. — KEATS 477:24
syrup pancake…when you pour the s. — WRIG 963:69
system American s. — HOOV 427:44
  automatic s. — MUMF 625:39
  came the turn of the nervous s. — RAMO 705:49
  communications s. — HAYEK 402:25
  empirical s. to be refuted — POPP 689:52
  every computer in the human s. — GIBS 367:15
  Every s. that we build — MINS 608:13
  false s. of government — PAINE 660:33
  got the North Pole out of my s. — PEARY 671:59
  greater and more equitable s. — MACA 544:5
  Love is just a s. — BARN 64:72
  Observe how s. into system runs — POPE 686:72
  patent s.…added — LINC 529:6
  science has…a s. of principles — PAINE 660:38
  self- epicentre of the solar s. — PHIL 677:56
  s. is benign — CRISP 255:8
  s. of existence…with no eye — WIEN 939:30
  s. of soft enterprise — ARNO 36:47
  s. of which they were the centre — DICK 280:27
  s. that we live in — WILL 945:94
  s. which has no purpose — FROMM 352:88
  they rocked the s. — ROBI 718:97
  tonic to the s. — LIVI 532:55
  true s. of the world — ALEM 12:56
  virtues of the s. — MCCA 548:93
systems After that, we had s. — HOPP 429:3
  are living s. — MONOD 612:2
  Atoms or s. into ruin hurled — POPE 686:73
  Away with s. — MERE 587:26
  number of symbol s. — HUXL 442:97
  Our little s. — TENN 873:56

T

ta thousand T.'s and Pardon's — BETJ 89:37
tabacco fumes of t. and liquors — LEWIS 527:66
  going to leave off t.! — LAMB 505:84
tabby Demurest of the t. kind — GRAY 383:50
tabernacle who shall abide in thy t.? — BIBLE 99:34
tabernacles holy place of the t. — BIBLE 100:68
  How amiable are thy t. — BIBLE 101:84
  t. of thy grace — SCOT 755:87
Tabitha T.…called Dorcas — BIBLE 124:81
table behave mannerly at t. — STEV 853:64
  clouds of the t. above — MONRO 612:5
  gets down from the t. — SITW 823:97
  In England…good t. manners — MIKES 590:86
  Miss Bolo rose from the t. — DICK 278:58
  patient etherized upon a t. — ELIOT 316:60
  preparest a t. before me — BIBLE 100:45
  reside at T. Mountain — HARTE 400:71
  sit at the t. — HUGH 434:9
  t. in a smoke-filled room — DAUG 263:62
  t. in Barchester Towers — BROY 169:89
  t. of brotherhood — KING 487:31
  this thy T. — BOOK 147:12
  Thou shalt prepare a t. — BOOK 149:10
  thrown from the t. — TUTU 901:32
tableau t. of crimes and misfortunes — VOLT 914:39
tablecloth Oedipus…over your t. — PAGE 659:14

tables creatures set upon t.	JOHN	462:40
furnish forth the marriage t.	SHAK	780:42
leave the word of God, and serve t.	BIBLE	124:77
My t.—meet it is	SHAK	781:67
sit at rich men's t.	BROW	166:89
sitting at their dressing t.	OSBO	655:84
table-talk Let it serve for t.-t.	SHAK	770:9
taboo t. birth control method	DALY	261:21
Tabor King Lear at the T. Grand	FIELD	335:12
tacit t., but constant and uniform	SMITH	827:80
tacks when you come to brass t.	ELIOT	319:26
tacky defines t. for all time	ANON	26:12
Toady, perhaps, even t.	ACHE	3:52
tact affection and t.	RUSS	734:31
tactful t. in audacity	COCT	233:84
tactics tolerate…only on t.	DULL	306:88
taedium vitae keep off the t. v.	JOHN	461:90
taffeta changeable t.	SHAK	786:98
tail Improve my shining t.	CARR	203:64
Nor knowst'ou wing from t.	POUND	692:26
porpoise…treading on my t.	CARR	203:80
such a little t.	BELL	76:52
t. hangs down behind!	KIPL	490:6
t. in its mouth	FERL	333:92
t. must wag the dog	KIPL	490:98
Their t. the rudder	DRYD	299:15
vanished…end of the t.	CARR	203:69
wags its t.	TOYN	895:73
waving his wild t.	KIPL	491:42
with its t. in its mouth	HOOD	426:26
tailor t. does not attempt	SMITH	827:85
t. make thy doublet	SHAK	786:98
there lived a t. in Gloucester	POTT	690:83
you t.'s yard	SHAK	771:47
tailors carpenters, or t.	SUN	860:96
off the list of living t.	MERE	588:29
tails Brushin' off my t.	BERL	84:39
stings in their t.	BIBLE	131:7
t. of tender thoughts	WOLFE	953:84
trains will run over their t.	SITW	823:98
We of the long t.!	GRASS	382:13
tainted see that the supply is not t.	SCOTT	751:98
take cannot, sir, t. from me anything	SHAK	782:82
can't t. that away	GERS	365:75
can't t. that away	GERS	365:76
easy to forget…and t. stock	ELIZ	322:13
Nay, t. my life and all	SHAK	770:17
t. away from our years	CRUZ	256:39
t. care of yourself	SPRIN	841:86
T. her up tenderly	HOOD	426:33
T. him for all in all	SHAK	780:43
t. the bull	GOLD	377:28
T. thou thy pound of flesh	SHAK	770:16
triple ways to t.	KIPL	490:2
taking t. them up one by one	HOMA	425:92
talcum t. Is always walcum	NASH	630:56
tale brings in a several t.	SHAK	761:50
could a t. unfold	SHAK	781:60
edge to the superstitious t.	PRIT	696:15
had a t. to tell	SCOTT	751:6
History is a t. of efforts	KISS	494:90
marvelous t.	HAWT	402:16
mere t. of a tub	WEBS	926:25
moral discovery…object of every t.	CONR	244:42
most tremendous t. of all	BETJ	88:36
No t. ever happened	BART	66:21
recalls a t.	AMADO	15:21
sad t.'s best for winter	SHAK	799:12
same t. repeat	WORD	959:7
speak out a plain t.	SCOTT	754:61
t. of arms	VIRG	913:11
t. should be judicious	COWP	250:89
t. Told by an idiot	SHAK	798:74
tedious as a twice-told t.	SHAK	768:58
tell the t. that I heard	HOUS	432:60
thereby hangs a t.	SUCK	858:70
Trust the t.	LAWR	513:65
With a t. forsooth he cometh	SIDN	820:56
talebearer where there is no t.	BIBLE	105:98
talent Brevity is the sister of t.	CHEK	218:13
Children's t. to endure	ANGE	18:84
creative t.…drained off	RICH	714:18
Even an attorney of modest t.	CAPO	197:21
Everybody has t. at twenty-five	DEGAS	269:89
Everyone has t.	JONG	466:29
extraordinary collection of t.	KENN	481:11
extraordinary t.	GOET	375:59

gilded tomb of a mediocre t.	SMITH	829:23
grand t. pour le silence	CARL	201:32
has a t. and cannot use it	WOLFE	953:69
infinite variety of t.	HAZL	403:30
make do with t.	BALC	56:11
must have t. too	KORDA	498:98
no substitute for t.	HUXL	441:64
OK, if you like t.	MERM	588:46
one really notable t.	MENC	586:94
snuffs out ten times more t.	HUGH	435:17
t., a glass, and some cracked ice	BARR	65:3
T. comes from originality	MAUP	582:13
t. for drama	VIDAL	912:82
t. instantly recognises genius	DOYLE	297:70
t. like a uniform	AUDEN	43:84
t. of our English nation	DRYD	302:96
t. to amuse	COWA	249:46
t. which is death to hide	MILT	601:26
T. wins games	JORD	467:45
t. without instruction	VITR	914:29
what every actor…wants: t.	GIEL	368:26
woman's particular t.	HUGO	437:77
wonder how many people of t.	STEV	854:92
writer of t. needs only	WINN	950:3
talents applied his t. to serving	ISHI	447:72
God-given t.	LEON	522:65
small t. might have use	CRAB	252:40
t.…howe'er designed	POPE	689:40
tales full of runic t.	FLEC	340:35
natural fear…is increased with t.	BACON	50:57
T., marvellous t.	FLEC	340:31
t. of others' griefs	SHAK	798:85
whereof t. are told	JONS	467:71
words seemed to them as idle t.	BIBLE	122:12
Taliban like living with the T.	LETTE	524:10
Taliesin Aneurin and T., cruel owls	BUNT	173:68
talk Bad t. drives out good	KNIG	494:11
beautiful family t.	COMP	239:99
do not t. of ourselves	TROL	897:25
English t. is a quadrille	JAMES	450:49
exercise is to t.	WILDE	942:26
good to t.	HOSK	430:27
hear anyone t. of culture	JOHST	465:11
how much my Ministers t.	THAT	881:67
If a lion could t.	WITT	951:29
loves to hear himself t.	SHAK	766:91
nor good t.	KIPL	492:51
nothing but t. of his horse	SHAK	769:77
no time to t.	BALD	56:14
No use to t. to me	HOUS	431:38
one cannot t. about after dinner	WILDE	941:72
People t. about the conscience	JAMES	450:50
People will always t.	GAGA	356:7
rather t. than work	BOYD	153:9
scientists who t.	WEIL	928:70
should be less t.	THER	882:83
shouldn't t. about art	JOHN	458:30
T. about those subjects	HOLM	424:72
t. a little wild	SHAK	804:40
t. but a tinkling cymbal	BACON	52:13
T.…commit an indiscretion	BIER	135:92
t. in this manner	JOHN	464:89
t. is of the weather	JOHN	460:82
t. like a lady	SHAW	810:95
t. slid north	KIPL	490:93
t. so like a waiting gentlewoman	SHAK	771:33
t.…tendeth only to penury	BIBLE	104:72
t. themselves mad	SHAK	774:34
T. to a hungry man	ADAMS	6:10
t. too much	DRYD	302:82
t. to the young people	JONES	466:24
t. was endless, compulsive	COUP	248:31
t. well but not too wisely	MAUG	582:3
t. with you, walk with you	SHAK	769:82
There is no one to t. to	PUTIN	700:95
very easy to t.	DICK	278:82
way not to be remembered is to t.	MAIL	560:54
wouldn't t. to you much	SALI	740:75
write or even to t.	THES	882:96
talked So much they t.	CHUR	224:54
t. about…not being t. about	WILDE	940:65
t. on for ever	HAZL	403:34
talkers present is an age of t.	HAZL	403:47
talking if you ain't t. about him	BRAN	156:68
opposite of t. is waiting	LEBO	518:64
stop people t.	ATTL	40:30
T. all the time	CABR	191:8

t. on paper	BAIN	55:90
The secret to t. is listening	JOHAN	456:70
tired the sun with t.	CORY	247:8
will still be t.	SHAK	773:19
t. to me?	DE	273:65
talks all right if the t. succeed	ZHOU	970:11
dead man…never t. back	CHAN	213:92
Licker t. mighty loud	HARR	399:47
Who t. of my nation?	SHAK	775:77
tall divinely t.	TENN	869:75
Let our children grow t.	THAT	881:49
once handsome and t. as you	ELIOT	318:7
she is t. and stately	TENN	876:22
T. as a crane	SITW	823:8
t., impossibly t., incomparably t.	CUMM	257:51
Tallard Monsieur T.	MARL	572:55
t. than other men	FEIB	331:54
taller biggest difference…she was t.	HARO	398:40
tallow-face Out…You t.-f.!	SHAK	766:4
Tallulah T. never bored anyone	LOOS	536:56
Talmud T., and the Alcoran	BACON	51:78
Tam T. was glorious	BURNS	179:24
tamarisks lowly t.	VIRG	913:23
tambourine Hey! Mr T. Man	DYLAN	309:57
shilling in my little t.	KIPL	491:22
Tamburlaine T.!—A Scythian	MARL	572:96
tame fox…ne'er so t.	SHAK	772:62
gentle, t., and meek	WYATT	964:90
heyday in the blood is t.	SHAK	784:40
Lions make leopards t.	SHAK	764:31
no man ever learned to t.	MEIL	584:38
though I seem t.	WYATT	963:88
which thou canst not t.	HERB	413:55
tamed not a bit t.	WHIT	937:96
tan of t. with henna hackles	STEV	849:72
tane smeddum t.	SMITH	831:64
tang t. of faintly scented urine	JOYCE	470:29
tangential God is the t. point	JARRY	452:95
tangere Noli me t.	BIBLE	133:48
tangled t. web we weave	SCOTT	752:24
tangles Pelt down through the t.	SITW	823:1
tangos sings outdated t.!	DIAZ	276:26
tank T. come down the stalls	SASS	745:80
tanks set the t. on them	MARC	569:54
wooden t. filled with water	GILL	370:77
tap on t., but not on top	CHUR	226:15
running t. of words	MOORE	615:58
tape complain about the 'red t.'	WEBER	925:14
leapt at the t.	BANN	62:33
taper t. of conviviality	DICK	279:89
tapes t., blemishes and all	NIXON	640:37
tapestry t. hanging on four…hooks	MILL	593:40
tape-tied t.-t. curtains	POPE	686:69
tapeworm t. in an intestine	GOLD	375:76
tappets t. that finally push men	ROTH	727:78
tar thumbnail dipped in t.	PATE	669:13
Tara T. rose so high	LAND	507:35
tarantula t. on a slice of angel food	CHAN	213:75
Tar-Baby T.-B., she stay still	HARR	398:45
tares sowed t. among the wheat	BIBLE	117:93
tarnish silver over this t.	LOWE	540:33
tarnished badge of t. braid	READ	708:95
man…who is neither t. nor afraid	CHAN	213:78
tarry Longer will t.	DRAY	299:94
why t. the wheels of his chariots?	BIBLE	95:12
Tarsus T.…no mean city	BIBLE	125:97
tart t. who has…married the mayor	BAXT	69:92
Tartar arrow from the T.'s bow	SHAK	767:37
Tartars T. made them a King	POLO	684:4
tarts action of two t.	MACM	556:69
Queen of Hearts…made some t.	CARR	204:84
Tarzan T. of the Apes	BURR	180:62
tase Don't t. me, bro	MEYER	589:62
task acceptance of a t.	GIDE	368:24
criticism that assumes this t.	DEWEY	276:20
definite t., an interest	POPP	689:59
Delightful t.!	THOM	887:98
enormity of the t.	ACHE	3:38
fed your hunger like an endless t.	CRANE	253:59
Good life be now my t.	DRYD	303:11
good never will be our t.	MILT	602:57
morning sees some t.	LONG	535:19
one t. for all	KIPL	493:72
performance of the t. itself	SHIP	818:13
sets love a t. like that	HUNT	439:27
t. begun so often	MACN	558:1
t. is smoothly done	MILT	599:80

tasks

t. is trying to determine	BART	66:29
t. of science can never end	PEAR	671:56
t. which I am trying to achieve	CONR	243:26
too useless a t.	KEYN	484:73
what he reads as a t.	JOHN	461:93
What is our t.?	LLOY	533:76
Women have but one t.	COUB	248:19
tasks have been my t.	KOLL	496:36
independent thoughts, or even t.	MCLU	556:56
sets us to the t.	SCHW	751:94
t. could not be limited	AREN	31:10
tassels fluttering of…silk t.	DICK	279:1
tassie fill it in a silver t.	BURNS	178:8
taste a matter of t.	STEV	851:24
arbiter of t.	TACI	866:8
bad t. of the smoker	ELIOT	316:56
but not t. thee	HERR	415:7
difference of t. in jokes	ELIOT	316:57
Ghastly Good T.	BETJ	88:17
ghetto of good t.	KEIL	479:55
good t. in women	BERL	85:54
Good t. is better than bad t.	BENN	81:75
How sweet are thy words unto my t.	BIBLE	103:27
Impartiality is an acquired t.	RIFK	715:35
no t. for reading	SMOL	831:67
nowhere worse t.	JOWE	469:16
once they get the t.	HAZZ	404:61
pandering to the public t.	BEAV	71:33
questions of t.	ADAMS	5:89
sense of t.	BALL	60:88
sheer lack of t.	FRY	354:41
splash of bad t.	VREE	915:56
suspect his t. in higher matters	LAMB	505:90
t. and see that the Lord is good	BIBLE	100:56
t. as lightly as the Bee	JONS	468:83
t. for French clothes	SCHL	747:37
t. for simplicity cannot endure	DELA	271:22
t. my Anno Domini	FARQ	330:26
T. not when the wine-cup glistens	SCOTT	754:64
t. of codfish	GRIEG	388:63
t. of death but once	SHAK	777:21
t. the barley bree	BURNS	178:12
Though t., though genius bless	COLL	238:75
tolerate any t.	THUR	891:2
undoubtedly wanted t.	WALP	919:68
value is not in its t.	FULB	355:62
writer…must…create the t.	WORD	961:32
taste-blind as a nation t.-b.	FISH	337:65
tastes artistic t.	DRAB	298:85
Nothing t. as good	MOSS	622:82
t. greatly alter	JOHN	461:14
t. its own innocence	UPDI	906:30
t. may not be the same	SHAW	808:59
t. no wise book-maker	LUCAS	541:49
tattered t. coat upon a stick	YEATS	966:26
tatters wallpaper…falling to t.	MILL	593:51
Tattle always despised Mr T.	CONG	241:49
tattoo t. soap bubbles	BROWN	164:30
tattooed Lydia The T. Lady	HARB	396:89
taught t. to be afraid	HAMM	395:67
what we call highly t.	ELIOT	316:54
tavern good t.	JOHN	462:43
no such joy in the t.	MCCA	547:76
t. for his friends	DOUG	295:10
taverns sat in t. while the tempest	HOUS	432:64
tawny T. are the leaves	RANS	706:68
tax argue for t. increases	KRUG	500:23
Bats…pay no t.	BERR	87:1
hateful t.	JOHN	460:74
keeps armies of t. lawyers	WRIS	963:80
lighten the t. burden	QUINE	702:22
put a t. on pianos	SITW	824:16
turned a t. into a diversion	STEE	844:44
taxation resists your t. in America	PITT	679:7
T. without representation	OTIS	656:92
taxed all the world should be t.	BIBLE	120:67
never t. for speech	SHAK	791:53
taxes certain as death and t.	DEFOE	269:81
death and t.	FRAN	348:19
death and t.	MITC	610:45
no new t.	BUSH	182:99
only President who raised t.	DOLE	290:98
Only the little people pay t.	HELM	408:52
people overlaid with t.	BACON	52:17
true…as t. is	DICK	280:49
taxi empty t. arrived at 10	CHUR	226:16
going in a t.	SHAW	810:1

taxicab ears make him look like a t.	HUGH	434:7
letting your dog vacation at the t.	PAGL	659:23
taxpayers only those t.	NUNN	642:74
Tay Bridge of the Silv'ry T.	MCGO	551:73
Tayler Chesterton down to…T.	WEST	933:95
TB TB or not TB	ALLEN	14:85
Tchaikovsky Tell T. the news	BERRY	87:94
Tching T. prayed on the mountain	POUND	692:27
tea afternoon or evening cup of t.	HOLM	424:85
after t. and cakes and ices	ELIOT	316:62
ain't going to be no t.	MANS	567:98
assaying of t. is an art	MO	611:67
best sweeteners of t.	FIEL	335:17
ceremony known as afternoon t.	JAMES	450:38
Drinking the best t.	SNOW	832:74
get a cup of t.	HYNDE	444:23
give the boys a little t.	ANDE	18:74
My t. is nearly ready	STEV	853:72
Retired to their t. and scandal	CONG	240:35
singles we played after t.	BETJ	88:24
sometimes counsel…sometimes t.	POPE	685:36
sooner the t.'s out of the way	REED	710:32
Take some more t.	CARR	203:72
T., although an Oriental	CHES	221:88
T. for two	CAES	191:10
t. is brought at five	MONRO	612:4
T. is like the East	CHES	221:87
t. is not healthy	GORO	379:67
The way you sip your t.	GERS	365:75
we drink too much t.	PRIE	695:88
we'll all have t.	DICK	279:97
When I makes t. I makes t.	JOYCE	470:23
woman is like a t. bag	ROOS	724:3
your t. you sip	CRAB	252:40
teabreaks t. and other manifestations	MISH	609:19
teach but t. high thought	TENN	877:57
can easier t. twenty	SHAK	769:75
fool has a lot to t.	RABE	704:18
how can they t.?	DAVI	264:71
I can t. thee	SHAK	771:49
in order to t. himself	KAZIN	474:52
learn what it had to t.	THOR	888:37
learn while they t.	SENE	757:23
t. him how to live	PORT	690:79
t. in song	SHEL	812:63
t. it round or flat	JOHN	458:20
T. me, my God and King	HERB	413:61
T. me to feel another's woe	POPE	688:28
t. that happiness	HARDY	397:13
T. the children under the…tree	QABO	701:1
t. thee in the way	BIBLE	100:54
t. the English how to talk	WILDE	942:13
t. the rest to sneer	POPE	687:3
t. the sea what it may do	DONNE	291:35
t. this stuff	RUSS	735:51
T. us to care	ELIOT	319:24
t. us to forget our own	SHAK	798:85
t. you to drink deep	SHAK	780:41
to t. and delight	SIDN	820:55
teacher Fear is a great t.	IGNA	445:15
greatest t. of morals	HOOV	427:52
My greatest T.	SINA	822:88
Nobody loves a bad t.	WRAGG	962:59
persuade the t.	TRIL	897:12
poor t. hurts	BOYER	154:16
sea is a t. of truth	BELL	77:69
t. affects eternity	ADAMS	5:91
t. is the most important	GATES	361:91
t., like every drill-sergeant	RYLE	736:61
t. who does not equip his pupils	PETE	675:39
Wine can be a better t.	FRY	354:49
Your best t. is your last mistake	NADER	629:26
teachers Believe false t.	SHAK	803:98
damage its t. did	STIG	854:97
Heston thinks America should arm its t.	RUSH	732:71
Love and delight are better t.	DURER	307:26
more understanding than all my t.	BIBLE	103:26
mountains are stern t.	TILM	891:17
rigorous t. seized my youth	ARNO	35:3
T.—a bunch of men	MISH	609:20
teaches He who cannot, t.	SHAW	808:39
High office t	KISS	494:92
T. the time	TOML	894:56
teaching environment and its t.	LAWR	514:85
follow mine own t.	SHAK	769:75
substituting indoctrination for t.	PETE	675:39
T. is not a lost art	BARZ	67:36

teachings no use for the t.	KHRU	485:95
team call it a t. game	ARLO	32:34
support their t.	BAIN	55:94
t. effort is a lot of people	WINN	950:5
t. gave a whistle	MOORE	616:65
t. of little atomi	SHAK	765:70
t.'s up against it	GIPP	372:21
why should…your t. object?	HEND	410:2
teams two great t.	SHAN	805:65
teamwork more than t.	SIKO	821:68
teapot warming the t.	MANS	567:98
tear cannot t. out a single page	SAND	741:8
fallen a splendid t.	TENN	876:28
furtive t.	ROMA	723:92
homage of a t.	BYRON	187:37
Of that divine t.	HUGO	438:89
shed one English t.	MACA	546:54
t. out a man's tongue	MART	576:80
t. them up	TYSON	904:9
t. to grace his obsequies	GRAY	385:85
unanswerable t.!	BYRON	188:78
tear-floods no t.-f.…move	DONNE	292:38
tearing t. up £5 notes	HEATH	405:91
tears bat with t. in your eyes	BRAD	155:45
Before my t. did drown it	HERB	414:76
bitter t. to shed	CORY	247:8
brings the t. into their eyes	CARR	205:20
cemented with t.	HERB	413:56
Come back in t.	ROSS	725:37
Creation's t. in shoulder blades	STEV	850:96
daffadillies fill their cups with t.	MILT	599:91
deal with your own t.	WYLIE	964:8
Deep in heart-wrung t.	BURNS	179:34
delivered…mine eyes from t.	BIBLE	102:20
did I wash you with my t.	HERB	414:84
dip their wings in t.	TENN	874:73
Dismiss…your feignèd t.	SHAK	762:86
doesn't like them he t. them up	HITC	419:86
Drew iron t.	MILT	598:55
Drops t. as fast	SHAK	790:51
enough of blood and t.	RABIN	704:24
eternal reciprocity of t.	OWEN	658:40
faded upholstery of t.	BROY	169:88
foolish t. upon my grave	TENN	873:53
fountains fraught with t.	KYD	501:49
frequently in t.	WEBS	926:21
gift of t.	SWIN	863:85
His big t.	SHEL	812:71
home, in a flood of t.	DICK	278:58
If you have t.	SHAK	777:62
I loved even the t.	RACI	704:28
in the midst of t.	THOM	886:81
in your t. ye'll droun	MACD	549:19
kiss again with t.!	TENN	872:36
lived…in t.	DESB	274:91
look through my t.	THOM	886:84
loosed our heart in t.	ARNO	34:75
loot the t. down fa'	SCOTT	753:45
Mine eyes are full of t.	SHAK	765:57
moistened it with t.	KEATS	477:12
more terrible than his t.	THUR	891:96
Mostly orphans' t.	BRAND	156:61
natural t. they dropped	MILT	607:74
Nothing is here for t.	MILT	608:3
now am full of t.	YEATS	965:3
remember with t.!	ALLI	14:7
salt of t.	KAIKO	472:11
scare me with thy t.	TENN	877:61
shall I let the t. run	OBRI	646:72
shed t. when they would devour	BACON	52:55
Smiles, t., of all my life	BROW	166:98
sow in t.	BIBLE	103:35
t. are but water	SPEN	839:44
t. are in my eyes	MASE	580:53
t. have overflowed his ground?	DONNE	291:28
T., idle t.	TENN	872:41
T. in his eyes	SHAK	782:99
t. in the true performing	SHAK	767:21
t. live in an onion	SHAK	794:47
T. may be intellectual	BELL	78:92
t. of friends	DRYD	301:49
t. of someone we do not know	DU	305:71
t. run down her cheeks	ANON	22:62
t. shall drown the wind	SHAK	790:25
t. Thaw not the frost	SHEL	815:27
T., then, for babes	SHAK	760:6
t. to pearl he turned	MARL	574:39

tender

t. wash out a word	FITZ 337:70	
that mine own t. Do scald	SHAK 793:30	
The bitterest t.	STOWE 856:33	
therefore I forbid my t.	SHAK 784:59	
The t. fall in my heart	VERL 910:57	
thoughts…too deep for t.	WORD 960:13	
vale of t.	FERRE 334:98	
waste of T.	STUD 858:63	
watered heaven with their t.	BLAKE 140:20	
weep barren t.	SHEL 814:10	
wipe away all t.	BIBLE 131:4	
wipe away all t.	BIBLE 132:24	
wipe away t. from off all faces	BIBLE 108:67	
wipe the t. for ever	MILT 600:95	
wiping away of t.	STER 848:39	
wish me to shed t.	HORA 430:18	
write of laughter than of t.	RABE 703:8	
tearsday All moanday, t.	JOYCE 470:37	
teas and had t.	CLIN 231:22	
tea-time every night at t.-t.	STEV 853:72	
teatray Like a t. in the sky	CARR 203:71	
technic our modern t. shows	OPPE 652:88	
technical after…your t. success	OPPE 651:83	
necessary t. skill	HOFF 421:24	
not a t. matter	JAMES 451:72	
too much t. ease	SLOAN 825:54	
technician absent-minded lab t.	BOYD 153:11	
technicians hundreds of t.	WELL 929:95	
women, gambling and t.	POMP 684:13	
technics modern science and t.	MUMF 625:36	
technique I never had t.	OERT 647:96	
most perfect t.…is not noticed	CASA 207:70	
pace of t.	FROMM 352:88	
style is not a question of t.	PROU 698:59	
thought and t.	RUSS 734:34	
techniques t. employed in seeking	KUHN 500:37	
tools, the ideals…or the painters' t.	RENO 711:57	
technological by no means anything t.	HEID 406:10	
For t. man it is time	MCLU 556:52	
If there is t. advance	HARR 398:43	
new direction to t. development	SCHU 750:74	
truism in t. development	STER 847:15	
technology advancing t. produced	MACL 555:41	
digital t. makes connecting possible	DOWD 296:33	
essence of t.	HEID 406:10	
For a successful t.	FEYN 334:8	
modern science and t.	GALB 357:20	
One t. doesn't replace another	FRY 354:46	
problems of the t. of today	GABOR 356:2	
Science and t.…are unpredictable	DYSON 309:60	
Science and t. multiply	BALL 60:68	
subsidy to the high t. industry	CHOM 222:28	
T. breaks the laws	OGDEN 648:3	
T. can be our best friend	SPIE 840:66	
T. feeds on itself	TOFF 893:39	
T.…is a queer thing	SNOW 832:79	
t. is indistinguishable from magic	CLAR 228:67	
T. is just a tool	GATES 361:91	
T. is not an image	PAZ 671:49	
t. is the art of using	HUXL 442:97	
t. of decentralization	MURP 627:77	
T.…the knack of so arranging	FRIS 351:82	
T., while adding daily	STEV 851:11	
Technopolis country called T.	WINN 950:99	
teddy T. Bears have their Picnic	BRAT 157:79	
tedious Life is as t.	SHAK 768:58	
Returning were as t.	SHAK 797:51	
So t. is this day	SHAK 766:96	
tedium long afternoons of t.	ROET 722:56	
T. is the worst disease	POMP 684:12	
teeming t. mistress	POPE 688:10	
teenage Gulf War was like t. sex	HARK 398:34	
Having a t. daughter	LETTE 524:10	
teenager buy a t. new clothes	WHITE 935:48	
teenagers t.…read us their poetry	STIPE 855:4	
teeth bared t. of stallions	CRANE 253:66	
bent low, gritting my t.	IGNA 445:17	
but he has iron t.	GROM 389:78	
children's t. are set on edge	BIBLE 110:32	
cut your t.	THOM 886:73	
Forty t.…twenty-four grinders	DICK 281:17	
irregular t.	WELLS 929:17	
Lies in the shape of false t.	WELLS 930:22	
lose our t. and eyelashes	LEAR 517:43	
old bitch gone in the t.	POUND 691:5	
peculiarly sharp white t.	STOK 855:8	
perpetually growing t.	GRASS 382:13	
ride roughshod over my t.	PERE 674:19	
Sans t., sans eyes…sans everything	SHAK 779:83	
shark has pretty t., dear	BREC 157:88	
skin of my t.	BIBLE 98:7	
take the bull between the t.	GOLD 377:28	
t. are like a flock of sheep	BIBLE 107:45	
t. like splinters	CAUS 209:14	
t. Lo. Lee. Ta.	NABO 628:4	
t. of splintered crystals?	BROW 168:54	
thing about him is his front t.	RUNY 731:56	
untying with the t.	BIER 134:65	
weeping and gnashing of t.	BIBLE 116:58	
weeping and gnashing of t.	BIBLE 119:34	
Writers, like t.	BAGE 54:65	
teetotaller easy as a t. walking	JACO 449:12	
no woman should marry a t.	STEV 852:37	
only a beer t.	SHAW 806:91	
Teflon just like T.	SCHR 749:67	
tekel Mene, Mene, T., Upharsin	BIBLE 111:42	
telegrams outer life of t. and anger	FORS 344:29	
telegraph t. are premises	NIET 638:93	
t. poles above a flood	NICO 637:85	
telekinetics Those who believe in t.	VONN 915:54	
Telemachus mine own T.	TENN 870:1	
telephone ask…your t. number	DACHE 260:1	
before he invented the t.	ISAAC 447:67	
cut off the t.	AUDEN 42:79	
I want t. numbers	BERL 85:57	
t. call from a director	PORT 690:71	
when you're on the t.	GIBS 367:16	
telescope t. to his ear	SMITH 827:73	
television animals…on British t. screens	ATTE 40:21	
art…imitates bad t.	ALLEN 14:2	
being on t.	MAIL 560:57	
hearth of t.	NEW 634:38	
largely on t. and radio	HUMP 439:14	
lies from…shock waves of t.	MAIL 559:38	
never be allowed on t.	GERV 365:82	
no plain women on t.	FORD 342:86	
opportunity in t.	SARN 743:55	
preoccupying myself with…t.	SELF 756:12	
T. brought…war	MCLU 556:60	
T. has brought back murder	HITC 419:84	
t. has killed the novel	FRAN 348:26	
T. has made dictatorship impossible	PERES 674:23	
T. has spread the habit	SCHL 748:38	
tell the truth in t.	MUGG 623:12	
thinking man's t.	HAMP 395:73	
until they see it on t.	NIXON 640:40	
When t. is good	MINOW 608:10	
Telfer It's I, Jamie T.	BALL 59:64	
tell could never t. why	GILB 368:31	
learn…to t. it well	RABAN 703:2	
Never t. anyone anything	SALI 740:82	
Nor at all can t.	TENN 877:69	
Sensible men never t.	DISR 289:71	
simply t. the most	KEATS 475:69	
'T. me a story'	CONR 244:56	
T. me, Muse	HOMER 425:9	
T. me the old, old story	HANK 395:81	
t. one that, would t. one anything	WILDE 941:87	
t. people you are	THAT 882:78	
To t. all would be	MAUP 582:14	
you never can t.	SHAW 806:93	
telling not arguing…I am t. you	WHIS 934:17	
still t. what is told	SHAK 801:64	
The art of t. a story	RUSH 732:75	
Why are you t. me this?	GALT 359:55	
Tempe vale of T.	RUSK 734:19	
temper good spirits and good t.	DICK 279:10	
hot t. leaps o'er a cold decree	SHAK 769:76	
Keep me in t.	SHAK 792:96	
One equal t.	TENN 870:2	
only keep your t.	STER 848:22	
science, t.	LONS 536:42	
tart t. never mellows	IRVI 447:57	
t. changed Into their t.	MILT 602:61	
t., naturally morose	DISR 288:46	
undertaken in a friendly t.	PEEL 672:66	
woman of…uncertain t.	AUST 45:54	
temperament Artistic t.	LENG 521:36	
by t.…a conquistador	FREUD 350:55	
greater premium on t.	BRAD 155:67	
have the satiric t.	BEER 73:76	
sanguine t.	MURP 626:74	
temperaments Human t.	LUCAS 541:53	
temperance less Her t. over appetite	MILT 605:28	
t.…the flower of old age	DEMO 272:49	
virtue of prosperity, is t.	BACON 51:3	
temperate in t. heat	SURR 860:4	
more lovely and more t.	SHAK 800:37	
t. affords me none	CAREW 199:59	
temperature light t. when I set out	CECIL 210:25	
not naturally its own	SCHU 750:77	
t.'s risin'	BERRY 87:94	
tempered t. with love's sighs	SHAK 763:18	
tempest covert from the t.	BIBLE 108:75	
here and there with a t.	BIBLE 112:77	
homeless, t.-tossed	LAZA 515:3	
t., a redundant energy	WORD 957:73	
t. came her tears	TENN 873:47	
t. of the gods	MARL 572:3	
we the t. fear	DRYD 299:9	
while the t. hurled	HOUS 432:64	
While the t. still is high	WESL 931:59	
tempests looks on t.	SHAK 802:80	
tempest-tossed Yet it shall be t.-t.	SHAK 795:1	
tempest-tost welcome to the t.-t.	BYRON 189:6	
temple body is the t.	BIBLE 126:39	
great t. of fiction	UPDI 906:32	
inquire in his t.	BIBLE 100:50	
my t. needs redecorating	RIVE 716:57	
Open the t. gates	SPEN 839:49	
t. bells they say	KIPL 489:80	
t., called his body	THOR 888:25	
t. in which the priest	SHAW 809:69	
t. of Jupiter	GIBB 366:2	
The Lord's anointed t.	SHAK 797:41	
train filled the t.	BIBLE 107:54	
vault of the T. of Peace	BRAM 156:57	
veil of the t. was rent	BIBLE 119:48	
veil of the t. was rent	BIBLE 122:9	
temples dwelleth not in t.	BIBLE 125:92	
mortal t. of a king	SHAK 764:52	
smote the nail into his t.	BIBLE 95:11	
solemn t.	SHAK 804:27	
t. are like a piece of a pomegranate	BIBLE 107:45	
t. of his God	MACA 545:45	
t. of the earth are to be overturned	DIDE 285:72	
t. stood on two pillars	HUGH 435:28	
t. th'upright heart and pure	MILT 601:31	
tempora O t.	CICE 227:38	
tempt shalt not t. the Lord thy God	BIBLE 114:23	
T. me no more	DAY 267:35	
temptation able…to resist t.	BRON 161:58	
enter not into t.	BIBLE 119:43	
indiscretion without t.	BIER 135:92	
It is always a t.	KIPL 492:65	
last t. is the greatest treason	ELIOT 319:47	
lead us not into t.	BIBLE 115:42	
maximum of t.	SHAW 808:40	
power of t.	TROL 897:32	
prepare thy soul for t.	BIBLE 112:80	
protections against t.	TWAIN 903:82	
resist everything except t.	WILDE 941:75	
say anything against t.	SAKI 739:68	
t. beset me	FOX 346:71	
t. in the wilderness	BIBLE 102:2	
t. of recklessly prophesying	WILDE 940:50	
t. to see all of society	LEWO 528:79	
Which of us can resist the t.	ATWO 41:49	
Why comes t.	BROW 169:75	
temptations In spite of all t.	GILB 368:35	
t. both in wine and women	KITC 494:94	
t. of a monopoly	SCOTT 751:98	
tempted one thing to be t.	SHAK 787:51	
t. to refuse it	CHAN 214:8	
When t. to say something	ITO 448:79	
tempter when the t. came to him	BIBLE 114:22	
ten In t. thousand years	SNYD 832:84	
one bullet in t. thousand	SPEN 837:4	
T. or twelve	HOPK 428:79	
t. thousand of those men	SHAK 775:86	
T. thousand saw I	WORD 960:25	
there is enough for t.	MOLI 611:83	
woman having t. pieces of silver	BIBLE 121:88	
tenacity our evolutionary t.	BANKS 62:22	
tenants T. of the house	ELIOT 317:86	
Ten Commandments aren't no T. C.	KIPL 489:83	
tendencies strong t. to rivalry	JAMES 451:69	
two simultaneous t.	BAUD 69:85	
tender beautiful, the t., the kind	MILL 592:27	
made t. to the heart	PROU 698:48	

tender-minded 1308

men had grown more t. STUD 858:64
such a t. voice BLAKE 139:86
tails of t. thoughts WOLFE 953:84
t. for another's pain GRAY 383:48
T. is the Night FITZ 338:91
t. is the North TENN 872:44
t. leaves of hopes SHAK 805:52
things that are t. BACON 52:2
tender-minded T.-m. and tough JAMES 451:73
tenderness Anger and t.: my selves RICH 713:7
its t., its joys WORD 960:13
knows not t. DRYD 301:54
strength lined with t. ANGE 18:85
t. gets no response NERVO 634:27
t. is not so oft BACON 51:74
t. of patient minds OWEN 657:26
tenders shoal of fools for t. CONG 241:64
tenement weak, frail, decayed t. ADAMS 5:6
tenements waste of modern t. THOR 889:51
Tennessee I was in T. 24 hours RAY 708:88
placed a jar in T. STEV 849:64
tennis already stuffed t. balls SHAK 774:45
Anybody...for a game of t.? SHAW 810:92
Conversation is like playing t. LODGE 534:96
die without having played enough t. BORO 151:66
old ladies in t. shoes MOSK 622:80
saw the King play at t. PEPYS 674:97
stars' t.-balls WEBS 927:64
taken up t. GULL 390:92
t. could be shorn HUGH 435:27
T....game of no use BACON 50:37
t. with the net down FROST 352:10
two hundred asphalt t. courts HUXL 442:76
What a polite game t. is BARR 65:94
tennis-girl t.-g.'s hand! BETJ 88:25
Tennyson dead!...T. PUNCH 699:82
Lawn T. JOYCE 470:25
tenor noiseless t. of their way GRAY 384:72
tens fold my t. KAUF 474:38
tension general sense of t. MACM 556:74
t. all human energies MUSS 627:91
Under the t., slip, slide, perish ELIOT 319:45
tent Caesar is in the t. YEATS 967:37
Came to my t. SHAK 761:52
inside the t. JOHN 458:11
little t. of blue WILDE 942:16
not a house or even a t. ATWO 41:35
t. made in linen LEON 522:71
tentacles t. that stifle and suffocate ARNO 36:47
tenth t. of mankind SHAK 799:10
t. time, lack of principle SIDM 819:33
tents dwelling in t. BIBLE 92:28
dwell in the t. of wickedness BIBLE 101:90
stately t. of war MARL 572:94
up their t. like Arabs LONG 535:23
tenure During my t. of power PEEL 672:67
Teresa I'm not Mother T. TYSON 904:11
term served a t. GILB 368:34
T., holidays, t., holidays LEWIS 526:48
To every nation a t. KORAN 497:61
terminations terrible as her t. SHAK 773:27
terms age conceived in spatial t. MIES 590:85
contradiction in t. SHAW 810:16
direct and unassuming t. ROCK 721:40
fair t. and a villain's mind SHAK 769:87
In good set t. SHAK 779:78
No t. except...surrender GRANT 381:7
part on better t. OTWAY 656:9
silken t. precise SHAK 763:24
T. of Endearment MCMU 557:81
t. too deep for me GILB 368:43
upon easier t. JOHN 464:91
Terpsichore grace of T. BARR 65:98
terrace sit on the t. remembering SASS 745:87
T. or lofty Tower LEAR 516:30
terraces statues on the t. KIPL 492:67
terrain fought...for such barren t. NOON 640:44
From a material and spiritual t. FULL 355:47
terrestrial confine our attention
to t. matters HAWK 401:92
terrible All strange and t. events SHAK 795:77
dying...is t. FIEL 335:26
it's got to be t.! PUZO 701:9
It's sometimes t. HUXL 442:94
t. is the place you hold BERN 85:63
t. things will happen BUEC 172:43
thee t. and dear. SHEL 816:65

terrier toothless t. on Valium SIKO 821:67
terrified t. and tight BETJ 89:39
terrifying in their briefcases is t. KHRU 485:96
territory all parts of this vast t. TOCQ 892:30
better...than to increase his t. ERAS 327:37
comes with the t. MILL 593:33
invade British t. HUNT 440:33
Not an inch of our t. FAVRE 331:50
Over all this t....an iron curtain GOEB 374:54
t. ahead of the rest TWAIN 903:68
terror even t. of their lives SHAR 806:71
fight t. with tyranny BUSH 183:41
flame of incandescent t. ELIOT 321:90
I would be in t. PRAT 694:66
no t., brother Toby STER 848:39
Our war on t. is well begun BUSH 183:19
perch, and let their t. SHAK 787:50
political figures fear...t. NOON 640:48
servile minds into t. TZARA 904:18
T....arises from...disestablishment KING 487:37
t. by night BIBLE 101:96
t. could it not repress SURR 860:2
t. for lowering a man's stamina DOUG 294:98
t. of his name BEAU 71:20
t. of the world GIBB 366:94
t. that paralyses ROOS 724:6
t., threats and dread KIPL 493:70
Thy t., O Christ HOPK 428:69
victory in spite of all t. CHUR 225:83
warfare, t., murder WELL 929:93
terrorism any nation that continues to
harbor...t. BUSH 183:17
Consensus T. COUP 248:28
make sure t. never prevails BLAIR 138:59
those engaged in t. BLAIR 138:69
We do not create t....We invite t. BUSH 183:34
Whatever else t. had achieved AMIS 17:58
terrorist cannot let t....nations hold this
nation hostile BUSH 182:15
One is a t. GORB 378:50
righted by the t.'s program JONAS 465:14
starve the t. THAT 881:62
t....from the same basket CONR 244:41
terrorists how we baptize t. PALIN 661:63
t. would...have abandoned the field CHEN 218:26
to get at t. GORE 379:59
with us, or...with the t. BUSH 183:17
terrors new t. of Death ARBU 30:3
t. of the earth SHAK 792:3
The Little T. GAVA 362:8
Tess ended his sport with T. HARDY 397:16
test Electric Kool-Aid Acid T. WOLFE 953:72
end and t. of art POPE 685:18
Habit...the t. of truth CRAB 252:41
Martyrdom is the t. JOHN 464:77
really decisive t. JAY 453:2
t. is a mere substitute MUSS 627:91
t. of a real comedian NATH 632:99
to a lie-detector t. KOES 495:28
universal t. of travel GELL 363:35
testament Than my T. fer that LOWE 539:5
testaments last wills and t. MELV 585:62
testimonies t. are my meditation BIBLE 103:26
testimony t. of a good conscience KEMP 480:75
testosterone awash in post-war t. SCHR 749:68
tests moral t. and tasks ELKIN 322:16
test tube baby made in a t. t. MAIL 560:57
tether world is at the end of its t. WELLS 930:40
Teutonic speech...free of T. guttural QUIL 702:13
Texas deeper than the skies of T. MCMU 557:83
part of the T. ritual FERB 332:68
state of T. KENN 482:33
T. wrestling match WRIS 963:83
text enrich My t. with many things BYRON 189:2
except the first t. GIRA 372:22
German t. of French operas WHAR 934:11
great t. in Galatians BROW 167:11
holy t. around she strews GRAY 384:73
listen to the wind's t. THOM 885:72
neat rivulet of t. SHER 817:87
paintings...to illustrate the t. WOLFE 953:74
square of t. TENN 877:49
t. book example TIME 892:20
textbook conspiracy among t. authors BRYS 171:16
texts difference of t. SPEN 839:42
texture closest, in t. THOM 884:44
t. and tone MORR 620:59

T. is the content POPO 689:51
t. of the soil SMITH 820:57
Thackeray T. and Dickens STEV 852:53
T. settled like a meat-fly RUSK 733:12
Thames Crossing the stripling T. ARNO 34:90
fished...from the stinking T. WINT 950:8
gaily as the sparkling T. ARNO 34:94
mouth of the T. GIBB 366:95
Sweet T., run softly ELIOT 318:3
Sweet T., run softly SPEN 839:59
T. is between me and the Duchess WALP 919:66
T....the noblest river ADDI 7:35
thrown in the T.? SHAK 773:12
upon the banks of T. JONS 468:81
where the charter'd T. does flow BLAKE 140:16
youthful T. ARNO 35:16
thane T. of Cawdor lives SHAK 796:9
T. of Fife SHAK 798:66
Your face, my t. SHAK 796:16
thank I want to t. everybody STOCK 855:6
not going to t. anybody MILL 595:3
not please but t. you DILL 286:93
only themselves to t. SAYE 746:10
t. all those who made this possible ANDR 18:81
t. me, love me, and reward me SHAK 789:10
t. we all our God WINK 950:98
thankful Be t. for what you have WINF 950:96
must be t. HAMM 394:58
t. that I am here to welcome you STAN 842:11
thankless have a t. child SHAK 792:95
thanks give solemn t. COLU 239:55
give t. unto thee BOOK 149:37
give t. unto the Lord BIBLE 103:41
ta'en with equal t. SHAK 783:21
T. for All the Fish ADAMS 4:78
T. for tomorrow ATKI 40:15
t. to you all KENN 482:42
to give t. is good SWIN 864:14
thanksgiving come...with t. BIBLE 102:1
With proud t. BINY 135:99
Thatcher better prospect than Mrs T. HESE 416:29
father, except perhaps Mrs T. WEST 933:99
If Margaret T. wins KINN 488:65
it was T., T., T. BENN 79:34
nobody scared me as much as Mrs T LIVI 532:58
plutonium blonde...T. SCAR 746:14
reappeared in the shape of...T. HOGG 423:44
talk with Mrs T. WEIG 927:68
[T.] has been charging around HEAL 404:65
[T.] has turned the...bulldog STEEL 844:81
T. is a...tyrant MACM 557:76
T. was perfect for me TOWN 895:69
thawed t. and gone KHAY 485:86
theatre devotes himself to the t. BEAU 70:7
Execrable English T. GOET 375:58
For the t. one needs long arms BERN 86:86
go to the t. to be entertained COOK 245:68
I left the t., dizzy and pale QUIR 703:27
I like the t., but never come late HART 400:67
in England nobody goes to the t. AGATE 9:90
interview that turned towards the T. PRIE 695:94
into the t. as a voyeur FRIS 351:86
laughter in the rear of the t. KAUF 474:41
most magical moment in the t. CRON 256:31
only desire...to construct a t. GENET 363:42
only regret in the t. BARR 65:2
people don't go to the t. JOUR 469:11
quit going to the t. SALI 740:86
remain in the t. TYNAN 904:99
talent...drained off into t. RICH 714:87
t. a place to scratch MUSC 627:86
t....can't and doesn't change society HYTN 444:25
t. has always been essential MAMET 564:77
t. has died in my lifetime MILL 593:47
t. is irresistible ARNO 36:39
t. is the primary evidence THUR 890:89
t. of man's life BACON 49:31
we t. folk MANK 566:75
what is happening in the t. TYNAN 904:2
what t. is all about STOP 856:21
theatres books are t. STEV 852:78
chain of moving picture t. DOSP 294:86
t. have had their day. BENN 81:81
towers, domes, t. WORD 960:73
theatrical fail to find happiness in t. life PAVL 670:42
theatricals game of private t. JAMES 451:70
thee my little jokes on T. FROST 353:19

think

Shakespeare—or t.	SCOTT	754:81
soul be required of t.	SMITH	830:43
theft Property is t.	PROU	697:35
there is boundless t.	SHAK	791:81
what would be t. in other poets	DRYD	300:21
them Let's be getting at t.	GRACE	380:83
theme Fools are my t.	BYRON	186:24
imperfection in the chosen t.	WORD	958:74
it is my t.!	DENH	272:60
must choose a mighty t.	MELV	585:64
My t. is always humanistic	WILS	947:43
so grave a t.	PRIOR	696:13
t., concept, structure	POUS	692:40
t. defeats structuralism	GOLD	375:79
t. too high doth seem	GURN	390:2
theme park Life is not a t. p.	BRAND	156:65
themes actions, and religious t.	POUS	692:40
leave great t. unfinished	MACB	546:62
muses on admirèdd t.	MARL	572:2
no transcendent t. in life	FORD	343:10
t. in a new light	LUCAS	541:56
t. men always have loved	DAY	267:2
themselves him rather than t.	WINT	950:9
ought to be doing for t.	JOHN	458:13
principal part of t.	HAZL	403:37
theologians if you believe the t.	SALI	740:87
invention of t. or priests	NIEB	637:87
theology hope of t.	INGE	445:31
keep history and t. apart	WELLS	930:36
reduce the glories of t.	FRY	354:47
schools of t.…are to be overturned	DIDE	285:72
t., philosophy, history, art	ARNO	35:8
T., sir, is a fortress	MILL	593:36
theorem T.—The acquisition	SART	744:63
theories come to nature with your t.	RENO	711:54
't.' and 'goals'	KIPL	492:59
theorist half-baked t.	TRUE	899:73
theorists armchair t.	ASHD	37:66
modern educational t.	RUSS	734:32
particularly economic t.	KNIG	494:10
talented economic t.	TOBIN	892:25
t. who can ruin your game	BOTH	152:80
theorize mistake to t.	DOYLE	296:39
theorizing t. about music	HEINE	407:16
theory All t.…is grey	GOET	375:63
Democracy is the t.	MENC	586:81
in t. if genius had not proved	LESS	524:4
life without t.	DISR	286:19
new t.…a discovery	POPP	689:54
new t. is attacked	JAMES	451:75
no good t. of what it is	MELL	584:49
not apply t. to history	STIN	854:1
nothing in the t. to indicate	SIMON	821:74
Plato divined in t.	WHIT	936:70
practical as the t.	OPPE	652:88
prop up their t.	TWAIN	903:93
t. and methods of revolution	MAO	568:27
T. is a good thing	KAPI	473:27
t. of modern education	WILDE	941:1
T. of Permanent Adolescence	CONN	242:5
t. of the Communists	MARX	579:32
t. of the subject is complete	MILL	591:95
t. that his wife is beautiful	MENC	586:5
without…a t.	POPP	689:58
wonders if it will work in t.	HELL	408:38
theosophy 'T.' is the essence	BLAV	142:50
T., on earth, is like	BLAV	142:51
therapy form of t.	GREE	386:25
psychoanalytic t. of hysteria	FREUD	350:56
there not t., t. is no t. t.	STEIN	845:69
thermodynamics Second Law of T.	SNOW	832:76
thermometer t. had been longer	MOOD	615:53
Thermopylae old man of T.	LEAR	517:46
The Scream This became T. S.	MUNCH	625:41
Thespian T. springs	DRAY	299:98
thick dashed through t. and thin	DRYD	302:94
grown t.	BIBLE	95:1
lay it on so t.	BUTL	185:97
T. and unwholesome	SHAK	784:52
t. as a plank	DIANA	276:23
thicker History gets t. and t.	TAYL	868:45
thicket t. of the world	JOHN	456:75
thick-jewelled t.-j. shone	TENN	870:84
thick-skinned t.-s. grown-ups	SHAW	807:18
writers…become t.-s.	WAUGH	924:85
thief apparel fits your t.	SHAK	788:75
come as a t.	BIBLE	130:76

come as a t.	BIBLE	132:15
come like a t. in the night	POE	683:83
cries out stop t.	CONG	240:44
grand t. into God's fold	MILT	604:95
have a t. or two	SHAK	787:52
He that steals…is a t.	SCOTT	753:37
in what watch the t. would come	BIBLE	118:32
Jean Cocteau thinks that I am poor t.	GENET	363:38
not the mouse who is the t.	JACO	449:10
Opportunity makes a t.	BACON	49:18
Pleasure is a t. to business	DEFOE	269:80
rather have been the good t.	BROW	165:80
steals something from the t.	SHAK	789:99
t. breaks into my house	PAINE	660:30
t. cometh not, but for to steal	BIBLE	123:44
t. in the night	BIBLE	130:76
Upon a dwarfish t.	SHAK	798:67
what a deformed t.	SHAK	774:46
which is the t.?	SHAK	793:24
thieves Beauty provoketh t.	SHAK	778:64
best of t.	DRYD	301:60
fell among t., which stripped him	BIBLE	120:80
made it a den of t.	BIBLE	118:23
so much gained upon the t.	STEV	851:26
T. for their robbery	SHAK	787:60
T. for want of Work	SWIFT	862:57
T. out, profit in!	ANON	20:24
T. respect property	CHES	220:72
T. think that I am a poor writer	GENET	363:38
Twenty Thousand T.	JOYCE	470:39
union of two t.	BIER	134:62
when t. cannot be true	SHAK	771:40
where t. do not break through	BIBLE	115:43
you are t. professed	SHAK	791:81
thigh bee with honied t.	MILT	598:58
happy dawning of her t.	HERR	415:8
on his t. a name written	BIBLE	132:20
smote them hip and t.	BIBLE	96:17
thimble silver t. lies cold	SITW	824:20
thimbles sought it with t.	CARR	206:31
thin Enclosing every t. man	WAUGH	924:87
how t. and clear	TENN	872:39
in every fat man a t. one	CONN	243:13
No matter how t.	SMITH	828:93
pallid and t. young man	GILB	369:48
t.…as a furled umbrella	EMERY	325:2
thine only call me T.	COLE	235:26
thing any manner of creeping t.	BIBLE	94:76
Being a t. immortal	SHAK	781:58
dear ravishing t.	BEHN	75:24
design…in a t. so small	FROST	352:11
do a t. in Israel	BIBLE	96:27
do only one t. at once	SMIL	827:70
excellent t. in woman	SHAK	793:38
far, far better t. that I do	DICK	282:1
fond t. vainly invented	BOOK	150:41
getting on with the bloody t.	EVANS	328:67
great To do that t.	SHAK	795:86
if a t. is worth doing	CHES	220:79
if they have a good t.	SHAK	772:74
it don't mean a t.	ELLI	322:22
it don't mean a t.	MILLS	595:9
least t. contains something	MAUP	583:16
life is the t.	SMITH	829:24
local t. called Christianity	HARDY	397:26
most important t. in life	PASC	667:86
most important t. in the world	SHAW	806:79
no new t. under the sun	BIBLE	105:11
one damned t. after another	HUBB	434:97
one t. we did right	ANON	26:94
palsy-stricken, churchyard t.	KEATS	477:19
poor virgin…an ill-favoured t.	SHAK	780:22
prettier the kind of a t.	LAMB	505:92
say that the t. is good	MOORE	616:66
sought to do the right t.	MCNA	557:93
Technology…is a queer t.	SNOW	832:79
t. about girls	SALI	740:74
t. depicted is less stationary	LEGER	519:7
t. fall down in peace	MAYB	583:24
too much of a good t.?	SHAK	779:11
unlike any other t.…in the universe	STEI	845:80
what t. is love	PEELE	672:70
what to make of a diminished t.	FROST	352:97
things accept…the t. that cannot	NIEB	637:18
all mortal t. doth sway	SPEN	839:60
all needful t.	WORD	959:99
All other t. must	SCHI	747:25

all the t. thou canst desire	BIBLE	104:55
All t. are artificial	BROW	165:58
all t. are become new	BIBLE	127:70
all t. are lawful for me	BIBLE	126:26
All t. are literally better	RUSK	733:87
all t. be done decently	BIBLE	127:54
All t. began in order	BROW	166:85
All t. bright and beautiful	ALEX	13:61
All t., by a law divine	SHEL	813:78
all t. work together for good	BIBLE	125:20
By whom all t. were made	BOOK	147:61
do all t. through Christ	BIBLE	128:7
ear of jealousy heareth all t.	BIBLE	112:72
faculty of seeing t.	SPEN	837:7
fairest t. have fleetest	THOM	886:80
fanatic for the externality of t.	LEWIS	527:72
habit…of correcting t.	BRADY	155:53
he that contemneth small t.	BIBLE	113:97
higher order of t.	MILL	594:71
impressions of external t.	RUSK	733:90
In the nature of t.	SPIN	840:71
leave great t. undone	GLAS	374:44
Little t. affect little minds	DISR	288:35
Many t. are formidable	SOPH	834:26
Mind not high t.	BIBLE	125:27
more t. are shewed unto thee	BIBLE	113:82
more t. in heaven and earth	SHAK	781:70
mystery of t.	SHAK	793:33
new way of looking at t.	MILL	594:89
power in small t.	SOPH	834:27
present state of t.	BAGE	54:63
remembrance of t. past	SHAK	801:47
sad vicissitude of t.	STER	848:49
Say not soft t.	SORL	834:33
science…interested in t.	CURIE	259:87
secret t. belong unto the Lord	BIBLE	95:96
sorts of t.	RYLE	736:60
These Foolish T.	MARV	578:12
T. are the sons	JOHN	460:68
T. fall apart	YEATS	966:24
T. have dropped from me	WOOLF	956:36
T. I'd been better without	PARK	664:12
T. in book's clothing	LAMB	506:11
t. in the world	RUSK	732:84
T. I once read	SNYD	832:89
t. made matter very little	CUMM	257:57
t. people have once held against her	SCHL	747:37
t. people make fools of themselves	SHAW	806:62
T. that are seen	JOHNS	457:86
t. that are tender and unpleasing	BACON	52:2
t. which have never yet been done	BACON	50:47
T. without all remedy	SHAK	797:45
t. you can do in a baseball game	STEN	847:8
think on these t.	BIBLE	128:5
those who say funny t.	DODD	289:89
thou hast created all t.	BIBLE	131:98
totality of facts, not of t.	WITT	951:22
to whom such t. are nothing	SOPH	834:32
useful or pleasurable t.	RUSK	733:97
value of the world of t.	MARX	578:25
wanted to be three t.	SCHU	750:76
way of doing t. rightly	RUSK	733:93
What t. have we seen	BEAU	70:11
why and wherefore in all t.	SHAK	776:96
thingummy no…but T.	DICK	280:35
think begin to t. about it	HEYE	417:40
cannot t. well, love well	WOOLF	955:25
can't t. and hit	BERRA	87:92
can't t. for you	DYLAN	309:52
can't t. without his hat	BECK	72:40
don't t. foolishly	JOHN	464:89
don't t. much of it	STRA	857:43
effort to t. clearly	JAMES	451:63
feel hot and t. cold	CARY	207:62
fellows whom it hurts to t.	HOUS	432:57
greatly t. or bravely die?	POPE	685:44
haven't got the money, so we've got to t.	RUSH	735:53
I am inclined to t.	DOYLE	297:69
if they t., they fasten	HOUS	432:66
If you can t.	KIPL	492:62
know more than you t.	SPOCK	841:84
might as well t. big	TRUMP	900:95
more clearly than you t.	BAKER	56:1
never expect a soldier to t.	SHAW	807:1
not so t. as you drunk	SQUI	841:91
pains to t. otherwise	HUME	438:97

thinker

problem is not whether machines t.	SKIN	825:47
talk who never t.	PRIOR	695:98
t. and t. for months and years	EINS	313:77
t. back through our mothers	WOOLF	955:31
T. before you speak	FORS	345:48
t. by fits and starts	HOUS	432:66
t. continually of those	SPEN	837:92
t....exclusively of others	WAUGH	924:93
t. he is growing old	IRVI	447:59
t. him so...t. him so	SHAK	758:57
t. is to be full	KEATS	478:43
t. like a man	SIMON	821:73
T. not of them	KEATS	478:33
t. out of the box	THARP	880:43
t. perhaps even less	BROW	168:40
t. so highly	STEV	852:52
t. that science can do anything	RAY	708:87
t. that we t.	BIER	134:67
t., therefore I am	DESC	274:96
t. too little	DRYD	302:82
t. with them	BENN	81:79
t. you are doing nothing	JULI	471:42
try to t. it again	GOET	375:64
'What do you t....?'	ATWO	41:52
What I t., I utter	SHAK	799:92
What will Mrs Grundy t.?	MORT	621:77
Whenever I t.	STEV	849:63
When I t., I must speak	SHAK	779:93
When I would pray and t.	SHAK	787:62
when we t. of thee, O America!'	WALP	919:73
thinker incompleteness as a t.	WEBB	925:6
thinkers masses of wishful t.	QUINE	702:22
thinking and then to t.!	HAZL	403:40
cannot prevent people from t.	SCHI	747:26
can't stop t. about it	HIRST	419:82
employment for a t. man	ADDI	7:58
expedient in the way of our t.	JAMES	451:76
explicit in my t.	RUSS	734:37
feverish after so much t.	CARR	205:24
hearing, t., writing	HAZL	404:54
instead of t.	JOHN	465:8
inventory of unfinished t.	RAND	706:55
It ain't t. about it	TROL	898:38
I, who was t. this	DESC	274:95
left hand is my t. hand	HEPW	412:30
live no longer by t.	SHAK	780:20
modes of t. are different	JOHN	464:79
much drinking, little t.	SWIFT	861:36
not a substitute for t.	STEV	851:10
not merely as t.	PLATH	681:29
originality...manner of t.	MAUP	582:13
science...a refinement of everyday t.	EINS	314:84
science fictional way of t.	ASIM	38:81
T. is the great enemy of perfection	CONR	244:48
t. it and not saying it	NOON	640:46
t. makes it so	SHAK	782:85
T. precisely and systematically	SOLOW	833:3
t. what nobody has thought	SZENT	865:29
t. what you really think	GINS	372:15
too busy t. about myself	SITW	824:13
usually a way of not t.	HELL	408:49
verbal t. is the most articulate	KOES	495:29
thinks person who reads or t.	YOUR	968:55
t. too much	SHAK	776:12
utter what he t. truth	JOHN	464:77
what his heart t.	SHAK	774:43
third deny that the T. Estate	SIEY	820:62
nothing new in T. World	AUNG	45:39
There is no t.!	SAINT	739:49
the t. day he rose again	BOOK	146:37
t. day comes a frost	SHAK	805:52
t. kind of knowledge	SPIN	841:82
t. who walks always beside you?	ELIOT	318:9
To make a t., she joined the....two	DRYD	303:19
third-rate what in the world is t.-r.?	HELL	407:32
thirst believeth...shall never t.	BIBLE	122:34
hunger, t....and death	GARI	360:73
man can raise a t.	KIPL	489:83
neither t. any more	BIBLE	131:4
nor a t. for water, but of hearing	BIBLE	111:54
pride which causes t.	DANTE	262:40
quench a country's t.	POPE	686:68
t. to be loved	RHYS	712:72
t. without quenching it	UPDI	906:21
without the provocation of t.	SWIFT	862:49
thirsteth Ho, every one that t.	BIBLE	109:96
thirstier t. than ever	SALA	739:70
thirsty t., and ye gave me drink	BIBLE	119:36
t. land springs of water	BIBLE	108:76
when I was t. they gave me vinegar	BOOK	149:26
thirteen clocks were striking t.	ORWE	655:71
T. wasted years	ANON	25:51
thirty American women over t.	FITZ	338:96
Between t. and forty	BENN	81:74
past t., and three parts iced	ARNO	34:83
t. pieces of silver	BIBLE	112:61
t. pieces of silver	BIBLE	119:39
t. years' experience	CARR	202:54
thirty-five between...t.-f. and forty	DIOR	286:3
thirty-seventh t.-s....situation	JARRY	452:96
Thisbe Death of Pyramus and T.	SHAK	767:20
love T.: very tragical	SHAK	768:46
thistle flew like the down of a t.	MOORE	616:65
t., O my soul	MACD	549:27
t. yet'll unite	MACD	549:24
thistles t. blinterin' white	MACD	549:31
thither transported hither and t.	OVID	657:21
Thomas John T. says goodnight	LAWR	513:73
T., because thou hast seen me	BIBLE	124:68
True T.	BALL	59:74
thorn Instead of the t....the fir tree	BIBLE	109:2
left the t. wi' me	BURNS	179:33
Oak, and Ash, and T.	KIPL	492:53
Oak, and Ash, and T.	KIPL	492:54
plant this t., this canker	SHAK	771:34
pricks like t.	SHAK	765:69
pull the t.	SCOTT	753:35
snail's on the t.	BROW	167:9
t. in the flesh	BIBLE	127:76
without t. the rose	MILT	604:97
thorns crackling of t. under a pot	BIBLE	106:21
impious hand to the Crown of T.	BRON	161:65
lily among t.	BIBLE	107:40
loops and t.	UPDI	906:28
no t. go as deep	SWIN	864:94
pain...of their t.	BERN	86:76
received seed among the t.	BIBLE	117:91
some fell among t.	BIBLE	117:90
t. of life	SHEL	813:82
thorny life is t.	COLE	235:34
t. way to heaven	SHAK	781:48
thoroughfare t. ful of wo	CHAU	217:86
thou eternal T.	BUBER	171:21
t. wilt not often be mistaken	PENN	673:82
Thus far t. shalt go	PARN	665:48
thought Action...the enemy of t.	CONR	244:37
All t., all passions, all delights	COLE	235:27
beautiful clean t.	LAWR	513:47
become our own t. police	MAMET	563:26
bud of t.	DARIO	262:45
but teach high t.	TENN	877:57
By t., word, and deed	BOOK	147:67
call it the stream of t.	JAMES	451:66
calmer of unquiet t.	WALT	920:92
can to sight or t.	MILT	606:51
carving and colouring of a t.	SITW	824:23
ceases to move in t.	ELIOT	319:28
certain dimensions of t.	STEI	846:98
closer the expression is to the t.	FLAU	339:17
community of t.	ADAMS	5:92
deep t., reason, or imagination	DARW	263:57
different from what we t.	HAVEL	401:85
dress of t.	POPE	685:21
end of man is...not a t.	CARL	200:95
Eternity!...dreadful t.!	ADDI	7:52
eternity of t.	WORD	957:69
Experience is the child of T.	DISR	287:15
greater cannot be t.	ANSE	29:71
great movements of human t.	BENN	81:81
habit of t.	SKEL	825:44
habits of metaphoric t.	FRYE	354:54
impartial in t. as well as in action	WILS	949:77
in a general honest t.	SHAK	778:57
inward world of t.	ARNO	35:22
Language is called the garment of t.	CARL	200:94
less permanent than t.	BUNT	173:65
liberty of t. perishes	ORWE	655:69
light of t.	SHEL	814:94
lived in pleasant t.	WORD	959:99
loftiness of t.	DRYD	303:19
man of yearning t.	ROSS	727:51
Ministers of t.	SHEL	815:30
never could divine his real t.	BYRON	190:14
Not a t. in all my rest	VAUG	909:38
nothing more than your t.	BACH	49:11
not the constant t. of their sins	BLOOM	143:65
odd t. strikes me	JOHN	464:99
once t. can never be unthought	DURR	308:39
optical form of t.	HUGO	436:56
Original t. is like original sin	LEBO	517:62
pale cast of t.	SHAK	782:7
Perish the t.	CIBB	227:26
possesses or possessed A t.	BYRON	187:38
reading of the history of t.	MERT	589:55
rear the tender t.	THOM	887:98
revelation of T.	EMER	325:91
seven thousand years of human t.	LABR	501:6
shoots of green t.	WHITE	935:50
sit alone with your t.	BOND	145:17
society in which t.	RUSS	734:34
songs...that tell of saddest t.	SHEL	814:97
spark of inextinguishable t.	SHEL	816:51
speech created t.	SHEL	814:15
splendour of a sudden t.	BROW	169:62
strange seas of T.	WORD	958:82
strive to express his t.	RYDER	736:58
sweet silent t.	SHAK	801:47
tease us out of t.	KEATS	478:39
t. frightens me greatly	SEVI	758:42
t. in the world	ARNO	35:13
t. is often original	HOLM	424:63
t. is viscous	ADAMS	5:97
t. it out with both hands	SAYE	746:8
t. it Pegasus	KEATS	475:68
t. moving in...complete abstraction	WHIT	936:67
t. of before	GOET	375:64
t. of his name	ELIOT	320:53
t. of Thee wakes	KIER	485:5
t. raised to heaven	LESS	524:5
t. rationally, acted	LIPP	531:43
T. shall be the harder	ANON	20:36
T....wed with T.	TENN	874:67
t. which could electrify	MILL	594:68
thousand minds the same t.	TOCQ	892:32
two people...hit upon the same t.	SHER	818:3
tyranny of conscious t.	BEEC	73:70
understandest my t.	BIBLE	103:43
unredeemed dreariness of t.	POE	683:80
utmost bound of human t.	TENN	870:99
vehicle for the t. of our day	FORD	343:93
wait without t.	ELIOT	320:57
what you t. you came for	ELIOT	321:82
whistled...for want of t.	DRYD	304:45
works of t. and intelligence	PAST	668:4
world of t.	HAMI	394:49
wrought by want of t.	HOOD	426:35
thoughtlessness t. is the weapon	CONN	243:8
thoughts appall your t.	MARL	572:95
As horrible t.	FULL	355:75
as thy t. in me	TENN	871:23
Beware t. that come in the night	HEAT	406:92
books...contain our very t.	CONR	244:40
censor one's own t.	WALEY	917:31
Cleanse the t. of our hearts	BOOK	147:58
cocoon of its own t.	LOWE	539:12
dark soul, and foul t.	MILT	594:68
decided by a person's t.	KIM	486:12
deep t. can be winnowed	SAGAN	737:26
extreme t. take hold	DIDE	285:78
for my t. are not your t.	BIBLE	109:98
generate misleading t.	SPEN	838:67
give them your love but not your t.	GIBR	367:13
images of t. refined	KEATS	475:65
In ernistfull t. and in studying	HENR	411:19
in their barks my t.	SHAK	779:86
joy of elevated t.	WORD	956:55
keep watch over my t.	HOUS	432:74
more offences...than I have t.	SHAK	783:11
Music is...your t.	PARK	663:93
My bloody t.	SHAK	790:29
my t. on white ships	COLUM	238:89
pained t. found	JEFF	453:12
pansies; that's for t.	SHAK	784:55
pleasant t. Bring sad t.	WORD	957:60
pleasures which my t.	LANY	508:58
printing our t.	JOHN	461:16
propriety of t. and words	DRYD	300:41
pursue independent t.	MCLU	556:56
recognize our own rejected t.	EMER	324:51
reveal their best t.	DESC	274:92
sad t. doth clear	VAUG	909:41

tie

Entry	Reference
sensations rather than of t.!	KEATS 475:74
shroud Of t.	BYRON 188:57
Style is the dress of t.	CHES 219:42
Suspicions amongst t.	BACON 52:18
than to his t.	HUGO 437:83
t. are my prostitutes	DIDE 285:70
t. are whirlèd	SHAK 759:74
t. began to burnish	HERB 413:73
t....come crowding in so fast	DRYD 304:38
t. dally with false surmise	MILT 599:92
T. die and are buried	LIND 529:12
t. go blowing through them	BROO 162:85
t. have any relation to reality	CHES 220:68
t. have eyes	LYLY 543:84
t. may startle well	MILT 598:69
t. of men are widened	TENN 871:19
t. of other men	COWP 251:21
t. remain below	SHAK 783:35
t. shall be established	BIBLE 105:78
t. smothering ye	KELM 479:70
t. that arise in me	TENN 871:3
T., that breathe	GRAY 385:91
t. to an end	SMITH 830:41
t....too deep for tears	WORD 960:13
troubled t.	MILT 603:89
turn your t. to becoming his equal	CONF 240:18
United t. and counsels	MILT 601:37
unwholesome in their t.	SHAK 784:56
whose second t. are good	BARR 65:90
worth a million t.	AI WEI 10:4
thought-woven tall t.-w. sails	YEATS 965:8
thousand After a t. victories	SHAK 800:44
better than a t.	BIBLE 101:90
bound him a t. years	BIBLE 132:21
I feel like a t. dollars	OCON 647:90
If we could all live a t. years	BERG 83:21
Not in a t. years	SMITH 829:8
t. a week	ALGR 13:69
t. natural shocks	SHAK 782:7
t. roads lead to Rome	ALAN 10:18
t. shall fall at thy side	BIBLE 101:96
T. T. Saints attending	WESL 932:64
t. years as one day	BIBLE 130:75
t. years in thy sight	BIBLE 101:93
thousands But t. die	POPE 686:66
Saul hath slain his t.	BIBLE 96:40
T. of little kids	SALI 740:81
T. of miles of wheat	RICH 714:23
thousand-year t.-y. conclusion	NIET 638:93
Thracian for the T. ships	SWIN 863:82
thraldom Europe from the t.	LLOY 533:74
highest step of t.	NASHE 632:97
thrall To none...I yield as t.	DYER 309:48
thrash t. the Spaniards too	DRAKE 298:88
thrashing t. your young woman	COOP 246:88
thread another t. in the web	PAGE 659:15
bind this line of scarlet t.	BIBLE 95:7
continuous t. of revelation	WELTY 931:48
division is a t.	BUCH 171:22
Feels at each t.	POPE 687:77
found by the right t.	JONS 468:97
held together by a common t.	JACK 448:3
t. from life's frayed mantle	ABU 1:16
t. loosened from the sky	ROSS 726:57
t. of his verbosity	SHAK 763:20
t. to bind the heart	GILM 371:95
t. we follow from one day	AUST 47:91
With a silken t.	KEATS 475:71
threat every one did t.	SHAK 761:52
I got a death t.	BENN 80:40
Whiles I t., he lives	SHAK 796:29
threaten t. to overrule him	PAXM 670:43
three Anyone who marries t. girls	STEIN 845:74
required t. necessaries	JONS 468:93
There are t. ways	DE 273:70
these t. have changed the whole face	BACON 50:45
T. be the things	PARK 664:12
T. days walking	SNYD 832:93
T. in One	ALEX 13:65
T. in One	DRYD 303:11
T. in One	SHAW 809:69
T. little maids	GILB 369:63
t. of us in this marriage	DIANA 276:24
t. things you can do	STEN 847:8
wanted to be t. things	SCHU 750:76
When shall we t. meet again?	SHAK 795:96
three-deckers well-appointed t.-d.	PALM 661:68
three-dimensional t.-d. drawing	HIRS 419:75
threefold t. cord	BIBLE 106:18
threepenny-bus t.-b. young man	GILB 369:47
three-personed t.-p. God	DONNE 292:54
three-pipe t.-p. problem	DOYLE 297:55
threescore of my t. years and ten	HOUS 431:34
t. years and ten	BIBLE 101:94
threshold Below this activity t.	WILL 944:73
by the happy t., he	TENN 873:51
like the t. of pain	GELL 363:35
thou goest over the t.	FULL 355:78
threesomes I like t.	BRAND 156:64
thrice T. welcome, darling	WORD 958:95
thrift virtue called 't.'	THOM 887:95
whatever may be happening to T.	KEYN 484:74
thrill experienced that subtle t.	SHIP 818:15
It does not t.	WILDE 941:95
Mere alcohol doesn't t. me	PORT 690:67
t. is very short	BRYAN 170:96
thrives t. in the dark	HUXL 441:57
throat air...clotted in my t.	THOM 887:9
'Amen'? Stuck in my t.	SHAK 797:33
blade of grass stuck in its t.	WODE 952:38
catch each other by the t.	SHAK 761:37
cut your own t.	THAT 881:64
cut your t.	PERE 674:20
Failure to examine the t.	OSLER 656:90
fishbone in the city's t.	LOWE 540:24
From heel to t.	YEATS 966:16
gash in its t.	HUGH 435:34
grandsire cut his t.	SWIFT 862:40
grips him warmly by the t.	WILS 948:60
in your sweet dividing t.	CAREW 199:57
one moistens one's t.	BARN 64:60
on the t. of Venice	TOME 894:55
passage in my t.	SHAK 785:82
razor that threatens the t.	ANGE 18:83
scuttled ship or cut a t.	BYRON 190:14
silent t.	GIBB 367:7
stomach thinks her t. is cut	RUNY 731:58
taking life by the t.	FROST 353:20
that youngster's t.	COWA 249:63
The t.: how strange	UPDI 906:31
t. cut With diamonds?	WEBS 927:58
t. of well-printed matter	MORR 620:51
Unto the sweet bird's t.	SHAK 778:75
throats witnesses...had their t. slit	PASC 667:92
Yellow River down our t.	PRIE 695:88
throne brother popped on to his t.	STOP 855:15
Famine never shall approach the t.	BYRON 190:20
great white t.	BIBLE 132:22
highest set his t.	SPEN 838:35
institution of the t.	ACHE 2:27
light which beats upon a t.	TENN 876:40
like a burnished t.	ELIOT 318:99
like a burnished t.	SHAK 794:55
living t., the sapphire-blaze	GRAY 385:90
married woman...put on a t.	BALZ 60:91
round about the t., were four beasts	BIBLE 131:96
Solomon's t. was supported by lions	BACON 51:67
Than is the t. of Denmark	SHAK 780:31
t. of bayonets	INGE 445:26
upon a t., high and lifted up	BIBLE 107:54
up to the T.	KIPL 489:74
wade through slaughter to a t.	GRAY 384:71
thrones T., dominations	MILT 604:19
t. in heaven	RUSK 732:85
throng fled from the mocking t.	GILB 370:70
Leaving the tumultuous t.	WORD 957:70
throttle turn the t.	TAYL 868:61
through came t. and...shall return	MACA 544:3
throw it's who you t. out	THOM 887:92
t. away the dearest thing	SHAK 796:11
T. away thy rod	HERB 414:85
t. myself down in my Chamber	DONNE 293:74
t. the entire book in the fire	SAND 741:8
want to t. up	GERG 365:65
throwing T. away food	FRAN 347:91
throws sometimes t. the dice	HAWK 401:87
thrush An aged t.	HARDY 397:23
pepper-pot breast of t.?	FRAME 346:75
That's the wise t.	BROW 167:21
t.'s song	THOM 885:72
thrust wherever it may t.	KAFKA 472:4
thumb angry only when I hit my t.	AMIS 16:83
no rules...except rules of t.	SHAW 810:23
thumbnail t. dipped in tar	PATE 669:13
thumbprint t. nowhere set	BARN 64:61
thumbs By the pricking of my t.	SHAK 797:53
Thummim Urim and the T.	BIBLE 94:68
thumps t. upon your back	COWP 251:3
thumpsday wailsday, t.	JOYCE 470:37
thunder all-shaking t.	SHAK 792:5
In t., lightning, or in rain?	SHAK 795:96
pass in t.	SHEL 813:75
powerful as the form of t.?	MACKE 553:9
says NO! in t.	MELV 585:71
sound like t.	WORD 959:96
steal my t.!	DENN 273:75
stunning as t.	KINS 488:67
t. and lightning of Desert Storm	SCHW 750:91
t. and the sunshine	TENN 870:2
t. of the captains	BIBLE 99:19
t.'s roar	SMART 826:67
t. to the tune of 'Greensleeves'	SHAK 773:14
trivial people should muse and t.	LAWR 514:79
When clouds are cursed by t.	THOM 883:11
thunderbolt like a t. he falls	TENN 875:4
thundered Volleyed and t.	TENN 875:12
thunders Below the t.	TENN 869:71
thunderstorm amaze us like a t.	AUDEN 43:84
plunging through the t.-s.	TENN 871:17
t. or blare of trumpets	MANN 566:82
thunderstorms hang of the t.	LOEN 534:3
standing out in t.	JARR 452:84
thunderstruck stood like one t.	DEFOE 269:74
thus Why is this t.?	WARD 920:5
thusness reason of this t.?	WARD 920:5
Thwackum T. was for doing justice	FIEL 335:23
thyme bank where the wild t. blows	SHAK 767:30
helps the mint and the t. grow	VERL 911:61
thymn desert caves, With wild t.	MILT 599:84
thyself Know then t.	POPE 687:80
only gift is a portion of t.	EMER 324:71
Tibbald in T.'s...breast	POPE 688:33
Tiber drop of allaying T.	SHAK 799:91
Let Rome in T. melt	SHAK 794:44
Tiberius in the reign of T.	TACI 866:7
Tibetanization de-T.	MACD 550:39
ticket return t.	GREE 386:11
t. to ride	LENN 522:50
ticking I am the very t.	FULL 355:76
t. movement of the human timepiece	ASLET 38:83
tickings ten t. of thy watch	WORD 957:67
tickle If you t. us	SHAK 769:1
No man can t. himself	BACON 53:47
t. her with a hoe	JERR 455:46
tiddely-pom more it SNOWS-t.-p.	MILNE 596:20
tide against t.	SMART 826:65
blood-dimmed t.	YEATS 966:24
But came the t.	SPEN 839:47
call of the running t.	MASE 580:51
hang his head, and view the lazy t.	CRAB 252:42
lively porpoise in a strong t.	DICK 277:47
never know what the t. will bring	HANKS 395:84
our t. ours overflows	WALL 918:60
resist both wind and t.	SHAK 760:14
rode that t. to Ararat	WILB 939:35
this filthy modern t.	YEATS 967:38
t. across a map	LOWE 540:38
t. in the affairs of men	SHAK 778:48
t. in the affairs of women	BYRON 190:19
t. of hours	YEATS 965:8
tremulous t.	YEATS 965:5
veer in the t.	SWIN 864:6
waiting for the t.	DU 306:94
wait until the t. is coming	HAGG 391:6
when the t. is going out	WOGAN 950:7
when the t.'s pretty nigh out	DICK 280:52
Why weep ye by the t.	SCOTT 753:45
tideless t. dolorous midland sea	SWIN 864:7
tides poinsettia meadows of her t.	CRANE 252:54
Push in their t.	THOM 883:4
salt t. seawards flow	ARNO 33:56
t. of grass break	SWIN 863:86
t. of men into my hands	LAWR 514:88
watch the t.	WADD 915:1
tidings good t. of great joy	BIBLE 120:69
tie father's old green t.	COLL 237:63
got a spot on your t.	GING 371:99
love endures no t.	DRYD 304:51
Tyin' up my white t.	BERL 84:39

tiempo

tiempo Salud, Dinero, Amor...y T. ANON 28:57
ties like a man trying on t. CURT 259:98
  t. only dissoluble by the annihilation SHEL 812:48
  t. which bind them together PLATO 682:66
tiger action of the t. SHAK 775:74
  Christ the t. ELIOT 317:83
  it's insane to blame the t. MUNG 625:46
  like riding a t. TRUM 900:92
  man wants to murder a t. SHAW 808:61
  of the tribe of T. SMART 826:63
  Once on the t.'s back BALL 58:46
  O t.'s heart SHAK 760:3
  slay the t. SHAK 762:96
  spontaneity of a mechanical t. ACHE 2:31
  there was one poor t. PUNCH 699:80
  t. of Bengal crouches MELV 585:67
  t. sniffs the rose SASS 746:95
  T.! T.! burning bright BLAKE 140:19
  T. will repay the trouble and expense BELL 76:54
tiger-moth t.-m.'s deep-damasked KEATS 477:20
tigers about the t. MACL 554:26
  catches t. STEV 850:78
  For tamed and shabby t. HODG 421:23
  There were no t. ELIOT 321:96
  t. of wrath BLAKE 140:1
  wilderness of t.? SHAK 760:24
tight terrified and t. BETJ 89:39
tights like a chorus girl's t. LAWR 514:87
  she played it in t. BEER 73:73
tile Dressed in style, brand new t. COLL 237:63
tiles t. on the roof LUTH 542:71
Tilman Not so T. SHIP 818:14
timber crooked t. of humanity KANT 473:22
  Knowledge and t. HOLM 424:72
  t. and irrigating rivers MUIR 624:25
Timbuctoo on the plains of T. WILB 939:33
time 10 years before its t. LAVER 512:33
  abyss of t.? SHAK 803:10
  achieve in t. GILB 370:66
  advantage of t. and place DRAKE 298:87
  after a t. they judge them WILDE 941:88
  ancient nobility is the act of t. BACON 52:93
  antidote against the opium of t. BROW 165:79
  any convenient t. for MITC 610:45
  any given t. or place WHIT 936:72
  Aphorisms...more for your t. DUDEK 305:73
  Art is long, and t. LONG 535:15
  Ask him what t. it is WYMAN 964:13
  as though for the first t. SPEN 837:7
  As t. goes by HUPF 440:35
  at any t. upon the earth WHIT 937:88
  at whatever t. PAZ 671:48
  At what t. KELV 479:71
  Bad girls don't have t. BANK 61:15
  bank and shoal of t. SHAK 796:19
  beat in T. GINS 372:5
  because it saves t. LERN 523:86
  besmeared with sluttish t. SHAK 801:53
  best means...of digesting t. AUDEN 44:21
  best t. to listen WHITE 936:57
  beyond Space and T. BROO 163:1
  bid t. return SHAK 764:48
  births of t. BACON 52:8
  blowing the new direction of T. LAWR 512:45
  books of all t. RUSK 733:3
  both meeting at one t. SPEN 838:39
  bourne of t. and place TENN 879:6
  Britain...on borrowed t. CALL 192:27
  burglar...takes his t. OHEN 648:22
  but for all t.! JONS 468:80
  but I am sick of T. TENN 873:53
  By the t. you say PARK 664:13
  camembert of t. and space DALI 261:15
  carried off by the wings of t. LAFO 504:64
  child of its t. KAND 473:16
  chronicles of the t. SHAK 782:97
  city of all t. HAWT 402:17
  closing t. in the gardens CONN 243:17
  comes a t. TWAIN 902:46
  conversing I forget all t. MILT 604:6
  cormorant devouring t. SHAK 763:99
  Crafts which require the most t. CANT 197:13
  crying, I spent all my t. LABE 501:4
  cursed from the t. our mothers SCHR 749:62
  dark t. the eye ROET 722:63
  death of t. GRAV 382:30
  die...for such a long t.! MOLI 611:72

doing nothing until the right t. BAKER 56:2
Doing t. is like climbing a mountain DEAN 267:41
do thy worst, old t. SHAK 800:38
drifting, waiting its t. MORG 619:30
dying...lasts so short a t. JOHN 462:19
employment for his idle t. WALT 920:92
events of the t. TIMES 892:23
expiration of that t. WARD 920:2
face the man of the t. STEV 850:81
Fate, T., Occasion, Chance SHEL 814:16
feet in ancient t. BLAKE 141:40
fill the t. available PARK 665:38
Fire Next T. BALD 57:22
fittest t. and place RUSK 733:97
flaming bounds of place and t. GRAY 385:90
fool all the people all of the t. LINC 529:5
foot of t. SHAK 791:73
Footprints on the sands of t. LONG 535:16
For a long t. UTTL 907:50
forefinger of all T. TENN 872:32
foremost files of t. TENN 871:22
for many a t. KEATS 478:46
For technological man it is t. MCLU 556:52
for the t. remained MILT 606:48
full t. work WELD 928:85
give gratitude constantly all the t. FAUL 331:37
Good T. was Had By All SMITH 830:33
great draughts of t. BERR 87:96
great lie of our t. POBE 683:77
Grown old before my t. ROSS 726:40
gude t. coming SCOTT 753:55
guest of one's t. KENN 480:87
'half as old as T.' BURG 175:5
half the t. WHITE 935:37
have not t. to say any more MARL 572:91
having a more enjoyable t. POWE 693:42
Health, Wealth, Love...and T. ANON 28:57
hear t. sliding past you RHYS 712:74
Heaven...is not a t. BACH 49:9
high t. we relit the stars APOL 29:85
hold back t. GRASS 382:11
holy t. is quiet WORD 959:96
How slowly does sad T. SPEN 839:51
Hurry up please it's t. ELIOT 318:2
I...may be some t. OATES 643:16
in a t. out-worn YEATS 965:9
inconceivable in our t. ROST 727:70
in his spare t. GILL 370:81
in his t. plays many parts SHAK 779:80
in love with the productions of t. BLAKE 140:98
In our t., political speech ORWE 655:61
In reality, killing t. SITW 824:24
in t. leave the body SMOL 831:68
in t. of affliction PASC 667:87
In t. the savage bull KYD 501:47
in t. 'twill grow into WEBS 927:48
I spend all my t. PLATO 681:43
Is this a fit t. STER 848:37
it was my t. HOLL 423:52
know the place for the first t. ELIOT 321:91
laws of space and t. CORY 247:11
length of t. that suggests PRIE 695:90
let not T. deceive you AUDEN 43:82
let the day be t. enough DANI 262:31
little t. while it is new BALL 60:79
long past the t. PETER 675:38
lot of t. to be a genius STEIN 845:68
loved the t. too well CLARE 228:56
Love is space and t. PROU 698:48
made manifest in t. MILL 594:85
make poor use of their t. LABR 502:28
Make use of t. SHAK 762:82
man is killing t. LOWE 540:27
martyred slaves of T. BAUD 68:73
masters...for a very long t. SHAW 811:36
men of our t. MACA 544:22
Men talk of killing t. BOUC 152:84
mist of t. THAT 881:53
mock the t. SHAK 796:25
moment in and out of t. ELIOT 320:77
most isolated way of having a bad t. CHER 219:31
Move in melodious t. MILT 597:35
Nae man can tether t. BURNS 179:26
neglects meditation, loses his t. CONF 240:22
no account of T. HOBB 420:2
nobody needs at any t. WILD 943:47
no dividend from t.'s to-morrows SASS 745:83

no enemy but t. YEATS 966:29
no precious t. at all SHAK 801:55
Not an easy t. for humorists BUCH 171:31
nothing but T. destroys us KORAN 498:85
no t. for eloquence PASC 666:67
no t. for the fine graces SMITH 828:2
no t. to bleed SHAK 763:29
no t. to labour ROGE 723:83
no t. to read BROO 163:4
no t. to stand and stare? DAVI 265:90
not in earth or t. recoverable PURDY 700:85
not redeemed from t. ELIOT 321:93
not t. or opportunity AUST 45:52
now is the accepted t. BIBLE 127:72
Old T. is still a flying HERR 415:12
once our t. devour MARV 577:93
on t.—No, you were late LERN 523:82
out of key with his t. POUND 691:99
out of t., out of space WELLS 930:20
own t. out of their work MASE 580:70
passage of t. WILL 945:99
pass away the t. SHAK 761:34
passed a hell of t. SHAK 802:82
peace for our t. CHAM 212:64
Plays...cut through t. MILL 593:45
play the fools with the t. SHAK 772:79
plenty of t. to win DRAKE 298:88
point free in t. DIDI 286:80
Popular in our t. HUGH 435:23
pure clay of t.'s mud MALA 562:88
puzzles me more than t. and space LAMB 505:81
rags of t. DONNE 291:25
really understands at the t. THOM 886:88
Redeeming the t. BIBLE 128:91
remember'd for a very long t. MCGO 551:73
repair t.'s faults MUIR 624:20
right notes at the right t. BACH 49:7
saltness of t. SHAK 772:71
same old druid T. ROSE 725:30
same t. in a thousand minds TOCQ 892:32
searched for myself across t. CIXO 227:45
seeds of t. SHAK 796:5
seen better faces in my t. SHAK 792:98
see the t.'s deformity JONS 466:43
sent before my t. SHAK 761:33
sequence in t. WELTY 931:48
She's the original good t. DAVIS 265:98
shipwreck of t. BACON 49:26
shook hands with t. FORD 343:2
short the t. to run DRYD 302:89
short t....does not make a man ARIS 31:20
signs of our own t. CARL 200:78
sing of T. or Eternity TENN 877:63
slap t. on their wrists KINC 486:14
slow and still the t. TWAIN 902:58
small bridge in t. STEI 846:85
something to do with the t. ROGE 723:79
somewhat before his t. HARDY 397:18
soul of the whole Past T. CARL 201:33
sounds in the movement of t. BUSO 184:54
Space-ships and t. machines KOES 495:28
speech is shallow as T. CARL 201:21
spend t. and ink GALS 358:49
sphere of leisure t. LOWE 540:91
spoils of t. GRAY 384:68
stars move still, t. runs MARL 573:30
strain, T.'s eunuch HOPK 429:96
strong necessity of t. SHAK 794:50
sunflower, weary of t. BLAKE 140:11
supreme cause of our t. SPEN 837:13
Suspended in t. ELIOT 321:80
Take a little t. DICK 282:84
tasks...to fulfil for our t. SCHW 751:94
That passed the t. BECK 72:41
That T. could turn up HEYW 417:43
that t. of night GINS 372:15
Then while t. serves HERR 415:11
there...existed, at some t. PALEY 661:57
there is t. for everything BOLD 145:5
There was a t. WORD 959:5
They reflect t. FULL 355:76
think of having such a good t. LOOS 536:50
this odd warp in t. RICH 713:6
This t....is a very good one EMER 324:49
thoughts are spurred on by t. LECO 518:81
Through the cold t. BIRN 136:20
through t. t. is conquered ELIOT 319:41

title

tied to their t.	PISS 679:99	T. the destroyer	ELIOT 320:74	different t. in the same country	RICA 712:79
till t. and times are done	YEATS 965:10	T. the devourer	OVID 657:20	discern the signs of the t.?	BIBLE 117:5
T., a maniac scattering dust	TENN 874:74	T., the world and the person	CIXO 227:44	fatness of these pursy t.	SHAK 784:44
t. and chance happeneth	BIBLE 106:29	t. to cultivate modesty	SITW 824:13	in all t. to come	SMITH 827:83
t. and death pinned human	FRAME 346:75	t. to do intensive…digging	LEAV 517:54	In t. of crisis	BALZ 60:94
t. and energy from	MORE 618:20	t. to every purpose	BIBLE 105:14	live in oppressive t.	MAMET 563:26
T. and the bell	ELIOT 319:42	t. to get married	EPST 327:33	mode of their t.	DAY 267:27
T. and the hour runs	SHAK 796:10	t. to make it shorter	PASC 668:95	not for the fashion of these t.	SHAK 778:72
t. appears to have been frozen	COUP 248:26	t. to think about it	FONT 342:78	not for you to know the t.	BIBLE 124:70
t. cannot destroy	MURP 626:75	T. travels in divers paces	SHAK 779:95	No t. were more dangerous	INOU 446:49
t. changes people	PROU 698:57	T. turns the old days	SWIN 864:94	old t.	GOLD 376:9
t. Craves that we taste	GREE 386:32	T. was away	MACN 558:4	ruins of forgotten t.	BROW 165:73
t. enough for everything	GUNN 390:94	t. was out of joint	STRA 856:37	Shall there be womanly t.?	MCEW 551:59
t. enough to sleep	HOUS 431:36	t. we may comprehend	BROW 165:54	sign of knowledge in our t.	WILL 946:17
T. flies and takes me	SEVI 758:42	t. we shall not know	PEAC 671:55	sundry t. and in divers manners	BIBLE 129:33
t. for such a word	SHAK 787:74	t. when all men walk proudly	RAND 706:58	T. are changed	STEV 852:40
t. goes about its immemorial work	AMIS 16:52	t. when the most powerful	MACA 545:41	t. begin to wax old	BIBLE 112:70
T. goes on crutches	SHAK 774:35	t. when thou mayest be found	BIBLE 100:53	t. have become vulgar	MOLI 611:75
T. goes…T. stays	DOBS 289:77	t. when too much seems to happen	COUP 248:25	t. long past	WORD 960:14
t. had come	PENI 673:80	t. when you have to let your clothes	MIDL 590:82	t. of faith as best	SMITH 830:38
t. has come…To talk of many things	CARR 204:1	T., which takes…Our youth	RALE 705:47	t. of preservation	SHAK 805:49
T. has no divisions	MANN 566:82	T. will change it	BRON 162:79	t. that try men's souls	PAINE 660:29
T. has three dimensions	HOPK 429:85	t. will come when you will hear me	DISR 287:22	time-stricken t.-s. willow	CALL 193:32
T. has transfigured them	LARK 509:81	T. will not be ours	JONS 467:56	timetable t. not necessarily	WELTY 931:48
t. hath…A wallet	SHAK 787:37	T. will run back	MILT 597:36	timetables imposed…by railway t.	TAYL 868:47
t. hath set a blot	SHAK 764:49	t. with a gift of tears	SWIN 863:85	timid t. requests, invites denial	SENE 757:25
t. held me green and dying	THOM 883:18	t. ylost may nought recovered be	CHAU 216:65	timidity in a young man is t.	HUGO 437:86
t. hovers o'er	JOHN 459:47	T., you old gipsy man	HODG 421:19	Timon Till I am T.	YEATS 967:34
t. in everybody's life	WILD 943:50	t. you see him	RUNY 731:57	Timotheus Let old T. yield the prize	DRYD 303:35
T. in hours, days, years	VAUG 909:39	t., you thief	HUNT 439:30	Timothy T. Winters…	CAUS 209:14
t. is all I lacked	DOUG 295:6	'Tis t. to fear	SHAK 798:82	tin cat on a hot t. roof	WILL 945:90
t. is eating away my life	BAUD 68:61	to be t.'s eunuch	HOPK 429:92	corrugated t. roof	BEEC 73:68
t. is long	DU 305:69	To choose t. is to save t.	BACON 52:10	eat cheese from a t.	PALT 662:10
T. is money	FRAN 348:12	to do with the t. of the day?	SHAK 770:27	Gershwin keeps pounding on t.	GERS 365:74
t. is no healer	ELIOT 320:75	to kill an admiral from t. to t.	VOLT 914:32	opened a t.	STEV 851:29
t. is now near at hand	WASH 921:27	tolling bell Measures t.	ELIOT 320:72	tincture Actions receive their t.	DEFOE 269:73
t. is on his side	BANKS 62:21	took t. to realize	HYDE 443:18	tinge t. of tawny yellow	SALA 739:70
T. is on our side	GLAD 373:37	too much change in too short a t.	TOFF 893:37	tingle ears of every one…shall t.	BIBLE 96:27
T. is our tedious song	MILT 597:38	too much of the t.	THUR 890:78	tinker do not matter a t.'s curse	SHIN 818:12
t. is out of joint	SHAK 781:71	too much t. talking	THOM 884:43	tinkering first rule of intelligent t.	EHRL 313:69
T. is the 101st Senator	DODD 289:87	torments…may in length of t.	MILT 602:61	The first rule of t.	MAMET 564:46
t. is the greatest innovator	BACON 52:9	Torture and T.	BYRON 188:64	tinklings drowsy t.	GRAY 384:62
T. is the great physician	DISR 287:21	to the end of t.	GAIN 356:9	tinsel Titles are t.	SHEL 812:51
t. is the longest distance	WILL 945:80	tower of my t.	NEME 633:18	tint t. ends and the orange t. begins?	MELV 585:76
t. is the medium of narration	MANN 566:84	ugly things…beautiful with t.	COCT 233:88	tinted in all his t. orders	FIRB 336:52
T. is the metre	WALC 916:16	understood in t.	KIER 485:4	TinyTim none of us forget poor T. T.	DICK 279:6
t. is tied to the wrist	RAINE 705:40	wake us T. and t. over	LARK 509:72	tip All t. and no iceberg	KEAT 475:57
T. kills us	SITW 824:24	warn't no t. to be	TWAIN 902:60	school-boy's t.	THAC 880:38
T. like a serpent	CRANE 253:62	wastes her t.	WALL 918:55	The t.'s a good one	POUND 691:7
T., Love, Beauty	MILL 593:52	weak by t. and fate	TENN 870:2	t. of every branch	PLATH 681:37
t. may cease	MARL 573:30	weight of this sad t.	SHAK 793:40	tipped t. with gold for this	JONS 467:58
T., not Corydon, hath conquered	ARNO 35:20	we shall die…'tis but the t.	SHAK 777:29	tippenny Wi' t., we fear nae evil	BURNS 179:27
t. not to become a father	WHITE 935:43	whatever t. of your life	SPARK 830:59	tips loyal to the t. of his stubby fingers	ACHE 3:43
t. of a man or woman	WHIT 937:99	what is t. but shadows	SASS 746:96	tiptoe t. on the misty mountaintops	SHAK 766:2
t. of awakening consciousness	RICH 713:6	What, then, is t.?	AUGU 44:29	tired busy, and the t.	FITZ 337:82
t. of life is short	SHAK 772:63	What's T. the next swan?	SLEZ 825:53	Give me your t., your poor	LAZA 515:3
t. of their growth	ROSE 725:32	when his t. is come	TWAIN 903:78	man is t. of London	JOHN 463:56
t. passes quicker	ALLEN 14:3	When our t.'s come	DIBD 276:31	soon get t. of them all	SHAW 809:89
t. past and t. future	ELIOT 319:40	When t. is broke	SHAK 765:63	Thou art t.	ARNO 35:24
t. present and t. past	ELIOT 319:36	When t. was open-eyed	LOWE 540:18	T., above all	GIRO 373:28
t. remembered	SWIN 863:83	when we meet at any t. again	DRAY 299:99	t. of being a woman	SEXT 758:48
t. rolls	SCOTT 752:30	whips and scorns of t.	SHAK 782:7	t. of giving in	PARKS 665:45
T.'s all-serving wave?	BRON 162:76	whirligig of t.	SHAK 786:23	T. of knocking	ARNO 34:89
't.'s arrow'	EDDI 311:24	whole t. the engine is at work	WATT 922:45	t. of living	WHITE 935:39
t.'s best jewel	SHAK 801:57	witching t. of night	SHAK 783:30	t. of the truth	ALBEE 11:23
t.'s deer is slain	MUIR 623:15	world enough, and t.	MARV 577:90	tires rain never t.	HUGH 436:44
T.'s devouring hand	BRAM 156:58	writer's t. is spent	JOHN 462:35	Tiresias I T., old man	ELIOT 318:4
T. seemeth…of the nature	BACON 49:25	wrong most of the t.	KURZ 501:46	tiresome Love…troublesome & t.	FLEM 340:49
t.'s eternal motion	FORD 343:6	timebo quem t.	BIBLE 132:30	t. for children	SAINT 738:35
t.'s furrows I behold	SHAK 800:40	time-honoured t.-h. bread-sauce	JAMES 450:48	tiring so damn t.	AGAS 9:85
T. shall not lose	DONNE 291:18	time-lag t.-l. of fifty years	WELLS 930:38	Titan like thy glory, T.	SHEL 815:20
T. shall turn those amber locks	DRAY 298:93	timepiece human t.	ASLET 38:83	Titania moonlight, proud T.	SHAK 767:26
T. shall unfold	SHAK 792:87	Times T. every morning	KING 488:50	Titanic deck of the T.	MORT 621:76
t. sic causis has repairit	ANON 22:63	The T. is…entitled	HAZL 403:41	inevitable the T. was going to set sail	HAGUE 391:10
T.'s most lethal weapon	SITW 824:18	times There are t. in politics	GALB 357:21	Titans we are T.	CARL 200:84
t. spent on any item	PARK 665:39	The T. They Are A' Changing	DYLAN 309:54	tithe the Personality T.: A price paid	COUP 248:35
T.'s thievish progress	SHAK 801:65	tincture from the t.	DEFOE 269:73	tithes Bring ye all the t.	BIBLE 112:63
T….strengthens friendship	LABR 502:12	What t.!	CICE 227:38	Titian cares much at heart about T.	RUSK 733:94
T.'s wheels runs back	BROW 168:60	when the t. were not hard	EMER 325:96	title appropriate t. of 'agnostic'	HUXL 443:4
T.'s winged chariot	LINK 530:30	times aesthetic principle of our t.	ROGE 722:66	courage prove my t.	SHAK 795:93
T. that is moved	SLES 825:52	All t. are his seasons	DONNE 293:72	does he feel his t.	SHAK 798:67
T., that takes survey	SHAK 792:66	all t. I have enjoyed	TENN 870:98	friends could only read the t.	WOOLF 955:11
T., that tireless gambler	BAUD 68:67	approaches recent t.	TAYL 868:49	guarantee of a t.	LISP 531:44
t. that we are living in	TOML 894:56	at all t. and in all cultures	WEBER 925:12	records prove the t. good	ARLO 32:31
t. that we love best	LAUD 511:16	bad t. at Anfield	PAIS 660:41	t. of…significance	LEVE 525:18
t….the author of authors	BACON 49:20	best of t.…worst of t.	DICK 282:94	vain t. of Trades Unions	RUSK 733:16
T., the deer	MACL 555:30	Different rhymes for different t.	BROD 160:59	whatever t. suit thee!	BURNS 177:83

titles

titles because there were no t. in it — HEMI 409:63
eskin-titles — BENET 79:23
hundred new t. of idiotism — NASHE 631:88
T. are tinsel — SHEL 812:51
T. distinguish the mediocre — SHAW 808:41
titwillow Willow, t., t.! — GILB 370:68
Tlön metaphysicians of T. — BORG 150:55
toad should I let the t. work — LARK 509:79
simply talked to T. — GRAH 381:91
Squat like a t. — MILT 604:11
t. beneath the harrow — KIPL 489:68
t. in fun — CRAS 254:88
t. or adder to catch — MUIR 624:17
t., ugly and venomous — SHAK 778:65
your arm, old t. — LARK 509:85
toady T., perhaps, even tacky — ACHE 3:52
toast faint flavour of t. — TRAV 896:94
let the t. pass — SHER 817:90
milk and t. and honey — MITC 609:36
my t. would be — ADAMS 5:4
smell of buttered t. — GRAH 381:91
t. of a' the town — BURNS 180:49
t. with three times three — GILB 369:59
Will Not Take this T. — ANON 23:96
toasted t., and buttered on both sides — JACK 448:1
toasted-cheese called him…'T.-c.' — CARR 205:28
tobacco Beer, t., and music — MANN 566:77
lives without t. — MOLI 611:79
T., divine, rare, superexcellent t. — BURT 181:83
tobacco-pipes dirty t.-p. — ELIOT 316:56
Toby uncle T. would never offer — STER 848:27
today All the poet can do t. — OWEN 657:30
beat them t. — STARK 843:26
down in the woods t. — BRAT 157:79
here t., and gone to-morrow — BEHN 75:20
Here t.—in next week tomorrow! — GRAH 380:90
Kind is my love t. — SHAK 802:75
live t. — MART 576:72
Living for t. — LENN 521:46
Maybe not t., maybe not tomorrow — EPST 327:30
Never do t. what you can put off — PUNCH 699:76
person who lives for t. — BELL 76:45
such a day tomorrow as t. — SHAK 799:7
technology of t. — GABOR 356:2
t. hidden by science! — NIET 639:14
t. I am fifty-five — REED 709:29
T. if ye will hear his voice — BOOK 149:31
t. is no longer news — RUSK 732:79
T., t., unhappy day — SHAK 764:48
T. we have naming of parts — REED 709:26
Tomorrow composts t. — STER 847:17
vibrant and the beautiful t. — MALL 562:94
Where are the warriors t.? — SITT 823:93
wiser t. than he was yesterday — POPE 686:54
toddle t. safely home and die — SASS 745:85
toe picking his nose with his t. — BOYC 153:8
t. of one shoe — TRAV 895:89
t. to t. — PEEL 672:68
Washington Post…with your big t. — LANCE 506:24
toenails makes my t. twinkle — THOM 884:25
toes Pobble who has no t. — LEAR 516:39
stepping on your t. — MOSS 622:81
t. grow big and black — THOM 884:41
tread in the bus on my t.? — AUDEN 43:83
turn out your t. as you walk — CARR 204:94
toff Me pal…does the t. — DENN 273:74
toga Idealism is the noble t. — HUXL 442:98
t., the kilt — MURR 627:80
together able to sit t. — KING 487:31
all hang t. — FRAN 348:17
Both bound t. — WALL 918:59
looking t. in the same direction — SAINT 738:32
toil cricket's manly t. — BYRON 186:23
fatuous sunbeams t. — OWEN 658:38
ferocious and endless t. — GARL 360:75
Horny-handed sons of t. — SALI 740:88
love and t. — KIPL 492:57
mock their useful t. — GRAY 384:66
more sweet than t. — TENN 870:93
necessary…to be worn with t. — EURI 328:59
Sleep after t. — SPEN 838:28
smeared with t. — HOPK 428:70
t. and trouble of acquiring it — SMITH 827:79
T. conquered the world — VIRG 914:26
t., envy, want — JOHN 459:46
t. in other men's extremes — KYD 501:31
t. its desolation — HAMM 394:59

t. obscure, and a' that — BURNS 180:52
t. Of dropping buckets — COWP 251:16
t. that is destroyed — MCCA 548:96
War…is t. and trouble — DRYD 303:33
waste their t. — SCOTT 752:14
Why t. to no avail? — LI 528:82
with his t. he won — DRYD 302:73
toiled forgot for which he t. — SHAK 800:44
toilet can be read only in the t. — MILL 593:56
toilette judged…through her t. — DE 268:46
toils prudently their t. upbraid — MARV 577:1
t., the conflicts, the sufferings — SCHW 751:94
token sending…small cash t. — CONN 242:97
told ate and drank as he was t. — HOFF 422:32
not t. even the half — POLO 684:5
the way it is t. here — PACH 658:1
tolerable Not a t. woman's part — AUST 47:67
scarcely t. and the…unbearable — DAFOE 260:3
tolerance excessive t. of suicide — DURK 308:29
Religious t. — ROMN 723:94
t. as uncertainty — BURKE 176:63
to practice t. — UNIT 905:9
tolerate cannot t. them — DE 270:96
Louisianans don't t. corruption — ANON 27:30
t. unlikely arguments — FORD 343:3
We are not going to t. — REAG 708:8
toll t. me back — KEATS 478:48
Tolstoy a T. or a Flaubert — WOLFE 953:83
in any ring with Mr T. — HEMI 410:84
T., Hugo, Dostoevsky — LESS 523:93
Tom Every T., Dick and Harry — GOLD 377:29
his name was T. — KING 487:46
more…than in all T. Jones — JOHN 462:25
So T. went home with Ellie — KING 488:53
T. bears logs — SHAK 763:27
tomahawks t., wi' blude red-rusted — BURNS 179:28
tomato You say t. — GERS 365:77
tomatoes if I grew t. — TREV 896:7
tomb a t. and a dungeon — HAWT 402:12
best-seller is the gilded t. — SMITH 829:23
buried in the silent t. — WORD 961:33
Claret on my T. — KEATS 476:95
erect…his own t. — SHAK 774:57
fair Fidele's grassy t. — COLL 237:70
ghost from the t. — SHEL 813:77
graces…blossom on the t. — CRAB 252:39
Kings for such a t. — MILT 597:40
made our land a t. — ORAH 652:91
Marriage is the grave or t. of wit — CAVE 210:20
Pyramus, at Ninny's T. — SHAK 767:34
smoking t. — GINS 372:6
straight and narrow as a t. — SMITH 830:35
this side the t. — BYRON 187:49
this side the t. — DAVI 265:91
t. remain uninscribed — EMMET 325:6
totter towards the t. — SAYE 746:12
toward the silent t. — WORD 961:43
world would smell…a t. — SHEL 813:74
tombs Faith…feeds among the t. — MELV 585:56
Nerves sit…like T. — DICK 284:36
rose from these stone t. — MORG 619:34
shovelled into the t. — SAND 742:17
upon our brazen t. — SHAK 763:99
tombstone The t. of capitalism — STILL 854:98
t. white — KIPL 490:99
tombstones Nothing sells t. like — APPEL 29:88
tomb-stones t.-s. where flowers — BLAKE 140:15
Tommy O it's T. this — KIPL 489:85
T. 'ow's yer soul? — KIPL 489:86
tomorrow Boast not thyself of t. — BIBLE 105:99
building…with t. inside — AKERS 10:11
die for him t. — BALL 58:50
for t. we die — BIBLE 127:59
For t. we shall die! — PARK 664:15
here to-day, and gone t.-m. — BEHN 75:20
History…start again t. — DURR 308:38
If scientists knew t.'s discovery — ZUCK 970:20
Kill me t. — SHAK 790:42
put off till t. — PUNCH 699:76
some good thing comes t. — SHAK 772:92
such a day t. as today — SHAK 799:7
Thanks for t. — ATKI 40:15
T., and t., and t. — SHAK 798:74
T. composts today — STER 847:17
T. country then — RICH 714:24
t. is another day — MITC 610:47
T. is Saint Crispian — SHAK 776:89

T.-m. let us do or die! — CAMP 194:67
t. morning, We shall have — REED 709:26
T. shall we strangers — TU 900:9
t.'s life's too late — MART 576:72
t. is the object — RUSK 732:79
t. we shall die — BIBLE 108:65
t. we will run faster — FITZ 338:87
t.…what he did today and yesterday — LABR 502:18
T. when thou leav'st — DONNE 291:22
what's going to happen t. — QUINN 703:24
tomorrows time's t. — SASS 745:83
tom-tit little t.-t. sang — GILB 370:64
tonality T. is a natural force — HIND 419:66
tone deep, autumnal t. — SHEL 813:83
ditties of no t. — KEATS 478:36
tones noble t. — GAUG 361:1
t. of a loved voice — ARNO 34:77
tongs t. and boniest doggerel — RUSK 733:18
tongue Before I taught my t. — VAUG 909:35
bridleth not his t. — BIBLE 110:51
bury my t. at Champmédy — BENET 79:26
calls with a cockerel's t. — LEE 519:95
cannot endure my Lady T. — SHAK 774:29
citizens speaking the same t. — MAZZ 583:31
Confounds the t. — SHAK 759:79
daily changing t.? — WALL 918:59
every t. should confess — BIBLE 128:97
eye to see nor t. — LENT 522:60
for mortal t. — GURN 390:2
hearing not my t. — SHAK 787:62
hidden even as a strange t. — DURER 307:25
hold your t. — DONNE 291:27
I have often given t. — YEATS 966:15
In a neat's t. — SHAK 769:72
knot that would not yield to the t. — BIER 134:65
knoweth and yet holdeth his t. — BIBLE 113:6
Lends the t. vows — SHAK 781:55
Letting the rank t. blossom — BROW 169:65
lost my t. from — NICH 636:72
made our English t. — SPEN 838:18
More than that t. — SHAK 800:42
Murder, though it have no t. — SHAK 782:3
music of his own vain t. — SHAK 763:6
mysmetre for defaute of t. — CHAU 216:68
my t. from…lying — BOOK 148:79
my t., the mystery — AQUI 30:96
never in the t. — SHAK 763:26
obnoxious to each carping t. — BRAD 155:50
of a slow t. — BIBLE 93:56
relation between the human t. — WAXM 925:4
sad words of t. or pen — WHIT 938:20
sharp t. in your head — PERE 674:20
sharp t. is the only — IRVI 447:57
shouldst give dust a t. — HERB 414:79
show you have a Scotch t. — SCOTT 754:61
snakes with double t. — SHAK 767:33
stick out your t. — MARQ 574:46
still the t. is wagging — SHER 817:86
stroke of the t. breaketh — BIBLE 113:2
sweet English t. — FLEC 340:30
tear out a man's t. — MART 576:80
thud of consonants in t. — BROY 169:88
t. acquire the Southern — STEV 853:76
t. and soul…be hypocrites — SHAK 783:31
t. Could scarcely cry — BLAKE 139:90
t. could utter — TENN 871:3
t. Dropped manna — MILT 602:18
t. is a fire — BIBLE 130:56
t. is a little member — BIBLE 130:55
t. is the clapper — SHAK 774:43
t. like the tail of a dog — NASHE 632:97
t. seeking out…a sore tooth — BURU 182:92
t. shall sing aloud — BIBLE 101:74
t.'s sweet air — SHAK 766:18
t. taking a trip — NABO 628:4
t.…tipped with gold — JONS 467:58
trippingly on the t. — SHAK 783:18
truth in every shepherd's t. — RALE 705:43
use of my oracular t. — SHER 817:76
when he's holding his t. — JAMES 450:39
While I have a t. — OCON 644:82
with stammering lips and another t. — BIBLE 108:69
with your heart and t. — SHEL 812:50
words of t. and pen — HARTE 400:75
Wounds…inflicted by the t. — RICH 714:22
write well in any t. — ASCH 37:52
you dried neat's t. — SHAK 771:47

Your hand, your t.	SHAK 796:17	no ordinary t.	PLATO 682:59	t. it, he fingers it, he feels it	SENG 757:28
tongued t. with fire	ELIOT 321:83	**topics** have but two t.	JOHN 463:53	**touching** danger in t.	BURNS 180:61
tongueless t. vigil and all the pain	SWIN 863:82	**tops** like whipping t.	HODG 421:22	**touch-line** kick…over the t.-l.	CHAR 216:49
tongues all nations…and t.	BIBLE 131:3	used to think their slender t.	HOOD 426:23	**touchstone** t. of the highest	RUSS 734:25
began to speak with other t.	BIBLE 124:72	**torch** bear the t. of truth	LICH 528:89	**tough** bloody t. being a legend	ATKI 40:17
clocks the t. of bawds	SHAK 770:27	king's t. throws its light	CYRA 260:12	gets t., the t. get	ROCK 721:41
Had I your t. and eyes	SHAK 793:37	lights the t. of war	HITL 420:92	She was too t.	TAYL 868:54
keep your t. well-omened	HORA 430:9	Man is a t. borne in the wind	CHAP 214:15	t. on crime	BLAIR 138:49
silence envious t.	SHAK 805:54	science…the t. which illuminates	PAST 668:4	Truth is t.	HOLM 424:68
sores on innocent t.	OWEN 657:31	t. has been passed	KENN 481:3	**tough-minded** Tender…t.-m.	JAMES 451:73
terror…the t. declare	ELIOT 321:90	**torches** as we with t. do	SHAK 787:47	**toujours** t. gai t. gai	MARQ 574:45
though fallen, and evil t.	MILT 605:27	one thousand burning t.	LABE 501:4	**tour** t. round the world	HARD 396:91
thousand several t.	SHAK 761:50	O, she doth teach the t.	SHAK 765:74	**Tourane** vulgar soul. Such is T.	MAUG 582:10
t. A dismal universal hiss	MILT 606:61	**toreador** T., en garde!	MEIL 584:40	**tourism** T. is the march of stupidity	DELI 271:38
t. in trees	SHAK 778:66	**Tories** better…party…than the T.	HITCH 420:90	**tourist** camera makes everyone a t.	SONT 834:17
t. of flame are in-folded	ELIOT 321:94	potential T.	ORWE 653:29	t. is an ugly human being	KINC 486:15
t. of men and of angels	BIBLE 126:52	sensible T.	WALP 919:78	**tourists** world's t. are coming here	WILS 948:67
t. of the French Council	SHAK 776:1	T. own no argument but force	BROW 166:87	**tous** T. pour un	DUMAS 306:89
t. recant like beaten weather vanes	CRANE 253:68	**torment** Christ perish in t.	SHAW 810:18	**toves** Twas brillig, and the slithy t.	CARR 204:89
t., that syllable men's	MILT 598:68	major writer…required major t.	BERG 84:28	**tow** death will take us in t.	DIBD 276:31
Walls have t.	SWIFT 862:55	More grievous t.	KEATS 476:6	should'st t. me after	SHAK 794:68
we loose wild t.	KIPL 490:17	more I feel T. within	MILT 605:44	**Tower** Eyefull T. is devine	LOOS 536:51
whispering t. can poison truth	COLE 235:34	smoke of their t. ascendeth	BIBLE 132:12	**tower** hawk of the t.	SKEL 824:29
tongue-tied t.-t.'s fighting	HARR 399:56	t. for our crimes	CHES 221:89	intending to build a t.	BIBLE 121:86
tonic hatred is a t.	BALZ 60:96	t. of the night's untruth	DANI 262:51	name of the Lord is a strong t.	BIBLE 105:83
t. to all save men	DOUG 295:12	**torments** t.…may in length of time	MILT 602:61	neck is like the t.	BIBLE 107:45
tonight fixed it t.	SNYD 832:92	will not have anybody's t.	CHES 219:45	stony t., nor walls	SHAK 776:14
soul be required of me t.	SMITH 830:43	**Toronto** T. is a kind of	USTI 907:48	tall building, with a t. and bells	CRAB 252:38
T. n. she'll hae but three	BALL 59:68	**torpedoes** Damn the t.!	FARR 330:31	Terrace or lofty T.	LEAR 516:29
T.—to you	NIXON 640:33	**torpor** woke me from the t.	WARR 921:21	to the dark t. came	SHAK 792:12
T. we sleep	MACN 558:3	**torrent** fiend for becoming a t.	LIGNE 529:98	t. of defence	ALCA 11:39
tons saves t. of explanation	SAKI 739:69	**torso** background to a t.	AUDEN 42:75	t. of my time	NEME 633:18
weighs a hundred t.	MACC 546:67	t. which has no face	YOUR 969:61	t. of strength	TENN 875:8
Tony T. will go on and on and on	PRES 694:07	**tortoise** writing for the t. market	BROO 163:4	yonder ivy-mantled t.	GRAY 384:63
took person you and I t. me for	CARL 199:68	**torture** Behaviourism…t.	AUDEN 44:19	**towers** and four grey t.	TENN 869:79
tool basic t. for the manipulation	DICK 277:37	condone t. of detainees	RICE 713:86	branchy between t.	HOPK 428:78
computer…only a t.	AMER 15:23	endure t.…for the national good	PANK 662:86	cloud-capped t.	SHAK 804:27
fashioned it with a graving t.	BIBLE 94:69	human cities t.	BYRON 187:53	hammered from a hundred t.	TENN 871:8
only edged t.	IRVI 447:57	T. and Time	BYRON 188:64	hills and t.	MUIR 623:14
T. Maker, Stacker of Wheat	SAND 741:13	t. in the country of the mind	WHITE 935:52	Ships, t., domes	WORD 959:3
worker uses a t.	MARX 579:42	t. into aught of the sublime	POE 683:80	thy palaces and t.	BURNS 178:96
tools filmmaker…afford his own t.	WELL 929:95	t. not again	SHEL 815:40	topless t. of Ilium?	MARL 573:29
Give us the t.	CHUR 225:89	t. of a lingering…passion	ETHE 327:47	ye antique t.	GRAY 383:45
persons using parties as t.	DISR 288:63	t.…of his fellow-creatures	FROU 353:27	**town** absent myself from the t.	MARP 574:42
rudimentary t. to discover	PETE 675:39	t. one poor word	DRYD 301:45	all the fools in t.	TWAIN 850:50
secrets are edged t.	DRYD 299:16	**tortured** We t. some folks	OBAMA 645:54	anyone lived in a pretty how t.	CUMM 258:69
Sin has many t.	HOLM 424:69	**Tory** born a T.…die a T.	POWE 693:59	architecture is also t. planning	LECO 518:82
t. of their t.	THOR 888:31	extinction of the T. Party	BEVAN 89:51	As the rain over the t.	VERL 910:57
t.…painters' techniques	RENO 711:57	hatred for the T. Party	BEVAN 89:53	A T. like Alice	SHUTE 819:31
t. that go together with culture	REYES 712:69	Let Whig and T. a' agree	SKIN 825:50	Bind t. to t.	CRANE 253:60
Unlikely adventures…unlikely t.	HOFF 422:30	neither a Whig nor a T.	DISR 287:32	bloody t.'s a bloody cuss	BLAIR 138:47
want to know which t.	SEXT 758:47	Voting T.	JOHN 457:91	circulating library in a t.	SHER 817:72
Without t. he is nothing	CARL 200:90	what is called the T.	CROK 257:13	Come sounding thro' the t.	BALL 58:54
tooth blue-black t. of sheer rock	BENU 83:9	wise T. and a wise Whig	JOHN 464:79	Country in the t.	MART 576:78
drill to the t. of America	CLIN 230:4	**Toryism** essence of T.	BAGE 54:63	Dear old Glasgow t.!	FYFFE 356:96
like a broken t.	BIBLE 105:94	**tosh** Never did I read such t.	WOOLF 955:13	Detroit is a one-trade t.	MAIL 560:55
moral truth is a hollow t.	MAST 581:82	**toss** t. him to My breast	HERB 414:83	direction to the t.	SWIFT 863:64
red in t. and claw	TENN 874:71	t. in the spray	ARNO 33:56	drummed them out of t.	CARR 205:15
red in t. and claw	TENN 874:80	**tossed** t. and gored several persons	BOSW 152:76	Duke takes a t.	POMP 684:10
sharper than a serpent's t.	SHAK 792:95	**totalitarian** t. and corrupt tyrannies	MO 611:66	foggy day in London T.	GERS 365:78
tongue seeking out…a sore t.	BURU 182:92	t. simplicities	LYND 543:92	girl in our t.	ANON 23:87
t. for a t.	BIBLE 115:35	**totalitarianism** friends of t.	ORWE 655:68	ideal t., clean, noble	LESS 524:95
t. for t.	BIBLE 94:67	West has not lived through t.	YELT 967:44	in the streets of the t.	PARN 665:46
toothache endure the t. patiently	SHAK 774:53	**totality** t. that I cannot suppress	ROSSO 727:68	Kercaldy my native t.	FLEM 340:48
Music helps not the t.	HERB 414:87	**totter** charming to t. into vogue	WALP 919:69	little marble cross below the t.	HAYES 403:27
toothless t. terrier on Valium	SIKO 821:67	t. towards the tomb	SAYE 746:12	majority of the t. were otherwise	LAWS 514:95
tooth-picker fetch you a t.-p. now	SHAK 774:28	**touch** dares not put it to the t.	MONT 615:50	man made the t.	COWP 251:11
toothpicks pear on top of two t.	ACHE 2:32	Do not let him t. you!	YEATS 967:42	midnight, in our little t.	LIND 530:20
top always room at the t.	WEBS 926:16	Do not t. me	BIBLE 133:48	moonless night in the small t.	THOM 884:31
carefully cleared at the t.	SHUL 819:27	exquisite t.…is denied to me	SCOTT 754:78	necessary to destroy the t.	ANON 25:61
dipped its t.	FROST 352:82	Gently its t. awoke him	OWEN 658:36	populous railway t.	THOR 889:52
from the naked t.	WORD 961:36	intercourse of t.	WORD 958:81	streets o' the t.	MACD 549:35
from this t. Of speculation	MILT 607:73	little t. of Harry	SHAK 775:79	studies in t.	COWP 250:93
I'm the bottom, you're the t.	PORT 690:69	mere t. of cold philosophy?	KEATS 477:9	surprise of a large t.	LARK 509:84
On her ingrateful t.!	SHAK 792:1	Of t. or marble	JONS 467:71	This t.'s a misnomer	QUIL 702:16
only way to get to the t.	ZATO 969:3	PLEASE DO NOT T.	PRAT 694:65	toast of a' the t.	BURNS 180:49
on tap, but not on t.	CHUR 226:15	shivering-sweet to the t.	CORN 247:3	t. among the trees	ROBI 718:89
started at the t. and worked down	WELL 929:96	T. me not	BIBLE 124:66	t., a place	JOHN 458:29
t. of admiration	SHAK 804:22	T. me with noble anger	SHAK 792:5	t.…buried its dead	SHAW 811:33
t. of the greasy pole	DISR 288:52	T.…most demystifying of all senses	BART 66:23	t. has two great teams	SHAN 805:65
You're the t.	PORT 690:69	t. of earthly years	WORD 957:64	t. is full of cozenage	SHAK 762:91
topaz gates of pearl and t.	LAUR 511:22	t. of holy bread	SHAK 775:13	t. of narrow streets	THOR 889:50
topee swell beneath a solar t.	HERB 414:90	t. of love	SHAK 759:65	t. of red brick	DICK 282:78
toper poor t. whose untutored sense	CRAB 251:24	t. of nature	SHAK 787:39	T. small-talk flows	CRAB 252:40
topic conflicting…on the same t.	ALTH 15:15	t., taste, smell your way	BUEC 172:42	t. surrounded by water	MOORE 616:72
constant t.	JOHN 461:16	wants the natural t.	SHAK 797:59	transport breaks upon the t.	DICK 283:31
most poetical t. in the world	POE 683:89	**touches** Nothing t.	HUGH 435:53	visit the ancient t. of Crieff	MCGO 551:74

town-crier

wale o' ilka t. — FERG 333:86
Washington is a resigning t. — SHUL 819:23
Washington is a t. — GERA 364:60
was the good t. once — MUIR 624:19
Winkie rins through the t. — MILL 155:98
town-crier as lief the t.-c. had spoke — SHAK 783:18
towns elephants for want of t. — SWIFT 863:63
gin joints in all the t. — EPST 327:26
industrial t. — MACM 556:65
London, thou art of t. — DUNB 306:2
Of t. and cities — WORD 956:53
run round in robot t. — BRAD 155:39
t. one can safely call 'her' — BETJ 88:30
t. or houses raised by poetry — COWL 250:72
Winter lies too long in country t. — CATH 208:88
townsmen soldiers into t. — WAUGH 924:81
townspeople teach you my t. — WILL 945:6
toxicologists unknown to t. — THOM 884:41
toy crammed in a monster t. — MACN 557:96
foolish thing was but a t. — SHAK 786:25
religion but a childish t. — MARL 572:7
their t. the world — COWP 251:20
woman…to be the t. of man — WOLL 954:89
toys all my t. beside me lay — STEV 853:68
babies like such t. — MORE 618:21
bundle of t. — MOORE 616:64
label our t. good and bad — DYSON 309:60
meddle with my t. — STEV 853:66
mind with all your t. — MILT 597:49
to be pretty t. — THOR 888:30
t. for your delight — STEV 853:84
toyshop T. of their heart — POPE 685:31
trace all t.…disappeared — WHIS 934:18
any t. of it in their hearts — REDON 709:24
No t. of pain — WORD 961:47
traces remove all t. of reality — PICA 677:58
track Around the ancient t. — MERE 588:37
beyond a railroad t. — LOWE 539:1
Come flying on our t. — THOM 887:6
forest with a golden t. — LIND 530:18
Jungle star or jungle t. — CULL 257:43
move us along the political t. — MCNA 557:91
on earth no t. — THOM 887:9
switching to their t. — WALE 917:28
T. twenty nine — GORD 378:55
tracks bright t. — GURN 390:99
cover up all the t. — FEYN 334:5
lies down on the t. of history — EISE 314:93
tractates reading all manner of t. — MILT 600:11
trade abolition of the slave t. — PITT 679:10
accident is not my t. — WORD 958:91
all is seared with t. — HOPK 428:70
among…articles of t. — FUSE 356:93
art…only is a t. — DRYD 300:35
as much a t. to write a book — LA 502:7
British t. unionist — BEVIN 90:65
effect of t. and commerce — HALL 393:40
fine thing for the t.! — DICK 278:66
first snarl of the t. unions — LLOY 532:68
functions of a t. union — LENIN 521:37
homely slighted Shepherd's t. — MILT 599:86
It is his t. — HEINE 407:18
live by t. — RUSK 733:16
master of his t. — DRAY 299:1
mysterious fluctuations of t. — ELIOT 315:31
no…association or t. union — OAKE 642:2
North-East t. — KIPL 490:2
People of the same t. — SMITH 827:81
port without t. — DEFOE 269:78
pride…in their daily t. — PRIT 696:25
principles of t. and business — HAZL 403:42
secrets of his t. — ORWE 654:42
serve his time to every t. — BYRON 186:25
t. and art is to live — MONT 614:26
T. could not be managed — JOHN 463:70
t. for the publick good — SMITH 828:86
t. union for pensioners — HEATH 405:84
T. Unionism of the married? — SHAW 808:31
t. unionists at heart — JEVO 455:54
traffic from the vulgar t. — MARL 573:9
us that t. in love — SHAK 794:60
War is the t. of kings — DRYD 303:21
Wheel that turned the T. — MAND 565:65
trader 55-year old t. — GREE 386:36
traders doomed t. — WRIG 963:71
free t. — PALM 661:69
trades best of t., to make songs — BELL 77:86

vain, superfluous t. — MORE 618:19
vain title of T. Unions — RUSK 733:16
tradesmen bow, ye t. — GILB 369:49
trading To preserve a t. state — STEU 849:60
tradition cultural t. — PARS 666:56
European philosophical t. — WHIT 936:69
History…It's t. — FORD 343:95
no t. of moral individual — MO 611:66
regard for it is a lost t. — BARZ 67:36
respect t. and to innovate — PEI 672:72
Science…opposed to history and t. — BORN 151:65
They are a great t. — ALLEN 13:74
t. Approves all forms of competition — CLOU 232:67
T. does not mean — MACM 556:72
T., if not constantly recreated — MACI 553:99
T. means giving votes — CHES 220:69
traditional atom of the t. novel — LODGE 534:95
justify t. custom — TWAIN 902:43
t. and popular sport — SITW 824:25
t. behavior — WIEN 939:29
t. fiction — GALB 357:19
t. stories and images — FRYE 354:54
You can't do t. work — BUFO 172:51
traditions Family t. — IGNA 445:16
T. are lovely things — MARC 569:50
Trafalgar go to T. Square — GEOR 364:52
traffic barbarous t. in slave — PITT 679:10
tragedies Let us have no ranting t. — AUST 46:67
t. are finished by a death — BYRON 190:13
why we like t. — GRAY 383:41
tragedy best actors…for t., comedy — SHAK 782:94
both comedy and t. — THUR 891:97
cannot balance t. in the scales — BENET 79:27
Comedy…is harder to do…than t. — MALA 561:86
Farce is nearer t. — COLE 236:52
first time as t. — BARN 64:70
first time as t. — MARX 579:36
five acts of Shakespeare's t. — FIELD 335:12
go, litel myn t. — CHAU 216:67
great t. has ended — MACA 544:5
great t. of Science — HUXL 443:6
inherent t. of things — STEV 853:81
most tremendous t. — BEER 73:73
our only real t. — PUZO 701:8
out of it is simply a t. — WILDE 941:90
participate in a t. — HUXL 442:89
perfect t. is the noblest production — ADDI 6:26
Religion is the t. — WILS 947:36
see a t. to be moved — VOLT 914:47
stress and t. of it all — WELLS 930:20
terrible t. and destiny of Cain — JOHN 456:78
That is their t. — WILDE 941:3
the food a t. — POWE 693:44
the word t. means…unpleasantness — BLIX 142:62
t., ecstasy, doom — ROTH 728:3
t.…in the very fact of frequency — ELIOT 316:52
T. is…a representation — ARIS 31:23
T. is if I cut my finger — BROO 163:14
t. of life is…that he almost wins — BROUN 163:18
t. of the age — DU 305:67
t. of the world that no one knows — CARY 207:68
t. paints the passions — HUGO 437:66
t. requires persons of heroic stature — AMIS 17:55
t. to those that feel — WALP 919:74
ultimate t. — HARL 398:36
worst t. for a poet — COCT 233:85
writers of t. have…insight — THUR 891:97
write you a t. — FITZ 338:99
tragic essentially a t. age — LAWR 513:72
t. mechanisms can't work — AMIS 17:55
who has experienced the t. — MAMET 563:30
tragically refuse to take it t. — LAWR 513:72
trail pull out on the Long T. — KIPL 493:74
t. has its own stern code — SERV 757:34
trails silver t. of inebriated slugs — JAMES 450:25
train all her negro t. — SMART 826:59
artist who has travelled on a steam t. — DAVIS 266:5
a runaway t. — SPIEL 840:67
car or an express t. — LEGER 519:7
caught the last t. — MCLE 554:23
father didn't buy me a t. set — BUFF 172:45
from the t., go running by — LAWS 514:97
funeral t. which the bridegroom sees — CLOU 232:59
hire an express t. — SPUR 841:89
in front of the…t. — SHAW 807:20
light of the oncoming t. — LOWE 540:36
pack, and take a t. — BROO 162:84

Runs the red electric t. — BETJ 89:37
shaves and takes a t. — WHITE 935:47
sneak into the house in her t. — LAMB 505:93
the next t. has gone — PUNCH 699:78
to Vietnam to take the t. — THER 882:88
t. filled the temple — BIBLE 107:54
t. of events has carried him — AMERY 15:25
t. of the future to run over him — EISE 314:93
t. passes through stations — LEWIS 526:40
T. up a child — BIBLE 105:89
triumph of His t. — WESL 932:64
Ultimate T. — MANS 567:27
we rush in the t. — THOM 887:6
whirligig wheels of the t. — SITW 823:98
Winter…Affrights thy shrinking t. — COLL 238:77
trained Then I t. hard — HEMI 410:84
t. folly — GERH 365:69
trainer animal t.…knows — RYLE 736:61
training not part of our t. — NORM 641:55
pitch of the highest t. — ROOS 724:15
t. which fits for labour! — SCHR 749:65
training-school democracy…a t.-s. — WHIT 938:11
trains Do people who wave at t. — MCGO 552:80
Fair t. of images — WORD 961:34
Garscadden T. — KENN 480:15
No bloody t. — BLAIR 138:47
rush through the fields in t. — CHES 221:8
t. will run over their tails — SITW 823:98
trait Death is an acquired t. — ALLEN 14:90
depend on this t. — JAMES 451:69
traitor Face of a t.! — HUGO 437:68
Thou art a t. — SHAK 761:43
t. Stands in worse — SHAK 803:99
traitors cowards flinch and t. sneer — CONN 242:84
doubts are t. — SHAK 787:49
fears do make us t. — SHAK 797:58
hate t. and the treason love — DRYD 303:17
more strong than t.' arms — SHAK 777:48
see a sort of t. — SHAK 765:57
t.…are a unfortunate class — WARD 920:99
tramp why the lady is a t. — HART 400:67
trample t. over their history — STREE 857:49
trams in the streets, in the t. — MAYA 583:22
tramways t., buses, aeroplanes — LARI 509:70
trance in mad t. — SHEL 815:39
tranquil anchored in t. waters — KENN 481:14
tranquillity chaos…in t. — THUR 891:98
divine T. — TENN 877:70
emotion recollected in t. — WORD 958:93
sinking down in its t. — WORD 959:96
Sorrow is t. — PARK 664:20
transactions t.…people expect — AUST 46:64
transcend write poems…to t. — SART 742:67
transcendent no t. themes in life — FORD 343:10
t. enlightenment — COND 240:14
t. memories — WHITE 934:31
t. passion — DRYD 301:52
transcendental T. Meditation — SHAR 806:74
transform t. honesty — SHAK 783:9
t. Men into monsters — FORD 343:8
transformation fluidity, t. — MARC 569:52
yearning for t. that underlies — MATH 581:86
transformed found himself t. — KAFKA 472:5
transgression where no law…no t. — BIBLE 125:7
transgressions acknowledge my t. — BIBLE 100:71
Remember not…my t. — BIBLE 100:48
so far hath he removed our t. — BIBLE 102:8
wounded for our t. — BIBLE 109:94
transgressors teach t. thy ways — BIBLE 101:73
transient Mirth is short and t. — ADDI 6:34
transitory t. in this vale of tears — FERRE 334:98
translate few…as cannot write, t. — DENH 272:61
t. beauty into his likeness — SHAK 765:7
t. pulsations into images — RICH 713:99
You've no right to t. — QUIL 702:16
translation book…merely needs t. — PROU 698:60
lose something in the t. — DRYD 300:19
T. is the paradigm — MATH 581:86
vanity of t. — SHEL 816:49
what is lost in t. — FROST 353:26
translations T.…are seldom faithful — CAMP 194:58
translunary those brave t. things — DRAY 299:98
transmission gears of a cycle t. — PIRS 679:89
transport hours of t. we shall spend! — AUST 46:61
t. breaks upon the town — DICK 283:31
t. in Los Angeles — LEBO 518:65
turned to share the t. — WORD 961:33

trees

yearn for the first available t.	GELL 363:35	so airy a t.	TENN 876:28	land where the Bong-t.	LEAR 516:36
transvestite about time a t. potter won	PERRY 675:28	tawny t. sublime	CRAIK 252:51	laughing leaves of the t.	SWIN 863:84
persecution of the t.	WHITE 934:27	We t. upon	SHAK 787:53	leaves grow on the t.	YEATS 965:3
trap after leaving the t.	HUXL 443:4	**treason** feel the t. sharply	SHAK 803:99	leaves to a t.	KEATS 476:79
T. of their own making	FLET 340:50	hate traitors and the t. love	DRYD 303:17	live on this Crumpetty T.	LEAR 517:42
trapeze man on the flying t.	LEYB 528:80	he harbours t.	SHAK 759:88	loved a t. or flower	MOORE 618:6
man on the flying t.	SARO 744:57	last temptation is the greatest t.	ELIOT 319:47	make a right Rose T.	YEATS 966:21
man on the flying t.	THUR 890:70	Music is a t.	KHOM 485:89	man, a madyn, and a t.	ANON 21:54
trappings goods and t. of your life	MOORE 616:59	popular humanity is t.	ADDI 7:49	marked a t.	STUA 858:57
t. and the suits of woe	SHAK 780:36	T. and murder	SHAK 775:67	On a t. by a river	GILB 370:68
Trappist credit to a T. nun	SHAR 806:73	t. can but peep	SHAK 784:53	on the T. of Life	MILT 604:95
diplomat is a deaf T.	LECA 518:74	T. doth never prosper	HARI 398:33	pine t. drops its dead	MERE 588:41
traps t. for eager and clever fools	SNYD 833:94	T. has done his worst	SHAK 797:46	problems of a t.	MAMET 564:38
trash Cash for t.	CLIN 230:98	T. is but trusted	SHAK 772:62	sat down under a juniper t.	BIBLE 97:66
white man is t.	LEE 519:91	t. is not owned	DRYD 302:1	sat under the T.	KIPL 490:97
traumatic Post T. Stress Disorder	SELL 756:16	t. to his country	JOHN 460:79	shade of a Coolibah t.	PATE 668:12
travail earth in t. and in pain	LONG 535:32	**treasons** From plots and t.	DRYD 302:91	shady cypress t.	ROSS 726:46
travel all that t. by land	SWIFT 863:73	t., stratagems, and spoils	SHAK 770:21	sings on yon pom'granate t.	SHAK 766:1
crime…you t. a lot	ALLEN 14:83	what care we For t.	WORD 956:57	smell thee on the t.	SHAK 790:40
effect of t. on a man	LIVI 532:55	**treasure** covetous man all his t.	MILT 600:16	some single herb or t.	MARV 577:1
Good t. books	RABAN 703:3	dig for hidden t.	TWAIN 902:46	somewhere in the Orange T.	NEIL 633:10
I cannot rest from t.	TENN 870:98	great t. and trouble therewith	BIBLE 104:75	spoils the growth of the t.	SHER 817:89
if one wishes to t. in peace	STARK 843:22	he that has stolen the t.	CONG 240:44	stands the lonely t.	MILL 592:24
most rewarding t.	THER 882:94	If love be t.	OTWAY 656:4	sticking in a t.	SCOTT 753:60
Most t.…involves	THER 882:93	Preserve it as your chiefest t.	BELL 76:50	swan-bosomed t.	SITW 823:10
Never to t. any road	IBN 444:6	purest t. mortal times afford	SHAK 764:32	take a t. from the forest	SCOTT 753:37
not to t. but to love	AUGU 45:35	Rich the t.	DRYD 303:30	Teach…under the nearest t.	QABO 701:1
real way to t.!	GRAH 380:90	She is your t.	SHAK 761:62	that's why the t.	ANON 24:11
The wish to t. seems…human	THER 882:95	Thine be ilka joy and t.	BURNS 179:36	thocht it was a trustie t.	BALL 60:79
To t. hopefully	STEV 852:48	t. in earthen vessels	BIBLE 127:86	three ravens sat on a t.	BALL 59:76
To t. is useful	CELI 211:36	t. in heaven	BIBLE 128:97	t., a house, a field	MONET 612:99
T. agents would be wiser	DE 268:55	t. is their only trust	DYER 309:49	t. Continues to be	KNOX 495:18
T. far enough you meet yourself	MITCH 609:32	t. may be hard to find	BRON 161:56	t. from which they spring	BIRD 136:10
t. for it too!	SHAK 779:7	t. on which we should live	HERZ 416:26	t. of knowledge	BIBLE 91:87
t. forth so far!	SHAK 778:64	Without glaidnes availis no t.	DUNB 306:99	t. of knowledge	BYRON 189:98
t. for t.'s sake	STEV 851:28	**treasures** accumulated t. of age	IRVI 447:56	t. of knowledge is not that of Life	BYRON 189:83
t. four hundred miles	WHITE 934:24	Better than all t.	SHEL 814:98	t. of liberty must be refreshed	JEFF 454:22
T. is fatal to prejudice	TWAIN 902:35	Not all the t. of the world	PAINE 660:30	t. of life	BIBLE 104:55
t., so broadening	THER 882:86	opened their t.	BIBLE 114:17	t. of life	BIBLE 104:68
t. the open road	WHIT 937:1	Strange T. lodg'd	TRAH 895:84	t. of life	BIBLE 91:1
t.…the sweetest and most delightful	CORY 247:13	t. upon earth	BIBLE 115:43	t. of life	BIBLE 91:87
two classes of t.	BENC 78:3	**treasury** cast into the t.	BIBLE 120:61	t. of life	BIBLE 132:28
universal test of t.	GELL 363:35	If the T. were to fill	KEYN 484:80	t. On fire by lightning	BYRON 187:54
Writing and t. broaden your ass	HEMI 410:85	well-filled t.	FRED 349:37	t. planted by the rivers of water	BIBLE 99:25
travelled care which way he t.	BEAV 71:29	wonder sitting on the T. Bench	CHUR 225:78	t. that fantasies had planted	HERZL 416:24
He who has not t.	ANON 26:76	**treat** always t. humanity…as an end	KANT 473:24	t. to be desired	BIBLE 91:93
I t. among unknown men	WORD 958:92	If you t. her gently	SNOW 832:84	Under the greenwood t.	SHAK 778:75
took the one less t. by	FROST 352:95	must t. them carefully	HIND 419:68	Virginia's aged t.	RANS 706:67
traveller Farewell, Monsieur T.	SHAK 779:8	Talk about a t.	COLL 237:63	Was there a t.	COWL 250:73
historian or a t.	HARR 398:42	way to t. her	FAUL 331:45	wisdom…is a t. of life	BIBLE 104:55
If a t. were informed	DISR 288:45	who gives a child a t.	MASE 580:64	wish I were a t.	HERB 413:64
'Is there anybody there?' said the T.	DELA 271:25	**treated** They're very well t.	CHEN 218:25	wither on the t.	JAY 453:2
no t. returns	TWAIN 902:63	**treaties** arising from t.	UNIT 905:9	**trees** all the t. are green	KING 487:48
Stand still, t., and read!	ANON 28:56	T. are like girls	DE 270:94	among the gusty t.	NOYES 642:70
to the t., a mountain	THOR 888:24	**treatise** T. of Human Nature	HUME 439:8	as fast as the Arabian t.	SHAK 790:51
t. between life and death	WORD 960:20	**treatment** diligent t.	PLATO 682:66	as winter changes the t.	BRON 162:79
t. from an antique land	SHEL 813:85	one sort of t. may serve for all	CARL 199:69	blasts the roots of t.	THOM 883:3
t. from the cradle to the grave	SHEL 814:19	scientific t. for all diseases	SHAW 809:80	childhood t. were green	MACN 558:5
t. is…recommended	BAED 54:61	Suitable Case for T.	MERC 587:21	country of birds and t.	WRIG 963:70
t. must have the back	NASHE 632:97	t. of a question is like	WITT 951:26	daffodils…beneath the t.	WORD 960:24
t. must…make himself…useless	GALT 359:56	**treaty** hand that signed the t.	THOM 883:9	die when the t. were green	CLARE 228:56
t.'s passport is sometimes asked for	BAED 54:60	not a peace t.	FOCH 341:68	filled the t. and flapped	HODG 421:20
t.…you have great reason	SHAK 779:6	**tree** almost insensitive t.	DARIO 263:46	fir t. dark and high	HOOD 426:23
when the t. reaches t.	STARK 843:24	as a t. bears apples	EMER 325:88	ghostly t. all dead and dry	LAWS 514:97
Where the t.'s journey is done	BLAKE 140:11	billboard lovely as a t.	NASH 630:63	Grass and t. wither	WU 963:84
travellers not be like other t.	AUST 46:61	birds still hopping on the t.	STEV 853:63	have fallen from the t.	WILH 943:56
sit outside at 'The T.' Rest'	HARDY 397:29	bomb the moth off a t.	JENS 454:34	heavy t. they climb	SPEN 838:39
t. and wanderers by nature	FERB 332:67	buss grew til a t.	YOUNG 968:53	Ice-scratched slabs and bent t.	SNYD 832:91
t. can use…editions	LEVIN 525:29	But a t. chiefly	THOM 885:60	in the end there were the t.	WHITE 935:50
t. in Europe	MELV 585:71	But there's a t., of many	WORD 959:7	Loveliest of t.	HOUS 431:33
t., who make too short	MONT 613:10	carve on every t.	SHAK 779:87	lyke as t. and erbys	MALO 563:14
travelling knowledge gained in t.	BAUD 68:70	Christmas t. is lighted	MOYN 623:1	music of its t. at dawn	ARNO 34:77
never t. less	WESL 932:71	climbing a birch t.	FROST 352:98	Of all the t.	KIPL 492:53
So it is in t.	JOHN 463:60	desire…a t. of life	BIBLE 104:55	peopled by tribes and t.	WRIG 963:71
t. in a straight line	MAIL 560:44	desire…a t. of life	BIBLE 104:68	procreate like t.	BROW 165:70
t. induces a feeling	THER 882:86	dew-bespangling herb and t.	HERR 415:10	river in the t.	HEAN 405:76
use of t.	JOHN 465:8	each t.…a tranced woman	FREE 350:48	see men as t., walking	BIBLE 119:58
travels In my t.…never felt	BOSW 152:67	evergreen t. of diabolical knowledge	SHER 817:72	Shade off the t.	CORY 247:12
sundry contemplation of my t.	SHAK 779:5	every t. of the garden	BIBLE 91:88	shady t. cover him	BIBLE 99:21
talk of my t. was to tarnish	THES 882:96	Eve, who tasted of the t.	LANY 508:53	snow fell, the t. stood	NEME 633:18
t. fastest who t. alone	KIPL 489:74	form as a t. has form	POUND 692:34	talking to t.	CHAR 216:43
treacherous none so t.	SHAW 807:17	fruit Of that forbidden t.	MILT 601:29	tall ancestral t.	HEMA 409:57
treachers t. by spherical	SHAK 792:89	gave me of the t.	BIBLE 91:95	The t. and the houses	THOM 887:6
treachery mother of all t.	PAIS 660:44	golden t. of actual life	GOET 375:83	The t. are the right height	ROMN 724:97
tread All that t.	BRYA 170:2	Hast thou eaten of the t.	BIBLE 91:94	thin t. in a city square	LOWE 539:1
face with an undaunted t.	STEV 853:73	hewing down a t.	JOHN 463:63	tongues in t.	SHAK 778:66
heavy is the t.	THOM 885:64	I'm like a t.	WEST 932:82	town among the t.	ROBI 718:89

trellises

T. cut to Statues	POPE 686:60
t. of noblest kind for sight	MILT 604:96
t. of the field shall clap	BIBLE 109:1
T.'re always a relief	MITCH 609:35
t....resigned to the way	CATH 208:86
t. shall be my books	SHAK 779:86
t. that yield to the flood	SOPH 834:28
t. were surfaced like flesh	LEE 519:98
t. with black marching boots	HARR 399:55
under t. by the eldritch light	DAY 267:37
vext garden t.	ARNO 35:18
walk, you lover of t.	BROW 168:46
with his lute made t.	SHAK 804:44
With rocks, and stones and t.	WORD 957:64

trellises Through gilded t. — SITW 823:1

tremble And make me t. — TENN 877:61
I t., I expire! — SHEL 816:48
Therefore t., and depart — SHAK 780:17
t. in this factory of books — SMITH 828:5

tremblers boding t. learned to trace — GOLD 376:1

trembling drink thy water with t. — BIBLE 110:31

trembly over t. and feverish — TWAIN 902:62

tremulous the t. tide — YEATS 965:5

trench t. warfare of World War I — NOON 640:44

trenches digging t. and trying on — CHAM 212:62
field between the t. — MACG 551:71

trepidation self-examination with t. — ICHI 445:13

trespass t. there and go — HOUS 432:73

trespasses forgive us our t. — BOOK 146:34

trespassing without t. upon others — BURKE 176:38

tresses bathe thy breathing t. — COLL 238:77
t. grey — SCOTT 752:9

trial Going to t. — THOM 887:91
no office...is a t. — SHAW 806:81
t., and t. is by what is contrary — MILT 600:8
t. by juries — JEFF 454:26
T. by jury — DENM 273:72

triangle lost its golden t. — MAIL 560:55

triangles Knights of the Isosceles T. — ROOS 725:21
t. had made a god — MONT 614:38

tribal constructing t. lays — KIPL 490:3
For t. man space — MCLU 556:52

tribalism t. and inquisitiveness — ALDI 12:51

tribe badge of all our t. — SHAK 769:85
customs of his t. — SHAW 807:10
may his t. increase! — HUNT 439:28
of the t. of Tiger — SMART 826:63
our t.'s complicity — HEAN 405:73
purify the dialect of the t. — ELIOT 321:86
Richer than all his t. — SHAK 790:51

tribeless T., lawless, homeless — HOMER 425:6

tribes peopled by t. and trees — WRIG 963:71
startled scaly t. — WORD 961:41
t. have left off eating each other — THOR 888:26
t....slumber in its bosom — BRYA 170:2
two mighty t., the Bores and Bored — BYRON 190:24

tribulation kept me in t. — MICH 590:68
out of great t. — BIBLE 131:4
ye shall have t. — BIBLE 123:57

tribunal new t. now — BROW 169:77

tributary how is she become t.! — BIBLE 110:23

tribute demands a heavy t. — INNO 446:47
feet thy t. bring — LYTE 543:93
Hypocrisy is a t. — LARO 510:4
t. of the current — FROST 352:7
t. to whom t. is due — BIBLE 126:30
vain t. of a smile — SCOTT 752:14

trice Change in a t. — SWIN 864:91

trick a confidence t. — WILS 947:40
because of a t. — THUR 890:83
conjuring t. with bones — JENK 454:31
served such another t. — SHAK 773:12
stuff that will do the t. — FORM 344:21
t. for t. — BEHN 75:19
T. is to Keep Breathing — GALL 358:42
t. of heaping obligations — SHAW 807:20
t. of making it appear — ORWE 654:42
t. of our English nation — SHAK 772:74
t. of that voice — SHAK 793:20
when the long t.'s over — MASE 580:52
wild t. of his ancestors — SHAK 772:62
win the t. — HOYLE 434:94

tricked t. and sold — SAND 742:23

trickling t. Of heart — PATC 668:6

tricks all t. are either knavish — JOHN 463:67
an underdog new t. — STEV 851:18
no more mean t. — TWAIN 902:61

old dog new t.	ONEI 651:78
Plays such fantastic t.	SHAK 787:58
rare t. of a Machiavellian	WEBS 926:35
shaped for sportive t.	SHAK 760:32
t. of sense	WILB 939:39
t. that are vain	HARTE 400:72
Women are like t.	CONG 240:45

tried adherence to the old and t. — LINC 529:7
not been t. and found wanting — CHES 220:77
number of people have t. — KERR 483:58

trifle As 'twere a careless t. — SHAK 796:11
disregard love, as a t. — HUNT 439:21
never t. with nature — AGAS 9:87

trifles observance of t. — DOYLE 297:51
She who t. with all — GAY 362:14
t. away out of a shamefaced — MORE 618:21
unconsidered t. — SHAK 799:15
with t. and jingles — BACON 52:22

trigger finger on the t. — MACM 556:68
Whose finger...on the t.? — ANON 24:29
Whose finger...on the t.? — DAILY 260:6

trillion ten, ten t. — LOWE 540:17

trilogy one-t. writer — ROTH 727:76

trim dressed in all his t. — SHAK 802:72

trimmed If only t. — ROTH 728:2

trinity strong name of the T. — ALEX 13:65
thanks to the Holy T. — COLU 238:91

trinkets returned to your t. — KIPL 492:49

trip fearful t. is done — WHIT 938:7
little t. to N.Y. — OHARA 648:13
long t. from all fours — THUR 890:79
t., hack and push their opponents — FRY 353:28
t. to Europe would be superfluous — SAAR 736:1

tripe fat t. finely broiled? — SHAK 762:74
mercy of bankers and t. sellers — MENC 586:89
Painch, t., or thairm — BURNS 178:94

triple t. ways to take — KIPL 490:2

triple-towered t.-t. sky — DAY 267:37

tripwire occasion, catalyst, or t. — ACKE 3:57

Trissotin Mithridates and half T. — MACA 546:53

triste jamais t. archy jamais t. — MARQ 575:52

tristesse Adieu t. — ELUA 324:45

Triton this T. of the minnows? — SHAK 799:96
T. blow his wreathèd horn — WORD 961:30

triumph contact before we can t. — NAPO 630:45
enjoy their t. — HAMM 394:56
first t. over Libya — PLUT 682:76
meet with T. and Disaster — KIPL 492:62
no t. in it — TROL 897:31
not the t. but the struggle — COUB 248:20
now is the Victor's t. won — POTT 690:81
pedestalled in t.? — BROW 169:75
Poor is the t. — THOM 887:2
tiny grunt of t. — NIGH 639:18
To t., and to die — GRAY 385:88
t. is somehow clouded — COMM 239:94
t. of Enlightenment — BELL 77:84
t. of failure — RYAN 736:54
t. of his heart — ADDI 7:35
t. of hope over experience — JOHN 462:21
t. of the embalmer's art — VIDAL 912:91
t. over death and sin — SPEN 839:43
t. over death and sin — SPEN 839:46
truth does not t. — PLAN 680:25
What t.! — ARNO 34:84
won a satisfaction and a t. — WOLFE 953:69
wrong would t. — BROW 169:85

triumphant militant and becomes t. — MORR 620:52

triumphs paints yet more glorious t. — CARL 200:77
t. of the Crusades — RUNC 731:50

trod Generations have t. — HOPK 428:70
T. beside me, close and dear — HOUS 431:53

Trojan left the T. shore — DRYD 304:37
never know what T. 'orses — BEVIN 90:66

trombone phrased on the t. — SINA 822:88

troop foreign t....in my country — PITT 679:9
over a t. of artists — WILL 945:6
preposterous t. of sons — SOME 833:9
run through a t. — BIBLE 99:38

troops admires its shock t. — LECA 518:75
die with t. — CHUR 225:93
Farewell the plumèd t. — SHAK 790:27
lead the t. out — WALE 917:29
T. always ready to act — FRED 349:37
t., and sweet societies — MILT 600:95
t. of friends — SHAK 798:69

trophies among a military one, t. — FUSE 356:93

Texas, the FBI, and hunting t.	KENN 482:33
trophy t. to magisterial interference	ANON 23:88
tropic between pole and t.	ELIOT 321:80
troth I wonder, by my t.	DONNE 291:21
thereto I plight thee my t.	BOOK 148:91
Trotsky done...by Lenin and T.	CHUR 224:70
trotter fastest t. in the Province	HALI 393:31
trouble Any wonder we're in t.?	DEMI 272:47
cause no t.	AESC 9:80
Double, double, toil and t.	SHAK 797:52
enough real causes of t.	ORWE 655:81
even I have t. doing it	BANK 61:16
full of t.	TWAIN 902:38
great treasure and t. therewith	BIBLE 104:75
help when in t.	STEV 850:1
if you wanted to view t.	RIDGE 715:32
if you will only take the t.	SHAW 810:4
In labour and t....more dignified	CHES 219:49
in time of t.	MARQ 575:56
Kindness in another's t.	GORD 378:52
Man...full of t.	BIBLE 98:5
man is born unto t.	BIBLE 98:97
may be t. ahead	BERL 84:40
repay the t. and expense	BELL 76:54
sit down with t.	GLAS 374:45
The t. with a book	WINT 950:16
toil and t. of acquiring it	SMITH 827:79
t. enough of its own	WILC 939:43
t. is that no devastating	GONC 377:40
T. t. and it will t. you!	TRAV 896:96
t. with children	CRISP 254:99
t. with girls	SALI 740:79
t. with me	SALI 740:77
t. with Moore	FRY 354:38
very present help in t.	BIBLE 100:67
War...is toil and t.	DRYD 303:33
When in t., delegate	WAGN 915:3
where all t. seems	SWIN 864:97
troubled Let not your heart be t.	BIBLE 123:51
Let not your heart be t.	BIBLE 123:54
t. on every side	BIBLE 127:67
troubles got over all its t.	JERO 454:42
help them through their t.	ALCO 12:45
t. are worse than your own	ALGR 13:68
t. of our proud and angry dust	HOUS 432:65
t. of the brain	SHAK 798:70
trough slip with the gravy t.	MACB 546:64
t. between the two world wars	LEWIS 527:75
trousers asked me for my t.	KRUG 500:71
bottoms of my t. rolled	ELIOT 316:67
Chinese nurse with green t.	MANS 567:96
cloud in t.	MAYA 583:03
covered...with the t. of decorum	LICH 528:85
involve taking the t. off	BENN 80:48
men's t....great modern things	WARH 920:8
Muses in striped t.	ORWE 654:53
never have your best t. on	IBSEN 444:8
t., jackets, shoes	LARI 509:70
t. of Winston Churchill	BREZ 158:5
trout find a t. in the milk	THOR 888:22
portrait of a t.	HUGH 435:25
Where the grey t. lies	HOGG 422:43
trowel lays it on with a t.	CONG 240:53
Troy against our crumbling T.	MACN 557:96
fields where T. once was	OVID 657:15
Homer...chronicled the siege of T.	CUOMO 257:01
Priam's sons of T.	SURR 860:1
sail from the land of T.	VIRG 913:11
Scare T. out of itself	SHAK 787:46
T.'s Chieftain	VIRG 913:13
T.'s sacred citadel	HOMER 425:9
Was there another T.	YEATS 966:14
Where's T.	BRAM 156:58
truant Biting my t. pen	SIDN 820:44
every t. knew	GOLD 376:1
t. in the law	SHAK 759:76
truce vacation, or a t.	WORD 961:38
truck t., a producer or a critic	LEMM 521:32
t. passing by a factory	CAGE 192:17
truckload equipment by the t.	WELL 929:95
trudged t. along unknowing	DRYD 304:45
true accept...as being t.	AYER 48:5
admitted to be t.	JAMES 451:15
All stereotypes...t.	CRON 256:27
always say what's t.	STEV 853:64
And is it t.?	BETJ 88:36

any less real and t. SHAW 806:88
Art for the sake of the t. SAND 741:11
art works because it is t. MART 575:68
as long as it isn't t. CAPO 197:23
as t....as taxes is DICK 280:49
be known to be t. RUSS 734:23
Be so t. to thyself BACON 52:4
brew that is t. PANA 662:80
But a t. man INGR 446:36
called Faithful and T. BIBLE 132:19
can the devil speak t.? SHAK 796:8
Change proves t. ICHI 444:12
common reproach is t. SOCR 833:96
dark and t. TENN 872:44
don't know they're t. BACH 49:14
equally happy, is not t. JOHN 461:12
errors that I had accepted as t. DESC 274:98
Every t. work of art FRIE 351:78
expected to go quite t. JOHN 464:96
false or t. YEATS 965:7
friends are t. BIER 134:79
Geometry is not t. PIRS 679:93
Hope, art thou t. SIDN 820:48
hope's t. gage RALE 705:44
if I know what t. love is TENN 877:53
If it be t. that good wine SHAK 780:27
keep on saying...it will be t. BENN 81:68
kept him falsely t. TENN 877:54
let God be t. BIBLE 125:5
Live pure, speak t. TENN 878:93
no matter how t. VIDAL 912:84
Nothing is t. ANOU 28:65
nothing t. except the exaggerations ADOR 8:72
nothing more t. LARK 510:95
old saying and a t. SWIFT 861:36
remain t. to himself KENN 482:26
ring in the t. TENN 875:95
rough appraisal, but curiously t. ACHE 2:35
said t. things...by wrong names BROW 168:42
say something t. JAMES 448:79
Some of these things are t. MANT 568:17
something is t. that isn't WILS 947:40
Some t., some light TENN 878:77
supposing thou art t. SHAK 802:68
sure they are t. SHAK 800:27
that which was prov'd t. before BUTL 185:83
'The t.'...is only the expedient JAMES 451:76
to haue t. lufe agane HENR 411:21
to thine own self be t. SHAK 781:54
t. and honourable wife SHAK 777:19
t. attribute of the soul STAEL 842:3
T. eloquence has no time PASC 666:67
T. Love...differs from gold SHEL 816:46
t. love hath my heart SIDN 820:40
t. lover of literature SOUT 835:52
t. nature of poetry RICH 713:5
t. that sin is the cause JULI 471:41
t., wise friend called Piggy GOLD 375:74
t. wood, of yew wood DOYLE 297:49
t. writers have experienced this feeling SARR 744:61
what a man would like to be t. BACON 50:43
whatever we conceive...is t. DESC 274:97
what is t. cannot always be proven HUMP 439:15
What I tell you three times is t. CARR 205:26
what people say of us is t.! SMITH 829:13
whatsoever things are t. BIBLE 128:5
what we believe is not necessarily t. BELL 75:37
when thieves cannot be t. SHAK 771:40
which may be the t. HAWT 402:6
truest those who paint 'em t. ADDI 6:20
t. poetry is the most feigning SHAK 779:98
truffle t. is not a true aphrodisiac BRIL 159:20
truffles where the t. are ALBEE 11:26
truism t. in technological STER 847:15
truisms box of t. MACN 558:9
Truman colleagues in the T. cabinet REST 711:61
Trump T. is the price of progress KRUG 500:23
trump at the last t. BIBLE 127:62
Lord with the sound of the t. BOOK 149:18
trumpet Blow t. TENN 878:76
do not sound a t. before thee BIBLE 115:40
great voice, as of a t. BIBLE 131:87
if the t. give an uncertain sound BIBLE 126:53
novel was not a t. LESS 524:98
Pride...his own t. SHAK 786:31
shifted his t. GOLD 377:19
t. and the steady drum MCCA 547:82

t. is sounding MCCA 547:74
t. of a prophecy! SHEL 813:84
t. shall sound BIBLE 127:62
t. shrill hath thrice SPEN 839:45
trumpets blow Your t., angels DONNE 292:50
eagles and the t.? ELIOT 317:87
eating...to the sound of t. SMITH 831:61
never been amid the blare of t. EUDA 328:52
priests blew with the t. BIBLE 95:8
saith among the t., Ha, ha BIBLE 99:19
silver, snarling t. KEATS 477:15
thunderstorm or blare of t. MANN 566:82
t., beat the drums! MORE 619:27
T. sounded for him BUNY 174:83
t. which sing to battle SHEL 816:53
trumps If dirt were t. LAMB 505:7
Let spades be t.! POPE 685:39
truncated in a world of t. sentences FIEN 336:37
truncheons extort their t. COWP 251:20
trunk perish, t. and all SOPH 834:28
Sin's rotten t. COWP 251:5
So large a t. BELL 76:52
trust absolute t. SHAK 796:12
all power is a t. DISR 287:16
brightness to hold in t. SPEN 837:95
children of men put their t. BIBLE 100:57
degree and a quality of t. SHAP 805:68
does still my t. renew BRID 158:9
do I put my t. BIBLE 101:83
don't t. anybody KAIKO 472:11
don't t. him, we are friends BREC 157:94
empire is...power in t. DRYD 302:80
equally unsound to t. everyone SENE 757:21
gift or t. MCCA 547:90
If you can t. yourself KIPL 492:62
In America few people will t. MAIL 560:45
knowing...about whom they can t. SHAP 805:68
man assumes a public t. JEFF 454:27
men dare t. themselves SHAK 791:74
Never t. a computer WOZNI 962:58
Never t. a husband too far ROWL 729:20
never t. an expert MAMET 564:36
never t. a woman who WILDE 941:87
Never t. the artist LAWR 513:65
only two lawyers...who t. each other DOLE 290:2
pains that conquer t. TENN 874:74
Put not your t. in money HOLM 424:66
put not your t. in princes BOOK 149:38
Quhome ye may t. HENR 411:21
Time, which takes in t. RALE 705:47
treasure is their only t. DYER 309:49
t. also in him BIBLE 100:58
T. him as much as...a rattlesnake ACHE 3:49
t. in Christ WESL 932:65
t. in God DENN 273:73
t. in God SMITH 830:52
t. in him BIBLE 108:78
t. in him BIBLE 98:4
t. in the basic fairness NIXON 640:37
T. in the Lord with all thine heart BIBLE 104:52
t. man on his oath SHAK 791:75
t. me not at all TENN 877:45
T. none, for oaths are straws SHAK 775:70
t. not the physician SHAK 791:82
t. that good shall fall TENN 874:77
t. that somehow good TENN 874:75
t. the very difference JORD 469:2
without the t. of the people CONF 240:21
You should not t. government CLEGG 229:83
trusted friend, in whom I t. BIBLE 100:62
not to be t. when he does HAMM 395:71
speaker is not to be t. EUDA 328:52
To be t. is a greater compliment MACD 550:50
t. like the fox SHAK 772:62
trustees t. of Posterity DISR 288:36
trusting never extended to t. him BULL 173:59
trusty T., dusky, vivid, true STEV 854:86
truth absolute t. HALD 392:25
Absolute t. is a very rare THOM 887:89
absolute t. is not attainable ORWE 655:68
absurd is...the first t. CAMUS 195:82
accepted as t. KING 487:34
according to t. BURB 174:85
admitted the t. LAUT 511:25
a little beyond exact t. STEE 844:51
Americans are polite by telling the t. BRAD 154:27
And love of t. TENN 877:57

And order, t., and beauty range SMART 826:64
Art...cheating t. RIDI 715:34
art is not t. PICA 677:63
astray as a premature t. ROST 727:71
authority and show of t. SHAK 774:51
bear the torch of t. LICH 528:89
Beauty is t., t. beauty KEATS 478:40
before the t. has got its boots on CALL 192:26
believe, falsely, to be the t. HAMP 395:74
blaze of t. and liberty MACA 544:24
books...contain...our fidelity to t. CONR 244:40
bright countenance of t. MILT 600:98
But it's the t. KESEY 483:63
category of t. and falsehood AYER 48:6
Celie, tell the t. WALK 917:39
certain basis of t. HERZ 416:23
Church which abandons the t. KUNG 500:39
closer to the t. HEAT 406:94
cold as t. RHYS 712:75
comfort of thy worth and t. SHAK 801:49
Communist must grasp the t. MAO 568:29
completely as too much t. TWAIN 904:97
concentrate to t. and liberty SHEL 812:59
confirmation of t. MILT 600:11
couldn't tell the t. LENO 522:56
cult of t. PIER 677:66
dared to speak the t. TROL 898:36
dearer still is t. ARIS 32:30
Death cancels everything but t. HAZL 403:46
distinguishing t. from falsehood DESC 274:93
do not seek for the t. BORG 150:55
doubt about the t. MARG 570:70
Doubt t. to be a liar SHAK 781:77
economical with the t. ARMS 33:53
enemies of t. than lies NIET 637:92
essence of all religion and of absolute t. BLAV 142:50
experience as our t. LEGU 520:15
fear mortal t. POIN 683:96
fight for freedom and t. IBSEN 444:8
first casualty...is t. JOHN 457:8
French t. ROCH 719:9
full of grace and t. BIBLE 122:18
function of t. LIPP 531:41
further to discover the t. BACON 49:20
God, the source of t. DESC 275:99
golden heresy of t. RUSS 735:44
good for testing the t. PIRS 679:94
gospel t. GREE 386:30
Granted we want t. NIET 638:6
grope for t. POPP 689:62
Habit...the test of t. CRAB 252:41
habitually tells the t. MENC 586:88
how one comes by the t. MILL 593:59
I am the way, the t. BIBLE 123:53
If religion is about t. SULL 859:75
I have told you the t. STEV 850:4
indifference to t. JOHN 460:83
I need never catch up with the t. MCGO 552:78
infinite source of t. HUXL 443:7
in seeking for T. PIUS 680:20
interprets the t. GIRA 372:25
in t. must own COWP 250:93
In t., the more I live LACL 503:33
in t. will the Good KIER 485:3
irrefutable t. POPP 689:55
Is the eternal t. man's fighting soul EBER 310:12
Is there in t. no beauty? HERB 413:72
is with the whole t. TRUM 899:78
It is a historical t. ANGE 19:89
joking is to tell the t. SHAW 809:65
judge of t., in endless error POPE 687:81
Justice is t. DISR 288:41
just tell the t. TRUM 899:84
know how to desire the t. DIDE 285:67
knowing the t. GRIS 389:76
knowledge of the t. of Propositions HOBB 420:96
language...speaking the t. MACL 555:28
lawyer's t. is not T. THOR 888:19
lies, even when...telling the t. ORWE 654:38
lies, thinking it is the t. SAFI 737:20
lie which is part a t. TENN 876:39
light of T. DICK 281:68
loins girt about with t. BIBLE 128:95
Lord God of t. BIBLE 100:52
lose belief in this t. DU 305:69
love of t. GOET 375:67
love of t. JOHN 460:84

truthful

love of t. and right	TENN	875:96
loving Christianity better than T.	COLE	236:46
Loving in t.	SIDN	820:43
loyalty to T.	JAMES	449:22
Mathematics possesses not only t.	RUSS	734:20
may we bring t.	THAT	881:54
melancholy t.	DICK	281:70
mind may rest on the intuition of t.	BACON	54:57
Monastery of Aesthetic T.	MAMET	564:34
moral t. is a hollow tooth	MAST	581:82
more readily swallow lies than t.	GELL	363:34
never to search for t.	LAVO	512:35
new scientific t.	ORTE	652:42
new scientific t.	PLAN	680:25
no longer afraid of the t.	BONH	146:22
No mask like open t.	CONG	240:40
not maintained for t.	SWIFT	862:47
no t. in him	BIBLE	123:42
oaths that make the t.	SHAK	791:65
one t., and many opinions	KURZ	501:46
One t. is clear	POPE	687:79
one way possible of speaking t.	BROW	169:79
on the face of t.	BROW	164:44
paint the cot, As t. will paint it	CRAB	252:31
path that leads to the t.	HUXL	443:5
path to general t.	LEWO	528:79
Photography is t.	GODA	374:52
Pilate saith...What is t.?	BIBLE	123:59
Plain t. to speak	BURNS	177:69
platitude is simply a t.	BALD	57:27
Politics determine...not who has the t.	KRUG	500:27
pretensions of final t.	NIEB	637:88
prime t. of woman	CHES	220:79
proper champion for t.	BROW	165:47
Pure t., and perfect change of will	CORY	247:10
pursuit of t.	DESC	274:94
put more t. and untruth together	BACON	52:12
queen of the t.	BAUD	69:75
reveals a way of t.	STEV	850:77
say no more than the plain t.	ROCH	720:21
Science has promised us t.	LEBON	517:55
Science is a search for t.	PAUL	670:34
Science is the only t.	GOUR	380:79
scrupulous fidelity to the t.	CONR	244:47
sea is a teacher of t.	BELL	77:69
secured by good nature and t.	ROCH	720:22
seldom...necessary to tell the whole t.	BALF	58:45
Simple t.	SHAK	801:59
sold the t.	TENN	875:10
Some t. there was	DRYD	301:70
speaketh the t. in his heart	BIBLE	99:34
speak every man t.	BIBLE	128:90
speak the t.	JERO	454:41
steal someone's right to the t.	HOSS	430:29
Strict Regard for t.	BELL	77:63
strife of T. with Falsehood	LOWE	539:3
subject is not t., but things like t.	CHAP	214:20
take the t. and just skew it	PARV	666:61
Tell all the T.	DICK	284:47
telling the t.	HAMM	395:70
telling the t.	RUIZ	730:39
telling the t. about them	STEV	850:3
tell me the t. about love	AUDEN	43:83
tell them the t. and they think it's hell	KEANE	475:55
tell the t. in television	MUGG	623:12
Tell t., and shame the devil	SHAK	771:49
that is the t.!	ARCH	30:6
that it was the t.	MOOD	615:56
that she is made of t.	SHAK	803:86
that's the only t.!	ONEI	651:69
The inquiry of t.	BACON	50:56
there are all kinds of t.	OCON	647:86
the t. will be there yet	MCCA	547:78
they worship T.	BROO	162:96
thing is to find a t.	KIER	485:98
This is t. the poet sings	TENN	871:14
This t.—to prove	ARNO	35:6
This t. within thy mind	TENN	872:25
tired of the t.	ALBEE	11:23
told the t. most constantly	TIMES	892:22
touch the t. by...fiction	PACH	658:1
t. about himself	JONES	466:23
t. and honour, fredom	CHAU	217:71
t. and shame the devil	LIPP	531:36
T. beareth away the victory	BIBLE	112:67
T. be veiled	SHEL	816:55
t. calls spade a spade!	BROW	169:80
T....came once into the world	MILT	600:17
t....credited to wine	PLIN	682:70
T. exists	BRAQ	156:76
T....fills me with astonishment	DAWK	266:15
t. has such a face	DRYD	303:10
T. hath a quiet breast	SHAK	764:33
t. hath better deeds	SHAK	758:60
t. hears him and runs away	BELL	77:79
t. in every shepherd's tongue	RALE	705:43
t. in masquerade	BYRON	190:21
t. in no man	BEAU	71:22
t. in philosophy	DIDE	285:61
t. in the inward parts	BIBLE	101:72
t. is a pathless land	KRIS	499:11
t. is, I'm tired	DIAZ	276:26
T. is its own standard	SPIN	840:73
t. is marching on	HOWE	433:92
t. is not always useful	BANKS	62:23
t. is not...a majority vote	BENE	79:20
t. is often unpopular	STEV	851:12
t. is pulling its boots on	SPUR	841:89
t. is rarely pure	WILDE	941:98
T. is strong next to the Almighty	MILT	600:9
t. is that I have anticipated	WELLS	930:37
T. is the cry of all	BERK	84:34
T. is the hyest thyng	CHAU	217:93
t. is the uncharted rock	CORN	247:6
T. is too simple	SAND	741:10
T. is tough	HOLM	424:68
T....is what makes him	SAINT	738:46
t. lay...undiscovered	NEWT	635:61
T., Lord	BIBLE	117:4
T. obeyed his call	YEATS	967:34
t. of a reflection	MONT	613:12
t. of art should never be	HUGO	436:54
t. of description	SCOTT	754:78
t. of God into a lie	BIBLE	125:3
t. of our faith	JOHN	456:79
t. of the Holocaust	WEIZ	928:78
t. of the imagination	KEATS	475:73
t. of the revelation of Mahomet	GIBB	366:95
t. shall be thy shield	BIBLE	101:96
t. shall make you free	BIBLE	123:40
t. shining from behind	MACD	550:49
T., Sir, is a cow	JOHN	461:97
t. sits upon the lips	ARNO	34:98
t....Stranger than fiction	BYRON	190:25
t. to deceive the public	STEF	844:53
t. universally acknowledged	AUST	45:53
t. was always hard as iron	GALL	358:44
t. with gold she weighs	POPE	688:30
two kinds of t.	BARRY	65:97
two to speak the t.	THOR	888:20
unclouded face of T.	SCOTT	751:98
utter what he thinks t.	JOHN	464:77
way of saying the t.	HELL	408:39
whatever remains...must be the t.?	DOYLE	297:46
What is t.?	BACON	50:55
When in doubt, tell the t.	TWAIN	903:77
when you tell the t.	BIDEN	133:55
Where t. is hid	SHAK	782:78
wherever the t. may be	FROST	352:8
whispering tongues can poison t.	COLE	235:34
white star of T.	ARNO	35:3
Wit has t. in it	PARK	664:23
worship him in spirit and in t.	BIBLE	122:28
truthful moderately t. towards men	HARDY	397:5
true Poet must be t.	OWEN	657:30
t. interpreter—in the eye	BRON	161:63
truthfulness from the vivid t.	HUMB	438:92
refining of the sense of t.	CATH	208:87
truths Abandon...to Nature's t.	RABE	704:22
All great t.	SHAW	810:11
bringing t. nearer	HENZE	412:24
common t. that round us lie	WORD	957:67
fate of new t.	HUXL	443:8
he speaks unseasonable t.	CONG	241:59
hold these t. to be sacred	JEFF	453:19
hold these t. to be self-evident	STAN	842:12
Irrationally held t.	HUXL	443:9
mixture of fact and t.	FRAME	346:76
no new t.	MCCA	548:95
not for spreading eternal t.	BLISS	142:57
Our lies reveal as much...as our t.	COET	233:90
Some t....so near and obvious	BERK	84:30
three fundamental t.	BELL	75:37
took one of the t.	ANDE	18:75
T. discovered by intelligence	FRAN	347:83
t. I had not dreamed	THOM	885:53
t....in and out of favour	FROST	352:89
t. of the heart	FAUL	331:35
t. that wake	WORD	960:11
try don't t. to make things nice!	IVES	448:82
get it if you t.	GERS	365:79
if you're willing to t.	OBAMA	644:46
just wish they'd t. harder	WINT	950:10
T. again...Fail again	BECK	72:52
t. hard to be succinct	HORA	417:5
t. to think it again	GOET	375:64
T., t. again	HICK	418:50
trying there is only the t.	ELIOT	320:67
Your duty is to keep t.	BAN	62:37
tryouts big one holds its t.	HEBB	406:97
tsar Pope and T., Metternich	MARX	579:33
tub mere tale of a t.	WEBS	926:25
puddling in t. continually	PERTH	675:31
tuba duet between a t. and a piccolo	DONA	290:6
tubby t. little chap	WODE	952:45
tuberculosis not leprosy or t.	THER	882:81
tuberose the sweet t.	SHEL	815:23
tuck you vile standing t.	SHAK	771:47
Tucson T. and Deadwood	BENET	79:23
Tudor Shakespeare and those T. critics	ACHE	2:28
Tuesday out of town T.	ALGR	13:69
Tuesdays passionately, on t.	SHER	817:84
tug crouch, swivel, t.	OBRI	646:73
tulips t. bloom as they are told	BROO	162:92
tumble Gibraltar may t.	GERS	365:80
t. on the heather	SCOTT	753:39
tumbled t. off a bus	GRAH	380:85
tumbler Bring in...a clean t.	DICK	278:86
t. of London Water	SMITH	830:50
tumour confronts the t.	HALD	392:26
when it ripens in a t.	ABSE	1:7
tumult sank in t. to a lifeless ocean	COLE	236:40
t. and the shouting dies	KIPL	490:16
t. dwindled to a calm	BYRON	191:33
t. of the masses	ALCU	12:46
t. of thy mighty harmonies	SHEL	813:83
tune angels...singing out of t.	BYRON	190:31
average guy who could carry a t.	CROS	256:33
complain about the t.	BEVAN	89:57
dancers dancing in t.	TENN	876:26
Every name is a t.	MOORE	617:82
forced to change their t.	BROD	160:30
good t. played on an old fiddle	BUTL	185:24
heavenly t. harsh sounding	SHAK	762:67
Hope...sings the t.	DICK	283:34
how it be in t.	SHAK	780:14
incapable of a t.	LAMB	505:95
lamentable t. is the sweetest music	SIDN	820:42
like a wayward t.	YEATS	965:5
melodise...sweetly play'd in t.	BURNS	180:50
Peter like a piper's t.	FARJ	330:20
sad raggy t.	HUGH	434:10
sudden springing of a t.	LOWE	539:1
Then murder's out of t.	SHAK	790:44
thunder to the t. of 'Greensleeves'	SHAK	773:74
we are out of t.	WORD	961:30
tunes all the good t.	HILL	418:57
beat out t. for bears	FLAU	339:20
only know two t.	GRANT	382:10
slow old t. of Spain	MASE	580:57
t. at which he was...working	DICK	280:31
tunic closest, all-concealing t.	SHEL	813:88
tunnel between two points was a t.	MANC	564:48
end of the t.	LOWE	540:36
one t., dark and solitary	SABA	736:2
On leaving the t.	LEVIN	525:29
perspective of a subway t.	TOOLE	894:58
some profound dull t.	OWEN	657:32
tunnels t. that re-wind themselves	CRANE	253:69
tuppence T. a Bag!	TRAV	896:29
t. for all of the rest!	FLAN	338:11
Wouldn't give you t.	COLL	237:63
turbid t. look the most profound	LAND	506:27
turbulent democracy...sometimes t.	CART	206:47
rid me of this t. priest?	HENR	411:11
turf At his head a grass-green t.	SHAK	784:48
blue ribbon of the t.	DISR	288:44
green t. beneath my feet	HAZL	403:40
pile of t. against the wall.	COLUM	238:90
shelving bank of t.	SHEL	816:59
t. such the honeyed showers	MILT	599:90

turf-dances t.-d. of…encounter	ALLEN 13:75	t. from the lecture	STEV 850:84	t. do defeat	SHAK 776:14
Turgenev beat Mr T.	HEMI 410:84	t.'s last gleaming	KEY 483:68	t. from policy	BURKE 176:43
Turk In heathen, T. or Jew	BLAKE 139:89	**twilights** ancient shadows and t.	RUSS 735:43	T. seldom want pretexts	BURKE 176:52
malignant and a turbaned T.	SHAK 790:51	**twin** ambition's ugly t.	KUSH 501:45	when t. seems to kiss	SHAK 798:82
Turkey Christians that travel in T.	BUTL 184:62	**twinkle** roguish t. in his eye	THOM 887:5	**tyre** Roosevelt's spare t.	GARN 360:77
In T. it was always 1952	THER 882:97	t. of a fading star	ELIOT 318:14	**tyres** everything but the air in the t.	CALD 192:23
T. carpet bears to a picture	MACA 545:32	**twinkling** in the t. of an eye	BIBLE 127:62	**tythe** t. o' what ye waste at cartes	BURNS 177:72
turkey It was a T.	DICK 279:7	Jew in the t.	SHAK 769:89		
secure all the myrtle and t.	AUST 46:68	**twins** threw the t. she nursed	GRAH 380:86	**u**	
turkish perpetual T. bath	SWET 861:11	two t. cleaving together	MILT 600:3	**Ubu** Mother U., you are very ugly	JARRY 452:93
Turks In those wicked T.	DICK 280:35	**twist** Let him t.…in the wind	EHRL 313:71	**udder** u. a swollen wobble	RAINE 705:38
turmoil with ceaseless t.	COLE 236:38	pale death your vital t. shall sever	DAVI 264:75	**UFO** convinced that U. exist	CART 206:44
turn could t., and live with animals	WHIT 937:93	**twitch** affected by every t.	TRUD 899:71	**ugliness** march of material u.	WHITE 935:54
do not hope to t.	ELIOT 318:22	**twits** Too many t. make a twat	CAM 193:39	see beneath both beauty and u.	ELIOT 319:30
painter must have a natural t.	DURER 307:26	**twitter** t. of sleepy canaries	GRAH 381:91	u. has a thousand	HUGO 436:51
requite thee with a shrewd t.	BIBLE 113:87	**two** being one and not t.	FLET 340:50	u., vice and unhappiness	BERN 86:75
t. away thy face	SHAK 778:55	Can t. walk together	BIBLE 111:50	**ugly** All Middlesex is u.	COBB 233:75
t. from Africa and live?	WALC 916:9	If ever t. were one	BRAD 155:51	Art produces u. things	COCT 233:88
t. of the road	FAWC 331:51	must have t. you know	CARR 205:18	better to be good than to be u.	WILDE 940:70
t. to little things	GIBS 367:14	sin ye do by t. and t.	KIPL 490:1	Mother Ubu, you are very u.	JARRY 452:93
wouldn't have left a t. unstoned	WIMP 949:88	think that t. and t. are four	HOUS 432:70	not more u.	SHAK 782:6
You t. if you want to	THAT 881:58	T. and t. is five	DOST 294:88	so very u. in persons of small means	ELIOT 315:16
Turnball Mr T. had predicted	TROL 898:41	T. are better than one	BIBLE 106:17	There is nothing u.	CONS 245:60
Turner T. looks a bit shaky	JOHN 465:10	t. for tea	CAES 191:10	toad, u. and venomous	SHAK 778:65
turning shadow of t.	BIBLE 130:49	t. ideas are more inseparable	SMITH 830:48	tourist is an u. human being	KINC 486:15
take the wrong t.	CONN 243:9	t. kinds of Arctic problems	STEF 844:52	u. mathematics	HARDY 396:97
The lady's not for t.	THAT 881:58	T. lads that thought	SHAK 799:7	u. woman is a blot	BRON 161:62
T. and t. in the widening gyre	YEATS 966:24	t. plus t. make four	ORWE 655:75	wish he were not so u.	BRON 161:57
turnings all its narrow t.	DICK 281:72	t. shall withstand him	BIBLE 106:18	**UK** enquiries about the UK climate	SAMU 741:3
t. intricate of verse	WORD 958:85	T. things are always the same	STEIN 845:70	**Ukraine** U. is not even a state	PUTIN 700:96
turnip noises like a t.	MACD 550:39	T. women placed together	SHAK 804:39	**Ulster** resistance to which U.	LAW 512:36
turnips type your t.	CAMP 194:53	went in t. and t.	BIBLE 92:8	U.'s honoured dead	PAIS 660:43
turn-up t.-u. in a million	BEVIN 90:68	**two-faced** not t.-f.	SNOW 832:78	U. will be right	CHUR 224:64
turpitude t. of incontinence	SCOTT 754:67	**Tyburn** has a damned T.-Face	CONG 240:41	**Ulsterman** armed Protestant U.	REDM 709:21
turret daily from the t. wall	MUIR 624:16	**Tyne** from the Severn to the T.!	KIPL 493:80	**ulterior** free of u. motives	JONG 466:31
Sultan's t.	FITZ 337:68	**type** grey paper with blunt t.!	BROW 167:12	**ultimate** u. mystery of nature	PLAN 680:24
washed me out of the t.	JARR 452:83	highest t. of human nature	SPEN 836:90	**Ulysses** Happy…like U.	BELL 76:44
turrets gorgeous t.	MAHO 559:34	megaphone of big t.	MAST 581:83	interest throughout U.	BOWL 153:5
t. split the sky	LAND 507:35	T. of the wise	WORD 961:45	nature of the sickness found, U.	SHAK 786:28
turtle Behold the t.	ANON 27:16	**types** certain t. of society	PARS 666:56	passages of U.	MILL 593:56
traces of the t. soup	DICK 282:80	device of Movable T.	CARL 200:89	U.…is a dogged attempt	FORS 344:39
t. lives 'twixt plated	NASH 630:60	only two t. of cases	BENN 80:48	**umbrella** fatal forgotten u.	MANS 567:98
tutor nurse and t. of eccentric minds	LAWS 514:94	T. and shadows have their ending	AQUI 30:97	good u. but a poor roof	LOWE 539:15
TV lecturers…should appear on TV	ZELD 969:4	**typewriter** acquires a new t.	AMIS 16:48	neat as a furled u.	EMERY 325:2
more interesting than TV	PIRS 679:91	needs only a t. and paper	WINN 950:3	you have got…an u.	FLET 341:61
TV and the Internet are good	COUP 248:37	t.…[judged by]…fingers	ANON 25:38	**umbrellas** audience…put up its u.	BEER 73:78
TV licence	THOM 888:11	t. needs only paper	WELL 929:95	**umpire** Never argue with an u.	BOTH 152:81
TV soap operas?	UPDI 906:26	**typical** hardly find a t. American	BARN 64:59	perched like an u.	AVIS 47:1
twaddle better far write t.	MANS 568:11	more t. and less exotic	ANON 25:36	u., the pavilion cat	LANG 507:41
Twain one book by Mark T.	HEMI 410:76	**typing** isn't writing…it's t.	CAPO 192:24	**umpiring** come to see you u.	GRACE 380:84
twain go with him t.	BIBLE 115:36	**tyrannical** most t. and oppressive	CALH 192:24	**unable** unwilling or u.	WILL 946:15
never the t. shall meet	KIPL 489:76	**tyrannies** totalitarian and corrupt t.	MO 611:66	**unacceptable** u. face of capitalism	HEATH 405:86
twat Too many twits make a t.	CAM 193:39	**tyrannous** love…so t. and rough	SHAK 765:66	**unadmitted** u. desire to undress	LIN 529:2
Tweed T. rins to the ocean	BURNS 179:41	**tyranny** Bolshevik t. is the worst	CHUR 224:70	**un-American** Solitude is u.-A.	JONG 466:32
Willie Wastle dwalt on T.	BURNS 179:39	burden of t.	SHAW 808:35	**unapproachable** u., the hard-bitten	MACD 550:40
tweed thread of good-class t.	BENN 80:46	call it t.	HOBB 420:3	**unarmed** rode all u.	SCOTT 752:21
Tweedledum T. and Tweedledee	CARR 204:96	dark night of t.	MURR 627:83	**unattainable** flight after the u.	WHIT 936:66
Twelfth Night T. N.…a silly play	PEPYS 673:95	equals, free from t.?	LANY 508:56	**unattended** only the u. Moment	ELIOT 320:77
twelve in the sworn t.	SHAK 787:52	expresses its t. by reducing	MILL 594:84	**unbalance** world is…in dynamic u.	BART 66:20
six nights when I was t.	THOM 884:46	fight terror with t.	BUSH 183:41	**unbearable** expressing lightly the u.	UPDI 906:35
There are only t. notes	HIND 419:68	liberty against t.	ROOS 725:22	tolerable and the absolutely u.	DAFOE 260:3
twelvemonth t. after The seven days	MUIR 624:23	modern democracy is a t.	MAIL 560:44	U. Lightness of Being	KUND 500:38
twenties dead by their late t.	GRAV 383:36	slow t. of moonlight	CRANE 253:57	**unbecoming** nothing more u.	CONG 240:36
twentieth horror of the T. Century	MAIL 560:56	struggled against t.	TUTU 901:25	u. for a cardinal	JOHN 456:77
t. will be happy	HUGO 437:87	Taxation…is t.	OTIS 656:92	**unbelief** Because of your u.	BIBLE 118:9
twentieth-century t.-c. Russia	HELL 408:46	t. begins	PITT 679:6	Blind u. is sure to err	COWP 250:86
twenty t. of t. years of life	SHAK 777:30	t. of conscious thought	BEEC 73:97	gained…by our u.	BROW 168:39
first t. years are the longest	SOUT 835:54	T. of Distance	BLAI 137:44	help thou mine u.	BIBLE 120:59
first t. years…still growing	THOM 886:73	t. of 'the rat race'	THOM 886:87	help thou my u.	FORS 345:45
love…means t. things	BENN 81:62	T. sets up…echo-chamber	CHAT 216:54	u., in denying them	EMER 324:74
one of the t.	SHAK 769:5	until this t. be over-past	BOOK 149:20	u. of what is false	MACD 550:49
T. Thousand Thieves	JOYCE 470:39	worst sort of t.	BURKE 175:31	**unbelievers** money…has no u.	GAUT 361:7
T. Volume Suicide Note	BARA 63:41	yoke of t.	PITT 680:12	**un-birthday** u.-b. present	CARR 205:9
T. will not come again	HOUS 431:34	**tyrant** by force or like a t.	PASC 667:84	**unborn** possible to talk to the u.	BARZ 67:38
twenty-four then we shall be t.-f.	HOUS 432:63	t. has in common	BROD 160:35	Ventriloquizing for the u.	GRAV 382:22
truth t.-f. times a second	GODA 374:32	t. spell has bound me	BRON 161:73	**uncertain** u. business of war	GERB 364:64
twice gives the poor man t. as much	PUBL 699:65	t., t. Jealousy	DRYD 303:27	U., coy, and hard to please	SCOTT 752:25
victory is t. itself	SHAK 773:15	vengeful t. stricken	SULL 859:80	**uncertainties** capable of being in u.	KEATS 475:75
twice-told tedious as a t.-t. tale	SHAK 768:45	**tyrants** abject intercourse between t.		**uncertainty** distribution of u.	STEIN 845:78
Twickenham T.…happy places	THOR 889:53	and slaves	GOLD 376:94	tolerance as a u.	BURKE 176:63
twigs man bent some t.	RUDO 730:35	all men would be t.	ADAMS 4:71	u.? Even ignorance?	NIET 638:6
twilight grey t. poured	TENN 870:96	As many councillors, so many t.	SALV 741:96	**uncharitableness** malice, and all u.	BOOK 146:47
in the grey t.	YEATS 965:9	barbarity of t.	SMITH 830:46	**uncivilized** very u. to invade	HUNT 440:33
lie…is a beautiful t.	CAMUS 196:99	blood of patriots and t.	JEFF 454:22	**uncle** her u. once taught her	HEAN 405:79
pilots of the purple t.	TENN 871:17	Rebellion against t.	DAVI 266:13	Mine u.?	SHAK 781:62
Suspicions…fly by t.	BACON 52:18	stuff of which t. are made	BEAV 71:24	My u. was famous	SPEN 837:9
T. and evening bell	TENN 879:6	t. and sensualists are…right	WOLL 953:88		

unclean

real live nephew of my U. Sam's	COHAN 234:93	no occasion to exert his u.	SMITH 828:89	**unhappiness** cause of man's u.	PASC 667:73
she wanted U. Tom	LEE 519:97	pains toward creating u.	NEWM 634:43	loyalty we all feel to u.	GREE 386:8
U. Matthew was saying	MITF 610:56	passeth all u.	BOOK 147:75	Man's u....comes of his greatness	CARL 200:98
u. who could never walk down	HOME 425:98	patient, sardonic u.	LESS 523:93	**unhappy** each u. family	TOLS 894:51
unclean all as an u. thing	BIBLE 110:7	pleasing to...the u.	ADDI 7:36	guy gets too complicated he's u.	CHAN 213:81
man of u. lips	BIBLE 107:55	presume yourself ignorant of his u.	COLE 236:43	if it makes you so u.	CARR 204:95
u. shall not pass	BIBLE 108:77	problem of u. the world	POPP 689:60	instinct for being u.	SAKI 739:60
unclubbable very u. man	JOHN 461:7	reputation of u.	DRYD 300:39	keeps the u. from thinking	DIBD 276:30
uncomfortable when he is only u.	SHAW 807:25	satisfied with not u.	DAWK 266:21	making one another u.	MENC 587:9
when it hardens does it become u.	ANGE 19:92	the limits of u.	DAWK 267:23	never as u. as one thinks	LARO 510:2
uncommitted live free and u.	THOR 888:36	too much u.	GOLD 375:78	some should be u.	JOHN 463:50
uncommon u. abilities	BAGE 55:80	u. can intuit nothing	KANT 473:18	speak when she is u.?	SMITH 830:40
very u. cook	SAKI 739:65	u. unto the simple	BIBLE 103:29	These u. people	SWIFT 862:47
unconceptualisable concrete and u.	KELM 479:67	with all thy getting get u.	BIBLE 104:54	unhappiest moment of the u. man	SCHO 749:57
unconcern looks with u.	JOHN 460:63	woman of mean u.	AUST 45:54	**unhealthy** u. for want of air	DICK 281:57
unconcerned Thou u. canst hear	POPE 687:98	women's...u. is freer and sharper	CHRI 223:47	**unheard** those u. Are sweeter	KEATS 478:36
unconscious u.....interpreter—in the eye	BRON 161:63	**understatement** That is an u.	SAMU 741:2	**unholy** Refrain from the u. pleasure	BELL 76:50
u. in us warns us	MOND 612:98	**understood** have ye not u.	BIBLE 109:84	sights u., Find out	MILT 597:41
u. unity with life	MILL 594:80	life must be u. backwards	KIER 485:4	**unicorn** Lion and the U....fighting	CARR 205:15
unconventional completely u. life	BIRD 136:8	never u. what music was	FAURE 331:49	rarer than the u.	JONG 466:31
uncouple consciously u.	PALT 662:79	no adolescent...wants to be u.	FRY 354:42	u. and lion wild	SHAK 762:96
uncouth Nothing...more u.	DISR 288:65	**understudies** slaughtered by their u.	STOP 855:16	**uniform** gaunt u.	ADAMS 4:73
U. unkist, said...Chaucer	SPEN 838:17	**undertaker** greeting...give an u.	BALD 57:26	good u. must work its way	DICK 278:59
undecided five who are u.	STEN 847:7	**undertaking** no such u.	CHAM 212:66	Should be more u.	HOOD 426:21
undeniable u. pretensions	PITT 679:10	prepared to join...the u.	MILL 592:15	talent like a u.	AUDEN 43:84
under-belly u.-b. of the Axis	CHUR 226:97	prosecution of any u.	JOHN 459:56	u. 'e wore	KIPL 489:90
undercurrent u. of emotion	UPDI 906:37	**undertakings** series of u.	SART 745:75	**uniformity** manageable u.	HUXL 442:97
undercurrents imperceptible u.	CUOMO 258:80	will to desperate u.	SHAK 781:73	u. of their means	FUSE 356:92
u., drifting, waiting	MORG 619:30	**undervalue** conspiracy to u. v. them	JAMES 450:36	**uniforms** buried in their u.	DOSP 294:86
u. of everlasting murmur	RUSK 733:94	**underwater** u. hazards	MORT 621:66	**unimaginable** nothing was u.	DIDI 286:83
underdog can't teach an u.	STEV 851:18	**underwear** in the rain in your u.	BRADY 155:52	**unimpeachable** u. orthodoxy	RAHN 705:36
on the side of the u.	PALEY 661:51	like...skid-marked u.	COUP 248:32	**uninformed** most unlearned and u.	AUST 46:71
underdogs among the u.	WAUGH 924:82	u. first, last and all the time	BREC 157:90	**uninstructed** plain to u. people	HUXL 443:11
under-dressed If you are u.-d.	RICE 713:88	Wearing u. is as formal	HEMI 410:96	**unintended** The law of u. consequences	FERG 333:81
undergarments old-fashioned u.	LEWIS 527:55	**underwhelmed** u. by the prospect	JAY 453:5	**union** impossible u.	ELIOT 320:79
undergraduate first modern u.	LEVE 525:18	**underwood** green u. and cover	SWIN 863:83	National U. of Mineworkers	MACM 556:73
undergraduates with the u.	HAZL 403:38	**underwrite** u. it with their lives	MILL 594:75	Only through their u.	KANT 473:18
underground best part of him is u.	ANON 27:21	**undisciplined** U. squads of emotion	ELIOT 320:66	proper u. of gin and vermouth	DE 275:9
Give me an u. laboratory	PERE 674:17	**undismayed** go forth to meet him u.	SHER 818:6	protesting against u.	GRAT 382:14
might well be u.	GILB 369:60	**undoing** u. of those human rights	KENN 481:3	remain in u. with England	SCOTT 754:76
not rest from taking u.	FRAME 346:75	**undone** John Donne...U.-d.	DONNE 292:48	Sail on, O U.	LONG 535:27
underlings we are u.	SHAK 776:9	leave great things u.	GLAS 374:44	u., before his citizenship	LEWIS 526:54
underlip u. protruded a little	MANS 567:99	Woe is me! for I am u.	BIBLE 107:55	u. between a man and a woman	BENE 79:16
underpants only has a pair of u. on	WENG 931:51	**undoomed** u. warrior	ANON 20:29	u. is perfect	DICK 284:58
word means u.	MURR 627:80	**undulate** forms of pleasure u.	FUSE 356:94	U. to be dissolved	LINC 529:4
underprivileged u. was over-used	FEIF 331:55	**undying** his passion is Infinite, u.	PARK 664:13	U. which never strikes	HICKS 417:48
understand Adults never u. anything	SAINT 738:35	**uneasy** no u. feeling	JOHN 461:90	u. with the universe	RUSS 734:23
believe so that I may u.	ANSE 29:70	U. lies the head	SHAK 772:85	war...which saved the U.	WILS 949:79
can't make somebody u.	GORE 379:60	**uneatable** full pursuit of the u.	WILDE 941:84	**unionism** u. is stronger than creed	LAWS 514:95
contempt for anything he didn't u.	WOOL 956:43	**unemployed** u....do not have the skills	CALL 192:28	**unions** aggregations of trade u.	DOSP 294:86
dogs who don't u.	CALV 193:35	**unemployment** creating u.	ROBI 718:78	Hitler attacked the u.	NIEM 637:91
don't believe...won't u.	AUGU 44:34	cure u. before Keynes	ROBI 718:95	**unique** Murder is a u. crime	JAMES 451:59
don't think I u. people	FORS 344:34	need be no more u.	KEYN 484:80	sonatas of Mozart are u.	SCHN 748:46
don't u. each other	DIDI 286:88	reduce u.	HEATH 405:85	u. to the level of the herd	MILL 594:84
hard to u.	GORB 378:46	u. only looks good	PASS 668:97	**uniqueness** poet reminds...u.	COUS 248:40
language I don't u.	APPL 30:91	**unexamined** u. life is not worth	PLATO 681:44	**unison** u. with this order	KANT 470:90
may not be made to u. it	CONF 240:17	u. life is not worth	SOCR 833:99	**unit** true middle-class u.	SHAW 808:48
people...who u. pictures	KIPL 490:96	**unexpected** By how much u.	SHAK 768:52	**united** country needs to be u.	JOHN 457:6
really don't u.	KENN 481:22	expect the u.	HERA 412:37	reminded him of Sheffield U.	HATT 400:82
Sex...I really don't u.	SALI 740:73	**unexplored** hitherto u. country	SHIP 818:15	u. by nothing	TOLS 894:53
shewed unto thee than men u.	BIBLE 113:82	**unexpressive** the chaste, and u. she	SHAK 779:87	u. in one person	HESS 417:34
striven...to u. them	SPIN 840:69	**unfairnesses** u. that were explained	GALL 358:43	**United Kingdom** Ireland and...U. K.	LLOY 533:77
talent is to u. a man	HUGO 437:77	**unfaithful** Confidence in an u. man	BIBLE 105:94	**United Nations** If the U. N. once	EISE 314:1
u. himself	KAZIN 474:52	ways of being u.	WYLIE 964:9	Peoples of the U. N.	UNIT 905:9
u. that a man	TROL 898:39	**unfashionable** Fashion is...u.	CHAN 214:98	The U. N. cannot do anything	OBRI 645:65
u. that you experience	KAFKA 472:4	u. is what other people wear	WILDE 942:12	turn the U. N. back into a talking shop	BLAIR 138:63
u. thy kisses	SHAK 771:51	**unfeathered** u. two-legged thing	DRYD 302:73	U. N. is not in a position	EDEN 311:31
understood as to u.	FRAN 347:99	**unfed** calls us, still u.	KIPL 490:9	When we started the U. N.	HARR 399:59
we could not u. him	WITT 951:29	**unfeeling** u. for his own	GRAY 383:48	**United States** defeat the U. S. aggressors	MAO 569:36
what they u. not	SHEL 816:53	**unfit** picked from the u.	HARK 398:35	few problems...the U.S. can solve	CLIN 231:36
When I do not u.	SOPH 834:31	u. for a nation of shopkeepers	SMITH 828:87	friendship of the U. S.	GEOR 364:48
wise enough to u.	SCHW 750:90	u. for power	FOOT 342:82	have our U. S.-mania	RODO 721:51
Women...we should not u.	CONG 240:45	**unfitness** personal u.	GLAD 373:36	In the U. S....more space	STEIN 845:65
understanding among men of u.	PLATO 681:47	**unfittest** survival of the u.	SUMN 859:82	In the U. S. there's a Puritan ethic	ECO 310:15
capable of u. each other	BERL 84:49	**unforeseen** contingent and the u.	FISH 337:62	lies about the U. S.	STEV 850:3
declare, if thou hast u.	BIBLE 98:13	**unforgetful** teach the u. to forget?	ROSS 726:62	loyalty to the U. S.	ROOS 725:31
experience and u. of life	MILL 593:60	**unforgiveness** an alp of u.	PLOM 682:72	mental illness of the U. S.	ATWO 41:36
eye of my u.	JULI 470:40	**unfruitful** he becometh u.	BIBLE 117:91	no major institution in the U. S.	FRIE 351:71
find you an u.	JOHN 464:94	unwarranted as they are u.	AYER 45:7	politics in the U. S.	TOCQ 892:29
for the clearer u. of English	WHAR 934:11	**ungartered** U., and down-gyvèd	SHAK 781:72	President of the U. S.	UPDI 905:20
for thy more sweet u.	SHAK 763:7	**ungodly** counsel of the u.	BIBLE 99:25	problem with the U. S. economy	KRUG 500:23
good u. with a new mistress	ETHE 327:44	the hope of the u.	BIBLE 112:77	prominent as the U. S.	MUNCH 625:42
in length of days u.	BIBLE 98:3	u. in great power	BOOK 149:13	so close to the U. S.	DIAZ 276:27
lack of u.	BIER 134:75	**ungracious** as some u. pastors do	SHAK 781:48	stand shoulder-to-shoulder with the	
lean not unto thine own u.	BIBLE 104:52	**unhandsome** she were u.	SHAK 773:22	U. S. of America	BLAIR 138:59
learn u., and to give answer	BIBLE 113:86	**unhanged** not three good men u.	SHAK 771:45	test case of U. S. capacity	MCNA 557:87
more u. than all my teachers	BIBLE 103:26	**unhappiest** u. moment	SCHO 749:57	there's the U. S. of America	OBAMA 643:19

unutterable

The U. S. today is an empire	FERG	333:78
the US edition of Time	BRYS	170:10
U. S. imperialism	MAO	569:33
U. S....is warm-hearted	FERB	332:67
U. S. and the British	CHUR	250:8
U. S., democratic and various	UPDI	906:38
U. S....global gendarme	MCNA	557:88
U. S....greatest poem	WHIT	937:88
U. S. is the best and fairest	BUSH	182:98
U. S. is the biggest business	ROGE	722:70
U. S. is...the great melting pot	MARS	575:65
U. S. is the only country	ROGE	723:80
U. S. must be neutral	WILS	949:77
U. S. of America	ROOS	724:96
U. S....the Jew among the nations	FERB	332:67
U. S. to the Monroe Doctrine	ROOS	724:16
U. S. will never again seek	WILS	949:76
Vice-President of the U. S.	GARN	360:77
women in the U. S.	BRYS	171:11
wouldn't have stood a chance in the U. S.	WOLFE	953:83
unity dwell together in u.!	BIBLE	103:40
rich, dark, organic u.	HOMA	425:92
unconscious u. with life	MILL	594:80
universal All partial evil, u. good	POPE	687:79
and u. peace lie	TENN	872:30
appetite, an u. wolf	SHAK	786:26
books...of u. appeal	FORD	343:91
'He never listens' is u.	MACK	553:8
if it is not u.	TOLK	893:44
[man] is a u. machine	REDT	709:25
maxim should become a u. law	KANT	473:23
mirror of the u. elements	STEI	845:58
old u. truths	FAUL	331:35
particular and u.	BERG	83:23
reach the u.	SART	744:65
u. as sea sickness	SHAW	807:28
u. darkness buries all	POPE	689:48
u. frame is without a mind	BACON	51:78
u. languages: love, music and sports	MOSES	622:79
u. pollution and u. frustration	ILLI	445:21
u. sickness	TRIL	897:14
u. suffrage prevails	PARE	663:89
u. test of travel	GELL	363:35
war tends to become u.	DU	305:70
universals Myth deals in false u.	CART	206:38
universe a little bit of the u.	BANKS	62:24
black hole of the u.	UMAS	905:2
boundless u.	TENN	872:25
by which the u. is regulated	PAINE	660:38
cement of the u.	SELF	756:10
circumscribe This u.	MILT	605:30
cold reaches of the u.	KENN	481:8
come to esteem the u.	FONT	341:74
corner of the u.	HUXL	442:85
cover the u. with mud	FORS	344:39
entire u....is Pure Accident	OATES	643:7
entities of which the u. is	KUHN	500:37
explain the u.	BERL	84:47
faintly through the u.	JOYCE	470:18
galaxies populating the u.	BRAUN	157:81
hell of a good u. next door	CUMM	258:68
In this u.	WORD	956:52
kingdom is as wide as the u.	FLAU	339:26
laws and nature of the U.	HARDY	397:25
Life, the U. and Everything	ADAMS	4:76
man said to the u.	CRANE	253:74
many wonderful things...in the u.	COLT	238:86
measure of the u.	SHEL	814:15
Miss U.'s buttocks	BENE	79:13
mock the u.	ARET	20:17
no intention in the u.	MONOD	612:3
no other u. except the human u.	SART	745:76
Not for all the u. contains	OCON	646:83
nothing dead in this U.	CARL	201:7
nothing in the whole u.	OVID	657:21
nothing is accidental in the u.	OATES	643:7
of her myriad u.	TENN	877:68
only objects in the material u.	FORS	345:44
On the stage of the u.	LAFO	504:61
otherwise kindly u.	HARDY	397:8
phenomenon of [the] u.	PEAR	671:56
plural, like the u.	PESS	675:32
protons in the u.	EDDI	311:27
Put back Thy u.	JONES	465:17
stole a page from the U.!	MARTI	576:70
sweet winds of the u.	MACD	550:46
tinker with the u.	MILL	593:60
transitory in the u.	GIRA	372:24
u. appears as an infinite	MUIR	624:26
u. had a beginning	MILL	592:10
u. is arranged like a cithera	HONO	426:16
u. is Copernican, not Ptolemaic	PHIL	677:56
u. is not only queerer	HALD	392:23
u. which philosophy contemplates	RUSS	734:23
unlike any other thing...in the u.	STEI	845:80
utmost limits of the u.	HUME	438:94
vast order of the u.	PAGE	659:16
Why does the u. go to...the bother of existing?	HAWK	401:89
Wisdom and Spirit of the u.!	WORD	957:69
universities As to our u.	LODGE	534:1
black market u.	ZELD	969:4
critics are like American u.	ALBEE	11:28
escape our u.	OPPE	652:87
u., and the public charities	MILL	591:4
university critic to the u.	BRAD	155:37
dismissed from a German u.	TILL	891:16
fools at a u.	GERH	365:69
no u. could pay	STIG	854:97
of that famous u.	HAZL	403:38
servant to be bred at an U.	CONG	241:48
this ancient U.	HOUS	432:61
true U....is a collection of books	CARL	201:34
u. has failed you	GOHE	375:73
U. of Oxford	GIBB	366:98
u. of Oxtail	JOYCE	470:28
U. should be a place of light	DISR	288:60
U. where he didn't inhale	DOWD	296:29
u. where...the Jews are hosts	SACH	736:3
unjust abhor...the u.	CURZ	260:5
Every u. man	PLATO	681:53
u. in the least	BIBLE	121:95
unjustified course was u.	HIRO	419:73
unkillable filthy, sturdy, u. infants	POUND	691:93
unkind Midlands...sodden and u.	BELL	77:68
None...deformed but the u.	SHAK	786:21
position is admittedly u.	STEV	851:24
Thou art not so u.	SHAK	779:84
u. or irreverential word	HAWT	402:17
when givers prove u.	SHAK	783:8
unkindled u., uncoffined	BYRON	188:72
unkindness by my u. shaken	SHAK	802:82
unkist Uncouth u., said...Chaucer	SPEN	838:17
unknown as One u.	SCHW	751:94
bird rising, unnamed, u.	REID	710:44
holier lot to be u.	HOPK	428:83
let nothing...be u. to you	RABE	704:22
route towards the u.	HUGO	438:88
She lived u.	WORD	957:62
she's also very u.	MIRR	609:18
To that u. and silent shore	LAMB	505:80
tread safely into the u.	HASK	400:81
uncertain, u., arbitrary rule	LOCKE	533:87
u. Prime Minister	ASQU	38:85
U., unkist, and lost	CHAU	216:58
ways that are still largely u.	REYES	712:69
unknowns there are known u.	RUMS	731:41
unlearned most u. and uninformed	AUST	46:71
what we have u.	TWAIN	903:85
unlessoned u. girl, unschooled	SHAK	770:6
unlucky U. the land	BREC	157:91
u. to sound off	ICHI	444:11
unmarried paid to them while u.	JOHN	462:45
u. guys in New York suck	BUSH	184:52
U. men are best friends	BACON	51:73
unmask u. her beauty to the moon	SHAK	781:47
unmeaning u. thing it is	HAZL	403:44
unmentionable Everything was u.	DIDI	286:83
unmourned are all u. and unknown	HORA	430:12
unmoved u. this place leaves one	SNYD	832:93
U. though witlings sneer	JOHN	459:39
unmusical Nothing can be more u.	DISR	288:65
no...u. person	HENZE	412:23
unnatural both equally u.	GRAT	382:14
everlastingly being u.	MITC	609:38
foul, strange, and u.	SHAK	781:61
nothing so u. as the commonplace	DOYLE	297:53
U., he called them	SHAR	806:72
unnebulous u. train of words	BISH	136:26
unnecessary eliminate the u.	HOFF	422:31
often utterly u.	TOLS	894:53
thou u. letter	SHAK	792:97
to do the u.	HARK	398:35
uncomfortable, u., and...useless	STEV	851:24
vain, u. things are men	ROCH	719:15
unnoble most u. swerving	SHAK	794:67
unnoticed that u. and that necessary	ATWO	41:43
unofficial u. magic becomes stronger	REED	710:34
unorthodox loopholes for an u.	ORWE	653:22
unpack u. my heart with words	SHAK	782:2
unpalatable disastrous and the u.	GALB	357:18
unparalleled lass u.	SHAK	795:95
u. elsewhere in our culture	SHAP	805:68
unpleasant enough u. things face...is so peculiarly u.	RENO	711:59
	SNOW	832:78
How u. to meet Mr Eliot!	ELIOT	319:49
u. way of saying the truth	HELL	408:39
unplumbed u., salt, estranging sea	ARNO	34:82
unpolished ignorant and u. people	DICK	283:17
unpopular safe to be u.	STEV	851:7
unpredictable never aim to be u.	JAY	453:4
unpremeditated u. lay	SCOTT	752:10
unprincipled sold by the u.	CAPP	197:32
unprofitable most idle and u.	GIBB	366:98
weary, stale, flat, and u.	SHAK	780:43
unprovoked It seemed u.	STEV	854:97
unquestionable one u. truth	TOLS	894:53
unquestioned u. law	WHAR	934:11
unravel can devise, another can u.	WRIS	963:80
unreal gunfire...sounded u.	USTI	906:46
this story is u.	PACH	658:1
unreality general atmosphere of u.	QUEN	702:5
unreason woman...element of u.	WRIG	962:63
unreasonable u. one persists	SHAW	808:49
unremarked legion of the u.	SAFI	737:22
unrequited Self-love...often u.	POWE	693:43
unrest root of the social u.	LECO	518:80
u. which men miscall delight	SHEL	815:40
unrighteousness cleanse...all u.	BIBLE	130:77
mammon of u.	BIBLE	121:94
unromantic u. poet	FROST	352:9
unsaid that which is u.	ANOU	28:65
unsatiable be not u.	BIBLE	113:4
unsatisfied leaves one u.	WILDE	940:69
unscathed guilty never escape u.	BAIL	55:85
unscotch if you u. us	SCOTT	754:79
unscrew u....from the practical words	WAITS	916:8
unscrupulous most u. kidney	FRY	353:28
unsearchable u. dispose Of highest	MILT	608:4
unseen all-seeing but u.	BYRON	188:65
Greet the u.	BROW	169:86
O friend u., unborn, unknown	FLEC	340:30
Of u. things above	HANK	395:81
unselfish u....are not the leaders	CONR	245:82
unselfishness u. of an oyster	SAKI	739:62
unsex u. me here	SHAK	796:15
unshackle u....transient desires	EINS	313:76
unshorn presents the god u.	HERR	415:9
unsightly grotesque, if not u.	VEBL	910:45
unsinkable u. air-craft carrier	MACA	544:6
unsophisticated u. can really go for	AMIS	16:32
unsorted u. stuff	GOLD	375:75
unsound notoriously u.	HOLM	424:65
unspeakable inedible raised to the u.	BASK	67:50
u. in full pursuit	WILDE	941:84
unspiritual conditions that are u.	MARX	578:24
unspontaneous I am u.	KENN	480:94
unspotted keep himself u.	BIBLE	130:52
unstable U. as water	BIBLE	93:49
unstoned left a turn u.	WIMP	949:88
unsubduable u. country	GILL	370:80
unsympathetic u. as butterflies	ELIOT	315:19
untalented product of the u.	CAPP	197:32
untell To u. the days	HEYW	417:43
unthinking Laughing...u. time	DRYD	304:56
painful process of U.	CUMM	257:50
untimely U. ripped	SHAK	798:77
untired against the new and u.	LINC	529:7
untouched expect to be u. by madness	BELL	77:77
untranslatable I too am u.	WHIT	937:96
untrodden among the u. ways	WORD	957:62
untrue blaming mirrors for being u.	LAFO	503:49
man who's u. to his wife	AUDEN	43:98
untruth torment of the night's u.	DANI	262:31
transfigured them into U.	LARK	509:81
why not rather u.?	NIET	638:6
untruths they have spoken u.	SHAK	774:55
untwist Not u....these last strands	HOPK	429:88
unusual moved by what is not u.	ELIOT	316:52
unutterable looked u. things	THOM	887:1
present u. things	THOR	888:23

unvisionary 1324

unvisionary u. language of farm ENGLE 326:16	skilled u. of blunt objects PEAR 671:58	v. man,' said she SPEN 839:47
unwanted feeling of being u. THER 882:81	u. alone that sanctifies expense POPE 686:63	V. matter is worse BACON 49:24
unwarrantable any u. belief RICH 714:15	U. every man SHAK 782:98	V. thy onset! ARNO 35:24
unwarranted u. as they are unfruitful AYER 47:3	u. him as he uses thee SHAK 791:57	v. to mislike the current fashion FULL 355:86
unwell begins to feel u. KIPL 489:77	u. of a new-born child? FRAN 348:20	v., unnecessary things are men ROCH 719:15
unwholesome u. in their thoughts SHAK 784:52	u. of travelling JOHN 465:8	youth is v. COLE 235:34
unwieldiness cumbersome u. DONNE 292:45	value in u. SMITH 827:78	**vainer** role of the critic…is v. DIDE 285:68
unwilling group of the u. HARK 398:35	**used** let them be well u. SHAK 782:97	**valanced** Thy face is v. SHAK 782:95
u. or unable WILL 946:15	shouldn't be much u. HOLM 424:72	**vale** after I depart this v. MENC 586:85
unwise sight of the u. BIBLE 112:74	**useful** both viable and u. HAYEK 402:26	cool sequestered v. of life GRAY 384:72
unworldliness out of u. MCCA 547:88	returns home wise and u. BELL 76:44	death's dark v. SCOT 754:85
unworthy opinion…is u. of him BACON 52:97	science is said to be u. HARDY 396:98	i' th' midst a horrid v. MILT 602:82
U. was what he did AESC 8:76	To be u.…hideous BAUD 69:83	Saimear's green v. MCCA 547:74
unwritten A book u. HARR 399:53	what is u. to oneself SPIN 840:78	shady sadness of a v. KEATS 477:28
unwrung our withers are u. SHAK 783:28	**useless** as u.…as possible GALT 359:56	v. in whose bosom MOORE 617:99
up cannot bear levelling up JOHN 461:1	let me not live to be u.! WESL 932:69	v. of soul-making KEATS 476:92
curtain was up KAUF 474:37	Protestations…are always u. COBB 233:74	v. of tears FERRE 334:98
more up and down than sideways HEMI 409:59	speech they know to be u. ELIOT 315:38	v. of Tempe RUSK 734:19
press the up button 50 336:42	wars are u. RICH 713:98	V., the three lone weirs ARNO 35:16
Up, all of us PEPYS 674:1	**uses** all the u. of this world! SHAK 780:38	violet-embroidered v. MILT 598:70
Up was the heartening EMPS 326:10	Usher's Well wife at U. W. BALL 60:82	**Valentine** Slander V. SHAK 759:69
UP YOURS DELORS SUN 859:85	**usquabae** Wi' u., we'll face BURNS 179:27	**vales** Making all the v. rejoice? BLAKE 139:86
upbringing result of my u. DYSON 309:59	**USSR** Back in the U. LENN 522:55	o'er v. and hills WORD 960:24
the u. a nun would envy ORTON 652:3	for the U. to reject Communism KHRU 485:90	**valet** to his very v. seemed a hero BYRON 189:85
upbringings u. that were so clean COUP 248:32	**usury** u. age-old POUND 691:4	**valiant** As he was v., I honour him SHAK 777:26
upgrowth germ and first u. KING 488:55	**utensil** every particle and u. SHAK 785:90	makes e'en the v. more brave DIBD 276:30
upharsin Mene, Mene, Tekel, U. BIBLE 111:42	**utilitarian** our u. world STARK 843:22	Ring in the v. man TENN 875:96
upholding u. all things by the word BIBLE 129:33	**utility** foundation of morals, U. MILL 591:8	v. and martial BACON 52:17
upholstery dogs had eaten the u. PERE 674:22	immediate practical u. HELM 408:51	v., but not too venturous LYLY 543:81
faded u. of tears BROY 169:88	neither gain nor loss of u. JEVO 455:52	v. man and true TENN 879:99
uplands thrilling over her u. DAY 267:36	u. of some particular object SMITH 827:78	v.…taste of death but once SHAK 777:21
upon Either with it or u. it ANON 20:17	view to future u. JEVO 455:53	**validity** If…God has any v. BALD 57:21
upper Have still the u. hand COWA 249:55	**utopia** u. remains forever closed MAIL 560:52	**Valium** Cricket is baseball on V. WILL 944:75
no longer u. classes TOCQ 892:26	view as an infernal U. LEWIS 527:74	toothless terrier on V. SIKO 821:67
uprising knowest…mine u. BIBLE 103:43	whatever U. of human virtue HAWT 402:4	**valley** bicker down a v. TENN 876:37
uproar amidst that joy and u. CAMP 194:66	**utopian** U.…romance WEBB 925:9	Every v. shall be exalted BIBLE 108:79
little u. as a jellyfish WODE 951:35	**Utopias** end all the static U. INGE 445:29	Green was my v. LLEW 532:63
set all the city on an u. BIBLE 124:88	**utter** ache to u. SAND 741:12	hill can't be a v. CARR 204:92
upset not u., are you? BANKS 62:18	Thou wilt not u. SHAK 771:43	in some such v. SHIP 818:15
upside autocracy turned u. down HERZ 416:23	What I think, I u. SHAK 799:92	journeys through the v. LEE 519:98
turned the world u. down BIBLE 124:89	**utterance** u. of the early Gods KEATS 477:31	love is of the v. TENN 873:51
upstairs labour going u. MUNDY 625:43	**utterances** by his own u. PARN 665:47	paweth in the v. BIBLE 99:18
u. into the world CONG 240:42	Deathbed u. PLOUT 682:74	V. and lowland, sing! OAKL 643:5
upstart curse…upon the sleek u. RANS 707:69	**uttered** u. it a hundred times HOLM 424:63	v. between Buxton RUSK 734:19
u. crow GREE 386:33	**U-turn** catchphrase, the U.-t. THAT 881:58	v. is his golden cup MERE 588:38
upwardly-mobile all pigs are u.-m. THOM 887:90	**Uzziah** year that king U. died BIBLE 107:54	v. of Death TENN 875:41
uranium nuclear reaction in u. EINS 313:78		v. of Death TENN 875:12
urban all u. and rural sounds LAMB 505:4	**V**	v. of…death BIBLE 100:45
Boston has become U. Renewal MAIL 560:55		v. sheep are fatter PEAC 671:54
incomplete in the u. compound MCLU 556:55	**vacancy** aught of blinder v. WORD 961:35	v. which was full of bones BIBLE 111:35
urchin ribald, inspired u. DAY 267:38	chaos of v. DELA 271:32	world a v. so sweet MOORE 617:99
urge absence of the u. to create MAMET 563:31	next v. for God CIAR 226:23	**valleys** below them in the v. TENN 870:92
something other than the u. SAND 742:35	v. which occupies the space TOOLE 894:60	descend into the v. again LLOY 533:72
U. that impels women THUR 891:95	which but for v. SHAK 794:56	listening V. hear BLAKE 139:79
urgency fierce u. of now KING 487:28	**vacant** v. into the v. ELIOT 320:62	Piping down the v. wild BLAKE 139:85
Life…having a sense of u. BURT 181:73	**vacation** v., or a truce WORD 961:38	stranger strayed into…their v. MONT 613:17
urgent assurance…that nothing was u. ACHE 2:29	**vacations** v. of the flesh TZARA 904:15	That v., groves, hills MARL 574:41
Egyptians were u. upon the people BIBLE 93:61	**vaccinated** v. with a phonograph GOLD 377:22	thou who passest through our v. BLAKE 139:81
urgings felt sexual u. COND 240:15	**vacuum** cannot work in a v. ROGE 722:67	Ye v. low where MILT 599:90
Uriah Set ye U. in the forefront BIBLE 96:44	nature hates a v. WILL 945:93	**valour** better part of v. SHAK 772:68
Uricon ashes under U. HOUS 431:48	They are void within a v. JOHN 457:89	contemplation he and v. formed MILT 604:99
Urim U. and the Thummim BIBLE 94:68	v. cleaner grazes over the carpet RAINE 705:38	fame, of v. MARL 572:3
urinal burnt match skating in a u. CRANE 253:69	v. that fills v. GALB 357:27	ideals, the v. and the sacrifices EISE 314:8
urine Cannot contain their u. SHAK 770:10	**vacuums** role is…filling v. CART 206:50	possess only strength and v. BRON 161:62
faintly scented u. JOYCE 470:29	**vagaries** correct the v. KEYN 484:78	report of v. SHAK 786:14
red wine of Shiraz into u. BLIX 142:61	v. of butlers ACHE 2:30	So full of v. SHAK 804:24
u. dump at sunset SCHW 750:93	**vague** woman's brain: v., slippery RICH 714:17	wonder at the desperate v. JONS 467:51
urn angel watching an u. TENN 875:18	**vailèd** with thy v. lids SHAK 780:34	**valuable** everything dear and v. PITT 680:11
bubbling and loud-hissing u. COWP 251:19	**vain** a' is done in v. BURNS 180:58	freedom is…supremely v. HUXL 442:95
dust falls to the u. VAUG 909:36	Call it not v. SCOTT 752:17	v. or even earnest THOR 888:32
Lean on a garden u. ELIOT 317:74	Destroy his fib…in v. POPE 687:99	**valuation** bias of v. KEYN 484:78
storied u. GRAY 384:67	full as v. DRYD 301:58	superstitious v. of Europe JAMES 450:34
u. Of bitter prophecy SHEL 811:58	head grown grey in v. SHEL 815:40	**value** absolute v. GREE 386:12
urs strew your pathway…dreadful u. HOLM 423:61	He is so v. DISR 288:63	any v. at all in the world LACL 503:53
us before they get at us GRACE 380:83	he seeks in v. HELM 408:51	consciousness of human v. DEWEY 276:19
usage dictionary of popular u. GREE 386:17	imagine a v. thing? BIBLE 99:26	Diamonds are of most precious v. WEBS 926:42
usages statutes or u. therein obtaining MILL 591:93	In v.—always in v. DAVI 267:67	economic v. of…women GILM 371:93
usances my moneys and my u. SHAK 769:85	in v. decry'd and curst POPE 688:29	enhance its v. MANN 566:84
use consumed by u. GILL 371:88	name of the Lord thy God in v. BIBLE 94:66	increase in v. of the world MARX 578:25
designed its u. PALEY 661:57	nothing is in v. HERB 413:54	lie…shows the v. of each object CAMUS 196:96
for the u. of his power HOBB 420:99	of Amber Snuff-box justly v. POPE 685:41	loses in descriptive v. LEGER 519:7
how to make the best u. of it SIMO 822:78	role of the author is v. enough DIDE 285:68	lose twenty-five percent of their v. STEN 846:2
keener with constant u. IRVI 447:57	Say not…the wounds are v. CLOU 232:47	maximum v. which he can consume HICKS 417:47
little u. for contraceptives SHAR 806:72	soul…made first in v. BROW 169:78	more permanent v. LAWR 514:85
no u. for the teachings KHRU 485:95	v. desire at last ROSS 726:62	no influence on the future v. JEVO 455:53
no u. save abuse SIMO 822:81	v., giddy, shallow, humorous youth SHAK 775:71	no more v. than their dress HAZL 403:82
Remains in u. with you SHAK 794:50	v. in verse SIDN 820:43	nothing has v. FORS 344:37

verse

nothing in the laws of v.	MILL 591:95
only a limited v.	ELIOT 320:59
Optimistic lies...therapeutic v.	SHAW 810:91
phonograph...commercial v.	EDIS 312:53
set a high v.	JOHN 464:83
v. depends on what is there	POUND 691:13
V....has two different meanings	SMITH 827:78
v. is not in its taste	FULB 355:62
v. is what can be counted	WEIL 928:74
v. judgments about the society	VAN 908:12
v. not a v.	KOHL 496:35
v. of a liberal education	BREW 158:4
v. of a man	ANON 26:76
v., or worth of a man	HOBB 420:99
v. upon it we do ourselves	MONT 613:11
very highest v.	RUSS 734:27
voice over wires...no practical v.	ANON 23:90
values a price for our v.	OBAMA 643:21
human imaginative v.	BRON 160:46
keep your v.	ALDA 12:47
lily-silver'd v.	POPE 689:43
sane balance of v.	POUND 692:21
the v. of art	OLSEN 650:48
v. and freedoms	THAT 881:50
v. far beyond...contracts	BROWN 164:25
v. of women differ	WOOLF 955:30
vampire like the v....dead	PATER 668:9
van Follow the v.	COLL 237:64
Vandyke V. is of the company	GAIN 357:10
vanes like beaten weather v.	CRANE 253:68
Van Gogh My V. G. is better	HAMM 394:61
vanished as rare things will, it v.	BROW 168:52
vanishest If thus thou v.	SHAK 795:94
vanitas V. vanitatum	BIBLE 133:39
vanities Guides us by v.	ELIOT 317:84
turn from these v.	BIBLE 124:86
vanity administering to the v. of others	AUST 47:85
a foolish v. to be gratified	SHER 817:95
Being an MP feeds your v.	PARR 666:52
day to find that it was v.	LAWR 514:89
drifted into sexual v.	WEBB 925:6
Envy itself, and V.	MAND 565:65
getting old was about v.	OATES 643:9
pomps and v.	BOOK 148:78
Pull down thy v.	POUND 692:24
Pull down thy v.	POUND 692:25
Pull down thy v.	POUND 692:26
speckled V. Will sicken	MILT 597:36
suppress one's v.	JAMES 449:21
v. doth very much corrupt	BAXT 69:94
V. in a newspaper man	ASSAN 39:96
v. of being seen	SMOL 831:67
v. of human hopes	JOHN 459:53
v. of person and of situation	AUST 47:86
v. of the writer	REES 710:38
v. of translation	SHEL 816:49
V. of vanities	BIBLE 105:9
V. of vanities	BIBLE 133:39
V. of vanities!	FRED 349:40
v., sets love a task	HUNT 439:27
Vanity-Fair name of V.-F.	BUNY 174:75
vanquished Macbeth...never v. be	SHAK 797:56
only Rome v. Rome	BELL 76:41
victor is often v.	SCHI 747:30
vans v. to beat the air	ELIOT 319:23
vantage from the v. point	PASS 668:97
vapour Floating, like a v.	FOST 345:55
life...even a v.	BIBLE 130:59
like v. over shrines	BROW 166:90
v. and fume	KIPL 490:94
vapours mystie v., cluddis and skyis	DUNB 306:5
pestilent congregation of v.	SHAK 782:88
v. or something worse	MONT 613:13
variable love prove likewise v.	SHAK 765:83
v. as the shade	SCOTT 752:25
variation each slight v....preserved	DARW 263:52
tunes...without any v.	DICK 280:31
varieties delineation of its v.	AUST 46:83
What v. man has found out	AUGU 44:32
variety almost endless v.	LOCKE 533:89
democracy...admits v.	FORS 345:47
Her infinite v.	SHAK 794:58
Simplicity, without v.	HOGA 422:40
V. is the soul of pleasure	BEHN 74:15
V.'s the spice of life	COWP 251:15
variousness precise account of v.	TRIL 897:13
varnishers v. and veneerers	MENC 587:14

vase like seeing a Sèvres v.	WAUGH 924:1
opaque v. fills to the brim	ROET 722:57
took murder out of the Venetian v.	CHAN 213:95
water poured into a v.	POUND 692:34
vasectomy v. of the vocal chords	ALTH 15:14
vassal God's silly v.	MELV 585:51
vassals his lithe bright v. tread	BLUN 143:73
Vassar old V. Girls	HEMI 409:63
vast wisdom, v., unwieldy	MILT 607:83
vat that it is a fermenting v.	HUNT 440:34
vatication deal much in v.	CARL 199:76
vats ate the cheeses out of the v.	BROW 167:16
minces among bad v.	THOM 884:41
spirited purple of the v.	TENN 873:51
vaudeville Terrible V.	ACE 2:19
Vaughan Here V. lies dead	SASS 746:1
vault heaven's v. should crack	SHAK 793:37
v. of the Temple of Peace	BRAM 156:57
vaunting V. aloud, but racked with	MILT 602:39
veal Bellamy's v. pies	PITT 680:15
Vega V. conspicuous overhead	AUDEN 42:73
vegetable adoption of v. diet	SHEL 812:53
Feminism...a catch-all v. drawer	PAGL 659:19
fruit Of v. gold	MILT 604:96
Mona Lisa of the v. world	HUGH 435:26
v., animal and mineral	GILB 368:39
v. love should grow	MARV 577:91
vegetables harvest...fruit and v.	MURR 627:84
without eating her v.	ALTH 15:13
your gods or your v.	GIRA 372:26
vegetarian I ate v. shepherd's pie	MELC 584:48
vegetarianism in favour of v.	INGE 445:25
vegetate v. in a village	COLT 238:85
vehicle v. for conveying ideas	MACB 546:63
v. for the thought of our day	FORD 343:93
vehicles robot v.	DAWK 266:15
veil beautiful girl in a diaphanous v.	PERE 674:17
that transparent v.	WORD 958:85
unzips the v. from beauty	WHITE 935:36
v. had been torn suddenly	MONET 612:1
v. of heaven	MARL 572:3
v. of the temple was rent	BIBLE 119:48
v. of the temple was rent	BIBLE 122:9
wrapped in a gauzy v.	SHEL 816:67
veils from the v. of the morning	YEATS 965:4
Religion blushing v.	POPE 689:47
vein not in the giving v.	SHAK 761:44
veins blood speaks to you in my v.	SHAK 770:7
bluest v. to kiss	SHAK 794:63
fear thrills through my v.	SHAK 766:8
floweth in your v.	TRAH 895:85
heats which my v. fill	DONNE 291:28
in its v. flows ink	KRAUS 499:6
love of...gardens Is running in your v.	MACK 553:10
of human v.	YEATS 967:31
v. are filled...with...carpet cleaner	CHEE 218:10
v. of rhyming mother-wits	MARL 572:94
v. that I may swim	MONT 615:51
v. that seemed to invite the lancet	SHER 817:81
velvet gold an' v.	ANON 23:87
hand of steel in a v. glove	WOOL 956:40
In v. collar-rolls	KIPL 492:59
loll on v. and satin	FRAN 348:23
v. of her paws	GRAY 383:51
veneer all fantasy and v.	GALL 358:44
veneerers varnishers and v.	MENC 587:14
venerable Beautiful city! so v.	ARNO 35:12
decrepit, without being v.	HAWT 402:10
like a v. battlewagon	TIME 891:18
Venetian plump V., fat, and lusty	FLET 341:58
vengeance but he's v. proud	SHAK 799:93
day of v. of our God	BIBLE 110:6
feeling of v.	DREN 299:2
instruments of v.	DONO 293:82
line a sudden v. waits	POPE 685:45
Tomorrow's v. on the head	SHAK 761:52
upon the Scots with a V.	FLET 340:50
V. is a personal reaction	RENO 711:50
V. is in my heart	SHAK 760:23
V. is mine	BIBLE 125:27
v. shall be taken...sevenfold	BIBLE 92:5
wreak their v.	TROL 897:35
vengeances stored v. of heaven fall	SHAK 792:1
vengefulness fainted on his v.	MERE 588:30
veni v., vidi, vici	CAES 192:14
Venice any man in all V.	SHAK 769:73
cunning whore of V.	SHAK 790:35

in V. they did not learn to draw well	VASA 909:28
Ocean's nursling, V.	SHEL 812:64
on the throat of V.	TOME 894:55
to see V., die first	DEBR 268:57
V. is like...chocolate liqueurs	CAPO 197:20
V., on the Bridge of Sighs	BYRON 188:58
V. will linger in your mind	MORR 620:46
venison turtle soup, and v.	DICK 282:80
v. pies and good wine	LOUI 537:64
venom v. of the reptile crew	BYRON 188:63
ventriloquist Facts are v.'s dummies	HUXL 442:87
ventriloquizing V. for the unborn	GRAV 382:22
venture drew a bow at a v.	BIBLE 97:70
each v....a new beginning	ELIOT 320:66
None wise dares hopeless v.	EURI 328:57
v. to hint	STEV 851:24
venturous valiant, but not too v.	LYLY 543:81
Venus blind boy, V.' baby	SPEN 839:48
embrace of the V. de Milo	DARIO 262:45
face of V.	BARR 65:98
Hero, V.' nun	MARL 574:35
Lady V. on the settee	SITW 823:94
putting lipstick on the V. de Milo	PICK 677:65
V. here will choose her dwelling	DRYD 303:22
V. in her naked glory	MARL 574:34
V., take my votive glass	PRIOR 696:5
veracity tell us...with v.	GRAY 385:96
of good men	EMER 325:78
verandahs houses there wear v.	MURR 627:79
verb God...is a v.	FULL 355:69
noun and a v.	SHAK 759:98
V. is God	HUGO 437:75
verbal v. contract	GOLD 377:32
verbatim V. I will quote it	PATE 669:13
verbosity exuberance of his own v.	DISR 288:67
thread of his v.	SHAK 763:20
verbs mix...rain with v.	BRAU 157:83
still studying v.	SAND 742:29
we are v.	FRY 354:51
verdict every royal v.	WHIT 934:24
fearlessly challenge the v.	PALM 662:72
Your v....will be less upon us	CLEM 229:86
verdure groves of ceaseless v.	MELV 585:67
verge ability to get to the v.	DULL 306:87
verges wanted your soft v.	HENRI 411:10
verifiability criterion of v.	AYER 48:5
verisimilitude do not seek...for v.	BORG 150:55
veritas v....attributa vino est	PLINY 682:70
verities old v. and truths of the heart	FAUL 331:35
verity in the cause of v.	BROW 165:47
Verlaine I'll stay off V., too	PARK 664:21
Vermeer V. gave to the sun's	LOWE 540:38
vermin humans...categorized as v.	CAREY 199:61
Tory Party...lower than v.	BEVAN 89:53
vermouth proper union of gin and v.	DE 275:9
vernacular v. is rare	STEV 851:12
Vernon Blanche V. occupied her time	BROO 163:6
impregnated by Brownie V.'s	QUIR 703:27
vers No v. is libre	ELIOT 320:55
Versailles V. of American	WOLFE 953:82
verse Become a v.	HERB 413:72
bombast out a blank v.	GREE 386:33
book of v.	FITZ 337:69
by v. seek fame	SIDN 820:51
chime his childish v.	BYRON 187:29
could not v. immortal save	BYRON 187:39
give up v., my boy	POUND 691:6
incarnation of thy v.	SHEL 813:84
in my v. ever live young	SHAK 800:38
Leave not a foot of v.	POPE 689:39
look upon this v.	SHAK 801:61
matter made for famous poet's v.	SPEN 838:37
now it's lyric v.	WAUGH 923:79
publish a volume of my v.	HOPK 428:83
quire of bad v.	MACA 546:53
still thy v. has charms	SCOTT 752:20
turnings intricate of v.	WORD 958:85
unmelodious v.	STEP 847:12
unpolished rugged v.	DRYD 302:2
unpremeditated v.	MILT 605:43
vain in v.	SIDN 820:43
v. again shall gild	DRAY 298:93
v. be a glorious adventure	VERL 911:61
V. calls them forth	LAND 507:29
v. hath a middle nature	DONNE 292:62
v. is a measured speech	BACON 49:30
V. is the optical form	HUGO 436:56

verses — 1326

v. represents a handle	NASH 631:85
V. thus design'd	WALL 918:61
v. you grave for me	STEV 853:62
whips my blood like v.	WILL 946:28
Who only thinks in v.	VIAN 911:74
Writing free v.	FROST 352:10
yet each v. of thine	HERR 416:18
you talk in blank v.	SHAK 779:8
verses false gallop of v.	SHAK 779:90
No one will get at my v.	WHIT 938:16
raptures…made his v. clear	DRAY 299:98
v. and the prophecy	WALL 918:59
v. from my heart	MARTI 576:71
vertebrate God…a gaseous v.	HAEC 391:4
vertue booste of conning nor v.	LYDG 542:79
vespers singing v. in the temple	GIBB 366:2
vessel In gallant trim the gilded v.	GRAY 385:86
Launch your v.	TENN 879:8
Let the Irish v. lie	AUDEN 43:92
like a potter's v.	BIBLE 99:28
make one v. unto honour	BIBLE 125:23
v. descending unto him	BIBLE 124:84
v. in which the powers of steam	WATT 922:45
v., puffs her sail	TENN 870:2
wife…the weaker v.	BIBLE 130:70
vessels inclined plane of little v.	DICK 281:76
treasure in earthen v.	BIBLE 127:66
v. of a potter	BIBLE 131:92
vestals into their lives aciduous v.	STEV 852:34
vet v. can't catch his patient	HERR 416:19
veteran as a v. may differ	HUXL 443:10
veterans world its v. rewards	POPE 688:15
veto Mercury should not have my V.	LEST 524:8
v. upon any mere aggression	LEES 519:4
vex tells me nothing that does not v.	AUST 46:84
V. not thou	TENN 869:73
vexation added v. of prayers	TWAIN 902:41
vexed knew by the blush…he was v.	SOME 833:8
viable and v. and useful	HAYEK 402:26
vials v. hermetically sealed	SWIFT 862:46
vibrant the v. and the beautiful	MALL 562:94
vibrations absolutely no v.	WILDE 941:95
vicars hundred v. down the lawn	BROO 162:93
vice between virtue and v.	JOHN 461:94
bounds into a v.	DRYD 301:48
difficult and nerve-racking v.	MAUG 582:6
exalted person's fall into v.	CANM 196:3
Extremism…is no v.	GOLD 377:20
Far from being a v.	SADE 737:14
frequently regarded as v.	FORD 342:90
good old-gentlemanly v.	BYRON 189:4
greatest v. in an actor	HAZL 403:31
ill-natur'd, baneful V.	MAND 565:65
in v. their law's their will	SHAK 798:80
knowledge and survey of v.	MILT 600:11
lost by not being v.	WALP 919:79
major v. and greatest pleasure	HEMI 410:90
moral restraint, v. and misery	MALT 563:20
Mutual forgiveness of each v.	BLAKE 140:5
nearer a v. than a virtue	JONS 467:68
no amusements…but v.	SMITH 831:62
no v. but beggary	SHAK 768:53
no v. so simple	SHAK 770:3
now called v.	SPEN 839:56
poverty, v., and misery	SUMN 859:81
prosperitie Upfosteris v.	BROWN 164:41
Prosperity doth best discover v.	BACON 51:66
Punctuality is the v.	PATR 670:30
quotation is a national v.	WAUGH 924:83
raptures and roses of v.	SWIN 864:91
sanction V., and hunt Decorum	BYRON 187:28
sensual pleasure without v.	JOHN 465:2
sole remaining v.	UPDI 906:35
subject…to this v. of lying!	SHAK 772:89
V. came in…the door of necessity	DEFOE 269:76
V. is a monster	POPE 687:82
v.…lost half its evil	BURKE 176:41
v. of meanness	THOM 887:96
v. of which no one boasts	NERV 634:25
v. pays to virtue	LARO 510:4
v. promises to her followers	MILT 600:10
v. to tiresome virtue	MOLI 611:82
v. with half its virtue	LOWE 540:34
Virtue itself turns v.	SHAK 766:88
Virtue…of v. must pardon beg	SHAK 784:44
When v. prevails	ADDI 7:41
whirled into folly and v.	TENN 875:15

vice-presidency v.-p. isn't worth	GARN 360:78
vice president Isn't it a bitch?…this	
v.p. thing?	BIDEN 134:56
vices discover his v. and virtues	CHAR 215:37
dishonour the v.	WILD 943:49
dwelt upon her v.	BELL 77:65
Go very light on v.	PAIGE 660:28
hating v. too much	BURKE 176:48
mean between two v.	ARIS 31:21
Neither our v. nor our virtues	DUNC 307:8
nursed up in those v.	ASTE 39:2
of our pleasant v.	SHAK 793:34
v. and follies of human kind	CONG 240:34
v.…fathered by our heroism	ELIOT 317:85
v. may be committed very genteelly	BOSW 152:78
V.…never change	BEAU 70:7
v. of authority	BACON 51:89
v. of his ancestors	FAUL 330:34
vicious can't expect a boy to be v.	SAKI 739:56
Football…a v. game	BADEN 54:59
never the truly v.	MARG 570:64
v.…to be a creative writer	LAWR 513:71
vicissitude no v. can find	WORD 961:33
sad v. of things	STER 848:49
victim fall v. to a big lie	HITL 420:91
fashion a v. of me	MERT 589:53
first insults the v.	CRAB 252:34
not help it, I am also a v.	LESS 523:91
refuse to be a v.	ATWO 41:39
shell of his v.	ANNAN 19:11
unsavoury role of v.	YOUR 968:58
v. and slave of his action	EMER 325:81
v. must be found	GILB 369:60
v. of creative suffering	KING 487:30
victimization safety in the state of v.	ANGE 19:94
victims Hibakusha, atomic v.	GEE 362:27
little v. play	GRAY 383:47
scrupulous and the just…are its v.	CONR 244:44
victis Vae v.	BREN 158:1
Vae v.	LIVY 532:61
victor Mighty v., mighty lord	GRAY 385:85
v. is often vanquished	SCHI 747:30
whichever side may call itself the v.	CHAM 212:61
Victoria admired…Queen V.	WILDE 942:31
Like Gladstone speaking to V.	MANC 564:52
Queen V. treats her prisoners	WILDE 942:14
rises in the V. Nyanza	SPEKE 836:81
Victorian antagonistic to the V. age	WILS 948:50
hats, as in V. days	SITW 824:12
history of the V. age	STRA 856:36
lost sense of V. regard	PRIT 696:25
Victorianism inverted V.	FORS 344:39
Victorians V. expected	CASS 207:74
victories After a thousand v.	SHAK 800:44
victors are by v. undone	DRYD 304:49
victorious come off always v.	CARL 200:80
licensings to make her v.	MILT 600:9
show themselves v.	BALZ 61:97
victors History is written for the v.	DREX 299:8
v. are by victories undone	DRYD 304:49
v., they left…not a few	DAVIS 266:9
victory advantage…is half the v.	DRAKE 298:87
authority of supreme v.	WHIT 936:71
Dig for V.	DORAM 294:84
fourth electoral v.	HESE 416:29
get anything by their v.	HALI 393:38
grave, where is thy v.?	BIBLE 127:63
great v. has been won	MACA 544:5
He judgement brings, and v.	OAKL 643:5
how to gain a v., Hannibal:	MARH 570:71
In v.: magnanimity	CHUR 224:69
In v., one deserves it	POL 684:8
in v., there is no beauty	LAO 508:62
in v. unbearable	CHUR 226:14
judgment unto v.	BIBLE 117:82
lose Life…to discover V.	APOL 29:86
No force to win the v.	DYER 309:48
no substitute for v.	MACA 544:7
One more such v.	PYRR 701:15
Or to v.!	BURNS 180:47
swallow up death in v.	BIBLE 108:67
swept on to V.	PRIE 695:86
Truth beareth away the v.	BIBLE 112:67
'twas a famous v.	SOUT 835:47
valour, and of v.	MARL 572:3
V. at all costs	CHUR 225:83
v.…celebrated with the funeral rite	LAO 508:63

v. for all the people of South Africa	MAND 564:55
v. is twice itself	SHAK 773:15
V. of a cat	WILL 945:90
V. of Samothrace	MARI 571:77
v. of sterility	BELL 77:74
v. of the children of light	BEND 78:12
V. sits on our helms!	SHAK 761:54
v. switches from man to man	HOMER 425:4
v. turns into a defeat	DE 268:47
what would be theft…is only v.	DRYD 300:21
where is thy V.?	BUNY 174:83
vie la v.…au pouvoir de la langue	CIXO 227:41
Viennesey waltz that is V.	GERS 365:74
Vietnam Gay V. Veteran	MATL 582:94
government of V. is Communist	GELL 363:36
not an invasion of V.	NIXON 640:34
Patriotism in V.	NGUY 636:69
see V. as a war	PILG 678:77
so compelling since the V. War	WHITE 934:29
to V. to take the train	THER 882:88
To win in V.	SPOCK 841:85
V. is somewhere near Panama	ANON 25:65
V. is the place	KENN 481:6
V. was what we had instead	HERR 415:96
wrong people remember V.	HERR 415:97
view America is in my v.	SCHAW 747:56
best v. is on the right	LEVIN 525:29
distance lends enchantment to the v.	CAMP 194:61
each has his own v.	TERE 879:15
if you wanted to v. trouble	RIDGE 715:32
illusion of a v. of life	ELIOT 319:77
never…see the same v. twice	STARK 843:24
point of v. has sadly changed	MACA 544:15
point of v. of participant	GALL 358:39
Room with a V.	FORS 344:23
slow, firm, inflexible v.	PASC 666:62
soar'd…quite out of reason's v.	DRYD 301:52
v. as an infernal Utopia	LEWIS 527:74
v. never changes	ANON 27:25
v. O'erlaid with black	MILT 598:50
v. On the clear hyaline	MILT 605:33
without any…purpose…in v.	PLAN 680:23
viewer modern…v.…is…overloaded	BELL 78:96
views false v.…do little harm	DARW 263:56
frightening v. of government	INOU 446:50
full of stately v.	KIPL 492:67
Hitler…held extreme v.	POUND 692:22
outdated v.	GORB 378:49
take short v.	SMITH 830:44
v. of the revolutionists	SCHL 747:33
Whenever you accept our v.	DAYAN 267:34
vigil yearly on the v.	SHAK 776:89
vigilance condition…is eternal v.	CURR 259:92
not so much eternal v.	ORWE 653:16
vigilant Be sober, be v.	BIBLE 130:73
v. as a cat	SHAK 771:56
vigilantes goose-stepping v.	LEWIS 526:53
vigils pensive poets painful v. keep	POPE 688:32
vigorous fresh and v. enough	WARD 920:2
vigour others which excite by their v.	GAUG 361:1
restore her to v.	BRON 162:80
vile be he ne'er so v.	SHAK 776:93
Makes nice of no v. hold	SHAK 768:60
make v. things precious	SHAK 792:8
nought so v.	SHAK 766:87
one v. antithesis	POPE 688:6
so v. a pun	DENN 273:76
this v. world	OTWAY 656:9
viler manners ne'er were v.	JONS 467:69
vilified v. by enemies	BIER 134:63
vilify v. a great man	POE 683:93
village above a bleached v.	WALC 916:19
Alpine v. passed	LONG 535:21
any v. in England	TROL 897:35
Black v. of gravestones	HUGH 436:43
came to the v. church	TENN 875:18
fast from every v.	MACA 546:52
greatest mere v. in England	DEFOE 269:77
life in the v. began	LEE 519:96
like to v. curs	SHAK 804:43
loveliest v.	GOLD 376:96
Model Boy of the v.	TWAIN 902:40
place for a V.	BATM 68:55
said he was a v. explainer	STEIN 845:76
simple v. green	TENN 874:83
vegetate in a v.	COLT 238:85
V. cricket spread fast	TREV 896:5

virtuous

Entry	Reference
world in the image of a global v.	MCLU 556:54
villages hill v. of Afghanistan	GLAD 373:38
V. and towns are now deserted	BERN 85:65
villain call rogue and v.	DRYD 303:24
condemns me for a v.	SHAK 761:50
fair terms and a v.'s mind	SHAK 769:87
hanged, if some eternal v.	SHAK 790:36
hungry lean-faced v.	SHAK 762:93
like a v. with a smiling cheek	SHAK 769:84
one murder made a v.	PORT 690:77
serviceable v.	SHAK 793:28
smile and smile and be a v.	SHAK 781:67
The more successful the v.	HITC 419:85
Turn out that eyeless v.	SHAK 793:15
v. and a bastard and a knave	SHAK 775:77
v. dwelling in all Denmark	SHAK 781:68
villainous newspapers...most v.	SHER 817:94
To hoard is a v. act	RABE 704:15
villains as if we were v. on necessity	SHAK 792:89
heroes and v. from fiction	AUDEN 44:17
villainy clothe my naked v.	SHAK 761:39
in the days of v.?	SHAK 771:55
Villiers Great V. lies	POPE 686:69
Villon V....brother's name	SWIN 864:15
Vinchy pronounce it V.	TWAIN 902:32
Vinci spell it V.	TWAIN 902:32
vindicate v. the ways of God to man	POPE 686:71
vindictiveness unfinished v.	ELIOT 315:32
v. of the female	CONN 243:8
vine foxlike in the v.	TENN 873:51
gadding v. o'ergrown	MILT 599:84
luscious clusters of the v.	MARV 577:4
Under his own v.	SHAK 805:58
wife shall be as a fruitful v.	BIBLE 103:38
vinegar dressed with pepper and v.	JOHN 462:32
how much oil...put with one's v.	WILDE 940:46
in him we see Oil, v.	GOLD 377:16
Marriage...like v. from wine	BYRON 190:11
mix like Oil and V.	GAIN 356:9
they gave me v. to drink	BOOK 149:26
V. he poured on me	OLSEN 650:44
vines advise his client to plant v.	WRIG 962:67
old house...covered with v.	BEME 78:98
With fruit the v.	KEATS 477:32
vino veritas...attribuia v. est	PLIN 682:70
vintage for a draught of v.!	KEATS 478:42
trampling out the v.	HOWE 433:92
vintager Since Ariadne was a v.	KEATS 476:88
violated dread the v.	JORD 469:1
violation conventional v.	NABO 629:21
self is so great a v.	LAWR 512:44
V. is a synonym	DWOR 308:46
v. of their natural birthright	MILT 601:24
violence because he had done no v.	BIBLE 109:95
danger of being torn with v.	ROSS 725:35
degenerate into physical v.	KING 487:19
energy...imparted by v.	LEON 522:70
essence of war is v.	MACA 545:38
friends...do such v.	BACON 53:53
heart and lost it to v.	RIVE 716:55
inconvenience of v.	WALK 917:35
In v., we forget	MCCA 548:97
I, too, will die by v.	MALC 562:90
Keep v. in the mind	ALDI 12:50
Least fancies into v.	WILB 939:39
machismo reeks of v.	WHITE 934:28
nation of v.	JORD 469:1
never...by v. constrained	ELIZ 321:99
pleasure in witnessing v.	ORWE 655:81
Snobbery with V.	BENN 80:46
v. and ferocity of our age	JAMES 450:32
v. in movies	TARA 867:26
v. in Northern Ireland	OROU 652:92
V. is a lie	JOHN 456:79
V. is fun	TARA 867:27
v. prevails	KYD 501:48
violent bloody thoughts with v. pace	SHAK 790:29
good sir, be not so v.	MIDD 590:73
more v. this last decade	ABSE 1:10
too v. for the body	JEFF 454:29
v. delights have v. ends	SHAK 766:92
v. revolution inevitable	KENN 481:10
V., vivid and of infinite possibility	EBER 310:10
violet cast a v. into a crucible	SHEL 816:49
humble v. under a cow pat	BARN 64:63
oxlips and the nodding v. grows	SHAK 767:30
perfume on the v.	SHAK 768:62

Entry	Reference
underfoot the v., Crocus	MILT 604:8
v. by a mossy stone	WORD 957:62
v.'s reclining head	DONNE 292:41
v., The musk-rose	MILT 599:91
violets beds of v. blue	MILT 597:42
covered in winter with v.	SHEL 815:26
Fast fading v.	KEATS 478:45
sweet v.	SHEL 816:63
the v. blow	TENN 875:98
upon a bank of v.	SHAK 785:77
violin Life is like playing a v. solo	BUTL 185:94
v. is wood and catgut	PRIE 695:84
whoever heard of an electric v.?	SEGO 756:4
violins Slow sobs of the v.	VERL 910:55
vipers extirpate the v.	AYTO 48:11
O generation of v.	BIBLE 114:20
O generation of v.	BIBLE 117:85
Virgil Jonson was the V.	DRYD 300:26
Oh V.! Oh poet!	HUGO 437:65
V. and Horace	DRYD 300:40
V. seems to have composed	ARNO 35:7
virgin born of the V. Mary	BOOK 146:37
everything brilliant and v.	DAY 267:38
memories come to you genuinely v.	ORWE 654:31
one's mother is a v.	JARRY 452:96
pale v. shrouded in snow	BLAKE 140:11
poor v....an ill-favoured thing	SHAK 780:22
see! the V. blessed	MILT 597:38
should have stayed a v.	CART 207:54
So though a v., yet a bride	CAREW 199:60
took the v. Truth	MILT 600:17
V. me no virgins!	MASS 581:80
v. shall be with child	BIBLE 114:15
v. shall conceive	BIBLE 107:57
V.'s womb	AQUI 30:96
v., the vibrant and the beautiful	MALL 562:94
virginals pair of v. in it	PEPYS 674:8
Virginia in V. creeper drown	BETJ 88:29
V. fox hunt	WASH 922:28
V.'s aged tree	RANS 706:67
Virginians Jackson with his V.	BEE 73:60
virginity for my v....I'll die	PRIOR 696:6
just a little more v.	TREE 896:97
long preserved v.	MARV 577:92
V., albeit some highly prize it	MARL 574:38
V. is peevish	SHAK 791:56
V., mysticism, melancholy!	GAUT 361:4
V., whom I thus long	MIDD 590:73
virgins holy v. in their ecstasies	TENN 878:78
narrating English v.	UPDI 906:23
virgin-widow v.-w....mourning	DRYD 304:55
virtue adversity...discover v.	BACON 51:66
air of noble v.	STRA 857:42
all men then did v. call	SPEN 839:56
Assume a v.	SHAK 784:45
be called 'v.' as, above	LUCAS 541:52
between v. and vice	JOHN 461:94
capacity and v.	SWIFT 862:47
compensate for lack of v.	PLATO 681:52
constituting of human v.	MILT 600:11
Contempt...has become a v.	OCON 647:91
Crime, like v.	RACI 704:30
crown enough to v.	JONS 468:84
defined as v.	MORE 619:22
despair, disguised as a v.	BIER 135:85
Drunkenness is his best v.	SHAK 791:69
everything but genius and v.	HAZL 403:46
every v....founded on compromise	BURKE 175:23
Expresseth v. fully	WEBS 926:19
find v....difficult to portray	PRIT 696:19
forms of v. are erect	FUSE 356:94
fugitive and cloistered v.	MILT 600:8
greatest offence against v.	HAZL 404:57
greatest v. of the mind	SPIN 841:79
her food, and her v.	NATI 632:4
if there be any v.	BIBLE 128:5
keep your v.	KIPL 492:63
latter stems from v.	HELO 408:54
let v. be as wax	SHAK 784:41
Liberty...mother of v.	WOLL 954:90
lilies and languors of v.	SWIN 864:91
long served v.	WEBS 927:46
manners, v., freedom, power	WORD 958:94
moderation...is no v.	GOLD 377:20
more v. than old men	JOHN 461:98
much v. in 'if'	SHAK 780:25
nearer a vice than a v.	JONS 467:68

Entry	Reference
negative v. of not	RUSS 734:32
no road or ready way to v.	BROW 165:66
no sign of v.	BIBLE 112:77
only reward of v. is v.	EMER 324:61
pass for v. in Constantinople	FORD 342:90
Patience is a v.	ANON 21:48
perhaps almost the chief v.	SCOTT 751:99
Progressive v.	THOM 887:99
ragged v.	OTWAY 656:3
royalty of v.	POTT 690:84
Self-denial is not a v.	SHAW 808:47
show v. her own feature	SHAK 783:19
sin which preaches v.	MARI 571:84
some by v. fall	SHAK 787:54
Some mark of v.	SHAK 770:3
That v. therefore	MILT 600:10
the very ingredients of v.	MILT 600:13
threatened to destroy...several types of v.	KENN 483:48
thy fair v.'s force	SHAK 767:36
To act...according to v.	SPIN 840:78
upgrowth of all v.	KING 488:55
vice pays to v.	LARO 510:4
vice to tiresome v.	MOLI 611:82
vice with half its v.	LOWE 540:34
V.? A fig!	SHAK 789:3
v., as you please	BAUD 68:73
v. at the testing point	LEWIS 527:76
v. called 'thrift'	THOM 887:95
V. could...do what V.	MILT 598:72
v. had gone out of him	BIBLE 119:56
V....is a state of character	ARIS 31:21
V. is bold	SHAK 788:71
V. is lacking	MOLI 611:80
V. is like a rich stone	BACON 52:27
V. is simply happiness	BURR 181:69
V. is the fount	MARL 572:1
v. is your greatest affectation	WYCH 964:95
V. itself turns vice	SHAK 766:88
V. knows to a farthing	WALP 919:79
v. of fools	BACON 50:51
V. of prosperity	BACON 51:63
V....of vice must pardon beg	SHAK 784:44
v. of weak minds	DRYD 299:13
v. sank the deeper	SURR 860:99
v., she alone is free	MILT 599:81
V. finds too painful	POPE 688:12
V.'s his path	DRYD 301:48
V.'s no more in womankind	CLEV 230:94
v. something that can be taught?	PLATO 681:15
v. that transgresses	SHAK 785:87
v. then shall be	SHAK 768:53
want women to specialise in v.	WEST 933:95
What is it that constitutes v.	BRON 161:58
What is v.	SHAW 808:31
With quickening v.	WORD 957:72
woman grows in v.	GOTT 379:70
virtues all the v. are of no avail	HUXL 441:64
American v. are daylight	RODR 722:52
brashness and noise are v.	AUDEN 44:16
cardinal v. of the sex	WOLL 954:89
circumscribed...their growing v.	GRAY 384:71
Curse on his v.!	ADDI 7:49
discover his vices and v.	CHAR 215:37
makes some v. impracticable	JOHN 464:85
Mentioned her v.	BELL 77:65
misfortune extinguishes our v.	BALZ 60:95
Neither our vices nor our v.	DUNC 307:8
one of the cardinal v.	FITZ 337:81
One of the v....of a newspaper	SCOTT 751:99
rural v.	GOLD 376:7
to her v. very kind	PRIOR 695:1
verse your v. rare	SPEN 839:77
V. Are forced upon us	ELIOT 317:85
v., are their own reward	FARQ 330:22
v. but the form	LEWIS 526:47
v. carry with it life and death	MARL 572:98
v. common to good	LUCAS 541:52
v. made or crimes	DEFOE 269:73
V. neglected then, adored become	CRAB 252:39
v. of their weaknesses	MENC 587:6
v. We write in water	SHAK 805:56
virtuoso produce one v.	VAUG 909:32
telling a v.	MALL 562:97
virtuous As for the v. poor	WILDE 941:73
be v.—be religious	SCOTT 754:84
learn...to be v.	PREV 694:77

virulent

lovers be v.	LYLY 543:85
Most plain girls are v.	ANGE 19:88
the v. who believe themselves	PASC 667:90
v. man	GREE 385:6
v. men pass mildly away	DONNE 292:38
When men grow v.	POPE 686:96
virulent in its most v. form	JERO 454:38
virus Conveyed the v. hither	WILB 939:38
If this is what v. pneumonia does	COOP 246:83
visage all his v. wanned	SHAK 782:99
Melancholy, Whose saintly v.	MILT 598:50
v. was so marred	BIBLE 109:92
viscous thought is v.	ADAMS 5:97
visible All things v.	BOOK 147:60
Art…makes v.	KLEE 494:5
too v. as sex objects	FRIE 350:65
v. self as its medium	HOLL 423:51
vision Boy, I got v.	GOLD 375:82
brightness of this v.	RAND 706:59
cried in a whisper…at some v.	CONR 243:30
devils to contest his v.	MAIL 560:46
distrust of its own v.	JEFF 454:25
faulty v. sees things as they are	BIER 134:73
In a v. once I saw	COLE 236:41
keen v. and feeling	ELIOT 316:51
man…without some v.	LAWR 514:81
nation's experience and his v.	KISS 494:93
no v., no foresight, no sight at all	DAWK 266:16
Poetry—tries to tell you about a v.	ENGLE 326:16
powerful v., formal and austere	PAGE 659:16
President's v.	SCHL 748:39
Science provides a v. of reality	PAGE 659:16
serving his v.	KENN 482:26
skull that…had v.	SASS 746:2
tinkering with moments of v.	BLUN 143:80
to Reagan the main fact was a v.	SHUL 819:30
unified v. of life	WILS 947:41
v. of an America	RODO 721:51
v. of a time	RAND 706:58
v. of our own	WORD 960:14
v. of the Commonwealth	MACM 556:63
v. of the holiness of God	BLOOM 143:65
v. of the world	TENN 871:17
v. sanctified	WORD 961:47
v. splendid	WORD 959:8
v. to recognize it as such	MILL 594:62
Where there is no v.	BIBLE 105:6
with his v.	SACK 737:10
young men's v.	DRYD 302:77
visionary The world has lost a v.	OBAMA 644:43
visions appear in v.	AUDEN 43:99
history of great v.	ADEL 8:61
lost in stormy v.	SHEL 815:39
My Oberon, what v.	SHAK 767:42
screwy v.	BELL 77:84
seen v. and had amazing	THOM 883:2
these v. did appear	SHAK 768:51
v. for a simple human delight	BARB 63:46
v. of sugarplums danced	MOORE 616:61
young men shall see v.	BIBLE 111:48
visit another country…we can v.	WINT 950:17
ever paying you a v.	MORT 621:70
going to v. every country	KEEN 478:52
If aliens v. us	HAWK 401:95
On every formal v.	AUST 45:51
visitant v. that…fans my cheek	WORD 957:72
visitation time of their v.	BIBLE 112:75
visiting-card v.-c. will answer	BAED 54:60
visitor any v. from outer space	BURR 181:65
caused the v.	KIPL 492:52
reels them off to every new v.	SHAW 809:89
subduing the impenitent v.	BIER 135:88
v. from Mars contemplating	LAVER 512:34
v. with a return ticket	GREE 386:11
visitors V. who wish to remain	LEBO 518:65
visits beauties…were but my v.	PRIOR 696:11
tendered their v.	JONS 468:89
vista at the end of every v.	BURKE 176:42
Hasta la v., baby	SCHW 750:86
visual v. aids, that sort of thing	NEWM 634:43
vitae V., non scholae discimus	SENE 757:24
vital No matter how v.	GLAS 374:46
vitality lowering the subject's v.	VEBL 910:44
not v. enough	JOHN 464:93
symptom of a deficient v.	STEV 852:50
V. in a woman	SHAW 807:16
vitalized highly v. persons	GALS 358:48
vitals red red v. of his heart	RANS 707:69
vitamins right proteins and v.	CART 207:57
vitriol lacy sleeve with a bottle of v.	WOOL 956:40
vituperation learn to accept v.	WAUGH 924:85
viva V. la the New Brigade!	DAVIS 266:11
vive V. l'amour!	STER 849:55
V. le Québec!	DE 270:97
vivid left the v. air	SPEN 837:93
vocabulary have a great v.	FEIF 331:55
mastery of v. and syntax	SAYE 746:10
Syntax and v.	MATH 581:87
to be a v.	UPDI 906:37
v. needs constant fertilizing	WAUGH 924:94
vocal vasectomy of the v. chords	ALTH 15:14
vocation dignity…the high v.	CARL 200:86
I have not felt the v.	CLOU 232:57
labour in his v.	SHAK 770:30
robs strength from my artistic v.	FUEN 354:59
'Tis my v., Hal	SHAK 770:30
vodka medium V. dry Martini	FLEM 340:42
vogue charming to totter into v.	WALP 919:69
voice as the v. of reason	LEGU 520:17
audible v. of the Past	CARL 201:33
broken v.	SHAK 782:99
certain what-is-it in his v.	WODE 952:50
confront the oppressor with one v.	MAKW 561:81
Conscience: the inner v.	MENC 586:82
echoes back the public v.	JOHN 459:44
every v. be song!	DODD 289:90
fill my mourning v.	SURR 860:3
gave v. to three words	LAMA 504:74
Give…few thy v.	SHAK 781:51
hard note crept into his v.	WALL 917:47
heard the still v. calling	LAWS 514:97
heard thy v. in the garden	BIBLE 91:94
Her v. was ever soft	SHAK 793:38
Imagination is the v.	MILL 594:72
In honoured poverty thy v.	SHEL 812:59
It was her v. that made	STEV 850:79
let thy v. rise	TENN 878:86
lift up your v.	WESL 931:61
Lord, hear my v.	BIBLE 133:38
Lord, hear my v.	BIBLE 103:39
make our v. audible	STEV 852:56
Methought I heard a v. cry	SHAK 797:34
Mistaken at the top of one's v.	BIER 135:89
moderate his v. at the same time	STER 847:21
Money speaks…with a male v.	DWOR 308:44
music…for the human v.	ANGE 19:1
No v., but oh! the silence sank	COLE 235:19
No v. or hideous hum	MILT 597:37
only v. I care to hear	CAMP 194:52
people's v. is odd	POPE 688:18
quality of v. that is…the writer's own	CATH 208:96
refuseth to hear the v. of the charmer	BOOK 149:21
reserve the more weighty v.	BACON 50:22
safe I sing with mortal v.	MILT 605:27
silence until any v. is heard	LEZA 528:81
Sink heart and v.	NEALE 632:7
sound of a v. that is still!	TENN 871:4
still small v.	BIBLE 97:67
such a tender v.	BLAKE 139:86
supplicating v.	JOHN 459:49
sweet and potent v.	COLE 235:30
Sweeter thy v.	TENN 873:52
sweet little rinky-dink of a v.	MAIL 560:58
The City's v.	SHEL 812:66
thundrous v.	WILL 946:20
till thou obey my v.	BLAKE 141:33
Today if ye will hear his v.	BOOK 149:31
tones of a loved v.	ARNO 34:72
top of your v.	BAKER 56:2
transmit the v. over wires	ANON 23:90
trick of that v.	SHAK 793:20
true v. arose in me	FOX 346:71
tune her sacred v.	JOHN 459:41
tune thy jolly v.	BLAKE 139:82
utter forth a glorious v.	ADDI 7:41
v., a mystery	WORD 958:95
v. as the sound of many waters	BIBLE 131:88
v. falls as they say love	LARK 509:76
v. in every wind	GRAY 383:46
v. in the darkness	LONG 536:37
v. is full of money	FITZ 337:84
v. less loud, through its joys	BROW 167:24
v.…like the sea	WORD 958:94
v. of dolorous pitch	HOOD 426:30
v. of freedom	SHAR 805:69
v. of high midsummer's heat	ROBE 717:72
v. of him that crieth	BIBLE 108:79
v. of the Bard!	BLAKE 140:8
v. of the dead	TENN 877:67
v., of the democracy	STEAD 843:30
v. of the people	ALCU 12:46
v. of the people	BACON 50:50
v. of the people	PITT 679:4
v. of those who suffer	CESA 211:50
v. said in mastery	BROW 166:92
v., so in a shapeless flame	DONNE 291:33
v., stunning as thunder	KINS 488:67
v. that tells him he is not	TRUM 900:88
v. the word 'nature'	REDON 709:24
v. which failed to sound	MILNE 595:11
With a monarch's v.	SHAK 777:34
with cheerful v.	KETHE 483:67
voiceless Science is v.	WEIL 928:70
voices Ancestral v. prophesying war!	COLE 236:40
Bubble their colourful v.	HUGH 435:36
clatter of high v.	DOYLE 297:48
Clear Cymric v.	BUNT 173:68
drowning out of false v.	DELI 271:40
English don't raise their v.	HELL 408:48
heart and hands and v.	WINK 950:98
hear v. in the air	KEYN 484:81
Moans round with many v.	TENN 870:2
Other V., Other Rooms	CAPO 197:18
soft v. die	SHEL 816:63
sounds of their v.	ANGE 19:99
Two v. are there	STEP 847:11
Two v. are there	WORD 961:31
unbearable v. of its announcers	ORWE 654:37
v. are heard among them	BOOK 148:9
v. dying with a dying fall	ELIOT 316:63
v. elected me of all men	LEE 519:98
v. of liberty be mute?	CUMM 257:59
v. of young people	SMITH 829:17
v. telling him that	TRUM 900:88
voice-trained v.-t. to speak	WATE 922:36
void All is without form and v.	HAZL 404:60
beating in the v.	ARNO 36:40
decorations over a v.	YOUR 968:56
No craving v.…in the breast	POPE 686:47
not enough…to be v.	BRAT 157:78
rubbish to the v.	TENN 874:76
shall not return unto me v.	BIBLE 109:99
terrors that flock to fill the v.	LEGU 520:10
They are v. within a vacuum	JOHN 457:89
v. in your life, fill it	NERVO 634:27
v. of noble rage	TENN 874:68
voids sins are attempts to fill v.	WEIL 928:72
volcanic v. landscapes a poor girl	CHEE 218:7
volcano erupt like a v.	MACD 550:42
like a slumbering v.	WHITE 936:58
volcanoes We are v.	LEGU 520:15
vole questing v.	WAUGH 924:74
volley fine v. of words	SHAK 758:61
volleys make her hit backhand v.	KING 486:18
Volsces Cut me to pieces, V.	SHAK 799:6
Voltaire always like V.	TALMA 866:21
mock on, V. Rousseau	BLAKE 140:22
Rousseau, V.…united in one person	HESS 417:34
V., Rousseau…fools, and madmen!	ONEI 651:70
V. smiled	HUGO 438:89
volume iron-clasped v. of despair	POE 683:91
take in our hand any v.	HUME 438:7
Twenty V. Suicide Note	BARA 63:41
v. can ever be written on the flea	MELV 585:64
v.…so far above the average	WILDE 940:50
world is a great v.	DONNE 293:79
volumes creators of odd v.	LAMB 505:3
Reticence, in three v.	GLAD 373:43
To their subsequent v.	SHAK 786:29
voluntary faith…become as fully v.	CUPI 258:86
volunteers brave York V.	BROCK 160:29
voluptuous Lush, calm and v.	BAUD 68:65
vomit dog is turned to his own v.	BIBLE 130:78
dog returneth to his v.	BIBLE 105:96
Dog returns to his v.	KIPL 493:79
giant pool of crapulous v.	BOYD 153:10
vortex bisection of a v.!	OCON 646:84
into the v. of immensity	DICK 280:24
v. of our grave	CRANE 252:55
vote against giving woman the v.	WRIG 962:61
Don't v. for bad people	KARZ 474:33

Fifty per cent...won't v.	VIDAL 912:98	never ta'en w. of her	WEBS 927:46	w. before me	BIBLE 92:20
fighting for the v.	PANK 662:86	rather than give them good w.	WEST 933:94	w....before they dance	POPE 688:23
I cast only one v.	ONAS 650:53	rise of w.	RICA 712:80	w. by faith, not by sight	BIBLE 127:69
It's not the v. women need	OBRI 645:67	took their w.	HOUS 432:71	W. by the shore	SITW 823:10
make it harder to v.	CLIN 231:20	w. may rise	MARX 579:35	W. cheerfully	FOX 346:72
man's decision on how to v.	SCHN 748:44	w. of sin is death	BIBLE 125:13	w. down the lane	FREED 349:42
my hearty v.	SWIFT 862:40	w. should be left to...competition	RICA 712:83	W.! Not bloody likely	SHAW 810:1
one dollar, one v.	KRIS 499:15	**waggon** Hitch your w. to a star	EMER 325:94	w. off proud	SAND 742:20
One man shall have one v.	CART 207:58	**waging** w. of peace	ELIZ 322:12	W. on the Wild Side	ALGR 13:69
Truth is not...a majority v.	BENE 79:20	**Wagner** like W.'s music better	WILDE 940:67	w. on, w. on	HAMM 394:65
v. for a woman	WATE 922:36	W. has good moments	ROSS 727:67	w. round it several times	SATIE 746:4
v. somebody into office	GERG 365:67	W.'s music is better	TWAIN 904:94	w. through the storm	HAMM 394:65
women...trying for the v.	PANK 662:82	write music like W.	GOLD 377:27	W. two Oscars behind	WARR 921:15
working classes...given the v.	WAUGH 924:96	**wags** how the world w.	SHAK 779:79	w. ye in it	BIBLE 108:74
voter v. who uses his money	SAMU 741:1	You w. that judge	OTWAY 656:95	w. your mystic way	GILB 368:43
what the v. receives	PRICE 695:82	**wail** suffice to w. their scorn	DANI 262:31	Will you w. a little faster?	CARR 203:80
woman v....pernicious to the State	WRIG 962:62	when I w.	SPEN 839:44	**walking** are ye w. yet?	SKIR 825:51
voters v. have no contact	PRICE 695:81	**wailing** fullers and their w.	ANON 20:25	as dancing is to w.	WAIN 915:4
votes asked men for v.	WEST 933:97	in w. there's nought availing	CURR 259:91	craves wary w.	SHAK 776:15
giving v. to the most obscure	CHES 220:69	**wailsday** tearsday, w.	JOYCE 470:37	hate w.	SMOL 831:67
speeches and majority v.	BISM 137:32	**waist** from the w. They're centaurs	SHAK 793:22	just w. dully along	AUDEN 42:80
voting It's not the v.	STOP 855:17	**waistcoat** fourth w. button	LICH 528:88	w., and leaping, and praising God	BIBLE 124:74
V.'s the best revenge	OBAMA 644:45	open your w.	HUNT 439:19	w. back towards yourself	MANT 568:16
V. Tory	JOHN 457:91	yolk runs down the w.	DICK 278:82	w. dead man	ANON 27:26
vow w....made to her in marriage	SHAK 781:63	**waistcoats** w. and...handkerchiefs	DICK 277:54	W. is a way of being somewhere	HILL 418:58
v. that is vowèd true	SHAK 791:65	**wait** I can w.	LISZT 531:46	W. so early	SCOTT 754:63
v. that to-morne	MALO 563:13	must w. until a shrimp	KHRU 485:90	**walks** luxuries...in my w.	KEATS 476:94
v. to thee, my country	SPRI 841:87	to w. is life	HUGO 437:62	w. up and down with me	SHAK 768:57
vowels Only consonants and v.	RANS 707:73	w. and not be tired	KIPL 492:62	**wall** auld grey w.	MACD 549:20
Scrabble with all the v. missing	ELLI 322:20	w. on wrinkled age!	SHAK 762:94	Before I built a w.	FROST 352:91
shifting of v. and consonants	UNTE 905:11	w., seated in a chair	VALE 907:2	behind its great w.	THUR 891:11
vows cancel all our v.	DRAY 299:99	w. until man comes around	FULL 355:70	daily from the turret w.	MUIR 624:16
constancy of its v.	SHAW 808:33	w. upon the Lord	BIBLE 109:85	had to put a w. up	KENN 481:23
Dismiss your v.	SHAK 762:86	You just w.	THOM 884:42	hanging on the w.	BETJ 88:23
falser than v. made in wine	SHAK 779:3	**waited** w. patiently for the Lord	BIBLE 100:61	interesting as a w. can be	SHAW 810:22
he w. his passion	PARK 664:13	**waiter** damn good head w.	GULB 390:91	Jackson...like a stone w.	BEE 73:60
Lends the tongue v.	SHAK 781:55	like the way a Swiss w. talks	CHAN 213:82	leaped over a w.	BIBLE 99:38
They fulfil their v.	KORAN 498:89	nothing but a head w.	USTI 906:44	lined up against a w.	TAYL 868:56
V., oaths, and all	JONS 468:87	**waiters** impulse exists among w.	WEBER 925:12	office of a w.	SHAK 764:40
voyage long, beautiful v.	TZARA 904:15	**waiting** pain of w.	GUY 390:7	picture on the w.	JOHN 458:18
v. and not a harbour	TOYN 895:74	The meaning is the w.	THOM 886:74	pile of turf against the w.	COLUM 238:90
v. is entirely imaginary	CELI 211:36	W. for the end	EMPS 326:11	Something...that doesn't love a w.	FROST 352:90
v. of their life	SHAK 778:48	**wake** doomed at last to w.	JOHN 460:71	stones into the Theban w.	COWL 250:72
v. of voyages	MUNDY 625:44	w. from ignorance	JOHN 459:41	To the top of the w.!	MOORE 616:63
voyeur into the theatre as a v.	FRIS 351:86	w. in a corner	KELM 479:70	to the w., dying, but fighting back!	MCKA 553:7
voyeurs the lethal v.	RUSH 732:69	w. in happiness	AUNG 45:42	walks through a w.	MALA 561:84
vulgar called wicked than v.	LEWIS 526:50	w. sleeping, and sleep	MONT 614:29	w. as solid as the earth	BUCH 171:22
Father is rather v.	DICK 282:91	w. slightly altered	UPDI 906:34	w. fell down flat	BIBLE 95:8
Funny without being v.	GILB 370:74	w. up and tell you	GAGA 356:5	w. is strong	WILDE 942:21
More is v.	SPARK 836:70	w. up one morning	HEYE 417:39	W. of China	PATM 669:25
rude remark or a v. action	WILL 945:81	w. us Time and time over	LARK 509:72	W. St. genes	THOM 885:69
shallow and v. view	WEBB 925:6	we w. eternally	DONNE 292:52	W. Street indexes predicted	SAMU 741:2
times have become v.	MOLI 611:75	when you w. in the morning	SAND 742:32	W. which separates you	DIDE 285:63
v. love...v. man	DRYD 301:52	**waked** w. herself with laughing	SHAK 774:33	Washes its w. on the southern side	BROW 167:15
v. sort of capacities	BACON 49:22	**wakeful** W. they lie	GRAV 382:30	Watch the w.	KIPL 492:56
v. to talk like a dentist	WILDE 941:97	**wakened** sleepeth, and must be w.	BIBLE 97:62	were not the W. itself extant	ADDI 7:37
work upon the v. with fine sense	POPE 686:53	**wakening** w. and uprising prove	KEBLE 478:51	When icicles hang by the w.	SHAK 763:27
vulgarest survival of the v.	WILDE 940:60	**wakes** He lives, he w.	SHEL 815:41	Without a city w.	ALEX 13:64
vulgarities may have other v.	HELL 408:48	w. in our hearts	KIER 485:5	with stones to build a w.	FROST 352:3
vulgarity mould of its v.	JEFF 453:10	w. or sleeps with the enduring dead	SHEL 815:38	wrote...upon the plaister of the w.	BIBLE 111:41
singularity and v.	HAZL 403:35	**Walden** W. the saxophone was	HOLM 423:57	**Wallace** Scots, wha hae wi' W. bled	BURNS 180:47
vulgarizing succeeded in...v.	HUXL 442:78	**Waldo** W. is one of those people	SAKI 739:66	**wallet** lump to my w.	WALL 918:53
vulnerable she is so v.	CURR 259:90	We are cursed, W.	SCHR 749:62	Time hath...A w.	SHAK 787:37
v. human beings	TURN 901:20	**Waldron** a song...to Mal W.	OHARA 648:10	**walling** w. in or w. out	FROST 352:91
		Wales Celtic genius of W.	ARNO 35:22	**wallow** let us w.	FLAN 338:8
W		give his soul...But for W.	BOLT 145:12	**wallowing** w. in low seriousness	BELL 78:89
wabe gyre and gimble in the w.	CARR 204:89	influence of W.	WAUGH 923:59	**wallpaper** audible w.	COOKE 245:76
wad leave him a w.	BALL 59:73	Mother of W.	FULL 355:79	Either that w. goes	WILDE 942:24
waddle flounce at a w. away	THOM 884:39	position of the artists of W.	THOM 884:43	w. with which the men	MILL 593:51
wade should I w. no more	SHAK 797:51	there were wolves in W.	THOM 884:47	**walls** cell whose w. are mirrors	ONEI 650:60
Wadman married to Mrs W.	STER 848:42	**walk** And w. among...grass	YEATS 965:10	dead w....Their ivy mantles	BYRON 188:65
wag How now, mad w.?	SHAK 770:28	before we have learnt to w.	CONN 243:9	floors of plaister, and the w. of dung	POPE 686:69
tail must w. the dog	KIPL 490:98	closer w. with God	COWP 250:88	four grey w.	TENN 869:79
wage One man's w. rise	WILS 948:68	country safe to w. in	THAT 881:52	four w. and a ring	HEAN 404:69
w. against the enmity	SHAK 792:2	do not w. so fast	BLAKE 139:91	four w. with tomorrow inside	AKERS 10:11
w. no war with women	SOUT 835:49	'Don't run, w.'	JOHAN 456:71	Hang on thy w.	JONS 467:72
wage-earner status of the w.-e.	SKEL 824:32	good w. spoiled	TWAIN 904:96	look into the stains of w.	LEON 523:77
wager w. that he does exist	PASC 667:78	make running water w.	RAYB 708:89	mute on Tara's w.	MOORE 618:4
wages better w. and shorter hours	ORWE 653:16	Men creep, Not w.	WHIT 938:21	noticed how many w. the room had	CHAN 213:93
common w. of labour	SMITH 827:80	me to w. doth make	SCOT 754:85	no w., no borders	ATWO 41:34
earneth w. to put it into a bag	BIBLE 111:57	never w. down the nave	HOME 425:98	on so many suburban w.	HUGH 435:26
floor under w. and a ceiling	WRIS 963:76	rise up and w.	BIBLE 124:73	on the w. of the world	KENN 482:31
Home...and ta'en thy w.	SHAK 803:60	stray Far as the solar w.	POPE 687:75	peopled labyrinth of w.	SHEL 812:64
labour and w. first	MANN 567:93	take up thy bed, and w.	BIBLE 122:30	phosphorescence out of the w.	MACD 549:20
like rent and w.	SMITH 827:82	talk, not to w.	WILDE 942:26	posts and w. with wine	SPEN 839:50
neither honours nor w.	GARI 360:73	those who like to w.	HILL 418:59	Stone w. do not a prison	LOVE 538:82
		w., and not faint	BIBLE 109:85	W. have ears	ANON 24:23

walnut

W. have ears	LINK 530:27	British way of w.	WAVE 925:3	never to go to w. with one another	CHAM 212:63
W. have tongues	SWIFT 862:55	bungled, unwise w.	PLOM 682:72	never understood this liking for w.	BENN 80:44
w., nor its ships	NICI 637:80	business of w.	GERB 364:64	never was a good w.	FRAN 348:16
w. of institutions	ROET 722:56	business of w.	WELL 928:11	no discharge in that w.	BIBLE 106:24
w. of spiders' legs	DRAY 299:1	calamities of W.	JOHN 460:84	No less renowned then w.	MILT 601:25
W., palaces, half-cities	BYRON 188:67	cardinal maxims of guerrilla w.	KISS 493:85	not at w. with Egypt	EDEN 311:32
w., the only sharers of secrets	AMMI 17:63	cast all weapons of w.	DEKA 270:7	not be involved in a European w	DAILY 260:4
w. with the heads of Bison	MACN 557:97	century…out of this w.	WALL 918:51	nothing of a sacredness of w.	BONH 145:21
Whose w. were high	SPEN 838:22	Civil w. is impossible	PAVL 670:40	not in fair w.	CHUR 224:70
within thy wicked w.	SURR 860:2	cold w. is getting warmer	BARU 67:34	no w. for domination	CHUR 225:81
wooden w. are the best	COVE 249:43	Communist 'w. of liberation'	MCNA 557:87	object of w. is not to die	PATT 670:31
walnut cradle of Spanish w.	PLATH 681:36	conscientious objection to	STRA 857:42	of the book of w.	MONT 615:47
walnuts you received 29 w.	STEE 844:39	consequent to a time of w.	HOBB 420:2	of w. I have slain men	SHAK 788:86
walrus W. and the Carpenter	CARR 204:99	convulsions of a great w.	LLOY 533:72	once w. is over	BEVE 90:63
Walter No repose for Sir W.	SCOTT 754:83	cruellest and most terrible w.	LLOY 533:75	Our w. on terror is well begun	BUSH 183:19
Sir W., being strangely surprised	AUBR 42:59	Dakotas, I am for w.	RED 709:19	painting…an instrument of w.	PICA 677:60
waltz w. that is Viennesey	GERS 365:74	dance and w.	STEIN 845:70	people taut for w.	THOM 885:70
waly O w., w. up the bank	BALL 60:79	dauntless in w.	SCOTT 752:21	permanently on a w. footing	HUXL 442:94
wan w. grass sea	SITW 823:10	declared w. on America	HIRO 419:71	playing golf during a w.	BUSH 183:44
wand all I have of magic w.	HARR 399:57	delays…in w.	DRYD 300:28	plumed w.-bonnet	BENET 79:23
body…straight as Circe's w.	MARL 574:36	desires peace prepare for w.	VEGE 910:48	Politics is w.	MAO 568:28
last possessors of the w.	DIOR 287:4	done very well out of the w.	BALD 57:25	Poor Brutus, with himself at w.	SHAK 776:6
stroke of the enchanter's w.	BYRON 188:58	Don't mention the w.	CLEE 229:80	Power and W.	KIPL 490:93
wander w. in that golden maze	DRYD 299:11	Ease after w.	SPEN 838:28	probabilities of peace or w.	PALM 662:74
wandered as I w. by the way	SHEL 816:59	easier to make w.	CLEM 229:88	profits of w. or office	TREV 896:10
we have w. all our ways	RALE 705:47	eighteen years before a w.	WHITE 935:43	purposes of the w.	LEES 519:4
wanderer do not we, W., await it too?	ARNO 34:93	Either w. is obsolete	FULL 355:71	quickest way of ending a w.	ORWE 655:70
foiled circuitous w.	ARNO 35:1	essence of w.	MACA 545:38	read about the w.	HEMI 409:65
wanderers As w. do	JONS 467:74	European w. thrust upon us	MARY 579:46	reasons for making w.	FRED 349:37
wandering forget the w. and pain	FLEC 340:36	even colder w.	KENN 481:8	responsibility for the w.	HIRO 419:73
W. between two worlds	ARNO 35:4	ever another w. in Europe	BISM 137:36	scourge of w.	UNIT 905:9
w. minstrel	GILB 369:58	everything possible to avoid w.	SCHW 750:90	seek to avoid w.	BLAIR 138:62
wanders w. and loses himself	CONF 240:22	Every time I have asked us to go to w.	BLAIR 138:61	seek…to avoid w.	CHAM 212:65
Wanstead W. drew me over	LEVE 525:23	Every US president has to have a w.	GORB 378:51	seen enough of one w.	JEFF 454:24
want die out for w. of simplicity	POUND 692:20	everywhere, I wage w.	CLEM 229:87	seven days w.	MUIR 624:23
for w. of better Knowledge	PATE 669:13	first casualty when w. comes	JOHN 457:8	sinews of w.	CICE 227:32
get what we don't…w.	KEIL 479:62	First World W. had begun	TAYL 868:47	single w.	GUST 390:3
get what you w.	SMITH 829:12	France has not lost the w.!	DE 270:91	some slain in w.	SHAK 764:52
giant evils of W.	BEVE 90:63	furnish the w.	HEAR 405:83	Spanish ships of w. at sea!	TENN 878:95
gittin all you w.	HARR 399:49	get out of the w. altogether	HELL 407:30	Stand up and take the w.	KIPL 493:71
hide…their w. of art	POPE 685:20	give a w. and nobody will come	SAND 742:27	stately tents of w.	MARL 572:94
if you w. it	WEAT 925:5	good w. makes a good peace	HERB 414:86	state of w. by nature	SWIFT 863:65
I w. it that way	IVES 448:82	government in peace and in w.	BEVE 90:62	success in w.	CHUR 225:88
no w. to them that fear him	BIBLE 100:56	green snot. There is w.	MITS 610:59	success in w.	CLARK 228:61
pleasantest preservative from w.	AUST 46:59	hashed over by nuclear w.	COUP 248:31	support an offensive w.	PAINE 660:30
signifies the w. of government	HOBB 420:3	how we began this w.	PRIE 695:86	surgical w.	ASHD 37:66
w. as an armed man	BIBLE 104:59	I am opposed to…a dumb w.	OBAMA 643:17	Sweets with sweets w. not	SHAK 800:34
w. of character	SHAW 807:5	I can't go to w.	RANK 706:64	take chances in w.	DULL 306:87
w. that pinches	VIRG 914:26	idealism, as in w. time	MENC 587:11	tell us all about the w.	SOUT 835:46
w. to be alone	GARBO 359:63	If there is w.	GREY 388:61	tempered by w.	KENN 481:3
w. to disappear	HUGO 437:67	If the w. didn't…kill you	ORWE 653:28	that first invented w.	MARL 572:97
What more can one w.?	WILDE 940:69	if they mean to have a w.	PARK 664:34	The art of w.	SUN 859:87
wanted Every man is w.	EMER 324:72	if w. did not include killing	ANGE 19:91	They had lost a w.	CLAV 229:77
everything I never w.	GARD 360:69	In a civil w., a general must know	REED 710:33	think hard before starting a w.	BISM 137:34
never really w. to	KING 488:60	In a pattern called a w.	LOWE 539:98	this country is at w. with Germany	CHAM 212:66
Not as we w. it	QUIL 702:10	infection and the hand of w.	SHAK 764:40	this damnable w.	ACHE 3:56
unless he w. something off you	SALI 740:75	in peace and…in w.	MONT 614:39	This is the w. room	KUBR 500:33
w. only one thing	HAZL 404:54	Instruments of W.	ALBE 11:33	this is w.	ADAMS 4:74
wanting Much w., so much w.	WORD 958:74	in the midst of a cold w.	BARU 67:33	Those who can win a w. well	CHUR 225:76
One being only is w.	LAMA 504:72	In the sex w.	CONN 243:8	though w. should rise against me	BIBLE 100:50
wanton As flies to w. boys	SHAK 793:17	In w.…all are losers	CHAM 212:61	throughout the w.	GILB 369:53
hath made me w.	JONS 467:54	In w.…no substitute for victory	MACA 544:7	through the Second World W.	BUSH 184:50
wantonness in clothes a w.	HERR 416:17	In w.: resolution	CHUR 224:69	time of w.	BIBLE 105:14
wantons Sleep, pretty w.	DEKK 270:10	justice, law and crime	NEME 633:18	To offer w.	SHAK 762:79
wants article which nobody w.	HONE 425:12	killing men at w.	MARG 570:69	torch of w. in Europe	HITL 420:92
social w. of the people	CHIS 222:24	know the w. prepared	KIPL 493:70	To w. and arms I fly	LOVE 538:85
supplying our w.	SWIFT 861:34	laws…silent in time of w.	CICE 227:30	truth…known at the end of the w.	WEIZ 928:78
to provide for human w.	BURKE 176:39	less than w. to waste	MILT 607:70	try to end the w.	EISE 314:94
w. have no limits	FLAU 339:26	let the Germans win the w.	MILE 590:88	under the shadow of w.	SPEN 837:99
wanworidly W., crazy, dinsome thing	FERG 333:85	Like a…holy w., a revolution	COOKE 245:74	used to be w.'s alarms	HOOD 426:19
war After each w.	ATKI 40:14	like to the morning's w.	SHAK 760:7	view of history…not of w.	CHILD 222:16
against this they made w.	SHER 816:69	little w. for a great nation	WELL 929:10	wage no w. with women	SOUT 835:49
America is not…at w. with Islam	OBAMA 644:35	living through w.	KRAM 499:3	wage w. against art	RODC 721:43
Ancestral voices prophesying w.!	COLE 236:40	lofty instruments of w.	SHAK 772:64	w. abhorrent to all real women	FOWL 345:61
army that we must train for w.	WILS 949:84	looks on w. as all glory	SHER 818:9	w. against the outsiders	GARI 360:47
arts of w.	MORE 618:10	Lord is a man of w.	BIBLE 93:63	W. alone can carry	MUSS 627:91
as if w. were a special circumstance	HOFS 422:37	lose the w. in an afternoon	CHUR 225:73	W. always finds a way	BREC 158:96
at w. over a few acres	VOLT 914:36	magnificent, but it isn't w.	BOSQ 151:73	w. and mutual slaughter	MILT 605:25
at w. you think about	WILD 943:43	Make love, not w.	ANON 25:50	W., and the pity of W.	OWEN 657:29
'a w. to end w.'	LEWIS 527:73	make w. on a kindred nation	BETH 87:11	w., as in love	NAPO 630:45
beating of w. drums	KOES 495:31	Mankind must put an end to w.	KENN 481:9	w. between civilised nations	GOOCH 378:44
Before the w.	ORWE 653:27	McNamara's w.	MCNA 557:86	w. between men and women	THUR 890:69
benefitted from prolonged w.	SUN 859:89	military struggle…a w.	SCHL 747:33	w. breeds w. again	DAVI 264:67
be prepared for w.	WASH 922:30	miners poured to w.	MACA 546:51	w. called murder	MACD 550:52
blast of w. blows	SHAK 775:74	Minstrel-boy to the w.	MOORE 618:2	w. every twenty-five years	MUSS 628:93
blossom of w.	TENN 876:35	neither shall they learn w.	BIBLE 107:51	w. for the emancipation	LLOY 533:74
British ships of w.	NELS 633:12	never fought a w. against a democracy	OBAMA 644:37	W. has its own sweetness	LAFO 504:55

W. has three handmaidens	HENR 411:12	mutual help...as often as w.	DOBZ 289:79	never comes out in the w.	KIPL 492:50
W. hath no fury	MONT 613:15	true method of w.	MAZZ 583:29	shores by the w.	YEATS 965:5
w. hath smoothed	SHAK 760:32	under the Borgias they had w.	WELL 929:93	w. all this scum off	DE 273:66
w. history...simple one	WODE 952:54	w. is based on deception	SUN 859:88	You cannot w. blood	AHMAD 10:99
w., I call it murder	LOWE 539:5	w. of men and machinery	WOLFE 953:70	washed w. in the brightness	RAND 706:59
w....I hate w.	ROOS 724:8	Warhol all about Andy W.	WARH 920:6	w. me out of the turret	JARR 452:83
w. in heaven	BIBLE 131:10	Waring What's become of W.?	BROW 167:14	w. their robes	BIBLE 131:4
w. in Spain is over	MUSS 628:95	warlike altogether w.	LUTH 542:75	washing grows...only w.	THOM 884:37
w. in Vietnam	MCCA 547:80	w. ironmongery	GILB 369:57	never...poured out my own w.	PU 701:3
W. is a condition of progress	RENAN 711:47	warm Being black is w. and gay	RHYS 712:73	seem thus w. her hands	SHAK 798:64
W. is, after all	RAE 705:35	Be w., but pure	BYRON 187:26	tattered w. on the line	MENC 587:17
w. is a necessary part	MOLT 612:92	in the w. hedge	SHEL 816:61	Washington dependence...on W.	BENN 79:32
W. is being deliberately prolonged	SASS 745:79	neither w. nor cold	GREER 387:45	didn't come to W.	GRAMM 381:94
W. is capitalism with	STOP 855:18	O, she's w.!	SHAK 800:32	first came to W.	TRUM 899:76
w. is natural	STALL 842:9	w. you up from the inside	MURAK 626:62	lawyers in W. who trust each other	DOLE 290:2
W....is not a relationship	ROUS 729:17	whenever he was getting w.	SELL 756:14	price on the W. Monument?	KENN 482:46
W. is peace	ORWE 655:73	while your hand is still w.	ROTH 728:97	shorter than the W. monument	REST 711:62
w. is preferable to...peace	TACI 866:6	yet so w., and yet so cold	LAWS 514:97	spotlight of public life in W.	FOST 345:57
w. is somewhat disappointing	GRIF 388:66	warmer cold war is getting w.	BARU 67:74	W. is a resigning town	SHUL 819:23
W. is the national industry	MIRA 608:14	creatures in w. countries	GUY 390:7	W. is a sieve	REAG 709:14
W. is the trade of kings	DRYD 303:21	warmonger w. put on my passport	BYRON 191:39	W. is a town	GERA 364:60
W....is toil and trouble	DRYD 303:33	warmth key to human w.	ISHI 447:73	W. is awash	SCHR 749:68
W. is to man	MUSS 628:94	No w., no cheerfulness	HOOD 426:37	W....like dull diamonds	MAIL 560:55
W. is too serious a business	CLEM 229:84	vigorous w. did...impart	DRYD 301:64	W. Post over with your big toe	LANCE 506:24
W. is, undoubtedly, hell	LEBO 518:68	yearned for w. and colour	TENN 877:58	W....where good ideas go to die	OBAMA 623:26
w. is what AD is elsewhere	TWAIN 902:49	warn w. you not to be ordinary	KINN 488:65	wash-out w.-o. of a cock-up	ANON 26:10
W. its thousands slays	PORT 689:78	warned be w. by me	BELL 76:60	Was-land furnishings of each W.-l.	FRAME 346:77
W. makes rattling good history	HARDY 397:27	Warner I'd like to thank...Jack W.	ANDR 18:81	wasps politicians are like crazed w.	JOHN 457:94
w. minus the shooting	ORWE 655:81	Working for W. Brothers	MIZN 610:61	w. and hornets break through	SWIFT 861:23
w. of eternal opposition	LYND 543:92	warning by w. to avoid his fate?	SPEN 838:38	Why stir the w.	RICK 715:29
w. of nature	DARW 263:53	come without w.	DAVIS 266:12	waste applied without any w.	LEUP 525:15
w. of races	MUIR 624:27	solemn word of w.	WILS 949:77	dead w. and middle	TWAIN 902:63
w. poet	GURN 390:1	warp Weave the w.	GRAY 385:84	don't intend to w. any	ARMS 33:52
w. raged about us	FRANK 347:2	warped w. and cracked	CRANE 252:52	I love all w.	SHEL 812:60
w. rather than a country	PILG 678:77	warping this odd w. in time	RICH 713:6	in the w. howling wilderness	BIBLE 95:99
W.'s a bloody game	SASS 745:93	warrant I signed my death w.	COLL 237:65	Life is too short to w.	SCOTT 751:8
w.'s a game	COWP 251:20	stag of w.	DAVI 264:69	utter w. is a coachload	HUNT 439:18
W. settles nothing	CHRI 223:44	Warren Miss W. is a great devotee	SHAW 807:9	w. has thinly strayed	ADAMS 4:73
W. springs from the love	RUNC 731:49	warrior brought her w. dead	TENN 873:46	W. is the highest virtue	MURAK 626:60
w. tends to become universal	DU 305:70	painful w.	SHAK 800:44	w. its stock	CRUZ 256:38
W. that will End W.	WELLS 930:30	priest, w., poet	BAUD 69:86	W. of Blood	STUD 858:63
W. That Would Not Boil	TAYL 868:45	This is the happy w.	READ 708:93	w. of seas	GALT 359:54
W. then, w. Open	MILT 602:52	undoomed w.	ANON 20:29	w. of white barren sand	SCHAW 747:20
w. they kill you	ROGE 723:78	w. eyes	HYDE 443:21	w. remains and kills	EMPS 326:8
w., three-quarters	NAPO 629:40	w. that is rapt with love	MARL 572:3	wasted Get w. all the time	CONN 242:91
W. to the castles	CHAM 212:69	warriors pale w., death-pale	KEATS 476:3	Nothing is w.	HERB 413:54
W. to the knife	PALA 661:48	w. here do not seek out	ANDR 18:77	presume to think her w.	EMPS 326:9
w. violates the order of nature	HERO 415:95	w. of Eternal Mind	RUSS 735:42	Thirteen w. years	ANON 25:51
W. was decided in the first twenty	CHUR 225:77	Where are the w. today?	SITT 823:93	wasting I was w. my life	BUFF 172:46
w....which saved the Union	WILS 949:79	wars All skilful in the w.	VAUG 909:37	wasteland observe a vast w.	MINOW 608:11
W. will never cease	MENC 587:10	all their w. are merry	CHES 220:81	Wastle W. dwalt on Tweed	BURNS 179:39
w. with rude Nature	CARL 200:80	All w. are planned	RICE 713:90	watch as a w. in the night	BIBLE 101:93
w. yield to peace	CICE 227:35	brotherhood of men-at-w.	PAZ 671:48	as much a trade...to make a w.	LA 502:7
W. yit with the Skottes	MINOT 608:9	divided by civil w.	MONT 614:36	Care keeps his w.	SHAK 766:89
weapons of w. perished!	BIBLE 96:42	from henceforth thou shalt have w.	BIBLE 98:86	done much better by a w.	BELL 77:73
weapon which will make w.	MORT 621:75	getting them killed in w.	HUGH 435:17	Set a w....before my mouth	BIBLE 104:47
We are against this w., Mr Bush	MOORE 617:93	History is littered with the w.	POWE 693:57	fat gold w.	PLATH 681:30
we glorify w.	MARI 571:76	holy w.	GUIB 389:86	gone by our w.	SHAK 780:29
we have lost this w.	MACD 549:17	maketh w. to cease	BIBLE 100:69	If you w. a game	HOPE 428:59
We have won the w.	CLEM 230:90	maketh w. to cease	BOOK 149:17	repair a w.	THUR 890:86
well that w. is so terrible	LEE 519:99	obviating of all future w.	FORD 343:94	Set a w....before my mouth	BIBLE 104:47
we prepare for w. like...giants	PEAR 671:57	sent into any foreign w.	ROOS 724:11	Suppose I had found a w.	PALEY 661:57
What if someone gave a w.	GINS 372:13	Since w. begin	UNES 905:8	tell you how the w. was made	WYMAN 964:13
What makes w. interesting	DALL 261:18	Soldiers find w.	DONNE 291:28	ten tickings of thy w.	WORD 957:67
What, then, was w.?	GRAV 382:21	subsequent w. have been lost	ORWE 654:35	tuppence for your old w. chain	COLL 237:63
when there was w.	AUDEN 43:85	thought of earthquakes, and of w.	BYRON 189:94	universe...resembles a w.	FONT 341:74
When the w. broke out	WAUGH 923:70	thousand w. of old	TENN 875:96	w. a grass or a leaf	GRAV 382:15
when w. is done	SASS 745:85	titanic w. had groined	OWEN 657:32	W. and pray	BIBLE 119:43
will not have another w.	GEOR 364:52	troops and the big w.	SHAK 790:27	w. each other w. each other	DURR 308:37
win a w. than you can win		W. are fought by children	LIVE 531:49	w....hirelings kick a ball	PRIE 695:84
an earthquake	RANK 706:65	w. are useless	RICH 713:98	w. of his wit	SHAK 804:19
witnesses to the desolation of w.	GEOR 364:49	w. brought nothing about	DRYD 304:58	W. out w'en you'er gittin all	HARR 399:49
wonderful time—the W.	HUGH 435:15	W. cannot be fought	MOUN 622:93	Wear your learning, like your w.	CHES 219:39
world ruled and led to w.?	KRAUS 499:9	w. of the European powers	ADAMS 5:5	watches Dictionaries are like w.	JOHN 464:96
wrong w., at the wrong place	BRAD 155:44	w. that are now afoot	GUST 390:3	famous soft w.	DALI 261:15
warbler Attic w.	GRAY 383:55	wear weapons, and serve in the w.	BOOK 150:43	watchful W. as fowlers	OTWAY 656:99
war-cries w.-c. arise	MCCA 547:74	We best avoid w.	EDEN 311:31	watching I remember w. myself	RHYS 712:78
wardrobe body like a w.	THOM 884:39	what care we...for w.?	WORD 956:57	observe...just by w.	BERRA 87:91
purple w. of thy side	CRAS 254:80	warship dark w. riding there below	SLES 825:52	watchmaker play the role of w.	DAWK 266:16
silken dalliance in the w.	SHAK 775:64	wartime w. decisions	TRUM 900:87	would have become a w.	EINS 314:88
war-drum w.-d. throbbed no longer	TENN 871:17	Warwickshire W. militia	EDGE 311:39	watchman duty of a w.	STEAD 843:33
wards deftly in the oiled w.	KEATS 476:91	war-wolf Desmond the w.-w.	MCCA 547:75	Like some melancholy w.	APOL 29:77
ware buy some other w.	BURNS 178:3	wary a lot to be w. about	WATE 922:37	w. waketh but in vain	BIBLE 103:36
left that fancy w.	DICK 280:28	I can't help feeling w.	PRIE 695:92	w. watches in vain	BIBLE 133:37
Scotland wants nae skinking w.	BURNS 178:95	wash Gonna W. That Man	HAMM 395:66	watchmen w. on the walls	KENN 482:31
wares w....harder to get rid of	FROST 352:1	Intellectually, most people never w.	DUDEK 305:77	w. shall lift up the voice	BIBLE 109:90
warfare general practice of w.	AUGU 44:33	may not w. it out	SIGO 821:64	watch springs like little w. s.	SPEN 837:5

water

Entry	Ref
water about her, of dead w.	MACN 557:94
asked for w....brought him milk	BIBLE 95:12
as w. spilt on the ground	BIBLE 96:47
back into the w.	ANON 26:78
barge-crowded w.	LARK 509:84
before it beat the w.	LONG 535:29
benison of hot w.	BROO 162:87
blade struck the w.	COKE 234:98
blood and w.	BIBLE 123:63
Blood may be thicker than w.	SOME 833:9
Brown bogs with black w.	COLUM 238:89
bubbles, as the w. has	SHAK 796:7
built under the w.	STEW 854:96
Burned on the w.	SHAK 794:55
by land, or by w.	SWIFT 863:73
by w. and the word	STONE 855:11
conscious w. saw its God	CRAS 253:77
covered by useless w.	DOUG 295:11
daughter of Earth and W.	SHEL 813:77
dead still w.	WORD 958:77
deeds Shall be in w. writ	BEAU 71:15
Differs...as much as wine and w.	MARL 574:38
drank rapidly a glass of w.	CUMM 257:59
Drink no longer w.	BIBLE 129:21
drink thy w. with trembling	BIBLE 110:31
fall away Like w.	SHAK 804:41
farre into the w.	MALO 563:15
fields and the w. shout	MERE 587:26
Flowing like clear w.	MACD 550:41
flowing on Of w.	FARJ 330:20
fountain of the w. of life	BIBLE 132:25
give him w. to drink	BIBLE 105:95
go across salt w.	DICK 282:96
hands and feet in the w.	CONR 244:32
hart panteth after the w. brooks	BIBLE 100:63
hear time...like w. running	RHYS 712:74
hit the w. and become so much pulp	CAMP 193:44
Jesus...out of the w.	BIBLE 114:21
Lay a great w.	TENN 878:81
led them to the w.	TORR 894:62
lifted oars like w.	MANS 567:5
like w. in the well	SMITH 828:2
like wine through w.	BRON 162:77
little w. clears us of this deed	SHAK 797:38
make running w. walk	RAYB 708:89
Minnehaha, Laughing W.	LONG 535:30
moonlight on still w.	SCOTT 751:2
moon Upon the w.	SHAK 799:23
native habitat was hot w.	ANON 26:93
neither w. nor any other substance	WATT 922:45
Not all the w.	SHAK 764:47
Nothing is more useful than w.	SMITH 827:78
not to go into the w.	MACA 545:25
one whose name was writ in w.	KEATS 478:50
only hot w.	GORO 379:67
patch of glassy w.	LAWS 514:97
Perrier or Malvern w.	BENN 80:57
poems have form...as w.	POUND 692:34
poured out like w.	BIBLE 99:43
pure air and w.	REES 710:38
Riveris...with w. broun	DOUG 294:1
rivers of w. in a dry place	BIBLE 108:75
run through fire and w.	SHAK 773:11
salt w. blinds them	SHAK 765:57
sight of salt w.	KIPL 491:45
skuttle fish...blackens all the w.	ADDI 7:43
slamming doors and slopping w.	MANS 567:95
Smoothly the w. kissed	MILT 597:32
Smooth runs the w.	SHAK 759:88
solidity of a w. buffalo	PERE 674:18
sound of w.	BASHO 67:44
sound of w.'s murmuring	SHEL 816:59
sports of the land And w.	REID 710:45
stone flung into the w.	LEON 523:78
stones with little w. drops	SHAK 762:96
struggling for life in the w.	JOHN 460:63
sullen w. far beneath	WORD 958:86
tanks filled with w.	GILL 370:77
tears are but w.	SPEN 839:44
Too much of w. hast thou	SHAK 784:59
town surrounded by w.	MOORE 616:72
tumbler of London W.	SMITH 830:50
Unstable as w.	BIBLE 93:49
used to sing in the w.	DICK 279:7
vegetable diet and pure w.	SHEL 812:53
virtues We write in w.	SHAK 805:56
walk on running w.	WILK 943:59
w. and the blood	TOPL 894:61
w. carries all the things	LEON 522:72
w. comes ashore	FROST 352:8
w. curves a stick	LAFO 504:65
W., for Heaven's sake	THAC 880:21
W. like a stone	ROSS 726:47
w. out of the wells of salvation	BIBLE 108:63
w. refreshes	HUME 438:97
w.'s care	YEATS 965:8
w. shrank, and shuddered	ROBE 717:73
W. suggest her clear	DONNE 291:18
w. that was made wine	BIBLE 122:22
w. this sorrow	SHAK 794:47
W. too pure breeds no fish	MAO 569:39
w. upon the stone	STEAD 843:31
W., w., everywhere	COLE 235:13
wetter w.	BROO 163:1
What is a wave without w.	PRAT 694:66
when I makes w. I makes w.	JOYCE 470:23
when she is in hot w.	ROOS 724:3
where no w. is	BIBLE 101:78
water-baby when he was a w.-b.	KING 488:53
water-bag leading a w.-b.	PATE 668:12
waterboarding w. is how we baptize terrorists	PALIN 661:63
watercolour W. is not especially	PISS 679:97
watercolourists pretty English w.	PISS 679:97
watercolours etchings, w.	RODC 721:43
waterfall From the w. he named her	LONG 535:30
water-lily saw the w.-l. bloom	TENN 870:85
Waterloo From Marathon to W.	GILB 369:43
heart as big as W. Station	AGATE 9:91
W. House young man!	GILB 369:48
world-earthquake, W.	TENN 875:9
watermelons He couldn't sell w.	RATH 707:77
waters as the w. cover the sea	BIBLE 108:62
beside the still w.	BIBLE 100:45
bosom the bright w. meet	MOORE 617:99
bread upon the w.	HAGG 391:6
By the w. of Babylon	WALP 919:73
cast my bread on the w.	JACK 448:1
Cast thy bread upon the w.	BIBLE 106:34
come ye to the w.	BIBLE 109:96
crept by me upon the w.	SHAK 803:15
depth Of w.	ROSS 726:49
different w. flow	HERA 412:33
effect of pent-up w.	SUN 859:91
Fades o'er the w. blue	BYRON 187:35
fen of stagnant w.	WORD 958:94
floods of great w.	BIBLE 100:53
in the wilderness shall w. break out	BIBLE 108:76
knowledge of man is as the w.	BACON 49:28
luminous home of w.	ARNO 35:1
Many w. cannot quench love	BIBLE 107:49
mighty w. rolling evermore	WORD 960:11
My native w. blue	OHAG 648:8
name is on your w.	SIGO 821:64
noise of w. in my ears	SHAK 761:40
Once more upon the w.!	BYRON 187:45
quiet w. by	SCOT 754:85
rolling w. go	TENN 872:37
see thee in our w.	JONS 468:81
spirit of God moved upon...the w.	BIBLE 90:80
still w. between walls	TENN 870:89
Stolen w. are sweet	BIBLE 104:62
troubled w. to whirlpool	LOWE 540:19
voice as the sound of many w.	BIBLE 131:88
w. aren't bound to anything	WINT 950:8
w. murmuring	MILT 598:58
w. Of the River Lee	MAHO 559:35
w. shall overflow the hiding place	BIBLE 108:71
w. were abated from off the earth	BIBLE 92:10
When thou passest through the w.	BIBLE 109:87
While the nearer w. roll	WESL 931:59
Who hath measured the w.	BIBLE 108:81
whore that sitteth upon many w.	BIBLE 132:16
wind makis w. overflow	ANON 22:63
yellow in the troubled w.	SALA 739:70
water's edge politics stops at the w. e.	CLIN 231:32
watershed prospect from the w.	STARK 843:24
waterside pair of stair by the w.	PEPYS 674:6
watersmooth-silver w.-s....stallion	CUMM 257:54
waterspouts noise of thy w.	BIBLE 100:65
watery w. noon	BROO 163:98
Watford woad began at W.	TALB 866:14
Watson Good old W.!	DOYLE 297:72
Wattle ever hear of Captain W.?	DIBD 276:29
wattles of clay and w.	YEATS 965:4
waukin W. still and weary	BURNS 178:13
wave brooding on the charmèd w.	MILT 597:32
Churchill on top of the w.	BEAV 71:24
Cross alone has flown the w.	CRANE 252:52
disdainful w. of a white	ANGE 19:99
heard the w.'s splash	BYRON 190:9
lift me as a w.	SHEL 813:82
like a w. of the sea	BIBLE 129:48
off the crested w.	SIGO 821:64
Swiftly walk o'er the western w.	SHEL 816:65
This mounting w.	TENN 870:88
Time's all-serving w.?	BRON 162:76
w. glittered the dew	MANS 567:5
w. of all her waves	KIPL 490:9
w. on w.	CRANE 253:56
w.'s intenser day	SHEL 813:81
w. that echoes round	TENN 876:43
What is a w. without water	PRAT 694:66
wind and w. and oar	TENN 870:93
wind, or swallowing w.	LOVE 538:83
Wish me luck, as you w.	PARR 665:50
Waverley continued to like W.	SCOTT 753:38
waves all thy w. and thy billows	BIBLE 100:65
Britannia, rule the w.	THOM 887:97
dash of w.	ARNO 35:1
Him that walked the w.	MILT 600:94
Like as the w.	SHAK 801:56
lute-resounding w.	POPE 689:44
portly pusher of w.	UPDI 905:14
proud w. be stayed	BIBLE 98:15
shines only on the w. behind us!	COLE 236:51
silver w. of thy sweet singing	SHEL 814:17
sparkling w.	WORD 960:26
spent w.' riot	SWIN 864:97
successive w. of dissent	SCHO 748:47
w. bound beneath me	BYRON 189:45
w. upon the shore	SHEL 812:67
w....washèd it away	SPEN 838:47
w. were always saying	DICK 280:29
w. work less and less	SURR 860:98
Wealdstone turned to w.	BETJ 89:38
waving not w. but drowning	SMITH 830:37
wax didn't w. his moustache	KIPL 489:73
girls with w. faces	WILD 943:44
heart is like w.	BIBLE 99:43
honey and w.	SWIFT 861:18
let virtue be as w.	SHAK 784:41
My faith shall w.	DANI 262:30
w. and wane	WATTS 923:47
W. to receive	BYRON 189:86
way ain't got you one w.	NAUG 632:5
All the W. with LBJ	HOLT 424:90
always be w.	TWAIN 903:67
best w. to suppose	HALI 393:37
catch the nearest w.	SHAK 796:3
certain w. to be wrong	STEI 846:87
cheer one on the tedious w.	ROSS 725:38
Commit thy w. unto the Lord	BIBLE 100:58
dirty, dangerous w.	GOLD 376:13
Every day, in every w.	COUE 248:21
Every w. of a man is right	BIBLE 105:87
except in such a w.	KANT 473:23
fall not out by the w.	BIBLE 93:47
going a long w.	TENN 878:87
go the longest w.	BUTL 185:98
heaven's wide pathless w.	MILT 598:53
here I go, on my w.	PARR 665:50
I am the w.	BIBLE 123:53
I don't know my w. about	WITT 951:25
individual w. of just seeing	JAMES 451:72
it's the w. they say it	STEI 845:82
knows the w. but can't drive	TYNAN 904:4
lead me in the w. everlasting	BIBLE 104:46
Long is the w. And hard	MILT 603:28
lose their w.	THOM 885:62
meet them on your w. down	MIZN 610:60
metaphoric w.	MALA 561:85
most difficult w.	MILL 594:86
My w. of life	SHAK 798:69
one certain w. for a woman	SPARK 835:62
on our w. to the line	SASS 745:86
pioneer a new w.	SHEL 811:97
plods his weary w.	GRAY 384:62
Rebellion lay in his w.	SHAK 771:37
safely by the middle w.	OVID 657:17
sees the world one w.	BARA 63:44

webs

shortest w....commonly the foulest	BACON	50:40
shortest w. to do many things	SMIL	827:70
take my endless w.	HOUS	431:50
That's the w. for Billy and me	HOGG	422:43
the end of the w.	PAST	668:98
This is the w.	BIBLE	108:74
this w. not to interfere	MURD	626:68
thorny w. to heaven	SHAK	781:48
up a sandy w.	BIBLE	113:1
War always finds a w.	BREC	158:96
w. guys yell when they're mad	STEI	845:83
w. is long	SENE	757:22
w. may be known upon earth	BIBLE	101:80
w. of all the earth	BIBLE	95:9
w. of all the earth	BIBLE	97:52
w. of a man with a maid	KIPL	490:2
w. of holiness	BIBLE	108:77
w. plain before my face	BOOK	148:4
w. that takes the town	HERB	413:62
w. to keep weeds	SHUL	819:24
w. to treat her	FAUL	331:45
w. was long	SCOTT	752:9
w. which seemeth right	BIBLE	104:70
w. you'd look at a chessman	JARR	452:87
we lost our w.	NEWS	635:55
whatsoe'er the w.	WORD	962:49
women I...give w. to	PEPYS	674:5
you get in his w.	TOSC	894:63
you'll find the w.	HEAN	405:81
wayfaring w. men	BIBLE	108:77
ways acquainted with all my w.	BIBLE	103:43
all w. do lie open	SHAK	773:5
crooked winding w.	HERB	414:77
fly in different w.	HEMI	409:69
good...In all the w.	WESL	932:68
great and gracious w.	PATM	669:19
Her w. are w. of pleasantness	BIBLE	104:55
know not well the subtle w.	EMER	325:85
learn her wanton w.	ROET	722:62
Let me count the w.!	BROW	166:97
look both w.	EDDI	311:25
maintain mine own w.	BIBLE	98:4
Most sure in all His w.	NEWM	635:49
neither are your w. my w.	BIBLE	109:98
nine and sixty w.	KIPL	490:3
the w. of God to man	POPE	686:71
w. are not as theirs	HOUS	432:67
w. deep and the weather sharp	ELIOT	318:17
w. of saying 'To hell with you'	FENW	332:64
whose w. are all discreet	PARK	663:96
weak arm the w.	FRAN	347:87
concessions of the w.	BURKE	175:14
entrust...freedom to the w.	EISE	314:96
eyesight has always been w.	GREG	387:52
flesh is w.	BIBLE	119:43
God hath chosen the w. things	BIBLE	126:36
How w. a thing	SHAK	777:25
let the w. say, I am strong	BIBLE	111:49
to be w. is miserable	MILT	602:40
w. alone repent!	BYRON	188:77
w. always have to decide	BONH	146:26
w. and feeble woman	ELIZ	321:4
w. and miserable men	CHOM	222:26
W. shall perish	SERV	757:33
w. spot or two in a character	HOLM	424:78
w., still tremulous	LEVE	525:25
weaker One is never w.	OLLI	650:43
wife...the w. vessel	BIBLE	130:70
weakest w. in nature	PASC	667:81
weakness childish w. to lament	SHAK	760:18
felt only his own w.	BELL	78:90
Marks of w.	BLAKE	140:16
means of w. and debility	SHAK	778:71
Power Girt round with w.	SHEL	815:36
sought her w. to reprove	LANY	508:55
strength and w. of human nature	MACA	546:53
strength is made perfect in w.	BIBLE	127:77
though it be a w.	JONS	467:87
w. for the stoic's pride	POPE	687:80
w. offered, strength	LANY	508:54
w. of our race	DELA	271:21
w. which impairs	ARNO	33:63
weaknesses pity...weakens our w.	BALZ	60:96
support two w. at the same time	WILD	943:49
virtues of their w.	MENC	587:6
w....into burnable energy	BELL	78:97
Wealdstone W. turned to waves	BETJ	89:38

wealth all that w. e'er gave	GRAY	384:66
all w. alchemy	DONNE	291:26
as their w. increaseth	MARL	573:9
Black love is Black w.	GIOV	372:17
born into w.	ROCK	720:29
by the acquisition of w.	MONT	614:44
cannot redistribute w.	TSON	900:8
carry the w. of the Indies	JOHN	463:60
consume w. without producing it	SHAW	806:87
cunning purchase of my w.	JONS	466:46
distribution of w.	HARDY	396:98
distribution of w. and income	KEYN	484:82
everything yields to w.	BLEST	142:52
excessive w. a libel	SHEL	812:51
Health, W., Love...and Time	ANON	28:57
heroic w.	WORD	958:94
how much w....in a country	SIDG	819:32
I have had w.	ALBE	11:30
insolence of w.	JOHN	463:61
Labour is the Father...of W.	PETTY	676:46
Large was his w.	DRYD	302:88
Nor that content surpassing w.	SHEL	812:68
nothing like w. for dulling desire	MCGU	552:89
no w. but life	RUSK	733:2
poor man's w.	SIDN	820:46
prevents the rule of w.	BAGE	54:69
prodigal of its w.	NORR	641:57
produce more w.	GILM	371:92
progress of society and w.	RICA	712:80
representative of w.	MILL	591:96
Republics end by w.	MONT	614:42
rich man's w. is his strong city	BIBLE	104:63
road to w.	TROL	897:22
Science...casts its w.	HERZ	416:21
the skill—the w.	ROOS	724:12
w. abides not	EURI	328:65
W. accumulates and men decay	GOLD	376:98
W. accumulates whatever	KEYN	484:74
W. and a good name	WALT	919:87
W. cannot make a life	HERR	415:4
W. does not bring goodness	PLATO	681:43
W. has more and more increased	CARL	200:81
W. I ask not	STEV	853:83
W., in a commercial age	POUND	692:39
w. is distributed in...society	MILL	591:93
w. is health	DYER	309:50
w....makes them doubly poor	CRAB	252:32
W. Of simple beauty	WHIT	938:19
w. of steaming phrases	SCHU	750:77
w. with our wisdom	KENN	482:28
What w....to me had brought	WORD	960:26
with w. and honour blest	DRYD	302:73
With w. your state...improve	DONNE	291:27
worker...poorer the more w.	MARX	578:25
wealthier To be w. or more powerful	HELO	408:54
wealthy Being w.	ALLEN	13:80
healthy and w. and dead	THUR	890:74
w. wife was she	BALL	60:82
weaned were we not w. till then?	DONNE	291:21
weans w. in their bed	MILL	595:98
weapon bayonet is a w.	ANON	24:18
buy an assault w.	CLIN	231:20
how steady you hold your w.	SIMP	822:84
most deadly w.	PARK	665:43
nobler w. than a wound	CRAS	254:86
Nostalgia IS A W.	COUP	248:36
other hand held a w.	BIBLE	98:88
religious and political w.	LEWIS	527:65
thoughtlessness is the w. of the male	CONN	243:8
Time's most lethal w.	SITW	824:18
trusty shield and w.	LUTH	542:73
w. had none	SCOTT	752:21
w. is starvation	STEV	854:92
w. which will make war	MORT	621:75
weapons Clothes are our w.	CART	206:36
do not build w. of mass destruction	HUSS	440:42
fought with nuclear w.	MOUN	622:93
hurt with the same w.	SHAK	769:1
into the cavity...cast all w.	DEKA	270:7
Iraq probably has no w. of mass destruction	COOK	245:70
lawful...to wear w.	BOOK	150:43
not only with w.	MANC	564:51
prevent...nuclear w.	AMIS	16:50
seeking w. of mass destruction	BUSH	183:18
w. against their capitalist exploiters	LENIN	521:39
W. grow rusty	HICKS	417:48

w. of mass destruction	BUSH	183:18
w. of mass destruction	BUSH	183:26
w. of mass destruction...in Iraq	BLIX	142:60
w. of mass extermination	RUSS	734:38
w. of war perished!	BIBLE	96:42
women...dropping their w.	OSBO	655:84
women's w., water-drops	SHAK	792:3
wearer merit of the w.!	SHAK	769:95
new w. of clothes	THOR	888:34
weariness Art thou pale for w.	SHEL	816:66
His W. the Prince	FIRB	336:52
hours of w.	WORD	956:53
labour w.	LYLY	543:86
study is a w.	BIBLE	107:37
W. Can snore	SHAK	803:3
w., the fever, and the fret	KEATS	478:43
yet w. May toss him	HERB	414:83
wearing meals that I...am w.	BUSH	182:95
wearisome monotonous, and w.	THOR	889:51
weary faint and be w.	BIBLE	109:85
fast asleep and w.	BIBLE	95:11
great rock in a w. land	BIBLE	108:75
How w., stale, flat, and unprofitable	SHAK	780:38
In me or, most w.	HOPK	429:88
lay his w. bones	SHAK	805:55
Let him be rich and w.	HERB	414:83
Let us not be w. in well doing	BIBLE	127:83
poor and the w. predominate	GARL	360:74
sae dowf and w.	BURNS	180:45
Say I'm w.	HUNT	439:30
Waukin still and w.	BURNS	178:13
w. be at rest	BIBLE	98:95
w. lot is thine	SCOTT	753:35
w. of these worldly bars	SHAK	776:14
weasel as a w. sucks eggs	SHAK	778:76
w. under the cocktail cabinet	PINT	678:83
weather Autumn's pleasant w.	BURNS	178:91
blue unclouded w.	TENN	870:84
calm or stormy w.	ROSS	725:38
Cricket w.	JOYCE	470:31
dry frigid w.	PIER	677:68
earthquakes are preceded by bright w.	CARL	200:4
fair w.: for the sky is red	BIBLE	117:5
french wine and fine w.	KEATS	476:96
he is also part of the w.	TRIL	897:17
Hillary...responsible for the w.	MCCU	549:16
If it prove fair w.	SUCK	858:72
in clear w.	SURR	860:4
in red w.	STEV	850:78
it's fruitcake w.!	CAPO	197:22
Jolly boating w.	CORY	247:12
makes cold w.	SHAK	804:39
more w....than anywhere else	SAMU	741:3
possible combination of w.	LODGE	534:94
promise of fair w.	DICK	280:27
protecting flat surfaces from the w.	SIER	135:84
reasonable summer w.	WAUGH	923:50
sad or singing w.	SWIN	864:4
season of calm w.	WORD	960:11
seven months of Arctic w.	ANON	23:93
sharp be the w.	SCOTT	753:39
talk is of the w.	JOHN	460:82
There is no bad w.	FIEN	336:39
waiting for the w. to break	PINT	678:82
ways deep and the w. sharp	ELIOT	318:17
W. abroad	RICH	713:93
W. and rain	KIPL	492:61
w. sharp	ANDR	18:79
w. that bringeth no gain	DEKK	270:8
w. the cuckoo likes	HARDY	397:29
won't hold up the w.	MACN	557:98
weave So did I w. my self	HERB	414:74
tangled web we w.	SCOTT	752:24
W. the warp	GRAY	385:84
weaving w. and unweaving	ELIOT	315:14
web as little w. as this	SHAK	789:7
She left the w.	TENN	870:85
take the w. back	BERN	86:84
tangled w. we weave	SCOTT	752:24
The original idea of the w.	BERN	86:82
The w....connects people	BERN	86:83
The w. is the most important book	BEZOS	90:70
w. do parents weave	NASH	631:71
w. of our grand illusion	PAGE	659:15
w. of our life	SHAK	791:68
wove a w. in childhood	BRON	161:59
webs Theoretical w., dirty w.	KELM	479:67

Webster

With swarthy w.	TENN 878:88	
Webster Like W.'s dictionary	BURKE 176:60	
wed December when they w.	SHAK 780:12	
w. a fair young man	CAMP 195:77	
w. itself with Speech	TENN 874:67	
w. ye to my youngest son	SCOTT 753:45	
With this kiss I w. thee	HEYW 417:44	
wedding barefoot on her w. day	SHAK 761:62	
Be well ware of w.	ANON 21:52	
bought her w. clothes	ADDI 7:42	
face...like a w.-cake	AUDEN 44:24	
Let's have a w.	DICK 283:12	
moldering like w.-cake	RICH 713:95	
till our w. day	COLUM 238:88	
where a w. has been	LENN 522:51	
white lies to ice a w. cake	ASQU 38:88	
wedding-guest W.-G. stood still	COLE 234:9	
weddings All w. are similar	BERG 83:25	
wedlock together in holy w.	BOOK 148:95	
W....hath oft compared been	DAVI 264:78	
Wednesday blue and white W. heart	HATT 400:82	
He that died o' W.	SHAK 771:61	
worked Monday....fired W.	ALGR 13:69	
weed on earth a vicious w.	DRYD 302:79	
O thou w.	SHAK 790:34	
salt w. sways in the stream	ARNO 33:57	
weeds all the idle w. that grow	SHAK 793:19	
grubbing w. from gravel paths	KIPL 492:68	
keep w. from overwhelming you	SHUL 819:24	
Long live the w.	HOPK 429:84	
smell far worse than w.	SHAK 802:70	
w. of peace...triumphs	MILT 597:47	
w. will overrun the fields	HOOV 427:42	
winter w. outworn	SHEL 816:57	
week £1 per w.	ANON 23:95	
accomplished in a w.	STEV 852:54	
any crisis next w.	KISS 494:91	
as much as a w.	TWAIN 901:31	
but a w. married	SHAK 774:34	
Christian on a Pound a W.?	HARD 396:92	
Englishman...there only a w.	FRAS 349:33	
go a w. without a drink	LEWIS 526:52	
lease for a w.	ANOU 28:60	
Middle of Next W.	CARR 206:33	
once a w. there should be	ORWE 654:48	
takes the rest of the w.	WALK 917:37	
That Was The W.	ANON 25:48	
tried...once a w.	JOHN 463:47	
w., a natural day	MARL 573:30	
w. is a long time in politics	WILS 948:63	
weekend the dirty w.	SMITH 828:1	
weekends plumber on w.	ALLEN 14:84	
weeks eight hours and w.	SHAK 802:80	
w. of watching the roof leak	SNYD 832:92	
weep better...to w. at joy	SHAK 773:16	
blame thee now to w.	SHAK 762:70	
No, I'll not w.	SHAK 792:3	
not to w. at them	SPIN 840:69	
O now you w.	SHAK 778:44	
O, w. for Adonais!	SHEL 815:27	
shepherds, w. no more	MILT 600:94	
That he should w. for her?	SHAK 782:99	
that I may not w.	BYRON 190:16	
time to w.	BIBLE 106:14	
To w. is to make less	SHAK 760:6	
w. and know why	HOPK 428:81	
w. for him	SHAK 777:36	
W. If you can	HAMM 394:58	
W. not for little Léonie	GRAH 380:88	
w. on your own grave	GRAV 382:22	
w. or she will die	TENN 873:46	
w. with them that w.	BIBLE 125:26	
w. with them that w.	SHAK 760:25	
when I w.	SPEN 839:44	
Why w. ye by the tide	SCOTT 753:45	
you w. alone	WILC 939:43	
weeping doth that bode w.?	SHAK 790:37	
full cause of w.	SHAK 792:43	
Her little boy w. sought	BLAKE 139:92	
joy at w.!	SHAK 773:16	
prove the w. philosopher	SHAK 769:78	
Rachel w. for her children	BIBLE 110:22	
w. and gnashing of teeth	BIBLE 116:58	
w. and gnashing of teeth	BIBLE 119:34	
w. over sins...never committed	WILDE 940:53	
weeps before we know...why he w.	DU 305:71	
Weetabix The W. Years	BENN 80:42	

weigh But w. this song	YEATS 966:11	
number, w. and measure	HALES 393:30	
'tis best to w.	SHAK 775:72	
weighs W. heavily on me	KEATS 475:64	
weight collapsed under the w.	CANN 196:5	
counter-opinion of...same w.	SPEN 837:9	
just w. is his delight	BIBLE 104:64	
Number, W., or Measure	PETTY 676:47	
'tis purchased by the w.	SHAK 770:4	
w. of the superincumbent hour	SHEL 815:36	
w. of this sad time	SHAK 793:40	
w. of womanhood	DANG 262:28	
w. were taken off the driving wheels	CANN 196:6	
weights clock with w. and chains	COLUM 238:90	
weighty drownth that which is w.	BACON 49:25	
weird home of the w.	LAWS 514:94	
weirs grass grows on the w.	YEATS 965:3	
three lone w.	ARNO 35:16	
welcome And W. To It	THUR 890:82	
Bear w. in your eye	SHAK 796:17	
effusive w. of the pier	AUDEN 42:74	
rest may reason and w.	BROW 168:58	
terrible events are w.	SHAK 795:77	
thankful that I am here to w. you	STAN 842:11	
W. to shuttle diplomacy!	SISCO 823:91	
w. was not excessive	USTI 907:49	
welcomest often w. when...gone	SHAK 759:75	
welcoming W., but not very	RANK 706:63	
welfare goes with the w.	WILS 947:47	
highest w. of your souls	PLATO 681:43	
most anxious for its w.	BURKE 175:8	
W. is hated by those	GOLD 376:83	
w....of the Irish nation	REDM 709:21	
W. should be a safety-net	ANON 27:31	
w. will be a hand-out	BLAIR 138:58	
welkin bow'd w....doth bend	MILT 599:80	
Hark! how all the w. rings	WESL 931:58	
let the w. roar	SHAK 772:81	
well All manner of thing shall be w.	ELIOT 321:94	
all shall be w.	JULI 471:41	
And did it very w.	GILB 369:53	
be alive, but to see w.	MART 576:76	
bed-time...and all w.	SHAK 771:58	
cannot think w., love w.	WOOLF 955:25	
confident I can do very w.	JOHN 460:64	
dark w.	PRIC 695:83	
do not feel quite w.	GALB 357:25	
don't dress w.	SHAW 806:94	
in some measure made me w.	SHAK 772:69	
Is it w. with thee?	BIBLE 97:74	
kingdom of the w.	SONT 834:20	
knew too w.	FROST 352:2	
like water in the w.	SMITH 828:2	
looks w. enough on the page	BUNT 173:67	
man lives w.	KIPL 489:77	
never speaks w. of me	CONG 240:24	
One's country is wherever one does w.	ANON 20:21	
They're very w. treated	CHEN 218:25	
things are going relatively w.	BROWN 164:32	
things that you don't do w.	BAN 62:37	
this is working very w. for them	BUSH 182:97	
valley of Baca make it a w.	BIBLE 101:89	
w. as long as I live on horseback	BIRD 136:8	
when looking w. can't	SUCK 858:66	
when things are going w.	BEAU 70:6	
worth doing w.	CHES 219:35	
Would all did so w. as I!	DYER 309:50	
well-appointed w.-a. three-deckers	PALM 661:68	
well-being responsible for its w.-b.	PORT 690:74	
well-bred w.-b. Captain	GILB 368:32	
well-educated w.-e. young women	AUST 46:59	
well-fed 60s face was w.-f.	WATE 922:37	
Wellington shoot three W. College boys	KING 488:50	
well-killed stab...A w.-k. Boche	READ 708:92	
well-looking one of my w.-l. days	GOLD 376:30	
well-off Awrish people are too w.-o.	SHAW 809:67	
well-rounded not a w.-r. person	BELL 77:82	
wells buckets into empty w.	COWP 251:16	
go about and poison w.	MARL 573:12	
w. of salvation	BIBLE 108:63	
well-spaced nothing is w.-s.	WILL 946:18	
well-to-do w.-t.-d. prosper	BRYAN 170:97	
well-written w.-w. life is almost as rare	CARL 201:19	
Welsh devil understands W.	SHAK 771:50	
Welshmen W. [are] Taffies	PAXM 670:45	
wench besides, the w. is dead	MARL 573:12	
fair hot w.	SHAK 770:27	

love a w.	SHIR 819:17	
O ill-starred w.	SHAK 790:49	
stuff fit only for a w.	MASE 580:58	
w....strays so from her kind	DEKK 270:12	
Wenonah called her name W.	LONG 535:28	
wept Caesar hath w.	SHAK 777:38	
He w. to hear	BLAKE 139:85	
I could have w.	HOLM 423:55	
Jesus w.	BIBLE 123:47	
Werther dies from excess...(like W.)	BART 66:26	
W. had a love	THAC 880:40	
Wesen Mensch ist das W	SCHI 747:25	
Weser river W., deep and wide	BROW 167:15	
Wesley W. and the Holy Ghost	MENC 587:14	
west As far as the east is from the w.	BIBLE 102:8	
blessed life was the W.'s future	TOLS 894:54	
daughter of the W.	TENN 875:5	
dearly like the W.	BURNS 178:9	
democracies of the W.	MASA 580:49	
east wind prevails over the w.	MAO 569:35	
falling down the w.	FROST 352:92	
for many people in the w.	SOLZ 833:7	
gardens of the W.	CONN 243:17	
Go W., young man	GREE 385:97	
Go W., young man	SOULE 834:38	
Iris of the W.	BYRON 188:60	
lady of the W. Country	DELA 271:29	
Lochinvar...out of the w.	SCOTT 752:21	
long the brightness of the w.	BRON 161:60	
men of the W.	WEIL 927:69	
oath on the plain at W. Point	MACA 544:8	
opium of the W.	FRAN 346:80	
planted another one down in the w.	BOUL 152:91	
room in the w. for wolves	BABB 48:2	
safeguard of the W.	WORD 959:4	
ship would not travel due W.!	CARR 206:30	
than they do in the W.	SNOW 832:81	
warm wind, the w. wind	MASE 580:53	
W. has not lived	YELT 967:47	
W. is W.	KIPL 489:76	
where the W. begins	CHAP 214:12	
who only the W. End know	POWE 693:61	
Westbury W....nasty odious	COBB 233:78	
Westen Im W. nichts Neues	REMA 710:46	
western All Quiet on the W. Front	REMA 710:43	
intellectual life...of w. society	SNOW 832:77	
music of the W. Hemisphere	GILL 370:87	
we have the w.	DUVA 308:41	
w. is not only the history of this country	LANG 507:42	
w. part of our European	TOLS 894:54	
Wind of the W. sea	TENN 872:24	
written in by a W. Union boy	DOSP 294:86	
Westerner typical W. wishes	RUSS 734:26	
Westerners W. are too self-absorbed	DALAI 261:9	
West Germany beat W. G.	RAMS 706:52	
West Indies an island in the W. I.	ONEI 650:58	
infant negroes in the W. I.	DICK 277:54	
Westminster the wine bars and brothels of W.	LIVI 532:56	
westward stepping w.?	WORD 960:17	
Then w. ho!	SHAK 786:10	
w....the land is bright	CLOU 232:49	
wet bereft Of w. and wildness?	HOPK 429:84	
in the dark and w.	STEV 853:65	
out of these w. clothes	ANON 24:14	
Petals on a w., black bough	POUND 691:95	
whacky Iraqi is really not w.	ACHE 3:52	
whale gull's way and the w.'s way	MASE 580:52	
impotent as a beached w.	TIME 891:19	
'No,' said the W.	KIPL 491:28	
th'enormous w.	SMART 826:65	
three nights in the w.'s belly	BIBLE 117:86	
whaleroad and the w.	LOWE 540:19	
w. ship was my Yale College	MELV 585:57	
whiteness of the w.	MELV 585:61	
whaleroad and the whale	LOWE 540:19	
whales great w. come sailing by	ARNO 33:58	
tub of male w.	UPDI 905:14	
whaling 'Scientific w.' is like the prostitution	WHIT 936:73	
w. a universal metaphor	LODGE 534:95	
what I know w.'s w.	WEST 933:91	
knew W. was W.	TRAV 896:93	
Now w.?	SARO 744:59	
W. ho!	WODE 951:34	
what-is-it spoke with a certain w.-i.-i.	WODE 952:50	
whaups w. are crying	STEV 854:87	

whole

wheat districts…like squares of w.	LARK 509:87	
fill his barn with w. or barley	BUNY 174:84	
separate the w. from the chaff	HUBB 434:1	
sowed tares among the w.	BIBLE 117:93	
Stacker of W.	SAND 741:13	
Thousands of miles of w.	RICH 714:23	
two grains of w.	SHAK 769:73	
w. is green	SHAK 766:18	
wheel before the w.	THOM 884:47	
ever-whirling w. of Change	SPEN 839:60	
every turn of the w.	BAUD 68:67	
Fortune from her w.	SHAK 778:58	
legalistic w. of fortune	CAPO 197:21	
man at the w.	MARI 571:76	
O, how the w. becomes it!	SHAK 784:54	
red w. barrow	WILL 946:10	
restoration of the w.	GAND 359:58	
shoulder to the w.	GINS 372:9	
spinning w. and the bronze axe	ENGE 326:15	
Upon a w. of fire	SHAK 793:30	
w. broken at the cistern	BIBLE 106:36	
w. in the middle of a w.	BIBLE 110:28	
w. is come full circle	SHAK 793:35	
w. of life	STER 848:38	
w.'s kick and the wind's song	MASE 580:50	
W. that turned the Trade	MAND 565:65	
whirlèd like a potter's w.	SHAK 759:74	
you who turn the w.	ELIOT 318:7	
wheeler-dealer called him a w.-d.	MANC 564:49	
wheel-horse third-rate…w.-h.	MENC 587:16	
wheels apparently rolled along on w.	HUXL 441:65	
bodies are under our w.	SHAW 807:20	
moved by little fidget w.	SLES 825:52	
Time's w. runs back	BROW 168:60	
use of w. within w.	MANC 564:49	
w. of Being slow	TENN 874:74	
w.…over my head	TENN 876:30	
whirligig w. of the train	SITW 823:98	
when distrust a man that says w.	HAMM 395:71	
forgotten to say 'W.!'	WODE 952:45	
whence W. are we	SHEL 815:35	
w., wherefore, whither	BRAH 156:56	
where never know w. you are	SALI 740:73	
no idea w. the world is going	SACKS 737:7	
W. is here?	FRYE 354:55	
w. I was born	SALI 739:71	
w. you are	GROS 389:81	
where'er w. you walk	POPE 685:15	
wherefore For every why he had a w.	BUTL 184:67	
why and w. in all things	SHAK 776:96	
whet kites to w. their beaks	RANS 707:69	
whiff w. of grapeshot	CARL 200:5	
whiffling make it the w.	HAZL 403:44	
whiffs in the air in bracing w.	FROST 353:22	
Whig Let W. and Tory a' agree	SKIN 825:50	
neither w. nor a Tory	DISR 287:32	
wise Tory and a wise W.	JOHN 464:79	
Whigism glorious spirit of W.	PITT 679:7	
whigmigmorum drop their w.	SKIN 825:50	
Whigs caught the W. bathing	DISR 288:37	
either Jacobites or became W.	WALP 779:81	
W. admit no force but argument	BROW 166:87	
while every once in a w.	ANDE 18:74	
whim every conviction begins as a w.	BROUN 163:19	
rule by w. or caprice	DOUG 295:21	
strangest w. has seized me	CHES 221:4	
whimper Henceforth I w. no more	WHIT 937:1	
Not with a bang but a w.	ELIOT 318:16	
whimsy Mountains of w.	ROCH 719:11	
whining w. schoolboy	SHAK 779:81	
whip bid him w.	STEV 849:66	
brings down the w.	LESS 523:90	
cossack's w.	TROT 899:62	
dark house and a w.	SHAK 779:96	
Do not forget the w.!	NIET 638:4	
God…hands you a w.	CAPO 197:25	
Lust carries her sharp w.	WEBS 926:23	
stroke of the w. maketh	BIBLE 113:2	
whipcord leader cut from w.	MANC 564:47	
whip-cut w.-c. that prevents	RENAN 711:47	
whipping get a good w.	VICT 912:76	
W. and abuse	STOWE 856:31	
who should scape w.?	SHAK 782:98	
whips chastised you with w.	BIBLE 97:58	
w. and scorns of time	SHAK 782:7	
w. and scorns of time	TWAIN 902:63	
w. to kennel The renegade	RANS 707:72	
whirl w., the excitement, the gaiety	SCHL 747:35	
whirligig w. of time	SHAK 786:23	
w. wheels of the train	SITW 823:98	
whirlpool w. of Cuba's political crisis	CAST 208:80	
w. of speculation	KEYN 484:79	
whirlwind comfort serves in a w.	HOPK 429:92	
Elijah went up by a w.	BIBLE 97:71	
reaping the w.	ELLI 323:33	
reap the w.	BIBLE 111:45	
Rides in the w.-w.	ADDI 6:19	
sweeping w.'s sway	GRAY 385:86	
w. hath blown the dust	DONNE 292:63	
whirr began to w. and chime	AUDEN 43:82	
whiskers crimson w.!	LEAR 516:41	
We of the presentient w.!	GRASS 382:13	
whiskey how to drink w.?	EDGE 311:39	
prayers…and some w.	ASHF 37:71	
w. polishes the copper	TWAIN 902:48	
whiskies after four or five w.	JACO 449:12	
extent of two w.	MONT 613:16	
had eighteen straight w.	THOM 884:30	
whisky drinkin' w. and rye	MCLE 554:22	
drunk on w. or religion	MENC 586:4	
education and w. the price it is	WAUGH 923:58	
fond of w.	WELLS 929:17	
FREEDOM and W. gang thegither	BURNS 177:82	
Great fury, like great w.	CAPO 197:27	
had enough w. there	TWAIN 902:57	
sin of w.	SPARK 835:64	
w. on their breath	UPDI 905:12	
whisper By all ye will or w.	KIPL 491:21	
cried in a w.	CONR 243:30	
Hush! W. who dares	MILNE 596:13	
I shall w.	STEV 849:68	
remonstrative w. to a mob	HUNT 439:20	
w. in her ear	WILB 939:34	
w. it in the kiss	ONEI 651:63	
w. of the south-wind	TENN 871:17	
w. 'Peace'	GROM 389:77	
whispered things that get w. about	BEAT 70:89	
whispering w. of fields unsown	OWEN 658:36	
whisperings keeps eternal w.	KEATS 475:70	
like moths among the w.	FITZ 337:80	
whispers good author…w.	SMITH 829:26	
mild w. use	MILT 599:90	
Picked his bones in w.	ELIOT 318:6	
whistle common as a train w.	KINS 488:67	
did na mind the storm a w.	BURNS 179:23	
maybe just w.	FURT 356:90	
until a shrimp learns to w.	KHRU 485:90	
w. all the airs	GILB 368:40	
w. as it will	SCOTT 752:22	
w. something of mine	BERN 86:88	
W. While You Work	MOREY 619:29	
whistleblower if we could find one…w.	ASSAN 39:99	
whistled w. as he went	DRYD 304:45	
whistling been worth the w.	SHAK 793:18	
ravished with the w. of a name	POPE 687:90	
W. to th'air	SHAK 794:56	
whit sleeps…now the w.	TENN 873:49	
white American w. man	BALD 56:13	
A w. American can orbit the earth	FOLL 341:72	
basic w. and with a roller	BROWN 164:36	
being w. is cold and sad	RHYS 712:73	
beside the w. chickens	WILL 946:10	
between black and w.	THOR 889:54	
black and w. entwine	NOON 641:50	
called the chess-board w.	BROW 168:39	
clothed with w. robes	BIBLE 131:3	
de w. men will	TRUTH 900:4	
dreaming of a W. Christmas	BERL 84:41	
either black or w.	TRAV 896:93	
enough w. lies to ice	ASQU 38:88	
flush o'er delicate w.	KEATS 475:63	
fought against w. domination	MAND 564:53	
give the w. man nothing	WALK 917:38	
Golf is a sport for w. men	WOODS 954:7	
I am black…my soul is w.	BLAKE 139:87	
I have seen the W. Raven	SMART 826:60	
look ahead up the w. road	ELIOT 318:9	
make the w. people…some money	DAVIS 265:2	
never spit on w. again	SHAK 772:73	
nightmare of elderly w. males	ABBO 1:1	
nor w. so very w.	CANN 197:8	
not black and w.	GREE 386:29	
No w. man ever had the blues	LEAD 516:26	
no w. person ever	GIOV 372:17	
phasing out the w. man	WALK 917:36	
prospering w. America	JORD 469:1	
shows them pearly w.	BREC 157:88	
skin…black or whether it is w.	MANS 568:14	
so-called w. races	FORS 344:35	
sound of the w. soldier's axe	RED 709:19	
that is W. Fang	MITF 610:53	
until you see the w. of their eyes	PUTN 700:2	
Wearing w. for Eastertide	HOUS 431:33	
whether a w. man likes him	MACI 553:2	
w. as driven snow	SHAK 800:25	
w. as snow	BIBLE 131:88	
w. as snow	BIBLE 107:50	
w. because you are rich	FANON 329:13	
w. dawn	SHEL 813:93	
w. face goes with a w. mind	GIOV 372:20	
w. girl instructed me to hate	ANON 20:23	
w. heat of this revolution	WILS 948:61	
w. in the blood of the Lamb	BIBLE 131:4	
w. man in Africa	LESS 523:90	
w. man's happiness	DOUG 296:24	
w. man's superior ideals	VASC 909:29	
W. Mariners	ONEI 650:58	
w. men cheat black men	LEE 519:91	
W. people…deal more with God	GIOV 372:19	
w. race does not really think	STEIN 845:66	
w. race is the cancer	SONT 834:16	
w. rose of Scotland	MACD 549:38	
w. rose weeps	TENN 876:28	
W. shall not neutralize the black	BROW 169:76	
w. to black	STEV 853:81	
w.—yet a part of me	HUGH 435:14	
wild w. horses play	ARNO 33:56	
Whitehall King beheaded at W.	PEPYS 673:87	
must not miss W.	APPL 30:90	
them rogues in W.	BROD 160:30	
W. generals	ASHD 37:66	
White House artists…at the W. H.	WHITE 936:59	
gathered in the W. H.	KENN 481:11	
halls of the W. H.	JOHN 457:4	
in control here in the W. H.	HAIG 391:13	
not going to take it to the W. H.	IACO 444:4	
silence in the W. H.	ACHE 2:34	
The W. H.…a palace	HOOV 427:49	
W. H. was a bad career move	BRYS 170:9	
whitewash in the W. H.	NIXON 640:36	
Why are we talking about this in the W.H.?	ASHCR 37:62	
white-livered booty, or turn w.-l.!	DICK 278:66	
whiteness w. she bears up my w.	BIRN 136:30	
w. is but an excremental w.	MILT 600:10	
whites Be nice to w.	TUTU 901:22	
Blacks should be used to play w.	ANGE 19:99	
w.…ignorant of blacks	ANGE 19:98	
W. must be made to realise	BIKO 135:94	
whitewash Clay blurs the w.	AVIS 47:1	
w. in the White House	NIXON 640:36	
whiting as the w. said	HOOD 426:26	
Whitman pact with you, Walt W.	POUND 691:94	
seen by W.'s astounded eyes	BORG 150:58	
The rest is yours, democratic Walt W.	DARIO 262:44	
W. and Poe? Whoremongers	ONEI 651:70	
W.'s mind	HOPK 429:98	
Whitson-ale W.-a. could ever yet	SUCK 858:70	
who w. am I?	RHYS 712:78	
And w. are you?	STER 848:44	
been in W.'s W.	WEST 933:91	
from w.'s w. to w.'s that	WRIS 963:75	
In reality, w. am I?	FANON 330:15	
W.—or what—put the question	HAMM 394:57	
whole animate the w.	SMITH 831:59	
A w. I planned	BROW 168:59	
beauty can lie…in a w.	FOWL 346:65	
call the w. thing off	GERS 365:77	
if she knew the w. of it	TROL 897:30	
love is the w.	CUMM 258:65	
participating in the w.	BEUYS 89:49	
parts of one stupendous w.	POPE 687:78	
parts, or they to w.	POPE 689:42	
parts shall slide into a w.	POPE 686:59	
prayers would make me w.	KIPL 490:95	
seeing the w. of them	RUSK 733:93	
she herself could be w. at last	GEE 362:28	
taking a speck for the w.	EDGE 311:45	
till thou inspire the w.	COLL 238:75	
w. in itself, and a prosperous one	SIEY 820:62	
w. is in every part	LEON 522:70	

wholes

w. is that which has a beginning	ARIS 31:24	opened it too w.	SPARK 836:70	Sic a w. as Willie's w.	BURNS 179:38
w. of experience	SCHO 748:53	world surely is w. enough	STER 848:31	single man...in want of a w.	AUST 45:53
wholes always forming new w.	ELIOT 317:94	**widow** become as a w.!	BIBLE 110:23	sleeping with someone else's w.	BRAD 154:23
wholesale that w. libel	PARK 663:8	become a w. in a painless...fashion	DIAZ 276:26	smirk with his w.	MARI 571:83
wholesome make the earth w.	EMER 325:78	bell rings and the w. weeps	SHAK 774:57	suburban w. struggled with it alone	FRIE 350:64
not w. to Our cause	SHAK 805:48	Black W., death	LOWE 540:17	take my w. to see Rochdale	SHAN 805:64
whooping after that out of all w.!	SHAK 779:92	delicious...be a young w.	SHER 817:85	take with them...the w.	CURR 259:94
whore concubine or w.	HELO 408:53	for the fatherless, and for the w.	BIBLE 95:93	Thane of Fife had a w.	SHAK 798:66
cunning w. of Venice	SHAK 790:35	or Molly Stark's a w.	STARK 843:26	Tib my w.	ANON 22:62
door of the private w.	PARK 664:32	there came a certain poor w.	BIBLE 120:61	to suit his w.?	TROL 898:45
each woman thy fond flexible w.	DEKK 270:16	till you are a much respected w.	ROCH 720:21	to the President, not to his w.	REGAN 710:41
Fortune's a right w.	WEBS 926:17	treated like an Indian w.	MITF 610:55	true and honourable w.	SHAK 777:19
Give...an Englishman his w.	OTWAY 656:7	w. and his orphan	LINC 529:11	waefu' w. and bairnies three	BALL 59:64
have a Madonna–w. complex	THER 882:85	W. at Windsor	KIPL 490:92	went in unto his brother's w.	BIBLE 93:40
judgment of the great w.	BIBLE 132:16	w. is the only complete	RUSS 735:48	Widowed w., and married maid	SCOTT 754:74
like a w., unpack my heart	SHAK 782:2	w. of fifty	SHER 817:90	widowhood...keeps up a w.'s spirits	GAY 362:18
morals of a w.	JOHN 459:59	w. woman	SYNGE 865:22	w....a kind of discipline	BACON 51:74
Protestant w.	GWYN 391:8	will be my w.	GUIT 389:90	w. and children	BACON 51:70
rolls about from w. to w.	ROCH 719:7	**widowhood** comfortable estate of w.	GAY 362:18	w. and children	BACON 51:71
Showed like a rebel's w.	SHAK 795:98	lives would be...improved by w.	SMITH 828:95	w. and children	BACON 51:74
Son of a w.	ROCH 720:20	**widow-maker** old grey W.-m.?	KIPL 492:55	w. at Usher's Well	BALL 60:82
'tis pity she's a w.?	FORD 343:7	**widows** judge of the w.	BIBLE 101:81	w. cries, auld Mahoun	BURNS 180:43
w. and gambler	BLAKE 141:28	New w. howl	SHAK 797:60	w. full of words	BIBLE 113:1
w. may be naked	KILP 486:11	visit the fatherless and w.	BIBLE 130:52	w. had an uncle	HOME 425:98
Why dost thou lash that w.?	SHAK 793:25	w. are crying	HOGG 422:41	w. has ever taken	SHAF 758:53
young man's w.	JOHN 461:14	w....perverse creatures	ADDI 6:33	w., I have sons	LUCAN 541:47
whorehouse song about a w.	GUTH 390:6	w. whose husbands are still alive	BERN 85:65	w. in this art of mine	MICH 590:68
whores make...not women w.	CAREW 198:56	**widthlessness** preposterous w.	CUMM 257:48	w. is beautiful and his children	MENC 586:5
of w. and murderers	WEBS 924:28	**wife** account w....as bills	BACON 51:71	w. left you in May	NORD 641:52
takes the physical out on w.	FROST 352:9	An ideal w.	TARK 867:31	w. looked back	BIBLE 92:24
The damned w.	CLARK 228:63	better off dead...your w.	CHAN 213:88	w. may suffer	EURI 328:55
W....are precious	WEBS 926:42	between man and w.	ANDR 18:78	w....must be dead	AUST 45:50
whoreson Thou w. Z	SHAK 792:97	Brutus' harlot, not his w.	SHAK 777:18	w. shall be as a fruitful vine	BIBLE 103:38
w. jackanapes must take me up	SHAK 803:89	but a w.	TENN 874:82	w. smiles, and lets it go	BARR 65:91
w. little tidy Bartholomew boar-pig	SHAK 772:82	Caesar's w. must be above suspicion	CAES 192:15	w., that he may live	PRIOR 696:9
why ask the question w.?	BENN 80:41	coming together of a man and w.	STOP 855:13	w. that I alone could love	WYCH 964:5
could never tell w.	GILB 368:31	covet thy neighbour's w.	BIBLE 94:66	w. to support	STEV 852:40
For every w. he had a wherefore	BUTL 184:67	did not come in on the w.'s side	LAMB 505:53	with ane wicket w.	DUNB 306:97
person who knows 'w.'	RAVI 707:85	disparagements of his w.'s fidelity	SHAW 811:29	**wifehood** w....incidental	STAN 842:13
see things, and you say, 'W.?'	SHAW 811:34	dwindle into w.	CONG 241:75	**wifie** wee w. waitin'	MORR 620:54
this is w. we read	MANG 565:67	established for the husband and w.	MONT 615:45	**wig** lady in the w.	DICK 280:24
W. am I me?	STEN 847:4	get thee a w.	SHAK 775:60	w. with the scorched foretop	MACA 545:36
w. and wherefore in all things	SHAK 776:96	Giant Despair had a w.	BUNY 174:77	**wigwam** Stood the w. of Nokomis	LONG 535:29
w. are we?	SHEL 815:35	Giving honour unto the w.	BIBLE 130:70	**wild** And the w. regrets	WILDE 942:20
W. is one of the most important words	AUNG 45:43	Have I a w.?	STRO 857:54	bore me in the southern w.	BLAKE 139:87
wicked be he never so w.	ETHE 327:45	health of his w.	CONN 243:14	Call of the W.	LOND 534:9
called w. than vulgar	LEWIS 526:50	hearkened unto the voice of thy w.	BIBLE 91:98	I had grown w.	YEATS 967:41
face should bear a w. mind	SHAK 763:98	how he may please his w.	BIBLE 126:42	I'm w. again	HART 400:68
live among w. people	RICH 714:12	husband frae the w. despises!	BURNS 179:21	made us nobly w.	HERR 416:18
love of w. friends	SHAK 765:59	I have experience: I have a w.	CONG 241:56	manner rude and w.	BELL 76:51
men of Sodom were w.	BIBLE 92:17	I have quarrelled with my w.	PEAC 671:53	never saw a w. thing	LAWR 514:78
mine is being w.	THUR 890:87	kill a w. with kindness	SHAK 762:73	now are w., and do not remember	WYATT 964:90
'...no God', the w. saith	CLOU 232:52	light w. doth make a heavy husband	SHAK 770:25	O w. West Wind	SHEL 813:80
no peace...to the w.	BIBLE 110:4	like Lot's w.	MOOD 615:52	rather rude and w.	BELL 77:64
no pleasure in the death of the w.	BIBLE 111:34	love your neighbour's w.	MACA 545:34	shoreless watery w.	ARNO 34:81
not that men are w.	DU 305:67	man and w. make one fool	JONS 467:65	talk a little w.	SHAK 804:40
pretending to be w.	WILDE 942:6	man lay down his w.	JOYCE 470:28	Walk on the W. Side	ALGR 13:67
prosperity of the w.	BIBLE 101:84	man who's untrue to his w.	AUDEN 43:98	w. and far away	HYDE 443:17
see if there be any w. way	BIBLE 104:46	many years with a good w.	HEMI 409:72	w. and rouch as ever	SMITH 831:64
sick and w.	AUST 46:82	married, but...no w.	CRAS 253:79	W. animals never kill	FROU 353:27
Something w. this way comes	SHAK 797:53	married to a w.	SHAK 770:15	w. are constant	POPE 687:95
w. and to be forbidden	STUB 858:60	marry his w.'s mother	EDGE 311:47	w. boys innocent	THOM 883:16
w....because my skin is red?	SITT 823:93	marry my w.	DALI 261:16	w. for to hold	WYATT 963:88
w. cease from troubling	BIBLE 98:95	Matched with an agèd w.	TENN 870:97	W. Spirit, which art moving	SHEL 813:80
w. man in the bathroom cupboard	EWART 328:72	Mistook his W. for a Hat	SACKS 737:6	w....the noble savage ran	DRYD 300:30
W. people means	SHAW 806:90	moderately faithful w.	SHAW 808:48	w. uncertain thee?	DONNE 290:12
w. to deserve such pain	BROW 168:35	more constant than a w.	RICK 715:28	W. white horses play	ARNO 33:56
wickedness consumed in...w.	BIBLE 112:77	most neglected w.	ROCH 720:21	**wildcats** w. in your kitchens	SHAK 789:6
dwell in the tents of w.	BIBLE 101:90	muzzled by a w.	OFLA 647:98	**Wilde** W.'s captors were the police	PARR 665:51
Hated w. that hinders loving	BROW 168:53	my first w. up there	THUR 890:64	**wilderness** cried in the w.	ATTL 40:26
history than human w.	TAYL 868:46	My w....poor wretch	PEPYS 673:94	crying in the w.	BIBLE 114:18
manifold sins and w.	BOOK 146:31	name of w. seems more blessed	HELO 408:53	day's journey into the w.	BIBLE 97:66
manifold sins and w.	BOOK 147:67	Nature meant me A w.	DRYD 301:59	empire of w. freight and rails	CRANE 253:61
men...are quite capable of every w.	CONR 244:45	neighed after his neighbour's w.	BIBLE 110:13	have brought us forth to this w.	BIBLE 93:64
neither shall w. deliver	BIBLE 106:24	nobody's w.	HERB 412:44	in the waste howling w.	BIBLE 95:99
spiritual w. in high places	BIBLE 128:95	no fury like an ex-w.	CONN 243:7	in the w. shall waters break out	BIBLE 108:76
standard of perfect w.	MACK 554:18	purse out of your w.'s ear	MORT 621:73	leave the ninety and nine in the w.	BIBLE 121:87
W. is always w.	AUST 46:76	Rearrange a 'W.'s' affection!	DICK 283:54	led up of the Spirit into the w.	BIBLE 114:22
w. of these nations	BIBLE 95:91	rejoice with the w. of thy youth	BIBLE 104:57	made the slovenly w.	STEV 849:64
wicket comes to the w. saying	TRAV 895:86	Remember Lot's w.	BIBLE 121:1	make a w.	TACI 865:2
fools at the w.	KIPL 492:49	riding to and from his w.	WHITE 935:47	out into the w.	BIBLE 116:77
slow W. of the Night	THOM 886:86	run away from his w.	SHAW 807:20	Rome is but a w.	SHAK 760:24
taking a man's w.	HORN 430:25	sanctified by the w.	BIBLE 126:41	scapegoat into the w.	BIBLE 94:77
Wickham Mr W. is blessed	AUST 45:57	Senate becomes the w.	TAYL 868:54	Science had married the w.	FERB 332:70
Widdicombe go to W. Fair	BALL 60:81	shall be my w.	SHAK 762:66	singing in the w.	FITZ 337:69
wide kingdom is as w. as the universe	FLAU 339:26	shall cleave unto his w.	BIBLE 91:90	suffered in the w. in vain	MOOD 615:54
Not deep..., but w.	ARNO 33:41	She's your w.	OGIL 648:6	temptation in the w.	BIBLE 102:2

window

To be a little w.	MARV 577:89
voice of him that crieth in the w.	BIBLE 108:79
wander in w.	MUIR 624:25
w. to the amenities	MACD 550:40
wildernesses shores, and desert w.	MILT 598:68
They're parks...not w.	RABAN 703:5
wildfowl hawk to fetch the w.	BALL 59:77
wildness bereft Of wet and w.?	HOPK 429:84
No artful w. to perplex	POPE 686:60
W. and silence disappeared	MACL 555:41
w. is a necessity	MUIR 624:25
wiles w. of the devil	BIBLE 128:95
Wilhelmine little grandchild W.	SOUT 835:45
will above all, the w.	ROOS 724:12
against his w.	MILL 591:99
arbitrary w. of men	ASTE 39:5
Architecture is the w. of the age	MIES 590:85
be his good w. and pleasure	LANC 506:23
bind me...to his absolute w.	PAINE 660:30
boy's w. is the wind's w.	LONG 535:31
bridle to her wanton w.	SPEN 838:34
brings peace and good w.	LLOY 533:77
but strong in w.	TENN 870:02
can't help people against their w.	FREE 349:46
cause is in my w.	SHAK 777:24
character is a...cultivated w.	NOVA 642:66
complies against his w.	BUTL 185:86
contrarious to his w. revealed w.	KNOX 495:14
contrary to the w. of God	JOHN 456:73
doing the w. of God from the heart	BIBLE 128:94
drape over their w. to power	HUXL 442:98
ewe obedient to the benders w.	SPEN 838:20
expression of the w. to power	PAZ 671:49
frame my w. to it	SHAK 759:76
his own sweet w.	WORD 959:3
holy rapes upon our w.	CAREW 198:50
In His w. is our peace	DANTE 262:41
interpret God's w.	RUNC 731:49
in truth, in the Good	KIER 485:3
know our w. is free	JOHN 462:18
law's their w.	SHAK 798:80
leafage worked his w.	ROBE 717:73
liberty to follow my own w.	LOCKE 533:87
love them—against my w.	ANON 20:23
Mariner hath his w.	COLE 234:9
mighty effort of w.	BENT 82:2
much against my w.	PEPYS 674:99
not my w., but thine, be done	BIBLE 122:5
of my own free w. I wore it	DICK 279:4
perfect change of w.	CORY 247:10
Perhaps it is God's w.	SMUTS 831:70
permissive w., through	MILT 603:88
poetry of the w.?	BALZ 61:4
Power into w.	SHAK 786:26
power of the w.	MORAN 618:9
rage of w.	DYER 309:49
rainbow of his w.	LOWE 540:20
rich in W.	SHAK 802:85
settled w. of the Scottish people	SMITH 829:9
Smaller and dryer than the w.	ELIOT 319:23
spiritual w. to power	NIET 638:8
summoned for w.	MORT 621:70
the w. of the people	PARE 663:89
thou hast thy W.	SHAK 802:84
To w. is present with me	BIBLE 125:14
unjust against his w.	PLATO 681:53
Weakening the w.	SPEN 837:94
weak of w., the strong of arm	MAST 581:81
what he has a w. to	HOBB 420:4
w. across the sky in stars	LAWR 514:88
w., And study of revenge	MILT 602:38
w. is excited	CLOU 232:58
w. made or suffered them	SHEL 814:18
w. of my Father	BIBLE 115:55
w. of my Father	BIBLE 117:89
w. of the gods	AESC 8:77
w....overruled by fate	MARL 574:37
w. that my maxim	KANT 473:21
w. to power must increase	LEGU 520:9
w. which fears nothing	BALZ 61:1
With all my w.	PATM 669:20
with half so good a w.	SHAK 778:56
without making his w.	LASS 510:12
Willey batsman's W.	JOHN 465:9
Will Honeycomb heard W. H. say	STEE 844:48
William Memory of King W.	ANON 23:96
Willie rattlin, roarin W.	BURNS 178:3
willing if you're w. to try	OBAMA 644:46
willow Beneath a w. left afloat	TENN 870:86
There is a w. grows aslant	SHAK 784:57
time-stricken w.	CALL 193:32
W., titwillow, titwillow!	GILB 370:68
w. worn of forlorn paramours	SPEN 838:20
willows harps upon the w.	BIBLE 103:42
w. of the brook compass him	BIBLE 99:21
W. whiten	TENN 869:78
wills last w. and testaments	MELV 585:62
man is the being who w.	SCHI 747:35
w. and fates...contrary run	SHAK 783:24
Wilson To read W.	ATLAS 40:20
Wiltshire fibres...unite in W.	FORS 344:22
wimps Lunch is for w.	DOUG 295:18
win A w. doesn't feel as good	AGAS 9:84
but she cannot w.	HUNT 439:21
desire to w.	CONN 242:90
doctor forbids...unless I w.	WOOL 956:46
even if you lose, you w.	WIES 939:31
great fight did w.	SOUT 835:47
if you w. you w. everything	PASC 667:78
let's w. there	KENN 482:42
never too bad to w.	MCEL 550:55
not called to w. battles	JENK 454:32
not necessarily to w.	THOM 887:90
Soldiers...must w.	SASS 745:83
To w. in Vietnam	SPOCK 841:85
We really w. if we w.	DOLE 290:1
w. a paradise?	SHAK 763:15
w. a war than you can w. an earthquake	RANK 706:65
W. her with gifts	SHAK 759:66
w....lose, or...rain	STEN 847:8
w., nothing hurts	NAMA 629:35
w....one for the Gipper	GIPP 372:21
w. the hand of woman	HAWT 402:5
w. the trick	HOYLE 434:94
w. the World Cup under...Labour	WILS 948:69
winced have not w. nor cried aloud	HENL 411:5
Winchelsea shall not lie easy at W.	BENET 79:26
wind Absence...what w. is to fire	BUSSY 184:55
agitate a bag of w.	WHITE 934:26
airts the w. can blaw	BURNS 178:9
all w. throughout	MONT 614:31
And the w. shall say	ELIOT 319:32
as nourishment to w.	MILT 605:28
Autumn w. rises	WU 963:84
Blow, blow, thou winter w.	SHAK 779:84
blowin' in the w.	DYLAN 309:51
blown away with the w.	BIBLE 112:77
Blows the w. to-day	STEV 854:87
Blow, thou w. of God!	KING 487:44
Blow w., swell billow	SHAK 778:52
boy's will is the w.'s	LONG 535:31
But swollen with w.	MILT 599:89
chaff which the w. driveth away	BIBLE 99:25
childhoods are sowing the w.	ELLI 323:33
devotion of the w. and seas	LANC 506:23
drees the w. and rain	SMITH 831:64
dust which the rude w. blows	SHAK 793:18
east w. made flesh	APPL 30:94
east w. may never blow	WALT 920:90
east w. prevails over the west w.	MAO 569:35
eye of the big w.	MAIL 559:39
Fair stood the w. for France	DRAY 298:94
fart in a gale of w.	BARN 64:63
Frosty w. made moan	ROSS 726:47
gentle w. does move	BLAKE 140:7
ghost of w.	WILL 946:22
give...solidity to pure w.	ORWE 655:65
God tempers the w.	STER 849:58
Gone with the w.	DOWS 296:36
Green w.	LORCA 537:58
hears him in the w.	POPE 687:75
hiding place from the w.	BIBLE 108:75
keen sea w.	STEV 854:90
keep the w. away	SHAK 784:65
let her down the w.	SHAK 789:22
Let him twist...in the w.	EHRL 313:71
likewise a w. on the heath	BORR 151:69
listen to the w.	WADD 915:1
listen to the w.'s text	THOM 885:72
Loose as the w.	HERB 414:75
Lord was not in the w.	BIBLE 97:67
motions of w. and cloud	LEE 519:98
no angles to the w.	TESS 880:20
Nor ever w. blows	TENN 878:87
nothing more than w.	ANON 21:58
no w., but pentecostal fire	ELIOT 321:81
O wild West W.	SHEL 813:79
paint the color of the w.	BODE 144:91
piffle before the w.	ASHF 38:72
Pity from blust'ring w.	LOVE 538:83
puff of w....out of the still night	CONR 244:34
resist both w. and tide	SHAK 760:14
rumpling Capework of the w.	WILB 939:40
rushing mighty w.	BIBLE 124:72
sighs like the autumn w.	CHEE 218:8
soft w. breathing through the grass	BRON 162:82
sown the w.	BIBLE 111:45
spit against the w.	WEBS 926:28
tears shall drown the w.	SHAK 796:20
There let the w. sweep	TENN 873:18
There was a fine gentle w.	DICK 277:47
This w. was old	THOM 885:49
throw the sand against the w.	BLAKE 140:22
to be sifted by the w.	BUNT 173:65
Unhelped by any w.	COLE 235:23
upset in a high w.	GOLD 375:75
Walk on through the w.	HAMM 394:65
warm w., the west w.	MASE 580:53
wash the w.!	ELIOT 319:48
western w.	KING 487:43
Westron w.	ANON 21:92
wheel's kick and the w.'s song	MASE 580:50
whenever the w. is high	STEV 853:65
when the w. blew due East	CARR 206:30
when the w. is southerly	SHAK 782:93
where the w.'s feet	SWIN 865:88
wild w. is roaring	BRON 161:55
w. and the rain	SHAK 786:25
w. and the rain	SHAK 776:25
w. and wave and oar	TENN 870:93
w. bloweth where it listeth	BIBLE 122:24
w. doth blow	SHAK 763:28
w. extinguishes candles	LARO 510:5
w. howls	BOWL 153:1
w. inflat in uther mennis eiris	HENR 412:22
w. is chill	SCOTT 752:22
w. it plies the saplings	HOUS 431:47
w. lifted into stinging clouds	PIER 677:68
w. makis waters overflow	ANON 22:63
w. of change is blowing	MACM 556:67
W. of the western sea	TENN 872:37
w. out of the bladder	ANON 22:83
w. passeth over it	BIBLE 102:10
w. sall blaw for evermair	BALL 60:78
w.'s in the east	DICK 281:60
w. so low	BYRON 190:9
w.'s twelve quarters	HOUS 431:50
w. sways in the pines	MERE 588:41
w. that blows through me!	LAWR 512:45
w. that breathes the spring	MILT 597:42
w. that follows fast	CUNN 258:74
w. thrashes God	HUID 438:91
w. was a torrent	NOYES 642:70
w. was cold	SCOTT 752:9
winter w. is loud and wild	BRON 161:74
with an east w.	LOWE 539:14
Woord is but w.	LYDG 543:80
words but w.	BUTL 185:79
winding one great w. river	RANJ 706:60
rising...by a w. stair	BACON 51:82
windings deep w. of the grove	BEAT 70:2
winding-sheet in a w. s.	SMART 826:59
w.-s. of Edward's race	GRAY 385:84
windmill fellow that lives in a w.	CONG 241:68
windmills his w. are ditches	USTI 907:47
window kick a hole in a stained glass w.	CHAN 213:76
light in the w.	SPEN 837:6
light through yonder w. breaks	SHAK 765:77
little w. where the sun	HOOD 426:22
Macy's w. at high noon	JOHN 458:15
mother of Sisera looked out at a w.	BIBLE 95:12
moth hanging on the w. pane	ONAS 650:50
open a w. into one's heart	MELBA 584:44
out at the w.	DICK 277:43
Outside the open w.	WILB 939:36
Prejudices...return through the w.	FRED 349:39
prose is like a w. pane	ORWE 654:59
scarlet thread in the w.	BIBLE 95:7
sheep out of the w.	WELD 928:87
stained-glass w.'s hue	BETJ 88:36

window-glass   1338

throw it out of the w.	BECK 72:47	ecstacy Of sun-fed w.	NEIL 633:11	weak-eyed bat...on leathern w.	COLL 238:76
time to take the w.	STEV 853:72	falser than vows made in w.	SHAK 779:3	White clouds on the w.	ALLI 14:7
Tirling at the w.	MILL 595:98	fetch to me a pint o' w.	BURNS 178:8	w. and a prayer	ADAM 6:13
turned from the w.	ROTH 729:79	Few things surpass old w.	BYRON 190:7	w. of friendship	DICK 279:89
upstairs w. to look out of	WILL 945:4	fine w. leaves you with	AMER 15:24	w. of friendship	DICK 279:90
Waits at the w.	LENN 522:51	flask of w.	FITZ 337:69	w. trails like a banner	JEFF 453:13
Whoever has opened the w.	SPARK 836:70	flown with insolence and w.	MILT 602:47	w. wherewith we fly to heaven	SHAK 760:99
w. has all the exuberance	HAMER 393:46	fond of Spanish w.	MASE 580:58	with as inconstant w.	SHEL 812:55
w. in the autumn evening	MORG 619:31	french w. and fine weather	KEATS 476:96	**winged** w. messenger of heaven	SHAK 765:58
w. of the railroad carriage	LEGER 519:7	From w....friendship springs!	GAY 362:24	**wings** angel...in his foreign w.	SMITH 828:3
w. on the world	UPDI 906:33	full of dewy w.	KEATS 478:45	beating...his luminous w.	ARNO 36:40
window-glass w.-g. to shivers!	SCOTT 753:43	giant refreshed with w.	BOOK 149:27	carried off by the w. of time	LAFO 504:64
windows baseballs through the w.	THUR 890:84	Good w., a friend	ALDR 12:53	clip an Angel's w.	KEATS 477:9
capitalism...with w.	STILL 854:98	good w. needs no bush	SHAK 780:27	cloudy w. expand	BYRON 188:58
cleaned the w.	GILB 368:34	have their strong w. diluted	SALI 740:89	contagion from her sable w.	MARL 573:10
Downy w., close	SHAK 795:95	he drinks no w.	SHAK 773:95	Creative Endeavour lost her w.	WAUGH 923:68
if we had glass w.	DICK 280:22	Here is w.	KEATS 476:88	deep-damasked w.	KEATS 477:20
no doors or w.	MALA 561:84	last drops of vintage w.	BOYLE 154:18	dip their w. in tears	TENN 874:73
not by eastern w. only	CLOU 232:49	Late at e'en, drinkin' the w.	BALL 58:59	divinity...breeding w.	MILT 606:55
old one of Gothic w.	KORN 498:99	like w. through water	BRON 162:77	each one had six w.	BIBLE 107:54
pigeons...hovered about the w.	PEPYS 674:6	lordliest in their w.	MILT 608:98	flapped its tinsel w.	MARV 577:95
shut up the w. and keep it	LEAC 515:13	man and his w.'s sae bewitching!	BURNS 180:61	flies with swallows' w.	SHAK 761:46
stared...through lighted w.	LEE 519:98	mouth do crush their w.	MARV 577:4	full of the linnet's w.	YEATS 965:4
through geranium w.	LEE 519:95	new friend is as new w.	BIBLE 113:89	gates she claps her w.	LYLY 543:83
Through w., and through curtains	DONNE 291:25	new w. into old bottles	BIBLE 116:64	giant w. prevent him from walking	BAUD 87:90
When I'm Cleaning W.	FORM 344:20	new w. intoxicated	MILT 606:55	God of Love...Beteth his w.	CHAU 217:90
w. need washing	CARA 198:34	Not given to w.	BIBLE 129:18	golden hours, on angel w.	BURNS 178:11
w. of the eyes of cats	DRAY 299:1	not look for w.	JONS 467:75	healing in his w.	BIBLE 112:65
w. richly dight	MILT 598:59	not to be rinsed with w.	HOPK 428:68	hear the beating of his w.	BRIG 159:13
w. to my breast	SHAK 800:43	no w. or good beer	GORO 379:67	indefatigable w.	MILT 603:65
winds And the w. blow	THOM 885:65	old w.	GOLD 376:9	lets grow her w.	MILT 598:72
as the w. change	SWIN 864:6	out-did the frolic w.	HERR 416:18	Liberty lends us her w.	BRON 161:69
Autumnal w. prevail	SMART 826:68	pass the rosy w.	DICK 279:90	May cricket...spread its w.	BRAD 155:47
battered by the w.	ADAMS 5:6	Pour out the w. without restraint	SPEN 839:50	mechanical birds with many w.	RAINE 705:39
beteem the w. of heaven	SHAK 780:39	press the rue for w.!	SCOTT 753:35	meer despair of w.	VAUG 909:33
birds and w. and streams	GIBS 367:14	red w. had brought red ruin	CHES 221:85	mount up with w. as eagles	BIBLE 109:85
Blow, w.	SHAK 792:4	red w. of Shiraz into urine?	BLIX 142:61	Oh that I had w. like a dove!	BIBLE 101:75
dead w.' and spent	SWIN 864:97	screw-top w.	AMIS 17:60	pair of fiery w. displayed	BEAU 71:21
floods came, and the w. blew	BIBLE 115:56	small people talk about w.	LEBO 519:63	pigeons...burned, their w.	PEPYS 674:6
great w. shorewards blow	ARNO 33:56	sops in w.	SPEN 838:15	Puts on swift w.	MILT 603:68
King, who ordainest Great w.	ELLE 322:18	spiced in the w. of sadness	MALA 561:86	riches certainly make themselves w.	BIBLE 105:90
leaf that lies rotting in moist w.	CARL 201:7	spoiled the bread and spilled the w.	PATM 669:15	Save w., for heaven	KEATS 477:21
make his bleak w. kiss	SHAK 768:65	Sure there was w.	HERB 414:76	soul has w.	DELA 271:21
motions of the viewless w.	WORD 958:84	Sweet is old w. in bottles	BYRON 189:97	to darkness, on extended w.	STEV 849:71
rebuked the w. and the sea	BIBLE 116:61	till w. inflame them?	BIBLE 107:53	under his w. shalt thou trust	BIBLE 101:96
roar Of w.	BEAT 70:2	truth...credited to w.	PLIN 682:70	under the shadow of thy w.	BIBLE 99:37
Rough w. do shake	SHAK 800:37	venison pies and good w.	LOUI 537:64	under the shadow of thy w.	BIBLE 101:57
scattered them to the four w.	MILT 600:17	water...into the w.	CHES 221:85	under the shadow of thy w.	BOOK 149:27
shades and wanton w.	MILT 599:90	water that was made w.	BIBLE 122:22	Upon her w. presents	HERR 415:9
summer w. that creep	SHEL 812:55	w. and wax	ANON 21:44	upon the w. Of silence	MILT 598:71
the sailor tells stories of the w.	PROP 697:30	W. and women will make men	BIBLE 113:98	while the w. aspire	WORD 961:44
The w. were love-sick	SHAK 794:55	w., be sure to drink it	TAO 867:25	w. are no longer w. to fly	ELIOT 319:23
westlin w.	BURNS 178:91	W. can be a better teacher	FRY 354:49	w. break into fire	BROW 166:94
wild w. coldly blow	BRON 161:73	w. can...the wise beguile	POPE 686:51	w. display and altars raise	DRYD 301:45
w. and sunbeams...convex gleams	SHEL 813:77	w. does but draw forth	SHER 815:91	w. like a dove	BOOK 149:19
w. are all asleep	ARNO 33:57	w. for thy stomach's sake	BIBLE 129:21	w. of gentle flush	KEATS 475:63
w. blew for or against	DICK 280:27	W. gives you liberty	WYCH 964:99	w. of the breeze	BRON 161:55
w....howling at all hours	WORD 961:30	w. in rivers	SCOTT 753:43	w. of the morning	BIBLE 103:44
w. of doctrine	MILT 600:7	W. is as good as life	BIBLE 113:5	w. outspread Dove-like	MILT 601:31
w. of heaven mix for ever	SHEL 813:78	W. is the strongest	BIBLE 112:67	w. with tireless feet	ROBE 717:72
w. of March	SHAK 799:19	W. makes a man better	JOHN 463:62	with ah! bright w.	HOPK 428:71
W. of the World	KIPL 490:94	w. maketh merry	BIBLE 106:32	with the shadow of his w.	SHAK 760:29
w. that blew!	TENN 875:8	w., oh how much sweeter	RABE 703:9	**wingtip** from w. to w.	BACH 49:11
w. will blow the profit	MACN 557:98	w. that maketh glad	BIBLE 102:11	**winner** crowning the w.	COUB 248:19
w., with wonder whist	MILT 597:32	w. that tasted of the tar?	BELL 77:70	**winners** there are no w.	CHAM 212:61
windshield w. of the car	LEGER 519:7	w. was a farce	POWE 693:44	where would the w. be?	STEN 847:9
Windsor as proud W.	SURR 860:1	w. was port	PRIOR 696:8	**winning** fallacy...about w.	BLAN 141:48
Free run of W. Forest	KING 488:50	w. which overflows	MERE 588:38	If the world be worth thy w.	DRYD 303:33
Widow at W.	KIPL 490:92	w. will burn our mouth	EMER 325:83	Never change a w. game	TILD 891:12
windward between w. and lee	SWIN 864:16	with w. dispense	CRAB 251:24	not the w. that matters	COOKE 245:75
look to w.	ELIOT 316:7	woman, w. and song	LUTH 542:76	not w. but taking part	COUB 248:20
windy w. side of the law	SHAK 786:18	**wine-cup** when the w.-c. glistens	SCOTT 754:64	the question as to whether we are w.	RUMS 731:44
wine Apostle's advice to use w.	BERN 85:62	**wine-less** thanks to w.-l.	BROW 169:80	W. isn't everything	LOMB 534:6
Be not drunk with w.	BIBLE 128:92	**wine-pots** castaway w.-p.	CLOU 232:55	W. isn't everything	PALM 661:65
blood and w. are red.	WILDE 942:15	**wines** importation of all foreign w.	SMITH 827:85	w. man's affection	GILB 368:38
both in w. and women	KITC 494:98	**wine-vaults** previously been to a w.-v.	DICK 279:18	**Winnipeg** Boy Meets Girl in W.	MACL 555:49
Botticelli isn't a w.	PUNCH 700:83	**wing** After the kingfisher's w.	ELIOT 319:43	**winnowed** deep thoughts can be w.	SAGAN 737:26
buy w. and milk without money	BIBLE 109:96	crept...on a broken w.	TENN 876:33	**wins** If Margaret Thatcher w.	KINN 488:65
cargo of...sweet white w.	MASE 580:55	crow Makes w.	SHAK 797:48	one who w.	SEXT 758:49
cup of full w.	FLET 341:58	flung the span on even w.	CRANE 253:67	teamwork w. championships	JORD 469:4
dark w. of Venice!	MORR 620:46	insect youth are on the w.	GRAY 384:58	Who dares, w.	ANON 24:21
days of w. and roses	DOWS 296:37	lark's on the w.	BROW 167:9	w. everyone's approval	HORA 430:20
Differs...as much as w. and water	MARL 574:38	left w....right w.	ASQU 38:94	**winter** age is as a lusty w.	SHAK 778:71
Drinking the blude-red w.	BALL 59:69	night...like a great dark w.	RAND 706:57	among the w. snows	GLAD 373:38
drink thy w. with a merry heart	BIBLE 106:27	Nor knowst'ou w. from tail	POUND 692:27	as w. changes the trees	BRON 162:79
drink w., and eat good cheer	MIDD 590:72	shade is on the brightest w.	SITW 823:6	as w. lies	MACD 549:33
Drink w....as you please	BAUD 68:73	space, an eaglet's w.	CRANE 253:62	Bare W....changed to Spring	SHEL 816:59

wishful

Entry	Ref
bleak mid-w.	ROSS 726:47
Blow, blow, thou w. wind	SHAK 779:83
Christmas...in the Middle of W.	ADDI 6:31
covered in w. with violets	SHEL 815:26
dead of w.	ELIOT 318:17
do we believe in w.?	ROTH 727:79
English w.	BYRON 190:23
especially in W.	SWIFT 862:59
every w. change to spring	TENN 878:77
Forget not bees in w.	SACK 737:8
For w., spring, and summer	ANON 22:67
from w. going into w.	BEDE 72:59
furious w. blowing	RANS 707:70
furious w.'s rages	SHAK 803:7
heel Of limping w.	SHAK 765:68
How like a w.	SHAK 802:71
If W. comes	SHEL 813:84
In w. I get up at night	STEV 853:63
ninetieth w. came	EGAN 313:65
Now is the w.	SHAK 760:31
O W.! bar thine adamantine doors	BLAKE 139:83
People live within w.	MUNRO 625:52
poor as w.	SHAK 789:20
sad tale's best for w.	SHAK 799:12
same w. and summer	SHAK 769:1
severest w....the spring	COWP 251:8
Summer in W.	CRAS 253:78
summer out of w.	DONNE 293:72
through the perils of w.	TROL 897:23
Thus in the w. stands	MILL 592:24
Twice a week the w.	HOUS 431:42
very dead of w.	ANDR 18:79
was the w. wild	MILT 597:31
when rivers are swollen in w.	SOPH 834:28
w. evening settles down	ELIOT 317:70
W. is come and gone	SHEL 815:32
W. is for women	PLATH 681:36
w. is past	BIBLE 107:43
W. lies too long	CATH 208:88
w. long, I am one	NASH 631:83
w., plague and pestilence	NASHE 632:95
W. scourged the meadow	ROBE 717:73
w.'s rains and ruins	SWIN 863:83
w. weeds outworn	SHEL 816:57
w., when men kill the fat swine	ANON 20:40
w. wind is loud and wild	BRON 161:74
W., yelling through the troublous air	COLL 238:77
Would seem a w.'s day	ROCH 720:25
winters Four lagging w.	SHAK 764:35
green end of one of civilization's hardest w.	FOWL 345:62
Of those four w.	GREE 386:10
sixteen w. cannot blow away	SHAK 800:31
wipe Gives it a w.	HOOD 426:38
wire fine w. around our s.	STEV 851:11
high w. of his own making	FERL 333:89
wireless message came on the w.	PENI 673:80
wires Along the electric w.	AUST 47:96
transmit the voice over w.	ANON 23:90
w. that span the mountain stream	CRANE 253:60
wisdom acquire that kind of w.?	ATWO 41:46
age of w.	DICK 282:94
apply our hearts unto w.	BIBLE 101:95
attained the sum Of w.	MILT 607:42
beginning in w.	LOWE 540:28
beginning of w.	BIBLE 102:19
beginning of w.	FLAU 339:24
but not to our w.	BANKS 62:22
but w. lingers	TENN 871:20
cannot myself give birth to w.	SOCR 833:96
contrivance of human w.	BURKE 176:39
dispose Of highest w.	MILT 608:4
double share Of w.	MILT 607:83
evidence of our w.	TROL 897:26
faith without w.	RUNC 731:50
famous then By w.	MILT 607:77
hard, ancient w.	WAUGH 924:81
highest w. and...beauty	EINS 313:80
idea of elder w.	UPDI 906:36
infallible criterion of w.	BURKE 176:51
infinite goodness and w.	WALL 917:45
in much w. is much grief	BIBLE 105:12
in respect of w.	PLATO 681:41
Jesus increased in w.	BIBLE 120:71
make me to know w.	BIBLE 101:72
more than W., Art, or Nature	HERR 415:6
Music is...your w.	PARK 663:93
nor w., in the grave	BIBLE 106:28
Of such w.	PATER 668:11
only w. ever to be attained	PRAT 694:67
only w. we can hope to acquire	ELIOT 320:61
our pocket w.	STEV 852:44
palace of w.	BLAKE 139:96
pray we have the w.	ALLEN 14:98
privilege of w. to listen	HOLM 424:83
profoundest w.	HAWT 402:13
Raphael paints w.	EMER 325:93
reputation for w. and honour	BIBLE 106:30
run to conceits or w.	BART 66:15
Science robs men of w.	UNAM 905:7
score of their w.	SWIFT 862:47
seek for knowledge and w.	SHEL 811:45
stage of w.	SKIN 825:49
staid W.'s hue	MILT 598:50
such w. as many of us have	TROL 897:32
that hopeless w. of experience	ONEI 651:63
There is a w. that is woe	MELV 585:63
There's more of w.	WORD 957:58
there's w. in women	BROO 162:85
those who love want w.	SHEL 814:10
thought...we had w.	BENET 79:28
turns W. to folly	MILT 605:28
utter words of w.	HUXL 442:87
We do not receive w.	PROU 698:44
what is bettre than w.?	CHAU 217:97
W. and policy dictate	NAPO 629:39
W. and Spirit of the universe!	WORD 957:69
w. at one entrance quite	MILT 603:75
w. begins at the end	WEBS 927:43
w. be put in a silver rod	BLAKE 139:84
w. can there be to choose	MILT 600:5
W. comes not from reason	GIDE 367:20
W. crieth without	BIBLE 104:51
W. denotes the pursuing	HUTC 441:48
W. hath builded her house	BIBLE 104:61
w. in discourse	MILT 605:41
W. in minds attentive	COWP 251:21
W. is a meditation	SPIN 841:80
W. is humble	COWP 251:22
w. is justified	BIBLE 116:80
W. is the principal thing	BIBLE 104:54
W....knowledge of good and evil	CHEE 218:6
W....lost in knowledge?	ELIOT 319:31
w....more precious than rubies	BIBLE 104:55
w. of a learned man	BIBLE 113:19
w. of God	BLAKE 126:35
w. of old men	ELIOT 320:60
w. of the crocodiles	BACON 52:7
w. of the sociologists	DYSON 309:59
w. shall die with you	BIBLE 98:2
W.'s heavenly Father	WORD 962:49
W.'s self Oft seeks	MILT 598:72
w. teaches us	KEYN 485:84
w. to distinguish the one	NIEB 637:89
W. without honesty	JONS 468:88
With the ancient is w.	BIBLE 98:3
world by w. knew not God	BIBLE 126:35
wisdoms w. of maturity	LIVE 531:50
wise A being darkly w.	POPE 687:80
all the rest, though fair and w.	SHEL 815:44
art of being w.	JAMES 451:68
as w. a snout on	FERG 333:84
as w. to cast a violet	SHEL 816:49
be lowly w.	MILT 605:36
Be not w. in your own conceits	BIBLE 125:27
Better is a poor and a w. child	BIBLE 106:19
better not to think ourselves w.	ELIOT 315:21
consider her ways, and be w.	BIBLE 104:58
cunning men pass for w.	BACON 52:3
discloses to be w.	BIER 134:75
folly to be w.	GRAY 383:48
fool doth think he is w.	SHAK 780:16
God only w.	SMITH 831:65
Great men are not always w.	BIBLE 98:11
heard a w. man say	HOUS 431:38
Histories make men w.	BACON 53:39
how vainly would the w.	ROCH 719:8
if you are w.	FOWL 345:60
in presence sad and w.	SURR 860:4
Is it the w. men or the fools?	IBSEN 444:7
liken him unto a w. man	BIBLE 115:56
make us happy make us w.	MASE 580:65
manly w.	MARL 572:5
more fools than w.	GIBB 367:7
more of the fool than of the w.	BACON 51:91
Neither a w. man nor a brave man	EISE 314:93
None w. dares hopeless venture	EURI 328:57
Nor ever did a w. one	ROCH 720:27
nor talk too w.	KIPL 492:62
No rules, however w.	RUSS 734:31
not w. to have either	GIRA 372:26
no w. man will undertake	CARL 200:87
O w. young judge	SHAK 770:14
puzzle all the w.	DRYD 301:70
reputed w. For saying nothing	SHAK 768:70
returns home w. and useful	BELL 76:44
should be w.	SHAK 792:93
Sitting on a w. man's knee	HUXL 442:87
Some deemed him wondrous w.	BEAT 70:1
spirits of the w.	SHAK 772:79
teach a w. man	RABE 704:18
the mighty, and the w.	WORD 961:42
The w. want love	SHEL 814:10
think as w. men do	ASCH 37:52
to love and to be w.	BACON 50:36
What fool is not so w.	SHAK 763:15
wherefore thou be w.	TENN 879:4
whether they be w. or simple	SCHW 751:94
wine can...the w. beguile	POPE 686:50
w. as serpents	BIBLE 116:69
w. course of prophylaxis	SILVA 821:70
w. enough to understand	SCHW 750:90
w. father that knows	SHAK 769:88
w., for cure, on exercise depend	DRYD 304:48
w. man keepeth it in	BIBLE 105:5
w. man proportions his belief	HUME 438:6
W. men come in all sizes	HERN 415:94
W. men fish here	STEL 846:1
w. men follow fools	BACON 52:98
W. men from the east	BIBLE 114:16
w. person is colour-blind	SCHW 751:95
w. shall shine	BIBLE 111:44
wisest of the w.	TENN 877:70
w. Tory and a w. Whig	JOHN 464:79
w. who soar	WORD 961:45
wise-cracking w.-c. and wit	PARK 664:23
wisely men and nations behave w.	EBAN 310:8
W. and slow	SHAK 766:90
Wiseman wise-manned...By W.	BROW 169:70
wiseness let thy w. fear	SHAK 784:67
wiser be w. than ourselves	TROL 897:26
but not the w. grow	POMF 684:9
ignorant man to be guided by the w.	CARL 201:26
looked w. when he was seated	KEYN 484:70
w....of the two sexes	GIBB 366:92
w. than their own	BROO 162:85
young man will be w.	TENN 878:74
wisest more than the w. man	COLT 238:84
Only the w. of mankind	SMITH 829:12
w., brightest, meanest of mankind	POPE 687:90
w. of men in all ages	STER 848:23
w. of them all professed	MILT 607:78
w., virtuousest, discreetest	MILT 605:40
wish As we can w.	WALL 918:58
constant and perpetual w.	JUST 471:51
every fear hides a w.	MAMET 564:45
man has a lurking w.	JOHN 462:23
man who granted his inmost w.	DAVI 265:85
momentary w.	ORWE 654:29
Thy w. nor prayer	VAUG 909:33
to w. to be remarkable	HOLM 424:75
virtue...the w. for it	PRIT 696:19
The w. to travel	THER 882:95
w. for prayer	BERN 85:59
w. for what I faintly hope	DRYD 299:11
w. it were impossible	JOHN 464:1
w. to admire	JOHN 463:73
w. to spread those opinions	BUTL 185:90
W. you were here	KAUF 475:17
wished w. him to talk on	HAZL 403:34
wishes all their country's w. blest!	COLL 237:71
archetypal w.	GABOR 355:82
good w. to the corpse	BARR 65:84
gratification of your w.	SHEL 811:45
hissing laboratory of his w.	THOM 884:67
sober w. never learned to stray	GRAY 384:72
w. that were fulfilled	KISS 494:90
w., vain as mine	WORD 960:21
wishful w. thinkers	QUINE 702:22
W. thinking...effective for	WEIN 928:77

wishing

wishing when we give up w. — ELIOT 315:33
wit although he had much w. — BUTL 184:64
an adequate substitute for w. — PRIE 695:94
baiting place of w. — SIDN 820:46
beams of w. — DRYD 300:44
Better...than a foolish w. — SHAK 785:86
blend of homespun tastes, acid w. — MCFA 551:67
by his strength and w. — HOBB 420:4
cannot say he wanted w. — DRYD 300:23
cause that w. is in other men — SHAK 772:70
comic w. degenerating into clenches — DRYD 300:20
conscience fools my w.! — JONS 467:53
Danes' w. — ROCH 719:9
does harm to my w. — SHAK 785:83
doors upon a woman's w. — SHAK 780:13
dream past the w. of man — SHAK 767:43
Drinking, to engender w. — ROCH 720:23
give wit to your characters — DIDE 284:59
had I w., before I kiss'd — BALL 60:80
has not w. enough — CONG 241:59
have a present w. — BACON 53:38
he shoots his w. — SHAK 780:26
high As metaphysic w. can fly — BUTL 184:68
His fine w. — SHEL 814:5
His w. invites you — COWP 250:91
Impropriety is the soul of w. — MAUG 582:4
little tiny w. — SHAK 792:9
liveliest effusions of w. — AUST 46:83
Love...doth show her w. — ANON 22:67
love's fine w. — SHAK 800:42
malice mingled with a little w. — DRYD 303:14
Marriage is the grave or tomb of w. — CAVE 210:20
marrow of w. — NASHE 631:89
more than w. to make an author — LA 502:7
neither a w. — CONG 240:47
no man's w. — DONNE 292:58
none in her sense and w. — BEHN 75:25
no pick-purse of another's w. — SIDN 820:50
not enough w. to keep it — JOHN 464:93
not his pointed w. — POPE 688:17
No wily w. to salve a sore — DYER 309:48
old man's w. may wander — TENN 878:74
Old Mother W. — DENH 272:62
only w. among Lords — JOHN 459:60
piety nor w. — FITZ 337:70
prize Of w. or arms — MILT 597:47
proud mind, a crafty w. — KNOX 495:15
quick in w. — ASCH 37:54
reaches of a human w. — MARL 572:2
Shakespeare the greater w. — DRYD 300:25
so much w., and mirth — ADDI 6:27
so silly a w. — WEBS 926:40
soul of w. — SHAK 782:4
sparks that are like w. — SHAK 774:39
Staircase w. — DIDE 285:74
'tis w. in them — SHAK 787:59
to mortify a w. — POPE 688:21
too proud for a w. — GOLD 377:17
True w. is Nature...dressed — POPE 685:20
universal monarchy of w. — CAREW 198:52
use my w. as a pitchfork — LARK 509:79
watch of his w. — SHAK 804:19
whole w. in a jest — BEAU 70:11
w. enough to run away — BUTL 185:87
W. has truth in it — PARK 664:29
with thy shallow w. — TENN 869:73
w. in all languages — DRYD 300:19
W. is more necessary than beauty — WYCH 964:2
w. is out — SHAK 774:49
W....is the unexpected copulation — JOHN 459:54
w. its soul — COLE 235:33
w. of man — WARN 921:11
w. should no more be sincere — CONG 241:58
w. with dunces — POPE 689:38
Words w. has not salted — ANON 21:58
worth, and w., and sense — TENN 872:28
witch Aroint thee, w. — SHAK 795:99
Beauty is a w. — SHAK 773:26
crabbed malice of a maundering w. — DISR 288:46
W. of Atlas — YEATS 967:39
witchcraft rebellion...sin of w. — BIBLE 96:33
Sans w. could not — SHAK 788:90
w. in your lips — SHAK 776:1
witches w. and sages — SMITH 830:38
Soul-killing w. that deform — SHAK 762:91
witching w. time of night — SHAK 783:30
with Either w. it or upon it — ANON 20:17

withdraw w....troops from Ireland — REDM 709:21
withdrawal emotional w. — COUP 248:33
wither Age cannot w. her — SHAK 794:58
w. on the tree — JAY 453:2
withered w. in the sod? — BRON 161:59
withers our w. are unwrung — SHAK 783:28
within need to look w. — SNYD 832:93
once it is w. thee — HERB 413:55
people to be w. at 9 — PEPYS 674:2
that w. which passeth show — SHAK 780:96
they that are w. — DAVI 264:78
without they that are w. — DAVI 264:78
witlings w. sneer — JOHN 459:39
witness as God is my w. — MITC 610:42
call heaven and earth to w. — BIBLE 94:87
Thou shalt not bear false w. — BIBLE 94:66
w. our own limits — THOR 888:27
witnesses histories told by w. — PASC 667:92
massed multitude of silent w. — GEOR 364:49
so great a cloud of w. — BIBLE 129:43
usually they want w. — DE 268:45
W. are expensive — RACI 704:27
w. laid down their clothes — BIBLE 124:78
w. unto me both in Jerusalem — BIBLE 124:70
wits at first for w....passed — POPE 685:17
at their w.'s end — BIBLE 102:16
cast on female w. — BRAD 155:50
drive a man out of his w. — ALCO 12:27
eloquence, native to famous w. — MILT 607:79
Great w....to madness near allied — DRYD 301:72
have ever homely w. — SHAK 758:55
of their w. the wise beguile — POPE 686:51
people in their right w. — LEST 524:8
poetry is conceived...in their w. — ARNO 36:42
recover his w. there — SHAK 784:62
stolen his w. away — DELA 271:28
when w. were fresh and clear — ARNO 34:94
witty Better a w. fool — SHAK 785:86
Conquered people tend to be w. — BELL 77:83
dogmatic, and ironically w. — REST 711:62
famous w. saying — THUR 890:90
intelligent, the w., the brave — MILL 592:27
not only w. in myself — SHAK 772:70
wive come to w. it wealthily — SHAK 761:60
wives bad...have very good w. — BACON 51:77
corpses or w. — SWIN 864:94
dumb goose-hiss of the w. — THOM 884:39
Husbands, love your w. — BIBLE 128:12
impart to w. and slaves — DRYD 301:64
lighten...our w.' heels — SHAK 775:59
Like strawberry w. — ELIZ 322:8
men...succeed through the help of their w. — LEE 519:1
night's lodging of their w. — WEBS 927:48
old w.' fables — BIBLE 129:19
old w. of both sexes — MACD 550:39
only my w. — GUIT 389:90
outraging their w. and daughters — GENG 363:43
poisoned by their w. — SHAK 764:52
preserve...our w. — LOVE 538:89
sky changes when they are w. — SHAK 780:12
That have revolted w. — SHAK 799:10
Their w. to all encounters! — JONS 467:51
toil of the farmers' w. — GARL 360:75
Translations, like w. — CAMP 194:58
we have w. — TENN 879:98
w. and daughters chaste — MOLI 611:74
W. are young men's mistresses — BACON 51:75
wonderful change from w. — EWART 328:73
wiving Hanging and w. — SHAK 769:96
Wixford Papist W. — ANON 24:32
wizards affairs of W. — TOLK 893:48
woad w. began at Watford — TALB 866:14
woe Ah, w. is me! — SHEL 815:32
balm of w. — SIDN 820:46
Cavalry of W. — DICK 283:30
charm his frantic w. — COLL 237:73
Cry w., destruction, ruin — SHAK 764:50
deep, unutterable w. — AYTO 48:13
deliver ye to w. — MILT 604:2
discover sights of w. — MILT 601:35
Europe made his w. her own — ARNO 35:5
feel another's w. — POPE 688:28
in joy and w. — SURR 860:98
Man was made for Joy and W. — BLAKE 141:26
marks of w. — BLAKE 140:16
never...parted, bliss or w. — MILT 606:52
O Sleep! the friend of W. — SOUT 835:51

story of more w. — SHAK 766:15
such a draught of w. — SHEL 815:37
suits of w. — SHAK 780:36
There is a wisdom that is w. — MELV 585:63
the song of w. — TENN 874:81
thine age of w. — BYRON 187:42
This world...a thurghfare ful of w. — CHAU 217:86
W. to those that pray and are heedless — KORAN 498:95
W. unto him that striveth — BIBLE 107:53
worse case of w. — SHAK 803:99
woes And with old w. — SHAK 801:47
bought with lasting w.! — MILT 606:62
detection of concrete human w. — DEWEY 276:19
easer of all w. — FLET 340:52
self-consumer of my w. — CLARE 228:54
To suffer w. — SHEL 815:20
w. at midnight rise — LYLY 543:82
worst of w. — BYRON 187:44
woke Happy till I w. again — HOUS 432:59
w. me from the torpor — WARR 921:21
w. to black flak — JARR 452:83
Woking playing for W. — BETJ 88:21
wold clothe the w. — TENN 869:77
wolf appetite, an universal w. — SHAK 786:26
comrade with the w. and owl — SHAK 792:2
Comrade w. knows who to eat — PUTIN 700:94
either a god or a w. — WEBS 926:21
grim w. with privy paw — MILT 599:89
let the w. into the sheepfold! — INGR 446:42
man is a w. — PLAU 682:69
naked child against hungry w. — DAVI 264:65
seeth the w. coming — BIBLE 123:45
spotted w. of sameness — SOYI 835:59
w. also shall dwell with the lamb — BIBLE 108:62
w. and the lamb shall feed together — BIBLE 110:10
w. and the lamb...united — ARIS 31:16
w. remains of a different opinion — INGE 445:25
W. that shall keep it — KIPL 490:37
w., the hyena, and the skunk? — BRYAN 170:98
wolves habitation for bears and w. — SCHAW 747:20
heard the w. scuffle — TATE 867:41
inwardly they are ravening w. — BIBLE 115:53
room in the west for w. — BABB 48:2
sheep in the midst of w. — BIBLE 116:69
there were w. in Wales — THOM 884:47
w. whose gospel — MILT 601:25
woman advice...to any young w. — CURR 259:95
Although w. has performed much — STAN 842:15
Anon...was often a w. — WOOLF 955:20
anything done, ask a w. — THAT 881:48
Any w.'s death — RICH 713:4
Any w. who understands — THAT 881:55
argument against giving w. the vote — WRIG 962:61
argument with men a w. — MILT 608:94
artist man and the mother w. — SHAW 807:17
As a w. I can't go to war — RANK 706:64
As to w.'s subjection — STAN 842:13
As w.'s love — SHAK 783:23
average man sees w. — MUIR 624:28
beautiful w....qualities of a gentleman — LABR 502:8
be a w. without thinking about it — CIXO 228:50
best w. painter — OKEE 649:24
better to love a w. — HARDY 397:32
bettre than a good w.? — CHAU 217:97
bettre than of wisedoom? W. — CHAU 217:97
between a man and a w. — GIBB 367:1
blessed with a w.'s brain — RICH 714:1
bloom on a w. — BARR 65:88
born of w. — TWAIN 902:32
brawling w. in a wide house — BIBLE 105:88
broken-hearted w. tends the grave — HAYES 403:27
but a w.'s reason — SHAK 758:57
But yet a w. — SHAK 771:43
called a w. in my own house — WAUGH 924:25
Can a w. forget her suckling child — BIBLE 109:89
cannot love a w. so well — ELIOT 316:55
cheeks of a young w. — DALI 261:14
child of our grandmother Eve...a w. — SHAK 763:8
civil and obliging young w. — AUST 45:49
clever w. to manage a fool — KIPL 489:70
constant w. — FORD 343:1
damnable w.'s trick — SHAW 807:20
Dear, dead w. — BROW 168:32
death...of a beautiful w. — POE 683:89
devil made himself a w. — HUGO 437:71
Did ever w., since the creation — STER 847:21
difference between one young w. — SHAW 809:77

woman

dispassionate w....has yet to see	LABR 502:11
does not the w. always suffer	BALZ 61:98
don't know a w. until	LEVE 525:20
doors upon a w.'s wit	SHAK 780:13
driving...with a pretty w.	JOHN 463:54
each tree...a tranced w.	FREE 350:48
each w. thy fond flexible whore	DEKK 270:16
either...your w.	WALK 917:38
every strong w.	FULL 355:67
Every w. adores a Fascist	PLATH 681:34
Every w. should marry	DISR 288:56
excellent thing in w.	SHAK 793:38
Except the American w.	BARR 64:81
expect that W.	MERE 587:25
experience...of the w. writer	WITT 951:30
fail as a w.	FRID 350:62
Farewell W.	ROCH 720:23
far from being half a w.	RUSS 735:48
fashionable w. wears clothes	QUANT 701:3
fat white w.	CORN 247:3
feeling a w.'s pulse	STER 849:57
football team is like a beautiful w.	WENG 931:50
For a w., she has...talent	GOET 375:59
For a w. to have	GRAV 382:28
furious about the W.'s Liberationists	LOOS 536:57
gentler sister W.	BURNS 178:93
Give not thy soul unto a w.	BIBLE 113:88
good-for-nothing w. on the streets	SHAW 808:62
good w. if I had	THAC 880:29
government of a w.	BACON 53:51
greatest glory of a w.	PERI 675:25
ground is like a beautiful w.	SNOW 832:84
hard for a w. to define	HARDY 397:6
Has a w. who knew	NIET 639:15
hate in a w.	SHAW 807:5
heart of a man that is lodged in a w.	CONG 241:68
heart of w.	SHAK 777:45
help and support of the w. I love	EDWA 312:61
he seduces a w.	POMP 684:10
historical repugnance to w.	PAGL 659:17
History, this old,...lying w.	MAUP 582:12
I am a w....of Africa	EMEC 324:47
if a w. have long hair	BIBLE 126:48
If I were a w..	VAN 908:17
I'm a w.. I want things	MANS 567:96
in a young w.	HUGO 437:86
in the shape of a w.	RICH 713:99
In w.'s eye the unanswerable tear	BYRON 188:78
is in w....element of unreason	WRIG 962:63
join together this man and this w.	BOOK 148:81
know that I am a w.?	SHAK 779:93
large-brained w.	BROW 166:88
lawful for a Catholic w.	MENC 587:7
Learn charity, w.	MILL 593:35
let not me play a w.	SHAK 767:22
Let still the w. take	SHAK 785:96
Let us have wine and w.	BYRON 190:7
Let w. share the rights	WOLL 954:95
likes a w. in a skirt	HEPB 412:26
lips of a strange w.	BIBLE 104:56
looketh on a w. to lust after her	BIBLE 114:33
look for the w.	DUMAS 306:90
loose with the worst w.	EDWA 313:64
lovely w. in a rural spot	HUNT 439:22
lovely w. stoops to folly	AUST 46:79
lovely w. stoops to folly	ELIOT 318:5
lovely w. stoops to folly	GOLD 376:93
loving one unattainable w.	FROST 352:9
loyal and faithful w.	NATH 632:98
made a w. cry	MACD 550:48
make love to every w.	KEEN 478:52
make love with a w.	ANOU 28:58
male...to accept a w.	PLATH 681:29
man and a w. in a garden	WILDE 941:83
man and a w. looking at a girl	WOOLF 955:23
Man delights not...nor w.	SHAK 782:90
man enough for a w.	DEKK 270:15
man or a w., old or young	WELTY 930:46
man's boots with a w.	MACC 546:65
man's commendation with w.	SHAK 786:14
Man that is born of a w.	BOOK 148:98
man wants what a w. has—sex	DWOR 308:43
Man was by Nature W.'s cully	CONG 240:25
Many a w. has a past	WILDE 941:76
married w. is a slave	BALZ 60:91
masculine figure created by a w.	MENC 585:83
masculine in the w.	KENT 483:50
mental relation with a w.	LAWR 513:70
middle-class w.	LURIE 542:65
millstone around a w.'s neck	GREER 387:40
misfortune it is to be born a w.!	EDGE 311:41
modern American w.	MCCA 548:98
more...sincere than a w. constant	CONG 241:58
most winning w. I ever knew	DOYLE 296:44
move a w.'s mind	SHAK 759:66
nakedness of w.	BLAKE 140:2
need to possess this w.	LACL 503:30
never trust a w. who	WILDE 941:87
never yet fair w.	SHAK 792:6
new w. is...above him	GRAND 381:97
Next to a w.	SHIR 819:17
none of w. born	SHAK 797:55
no other purgatory but a w.	BEAU 71:17
no sane w. would marry	BIRD 135:6
Not a tolerable w.'s part	AUST 46:67
not given to a w.	LISP 531:44
No w. can be a beauty	FARQ 330:30
No w. can look	TWAIN 901:30
No w. has ever invented	FLAU 339:18
No w. has to prove herself	PAGL 659:18
No w. in my time	THAT 880:46
No w. should have a memory	WILDE 941:91
no w. who does not dream	ANON 24:12
no young w. ugly that has it	WYCH 964:2
occupation of a w. writer	WOOLF 956:75
older w. knows	ATWO 41:46
Old Testament makes w.	STAN 843:17
old w. to outlive her dogs	WILL 945:84
one becomes a w.	DE 268:4
one w. differs from another	MENC 586:98
only comfort about being a w.	STARK 843:21
opinion is about a w.	JAMES 450:46
os cervix of w.	SCHR 749:66
overmuch...in a w.	CRUZ 256:40
O W.!	SCOTT 752:25
paid for a w.	GREE 386:18
parent...a w. cannot	MUIR 624:29
passion for any w.	RIVE 716:55
pity any w. who is married to	WILDE 941:65
place where w. never smiled	CLARE 228:55
play without a w.	KYD 501:52
prime truth of w.	CHES 220:79
print a w.'s age	CHRI 223:35
product of every other black w.	WINF 949:90
Prudence is the other w.	ANON 27:39
public is an old w.	CARL 200:3
questions...put to a defenseless w.	CHOP 223:34
rainy day and a contentious w.	BIBLE 105:3
recalls...a w.	AMADO 15:21
recently murdered w.	SHAR 806:77
responsibility...to be a w.	PALEY 661:55
restrictions on w.	FULL 355:66
rich w. as a poor w.	THAC 880:33
routinely silly w.	BYATT 186:16
roving w. gives rise to gossip	ANON 20:33
saw a w. flayed	SWIFT 861:22
scarce Another w.	JONS 467:55
scarce be a contented w.	ROCH 720:21
Self-development...w.'s motto	STAN 843:18
separates a man from a w.	ROBBE 716:61
Sexually, W. is Nature's contrivance	SHAW 808:29
sex was something no w.	MUNRO 625:48
She is always the w.	DOYLE 297:56
She is only a w.	SIXT 824:26
sign of despair in a w.	WILDE 942:10
Solitude...is a w.'s life	CART 206:37
soul-sides...One to show a w.	BROW 168:56
story of a w.'s life	STAEL 841:92
Success is...like a w.	FAUL 331:45
take some savage w.	TENN 871:21
tell a w.'s age	GILB 369:56
thanks of man and w.	PAINE 660:29
that immaculate w.	JOHN 457:2
that she is a w.	SHAK 800:30
That w. speaks eighteen languages	PARK 663:7
there shone one w.	SWIN 864:7
think myself a very bad w.	ADDI 7:56
Though I be a w.	ELIZ 321:99
thrashing your young w.	COOP 246:88
th' wondher of a w. wears off	OCAS 646:78
thy name is w.	SHAK 780:40
time of a man or w.	WHIT 937:79
tired of being a w.	SEXT 758:48
'Tis w.'s whole existence	BYRON 189:1
Two for a w.	BEEC 73:65
unbecoming to a w.	WILDE 941:79
Until a w. is free to be as incompetent	CUNN 258:76
virtuous w. is a crown	BIBLE 104:66
Vitality in a w.	SHAW 807:16
vote for a w.	WATE 922:36
wasteful w.	PATM 669:15
weak and feeble w.	ELIZ 321:4
were I a w.	SHAK 786:99
What is a w.	KIPL 492:55
what is w.?	COWL 250:78
what w. having ten pieces of silver	BIBLE 121:88
When a w. isn't beautiful	CHEK 218:18
When I find a w. attractive	SAINT 738:33
When we love a w.	PICA 677:59
Who can find a virtuous w.?	BIBLE 105:7
widow w.	SYNGE 865:22
win the hand of w.	HAWT 402:5
w. always a w.	WOLL 954:92
w. a man loves	STEV 851:31
w. at last appearing	MERE 588:40
w. be more like a man?	LERN 523:85
w. beyond her change	HOPE 427:57
w. can always place her lover	BALZ 60:89
w. can become a man's friend	CHEK 218:17
w. can hardly ever choose	ELIOT 316:42
w. can look both moral and exciting	FERB 332:69
w. ceases to alter...her hair	AUST 47:97
w. clothed with the sun	BIBLE 131:9
w. dictates before marriage	ELIOT 316:45
w. grows in virtue	GOTT 379:70
w. in a crinoline	LAVER 512:34
w. in a last month's	NASH 630:61
w. in this humour wooed?	SHAK 761:36
w. into a sex object	MORG 619:35
w. is a foreign land	PATM 669:18
w. is asked out	WHAR 933:3
w. is as young as her knee	QUANT 701:5
w. is at heart a rake	POPE 688:14
w. is beautiful...when she is loved	EPST 327:32
w. is his game	TENN 872:33
w. is like a tea bag	ROOS 724:3
w. is like the same teetotaller	JACO 449:12
W. is natural	BAUD 69:81
w. is not 'giving'	JONG 466:31
W. is often fickle	FRAN 347:96
w. is so hard	TENN 872:34
w. is stripped of everything	NATI 632:4
W. is thought to be a Comet	MAKIN 561:80
w....keeps her own secrets	LABR 502:10
W...knows that when she is looked at	DE 268:46
w., let her be as good	ELIOT 316:53
w. loses a charm	JOYCE 470:30
w. loves her lover	BYRON 190:10
W. monogamous	JAMES 452:78
w. much missed	HARDY 397:28
w. must have money	WOOLF 955:26
w. must wear chains	FARQ 330:29
w. needs a man	STEI 846:91
w....not exactly a lady	RIDGE 715:31
w. of easy virtue	HAIL 392:18
w. of the world	SHAW 810:4
w....one would...bury for nothing	DICK 280:20
W.'s at best a contradiction	POPE 688:16
w. sat, in unwomanly rags	HOOD 426:30
w. saw that the tree was good	BIBLE 91:93
w. says what pleases	ROUS 729:16
w.'s desire...for the desire of the m.	COLE 236:49
w....sees much more than a man	MILL 592:14
w. seldom asks advice	ADDI 7:42
W. seldom Writes her M.	STEE 844:48
w.'s face with nature's own hand	SHAK 800:39
w.'s friendship ever ends in love	GAY 362:12
W., silence makes a w.	SOPH 834:24
w.'s particular talent	HUGO 437:77
w.'s preaching is like a dog	JOHN 461:5
w.'s true position in the home	STAN 842:13
w.'s whole life	IRVI 447:58
w. that deliberates is lost	ADDI 7:48
w. that feareth the Lord	BIBLE 105:8
w., therefore to be won	SHAK 759:80
w....to be the toy of man	WOLL 954:93
w. to hold a man	SPARK 835:62
W. to man	WEBS 926:31
w. to provide for herself	SHAW 806:6
w. touches another's heart	LACL 503:29
w. trying to stay half pregnant	BOHL 144:98

womanhood

w. voter...pernicious to the State	WRIG 962:62
w. wailing for her demon-lover!	COLE 236:37
w. wakes to love	TENN 877:46
w. was full of good works	BIBLE 124:81
W., what have I to do with thee?	BIBLE 122:21
w. who cannot be a governess	OLIP 649:35
woman...who cheats a w.!	GAY 362:21
w. who is really kind to dogs	BEER 73:83
w. who is very anxious	FREUD 350:58
w. who lives for others	LEWIS 526:45
w. whom thou gavest	BIBLE 91:95
w. who walks rather well	MONT 614:35
W., why weepest thou?	BIBLE 124:66
w., wine and song	LUTH 542:76
w. with fair opportunities	THAC 880:22
w. would run through fire	SHAK 773:11
w. yet think him an angel	THAC 880:37
worser spirit a w.	SHAK 803:87
would like to be a w.	SCHR 749:61
wrapped in a w.'s hide!	SHAK 760:3
wrecks a w.'s reputation	COLE 236:57
wrong man the w.	HARDY 397:15
womanhood body of its w.	SCHR 749:66
Heroic w.	LONG 535:33
w. is a heavy burden	DANG 262:28
W. is the great fact	STAN 842:13
womanizers a step beyond w.	BUSH 184:53
womankind all things else, from w.	ROCH 719:17
packs off its w.	SHAW 808:30
Virtue's no more in w.	CLEV 230:94
womanly Shall there be w. times?	MCEW 551:59
w. feeling and propriety	VICT 912:76
womb child from the w.	SHEL 813:77
comes with us from the w.	SMITH 827:84
filled her w.	SPEN 839:61
foul w. of night	SHAK 775:78
from his mother's w.	SHAK 798:77
fruit of the w.	BIBLE 103:37
Immensity cloistered in thy dear w.	DONNE 292:49
Naked came I out of my mother's w.	BIBLE 96:91
out of my mother's w.	CRISP 254:99
out of the w.	BIBLE 98:99
O w.! O bely!	CHAU 217:94
trusted the servile w.	HOPE 427:56
Unsatiate as the barren w.	DRYD 302:91
Virgin's w.	AQUI 30:96
wide w. of uncreated night	MILT 602:59
within the w. is dry	HOPE 427:57
with summer in her w.	SACK 737:8
wombs Our mothers' w.	RALE 705:45
women 22 w. having babies	BARB 63:48
accused of kissing w.	PACK 659:11
all the w. are strong	KEIL 479:53
all w. are born slaves	ASTE 39:5
All w. do	ASTOR 39:10
All w.'s dresses	LIN 529:2
American w. over thirty	FITZ 338:96
And of w.	SHAK 775:69
ashamed that w.	SHAK 762:79
backlash against w.'s rights	FALU 329:12
Bah! I have sung w.	POUND 691:87
better time of it than w.	MENC 586:99
black W. from whose loins I sprang	CULL 257:43
blessed art thou among w.	BIBLE 120:64
both in wine and w.	KITC 494:98
called the book Men Without W.	HEMI 409:63
chilly w.	BYRON 189:87
Christianity...not much in it for w.	WELD 928:83
class of declassed w.	DUMAS 306:91
condition left to w.	LEGU 520:11
convent for unloved w.	BROY 169:91
danced with beautiful w.	WHITE 936:59
deep love for w.	HAGG 391:9
defiance in w.	ROWB 729:18
de w. at de Norf	TRUTH 900:4
discuss w.'s rights	CLIN 231:24
domestic industry of w.	GILM 371:93
do not bear like w. dogs	FLEM 340:46
do not like w.	LAUT 511:27
dotages of...wine and w.	BURT 181:87
eat the power out of w.	WEST 933:96
economic status of w.	GILM 371:91
Empires and old w.	BACON 50:41
England is the paradise of w.	FLOR 341:62
Fatigue makes w. talk	LEWIS 526:46
fifty men and w.	BROW 168:51
folly of 'W.'s Rights'	VICT 912:76

for the amusement of w.	MONT 613:13
For w. are as roses	SHAK 786:97
girls turn into American w.	HAMP 395:75
given w. so much power	JOHN 461:6
God's police...good and virtuous w.	CHIS 222:24
Good w. always think	BROO 163:5
grown-up w. have to deal with	STEI 846:94
Half the sorrows of w.	ELIOT 315:38
happiest w....have no history	ELIOT 315:35
Hardly any of the w.	MORE 618:18
hard to be...a lover of w.	WYCH 964:98
hindrances w. have broken through	WOLF 962:60
history...hardly any w.	AUST 46:84
how w. pass the time	OHEN 648:16
if w. be...slaves	WOLL 954:90
indulging...in the company of w.	CENN 211:43
infernal w.-folk	MACD 550:39
In the hands of w., money	DWOR 308:44
in their relations with w.	FREN 350:53
in w. to appear?	SPEN 838:37
It's not the vote w. need	OBRI 645:67
kill more w. and children	BALD 57:31
kinder to the brutes...than to the w.	ELIOT 315:18
labor of w.	GILM 371:92
lamps that shone o'er fair w.	BYRON 187:50
Leave the pretty w.	PROU 698:54
little questions from w.	ROTH 727:78
looked on a lot of w. with lust	CART 206:46
make...not w. whores	CAREW 198:57
make pale w. swoon	PISS 679:96
make w. more affectionate	BRIL 159:20
make w. unhappy	PUCK 699:67
Married w. are kept w.	SMITH 829:22
maternity to w.	MUSS 628:94
mature w., dancing?	FRIEL 351:80
men and w. and the society	JAMES 451:58
men and w. are created equal	STAN 842:12
men and w. are not so...enslaved	SHAW 809:87
men and w. laughing	SAND 742:15
men and w. merely players	SHAK 799:80
men and w. of this generation	LLOY 533:72
Men don't know w.	TROL 898:36
men like—not w.	NORR 641:56
menstruate and w. could not?	STEI 846:93
men that w. marry	LONG 536:39
men, w., and clergymen	SMITH 830:55
mettlesome w.	ANDR 18:77
middle-aged and elderly w.	LESS 524:94
mob of scribbling w.	HAWT 402:14
Monstrous Regiment of W.	KNOX 495:13
more w. are paid	FALU 329:10
more w. in the rock scene	HARV 400:77
Most w. are not so young	BEER 73:72
Most w. know that sex	WILB 939:42
Music and w. I...give way to	PEPYS 674:5
must have w.	GAY 362:20
no place for w.'s plans	AESC 9:80
no plain w. on television	FORD 342:86
noticed how noisy w. are?	OSBO 655:84
not with w. but with models	BUSH 184:53
Of all those young w.	POUND 691:98
offensive to many w.	LEWIS 527:66
of w. this I say	DUNB 306:98
owe nothing to W.'s Lib	THAT 880:47
passing the love of w.	BIBLE 96:42
patriotism that has nerved w.	PANK 662:86
Plain w....to be faced	ELIOT 316:48
portraits I paint of w.	LAUR 511:24
power over w.	LEGU 520:13
Priests, princes, w.	POPE 687:95
proper function of w.	ELIOT 315:36
rather second-rate w.	WEBB 925:6
reduce w. of a certain age	BROO 163:10
sadness of the w.'s movement	ANGE 19:93
save w. and girls	WEBB 925:7
sayings are generally like w.'s letters	HAZL 404:51
secure the good conduct of w.	WOLL 953:87
; She looks at other w.	FIRB 336:57
simple w. only fit	LEWIS 526:51
Single w....propensity for being poor	AUST 46:81
sleep with w. we do not love	DIDE 285:73
society w. never serve chilli	RAYB 708:90
Solomon loved many strange w.	BIBLE 97:57
some w. govern their husbands	WOLL 953:85
Some w.'ll stay	KIPL 492:51
strength...in black w.	ANGE 19:90
such a place for...[wanton w.]	BORR 151:71

Sweet is revenge—especially to w.	BYRON 189:96
taken for a ride by his w.	JOSE 469:7
there's wisdom in w.	BROO 162:85
though w. all above	SHAK 793:22
three w. I have admired most	WILDE 942:31
through our mothers if we are w.	WOOLF 955:31
tide in the affairs of w.	BYRON 190:19
to w. [I speak] Italian	CHAR 215:38
to w. lied like a Cretan	HARDY 397:5
trouble with w. like me	MANS 567:95
trumpet for W.'s Liberation	LESS 524:98
Two w. placed together	SHAK 804:39
values of w. differ	WOOLF 955:30
wage no war with w.	SOUT 835:49
want w. to specialise in virtue	WEST 933:95
war between men and w.	THUR 890:69
war...between men and w.	LYND 543:92
well-educated young w.	AUST 46:59
what all w. do	SHAW 807:20
Whatever w. do	WHIT 938:25
when we are grown w.	SCHR 749:63
When will w. begin to have	JAMES 449:22
when w. are free to make...decisions	FRIE 350:66
When w. kiss	MENC 586:97
when w. succeed, america succeeds	OBAMA 645:52
where w. are concerned?	SHAW 810:96
why God created w.?	WALL 917:45
why young w. should marry	JOHN 462:45
Wine and w. will make men	BIBLE 113:98
Winter is for w.	PLATH 681:36
With many w.	TROL 897:34
w. and gear are at the bottom	SCOTT 753:57
W. and Horses	KIPL 490:93
W. and men do not	VIAN 911:73
W. are all in extremes	LABR 502:9
w. are brighter than men	LOOS 536:55
W. are from their very Infancy	ASTE 39:2
w. are in furious secret rebellion	SHAW 809:86
W....are invisible people	FRIE 350:65
W. are like elephants	FIEL 335:31
W. are like tricks	CONG 240:45
W. are most fascinating	DIOR 286:3
w. are not merely tolerated, they are valued	AUNG 45:41
W. are soft, mild, pitiful	SHAK 760:4
W. are strongest	BIBLE 112:67
W. are supposed to be very calm	BRON 161:61
W. are the last group...in Hollywood	STREE 857:48
W. are the...most underused resource	CLIN 231:35
W. are the only exploited group	JONG 466:39
W....as looking-glasses	WOOLF 955:27
W. become like their mothers	WILDE 941:3
W....behave like men	MACK 554:15
W....born three thousand years old	DELA 271:36
w. breached the power structure	WOLF 952:62
W. cannot be expected	MILL 592:15
w. cannot escape it	GIBB 367:9
W. can't forgive failure	CHEK 218:15
W. come out	KIPL 489:88
W. complain about sex	LAND 506:25
w. do not count in the State	DAVI 266:13
w.? Do not forget	NIET 638:4
w. do the hod carrying	NEVI 634:32
W. enjoyed	SUCK 858:69
W. fond of dress	DE 268:45
w. for escape from this death	NIGH 639:22
W. had always fought for men	PANK 662:85
w. have but one task	COUB 248:19
w. have dominion over you	BIBLE 112:68
w. have no character	POPE 688:8
W. have no wideness in them	BOGAN 144:93
w. have read only the novel	GAUT 361:5
w. have taken it upon themselves	MARG 570:63
w. have walked past mirrors	ALLEN 13:77
w. highly hold in hate	SHAK 759:69
w. in the United States	BRYS 171:11
w. into darling little slaves	MILLS 595:7
W....keep men from better company	WYCH 964:96
W. know the damnation of charity	WEST 933:94
W. leave the Royal Family	YORK 968:49
W. like to sit down	GLAS 374:45
W....love completely	BAIN 55:96
W. MPs	JOWE 469:5
W. Must be half-workers?	SHAK 803:94
w. never took a single step forward	PANK 662:83
w. offer our experience	LEGU 520:15
w. of her type	WAUGH 923:61

word

W., of kynde, desiren	CHAU	217:91
w. Passion, intellect	NIGH	639:19
w. prudes if they don't	MILL	595:1
w....remained thirty-five years	WILDE	942:9
w....rendered systematically vicious	WOLL	954:94
w. rule us	CATO	208:98
w. see the relationship	FOWL	345:61
w.'s eyes this doctrine	SHAK	763:19
w. shall put on	TROL	898:45
w.'s happiest knowledge	MILT	604:6
w.'s horrifying sexuality	MILT	593:49
W. should be obscene	LENN	521:47
w. should be struck	COWA	249:49
W. should be trained	ANON	20:39
W.'s love is for their men	EURI	328:56
w.'s parts be acted by w.	CHAR	215:32
w....succeed in spite of their husbands	LEE	519:1
w. suffered...in the United States	FRIE	350:64
w.'s unnatural, unsatiable lust	BURT	181:86
w.'s weapons, water-drops	SHAK	792:3
w....Talking of Michelangelo	ELIOT	316:61
w., than to study household	MILT	606:46
w., their rights and nothing less	ANTH	29:73
w. themselves help to make laws	ANTH	29:74
w. the Pariahs	STAN	842:14
W. They are a complete mystery	HAWK	401:96
w. to bear rule	KNOX	495:14
w. today	PANK	662:87
w....trying for the vote	PANK	662:82
w., two almost divide	POPE	688:13
w. understand by emancipation	GREER	387:42
W. were brought up to believe	BARN	64:69
W. were ever things	VIRG	913:19
W. were expected to have weak	ELIOT	316:44
w. who do not dress modestly	SEDI	755:98
w. who don't help other w.	ALBR	11:34
W. who love the same man	BEER	73:82
w. whom I really think	KEATS	476:93
W. Whose Lives Are Food	OATES	643:8
w. who wear ankle socks	BENN	80:49
W. will love her	SHAK	800:30
w. within these marginal	RUET	730:37
w. won't buy anything	RUBE	730:32
W. would rather be	NASH	631:78
work its way with the w.	DICK	278:59
Yes, Sir...many w.	JOHN	461:91
You should be w.	SHAK	795:4
women-folk moo and coo with w.-f.	KIPL	492:59
won heaven on earth I have w.	SHAK	791:67
in the sun and have w. it	WILH	943:55
IT'S THE SUN WOT W. IT	SUN	859:86
life will not be w.	HEIS	407:23
not that you w. or lost	RICE	713:89
talk about who w.	KHRU	485:94
too quickly w.	SHAK	765:82
until they w. her	TENN	877:57
woman in this humour w.?	SHAK	761:36
woman, therefore to be w.	SHAK	759:80
w. first prize in the lottery	RHOD	712:71
w. on the playing fields of Eton	WELL	929:13
wonder all a w. and a wild desire	BROW	169:72
all knowledge and w.	BACON	49:19
all the w. that would be	TENN	871:17
capacity for w.	FITZ	338:86
common w. of all men	BROW	165:69
Hidden in w.	SCOTT	751:3
it is a w. what will be	PEPYS	674:3
longer the shoreline of w.	MACI	553:4
miles around the w. grew	HOUS	431:39
no longer w. and stand...in awe	EINS	313:80
sense of w.	LAWR	514:86
sense of w.	SOCR	833:97
sign or a w.	BIBLE	95:92
state of w.	GOULD	379:73
still the w. grew	GOLD	376:2
strangeness and w. lying	RUSS	734:21
struck with w.	LAWR	514:79
through w. that men...philosophize	ARIS	31:18
th' w. of a woman wears off	OCAS	646:78
with a sense of w.	JOVA	469:13
w. how long this is going	KEIL	479:57
w. of our stage!	JONS	468:78
w. what he meant by that	LOUIS	537:72
Worship is transcendent w.	CARL	201:31
wondered w. why young women	JOHN	462:45
wonderful after...it was w.	WILD	942:33
most w. in the world	SIHA	821:66

name shall be called W.	BIBLE	107:60
O w., w., and most w.	SHAK	779:92
reality was no less w.	SHIP	818:15
What a w. boy he is!	HOGG	422:42
w. time—the War	HUGH	435:15
w. to listen to	HARDY	396:2
wondering w. what lay round	KAVA	474:50
w. whether it would take spin	HOME	425:98
wonders all W. in one sight!	CRAS	253:78
Everything has its w.	KELL	479:65
His w. to perform	COWP	250:85
left us surmising w.	QUIL	702:17
lost w. of the ancient world	AUCH	42:65
Of all the w.	SHAK	777:22
Seven W. of the World	ADDI	7:35
Signs and tokens w.	ELIOT	317:83
We carry with us the w.	BROW	165:55
w. in the deep	BIBLE	102:15
w. Of common things	MIDD	590:74
w. of the western world	SYNGE	865:23
wondrous we'll be w. rich	OTWAY	656:4
woo April when they w.	SHAK	780:12
cannot w. in festival terms	SHAK	774:56
Come, w. me, w. me	SHAK	779:9
forced to w.	WEBS	927:47
So thou wilt w.	SHAK	765:82
were not made to w.	SHAK	767:29
when a married man doth w.	DONNE	291:34
w. not like a babe	SHAK	761:63
wood bit about nudism in the w.	JOYCE	470:34
bows down to w.	KIPL	490:13
correct in cypress w.	PARK	664:16
courtiers'-and-rabbits' w.	THOM	884:31
creeping ivy clings to w.	COWP	251:5
dark impenetrable w.	SCOTT	752:26
enclosing it in a case of w.	WATT	922:45
Far off the w.	FREE	350:48
found myself in a dark w.	DANTE	262:36
goblets for a dish of w.	SHAK	764:54
harbour and neighbour w.	THOM	883:20
Heap on more w.!	SCOTT	752:22
impulse from a vernal w.	WORD	957:59
in the w. the furious winter	RANS	707:70
Land of...shaggy w.	SCOTT	752:17
maker of worn w.	UPDI	905:14
piles of dry w. with red-hot coals	CISN	227:39
Proud Maisie is in the w.	SCOTT	754:63
rooky w.	SHAK	797:48
Sit...in this w.	BRON	161:60
springth the w. nu	ANON	21:43
strange odours...of aromatic w.	CONR	244:34
that piece of w.	MANN	567:92
Through w. and dale	COLE	236:40
true w., of yew w.	DOYLE	297:49
two pieces of w.	MITF	610:50
Two roads diverged in a w.	FROST	352:95
violin is w. and catgut	PRIE	695:84
Where no w. is...the fire goeth out	BIBLE	105:98
whiffling through the tulgey w.	CARR	204:90
w. a Piggy-wig stood	LEAR	516:36
w. found on a beach	ROSE	725:28
w. of Hallaig	MACL	555:30
w.'s in trouble	HOUS	431:47
woodbine luscious w.	SHAK	767:30
well attir'd w.	MILT	599:91
w. spices are wafted	TENN	876:25
woodcock Spirits of well-shot w.	BETJ	88:19
woodcocks springes to catch w.	SHAK	781:55
wooden W. legs are not inherited	CONK	242:79
W. Shoes	ANON	23:96
woodland stands about the w. ride	HOUS	431:33
woodlands about the w. I will go	HOUS	431:35
wood-pigeons brassy w.-p.	HUGH	435:36
woods Enter these enchanted w.	MERE	588:36
Flow down the w.	SACK	737:10
for the w. against the world	BLUN	143:81
If you go down in the w.	BRAT	157:79
in the deep green w.	HOLM	423:18
in w. the noble savage ran	DRYD	300:30
let it loose in the w.	SHAW	809:88
Love-whispering w.	POPE	689:44
never knew the summer w.	TENN	874:68
ordered w. and gardens	MACK	553:10
pleasure in the pathless w.	BYRON	188:70
shepherd, thee the w.	MILT	599:84
shut the road through the w.	KIPL	492:61
these hoary w. are grand	GALT	359:54

The w. decay	TENN	877:60
through the Wet Wild W.	KIPL	491:42
Tomorrow to fresh w.	MILT	600:96
went to the w.	THOR	888:37
w. are lovely	FROST	352:5
w. as deep and cool	COWL	250:82
W., or steepy mountain	MARL	574:41
worked in the w.	SNYD	833:95
woodshed Something nasty in the w.	GIBB	367:10
wooed therefore to be w.	SHAK	759:80
woman in this humour w.?	SHAK	761:36
wooer knight to be their w.	BALL	58:52
wooing a fresh w.	STOP	855:13
won by w. thee	SHAK	791:67
Young men a w.	ANON	21:52
wool jeweller's cotton and fine w.	DICK	281:57
lots of screams but little w.	PUTIN	700:97
shall be as w.	BIBLE	107:50
Woolf afraid of Virginia W.?	ALBEE	11:24
woollen Odious! in w.!	POPE	687:96
rather lie in the w.	SHAK	773:23
word according to thy w.	BIBLE	133:44
according to thy w.	BIBLE	120:65
according to thy w.	BIBLE	120:70
according to thy w.	BIBLE	103:24
ages for the wrong w.	USTI	906:43
ancient w. of courage	SHAK	761:54
At ev'ry w. a reputation	POPE	685:37
bad-weather kind of w.	BUFO	172:50
before thy uncreating w.	POPE	689:48
Bilbo's the w.	CONG	240:26
bring out of each w.	JAMES	451:74
By any other w.	SHAK	765:80
By thought, w., and deed	BOOK	147:67
by water and the w.	STONE	855:11
cannot utter a w.	SHAW	806:90
changed...to past Without a w.	LARK	509:82
choke the w.	BIBLE	117:91
Closure is a greasy little w.	AMIS	17:57
Conscience is but a w.	SHAK	761:53
contempt of thy w.	BOOK	147:53
discouraging w.	HIGL	418:54
eaten thee for a w.	SHAK	763:21
every w. has its marrow	SMART	826:61
every w. she writes is a lie	MCCA	548:2
every w. stabs	SHAK	773:27
every w. that proceedeth	BIBLE	95:90
every w. that proceedeth	BIBLE	114:22
falling cadence of the lovely w.	MAUG	582:8
final w., before I'm done	HALD	392:26
Fine w., 'legitimate'	SHAK	792:88
first w. on everything	HUGO	438:90
gone without a w.?	SHAK	758:60
Good isn't the w.	GILB	370:76
great actor or a household w.?	OLIV	649:37
great deal to make one w. mean	CARR	205:11
Greeks Had a W. for It	AKINS	10:13
hard, brown, nutlike w.	BART	66:15
hast kept my w.	BIBLE	131:93
have not the w.	ARNO	35:14
heareth the w.	BIBLE	117:91
heareth the w.	BIBLE	117:92
horror of the w. 'flesh'	RENO	711:55
How the w. rolls—Leonora	CRAIK	252:51
If thou hast heard a w.	BIBLE	113:99
In one w.	PASC	667:89
In one w. he told me the secret	LEHR	520:26
In the beginning was the W.	BIBLE	122:15
In the beginning was the W.	ELIOT	317:79
kens a w. Burns	MACD	549:22
leave for the w. of God	BIBLE	124:7
Let the w. go forth	KENN	481:3
lies in one little w.!	SHAK	764:35
Lord's First W.	FARJ	330:20
Love in search of a w.	LANI	508:52
Man's w. is God in man	TENN	878:72
most important sense of the w.	MOORE	616:66
my most painted w.	SHAK	782:6
never will speak w.	SHAK	790:50
No man would set a w.	MILL	594:69
No simple w.	JONS	467:70
not one w. is said	STAN	843:16
no w. in their language	SWIFT	862:49
No w. like 'Pardon'	SHAK	765:61
Observant of the heavenly w.	DODD	289:92
ordinary sense of the w.	MILL	593:52
people answered him not a w.	BIBLE	97:61

wordless

pleynly, at a w.	CHAU 217:95	comfortable w. our Saviour	BOOK 147:68	Thy w. are too precious	SHAK 778:62
polite w. for dead…imagination	CUMM 258:70	complete an incomplete self with w.	GASS 361:87	tune without the w.	DICK 283:34
Polyester…the most valuable w.	ANON 26:12	comprehending much in few w.	BIBLE 113:6	two most beautiful w.	JAMES 451:55
power of the written w.	CONR 243:26	danced on a plume of w.	DAY 267:38	two truly expressive w.	DERBY 274:86
Preach the w.	BIBLE 129:29	Dance, little w.	WORL 962:53	unnebulous train of w.	BISH 136:26
precise meaning of a w.	BAND 61:10	Deeds, not w.	EDGE 311:44	unpack my heart with w.	SHAK 782:2
proud Victorian w.	PRIT 696:25	draftsman of w.	CUMM 258:73	unscrew…from the practical w.	WAITS 916:8
run to and fro to seek the w.	BIBLE 111:54	embarrassed by the w.	HEMI 409:64	used big w. in dealing	RAMOS 705:50
say a w. against G.	SHAW 809:71	end to end w.	LODGE 534:95	use w. as they are used	COMP 239:3
single w. even may be a spark	SHEL 816:51	entrance of thy w. giveth light	BIBLE 103:29	using only comparative W.	PETTY 676:47
solemn w. of warning	WILS 949:77	exchanged many frank w.	COOK 245:67	vital w. were once slangy	GALS 358:52
So shall my w. be	BIBLE 109:99	fair w.…in foulest letters?	SHAK 773:96	weighing w.	FLAU 339:26
speaks to us the same w.	SCHW 751:94	few odd w. in Hebrew	DAY 267:30	weigh'st thy w.	SHAK 789:17
speak the w. only	BIBLE 116:57	few of the unpleasant'st w.	SHAK 770:8	What grows by the w.?	SIDN 820:39
spoken the foremost w.	BALL 59:62	fine volley of w.	SHAK 758:61	which is but saying, in other w.	POPE 686:54
squeeze it w. till it hurts	MACL 555:45	Fine w.!	SWIFT 862:41	Why is one of the most important w.	AUNG 45:43
sweeter…will be the w. lover	HELO 408:53	food and not fine w.	MOLI 611:88	wife full of w.	BIBLE 113:1
Taäke my w. for it	TENN 878:90	forgets w. as one forgets names	WAUGH 924:94	With high w., that bore	MILT 602:48
take thy w. for faith	SHAK 798:84	For w., like Nature	TENN 873:58	w. are a very fantastical banquet	SHAK 774:36
tears wash out a w.	FITZ 337:70	four most dramatic w.	HART 400:70	w. are beautiful things	MUSS 628:92
Tell them…I kept my w.	DELA 271:26	frames in all but w.	FROST 352:97	W. are…from a defunct language	CIXO 227:46
that w. 'hummy', my darlings	PARK 663:1	fresh, usual w.	FORD 343:92	w. are idle	WEBS 926:25
there is not a w. of fear	LAND 507:33	gave voice to three w.	LAMA 504:74	w. are images of thoughts	KEATS 475:65
The w. is life	SASS 746:97	glorious sense of w.	ACHE 2:28	W. are, of course	KIPL 493:78
the w. of a noble Messenger	KORAN 498:92	gloten of w.	LANG 507:45	w. are of less weight	BACON 52:2
The w. VALUE	SMITH 827:78	Good w. are better	SHAK 778:51	w. are quick and vain	SHEL 814:8
This is my final w.	BEAV 71:31	grievous w. stir up anger	BIBLE 104:73	w. are slippery	ADAMS 5:97
thru the nicht we spak nae w.	SOUT 835:40	heaven hath my empty w.	SHAK 787:62	W. are the bugles	HANDY 395:80
torture one poor w.	DRYD 301:45	Hold fast the form of sound w.	BIBLE 129:27	w. are the daughters	JOHN 460:68
Turning the w. to sword	SHAK 772:91	house of w.	GALE 357:28	w. are the passkeys to our souls	ACKER 3:59
unkind or irreverential w.	HAWT 402:17	How often misused w.	SPEN 836:88	w. are true and faithful	BIBLE 132:24
unto me according to thy w.	BIBLE 133:44	how you use proud w.	SAND 742:20	w. burst from him	SCOTT 754:73
upholding all things by the w.	BIBLE 129:33	huffing of hyphenated w.	BROY 169:68	w. came halting forth	SIDN 820:47
use no w.…under stress	POUND 692:37	hundred and twenty w.	LINK 530:28	W. can keep people apart	MARC 569:52
utter and see in w.	SAND 741:12	If I write four w.	BOIL 144:1	w. can outlive us	PLOUT 682:74
voice for my 'nature'	REDON 709:24	if she respects not w.	SHAK 759:66	w. clothed in reason's garb	MILT 602:60
What is honour? A w.	SHAK 771:60	if you have the w.	HEAN 405:81	w. come more readily	GREE 385:99
When I hear that w.	GINS 372:10	I have few w.	CIXO 227:43	w. could never utter	THAC 880:40
whose lightest w.	SHAK 781:60	Immodest w. admit of no defence	DILL 286:96	w. divested of their magic	MILL 594:88
whose w. one cannot believe	VICT 912:77	In W., as Fashions	POPE 685:22	w. divide and rend	SWIN 863:87
with a flattering w.	WILDE 942:17	language without w.	STEV 850:85	w. echo…in your mind	ELIOT 319:37
without adding a w.	TROL 898:47	let thy w. be few	BIBLE 106:20	w. filling yer head	KELM 479:70
w. alone shall fit	CHES 221:83	like others been all w.	MASS 581:73	w. fly up	SHAK 783:35
w. 'civilization' to my mind	MILL 594:92	long w. and exhausted idioms	ORWE 654:36	w. in their best order	COLE 236:48
W. climbs upward	DUNC 307:10	long w. Bother me.	MILNE 596:17	w. into life	SENG 757:27
w. fitly spoken	BIBLE 105:93	long w. to cover the errors	CHES 220:60	w. into the ends of the world	BOOK 148:9
w. for w. without book	SHAK 785:80	manipulation of w.	DICK 277:37	w. just say what you want	KENN 480:90
w. from the content	FLAU 339:17	multiplieth w. without knowledge	BIBLE 98:12	w. left unsaid	STOWE 856:43
W. has somehow got around	THUR 891:5	mystery of w.	WORD 958:84	w., like children	NOON 640:45
w. have I hid in mine heart	BIBLE 103:25	my w. among mankind!	SHEL 813:84	w. most wonderful	NEWM 635:49
w. is a lamp	BIBLE 103:28	my w. are my own	CHAR 215:34	w. no virtue can digest	MARL 572:2
W. is but wynd	LYDG 543:80	never yet was put into w. or books	MELV 585:65	w. of learned length	GOLD 376:2
w. is dead	DICK 284:48	nor hear your w.	BIBLE 116:68	w. of my love	ROET 722:60
w. is like a bell	KEATS 478:48	oaths are but w.	BUTL 185:79	W. of the world	STEV 850:98
w. is the carving	SITW 824:23	of all w. of tongue and pen	HARTE 400:75	W. pay no debts	SHAK 787:34
w. is the Verb	HUGO 437:75	pain of history w. contain	WALC 916:12	w. prevail not	KYD 501:48
w.…means just what I choose	CARR 205:14	palm-oil with which w. are eaten	ACHE 2:20	w. reign over ideas	SAND 741:5
w. means underpants	MURR 627:80	play…some ten w. long	SHAK 768:47	w. seemed to them as idle tales	BIBLE 122:12
w. 'Now' is like a bomb	MILL 593:40	Poets paint with w.	CARR 202:59	w. shall not pass away	BIBLE 118:30
w. of Caesar	SHAK 777:41	poets…write in w.	FOWL 345:63	W. should be an intense	WAUGH 924:84
w. of God is quick	BIBLE 129:34	power to master w.	SCAR 746:13	W. spoken on the road	MO 610:63
w. of our God shall stand for ever	BIBLE 108:79	preoccupation with w.	CHAN 213:89	W. strain	ELIOT 319:45
w. of worlds	CURN 259:88	Proper w. in	SWIFT 861:37	w. tend to be blunt	MURR 627:85
w.…out of a ladys lips	FLEM 340:45	propriety of thoughts and w.	DRYD 300:41	w. that are only forms	WILS 947:45
w. spoken in due season	BIBLE 104:76	put my w. in thy mouth	BIBLE 110:11	w., that burn	GRAY 385:91
w. stung him	SITW 823:2	quench the fire…with w.	SHAK 759:65	w. that I speak…are life	BIBLE 123:37
w. that may not be there	WILB 939:41	Read out my w.	FLEC 340:30	W.…the great foes of reality	CONR 244:43
W. was made flesh	BIBLE 122:18	rhubarb. w.	SIDN 820:45	w. the head does not shape	ANON 21:58
w. within the w.	ELIOT 317:83	roof in w. deceiving	MILT 597:37	w. thou canst not understand	BIBLE 110:29
wordless set of w. symbols	UPDI 906:22	running tap of w.	MOORE 615:58	W. to the heat of deeds	SHAK 796:29
words alms-basket of w.	SHAK 763:21	see and imitate…by w.	CUMM 257:50	w. which express	SHEL 816:53
and aimable w.	TENN 877:57	shut up the w.	BIBLE 111:44	w. which he of God	LANY 508:55
any relation to the w.	ROSE 725:28	significations of their w.	HOBB 420:97	w. will break cement	PUSSY 700:90
apt w. have power	MILT 607:88	Some…find those w. mis-placed	CONG 240:31	w. will follow	CATO 209:1
ate and drank the precious W.	DICK 284:50	sought out quaint w.	HERB 413:73	w. without knowledge?	BIBLE 98:12
bad poet dwells…in a world of w.	ELIOT 317:91	sounds called w. may be strung	FROST 352:94	w. without knowledge?	BIBLE 98:13
believed not the w.	BIBLE 97:56	spite and hard w.	MORR 620:51	W., w., mere w.	SHAK 787:45
Be not the slave of w.	CARL 200:93	still at the mercy of w.	THOM 884:26	W., w., w.	SHAK 782:80
bereft me of all w.	SHAK 770:7	such abominable w.	SHAK 759:98	worse than vain w.	BACON 49:47
better deeds than w.	SHAK 758:60	such a hail of w.	JONS 467:55	worst…one can do with w.	ORWE 655:64
big w. to talk about dirty things	DOCT 289:82	Such w. as 'chain' or 'train'	JAMES 451:66	worth ten thousand w.	BARN 63:57
But w. are w.	SHAK 789:1	Th' artillery of w.	SWIFT 861:15	wrote the magnificent w.	KING 487:27
callisthenics with w.	PARK 664:23	that make up w.	UPDI 906:28	**Wordsworth** Let simple W. chime	BYRON 187:29
can drug, with w.	LOWE 539:97	the magic of w.	PAGL 659:21	Mr W.'s genius	HAZL 404:49
can express in w.	NABO 628:12	the W. of my Lord	KORAN 498:76	seen W. drunk	HOUS 432:61
change the world into w.	GASS 361:88	Three unknown w.	GAUT 361:4	what daffodils were for W.	LARK 510:98
coiner of sweet w.!	ARNO 34:96	threw w. like stones	SPEN 837:98	W., both are thine.	STEP 847:11

W....crazed beyond all hope	BYRON 189:3	not the w. of other singers	SINA 822:88
W. says somewhere	ARNO 35:7	now....in the grave	BIBLE 106:28
work Acting is not hard w.	CLOO 231:42	obviously unfit for w.	VEBL 910:44
All buildings w.	JOHN 458:27	off to w. we go	MOREY 619:28
all hope of genuine good w.	BUTL 186:3	outside this w. relationship	MARX 578:26
Art is the only w.	GRAY 383:42	over, and our w. is done!	NEWM 635:46
being dead is hard w.	RILKE 715:38	own time out of their w.	MASE 580:70
Better the rudest w.	RUSK 732:82	People out of w.	EVANS 328:69
break a man's spirit is devil's w.	SHAW 806:89	perfectly equipped for its w.	ELIOT 317:94
breed one w. that wakes	HOPK 429:96	Perseverance is....hard w.	GING 371:3
buy his w.	RENO 711:56	Plato...in the body of his w.	SIDN 820:53
Canst w. i'th' earth so fast?	SHAK 781:69	plenty of w. to do	JERO 454:35
change from wives and w.	EWART 328:73	poor pay, and easy w.	LOND 534:10
classical mind at w.	PIRS 679:95	prime w. of God	MILT 607:84
composing a w.	PASC 666:68	protracted my w.	JOHN 460:69
continuous administrative w.	WEBER 925:14	puts off my w. for days	WODE 952:46
country safe to w. in	THAT 881:52	rather talk than w.	BOYD 153:9
creature's at his dirty w.	POPE 687:99	sad as going to w.	ANOU 28:58
curse...finishes its w.	SCHR 749:63	said about her w.	SARR 744:60
day's hard w. in thy life	LAWR 513:69	scan his w. in vain	COWP 250:86
days when w. was scrappy	CHES 221:2	six days' w., a world	MILT 605:32
Did he smile his w. to see?	BLAKE 140:20	society built on w.	MAMET 564:39
dirty w. for the rest	RUSK 733:5	spits...and goes to w.	SAND 742:31
done your w. and may go play	ASTL 39:9	splendid w. for the blind	SASS 745:87
do no w. today	SHAK 775:86	stomach sets us to w.	ELIOT 316:43
embark upon any w.	STEV 852:53	success comes before w.	KIMB 486:13
'ergophobia', meaning 'fear or hatred of'	TYNAN 904:2	test of a first-rate w.	BENN 81:70
Every w. of art	KAND 473:16	they must hate to w. for a living	ROWL 729:19
Faints the cold w.	COLL 238:75	time goes about its immemorial w.	AMIS 16:52
finish the w. we are in	LINC 529:11	'Tis not your w.	TENN 871:5
fit...only for w.	BERG 84:28	To be Modern Art a w.	ROSE 725:28
flowery w. doth sing	MILT 598:58	trade, but by w.	RUSK 733:16
full time w.	WELD 928:85	What a piece of w. is a man!	SHAK 782:89
future...does not w.	TOYN 895:76	when your w. is finished	KIPL 493:69
get home from w.	PARKS 665:44	Whistle While You W.	MOREY 619:29
get them at w. again	EDWA 312:60	Who first invented w.	LAMB 505:89
get your w. done	HEMI 410:74	who is not allowed to w.	STEV 854:93
God ended his w.	BIBLE 91:81	Why do we w. so hard	KEIL 479:62
going to me w.	STRO 857:54	willing to w., and unable to find w.	CARL 201:25
Good w., Mary	PARK 664:9	women who do the most w.	GILM 371:93
Go to w. on an egg	WELD 928:79	W. alone	WOZNI 962:56
half of the population, w.	MORE 618:18	w. as finished as possible	FEYN 334:5
hands employed in w.	STEU 849:60	w. as much	TRUTH 900:5
hands wrought in the w.	BIBLE 98:88	W. done least rapidly	BROW 168:55
her or his own w.	KELM 479:68	W. earnestly at anything	CARL 201:37
holidays...interfere with one's w.	EDWA 312:62	W. expands	PARK 665:38
housing, w., leisure	LECO 518:82	w. for their honest livelihood	SWIFT 862:57
How hard you w.	OBAMA 645:58	w. goes on merrily	BICK 133:50
how things really w.	GIBS 367:17	working on the w.	MOTH 622:87
If any would not w.	BIBLE 129:16	w. in the dark	JAMES 450:47
if I could but produce a w.	HOPK 429:93	w. is a commentary	KAZA 474:51
If you w. at it	HOPE 428:59	w. is less boring	BAUD 69:84
If you w. very hard	YOST 968:50	w. is play	SHAW 809:69
If you would w. any man	BACON 53:33	w. is sometimes less	LOUI 537:69
I like w.	JERO 454:40	W. is the curse of	WILDE 942:29
impassioned, at the birth of his w.	ERNST 327:39	w. is to present things	FRED 349:36
individual w. serves as an expression	FEIN 332:57	W. is x	EINS 314:86
In every w. of genius	EMER 324:51	w. itself shall not be lost	FRAN 348:7
inside w. with no heavy lifting	DOLE 290:95	W. liberates	ANON 24:20
invent for himself a w.	ROBBE 716:64	w. like a dog	SIMON 821:73
I want w.	SHAK 771:44	w. of fifty ordinary men	HUBB 434:99
Justice is doing one's w.	PLATO 682:62	w. of God	BLAKE 140:2
let me w.	SAND 742:18	w. of his hands	LOCKE 533:86
literary w.	JOHN 460:64	w. of noble note	TENN 870:2
looked for w.	TEBB 869:63	w. of rich entail	SPEN 838:30
make a world do a lot of w.	CARR 205:11	w. of the individual	SIKO 821:68
make them capable of doing the w.	DRUC 299:7	w. of the master	LEON 522:66
manage to get so much w. done	BENC 78:8	w. of the master is his self	WERE 931:54
man and his w. existed	MEYER 589:63	w. of thy fingers	BIBLE 99:31
Man goeth forth unto his w.	BIBLE 102:12	w. ought to speak for itself	ASIM 38:80
Man...grows beyond his w.	STEI 845:80	W. out your own salvation	BIBLE 128:98
Man hath his daily w.	MILT 604:5	w. shall with the world remain	WALL 918:59
man who lives by his own w.	COLL 237:59	w. such as Pasteur's	ROST 727:70
matter of the w.	GLAS 374:44	w. that aspires...condition of art	CONR 243:25
maun to our w. again	SCOTT 753:50	w. that results dies	LEON 522:68
million and a quarter people lack w.	CHUR 225:71	w. that should have for its purpose	FORD 343:94
monotony, w. or leisure	POMP 684:18	w. to keep alive	BELL 77:72
most important aspect of the w.	LEWI 526:77	W. was like cats	AMIS 16:33
my w. or ye reprief	DOUG 294:99	w. with your own hands	BIBLE 128:14
never done any w. cold	KOLL 496:37	w., w., w. till we die	LEWIS 526:48
Nice w. if you can get it	GERS 365:79	world's w....done by men	GALB 357:25
noblest w. of man	INGE 445:32	You w. hard making...films	JOHAN 456:69
noble w. of GOD	BURNS 177:76	you w. not	SHAK 791:81
no success without hard w.	SOPH 834:30	**worker** material position of the w.	MARX 579:35
not enough to his w.	BOWL 153:99	unoccupied w., the working	MARX 578:26
Nothing will w. unless you do	ANGE 19:8	w. at each end	ANON 24:18
		w. becomes poorer	MARX 578:25

w. is the slave of capitalist society	CONN 243:22
w. uses a tool	MARX 579:42
w. would sooner have a £5 note	BLYT 144:87
workers claim the mission w.	RUNY 732:62
experienced and hardened w.	LENIN 521:37
men the w.	TENN 871:17
organized w. of the country	SHIN 818:12
W., all demand	SERV 757:37
workhouse born in the w.	THOM 884:35
Home is the...woman's w.	SHAW 808:53
w. from the horizon	LLOY 532:71
working can't be alwayth a w.	DICK 282:82
choice of w. or starving	JOHN 461:89
condition...of the W. Class	CARL 201:22
in his w. time	GILL 370:81
Labour isn't w.	ANON 26:81
necessary to exclude...the w. classes	GLAD 373:36
produce without w.	INGR 446:40
self-help created among w. people	SMIL 827:71
swell way to keep from w.	HEMI 409:62
vast portion...of the w.-class	ARNO 36:29
When I have them w. together	COLE 234:5
w. for 16th Century Fox	RENO 711:53
working class the can't-be-bothered w. c.	GALL 358:36
workings tracings of her w.	HARV 400:78
workman w. in the land	LLOY 532:71
workmanship dark Inscrutable w.	WORD 958:76
workmen w. and menial servants	MALT 563:23
works all her w. gave signs of woe	MILT 606:50
all just w.	BOOK 146:42
all the w. of the Lord	BIBLE 133:41
body and substance of his w.	COLE 236:53
children shall be the w.	MICH 590:68
Commit thy w. unto the Lord	BIBLE 105:78
Faith without w. is dead	BIBLE 130:54
full of good w.	BIBLE 124:81
have seen the future and it w.	STEF 844:55
hope to create a few great w.	BEET 74:4
inspire These wond'rous w.	POPE 688:29
judged...according to their w.	BIBLE 132:22
know thy w.	BIBLE 131:94
Look on my w.	SHEL 813:86
marvellous are thy w.	BOOK 149:37
Merit and good w.	BACON 51:88
most beautiful w.	FLAU 339:17
move immediately upon your w.	GRANT 381:7
Of all God's w.	SPEN 838:32
painters speak with w.	CARR 202:59
poets...reading from their own w.	WHITE 935:33
praise those w.	MART 576:74
selling my own w.	POUND 691:7
so too are my other w.	KOLL 496:36
thro' her w.	SMART 826:68
To her fair w.	WORD 957:61
w. by contemporary composers	HEIF 407:12
w. do follow them	BIBLE 132:13
w. harder to convince himself	FRAS 349:32
w. in the social sciences	NISB 639:27
w. is a fool	MORL 620:43
w. of a great genius	ADDI 7:55
W. of art	FORS 345:44
w. of love or enmity fulfil	MILT 602:46
w. of the Lord	BIBLE 133:41
w. of thought and intelligence	PAST 668:4
workshop nation may be its w.	CHAM 212:59
no room in his w.	FAUL 331:35
not a temple, but a w.	TURG 901:17
w. for world peace	HARR 399:59
world about the end of the w.	GARD 360:68
active and creative w.	SPEN 837:12
adapts himself to the w.	SHAW 808:49
advice on the affairs of the w.	FLAU 339:23
Affairs of the w.	MERE 588:40
agency in the w.	WHIT 936:71
all country people, in the w.	SENG 757:26
all-eclipsing Soviet w.	THUB 890:60
alleged, from the beginning of the w.	EMER 325:75
all museums throughout the w.	PATE 669:14
All's right with the w.	BROW 167:9
all the kingdoms of the w.	BIBLE 114:24
all the Tartars in the w.	POLO 684:5
all the towns in all the w.	EPST 327:26
all the uses of this w.!	SHAK 780:38
all the wide w. over	IBSEN 444:3
all the w. as my parish	WESL 932:67
all the w. in ev'ry corner sing	HERB 413:58

world

all the w. is queer	OWEN 657:24	delights of this w.	TWAIN 903:92
All the w. over	GLAD 373:40	deliver the w.	LEE 519:98
All the w.'s a stage	SHAK 779:80	democratic in the w.	MACA 546:58
all the w.'s was gay	POPE 685:34	departure from this w.	EMMET 325:6
America...curse...upon the w.	MILL 593:58	destruction of the whole w.	HUME 438:99
amidst a bursting w.	POPE 687:98	devaluation of the human w.	MARX 578:25
And round the w. away	KING 487:48	disasters of the w.	CONN 243:12
another w., the happy seat	MILT 602:62	dominate the w.	WILDE 941:93
antagonisms of the Old W.	BORAH 150:53	do something...w. may talk of	COLL 236:58
any game in the w.	TRUE 899:73	drives him to the w.	ARNO 34:79
any service to the w.'s end?	SHAK 774:28	drowsy syrups of the w.	SHAK 789:25
any value at all in the w.	LACL 503:33	dying w. I come from	WAUGH 924:83
any way to perpetuate the W.	BROW 165:70	Each creature of the w.	ALAN 10:15
appear before the w.	PARK 665:37	earth is nobler than the w.	PRIE 695:85
appear to the w.	NEWT 635:61	echoes round the w.	TENN 876:43
apply to the real w.	MINS 608:12	edge of the w.	SITW 824:22
architecture of the w.	MARL 572:99	Eggheads of the w. unite	STEV 851:8
arrangement with the w.	MOLT 612:92	Encyclopedia behind...the w.	LAMB 505:91
arrange the w.	HEAN 404:69	end is in the other w.	MONT 614:30
Artist of the Floating W.	ISHI 447:71	England...workshop of the w.	DISR 287:23
As round as the w.	SITW 823:98	enough unpleasant things in the w.	RENO 711:59
a' the mischief in this w.	SCOTT 753:57	enter the new w. naked	WILL 946:8
at the summit of the w.	PEARY 671:60	entrances of this w.	BIBLE 112:69
Away with a corrupt w.	MERE 587:26	epoch unrivalled in w. history	LARI 509:70
awe for the natural w.	WILS 947:44	even unto the end of the w.	BIBLE 119:49
babies begin to come into the w.	MENC 587:10	every country in the w.	KEEN 478:52
bade the w. farewell	CAMP 194:62	everything else in the w.	MONT 614:40
bathe the w. in light	WORD 961:36	Everything in the w.	LAFO 504:55
beauty made The bright w. dim	SHEL 815:25	evil in this w.	PECK 672:62
beauty of the w.	SHAK 782:89	Example moves the w.	MILL 594:61
beauty of the w.	WEIL 928:73	excellent thing in w.	WILD 943:45
before the eyes of the w.	JOHN 456:81	eyes of the w. are upon you	EISE 314:92
before the w. confess'd	HOW 433:84	face of the w.	LAUT 512:30
Before the w. was made	YEATS 967:30	fairest order in the w.	HERA 412:38
Before you save the w.	ANON 26:3	fall in love with the w.	WALC 916:21
begin saving the w.	BUKO 173:54	false map of the w.	ORWE 654:55
best actors in the w.	SHAK 782:94	far fairer w.	DONNE 291:19
best game in the w. to watch	TREV 896:5	Federation of the w.	TENN 871:17
best minds in the w.	ACHE 3:56	feelings of a heartless w.	MARX 578:24
bestride the narrow w.	SHAK 776:9	fertilize the whole w.	TOCQ 892:27
best tea in the w.	SNOW 832:74	field of w. policy	ROOS 724:5
better w. than this	SHAK 778:61	fight...against...the w.	BOOK 147:77
birth of the modern w.	MCCA 548:93	fill the w. at once	MILT 606:64
blackguard made the w.	HOUS 432:64	first act on entering this w.	BOYD 154:12
blithely handing over the w.	COUP 248:32	foolish w.	DRYD 301:54
blowing round the w.	BALD 57:33	For all the w.	SHAK 772:90
born into the w. alive	GILB 369:52	force maintaining...the w.	DOST 294:91
brave w.	BEHN 75:18	For God so loved the w.	BIBLE 122:25
breath...can move a w.	WORD 956:52	forgotten the w.	AURE 45:46
bridge between the w.	RUSS 734:37	for the woods against the w.	BLUN 143:81
brings him into the w. poor	INNO 446:46	free w. and the Communist w.	KENN 481:22
broad highway of the w.	SHEL 815:45	fresh, green breast of the new w.	FITZ 338:86
brought nothing into this w.	BIBLE 129:22	funniest joke in the w.	SHAW 809:65
brought the whole w.	PLUT 682:76	gain the whole w.	BIBLE 118:8
bubble burst, and now a w.	POPE 686:73	garden of the w.	MARV 578:10
business institution in the w.	ROGE 722:70	gates of the w.	HARDY 397:14
busy w. is hushed	NEWM 635:46	gem of the western w.	MOORE 617:1
called the New W. into existence	CANN 197:11	genius appears in the w.	SWIFT 861:32
call man a little w.	DONNE 293:66	Gid, the w. is not like	MO 611:68
Call the w. if you please	KEATS 476:92	girdled with the gleaming w.	TENN 870:92
Canada...the only country in the w.	MCLU 556:58	give his soul for the whole w.	BOLT 145:12
caught the w.'s great hands	HUNT 439:23	gives me all the w.	LEGU 520:18
cause of the w.	POUND 691:98	gleams that untravelled w.	TENN 870:98
change the w. into words	GASS 361:88	glory of the w. passes	KEMP 479:75
characterizes the animal w.	MILL 594:80	god going thro' his w.	BROW 167:10
citizen of the w.	BOSW 152:77	God...had created a perfect w.	SHAR 806:75
civilized nations of the w.	PEARY 671:59	God heard before creating the w.	FERN 334:97
clothes go out in the w.	MIDL 590:82	God's works...this w. adorn	SPEN 838:32
come into the w.	DICK 281:62	go forth into a w.	FORS 344:40
coming into the w.	SWIFT 861:19	going round the w.	HERZ 416:22
constant in a changing w.	JOUV 469:12	gone into the w. of light	VAUG 909:41
contagion of the w.'s slow stain	SHEL 815:40	good deed in a naughty w.	SHAK 770:22
contagion on the w.	TWAIN 902:63	Go ye into all the w.	BIBLE 120:63
Contagion to this w.	SHAK 783:30	great allegory—the w.	MELV 585:73
continue being leaders in the w.	IACO 444:3	greatest deliberative body in the w.	SMITH 829:27
could electrify the w.	MILL 594:68	greatest man in the w.	TRUM 900:88
country is the w.	PAINE 660:36	greatest obloquy i' th' w.	SHAK 791:66
covered the w. of reality	MILL 593:51	greatest powers of the w.	PALM 662:74
Crested the w.	SHAK 795:88	greatest secrets...preserved in our w.	FAWC 331:51
crossroads of all the evil in the w.	GENET 363:40	greatest thing in the w.	FORS 344:33
Dark as the w. of man	SITW 823:11	greatest thing in the w.	MONT 614:24
Days That Shook The W.	REED 710:36	great morning of the w.	SHEL 815:33
dearest to the w.	SHAK 804:22	great w.'s altar-stairs	TENN 874:79
Dear W., I am leaving	SAND 742:38	great w. spin for ever	TENN 871:23
death into the w.	BIBLE 112:73	Had we but w. enough	MARV 577:90
death shall all the w. subdue	SPEN 839:47	half-brother of the w.	BAIL 55:88
defies the w.	DRYD 301:47	half of the w. cannot understand	AUST 46:74

hands...that would light the w.	MILL 593:34	I am the light of the w.	BIBLE 123:18
hand that rules the w.	WALL 918:52	ideal view of the w.	NAIP 629:31
happiest Africans in the w.	SMITH 829:7	If all the economists in the w.	SHAW 811:32
happiness of the next w.	BROW 165:74	If all the w....were young	RALE 705:43
happy in this w.?	THAC 880:30	if I reprehend anything in this w.	SHER 817:76
happy state in this w.	LOCKE 534:47	If the w. be worth thy winning	DRYD 303:33
hated and despised the w.	HAZL 404:50	ignorance the Western W.	JOHN 459:41
have a w. to win	MARX 579:34	image of the w.	PAZ 671:49
have not loved the w.	BYRON 187:56	imagination created the w.	BAUD 69:76
have overcome the w.	BIBLE 123:57	immorality...in our utilitarian w.	STARK 843:23
head is...map of the whole w.	FIEL 335:18	in a w. gone blind	RUSS 735:42
hidden in the Western w.	MATT 582:1	independence recreates the w.	MCLU 556:54
hill of beans in this crazy w.	EPST 327:29	influence moves our w.	ARNO 36:30
Hispanic w. never crumbled	REYES 712:69	ingress into the w.	LONG 536:36
history of the w.	GIBB 366:90	insignificant chatter of the w.	TROL 897:25
history of the w.	POPP 689:57	interesting discovery about the w.	BRAD 154:24
Hog Butcher for the W.	SAND 741:13	interest of the w.	RUSS 734:21
hold the w. but as the w.	SHAK 768:68	in the w....as a Spectator	ADDI 6:24
hope of establishing a w. order	EISE 314:1	in the w. climbs	WILD 943:39
hope the w. can show	DONNE 291:24	in the w.'s eyes	YEATS 966:16
house in the w.	RYBC 736:55	In this dull w.	SHAK 795:83
How beautiful...this visible w.!	BYRON 189:84	in this fair w. appear	TRAH 895:84
how dry a cinder this w. is	DONNE 292:61	in this harsh w.	SHAK 785:73
how the w. wags	SHAK 779:79	In this w.	FRAN 348:94
I am a little w.	DONNE 292:56	in this w. is concerned	RUNY 731:61
I am the light of the w.	BIBLE 123:48	In this w., one must	MARI 571:84
		Into the dangerous w. I leapt	BLAKE 140:18
		Into this breathing w.	SHAK 761:33
		In whom his w. rejoices	WINK 950:98
		Is the w. reform'd	OTWAY 656:5
		It is a fine w.	THOM 885:58
		It will be a gay w.	READ 708:96
		jest, and riddle of the w.	POPE 687:81
		joy the w. can give	BYRON 189:81
		just circumference, O w.	MILT 605:30
		king of the w.	CAME 193:43
		knack of so arranging the w.	FRIS 351:82
		knowledge of the physical w.	LEVI 525:26
		knowledge of...the w.	LURIE 542:65
		knyght of the w.	MALO 563:12
		labor of the w.	STAN 842:15
		launch through the w.	MARI 571:78
		law of the musical w.	WHAR 934:12
		laws of the fallen w.	BLOOM 143:66
		leans away from the w.	SCOTT 751:3
		Learn of the green w.	POUND 692:25
		leaves the w. to darkness	GRAY 384:62
		leave the w. unseen	KEATS 478:42
		let nothing in this w.	RABE 704:22
		lie can travel halfway round the w.	CALL 192:29
		life...and all the w.	SHAK 770:15
		light of the bright w. dies	BOUR 153:94
		light of the w.	BIBLE 114:29
		light of the w.	BIBLE 123:39
		lip Of his w.	DAY 267:34
		Literature...makes justice in the w.	PALEY 661:51
		Little Friend of all the W.	KIPL 491:25
		little friendship in the w.	BACON 53:34
		little w. in which the big one	HEBB 406:97
		little w. of thee	MONT 615:49
		lived long enough in the w.	WALP 919:83
		live in a w. ruined by Reason	MAMET 564:33

world

living in a material w.	MADO 558:19	on the walls of the w.	KENN 482:31	state of things throughout the w.	BACON 50:45
look forward to a w.	ROOS 724:13	Out of the w.!	HOOD 426:34	stay of the whole w.?	HOOK 427:39
lords, a spacious w.	MILT 606:60	out of the w.	THOM 885:54	still point of the turning w.	ELIOT 319:39
lost the w. for love	DRYD 304:52	outward and visible w.	ARNO 35:22	still point of the turning w.	ELIOT 319:43
lost wonders of the ancient w.	AUCH 42:65	over the bent W. broods	HOPK 428:71	stood against the w.	SHAK 777:41
lover's quarrel with the w.	FROST 353:16	over the roofs of the w.	WHIT 937:96	Stop The W.	ANON 25:45
loyalty to the w. organization	CHUR 226:3	O w. invisible	THOM 886:83	surrender the whole w.	BARB 63:46
magic to change the w.	ROWL 730:26	passage to the intellectual W.	STER 848:40	survey of all the w.	SHAK 772:66
makes the whole w. kin	SHAK 787:39	pass current in the w.	LAMB 505:93	survive in this modern w.	GOLD 375:76
making the private w. public	GINS 372:15	passing w.	JOHN 459:46	symphony must be like the w.	MAHL 559:31
making the w. safe for hypocrisy	WOLFE 953:67	pass through this w.	GREL 387:54	taken a lead in w. affairs	THAT 881:68
Man is one w.	HERB 413:71	pattern for the future of the w.	CHUR 225:80	taketh away the sin of the w.	BIBLE 122:19
mankind throughout the w.	STEI 845:58	peace which the w. cannot give	BOOK 146:42	taste Brought death into the w.	MILT 601:29
man…surges up in the w.	SART 744:72	peopled half the w.	SEEL 756:2	teach the w. new love	PHIL 676:53
Man to Man the w. o'er	BURNS 180:54	people in the w. are fools	WILD 943:48	terror of the w.	GIBB 366:94
man who convinces the w.	DARW 263:61	people in the w. more fond	MELV 585:62	Than this w. dreams of	TENN 878:86
man who has seen the w.	MACA 545:26	People of the w., unite	MAO 569:36	that all the w. should be taxed	BIBLE 120:67
man who is born into a w.	MALT 563:22	personalities in the w. reappear	MARX 579:36	that ever happened in the w.	FOX 346:68
masculine w.	WARN 921:10	philosophers…interpreted the w.	MARX 579:28	the w. has lost a visionary	OBAMA 644:43
menace to the whole w.	ROOS 725:22	phonograph of the w.	STEAD 843:30	the w. is a mess	ALBR 11:38
men are rolling round the w.	WEST 933:95	physicists have changed our w.	SNOW 832:82	the w. looks like the photograph	HOCK 421:17
men of the w.	DICK 278:59	pillars of the w.	BETH 87:13	thicket of the w.	JOHN 456:75
men's watch upon the w.	MACL 555:37	place from which to view the w.	ANON 26:87	thick rotundity o' th' w.	SHAK 792:5
microcosm of little w.	BROW 165:72	Playboy of the Western W.	SYNGE 865:20	things in the w.	RUSK 732:84
mighty frame of the w.	BERK 84:30	pleasures in the w.	CORY 247:13	things that in the great w. be	WORD 959:97
mighty w.	WORD 956:56	pleasures, of a free w.	LURIE 542:66	This gewgaw w.	DRYD 301:51
milk the cow of the w.	WILB 939:34	poised between this w. and the next	DICK 278:63	This great w. Shall so wear out	SHAK 793:23
mind o'er all the w.	MILT 607:77	portion of the foreign w.	WASH 922:31	this Is a w. of sweets	POE 683:87
miserable w.!	SHAK 779:78	power or respect in the w.	BAGE 54:76	this little w.	SHAK 764:40
modern w. is a dreary business	PERCY 674:10	power to make the w. a desert	STEV 850:5	This pendent w.	MILT 603:72
more fantastic the w. becomes	HUXL 441:58	problem of understanding the w.	POPP 689:60	This various w.	SHEL 812:55
most governed people in the w.	EDIN 312:48	problems of the w.	MAMET 564:38	this vile w.	OTWAY 656:9
most important thing in the w.	SHAW 806:79	promotion…to a better w.	WEST 933:95	this wicked w.	BOOK 148:78
most incomprehensible…w.	EINS 314:87	prudent to gain the whole w.	SHAW 810:5	This w.…a thurghfare ful of wo	CHAU 217:86
Most of the w.'s troubles	WAUGH 924:90	Queens of this w.	DONNE 293:73	This w.'s no blot	BROW 167:29
most perverse creatures in the w.	ADDI 6:33	quiet limit of the w.	TENN 877:60	this w.'s ransoming	AQUI 30:96
most poetical topic in the w.	POE 683:89	random element in the w.	EDDI 311:24	thought in the w.	ARNO 35:13
most wonderful in the w.	SIHA 821:66	real w. is not easy to live in	DAY 267:28	Though we travel the w.	EMER 324:65
mothers bring us into the w.	SCHR 749:62	receive a ready-made w.	ROBBE 716:64	Thro' the w. we safely go	BLAKE 141:26
music…the w. is full of it	ELGAR 314:12	reduce the w. to…a chessboard	ORWE 653:17	throw me off the w.	NASH 631:85
mystery to the w.	LONG 536:39	reform a w.	CARL 200:87	thrust me out to the wide w.	DRYD 301:59
My W.	THUR 890:82	remembered around the w.	DISN 287:14	Till the w. is wrought	SHEL 814:94
naked shingles of the w.	ARNO 33:66	rest of the w. wears bifocals	GOLD 375:82	Time, the w. and the person	CIXO 227:44
nation which exploits the whole w.	ENGE 326:12	retire from the w.	DISR 288:55	To be honest, as this w. goes	SHAK 782:79
natural w. is full of irregularity	BOYD 154:13	reunite…with the w.	ARNO 35:23	Toil conquered the w.	VIRG 914:26
[Nature's] w. is brazen	SIDN 820:54	riches of this w. enjoy'dst	MILT 607:72	top of the w.	CAGN 192:19
needs of the material w.	UPDI 906:31	right…brought into the w.	SHEL 812:50	torch which illuminates the w.	PAST 668:4
never enjoy the w. aright	TRAH 895:85	Ringed with the azure w.	TENN 875:4	torments in this w. or the next	CHES 219:45
never merry w. in England	SHAK 759:94	rising in the w.	JOHN 462:39	To save your w.	AUDEN 43:4
new found w.	MARL 573:23	Romans conquered the w.	SWEE 861:9	to seek a newer w.	TENN 870:2
no idea where the w. is going	SACKS 737:7	Rose of all the W.!	YEATS 965:8	to the ending of the w.	SHAK 776:92
no longer a chaos, but a w.	CARL 200:99	rose of all the w.	MACD 549:38	tragic a place this w.	LYND 543:91
no love-broker in the w.	SHAK 786:14	Round the w. for ever and aye	ARNO 33:58	tremendous w. in my head	HEWE 417:37
No one in this w.	MENC 586:92	saddest features of the real w.	ECON 310:22	triple pillar of the w.	SHAK 794:42
no other ambition in the w.	SHIP 818:14	same w. then as now	PRATT 694:68	trough between the two w. wars	LEWIS 527:75
Not all the treasures of the w.	PAINE 660:30	sceptre to control the w.	SHAK 760:22	true system of the W.	ALEM 12:56
not as the w. giveth	BIBLE 123:54	scorching w.'s opinion	FLET 341:61	Truth indeed came once into the w.	MILT 600:17
Nothing in the w.	LOWRY 541:41	see and imitate…this so-called w.	CUMM 257:50	truth to go round the w.	SPUR 841:89
Nothing in the w. is single	SHEL 813:78	see a w. in a grain of sand	BLAKE 140:24	turned the w. upside down	BIBLE 124:89
nothing in this w. constant	SWIFT 861:24	sees the w. one way	BARA 63:44	two axes of the w.	FRAN 346:81
nothing in…w. so unbecoming	WILDE 941:79	send us a merry meeting in this w.	LANC 506:23	two divinest things this w. has	HUNT 439:22
not innocence into the w.	MILT 600:8	sentiments in the w.	LOWE 539:11	two qualities in the w.	SHAW 809:68
not necessary…that the w. is good	CONR 244:39	set the w. ablaze	GILB 369:53	unacknowledged legislators of the w.	SHEL 816:53
not the clear-sighted who rule the w.	CONR 244:49	Shadows of the w. appear	TENN 869:81	Undulate round the w.	WHIT 938:9
nourish all the w.	SHAK 763:19	Shall give the w. to note	MARL 572:47	unknown w. t'explore	WENT 931:53
objective was the w.	DULL 306:88	shape the w.	RUSH 732:65	unreasonable silence of the w.	CAMUS 195:84
O brave new w.	SHAK 804:33	shore Of the wide w.	KEATS 475:78	unseen w. all around us	KING 487:38
of all the w.!	HAWT 402:17	shot heard around the w.	EMER 324:48	upstairs into the w.	CONG 240:42
Off all this w.	HENR 411:16	should corrupt the w.	TENN 878:85	value in my w.	GREE 386:12
offence to the w.	MOLI 611:78	sight of all the w.	LOUI 537:63	vice is in this w. so necessary	MILT 600:11
official w.	SNOW 832:75	since the creation of the w.	STER 847:21	visible w. seems formed in love	MELV 585:60
Of the wide w. dreaming	SHAK 802:76	single artificer of the w.	STEV 850:79	visible w. to love or reject	AUDEN 42:78
Of this hard w.	SHAK 765:62	sins of the whole w.	BOOK 147:71	vision of the w.	TENN 871:17
Oh w., no w.	KYD 501:49	Sioux owned the w.	SITT 823:93	wakes he will move the w.	NAPO 629:38
Oh, w., Oh, death?	SPEN 837:4	six days' work, a w.	MILT 605:32	Walk cheerfully over the w.	FOX 346:72
on any map of the w.	ROOS 724:2	Slavery broke the w.	MORR 620:58	warm kind w. is all I know	CORY 247:10
One had as good be out of the W.	CIBB 227:25	slip out of the w.	DRYD 299:17	warning to the w.	SHAK 801:61
One knows nothing of the w.	SCOTT 754:80	Sob, heavy w.	AUDEN 43:1	war that put the w. to sleep	MUIR 624:23
one of the capitals of the w.	MAIL 560:55	So in the w.	SHAK 777:26	way the w. ends	ELIOT 318:16
one should scour the w.	WILL 945:6	sole heir of the whole w.	TRAH 895:85	wears a mask in the w.	MARI 571:83
one thing in the w. worse	WILDE 940:65	something that infects the w.	ARNO 33:61	Well, W., you have kept faith	HARDY 397:30
one to face the w. with	BROW 168:56	sordid bourgeois w.	MISH 609:22	What about the w., Mr Cummings?	CUMM 258:63
one wants in this w.	MERR 589:50	soul ever does in this w.	RUSK 733:14	What Art was to the Ancient w.	DISR 287:28
only animal in the w. to fear	LAWR 513:61	spectacle unto the w.	BIBLE 126:38	What a w. is this	BOLI 145:7
only institution in the w.	SAMU 741:98	spinning in a w. of words	CURN 259:88	what is happening in the w.	PRIT 696:22
only people in the w.	SLOAN 825:55	spoil…their toy the w.	COWP 251:20	What is this w.?	CHAU 217:85
only saved the w.	CHES 221:5	statements about the w.	BOYD 154:14	what it does in the w.	KENN 482:32

World Cup

what once it was, the w.	MARV 578:9	w. is now as it was	BROW 165:50	w. would go round a deal faster	CARR 203:67
What would the w. be	HOPK 429:84	w. is richer for a new beauty	MARI 571:76	w. would have been	HALI 393:33
when all the w. dissolves	MARL 573:25	w. is ruled by little else	KEYN 484:81	w. would smell...a tomb	SHEL 814:3
When all the w. is young	KING 487:48	w. is run quite out	SPEN 839:55	w. wrapped up in...jeweller's cotton	DICK 281:57
when Rome falls—the W.	BYRON 188:68	w. is sagging	BART 66:20	worst woman in the w.	EDWA 313:64
When the w. was made	ANON 28:55	w. is so full	STEV 853:70	yearning for the wider w.	MUSC 627:86
When the w. was young	BACON 52:21	w. is the mirror	MILL 593:57	your whole w. is bereft	LAMA 504:72
When will the w. know	WALP 919:76	w. is the totality of facts	WITT 951:22	**World Cup** in the W. C. Final	RAMS 706:52
Where in this small-talking w.	FRY 353:33	w. is too much with us	WORD 961:30	win the W. C. under...Labour	WILS 948:69
where the w. is quiet	SWIN 864:97	w. is upheld by...veracity	EMER 325:78	**world-earthquake** w.-e., Waterloo!	TENN 875:9
whole new democratic w.	CARL 200:89	w. is weary of the past	SHEL 816:58	**worldkin** world, or even w.	CARL 200:99
whole wide w.	PAST 668:99	w. is white with May	TENN 878:76	**worldly** most loathed w. life	SHAK 788:70
whole w. hallucinated	RUSS 735:47	w. is wounded	KELL 479:66	**worlds** best of all possible w.	CABE 191:6
whole w. in the face	LONG 535:18	w. its veterans rewards	POPE 688:15	best of all possible w.	VOLT 914:33
whole w. is a place of exile	HUGH 434:6	w. knew him not	BIBLE 122:17	Between two w. life hovers	BYRON 190:28
whole w. is frightened to death!	SHER 818:10	w. locks up its spoons	SHAW 808:30	diverting and stimulating of w.	MENC 586:4
whole w. needs restructuring	GORB 378:47	w. market...computers	WATS 922:42	Dream not of other w.	MILT 605:36
whole w.'s in a state	OCAS 646:76	w. may perish	FERD 332:73	so many w.	TENN 874:84
wide in this w.	LANG 507:44	w. might gain	GREE 386:19	Wandering between two w.	ARNO 35:4
wildest beauty in the w.	OWEN 657:34	w. might now be a better place	DOWN 296:35	What w. delight	SPEN 838:26
will leave to the w.	NASHE 632:90	w. mirrored in the newspapers	LESS 524:97	w. not realised	WORD 959:10
window on the w.	UPDI 906:33	w. must be made safe for democracy	WILS 949:83	w. of wanwood leafmeal	HOPK 428:81
Winds of the W.	KIPL 490:94	w. must reel	BERR 87:96	worst of both w.	MACL 556:51
wiser w. doth greater thee confess	CAREW 198:47	w. now stands on the brink	MOUN 622:93	**worldview** w. a compound of	TOOLE 894:58
Witness this new-made w.	MILT 605:33	w. Of all of us	WORD 958:87	**WorldWar** before W. W. II	HOPP 429:3
woman of the w.	SHAW 810:4	w. of gammon and spinnage	DICK 280:50	passing resemblance to W. W. II	BARR 64:82
wonders of the western w.	SYNGE 865:23	w. of gutterals	STEV 849:68	warfare of W. W. I	NOON 640:44
Words of the w.	STEV 850:94	w. of his own making	WRIG 962:65	**worm** bird, insect, or w.	MILT 604:8
working economy in the w.	MARS 575:63	w. of objects...w. of words	ELIOT 317:91	channerin' w. doth chide	BALL 60:83
work shall with the w. remain	WALL 918:59	w. of profit and delight	MARL 573:21	Hast thou the pretty w.	SHAK 795:90
w....a kind of kindergarten	ROBI 718:87	w. of the dead	FORS 345:43	I am a w.	BIBLE 99:42
w. an honest man	LICH 528:91	w. of the emotions	COLE 236:56	like a w. i' th' bud	SHAK 786:1
w. a valley so sweet	MOORE 617:99	w. of thought	HAMI 394:49	loss of a w.?	SIDN 820:47
w. becomes stranger	ELIOT 320:68	w. of vile ill-favoured faults	SHAK 773:10	Of man or w.	MILT 607:84
w. being seldom visited	MONT 613:10	w. owes all its onward impulse	HAWT 402:11	physicists could create a w.	KRUT 500:30
w. be made fit and safe	WILS 949:85	W.-politics stepped in	LEWIS 527:73	remorse, my w.	RIMB 716:51
w. breaks everyone	HEMI 409:66	w. proletarian army	LENIN 521:39	The invisible w.	BLAKE 140:12
w. by wisdom knew not God	BIBLE 126:35	w....ranged against an aggressor	ATTL 40:24	w'en he fine a w.	HARR 399:48
w. can only be richer for it	BRAD 155:47	w. rolls under	HUGH 435:30	w. at one end	JOHN 465:7
w. continues to offer glittering prizes	BIRK 136:12	w. ruled and led to war?	KRAUS 499:9	w. of death	GRAV 382:25
w. could become socialist	MAO 568:32	w.'s a bubble	BACON 53:49	w. sucking an envenomed sore?	DONNE 290:16
w. dawns on unrecognizing...eyes	REID 710:44	w.'s anguish is caused by people	FAUL 331:38	w. that hath eat of a king	SHAK 784:47
w....does not owe us a living	EDIN 312:49	w.'s an inn	DRYD 304:54	w. that never dies	BROO 163:2
w. empty of people	LAWR 513:47	w.'s a scene of changes	COWL 250:71	**worms** among the hungry w. I sleep	BALL 58:57
w. forgetting, by the w. forgot	POPE 686:50	w. seemed none so bad	HOUS 432:59	exclusive w.	PARK 664:16
w. goes on because	MILL 594:75	w.'s going to be...one huge gallows	BRAU 157:84	filled with the ends of w.	TOLK 893:42
w. goes on out there	KRAM 499:3	w.'s great age begins anew	SHEL 816:57	food for w.!	FRAN 348:7
w. has grown grey	SWIN 864:99	w. great day	MUIR 624:24	gone into W.	LUTH 542:71
w. has not to be put in order	MILL 594:70	w.'s great sorrows	RUSS 735:43	grubs, or w.!	POPE 687:1
w. has turned over	MACA 544:8	w.'s grown honest	SHAK 782:84	have made w.' meat of me	SHAK 766:94
w. hath lost his youth	BIBLE 112:70	w. shall find this miracle	DANI 262:30	silk dresses out of w.	STEV 850:92
w. haunted by the hydrogen	ROUS 729:8	w. should listen then	SHEL 814:99	The more the w. writhe	BRON 162:81
w. holdith with Arthure	MALO 563:11	w.'s last night?	DONNE 292:57	the one that the editor gives to the w.	MACH 552:90
w. in arms	MACA 546:53	w.'s magnificence	MARI 571:77	vilest w. to dwell	SHAK 801:61
w. in endlessly different ways	NUTT 642:75	w.'s mine oyster	SHAK 773:3	will surely become w.	MILL 594:67
w. I never made	HOUS 432:68	w.'s new fashion	SHAK 763:6	w. destroy this body	BIBLE 98:8
w. in flames	VOLT 914:38	w.'s riches, which dispersèd lie	HERB 414:82	w. have eaten them	SHAK 779:10
w. in general knows	LEAR 519:39	w.'s sharpness like	BROW 166:95	w. shall try	MARV 577:92
W., in hounding me	CRUZ 256:38	w.'s storm-troubled sphere	BRON 162:75	w. that are thy chambermaids	SHAK 766:14
w. in its own image	NIET 638:8	w.'s tempestuous sea	EDME 312:55	**wormwood** end is bitter as w.	BIBLE 104:56
w. into a welter of bloodshed	LLOY 533:74	w.'s tourists are coming here	WILS 948:67	w. and the gall	BIBLE 110:25
w. in which children	DICK 282:5	w. surely is wide enough	STER 848:31	**worn** necessary...to be w. with toil	EURI 328:59
w. in which he found himself	HOLM 423:57	w.'s work...done by men	GALB 357:25	w. some twenty yeare agoe	FLET 341:60
w. in which this unconquerable	LAMB 505:84	w.'s worst son of a bitch	PARK 664:32	**worried** w. into being	FROST 353:13
w. is a comedy	WALP 919:74	w., that grey-bearded...profligate	HAWT 402:10	**worries** leaving you with your w.	SAND 742:38
w. is a funny paper	WILL 945:96	w. that is ours no more	BINY 135:3	money has dissolved more w.	BLEST 142:52
w. is a global campus	LODGE 534:97	w., to offer for their sin	MARV 576:87	**worrisome** night of this w. day	BERN 86:77
w. is a great volume	DONNE 293:79	w. understands my language	HAYDN 402:22	**worry** any one he wanted to w. about	HELL 407:29
w. is all that is the case	WITT 951:21	w. was all before them	MILT 607:74	cakes...looked green with w.	FIRB 336:54
w. is an ever-living fire	HERA 412:34	w. was before the creation	BROW 165:67	don't need to w.	HUTC 441:50
w. is at the end of its tether	WELLS 930:40	w. was headed	SZIL 865:31	friends are beginning to w.	EPST 327:34
w. is bad enough	CLOU 232:51	w. was not worthy	BIBLE 129:42	nothing much to w. about	HERR 416:19
w. is charged	HOPK 428:70	w. we find terrifying	MAMET 563:28	w. about is bad luck	TRUM 899:79
W. is crazier	MACN 557:95	w. well-tried and old	HUGH 435:36	w. incessantly	GREE 387:37
w. is diminished by the experience	SHAW 811:39	w. where action is not sister	BAUD 68:68	w. on the doorstep	FIEL 335:28
w. is disgracefully managed	FIRB 336:47	w. where it is so easy to neglect	CORN 247:6	you don't have to w.	DENN 273:73
w. is full of middle-class people	SHAR 806:78	w. will disagree	POPE 687:85	**worse** do w. than be a swinger	FROST 352:48
w. is grievously given to lying	TWAIN 903:88	w. will end in fire	FROST 352:4	everything...will get w. over time	COUL 248:21
w. is growing old	HAZL 403:47	w. will give their credit	CHUR 220:81	for better for w.	BOOK 148:91
w. is in flames today	WITTE 950:19	w. will little note	LINC 529:10	from w. to better	JOHN 460:59
w. is made up	BUCK 172:40	w. without end	BOOK 149:29	I follow the w.	OVID 657:19
w. is more and more	TENN 871:20	w. without end	RHYS 712:76	inflicting one that is w.	BOIL 144:2
w. is never the same	THOM 884:45	w. without end. Amen	BIBLE 128:89	More will mean w.	AMIS 16:34
w. is not black and white	GREE 386:29	w. without end. Amen	BOOK 146:35	person for the w.	SWIFT 861:22
w. is not thy friend	SHAK 766:12	w. without our pain	LANY 508:56	The w. the country	HORN 430:24
w. is not with us	LEVE 525:24	W., w., I cannot get	MILL 592:18	w. appear The better reason	MILT 602:58
w. is not yet prepared	DOYLE 297:74	w. worth working for	MITC 610:39	w. case of woe	SHAK 803:99

write

w. occupations in this world	STER 849:57	
w. than being talked about	WILDE 940:65	
w. things in life	SCOTT 753:39	
w. when it comes late	JERR 455:47	
worship condesended to w. her	FORS 344:22	
even in the house of w.	PARN 665:46	
find someone to w.	DOST 294:93	
if thou wilt fall down and w. me	BIBLE 114:24	
machines we w.	PRIE 695:89	
not dressed for w.	UPDI 906:32	
O w. the King	GRANT 381:5	
religion without…death w.	REED 710:35	
traditional w. of progress	WIEN 939:29	
w. and great honoring	DUNB 306:98	
w. her by…noble deeds	TENN 877:57	
w. him in spirit and in truth	BIBLE 122:28	
W. is transcendent wonder	CARL 201:31	
w. of God	WHIT 936:66	
w. of…second-rate women	WEBB 925:6	
w. the Caesars and Napoleons	HUXL 442:81	
w. the Lord	BIBLE 102:3	
w. this dull fool	SHAK 804:34	
Your w. is your furnaces	BOTT 152:83	
worshipful neither articulate or w.	SNYD 832:93	
worshipper Nature mourns her w.	SCOTT 752:15	
priest is the w.	SHAW 809:69	
worships he w. in his way	SMART 826:62	
worst At w., one is in motion	GUNN 390:96	
best and the w. of this	SWIN 864:3	
do thy w., old time	SHAK 800:38	
exacts a full look at the w.	HARDY 397:24	
favour of the w.	MILL 592:11	
good to know the w.	BRAD 155:42	
learn, at best and w.	RABAN 703:2	
Let's reason with the w.	SHAK 778:53	
No w., there is none	HOPK 429:90	
only believe the w.	LAFO 503:47	
This is the w.	SHAK 793:16	
very best and the very w.	FORD 343:91	
What America…does w.	FUEN 354:60	
world's w. son of a bitch	PARK 664:32	
w. are…passionate intensity	YEATS 966:24	
w. comes in the end	SYNGE 865:22	
w. is better than any other person	HAZL 403:48	
w. is better than none	JOHN 464:96	
w. is death	SHAK 764:50	
w. is yet to come	JOHN 458:25	
w. of madmen	POPE 688:25	
w. of prison life	STEN 847:5	
w. of worse journeys	WOOD 954:1	
w. possible location in the world	ACHE 3:56	
w. sin towards our fellow creatures	SHAW 807:98	
w. thing is that we live in	HAVEL 401:83	
w. time of the year	ELIOT 318:17	
worsted though right were w.	BROW 169:85	
worth been w. the whistling	SHAK 793:18	
comfort of thy w. and truth	SHAK 801:49	
for what they are w.	FORB 342:85	
grow in w., and wit	TENN 872:28	
honest w. must wait outside	CHAO 214:9	
matter of more w.	SHAK 759:82	
measured by his w.	SHAK 798:79	
More w. than any man	SHAK 800:30	
not w. going to see	JOHN 463:68	
prove…their commercial w.	ROCK 720:32	
Small is the w.	WALL 918:56	
two things w. aiming for	HIND 419:67	
w. a great deal	WEBB 925:7	
w. doing well	CHES 219:35	
w. of the State	MILL 591:6	
worthier not necessarily to be w.	HELO 408:54	
Worthington Mrs W.	COWA 249:54	
worthwhile never does anything w.	CHAR 215:26	
worthy he is also w.	PASC 667:89	
not w. of me	BIBLE 116:73	
Who is w. to open the book	BIBLE 131:99	
world was not w.	BIBLE 129:42	
w., O Lord, to receive glory	BIBLE 131:98	
w. was what he suffered	AESC 8:76	
Wotton W.…a most dear lover	WALT 920:92	
woulda w. shoulda, coulda	HOFF 422:27	
wound always w. up and going	LOWE 539:9	
bleeding in the bitter w.	SPEN 838:20	
books that w.	KAFKA 472:3	
heal me of my grievous w.	TENN 878:87	
later return to w.	MURR 627:85	
Makes such a w.	SHEL 814:6	

Most writers need a w.	AMIS 16:49	
nobler weapon than a w.	CRAS 254:86	
not the w. that caused the scream	ELTIT 323:40	
purple with love's w.	SHAK 767:27	
Safe with his w.	SASS 745:81	
stain like a w.	BURKE 176:41	
taken an immortal w.	FROST 353:25	
What w. did ever heal	SHAK 789:15	
Willing to w.	POPE 687:3	
w. for w.	BIBLE 94:67	
w. is incurable	LACL 503:39	
wounded Bury my heart at W. Knee	BENET 79:26	
forgive last the delicately w.	CIAR 226:23	
When you're w.	KIPL 489:88	
w. for our transgressions	BIBLE 109:94	
w. surgeon plies the steel	ELIOT 320:64	
wounding guardianship…against w.	PATR 669:29	
heart's deep-sore w.	SHAK 762:87	
wounds Balm to fester'd w.	MILT 607:88	
balm to heal their w.	SHAK 760:16	
Bind up my w.!	SHAK 761:48	
bind up the nation's w.	LINC 529:11	
bound up his w.	BIBLE 121:81	
Faithful are the w. of a friend	BIBLE 105:2	
Say not…labour and the w. are vain	CLOU 232:47	
shall make my w. all sound	LAYA 515:98	
the soldier lists his w.	PROP 697:30	
too much attainted by w.	HOFS 422:38	
With balmy hands his w. to bind	COLL 237:73	
W. are an essential part of life	AUST 47:94	
w. are in his breast and face	DAVIS 266:10	
w. I had on Crispin's day	SHAK 776:90	
W. inflicted by the sword	RICH 714:22	
w. of deadly hate	MILT 604:94	
woven Joy and Woe are w. fine	BLAKE 141:26	
w. and held together	JACK 448:3	
wow Oh w., oh w., oh w.	JOBS 455:67	
wrath chariots of w.	GRANT 381:6	
Envy and w. shorten the life	BIBLE 113:3	
eternal w. Burnt after them	MILT 605:26	
give place unto w.	BIBLE 125:27	
in w. remember mercy	BIBLE 111:56	
my w. did end	BLAKE 140:17	
Nursing her w.	BURNS 179:19	
provoke not your children to w.	BIBLE 128:93	
soft answer turneth away w.	BIBLE 104:73	
sun go down upon your w.	BIBLE 128:90	
sware in my w.	BIBLE 102:2	
Throw away thy w.	HERB 414:85	
tygers of w.	BLAKE 140:1	
warned you to flee from the w.	BIBLE 114:20	
w. and indignation against us	BOOK 147:52	
W. brings…gravest hurt	EURI 328:62	
W. is cruel	BIBLE 105:1	
w. of the Lamb	BIBLE 131:2	
w. of the lion	BLAKE 140:2	
w. which thou condemnest	BLAKE 141:33	
wreaths laurel w. entwine	HARTE 400:74	
w. of fame and interest	MARV 577:98	
wreck Amid the w.…of nations	PITT 680:12	
decay Of that colossal w.	SHEL 813:86	
From its own w.	SHEL 815:20	
playing bowls upon a splitting w.	DAVI 264:65	
rock on which thou art to w.	DRYD 302:95	
worthless check, a total w.	PORT 690:69	
w. and not the story of the w.	RICH 713:2	
w. of Paradise	SHEL 816:41	
wreckage w. of men	WOOLF 955:29	
wrecks thousand fearful w.	SHAK 761:40	
Vomits its w.	SHEL 814:2	
w. of a dissolving dream	SHEL 816:57	
w. will surface over the sea	EWART 328:76	
Wren Sir Christopher W. said	BENT 82:99	
wren Four Larks and a W.	LEAR 516:2	
No, the w. goes to't	SHAK 793:21	
robin-red-breast and the w.	WEBS 926:36	
wrest w. the ball from your neighbour	ANON 23:91	
wrestle w. not against flesh	BIBLE 128:95	
w.…words and meanings	ELIOT 320:58	
wrestling lay w. with…my God	HOPK 429:89	
Light w. there incessantly with light	CRANE 253:56	
Texas w. match	WRIS 963:83	
wretch Excellent w.!	SHAK 789:16	
My well…poor w.	PEPYS 673:94	
on a w. wilt thou be revenged?	SIDN 820:41	
Perfidious w.!	TREI 896:2	
poor w. whose one d.	SHAW 809:20	

Pulled the poor w.	SHAK 784:58	
Saucy pedantic w.	DONNE 291:25	
saved a w. like me!	NEWT 635:63	
sharp-looking w.	SHAK 762:93	
W., under a comfort	HOPK 429:92	
w. who supports	JOHN 460:78	
wretched All men hate the w.	SHEL 812:48	
how w. I should be	ALBE 11:30	
make every one w.	JAMES 450:23	
man…a w. thing	DAVI 264:77	
Most w. men	SHEL 812:63	
O w. state of man	SIDN 820:36	
This rortie w. city	SMITH 831:64	
w. man that I am!	BIBLE 125:15	
w., rash, intruding fool	SHAK 784:39	
wretchedness so bare and full of w.	SHAK 766:12	
w. is irremediable	EDGE 311:41	
wretches Poor naked w.	SHAK 792:11	
w. hang	POPE 685:28	
Wright W.'s limp sentences	WEST 933:98	
wring w. under the load of sorrow	SHAK 774:52	
wrinkle out…with the first w.	DRYD 299:17	
What stamps the w.	BYRON 187:44	
wrinkles let old w. come	SHAK 786:69	
w. will devour	NASHE 632:96	
wrist time is tied to the w.	RAINE 705:40	
tread her w.	DUNC 307:11	
wrists slap time on their w.	KINC 486:14	
writ censure this mysterious w.	DRYD 303:14	
One w. with me	SHAK 766:13	
stol'n forth of Holy W.	SHAK 761:39	
w. your annals true	SHAK 799:6	
write allow them to sing and to w.	MAZA 583:28	
always w. of you	SHAK 801:63	
as a man ought to w.	TROL 898:56	
as much of a labour to w.	HUXL 441:63	
better to w. of laughter	RABE 703:8	
cause to w. about me	GIOV 372:17	
difficult not to w. satire	JUVE 471:52	
do not w. on a computer	OROU 652:96	
Don't w. anything down	DOWD 296:30	
Don't you like to w. letters?	HEMI 409:62	
engender in those who w.	GOWE 380:81	
few…as cannot w.	DENH 272:61	
For a man to w. well	JONS 468:93	
If a man w. little	BACON 53:38	
invoked, sit down to w.	SWIFT 862:61	
isn't much to w. home about	HYDE 443:20	
I w. because	GALL 358:43	
like to w. standing up	HEMI 410:85	
look in thy heart, and w.	SIDN 820:44	
make me w. too much	DANI 262:35	
may w. at any time	JOHN 459:50	
necessary to w. for oneself	FLAU 339:22	
never w. another	WELD 928:88	
No man can w.	FAUL 331:46	
not easy to w. well	JAMES 451:58	
number who can w.	MACD 559:32	
people who do not w.	GREE 386:25	
those who cannot w.	POPE 688:19	
took him seventeen years to w.	PRIE 695:90	
to w. a really funny book	HEMI 409:60	
To w. music is to	HONE 425:14	
to w. or even to talk	THES 882:96	
try to w. as good	HEMI 410:92	
watches over us when we w.	AMIS 16:51	
What I feel most moved to w.	MELV 585:72	
When I do not w.	CIXO 227:48	
when you w. or when you fight	HEMI 410:77	
would have liked to w.	KAVA 474:47	
w. a book a year	TARTT 867:34	
w. about it if I like	STEIN 845:69	
w. against your name	RICE 713:89	
w. enough to sign contracts	GING 371:98	
w.…exclusively of others	WAUGH 924:93	
w. for money or fame	MOORE 617:83	
w. for the adults	WALK 917:34	
W.: for these words are true	BIBLE 132:24	
w. his thoughts upon a slate	HOOD 426:38	
W. me as one that loves	HUNT 439:29	
w. music like Wagner	GOLD 377:27	
w. of Hell	HERR 415:98	
w. straight honest prose	HEMI 410:75	
w. the beauty of your eyes	SHAK 800:35	
w.…too early in your life	RILKE 715:36	
w. whatever story	KELM 479:68	
w. when I feel spiteful	LAWR 512:41	

writer

w. when there is something	HEMI 410:74	bad w. must start with plain heroines	FITZ 338:2	W. is turning one's worst moments	DONL 290:11
w. with no dinner	RANS 707:73	cause of poets and of w.	SPEN 837:13	W. is…waiting for the word	WILB 939:41
yet could w. of thee?	JONS 468:85	comic w. to have a hate figure	TOWN 895:69	w. on what pleased me best	HAZL 404:54
writer Aboriginal w. is a Janus-type	NARO 630:53	Creative w. are always greater	FORS 345:49	w. paper thinner	MITF 610:57
advertisement w. uses his mastery	SAYE 746:10	Derivative w. seem	NABO 628:16	w.…remaining vice	UPDI 906:35
art of the w.	APOL 29:80	English…the best dull w.	CHAN 213:79	W. saved me from	WALK 917:35
as a w. or artist	STEV 854:92	few w. can prostitute	FORS 345:42	w. something like it tomorrow	MERI 588:42
Asking a working w.	HAMP 395:76	give young w. advice	HELL 408:45	W. stopped being fun	CAPO 197:26
ask the w. to censor	KELM 479:68	great Victorian w.	WILS 948:50	w. that was…black	MORR 620:59
A w. leaves you with everything	JAMES 450:29	hold w. in contempt	BELL 77:81	W. today is like being	DE 268:48
basic material a w. works with	CATH 208:93	I don't think w. choose the genre	JAMES 451:61	W., when properly managed	STER 848:30
being a professional w.	ROST 727:73	I suppose all w. are crazy	CHAN 213:94	**writings** blanks in their w.	POUND 691:11
being a w. here means nothing	GOLD 375:80	Make way, Roman w.	PROP 697:31	**writs** issue w. for libel	PROF 697:28
concealed beauties of a w.	ADDI 6:32	men trying to be w.	JONES 465:19	**written** already w. before it started	HESE 416:27
danger of its tricking the w.	SAND 742:35	Most w. in…their careers	WAUGH 924:85	apparent in whatever is w.	WOOLF 956:38
Detach the w.	ROTH 727:76	Most w. need a wound	AMIS 16:49	Everything has been w.	FERN 334:97
duty of the w.	KENN 482:26	no different from other w.	BARN 64:73	most of the w. word	WILL 947:32
Every w. is a frustrated actor	SERL 757:52	rare…to take w. seriously	POWE 693:50	not what you have w.	FENT 332:59
experience…of the woman w.	WITT 951:30	self-limited w.	WOOLF 955:18	Not w. on by history	SCOTT 751:3
For the w.…as for the painter	PROU 698:59	severest w. of the severest age	DRYD 300:40	our destiny is not w. for us	OBAMA 644:29
function of a w.	CONN 243:6	some w. are lost	HAWT 401:2	paper it's w. on	GOLD 377:32
good w. always works	STEI 846:90	such great w. in the past	HEMI 410:88	people not w. about	GEE 362:27
good w. is not…a good book critic	BISH 137:30	true w. have experienced this feeling	SARR 744:61	poor man's life is w.	ADIGA 8:65
great and original w.	WORD 961:32	w. and the bardies	FERG 333:87	sat in my chair and w.	WODE 952:54
greatest part of a w.'s time	JOHN 462:36	W. are always envious	CAREY 199:64	until he has w. a book	JOWE 469:15
great w.…always the plodder	POUND 692:35	W. are much more esteemed	SNOW 832:81	well w., or badly w.	WILDE 940:62
great w. creates a world of his own	CONN 242:94	w. are there to overhear	BEAT 70:98	What I have w. I have w.	BIBLE 123:60
great w. does not…invent	PROU 698:60	w. could live in their own minds	BRAD 155:35	w. by a committee	GRIS 389:75
housewife nor a complete w.	PLATH 680:28	W. do not come out of	LESS 524:3	w. for the purpose of narrative	QUIN 703:26
If any w. thinks	SHAR 806:78	w., like clear fountains	LAND 506:27	w. with beautiful sentiments	GIDE 368:23
If I were a w.	DELI 271:39	W., like teeth	BAGE 54:65	w.…with mine own hand	BIBLE 127:84
if Mr Kissinger is a great w.	ANON 27:22	w.' lives	GIBB 367:6	**wrong** absent are always in the w.	DEST 275:4
it is the w.	ASIM 38:80	w.…make their language convey more	CONN 242:4	against injustice and w.	PALM 662:72
lesser w. may entice…for a moment	CONN 242:94	w. of the same age	COWL 250:80	all his life…in the w.	ROCH 719:12
loopholes for an unorthodox w.	ORWE 653:22	w. the young like	BURG 174:96	always in the w.	DRYD 302:83
major w.…required major torment	BERG 84:28	W. who drew	HIRS 419:77	authors could not endure being w.!	CAMUS 196:98
memorandum…to protect the w.	ACHE 3:47	w. who write about their childhood	PARK 664:24	brutal w. and deeds	NOON 641:50
modern hardback w.	MORT 621:68	**writes** say a man w. badly	JACK 450:28	certain way to be w.	STEI 846:87
No modern Irish w.	ORWE 654:51	w. as fast as they can read	HAZL 403:48	clearly and definitely w.	HUXL 443:12
not an easy country for a fiction-w.	UPDI 906:38	w. verses	SHAK 773:9	cradled into poetry by w.	SHEL 812:63
No w. before the…19th century	WAUGH 924:96	**writing** All w. is a disease	WILL 946:27	different kinds of w.	COMP 239:6
No w., sacred or profane	PATM 669:22	American w. comes from that	HEMI 410:76	do right or w.	TWAIN 903:66
occupation of a woman w.	WOOLF 956:35	art of w. something…read twice	CONN 242:95	do right or w.	TWAIN 903:67
plain, rude w.	BURT 181:75	difference between w. a book	MAIL 560:57	Eating people is w.!	FLAN 338:9
present or any future w.	MILL 591:95	discourage the composer from w.	HEIF 407:12	egotism w. side out	HOLM 424:79
primarily a w.	GENET 363:38	ease in w. comes from art	POPE 685:24	egregiously w.	SAFI 737:23
primary requirement for a w.	STAEL 842:99	fairy kind of w.	DRYD 303:20	Englishman in the w.	SHAW 807:97
responsibility of the w.	ALGR 13:70	going back to w.	SARD 743:51	From w. to w.	ELIOT 321:87
role of the w. and critic divided	BRAD 155:37	good w. is knowing when to stop	MONT 615:48	getting things w.	VIDAL 912:99
something of the w. in the work	STIPE 855:5	idea of w. the decline and fall	GIBB 366:2	great right of an excessive w.	BROW 169:73
stink…of the w.'s pride	SALI 740:85	in a w. unexpected	PATE 669:13	Had anything been w.	AUDEN 43:86
success happens to an English w.	AMIS 16:48	in his w.	JONS 468:90	hindsight proves us w.	MCNA 557:93
To a w., madness is a final distillation	DELI 271:40	isn't w.…it's typing	CAPO 197:19	hold them the w. way round	RIDGE 715:21
Too much importance is given the w.	BOWL 153:99	laws of prose w.	HEMI 410:83	if you w. us	SHAK 769:1
tragic w. does not have to believe	KRUT 500:29	live and despise w.	SMITH 830:40	I know when I'm w.	SOROS 834:37
true friend and a good w.	WHITE 935:42	Looking back…I was always w.	MANS 568:11	I think the world is w.	STARK 843:22
understand a w.'s ignorance	COLE 236:43	more than all the w. of critics	DU 305:72	know when I'm doing w.	WILS 947:38
vanity of the w.	REES 710:38	Most of my w.	FRYE 354:56	My country right or w.	CHES 220:54
vicious…to be a creative w.	LAWR 513:71	much arguing, much w.	MILT 600:4	ne'er pardon, who have done the w.	DRYD 300:31
When a w. calls his work	HAWT 402:7	only end of w.	JOHN 460:80	nets of w.	YEATS 965:9
wise w.…writes for the youth	FITZ 337:74	pattern of elaborate w.	DRYD 300:26	not between right and w.	JUNG 471:46
w. and nothing else	HUTC 441:47	political speech and w.	ORWE 655:61	Nothing really w. with him	HILT 418:64
w.…at the White House	WHITE 936:59	profession of book w.	STEI 846:89	one who does, not suffers w.	SHEL 814:7
w. by profession	GRASS 382:11	Ready w. makes not good w.	JONS 468:94	own he has been in the w.	POPE 686:54
w. enters into a structure	FRYE 354:54	seek in my w.	GRASS 382:11	people who don't are the w. ones	SHAW 810:10
w. has to rob his mother	FAUL 331:41	sounds like w.	LEON 522:63	petty right or w.	THOM 885:55
w. have a social responsibility?	NABO 629:22	talking about w. or themselves	HELL 408:45	Philosophy was w.	RANS 707:71
w.…if you copy others	BERN 86:78	This manner of w.	MILT 600:97	players have been all w.	QUIN 702:18
w. must eventually write	ROY 730:30	thought nothing of her w.	SITW 824:14	positions which, if w.	KENN 482:44
w. of dictionaries	JOHN 460:67	Translation…the exemplar of all w.	MATH 581:86	precisely w.	BUFF 172:44
w. of dictionaries	JOHN 460:75	w. a book	GERA 364:60	protest against w.	MACL 554:27
w. of talent needs only	WINN 950:3	w. a detective story	JAMES 451:58	responsible and w.	CHUR 226:8
w. or a good public servant	MACM 557:79	w. a good play is difficult	PRIE 695:94	right now is w.	SPEN 839:56
w. overwhelmingly honest	MOORE 617:87	w. a line	GERG 365:65	Right…of Kings to govern w.	POPE 689:41
w. risks sterility	HOLM 423:59	W. and travel broaden your ass	HEMI 410:85	right out of w.	JONS 467:67
w.'s ambition	KOES 495:27	W. a novel	GREE 386:24	solve it right or w.	WATS 922:43
w.'s greed is appalling	BALD 56:16	W. a novel	SPARK 836:76	sometimes in the w.	DRYD 300:22
w.'s only responsibility	FAUL 331:40	w. as an escape from	WILL 945:95	take the w. course	KENN 481:13
w. thinks from…cliché	POUND 691:88	w. bears…to poetry	MACA 545:32	that is a w. one	JOHN 462:20
w.…universal in sympathy	BARN 64:66	W. books is the closest men	MAIL 560:49	the w. way	DE 273:70
w. who has nothing to say	BIER 134:69	W. free verse	FROST 352:10	think something is…right or w.	STEV 851:11
w. writes in order to teach	KAZIN 474:52	w. has become your major vice	HEMI 410:90	to be proved w.	HUXL 442:93
writers All w. are either 29	PARK 664:30	W. has laws of perspective	CAPO 197:24	To do w.	PLATO 681:44
All w. are vain	ORWE 654:60	w. is a craft	PORT 690:73	too many w. mistakes	BERRA 87:90
ancient w.	YEATS 966:28	W. is a form of therapy	GREE 386:25	to win and do the w. thing	BLAIR 138:71
and of all w.	TIMES 892:22	w. is a sheer paring away	FITZ 338:95	Truth suffer w.	SCOTT 751:98
as many good w.	VIDAL 912:3	w. is nothing	HEMI 410:97	we do him w.	TENN 874:81

what bitter w.	BROW	166:94
when things are w.	GIPP	372:21
When things go w.	OBRI	646:68
w. because not all was right	CRAB	252:44
w. for me to love my own?	SITT	823:93
w. in its conclusions	REGAN	710:42
w. man the woman	HARDY	397:15
w. notes are right	IVES	448:82
w. people remember Vietnam	HERR	415:97
w. war, at the w. place	BRAD	155:44
w. would triumph	BROW	169:85
years hath done this w.	DANI	262:35
You do me w.	SHAK	793:30
wrongdoing cases of w.	ROOS	724:16
wrongfully to be w. accused	WINT	950:13
wrongs Bill of W.	MORR	620:53
forgive w. darker than death	SHEL	815:20
if two w. don't make a right	COUS	248:41
like w. hushed-up	OWEN	658:39
many w. in the world	JONAS	465:14
people's w. his own	DRYD	302:85
wrote about the prow she w.	TENN	870:86
as I w. it	HAND	395:79
blockhead ever w.	JOHN	463:49
w. like an angel	GARR	360:79
wroth Gave way to w.	SITW	823:3
to be w. with one we love	COLE	235:34
wrought What hath God w.!	BIBLE	94:85
Wyatt W. resteth here	SURR	860:99
Wye half the babbling W.	TENN	873:65
Wykehamist rather dirty W.	BETJ	88:16
Wynken W., Blynken, and Nod	FIELD	335:13

X

Xanadu In X. did Kubla Khan	COLE	236:36
one does not 'live' at X.	DIDI	286:81
Xerox x. makes everybody	MCLU	556:61

Y

yacht y. on the sea	REID	710:45
Yale for Country and for Y.	THUR	890:88
libel on a Y. prom	PARK	663:8
whale ship was my Y. College	MELV	585:57
Yankee brain of a Y. entrepreneur	ONET	651:82
One of them is 'Y. Doodle'	GRANT	382:10
that lanky Y. finger	CONN	242:83
Y. Doodle Dandy	COHAN	234:93
Y. to the south of us	JOHN	458:24
Yankees Four and twenty Y.	ANON	24:9
yanking y. and hauling	POUND	692:31
yaptown that Y….called New York	OHEN	648:19
yard into your front y.	JOHN	458:12
yarn merry y. from a laughing	MASE	580:52
web…is of mingled y.	SHAK	790:68
Yarrow dowie houms o' Y.	BALL	58:59
dowie houms o' Y.	BALL	59:60
such a place as Y.	WORD	960:14
yawn heard thy everlasting y.	POPE	689:45
When churchyards y.	SHAK	783:30
y. or 'Pooh!'	BYRON	190:26
yawp barbaric y.	WHIT	937:96
ydrad fiend of gods and men y.	SPEN	839:54
yea let your y. be y.	BIBLE	130:61
year at this time of the y.	ANDR	18:79
before the mellowing y.	MILT	599:82
beginning of a new month or y.	MANN	566:82
beri-beri y. is as lonely	NASH	630:61
Birmingham in a lean y.	LLOY	533:80
bright soul of the sad y.	NASHE	632:94
circle of the golden y.	TENN	872:30
consumes each y.	UPDI	905:16
creator in the y. 1902	MORT	621:72
crownest the y.	BIBLE	101:79
dark time of the y.	ELIOT	321:81
death-struck y.	HOUS	431:53
distance of about one y.	REED	709:28
does not give you a y.	STEV	852:54
finish up the y.	SHAK	760:9
five thousand a y.	THAC	880:29
for a y., for a day	LEAR	516:36
For many an ardent y.	DICK	284:55
grief returns with the revolving y.	SHEL	815:32
haven't…sleep for over a y.	WAUGH	923:63
hour be but A y.	MARL	573:30
juvescence of the y.	ELIOT	317:83
last y. I was fifty-four	REED	709:29
lease for a y.	ANOU	28:60
love in a single y.	RILKE	715:39
needs at least once a y.	WILD	943:47
one y. we came second	PAIS	660:41
on Nothing a Y.	THAC	880:28
pleasure of the fleeting y.!	SHAK	802:71
remember me just once a y.	RUNY	732:63
shortest knight of the y.	RICH	714:14
sword has won in half a y.	MOLT	612:93
That night, that y.	HOPK	429:89
That time of y.	SHAK	801:62
three hundred pounds a y.!	SHAK	773:10
'Tis the y.'s midnight	DONNE	291:29
world too beautiful this y.	MILL	592:18
worst time of the y.	ELIOT	318:17
Y. by y.	BASHO	67:45
y. is going	TENN	875:95
y. passed; a y. of art	MOORE	616:68
y.'s at the spring	BROW	167:9
y. Seasons return	MILT	603:75
Y.'s end—still in straw hat	BASHO	67:46
y. to be said goodbye to	HARD	396:93
y. whose days are l.	WILDE	942:21
yearly y. on the vigil	SHAK	776:89
yearning girl solid with y.	LOWE	540:38
mother's y.	ELIOT	315:27
y. like a God in pain	KEATS	477:17
yearnings different y., different hopes	CART	206:45
years 10 y. before its time	LAVER	512:33
24 hours and got 99 y.	RAY	708:88
30 y. ago…I made the decision	MCKE	554:11
arches of the y.	THOM	886:81
beginning of y.	SWIN	863:85
buried for many y.	FRIE	350:64
caves for thousands of y.	NIET	638:94
comfortable y. allowed to man!	SASS	745:81
do not count a man's y.	EMER	325:97
do that for hundreds of y.	MORR	620:58
down the Lachlan, y. ago	PATE	669:13
earthly y.	WORD	957:64
first ten million y. were the worst	ADAMS	4:77
fleeting y. are slipping by	HORA	429:8
for months, for y.	ROBBE	716:63
For three y.…He strove	POUND	691:99
forty long y. of good rhyme	OBRU	646:75
forty-six y. old	LEWIS	527:56
For y. I have let dentists	PERE	674:17
Four score and seven y.	LINC	529:9
[Gladstone] spent his declining y.	SELL	756:14
golden y. return	SHEL	816:57
great number of y. are elapsed	WALP	918:65
gulf of y. and pathos	MARQ	574:43
Heaven preserve my y.	DRYD	302:91
hopes of future y.	LONG	535:27
hundred y. as a sheep	MUSS	617:90
In ten thousand y.	SNYD	832:91
in the midst of the y.	BIBLE	111:56
I've been using it for y.	BANK	61:12
known each other for y.	THUR	891:9
like y. and ages creep	THOM	887:7
love of finished y.	ROSS	725:37
more wise, than…6,000 y. ago	POE	683:85
not…wanted these ten y.	PITT	680:13
O for ten y.	KEATS	475:67
old and stricken in y.	BIBLE	97:51
Our noisy y.	WORD	960:11
persecuted for 2,000 y.	KISS	494:96
played 33 y.	MATT	582:98
promise of their early y.	POWE	693:41
remember for y.	ALLI	14:7
senior y. are reached	RAND	706:55
speaking prose for forty y.	MOLI	611:86
take away from our y.	CRUZ	256:39
think for months and y.	EINS	313:77
Thirteen wasted y.	ANON	25:51
thirty y. of struggle	LOOS	536:43
threescore y. and ten	BIBLE	101:94
Three y. she grew	WORD	957:63
through y. of darkness	MANS	567:3
Time in hours, days, y.	VAUG	909:39
took him seventeen y. to write	PRIE	695:90
took me 25 y. to do it	BELL	76:49
two y. in Holiday Inns	MOND	612:94
undone y.	OWEN	657:34
where all past y. are	DONNE	291:23
will keep for y.	LEAC	515:13
with all their thousands of y.	DONNE	293:73
y. before and after	LEGU	520:11
y. hath done this wrong	DANI	262:35
y. have not brought…effacement	RANS	707:71
y. of missing each other	RICH	713:6
y. of my pilgrimage	BIBLE	93:48
y. should go to praise	MARV	577:91
Y. steal Fire from the mind	BYRON	187:47
y. that the locust hath eaten	BIBLE	111:47
you measured your y. in theirs	ATKIN	40:16
yeast as some immense y. culture	BOYD	153:11
he thinks he's Y.	EWART	328:75
Mr Y.'s Wanderings of Oisin	WILDE	940:50
of the stature of Y.	ORWE	654:51
understood Y.'s poems	SAKI	739:58
Y. is laid	YEATS	967:40
Y. is laid to rest	AUDEN	43:92
yellow come to her in y. stockings	SHAK	786:5
green and y. melancholy	SHAK	786:2
leaves…turn y.	ANON	20:32
lemon y. or sun y.	GALE	357:28
no blue without y.	VAN	908:18
Not y. like a daisy	TRUMP	900:97
put on the y. star	FACK	329:1
tawdry y. strove with dirty red	POPE	686:69
the sere, the y. leaf	SHAK	798:69
This y. slave	SHAK	791:80
tinge of tawny y.	SALA	739:70
Y. River down our throats	PRIE	695:20
your y. hair	YEATS	967:33
yellow-bosomed y.-b. basset-hounds	MORG	619:31
yellows y., as violent as can be	CARRA	202:57
yells stale bean-soup, of college y.	MENC	587:17
yelp puppy's insolent y.	ANON	21:58
yelps y. for liberty	JOHN	462:41
yes answer Y. to Someone	HAMM	394:57
approach it by first saying y.	EVANS	328:67
I did say y.	HOPK	428:69
say no when they mean y.	ALCO	12:44
we say y.—and we are the people	WRIG	963:72
y. I said y. I will Y.	JOYCE	470:33
Y., we can	OBAMA	643:21
yes-sayer wish to be only a Y.-s.	NIET	638:96
yesterday art of keeping up with y.	MARQ	574:47
as y. when it is past	BIBLE	101:93
behind the doors of y.	HYDE	443:17
give me y.	JONES	465:17
O, call back y.	SHAK	764:48
person we were y.	UPDI	906:34
same y., and to day	BIBLE	129:47
technology of y.	GABOR	356:2
wiser to-day than he was y.	POPE	686:54
Y., December 7, 1941	ROOS	724:14
y. of my disease	PRIOR	696:4
Y.'s men	ANON	25:71
Y., We had daily cleaning	REED	709:26
yesterdays And all our y.	SHAK	798:74
no more tomorrows, only y.	PARF	663:90
yew true wood, of y. wood	DOYLE	297:49
yewberries the y.	MERE	587:24
y.-tree's shade	GRAY	384:64
yid ID BACK IN Y.	ROTH	728:81
Yiddish look Irish, think Y.	KOFF	496:32
Y. is a household tongue	OZICK	658:42
yield perish if we y.	KIPL	493:70
probable y.	KEYN	484:78
to find, and not to y.	TENN	870:2
yielded saw me, and y.	SHAK	792:8
yoga lotus position at her y. class	SHAR	806:74
yoghurt between butter and y.	TRIL	897:11
milk and the y.	MORT	621:68
yoke add to your y.	BIBLE	97:58
Bear his mild y.	MILT	601:26
bear the y. in his youth	BIBLE	110:27
bending under the y. of tyranny	PITT	680:12
y. is easy	BIBLE	116:81
yoked Irish…cruelly y.	BUCH	171:25
yoke-devils y.-d. sworn	SHAK	775:67
Yokoi is Y. correct	ASAHI	37:51
yolk y. runs down the waistcoat	DICK	278:82
yolks nothing to lose but your y.	STEV	851:8
yore as in the days of y.	GREN	388:56
as it hath been of y.	WORD	959:5
fought and drank as of y.	DAVIS	266:9
Yorick Alas, poor Y.	SHAK	784:63
York brave Y. volunteers	BROCK	160:29
by this son of Y.	SHAK	760:31
tumble…from London to Y.	KING	488:52

Yossarian

Yossarian hell kind of a name is Y.? — HELL 407:28
 Y. was moved very deeply — HELL 407:27
you I'm afraid it's y. — COPE 246:95
 Now that I know y. — GOET 375:72
 see y. umpiring — GRACE 380:84
 things perish, and y. along — KEMP 480:78
 what no one knows about y. — DELI 272:44
 Y. are your possibilities — WINF 949:92
Young [Brigham Y.] is dreadfully — WARD 920:4
 How gently...G M Y. deals — ACHE 3:50
young Alligators...eat their y. — MACD 550:54
 Angry Y. Man — PAUL 670:32
 an old man y. — TENN 871:6
 apple that isn't y. anymore — GARBO 359:64
 being y. until you retire — LARK 510:93
 Bowls is a y. man's game — BRYA 170:1
 call her a y. country — HOPE 427:57
 can be y. without money — WILL 945:91
 compliment him about looking y. — IRVI 447:59
 corrupting the minds of the y. — PLATO 681:42
 crime of being a y. man — PITT 679:1
 death of one so y. — SPEN 837:4
 denunciation of the y. — SMITH 829:11
 dies married y. — SHAK 766:10
 die so y. — AUDEN 43:84
 everything...we do for the y. — ELIZ 322:14
 fashion for the y.? — CHAN 214:1
 For to be y. I wald not — HENR 411:16
 Go West, y. man — SOULE 834:38
 granted to the aged or the y. — LAUR 511:21
 have been y. — BIBLE 100:60
 head bit off by it y. — SHAK 792:92
 how y. the policemen look — HICKS 417:45
 I, being y. and foolish — YEATS 965:3
 If...love were y. — RALE 705:43
 in my verse ever live y. — SHAK 800:38
 I was y. — FLEC 340:30
 life-chances of the y. — MUSG 627:87
 Like all the very y. — MITF 610:51
 Like all y. men — SHAW 809:7
 look y. till forty — DRYD 299:17
 misery peculiar to the y. — LESS 523:92
 most perish y. — ETHE 327:42
 never an Angry Y. Man — AMIS 16:38
 not so y. as they are painted — BEER 73:72
 Now as I was y. and easy — THOM 883:17
 Old and y. — STEV 852:45
 old heads on your y. shoulders — SPARK 836:67
 old [might as well speak] to the y. — CATH 208:89
 one so y. — FORD 343:7
 persuade you, y. and old — PLATO 681:43
 radical when y. — FROST 352:12
 seventy years y. — HOLM 424:84
 she died y. — WEBS 927:62
 Since we're not y. — RICH 713:6
 So wise so y. — SHAK 761:42
 still y. an' believing — WILL 945:92
 their y. dying for...oil — POWE 693:53
 to be y., gifted and black — HANS 396:86
 to be y. was very heaven! — WORD 960:23
 too y. to fall asleep — SASS 745:91
 voices of y. people — SMITH 829:17
 warn you not to be y. — KINN 488:65
 We that are y. — SHAK 793:40
 When I was a y. man — SCHU 750:76
 When the world was y. — BACON 52:21
 When thou wast y. — BIBLE 124:69
 where she may lay her y. — BIBLE 101:88
 whom the gods love dies y. — MENA 586:78
 woman is as y. as her knee — QUANT 701:5
 writers the y. like — BURG 174:96
 y. and inexperienced house — JERO 454:42
 Y., and so fair! — HOOD 426:33
 y. girl's skin — RENO 711:55
 y. have aspirations — SAKI 739:53
 y. man can bring off — UPDI 906:27
 y. man carbuncular — ELIOT 318:4
 y. man not yet — BACON 51:76
 y. men can possibly imagine — SMITH 829:16
 Y. men have more virtue — JOHN 461:98
 Y. men need not their sight — DONNE 293:76
 y. men shall see visions — BIBLE 111:48
 y. men shall utterly fall — BIBLE 109:85
 y. ones carry pistols — SHAW 806:84
 Y. players, y. boys — CAPEL 197:17
 y. things that marry for love — SHAW 809:84
 y., too stupid — RYLE 736:61
 you're only too y. — THOR 889:48
younger something y. than she looks — FIRB 336:49
 we do not get any y. — REED 709:29
 y. than that now — DYLAN 309:53
youngling y. in the contemplation — MILT 600:10
youngman Let me die a y.'s death — MCGO 552:76
youngster that y.'s throat — COWA 249:63
yourself have to go do it y. — WOODS 954:6
 looking out for y. — COOL 246:82
 more interested in y. — GIDE 367:19
 more interesting than being y. — GIEL 368:27
 Nothing can bring you peace but y. — EMER 324:56
 to y., that husband — JAMES 449:22
 two topics, y. and me — JOHN 463:53
youth All the flattering y. defy — ROCH 720:26
 anything to do with y. clubs — SPARK 836:65
 bear the yoke in his y. — BIBLE 110:27
 blessings of y. — DEMO 272:49
 cased up...have y. — WEBS 927:53
 cheerful bird of y. — KHAY 485:88
 corrupted the y. of the realm — SHAK 759:98
 crudity of y., disdaining — NORR 641:57
 days of my y. — SOUT 835:44
 days of our y. — BYRON 190:30
 deeds of y. — SHAK 801:49
 differences between y. and age — BARN 64:77
 done it from my y. — CRAB 252:41
 eagle mewing her mighty y. — MILT 601:20
 Farewell y.! — FRANZ 348:24
 full of unmannerly sadness in his y. — SHAK 769:78
 giddy, shallow, humorous y. — SHAK 775:71
 green suckers of y. — SHER 817:89
 had been friends in y. — COLE 235:34
 has eyes of y. — SHAK 773:9
 Her Aunt...from her Earliest Y. — BELL 77:63
 Home-keeping y. — SHAK 758:55
 hour of thoughtless y. — WORD 956:55
 Immortal y. to mortal maids — LAND 507:29
 infirmities...I had in my y. — WESL 932:71
 in my y. I never did apply — SHAK 778:71
 in y. man is...depraved — MITC 609:25
 In y. open your mind — ANON 21:58
 joy...in my y. — AUDEN 44:20
 laugh uproariously in y. — BROO 162:96
 less of an affair of y. — FITZ 338:89
 Let age approve of y. — BROW 168:61
 Let no man despise thy y. — BIBLE 129:20
 misspent y. and middle age — THUR 891:4
 morn of y. — WORD 961:42
 noble y. did dress — SHAK 772:80
 no danger in sweetness and y. — ROCH 720:22
 not clean past your y. — SHAK 772:71
 outlive Thy y., thy strength — MILT 607:68
 pass over y. — CONG 241:61
 poets in our y. — WORD 959:1
 Rejoice...in thy y. — BIBLE 106:35
 rejoice with the wife of thy y. — BIBLE 104:57
 rigorous teachers seized my y. — ARNO 35:3
 rose Of y. — SHAK 794:70
 roses for the flush of y. — ROSS 726:40
 sign of an ill-spent y. — SPEN 837:91
 sins of my y. — BIBLE 100:48
 So long as y. — SHAK 800:40
 sowed in y. a mustard seed — BRON 161:59
 spirit of y. in everything — SHAK 802:72
 strong disposition in y. — POWE 693:42
 thoughtless y....with vain desires — DRYD 303:11
 Time, which takes...Our y. — RALE 705:47
 To flaming y. — SHAK 784:41
 to living y. denied — WORD 961:47
 transitory as your y. — THOM 886:77
 What one knows...in y. — ADAMS 5:93
 Where y. grows pale — KEATS 478:43
 whose follies cease with their y. — PITT 679:1
 world hath lost his y. — BIBLE 112:70
 y. and the feeling — CONR 244:36
 Y. are boarded, clothed, booked — DICK 278:75
 y. are long, long thoughts — LONG 535:31
 Y., beauty, graceful action — DRYD 302:85
 y., before I waxèd old — SPEN 839:48
 Y....forgives itself nothing — SHAW 808:55
 y. full of grace — WHIT 938:14
 y. had seemed to teach — HARDY 397:13
 Y. is a blunder — DISR 287:26
 y. is bent by...wintry fever — THOM 883:3
 y. is bliss — BETJ 89:40
 y. is renewed like the eagle's — BIBLE 102:6
 Y. is something very new — CHAN 214:99
 y. is vain — COLE 235:34
 Y. may be forgiven — AUDEN 44:16
 y. may wear and waste — CONG 241:61
 Y. means love — BROW 169:71
 y....Must travel — WORD 959:8
 y. of America — WILDE 941:86
 Y. of a Nation — DISR 288:36
 y. of a state — BACON 53:43
 y. of England are on fire — SHAK 775:64
 y. of frolics — POPE 688:15
 y. of his own generation — FITZ 337:74
 Y. on the prow — GRAY 385:86
 y. pined away with desire — BLAKE 140:11
 y.'s eyes burned — ROSS 726:58
 Y. shows but half — BROW 168:59
 y.'s most precious years — STUD 858:63
 y. stone dead — SASS 745:85
 y. to fortune...unknown — GRAY 384:77
 y. unkind — BAST 67:51
 Y., what man's age is like — DENH 272:63
youths Even the y. shall faint — BIBLE 109:85
 two noble y., stand prisoners — WILDE 939:44
 y. at cricks did play — JOSE 469:9
Yukon law of the Y. — SERV 757:33
yuppies Y. as a class — ADLER 8:69

Z

zany mountebank and his z. — WALP 919:77
Zarathustra Z., sometime regius — JOYCE 470:28
zeal holy mistaken z. in politics — JUNI 471:48
 with half the z. — SHAK 805:53
 z. of the Lord of hosts — BIBLE 107:60
zealots murmur among the z. — HUME 439:8
zealous z. citizen — BURKE 176:49
zebra Striped like a z. — KEATS 476:4
 z. stripes along his jaw — ELIOT 317:80
Zembla gives to Z. fruits — POPE 688:31
zenith z. doth depend upon — SHAK 803:11
zephyr soft the z. blows — GRAY 385:86
 z. and khaki shorts — BETJ 88:21
 Z. with Aurora — MILT 597:42
zero Global double z. — ANON 26:96
 z. and the infinite — JARRY 452:95
Zerubbabel word...unto Z. — BIBLE 112:60
zest tell with such high z. — OWEN 657:31
Zidane What Z. does with a ball — PLAT 681:39
ziggurats later came z. — GILL 370:77
Zimbabwe play cricket in Z. — MUGA 623:7
Zimmermann Z. in bright lights? — MERM 588:47
Zion every one of them in Z. — BIBLE 101:89
 lay in Z. for a foundation — BIBLE 108:71
 Lord shall bring again Z. — BIBLE 109:90
 mount Z., on the sides — BIBLE 100:70
 shall be as mount Z. — BIBLE 103:34
 when we remembered Z. — BIBLE 103:42
 Z., city of our God! — NEWT 636:64
Zionism with criminal Z. — HUSS 440:38
zip remorseless Z. — CHRI 223:42
zipless z. fuck is absolutely pure — JONG 466:31
zodiac never give out my z. sign — PEACE 671:50
zombies political z. — WILS 948:71
zone with the Heavenly z. — LOVE 538:87
 yesterdays, for the Canal Z. — PARF 663:90
zones dwellers in different z. — DISR 288:34
zoo city is...a human z. — MORR 620:45
 may see at the Z. — KIPL 491:31
 return the giraffes to the z. — NASH 631:86
 The Human Z. — MORR 620:44
zoological beings in the z. scale — CARB 198:36
Zoroaster Z., my dead child — SHEL 814:6
Zuleika Z., on a desert island — BEER 73:71
Zurich little gnomes in Z. — WILS 948:59